LITERARY MARKET PLACE™

LMP
2021

Literary Market Place™
81st Edition

Publisher
Thomas H. Hogan

Senior Director, ITI Reference Group
Owen O'Donnell

Managing Editor
Karen Hallard

Assistant Editor
Karen DiDario

Tampa Operations:

Manager, Tampa Editorial Operations
Debra James

Project Coordinator, Tampa Editorial
Carolyn Victor

Graphics & Production:

Production Manager
Tiffany Chamenko

Production
Dana Stevenson
Jackie Crawford

LITERARY MARKET PLACE™

LMP 2021

THE DIRECTORY OF THE AMERICAN BOOK PUBLISHING INDUSTRY WITH INDUSTRY INDEXES

Volume

Published by

Information Today, Inc.
143 Old Marlton Pike
Medford, NJ 08055-8750
Phone: (609) 654-6266
Fax: (609) 654-4309
E-mail (Orders): custserv@infotoday.com
Web site: www.infotoday.com

ISSN 0000-1155
ISBN 978-1-57387-567-7 (set)
Library of Congress Catalog Card Number 41-51571

Information Today, Inc.
143 Old Marlton Pike
Medford, NJ 08055-8750
Phone: 800-300-9868 (Customer Service)
         800-409-4929 (Editorial)
Fax: 609-654-4309
E-mail (orders): custserv@infotoday.com
Web Site: www.infotoday.com

Printed in the United States of America

US $459.50
ISBN 13: 978-1-57387-567-7
45950>

9 781573 875677

CONTENTS

VOLUME 2

SERVICES & SUPPLIERS

INDEXES

Preface

The 2021 edition marks the 81st annual publication of *Literary Market Place*™—the leading directory of the American and Canadian book publishing industry. Covering publishers and literary agents to manufacturers and shipping services, *LMP* is the most comprehensive directory of its kind. The revised 2021 edition contains over 8,000 entries. Of these listings 2,204 are publishers—including Canadian houses and small presses. Together with its companion publication, *International Literary Market Place*™, these directories cover the global book publishing industry.

Organization & Content

Volume 1 covers core publishing industry information: Book Publishers; Editorial Services and Agents; Associations, Events, Courses and Awards; and Books and Magazines for the Trade.

Volume 2 contains information on service providers and suppliers to the publishing industry. Advertising, Marketing and Publicity; Book Manufacturing; Sales and Distribution; and Services and Suppliers can be found in this volume.

Entries generally contain name, address, telephone and other telecommunications data, key personnel, company reportage, branch offices, brief statistics and descriptive annotations. Where applicable, Standard Address Numbers (SANs) have been included. SANs are unique numbers assigned to the addresses of publishers, wholesalers and booksellers. Publishers' entries also contain their assigned ISBN prefixes. Both the SAN and ISBN systems are administered by R.R. Bowker LLC, 630 Central Avenue, New Providence, NJ 07974.

Indexes

In addition to the numerous section-specific indexes appearing throughout, each volume of *LMP* contains four indexes that reference listings appearing in that volume. The Industry Indexes cover two distinct areas of data: a Company Index that includes the name, address, communications information and page reference for company listings and a separate Personnel Index that includes the main personnel associated with each entry as well as the page reference. Other indexes include the Index to Sections for quickly finding specific categories of information and the Index to Advertisers.

A Note to Authors

Prospective authors seeking a publisher should be aware that there are publishers who, as a condition for publishing and marketing an individual's work, may require a significant sum of money be paid to the publisher. This practice is known by a number of terms including author subsidized publishing, author investment, and co-operative publishing. Before entering an agreement involving such a payment, the author is advised to make a careful investigation to determine the standing of the publisher's imprint in the industry.

Similarly, authors seeking literary representation are advised that some agents request a nominal reading fee that may be applied to the agent's commission upon representation. Other agencies may charge substantially higher fees which may not be applicable to a future commission and which are not refundable. The recommended course is to first send a query letter with an outline, sample chapter, and a self-addressed stamped envelope (SASE). Should an agent express interest in handling the manuscript, full details of fees and commissions should be obtained in writing before the complete manuscript is sent. Should an agency require significant advance payment from an author, the author is cautioned to make a careful investigation to determine the agency's standing in the industry before entering an agreement. The author should always retain a copy of the manuscript in his or her possession.

Occasionally, the editors of *LMP* will receive complaints against publishers or agents listed in the work. If, after investigation and review, the editors determine that the complaints are significant and justified, we may exclude the company or individual in question. However, the absence of a listing in *LMP* for any particular publisher or agent should not be construed as a judgment on the legitimacy or integrity of that organization or individual.

Compilation

LMP is updated throughout the year via a number of methods. A request for updated information is sent to current entrants to corroborate and update the information contained on our database. All updates received are edited for the next product release. Those entrants who do not respond to our request may be verified through telephone interviews or online research. Entrants who cannot be verified or who fall short of entry criteria are dropped from the current edition.

Information for new listings is gathered in a similar method. Possible new listings are identified through ongoing research, or when a listing request is received either from the organization itself or from a third party. If sufficient information is not initially gathered to create a listing, a data collection form is provided to the organization to submit essential listing information.

Updated information or suggestions for new listings can be submitted by mail to:

> *Literary Market Place*
> Information Today, Inc.
> 121 Chanlon Rd, Suite G-20
> New Providence, NJ 07974-2195

An updating method using the Internet is also available for *LMP* listings:

Visit the *Literary Market Place* web site to update an *LMP* listing. **Literarymarketplace.com** allows you the opportunity to provide new information for a listing by clicking on the "Update or Correct Your Entry" option. The Feedback option on the home page of the web site can be used to suggest new entries as well.

Related Services

Literary Market Place, along with its companion volume *International Literary Market Place*, is available through the Internet at **www.literarymarketplace.com**. Designed to give users simple, logical access to the information they require, the site offers users the choice of searching for data alphabetically, geographically, by type, or by subject. Continuously updated by Information Today's team of editors, this is a truly enhanced version of the *LMP* and *ILMP* databases, incorporating features that make "must-have" information easily available.

Arrangements for placing advertisements in *LMP* can be coordinated through Lauri Rimler by telephone at 800-409-4929 (press 1) or 908-219-0088, or by e-mail at lwrimler@infotoday.com.

Your feedback is important to us. We strongly encourage you to contact us with suggestions or comments on the print edition of *LMP*, or its web site. Our editorial office can be reached by telephone at 800-409-4929 (press 3) or 908-219-0277, or by e-mail at khallard@infotoday.com.

The editors would like to thank those entrants who took the time to respond to our requests for current information.

Abbreviations & Acronyms

The following is a list of acronyms & abbreviations used throughout *LMP*.

AAR - Association of Authors' Representatives
AB - Alberta
Acct(s) - Account(s)
Acctg - Accounting
Acq(s) - Acquisition(s)
Ad - Advertising
Admin - Administrative, Administration, Administrator
Aff - Affairs
AK - Alaska
AL - Alabama
appt - appointment
Apt - Apartment
AR - Arkansas
Assoc - Associate
Asst - Assistant
AV - Audiovisual
Ave - Avenue
AZ - Arizona

B&W - Black & White
BC - British Columbia
Bd - Board
bio - biography
BISAC - Book Industry Standards and Communications
Bldg - Building
Blvd - Boulevard
Br - Branch
Busn - Business

CA - California
CEO - Chief Executive Officer
CFO - Chief Financial Officer
Chmn - Chairman
Chpn - Chairperson
CIO - Chief Information Officer
Circ - Circulation
CN - Canada
CO - Colorado
Co(s) - Company(-ies)
Co-edns - Co-editions
Coll(s) - College(s)
Comm - Committee
Commun(s) - Communication(s)
Comp - Compiler
Compt - Comptroller
Cont - Controller
Contrib - Contributing
COO - Chief Operating Officer
Coord - Coordinator
Corp - Corporate, Corporation
Coun - Counsel
CT - Connecticut
Ct - Court
CTO - Chief Technical / Technology Officer

Ctr - Center
Curr - Current
Cust - Customer
CZ - Canal Zone

DC - District of Columbia
DE - Delaware
Dept - Department
Devt - Development
Dir(s) - Director(s)
Dist - Distributed, Distribution, Distributor
Div - Division
Dom - Domestic
Dr - Drive

ed - edition
Ed(s) - Editor(s)
Edit - Editorial
Educ - Education, Educational
El-hi - Elementary-High School
Elem - Elementary
Ency - Encyclopedia
Eng - English
Engg - Engineering
Engr - Engineer
Equip - Equipment
ESL - English as a Second Language
Est - Established
EVP - Executive Vice President
exc - except
Exec - Executive
Expwy - Expressway
ext - extension

Fed - Federal
Fin - Finance, Financial
fl - floor
FL - Florida
Freq - Frequency
Fwy - Freeway

GA - Georgia
Gen - General
Govt - Government
GU - Guam

HD - High-definition
HI - Hawaii
HR - Human Resources
HS - High School
Hwy - Highway

IA - Iowa
ID - Idaho
IL - Illinois
Illus - Illustrator
IN - Indiana
Inc - Incorporated

indiv(s) - individual(s)
Indus - Industrial, Industry
Info - Information
Instl - Institutional
Instn(s) - Institution(s)
Instrl - Instructional
Intl - International
ISBN - International Standard Book Number
ISSN - International Standard Serial Number
IT - Information Technology

Jr - Junior
Jt - Joint
Juv - Juvenile

K - Kindergarten
KS - Kansas
KY - Kentucky

LA - Louisiana
Lang(s) - Language(s)
Lib(s) - Library(-ies)
Libn - Librarian
Lit - Literature

MA - Massachusetts
MB - Manitoba
MD - Maryland
Mdse - Merchandise
Mdsg - Merchandising
ME - Maine
Med - Medical
memb(s) - member(s)
Metro - Metropolitan
Mfg - Manufacturing
Mgmt - Management
Mgr - Manager
MI - Michigan
Mkt(s) - Market(s)
Mktg - Marketing
MN - Minnesota
Mng - Managing
MO - Missouri
mo - month
MS - Mississippi
ms(s) - manuscript(s)
MT - Montana

Natl - National
NB - New Brunswick
NC - North Carolina
ND - North Dakota
NE - Nebraska
NH - New Hampshire
NJ - New Jersey
NL - Newfoundland and Labrador
NM - New Mexico
No - Number

ABBREVIATIONS & ACRONYMS

NS - Nova Scotia
NT - Northwest Territories
NU - Nunavut
NV - Nevada
NY - New York

Off(s) - Office(s)
Offr - Officer
OH - Ohio
OK - Oklahoma
ON - Ontario
Oper(s) - Operation(s)
OR - Oregon

PA - Pennsylvania
Pbk(s) - Paperback(s)
PE - Prince Edward Island
Perms - Permissions
Photo - Photograph
Photog - Photographer, Photography
Pkwy - Parkway
pp - pages
PR - Public Relations
PR - Puerto Rico
Pres - President
Proc - Processing
Prod(s) - Product(s)
Prodn - Production
Prodr - Producer
Prof - Professional, Professor
Prog(s) - Program(s)
Proj(s) - Project(s)
Promo(s) - Promotion(s)
Prop - Proprietor
Pub Aff - Public Affairs

Publg - Publishing
Publr - Publisher
Pubn(s) - Publication(s)
Purch - Purchasing

QC - Quebec

R&D - Research & Development
Rd - Road
Ref - Reference
Reg - Region
Regl - Regional
Rel - Relations
Rep(s) - Representative(s)
Res - Research
RI - Rhode Island
Rm - Room
Rte - Route
Rts - Rights

SAN - Standard Address Number
SASE - Self-Addressed Stamped Envelope
SC - South Carolina
Sci - Science
SD - South Dakota
Secy - Secretary
Serv(s) - Service(s)
SK - Saskatchewan
Soc - Social, Sociology
Spec - Special
Sq - Square
Sr - Senior
St - Saint, Street
Sta - Station
Ste - Sainte

Subn(s) - Subscription(s)
Subs - Subsidiary
Supv - Supervisor
SVP - Senior Vice President
Synd - Syndicated, Syndication

Tech - Technical
Technol - Technology
Tel - Telephone
Terr - Terrace
TN - Tennessee
Tpke - Turnpike
Treas - Treasurer
TX - Texas

UK - United Kingdom
Univ - University
unsol - unsolicited
UT - Utah

V - Vice
VA - Virginia
VChmn - Vice Chairman
VI - Virgin Islands
vol(s) - volume(s)
VP - Vice President
VT - Vermont

WA - Washington
WI - Wisconsin
WV - West Virginia
WY - Wyoming

yr - year
YT - Yukon Territory

Book Publishers

U.S. Publishers

Listed in alphabetical order are those U.S. publishers that have reported to *LMP* that they produce an average of three or more books annually. Publishers that have appeared in a previous edition of *LMP*, but whose output currently does not meet our defined rate of activity, will be reinstated when their annual production reaches the required level. It should be noted that this rule of publishing activity does not apply to publishers of dictionaries, encyclopedias, atlases or Braille books or to university presses.

The definition of a book excludes charts, pamphlets, folding maps, sheet music and material with stapled bindings. Publishers that make their titles available only in electronic or audio format are included if they meet the stated criteria. In the case of packages, the book must be of equal or greater importance than the accompanying piece. With few exceptions, new publishers are not listed prior to having published at least three titles within a year.

§ before the company name indicates publishers involved in electronic publishing.

The following indexes can be found immediately after the publishers' listings:

    U.S. Publishers–Geographic Index
    U.S. Publishers–Type of Publications Index
    U.S. Publishers–Subject Index

See **Imprints, Subsidiaries & Distributors** for additional information on the companies listed herein. This section should also be checked for apparently active companies that are no longer listed in the U.S. Publishers section. In many cases, they have been acquired as an imprint or subsidiary of a larger entity and no longer have a discrete listing.

§A-R Editions Inc
1600 Aspen Commons, Suite 100, Middleton, WI 53562
Tel: 608-836-9000 *Toll Free Tel:* 800-736-0070 (North America book orders only) *Fax:* 608-831-8200
E-mail: info@areditions.com; orders@areditions.com
Web Site: www.areditions.com
Key Personnel
Pres & CEO: Patrick Wall *Tel:* 608-203-2575
    E-mail: patrick.wall@areditions.com
Dir, Spec Projs: James Zychowicz *Tel:* 608-203-2580 *E-mail:* james.zychowicz@areditions.com
Founded: 1962
Scholarly critical editions of music for performance & study; computer music & digital audio professional books, electronics & Internet technology, online music anthology (www.armusicanthology.com) & co-published series with MLA: Index & Bibliography, Basic Manual & Technical Reports Series.
ISBN Prefix(es): 978-0-89579
Number of titles published annually: 25 Print
Total Titles: 500 Print
Imprints: Greenway Music Press
Distributor for AIM (American Institute of Musicology)

A 2 Z Press LLC
3670 Woodbridge Rd, Deland, FL 32720
Mailing Address: PO Box 582, Deleon Springs, FL 32130
Tel: 440-241-3126
E-mail: sizemore3630@aol.com
Web Site: www.a2zpress.com; www.bestlittleonlinebookstore.com
Key Personnel
CEO: Terrie Sizemore
Proofreader/Asst: Holly Westfall
Founded: 2016

Small publishing press that has the vision to receive submissions from writers who have quality titles that meet our submission guidelines but have been rejected by other publishing houses.
ISBN Prefix(es): 978-0-9976407; 978-1-946908
Number of titles published annually: 30 Print; 30 Online; 20 E-Book
Total Titles: 50 Print; 15 E-Book
Distribution Center: Ingram Wholesale

AAAI Press
Imprint of Association for the Advancement of Artificial Intelligence
2275 E Bayshore Rd, Suite 160, Palo Alto, CA 94303
Tel: 650-328-3123 *Fax:* 650-321-4457
E-mail: publications20@aaai.org
Web Site: www.aaai.org/Press/press.php
Key Personnel
Exec Dir: Carol Hamilton
Pubns Dir: David M Hamilton
Ed: Anthony G Cohn
Founded: 1989
Publishing books on all aspects of artificial intelligence.
ISBN Prefix(es): 978-0-929280; 978-1-57735
Number of titles published annually: 30 Print; 4 Online; 40 E-Book
Total Titles: 550 Print; 4 Online; 50 E-Book

AACC International
3340 Pilot Knob Rd, St Paul, MN 55121
Tel: 651-454-7250 *Fax:* 651-454-0766
E-mail: aacc@scisoc.org
Web Site: www.aaccnet.org
Key Personnel
Mktg Coord: Dawn Wuest *E-mail:* dwuest@scisoc.org
Dir, Pubns: Greg Grahek *E-mail:* ggrahek@scisoc.org
Founded: 1920

Source for cereal science information.
ISBN Prefix(es): 978-1-891127; 978-0-9624407
Number of titles published annually: 5 Print; 1 CD-ROM
Total Titles: 100 Print; 1 CD-ROM; 1 Online; 1 E-Book

AACC Press, see AACC International

AAPC Publishing, see Autism Asperger Publishing Co

§AAPG (American Association of Petroleum Geologists)
1444 S Boulder Ave, Tulsa, OK 74119
Mailing Address: PO Box 979, Tulsa, OK 74101-0979
Tel: 918-584-2555 *Toll Free Tel:* 800-364-AAPG (364-2274) *Fax:* 918-580-2665
E-mail: info@aapg.org
Web Site: www.aapg.org
Key Personnel
Mng Ed, Tech Pubns: Beverly Molyneux
    Tel: 918-560-2670 *E-mail:* molyneux@aapg.org
Founded: 1917
Peer-reviewed geological science tomes.
ISBN Prefix(es): 978-0-89181; 978-1-58861
Number of titles published annually: 10 Print; 10 CD-ROM
Total Titles: 100 Print; 80 CD-ROM
Distributed by Affiliated East-West Press Private Ltd; Canadian Society of Petroleum Geologists; Geological Society of London
Distributor for Geological Society of London
Shipping Address: 125 W 15 St, Tulsa, OK 74119

AAVIM, see American Association for Vocational Instructional Materials

Abaris Books
Division of Opal Publishing Corp

70 New Canaan Ave, Norwalk, CT 06850
Tel: 203-838-8402 *Fax:* 203-857-0730
E-mail: abaris@abarisbooks.com
Web Site: abarisbooks.com
Key Personnel
Publr: Anthony S Kaufmann
Mng Ed: J C West *Tel:* 203-838-8625
Founded: 1973
Art, art history, art reference, philosophy & meta-physics.
ISBN Prefix(es): 978-0-913870; 978-0-89835
Number of titles published annually: 7 Print
Total Titles: 185 Print

§Abbeville Press
Imprint of Abbeville Publishing Group
655 Third Ave, New York, NY 10017
Tel: 212-366-5585 *Toll Free Tel:* 800-ART-BOOK (278-2665); 800-343-4499 (orders)
Fax: 646-375-2359 *Toll Free Fax:* 800-351-5073 (orders)
E-mail: abbeville@abbeville.com; sales@abbeville.com; marketing@abbeville.com; rights@abbeville.com
Web Site: www.abbeville.com
Key Personnel
Pres & Publr: Robert E Abrams
Cust Serv Mgr: Nadine Winns
Rts & Perms: David Fabricant
Founded: 1977
Fine arts publisher.
ISBN Prefix(es): 978-0-89659; 978-1-55859; 978-0-7892
Number of titles published annually: 25 Print
Distribution Center: W W Norton & Company Inc, 500 Fifth Ave, New York, NY 10110-0017 *Tel:* 212-354-5500 *Fax:* 212-869-0856 *E-mail:* orders@wwnorton.com *Web Site:* books.wwnorton.com

Abbeville Publishing Group
655 Third Ave, New York, NY 10017
SAN: 211-4755
Tel: 646-375-2136 *Fax:* 646-375-2359
E-mail: abbeville@abbeville.com; marketing@abbeville.com; sales@abbeville.com; rights@abbeville.com
Web Site: www.abbeville.com
Key Personnel
Pres & Publr: Robert E Abrams
Dir, Fin Analysis: John Olivieri
Cust Serv Mgr: Nadine Winns *E-mail:* nwinns@abbeville.com
Rts & Perms: David Fabricant
Founded: 1977
Publishers of high-quality, fine art books, nonfiction illustrated books, children's books, limited editions, prints, gift line.
ISBN Prefix(es): 978-0-89659; 978-1-55859; 978-0-89660; 978-0-7892
Number of titles published annually: 40 Print
Total Titles: 700 Print
Imprints: Abbeville Kids; Abbeville Press; Artabras; Modern Masters
Foreign Rep(s): Book Promotions (Nicky Stubbs) (South Africa); Gilles Fauveau (Japan, Korea); Jaime Gregorio (Philippines); Sharad Mohan (Bangladesh, India, Maldives, Nepal, Pakistan, Sri Lanka); Peribo Pty Ltd (Eddie Coffey) (Australia); Perseus Books Group UK (Europe, Ireland, UK); June Poonpanich (Cambodia, Indonesia, Laos, Thailand, Vietnam); Publishers Group Canada (Canada); Steimatzky (2005) Ltd (Diane Levy) (Israel); Wei Zhao (China, Hong Kong, Taiwan)
Foreign Rights: Bookbank, SA (Latin America, Mexico, Spain); Motovun Tokyo (Japan); Ultreya srl (Italy)
Orders to: Publishers Group Worldwide, 250 W 57 St, 15th fl, New York, NY 10107 *Tel:* 212-581-7839 *E-mail:* intlorders@pgw.com

Warehouse: Client Distribution Services, 193 Edwards Dr, Jackson, TN 38301 *Toll Free Tel:* 800-343-4499 *Toll Free Fax:* 800-351-5073
See separate listing for:
Abbeville Press

§ABC-CLIO
130 Cremona Dr, Santa Barbara, CA 93117
Tel: 805-968-1911 *Toll Free Tel:* 800-368-6868 *Fax:* 805-685-9685 *Toll Free Fax:* 866-270-3856
E-mail: customerservice@abc-clio.com
Web Site: www.abc-clio.com
Key Personnel
CEO: Ronald Boehm
Pres: Becky Snyder
Founded: 1955
A privately held corporation which has for many years enjoyed an international reputation for high quality & innovation. As an educational reference publisher, the company has received critical acclaim for its computer assisted abstracting & indexing services, world renowned book program & cutting-edge online products.
ISBN Prefix(es): 978-0-87436; 978-1-57607
Number of titles published annually: 300 Print; 300 Online; 300 E-Book
Total Titles: 20,000 Print; 15,000 Online; 15,000 E-Book
Imprints: Greenwood Publishing Group; Libraries Unlimited; Praeger
See separate listing for:
Libraries Unlimited

ABDO Publishing Co Inc
Subsidiary of Abdo Consulting Group Inc (ACGI)
8000 W 78 St, Suite 310, Edina, MN 55439
Mailing Address: PO Box 398166, Minneapolis, MN 55439-8166
Tel: 952-698-2403 *Toll Free Tel:* 800-800-1312 *Fax:* 952-831-1632 *Toll Free Fax:* 800-862-3480
E-mail: customerservice@abdopublishing.com; info@abdopublishing.com
Web Site: abdopublishing.com
Key Personnel
CEO: Melody Borth
Pres & Dir: Jill Hansen
Publr: Jim Abdo *E-mail:* jim@abdopublishing.com
VP, Sales & Mktg: Paul Skaj *E-mail:* pskaj@abdopublishing.com
Natl Sales Dir: Monte Kuehl *E-mail:* mkuehl@abdopublishing.com
Mktg & Communs Mgr: BreAnn Rumsch
Ed-in-Chief: Paul Abdo *E-mail:* pabdo@abdopublishing.com
Founded: 1985
Children's PreK-12 educational publishing for school & public libraries.
ISBN Prefix(es): 978-1-56239; 978-1-57765
Number of titles published annually: 350 Print; 350 Online
Total Titles: 3,000 Print; 2,000 Online; 500 E-Book
Imprints: A&D Xtreme (grades 3-9 bold hi-lo nonfiction); Abdo & Daughters (grades 5-9 nonfiction); Abdo Digital (interactive products); Abdo Kids (grades PreK-2 beginning readers); Abdo Kids Jumbo (grades PreK-2 oversized nonfiction); Abdo Kids Junior (grades PreK-2 nonfiction); Abdo Publishing (grades PreK-12 educational nonfiction); Abdo Zoom (engaging nonfiction); Beginning Readers (grades PreK-4 early fiction); Big Buddy Books (grades 2-5 oversized nonfiction); Bolt! (grades 2-8 hi-lo nonfiction); Buddy Books (grades 2-5 nonfiction); Calico (grades 2-5 chapter books); Calico Kid (grades PreK-3 chapter books); Chapter Books (grades K-8 intermediate stories); Checkerboard Library (grades 3-6 curriculum-based nonfiction); Classics (grades 3-8 illustrated literature); Core Library (grades 3-6

Common Core nonfiction); Dash! (grades K-4 leveled readers); EPIC Edge (grades 8+ bold young adult stories); EPIC Escape (grades 6+); EPIC Extreme (grades 10+ intense young adult reading); EPIC Press (hi-lo young adult fiction); Essential Library (grades 6-12 research & reference); Graphic Novels (grades 2-12 comic book stories); Graphic Planet (grades 2-8 graphic novels); Launch! (grades PreK-2 beginning research); Leveled Readers (grades PreK-4 emerging readers); Looking Glass Library (grades PreK-4 picture books); Magic Readers (grades K-3 leveled readers); Magic Wagon (grades PreK-8 illustrated); Marvel Illustrated (grades 2-12); Marvel Picture Books (grades PreK-6 Marvel storytime favorites); Picture Books (grades PreK-6 storytime favorites); Sandcastle (grades PreK-3 beginning nonfiction); Short Tales (grades 1-6 adapted stories); Spellbound (grades 2-8 hi-lo chapter books); SportsZone (grades 2-12); Spotlight (grades PreK-8 popular fiction); Super Sandcastle (grades K-4 oversized early nonfiction)
Distributed by Rockbottom Book Co
Warehouse: 1920 Lookout Dr, North Mankato, MN 56003
Distribution Center: Baker & Taylor Global Publishers Services (GPS), 2550 W Tyvola Rd, Suite 300, Charlotte, NC 28217 (intl mkts worldwide) *Tel:* 704-998-3100 *Toll Free Tel:* 800-775-1800 *E-mail:* gps@baker-taylor.com *Web Site:* www.baker-taylor.com

§Abingdon Press
Imprint of The United Methodist Publishing House
2222 Rosa L Parks Blvd, Nashville, TN 37228
SAN: 201-0046
Mailing Address: PO Box 280988, Nashville, TN 37228-0988
Tel: 615-749-6000 (academic books) *Toll Free Tel:* 800-251-3320 (orders) *Fax:* 615-749-6056 (academic books) *Toll Free Fax:* 800-836-7802 (orders)
E-mail: orders@abingdonpress.com; permissions@abingdonpress.com
Web Site: www.abingdonpress.com
Key Personnel
Pres & Publr: Brian Milford
Exec Dir, Mktg: Tamara Crabtree *E-mail:* tcrabtree@umpublishing.org
Dir, Trade Sales: Robin Glennon *E-mail:* rglennon@abingdonpress.com
Assoc Publr & Ed-in-Chief: Mary Catherine Dean *E-mail:* mdean@umpublishing.org
Founded: 1789
Religion/ecumenical Christianity; general interest, children's, family, church professional, academic, reference, lay spiritual; United Methodist history, doctrine, polity.
ISBN Prefix(es): 978-0-687; 978-1-4267; 978-1-63088; 978-1-5018
Number of titles published annually: 175 Print
Total Titles: 270 Print; 10 CD-ROM; 3 Online
Imprints: Upper Room Books
Distributor for Church Publishing Inc; Judson Press; Upper Room Books
Foreign Rep(s): Canaanland Distributors (Malaysia); CLC Wholesale (UK); KCBS (Korea); MediaCom Education Inc (Australia); Parasource Marketing & Distribution (Canada); SKS Books (Singapore)
Foreign Rights: Riggins International Rights Services
Returns: 700 Airtech Pkwy, Plainfield, IL 46168

Harry N Abrams Inc
Subsidiary of La Martiniere Groupe
195 Broadway, 9th fl, New York, NY 10007
SAN: 200-2434
Tel: 212-206-7715 *Toll Free Tel:* 800-345-1359 *Fax:* 212-519-1210
E-mail: abrams@abramsbooks.com

Web Site: www.abramsbooks.com
Key Personnel
Pres & CEO: Michael Jacobs
SVP & COO: Michelle R Ferguson
SVP & Publr, Children's Books: Andrew Smith
SVP, Intl Sales: Mary Wowk
SVP, Mktg & Publicity: Melanie Chang
SVP, Strategic Devt & Busn Analytics: Steve Tager
VP & CFO: Thomas Moloney
VP, Publg Opers: Anet Sirna-Bruder
VP, Publr, Adult Trade: Michael Sand
VP, Ed-in-Chief, Adult Trade: Eric Himmel
VP, Sales, North America: Elisa Gonzalez
VP, Subs Rts & Export Sales: Yulia Borodyanskaya
Assoc Publr, Abrams Plus, Digital Publg: Lindy Humphreys
Assoc Publr, Adult Trade: Shawna Mullen
Assoc Publr, Children's Books: Jody Mosley
Exec Dir, Adult Trade Publicity: Jennifer Brunn
Exec Dir, Natl Accts: Mark Harrington
Exec Dir, Spec Mkts & Natl Accts: Monica Shah
Sr Dir, Mktg, Adult Books: Jessica Wiener
Sr Dir, Mktg, Children's Books: Kim Lauber
Art Dir, Children's Books & ComicArts: Pam Notarantonio
Contracts Dir: Peggy Garry
Dir, Children's Publicity: Hallie Patterson
Dir, Franchise Mktg, Children's Books: Elizabeth Fithian
Dir, Mng Edit, Adult Trade: Mary O'Mara
Dir, Online Mktg Opers: Chris Blank
Edit Dir, Abrams Press: Jamison Stoltz
Edit Dir, Calendars: Miriam Tribble
Edit Dir, Children's Fiction: Maggie Lehrman
Edit Dir, ComicArts: Charles Kochman
Edit Dir, Food & Drink/Exec Ed, Adult Trade: Holly Dolce
Edit Dir, Noterie: Karrie Witkin
Edit Dir, PreK, Abrams Children's: Meredith Mundy
Natl Accts Dir: Stefanie Lindner; Andy Weiner
Assoc Art Dir, Calendars & Children's Licensing: John Passineau
Assoc Art Dir, Children's Books & ComicArts: Brenda Angelilli
Assoc Dir, Spec Sales: Nadine Sferratore
Ed-in-Chief: Rebecca Kaplan
Exec Ed, Adult Trade: David Cashion
Exec Ed, Amulet/Abrams Children's: Anne Heltzel
Sr Mng Ed, Children's Books: Amy Vreeland
Sr Ed, Adult Trade: Laura Dozier; Eric Klopfer
Sr Ed, Amulet/Abrams Children's: Erica Finkel
Sr Ed, Children's Entertainment & Licensed Publg: Russell Busse
Assoc Mng Ed, Children's: Megan Carlson
Ed, Children's: Courtney Code
Assoc Ed, Adult Books: Shannon Kelly
Asst Ed, Amulet/Abrams Children's: Emily Daluga
Ed-at-Large, Children's Books: Howard Reeves
Sr Mgr, Digital & Soc Media Mktg, Children's Books: Trish McNamara O'Neill
Sr Mgr, Mktg, Adult Books: Kim Lew
Sr Mgr, Spec Sales: Wayne Gurreri
Sr Subs Rts Mgr: Karin Schulze
Mgr, Corp Events & Exec Asst to CEO: Merle Brown
Mktg Mgr: Borana Greku
Publicity Mgr, Children's: Brooke Shearouse
Subs Rts Mgr: Talia Behrend-Wilcox
Trade Sales Mgr: Kay Makanju
Mktg Coord: Natali Cavanagh; Megan Evans
Sales Coord, Spec Sales: Shelby Ozer
Mktg & Publicity Asst: Gabriella Paez
Sr Designer: Heather Kelly
Sr Marketing Designer, Children's: Lora Grisafi
Designer, Children's Books & ComicArts: Steph Stillwell
Asst Designer: Max Temescu
Jr Designer, Children's: Megan Kelchner
Publicist, Adult: Andrew Gibeley

Publicist, Children's: Mary Marolla
Founded: 1949
Art & architecture, photography, natural sciences, performing arts & children's books, gifts, calendars & stationary.
ISBN Prefix(es): 978-0-8109
Number of titles published annually: 300 Print
Total Titles: 2,600 Print
Imprints: Abrams Appleseed; Abrams Books; Abrams Books for Young Readers; Abrams ComicArts; Abrams Image; Abrams Noterie; Abrams Plus (ebooks); Abrams Press; Amulet Books; The Overlook Press
Distributed by Abrams & Chronicle Books (Great Britain); Editions Alain
Distributor for Booth-Clibborn Editions; Cameron + Company Inc; Cernunnos; Editions Alain Ducasse; 5 Continents Editions; Getty Publications; Lucky Spool Media (Australia, New Zealand & North America); Museum of Modern Art Children's Books; SelfMadeHero; Tate Publishing; V&A Publishing; The Vendome Press
Foreign Rep(s): Canadian Manda Group
Orders to: Hachette Book Group (North America) *Toll Free Tel:* 800-759-0190 *Toll Free Fax:* 800-286-9471; Hachette UK Distribution Limited, Hely Hutchinson Centre, Milton Rd, Didcot, Oxon OX11 7HH, United Kingdom (UK, Africa, Asia, Europe & Middle East) *Tel:* (01235) 759500 *E-mail:* enquiries@hachette.co.uk *Web Site:* www.hachetteukdistribution.co.uk
Distribution Center: Baker & Taylor Global Publishers Services (GPS), 2550 W Tyvola Rd, Suite 300, Charlotte, NC 28217 (Asia (exc India), Caribbean & Latin America) *Tel:* 704-998-3100 *Toll Free Tel:* 800-775-1800 *E-mail:* gps@baker-taylor.com *Web Site:* www.baker-taylor.com
Hachette UK Distribution Limited, Hely Hutchinson Centre, Milton Rd, Didcot, Oxon OX11 7HH, United Kingdom (UK, Africa, Asia, Europe & Middle East) *Tel:* (01235) 759500 *E-mail:* enquiries@hachette.co.uk *Web Site:* www.hachetteukdistribution.co.uk
Membership(s): Association of American Publishers (AAP)
See separate listing for:
The Overlook Press
Stewart, Tabori & Chang

§Abrams Learning Trends
Subsidiary of Learning Trends LLC
16310 Bratton Lane, Suite 250, Austin, TX 78728-2403
Toll Free Tel: 800-227-9120 *Toll Free Fax:* 800-737-3322
E-mail: customerservice@abramslearningtrends.com (orders, cust serv); contactus@abramslearningtrends.com
Web Site: www.abramslearningtrends.com (orders, cust serv)
Key Personnel
Pres & CEO: Aaron Mayers
EVP & Publr: Tina Posner
EVP & Gen Mgr: William Thomas
EVP, Sales & Mktg: Erin King
VP, Sales: Bruce Warren
Founded: 2008
PreK-5 educational materials.
ISBN Prefix(es): 978-0-7665; 978-0-7664
Number of titles published annually: 100 Print; 6 CD-ROM; 15 Audio
Total Titles: 1,000 Print; 36 CD-ROM; 36 Audio
Imprints: The Letter People®
Distributor for General Education Services (New Zealand)

§Academic Press
Imprint of Elsevier BV
50 Hampshire St, 5th fl, Cambridge, MA 02139
Tel: 781-663-5200 *Fax:* 937-247-0808

Web Site: www.elsevier.com/books-and-journals/academic-press
Founded: 1942
Scientific, technical & professional information in multiple media formats.
ISBN Prefix(es): 978-0-12
Number of titles published annually: 375 Print; 25 E-Book
Total Titles: 4,700 Print; 200 E-Book

Academica Press
1727 Massachusetts Ave NW, Suite 507, Washington, DC 20036
Tel: 978-829-2577
E-mail: editorial@academicapress.com
Web Site: www.academicapress.com
Key Personnel
Publr & Dir: Dr Paul du Quenoy
Founded: 2002
Publish scholarly research, monographs & collections in humanities, social sciences, education & law.
ISBN Prefix(es): 978-1-933146; 978-1-930901
Number of titles published annually: 40 Print
Total Titles: 250 Print; 50 Online
Imprints: Maunsel & Co Publishers (Dublin); W B Sheridan (law books)
Foreign Rep(s): Eurospan Group (London) (Europe, Middle East, UK)
Orders to: PSSC, 46 Development Rd, Fitchburg, MA 01420, Contact: Erika Wilson *Tel:* 978-345-2121 *E-mail:* ewilson@pssc.com
Returns: Books International Inc, 22883 Quicksilver Dr, Dulles, VA 20166 *Tel:* 703-661-1500 *Fax:* 703-661-1501 *E-mail:* todd@booksintl.com
Shipping Address: PSSC, 46 Development Rd, Fitchburg, MA 01420, Contact: Erika Wilson *Tel:* 978-345-2121 *E-mail:* ewilson@pssc.com
Warehouse: PSSC, 46 Development Rd, Fitchburg, MA 01420, Contact: Erika Wilson *Tel:* 978-345-2121 *E-mail:* ewilson@pssc.com
Distribution Center: PSSC, 46 Development Rd, Fitchburg, MA 01420, Contact: Erika Wilson *Tel:* 978-345-2121 *E-mail:* ewilson@pssc.com
Membership(s): American Conference on Irish Studies (ACIS)

Academy Chicago
Imprint of Chicago Review Press
814 N Franklin St, Chicago, IL 60610
Tel: 312-337-0747 *Toll Free Tel:* 800-888-4741 (orders) *Fax:* 312-337-5110
E-mail: frontdesk@chicagoreviewpress.com
Web Site: www.chicagoreviewpress.com
Key Personnel
Acqs Ed: Cynthia Sherry *E-mail:* csherry@chicagoreviewpress.com
Founded: 1975
Fiction, nonfiction, history, mysteries, women's studies; emphasis on neglected classics & books for women.
ISBN Prefix(es): 978-0-915864; 978-0-89733
Number of titles published annually: 12 Print
Total Titles: 367 Print
Distribution Center: Independent Publishers Group, 814 N Franklin St, Chicago, IL 60610 *Tel:* 312-337-0747 *Toll Free Tel:* 800-888-4741 (orders) *Fax:* 312-337-5985

The Academy of Northwest Writers & Publishers, see Lost Horse Press

Academy of Nutrition & Dietetics
120 S Riverside Plaza, Suite 2190, Chicago, IL 60606-6995
Tel: 312-899-0040 (ext 5000) *Toll Free Tel:* 800-877-1600
E-mail: sales@eatright.org
Web Site: www.eatright.org
Key Personnel
Dir, Prodn: Erin Faley
Dir, Pubns: Ryan Baechler

Founded: 1917
Information on food, nutrition & fitness for dieticians & other allied health professionals.
ISBN Prefix(es): 978-0-88091; 978-0-9837255 (Eat Right Press)
Number of titles published annually: 12 Print; 4 Online
Total Titles: 70 Print
Branch Office(s)
1120 Connecticut Ave NW, Suite 460, Washington, DC 20036 *Tel:* 202-775-8277 *Toll Free Tel:* 800-877-0877
Distributed by Small Press United (Eat Right Press)

ACC Art Books
Division of ACC Art Books (England)
6 W 18 St, Suite 4B, New York, NY 10011
Tel: 212-645-1111 *Toll Free Tel:* 800-252-5231
Fax: 212-989-3205
E-mail: ussales@accpublishinggroup.com
Web Site: www.accartbooks.com/us/
Founded: 1966
Books on fine & decorative arts, gardening, architecture & antiques, multicultural.
ISBN Prefix(es): 978-1-85149; 978-0-907462; 978-0-902028
Number of titles published annually: 300 Print
Total Titles: 1,500 Print
Imprints: ACC Editions; Garden Art Press
Divisions: ACC Distribution
Foreign Office(s): Sandy Lane, Old Martlesham, Woodbridge, Suffolk 1P12 4SD, United Kingdom *Tel:* (01394) 389950 *Fax:* (01394) 389999 *E-mail:* sales@antique-acc.com *Web Site:* www.antiquecollectorsclub.com
Foreign Rep(s): Jenny Gosling (Belgium, London, Luxembourg, Netherlands); Lilian Koe (Malaysia); Clive & Moira Malins (Northeast England, Scotland); Michael Morris (Middle East, Near East); Penny Padovani (Italy, Portugal, Spain); David Pearson (France); Ian Pringle (Brunei, Indonesia, Singapore, Thailand); Ed Summerson (China, Hong Kong, Philippines, South Korea, Taiwan); Ralph & Sheila Sumners (Japan); Robert Towers (Ireland, Northern Ireland)

§Accuity
Division of Reed Business Information Ltd
1007 Church St, 6th fl, Evanston, IL 60201
Tel: 847-676-9600 *Toll Free Tel:* 800-321-3373
Fax: 847-933-8101
E-mail: customerservice@accuity.com
Web Site: www.accuity.com
Key Personnel
Pres & CEO: Hugh Jones
EVP: Brent Newman
Sr Dir, HR: Patty Pickett
Head, Communs: Heather Smith *E-mail:* heather.smith@accuity.com
Founded: 1876
Leading worldwide provider of information on depository financial institutions throughout the world. Specialize in Internet references/directories; software; databases.
ISBN Prefix(es): 978-1-56310
Number of titles published annually: 30 Print; 1 CD-ROM; 2 E-Book
Total Titles: 30 Print; 4 CD-ROM; 3 E-Book
Foreign Office(s): Level 10, 10 Help St, Chatswood, NSW 2067, Australia *Tel:* (02) 8006 0584 *E-mail:* asiasales@accuity.com
Digital China Centre, 5F Unit A, No 567 Tianshan W Rd, Changning District, Shanghai 200335, China *Tel:* (021) 6010 7250 *Fax:* (021) 6010 7249 *E-mail:* asiasales@accuity.com
Rm 1204-6, Tai Tung Bldg, 8 Fleming Rd, Wanchai, Hong Kong *Tel:* 2280 9572 *Fax:* 2813 6357 *E-mail:* asiasales@accuity.com
Chennai Ragus Citi Centre, Off No 664, Level 6, 10/11, Dr Radhakrishnan, Salai Mylapore,

Chennai 600 004, India *Tel:* (044) 4221 8530
E-mail: asiasales@accuity.com
Phoenix Paragon Plaza, 3rd fl, LBS Marg, Kurla W, Mumbai 400 070, India *Tel:* (022) 6229 2828 *E-mail:* asiasales@accuity.com
1-9-15 Higashi-Azabu, 6F, One Cho-me Bldg, Minato-ku, Tokyo 106-0044, Japan *Tel:* (03) 5561 5363 *Fax:* (065) 6544 1171 *E-mail:* asiasales@accuity.com *Web Site:* www.accuity.co.jp
Killiney Rd, No 08-01, Winsland House 1, Singapore 239519, Singapore *Tel:* 6780 4814 *Fax:* 6544 1171 *E-mail:* asiasales@accuity.com
Proctor House, 110 High Hilborn, London WC1V 6EU, United Kingdom *Tel:* (020) 7653 3800 *Fax:* (020) 7653 3828 *E-mail:* sales@accuity.com

Acres USA
Division of Acres USA Inc
501 Eighth Ave, Greenley, CO 80631
Mailing Address: PO Box 1690, Greeley, CO 80632-1690
Tel: 512-892-4400 *Toll Free Tel:* 800-355-5313
E-mail: orders@acresusa.com; editor@acresusa.com; info@acresusa.com
Web Site: www.acresusa.com
Founded: 1970
Books & a monthly periodical on organic & sustainable agriculture.
ISBN Prefix(es): 978-0-911311; 978-1-60173
Number of titles published annually: 6 Print; 10 Audio
Total Titles: 100 Print; 100 Audio

ACTA Publications
4848 N Clark St, Chicago, IL 60640
Toll Free Tel: 800-397-2282
E-mail: actapublications@actapublications.com
Web Site: www.actapublications.com
Key Personnel
Pres & Publr: Gregory Pierce
Founded: 1957
ACTA stands for "A Commitment to All." Books & media that are "gifts that compel" on a variety of topics.
ISBN Prefix(es): 978-0-87946; 978-0-914070; 978-0-915388
Number of titles published annually: 10 Print; 5 E-Book; 1 Audio
Total Titles: 300 Print; 25 E-Book; 10 Audio
Imprints: ACTA Sports; In Extenso Press
Distributor for Grief Watch; Pilgrim's Guide Books; Veritas
Foreign Rep(s): John Garratt Publishing (Australia); Veritas (Ireland, UK)
Membership(s): Association of Catholic Publishers Inc; Independent Book Publishers Association (IBPA)

ACU Press
Affiliate of Abilene Christian University
1648 Campus Ct, Abilene, TX 79601
SAN: 207-1681
Tel: 325-674-2720 *Toll Free Tel:* 877-816-4455
Web Site: www.acupressbooks.com; www.leafwoodpublishers.com
Key Personnel
Dir, Opers: Duane Anderson
Founded: 1984
Religion & ethics.
ISBN Prefix(es): 978-0-915547; 978-0-89112
Number of titles published annually: 35 Print; 30 E-Book
Total Titles: 480 Print; 170 E-Book
Imprints: Leafwood Publishers (Christian trade imprint)

Adams & Ambrose Publishing
PO Box 259684, Madison, WI 53725-9684
SAN: 655-5624
Tel: 608-977-1825

E-mail: info@adamsambrose.com
Key Personnel
Mktg Dir & Intl Rts: Joyce Harrington *E-mail:* jharrington@adamsambrose.com
Sr Ed: Jill Robinson Wren *E-mail:* jrwren@adamsambrose.com
Edit: Roger B Oakes *E-mail:* rboakes@adamsambrose.com
Founded: 1983
Publication of nonfiction books. Specialize in academic, professional & how-to books.
ISBN Prefix(es): 978-0-916951
Number of titles published annually: 6 Print
Total Titles: 6 Print
Returns: c/o United Parcel Service, 8350 Murphy Dr, Middleton, WI 53562 (hold for pick up)

§Adams Media
Imprint of Simon & Schuster
57 Littlefield St, Avon, MA 02322
Tel: 508-427-7100
Web Site: www.simonandschuster.com
Key Personnel
VP & Publr: Karen Cooper
Mktg & Publicity Dir: Beth Gissinger-Rivera
Ed-in-Chief: Brendan O'Neill
Dir of Mng Edit: Meredith O'Hayre
Sr Content Ed: Lisa Laing
Assoc Publr: Stephanie McKenna
Sr Devt Mgr: Katherine Corcoran-Lytle
Sr Ed: Jacqueline Musser; Cate Prato; Laura Daly; Brett Palana-Shanahan
Ed: Rebecca Tarr Thomas; Eileen Mullan; Julia Jacques; Peter Archer
Assoc Devt Ed: Sarah Doughty
Assoc Ed: Rachael Thatcher
Edit Asst: Leah D'Sa
Mgr, Publicity: Sarah Armour
Publicist: Mary Kate Schulte
Creative Dir & Design Mgr: Frank Rivera
Natl Sales Dir: Janice Fryer
Founded: 1980
General nonfiction publisher, with emphasis on business, self-help, careers, health, New Age, cooking, parenting, reference, & relationships.
ISBN Prefix(es): 978-0-937860; 978-1-55850; 978-1-58062; 978-1-59337; 978-1-59869; 978-1-60550; 978-1-4405; 978-1-5072
Number of titles published annually: 125 Print; 110 E-Book
Total Titles: 1,200 Print; 20 CD-ROM; 1,100 E-Book
Imprints: Adams Business (busn); Everything (series)
Foreign Rights: Bardon-Chinese Media Agency (China, Hong Kong, Taiwan); Julio F-Yanez Agencia Literaria SL (Spain); Graal Literary Agency (Poland); Imprima Korea Agency (Korea); Japan UNI Agency (Japan); Alexander Korzhenevski Agency (Russia); Michael Meller Literary Agency GmbH (Germany); Silkroad Publishers Agency (Jane Vejjajiva) (Thailand)

Addicus Books Inc
PO Box 45327, Omaha, NE 68145
Tel: 402-330-7493 *Fax:* 402-330-1707
E-mail: info@addicusbooks.com; addicusbks@aol.com
Web Site: www.addicusbooks.com
Key Personnel
Publr: Rod Colvin *E-mail:* rod@addicusbooks.com
Assoc Publr: Jack Kusler *E-mail:* jackaddicusbks@aol.com
Founded: 1994
Independent press, publishing high-quality trade paperbacks. Submissions by mail only, no phone inquiries.
ISBN Prefix(es): 978-1-886039; 978-1-936374; 978-1-938803; 978-1-940495
Number of titles published annually: 9 Print; 10 E-Book
Total Titles: 200 Print; 200 Online; 185 E-Book

Billing Address: IPG Books, 814 Franklin St, Chicago, IL 60610 *Tel:* 312-337-0747 *Toll Free Tel:* 800-888-4741 *Fax:* 312-337-5985 *Web Site:* ipgbook.com
Returns: IPG Warehouse, 600 N Pulaski, Chicago, IL 60624, Contact: Tom Greene
Warehouse: IPG Warehouse, 600 N Pulaski, Chicago, IL 60624, Contact: Tom Greene
Distribution Center: IPG Books, 814 Franklin St, Chicago, IL 60610 *Tel:* 312-337-0747 *Toll Free Tel:* 800-888-4741 *Fax:* 312-337-5985 *Web Site:* ipgbook.com
Membership(s): Association of American Publishers (AAP); The Imaging Alliance; Independent Book Publishers Association (IBPA); National Association of Independent Publishers (NAIP)

Adirondack Mountain Club (ADK)
814 Goggins Rd, Lake George, NY 12845-4117
SAN: 204-7691
Tel: 518-668-4447 *Toll Free Tel:* 800-395-8080 *Fax:* 518-668-3746
E-mail: info@adk.org
Web Site: www.adk.org
Key Personnel
Pres: John Gilewicz
VP: Robert Manning
Exec Dir: Neil Woodworth *Tel:* 518-449-3870 *Fax:* 518-669-0128
Founded: 1922
Wall calendar; trade, hiking, canoeing, skiing & climbing guidebooks & maps for New York State; natural history field guides; cultural & literary works on the Adirondacks, members journals, *Adirondac.*
ISBN Prefix(es): 978-0-935272; 978-1-931951; 978-0-9896073
Number of titles published annually: 4 Print
Total Titles: 39 Print

Advance Publishing Inc
6950 Fulton St, Houston, TX 77022
SAN: 263-9572
Tel: 713-695-0600 *Toll Free Tel:* 800-917-9630 *Fax:* 713-695-8585
E-mail: info@advancepublishing.com
Web Site: www.advancepublishing.com
Key Personnel
VP: John Sommer
Founded: 1984
Publish children's picture books, junior biographies & general nonfiction, technical books & current events.
ISBN Prefix(es): 978-1-57537; 978-0-9610810
Number of titles published annually: 20 Print
Total Titles: 150 Print; 72 CD-ROM; 75 Online
Imprints: Another Great Achiever Series (biographies of men & women of inspiring accomplishment); Number Success (online video practical mathematics program for adult & children); Phonics Adventure (motivational phonics literature-based children's reading program); Quest for Success (short stories for upper elementary & reluctant middle & high school readers); Reading Success (adult intensive phonics literature-based reading program); Sommer-Time Story Classics Series (inspirational picture books with a fun & modern take on timeless folktales & fables); Sommer-Time Story Series (character-building books for children)
Membership(s): The Children's Book Council (CBC); Independent Book Publishers Association (IBPA)

Adventure House
914 Laredo Rd, Silver Spring, MD 20901
Tel: 301-754-1589
Web Site: www.adventurehouse.com
Key Personnel
Publr & Ed: John P Gunnison *E-mail:* gunnison@adventurehouse.com

Founded: 1985
Special reprints; fiction from the pulp fiction era.
ISBN Prefix(es): 978-1-886937; 978-1-59798
Number of titles published annually: 60 Print
Total Titles: 300 Print

AdventureKEEN
2204 First Ave S, Suite 102, Birmingham, AL 35233
SAN: 212-7199
Tel: 763-689-9800 *Toll Free Tel:* 800-678-7006 *Fax:* 763-689-9039 *Toll Free Fax:* 877-374-9016
E-mail: info@adventurewithkeen.com
Web Site: adventurewithkeen.com
Key Personnel
Owner & Publr: Robert W Sehlinger
COO: Molly Merkle
Pres: Richard Hunt
Dir, Mktg & PR: Liliane Opsomer *E-mail:* liliane@adventurewithkeen.com
Sales Mgr: Meredith Hutchins
Founded: 1988
General trade & regional.
ISBN Prefix(es): 978-0-934860; 978-1-885061; 978-1-59193
Number of titles published annually: 30 Print
Total Titles: 435 Print; 12 CD-ROM
Imprints: Adventure Publications; Clerisy Press; Menasha Ridge Press; Nature Study Guides; Unofficial Guides; Wilderness Press
Distributor for Blacklock Nature Photography; Kollath-Stensaas; Nodin Press; Pocket Guides Publishing
Distribution Center: Ingram Content Group LLC, One Ingram Blvd, La Vergne, TN 37086 *Tel:* 615-793-5000
See separate listing for:
Clerisy Press

§Adventures Unlimited Press (AUP)
One Adventure Place, Kempton, IL 60946
Mailing Address: PO Box 74, Kempton, IL 60946-0074
Tel: 815-253-6390 *Fax:* 815-253-6300
E-mail: info@adventuresunlimitedpress.com
Web Site: www.adventuresunlimitedpress.com
Key Personnel
Pres & Intl Rts Contact: David H Childress
Mng Dir: Jennifer Bolm
Founded: 1983
Eclectic variety of books on mysteries of the past, alternative technologies & conspiracy theories.
ISBN Prefix(es): 978-0-932813; 978-1-931882; 978-1-935487; 978-1-939149
Number of titles published annually: 11 Print
Total Titles: 215 Print
Distributor for Eagle Wing Books; EDFU Books; Yelsraek Publishing
Foreign Rep(s): Brumby Books (Australia); Speaking Tree (UK)
Foreign Rights: Il Caduceo (Italy)

The AEI Press
Division of American Enterprise Institute
1789 Massachusetts Ave NW, Washington, DC 20036
SAN: 202-4527
Tel: 202-862-5800 *Fax:* 202-862-7177
Web Site: www.aei.org
Key Personnel
Co-Chmn of the Bd: Tully M Friedman
Pres: Arthur Brooks
Founded: 1943
Public policy economics, foreign affairs & defense, government & politics, law; research on education, energy, government regulation & tax policy.
ISBN Prefix(es): 978-0-8447
Number of titles published annually: 15 Print
Total Titles: 300 Print
Distributed by MIT (selected titles)

Foreign Rep(s): Europspan
Orders to: c/o National Book Network, 4501 Forbes Blvd, Suite 200, Lantham, MD 20706 *Toll Free Tel:* 800-462-6420 *Toll Free Fax:* 800-338-4550 *E-mail:* custserv@nbnbooks.com

§AFB Press
Imprint of American Foundation for the Blind (AFB)
1401 S Clark St, Suite 730, Arlington, VA 22202
Tel: 304-710-3043 *Toll Free Tel:* 800-232-3044 (orders) *Fax:* 917-210-3979 (orders)
E-mail: afbpress@afb.net
Web Site: www.afb.org
Key Personnel
Dir, AFB Press & Prof Devt: George Abbott
Rts & Admin Dir: Jenese Griffiths
Mgr, Fulfillment & Cust Serv: Heather Spence *Tel:* 304-710-3027 *E-mail:* hspence@afb.net
Founded: 1921
Text & professional books in the fields of visual impairment & blindness.
ISBN Prefix(es): 978-0-89128; 978-1-68413
Number of titles published annually: 4 Print; 4 Online
Total Titles: 100 Print; 70 Online
Branch Office(s)
AFB Atlanta, 739 W Peachtree St NW, Suite 250, Atlanta, GA 30308 *Tel:* 404-525-2303 *Fax:* 646-478-9260 *E-mail:* literacy@afb.net
AFB Center on Vision Loss, 11030 Ables Lane, Dallas, TX 75229 *Tel:* 214-352-7222 *Fax:* 646-478-9260 *E-mail:* dallas@afb.net
AFB Huntington, 1000 Fifth Ave, Suite 350, Huntington, WV 25701 *Tel:* 304-523-8651 *Fax:* 646-478-9260
Membership(s): Association of American Publishers (AAP)

Africa World Press Inc
541 W Ingham Ave, Suite B, Trenton, NJ 08638
Tel: 609-695-3200 *Fax:* 609-695-6466
E-mail: customerservice@africaworldpressbooks.com
Web Site: www.africaworldpressbooks.com
Key Personnel
Owner: Kassahun Checole *E-mail:* kchecole@awprsp.com
Founded: 1983
Research on Latin America, the Caribbean, Africa, Afrocentric children's books.
ISBN Prefix(es): 978-0-86543; 978-1-59221
Number of titles published annually: 100 Print
Total Titles: 2,350 Print; 10 Online; 10 E-Book
Foreign Rights: Turnaround Publisher Services Ltd (Europe, London)

§African American Images
PO Box 1799, Chicago Heights, IL 60412
Tel: 708-672-4909 (cust serv) *Fax:* 708-672-0466
E-mail: customersvc@africanamericanimages.com
Web Site: www.africanamericanimages.com
Key Personnel
Pres & Intl Rts: Dr Jawanza Kunjufu, PhD
Founded: 1983
Publish & distribute books of an Africentric nature that promote self-esteem, collective values, liberation & skill development.
ISBN Prefix(es): 978-0-913543; 978-0-9749000; 978-1-934155
Number of titles published annually: 8 Print
Total Titles: 130 Print; 2 CD-ROM

AGU, see American Geophysical Union (AGU)

Ahsahta Press
Boise State University, Mail Stop 1580, 1910 University Dr, Boise, ID 83725-1580
Tel: 208-519-6726
E-mail: ahsahta@boisestate.edu
Web Site: ahsahtapress.org

Key Personnel
Dir & Ed: Prof Janet Holmes *E-mail:* jholmes@
   boisestate.edu
Founded: 1974
Trade paperback books. Specialize in American
   poetry. Accept editorial submissions through
   our submissions manager.
ISBN Prefix(es): 978-0-916272; 978-1-934103
Number of titles published annually: 8 Print
Total Titles: 118 Print; 47 Online; 2 E-Book
Orders to: Small Press Distribution, 1341 Seventh
   St, Berkeley, CA 94710-1409, Contact: Nicole
   Trigg *Tel:* 510-524-1668 *Toll Free Tel:* 800-
   869-7553 *Fax:* 510-524-0852 *E-mail:* spd@
   spdbooks.org *Web Site:* www.spdbooks.org
Membership(s): Community of Literary Maga-
   zines & Presses (CLMP)

§AICPA Professional Publications
Subsidiary of American Institute of Certified Pub-
   lic Accountants
220 Leigh Farm Rd, Durham, NC 27707
SAN: 202-4578
Tel: 919-402-4500 *Toll Free Tel:* 888-777-
   7077 (memb serv ctr) *Fax:* 919-402-4505
   Toll Free Fax: 800-362-5066 (memb serv ctr)
E-mail: acquisitions@aicpa.org; service@aicpa.
   org
Web Site: www.aicpa.org
Key Personnel
Pres & CEO: Barry C Melancon
   E-mail: bmelancon@aicpa.org
Founded: 1959
Technical guidance for accountants & auditors,
   books on practice management & specialized
   topics, research & practice development tools,
   magazines, newsletters, online & downloadable
   products.
ISBN Prefix(es): 978-0-87051; 978-1-937350;
   978-1-937351; 978-1-937352; 978-1-940235;
   978-1-941651
Number of titles published annually: 150 Print;
   10 CD-ROM; 20 Online; 100 E-Book
Total Titles: 600 Print; 20 CD-ROM; 50 Online;
   200 E-Book
Branch Office(s)
1455 Pennsylvania Ave NW, Washington, DC
   20004-1081 *Tel:* 202-737-6600 *Fax:* 202-638-
   4512
Princeton South Corporate Ctr, Suite 200, 100
   Princeton S, Ewing, NJ 08628 *Tel:* 609-671-
   2902 *Fax:* 609-671-2922
1211 Avenue of the Americas, New York, NY
   10036-8775 *Tel:* 212-596-6200 *Fax:* 212-596-
   6213
Distributed by Practitioners Publishing Co; Thomson Reuters
Distributor for Wiley
Membership(s): Association for Talent Development (ATD); EBSCO; ISO

AIP Publishing, see American Institute of
   Physics

AK Press Distribution
Subsidiary of AK Press Inc
370 Ryan Ave, Unit 100, Chico, CA 95973
Tel: 510-208-1700 *Fax:* 510-208-1701
E-mail: info@akpress.org
Web Site: www.akpress.org
Key Personnel
Ed: Charles Weigl
Founded: 1990
Specialize in publishing & distribution of radical
   & small press nonfiction.
ISBN Prefix(es): 978-1-873176; 978-1-902593;
   978-1-904859
Number of titles published annually: 20 Print
Total Titles: 500 Print
Distributor for Arbeiter Ring; Autonomedia;
   Crimethinc; Freedom Press; Charles H Kerr;
   Kersplebedelo

Akashic Books
232 Third St, Suite A-115, Brooklyn, NY 11215
Tel: 718-643-9193 *Fax:* 718-643-9195
E-mail: info@akashicbooks.com
Web Site: www.akashicbooks.com
Key Personnel
Publr & Ed-in-Chief: Johnny Temple
Mng Ed & Dir, Foreign Rts: Johanna Ingalls
Dir, Publicity & Soc Media: Susannah Lawrence
Edit Dir: Ibrahim Ahmad
Prodn Mgr, Ebook Developer & Assoc Ed: Aaron
   Petrovich
Publicity Asst: Alice Wertheimer
Founded: 1997
Specialize in urban literary fiction & political
   nonfiction.
ISBN Prefix(es): 978-1-888451; 978-0-9719206;
   978-1-933354; 978-1-936070; 978-1-61775
Number of titles published annually: 35 Print; 35
   E-Book
Total Titles: 500 Print; 500 E-Book
Imprints: Black Sheep Books for Young Readers;
   Edge of Sports (Dave Zirin's imprint); Gra-
   cie Belle (Ann Hood's imprint); Kaylie Jones
   Books; Open Lens
Orders to: Consortium Book Sales & Distri-
   bution, The Keg House, Suite 101, 34 13
   Ave NE, Minneapolis, MN 55413 *Toll Free
   Tel:* 866-400-5351 *E-mail:* ips@ingramcontent.
   com *Web Site:* www.cbsd.com SAN: 200-6049
Returns: Consortium Book Sales & Distribu-
   tion, c/o Ingram Publishing Services, 1210
   Ingram Dr, Chambersburg, PA 17202 (return
   address for orders from Jackson, TN) *Toll Free
   Tel:* 866-400-5351 *E-mail:* ips@ingramcontent.
   com *Web Site:* www.cbsd.com SAN: 200-6049
Warehouse: Consortium Book Sales & Dis-
   tribution, c/o Ingram Publishing Services,
   210 American Dr, Jackson, TN 38301 *Toll
   Free Tel:* 866-400-5351 *Fax:* 731-424-
   0988 *E-mail:* ips@ingramcontent.com *Web
   Site:* www.cbsd.com SAN: 200-6049
Distribution Center: Consortium Book Sales &
   Distribution, The Keg House, Suite 101, 34 13
   Ave NE, Minneapolis, MN 55413 *Tel:* 612-
   746-2600 *Fax:* 612-746-2606 *E-mail:* info@
   cbsd.com *Web Site:* www.cbsd.com SAN: 200-
   6049

ALA, see The American Library Association
   (ALA)

§ALA Neal-Schuman
Imprint of The American Library Association
   (ALA)
50 E Huron St, Chicago, IL 60611
Toll Free Tel: 800-545-2433 *Fax:* 312-280-5860
E-mail: editionsmarketing@ala.org
Web Site: www.alastore.ala.org
Key Personnel
Mktg Coord: Rob Christopher *Tel:* 312-280-5052
   E-mail: rchristopher@ala.org
Founded: 1976
How-to manuals, technology, library & informa-
   tion science texts.
ISBN Prefix(es): 978-0-918212; 978-1-55570
Number of titles published annually: 65 Print; 30
   E-Book
Total Titles: 320 Print; 300 E-Book

Aladdin Books, see Simon & Schuster Children's
   Publishing

Alaska Native Language Center
Division of University of Alaska Fairbanks
PO Box 757680, Fairbanks, AK 99775-7680
SAN: 692-9796
Fax: 907-474-6586
E-mail: uaf-anlc@alaska.edu (orders)
Web Site: www.uaf.edu/anlc

Key Personnel
Dir: Lawrence D Kaplan *Tel:* 907-474-6582
   E-mail: ldkaplan@alaska.edu
Ed: Leon Unruh *Tel:* 907-474-6577
   E-mail: ldunruh@alaska.edu
Founded: 1972
Publish books in & about Alaska's 20 indigenous
   languages, including dictionaries, grammars &
   collections of folktales & oral history, language
   maps.
ISBN Prefix(es): 978-1-55500; 978-0-933769
Number of titles published annually: 3 Print
Total Titles: 200 Print; 3 Audio

Albert Whitman & Co
250 S Northwest Hwy, Suite 320, Park Ridge, IL
   60068
SAN: 201-2049
Tel: 847-232-2800 *Toll Free Tel:* 800-255-7675
   Fax: 847-581-0039
E-mail: mail@albertwhitman.com
Web Site: www.albertwhitman.com
Key Personnel
Pres & Co-Owner: John Quattrocchi
VP & Co-Owner: Pat McPartland
Busn Dir: Joe Campbell
Publg Dir: Sue Tarsky
Assoc Art Dir: Ellen Kokontis
Assoc Ed: Andrea Hall
Metadata & Contracts Supv: Caity Anast
Assoc Graphic Designer: Morgan Avery
Founded: 1919
Juveniles, language arts, fiction & nonfiction.
ISBN Prefix(es): 978-0-8075
Number of titles published annually: 50 Print
Total Titles: 800 Print
Distribution Center: Baker & Taylor Publisher
   Services, 30 Amberwood Pkwy, Ashland, OH
   44805 *Tel:* 567-215-0030 *Toll Free Tel:* 888-
   814-0208 *E-mail:* orders@btpubservices.com
   Web Site: www.btpubservices.com

**The Alexander Graham Bell Association for
   the Deaf & Hard of Hearing**
3417 Volta Place NW, Washington, DC 20007
SAN: 203-6924
Tel: 202-337-5220 *Toll Free Tel:* 866-337-5220
   (orders) *Fax:* 202-337-8314
E-mail: info@agbell.org; publications@agbell.org
Web Site: www.agbell.org
Key Personnel
CEO: Emilio Alonso-Mendoza
   E-mail: ealonsomendoza@agbell.org
Chief Devt Offr: Lisa Chutjian
   E-mail: lchutjian@agbell.org
Chief Strategy Offr: Gayla Guignard
   E-mail: gguignard@agbell.org
Dir, Communs: Chris Gensch *E-mail:* cgensch@
   agbell.org
Mgr, Association Rel: Gary Yates *Tel:* 202-204-
   4683 *E-mail:* gyates@agbell.org
Founded: 1890
Resource, support network & advocate for listen-
   ing, learning, talking & living independently
   with hearing loss. Through publications, out-
   reach, training, scholarships & financial aid,
   AG Bell promotes the use of spoken language
   & hearing technology. Headquarted in Washington, DC with chapters located in the US &
   CN & a network of international affiliates. AG
   Bell's global presence provides its members &
   the public with the support they need close to
   home. With over a century of service, AG Bell
   supports it's mission, advocating independence
   through listening & talking.
ISBN Prefix(es): 978-0-88200
Number of titles published annually: 9 Print
Total Titles: 70 Print

Alexander Street, a ProQuest Company
99 Canal Center Plaza, Suite 200, Alexandria, VA
   22314

SAN: 858-5512
Tel: 703-212-8520 *Toll Free Tel:* 800-889-5937
E-mail: sales@alexanderstreet.com; marketing@
alexanderstreet.com; info@alexanderstreet.com
Web Site: alexanderstreet.com
Key Personnel
VP, Licensing: Will Whalen *E-mail:* whalen@
alexanderstreet.com
Sr Dir, Prod Mktg: Bradley Cigich
E-mail: bradley.cigich@proquest.com
Dir, Prod Mgmt: Nathalie Duval *E-mail:* nathalie.
duval@proquest.com
Dir, Prod Mktg: Barbara Olson *E-mail:* barbara.
olson@proquest.com
Founded: 2000
Publish large-scale digital collections of works in
the humanities & social sciences.
ISBN Prefix(es): 978-1-4631; 978-1-5016; 978-1-
5034
Number of titles published annually: 30 Print; 6
Online; 2,000 E-Book; 4 Audio
Total Titles: 34 Online; 10,000 E-Book; 6 Audio
Imprints: Filmakers Library; Insight Media; Mi-
crotraining Associates
Foreign Office(s): 2123 Pudong Ave, Rm 805,
Shanghai 200135, China *Tel:* (021) 386875
Business & Technology Ctr, Unit G04, Besse-
mer Dr, Stevenage SG1 2DX, United Kingdom
Tel: (01438) 310193
Membership(s): American Library Association
(ALA)

§Alfred Music
PO Box 10003, Van Nuys, CA 91410
Tel: 818-891-5999 (dealer sales, intl)
Toll Free Tel: 800-292-6122 (dealer sales, US
& CN); 800-628-1528 (cust serv) *Fax:* 818-
893-5560 (dealer sales); 818-830-6252 (cust
serv) *Toll Free Fax:* 800-632-1928 (dealer
sales)
E-mail: customerservice@alfred.com; sales@
alfred.com
Web Site: www.alfred.com
Key Personnel
Chief Busn Devt Offr: Ron Manus
SVP, Busn Opers: Doug Fraser
VP, Busn Aff: Teveyah Dovbish
VP, Fin/Cont: Un Chu Kim
VP, IT: Lynnda Hullinger
VP, Mktg: Alex Ordonez
VP, Prodn & Edit: Derek Richard
VP, Sales: Johann Gouws
Gen Mgr: Keith Watson
Founded: 1922
Publisher of music education; music books &
software, performance & instructional.
ISBN Prefix(es): 978-0-88284; 978-0-87487; 978-
0-7390; 978-1-58951; 978-1-4574; 978-1-4706
Number of titles published annually: 500 Print; 4
CD-ROM
Total Titles: 18,000 Print; 20 CD-ROM
Imprints: Belwin; Highland/Etling; Kalmus; Mu-
sic Inc; Warner/Chappell Music Inc
Foreign Office(s): Lutzerathstr 127, 51107
Cologne, Germany *Tel:* (0221) 933539
0 *E-mail:* info@alfredverlag.de *Web
Site:* alfredverlag.de
20 Sin Ming Lane, No 05-54 Midview City, 5th
fl, Singapore 573968, Singapore *Tel:* 6659
8919 *E-mail:* music@alfred.com.sg
Burnt Mill, Elizabeth Way, Harlow, Essex
CM20 2HX, United Kingdom *Tel:* (01279)
828960 *E-mail:* music@alfred.uk.com *Web
Site:* alfreduk.com
Distributor for Daisy Rock Girl Guitars; Dover
Publications Inc; Drum Channel; Faber Music
Ltd; MakeMusic Inc; Penguin; WEA
Foreign Rep(s): Dave Bolden (Australia, New
Zealand); Larry Bong (Asia); Gerry Mooney
(UK); Thomas Petzold (Europe)
Membership(s): MPA - The Association of Maga-
zine Media

Alfred Publishing LLC, see Alfred Music

Algonquin Books
Division of Workman Publishing Co Inc
400 Silver Cedar Ct, Suite 300, Chapel Hill, NC
27514-1585
SAN: 282-7506
Mailing Address: PO Box 2225, Chapel Hill, NC
27515-2225
Tel: 919-967-0108 *Fax:* 919-933-0272
E-mail: inquiry@algonquin.com
Web Site: www.workman.com/algonquin
Key Personnel
Publr: Betsy Gleick
Publr, Young Adult & Middle Grade: Elise
Howard
Assoc Publr: Michael McKenzie
Art & Creative Dir: Anne Winslow *Tel:* 919-967-
0108 ext 29
Creative Dir (NY): Christopher Moisan
Dir, Digital Mktg: Debra Linn
Dir, Mktg & Sales: Randall Lotowycz
Dir, Mktg, Algonquin Young Readers: Jodie Co-
hen
Assoc Dir, Mktg: Lauren Moseley
Mng Ed & ISBN Contact: Brunson Hoole
Tel: 919-967-0108 ext 22 *E-mail:* brunson@
algonquin.com
Exec Ed: Amy Gash; Kathy Pories
Ed: Chuck Adams
Ed, Algonquin Young Readers: Krestyna Lypen
Assoc Ed, Algonquin Young Readers: Sarah
Alpert
Sr Mgr, Foreign Rts & Co-Editions: Allison Hug-
gins
Mktg Mgr, Algonquin Young Readers: Megan
Harley
Publicity Mgr: Jackie Burke; Stephanie Mendoza
Asst Mgr, Trade Sales & Retail Mktg: Christian
Westermann
Sr Publicist: Carla Bruce-Eddings; Brooke Csuka;
Brittani Hilles
Publicity Asst: Kelly Doyle
Intl Rts: Kendra Poster *Tel:* 212-614-7506
Founded: 1982
Trade books, fiction & nonfiction.
ISBN Prefix(es): 978-0-912697; 978-0-945575;
978-1-56512
Number of titles published annually: 38 Print
Imprints: Algonquin Young Readers
Sales Office(s): Workman Publishing Co Inc,
225 Varick St, New York, NY 10014-4381
Tel: 212-254-5900 *Fax:* 212-254-8098
Distributed by Workman Publishing Co Inc
Distributor for Fearless Critic Media; Greenwich
Workshop Press; HighBridge Audio
Foreign Rep(s): Thomas Allen & Son Ltd
(Canada); Bill Bailey Publishers' Represen-
tatives (Europe); Bookreps NZ Ltd (New
Zealand); Michelle Morrow Curreri (Asia);
Hardie Grant (Australia); InterMediaAmericana
Ltd (David Williams) (Caribbean, Latin Amer-
ica, South America); Melia Publishing Services
Ltd (UK); Real Books (South Africa)
Foreign Rights: Big Apple Agency Inc (China,
Taiwan); Copenhagen Literary Agency ApS
(Scandinavia); Julio F-Yanez Agencia Literaria
SL (Portugal, Spain); Graal Literary Agency
(Poland); The Deborah Harris Agency (Israel);
The Italian Literary Agency srl (Italy); Japan
UNI Agency Inc (Japan); JLM Literary Agency
(Greece); Katai & Bolza Literary Agency
(Hungary); Korea Copyright Center Inc (KCC)
(Korea); Alexander Korzhenevski Agency
(Russia); Kristin Olson Literary Agency SRO
(Czechia, Slovakia); Plima Literary Agency
(Bulgaria, Croatia, North Macedonia, Serbia,
Slovenia); Sebes & Bisseling Literary Agency
(Netherlands)
Billing Address: Workman Publishing Co Inc,
225 Varick St, New York, NY 10014-4381
Tel: 212-254-5900 *Fax:* 212-254-8098

Orders to: Workman Publishing Co Inc, 225
Varick St, New York, NY 10014-4381
Tel: 212-254-5900 *Toll Free Tel:* 800-722-7202
Fax: 212-254-8098
Returns: Workman Publishing Co Inc, c/o RR
Donnelly, 677 Brighton Beach Rd, Menasha,
WI 54952-2998
Warehouse: Workman Publishing Co Inc, c/o RR
Donnelly, 677 Brighton Beach Rd, Menasha,
WI 54952-2998

Algora Publishing
1732 First Ave, No 20330, New York, NY 10128
Tel: 212-678-0232 *Fax:* 212-666-3682
E-mail: editors@algora.com
Web Site: www.algora.com
Key Personnel
Publr: Claudiu A Secara
Ed: Martin De Mers
Author Rel: Andrea Secara
Founded: 1992
Books on subjects of history, international affairs,
current issues, political economy, philosophy,
etc in the tradition of independent progressive
thinking.
ISBN Prefix(es): 978-0-87586; 978-0-9646073;
978-1-892941; 978-1-62894
Number of titles published annually: 25 Print; 25
E-Book
Total Titles: 600 Print; 600 E-Book
Imprints: Agathon Press
Membership(s): Association of American Pub-
lishers (AAP); Independent Book Publishers
Association (IBPA)

Alice James Books
Division of Alice James Poetry Cooperative Inc
114 Prescott St, Farmington, ME 04938
SAN: 201-1158
Tel: 207-778-7071 *Fax:* 207-778-7766
E-mail: info@alicejamesbooks.org
Web Site: alicejamesbooks.org
Key Personnel
Exec Dir: Carey Salerno
Mng Ed: Alyssa Neptune
Edit Asst: Alicia Hynes
Bookkeeper: Debra Norton
Founded: 1973
ISBN Prefix(es): 978-0-914086; 978-1-882295;
978-1-938584
Number of titles published annually: 6 Print
Total Titles: 115 Print; 3 Audio
Distribution Center: Consortium Book Sales &
Distribution, The Keg House, Suite 101, 34 13
Ave NE, Minneapolis, MN 55413 *Tel:* 612-
746-2600 *Toll Free Tel:* 800-283-3572 (cust
serv) *Fax:* 612-746-2606 *E-mail:* info@cbsd.
com *Web Site:* www.cbsd.com SAN: 200-6049

§All About Kids Publishing
PO Box 159, Gilroy, CA 95021
Tel: 408-337-1152
E-mail: info@allaboutkidspub.com
Web Site: www.allaboutkidspub.com
Key Personnel
Ed: Linda L Guevara *E-mail:* lguevara@
allaboutkidspub.com
Founded: 2000
Strives to set the standards in children's book
publishing by creating innovative books of the
highest quality with beautiful art work for chil-
dren of all walks of life. See submission guide-
lines on web site.
ISBN Prefix(es): 978-0-9700863; 978-0-9710278;
978-0-9744446
Number of titles published annually: 6 Print
Total Titles: 20 Print
Imprints: Talking Donkey Press
Warehouse: 34 Production Ave, Keene, NH 03431
Tel: 603-357-0236 *Toll Free Tel:* 800-345-6665
Fax: 603-965-2181
Membership(s): Independent Book Publishers As-
sociation (IBPA)

§All Things That Matter Press
79 Jones Rd, Somerville, ME 04348
E-mail: allthingsthatmatterpress@gmail.com
Web Site: www.allthingsthatmatterpress.com
Key Personnel
CEO: Debra Harris
Founded: 2008
ISBN Prefix(es): 978-0-9966634
Number of titles published annually: 10 Print; 10
   E-Book; 4 Audio
Total Titles: 245 Print; 245 E-Book; 70 Audio

§Allium Press of Chicago
1530 Elgin Ave, Forest Park, IL 60130
SAN: 858-3331
Tel: 708-689-9323
E-mail: info@alliumpress.com
Web Site: www.alliumpress.com
Key Personnel
Publr: Emily Victorson
Founded: 2009
Small independent press publishing fiction with
   a Chicago connection. Publish literary fiction,
   historical fiction, mysteries, thrillers & young
   adult fiction.
ISBN Prefix(es): 978-0-9840676; 978-0-9831938;
   978-0-9890535; 978-0-9967558; 978-0-
   9996982
Number of titles published annually: 5 Print; 5 E-
   Book
Total Titles: 20 Print; 20 E-Book
Membership(s): Historical Novel Society (HNS);
   Independent Book Publishers Association
   (IBPA); Mystery Writers of America (MWA);
   Sisters in Crime; Society of Midland Authors

Alloy Entertainment LLC
Member of Warner Bros Entertainment Group
30 Hudson Yards, 22nd fl, New York, NY 10001
E-mail: collaborative@alloyentertainment.com
Key Personnel
Pres: Leslie Morgenstein
EVP: Josh Bank
SVP, Edit: Sara Shandler
VP & Exec Ed: Lanie Davis
VP, Book Devt: Joelle Hobeika
Ed: Viana Siniscalchi
Asst Ed: Laura Barbiea
Founded: 1987
Hardcover, trade, mass market juvenile & young
   adult fiction & nonfiction; adult trade fiction &
   mass market fiction.
ISBN Prefix(es): 978-0-9850261; 978-1-939106
Number of titles published annually: 50 Print
Distributed by Avon Books; HarperCollins; Hy-
   perion; Little, Brown & Company; Penguin
   Group USA, A Penguin Random House Com-
   pany; Penguin Random House Inc; Scholastic
   Books; Simon & Schuster
Foreign Rep(s): Rights People (UK)

§Allworth Press
Imprint of Skyhorse Publishing Inc
307 W 36 St, 11th fl, New York, NY 10018
Tel: 212-643-6816 *Fax:* 212-643-6819
Web Site: www.allworth.com
Key Personnel
Founder & Publr: Tad Crawford
   E-mail: crawford@allworth.com
Founded: 1989
Business & self-help books for artists, crafters,
   designers, photographers, authors & film &
   performing artists; books about business & law
   for the general public.
ISBN Prefix(es): 978-0-927629; 978-0-9607118;
   978-1-880559; 978-1-58115; 978-1-62153
Number of titles published annually: 20 Print; 20
   E-Book
Total Titles: 400 Print; 400 E-Book
Sales Office(s): Perseus Book Distribution, 1400
   Broadway, New York, NY 10018

Foreign Rights: Jean V Naggar Literary Agency
   (worldwide)
Distribution Center: Perseus Book Distribution,
   1400 Broadway, New York, NY 10018

AllWrite Advertising & Publishing
3300 Buckeye Rd, Suite 264, Atlanta, GA 30341
Mailing Address: PO Box 1071, Atlanta, GA
   30301
Tel: 770-284-8983 *Fax:* 770-284-8986
E-mail: questions@allwritepublishing.com;
   support@allwritepublishing.com (orders &
   returns)
Web Site: allwritepublishing.com
Key Personnel
Pres & Publr: Annette R Johnson
   E-mail: annette@allwritepublishing.com
Founded: 2003
A conventional small press. Books that we do not
   decide to publish are given thorough feedback.
ISBN Prefix(es): 978-0-9744935
Number of titles published annually: 5 Print
Membership(s): Independent Book Publishing
   Professionals Group (IBPPG); Writers Guild of
   America, East (WGAE)

§Alpha Books
Subsidiary of DK Publishing
6081 E 82 St, 4th fl, Indianapolis, IN 46250
Tel: 212-366-2000
E-mail: ecommerce@us.penguingroup.com
Web Site: www.dk.com
Key Personnel
Publr: Michael Sanders
Founded: 2003
Publisher of *Idiot's Guides*®.
Penguin Random House & its publishing entities
   are not accepting unsol submissions, proposals,
   mss, or submission queries via e-mail at this
   time.
Number of titles published annually: 88 Print
Total Titles: 580 Print

Amadeus Press
Imprint of Rowman & Littlefield Publishing
   Group
200 Park Ave S, Suite 1109, New York, NY
   10003
Tel: 212-529-3888 *Fax:* 212-529-4223
Web Site: www.rowman.com
Key Personnel
Sr Exec Ed, Performing Arts, Music & Digital
   Publg: John Cerullo
Founded: 1987
Full service trade publisher that produces books,
   book/CDs & DVDs about classical music &
   opera.
ISBN Prefix(es): 978-1-57467
Number of titles published annually: 40 Print; 30
   E-Book
Total Titles: 1,200 Print; 1,000 E-Book
Foreign Rep(s): Publishers Group UK (Europe,
   UK)

§Amakella Publishing
PO Box 9445, Arlington, VA 22219
Tel: 202-239-8660
E-mail: info@amakella.com
Web Site: www.amakella.com
Independent publisher interested in publishing
   books in areas such as social sciences, inter-
   national development, environmental conserva-
   tion, investing & current affairs.
ISBN Prefix(es): 978-1-63387
Number of titles published annually: 2 Print; 2 E-
   Book
Total Titles: 7 Print; 8 E-Book
Membership(s): Independent Book Publishers As-
   sociation (IBPA)

Frank Amato Publications Inc
4040 SE Wister St, Milwaukie, OR 97222

Mailing Address: PO Box 82112, Portland, OR
   97282
Tel: 503-653-8108 *Toll Free Tel:* 800-541-9498
   Fax: 503-653-2766
E-mail: customerservice@amatobooks.com;
   info@amatobooks.com
Web Site: www.amatobooks.com
Key Personnel
Publr: Frank W Amato
Co-Publr & Ed: Nick S Amato *E-mail:* n.amato@
   comcast.net
Co-Publr: Tony F Amato *E-mail:* tony@
   amatobooks.com
Ad & Inquiries: Dave Eng *E-mail:* deng@
   amatobooks.com
Founded: 1967
Fishing books & magazines, some outdoor sport
   titles & cookbooks.
ISBN Prefix(es): 978-0-936608; 978-1-878175;
   978-1-57188
Number of titles published annually: 30 Print
Total Titles: 800 Print
Distributor for Haugen Enterprises (cooking &
   hunting titles)
Membership(s): Pacific Northwest Booksellers
   Association (PNBA)

§Ambassador International
Division of Emerald House Inc
411 University Ridge, Suite B14, Greenville, SC
   29601
Tel: 864-751-4844
E-mail: info@emeraldhouse.com; publisher@
   emeraldhouse.com; sales@
   emeraldhouse.com (orders/order inquiries);
   media@emeraldhouse.com
Web Site: ambassador-international.com; www.
   facebook.com/AmbassadorIntl; twitter.com/
   ambassadorintl
Key Personnel
Pres & CEO: Dr Samuel Lowry
COO: Anna Raats *E-mail:* araats@emeraldhouse.
   com
Creative Dir: Hannah Nichols
Ed: Katie Cruice Smith
Publicist: Liz Burgdorf
Founded: 1980 (UK, 1996 US)
Christian publisher. Works with authors to create quality Christian literature of several gen-
   res - fiction, devotional & children's books.
   The company's vision has always been to cre-
   ate products that strengthen believers in their
   Christian walk & direct the lost to the way of
   salvation. New titles each year in both print &
   ebook format. Offices in the US & Northern
   Ireland, distribution partnerships on four conti-
   nents & books in the hands of readers around
   the world.
ISBN Prefix(es): 978-1-889893; 978-1-932307;
   978-1-620202; 978-1-64960
Number of titles published annually: 45 Print; 45
   E-Book; 45 Audio
Total Titles: 400 E-Book; 200 Audio
Foreign Office(s): Ambassador Books & Me-
   dia, The Mount, 2 Woodstock Link, Belfast
   BT6 8DD, United Kingdom *Tel:* (028) 9073
   0184 *Fax:* (028) 9073 0199 *Web Site:* www.
   ambassadormedia.co.uk
Distribution Center: Baker & Taylor, 2550 W
   Tyvola Rd, Suite 300, Charlotte, NC 28217
   (US dist) *Tel:* 704-998-3100 *Toll Free Tel:* 800-
   775-1800 *Web Site:* www.baker-taylor.com
Ingram/Spring Arbor, One Ingram Blvd, La
   Vergne, TN 37086 (US dist) *Tel:* 615-793-5000
   Web Site: www.ingramcontent.com

Amber Lotus Publishing
PO Box 11329, Portland, OR 97211
SAN: 247-6819
Tel: 503-284-6400 *Toll Free Tel:* 800-326-2375
   (orders only) *Fax:* 503-284-6417
E-mail: info@amberlotus.com
Web Site: www.amberlotus.com

Key Personnel
Co-Owner & Pres: Lawson Day
Co-Owner & Creative Dir: Leslie Gignilliat-Day
VP, Sales: Tim Campbell
Prodn Mgr: Aleta Florentin
Mktg: Dianne Foster
Opers: Ethan Disbrow
Founded: 1988
Calendars, greeting cards, journals & books.
ISBN Prefix(es): 978-1-885394; 978-1-56937; 978-1-60237
Number of titles published annually: 65 Print

AMC Books, see Appalachian Mountain Club Books

America West Publishers
Subsidiary of Global Insights Inc
5872 Government Way, Unit 1-10, Dalton Gardens, ID 83814
Mailing Address: PO Box 599, Hayden, ID 83835
Tel: 208-762-0633 *Toll Free Tel:* 800-729-4131
Web Site: www.nohoax.com
Key Personnel
Pres: George Green *E-mail:* geo@nohoax.com
Founded: 1986
New science, UFOs, healing, metaphysics, spiritual, political & economic.
ISBN Prefix(es): 978-0-922356
Number of titles published annually: 5 Print; 1 CD-ROM
Total Titles: 100 Print; 20 CD-ROM; 5 Audio

American Academy of Environmental Engineers & Scientists®
147 Old Solomons Island Rd, Suite 303, Annapolis, MD 21401
Tel: 410-266-3311 *Fax:* 410-266-7653
E-mail: info@aaees.org
Web Site: www.aaees.org
Key Personnel
Exec Dir: Burk Kalweit *E-mail:* bkalweit@aaees.org
Mgr, Spec Projs: J Sammi Olmo
    E-mail: jsolmo@aaees.org
Mktg Mgr: Marisa Waterman
    E-mail: mwaterman@aaees.org
Pubns Mgr: Yolanda Y Moulden
    E-mail: ymoulden@aaees.org
Founded: 1955
Journals & textbooks for the environmental engineering & science professions.
ISBN Prefix(es): 978-1-883767
Number of titles published annually: 5 Print
Total Titles: 49 Print
Distributor for The ABS Group; CRC Press; McGraw-Hill; Pearson Education; Prentice Hall; John Wiley & Sons Inc

American Academy of Pediatrics
345 Park Blvd, Itasca, IL 60143
Toll Free Tel: 888-227-1770 *Fax:* 847-228-1281
Web Site: www.aap.org; shop.aap.org; publishing.aap.org
Key Personnel
VP, Publg: Mark Grimes *E-mail:* mgrimes@aap.org
Founded: 1930
Patient educational material, medical textbooks, professional textbook, patient education & practice management materials; pediatrics; family & emergency medicine.
ISBN Prefix(es): 978-0-910761; 978-0-87493; 978-0-915473; 978-0-87553; 978-0-553; 978-0-89707; 978-1-56055; 978-1-58110
Number of titles published annually: 40 Print; 5 CD-ROM; 10 Online; 120 E-Book
Total Titles: 400 Print; 10 CD-ROM; 10 Online; 120 E-Book
Foreign Rights: John Scott & Co
Orders to: PO Box 776442, Chicago, IL 60677-6442

Distribution Center: Independent Publishers Group (IPG), 814 N Franklin St, Chicago, IL 60610 *Toll Free Tel:* 800-888-4741 *E-mail:* orders@ipgbook.com *Web Site:* www.ipgbook.com

The American Alpine Club Press
Division of The American Alpine Club
710 Tenth St, Suite 100, Golden, CO 80401
Tel: 303-384-0110 *Fax:* 303-384-0111
E-mail: info@americanalpineclub.org
Web Site: americanalpineclub.org
Key Personnel
Exec Ed: Dougald MacDonald
    E-mail: dmacdonald@americanalpineclub.org
Founded: 1902
Mountaineering: general, regional guides, safety, medical & scientific, annual journals & historical.
ISBN Prefix(es): 978-0-930410
Number of titles published annually: 3 Print; 2 E-Book
Total Titles: 57 Print
Distributed by The Mountaineers Books
Foreign Rep(s): Mountaineers Books (worldwide)
Foreign Rights: Mountaineers Books (worldwide)

§American Anthropological Association (AAA)
2300 Clarendon Blvd, Suite 1301, Arlington, VA 22201
Tel: 703-528-1902 *Fax:* 703-528-3546
E-mail: pubs@americananthro.org
Web Site: www.americananthro.org
Key Personnel
Dir, Publg: Janine Chiappa McKenna *Tel:* 703-528-1902 ext 1174 *E-mail:* jmckenna@americananthro.org
Asst to Dir, Publg: Chelsea Horton *Tel:* 703-528-1902 ext 1181 *E-mail:* chorton@americananthro.org
Mng Ed: Natalie Konopinski *Tel:* 703-528-1902 ext 1184 *E-mail:* nkonopinski@americananthro.org
Founded: 1902
Publish scholarly journals.
ISBN Prefix(es): 978-0-913167; 978-1-931303; 978-0-9799094; 978-0-9826767; 978-0-9836822
Number of titles published annually: 100 Print
Total Titles: 27 Print
Distributed by Wiley-Blackwell
Membership(s): Association of American Publishers (AAP); World Council of Anthropological Associations (WCAA)

§American Association for Vocational Instructional Materials
220 Smithonia Rd, Winterville, GA 30683
Tel: 706-742-5355 *Fax:* 706-742-7005
E-mail: sales@aavim.com
Key Personnel
Dir: Gary Farmer
Founded: 1949
Consortium formed for development, publishing & distribution of instructional materials for vocational education.
ISBN Prefix(es): 978-0-89606
Number of titles published annually: 4 Print
Total Titles: 182 Print; 10 CD-ROM
Distributor for Southeastern Cooperative Wildlife Disease Study

§American Association of Blood Banks
North Tower, 4550 Montgomery Ave, Suite 700, Bethesda, MD 20814
Tel: 301-907-6977 *Toll Free Tel:* 866-222-2498 (sales) *Fax:* 301-907-6895
E-mail: aabb@aabb.org; sales@aabb.org (ordering); publications1@aabb.org (catalog)
Web Site: www.aabb.org

Key Personnel
Dir, Pubns: Laurie Munk *Tel:* 301-215-6595
    E-mail: laurie@aabb.org
Mgr, Pubns: Jennifer Boyer *Tel:* 301-215-6596
    E-mail: jboyer@aabb.org
Founded: 1947
Texts in blood banking standards, transfusion medicine, transplantation & cellular therapy.
ISBN Prefix(es): 978-0-915355
Number of titles published annually: 20 Print; 14 Audio
Total Titles: 73 Print; 42 Online; 60 Audio
Returns: BrightKey Inc, Attn: AABB Returns, 1780 Crossroads Dr, Odenton, MD 21113

American Association of Cereal Chemists, see AACC International

American Association of Collegiate Registrars & Admissions Officers (AACRAO)
One Dupont Circle NW, Suite 520, Washington, DC 20036
Tel: 202-293-9161 *Fax:* 202-872-8857
Web Site: www.aacrao.org
Key Personnel
Exec Dir: Michael Reilly *E-mail:* reillym@aacrao.org
Dir, Opers, Membership & Pubns: Martha Henebry *Tel:* 202-263-0285 *E-mail:* henebrym@aacrao.org
Founded: 1910
Periodicals, monograph series, higher education-general, international, technology & higher education.
ISBN Prefix(es): 978-0-929851; 978-0-910054
Number of titles published annually: 4 Print; 4 E-Book
Total Titles: 118 Print; 11 E-Book
Distribution Center: AACRAO Distribution Center, PO Box 231, Annapolis Junction, MD 20701 *Tel:* 301-263-0292 *Fax:* 240-396-5986 *E-mail:* pubs@aacrao.org *Web Site:* www.aacrao.org/bookstore

American Bar Association
321 N Clark St, Chicago, IL 60654
Tel: 312-988-5000 *Toll Free Tel:* 800-285-2221 (orders) *Fax:* 312-988-6281
E-mail: orders@abanet.org
Web Site: www.americanbar.org
Key Personnel
Dir, Publg: Donna Gollmer
Founded: 1878
Books, magazines, journals, newsletters & AV materials.
ISBN Prefix(es): 978-1-57073; 978-1-59031; 978-1-60442
Number of titles published annually: 170 Print; 25 CD-ROM; 100 Online; 100 E-Book
Total Titles: 1,000 Print; 150 CD-ROM; 250 Online; 250 E-Book
Branch Office(s)
1050 Connecticut Ave NW, Suite 400, Washington, DC 20036 *Tel:* 202-662-1000
Warehouse: Thomson Reuters, 610 Opperman Dr, Eagan, MN 55123 *Tel:* 651-687-7000
Distribution Center: National Book Network, 4501 Forbes Blvd, Suite 200, Lanham, MD 20706
Membership(s): Independent Book Publishers Association (IBPA)

§American Bible Society
101 N Independence Mall E, 8th fl, Philadelphia, PA 19106-2112
SAN: 203-5189
Tel: 215-309-0900 *Toll Free Tel:* 800-322-4253 (cust serv); 888-596-6296
E-mail: info@americanbible.org
Web Site: www.americanbible.org
Key Personnel
Mng Dir, Opers: John Greco

Founded: 1816
Publisher, producer & distributor of Bibles, books, audio, video & software products emphasizing Christian, inspirational & family values.
ISBN Prefix(es): 978-1-58516
Number of titles published annually: 20 Print
Total Titles: 800 Print
Warehouse: PO Box 2854, Tulsa, OK 74101-9921
Toll Free Fax: 866-570-1777

§American Carriage House Publishing
400 Idaho Maryland Rd, Grass Valley, CA 95945
Tel: 530-432-8860 *Toll Free Tel:* 866-986-2665
E-mail: editor@carriagehousepublishing.com
Web Site: www.americancarriagehousepublishing.com
Founded: 2003
Focused on providing traditional & family values in a new fresh approach.
ISBN Prefix(es): 978-0-970
Number of titles published annually: 8 Print; 20 CD-ROM; 8 Online; 14 E-Book; 68 Audio
Total Titles: 16 E-Book; 240 Audio
Distributed by Faith Works Books
Distribution Center: Baker & Taylor
Ingram Book Group
Quality Books Inc
Membership(s): The Association of Publishers for Special Sales (APSS); Independent Book Publishers Association (IBPA)

American Catholic Press (ACP)
16565 S State St, South Holland, IL 60473
SAN: 162-4989
Tel: 708-331-5485 *Fax:* 708-331-5484
E-mail: acp@acpress.org
Web Site: www.acpress.org
Key Personnel
Exec Dir: Rev Michael Gilligan, PhD
Devt Dir: Peter Ruhl
Subscriber Serv Dir: Michael Yukich
Founded: 1967
Christian liturgy, especially in the Roman Catholic Church including music resources for churches. No poetry or fiction.
ISBN Prefix(es): 978-0-915866
Number of titles published annually: 5 Print; 1 Audio
Total Titles: 25 Print; 1 CD-ROM; 4 Audio

§The American Ceramic Society
550 Polaris Pkwy, Suite 510, Westerville, OH 43082
Tel: 240-646-7054 *Toll Free Tel:* 866-721-3322
Fax: 240-396-5637
E-mail: customerservice@ceramics.org
Web Site: ceramics.org
Key Personnel
Exec Dir: Mark Mecklenborg
E-mail: mmecklenborg@ceramics.org
Dir, Tech Content & Communs: Eileen De Guire
E-mail: edeguire@ceramics.org
Mng Dir, Ceramics Publishing Co: Bill Janeri
E-mail: bjaneri@ceramics.org
Founded: 1898
Dedicated to the advancement of ceramics, serving more than 8,000 members & subscribers. Members include engineers, scientists, researchers & others in the ceramics & materials industry. Provides the latest technical, scientific & educational information.
ISBN Prefix(es): 978-0-944904; 978-1-57498; 978-0-916094
Number of titles published annually: 25 Print
Total Titles: 250 Print; 8 CD-ROM

The American Chemical Society
1155 16 St NW, Washington, DC 20036
SAN: 201-2626
Tel: 202-872-4600 *Toll Free Tel:* 800-227-5558 (US) *Fax:* 202-872-6067

E-mail: help@acs.org
Web Site: www.acs.org
Key Personnel
Pres, Pubns Div: James Milne
Asst Dir: Joseph Graham *E-mail:* j_graham@acs.org
Sr Mng Ed: Sai Konda
Founded: 1876
Serials, proceedings, reprint collections, monographs & other professional & reference books; specializes in food chemistry, environmental sciences & green chemistry, analytical, inorganic, medicinal, organic & physical chemistries, biochemistry, polymer & materials science & nanotechnology.
ISBN Prefix(es): 978-0-8412
Number of titles published annually: 31 Print
Total Titles: 500 Print; 1 CD-ROM
Distributed by Oxford University Press USA
Distributor for Royal Society of Chemistry
Foreign Rep(s): Maruzen Co Ltd (Japan); Sonya Nickson (UK); Andrew Pitts (UK)
Membership(s): Association of American Publishers (AAP)

American College
270 S Bryn Mawr Ave, Bryn Mawr, PA 19010
SAN: 240-5822
Tel: 610-526-1000 *Toll Free Tel:* 888-263-7265
Fax: 610-526-1310
Web Site: www.theamericancollege.edu
Key Personnel
Pres: Bob Johnson
Chief Academic Offr: Michael Finke
Founded: 1927
An independent, accredited nonprofit educational institution offering financial services texts & course guides online & life insurance for students in financial services programs at colleges & universities including American College programs: CLU, ChFC, CLF, LUTCF, RHU, REBC, CASL & CFP certification curriculum & MSFS degree for professionals in the financial services industry. Subject specialties: business, finance, insurance & securities.
ISBN Prefix(es): 978-0-943590; 978-1-57996; 978-1-932819
Number of titles published annually: 42 Print; 60 Online; 11 Audio
Total Titles: 42 Print; 15 CD-ROM; 60 Online; 11 Audio

American College of Surgeons
633 N Saint Clair St, Chicago, IL 60611-3211
Tel: 312-202-5000 *Fax:* 312-202-5001
E-mail: postmaster@facs.org
Web Site: www.facs.org
Key Personnel
Gen Pubns Mgr: Katie McCauley
E-mail: kmccauley@facs.org
Founded: 1913
Publishes reference books & manuals. Specialize in surgery, trauma, cancer & professional liability. Also publishes the *Journal of the American College of Surgeons* (monthly) & the *Bulletin of the American College of Surgeons* (monthly).
ISBN Prefix(es): 978-0-9620370
Number of titles published annually: 5 Print; 10 Online
Total Titles: 20 Print; 2 CD-ROM
Distributed by Cine-Med Inc; Scientific American Medicine

American Correctional Association
206 N Washington St, Suite 200, Alexandria, VA 22314
Tel: 703-224-0000 *Toll Free Tel:* 800-222-5646
Fax: 703-224-0179
E-mail: publications@aca.org
Web Site: www.aca.org
Founded: 1870
Corrections professionals.

ISBN Prefix(es): 978-1-56991
Number of titles published annually: 6 Print
Total Titles: 200 Print

American Council on Education
One Dupont Circle NW, Washington, DC 20036
Tel: 202-939-9300; 202-939-9452 (publg dept); 301-632-6757 (orders)
E-mail: pubs@acenet.edu
Web Site: www.acenet.edu
Key Personnel
Pres: Ted Mitchell
Dir, Pubns: Felicia Carr
Founded: 1917
Books, directories & handbooks in higher education, monographs.
ISBN Prefix(es): 978-0-8268; 978-0-89774
Number of titles published annually: 70 Print
Total Titles: 200 Print
Distributed by Rowman & Littlefield

American Counseling Association
6101 Stevenson Ave, Suite 600, Alexandria, VA 22304
Tel: 703-823-9800 *Toll Free Tel:* 800-298-2276
Fax: 703-823-0252 *Toll Free Fax:* 800-473-2329
E-mail: membership@counseling.org (book orders)
Web Site: www.counseling.org
Key Personnel
Assoc Publr: Carolyn C Baker *Tel:* 703-823-9800 ext 356 *Fax:* 703-823-4786 *E-mail:* cbaker@counseling.org
Digital & Print Devt Ed, Rts & Perms: Nancy Driver *Tel:* 703-823-9800 ext 253 *Fax:* 703-823-4786 *E-mail:* ndriver@counseling.org
Founded: 1952
More than 55,000 members from the school counseling, mental health & human development professions at all educational levels. Publishes 10 scholarly journals, a magazine & approximately 8-10 new professional book titles a year for members & nonmembers.
ISBN Prefix(es): 978-1-55620
Number of titles published annually: 10 Print; 10 E-Book
Total Titles: 100 Print; 60 E-Book
Imprints: ACA

§American Diabetes Association
2451 Crystal Dr, Suite 900, Arlington, VA 22202
Toll Free Tel: 800-342-2383
E-mail: booksinfo@diabetes.org
Web Site: www.diabetes.org
Key Personnel
Assoc Publr, Books: Abraham Ogden
Dir, Books: Victor Van Beuren
Founded: 1945
Books, handouts & collateral materials pertaining to diabetes for patients & health care professionals.
ISBN Prefix(es): 978-1-58040; 978-0-94544
Number of titles published annually: 20 Print; 15 E-Book
Total Titles: 180 Print; 80 E-Book
Distribution Center: Publishers Group West (PGW), 1700 Fourth St, Berkeley, CA 94710
Toll Free Tel: 800-788-3123 (cust serv)
SAN: 202-8522

American Federation of Arts
305 E 47 St, 10th fl, New York, NY 10017
Tel: 212-988-7700 *Toll Free Tel:* 800-232-0270
Fax: 212-861-2487
E-mail: pubinfo@amfedarts.org
Web Site: www.amfedarts.org
Key Personnel
Mgr of Pubns: Anna Kyoko Barnet
E-mail: abarnet@amfedarts.org
Head of Communs & Mktg: Shawna C Gallancy
E-mail: sgallancy@amfedarts.org
Founded: 1909

Publisher of exhibition catalogues (books) that accompany art exhibitions organized by the AFA.
ISBN Prefix(es): 978-0-917418; 978-1-885444
Number of titles published annually: 4 Print
Total Titles: 47 Print
Distributed by Harry N Abrams Inc; Distributed Art Publishers; D Giles Ltd; Hudson Hills Press Inc; Scala Publishers; University of Washington Press; Yale University Press

American Federation of Astrologers Inc
6535 S Rural Rd, Tempe, AZ 85283-3746
Tel: 480-838-1751 *Toll Free Tel:* 888-301-7630
Fax: 480-838-8293
Web Site: www.astrologers.com
Key Personnel
Exec Dir: Kris Brandt Riske
Founded: 1938
Astrology book publisher & membership organization.
ISBN Prefix(es): 978-0-86690
Number of titles published annually: 25 Print
Total Titles: 250 Print

American Fisheries Society
425 Barlow Place, Suite 110, Bethesda, MD 20814-2144
Tel: 301-897-8616; 703-661-1570 (book orders)
Fax: 301-897-8096; 703-996-1010 (book orders)
E-mail: main@fisheries.org
Web Site: www.fisheries.org
Key Personnel
Dir, Pubns: Aaron Lerner *Tel:* 301-897-8616 ext 231 *E-mail:* alerner@fisheries.org
Off & Admin Mgr: Denise Spencer *Tel:* 301-897-8616 ext 212 *E-mail:* dspencer@fisheries.org
Founded: 1870
Fisheries science, aquaculture & management materials, aquatic ecology, fisheries law, fisheries history, conservation biology & publishing.
ISBN Prefix(es): 978-0-913235; 978-1-888569; 978-1-934874
Number of titles published annually: 10 Print; 5 Online
Total Titles: 180 Print
Advertising Agency: Media West Inc, 230 Kings Hwy E, Suite 316, Haddonfield, NJ 08033 (Fisheries Magazine only), Contact: Steve West *Tel:* 856-432-1501 *Fax:* 856-494-1455
E-mail: steve@afs-fisheries.com

American Foundation for the Blind Press, see AFB Press

American Geophysical Union (AGU)
2000 Florida Ave NW, Washington, DC 20009
SAN: 202-4489
Tel: 202-462-6900 *Toll Free Tel:* 800-966-2481 (North America) *Fax:* 202-328-0566
E-mail: service@agu.org (cust serv); earthspacescience@agu.org
Web Site: www.agu.org
Key Personnel
SVP, Pubns: Brooks Hanson *E-mail:* bhanson@agu.org
Dir, Pubns: Jenny Lunn *E-mail:* jlunn@agu.org; Jeanette Panning *E-mail:* jpanning@agu.org
Founded: 1919
International scientific society with more than 50,000 members in over 135 countries. For over 80 years, AGU researchers, teachers & science administrators have dedicated themselves to advancing the understanding of earth & its environment in space. AGU now stands as a leader in the increasingly interdisciplinary global endeavor that encompasses the geophysical sciences.
ISBN Prefix(es): 978-0-87590
Number of titles published annually: 15 Print; 20 Online

Total Titles: 500 Print
Membership(s): Association of American Publishers (AAP); Society for Scholarly Publishing (SSP)

§American Geosciences Institute (AGI)
4220 King St, Alexandria, VA 22302-1502
Tel: 703-379-2480 (ext 246) *Fax:* 703-379-7563
E-mail: agi@americangeosciences.org
Web Site: www.americangeosciences.org
Key Personnel
Exec Dir: Allyson K Anderson Book *Tel:* 703-379-2480 ext 202 *E-mail:* aandersonbook@americangeosciences.org
Fin & Admin Dir: Walter R Sisson *Tel:* 703-379-2480 ext 209 *E-mail:* wsisson@americangeosciences.org
Info Servs Dir: Sharon Tahirkheli *Tel:* 703-379-2480 ext 231 *E-mail:* snt@americangeosciences.org
Mktg Dir: John P Rasanen *Tel:* 703-379-2480 ext 224 *E-mail:* jr@americangeosciences.org
Technol & Communs Dir: Christopher Keane *Tel:* 703-379-2480 ext 219 *E-mail:* keane@americangeosciences.org
Founded: 1948
Geoscience reference books.
ISBN Prefix(es): 978-0-922152; 978-0-913312; 978-1-941878
Number of titles published annually: 5 Print; 3 E-Book
Total Titles: 60 Print; 10 CD-ROM; 2 Online; 5 E-Book
Distributed by W H Freeman; It's About Time Inc; Prentice Hall
Orders to: AGI Book Center *Web Site:* www.agiweb.org/pubs

American Girl Publishing
Subsidiary of Mattel
8400 Fairway Place, Middleton, WI 53562
Mailing Address: PO Box 620497, Middleton, WI 53562-0497
Tel: 608-836-4848; 608-831-5210 (outside US & CN) *Toll Free Tel:* 800-233-0264; 800-360-1861; 800-845-0005 (US & CN) *Fax:* 608-836-1999
Web Site: www.americangirl.com
Key Personnel
Pres: Jean McKenzie
Founded: 1986
Children's fiction & nonfiction.
ISBN Prefix(es): 978-0-937295; 978-1-56247; 978-1-58485
Number of titles published annually: 40 Print; 1 CD-ROM; 6 Audio
Total Titles: 350 Print; 3 CD-ROM; 18 Audio
Imprints: A G Fiction™; American Girl Library®; The American Girls Collection®
Membership(s): The Children's Book Council (CBC)

§American Historical Association (AHA)
400 "A" St SE, Washington, DC 20003
Tel: 202-544-2422 *Fax:* 202-544-8307
E-mail: aha@historians.org; awards@historians.org
Web Site: www.historians.org
Key Personnel
Exec Dir: Jim Grossman
Founded: 1884
The umbrella organization for the history profession.
ISBN Prefix(es): 978-0-87229
Number of titles published annually: 5 Print; 3 Online
Total Titles: 100 Print

American Industrial Hygiene Association - AIHA
3141 Fairview Park Dr, Suite 777, Falls Church, VA 22042

Tel: 703-849-8888 *Fax:* 703-207-3561
E-mail: infonet@aiha.org
Web Site: www.aiha.org
Key Personnel
Sr Mgr, Memb & Cust Rel: Wanda Barbour *Tel:* 703-846-0782 *E-mail:* wbarbour@aiha.org
Mgr, Prod Devt: Katie Robert *Tel:* 703-846-0738 *E-mail:* krobert@aiha.org
Founded: 1939
Serves the needs of occupational & environmental health professionals practicing industrial hygiene in industry, government, labor, academic institutions & independent organizations.
ISBN Prefix(es): 978-1-931504
Number of titles published annually: 15 Print; 15 E-Book
Total Titles: 150 Print

§American Institute for Economic Research (AIER)
250 Division St, Great Barrington, MA 01230
Mailing Address: PO Box 1000, Great Barrington, MA 01230-1000
Tel: 413-528-1216 *Toll Free Tel:* 888-528-1216 (orders)
E-mail: info@aier.org
Web Site: www.aier.org
Key Personnel
Pres & CEO: Edward Stringham
COO: John Sylbert
Libn: Suzanne Hermann *Tel:* 413-528-1216 ext 3116
Founded: 1933
Conducts independent, scientific, economic research to educate individuals, thereby advancing their personal interests & those of the nation.
ISBN Prefix(es): 978-0-913610
Number of titles published annually: 3 Print; 8 Online; 4 E-Book
Total Titles: 50 Print; 46 Online; 4 E-Book

American Institute of Aeronautics & Astronautics (AIAA)
12700 Sunrise Valley Dr, Suite 200, Reston, VA 20191-5807
Tel: 703-264-7500 *Toll Free Tel:* 800-639-AIAA (639-2422) *Fax:* 703-264-7551
E-mail: custserv@aiaa.org
Web Site: www.aiaa.org
Key Personnel
Exec Dir: Dr Sandra Magnus *Tel:* 703-264-7512 *E-mail:* sandym@aiaa.org
Dir, Communs: John Blacksten *Tel:* 703-264-7532 *E-mail:* johnb@aiaa.org
Ed-in-Chief, Aerospace America: Ben Iannotta *Tel:* 703-264-7528 *E-mail:* beni@aiaa.org
Mgr, Journal Opers: Karina Bustillo *Tel:* 703-264-7525 *E-mail:* karinab@aiaa.org
Founded: 1963
Professional technical books; member magazine; archival journals & technical meeting papers in the science & technology of aerospace engineering & systems, print CD-ROMs & online delivery.
ISBN Prefix(es): 978-0-915928; 978-0-930403; 978-1-56347; 978-1-60086; 978-1-62410
Number of titles published annually: 20 Print
Total Titles: 600 Print
Foreign Rep(s): ACCUCOMS BV (Europe); ACCUCOMS India (India); ACCUCOMS MENA (Eyad Mohammad) (Middle East, North Africa); Publishers Communication Group (Rebekah Matthews) (North America, South America); Transatlantic Publishers Group (Europe)
Distribution Center: AIAA Publications Customer Service, PO Box 960, Herndon, VA 20172-0960 *Tel:* 703-661-1595 *Toll Free Tel:* 800-682-2422 *Fax:* 703-661-1501
E-mail: aiaamail@presswarehouse.com

American Institute of Certified Public Accountants, see AICPA Professional Publications

§American Institute of Chemical Engineers (AIChE)
120 Wall St, 23rd fl, New York, NY 10005-4020
Tel: 203-702-7660 *Toll Free Tel:* 800-242-4363
  Fax: 203-775-5177
E-mail: customerservice@aiche.org
Web Site: www.aiche.org
Key Personnel
Pres: Christine Seymour
Exec Dir: June C Wispelwey *Tel:* 646-495-1310
  E-mail: junew@aiche.org
Sr Dir, Pubns: Cynthia Mascone *Tel:* 646-495-1360 *E-mail:* cyntm@aiche.org
Dir, Meeting & Conference Programming: Kristine Chin *Tel:* 646-495-1366 *E-mail:* krisc@aiche.org
Founded: 1908
Chemical engineering books & journals, technical manuals, symposia proceedings, directories.
ISBN Prefix(es): 978-0-8169
Number of titles published annually: 15 Print
Total Titles: 300 Print; 4 CD-ROM
Distributed by Dechema (selected titles)
Distributor for ASM International (selected titles); Dechema (selected titles); Engineering Foundation; IchemE (selected titles)
Distribution Center: Institution of Chemical Engineers, Davis Bldg, 165-189 Railway Terr, Rugby CV21 3HQ, United Kingdom

American Institute of Physics
One Physics Ellipse, College Park, MD 20740-3843
Mailing Address: 1305 Walt Whitman Rd, Suite 300, Melville, NY 11747
Tel: 516-576-2200; 301-209-3100 (orders)
E-mail: help@aip.org
Web Site: www.aip.org
Key Personnel
CEO: Alexandra (Alix) Vance
Founded: 1931
Publisher of conference proceedings, professional journals, magazines & books.
ISBN Prefix(es): 978-0-88318; 978-1-56396; 978-0-7354
Number of titles published annually: 13 Print; 8 CD-ROM; 3 Online
Total Titles: 700 Print; 200 Online
Distributed by Springer-Verlag
Membership(s): Association of American Publishers (AAP)

§American Law Institute
4025 Chestnut St, Philadelphia, PA 19104-3099
SAN: 204-756X
Tel: 215-243-1600 *Toll Free Tel:* 800-253-6397
  Fax: 215-243-1636
E-mail: ali@ali.org; custserv@ali.org
Web Site: www.ali.org
Key Personnel
Pubns Dir: Deanne Dissinger
Edit Dir: Marianne M Walker
Sr Ed: Todd David Feldman
Ed & Pubns Mgr: Karen Van Gorder
Ed: Elizabeth T Brown
Founded: 1923
Professional & scholarly legal books & treatises.
ISBN Prefix(es): 978-0-8318
Number of titles published annually: 10 Print

§American Law Institute Continuing Legal Education (ALI CLE)
Affiliate of American Law Institute
4025 Chestnut St, Philadelphia, PA 19104
Tel: 215-243-1600 *Toll Free Tel:* 800-CLE-NEWS (253-6397) *Fax:* 215-243-1664; 215-243-1608
Web Site: www.ali-cle.org

Key Personnel
Deputy Dir, ALI: Stephanie Middleton
Founded: 1947 (as ALI-ABA; reconstituted as ALI CLE in 2012)
Publish law books & legal periodicals.
ISBN Prefix(es): 978-0-8318
Number of titles published annually: 2 Print; 2 Online

§The American Library Association (ALA)
225 N Michigan Ave, Suite 1300, Chicago, IL 60601
Tel: 312-944-6780 *Toll Free Tel:* 800-545-2433
  Fax: 312-280-5275
E-mail: editionsmarketing@ala.org
Web Site: www.alastore.ala.org
Key Personnel
Exec Dir: Tracie D Hall
Assoc Exec Dir, Publg: Mary Mackay
Sr Ed, Lib Technol: Patrick Hogan *Tel:* 800-545-2433 ext 3240 *E-mail:* phogan@ala.org
Acqs Ed, Prof Devt & Librarianship: Jamie Santoro *Tel:* 800-545-2433 ext 5107
  E-mail: jsantoro@ala.org
Acqs Ed, Textbooks: Rachel Chance *Tel:* 800-545-2433 ext 1548 *E-mail:* rchance@ala.org
Mktg Dir: Jill Hillemeyer *Tel:* 800-545-2433 ext 5418 *E-mail:* jhillemeyer@ala.org
Mktg Coord: Rob Christopher *Tel:* 800-545-2433 ext 5052 *E-mail:* rchristopher@ala.org
Rts & Perms: Mary Jo Bolduc *Tel:* 312-280-5416
  E-mail: mbolduc@ala.org
Founded: 1876
Publisher of titles for librarians & educators; library & information science, professional books.
ISBN Prefix(es): 978-0-8389; 978-1-937589
Number of titles published annually: 36 Print; 1 CD-ROM; 1 Online
Total Titles: 400 Print; 2 CD-ROM; 1 Online
Imprints: ALA Neal-Schuman
Foreign Rep(s): Eurospan (Africa, Europe, Israel, UK)
Foreign Rights: Inbooks (James Bennett) (Australia); Ontario Library Association (Canada)
Orders to: PO Box 117219, Atlanta, GA 30368-7219 *Toll Free Tel:* 866-SHOP-ALA (746-7252) *Fax:* 312-280-5860 *E-mail:* alastore@ala.org
Returns: 3280 Summit Ridge Pkwy, Duluth, GA 30096
See separate listing for:
ALA Neal-Schuman
Association of College & Research Libraries (ACRL)

American Map Corp
Member of Kappa Map Group LLC
36-36 33 St, 4th fl, Long Island City, NY 11106
SAN: 202-4624
Tel: 718-784-0055 *Toll Free Tel:* 888-774-7979
  Fax: 718-784-0640 (admin); 718-784-1216 (sales & orders)
E-mail: info@kappamapgroup.com
Web Site: www.kappamapgroup.com
Founded: 1923
Maps & atlases; charts.
ISBN Prefix(es): 978-0-8416
Number of titles published annually: 30 Print
Total Titles: 1 CD-ROM
Imprints: Cleartype American Map Corp; Colorprint American Map Corp
Subsidiaries: ADC the Map People; Arrow Maps Inc; Creative Sales Corp; Hagstrom Map Co Inc; Hammond World Atlas Corp; Trakker Maps Inc
Distributed by Arrow Maps Inc; Creative Sales Corp
Distributor for De Lorme Atlas; Kappa Map Group LLC; RV Guides; Stubs Magazine
Advertising Agency: ATL/SD, 46-35 54 Rd, Maspeth, NY 11378, Contact: Sara Ascalon

Tel: 718-784-0555 *Fax:* 718-784-0640
E-mail: sascalon@americanmap.com
See separate listing for:
Hagstrom Map

American Mathematical Society
201 Charles St, Providence, RI 02904-2213
SAN: 201-1654
Tel: 401-455-4000 *Toll Free Tel:* 800-321-4267
  Fax: 401-331-3842; 401-455-4046 (cust serv)
E-mail: ams@ams.org; cust-serv@ams.org
Web Site: www.ams.org
Key Personnel
Exec Dir: Dr Catherine A Roberts
Publr: Dr Sergei Gelfand
Assoc Exec Dir: Dr Robert M Harrington
Assoc Exec Dir, Washington, DC: Dr Karen Saxe
Founded: 1888
Membership society & publisher of mathematics.
ISBN Prefix(es): 978-0-8218; 978-0-8284; 978-1-4704
Number of titles published annually: 100 Print
Total Titles: 3,400 Print; 2 CD-ROM; 28 Online
Imprints: Chelsea Publishing Co Inc
Branch Office(s)
1527 18 St NW, Washington, DC 20036-1358 (govt rel & sci policy) *Tel:* 202-588-1100
  Fax: 202-588-1853 *E-mail:* amsdc@ams.org
Mathematical Reviews®, 416 Fourth St, Ann Arbor, MI 48103-4820 (edit) *Tel:* 734-996-5250
  Fax: 734-996-2916 *E-mail:* mathrev@ams.org
Secretary of the AMS - Society Governance, Dept of Computer Science, North Carolina State University, Box 8206, Raleigh, NC 27695-8206 *Tel:* 919-515-7863 *Fax:* 919-515-7896
  E-mail: secretary@ams.org
Distributor for Annales de la faculte des sciences de Toulouse mathematiques; Bar-Ilan University; Brown University; European Mathematical Society; Hindustan Book Agency; Independent University of Moscow; International Press; Mathematica Josephina; Mathematical Society of Japan; Narosa Publishing House; Ramanujan Mathematical Society; Science Press USA Inc; Societe Mathematique de France; Tata Institute of Fundamental Research; Theta Foundation of Bucharest; University Press; Vieweg Verlag Publications
Foreign Rep(s): Eurospan Australia (Australia, New Zealand, Oceania); Eurospan Group (Africa, Europe, Middle East, Southeast Asia); Hindustan Book Agency (India); IBH Book & Magazines Distributors Pvt Ltd (India); Maruzen Co Ltd (Japan); Neutrino Inc (Japan); Segment Book Distributors (India)
Returns: Pawtucket Warehouse, 35 Monticello Place, Pawtucket, RI 02861
Warehouse: Pawtucket Warehouse, 35 Monticello Place, Pawtucket, RI 02861, Contact: Donald Proulx *Tel:* 401-729-4184 *Fax:* 401-728-3564
  E-mail: dap@ams.org
Distribution Center: Pawtucket Warehouse, 35 Monticello Place, Pawtucket, RI 02861, Contact: Donald Proulx *Tel:* 401-729-4184
  Fax: 401-728-3564 *E-mail:* dap@ams.org
Membership(s): Society for Scholarly Publishing (SSP)

American Medical Association
AMA Plaza, 330 N Wabash, Suite 39300, Chicago, IL 60611-5885
Tel: 312-464-5000 *Toll Free Tel:* 800-621-8335
Web Site: www.ama-assn.org
Key Personnel
CEO & EVP: James L Madara, MD
SVP & Publr, Periodic Pubns: Thomas J Easley
SVP & Ed-in-Chief, Scientific Pubns: Howard C Bauchner, MD
VP/Exec Mng Ed, Edit Opers: Annette Flanagin
Founded: 1847
Medical profession.
ISBN Prefix(es): 978-0-89970; 978-1-57947; 978-1-60359; 978-1-62202

Number of titles published annually: 30 Print
Total Titles: 150 Print
Advertising Agency: GSP Marketing Services Inc
Warehouse: Catalog Resources Inc, 100 Enterprise Dr, Dover, DE 19901
Membership(s): Association of American Publishers (AAP)

American Numismatic Society
75 Varick St, 11th fl, New York, NY 10013
Tel: 212-571-4470 *Fax:* 212-571-4479
E-mail: ans@numismatics.org
Web Site: www.numismatics.org
Key Personnel
Exec Dir: Ute Wartenberg Kagan
Ad Ed, ANS Magazine: Joanne Isaac *Tel:* 212-571-4470 ext 112 *E-mail:* isaac@numismatics.org
Founded: 1858
Scholarly materials.
ISBN Prefix(es): 978-0-89722
Number of titles published annually: 5 Print
Total Titles: 100 Print

American Oil Chemists' Society, see AOCS Press

American Philosophical Society
104 S Fifth St, Philadelphia, PA 19106
SAN: 206-9016
Tel: 215-440-3425 *Fax:* 215-440-3450
E-mail: orders@dianepublishing.net
Web Site: www.amphilsoc.org
Key Personnel
Pres: Linda Greenhouse
Exec Offr: Robert M Hauser
Ed: Mary McDonald *E-mail:* mmcdonald@amphilsoc.org
Founded: 1743
Nonprofit educational institution for promotion of useful knowledge in humanities & sciences.
ISBN Prefix(es): 978-0-87169; 978-1-60618
Number of titles published annually: 13 Print
Total Titles: 1,150 Print
Imprints: Lightning Rod Press; Memoirs; Proceedings; Transactions
Distributed by Diane Publishing Co
Billing Address: Diane Publishing Co, APS Fulfillment, 330 Pusey Ave, Unit 3 (rear), Collingdale, PA 19023 *Tel:* 610-461-6200 *Toll Free Tel:* 800-782-3833 *Fax:* 610-461-6130 *E-mail:* orders@dianepublishing.net
Orders to: Diane Publishing Co, APS Fulfillment, 330 Pusey Ave, Unit 3 (rear), Collingdale, PA 19023 *Tel:* 610-461-6200 *Toll Free Tel:* 800-782-3833 *Fax:* 610-461-6130 *E-mail:* orders@dianepublishing.net
Warehouse: Diane Publishing Co, Contact: Herman Baron *Tel:* 610-461-6200 *Toll Free Tel:* 800-782-3833

American Press
60 State St, Suite 700, Boston, MA 02109
SAN: 210-7007
Tel: 617-247-0022
E-mail: americanpress@flash.net
Web Site: www.americanpresspublishers.com
Key Personnel
Publr: R K Fox
Ed: Marci Taylor
Founded: 1911
College textbooks, study guides, lab manuals & handbooks.
ISBN Prefix(es): 978-0-89641
Number of titles published annually: 20 Print
Total Titles: 300 Print

§American Printing House for the Blind Inc
1839 Frankfort Ave, Louisville, KY 40206
SAN: 203-5235

Mailing Address: PO Box 6085, Louisville, KY 40206-0085
Tel: 502-895-2405 *Toll Free Tel:* 800-223-1839 (cust serv) *Fax:* 502-899-2274
E-mail: info@aph.org
Web Site: www.aph.org; shop.aph.org
Key Personnel
Pres: Craig Meador *E-mail:* cmeador@aph.org
VP, Pub Aff: Gary Mudd *E-mail:* gmudd@aph.org
PR Mgr: Rebecca Snider *Tel:* 502-899-2357 *E-mail:* rsnider@aph.org
Founded: 1858
Literature & aids for people who are visually impaired: braille text books, magazines & other items, large-type textbooks, talking books & magazines, educational & miscellaneous aids, talking PC hardware & software. Publisher of braille & reprints in braille.
ISBN Prefix(es): 978-1-61648
Number of titles published annually: 4,500 Print
Total Titles: 6,300 Print

§American Psychiatric Association Publishing
Division of American Psychiatric Association (APA)
800 Maine Ave SW, Suite 900, Washington, DC 20024
SAN: 293-2288
Tel: 202-459-9722 *Toll Free Tel:* 800-368-5777 *Fax:* 202-403-3094
E-mail: appi@psych.org
Web Site: www.appi.org; www.psychiatryonline.org
Key Personnel
Publr: John D McDuffie *E-mail:* jmcduffie@psych.org
Dir, Sales & Mktg: Patrick Hansard *E-mail:* phansard@psych.org
Edit Dir, American Journal of Psychiatry: Michael Roy
Ed-in-Chief, Books: Laura Weiss Roberts, MD
Mng Ed, Books: Greg Kuny
Acqs Mgr: Erika Parker *E-mail:* eparker@psych.org
Opers Mgr: Debra Eubanks
Founded: 1981
Professional, reference & general trade books, college textbooks; behavioral & social sciences, psychiatry, medicine.
ISBN Prefix(es): 978-0-88048; 978-0-89042; 978-0-87318; 978-1-58562; 978-1-61537
Number of titles published annually: 30 Print; 3 Online; 30 E-Book
Total Titles: 750 Print; 30 Online; 350 E-Book; 1 Audio
Distributor for American Psychiatric Association (APA); Group for the Advancement of Psychiatry
Foreign Rep(s): Catamount (Latin America); CBS Publishers (India); Europsan (Central Asia, China, East Asia, Singapore, South Korea); Footprint Books Pty Ltd (Australia, New Zealand); International Publishers Representatives (Africa, Middle East); Login Canada (Canada); Nankodo (Japan); NBN International (Europe, UK); Oxford University Press (Southern Africa)
Foreign Rights: John Scott Agency
Warehouse: Ware-Pak, 2427 Bond St, University Park, IL 60484-3170
Membership(s): American Association of University Presses (AAUP); Association of American Publishers (AAP)

American Psychological Association
750 First St NE, Washington, DC 20002-4242
Tel: 202-336-5510 *Toll Free Tel:* 800-374-2721 *Fax:* 202-336-5502
E-mail: order@apa.org
Web Site: www.apa.org/books

Key Personnel
Exec Publr: Jasper Simons *E-mail:* jsimons@apa.org
Publr, APA Books: Brenda Carter *E-mail:* bcarter@apa.org
Publr, APA Journals: Rose Sokol-Chang *E-mail:* rsokol-chang@apa.org
Busn Devt Dir, APA Style: Emily Ayubi *E-mail:* eayubi@apa.org
Dir, Books Mktg: Jason Wells
Dir, Edit Acqs, Academic & Prof Books: Emily Ekle
Dir, Video Media: Edward Meidenbauer *E-mail:* emeidenbauer@apa.org
Edit Dir, Magination Press: Kristine Enderle *E-mail:* kenderle@apa.org
Sales Dir, APA Books & Magination Press: Kerry Cahill
Sales Specialist, APA Books & Magination Press: Emma All
Sr Acqs Ed (Clinical & Counseling): Susan Reynolds *E-mail:* sreynolds@apa.org
Sr Acqs Ed (LifeTools; Methodology; Student, Faculty & Career Resources): Linda Malnasi McCarter *E-mail:* lmccarter@apa.org
Sr Acqs Ed (Res Vols): Christopher Kelaher *E-mail:* ckelaher@apa.org
Sr Ed, Magination Press: Sarah Fell
Books Mktg Mgr: Chi Wang
Busn Devt Mgr, Magination Press: Jenna Vaccaro
Content Devt Mgr, APA Style: Hayley Kamin
Asst Mktg Mgr, Magination Press: Monet A Stevens
Graphic Designer: Rachel Ross
Founded: 1892
Scholarly & professional works on psychology & related fields, including books, journals, videos, databases; trade books for general audiences (LifeTools); children's books (Magination Press®); APA Style Central®, a suite of integrated services & tools for writing & teaching APA Style; *American Psychologist*® (flagship quarterly journal) & *Monitor on Psychology*, a monthly magazine.
ISBN Prefix(es): 978-0-912704; 978-1-55798; 978-0-945354; 978-0-9792125; 978-1-59147; 978-1-4338
Number of titles published annually: 65 Print
Total Titles: 700 Print
Imprints: APA Books®; APA Style; APA Video®; LifeTools; Magination Press®
Foreign Rep(s): Aditya Books Pvt Ltd (India); Booknet Co Ltd (Brunei, Cambodia, China, Hong Kong, Indonesia, Korea, Laos, Macau, Malaysia, Myanmar, Singapore, Taiwan, Thailand, Vietnam); EUROSPAN Group (Africa, Europe, India, Middle East, Nepal, Pakistan, Sri Lanka, UK); Footprint Books (Australia, Fiji, New Zealand, Papua New Guinea); IMEDISA (Mexico); Login Canada (Canada); Taylor & Francis Asia Pacific (Brunei, China, Hong Kong, Indochina, Indonesia, Malaysia, Philippines, Singapore, Taiwan, Thailand, Vietnam)
Warehouse: APA Order Dept, PO Box 92984, Washington, DC 20090-2984

American Public Works Association (APWA)
1200 Main St, Suite 1400, Kansas City, MO 64105-2100
Tel: 816-472-6100 *Toll Free Tel:* 800-848-APWA (848-2792) *Fax:* 816-472-1610
Web Site: www.apwa.net
Key Personnel
Dir, Mktg & Web Servs: David Dancy *Tel:* 816-595-5250 *E-mail:* ddancy@apwa.net
Ed, APWA Reporter: Kevin Clark *Tel:* 816-595-5230 *E-mail:* kclark@apwa.net
Founded: 1894
Public work related publications. Also publishes *APWA Reporter* magazine.
ISBN Prefix(es): 978-0-917084; 978-1-60675
Number of titles published annually: 12 Print

Total Titles: 12 Print
Branch Office(s)
25 Massachusetts Ave NW, Suite 500A, Washington, DC 20001 *Tel:* 202-408-9541

American Quilter's Society
5801 Kentucky Dam Rd, Paducah, KY 42003-9323
Mailing Address: PO Box 3290, Paducah, KY 42002-3290
Tel: 270-898-7903 *Toll Free Tel:* 800-626-5420 (orders) *Fax:* 270-898-1173
E-mail: orders@americanquilter.com
Web Site: www.americanquilter.com
Key Personnel
Co-Founder & Pres: Meredith Schroeder
Mktg Dir: Katherine Rupp *E-mail:* katherine.rupp@americanquilters.com
Dir, Prod Devt: Lynn Loyd
Founded: 1983
Publish books & magazines, distributes books & operates quilting shows.
ISBN Prefix(es): 978-0-89145; 978-1-57432; 978-1-60460
Number of titles published annually: 20 Print; 10 CD-ROM; 4 E-Book
Total Titles: 300 Print; 20 CD-ROM; 7 E-Book

American Society for Nondestructive Testing
1711 Arlingate Lane, Columbus, OH 43228-0518
Mailing Address: PO Box 28518, Columbus, OH 43228-0518
Tel: 614-274-6003 *Toll Free Tel:* 800-222-2768 *Fax:* 614-274-6899
Web Site: www.asnt.org
Key Personnel
Sr Mgr, Pubns: Tim Jones *Tel:* 614-274-6003 ext 204 *E-mail:* tjones@asnt.org
Founded: 1941
Nonprofit association producing educational materials for members & nonmembers engaged in nondestructive testing.
ISBN Prefix(es): 978-0-931403; 978-1-57117
Number of titles published annually: 12 Print; 6 CD-ROM
Total Titles: 250 Print; 6 CD-ROM
Distributed by American Ceramic Society (ACerS); American Society for Mechanical Engineers (ASME); American Society for Metals (ASM); The American Welding Society (AWS); ASTM; Edison Welding Institute; Mean Free Path

§American Society for Quality (ASQ)
600 N Plankinton Ave, Milwaukee, WI 53203
Mailing Address: PO Box 3005, Milwaukee, WI 53201-3005
Tel: 414-272-8575 *Toll Free Tel:* 800-248-1946 (US & CN); 800-514-1564 (Mexico) *Fax:* 414-272-1734
E-mail: help@asq.org
Web Site: www.asq.org
Founded: 1983
Publisher of technical books: quality, statistical process control, ISO9000, six sigma, QS9000, ISO14000, statistics, reliability, auditing, sampling, standards' supplier quality & quality costs. Also management topics: total quality management, human resources & teamwork, health care, government, education & benchmarking, quality tools.
ISBN Prefix(es): 978-0-87389
Number of titles published annually: 25 Print; 5 E-Book
Total Titles: 300 Print; 5 CD-ROM; 15 E-Book
Distributed by GOAL/QPC; IEEE Computer Society Press; McGraw-Hill Professional Publishing; Productivity Press
Distribution Center: PBD Worldwide Inc, 905 Carlow Dr, Unit B, Bolingbrook, IL 60490

§American Society of Agricultural & Biological Engineers (ASABE)
2950 Niles Rd, St Joseph, MI 49085-9659
Tel: 269-429-0300 *Toll Free Tel:* 800-371-2723 *Fax:* 269-429-3852
E-mail: hq@asabe.org
Web Site: www.asabe.org
Key Personnel
Exec Dir: Darrin Drollinger *Tel:* 269-932-7007 *E-mail:* drollinger@asabe.org
Dir, Pubns: Joe Walker *Tel:* 269-932-7026 *E-mail:* walker@asabe.org
Book & Journal Ed: Peg McCann *Tel:* 269-932-7019 *E-mail:* mccann@asabe.org
Journal Ed: Glenn Laing *Tel:* 269-932-7014 *E-mail:* laing@asabe.org; Melissa Miller *Tel:* 269-932-7017 *E-mail:* miller@asabe.org
Pubns Asst: Sandy Rutter *Tel:* 269-932-7004 *E-mail:* rutter@asabe.org
Founded: 1907
Agricultural, biological & food systems, books & journals.
ISBN Prefix(es): 978-0-916150; 978-0-929355; 978-1-892769
Number of titles published annually: 4 Print
Total Titles: 150 Print; 1 CD-ROM; 2 Online

American Society of Agronomy
5585 Guilford Rd, Madison, WI 53711-5801
Tel: 608-273-8080 *Fax:* 608-273-2021
E-mail: headquarters@sciencesocieties.org
Web Site: www.agronomy.org
Key Personnel
CEO: Nichols J Goeser, PhD *Tel:* 608-327-9034
Dir of Publns: Matt Wascavage *Tel:* 608-819-3916
Founded: 1907
Technical books for professionals in agronomy; crop science, soil science, environmental sciences & related fields.
ISBN Prefix(es): 978-0-89118
Number of titles published annually: 12 Print
Total Titles: 90 Print

§American Society of Civil Engineers (ASCE)
1801 Alexander Bell Dr, Reston, VA 20191-4400
SAN: 204-7594
Tel: 703-295-6300 *Toll Free Tel:* 800-548-ASCE (548-2723) *Toll Free Fax:* 866-913-6085
E-mail: ascelibrary@asce.org; pubsful@asce.org
Web Site: www.asce.org
Key Personnel
Publr & Mng Dir: Angela Cochran *Tel:* 703-295-6133
Dir, Pubns Busn Opers: Gina Lindquist
Dir, Pubns Mktg: William Nara
Founded: 1852
Books, technical journals, information products on civil engineering & related fields; online & print.
ISBN Prefix(es): 978-0-87262; 978-0-7844
Number of titles published annually: 60 Print; 25 E-Book
Total Titles: 1,400 Print; 425 E-Book
Imprints: ASCE Press
Foreign Rep(s): Aditya Books (P) Ltd (Bangladesh, Bhutan, India, Nepal, Pakistan, Sri Lanka); Allied Book Co (Pakistan); Apex Knowledge Sdn Bhd (Brunei, Malaysia); Areesh Education & Trading Sdn Bhd (Brunei, Malaysia); Booknet Co Ltd (Suphaluck Sattabuz) (Cambodia, Laos, Myanmar, Thailand, Vietnam); Capital Books Pvt Ltd (India); ChoiceTEXTS (Asia) Pte Ltd (Phillip Ang) (Indonesia, Singapore); Grupo Difusion Cientifica (Mexico, South America); Eurospan Group (Africa, Continental Europe, Middle East, UK); ICaves Ltd (Eddy Lam) (China, Hong Kong, Macau); International Book House Pvt Ltd (India); MegaTEXTS Phil Inc (Jean Tiu Lim) (Philippines); Multi-Line Books (Bangladesh, Bhutan, Nepal, Pakistan); PT Ina Publikatama (Indonesia); Shankar's Book Agency Pvt Ltd (India); Taiwan Publishers Marketing Services Ltd (George Liu) (Taiwan); Unique Sellers (India)
Orders to: PO Box 79162, Baltimore, MD 21279-0162
Returns: 9050 Junction Dr, Annapolis Junction, MD 20701

American Society of Electroneurodiagnostic Technologists Inc, see ASET - The Neurodiagnostic Society

§American Society of Health-System Pharmacists (ASHP)
4500 East-West Hwy, Suite 900, Bethesda, MD 20814
Tel: 301-657-3000; 301-664-8700 *Toll Free Tel:* 866-279-0681 (orders) *Fax:* 301-657-1251 (orders)
E-mail: custserv@ashp.org
Web Site: www.ashp.org
Key Personnel
Mktg Mgr: Rachel Gellman
Founded: 1943
Medical scholarly books.
ISBN Prefix(es): 978-0-930530; 978-1-879907; 978-1-58528
Number of titles published annually: 20 Print
Total Titles: 115 Print
Foreign Rep(s): APAC (Asia); L Horvath (Eastern Europe); LPR (Middle East); LR International (Brazil); R Seshadri (India)
Advertising Agency: Cunningham Associates, 180 Old Tappan Rd, Old Tappan, NJ 07675, Contact: Jim Pattis *Tel:* 201-767-4170 *E-mail:* jpattis@cunnasso.com

§American Society of Mechanical Engineers (ASME)
2 Park Ave, New York, NY 10016-5990
SAN: 201-1379
Tel: 212-591-7000 *Toll Free Tel:* 800-843-2763 (cust serv-US, CN & Mexico) *Fax:* 973-882-1717 (orders & inquiries)
E-mail: customercare@asme.org
Web Site: www.asme.org
Key Personnel
Exec Dir: Thomas G Loughlin *E-mail:* execdirector@asme.org
Mng Dir, Publg: Philip DiVietro *Tel:* 212-591-7696 *E-mail:* divietrop@asme.org
Dir, Public Info: Michael Cowan *Tel:* 212-591-7303 *E-mail:* cowanm@asme.org
Mgr, Media Rel: Deborah Wetzel *Tel:* 212-591-7085 *E-mail:* wetzeld@asme.org
Founded: 1880
Publisher of codes & standards, journals, conference proceedings, professional references, *Mechanical Engineering* magazine, technical papers & reports.
ISBN Prefix(es): 978-0-7918
Number of titles published annually: 185 Print
Total Titles: 1,500 Print
Imprints: ASME Press
Branch Office(s)
1828 "L" St NW, Suite 510, Washington, DC 20036-5104 *Tel:* 202-785-3756 *Fax:* 202-429-9417 *E-mail:* grdept@asme.org
Warehouse: 150 Clove Rd, Little Falls, NJ 07424-2100 *Tel:* 973-882-1170

American Society of Plant Taxonomists
University of Wyoming, Dept of Botany 3165, 1000 E University Ave, Laramie, WY 82071
SAN: 282-969X
Tel: 307-766-2556 *Fax:* 307-766-2851
E-mail: aspt@uwyo.edu
Web Site: www.aspt.net
Key Personnel
Contact: Linda Brown
Founded: 1980
Botanical monographs.
ISBN Prefix(es): 978-0-912861

Number of titles published annually: 3 Print
Total Titles: 102 Print

American Technical Publishers Inc
10100 Orland Pkwy, Suite 200, Orland Park, IL
60467-5756
SAN: 206-8141
Toll Free Tel: 800-323-3471 *Fax:* 708-957-1101
E-mail: service@atplearning.com; order@
atplearning.com
Web Site: www.atplearning.com
Key Personnel
Pres: Robert D Deisinger *E-mail:* robert.
deisinger@atplearning.com
SVP: J David Holloway *E-mail:* david.holloway@
atplearning.com
Ed-in-Chief: Jonathan F Gosse *E-mail:* jonathan.
gosse@atplearning.com
Founded: 1898
Technical, industrial & vocational textbooks, ref-
erence books & related materials.
ISBN Prefix(es): 978-0-8269
Number of titles published annually: 8 Print; 2
CD-ROM; 25 Online; 3 E-Book
Total Titles: 200 Print; 10 CD-ROM; 25 Online;
3 E-Book
Distributor for Craftsman Book Co
Orders to: Nelson Publishing, 1120 Birchmount
Rd, Toronto, ON M1K 5G4, Canada (CN
school orders) *Tel:* 416-752-9448 *Toll Free
Tel:* 800-268-2222
Returns: 1155 W 175 St, Homewood, IL 60430,
Contact: Gail Prohaska *E-mail:* gail.prohaska@
atplearning.com

American Traveler Press, see Golden West
Cookbooks

§American Water Works Association (AWWA)
6666 W Quincy Ave, Denver, CO 80235-3098
Tel: 303-794-7711 *Toll Free Tel:* 800-926-7337
E-mail: service@awwa.org (cust serv)
Web Site: www.awwa.org
Key Personnel
CEO: David B LaFrance
Deputy CEO: Paula I MacIlwaine *Tel:* 303-347-
6135
CFO: Kevin Mann
CIO: Joe Thielen
Chief Membership Offr: Susan Franceschi
Dir, Communs: Greg Kail
Dir, Pubns: Zsolt Silberer
Dir, Sales: JoAnn Spinnato
Founded: 1881
Water works technology & management.
ISBN Prefix(es): 978-0-89867; 978-1-58321; 978-
1-61300; 978-1-62576
Number of titles published annually: 50 Print
Total Titles: 500 Print; 12 CD-ROM; 2 Online
Imprints: AWWA
Distributor for CRC Press; McGraw-Hill; John
Wiley & Sons
Foreign Rep(s): Australian Water Association
(Australia); Canadian Water & Wastewater As-
sociation (Canada)
Membership(s): Association Media & Publishing;
Publishers Association of the West (PubWest)

§Amherst Media Inc
PO Box 538, Buffalo, NY 14213
Tel: 716-874-4450
E-mail: marketing@amherstmedia.com
Web Site: www.amherstmedia.com
Key Personnel
Owner, Pres & Publr: Craig Alesse
Assoc Publr: Katie Loder-Kiss *E-mail:* kkiss@
amherstmedia.com
Founded: 1979
Publisher of photography books & more.
ISBN Prefix(es): 978-0-936262; 978-1-58428
Number of titles published annually: 36 Print; 24
E-Book

Total Titles: 500 Print; 500 E-Book
Foreign Rep(s): Peribo (Australia, New Zealand);
Publishers Group West (worldwide
exc Australia, Ireland, New Zealand & UK);
Turnaround Publisher Services (England, Ire-
land, UK)
Foreign Rights: Publishers Group West (PGW)
(worldwide)
Distribution Center: Publishers Group West
(PGW), 1700 Fourth St, Berkeley, CA
94710 *Tel:* 510-809-3700 *Fax:* 510-809-3777
E-mail: info@pgw.com *Web Site:* www.pgw.
com
Peribo Pty Ltd, 58 Beaumont Rd, Mount Kuring-
gai NSW 2080, Australia *Tel:* (02) 9457 0011
Fax: (02) 9457 0022 *E-mail:* info@peribo.com.
au *Web Site:* www.peribo.com.au
Turnaround Publisher Services, Unit 3, Olympia
Trading Estate, Coburg Rd, Wood Green, London N22 6TZ, United Kingdom *Tel:* (020)
8829 3002 *E-mail:* customercare@turnaround-
uk.com *Web Site:* www.turnaround-uk.com

Amicus
PO Box 1329, Mankato, MN 56002
Tel: 507-388-9357 *Fax:* 507-388-9357
E-mail: info@amicuspublishing.us; orders@
amicuspublishing.us
Web Site: www.amicuspublishing.us
Key Personnel
Assoc Publr: Rebecca Glaser *E-mail:* rglaser@
amicuspublishing.us
Founded: 2010
Publish books for children that educate & inspire
young readers. Our library imprints—Spot,
Amicus Readers, Amicus Illustrated & Amicus High Interest—offer informational books
in a variety of formats that make reading to
learn fun & encourage life-long learning. Our
trade imprint, Amicus Ink, features original
picture books & board books, each sharing a
child's-eye view of the world. Amicus: Friend
of education. Friend for life.
ISBN Prefix(es): 978-1-60753; 978-1-68151; 978-
1-68152
Number of titles published annually: 130 Print;
120 E-Book
Total Titles: 650 Print; 450 E-Book
Imprints: Amicus Ink (children's board books,
picture books & paperbacks)
Foreign Rights: Lorena Vazzola (worldwide)
Distribution Center: Saunders Book Co, PO
Box 308, Collingwood, ON L9Y 3Z7, Canada
Tel: 705-445-4777 *Toll Free Tel:* 800-461-9120
Fax: 705-445-9569 *Toll Free Fax:* 800-561-
1763 *E-mail:* info@saundersbooks.ca

AMMO Books LLC
5022 N Eagle Rock Blvd, Los Angeles, CA
90041
Mailing Address: PO Box 412402, Los Angeles,
CA 90041
Tel: 323-223-AMMO (223-2666) *Fax:* 323-978-
4200
E-mail: weborders@ammobooks.com; orders@
ammobooks.com
Web Site: ammobooks.com
Key Personnel
Co-Founder & Pres: Paul Norton *E-mail:* paul@
ammobooks.com
Founded: 2006
Provocative, one-of-a-kind titles that highlight the
best of the visual arts & pop culture.
ISBN Prefix(es): 978-0-9786076; 978-1-934429;
978-1-62326
Number of titles published annually: 50 Print

**§Ampersand Inc/Professional Publishing
Services**
515 Madison St, New Orleans, LA 70116
Tel: 312-280-8905 *Fax:* 312-944-1582
E-mail: info@ampersandworks.com

Web Site: www.ampersandworks.com
Key Personnel
Pres & Publr: Suzanne Talbot Isaacs
E-mail: suzie@ampersandworks.com
Founded: 1995 (began publishing in 2005)
Private publisher. Highly customized books, tailored to the author's specific objectives & developed by professionals with over 30 years of
publishing experience. We take your ms to fin-
ished book in a matter of weeks, on time & on
budget, support your marketing efforts, ware-
house & distribute your book. Branch office in
Chicago, IL.
This publisher has indicated that 90% of their
product line is author subsidized.
ISBN Prefix(es): 978-1-7340; 978-1-4507; 978-0-
9818126; 978-0-9761235; 978-0-873671; 978-
1-4675; 978-0-9962525; 978-0-9722529; 978-0-
9994; 978-0-9985; 978-0-9974; 978-0-9905
Number of titles published annually: 10 Print; 5
E-Book
Total Titles: 80 Print; 19 E-Book
Membership(s): Association of Independent Authors (AIA); The Association of Publishers for
Special Sales (APSS); Independent Book Pub-
lishers Association (IBPA); Society of Children's Book Writers & Illustrators (SCBWI)

Anaphora Literary Press
1108 W Third St, Quanah, TX 79252
Tel: 470-289-6395
Web Site: anaphoraliterary.com
Key Personnel
Dir: Dr Anna Faktorovich *E-mail:* director@
anaphoraliterary.com
Founded: 2009
Established publisher of paperback, hardcover &
ebook originals in poetry, fiction & nonfiction,
scholarly & business. Anaphora has released
books by best-selling/award-winning novelists
(Bob Van Laerhoven), academic books by Ivy
League professors & works by innovative new
writers. 50/50% split of royalties. E-mail sub-
mission with ms & paragraph bio, summary &
marketing plan. Anaphora helps with marketing
via press releases, reviews in *Library Journal*
& Publishers Weekly, designing releases & ex-
hibiting titles at conventions (ALA/SIBA).
ISBN Prefix(es): 978-1-937536; 978-1-68114
Number of titles published annually: 30 Print; 30
E-Book
Total Titles: 300 Print; 300 E-Book
Distribution Center: Lightning Source, 1246 Heil
Quaker Blvd, La Vergne, TN 37086
Membership(s): Community of Literary Maga-
zines & Presses (CLMP); Independent Book
Publishers Association (IBPA); Independent
Book Publishing Professionals Group (IBPPG);
Modern Language Association (MLA)

Anchor Books
Imprint of Knopf Doubleday Publishing Group
c/o Penguin Random House Inc, 1745 Broadway,
New York, NY 10019
Tel: 212-572-2420
E-mail: vintageanchorpublicity@randomhouse.
com
Web Site: knopfdoubleday.com/imprint/anchor
Key Personnel
Publr: Suzanne Herz
SVP & Edit Dir: Luann Walther
VP & Assoc Publr: Beth Lamb
VP & Exec Ed: Edward Kastenmeier
Exec Dir, Publicity & Soc Media: James Meader
Sr Dir, Sales Mktg & Busn Devt: Laura Crisp
Design Dir: Claudia Martinez
Dir, Ad & Promo: Irena Vukov-Kendes
Dir, Digital Mktg: Paige Smith
Assoc Dir, Publicity: Angie Venezia
Mng Ed: Barbara Richard
Ed: Margaux Weisman
Mktg Mgr: Laura Chamberlain; Jessica Deitcher
Publicity Mgr: Julie Ertl

Founded: 1953

Penguin Random House & its publishing entities are not accepting unsol submissions, proposals, mss, or submission queries via e-mail at this time.

Number of titles published annually: 175 Print; 190 E-Book

Total Titles: 2,650 Print; 1,750 E-Book

Foreign Rights: Anthea Agency (Katalina Sabeva) (Bulgaria); Bardon-Chinese Media Agency (Xu Weiguang) (China); Bardon-Chinese Media Agency (Yu Shiuan Chen & David Tsai) (Taiwan); The English Agency (Hamish Macaskill & Junzo Sawa) (Japan); Graal Literary Agency (Maria Strarz-Kanska) (Poland); The Deborah Harris Agency (Ilana Kurshan) (Israel); JLM Literary Agency (Nelly Moukakou) (Greece); Katai & Bolza Literary (Peter Bolza) (Croatia, Hungary, Serbia); Simona Kessler Agency (Simona Kessler) (Romania); Korea Copyright Center (MiSook Hong) (Korea); Licht & Burr Literary Agency (Trine Licht) (Scandinavia); La Nouvelle Agence (Vanessa Kling) (France); Kristin Olson Literary Agency (Kristin Olson) (Czechia); Agenzia Letteraria Santachiara (Roberto Santachiara) (Italy); Sebes & Bisseling Literary Agency (Holland)

Ancient Faith Publishing

Division of Ancient Faith Ministries

2427 Bond St, University Park, IL 60484

Mailing Address: PO Box 748, Chesterton, IN 46304

Tel: 219-728-2216 *Toll Free Tel:* 800-967-7377 *Toll Free Fax:* 866-599-5208

E-mail: info@ancientfaith.com; orders@ancientfaith.com

Web Site: www.ancientfaith.com/publishing

Key Personnel

CEO: John Maddex *E-mail:* jmaddex@ancientfaith.com

Edit Dir: Katherine Hyde *E-mail:* khyde@ancientfaith.com

Mktg Dir: Melinda Johnson *E-mail:* mjohnson@ancientfaith.com

Founded: 1978

Books, booklets, brochures, greeting cards, icons.

ISBN Prefix(es): 978-0-9622713; 978-0-888212; 978-0-9822770; 978-1-936270; 978-1-944967

Number of titles published annually: 12 Print; 10 E-Book; 2 Audio

Total Titles: 160 Print; 133 E-Book; 6 Audio

Distributed by St Tikhon's; St Vladimir's

Foreign Rep(s): Crossroad Books (Australia)

Sara Anderson Children's Books

PO Box 47182, Seattle, WA 98146

Tel: 206-285-1520

Web Site: www.saranderson.com

Key Personnel

Founder & CEO: Sara Anderson *E-mail:* sara@saranderson.com

Founded: 2008

Specialize in colorful, innovatively designed early-concept books for babies & toddlers, picture books & a line of bilingual (Spanish-English) children's books.

ISBN Prefix(es): 978-0-9702784; 978-0-9911933; 978-1-943459

Number of titles published annually: 5 Print

Total Titles: 18 Print

§Andrews McMeel Publishing LLC

Division of Andrews McMeel Universal

1130 Walnut St, Kansas City, MO 64106-2109

Toll Free Tel: 800-851-8923; 800-943-9839 (cust serv) *Toll Free Fax:* 800-943-9831 (orders)

E-mail: sales@amuniversal.com

Web Site: www.andrewsmcmeel.com; publishing.andrewsmcmeel.com

Key Personnel

Chmn, Andrews McMeel Universal: John P McMeel

VChmn, Andrews McMeel Universal: Hugh Andrews

Pres, Book Div: Kirsty Melville

VP, Licensing: James Andrews

VP, Mktg: Kathy Hilliard

VP, Opers: Brent Bartram

VP, Prodn: Cliff Koehler

VP of Sales, Books: Lynne McAdoo

Exec Design Dir: Julie Phillips

Asst Art Dir: Sierra Stanton

Exec Ed: Patty Rice

Sr Ed: Allison Adler

Sr Ed, Calendars: Ben Accardi

Sr Prodn Ed: Julie Railsback; Amy Strassner

Ed: Lucas Wetzel

Prodn Ed: Jasmine Lim

Assoc Ed: Melissa Rhodes

Founded: 1973

Publish calendars & humor.

ISBN Prefix(es): 978-0-8362; 978-88-7407; 978-1-4494

Number of titles published annually: 300 Print

Imprints: Accord Publishing; Udig (ebooks)

Distributor for Gooseberry Patch (North America); Signatures Network; Sporting News; Universe Publishing Calendars; Vegan Heritage Press

Foreign Rights: Big Apple Agency Inc (China, Taiwan); The Book Publishers' Association of Israel, International Promotion & Literary Rights Department (Israel); DS Druck und Verlag (Eastern Europe); Europa Press (Scandinavia); Julio F-Yanez Agencia Literaria SL (Brazil, Latin America, Portugal, Spain); Gamma Medya Agency (Turkey); The Italian Literary Agency srl (Italy); Japan UNI Agency Inc (Japan); JLM Literary Agents (Greece); Korea Copyright Center Inc (KCC) (Korea); Andrew Nurnberg Associates Ltd (Bulgaria); Abner Stein Agency (Australia, UK); Tuttle-Mori Agency Inc (Thailand); VVV Agency (France)

Orders to: c/o Simon & Schuster Inc, 100 Front St, Riverside, NJ 08075 *Toll Free Tel:* 800-943-9839 (US orders); 800-268-3216 (CN orders)

Returns: Simon & Schuster, c/o Arnold Logistics, 4406 Industrial Park Rd, Bldg 7, Camp Hill, PA 17011

Distribution Center: Simon & Schuster, Inc, 100 Front St, Riverside, NJ 08075 *Toll Free Tel:* 800-943-9839 (US orders); 800-268-3216 (CN orders)

Vearsa, 79 Madison Ave, New York, NY 10016 (digital dist) *Tel:* 646-568-7797 *E-mail:* info@vearsa.com *Web Site:* www.vearsa.com

Andrews University Press

Division of Andrews University

Sutherland House, 8360 W Campus Circle Dr, Berrien Springs, MI 49104-1700

SAN: 241-0958

Tel: 269-471-6134 *Toll Free Tel:* 800-467-6369 (Visa, MC & American Express orders only) *Fax:* 269-471-6224

E-mail: aupo@andrews.edu; aup@andrews.edu; aupress@andrews.edu

Web Site: www.universitypress.andrews.edu

Key Personnel

Dir: Ronald Knott *E-mail:* knott@andrews.edu

Edit & Mktg Coord: Scottie Baker *Tel:* 269-471-6133 *E-mail:* aup@andrews.edu

Ed: Deborah L Everhart *E-mail:* aupress@andrews.edu

Selected areas of theology, education, philosophy, science, faith & learning.

ISBN Prefix(es): 978-0-943872; 978-1-883925; 978-1-936337; 978-1-940980

Number of titles published annually: 7 Print

Total Titles: 100 Print; 1 CD-ROM; 1 Online

Angel City Press

2118 Wilshire Blvd, Suite 880, Santa Monica, CA 90403

Tel: 310-395-9982 *Toll Free Tel:* 800-949-8039 *Fax:* 310-395-3353

E-mail: info@angelcitypress.com

Web Site: www.angelcitypress.com

Key Personnel

Co-Founder & CEO: Paddy Calistro

Co-Founder & CFO: Scott McAuley

Founded: 1993

Publish books on California & Southern California social & cultural history.

ISBN Prefix(es): 978-1-883318; 978-1-62640

Number of titles published annually: 8 Print

Total Titles: 100 Print

Distributed by Gibbs Smith Publisher

Foreign Rep(s): Turnaround Publishing Services (London)

§Angelus Press

Subsidiary of The Society of Saint Pius X, Southwest District

2915 Forest Ave, Kansas City, MO 64109

Mailing Address: PO Box 217, St Marys, KS 66536

Tel: 816-753-3150 *Toll Free Tel:* 800-966-7337 *Fax:* 816-753-3557

E-mail: support@angeluspress.org

Web Site: www.angeluspress.org

Key Personnel

Ed: James Vogel

Founded: 1978

Monthly journal of Catholic Tradition; traditional Roman Catholic books.

ISBN Prefix(es): 978-0-935952; 978-1-892331; 978-1-937843

Number of titles published annually: 10 Print

Total Titles: 150 Print

Imprints: Sarto House

Branch Office(s)

907 E Jesuit Lane, St Marys, KS 66536 *E-mail:* accounts@angeluspress.org

Sales Office(s): 907 E Jesuit Lane, St Marys, KS 66536, Contact: Ben Bielinski *E-mail:* bbielinski@angeluspress.org

Distributed by Fatima Crusader

Anhinga Press

PO Box 3665, Tallahassee, FL 32315

Tel: 850-577-0745

E-mail: info@anhinga.org

Web Site: www.anhingapress.org; www.facebook.com/anhingapress

Key Personnel

Co-Dir: Carol Lynne Knight *E-mail:* lynne.knight@comcast.net; Jay Snodgrass, PhD *E-mail:* jaysnod@gmail.com; Kristine Snodgrass *E-mail:* kristine.snodgrass@gmail.com

Founded: 1972

ISBN Prefix(es): 978-0-938078; 978-1-934695

Number of titles published annually: 8 Print

Total Titles: 70 Print

Animal Media Group LLC

Subsidiary of Animal Inc

100 First Ave, Suite 1100, Pittsburgh, PA 15222-1519

Tel: 412-566-5656 *Fax:* 412-566-5656

E-mail: info@animalmediagroup.com

Web Site: www.animalmediagroup.com

Key Personnel

Dir, Publg: Howard Shapiro

Founded: 2012

ISBN Prefix(es): 978-0-9912550

Number of titles published annually: 4 Print; 4 Online; 4 E-Book

Total Titles: 12 Print; 10 Online; 4 E-Book

Distribution Center: Consortium Book Sales & Distribution, The Keg House, 34 13 Ave, Suite 101, Minneapolis, MN 55413-1007 *Tel:* 612-746-2600 *Toll Free Tel:* 800-283-3572

(cust serv, Jackson, TN) *Fax:* 612-746-2606
E-mail: info@cbsd.com *Web Site:* www.cbsd.
com SAN: 200-6049

Annual Reviews
4139 El Camino Way, Palo Alto, CA 94306
SAN: 201-1816
Mailing Address: PO Box 10139, Palo Alto, CA
94303-0139
Tel: 650-493-4400 *Toll Free Tel:* 800-523-8635
Fax: 650-424-0910; 650-855-9815
E-mail: service@annualreviews.org
Web Site: www.annualreviews.org
Key Personnel
CFO: Steve Castro *E-mail:* scastro@
annualreviews.org
Pres & Ed-in-Chief: Richard Gallagher
Dir, HR: Lisa Wucher *E-mail:* lwucher@
annualreviews.org
Dir, Prodn: Jennifer Jongsma *E-mail:* jjongsma@
annualreviews.org
Dir, Technol: Paul Calvi *E-mail:* pcalvi@
annualreviews.org
Mktg Mgr: Jenni Rankin *E-mail:* jrankin@
annualreviews.org
Founded: 1932
Scientific review literature, in print & online, in
the biomedical, life, physical & social sciences.
ISBN Prefix(es): 978-0-8243
Number of titles published annually: 20 Print; 50
Online
Total Titles: 50 Online
Foreign Rep(s): Gazelle Book Services Ltd
(Africa, Continental Europe, Ireland, Middle
East, UK); SARAS Books (Bangladesh, India,
Pakistan, Sri Lanka)
Returns: 526 N Earl Ave, PO Box 5685,
Lafayette, IN 47903 (return authorization re-
quired)
Membership(s): American Library Association
(ALA); International Federation of Library
Associations & Institutions (IFLA); Medical
Library Association; National Information Stan-
dards Organization (NISO); Society for Schol-
arly Publishing (SSP); Special Libraries Asso-
ciation (SLA); STM

§ANR Publications University of California
Division of Agriculture & Natural Resources,
University of California
2801 Second St, Davis, CA 95618
Tel: 530-400-0725 (cust serv) *Toll Free Tel:* 800-
994-8849
E-mail: anrcatalog@ucanr.edu
Web Site: anrcatalog.ucanr.edu
Key Personnel
Dir, Publg: Jim Downing *Tel:* 530-750-1352
E-mail: jdowning@ucanr.edu
Mktg Dir & Foreign Rts: Cynthia Kintigh
Tel: 530-750-1217 *E-mail:* cckintigh@ucanr.
edu
Founded: 1914
Peer-reviewed publications on agriculture, gar-
dening, integrated pest management, nutrition,
childhood obesity & natural resources.
ISBN Prefix(es): 978-0-931876; 978-1-879906;
978-1-60107
Number of titles published annually: 4 Print; 30
Online; 5 E-Book
Total Titles: 350 Print; 500 Online; 5 E-Book
Returns: Elite Fulfillment & Logistics, 305 Se-
quoia Ave, Ontario, CA 91761 (contact mv-
comtois@ucanr.edu for A/R prior to making
a return) *Tel:* 951-405-2978 *E-mail:* alma.
anaya@elitelf.com
Distribution Center: Elite Fulfillment & Logistics,
305 Sequoia Ave, Ontario, CA 91761 *Tel:* 951-
405-2978 *E-mail:* kuulei.reyes@elitelf.com
Membership(s): Publishers Association of the
West (PubWest)

Antrim House
21 Goodrich Rd, Simsbury, CT 06070-1804

Tel: 860-217-0023
E-mail: eds@antrimhousebooks.com
Web Site: www.antrimhousebooks.com
Key Personnel
Publr & Ed: Robert Rennie McQuilkin
Founded: 1990
Publish cloth bound editions, perfect bound pa-
perbacks & saddle stitched chapbooks by poets.
This publisher has indicated that 100% of their
product line is author subsidized.
ISBN Prefix(es): 978-0-9662783; 978-0-9792226;
978-0-9770633; 978-0-9762091; 978-0-
9798451; 978-0-9817883; 978-0-9823970; 978-
0-9843418; 978-1-936482
Number of titles published annually: 17 Print; 1
Audio
Total Titles: 140 Print; 3 E-Book; 3 Audio

AOCS Press
Division of American Oil Chemists' Society
2710 S Boulder Dr, Urbana, IL 61802-6996
Mailing Address: PO Box 17190, Urbana, IL
61803-7190
Tel: 217-693-4838 *Fax:* 217-351-8091
E-mail: general@aocs.org
Web Site: www.aocs.org
Key Personnel
CEO: Patrick Donnelly *Fax:* 217-693-4881
E-mail: patrick.donnelly@aocs.org
Founded: 1909
Journals & monographs.
ISBN Prefix(es): 978-0-935315; 978-1-893997;
978-0-9818936
Number of titles published annually: 5 Print; 5
CD-ROM
Total Titles: 100 Print; 21 CD-ROM; 2 Audio

AOTA Press
Imprint of The American Occupational Therapy
Association Inc (AOTA)
6116 Executive Blvd, Suite 200, North Bethesda,
MD 20852-4929
Tel: 301-652-6611 *Toll Free Tel:* 877-404-AOTA
(404-2682, orders) *Fax:* 770-238-0414 (orders)
E-mail: aotapress@aota.org; customerservice@
aota.org
Web Site: www.aota.org/Publications-News/
AOTAPress.aspx; www.aota.org; store.aota.org
Key Personnel
Developmental/Prodn Ed: Ashley Hofmann
E-mail: ahofmann@aota.org
Prodn Ed: Barbara Dickson *E-mail:* bdickson@
aota.org
Founded: 1917
Single titles, newsletters, journals & magazines.
ISBN Prefix(es): 978-0-910317; 978-1-56900
Number of titles published annually: 25 Print
Total Titles: 150 Print
Orders to: PO Box 347036, Pittsburgh, PA
15251-4036 *Toll Free Tel:* 800-729-2682

APC Publishing
PO Box 461166, Aurora, CO 80046-1166
Tel: 303-660-2158 *Toll Free Tel:* 800-660-5107
(sales & orders)
E-mail: mail@4wdbooks.com; orders@4wdbooks.
com
Web Site: www.4wdbooks.com
Key Personnel
Publr: Peter Massey
Mktg Dir: Jeanne Massey
Founded: 1999
ISBN Prefix(es): 978-0-930657; 978-0-9665675;
978-1-930193
Number of titles published annually: 5 Print
Total Titles: 70 Print
Imprints: Outdoor Books & Maps

Aperture Books
Division of Aperture Foundation Inc
547 W 27 St, 4th fl, New York, NY 10001
SAN: 201-1832

Tel: 212-505-5555 *Toll Free Fax:* 888-623-6908
E-mail: customerservice@aperture.org
Web Site: aperture.org
Key Personnel
Creative Dir & Publr: Lesley Martin
Exec Dir: Chris Boot
Dir, Sales & Mktg: Kellie McLaughlin
E-mail: kmclaughlin@aperture.org
Sales Dir, Books: Richard Gregg
E-mail: rgregg@aperture.org
Exec Mng Ed: Amelia Lang
Ed-in-Chief: Melissa Harris
Sr Ed: Denise Wolff
Communs Mgr: Joshua Machat *E-mail:* jmachat@
aperture.org
Founded: 1952
Quarterly magazine; books on photography as
fine art, history of photography, photojournal-
ism, environment.
ISBN Prefix(es): 978-0-89381
Number of titles published annually: 25 Print
Total Titles: 250 Print
Imprints: Aperture Monographs; Masters of Pho-
tography; Writers & Artists on Photography
Series
Foreign Rep(s): Thames & Hudson Ltd (world-
wide exc Canada & USA)
Distribution Center: Ingram Publisher Services,
Cust Serv, Box 631, 14 Ingram Blvd, La
Vergne, TN 37086 *Toll Free Tel:* 844-841-
0255 *E-mail:* ips@ingramcontent.com *Web
Site:* ipage.ingrambook.com

The Apocryphile Press
1700 Shattuck Ave, Suite 81, Berkeley, CA 94709
Tel: 510-290-4349
E-mail: apocryphile@me.com
Web Site: www.apocryphilepress.com
Key Personnel
Publr & Ed: John R Mabry
Assoc Ed: Michael Asteriou
Founded: 1994
Publishes edgy spirituality, liberal religious fiction
& mystical poetry.
ISBN Prefix(es): 978-1-933993; 978-0-9747623;
978-0-9764025; 978-0-9771461; 978-1-937002;
978-1-940671
Number of titles published annually: 12 Print
Total Titles: 200 Print

Apogee Press
2308 Sixth St, Berkeley, CA 94710
E-mail: editors.apogee@gmail.com
Web Site: www.apogeepress.com
Key Personnel
Ed: Alice Jones; Edward Smallfield *Tel:* 510-845-
8800
Founded: 1998
Publishes innovative poetry with an emphasis on
West Coast writers.
ISBN Prefix(es): 978-0-9669937; 978-0-9744687;
978-0-9787667; 978-0-9851007
Number of titles published annually: 3 Print
Total Titles: 38 Print; 2 E-Book
Orders to: Small Press Distribution, 1341 Sev-
enth St, Berkeley, CA 94710-1409, Deputy Dir:
Laura Moriarty *Toll Free Tel:* 800-869-7553
Fax: 510-524-1563 *E-mail:* spd@spdbooks.org
Web Site: www.spdbooks.org
Returns: Small Press Distribution, 1341 Seventh
St, Berkeley, CA 94710-1409, Deputy Dir:
Laura Moriarty *Toll Free Tel:* 800-869-7553
Fax: 510-524-1563 *E-mail:* spd@spdbooks.org
Web Site: www.spdbooks.org
Shipping Address: Small Press Distribution,
1341 Seventh St, Berkeley, CA 94710-1409,
Deputy Dir: Laura Moriarty *Toll Free Tel:* 800-
869-7553 *E-mail:* spd@spdbooks.org *Web
Site:* www.spdbooks.org
Warehouse: Small Press Distribution, 1341 Sev-
enth St, Berkeley, CA 94710-1409 *Toll Free
Tel:* 800-869-7553 *E-mail:* spd@spdbooks.org
Web Site: www.spdbooks.org

Distribution Center: Small Press Distribution, 1341 Seventh St, Berkeley, CA 94710-1409, Deputy Dir: Laura Moriarty *Toll Free Tel:* 800-869-7553 *Fax:* 510-524-1563 *E-mail:* spd@spdbooks.org *Web Site:* www.spdbooks.org
Membership(s): Community of Literary Magazines & Presses (CLMP)

Apollo Managed Care Inc
1100 Town & Country Rd, Suite 1250, Orange, CA 92868
Toll Free Tel: 888-276-5563
E-mail: info@apollomanagedcare.com
Web Site: www.apollomanagedcare.com
Key Personnel
Chief Med Offr: Dr Margaret Bischel
E-mail: mbischel@cox.net
Founded: 1987
Publish comprehensive evidence-based healthcare review criteria & clinical guidelines.
ISBN Prefix(es): 978-1-893826; 978-1-939209
Number of titles published annually: 35 Print; 1 CD-ROM; 5 Online
Total Titles: 40 Print; 1 CD-ROM; 40 Online

APPA: The Association of Higher Education Facilities Officers
1643 Prince St, Alexandria, VA 22314-2818
Tel: 703-684-1446 *Fax:* 703-549-2772
Web Site: www.appa.org
Key Personnel
Dir, Knowledge Mgmt: Steve Glazner
E-mail: steve@appa.org
Pubn Mgr: Anita Dosik *E-mail:* anita@appa.org
Founded: 1914
All titles seek to enhance the development of leadership & professional management applicable to the planning, design, construction & operation of higher education facilities.
ISBN Prefix(es): 978-0-913359; 978-1-890956
Number of titles published annually: 5 Print
Total Titles: 60 Print

Appalachian Mountain Club Books
Division of Appalachian Mountain Club
5 Joy St, Boston, MA 02114
SAN: 203-4808
Tel: 617-523-0655 *Toll Free Tel:* 800-262-4455 (orders) *Fax:* 617-523-0722
E-mail: amcbooks@outdoors.org
Web Site: www.outdoors.org
Key Personnel
VP, Commns & Mktg: Kevin Breunig
Dir, Media & Pub Aff: Rob Burbank *Tel:* 603-466-8155 *E-mail:* rburbank@outdoors.org
Founded: 1897
Guidebooks, maps, outdoor recreation & conservation, mountain history, nature & travel for Northeast US.
ISBN Prefix(es): 978-0-910146; 978-1-878239; 978-1-929173; 978-1-934028; 978-1-62842
Number of titles published annually: 20 Print
Total Titles: 110 Print
Foreign Rep(s): Canadian Manda Group (Canada); Windsor Books Ltd (Europe)
Distribution Center: National Book Network (NBN), 15200 NBN Way, Blue Ridge Summit, PA 17214 *Tel:* 717-794-3800 *Toll Free Tel:* 800-462-6420 *Fax:* 717-794-3828 *Toll Free Fax:* 800-338-4550 *E-mail:* customercare@nbnbooks.com *Web Site:* www.nbnbooks.com

Appalachian Trail Conservancy (ATC)
799 Washington St, Harpers Ferry, WV 25425
Mailing Address: PO Box 807, Harpers Ferry, WV 25425-0807
Tel: 304-535-6331 *Toll Free Tel:* 888-287-8673 (orders only) *Fax:* 304-535-2667
E-mail: publisher@appalachiantrail.org
Web Site: www.appalachiantrail.org; www.atctrailstore.org

Key Personnel
Pres & CEO: Sandra Marra
Publr: Brian B King *Tel:* 304-885-0823
E-mail: bking@appalachiantrail.org
Founded: 1925
Books & maps related to the Appalachian Trail.
ISBN Prefix(es): 978-0-917953; 978-1-889386; 978-1-944958
Number of titles published annually: 5 Print
Total Titles: 46 Print
Sales Office(s): 179 E Burr Blvd, Unit N, Kearneysville, WV 25430, Sales Mgr: Renee M Rodgers *Tel:* 304-728-5143 *Fax:* 304-724-8386 *E-mail:* sales@appalachiantrail.org
Distributed by Mountaineers Books
Distributor for Appalachian Trail Museum Society; Keystone Trails Association; Maine Appalachian Trail Club; Potomac Appalachian Trail Club
Billing Address: PO Box 807, Harpers Ferry, WV 25425-0807
Orders to: 179 East Burr Blvd, Unit N, Kearneysville, WV 25430, Sales Mgr: Renee M Rodgers *Tel:* 304-728-5143 *Fax:* 304-724-8386 *E-mail:* sales@appalachiantrail.org
Warehouse: 179 E Burr Blvd, Unit N, Kearneysville, WV 25430, Sales Mgr: Renee M Rodgers *Tel:* 304-728-5143 *Fax:* 304-724-8386 *E-mail:* sales@appalachiantrail.org
Distribution Center: 179 E Burr Blvd, Unit N, Kearneysville, WV 25430, Sales Mgr: Renee M Rodgers *Tel:* 304-728-5143 *E-mail:* sales@appalachiantrail.org

Applause Theatre & Cinema Books
Imprint of The Globe Pequot Press
PO Box 1520, Wayne, NJ 07470-1520
Tel: 973-987-5363
E-mail: info@applausepub.com
Web Site: www.applausepub.com
Key Personnel
Sr Acq Ed: Carol Flannery *E-mail:* cflannery@rowman.com
Founded: 1983
Plays, theatre books, cinema books, entertainment, television; including DVDs.
ISBN Prefix(es): 978-0-936839; 978-1-55783
Number of titles published annually: 25 Print; 20 E-Book; 10 Audio
Total Titles: 1,000 Print; 700 E-Book; 50 Audio
Sales Office(s): National Book Network, 15200 NBN Way, Blue Ridge Summit, PA 17214 *Toll Free Tel:* 800-462-6420
Distributor for The Working Arts Library; Glenn Young Books
Foreign Rep(s): National Book Network International (worldwide exc Canada, Ireland, UK & USA); Publishers Group UK (UK); Woodslane (Australia, New Zealand)
Foreign Rights: Clare Cox (worldwide)
Orders to: National Book Network, 15200 NBN Way, Blue Ridge Summit, PA 17214 *Toll Free Tel:* 800-462-6420
Warehouse: National Book Network, 15200 NBN Way, Blue Ridge Summit, PA 17214 *Toll Free Tel:* 800-462-6420
Distribution Center: National Book Network, 15200 NBN Way, Blue Ridge Summit, PA 17214 *Toll Free Tel:* 800-462-6420

Applewood Books Inc
One River Rd, Carlisle, MA 01741
SAN: 210-3419
Mailing Address: PO Box 27, Carlisle, MA 01741
Tel: 781-271-0055 *Toll Free Tel:* 800-277-5312 (orders) *Fax:* 781-271-0056
E-mail: bookorder@awb.com; customercare@awb.com
Web Site: www.awb.com
Key Personnel
Founder, Pres & ISBN Contact: Phil Zuckerman
E-mail: philz@awb.com

VP, Opers: Sue Cabezas *E-mail:* suec@awb.com
Founded: 1976
Americana reprints.
ISBN Prefix(es): 978-0-918222; 978-1-55709; 978-1-889833; 978-1-933212; 978-1-4290; 978-0-9819430; 978-1-60889; 978-0-9844156; 978-0-9836416; 978-1-938700; 978-0-9882885; 978-1-5162
Number of titles published annually: 500 Print
Total Titles: 2,500 Print
Imprints: Commonwealth Editions; Grab a Pencil Press
Orders to: PO Box 27, Carlisle, MA 01741
Warehouse: Ingram Publishers Services, 1280 Ingram Dr, Chambersburg, PA 17201
See separate listing for:
Commonwealth Editions

Appraisal Institute
200 W Madison, Suite 1500, Chicago, IL 60606
Tel: 312-335-4100 *Toll Free Tel:* 888-756-4624 *Fax:* 312-335-4400
E-mail: aiservice@appraisalinstitute.org
Web Site: www.appraisalinstitute.org
Key Personnel
Sr Mgr, Pubns: Tep Shea-Joyce *E-mail:* tshea-joyce@appraisalinstitute.org
Founded: 1932
Professional real estate appraisal books, monographs, periodicals & videos.
ISBN Prefix(es): 978-0-911780; 978-0-922154
Number of titles published annually: 6 Print
Total Titles: 60 Print
Branch Office(s)
440 First St NW, Suite 880, Washington, DC 20001 *Tel:* 202-298-6449
Distributed by Dearborn Trade
Foreign Rep(s): Royal Institution of Chartered Surveyors (Africa, Caribbean, Commonwealth, Ethiopia, Europe, Far East)

Apress Media LLC
Division of Springer Nature
233 Spring St, 6th fl, New York, NY 10013
Tel: 212-460-1500
E-mail: editorial@apress.com; customerservice@springernature.com
Web Site: www.apress.com
Key Personnel
Mng Dir: Welmoed Spahr *Tel:* 212-460-1622
E-mail: welmoed.spahr@springer.com
Edit Dir: Todd Green *E-mail:* todd.green@apress.com
Mng Devt Ed: Matthew Moodie
E-mail: matthewmoodie@apress.com
Edit Opers Mgr: Mark Powers
E-mail: markpowers@apress.com
Technical publisher devoted to meeting the needs of IT professionals, software developers & programmers with books in print & electronic format.
ISBN Prefix(es): 978-1-893115; 978-1-59059; 978-1-4302
Total Titles: 1,000 Print

§APS PRESS
Imprint of The American Phytopathological Society (APS)
3340 Pilot Knob Rd, St Paul, MN 55121
Tel: 651-454-7250 *Toll Free Tel:* 800-328-7560 *Fax:* 651-454-0766
E-mail: aps@scisoc.org
Web Site: www.shopapspress.org
Key Personnel
EVP: Amy Hope *E-mail:* ahope@scisoc.org
Pubns Mktg Dir: Greg Grahek *Tel:* 651-454-7250 ext 141 *E-mail:* ggrahek@scisoc.org
Pubns Mktg Coord: Dawn Wuest
E-mail: dwuest@scisoc.org
Founded: 1908

Publishers of key reference books, field guides, laboratory manuals & other scientific titles related to plant health.
ISBN Prefix(es): 978-0-89054
Number of titles published annually: 10 Print; 2 CD-ROM; 4 Online
Total Titles: 300 Print; 40 CD-ROM; 2 Online

§Arbordale Publishing
612 Johnnie Dodds Blvd, Suite A2, Mount Pleasant, SC 29464
SAN: 256-6109
Tel: 843-971-6722 *Toll Free Tel:* 877-243-3457
  Fax: 843-216-3804
E-mail: info@arbordalepublishing.com
Web Site: www.arbordalepublishing.com
Key Personnel
Publr: Lee German *E-mail:* leegerman@arbordalepublishing.com
Ed: Donna German *E-mail:* donna@arbordalepublishing.com
PR: Heather Williams *E-mail:* heather@arbordalepublishing.com
Off Mgr: Elma Haley *E-mail:* elma@arbordalepublishing.com
Founded: 2005
Company on a mission to create picture books that will excite children's imagination, are artistically spectacular & have educational value. Most of our stories are fictional but relate to a nonfictional theme of science, nature or animals. Each book is seriously vetted for scientific accuracy before publication. We reserve 3-5 pages in the back of each book to add our "Creative Minds" section, loaded with fun facts, crafts & games to supplement the educational thread of the book. Ebooks with auto read, auto flip & selectable English & Spanish text in audio.
ISBN Prefix(es): 978-0-9777423; 978-1-60718; 978-1-62855; 978-1-934358; 978-0-9764943; 978-0-9768823
Number of titles published annually: 36 Print; 24 Online; 27 E-Book; 27 Audio
Total Titles: 228 Print; 303 Online; 303 E-Book; 303 Audio
Foreign Rep(s): Ediciones Enlace de PR (Puerto Rico); Fitzhenry & Whiteside (Canada)
Foreign Rights: Sylvia Hayes Literary Agency
Distribution Center: The Reading Warehouse, PO Box 41328, North Charleston, SC 29423 *E-mail:* customerservice@thereadingwarehouse.com *Web Site:* www.thereadingwarehouse.com
Bound to Stay Bound, 1880 W Morton Ave, Jacksonville, IL 62650 *Toll Free Tel:* 800-637-6586 *Toll Free Fax:* 800-747-2872 *E-mail:* btsb@btsb.com *Web Site:* www.btsb.com
Perma-Bound, 617 E Vandalia Rd, Jacksonville, IL 62650 *Tel:* 217-243-5451 *Toll Free Tel:* 800-637-9581 *Fax:* 217-243-7505 *Toll Free Fax:* 800-551-1169 *E-mail:* books@perma-bound.com *Web Site:* www.perma-bound.com
Follett School Solutions Inc, 1340 Ridgeview Dr, McHenry, IL 60050 *Tel:* 815-759-1700 *Toll Free Tel:* 888-511-5114 (cust serv) *Fax:* 815-459-9831 *Toll Free Fax:* 800-852-5458 *E-mail:* info@follettlearning.com *Web Site:* www.follettlearning.com SAN: 169-1902
Mackin Educational Resources, 3505 County Rd 42 W, Burnsville, MN 55306 *Tel:* 952-895-9540 *Toll Free Tel:* 800-245-9540 *Fax:* 952-894-8806 *Toll Free Fax:* 800-369-5490 *E-mail:* customerservice@mackin.com *Web Site:* www.mackin.com
The Booksource Inc, 1230 Macklind Ave, St Louis, MO 63110 *Toll Free Tel:* 800-444-0435 *Toll Free Fax:* 800-647-1923 *E-mail:* service@booksource.com *Web Site:* www.booksource.com
Baker & Taylor, 2550 W Tyvola Rd, Suite 300, Charlotte, NC 28217 *Toll Free Tel:* 800-775-1800 *Fax:* 704-998-3100 *E-mail:* btinfo@baker-taylor.com *Web Site:* www.baker-taylor.com
Brodart, 500 Arch St, Williamsport, PA 17701 *Tel:* 570-326-2461 *Toll Free Tel:* 800-233-8487 *Fax:* 570-326-1479 *E-mail:* support@brodart.com *Web Site:* www.brodart.com
Ingram, One Ingram Blvd, La Vergne, TN 37086 *Tel:* 615-793-5000 *Toll Free Tel:* 800-937-8200 *E-mail:* customer.service@ingrambook.com *Web Site:* www.ingrambook.com
Penworthy, 219 N Milwaukee St, Milwaukee, WI 53202 *Tel:* 414-287-4600 *Toll Free Tel:* 800-262-2665 *Fax:* 414-287-4602 *E-mail:* info@penworthy.com *Web Site:* www.penworthy.com
Membership(s): American Booksellers Association (ABA); BookSense Publisher Partner; The Children's Book Council (CBC); Florida Authors & Publishers Association Inc (FAPA); Independent Book Publishers Association (IBPA); International Literacy Association (ILA); National Association for Bilingual Education; National Association of Book Entrepreneurs (NABE)

Arbutus Press
2364 Pinehurst Trail, Traverse City, MI 49696
Tel: 231-946-7240
E-mail: info@arbutuspress.com
Web Site: www.arbutuspress.com
Key Personnel
Publr: Susan Bays
Founded: 1998
Midwest regional history & travel related.
ISBN Prefix(es): 978-0-9665316; 978-0-9766104; 978-1-933926
Number of titles published annually: 12 Print
Total Titles: 90 Print; 25 E-Book; 3 Audio

Arcade Publishing Inc
Imprint of Skyhorse Publishing Inc
307 W 36 St, 11th fl, New York, NY 10018
Tel: 212-643-6816 *Fax:* 212-643-6819
E-mail: info@skyhorsepublishing.com (subs & foreign rts)
Web Site: www.arcadepub.com
Key Personnel
Pres & Publr: Tony Lyons
VP: Bill Wolfsthal *E-mail:* bwolfsthal@skyhorsepublishing.com
Founded: 1988
Trade fiction & nonfiction; adult & juvenile.
ISBN Prefix(es): 978-1-61145; 978-1-62872
Number of titles published annually: 100 Print; 100 E-Book
Total Titles: 700 Print
Foreign Rights: Biagi Literary Management
Distribution Center: Perseus Book Distribution/Ingram Content Group, 1400 Broadway, New York, NY 10018 *E-mail:* orderentry@perseusbooks.com

Arcadia Publishing Inc
420 Wando Park Blvd, Mount Pleasant, SC 29464
SAN: 255-268X
Tel: 843-853-2070 *Toll Free Tel:* 888-313-2665 (orders only) *Fax:* 843-853-0044
E-mail: sales@arcadiapublishing.com
Web Site: www.arcadiapublishing.com
Key Personnel
Pres & CEO: David Steinberger
COO: Charles Gallagher
Cont: Kristen Crawford
Publr, Pelican Publishing: Scott Campbell
Dir, IT: William Brandt
Dir, Natl Sales & Mktg: Amy Kaneko
Dir, Publicity, Pelican Publishing: Antoinette de Alteriis
Dir, Spec Projs: Christen Thompson
Ed-in-Chief, Pelican Publishing: Nina Kooij
Ed-in-Chief, Wildsam: Taylor Bruce
Acqs Ed: Katelyn Jenkins
Sr Prodn Ed & Design Coord, Pelican Publishing: Kevin Johnson
Prodn Ed: Cameron Haines
Prodn Ed, History Press: Hayley Behal; Ashley Hill
Prodn Ed & Design Coord, Pelican Publishing: Cassie Zimmerman
Asst Ed, Pelican Publishing: Devinn Adams
Ed-at-Large & Sr Advisor: Walter Isaacson
Busn Devt Mgr: Matthew Gildea
Independent Sales Mgr, East: Mike Nieken
Independent Sales Mgr, Strategic Growth: Leigh Scott
Independent Sales Mgr, West: Elysia Walton
Sales Mgr, Pelican Publishing: John Scheyd
Scan-Based Trading Data Mgr: Sam Jones
Field Sales Rep: Hampton Ryan
Sales Specialist: Shane Hennigan
Founded: 1992
Local history & vintage images.
ISBN Prefix(es): 978-0-7385; 978-1-4396; 978-1-4671
Number of titles published annually: 600 Print
Total Titles: 14,500 Print; 6,000 E-Book
Imprints: Arcadia Children's Books; History Press; Legendary Locals; Pelican Publishing Co; Wildsam (field guides)
See separate listing for:
Pelican Publishing Co

Arcana Publishing, see Lotus Press

ARE Press
Division of The Association for Research & Enlightenment Inc (ARE)
215 67 St, Virginia Beach, VA 23451
Tel: 757-428-3588 *Toll Free Tel:* 800-333-4499
Web Site: www.edgarcayce.org
Key Personnel
Mktg Dir: Jennie Taylor Martin *Tel:* 757-457-7249 *E-mail:* jennie@edgarcayce.org
Dir, Prodn, Cust Serv, Rts & Perms: Cassie McQuagge *Tel:* 757-457-7239 *E-mail:* cassie@edgarcayce.org
Founded: 1931
Holistic health & spiritual development, based on Edgar Cayce material.
ISBN Prefix(es): 978-0-87604
Number of titles published annually: 1 Print; 4 E-Book
Imprints: 4th Dimension Press

Ariadne Press
270 Goins Ct, Riverside, CA 92507
Tel: 951-684-9202 *Fax:* 951-779-0449
E-mail: ariadnepress@aol.com
Web Site: www.ariadnebooks.com
Key Personnel
Partner: Jorun Johns
Founded: 1988
Studies in Austrian literature, culture & thought.
ISBN Prefix(es): 978-0-929497; 978-1-57241
Number of titles published annually: 12 Print
Total Titles: 205 Print
Foreign Rep(s): Gazelle Book Services Ltd (UK); Schaden (Austria)
Foreign Rights: Gazelle Book Services Ltd (UK)

§Ariel Press
Subsidiary of Light
2317 Quail Cove Dr, Jasper, GA 30143
Mailing Address: PO Box 251, Marble Hill, GA 30148
Tel: 770-894-4226
E-mail: lig201@lightariel.com
Web Site: www.lightariel.com
Key Personnel
Pres & Publr: Carl Japikse
Art Dir: Nancy Maxwell
Founded: 1976
Nonfiction hardcover & paperbound books; essays & subscription series on personal growth, cre-

ativity, holistic health & psychic phenomena; esoteric fiction; reprints.
ISBN Prefix(es): 978-0-89804
Number of titles published annually: 11 Print; 10 E-Book
Total Titles: 200 Print; 25 E-Book
Imprints: Enthea Press; Kudzu House
Distributor for Enthea Press; Kudzu House

The Arion Press
Division of Lyra Corp
The Presidio, 1802 Hays St, San Francisco, CA 94129
SAN: 203-1361
Tel: 415-668-2542 *Fax:* 415-668-2550
E-mail: arionpress@arionpress.com
Web Site: www.arionpress.com
Key Personnel
Dir, Mktg & Sales: Chris Dunlap
Founded: 1974
Fine, limited edition illustrated books of fiction, literature & poetry.
ISBN Prefix(es): 978-0-910457
Number of titles published annually: 3 Print
Total Titles: 110 Print
Divisions: M & H Type

Arkham House Publishers Inc
PO Box 546, Sauk City, WI 53583
SAN: 206-9741
Tel: 608-643-4500 *Fax:* 608-643-5043
E-mail: sales@arkhamhouse.com
Web Site: www.arkhamhouse.com
Key Personnel
Pres: Danielle Hackett
VP: Damon Derleth
Founded: 1939
Fantasy fiction, horror, macabre, science fiction.
ISBN Prefix(es): 978-0-87054
Number of titles published annually: 3 Print
Total Titles: 54 Print; 54 Online; 54 E-Book
Imprints: Mycroft & Moran

Aro Book Publishing Co
130 S 800 W, Salt Lake City, UT 84104-1120
Tel: 801-637-9115 *Fax:* 801-419-0125
E-mail: arobook@yahoo.com
Web Site: www.arobookpublishing.com
Key Personnel
Pres: Bob Reese
Founded: 1973
K-4 beginning to read.
ISBN Prefix(es): 978-0-89868
Number of titles published annually: 30 Print
Total Titles: 35 Print; 65 Online; 35 E-Book

Jason Aronson Inc
Imprint of Rowman & Littlefield Publishing Group
4501 Forbes Blvd, Suite 200, Lanham, MD 20706
SAN: 201-0127
Tel: 301-459-3366 *Toll Free Tel:* 800-462-6420 ext 3024 (cust serv) *Fax:* 301-429-5748
Toll Free Fax: 800-338-4550 (cust serv)
E-mail: orders@rowman.com; customercare@rowman.com
Web Site: www.rowman.com
Key Personnel
SVP & Publr: Julie E Kirsch *Tel:* 301-459-3366 ext 5309 *E-mail:* jkirsch@rowman.com
Exec Channel Mgr, Academic & Spec Libs: Kim Lyons *Tel:* 301-459-3366 ext 5602 *E-mail:* klyons@rowman.com
Perms & Alternate Format for Students with Disabilities: Rachel Twombly *Tel:* 301-459-3366 ext 5420 *E-mail:* rtwombly@rowman.com
Founded: 1965
Professional books in psychotherapy, psychoanalysis & psychology.
ISBN Prefix(es): 978-0-87668; 978-1-56821; 978-0-7657; 978-1-4425

Number of titles published annually: 25 Print; 25 E-Book
Total Titles: 1,700 Print
Foreign Rep(s): Academic Marketing Services Pty Ltd (Botswana, Namibia, South Africa, Zimbabwe); APD Singapore Pte Ltd (Brunei, Cambodia, Indonesia, Laos, Malaysia, Singapore, Thailand, Vietnam); Asia Publishers Service Ltd (China, Hong Kong, Korea, Philippines, Taiwan); Avicenna Partnership Ltd (Afghanistan, Algeria, Armenia, Bahrain, Cyprus, Egypt, Iran, Iraq, Jordan, Kuwait, Lebanon, Libya, Morocco, Oman, Palestine, Qatar, Saudi Arabia, Sudan, Syria, Tunisia, United Arab Emirates, Yemen); Cranbury International LLC (Caribbean, Central America, Mexico, Pakistan, Puerto Rico, South America); Durnell Marketing Ltd (Austria, Baltic States, Belgium, Czechia, Denmark, Finland, France, Germany, Greece, Hungary, Iceland, Italy, Malta, Netherlands, Norway, Poland, Portugal, Slovakia, Slovenia, Spain, Sweden, Switzerland); NBN International; Overleaf (Bangladesh, Bhutan, India, Nepal, Sri Lanka); United Publishers Service Ltd (Japan, South Korea)

Art Image Publications
Division of GB Publishing Inc
PO Box 160, Derby Line, VT 05830
Toll Free Tel: 800-361-2598 *Toll Free Fax:* 800-559-2598
E-mail: info@artimagepublications.com; customer.service@artimagepublications.com
Web Site: www.artimagepublications.com
Key Personnel
Pres: Yvan Boulerice
Secy: Francoise Desjardins
Founded: 1980
ISBN Prefix(es): 978-1-896876; 978-1-55292
Number of titles published annually: 12 Print
Total Titles: 52 Print

The Art Institute of Chicago
111 S Michigan Ave, Chicago, IL 60603-6404
SAN: 204-479X
Tel: 312-443-3600; 312-443-3540 (pubns) *Fax:* 312-443-1334 (pubns)
Web Site: www.artic.edu; www.artinstituteshop.org
Key Personnel
Pres & Dir: James Rondeau *Tel:* 312-443-3632
Exec Dir, Pubns: Gregory Nosan *Tel:* 312-443-4964 *E-mail:* gnosan@artic.edu
Dir, Prodn: Joseph Mohan *Tel:* 312-443-4955 *E-mail:* jmohan@artic.edu
Asst Dir, Prodn: Lauren Makholm *Tel:* 312-443-3539 *E-mail:* lmakholm@artic.edu
Ed: Amy Peltz *Tel:* 312-443-4963 *E-mail:* apeltz@artic.edu; Maia M Rigas *Tel:* 312-443-4774 *E-mail:* mrigas@artic.edu
Photo Ed: Katie Levi *Tel:* 312-443-4974 *E-mail:* klevi@artic.edu
Asst Ed: Sara Carminati *Tel:* 312-857-7612 *E-mail:* scarmi@artic.edu
Fin & Admin Coord: Jessica Applebee *Tel:* 312-443-4962 *E-mail:* japplebee@artic.edu
Prodn Coord: Rachel Edsill *Tel:* 312-443-1334 *E-mail:* redsill@artic.edu
Digital Catalog Designer: Beata Hosea *Tel:* 312-443-3727 *E-mail:* bhosea@artic.edu
Founded: 1879
Exhibition catalogues, popular & scholarly art books on the museum's permanent collection: African art & Indian art of the Americas; American art; Ancient & Byzantine art; architecture & design; Asian art; contemporary art; European painting, sculpture & decorative arts; photography; prints & drawings; textiles.
ISBN Prefix(es): 978-0-86559
Number of titles published annually: 10 Print; 1 Online

Total Titles: 60 Print; 10 Online; 1 E-Book
Distributed by Yale University Press

Art of Living, PrimaMedia Inc
1050 Second St Pike, Unit 1373, Southampton, PA 18966
SAN: 299-8858
Tel: 215-660-5045
E-mail: primamedia4@yahoo.com
Key Personnel
Ed: Gia Carispat *E-mail:* primamedia12@yahoo.com
Billing: Joan Campo *E-mail:* primamedia40@gmail.com
Orders & Cust Serv: Sue Thomson
Orders & Returns: Sue Timmons Thomas
Contact: Katherine Rafter *E-mail:* primamedia9@yahoo.com
Founded: 2005
Boutique publishing company. Publisher of the award-winning book series *The Basic Art of Italian Cooking* & *The Basic Art.* Can place orders by telephone or e-mail, but prefer e-mail.
ISBN Prefix(es): 978-1-928911
Number of titles published annually: 20 Print; 10 E-Book
Total Titles: 25 Print; 35 Online; 35 E-Book
Foreign Rep(s): Rebecca Ferrone (Australia, Canada, Europe)
Distribution Center: Amazon.com
Follett School Solutions Inc, 1340 Ridgeview Dr, McHenry, IL 60050 *Tel:* 815-759-1700 *Toll Free Tel:* 888-511-5114 (cust serv) *Fax:* 815-759-9831 *Toll Free Fax:* 800-852-5458 *E-mail:* info@follettlearning.com *Web Site:* www.follettlearning.com SAN: 169-1902

ArtAge Publications
PO Box 19955, Portland, OR 97280
Tel: 503-246-3000 *Toll Free Tel:* 800-858-4998
Web Site: www.seniortheatre.com
Key Personnel
Pres: Bonnie L Vorenberg *E-mail:* bonniev@seniortheatre.com
Founded: 1997
The Senior Theatre Resource Center has the largest collection of plays, books & information for older performers. We help older performers fulfill their theatrical dreams.
ISBN Prefix(es): 978-0-9669412
Number of titles published annually: 45 Print; 45 Online; 27 E-Book; 5 Audio
Total Titles: 400 Print; 300 Online; 275 E-Book; 11 Audio
Returns: 7845 SW Capitol Hwy, Suite 12, Portland, OR 97219

Arte Publico Press
Affiliate of University of Houston
University of Houston, Bldg 19, Rm 100, 4902 Gulf Fwy, Houston, TX 77204-2004
Tel: 713-743-2998 (sales) *Toll Free Tel:* 800-633-2783 *Fax:* 713-743-2847 (sales)
E-mail: appinfo@uh.edu; bkorders@uh.edu
Web Site: artepublicopress.com
Key Personnel
Publr: Nicolas Kanellos
Founded: 1979
Books by American Hispanic authors.
ISBN Prefix(es): 978-0-934770; 978-1-55885
Number of titles published annually: 30 Print
Total Titles: 400 Print
Imprints: Pinata Books
Subsidiaries: The Americas Review
Distributor for Bilingual Review Press; Latin American Review Press
Foreign Rights: Raquel de la Concha (Spain); Agencia Literaria Virginia Lopez-Ballesteros (Spain)
Membership(s): Association of American Publishers (AAP)

§Artech House®

Subsidiary of Horizon House Publications Inc
685 Canton St, Norwood, MA 02062
SAN: 201-1441
Tel: 781-769-9750 *Toll Free Tel:* 800-225-9977
 Fax: 781-769-6334
E-mail: artech@artechhouse.com
Web Site: www.artechhouse.com
Key Personnel
COO: Christopher D Ernst *E-mail:* cernst@
 artechhouse.com
Publr: William M Bazzy *E-mail:* wmbazzy@
 artechhouse.com
Dir, Edit & Prodn: Darrell Judd
Exec Ed: Judi Stone
Acq Ed: David Michelson *E-mail:* dmichelson@
 artechhouse.com
Sales & Mktg Mgr: Kate Skypeck
 E-mail: kskypeck@artechhouse.com
Founded: 1970
Technical & engineering.
ISBN Prefix(es): 978-0-89006; 978-1-58053; 978-
 1-59693; 978-1-60807; 978-1-60783; 978-1-
 63081
Number of titles published annually: 35 Print; 35
 E-Book
Total Titles: 1,500 Print; 600 E-Book
Foreign Office(s): 16 Sussex St, London SW1V
 4RW, United Kingdom, Acqs Dir: Merlin Fox
 Tel: (020) 7596 8750 *Fax:* (020) 7630 0166
 E-mail: artech-uk@artechhouse.com
Foreign Rep(s): Akateeminen (Finland); Anglo-
 American Book Co (Italy); Asian Books Pvt
 Ltd (India, Pakistan); C V Toko Buku Topen
 (Indonesia); Clarke Associates Ltd (Pacific
 Basin); Computer Press (Sweden); D A Book
 Pty Ltd (Australia, New Zealand); Dai-Iti Pub-
 lications Trading Co Ltd (Japan); Diaz de San-
 tos (Spain); Dietmar Dreier (Germany); DK
 Book House Co Ltd (Thailand); Freihofer AG
 (Switzerland); Kumi Trading Co Ltd (South
 Korea); Librairie Lavoisier (France); Login
 Canada (Canada); Julio Logrado de Figueiredo
 Lda (Portugal); The Modern Book Co (UK);
 Pak Book Corp (Pakistan); Polyteknisk (Den-
 mark); Sejong (Korea); Ta Tong Book Co Ltd
 (Taiwan); Tapir (Norway); Tecmedd (Brazil);
 UBS Library Services (Singapore); United Pub-
 lishers Services Ltd (Japan, South Korea); L
 Wouters (Belgium)
Foreign Rights: ABE Marketing (Poland); BSB
 Distribution (Germany); Fleet Publications
 (Chile); Foyles (UK); Hoepli (Italy); Kuwkab
 (Mideast); Livraria Canuto (Brazil); Papsotiriou
 (Greece)
Returns: NBN International, Airport Busn Ctr,
 10 Thornbury Rd, Plymouth PL6 7PP, United
 Kingdom; Publishers Storage & Shipping Corp
 (US only), 231 Industrial Park, 46 Develop-
 ment Rd, Fitchburg, MA 01420 *Tel:* 978-345-
 2121 *Fax:* 978-348-1233
Warehouse: Publishers Storage & Shipping Corp
 (US only), 231 Industrial Park, 46 Develop-
 ment Rd, Fitchburg, MA 01420 *Tel:* 978-345-
 2121 *Fax:* 978-348-1233

Artisan

Division of Workman Publishing Co Inc
225 Varick St, New York, NY 10014-4381
Tel: 212-254-5900 *Toll Free Tel:* 800-722-7202
 Fax: 212-677-6692
E-mail: artisaninfo@artisanbooks.com
Web Site: www.artisanbooks.com; www.workman.
 com/artisanbooks
Key Personnel
Publr: Lia Ronnen
Assoc Publr: Allison McGeehon
Creative Dir: Michelle Ishay-Cohen
Prodn Dir: Nancy Murray
Asst Dir, Publicity & Mktg: Theresa Collier
Mng Ed: Zachary Greenwald
Sr Ed: Shoshana Gutmajer; Bridget Monroe Itkin

Sr Mgr, Foreign Rts & Co-Editions: Allison Hug-
 gins
Founded: 1993
Illustrated books & calendars to the trade.
ISBN Prefix(es): 978-1-885183; 978-1-57965
Number of titles published annually: 15 Print
Distributor for Greenwich Workshop Press
Foreign Rep(s): Thomas Allen & Son Ltd
 (Canada); Bookreps New Zealand (New
 Zealand); Hardie Grant Books (Australia);
 Melia Publishing Services (UK)
Foreign Rights: Big Apple Agency Inc (China,
 Taiwan); Julio F-Yanez Agencia Literaria SL
 (Latin America, Portugal, Spain); Graal Lit-
 erary Agency (Poland); The Deborah Harris
 Agency (Israel); The Italian Literary Agency
 srl (Italy); Japan UNI Agency Inc (Japan); JLM
 Literary Agency (Greece); Katai & Bolza Lit-
 erary Agents (Hungary); Korea Copyright Cen-
 ter Inc (KCC) (Korea); Kristin Olson Literary
 Agency SRO (Czechia); Plima Literary Agency
 (Bulgaria, Croatia, North Macedonia, Serbia,
 Slovenia); Sebes & Bisseling Literary Agency
 (Netherlands)
Shipping Address: RR Donnelley, 1077 Prospect
 Lane, Kaukauna, WI 54130

§Artisan Bookworks

921 S Third Ave, No 8, Sequim, WA 98382
Mailing Address: PO Box 1972, Sequim, WA
 98382
Tel: 425-954-5277
E-mail: books@artisanbookworks.com
Web Site: www.artisanbookworks.com
Key Personnel
Publr: Kelly Lenihan
Founded: 2012
Artisan Bookworks mission is to assist emerging
 writers on their publishing journey. Publishing
 services include book design (print & digital),
 copy-editing/proofreading for children's books,
 picture books & general fiction. Some nonfic-
 tion & memoirs will be considered.
This publisher has indicated that 75% of their
 product line is author subsidized.
ISBN Prefix(es): 978-0-9898692; 978-0-9911747;
 978-0-9979578
Number of titles published annually: 15 Print; 10
 E-Book
Shipping Address: Ingram Books Direct Distribution Services, 1246 Heil Quaker Blvd, La
 Vergne, TN 37086
Membership(s): The Association of Publishers for
 Special Sales (APSS); Book Publishers of the
 Northwest (BPNW); Pacific Northwest Book-
 sellers Association (PNBA)

ArtWrite Productions

1555 Gardena Ave NE, Minneapolis, MN 55432-
 5848
Tel: 612-803-0436
E-mail: artwriteprod@gmail.com
Web Site: artwriteproductions.com;
 adaptedclassics.com
Key Personnel
Owner: Jerome Tiller *E-mail:* jtiller@
 adaptedclassics.com
Founded: 2003
Publishes books using humorous storytelling to
 enhance lessons in natural & social sciences.
 Under the imprint, Adapted Classics, we adapt
 stories by the world's greatest authors, using
 gallery-worthy illustrations to entice young
 adults to discover & embrace classic literature.
ISBN Prefix(es): 978-1-939846; 978-0-9777693
Number of titles published annually: 2 Print; 2 E-
 Book
Total Titles: 9 Print; 8 E-Book
Imprints: Adapted Classics
Distribution Center: Follett School Solutions,
 1340 Ridgeview Dr, McHenry, IL 60050, Con-
 tact: Liz Michmershuizen *Tel:* 708-884-6564

Fax: 815-759-9552 *E-mail:* lmichmershuizen@
 follett.com
Baker & Taylor Books, 2550 W Tyvola Rd,
 Suite 300, Charlotte, NC 28217, Sr Buyer: Ms
 Robin Bright *Tel:* 908-541-7425 *E-mail:* robin.
 bright@baker-taylor.com *Web Site:* btol.com
Membership(s): Independent Book Publishers Association (IBPA); Midwest Independent Publishing Association (MIPA); Society of Children's Book Writers & Illustrators (SCBWI)

ASBO International, see Association of School
Business Officials International

§ASCD

1703 N Beauregard St, Alexandria, VA 22311-
 1714
SAN: 201-1352
Tel: 703-578-9600 *Toll Free Tel:* 800-933-2723
 Fax: 703-575-5400
E-mail: member@ascd.org
Web Site: www.ascd.org
Key Personnel
Publr: Stefani Roth
Dir, Book Editing & Prodn: Julie Houtz *Tel:* 703-
 575-5706 *E-mail:* jhoutz@ascd.org
Dir, Acqs: Genny Ostertag *Tel:* 703-575-5469
 E-mail: gostertag@ascd.org
Founded: 1943
Professional books for educators.
ISBN Prefix(es): 978-0-87120; 978-1-4166
Number of titles published annually: 50 Print; 35
 E-Book
Total Titles: 480 Print; 460 E-Book
Orders to: PO Box 17035, Baltimore, MD 21297-
 8431

Ascend Books LLC

7221 W 79 St, Suite 206, Overland Park, KS
 66204
SAN: 856-3454
Tel: 913-948-5500
Web Site: www.ascendbooks.com
Key Personnel
Publr & CEO: Robert Snodgrass
 E-mail: bsnodgrass@ascendbooks.com
Mng Ed: Aaron Cedeno *E-mail:* acedeno@
 ascendbooks.com
Pubn Sales Mgr: Christine Drummond
 Tel: 913-948-7635 *Fax:* 913-948-7770
 E-mail: cdrummond@ascendbooks.com
Founded: 2008
Publisher of books on sports & entertainment top-
 ics & children's books by celebrity authors &
 educators.
ISBN Prefix(es): 978-0-9830619
Number of titles published annually: 12 Print; 10
 E-Book
Total Titles: 80 Print; 35 E-Book
Distribution Center: Ingram Book Co, One
 Ingram Blvd, La Vergne, TN 37086, Con-
 tact: Kitti McConnell *Tel:* 615-213-5335
 Toll Free Tel: 800-937-8200 *E-mail:* kitti.
 mcconnell@ingramcontent.com *Web
 Site:* www.ingrambook.com
APG, 1501 County Hospital Rd, Nashville,
 TN 37218, Sales Mgr: Debbie Felt *Tel:* 615-
 254-2488 *E-mail:* dfelt@apgbooks.com *Web
 Site:* apgbooks.com
Membership(s): Independent Book Publishers As-
 sociation (IBPA)

Ascension Press

PO Box 1990, West Chester, PA 19380
Tel: 610-696-7795; 484-875-4550 (admin)
 Toll Free Tel: 800-376-0520 (sales & cust serv)
Web Site: ascensionpress.com
Key Personnel
Pres: Matthew Pinto
Dir, Mktg: Chris Michalski *E-mail:* cmichalski@
 ascensionpress.com

Dir, Sales: Deb Varnado *E-mail:* dvarnado@ ascensionpress.com

Exec Prodr: Steve Motyl *E-mail:* smotyl@ ascensionpress.com

Exec Ed: Mike Flickinger *E-mail:* mflickinger@ ascensionpress.com

Assoc Ed: Lora Brecker *E-mail:* lbrecker@ ascensionpress.com

Religious educational publishers.

ISBN Prefix(es): 978-1-932645; 978-0-9742238; 978-0-9659228; 978-0-9744451; 978-1-932631; 978-1-932927; 978-1-934217; 978-1-935940

Number of titles published annually: 15 Print

Total Titles: 250 Print; 200 Online; 40 Audio

Sales Office(s): 4001 W Greentree Rd, Milwaukee, WI 53209 *Toll Free Tel:* 800-376-0520

Orders to: 4001 W Greentree Rd, Milwaukee, WI 53209 *Toll Free Tel:* 800-376-0520

Returns: 4001 W Greentree Rd, Milwaukee, WI 53209 *Toll Free Tel:* 800-376-0520

Warehouse: 4001 W Greentree Rd, Milwaukee, WI 53209 *Toll Free Tel:* 800-376-0520

Distribution Center: 4001 W Greentree Rd, Milwaukee, WI 53209 *Toll Free Tel:* 800-376-0520

ASCP Press

Subsidiary of American Society for Clinical Pathology

33 W Monroe St, Suite 1600, Chicago, IL 60603

SAN: 207-9429

Tel: 312-541-4999 *Toll Free Tel:* 800-267-2727 *Fax:* 312-541-4998

Web Site: www.ascp.org

Key Personnel

Publr: Joshua R Weikersheimer *Tel:* 312-541-4866 *E-mail:* joshua.weikersheimer@ascp.org

Founded: 1959

Books, multimedia, slide sets, atlases, audiovisual seminars, videotapes, manuals, interactive software & videodiscs for lab professionals. Subjects include continuing education.

ISBN Prefix(es): 978-0-89189

Number of titles published annually: 21 Print; 10 Online

Total Titles: 238 Print; 112 Online

ASCSA Publications

6-8 Charlton St, Princeton, NJ 08540-5232

Tel: 609-683-0800 *Fax:* 609-924-0578

Web Site: www.ascsa.edu.gr/publications

Founded: 1881

Publishing office for the American School of Classical Studies at Athens, an advanced research & teaching institution focused on the history & culture of Greece & the wider Greek world.

ISBN Prefix(es): 978-0-87661 (print titles); 978-1-62139 (e-book titles)

Number of titles published annually: 12 Print; 5 E-Book

Total Titles: 300 Print; 1 Online; 25 E-Book

Imprints: American School of Classical Studies at Athens; Gennadeion Monographs; Hesperia

Billing Address: Casemate | academic, 1950 Lawrence Rd, Havertown, PA 19083 *Tel:* 610-853-9131 *Fax:* 610-853-9146 *E-mail:* info@ casemateacademic.com *Web Site:* www. oxbowbooks.com/dbbc

Orders to: Casemate | academic, 1950 Lawrence Rd, Havertown, PA 19083 *Tel:* 610-853-9131 *Fax:* 610-853-9149 *E-mail:* info@ casemateacademic.com *Web Site:* www. oxbowbooks.com/dbbc

Returns: Casemate | academic, 1950 Lawrence Rd, Havertown, PA 19083 *Tel:* 610-853-9131 *Fax:* 610-853-9146 *E-mail:* info@ casemateacademic.com *Web Site:* www. oxbowbooks.com/dbbc

Shipping Address: Casemate | academic, 1950 Lawrence Rd, Havertown, PA 19083 *Tel:* 610-853-9131 *Fax:* 610-853-9146 *E-mail:* info@ casemateacademic.com *Web Site:* www. oxbowbooks.com/dbbc

Warehouse: Casemate | academic, 1950 Lawrence Rd, Havertown, PA 19083 *Tel:* 610-853-9131 *Fax:* 610-853-9146 *E-mail:* info@ casemateacademic.com *Web Site:* www. oxbowbooks.com/dbbc

Distribution Center: Casemate | academic, 1950 Lawrence Rd, Havertown, PA 19083 *Tel:* 610-853-9131 *Fax:* 610-853-9146 *E-mail:* info@ casemateacademic.com *Web Site:* www. oxbowbooks.com/dbbc

Membership(s): American Association of University Presses (AAUP); Association of American Publishers Professional & Scholarly Publishing Division; Society for Scholarly Publishing (SSP)

ASET - The Neurodiagnostic Society

402 E Bannister Rd, Suite A, Kansas City, MO 64131-3019

Tel: 816-931-1120 *Fax:* 816-931-1145

E-mail: info@aset.org

Web Site: www.aset.org

Key Personnel

Exec Dir: Kevin Helm *Tel:* 816-945-9226 *E-mail:* kevin@aset.org

Dir, Pubns: Anna M Bonner *Tel:* 816-945-9224 *E-mail:* anna@aset.org

Founded: 1959

Books on EEG, evoked potentials, nerve conduction studies, long-term monitoring for epilepsy, intraoperative neuromonitoring & polysomnography/sleep technology.

ISBN Prefix(es): 978-1-57797

Number of titles published annually: 8 Print

Total Titles: 100 Print; 75 CD-ROM

Ash Tree Publishing

PO Box 64, Woodstock, NY 12498

Tel: 845-246-8081 *Fax:* 845-246-8081

Web Site: www.ashtreepublishing.com

Key Personnel

Founder & Owner: Susun Weed *E-mail:* wisewoman@herbshealing.com

Orders: Michael Dattorre

Founded: 1985

ISBN Prefix(es): 978-1-888123; 978-0-9614620

Number of titles published annually: 3 Print; 2 Audio

Total Titles: 14 Print; 3 Audio

Distributed by Brumby Sunstate; Dempsey Your Distributor; Nutri-Books

Distribution Center: New Leaf Distributing Co, 401 Thornton Rd, Lithia Springs, GA 30122-1557 *Tel:* 770-948-7845 *Fax:* 770-944-2313 *Web Site:* www.newleafdist.com

Ashland Creek Press

2305 Ashland St, Suite C417, Ashland, OR 97520

Tel: 760-300-3620

E-mail: editors@ashlandcreekpress.com

Web Site: www.ashlandcreekpress.com

Key Personnel

Founder & Ed: Midge Raymond *E-mail:* midge@ ashlandcreekpress.com; John Yunker *E-mail:* john@ashlandcreekpress.com

Founded: 2011

Small, independent publisher of books with a worldview. Our mission is to publish a range of books that foster an appreciation for worlds outside our own, for nature & the animal kingdom & for the ways in which we all connect.

ISBN Prefix(es): 978-0-9796475; 978-1-61822

Number of titles published annually: 3 Print; 3 E-Book; 3 Audio

Total Titles: 36 Print; 36 E-Book; 3 Audio

Imprints: Byte Level Books

Membership(s): Independent Book Publishers Association (IBPA)

Ashland Poetry Press

Affiliate of Ashland University

Bixler Center for the Humanities, Ashland University, 401 College Ave, Ashland, OH 44805

Tel: 419-289-5098

E-mail: app@ashland.edu

Web Site: www.ashland.edu/aupoetry

Key Personnel

Dir & Ed: Dr Deborah Fleming *E-mail:* dfleming@ashland.edu

Mng Ed: Paige Webb *E-mail:* pwebb@ashland. edu

Assoc Ed: Jennifer Rathbun

Founded: 1969

ISBN Prefix(es): 978-0-912592

Number of titles published annually: 3 Print

Total Titles: 100 Print

Distribution Center: Small Press Distribution, 1341 Seventh St, Berkeley, CA 94710-1409 *Web Site:* www.spdbooks.org

Membership(s): Community of Literary Magazines & Presses (CLMP); Independent Book Publishers Association (IBPA)

ASIS International

1625 Prince St, Alexandria, VA 22314

Tel: 703-519-6200 *Fax:* 703-519-6299

E-mail: asis@asisonline.org

Web Site: www.asisonline.org

Founded: 1955

Organization for security professionals, with more than 33,000 members worldwide. Dedicated to increasing the effectiveness & productivity of security professionals by developing educational programs & certification reference materials that address broad security interests, such as the annual seminar & exhibits, as well as specific security topics. Also advocates the role & value of the security management profession to business, the media, government entities & the public.

ISBN Prefix(es): 978-1-887056

Number of titles published annually: 3 Print; 2 CD-ROM

Total Titles: 35 Print; 2 CD-ROM

§ASM International

9639 Kinsman Rd, Materials Park, OH 44073-0002

SAN: 204-7586

Tel: 440-338-5151 *Toll Free Tel:* 800-336-5152; 800-368-9800 (Europe) *Fax:* 440-338-4634

E-mail: memberservicecenter@asminternational. org

Web Site: www.asminternational.org

Key Personnel

Mgr, Prodn: Madrid Tramble *Tel:* 440-338-5151 ext 5241

Founded: 1913

Technical & reference books.

ISBN Prefix(es): 978-0-87170

Number of titles published annually: 10 Print; 1 CD-ROM; 35 Online

Total Titles: 210 Print; 1,000 Online

§ASM Press

Division of American Society for Microbiology

1752 "N" St NW, Washington, DC 20036-2904

Tel: 202-737-3600 *Fax:* 202-942-9342

E-mail: books@asmusa.org

Web Site: www.asmscience.org

Key Personnel

Dir: Christine Charlip *E-mail:* ccharlip@asmusa. org

Edit & Rts Coord: Lindsay Williams *E-mail:* lwilliams@asmusa.org

Founded: 1899

Microbiology, cell biology, medicine, books, journals, proceedings & abstracts.

ISBN Prefix(es): 978-1-55581

Number of titles published annually: 14 Print; 15 Online

Total Titles: 250 Print; 25 Online

Foreign Rep(s): Cranbury International LLC (Latin America); Information & Culture Ko-

rea (ICK) (South Korea); Donald MacIvor & Associates (Canada); Taylor & Francis Group (UK)
Foreign Rights: Aditya Books Pvt Ltd (Bangladesh, India, Nepal, Pakistan, Sri Lanka); Apex Knowledge Sdn Bhd (Brunei, Malaysia); Booknet Co Ltd (Cambodia, Laos, Myanmar, Thailand, Vietnam); iCaves Ltd (China, Hong Kong, Macau); IG Knowledge Services Ltd (Taiwan); MegaTEXTS Phil Inc (Philippines); United Publishers Services Ltd (Japan); John Wiley & Sons Ltd (Africa, Europe, Middle East); Woodslane (Australia, Fiji, New Zealand, Papua New Guinea, Solomon Islands)
Orders to: PO Box 605, Herndon, VA 20172
Tel: 703-661-1593 *Fax:* 703-661-1501
E-mail: asmmail@presswarehouse.com
Returns: PO Box 605, Herndon, VA 20172
Tel: 703-661-1593 *Fax:* 703-661-1501
E-mail: asmmail@presswarehouse.com
Warehouse: 22883 Quicksilver Dr, Dulles, VA 20166 *Toll Free Tel:* 800-546-2416

§Aspatore Books
Division of Thomson Reuters
610 Opperman Dr, Eagan, MN 55123
Tel: 651-687-7000 *Toll Free Tel:* 844-209-1086
E-mail: globallegalproducts@thomson.com
Web Site: store.legal.thomsonreuters.com
Founded: 1999
Legal tips from leading executives & lawyers to help attorneys expand their practice.
ISBN Prefix(es): 978-0-314; 978-1-58762; 978-1-59622
Number of titles published annually: 150 Print
Total Titles: 500 Print

Aspen Publishers Inc, see Wolters Kluwer Law & Business

§Association for Computing Machinery
2 Penn Plaza, Suite 701, New York, NY 10121-0701
SAN: 267-7784
Mailing Address: PO Box 30777, New York, NY 10087-0777
Tel: 212-869-7440 *Toll Free Tel:* 800-342-6626
Fax: 212-944-1318 (memb servs)
E-mail: acmhelp@acm.org
Web Site: www.acm.org
Key Personnel
Publg Dir: Scott Delman *E-mail:* scott.delman@hq.acm.org
Founded: 1947
Computer science.
ISBN Prefix(es): 978-0-89791; 978-1-58113; 978-1-59593; 978-1-60558; 978-1-4503
Number of titles published annually: 150 Print
Total Titles: 500 Print
Foreign Office(s): FIT Bldg 1-118, Tsinghua University, Beijing 100084, China *Tel:* (010) 62783549 *E-mail:* acmchina@tsinghua.edu.cn
Membership(s): Association of American Publishers (AAP)

Association for Information Science & Technology (ASIS&T)
8555 16 St, Suite 850, Silver Spring, MD 20910
Tel: 301-495-0900 *Fax:* 301-495-0810
E-mail: asist@asist.org
Web Site: www.asist.org
Key Personnel
Exec Dir: Lydia Middleton *E-mail:* lmiddleton@asist.org
Founded: 1937
Provides high-quality conference programs & publications for information systems developers, online professionals, information resource managers, librarians, records managers, academics & others who "bridge the gap".
ISBN Prefix(es): 978-0-87715

Number of titles published annually: 12 Print; 1 CD-ROM; 1 Online
Total Titles: 12 Print; 1 CD-ROM; 1 Online
Distributed by Information Today, Inc; John Wiley & Sons Inc

Association for Talent Development (ATD) Press
1640 King St, Box 1443, Alexandria, VA 22313-1443
SAN: 224-8972
Tel: 703-683-8100 *Toll Free Tel:* 800-628-2783
Fax: 703-299-8723; 703-683-1523 (cust care)
E-mail: customercare@td.org
Web Site: www.astd.org; www.td.org
Key Personnel
Pres & CEO: Tony Bingham
Dir, Pubns & Edit: Kristine Luecker
E-mail: kluecker@td.org
Mktg Mgr, Pubns: Deborah Orgel Hudson
E-mail: dhudson@td.org
Founded: 1944
Internationally renowned source of insightful & practical information for professionals & general readers on workplace learning & performance topics, including training basics, evaluation & return-on investment, instructional systems development, e-learning, leadership & career development.
ISBN Prefix(es): 978-1-56286; 978-1-60728
Number of titles published annually: 25 Print; 4 CD-ROM
Total Titles: 200 Print
Distributed by Cengage Learning Asia Pte Ltd (Asia); Eurospan Group (Europe, Middle East & the former Soviet Bloc); Knowledge Resources (South Africa); National Book Network (NBN) (US, CN, Australia & New Zealand)
Membership(s): Association Media & Publishing; Association of American Publishers (AAP)

Association of College & Research Libraries (ACRL)
Division of The American Library Association (ALA)
50 E Huron St, Chicago, IL 60611
Tel: 312-280-2523 *Toll Free Tel:* 800-545-2433 (ext 2523) *Fax:* 312-280-2520
E-mail: acrl@ala.org
Web Site: www.ala.org/acrl
Key Personnel
Assoc Dir: Mary Jane Petrowski
E-mail: mpetrowski@ala.org
Founded: 1938
Higher education association for librarians. Representing more than 11,000 academic & research librarians & interested individuals, ACRL develops programs, products & services to help academic & research librarians learn, innovate & lead within the academic community. ACRL is the largest division of the American Library Association (ALA).
ISBN Prefix(es): 978-0-8389
Number of titles published annually: 15 Print; 15 E-Book
Total Titles: 125 Print; 70 E-Book
Foreign Rep(s): Baker & Taylor International; Booknet Co Ltd (Cambodia, Laos, Thailand); Cranbury International (Caribbean, Latin America, Mexico, Puerto Rico); Eurospan (Africa, Europe, Israel, UK); iGroup (Asia-Pacific); Ontario Library Association (Canada); PMS Publishers Services Pte Ltd (Singapore)
Orders to: American Library Association, PO Box 17219, Atlanta, GA 30368-7219 *Toll Free Tel:* 866-746-7252 *Fax:* 312-280-5860 *E-mail:* alastore@ala.org *Web Site:* www.alastore.ala.org
Returns: American Library Association, Attn: Receiving Dept, 3280 Summit Ridge Pkwy, Duluth, GA 30096-1616
Membership(s): American Library Association (ALA); Association for Information Science

& Technology (ASIS&T); Association of Research Libraries (ARL); Modern Language Association (MLA)

Association of Research Libraries (ARL)
21 Dupont Circle NW, Suite 800, Washington, DC 20036
Tel: 202-296-2296 *Fax:* 202-872-0884
E-mail: webmgr@arl.org
Web Site: www.arl.org
Key Personnel
Sr Dir, Communs: Jessica Aiwuyor
E-mail: jaiwuyor@arl.org
Founded: 1932
Serial, occasional paper series & special topics of interest.
ISBN Prefix(es): 978-0-918006; 978-1-59407
Number of titles published annually: 4 Print; 8 Online; 4 E-Book
Total Titles: 618 Print; 188 Online; 125 E-Book
Distribution Center: ARL Publications Distribution Center, PO Box 531, Annapolis Junction, MD 20701-0531 *Tel:* 301-362-8196 *Fax:* 240-396-2479 *E-mail:* arl@brightkey.net

Association of School Business Officials International
11401 N Shore Dr, Reston, VA 20190
Tel: 703-478-0405 *Toll Free Tel:* 866-682-2729
Fax: 703-708-7060
E-mail: asboreq@asbointl.org; asbosba@asbointl.org
Web Site: www.asbointl.org
Founded: 1910
Professional books co-published with Rowman & Littlefield Education.
ISBN Prefix(es): 978-0-910170; 978-0-810847; 978-1-1578860
Number of titles published annually: 8 Print
Total Titles: 40 Print

Asta Publications LLC
275 W Clarkstown Rd, New City, NY 10956
Tel: 678-814-1320 *Toll Free Tel:* 800-482-4190
Fax: 678-814-1370
E-mail: info@astapublications.com
Web Site: www.astapublications.com
Key Personnel
CEO: Assuanta Howard *E-mail:* ahoward@astapublications.com
Founded: 2004
Delivering first-class book publishing services for corporations, entrepreneurs & individuals who understand the power of being a published author.
This publisher has indicated that 30% of their product line is author subsidized.
ISBN Prefix(es): 978-0-9777060; 978-1-934947
Number of titles published annually: 200 Print; 200 Online; 200 E-Book
Total Titles: 500 Print; 500 Online; 500 E-Book
Membership(s): The Association of Publishers for Special Sales (APSS); The Imaging Alliance

§ASTM International
100 Barr Harbor Dr, West Conshohocken, PA 19428-2959
Mailing Address: PO Box C700, West Conshohocken, PA 19428-0700
Tel: 610-832-9500; 610-832-9585 (intl)
Toll Free Tel: 877-909-2786 (sales & cust support) *Fax:* 610-832-9555
E-mail: service@astm.org
Web Site: www.astm.org
Key Personnel
Pres: Katharine E Morgan *Tel:* 610-832-9721
E-mail: kmorgan@astm.org
VP, Sales & Mktg: James S Thomas *Tel:* 610-832-9651 *E-mail:* jsthomas@astm.org
Mgr, Sales: George Zajdel *Tel:* 610-832-9614
E-mail: gzajdel@astm.org
Founded: 1898

Standards, technical publications, data series manuals & journals on engineering, science, materials testing, safety, quality control.
ISBN Prefix(es): 978-0-8031
Number of titles published annually: 176 Print; 125 CD-ROM
Total Titles: 1,500 Print; 125 CD-ROM; 80 On-line
Branch Office(s)
1850 "M" St NW, Suite 1030, Washington, DC 20036, Contact: Jeffrey Grove *Tel:* 202-223-8505 *E-mail:* jgrove@astm.org
171 Nepean St, Suite 400, Ottawa, ON K2P 0B4, Canada, Contact: Diane VC Thompson *Tel:* 613-751-3409 *E-mail:* dthompson@astm.org
Foreign Office(s): Rue de la Loi 67, 1040 Brussels, Belgium, Contact: Sara Gobbi *Tel:* (02) 8405127 *E-mail:* sgobbi@astm.org
Suite EF02, Twin Towers E, B-12 Jianguomenwai Ave, Chaoyang District, Beijing 100022, China, Contact: H U Yanan *Tel:* (010) 5109-6033 *Fax:* (010) 5109-6039 *E-mail:* rhu@astm.org
EnginZone, Monterosa 233, of 402 Chacarilla del Estanque, Surco, Lima 33, Peru, Contact: Maria Isabel Barrios *Tel:* (01) 205-5502 *E-mail:* astmlatinamerica@astm.org

Astragal Press
Imprint of Rowman & Littlefield Publishing Group
4501 Forbes Blvd, Suite 200, Lanham, MD 20706
Tel: 301-459-3366 *Fax:* 301-429-5748
Web Site: rowman.com
Founded: 1983
Early tools, trades & technology.
ISBN Prefix(es): 978-0-9618088; 978-1-879335; 978-1-931626
Number of titles published annually: 5 Print
Total Titles: 89 Print; 89 Online
Distribution Center: National Book Network (NBN), 15200 NBN Way, Blue Ridge Summit, PA 17214 *Tel:* 717-794-3800 *E-mail:* customercare@nbnbooks.com

The Astronomical Society of the Pacific
390 Ashton Ave, San Francisco, CA 94112
Tel: 415-337-1100 *Fax:* 415-337-5205
Web Site: www.astrosociety.org
Key Personnel
Exec Dir: Dr Linda Shore *Tel:* 415-715-1411 *E-mail:* lshore@astrosociety.org
Mng Ed: Joseph Jensen *E-mail:* jjensen@aspbooks.org
Assoc Ed: Jonathan Barnes *E-mail:* jonathan@aspbooks.org
Pubns Mgr, ASP Conference Series: Cindy Moody *E-mail:* publicationmanager@aspbooks.org
Founded: 1889
Books, booklets, tapes, slide sets, software & other educational materials about astronomy; conference proceedings. Publisher of *Mercury Magazine* & *Publications of the Astronomical Society of the Pacific* journal.
ISBN Prefix(es): 978-0-937707; 978-1-886733; 978-1-58381
Number of titles published annually: 20 Print; 1 CD-ROM; 20 E-Book
Total Titles: 360 Print; 1 CD-ROM; 60 E-Book; 1 Audio

ATD Press, see Association for Talent Development (ATD) Press

Atheneum Books for Young Readers, see Simon & Schuster Children's Publishing

Atlantic Law Book Co
Division of Peter Kelsey Publishing Inc

22 Grassmere Ave, West Hartford, CT 06110-1215
Tel: 860-231-9300 *Toll Free Tel:* 800-259-5534
E-mail: atlanticlawbooks@aol.com
Web Site: www.atlanticlawbooks.com
Key Personnel
VP: Richard Epstein
Founded: 1945
Law books for Connecticut legal practice. Marketed in Connecticut & other states & used by practitioners & judges in this state. The books are all written by law professors, lawyers or judges who are recognized experts in their respective fields. The material is updated regularly, usually by annual pocket supplements. This publisher has indicated that 100% of their product line is author subsidized.
ISBN Prefix(es): 978-1-878698
Number of titles published annually: 12 Print; 2 CD-ROM
Total Titles: 12 Print; 2 CD-ROM

§Atlantic Publishing Group Inc
1405 SW Sixth Ave, Ocala, FL 34471
Tel: 352-622-1825 *Fax:* 352-622-1875
E-mail: sales@atlantic-pub.com
Web Site: www.atlantic-pub.com
Key Personnel
Pres: Douglas R Brown
VP: Sherri L Brown
Founded: 1982
Provides millions of readers information to jump-start their careers, start businesses, manage employees, invest, plan for retirement, learn technologies, build relationships & live rewarding, fulfilling lives.
ISBN Prefix(es): 978-0-910627; 978-1-60138; 978-1-62023
Number of titles published annually: 100 Print; 25 CD-ROM
Total Titles: 500 Print; 150 CD-ROM
Membership(s): American Booksellers Association (ABA); American Publishers Association; Association of American Publishers (AAP); The Association of Publishers for Special Sales (APSS); Florida Authors & Publishers Association Inc (FAPA); Independent Book Publishers Association (IBPA); Young Adult Library Services Association (YALSA)

§Atlas Publishing
25185 Madison Ave, Suite A, Murrieta, CA 92562
Tel: 858-222-3747
E-mail: permissions@atlaspublishing.biz
Web Site: www.atlaspublishing.biz
Key Personnel
Mng Ed: Brent D Tharp *E-mail:* brent@atlaspublishing.biz
Founded: 2011
Traditional publisher of children's & nonfiction titles. Author services also available for books not printed under our imprint. Please note that the only fiction titles that we print under our imprint are children's books. We can provide editing services for all genres, but publish only children's books & nonfiction titles. Writers interested in submitting materials may do so directly, but initial submissions should be limited to query letters, sell sheets, & synopses. Please do not submit full mss or attachments at the initial query stage as they will not be reviewed.
ISBN Prefix(es): 978-0-9969679; 978-1-945033
Number of titles published annually: 4 Print; 3 E-Book
Total Titles: 10 Print; 10 E-Book
Distribution Center: Ingram
Membership(s): Editorial Freelancers Association (EFA); Independent Book Publishers Association (IBPA)

Atria Books
Imprint of Atria Publishing Group

1230 Avenue of the Americas, New York, NY 10020
Tel: 212-698-7000 *Fax:* 212-698-7007
Web Site: www.simonandschuster.com
Key Personnel
SVP, Publr: Libby McGuire *Tel:* 212-698-7675 *E-mail:* libby.mcguire@simonandschuster.com
SVP & Ed-in-Chief, Emily Bestler Books: Emily Bestler *Tel:* 212-698-7685 *E-mail:* emily.bestler@simonandschuster.com
VP & Ed-in-Chief: Peter Borland *Tel:* 212-698-7569 *E-mail:* peter.borland@simonandschuster.com
VP & Dir, Subs Rts: Nicole Bond *Tel:* 212-698-7397 *E-mail:* nicole.bond@simonandschuster.com
VP, Publr, One Signal Publishers: Julia Cheiffetz *Tel:* 212-698-7339 *E-mail:* julia.cheiffetz@simonandschuster.com
VP, Dir of Integrated Mktg: Kristin Fassler *E-mail:* kristin.fassler@simonandschuster.com
VP, Edit Dir: Lindsay Sagnette *Tel:* 212-698-7057 *E-mail:* lindsay.sagnette@simonandschuster.com
VP, Exec Ed: Trish Todd *Tel:* 212-698-4659 *E-mail:* trish.todd@simonandschuster.com
Dir, Mktg: Dana Trocker *E-mail:* dana.trocker@simonandschuster.com
Exec Ed: Leah Miller *Tel:* 212-698-7172 *E-mail:* leah.miller@simonandschuster.com
Sr Ed: Michelle Herrera Mulligan *Tel:* 212-698-7696 *E-mail:* michelle.herreramulligan@simonandschuster.com; Stephanie Hitchcock *E-mail:* stephanie.hitchcock@simonandschuster.com
Ed: Daniella Wexler *Tel:* 212-698-2822 *E-mail:* daniella.wexler@simonandschuster.com; Kaitlin Olson *Tel:* 212-698-7342 *E-mail:* kaitlin.olson@simonandschuster.com; Amar Deol *Tel:* 212-698-7238 *E-mail:* amar.deol@simonandschuster.com; Loan Le
Ed, One Signal Publishers: Nicholas Ciani
Founded: 2002
ISBN Prefix(es): 978-0-671; 978-0-7434; 978-0-7432
Imprints: Atria Trade Paperback; Emily Bestler Books; Beyond Words; Howard Books; Keywords Press; Marble Arch; One Signal Publishers; Washington Square Press
Foreign Rights: Akcali Copyright Agency (Turkey); Bardon-Chinese Media Agency (China, Thailand); Book/lab (Poland); The Book Publishers' Association of Israel, International Promotion & Literary Rights Department (Israel); The Italian Literary Agency (Italy); JLM Literary Agency (Greece); Mohrbooks AG Literary Agency (Germany); La Nouvelle Agency (France); Andrew Nurnberg Associates Ltd (Bulgaria, Croatia, Estonia, Hungary, Latvia, Lithuania, Montenegro, North Macedonia, Romania, Russia, Serbia, Slovakia, Slovenia, Ukraine); Sane Toregard Agency (Denmark, Finland, Iceland, Norway, Sweden); Tuttle-Mori Agency Inc (Japan); Eric Yang Agency (Korea)

Atwood Publishing
PO Box 3185, Madison, WI 53704
Tel: 608-242-7101 *Toll Free Tel:* 888-242-7101 *Fax:* 608-242-7102
E-mail: customerservice@atwoodpublishing.com
Web Site: www.atwoodpublishing.com
Key Personnel
Publr: Linda Babler *E-mail:* lindab@atwoodpublishing.com
Founded: 1997
Book publishing for higher education market: teaching improvement, distance, education, student affairs, semiotics & administration.
ISBN Prefix(es): 978-1-891859
Number of titles published annually: 6 Print
Total Titles: 60 Print; 2 CD-ROM; 8 E-Book
Returns: 2095 Winnebago St, Suite B, Madison, WI 53704

§Augsburg Fortress Publishers, Publishing House of the Evangelical Lutheran Church in America
510 Marquette Ave S, Minneapolis, MN 55402
SAN: 169-4081
Mailing Address: PO Box 1209, Minneapolis, MN 55440-1209
Tel: 612-330-3300 *Toll Free Tel:* 800-426-0115 (ext 639, subns); 800-328-4648 (orders)
Fax: 612-330-3455
E-mail: info@augsburgfortress.org; copyright@ augsburgfortress.org (reprint permission requests); customercare@augsburgfortress.org
Web Site: www.augsburgfortress.org; www.1517. media
Key Personnel
Pres & CEO: Tim Blevins *Tel:* 612-330-3300 ext 400 *E-mail:* blevinst@1517.media
CFO: John Rahja *E-mail:* rahjaj@1517.media
VP, HR: Sandy Amundson *E-mail:* amundsons@ 1517.media
VP & Publr, Fortress Press: Will Bergkamp *E-mail:* bergkampw@1517.media
Publr, Worship & Music: Martin Seltz *E-mail:* seltzm@1517.media
Perms, Pubns: Michael Moore *E-mail:* moorem@ 1517.media
Founded: 1855
ISBN Prefix(es): 978-0-8066; 978-0-8006
Number of titles published annually: 100 Print
Total Titles: 4,600 Print; 1,700 E-Book; 3,500 Audio
Imprints: Augsburg Fortress; Beaming Books; Fortress Press; Sparkhouse
Sales Office(s): PO Box 1209, Minneapolis, MN 55440-1209
Foreign Rep(s): Asian Trading Corp (India); Australian Church Resources (Australia); Canaanland Distributors Sdn Bhd (Malaysia); Cross Communications Ltd (Hong Kong); Durnell Marketing (Israel); John Garratt Publishing (Australia); Glad Sounds Sdn Bhd (Malaysia); KCBS Inc (Korea); Kyo Bun Kwan Inc (Japan); Logos Publishers Ltd (Hong Kong); MediaCom Education (Australia); N-Online Co Ltd (Japan); NBN International (Europe, UK); Pustaka Sufes Sdn Bhd (Malaysia); SKS Books Warehouse (Singapore); Soul Distributors Ltd (New Zealand); Taosheng Publishing House (Hong Kong); Tecman Management Services (Singapore)
Foreign Rights: Rowman & Littlefield Publishing Group (worldwide exc Korea)
Billing Address: PO Box 1209, Minneapolis, MN 55440-1209
Orders to: PBD Worldwide, c/o AF Distribution, 905 Carlow Dr, Unit B, Bolingbrook, IL 60490
Warehouse: PBD Worldwide, c/o AF Distribution, 905 Carlow Dr, Unit B, Bolingbrook, IL 60490
Distribution Center: PBD Worldwide, c/o AF Distribution, 905 Carlow Dr, Unit B, Bolingbrook, IL 60490

August House Inc
3500 Piedmont Rd NE, Suite 310, Atlanta, GA 30305
Tel: 404-442-4420 *Toll Free Tel:* 800-284-8784 *Fax:* 404-442-4435
E-mail: ahinfo@augusthouse.com
Web Site: www.augusthouse.com
Key Personnel
CEO: Steve Floyd *E-mail:* steve@augusthouse. com
EVP: Graham Anthony *E-mail:* graham@ augusthouse.com
Dir, Devt: Rob Cleveland *E-mail:* rob@ augusthouse.com
Founded: 1979
Folklore, multicultural folktales & storytelling.
ISBN Prefix(es): 978-0-87483
Number of titles published annually: 15 Print; 30 Online; 15 E-Book

Total Titles: 350 Print; 300 Online; 15 E-Book; 71 Audio
Imprints: August House Audio; August House Little Folk; August House Story Cove
Foreign Rights: The Fielding Agency (Whitney Lee)

Aum Publications
86-10 Parsons Blvd, Jamaica, NY 11432-3314
SAN: 201-128X
Tel: 347-744-3199
Key Personnel
Pres: Carl Brown
Founded: 1973
Trade paperbacks; literature, Eastern philosophy, theology, occult, poetry, meditation; only books on or by Sri Chinmoy.
ISBN Prefix(es): 978-0-88497
Number of titles published annually: 5 Print
Total Titles: 53 Print; 2 CD-ROM
Distribution Center: Heart-Light Distributors, PO Box 85464, Seattle, WA 98145 *Toll Free Tel:* 800-739-2885 *Fax:* 206-523-5637

AuthorHouse
Division of Author Solutions LLC
1663 Liberty Dr, Bloomington, IN 47403
Tel: 812-339-6000 (outside US)
Toll Free Tel: 888-519-5121
E-mail: authorsupport@authorhouse.com
Web Site: www.authorhouse.com
Key Personnel
CEO: Mitchell Black
SVP, Mktg: Ben Crum
SVP, Prodn Servs & Output Opers: Bill Becher
VP, Sales Opers: Bruce Bunner
Pres, Author Learning Center: Keith Ogorek
Dir, Fin: William Elliott
Exec Asst: Vickie Breeden
Founded: 1997
The leading provider of indie book publishing, marketing & bookselling services for authors around the globe. Committed to providing the highest level of customer service. Assign each author personal publishing & marketing consultants who provide guidance throughout the process.
This publisher has indicated that 100% of their product line is author subsidized.
ISBN Prefix(es): 978-1-58500; 978-0-9675669; 978-1-58721; 978-1-58820; 978-0-7596; 978-1-4033; 978-1-4107; 978-1-4140; 978-1-4184; 978-1-4208
Number of titles published annually: 7,500 Print
Total Titles: 80,000 Print
Distribution Center: Baker & Taylor LLC, 2550 W Tyvola Rd, Suite 300, Charlotte, NC 28217
Ingram Book Group, One Ingram Blvd, La Vergne, TN 37086-1986
Membership(s): American Booksellers Association (ABA)

Authorlink® Press
Imprint of Authorlink®
103 Guadalupe Dr, Irving, TX 75039-3334
Tel: 972-402-0101
E-mail: admin@authorlink.com
Web Site: www.authorlink.com
Key Personnel
Founder, CEO & Ed-in-Chief: Doris Booth *E-mail:* dbooth@authorlink.com
Founded: 1996
Provides production & consulting services for ebooks & print-on-demand titles for about 150 self-published & small press clients per year. The parent company's new Authorlink® Books N' Flix system offers an inexpensive big data research platform for authors & small presses. *Authorlink® Writers & Readers Magazine* provides news & information about the publishing & film industry. In addition, Authorlink® pub-

lishes & represents several leading authors but is not accepting new authors at this time.
ISBN Prefix(es): 978-1-928704
Number of titles published annually: 10 Print; 150 E-Book
Total Titles: 10 Print; 150 E-Book
Orders to: Lightning Source, 1246 Heil Quaker Blvd, La Vergne, TN 37086 *Tel:* 615-213-5815 *Fax:* 615-213-4426 *E-mail:* inquiry@ lightningsource.com *Web Site:* www. lightningsource.com
Distribution Center: Lightning Source, 1246 Heil Quaker Blvd, La Vergne, TN 37086 *Tel:* 615-213-5815 *Fax:* 615-213-4426 *E-mail:* inquiry@lightningsource.com *Web Site:* www.lightningsource.com
Membership(s): Independent Book Publishers Association (IBPA)

Autism Asperger Publishing Co
6448 Vista Dr, Shawnee, KS 66218
Tel: 913-897-1004 *Toll Free Tel:* 877-277-8254 *Fax:* 913-681-9473
E-mail: support@aapcpublishing.net
Web Site: www.aapcpublishing.net
Key Personnel
Dir, Opers: James Jones *Tel:* 913-232-4501 *E-mail:* james.jones@aapcpublishing.net
Gen Mgr: Serdar Marun *Tel:* 913-232-4505 *E-mail:* serdar.marun@aapcpublishing.net
Specialize in books & multimedia in autism spectrum disorders (ASD) & related exceptionalities for individuals on the spectrum, their parents, families, peers, educators & other professionals.
ISBN Prefix(es): 978-0-9672514; 978-1-931282; 978-1-937473; 978-1-934575
Number of titles published annually: 24 Print

Autumn House Press
5530 Penn Ave, Pittsburgh, PA 15206
Tel: 412-362-2665
E-mail: info@autumnhouse.org
Web Site: www.autumnhouse.org
Key Personnel
Ed-in-Chief: Christine Stroud *E-mail:* cstroud@ autumnhouse.org
Founded: 1998
Nonprofit corporation with the mission of publishing poetry, fiction & nonfiction. Submissions should be through one of the annual contests. Guidelines are posted on the web site.
Publish the online journal *Coal Hill Review.*
ISBN Prefix(es): 978-0-9669419; 978-1-932870
Number of titles published annually: 8 Print; 4 E-Book
Total Titles: 100 Print; 50 E-Book
Distribution Center: Chicago Distribution Center (CDC), 11030 S Langley Ave, Chicago, IL 60628 *Tel:* 773-702-7010 *Toll Free Fax:* 800-621-8476

Avant-Guide
Unit of Empire Press Media Inc
244 Fifth Ave, Suite 2053, New York, NY 10001-7604
Tel: 917-512-3881 *Fax:* 212-202-7757
E-mail: info@avantguide.com; communications@ avantguide.com; editor@avantguide.com
Web Site: www.avantguide.com
Key Personnel
Dir: Scott Walker
Founded: 1999
Publisher of nonfiction books on marketing, keynote speakers, travel, business as well as handbooks for keynote speakers & trends by the global trends expert Daniel Levine.
ISBN Prefix(es): 978-1-891603
Number of titles published annually: 50 Print; 50 E-Book
Total Titles: 224 Print; 400 E-Book

Imprints: Empire; Keynote Speakers Today; Top Keynote Speakers; Trends Experts
Foreign Rep(s): Hi Marketing (Europe, UK)
Foreign Rights: PGW (Canada)
Distribution Center: Publishers Group West, 1700 Fourth St, Berkeley, CA 94710 *Tel:* 510-809-3700 *Toll Free Tel:* 866-400-5351 *Fax:* 510-809-3777

Ave Maria Press
PO Box 428, Notre Dame, IN 46556
SAN: 201-1255
Toll Free Tel: 800-282-1865 *Toll Free Fax:* 800-282-5681
E-mail: avemariapress.1@nd.edu
Web Site: www.avemariapress.com
Key Personnel
Publr & CEO: Karey Circosta *Tel:* 574-287-2831 ext 219 *E-mail:* kcircosta@nd.edu
VP & Creative Dir: Kristen Bonelli *Tel:* 574-287-2831 ext 240 *E-mail:* hornyak.3@nd.edu
VP & Dir, Fin & Opers: Kyle Marscola
VP & Edit Dir: Daniel Marrs
Exec Ed, Ministry Resources: Eileen Ponder
Sr Acqs Ed: Heidi Hess Saxton
Sales Mgr: Kay Luther *Tel:* 574-287-2831 ext 232 *E-mail:* k.luther.8@nd.edu
Founded: 1865
Adult paperback books of religious interest; prayer books & religious education materials, programs & textbooks.
ISBN Prefix(es): 978-0-87793 (Ave Maria Press); 978-0-939516 (Forest of Peace); 978-0-87061 (Christian Classics); 978-1-893732 (Sorin Books); 978-1-59471 (Ave Maria Press); 978-1-933495 (Sorin Books)
Number of titles published annually: 40 Print
Total Titles: 550 Print
Imprints: Christian Classics; Forest of Peace; Sorin Books
Foreign Rep(s): Alban Books Ltd (UK); John Garratt Publishing (Australia); Novalis (Canada); Pleroma Christian Supplies (New Zealand)
Returns: 1865 Moreau Dr, Notre Dame, IN 46556

Avery
Imprint of Penguin Group USA, A Penguin Random House Company
1745 Broadway, New York, NY 10019
Tel: 212-366-2000 *Fax:* 212-366-2636
E-mail: averypublicity@penguinrandomhouse.com
Web Site: www.penguin.com/publishers/avery; www.penguinrandomhouse.com
Key Personnel
VP & Publr: Megan Newman
Assoc Publr & Dir, Publicity & Mktg: Lindsay Gordon
Exec Ed: Lucia Watson
Ed-in-Chief: Caroline Sutton
Sr Ed: Nina Shield
Publicity Dir: Anne Kosmoski
Assoc Publicity Dir: Casey Maloney
Asst Mktg Dir, Avery & Tarcher Perigee: Farin Schlussel
Founded: 1976 (acquired by The Penguin Group in the fall of 1999)
The imprint is dedicated to publishing books on health & nutrition with a complimentary, natural, or alternative focus.
Penguin Random House & its publishing entities are not accepting unsol submissions, proposals, mss, or submission queries via e-mail at this time.
Number of titles published annually: 35 Print
Total Titles: 247 Print
Imprints: Pam Krauss Books

Avery Color Studios
511 "D" Ave, Gwinn, MI 49841
Tel: 906-346-3908 *Toll Free Tel:* 800-722-9925 *Fax:* 906-346-3015

E-mail: averycolor@averycolorstudios.com
Web Site: www.averycolorstudios.com
Key Personnel
Pres: Wells Chapin
Busn Mgr: Amy Chapin
Founded: 1956
Regional publisher. Specialize in nautical books.
ISBN Prefix(es): 978-0-932212; 978-1-892384
Number of titles published annually: 4 Print
Total Titles: 50 Print

Avid Reader Press
Imprint of Simon & Schuster, Inc
1230 Avenue of the Americas, New York, NY 10020
Web Site: avidreaderpress.com
Key Personnel
VP & Publr: Jofie Ferrari-Adler
VP & Ed-in-Chief: Ben Loehnen
Edit Dir: Lauren Wein
Deputy Dir of Publicity: Jordan Rodman
Assoc Ed: Julianna Haubner
Assoc Publr: Meredith Vilarello
Number of titles published annually: 30 Print

AVKO Educational Research Foundation Inc
3084 Willard Rd, Birch Run, MI 48415-9404
Tel: 810-686-9283 (orders & billing) *Fax:* 810-686-1101
E-mail: info@avko.org (gen inquiry)
Web Site: www.avko.org; www.avko.blogspot.org
Key Personnel
Res Dir: Don McCabe *Tel:* 810-686-9283 ext 203 *E-mail:* donmccabe@aol.com
Opers Mgr: Robert McCabe *Tel:* 810-686-9283 ext 202 *E-mail:* brian@avko.org
Accts Receivable & Accts Payable: Sue Johnson *Tel:* 810-686-9283 ext 201 *E-mail:* avkosueat@aol.com
Founded: 1974
Nonprofit organization devoted to providing free & low-cost materials for teaching language arts, keyboarding & reference. Our materials work great for dyslexics, homeschoolers & school teachers.
ISBN Prefix(es): 978-1-56400
Total Titles: 49 Print; 6 CD-ROM; 60 E-Book

AVKO Foundation, see AVKO Educational Research Foundation Inc

Avotaynu Inc
794 Edgewood Ave, New Haven, CT 06515
Tel: 475-202-6575 *Toll Free Tel:* 800-AVOTAYNU (286-8296)
E-mail: info@avotaynu.com
Web Site: www.avotaynu.com
Key Personnel
Publr: Gary Mokotoff *E-mail:* garymokotoff@avotaynu.com
Founded: 1984
Publisher of information & products of interest to persons researching their Jewish family history. This includes the journal & books.
ISBN Prefix(es): 978-0-9626373; 978-1-886223; 978-0-9836975
Number of titles published annually: 3 Print
Total Titles: 75 Print

Azro Press
1704 Llano St B, PMB 342, Santa Fe, NM 87505
Tel: 505-989-3272 *Fax:* 505-989-3832
E-mail: books@azropress.com
Web Site: www.azropress.com
Key Personnel
CEO: Gae Eisenhardt
Founded: 1997
Publish illustrated children's books with a Southwestern flavor.
ISBN Prefix(es): 978-1-929115
Number of titles published annually: 3 Print

Total Titles: 20 Print
Imprints: Green Knees

Baby Tattoo Books
6045 Longridge Ave, Van Nuys, CA 91401
Tel: 818-416-5314
E-mail: info@babytattoo.com
Web Site: www.babytattoo.com
Key Personnel
Pres & Publr: Robert Self *E-mail:* bob@babytattoo.com
Founded: 2003
Publisher of art books by contemporary artists.
ISBN Prefix(es): 978-0-9729388; 978-0-9778949; 978-0-9793307; 978-0-9845210; 978-1-61404
Number of titles published annually: 4 Print
Total Titles: 30 Print
Orders to: SCB Distributors Inc, 15608 S New Century Dr, Gardena, CA 90248 *Toll Free Tel:* 800-729-6423
Returns: SCB Distributors Inc, 15608 S New Century Dr, Gardena, CA 90248 *Toll Free Tel:* 800-729-6423
Shipping Address: SCB Distributors Inc, 15608 S New Century Dr, Gardena, CA 90248 *Toll Free Tel:* 800-729-6423
Warehouse: SCB Distributors Inc, 15608 S New Century Dr, Gardena, CA 90248 *Toll Free Tel:* 800-729-6423
Distribution Center: SCB Distributors Inc, 15608 S New Century Dr, Gardena, CA 90248 *Toll Free Tel:* 800-729-6423

Back to Eden Books, see Lotus Press

Backbeat Books
Imprint of The Globe Pequot Press
PO Box 1520, Wayne, NJ 07042-1520
Tel: 973-987-5363
E-mail: submissions@halleonardbooks.com
Web Site: www.backbeatbooks.com
Key Personnel
Sr Exec Ed: John Cerullo *E-mail:* jcerullo@rowman.com
Founded: 1991
Books about popular music & musical instruments.
ISBN Prefix(es): 978-0-87930
Number of titles published annually: 30 Print; 20 E-Book
Total Titles: 400 Print; 300 E-Book
Foreign Rep(s): National Book Network (Europe, India, Latin America, Mexico, Middle East, Pacific Rim, Russia & former USSR, South America); Publishers Group UK (UK); Woodslane (Australia, New Zealand)
Foreign Rights: Clare Cox (worldwide)
Distribution Center: National Book Network, 15200 NBN Way, Blue Ridge Summit, PA 17214

Baen Publishing Enterprises
PO Box 1188, Wake Forest, NC 27588
Tel: 919-570-1640 *Fax:* 919-570-1644
E-mail: info@baen.com
Web Site: www.baen.com
Key Personnel
Publr: Toni Weisskopf *E-mail:* toni@baen.com
Founded: 1984
Only science fiction & fantasy.
ISBN Prefix(es): 978-0-671; 978-0-7434; 978-1-4165
Number of titles published annually: 70 Print; 50 Online; 48 E-Book
Total Titles: 700 Print; 250 Online; 200 E-Book
Distributed by Simon & Schuster
Foreign Rep(s): EYA (South Korea); Lora Fountain (France); Grayhawk Agency (China, Taiwan); Alex Korzhenevshi (Russia); Kristin Olson (Czechia); PNLA (Italy); Thomas Schlueck GmbH (Germany); Tuttle-Mori Agency Inc (Japan)

Baha'i Publishing
Subsidiary of The National Spiritual Assembly of
the Baha'is of the United States
401 Greenleaf Ave, Wilmette, IL 60091
Tel: 847-853-7899 *Toll Free Tel:* 800-999-9019
(orders)
E-mail: bds@usbnc.org
Web Site: books.bahai.us; www.bahaibookstore.
com
Founded: 1902
Religion (Baha'i).
ISBN Prefix(es): 978-0-87743; 978-1-931847
Number of titles published annually: 15 Print
Total Titles: 2,000 Print; 250 Audio

§Baker Books
Division of Baker Publishing Group
6030 E Fulton Rd, Ada, MI 49301
Mailing Address: PO Box 6287, Grand Rapids,
MI 49516 SAN: 299-1500
Tel: 616-676-9185 *Toll Free Tel:* 800-877-2665
(orders) *Fax:* 616-676-9573 *Toll Free Fax:* 800-
398-3111 (orders)
E-mail: media@bakerpublishinggroup.com;
orders@bakerpublishinggroup.com; sales@
bakerpublishinggroup.com
Web Site: www.bakerpublishinggroup.com
Key Personnel
Pres & CEO: Dwight Baker
EVP, Academic Publg: Jim Kinney
E-mail: jkinney@bakerpublishinggroup.com
EVP, Sales & Mktg: Dave Lewis
E-mail: dlewis@bakerpublishinggroup.com
Dir, Rts & Contracts: Marilyn Gordon
E-mail: mgordon@bakerpublishinggroup.com
Founded: 1939
Religion (Protestant).
ISBN Prefix(es): 978-0-8010
Number of titles published annually: 75 Print; 1
CD-ROM; 1 Audio
Total Titles: 1,000 Print
Imprints: Hamewith; Hourglass
Foreign Rep(s): Christian Art Distributors
(South Africa); Manna Christian Stores (New
Zealand); Parasource (Canada); SPCK (Ireland,
UK)

Balance Sports Publishing LLC
195 Lucero Way, Portola Valley, CA 94028
SAN: 857-3298
Tel: 650-561-9586 *Fax:* 650-391-9850
E-mail: info@balancesportspublishing.com
Web Site: www.balancesportspublishing.com
Key Personnel
Founder & Publr: Jim Lobdell *E-mail:* jlobdell@
balancesportspublishing.com
Founder & Dir, Prod Devt: Steve Seely
E-mail: sseely@balancesportspublishing.com
Founded: 2008
Publishes high-quality youth sports books for
youth sports coaches, parents, athletes & organi-
zation leaders. Our mission is to create titles
that ensure every child has a positive youth
sports experience & that every coach is in-
spired to help youngsters achieve their goals
in sports while developing important life skills
& character traits.
ISBN Prefix(es): 978-0-9821317
Number of titles published annually: 3 Print
Total Titles: 12 Print
Returns: 3623 Munster St, Suite B, Hayward,
CA 94545, Contact: Bill Armor *Tel:* 510-732-
6521 *Fax:* 510-732-6523 *E-mail:* orders@
balancesportspublishing.com
Shipping Address: 3623 Munster St, Suite B,
Hayward, CA 94545, Contact: Bill Armor
Tel: 510-732-6521 *Fax:* 510-732-6523
Warehouse: 3623 Munster St, Suite B, Hayward,
CA 94545, Contact: Bill Armor *Tel:* 510-
732-6521 *Fax:* 510-732-6523

Distribution Center: 3623 Munster St, Suite B,
Hayward, CA 94545, Contact: Bill Armor
Tel: 510-732-6521 *Fax:* 510-732-6523
Membership(s): Independent Book Publishers As-
sociation (IBPA)

Ballinger Publishing
314 N Spring St, Suite A, Pensacola, FL 32501
Mailing Address: PO Box 12665, Pensacola, FL
32591-2665
Tel: 850-433-1166 *Fax:* 850-435-9174
E-mail: info@ballingerpublishing.com
Web Site: www.ballingerpublishing.com
Key Personnel
Owner & Publr: Malcolm Ballinger *Tel:* 850-
433-1166 ext 27 *E-mail:* malcolm@
ballingerpublishing.com
Owner: Glenys Ballinger *Tel:* 850-433-1166 ext
22 *E-mail:* glenys@ballingerpublishing.com
Exec Ed: Kelly Oden *Tel:* 850-433-1166 ext 23
E-mail: kelly@ballingerpublishing.com
Founded: 2001
Publishers of local & regional magazines.
This publisher has indicated that 100% of their
product line is author subsidized.
ISBN Prefix(es): 978-0-9791103
Number of titles published annually: 80 Print

Bancroft Press
3209 Bancroft Rd, Baltimore, MD 21215
Mailing Address: PO Box 65360, Baltimore, MD
21209-9945
Tel: 410-358-0658
Web Site: www.bancroftpress.com
Key Personnel
Publr & Ed, Fiction & Nonfiction: Bruce L Bortz
E-mail: bruceb@bancroftpress.com
Deputy Publr, Lead Designer: Jen Herchenroeder
E-mail: jen@bancroftpress.com
Tech Consultant: Andrew Bortz *E-mail:* abortz@
bancroftpress.com
Founded: 1995
General interest trade book publisher; has re-
ceived special recognition & ranks among the
nation's top 100 independent presses. World-
wide rights & distribution.
ISBN Prefix(es): 978-1-890862
Number of titles published annually: 5 Print; 1
Audio
Total Titles: 60 Print; 1 Audio
Foreign Rights: Barbara Newman
Distribution Center: Baker & Taylor Publisher
Services, 30 Amberwood Pkwy, Ashland, OH
44805 *Tel:* 567-215-0030 *Toll Free Tel:* 888-
814-0208 *E-mail:* info@btpubservices.com *Web
Site:* www.btpubservices.com

Bandanna Books
1212 Punta Gorda St, No 13, Santa Barbara, CA
93103
SAN: 238-7956
E-mail: bandanna@cox.net
Web Site: www.bandannabooks.com; www.
mudbornpress.us; www.betabooks.us; www.
shakespeareplaybook.com; www.bookdoc.us;
catandbirdiebooks.com
Key Personnel
Publr: Sasha "Birdie" Newborn *E-mail:* birdie.
newborn@gmail.com
Founded: 1981 (outgrowth of Mudborn Press)
College market in literature, poetry, history, translations. Also BetaBooks imprint for DIY authors.
ISBN Prefix(es): 978-0-942208; 978-0-930012;
978-1-944371
Number of titles published annually: 12 Print
Total Titles: 110 Print; 35 E-Book; 5 Audio
Imprints: Beta Books (pre-publishing option of
mini-editions for DIY authors & modern poetry); Dictionary Series (series of little dictionaries: Italian for Opera Lovers, French
for Food Lovers, Yiddish, You Say? Nu?,

Doctorese for the imPatient); Gender Genre
(classic transgender literature, 8 variants for
third-person singular unknown or hypothetical); Mudborn Press (reprints, poetry, bilingual
Portuguese, Nahuatl, Latvian); Shakespeare
Playbooks (series of playbooks designed for
directors to envision a play & to keep track of
production details); Supplement Editions (texts
with supplementary background materials for
teachers)

B&H Publishing Group
Imprint of LifeWay Christian Resources
One LifeWay Plaza, Nashville, TN 37234
SAN: 201-937X
Toll Free Tel: 800-251-3225 (retailers); 800-448-
8032 (consumers); 800-458-2772 (churches)
Fax: 615-251-3914 (consumers); 615-251-5933
(churches) *Toll Free Fax:* 800-296-4036 (retail-
ers)
E-mail: customerservice@lifeway.com;
bhcustomerservice@lifeway.com;
bhtradesales@lifeway.com
Web Site: www.bhpublishinggroup.com
Key Personnel
Pres & CEO, LifeWay Christian Resources:
Thom S Rainer
Founded: 1934
Religious trade publisher of nonfiction (Christian
living, inspirational, devotional, contemporary
issues); fiction; children's books; Bibles; Bibli-
cal reference; Biblical commentaries.
ISBN Prefix(es): 978-0-8054; 978-1-5359; 978-1-
4300; 978-1-0877
Number of titles published annually: 95 Print
Total Titles: 700 Print; 5 Audio
Imprints: B&H Academic; B&H Espanol; B&H
kids; B&H Publishing; Holman Bibles
Foreign Rep(s): Parasource Marketing & Distribu-
tion (Canada)
Foreign Rights: Riggins International Rights Ser-
vices Inc (worldwide exc USA)
Returns: LifeWay Christian Resources, 535
Maddox-Simpson Pkwy, Lebanon, TN 37090

Banner of Truth
63 E Louther St, Carlisle, PA 17013
Mailing Address: PO Box 621, Carlisle, PA
17013-0621
Tel: 717-249-5747 *Toll Free Tel:* 800-263-8085
(orders) *Fax:* 717-249-0604
E-mail: info@banneroftruth.org
Web Site: www.banneroftruth.org
Key Personnel
Mgr: Patrick Daly
Founded: 1957
Not-for-profit Evangelical Christian publisher.
ISBN Prefix(es): 978-0-85151
Number of titles published annually: 15 Print
Total Titles: 802 Print
Foreign Office(s): The Banner of Truth Trust, PO
Box 29, Sylvania Southgate, NSW 2224, Aus-
tralia
The Banner of Truth Trust, The Grey House, 3
Murrayfield Rd, Edinburgh EH12 6EL, United
Kingdom *Tel:* (0131) 337 7310 *Fax:* (0131)
346 7484 *E-mail:* info@banneroftruth.co.uk
Membership(s): Evangelical Christian Publishers
Association (ECPA)

Baptist Spanish Publishing House, see Casa
Bautista de Publicaciones

Barbour Publishing Inc
1810 Barbour Dr, Uhrichsville, OH 44683
Tel: 740-922-6045 *Fax:* 740-922-5948
E-mail: info@barbourbooks.com
Web Site: www.barbourbooks.com
Key Personnel
Pres & COO: Mary Burns
VP, Edit: Kelly McIntosh *E-mail:* kmcintosh@
barbourbooks.com

VP, Mktg: Shalyn Sattler
VP, Sales: William Westfall *E-mail:* bwestfall@
barbourbooks.com
Founded: 1981
Christian books, Bibles, fiction, gift books, devotional journals, reference.
ISBN Prefix(es): 978-1-57748; 978-0-916441; 978-1-55748; 978-1-58660; 978-1-59310; 978-1-59789; 978-1-60260; 978-1-61626; 978-1-63058; 978-1-63409; 978-1-62416; 978-1-62836; 978-1-68322; 978-1-64352
Number of titles published annually: 244 Print
Total Titles: 793 Print
Imprints: Barbour Books; Shiloh Kidz; Shiloh Run Press

Barcelona Publishers LLC
10231 N Plano Rd, Dallas, TX 75238
Tel: 214-553-9785
E-mail: warehouse@barcelonapublishers.com
Web Site: www.barcelonapublishers.com
Key Personnel
Dir: Kenneth E Bruscia
Founded: 1989
Music therapy books & materials.
ISBN Prefix(es): 978-0-9624080; 978-1-891278; 978-1-937440; 978-1-945411
Number of titles published annually: 8 Print; 5 Audio
Total Titles: 95 Print; 70 Online; 70 E-Book
Foreign Rep(s): Eurospan Group (worldwide exc North America)
Distribution Center: Eurospan Group, Gray's Inn House, 127 Clerkenwell Rd, London EC1R 5DB, United Kingdom *Web Site:* www.eurospanbookstore.com/barcelona

Barefoot Books
2067 Massachusetts Ave, 5th fl, Cambridge, MA 02140
Tel: 617-576-0660 *Toll Free Tel:* 866-215-1756 (cust serv); 866-417-2369 (orders) *Fax:* 617-576-0049
E-mail: help@barefootbooks.com
Web Site: www.barefootbooks.com
Key Personnel
CEO: Nancy Traversy *E-mail:* nancy.traversy@
barefootbooks.com
Group Opers Dir: Karen Janson *E-mail:* karen.
janson@barefootbooks.com
Sr Ed: Lisa Rosinsky *E-mail:* lisa.rosinsky@
barefootbooks.com
Founded: 1993
Publishes high quality picture books for children of all ages specializing in the work of authors & artists from many cultures, wrapping paper, artists prints & cards.
ISBN Prefix(es): 978-1-898000; 978-1-901223; 978-1-902283; 978-1-84148; 978-1-84686; 978-1-905236; 978-1-78285
Number of titles published annually: 30 Print; 12 Audio
Total Titles: 300 Print
Returns: LSC Communications, 655 Brighton Beach Rd, Menasha, WI 54952
Warehouse: LSC Communications, 655 Brighton Beach Rd, Menasha, WI 54952
Membership(s): American Library Association .(ALA); The Children's Book Council (CBC)

Barnhardt & Ashe Publishing Inc
444 Brickell Ave, Suite 51, PMB 432, Miami, FL 33131
Toll Free Tel: 800-283-6360 (orders)
E-mail: barnhardtashe@aol.com
Founded: 2001
ISBN Prefix(es): 978-0-9715402; 978-0-9801744
Number of titles published annually: 10 Print
Total Titles: 9 Print
Membership(s): Association of American Publishers (AAP)

Barranca Press
17 Rockridge Rd, Mount Vernon, NY 10552
Tel: 347-820-2363
E-mail: editor@barrancapress.com
Web Site: www.barrancapress.com
Key Personnel
Ed: Lisa Noudehou *E-mail:* lisa@barrancapress.
com
Founded: 2012
Booklist includes photojournalism, novels, literary collections, children's books & memoirs. Unsol mss accepted March-Aug annually. E-mail submissions preferred.
ISBN Prefix(es): 978-1-939604
Number of titles published annually: 3 Print
Total Titles: 21 Print
Membership(s): Independent Book Publishers Association (IBPA)

Barricade Books Inc
2037 LeMoine Ave, Fort Lee, NJ 07024
Tel: 201-944-7600
E-mail: info@barricadebooks.com
Web Site: www.barricadebooks.com
Key Personnel
Owner & Publr: Jonathan Bernstein
Founded: 1992
ISBN Prefix(es): 978-1-56980
Number of titles published annually: 6 Print; 100 E-Book; 50 Audio
Total Titles: 100 Print; 200 E-Book; 50 Audio
Imprints: Barricade Books
Foreign Rights: Waterside (Europe exc UK)
Returns: National Book Network, 4501 Forbes Blvd, Suite 200, Lanham, MD 20706 *Tel:* 301-459-3366 *Toll Free Tel:* 800-462-6420 *Fax:* 301-429-5746
Warehouse: National Book Network, 4501 Forbes Blvd, Suite 200, Lanham, MD 20706 *Tel:* 301-459-3366 *Toll Free Tel:* 800-462-6420 *Fax:* 301-429-5746
Distribution Center: National Book Network, 4501 Forbes Blvd, Suite 200, Lanham, MD 20706 *Tel:* 301-459-3366 *Toll Free Tel:* 800-462-6420 *Fax:* 301-429-5746
Membership(s): Association of American Publishers (AAP)

Barringer Publishing
Division of Schlesinger Advertising & Marketing
770 Glendale Ave, Naples, FL 34110
Tel: 239-293-1289
E-mail: schlesadv@gmail.com
Web Site: www.barringerpublishing.com
Key Personnel
Owner: Jeff Schlesinger *E-mail:* js@
barringerpublishing.com
Founded: 2009
Full service: cover & book design, editing, printing, marketing, advertising & public relations, web sites, graphics, displays & illustrations.
ISBN Prefix(es): 978-0-9825109
Number of titles published annually: 15 Print
Total Titles: 120 Print
Membership(s): Independent Book Publishers Association (IBPA)

Barrytown/Station Hill Press
120 Station Hill Rd, Barrytown, NY 12507
SAN: 214-1485
Tel: 845-758-5293
E-mail: publishers@stationhill.org
Web Site: www.stationhill.org
Key Personnel
Publr: George Quasha
Co-Publr: Susan Quasha
Dir: Sam Truitt
Founded: 1977
General trade books, quality paperbacks & fine editions; poetry, fiction & discourse; visual arts; studies in literature & psychology, clas-

sics, translations, theater, creative nonfiction, health/New Age.
ISBN Prefix(es): 978-0-930794; 978-0-88268
Number of titles published annually: 6 Print
Total Titles: 300 Print
Foreign Rep(s): Lora Fountain (France); Gara Media (Germany); Japanville (Japan); Kerrigan (Spain); Living Weary (Italy)
Distribution Center: Midpoint Trade Books, 814 N Franklin St, Suite 100, Chicago, IL 60610 *Tel:* 312-337-0747 *Toll Free Tel:* 800-888-4741 *Fax:* 312-337-5985 *E-mail:* orders@ipgbook.
com *Web Site:* www.midpointtrade.com

Bartleby Press
Subsidiary of Jackson Westgate Publishing Group
8926 Baltimore St, No 858, Savage, MD 20763
SAN: 241-2098
Tel: 301-589-5831 *Toll Free Tel:* 800-953-9929
E-mail: inquiries@bartlebythepublisher.com
Web Site: www.bartlebythepublisher.com
Key Personnel
Publr: Jeremy Kay *E-mail:* publisher@
bartlebythepublisher.com
Proj Ed: Greg Giroux
Founded: 1981
ISBN Prefix(es): 978-0-910155; 978-0-9625963; 978-0-935437
Number of titles published annually: 7 Print; 10 E-Book
Total Titles: 58 Print; 22 E-Book
Imprints: Elstreet Educational; Eshel Books; PS&E Publications
Distribution Center: Casemate | IPM, 1950 Lawrence Rd, Havertown, PA 19083, Contact: Christine Wolf *Tel:* 610-853-9131 *Fax:* 610-853-9146 *E-mail:* casemate@
casematepublishers.com *Web Site:* www.
casemateipm.com
Membership(s): Independent Book Publishers Association (IBPA)

Basic Health Publications
Imprint of Turner Publishing Co
4507 Charlotte Ave, Suite 100, Nashville, TN 37209
Tel: 615-255-2665
E-mail: marketing@turnerpublishing.com
Key Personnel
Mktg: Kathleen Timberlake
Founded: 2001
ISBN Prefix(es): 978-1-59120
Number of titles published annually: 15 Print; 15 Online; 15 E-Book
Total Titles: 250 Print; 250 Online; 250 E-Book
Imprints: Basic Health Guides; User's Guides
Foreign Rights: Athena Productions Inc (worldwide)
Distribution Center: Ingram Content Group, One Ingram Blvd, La Vergne, TN 37086 *Tel:* 615-793-5000 *Web Site:* www.ingramcontent.com

Bay Tree Publishing LLC
225 E Richmond Ave, Point Richmond, CA 94801
Tel: 510-619-6338
Web Site: www.baytreepublish.com
Key Personnel
Publr: David Cole *E-mail:* dcole@baytreepublish.
com
Founded: 2002
ISBN Prefix(es): 978-0-9801758; 978-0-9720021; 978-0-9819577; 978-0-9836179; 978-0-9859399; 978-0-9966765
Number of titles published annually: 4 Print; 4 E-Book
Total Titles: 25 Print; 8 E-Book
Foreign Rep(s): National Book Network (Les Petriw) (Australia, Canada, New Zealand, UK)
Orders to: National Book Network (NBN), 15200 NBN Way, Blue Ridge Summit, PA 17214 *Toll Free Tel:* 800-462-6420

Returns: National Book Network (NBN), 15200 NBN Way, Blue Ridge Summit, PA 17214

Shipping Address: National Book Network (NBN), 15200 NBN Way, Blue Ridge Summit, PA 17214

Warehouse: National Book Network (NBN), 15200 NBN Way, Blue Ridge Summit, PA 17214

Distribution Center: National Book Network (NBN), 15200 NBN Way, Blue Ridge Summit, PA 17214

Membership(s): Bay Area Independent Publishers Association (BAIPA); Independent Book Publishers Association (IBPA)

Baylor University Press
Baylor University, One Bear Place, Waco, TX 76798-7363
SAN: 685-317X
Tel: 254-710-3164
Web Site: www.baylorpress.com
Key Personnel
Assoc Dir/Dir, Prodn & Design: Diane E Smith *Tel:* 254-710-2563 *E-mail:* diane_smith@ baylor.edu
Interim Dir, Mktg, Sales & Publicity: David Aycock *Tel:* 254-710-1465 *E-mail:* david_aycock@baylor.edu
Founded: 1897
Scholarly books & monographs.
ISBN Prefix(es): 978-0-918954; 978-1-932792
Number of titles published annually: 30 Print
Total Titles: 110 Print
Shipping Address: 1920 S Fourth St, Waco, TX 76706
Distribution Center: Longleaf Services Inc, 116 S Boundary St, Chapel Hill, NC 27514-3808 *Toll Free Tel:* 800-848-6224 ext 1 *Fax:* 919-962-2704 *E-mail:* customerservice@ longleafservices.org *Web Site:* www. longleafservices.org
Membership(s): American Association of University Presses (AAUP)

Beach Lane Books, see Simon & Schuster Children's Publishing

Beach Lloyd Publishers LLC
231 Sunnyside Rd, West Grove, PA 19390
SAN: 255-4992
Tel: 215-407-4570 (cell)
E-mail: beachlloyd@erols.com
Web Site: www.beachlloyd.com
Key Personnel
Owner & Mgr: Joanne S Silver
Founded: 2002
ISBN Prefix(es): 978-0-9743158; 978-0-9792778
Number of titles published annually: 3 Print; 1 Audio
Total Titles: 18 Print
Distributed by Tralco (CN)
Distributor for Le Chambon-sur-Lignon; CIDEB (Italy); Fondation pour la Memoire de la Shoah (Paris); Kar-Ben Publishing; Kiron Editions du Felin (Paris); JP Lattes (Paris); Le Manuscrit (Paris); Oxford University Press (NYC)
Distribution Center: Baker & Taylor
Membership(s): Alliance Francaise; American Association of Teachers of French

Beacon Hill Press of Kansas City
Subsidiary of The Foundry Publishing
PO Box 419527, Kansas City, MO 64141
SAN: 202-9022
Tel: 816-931-1900 *Toll Free Tel:* 800-877-0700 (cust serv) *Fax:* 816-531-0923
Toll Free Fax: 800-849-9827
E-mail: orders@thefoundrypublishing.com; customercare@thefoundrypublishing.com
Web Site: www.thefoundrypublishing.com
Key Personnel
CEO: Mark Brown

Dir: Bonnie Perry
Ministry Prod Line Ed: Richard E Buckner
Founded: 1912
Religion (Nazarene), ministry resources, Christian care & spiritual growth.
ISBN Prefix(es): 978-0-8341
Number of titles published annually: 30 Print
Total Titles: 700 Print

Beacon Press
24 Farnsworth St, Boston, MA 02210-1409
SAN: 201-4483
Tel: 617-742-2110 *Fax:* 617-723-3097; 617-742-2290
Web Site: www.beacon.org
Key Personnel
CFO: Cliff Manko
Dir: Helene Atwan
Dir, Communs: Pamela MacColl
Dir, Sales & Mktg: Sanj Kharbanda
Edit Dir & Assoc Dir: Gayatri Patnaik
Assoc Edit Dir: Amy Caldwell
Assoc Publicity Dir: Caitlin Meyer
Prodn Dir: Marcy Barnes
Prodn Mgr: Beth Collins
Reprint & Digital Prodn Mgr: Daniel Barks
Sr Ed: Joanna Green
Assoc Ed: Catherine Tung
Mktg Mgr: Emily Powers
Publicist: Nicholas DiSabatino
Asst Publicist: Michelle Betters
Sales Devt Coord: Jennifer Canela
Founded: 1854
General nonfiction, religion & theology, current affairs, anthropology, women's studies, history, gay & lesbian studies, African-American studies, Latino studies, education, hardcover, paperback, ebook & audio.
ISBN Prefix(es): 978-0-8070
Number of titles published annually: 60 Print; 35 E-Book
Total Titles: 800 Print; 350 E-Book; 5 Audio
Imprints: Concord Library; The King Legacy (writings of Dr Martin Luther King Jr)
Foreign Rep(s): New South Books (Australia, New Zealand); Publishers Group UK (UK)
Foreign Rights: Akcali Copyright Agency (Mustafa Urgen) (Turkey); Eliane Benisti Literary Agency (Noemie Rollet) (France); Chinese Connection Agency (Mei Yao) (China); The Deborah Harris Agency (Rene Rossner) (Israel); International Editors' Co (Isabel Monteagudo) (Portugal, Spain); Agenzia Internazionale Literaria (Stefania Fietta) (Italy); Maxima Creative Agency (Santo Manurung) (Indonesia); Prava i prevodi (Milena Lukic) (Eastern Europe exc Estonia, Latvia, Lithuania & Russia, Greece); Agencia Riff (Roberto Matos) (Brazil); Sebes & Bisseling Literary Agency (Netherlands, Scandinavia); Synopsis Literary Agency (Olga Zasetskaya) (Russia); Tuttle-Mori Agency Inc (Shoko Kobayashi & Youthapong Charoenpan) (Japan); Eric Yang Agency (Jackie Yang) (Korea)
Returns: Penguin Random House Returns Dept, 1019 N State Rd 47, Crawfordsville, IN 47933
Warehouse: Penguin Random House Publisher Services (PRHPS), 400 Hahn Rd, Westminster, MD 21157 *Toll Free Tel:* 800-733-3000 *Toll Free Fax:* 800-659-2436 *E-mail:* customerservice@ penguinrandomhouse.com
Distribution Center: Penguin Random House Publisher Services (PRHPS), 400 Hahn Rd, Westminster, MD 21157 *Toll Free Tel:* 800-733-3000 *Toll Free Fax:* 800-659-2436 *E-mail:* customerservice@ penguinrandomhouse.com
Membership(s): American Association of University Presses (AAUP); New England Independent Booksellers Association (NEIBA)

Beaming Books, see Augsburg Fortress Publishers, Publishing House of the Evangelical Lutheran Church in America

Bear & Bobcat Books
Imprint of Hameray Publishing Group Inc
5212 Venice Blvd, Los Angeles, CA 90019
Toll Free Tel: 866-918-6173 *Fax:* 858-369-5201
E-mail: info@hameraypublishing.com (cust serv); sales@hameraypublishing.com (sales)
Web Site: www.bearandbobcat.com
Founded: 2018
Bear & Bobcat Books feature works by internationally renowned authors & illustrators whose stories inspire laughter & a love of reading among children. As a part of the Hameray Publishing Group, Bear & Bobcat Books is dedicated to sparking imaginations & success of children through the powerful act of reading.
ISBN Prefix(es): 978-1-7324300
Number of titles published annually: 4 Print
Total Titles: 4 Print
Distributed by Hameray Publishing Group Inc

Bear & Co Inc
Imprint of Inner Traditions International Ltd
One Park St, Rochester, VT 05767
Mailing Address: PO Box 388, Rochester, VT 05767-0388
Tel: 802-767-3174 *Toll Free Tel:* 800-932-3277 *Fax:* 802-767-3726
E-mail: customerservice@InnerTraditions.com
Web Site: InnerTraditions.com
Key Personnel
Pres: Ehud C Sperling *E-mail:* prez@ InnerTraditions.com
VP, Opers: Diane Shepard *E-mail:* dianes@ InnerTraditions.com
Dir, Content & Consumer Sales: Rob Meadows *E-mail:* robm@InnerTraditions.com
Dir, Sales & Mktg: John Hays *E-mail:* johnh@ InnerTraditions.com
Ed-in-Chief: Jeanie Levitan *E-mail:* jeaniel@ InnerTraditions.com
Acqs Ed: Jon Graham *E-mail:* jong@ InnerTraditions.com
Audiobook Mgr: Megan Rule *E-mail:* meganr@ InnerTraditions.com
Print Mgr: Jon Desautels *E-mail:* jond@ InnerTraditions.com
Foreign Rts & Perms: Maria Loftus *E-mail:* marial@InnerTraditions.com
Publicity: Manzanita Carpenter *E-mail:* manzanitac@InnerTraditions.com
Sales & Mktg: Andrea Raymond *E-mail:* andyr@ InnerTraditions.com
Spec Sales: Jessica Arsenault *E-mail:* jessa@ InnerTraditions.com
Founded: 1980
Mysticism, philosophy, spirituality & medieval studies, contemporary prophecy, earth sciences, indigenous wisdom, new thought, alternative healing.
ISBN Prefix(es): 978-1-879181; 978-0-939680; 978-1-59143
Number of titles published annually: 15 Print; 15 E-Book
Total Titles: 359 Print; 313 E-Book
Foreign Rights: Akcali Copyright Agency (Turkey); Big Apple Agency Inc (China, Taiwan); Blackbird Literary Agency (Netherlands); The Book Publishers' Association of Israel, International Promotion & Literary Rights Department (Israel); Graal Literary Agency (Poland); International Editors' Co SA (Spain); The Italian Literary Agency (Italy); Simona Kessler International Copyright Agency Ltd (Romania); Alexander Korzhenevski Agency (Russia); Ilidio Matos Agency (Portugal); Montreal-Contacts/The Rights Agency (Canada); Andrew Nurnberg Associates (Baltic States, Bulgaria, Czechia, Hungary); Plima doo (Croatia); Read n Right Agency (Greece);

Schindler's Literary Agency (Brazil); Thomas Schlueck GmbH (Germany); Agence Schweiger (France); Tuttle-Mori Agency Inc (Indonesia, Japan, Thailand); Eric Yang Agency (Korea)
Orders to: Inner Traditions International - Bear & Co, c/o Simon & Schuster, 100 Front St, Riverside, NJ 08075 *Toll Free Tel:* 800-223-2336 *Toll Free Fax:* 800-943-9831 *E-mail:* purchaseorders@simonandschuster.com
Returns: Simon & Schuster, c/o Jacobson Logistics, 4406 Industrial Park Rd, Bldg 7, Camp Hill, PA 17011 (truckload shipments must call for an appt: 800-967-3914 ext 5318)
Warehouse: Inner Traditions International - Bear & Co, c/o Simon & Schuster, 100 Front St, Riverside, NJ 08075 *Toll Free Tel:* 800-943-9831 *E-mail:* purchaseorders@simonandschuster.com

§BearManor Media
PO Box 71426, Albany, GA 31708
Tel: 580-252-3547
E-mail: orders@benohmart.com; books@benohmart.com
Web Site: www.bearmanormedia.com
Key Personnel
Pres & Owner: Ben Ohmart
ISBN Prefix(es): 978-0-9714570; 978-1-59393; 978-1-62933
Number of titles published annually: 70 Print; 1 CD-ROM; 90 E-Book; 20 Audio
Total Titles: 1,100 Print; 2 CD-ROM; 1,100 Online; 900 E-Book; 60 Audio
Imprints: BearManor Bare (adult film biographies); BearManor Fiction (fiction about or by Hollywood stars)
Membership(s): Independent Book Publishers Association (IBPA)

Bearport Publishing Co Inc
45 W 21 St, Suite 3B, New York, NY 10010
Tel: 212-337-8577 *Toll Free Tel:* 877-337-8577 *Fax:* 212-337-8557 *Toll Free Fax:* 866-337-8557
E-mail: service@bearportpublishing.com; info@bearportpublishing.com
Web Site: www.bearportpublishing.com
Key Personnel
Pres & Publr: Kenn Goin
VP, Design & Prodn: Spencer Brinker
Sr Ed: Joyce Tavolacci
Natl Sales Mgr: Linda McGee
Founded: 2003
Curriculum-aligned, high-interest nonfiction for the library market.
ISBN Prefix(es): 978-1-59716; 978-1-936087; 978-1-61772
Number of titles published annually: 68 Print; 440 E-Book
Total Titles: 570 Print
Distributor for Ruby Tuesday Books
Returns: Corporate Graphics International, 1885 Northway Dr, North Mankato, MN 56003 *Toll Free Tel:* 800-851-8767 (sales & mktg); 800-247-2751 (cust serv) *E-mail:* marketing@cgintl.com *Web Site:* cgintl.com
Shipping Address: Corporate Graphics International, 1885 Northway Dr, North Mankato, MN 56003 *Toll Free Tel:* 800-851-8767 (sales & mktg); 800-247-2751 (cust serv) *E-mail:* marketing@cgintl.com *Web Site:* cgintl.com
Warehouse: Corporate Graphics International, 1885 Northway Dr, North Mankato, MN 56003 *Toll Free Tel:* 800-851-8767 (sales & mktg); 800-247-2751 (cust serv) *E-mail:* marketing@cgintl.com *Web Site:* cgintl.com
Membership(s): American Library Association (ALA); The Children's Book Council (CBC)

Beaver's Pond Press Inc
939 Seventh St W, St Paul, MN 55102

Tel: 952-829-8818
E-mail: info@beaverspondpress.com
Web Site: www.beaverspondpress.com
Key Personnel
CEO: Lily Coyle *E-mail:* lily@beaverspondpress.com
Ed: Alicia Ester *E-mail:* alicia@beaverspondpress.com; Laurie Herrmann *E-mail:* laurieh@beaverspondpress.com; Hanna Kjeldbjerg *E-mail:* hanna@beaverspondpress.com
Coord: Becca Hart *E-mail:* becca@beaverspondpress.com
Founded: 1998
Veteran-owned, woman-owned company for independent authors. Specialize in children's & coffee table books.
This publisher has indicated that 100% of their product line is author subsidized.
ISBN Prefix(es): 978-1-59298; 978-1-64343; 978-1-890676; 978-1-931646
Number of titles published annually: 60 Print; 15 E-Book
Total Titles: 1,000 Print; 150 E-Book
Orders to: Itasca Books, 5120 Cedar Lake Rd, Minneapolis, MN 55416, Contact: Mark Jung *Tel:* 952-345-4488 *Toll Free Tel:* 800-901-3480 ext 118 *Fax:* 952-920-0541 *E-mail:* orders@itascabooks.com *Web Site:* itascabooks.com
Returns: Itasca Books, 5120 Cedar Lake Rd, Minneapolis, MN 55416, Contact: Mark Jung *Tel:* 952-345-4488 *Toll Free Tel:* 800-901-3480 ext 118 *Fax:* 952-920-0541 *E-mail:* orders@itascabooks.com *Web Site:* itascabooks.com
Warehouse: Itasca Books, 5120 Cedar Lake Rd, Minneapolis, MN 55416, Contact: Mark Jung *Tel:* 952-345-4488 ext 118 *E-mail:* mark@itascabooks.com *Web Site:* itascabooks.com
Distribution Center: Itasca Books, 5120 Cedar Lake Rd, Minneapolis, MN 55416, Contact: Mark Jung *Tel:* 952-345-4488 *Toll Free Tel:* 800-901-3480 ext 118 *Fax:* 952-920-0541 *E-mail:* orders@itascabooks.com *Web Site:* itascabooks.com
Membership(s): The Dramatists Guild of America; Independent Book Publishers Association (IBPA); Midwest Independent Booksellers Association (MIBA); Midwest Independent Publishing Association (MIPA); PEN American Center; Society of Children's Book Writers & Illustrators (SCBWI)

Bedford, Freeman & Worth Publishing Group, LLC, see Macmillan Learning

Bedford/St Martin's
Imprint of Macmillan Learning
One New York Plaza, 46th fl, New York, NY 10004
Tel: 212-576-9400; 212-375-7000
E-mail: press.inquiries@macmillan.com
Web Site: www.macmillanlearning.com/college/us
Founded: 1981
Humanities publisher specializing in English composition, literature, history, communication & college success.
ISBN Prefix(es): 978-0-312; 978-1-457
Number of titles published annually: 200 Print; 50 E-Book
Warehouse: MPS Distribution Center, 16365 James Madison Hwy (US Rte 15), Gordonsville, VA 22942 *Toll Free Tel:* 888-330-8477 *Fax:* 540-672-7540 (cust serv) *Toll Free Fax:* 800-672-2054 (orders) SAN: 631-5011
Membership(s): Association of American Publishers (AAP)

Beehive Books
4700 Kingsessing Ave, Suite C, Philadelphia, PA 19143
E-mail: beehivebook@gmail.com
Web Site: www.beehivebooks.net

Key Personnel
Co-Founder: Maelle Doliveux; Josh O'Neill
Founded: 2017
A boutique visual arts press specializing in the odd, inventive, lovely & quixotic. Artist's books, monographs, magazines, graphic novels, prints & more.
ISBN Prefix(es): 978-1-948886
Number of titles published annually: 5 Print
Total Titles: 8 Print
Foreign Rights: Sequential Rights (Amber Garza) (worldwide)
Distribution Center: Consortium Book Sales & Distribution, 34 13 Ave NE, Suite 101, Minneapolis, MN 55413 *Tel:* 612-746-2600

Beekman Books Inc
300 Old All Angels Hill Rd, Wappingers Falls, NY 12590
Tel: 845-297-2690
E-mail: beekmanbooks@yahoo.com
Web Site: www.beekmanbooks.com
Key Personnel
Pres: Michael Arthur
Founded: 1972
New titles, reprints & imported titles from England, Wales, India & Russia in all subject areas, particularly music, holistic healing, homeopathic medicine, business, medical & computer books.
ISBN Prefix(es): 978-0-8464
Number of titles published annually: 3 Print
Total Titles: 3,026 Print
Distributor for C W Daniel; Gomer Press; Music Sales Corp; Kogan Page

Begell House Inc Publishers
50 North St, Danbury, CT 06810
Tel: 203-456-6161 *Fax:* 203-456-6167
E-mail: orders@begellhouse.com
Web Site: www.begellhouse.com
Key Personnel
VP & COO: Vicky Lipowski *E-mail:* vicky@begellhouse.com
Pres: Yelena Shafeyeva *E-mail:* elena@begellhouse.com
Mktg Dir: Peter White *E-mail:* peterw@begellhouse.com
Founded: 1992
Science books & journals.
ISBN Prefix(es): 978-1-56700
Number of titles published annually: 43 Print; 43 Online
Total Titles: 200 Print; 105 E-Book
Subsidiaries: Begell-Atom LLC
Membership(s): Association of American Publishers (AAP)

Behrman House Inc
11 Edison Place, Springfield, NJ 07081
SAN: 201-4459
Tel: 973-379-7200 *Toll Free Tel:* 800-221-2755 *Fax:* 973-379-7280
E-mail: customersupport@behrmanhouse.com
Web Site: store.behrmanhouse.com
Key Personnel
Pres & CEO: David Behrman
VP & Dir: Terry Kaye
Exec Ed: Dena Neusner
Founded: 1921
Synagogue school textbooks & trade books (Jewish).
ISBN Prefix(es): 978-0-87441
Number of titles published annually: 212 Print
Total Titles: 500 Print; 3 CD-ROM
Imprints: Apples & Honey Press
Distributor for Rossel Books
Distribution Center: Baker & Taylor Publisher Services, 30 Amberwood Pkwy, Ashland, OH 44805 *Tel:* 567-215-0030 *Toll Free Tel:* 888-814-0208 *E-mail:* info@btpubservices.com *Web Site:* www.btpubservices.com

Beignet Books, see BrickHouse Books Inc

Frederic C Beil Publisher Inc
609 Whitaker St, Savannah, GA 31401
Tel: 912-233-2446
E-mail: fcb@beil.com
Web Site: www.beil.com
Key Personnel
Pres & Publr: Frederic C Beil
Founded: 1982
Biography, history & fiction.
ISBN Prefix(es): 978-0-913720; 978-1-929490
Number of titles published annually: 4 Print
Total Titles: 145 Print
Imprints: Hypermedia Inc; The Sandstone Press
Foreign Rep(s): Gazelle Book Services Ltd (Europe, UK)

Bell Pond Books, see SteinerBooks Inc

Bell Springs Publishing
PO Box 1240, Willits, CA 95490-1240
SAN: 209-3138
Tel: 707-272-3472
E-mail: publisher@bellsprings.com
Web Site: bellsprings.com; aboutpinball.com
Key Personnel
Publr: Sam Leandro *E-mail:* sam@bellsprings.
  com
Ed: Bernard Kamoroff *E-mail:* bk@bellsprings.
  com
Founded: 1976
Books, small business, pinball machines.
ISBN Prefix(es): 978-0-917510
Number of titles published annually: 10 Print
Total Titles: 20 Print
Shipping Address: 106 State St, Willits, CA
  95490

Bella Books
PO Box 10543, Tallahassee, FL 32302
Tel: 850-576-2370 *Toll Free Tel:* 800-729-4992
  Fax: 850-576-3498
E-mail: info@bellabooks.com; orders@
  bellabooks.com; ebooks@bellabooks.com
Web Site: www.bellabooks.com
Key Personnel
Publr & CEO: Linda Hill *E-mail:* linda@
  bellabooks.com
Founded: 1991
Publish books for, by & about women; fiction &
  nonfiction.
ISBN Prefix(es): 978-0-9628938; 978-1-883061
Number of titles published annually: 10 Print
Total Titles: 35 Print
Imprints: Spinsters Ink
Distributed by Turnaround (London)
See separate listing for:
Spinsters Ink

BelleBooks
PO Box 300921, Memphis, TN 38130
Tel: 901-344-9024 *Fax:* 901-344-9068
E-mail: bellebooks@bellebooks.com
Web Site: www.bellebooks.com
Key Personnel
Pres & CEO: Debra Dixon
Dir, Mktg: Deborah Smith
Edit Dir, ImaJinn: Brenda Chin
Opers Mgr: Pamela Ireland
Founded: 1999
ISBN Prefix(es): 978-0-9768760
Number of titles published annually: 100 Print
Total Titles: 500 Print
Imprints: Bell Bridge Books; ImaJinn Books
See separate listing for:
ImaJinn Books

Bellerophon Books
PO Box 21307, Santa Barbara, CA 93121-1307
SAN: 202-392X

Tel: 805-965-7034 *Toll Free Tel:* 800-253-9943
  Fax: 805-965-8286
E-mail: sales.bellerophon@gmail.com
Web Site: www.bellerophonbooks.com
Key Personnel
Pres: Ellen Knill
Founded: 1969
Children's art & history.
ISBN Prefix(es): 978-0-88388
Number of titles published annually: 6 Print
Total Titles: 142 Print
Returns: 6685 El Pomar Dr, Templeton, CA
  93465

§Bellevue Literary Press
90 Broad St, Suite 2100, New York, NY 10004
Tel: 917-732-3603
Web Site: blpress.org
Key Personnel
Publr & Edit Dir: Erika Goldman *E-mail:* erika@
  blpress.org
Publg Asst: Laura Hart *E-mail:* laura@blpress.org
Founded: 2007
Bellevue Literary Press is a nonprofit, mission-
  driven press devoted to publishing literary fic-
  tion & nonfiction at the intersection of the arts
  & sciences because we believe that science &
  the humanities are natural companions for un-
  derstanding the human experience. With each
  book we publish, our goal is to foster a rich,
  interdisciplinary dialogue that will forge new
  tools for thinking & engaging with the world.
ISBN Prefix(es): 978-1-942658; 978-1-934137
Number of titles published annually: 8 Print; 8 E-
  Book
Total Titles: 80 Print; 76 E-Book
Foreign Rights: Kaplan/DeFiore Rights (Linda
  Kaplan) (worldwide)
Distribution Center: Consortium Book Sales
  & Distribution, The Keg House, 34 13 Ave
  NE, Suite 101, Minneapolis, MN 55413-1007
  Tel: 612-746-2600 *Toll Free Tel:* 800-283-3572
  (cust serv, Jackson, TN) *Fax:* 612-746-2606
  E-mail: info@cbsd.com *Web Site:* www.cbsd.
  com SAN: 200-6049
Membership(s): Community of Literary Maga-
  zines & Presses (CLMP); PEN American Cen-
  ter

Ben Yehuda Press
122 Ayers Ct, No 1B, Teaneck, NJ 07666
E-mail: orders@benyehudapress.com; yudel@
  benyehudapress.com
Web Site: www.benyehudapress.com
Key Personnel
Owner & Edit Dir: Larry Yudelson
  E-mail: larry@benyehudapress.com
Founded: 2005
Pluralistic Jewish publisher. Accept agented &
  unagented material. Prefer to see queries of a
  short synopsis (less than a page), table of con-
  tents & complete ms by electronic submission
  in Word format.
ISBN Prefix(es): 978-0-9769862; 978-0-9789980
Number of titles published annually: 6 Print; 2 E-
  Book
Total Titles: 50 Print; 12 E-Book
Membership(s): Independent Book Publishers As-
  sociation (IBPA)

§BenBella Books Inc
10300 N Central Expwy, Suite 400, Dallas, TX
  75231
Tel: 214-750-3600
E-mail: feedback@benbellabooks.com
Web Site: www.benbellabooks.com; www.
  smartpopbooks.com
Key Personnel
Publr: Glenn Yeffeth *Tel:* 214-750-3628
  E-mail: glenn@benbellabooks.com
Deputy Publr: Adrienne Lang *E-mail:* adrienne@
  benbellabooks.com

Admin Dir: Aida Herrera *Tel:* 214-361-7901
  E-mail: aida@benbellabooks.com
Mktg Dir: Jennifer Canzoneri *Tel:* 214-750-3600
  ext 104 *E-mail:* jennifer@benbellabooks.com
Ed-in-Chief: Leah Wilson *E-mail:* leah@
  benbellabooks.com
Ed-in-Chief, Matt Holt Books: Matt Holt
Ed-in-Chief, Smart Pop Books: Robb Pearlman
Prod Mgr: Monica Lowry *E-mail:* monica@
  benbellabooks.com
Founded: 2001
The best of health & nutrition, pop culture &
  smart nonfiction.
ISBN Prefix(es): 978-1-932100; 978-1-933771
Number of titles published annually: 40 Print
Total Titles: 150 Print
Imprints: BenBella Vegan; Matt Holt Books;
  Smart Pop
Foreign Rep(s): Jonathan Ball Publishers (South
  Africa); Canadian Manda Group (Canada); Edi-
  son Garcia (Asia); Grantham Book Services
  (Europe, Ireland, UK); NewSouth Books (Aus-
  tralia); Penguin Books India Pvt Ltd (India)
Orders to: Ingram Publisher Services, 210
  American Dr, Jackson, TN 38301 *Toll Free
  Tel:* 800-343-4499 *E-mail:* ipsjacksonorders@
  ingramcontent.com
Distribution Center: Two Rivers Distribution, an
  Ingram Brand, 1400 Broadway, Suite 520, New
  York, NY 10018
Membership(s): Independent Book Publishers As-
  sociation (IBPA)

Matthew Bender & Co Inc, see LexisNexis®
  Matthew Bender®

R James Bender Publishing
PO Box 23456, San Jose, CA 95153-3456
Tel: 408-225-5777 *Fax:* 408-225-4739
Web Site: www.bender-publishing.com
Key Personnel
Prop & Dir: Roger J Bender *E-mail:* rbender@
  bender-publishing.com
Founded: 1967
Military books & magazines.
ISBN Prefix(es): 978-0-912138
Number of titles published annually: 6 Print
Total Titles: 35 Print

John Benjamins Publishing Co
10 Meadowbrook Rd, Brunswick, ME 04011
SAN: 219-7677
Toll Free Tel: 800-562-5666 (orders)
Web Site: www.benjamins.com
Key Personnel
Consultant: Paul Peranteau *E-mail:* paul@
  benjamins.com
Founded: 1981
Linguistics, language studies, ESL, terminology
  & art; translation studies; literacy; scientific
  study of consciousness & communication.
ISBN Prefix(es): 978-1-55619; 978-0-915027;
  978-90-272; 978-1-58811
Number of titles published annually: 165 Print; 1
  CD-ROM; 2 Online; 165 E-Book
Total Titles: 4,500 Print; 10 CD-ROM; 4 Online;
  5,000 E-Book
Imprints: B R Gruener Publishing Co
Subsidiaries: John Benjamins North America Inc
Foreign Office(s): Box 36224, 1020 ME Amster-
  dam, Netherlands
Orders to: John Benjamins, PO Box 960,
  Herndon, VA 20172 *E-mail:* benjamins@
  presswarehouse.com
Returns: Books International, 22883 Quicksilver
  Dr, Dulles, VA 20166
Shipping Address: Books International, 22883
  Quicksilver Dr, Dulles, VA 20166, Con-
  tact: Todd Riggelman *E-mail:* benjamins@
  presswarehouse.com

Warehouse: Books International, 22883 Quicksilver Dr, Dulles, VA 20166 *Fax:* 703-661-1501
Distribution Center: Books International, 22883 Quicksilver Dr, Dulles, VA 20166

§Bentley Publishers
Division of Robert Bentley Inc
1734 Massachusetts Ave, Cambridge, MA 02138-1804
SAN: 213-9839
Tel: 617-547-4170 *Toll Free Tel:* 800-423-4595
Fax: 617-876-9235
E-mail: sales@bentleypublishers.com
Web Site: www.bentleypublishers.com
Key Personnel
Chmn & Pres: Michael Bentley
Dir, Publg: Janet Barnes
Founded: 1949
Technical automotive reference, automotive repair manuals, automotive history, automotive performance driving & motorsports.
ISBN Prefix(es): 978-0-8376
Number of titles published annually: 35 Print
Total Titles: 400 Print; 30 CD-ROM; 30 Online
Imprints: Linnaean Press

BePuzzled
Division of University Games
2030 Harrison St, San Francisco, CA 94110
Tel: 415-503-1600 *Toll Free Tel:* 800-347-4818
Fax: 415-503-0085
E-mail: info@ugames.com
Web Site: www.ugames.com
Key Personnel
Pres: Bob Moog
Gen Mgr: Stacy Cheregotis *E-mail:* stacyc@ugames.com
Puzzle Plus & Brain Teaser collections including Original 3D Crystal Puzzles, 3D Pixel Puzzles, Hanayama Cast Puzzles, Smart Egg Labyrinth Puzzles, Classic Mystery Jigsaw Puzzles & Preschool Jigsaw Puzzles.
ISBN Prefix(es): 978-1-57528; 978-1-57561
Number of titles published annually: 15 Print
Total Titles: 50 Print

Berghahn Books
20 Jay St, Suite 512, Brooklyn, NY 11201
Tel: 212-233-6004 *Fax:* 212-233-6007
E-mail: info@berghahnbooks.com; salesus@berghahnbooks.com; editorial@journals.berghahnbooks.com
Web Site: www.berghahnbooks.com
Key Personnel
Publr & Ed-in-Chief: Dr Marion Berghahn *E-mail:* publisher@berghahnbooks.com
Publg Opers Dir, Books & Journals: Melissa Gannon *E-mail:* melissa.gannon@berghahnbooks.com
Mng Dir & Journals Edit Dir: Vivian Berghahn *E-mail:* vivian.berghahn@berghahnbooks.com
Sr Ed, History & Film: Chris Chappell *E-mail:* chris.chappell@berghahnbooks.com
Mktg Mgr, Journals: Young Lee *E-mail:* young.lee@berghahnbooks.com
Founded: 1994
Scholarly books & journals in humanities & social sciences.
ISBN Prefix(es): 978-1-57181; 978-1-84545
Number of titles published annually: 150 Print; 1,000 E-Book
Total Titles: 2,800 Print; 1,500 E-Book
Divisions: Berghahn Books Ltd (UK)
Foreign Office(s): 3 Newtec Place, Magdalen Rd, Oxford OX4 1RE, United Kingdom *Tel:* (01865) 250011 *Fax:* (01865) 250056
Foreign Rep(s): About3 Pty Ltd (Australia, New Zealand); Avicenna (Middle East, North Africa); Iberian Book Services (Peter Prout) (Portugal, Spain); Jacek Lewinson (Central Europe, Eastern Europe); MHM Ltd (Japan); Missing Link (Germany); Ian Taylor Associates

Ltd (China); David Towle International (David Towle) (Scandinavia); Unifacmanu Trading Co Ltd (Celine Li) (Taiwan); Andrew White (India, Malaysia, Southeast Asia)
Foreign Rights: Afroditi Forti (worldwide)
Warehouse: Ingram, Jackson, TN

Berkley Publishing Group
Division of Penguin Group USA, A Penguin Random House Company
1745 Broadway, 19th fl, New York, NY 10019
Tel: 212-366-2000
Web Site: www.penguin.com
Key Personnel
SVP & Publr: Christine Ball
VP & Assoc Publr: Jeanne-Marie Hudson
VP & Ed-in-Chief: Claire Zion
VP & Edit Dir: Tom Colgan; Cindy Hwang
VP & Exec Dir, Publicity: Craig Burke
Exec Dir, Ad & Promo: Jaime Mendola-Hobbie
Sr Art Dir: Anthony Ramondo
Dir, Contracts: Robin Simon
Deputy Dir, Mktg: Jin Yu
Deputy Publicity Dir: Erin Galloway
Assoc Publicity Dir: Diana Franco
Assoc Dir, Publg, Putnam/Dutton/Berkley: Liza Cassity
Exec Ed: Amanda Bergeron; Anne Sowards
Sr Ed: Jen Monroe; Kristine Swartz
Assoc Ed: Sarah Blumenstock
Sr Mktg Mgr: Fareeda Bullert
Mktg Mgr: Bridget O'Toole
Founded: 1954
An industry leader in commercial & genre fiction, Berkley has a rich tradition of discovering new talent, defining emerging trends & building authors & series into global franchises. With Berkley's dedicated focus & guidance, many bestselling authors have grown into international brand names, including Nora Roberts, William Gibson, Laurell K Hamilton, Jim Butcher & Charlaine Harris. We're proud to publish Jasmine Guillory, Jayne Ann Krentz, Karen White, Patricia Briggs, Christine Feehan, Mark Greaney, Susan Meissner, Kristan Higgins & Chanel Cleeton, among others.
Number of titles published annually: 350 Print
Imprints: Ace Books; Berkley Books; Jove; Prime Crime; Signet

Berkshire Publishing Group LLC
PO Box 177, Great Barrington, MA 01230
E-mail: info@berkshirepublishing.com
Web Site: www.berkshirepublishing.com
Key Personnel
CEO: Karen Christensen
Founded: 2005
Specialize in international relations, cross-cultural communication, global business & economic information, environmental sustainability.
ISBN Prefix(es): 978-1-933782
Number of titles published annually: 7 Print; 6 E-Book

Bernan
Imprint of Rowman & Littlefield Publishing Group
4501 Forbes Blvd, Suite 200, Lanham, MD 20706
Mailing Address: PO Box 191, Blue Ridge Summit, PA 17214-0191
Tel: 717-794-3800 (cust serv & orders) *Toll Free Tel:* 800-462-6420 (cust serv & orders) *Fax:* 717-794-3803 *Toll Free Fax:* 800-338-4550
E-mail: customercare@bernan.com
Web Site: rowman.com/page/bernan
Key Personnel
Mktg Mgr: Veronica M Dove *Tel:* 301-459-2255 ext 5716 *Fax:* 301-459-0056 *E-mail:* vdove@bernan.com
Founded: 1952

Publishes original government-related reference works & provides a wide range of services to help librarians build their government information collections.
ISBN Prefix(es): 978-1-59888
Number of titles published annually: 45 Print
Total Titles: 336 Print
Distribution Center: National Book Network, 15200 NBN Way, Blue Ridge Summit, PA 17214 *Tel:* 301-459-7666 *Toll Free Tel:* 800-865-3457 *Fax:* 301-459-6988 *Toll Free Fax:* 800-865-3450

§Berrett-Koehler Publishers Inc
1333 Broadway, Suite 1000, Oakland, CA 94612
Tel: 510-817-2277 *Fax:* 510-817-2278
E-mail: bkpub@bkpub.com
Web Site: www.bkconnection.com
Key Personnel
CEO & CFO: David Marshall
Pres & Publr: Johanna Vondeling
VP, Sales & Mktg: Kristen Frantz
Mng Dir, Edit: Jeevan Sivasubramaniam
Edit Dir: Neal Maillet
Dir, Subs Rts: Maria Jesus Aguilo
Sr Communs Mgr, Digital Communs: Katie Sheehan
Sr Sales Mgr: Leslie Crandell
Assoc Dir, Sales & Mktg: Michael Crowley
Online Mktg & Intl Sales Mgr: Zoe Mackey
Assoc Ed: Anna Leinberger
Founded: 1992
Publications on business, work, stewardship, leadership, management, career development, human resources, entrepreneurship & global sustainability for the trade, scholarly, text & professional reference markets.
ISBN Prefix(es): 978-1-881052; 978-1-57675; 978-1-62656
Number of titles published annually: 40 Print
Total Titles: 320 Print
Foreign Rep(s): Eurospan Australia (Australia, New Zealand); HarperCollins Publishers India (Bangladesh, Bhutan, India, Maldives, Nepal, Pakistan, Sri Lanka); McGraw-Hill Education (Africa, Europe, Middle East, UK); McGraw-Hill Education Asia (East Asia, South Asia, Southeast Asia); Raincoast Books (Canada)
Warehouse: American International Distribution Corp (AIDC), 82 Winter Sport Lane, Williston, VT 05495 *Toll Free Tel:* 800-929-2929 *Toll Free Fax:* 800-864-7626 *E-mail:* urgent@aidcvt.com *Web Site:* www.aidcvt.com
Distribution Center: Penguin Random House Publisher Services, 400 Hahn Rd, Westminster, MD 21157 *Tel:* 410-848-1900 *Toll Free Tel:* 800-733-3000 (US); 888-523-9292 (CN) *E-mail:* customerservice@penguinrandomhouse.com *Web Site:* penguinrandomhouse.biz/publisherservices

§Bess Press
3565 Harding Ave, Honolulu, HI 96816
Tel: 808-734-7159 *Fax:* 808-732-3627
E-mail: customerservice@besspress.com
Web Site: www.besspress.com
Key Personnel
Owner & Publr: Benjamin E Bess
Exec Dir: David DeLuca *E-mail:* deluca@besspress.com
Founded: 1979
Books about the Pacific Islands, with a special emphasis on Hawaii. Includes elementary & secondary level textbooks in Hawaiian & Pacific Island history, geography & environment, Hawaiian & Pacific bilingual language materials, popular regional trade paperbacks, cookbooks, anthologies, humor, Christmas, guides, how-to & children's books on Hawaii & Oceania.
ISBN Prefix(es): 978-0-935848; 978-1-880188; 978-1-57306
Number of titles published annually: 17 Print

Total Titles: 285 Print; 12 Audio
Distributed by The Islander Group (TIG) (Hawaii wholesaler/book dist)

A M Best Co
One Ambest Rd, Oldwick, NJ 08858
Tel: 908-439-2200 (ext 5311, sales); 908-439-2200
E-mail: customer_service@ambest.com; sales@ambest.com
Web Site: www.ambest.com
Founded: 1899
Insurance industry statistics & supporting material, rate & provide financial information about insurance companies.
ISBN Prefix(es): 978-0-89408
Number of titles published annually: 3 Print
Total Titles: 17 Print
Foreign Office(s): A M Best Asia-Pacific, Central Plaza, Suite 4004, 18 Harbour Rd, Hong Kong, Hong Kong *Tel:* 2827 3400
A M Best American Latina SA de CV, Paseo de la Reforma 412, Piso 23, Col Juarez, Mexico, DF, Mexico *Tel:* (0155) 1102-2720
A M Best MENA South & Central Asia, Off 102, Tower 2, Currency House, DIFC, PO Box 506617, Dubai, United Arab Emirates *Tel:* (04) 375 2780
A M Best Europe, 12 Arthur St, 6th fl, London EC4R 9AB, United Kingdom *Tel:* (020) 7626 6264

Bethany House Publishers
Division of Baker Publishing Group
11400 Hampshire Ave S, Bloomington, MN 55438
SAN: 201-4416
Tel: 952-829-2500 *Toll Free Tel:* 800-877-2665 (orders) *Fax:* 952-829-2568 *Toll Free Fax:* 800-398-3111 (orders)
Web Site: www.bethanyhouse.com; www.bakerpublishinggroup.com
Key Personnel
EVP & Dir: Jim Parrish
VP, Edit: David Horton
VP, Mktg: Steve Oates
Pres, Baker Publishing Group: Dwight Baker
EVP, Sales & Mktg, Baker Publishing Group: Dave Lewis
Natl Sales Mgr: Rod Jantzen
Founded: 1956
Religion (Evangelical).
ISBN Prefix(es): 978-0-87123; 978-1-55661; 978-0-7642; 978-0-76428
Number of titles published annually: 90 Print; 90 E-Book
Total Titles: 1,500 Print
Foreign Rep(s): Challenge Bookshops Enterprises of Ghana (Nigeria); Christian Literature Center (Hong Kong); Christian Literature Crusade (Japan); Glad Sounds (Malaysia); Manna Christian Stores (New Zealand); Parasource (Canada); Salvation Book Center (Malaysia); Scripture Union (Singapore); SPCK (Netherlands, Norway, Sweden, UK); Word of Life Press (Japan, Korea)

Bethlehem Books
Affiliate of Bethlehem Community
10194 Garfield St S, Bathgate, ND 58216
Toll Free Tel: 800-757-6831 *Fax:* 701-265-3716
E-mail: contact@bethlehembooks.com
Web Site: www.bethlehembooks.com
Key Personnel
Pres: Jim Rasmussen
Gen Mgr & Publr: Jack Sharpe *E-mail:* jsharpe@bethlehembooks.com
Founded: 1993
Children's & youth books.
ISBN Prefix(es): 978-1-883937; 978-1-932350
Number of titles published annually: 8 Print; 10 E-Book; 4 Audio

Total Titles: 100 Print; 100 E-Book; 22 Audio
Distributed by Ignatius Press
Foreign Rights: Canadian Home Education Resources (Canada); St Andrews Books (Canada); Saint Benedicts Book Centre (Australia); Sunrise Marian Distributors (Canada)
Distribution Center: Amazon.com

Betterway Books
Imprint of Penguin Random House LLC
1745 Broadway, New York, NY 10019
Tel: 212-782-9000
Web Site: www.penguinrandomhouse.com
Founded: 1981
Instructional & self-help books for creative people in the areas of home maintenance, repair, woodworking, home-based business, sports & recreation, theater, arts, genealogy & gardening.
Penguin Random House & its publishing entities are not accepting unsol submissions, proposals, mss, or submission queries via e-mail at this time.
Number of titles published annually: 10 Print
Total Titles: 130 Print

§Bhaktivedanta Book Trust (BBT)
9701 Venice Blvd, Suite 3, Los Angeles, CA 90034
Mailing Address: PO Box 341445, Los Angeles, CA 90034
Tel: 310-837-5283 *Toll Free Tel:* 800-927-4152 *Fax:* 310-837-1056
E-mail: store@krishna.com
Web Site: www.krishna.com
Key Personnel
Mktg & Dist Mgr: Stuart Kadetz *E-mail:* sura108@gmail.com
Founded: 1972
Books of Vedic culture & philosophy, vegetarianism, reincarnation & karma.
ISBN Prefix(es): 978-0-89213; 978-0-912776
Number of titles published annually: 3 Print; 2 CD-ROM
Total Titles: 96 Print; 1 CD-ROM; 2 E-Book; 84 Audio
Warehouse: 13569 Larwin Circle, Santa Fe Springs, CA 90670-5032, Contact: Efren Gonzalez *Tel:* 562-229-1234 *Fax:* 562-229-1080

BHB, see BrickHouse Books Inc

Bick Publishing House
75 Mungertown Rd, Madison, CT 06443
Tel: 203-245-0341 *Fax:* 203-208-5253
E-mail: bickpubhse@aol.com
Web Site: www.bickpubhouse.com
Key Personnel
Pres & Owner: Hannah Carlson Jurewicz
Edit Dir: Dale Carlson
Founded: 1993
Adult & young adult professional information for general audience & teens on health & recovery, adult & teenage psychology, meditation, neuroscience, general science, special needs & wildlife rehabilitation.
ISBN Prefix(es): 978-1-884158
Number of titles published annually: 4 Print
Total Titles: 36 Print
Foreign Rep(s): Bob Erdmann (worldwide)
Foreign Rights: Bob Erdmann (worldwide)
Membership(s): Independent Book Publishers Association (IBPA)

Big Guy Books
6866 Embarcadero Lane, Carlsbad, CA 92011
SAN: 253-0392
Tel: 760-652-5360 *Toll Free Tel:* 800-536-3030 (booksellers' cust serv) *Fax:* 760-652-5361
E-mail: info@bigguybooks.com
Web Site: www.bigguybooks.com

Key Personnel
Pres: Robert Gould *E-mail:* robert@bigguybooks.com
Founded: 2000
Publishes high quality adventure stories for children. Combine cutting-edge graphics & old fashioned values to increase literacy as well as confidence & self-respect in young readers.
ISBN Prefix(es): 978-1-929945
Number of titles published annually: 3 Print
Membership(s): American Booksellers Association (ABA); American Library Association (ALA); Independent Book Publishers Association (IBPA)

Biographical Publishing Co
95 Sycamore Dr, Prospect, CT 06712-1011
Tel: 203-758-3661 *Fax:* 253-793-2618
E-mail: biopub@aol.com
Web Site: www.biopub.us
Key Personnel
Ed: John R Guevin
Founded: 1991
Pre-print, printing & marketing services.
ISBN Prefix(es): 978-0-9637240; 978-1-929882; 978-1-7338120; 978-0-9976028
Number of titles published annually: 10 Print; 5 E-Book
Total Titles: 115 Print; 98 Online; 30 E-Book
Distributor for Eagles Landing Publishing; Spyglass Books LLC
Distribution Center: Pathway Book Service, 34 Production Ave, Keene, NH 03431, Serv Contact: Bob Zipoli *Tel:* 603-357-0236 *Toll Free Tel:* 800-345-6665 *Fax:* 603-357-2073 *E-mail:* pbs@pathwaybook.com *Web Site:* www.pathwaybook.com

Bird Dog Publishing, see Bottom Dog Press

§George T Bisel Co Inc
710 S Washington Sq, Philadelphia, PA 19106-3519
Tel: 215-922-5760 *Toll Free Tel:* 800-247-3526 *Fax:* 215-922-2235
E-mail: gbisel@bisel.com
Web Site: www.bisel.com
Key Personnel
Pres: Franklin Jon Zuch *E-mail:* fjzuch@bisel.com
Ed-in-Chief: Tony Di Gioia *E-mail:* tonyd@bisel.com
Ed: Frank Coyne *E-mail:* fcoyne@bisel.com
Sales & Mktg: Paul Roberts *E-mail:* proberts@bisel.com
Founded: 1876
Pennsylvania, New Jersey, Florida law practice subjects.
ISBN Prefix(es): 978-1-887024
Number of titles published annually: 8 Print
Total Titles: 75 Print; 10 CD-ROM; 1 Audio

§Bisk Education
9417 Princess Palm Ave, Suite 400, Tampa, FL 33619
Tel: 813-621-6200 *Toll Free Tel:* 800-280-9718 (cust serv)
E-mail: customerservice@bisk.com
Web Site: www.bisk.com
Key Personnel
CEO: Michael Bisk
CFO: William Geary, III
Chief Growth Offr: Chad Bandy
Chief Corp Advisor: Andrew Titen
VP & Corp Coun: Alison L Bisk
Assoc VP, Learning Experience, Design & Media: Cherie Mazer
Dir, Mktg: Kimberly Simon
Founded: 1971
One of the leading providers of online, interactive continuing professional education, including continuing education for accountants, attorneys,

physicians & nurses, CPA Exam preparation materials & web-based certificate, associate's, bachelor's & master's degree programs from nationally known, regionally accredited universities, including Villanova University, Regis University, the University of South Florida, Saint Leo University & Jacksonville University.
ISBN Prefix(es): 978-1-57961
Number of titles published annually: 50 Print
Total Titles: 500 Print; 50 CD-ROM; 150 Online; 9 E-Book; 90 Audio

Bisk Publishing Co, see Bisk Education

§Bitingduck Press LLC
1262 Sunnyoaks Circle, Altadena, CA 91001
Tel: 626-507-8033
E-mail: notifications@bitingduckpress.com
Web Site: bitingduckpress.com
Key Personnel
Ed-in-Chief: Jay Nadeau *E-mail:* jay@ bitingduckpress.com
Creative Dir: Dena Eaton *E-mail:* dena@ bitingduckpress.com
Technol Dir: Chris Lindensmith *E-mail:* chris@ bitingduckpress.com
Ed: Susan Foster
Acqs Ed: Marie Nadeau *E-mail:* marie@ bitingduckpress.com
Founded: 2012
Quality electronic publishing for a digital world.
ISBN Prefix(es): 978-1-938463
Number of titles published annually: 8 Print; 12 E-Book
Total Titles: 50 Print; 140 E-Book
Imprints: Boson Books™
Distribution Center: Independent Publishers Group (IPG), 814 N Franklin St, Chicago, IL 60610 *Tel:* 312-337-0747 *Toll Free Tel:* 800-888-4741 *Fax:* 312-337-5985 *E-mail:* orders@ ipgbook.com *Web Site:* www.ipgbook.com
Ingram Book Group, One Ingram Blvd, La Vergne, TN *Tel:* 615-793-5000
Membership(s): The Authors Guild; Independent Book Publishing Professionals Group (IBPPG)
See separate listing for:
Boson Books™

§BJU Press
Unit of BJU Education Group
1430 Wade Hampton Blvd, Greenville, SC 29609-5046
SAN: 223-7512
Tel: 864-770-1317; 864-546-4600
Toll Free Tel: 800-845-5731
E-mail: bjuinfo@bju.edu
Web Site: www.bjupress.com
Key Personnel
Pres: Bill Apelian
Exec Asst: Jennifer Headley
Founded: 1974
El-hi textbooks & trade media.
ISBN Prefix(es): 978-0-89084; 978-1-57924; 978-1-59166
Number of titles published annually: 50 Print
Total Titles: 2,500 Print
Imprints: JourneyForth Books; ShowForth Videos
Divisions: JourneyForth Books; ShowForth Videos
Warehouse: 134 White Oak Dr, Greenville, SC 29607-1218

BkMk Press - University of Missouri-Kansas City
University House, 5101 Rockhill Rd, Kansas City, MO 64110-2499
Tel: 816-235-2558 *Fax:* 816-235-2611
E-mail: bkmk@umkc.edu
Web Site: www.umkc.edu/bkmk
Key Personnel
Exec Ed: Robert Stewart *Tel:* 816-235-2610
E-mail: stewartr@umkc.edu

Mng Ed: Ben Furnish *E-mail:* furnishb@umkc. edu
Founded: 1971
Fine literature & essays.
ISBN Prefix(es): 978-0-933532; 978-1-886157
Number of titles published annually: 8 Print
Total Titles: 130 Print
Distribution Center: Small Press Distribution, 1341 Seventh St, Berkeley, CA 94710 (recent titles) *Toll Free Tel:* 800-869-7553
Membership(s): Association of American Publishers (AAP); Association of Writers & Writing Programs (AWP); Community of Literary Magazines & Presses (CLMP)

Black Classic Press
3921 Vero Rd, Suite F, Baltimore, MD 21203-3414
SAN: 219-5836
Mailing Address: PO Box 13414, Baltimore, MD 21203-3414
Tel: 410-242-6954 *Toll Free Tel:* 800-476-8870
Fax: 410-242-6959
E-mail: email@blackclassicbooks.com; blackclassicpress@yahoo.com
Web Site: www.blackclassicbooks.com; www. bcpdigital.com
Key Personnel
Pres: W Paul Coates
Publr: Natalie Stokes-Peters
Digital Print Consultant: Damani Coates
Founded: 1978
Publishing obscure & significant works by & about people of African descent.
ISBN Prefix(es): 978-0-933121; 978-1-57478
Number of titles published annually: 20 Print
Total Titles: 100 Print
Imprints: Inprint Editions
Distributed by Publishers Group West (PGW)
Membership(s): Independent Book Publishers Association (IBPA)

Black Dome Press Corp
649 Delaware Ave, Delmar, NY 12054
Tel: 518-439-6512
E-mail: blackdomep@aol.com
Web Site: www.blackdomepress.com
Key Personnel
Publr: Steve Hoare
Founded: 1990
Regional small press publishing New York State history & guide books.
ISBN Prefix(es): 978-1-883789; 978-0-9628523
Number of titles published annually: 5 Print
Total Titles: 80 Print

Black Heron Press
PO Box 614, Anacortes, WA 98221
Tel: 360-899-9335
Web Site: blackheronpress.com
Key Personnel
Publr & Lib Sales Dir: Jerry Gold
E-mail: jgoldberon@aol.com
Founded: 1984
Literary fiction & nonfiction pertaining to independent publishing & the writing craft; literature, science fiction (not dungeons & dragons).
ISBN Prefix(es): 978-0-930773; 978-1-936364
Number of titles published annually: 4 Print
Total Titles: 80 Print
Foreign Rep(s): Eulama International Literary Agency (Pina von Prellwitz) (worldwide)
Foreign Rights: Eulama International Literary Agency (Pina von Prellwitz) (worldwide)
Distribution Center: Independent Publishers Group (IPG), 814 N Franklin St, Chicago, IL 60610 *Tel:* 312-337-0747 *Toll Free Tel:* 800-888-4741 *Fax:* 312-337-5985 *E-mail:* orders@ ipgbook.com *Web Site:* www.ipgbook.com

§Black Mountain Press
PO Box 9907, Asheville, NC 28815

Tel: 828-273-3332
Web Site: www.theblackmountainpress.com
Key Personnel
Publr: Carlos Steward *E-mail:* carlos@ theblackmountainpress.com
Ed: Joline Mechanic *E-mail:* jolene99@bellsouth. net
Founded: 1994
Literary press for emerging & established creative writers, with or without literary agents. Specialize in literary novels, short story collections, poetry & creative nonfiction.
ISBN Prefix(es): 978-0-9700165; 978-1-940605
Number of titles published annually: 12 Print; 10 E-Book
Total Titles: 25 Print; 10 E-Book

Black Rabbit Books
2140 Howard Dr W, North Mankato, MN 56003
Mailing Address: PO Box 3263, Mankato, MN 56002-3263
Tel: 507-388-1609 *Fax:* 507-388-2746
E-mail: info@blackrabbitbooks.com; orders@ blackrabbitbooks.com
Web Site: www.blackrabbitbooks.com
Key Personnel
Assoc Publr: Jen Besel
VP, Sales: Jonathan Strickland
Founded: 2006
Founded on the principle that quality books produce quality readers. Our list of K-12 books has a wide variety of topics, innovative approaches & multiple reading levels to serve all facets of the school library market.
ISBN Prefix(es): 978-1-84234; 978-1-84193; 978-1-59920; 978-1-58340; 978-1-59771; 978-1-59566; 978-1-59604; 978-1-93288; 978-8-86098; 978-1-93383; 978-1-93279; 978-1-84837
Number of titles published annually: 375 Print
Total Titles: 2,000 Print
Imprints: Bolt; Book House; Brown Bear Books; Hi Jinx; Smart Apple Media
Foreign Rep(s): Saunders Book Co (Canada)
Distribution Center: The Creative Co, PO Box 227, Mankato, MN 56002 *Toll Free Tel:* 800-445-6209 *Fax:* 507-388-2746 *E-mail:* sales@thecreativecompany.us *Web Site:* thecreativecompany.us
Saunders Book Co, PO Box 308, Collingwood, AB L9Y 3Z7, Canada *Tel:* 705-445-4777 *Toll Free Tel:* 800-461-9120 *Fax:* 705-445-9569 *Toll Free Fax:* 800-561-1763 *E-mail:* info@ saundersbooks.ca

The Blackburn Press
PO Box 287, Caldwell, NJ 07006-0287
Tel: 973-228-7077 *Fax:* 973-228-7276
Web Site: www.blackburnpress.com
Key Personnel
Edit Dir & Publr: Frances Reed *E-mail:* freed@ blackburnpress.com
Gen Mgr: Maryanne Kenny *E-mail:* mkenny@ blackburnpress.com
Mktg & Cust Serv: Barbara R Chmiel
E-mail: bchmiel@blackburnpress.com
Founded: 1999
Book titles, largely reprints, of classics in science & technology. Worldwide distributors.
ISBN Prefix(es): 978-1-930665; 978-1-932846
Number of titles published annually: 20 Print
Total Titles: 100 Print
Distribution Center: Baker & Taylor, 2550 W Tyvola Rd, Charlotte, NC *Tel:* 800-775-1800 *Toll Free Fax:* 800-998-3316 *E-mail:* btinfo@baker-taylor.com *Web Site:* www.baker-tayor.com
Barnes & Noble, One Barnes & Noble Way, Monroe, NJ 08831 *Tel:* 732-656-7400
indiCo, 528 E Lorain St, Oberlin, OH 44074-1298 *Toll Free Tel:* 800-321-3883 (orders) *E-mail:* orders@goindico.com *Web Site:* www. goindico.com

Ingram, One Ingram Blvd, La Vergne, TN
Tel: 615-793-5000 *Toll Free Tel:* 800-937-8200
E-mail: customer.service@ingrambook.com
Web Site: www.ingrambook.com

Amazon.com, 440 Terry Ave N, Seattle, WA
E-mail: amazonpublishing-pr@amazon.com
Web Site: www.amazon.com

Adlibris.com, Box 3367, 103 59 Stockholm, Sweden

Amazon.co.uk

Ingram International

Mallory International Ltd, Aylesbeare Common
Business Park, Exmouth Rd, Aylesbeare, Devon
EX5 2DG, United Kingdom, Contact: Julian
Hardinge *Tel:* (01395) 239199 *Fax:* (01395)
239168 *E-mail:* julian@malloryint.co.uk *Web
Site:* www.malloryint.co.uk

Blackwell, Unipart House, Garsington Rd,
Cowley, Oxford OX4 2PG, United Kingdom *Tel:* (01865) 382 524 *Fax:* (01865)
382 790 *E-mail:* sales@blackwell.co.uk *Web
Site:* bookshop.blackwell.co.uk

Gardners Books, One Whittle Dr, Eastbourne, East Sussex, United Kingdom
Tel: (01323) 521777 *Fax:* (01323) 521666
E-mail: custcare@gardners.com *Web
Site:* www.gardners.com

Paperback Shop, Horcott Industrial Estate, Unit
22, Horcott Rd, Fairford, Glos GL7 4BX,
United Kingdom *Tel:* (01285) 712 917

Coutts & Co, 440 Stand, London WC2R 0QS,
United Kingdom *Tel:* (020) 7753 1000 *Web
Site:* www.coutts.com

Book Depository, PO Box 91, St Peter Port GY1
3EG, United Kingdom, Contact: Steve Potter
E-mail: steve@bookdepository.co.uk

Aphrohead, 277-A Wennington Rd, Southport,
Merseyside PR9 7TW, United Kingdom,
Mng Dir: Paul Anderson *E-mail:* enquiries@
aphrohead.com *Web Site:* aphrohead.com

Bertrams, Wakefield House, Pipers Way, Swindon, Wilts SN3 1RF, United Kingdom
Tel: (0871) 803 6666 *Web Site:* www.bertrams.com

§Blair

905 W Main St, Suite 19 D-1, Durham, NC
27701
Tel: 919-682-0555
E-mail: customersupport@blair.com
Web Site: www.blairpub.com
Key Personnel
Publr: Lynn York
Assoc Publr & Sr Ed: Robin Miura
Founded: 2018 (combined list of Carolina Wren
Press & John F Blair, Publisher)
Prose & poetry.
ISBN Prefix(es): 978-0-910244; 978-0-89587;
978-0-932112
Number of titles published annually: 9 Print
Total Titles: 159 Print
Distribution Center: Consortium Book Sales
& Distribution, The Keg House, 34 13 Ave
NE, Suite 101, Minneapolis, MN 55413-1007
Tel: 612-746-2600 *Toll Free Tel:* 800-283-3572
Fax: 612-746-2606 *E-mail:* info@cbsd.com
Web Site: www.cbsd.com SAN: 200-6049

Blood Moon Productions Ltd

75 Saint Marks Place, Staten Island, NY 10301-
1606
Tel: 718-556-9410
E-mail: danforthprince@gmail.com
Web Site: bloodmoonproductions.com
Key Personnel
Pres & Publr: Danforth Prince *E-mail:*
danforthprince@bloodmoonproductions.com
Founded: 2004
A New York-based publishing enterprise dedicated to researching, salvaging & indexing the
oral histories of America's entertainment industry.

ISBN Prefix(es): 978-0-9748118; 978-0-9786465;
978-1-936003
Number of titles published annually: 4 Print; 4 E-Book
Total Titles: 50 Print; 50 E-Book
Distribution Center: National Book Network,
4501 Forbes Blvd, Suite 200, Lanham, MD
20706 (Australia, New Zealand, North America & UK) *Tel:* 301-459-3366 *Toll Free*
Tel: 800-462-6420 *Fax:* 301-429-5746 *Toll Free*
Fax: 800-338-4550 *E-mail:* customercare@
nbnbooks.com *Web Site:* www.nbnbooks.com
Membership(s): American Booksellers Association (ABA); Independent Book Publishers Association (IBPA); New Atlantic Independent
Booksellers Association (NAIBA); Southern
Independent Booksellers Alliance (SIBA)

Bloomberg Law Book Division

Division of Bloomberg BNA
1801 S Bell St, Arlington, VA 22202
SAN: 201-4262
Tel: 732-476-6397 *Toll Free Tel:* 800-960-1220
Fax: 732-346-1624
E-mail: books@bloomberglaw.com
Web Site: www.bna.com/bloomberglaw/
Key Personnel
CEO: Josh Eastright
Pres: Scott Mozarsky
Publr: Margret S Hullinger *Tel:* 703-341-5742
E-mail: mhullinger@bna.com
Acqs Mgr: Robert Anderson *Tel:* 703-341-5765
E-mail: randerson@bna.com
Founded: 1929
Employment law: labor law, labor relations, employee benefits, labor arbitration, intellectual
property law; tax law: estate & insurance company tax; health law: legal practice & reference.
ISBN Prefix(es): 978-0-87179; 978-1-57018
Number of titles published annually: 60 Print
Total Titles: 160 Print; 120 Online
Orders to: 2500 Main St, Unit 12, Sayreville, NJ
08872
Returns: 2500 Main St, Unit 12, Sayreville, NJ
08872
Warehouse: 2500 Main St, Unit 12, Sayreville, NJ
08872

Bloom's Literary Criticism

Imprint of Infobase Learning
132 W 31 St, 17th fl, New York, NY 10001
Toll Free Tel: 800-322-8755 *Toll Free Fax:* 800-
678-3633
E-mail: custserv@factsonfile.com
Web Site: www.infobasepublishing.com
Key Personnel
Pres & CEO, Infobase Learning: Mark McDonnell
CFO, Infobase Learning: Jim Housley
Edit Dir, Infobase Learning: Laurie Likoff
Dir, Licensing & Busn Devt, Infobase Learning: Ben Jacobs *Tel:* 212-896-4268
E-mail: bjacobs@factsonfile.com
Dir, Mktg, Infobase Learning: Zina Scarpulla
Dir, Publicity, Infobase Learning: Laurie Katz
Tel: 800-322-8755 ext 4269 *E-mail:* lkatz@
infobaselearning.com
Dir, Sales & Opers, Infobase Learning: Mark
Zielinski
Offers hundreds of volumes of literary criticism
edited by Harold Bloom, focusing on the writers & works most often studied in high schools
& universities.
ISBN Prefix(es): 978-0-7910; 978-1-4381
Number of titles published annually: 67 Print; 67
E-Book
Total Titles: 453 Print; 525 E-Book
Returns: Maple Logistics Solutions, Lebanon Distribution Ctr, 704 Legionaire Dr, Fredericksburg, PA 17026

Warehouse: Maple Logistics Solutions, Lebanon
Distribution Ctr, 704 Legionaire Dr, Fredericksburg, PA 17026
Distribution Center: Maple Logistics Solutions,
Lebanon Distribution Ctr, 704 Legionaire Dr,
Fredericksburg, PA 17026

Bloomsbury Academic

1385 Broadway, 5th fl, New York, NY 10018
SAN: 213-8220
Tel: 212-419-5300
Web Site: www.bloomsbury.com/us/academic
Key Personnel
Mng Dir, Digital Resources Div: Kathryn Earle
Assoc Dir, Sales: Mat Nichols
Mktg Mgr: Joe Kreuser *E-mail:* joseph.kreuser@
bloomsbury.com
Mktg Assoc: Laura Ewen *E-mail:* laura.ewen@
bloomsbury.com
Conference & Events Coord: Jessica Tackett
Founded: 1999 (result of a merger between The
Continuum Publishing Company of NY & the
academic & religious publishing programs of
Cassell plc in London)
Hardcover & paperbacks; scholarly & professional & general interest; music, film, literature, media studies, the arts & popular culture;
philosophy, religion, biblical studies, theology
& spirituality, history, politics & contemporary
issues, education; women's studies & reference.
ISBN Prefix(es): 978-0-304; 978-0-7201; 978-0-
8264; 978-1-56338; 978-0-7136; 978-0-86012;
978-0-225; 978-0-264; 978-0-7185; 978-0-
86187; 978-1-85567; 978-0-7220; 978-0-567;
978-0-485; 978-1-84127; 978-1-85805; 978-1-
84371; 978-0-8044; 978-0-223
Number of titles published annually: 1,200 Print
Total Titles: 6,000 Print
Distributor for Paragon House; Spring Publications
Foreign Rights: Allen & Unwin Pty Ltd (Australia); APD (Brunei, Indonesia, Malaysia, Singapore, Thailand, Vietnam); APS Ltd (China,
Hong Kong, Philippines, South Korea, Taiwan); Robert Barnett (USA); BCR University
Bookstore (Jamaica); Bounty Press Ltd (Nigeria); Continuum (Africa exc North & South
Africa, Caribbean, Germany, Israel, Netherlands, North America); Cranbury International
LLC (Central America, Mexico, South America); Durnell Marketing Ltd (Europe); Horizon
Books (Botswana, Lesotho, Namibia, South
Africa, Swaziland); IPS (Middle East exc Israel, North Africa); Richard Lyle (London);
Maya Publishers Pvt Ltd (Bangladesh, India,
Sri Lanka); Richard McNeace (USA); Natoli
Stefan & Oliva Literary Agency (Italy); Novalis
(Canada); Nick Pepper (Northern England,
Scotland); Publishers Consultants & Representatives (Pakistan); Jonathan Rhodes (England,
Midlands); Andrew Toal (England); United
Publishers Services Ltd (Japan)

Bloomsbury Publishing Inc

1385 Broadway, 5th fl, New York, NY 10018
Tel: 212-419-5300
E-mail: marketingusa@bloomsbury.com;
adultpublicityusa@bloomsbury.com;
askacademic@bloomsbury.com
Web Site: www.bloomsbury.com
Key Personnel
VP, US Sales & Mktg: Valentina Rice
Sr Dir, Mktg & Publicity, Children's Trade: Erica
Barmash
Sr Dir, Publicity & Communs: Marie Coolman
Sr Dir, School & Lib Mktg & Dom Subs Rts:
Beth Eller
Publg Dir, Bloomsbury Children's Books USA &
Bloomsbury USA: Cindy Loh
Assoc Publr & Edit Dir: Nancy Miller
Mng Edit Dir, Children's: Melissa Kavonic
Edit Dir, Children's: Mary Kate Castellani; Annette Pollert-Morgan

Edit Dir, Fiction: Liese Mayer
Mng Dir, Digital Resources Div: Kathryn Earle
Sr Dir, Mktg & Publicity, Adult Trade: Laura Keefe
Dir, Adoption Sales, Bloomsbury Academic & Professional: Liza Murphy
Dir, Children's Publicity: Faye Bi
Dir, Mktg Design & Opers: Alona Fryman
Dir Sales, US & CN: Frank Bumbalo
Publicity Dir: Tara Kennedy
Sales Dir, Latin America, Caribbean & Canada: Nick Parker
Asst Art Dir: Katya Mezhibovskaya
Asst Art Dir, Children's: Jeanette Levy
Head, Academic Mktg (Americas): Abigail Naqvi
Exec Mng Ed, Bloomsbury Children's Books: Melissa Kavonic
Exec Ed: Anton Mueller
Exec Ed, Bloomsbury Children's Books: Sarah Shumway; Noa Wheeler
Mng Ed: Laura Phillips
Sr Ed: Daniel Loedel
Sr Ed, Bloomsbury USA: Lea Beresford
Sr Ed/Brand Mgr, Bloomsbury Children's Books: Kamilla Benko
Sr Ed, Nonfiction: Ben Hyman
Sr Ed, Nonfiction, Bloomsbury Children's: Susan Dobinick
Sr Prodn Ed: Oona Patrick
Ed: Callie Garnett
Assoc Ed: Grace McNamee
Assoc Ed, Bloomsbury Children's Books: Hali Baumstein; Allison Moore
Asst Ed: Morgan Jones
Asst Ed, Children's: Kate Sederstrom
Asst Prodn Ed: Nick Sweeney
Sr Sales Mgr: Daniel O'Connor
Inventory Mgr, Bloomsbury USA: Donna Gautier
Mktg Mgr, Adult Trade Div: Nicole Jarvis
Mktg Mgr, Bloomsbury Children's Books: Lily Yengle
US Trade Sales Opers Mgr: Doug White
Asst Mktg Mgr for School & Lib, Children's Trade Group: Brittany Mitchell
Sr Designer: Tree Abraham
Sr Publicist: Rosie Mahorter
Sr Publicist, Children's: Ksenia Winnicki
Publicist: Lauren Hill
Publicist, Children's: Courtney Griffin; Alexa Higbee
Mktg Assoc: Ellen Whitaker
Mktg Assoc, Children's: Phoebe Dyer
Founded: 1998
No unsol mss.
ISBN Prefix(es): 978-1-58234; 978-1-61963; 978-1-62040; 978-1-63286; 978-1-68119; 978-1-59691; 978-1-59990; 978-1-60819
Number of titles published annually: 100 Print
Imprints: Bloomsbury; Bloomsbury Press (nonfiction); Bloomsbury USA (adult); Osprey Publishing
Distributed by Macmillan
Orders to: MPS Distribution Center, 16365 James Madison Hwy, Gordonsville, VA 22942-8501 *Toll Free Tel:* 888-330-8477 *Toll Free Fax:* 800-672-2054
Returns: MPS Returns Center, 14301 Litchfield Rd, Orange, VA 22960
Distribution Center: MPS Distribution Center, 16365 James Madison Hwy, Gordonsville, VA 22942-8501 *Toll Free Tel:* 888-330-8477 *Toll Free Fax:* 800-672-2054

§BLR®—Business & Legal Resources
Division of Simplify Compliance LLC
100 Winners Circle, Suite 300, Brentwood, TN 37027
Tel: 860-510-0100 *Toll Free Tel:* 800-727-5257
E-mail: service@blr.com
Web Site: www.blr.com
Key Personnel
Founder: Robert L Brady
Pres: Rafael Cardoso

VP, Content & Prod Devt: Patricia M Trainor
VP, Learning & Devt: David Gomes
VP, Mktg: Amy Wieman
VP, Sales: Beth Greene
Dir, Media Sales: Paul Manko
Dir, Proj Mgmt: Jane Murphy
Sr Mng Ed: Catherine Moreton Gray
    E-mail: cgray@blr.com
Mng Ed: Celeste Duke *E-mail:* cduke@blr.com
Founded: 1977
Business newsletters, books, booklets, films & CD-ROMs. Specialize in safety, human resource & environmental training & compliance.
ISBN Prefix(es): 978-1-55645
Number of titles published annually: 100 Print
Total Titles: 380 Print; 113 CD-ROM; 4 Online; 4 E-Book
Divisions: HCPro; HealthLeaders Media; M Lee Smith Publishers
Membership(s): NEPA
See separate listing for:
HCPro
M Lee Smith Publishers

Blue Apple Books
515 Valley St, Suite 170, Maplewood, NJ 07040
Tel: 973-763-8191
E-mail: info@blueapplebooks.com
Web Site: blueapplebooks.com
Key Personnel
Publr: Harriet M Ziefert
Dir, Opers: Kip Jacobson
Founded: 2003
Publisher of innovative children's books. No unsol mss accepted at this time.
ISBN Prefix(es): 978-1-59354; 978-1-934706; 978-1-60905
Number of titles published annually: 60 Print
Total Titles: 300 Print
Distribution Center: Consortium Book Sales & Distribution, The Keg House, 34 13 Ave NE, Suite 101, Minneapolis, MN 55413-1007
Tel: 612-746-2600 *Toll Free Tel:* 800-283-3572 (cust serv, Jackson, TN) *Fax:* 612-746-2606
E-mail: info@cbsd.com *Web Site:* www.cbsd.com SAN: 200-6049

Blue Book Publications Inc
8009 34 Ave S, Suite 250, Minneapolis, MN 55425
Tel: 952-854-5229 *Toll Free Tel:* 800-877-4867 *Fax:* 952-853-1486
E-mail: support@bluebookinc.com
Web Site: www.bluebookofgunvalues.com; www.bluebookofguitarvalues.com
Key Personnel
Publr & Author: S P Fjestad *Tel:* 952-853-1486 ext 13 *E-mail:* stevef@bluebookinc.com
Sales Mgr: Tom Toupin *Tel:* 952-253-2932 *E-mail:* tomt@bluebookinc.com
Founded: 1989
Industry leader in up-to-date & accurate values & information for firearms, airguns, modern black powder replicas, amplifiers & fretted instruments. Publisher of reference books, consumer pricing guides, encyclopedias & coffee table books. Online information provider/appraisals.
ISBN Prefix(es): 978-1-936120
Number of titles published annually: 20 Print; 8 Online; 2 E-Book
Total Titles: 36 Print; 8 Online; 2 E-Book
Membership(s): American Booksellers Association (ABA); Midwest Independent Booksellers Association (MIBA); Outdoor Writers Association of America (OWAA)

Blue Crane Books Inc
36 Hazel St, Watertown, MA 02472
Tel: 617-926-8989
Key Personnel
Pres: Alvart Badalian
Secy: Mr Aramais Andonian

Founded: 1991
Publish adult trade fiction & nonfiction, history, political & social sciences, culture & art. Special line of adult & children's books in Armenian & English translations of Armenian originals. No unsol mss.
ISBN Prefix(es): 978-0-9628715; 978-1-886434
Number of titles published annually: 3 Print
Total Titles: 20 Print

Blue Mountain Arts Inc
2905 Wilderness Place, Suite 100, Boulder, CO 80301
Mailing Address: PO Box 4549, Boulder, CO 80306-4549 SAN: 299-9609
Tel: 303-449-0536 *Toll Free Tel:* 800-525-0642 *Fax:* 303-417-6472 *Toll Free Fax:* 800-545-8573
E-mail: info@sps.com
Web Site: www.sps.com
Key Personnel
Pres: James Gurney
Founded: 1971
Publisher of trade books: inspirational, poetry, juvenile, young adult & gift books & sidelines.
ISBN Prefix(es): 978-0-88396; 978-1-58786; 978-1-59842
Number of titles published annually: 20 Print; 20 Online
Total Titles: 120 Print; 120 Online
Imprints: Artes Monte Azul; Blue Mountain Press®; Orphiflamme Press™; Rabbit's Foot Press™
Editorial Office(s): PO Box 1007, Boulder, CO 80301, Contact: P Wayant
Returns: 6455 Spine Rd, Boulder, CO 80301
Shipping Address: 6455 Spine Rd, Boulder, CO 80301, Contact: Wayne Ivers
Membership(s): American Booksellers Association (ABA); National Association of College Stores (NACS)

Blue Note Books, see Blue Note Publications Inc

Blue Note Publications Inc
721 North Dr, Suite D, Melbourne, FL 32934
Tel: 321-799-2583; 321-622-6289
    Toll Free Tel: 800-624-0401 (orders) *Fax:* 321-799-1942; 321-622-6830
E-mail: bluenotebooks@gmail.com
Web Site: bluenotepublications.com
Key Personnel
Pres: Paul Maluccio
Founded: 1988
Small press book publishing, production, printing, distribution, marketing.
ISBN Prefix(es): 978-1-878398; 978-0-9963066
Number of titles published annually: 25 Print; 20 Online; 15 E-Book
Total Titles: 180 Print; 2 CD-ROM; 80 Online; 40 E-Book
Imprints: Blue Note; Blue Note Books
Membership(s): Independent Book Publishers Association (IBPA)

§Blue Poppy Press
Division of Blue Poppy Enterprises Inc
3275-B Prairie Ave, Boulder, CO 80301
Tel: 303-447-8372 *Toll Free Tel:* 800-487-9296 *Fax:* 303-245-8362
E-mail: info@bluepoppy.com
Web Site: www.bluepoppy.com
Founded: 1982
Books on acupuncture & Chinese medicine.
ISBN Prefix(es): 978-0-936185; 978-1-891845
Number of titles published annually: 10 Print; 3 E-Book
Total Titles: 12 Print; 100 E-Book
Distributed by China Books; New Leaf Books; Partner's Book Distributing Inc; Partner's/West Book Distributing Inc; Redwing Book Co; Satas

Blue Whale Press

237 Rainbow Dr, No 13702, Livingston, TX
77399-2037
SAN: 855-7004
Toll Free Tel: 800-848-1631
E-mail: info@bluewhalepress.com; sales@
bluewhalepress.com
Web Site: www.bluewhalepress.com
Key Personnel
Content & Developmental Ed: Alayne Kay Chris-
tian *E-mail:* submissions@bluewhalepress.com
Publr: Steve Kemp *E-mail:* steve@
bluewhalepress.com
Founded: 2008
ISBN Prefix(es): 978-0-9814938; 978-1-7328935
Number of titles published annually: 4 Print
Total Titles: 3 Print
Distribution Center: Follett School Solu-
tions Inc, 1340 Ridgeview Dr, McHenry,
IL 60050 *Tel:* 815-759-1700 *Toll Free
Tel:* 888-511-5114 (cust serv) *Fax:* 815-
759-9831 *Toll Free Fax:* 800-852-5458
E-mail: info@follettlearning.com *Web
Site:* www.follettlearning.com SAN: 169-1902
Ingram Content Group LLC, One Ingram Blvd,
La Vergne, TN 37086-1986 *Tel:* 615-793-5000
Web Site: www.ingramcontent.com

BlueBridge

Imprint of United Tribes Media Inc
PO Box 601, Katonah, NY 10536
Tel: 914-301-5901
Web Site: www.bluebridgebooks.com
Key Personnel
Founder & Publr: Jan-Erik Guerth
E-mail: janguerth@aol.com
Founded: 2004
Independent publisher of international nonfiction
based near New York City. Subjects include
culture, history, biography, nature & science,
inspiration & self-help.
ISBN Prefix(es): 978-1-933346; 978-0-9742405;
978-1-62919
Number of titles published annually: 4 Print
Total Titles: 40 Print
Distribution Center: Publishers Group West, 1700
Fourth St, Berkeley, CA 94710 *Tel:* 510-809-
3700 *Toll Free Tel:* 866-400-5351 (cust serv)
Fax: 510-809-3777 *Web Site:* www.pgw.com

Bluestocking Press

3045 Sacramento St, No 1014, Placerville, CA
95667-1014
SAN: 667-2981
Mailing Address: PO Box 1014, Placerville, CA
95667-1014
Tel: 530-622-8586 *Toll Free Tel:* 800-959-8586
Fax: 530-642-9222
E-mail: customerservice@bluestockingpress.com;
orders@bluestockingpress.com
Web Site: www.bluestockingpress.com
Key Personnel
Owner & Pres: Jane A Williams *E-mail:* jane@
bluestockingpress.com
Founded: 1987
Among subjects offered: free market economics,
business, finance, justice, ancient Rome, World
Wars, Mideast War. Sell on nonreturnable ba-
sis (except for books received damaged) to the
reseller market.
ISBN Prefix(es): 978-0-942617
Number of titles published annually: 21 Print
Total Titles: 23 Print
Sales Office(s): PO Box 1014, Placerville,
CA 95667-1014, Contact: Ann Marie
E-mail: annmarie@bluestockingpress.com
Billing Address: PO Box 1014, Placerville, CA
95667-1014, Accts Payable: Jane Williams
E-mail: jane@bluestockingpress.com
Orders to: PO Box 1014, Placerville, CA 95667-
1014, Contact: Ann Marie *E-mail:* annmarie@
bluestockingpress.com

BNi Building News

990 Park Center Dr, Suite E, Vista, CA 92081-
8352
Tel: 760-734-1113 *Toll Free Tel:* 888-BNI-BOOK
(264-2665)
Web Site: www.bnibooks.com
Key Personnel
Gen Mgr: John Moore *Tel:* 760-734-1134
E-mail: johnmoore@bnibooks.com
Founded: 1946
Construction & engineering.
ISBN Prefix(es): 978-1-55701; 978-1-878088
Number of titles published annually: 100 Print
Total Titles: 120 Print

BOA Editions Ltd

250 N Goodman St, Suite 306, Rochester, NY
14607
Tel: 585-546-3410 *Fax:* 585-546-3913
E-mail: contact@boaeditions.org
Web Site: www.boaeditions.org
Key Personnel
Publr: Peter Conners *E-mail:* conners@
boaeditions.org
Devt Dir & Off Mgr: Kelly Hatton
E-mail: hatton@boaeditions.org
Dir, Mktg & Prodn: Ron Martin-Dent
E-mail: martindent@boaeditions.org
Founded: 1976
Publication of books of poetry, poetry in transla-
tion & fiction.
ISBN Prefix(es): 978-0-918526; 978-1-880238;
978-1-929918; 978-1-934414
Number of titles published annually: 12 Print; 12
E-Book
Total Titles: 215 Print; 100 E-Book
Orders to: Consortium Book Sales & Distri-
bution, The Keg House, Suite 101, 34 13
Ave NE, Minneapolis, MN 55413-1007
Tel: 612-746-2600 *Toll Free Tel:* 800-283-3572
(cust serv, Jackson, TN) *Fax:* 612-746-2606
E-mail: info@cbsd.com *Web Site:* www.cbsd.
com SAN: 200-6049
Shipping Address: Consortium Book Sales &
Distribution, The Keg House, Suite 101, 34
13 Ave NE, Minneapolis, MN 55413-1007
Tel: 612-746-2600 *Toll Free Tel:* 800-283-3572
(cust serv, Jackson, TN) *Fax:* 612-746-2606
E-mail: info@cbsd.com *Web Site:* www.cbsd.
com SAN: 200-6049
Warehouse: Consortium Book Sales & Distribu-
tion, The Keg House, Suite 101, 34 13 Ave
NE, Minneapolis, MN 55413-1007 *Tel:* 612-
746-2600 *Toll Free Tel:* 800-283-3572 (cust
serv, Jackson, TN) *Fax:* 612-746-2606 *Web
Site:* www.cbsd.com SAN: 200-6049
Distribution Center: Consortium Book Sales &
Distribution, The Keg House, Suite 101, 34
13 Ave NE, Minneapolis, MN 55413-1007
Tel: 612-746-2600 *Toll Free Tel:* 800-283-3572
(cust serv, Jackson, TN) *Fax:* 612-746-2606
E-mail: info@cbsd.com *Web Site:* www.cbsd.
com SAN: 200-6049

§BoardSource

750 Ninth St NW, Suite 650, Washington, DC
20001-4793
Tel: 202-349-2580 *Toll Free Tel:* 877-892-6273
E-mail: members@boardsource.org
Web Site: www.boardsource.org
Key Personnel
Pres & CEO: Anne Wallestad
VP, Mktg & Communs: Erin Berry
Dir, Communs: Ann Atwood Mead
E-mail: mediarelations@boardsource.org
Founded: 1988
Premier resource for practical information, tools
& best practices, training & leadership devel-
opment for board members of nonprofit orga-
nizations. Enables organizations to fulfill their
missions by helping build effective nonprofit
boards, offering credible support in solving
tough problems.

ISBN Prefix(es): 978-0-925299; 978-1-58686
Number of titles published annually: 6 Print; 3
CD-ROM; 2 E-Book
Total Titles: 100 Print; 6 E-Book

§Bolchazy-Carducci Publishers Inc

1570 Baskin Rd, Mundelein, IL 60060
SAN: 219-7685
Tel: 847-526-4344 *Fax:* 847-526-2867
E-mail: info@bolchazy.com; orders@bolchazy.
com
Web Site: www.bolchazy.com
Key Personnel
Pres: Bridget Dean, PhD *E-mail:* bridget@
bolchazy.com
Founded: 1978
Scholarly books, textbooks, self-teaching Latin
series, Latin music CDs & Slovak publications.
ISBN Prefix(es): 978-0-86516; 978-1-61041
Number of titles published annually: 10 Print; 5
Online; 10 E-Book; 1 Audio
Total Titles: 450 Print; 5 Online; 250 E-Book; 20
Audio
Returns: 1576 Baskin Rd, Mundelein, IL
60060 *Tel:* 847-526-4344 *Fax:* 847-526-2867
E-mail: returns@bolchazy.com
Warehouse: 1576 Baskin Rd, Mundelein, IL
60060 *Tel:* 847-526-4344 *Fax:* 847-526-2867
Distribution Center: 1576 Baskin Rd, Mundelein,
IL 60060 *Tel:* 847-526-4344 *Fax:* 847-526-
2867

§Bold Strokes Books Inc

648 S Cambridge Rd, Bldg A, Johnsonville, NY
12094
Tel: 518-677-5127
E-mail: service@boldstrokesbooks.com
Web Site: www.boldstrokesbooks.com
Key Personnel
Pres: Len Barot *E-mail:* publisher@
boldstrokesbooks.com
Sr Ed: Sandy Lowe
Founded: 2004
Independent publishing company publishing
works of gay, lesbian & feminist themed fic-
tion in all genres, including general, genre &
young adult fiction. Readership is international
& all titles are released in print & multi-format
ebook version. Employs conventional distri-
bution channels to bring products to the cus-
tomers.
ISBN Prefix(es): 978-1-9331100; 978-1-60282;
978-1-62639
Number of titles published annually: 110 Print;
110 Online; 110 E-Book; 25 Audio
Total Titles: 850 Print; 950 Online; 950 E-Book;
75 Audio
Orders to: Bella Distribution, 1041 Aenon
Church Rd, Tallahassee, FL 32304
Returns: Bella Distribution, 1041 Aenon Church
Rd, Tallahassee, FL 32304
Shipping Address: Bella Distribution, 1041 Aenon
Church Rd, Tallahassee, FL 32304
Warehouse: Bella Distribution, 1041 Aenon
Church Rd, Tallahassee, FL 32304
Distribution Center: Bella Distribution, 1041
Aenon Church Rd, Tallahassee, FL 32304,
Contact: Becky Arbogast *Toll Free Tel:* 800-
533-1973 *Fax:* 850-576-3498 *E-mail:* info@
belladistribution.com
Membership(s): Independent Book Publishers As-
sociation (IBPA); Romance Writers of America
(RWA)

Book Marketing Works LLC

50 Lovely St (Rte 177), Avon, CT 06001
Mailing Address: PO Box 715, Avon, CT 06001-
0715
Tel: 860-675-1344
Web Site: www.bookmarketingworks.com
Key Personnel
Pres: Brian Jud *E-mail:* brianjud@
bookmarketingworks.com

Founded: 1990
ISBN Prefix(es): 978-1-928782
Number of titles published annually: 10 Print
Total Titles: 26 Print
Imprints: Strong Books
Subsidiaries: Book Marketing Works

Book Peddlers
18925 Lake Ave, Deephaven, MN 55391
Tel: 952-544-1154
Web Site: www.bookpeddlers.com
Key Personnel
Owner & Publr: Diane Schwarze *E-mail:* diane@
bookpeddlers.com
Founded: 1985
Nonfiction hardcover & CDs; gift-giving occasion
books.
ISBN Prefix(es): 978-0-916773; 978-1-931863
Number of titles published annually: 1 Print; 2 E-
Book
Total Titles: 20 Print; 3 CD-ROM; 15 E-Book
Orders to: Publishers Group West (PGW), 1094
Flex Dr, Jackson, TN 38301 *Toll Free Tel:* 800-
788-3123 *Toll Free Fax:* 800-351-5073
Distribution Center: Publishers Group West
(PGW), 1700 Fourth St, Berkeley, CA 94710

Book Publishing Co, see BPC

Book Sales
Imprint of Quarto Publishing Group USA Inc
142 W 36 St, 4th fl, New York, NY 10018
SAN: 299-4062
Tel: 212-779-4972; 212-779-4971 *Fax:* 212-779-
6058
Web Site: www.quartoknows.com
Key Personnel
Sales Dir: Steven Wilson *Tel:* 212-779-4973
E-mail: steve.wilson@quarto.com
Founded: 1952
Publisher & supplier of books to wholesalers,
mail order companies & retail stores.
ISBN Prefix(es): 978-0-89009; 978-1-55521; 978-
0-7858
Number of titles published annually: 300 Print
Total Titles: 2,500 Print
Imprints: Blue & Gray; Castle Books; Chartwell
Books; Crestline; Poplar Books
Orders to: Hachette Book Group, 53 State St,
Boston, MA 02109 *Toll Free Tel:* 800-759-
0190
Returns: Hachette Book Group, 322 S Enterprise
Blvd, Lebanon, IN 46052 (accepted only with
pre-approval prior to return)
Warehouse: Hachette Book Group, 121 N Enter-
prise Blvd, Lebanon, IN 46052
Membership(s): American Booksellers Associa-
tion (ABA)

The Book Tree
3316 Adams Ave, Suite A, San Diego, CA 92116
Mailing Address: PO Box 16476, San Diego, CA
92176
Tel: 619-280-1263 *Toll Free Tel:* 800-700-8733
(orders) *Fax:* 619-280-1285
E-mail: orders@thebooktree.com; info@
thebooktree.com
Web Site: thebooktree.com
Key Personnel
Owner: Paul Willey
Founded: 1992
Metaphysical, spiritual & controversial books; do
not accept, respond to or return unsol mss.
ISBN Prefix(es): 978-1-885395; 978-1-58509
Number of titles published annually: 10 Print
Total Titles: 300 Print
Membership(s): Independent Book Publishers As-
sociation (IBPA)

Bookhaven Press LLC
302 Scenic Ct, Moon Township, PA 15108

SAN: 668-7075
Tel: 412-494-6926
E-mail: info@bookhavenpress.com; orders@
bookhavenpress.com
Web Site: bookhavenpress.com
Key Personnel
Pres & Publr: Dennis V Damp *E-mail:* ddamp@
aol.com
Assoc Publr: Victor Richards *E-mail:* vrichards@
bookhavenpress.com
Founded: 1985
Independent publishing house dedicated to pro-
ducing award-winning business, career & fi-
nance books & companion web sites. *The Book
of U.S. Government Jobs* was awarded "Best
Career Title" by the Benjamin Franklin Awards
Committee. Our 4th edition of *Health Care Job
Explosion* was nominated for Best Books 2006
(Business-Career) title by USA Book News.
Bookhaven's titles have been reviewed & rec-
ommended by Library Journal, Booklist, the
New York Times & Washington Post, Career
Opportunities News & over 100 magazines,
newspapers & journals. We also publish envi-
ronmental compliance books & comprehensive
web sites for our titles.
ISBN Prefix(es): 978-0-943641
Number of titles published annually: 1 Print; 2 E-
Book
Total Titles: 5 Print; 3 E-Book
Membership(s): Independent Book Publishers As-
sociation (IBPA)

§BookLogix
1264 Old Alpharetta Rd, Alpharetta, GA 30005
SAN: 860-0376
Tel: 470-239-8547 *Toll Free Fax:* 888-564-7890
E-mail: publishing@booklogix.com
Web Site: www.booklogix.com
Key Personnel
CEO: Angela DeCaires
Founded: 2009
This publisher has indicated that 80% of their
product line is author subsidized.
ISBN Prefix(es): 978-1-61005
Number of titles published annually: 60 Print;
100 E-Book
Total Titles: 800 Print; 300 E-Book
Distribution Center: Baker & Taylor, 2550 W
Tyvola Rd, Suite 300, Charlotte, NC 28217
Tel: 704-998-3100 *Toll Free Tel:* 800-775-1800
Web Site: www.baker-taylor.com

Books In Motion
Division of Classic Ventures Ltd
9922 E Montgomery, Suite 31, Spokane Valley,
WA 99206
Tel: 509-922-1646 *Toll Free Tel:* 800-752-3199
Fax: 509-922-1445
E-mail: info@booksinmotion.com
Web Site: www.booksinmotion.com
Key Personnel
Pres: Gary Challender
Founded: 1980
Produce fiction books on CD & MP3. Does not
accept unsol mss. Criteria is exceptionally high
for acceptance. There is no cost to the authors.
Currently seeking subsidiary audio rights on
previously print published titles.
ISBN Prefix(es): 978-1-55686; 978-1-58116; 978-
1-59607; 978-1-60548
Number of titles published annually: 24 Print; 60
Audio
Total Titles: 2,000 Audio

Books on Tape™
Imprint of Penguin Random House Audio Pub-
lishing
1745 Broadway, New York, NY 10019
Toll Free Tel: 800-733-3000 (cust serv)
Toll Free Fax: 800-940-7046
Web Site: www.booksontape.com

Key Personnel
Pres & Publr, Penguin Random House Audio
Group: Amanda D'Acierno
VP, Lib & Academic Sales: Skip Dye
Mktg Dir: Cheryl Herman
Ed, Listening Library®: Emily Parliman
Asst Acqs Ed, Listening Library®: Megan Mills
Coord, Digital Opers, Listening Library®: Renee
Watson
Founded: 1975
For over 40 years Books on Tape® has offered
the best in unabridged audiobooks. Our best
selling & award-winning titles are produced
in NY & LA studios & read by the finest nar-
rators in the industry. Select from over 3,000
titles available, durable library packaging & delivered with a complement of services tailored
to meet special needs of librarians & educators.
Flexible standing order plans, featuring the
freedom to choose your titles & free lifetime
replacement guarantees. Books on Tape® is
proud to exclusively have Listening Library®,
the premier audio book publisher of children's
& young adult literature, as its children's imprint.
Number of titles published annually: 300 Audio
Total Titles: 3,000 Audio
Imprints: Listening Library®
Distributor for Listening Library®
Orders to: Penguin Random House Publisher Ser-
vices (PRHPS), Library & School Services,
400 Hahn Rd, Westminster, MD 21157
Returns: Penguin Random House Inc, 1019 N
State Rd 47, Crawfordville, NJ 47933
Membership(s): AASL; ALSC; American Li-
brary Association (ALA); California Library
Association; National Council of Teachers of
English (NCTE); Public Library Association
(PLA); Young Adult Library Services Associa-
tion (YALSA)

Boom! Studios
5670 Wilshire Blvd, Suite 400, Los Angeles, CA
90036
Web Site: www.boom-studios.com
Key Personnel
Founder & CEO: Ross Richie
Pres, Publg & Mktg: Filip Sablik
VP, Licensing & Mdsg: Lance Kreiter
Ed-in-Chief: Matt Gagnon
Founded: 2005
ISBN Prefix(es): 978-1-934506; 978-1-60886;
978-1-61398; 978-1-932386; 978-1-936393;
978-1-68159; 978-1-939867
Number of titles published annually: 80 Print
Distributed by Simon & Schuster Sales Division

§Boson Books™
Imprint of Bitingduck Press LLC
1262 Sunnyoaks Circle, Altadena, CA 91001
Tel: 626-507-8033 *Fax:* 626-818-1842
Web Site: bitingduckpress.com
Key Personnel
Ed-in-Chief: Jay Nadeau *E-mail:* jay@
bitingduckpress.com
Publr & Ed: Chris Lindensmith *E-mail:* chris@
bitingduckpress.com
Founded: 1994
Publish ebooks & selected print books. First com-
mercial general ebook publisher.
ISBN Prefix(es): 978-1-886420; 978-0-917990;
978-1-932482
Number of titles published annually: 8 Print; 13
E-Book
Total Titles: 100 Print; 350 E-Book
Distribution Center: Independent Publishers
Group (IPG), 814 N Franklin St, Chicago, IL
60610 *Tel:* 312-337-0747 *Toll Free Tel:* 800-
888-4741 *Fax:* 312-337-5985 *E-mail:* orders@
ipgbook.com *Web Site:* www.ipgbook.com
Membership(s): The Authors Guild

Bottom Dog Press
813 Seneca Ave, Huron, OH 44839
SAN: 689-5492
Mailing Address: PO Box 425, Huron, OH
  44839-0425
Tel: 419-602-1556 *Fax:* 419-616-3966
Web Site: smithdocs.net
Key Personnel
Dir & Publr: Larry Smith *E-mail:* lsmithdog@
  smithdocs.net
Assoc Ed: Susanna Sharp Schwacke; Laura Smith
Founded: 1985
ISBN Prefix(es): 978-0-933087; 978-1-933960;
  978-1-947504
Number of titles published annually: 6 Print; 6 E-
  Book; 2 Audio
Total Titles: 210 Print; 2 CD-ROM; 18 E-Book; 4
  Audio
Imprints: Bird Dog Publishing
Distribution Center: Baker & Taylor, 501 Gladio-
  lus St, Momence, IL 60954
Ingram Publisher Services, One Ingram
  Blvd, La Vergne, TN 37086 *Tel:* 615-793-
  5000 *Toll Free Tel:* 866-400-5351 (or-
  ders) *E-mail:* ips@ingramcontent.com *Web
  Site:* www.ingramcontent.com
Membership(s): Appalachian Studies Association;
  Community of Literary Magazines & Presses
  (CLMP); PEN American Center; Working-
  Class Studies Association

R R Bowker LLC
Subsidiary of ProQuest LLC
789 E Eisenhower Pkwy, Ann Arbor, MI 48106
SAN: 214-1191
Tel: 908-286-1090 *Toll Free Tel:* 888-269-5372
  (edit & cust serv, press 2 for returns) *Fax:* 908-
  219-0098; (020) 7832 1710 (UK for intl)
  Toll Free Fax: 877-337-7015 (US & CN)
E-mail: orders@proquest.com (domestic orders);
  isbn-san@bowker.com
Web Site: www.bowker.com
Founded: 1872
Leading provider of bibliographic information &
  management solutions designed to help publishers, booksellers & libraries better serve
  their customers. Creators of products & services that make books easier for people to discover, evaluate, order & experience. The company also generates research & resources for
  publishers, helping them understand & meet
  the interests of readers worldwide. Bowker, an
  affiliated business of ProQuest & the official
  ISBN Agency for Australia, US & US territories, is headquartered in New Providence, NJ
  with additional operations in England & Australia.
ISBN Prefix(es): 978-0-8352
Number of titles published annually: 13 Print; 8
  Online
Total Titles: 29 Print; 8 Online
Editorial Office(s): 630 Central Ave, New Providence, NJ 07974
Foreign Office(s): Thorpe-Bowker, Level
  One, 607 St Kilda Rd, Melbourne, Victo-
  ria 3004, Australia, Mng Dir: Gary Pen-
  gelly *Tel:* (03) 8517 8345 *Fax:* (03) 8517-
  8399 *E-mail:* yoursay@thorpe.com.au *Web
  Site:* www.thorpe.com.au
Bowker, an affiliate of ProQuest, 3 Dorset Rise,
  5th floor, London EC4Y 8EN, United King-
  dom, Mng Dir: Doug McMillan *Tel:* (020)
  7832 1700 *E-mail:* sales@bowker.co.uk
Membership(s): American Library Association
  (ALA); Association of American Publishers
  (AAP); Book Industry Study Group (BISG);
  Evangelical Christian Publishers Associa-
  tion (ECPA); National Association of College
  Stores (NACS)

Boydell & Brewer Inc
Affiliate of Boydell & Brewer Ltd (UK)
668 Mount Hope Ave, Rochester, NY 14620-2731

Tel: 585-275-0419 *Fax:* 585-271-8778
E-mail: boydell@boydellusa.net
Web Site: www.boydellandbrewer.com
Key Personnel
Mng Dir: Sue Smith *Tel:* 585-273-2817
  E-mail: smith@boydellusa.net
Edit Dir: Sonia Kane *Tel:* 585-273-5778
Sales & Mktg Mgr: Sue Miller *Tel:* 585-273-5787
Accts Asst: Olga Reshota *Tel:* 585-273-5777
Founded: 1989
Publisher of scholarly books.
ISBN Prefix(es): 978-0-85115; 978-0-85991; 978-
  0-86193; 978-0-7293; 978-0-900411; 978-1-
  85566; 978-1-878822; 978-1-58046; 978-1-
  57113; 978-1-900639; 978-1-64014
Number of titles published annually: 200 Print
Total Titles: 3,100 Print
Imprints: Boydell Press; DS Brewer; Camden
  House; Companion Guides; James Curry Ltd;
  Early English Text Society; Plumbago Books;
  Royal Historical Society; Scholarly Digital Edi-
  tions; Scottish Text Society; Suffolk Records
  Society; Tamesis Books; Toccata Press; Univer-
  sity of Rochester Press; Victory History of the
  Counties of England; York Medieval Press
Foreign Office(s): Boydell & Brewer Ltd, Bridge
  Farm Business Park, Top St, Martlesham, Suf-
  folk 1P12 4RB, United Kingdom, Mng Ed: Pe-
  ter Clifford *Tel:* (01394) 610600 *Fax:* (01394)
  610316 *E-mail:* editorial@boydell.co.uk
Distributed by Casemate | publishers (North &
  South America)
Distributor for Pendragon Press
Orders to: Boydell & Brewer Ltd, Bridge
  Farm Business Park, Top St, Martle-
  sham, Suffolk 1P12 4RB, United Kingdom
  Tel: (01394) 610600 *Fax:* (01394) 610316
  E-mail: editorial@boydell.co.uk
Returns: c/o Books International Inc, 22883
  Quicksilver Dr, Dulles, VA 20166
Warehouse: c/o Books International Inc, 22883
  Quicksilver Dr, Dulles, VA 20166
College Farm, Forward Green, Stawmarket, Suf-
  folk IP14 5EH, United Kingdom

Boyds Mills & Kane
250 Park Ave, 7th fl, New York, NY 10177
E-mail: info@bmkbooks.com
Web Site: www.boydsmillsandkane.com
Key Personnel
Pres & CFO: Leying Jiang
COO: Ben Schrank
Publr: Juliana Lauletta
Founded: 1990
Books for children of all ages.
ISBN Prefix(es): 978-1-56397; 978-1-57565; 978-
  1-59078; 978-1-63592; 978-1-87809
Number of titles published annually: 40 Print
Total Titles: 800 Print
Imprints: Boyds Mills Press; Calkins Creek (his-
  tory); Kane Press (STEM/education fiction &
  nonfiction); minedition; StarBerry Books (pic-
  ture books); WordSong (poetry)
Returns: Penguin Random House, Attn Returns
  Dept, 1019 N State Rd 47, Crawfordsville, IN
  47933; Penguin Random House Canada, Attn
  Returns Dept, 6971 Columbus Rd, Mississauga,
  ON L5T 1K1, Canada
Distribution Center: Penguin Random House,
  400 Hahn Rd, Westminster, MD 21157 *Toll
  Free Tel:* 800-733-3000 *E-mail:* csorders@
  penguinrandomhouse.com
Penguin Random House Canada, 320 Front
  St W, Suite 1400, Toronto, ON M5V 3B6,
  Canada *Toll Free Tel:* 888-523-9292 *Toll Free
  Fax:* 888-562-9924

Boys Town Press
Division of Father Flanagan's Boys' Home
13603 Flanagan Blvd, 2nd fl, Boys Town, NE
  68010
Tel: 531-355-1320 *Toll Free Tel:* 800-282-6657
  Fax: 531-355-1310

E-mail: btpress@boystown.org
Web Site: www.boystownpress.org
Key Personnel
Dir: Erin Green *E-mail:* erin.green@boystown.org
Sales & Mktg Mgr: Patricia Martens *Tel:* 531-
  355-1334 *E-mail:* patricia.martens@boystown.
  org
Founded: 1992
Publisher of books for counselors, children, edu-
  cators, youth care professionals & parents. Also
  inspirational titles.
ISBN Prefix(es): 978-0-938510; 978-1-889322;
  978-1-934490; 978-1-944882
Number of titles published annually: 14 Print; 10
  E-Book
Total Titles: 110 Print; 2 CD-ROM; 50 E-Book; 7
  Audio
Distributed by CSH Educational Resources
  Pte Ltd (Singapore); Deep Books Ltd (Eu-
  rope & UK); Silvereye Learning Resources
  (NSW, Australia); University of Toronto Press
  (Canada)
Foreign Rights: DropCap (worldwide exc North
  America)
Returns: 250 Monsky Dr, Boys Town, NE 68010
Warehouse: 250 Monsky Dr, Boys Town, NE
  68010
Distribution Center: Follett School Solu-
  tions Inc, 1340 Ridgeview Dr, McHenry,
  IL 60050 *Tel:* 815-759-1700 *Toll Free
  Tel:* 888-511-5114 (cust serv) *Fax:* 815-
  759-9831 *Toll Free Fax:* 800-852-5458
  E-mail: info@follettlearning.com *Web
  Site:* www.follettlearning.com SAN: 169-1902
Baker & Taylor, 2550 W Tyvola Rd, Suite 300,
  Charlotte, NC 28217 *Tel:* 815-802-2479 *Toll
  Free Fax:* 800-411-8433 *Web Site:* www.baker-
  taylor.com
Ingram Book Co, One Ingram Blvd, La Vergne,
  TN 37086-3650
Membership(s): Independent Book Publishers As-
  sociation (IBPA)

BPC
Formerly Book Publishing Co
415 Farm Rd, Summertown, TN 38483
Mailing Address: PO Box 99, Summertown, TN
  38483-0099
Tel: 931-964-3571 *Toll Free Tel:* 888-260-8458
  Fax: 931-964-3518
E-mail: info@bookpubco.com
Web Site: www.bookpubco.com
Key Personnel
Pres: Robert Holzapfel
Ed: Cynthia Holzapfel
Mktg: Anna Pope *E-mail:* annap@bookpubco.
  com
Founded: 1974
Community-owned independent press commit-
  ted to promoting books that educate, inspire &
  empower. Topics include plant-based cooking
  & nutrition, sustainable living, natural health
  care, gardening, sci-fi & fantasy novels, Na-
  tive American culture & hi-lo novels for young
  adults.
ISBN Prefix(es): 978-0-913990; 978-1-57067;
  978-1-55312
Number of titles published annually: 8 Print
Total Titles: 450 Print; 2 Audio
Imprints: Books Alive; Botanica Press;
  GroundSwell; Healthy Living; Native Voices;
  Norwalk Press; 7th Generation
Distributor for Cherokee Publications; Crazy
  Crow; CRCS Publications; Critical Path; Gen-
  tle World; Hippocrates Publications; Magni
  Co; Moon River Publishing; Second Nature;
  Sproutman Publications; Uproar Books
Foreign Rep(s): Brumby Books (Australia);
  Faradawn (South Africa); Publishers Group
  UK (England)

Brandylane Publishers Inc
5 S First St, Richmond, VA 23219

Tel: 804-644-3090 *Fax:* 804-644-3092
Web Site: brandylanepublishers.com
Key Personnel
Publr: Robert H Pruett *E-mail:* rhpruett@
brandylanepublishers.com
Sr Ed: Mary A Tobey
Founded: 1985
Publisher & packager of books. Work with previously unpublished writers.
ISBN Prefix(es): 978-1-883911
Number of titles published annually: 15 Print; 15 Online; 15 E-Book
Total Titles: 60 Print; 40 Online; 7 E-Book
Imprints: Belle Isle Books
Billing Address: PO Box 274, Kilmarnock, VA 22482 *Tel:* 804-435-6900
Membership(s): Independent Book Publishers Association (IBPA)

George Braziller Inc
277 Broadway, Suite 708, New York, NY 10007
SAN: 201-9310
Tel: 212-260-9256 *Fax:* 212-267-3165
E-mail: submissions@georgebraziller.com
Web Site: www.georgebraziller.com
Key Personnel
Pres & Ed: Michael Braziller
E-mail: mbraziller@georgebraziller.com
Founded: 1955
Publishers of fine illustrated art books.
ISBN Prefix(es): 978-0-8076
Number of titles published annually: 12 Print
Total Titles: 300 Print
Distributed by ACC Art Books; W W Norton & Company Inc
Foreign Rep(s): ACC Art Books (Australia, England, Europe, India, New Zealand)
Orders to: W W Norton & Company Inc, 500 Fifth Ave, New York, NY 10110-0017 *Toll Free Tel:* 800-233-4830 *Toll Free Fax:* 800-458-6515

Breakaway Books
PO Box 24, Halcottsville, NY 12438-0024
Tel: 607-326-4805
E-mail: breakawaybooks@gmail.com
Web Site: www.breakawaybooks.com
Key Personnel
Publr: Garth Battista
Founded: 1994
Sports literature & books.
ISBN Prefix(es): 978-1-891369; 978-1-55821; 978-1-62124
Number of titles published annually: 10 Print
Total Titles: 100 Print; 1 E-Book
Distribution Center: Consortium Book Sales & Distribution, 34 13 Ave NE, Suite 101, Minneapolis, MN 55413-1007 *Tel:* 612-746-2600 *Toll Free Tel:* 800-283-3572 (cust serv, Jackson, TN) *Fax:* 612-746-2606 *E-mail:* info@cbsd.com *Web Site:* www.cbsd.com SAN: 200-6049

Breakthrough Publications Inc
3 Iroquois St, Barn, Emmaus, PA 18049
Toll Free Tel: 800-824-5001 (ext 12) *Fax:* 610-928-4064
E-mail: dot@booksonhorses.com; ruth@booksonhorses.com
Web Site: www.booksonhorses.com
Key Personnel
Pres & Publr: Peter E Ognibene *E-mail:* peter@workkplace.com
Founded: 1980
Career & equestrian.
ISBN Prefix(es): 978-0-914327
Number of titles published annually: 30 Print
Total Titles: 50 Print
Imprints: Breakthrough Publications

Nicholas Brealey Publishing
Imprint of John Murray (Publishers) Ltd (UK)

53 State St, 9th fl, Boston, MA 02109
Tel: 617-523-3801
E-mail: info@nicholasbrealey.com; sales-us@nicholasbrealey.com
Web Site: www.nicholasbrealey.com
Key Personnel
Dir, Prodn: Michelle Morgan
Sales Mgr: Melissa Carl
Founded: 1992
Professional/trade business book (hardcover & original paperback) publisher. Additional subjects include: international business & culture, training & human resources.
ISBN Prefix(es): 978-0-89106 (Davies-Black); 978-1-85788; 978-1-90483; 978-1-93193 (Intercultural Press); 978-1-87786 (Intercultural Press); 978-0-93366 (Intercultural Press)
Number of titles published annually: 50 Print
Total Titles: 330 Print
Imprints: Davies-Black; Intercultural Press
Divisions: Intercultural Press Inc
Distributed by Hachette Book Group
Membership(s): Association of American Publishers (AAP)
See separate listing for:
Intercultural Press Inc

Brentwood Christian Press
PO Box 4773, Columbus, GA 31914-4773
Toll Free Tel: 800-334-8861
E-mail: brentwood@aol.com
Web Site: www.brentwoodbooks.com
Key Personnel
Owner: U D Roberts
Founded: 1982
Custom self-publishing of Christian books.
This publisher has indicated that 100% of their product line is author subsidized.
ISBN Prefix(es): 978-1-55630
Number of titles published annually: 220 Print
Total Titles: 9,000 Print

Brethren Press
Division of Church of the Brethren
1451 Dundee Ave, Elgin, IL 60120
SAN: 201-9329
Tel: 847-742-5100 *Toll Free Tel:* 800-323-8039 *Toll Free Fax:* 800-667-8188
E-mail: brethrenpress@brethren.org
Web Site: www.brethrenpress.com
Key Personnel
Publr: Wendy McFadden *Tel:* 847-742-5100 ext 307 *E-mail:* wmcfadden@brethren.org
Dir, Mktg & Sales: Jeff Lennard *Tel:* 847-742-5100 ext 321 *E-mail:* jlennard@brethren.org
Founded: 1897
Trade books, church school curriculum, tracts & pamphlets & various media resources. Specialize in Bible study, theology, church history, practical discipleship, personal lifestyle issues, social concerns, peace & justice, devotional life & personal growth.
ISBN Prefix(es): 978-0-87178
Number of titles published annually: 6 Print
Total Titles: 100 Print
Imprints: faithQuest
Membership(s): Protestant Church-Owned Publishers Association (PCPA)

Brewers Publications
Division of Brewers Association
1327 Spruce St, Boulder, CO 80302
Mailing Address: PO Box 1679, Boulder, CO 80306
Tel: 303-447-0816 *Toll Free Tel:* 888-822-6273 (CN & US) *Fax:* 303-447-2825
E-mail: info@brewersassociation.org
Web Site: www.brewersassociation.org
Key Personnel
Publr: Kristi Switzer *Tel:* 720-473-7660
E-mail: kristi@brewersassociation.org
Founded: 1986

Not-for-profit educational publishing house & the foremost publisher of books on the art, science, history & culture of brewing for professional & amateur brewers & serious beer enthusiasts. Must know at least 10 brewers to query.
ISBN Prefix(es): 978-0-937381
Number of titles published annually: 3 Print; 2 E-Book
Total Titles: 50 Print
Foreign Rep(s): Sylvia Hayse Literary Agency (Sylvia Hayse) (worldwide exc North America)
Foreign Rights: Sylvia Hayse Literary Agency (Sylvia Hayse) (worldwide exc North America)
Shipping Address: National Book Network, 15200 NBN Way, Blue Ridge Summit, PA 17214 *Toll Free Tel:* 800-462-6420 *Toll Free Fax:* 800-338-4550 *E-mail:* custserv@nbnbooks.com
Warehouse: National Book Network, 15200 NBN Way, Blue Ridge Summit, PA 17214 *Tel:* 717-794-3800 *Toll Free Tel:* 800-462-6420 *Toll Free Fax:* 800-338-4550 *E-mail:* custserv@nbnbooks.com

§Brick Mantel Books
Imprint of Pen & Publish LLC
4719 Holly Hills Ave, St Louis, MO 63116
Tel: 314-827-6567
E-mail: info@brickmantelbooks.com
Web Site: brickmantelbooks.com
Key Personnel
Owner & Publr: Jennifer Geist *E-mail:* jennifer@brickmantelbooks.com
Founded: 2015
Publishes innovative works of literary excellence by new & established writers. We value literature as an art & publish literary fiction & thought-provoking poetry that leave a lasting impression. We want to help readers gain a stronger sense of the world & humanity through literature.
ISBN Prefix(es): 978-1-941799
Number of titles published annually: 2 Print; 2 E-Book
Total Titles: 8 Print; 8 E-Book
Membership(s): Independent Book Publishers Association (IBPA); St Louis Publishers Association; St Louis Writers Guild

Brick Tower Press
Subsidiary of J T Colby & Co Inc
Manhanset House, PO Box 342, Shelter Island Heights, NY 11965-0342
Tel: 212-427-7139 *Toll Free Tel:* 800-68-BRICK (682-7425)
E-mail: bricktower@aol.com
Web Site: bricktowerpress.com
Key Personnel
Publr: John T Colby, Jr
Founded: 1993
ISBN Prefix(es): 978-1-883283; 978-0-9531737; 978-1-899694
Number of titles published annually: 20 Print; 10 E-Book
Total Titles: 150 Print; 50 E-Book
Foreign Rep(s): Gazelle Book Services Ltd (Europe, UK); Ingram Content Group LLC (Australia, Canada, European Union)
Foreign Rights: Creative Management Partners (Canada, USA); D4EO Literary Agency (Bob Diforio) (worldwide)
Warehouse: Ingram Content Group LLC, One Ingram Blvd, La Vergne, TN 37086 *Tel:* 615-793-5000
Distribution Center: Ingram Content Group LLC, One Ingram Blvd, La Vergne, TN 37086 *Tel:* 615-793-5000

BrickHouse Books Inc
306 Suffolk Rd, Baltimore, MD 21218
Fax: 410-235-7690
Web Site: brickhousebooks.wordpress.com

Key Personnel
Publr & Ed-in-Chief: Clarinda Harriss
  E-mail: charriss@towson.edu
Founded: 1970
Poetry; mixed genres by gay & lesbian (Stonewall only); artistic prose, experimental, memoir, plays.
ISBN Prefix(es): 978-1-938144
Number of titles published annually: 6 Print
Total Titles: 246 Print
Imprints: Beignet Books; Chestnut Hills Press; New Poets Series; Side Street; Stonewall
Foreign Rep(s): Salmon Publishing (Ireland)
Distribution Center: Itasca Books, 5120 Cedar Lake Rd, Minneapolis, MN 55416, Dist Mgr: Mark Jung *Tel:* 952-345-4488 ext 118 *Toll Free Tel:* 800-901-3480 ext 118 *Fax:* 952-920-0541 *E-mail:* orders@itascabooks.com *Web Site:* www.itascabooks.com
Membership(s): Academy of American Poets; Association of American Publishers (AAP)

Bridge-Logos
1426W Newberry Rd, No 409, Newberry, FL 32669-2765
Toll Free Tel: 800-320-4108
Web Site: www.bridgelogos.com
Key Personnel
Pres & CEO: Suzi Wooldridge
Founded: 1969
Bibles, Christian classics, spirit-filled life, Christian books, parenting, family, Eschatological, evangelism, revival, children's bibles.
ISBN Prefix(es): 978-0-88270; 978-0-61036
Number of titles published annually: 20 Print
Total Titles: 216 Print
Imprints: Bridge; Haven; Logos; Open Scroll; Synergy
Foreign Office(s): The Coach House Annexe, Wellington Lane, Cheltenham, Glos GL50 4JF, United Kingdom *Tel:* (01242) 300860
Distributor for Warboys LLC
Foreign Rep(s): Winfried Bluth (Germany)
Foreign Rights: Winfried Bluth (Germany)
Orders to: Anchor Distributors, 1030 Hunt Valley Circle, New Kensington, PA 15058 *Tel:* 724-334-7000 *Toll Free Tel:* 800-444-4484 *Fax:* 724-334-1200 *Toll Free Fax:* 800-765-1960 *E-mail:* anchor.customerservice@anchordistributors.com *Web Site:* www.anchordistributors.com
Returns: Anchor Distributors, 1030 Hunt Valley Circle, New Kensington, PA 15058 *Tel:* 724-334-7000 *Toll Free Tel:* 800-444-4484 *Fax:* 724-334-1200 *Toll Free Fax:* 800-765-1960 *E-mail:* anchor.customerservice@anchordistributors.com *Web Site:* www.anchordistributors.com
Shipping Address: Anchor Distributors, 1030 Hunt Valley Circle, New Kensington, PA 15058 *Tel:* 724-334-7000 *Toll Free Tel:* 800-444-4484 *Fax:* 724-334-1200 *Toll Free Fax:* 800-765-1960 *E-mail:* anchor.customerservice@anchordistributors.com *Web Site:* www.anchordistributors.com
Distribution Center: Anchor Distributors, 1030 Hunt Valley Circle, New Kensington, PA 15058 *Tel:* 724-334-7000 *Toll Free Tel:* 800-444-4484 *Fax:* 724-334-1200 *Toll Free Fax:* 800-765-1960 *E-mail:* anchor.customerservice@anchordistributors.com *Web Site:* www.anchordistributors.com

Bridge Publications Inc
5600 E Olympic Blvd, Commerce, CA 90022
SAN: 208-3884
Tel: 323-888-6200 *Toll Free Tel:* 800-722-1733
  Fax: 323-888-6202
E-mail: info@bridgepub.com
Web Site: www.bridgepub.com
Key Personnel
Pres: Blake Silber

Dir, Trade Opers: Ann Arnow
  E-mail: annarnow@bridgepub.com
Trade Sales Mgr: Don Arnow *E-mail:* darnow@bridgepub.com
Founded: 1981
US & international nonfiction publisher of L Ron Hubbard's Dianetics & Scientology materials.
ISBN Prefix(es): 978-0-88404; 978-1-57318; 978-1-4031
Number of titles published annually: 3,200 Print; 400 CD-ROM; 52 Online; 5 Audio
Total Titles: 32,400 Print; 3,500 CD-ROM; 257 Online; 288 Audio
Imprints: BPI Records; Bridge Audio; Theta Books
Branch Office(s)
Bridge Publications Canada, 696 Yonge St, Toronto, ON M4Y 2A7, Canada, Contact: Emily Harris *Tel:* 416-964-8927 *Fax:* 416-964-3201
Foreign Office(s): Era Dinamica Editores SA de CV, Pablo U Cello, No 16, Colonia de los Deportes, 03710 Mexico, CDMX, Mexico, Contact: Irma Macias *Tel:* (0155) 5984487 *Fax:* (0155) 5984624
Foreign Rep(s): New Era Publications International (Copenhagen, Europe, Russia & former USSR)
Distribution Center: Amazon.com (house acct)
Follett School Solutions Inc, 1340 Ridgeview Dr, McHenry, IL 60050 *Tel:* 815-759-1700 *Toll Free Tel:* 888-511-5114 (cust serv) *Fax:* 815-759-9831 *Toll Free Fax:* 800-852-5458 *E-mail:* info@follettlearning.com *Web Site:* www.follettlearning.com
Baker & Taylor, 2550 Tyvola Rd, Suite 300, Charlotte, NC 28217 (house acct) *Tel:* 815-802-2479 *Fax:* 815-411-8433 *Web Site:* www.baker-taylor.com
Ingram Content Group LLC, One Ingram Blvd, La Vergne, TN 37086 *Tel:* 615-793-5000
Membership(s): Independent Book Publishers Association (IBPA)

Brigantine Media
211 North Ave, St Johnsbury, VT 05819
Tel: 802-751-8802 *Fax:* 802-751-8804
Web Site: brigantinemedia.com
Key Personnel
Acqs Ed: Neil Raphel *E-mail:* neil@brigantinemedia.com
Edit Chief: Janis Raye
Founded: 1990
ISBN Prefix(es): 978-0-9826644
Number of titles published annually: 12 Print; 2 Online; 12 E-Book
Total Titles: 50 Print; 2 Online; 40 E-Book
Imprints: Compass (educational materials for teachers); Voyage (fiction, primarily from VT & regional authors)

Bright Connections Media, A World Book Encyclopedia Company
Imprint of World Book Inc
180 N LaSalle St, Suite 900, Chicago, IL 60601
Tel: 312-729-5800
Web Site: www.brightconnectionsmedia.com
Key Personnel
VP, Mktg: Jean Lin *E-mail:* jean.lin@worldbook.com
Founded: 2012
Nonfiction & playful educational material for young children through young adults.
ISBN Prefix(es): 978-1-62267
Number of titles published annually: 8 Print
Total Titles: 20 Print

§Brill Inc
Subsidiary of Koninklijke Brill NV
2 Liberty Sq, 11th fl, Boston, MA 02109

Tel: 617-263-2323 *Toll Free Tel:* 800-962-4406; 800-337-9255 (orders - USA & CN) *Fax:* 617-263-2324
E-mail: sales-us@brill.com
Web Site: www.brill.com
Key Personnel
Sales Mgr: Eleanor Kerrissey *E-mail:* kerrissey@brill.com
Off Mgr: Rose Luongo
Founded: 1683
Publishes high-level, specialized, academic titles.
ISBN Prefix(es): 978-90-04
Number of titles published annually: 600 Print
Total Titles: 6,000 Print
Returns: Books International Inc, c/o Brill Academic Publishers Inc, 22883 Quicksilver Dr, Sterling, VA 20166
Warehouse: PO Box 605, Herndon, VA 20172 *Tel:* 703-661-1500 *Toll Free Tel:* 800-337-9255 *Fax:* 703-661-1501
Distribution Center: Books International Inc, 22883 Quicksilver Dr, Sterling, VA 20166 *Tel:* 703-661-1500

Brilliance Audio
Subsidiary of Amazon Publishing
1704 Eaton Dr, Grand Haven, MI 49417
Tel: 616-846-5256 *Toll Free Tel:* 800-648-2312 (orders only) *Fax:* 616-846-0630
E-mail: customerservice@brillianceaudio.com
Web Site: www.brillianceaudio.com
Key Personnel
Gen Mgr/Publr: Mark Pereira *E-mail:* mpereira@brillianceaudio.com
Acq Ed: Sheryl Zajechowski *Tel:* 616-846-5256 ext 726 *E-mail:* szajechowski@brillianceaudio.com
Founded: 1984
Country's leading independent audiobook publisher. Brilliance Audio is a trademark of Brilliance Publishing Inc.
ISBN Prefix(es): 978-0-930435; 978-1-56100; 978-1-56740; 978-1-58788; 978-1-59086; 978-1-59355; 978-1-59600; 978-1-59710; 978-1-59737; 978-1-4233; 978-1-4418; 978-1-61106; 978-1-4558
Number of titles published annually: 700 Audio
Total Titles: 6,500 Audio
Imprints: Grand Harbor Press; Waterfall Press
Membership(s): Audio Publishers Association

Bristol Park Books
252 W 38 St, Suite 206, New York, NY 10018
Tel: 212-842-0700 *Fax:* 212-842-1771
E-mail: info@bristolparkbooks.com
Web Site: bristolparkbooks.com
Key Personnel
Pres: Richard Alexander
Promotional hardcover reprints.
ISBN Prefix(es): 978-0-88365; 978-0-88486; 978-1-57866
Number of titles published annually: 50 Print
Total Titles: 200 Print
Orders to: National Book Network, 4501 Forbes Blvd, Suite 200, Lantham, MD 20706 *Tel:* 301-459-3366 *Web Site:* nbnbooks.com
Distribution Center: National Book Network, 4501 Forbes Blvd, Suite 200, Lantham, MD 20706 *Tel:* 301-459-3366 *Web Site:* nbnbooks.com

Broden Books LLC
3824 Sunset Dr, Spring Park, MN 55384
SAN: 920-0614
Tel: 952-471-1066
E-mail: media@brodenbooks.com
Web Site: www.brodenbooks.com
Key Personnel
Pres & CEO: Kathy La Pointe
Founded: 1999
Early childhood literacy resources for parents, schools & libraries. We are engaged in ongoing

research into issues impacting literacy in the US. Our resources are sold worldwide through online & retail stores.
ISBN Prefix(es): 978-0-9832023
Number of titles published annually: 3 Print
Total Titles: 3 Print
Imprints: REAL Phonics™

§Paul H Brookes Publishing Co Inc
PO Box 10624, Baltimore, MD 21285-0624
SAN: 212-730X
Tel: 410-337-9580 (outside US & CN)
 Toll Free Tel: 800-638-3775 (US & CN)
 Fax: 410-337-8539
E-mail: custserv@brookespublishing.com
Web Site: www.brookespublishing.com
Key Personnel
Chmn of the Bd: Paul H Brookes
Pres: Jeffrey D Brookes *E-mail:* jbrookes@ brookespublishing.com
EVP: Melissa A Behm *E-mail:* mbehm@ brookespublishing.com
EVP & Publr: George S Stamathis
 E-mail: gstamathis@brookespublishing.com
VP, Fin: Kathy Harris *E-mail:* kharris@ brookespublishing.com
VP, Opers: Erika Kinney *E-mail:* ekinney@ brookespublishing.com
Dir, Assessment & Content Solutions: Heather Shrestha *Tel:* 410-337-9580 ext 102
 E-mail: hshrestha@brookespublishing.com
Dir, Mktg: Jessica Reighard *E-mail:* jreighard@ brookespublishing.com
Dir, Prodn: Dana Battaglia *E-mail:* dbattaglia@ brookespublishing.com
Dir, Sales: Robert Miller *E-mail:* rmiller@ brookespublishing.com
Assoc Dir, Rts & Intellectual Property: Heather Lengyel *Tel:* 410-491-3311 *E-mail:* hlengyel@ brookespublishing.com
Founded: 1978
Publishes professional books, textbooks, assessments, curricula & web-based products in the areas of: early childhood, early intervention, social-emotional development, literacy, learning disabilities, autism, behavior, special education, developmental disabilities, communication & language.
ISBN Prefix(es): 978-0-933716; 978-1-55766; 978-1-59857; 978-1-68125
Number of titles published annually: 50 Print; 5 CD-ROM; 5 Online; 40 E-Book
Total Titles: 642 Print; 20 CD-ROM; 10 Online; 107 E-Book
Subsidiaries: Health Professions Press (specialist publisher focused on the broad range of issues in gerontology, long-term care & health administration)
Foreign Rep(s): Cranbury International LLC (Caribbean, Latin America); Eurospan Ltd (Africa, Asia, Europe, Middle East, UK); Footprint Books Pty Ltd (Australia, Fiji, New Zealand, Papua New Guinea)
Returns: Maple Logistics Solutions, 60 Grumbacher Rd, I-83 Industrial Park, York, PA 17406
Warehouse: Maple Logistics Solutions, PO Box 15100, York, PA 17405 *Web Site:* www.maplelogisticssolutions.com
See separate listing for:
Health Professions Press

§The Brookings Institution Press
Division of The Brookings Institution
1775 Massachusetts Ave NW, Washington, DC 20036-2188
SAN: 201-9396
Tel: 202-797-6000
E-mail: permissions@brookings.edu
Web Site: www.brookings.edu
Key Personnel
Pres: John R Allen
Dir: Bill Finan

Asst Dir: Yelba Quinn
Mng Ed: Cecilia Gonzalez *Tel:* 202-238-3510
 E-mail: cgonzalez@brookings.edu
Digital & Mktg Mgr: Steven Roman *Tel:* 202-536-3609 *E-mail:* sroman@brookings.edu
Prodn Mgr: Elliott Beard *Tel:* 202-797-6303
 E-mail: cbeard@brookings.edu
Publicity Mgr: Robert Wicks *Tel:* 202-238-3690
 E-mail: rwicks@brookings.edu
Rts Mgr: Kristen Harrison *Tel:* 202-536-3604
 E-mail: kharrison@brookings.edu
Dist Mgr: Terrence Melvin
Founded: 1916
Economics, foreign policy & government affairs.
ISBN Prefix(es): 978-0-8157
Number of titles published annually: 35 Print; 35 E-Book
Total Titles: 1,600 Print; 1,400 E-Book
Foreign Rep(s): APD Singapore Pte Ltd (Brunei, Indonesia, Korea, Malaysia, Singapore, Thailand, Vietnam); Eurospan Group (Africa, China, Europe, Hong Kong, Middle East, Taiwan, UK); Far Eastern Booksellers (Mr Nobuyuki Namekawa) (Japan); MHM Ltd (Japan); NewSouth Books (Australia, New Zealand); Publishers Group Canada (Canada); Viva Books Pvt Ltd (Bangladesh, India, Nepal, Pakistan, Sri Lanka)
Foreign Rights: Agency Literaria Internazionale (Italy); Big Apple Agency (China); Tuttle-Mori Agency Inc (Japan)
Distribution Center: Ingram Academic Services, 210 American Dr, Jackson, TN 38301 (US)
 E-mail: ipsjacksonorders@ingramcontent.com
Membership(s): American Association of University Presses (AAUP); Association of American Publishers (AAP)

Brookline Books
8 Trumbull Rd, Suite B-001, Northampton, MA 01060
Tel: 603-669-7032 (orders) *Toll Free Tel:* 800-666-2665 (orders) *Fax:* 413-584-6184
E-mail: brbooks@yahoo.com
Founded: 1985
Education, special needs, readings, general trade.
ISBN Prefix(es): 978-0-914797; 978-1-57129
Number of titles published annually: 5 Print
Total Titles: 125 Print

Brooklyn Publishers LLC
PO Box 248, Cedar Rapids, IA 52406
Tel: 319-368-8012 *Toll Free Tel:* 888-473-8521
 Fax: 319-368-8011
E-mail: customerservice@brookpub.com
Web Site: www.brookpub.com
Key Personnel
Sr Ed: David Burton
ISBN Prefix(es): 978-1-930961; 978-1-931000; 978-1-931805; 978-1-932404; 978-1-60003
Number of titles published annually: 100 Print
Total Titles: 1,800 Print

Brown Books Publishing Group
16250 Knoll Trail, Suite 205, Dallas, TX 75248
Tel: 972-381-0009 *Fax:* 972-248-4336
E-mail: publishing@brownbooks.com
Web Site: www.brownbooks.com
Key Personnel
Publr & CEO: Milli Brown
Pres: Tom Reale
EVP, Mktg: Kathy Williams
Founded: 1994
Full service independent publisher. Committed to producing high quality books of all genres for authors who choose to retain the rights to their intellectual property.
This publisher has indicated that 85% of their product line is author subsidized.
ISBN Prefix(es): 978-1-933285; 978-1-934812
Number of titles published annually: 150 Print
Total Titles: 1,000 Print

Divisions: The Agency at Brown Books; Brown Books Kids; Christian Press; Personal Profiles
Distribution Center: Ingram Content Group Inc, One Ingram Blvd, La Vergne, TN 37086
Membership(s): Independent Book Publishers Association (IBPA)

§Karen Brown Guides LLC
PO Box 70, San Mateo, CA 94401-0070
Fax: 650-342-9153
Web Site: www.karenbrown.com
Key Personnel
Pres: Karen Brown Herbert *E-mail:* karen@ karenbrown.com
Founded: 1977
Electronic travel guides & itineraries.
ISBN Prefix(es): 978-0-930328; 978-1-928901; 978-1-933810; 978-1-63371
Number of titles published annually: 16 E-Book
Total Titles: 16 E-Book

Bucknell University Press
One Dent Dr, Lewisburg, PA 17837
Tel: 570-577-3674
E-mail: universitypress@bucknell.edu
Web Site: www.bucknell.edu/universitypress
Key Personnel
Dir: Suzanne Guiod *Tel:* 570-577-1552
 E-mail: suzanne.guiod@bucknell.edu
Mng Ed: Pam Dailey *E-mail:* pad024@bucknell.edu
Founded: 1968
ISBN Prefix(es): 978-0-8387; 978-1-61148
Number of titles published annually: 25 Print
Total Titles: 1,200 Print
Distributed by Rutgers University Press

§BuilderBooks
Division of National Association of Home Builders (NAHB)
1201 15 St NW, Washington, DC 20005
SAN: 207-7035
Tel: 202-822-0200 *Toll Free Tel:* 800-223-2665
 Fax: 202-266-8096 (edit)
E-mail: info@nahb.com
Web Site: builderbooks.com
Key Personnel
Sr Dir, Print Mktg: Patricia Potts *E-mail:* ppotts@ nahb.org
Art Dir: Joe Rudden
Dir, Mktg Opers: Stephanie Thomas
Acqs & Mng Ed: Elizabeth Hartke
Mgr, Mktg: Tiffany Scott
Founded: 1943
Publish books about home construction & design, remodeling, land development, housing & construction management, sales & marketing of new homes, safety & seniors housing.
ISBN Prefix(es): 978-0-86718
Number of titles published annually: 7 Print
Total Titles: 150 Print
Orders to: PO Box 759290, Baltimore, MD 21275-9290
Returns: c/o Returns, National Association of Home Builders, 905 Carlow Dr, Unit B, Bolingbrook, IL 60490

Bull Publishing Co
PO Box 1377, Boulder, CO 80306
SAN: 208-5712
Tel: 303-545-6350 *Toll Free Tel:* 800-676-2855
 Fax: 303-545-6354
E-mail: bullpublishing@msn.com
Web Site: www.bullpub.com
Key Personnel
CFO: Emily Sewell
Pres & Publr: James Bull
Dir, Mktg: Claire Cameron
Founded: 1974
Self-care, nutrition & health care, physical fitness, weight loss, mental health, parenting & child care, psychology, self-help.

ISBN Prefix(es): 978-0-915950; 978-0-923521; 978-1-933503
Number of titles published annually: 6 Print; 1 Audio
Total Titles: 70 Print; 6 Audio
Foreign Rep(s): Gazelle Book Services Ltd (UK & the continent)
Warehouse: A & A Quality Shipping Services, 3623 Munster Ave, Unit B, Hayward, CA 94545
Distribution Center: Independent Publishers Group, 814 N Franklin St, Chicago, IL 60610 *Toll Free Tel:* 800-888-4741 *Web Site:* www. ipgbook.com

§The Bureau for At-Risk Youth
40 Aero Rd, Unit 2, Bohemia, NY 11716
Mailing Address: PO Box 170, Farmingville, NY 11738
Toll Free Tel: 800-99YOUTH (999-6884)
Toll Free Fax: 800-262-1886
Web Site: www.at-risk.com
Key Personnel
Owner: Carmine Russo
Founded: 1988
Educational materials on at-risk children's issues for educators, counselors, parents & children.
ISBN Prefix(es): 978-1-56688
Number of titles published annually: 15 Print
Total Titles: 250 Print

§Bureau of Economic Geology
Unit of University of Texas at Austin, Jackson School of Geosciences
c/o The University of Texas at Austin, 10100 Burnet Rd, Bldg 130, Austin, TX 78758
Mailing Address: c/o The University of Texas at Austin, PO Box X, University Sta, Austin, TX 78713-8924
Tel: 512-471-1534 *Fax:* 512-471-0140
E-mail: pubsales@beg.utexas.edu
Web Site: www.beg.utexas.edu
Key Personnel
Dir: Scott W Tinker
Mgr, Pubn Sales/The Bureau Store: Amanda Masterson *E-mail:* amanda.masterson@beg.utexas. edu
Founded: 1909
Scientific & technical books in geosciences.
ISBN Prefix(es): 978-1-970007
Number of titles published annually: 6 Print; 1 CD-ROM; 3 Online
Total Titles: 1,800 Print; 8 CD-ROM; 900 Online
Distributor for Gulf Coast Association of Geological Societies; Gulf Coast Section SEPM; Texas Memorial Museum (selected titles)
Orders to: The Bureau Store, c/o The University of Texas at Austin, PO Box X, University Sta, Austin, TX 78713-8924, Mgr: Amanda Masterson *Tel:* 512-471-3794 *Fax:* 512-471-0140 *Web Site:* store.beg.utexas.edu

Burford Books
101 E State St, No 301, Ithaca, NY 14850
Tel: 607-319-4373 *Fax:* 607-319-4373
Toll Free Fax: 866-212-7750
E-mail: info@burfordbooks.com
Web Site: www.burfordbooks.com
Key Personnel
Pres: Peter Burford
Founded: 1997
Publisher of books on the outdoors, sports, food & wine, fitness, nature, travel, fishing, military, Finger Lakes area.
ISBN Prefix(es): 978-1-58080
Number of titles published annually: 6 Print; 6 E-Book
Total Titles: 125 Print; 54 E-Book
Foreign Rep(s): Gazelle Book Services Ltd (UK)

Distribution Center: National Book Network, 15200 NBN Way, Blue Ridge Summit, PA 17214 *Tel:* 717-794-3800
Membership(s): Independent Publishers Association

Burns Archive Press
Imprint of Burns Archive Photographic Distributors Ltd
140 E 38 St, New York, NY 10016
Tel: 212-889-1938
E-mail: info@burnsarchive.com
Web Site: www.burnsarchive.com
Key Personnel
Pres & CEO: Stanley B Burns, MD
E-mail: burns@inch.com
Founded: 1979
Renowned for images of the darker side of life: death, disease, crime, racism, revolution & war. Provides a unique source of historic visual documentation containing over 700,000 vintage photographs. The Archive houses world-class holdings of African-American imagery & Judaica, as well as the foremost collection of early medical photography. More than a century of iconographic & historic photographs from the 1840s through the 1950s are available as stock photography. In addition, The Archive provides consultation, prepares exhibitions & publishes books on photographic history.
ISBN Prefix(es): 978-0-9612958; 978-0-9748688; 978-0-9748688; 978-0-9764495; 978-0-9764495; 978-1-934421; 978-1-936002
Number of titles published annually: 4 Print
Total Titles: 35 Print

Business & Legal Resources, see BLR®—Business & Legal Resources

Business Expert Press
222 E 46 St, Suite 203, New York, NY 10017-2906
Tel: 919-612-6706
E-mail: sales@businessexpertpress.com
Web Site: www.businessexpertpress.com
Key Personnel
COO: Sung Tinnie *E-mail:* stinnie@ businessexpertpress.com
Mktg Dir: Sheri E Dean *E-mail:* sheri.dean@ businessexpertpress.com
Founded: 2008
Providing MBA level students, as well as practitioners & executive education classes, with applied, concise textbooks that can be used in & out of the classroom.
ISBN Prefix(es): 978-1-60649; 978-1-63157; 978-1-94784
Number of titles published annually: 100 Print; 100 Online; 100 E-Book
Total Titles: 600 Print; 600 Online; 600 E-Book
Membership(s): American Library Association (ALA); Special Libraries Association (SLA)

Business Research Services Inc
PO Box 42674, Washington, DC 20015
SAN: 691-8522
Tel: 301-229-5561 *Toll Free Fax:* 877-516-0818
E-mail: brspubs@sba8a.com
Web Site: www.sba8a.com; www.setasidealert.com
Key Personnel
Pres & Publr: Thomas D Johnson
E-mail: tjohnson@setasidealert.com
Founded: 1984
Directories/lists of minority & women's businesses; small business newsletters & contract opportunities services.
ISBN Prefix(es): 978-0-933527
Number of titles published annually: 2 Print; 1 Online
Total Titles: 7 Print; 1 Online
Distributor for Riley & Johnson

By Design Press, see Quite Specific Media Group Ltd

Bywater Books Inc
PO Box 3671, Ann Arbor, MI 48106-3671
Tel: 734-662-8815
Web Site: bywaterbooks.com
Key Personnel
Owner & Ed-in-Chief: Kelly Smith
Publr: Salem West *E-mail:* salemwestbywater@ gmail.com
Dir, Opers: Marianne K Martin
E-mail: mkmbywater@aol.com
Dir, Creative Servs: Ann McMan
Mng Ed, Amble Press: Michael Nava
Founded: 1992
Publish top quality lesbian fiction. Our Bloody Brits imprint publishes the finest mainstream British mysteries in the US.
ISBN Prefix(es): 978-1-932859
Number of titles published annually: 10 Print
Total Titles: 42 Print
Imprints: Amble Press; Bloody Brits Press

Caissa Editions
Affiliate of Dale A Brandreth Books
PO Box 151, Yorklyn, DE 19736-0151
Tel: 302-239-4608
Web Site: www.chessbookstore.com
Key Personnel
Owner & Pres: Dale Brandreth
E-mail: dbrandreth3@comcast.net
Founded: 1971
Publisher of books that are primarily on chess.
ISBN Prefix(es): 978-0-939433
Number of titles published annually: 3 Print
Total Titles: 23 Print

§Cambridge University Press
Division of University of Cambridge
One Liberty Plaza, 20th fl, New York, NY 10006
SAN: 200-206X
Tel: 212-924-3900; 212-337-5000 *Fax:* 212-691-3239; 845-353-4141
E-mail: newyork@cambridge.org; customer_service@cambridge.org
Web Site: www.cambridge.org/us
Key Personnel
SVP, Academic Publg, Americas: Brigitte Shull
Mng Dir, Americas & Global Mng Dir, Eng Lang Teaching: Michael Peluse
HR Dir: Nick Correa
Press Dist Dir: Ian R Bradie
Publr, Economics & Political Sci: Robert Dreesen
Publg Dir, Humanities & Soc Sci: Dr Beatrice Rehl *E-mail:* brehl@cambridge.org
Head, Retail Sales: Tom Willshire
Journals Mktg Mgr: Susan Soule
Mktg Mgr, Humanities, Law & Psychology: Michael Duncan
Mktg Communs Mgr: Carine Mitchell
Journals Ed: Mark Zadrozny
Sr Ed, Engg: Peter Gordon
Sr Ed, Law: Dr John Berger
Sr Ed, Soc Sci: Lewis Bateman
Sr Ed, US & Latin American History: Cecelia Cancellaro
Sr Commissioning Ed: Marigold Acland
E-mail: macland@cambridge.org
Ed, Math & Computer Sci: Lauren Cowles
Founded: 1534
Scholarly & trade books, college textbooks & journals.
ISBN Prefix(es): 978-0-521
Number of titles published annually: 2,400 Print
Total Titles: 45,000 Print; 160 Online
Foreign Office(s): The Edinburgh Bldg, Shaftesbury Rd, Cambridge CB2 8BS, United Kingdom *Tel:* (01223) 358331
Warehouse: One Ingram Blvd, La Vergne, TN 17202
Distribution Center: Ingram Academic Services (US & CN)

Membership(s): Association of American Publishers (AAP); Association of University Presses (AUPresses); Book Industry Study Group (BISG)

Camino Books Inc
PO Box 59026, Philadelphia, PA 19102-9026
Tel: 215-413-1917 *Fax:* 215-413-3255
E-mail: camino@caminobooks.com
Web Site: www.caminobooks.com
Key Personnel
Pres & Publr: Edward Jutkowitz
  E-mail: ejutkowitz@caminobooks.com
Founded: 1987
Regional trade books for the Mid-Atlantic states.
ISBN Prefix(es): 978-0-940159; 978-1-933822; 978-1-68098
Number of titles published annually: 10 Print; 10 E-Book
Total Titles: 90 Print; 75 E-Book
Returns: Whitehurst & Clark Book Fulfillment Inc, 1200 County Rd, Rte 523, Flemington, NJ 08822
Warehouse: Whitehurst & Clark Book Fulfillment Inc, 1200 County Rd, Rte 523, Flemington, NJ 08822 *Tel:* 908-782-2323

Campfield & Campfield Publishing LLC
6521 Cutler St, Philadelphia, PA 19126
Toll Free Tel: 888-518-2440 *Fax:* 215-224-6696
E-mail: info@campfieldspublishing.com
Web Site: www.campfieldspublishing.com
Key Personnel
Publr: Charlene M Campfield
Founded: 2009
Publisher of Christ-centered books for children, teens & young adults.
ISBN Prefix(es): 978-0-9817025
Number of titles published annually: 2 Print; 2 Online
Total Titles: 10 Print; 10 Online; 4 E-Book
Membership(s): Independent Book Publishers Association (IBPA)

Candied Plums
Imprint of Paper Republic LLC
7548 Ravenna Ave NE, Seattle, WA 98115
Mailing Address: 2301 N 65 St, Seattle, WA 98103
E-mail: candiedplums@gmail.com
Web Site: www.candiedplums.com
Key Personnel
Publr: Eric Abrahamsen *E-mail:* eric@candiedplums.com
Publg Consultant: Roxanne Feldman
  E-mail: roxannefeldman@gmail.com
Edit Coord: Lisa Lee *E-mail:* lisa.candiedplums@gmail.com
Ed: Nancy Zhang *E-mail:* nancy.candiedplums@gmail.com
Founded: 2016
ISBN Prefix(es): 978-1-945295
Number of titles published annually: 20 Print
Total Titles: 20 Print
Orders to: Pathway Book Service, 34 Production Ave, Keene, NH 03431, Contact: George Corrette *Toll Free Tel:* 800-345-6665 *Fax:* 603-965-2181 *E-mail:* george.corrette@pathwaybook.com
Returns: Pathway Book Service, 34 Production Ave, Keene, NH 03431, Contact: George Corrette *Toll Free Tel:* 800-345-6665 *Fax:* 603-965-2181 *E-mail:* george.corrette@pathwaybook.com
Warehouse: Global Union International Inc, 16801 Gale Ave, Unit C, City of Industry, CA 91745, Contact: Allen Wang *Tel:* 626-965-8878 *Fax:* 626-965-8877 *E-mail:* allenwang@globaluniontintl.com
Distribution Center: Pathway Book Service, 34 Production Ave, Keene, NH 03431, Contact:

George Corrette *Toll Free Tel:* 800-345-6665 *Fax:* 603-965-2181 *E-mail:* george.corrette@pathwaybook.com

§Candlewick Press
Subsidiary of Trustbridge Global Media
99 Dover St, Somerville, MA 02144-2825
Tel: 617-661-3330 *Fax:* 617-661-0565
E-mail: bigbear@candlewick.com; salesinfo@candlewick.com
Web Site: www.candlewick.com
Key Personnel
Pres & Publr: Karen Lotz
EVP, Exec Edit Dir & Assoc Publr: Liz Bicknell
SVP & Group Sales Dir: John Mendelson
SVP, Commercial Opers: Susan Batcheller
SVP, Fin: Hilary Berkman
VP, Contracts, Rts & Royalties: Becky S Hemperly
VP, Publicity & Exec Dir, Mktg Campaigns: Jennifer Roberts
Assoc Publr & Creative Dir: Chris Paul
Exec Art Dir: Nancy Brennan
Exec Dir, Educ Sales & Mktg: Kathleen Rourke
Exec Dir, Independent Retail & CN Sales: Elise Supovitz
Exec Dir, Publicity: Karen Walsh
Exec Edit Dir, Walker Books US: Susan Van Metre
Dir, Edit Opers & Edit Dir: Mary Lee Donovan
Group Edit Dir, Candlewick Entertainment & Walker Entertainment: Joan Powers
Publicity & Mktg Campaigns Dir: Tracy Miracle
Publicity, Brands & Consumer Outreach Dir: Laura Rivas
Sr Exec Ed: Sarah Ketchersid
Exec Ed: Hilary Van Dusen
Founded: 1992
ISBN Prefix(es): 978-1-56402; 978-0-7636
Number of titles published annually: 300 Print
Total Titles: 2,250 Print; 230 E-Book
Imprints: Big Picture Press; Candlewick Entertainment; Candlewick Studio; MIT Kids Press; MITeen Press; Nosy Crow; Templar Books
Foreign Rights: Walker Books Australia; Walker Books London
Returns: Penguin Random House LLC, 1019 N State Rd 47, Crawfordsville, IN 47933; Penguin Random House Canada, 6971 Columbus Rd, Mississauga, ON L5T 1K1, Canada
Distribution Center: Penguin Random House Publisher Services (PRHPS), 400 Hahn Rd, Westminster, MD 21157 *Toll Free Tel:* 800-733-3000 *Toll Free Fax:* 800-659-2436
  E-mail: customerservice@randomhouse.com
Penguin Random House Canada, 75 Sherbourne St, 5th fl, Toronto, ON M5A 2P9, Canada *Toll Free Tel:* 888-523-9292 *Toll Free Fax:* 888-562-9924
Membership(s): The Children's Book Council (CBC)

C&T Publishing Inc
1651 Challenge Dr, Concord, CA 94520-5206
Tel: 925-677-0377 *Toll Free Tel:* 800-284-1114
  Fax: 925-677-0373
E-mail: support@ctpub.com
Web Site: www.ctpub.com
Key Personnel
CEO: Todd Hensley
CFO: Tony Hensley
Edit Dir: Gailen Runge
Publr: Amy Marson
Founded: 1983
Specialize in fiber & paper craft books & products.
ISBN Prefix(es): 978-0-914881; 978-1-57120
Number of titles published annually: 45 Print
Total Titles: 400 Print
Distributed by National Book Network
Membership(s): Independent Book Publishers Association (IBPA)

Capitol Enquiry Inc
1034 Emerald Bay Rd, No 435, South Lake Tahoe, CA 96150
Tel: 916-442-1434 *Toll Free Tel:* 800-922-7486
  Fax: 916-244-2704
E-mail: info@capenq.com
Web Site: govbuddy.com
Key Personnel
Owner & Mktg Dir: Bruce Campbell
Founded: 1973
Legislative directories, information, interactive maps (CA) zip code directory, mobile apps & *US Congress Directory*.
ISBN Prefix(es): 978-0-917982
Number of titles published annually: 7 Print
Total Titles: 15 Print
Distributor for Center for Investigative Reporting

CAPPA, see University of Texas at Arlington College of Architecture, Planning & Public Affairs

Capstone Publishers™
1710 Roe Crest Dr, North Mankato, MN 56003
Toll Free Tel: 800-747-4992 (cust serv)
  Toll Free Fax: 888-262-0705
E-mail: customer.service@capstonepub.com
Web Site: www.capstonepub.com
Key Personnel
Owner: Robert Coughlan
CEO: G Thomas Ahern
COO & CFO: William R Rouse
VP, Digital Prod Devt & Mgmt: Darin Rasmussen
Publr: Patricia Stockland
Sr Mng Ed: Nick Healy
Book Trade Sales Mgr: Larry Dorfman
Founded: 1991
Provides new & struggling readers with a strong foundation on which to build reading success. Our broad range of nonfiction titles for grades PreK-8 easily blends a world of books with the world children experience every day.
ISBN Prefix(es): 978-1-56065; 978-0-7368
Number of titles published annually: 250 Print
Total Titles: 2,100 Print
Imprints: Capstone Press; Capstone Young Readers; Compass Point Books; Heinemann Raintree; Picture Window Books; Stone Arch Books
Divisions: Heinemann Raintree
Branch Office(s)
5050 Lincoln Dr, Suite 200, Edina, MN 55436
Billing Address: 3680 Momentum Place, Chicago, IL 60689-5336
Distribution Center: 1905 Lookout Dr, North Mankato, MN 56003

Captain Fiddle Music & Publications
94 Wiswall Rd, Lee, NH 03861
Tel: 603-659-2658
E-mail: cfiddle@tiac.net
Web Site: captainfiddle.com
Key Personnel
Owner: Ryan J Thomson
Founded: 1985
ISBN Prefix(es): 978-0-931877
Number of titles published annually: 3 Print
Total Titles: 24 Print

§Cardiotext Publishing
3405 W 44 St, Minneapolis, MN 55410
SAN: 852-2251
Tel: 612-925-2053 *Toll Free Tel:* 888-999-9174
  Fax: 612-922-7556
E-mail: info@cardiotext.com
Web Site: www.cardiotextpublishing.com
Key Personnel
Pres: Mike Crouchet *Tel:* 612-925-2053
  E-mail: mike.crouchet@cardiotext.com
Founded: 2007
Independent print & digital publisher. Specialize in the field of cardiovascular medicine.
ISBN Prefix(es): 978-1-935395; 978-1-942909; 978-0-979016

Number of titles published annually: 10 Print; 10 Online; 10 E-Book

Total Titles: 35 Print; 35 Online; 35 E-Book

Foreign Rights: John Scott & Co (worldwide exc North America)

Distribution Center: NBN International, 10 Thornbury Rd, Plymouth PL6 7PP, United Kingdom *Tel:* (01752) 202 301 *E-mail:* cservs@nbninternational.com *Web Site:* distribution.nbni.co.uk

Cardoza Publishing

1916 E Charleston Blvd, Las Vegas, NV 89104

Tel: 702-870-7200 *Toll Free Tel:* 800-577-WINS (577-9467)

E-mail: info@cardozabooks.com

Web Site: www.cardozabooks.com

Key Personnel

Publr & Author: Avery Cardoza

Founded: 1981

Independent publisher. Specialize in gaming, gambling, poker, backgammon & chess titles.

ISBN Prefix(es): 978-1-58042

Number of titles published annually: 15 Print

Total Titles: 200 Print

Distributed by Simon & Schuster, Inc; Simon & Schuster Sales Division

Orders to: Simon & Schuster, 100 Front St, Riverside, NJ 08075, Order Processing Dept *Toll Free Tel:* 800-223-2336 *Toll Free Fax:* 800-943-9831 *E-mail:* order_desk@distican.com

Carlisle Press - Walnut Creek

2673 Township Rd 421, Sugarcreek, OH 44681

Tel: 330-852-1900 *Toll Free Tel:* 800-852-4482 *Fax:* 330-852-3285

Key Personnel

Publr: Marvin Wengerd

Founded: 1992

Amish books & cookbooks, *Keeper's at Home* Magazine.

ISBN Prefix(es): 978-1-890050; 978-0-9642548; 978-1-933753

Number of titles published annually: 6 Print

Total Titles: 60 Print

Carnegie Mellon University Press

5032 Forbes Ave, Pittsburgh, PA 15289-1021

SAN: 211-2329

Tel: 412-268-2861 *Fax:* 412-268-8706

E-mail: carnegiemellonuniversitypress@gmail.com

Web Site: www.cmu.edu/universitypress

Key Personnel

Dir: Gerald Costanzo *E-mail:* gc3d@andrew.cmu.edu

Sr Ed: Cynthia Lamb *E-mail:* cynthial@andrew.cmu.edu

Prodn Mgr: Connie Amoroso *E-mail:* camoroso@andrew.cmu.edu

Accts Admin: Anna Houck *E-mail:* am2x@andrew.cmu.edu

Founded: 1974

ISBN Prefix(es): 978-0-915604; 978-0-88748

Number of titles published annually: 15 Print

Total Titles: 308 Print

Distribution Center: Chicago Distribution Center (CDC), 11030 S Langley Ave, Chicago, IL 60628 *Tel:* 773-702-7010 *Toll Free Fax:* 800-621-8476

Membership(s): Association of University Presses (AUPresses)

Carolina Academic Press

700 Kent St, Durham, NC 27701

SAN: 210-7848

Tel: 919-489-7486 *Toll Free Tel:* 800-489-7486 *Fax:* 919-493-5668

E-mail: cap@cap-press.com

Web Site: www.cap-press.com; www.caplaw.com

Key Personnel

Publr: Keith R Sipe *Tel:* 919-489-7486 ext 120 *E-mail:* ksipe@cap-press.com

Assoc Publr, List Devt: Scott Sipe *Tel:* 919-489-7486 ext 129 *E-mail:* css@cap-press.com

Mng Ed: Ryland Bowman *Tel:* 919-489-7486 ext 133 *E-mail:* rbowman@cap-press.com

Sr Ed: Linda M Lacy *Tel:* 919-489-7486 ext 128 *E-mail:* linda@cap-press.com

Founded: 1974

Scholarly books & journals; anthropology, archaeology, criminal justice, economics, government, political science, history, reference, law, social science, african studies.

ISBN Prefix(es): 978-0-89089; 978-1-59460; 978-1-61163

Number of titles published annually: 150 Print; 150 E-Book

Total Titles: 1,100 Print; 350 E-Book

Returns: 101 Tobacco Rd, Oxford, NC 27565

Warehouse: 101 Tobacco Rd, Oxford, NC 27565

Carolrhoda Books Inc

Imprint of Lerner Publishing Group Inc

241 First Ave N, Minneapolis, MN 55401

Tel: 612-332-3344 *Toll Free Tel:* 800-328-4929 *Fax:* 612-332-7615 *Toll Free Fax:* 800-332-1132

E-mail: info@lernerbooks.com; custserve@lernerbooks.com

Web Site: www.lernerbooks.com; www.facebook.com/lernerbooks

Key Personnel

Chmn: Harry J Lerner

Pres & Publr: Adam Lerner

EVP & COO: Mark Budde

EVP & CFO: Margaret Thomas

EVP, Sales: David Wexler

VP & Ed-in-Chief: Andy Cummings

VP, Mktg: Rachel Zugschwert

Edit Dir, Millbrook & Carolrhoda: Carol Hinz

Dir, HR: Cyndi Radant

Dir, Rts, Spec Sales & Intl Dist: Maria Kjoller

Ed: Amy Fitzgerald

Founded: 1969

Children's picture books & middle grade fiction.

Number of titles published annually: 20 Print

Total Titles: 70 Print; 334 E-Book

Foreign Rep(s): Thomas Allen & Son (trade) (Canada); Bounce Sales & Marketing Ltd (UK); INT Books (Australia); J Appleseed, A Division of Saunders (Canada); Phambili Agencies (Botswana, Lesotho, Namibia, Southern Africa); Publishers Marketing Services (Brunei, Malaysia, Singapore); Saunders Book Co (education) (Canada); South Pacific Books (New Zealand); Walker Books (Australia)

Foreign Rights: Japan Foreign-Rights Centre (Japan); Korea Copyright Center (KCC) (Korea); Agence Michelle Lapautre (France); Literarische Agentur Silke Weniger (Germany)

Warehouse: 1251 Washington Ave N, Minneapolis, MN 55401, Mgr: Ken Rued

Carolrhoda Lab™

Imprint of Lerner Publishing Group Inc

241 First Ave N, Minneapolis, MN 55401

Tel: 612-332-3344 *Toll Free Tel:* 800-328-4929 *Fax:* 612-332-7615 *Toll Free Fax:* 800-332-1132

E-mail: info@lernerbooks.com; custserve@lernerbooks.com

Web Site: www.lernerbooks.com; www.facebook.com/lernerbooks

Key Personnel

Chmn: Harry J Lerner

Pres & Publr: Adam Lerner

EVP & COO: Mark Budde

EVP & CFO: Margaret Thomas

EVP, Sales: David Wexler

VP & Ed-in-Chief: Andy Cummings

VP, Mktg: Rachel Zugschwert

Dir, HR: Cyndi Radant

Dir, Rts, Spec Sales & Intl Dist: Maria Kjoller

Edit Dir: Amy Fitzgerald

School & Lib Mktg Dir: Lois Wallentine

Founded: 2010

Dedicated to distinctive, provocative, boundary-pushing fiction for teens & their sympathizers.

Number of titles published annually: 10 Print

Total Titles: 95 E-Book

Foreign Rep(s): Thomas Allen & Son (trade) (Canada); Bounce Sales & Marketing Ltd (UK); INT Books (Australia); J Appleseed, A Division of Saunders (Canada); Phambili Agencies (Botswana, Lesotho, Namibia, Southern Africa); Publishers Marketing Services (Brunei, Malaysia, Singapore); Saunders Book Co (education) (Canada); South Pacific Books (New Zealand); Walker Books (Australia)

Foreign Rights: Japan Foreign-Rights Centre (Japan); Korea Copyright Center (KCC) (Korea); Agence Michelle Lapautre (France); Literarische Agentur Silke Weniger (Germany)

Warehouse: 1251 Washington Ave N, Minneapolis, MN 55401, Mgr: Ken Rued

Carroll Publishing

4701 Sangamore Rd, Suite S-155, Bethesda, MD 20816

SAN: 237-6334

Tel: 301-263-9800 *Fax:* 301-263-9805

E-mail: info@carrollpub.com; customersvc@carrollpub.com

Web Site: www.carrollpublishing.com

Key Personnel

VP, Fin & Admin: Shirley Paris *Tel:* 301-263-9800 ext 107 *E-mail:* smparis@carrollpub.com

Founded: 1973

Number of titles published annually: 15 Print; 11 Online

Total Titles: 15 Print; 11 Online

Carson Dellosa Publishing LLC

PO Box 35665, Greensboro, NC 27425-5665

Tel: 336-632-0084 *Toll Free Tel:* 800-321-0943 *Fax:* 336-632-0087 *Toll Free Fax:* 800-535-2669

E-mail: custsvc@carsondellosa.com

Web Site: www.carsondellosa.com

Key Personnel

CEO: Al Greco

Founded: 1976

Publishes supplementary educational materials, including activity books, resource guides, classroom materials & reproducibles, toddler-grade 8. Topics include reading, language arts, mathematics, science, the arts, social studies, English language learners, early childhood learning, Christian books & crafts.

ISBN Prefix(es): 978-0-513; 978-0-7424; 978-1-56822; 978-0-88012; 978-0-88724; 978-1-59441; 978-1-60022; 978-1-60418

Number of titles published annually: 80 Print; 10 E-Book

Total Titles: 700 Print

Imprints: DJ Inkers; Rainbow Bridge Publishing; Kelley Wingate Publications

Branch Office(s)

8720 Orion Place, Suite 200, Columbus, OH 43240, Cust Serv Mgr: Alba Jaimes *Toll Free Tel:* 800-228-6898

Distributor for Key Education; Mark Twain Media

CarTech Inc

838 Lake St S, Forest Lake, MN 55025

Tel: 651-277-1200 *Toll Free Tel:* 800-551-4754 *Fax:* 651-277-1203

E-mail: info@cartechbooks.com

Web Site: www.cartechbooks.com

Key Personnel

Owner & Publr: David Arnold

Founded: 1993

Automotive books.

ISBN Prefix(es): 978-1-884089; 978-1-932494; 978-1-61325
Number of titles published annually: 25 Print
Total Titles: 100 Print
Imprints: S-A Design Books
Distributor for Behemoth Publishing; Brooklands Books Ltd; California Bill's; Wolfgang Publications
Foreign Rights: Publishers Group UK (PGUK) (Australia, England)
Returns: Publishers Storage & Shipping, 660 S Mansfield, Ypsilanti, MI 48197 *Tel:* 734-487-9720
Warehouse: Publishers Storage & Shipping, 660 S Mansfield, Ypsilanti, MI 48197 *Tel:* 734-487-9720

Casa Bautista de Publicaciones
Affiliate of Southern Baptist Convention
7000 Alabama St, El Paso, TX 79904
Tel: 915-566-9656 *Toll Free Tel:* 800-755-5958 (cust serv & orders) *Fax:* 915-565-9008 (orders)
E-mail: orders@editorialmh.org
Web Site: www.editorialmh.org
Key Personnel
CEO: Raquel Contreras
Secy: Cecilia Nevarez *Tel:* 915-566-9656 ext 288 *E-mail:* cnevarez@editorialmh.org
Founded: 1905
Religious publications in Spanish. Foreign distributors also located in all Latin countries.
ISBN Prefix(es): 978-0-311
Number of titles published annually: 16 Print
Total Titles: 895 Print; 895 E-Book
Imprints: CBP/EMH
Distributed by LifeWay Christian Resources

Casemate | publishers
Division of Casemate Group
1950 Lawrence Rd, Havertown, PA 19083
Tel: 610-853-9131 *Fax:* 610-853-9146
E-mail: casemate@casematepublishers.com
Web Site: www.casematepublishers.com
Key Personnel
Pres/CEO, Casemate Group: David Farnsworth
VP: Sarah Farnsworth
VP, Busn Devt: Simone Drinkwater
VP, Digital Servs & Publg Opers: Curtis Key
VP, Sales, Mktg & Client Rel: Michaela Goff
US Group Mktg & Publicity Dir: Samuel M Caggiula
Sales Dir: Kate Stein
Mktg Exec: Jenna Faccenda; Daniel Yesilonis
Cust Serv Mgr: Jill Tanenbaum
Founded: 2001
Publisher & distributor of military history, defense & travel books.
ISBN Prefix(es): 978-0-9711709; 978-1-932033; 978-1-935149; 978-1-61200
Number of titles published annually: 30 Print; 30 E-Book; 5 Audio
Total Titles: 175 Print; 175 E-Book
Distributor for AF Editions; AVF Modeller; Air Sea Media; Air War Publications; Airfile Publications; Andrea Press; Aviaeology; Big Sky Publishing; Birlinn (UK); Boydell & Brewer Inc; Casemate (USA); Chipotle Publishing; Claymore Press; Clear Vue Publishing; Colourpoint; Compendium (UK); Compendium Films; D-Day Publishing (Belgium); Fighting High Publishing; Fonthill Media; Formac (Canada); Foundry; Front Street Press (USA); Frontline Books; Greenhill Books; Grub Street Publishing (UK); Harpia Publishing; Heimdal; Helion & Co Ltd (UK); Editions Charles Herissey (France); Histoire & Collections (France); Historical Indexes (USA); History Facts; Histria Books; Kagero; De Krijger (Belgium); Lombardy Studios; Lorimer; LRT Editions; Military History Press; MMPBooks (UK/Poland); Model Centrum Progres; Mortons Media Group; Moselle River; Panzerwrecks; PeKo

Publishing; PelikaanPers; Pen & Sword (UK); Pen & Sword Digital; Philedition; Pool of London Press; Pritzker Military Museum & Library; Riebel-Roque; RN Publishing (USA); S I Publicaties BV; Sabrestorm Publishing; Savas Beatie (USA); Savas Publishing; Scarab Miniatures; Seaforth Publishing; Tattered Flag; 30 Degrees South Publishers; WAG Books; Warlord Games
Foreign Rep(s): Casemate UK (UK & Commonwealth)
Returns: c/o Casemate, 22883 Quicksilver Dr, Dulles, VA 20166
Shipping Address: c/o Casemate, 22883 Quicksilver Dr, Dulles, VA 20166
Membership(s): The Imaging Alliance

Castle Connolly Medical Ltd
42 W 24 St, 2nd fl, New York, NY 10010
Tel: 212-367-8400 *Fax:* 212-367-0964
Web Site: www.castleconnolly.com
Key Personnel
Founder & Chmn: John K Castle
Founder, Pres & CEO: John J Connolly, EdD
VP, Chief Strategy & Opers Offr: William Liss-Levinson, PhD *E-mail:* bliss-levinson@castleconnolly.com
VP, Chief Med & Res Offr: Dr Jean Morgan
Mgr, Client Rel & Res Opers: Nicki Hughes LaMonica *Tel:* 212-367-8400 ext 138 *E-mail:* nhughes@castleconnolly.com
Founded: 1991
Publishing company whose mission is to help consumers find the best healthcare with its "Top Doctors" guides.
ISBN Prefix(es): 978-1-883769; 978-1-935036; 978-0-984
Number of titles published annually: 3 Print
Total Titles: 10 Print
Membership(s): The Association of Publishers for Special Sales (APSS)

§Catholic Book Publishing Corp
77 West End Rd, Totowa, NJ 07512
Tel: 973-890-2400 *Toll Free Tel:* 877-228-2665 *Fax:* 973-890-2410
E-mail: info@catholicbookpublishing.com
Web Site: www.catholicbookpublishing.com
Founded: 1911
For over 115 years, the leading publisher of quality Catholic resources—including Bibles, Missals, Prayer books, liturgical books, spirituality books, Spanish titles & children's books. The company's trademark St Joseph Editions are distinctive for their large, easy-to-read typefaces; magnificent, full-color illustrations; & helpful & plentiful guides, summaries, notes, indices & photographs.
ISBN Prefix(es): 978-0-89942; 978-1-878718 (Resurrection Press); 978-0-529 (World Catholic Press); 978-1-933066 (Resurrection Press)
Number of titles published annually: 25 Print
Total Titles: 750 Print; 9 Audio
Imprints: Regina Press; Resurrection Press (spirituality & personal growth titles); World Catholic Press (complements the company's rich tradition of Bible publishing)

The Catholic Health Association of the United States
4455 Woodson Rd, St Louis, MO 63134-3797
SAN: 201-968X
Tel: 314-427-2500 *Fax:* 314-427-0029
E-mail: servicecenter@chausa.org
Web Site: www.chausa.org
Key Personnel
Dir, Communs & Mktg: Kimberly Van Oosten *E-mail:* kvanoosten@chausa.org
Founded: 1915
Catholic health care resources, Catholic ministry, health, labor, medicine & nursing.

ISBN Prefix(es): 978-0-87125
Number of titles published annually: 2 Print; 9 Audio
Total Titles: 58 Print
Branch Office(s)
1875 Eye St NW, Suite 1000, Washington, DC 20006 *Tel:* 202-296-3993 *Fax:* 202-296-3997

The Catholic University of America Press
Division of The Catholic University of America
240 Leahy Hall, 620 Michigan Ave NE, Washington, DC 20064
SAN: 203-6290
Tel: 202-319-5052 *Toll Free Tel:* 800-537-5487 (orders only) *Fax:* 202-319-4985
E-mail: cua-press@cua.edu
Web Site: cuapress.org
Key Personnel
Dir & Ed-in-Chief: Trevor C Lipscombe *E-mail:* lipscombe@cua.edu
Sales & Mktg Dir: Brian Roach *E-mail:* roach@cua.edu
Mng Ed: Theresa Walker *E-mail:* walkert@cua.edu
Acqs Ed, Philosophy & Theology: John B Martino *E-mail:* martinoj@cua.edu
Founded: 1939
ISBN Prefix(es): 978-0-8132
Number of titles published annually: 38 Print; 25 Online; 25 E-Book
Total Titles: 580 Print; 300 Online; 300 E-Book
Distributor for The Academy of American Franciscan History; American Maritain Association; Franciscan University Press; Humanum Academic Press; Institute for the Psychological Sciences Press (IPS); Sapientia Press
Foreign Rep(s): Brunswick Books (Canada); Eurospan University Press Group (Africa, Asia, Australia, Europe, Middle East, New Zealand, South America, UK)
Orders to: HFS, PO Box 50370, Baltimore, MD 21211-4370 *Fax:* 410-516-6998 *E-mail:* hfscustserv@mail.press.jhu.edu
Returns: HFS, c/o Maple Logistics Solutions, Lebanon Distribution Ctr, PO Box 1287, Lebanon, PA 17042-1287
Warehouse: Maple Logistics Solutions, Lebanon Distribution Ctr, 704 Legionaire Dr, Fredricksburg, PA 17042
Membership(s): Association of University Presses (AUPresses)

Cato Institute
1000 Massachusetts Ave NW, Washington, DC 20001-5403
Tel: 202-842-0200 *Toll Free Tel:* 800-767-1241 *Fax:* 202-842-3490
E-mail: catostore@cato.org
Web Site: www.cato.org
Key Personnel
Pres: Peter Goettler
Pubns Dir: Eleanor O'Connor *Tel:* 202-789-5266
Founded: 1977
Non-partisan, public-policy think tank.
ISBN Prefix(es): 978-0-932790; 978-1-882577; 978-1-930865; 978-1-933995
Number of titles published annually: 15 Print
Total Titles: 150 Print
Foreign Rights: Rights & Distribution Inc (worldwide)
Distribution Center: National Book Network, 15200 NBN Way, Blue Ridge Summit, PA 17214, VP, Opers: Mike Cornell *Tel:* 717-794-3800 *Toll Free Tel:* 800-462-6420 *Fax:* 717-794-3828 *Web Site:* www.nbnbooks.com

Frank W Cawood & Associates Inc, see FC&A Publishing

Caxton Press
Division of The Caxton Printers Ltd
312 Main St, Caldwell, ID 83605-3299
SAN: 201-9698

Tel: 208-459-7421 *Toll Free Tel:* 800-657-6465
 Fax: 208-459-7450
E-mail: publish@caxtonpress.com
Web Site: www.caxtonpress.com
Key Personnel
Pres & Publr: Scott Gipson *E-mail:* sgipson@
 caxtonpress.com
Founded: 1925
Founded by J H Gipson, Caxton Press is still
 owned & managed by the Gipson family.
ISBN Prefix(es): 978-0-87004
Number of titles published annually: 6 Print; 5 E-
 Book
Total Titles: 215 Print; 75 E-Book
Distributor for Hambleton Publishing; Historic
 Idaho Series; Photosmith Books; Snake Coun-
 try Publishing; University of Idaho Asian
 American Comparative Collection; University
 of Idaho Press
Membership(s): Association of American Pub-
 lishers (AAP); Pacific Northwest Booksellers
 Association (PNBA); Western Writers of Amer-
 ica (WWA)

CCAR Press, see Central Conference of
 American Rabbis/CCAR Press

§CCH, a Wolters Kluwer business
Subsidiary of Wolters Kluwer
2700 Lake Cook Rd, Riverwoods, IL 60015
SAN: 202-3504
Tel: 847-267-7000
Web Site: www.cch.com
Key Personnel
Dir, Communs: Leslie Bonacum *Tel:* 847-267-
 7153 *E-mail:* mediahelp@cch.com
Founded: 1913
Current US international tax law, business, human
 resources, securities & health care law, tax,
 small business, home office human resources &
 health care.
ISBN Prefix(es): 978-0-8080
Number of titles published annually: 100 Print
Total Titles: 400 Print
Subsidiaries: CCH Peterson; CCH Riverwoods;
 CCH St Petersburg; CCH Tax Compliance;
 CCH Washington DC; LIS (Legal Information
 Services); Washington Service Bureau
Foreign Office(s): Wolters Kluwer nv, Zuid-
 poolsingel 2, Postbus 1030, 2400 BA Alphen
 aan den Rijn, Netherlands *Tel:* (0172) 641
 400 *Fax:* (0172) 474 889 *E-mail:* info@
 wolterskluwer.com *Web Site:* www.
 wolterskluwer.com
Billing Address: PO Box 4307, Carol Stream, IL
 60197-4307
Returns: 7201 McKinney Circle, Frederick, MD
 21704-8356
Warehouse: 4025 Peterson Ave, Chicago, IL
 60646-6085

CCL - Americas, see Center for Creative
 Leadership LLC

Cedar Fort Inc
2373 W 700 S, Springville, UT 84663
Tel: 801-489-4084 *Toll Free Tel:* 800-SKY-BOOK
 (759-2665)
Web Site: cedarfort.com
Key Personnel
Owner & Chmn: Bryce Mortimer
 E-mail: bmortimer@cedarfort.com
Sr Commodities Mgr: Kim Clemons *Tel:* 801-
 477-9029 *E-mail:* kclemons@cedarfort.com
Founded: 1986
Christian (primarily Latter-Day Saints), inspira-
 tional, motivational, LDS fiction & doctrinal.
ISBN Prefix(es): 978-1-55517
Number of titles published annually: 120 Print;
 50 E-Book; 5 Audio
Total Titles: 500 Print

Imprints: Bonneville Books; CFI; Front Table
 Books; Hobble Creek Press; Horizon Pub-
 lishers; Pioneer Press; Plain Sight Publishing;
 Sweetwater Books

Cedar Grove Books, see Cedar Grove Publishing

§Cedar Grove Publishing
Subsidiary of WRTB LLC
3205 Elmhurst St, Rowlett, TX 75088
SAN: 255-3732
Mailing Address: 236 W Portal Ave, No 118, San
 Francisco, CA 94127
Tel: 415-364-8292
E-mail: queries@cedargrovebooks.com
Web Site: www.cedargrovebooks.com
Key Personnel
Pres & Publr: Rochon Perry *E-mail:* rperry@
 cedargrovebooks.com
Edit Dir: J Cameron McClain *E-mail:* j.cameron.
 mcclain.stories@gmail.com
Dir, Soc Media: Rebecca Sims-Nichols
 E-mail: bexlnichols@gmail.com
Founded: 2010
Publish diverse & inclusive books across genres
 with protagonists that overcome adversity by
 staying true to themselves.
ISBN Prefix(es): 978-0-9835077; 978-1-941958
Number of titles published annually: 9 Print; 9
 Online; 9 E-Book; 1 Audio
Total Titles: 9 Print; 9 Online; 9 E-Book; 1 Audio
Distribution Center: Independent Publishers
 Group (IPG), 814 N Franklin St, Chicago, IL
 60610 *Web Site:* www.ipgbook.com
Membership(s): American Library Association
 (ALA); Bay Area Independent Publishers As-
 sociation (BAIPA); Book Industry Study Group
 (BISG); Book Promotion Forum; The Chil-
 dren's Book Council (CBC); Independent Book
 Publishers Association (IBPA); Publishers As-
 sociation of the West (PubWest)

Cedar Tree Books
PO Box 4256, Wilmington, DE 19807
Tel: 302-998-4171 *Fax:* 302-998-4185
E-mail: books@ctpress.com
Web Site: www.cedartreebooks.com
Founded: 1925
This publisher has indicated that 100% of their
 product line is author subsidized.
ISBN Prefix(es): 978-1-892142
Number of titles published annually: 3 Print; 2 E-
 Book
Total Titles: 60 Print; 2 E-Book

CEF Press
Subsidiary of Child Evangelism Fellowship Inc
17482 State Hwy M, Warrenton, MO 63383-0348
Mailing Address: PO Box 348, Warrenton, MO
 63383-0348
Tel: 636-456-4321 *Toll Free Tel:* 800-748-7710
 (cust serv); 800-300-4033 (USA ministries)
 Fax: 636-456-2078 (cust serv)
E-mail: custserv@cefonline.com
Web Site: www.cefonline.com
Founded: 1937
Christian education curriculum.
ISBN Prefix(es): 978-1-55976
Number of titles published annually: 30 Print
Total Titles: 300 Print
Foreign Rep(s): CEFMARK (Australia)

Celebra
Imprint of Penguin Group USA, A Penguin Ran-
 dom House Company
375 Hudson St, New York, NY 10014
Tel: 212-366-2000
E-mail: ecommerce@us.penguingroup.com
Web Site: www.penguin.com
Penguin Random House & its publishing entities
 are not accepting unsol submissions, proposals,

mss, or submission queries via e-mail at this
 time.
Number of titles published annually: 10 Print

§Cengage Learning
20 Channel Center St, Boston, MA 02210
Tel: 617-289-7700 *Toll Free Tel:* 800-354-9706
 Fax: 617-289-7844
E-mail: esales@cengage.com
Web Site: www.cengage.com
Key Personnel
CEO: Michael Hansen
EVP & CFO: Bob Munro
CTO: George Moore
Chief Integration Offr: Rebecca McNamara
Chief Mktg Offr: Sharon Loeb
Chief People Offr & Gen Coun: Ken Carson
Chief People Offr: Gary Fortier
Chief Sales & Mktg Offr: Kevin Stone
Pres, Intl: Alexander Broich
EVP & Chief Strategy Offr: Todd Markson
SVP & Treas: Richard Veith
SVP, Brand Strategy: Daniel Sieger
SVP, Pub Aff: Susan Aspey
VP, Public & Media Rel: Lindsay Stanley
Sr Educ Advisor: George Miller
Cengage Learning delivers highly-customized
 learning solutions for colleges, universities, in-
 structors, students, libraries, government agen-
 cies, corporations & professionals around the
 world. These solutions are delivered through
 specialized content, applications & services
 that foster academic excellence & professional
 development, as well as provide measurable
 learning outcomes to its customers.
Number of titles published annually: 150 Print
Subsidiaries: Gale (www.gale.com); Thorndike
 Press
Billing Address: Cengage Learning Distribution
 Center, 10650 Toebben Dr, Independence, KY
 41051 *Tel:* 859-525-2230
Orders to: Cengage Learning Distribution Center,
 10650 Toebben Dr, Independence, KY 41051
 Tel: 859-525-2230
Returns: Cengage Learning Distribution Center,
 10650 Toebben Dr, Independence, KY 41051
 Tel: 859-525-2230
Warehouse: Cengage Learning Distribution Cen-
 ter, 10650 Toebben Dr, Independence, KY
 41051 *Tel:* 859-525-2230
Distribution Center: Cengage Learning Distribu-
 tion Center, 10650 Toebben Dr, Independence,
 KY 41051 *Tel:* 859-525-2230
Membership(s): Association of American Publish-
 ers (AAP)
See separate listing for:
Charles River Media
Gale
Milady
National Geographic Learning

Center for Creative Leadership LLC
Affiliate of Smith Richardson Foundation
One Leadership Place, Greensboro, NC 27410-
 9427
Tel: 336-545-2810; 336-288-7210 *Fax:* 336-282-
 3284
E-mail: info@ccl.org
Web Site: www.ccl.org/publications
Key Personnel
Pres & CEO: John R Ryan
EVP & CFO: Bradley E Shumaker
EVP & Mng Dir, CCL-EMEA: David G Altman
Founded: 1970
Books on leadership & leadership development.
ISBN Prefix(es): 978-0-912879; 978-0-9638301;
 978-1-882197
Number of titles published annually: 10 Print
Total Titles: 123 Print
Foreign Office(s): CCL-Europe, Rue Neerveld
 101-103 Neerveldstr, 1200 Brussels, Bel-
 gium *Tel:* (02) 679 0910 *Fax:* (02) 673 6306
 E-mail: ccl.emea@ccl.org

CCL-Asia, The Rutherford, Lobby B, No 03-07/08, 89 Science Park Dr 1, Singapore 118261, Singapore *Tel:* 6854 6000 *Fax:* 6854 6001 *E-mail:* ccl.apac@ccl.org
Distributed by Jossey-Bass; John Wiley & Sons Inc
Distributor for Free Press; Harvard Business School Press; Jossey-Bass; Lominger Inc; John Wiley & Sons Inc

Center for East Asian Studies (CEAS)
Subsidiary of Western Washington University
Western Washington University, 516 High St, Bellingham, WA 98225
Tel: 360-650-3339 *Fax:* 360-650-6110
E-mail: eas@wwu.edu
Web Site: www.wwu.edu/eas
Key Personnel
Dir: Prof Massimiliano Tomasi
   E-mail: massimiliano.tomasi@wwu.edu
Mng Ed: Dr Scott Pearce *Tel:* 360-650-3897
   E-mail: scott.pearce@wwu.edu
Founded: 1971
East Asia & Iran; Asia mainly monographs.
ISBN Prefix(es): 978-0-914584
Number of titles published annually: 3 Print
Total Titles: 30 Print

§Center for Futures Education Inc
345 Erie St, Grove City, PA 16127
Mailing Address: PO Box 309, Grove City, PA 16127
Tel: 724-458-5860 *Fax:* 724-458-5962
E-mail: info@thectr.com
Web Site: www.thectr.com
Key Personnel
Treas: Lyn M Sennholz *E-mail:* lyn@thectr.com
Founded: 1981
Print & online books on commodity futures & securities.
ISBN Prefix(es): 978-0-915513
Number of titles published annually: 12 Print
Total Titles: 50 Print; 15 E-Book

The Center for Learning
Division of Social Studies School Service
10200 Jefferson Blvd, Culver City, CA 90232
Mailing Address: PO Box 802, Culver City, CA 90232
Tel: 310-839-2436 *Toll Free Tel:* 800-421-4246
   Fax: 310-839-2249 *Toll Free Fax:* 800-944-5432
E-mail: access@socialstudies.com
Web Site: www.centerforlearning.org
Key Personnel
HR Mgr: Russell Kantor
Founded: 1965
Founded to publish values based curriculum materials. All materials are written by master teachers who integrate academic objectives & ethical values. Nonprofit educational publisher of value based curriculum units with reproducible handouts for teachers of English/Language Arts, social studies, novel/dramas, biographies & religion. Specialize in advanced placement, genres; American, British & World novels & literature; skills, supplementary topics, writing; economics, social & global issues, US government & history, world history; Catholic teaching, ministry, retreats, adult faith resources, marriage & parenting, divorce & blended families, abstinence education & chastity; publish lesson plans for elementary & secondary grades.
ISBN Prefix(es): 978-1-56077
Number of titles published annually: 20 Print
Total Titles: 600 Print

Center for the Collaborative Classroom
1001 Marina Village Pkwy, Suite 110, Alameda, CA 94501-1042

Tel: 510-533-0213 *Toll Free Tel:* 800-666-7270
   Fax: 510-464-3670
E-mail: info@collaborativeclassroom.org; clientsupport@collaborativeclassroom.org
Web Site: www.collaborativeclassroom.org
Key Personnel
Founder: Eric Schaps
Pres & CEO: Roger King *E-mail:* rking@collaborativeclassroom.org
SVP & CFO: Brent Welling *E-mail:* bwelling@collaborativeclassroom.org
COO: Kelly Stuart *E-mail:* kstuart@collaborativeclassroom.org
CTO: Tim Millen
VP, Communs: Peter Brunn
VP, Prog Devt: Lana Costantini MFA
Founded: 1980
Books, teacher study packages, literature guides, in school & after school curricula in character education, reading & mathematics.
ISBN Prefix(es): 978-1-885603; 978-1-57621; 978-0-439
Number of titles published annually: 15 Print
Total Titles: 450 Print

Centering Corp
7230 Maple St, Omaha, NE 68134
SAN: 298-1815
Tel: 402-553-1200 *Toll Free Tel:* 866-218-0101
   Fax: 402-553-0507
E-mail: orders@centering.org
Web Site: www.centering.org
Key Personnel
Founder & Pres: Joy Johnson
Exec Dir: Janet Roberts *E-mail:* centeringcorp@aol.com
Busn Dir: Marc Roberts
Dir, Devt: Ben Schroeder
Founded: 1977
Bereavement support; specializes in divorce, grief & loss. Nonprofit organization.
ISBN Prefix(es): 978-1-56123
Number of titles published annually: 10 Print
Total Titles: 150 Print

Centerstream Publishing LLC
PO Box 17878, Anaheim Hills, CA 92817-7878
SAN: 683-8022
Tel: 714-779-9390
E-mail: centerstrm@aol.com
Web Site: www.centerstream-usa.com
Key Personnel
Owner: Ron Middlebrook
Founded: 1971
Music history, bios, music instruction books, videos & DVDs: all instruments.
ISBN Prefix(es): 978-0-931759; 978-1-57467
Number of titles published annually: 20 Print; 10 CD-ROM
Total Titles: 250 Print; 30 CD-ROM
Subsidiaries: Centerbrook Publishing
Distributed by Hal Leonard Corp
Membership(s): Independent Book Publishers Association (IBPA)

Central Conference of American Rabbis/CCAR Press
355 Lexington Ave, New York, NY 10017
SAN: 204-3262
Tel: 212-972-3636 *Fax:* 212-692-0819
E-mail: info@ccarpress.org
Web Site: www.ccarpress.org
Key Personnel
Chief Exec: Steven A Fox *Tel:* 212-542-8777
   E-mail: sfox@ccarnet.org
Publr & Dir, Press: Hara Person *Tel:* 212-542-8799 *E-mail:* hperson@ccarnet.org
Founded: 1889
Books on liturgy & Jewish practices from a liberal point of view.
ISBN Prefix(es): 978-0-88123; 978-0-916694

Number of titles published annually: 10 Print; 10 E-Book
Total Titles: 102 Print; 59 E-Book
Imprints: Reform Judaism Publishing
Shipping Address: PBD Worldwide, 1650 Bluegrass Lakes Pkwy, Alpharetta, GA 30004
Warehouse: PBD Worldwide, 1650 Bluegrass Lakes Pkwy, Alpharetta, GA 30004

§Central Recovery Press (CRP)
Unit of Central Recovery Treatment
3321 N Buffalo Dr, Suite 275, Las Vegas, NV 89129
Tel: 702-868-5830 *Fax:* 702-868-5831
E-mail: sales@centralrecovery.com
Web Site: centralrecoverypress.com
Key Personnel
Exec Ed: Nancy Schenck *E-mail:* nschenck@centralrecovery.com
Mng Ed: Valerie Killeen *E-mail:* vkilleen@centralrecovery.com
Sales & Mktg Mgr: Patrick Hughes
   E-mail: phughes@centralrecovery.com
Spec Sales Mgr: John Davis
Committed to building lasting & meaningful connections based on shared values & principles. Library of quality materials across the full spectrum of behavioral healthcare topics, including addiction treatment & recovery, addiction & the family, parenting, relationships, trauma, grief & loss & mindfulness. Mission is to shift the prevailing perception of addiction, co-occurring & other behavioral health issues as moral failing, character weakness, or vice, offering materials that promote a broader view of recovery & encourage a holistic approach to emotional, physical, mental & spiritual well-being.
ISBN Prefix(es): 978-0-9799869
Number of titles published annually: 12 Print; 12 E-Book; 8 Audio
Total Titles: 140 Print; 125 E-Book; 29 Audio

§Chain Store Guide (CSG)
3710 Corporex Park Dr, Suite 310, Tampa, FL 33619
Toll Free Tel: 800-927-9292 (orders) *Fax:* 813-627-6888
E-mail: webmaster@csgis.com
Web Site: www.csgis.com
Key Personnel
EVP: Carmen Vasquez-Perez
IT Dir: Scott Mitchell
Founded: 1934
Directories of retail & wholesale companies.
ISBN Prefix(es): 978-0-86730
Number of titles published annually: 5 Print
Total Titles: 21 Print; 21 Online

Chalice Press
Division of Christian Board of Publications
483 E Lockwood Ave, Suite 100, St Louis, MO 63119
SAN: 201-4408
Tel: 314-231-8500 *Toll Free Tel:* 800-366-3383
   Fax: 314-231-8524; 770-280-4039 (orders)
E-mail: customerservice@chalicepress.com
Web Site: www.chalicepress.com
Key Personnel
Pres & Publr: Brad Lyons *E-mail:* blyons@chalicepress.com
Assoc Publr & Opers Dir: Corinne Lattimer
   E-mail: clattimer@chalicepress.com
Sales & Mktg Dir: Deborah Arca *E-mail:* darca@chalicepress.com
Founded: 1911
Religion (Protestant) & hymnals.
ISBN Prefix(es): 978-0-8272
Number of titles published annually: 15 Print
Total Titles: 300 Print
Orders to: PO Box 933119, Atlanta, GA 31193-3119

Returns: 3280 Summit Ridge Pkwy, Suite 100, Duluth, GA 30096 *Fax:* 770-280-4039
Warehouse: 3280 Summit Ridge Pkwy, Suite 100, Duluth, GA 30096 *Fax:* 770-280-4039
Distribution Center: Baker & Taylor Publisher Services, 30 Amberwood Pkwy, Ashland, OH 44805 *Tel:* 567-215-0030 *Toll Free Tel:* 888-814-0208 *E-mail:* info@btpubservices.com *Web Site:* www.btpubservices.com
Sperlings Church Supply, 85 Bathurst Dr, Waterloo, ON N2V 1Z4, Canada *Toll Free Tel:* 888-838-6626 *Fax:* 519-725-0668
Rainbow Book Agencies, 303 Arthur St, Fairfield, Victoria 3078, Australia *Tel:* 9481-6611 *Fax:* 9481-2371 *E-mail:* rba@rainbowbooks.com.au

§Channel Photographics
980 Lincoln Ave, Suite 200-B, San Rafael, CA 94901
Tel: 415-456-2934 *Fax:* 415-456-4124
Web Site: www.channelphotographics.com
Key Personnel
Co-Publr: Adrianne Casey *E-mail:* adrianne@channelphotographics.com
Publr: Steven Goff *E-mail:* steven@channelphotographics.com
This publisher has indicated that 50% of their product line is author subsidized.
ISBN Prefix(es): 978-0-9819942; 978-0-9744029; 978-0-9766708; 978-0-9773399; 978-0-9826137; 978-0-9832983
Number of titles published annually: 10 Print
Total Titles: 50 Print
Branch Office(s)
244 Fifth Ave, Suite 2464, New York, NY 10001 *Tel:* 212-627-1400 *Toll Free Fax:* 866-729-2725
16510 203 Place NE, Woodinville, WA 98077 *Tel:* 425-354-3690; 206-390-9617 (cell) *Fax:* 425-354-3664
Foreign Office(s): 8 Commercial Tower, 30/F, Unit 06-07, 8 Sun Yip St, Chai Wan, Hong Kong
Via Meucci 24, 37036 San Martino Buon Albergo, Verona VR, Italy *Tel:* (045) 994855 *Fax:* (045) 994746

Chaosium Inc
3450 Wooddale Ct, Ann Arbor, MI 48104
SAN: 692-6460
Tel: 734-972-9551
E-mail: customerservice@chaosium.com
Web Site: www.chaosium.com
Key Personnel
Pres: Rick Meints *E-mail:* rick@chaosium.com
Founded: 1975
Publisher of horror anthologies & role playing games.
ISBN Prefix(es): 978-0-933635; 978-1-56882
Number of titles published annually: 15 Print; 12 E-Book
Total Titles: 241 Print; 60 E-Book
Orders to: 719 E Murray St, Rockport, TX 78382, Contact: Dustin Wright *Tel:* 361-727-9458 *E-mail:* dustin@chaosium.com
Warehouse: Bang Fulfillment Service, 217 Etak Dr, Brainerd, MN 56401

Charisma Media
600 Rinehart Rd, Lake Mary, FL 32746
Tel: 407-333-0600 (all imprints)
Toll Free Tel: 800-283-8494 (Charisma Media, Siloam Press, Creation House); 800-665-1468 *Fax:* 407-333-7100 (all imprints)
E-mail: charisma@charismamedia.com
Web Site: www.charismamedia.com
Key Personnel
Owner & Pres: Stephen Strang
Founded: 1975
Christianity.
ISBN Prefix(es): 978-0-88419
Number of titles published annually: 200 Print

Total Titles: 500 Print; 2 Audio
Imprints: Casa Creation (international publishing group); Creation House (co-publishing group); Siloam Press (health publishing group)
Membership(s): Evangelical Christian Publishers Association (ECPA)

§Charles Press Publishers
Subsidiary of Oxbridge Corporation
230 N 21 St, Suite 312, Philadelphia, PA 19103
Tel: 215-470-5977
E-mail: mail@charlespresspub.com
Web Site: charlespresspub.com
Key Personnel
Publr: Lauren Meltzer *E-mail:* lauren@charlespresspub.com
Founded: 1974
Independent traditional publishing house specializing in social & behavioral science books for the academic, professional & trade markets.
ISBN Prefix(es): 978-0-914783
Number of titles published annually: 10 Print; 1 CD-ROM; 2 E-Book
Total Titles: 125 Print; 6 CD-ROM; 2 E-Book
Returns: c/o Self-Service Storage, 2000 Hamilton St, No 2884, Philadelphia, PA 19130 (permission must be requested in advance of returns)

Charles River Media
Imprint of Cengage Learning
20 Channel Center St, Boston, MA 02210
Tel: 617-289-7700 *Fax:* 617-289-7844
Web Site: www.cengage.com; www.delmarlearning.com/charlesriver
Founded: 1994
Publishing computer books for web development, music technology, game development, graphic design & digital video.
ISBN Prefix(es): 978-1-886801; 978-1-58450
Number of titles published annually: 50 Print; 2 CD-ROM; 150 Online; 100 E-Book
Total Titles: 200 Print; 5 CD-ROM; 150 Online; 100 E-Book
Foreign Rep(s): IPR (Middle East); Login Canada (Canada); Thomson Learning (Asia); Transatlantic (Europe); Woodslane (Australia)
Foreign Rights: David Pallai

Charles Scribner's Sons®
Imprint of Gale
27500 Drake Rd, Farmington Hills, MI 48331-3535
Toll Free Tel: 800-877-4253 *Toll Free Fax:* 800-414-5043
E-mail: gale.galeord@cengage.com
Web Site: www.gale.com/scribners
Founded: 1846
Publishes reference books in fields of history, science & literature for audiences ranging from high school students to professional researchers.
ISBN Prefix(es): 978-0-684
Number of titles published annually: 4 E-Book

Charlesbridge Publishing Inc
85 Main St, Watertown, MA 02472
Tel: 617-926-0329 *Toll Free Tel:* 800-225-3214 *Fax:* 617-926-5720 *Toll Free Fax:* 800-926-5775
E-mail: books@charlesbridge.com
Web Site: www.charlesbridge.com
Key Personnel
Pres & CEO: Brent Farmer *E-mail:* bfarmer@charlesbridge.com
Publr & COO: Mary Ann Sabia *E-mail:* masabia@charlesbridge.com
CFO: Brent Farmer, Jr *E-mail:* brent.farmer@charlesbridge.com
VP, Prodn: Brian Walker *E-mail:* bwalker@charlesbridge.com
Assoc Publr & Edit Dir: Yolanda Scott *E-mail:* yolanda@charlesbridge.com

Art Dir: Diane Earley *E-mail:* dearley@charlesbridge.com
Founded: 1980
Children's illustrated picture books, board books, early readers, chapter books, middle grade & young adult fiction & nonfiction. Adult imprint, Imagine Publishing: general trade, cookbooks, puzzle/game, humor & nonfiction.
ISBN Prefix(es): 978-0-88106; 978-1-57091; 978-1-56566; 978-0-934738; 978-1-890674; 978-1-879085; 978-1-58089; 978-1-936140 (Imagine)
Number of titles published annually: 60 Print; 50 E-Book
Total Titles: 750 Print; 500 E-Book
Imprints: CharlesbridgeTEEN; Imagine Publishing (www.imaginebooks.net)
Orders to: Penguin Random House Publisher Services (PRHPS), 400 Hahn Rd, Westminster, MD 21157 *Toll Free Tel:* 800-733-3000
Returns: Penguin Random House Inc, 1019 N State Rd 47, Crawfordsville, IN 47933
Distribution Center: Penguin Random House Publisher Services (PRHPS), 400 Hahn Rd, Westminster, MD 21157 *E-mail:* distribution@randomhouse.com
Membership(s): American Booksellers Association (ABA); American Library Association (ALA); Association of Booksellers for Children; Bookbuilders of Boston; The Children's Book Council (CBC); Education Market Association; International Literacy Association (ILA); MSA; NCBA; NEBA; TLA

§Chelsea Green Publishing Co
85 N Main St, Suite 120, White River Junction, VT 05001
SAN: 669-7631
Tel: 802-295-6300 *Toll Free Tel:* 800-639-4099 (cust serv & orders) *Fax:* 802-295-6444
E-mail: customerservice@chelseagreen.com; editorial@chelseagreen.com; publicity@chelseagreen.com; rights@chelseagreen.com
Web Site: www.chelseagreen.com
Key Personnel
Pres & Publr: Margo Baldwin *E-mail:* mbaldwin@chelseagreen.com
Busn & Dist Dir: Sandi Eaton *E-mail:* seaton@chelseagreen.com
Dir, Mktg: Sean Maher *E-mail:* smaher@chelseagreen.com
Prodn Dir: Patricia Stone *E-mail:* pstone@chelseagreen.com
Sr Ed: Fern Marshall Bradley *E-mail:* fbradley@chelseagreen.com; Brianne Goodspeed *E-mail:* bgoodspeed@chelseagreen.com; Michael Metivier *E-mail:* mmetivier@chelseagreen.com; Ben Watson *E-mail:* bwatson@chelseagreen.com
Author Events Mgr: Jenna Dimmick Stewart *E-mail:* jstewart@chelseagreen.com
Spec & Corp Sales Mgr: Darrell Koerner *E-mail:* dkoerner@chelseagreen.com
Trade Sales Mgr: Michael Weaver *E-mail:* mweaver@chelseagreen.com
Prodn Coord: Alexander Bullett *E-mail:* abullet@chelseagreen.com
Founded: 1984
Books for sustainable living including: environment, building, nature, outdoors, sustainability, organic gardening, home, renewable energy, homesteading, politics & current events.
ISBN Prefix(es): 978-0-930031; 978-1-890132; 978-1-933392; 978-1-60358
Number of titles published annually: 35 Print; 35 E-Book
Total Titles: 300 Print; 250 E-Book
Foreign Office(s): Chelsea Green Publishing UK Ltd, South Wing, Somerset House, Strand, London WC2R 1LA, United Kingdom, Mng Dir: Matt Haslum *E-mail:* mhaslum@chelseagreen.com
Distributor for AATEC Publications; American Council for an Energy Efficient Economy

(ACEEE); Anomaly Press; Avalon House; Boye Knives Press; Cal-Earth; Earth Pledge; Eco Logic Books; Ecological Design Institute; Ecological Design Press; Empowerment Institute; Filaree Productions; Flower Press; Foundation for Deep Ecology; Fox Maple Press; Green Books; Green Building Press; Green Man Publishing; Groundworks; Hand Print Press; Holmgren Design Services; Jenkins Publishing; Knossus Project; Left To Write Press; Madison Area Community Supported Agriculture Coalition; Marion Institute; marketumbrella.org; Metamorphic Press; Moneta Publications; Ottographics; Peregrinzilla; Permanent Publications; Daniela Piazza Editore; Polyface; Propriometrics Press; Rainsource Press; Raven Press; Anita Roddick Publications; Rural Science Institute; Seed Savers; Service Employees International Union; Slow Food Editore; Solar Design Association; Stone Pier Press; Stonefield Publishing; Sun Plans Inc; Sustainability Press; Trailblazer Press; Trust for Public Land; Yes Books
Foreign Rep(s): Booktopia Publisher Services (Australia, New Zealand); Grantham Book Services (UK); SG Distributors (South Africa); University of Toronto Press Distribution (Canada)
Returns: 22880 Quicksilver Dr, Dulles, VA 20166

Chelsea House
Imprint of Infobase Learning
132 W 31 St, 17th fl, New York, NY 10001
SAN: 169-7331
Toll Free Tel: 800-322-8755 *Toll Free Fax:* 800-678-3633
E-mail: custserv@factsonfile.com; info@infobase.com
Web Site: www.infobasepublishing.com; www.infobase.com
Key Personnel
Pres & CEO: Mark McDonnell
CFO: Jim Housley
Dir, Publicity: Laurie Katz
Dir, Opers & Sales: Mark Zielinski
Dir, Mktg: Zina Scarpulla
Edit Dir: Laurie Likoff
Dir, Licensing & Intl Sales: Ben Jacobs
Founded: 1966
Offers timely & engaging young adult sets & series ebooks spanning a wide variety of subject areas. Chelsea Clubhouse, its elementary imprint, presents easy-to-read, full-color books for young readers in grades 2-6.
ISBN Prefix(es): 978-0-87754; 978-0-7910; 978-1-55546; 978-1-60413; 978-1-4381; 978-1-61753
Number of titles published annually: 230 E-Book
Total Titles: 1,866 Print; 1,680 E-Book
Imprints: Chelsea Clubhouse
Returns: Chelsea House Publishers Returns Dept, c/o Maple Press Distribution Ctr, 704 Legionaire Dr, Fredericksburg, PA 17026
Warehouse: Maple Logistics Solutions, Lebanon Distribution Ctr, 704 Legionaire Dr, Fredericksburg, PA 17026
Distribution Center: Maple Logistics Solutions, Lebanon Distribution Ctr, 704 Legionaire Dr, Fredericksburg, PA 17026
Membership(s): American Library Association (ALA); Association of American Publishers (AAP)

§Cheng & Tsui Co Inc
25 West St, 2nd fl, Boston, MA 02111-1213
Tel: 617-988-2400 *Toll Free Tel:* 800-554-1963
Fax: 617-426-3669; 617-556-8964
E-mail: service@cheng-tsui.com; orders@cheng-tsui.com
Web Site: www.cheng-tsui.com
Key Personnel
Pres: Jill Cheng
Founded: 1979

Publisher, importer & exporter of Asian books in English. Publish & distribute Asia related books & Chinese, Japanese & Korean language learning textbooks.
ISBN Prefix(es): 978-0-917056; 978-0-88727
Number of titles published annually: 30 Print
Total Titles: 640 Print; 75 CD-ROM; 4 Online; 4 E-Book
Distributor for Action Language Learning; aha! Chinese; Bider Technology; Cengage Learning Australia; China International Book Trading Co (Beijing, selected titles only); China Soft; China Sprout; Crabtree Publishing Co; Curriculum Corp; Facets Video; Ilchokak Publishers; Italian School of East Asian Studies; JPT America Inc; Oxford University Press; Pan Asian Publications; Panmun Academic Services; Panpac Education; Paradigm Busters; Pearson Education Australia; Royal Asiatic Society (Korea Branch); SMC Publishing; Sogang University Institute; SUP Publishing Logistics; US International Publishing; White Rabbit Press; Zeitgeist Films
Returns: Publishers Storage & Shipping Corp, 46 Development Rd, Fitchburg, MA 01420
Warehouse: Publishers Storage & Shipping Corp, 46 Development Rd, Fitchburg, MA 01420
Tel: 978-345-2121 ext 223 *Fax:* 978-348-1233
Web Site: www.pssc.com

Cherry Hill Publishing LLC
24344 Del Amo Rd, Ramona, CA 92065
SAN: 255-0075
Tel: 858-829-5550 *Toll Free Tel:* 800-407-1072
Fax: 760-203-1200
E-mail: operations@cherryhillpublishing.com; sales@cherryhillpublishing.com
Web Site: www.cherryhillpublishing.com
Key Personnel
Pres: Rick Roane *E-mail:* rick@cherryhillpublishing.com
Returns: Sharon Roane *Tel:* 858-735-5397
E-mail: sharon@cherryhillpublishing.com
Founded: 2002
Publisher of audiobook titles.
ISBN Prefix(es): 978-0-9843759; 978-0-9723298; 978-0-9830086; 978-1-937028; 978-1-62079
Number of titles published annually: 5 CD-ROM; 20 Online; 5 E-Book; 15 Audio
Total Titles: 1 Print; 10 CD-ROM; 150 Online; 40 E-Book; 90 Audio
Distribution Center: Baker & Taylor, 2550 W Tyvola Rd, Suite 300, Charlotte, NC 28217
Toll Free Tel: 800-775-1800 *Fax:* 704-998-3100
Web Site: www.baker-taylor.com
Midwest Tape, 6950 Hall St, Holland, OH 43528 *Toll Free Tel:* 800-875-2785 *Toll Free Fax:* 800-444-6645 *E-mail:* info@midwesttapes.com *Web Site:* www.midwesttapes.com
Membership(s): Audio Publishers Association

Chestnut Hills Press, see BrickHouse Books Inc

Chicago Review Press
814 N Franklin St, Chicago, IL 60610
Tel: 312-337-0747 *Toll Free Tel:* 800-888-4741
Fax: 312-337-5110
E-mail: frontdesk@chicagoreviewpress.com
Web Site: www.chicagoreviewpress.com
Key Personnel
Group Publr: Cynthia Sherry
Dir, Mktg: Andrea Baird
Dir, Prodn: Allison Felus
Dir, Publicity: Caitlin Eck
Mng Ed: Michelle Williams
Sr Ed: Jerome Pohlen; Lisa Reardon; Kara Rota; Yuval Taylor
Edit, Amberjack Publishing: Cherrita Lee
Mktg & Publicity, Amberjack Publishing: Jana Good
Founded: 1973

ISBN Prefix(es): 978-1-56976; 978-1-55652; 978-1-88305 (Ball Publishing)
Number of titles published annually: 65 Print; 65 E-Book
Total Titles: 1,000 Print; 1,000 E-Book
Imprints: Academy Chicago; Amberjack Publishing; Ball Publishing; Bright Ring; Council Oak Books; Lawrence Hill Books; Parenting Press; Zephyr Press
Divisions: Independent Publishers Group
Foreign Rights: The Susan Schulman Agency (worldwide)
Distribution Center: Independent Publishers Group, 814 N Franklin St, Chicago, IL 60610
Tel: 312-337-0747 *Toll Free Tel:* 800-888-4741 *Fax:* 312-337-5985 *E-mail:* frontdesk@ipgbook.com *Web Site:* www.ipgbook.com
See separate listing for:
Academy Chicago
Parenting Press

Chickadee Prince Books
378 Fourth St, Brooklyn, NY 11215
Tel: 917-854-6073
E-mail: submissions@chickadeeprince.com
Web Site: chickadeeprince.com
Founded: 2013
We are a small press that publishes acclaimed fiction & nonfiction of all genres. Books include Donna Levin's contemporary women's fiction novel, *There's More Than One Way Home* & Jay Greenfield's post-war saga, *Max's Diamonds*. We are not a subsidy or hybrid press; we pay a small advance & cover all costs of publication, publicity & bookstores marketing/outreach. After publication, authors assist in nonfinancial ways to help to bring more CPB books into print, which allows us to publish books other presses would not & also creates a true community of writers. Distributed through Ingram, we employ our own bookstore representatives.
ISBN Prefix(es): 978-0-9913274; 978-0-9997569
Number of titles published annually: 5 Print; 5 Online; 5 E-Book
Total Titles: 16 Print; 18 Online; 18 E-Book

Child Welfare League of America (CWLA)
727 15 St NW, Suite 1200, Washington, DC 20005
SAN: 201-9876
Tel: 202-688-4200
E-mail: cwla@cwla.org
Web Site: www.cwla.org/pubs
Key Personnel
Dir, Pubns: Marlene Saulsbury *Tel:* 202-590-8748
E-mail: msaulsbury@cwla.org
Founded: 1920
Provide relevant & timely publications that enable CWLA members & the child welfare field at large to improve services to children & their families.
ISBN Prefix(es): 978-0-87868; 978-1-58760
Number of titles published annually: 9 Print
Total Titles: 167 Print
Imprints: CWLA Press

Children's Book Press
Imprint of Lee & Low Books
95 Madison Ave, Suite 1205, New York, NY 10016
Tel: 212-779-4400 *Fax:* 212-683-1894
E-mail: general@leeandlow.com; orders@leeandlow.com; sales@leeandlow.com
Web Site: www.leeandlow.com
Key Personnel
Pres: Craig Low
Opers: John Man
Founded: 1975
Multicultural & bilingual picture books for children. Central American, African-American, Asian-American, Hispanic-American, Native

American tales, folklore, contemporary fiction & nonfiction.
ISBN Prefix(es): 978-0-89239
Number of titles published annually: 6 Print
Total Titles: 30 Print
Distribution Center: Ingram Books, One Ingram Blvd, La Vergne, TN 37086 *Tel:* 615-793-5000 *Toll Free Tel:* 800-932-8200 *E-mail:* customerservice@ingrambook.com *Web Site:* www.ingrambook.com

Child's Play®
Affiliate of Child's Play (International) Ltd
250 Minot Ave, Auburn, ME 04210
Tel: 207-784-7252 *Toll Free Tel:* 800-639-6404 *Fax:* 207-784-7358 *Toll Free Fax:* 800-854-6989
E-mail: chpmaine@aol.com
Web Site: www.childs-play.com
Key Personnel
VP, Sales & Mktg: Joseph Gardner *E-mail:* joe@childsplayusa.com
Gen Mgr: Laurie Reynolds *E-mail:* laurie@childsplayusa.com
Founded: 1972
Children's books, games, toys & AV materials.
ISBN Prefix(es): 978-0-85953; 978-1-904550; 978-1-84643
Number of titles published annually: 30 Print
Total Titles: 450 Print; 8 Audio

§The Child's World Inc
1980 Lookout Dr, North Mankato, MN 56003-1705
Tel: 507-385-1044 *Toll Free Tel:* 800-599-READ (599-7323) *Toll Free Fax:* 888-320-2329
E-mail: sales@childsworld.com
Web Site: childsworld.com
Key Personnel
Pres: Mike Peterson
Off Mgr: Amy Dols
Founded: 1968
K-8 library books for childhood education; social studies.
ISBN Prefix(es): 978-0-89565; 978-0-913778; 978-1-56766; 978-1-59296; 978-1-60253; 978-1-60954; 978-1-60973; 978-1-61473; 978-1-62323; 978-1-62687; 978-1-63143; 978-1-63407; 978-1-5038
Number of titles published annually: 200 Print; 100 E-Book
Total Titles: 850 Print; 1,018 E-Book
Imprints: Tradition Books
Distributor for Tradition Books

§China Books
Division of Sinomedia International Group
360 Swift Ave, Suite 48, South San Francisco, CA 94080
SAN: 169-0167
Fax: 650-872-7808
E-mail: editor.sinomedia@gmail.com
Key Personnel
Edit Dir: Chris Robyn *Tel:* 650-872-7718 ext 312 *E-mail:* chris@sinomediausa.com
Sales Mgr: Kelly Feng *Tel:* 650-872-7076 ext 310 *E-mail:* kelly@chinabooks.com
Founded: 1960
Fiction, trade, nonfiction, dictionaries, encyclopedias, maps, atlases, periodicals, sidelines, foreign language, secondary textbooks, juvenile & young adult, subscription & mail order, hardcover & paperback trade books; government, language arts, travel.
ISBN Prefix(es): 978-0-8351
Number of titles published annually: 12 Print
Total Titles: 230 Print

China Books & Periodicals Inc, see China Books

Chosen Books
Division of Baker Publishing Group
11400 Hampshire Ave S, Bloomington, MN 55438-2852
Tel: 952-829-2500 *Toll Free Tel:* 800-877-2665 (orders only) *Fax:* 616-676-9573 *Toll Free Fax:* 800-398-3111 (orders only)
Web Site: www.chosenbooks.com
Key Personnel
Pres, Baker Publishing Group: Dwight Baker
Edit Dir: Jane Campbell *E-mail:* jcampbell@chosenbooks.com
Founded: 1971
Christian.
ISBN Prefix(es): 978-0-8007
Number of titles published annually: 33 Print; 33 E-Book
Total Titles: 800 Print
Foreign Rep(s): Christian Art (South Africa); Koorong Books Ltd (Australia); Macmillan Distribution (MDL) (Europe, UK); Parasource (Canada); Soul Distributors Ltd (New Zealand)

§Christian Liberty Press
502 W Euclid Ave, Arlington Heights, IL 60004-5402
Toll Free Tel: 800-348-0899 *Fax:* 847-259-2941
E-mail: custserv@christianlibertypress.com
Web Site: www.shopchristianliberty.com
Key Personnel
Dir: Lars Johnson *E-mail:* larsj@christianlibertypress.com
Founded: 1984
Publisher of Christian education materials.
ISBN Prefix(es): 978-1-930092; 978-1-930367; 978-1-932971; 978-1-935796; 978-1-62982
Number of titles published annually: 6 Print; 3 CD-ROM; 4 Audio
Total Titles: 150 Print; 8 CD-ROM; 38 Audio

Christian Light Publications Inc
1051 Mount Clinton Pike, Harrisonburg, VA 22802
Mailing Address: PO Box 1212, Harrisonburg, VA 22803-1212
Tel: 540-434-1003 *Toll Free Tel:* 800-776-0478 *Fax:* 540-433-8896
E-mail: info@clp.org; orders@clp.org
Web Site: www.clp.org
Key Personnel
Gen Mgr & Secy, Bd of Dirs: Andrew K Crider
Founded: 1969
Books, booklets, tracts, Sunday school, vacation Bible school & Christian day school curriculum.
ISBN Prefix(es): 978-0-87813
Number of titles published annually: 17 Print
Total Titles: 160 Print

Christian Schools International
3350 E Paris Ave SE, Grand Rapids, MI 49512-3054
SAN: 204-1804
Tel: 616-957-1070 *Toll Free Tel:* 800-635-8288 *Fax:* 616-957-5022
E-mail: info@csionline.org
Web Site: www.csionline.org
Key Personnel
Pres & CEO: Joel Westa *Tel:* 616-957-1070 ext 254 *E-mail:* jwesta@csionline.org
COO: Darryl Shelton *Tel:* 616-957-1070 ext 257 *E-mail:* dshelton@csionline.org
Exec to Pres: Deb Lantz *Tel:* 616-957-1070 ext 253 *E-mail:* dlantz@csionline.org
Founded: 1920
Classroom curriculum resources for students & teachers.
ISBN Prefix(es): 978-0-87463; 978-1-935876
Number of titles published annually: 18 Print; 2 CD-ROM
Total Titles: 172 Print; 11 CD-ROM
Imprints: CSI Publications

§The Christian Science Publishing Society
Division of The First Church of Christ, Scientist
210 Massachusetts Ave, Boston, MA 02115
Tel: 617-450-2000
E-mail: info@christianscience.com
Web Site: christianscience.com
Founded: 1879
Books on healing, health & spirituality; major title: *Science & Health with Key to the Scriptures* by Mary Baker Eddy, available in 16 languages & English braille.
ISBN Prefix(es): 978-0-87952
Number of titles published annually: 17 Print
Total Titles: 17 Print

Chronicle Books
680 Second St, San Francisco, CA 94107
SAN: 202-165X
Tel: 415-537-4200 *Toll Free Tel:* 800-759-0190 (cust serv) *Fax:* 415-537-4460 *Toll Free Fax:* 800-858-7787 (orders); 800-286-9471 (cust serv)
E-mail: frontdesk@chroniclebooks.com
Web Site: www.chroniclebooks.com
Key Personnel
Chmn & CEO: Nion McEvoy
Pres: Tyrrell Mahoney
VP, Opers & Fin: Tom Fernald
VP, Sales & Mktg: Kim Anderson
Publr: Christine Carswell
Exec Dir, Dom Sales: Rachel Geiger
Exec Dir, HR: Todd Presley
Exec Dir, IT: Mike Conway
Exec Dir, Mktg & Publicity: Liza Algar
Exec Dir, Opers: John Carlson
Exec Dir, Prodn: Lindsay Sablosky
Exec Publg Design Dir: Sara Schneider
Exec Publg Dir, Adult Trade: Christina Amini
Exec Publg Dir, Children's: Ginee Seo
Mng Dir, Chronicle Prism: Mark Tauber
Exec Ed, Art: Bridget Watson Payne
Edit Dir, Children's: Kelli Chipponeri
Edit Dir, Entertainment: Rebecca Hunt
Edit Dir, Food & Lifestyle: Sarah Billingsley
Sr Dir, Mktg, Adult Trade: Christina Loff
Children's Mktg Dir: Andie Krawczyk
Design Dir: Kristen Hewitt
Design Dir, Children's Publg: Jennifer Tolo Pierce
Design Dir, Mktg Communs: Liz Rico
Dir, Intl & Subs Rts Sales: Lynda Zuber Sassi
Dir, Mng Edit: Beth Weber
Dir, Natl Specialty & Mass Mkt Sales: Shelley Sanders
Dir, Spec Sales: Lisa Bach
Prodn Dir, Creative Devt: Erin Thacker
Prodn Dir, Purch & Vendor Mgmt: Beth Steiner
Assoc Dir, Intl Sales: Tessa Ingersoll
Assoc Dir, Mktg, Chronicle Prism: Jennifer Jensen
Assoc Dir, Trade Sales: Courtney Payne
Sr Sales Mgr, Spec Mkts: Julia Carvalho
Natl Acct Mgr, Barnes & Noble & Ingram: Karen Finlay
Natl Accts Mgr: Genny McAuley; Samantha Steele
Sr Prodn Mgr: Wendy Thorpe
Sr Prodn Mgr, Prodn Servs: Leslie Cohen
Sr Proj & Busn Process Mgr: Elke Olson
Sr Sales Mgr: Kate Herman; Liz Marotte
Sr Web Mgr: Viniita Moran
Compliance Mgr: Eliz Fink
Digital Mktg Mgr, Adult: Jenna Homen
Digital Mktg Mgr, Children's: Madison Killen
Dist Client Acct Mgr: Graham Barry; Mercury Ellis; Christina Mott
HR Mgr: Scott Haney
Inventory Planning Mgr: Mary O'Hara
Food & Drink Mktg & Publicity Mgr: Joyce Lin
Mktg & Publicity Mgr, Lifestyle: Alexandra Brown
Mktg Mgr, Children's: Mary Duke; Jaime Wong
Mktg Mgr, Entertainment: Brittany Boughter
Mktg Mgr, Food & Lifestyle: Cynthia Shannon

Mgr, Prodn & Creative Systems: Tim Wudurski
Natl Accts Mgr: Samantha Steele
Oracle Tech Mgr: Hari Ram
Prodn Mgr, Chronicle Chroma: Kayleigh Jankowski
Proj Mgr: Victoria Chao
Sales Mgr: Morgan Amer
Sales Mgr, Independent Specialty: Vanessa Navarrete
Sales Mgr, Specialty Dept: Alice Robertson
Sales Mgr, Specialty Mkts: Miriam Keil
Soc Media Mgr, Adult Trade: Aubrey Rojas
Subs Rts Mgr: Samantha Allen; Joya Anthony; Rachel Nuzman
Assoc Sales Mgr: Ian Delaney; Kathleen Miller
Prodn Developer: Freesia Blizard
Prodn Developer, Art: Janine Sato
Prodn Developer, Children's: Ashley Despain
Prodn Developer, Food & Lifestyle: Madeleine Moe
Trade Sales Rep, New England: Emily Cervone
Trade Sales Rep, Pacific Northwest: Jamil Zaidi
Sr Mng Ed, Children's: Claire Fletcher
Mng Ed, Entertainment: Alison Petersen
Mng Ed, Food & Lifestyle: Magnolia Molcan
Asst Mng Ed, Children's: Jamie Real
Exec Ed: Cara Bedick
Sr Ed, Children's: Naomi Kirsten; Melissa Manlove
Sr Ed, Entertainment: Brittany McInerney; Frank Parisi
Sr Ed, Entertainment & Lifestyle: Kim Romero
Sr Ed, Food & Lifestyle: Christina Garces; Rachel Hiles
Ed: Mirabelle Korn
Ed, Art: Caitlin Kirkpatrick
Ed, Children's Group: Taylor Norman; Ariel Richardson
Ed, Entertainment: Julia Patrick
Assoc Ed, Food & Lifestyle: Deanne Katz
Asst Ed: Eva Avery; Zaneta Jung; Dena Rayess
Asst Ed, Art: Natalie Butterfield
Asst Ed, Entertainment: Sahara Clement; Olivia Roberts
Sr Publicist: Diane Levinson
Sr Publicist, Children's Publg: Lara Starr
Sr Publicist, Entertainment: April Whitney
Children's Publicist: Eva Zimmerman
Food & Lifestyle Publicist: Joyce Lin
Contracts & Perms Assoc: Madeline Carruthers
Design Mgr: Allison Weiner
Design Mgr, Entertainment: Neil Egan
Mktg Mgr, Art: Sarah Lin Go
Mktg Mgr, Entertainment: Natalie Nicolson
Assoc Mktg Mgr, Events & Retail Mktg: Eden Sugay
Assoc Mktg Mgr, School & Lib: Kaitlyn Spotts
Sr Children's Book Designer: Ryan Hayes
Sr Designer: Jenna Huerta; Allison Weiner
Sr Designer, Children's: Lydia Ortiz
Sr Designer, Entertainment: Jon Glick
Sr Prodn Designer: Kevin Armstrong
Sr Prodn Designer, Tech Lead: Steve Kim
Sr Prodn Developer: Michelle Clair
Children's Book Designer: Alice Seiler
Designer: Kayla Ferriera
Designer, Children's: Julia Marvel; Mariam Quraishi
Designer, Entertainment: Evelyn Furuta
Designer, Entertainment Group: Maggie Edelman
Designer, Food & Lifestyle: Rachel Harrell
Designer, Mktg Communs: Alina Buevich
Indus Designer: Lauren Grand Lubell
Jr Prodn Designer, Children's: Aki Neumann
Jr Prodn Developer: Morgan Gutierrez
Sr Busn Analyst: Molly Krauss
Sr Fin Analyst: Barrett Hooper
Export Sales Coord: Stephanie Cargill-Greer
Mktg & Publicity Coord, Children's: Jennifer Yim
Mktg Photog & Visual Content Coord: Patrick Rafanan
Opers Coord: Elizabeth Hambrick; Chelsea Masquelier

Prodn Coord, Reprints: Terri Lancaster
Sales & Lib Mktg Coord: Michaela Whatnall
Sales & Mktg Materials Coord: Eve Brodsly
Sales Coord, Independent Specialty: Emily Malter
Sales Opers Coord: Bebe Barrow
Trade Sales Coord: Camille Geeter
Web & E-Commerce Coord: Maggie Haas
Export Sales Asst, Intl Sales: Kimiko Vann
Mktg & Publicity Asst, Adult: Julia Hass
Mktg & Publicity Asst, Children's: Samantha Chambers
Mktg Asst, Spec Projs: Carrie Gao
Sales Asst: Maddy Boles
Founded: 1967
General nonfiction & fiction, cloth & paperbound: fine arts, gift, nature, outdoors, nationwide regional guidebooks, stationery, calendars & ancillary products.
ISBN Prefix(es): 978-0-87701; 978-0-8118; 978-0-938491; 978-1-4521
Number of titles published annually: 300 Print
Total Titles: 1,500 Print
Imprints: Chronicle Bridge (Chinese-language children's books); Chronicle Chroma (visual arts & pop culture); Chronicle Prism
Distributor for Amicus Ink; Blue Apple Books; Handprint Books Inc; Hardie Grant Books; Laurence King Publishing; Levine Querido; Moleskine; Princeton Architectural Press; Quadrille Publishing; SmartLab; SmartsCo
Foreign Rep(s): A-Z Africa Book Services (Anita Zih-De Haan) (Eastern Africa, West Africa); Abrams & Chronicle Books (Europe, UK); Ampersand Inc (British Columbia, CN, Ontario, CN); Melanie Boesen (Denmark, Faroe Islands, Finland, Greenland, Iceland, Norway, Sweden); Bookreps NZ Ltd (New Zealand); Michelle Curreri & Sonja Merz (Asia exc China & Japan, India); Everest Int'l Publishing (Wei Zhao) (China); John Fitzpatrick (Ireland); Tiffany Georges (France); Hachette UK Ltd (Matthew Cowdery) (Algeria, Bahrain, Egypt, Iran, Iraq, Israel, Jordan, Kuwait, Lebanon, Libya, Morocco, Oman, Palestine, Saudi Arabia, Sudan, Syria, Tunisia, United Arab Emirates, Yemen); Hardie Grant Books (Australia); Hornblower Group Inc (Atlantic Canada, New Brunswick, CN, Nova Scotia, CN, Prince Edward Island, CN, Quebec, CN); JCC Enterprises Inc (Jerry C Carrillo) (Bermuda, Caribbean, Latin America); Cristian & Adriana Juncu (Eastern Europe, Russia); Laurence King Publishing (Asia exc Japan); Padovani Books (Penny Padovani) (Italy, Portugal); Padovani Books (Isabella Curtis) (Greece); Padovani Books (Jenny Padovani Frias) (Spain); Publishers Group UK (Melanie Boesen) (Denmark, Faroe Islands, Finland, Greenland, Iceland, Norway, Sweden); Publishers Group UK (John Fitzpatrick) (Ireland); Publishers Group UK (Deborah Dyson) (Midlands, Northern England, Northern Wales, Scotland, Southern England, Southern Wales); Publishers Services (Gabriele Kern) (Austria, Germany, Switzerland); Raincoast Books (Canada); Real Books (South Africa); 62Damrak (Francine Siemer-Ankersmit) (Netherlands)
Foreign Rights: Bettina Nibbe (Germany); Nordin Agency (Netherlands, Scandinavia); Frederique Porretta (France); Tao Media (China)
See separate listing for:
Handprint Books Inc

Cider Mill Press Book Publishers LLC
12 Spring St, Kennebunkport, ME 04046
Mailing Address: PO Box 454, Kennebunkport, ME 04046
Tel: 207-967-8232 *Fax:* 207-967-8233
Web Site: www.cidermillpress.com
Key Personnel
Founder & Publr: John F Whalen, Jr
  E-mail: johnwhalen@cidermillpress.com
Founded: 2005

Publish creative, innovative, inspiring & visually stunning books & gift books.
ISBN Prefix(es): 978-1-933662; 978-1-60433; 978-1-941868
Number of titles published annually: 50 Print; 4 Audio
Total Titles: 135 Print
Imprints: Applesauce Press; Cider Mill Press
Distributed by Simon & Schuster, Inc; Simon & Schuster Sales Division
Foreign Rights: Print Co Verlagsgesellschaft (Gabriella Scolik) (Europe)
Membership(s): American Booksellers Association (ABA)

Cinco Puntos Press
701 Texas Ave, El Paso, TX 79901
Tel: 915-838-1625 *Toll Free Tel:* 800-566-9072
  Fax: 915-838-1635
E-mail: info@cincopuntos.com
Web Site: www.cincopuntos.com
Key Personnel
Pres & CFO: John Byrd
Publr & Ed-in-Chief: Lee Byrd *E-mail:* leebyrd@cincopuntos.com
Edit & Foreign Rts Dir: Jessica Powers
Publicity Dir: Stephanie Frescas Macias
Founded: 1985
Books of the Southwest US & bilingual children's literature.
ISBN Prefix(es): 978-0-938317
Number of titles published annually: 23 Print
Total Titles: 130 Print; 9 Audio
Foreign Rep(s): Publishers Group Canada (Canada)
Distribution Center: Consortium Book Sales & Distribution, The Keg House, Suite 101, 34 13 Ave NE, Minneapolis, MN 55413-1007, VP, Sales: Jim Nichols *Tel:* 612-746-2600 *Toll Free Tel:* 800-283-3572 (cust serv, Jackson, TN) *Fax:* 612-746-2606 *E-mail:* info@cbsd.com
Web Site: www.cbsd.com SAN: 200-6049

§Circlet Press
Imprint of Riverdale Avenue Books
39 Hurlbut St, Cambridge, MA 02138
Toll Free Tel: 800-729-6423
E-mail: customerservice@riverdaleavebooks.com
Web Site: www.circlet.com
Key Personnel
Ed: Cecilia Tan
Founded: 1992
Anthologies of erotic science fiction/fantasy, paranormal romance, alternative sexuality & fiction with transgender themes.
ISBN Prefix(es): 978-0-9633970; 978-1-885865
Number of titles published annually: 10 Print; 2 Online; 12 E-Book; 5 Audio
Total Titles: 125 Print; 2 Online; 150 E-Book; 5 Audio
Foreign Rep(s): Bulldog Books (Australia); Turnaround Ltd (Europe, UK)
Foreign Rights: Lawrence Schimel (all other territories)

Cistercian Publications
Imprint of Liturgical Press
Saint John's Abbey, PO Box 7500, Collegeville, MN 56321
SAN: 202-1668
Tel: 320-363-2213 *Toll Free Tel:* 800-436-8431
  Fax: 320-363-3299 *Toll Free Fax:* 800-445-5899
E-mail: sales@litpress.org
Web Site: www.cistercianpublications.org
Key Personnel
Dir: Peter Dwyer
Sales & Mktg Mgr: Brian Woods
Founded: 1969
Religion (Roman Catholic) & history.
ISBN Prefix(es): 978-0-87907
Number of titles published annually: 10 Print
Total Titles: 260 Print

Distributed by Liturgical Press
Returns: Liturgical Press, 2950 St John's Rd, Collegeville, MN 56321 *Tel:* 320-363-2213 *Fax:* 320-363-3299 *Web Site:* www.litpress.org
Shipping Address: Liturgical Press, 2950 St John's Rd, Collegeville, MN 56321 *Tel:* 320-363-2213 *Fax:* 320-363-3299 *Web Site:* www.litpress.org

Citadel Press, see Kensington Publishing Corp

City Lights Publishers
261 Columbus Ave, San Francisco, CA 94133
SAN: 202-1684
Tel: 415-362-8193 *Fax:* 415-362-4921
E-mail: staff@citylights.com
Web Site: www.citylights.com
Key Personnel
Exec Dir & Publr: Elaine Katzenberger
PR & Mktg Dir: Stacey Lewis
Open Media Series Founder & Ed: Greg Ruggiero
Publicity & Mktg Assoc: Chris Carosi
Founded: 1955
Publisher of progressive political nonfiction, innovative literature & poetry.
ISBN Prefix(es): 978-0-87286
Number of titles published annually: 15 Print
Total Titles: 200 Print
Foreign Rights: Agencia Literaria Carmen Balcells SA (Portugal, Spain); Bardon-Chinese Media Agency (China, Taiwan); BC Agency (Korea); Agence Hoffman (France, Germany); International Editor's Co (Brazil); Japan UNI Agency (Japan); Agenzia Letteraria Internazionale (Italy); ONK Agency Ltd (Turkey); Owls Agency Inc (Japan); Plima Agency (Bosnia and Herzegovina, Croatia, Czechia, Poland, Serbia); PubHub Literary Agency (Korea)
Distribution Center: Consortium Book Sales & Distribution, The Keg House, Suite 101, 34 13 Ave NE, Minneapolis, MN 55413-1007 *Tel:* 612-746-2600 *Toll Free Tel:* 800-283-3572 (cust serv, Jackson, TN) *Fax:* 612-746-2606 *E-mail:* info@cbsd.com *Web Site:* www.cbsd.com SAN: 200-6049

Clarion Books
Imprint of Houghton Mifflin Harcourt
3 Park Ave, New York, NY 10016
Tel: 212-420-5800 *Toll Free Tel:* 800-225-3362 (orders) *Fax:* 212-420-5855 *Toll Free Fax:* 800-634-7568 (orders)
Web Site: www.hmhco.com
Key Personnel
VP & Assoc Publr: Anne Hoppe
Subs Rts Mgr: Candace Finn
Sr Ed: Jennifer Greene; Lynne Polvino
Founded: 1965
Picture, chapter, middle grade & young adult books, fiction & nonfiction.
ISBN Prefix(es): 978-0-547; 978-0-544; 978-1-328
Number of titles published annually: 40 Print
Distributed by Houghton Mifflin Harcourt

Clarity Press Inc
2625 Piedmont Rd NE, Suite 56, Atlanta, GA 30324
SAN: 688-9530
Tel: 404-647-6501
E-mail: claritypress@usa.net (foreign rts & perms)
Web Site: www.claritypress.com
Key Personnel
Edit Dir: Diana G Collier
Busn Mgr: Annette Gordon
    E-mail: businessmanager@claritypress.com
Founded: 1984
Scholarly works on contemporary justice & human rights issues.

ISBN Prefix(es): 978-0-9845255; 978-0-9860362; 978-0-9972870; 978-0-9986947; 978-0-9833539
Number of titles published annually: 6 Print; 6 E-Book
Total Titles: 103 Print; 78 E-Book; 4 Audio
Imprints: Clear Day Books (print-on-demand, rare books)
Foreign Rep(s): Marston Books (UK & the continent)
Foreign Rights: Chengdu Rightol Media (China)
Distribution Center: SCB Distributors, 15608 S New Century Dr, Gardena, CA 90248, Contact: Victor Duran *Tel:* 310-532-9400 *Toll Free Tel:* 800-729-6423 *Fax:* 310-532-7001 *E-mail:* victor@scbdistributors.com *Web Site:* www.scbdistributors.com
Marston Book Services Ltd, 160 Milton Park, Abingdon, Oxon OX14 4SD, United Kingdom (includes Europe) *Tel:* (01235) 465576 *Fax:* (01235) 465555 *E-mail:* trade.orders@marston.co.uk
Membership(s): Association of American Publishers (AAP); Society for Scholarly Publishing (SSP)

Classical Academic Press
515 S 32 St, Camp Hill, PA 17011
Tel: 717-730-0711 *Toll Free Tel:* 866-730-0711 *Fax:* 717-730-0721 *Toll Free Fax:* 866-730-0721
E-mail: info@classicalsubjects.com; orders@classicalsubjects.com
Web Site: classicalacademicpress.com
Key Personnel
CEO: Christopher Perrin
Pres: Greg Lowe
VP, Prod Devt: Jesse Hake
VP, Sales, Mktg & Opers: Joelle Hodge
Mng Ed & Creative Designer: Lauraine Gustafson
Sales & Mktg Mgr: Tristin Schambach
    E-mail: tschambach@classicalsubjects.com
Founded: 2001
K-12 educational textbooks & media. Focus on classical education.
ISBN Prefix(es): 978-1-60051
Number of titles published annually: 12 Print; 2 Online; 12 E-Book; 3 Audio
Total Titles: 150 Print; 1 Online; 12 E-Book; 10 Audio
Imprints: Plum Tree Books
Foreign Rep(s): Baker & Taylor (New Zealand, UK)
Returns: Maple Distribution Center, 60 Grumbacher Rd, York, PA 17406
Shipping Address: Baker & Taylor, 2550 W Tyvola Rd, Charlotte, NC 28217 *Tel:* 704-998-3100
Membership(s): Independent Book Publishers Association (IBPA)
See separate listing for:
Plum Tree Books

Clear Light Publishers
823 Don Diego Ave, Santa Fe, NM 87505
Tel: 505-989-9590 *Toll Free Tel:* 800-253-2747 (orders)
E-mail: info@clearlightbooks.com
Web Site: www.clearlightbooks.com
Key Personnel
Publr: Harmon Houghton
Founded: 1981
ISBN Prefix(es): 978-0-940666; 978-1-57416
Number of titles published annually: 18 Print
Total Titles: 200 Print
Foreign Rights: Harmon Houghton Clear Light Books
Membership(s): American Booksellers Association (ABA); American Library Association (ALA); Mountains & Plains Booksellers Association (MPBA); New Mexico Book Association

§Clearfield Co Inc
Subsidiary of Genealogical Publishing Co
3600 Clipper Mill Rd, Suite 229, Baltimore, MD 21211
Tel: 410-837-8271 *Toll Free Tel:* 800-296-6687 (orders & cust serv) *Fax:* 410-752-8492
E-mail: sales@genealogical.com
Web Site: www.genealogical.com
Key Personnel
Mktg Dir: Joe Garonzik *E-mail:* jgaronzi@genealogical.com
Founded: 1989
Leading publisher of short-run genealogy how-to books, reference books & CD-ROM publications in the US.
ISBN Prefix(es): 978-0-8063
Number of titles published annually: 20 Print; 1 CD-ROM
Total Titles: 1,000 Print; 10 CD-ROM
Membership(s): American Booksellers Association (ABA); American Name Society; National Genealogical Society

Cleis Press
Imprint of Start Publishing LLC
101 Hudson St, 37th fl, Suite 3705, Jersey City, NJ 07302
Tel: 646-257-4343
E-mail: cleis@cleispress.com
Web Site: www.cleispress.com; www.vivaeditions.com
Key Personnel
Mktg Mgr: Allyson Fields *E-mail:* afields@cleispress.com
Acqs Ed: Hannah Bennett
Founded: 1980
Outriders. Outwriters. Outliers. Cleis Press publishes works in the areas of fiction & LGBTQ studies, as well as romance, erotica, how-to sex guides, human rights, memoirs & women's studies. Viva Editions are books that inform, entertain & enlighten. Books contain inspiration, self-help, women's issues, lifestyle, health, parenting, reference, gift & relationship advice.
ISBN Prefix(es): 978-0-939416; 978-1-57344
Number of titles published annually: 30 Print; 30 E-Book; 150 Audio
Total Titles: 600 Print; 400 E-Book
Distribution Center: Red Wheel/Weiser/Conari, 65 Parker St, Suite 7, Newburyport, MA 01950 *Toll Free Tel:* 800-423-7087 *E-mail:* customerservice@rwwbooks.com *Web Site:* redwheelweiser.com

Clerisy Press
Imprint of AdventureKEEN
306 Greenup St, Covington, KY 41011
Tel: 859-815-7204
E-mail: info@clerisypress.com
Web Site: www.clerisypress.com
Key Personnel
Pres, AdventureKEEN: Richard Hunt *Tel:* 859-815-7204 *E-mail:* richard@clerisypress.com
Founded: 2006
Trade & custom publisher.
ISBN Prefix(es): 978-1-57860
Number of titles published annually: 10 Print; 10 E-Book
Total Titles: 100 Print; 100 E-Book
Billing Address: 2204 First Ave S, Suite 102, Birmingham, AL 35233, Contact: Lisa Myers *Tel:* 205-443-7992 *Fax:* 205-326-1012 *E-mail:* lisa@adventurewithkeen.com
Distribution Center: Publishers Group West (PGW), 1700 Fourth St, Berkeley, CA 94710, Contact: Kevin Votel
Membership(s): American Booksellers Association (ABA)

§Clinical & Laboratory Standards Institute (CLSI)
950 W Valley Rd, Suite 2500, Wayne, PA 19087

Tel: 610-688-0100 *Toll Free Tel:* 877-447-1888
(orders) *Fax:* 610-688-0700
E-mail: customerservice@clsi.org
Web Site: www.clsi.org
Founded: 1968
Voluntary consensus standards & guidelines for
medical testing & in vitro diagnostic products
& healthcare services.
ISBN Prefix(es): 978-1-56238
Number of titles published annually: 25 Print
Total Titles: 200 Print

Close Up Publishing
Division of Close Up Foundation
1330 Braddock Place, Suite 400, Alexandria, VA
22314
Tel: 703-706-3300 *Toll Free Tel:* 800-CLOSE-UP
(256-7387)
E-mail: info@closeup.org
Web Site: www.closeup.org
Key Personnel
Pres & CEO: Timothy S Davis, Esq
Sr Dir, Prodr & Teacher Prog Specialist: Joe Ger-
aghty
Academic Outreach Coord: Ian Fried
Founded: 1971
Publish supplemental texts, videos, teachers'
guides & simulation activities for secondary
school & college social studies, political sci-
ence, government, economics, international
relations & history courses & for general read-
ership.
ISBN Prefix(es): 978-0-932765; 978-1-930810
Number of titles published annually: 1 Print; 12
Online; 3 Audio
Total Titles: 56 Print; 20 Online; 19 Audio

Closson Press
257 Delilah St, Apollo, PA 15613-1933
Tel: 724-337-4482 *Fax:* 724-337-9484
E-mail: clossonpress@comcast.net
Web Site: www.clossonpress.com
Key Personnel
Founder & Owner: Bob Closson; Marietta Clos-
son
Founded: 1976
Printer & publisher of history, family history &
genealogy books.
ISBN Prefix(es): 978-0-933227; 978-1-55856
Number of titles published annually: 40 Print
Total Titles: 800 Print
Distributed by Janaway Publishing; Masthof Press
Distributor for Hearthside Books; Darvin Martin
CDs; Retrospect Publishing
Foreign Rep(s): Brian Mitchell (Ireland); Cornelia
Schrader (France, Germany)

CMF Press, see Country Music Foundation Press

§CN Times Books
Imprint of CN Times Inc
100 Jericho Quadrangle, Suite 337, Jericho, NY
11791
Tel: 516-719-0886
E-mail: yanliu@cntimesbooks.com
Web Site: www.cntimesbooks.com
Key Personnel
Pres & Publr: George Zhu
Sales & Mktg Mgr: Paul Myatovich
Founded: 2013
ISBN Prefix(es): 978-1-62774
Number of titles published annually: 21 Print
Total Titles: 55 Print; 7 E-Book
Distributor for Bashu Publishing; Foreign Lan-
guage Press; Intercontinental Press; Phoenix
Publishing
Orders to: Ingram Publisher Services (IPS), One
Ingram Blvd, La Vergne, TN 37086 *Toll Free
Tel:* 855-802-8317 *Toll Free Fax:* 800-838-
1149 *E-mail:* ips@ingramcontent.com *Web
Site:* ipage.ingramcontent.com

Returns: Ingram Publisher Services, 1210 Ingram
Dr, Chambersburg, PA 17202
Distribution Center: Ingram Publisher Services
(IPS), One Ingram Blvd, La Vergne, TN
37086 *Toll Free Tel:* 855-802-8317 *Toll Free
Fax:* 800-838-1149 *E-mail:* ips@ingramcontent.
com *Web Site:* ipage.ingramcontent.com
Membership(s): American Booksellers Associa-
tion (ABA)

Coaches Choice
5 Harris Ct, Bldg N, Suite 4, Monterey, CA
93940
Mailing Address: PO Box 1828, Monterey, CA
93942-1828
Toll Free Tel: 888-229-5745 *Fax:* 831-372-6075
E-mail: info@coacheschoice.com
Web Site: www.coacheschoice.com
Key Personnel
Pres: James Peterson
Edit Mgr: Kristi Huelsing *E-mail:* kristih@
coacheschoice.com
Founded: 1999
Instructional books & DVDs for coaches (foot-
ball, basketball, baseball, softball, volleyball,
soccer, track & field, etc); health, fitness &
sports medicine professionals & camp profes-
sionals.
ISBN Prefix(es): 978-1-57167; 978-1-58518; 978-
1-60679
Number of titles published annually: 40 Print

§Coachlight Press LLC
1704 Craig's Store Rd, Afton, VA 22920-2017
SAN: 254-2579
Tel: 434-823-1692
E-mail: sales@coachlightpress.com
Web Site: www.coachlightpress.com
Key Personnel
Mng Memb: Kim Murphy
Founded: 2001
ISBN Prefix(es): 978-0-9716790; 978-1-936785
Number of titles published annually: 1 Print; 2 E-
Book
Total Titles: 9 Print; 8 E-Book
Membership(s): Independent Book Publishers As-
sociation (IBPA)

Codhill Press
One Arden Lane, New Paltz, NY 12561
E-mail: codhillpress@aol.com
Web Site: www.codhill.com
Key Personnel
Ed: David Appelbaum *E-mail:* appelbad@gmail.
com
Founded: 1998
Literary small press.
ISBN Prefix(es): 978-1-930337
Number of titles published annually: 12 Print; 2
Online; 2 E-Book
Total Titles: 100 Print; 6 Online; 6 E-Book
Distributed by State University of New York
Press
Orders to: State University of New York Press,
PO Box 960, Herndon, VA 20172 *Tel:* 703-
661-1575 *Toll Free Tel:* 877-204-6073
Fax: 703-996-1010 *Toll Free Fax:* 877-204-
6074
Warehouse: Books International, 22883 Quicksil-
ver Dr, Dulles, VA 20166 *Tel:* 703-661-1500
Membership(s): Community of Literary Maga-
zines & Presses (CLMP)

Coffee House Press
79 13 Ave NE, Suite 110, Minneapolis, MN
55413
SAN: 206-3883
Tel: 612-338-0125 *Fax:* 612-338-4004
E-mail: info@coffeehousepress.org
Web Site: coffeehousepress.org

Key Personnel
Publr: Christopher Fischbach *E-mail:* fish@
coffeehousepress.org
Dir, Opers & Mng Ed: Carla Valadez
E-mail: carla@coffeehousepress.org
Devt Dir: Enrique Olivarez *E-mail:* enrique@
coffeehousepress.org
Sr Ed: Erika Stevens *E-mail:* erika@
coffeehousepress.org
Ed: Lizzie Davis *E-mail:* lizzie@
coffeehousepress.org
Mktg & Sales Mgr: Marit Swanson
E-mail: marit@coffeehousepress.org
Publicist: Daley Farr *E-mail:* daley@
coffeehousepress.org
Publicity & Opers Assoc: Claire Fallon
E-mail: claire@coffeehousepress.org
Founded: 1984
Fine editions & trade books; contemporary po-
etry, short fiction, novels, literary essays &
memoirs.
ISBN Prefix(es): 978-0-918273; 978-1-56689
Number of titles published annually: 14 Print
Total Titles: 250 Print
Distribution Center: Consortium Book Sales &
Distribution, The Keg House, 34 13 Ave NE,
Suite 101, Minneapolis, MN 55413 *Tel:* 612-
746-2600 *Fax:* 612-746-2606 *E-mail:* info@
cbsd.com *Web Site:* www.cbsd.com SAN: 200-
6049

Cognizant Communication Corp
18 Peekskill Hollow Rd, Putnam Valley, NY
10579-0037
Mailing Address: PO Box 37, Putnam Valley, NY
10579-0037
Tel: 845-603-6440; 845-603-6441 (warehouse &
orders) *Fax:* 845-603-6442
E-mail: inquiries@cognizantcommunication.com;
sales@cognizantcommunication.com
Web Site: www.cognizantcommunication.com
Key Personnel
Chmn & Publr: Robert N Miranda
Pres: Lori Miranda
Founded: 1992
STM & social science books & journals. Subjects
include: tourism research & leisure studies,
medical research, engineering & psychology.
ISBN Prefix(es): 978-1-882345; 978-0-971587
Number of titles published annually: 11 Print; 23
Online
Total Titles: 53 Print; 1 CD-ROM; 1 Audio
Imprints: Innovation & Tourisms (INTO); Mi-
randa Press Trade Division; Tourism Dynamic

Cokesbury, see Abingdon Press

§Cold Spring Harbor Laboratory Press
Division of Cold Spring Harbor Laboratory
One Bungtown Rd, Cold Spring Harbor, NY
11724
SAN: 203-6185
Tel: 516-422-4100 *Toll Free Tel:* 800-843-4388
Fax: 516-422-4097; 516-422-4092 (submis-
sions)
E-mail: cshpress@cshl.edu
Web Site: www.cshlpress.com
Key Personnel
Exec Dir: John Inglis *Tel:* 516-422-4005
E-mail: inglis@cshl.edu
Dir, Edit Devt: Jan Argentine *E-mail:* argentin@
cshl.edu
Dir, Prod Devt & Mktg: Wayne Manos
E-mail: manos@cshl.edu
Dir, Pubns: Linda Sussman *E-mail:* sussman@
cshl.edu
Sr Mktg Mgr: Stephanie Novara *E-mail:* novara@
cshl.edu
Mktg Mgr: Robert Redmond *Tel:* 516-422-4101
E-mail: rredmond@cshl.edu
Opers Mgr: Nancy Hodson *E-mail:* hodson@cshl.
edu

Prodn Mgr: Denise Weiss *E-mail:* weiss@cshl.edu
Head, Ad & Sponsorship Sales: Marcie Siconolfi *Tel:* 516-422-4010 *E-mail:* siconolf@cshl.edu
Founded: 1933
Scholarly & scientific books, journals & electronic media.
ISBN Prefix(es): 978-0-87969
Number of titles published annually: 20 Print
Total Titles: 220 Print; 1 CD-ROM; 15 E-Book; 2 Audio
Foreign Rep(s): Academic Books (Austria, Europe, Germany, Switzerland); Maruzen Co Ltd (Japan); NBN International (Europe exc Austria, Germany & Switzerland, UK); Viva Books Pvt Ltd (Indian subcontinent)
Distribution Center: Oxford University Press, 2001 Evans Rd, Cary, NC 27513

§The College Board
250 Vesey St, New York, NY 10281
SAN: 269-0829
Tel: 212-713-8000 *Toll Free Tel:* 866-630-9305
Web Site: www.collegeboard.com
Key Personnel
CEO: David Coleman
Pres: Jeremy Singer
Founded: 1900
Educational & trade books in the fields of college admission, continuing education, guidance, curriculum, financial aid, educational research, college-level & advanced placement examinations & school reform.
ISBN Prefix(es): 978-0-87447
Number of titles published annually: 7 Print
Total Titles: 100 Print; 7 CD-ROM; 4 E-Book; 1 Audio
Branch Office(s)
1919 "M" St NW, Suite 300, Washington, DC 20036 *Tel:* 202-741-4700
11955 Democracy Dr, Reston, VA 20190-5662 *Tel:* 571-485-3000 *Fax:* 571-485-3099
Distributed by Macmillan

College Publishing
12309 Lynwood Dr, Glen Allen, VA 23059
Tel: 804-364-8410 *Fax:* 804-364-8408
E-mail: collegepub@mindspring.com
Web Site: www.collegepublishing.us
Key Personnel
Publr: Stephen R Mosberg
Founded: 2001
Publish college textbooks in engineering, literature, linguistics & scholarly journals in engineering.
ISBN Prefix(es): 978-0-9679121; 978-1-932780
Number of titles published annually: 10 Print; 10 Online; 8 E-Book
Total Titles: 30 Print; 10 Online; 8 E-Book

The Colonial Williamsburg Foundation
PO Box 1776, Williamsburg, VA 23187-1776
SAN: 203-297X
Tel: 757-229-1000 *Toll Free Tel:* 800-HISTORY (447-8679)
E-mail: geninfo@cwf.org
Web Site: www.colonialwilliamsburg.org
Key Personnel
Pres & CEO: Mitchell Reiss
Dir & Mng Ed, Pubns & Rts/Perms: Paul Aron *Tel:* 757-220-7341 *E-mail:* paron@cwf.org
Founded: 1930
Trade & scholarly nonfiction, children's, young adult, juveniles & regional books specializing in aspects of 18th century history in Virginia's colonial capital.
ISBN Prefix(es): 978-0-87935; 978-0-910412
Number of titles published annually: 5 Print
Total Titles: 115 Print; 28 Audio
Imprints: Colonial Williamsburg
Distributed by Harry N Abrams Inc; John F Blair Publisher; Clarkson Potter Publishers; Lexing-

ton Books; National Geographic; Ohio University Press; Quite Specific Media Group Ltd; Rowman & Littlefield; Scholastic Inc; Stackpole Books; Texas Tech University Press; The University of Virginia Press; Yale University Press
Shipping Address: c/o Coastal Forms & Data Products, 141 Enterprise Dr, Newport News, VA 23603 *Tel:* 757-873-8806 *Toll Free Tel:* 800-241-4067 *Fax:* 757-873-7619
Distribution Center: 201 Fifth Ave, Williamsburg, VA 23185

§Columbia Books & Information Services (CBIS)
4340 East-West Hwy, Suite 300, Bethesda, MD 20814
Tel: 202-464-1662 *Fax:* 301-664-9600
E-mail: info@columbiabooks.com
Web Site: www.columbiabooks.com; www.lobbyists.info; www.associationexecs.com
Key Personnel
Pres: Brittany Carter *E-mail:* bcarter@columbiabooks.com
Dir, Edit & Data Servs: Duncan Bell
Dir, Fin: Anna Magallanes
Dir, Opers: Renee Cannady
Dir, Sales & Mktg: Jamie Herring *Tel:* 240-235-0271
Founded: 1965
Publish print directories, reference books, newsletters & reports. Do not accept mss.
ISBN Prefix(es): 978-0-910416; 978-1-880873; 978-0-9715487; 978-0-9747322; 978-1-938939
Number of titles published annually: 10 Print; 2 Online; 1 E-Book
Total Titles: 10 Print; 2 Online; 1 E-Book

§Columbia University Press
61 W 62 St, New York, NY 10023
SAN: 212-2472
Tel: 212-459-0600 *Toll Free Tel:* 800-944-8648 *Fax:* 212-459-3678
Web Site: cup.columbia.edu
Key Personnel
CFO: Robert Abrams
Assoc Provost & Dir: Jennifer Crewe
Dir, Editing, Design & Prodn: Marielle Poss
Dir, Sales & Opers: Brad Hebel
Edit Dir: Eric Schwartz
Promos Dir: Meredith Howard
Publr, Fin & Economics: Myles Thompson
Publr, Philosophy & Religion: Wendy Lochner
Sr Ed: Philip Leventhal
Ed, Global History & Politics: Caelyn Cobb
Ed, Life & Physical Sciences: Miranda Martin
Founded: 1893
Books of scholarly value, including nonfiction, general interest, scientific & technical books, textbooks in special fields at the university level & reference books.
ISBN Prefix(es): 978-0-231
Number of titles published annually: 500 Print; 120 E-Book
Total Titles: 7 CD-ROM; 4 Online; 350 E-Book
Imprints: Columbia Business School Publishing (business, finance & economics titles); Wallflower Press (film titles)
Distributor for Agenda Publishing; American Institute of Buddhist Studies; Austrian Film Museum Books; Auteur Publishing; Barbara Budrich Publishers; Chinese University Press; Columbia Books on Architecture & the City; Maria Curie-Sklodowska University Press; Harrington Park Press (frontlist titles); ibidem Press (English language titles exc China & India); Jagiellonian University Press; Peterson Institute for International Economics; Slovenian Cinematheque; Transcript Verlag; Tulika Books; University of Tokyo Press
Foreign Rep(s): Apex Knowledge Sdn Bhd (Simon Tay) (Brunei, Malaysia); Avicenna Partnership Ltd (Claire de Gruchy) (Algeria,

Cyprus, Jordan, Malta, Morocco, Palestine, Tunisia, Turkey); Avicenna Partnership Ltd (Bill Kennedy) (Bahrain, Egypt, Iran, Iraq, Kuwait, Lebanon, Libya, Oman, Qatar, Saudi Arabia, Syria, United Arab Emirates); Dominique Bartshukoff (Austria, Croatia, Czechia, Eastern Europe, Germany, Greece, Holland, Portugal, Russia, Slovenia, Spain); Booknet Co Ltd (Suphaluck Sattabuz) (Thailand); Everest International Publishing Services (Wei Zhao) (China); Footprints Books (Australia, New Zealand); Information & Culture Korea (Se-Yung Jun) (Korea); Peter Jacques (Belgium, Denmark, Finland, France, Italy, Norway, Poland, Sweden, Switzerland); MegaTEXTS Phil Inc (Jean Lim) (Philippines); MHM Limited (Mark Gresham) (Japan); B K Norton Ltd (Chiafeng Peng) (Singapore, Taiwan); Penguin Random House India (Bangladesh, Bhutan, India, Nepal, Pakistan, Sri Lanka); Rockbook (Akiko Iwamoto & Gilles Fauveau) (Japan); The University Press Group Ltd (Lois Edwards) (Europe, South Africa, UK); Kelvin van Hasselt Publishing Services (Africa); Wiley Distribution Services Ltd (Africa, Europe, Middle East, South Africa, UK)
Foreign Rights: Akcali Copyright Agency (Mustafa Urgen) (Turkey); L'Autre Agence (Corinne Marotte) (France); Bardon-Chinese Media Agency (Simplified-Ivan Zhang) (China); Bardon-Chinese Media Agency (Complex-Luisa Yeh) (China); Bestun Korea (Ms Yumi Chun) (Korea); Dar Cherlin (Amelie Cherlin) (Arab Middle East); Agencia Literaria Raquel de la Concha (Spain); The English Agency (Tsutomu Yawata) (Japan); Paul & Peter Fritz AG (Germany); Graal Literary Agency (Lukasz Wrobel) (Poland); Danny Hong Agency (Danny Hong) (Korea); Korea Copyright Center Inc (Joeun Lee) (Korea); Alexander Korzhenevski Agency (Alexander Khorzhenevski) (Russia & former USSR); Andrew Nurnberg Associates International (Complex-Whitney Hsu & Jackie Huang) (China); Oxford Literary & Rights Agency (Hana Whitton) (Croatia, Czechia, Hungary, North Macedonia); Reiser Literary Agency (Roberto Gilodi) (Italy); Sebes & Bisseling Literary Agency (Paul Sebes) (Denmark, Finland, Netherlands, Norway, Sweden); Seibel Publishing Services (Patricia Seibel) (Brazil, Portugal); Tuttle-Mori Agency Inc (Fumika Ogihara) (Japan); Eric Yang Agency (Jackie Yang) (Korea)
Orders to: Ingram Academic, 1094 Flex Dr, Jackson, TN 38301 *Tel:* 731-988-4440 *Toll Free Tel:* 800-343-4499 *Toll Free Fax:* 800-351-5073 *E-mail:* ordersupport@ingramcontent.com
Membership(s): American Association of University Presses (AAUP); Association of American Publishers (AAP)

§Comex Systems Inc
9380 Nastrand Circle, Port Charlotte, FL 33981
Tel: 908-881-6301
E-mail: mail@comexsystems.com
Web Site: www.comexsystems.com
Founded: 1973
Publish test preparation & other educational books.
ISBN Prefix(es): 978-1-56030
Number of titles published annually: 5 Print; 10 CD-ROM; 5 E-Book
Total Titles: 30 Print; 50 CD-ROM; 5 E-Book

Commonwealth Editions
Imprint of Applewood Books Inc
One River Rd, Carlisle, MA 01741
Tel: 781-271-0055 *Toll Free Tel:* 800-277-5312 *Fax:* 781-271-0056
E-mail: customercare@awb.com
Web Site: www.awb.com

Key Personnel
Founder, Pres & Publr: Phil Zuckerman
   E-mail: philz@awb.com
Founded: 1988
Publisher of nonfiction books about New England & its historic places.
ISBN Prefix(es): 978-1-889833; 978-1-933212
Number of titles published annually: 12 Print
Total Titles: 125 Print
Membership(s): NEBA

Concordia Publishing House
Subsidiary of The Luthern Church, Missouri Synod
3558 S Jefferson Ave, St Louis, MO 63118-3968
SAN: 202-1781
Tel: 314-268-1000; 314-268-1268 (bookshop)
   Toll Free Tel: 800-325-3040 (cust serv)
   Toll Free Fax: 800-490-9889 (cust serv)
E-mail: order@cph.org
Web Site: www.cph.org
Key Personnel
Pres & CEO: Dr Bruce G Kintz *Tel:* 314-268-1190 *E-mail:* bruce.kintz@cph.org
VP & Corp Coun: Jonathan D Schultz
   E-mail: jonathan.schultz@cph.org
Publr & Exec Dir: Rev Paul T McCain
   E-mail: paul.mccain@cph.org
Exec Dir, Innovation Technologies: Steve Harris
   E-mail: steve.harris@cph.org
Exec Dir, Mktg & E-Commerce: Mr Loren Pawlitz *E-mail:* loren.pawlitz@cph.org
Exec Dir, Prodn Control & Quality Systems: Karen Capps *E-mail:* karen.capps@cph.org
Dir, Graphic Design: Tim Agnew *E-mail:* tim.agnew@cph.org
Dir, HR: Dana Neuhaus *E-mail:* dana.neuhaus@cph.org
Dir, Opers: Bob Rothmeyer *E-mail:* bob.rothmeyer@cph.org
Dir, Sales: Paul Brunette *E-mail:* paul.brunette@cph.org
Founded: 1869
Theological works, sacred & family, devotional music, curriculum, computer software, bulletins, envelopes.
ISBN Prefix(es): 978-0-570; 978-0-7586
Number of titles published annually: 150 Print; 2 CD-ROM
Total Titles: 1,000 Print; 10 CD-ROM
Divisions: Concordia Gospel Outreach; Concordia Technology Solutions; Editorial Concordia
Membership(s): Evangelical Christian Publishers Association (ECPA); Protestant Church-Owned Publishers Association (PCPA)

The Conference Board Inc
845 Third Ave, New York, NY 10022-6600
SAN: 202-179X
Tel: 212-759-0900; 212-339-0345 (cust serv)
E-mail: customer.service@conferenceboard.org; membership@conferenceboard.org
Web Site: www.conference-board.org; www.linkedin.com/company/the-conference-board
Key Personnel
CEO: Jon Spector
SVP: Janet Etsch
Exec Dir, Knowledge Content & Quality: Chuck Mitchell
Exec Dir, Governance Ctr: Douglas Chia
Founded: 1916
Periodic studies in management practices, economics & public affairs.
ISBN Prefix(es): 978-0-8237
Number of titles published annually: 25 Print; 25 Online
Branch Office(s)
1530 Wilson Blvd, Suite 400, Arlington, VA 22209
The Conference Board of Canada, 255 Smyth Rd, Ottawa, ON, Canada (affiliate), Pres & CEO: Daniel Muzyka *Tel:* 613-526-3280 *Toll Free Tel:* 866-711-2262 *Fax:* 613-526-4857

E-mail: contactcboc@conferenceboard.ca *Web Site:* www.conferenceboard.ca
Foreign Office(s): Chaussee de La Hulpe 130, 6th fl, 1170 Brussels, Belgium, VP & Mng Dir: Rainer Schultheis *Tel:* (02) 675 5405 *E-mail:* brussels@conferenceboard.org
7-2-72 Qijiayuan, 9 Jianwai St, Beijing 100600, China, VP & Mng Dir: David Hoffman *Tel:* (010) 8532 4688 *E-mail:* david.hoffman@conferenceboard.org
Room 1213, 12/F, Tai Yau Bldg, 181 Johnston Rd, Wanchai, Hong Kong, Exec Dir, Asia Pacific Region: Nick Sutcliffe *Tel:* 2804 1000 *E-mail:* service.ap@conferenceboard.org
22-81 The Central, 8 Eu Tong Sen St, Singapore 059818, Singapore, Exec Dir, Asia Pacific Region: Nick Sutcliffe *Tel:* 6325 3121 *E-mail:* service.ap@conferenceboard.org

§The Connecticut Law Tribune
Division of ALM Media LLC
201 Ann Uccello St, 4th fl, Hartford, CT 06103
Tel: 860-527-7900 *Toll Free Tel:* 877-256-2472
Web Site: www.law.com/ctlawtribune/
Key Personnel
Ed-in-Chief: Michael Marciano
   E-mail: mmarciano@alm.com
Founded: 1974
Publisher of books, newspapers & other materials for the legal community & the public.
ISBN Prefix(es): 978-0-910051; 978-1-62881; 978-1-57625
Number of titles published annually: 5 Print
Total Titles: 40 Print; 1 E-Book

Consumer Press
13326 SW 28 St, Suite 102, Fort Lauderdale, FL 33330-1102
SAN: 297-7888
Tel: 954-370-9153 *Fax:* 954-472-1008
E-mail: info@consumerpress.com
Web Site: www.consumerpress.com
Key Personnel
Pres: Diana Gonzalez
Edit Dir: Joseph J Pappas
Publicity Dir: Linda Muzzarelli
Founded: 1989
Consumer-oriented self-help & how-to titles. Specialize in nutrition, health & homeowner issues.
ISBN Prefix(es): 978-0-9628336; 978-1-891264; 978-0-9637641
Number of titles published annually: 9 Print
Total Titles: 12 Print
Imprints: Women's Publications
Membership(s): Independent Book Publishers Association (IBPA)

Contemporary Publishing Co of Raleigh Inc
5849 Lease Lane, Raleigh, NC 27617
Tel: 919-851-8221 *Fax:* 919-851-6666
E-mail: questions@contemporarypublishing.com
Web Site: www.contemporarypublishing.com
Key Personnel
Publr: Charles E Grantham *E-mail:* chuck246cp@aol.com
Lib Sales Dir & Prodn Mgr: Erika Kessler
   E-mail: erikacpc@aol.com
Mktg Dir: Sherri Powell
Founded: 1977
Laboratory textbooks for college.
ISBN Prefix(es): 978-0-89892
Number of titles published annually: 10 Print
Total Titles: 120 Print; 1 CD-ROM

Continental AfrikaPublishers
Division of Afrikamawu Miracle Mission, AMI Inc
182 Stribling Circle, Spartanburg, SC 29301
E-mail: afrikalion@aol.com; profafrikadzatadeku@yahoo.com; profafrikadzatadeku@facebook.com
Web Site: www.afrikacentricity.com

Key Personnel
Publr: Prof Afrikadzata Deku, PhD
Founded: 1990
Afrikacentric books, booklets & video documentaries, calendars, films on Continental Afrikan studies, Afrika Centricity, Pan-Continental Afrikanism, Continental Afrikan Government MIRACLE Project of the Century-its what, why, how & when.
ISBN Prefix(es): 978-1-56454
Number of titles published annually: 20 Print; 260 Online; 500 E-Book; 20 Audio
Total Titles: 260 Print; 260 Online; 638 E-Book; 20 Audio
Foreign Office(s): PO Box 209, Dansoman-Accra, Ghana, Chmn: Afrikanenyo Deku
Foreign Rep(s): Continental/Diaspora Afrikan (worldwide)

David C Cook
4050 Lee Vance Dr, Colorado Springs, CO 80918
Tel: 719-536-0100 *Toll Free Tel:* 800-708-5550; 800-323-7543 (orders & cust serv)
   Toll Free Fax: 800-430-0726 (cust serv)
Web Site: www.davidccook.org
Key Personnel
CEO: Cris Doornbos
COO: Scott Miller
CIO: Sean Everhart
Chief Global Offr: Gary Hopwood
Chief Publg Offr: Jon Burgess
Pres, Integrity Music: Jonathan Brown
VP & Publr, Learning Resources Group: Wendi Lord
VP, Sales: Dave Thornton
Publr, Traditional Children's Resources: Lindsay Black
Sr Dir, Mktg: Michele Baird
Founded: 1875
Publish & distribute leadership & discipleship resources.
ISBN Prefix(es): 978-0-912692; 978-0-89191; 978-1-55513; 978-1-56476; 978-0-89693; 978-0-7814; 978-0-88207; 978-1-4347
Number of titles published annually: 50 Print
Total Titles: 2,500 Print
Imprints: Standard Publishing
Divisions: Integrity Music (music publg & recording)
Foreign Rep(s): Ian Matthews (UK)
Foreign Rights: Paige Walton (worldwide)
Returns: 850 N Grove, Elgin, IL 60120
Membership(s): Evangelical Christian Publishers Association (ECPA)
See separate listing for:
Standard Publishing

§Copper Canyon Press
Fort Worden State Park, Bldg 313, Port Townsend, WA 98368
SAN: 206-488X
Mailing Address: PO Box 271, Port Townsend, WA 98368
Tel: 360-385-4925 *Toll Free Tel:* 877-501-1393 (orders) *Fax:* 360-385-4985
E-mail: poetry@coppercanyonpress.org
Web Site: www.coppercanyonpress.org
Key Personnel
Co-Publr: Joseph Bednarik *E-mail:* joseph@coppercanyonpress.org; George Knotek
   E-mail: george@coppercanyonpress.org
Ed-in-Chief & Co-Publr: Michael Wiegers
   E-mail: michael@coppercanyonpress.org
Ed: Elaina Ellis *E-mail:* elaina@coppercanyonpress.com
Fin Mgr: Randy Sturgis *E-mail:* randy@coppercanyonpress.org
Digital Content Mgr: Emily Grise
   E-mail: emilygrise@coppercanyonpress.com
Reader Servs Coord: Janeen Armstrong
   E-mail: janeen@coppercanyonpress.com
Fin/Opers: Margaret Kirk *E-mail:* margaret@coppercanyonpress.org

Publicist: Laura Buccieri *E-mail:* laura@
coppercanyonpress.org
Founded: 1972
Hardcover & paperback trade books of poetry.
ISBN Prefix(es): 978-0-914742; 978-1-55659;
978-1-61932
Number of titles published annually: 32 Print
Total Titles: 400 Print
Branch Office(s)
216 First Ave, Suite 480, Seattle, WA 98104
Distributor for American Poetry Review/Honick-
man
Distribution Center: Consortium Book Sales &
Distribution, The Keg House, Suite 101, 34
13 Ave NE, Minneapolis, MN 55413-1007
Tel: 612-746-2600 *Toll Free Tel:* 800-283-3572
(cust serv, Jackson, TN) *Fax:* 612-746-2606
E-mail: info@cbsd.com *Web Site:* www.cbsd.
com SAN: 200-6049

Cornell Maritime Press
Imprint of Schiffer Publishing Ltd
4880 Lower Valley Rd, Atglen, PA 19310
SAN: 203-5901
Tel: 610-593-1777 *Fax:* 610-593-2002
E-mail: info@schifferbooks.com
Web Site: www.schifferbooks.com
Key Personnel
Pres: Pete Schiffer
Founded: 1938
Professional, technical books in maritime arts &
sciences; boats & boat building; related hobbies
& crafts.
ISBN Prefix(es): 978-0-87033
Number of titles published annually: 5 Print
Total Titles: 300 Print
Imprints: Tidewater Publishers
Distributor for Chesapeake Bay Maritime Mu-
seum; Independent Seaport Museum; Literary
House Press; Maryland Historical Trust Press;
Maryland Sea Grant Program

Cornell University Press
Division of Cornell University
Sage House, 512 E State St, Ithaca, NY 14850
SAN: 202-1862
Tel: 607-253-2338 *Fax:* 607-253-2374
E-mail: cupressinfo@cornell.edu; cupress-sales@
cornell.edu
Web Site: www.cornellpress.cornell.edu
Key Personnel
Edit Dir: Mr Mahinder S Kingra *Tel:* 607-882-
2239 *E-mail:* msk55@cornell.edu
Edit Dir, ILR Press: Ms Frances Benson *Tel:* 607-
882-2255 *E-mail:* fgb2@cornell.edu
Edit Dir, Three Hills: Michael J McGandy
Tel: 607-882-2250 *E-mail:* mjm475@cornell.
edu
Mktg & Sales Dir: Martyn Beeny *Tel:* 402-840-
9930 *E-mail:* mb2545@cornell.edu
Press Dir: Jane Bunker *Tel:* 607-253-2356
E-mail: jfb324@cornell.edu
Exec Ed: Roger Haydon *Tel:* 607-882-2236
E-mail: rmh11@cornell.edu
Mng Ed, Southeast Asia Program Publications:
Sarah E M Grossman *Tel:* 607-255-4359
E-mail: sg265@cornell.edu
Sr Ed: Emily Andrews *Tel:* 607-277-2338 ext
222 *E-mail:* ea424@cornell.edu; James Lance
E-mail: jml554@cornell.edu
Acqs Ed, Northern Illinois University Press: Amy
Farranto *E-mail:* afarranto@niu.edu
Ed, Comstock Publishing Associates: Kitty Liu
Tel: 607-882-2247 *E-mail:* khl8@cornell.edu
Design & Prod Mgr: Lynn Benedetto *Tel:* 607-
253-2310 *E-mail:* lad23@cornell.edu
Subs Rts Mgr: Tonya Cook *Tel:* 607-882-2252
E-mail: tcc6@cornell.edu
Founded: 1869 (reconstituted in 1930)
General nonfiction, scholarly books & mono-
graphs; hardcover & paperbacks.
ISBN Prefix(es): 978-0-8014; 978-0-87546; 978-
1-5017

Number of titles published annually: 190 Print;
188 E-Book
Total Titles: 4,400 Print; 2,700 E-Book
Imprints: Comstock Publishing Associates; Cor-
nell East Asia Series; ILR Press; Northern Illi-
nois University Press; Southeast Asia Program
Publications; Three Hills
Distributor for Leuven University Press
Foreign Rep(s): Combined Academic Publish-
ers (CAP) (Africa, Asia, Europe, Middle East,
UK); Footprint Books Pty Ltd (Australia, Fiji,
New Zealand, Papua New Guinea); US PubRep
Inc (Craig Falk) (Latin America)
Foreign Rights: EULAMA (Alexander von Prell-
witz) (Italy); Graal Literary Agency (Lukasz
Wrobel) (Eastern Europe); Maya Publishers
(Mr Surit Mitra) (India); La Nouvelle Agence
(Vanessa Kling) (France); RDC Agencia Liter-
aria (Beatriz Coll) (Portugal, Spain); Thomas
Schlueck GmbH (Franka Zastrow) (Germany)
Returns: Longleaf Services, c/o Ingram Publisher
Services, 1210 Ingram Dr, Chambersburg, PA
17202 *E-mail:* credit@longleafservices.org
Distribution Center: Longleaf Services Inc,
116 S Boundary St, Chapel Hill, NC 27514-
3808 *Toll Free Tel:* 800-848-6224 *Toll Free
Fax:* 800-272-6817 *E-mail:* customerservice@
longleafservices.org SAN: 203-3151
University of Toronto Distribution, 5201 Duf-
ferin St, Downsview, Toronto, ON M3H
5T8, Canada *Tel:* 416-667-7791 *Toll Free
Tel:* 800-565-9523 *Fax:* 416-667-7832 *Toll Free
Fax:* 800-221-9985
Footprint Books Pty Ltd, 1/6a Prosperity Parade,
Warriewood, NSW 2102, Australia *Tel:* (02)
9997 3973; 1300 260 090 (toll free) *Fax:* (02)
9997 3185
Combined Academic Publishers (CAP), 39
E Parade, Harrogate, N Yorks HG1 5LQ,
United Kingdom *Tel:* (01423) 526350
E-mail: enquiries@combinedacademic.co.uk
Web Site: www.combinedacademic.co.uk
Membership(s): Association of University Presses
(AUPresses)
See separate listing for:
Northern Illinois University Press

Cornerstone Book Publishers
PO Box 24652, New Orleans, LA 70184
E-mail: info@cornerstonepublishers.com;
1cornerstonebooks@gmail.com
Web Site: www.cornerstonepublishers.com
Key Personnel
Owner: Michael R Poll
Founded: 1995
Masonic, Scottish Rite, Rosicrucian, metaphys-
ical, Louisiana themed & classic outdoor &
bushcraft books.
ISBN Prefix(es): 978-1-887560
Number of titles published annually: 6 Print; 10
E-Book
Total Titles: 33 Print; 65 E-Book
Foreign Rep(s): Ingram (UK)

§Corwin
Division of SAGE Publishing
2455 Teller Rd, Thousand Oaks, CA 91320
Tel: 805-499-9734 *Toll Free Tel:* 800-233-9936
Fax: 805-499-5323 *Toll Free Fax:* 800-417-
2466
E-mail: info@corwin.com; order@corwin.com
Web Site: www.corwin.com
Key Personnel
Pres: Mike Soules
SVP & Mng Dir: Lisa Shaw
VP, Mktg & Channel Devt: Elena Nikitina
VP, Prof Learning, Servs & Sales: Dave West
Dir, Prof Learning: Sonja Hollins-Alexander, EdD
Founded: 1990
Offers practical, research-based books, journals &
multimedia resources specifically developed for
principals, administrators, teachers, staff devel-
opers, curriculum developers, special & gifted

educators & other PreK-12 education profes-
sionals.
ISBN Prefix(es): 978-0-7619; 978-0-8039; 978-1-
4129; 978-1-8904; 978-1-57517; 978-1-5697;
978-1-879179
Number of titles published annually: 120 Print
Total Titles: 1,900 Print
Distributor for SAGE UK Resources for Educa-
tors
Foreign Rep(s): SAGE India (India); SAGE Lon-
don (Europe, UK); SAGE Singapore (Asia-
Pacific)

§Cosimo Inc
Old Chelsea Sta, PO Box 416, New York, NY
10011-0416
Tel: 212-989-3616 *Fax:* 212-989-3662
E-mail: info@cosimobooks.com
Web Site: www.cosimobooks.com
Founded: 2005
Specialty publisher for independent authors, not-
for-profit organizations & innovative busi-
nesses, dedicated to publishing books that in-
spire, inform & engage readers around the
world. We offer authors & organizations full
publishing support, while using the newest
technologies to present their works in the most
timely & effective way.
ISBN Prefix(es): 978-1-931044 (Paraview print on
demand titles); 978-1-4165 (Paraview Pocket
Books); 978-1-59605; 978-1-60206; 978-1-
60520; 978-1-61640
Number of titles published annually: 12 Print; 12
E-Book
Total Titles: 45 Print
Imprints: Cosimo Books; Cosimo Classics;
Cosimo Reports; Paraview Pocket Books; Par-
aview Special Editions
Divisions: Paraview Press

Costume + Fashion Press, see Quite Specific
Media Group Ltd

Cotsen Institute of Archaeology Press
Division of University of California, Los Angeles
308 Charles E Young Dr N, Fowler A163, Box
951510, Los Angeles, CA 90095
Tel: 310-206-9384 *Fax:* 310-206-4723
E-mail: cioapress@ioa.ucla.edu
Web Site: www.ioa.ucla.edu
Key Personnel
Dir, Institute: Willeke Wendrich
Dir, Pubns: Randi Danforth
Founded: 1974
Books, monographs & occasional papers in the
field of archaeology.
ISBN Prefix(es): 978-0-917956; 978-1-938770;
978-1-931745
Number of titles published annually: 5 Print; 5 E-
Book
Total Titles: 100 Print; 50 E-Book
Distribution Center: ISD, 70 Enterprise Dr,
Suite 2, Bristol, CT 06010, Pres: Ian Stevens
Tel: 860-584-6546 *E-mail:* ian@isdistribution.
com *Web Site:* www.isdistribution.com

§Council for Exceptional Children (CEC)
2900 Crystal Dr, Suite 100, Arlington, VA 22202
Toll Free Tel: 888-232-7733; 866-915-5000
(TTY)
E-mail: service@cec.sped.org
Web Site: www.cec.sped.org
Key Personnel
Exec Dir: Alexander T Graham *Tel:* 703-264-
9415 *E-mail:* agraham@cec.sped.org
Mgr, Prof Pubns: Lorraine Sobson *Tel:* 703-264-
9466 *E-mail:* lorraines@cec.sped.org
Founded: 1922
Mail order books & other products to improve the
educational success of individuals with disabili-
ties +/or gifts & talents.
ISBN Prefix(es): 978-0-86586
Number of titles published annually: 6 Print

Total Titles: 75 Print
Branch Office(s)
CEC Publications, PO Box 79026, Baltimore, MD 21279-0026
Distributed by ASCD; National Professional Resources (selected titles)
Distributor for Brookes (selected titles); Free Spirit (selected titles); Guilford (selected titles); National Professional Resources (selected titles)
Distribution Center: Amazon
Baker & Taylor
Barnes & Noble

Council for Research in Values & Philosophy
The Catholic University of America, Gibbons Hall, Rm B-12, 620 Michigan Ave NE, Washington, DC 20064
Mailing Address: PO Box 261, Cardinal Sta, Washington, DC 20064-0261
Tel: 202-319-6089 *Fax:* 202-319-6089
E-mail: cua-rvp@cua.edu
Web Site: www.crvp.org
Key Personnel
Exec Dir: Hu Yeping *E-mail:* mclean@cua.edu
Ed: John P Hogan *E-mail:* jhogan4020@yahoo.com
Founded: 1982
Works on philosophy, values, education, civil society, culture.
ISBN Prefix(es): 978-1-56518
Number of titles published annually: 12 Print; 12 Online
Total Titles: 300 Print; 300 Online
Orders to: Oblate School of Theology (OST), 285 Oblate Dr, San Antonio, TX 78216, Contact: Mathew C Martin *Tel:* 210-341-1366 ext 205 *E-mail:* mmartin@ost.edu

Council of State Governments
1776 Avenue of the States, Lexington, KY 40511
Tel: 859-244-8000 *Toll Free Tel:* 800-800-1910
Fax: 859-244-8001
E-mail: sales@csg.org
Web Site: www.csg.org; csgstore.org
Key Personnel
Exec Dir & CEO: David Adkins
E-mail: dadkins@csg.org
Founded: 1933
Nonprofit association representing state government officials in all three branches. Publish reference guides, books, directories, journals, newsletters & conference proceedings & hold major regional & special topical conferences. Will contract or do grant-funded topic research. Specialize in corrections & public safety.
ISBN Prefix(es): 978-0-87292
Number of titles published annually: 10 Print
Total Titles: 72 Print
Branch Office(s)
1107 Ninth St, Suite 730, Sacramento, CA 95814, Exec Dir: Edgar E Ruiz *Tel:* 916-553-4423 *Fax:* 916-446-5760 *E-mail:* csgw@csg.org *Web Site:* www.csgwest.org
444 N Capitol St NW, Suite 401, Washington, DC 20001 *Tel:* 202-624-5460 *Web Site:* www.csgdc.org
PO Box 98129, Atlanta, GA 30359, Dir: Colleen Cousineau *Tel:* 404-633-1866 *Fax:* 404-633-4896 *E-mail:* slc@csg.org *Web Site:* www.slcatlanta.org
701 E 22 St, Suite 110, Lombard, IL 60148, Dir: Michael H McCabe *Tel:* 630-925-1922 *E-mail:* csgm@csg.org *Web Site:* www.csgmidwest.org
22 Cortlandt St, 22nd fl, New York, NY 10007, Dir: Wendell Hannaford *Tel:* 212-482-2320 *Fax:* 212-482-2344 *E-mail:* info@csg-erc.org *Web Site:* www.csgeast.org

Council on Foreign Relations Press
Division of Council on Foreign Relations

The Harold Pratt House, 58 E 68 St, New York, NY 10065
SAN: 201-7784
Tel: 212-434-9400 *Fax:* 212-434-9800
E-mail: publications@cfr.org
Web Site: www.cfr.org
Key Personnel
Edit Dir: Patricia Dorff *Tel:* 212-434-9514 *Fax:* 212-434-9807 *E-mail:* pdorff@cfr.org
Founded: 1922
Scholarly books on foreign policy, international economics, international affairs.
ISBN Prefix(es): 978-0-87609
Number of titles published annually: 10 Print
Total Titles: 245 Print
Branch Office(s)
1777 "F" St NW, Washington, DC 20006 *Tel:* 202-509-8400 *Fax:* 202-509-8490
Membership(s): Association of American Publishers (AAP)

Council on Social Work Education (CSWE), see CSWE Press

Counterpath Press
7935 E 14 Ave, Denver, CO 80220
E-mail: counterpath@counterpathpress.org
Web Site: www.counterpathpress.org
Key Personnel
Assoc Dir & Co-Founder: Julie Carr
Dir: Tim Roberts
Founded: 2006
Independent, nonprofit, literary publisher of poetry, fiction, drama, cross-genre work, literary & cultural theory & criticism, translations, reprints & high-quality Internet material.
ISBN Prefix(es): 978-1-933996
Number of titles published annually: 6 Print
Total Titles: 60 Print
Distribution Center: Small Press Distribution, 1341 Seventh St, Berkeley, CA 94710-1409, Deputy Dir: Laura Moriarty *Tel:* 510-524-1668 *Fax:* 510-524-0852 *E-mail:* laura@spdbooks.org *Web Site:* www.spdbooks.org
Membership(s): Community of Literary Magazines & Presses (CLMP)

Counterpoint Press LLC
2560 Ninth St, Suite 318, Berkeley, CA 94710
Tel: 510-704-0230 *Fax:* 510-704-0268
E-mail: info@counterpointpress.com
Web Site: counterpointpress.com; softskull.com
Key Personnel
Publr: Andy Hunter
VP/Assoc Publr, Publicity, Catapult/Counterpoint Press/Soft Skull: Megan Fishmann
Assoc Publr & Exec Dir, Mktg, Counterpoint Press/Catapult/Soft Skull: Rachel Fershleiser
Assoc Publr & Head, Sales, Counterpoint Press/Catapult/Soft Skull: Alyson Forbes
VP & Edit Dir: Jack Shoemaker
VP, Company Culture/Sr Mng Ed, Books, Catapult/Counterpoint/Soft Skull: Wah-Ming Chang
Creative Dir & Art Dir: Nicole Caputo
Opers & Fin Assoc, Catapult/Counterpoint/Soft Skull: Alexis Aceves Garcia
Exec Ed: Dan Smetanka
Exec Ed, Catapult: Mensah Demary
Ed-in-Chief, Soft Skull Press: Yuka Igarashi
Web Ed-in-Chief, Catapult: Nicole Chung
Digital Mng Ed: Matt Ortile
Ed, Catapult: Megha Majumdar; Leigh Newman
Soc Media Ed, Catapult/Counterpoint/Soft Skull: Dustin Kurtz
Assoc Ed, Publg Mgr & Foreign Rts Mgr, Catapult/Counterpoint/Soft Skull: Kendall Storey
Asst Ed, Catapult: Alicia Kroell
Ed-at-Large: Julie Buntin; Charlie Winton
Sr Publicity Mgr, Catapult/Counterpoint/Soft Skull: Sarah Jean Grimm; Lena Moses-Schmitt
Busn Mgr: Kelli Adams

Events & Programming Mgr, Books, Catapult/Counterpoint/Soft Skull: Katie Boland
Mktg & Spec Sales Mgr, Catapult/Counterpoint/Soft Skull: Dory Athey
Publicity Mgr: Lena Moses-Schmitt
Sr Publicist, Counterpoint/Catapult/Soft Skull: Carla Bruce-Eddings; Alisha Gorder
Sales & Mktg Mgr, Catapult & Soft Skull Press: Elizabeth Ireland
Mktg Coord, Catapult/Counterpoint/Soft Skull: Arriel Vinson
Sales & Mktg Coord, Catapult/Counterpoint/Soft Skull Press: Hope Levy
Designer, Catapult/Counterpoint: Dana Li
Founded: 2007 (through acquisition of Counterpoint, Shoemaker & Hoard, & Soft Skull Press)
Publish literary work with an emphasis on fiction, natural history, philosophy & contemporary thought, history, art, poetry, narrative & nonfiction.
ISBN Prefix(es): 978-1-887178; 978-1-58243; 978-1-61902 (Counterpoint); 978-1-933368 (Soft Skull Press); 978-1-57805 (Sierra Club Books); 978-0-9796636 (Soft Skull Press); 978-1-932360 (Soft Skull Press); 978-1-887128 (Soft Skull Press)
Number of titles published annually: 60 Print
Total Titles: 60 Print
Imprints: Catapult; Counterpoint; Sierra Club Books; Soft Skull Press
Foreign Rep(s): Ingram Publisher Services International (worldwide exc Australia, Canada, Europe & USA); Ingram Publisher Services UK/Grantham Book Services (Europe); NewSouth Books (Australia); Publishers Group Canada/Raincoast (Canada)
Foreign Rights: Kleinworks Agency (Judy Klein)
Distribution Center: Publishers Group West, 1700 Fourth St, Berkeley, CA 94710 *Toll Free Tel:* 866-400-5351 *E-mail:* ips@ingramcontent.com *Web Site:* www.pgw.com

Country Music Foundation Press
Division of Country Music Hall of Fame® & Museum
222 Fifth Ave S, Nashville, TN 37203
Tel: 615-416-2001 *Fax:* 615-255-2245
E-mail: info@countrymusichalloffame.org
Web Site: www.countrymusichalloffame.org
Key Personnel
Writer/Ed: Michael McCall
Founded: 1967
Publish books & calendars. Also author books for trade publications & co-publish with Vanderbilt University Press.
ISBN Prefix(es): 978-0-8265; 978-0-915608
Number of titles published annually: 3 Print
Total Titles: 40 Print
Distributed by Chronicle; Oxford University Press USA; Providence Publishing; Universe; Vanderbilt University Press

§The Countryman Press
Division of W W Norton & Company Inc
c/o W W Norton & Company Inc, 500 Fifth Ave, New York, NY 10110
SAN: 206-4901
Tel: 212-354-5500 *Fax:* 212-869-0856
E-mail: countrymanpress@wwnorton.com
Web Site: wwnorton.com/the-countryman-press
Key Personnel
Edit Dir: Ann Treistman
Founded: 1973
ISBN Prefix(es): 978-0-936399; 978-1-58157; 978-0-914378; 978-0-88150; 978-0-942440
Number of titles published annually: 70 Print
Total Titles: 350 Print
Distributed by Penguin Books (CN only)
Foreign Rep(s): W W Norton & Co Inc
Foreign Rights: Casanovas & Lynch (Portugal, Spain)
Warehouse: National Book Co Inc, 800 Keystone Industrial Park, Scranton, PA 18512-4601

§Covenant Communications Inc
1226 S 630 E, Suite 4, American Fork, UT 84003
Mailing Address: PO Box 416, American Fork,
UT 84003-0416
Tel: 801-756-1041
E-mail: info@covenant-lds.com
Web Site: www.covenant-lds.com
Key Personnel
VP, Mktg: Robby Nichols *Tel:* 801-756-1041 ext
106 *E-mail:* robbyn@covenant-lds.com
Mng Ed, Multimedia & Electronic Publg: Phil
Reschke *Tel:* 801-756-1041 ext 114
Sales Mgr: Tammy Kolkman *Tel:* 801-756-1041
ext 122
Founded: 1958
Publish for the LDS (Mormon) market.
ISBN Prefix(es): 978-1-55503; 978-1-57734; 978-
1-59156; 978-1-59811; 978-1-60681; 978-1-
62108; 978-1-68047
Number of titles published annually: 60 Print; 60
E-Book; 50 Audio
Total Titles: 300 Print; 500 E-Book; 450 Audio

Coyote Press
Affiliate of Archaeological Consulting
PO Box 3377, Salinas, CA 93912-3377
Tel: 831-422-4912 *Fax:* 831-422-4913
E-mail: orders@coyotepress.com
Web Site: www.coyotepress.com
Key Personnel
Owner & Ed: Gary Breschini, PhD
Founded: 1980
Archaeology, history, pre-history, ethnography,
linguistics, rock art & Native American studies
of Western North America.
ISBN Prefix(es): 978-1-55567; 978-1-4044
Number of titles published annually: 50 Print
Total Titles: 3,000 Print

CQ Press
Imprint of SAGE Publishing
2600 Virginia Ave NW, Suite 600, Washington,
DC 20037
Tel: 202-729-1900; 202-729-1800
Toll Free Tel: 866-4CQ-PRESS (427-7737)
E-mail: customerservice@cqpress.com
Web Site: www.cqpress.com; library.cqpress.com
Founded: 1959
Publisher of reference & text books, directories,
periodicals & online products on American
government & politics, journalism & mass
communication.
ISBN Prefix(es): 978-0-87187; 978-1-56802; 978-
0-9625531; 978-1-56692; 978-0-7401; 978-1-
933116; 978-1-60426; 978-0-9823537; 978-1-
60871
Number of titles published annually: 50 Print
Total Titles: 300 Print; 4 CD-ROM; 1 Online; 3
E-Book
Foreign Rep(s): SAGE Publications (Amanda
Fox); SAGE Publications (Sarah Broomhead);
SAGE Publications Asia-Pacific Pte Ltd (Ros-
alia da Garcia)

§Crabtree Publishing Co
347 Fifth Ave, Suite 1402-145, New York, NY
10016
Tel: 212-496-5040 *Toll Free Tel:* 800-387-7650
Toll Free Fax: 800-355-7166
E-mail: custserv@crabtreebooks.com
Web Site: www.crabtreebooks.com
Key Personnel
Pres: Peter A Crabtree *Tel:* 212-496-5040 ext 225
E-mail: peter_c@crabtreebooks.com
Publr: Bobbie Kalman *E-mail:* bobbiek@
crabtreebooks.com
VP, Edit: Kathy Middleton *Tel:* 212-496-5040 ext
226 *E-mail:* kathy_m@crabtreebooks.com
VP, Mktg: Julie Alguire *Tel:* 212-496-5040 ext
235 *E-mail:* julie_a@crabtreebooks.com
VP, Opers: Craig Culliford *Tel:* 212-496-5040 ext
236 *E-mail:* craig_c@crabtreebooks.com

Dir, Art & New Media: Robert MacGregor
Tel: 212-496-5040 ext 231 *E-mail:* rob_m@
crabtreebooks.com
Sales Dir: Andrea Crabtree *Tel:* 212-496-5040 ext
265 *E-mail:* andrea_c@crabtreebooks.com
Warehouse Mgr: Karl Kasper *Tel:* 212-496-5040
ext 237 *E-mail:* warehouse@crabtreebooks.com
Cust Serv: Candice Pinkerton *Tel:* 212-496-5040
ext 221 *E-mail:* candice_c@crabtreebooks.com
Founded: 1978
Publisher of children's nonfiction & fiction; li-
brary binding & paperback for school & trade.
ISBN Prefix(es): 978-0-86505; 978-0-7787; 978-
1-4271
Number of titles published annually: 524 Print;
262 E-Book
Total Titles: 5,964 Print; 2,276 E-Book; 105 Au-
dio
Subsidiaries: Crabtree Publishing Co Ltd (CN)
Distributor for Bayard; Maren Green Publishing
Inc
Foreign Rep(s): Everybody's Books (Namibia,
South Africa); Novella (Australia, New
Zealand); Roundhouse Group (European Union,
UK)
Warehouse: 2321 Kenmore Ave, Buffalo, NY
14207
Membership(s): American Alliance of Muse-
ums (AAM); American Booksellers Associ-
ation (ABA); American Library Association
(ALA); Educational Book & Media Association
(EBMA); Museum Store Association (MSA);
National Science Teachers Association (NSTA)

§Craftsman Book Co
6058 Corte Del Cedro, Carlsbad, CA 92011
SAN: 159-7000
Tel: 760-438-7828 *Toll Free Tel:* 800-829-8123
Fax: 760-438-0398
Web Site: www.craftsman-book.com
Key Personnel
Chmn & Intl Rts: Gary Moselle *E-mail:* gary@
costbook.com
Publr, Data Licensing: Ben Moselle *Tel:* 760-438-
7828 ext 122 *E-mail:* ben@costbook.com
Dir, Lib Sales & Mgr, Sales & Ad: Jen-
nifer Johnson *Tel:* 760-438-7828 ext 105
E-mail: johnson@costbook.com
Edit Mgr & Rts & Perms: Laurence Jacobs
Tel: 760-438-7828 ext 108 *E-mail:* jacobs@
costbook.com
Founded: 1952
Estimating software, trade & professional, state-
specific contract-writing software, subscription,
mail order & download, reference; construction
industry.
ISBN Prefix(es): 978-0-934041; 978-0-910460;
978-1-57218
Number of titles published annually: 8 Print; 2
CD-ROM; 150 Online; 11 E-Book
Total Titles: 150 Print; 2 CD-ROM; 150 Online;
100 E-Book
Distributed by The Aberdeen Group; BNI Publi-
cations; Builders Book Inc
Distributor for BNI Publications; Builders Book
Inc; Building News Inc; Home Builders Press
Foreign Rep(s): Gauge Publications (Canada)
Distribution Center: Quality Books Inc, 103 W
Pines Rd, Oregon, IL 61061-9680 *Tel:* 815-
732-4450 *Toll Free Tel:* 800-323-4241
Fax: 815-732-4499 *E-mail:* info@quality-
books.com *Web Site:* www.quality-books.com

§CRC Press
Imprint of Taylor & Francis Group, an Informa
Business
6000 Broken Sound Pkwy NW, Suite 300, Boca
Raton, FL 33487
Toll Free Tel: 800-272-7737 (orders)
Toll Free Fax: 800-374-3401 (orders)
E-mail: orders@taylorandfrancis.com
Web Site: www.crcpress.com

Key Personnel
CEO: Annie Callahan
SVP, Sales: Dennis Weiss *Tel:* 561-998-2510
E-mail: dennis.weiss@taylorandfrancis.com
Founded: 1913
Premier publisher of science, technology & med-
ical reference books, textbooks & online con-
tent.
ISBN Prefix(es): 978-0-8493; 978-0-935184; 978-
1-57491; 978-0-87762; 978-1-56676; 978-0-
87819; 978-1-58488; 978-1-58716; 978-1-4200;
978-1-4398; 978-1-4665; 978-1-4822; 978-1-
4987
Number of titles published annually: 1,300 Print
Total Titles: 23,000 Print
Warehouse: Taylor & Francis, 7625 Empire Dr,
Florence, KY 41042
See separate listing for:
Productivity Press

§Creative Editions
Imprint of The Creative Co
PO Box 227, Mankato, MN 56002
Tel: 507-388-6273 *Toll Free Tel:* 800-445-6209
Fax: 507-388-2746
E-mail: info@thecreativecompany.us; orders@
thecreativecompany.us
Web Site: www.thecreativecompany.us
Key Personnel
Owner & Publr: Tom Peterson *Tel:* 507-388-6273
ext 225
Publicity: Anna Erickson *Tel:* 415-728-1566
E-mail: aerickson@thecreativecompany.us
Founded: 1932
Gift books.
ISBN Prefix(es): 978-0-87191; 978-0-88682; 978-
0-89812; 978-1-56660; 978-1-56846; 978-1-
60818; 978-1-62832; 978-1-58341
Number of titles published annually: 110 Print
Total Titles: 3,500 Print
Imprints: Creative Digital; Creative Education;
Creative Paperbacks
Foreign Rep(s): Ampersand Inc (British
Columbia, CN, Ontario, CN); Hachette Book
Group (Carlos Azula); Hornblower Group Inc
(Atlantic Canada); Raincoast Books (Canada)
Returns: c/o Hachette Book Group USA, 322 S
Enterprise Blvd, Lebanon, IN 46052
Warehouse: 2140 Howard Dr W, North Mankato,
MN 56003

Creative Homeowner
Imprint of Fox Chapel Publishing Co Inc
1970 Broad St, East Petersburg, PA 17520
Tel: 717-560-4703 *Toll Free Tel:* 844-307-3677
Toll Free Fax: 888-369-2885
E-mail: customerservice@foxchapelpublishing.
com; sales@foxchapelpublishing.com
Web Site: www.foxchapelB2B.com
Founded: 1978
Quality trade paperbacks for kitchen & bath de-
sign & decor, gardening, landscaping, outdoor
hobbies & home improvement.
ISBN Prefix(es): 978-0-932944; 978-1-880029;
978-1-58011
Number of titles published annually: 25 Print
Total Titles: 220 Print

§Cricket Cottage Publishing LLC
Unit of Justice & Chaos Entertainment LLC
1500 Beville Rd, Suite 606-346, Daytona Beach,
FL 32114
Tel: 323-207-6213
E-mail: thecricketpublishing@gmail.com
Web Site: thecricketpublishing.com; www.
facebook.com/CricketCottagePublishing
Key Personnel
Partner: Michael Murray
Soc Media & Mktg Dir: Josh Jones *E-mail:* j@
thecricketpublishing.com
Founded: 2012

Micro-publisher combining the best of traditional & modern publishing. Strictly royalty-based, giving authors a new chance & making use of social media to help promote the company & its books. Basic editing/proofing, book formatting & cover design. Online distribution for paperback & ebook versions.
ISBN Prefix(es): 978-0-9991224
Number of titles published annually: 15 Print; 12 Online; 15 E-Book
Total Titles: 28 Print; 24 Online; 24 E-Book

§Cross-Cultural Communications
Division of Cross-Cultural Literary Editions Inc
239 Wynsum Ave, Merrick, NY 11566-4725
SAN: 208-6122
Tel: 516-868-5635 *Fax:* 516-379-1901
E-mail: cccbarkan@optonline.net; cccpoetry@aol.com
Web Site: www.facebook.com/CrossCulturalCommunications.NY/
Key Personnel
Publr & Ed-in-Chief: Stanley H Barkan
Art Ed: Bebe Barkan
Asst Ed: Mia Barkan Clarke
Founded: 1971
Traditionally neglected languages & cultures in bilingual format, primarily poetry, some fiction, drama, music & art. Cross-cultural review series of world literature & art in sound, print & motion.
ISBN Prefix(es): 978-0-89304
Number of titles published annually: 20 Print; 1 CD-ROM; 100 Online; 1 Audio
Total Titles: 450 Print; 3 CD-ROM; 400 Online; 16 Audio
Imprints: ARC (Magazine & Press) (Israel); Cross-Cultural Prototypes; Expressive Editions; Fact Publishers (Ukraine); Midrashic Editions; Nightingale Editions; Ostrich Editions; The Seventh Quarry (Wales, Seventh Quarry Chapbook Series); The Seventh Quarry Press (Wales)
Subsidiaries: Bulgarian-American Cultural Society ALEKO (Chicago/Sofia, Bulgaria); Varlik (Turkey)
Branch Office(s)
3131 Mott Ave, Far Rockaway, NY 11691, Contact: Roy Cravzow *Tel:* 718-327-4714
HC 67, Box 1206, Big Sur, CA 93920-9629, Contact: Patricia Holt *Tel:* 831-667-2433 *E-mail:* surph8@yahoo.com
Foreign Office(s): Antigruppo Siciliano, Via Mogia 8, 90138 Palermo, Sicily PA, Italy, Contact: Nicolo D'Alessandro *Tel:* (091) 322030 *E-mail:* nicolodalessandro@virgilio.it
Distributed by Ad Infinitum Books; Hochelaga (Canada)
Distributor for Ad Infinitum Press; Arba Sicula (Magazine, US); Center of Emigrants from Serbia (Serbia); Decalogue Books (US); The Feral Press (US); Greenfield Review Press (US); Hochelaga (Canada); Immagine&Poesia (Italy); Legas Publishers (CN); Lips (Magazine & Press) (US); Pholiota Press Inc (England); The Seventh Quarry Press (Wales); Shabdaguchha (Magazine & Press) (Bangladesh & US); Sicilia Parra (Magazine, US); Word & Quill Press (US)
Foreign Rep(s): Hassanal Abdullah (Bangladesh, USA); Karen Alkalay-Gut (Israel); Max Babi (India); Vahe Baladouni (Armenia, USA); Raymond Beauchemin (Canada); August Bover (Spain); Bohdan Boychuk (Ukraine); Gaetano Cipolla (Italy, USA); Nicolo D'Alessandro (Italy); Kristine Doll (Spain, USA); Christopher Fauske (Norway, USA); Isaac Goldemberg (Peru, USA); Theofil Halama (Czechia, USA); Luisa A Igloria (Philippines, USA); Vladimir Kandelaki (Georgia); Dovid Katz (UK); Naoshi Koriyama (Japan); Dariusz Thomasz Lebioda (Poland); Vladimir Levchev (Bulgaria, USA); Bijana D Obradovic (Mon-

tenegro, Serbia, USA); Ritva Poom (Estonia, Finland, USA); Kyung-Nyun "Kay" Kim Richards (South Korea, USA); Stephen A Sadow (Argentina, USA); Marco Scalabrino (Italy); Stoyan "Tchouki" Tchoukanov (Bulgaria); Peter Thabit Jones (UK); Tino Villanueva (Mexico, USA); Claire Nicolas White (Netherlands, USA); Sara Wolosker (Brazil)
Membership(s): American Literary Translators Association (ALTA)

Crossquarter Publishing Group
PO Box 23749, Santa Fe, NM 87502
Tel: 505-690-3923 *Fax:* 214-975-9715
E-mail: sales@crossquarter.com; info@crossquarter.com
Web Site: www.crossquarter.com
Key Personnel
Exec Dir: Therese Francis
Founded: 1986
Small book press with some sidelines. Publishes books, ebooks & information packages. No longer accept fiction queries.
ISBN Prefix(es): 978-1-890109
Number of titles published annually: 25 Print; 3 E-Book
Total Titles: 57 Print; 2 E-Book
Imprints: Crossquarter Breeze; CrossTIME; Fenris Brothers; Herb & Spice; Xemplar
Membership(s): The Association of Publishers for Special Sales (APSS); Independent Book Publishers Association (IBPA)

§The Crossroad Publishing Co
831 Chestnut Ridge Rd, Chestnut Ridge, NY 10977
SAN: 287-0118
Tel: 845-517-0180 *Toll Free Tel:* 800-888-4741 (orders)
E-mail: info@crossroadpublishing.com
Web Site: www.CrossroadPublishing.com
Key Personnel
Publr & CEO: Dr Gwendolin Herder
Off Mgr: Stephanie Marchese
Founded: 1980
Independent book publisher in religion, spirituality, theology, personal growth, leadership & parenting.
ISBN Prefix(es): 978-0-8245
Number of titles published annually: 30 Print; 1 CD-ROM; 1 Online; 20 E-Book; 1 Audio
Total Titles: 550 Print; 1 CD-ROM; 1 Online; 20 E-Book; 4 Audio
Imprints: Crossroad (trade secular & religious); Herder & Herder (Catholic parish & academic)
Foreign Rep(s): John Garratt (Australia); Novalis (Canada)
Billing Address: Independent Publishers Group, 814 N Franklin St, Chicago, IL 60610
E-mail: orders@ipgbook.com *Web Site:* www.ipgbook.com
Membership(s): Association of Catholic Publishers Inc

Crossway
Division of Good News Publishers
1300 Crescent St, Wheaton, IL 60187
SAN: 211-7991
Tel: 630-682-4300 *Toll Free Tel:* 800-635-7993 (orders); 800-543-1659 (cust serv) *Fax:* 630-682-4785
E-mail: info@crossway.org
Web Site: www.crossway.org
Key Personnel
Pres: Josh Dennis
EVP, Book Publg: Justin Taylor
EVP, Busn Opers: Anthony Gosling
EVP, Creative: Dan Farrell
EVP, Publg: Dane Ortlund
SVP, Fin: Paul Thomas
SVP, Ministry & Licensing: Randy Jahns

Edit Admin & ISBN Contact: Jill Carter
E-mail: jcarter@crossway.org
Intl Rts: Aaron Camp *E-mail:* acamp@crossway.org
Perms: Nicole Gosling *E-mail:* ngosling@crossway.org
Founded: 1969
Books with an evangelical Christian perspective aimed at the religious market.
ISBN Prefix(es): 978-0-89107; 978-1-58134; 978-1-4335
Number of titles published annually: 80 Print
Total Titles: 354 Print; 9 Audio

§Crown House Publishing Co LLC
Division of Crown House Publishing Ltd (UK Co)
81 Brook Hills Circle, White Plains, NY 10605
SAN: 013-9270
Tel: 914-946-3517 *Toll Free Tel:* 877-925-1213 (cust serv) *Fax:* 914-946-1160
E-mail: info@chpus.com
Web Site: www.crownhousepublishing.com
Key Personnel
Pres: Mark Tracten *E-mail:* mtracten@chpus.com
Founded: 1996
Publisher of quality books in psychology & education.
ISBN Prefix(es): 978-1-89983; 978-1-90442; 978-1-84590; 978-0-98235
Number of titles published annually: 30 Print; 1 CD-ROM; 6 Audio
Total Titles: 330 Print; 2 CD-ROM; 30 Audio
Distributor for Developing Press Co; Human Alchemy Publications; Institute Press; Transforming Press
Foreign Rep(s): Footprint Books Pty Ltd (Australia, New Zealand)
Foreign Rights: Anglo-American Book Co Ltd (Europe, UK)
Billing Address: PO Box 2223, Williston, VT 05495
Orders to: PO Box 2223, Williston, VT 05495, Contact: Matt Drake *Fax:* 802-864-7626 *E-mail:* mdrake@aidcvt.com
Returns: American International Distribution Corp (AIDC), 82 Winter Sport Lane, Williston, VT 05495, Contact: Matt Drake *E-mail:* mdrake@aidcvt.com
Shipping Address: PO Box 2223, Williston, VT 05495, Contact: Laurie Kenyon *Tel:* 802-862-0095 ext 113 *Fax:* 802-864-7626
Warehouse: PO Box 2223, Williston, VT 05495
Distribution Center: American International Distribution Corp (AIDC), 82 Winter Sport Lane, Williston, VT 05495, Contact: Laurie Kenyon *Tel:* 802-862-0095 *Toll Free Tel:* 800-678-2432 *Fax:* 802-864-7749 *E-mail:* lkenyon@aidcvt.com *Web Site:* www.aidcvt.com

Crown Publishing Group
Imprint of Random House Publishing Group
1745 Broadway, New York, NY 10019
Tel: 212-782-9000 *Toll Free Tel:* 888-264-1745 *Fax:* 212-940-7408
E-mail: crownosm@penguinrandomhouse.com
Web Site: crownpublishing.com
Founded: 1933
Leading publisher of bestselling fiction & critically acclaimed narrative nonfiction in categories that include biography & memoirs, history, science, politics & current events.
Penguin Random House & its publishing entities are not accepting unsol submissions, proposals, mss, or submission queries via e-mail at this time.
Number of titles published annually: 400 Print
Imprints: Amphoto Books; Broadway Books; Clarkson Potter; Convergent Books; Crown Archetype; Crown Business; Crown Forum; Crown Publishers; Currency; Harmony Books; Hogarth; Image Books; Multnomah; Rodale

Books; Ten Speed Press; Three Rivers Press; WaterBrook; Watson-Guptill
See separate listing for:
Clarkson Potter Publishers
Ten Speed Press
WaterBrook
Watson-Guptill Publications

§Crystal Clarity Publishers
14618 Tyler Foote Rd, Nevada City, CA 95959
Tel: 530-478-7600 *Toll Free Tel:* 800-424-1055
Fax: 530-478-7562
E-mail: clarity@crystalclarity.com
Web Site: www.crystalclarity.com
Key Personnel
Pres & Publr: Richard Salva *Tel:* 530-478-7600 ext 7606
Founded: 1968
Self-help, psychology, philosophy, religion, business, books, tapes, videos, sidelines, metaphysical, health/healing.
ISBN Prefix(es): 978-0-916124; 978-1-878265; 978-1-56589
Number of titles published annually: 6 Print
Total Titles: 125 Print; 15 Audio
Imprints: Clarity Sound & Light
Foreign Rep(s): Brumby Books (Australia); Deep Books Ltd (England, Europe); National Book Network (Canada, New Zealand); New Horizons (South Africa)
Foreign Rights: Alexandra McGilloway

CSHL Press, see Cold Spring Harbor Laboratory Press

The CSIS Press
Division of Center for Strategic & International Studies
1616 Rhode Island Ave NW, Washington, DC 20036
Tel: 202-887-0200 *Fax:* 202-775-3199
E-mail: books@csis.org
Web Site: www.csis.org
Key Personnel
Pres & CEO: John J Hamre
Sr Pubns Mgr: Jeeah Jehanne Lee *Tel:* 202-775-3160 *E-mail:* jelee@csis.org
Founded: 1962
Public policy research organization.
ISBN Prefix(es): 978-0-89206; 978-1-44228
Number of titles published annually: 65 Print; 65 Online; 25 E-Book
Total Titles: 250 Print; 100 Online; 200 E-Book
Distributed by Rowman & Littlefield
Membership(s): Association of American Publishers (AAP)

§CSLI Publications
Stanford University, Cordura Hall, 220 Panama St, Stanford, CA 94305-4115
Tel: 650-723-1839 *Fax:* 650-725-2166
E-mail: pubs@csli.stanford.edu
Web Site: cslipublications.stanford.edu
Key Personnel
Dir: Dikran Karagueuzian *Tel:* 650-723-1712 *E-mail:* dikran@csli.stanford.edu
Founded: 1985
Subjects include computer science, computational linguistics, linguistics & philosophy.
ISBN Prefix(es): 978-0-937073; 978-1-881526; 978-1-57586; 978-0-226
Number of titles published annually: 6 Print
Total Titles: 375 Print; 7 Online
Distributed by University of Chicago Press

CSWE Press
Division of Council on Social Work Education
1701 Duke St, Suite 200, Alexandria, VA 22314-3457
Tel: 703-683-8080 *Fax:* 703-683-8493
E-mail: publications@cswe.org; info@cswe.org

Web Site: www.cswe.org
Key Personnel
Pres & CEO: Darla Spence Coffey, PhD
Pubns Mgr: Elizabeth Simon *Tel:* 703-519-2076 *E-mail:* esimon@cswe.org
Founded: 1952
Professional books.
ISBN Prefix(es): 978-0-87293
Number of titles published annually: 3 Print
Total Titles: 33 Print
Orders to: c/o Ware-Pak, 2427 Bond St, University Park, IL 60484 *Toll Free Tel:* 877-751-5053 *E-mail:* cswe@ware-pak.com
Returns: c/o Ware-Pak, 2427 Bond St, University Park, IL 60484 *Toll Free Tel:* 877-751-5053 *E-mail:* cswe@ware-pak.com
Membership(s): Copyright Clearance Center (CCC)

CUA Press, see The Catholic University of America Press

§Cup of Tea Books
Imprint of PageSpring Publishing
PO Box 21133, Columbus, OH 43221
E-mail: sales@pagespringpublishing.com; weditor@pagespringpublishing.com; submissions@pagespringpublishing.com
Web Site: www.cupofteabooks.com
Key Personnel
Publr & Ed: Rebecca Seum
Founded: 2012
Independent publisher. Specialize in quality women's fiction.
ISBN Prefix(es): 978-1-939403
Number of titles published annually: 2 Print; 2 E-Book
Total Titles: 9 Print; 8 E-Book

Curious Cat Books, see Legacy Bound

Cycle Publishing LLC
1282 Seventh Ave, San Francisco, CA 94122-2526
Tel: 415-665-8214 *Fax:* 415-753-8572
Web Site: www.cyclepublishing.com
Key Personnel
Principal & Publr: Rob van der Plas
Founded: 1997
Books on sports, fitness, home building & home buying; emphasis on cycling.
ISBN Prefix(es): 978-1-892495
Number of titles published annually: 3 Print
Total Titles: 30 Print
Imprints: Cycle Publishing; Van der Plas Publications
Foreign Rights: Bicycling (Australia); Fahrradbuch.de (Austria, Germany); Orca Book Services (UK)
Warehouse: PCFS, 35 Ash Dr, Kimball, MI 48074
Membership(s): The Association of Publishers for Special Sales (APSS); Independent Book Publishers Association (IBPA)

Cypress House
Imprint of Comp-Type Inc
155 Cypress St, Fort Bragg, CA 95437
Tel: 707-964-9520 *Toll Free Tel:* 800-773-7782 *Fax:* 707-964-7531
Web Site: www.cypresshouse.com
Key Personnel
Pres: Cynthia Frank *E-mail:* cynthia@cypresshouse.com
Mng Ed: Joe Shaw *E-mail:* joeshaw@cypresshouse.com
ISBN Prefix(es): 978-1-879384
Number of titles published annually: 10 Print; 4 E-Book; 1 Audio
Total Titles: 140 Print; 20 E-Book; 1 Audio
Imprints: Lost Coast Press; QED Press

Membership(s): American Booksellers Association (ABA); California Independent Booksellers Alliance (CALIBA); Independent Book Publishers Association (IBPA); Pacific Northwest Booksellers Association (PNBA)

Dafina Books, see Kensington Publishing Corp

Dalkey Archive Press
University of Houston-Victoria, 3402 N Ben Wilson, Victoria, TX 77901
E-mail: contact@dalkeyarchive.com
Web Site: www.dalkeyarchive.com
Key Personnel
Dir: John O'Brien
Assoc Dir: Jake Snyder
Founded: 1984
Literary fiction, translations & criticism. We keep works of literary value in print.
ISBN Prefix(es): 978-0-916583; 978-1-56478; 978-1-62897; 978-1-943150
Number of titles published annually: 60 Print
Total Titles: 750 Print
Foreign Rep(s): Canadian Manda Group (Canada); John Toomey (Europe, UK & Commonwealth)
Distribution Center: Ingram Publisher Services, One Ingram Blvd, La Vergne, TN 37086 (worldwide exc Europe) *Toll Free Tel:* 866-400-5351 (orders)
Central Books Ltd, 50 Freshwater Rd, Chadwell Heath RM8 1RX, United Kingdom (Europe), Contact: Bill Norris *Tel:* (020) 8525 8800 *Fax:* (020) 8599 2694 *E-mail:* contactus@centralbooks.com *Web Site:* www.centralbooks.com

Dancing Dakini Press
77 Morning Sun Dr, Sedona, AZ 86336
Tel: 505-466-1887
E-mail: editor@dancingdakinipress.com
Web Site: www.dancingdakinipress.com
Key Personnel
CFO: Ben Long *Tel:* 503-415-0229 *E-mail:* ben@benllong.com
Founded: 2012
Small publisher creating well-crafted books to inspire compassionate awareness, skillful means, authentic lives & a deep respect for all.
ISBN Prefix(es): 978-0-9836333
Number of titles published annually: 3 Print; 2 E-Book
Total Titles: 7 Print; 5 E-Book
Imprints: Dancing Ants Press
Orders to: New Leaf Distributing Co, 401 Thornton Rd, Lithia Springs, GA 30122-1557, Contact: Lenora Whitmire *Tel:* 770-948-7845 *Fax:* 770-944-2313 *E-mail:* domestic@newleafdist.com *Web Site:* newleafdist.com
Returns: New Leaf Distributing Co, 401 Thornton Rd, Lithia Springs, GA 30122-1557, Contact: Lenora Whitmire *Tel:* 770-948-7845 *Fax:* 770-944-2313 *E-mail:* lwhitmire@newleaf-dist.com *Web Site:* newleafdist.com
Shipping Address: New Leaf Distributing Co, 401 Thornton Rd, Lithia Springs, GA 30122-1557 *Tel:* 770-948-7845 *Fax:* 770-944-2313 *Web Site:* newleafdist.com
Warehouse: New Leaf Distributing Co, 401 Thornton Rd, Lithia Springs, GA 30122-1557 *Tel:* 770-948-7845 *Fax:* 770-944-2313 *Web Site:* newleafdist.com
Distribution Center: New Leaf Distributing Co, 401 Thornton Rd, Lithia Springs, GA 30122-1557, Contact: Lenora Whitmire *Tel:* 770-948-7845 *Fax:* 770-944-2313 *E-mail:* lwhitmire@newleaf-dist.com *Web Site:* newleafdist.com

Dancing Lemur Press LLC
PO Box 383, Pikeville, NC 27863-0383
E-mail: inquiries@dancinglemurpressllc.com
Web Site: www.dancinglemurpressllc.com
Founded: 2008

Dedicated to bringing outstanding & inspiring science fiction & fantasy, new adult/young adult, mystery, paranormal, middle grade, nonfiction, Christian & more to readers.
ISBN Prefix(es): 978-0-9816210; 978-0-9827139; 978-1-939844
Number of titles published annually: 5 Print; 6 E-Book; 2 Audio
Total Titles: 45 Print; 51 E-Book; 12 Audio
Imprints: Freedom Fox Press
Distribution Center: Ingram Content Group, One Ingram Blvd, La Vergne, TN 37086 (US) *Tel:* 615-793-5000 *Web Site:* www.ingramcontent.com
Membership(s): Independent Book Publishers Association (IBPA)

John Daniel & Co
Division of Daniel & Daniel Publishers Inc
PO Box 2790, McKinleyville, CA 95519-2790
SAN: 215-1995
Tel: 707-839-3495 *Toll Free Tel:* 800-662-8351
E-mail: dandd@danielpublishing.com
Web Site: www.danielpublishing.com
Key Personnel
Owner & Publr: John Daniel *E-mail:* john@danielpublishing.com
Owner & Sales Mgr: Susan Daniel *E-mail:* susan@danielpublishing.com
Founded: 1985
ISBN Prefix(es): 978-1-56474
Number of titles published annually: 5 Print
Total Titles: 200 Print
Branch Office(s)
2611 Kelly Ave, McKinleyville, CA 95519
Distributor for Fithian Press; Perseverance Press
Returns: 2611 Kelly Ave, McKinleyville, CA 95519
Distribution Center: SCB Distributors, 15608 S New Century Dr, Gardena, CA 90248, Contact: Aaron Silverman *Toll Free Tel:* 800-729-6423
Membership(s): Independent Book Publishers Association (IBPA)

Dark Horse Comics
Affiliate of Dark Horse Entertainment
10956 SE Main St, Milwaukie, OR 97222
Tel: 503-652-8815 *Fax:* 503-654-9440
E-mail: dhcomics@darkhorse.com
Web Site: www.darkhorse.com
Key Personnel
Founder & Pres: Michael Richardson
VP, Mktg: Matt Parkinson
Head, Berger Books: Karen Berger
Founded: 1986
Primary area is graphic novels; pop culture; limited edition hardcovers & comics.
ISBN Prefix(es): 978-1-56971
Number of titles published annually: 200 Print
Total Titles: 600 Print
Imprints: Berger Books; Dark Horse Books; The M Press
Distributed by LPC Group Inc
Foreign Rights: Anita Nelson
Distribution Center: Penguin Random House Publisher Services (PRHPS), 1745 Broadway, New York, NY 10019 *E-mail:* distribution@penguinrandomhouse.com

§The Dartnell Corporation
Subsidiary of Eli Research Inc
2222 Sedwick Dr, Durham, NC 27713
Toll Free Tel: 800-223-8720; 800-472-0148 (cust serv) *Toll Free Fax:* 800-508-2592
E-mail: customerservice@dartnellcorp.com
Web Site: www.dartnellcorp.com
Founded: 1916
Business information, training, motivation.
ISBN Prefix(es): 978-0-85013
Number of titles published annually: 20 Print
Total Titles: 150 Print

§Data Trace Publishing Co (DTP)
110 West Rd, Suite 227, Towson, MD 21204-2316
Mailing Address: PO Box 1239, Brooklandville, MD 21022-1239
Tel: 410-494-4994 *Toll Free Tel:* 800-342-0454 *Fax:* 410-494-0515
E-mail: info@datatrace.com; customerservice@datatrace.com; salesandmarketing@datatrace.com; editorial@datatrace.com
Web Site: www.datatrace.com
Key Personnel
VP, Edit & Client Servs: Kimberly Collignon
Dir, Mktg: Holly Ballard
Ad Mgr: Frank Tufariello
Founded: 1987
Full service specialty publisher with interest in science, technical, law & medicine.
ISBN Prefix(es): 978-0-9637468; 978-1-57400
Number of titles published annually: 20 Print; 25 E-Book
Total Titles: 125 Print; 15 CD-ROM; 30 Online; 15 E-Book
Foreign Rep(s): Eurospan (worldwide exc Canada & USA)

Daughters of St Paul, see Pauline Books & Media

May Davenport Publishers
26313 Purissima Rd, Los Altos Hills, CA 94022
Tel: 650-947-6499
E-mail: mdbooks@earthlink.net
Web Site: www.maydavenportpublishers.org
Key Personnel
Ed & Publr: May Davenport
Founded: 1975
Publish & distribute books for children/young adults (grades K-12). Books are written by teachers, writers, social workers, mental clinicians & counselors. We sell books by direct mail. Remainders are donated to schools in depressed areas who ask for free copies for their students to take home. The company originally created *Comic Tales* to read-aloud happy stories for children to color the illustrations. Titles include *Comic Tales Anthology No 1*, *Pogo Sticks* by Andrea Ross plus two others, *Comic Tales No 2* by five authors, *The Runaway Game* by Kevin Casey, *A Time to Fantasize* by May Davenport, *Windriders* by Blake F Grant & *Comic Tales No 3* by 31 authors.
ISBN Prefix(es): 978-0-9603118; 978-0-943864; 978-0-9794140
Number of titles published annually: 3 Print; 8 Online
Total Titles: 32 Print; 32 Online
Imprints: Md Books

The Davies Group Publishers
PO Box 440140, Aurora, CO 80044-0140
Tel: 303-750-8374
E-mail: daviesgroup@msn.com (orders)
Web Site: www.thedaviesgrouppublishers.com
Founded: 1991
Scholarly publisher; philosophy, humanities & social sciences.
ISBN Prefix(es): 978-1-888570; 978-0-9630076; 978-1-934542; 978-1-935790; 978-1-943047
Number of titles published annually: 6 Print; 2 E-Book
Total Titles: 109 Print; 85 E-Book
Imprints: Noesis Press; PenMark Press

§Davies Publishing Inc
32 S Raymond Ave, Suites 4 & 5, Pasadena, CA 91105-1961
SAN: 217-3255
Tel: 626-792-3046 *Toll Free Tel:* 877-792-0005 *Fax:* 626-792-5308
E-mail: info@daviespublishing.com
Web Site: daviespublishing.com

Key Personnel
Pres & Publr: Michael Davies *E-mail:* mikedavies@daviespublishing.com
Edit Dir: Christina Moose *E-mail:* chrismoose@daviespublishing.com
Corp Secy & Opers Mgr: Janet Heard *E-mail:* janetheard@daviespublishing.com
Prodn Mgr: Charlene Locke *E-mail:* charlenelocke@daviespublishing.com
Founded: 1981
Ultrasound education & test preparation: books, software, DVDs, mock examinations & flashcards.
ISBN Prefix(es): 978-0-941022
Number of titles published annually: 2 Print; 2 CD-ROM
Total Titles: 48 Print; 7 CD-ROM
Membership(s): Association of American Publishers (AAP); Independent Book Publishers Association (IBPA)

§F A Davis Co
1915 Arch St, Philadelphia, PA 19103
SAN: 200-2078
Tel: 215-568-2270; 215-440-3001 *Toll Free Tel:* 800-523-4049 *Fax:* 215-568-5065; 215-440-3016
E-mail: info@fadavis.com; orders@fadavis.com
Web Site: www.fadavis.com
Key Personnel
Chmn of the Bd: Robert H Craven, Sr
Pres: Robert H Craven, Jr
Exec Dir, Sales: Neil K Kelly
Publr: Lisa Deitch; Robert Martone
Ed-in-Chief, Nursing: Jean Rodenberger
Founded: 1879
Publisher of nursing, medical & health profession texts, podcasts & clinical simulations.
ISBN Prefix(es): 978-0-8036
Number of titles published annually: 75 Print; 1 Online; 65 E-Book; 5 Audio
Total Titles: 399 Print; 150 E-Book; 10 Audio
Foreign Rep(s): ChoiceTEXTS (Brunei, Cambodia, China, Hong Kong, Indonesia, Laos, Malaysia, Myanmar, Palau, Philippines, Saipan, Singapore, South Korea, Taiwan, Thailand, Vietnam); Elsevier Australia (Australia, New Zealand); International Publishers Representatives Ltd (Algeria, Cyprus, Egypt, Ethiopia, Iran, Iraq, Israel, Jordan, Kuwait, Lebanon, Libya, Malta, Morocco, Oman, Pakistan, Qatar, Saudi Arabia, Sudan, Syria, Tunisia, United Arab Emirates, Virgin Islands, West Bank, Yemen); Jaypee Bros Medical Publishers (Bangladesh, India, Nepal, Sri Lanka); Medicus Media (Albania, Austria, Belarus, Belgium, Bulgaria, Canary Islands, Channel Islands, Croatia, Czechia, Denmark, Georgia, Germany, Gibraltar, Greece, Hungary, Iceland, Ireland, Italy, Kazakhstan, Latvia, Liechtenstein, Luxembourg, Monaco, Netherlands, North Macedonia, Northern Isles, Norway, Poland, Portugal, Romania, Russia, San Marino, Scotland, Serbia, Slovakia, Slovenia, Spain, Sweden, Switzerland, Turkey, Ukraine, UK, Uzbekistan, Wales)
Returns: Attn: Returns Dept, 404 S Second St, Philadelphia, PA 19123 *Tel:* 215-440-3002 *Toll Free Tel:* 800-323-3555 *E-mail:* credits@fadavis.com
Distribution Center: 404 N Second St, Philadelphia, PA 19123 *Tel:* 215-440-3002 *Toll Free Tel:* 800-323-3555 *Fax:* 215-440-3016
Matthews Book Co, 11559 Rock Island Ct, Maryland Heights, MO 63043 *Tel:* 314-432-1400 *Toll Free Tel:* 800-633-2665 *Fax:* 314-432-7044 *Toll Free Fax:* 800-421-8816 *Web Site:* www.matthewsbooks.com
Baker & Taylor LLC, 2550 W Tyvola Rd, Suit 300, Charlotte, NC 28217 *Tel:* 704-998-3100 *Toll Free Tel:* 800-775-1800 *E-mail:* btinfo@baker-taylor.com *Web Site:* www.baker-taylor.com

Rittenhouse Book Distributors, 511 Feheley Dr, King of Prussia, PA 19406 *Toll Free Tel:* 800-345-6425 *Toll Free Fax:* 800-223-7488 *Web Site:* www.rittenhouse.com

Login Canada, 300 Saulteaux Crescent, Winnipeg, MB R3J 3T2, Canada *Tel:* 204-837-2987 *Toll Free Tel:* 800-665-1148 *Web Site:* lb.ca

§DAW Books Inc
Imprint of Penguin Group USA, A Penguin Random House Company
375 Hudson St, New York, NY 10014
Tel: 212-366-2096 *Fax:* 212-366-2090
E-mail: daw@penguinrandomhouse.com
Web Site: www.dawbooks.com; www.penguin.com; www.penguinrandomhouse.com
Key Personnel
Publr: Sheila E Gilbert; Elizabeth R Wollheim
Submission Ed: Peter Stampfel
E-mail: submissions@us.penguingroup.com
Founded: 1971
Science fiction; fantasy; paperbound originals & reprints; hardcover editions, trade paperbacks & ebooks.
Penguin Random House & its publishing entities are not accepting unsol submissions, proposals, mss, or submission queries via e-mail at this time.
Number of titles published annually: 60 Print; 60 E-Book
Total Titles: 325 Print
Imprints: DAW/Fantasy; DAW/Fiction; DAW/Science Fiction
Distributed by Penguin Group USA, A Penguin Random House Company

The Dawn Horse Press
Division of The Adidam Holy Institution
12040 N Seigler Rd, Middletown, CA 95461
Mailing Address: PO Box 70, Lower Lake, CA 95457
Tel: 707-928-6590 *Toll Free Tel:* 877-770-0772
Fax: 707-928-5068
E-mail: dhp@adidam.org
Web Site: www.dawnhorsepress.com
Key Personnel
Publr: James Minkin
Founded: 1972
Produces & markets books, CDs & AV materials on every aspect of authentic spiritual life & human development based upon the wisdom & teaching of Avatar Adi Da Samraj.
ISBN Prefix(es): 978-0-913922; 978-0-918801; 978-0-918801; 978-1-57097; 978-0-929929
Number of titles published annually: 8 Print; 5 CD-ROM; 12 Online; 4 Audio
Total Titles: 100 Print; 40 CD-ROM; 65 Online; 1 E-Book; 33 Audio
Shipping Address: 12312 Hwy 175, Cobb Mountain, CA 95426, Contact: Patrick Forristal
Distribution Center: New Leaf Distributing Co, 401 Thorton Rd, Lithia Springs, GA 30122-1557 *Tel:* 770-948-7845 *Fax:* 770-944-2313 *E-mail:* newleaf@newleaf-dist.com *Web Site:* newleafdist.com
Membership(s): Independent Book Publishers Association (IBPA)

Dawn Publications Inc
Imprint of Sourcebooks Inc
12402 Bitney Springs Rd, Nevada City, CA 95959
Tel: 530-274-7775 *Toll Free Tel:* 800-545-7475
Fax: 530-274-7778
E-mail: nature@dawnpub.com; orders@dawnpub.com
Web Site: www.dawnpub.com
Key Personnel
Co-Publr/Ed & Art Dir: Carol Malnor
E-mail: carol@dawnpub.com
Co-Publr/Mktg Dir: Bruce Malnor
E-mail: bruce@dawnpub.com

Co-Publr/Fin & Rts Mgr: Richard Rodrigue
E-mail: richard@dawnpub.com
Founded: 1979
Nature awareness nonfiction picture books for children, teachers, naturalists & parents; character value education; natural science.
ISBN Prefix(es): 978-0-916124; 978-1-883220; 978-1-58469
Number of titles published annually: 4 Print; 4 E-Book
Total Titles: 95 Print; 85 E-Book
Foreign Rep(s): Deep Books Ltd (UK); Fitzhenry & Whiteside (Canada); SULA Book Distributors (South Africa)
Membership(s): American Booksellers Association (ABA); APPL; Independent Book Publishers Association (IBPA); Publishers Association of the West (PubWest)

DawnSignPress
6130 Nancy Ridge Dr, San Diego, CA 92121-3223
Tel: 858-625-0600 *Toll Free Tel:* 800-549-5350
Fax: 858-625-2336
E-mail: contactus@dawnsign.com
Web Site: www.dawnsign.com
Key Personnel
Founder & Pres: Joe Dannis
Mktg & Lib Sales Dir: Becky Ryan
Founded: 1979
Specialty publisher of instructional sign language & educational deaf studies materials for both children & adults.
ISBN Prefix(es): 978-0-915035; 978-1-58121
Number of titles published annually: 5 Print
Total Titles: 65 Print; 1 CD-ROM
Distributed by Gryphon House
Distributor for Gallaudet University Press; MIT Press; Penguin Random House Inc
Foreign Rights: Gloval Interprint (Hong Kong)

dbS Productions
PO Box 94, Charlottesville, VA 22902
Tel: 434-293-5502 *Toll Free Tel:* 800-745-1581
E-mail: info@dbs-sar.com
Web Site: www.dbs-sar.com
Key Personnel
CEO & Sr Scientist: Robert J Koester
E-mail: robert@dbs-sar.com
Founded: 1989
Search & rescue.
ISBN Prefix(es): 978-1-879471
Number of titles published annually: 5 Print
Total Titles: 17 Print; 2 CD-ROM
Distributed by CMC

DC Comics Inc
Unit of DC Entertainment
4000 Warner Blvd, Burbank, CA 91522
Web Site: www.dccomics.com; www.dcentertainment.com; www.madmag.com
Key Personnel
EVP, Busn & Mktg Strategy, Direct to Consumer & Global Franchise Mgmt: Amit Desai
Co-Publr: Dan Didio
Co-Publr & Chief Creative Offr: Jim Lee
Founded: 1935
Innovative comics publishing in periodical & book formats. In addition to the world's most popular superheroes, Superman, Batman & Wonder Woman, DC publishes cutting edge fantasy, horror, mystery, adventure, humor, nonfiction & general interest titles & maintains a 500+ title backlist in print. *MAD* Books is based on the classic magazine featuring Alfred E Neuman, Spy vs Spy & other icons. DC/MAD properties are also licensed for various publishing formats, as well as media, promotions & consumer products. DC Comics does not accept unsol mss. For more information, visit our web site at www.dcentertainment.com.

ISBN Prefix(es): 978-0-930289; 978-1-56389; 978-1-4012
Number of titles published annually: 240 Print
Total Titles: 2,778 Print
Imprints: DC (readers 13 years & older); DC Black Label (readers 17 years & older); DC Comics; DC Kids (middle grade); MAD Books
Distribution Center: Penguin Random House Publisher Services (PRHPS), 1745 Broadway, New York, NY 10019 *E-mail:* distribution@randomhouse.com

§Walter De Gruyter Inc
Division of Walter de Gruyter GmbH
121 High St, 3rd fl, Boston, MA 02110
Tel: 857-284-7073 *Fax:* 857-284-7358
E-mail: service@degruyter.com
Web Site: www.degruyter.com
Key Personnel
VP, De Gruyter Americas: Paul Manning
E-mail: paul.manning@degruyter.com
Founded: 1749
Scholarly & scientific books, journals, paperbacks & hardcover reprints.
ISBN Prefix(es): 978-0-311; 978-0-89925; 978-3-11; 978-1-56445; 978-1-934078; 978-1-61451; 978-1-5015
Number of titles published annually: 200 Print; 5 CD-ROM
Total Titles: 8,500 Print; 20 CD-ROM; 15 Online; 10 E-Book
Foreign Office(s): Walter de Gruyter GmbH, Genthinerstr 13, 10785 Berlin, Germany *Tel:* (030) 260 05 0 *Fax:* (030) 260 05 251
Foreign Rep(s): Allied Publishers (India, Nepal, Sri Lanka); Book Club International (Bangladesh); Combined Representatives Worldwide Inc (Philippines); D A Books & Journals (Australia, New Zealand); Verlags und Kommissionsbuchhandlung Dr Franz Hain (Austria); Kumi Trading (South Korea); Kweilin Bookstore (Taiwan); Maruzen Co Ltd (Japan); Pak Book Corp (Pakistan); Parry's Book Center (Sendjrjan Berhad) (Brunei, Malaysia, Singapore); Swinden Book Co Ltd (Hong Kong)
Orders to: TriLiteral, 100 Maple Ridge Dr, Cumberland, RI 02864 *Tel:* 401-531-2800 *Toll Free Tel:* 800-405-1619 *Fax:* 401-531-2801 *Toll Free Fax:* 800-406-9145 *E-mail:* orders@triliteral.org

§Deep River Books LLC
PO Box 310, Sisters, OR 97759
Tel: 541-549-1139
E-mail: info@deepriverbooks.com
Web Site: deepriverbooks.com
Key Personnel
Publr: Bill Carmichael; Nancie Carmichael
Founded: 2001
Publisher of Christian/inspirational books.
This publisher has indicated that 70% of their product line is author subsidized.
ISBN Prefix(es): 978-1-940269; 978-1-63269
Number of titles published annually: 40 Print; 40 E-Book
Total Titles: 500 Print; 300 E-Book
Imprints: Deep River Books; Fish Pond; Trusted Books; WaterLife Books
Orders to: Baker & Taylor Publisher Services, 30 Amberwood Pkwy, Ashland, OH 44805 *Tel:* 567-215-0030 *Toll Free Tel:* 888-814-0208 *E-mail:* info@btpubservices.com *Web Site:* www.btpubservices.com
Returns: Baker & Taylor Publisher Services, 30 Amberwood Pkwy, Ashland, OH 44805 *Tel:* 567-215-0030 *Toll Free Tel:* 888-814-0208 *E-mail:* info@btpubservices.com *Web Site:* www.btpubservices.com
Distribution Center: Baker & Taylor Publisher Services, 30 Amberwood Pkwy, Ashland, OH 44805 *Tel:* 567-215-0030 *Toll Free Tel:* 888-

814-0208 *E-mail:* info@btpubservices.com *Web Site:* www.btpubservices.com
Membership(s): Evangelical Christian Publishers Association (ECPA)

Delphinium Books
16350 Ventura Blvd, Suite D, Encino, CA 91436
Tel: 917-301-7496 (e-mail first)
Web Site: www.delphiniumbooks.com
Founded: 1986
ISBN Prefix(es): 978-1-883285
Number of titles published annually: 5 Print; 5 E-Book; 5 Audio
Total Titles: 60 Print; 35 E-Book; 7 Audio
Distributed by HarperCollins
Foreign Rights: David Marshall (worldwide exc Canada)

Demos Medical Publishing
Imprint of Springer Publishing Co
11 W 42 St, 15th fl, New York, NY 10036
Tel: 212-683-0072
E-mail: cs@springerpub.com
Web Site: www.springerpub.com/medicine; www.springerpub.com/consumer-health
Key Personnel
Publr: Beth Barry *E-mail:* bbarry@springerpub.com
Founded: 1985
Publish professional medical & consumer health titles.
ISBN Prefix(es): 978-1-888799; 978-0-939957; 978-1-932603; 978-1-933864; 978-1-934559; 978-1-935281; 978-1-936287; 978-1-936303; 978-1-61705; 978-1-62070
Number of titles published annually: 40 Print
Total Titles: 150 Print; 100 E-Book
Imprints: Demos Health
Foreign Rep(s): Eurospan Group (Africa, Europe, Middle East, UK); Footprint Books Pty Ltd (Australia, New Zealand); Login Canada (Canada); Taylor & Francis Books Pvt Ltd (Ritesh Kumar) (Asia)
Foreign Rights: Viva Books (India)
Membership(s): Association of American Publishers (AAP)

§Deseret Book Co
Subsidiary of Deseret Management Corp
57 W South Temple, Salt Lake City, UT 84101-1511
SAN: 201-3185
Mailing Address: PO Box 30178, Salt Lake City, UT 84130
Tel: 801-517-3369; 801-534-1515 (corp)
Toll Free Tel: 800-453-4532 (orders); 888-846-7302 (orders) *Fax:* 801-517-3126
E-mail: service@deseretbook.com
Web Site: www.deseretbook.com
Key Personnel
Pres: Jeff Simpson
Publr: Lisa Mangum *E-mail:* lmangum@deseretbook.com
Founded: 1886
Juveniles & young adults, trade paperbacks; fiction, general nonfiction, religion (Mormon).
ISBN Prefix(es): 978-0-87747; 978-1-59038; 978-1-57345; 978-0-87579; 978-1-60908; 978-1-60641; 978-1-60907; 978-1-62972; 978-1-62973
Number of titles published annually: 150 Print
Total Titles: 1,100 Print; 1 CD-ROM; 120 Audio
Imprints: Deseret Book; Ensign Peak; Shadow Mountain
Shipping Address: 2240 W 1500 S, Salt Lake City, UT 84104 *Tel:* 801-517-3285

§DEStech Publications Inc
439 N Duke St, Lancaster, PA 17602-4967
SAN: 990-6916
Tel: 717-290-1660 *Toll Free Tel:* 877-500-4DES (500-4337) *Fax:* 717-509-6100

E-mail: info@destechpub.com
Web Site: www.destechpub.com
Key Personnel
Pres & Owner: Anthony A Deraco *Tel:* 717-290-1660 ext 101 *E-mail:* aderaco@destechpub.com
Art Dir: Holly High *E-mail:* hhigh@destechpub.com
Edit Dir: Susan Farmer *Tel:* 717-290-1660 ext 103 *E-mail:* sfarmer@destechpub.com
Prodn Dir: Stephen Spangler *Tel:* 717-290-1660 ext 102 *E-mail:* sspangler@destechpub.com
Edit Asst: Alexandra Cahill *Tel:* 717-290-1660 ext 105 *E-mail:* acahill@destechpub.com
Founded: 2001
Science, technical & medical publisher; proceedings publishing.
ISBN Prefix(es): 978-1-605950
Number of titles published annually: 15 Print; 2 Online; 15 E-Book
Total Titles: 175 Print; 15 E-Book
Foreign Rep(s): Areesh Education & Trading Sdn Bhd (Malaysia); CRW Marketing Services for Publishers Inc (American Samoa, Guam, Philippines, Virgin Islands); DKG Info Systems (China, Hong Kong, Indonesia, Japan, Malaysia, Singapore, South Korea, Taiwan, Thailand); LSR Libros Servicios y Representaciones (Caribbean, Central America, Mexico, South America); Publisher's Representatives (Pakistan); Shankars Book Agency Pvt Ltd (India); Transatlantic Publishers Group Ltd (Europe, Middle East, North Africa, UK)

§Destiny Image Inc
Subsidiary of Nori Media Group
167 Walnut Bottom Rd, Shippensburg, PA 17257-0310
SAN: 253-4339
Mailing Address: PO Box 310, Shippensburg, PA 17257-0310
Tel: 717-532-3040 *Toll Free Tel:* 800-722-6774 (orders only) *Fax:* 717-532-9291
Web Site: www.destinyimage.com
Key Personnel
Pres & CEO: Don Nori
Founded: 1983
Publisher of Christian books.
ISBN Prefix(es): 978-0-914903; 978-1-56043; 978-0-938612; 978-0-7684
Number of titles published annually: 60 Print
Total Titles: 1,500 Print
Foreign Rep(s): Koorong (Australia)
Membership(s): American Booksellers Association (ABA); Evangelical Christian Publishers Association (ECPA)

Development Concepts Inc, see Impact Publications/Development Concepts Inc

DeVorss & Co
553 Constitution Ave, Camarillo, CA 93012-8510
SAN: 168-9886
Mailing Address: PO Box 1389, Camarillo, CA 93011-1389
Tel: 805-322-9010 *Toll Free Tel:* 800-843-5743 *Fax:* 805-322-9011
E-mail: service@devorss.com
Web Site: www.devorss.com
Key Personnel
Pres: Gary R Peattie *Tel:* 805-322-9010 ext 14 *E-mail:* gpeattie@devorss.com
Off & Cust Serv Mgr: Debbie Krovitz *E-mail:* dkrovitz@devorss.com
Buyer: Sonia Dominguez *E-mail:* sdominguez@devorss.com
Founded: 1929
Publisher & distributor of metaphysical, spiritual, inspirational, self-help, body/mind/spirit & New Thought books & sidelines.
ISBN Prefix(es): 978-0-87516
Number of titles published annually: 10 Print
Total Titles: 270 Print; 85 E-Book; 4 Audio

Imprints: DeVorss Publications
Distributor for Acropolis Books (Joel S Goldsmith titles); Touch for Health; White Eagle Publishing Trust (England)
Foreign Rep(s): Brumby Books (Australia); Deep Books (UK); Dempsey Canada (Canada); New Horizons (South Africa)
Billing Address: PO Box 1389, Camarillo, CA 93011-1389

§Dewey Publications Inc
1840 Wilson Blvd, Suite 203, Arlington, VA 22201
SAN: 694-1451
Tel: 703-524-1355 *Fax:* 703-524-1463
E-mail: deweypublications@gmail.com
Web Site: www.deweypub.com
Key Personnel
Owner & Author: Peter Broida
Busn Mgr: Karen Troutman
Founded: 1984
ISBN Prefix(es): 978-1-878810; 978-1-932612
Number of titles published annually: 8 Print; 4 CD-ROM; 8 E-Book
Total Titles: 36 Print; 8 CD-ROM; 36 E-Book; 5 Audio

Dharma Publishing
35788 Hauser Bridge Rd, Cazadero, CA 95421
SAN: 201-2723
Tel: 707-847-3717 *Fax:* 707-847-3380
E-mail: contact@dharmapublishing.com
Web Site: www.dharmapublishing.com
Key Personnel
Dir: Arnaud Maitland
Sales Dir: Rima Tamar *Tel:* 707-847-3717 ext 210 *E-mail:* rimat@dharmapublishing.com
Founded: 1975
Asian art, Eastern philosophy & psychology, Tibetan meditation & yoga, scholarly, history, biography, cosmology, juveniles, Asian culture.
ISBN Prefix(es): 978-0-913546; 978-0-89800
Number of titles published annually: 10 Print; 6 E-Book; 36 Audio
Total Titles: 120 Print; 12 E-Book; 48 Audio
Sales Office(s): 2210 Harold Way, Berkeley, CA 94704 *Tel:* 510-809-1540
Foreign Rep(s): Ka-Nying (India, Nepal); Nyingma Centrum Nederland (Netherlands); Nyingma Do Brazil (Brazil); Nyingma Gemeinschaft (Germany); Windhorse (Australia); Wisdom Publications (UK)
Membership(s): Association of American Publishers (AAP)

Dial Books for Young Readers
Imprint of Penguin Young Readers Group
345 Hudson St, New York, NY 10014
Tel: 212-366-2000 *Toll Free Tel:* 800-733-3000 (orders) *Fax:* 212-414-3396
Web Site: www.penguin.com/publishers/dialbooksforyoungreaders/
Key Personnel
Pres & Publr: Lauri Hornik
Assoc Publr & Edit Dir: Nancy Mercado
VP & Exec Art Dir: Lily Malcom
Exec Ed: Kate Harrison; Jessica Dandino Garrison
Sr Ed: Lucia Monfried
Assoc Ed: Dana Chidiac; Ellen Cormier
Founded: 1961
Penguin Random House & its publishing entities are not accepting unsol submissions, proposals, mss, or submission queries via e-mail at this time.
ISBN Prefix(es): 978-0-8037
Number of titles published annually: 70 Print
Total Titles: 383 Print

DiscoverNet Publishing
Division of DiscoverNet
2474 Walnut St, Suite 105, Cary, NC 27518
Tel: 919-301-0109 *Fax:* 919-557-2261

E-mail: info@discovernet.com
Web Site: www.discovernet.com
Founded: 2002
ISBN Prefix(es): 978-0-9728053; 978-0-9742787;
  978-0-9746943; 978-1-932813
Number of titles published annually: 50 Print; 45
  Online; 45 E-Book
Total Titles: 140 Print; 130 Online; 130 E-Book

§Discovery House Publishers
Division of Our Daily Bread Ministries
3000 Kraft Ave SE, Grand Rapids, MI 49512
Mailing Address: PO Box 3566, Grand Rapids,
  MI 49501-3566
Tel: 616-942-2803 *Toll Free Tel:* 800-653-8333
  (cust serv)
E-mail: support@dhp.org; customerservice@dhp.
  org
Web Site: www.dhp.org
Key Personnel
Publr: Ken Petersen
Mng Ed: Joyce Dinkins
Founded: 1987
Religious trade books; audio CDs (recorded mu-
  sic); DVDs.
ISBN Prefix(es): 978-0-929239; 978-1-57293
Number of titles published annually: 12 Print; 1
  Audio
Total Titles: 3 CD-ROM; 150 Online; 1 Audio
Membership(s): Evangelical Christian Publishers
  Association (ECPA)

Disney-Hyperion Books
Imprint of Disney Book Group
1101 Flower St, Glendale, CA 91201
Web Site: books.disney.com
Key Personnel
VP & Publr: Emily Thomas Meehan
Edit Dir: Jennifer Levesque
Exec Ed: Tracey Kevin
Mng Ed: Sara Liebling
Sr Ed: Kieran Viola
Assoc Ed: Julie Rosenberg
Ed-at-Large: Stephanie Owens Lurie
Publg Coord: Liz Usuriello
Lead Designer: Marci Senders
Sr Mgr, Design: Joann Hill
Sr Designer: Tyler Nevins
Designer: Phil Caminiti
Founded: 1991
Publish high quality picture books, young adult
  fiction & nonfiction.
ISBN Prefix(es): 978-0-7868
Number of titles published annually: 250 Print
Total Titles: 2,200 Print
Imprints: Michael di Capua Books; Jump at the
  Sun; Rick Riordan Presents; Volo
Foreign Rep(s): Little, Brown Canada Ltd; Little,
  Brown International
Foreign Rights: ACER Agencia Literaria (Spain);
  Big Apple Agency Inc (China); BMSR Agen-
  cia Literaria (Brazil); The English Agency
  (Japan) Ltd (Japan); Harris/Elon Agency (Is-
  rael); The Italian Literary Agency SRL (Italy);
  Jacqueline Miller (France); Sebes & Bisseling
  (Netherlands)
Membership(s): The Children's Book Council
  (CBC)
See separate listing for:
Jump at the Sun

Disney Press
Division of The Walt Disney Co
1101 Flower St, Glendale, CA 91201
Web Site: books.disney.com
Key Personnel
Global Publr, Franchise: Lynn Waggoner
Edit Dir: Wendy Lefkon
Dir, Subs Rts: Molly Kong
Exec Ed: Nachie Marsham
Sr Ed: Brooke Dworkin
Founded: 1990

Publish fiction & fantasy.
ISBN Prefix(es): 978-1-56282; 978-0-7868
Number of titles published annually: 55 Print
Total Titles: 1,000 Print
Distributed by Hachette Book Group (USA)
Foreign Rep(s): Little, Brown Canada Ltd; Little,
  Brown International
Foreign Rights: ACER Agencia Literaria (Spain);
  Big Apple Agency Inc (China); BMSR Agen-
  cia Literaria (Brazil); The English Agency Ltd
  (Japan); Harris/Elon Agency (Israel); A M
  Heath & Co Ltd (England); Monica Heyum
  Agency (Denmark, Finland, Iceland, Norway,
  Sweden); The Italian Literary Agency SRL
  (Italy); Agence Michelle Lapautre (France);
  Sebes & Bisseling (Netherlands)
Warehouse: 53 State St, Boston, MA 02109

Disney Publishing Worldwide
Subsidiary of The Walt Disney Co
1101 Flower St, Glendale, CA 91201
Web Site: books.disney.com
Key Personnel
Pres, Disney Consumer Prods: James Pitaro
EVP: Andrew Sugerman
SVP Fin, IT & Global Opers: Raj Murari
VP & Publr, Hyperion: Emily Thomas Meehan
VP, Digital Media: Yves Saada
VP, Publg Opers: Terry Downes
Global Publr, Franchise: Lynn Waggoner
Publicity Dir: Seale Ballenger
Publicity Mgr: Mary Ann Zissimos
Exec Ed, Disney Lucasfilm Press: Jennifer Heddle
Mng Ed: Sara Liebling
Founded: 1930
Publisher of children's books, comics & maga-
  zines.
ISBN Prefix(es): 978-1-56115
Number of titles published annually: 275 Print
Total Titles: 1,000 Print
Imprints: Disney Editions; Disney-Hyperion; Dis-
  ney Lucasfilm Press; Disney Press; Freeform;
  Hyperion Books for Children; Jump at the Sun;
  Kingswell; Marvel
Divisions: Disney Children's Book Group
Branch Office(s)
500 S Buena Vista St, Burbank, CA 91521
  Tel: 914-288-4100
Foreign Rights: Sebes & Bisseling (Netherlands)

Dissertation.com
Imprint of Universal-Publishers Inc
200 Spectrum Center Dr, 3rd fl, Irvine, CA 92618
SAN: 299-3635
Tel: 561-750-4344 *Toll Free Tel:* 800-636-8329
  Fax: 561-750-6797
Web Site: www.dissertation.com
Key Personnel
Publr & CEO: Dr Jeffrey Young
Artistic & Edit Dir: Shereen Siddiqui
Founded: 1997
Academic books.
This publisher has indicated that 50% of their
  product line is author subsidized.
ISBN Prefix(es): 978-1-58112; 978-0-9658564;
  978-1-59942; 978-1-61233; 978-1-62734
Number of titles published annually: 50 Print; 50
  Online; 50 E-Book
Total Titles: 500 Print; 300 Online; 500 E-Book
Distributed by Bertrams UK

Diversion Books
Division of Diversion Publishing Corp
443 Park Ave S, Suite 1008, New York, NY
  10016
SAN: 990-6304
Tel: 212-961-6390
E-mail: info@diversionbooks.com
Web Site: www.diversionbooks.com
Key Personnel
Co-Founder: Charles Platkin
Co-Founder & CEO: Scott Waxman

Exec Ed & Ed-in-Chief: Keith Wallman
Sr Acqs Ed, EverAfter Romance: Shannon Criss
Acqs Ed: Lia Ottaviano
Ed, Nonfiction: Melanie Madden
Mktg Mgr: Shannon Donnelly
Founded: 2010
An innovative indie publisher, combining decades
  of traditional experience with new, digital
  strategies. In publishing a mix of original titles & giving old titles a digital life, our high
  royalties, quick turnaround & tailored marketing plans are helping us to create a space
  between legacy publishing & the uneven field
  of self-publishing. We are taking advantage of
  the abundance of opportunities that new models of distribution & purchasing provide, while
  executing our core publishing capabilities, ultimately connecting great books with avid readers.
ISBN Prefix(es): 978-0-9845151; 978-0-9829050;
  978-0-9838395; 978-0-9839885; 978-0-
  9833371; 978-1-938120
Number of titles published annually: 50 Print;
  350 E-Book
Total Titles: 50 Print; 1,000 E-Book
Distributor for Zubaan Books
Foreign Rights: Craig Literary (Jessica Craig)
  (worldwide)
Distribution Center: Ingram Publisher Services,
  One Ingram Blvd, La Vergne, TN 37086 *Toll
  Free Tel:* 866-400-5351 (orders)
Membership(s): Association of American Pub-
  lishers (AAP); Independent Book Publishers
  Association (IBPA); International Thriller Writ-
  ers Inc (ITW); Media Women's Association
  (MWA)

DK Publishing
Division of Penguin Group USA, A Penguin Ran-
  dom House Company
1450 Broadway, Suite 801, New York, NY 10018
Tel: 646-674-4000 *Toll Free Tel:* 800-733-3000
  Fax: 646-674-4020
E-mail: marketing@dk.com; publicity@dk.
  com; csorders@penguinrandomhouse.com;
  ecustomerservice@randomhouse.com
Web Site: www.dk.com; www.penguin.com
Key Personnel
CEO: Carsten Coesfeld
SVP, DK North America: Mary Marotta
VP, Mktg & Publicity: Gayley Avery
VP, Sales: Carol Stokke
Dir, Custom Publg: Meghan Marton
Dir, Opers: Sheila Phelan
Sr Mktg Mgr, Educ & Lib: Kristin Pozzuoli
Adult Mktg Mgr: Victoria Verhowsky
Brand Mgr: Katie Schloss
Digital Mktg Mgr: Hillary Brady
Sales Mgr: Shawn Sarles
Assoc Mktg Mgr, Children's: Michael Ploetz
Assoc Mktg Mgr, DK Travel: Lauren Paley
Sr Publicist: Kelsey Curtis
Publicist: Kristen Fisher
Founded: 1974 (in UK)
Illustrated reference books on a wide range of
  topics for adults & children, including travel,
  health, history, sports, pets, atlases, dictionaries,
  music, art, decorating, astrology, sex & cook-
  ing.
Penguin Random House & its publishing entities
  are not accepting unsol submissions, proposals,
  mss, or submission queries via e-mail at this
  time.
Number of titles published annually: 392 Print
Total Titles: 1,850 Print
Subsidiaries: Alpha Books
Foreign Rep(s): Dorling Kindersley Ltd (UK)
Advertising Agency: Spier NY
Membership(s): American Booksellers Association (ABA); American Library Association
  (ALA); The Children's Book Council (CBC);
  International Association of Culinary Profes-
  sionals (IACP); International Literacy Associ-
  ation (ILA); National Council of Teachers of

English (NCTE); National Science Teachers Association (NSTA)
See separate listing for:
Alpha Books

Caitlyn Dlouhy Books, see Simon & Schuster Children's Publishing

§Dogwise Publishing
Division of Direct Book Service Inc
403 S Mission St, Wenatchee, WA 98801
SAN: 132-9545
Tel: 509-663-9115 *Toll Free Tel:* 800-776-2665
E-mail: mail@dogwise.com
Web Site: www.dogwise.com
Key Personnel
Owner & Publr: Charlene Woodward
Owner: Larry Woodward
Founded: 2000
Publish how-to books on dog care, training, behavior, health & competition.
ISBN Prefix(es): 978-1-929242; 978-1-61781
Number of titles published annually: 10 Print
Total Titles: 90 Print; 260 E-Book
Membership(s): Book Publishers of the Northwest (BPNW); Dogwise Association of America (DWAA); Independent Book Publishers Association (IBPA)

Tom Doherty Associates, LLC
Subsidiary of Macmillan
120 Broadway, New York, NY 10271
Tel: 646-307-5511 *Toll Free Tel:* 800-455-0340
Web Site: us.macmillan.com/torforge
Key Personnel
Chmn: Thomas Doherty *E-mail:* thomas.doherty@tor.com
Pres & Publr: Fritz Foy
VP & Publr, Tor, Tor Teen & Starscape: Devi Pillai *E-mail:* devi.pillai@tor.com
VP, Assoc Publr, Dir Mktg & Publicity: Lucille Rettino
VP & Ed-in-Chief, Tor Books: Patrick Nielsen Hayden *E-mail:* patrick.hayden@tor.com
Exec Dir, Mktg: Eileen Lawrence
Exec Dir, Publicity: Sarah Reidy
Sr Dir, Trade & Inside Sales, Tor/Forge: Christine Jaeger
Art Dir, Mass Market/Forge Books: Seth Lerner *E-mail:* seth.lerner@tor.com
Creative Dir, Publr Tor.com: Irene Gallo *E-mail:* irene.gallo@tor.com
Sr Assoc Dir, Mktg, Tor/Forge/Nightfire: Theresa DeLucci
Sr Assoc Dir, Publicity, Forge: Alexis Saarela
Dir, Intl Rts: Marta Fleming
Assoc Dir, Ad, Promo & Trade Opers: Stephanie Sirabian
Assoc Dir, Tor Teen/Starscape & School & Lib Mktg: Anthony Parisi
Ad Promo Asst Creative Dir: Megan Bernard
Exec Ed: Bob Gleason *E-mail:* bob.gleason@tor.com; Beth Meacham *E-mail:* beth.meacham@tor.com
Exec Ed, Forge: Kristin Sevick
Exec Ed, Tor/Forge Books: Claire Eddy
Sr Ed, Nightfire: Kelly O'Connor Lonesome
Sr Ed, Tor: Lindsey Hall
Sr Ed, Tor Teen/Starscape: Susan Chang; Ali Fisher
Sr Mktg Mgr, Tor: Renata Sweeney
Ad & Promos Mgr: Rebecca Yeager
Brand Mgr: Alex Cameron
Mgr, Admin: Robert Davis *E-mail:* robert.davis@tor.com
Mktg Mgr, Forge Books: Jennifer McClelland-Smith
Mktg Mgr, Nightfire: Jordan Hanley
Mktg Mgr, Tor Teen/Starscape & School & Lib Mktg: Isa Caban
Publicity Mgr: Saraciea Fennell

Sr Publicist, Tor: Desirae Friesen *E-mail:* desirae.friesen@tor.com
Publicist: Laura Etzkorn
Ad Promo Assoc Mktg Mgr: Julia Bergen
Digital Mktg Coord, Nightfire/Forge/Tor Teen/Starscape: Sarah Pannenberg
Mktg Asst, Tor Teen/Starscape & School & Lib Mktg: Sara Di Blasi
Founded: 1980
Mass market & trade paperbacks; trade hardcover: fiction, horror, science fiction, fantasy, mystery, suspense, techno-thrillers, western fiction, American historicals, nonfiction, paranormal romance, true crime & biography.
ISBN Prefix(es): 978-0-8125; 978-0-7653
Number of titles published annually: 425 Print
Total Titles: 2,224 Print
Imprints: Aerie Books; Forge Books; Nightfire; Orb Books; Starscape; Tor; Tor Classics; Tor Teen
Distributed by Macmillan
Foreign Rights: St Martin's Press
Advertising Agency: Slocum Advertising Agency
Distribution Center: MPS Distribution Center, 16365 James Madison Hwy, Gordonsville, VA 22942-8501 *Toll Free Tel:* 888-330-8477 *Fax:* 540-672-7540 (cust serv) *Toll Free Fax:* 800-672-2054 (orders) *E-mail:* firstinitial.lastname@mpsvirginia.com

The Donning Company Publishers
Subsidiary of Walsworth
731 S Brunswick St, Brookfield, MO 64628
Toll Free Tel: 800-369-2646 (ext 3377)
Web Site: www.donning.com
Key Personnel
Gen Mgr: Lex Cavanah
Ed: Anne Burns
Prodn Supv: Nathan Stufflebean *E-mail:* nathan.stufflebean@donning.com
Founded: 1974
Specialty book publisher of limited-edition commemorative volumes, pictorial histories & contemporary portraits.
ISBN Prefix(es): 978-0-915442; 978-0-89865
Number of titles published annually: 80 Print
Imprints: Portraits of America
Foreign Rights: Writers House Inc

Doodle and Peck Publishing
413 Cedarburg Ct, Yukon, OK 73099
Mailing Address: PO Box 852105, Yukon, OK 73085
Tel: 405-354-7422
E-mail: contact@doodleandpeck.com
Web Site: www.doodleandpeck.com
Key Personnel
Publr & Ed: Marla F Jones *E-mail:* iluvrocksmj@yahoo.com
Founded: 2015
Pairs talented authors & illustrators to create family-friendly books.
ISBN Prefix(es): 978-0-9966205; 978-0-9972351
Number of titles published annually: 7 Print; 5 E-Book
Total Titles: 40 Print; 30 E-Book
Membership(s): Independent Book Publishers Association (IBPA); Society of Children's Book Writers & Illustrators (SCBWI)

Dordt College Press, see Dordt Press

Dordt Press
Formerly Dordt College Press
Affiliate of Dordt University
700 Seventh St NE, Sioux Center, IA 51250-1671
Tel: 712-722-6420 *Toll Free Tel:* 800-343-6738 *Fax:* 712-722-6035
E-mail: dordtpress@dordt.edu; bookstore@dordt.edu
Web Site: www.dordt.edu/about-dordt/publications/dordt-press-catalog

Key Personnel
Mng Ed: John H Kok *Tel:* 712-722-2254 *E-mail:* jkok@dordt.edu
Founded: 1978
Publishes primarily academic books & monographs, plus a quarterly journal.
ISBN Prefix(es): 978-0-932914; 978-1-940567
Number of titles published annually: 6 Print
Total Titles: 75 Print; 1 E-Book

Dorrance Publishing Co Inc
585 Alpha Dr, Suite 103, Pittsburgh, PA 15238
Toll Free Tel: 800-695-9599; 800-788-7654 (gen cust orders) *Fax:* 412-387-1319
E-mail: dorrinfo@dorrancepublishing.com; dorrordr@dorrancepublishing.com (book orders)
Web Site: www.dorrancepublishing.com
Key Personnel
Pres: David Zeolla
Founded: 1920
Full service author services company.
This publisher has indicated that 100% of their product line is author subsidized.
ISBN Prefix(es): 978-0-8059; 978-1-4349; 978-1-4809
Number of titles published annually: 1,000 Print; 1,000 Online; 1,000 E-Book; 10 Audio
Total Titles: 6,000 Print; 6,000 Online; 4,000 E-Book; 5 Audio
Imprints: Rose Dog Books

§Doubleday
Imprint of Knopf Doubleday Publishing Group
c/o Penguin Random House Inc, 1745 Broadway, New York, NY 10019
Tel: 212-751-2600 *Fax:* 212-572-2662 (foreign rts)
E-mail: ddaypub@randomhouse.com
Web Site: knopfdoubleday.com
Key Personnel
EVP & Exec Dir, Publg, Knopf Doubleday Publishing Group: Suzanne Herz
SVP & Deputy Publr: Todd Doughty
VP & Group Sales Dir: Christopher Dufault
VP & Exec Dir, Sales Mgmt & Planning: Beth Meister
Mktg Mgr, Knopf Doubleday Publishing Group: Sarah Engelmann
SVP, Publr & Ed-in-Chief: William Thomas
SVP & Creative Dir: John Fontana
VP & Exec Dir, Mktg: John Pitts
VP & Creative Mktg Dir: Judy Jacoby
VP & Exec Ed: Lee Boudreaux; Gerry Howard; Jason Kaufman
Dir, Publicity: Michael Goldsmith
Assoc Dir, Mktg: Lauren Weber
Asst Dir, Publicity: Elena Hershey
Sr Publicist: Tricia Cave
Assoc Publicist: Emma Joss; Mark Lee
Mktg Assoc: Hannah Engler
Exec Ed: Kristine Puopolo
Mng Ed: Katherine Hourigan
Sr Ed: Jennifer Jackson; Yaniv Soha
Ed: Margo Shickmanter
Assoc Ed: Dan Meyer
Asst Ed: Nora Grubb; Cara Reilly
Asst Mgr, Digital Mktg: Daniela Ayuso
Founded: 1897
Penguin Random House & its publishing entities are not accepting unsol submissions, proposals, mss or submission queries via e-mail at this time.
Foreign Rights: ALS-Agenzia Letteraria Santachiara (Roberto Santachiara) (Italy); Anthea Agency (Katalina Sabeva) (Bulgaria); Bardon-Chinese Media Agency (Xu-Weiguang) (China); Bardon-Chinese Media Agency (Yu-Shiuan Chen) (Taiwan); The English Agency (Junzo Sawa) (Japan); Graal Literary Agency (Maria Strarz-Kanska) (Poland); The Deborah Harris Agency (Ilana Kurshan) (Israel); JLM Literary Agency (Nelly Moukakos) (Greece);

Katai & Bolza Literary (Peter Bolza) (Croatia, Hungary); KCC (MiSook Hong) (Korea); Simona Kessler International (Simona Kessler) (Romania); Licht & Burr Literary Agency (Trine Licht) (Scandinavia); La Nouvelle Agence (Vanessa Kling) (France); Kristin Olson Literary Agency (Kristin Olson) (Czechia); Sebes & Bisseling Literary Agency (Paul Sebes) (Netherlands)

§Dover Publications Inc
31 E Second St, Mineola, NY 11501-3852
Tel: 516-294-7000 *Toll Free Tel:* 800-223-3130 (orders) *Fax:* 516-742-6953
E-mail: rights@doverpublications.com; service@doverpublications.com; doversales@doverpublications.com
Web Site: store.doverdirect.com; www.doverpublications.com
Key Personnel
Publr: Jennifer Feldman *E-mail:* jennifer.r.feldman@lsccom.com
Mktg Dir: Philip Dominici *Tel:* 978-251-6025 *E-mail:* philip.dominici@lsccom.com
Sales Dir: Tim McCall *E-mail:* tim.e.mccall@lsccom.com
Acqs Ed: Jeff Golick *E-mail:* jgolick@doverpublications.com
Spec Mkts: Laurie Smith *E-mail:* laurie.l.smith@lsccom.com
Founded: 1941
Trade adult & children's, crafts, art, music; higher education.
ISBN Prefix(es): 978-0-486; 978-1-60660
Number of titles published annually: 600 Print; 400 E-Book
Total Titles: 10,000 Print; 36 CD-ROM; 6,500 E-Book; 22 Audio
Foreign Rep(s): Bill Baily Group (Eastern Europe); F&W Media (UK); HarperCollins India (Indian subcontinent); International Publishers Representatives (Mideast); JCC Enterprises Inc (Caribbean, Central America, Mexico); Peribo (Australia); Publishers International Marketing (Asia exc Japan)
Foreign Rights: Biagi Literary Management (worldwide exc North America)
Shipping Address: 11 E Second St, Mineola, NY 11501
Membership(s): American Booksellers Association (ABA)

Down East Books
Imprint of Rowman & Littlefield Publishing Group
4501 Forbes Blvd, Suite 200, Lanham, MD 20706
Tel: 301-459-3366 *Fax:* 301-429-5748
E-mail: orders@rowman.com; customercare@rowman.com
Web Site: rowman.com/page/downeastbooks
Founded: 1954
ISBN Prefix(es): 978-0-924357; 978-0-89272
Number of titles published annually: 15 Print; 16 E-Book
Total Titles: 350 Print; 50 E-Book
Sales Office(s): National Book Network, 15200 NBN Way, Bldg C, Blue Ridge Summit, PA 17214 *Toll Free Tel:* 800-462-6420 ext 3024
Distributor for Nimbus Publishing Ltd (selected titles, CN sales only)
Distribution Center: National Book Network, 15200 NBN Way, Bldg C, Blue Ridge Summit, PA 17214, VP, Opers: Mike Cornell *Tel:* 717-794-3800 *Toll Free Tel:* 800-462-6420 ext 3024 *Fax:* 717-794-3803 *Toll Free Fax:* 800-338-4550 *E-mail:* mcornell@nbnbooks.com

Down The Shore Publishing Corp
106 Stafford Forge Rd, West Creek, NJ 08092
SAN: 661-082X

Mailing Address: PO Box 100, West Creek, NJ 08092
Tel: 609-812-5076 *Fax:* 609-812-5098
E-mail: dtsbooks@comcast.net; info@down-the-shore.com
Web Site: www.down-the-shore.com
Key Personnel
Founder & Pres: Raymond G Fisk
Founded: 1984
Regional books, history; calendars; videos; note cards.
ISBN Prefix(es): 978-0-9615208; 978-0-945582; 978-1-59322
Number of titles published annually: 6 Print
Total Titles: 95 Print
Imprints: Bufflehead Books; Cormorant Books; Cormorant Calendars; Terrapin Greetings
Membership(s): Independent Book Publishers Association (IBPA)

Downtown Press, see Gallery Books

§Dragon Door Publications
2999 Yorkton Blvd, Suite 2, Little Canada, MN 55117
Tel: 651-487-2180
E-mail: support@dragondoor.com
Web Site: www.dragondoor.com
Key Personnel
Publr & Ed-in-Chief: John Du Cane
ISBN Prefix(es): 978-0-938045
Number of titles published annually: 5 Print
Total Titles: 115 Print; 35 E-Book

Drama Publishers, see Quite Specific Media Group Ltd

Dramatic Publishing Co
311 Washington St, Woodstock, IL 60098-3308
SAN: 201-5676
Tel: 815-338-7170 *Toll Free Tel:* 800-448-7469 *Fax:* 815-338-8981 *Toll Free Fax:* 800-334-5302
E-mail: plays@dramaticpublishing.com; customerservice@dpcplays.com
Web Site: www.dramaticpublishing.com
Key Personnel
Pres: Christopher Sergel, III
VP: Gayle Sergel; Susan Sergel
Dir: Kent Brown
Founded: 1885
Acting editions of plays & musicals & licensing productions of same.
ISBN Prefix(es): 978-0-87129; 978-1-58342; 978-1-61959
Number of titles published annually: 55 Print
Total Titles: 2,000 Print
Foreign Rep(s): DALRO Pty Ltd (Southern Africa); Origin Theatrical Pty Ltd (Australia); The Play Bureau NZ Ltd (New Zealand)

Dramatists Play Service Inc
440 Park Ave S, New York, NY 10016
Tel: 212-683-8960 *Fax:* 212-213-1539
E-mail: postmaster@dramatists.com; orders@dramatists.com; publications@dramatists.com
Web Site: www.dramatists.com
Key Personnel
Pres: Peter Hagan *E-mail:* hagan@dramatists.com
VP: David Moore
Edit Dir: Haleh Roshan Stilwell *E-mail:* stilwell@dramatists.com
Edit Assoc: Ben Keiper *E-mail:* keiper@dramatists.com
Edit Asst: Leah Barker *E-mail:* barker@dramatists.com
Founded: 1936
Publisher & licensor of plays & musicals.
ISBN Prefix(es): 978-0-8222
Number of titles published annually: 60 Print

Total Titles: 4,000 Print
Foreign Rights: DALRO (South Africa); Hal Leonard Australia Pty Ltd (Australia, New Zealand); Josef Weinberger (UK)

Dreaming Robot Press
Imprint of Studio Weaver
1214 San Francisco Ave, Las Vegas, NM 87701
Tel: 505-264-3830
E-mail: books@dreamingrobotpress.com
Web Site: dreamingrobotpress.com
Founded: 2013
Quality middle grade & young adult science fiction & fantasy novels.
ISBN Prefix(es): 978-1-940924
Number of titles published annually: 2 Print; 20 E-Book
Total Titles: 7 Print; 3 E-Book
Membership(s): Independent Book Publishers Association (IBPA)

Dreamscape Media LLC
Division of Midwest Tapes
1417 Timberwolf Dr, Holland, OH 43528
Tel: 419-867-6965 *Toll Free Tel:* 877-983-7326
E-mail: info@dreamscapeab.com
Web Site: www.dreamscapepublishing.com
Key Personnel
Publr: Levine Querido
Publr & EVP, Film & TV: Catherine Zappa
Audiobook Acqs Ed: Michael Olah *E-mail:* molah@dreamscapeab.com
Founded: 2010
Audio & video media publisher.
ISBN Prefix(es): 978-0-9745563; 978-0-9747118; 978-0-9760996; 978-0-9761981; 978-0-9771510; 978-0-9772338; 978-0-9774680; 978-0-9776262; 978-0-9777098; 978-1-933938; 978-1-61120; 978-1-62406; 978-1-62923; 978-1-63379
Number of titles published annually: 50 E-Book; 250 Audio
Total Titles: 600 E-Book; 1,500 Audio
Editorial Office(s): 150 N Wacker Dr, Suite 2250, Chicago, IL 60606
Distributor for Berrett-Koehler Publishers; Gildan Media; Hallmark Publishing; HarperCollins; Ideal Audiobooks; Penguin Random House Inc; Radio Archives
Foreign Rep(s): CVS Midwest Tape (Canada)
Membership(s): Audio Publishers Association

Dufour Editions Inc
PO Box 7, Chester Springs, PA 19425
SAN: 201-341X
Tel: 610-458-5005
E-mail: info@dufoureditions.com
Web Site: www.dufoureditions.com
Key Personnel
Pres & Publr: Christopher May
Ed, Sales Dir: Duncan May
Publicity & Prodn Dir: Miranda Elliott
Founded: 1949
Literary fiction, general nonfiction, literature, poetry, philosophy, history, drama & criticism, Irish.
ISBN Prefix(es): 978-0-8023
Number of titles published annually: 400 Print
Total Titles: 6,000 Print
Distribution Center: Casemate | IPM, 1950 Lawrence Rd, Havertown, PA 19083 (North America) *Tel:* 610-853-9131 *E-mail:* casemate@casematepublishers.com *Web Site:* www.casemateipm.com

Duke University Press
905 W Main St, Suite 18B, Durham, NC 27701
SAN: 201-3436
Mailing Address: PO Box 90660, Durham, NC 27708-0660

Tel: 919-688-5134 *Toll Free Tel:* 888-651-0122 (US) *Fax:* 919-688-2615 *Toll Free Fax:* 888-651-0124
E-mail: orders@dukeupress.edu
Web Site: www.dukeupress.edu
Key Personnel
Dir: Dean Smith
Dir, Digital Strategy & Systems: Allison Belan
   E-mail: allison.belan@dukeupress.edu
Dir, Editing, Design & Prodn: Nancy Hoagland
Dir, Mktg & Sales: Cason Lynley
Edit Dir: Gisela Fosado *E-mail:* gisela.fosado@dukeupress.edu
Journals Dir: Rob Dilworth
   E-mail: journalsdirector@dukeupress.edu
Sr Exec Ed: Ken Wissoker *E-mail:* kwiss@duke.edu
Exec Ed: Courtney Berger *E-mail:* cberger@dukeupress.edu
Sr Ed, Journals: Erich Staib *E-mail:* erich.staib@dukeupress.edu
Ed: Elizabeth Ault *E-mail:* elizabeth.ault@dukeupress.edu
Assoc Ed: Miriam Angress *E-mail:* miriam.angress@dukeupress.edu
Asst Ed: Sandra Korn *E-mail:* sandra.korn@dukeupress.edu; Joshua Gutterman Tranen
   E-mail: joshua.tranen@dukeupress.edu
Sales Mgr: Jennifer Schaper *E-mail:* jennifer.schaper@dukeupress.edu
Founded: 1921
Scholarly, trade & textbooks.
ISBN Prefix(es): 978-0-8223
Number of titles published annually: 120 Print
Total Titles: 1,300 Print
Distributor for Forest History Society
Foreign Rep(s): Academic Marketing Services (Pty) Ltd (Mike Brightmore) (Southern Africa); AfricaConnection.co.uk (Guy Simpson) (Africa exc South Africa); Avicenna Partnership Ltd (Bill Kennedy) (Bahrain, Egypt, Iran, Iraq, Kuwait, Lebanon, Oman, Qatar, Saudi Arabia, Syria, United Arab Emirates, Yemen); Avicenna Partnership Ltd (Claire de Gruchy) (Algeria, Israel, Jordan, Malta, Morocco, Tunisia, Turkey); China Publishers Marketing (Benjamin Pan) (China, Hong Kong, Taiwan); CoInfo Ltd (Debra Triplett) (Australia, Fiji, New Zealand, Papua New Guinea); Leonidas Diamantopoulos (Cyprus, Greece); Charles Gibbs (Cyprus, Greece); Ben Greig (Denmark, Iceland, Southern Sweden); Steven Haslemere (Sweden); Wilf Jones (Finland, Norway); Jacek Lewinson (Eastern Europe, Russia); Lexa Publishers Representatives (Mical Moser) (Canada); Mare Nostrum (Lauren Keane) (Belgium, France, Luxembourg, Netherlands); Mare Nostrum (Frauke Feldmann) (Austria, Germany, Switzerland); Mare Nostrum (Francesca Pollard) (Italy); Publishers International Marketing (Chris Ashdown) (Brunei, Cambodia, Indonesia, Japan, Laos, Malaysia, Philippines, Singapore, South Korea, Thailand, Timor-Leste, Vietnam); Quantum Publishing Solutions Ltd (James Wickham) (UK); Cristina De Lara Ruiz (Portugal, Spain); Viva Books Pvt Ltd (Bangladesh, Bhutan, India, Maldives, Nepal, Sri Lanka); World Press (Saleem A Malik) (Pakistan)
Returns: 120 Golden Dr, Durham, NC 27705
Distribution Center: Combined Academic Publishers, 39 E Parade, Harrogate, N Yorks HG1 5LQ, United Kingdom (Africa, Asia, Europe, Middle East, Pacific & UK) *Tel:* (01423) 526350 *E-mail:* enquiries@combinedacademic.co.uk *Web Site:* www.combinedacademic.co.uk

Dumbarton Oaks
1703 32 St NW, Washington, DC 20007
Tel: 202-339-6400 *Fax:* 202-339-6401; 202-298-8407
E-mail: doaksbooks@doaks.org; press@doaks.org
Web Site: www.doaks.org

Key Personnel
Dir, Pubns: Kathy Sparkes
Mng Ed, Art & Archaeology: Sara Taylor
ISBN Prefix(es): 978-0-88402
Number of titles published annually: 8 Print
Total Titles: 260 Print
Distributed by Harvard University Press

§Dun & Bradstreet
103 JFK Pkwy, Short Hills, NJ 07078
Tel: 973-921-5500 *Toll Free Tel:* 844-869-8244; 800-234-3867 (cust serv)
Web Site: www.dnb.com
Key Personnel
CEO: Anthony Jabbour
Pres: Stephen C Daffron
CFO: Richard H Veldran
Chief Content & Technol Offr: Curtis Brown
Chief Data Offr: Gary Kotovets
Chief People Offr: Roslynn Williams
Business & business reference; US & international coverage, country information.
ISBN Prefix(es): 978-1-56203
Total Titles: 31 Print; 20 CD-ROM
Subsidiaries: Hoover's Inc
See separate listing for:
Hoover's Inc

§Dustbooks
PO Box 100, Paradise, CA 95967-0100
SAN: 204-1871
Tel: 530-877-6110 *Fax:* 530-877-0222
E-mail: inquiries@dustbooks.com; info@dustbooks.com
Web Site: www.dustbooks.com
Key Personnel
Ed: Neil McIntyre
Founded: 1964
Full service publishing company founded by Len Fulton.
ISBN Prefix(es): 978-0-913218; 978-0-916685; 978-1-935742
Number of titles published annually: 3 Print
Total Titles: 1 CD-ROM; 4 Online
Distributor for American Dust Publications

Dutton
Division of Penguin Group USA, A Penguin Random House Company
1745 Broadway, New York, NY 10019
Tel: 212-366-2000 *Fax:* 212-366-2262
E-mail: duttonpublicity@us.penguingroup.com
Web Site: www.penguin.com
Key Personnel
Pres: Ivan Held
Pres & Publr, Dutton Children's: Julie Strauss-Gabel
SVP & Publr, Dutton, Plume & Tiny Reparations Books: Christine Ball
VP & Assoc Publr, Pbks: Benjamin Lee
VP & Exec Ed: Stephen Morrow
VP & Ed-in-Chief: John Parsley
Exec Dir, Ad & Promo: Jaime Mendola-Hobbie
Edit Dir: Jill Schwartzman
Mktg Dir: Stephanie Cooper
Dir, Publicity: Amanda Walker
Assoc Dir, Publicity: Jamie Knapp
Assoc Dir, Publg, Putnam/Dutton/Berkley: Liza Cassity
Exec Mng Ed: Susan Schwartz
Exec Ed: Brent Howard; Lindsey Rose; Maya Ziv
Ed: Stephanie Kelly; Amber Oliver
Assoc Ed: Katie Zaborsky
Asst Ed: Lexy Cassola; Marya Pasciuto; Cassidy Sachs
Edit Asst: Hannah Feeney
Mktg Mgr, Putnam/Dutton: Katie Parry
Asst Mktg Mgr: Natalie Church; Leila Siddiqui
Sr Publicity Mgr: Emily Canders
Sr Publicist: Emily Brock; Sarah Thegeby
Publicist: Becky Odell
Mktg Coord: Caroline Payne

Founded: 1864
Penguin Random House & its publishing entities are not accepting unsol submissions, proposals, mss, or submission queries via e-mail at this time.
Number of titles published annually: 12 Print
Total Titles: 130 Print
Advertising Agency: Spier NY

Dutton Children's Books
Imprint of Penguin Young Readers Group
345 Hudson St, New York, NY 10014
Tel: 212-366-2000
Web Site: www.penguin.com/publishers/duttonchildrensbooks/
Key Personnel
Pres & Publr, Dutton Children's: Julie Strauss-Gabel
Exec Ed: Andrew Karre
Assoc Publg Mgr: Melissa Faulner
Founded: 1852 (as Dutton)
Penguin Random House & its publishing entities are not accepting unsol submissions, proposals, mss, or submission queries via e-mail at this time.
Number of titles published annually: 12 Print
Total Titles: 355 Print

Eakin Press
Imprint of Wild Horse Media Group
PO Box 331779, Fort Worth, TX 76163
Tel: 817-344-7036 *Toll Free Tel:* 888-982-8270
   Fax: 817-344-7036
Web Site: www.eakinpress.com
Key Personnel
CEO: Billy Huckaby
Founded: 1979
ISBN Prefix(es): 978-0-89015; 978-1-57168
Number of titles published annually: 25 Print
Total Titles: 1,000 Print; 220 E-Book; 1 Audio
Membership(s): Independent Publishers Association

East Asian Legal Studies Program (EALSP)
Division of University of Maryland School of Law
500 W Baltimore St, Rm 254, Baltimore, MD 21201-1786
Tel: 410-706-3870 *Fax:* 410-706-0407
E-mail: eastasia@law.umaryland.edu
Web Site: www.law.umaryland.edu/programs/international/eastasia
Key Personnel
Dir: Dr Michael Van Altine
Assoc Dir: Chih-Yu T Wu
Founded: 1977
East Asian legal studies, political, economic & legal.
ISBN Prefix(es): 978-0-942182; 978-0-925153; 978-1-932330
Number of titles published annually: 4 Print
Total Titles: 240 Print

East West Discovery Press
PO Box 3585, Manhattan Beach, CA 90266
Tel: 310-545-3730 *Fax:* 310-545-3731
E-mail: info@eastwestdiscovery.com
Web Site: www.eastwestdiscovery.com
Key Personnel
Publr & Ed: Icy Smith
Dir: Michael Smith
Founded: 2000
Independent publisher & distributor of multicultural & bilingual books in 50+ languages.
ISBN Prefix(es): 978-0-9701654; 978-0-9669437; 978-0-9799339; 978-0-9821675; 978-0-9856237; 978-0-9913454; 978-0-9832278; 978-0-9973947
Number of titles published annually: 5 Print
Total Titles: 60 Print
Membership(s): APALA; The Children's Book Council (CBC); Independent Book Publishers Association (IBPA)

Eastland Press
2421 29 Ave W, Seattle, WA 98199
Mailing Address: PO Box 99749, Seattle, WA 98139
Tel: 206-931-6957 (cust serv) *Fax:* 206-283-7084 (orders)
E-mail: info@eastlandpress.com; orders@eastlandpress.com
Web Site: www.eastlandpress.com
Key Personnel
Mng Ed: John O'Connor
Med Ed: Dan Bensky
Art Dir/Prodn Mgr: Patricia O'Connor
Founded: 1981
Chinese medicine, osteopathic & manual medicine, yoga.
ISBN Prefix(es): 978-0-939616
Number of titles published annually: 4 Print; 10 E-Book
Total Titles: 60 Print; 20 E-Book
Distributor for Journal of Chinese Medicine Publications
Warehouse: PSSC, 660 S Mansfield St, Ypsilanti, MI 48197
Membership(s): Publishers Association of the West (PubWest)

§Easy Money Press
Subsidiary of Wolford & Associates
82-5800 Napo'opo'o Rd, Captain Cook, HI 96704
Tel: 808-313-2808
E-mail: easymoneypress@yahoo.com
Key Personnel
Creative Dir: Henry Wolford *E-mail:* hcwolford@yahoo.com
Mktg Dir: Sheri Kephart
Prodn Dir: P J Max
Founded: 1996
ISBN Prefix(es): 978-0-9654563; 978-1-929714
Number of titles published annually: 1 Print; 3 E-Book
Total Titles: 12 Print; 21 E-Book
Imprints: Big Tree Books; EMP; Haase House

Eclectic Book Press
Imprint of Endless Mountains Publishing Co
72 Glenmaura National Blvd, Suite 104B, Moosic, PA 18507
Tel: 862-251-2296; 570-878-7960
E-mail: info@endlessmountainspublishing.com
Web Site: endlessmountainspublishing.com
Key Personnel
Publr & Creative Dir: Lilian Rosenstreich *E-mail:* lili@endlessmountainspublishing.com
Publr & Busn Mgr: Mitchel Weiss *E-mail:* mitchel@endlessmountainspublishing.com
Founded: 2016
Publish a variety of children's books with a focus on redesign & reissue of vintage books.
ISBN Prefix(es): 978-0-9988527
Number of titles published annually: 3 Print
Total Titles: 3 Print
Distribution Center: Ingram Spark, 14 Ingram Blvd, La Vergne, TN 37086 *Toll Free Tel:* 855-997-7275 *E-mail:* ingramsparksupport@ingramcontent.com

ECS, see The Electrochemical Society (ECS)

ECS Publishing Group
1727 Larkin Williams Rd, Fenton, MO 63026
Tel: 636-305-0100 *Toll Free Tel:* 800-647-2117
Web Site: ecspublishing.com; www.facebook.com/ecspublishing
Key Personnel
Pres: Mark Lawson
Dir, Mktg & Communs: Caitlin Custer *E-mail:* ccuster@ecspublishing.com
Founded: 2014 (first imprint was E C Shirmer, dating back to 1921)
Music publishing (sheet music).

ISBN Prefix(es): 978-0-911318
Number of titles published annually: 125 Print
Total Titles: 10,200 Print
Imprints: ARSIS Audio; Aureole Editions; Galaxy Music Corp; Highgate Press; Ione Press; MorningStar Music Publishers; E C Schirmer Music Co
Distributor for Randol Bass Music; Consort Press; Dunstan House; Edition Delrieu; Gaudia Music & Arts; Laurendale Associates; Layali Music Publishing; Prime Music; Evelyn Simpson-Curenton; Stainer & Bell Ltd; Vireo Press
Orders to: Canticle Distributing, 1727 Larkin Williams Rd, St Louis, MO 63026-2024
Tel: 636-305-0100 *Toll Free Tel:* 800-647-2117 (US & CN only) *Fax:* 636-305-0121
E-mail: morningstar@morningstarmusic.com
Distribution Center: Canticle Distributing, 1727 Larkin Williams Rd, Fenton, MO 63026-2024
Tel: 636-305-0100 *Toll Free Tel:* 800-647-2117 (US & CN only) *Fax:* 636-305-0121
E-mail: morningstar@morningstarmusic.com
Membership(s): Music Publishers Association (MPA); National Music Publishers' Association (NMPA)

EDC Publishing
Division of Educational Development Corp
5402 S 122 E Ave, Tulsa, OK 74146
Mailing Address: PO Box 470663, Tulsa, OK 74147-0663
Tel: 918-622-4522 *Toll Free Tel:* 800-475-4522 *Fax:* 918-665-7919 *Toll Free Fax:* 800-743-5660
E-mail: edc@edcpub.com
Web Site: www.edcpub.com
Key Personnel
Pres & CEO: Randall White *E-mail:* rwhite@edcpub.com
CFO: Dan O'Keefe *E-mail:* dan.okeefe@edcpub.com
COO: Craig M White *E-mail:* craig.white@edcpub.com
Founded: 1978
Children's books (fiction & nonfiction).
ISBN Prefix(es): 978-0-88110; 978-0-7460; 978-0-86020; 978-0-7945; 978-1-58086; 978-1-60130
Number of titles published annually: 200 Print
Total Titles: 1,800 Print
Imprints: Kane Miller Books; Usborne Books
Distributor for Usborne Publishing Ltd
See separate listing for:
Kane Miller Books

Edgewise Press Inc
24 Fifth Ave, Suite 224, New York, NY 10011
Tel: 212-982-4818 *Fax:* 212-982-1364
E-mail: epinc@mindspring.com
Web Site: www.edgewisepress.org
Key Personnel
Co-Publr & CEO: Howard Johnson, Jr
Co-Publr & Mng Ed: Joy L Glass
Co-Publr & Ed: Richard Milazzo
Founded: 1995
Publisher of serious art & literary books.
ISBN Prefix(es): 978-0-9646466; 978-1-893207
Number of titles published annually: 3 Print
Total Titles: 40 Print
Distributor for Editions d'Afrique du Nord; Libri Canali Bassi; Paolo Torti degli Alberti

ediciones Lerner
Imprint of Lerner Publishing Group Inc
241 First Ave N, Minneapolis, MN 55401
Tel: 612-332-3344 *Toll Free Tel:* 800-328-4929 *Fax:* 612-332-7615 *Toll Free Fax:* 800-332-1132
E-mail: info@lernerbooks.com; custserve@lernerbooks.com
Web Site: www.lernerbooks.com; www.facebook.com/lernerbooks

Key Personnel
Chmn: Harry J Lerner
EVP & COO: Mark Budde
EVP & CFO: Margaret Thomas
Pres & Publr: Adam Lerner
EVP, Sales: David Wexler
VP & Ed-in-Chief: Andy Cummings
VP, Mktg: Rachel Zugschwert
Publg Dir, School & Lib: Jenny Krueger
Dir, HR: Cyndi Radant
Dir of Rts, Spec Sales & Intl Dist: Maria Kjoller
School & Lib Mktg Dir: Lois Wallentine
Publishes fiction & nonfiction books for PreK-4 in Spanish.
ISBN Prefix(es): 978-0-8225; 978-0-7613
Number of titles published annually: 20 Print; 20 E-Book
Total Titles: 150 Print; 100 E-Book
Foreign Rep(s): Thomas Allen & Son Ltd (trade) (Canada); Bounce (UK); INT Books (Australia); Phambili Agencies (Botswana, Lesotho, Namibia, Southern Africa); Publishers Marketing Services (Brunei, Malaysia, Singapore); Saunders Book Co (school & library) (Canada); Saunders Book Co (education) (Canada); South Pacific Books (New Zealand); Walker Books (Australia, New Zealand)
Foreign Rights: Japan Foreign-Rights Centre (Japan); Korea Copyright Center (KCC) (Korea); Agence Michelle Lapautre (France); Literarische Agentur Silke Weniger (Germany)
Warehouse: 1251 Washington Ave N, Minneapolis, MN 55401, Mgr: Ken Rued

Editorial Bautista Independiente
Division of Baptist Mid-Missions
3417 Kenilworth Blvd, Sebring, FL 33870-4469
Tel: 863-382-6350 *Toll Free Tel:* 800-398-7187 (US) *Fax:* 863-382-8650
E-mail: info@ebi-bmm.org; ebiweb@ebi-bmm.org
Web Site: www.ebi-bmm.org
Key Personnel
Gen Dir & Busn Mgr: Bruce Burkholder
Founded: 1950
Sunday school materials, extension materials, Bible study-all in Spanish.
ISBN Prefix(es): 978-1-879892
Number of titles published annually: 5 Print
Total Titles: 200 Print
Distributor for Casa Bautista; CLIE; Portavoz

Editorial de la Universidad de Puerto Rico, see University of Puerto Rico Press

Editorial Mundo Hispano, see Casa Bautista de Publicaciones

Editorial Portavoz
Division of Kregel Publications
2450 Oak Industrial Dr NE, Grand Rapids, MI 49505
SAN: 298-9115
Toll Free Tel: 877-733-2607 (ext 206) *Fax:* 616-493-1790
E-mail: portavoz@portavoz.com
Web Site: www.portavoz.com
Key Personnel
Pres: Jerold W Kregel *E-mail:* jerry@kregel.com
Publr: Tito Mantilla *E-mail:* tito@portavoz.com
Founded: 1970
Christian products.
ISBN Prefix(es): 978-0-8254
Number of titles published annually: 30 Print
Total Titles: 500 Print
Membership(s): Evangelical Christian Publishers Association (ECPA); SEPA

Educational Insights
Subsidiary of Learning Resources
152 W Walnut St, Suite 201, Gardena, CA 90248
SAN: 282-762X

Toll Free Tel: 800-995-4436 *Toll Free Fax:* 888-892-8731
E-mail: cs@educationalinsights.com
Web Site: www.educationalinsights.com
Key Personnel
Gen Mgr: Lisa Guili *Tel:* 847-968-3719
Founded: 1962
El-hi instructional materials; teacher's aids, teaching machines & games.
ISBN Prefix(es): 978-1-56767; 978-0-88679
Number of titles published annually: 4 Print; 2 Audio
Total Titles: 92 Print
Distribution Center: Learning Resources, 380 N Fairway Dr, Vernon Hills, IL 60061

Educator's International Press Inc (EIP)
756 Linderman Ave, Kingston, NY 12401
Tel: 518-334-0276 *Toll Free Tel:* 800-758-3756
Fax: 703-661-1547
E-mail: info@edint.com
Web Site: edint.presswarehouse.com
Key Personnel
Publr: William Clockel
Founded: 1997
Educational foundations, teacher research, curriculum, special education.
ISBN Prefix(es): 978-0-9658339; 978-1-891928
Number of titles published annually: 4 Print; 4 E-Book
Total Titles: 40 Print; 4 E-Book

Edupress Inc
Division of Teacher Created Resources Inc
12621 Western Ave, Garden Grove, CA 92841
Toll Free Tel: 800-662-4321 *Toll Free Fax:* 800-525-1254
E-mail: custserv@teachercreated.com
Web Site: www.teachercreated.com
Founded: 1956
Publisher of teacher resource materials.
ISBN Prefix(es): 978-1-56472
Number of titles published annually: 20 Print
Total Titles: 220 Print

Wm B Eerdmans Publishing Co
4035 Park East Ct SE, Grand Rapids, MI 49546
SAN: 220-0058
Tel: 616-459-4591 *Toll Free Tel:* 800-253-7521
Fax: 616-459-6540
E-mail: customerservice@eerdmans.com; sales@eerdmans.com
Web Site: www.eerdmans.com
Key Personnel
Chmn of the Bd: William B Eerdmans, Jr
Pres & Publr: Anita Eerdmans
VP & Ed-in-Chief: James Ernest
Dir, Mktg & Publicity: Laura Bardolph Hubers
E-mail: lbhubers@eerdmans.com
Mng Ed, EBYR: Kathleen Merz
Asst Mng Ed, EBYR: Courtney Zonnefeld
E-mail: czonnefeld@eerdmans.com
Sr Acct Mgr: Natalie Kompik *E-mail:* nkompik@eerdmans.com
Digital Mktg Mgr: Michael Beachy
E-mail: mbeachy@eerdmans.com
Subs Rts Mgr: Tom DeVries *E-mail:* tdevries@eerdmans.com
Sales & Exhibits Coord: Ingrid Wolf
E-mail: iwolf@eerdmans.com
Edit Assoc: Amy R Kent *E-mail:* akent@eerdmans.com
Acctg Specialist: Karl Eerdmans
Prodn Buyer: Karen Stange *E-mail:* kstange@eerdmans.com
Founded: 1911
Scholarly religious & religious reference, religion & social concerns, children's books.
ISBN Prefix(es): 978-0-8028; 978-1-4674
Number of titles published annually: 130 Print
Total Titles: 1,200 Print
Imprints: Eerdmans Books for Young Readers

Distributed by Fitzhenry & Whiteside
Foreign Rep(s): Acts TCCN Bookshop (Nigeria); Asian Trading Corp (India); Bethesda Book Centre (East Asia, Singapore); Challenge Enterprises of Ghana (Ghana); Christian Art Distributors (South Africa); Christian Book Discounters (South Africa); Co Info Pty Ltd (Australia); Cru Asia Ltd (East Asia, Singapore); Culturasia (East Asia, Singapore); Evangelical Outreach (Philippines); Foundation Distributing Inc (Canada); John Garratt Publishing (Australia); KCBS (Korea); Kyo Bun Kwan Inc (Japan); Manna Christian Stores (New Zealand); Momentum Christian Literature (Indonesia); OM Books Foundation (India); OMF Literature (Philippines); Pustaka Sufes Sdn Bhd (Malaysia); SKS Books Warehouse (East Asia, Singapore); SPCK Publishing (Europe, UK); Tien Dao Publishing House (Hong Kong)
Warehouse: LSC-BFS Plainfield, 716 Airtech Pkwy, Plainfield, IN 46168
Distribution Center: Baker & Taylor Publisher Services, 30 Amberwood Pkwy, Ashland, OH 44805 (select intl mkts only) *Tel:* 567-215-0030 *Toll Free Tel:* 888-814-0208 *E-mail:* orders@btpubservices.com *Web Site:* www.btpubservices.com

§Eifrig Publishing LLC
PO Box 66, Lemont, PA 16851
Toll Free Tel: 888-340-6543
E-mail: info@eifrigpublishing.com
Web Site: www.eifrigpublishing.com
Key Personnel
Founder & Ed-in-Chief: Penelope Eifrig
E-mail: penny@eifrigpublishing.com
Founded: 2006
Primarily children's titles with social, ecological, community & self-esteem emphasis.
ISBN Prefix(es): 978-1-63233
Number of titles published annually: 12 Print; 1 CD-ROM; 12 Online; 12 E-Book; 1 Audio
Total Titles: 102 Print; 3 CD-ROM; 102 Online; 102 E-Book; 5 Audio
Imprints: Berry Street Books; Eifrig Publishing; Getting Smart; Mt Nittany Press; YACK!
Foreign Office(s): Knobelsdorffstr 44, 14059 Berlin, Germany *Tel:* (030) 37448085
Foreign Rep(s): Sylvia Hayse Literary Agency (worldwide)
Foreign Rights: Sylvia Hayse Literary Agency (worldwide)
Membership(s): Independent Book Publishers Association (IBPA)

Eisenbrauns
Imprint of The Pennsylvania State University Press
820 N University Dr, USB 1, Suite C, University Park, PA 16802
SAN: 200-7835
Tel: 814-865-1327 *Toll Free Tel:* 800-326-9180
Fax: 814-863-1408 *Toll Free Fax:* 877-778-2665
E-mail: orders@eisenbrauns.org
Web Site: www.eisenbrauns.org
Key Personnel
Publr: James E Eisenbraun *E-mail:* jeisenbraun@press.psu.edu
Founded: 1975
Educational books, books on the Ancient Near East.
ISBN Prefix(es): 978-0-931464; 978-1-57506
Number of titles published annually: 40 Print; 40 E-Book
Total Titles: 615 Print; 10 CD-ROM; 432 E-Book

§Elderberry Press Inc
1393 Old Homestead Dr, Oakland, OR 97462-9690
Tel: 541-459-6043
Web Site: www.elderberrypress.com

Key Personnel
Co-Owner & Exec Ed: Valerie St John
E-mail: editor@elderberrypress.com
Co-Owner: Asia St John
Founded: 1997
Works closely with authors, from first reading of their ms to publishing & long after to ensure their book finds up to 50,000 or more readers. This publisher has indicated that 100% of their product line is author subsidized.
ISBN Prefix(es): 978-0-9658407; 978-1-930859; 978-1-932762; 978-1-934956
Number of titles published annually: 6 Print; 12 Online; 12 E-Book
Total Titles: 300 Print; 120 Online; 100 E-Book; 1 Audio
Foreign Rep(s): Ingram Book Co (worldwide)

§The Electrochemical Society (ECS)
65 S Main St, Bldg D, Pennington, NJ 08534-2839
Tel: 609-737-1902 *Fax:* 609-737-0629
E-mail: publications@electrochem.org; customerservice@electrochem.org
Web Site: www.electrochem.org
Key Personnel
Chief Content Offr/Publr: Mary E Yess *Tel:* 609-737-1902 ext 119 *E-mail:* mary.yess@electrochem.org
Exec Dir: Christopher J Jannuzzi *Tel:* 609-737-1902 ext 101 *E-mail:* chris.jannuzzi@electrochem.org
Dir, Mktg & Communs: Rob Gerth *Tel:* 609-737-1902 ext 114 *E-mail:* rob.gerth@electrochem.org
Dir, Pubns: Beth Craanen *Tel:* 609-737-1902 ext 103 *E-mail:* beth.craanen@electrochem.org
Assoc Dir, Pubns: Annie Goedkoop *Tel:* 609-737-1902 ext 118 *E-mail:* ann.goedkoop@electrochem.org
Edit Mgr: Paul B Cooper *E-mail:* paul.cooper@electrochem.org
Pubns Specialist: Andrea L Guenzel
E-mail: andrea.guenzel@electrochem.org; Beth Schademann *E-mail:* beth.schademann@electrochem.org
Founded: 1902
Technical journals, membership magazine, proceedings volumes, monographs, ECS Digital Library.
ISBN Prefix(es): 978-1-56677; 978-1-60768; 978-1-62332
Number of titles published annually: 1 Print; 1 CD-ROM; 4 Online
Total Titles: 1 Print; 1 CD-ROM; 4 Online
Distributed by John Wiley & Sons (monographs)
Membership(s): American Society of Association Executives (ASAE)

Edward Elgar Publishing Inc
The William Pratt House, 9 Dewey Ct, Northampton, MA 01060-3815
SAN: 299-4615
Tel: 413-584-5551 *Toll Free Tel:* 800-390-3149 (orders) *Fax:* 413-584-9933
E-mail: elgarinfo@e-elgar.com; elgarsales@e-elgar.com; elgarsubmissions@e-elgar.com (edit)
Web Site: www.e-elgar.com; www.elgaronline.com (ebooks & journals)
Key Personnel
Sales & Mktg Mgr: Katy Wight *E-mail:* kwight@e-elgar.com
Exec Ed: Alan Sturmer *E-mail:* asturmer@e-elgar.com
Founded: 1986
Leading international publisher of academic books, ebooks & journals in economics, finance, business & management, law, environment, public & social policy.
ISBN Prefix(es): 978-1-85898; 978-1-85278; 978-1-84064; 978-1-84376; 978-1-84542; 978-1-84720; 978-1-84844; 978-1-78536; 978-

1-78471; 978-1-78347; 978-1-78100; 978-1-78254; 978-1-84980
Number of titles published annually: 350 Print; 300 E-Book
Total Titles: 5,600 Print; 3,000 E-Book
Foreign Office(s): Edward Elgar Publishing Ltd, the Lypiatts, 15 Lansdown Rd, Cheltenham, Glos GL50 2JA, United Kingdom, Mng Dir: Tim Williams *Tel:* (01242) 226934 *Fax:* (01242) 262111 *E-mail:* info@e-elgar.co.uk *Web Site:* www.e-elgar.co.uk
Warehouse: Books International Inc, 22883 Quicksilver Dr, Dulles, VA 20166, Cust Serv: Todd Riggleman *Tel:* 703-661-1596 *Toll Free Tel:* 800-390-3149 *Fax:* 703-996-1010 *E-mail:* elgar.orders@presswarehouse.com

Elite Books
PO Box 442, Fulton, CA 95439
Tel: 707-525-9292 *Toll Free Fax:* 800-330-9798
E-mail: support@eftuniverse.com
Web Site: www.elitebooksonline.com
Key Personnel
Ed: Stephanie Marohn *E-mail:* angel@stephaniemarohn.com
ISBN Prefix(es): 978-0-9720028; 978-0-9710888; 978-1-60070
Number of titles published annually: 5 Print
Total Titles: 40 Print
Distribution Center: Hay House, 2776 Loker Ave W, Carlsbad, CA 92010 *Tel:* 760-431-7695 *E-mail:* orders@hayhouse.com *Web Site:* www.hayhouse.com
Membership(s): Independent Book Publishers Association (IBPA)

Elsevier Engineering Information (Ei)
Subsidiary of Elsevier Inc
230 Park Ave, 8th fl, New York, NY 10169-0123
Tel: 212-989-5800 *Fax:* 212-633-3990
E-mail: eicustomersupport@elsevier.com
Web Site: www.elsevier.com/solutions/engineering-village
Key Personnel
Dir & Prod Mgmt, EV Content: Judy Salk
Founded: 1884
Provides online information, knowledge & support to engineering researchers. Flagship platform is Engineering Village & the primary database is Compendex.
ISBN Prefix(es): 978-0-87394
Number of titles published annually: 8 Online
Total Titles: 8 Online

Elsevier, Health Sciences Division
Division of RELX Group PLC
1600 John F Kennedy Blvd, Suite 1800, Philadelphia, PA 19103-2899
Tel: 215-239-3900 *Toll Free Tel:* 800-523-1649 *Fax:* 215-239-3990
Web Site: www.us.elsevierhealth.com
Founded: 1906
ISBN Prefix(es): 978-0-7506; 978-0-443; 978-0-444; 978-0-932883; 978-1-56053; 978-0-8016; 978-0-8151; 978-0-7216; 978-0-7020; 978-0-7234; 978-0-323; 978-0-7236; 978-1-4160; 978-1-55664; 978-0-920513; 978-1-898507; 978-1-932141; 978-1-4377; 978-1-4557
Number of titles published annually: 2,000 Print
Imprints: Churchill Livingstone; Mosby; WB Saunders Co
Distributor for G W Medical Publisher
Foreign Rights: John Scott & Co (Jake Scott)
Shipping Address: PO Box 437, Linn, MO 65051-0437
Distribution Center: 1799 Hwy 50 E, Linn, MO 65051 *Tel:* 573-897-3694 *Fax:* 573-897-4387

§Elsevier Inc
Subsidiary of RELX Group PLC
230 Park Ave, Suite 800, New York, NY 10169
Tel: 212-989-5800 *Fax:* 212-633-3990

Web Site: www.elsevier.com
Founded: 1880
Books for professionals, researchers & students in the sciences, technology, engineering, business & media. Also research monographs, major reference works & serials.
Number of titles published annually: 2,500 Print; 400 E-Book
Total Titles: 40,000 Print
Branch Office(s)
2171 Monroe Ave, Suite 203, Rochester, NY 14618 *Tel:* 585-442-8170 *Fax:* 585-442-8171
24422 Avenida De La Carlota, Suite 235, Leguna Hills, CA 92653 *Tel:* 801-485-6500
Marquis One, 245 Peachtree Ctr Ave, Suite 1900, Atlanta, GA 30303 *Tel:* 404-669-9400 *Toll Free Tel:* 800-999-6274 *Fax:* 404-669-9339
5635 Fishers Lane, Suite 510, Rockville, MD 20852
50 Hampshire St, 5th fl, Cambridge, MA 02139 *Tel:* 617-661-7057 *Fax:* 617-661-7061
Glenwood Hills Bldg, 3196 Kraft Ave, Suite 305, Grand Rapids, MI 49512 *Tel:* 616-530-9206 *Fax:* 616-530-9245
3251 Riverport Lane, Maryland Heights, MO 63043 *Tel:* 314-447-8000 *Fax:* 314-447-8033
1600 John F Kennedy Blvd, Suite 1800, Philadelphia, PA 19103-2398 *Tel:* 215-239-3900 *Fax:* 215-239-3990
111 Center Park Dr, Suite 175, Knoxville, TN 37922 *Toll Free Tel:* 800-999-6274
11011 Richmond Ave, Suite 450, Houston, TX 77042 *Toll Free Tel:* 800-950-2728 *Fax:* 713-838-7787
Foreign Office(s): Elsevier Ltd, The Boulevard, Langford Lane, Kidlington, Oxford OX5 1GB, United Kingdom *Tel:* (01865) 843000 *Fax:* (01865) 843010
Foreign Rep(s): Elsevier Ltd (Europe)
Membership(s): Association of American Publishers (AAP)
See separate listing for:
Elsevier Engineering Information (Ei)
Morgan Kaufmann

Elva Resa Publishing
8362 Tamarack Village, Suite 119-106, St Paul, MN 55125
Tel: 651-357-8770 *Fax:* 501-641-0777
E-mail: staff@elvaresa.com
Web Site: www.elvaresa.com; www.militaryfamilybooks.com
Founded: 1997
Books for & about military families.
ISBN Prefix(es): 978-1-934617; 978-0-9657483
Number of titles published annually: 4 Print
Total Titles: 34 Print; 5 E-Book
Imprints: Alma Little (children's books); Elva Resa (books for & about military families); Juloya (inspirational works that help people celebrate life)
Distribution Center: Independent Publishers Group (IPG), 814 N Franklin St, Chicago, IL 60610 *Toll Free Tel:* 800-888-4741 *E-mail:* orders@ipgbook.com *Web Site:* www.ipgbook.com
Membership(s): Independent Book Publishers Association (IBPA); Midwest Independent Publishing Association (MIPA)

§EMC Publishing LLC
Division of Carnegie Learning Inc
875 Montreal Way, St Paul, MN 55102
SAN: 201-3800
Tel: 651-290-2800 (corp) *Toll Free Tel:* 888-851-7094
E-mail: info@carnegielearning.com
Web Site: www.emcp.com
Key Personnel
CEO: Eric Cantor
Founded: 1954
Paper & hardbound textbooks, audio, video, online Internet, CD-ROM, software microcom-

puter instructional materials in world language, business education, literature & language arts, social studies, medical, computer technology.
ISBN Prefix(es): 978-0-8219; 978-1-56118; 978-0-7638; 978-0-88436; 978-0-912022
Number of titles published annually: 100 Print; 75 CD-ROM; 20 Online; 100 E-Book; 80 Audio
Total Titles: 3,700 Print; 300 CD-ROM; 75 Online; 3,500 E-Book; 1,035 Audio
Divisions: JIST Publishing; Paradigm Education Solutions
Distributor for Sybex Inc
Foreign Rep(s): Wolfgang Kraft (worldwide)
Foreign Rights: Wolfgang Kraft (worldwide)
See separate listing for:
JIST Publishing

Emerald Books
Affiliate of YWAM Publishing
PO Box 55787, Seattle, WA 98155
Tel: 425-771-1153 *Toll Free Tel:* 800-922-2143 *Fax:* 425-775-2383
E-mail: books@ywampublishing.com
Web Site: www.ywampublishing.com
Founded: 1992
Christian theme.
ISBN Prefix(es): 978-1-883002; 978-1-932096; 978-1-62486
Number of titles published annually: 15 Print
Total Titles: 364 Print
Distributed by YWAM Publishing
Shipping Address: 7825 230 St SW, Edmonds, WA 98026 *Web Site:* ywampublishing.com

Emmaus Road Publishing Inc
Division of St Paul Center for Biblical Theology
1468 Parkview Circle, Steubenville, OH 43952
Tel: 740-283-2880 (outside US)
Toll Free Tel: 800-398-5470 (orders) *Fax:* 740-283-4011 (orders)
E-mail: questions@emmausroad.org
Web Site: www.emmausroad.org
Key Personnel
VP, Opers: Nate Roberts
Publr: Andrew Jones
Order Processing: Michelle Olenick *E-mail:* molenick@emmausroad.org
Founded: 1998
Bible studies, biblically based apologetics & other materials faithful to the teaching of the Catholic church. Restocking fee of 20% for returns.
ISBN Prefix(es): 978-0-9663223; 978-1-931018; 978-1-937155; 978-1-941447; 978-1-940329; 978-1-63446
Number of titles published annually: 12 Print; 12 E-Book
Total Titles: 80 Print; 1 CD-ROM; 50 E-Book; 10 Audio

Empire Publishing Service
PO Box 1344, Studio City, CA 91614-0344
Tel: 818-784-8918 *Fax:* 818-990-2477
E-mail: empirepubsvc@att.net
Founded: 1960
Publisher & distributor of entertainment books, plays & musicals, specialty books & printed music.
ISBN Prefix(es): 978-1-58690; 978-0-934468
Number of titles published annually: 25 Print
Total Titles: 4,365 Print
Imprints: Arsis Press (music); Classics With a Twist; Gaslight Publications; Paul Mould Publishing; Phantom Books & Music; Sisra Music Publishing; Spotlight Books; Jack Spratt Choral Music
Subsidiaries: Best Books International
Distributor for Arsis Press; Arte Publico Press; Ian Henry Publications; ISH Group (worldwide exc Australia); Paul Mould Publishing

Enchanted Lion Books

67 West St, Studio 317A, Brooklyn, NY 11222
Tel: 646-785-9272
E-mail: enchantedlion.community@gmail.com
Web Site: www.enchantedlion.com
Key Personnel
Publr: Claudia Bedrick
Founded: 2002
Publish illustrated nonfiction picture books for
children in the categories of art, biography &
history, science & nature, folktales & mythol-
ogy.
ISBN Prefix(es): 978-1-59270
Number of titles published annually: 20 Print
Total Titles: 100 Print
Distributed by Consortium; Farrar, Straus &
Giroux, LLC
Orders to: Ingram, 1094 Flex Dr, Jackson, TN
38301-5070 *Toll Free Tel:* 800-283-3572 *Toll
Free Fax:* 800-351-5073 *E-mail:* orderentry@
perseusbooks.com
Returns: Ingram, 193 Edwards Dr, Jackson, TN
38301-5070 *Toll Free Tel:* 800-343-4499
Distribution Center: Consortium Book Sales &
Distribution, The Keg House, Suite 101, 34
13 Ave NE, Minneapolis, MN 55413-1007
Tel: 612-746-2600 *Toll Free Tel:* 800-283-3572
(cust serv, Jackson, TN) *Fax:* 612-746-2606
E-mail: info@cbsd.com *Web Site:* www.cbsd.
com SAN: 200-6049

Encounter Books

900 Broadway, Suite 601, New York, NY 10003
Tel: 212-871-6310 *Toll Free Tel:* 800-343-4499
Fax: 212-871-6311
E-mail: publicity@encounterbooks.com
Web Site: www.encounterbooks.com
Key Personnel
Pres & Publr: Roger Kimball *E-mail:* kimball@
encounterbooks.com
Exec Dir, Opers: Nola Tully *E-mail:* ntully@
encounterbooks.com
Dir, Mktg: Sam Schneider
Dir, Prodn: Katherine Wong *E-mail:* kwong@
encounterbooks.com
Publicity Dir: Lauren Miklos *E-mail:* lmiklos@
encounterbooks.com
Founded: 1998
Serious nonfiction books about history, culture,
current events, religion, politics, social criticism
& public policy.
ISBN Prefix(es): 978-1-893554; 978-1-59403
Number of titles published annually: 30 Print; 30
E-Book
Total Titles: 400 Print; 250 E-Book
Orders to: Two Rivers Distribution, 210 Amer-
ican Dr, Jackson, TN 38301 (US, CN &
Australia) *Toll Free Tel:* 800-343-4499 *Toll
Free Fax:* 800-351-5073 *Web Site:* www.
tworiversdistribution.com
Returns: PSSC-Returns, 660 S Mansfield, Ypsi-
lanti, MI 48197
Distribution Center: Two Rivers Distribution,
210 American Dr, Jackson, TN 38301 (US,
CN & Australia) *Toll Free Tel:* 800-343-4499
Toll Free Fax: 800-351-5073 *Web Site:* www.
tworiversdistribution.com
Membership(s): American Booksellers Associ-
ation (ABA); American Library Association
(ALA); Independent Book Publishers Associa-
tion (IBPA)

§Encyclopaedia Britannica Inc

325 N La Salle St, Suite 200, Chicago, IL 60654
Tel: 312-347-7000 (all other countries)
Toll Free Tel: 800-323-1229 (US & CN)
Fax: 312-294-2104
E-mail: contact@eb.com
Web Site: www.britannica.com
Key Personnel
Global CEO: Karthik Krishnan
EVP, Corp Secy & Gen Coun: Douglas Eveleigh
SVP & CFO: Jim Conners

SVP, Britannica Digital Learning Intl: Leah Man-
soor
VP, Consumer Mkts: Chris Mayland
VP, Mktg & Channel Devt: Sal De Spirito
VP, Sales: Matthew Krise
Exec Dir, Cust Success: Rick Lumsden
Founded: 1768
Reference works, print & online for consumers &
institutions.
ISBN Prefix(es): 978-0-87827; 978-0-8347; 978-
0-85229; 978-1-61535; 978-0-9823824; 978-
1-62513; 978-1-59339; 978-1-60835; 978-0-
9823823; 978-0-9823819; 978-0-7826; 978-0-
9823820; 978-0-9823821; 978-0-9823822
Subsidiaries: Merriam-Webster Inc
Foreign Office(s): Encyclopaedia Britannica Aus-
tralia Ltd, Level 1, 9 Help St, Chatswood,
NSW 2067, Australia (Australia & Asia Pa-
cific) *Tel:* (02) 9915 8800 *Fax:* (02) 9419 5247
E-mail: sales@eb.com.au *Web Site:* www.
britannica.com.au
Britannica.com Israel Ltd, 16 Tozeret Ha'aretz
St, Tel Aviv 67891, Israel *Tel:* (03) 607 0400
Fax: (03) 607 0401 *Web Site:* www.britannica.
co.il
Britannica Japan Co Ltd, Nishi-Gotanda 8 Chome
Bldg, 8-3-16 Nishi-Gotanda, Shinagawa-ku,
Tokyo 141-0031, Japan *Tel:* (03) 5436 1388
Fax: (03) 5436 1380 *E-mail:* info@britannica.
co.jp *Web Site:* www.britannica.co.jp
Encyclopaedia Britannica (UK) Ltd, Unity
Wharf, 2nd fl, Mill St, London SE1 2BH,
United Kingdom (Africa, Europe & Middle
East) *Tel:* (020) 7500 7800 *Fax:* (020) 7500
7878 *E-mail:* enquiries@britannica.co.uk *Web
Site:* www.britannica.co.uk
See separate listing for:
Merriam-Webster Inc

Endless Mountains Publishing Co

72 Glenmaura National Blvd, Suite 104B,
Moosic, PA 18507
Tel: 862-251-2296; 570-878-7960
E-mail: info@endlessmountainspublishing.com
Web Site: www.endlessmountainspublishing.com
Key Personnel
Publr & Creative Dir: Lilian Rosenstreich
E-mail: lili@endlessmountainspublishing.com
Publr & Busn Mgr: Mitchel Weiss
E-mail: mitchel@endlessmountainspublishing.
com
Founded: 2017
We are a niche publisher focusing on books of
interest to Jewish children. We also publish
books of regional interest to Northeast Pennsyl-
vania.
ISBN Prefix(es): 978-0-9988527
Number of titles published annually: 4 Print
Total Titles: 2 Print
Imprints: Eclectic Book Press (books of general
interest to children); Kalaniot Books (books of
interest to Jewish children)
See separate listing for:
Eclectic Book Press
Kalaniot Books

Energy Psychology Press

Division of Energy Psychology Group
1490 Mark West Springs Rd, Santa Rosa, CA
95404
Mailing Address: 3340 Fulton Rd, No 442, Ful-
ton, CA 95439
Tel: 707-525-9292 *Toll Free Fax:* 800-330-9798
E-mail: energypsychologypress@gmail.com;
support@eftuniverse.com
Web Site: www.energypsychologypress.com;
www.elitebooksonline.com
Key Personnel
Publr: Dawson Church
Ed-in-Chief: Stephanie Marohn
E-mail: stephanie@eftuniverse.com
Prodn Coord: Heather Montgomery
E-mail: heather@eftuniverse.com

Founded: 1994
ISBN Prefix(es): 978-1-60415
Number of titles published annually: 5 Print
Total Titles: 40 Print
Distribution Center: Hay House, 2750 Progress
St, Vista, CA 92081, Contact: Joe Koburn
Tel: 760-419-1715 *E-mail:* jcoburn@hayhouse.
com *Web Site:* www.hayhouse.com
Membership(s): Independent Book Publishers As-
sociation (IBPA)

§Enslow Publishing LLC

101 W 23 St, Suite 240, New York, NY 10011
Toll Free Tel: 800-398-2504 *Fax:* 908-771-0925
Toll Free Fax: 877-980-4454
E-mail: customerservice@enslow.com
Web Site: www.enslow.com
Key Personnel
Pres: Roger Rosen
Founded: 1976
Educational nonfiction books for children &
young adults.
ISBN Prefix(es): 978-0-89490; 978-0-7760; 978-
1-59845; 978-1-4644; 978-1-4645; 978-1-4646;
978-1-62285; 978-1-62293; 978-1-62324; 978-
1-62400
Number of titles published annually: 200 Print;
200 E-Book
Total Titles: 2,400 Print
Imprints: Enslow (middle & high school
books); Enslow Elementary (PreK-5); MyRe-
portLinks.com Books (Internet supported
books); West 44 Books (hi-lo middle grade
& young adult fiction)
Foreign Rep(s): CrossCan Educational Services
Inc (Canada); EduCan Media (Canada); Everybody's Books (Warren Halford) (South Africa);
Read Pacific (New Zealand)
Membership(s): AASL; American Library Association (ALA); Educational Book & Media
Association (EBMA); TLA

Entangled Publishing LLC

2614 S Timberline Rd, Suite 105, Fort Collins,
CO 80525
Toll Free Tel: 877-677-9451
E-mail: publisher@entangledpublishing.com
Web Site: www.entangledpublishing.com
Key Personnel
Publr & CEO: Liz Pelletier
CFO: Peter DeGiglio
Fin Dir & Mng Ed: Melanie Smith
Mktg Dir: Jessica Turner
Sales & Publicity Dir: Shayla Fereshetian
ISBN Prefix(es): 978-1-937044; 978-1-62266;
978-1-62061
Number of titles published annually: 48 Print;
312 E-Book
Imprints: Amara (upmarket single title romance);
Bliss (sweet romance, with small-town, fam-
ily vibe); Brazen (sexy contemporary category
romance); Covet (contemporary category romance with a paranormal twist); Embrace (new
adult romance); Entangled Select (adult single
title romance); Entangled Teen (young adult
single title romance); Ignite (suspenseful category romance); Indulgence (rich & powerful
alpha heroes); Lovestruck (romantic comedy
& fun, flirty romance); Scandalous (historical
category romance); Scorched (erotic romance);
TEEN Crave (teen contemporary category romance with a paranormal twist); TEEN Crush
(teen contemporary category romance)
Distributed by Macmillan

EntertainmentPro, see Quite Specific Media
Group Ltd

Entomological Society of America

3 Park Place, Suite 307, Annapolis, MD 21401-
3722
Tel: 301-731-4535 *Fax:* 301-731-4538
E-mail: esa@entsoc.org

Web Site: www.entsoc.org
Key Personnel
Exec Dir: David Gammel *E-mail:* dgammel@
entsoc.org
Dir, Pubns: Lisa Junker *Tel:* 301-731-4535 ext
3020 *E-mail:* ljunker@entsoc.org
Dir, Strategic Initiatives: Christopher Stelzig
E-mail: cstelzig@entsoc.org
Founded: 1889
Professional scientific society for entomologists.
Publish research journals on all areas of ento-
mology.
ISBN Prefix(es): 978-0-938522; 978-0-9776209;
978-0-9966674
Number of titles published annually: 3 Print
Total Titles: 25 Print
Distributed by Oxford University Press

§Environmental Law Institute
1730 "M" St NW, Suite 700, Washington, DC
20036
Tel: 202-939-3800 *Toll Free Tel:* 800-433-5120
Fax: 202-939-3868
E-mail: law@eli.org
Web Site: www.eli.org
Key Personnel
Pres: Scott Fulton *E-mail:* sfulton@eli.org
Ed, The Environmental Forum: Stephen Dujack
E-mail: dujack@eli.org
Founded: 1969
Environmental studies, references, online database
services, monographs, policy studies.
ISBN Prefix(es): 978-0-911937; 978-1-58576
Number of titles published annually: 6 Print; 30
Online
Total Titles: 53 Print; 1 CD-ROM; 200 Online
Distributed by Island Press

Epicenter Press Inc
6524 NE 181 St, Suite 2, Kenmore, WA 98028
Tel: 425-485-6822 (edit, mktg, busn off)
Fax: 425-481-8253
E-mail: info@epicenterpress.com
Web Site: www.epicenterpress.com
Key Personnel
Pres: Phil Garrett *E-mail:* phil@epicenterpress.
com
Exec Ed/Assoc Publr: Jennifer McCord
E-mail: jennifer@coffeetownpress.com
Acqs Ed: Lael Morgan *E-mail:* lael@
epicenterpress.com
Founded: 1988
Regional nonfiction trade publisher. Specialize in
titles about Alaska & the Pacific Northwest.
Trade distributor of titles by other publishers.
Packager, print-broker & book publishing con-
sultant.
ISBN Prefix(es): 978-0-945397; 978-0-9708493;
978-0-9724944; 978-0-9800825; 978-1-935347
Number of titles published annually: 20 Print; 20
E-Book
Total Titles: 425 Print
Imprints: Camel Press (genre fiction: mystery &
romance); Coffeetown Press (memoir & liter-
ary fiction); Emerald Point Press; Fanny Press
(erotica); Northwest Corner Books
Divisions: Aftershocks Media (book packager,
contract publishing services, consulting, book
distribution)
Distributor for Coastal Publishing; Documentary
Media
Foreign Rights: Susan Schulman Agency (Camel
Press & Coffeetown Press) (worldwide); Wales
Literary Agency (worldwide)
Membership(s): Independent Book Publishers
Association (IBPA); Pacific Northwest Book-
sellers Association (PNBA)

EPS/School Specialty Literacy & Intervention
Division of School Specialty Inc
625 Mount Auburn St, 3rd fl, Cambridge, MA
02138-3039

SAN: 201-8225
Mailing Address: PO Box 9031, Cambridge, MA
02139-9031
Toll Free Tel: 800-225-5750 *Toll Free Fax:* 888-
440-2665
E-mail: customerservice.eps@schoolspecialty.com
Web Site: eps.schoolspecialty.com
Key Personnel
VP, Fin: Dave Ciommo
Founded: 1952
Technology & print educational materials for
grades K-12, with particular emphasis on lan-
guage arts, remedial reading skills, materials
for the child with specific language disabil-
ity, workbooks - elementary; workbooks - sec-
ondary, learning differences.
ISBN Prefix(es): 978-0-8388; 978-1-4293
Number of titles published annually: 25 Print
Total Titles: 800 Print
Imprints: Modern Learning Press
Branch Office(s)
555 Legget Dr, Suite 900, Tower B, Ottawa, ON
K2K 2X3, Canada
Returns: 80 Northwest Blvd, Nashua, NH 03063

§Etruscan Press
Wilkes University, 84 W South St, Wilkes-Barre,
PA 18766
Tel: 570-408-4546 *Fax:* 570-408-3333
E-mail: books@etruscanpress.org
Web Site: www.etruscanpress.org
Key Personnel
Exec Dir: Dr Philip Brady
Exec Ed: Dr Robert Mooney
Mng Ed: Bill Schneider *E-mail:* bill@
etruscanpress.org
Founded: 2001
Housed at Wilkes University & partnering with
Youngstown State University, Etruscan is a
nonprofit literary press working to produce &
promote books that nurture the dialogue among
genres, cultures & voices. We publish books of
poems, novels, short stories, creative nonfiction,
criticism, translation & anthologies.
ISBN Prefix(es): 978-0-9832944; 978-0-9797450;
978-0-9833294; 978-0-9897532; 978-0-
9886922; 978-0-9903221; 978-0-9987508; 978-
0-9977455
Number of titles published annually: 6 Print
Total Titles: 83 Print
Distribution Center: Consortium Book Sales &
Distribution, The Keg House, Suite 101, 34
13 Ave NE, Minneapolis, MN 55413-1007
Tel: 612-746-2600 *Toll Free Tel:* 800-283-3572
(cust serv, Jackson, TN) *Fax:* 612-746-2606
E-mail: info@cbsd.com *Web Site:* www.cbsd.
com SAN: 200-6049
Membership(s): Community of Literary Maga-
zines & Presses (CLMP); Independent Book
Publishers Association (IBPA)

Europa Editions
Subsidiary of E/O Edizioni SRL
214 W 29 St, Suite 1003, New York, NY 10001
Tel: 212-868-6844 *Fax:* 212-868-6845
E-mail: info@europaeditions.com
Web Site: www.europaeditions.com
Key Personnel
Publr & Co-Founder: Sandro Ferri
Publr, Pres & Co-Founder: Sandra Ozzola Ferri
Dir, Sales, Mktg & Busn Devt: Kathy Wiess
Ed-in-Chief: Michael Reynolds
Publr-at-Large: Kent Carroll
Sr Publicist: Rachael Small
Founded: 2005
Publisher of international literary fiction in trans-
lation, domestic literary fiction, crime & narra-
tive nonfiction.
ISBN Prefix(es): 978-1-933372; 978-1-60945
Number of titles published annually: 35 Print
Total Titles: 300 Print
Imprints: Europa Compass; Tonga Books; World
Noir

Foreign Office(s): via Camozzi 1, 00195 Rome
RM, Italy, Mng Ed: Leonella Basiglini
Tel: (06) 3722829 *Fax:* (06) 37351096
Distributed by Jonathan Ball Publishers; New-
South Books
Distribution Center: Publishers Group West, 1400
Fourth St, Berkeley, CA 94710 *Tel:* 510-528-
1444 *E-mail:* ips@ingramcontent.com
Publishers Group Canada, 300-76 Stafford St,
Toronto, ON M6J 2S1, Canada *Tel:* 416-934-
9900 *Toll Free Tel:* 800-747-8147 *Fax:* 416-
934-1410 *E-mail:* info@pgcbooks.ca
Turnaround Publisher Services Ltd, Unit 3,
Olympia Trading Estate, Coburg Rd, Wood
Green, London N22 6TZ, United King-
dom (UK & Ireland) *Tel:* (020) 8829 3000
E-mail: orders@turnaround-uk.com *Web
Site:* www.turnaround-uk.com

§Evan-Moor Educational Publishers
18 Lower Ragsdale Dr, Monterey, CA 93940-
5746
Tel: 831-649-5901 *Toll Free Tel:* 800-777-4362
(orders) *Fax:* 831-649-6256 *Toll Free Fax:* 800-
777-4332 (orders)
E-mail: sales@evan-moor.com; marketing@evan-
moor.com
Web Site: www.evan-moor.com
Key Personnel
Founder & CEO: William Evans *E-mail:* bill@
evan-moor.com
VP, Sales: James O'Donnell, III
Exec Ed: Lisa Vitarisi Mathews
Dir, Fin: David Miller
Dir, Technol Prods: Keli Winters
Dir, Opers & Fulfillment: Anney Banales
Founded: 1979
Supplemental educational materials in print &
digital formats for parents & teachers of chil-
dren ages 3-14. Subjects include reading, math,
writing, science, social studies, arts & crafts &
literature.
ISBN Prefix(es): 978-1-55799; 978-1-62938; 978-
1-61367; 978-1-61366; 978-1-59673; 978-1-
4409; 978-1-60792; 978-1-61368; 978-1-61365;
978-1-60793; 978-1-935353; 978-1-60823; 978-
1-60963
Number of titles published annually: 25 Print; 60
Online; 25 E-Book
Total Titles: 450 Print; 450 Online; 450 E-Book
Membership(s): American Booksellers Association (ABA); American Library Association
(ALA); Association of American Publishers
PreK-12 Learning Group; Education Market
Association

M Evans & Company
Imprint of Rowman & Littlefield Publishing
Group
c/o Rowman & Littlefield Publishing Group, 4501
Forbes Blvd, Suite 200, Lanham, MD 20706
Tel: 301-459-3366 *Fax:* 301-429-5748
Web Site: rowman.com
Key Personnel
Ed: Rick Rinehart *Tel:* 203-458-4656
E-mail: rrinehart@rowman.com
Founded: 1963
Health, medical & business books.
ISBN Prefix(es): 978-0-87131; 978-1-59077
Number of titles published annually: 30 Print
Total Titles: 250 Print
Foreign Rights: Rights Unlimited
Shipping Address: National Book Network, 15200
NBN Way, Blue Ridge Summit, PA 17214
Tel: 717-794-3800 *Toll Free Tel:* 800-462-6420
Fax: 717-794-4801 *Toll Free Fax:* 800-338-
4550
Distribution Center: National Book Network,
15200 NBN Way, Blue Ridge Summit, PA
17214 *Tel:* 717-794-3800 *Toll Free Tel:* 800-
462-6420 *Fax:* 717-794-4801 *Toll Free
Fax:* 800-338-4550

Evergreen Pacific Publishing Ltd
4204 Russell Rd, Suite M, Mukilteo, WA 98275-5424
Tel: 425-493-1451 *Fax:* 425-493-1453
E-mail: sales@evergreenpacific.com
Web Site: www.evergreenpacific.com
Key Personnel
Pres: Paul Hamstra
Founded: 1996
Books, charts & guides for water related recreations.
ISBN Prefix(es): 978-0-945265; 978-0-9609036; 978-1-934707
Number of titles published annually: 4 Print
Total Titles: 25 Print
Imprints: Evergreen Pacific Publishing

§Everyman's Library
Imprint of Knopf Doubleday Publishing Group
c/o Penguin Random House Inc, 1745 Broadway, New York, NY 10019
Tel: 212-751-2600 *Fax:* 212-572-2662 (foreign rts)
Web Site: knopfdoubleday.com
Key Personnel
SVP & Edit Dir: LuAnn Walther
Founded: 1906
Penguin Random House & its publishing entities are not accepting unsol submissions, proposals, mss or submission queries via e-mail at this time.
Foreign Rights: ALS-Agenzia Letteraria Santachiara (Roberto Santachiara) (Italy); Anthea Agency (Katalina Sabeva) (Bulgaria); Bardon-Chinese Media Agency (Xu-Weiguang) (China); Bardon-Chinese Media Agency (Yu-Shiuan Chen) (Taiwan); The English Agency (Junzo Sawa) (Japan); Graal Literary Agency (Maria Strarz-Kanska) (Poland); The Deborah Harris Agency (Ilana Kurshan) (Israel); JLM Literary Agency (Nelly Moukakos) (Greece); Katai & Bolza Literary (Peter Bolza) (Croatia, Hungary); KCC (MiSook Hong) (Korea); Simona Kessler International (Simona Kessler) (Romania); Licht & Burr Literary Agency (Trine Licht) (Scandinavia); La Nouvelle Agency (Vanessa Kling) (France); Kristin Olson Literary Agency (Kristin Olson) (Czechia); Sebes & Bisseling Literary Agency (Paul Sebes) (Netherlands)

Everything Goes Media LLC
PO Box 1524, Milwaukee, WI 53201
Tel: 312-226-8400
E-mail: info@everythinggoesmedia.com
Web Site: www.everythinggoesmedia.com
Key Personnel
Owner & Publr: Sharon Woodhouse
 E-mail: sharon@everythinggoesmedia.com
Founded: 1994
"The book is the medium." Traditional publisher with unconventional approaches.
ISBN Prefix(es): 978-1-893121
Number of titles published annually: 5 Print; 4 E-Book
Total Titles: 40 Print; 12 E-Book
Imprints: Everything Goes Media (nonfiction-lifestyle, hobby, gift & business); Lake Claremont Press (nonfiction-Chicago guidebooks & histories); S Woodhouse Books (nonfiction-ideas, history, trends & current events)
Subsidiaries: Tiny Golem Press
Divisions: Conspire Creative

Excalibur Publications
PO Box 89667, Tucson, AZ 85752-9667
Tel: 520-575-9057
E-mail: excaliburpublications@centurylink.net
Key Personnel
Ed-in-Chief: Alan M Petrillo
Founded: 1990
ISBN Prefix(es): 978-1-880677

Number of titles published annually: 5 Print
Total Titles: 16 Print
Distribution Center: Barnes & Noble, One Barnes & Noble Way, Suite B, Monroe, NJ 08831
Baker & Taylor, 2550 W Tyvola Rd, Suite 300, Charlotte, NC 28217
Amazon.com, 1200 12 Ave S, Suite 1200, Seattle, WA 98144-2734

Excelsior Editions
Imprint of State University of New York Press
10 N Pearl St, 4th fl, Albany, NY 12207
SAN: 760-7261
Tel: 518-944-2800 *Toll Free Tel:* 866-430-7869
 Fax: 518-320-1592
E-mail: info@sunypress.edu
Web Site: www.sunypress.edu
Key Personnel
Co-Dir: James Peltz *Tel:* 518-944-2815
 E-mail: james.peltz@sunypress.edu
Founded: 2008
Publish regional & trade books.
ISBN Prefix(es): 978-0-7914; 978-1-929373 (Hudson Valley region); 978-1-4384; 978-0-9722977 (Uncrowned Queens)
Number of titles published annually: 25 Print
Total Titles: 272 Print; 222 E-Book; 1 Audio
Distributor for Albany Institute of History & Art; Uncrowned Queens
Foreign Rep(s): Lexa Publishers' Representatives (Elise & Mical Moser) (Canada); MHM Ltd (Japan); NBN International (UK & the continent); US PubRep Inc (Craig Falk) (Caribbean, Central America, Mexico, Puerto Rico, South America)
Orders to: SUNY Press, PO Box 960, Herndon, VA 20172-0960, Cust Serv *Tel:* 703-661-1575 *Toll Free Tel:* 877-204-6073 *Fax:* 703-996-1010 *Toll Free Fax:* 877-204-6074 *E-mail:* suny@presswarehouse.com
Returns: SUNY Press, Returns Dept, 22883 Quicksilver Dr, Dulles, VA 20166, Cust Serv *Tel:* 703-661-1575 *Toll Free Tel:* 877-204-6073 *Fax:* 703-996-1010 *Toll Free Fax:* 877-204-6074 *E-mail:* suny@presswarehouse.com
Shipping Address: SUNY Press, 22835 Quicksilver Dr, Dulles, VA 20166, Cust Serv *Tel:* 703-661-1575 *Toll Free Tel:* 877-204-6073 *Fax:* 703-996-1010 *Toll Free Fax:* 877-204-6074 *E-mail:* suny@presswarehouse.com
Warehouse: SUNY Press, PO Box 960, Herndon, VA 20172-0960, Cust Serv *Tel:* 703-661-1575 *Toll Free Tel:* 877-204-6073 *Fax:* 703-996-1010 *Toll Free Fax:* 877-204-6074 *E-mail:* suny@presswarehouse.com

The Experiment
220 E 23 St, Suite 600, New York, NY 10010-4658
Tel: 212-889-1659
E-mail: info@theexperimentpublishing.com
Web Site: www.theexperimentpublishing.com
Key Personnel
Pres, Publr & CEO: Matthew Lore
COO & CFO: Peter Burri
Exec Dir, Mktg, Publicity & Sales: Jennifer Hergenroeder
Exec Dir, Publg & Prodn: Pamela Schechter
Contracts & Rts Dir: Margie Guerra
Creative Dir: Beth Bugler
Gen Mgr & Roving Ed: Karen Giangreco
Mng Ed: Zachary Pace
Exec Ed: Nick Cizek
Sr Ed: Batya Rosenblum
Assoc Ed: Olivia Peluso; Liana Willis
Digital Opers Mgr: Grace Rambo
Publicist: Ashley Yepsen
Designer: Jack Dunnington
Sales & Mktg Asst: Will Rhino
Founded: 2008
ISBN Prefix(es): 978-1-61519
Number of titles published annually: 50 Print; 50 E-Book

Total Titles: 250 Print; 230 E-Book
Sales Office(s): Workman Publishing Co Inc, 225 Varick St, New York, NY 10014-4381
SAN: 631-760X
Distributed by Workman Publishing Co Inc
Foreign Rep(s): Maribeth Casey (worldwide exc Australia, Brazil, New Zealand & UK); Gregory Messina (Australia, New Zealand, UK & Commonwealth); Agencia Riff (Brazil)
Foreign Rights: Linwood Messina Literary Agency (Australia, India, New Zealand, UK); Agencia Riff (Brazil); Storey Publishing (Maribeth Casey) (worldwide exc Australia, Brazil, India, New Zealand & UK)
Orders to: Workman Publishing Co Inc, 225 Varick St, New York, NY 10014-4381 *Toll Free Tel:* 800-722-7202 *E-mail:* orders@workman.com SAN: 631-760X
Returns: Workman Publishing Co Inc, c/o RR Donnelley, 677 Brighton Beach Rd, Menasha, WI 54952
Membership(s): Association of American Publishers (AAP)

Eye in the Ear Children's Audio
5 Crescent St, Portland, ME 04102
Toll Free Tel: 855-99-STORY (997-8679)
 Fax: 207-699-1380 (attn: Laurence Kelly)
E-mail: info@eyeintheear.com
Web Site: www.eyeintheear.com
Key Personnel
Owner: Frances Kelly
Pres: Laurence A Kelly *E-mail:* lk@usanswer.com
Founded: 1985
Production & distribution of quality classic children's audio stories. Titles available from Amazon.com, Chinaberry & TEI Landmark Audio.
ISBN Prefix(es): 978-0-944168
Number of titles published annually: 3 Audio
Total Titles: 31 Online; 31 Audio
Editorial Office(s): c/o MBC, 415 Congress St, Portland, ME 04101
Returns: Fleetwood MultiMedia, 20 Wheeler St, St Lynn, MA 01910, Contact: Wayne Terminello *Toll Free Tel:* 800-353-1830 *Fax:* 781-599-2440 *E-mail:* wayne@fltwood.com
Shipping Address: Fleetwood MultiMedia, 20 Wheeler St, St Lynn, MA 01910, Contact: Wayne Terminello *Toll Free Tel:* 800-353-1830 *Fax:* 781-599-2440 *E-mail:* wayne@fltwood.com
Warehouse: Fleetwood MultiMedia, 20 Wheeler St, St Lynn, MA 01910, Contact: Wayne Terminello *Toll Free Tel:* 800-353-1830 *Fax:* 781-599-2440 *E-mail:* wayne@fltwood.com
Distribution Center: Christianbook Inc, 1400 Summit St, Peabody, MA 01960-5156 *Toll Free Tel:* 800-CHRISTIAN (247-4784)
 E-mail: customer.service@christianbook.com
Fleetwood MultiMedia, 20 Wheeler St, St Lynn, MA 01910, Contact: Wayne Terminello *Toll Free Tel:* 800-353-1830 *Fax:* 781-599-2440 *E-mail:* wayne@fltwood.com

Facts Cures & Answers, see FC&A Publishing

§Facts On File
Imprint of Infobase Learning
132 W 31 St, 17th fl, New York, NY 10001
SAN: 201-4696
Tel: 212-967-8800 *Toll Free Tel:* 800-322-8755
 Toll Free Fax: 800-678-3633
E-mail: custserv@factsonfile.com
Web Site: infobasepublishing.com
Key Personnel
Pres & CEO: Mark McDonnell
CFO: Jim Housley
Dir, Book & Ebook Sales: Justyna Pawluk
 E-mail: jpawluk@infobaselearning.com
Edit Dir, Print: Laurie Likoff

Dir, Licensing & Busn Devt: Ben Jacobs
 E-mail: bjacobs@infobaselearning.com
Dir, Mktg: Zina Scarpulla
Dir, Publicity: Laurie Katz *E-mail:* lkatz@
 infobaselearning.com
Dir, Sales & Opers: Mark Zielinski
Founded: 1941
Award-winning publisher of authoritative
 curriculum-related print & online reference ma-
 terials for schools & libraries.
ISBN Prefix(es): 978-0-8160; 978-0-87196; 978-
 1-60057; 978-1-60413; 978-1-4381; 978-1-
 57852; 978-1-61753
Number of titles published annually: 135 Print;
 28 Online; 135 E-Book
Total Titles: 940 Print; 37 Online; 934 E-Book
Returns: Maple Logistics Solutions, Lebanon Dis-
 tribution Center, 704 Legionaire Dr, Fredericks-
 burg, PA 17026
Warehouse: Maple Logistics Solutions, Lebanon
 Distribution Center, 704 Legionaire Dr, Freder-
 icksburg, PA 17026
Distribution Center: Maple Logistics Solutions,
 Lebanon Distribution Center, 704 Legionaire
 Dr, Fredericksburg, PA 17026

Fair Winds Press
Imprint of Quarto Publishing Group USA Inc
100 Cummings Ctr, Suite 265-D, Beverly, MA
 01915
Tel: 978-282-9590 *Fax:* 978-282-7765
E-mail: sales@quarto.com
Web Site: www.quartoknows.com
Key Personnel
VP & Group Publr: Winnie Prentiss
 E-mail: winnie.prentiss@quarto.com
Founded: 2001
Offer nonfiction books in a range of practical cat-
 egories, including nutrition & cookery, fitness,
 parenting, beauty, treating sickness, mental
 health & using new medicine.
ISBN Prefix(es): 978-1-59233
Number of titles published annually: 50 Print
Total Titles: 200 Print

Fairchild Books
Division of Bloomsbury Publishing PLC
1385 Broadway, 5th fl, New York, NY 10018
SAN: 201-470X
Tel: 212-419-5300 *Toll Free Tel:* 800-932-4724;
 888-330-8477 (orders)
Web Site: bloomsbury.com/us/academic/
 fairchildbooks
Key Personnel
Dir, Sales & Sr Devt Ed: Joseph Miranda
 E-mail: joseph.miranda@bloomsbury.com
Head, Children's Prodn: Claire Henry
Acqs Ed: Emily Samulski *E-mail:* emily.
 samulski@bloomsbury.com
Higher Educ Rep: Kirby Pendergast
 E-mail: kirby.pendergast@bloomsbury.com
Edit Asst: Jenna Lefkowitz *Tel:* 212-419-5404
 E-mail: jenna.lefkowitz@bloomsbury.com
Founded: 1910
Interior design, fashion, merchandising, market-
 ing, management, retailing, careers market, re-
 search art foundation, clothing, textiles.
Membership(s): Interior Design Educators Coun-
 cil (IDEC); International Textiles Apparel As-
 sociation (ITAA)
ISBN Prefix(es): 978-0-87005; 978-1-56367; 978-
 1-60901
Number of titles published annually: 40 Print; 30
 CD-ROM
Total Titles: 375 Print; 60 CD-ROM
Orders to: MPS Distribution Center, 16365 James
 Madison Hwy, Gordonsville, VA 22942-8501
Returns: MPS Distribution Center, 16365 James
 Madison Hwy, Gordonsville, VA 22942-8501

Warehouse: MPS Distribution Center, 16365
 James Madison Hwy, Gordonsville, VA 22942-
 8501
Distribution Center: MPS Distribution Center,
 16365 James Madison Hwy, Gordonsville, VA
 22942-8501

The Fairmont Press Inc
700 Indian Trail, Lilburn, GA 30047
SAN: 207-5946
Tel: 770-925-9388 *Fax:* 770-381-9865
Web Site: www.fairmontpress.com
Key Personnel
VP: Linda Hutchings *E-mail:* linda@
 fairmontpress.com
Book Prodn Mgr: Brenda Powell
 E-mail: brenda@aeecenter.org
Founded: 1973
Professional & reference books on energy, safety,
 environment, how-to & facility management.
ISBN Prefix(es): 978-0-915586; 978-0-88173
Number of titles published annually: 10 Print; 1
 CD-ROM; 10 E-Book
Total Titles: 500 Print; 8 CD-ROM; 150 E-Book
Distributed by Taylor & Francis
Foreign Rep(s): Taylor & Francis

Faith & Fellowship Publishing
Subsidiary of Church of the Lutheran Brethren
1020 W Alcott Ave, Fergus Falls, MN 56537
Tel: 218-736-7357 *Toll Free Tel:* 800-332-9232
E-mail: ffpublishing@clba.org
Web Site: www.clba.org
Key Personnel
Dir: Troy Tysdol
Religious books, newsletters.
ISBN Prefix(es): 978-0-943167
Number of titles published annually: 6 Print
Total Titles: 59 Print

§Faith Library Publications
Subsidiary of RHEMA Bible Church
PO Box 50126, Tulsa, OK 74150-0126
Tel: 918-258-1588 (ext 2218) *Toll Free Tel:* 888-
 258-0999 (orders) *Fax:* 918-872-7710 (orders)
E-mail: flp@rhema.org
Web Site: www.rhema.org/store
Key Personnel
Dept Head, Kenneth Hagin Ministries: Brian
 Cumberland
Founded: 1963
ISBN Prefix(es): 978-0-89276; 978-1-60616
Number of titles published annually: 4 Print; 15
 CD-ROM
Total Titles: 185 Print; 115 CD-ROM; 185 E-
 Book
Distributed by Harrison House; Whitaker

§Faithlife Corp
1313 Commercial St, Bellingham, WA 98225
Tel: 360-527-1700 *Toll Free Tel:* 800-875-6467
 Fax: 360-527-1707
E-mail: sales@faithlife.com; customerservice@
 faithlife.com
Web Site: faithlife.com
Founded: 1992
Electronic & ebook publisher & technology
 provider.
ISBN Prefix(es): 978-1-57799
Number of titles published annually: 30 CD-
 ROM; 200 E-Book
Total Titles: 200 CD-ROM; 4,000 E-Book
Membership(s): Evangelical Christian Publishers
 Association (ECPA); Society of Bible Litera-
 ture (SBL)

FaithWalk Publishing
Imprint of CSS Publishing Co Inc
5450 N Dixie Hwy, Lima, OH 45807
Tel: 419-227-1818 *Toll Free Tel:* 800-537-1030
 (orders, non-bookstore mkts) *Fax:* 419-224-
 9184

E-mail: orders@csspub.com
Web Site: www.faithwalkpub.com
Key Personnel
Pres: David Runk *Tel:* 419-516-4205
 E-mail: david@csspub.com
Prodn Mgr: Karyl Corson *E-mail:* kcorson@
 csspub.com
Acctg: Patti Furr *E-mail:* pfurr@csspub.com
Founded: 2002
ISBN Prefix(es): 978-0-9724196; 978-1-932902
Number of titles published annually: 10 Print
Total Titles: 31 Print
Membership(s): Independent Book Publishers As-
 sociation (IBPA)

§Familius
1254 Commerce Way, Sanger, CA 93657
Tel: 559-876-2170 *Fax:* 559-876-2180
E-mail: orders@familius.com
Web Site: www.familius.com
Key Personnel
Founder & CEO: Christopher Robbins
Founder & Acqs: Michele Robbins
Mng Ed: Brooke Jorden *E-mail:* brooke@
 familius.com
Founded: 2012
ISBN Prefix(es): 978-1-938301; 978-1-939629;
 978-1-942672
Number of titles published annually: 60 Print; 50
 E-Book; 40 Audio
Total Titles: 170 Print; 120 E-Book; 100 Audio
Distributed by Workman Publishing (worldwide
 exc CN)
Foreign Rep(s): Baker & Taylor (worldwide exc
 Australia, Canada, New Zealand, UK & USA)
Foreign Rights: Letter Soup Rights Agency
 (worldwide exc USA)
Membership(s): Independent Book Publishers As-
 sociation (IBPA)

§Farcountry Press
2750 Broadwater Ave, Helena, MT 59602-9202
Mailing Address: PO Box 5630, Helena, MT
 59604-5630
Tel: 406-422-1263 *Toll Free Tel:* 800-821-3874
 (sales off) *Fax:* 406-443-5480
E-mail: books@farcountrypress.com; sales@
 farcountrypress.com
Web Site: www.farcountrypress.com
Key Personnel
Publr: Linda Netschert *E-mail:* linda.netschert@
 farcountrypress.com
Pubns Dir: Kathy Springmeyer *E-mail:* kathy@
 farcountrypress.com
Publicist: Shannon Johnston
Founded: 1980
Softcover & hardcover color photography books
 showcasing the nation's cities, states, national
 parks & wildlife. Also publish nonfiction chil-
 dren's series, guidebooks, cookbooks & re-
 gional history titles nationwide.
ISBN Prefix(es): 978-0-93814; 978-1-56037; 978-
 1-59152 (Sweetgrass Books)
Number of titles published annually: 25 Print
Membership(s): APPL; The Association of Publishers for Special Sales (APSS); Independent
 Book Publishers Association (IBPA); Publishers Association of the West (PubWest)

**Farrar, Straus & Giroux Books for Young
 Readers**
Imprint of Macmillan Children's Publishing
 Group
120 Broadway, New York, NY 10271
Tel: 212-741-6900 *Toll Free Tel:* 888-330-8477
 (orders) *Fax:* 212-633-9385
Web Site: us.macmillan.com/mackids; www.
 mackidsbooks.com
Key Personnel
Pres & Publr, Macmillan Children's Publishing
 Group: Jon Yaged
SVP & Publg Dir: Jennifer Besser

SVP & Deputy Publr: Allison Verost
VP & Assoc Publr: Angus Killick
VP & Sr Creative Dir: Beth Clark
VP & Edit Dir: Joy Peskin *Tel:* 646-307-5187
   E-mail: joy.peskin@macmillan.com
VP, Subs Rts: Kristin Dulaney
Exec Dir, Ad & Promo: Mariel Dawson
Exec Dir, Publicity: Molly Ellis
Sr Art Dir: Sharismar Rodriguez
Art Dir: Jen Keenan
Asst Dir, Publicity: Morgan Kane
Exec Ed: Wesley Adams *Tel:* 646-307-5673
   E-mail: wesley.adams@fsgbooks.com; Janine
   O'Malley *Tel:* 646-307-5598 *E-mail:* janine.
   omalley@fsgbooks.com
Sr Mng Ed: Hayley Jozwiak
Sr Prodn Ed: Ilana Worrell
Sr Ed: Grace Kendall
Assoc Ed: Trisha de Guzman; Melissa Warten
Asst Ed: Nicholas Henderson; Elizabeth Lee
Mktg Mgr: Katie Quinn
Studio Mgr: Ginny Dominguez
Designer: Cassie Gonzales
Publicist: Morgan Rath
Assoc Publicist: Madison Furr
Sr Coord: Debbie Cobb
Founded: 1953
Preschool through young adult fiction & nonfiction, hardcover & paperback.
ISBN Prefix(es): 978-0-374
Number of titles published annually: 80 Print
Total Titles: 700 Print
Imprints: Frances Foster Books
Membership(s): The Children's Book Council
   (CBC)

Farrar, Straus & Giroux, LLC
Subsidiary of Macmillan
175 Varick St, 9th fl, New York, NY 10014
SAN: 206-782X
Tel: 212-741-6900
E-mail: fsg.publicity@fsgbooks.com
Web Site: us.macmillan.com/fsg.aspx
Key Personnel
Pres: Jonathan Galassi
EVP & COO: Andrew Mandel *Tel:* 212-206-5354
EVP & Publr: Mitzi Angel
SVP & Dir, Mktg & Publicity: Sheila O'Shea
SVP & Dir, Spec Projs: Jeff Seroy *Tel:* 212-206-5323
SVP & Ed-in-Chief: Eric Chinski
SVP & Sales Dir: Spenser Lee
VP & Cont, Rts & Perms: Erika Seidman
VP & Dir, Publicity: Sarita Varma *Tel:* 212-206-5327 *E-mail:* svarma@fsgbooks.com
VP & Exec Ed: Colin Dickerman
Publr, MCD & FSG Originals: Sean McDonald
Ad Dir: Victoria Genna
Creative Dir: Rodrigo Corral
Design Dir: Abby Kagan
Mktg Dir, Digital Strategy & Technol: Daniel Del Valle
Exec Mng Ed: Debra Helfand
Exec Ed: Jenna Johnson; Alex Star
Exec Ed, MCD: Daphne Durham
Sr Ed: Emily Bell
Ed: Jeremy Davies
Ed-at-Large: Ileene Smith
Assoc Ed: Laird Gallagher; Julia Ringo
Asst Ed: Jackson Howard
Digital Mktg Mgr MCD/FSG Originals: Naomi Huffman
Founded: 1946
General fiction, nonfiction, poetry & juveniles.
ISBN Prefix(es): 978-0-374
Number of titles published annually: 150 Print
Total Titles: 1,400 Print
Imprints: Farrar, Straus & Giroux Books for Young Readers; Hill & Wang; MCD/FSG; North Point Press; Picador; Scientific American
Distributor for Drawn & Quarterly; Gray Wolf Books

Foreign Rep(s): Pan Macmillan Ltd (UK); Raincoast Books (Canada)
Foreign Rights: ANA Baltic (Tatjana Zoldnere) (Estonia, Latvia, Lithuania); AnatoliatLit Agency (Amy Spangler & Eda Caca) (Turkey); Anthea Agency (Katalina Sabeva) (Bulgaria); L'Autre Agence (Corinne Marotte & Marie Lannurien) (France); Bardon-Chinese Media (David Tsai) (China, Taiwan); Anoukh Foerg Agency (Germany); Deborah Harris Agency (Geula Geurts) (Israel); International Copyright Agency (Simon Kessler & Marina Adriana) (Romania); The Italian Literary Agency srl (Claire Sabatie-Garat) (Italy); Anna Jarota Agency (Dominika Bojanowska) (Poland); Katai & Bolza (Peter Bolza) (Hungary); KCC (Kyung Kang) (Korea); MB Agencia Literaria (Monica Martin & Ines Planells) (Latin America, Spain); Kristin Olson Literarni Agentura (Czechia); Plima Literary Agency (Vuk Perisic) (Albania, Croatia, Serbia, Slovenia); Read 'n Right Agency (Nike Davarinou) (Greece); Riff Agency (Laura & Joao Paulo Riff) (Brazil); Sebes & Bisseling Literary Agency (Paul Sebes) (Netherlands); Synopsis Literary Agency (Olga Zasetskaya) (Russia); Tuttle-Mori Agency Inc (Asako Kawachi) (Japan)
Advertising Agency: Verso Advertising
Warehouse: MPS Distribution Center, 16365 James Madison Hwy, Gordonsville, VA 22942
   Toll Free Tel: 888-330-8477
Membership(s): The Children's Book Council
   (CBC)
See separate listing for:
Hill & Wang
North Point Press
Picador

§Father & Son Publishing Inc
4909 N Monroe St, Tallahassee, FL 32303-7015
Tel: 850-562-2712 *Toll Free Tel:* 800-741-2712
   (orders only) *Fax:* 850-562-0916
Web Site: www.fatherson.com
Key Personnel
Pres: Lance Coalson *E-mail:* lance@fatherson.
   com
Founded: 1982
Publishers of nonfiction, historical fiction, cookbooks, giftbooks & children's books.
ISBN Prefix(es): 978-0-942407; 978-1-935802
Number of titles published annually: 12 Print; 3 Audio
Total Titles: 212 Print; 15 Audio
Distributor for BADM Books
Membership(s): American Booksellers Association (ABA); Florida Authors & Publishers Association Inc (FAPA); National Association of Independent Publishers (NAIP)

FC&A Publishing
103 Clover Green, Peachtree City, GA 30269
Tel: 770-487-6307 *Toll Free Tel:* 800-226-8024
E-mail: customer_service@fca.com
Web Site: www.fca.com
Key Personnel
CFO: Tim Anders
Founded: 1969
ISBN Prefix(es): 978-0-915099; 978-1-890957; 978-1-932470; 978-1-935574
Number of titles published annually: 3 Print; 3 Online
Total Titles: 36 Print; 30 Online

§Federal Bar Association
1220 N Filmore St, Suite 444, Arlington, VA 22201
Tel: 571-481-9100 *Fax:* 571-481-9090
E-mail: fba@fedbar.org
Web Site: www.fedbar.org
Key Personnel
Exec Dir: Stacy King *E-mail:* sking@fedbar.org

Dir, Mktg & Communs: Dominick Alcid
   E-mail: dalcid@fedbar.org
Founded: 1920
Publish course materials, newsletters & *The Federal Lawyer* magazine.
ISBN Prefix(es): 978-1-56986
Number of titles published annually: 15 Print; 1 CD-ROM
Total Titles: 350 Print; 1 CD-ROM; 2 Audio

Federal Street Press
Division of Merriam-Webster Inc
25-13 Old Kings Hwy N, No 277, Darien, CT 06820
Tel: 203-852-1280 *Toll Free Tel:* 877-886-2830
   Fax: 203-852-1389
E-mail: info@federalstreetpress.com; sales@federalstreetpress.com; customerservice@federalstreetpress.com; orders@federalstreetpress.com
Web Site: federalstreetpress.com
Key Personnel
Mng Dir: Virginia Guilfoyle *E-mail:* vguilfoyle@federalstreetpress.com
Founded: 1998
Offers up-to-date, quality, value-priced language reference titles created in cooperation with the editors of Merriam-Webster Inc.
ISBN Prefix(es): 978-1-892859; 978-1-59695
Number of titles published annually: 5 Print
Total Titles: 45 Print

Philipp Feldheim Inc, see Feldheim Publishers

Feldheim Publishers
208 Airport Executive Park, Nanuet, NY 10954
SAN: 207-0545
Tel: 845-356-2282 *Toll Free Tel:* 800-237-7149
   (orders) *Fax:* 845-425-1908
E-mail: sales@feldheim.com
Web Site: www.feldheim.com
Key Personnel
Pres: Yitzchak Feldheim
Mng Dir: Eli M Hollander *E-mail:* eli@feldheim.com
Sales Mgr: Suzanne Brandt *E-mail:* suzanne@feldheim.com
Founded: 1939
Translations from Hebrew of Jewish classical works & works of contemporary authors in the field of Orthodox Jewish thought & contemporary Jewish literature for ages three & up.
This publisher has indicated that 50% of their product line is author subsidized.
ISBN Prefix(es): 978-0-87306; 978-1-58330; 978-1-59826; 978-1-68025
Number of titles published annually: 80 Print
Total Titles: 800 Print
Imprints: Ayal Press
Foreign Office(s): F Books Ltd, Box 43163, 91431 Jerusalem, Israel
Distributor for Adir Press; Jerusalem Publications; Mosaica Press

The Feminist Press at The City University of New York
365 Fifth Ave, Suite 5406, New York, NY 10016
SAN: 213-6813
Tel: 212-817-7915 *Fax:* 212-817-1593
E-mail: info@feministpress.org
Web Site: www.feministpress.org
Key Personnel
Exec Dir & Publr: Jamia Wilson
Art Dir: Drew Stevens *Tel:* 212-817-7931
   E-mail: drew@feministpress.org
Sr Ed: Lauren Rosemary Hook *Tel:* 212-817-7922
   E-mail: lauren@feministpress.org
Assoc Ed: Alyea Canada *Tel:* 212-817-7926
   E-mail: alyea@feministpress.org
Sr External Rel Mgr: Lucia Brown *Tel:* 212-817-7928 *E-mail:* lucia@feministpress.org

Sr Mktg & Sales Mgr/Publicity: Jisu Kim *Tel:* 212-817-7918 *E-mail:* jisu@feministpress. org

Sr Graphic Designer: Suki Boynton *Tel:* 212-817-7924 *E-mail:* suki@feministpress.org

Devt Mgr: Sophia Booth Magnone *Tel:* 212-817-7930 *E-mail:* sophia@feministpress.org

Outreach & Opers Mgr: Hannah Goodwin *Tel:* 212-817-7929 *E-mail:* hannah@feministpress.org

Founded: 1970

Popular culture, African studies, Asian American studies, international studies, history of feminism, women's studies, working class studies, current issues & women's literature from the Middle East, Africa, Asia & Latin America & US women writers.

ISBN Prefix(es): 978-0-912670; 978-0-935312; 978-1-55861; 978-1-936932

Number of titles published annually: 18 Print; 10 E-Book

Total Titles: 400 Print; 50 E-Book

Foreign Rights: AnatoliaLit Agency (Amy Spangler) (Turkey); The Foreign Office (Teresa Vilarrubla) (Latin America, Spain); The Deborah Harris Agency (Geula Geurts) (Israel); Japan UNI Agency (Miko Yamanouchi) (Japan); Natoli, Stefan & Oliva (Roberta Oliva) (Italy); VBMLitag (Luciana Villas-Boas) (Brazil, Portugal); Literary Agent Silke Weniger (Germany)

Distribution Center: Consortium Book Sales & Distribution, The Keg House, Suite 101, 34 13 Ave NE, Minneapolis, MN 55413-1007 *Tel:* 612-746-2600 *Toll Free Tel:* 800-283-3572 (cust serv, Jackson, TN) *Fax:* 612-746-2606 *E-mail:* info@cbsd. com SAN: 200-6049

Baker & Taylor International, 652 E Main St, PO Box 6920, Bridgewater, NJ 08807-0920 (worldwide exc Africa, Asia, Canada, Continental Europe, Middle East, UK & US) *Tel:* 908-218-0400 *Fax:* 908-707-4387 *E-mail:* btinfo@btol. com *Web Site:* btol.com/international.cfm

Turnaround Publisher Services Ltd, Unit 3, Olympia Trading Estate, Coburg Rd, Wood Green, London, United Kingdom (UK, Africa, Asia, Continental Europe & Middle East) *Tel:* (020) 8829 3000 *Fax:* (020) 8881 5088 *E-mail:* orders@turnaround-uk.com *Web Site:* www.turnaround-uk.com

Membership(s): Association of American Publishers (AAP); Community of Literary Magazines & Presses (CLMP); National Council for Research on Women (NCRW)

Fence Books
Imprint of Fence Magazine Inc
University at Albany, Science Library 320, 1400 Washington Ave, Albany, NY 12222
Tel: 518-567-7006
Web Site: www.fenceportal.org
Key Personnel
Publr & Ed: Rebecca Wolff
  E-mail: rebeccafence@gmail.com
Founded: 2001
ISBN Prefix(es): 978-1-934200; 978-0-9771064; 978-0-9713189; 978-0-9663324; 978-0-9740909; 978-0-9864373; 978-1-944380
Number of titles published annually: 6 Print
Total Titles: 90 Print
Imprints: Fence Digital; La Presse
Distribution Center: Small Press Distribution, 1341 Seventh St, Berkeley, CA 94710-1409 *Tel:* 510-524-1668 *Toll Free Tel:* 800-869-7553 *E-mail:* spd@spdbooks.org *Web Site:* www. spdbooks.org
Consortium Book Sales & Distribution, The Keg House, 34 13 Ave NE, Suite 101, Minneapolis, MN 55413 *Tel:* 612-746-2600 *Fax:* 612-746-2606 *E-mail:* info@cbsd.com *Web Site:* www. cbsd.com

Feral House
1240 W Sims Way, Suite 124, Port Townsend, WA 98368
Tel: 323-666-3311
E-mail: info@feralhouse.com
Web Site: feralhouse.com
Key Personnel
Pres & Publr: Adam Parfrey
Founded: 1989
Pop culture, alternative, art, nonfiction, religion, sociology & social sciences.
ISBN Prefix(es): 978-0-922915; 978-1-932595
Number of titles published annually: 12 Print
Total Titles: 120 Print
Imprints: Process Media Inc
Distribution Center: Consortium Book Sales & Distribution/Ingram, The Keg House, Suite 101, 34 13 Ave NE, Minneapolis, MN 55413-1007 *Tel:* 612-746-2600 *Toll Free Tel:* 800-283-3572 (cust serv, Jackson, TN) *Fax:* 612-746-2606 *E-mail:* info@cbsd.com *Web Site:* www.cbsd.com SAN: 200-6049
Turnaround Publisher Services, Olympia Trading Estate, Unit 3, Coburg Rd, London N22 6TZ, United Kingdom *Tel:* (020) 8829 3000 *Fax:* (020) 8881 5088 *E-mail:* orders@turnaround-uk.com

§Ferguson Publishing
Imprint of Infobase Learning
132 W 31 St, 17th fl, New York, NY 10001
Tel: 212-967-8800 *Toll Free Tel:* 800-322-8755
  Toll Free Fax: 800-678-3633
E-mail: custserv@factsonfile.com
Web Site: infobasepublishing.com
Key Personnel
Pres & CEO: Mark McDonnell
CFO: Jim Housley
Dir, Book & Ebook Sales: Justyna Pawluk
  E-mail: jpawluk@infobaselearning.com
Dir, Licensing & Busn Devt: Ben Jacobs
  E-mail: bjacobs@infobaselearning.com
Dir, Mktg: Tara McCaffrey
Dir, Sales: Mark Zielinski
Dir, Publicity: Laurie Katz *E-mail:* lkatz@infobaselearning.com
Edit Dir: Laurie Likoff
With its acclaimed career guidance & reference materials, Ferguson Publishing is known among librarians & guidance counselors as the premier publisher in the career education field.
ISBN Prefix(es): 978-0-8160; 978-0-87196; 978-0-89434; 978-1-60413; 978-1-4381
Number of titles published annually: 74 Print; 74 E-Book
Total Titles: 333 Print; 363 E-Book

Fiction Collective Two Inc (FC2)
Imprint of University of Alabama Press
c/o University of Alabama Press, Box 870380, Tuscaloosa, AL 35487-0380
Tel: 773-702-7000
Web Site: www.fc2.org
Founded: 1974
Publish formally innovative fiction.
ISBN Prefix(es): 978-1-57366
Number of titles published annually: 6 Print
Total Titles: 200 Print
Distributed by University of Alabama Press
Returns: University of Alabama Press, Chicago Distribution Center, 11030 S Langley Ave, Chicago, IL 60628 *Tel:* 773-702-7000 *Toll Free Tel:* 800-621-2736 *Fax:* 773-702-7212 *Toll Free Fax:* 800-621-8476
Membership(s): Community of Literary Magazines & Presses (CLMP)

1517 Media, see Augsburg Fortress Publishers, Publishing House of the Evangelical Lutheran Church in America

Fifth Estate Publishing
2795 County Hwy 57, Blountsville, AL 35031
SAN: 852-6419
Tel: 256-631-5107 *Toll Free Tel:* 855-299-2160
E-mail: josephlumpkin@hotmail.com
Web Site: fifthestatepub.com
Founded: 2003
Publisher & distributor.
ISBN Prefix(es): 978-0-9746336; 978-0-9760992; 978-0-9768233; 978-1-933580; 978-1-936533
Number of titles published annually: 6 Print; 6 Online; 6 E-Book
Total Titles: 136 Print; 136 Online; 75 E-Book

Filter Press LLC
PO Box 95, Palmer Lake, CO 80133
SAN: 201-484X
Tel: 719-481-2420 *Toll Free Tel:* 888-570-2663
  Fax: 719-481-2420
E-mail: info@filterpressbooks.com; orders@filterpressbooks.com
Web Site: filterpressbooks.com
Key Personnel
Pres: Doris Baker *E-mail:* doris@filterpressbooks. com
Founded: 1957
Publisher of books on the American West, Western expansion, children's historical fiction, Colorado history & biography.
ISBN Prefix(es): 978-0-910584; 978-0-86541
Number of titles published annually: 3 Print; 1 Audio
Total Titles: 110 Print; 2 CD-ROM; 67 E-Book; 2 Audio
Returns: 19980 Top O'Moor W, Monument, CO 80132
Shipping Address: 19980 Top O'Moor W, Monument, CO 80132
Membership(s): Colorado Association of Libraries; Colorado Independent Publishers Association (CIPA); Women Writing the West

Financial Executives Research Foundation Inc (FERF)
Affiliate of Financial Executives International (FEI)
West Tower, 7th fl, 1250 Headquarters Plaza, Morristown, NJ 07960-6837
Tel: 973-765-1000 *Fax:* 973-765-1018
Web Site: www.financialexecutives.org
Key Personnel
Dir, Devt: Kit Hall
Dir, Fin Servs & Devt: Lorna Raagas *Tel:* 973-765-1033 *E-mail:* lraagas@financialexecutives. org
Mgr, Tech Activities: Tom Thompson
Founded: 1944
Executive reports & full-length monographs of research related to financial topics. All publications available on PDF.
This publisher has indicated that 50% of their product line is author subsidized.
ISBN Prefix(es): 978-0-910586; 978-1-885065; 978-1-61509; 978-1-933130
Number of titles published annually: 20 Print; 20 Online
Total Titles: 120 Print; 120 Online

Financial Times Press
Imprint of Pearson Education Ltd
800 E 96 St, Indianapolis, IN 46240
E-mail: customer-service@informit.com; community@informit.com
Web Site: www.informit.com/ftpress
Publisher of business, management, investment & finance books for general consumers, professionals & students.
ISBN Prefix(es): 978-0-13; 978-1-292
Number of titles published annually: 165 Print
Total Titles: 5,143 Print; 6,580 E-Book
Imprints: FT Press

§Finding My Way Books
3512 SW Huntoon St, Topeka, KS 66604-1748
Tel: 785-273-6239
E-mail: findingmywaybooks@gmail.com
Web Site: www.findingmywaybooks.net
Key Personnel
Author & Publr: Jo Meserve Mach *Tel:* 785-273-6329 *E-mail:* jo.mach@findingmywaybooks.com
Author: Vera Lynne Stroup-Rentier, PhD
    E-mail: verafindingmywaybooks@gmail.com
Photog, Author & Designer: Mary Birdsell
    E-mail: maryb.birdsell@gmail.com
Founded: 2014
Finding My Way Books honors children & adults with special needs or disabilities by sharing their stories. It supports educational inclusion through publications that are easy to read, with large print & easy to understand, with photographs. All books include tools for educators to promote learning & inclusion.
This publisher has indicated that 75% of their product line is author subsidized.
ISBN Prefix(es): 978-0-9968357; 978-1-944764; 978-1-947541
Number of titles published annually: 10 Print
Total Titles: 38 Print; 35 E-Book
Distributed by Brown Books Publishing Group
Distribution Center: Perma-Bound Books, 617 E Vandalia Rd, Jacksonville, FL 62650 *Toll Free Tel:* 800-637-6581 *E-mail:* emailbooks@perma-bound.com
Red Clover Reader Inc, 306 Foxwell Ct, Champaign, IL 61820 *Tel:* 970-818-2415 *E-mail:* contact@redcloverreader.com *Web Site:* www.redcloverreader.com
Follett Educational Products, 3 Westbrook Corporate Ctr, Suite 200, Westchester, IL 60154 *Toll Free Tel:* 800-365-3588 *Web Site:* www.follett.com
Mackin Educational Resources, 3505 County Rd 42, Burnsville, MN 55306 (print & ebook) *Toll Free Tel:* 800-245-9540 *E-mail:* mackin@mackin.com *Web Site:* www.mackin.com
Ingram, One Ingram Blvd, La Vergne, TN 37086 *Tel:* 615-793-5000 *Web Site:* www.ingramcontent.com
Inclusion Press, 47 Indian Trail, Toronto, ON M6R 128, Canada, Contact: Cathy Holland *Tel:* 416-658-5363 *Web Site:* inclusion.com
Membership(s): Independent Book Publishers Association (IBPA)

Fine Creative Media, Inc
589 Eighth Ave, 6th fl, New York, NY 10018
Tel: 212-595-3500 *Fax:* 212-202-4195
E-mail: info@mjfbooks.com
Web Site: www.mjfbooks.com
Key Personnel
Founder & CEO, MJF Books, Barnes & Noble Classics: Michael J Fine *E-mail:* mjf@mjfbooks.com
VP, Acqs, MJF Books: Antony Fine
Dir, Admin & HR: Steven Fine
Dir, Fin & Acctg: Ian Teixeira
Dir, Mktg: Keren Unrad
Dir, Prodn: Benjamin Lee
Acqs Ed, MJF Books: Kaethe Fine
Reprint Mgr: Colin Warnock
Bookkeeper: Cindy Lew
Founded: 1991
Leading independent publisher of hardcover & paperback promotional reprints of fiction & nonfiction under the MJF Books imprint. Subject categories include self-improvement, mind/body/spirit, business, history & reference. Also publisher of the Barnes & Noble Classics series, produced in conjunction with Barnes & Noble Inc.
ISBN Prefix(es): 978-1-56731 (MJF Books); 978-1-59308 (Barnes & Noble Classics); 978-1-60671 (MJF Books)
Number of titles published annually: 80 Print

Total Titles: 1,500 Print
Imprints: Barnes & Noble Classics; MJF Books

FineEdge.com LLC
902 Eighth St, Anacortes, WA 98221
Tel: 360-299-8500 *Fax:* 360-299-0535
E-mail: orders@fineedge.com
Web Site: www.fineedge.com; waggonerguide.com
Key Personnel
Publr: Mark Bunzel *E-mail:* mark@fineedge.com
Founded: 1986
Publishing, wholesaling, outdoor guidebooks & maps. Specialize in nautical books & mountain biking publications.
ISBN Prefix(es): 978-0-938665; 978-1-932310
Number of titles published annually: 3 Print
Total Titles: 50 Print; 2 Online
Distributed by Heritage House; Sunbelt Publications Inc

Fire Engineering Books & Videos
Division of PennWell Books
1421 S Sheridan Rd, Tulsa, OK 74112
Tel: 918-831-9421 *Toll Free Tel:* 800-752-9764 *Fax:* 918-831-9555
E-mail: sales@pennwell.com
Web Site: www.pennwellbooks.com
Key Personnel
Mktg Coord: Holly Fournier *Tel:* 918-832-9380 *E-mail:* hollyf@pennwell.com
Founded: 1877
Fire science, suppression & protection, petroleum, electric power, water, hazardous materials books & videos.
ISBN Prefix(es): 978-1-57340; 978-0-912212; 978-0-87814
Number of titles published annually: 10 Print; 5 CD-ROM
Total Titles: 120 Print; 10 CD-ROM
Distributed by David Publishing; Fire Protection Publications
Distributor for Brady; Idea Bank; IFSTA; Mosby
Foreign Rep(s): Cranbury International LLC (Ethan Atkin) (Caribbean, Central America, South America); Disvan Enterprises (Ish Dawar) (India); Eurospan (Africa, Asia, Australasia, Europe, Middle East); Tony Poh (Southeast Asia); Publishers Representatives (Tahir M Lodhi) (Pakistan)

§Firefall Editions
Imprint of Firefallmedia
4905 Tunlaw St, Alexandria, VA 22312
Tel: 510-549-2461
E-mail: literary@att.net
Web Site: www.firefallmedia.com
Key Personnel
Mng Dir: Robinson Joyce
Mktg Dir: Kathryn DeLappe *E-mail:* prize@att.net
Founded: 1996
Specialize in fiction, photography, art, autobiographies, textbooks, audiobooks & documentary films.
ISBN Prefix(es): 978-0-915090; 978-1-939434
Number of titles published annually: 7 Print; 2 E-Book; 5 Audio
Total Titles: 111 Print; 10 E-Book; 32 Audio
Imprints: Firefall Originals
Foreign Office(s): Firefallmedia, 17 Shore Rd, Drummore, by Stranraer, Dumfries & Galloway DG9 9PU, United Kingdom
Distribution Center: Brodart, 500 Arch St, Williamsport, PA 17701

First Avenue Editions
Imprint of Lerner Publishing Group Inc
241 First Ave N, Minneapolis, MN 55401
Tel: 612-332-3344 *Toll Free Tel:* 800-328-4929 *Fax:* 612-332-7615 *Toll Free Fax:* 800-332-1132

E-mail: info@lernerbooks.com; custserve@lernerbooks.com
Web Site: www.lernerbooks.com; www.facebook.com/lernerbooks
Key Personnel
Chmn: Harry J Lerner
EVP & COO: Mark Budde
EVP & CFO: Margaret Thomas
Pres & Publr: Adam Lerner
EVP, Sales: David Wexler
VP & Ed-in-Chief: Andy Cummings
VP, Mktg: Rachel Zugschwert
Publg Dir, School & Lib: Jenny Krueger
Dir, HR: Cyndi Radant
Dir, Rts, Spec Sales & Intl Dist: Maria Kjoller
School & Lib Mktg Dir: Lois Wallentine
Social studies, picture storybooks, art, multicultural issues, activity books & beginning readers.
Number of titles published annually: 3 Print; 8 E-Book
Total Titles: 240 Print; 65 E-Book
Foreign Rep(s): Thomas Allen & Son (trade) (Canada); Bounce Sales & Marketing Ltd (UK); J Appleseed, A Division of Saunders (Canada); Phambili Agencies (Botswana, Lesotho, Namibia, Southern Africa); Publishers Marketing Services (Brunei, Malaysia, Singapore); Saunders Book Co (education) (Canada); South Pacific Books (New Zealand)
Foreign Rights: Japan Foreign-Rights Centre (Japan); Korea Copyright Center (KCC) (Korea); Agence Michelle Lapautre (France); Literarische Agentur Silke Weniger (Germany)
Warehouse: 1251 Washington Ave N, Minneapolis, MN 55401, Mgr: Ken Rued

Fitzroy Books
Imprint of Regal House Publishing
c/o Regal House Publishing, 806 Oberlin Rd, No 12094, Raleigh, NC 27605
E-mail: info@regalhousepublishing.com
Web Site: fitzroybooks.com
Key Personnel
Founder, Publr & Ed-in-Chief: Jaynie Royal
Mng Ed: Pam Van Dyk
Sr Ed: Ruth Feiertag
Ed: Elizabeth Lowenstein
Founded: 2014
Fitzroy Books is dedicated to the publication & promotion of high-quality literature in the children's, young adult, & middle grade fiction categories. We provide extensive editorial support to our authors & strong pre- & post-release digital marketing campaigns to further amplify our authors' outreach efforts. We seek authors with whom we can form meaningful partnerships, working together in a collaborative fashion to best polish & promote their work. We are delighted to accept submissions directly from authors at: regalhousepublishing.submittable.com/submit.
ISBN Prefix(es): 978-0-9912612; 978-0-9988398; 978-1-947548
Number of titles published annually: 11 Print; 11 E-Book
Orders to: Independent Publishers Group, 814 N Franklin St, Chicago, IL 60610 *Toll Free Tel:* 800-888-4741 *Web Site:* www.ipgbook.com
Distribution Center: Independent Publishers Group, 814 N Franklin St, Chicago, IL 60610 *Tel:* 312-337-0747 *Fax:* 312-337-5085 *Web Site:* www.ipgbook.com
Membership(s): American Booksellers Association (ABA); The Children's Book Council (CBC); Community of Literary Magazines & Presses (CLMP); Independent Book Publishers Association (IBPA); Southern Independent Booksellers Alliance (SIBA)

FJH Music Co Inc
2525 Davie Rd, Suite 360, Fort Lauderdale, FL 33317-7424

Tel: 954-382-6061 *Toll Free Tel:* 800-262-8744 *Fax:* 954-382-3073
E-mail: custserv@fjhmusic.com; sales@fjhmusic. com
Web Site: www.fjhmusic.com
Key Personnel
Pres & CEO: Frank J Hackinson
VP: Kevin Hackinson; Kyle Hackinson
  E-mail: kyleh@fjhmusic.com
Founded: 1988
Educational music publications.
ISBN Prefix(es): 978-0-929666; 978-1-56939
Number of titles published annually: 100 Print

Flashlight Press
527 Empire Blvd, Brooklyn, NY 11225
Tel: 718-288-8300 *Fax:* 718-972-6307
Web Site: www.flashlightpress.com
Key Personnel
Publr: Harry Mauer *E-mail:* publisher@ flashlightpress.com
Ed: Shari Dash Greenspan *E-mail:* editor@ flashlightpress.com
Founded: 2004
Children's picture books that explore & illuminate.
ISBN Prefix(es): 978-0-9729225; 978-0-9799746; 978-1-993612; 978-1-936261
Number of titles published annually: 3 Print
Total Titles: 32 Print; 33 E-Book
Returns: Independent Publishers Group (IPG), c/o Returns Dept, 814 N Franklin St, Chicago, IL 60610 *Tel:* 312-337-0747 *Toll Free Tel:* 800-888-4741 *Fax:* 312-337-5985 *E-mail:* frontdesk@ipgbook.com *Web Site:* www.ipgbook.com
Distribution Center: Independent Publishers Group (IPG), 814 N Franklin St, Chicago, IL 60610 *Tel:* 312-337-0747 *Toll Free Tel:* 800-888-4741 *Fax:* 312-337-5985 *E-mail:* frontdesk@ipgbook.com *Web Site:* www.ipgbook.com

FleetSeek
6190 Powers Ferry Rd, Suite 320, Atlanta, GA 30339
Tel: 540-899-9872 *Toll Free Tel:* 888-ONLY-TTS (665-9887) *Fax:* 540-899-1948
E-mail: fleetseek@fleetseek.com
Web Site: www.fleetseek.com
Founded: 1980
Directories online relating to data in the trucking industry.
ISBN Prefix(es): 978-1-880701
Number of titles published annually: 4 Online
Total Titles: 4 Online

§Focus
Imprint of Hackett Publishing Co Inc
PO Box 390007, Cambridge, MA 02139-0001
Tel: 317-635-9250 *Fax:* 317-635-9292
E-mail: customer@hackettpublishing.com; editorial@hackettpublishing.com
Web Site: focusbookstore.com; www. hackettpublishing.com
Key Personnel
Pres, Publr & CEO: Deborah Wilkes
Edit Dir: Brian Rak
Rts Mgr: Maura Gaughan
Founded: 1985
Publisher of textbooks in modern languages, classical languages, philosophy & classics.
ISBN Prefix(es): 978-0-941051; 978-1-58510
Number of titles published annually: 30 Print; 30 E-Book
Total Titles: 900 Print; 500 E-Book
Distributor for Domus Latina Publishing
Foreign Rep(s): Accademia Vivarium Novum (Lingua Latina titles) (Continental Europe exc Portugal & Spain); Cultura Clasica SL (Lingua Latina titles) (Portugal, Spain); Gazelle Book

Services Ltd (Europe, UK); NewSouth Books (Australia, New Zealand)
Orders to: PO Box 44937, Indianapolis, IN 46244-0937
Returns: 3333 Massachusetts Ave, Indianapolis, IN 46218
Shipping Address: 3333 Massachusetts Ave, Indianapolis, IN 46218

Focus on the Family
8605 Explorer Dr, Colorado Springs, CO 80920-1051
Tel: 719-531-5181 *Toll Free Tel:* 800-A-FAMILY (232-6459) *Fax:* 719-531-3424
Web Site: www.focusonthefamily.com; www. facebook.com/focusonthefamily
Key Personnel
VP, Communs: Paul Batura
Founded: 1986
Case bound & soft cover books (adult & children) dealing with family relationships & emphasizing the importance of values & Christian principles in people's lives.
ISBN Prefix(es): 978-0-929608; 978-1-56179; 978-1-58997; 978-1-60482; 978-1-62405; 978-1-62471
Number of titles published annually: 25 Print
Total Titles: 300 Print; 25 CD-ROM; 60 Audio
Imprints: Adventures in Odyssey; Heritage Builders; Life on the Edge; Radio Theatre; Ribbits; That the World May Know
Distributed by Baker Books; Moody Press; Tyndale House Publishers Inc; Zondervan

Fodor's Travel
Division of Internet Brands Inc
909 N Sepulveda Blvd, El Segundo, CA 90245
E-mail: marketing@fodors.com
Web Site: www.fodors.com
Key Personnel
Dir, Publg Opers: Tara McCrillis
Edit Dir: Doug Stallings
Gen Mgr: Joy Lai
Mktg Mgr: Esther Su
Founded: 1936
Travel guides, foreign & domestic.
ISBN Prefix(es): 978-1-101; 978-0-307; 978-0-676; 978-1-4000
Number of titles published annually: 100 Print
Total Titles: 800 Print; 800 E-Book
Imprints: Compass American Guides; Fodor's
Warehouse: Ingram Publisher Services, One Ingram Blvd, La Vergne, TN 37086

Fons Vitae
49 Mockingbird Valley Dr, Louisville, KY 40207-1366
Tel: 502-897-3641 *Fax:* 502-893-7373
E-mail: fonsvitaeky@aol.com
Web Site: www.fonsvitae.com
Key Personnel
Dir: Gray Henry *E-mail:* grayh101@aol.com
Proj Dir: Elena Lloyd-Sidle
Busn Mgr: Lucy Langman
Mktg & Multimedia: Paul T Carney
Founded: 1997
Fons Vitae is both an academic charity with 501(c)(3) charitable status & a peer-reviewed publishing house which ensures the highest scholarly standards for its publications. Authentic text, impeccably translated & exquisitely produced, make these volumes useful for both the university classroom & for those interested in the eternal verities with no compromise to a recent soft focus on spirituality.
ISBN Prefix(es): 978-1-887752
Number of titles published annually: 10 Print; 5 CD-ROM
Total Titles: 130 Print; 5 CD-ROM
Distributor for African American Islamic Institute; Anqa Press (UK); Aperture (NY); Archetype (UK); Broadstone Books; Dar Nun;

Golganooza Press (UK); Islamic Texts Society (UK); Matheson Trust; Parabola; Paragon; Parvardigar Press; Pir Press (NY); Qiblah Books; Quilliam Press (UK); Sandala Productions; Sophia Perennis; Sri Lanka Institute of Traditional Studies; Thesaurus Islamicus Foundation; Tradigital; White Thread Press (US); Wisdom Foundation; World Wisdom (US); Zaytuna Institute Press (US)
Foreign Rep(s): American University in Cairo Press (AUC) (Middle East)
Distribution Center: Independent Publishers Group (IPG), 814 N Franklin St, Chicago 60610, IL *Tel:* 312-337-0747 *Toll Free Tel:* 800-888-4741 *Fax:* 312-337-5985 *E-mail:* frontdesk@ipgbook.com *Web Site:* www.ipgbook.com

Fordham University Press
Joseph A Martino Hall, 45 Columbus Ave, New York, NY 10023
SAN: 201-6516
Fax: 347-842-3083
Web Site: www.fordhampress.com
Key Personnel
Dir: Fredric Nachbaur *E-mail:* fnachbaur@ fordham.edu
Edit Dir: Richard Morrison *E-mail:* morrison7@ fordham.edu
Mktg Dir: Kathleen O'Brien-Nicholson *Tel:* 646-868-4204 *E-mail:* bkaobrien@fordham.edu
Mng Ed: Eric Newman *Tel:* 646-868-4210 *E-mail:* ernewman@fordham.edu
Acqs Ed: Tom Lay *E-mail:* tlay@fordham.edu
Ed, Rts & Perms Mgr: Will Cerbone *E-mail:* wcerbone@fordham.edu
Busn Mgr: Margaret Noonan *E-mail:* mnoonan@ fordham.edu
Asst Busn Mgr: Marie Hall *E-mail:* mhall21@ fordham.edu
Mktg Mgr: Katie Sweeney *Tel:* 646-868-4205 *E-mail:* kasweeney@fordham.edu
Prodn & Design Mgr: Ann-Christine Racette *E-mail:* aracette@fordham.edu
Founded: 1907
Scholarly books & journals, New York regional books, general trade books & videos.
ISBN Prefix(es): 978-0-8232
Number of titles published annually: 42 Print
Total Titles: 450 Print
Imprints: American Literatures Initiative; Empire State Editions; The Modern Language Initiative
Distributed by Oxford University Press (US & CN)
Distributor for Creighton University Press; Institute for Advanced Study in the Theatre Arts (IASTA); Little Room Press; Rockhurst University Press; St Bede's Publications; University of San Francisco Press
Foreign Rep(s): AfricaConnection.co.uk (Guy Simpson) (Africa exc South Africa); The African Moon Press (Chris Reinders) (Southern Africa); Avicenna Partnership Ltd (Bill Kennedy) (Middle East); Canadian Manda Group (Canada); China Publishers Marketing (Benjamin Pan) (China, Hong Kong, Taiwan); CoInfo Ltd (Debra Triplett) (Australia, Fiji, New Zealand, Papua New Guinea); Combined Academic Publishers Ltd (Africa, Australia, Europe, Middle East, New Zealand, Pacific Region, UK); Claire De Gruchy (Middle East); Cristina De Lara Ruiz (Portugal, Spain); Rupinder Gahle (Kenya); Charles Gibbes & Leonidas Diamantopoulos (Cyprus, Greece); Ben Greig (Denmark, Iceland, Sweden); Steven Haslemere (Sweden); Ingram Publisher Services International (Denise Lourenco) (Latin America); Wilf Jones (Finland, Norway); Jacek Lewinson (Eastern Europe, Russia); Mare Nostrum (Lauren Keane) (Belgium, Benelux, Luxembourg, Netherlands); Mare Nostrum (Frauke Feldmann) (Austria, Central Europe, Germany, Switzerland); Mare Nostrum (Alice Scott)

(France); Mare Nostrum (Francesca Pollard) (Italy); Greggory Oluma (Rwanda, Southern Sudan, Tanzania, Uganda); Publishers International Marketing (Chris Ashdown) (Brunei, Cambodia, Indonesia, Japan, Laos, Malaysia, Philippines, Singapore, South Korea, Thailand, Vietnam); Viva Books Pvt Ltd (Bangladesh, Bhutan, India, Maldives, Nepal, Sri Lanka); World Press (Saleem A Malik) (Pakistan)
Returns: Maple Logistics Solutions, Lebanon Distribution Ctr, 704 Legionaire Dr, Fredricksburg, PA 17026
Distribution Center: Ingram Publisher Services, One Ingram Blvd, La Vergne, TN 37086 *Toll Free Tel:* 866-400-5351 *E-mail:* ips@ingramcontent.com *Web Site:* www.ingramcontent.com SAN: 631-8630
IPS-Jackson, 210 American Dr, Jackson, TN 38301 *Toll Free Tel:* 800-343-4499 *E-mail:* ipsjacksonorders@ingramcontent.com
Ingram Content Group LLC, One Ingram Blvd, La Vergne, TN 37086 *Toll Free Tel:* 866-400-5351 *E-mail:* ips@ingramcontent.com
Membership(s): Association of American Publishers (AAP); Association of Jesuit University Presses; Association of University Presses (AUPresses)

Fortress Press, see Augsburg Fortress Publishers, Publishing House of the Evangelical Lutheran Church in America

§Forum Publishing Co
383 E Main St, Centerport, NY 11721
Tel: 631-754-5000 *Toll Free Tel:* 800-635-7654
Fax: 631-754-0630
E-mail: forumpublishing@aol.com
Web Site: www.forum123.com
Key Personnel
Publr & CEO: Martin Stevens
Founded: 1981
Business magazines & books.
ISBN Prefix(es): 978-0-9626141
Number of titles published annually: 5 Print
Total Titles: 15 Print; 6 CD-ROM

Forward Movement
Affiliate of The Episcopal Church
412 Sycamore St, Cincinnati, OH 45202-4110
Tel: 513-721-6659 *Toll Free Tel:* 800-543-1813
Fax: 513-721-0729 (orders)
E-mail: orders@forwardmovement.org (orders & cust serv)
Web Site: www.forwardmovement.org
Key Personnel
Deputy Dir & Mng Ed: Richelle Thompson
E-mail: rthompson@forwardmovement.org
Dir, Busn Opers: Jane Paraskevopoulos
E-mail: jparaskevo@forwardmovement.org
Dir, Mktg: Jason Merritt *E-mail:* jmerritt@forwardmovement.org
Founded: 1935
Inspires disciples & empowers evangelists around the globe through offerings that encourage spiritual growth in individuals & congregations.
ISBN Prefix(es): 978-0-88028
Number of titles published annually: 12 Print
Total Titles: 60 Print; 1 Audio
Imprints: FMP
Distributor for Anglican Book Centre
Warehouse: 10001 Alliance Rd, Cincinnati, OH 45242

Walter Foster Jr, see Walter Foster Publishing Inc

Walter Foster Publishing Inc
Imprint of Quarto Publishing Group USA Inc
6 Orchard Rd, Suite 100, Lake Forest, CA 92630
SAN: 249-051X

Tel: 949-380-7510 *Toll Free Tel:* 800-426-0099; 800-759-0190 (orders) *Fax:* 949-380-7575
E-mail: walterfoster@quarto.com
Web Site: www.quartoknows.com/walter-foster
Key Personnel
Group Publr: Anne Landa *E-mail:* anne.landa@quarto.com
US Adult Mktg Dir: Kristine Anderson
E-mail: kristine.anderson@quarto.com
Founded: 1922
Instructional art books, specialty art & creative products.
ISBN Prefix(es): 978-0-929261; 978-1-56010; 978-1-60058; 978-1-63322
Number of titles published annually: 100 Print
Total Titles: 600 Print

Foundation Center
32 Old Slip, 24th fl, New York, NY 10005-3500
SAN: 207-5687
Tel: 212-620-4230 *Toll Free Tel:* 800-424-9836
Fax: 212-807-3677
E-mail: customerservice@foundationcenter.org
Web Site: foundationcenter.org
Key Personnel
Pres: Bradford K Smith *Tel:* 212-807-3602
E-mail: bks@foundationcenter.org
Founded: 1956
Reference books on US foundations, corporations & their grant-making activities & books about philanthropy & nonprofit management.
ISBN Prefix(es): 978-0-87954; 978-1-931923; 978-1-59542
Number of titles published annually: 12 Print; 3 Online
Total Titles: 292 Print; 3 Online; 25 E-Book
Branch Office(s)
312 Sutter St, Suite 606, San Francisco, CA 94108-4314 *Tel:* 415-397-0902
1627 "K" St NW, 3rd fl, Washington, DC 20006-1708 *Tel:* 202-331-1400
133 Peachtree St NE, Lobby Suite 350, Atlanta, GA 30303-1804 *Tel:* 404-880-0094
1422 Euclid Ave, Suite 1600, Cleveland, OH 44115-2001 *Tel:* 216-861-1933

Foundation Press
Imprint of West Academic
c/o West Academic, 444 Cedar St, Suite 700, St Paul, MN 55101
Toll Free Tel: 877-888-1330
E-mail: customerservice@westacademic.com
Web Site: www.westacademic.com
Key Personnel
VP & Publr: Pamela Siege Chandler
E-mail: pamela.siege@westacademic.com
Dir, Mktg: Julie Flower *Tel:* 651-202-4821
E-mail: julie.flower@westacademic.com
Founded: 1931
Law, business, political science, criminal justice, curriculum books, graduate & undergraduate, primarily in law.
ISBN Prefix(es): 978-0-88277; 978-1-56662; 978-1-58778; 978-1-59941
Number of titles published annually: 120 Print
Total Titles: 500 Print

Foundation Publications
900 S Euclid St, La Habra, CA 90631
Mailing Address: PO Box 2935, La Habra, CA 90632-2935
Tel: 714-879-2286
E-mail: info@foundationpublications.com
Web Site: www.foundationpublications.com
Key Personnel
EVP: Pike Lambeth *E-mail:* pike@foundationpublications.com
Founded: 1971
Publish New American Standard Bible, La Biblia de Las Americas & Nueva Biblia Latinoamericana de Hoy.

ISBN Prefix(es): 978-0-910618; 978-1-58135; 978-1-885217
Number of titles published annually: 2 Print
Total Titles: 13 Print
Distribution Center: Anchor Distributors, 1030 Hunt Valley Circle, New Kensington, PA 15068 *Toll Free Fax:* 800-444-4484
Ingram, One Ingram Blvd, La Vergne, TN 37086 *Tel:* 615-793-5000 *Web Site:* www.ingramcontent.com
Membership(s): Evangelical Christian Publishers Association (ECPA)

Fowler Museum at UCLA
PO Box 951549, Los Angeles, CA 90095-1549
Tel: 310-825-4361 *Fax:* 310-206-7007
E-mail: fowlerws@arts.ucla.edu
Web Site: www.fowler.ucla.edu
Key Personnel
Mng Ed: Marina Belozerskaya *Tel:* 310-794-9582
E-mail: mbelozerskaya@arts.ucla.edu
Founded: 1963
Active publisher of African, Southeast Asian & Latin American arts publications.
ISBN Prefix(es): 978-0-930741; 978-0-9748729
Number of titles published annually: 4 Print
Total Titles: 146 Print
Distributed by University of Washington Press
Shipping Address: 308 Charles E Young Dr N, Los Angeles, CA 90095

Fox Chapel Publishing Co Inc
1970 Broad St, East Petersburg, PA 17520
Tel: 717-560-4703 *Toll Free Tel:* 800-457-9112
Fax: 717-560-4702
E-mail: customerservice@foxchapelpublishing.com
Web Site: www.foxchapelpublishing.com
Key Personnel
CFO: Jeff Baughman *E-mail:* baughman@foxchapelpublishing.com
Pres: Alan Giagnocavo *E-mail:* alan@foxchapelpublishing.com
VP, Content: Chris Reggio *E-mail:* reggio@foxchapelpublishing.com
Founded: 1991
Publisher of illustrated nonfiction books, magazines, patterns & videos for craft, hobby & do-it-yourself enthusiasts, as well as children's books, journals & other stationery book products. Fox Chapel Publishing inspires & informs readers who enjoy woodworking, needlework, pyrography, home & garden, cooking, outdoor recreation, coloring, Zentangle®, kids crafts & more. Fox Chapel publishes 3 magazines, *Woodcarving Illustrated, Scroll Saw, Woodworking & Crafts* & *DO Magazine.*
ISBN Prefix(es): 978-1-58011 (Creative Homeowner); 978-1-56523 (Fox Chapel); 978-1-4972 (Design Originals); 978-1-5048 (IMM Lifestyle); 978-1-64178 (Quiet Fox); 978-1-64124 (Happy Fox); 978-1-62008 (CompanionHouse); 978-1-62187 (CompanionHouse); 978-1-912158 (Old Pond)
Number of titles published annually: 200 Print
Total Titles: 3,000 Print
Imprints: CompanionHouse Books; Creative Homeowner; Design Originals; Happy Fox; Heliconia Press; IMM Lifestyle Books; Landauer Publishing; Old Pond; Quiet Fox
Distributor for Reader's Digest; Taunton Sterling Dover
Membership(s): Craft Hobby Association (CHA); Publishers Association of the West (PubWest)
See separate listing for:
Creative Homeowner
Landauer Publishing

Franciscan Media
28 W Liberty St, Cincinnati, OH 45202
SAN: 204-6237
Tel: 513-241-5615 *Toll Free Tel:* 800-488-0488

E-mail: admin@franciscanmedia.org
Web Site: www.franciscanmedia.org
Key Personnel
Publr & CEO: Rev Dan Kroger, OFM
E-mail: dkroger@franciscanmedia.org
Pres: Kelly McCracken *E-mail:* kmccracken@
franciscanmedia.org
Dir, Design & Prodn: Mark Sullivan
E-mail: msullivan@franciscanmedia.org
Dir, Mktg: Ray Taylor *E-mail:* rtaylor@
franciscanmedia.org
Founded: 1893
Religion-Catholic. Nonprofit ministry of the
Franciscan Friars of the St John the Baptist Province, publishing books, audiobooks,
ebooks, weekly & Sunday homily programs;
monthly subscription newsletters, *St Anthony
Messenger*, monthly magazine.
ISBN Prefix(es): 978-0-912228; 978-0-86716;
978-1-61636; 978-1-63253; 978-1-63254
Number of titles published annually: 30 Print; 35
E-Book; 25 Audio
Total Titles: 550 Print; 100 E-Book; 200 Audio
Imprints: Fisher Productions; Franciscan Communications; Ikonographics; Servant Books
Foreign Rep(s): Redemptorist Publications Book
Service (UK)
Membership(s): Association of Catholic Publishers Inc; Catholic Press Association (CPA); Society of Professional Journalists

§Franklin, Beedle & Associates Inc
2154 NE Broadway, Suite 100, Portland, OR
97232
Tel: 503-284-6348 *Toll Free Tel:* 800-322-2665
Fax: 503-625-4434
Web Site: www.fbeedle.com
Key Personnel
Ed: Tom Sumner *E-mail:* tsumner@fbeedle.com
Founded: 1985
College textbooks in computer science, information systems & computers in education, educational software, computer engineering, computer information systems, information technology.
ISBN Prefix(es): 978-0-938661; 978-1-887902;
978-1-59028
Number of titles published annually: 10 Print; 5
E-Book
Total Titles: 50 Print; 5 E-Book
Imprints: William, James & Co (humanities
publr); Xpat Fiction
Distributor for Arcus; Battlebridge; Blue Sky
Gallery; Photolucida Book; Ringing Bell Press;
Tayo Press; Wordstock
Foreign Rep(s): Transatlantic Publishers (Europe,
Middle East, UK)
Membership(s): Association for Computing Machinery (ACM)

Frederick Fell Publishers Inc
7519 LaPaz Blvd, Suite C303, Boca Raton, FL
33433
SAN: 208-2365
Tel: 954-925-5242
E-mail: fellpub@aol.com (admin only)
Web Site: www.fellpub.com
Key Personnel
Pres & Publr: Donald L Lessne
E-mail: donlessne@aol.com
Ed-in-Chief: Barbara Newman
E-mail: felleditor@aol.com
Founded: 1943
An award-winning publisher of general trade
books. Series published include the Know-It-All Guides, Top 100 series, Heroes & Heroines
series & So You Want To Be series.
ISBN Prefix(es): 978-0-88391
Number of titles published annually: 24 Print; 50
E-Book
Total Titles: 150 Print; 150 E-Book
Foreign Rep(s): Gazelle Book Services Ltd
(UK & the continent); Jarir Bookstore (Tony

Herold) (Saudi Arabia); Parrot Reads Publishers (Indian subcontinent); USBD Distribution
(Singapore)
Foreign Rights: Akcali Copyright Agency
(Turkey); Agencia Literaria Carmen Balcells SA (Latin America exc Brazil, Portugal,
Spain); Lorella Belli Literary Agency (UK);
Big Apple Agency (Maggie Han) (China);
Big Apple Agency (Taiwan); Book Publishers Association of Israel (Beverley Levit) (Israel); Graal Literary Agency (Marcin Biegaj)
(Poland); Imprima Korea Agency (Korea);
International Copyright Agency Ltd (Simona
Kessler) (Romania); Christiane Janssen (Germany); Japan UNI Agency Inc (Japan); Jarir
Bookstore (Tony Herold) (Saudi Arabia); LEX
Copyright Office (Norbert Uzseka) (Hungary);
Maxima Creative Agency (Santo Manurung)
(Indonesia); Nova Littera S L (Konstantin
Paltchikov) (Russia); Andrew Nurnberg Associates Ltd (Tatjana Zoldnere) (Latvia, Lithuania, Ukraine); Andrew Nurnberg Associates
Prague (Petra Tobiskova) (Czechia); Andrew
Nurnberg Associates Sofia (Anna Droumeva)
(Bulgaria); OA Literary Agency (Greece);
Plima Literary Agency (Mila Perisic) (Croatia,
Serbia, Slovenia); Schindler's Literary Agency
(Brazil); Tuttle-Mori Agency Inc (Japan, Thailand)
Distribution Center: Independent Publishers
Group (IPG), 814 N Franklin St, No 100,
Chicago, IL 60610, VP: Alex Kampmann
Tel: 312-337-0747 *Fax:* 312-337-5985 *Web
Site:* www.ipg.com
Gazelle Book Services Ltd, White Cross Mills,
Hightown, Lancaster, Lancs LA1 4XS, United
Kingdom *Tel:* (01524) 528500 *Fax:* (01524)
528510 *E-mail:* sales@gazellebookservices.co.
uk *Web Site:* www.gazellebookservices.co.uk

§Free Spirit Publishing Inc
6325 Sandburg Rd, Suite 100, Minneapolis, MN
55427
Tel: 612-338-2068 *Toll Free Tel:* 800-735-7323
Fax: 612-337-5050 *Toll Free Fax:* 866-419-
5199
E-mail: help4kids@freespirit.com
Web Site: www.freespirit.com
Key Personnel
Pres & Publr: Judy Galbraith
Intl Rts Asst: Kiera Cato
Founded: 1983
Offer books & learning materials for parents, educators, children & teens. Topics include: self-esteem, stress management, school success,
creativity, relationships with friends & family,
social action, special needs (i.e. children with
LD/learning differences, gifted & talented &
at-risk youth), bullying & conflict resolution.
ISBN Prefix(es): 978-0-915793; 978-1-57542;
978-0-9665988
Number of titles published annually: 25 Print; 1
CD-ROM
Total Titles: 170 Print; 2 CD-ROM; 3 Audio
Foreign Rep(s): Educational Distributors (New
Zealand); Georgetown Publications (Canada);
Incentive Plus (UK)

§W H Freeman
Imprint of Macmillan Learning
41 Madison Ave, New York, NY 10010
Tel: 212-576-9400 *Fax:* 212-689-2383
Web Site: www.macmillanlearning.com
Founded: 1946
Science & mathematics texts for the higher education market & high school advanced courses.
ISBN Prefix(es): 978-1-57259; 978-1-4292; 978-
0-7167; 978-0-9747077; 978-1-936221
Number of titles published annually: 25 Print; 20
Online; 20 E-Book
Total Titles: 500 Print
Foreign Rep(s): Macmillan Education East
Asia (China, Hong Kong, Indonesia, Korea,

Malaysia, Philippines, Singapore, Taiwan, Thailand, Vietnam); Palgrave Macmillan Australia
(Australia, New Zealand); Palgrave Macmillan
Ltd (Africa, Caribbean, Europe, India, Japan,
Latin America, Middle East, Pakistan, UK)
Warehouse: MPS Distribution Center, 16365
James Madison Hwy, Gordonsville, VA 22942
Toll Free Tel: 888-330-8477 *Fax:* 540-672-7540
(cust serv) *Toll Free Fax:* 800-672-2054 (orders)

Samuel French Inc
235 Park Ave S, 5th fl, New York, NY 10003
Tel: 212-206-8990 *Toll Free Tel:* 866-598-8449
Fax: 212-206-1429
E-mail: info@samuelfrench.com
Web Site: www.samuelfrench.com
Key Personnel
Pres: Nate Collins *E-mail:* ncollins@
samuelfrench.com
Literary Dir: Amy Rose Marsh *E-mail:* amarsh@
samuelfrench.com
Dir, Music & Pubns: David Geer *E-mail:* dgeer@
samuelfrench.com
Founded: 1830
Plays.
ISBN Prefix(es): 978-0-573
Number of titles published annually: 70 Print
Foreign Office(s): Samuel French Ltd, 24-
32 Stephenson Way, London NW1 2HD,
United Kingdom *Tel:* (020) 7387 9373
E-mail: customerservices@samuelfrench.co.uk
Web Site: www.samuelfrench.co.uk
Distributed by Baker's Plays; Samuel French Ltd
(UK)
Distributor for Baker's Plays; Samuel French Ltd
(UK)
Foreign Rights: DALRO Pty Ltd (Botswana,
Lesotho, Namibia, South Africa, Swaziland);
Drama League of Ireland (Ireland); Origin Theatrical (Australia); Play Bureau (NZ) Ltd (New
Zealand)

Fresh Air Books
Imprint of Upper Room Books
1908 Grand Ave, Nashville, TN 37212
Tel: 615-340-7200 *Toll Free Tel:* 800-972-0433
(orders)
Web Site: books.upperroom.org
Key Personnel
Acq Ed: Joanna Bradley *Tel:* 615-340-7256
E-mail: jbradley@upperroom.org
Founded: 2009
Nonprofit publisher of religious materials.
ISBN Prefix(es): 978-1-935205
Number of titles published annually: 1 Print; 2 E-Book
Total Titles: 14 Print; 10 E-Book
Returns: PBD Worldwide Fulfillment Services,
Discipleship Resources, Upper Rm, Return Door 16, 1650 Bluegrass Lakes Pkwy,
Alpharetta, GA 30004 *Tel:* 770-442-8633
Fax: 770-442-9742
Warehouse: PBD Worldwide Fulfillment Services,
1650 Bluegrass Lakes Pkwy, Alpharetta, GA
30004 *Tel:* 770-442-8633 *Fax:* 770-442-9742
Distribution Center: PBD Worldwide Fulfillment Services, 1650 Bluegrass Lakes Pkwy,
Alpharetta, GA 30004 *Tel:* 770-442-8633
Fax: 770-442-9742

Friends United Press
Subsidiary of Friends United Meeting
101 Quaker Hill Dr, Richmond, IN 47374
SAN: 201-5803
Tel: 765-962-7573 *Fax:* 765-966-1293
E-mail: friendspress@fum.org; orders@fum.org
Web Site: www.friendsunitedmeeting.org;
bookstore.friendsunitedmeeting.org
Founded: 1969
Religion; Quaker history; Quakerism; Christian
Curriculum.
ISBN Prefix(es): 978-0-913408; 978-0-944350

Number of titles published annually: 3 Print; 3 Online; 2 E-Book
Total Titles: 110 Print; 70 Online; 2 E-Book
Membership(s): Christian Small Publishers Association; Independent Book Publishers Association (IBPA); Quakers Uniting in Publications

FT Press, see Financial Times Press

Fulcrum Publishing Inc
4690 Table Mountain Dr, Suite 100, Golden, CO 80403
SAN: 200-2825
Tel: 303-277-1623 *Toll Free Tel:* 800-992-2908 *Fax:* 303-279-7111 *Toll Free Fax:* 800-726-7112
E-mail: info@fulcrumbooks.com; orders@fulcrumbooks.com
Web Site: www.fulcrumbooks.com
Key Personnel
Pres: Sam Scinta
Dir, Sales & Mktg: Melanie Roth *Tel:* 800-922-2908 ext 213 *E-mail:* melanie@fulcrumbooks.com
Ed-in-Chief: Rebecca McEwen
Founded: 1984
Nonfiction trade: Western culture & history, Native American culture & history, environment & nature, popular culture, lifestyle, outdoor recreation, public policy & gardening.
ISBN Prefix(es): 978-1-55591; 978-1-56373; 978-0-912347; 978-1-936218; 978-1-938486
Number of titles published annually: 15 Print; 15 E-Book
Total Titles: 600 Print; 250 E-Book
Distribution Center: Consortium Book Sales & Distribution, The Keg House, Suite 101, 34 13 Ave NE, Minneapolis, MN 55413-1007, VP, Sales: Jim Nichols *Tel:* 612-746-2600 *Toll Free Tel:* 800-283-3572 (cust serv, Jackson, TN) *Fax:* 612-746-2606 *E-mail:* info@cbsd.com *Web Site:* www.cbsd.com SAN: 200-6049
Membership(s): American Booksellers Association (ABA); Association of American Publishers (AAP); Midwest Independent Booksellers Association (MIBA); Mountains & Plains Independent Booksellers Association (MPIBA); Pacific Northwest Booksellers Association (PNBA)

FurnitureCore
1389 Peachtree St NE, Suite 310, Atlanta, GA 30309
Tel: 404-961-3734 *Toll Free Tel:* 800-826-8868 *Fax:* 404-961-3749
E-mail: info@furniturecore.com
Web Site: www.furniturecore.com
Key Personnel
Owner & Pres: Bob George
Founded: 1985 (acquired in 2008)
Specialize in business, industry & statistical reports.
ISBN Prefix(es): 978-0-921577; 978-1-894330; 978-1-894960
Number of titles published annually: 12 Print; 10 Online
Total Titles: 56 Print; 30 Online
Distributor for AMA Research; Business & Research Associates

§Future Horizons Inc
721 W Abram St, Arlington, TX 76013
Tel: 817-277-0727 *Toll Free Tel:* 800-489-0727 *Fax:* 817-277-2270
E-mail: info@fhautism.com
Web Site: www.fhautism.com
Founded: 1996
Resources on Autism/Asperger's Syndrome, including books, CDs, DVDs, magazines & conferences.
ISBN Prefix(es): 978-1-885477; 978-1-932565; 978-1-935274

Number of titles published annually: 7 Print
Total Titles: 20 Print

Gagosian Gallery
980 Madison Ave, New York, NY 10075
Tel: 212-744-2313 *Fax:* 212-772-7962
E-mail: newyork@gagosian.com
Web Site: www.gagosian.com
Key Personnel
Publg Dir: Alison McDonald
Founded: 1989
Publish fine editions & illustrated books on contemporary & modern art.
ISBN Prefix(es): 978-1-880154
Number of titles published annually: 30 Print
Total Titles: 40 Print
Branch Office(s)
456 N Camden Dr, Beverly Hills, CA 90210
Tel: 310-271-9400 *Fax:* 310-271-9420
E-mail: losangeles@gagosian.com

§Galaxy Press
7051 Hollywood Blvd, Hollywood, CA 90028
SAN: 254-6906
Tel: 323-466-3310 *Toll Free Tel:* 877-8GALAXY (842-5299)
E-mail: info@galaxypress.com; customers@galaxypress.com
Web Site: www.galaxypress.com
Key Personnel
Pres: John Goodwin *Tel:* 323-466-7812 *E-mail:* jgoodwin@galaxypress.com
SVP, Sales & Rts: Kim Catalano *Tel:* 323-466-7815 ext 1740 *E-mail:* kcatalano@galaxypress.com
VP, Trade Sales: Juliet Wills *E-mail:* jwills@galaxypress.com
Dir, Intl Sales/Rts: Claude Sandoz *E-mail:* claude@asirights.com
Consumer Sales: Sarah Toth *E-mail:* sarahc@galaxypress.com
Founded: 2002
Publisher of the fiction works of L Ron Hubbard.
ISBN Prefix(es): 978-1-59212
Number of titles published annually: 10 Print; 10 E-Book; 6 Audio
Total Titles: 110 Print; 110 E-Book; 100 Audio
Imprints: Galaxy Audio
Returns: 6131 Malburg Way, Vernon, CA 90058 *Tel:* 323-588-8777
Warehouse: 6131 Malburg Way, Vernon, CA 90058 *Tel:* 323-588-8777
Distribution Center: 6131 Malburg Way, Vernon, CA 90058 *Tel:* 323-588-8777

Galde Press Inc
PO Box 774, Hendersonville, NC 28793
Tel: 828-702-3032
Web Site: www.galdepress.com
Key Personnel
Founder & Pres: Phyllis Galde *E-mail:* phyllis@galdepress.com
Founded: 1991
Independent publisher of books on a variety of subjects with over 100 titles in print.
ISBN Prefix(es): 978-1-880090; 978-1-931942
Number of titles published annually: 11 Print
Total Titles: 108 Print

§Gale
Division of Cengage Learning
27500 Drake Rd, Farmington Hills, MI 48331-3535
SAN: 213-4373
Tel: 248-699-4253 *Toll Free Tel:* 800-877-4253 *Toll Free Fax:* 800-414-5043 (orders)
E-mail: gale.customercare@cengage.com
Web Site: www.gale.com
Key Personnel
SVP, Mng Dir, Intl: Terry Robinson
SVP & Gen Mgr: Paul Gazzolo
SVP, North American Sales: Brian McDonough

VP, Mktg & Communs: Harmony Faust
Founded: 1954
Gale, a Cengage company, partners with librarians & educators around the world to connect learners to essential content through user-friendly technology that enhances experiences & improves learning outcomes. For more than 65 years, Gale has collaborated with academic institutions, schools & public libraries around the world to empower the discovery of knowledge & insights that push the boundaries of traditional research & advance learners in all areas of life.
ISBN Prefix(es): 978-0-8103; 978-0-7876
Number of titles published annually: 50 Print
Total Titles: 4,099 Print
Imprints: Charles Scribner's Sons®; Christian Large Print; Five Star™; Large Print Press™; Macmillan Reference USA™; Primary Source Media™; St James Press®; Schirmer Reference™; Scholarly Resources Inc; The TAFT Group®; Thorndike Press®; U X L™; Wheeler Publishing™
Distribution Center: 10650 Toebben Dr, Independence, KY 41051 *Tel:* 859-525-2230
See separate listing for:
Charles Scribner's Sons®
Macmillan Reference USA™
St James Press®
Thorndike Press®

§Galen Press Ltd
PO Box 64400-WB, Tucson, AZ 85728-4400
Tel: 520-577-8363 *Fax:* 520-529-6459
E-mail: sales@galenpress.com
Web Site: www.galenpress.com
Key Personnel
Owner, CFO & Publr: Mary Lou Iserson
VP, Mktg & Spec Sales: Mary Lou Sherk *E-mail:* ml@galenpress.com
Ed: Jennifer G Gilbert *E-mail:* jennifer@galenpress.com
Founded: 1993
Publish non-clinical health related books in medical education, death & dying & bioethics.
ISBN Prefix(es): 978-1-883620
Number of titles published annually: 2 Print; 1 CD-ROM; 3 E-Book
Total Titles: 32 Print; 1 CD-ROM; 6 E-Book
Membership(s): The Association of Publishers for Special Sales (APSS)

§Gallaudet University Press
800 Florida Ave NE, Washington, DC 20002-3695
SAN: 205-261X
Tel: 202-651-5488 *Fax:* 202-651-5489
E-mail: gupress@gallaudet.edu
Web Site: gupress.gallaudet.edu
Key Personnel
Exec Dir: Gary Aller
Dir: Angela Leppig
Founded: 1980
Reference books, scholarly, educational & general interest books on deaf studies, deaf culture & issues, sign language textbooks.
ISBN Prefix(es): 978-0-913580; 978-0-930323; 978-1-56368; 978-1-944838
Number of titles published annually: 16 Print
Total Titles: 250 Print; 4 CD-ROM
Imprints: Clerc Books; Kendall Green
Warehouse: Chicago Distribution Center, 11030 S Langley Ave, Chicago, IL 60628, Contact: Karen Hyzy *Tel:* 773-702-7000 *Toll Free Tel:* 800-621-2736 *Fax:* 773-702-7212 *Toll Free Fax:* 800-621-8476 *E-mail:* orders@press.uchicago.edu
Membership(s): Association of University Presses (AUPresses)

Gallery Books
Imprint of Gallery Publishing Group

1230 Avenue of the Americas, New York, NY 10020
Toll Free Tel: 800-456-6798 *Fax:* 212-698-7284
E-mail: consumer.customerservice@ simonandschuster.com
Web Site: www.simonandschuster.com
Key Personnel
SVP & Publr, Gallery Books Group: Jennifer Bergstrom *Tel:* 212-698-2117 *E-mail:* jennifer. bergstrom@simonandschuster.com
VP, Assoc Publr, Gallery Books Group; Publisher of Pocket Books: Jennifer Long *E-mail:* jennifer.long@simonandschuster.com
Publg Mgr, Gallery Books & Pocket Books: Eliza Hanson *E-mail:* eliza.hanson@ simonandschuster.com
VP, Edit Dir, Gallery Books Group: Aimee Bell *Tel:* 212-698-7234 *E-mail:* aimee.bell@ simonandschuster.com
Edit Dir, Saga Press: Joe Monti *Tel:* 212-698-2104 *E-mail:* joe.monti@simonandschuster.com
VP, Exec Ed, Gallery Books/Scout Press: Alison Callahan *Tel:* 212-698-2442 *E-mail:* alison. callahan@simonandschuster.com
Exec Ed, Gallery Books, Threshold Editions: Natasha Simons *Tel:* 212-698-7287 *E-mail:* natasha.simons@simonandschuster.com
Exec Ed, Gallery Books: Jeremie Ruby-Strauss *Tel:* 212-698-7683 *E-mail:* jeremie. rubystrauss@simonandschuster.com; Lauren Spiegel *Tel:* 212-698-7678 *E-mail:* lauren. spiegel@simonandschuster.com; Karyn Marcus *Tel:* 212-698-2329 *E-mail:* karyn.marcus@ simonandschuster.com
Sr Ed, Gallery Books & Gallery 13: Edward Schlesinger *Tel:* 212-698-7463 *E-mail:* ed. schlesinger@simonandschuster.com
Sr Ed, Gallery Books: Jackie Cantor *Tel:* 212-698-4382 *E-mail:* jackie.cantor@ simonandschuster.com; Hannah Braaten *Tel:* 212-698-2729 *E-mail:* hannah.braaten@ simonandschuster.com; Kate Dresser *Tel:* 212-698-7575 *E-mail:* kate.dresser@ simonandschuster.com
Asst Ed, Gallery Books: Rebecca Strobel *Tel:* 212-698-2476 *E-mail:* rebecca.strobel@ simonandschuster.com; Sara Quaranta *Tel:* 212-698-2493 *E-mail:* sara.quaranta@ simonandschuster.com; Molly Gregory *Tel:* 212-698-2125 *E-mail:* molly.gregory@ simonandschuster.com; Max Meltzer *Tel:* 212-698-7401 *E-mail:* max.meltzer@ simonandschuster.com; Maggie Loughran *Tel:* 212-698-7490 *E-mail:* maggie.loughran@ simonandschuster.com
VP, Dir of Mktg & Publicity, Gallery Books: Sally Marvin *Tel:* 212-698-2360 *E-mail:* sally. marvin@simonandschuster.com
VP & Exec Publicist, Gallery Books Group: Jennifer Robinson *Tel:* 212-698-2719 *E-mail:* jennifer.robinson@simonandschuster. com
Assoc Dir, Publicity, Gallery Books: Jessica Roth *Tel:* 212-698-4665 *E-mail:* jessica.roth@ simonandschuster.com
Assoc Dir, Mktg, Gallery Books: Abby Zidle *Tel:* 212-698-2898 *E-mail:* abby.zidle@ simonandschuster.com
Assoc Dir of Publicity, Gallery Books: Lauren Truskowski *Tel:* 212-698-4792 *E-mail:* lauren. truskowski@simonandschuster.com
Sr Mktg & Publicity Mgr, Saga Press: Lauren Jackson *Tel:* 212-698-7645 *E-mail:* lauren. jackson@simonandschuster.com
Sr Publicist, Gallery Books: Michelle Podberezniak *Tel:* 212-698-2807 *E-mail:* michelle. podberezniak@simonandschuster.com
VP & Dir, Rts, Gallery Books Group: Paul O'Halloran *Tel:* 212-698-7367 *E-mail:* paul. o'halloran@simonandschuster.com
Asst Mgr, Subs Rts, Gallery Books, Pocket Books: Elizabeth Lotto *Tel:* 212-698-7446 *E-mail:* elizabeth.lotto@simonandschuster.com

Sr Art Dir, Gallery Books, Pocket Books: Lisa Litwack *E-mail:* lisa.litwack@ simonandschuster.com
Founded: 1939
Trade paperbacks & hardcovers; mass market, reprints & originals.
ISBN Prefix(es): 978-0-671; 978-0-7434; 978-1-4165
Imprints: Downtown Press; Gallery 13; Jeter Publishing; MTV Books; Pocket Books; Saga Press (adult science fiction/fantasy/horror); Scout Press; Star Trek®; VH1 Books
Foreign Rights: Akcali Copyright Agency (Atilla Izgi Turgut & Begum Ayfer) (Turkey); Berla & Griffini Rights Agency (Italy); Book Publishers Association of Israel (Beverley Levit) (Israel); International Editors Co (Amaiur Fernandez) (Portugal, Spain); Japan UNI Agency (Miko Yamanouchi & Ayako Sasamoto) (Japan); JLM Literary Agency (John Moukakos) (Greece); Korea Copyright Center Inc (KCC) (Sangeun Lee) (Korea); Mohrbooks AG Literary Agency (Sebastian Ritscher) (Germany); La Nouvelle Agence (Vanessa Kling & Anne Maizeret) (France); Andrew Nurnberg Associates (Ludmilla Sushkova) (Russia); Andrew Nurnberg Associates (Whitney Hsu) (Taiwan); Andrew Nurnberg Associates (Mira Droumeva) (Bulgaria, Montenegro, Romania, Serbia); Andrew Nurnberg Associates (Jackie Huang) (China); Andrew Nurnberg Associates (Judit Hermann) (Croatia, Hungary); Andrew Nurnberg Associates (Marta Soukopova) (Czechia, Slovakia, Slovenia); Andrew Nurnberg Associates (Tatjana Zoldnere) (Estonia, Latvia, Lithuania); Andrew Nurnberg Associates (Marcin Biegaj) (Poland); Andrew Nurnberg Associates International (Helen Lin) (Taiwan); Agencia Riff (Brazil); Sebes & Bisseling Literary Agency (Paul Sebes & Willem Bisseling) (Netherlands); Ulf Toregard Agency (Ulf Toregard) (Denmark, Finland, Iceland, Norway, Sweden); Tuttle-Mori Agency Inc (Pumi Boonyatud) (Thailand)

Gallery 13, see Gallery Books

§Gallopade International Inc
611 Hwy 74 S, Suite 2000, Peachtree City, GA 30269
SAN: 213-8441
Mailing Address: PO Box 2779, Peachtree City, GA 30269
Tel: 770-631-4222 *Toll Free Tel:* 800-536-2GET (536-2438) *Fax:* 770-631-4810
Toll Free Fax: 800-871-2979
E-mail: customerservice@gallopade.com
Web Site: www.gallopade.com
Key Personnel
Owner & CEO: Carole Marsh *E-mail:* carole@ gallopade.com
Pres & Intl Rts: Michele Yother *E-mail:* michele@gallopade.com
Pres: Michael Longmeyer *E-mail:* michael@ gallopade.com
Dir, Mktg: Gabby Shaw *E-mail:* gabby@ gallopade.com
Founded: 1979
"State stuff" for all 50 states including activity books, games, maps, posters, stickies, etc. Subjects include travel, regional, school travel supply, home school, juvenile mysteries, human sex education, multicultural, preschool through adult.
ISBN Prefix(es): 978-0-935326; 978-1-55609; 978-0-7933; 978-0-635
Number of titles published annually: 500 Print; 50 CD-ROM; 200 Online; 200 E-Book
Total Titles: 15,000 Print; 200 CD-ROM; 10,050 Online; 10,050 E-Book; 13 Audio
Imprints: American Milestones; Black Heritage: Celebrating Culture; The Day That Was Different; Here & Now; Heroes & Helpers; Carole Marsh Books; Carole Marsh Mysteries; New

Traditions; 1000 Readers; Smart Sex Stuff for Kids; State Experience; State Stuff
Subsidiaries: Six House; The World's Largest Publishing Co
Membership(s): Education Market Association

Gareth Stevens Publishing
Imprint of The Rosen Publishing Group Inc
111 E 14 St, Suite 349, New York, NY 10003
Mailing Address: PO Box 29088, New York, NY 10087-9088
Toll Free Tel: 800-542-2595 *Toll Free Fax:* 877-542-2596 (cust serv)
E-mail: customerservice@gspub.com
Web Site: garethstevens.com
Founded: 1983
ISBN Prefix(es): 978-0-918831; 978-1-55532; 978-0-8368; 978-1-4339
Number of titles published annually: 400 Print
Total Titles: 1,500 Print
Returns: Maple Logistics Solutions, York Distribution Center, 60 Grumbacher Rd, York, PA 17406

Gatekeeper Press
2167 Stringtown Rd, Suite 109, Columbus, OH 43123
Toll Free Tel: 866-535-0913 *Fax:* 216-803-0350
E-mail: info@gatekeeperpress.com
Web Site: www.gatekeeperpress.com
Key Personnel
Pres: Robert Price *Tel:* 866-535-0913 ext 713 *E-mail:* rprice@gatekeeperpress.com
Founded: 2015
Full service publishing house that partners with authors & publishers to produce & distribute high quality books in digital & print formats. Authors earn 100% of their royalties. Distribution networks reach readers worldwide. Provide services for all subjects & types of books, including ebook conversion & distribution, book cover design, paperback publishing & distribution, editing & proofreading.
This publisher has indicated that 100% of their product line is author subsidized.
ISBN Prefix(es): 978-1-61984
Number of titles published annually: 500 Print
Membership(s): Independent Book Publishers Association (IBPA)

§Gateways Books & Tapes
Division of Institute for the Development of the Harmonious Human Being Inc
PO Box 370, Nevada City, CA 95959
SAN: 211-3635
Tel: 530-271-2239 *Toll Free Tel:* 800-869-0658
E-mail: info@gatewaysbooksandtapes.com
Web Site: www.gatewaysbooksandtapes.com; www.retrosf.com (Retro Science Fiction imprint)
Key Personnel
Sr Ed & Intl Rts: Iven Lourie *E-mail:* ilourie@ oro.net
Founded: 1971
Trade & fine art book publisher. Categories include psychology, spirituality, metaphysics, Judaica, science fiction & limited editions.
ISBN Prefix(es): 978-0-89556
Number of titles published annually: 6 Print; 4 CD-ROM; 4 Audio
Total Titles: 35 Print; 8 CD-ROM; 300 Audio
Imprints: Artemis Books (2 titles); Consciousness Classics; Gateways Fine Art Series; Retro Science Fiction
Distributor for Cloister Recordings (audio & video tapes)

Gauthier Publications Inc
PO Box 806241, St Clair Shores, MI 48080
SAN: 857-2119
Tel: 313-458-7141 *Fax:* 586-279-1515
E-mail: info@gauthierpublications.com
Web Site: www.gauthierpublications.com

Key Personnel
CEO: Daniel J Gauthier *E-mail:* daniel@
gauthierpublications.com
Creative Dir: Elizabeth Gauthier
E-mail: elizabeth@gauthierpublications.com
Founded: 2008
Devoted to printing high quality literary work.
Our mission is simple, to introduce reading
early & help promote a lifetime love for the
written word by putting out captivating &
unique titles that are tailored to their audi-
ence. We are proud to say all of our books are
printed & bound in the US & our Hungry Goat
Press line is made with 100% post consumer
recycled paper because we think a good book
means more than an exciting plot-line. Distri-
bution also by Amazon.
ISBN Prefix(es): 978-0-9820812; 978-0-9833593
Number of titles published annually: 15 Print
Total Titles: 65 Print
Imprints: DragonFish Comics (graphic novels);
Frog Legs Ink (children's books); Hungry Goat
Press (young adult books)
Distribution Center: Follett School Solu-
tions Inc, 1340 Ridgeview Dr, McHenry,
IL 60050 *Tel:* 815-759-1700 *Toll Free
Tel:* 888-511-5114 (cust serv) *Fax:* 815-
759-9831 *Toll Free Fax:* 800-852-5458
E-mail: info@follettlearning.com *Web
Site:* www.follettlearning.com SAN: 169-1902
Diamond, 1966 Greenspring Dr, Suite 300, Timo-
nium, MD 21093 *Toll Free Tel:* 800-452-6642
Membership(s): American Booksellers Associa-
tion (ABA)

Gefen Books
c/o Storch, 255 Central Ave, B-206, Lawrence,
NY 11559
Tel: 516-593-1234 *Toll Free Tel:* 800-477-5257
Fax: 516-295-2739
E-mail: gefenny@gefenpublishing.com; info@
gefenpublishing.com
Web Site: www.gefenpublishing.com
Key Personnel
Contact: Maury Storch
Founded: 1981
General interest, mainly books from Israel. Spe-
cialize in Judaic interest, Israel, art, Holocaust
& Jewish history. Can supply any books pub-
lished in Israel +/or in the Hebrew language.
ISBN Prefix(es): 978-0-86343
Number of titles published annually: 25 Print
Total Titles: 425 Print; 400 Online; 400 E-Book
Subsidiaries: IsraBook
Divisions: Medical Publishing (Gefen)
Foreign Office(s): Gefen Publishing House Ltd,
6 Hatzvi St, 94386 Jerusalem, Israel *Tel:* (02)
538-0247 *Fax:* (02) 538-8423
Distributor for Bar Ilan; Magnes Press
Shipping Address: 11 Edison Place, Springfield,
NJ 07081
Warehouse: 11 Edison Place, Springfield, NJ
07081

Gem Guides Book Co
1155 W Ninth St, Upland, CA 91786
Tel: 626-855-1611 *Toll Free Tel:* 800-824-5118
(orders) *Fax:* 626-855-1610
E-mail: info@gemguidesbooks.com; sales@
gemguidesbooks.com (orders)
Web Site: www.gemguidesbooks.com
Key Personnel
Opers Mgr: Matt Warner
Ed: Nancy Fox
Off Mgr: Nannette Becerra
Sales: Michael Moran
Founded: 1965
Publisher & distributor of regional & specialty
trade books; rocks, minerals, crystals, Old
West, western & southwestern region & local
interests.
ISBN Prefix(es): 978-0-935182; 978-1-889786
Number of titles published annually: 7 Print

Total Titles: 45 Print
Imprints: Gembooks
Distributed by Nevada Publications
Distributor for Abedus Press; AdventureKEEN;
Aerolite Meteorites LLC; Ahhh Muse; Alpine
Views Publishing Co; American Travelers
Press; AMI-Ascension Mastery; APC Enter-
prise LLC; Arbordale Publishing; Aurora Press;
Bazic Products; Bellerophon Books; Bench-
mark Maps; Blossom Hill Books; Bobolink
Media Inc; Book Publishing Co; Borden Pub-
lishing; Bourget Bros; Brynmorgen Press;
Jasper Burns; Chronicle Books; Clear Creek
Publisher; CPFS CA Princeton Fulfillment Ser-
vice; Crabtree Publishing Co; Crystal Lotus;
Crystalis Institute Press; Diamond Dan Pub-
lications; DK/Penguin; Dover Publications
Inc; Educational Development; EMB Fulfill-
ment/Consignment; LJ Ettinger; F+W Media
Inc; FACETS; Firefly Books; Fossil News; Free
Wheel Publications; FunTreks Inc; Garden-
Guy.Com; Garret Metal Detectors; Gem Book
Publishers; The Gem Shop; Gitche Gumee
Agate & History Museum; Global Graph-
ics; Golden West Books; Good Karma Fac-
tory; Grand Canyon Association; Hachette
Book Group; Hancock House; HarperCollins
Publishers; Tom Harrison Maps; Hay House;
Le Hayes; Heaven & Earth LLC; Heyday;
Houghton Mifflin; Impactika; Independent
Publishers Group; Infobase Publishing; In-
gram Publisher Services; Ingram Publisher
Services/Two Rivers; Inner Traditions; Inter-
national Jewelry Publications; Journal Publica-
tions; Shelley Kaehr; KC Publications; Keene
Engineering; Konecky & Konecky; Leaning
Tree Tales LLC; Light Technology Publish-
ing; Llewellyn Worldwide; Majestic Press;
Maturango Museum; Mineral Land Publica-
tions; Mojave River Valley Museum; Mountain
Press Publishing; The Mountaineers Books;
MPS; Museon Publishing; National Book
Network; National Historic Route 66 Federa-
tion; Natural Inspirations/Brush Creek; Nature
Trails Press; Naturegraph; Nevada Publica-
tions; New Era Productions; Northwest Dis-
tributors LLC; W W Norton & Company Inc;
Park Partners Inc; Penguin Random House;
Pentrex; Pinyon Publishing; Quarto Pub-
lishing Group/Hachette Book Group; Quest
Publishing; Quick Reference Publishing Inc;
Chris Ralph; Katrina Raphaell; Reading With
Peaches LLC; Real Adventure Publishing;
Red Wheel/Weiser/Conari; Ronald Ringsrud
Co; Riverbend Publishing; Ryland Peters &
Small; San Gabriel Mountains Regional Con-
servancy; Schiffer Publishing Ltd; Scholastic;
Scholastic Library Publishing; Sierra Outdoor
Products; Edition du Signe; Mark Silva; Simon
& Schuster; Gibbs Smith; Sounds True Inc;
Spotted Dog Press; Sterling Publishing Co Inc;
Leighton Stone; Storey Publishing LLC; Delos
Toole Gold Books; Track & Trail Publications;
Treasure Chest Books; Trees Company Press;
TVL VIDEO; University of Nebraska; Water-
ford Press; Wesanne Publications; Ronald S
Wielgus; WolfWalker Collection
Membership(s): American Booksellers Associa-
tion (ABA); Independent Book Publishers As-
sociation (IBPA)

GemStone Press
Imprint of Turner Publishing Co
4507 Charlotte Ave, Suite 100, Nashville, TN
37209
SAN: 134-5621
Tel: 615-255-BOOK (255-2665) *Fax:* 615-255-
5081
E-mail: marketing@turnerpublishing.com
Web Site: gemstonepress.com; www.
turnerpublishing.com

Key Personnel
Pres & Publr, Turner Publishing Co: Todd Bot-
torff
Founded: 1987
Books on buying, enjoying, identifying & selling
jewelry & gems for the consumer, collector,
hobbyist, investor & jewelry trade.
ISBN Prefix(es): 978-0-943763
Number of titles published annually: 5 Print; 1 E-
Book
Total Titles: 15 Print

§Genealogical Publishing Co
Subsidiary of Genealogical.com
3600 Clipper Mill Rd, Suite 229, Baltimore, MD
21211
Tel: 410-837-8271 *Toll Free Tel:* 800-296-6687
Fax: 410-752-8492 *Toll Free Fax:* 800-599-
9561
E-mail: info@genealogical.com; web@
genealogical.com
Web Site: www.genealogical.com
Key Personnel
VP & Ed-in-Chief: Michael Tepper
E-mail: mtepper@genealogical.com
Mktg Dir: Joe Garonzik *E-mail:* jgaronzi@
genealogical.com
Data Processing Mgr: Roger Sherr
E-mail: rsherr@genealogical.com
Founded: 1959
Genealogy, local history, immigration history &
source records. Products are nonreturnable, un-
less mis-shipped or damaged in shipment.
ISBN Prefix(es): 978-0-8063
Number of titles published annually: 50 Print; 1
CD-ROM; 30 E-Book
Total Titles: 2,000 Print; 84 CD-ROM; 100 On-
line; 800 E-Book
Subsidiaries: Clearfield Co Inc
See separate listing for:
Clearfield Co Inc

§Genesis Press Inc
PO Box 101, Columbus, MS 39701
Toll Free Tel: 888-463-4461 (orders only)
Key Personnel
Pres & Co-Founder: Wilbur O Colom
Off Mgr: Diane Blair
Founded: 1993
Privately owned African-American book pub-
lisher.
ISBN Prefix(es): 978-1-885478; 978-1-58571
Number of titles published annually: 26 Print
Total Titles: 160 Print
Imprints: Black Coral; Indigo; Indigo Love Spec-
trum; Indigo Vibe; Mount Blue; Obsidian; Sage
Membership(s): Association of American Publish-
ers (AAP)

Geological Society of America (GSA)
3300 Penrose Place, Boulder, CO 80301-1806
SAN: 201-5978
Mailing Address: PO Box 9140, Boulder, CO
80301-9140
Tel: 303-357-1000 *Fax:* 303-357-1070
E-mail: pubs@geosociety.org (prodn); editing@
geosociety.org (edit)
Web Site: www.geosociety.org
Key Personnel
Exec Dir: Vicki McConnell *E-mail:* vmcconnell@
geosociety.org
Ad Mgr: Ann H Crawford *Tel:* 303-357-1053
E-mail: acrawford@geosociety.org
Founded: 1888
General earth sciences, cover such areas as geol-
ogy, economic geology, engineering geology,
geochemistry, geomorphology, marine geology,
mineralogy, paleontology, petrology, seismol-
ogy, solid earth geophysics, structural geology,
tectonics & environmental geology.
ISBN Prefix(es): 978-0-8137
Number of titles published annually: 9 Print

Total Titles: 200 Print
Branch Office(s)
1200 New York Ave NW, Suite 400, Washington, DC 20005, Dir, Geoscience Policy: Kasey White *Tel:* 202-669-0466 *E-mail:* kwhite@geosociety.org
Foreign Rep(s): Geological Society of London (UK)

§GeoLytics Inc
3322 Rte 22, Suite 806, Branchburg, NJ 08876
Mailing Address: PO Box 5336, East Brunswick, NJ 08876
Tel: 908-707-1505 *Toll Free Tel:* 800-577-6717
   Fax: 908-707-1595
E-mail: support@geolytics.com; questions@geolytics.com
Web Site: www.geolytics.com
Key Personnel
Mktg Dir: Katia Segre Cohen
Founded: 1996
Provider of census, demographic & geographic data for academic & business researchers.
ISBN Prefix(es): 978-1-892445
Number of titles published annually: 7 CD-ROM; 7 Online
Total Titles: 55 CD-ROM; 55 Online

Georgetown University Press
3520 Prospect St NW, Suite 140, Washington, DC 20007
Tel: 202-687-5889 (busn) *Fax:* 202-687-6340 (edit)
E-mail: gupress@georgetown.edu
Web Site: press.georgetown.edu
Key Personnel
Dir: Alfred Bertrand *Tel:* 202-687-5912
   E-mail: ab3463@georgetown.edu
Mktg & Sales Dir: Virginia Veiga Bryant
   Tel: 202-687-9856 *E-mail:* vvb6@georgetown.edu
Asst Dir of Press & Busn Mgr: Ioan Suciu
   Tel: 202-687-5641 *E-mail:* suciui@georgetown.edu
Sr Acqs Ed & Intl Aff, Public Policy: Donald Jacobs *Tel:* 202-687-5218 *E-mail:* dpj5@georgetown.edu
Edit Designer & Prodn Mgr: Glenn Saltzman
   Tel: 202-687-6251 *E-mail:* gls43@georgetown.edu
Founded: 1964
Bioethics; international affairs & human rights; languages & linguistics; political science, public policy & public management; religion & ethics.
ISBN Prefix(es): 978-0-87840; 978-1-58901; 978-1-62616
Number of titles published annually: 40 Print; 2 Audio
Total Titles: 500 Print; 9 Audio
Foreign Rep(s): Apex Knowledge Sdn Bhd (Simon Tay) (Brunei, Malaysia); Avicenna Partnership Ltd (Middle East); Booknet Co Ltd (Ms Suphaluck Sattabuz) (Cambodia, Laos, Myanmar, Thailand, Vietnam); ChoiceTEXTS (Asia) Pte Ltd (Philip Ang) (Indonesia, Singapore); Columbia University Sales Consortium (Catherine Hobbs) (Canada); Durnell Marketing Ltd (Andrew Durnell) (Continental Europe); Footprint Books (Australia, New Zealand); iCaves Ltd (Eddy Lam) (China, Hong Kong, Macau); iGroup (Asia Pacific) Ltd (Estela Suyat) (Philippines); iGroup Korea (IDC Asia) (Mr DJ Kim) (Korea); KW Publishers Pvt Ltd (Bangladesh, Bhutan, India, Nepal); MHM Ltd (Mark Gresham) (Japan); The Oxford Publicity Partnership Ltd (Matthew Surzyn) (UK exc Ireland); Taiwan Publisher Marketing Service Ltd (George Liu) (Taiwan)
Orders to: HFS, PO Box 50370, Baltimore, MD 21211-4370 *Tel:* 410-516-6965 *Toll Free Tel:* 800-537-5487 *Fax:* 410-516-6998 *E-mail:* hfscustserv@press.jhu.edu; NBN International Business Center, 10 Thornbury Rd, Plymouth PL6 7PP, United Kingdom (Africa, Europe, Middle East & UK) *Tel:* (01752) 202301 *Fax:* (01752) 202333 *E-mail:* orders@nbninternational.com *Web Site:* distribution.nbni.co.uk
Returns: HFS, c/o Maple Logistics Solutions, Lebanon Distribution Ctr, 704 Legionaire Dr, Fredericksburg, PA 17026
Warehouse: Maple Logistics Solutions, Lebanon Distribution Ctr, 704 Legionaire Dr, Fredericksburg, PA 17026
Distribution Center: Brunswick Books, 20 Maud St, Suite 303, Toronto, ON M5V 2M5, Canada *Tel:* 416-703-3598 *Fax:* 416-703-6561 *E-mail:* orders@brunswickbooks.ca *Web Site:* www.brunswickbooks.ca

§Gestalt Journal Press
PO Box 278, Gouldsboro, ME 04607-0278
Tel: 207-404-9954 *Fax:* 207-510-4889
E-mail: press@gestalt.org
Web Site: gestalt.org
Founded: 1975
Mental health, gestalt therapy specifically.
ISBN Prefix(es): 978-0-939266
Number of titles published annually: 5 Print; 11 E-Book
Total Titles: 41 Print; 5 E-Book; 6 Audio

§Getty Publications
1200 Getty Center Dr, Suite 500, Los Angeles, CA 90049-1682
SAN: 208-2276
Tel: 310-440-7365 *Toll Free Tel:* 800-223-3431 (orders) *Fax:* 310-440-7758
E-mail: pubsinfo@getty.edu
Web Site: www.getty.edu/publications
Key Personnel
Publr: Kara Kirk *Tel:* 310-440-6066
   E-mail: kkirk@getty.edu
Assoc Publr: Maureen Winter *Tel:* 310-440-6117
   E-mail: mwinter@getty.edu
Ed-in-Chief: Karen Levine *Tel:* 310-440-6525
   E-mail: klevine@getty.edu
Gen Mgr: Carolyn Simmons *Tel:* 310-440-7130
   E-mail: csimmons@getty.edu
Rts Mgr: Leslie Rollins *Tel:* 310-440-7102
   E-mail: lrollins@getty.edu
Founded: 1982
Produces a wide variety of books in the fields of art, photography, archaeology, architecture, conservation & the humanities for both general & specialized audiences. These award-winning publications complement & often result from the work of the J Paul Getty Museum, the Getty Conservation Institute & the Getty Research Institute. Publications include illustrated exhibition catalogues, illustrated works on single artists & art history, works on cultural history, scholarly monographs, critical editions of translated works, comprehensive studies of the Getty's collections, educational books to interest children of all ages in art & gift books.
ISBN Prefix(es): 978-0-89236; 978-1-60606
Number of titles published annually: 50 Print; 2 Online; 3 E-Book
Total Titles: 500 Print; 5 Online; 5 E-Book
Distributed by University of Chicago Press (US only)
Foreign Rep(s): Canadian Manda Group (Canada); Orca Book Services (Europe, UK); Roundhouse Group (Europe, UK)
Distribution Center: Chicago Distribution Center, 11030 S Langley Ave, Chicago, IL 60628 *Tel:* 773-702-7000 *Toll Free Tel:* 800-621-2736 *Fax:* 773-702-7212 *Toll Free Fax:* 800-621-8476 *E-mail:* custserv@press.uchicago.edu *Web Site:* www.press.uchicago.edu
Membership(s): Association of American Publishers (AAP); Association of University Presses (AUPresses); CAA; International Association of Museum Publishers (IAMP)

GIA Publications Inc
7404 S Mason Ave, Chicago, IL 60638
Tel: 708-496-3800 *Toll Free Tel:* 800-GIA-1358 (442-1358) *Fax:* 708-496-3828
E-mail: custserv@giamusic.com
Web Site: www.giamusic.com
Key Personnel
COO & Pres: Alec Harris *E-mail:* alech@giamusic.com
Founded: 1941
Publish sacred choral music, hymnals, books, recordings & music education materials.
ISBN Prefix(es): 978-0-941050; 978-1-57999
Number of titles published annually: 200 Print
Total Titles: 6,000 Print; 250 Audio

§Gibbs Smith Publisher
1877 E Gentile St, Layton, UT 84041
Mailing Address: PO Box 667, Layton, UT 84041-0667 SAN: 201-9906
Tel: 801-544-9800 *Toll Free Tel:* 800-748-5439; 800-835-4993 (orders) *Fax:* 801-544-5582 *Toll Free Fax:* 800-213-3023 (orders only)
E-mail: info@gibbs-smith.com; tradeorders@gibbs-smith.com
Web Site: www.gibbs-smith.com
Key Personnel
CEO: Brad Farmer *E-mail:* brad.farmer@gibbs-smith.com
Dir, Trade Sales: Sarah Rucker *E-mail:* sarah.rucker@gibbs-smith.com
Founded: 1969
ISBN Prefix(es): 978-0-87905; 978-1-58685
Number of titles published annually: 80 Print; 50 Online; 80 E-Book
Total Titles: 350 Print; 200 Online; 350 E-Book
Imprints: Ancient City Press; Wyrick & Co
Distributor for Angel City Press
Foreign Rep(s): Jonathan Ball & Nicky Stubbs (South Africa); Gilles Fauveau (Japan, Korea); Jaime Gregorio (Philippines); Penguin Books India Pvt Ltd (Sharad Mohan) (Bangladesh, India, Maldives, Nepal, Pakistan, Sri Lanka); Peribo (Australia, New Zealand); Perseus Book Group UK (Europe exc UK); Perseus International (Edison Garcia) (Caribbean, Latin America, Middle East, North Africa, Singapore); Perseus International (Suk Lee) (Malaysia, Singapore); June Poonpanich (Cambodia, Indonesia, Laos, Thailand, Vietnam); Publishers Group UK (UK); Raincoast Books (Canada); Wei Zhao (China, Hong Kong, Taiwan)
Returns: 570 N Sportsplex Dr, Kaysville, UT 84037
Shipping Address: 570 N Sportsplex Dr, Kaysville, UT 84037
Distribution Center: Baker & Taylor Global Publishers Services (GPS), 2550 W Tyvola Rd, Suite 300, Charlotte, NC 28217 (worldwide exc Australia, CN & UK) *Tel:* 704-998-3100 *Toll Free Tel:* 800-775-1800 *E-mail:* gps@baker-taylor.com *Web Site:* www.baker-taylor.com
Membership(s): Association of American Publishers (AAP)

Gifted Education Press
10201 Yuma Ct, Manassas, VA 20109
Tel: 703-369-5017
Web Site: www.giftededpress.com
Key Personnel
Publr & Dir: Maurice D Fisher
   E-mail: mfisher345@comcast.net
Founded: 1981
Books, quarterly newsletter, *Gifted Education News-Page* published 6 times a year, teaching guides & supplemental materials for students. Education of gifted children.
ISBN Prefix(es): 978-0-910609
Number of titles published annually: 10 Print
Total Titles: 80 Print

Gifted Unlimited LLC
Formerly Great Potential Press Inc
12340 US Hwy 42, No 453, Goshen, KY 40026
Tel: 502-715-6306
E-mail: info@giftedunlimitedllc.com; orders@
giftedunlimitedllc.com
Web Site: www.giftedunlimitedllc.com
Founded: 1982
Educational guide books & books for parents
& adults relating to social/emotional needs &
other characteristics of gifted children & adults.
ISBN Prefix(es): 978-0-910707
Number of titles published annually: 5 Print
Total Titles: 58 Print; 4 CD-ROM; 1 Audio
Membership(s): Independent Book Publishers Association (IBPA)

Gingko Press Inc
1321 Fifth St, Berkeley, CA 94710
Tel: 510-898-1195 *Fax:* 510-898-1196
E-mail: books@gingkopress.com
Web Site: www.gingkopress.com
Key Personnel
VP & Publr: David Lopes *E-mail:* david@
gingkopress.com
VP, Sales & Mktg: Rick Markell *E-mail:* rick@
gingkopress.com
Founded: 1991
Publisher & distributor.
ISBN Prefix(es): 978-1-58423; 978-1-934471
Number of titles published annually: 100 Print; 1
E-Book
Total Titles: 450 Print; 2 E-Book
Imprints: Rebel Arts
Foreign Office(s): Gingko Press Verlags GmbH,
Schulterblatt 58, 20357 Hamburg, Germany,
Contact: Anika Heusermann *Tel:* (040) 29 14
25 *Fax:* (040) 29 10 55 *E-mail:* gingkopress@
t-online.de
Distributor for All Rights Reserved Ltd;
Archimap; Art Power; Basheer; Choi's Gallery;
CYPI; Gingko Press; Rebel Arts; Sandu Publications; Sendpoints Books Co Ltd; Upper Playground; Victionary; Wax Facts Press; Zero+
Publishing
Distribution Center: Ingram Publisher Services,
One Ingram Blvd, La Vergne, TN 37086
Tel: 615-793-5000 *Toll Free Tel:* 866-400-5351
(orders) *E-mail:* ips@ingramcontent.com *Web
Site:* www.ingramcontent.com

Gival Press
Imprint of Gival Press LLC
5200 N First St, Arlington, VA 22203
Mailing Address: PO Box 3812, Arlington, VA
22203 SAN: 852-9787
Tel: 703-351-0079 *Fax:* 703-351-0079 (call first)
E-mail: givalpress@yahoo.com
Web Site: www.givalpress.com
Key Personnel
Publr & Ed: Robert L Giron
Founded: 1998
Small, independent literary press.
ISBN Prefix(es): 978-1-928589
Number of titles published annually: 3 Print; 3 E-Book
Total Titles: 80 Print; 40 E-Book
Distribution Center: Follett Higher Education
Group, 3 Westbrook Corporate Ctr, Suite 200,
Westchester, IL 60154 *Tel:* 708-884-0000 *Toll
Free Tel:* 800-FOLLETT (365-5388) *Web
Site:* www.follett.com/higher-ed
Membership(s): The Association of Publishers for
Special Sales (APSS); Community of Literary
Magazines & Presses (CLMP); Independent
Book Publishers Association (IBPA); Publishing Triangle

§Peter Glenn Publications
Division of Blount Communications Corp
306 NE Second St, 2nd fl, Delray Beach, FL
33483

Web Site: pgdirect.com
Key Personnel
Publr & CEO: Gregory James Blount
E-mail: gregjames@pgdirect.com
Dir: L Chip Brill; Umberto Guido, III
Ed: Todd Heustess
Founded: 1956
Directories for the world of advertising, TV &
film publicity; directories & how-to books for
performing arts, fashion & modeling industry.
ISBN Prefix(es): 978-0-87314
Number of titles published annually: 9 Print
Total Titles: 9 Print; 6 E-Book

Glitterati Editions
311 W 43 St, 12th fl, New York, NY 10036
Tel: 646-584-6382 *Fax:* 646-607-4433
E-mail: media@glitteratieditions.com
Web Site: glitteratieditions.com
Key Personnel
Pres & CEO: Marta Hallett *E-mail:* mhallett@
glitteratiincorporated.com
Assoc Publr: Brandon Schultz *E-mail:* bschultz@
glitteratiincorporated.com
Independent producer & publisher of distinctive
illustrated books, ancillary gift products &
electronic media for domestic & international
markets.
ISBN Prefix(es): 978-0-9721152; 978-0-9765851;
978-0-9777531; 978-0-9793384; 978-0-
9801557; 978-0-9822669; 978-0-9823412; 978-
0-9823799; 978-0-9832702; 978-0-9851696;
978-0-9881745; 978-0-9891704; 978-0-
9913419; 978-0-9905320; 978-0-9862500; 978-
0-9962930; 978-1-943876; 978-0-9903808
Number of titles published annually: 9 Print
Total Titles: 58 Print; 1 Audio
Foreign Office(s): One Rona Rd, London
NW3 2HY, United Kingdom, Edit: Chris
Fagg *Tel:* (020) 7267 8339 *E-mail:* cfagg@
glitteratiincorporated.com
Distribution Center: Baker & Taylor Global Publishers Services (GPS)

Global Authors Publications (GAP)
38 Bluegrass, Middleberg, FL 32068
Tel: 904-425-1608
E-mail: gapbook@yahoo.com
Web Site: www.globalauthorspublications.com
Key Personnel
Co-Owner & Publr: Kathleen Walls
Co-Owner: Tammy C McMullen
Founded: 2003
Offer complete subsidy publishing services &
consider any genre except pornography or textbooks. Books must be at least 48 pages & not
more than 700. We have set a literary standard
with all the books we have published already
& we do not plan to change our reputation.
We won't publish everything that is offered us.
Provide an affordable alternative to traditional
publishing.
This publisher has indicated that 100% of their
product line is author subsidized.
ISBN Prefix(es): 978-0-97
Number of titles published annually: 6 Print
Total Titles: 30 Print

§Global Publishing, Sales & Distribution
135 Third St, Suite 150, San Rafael, CA 94901
Tel: 415-456-2934 *Fax:* 415-456-4124
E-mail: info@globalpsd.com
Web Site: www.globalpsd.com
Key Personnel
Publr: Adrianne Casey *E-mail:* adrianne@
globalpsd.com; Steven Goff *E-mail:* steven@
globalpsd.com
ISBN Prefix(es): 978-0-9819942
Number of titles published annually: 50 Print; 50
CD-ROM; 100 Online
Total Titles: 50 Print; 50 CD-ROM; 100 Online

Branch Office(s)
244 Fifth Ave, Suite 2464, New York, NY 10001
Tel: 212-627-1400 *Toll Free Fax:* 866-729-2725
16510 203 Place NE, Woodinville, WA 98077
Tel: 425-354-3690 *Fax:* 425-354-3664
Foreign Office(s): 8 Commercial Tower, 30/F,
Unit 06-07, 8 Sun Yip St, Chai Wan, Hong
Kong *Tel:* 3576 3239 *Fax:* 3184 0728
Via Meucci 24, 37036 San Martino Buon
Albergo, Verona, Italy *Tel:* (045) 994855
Fax: (045) 994746

Global Training Center Inc
550 S Mesa Hills Dr, Suite E4, El Paso, TX
79912
Mailing Address: PO Box 221977, El Paso, TX
79913
Tel: 915-534-7900 *Toll Free Tel:* 800-860-5030
Fax: 915-534-7903
E-mail: contact@globaltrainingcenter.com
Web Site: www.globaltrainingcenter.com
Key Personnel
Pres: Elsa Solorzano
Founded: 1992
Training seminar/workshops covering International Documentation, NAFTA, Importing, etc.
ISBN Prefix(es): 978-1-891249
Number of titles published annually: 23 Print
Total Titles: 23 Print

The Globe Pequot Press
Division of Rowman & Littlefield Publishing
Group
246 Goose Lane, Guilford, CT 06437
SAN: 201-9892
Tel: 203-458-4500 *Toll Free Tel:* 800-243-0495
(orders only); 888-249-7586 (cust serv)
Fax: 203-458-4601 *Toll Free Fax:* 800-820-
2329 (orders & cust serv)
E-mail: editorial@globepequot.com; info@
rowman.com; orders@rowman.com
Web Site: rowman.com
Key Personnel
Edit Dir, TwoDot Books: Erin Turner *Tel:* 406-
442-6708 *E-mail:* eturner@rowman.com
Mgr, Dist Busn: Andrea Jacobs *Tel:* 203-458-
4552 *E-mail:* ajacobs@rowman.com
Founded: 1947
Travel guidebooks, regional books, sports, how-to,
outdoor recreation, personal finance, self-help,
sports, cooking, entertaining, military history,
fishing, hunting, gift books.
ISBN Prefix(es): 978-0-937959; 978-1-56044;
978-1-57380; 978-1-57540; 978-1-882997;
978-0-87842; 978-0-87106; 978-0-7627; 978-
0-89933; 978-0-934641; 978-1-56440; 978-0-
912367; 978-0-933469; 978-0-934802; 978-
0-934318; 978-1-57034; 978-1-58592; 978-1-
901970 (Sawday)
Number of titles published annually: 500 Print;
500 E-Book
Total Titles: 2,800 Print; 1,000 E-Book
Imprints: Applause Theatre & Cinema Books;
Backbeat Books; Cheap Bastards; Down East
Books; Falcon®; Globe Pequot; Gooseberry
Patch; GPP® Travel; The Lyons Press; Pineapple Press; Prometheus Books; Taylor Trade;
TwoDot®; Western Horseman
Foreign Rep(s): Faradawn (South Africa); Pansing
(Singapore); Les Petriw (Canada); Woodslane
NZ Ltd (New Zealand); Woodslane Pty Ltd
(Australia)
Returns: National Book Network (NBN), 15200
NBN Way, Blue Ridge Summit, PA 17214
Warehouse: National Book Network (NBN),
15200 NBN Way, Blue Ridge Summit, PA
17214
Distribution Center: National Book Network
(NBN), 15200 NBN Way, Blue Ridge Summit,
PA 17214
Membership(s): American Booksellers Association (ABA); Association of American Publishers (AAP); Book Industry Study Group

(BISG); New England Independent Booksellers Association (NEIBA)
See separate listing for:
Applause Theatre & Cinema Books
Backbeat Books
The Lyons Press
Pineapple Press
Prometheus Books

David R Godine Inc
15 Court Sq, Suite 320, Boston, MA 02108-2536
SAN: 213-4381
Tel: 617-451-9600 *Fax:* 617-350-0250
E-mail: info@godine.com
Web Site: www.godine.com
Key Personnel
Pres & Publr: David R Godine
Publr, Black Sparrow: Chelsea Bingham
Mng Dir: David Allender
Prodn & Design Mgr: Michael Babcock
Founded: 1970
Fiction & nonfiction, history, biography, typography, art & photography, poetry, horticulture, Americana, cooking, regional, mysteries, juveniles.
ISBN Prefix(es): 978-0-87923; 978-1-56792; 978-0-87685; 978-1-57423
Number of titles published annually: 40 Print
Total Titles: 500 Print
Imprints: Black Sparrow; David R Godine, Publisher; Imago Mundi; Nonpareil Books; Pocket Paragons; Verba Mundi
Sales Office(s): 426 Nutting Rd, PO Box 450, Jaffrey, NH 03452
Foreign Rep(s): Big Apple Agency Inc (Kelly Chang) (Taiwan); Sandra Bruna Agency (Spain); The English Agency (Hamish Macaskill) (Japan); Paul & Peter Fritz Agency (Peter Fritz) (Switzerland); Graal Literary Agency (Magda Koceba) (Poland); Korea Copyright Center (Jae-Yeon Ryu) (Korea); Agence Michelle Lapautre (France); Natoli Stefan & Oliva Agenzia (Roberta Oliva) (Italy); Agencia Literara SUN (Crina Chitan) (Romania)
Foreign Rights: Sandra Bruna Agency (Spain); The English Agency (Japan); Paul & Peter Fritz (Germany); Korea Copyright Center (Korea); Agence Michelle Lapautre (Catherine Lapautre) (France); Natoli, Stefan & Oliva (Italy)
Orders to: 426 Nutting Rd, PO Box 450, Jaffrey, NH 03452 *Toll Free Tel:* 800-344-4771 *Toll Free Fax:* 800-226-0934 *E-mail:* order@godine.com
Returns: 426 Nutting Rd, PO Box 450, Jaffrey, NH 03452 *Toll Free Tel:* 800-344-4771 *Toll Free Fax:* 800-226-0934
Warehouse: 426 Nutting Rd, PO Box 450, Jaffrey, NH 03452 *Tel:* 603-532-4100 *Toll Free Tel:* 800-344-4771 *Fax:* 603-532-5940 *Toll Free Fax:* 800-226-0934 *E-mail:* order@godine.com
Distribution Center: Two Rivers Distribution, an Ingram brand, Ingram Content Group LLC, One Ingram Blvd, La Vergne, TN 37086 *Toll Free Tel:* 866-400-5351 *E-mail:* ips@ingramcontent.com
Membership(s): Association of American Publishers (AAP)

Golden West Cookbooks
Division of American Traveler Press
5738 N Central Ave, Phoenix, AZ 85012-1316
Tel: 602-234-1574 *Toll Free Tel:* 800-521-9221
Fax: 602-234-3062
E-mail: info@americantravelerpress.com
Web Site: www.americantravelerpress.com
Key Personnel
Gen Mgr: Bill Fessler
Founded: 1973
Cookbooks & nonfiction books on the Southwest & the Rocky Mountains.
ISBN Prefix(es): 978-0-914846; 978-1-885590
Number of titles published annually: 5 Print

Total Titles: 150 Print
Membership(s): Publishers Association of the West (PubWest)

Goodheart-Willcox Publisher
18604 W Creek Dr, Tinley Park, IL 60477-6243
SAN: 203-4387
Tel: 708-687-5000 *Toll Free Tel:* 800-323-0440 *Toll Free Fax:* 888-409-3900
E-mail: custserv@g-w.com; orders@g-w.com
Web Site: www.g-w.com
Key Personnel
Pres & CEO: John F Flanagan
VP, Admin & Treas: Robert Kelly
VP, Sales & Mktg: Todd Scheffers
Graphic Designer: Mary Lynn Griffin *Tel:* 708-623-1813 *E-mail:* mgriffin@g-w.com
Founded: 1921
Industrial technical; family & consumer sciences; career; health & health sciences; agriculture textbooks.
ISBN Prefix(es): 978-0-87006; 978-1-56637; 978-1-59070; 978-1-60525; 978-1-63126
Number of titles published annually: 50 Print
Total Titles: 150 Print; 100 CD-ROM; 150 Online
Foreign Rep(s): Baker & Taylor International (Europe)

Goose River Press
3400 Friendship Rd, Waldoboro, ME 04572-6337
Tel: 207-832-6665
E-mail: gooseriverpress@gmail.com
Web Site: gooseriverpress.com
Key Personnel
Owner & Ed: Deborah J Benner
Acct Exec: Meredith K Sanders
E-mail: mksanders@roadrunner.com
Founded: 1999
Traditional publisher, but also offers self-publishing services to the authors of books that do not meet literary quality or who would prefer to self-publish.
This publisher has indicated that 25% of their product line is author subsidized.
ISBN Prefix(es): 978-1-930648; 978-1-59713
Number of titles published annually: 15 Print; 10 E-Book
Total Titles: 100 Print; 30 E-Book
Distribution Center: Ingram Content Group, 1246 Heil Quaker Blvd, La Vergne, TN 37086, Contact: Jim Patterson *Tel:* 615-213-4475 *Fax:* 615-213-4725 *E-mail:* jim.patterson@lightningsource.com
Membership(s): Maine Writers & Publishers Alliance (MWPA)

Goosebottom Books
Imprint of Goosebottom Books LLC
PO Box 150764, San Rafael, CA 94915-0764
SAN: 859-8029
Tel: 415-717-6300
E-mail: info@goosebottombooks.com
Web Site: goosebottombooks.com
Key Personnel
Publr: Pamela Livingston *E-mail:* mamagoose@goosebottombooks.com
Founded: 2010
A small press dedicated to education of the histories of under represented persons via fun nonfiction.
ISBN Prefix(es): 978-0-9845098 (Real Princesses series); 978-0-9834256 (Dastardly Dames series); 978-1-937463 (all others)
Number of titles published annually: 6 Print; 6 Online; 6 E-Book; 4 Audio
Total Titles: 19 Print; 19 Online; 19 E-Book; 17 Audio
Imprints: Golden Egg Press; Gosling Press
Foreign Rights: Perseus (worldwide)
Orders to: Publishers Group West (PGW), 1700 Fourth St, Berkeley, CA 94710 *Toll Free Tel:* 800-788-3123 *Toll Free Fax:* 800-351-5073

E-mail: orderentry@perseusbooks.com *Web Site:* www.pgw.com
Distribution Center: Publishers Group West (PGW), 1700 Fourth St, Berkeley, CA 94710 *Toll Free Tel:* 800-788-3123 *Toll Free Fax:* 800-351-5073 *E-mail:* orderentry@perseusbooks.com *Web Site:* pgw.com
Membership(s): The Children's Book Council (CBC)

Gorgias Press LLC
PO Box 6939, Piscataway, NJ 08854-6939
Tel: 732-885-8900 *Fax:* 732-885-8908
E-mail: helpdesk@gorgiaspress.com
Web Site: www.gorgiaspress.com
Key Personnel
Co-Founder & Pres: George Anton Kiraz, PhD
Co-Founder & VP: Christine Kiraz, PhD
Acqs Ed: Melonie Schmierer-Lee, PhD
Founded: 2001
Academic publishers of specialty books; provides for author/small publisher's digitization & publishing services needs.
ISBN Prefix(es): 978-1-59333; 978-0-9713097; 978-0-9715986; 978-1-931956; 978-1-60724
Number of titles published annually: 75 Print
Total Titles: 3,000 Print
Distributor for Yeshiva University Museum Press
Membership(s): Independent Book Publishers Association (IBPA)

Gospel Publishing House
Division of General Council of the Assemblies of God
1445 Boonville Ave, Springfield, MO 65802
SAN: 206-8826
Tel: 417-862-2781; 417-831-8000 (outside US) *Toll Free Tel:* 800-641-4310 *Fax:* 417-862-5881 *Toll Free Fax:* 800-328-0294
E-mail: custsrvorders@ag.org
Web Site: www.gospelpublishing.com
Founded: 1914
Religion (Assemblies of God); sign language textbooks & curricular materials.
ISBN Prefix(es): 978-0-88243
Number of titles published annually: 6 Print
Total Titles: 250 Print
Imprints: Logion Press; My Healthy Church; Radiant Life Curriculum
Distribution Center: Baker & Taylor Publisher Services, 30 Amberwood Pkwy, Ashland, OH 44805 *Tel:* 567-215-0030 *Toll Free Tel:* 888-814-0208 *E-mail:* info@btpubservices.com *Web Site:* www.btpubservices.com

GPH, see Gospel Publishing House

The Graduate Group/Booksellers
86 Norwood Rd, West Hartford, CT 06117-2236
Mailing Address: PO Box 370351, West Hartford, CT 06137-0351
Tel: 860-233-2330
E-mail: graduategroup@hotmail.com
Web Site: www.graduategroup.com
Key Personnel
Partner: Mara Whitman
Lib Sales Dir: Robert Whitman *Tel:* 860-232-3100
Founded: 1964
Publish career oriented reference books & self-help books for libraries, career & placement offices in the US & abroad, law enforcement, career series, exam preparation.
ISBN Prefix(es): 978-0-938609
Number of titles published annually: 20 Print; 1 Online
Total Titles: 100 Print; 2 Online

§Grand & Archer Publishing
463 Coyote, Cathedral City, CA 92234
Tel: 323-493-2785
E-mail: grandandarcher@gmail.com

Key Personnel
Owner & CEO: Will Tom Shoaff
Chief Content Offr: Max Visconti
Founded: 2016
Boutique publishing agency.
ISBN Prefix(es): 978-1-929730
Number of titles published annually: 3 Print; 5 E-Book; 3 Audio
Total Titles: 3 Print
Membership(s): Independent Book Publishers Association (IBPA)

Grand Central Publishing
Division of Hachette Book Group
1290 Avenue of the Americas, New York, NY 10104
Tel: 212-364-1100
Web Site: www.hachettebookgroup.com
Key Personnel
SVP & Publr: Ben Sevier
VP, Ed-in-Chief: Karen Kosztolnyik
Edit, Grand Central Publishing/VP & Publr, Twelve: Sean Desmond
VP, Digital & Pbk Publr: Beth de Guzman
VP, Exec Ed, Grand Central Publishing: Gretchen Young
VP, Assoc Publr & Mktg Dir, Grand Central Publishing & Twelve: Brian McLendon
Exec Ed, Ed-in-Chief, Forever & Forever Yours: Amy Pierpont
VP, Exec Dir, Publicity, Grand Central Publishing: Matthew Ballast
Sr Publicity Dir: Jimmy Franco
Sr Dir, HBG Multicultural Publicity: Linda Duggins
Publicity Dir, Twelve: Paul Samuelson
Publicity & Mktg Dir, Forever & Forever Yours: Jodi Rosoff
Assoc Dir, Publicity (best-selling fiction brand authors): Andy Dodds
Assoc Publicist: Jordan Rubinstein
Dir, Mktg & Campaign Strategy: Amanda Pritzker
Dir, Digital Mktg & Content Strategy: Andrew Duncan
Asst Dir, Ad & Promos: Alexis Gilbert
Creative Dir: Albert Tang
Exec Art Dir: Flamur Tonuzi
Founded: 1961
Hardcover, trade paperback & mass market paperback, reprint & original, fiction & nonfiction, audiobooks. Unsol/unagented mss not accepted.
ISBN Prefix(es): 978-0-445; 978-0-446; 978-0-89296
Number of titles published annually: 360 Print
Total Titles: 3,392 Print
Imprints: Forever; Forever Yours; goop press; Twelve; Vision
Foreign Rights: Antonella Antonelli Agenzia (Italy); Bardon Far Eastern Agents (Taiwan); Graal Literary Agency (Poland); Imprima Korea Agency (Korea); Katai & Bolza Literary Agents (Hungary); Simona Kessler International Copyright Agency Ltd (Romania); La Nouvelle Agence (France); Andrew Nurnberg Associates Ltd (Baltic States, Bulgaria, Mainland China, Russia); OA Literary Agency (Greece); Kristin Olson Literary Agency SRO (Czechia, Slovakia); Pikarski Agency (Israel); Prava i prevodi (Croatia, Slovenia); RDC Agencia Literaria (Brazil, Latin America, Spain); Sane Toregard Agency (Denmark, Finland, Iceland, Norway, Sweden); Thomas Schlueck GmbH (Germany)
Advertising Agency: Publishers Advertising
Shipping Address: Hachette Book Group Distribution Center, 121 N Enterprise Blvd, Lebanon, IN 46052 *Tel:* 765-483-9900 *Fax:* 765-483-0706
Membership(s): Association of American Publishers (AAP); Book Industry Study Group (BISG)

Donald M Grant Publisher Inc
PO Box 187, Hampton Falls, NH 03844-0187
Tel: 603-778-7191 *Fax:* 603-778-7191
E-mail: office@grantbooks.com
Web Site: secure.grantbooks.com
Key Personnel
Pres: Robert K Wiener *E-mail:* robert@grantbooks.com
Founded: 1964
Horror, science fiction, art & fantasy illustrated books.
ISBN Prefix(es): 978-0-937986; 978-1-880418
Number of titles published annually: 6 Print
Total Titles: 50 Print
Distributor for Archival; Oswald Train

Graphic Universe™
Imprint of Lerner Publishing Group Inc
241 First Ave N, Minneapolis, MN 55401
Tel: 612-332-3344 *Toll Free Tel:* 800-328-4929 *Fax:* 612-332-7615 *Toll Free Fax:* 800-332-1132
E-mail: info@lernerbooks.com; custserve@lernerbooks.com
Web Site: www.lernerbooks.com; www.facebook.com/lernerbooks
Key Personnel
Chmn: Harry J Lerner
Pres & Publr: Adam Lerner
EVP & COO: Mark Budde
EVP & CFO: Margaret Thomas
EVP, Sales: David Wexler
VP & Ed-in-Chief: Andy Cummings
VP, Mktg: Rachel Zugschwert
Publg Dir, School & Lib: Jenny Krueger
Dir, HR: Cyndi Radant
Dir, Rts, Spec Sales & Intl Dist: Maria Kjoller
Edit Dir: Greg Hunter
School & Lib Mktg Dir: Lois Wallentine
Founded: 2006
Publish fiction & nonfiction graphic novels for beginning readers, middle grade readers & young adults.
Number of titles published annually: 24 Print; 24 E-Book
Total Titles: 150 Print; 520 E-Book
Foreign Rep(s): Thomas Allen & Son (trade) (Canada); Bounce Sales & Marketing Ltd (UK); J Appleseed, A Division of Saunders (Canada); Phambili Agencies (Botswana, Lesotho, Namibia, Southern Africa); Publishers Marketing Service (Brunei, Malaysia, Singapore); Saunders Book Co (educ) (Canada); South Pacific Books (New Zealand); Walker Books (Australia)
Foreign Rights: Japan Foreign-Rights Centre (Japan); Korea Copyright Center (KCC) (Korea); Agence Michelle Lapautre (France); Literarische Agentur Silke Weniger (Germany)
Warehouse: 1251 Washington Ave N, Minneapolis, MN 55401, Mgr: Ken Rued

Gray & Company Publishers
1588 E 40 St, Suite 1B, Cleveland, OH 44103
Tel: 216-431-2665 *Toll Free Tel:* 800-915-3609
E-mail: sales@grayco.com; editorial@grayco.com; support@grayco.com; publicity@grayco.com
Web Site: www.grayco.com
Key Personnel
Pres: David Gray
Founded: 1991
Books about Cleveland, Northeast Ohio & Ohio.
ISBN Prefix(es): 978-1-886228; 978-0-9631738; 978-1-59851; 978-1-938441
Number of titles published annually: 4 Print; 4 E-Book
Total Titles: 110 Print; 60 E-Book

Graywolf Press
250 Third Ave N, Suite 600, Minneapolis, MN 55401

Tel: 651-641-0077 *Fax:* 651-641-0036
E-mail: wolves@graywolfpress.org (no ms queries, sample chapters or proposals)
Web Site: www.graywolfpress.org
Key Personnel
Dir & Publr: Fiona McCrae
Assoc Dir: Katie Dublinski
Mng Dir: Leslie Johnson
Dir, Mktg & Engagement: Marisa Atkinson
Sales Dir: Casey O'Neil
Exec Ed: Jeffrey Shotts
Assoc Ed: Steve Woodward
Contrib Ed: Brigid Hughes
Sr Publicity Mgr: Caroline Nitz
Publicity Assoc: Elizabeth Bryant; Morgan LaRocca
Mktg & Events Asst: Shaina Robinson
Founded: 1974
Graywolf Press publishes 21st century American & international literature in the form of poetry, fiction & nonfiction. Due to the volume of submissions & the size of their list, Graywolf Press no longer accepts unsol queries, book proposals or mss.
ISBN Prefix(es): 978-1-55597
Number of titles published annually: 30 Print
Total Titles: 200 Print; 30 E-Book
Foreign Rights: Agence Michelle Lapautre (France); Michael Meller Literary Agency GmbH (Germany)
Billing Address: MPS Distribution Center, 16365 James Madison Hwy, Gordonsville, VA 22942
Orders to: MPS Distribution Center, 16365 James Madison Hwy, Gordonsville, VA 22942
Warehouse: MPS Distribution Center, 16365 James Madison Hwy, Gordonsville, VA 22942
Distribution Center: MPS Distribution Center, 16365 James Madison Hwy, Gordonsville, VA 22942 *Tel:* 212-206-5311 *Toll Free Tel:* 888-330-8477 *Fax:* 540-672-7703

Great Potential Press Inc, see Gifted Unlimited LLC

Green Dragon Books
2275 Ibis Isle Rd W, Palm Beach, FL 33480
Mailing Address: PO Box 1608, Lake Worth, FL 33460
Tel: 561-533-6231 *Toll Free Tel:* 800-874-8844 *Fax:* 561-533-6233 *Toll Free Fax:* 888-874-8844
E-mail: info@greendragonbooks.com
Web Site: greendragonbooks.com
Key Personnel
Chmn & Publr: Gary Wilson *Tel:* 404-409-1930
Mng Dir: Jennifer Wilson *E-mail:* jennifer@greendragonbooks.com
Founded: 1969
Publications include Learning Center guides, early learning activity guides, children's picture books, general trade books, Legacies memoir series & SleuthHound mystery series.
ISBN Prefix(es): 978-1-62386; 978-0-89334
Number of titles published annually: 25 Print; 25 Online; 30 E-Book; 10 Audio
Total Titles: 475 Print; 475 Online; 500 E-Book; 10 Audio
Foreign Rights: Montreal-Contacts/The Rights Agency (worldwide)
Distribution Center: Baker & Taylor
Ingram Book Co
New Leaf Distributing Co, 401 Thornton Rd, Lithia Springs, GA 30122-1557 *Tel:* 704-948-7845 *Fax:* 704-944-2313 *Web Site:* newleafdist.com
Membership(s): American Booksellers Association (ABA); American Marketing Association; ASCD; Independent Book Publishers Association (IBPA); National Education Association (NEA); National Press Club; Southern Independent Booksellers Alliance (SIBA); Toastmasters International

Green Integer

6210 Wilshire Blvd, Suite 211, Los Angeles, CA 90048
SAN: 216-3063
E-mail: info@greeninteger.com
Web Site: www.greeninteger.com
Key Personnel
Publr: Douglas Messerli *E-mail:* douglas.
messerli@gmail.com
Founded: 1978
Contemporary fiction, criticism, drama & poetry.
ISBN Prefix(es): 978-0-940650; 978-1-55713
Number of titles published annually: 15 Print
Total Titles: 300 Print
Imprints: New American Fiction Series; New American Poetry Series; Sun & Moon Classics; Zerogram Press
Foreign Rights: Eliane Benesti Literary Agency (France); Bookbank SA (Spain); Copenhagen Literary Agency ApS (Scandinavia); Paul & Peter Fritz AG Literary Agency (Germany, Switzerland); Japan UNI Agency Inc (Japan); Natoli, Stefan & Oliva Literary Agency (Italy); Rogan Pikarski Literary Agency (Israel)
Distribution Center: Consortium Book Sales & Distribution, The Keg House, Suite 101, 34 13 Ave NE, Minneapolis, MN 55413-1007
Tel: 651-746-2600 *Toll Free Tel:* 800-283-3572 (cust serv, Jackson, TN) *Fax:* 651-746-2606
E-mail: info@cbsd.com *Web Site:* www.cbsd.
com SAN: 200-6049

Greenhaven Press®

Imprint of The Rosen Publishing Group Inc
29 E 21 St, New York, NY 10010
Toll Free Tel: 800-237-9932 *Toll Free Fax:* 888-436-4643
Web Site: www.rosenpublishing.com
Founded: 1970
High school, college & secondary nonfiction social studies & debate books for classrooms & libraries: social studies reference series; library & paper bound books in area studies, criminal justice, the environment, health, Literary Companion & American History series & AT Issues series.
ISBN Prefix(es): 978-0-89908; 978-1-56510; 978-0-7377
Number of titles published annually: 200 Print
Total Titles: 3,500 Print

Greenleaf Book Group LLC

3 Park Place, 4005 Banister Lane, Suite B, Austin, TX 78704
Mailing Address: PO Box 91869, Austin, TX 78709
Tel: 512-891-6100 *Fax:* 512-891-6150
E-mail: contact@greenleafbookgroup.com
Web Site: www.greenleafbookgroup.com
Key Personnel
Founder: Clint Greenleaf
CEO: Tanya Hall
Gen Coun: Sujan Trivedi
CFO: Brian Viktorin
Art Dir: Neil Gonzalez
Dir, Consulting: Justin Branch
Dir, Dist: Steve Elizalde
Dir, Mktg & Branding: Corrin Foster
Dir, Prodn: Carrie Jones
Mgr, Busn Devt: Kesley Smith *E-mail:* ksmith@greenleafbookgroup.com
Sr Ed: Nathan True
Founded: 1997
Publisher & distributor specializing in the development of independent authors & the growth of small presses. Our publishing model was designed to support independent authors & allow writers to retain the rights to their work & still compete with major publishing houses. We also distribute select titles from small & independent publishers to major trade outlets, including bookstores, libraries & airport retailers. We serve the small & independent publishing com-munity by offering industry guidance, business development, production, distribution & marketing services.
ISBN Prefix(es): 978-0-9665319; 978-1-929774; 978-0-9790842; 978-1-60832; 978-1-61486; 978-1-62634
Number of titles published annually: 100 Print
Total Titles: 350 Print
Imprints: An Inc Original; Greenleaf Book Group Press; River Grove Books
Returns: Archway, 20770 Westwood Dr, Strongsville, OH 44149
Membership(s): American Library Association (ALA); American Society of Journalists & Authors (ASJA); Association of American Publishers (AAP); BookSense Publisher Partner; Independent Book Publishers Association (IBPA); National Speakers Association (NSA)

Greenleaf Book Group Press, see Greenleaf Book Group LLC

§Grey House Publishing Inc™

4919 Rte 22, Amenia, NY 12501
Mailing Address: PO Box 56, Amenia, NY 12501-0056
Tel: 518-789-8700 *Toll Free Tel:* 800-562-2139
Fax: 518-789-0556
E-mail: books@greyhouse.com; customerservice@greyhouse.com
Web Site: greyhouse.com
Key Personnel
Pres: Richard Gottlieb *E-mail:* rhg@greyhouse.com
VP, Mktg: Jessica Moody *Tel:* 518-789-8700 ext 101 *E-mail:* jmoody@greyhouse.com
Publr: Leslie Mackenzie *E-mail:* lmackenzie@greyhouse.com
Edit Dir: Laura Mars *E-mail:* lmars@greyhouse.com
Founded: 1981
Directories, reference books & encyclopedias in history, business, economics, health & demographic areas.
ISBN Prefix(es): 978-1-930956; 978-1-891482; 978-0-939300; 978-1-59237; 978-1-61925
Number of titles published annually: 185 Print; 50 E-Book
Imprints: R R Bowker's Books in Print Series; Grey House; Financial Ratings Series; Salem Press; H W Wilson
Divisions: Grey House Publishing Canada
Returns: 5979 N Elm Ave, Suite 113, Millerton, NY 12546
Warehouse: 5979 N Elm Ave, Suite 113, Millerton, NY 12546
Membership(s): American Library Association (ALA)
See separate listing for:
Salem Press

Group Publishing Inc

1515 Cascade Ave, Loveland, CO 80538
Tel: 970-669-3836 *Toll Free Tel:* 800-447-1070
E-mail: puorgbus@group.com (submissions)
Web Site: www.group.com
Key Personnel
Founder & Chmn: Thom Schultz
Founded: 1974
ISBN Prefix(es): 978-1-55945; 978-0-7644; 978-1-4707
Number of titles published annually: 40 Print
Total Titles: 300 Print; 20 CD-ROM; 30 E-Book
Foreign Rights: Canaanland (Malaysia); CLC Wholesale (UK); Group Canada (Canada); KCBS Inc (Korea); Koorung Books Pty Ltd (Australia); Manna Christian Stores (New Zealand); SKS (Singapore); Word Bookstores (Australia)
Returns: 1615 Cascade Ave, Loveland, CO 80538
Membership(s): Evangelical Christian Publishers Association (ECPA)

Grove Atlantic Inc

154 W 14 St, 12th fl, New York, NY 10011
SAN: 201-4890
Tel: 212-614-7850 *Toll Free Tel:* 800-521-0178
Fax: 212-614-7886
E-mail: info@groveatlantic.com; sales@groveatlantic.com; publicity@groveatlantic.com; rights@groveatlantic.com
Web Site: www.groveatlantic.com
Key Personnel
Publr & CEO: Morgan Entrekin *E-mail:* mentrekin@groveatlantic.com
Assoc Publr: Judy Hottensen *E-mail:* jhottensen@groveatlantic.com
VP & Dir, Publicity: Deb Seager *E-mail:* dseager@groveatlantic.com
VP & Edit Dir: Elisabeth Schmitz *E-mail:* eschmitz@groveatlantic.com
Rts Dir & Sr Ed: Amy Hundley *E-mail:* ahundley@groveatlantic.com
Exec Ed: George Gibson
Sr Ed: Peter Blackstock
Ed: Katie Raissian
Assoc Ed: Emily Burns
Sr Publicity Mgr: John Mark Boling
Publicity Mgr: Justina Batchelor
Digital Mktg Mgr: Nick Stewart
Rts Mgr: Erica Nunez *E-mail:* enunez@groveatlantic.com
Assoc Publicist: Kait Astrella
Sales & Mktg Asst: Andrew Unger *E-mail:* aunger@groveatlantic.com
Founded: 1917
General fiction & nonfiction, hardcover & paperbound.
ISBN Prefix(es): 978-0-8021; 978-1-55584; 978-0-87113; 978-1-61185
Number of titles published annually: 120 Print; 90 E-Book
Total Titles: 2,700 Print; 3,000 E-Book
Imprints: Atlantic Monthly Press; Black Cat; Grove Press; Grove Press UK
Foreign Rep(s): Jonathan Ball Publishers (South Africa); Book Promotions (Nicky Stubbs) (South Africa); Gilles Fauveau (Japan, Korea); Jaime Gregorio (Philippines); Ingram Publisher Services (Edison Garcia) (Asia); Ingram Publisher Services UK (Matthew Dickie) (Europe, Ireland, Latin America, UK); Sharad Mohan (Bangladesh, India, Maldives, Nepal, Pakistan, Sri Lanka); NewSouth Books (Australia, New Zealand); June Poonpanich (Cambodia, Indonesia, Laos, Thailand, Vietnam); Wei Zhao (China, Hong Kong, Taiwan)
Foreign Rights: AnatoliaLit Agency (Amy Spangler) (Turkey); Eliane Benisti Agency (Eliane Benisti) (France); Casanovas & Lynch Agencia Literaria (Maria Lynch) (Latin America, Portugal, Spain); Ersilia Literary Agency (Evangelia Avloniti) (Greece); Graal Literary Agency (Filip Wojciechowski) (Poland); International Copyright Agency (Simona Kessler) (Romania); The Italian Literary Agency srl (Claire Sabatie-Garat) (Italy); Japan UNI Agency Inc (Miko Yamanouchi) (Japan); Katai & Bolza (Peter Bolza) (Hungary); Korea Copyright Center (Rockyoung Lee) (Korea); Andrew Nurnberg Associates (Tatjana Zoldnere) (Estonia, Latvia, Lithuania); Andrew Nurnberg Associates, Beijing Representative Office (Jackie Huang) (China); Andrew Nurnberg Associates, Taiwan Representative Office (Whitney Hsu) (Taiwan); Kristin Olson Literary Agency (Kristin Olson) (Czechia); Plima Literary Agency (Vuk Perisic) (Bosnia and Herzegovina, Bulgaria, Croatia, North Macedonia, Serbia, Slovenia); The Riff Agency (Laura Riff & Joao Paulo Riff) (Brazil); Elisabeth Ruge Agentur GmbH (Elisabeth Ruge) (Germany); Synopsis Literary Agency (Natalia Sanina) (Russia); Ulf Toregard Agency (Ulf Toregard) (Netherlands, Scandinavia); Tuttle-Mori Agency Inc (Ken Mori) (Japan)

Orders to: Ingram Publisher Services International, 1400 Broadway, Suite 520, New York, NY 10018 *Tel:* 212-714-9000 *E-mail:* ips_internationalsales@ingramcontent.com; Ingram Content Group LLC, One Ingram Blvd, La Vergne, TN 37086 *Tel:* 615-793-5000 *E-mail:* ips@ingramcontent.com; Publishers Group Canada, c/o Raincoast Books, 2440 Viking Way, Richmond, BC V6V IN2, Canada *Toll Free Tel:* 800-663-5714 *E-mail:* customerservices@raincoast.com; Grantham Book Services, Trent Rd, Grantham. Lincs NG31 7XQ, United Kingdom *Tel:* (01476) 541000 *Fax:* (01476) 541060

Returns: Ingram Publisher Services, Returns Dept, 1210 Ingram Dr, Chambersburg, TN 17202; Raincoast Books, 2440 Viking Way, Richmond, BC V6V 1N2, Canada *Toll Free Tel:* 800-663-5714 *Toll Free Fax:* 800-565-3770 *E-mail:* customerservice@raincoast.com

Distribution Center: Ingram Content Group, One Ingram Blvd, La Vergne, TN 37086

Membership(s): Association of American Publishers (AAP)

Gryphon Editions
PO Box 241823, Omaha, NE 68124
Tel: 402-298-5385 (intl) *Toll Free Tel:* 888-655-0134 (US & CN)
E-mail: customerservice@gryphoneditions.com
Web Site: www.gryphoneditions.com
Founded: 1977
Reprints: medicine, law, political philosophy, science; fine editions.
Number of titles published annually: 25 Print
Total Titles: 750 Print

Gryphon House Inc
Subsidiary of Kaplan Early Learning Co
6848 Leon's Way, Lewisville, NC 27023
Mailing Address: PO Box 10, Lewisville, NC 27023
Toll Free Tel: 800-638-0928 *Toll Free Fax:* 877-638-7576
E-mail: info@ghbooks.com
Web Site: www.gryphonhouse.com
Key Personnel
Acct Exec: Whitley Vogler *E-mail:* whitley@ghbooks.com
Dir, Mktg: Ashleigh Craven *E-mail:* ashleigh@ghbooks.com
Gen Mgr: Jennifer Lewis *E-mail:* jennifer@ghbooks.com
Founded: 1971
Publishes & distributes books for teachers & parents of young children.
ISBN Prefix(es): 978-0-87659
Number of titles published annually: 12 Print; 12 E-Book
Total Titles: 310 Print; 300 E-Book
Distributor for Aha Communications; Book Peddlers; Deya Brashears; Bright Ring Publishing; Building Blocks; Center for the Child Care Workforce; Chatterbox Press; Chicago Review Press; Children's Resources International; Circle Time Publishers; Sydney Gurewitz Clemens; Conari Press; Council Oak Books; DawnSignPress; Delmar Publishers Inc; Early Educator's Press; Educators for Social Responsibility; Family Center of Nova University; Jean Feldman; Floris Books; Hawthorne Press; Hunter House Publishers; Kaplan Press; Miss Jackie Inc; Monjeu Press; National Center Early Childhood Workforce; New England AEYC; Nova Southeastern University; Pademelon Press; Partner Press; Pollyanna Productions; Robins Lane Press; School Renaissance; Southern Early Childhood Association; Steam Press; Syracuse University Press; Teaching Strategies LLC; Telshare Publishing
Foreign Rep(s): Monarch Books (Canada); Pademelon Press (Australia)

Guideposts Book & Inspirational Media
110 William St, Suite 901, New York, NY 10038
Mailing Address: PO Box 5815, Harlan, IA 51593-1315
Tel: 212-251-8100 *Toll Free Tel:* 800-932-2145 (cust serv) *Fax:* 212-587-4282
E-mail: gpsprod@cdsfulfillment.com
Web Site: guideposts.org
Key Personnel
Pres & CEO: John F Temple
Founded: 1945
Inspirational books & videos.
ISBN Prefix(es): 978-0-9661766
Number of titles published annually: 30 Print

§The Guilford Press
370 Seventh Ave, Suite 1200, New York, NY 10001-1020
SAN: 212-9442
Tel: 212-431-9800 *Toll Free Tel:* 800-365-7006 *Fax:* 212-966-6708
E-mail: info@guilford.com
Web Site: www.guilford.com
Key Personnel
Pres & Gen Mgr: Robert Matloff *E-mail:* bob.matloff@guilford.com
Lib Sales Dir & Sales Mgr: Anne Patota *Tel:* 212-431-9800 ext 217 *E-mail:* anne.patota@guilford.com
Mktg Dir: Marian Robinson *E-mail:* marian.robinson@guilford.com
Ed-in-Chief: Seymour Weingarten *E-mail:* seymour.weingarten@guilford.com
Mng Ed: Judith Grauman *E-mail:* judith.grauman@guilford.com
Busn Mgr: David Mitchell *E-mail:* david.mitchell@guilford.com
Credit Mgr: Vernita Hurston *Tel:* 212-431-9800 ext 230 *E-mail:* vernita.hurston@guilford.com
Fulfillment Mgr: Christopher Etsell *Tel:* 800-365-7006 ext 260 *E-mail:* christopher.etsell@guilford.com
Prodn Mgr: Katya Edwards *E-mail:* katya.edwards@guilford.com
Intl Rts, Perms & ISBN Contact: Kathy Kuehl *E-mail:* kathy.kuehl@guilford.com
Founded: 1973
Professional & reference books, videos, journals & software in psychology, psychiatry & the behavioral sciences, neuroscience, research methods, education & literacy & geography.
ISBN Prefix(es): 978-0-89862; 978-1-57230; 978-1-59385; 978-1-60623; 978-1-60918; 978-1-4625
Number of titles published annually: 90 Print; 90 E-Book
Total Titles: 1,350 Print; 2 CD-ROM; 850 E-Book
Foreign Rep(s): Avicenna Partnership (Middle East); Cranbury International LLC (Caribbean, Central America, Mexico, South America); Footprint Books (Australia, New Zealand); Juta (South Africa); MHM Ltd (Japan); Taylor & Francis Asia Pacific (Asia, China); Taylor & Francis India (India); Taylor & Francis Informa UK (Europe, UK); Unifacmanu (Taiwan)
Returns: Maple Logistics Solutions, York Distribution Ctr, 60 Grumbacher Rd, York, PA 17406
Warehouse: Maple Logistics Solutions, York Distribution Ctr, 60 Grumbacher Rd, York, PA 17406

Guilford Publications Inc, see The Guilford Press

§Gulf Energy Information
2 Greenway Plaza, Suite 1020, Houston, TX 77046
Mailing Address: PO Box 2608, Houston, TX 77252
Tel: 713-529-4301

E-mail: store@gulfpub.com; customerservice@energyinfo.com
Web Site: www.gulfenergyinfo.com
Key Personnel
Pres & CEO: John T Royall
VP, Prodn: Sheryl Stone
Publr, Hydrocarbon Processing: Catherine Watkins
Publr, World Oil Magazine: Andy McDowell
Founded: 1916
Communications company dedicated to the petrochemical industry & related industries.
ISBN Prefix(es): 978-1-933762; 978-0-9765113
Number of titles published annually: 10 Print; 3 CD-ROM
Total Titles: 20 Print; 30 CD-ROM
Distributor for Editions Technip; Elsevier; Pennwell; Simon & Schuster; Wiley

Hachai Publishing
527 Empire Blvd, Brooklyn, NY 11225
SAN: 251-3749
Tel: 718-633-0100 *Fax:* 718-633-0103
E-mail: info@hachai.com
Web Site: www.hachai.com
Key Personnel
Pres: Yerachmiel Binyominson
Publr & Sales: Yossi Leverton *E-mail:* yossi@hachai.com
Ed: Dina Rosenfeld *E-mail:* dlr@hachai.com
Founded: 1988
Full color children's Judaica books.
ISBN Prefix(es): 978-0-922613; 978-1-929628; 978-1-945560
Number of titles published annually: 6 Print
Total Titles: 110 Print; 1 E-Book
Distributor for Attara; Kerem; Living Lessons
Membership(s): Association of Jewish Libraries; Independent Book Publishers Association (IBPA)

Hachette Audio
Division of Hachette Book Group
1290 Avenue of the Americas, New York, NY 10104
Tel: 212-364-1100
Web Site: www.hachetteaudio.com
Key Personnel
SVP, Content Devt & Publr, Hachette Audio & Large Print: Anthony Goff
VP, Assoc Publr: Kim Sayle
Exec Dir, Prodn: Michele McGonigle
Sr Audio Coord: Mishell Velez
Sr Dir, Audio Mktg & Publicity: Megan Fitzpatrick
Mgr, Mktg & Publicty: Nita Basu
Assoc Art Dir: Cynthia Joy
Number of titles published annually: 470 Audio
Total Titles: 4,421 Audio

Hachette Book Group
Division of Hachette Livre
1290 Avenue of the Americas, New York, NY 10104
Tel: 212-364-1100 *Toll Free Tel:* 800-759-0190 (cust serv) *Fax:* 212-364-0933 (intl orders) *Toll Free Fax:* 800-286-9471 (cust serv)
Web Site: www.hachettebookgroup.com
Key Personnel
CEO: Michael Pietsch
EVP & COO: Joe Mangan
EVP, Publr, Little, Brown Books for Young Readers: Megan Tingley
EVP, Group Sales Dir: Alison Lazarus
SVP & Gen Coun: Min Lee
SVP, Corp Communs Dir: Sophie Cottrell
SVP, CFO: Stephen Mubarek
SVP, Chief Mktg Offr: Wibke Grutjen
SVP, CIO: Mike Ballanco
SVP, HR: Andrea Weinzimer
SVP, Publr, Grand Central Publishing: Ben Sevier
SVP, Publr, Orbit: Tim Holman

SVP, Publr, Perseus Books: Susan Weinberg
SVP, Publr, Hachette Audio: Anthony Goff
SVP, Intl, Canada, Spec Mkts: Jean Griffin
SVP, Retail Sales: Christopher Murphy
SVP, Publg Opers & Strategy: Dylan Hoke
VP, Busn Devt: Todd McGarity
VP, Exec Mng Ed, Hachette: Rena Kornbluh
VP, Contracts: Andrea Shallcross
VP, Subs Rts: Nancy Wiese
VP, Dist: Frank Casolaro
VP, Progs & Prods: Lee Huang
VP, Opers Planning & Corp Facilities: Mark Kent
Assoc Dir, Consumer Mktg: Erica Nelson
Assoc Dir, Communs: Matt Hooban
Founded: 2006 (when Time Warner Book Group was purchased by Hachette Livre)
Hachette Book Group is a leading trade publisher based in New York & a division of Hachette Livre (a Lagardere company), the third largest trade & educational publisher in the world. HBG is made up of 8 publishing groups: Little, Brown and Company; Little, Brown Books for Young Readers; Grand Central Publishing; Perseus Books; Orbit; Hachette Books; Hachette Nashville; Hachette Audio.
ISBN Prefix(es): 978-1-56282; 978-0-7868; 978-0-316; 978-1-4013
Divisions: Grand Central Publishing; Hachette Audio; Hachette Nashville; Little, Brown and Company; Little, Brown Books for Young Readers; Orbit; Perseus Books
Distributor for Harry N Abrams Inc; Nicholas Brealey Publishing; Chronicle Books; Disney Book Group; Gildan Media; Hachette UK; Houghton Mifflin Harcourt; Kids Can Press; Lonely Planet; Marvel Worldwide Inc; Moleskine; Octopus Books; Peterson's; Phaidon Press; Phoenix International Publications (PiKids); Quarto Publishing Group; Quercus Books; Sheldon Press (all print & digital); Time Inc Books; Yen Press
Orders to: Order Dept, 53 State St, Boston, MA 02109 (US orders) *Toll Free Tel:* 800-759-0190 *Toll Free Fax:* 800-286-9471
Returns: Returns Dept, 322 S Enterprise Blvd, Lebanon, IN 46052
Shipping Address: Hachette Book Group Distribution Center, 121 N Enterprise Blvd, Lebanon, IN 46052 *Tel:* 765-483-9900 *Fax:* 765-483-0706
See separate listing for:
Grand Central Publishing
Hachette Audio
Hachette Nashville
Little, Brown and Company
Little, Brown Books for Young Readers
Orbit
Perseus Books

Hachette Nashville
Division of Hachette Book Group
6100 Tower Circle, Room 210, Franklin, TN 37067
Tel: 615-221-0996 *Fax:* 615-221-0962
Web Site: www.hachettebookgroup.com
Key Personnel
VP & Publr: Daisy Blackwell Hutton
VP, Mktg & Publicity: Patsy Jones
VP, Nashville & Client Opers: Billy Clark
VP, Christian Booksellers Assn Sales: Gary Davidson
Exec Ed, Center Street: Kate Hartson
Mktg Dir: Rudy Kish
Channel Dir, Clients & Nashville: Gina Wynn
Art Dir: Jody Waldrup
Fin Dir: Deirdre Baule
Assoc Art Dir: Edward Crawford
Edit Asst, FaithWords: Karin Mathis
Sr Publicist: Katie Broaddus
Sr Publicist, FaithWords: Laini Brown
Dir, Online Mktg: Katie Norris
Mktg Dir, Ad: Caroline Green
Mktg Mgr: Amy Biter

Mktg Mgr, Specialty: Cat Hoort
Sr Dir, Assoc Publr, Worthy: Jeana Ledbetter; Peggy Schaefer
Edit Dir, Specialty, Ellie Claire: Marilyn Jansen
Creative Dir, Specialty, Ellie Claire: Melissa Reagan
Mgr, Interior Design, Ellie Claire: Bart Dawson
Sr Ed, WorthyKids: Melinda Rathjen
Assoc Ed, WorthyKids: Kristi Breeden
Asst Ed, WorthyKids: Rebekah Moredock
Art Dir, WorthyKids: Georgina Chidlow-Irvin
Founded: 2001
Publish books for the growing inspirational market. No unsol mss.
ISBN Prefix(es): 978-0-446
Number of titles published annually: 95 Print
Total Titles: 556 Print
Imprints: Center Street (nonfiction conservative political & military titles); FaithWords; Worthy Publishing (includes Ellie Claire Gifts, Museum of the Bible Books, Worthy Inspired & WorthyKids/Ideals)
Orders to: Hachette Book Group, 53 State St, Boston, MA 02109 *Toll Free Tel:* 800-759-0190 *Toll Free Fax:* 800-286-9471
Membership(s): Evangelical Christian Publishers Association (ECPA)

Hackett Publishing Co Inc
3333 Massachusetts Ave, Indianapolis, IN 46218
SAN: 201-6044
Mailing Address: PO Box 390007, Cambridge, MA 02139
Tel: 317-635-9250 (orders & cust serv); 617-497-6303 (edit off & sales) *Fax:* 317-635-9292; 617-661-8703 (edit off) *Toll Free Fax:* 800-783-9213
E-mail: customer@hackettpublishing.com; editorial@hackettpublishing.com
Web Site: www.hackettpublishing.com
Key Personnel
Pres, Publr & CEO: Deborah Wilkes
VP, Mktg Dir & Dir, Opers: John Pershing *Tel:* 617-234-0371 *E-mail:* johnp@hackettpublishing.com
Secy & Treas: Cheri Brown
Promos Mgr: Mr Ryan Picazio *Tel:* 617-497-6307 *E-mail:* ryanp@hackettpublishing.com
Founded: 1972
College textbooks & scholarly books; emphasis on philosophy, political theory, political science, classics, history & literature.
ISBN Prefix(es): 978-0-915144; 978-0-915145; 978-0-87220; 978-1-60384
Number of titles published annually: 30 Print; 30 E-Book
Total Titles: 840 Print; 300 E-Book
Imprints: Focus
Distributor for Bryn Mawr Commentaries
Foreign Rep(s): Gazelle Book Services Ltd (Europe, UK); UNIREPS (Australia, New Zealand)
Foreign Rights: Eulama
See separate listing for:
Focus

§Hagstrom Map
Subsidiary of American Map Corp
1800 Lovering Ave, Wilmington, DE 19806
Toll Free Tel: 800-432-MAPS (432-6277)
 Toll Free Fax: 888-210-9654
Founded: 1916
Three million maps, atlases, guides.
ISBN Prefix(es): 978-0-88097; 978-0-910684; 978-1-59245
Total Titles: 1 CD-ROM
Distributor for ADC The Map People; American Map Corp; Arrow Maps Inc; Creative Sales Corp; De Lorme Atlas; Hammond World Atlas Corp; RV International Maps & Atlases; Stubs Guides; Trakker Maps Inc

§Hal Leonard Corp
7777 W Bluemound Rd, Milwaukee, WI 53213

Mailing Address: PO Box 13819, Milwaukee, WI 53213-0819
Tel: 414-774-3630 *Fax:* 414-774-3259
E-mail: halinfo@halleonard.com
Web Site: www.halleonard.com
Key Personnel
Chmn & CEO: Keith Mardak
Pres: Larry Morton
Sr Sales & Mktg Mgr, Book Trade & Ebooks: Mike Hansen
Sr Key Accts Mgr: David Cywinski
Founded: 1947
The world's largest music print publisher, with an incomparable selection of sheet music, songbooks, music related books, self-instruction books, CD packs & videos, music reference & special interest titles, music biographies, children's music products; CD-ROMs, DVDs, performance videos & more. Additional offices in Minnesota, New York, Nashville, Australia, Belgium, France, Germany, Holland, Italy, Switzerland & the UK.
ISBN Prefix(es): 978-1-57467; 978-0-88188; 978-0-7935; 978-0-87910; 978-0-87930; 978-0-634; 978-0-9607350; 978-1-56516; 978-1-61713; 978-1-61774; 978-1-61780; 978-1-4584; 978-1-4768; 978-1-4803; 978-0-931340; 978-1-4950
Number of titles published annually: 2,000 Print
Total Titles: 200,000 Print; 15 CD-ROM
Imprints: Berklee Press; Cherry Lane Music Co; Ashley Mark Publishing Co; Musicians Institute Press; G Shirmer; Vintage Guitar
Divisions: Hal Leonard Performing Arts Publishing Group
Distributor for Ableton; Acoustica; AirTurn; Amadeus Press; Antares; Apogee; Aquarius; Arrangers Publishing LLC; Art String Publishing; Ashley Music; Avid; Axe Heauen; Berklee Press; Leonard Bernstein; Blue Microphones; Fred Bock Music Company; Boosey & Hawkes; CD Sheet Music; Cakewalk; Centerstream Publishing LLC; Cherry Lane Music Co; ChordBuddy; Curnow Music; De Haske Publications; Dots & Lines Inc; Editions Durand; Editions Max Eschig; Editions Salabert; EM Books; EMI Christian; Faber Music Ltd; Family Communications; Fleamarket Music; Griffin Technology; Guitar World; Hamilton Stands; Hartke; G Henle Verlag; Homespun Tapes; Hudson Music; IK Multimedia; Lauren Keiser Music; Lorie Lane; Line 6; M-Audio; Ashley Mark Publishing Co; Edward B Marks Music; Meredith Music; Mighty Bright; Modern Drummer Publications; Music Minus One; Music Sales America; Musicians Institute Press; Noteflight; Peermusic Classical; PreSonus; Professional Music Institute; Propellerhead; PWM Editions; QSC; Ricordi; Lee Roberts Publications; Rock House; Rubank Publications; St Nicolas Music Inc; Samson Audio; G Schirmer Inc/Associated Music Publishers Ltd; Schott Music; Shawnee Press; Sibelius; Sikorski; Sony; Steinberg; Sterling Publishing Co Inc; String Letter Publishing; Tara Publications; Tycoon Percussion; Vintage Guitar; Voyageur Press; XLN Audio; Waltons Irish Music; Willis Music; Yamaha
Foreign Rep(s): Publishers Group UK (Europe, UK)
Foreign Rights: Robert Lecker Agency Inc
Returns: 1210 Innovation Dr, Winona, MN 55987
Shipping Address: 1210 Innovation Dr, Winona, MN 55987 *Tel:* 507-454-2920 *Fax:* 507-454-4042
Warehouse: 960 E Mark St, Winona, MN 55987
Distribution Center: 1210 Innovation Dr, Winona, MN 55987

Hameray Publishing Group Inc
5212 Venice Blvd, Los Angeles, CA 90019
Toll Free Tel: 866-918-6173 *Fax:* 858-369-5201
E-mail: info@hameraypublishing.com (cust serv); sales@hameraypublishing.com (sales)
Web Site: www.hameraypublishing.com

Founded: 2008

Hameray Publishing Group's mission is to help inspire budding readers with leveled books that make the learning process more pleasurable. We strive to help teachers foster a love of reading that will last a lifetime with fun & immersive stories from leading authors like Joy Cowley.

For US customers, our shipping & handling is $6 or 10% (whichever is greater). For international customers, shipping & handling rates will vary depending on your location. We typically process & ship orders within 2 business days of receipt. Our warehouse is in California, so packages can take 1 to 5 business days to arrive once shipped. Hameray Publishing Group is a sole-source vendor & an approved New York City vendor (# HAM736846).

ISBN Prefix(es): 978-1-60559; 978-1-62817; 978-1-64039

Number of titles published annually: 200 Print

Total Titles: 1,000 Print

Imprints: Bear & Bobcat Books

Membership(s): Reading Recovery Council of North America

See separate listing for:

Bear & Bobcat Books

Hamilton Books

Imprint of Rowman & Littlefield Publishing Group

4501 Forbes Blvd, Suite 200, Lanham, MD 20706

Tel: 301-459-3366 *Toll Free Tel:* 800-462-6420 (cust serv) *Fax:* 301-429-5748

Toll Free Fax: 800-388-4550 (cust serv)

Key Personnel

Dir, Edit: Nicolette Amstutz *E-mail:* namstutz@rowman.com

Acqs Ed: Brooke Bures *E-mail:* bbures@rowman.com

Founded: 2002

Provides authors of serious nonfiction titles, including corporate leaders, politicians, scholars, war veterans & family historians, the opportunity to sign with a top-quality publisher without the typical hassles & extreme selectivity enforced by other publishers.

ISBN Prefix(es): 978-0-7618

Number of titles published annually: 40 Print; 40 E-Book

Total Titles: 500 Print; 500 E-Book

Hamilton Stone Editions

PO Box 43, Maplewood, NJ 07040

Tel: 973-378-8361

E-mail: hstone@hamiltonstone.org

Web Site: www.hamiltonstone.org

Key Personnel

Edit Dir: Meredith Sue Willis

E-mail: meredithsuewillis@gmail.com

Artistic Dir: Lynda Schor *E-mail:* lynda.schor@gmail.com

Dir: Nathan Leslie *E-mail:* nleslie@nvcc.edu; Carole Rosenthal *E-mail:* crlrosenthal@gmail.com

Founded: 2003

Independent press for independent literary writing. Dedicated to vivid writing that probes the hidden realities of the everyday, valuing most highly the kind of writing that displays a multifaced vision. Interested in keeping new books in print & bringing forgotten, excellent old books back into print.

ISBN Prefix(es): 978-0-9654043; 978-0-9714873

Number of titles published annually: 4 Print; 4 E-Book

Total Titles: 50 Print; 50 E-Book

Imprints: Irene Weinberger Books (literary books in ebook & trade paperback format, often in collaboration with other presses)

Shipping Address: 447 Tremont Place, Orange, NJ 07050

Hampton Press Inc

307 Seventh Ave, Suite 506, New York, NY 10001

Tel: 646-638-3800 *Toll Free Tel:* 800-894-8955 *Fax:* 646-638-3802

E-mail: hamptonpr1@aol.com

Web Site: www.hamptonpress.com

Key Personnel

Pres: Barbara Bernstein

Founded: 1992

ISBN Prefix(es): 978-1-881303; 978-1-57273; 978-1-61289

Number of titles published annually: 20 Print

Total Titles: 775 Print

Foreign Rep(s): Eurospan Group (Asia, Australia, Europe, Far East, Latin America, UK)

Hampton Roads Publishing

Imprint of Red Wheel/Weiser

65 Parker St, Suite 7, Newburyport, MA 01950-4600

Tel: 978-465-0504 *Toll Free Tel:* 800-423-7087 (orders) *Fax:* 978-465-0243 *Toll Free Fax:* 877-337-3309

E-mail: orders@rwwbooks.com

Web Site: redwheelweiser.com

Key Personnel

Exec Dir, Busn Devt: Bonni Hamilton

E-mail: bhamilton@rwwbooks.com

Publicity Mgr: Eryn Carter Eaton

E-mail: ecarter@rwwbooks.com

Founded: 1989

Trade publishing. Specialize in metaphysics, self-help, integrative medicine, visionary fiction & paranormal phenomena.

ISBN Prefix(es): 978-1-878901; 978-1-57174; 978-1-61283

Number of titles published annually: 30 Print

Total Titles: 350 Print; 2 Audio

Distributed by Red Wheel/Weiser

Foreign Rep(s): Brumby Sunstate (Australia); Deep Books Ltd (Europe, UK); Georgetown Publications (Canada); Publishers International Marketing (Asia, Middle East)

Foreign Rights: Biagi Rights Management (Linda Biagi) (worldwide)

§Hancock House Publishers

4550 Birch Bay Lynden Rd, Suite 104, Blaine, WA 98230-9436

Tel: 604-538-1114 *Toll Free Tel:* 800-938-1114 *Fax:* 604-538-2262 *Toll Free Fax:* 800-983-2262

E-mail: sales@hancockhouse.com

Web Site: www.hancockhouse.com

Key Personnel

Publr & Intl Rts: Myles Lamont

Founded: 1975

Specialize in natural history (world), regional northwest history & Native art.

ISBN Prefix(es): 978-0-88839

Number of titles published annually: 15 Print

Total Titles: 600 Print

Branch Office(s)

19313 Zero Ave, Surrey, BC V3Z 9R9, Canada

Handprint Books Inc

Imprint of Chronicle Books

413 Sixth Ave, Brooklyn, NY 11215-3310

Tel: 718-768-3696 *Toll Free Tel:* 800-722-6657 (orders) *Fax:* 718-369-0844 *Toll Free Fax:* 800-858-7787 (orders)

E-mail: info@handprintbooks.com

Web Site: www.handprintbooks.com

Key Personnel

Pres & Publr: Christopher Franceschelli

E-mail: cmf@handprintbooks.com

Founded: 2000

Publisher of high-quality books for children.

ISBN Prefix(es): 978-1-929766; 978-1-59354

Number of titles published annually: 12 Print

Distributed by Chronicle Books

Returns: Chronicle Books, c/o Genco Fulfillment, 1585 Linda Way, Door 1, Sparks, NV 89431

Hanging Loose Press

231 Wyckoff St, Brooklyn, NY 11217

SAN: 206-4960

Tel: 347-529-4738 *Fax:* 347-227-8215

E-mail: print225@aol.com

Web Site: www.hangingloosepress.com

Key Personnel

Ed & Intl Rts: Robert Hershon

Ed: Dick Lourie; Mark Pawlak

Founded: 1966

Poetry & short fiction.

ISBN Prefix(es): 978-0-914610; 978-1-882413; 978-1-931236

Number of titles published annually: 8 Print

Total Titles: 225 Print

Membership(s): Community of Literary Magazines & Presses (CLMP)

§Hannacroix Creek Books Inc

1127 High Ridge Rd, No 110-B, Stamford, CT 06905-1203

SAN: 299-9560

Tel: 203-968-8098

Web Site: www.hannacroixcreekbooks.com

Key Personnel

Pres & CEO: Dr Jan Yager

Founded: 1996

Trade publisher of quality & innovative fiction & nonfiction books & journals that entertain, educate & inform.

ISBN Prefix(es): 978-1-889262; 978-1-938998

Number of titles published annually: 7 Print; 10 E-Book

Total Titles: 38 Print; 18 E-Book

Foreign Rep(s): International Editors' Co (Flavia Sala) (Brazil)

Foreign Rights: Guiliana Bernardi Literary Agent (Italy); DS Rights (Eastern Europe); Antonia Kerrigan Literary Agency (Spain); Eric Yang Agency (Korea)

Membership(s): Association of American Publishers (AAP); Independent Book Publishers Association (IBPA); Women's Media Group

§Hanser Publications LLC

Subsidiary of Carl Hanser Verlag GmbH & Co KG

414 Walnut St, Suite 323, Cincinnati, OH 45202

Toll Free Tel: 800-950-8977; 888-558-2632 (orders)

E-mail: info@hanserpublications.com

Web Site: www.hanserpublications.com

Key Personnel

Mktg Mgr: Valerie Lauer *Tel:* 513-527-8896

E-mail: valerie.lauer@hanserpublications.com

Founded: 1993

Technical & reference books & related products in manufacturing, metalworking & products finishing. Hanser Publishers: technical, engineering & science reference books, monographs, textbooks & journals in plastics technology, polymer & materials science.

ISBN Prefix(es): 978-1-56990

Number of titles published annually: 17 Print

Total Titles: 312 Print; 250 Online

Foreign Office(s): Carl Hanser Verlag, Kolbergerstr 22, 81679 Munich, Germany *Tel:* (089) 99 93 00 *Fax:* (089) 98 48 09

Foreign Rep(s): Aalborg Centerboghandel (Denmark); Alkem Co (S) Pte Ltd (Mr Adrian Tan) (Singapore); Allied Publishers Pvt Ltd (Mr R N Purwar) (India); Applied Market Information Ltd (Phil Cotterell) (Ireland, UK); Book Editions Pte Ltd (Brunei, Indonesia, Malaysia, Philippines, Singapore, Thailand, Vietnam); Booknet Co Ltd (Muntima Warangkanakooln) (Thailand); Bookshop Lux Libris (Andrej Pucnik) (Slovenia); Co Info Pty Ltd (Australia);

Com.books Ltd (Eliad Sofi) (Israel); Faravaran Publication Distributor Co (Iran); Carl Hanser Verlag GmbH & Co KG (Germany); Inspirees International (China); Interempresas Media SL (Portugal, Spain); Levant Distributors Sarl (Lebanon, Syria); Kuba Libri Ltd (Czechia, Slovakia); Male centrum sro (Slovakia); MeBS (Maurizio Modugno) (Italy); Mirza Book Agency (Qasim Mahmood Mirza) (Pakistan); Progressive International Agencies (Pvt) Ltd (Pakistan); Prospero's Konyvei Budapest KFT (Hungary); Publishers Consultants & Representatives (Tahir M Lodhi) (Pakistan); UBSD Distribution Sdn Bhd (Malaysia); Unifacmanu Trading Co Ltd (Ariel Lai) (Taiwan); Yuha Associates Sdn Bhd (Malaysia)
Returns: Ingram Publisher Services, 1210 Ingram Dr, Chambersburg, PA 17202 *Toll Free Tel:* 888-558-2632 *E-mail:* ips@ingramcontent. com
Distribution Center: Ingram Publisher Services, One Ingram Blvd, La Vergne, TN 37086 *Toll Free Tel:* 888-558-2632 (orders) *E-mail:* ips@ ingramcontent.com

Harlequin Enterprises Ltd
Division of HarperCollins
195 Broadway, 24th fl, New York, NY 10007
SAN: 200-2450
Tel: 212-207-7000 *Toll Free Tel:* 888-432-4879
E-mail: customerservice@harlequin.com
Web Site: www.harlequin.com
Key Personnel
VP & Assoc Publr, Adult Books: Rachel Bressler
VP, Edit, Harlequin Trade Publishing: Margaret Marbury *E-mail:* margaret.marbury@ harpercollins.com
VP, Publicity & Trade Communs, Harlequin Trade Publishing: Heather Connor
Publg Dir, Inkyard Press: Bess Braswell
Edit Dir, Park Row Books: Erika Imranyi
Edit Dir, TK: Peter Joseph
Sr Exec Ed: Glenda Howard
Exec Ed, Love Inspired: Tina James
Sr Mng Ed: Kathleen Reed
Asst Mng Ed: Kristin Errico
Sr Acqs Ed, MIRA: Kathy Sagan
Sr Ed: Gail Chasan; Patience Bloom; Denise Zaza
Sr Ed, Carina Press: Kerri Buckley
Sr Ed, Hanover Square Press: John Glynn
Ed, HQN/Graydon House: Cat Clyne
Ed, Inkyard Press: Rebecca Kuss
Ed, MIRA: April Osborn
Ed, Park Row Books: Laura Brown
Assoc Ed, Harlequin Romantic Suspense: Carly Silver
Assoc Ed, Inkyard Press: Lauren Smulski
Assoc Ed, Love Inspired & Love Inspired Suspense: Dina Davis
Asst Ed, Park Row Books & Hanover Square Press: Natalie Hallak
Sr Publicity Mgr, Fiction: Meredith Barnes
Sr Publicity Mgr, Hanover Square Press, Park Row Books & MIRA: Emer Flounders
Sr Publicist, MIRA, Park Row Books & Hanover Square Press: Roxanne Jones
Publicist: Samantha McVeigh
Assoc Publicist: Jessica Rosenberg
Mgr, Subs Rts: Jennifer Choi
Founded: 1980
Adult contemporary, historical romance novels & women's fiction.
ISBN Prefix(es): 978-0-373
Number of titles published annually: 1,400 Print
Imprints: Carina Press; Graydon House Books; Hanover Square Press; Harlequin; Harlequin Audio; HQ; HQN Books; Inkyard Press; Love Inspired®; Luna Books; MIRA; Park Row Books; Red Dress Ink; Silhouette; Steeple Hill; Worldwide Mystery
Distributed by Simon & Schuster

Distribution Center: 3010 Walden Ave, Depew, NY 14043
Membership(s): Association of American Publishers (AAP); Association of Canadian Publishers (ACP); Book Industry Study Group (BISG)

HarperCollins Children's Books
Division of HarperCollins Publishers
195 Broadway, New York, NY 10007
SAN: 200-2086
Tel: 212-207-7000
Web Site: www.harpercollins.com/childrens
Key Personnel
Pres & Publr: Suzanne Murphy
VP & Publr: Alessandra Balzer; Donna Bray; Virginia Duncan; Katherine Tegen
SVP, Children's Sales: Andrea Pappenheimer *E-mail:* Andrea.Pappenheimer@HarperCollins. com
VP & Edit Dir: Rosemary Brosnan; Nancy Inteli; Tara Welkum
VP & Publg Dir: Erica Sussman; Rich Thomas
VP, Fin & Admin: Tara Feehan
VP, Mktg & Publicity: Nellie Kurtzman
Sr Dir, Digital Mktg: Colleen O'Connell
Sr Dir, Mktg: Ann Dye
Sr Dir, Publicity: Jennifer Corcoran; Cindy Hamilton
Sr Dir, Subs Rts: Rachel Horowitz
Dir, Mktg Design: Audrey Steuerwald
Dir, School & Lib Mktg: Patty Rosati
Edit Dir: Claudia Gabel
Exec Ed: Alyson Day; Kristen Pettit; Andrew Harwell
Board books, novelty books, early readers, picture books, chapter books, juvenile fiction, young adult novels & nonfiction across all categories.
ISBN Prefix(es): 978-0-06; 978-0-688; 978-0-380; 978-0-694; 978-0-690
Imprints: Balzer + Bray; Greenwillow Books; HarperAlley; HarperAudio; HarperCollins; HarperCollins e-books; Heartdrum Books; Quill Tree Books; Katherine Tegen Books; Walden Pond Press
Membership(s): The Children's Book Council (CBC)

HarperCollins General Books Group
Division of HarperCollins Publishers
195 Broadway, New York, NY 10007
SAN: 200-2086
Tel: 212-207-7000
Web Site: www.harpercollins.com
Key Personnel
Pres & Publr, Ecco, EVP: Daniel Halpern
Pres & Publr, Harper: Jonathan Burnham
Pres & Publr, HarperOne/HarperVia/Amistad/Rayo/HarperCollins Espanol: Judith Curr
Pres & Publr, William Morrow/Avon: Liate Stehlik
SVP & Publr, Harper Business: Hollis Heimbouch
SVP & Publr, Harper Wave: Karen Rinaldi
SVP & Deputy Publr, Harper Group/Publr, Harper Perennial: Doug Jones
SVP & Exec Ed, Harper: Jennifer Barth
SVP & Exec Ed, Morrow/Avon: Carrie Feron
SVP, Fin & Publg Opers: Len Marshall *E-mail:* Len.Marshall@HarperCollins.com
SVP, Publicity: Tina Andreadis
VP & Publr, Harper Design: Marta Schooler
VP & Assoc Publr, Harper Perennial: Amy Baker
VP & Assoc Publr, HarperOne: Laina Adler
VP, Edit Dir & Gen Mgr: Gideon Weil
VP & Edit Dir, Custom House: Peter Hubbard
VP & Edit Dir, Dey Street Books: Carrie Thornton
VP & Edit Dir, Ecco: Helen Atsma
VP & Edit Dir, Harper Wave: Julie Will
VP & Exec Ed: Noah Eaker; Jonathan Jao; Sara Nelson
VP & Sr Art Dir, William Morrow: Jeanne Reina
VP & Dir, Sales: Andy LeCount

VP & Deputy Dir, Sales: Mary Beth Thomas
VP, Deputy Gen Coun: Beth Silfin
VP, Exec Ed, Edit Dir, William Morrow: Cassie Jones
VP, Children's Mktg & Publicity: Nellie Kurtzman
VP, Mktg: Leah Wasielewski
VP, Mktg, Harper Wave & Harper Business: Brian Perrin
VP, Prodn & Creative Opers: Tracey Menzies
VP, Sales: Kathy Faber
Assoc Publr, Amistad, Harper Espanol & Intl Fiction Prog: Tara Parsons
Assoc Publr, Ecco: Miriam Parker
Sr Dir, Digital Sales & Mktg: Jim Hanas
Sr Dir, Mktg, Ecco: Meghan Deans
Sr Dir, Mktg, William Morrow: Tavia Kowalchuk
Sr Group Publicity Dir: Kelly Rudolph
Sr Dir, Publicity, Avon/Voyager: Pamela Jaffee
Sr Dir, Publicity, Ecco: Sonya Cheuse
Sr Dir, Publicity, HarperOne: Melinda Mullin
Sr Dir, Publicity, William Morrow: Anwesha Basu; Heidi Richter
Sr Dir, Video & Group Exec Prodr: David Heydt
Sr Mktg Dir, Dey Street Books: Kendra Newton
Sr Mktg Dir, William Morrow: Kaitlin Harri
Art Dir, HarperVia/Amistad/HarperCollins Espanol: Stephen Brayda
Edit Dir, Amistad: Tracy Sherrod
Edit Dir, Harper Voyager: David Pomerico
Edit Dir, William Morrow/Avon: Erika Tsang
Dir, Brand Devt, William Morrow: Kathryn Gordon
Dir, Foreign Rts: Catherine Barbosa Ross
Dir, Prodn Edit, Harper, Harper Business & Collins Reference: John Jusino
Mktg Dir, Harper Perennial & Harper Paperbacks: Lisa Erickson
Mktg Dir, HarperOne: Aly Mostel
Mktg Dir, William Morrow: Kayleigh George
Dir, Mktg: Katie O'Callaghan
Dir, Publicity, Ecco: Caitlin Mulrooney-Lyski
Dir, Publicity, Morrow/Avon: Danielle Bartlett
Dir, Publicity, William Morrow: Maureen Cole
Dir of Sales, General Books, Natl Accts & Amazon: Ashley Mihlebach
Assoc Art Dir, Ecco: Sara Wood
Assoc Dir, Mktg, Harper Wave & Harper Business: Penny Makras
Assoc Dir, Publg, Harper Group: Jennifer Civiletto
Exec Mng Ed, William Morrow: Pamela Barricklow
Exec Ed: Luke Dempsey; Emily Griffin
Exec Ed, Creative Devt: Matt Harper
Exec Ed, Custom House: Katherine Nintzel
Exec Ed, Ecco: Denise Oswald
Exec Ed, HarperOne: Rakesh Satyal; Juan Mila Valcarcel
Exec Ed, HarperVia: Juan Mila
Exec Ed, William Morrow: Rachel Kahan; Emily Krump; Jessica Williams
Exec Ed, William Morrow/Avon: May Chen
Sr Ed, Amistad: Patrik Bass
Sr Ed, Dey Street Books: Matthew Daddona; Jessica Sindler
Sr Ed, Harper: Sarah Stein
Sr Ed, HarperElixir: Libby Edelson
Sr Ed, HarperOne: Miles Doyle; Hilary Swanson
Sr Ed, William Morrow: Liz Stein
Sr Ed, William Morrow/Avon: Tessa Woodward
Ed, Ecco: Gabriella Doob
Ed, Harper: Erin Wicks
Ed, HarperOne: Anna Paustenbach; Sydney Rogers
Ed, William Morrow: Nick Amphlett
Ed, William Morrow/Avon: Nicole Fischer
Assoc Ed, Ecco: Sara Birmingham
Assoc Ed, Harper & Harper Perennial: Mary Gaule
Assoc Ed, Harper Wave: Haley Swanson
Assoc Ed, William Morrow/Avon: Elle Keck
Asst Ed, Dey Street Books: Peter Kispert
Asst Ed, Harper: Alicia Tan

Asst Ed, Harper Wave & Harper Business: Rebecca Raskin
Sr Mktg Mgr, Harper: Becca Putman
Sr Publicity Mgr, Ecco: Martin Wilson
Sr Publicity Mgr, William Morrow: Erin Reback; Eliza Rosenberry
Publicity Mgr: Camille Collins; Theresa Dooley
Sales Mgr: Ronnie Kutys
Sales Support Coord: Raven Andrus
ISBN Prefix(es): 978-0-06
Imprints: Amistad; Avon; Avon Impulse (digital only); Broadside Books; Custom House; Dey Street Books; Ecco; Harper; Harper Business; Harper Design; Harper Luxe (large print); Harper Perennial; Harper Voyager; Harper Wave; HarperAudio; HarperCollins Espanol; HarperLegend; HarperOne; HarperVia; Morrow Gift; William Morrow; William Morrow Paperbacks; Rayo; Witness Impulse

§HarperCollins Publishers
Subsidiary of News Corp
195 Broadway, New York, NY 10007
SAN: 200-2086
Tel: 212-207-7000 *Fax:* 212-207-7145
Web Site: www.harpercollins.com
Key Personnel
Pres & CEO: Brian Murray *E-mail:* Brian.Murray@HarperCollins.com
SVP & CFO: Janet Gervasio *E-mail:* Janet.Gervasio@HarperCollins.com
Chief Digital Offr & EVP, Intl: Chantal Restivo-Alessi
Global CIO: Rick Schwartz *E-mail:* Rick.Schwartz@HarperCollins.com
EVP, Opers: Larry Nevins
SVP, Corp Communs: Erin Crum
SVP, Dist Opers: Joe Franceschelli
SVP, Foreign & Dom Rts: Juliette Shapland
SVP, HR: Diane Bailey
SVP, Intl Sales: David Wolfson
SVP, Mkt Insight & Sales Opers: Frank Albanese
SVP, Sales: Christine Edwards
VP, Assoc Gen Coun: Kyran Cassidy
VP, Prodn & Creative Opers: Tracey Menzies
Affiliate Publr, HarperCollins 360: Jean Marie Kelly
Pres, Sales: Josh Marwell *E-mail:* Josh.Marwell@HarperCollins.com
Sr Dir, Digital Sales & Mktg: Jim Hanas
Dir, Publicity: Kate D'Esmond; Rachel Elinsky
Sr Mgr, Corp Communs: Katie Bennett
Founded: 1817
HarperCollins Publishers is one of the largest consumer book publisher in the world, with operations in 17 countries. With 200 years of history & more than 120 branded imprints around the world, HarperCollins publishes approximately 10,000 new books every year in 16 languages & has a print & digital catalog of more than 200,000 titles. Writing across dozens of genres, HarperCollins authors include winners of the Nobel Prize, the Pulitzer Prize, the National Book Award, the Newbery & Caldecott Medals & the Man Booker Prize. HarperCollins, headquartered in New York, is a subsidiary of News Corp (NASDAQ: NWS, NWSA; ASX: NWS, NWSLV).
ISBN Prefix(es): 978-0-06; 978-0-688; 978-0-380; 978-0-694
Number of titles published annually: 10,000 Print
Membership(s): Association of American Publishers (AAP); Book Industry Study Group (BISG)
See separate listing for:
HarperCollins Children's Books
HarperCollins General Books Group

Harper's Magazine Foundation
666 Broadway, 11th fl, New York, NY 10012
Tel: 212-420-5720 *Toll Free Tel:* 800-444-4653
Fax: 212-228-5889
E-mail: harpers@harpers.org
Web Site: www.harpers.org

Key Personnel
VP & Gen Mgr: Lynn Carlson *E-mail:* lynn@harpers.org
VP, PR: Giulia Melucci
Edit Dir: Ellen Rosenbush
Founded: 1850
General trade.
ISBN Prefix(es): 978-1-879957
Number of titles published annually: 12 Print
Total Titles: 40 Print

Harrington Park Press
9 E Eighth St, Box 331, New York, NY 10003
Tel: 347-882-3545 (edit & publicity) *Fax:* 646-602-1349 (edit & publicity)
Web Site: harringtonparkpress.com
Key Personnel
Publr & Ed-in-Chief: Bill Cohen *E-mail:* bcohen@harringtonparkpress.com
Founded: 2010
Privately owned small scholarly LBGTQ press. Inquiries regarding distribution, such as discounts, shipping, publication date updates, etc, should go directly to Columbia University Press.
ISBN Prefix(es): 978-1-939594
Number of titles published annually: 4 Print; 4 E-Book
Total Titles: 11 Print; 11 E-Book
Distributed by Columbia University Press
Membership(s): American Association of Law Libraries; American Library Association (ALA); Association of American Publishers (AAP); Association of American Publishers Professional & Scholarly Publishing Division; Crossref; Medical Library Association; Society for Scholarly Publishing (SSP); Special Libraries Association (SLA)

§Harrison House Publishers
Subsidiary of Nori Media Group
167 Walnut Bottom Rd, Shippensburg, PA 17257
SAN: 253-4339
Tel: 717-532-3040
Web Site: www.harrisonhouse.com
Founded: 1975
Charismatic/Christian publishing house.
ISBN Prefix(es): 978-1-57794; 978-0-89274
Number of titles published annually: 50 Print
Total Titles: 400 Online

Hartman Publishing Inc
1313 Iron Ave SW, Albuquerque, NM 87102
Tel: 505-291-1274 *Toll Free Tel:* 800-999-9534
Toll Free Fax: 800-474-6106
E-mail: info@hartmanonline.com
Web Site: www.hartmanonline.com
Key Personnel
Publr: Mark Hartman
Mng Ed: Susan Alvare Hedman
Founded: 1994
Publish a variety of in-service training materials & textbooks for certified nursing assistants & home health aides. Subjects include Alzheimer's disease, infection control, body mechanics, abuse & neglect, AIDS/HIV & communication skills.
ISBN Prefix(es): 978-1-888343
Number of titles published annually: 12 Print; 1 CD-ROM; 1 Audio
Total Titles: 40 Print; 1 CD-ROM; 1 Audio
Membership(s): New Mexico Book Association

Harvard Art Museums
32 Quincy St, Cambridge, MA 02138
Tel: 617-495-9400; 617-496-6529 (edit)
Web Site: www.harvardartmuseums.org
Key Personnel
Dir, Communs: Daron Manoogian
Assoc Dir, Publg & Mng Ed: Micah Buis
Ed: Cheryl Pappas
Asst Ed: Sarah Kuschner

Founded: 1901
Art history.
ISBN Prefix(es): 978-0-916724; 978-1-891771
Number of titles published annually: 5 Print
Total Titles: 70 Print
Distributed by Yale University Press

Harvard Business Review Press
Division of Harvard Business Publishing
20 Guest St, Suite 700, Brighton, MA 02135
Tel: 617-783-7400 *Fax:* 617-783-7489
E-mail: custserv@hbsp.harvard.edu
Web Site: www.harvardbusiness.org
Key Personnel
Commercial Dir & Assoc Publr: Erika Heilman
Edit Dir & Assoc Publr: Melinda Merino
Mktg Dir: Julie Devoll
Ed-in-Chief: Adi Ignatius
Exec Ed: Jeff Kehoe
Assoc Ed: Ania Wieckowski
Founded: 1984
Trade & professional books for the business management & academic audiences in the areas of strategy, leadership, innovation, organizational behavior/human resource management, finance management, marketing, production & operations management. *Harvard Business Review*, reference books & Internet.
ISBN Prefix(es): 978-0-87584; 978-1-57851; 978-1-4221; 978-1-59139
Number of titles published annually: 70 Print
Total Titles: 700 Print
Imprints: Harvard Business Reference
Foreign Rep(s): McGraw-Hill Education (Africa, Asia, Australia, Canada, Europe, Middle East, New Zealand); United Publishers Services Ltd (Japan)
Distribution Center: Perseus Distribution, 250 W 57 St, 15th fl, New York, NY 10107 *Tel:* 212-340-8100 *Fax:* 212-340-8105

Harvard Common Press
Imprint of Quarto Publishing Group USA Inc
100 Cummings Ctr, Suite 265-D, Beverly, MA 01915
Tel: 978-282-9590 *Fax:* 978-282-7765
Web Site: www.quartoknows.com/harvard-common-press
Key Personnel
VP & Group Publr: Winnie Prentiss *E-mail:* winnie.prentiss@quarto.com
Edit Dir: Dan Rosenberg *E-mail:* dan.rosenberg@quarto.com
Founded: 1976
General nonfiction: cookbooks, health, self-help, child care & parenting.
ISBN Prefix(es): 978-0-916782; 978-0-87645; 978-1-55832
Number of titles published annually: 24 Print
Total Titles: 150 Print

§Harvard Education Publishing Group
Division of Harvard Graduate School of Education
8 Story St, 1st fl, Cambridge, MA 02138
Tel: 617-495-3432 *Fax:* 617-496-3584
Web Site: www.hepg.org
Key Personnel
Dir: Douglas Clayton *Fax:* 978-348-1233 *E-mail:* douglas_clayton@gse.harvard.edu
Assoc Dir & Ed-in-Chief: Caroline Chauncey *E-mail:* caroline_chauncey@harvard.edu
Dir, Sales & Mktg: Christina DeYoung *E-mail:* christina_deyoung@gse.harvard.edu
Edit & Prodn Dir: Sumita Mukherji *E-mail:* sumita_mukherji@gse.harvard.edu
Publisher of books & journals on education practice, research & policy.
ISBN Prefix(es): 978-1-891792; 978-1-883433; 978-0-916690; 978-1-934742; 978-1-61250; 978-1-68253
Number of titles published annually: 30 Print; 1 CD-ROM; 20 E-Book

Total Titles: 285 Print; 1 CD-ROM; 120 E-Book
Imprints: Harvard Education Press; Harvard Educational Review
Foreign Rep(s): Eurospan Group (worldwide exc Canada & USA)
Orders to: Publishers Shipping & Storage, 46 Development Rd, Fitchburg, MA 01420 *Tel:* 978-345-2121 *Toll Free Tel:* 888-437-1437 *Fax:* 978-348-1233 *E-mail:* orders@pssc.com *Web Site:* pssc.com
Returns: Publishers Shipping & Storage, 46 Development Rd, Fitchburg, MA 01420 *Toll Free Tel:* 888-437-1437 *Fax:* 978-348-1233 *E-mail:* orders@pssc.com *Web Site:* pssc.com
Warehouse: Publishers Shipping & Storage, 46 Development Rd, Fitchburg, MA 01420 *Tel:* 978-345-2121 *Toll Free Tel:* 888-437-1437 *Fax:* 978-348-1233 *E-mail:* orders@pssc.com *Web Site:* pssc.com

Harvard Square Editions
Beachwood Terr, Hollywood, CA 90068
Tel: 323-203-0233
E-mail: submissions@harvardsquareeditions.org
Web Site: harvardsquareeditions.org
Key Personnel
Outreach Dir: Simone Weingarten *E-mail:* sw@harvardsquareeditions.org
Founded: 2000
Run by Harvard alumni, Harvard Square Editions publishes authors of literary fiction of environmental, spiritual or social value. Harvard Square Editions books have won National Book Foundation, Nautilus & other awards. Its mission is to publish fiction that transcends national boundaries, especially mss that are international, political, literary, diverse, multicultural, science fiction, climate fiction, fantasy, utopia & dystopia. They appreciate aesthetic value & constructive social & political content, especially mss related to climate change, deforestation & conservation, but have a low tolerance for profanity & graphic violence.
ISBN Prefix(es): 978-0-9833216; 978-0-9895960; 978-1-941861
Number of titles published annually: 10 Print; 10 E-Book
Total Titles: 55 Print; 58 E-Book
Distribution Center: Gardners Books, One Whittle Dr, Eastbourne, East Sussex BN23 6QH, United Kingdom *Tel:* (01323) 521555 *Web Site:* www.gardners.com

Harvard Ukrainian Research Institute
Subsidiary of Harvard University
34 Kirkland St, Cambridge, MA 02138
SAN: 208-967X
Tel: 617-495-4053 *Fax:* 617-495-8097
E-mail: huri@fas.harvard.edu
Web Site: www.huri.harvard.edu
Key Personnel
Mgr, Pubns: Oleh Kotsyuba *E-mail:* kotsyuba@fas.harvard.edu
Founded: 1973
ISBN Prefix(es): 978-0-916458; 978-1-932650
Number of titles published annually: 5 Print; 3 Online
Total Titles: 100 Print; 6 Online
Distributed by Harvard University Press

Harvard University Press
79 Garden St, Cambridge, MA 02138-1499
SAN: 200-2043
Tel: 617-495-2600; 401-531-2800 (intl orders) *Toll Free Tel:* 800-405-1619 (orders) *Fax:* 617-495-5898 (gen); 617-496-4677 (edit & rts); 401-531-2801 (intl orders) *Toll Free Fax:* 800-406-9145 (orders)
E-mail: contact_hup@harvard.edu
Web Site: www.hup.harvard.edu

Key Personnel
CFO: Dan Wackrow *E-mail:* dan_wackrow@harvard.edu
Dir: George Andreou
Promo & Ad Dir: Sheila Barrett *E-mail:* sheila_barrett@harvard.edu
Dir, Design & Prodn: Tim Jones *E-mail:* tim_jones@harvard.edu
Dir, Intellectual Property: Stephanie Vyce *E-mail:* stephanie_vyce@harvard.edu
Asst Dir/Ed-in-Chief: Susan Wallace Boehmer *E-mail:* susan_boehmer@harvard.edu
Asst Dir, Sales & Mktg: Susan Donnelly *E-mail:* susan_donnelly@harvard.edu
Exec Ed: Joy de Menil
Exec Ed-at-Large: Thomas LeBien *E-mail:* thomas_lebien@harvard.edu; Sharmila Sen *E-mail:* sharmila_sen@harvard.edu
Exec Ed-at-Large, Global: Ian Malcolm *E-mail:* imalcolm@harvardup.co.uk
Exec Ed-at-Large, History: Kathleen McDermott *E-mail:* kathleen_mcdermott@harvard.edu
Sr Exec Ed, History & Contemporary Aff: Joyce Seltzer *E-mail:* joyce_seltzer@harvard.edu
Exec Ed, Humanities: Lindsay Waters *E-mail:* lindsay_waters@harvard.edu
Exec Ed, Life Sciences: Janice Audet
Exec Ed, Physical Sciences & Technol: Jeff Dean
Gen Ed, Human Behavior, Educ & the Humanities: Andrew Kinney *E-mail:* andrew_kinney@harvard.edu
Sales Mgr & Digital Content Mgr: Vanessa Vinarub *E-mail:* vanessa_vinarub@harvard.edu
Founded: 1913
General scholarly, humanities, social sciences, life/physical sciences.
ISBN Prefix(es): 978-0-674
Number of titles published annually: 200 Print
Total Titles: 8,000 Print
Imprints: Belknap Press
Foreign Office(s): Vernon House, 23 Sicilian Ave, London WC1A 2QS, United Kingdom, Exec Ed-at-Large, Global: Ian Malcolm *Tel:* (020) 3463 2350 *Fax:* (020) 7831 9261 *E-mail:* imalcolm@harvardup.co.uk
Distributed by HarperCollins Publishers India Ltd (Indian subcontinent)
Distributor for Harvard Center for Middle Eastern Studies; Harvard Center for Population Studies; Harvard Center for the Study of World Religions; Harvard College Library (including Houghton Library Judaica div); Harvard Department of Sanskrit & Indian Studies; Harvard Department of the Classics; Harvard Ukrainian Research Institute; Harvard University Asia Center; Harvard University David Rockefeller Center for Latin American Studies; Harvard-Yenching Institute; Peabody Museum of Archaeology & Ethnology
Foreign Rep(s): Academic Book Promotions (Benelux); Aromix Books (Hong Kong); Avicenna Ltd (Bill Kennedy) (Bahrain, Egypt, Iran, Iraq, Kuwait, Lebanon, Libya, Oman, Qatar, Saudi Arabia, Sudan, Syria, United Arab Emirates, Yemen); Avicenna Ltd (Claire de Gruchy) (Algeria, Cyprus, Jordan, Malta, Morocco, Palestine, Tunisia, Turkey); Amos Bampisaki (Burundi, Rwanda, Sudan, Tanzania, Uganda); John Eklund (Canada exc British Columbia, Midwestern States); Everest International Publishing Services (Wei Zhao) (China); Harvard Business Review Press (Bangladesh, Bhutan, India, Maldives, Nepal, Pakistan, Sri Lanka); Harvard University Press London (Greece, Ireland, Israel, UK); Havilah Procurement & Library Services (Ghana, Nigeria); In-Books/James Bennett Pty Ltd (Australia, New Zealand); Information & Culture, Korea (South Korea); Ewa Ledochiwicz (Albania, Bosnia and Herzegovina, Croatia, Czechia, Estonia, Hungary, Kazakhstan, Latvia, Lithuania, Poland, Romania, Russia, Serbia, Slovakia, Slovenia); Uwe Ludemann (Austria, France, Germany, Italy, Portugal, Spain, Switzerland); Patricia

Nelson (British Columbia, CN, Southwest, Western USA); B K Norton Ltd (Taiwan); Palgrave (Cory Voigt) (Southern Africa); Rockbook Inc (Japan); Joan Wamae (Kenya); Yuha Associates (Malaysia); Zimpfer Global Services (Caribbean, Central America)
Foreign Rights: Akcali Agency (Turkey); L'Autre Agence (France); Bardon-Chinese Media Agency (China, Hong Kong, Taiwan); Bookman Literary Agency (Denmark, Finland, Iceland, Norway, Sweden); Dar Cherlin (Arab Middle East); The English Agency (Japan); Graal Literary Agency (Bulgaria, North Macedonia, Poland, Romania, Serbia, Slovakia); The Deborah Harris Agency (Israel); International Editors' Co (Central America, Latin America, South America, Spain); Alexander Korzhenevski Agency (Russia); Liepman Agency AG (Germany, Switzerland); Ilidio Matos Agencia (Portugal); OA Literary Agency (Greece); Oxford Literary & Rights Agency (Croatia, Czechia, Ukraine); Seibel Publishing Services (Brazil); Suzanna Zevi Agenzia Letteraria (Italy)
Shipping Address: Triliteral LLC, 100 Maple Ridge Dr, Cumberland, RI 02864-1769
Membership(s): American Association of University Presses (AAUP); Association of American Publishers (AAP); Book Industry Study Group (BISG)

Harvest House Publishers Inc
PO Box 41210, Eugene, OR 97404-0322
SAN: 207-4745
Tel: 541-343-0123 *Toll Free Tel:* 888-501-6991 *Fax:* 541-342-6410
E-mail: admin@harvesthousepublishers.com; permissions@harvesthousepublishers.com
Web Site: harvesthousepublishers.com
Key Personnel
Pres: Bob Hawkins, Jr
Intl Rts: Sharon Shook
Founded: 1974
Evangelical Christian books; no unsol mss.
ISBN Prefix(es): 978-0-89081; 978-1-56507; 978-0-7369
Number of titles published annually: 120 Print
Total Titles: 1,400 Print
Membership(s): Book Industry Study Group (BISG)

§Hatherleigh Press Ltd
62545 State Hwy 10, Hobart, NY 13788
Toll Free Tel: 800-528-2550
E-mail: info@hatherleighpress.com; publicity@hatherleighpress.com
Web Site: www.hatherleighpress.com
Key Personnel
Pres & CEO: Andrew Flach
Assoc Publr: Ryan Tumambing
Mng Ed: Ryan Kennedy
Founded: 1995
Motto: "Improve your life. Change your world." Expert content in health, wellness, fitness, exercise, nutrition, inspiration, healthy living & sustainability. Print books, ebooks, audio, digital & filmed entertainment.
ISBN Prefix(es): 978-1-886330; 978-1-57826
Number of titles published annually: 30 Print; 30 E-Book
Total Titles: 300 Print; 100 E-Book; 4 Audio
Imprints: GetFitNow.com Books; Healthy Living Books
Distributed by Penguin Random House Inc
Foreign Rep(s): Nigel Yorweth (worldwide)
Distribution Center: Penguin Random House Publisher Services (PRHPS) *Toll Free Tel:* 800-733-3000; 888-523-9292 (CN sales) *Toll Free Fax:* 800-659-2436; 888-562-9924 (CN sales) *E-mail:* csorders@randomhouse.com

§Hay House Inc
2776 Loker Ave W, Carlsbad, CA 92010

Mailing Address: PO Box 5100, Carlsbad, CA 92018-5100

Tel: 760-431-7695 (ext 2, intl) *Toll Free Tel:* 800-654-5126 (ext 2, US) *Toll Free Fax:* 800-650-5115

E-mail: info@hayhouse.com; editorial@hayhouse.com

Web Site: www.hayhouse.com

Key Personnel

Founder & Chmn: Louise Hay

Pres & CEO: Reid Tracy

COO: Margarete Nielsen

Publr & VP: Patricia Gift

Founded: 1984

Self-help/New Age, health, philosophy, spiritual growth & awareness, mental & environmental harmony books; also self-healing; biography, producers & distributors of recordings & video pertaining to health of mind, body & spirit. Accept agented submissions only; SASE required.

ISBN Prefix(es): 978-0-937611; 978-1-56170; 978-1-4019

Number of titles published annually: 50 Print; 50 Audio

Total Titles: 1,000 Print; 1,000 Audio

Imprints: Hay House Business

Divisions: Balboa Press

Branch Office(s)

665 Broadway, Suite 1200, New York, NY 10012 *Tel:* 646-484-4950 *Fax:* 646-484-4956

Foreign Office(s): Hayhouse Australia Pty Ltd, 18/36 Ralph St, Alexandria, NSW 2015, Australia *Tel:* (02) 9669 4299 *Fax:* (02) 9669 4144 *Web Site:* www.hayhouse.com.au

Hayhouse Publishers India, Muskaan Complex, Plot No 3, B-2, Vasant Kunj, New Delhi 110 070, India *Tel:* (011) 4176 1620 *Fax:* (011) 4176 1630 *Web Site:* www.hayhouse.co.in

Hayhouse SA Pty Ltd, PO Box 990, Witkoppen 2068, South Africa *Tel:* (011) 326 3449 *Web Site:* www.hayhouse.co.za

Hayhouse UK Ltd, 33 Notting Hill Gate, London W11 3JQ, United Kingdom *Tel:* (020) 3675 2460 *Fax:* (020) 3675 2451 *Web Site:* www. hayhouse.co.uk

Returns: 2750 Progress St, Vista, CA 92081 *Toll Free Tel:* 800-654-5126

Warehouse: 2750 Progress St, Suite B, Vista, CA 92081 *Fax:* 760-431-6948

Distribution Center: Penguin Random House Publisher Services (PRHPS), 1745 Broadway, New York, NY 10019 *E-mail:* distribution@randomhouse.com *Web Site:* www. penguinrandomhouse.biz/publisherservices

Raincoast Books, 2440 Viking Way, Richmond, BC V6V 1N2, Canada *Toll Free Tel:* 800-663-5714 *Toll Free Fax:* 800-565-3770 *E-mail:* customerservice@raincoast.com

Haynes North America Inc

Division of The Haynes Publishing Group

859 Lawrence Dr, Newbury Park, CA 91320-1514

Tel: 805-498-6703 *Toll Free Tel:* 800-4-HAYNES (442-9637) *Fax:* 805-498-2867

E-mail: cstn@haynes.com

Web Site: www.haynes.com

Key Personnel

Chmn: E Bell

SVP: Harvey Wolff

Mktg Dir: Reed Trueblood

Founded: 1960

Publisher & importer of books on domestic & foreign autos & motorcycles & historical & technical motoring.

ISBN Prefix(es): 978-0-946609; 978-1-56392

Number of titles published annually: 13 Print

Total Titles: 690 Print

Distributed by Motorbooks

Distributor for G T Foulis; Haynes Owners Workshop Manuals; Oxford Illustrated Press

Warehouse: Eastern Warehouse, 1299 Bridgestone Pkwy, La Vergne, TN 37086 *Fax:* 615-793-5325

§Hazelden Publishing

Division of The Hazelden Betty Ford Foundation

15251 Pleasant Valley Rd, Center City, MN 55012-0011

SAN: 125-1953

Mailing Address: PO Box 176, Center City, MN 55012-0176

Tel: 651-213-4200 *Toll Free Tel:* 800-257-7810; 866-328-9000 *Fax:* 651-213-4793

E-mail: productionformation@hazeldenbettyford. org

Web Site: www.hazelden.org

Key Personnel

Publr: Joseph Jaksha

Founded: 1954

Adult trade hardcover & paperbacks; curriculum, workbooks; gift books, video & audio; self-help, addiction & recovery, personal & spiritual growth; computer based products, wellness products, young adult nonfiction.

ISBN Prefix(es): 978-0-89486; 978-1-56838; 978-0-89638; 978-0-942421; 978-0-935908; 978-1-56246; 978-0-934125

Number of titles published annually: 12 Print

Total Titles: 500 Print; 500 E-Book; 10 Audio

Imprints: Hazelden/Johnson Institute; Hazelden/Keep Coming Back; Hazelden-Pittman Archives Press

Distributed by Health Communications Inc (trade); Simon & Schuster

Distributor for Obsessive Anonymous

Foreign Rep(s): Eurospan (Europe, Ireland, UK); RecoverOz (Australia, New Zealand)

Hazy Dell Press

1001 SE Water Ave, Suite 132, Portland, OR 97214

Tel: 971-279-5779

E-mail: info@hazydellpress.com

Web Site: www.hazydellpress.com

Key Personnel

Edit Dir: Kyle Sullivan

Art Dir: Derek Sullivan

Mktg Dir: Renee Yama

Founded: 2015

Headquartered in the Pacific Northwest with offices in Portland & Seattle, Hazy Dell Press publishes quirky, grown-up-friendly children's books that promote empathy, diversity & imagination.

ISBN Prefix(es): 978-0-9965787; 978-1-948931

Number of titles published annually: 5 Print; 4 E-Book

Total Titles: 14 Print; 10 E-Book

Orders to: Consortium Book Sales & Distribution, 210 American Dr, Jackson, TN 38301 *Toll Free Tel:* 800-283-3572 *E-mail:* ipsjacksonorders@ingramcontent. com; Publishers Group Canada, c/o Raincoast Books, 2440 Viking Way, Richmond, BC V6V 1N2, Canada *Toll Free Tel:* 800-663-5714 *E-mail:* customerservice@raincoast.com

Distribution Center: Consortium Book Sales & Distribution, 210 American Dr, Jackson, TN 38301 *Toll Free Tel:* 800-283-3572 *E-mail:* ipsjacksonorders@ingramcontent.org

Membership(s): Publishers Association of the West (PubWest)

§HCPro

Division of BLR®—Business & Legal Resources

35 Village Rd, Suite 200, Middleton, MA 01949

Toll Free Tel: 800-650-6787 *Toll Free Fax:* 800-785-9212

E-mail: customerservice@hcpro.com

Web Site: www.hcpro.com

Founded: 1986

Specialize in healthcare administration & management.

ISBN Prefix(es): 978-1-885829; 978-1-55645

Number of titles published annually: 110 Print; 4 CD-ROM; 30 Online; 5 E-Book; 60 Audio

Total Titles: 125 Print; 5 CD-ROM; 40 Online; 25 E-Book; 75 Audio

Imprints: Opus Communications

Subsidiaries: The Greeley Co

Membership(s): NEPA

Health Administration Press

Division of Foundation of the American College of Healthcare Executives

One N Franklin St, Suite 1700, Chicago, IL 60606-3491

SAN: 207-0464

Tel: 312-424-2800 *Fax:* 312-424-0014

E-mail: hapbooks@ache.org

Web Site: www.ache.org/hap (orders)

Key Personnel

Pres & CEO: Deborah J Bowen

VP, Pubns: Michael Cunningham *Tel:* 312-424-9470 *E-mail:* mcunningham@ache.org

Acqs Ed: Janet Davis *Tel:* 312-424-9460 *E-mail:* jdavis@ache.org

Mktg Mgr: Nancy Vitucci *Tel:* 312-424-9450 *E-mail:* nvitucci@ache.org

Founded: 1972

Health administration, health care, law & medicine, medical care organization.

ISBN Prefix(es): 978-0-910701; 978-1-56793

Number of titles published annually: 20 Print

Total Titles: 200 Print; 1 E-Book

Imprints: American College of Healthcare Executives Management Series; AUPHA Press/Health Administration Press; Executive Essentials; Gateway to Healthcare Management

Branch Office(s)

PO Box 75145, Baltimore, MD 21275, Contact: Jessica Dunkerly *Tel:* 301-362-6905 *Fax:* 240-396-5907

Foreign Rep(s): ELEA doo (Europe); iGroup (Asia); Login Bros (Canada)

Billing Address: 9050 Junction Dr, Annapolis Junction, MD 20701

Orders to: 9050 Junction Dr, Annapolis Junction, MD 20701 *Tel:* 301-362-6905 *Fax:* 240-396-5907 *E-mail:* hap@brightkey.net

Returns: 9050 Junction Dr, Annapolis Junction, MD 20701

Shipping Address: 9050 Junction Dr, Annapolis Junction, MD 20701 *Tel:* 301-362-6905 *E-mail:* hap@brightkey.net

Warehouse: 9050 Junction Dr, Annapolis Junction, MD 20701, Contact: Jessica Dunkerly *Tel:* 301-362-6905 *Fax:* 240-396-5907

Distribution Center: Independent Publishers Group (IPG), 814 N Franklin St, Chicago, IL 60610 *Toll Free Tel:* 800-888-4741 *E-mail:* orders@ipgbook.com *Web Site:* www. ipgbook.com

9050 Junction Dr, Annapolis Junction, MD 20701

§Health Communications Inc

3201 SW 15 St, Deerfield Beach, FL 33442

SAN: 212-100X

Tel: 954-360-0909 *Toll Free Tel:* 800-851-9100; 800-441-5569 (cust serv & orders) *Fax:* 954-360-0034 *Toll Free Fax:* 800-424-7652 (cust serv & orders)

E-mail: customerservice2@hcibooks.com

Web Site: www.hcibooks.com

Key Personnel

CEO: Christian Blonshine *E-mail:* christian. blonshine@hcibooks.com

CFO: Craig Jarvie *E-mail:* craig.jarvie@hcibooks. com

Pres & Publr: Peter Vegso

Art Dir: Larissa Henoch

Edit Dir: Christine Belleris; Candace Johnson

Dir, PR: Kim Weiss *E-mail:* kim.weiss@ hcibooks.com

Dir, Trade Sales, Intl Sales & Dist: Lori Golden *E-mail:* lori.golden@hcibooks.com

Founded: 1977

Publisher of nonfiction paperbacks & hardcover books on self-help, personal growth, diet, fit-

ness, inspiration, health, parenting, women's issues, teens, religion, psychology, addiction & recovery.
ISBN Prefix(es): 978-0-932194; 978-1-55874; 978-0-7573; 978-0-9910732
Number of titles published annually: 50 Print; 50 E-Book
Total Titles: 500 Print; 500 E-Book; 18 Audio
Imprints: HCI Books; HCI Teens
Divisions: HCI Printing & Publishing
Distributed by Simon & Schuster Inc
See separate listing for:
Simcha Press

§Health Forum Inc
Subsidiary of American Hospital Association
155 N Wacker Dr, Suite 400, Chicago, IL 60606
SAN: 216-5872
Tel: 312-893-6800 *Toll Free Tel:* 800-242-2626 *Fax:* 312-422-4500
E-mail: hfcustsvc@healthforum.com
Web Site: www.ahaonlinestore.com; www. healthforum.com
Key Personnel
Sr Ed: Rick Hill *Tel:* 312-893-6863
    E-mail: rhill@aha.org
Founded: 1986
Publisher of professional books & textbooks for health care professionals. Specialize in books that help hospital executives & department heads manage their business better & achieve improved patient satisfaction. Also provide ICD-10-CM/PCS & data information from the AHA Central Office & the American Hospital Association annual survey of hospitals.
ISBN Prefix(es): 978-1-55648; 978-0-87258
Number of titles published annually: 10 Print; 2 CD-ROM; 2 E-Book
Total Titles: 30 Print; 2 CD-ROM; 3 E-Book
Imprints: AHA (American Hospital Association)
Billing Address: AHA Services Inc, Contact: Francine Adcock *Tel:* 312-422-3238 *Fax:* 312-422-4597 *E-mail:* fadcock@aha.org
Orders to: AHA Services Inc, PO Box 933283, Atlanta, GA 31193-3283 *Toll Free Fax:* 866-516-5817 *E-mail:* aha-orders@pbd.com
Returns: AHA Services Inc, Cust Returns, 3280 Summit Ridge Pkwy, Duluth, GA 30096
Warehouse: AHA Services Inc, 3280 Summit Ridge Pkwy, Duluth, GA 30096 (AHA order servs) *Toll Free Tel:* 866-516-5817 *E-mail:* aha-orders@pbd.com
Distribution Center: Rittenhouse Book Distributors, 511 Feheley Dr, King of Prussia, PA 19406, Contact: Nicole Gallo *Toll Free Tel:* 800-345-6425 *Fax:* 610-277-0390 *E-mail:* n.gallo@rittenhouse.com *Web Site:* www.rittenhouse.com
Majors Education Solutions, 500 E Corporate Dr, Suite 600, Lewisville, TX 75057, Contact: Martha Yeahquo *Tel:* 972-353-1100 *Toll Free Tel:* 800-633-1851 *Fax:* 972-353-1300 *E-mail:* customerservice@majors.com *Web Site:* www.majors.com
Membership(s): American Hospital Association; Independent Book Publishers Association (IBPA)

§Health Professions Press
Subsidiary of Paul H Brookes Publishing Co Inc
409 Washington Ave, Suite 500, Towson, MD 21204
SAN: 297-7338
Mailing Address: PO Box 10624, Baltimore, MD 21285-0624
Tel: 410-337-9585 *Toll Free Tel:* 888-337-8808 *Fax:* 410-337-8539
Web Site: www.healthpropress.com
Key Personnel
Pres: Melissa Behm *E-mail:* mbehm@ healthpropress.com
Dir, Pubns: Mary H Magnus *E-mail:* mmagnus@ healthpropress.com

Mktg Mgr: Kaitlin Konecke *E-mail:* kkonecke@ healthpropress.com
Founded: 1989
Hardcover, paperback & digital professional resources & textbooks in aging, Alzheimer's disease, long-term care & health administration.
ISBN Prefix(es): 978-1-878812; 978-1-932529; 978-1-938870
Number of titles published annually: 6 Print; 5 E-Book
Total Titles: 105 Print; 5 CD-ROM; 37 E-Book
Foreign Rep(s): Cranbury International Books LLC (Caribbean, Latin America); Eurospan Ltd (Africa, Asia, Europe, Middle East, UK); Footprint Books Pty Ltd (Australia, Fiji, New Zealand, Papua New Guinea); Login Brothers (Canada); Unifacmanu Trading Co Ltd (Taiwan)
Warehouse: Maple Logistics Solutions, 60 Grumbacher Rd I-83 Industrial Park, PO Box 15100, York, PA 17406
Membership(s): Independent Book Publishers Association (IBPA)

Healthy Learning, see Coaches Choice

§HeartMath LLC
14700 W Park Ave, Boulder Creek, CA 95006
Tel: 831-338-8500 *Toll Free Tel:* 800-711-6221 *Fax:* 831-338-8504
E-mail: info@heartmath.org; inquiry@heartmath. org
Web Site: www.heartmath.org
Key Personnel
Sr Advisor: Bruce Cryer
EVP, Strategic Devt: Howard Martin
VP, Fin/COO: Chris Jacob
Dir, PR: Gabriella Boehmer *E-mail:* gboehmer@ heartmath.org
Founded: 1998
Publishers of The HeartMath System.
ISBN Prefix(es): 978-1-879052; 978-0-9700286
Number of titles published annually: 16 Print
Total Titles: 2 CD-ROM; 7 Audio

Hearts 'n Tummies Cookbook Co
Division of Quixote Press
3544 Blakslee St, Wever, IA 52658
Tel: 319-372-7480 *Toll Free Tel:* 800-571-2665 *Fax:* 319-372-7485
E-mail: quixotepress@gmail.com; heartsntummies@gmail.com
Web Site: www.heartsntummies.com
Key Personnel
Pres & Intl Rts: Bruce Carlson
Founded: 1982
Cookbooks.
ISBN Prefix(es): 978-1-878488; 978-1-57166
Number of titles published annually: 20 Print
Total Titles: 400 Print

Hebrew Union College Press
Division of Hebrew Union College
3101 Clifton Ave, Cincinnati, OH 45220
Tel: 513-221-1875 *Fax:* 513-221-0321
Web Site: press.huc.edu
Key Personnel
Co-Dir: David H Aaron *Tel:* 513-487-3265 *E-mail:* daaron@huc.edu; Jason Kalman *Tel:* 513-221-1875 ext 3248 *E-mail:* jkalman@ huc.edu
Edit Dir: David Ellenson *Tel:* 800-424-1336 ext 2201 *E-mail:* dellenson@huc.edu; Sharon Gillerman *Tel:* 213-765-2152 *E-mail:* sgillerman@huc.edu; Alyssa Gray *Tel:* 212-824-2284 *E-mail:* agray@huc.edu; Richard Saranson *Tel:* 513-221-1875 ext 3245 *E-mail:* rsaranson@huc.edu; Adam Shear; Yaron Tsur
Mng Ed: Sonja Rethy
Founded: 1921
Scholarly Jewish books.

ISBN Prefix(es): 978-0-87820
Number of titles published annually: 11 Print
Total Titles: 100 Print
Distribution Center: ISD, 70 Enterprise Dr, Bristol, CT 06010 *Tel:* 860-584-6546 *E-mail:* orders@isdistribution.com *Web Site:* isdistribution.com

Heimburger House Publishing Co
7236 W Madison St, Forest Park, IL 60130
Tel: 708-366-1973 *Fax:* 708-366-1973
E-mail: info@heimburgerhouse.com
Web Site: www.heimburgerhouse.com
Key Personnel
Publr: Donald J Heimburger
Founded: 1962
Publish books & magazines on railroad & other transportation subjects; list includes more than 350 book titles.
ISBN Prefix(es): 978-0-911581
Number of titles published annually: 3 Print
Total Titles: 50 Print
Distributor for Child's Play International; Evergreen Press; Firefly Books Ltd; Fordham University Press; Globe Pequot Press; HarperCollins; Johns Hopkins University Press; Houghton Mifflin Harcourt; Iconografix; Indiana University Press; Kalmbach Publishing Co; Krause Publications; Motorbooks; National Book Network; New York University Press; W W Norton & Company Inc; Penguin Putnam Inc; Pictorial Histories Publishing Co; Steam Passages Publishing; Sterling Publishing Co Inc; Sugar Cane Press; Syracuse University Press; Thunder Bay Press; University of Minnesota Press; John Wiley & Sons

§William S Hein & Co Inc
2350 N Forest Rd, Getzville, NY 14068
Tel: 716-882-2600 *Toll Free Tel:* 800-828-7571 *Fax:* 716-883-8100
E-mail: mail@wshein.com; marketing@wshein. com
Web Site: www.wshein.com
Key Personnel
Chmn of the Bd: William S Hein, Jr *E-mail:* whein@wshein.com
Pres & CEO: Shane P Marmion *Tel:* 716-882-2600 ext 129 *E-mail:* smarmion@wshein.com
Chief Resource Offr: Daniel P Rosati *E-mail:* drosati@wshein.com
VP, Sales: W Shannon Hein *E-mail:* shein@ wshein.com
VP, Technol: Kyle Daving
Dir, Mktg: Shannon Furtak *E-mail:* sfurtak@ wshein.com
Founded: 1961
Publish & reprint law & related materials, hard copy, micro, CDs & online products.
ISBN Prefix(es): 978-0-8377; 978-0-89941; 978-1-57588
Number of titles published annually: 30 Print; 2 CD-ROM; 1 Online
Total Titles: 5,000 Print; 5 CD-ROM; 2 Online
Distributor for Ashgate; Aspen; Butterworths; Sweet & Maxwell; John Wiley & Sons Inc
Membership(s): American Association of Law Libraries; Canadian Association of Law Libraries

§Heinemann
Division of Houghton Mifflin Harcourt
361 Hanover St, Portsmouth, NH 03801-3912
SAN: 210-5829
Mailing Address: PO Box 6926, Portsmouth, NH 03802-6926
Tel: 603-431-7894 *Toll Free Tel:* 800-225-5800 (US) *Fax:* 603-431-2214 *Toll Free Fax:* 877-231-6980 (US)
E-mail: custserv@heinemann.com
Web Site: www.heinemann.com
Key Personnel
SVP, Gen Mgr: Vicki Boyd *E-mail:* vicki.boyd@ heinemann.com

Mng Ed: Sarah Fournier *Tel:* 603-431-7894 ext 1195 *E-mail:* sarah.fournier@heinemann.com
Founded: 1978
Education - professional books for teachers K-college. Literacy, math, social studies, drama, art & English teaching. Hardcover & paperbound. Trade - drama, world literature, education, African studies. Hardcover & paperbound class.
ISBN Prefix(es): 978-0-86709; 978-0-325; 978-0-435
Number of titles published annually: 50 Print; 40 E-Book
Total Titles: 2,500 Print; 225 E-Book
Distributed by Pearson (Canada, Australia & New Zealand)

§Hellgate Press
Imprint of L & R Publishing
PO Box 3531, Ashland, OR 97520
Tel: 541-973-5154 *Toll Free Tel:* 800-795-4059
E-mail: sales@hellgatepress.com
Web Site: www.hellgatepress.com
Key Personnel
Owner: Harley B Patrick *E-mail:* harley@hellgatepress.com
Founded: 1997
Military history, adventure travel, veteran memoirs, historical & adventure fiction.
ISBN Prefix(es): 978-1-55571
Number of titles published annually: 15 Print
Total Titles: 80 Print
Distribution Center: Independent Publishers Group (IPG), 814 N Franklin St, Chicago, IL *Tel:* 312-337-0747 *Toll Free Tel:* 800-888-4741 *Fax:* 312-337-5985 *E-mail:* orders@ipgbook.com *Web Site:* www.ipgbook.com

Hendrickson Publishers Inc
PO Box 3473, Peabody, MA 01961-3473
Tel: 978-532-6546 *Toll Free Tel:* 800-358-3111 *Fax:* 978-573-8111
E-mail: customerservice@hendricksonrose.com; info@hendricksonrose.com
Web Site: www.hendricksonrose.com
Key Personnel
Dir, Mktg & Communs: Meg Rusick *E-mail:* mrusick@hendricksonrose.com
Contract & Licensing/Digital Publg/Systems Mgr: Kris Orlando
Founded: 1978
Religious reference, language, history & theology.
ISBN Prefix(es): 978-0-913573; 978-0-943575; 978-0-917006; 978-1-56563
Number of titles published annually: 80 Print; 3 CD-ROM
Total Titles: 450 Print
Imprints: Aspire Press; Rose Kidz; Rose Publishing
Foreign Rep(s): Alban Books Ltd (Europe, UK)
Foreign Rights: KCBS (Korea)
Orders to: Parasource Distribution, 55 Woodslee Ave, PO Box 98, Paris, ON N3L 3E5, Canada (CN) *Toll Free Tel:* 800-263-2664 *Toll Free Fax:* 800-461-8575 *E-mail:* custserv@davidccook.ca *Web Site:* www.davidccook.ca; Alban Books Ltd, 14 Belford Rd, Edinburgh, Scotland EH4 3BL, United Kingdom *Tel:* (0131) 226 2217 *Fax:* (0131) 225 5999 *E-mail:* sales@albanbooks.com *Web Site:* www.albanbooks.com

Her Own Words LLC
PO Box 5264, Madison, WI 53705-0264
Tel: 608-271-7083 *Fax:* 608-271-0209
Web Site: www.herownwords.com; www.nontraditionalcareers.com
Key Personnel
Mgr: Jocelyn Riley *E-mail:* jocelynriley@herownwords.com
Founded: 1986

Women's history, literature, arts & women in non-traditional careers.
ISBN Prefix(es): 978-1-60118
Number of titles published annually: 3 Print
Total Titles: 36 Print
Imprints: Her Own Words; Literature & Arts; Women In Nontraditional Careers; Women's History

Herald Press
Imprint of MennoMedia
PO Box 866, Harrisonburg, VA 22803
SAN: 202-2915
Toll Free Tel: 800-245-7894 (orders) *Fax:* 540-242-4476 *Toll Free Fax:* 877-271-0760
E-mail: info@mennomedia.org; customerservice@mennomedia.org
Web Site: www.heraldpress.com; store.mennomedia.org
Key Personnel
Exec Dir & Publr: Amy Gingerich *E-mail:* amyg@mennomedia.org
Mng Ed: Meghan Florian *Tel:* 540-574-4874 *E-mail:* meghanf@mennomedia.org
Acqs Ed: Dayna Olson-Getty *E-mail:* daynaog@mennomedia.org
Founded: 1908
General Christian trade books, family, devotional, cookbooks, juveniles, adult fiction, Bible study, theology, peace & social concerns, missions, Amish & Mennonite history & culture, songbooks.
ISBN Prefix(es): 978-0-8361
Number of titles published annually: 20 Print
Total Titles: 500 Print
Membership(s): Evangelical Christian Publishers Association (ECPA)

Herald Publishing House
Division of Community of Christ
1001 W Walnut St, Independence, MO 64050-3562
SAN: 202-2907
Tel: 816-521-3015 *Toll Free Tel:* 800-767-8181 *Fax:* 816-521-3066
E-mail: sales@heraldhouse.org
Web Site: www.heraldhouse.org
Key Personnel
Fiscal Servs Specialist: Suzan Hudson
Founded: 1860
ISBN Prefix(es): 978-0-8309
Number of titles published annually: 12 Print
Total Titles: 360 Print
Imprints: Independence Press

Heritage Books Inc
5810 Ruatan St, Berwyn Heights, MD 20740
Toll Free Tel: 800-876-6103 *Toll Free Fax:* 800-876-6103; 800-297-9954
E-mail: orders@heritagebooks.com; submissions@heritagebooks.com
Web Site: www.heritagebooks.com
Key Personnel
Pres & CEO: Craig R Scott *Tel:* 800-876-6103 ext 700 *E-mail:* crscott@heritagebooks.com
Founded: 1978
Books on local history, genealogy & Americana.
ISBN Prefix(es): 978-0-917890; 978-1-55613; 978-0-7884; 978-1-58549; 978-0-940907; 978-1-888265; 978-1-68034
Number of titles published annually: 200 Print; 200 E-Book
Total Titles: 8,500 Print; 1,200 CD-ROM; 4,000 E-Book
Imprints: Antient Press; Colonial Roots; Delmarva Roots; Eagle Editions; Fireside Fiction; Heritage Books; Willow Bend Books
Distributor for Fairfax Genealogical Society; National Genealogical Society; Virginia Genealogical Society

§The Heritage Foundation
214 Massachusetts Ave NE, Washington, DC 20002-4999
Tel: 202-546-4400 *Toll Free Tel:* 800-544-4843 *Fax:* 202-546-8328
E-mail: info@heritage.org
Web Site: www.heritage.org
Key Personnel
Pres: Kay Coles James
Creative Dir: Melissa Bluey
Founded: 1973
Domestic policy, foreign policy & defense.
ISBN Prefix(es): 978-0-89195
Number of titles published annually: 10 Print; 2 CD-ROM
Total Titles: 19 Print; 2 CD-ROM; 8 E-Book

Heuer Publishing LLC
PO Box 248, Cedar Rapids, IA 52406
Tel: 319-368-8008 *Toll Free Tel:* 800-950-7529 *Fax:* 319-368-8011
E-mail: orders@heuerpub.com; customerservice@heuerpub.com
Web Site: www.hitplays.com
Key Personnel
Publr: Steven S Michalicek
Ed: Ms Geri Albrecht
Founded: 1928
Publishes plays, musicals, operas/operettas & guides (choreography, costume, production/staging) for amateur & professional markets including junior & senior high schools, college/university & community theatres. Focus includes comedy, drama, fantasy, mystery & holiday with special interest focus in multicultural, historic, classic literature, Shakespearian theatre, interactive, teen issues & biographies. Pays by percentage royalty or outright purchase.
ISBN Prefix(es): 978-1-61588
Number of titles published annually: 25 Print
Total Titles: 150 Print

Hewitt Homeschooling Resources
Division of Hewitt Research Foundation
8117 N Division, Suite D, Spokane, WA 99208
Mailing Address: PO Box 28010, Spokane, WA 99228
Toll Free Tel: 800-348-1750 *Fax:* 360-835-8697
E-mail: sales@hewitthomeschooling.com
Web Site: hewitthomeschooling.com
Key Personnel
Pres: Jack Lewis
Founded: 1964
Homeschooling, curriculum.
ISBN Prefix(es): 978-0-913717; 978-1-57896
Number of titles published annually: 6 Print
Total Titles: 150 Print

Heyday
1808 San Pablo Ave, Suite A, Berkeley, CA 94702
SAN: 207-2351
Mailing Address: PO Box 9145, Berkeley, CA 94709-0145
Tel: 510-549-3564
E-mail: heyday@heydaybooks.com
Web Site: heydaybooks.com
Key Personnel
Publr & Exec Dir: Steve Wasserman
Edit Dir: Gayle Wattawa
Acqs Ed: Marthine Satris
Founded: 1974
Nonprofit publisher of nonfiction in the following subject areas: history, nature, social justice & California Indians (preference for Native writers). Publishes the quarterly magazine *News from Native California*.
ISBN Prefix(es): 978-0-930588; 978-1-890771; 978-0-9666691; 978-1-59714
Number of titles published annually: 20 Print
Total Titles: 225 Print

Imprints: Sierra College Press
Returns: Ingram Publisher Services, 1210 Ingram Dr, Chambersburg, TN 17202
Distribution Center: Publishers Group West, 1700 Fourth St, Berkeley, CA 94710 *Tel:* 510-809-3700 *Toll Free Tel:* 800-788-3123 *Fax:* 510-809-3777 *E-mail:* info@pgw.com *Web Site:* www.pgw.com

Hi Willow Research & Publishing
123 E Second Ave, Suite 1106, Salt Lake City, UT 84103
Tel: 801-755-1122
E-mail: lmcsourcesales@gmail.com
Web Site: www.lmcsource.com; www.davidvl.org
Key Personnel
Owner: David V Loertscher
Founded: 1978
Books for schools & libraries.
ISBN Prefix(es): 978-0-931510; 978-1-933170
Number of titles published annually: 8 Print
Total Titles: 35 Print

Higginson Book Co
10 Colonial Rd, Suite 5-6, Salem, MA 01970
Mailing Address: PO Box 778, Salem, MA 01970
Tel: 978-745-7170 *Fax:* 978-745-8025
E-mail: higginsonbookcompany@gmail.com
Web Site: www.higginsonbooks.com
Founded: 1969
Publish reprints of rare & out of print genealogies, local history & Civil War regimentals.
ISBN Prefix(es): 978-0-8328; 978-0-7404
Number of titles published annually: 400 Print
Total Titles: 15,000 Print

High Plains Press
PO Box 123, Glendo, WY 82213
Tel: 307-735-4370 *Toll Free Tel:* 800-552-7819
Fax: 307-735-4590
E-mail: editor@highplainspress.com
Web Site: highplainspress.com
Key Personnel
Publr & Primary Ed: Nancy Curtis
Founded: 1984
Books about Wyoming & the American West.
ISBN Prefix(es): 978-0-931271
Number of titles published annually: 3 Print; 3 E-Book
Total Titles: 70 Print; 15 E-Book; 1 Audio
Membership(s): Independent Book Publishers Association (IBPA); Publishers Association of the West (PubWest)

High Tide Press
Subsidiary of The Trinity Foundation
301 Veterans Pkwy, New Lenox, IL 60451
E-mail: orders@cherryhillhightide.com
Web Site: www.cherryhillhightide.com
Key Personnel
Dir: Anne C Ward *Tel:* 800-235-6009
E-mail: award@hightidepress.com
Founded: 1995
Full service publisher of hardcover & paperback books & one quarterly magazine for the book trade & professional niche markets. Specialize in the fields of developmental & intellectual disabilities, behavioral health, nonprofit management, social enterprise, leadership. The High Tide Monograph Series imprint focuses on high quality management practices in behavioral health & developmental disability services while the Midewin Series focuses on the prevention of abuse & neglect of persons with disabilities.
ISBN Prefix(es): 978-0-9653744; 978-1-892696
Number of titles published annually: 12 Print; 4 Online; 4 E-Book
Total Titles: 46 Print; 1 E-Book
Imprints: High Tide Monograph Series; Midewin Series

Orders to: Cherry Hill Bookstore, 1805 Ferro Dr, New Lenox, IL 60451, Cust Serv: Terra Radetski *Tel:* 815-723-0898 *Toll Free Tel:* 800-235-6009 *Fax:* 815-723-2760
Membership(s): Independent Book Publishers Association (IBPA)

Highlights for Children Inc
815 Church St, Honesdale, PA 18431
Tel: 570-253-1164 *Toll Free Tel:* 800-490-5111
Fax: 570-253-0179
E-mail: salesandmarketing@highlightspress.com
Web Site: www.highlightspress.com; www.highlights.com; www.facebook.com/HighlightsforChildren
Key Personnel
Pres, Consumer Busn: Lece Lohr
VP & Publr, Highlights Book Group: Michael Eisenberg *E-mail:* michael.eisenberg@highlights.com
Dir, Specialty & Gift Sales, Highlights Book Group: Janine G Webb *E-mail:* janine.webb@highlights.com
Sales Dir, Highlights Book Group: Jon Ackerman *E-mail:* jon.ackerman@highlights.com
Asst Ed, Highlights Press: Christy Thomas
Retail Mktg Mgr, Highlights Press: Monica Jankauskas
Founded: 1946
ISBN Prefix(es): 978-0-87534
Number of titles published annually: 150 Print
Imprints: Highlights Learning; Highlights Press
Orders to: Penguin Random House, 400 Hahn Rd, Westminster, MD 21157 *Toll Free Tel:* 800-733-3000; Penguin Random House Inc International Dept, 1745 Broadway, New York, NY 10019 *Tel:* 212-572-6083 *Fax:* 212-572-6045 *E-mail:* international@penguinrandomhouse.com; Penguin Random House Canada, 320 Front St W, Suite 1400, Toronto, ON M5V 3B6, Canada *Toll Free Tel:* 888-523-9292 *Toll Free Fax:* 888-562-9924
Returns: Penguin Random House, Attn: Returns Dept, 1019 N State Rd 47, Crawfordsville, IN 47933; Penguin Random House Canada, Attn: Returns Dept, 6971 Columbus Rd, Mississauga, ON L5T 1K1, Canada

Hill & Wang
Division of Farrar, Straus & Giroux, LLC
175 Varick St, New York, NY 10014
SAN: 201-9299
Tel: 212-741-6900 *Fax:* 212-633-9385
E-mail: fsg.publicity@fsgbooks.com; fsg.editorial@fsgbooks.com; sales@fsgbooks.com
Web Site: us.macmillan.com/hillandwang.aspx
Key Personnel
VP & Contracts Dir, FSG: Erika Seidman
VP & Dir, Publicity, FSG: Sarita Varma
Dir, Ad & Promo, FSG: Victoria Genna
Founded: 1956
General nonfiction, history & drama.
ISBN Prefix(es): 978-0-8090
Number of titles published annually: 10 Print
Foreign Rights: ANA Baltic (Tatjana Zoldnere) (Estonia, Latvia, Lithuania); AnatoliaLit Agency (Amy Spangler & Eda Caca) (Turkey); Anthea Agency (Katalina Sabeva) (Bulgaria); L'Autre Agency (Corinne Marotte & Marie Lannurien) (France); Bardon-Chinese Media (David Tsai) (China, Taiwan); Anoukh Foerg Agency (Germany); Deborah Harris Agency (Geula Geurts) (Israel); International Copyright Agency (Simon Kessler & Marina Adriana) (Romania); The Italian Literary Agency srl (Claire Sabatie-Garat) (Italy); Anna Jarota Agency (Dominika Bojanowska) (Poland); Katai & Bolza (Peter Bolza) (Hungary); KCC (Kyung Kang) (Korea); MB Agencia Literaria (Monica Martin & Ines Planells) (Latin America, Spain); Kristin Olson Literarni Agentura (Czechia); Plima Literary Agency (Vuk Perisic) (Albania, Croatia, Serbia, Slove-

nia); Read 'n Right Agency (Nike Davarinou) (Greece); Riff Agency (Laura & Joao Paulo Riff) (Brazil); Sebes & Bisseling Literary Agency (Paul Sebes) (Netherlands); Synopsis Literary Agency (Olga Zasetskaya) (Russia); Tuttle-Mori Agency Inc (Asako Kawachi) (Japan)
Warehouse: MPS Distribution Center, 16365 James Madison Hwy, Gordonsville, VA 22942 *Toll Free Tel:* 888-330-8477

Hillsdale College Press
Division of Hillsdale College
33 E College St, Hillsdale, MI 49242
Tel: 517-437-7341 *Toll Free Tel:* 800-437-2268
Fax: 517-607-2658
E-mail: pr@hillsdale.edu
Web Site: www.hillsdale.edu
Key Personnel
Ed & VP, External Aff: Douglas A Jeffrey
Founded: 1974
Single author books & collected essays of historical, political & economic interest.
ISBN Prefix(es): 978-0-916308

Hillsdale Educational Publishers Inc
39 North St, Hillsdale, MI 49242
SAN: 159-8759
Tel: 517-437-3179 *Fax:* 517-437-0531
E-mail: davestory@aol.com
Web Site: www.hillsdalepublishers.com; michbooks.com
Key Personnel
Pres & Author: David B McConnell
Founded: 1965
Publish & distribute regional titles for schools & libraries.
ISBN Prefix(es): 978-0-910726; 978-1-931466
Number of titles published annually: 4 Print; 1 CD-ROM; 1 Audio
Total Titles: 18 Print; 1 CD-ROM; 1 Audio

§Hilton Publishing Co
Division of HPC
1630 45 St, Suite B101, Munster, IN 46321
Tel: 219-922-4868 *Fax:* 219-924-6811
E-mail: info@hiltonpub.com
Web Site: www.hiltonpub.com
Key Personnel
EVP: Megan Lippert *E-mail:* mlippert@hiltonpub.com
Sr Dir, Fin & Acctg: Tammy Gauthier *E-mail:* tgauthier@hiltonpub.com
Founded: 1996
Publish books in health & wellness, minority health, religion (health-related). Consistent themes of publications include living with & preventing various disease states, illustrating & promoting components of healthy living, embracing & illuminating cultural diversity related to health & well-being & fostering health in the Christian community. Books are peer-reviewed by experts in the appropriate fields to insure we have included the most current, accurate & relevant information. We publish informative & educational books for the general public as well as books aimed at the medical community.
ISBN Prefix(es): 978-0-9654553; 978-0-9675258; 978-0-9716067; 978-0-9743144; 978-0-9764443; 978-0-9777779; 978-0-9800649; 978-0-9815381; 978-0-9841447; 978-0-9847566
Number of titles published annually: 12 Print; 10 E-Book
Total Titles: 50 Print; 3 CD-ROM; 50 Online; 20 E-Book; 3 Audio
Foreign Rep(s): Gabriel Wilmoth (Canada, Germany, USA)
Foreign Rights: Nigel Yorwerth (worldwide)
Membership(s): Indiana Minority Supplier Development Council (INMSDC); National Minor-

ity Supplier Development Council (NMSDC); North Carolina Ministry Supplier Development Council (NCMSDC)

Himalayan Institute Press
Division of Himalayan International Institute of Yoga Science & Philosophy
952 Bethany Tpke, Honesdale, PA 18431
Tel: 570-253-5551 *Toll Free Tel:* 800-822-4547
E-mail: trade@himalayaninstitute.org
Web Site: www.himalayaninstitute.org
Key Personnel
Chmn & Spiritual Head: Pandit Rajmani Tigunait, PhD
Dir: Stephen Moulton *E-mail:* smoulton@ himalayaninstitute.org
Founded: 1971
Publish CDs, DVDs & books on yoga, meditation, holistic health, philosophy, psychology & stress management.
ISBN Prefix(es): 978-0-89389
Number of titles published annually: 4 Print; 3 E-Book; 2 Audio
Total Titles: 60 Print; 10 Audio

§Hippocrene Books Inc
171 Madison Ave, Suite 1605, New York, NY 10016
Tel: 212-685-4373
E-mail: info@hippocrenebooks.com; orderdept@ hippocrenebooks.com (orders)
Web Site: www.hippocrenebooks.com
Key Personnel
Publr & Edit Dir: Priti Chitnis Gress
E-mail: pgress@hippocrenebooks.com
Fin Offr: Awilda Alvarez
Publicity Mgr & Ed: Colette Laroya *Tel:* 212-685-4371 ext 4
Founded: 1971
Foreign language dictionaries & self-study guides in over 120 languages; international cookbooks, history & travel.
ISBN Prefix(es): 978-0-87052; 978-0-7818
Number of titles published annually: 25 Print
Total Titles: 500 Print; 150 E-Book
Foreign Rights: A B E Marketing (Poland); Bookery Pty Ltd (Australia); Gazelle Book Services Ltd (England); Publishers Group Canada (Canada)
Shipping Address: Whitehurst & Clark Book Services, 1200 County Rd, Rte 523, Flemington, NJ 08822
Warehouse: Whitehurst & Clark Book Services, 1200 County Rd, Rte 523, Flemington, NJ 08822
Membership(s): Independent Book Publishers Association (IBPA)

The Historic New Orleans Collection
533 Royal St, New Orleans, LA 70130
Tel: 504-523-4662 *Fax:* 504-598-7108
E-mail: wrc@hnoc.org
Web Site: www.hnoc.org
Key Personnel
Pres & CEO: Daniel Hammer *Tel:* 504-598-7112
E-mail: daniel.hammer@hnoc.org
Dir, Pubns & Mktg: Dr Jessica Dorman *Tel:* 504-598-7174 *E-mail:* jessicad@hnoc.org
Founded: 1966
Publications related to Louisiana history & to the holdings of The Historic New Orleans Collection; preservation manuals for family papers, photographs, etc.
ISBN Prefix(es): 978-0-917860
Number of titles published annually: 3 Print
Total Titles: 74 Print; 3 E-Book

§History Publishing Co LLC
PO Box 700, Palisades, NY 10964
SAN: 850-5942
Tel: 845-359-1765 *Fax:* 845-818-3730 (sales)
E-mail: info@historypublishingco.com

Web Site: www.historypublishingco.com
Key Personnel
Owner & Publr: Don Bracken *E-mail:* djb@ historypublishingco.com
Sr Ed: Alexis Starke *E-mail:* alex@ historypublishingco.com
Founded: 2007
Trade book publisher. HPC imprint for early & recent history. Chronology books for history from a third party perspective, *Today's Books* for current issues. Introduced 2 new imprints in 2017 one for historical fiction & one for issues dealing with contemporary issues.
ISBN Prefix(es): 978-19339-09; 978-19407-73
Number of titles published annually: 12 Print; 75 Online; 100 E-Book
Total Titles: 75 Print; 75 Online; 100 E-Book
Imprints: Chronology Books; History Publishing Company (early & recent history); Today's Books; Today's Titles
Warehouse: Whitehurst & Clark, 1200 County Rte 523, Flemington, NJ 08822 *Tel:* 908-782-2323 *Fax:* 908-237-2407 *Web Site:* www.wcbks.com
Distribution Center: INscribe Digital, 444 Spear St, Suite 213, San Francisco, CA 94105
Membership(s): Association of American Publishers (AAP); Independent Book Publishers Association (IBPA)

Histria Books
Division of Histria LLC
7181 N Hualapai Way, Suite 130-86, Las Vegas, NV 89166
Tel: 561-299-0802
E-mail: info@histriabooks.com; orders@ histriabooks.com; rights@histriabooks.com
Web Site: histriabooks.com
Key Personnel
Dir: Kurt Brackob
Mgr: Dana Brackob; Dana Ungureanu
E-mail: dana@histriabooks.com
Asst Mgr: J D Mabbot
Founded: 1996
Publishes general interest books, fiction & literature, children's books, as well as scholarly books in a broad range of categories. Originally established as an academic publisher, Histria Books is now an independent publishing house with offices in Las Vegas, NV & Palm Beach, FL.
ISBN Prefix(es): 978-973-9432 (Center for Romanian Studies); 978-973-98091 (Center for Romanian Studies); 978-973-98392 (Center for Romanian Studies); 978-1-59211
Number of titles published annually: 28 Print; 20 E-Book
Total Titles: 115 Print; 25 E-Book
Imprints: Addison & Highsmith Publishers (high quality works of fiction); Center for Romanian Studies (history & culture of Romania); Gaudium Publishing (contemporary lifestyle, culture, sports, politics, biography & autobiography); Histria Kids (children & young adults); Vita Histria (academic books)
Branch Office(s)
931 Village Blvd, No 905-269, West Palm Beach, FL 33409
Sales Office(s): Casemate | publishers, 1950 Lawrence Rd, Havertown, PA 19083
Tel: 610-853-9131 *E-mail:* casemate@ casematepublishers.com
Casemate UK, The Old Music Hall, 106-108 Cowley Rd, Oxford OX4 1JE, United Kingdom *Tel:* (01865) 241249 *Fax:* (01865) 794449
E-mail: casemate-uk@casematepublishers.co.uk
Web Site: www.casematepublishing.co.uk
Distributed by Casemate | publishers
Foreign Rights: Pubmatch (worldwide exc North America & UK)
Orders to: Casemate | publishers, 1950 Lawrence Rd, Havertown, PA 19083 *Tel:* 610-853-9131
E-mail: casemate@casematepublishers.com

Web Site: www.casematepublishers.com; Lightning Source Inc, 1246 Heil Quaker Blvd, La Vergne, TN 37086 *Toll Free Tel:* 800-509-4156 *Fax:* 615-213-4725 *E-mail:* inquiry@ lightningsource.com; Casemate UK, The Old Music Hall, 106-108 Cowley Rd, Oxford OX4 1JE, United Kingdom *Tel:* (01865) 241249 *Fax:* (01865) 794449 *E-mail:* casemate-uk@ casematepublishers.co.uk *Web Site:* www. casematepublishing.co.uk
Shipping Address: Lightning Source Inc, 1246 Heil Quaker Blvd, La Vergne, TN 37086 *Toll Free Tel:* 800-509-4156 *Fax:* 615-213-4725 *E-mail:* inquiry@lightningsource.com; Books International, 22883 Quicksilver Dr, Dulles, VA 20166; POD Worldwide, 9 Culley Ct, Orton Southgate, Peterborough PE2 6XD, United Kingdom
Warehouse: Books International, 22883 Quicksilver Dr, Dulles, VA 20166 (Casemate | publishers US) *Tel:* 703-661-1500 *Fax:* 703-661-1501
Web Site: booksintl.presswarehouse.com
Orca Book Services Ltd, Unit A3, Fleets Corner Industrial Estate, Off Nuffield Rd, Fleetsbridge, Poole, Dorset BH17 0HL, United Kingdom (Casemate UK) *Tel:* (01235) 465500
E-mail: tradeorders@orcabookservices.co.uk
Web Site: www.orcabookservices.co.uk
Distribution Center: Casemate | publishers, 1950 Lawrence Rd, Havertown, PA 19083 (North America) *Tel:* 610-853-9131
E-mail: casemate@casematepublishers.com
Web Site: www.casematepublishers.com
Casemate UK, The Old Music Hall, 106-108 Cowley Rd, Oxford OX4 1JE, United Kingdom (worldwide exc North America) *Tel:* (01865) 241249 *Fax:* (01865) 794449
E-mail: casemate-uk@casematepublishers.co.uk
Web Site: www.casematepublishing.co.uk
Membership(s): American Association for the Advancement of Slavic Studies (AAASS); Independent Book Publishers Association (IBPA); Publishers Association of the West (PubWest)

HMH Assessments, see Houghton Mifflin Harcourt Assessments

W D Hoard & Sons Co
28 W Milwaukee Ave, Fort Atkinson, WI 53538
Mailing Address: PO Box 801, Fort Atkinson, WI 53538-0801
Tel: 920-563-5551 *Fax:* 920-563-7298
E-mail: hdbooks@hoards.com; editors@hoards.com
Web Site: www.hoards.com
Key Personnel
Assoc Ed: Maggie Seiler
Book Ed: Aisha Liebenow
Founded: 1870
Dairy oriented & some agricultural, regional publications, catalogs & specialty projects.
ISBN Prefix(es): 978-0-932147
Number of titles published annually: 5 Print
Total Titles: 22 Print
Imprints: Hoard's Dairyman Magazine

Hobblebush Books
17-A Old Milford Rd, Brookline, NH 03033
Tel: 603-672-4317 *Fax:* 603-672-4317
E-mail: info@hobblebush.com
Web Site: www.hobblebush.com
Key Personnel
Owner: Mr Sidney Hall, Jr
Pres: Kirsty Walker
Founded: 1993
Independent publisher of both literary & non-literary titles.
ISBN Prefix(es): 978-0-9636413; 978-0-9760896; 978-0-9801672; 978-1-939449
Number of titles published annually: 3 Print; 3 E-Book
Total Titles: 45 Print; 3 E-Book

Orders to: Small Press Distributors, 1341 Seventh St, Berkeley, CA 94710-1409 (bookstores & libs) *Toll Free Tel:* 800-869-7553 *Fax:* 510-524-0852 *Web Site:* www.spdbooks.org; Baker & Taylor, 2550 W Tyvola Rd, Suite 300, Charlotte, NC 28217 (trade) *Tel:* 704-998-3100 *Toll Free Tel:* 800-775-1800 *E-mail:* btinfo@btol.com *Web Site:* www.btol.com

Distribution Center: Small Press Distributors, 1341 Seventh St, Berkeley, CA 94710-1409 (bookstores & libs) *Toll Free Tel:* 800-869-7553 *Fax:* 510-524-0852 *Web Site:* www.spdbooks.org

Baker & Taylor, 2550 W Tyvola Rd, Suite 300, Charlotte, NC 28217 (trade) *Tel:* 704-998-3100 *Toll Free Tel:* 800-775-1800 *Web Site:* www.baker-taylor.com

Membership(s): Community of Literary Magazines & Presses (CLMP); Independent Publishers of New England (IPNE); New Hampshire Writers Project (NHWP)

§Hogrefe Publishing Corp
Subsidiary of Hogrefe Verlag GmbH & Co Kg
361 Newbury St, 5th fl, Boston, MA 02115
SAN: 293-2792
Tel: 857-880-2002
E-mail: customerservice@hogrefe.com
Web Site: us.hogrefe.com
Key Personnel
Publg Mgr: Robert Dimbleby *E-mail:* robert.dimbleby@hogrefe.com
Founded: 1978
Books, journals & online resources in the fields of psychiatry, psychology, psychotherapy, medicine.
ISBN Prefix(es): 978-0-88937; 978-0-920887; 978-1-61676 (ebooks); 978-1-61334 (EPUB)
Number of titles published annually: 15 Print
Foreign Office(s): Hogrefe Verlag GmbH & Co Kg, Merkelstr 3, 37085 Goettingen, Germany *Tel:* (0551) 999 50-0 *Fax:* (0551) 999 50
Distributor for Hogrefe AG (Switzerland); Hogrefe Verlag (Germany)
Orders to: Baker & Taylor Publisher Services, 30 Amberwood Pkwy, Ashland, OH 44805, Dist Servs Mgr: Cheryl Householder *Tel:* 567-215-0030 *Toll Free Tel:* 888-814-0208 *E-mail:* info@btpubservices.com *Web Site:* www.btpubservices.com
Returns: Baker & Taylor Publisher Services, 30 Amberwood Pkwy, Ashland, OH 44805, Dist Servs Mgr: Cheryl Householder *Tel:* 567-215-0030 *Toll Free Tel:* 888-814-0208 *E-mail:* info@btpubservices.com *Web Site:* www.btpubservices.com
Distribution Center: Baker & Taylor Publisher Services, 30 Amberwood Pkwy, Ashland, OH 44805, Dist Servs Mgr: Cheryl Householder *Tel:* 567-215-0030 *Toll Free Tel:* 888-814-0208 *E-mail:* info@btpubservices.com *Web Site:* www.btpubservices.com
Membership(s): Association of American Publishers (AAP); STM

Hohm Press
Subsidiary of HSM LLC
PO Box 4410, Chino Valley, AZ 86323
Tel: 928-636-3331 *Toll Free Tel:* 800-381-2700
Fax: 928-636-7519
E-mail: publisher@hohmpress.com
Web Site: www.hohmpress.com
Key Personnel
Gen Mgr & Publr: Dasya Anthony Zuccarello
Mng Ed: Regina Sara Ryan
Prodn Mgr: Joe Bala Zuccarello
Founded: 1975
Independent publisher of books on spirituality & consciousness studies.
ISBN Prefix(es): 978-0-934252; 978-1-890772
Number of titles published annually: 8 Print; 8 E-Book
Total Titles: 250 Print; 65 E-Book; 6 Audio

Imprints: Kalindi Press (books on natural health & nutrition, children's & family health)
Foreign Rep(s): Gazelle Book Services Ltd (Europe)
Foreign Rights: HBC Productions (Deanna Leah) (worldwide)
Shipping Address: 860 Staley Lane, Chino Valley, AZ 86323
Warehouse: 860 Staley Lane, Chino Valley, AZ 86323
Distribution Center: SCB Distributors, 15608 S New Century Dr, Gardena, CA 90248 (US & CN) *Toll Free Tel:* 800-729-6423 *Web Site:* www.scbdistributors.com

Holiday House Publishing Inc
50 Broad St, New York, NY 10004
SAN: 202-3008
Tel: 212-688-0085 *Fax:* 212-421-6134
E-mail: info@holidayhouse.com
Web Site: www.holidayhouse.com
Key Personnel
EVP & Gen Mgr: Derek Stordahl
VP & Ed-in-Chief: Mary Cash *E-mail:* mcash@holidayhouse.com
VP & Dir, Prodn: Lisa Lee *E-mail:* llee@holidayhouse.com
VP, Mktg: Terry Borzumato-Greenberg *E-mail:* tborzumato@holidayhouse.com
VP, Rts, Perms & Digital Publg: Julia Gallagher *E-mail:* jgallagher@holidayhouse.com
Publr, Margaret Ferguson Books: Margaret Ferguson *E-mail:* mferguson@holidayhouse.com
Publr, Neal Porter Books: Neal Porter *E-mail:* nporter@holidayhouse.com
Exec Dir, Mktg: Michelle Montague
Dir, Art & Design: Kerry Martin *E-mail:* kmartin@holidayhouse.com
Exec Ed: Grace Maccarone *E-mail:* gmaccarone@holidayhouse.com
Mng Ed: Raina Putter
Ed: Mora Couch; Elizabeth Law; Sally Morgridge
Sr Rts Mgr: Miriam Miller *E-mail:* mmiller@holidayhouse.com
Data Mgr: Hannah Finne
Sr Publicist: Cheryl Lew
Mktg Coord: Emily Mannon
School & Lib Mktg Coord: Nicole Benevento
Founded: 1935
Juvenile & young adult books.
ISBN Prefix(es): 978-0-8234
Number of titles published annually: 90 Print
Total Titles: 800 Print; 300 E-Book
Imprints: Margaret Ferguson Books; Neal Porter Books
Distributed by Pengin Random House
Foreign Rights: Big Apple Agency (Vincent Lin) (China); Sandra Bruna Agencia Literaria (Sandra Bruna) (Spanish-speaking countries); The Deborah Harris Agency (Efrat Lev) (Israel); The Italian Agency (Chiara Piovan) (Italy); Japan UNI Agency (Takeshi Oyama) (Japan); Korea Copyright Center (Hansol Lee) (Korea); Agence Michelle Lapautre (Catherine Lapautre) (French-speaking countries); Seibel Publishing Services (Patricia Natalia Seibel) (Brazil, Portugal); Tuttle-Mori Thailand (Nawara Hirankan) (Indonesia, Thailand, Vietnam); Watson Little Ltd (Rachel Richardson) (British Commonwealth, Eastern Europe, Greece, Hungary, Netherlands); Literarische Agentur Silke Weniger (Silke Weniger, Alexandra Legath & Sabrina Gold) (Austria, Germany, Switzerland (German-speaking))
Orders to: Penguin Random House (US) *Toll Free Tel:* 800-733-3000
Shipping Address: Penguin Random House (US)
Distribution Center: Penguin Random House Publisher Services (PRHPS)
Membership(s): The Children's Book Council (CBC)

Hollym International Corp
2647 Gateway Rd, No 105-223, Carlsbad, CA 92009
SAN: 211-0172
Tel: 760-814-9880 *Fax:* 908-353-0255
E-mail: contact@hollym.com
Web Site: www.hollym.com
Key Personnel
Pres: Gene S Rhie
Founded: 1977
Publish & distribute books in English on Korea related topics.
ISBN Prefix(es): 978-0-930878; 978-1-56591
Number of titles published annually: 10 Print
Total Titles: 155 Print
Foreign Office(s): Hollym Corp, 13-13 Gwancheol-dong, Jongno-gu, 110-111 Seoul, South Korea, Contact: Kim-Man Ham *Tel:* (02) 735-7551 *Fax:* (02) 730-5149 *E-mail:* info@hollym.co.kr *Web Site:* www.hollym.co.kr

Hollywood Film Archive
8391 Beverly Blvd, No 321, Los Angeles, CA 90048
Web Site: hfarchive.com
Key Personnel
Founder: D Richard Baer
Founded: 1972
Publication, sales & distribution of comprehensive movie, video & TV reference books.
ISBN Prefix(es): 978-0-913616
Number of titles published annually: 3 Print
Total Titles: 54 Print
Advertising Agency: Tartan Advertising

Holmes Publishing Group LLC
PO Box 2370, Sequim, WA 98382
Tel: 360-681-2900
E-mail: holmespub@fastmail.fm
Web Site: www.jdholmes.com
Key Personnel
Pres & CEO: J D Holmes *E-mail:* jdholmes@fastmail.fm
Founded: 1971
Specialize in books, both Holmes published & distributed private press titles, in alchemy, magic & esoteric subjects.
ISBN Prefix(es): 978-1-55818; 978-0-916411
Number of titles published annually: 4 Print
Total Titles: 588 Print
Imprints: Alchemical Press; Alexandrian Press; Contra/Thought; Holmes Publishing Group; Near Eastern Press; Sure Fire Press
Distributor for Jerusalem Press (UK); Starfire Publishing (UK); Theion Publishing (Germany); Three Hands Press (US); Von Zos Publishing; Xoanon Publishing (US)
Distribution Center: New Leaf Distributing Co, 401 Thornton Rd, Lithia Springs, GA 30122-1557 *Tel:* 770-948-7845 *Fax:* 770-944-2313 *Web Site:* newleafdist.com

Henry Holt and Company, LLC
Division of Macmillan
120 Broadway, 23rd fl, New York, NY 10271
SAN: 200-2108
Tel: 646-307-5151 *Toll Free Tel:* 888-330-8477 (orders) *Fax:* 646-307-5285
Web Site: www.henryholt.com
Key Personnel
Pres & Publr: Amy Einhorn
SVP & Publr, Metropolitan Books: Sara Bershtel
SVP & Assoc Publr: Maggie Richards
VP & Exec Dir, Publicity, Adult Trade: Patricia Eisemann
VP & Group Creative Dir: Christopher Sergio
VP & Sr Creative Dir, Children's: Beth Clark
VP & Ed-in-Chief: Sarah Crichton
Publr, Godwin Books: Laura Godwin
Exec Dir, Mktg & Brand Strategy: Caitlin O'Shaughnessy
Sr Art Dir: Sharismar Rodriguez

Asst Dir, Mktg: Allison Carney
Exec Mng Ed, Adult Trade: Kenn Russell
Edit Dir, Holt Children's: Christian Trimmer
Deputy Dir, Publicity: Carolyn O'Keefe
Exec Ed: Serena Jones
Sr Ed: James Melia; Caroline Zancan
Sr Ed, Henry Holt Books for Young Readers:
  Tiffany Liao
Sr Ed, Metropolitan Books: Riva Hocherman;
  Grigory Tovbis
Ed, Henry Holt Books for Young Readers: Brian
  Geffen
Ed, Henry Holt Books for Younger Readers/God-
  win Books: Julia Sooy
Ed-at-Large: Retha Powers
Assoc Ed: Madeline Jones; Conor Mintzer
Assoc Ed, Henry Holt Books for Younger Read-
  ers: Rachel Murray
Assoc Ed, Henry Holt Books for Younger Read-
  ers/Christy Ottaviano Books: Jessica Anderson
Asst Ed: Kerry Cullen; Ruby Rose Lee
Asst Ed, Henry Holt Books for Young Readers:
  Mark Podesta
Asst Ed, Metropolitan Books: Brian Lax
Ed-at-Large: Retha Powers
Sr Natl Accts Mgr: Cristina Cushing
Studio Mgr: Ginny Dominguez
Asst Mktg Mgr: Maia Sacca-Schaeffer
Publicity Coord, Adult Trade Div: Catryn Silber-
  sack
Publicist-at-Large: Marian Brown
Founded: 1866
ISBN Prefix(es): 978-0-8050 (Holt)
Number of titles published annually: 56 Print
Total Titles: 3,000 Print
Imprints: Andy Cohen Books; Godwin Books;
  Henry Holt; Henry Holt Books for Younger
  Readers; Holt Paperbacks; John Macrae Books;
  Metropolitan Books; Christy Ottaviano Books;
  Times Books
Foreign Rep(s): Raincoast (Canada)
Foreign Rights: A/S Bookman Literary Agency
  (Denmark, Finland, Iceland, Norway, Sweden);
  AnatoliaLit Agency (Turkey); Anthea Agency
  (Bulgaria); Author Rights Agency Ltd (Rus-
  sia); Bardon-Chinese Media Agency (Mainland
  China, Taiwan); Eliane Benisti Literary Agency
  (France); Copenhagen Literary Agency ApS
  (Scandinavia); The English Agency (Japan)
  Ltd (Japan); Farrar, Straus and Giroux (USA);
  Graal Literary Agency (Maria Strarz-Kanska)
  (Poland); The Deborah Harris Agency (Israel);
  Internationaal Literatuur Bureau BV (Nether-
  lands); International Copyright Agency Ltd
  (Simona Kessler) (Romania); The Italian Liter-
  ary Agency srl (Italy); Katai & Bolza Literary
  Agents (Hungary); Korea Copyright Center Inc
  (KCC) (Korea); Liepman Agency (Eva Ko-
  ralnik & Ronit Zafran) (Germany); Literarni
  Aventura sro (Czechia, Slovakia); MB Agen-
  cia Literaria (Portugal, Spain); Plima Liter-
  ary Agency (Croatia, Serbia, Slovenia); RIFF
  (Brazil)
Advertising Agency: Verso Advertising, 50 W 17
  St, New York, NY 10010 Tel: 212-292-2990
  Web Site: www.versoadvertising.com
Warehouse: MPS, 16365 James Madison Hwy,
  Gordonsville, VA 22942 Tel: 540-672-7698
  SAN: 631-5011
Membership(s): Association of American Publish-
  ers (AAP)

Holy Cow! Press
PO Box 3170, Mount Royal Sta, Duluth, MN
  55803
Tel: 218-724-1653
E-mail: holycow@holycowpress.org
Web Site: www.holycowpress.org
Key Personnel
Publr & Ed: Jim Perlman
Founded: 1977
ISBN Prefix(es): 978-0-930100; 978-0-9779458

Number of titles published annually: 4 Print; 3 E-
  Book
Total Titles: 120 Print; 8 E-Book
Distribution Center: Consortium Book Sales &
  Distribution, The Keg House, Suite 101, 34
  13 Ave NE, Minneapolis, MN 55413-1007
  Tel: 612-746-2600 *Toll Free Tel:* 800-283-3572
  (cust serv, Jackson, TN) *Fax:* 612-746-2606
  E-mail: info@cbsd.com *Web Site:* www.cbsd.
  com SAN: 200-6049

Holy Cross Orthodox Press
Division of Hellenic College Holy Cross
50 Goddard Ave, Brookline, MA 02445
Tel: 617-731-3500; 617-850-1321
E-mail: press@hchc.edu
Web Site: www.hchc.edu
Key Personnel
Contact: Rev Michael Monos
Founded: 1974
Books on Orthodox Christian religion.
This publisher has indicated that 25% of their
  product line is author subsidized.
ISBN Prefix(es): 978-0-917651; 978-1-885652;
  978-0-916586; 978-1-935317
Number of titles published annually: 10 Print
Total Titles: 120 Print

§Homa & Sekey Books
140 E Ridgewood Ave, Paramus, NJ 07652
Tel: 201-261-8810 *Toll Free Tel:* 800-870-HOMA
  (870-4662 orders) *Fax:* 201-261-8890
E-mail: info@homabooks.com
Web Site: www.homabooks.com
Key Personnel
Publr: Shawn Ye
Founded: 1997
Publisher & distributor of books on Asia.
ISBN Prefix(es): 978-1-931907; 978-0-966542
Number of titles published annually: 15 Print
Distributor for China Encyclopedia Publishing
  House; China Intercontinental Press; China
  Zhejiang Publishing United Group
Foreign Rights: Eric Yang Agency (Korea)
Membership(s): Independent Book Publishers As-
  sociation (IBPA)

Homestead Publishing
Affiliate of Book Design Ltd
Box 193, Moose, WY 83012-0193
Tel: 307-733-6248 *Fax:* 307-733-6248
E-mail: orders@homesteadpublishing.net
Web Site: www.homesteadpublishing.net
Key Personnel
Publr: Carl Schreier *Tel:* 760-832-7152
Contact: Diane Henderson
Founded: 1980
Publisher of guide books.
ISBN Prefix(es): 978-0-943972
Number of titles published annually: 12 Print;
  2,000 Online; 6 E-Book
Total Titles: 268 Print; 4,500 Online; 16 E-Book
Branch Office(s)
4388 17 St, San Francisco, CA 94114 *Tel:* 760-
  832-7152
Returns: 4030 W Lake Creek Dr, Wilson, WY
  83014
Warehouse: 4030 W Lake Creek Dr, Wilson, WY
  83014

Hoover Institution Press
Subsidiary of Hoover Institution on War, Revolu-
  tion & Peace
Stanford University, 434 Galvez Mall, Stanford,
  CA 94305-6003
SAN: 202-3024
Tel: 650-723-3373 *Toll Free Tel:* 800-935-2882
  Fax: 650-723-8626
E-mail: hooverpress@stanford.edu
Web Site: www.hooverpress.org; www.hoover.org

Key Personnel
Sr Pubn Mgr: Barbara Arellano *Tel:* 650-725-
  5630
Book Prodn Mgr: Marshall Blanchard *Tel:* 650-
  725-3460
Founded: 1962
Studies on domestic & international policy, stud-
  ies of nationalities in Central & Eastern Eu-
  rope, history & political science; bibliographies
  & surveys of Hoover Institution's resources.
ISBN Prefix(es): 978-0-8179
Number of titles published annually: 20 Print
Total Titles: 700 Print; 100 Online; 700 E-Book
Foreign Rep(s): Europspan (Europe)
Orders to: Independent Publishers Group
  (IPG), 814 N Franklin St, Chicago, IL 60610
  Tel: 312-337-0747 *Toll Free Tel:* 800-888-4741
  Fax: 312-337-5985 *E-mail:* orders@ipgbook.
  com *Web Site:* www.ipgbook.com
Returns: Independent Publishers Group (IPG),
  814 N Franklin St, Chicago, IL 60610
  Tel: 312-337-0747 *Toll Free Tel:* 800-888-4741
  Fax: 312-337-5985 *E-mail:* orders@ipgbook.
  com *Web Site:* www.ipgbook.com
Distribution Center: Independent Publishers
  Group (IPG), 814 N Franklin St, Chicago, IL
  60610 *Tel:* 312-337-0747 *Toll Free Tel:* 800-
  888-4741 *Fax:* 312-337-5985 *E-mail:* orders@
  ipgbook.com *Web Site:* www.ipgbook.com

Hoover's Inc
Subsidiary of Dun & Bradstreet
7700 W Parmer Lane, Bldg A, Austin, TX 78729
Tel: 512-374-4500 *Toll Free Tel:* 855-858-5974
Web Site: www.hoovers.com
Founded: 1990
Business reference books & online services.
ISBN Prefix(es): 978-1-878753; 978-1-57311;
  978-1-59274; 978-1-63053
Number of titles published annually: 7 Print
Total Titles: 7 Print; 3 Online
Imprints: Hoover's Business Press; Hoover's
  Handbooks

Hope Publishing Co
380 S Main Place, Carol Stream, IL 60188
Tel: 630-665-3200 *Toll Free Tel:* 800-323-1049
E-mail: hope@hopepublishing.com
Web Site: www.hopepublishing.com
Key Personnel
Pres: John Shorney *E-mail:* john@
  hopepublishing.com
VP: Scott A Shorney *E-mail:* scott@
  hopepublishing.com; Steve Shorney
  E-mail: steve@hopepublishing.com
Founded: 1892
Choir music, hymnals, instrumental music books
  & hand bell music.
ISBN Prefix(es): 978-0-916642
Number of titles published annually: 50 Print
Divisions: Agape; Providence Press; Somerset
  Press; Tabernacle Publishing
Advertising Agency: Lamplighter Agency

Horizon Publishers & Distributors Inc
191 N 650 E, Bountiful, UT 84010-3628
Tel: 801-292-7102
E-mail: ldshorizonpublishers1@gmail.com
Web Site: www.ldshorizonpublishers.com
Key Personnel
Owner & CEO: Duane S Crowther; Jean D
  Crowther
Founded: 1971
Christian (primarily Latter-day Saints), inspira-
  tional, health foods, self-sufficient living, mu-
  sic, marriage & family, children's activities,
  needlework, nonfiction, biography paperbacks
  & hardbound.
ISBN Prefix(es): 978-0-88290
Number of titles published annually: 15 Print
Total Titles: 521 Print; 35 CD-ROM; 40 Audio
Distributed by Cedar Fort Inc

Hospital & Healthcare Compensation Service
Subsidiary of John R Zabka Associates Inc
3 Post Rd, Suite 3, Oakland, NJ 07436
Mailing Address: PO Box 376, Oakland, NJ 07436-0376
Tel: 201-405-0075 *Fax:* 201-405-2110
E-mail: allinfo@hhcsinc.com
Web Site: www.hhcsinc.com
Key Personnel
Dir, Reports: Rosanne Zabka *Tel:* 201-405-0075 ext 11 *E-mail:* rzabka@hhcsinc.com
Client Servs: Tracy Schilling *Tel:* 201-405-0075 ext 13 *E-mail:* tschilling@hhcsinc.com
Founded: 1971
Publisher of salary & benefits reports for hospital, nursing home, assisted living, CCRC, home care, hospice & rehabilitation employees.
ISBN Prefix(es): 978-0-939326; 978-1-934847
Number of titles published annually: 11 Print; 11 CD-ROM
Total Titles: 10 Print; 11 CD-ROM

Host Publications
3408 West Ave, Austin, TX 78705
Mailing Address: 3507 N Lamar Blvd, PO Box 302920, Austin, TX 78703
Tel: 512-236-1290 *Fax:* 512-236-1208
Web Site: www.hostpublications.com
Key Personnel
Pres: Joe W Bratcher, III *E-mail:* jbratcher@hostpublications.com
Dir, Fulfillment: Susan Lesak *E-mail:* slesak@hostpublications.com
Founded: 1987
ISBN Prefix(es): 978-0-924047
Number of titles published annually: 6 Print
Total Titles: 50 Print
Distribution Center: Small Press Distribution, 1341 Seventh St, Berkeley, CA 94710-1409, Opers Dir: Dr Brent Cunningham *Tel:* 510-524-1668 ext 308 *Toll Free Tel:* 800-869-7553 *E-mail:* spd@spdbooks.org *Web Site:* www.spdbooks.org
Membership(s): Independent Book Publishers Association (IBPA)

§Houghton Mifflin Harcourt
125 High St, Boston, MA 02110
SAN: 200-2388
Tel: 617-351-5000 *Toll Free Tel:* 855-969-4642; 800-225-5425 (K-12 educ materials); 800-323-9540 (assessment materials); 877-219-1537 (SkillsTutor); 888-242-6747 (Innovation in Educ Group); 800-225-3362 (Trade & Ref Div) *Toll Free Fax:* 800-269-5232
E-mail: myhmhco@hmhco.com
Web Site: www.hmhco.com
Key Personnel
Pres & CEO: John (Jack) J Lynch, Jr
CFO: Joseph P Abbott, Jr
Chief Revenue Offr: Mike Evans
CTO: Peter George
Chief Platform Architect & EVP, Engg: Martin Davy
Pres, Trade Publg: Ellen Archer
EVP & Gen Coun: William Bayers
EVP & CTO: Brook Colangelo
EVP & Chief, Consumer Brands & Strategy: CJ Kettler
EVP & Gen Mgr, Core Curriculum: Jim O'Neill
EVP & Gen Mgr, Heinemann: Vicki Boyd
EVP & Gen Mgr, Prof Servs: Amy Dunkin
EVP & Gen Mgr, Supplemental Curriculum: Matthew Mugo Fields
EVP, Global Strategic Alliances: Timothy L Cannon
EVP, Intervention Solutions: Margery Mayer
EVP, HR & Chief People Offr: Bridgett Paradise
SVP & CIO: Trish Torizzo
SVP & Chief People Offr: Alejandro Reyes
SVP & Gen Mgr, Specialized Curriculum Group: Scott Bowker
SVP, Corp Aff: Bianca Olson

SVP, Consumer Digital Prods & Platforms: Leigh Zarelli Lewis
SVP, Mktg: Matt Schweitzer
SVP, Prog Devt & Acq: Caroline Fraser
VP, Natl Accts, Trade Sales & Strategy: Ed Spade
VP, Spec Mkts, Mass Mkt Sales & Prod Devt: Colleen Murphy
Exec Dir, Spec Sales: James Phirman
Sr Dir, Publg Opers: Cara Coggins
Dir, Field Sales: Jen Reynolds
Dir, Field Sales & Events: Rachel Sanders
Dir, Sales Analytics: Christine Sikule
Assoc Dir, Publicity: Megan Wilson
Sr Mktg Mgr: Elizabeth Anderson; Michael Dudding; Katrina Kruse
Dist Client Mgr & Natl Accts: Morgan Gould
Mktg Mgr: Liz Anderson
Mktg Assoc: Lisa McAuliffe
Natl Acct Mgr: Emily Logan
Sales Mgr: Carissa Ray
Subs Rts Mgr, General Interest Books: Marleen Reimer
Sr Publicity Mgr: Sari Kamin
Publicity Mgr: Breanne Sommer
Publicist: Stephanie Buschardt
Publicity Assoc: Samantha Trovillion
Assoc Sales Rep: Jaclyn Sassa
Founded: 1832
With education products & services used by more than 50 million students in more than 150 countries, Houghton Mifflin Harcourt is a global education & learning company. The world's largest provider of materials for PreK-12 learning, HMH is leading the way with innovative solutions & approaches to the challenges facing education today. Through curricula excellence coupled with technology innovations & professional services, HMH collaborates with school districts, administrators, teachers, parents & students, providing interactive, results-driven learning solutions. Its Educational Consulting Services group works to increase student achievement in underperforming schools by developing, implementing & supporting education transformation through sustained district partnerships. With origins dating back to 1832, the company also publishes an extensive line of reference works & award-winning literature for adults & young readers.
ISBN Prefix(es): 978-0-395; 978-0-618; 978-0-547; 978-0-544; 978-0-9709455; 978-0-9747343; 978-1-933196; 978-1-935588
Divisions: Houghton Mifflin Harcourt K-12 Publishers; Houghton Mifflin Harcourt Trade & Reference Division; The Learning Company; SkillsTutor
Branch Office(s)
2180 S McDowell Blvd, Suite B, Petaluma, CA 94954 *Tel:* 707-769-2222
One Harbor Dr, Sausalito, CA 94965 *Tel:* 415-332-4181
5680 Greenwood Plaza Blvd, Suite 550, Greenwood Village, CO 80111 *Tel:* 303-504-9312
9400 Southpark Ctr Loop, Orlando, FL 32819 *Tel:* 407-345-2000
7584 Presidents Way, Orlando, FL 32809 *Tel:* 407-345-2000
909 Davis St, Suite 300, Evanston, IL 60201 *Toll Free Tel:* 800-225-5425
1900 S Batavia Ave, Geneva, IL 60134-3399 *Tel:* 630-232-2550
One Pierce Place, Suite 900W, Itasca, IL 60143 *Toll Free Tel:* 800-767-8420
761 District Dr, Itasca, IL 60143
255 38 Ave, Suite L, St Charles, IL 60174 *Tel:* 630-659-1200
2700 N Richardt Ave, Indianapolis, IN 46219 *Tel:* 317-359-5585
465 S Lincoln Dr, Troy, MO 63379 *Tel:* 636-528-8110
361 Hanover St, Portsmouth, NH 03801 *Tel:* 630-467-7000

3 Park Ave, New York, NY 10016 *Tel:* 212-420-5800
132 W 31 St, New York, NY 10001
1587 Rte 146, Rexford, NY 12148 *Tel:* 518-399-2776
2270 Spring Lake Rd, Suite 600, Farmers Branch, TX 75234 *Toll Free Tel:* 800-225-5425
2700 La Frontera Blvd, Round Rock, TX 78681 *Tel:* 512-721-7000
4200 Blvd St Laurent, Suite 1203, Montreal, QC H2W 2R2, Canada *Tel:* 514-598-0444
B7 Calle Tabonuco, Suite 1410, Guaynabo 00968-3003, Puerto Rico *Tel:* 787-520-9599; 787-520-9585
Foreign Office(s): 59 Zhongguancun St, Rm 1004, Haidian District, Beijing 100872, China *Tel:* (010) 62602236
152-160 Pearse St, Dublin 2, Ireland *Tel:* (01) 240 5900
67 Ubi Rd, No 05-08 Oxley Bizhub, Singapore 408730, Singapore *Tel:* 6635 6825
No 501 KGIT SangAm Ctr, 1601, SangAm-dong, Mapo-gu, Seoul 123-913, South Korea *Tel:* (02) 6393 5790; (02) 6393 5792
Distributor for Old Farmer's Almanac
Membership(s): American Bar Association (ABA); American Booksellers Association (ABA); American Library Association (ALA); Association of American Publishers (AAP); Association of American Publishers PreK-12 Learning Group; Association of Booksellers for Children; Association of Catholic Publishers Inc; Association of Test Publishers; The Children's Book Council (CBC); Dictionary Society of North America; National Catholic Education Association (NCEA); Society of Printers; Software & Information Industry Association (SIIA)
See separate listing for:
Clarion Books
Heinemann
Houghton Mifflin Harcourt Assessments
Houghton Mifflin Harcourt K-12 Publishers
Houghton Mifflin Harcourt Trade & Reference Division
Math Solutions®

Houghton Mifflin Harcourt Assessments
Subsidiary of Houghton Mifflin Harcourt
One Pierce Place, Itasca, IL 60143
Tel: 630-467-7000 *Toll Free Tel:* 800-323-9540 *Fax:* 630-467-7192 (cust serv)
E-mail: assessmentsorders@hmhco.com
Web Site: www.hmhco.com/classroom-solutions/assessment
Key Personnel
Assessment Consultant Exec: Sue Rawls *E-mail:* sue.rawls@hmhco.com
Founded: 1852 (as Riverside Press)
Develops & sells print & digital assessment tools for the education market.
ISBN Prefix(es): 978-0-8292
Number of titles published annually: 20 Print

Houghton Mifflin Harcourt K-12 Publishers
Division of Houghton Mifflin Harcourt
125 High St, Boston, MA 02110
SAN: 200-2388
Tel: 617-351-5020
E-mail: corporate.communications@hmhco.com
Web Site: www.hmhco.com/classroom (solutions); www.hmhco.com
K-12 textbooks, educational materials & services.
Imprints: Rigby; Saxon
Sales Office(s): 9205 Southpark Center Loop, Orlando, FL 32819 *Toll Free Tel:* 800-225-5425 *Toll Free Fax:* 800-269-5232 *E-mail:* k-12orders@hmhco.com

§Houghton Mifflin Harcourt Trade & Reference Division
Division of Houghton Mifflin Harcourt

125 High St, Boston, MA 02110
SAN: 200-2388
Tel: 617-351-5000
Web Site: www.hmhco.com
Key Personnel
Pres & CEO: John (Jack) J Lynch, Jr
Pres, Trade Publg Group: Ellen Archer
SVP & Publr, Books for Young Readers: Catherine Onder
SVP & Trade Assoc Publr: Becky Saikia-Wilson
SVP & Exec Dir, Publicity: Lori Glazer
SVP, Mktg: Matt Schweitzer
VP & Publr, Adult Trade: Deb Brody
VP & Creative Dir: Michaela Sullivan
VP & Dir, Publicity: Taryn Roeder
VP & Ed-in-Chief, Children's: Mary Wilcox
VP, Mktg & Communs: Adriana Rizzo
VP, Prodn: Jill Lazer
Exec Dir, Mktg & Brand Strategy, Children's: Veronica Wasserman
Exec Dir, Mktg, Books for Young Readers: Lisa DiSarro
Sr Mktg Dir, Gen Interest, Lifestyle & Culinary: Andrea DeWerd
Creative Dir, Books for Young Readers: Jessica Handelman
Dir, School Supply & Ref Sales: Cheryl Dickemper
Sr Edit Dir, Versify & Books for Young Readers: Margaret Raymo
Edit Dir: Millicent Bennett
Edit Dir, Etch & Books for Young Readers: Emilia Rhodes
Edit Dir, Lifestyle: Karen Murgolo
Edit Dir, Rux Martin Books: Rux Martin
Mktg Dir, Children's: Ann Dye
Publicity Dir, Books for Young Readers: John Sellers
Assoc Art Dir: Whitney Leader-Picone; Brian Moore
Assoc Dir, Children's Publicity: Tara Shanahan
Assoc Dir, Publicity: Shara Alexander
Assoc Dir, Subs Rts: Candace Finn
Asst Dir, Mktg: Julie Yeater
Sr Exec Ed: Deanne Urmy; Rick Wolff
Sr Exec Ed, Children's: Kate O'Sullivan
Exec Ed: Sarah Pelz
Exec Ed, CliffsNotes: Greg Tubach
Sr Mng Ed: Marina Padakis
Mng Ed, Digital Formats: Kristin Brodeur
Mng Ed, Publg Workflow Specialist: Rebecca Springer
Sr Ed: Rakia Clark; Stephanie Fletcher; Naomi Gibbs; Jaime Levine; Alex Littlefield
Sr Ed, Children's: Amy Cloud; Alessandra Preziosi; Bethany Vinhateiro
Sr Ed, Versify: Erika Turner
Ed: Pilar Garcia-Brown
Ed, Children's: Christine Krones
Assoc Ed: Tim Mudie; Jenny Xu
Assoc Ed, Children's: Lily Kessinger; Nicole Sclama
Ed-at-Large: David Rosenthal
Ed-at-Large, Clarion Books: Dinah Stevenson
Lead Designer: Lyndsay Calusine
Sr Mktg Designer, Children's: Abigail Stahlman
Sr Mktg Mgr: Zoe Del Mar
Sr Publicity Mgr: Michelle Bonanno Triant
Sr Publicity Mgr, Culinary & Lifestyle Books: Sari Kamin
Culinary Publicity Mgr: Brittany Edwards
Mktg Mgr, Books for Young Readers: Alia Almeida
Mktg Mgr, Children's: Nadia Almahdi
Mktg Mgr, School & Lib, Books for Young Readers: Amanda Acevedo
Sales Mgr, Specialty Retail & Intl: Olivia Wilson
Subs Rts Mgr, General Interest Books: Marleen Reimer
Assoc Mktg Mgr, Lifestyle: Samantha Simon
Sr Prodn Coord: Kim Kiefer
Lead Sales Coord, Natl Accts: Jackie Sassa
Digital Mktg & Publicity Specialist: Tara Sonin Schlesinger

Mktg Specialist, School & Lib, Books for Young Readers: Taylor McBroom
Edit Assoc: Olivia Bartz
Edit Assoc, Children's: Gabriella Abbate; Elizabeth Agyemang; Harriet Low; Allison Vroegop
Publicist: Emma Gordon
Publicist, Books for Young Readers: Sammy Brown
Publicist, Culinary & Lifestyle Books: Bridget Nocera
Publicity Assoc: Maria Mann; Marissa Page
Publicity Asst: Emily Moon
Publicity Assoc, Children's: Anna Ravenelle
General literature, fiction, nonfiction, biography, autobiography, history, poetry & juvenile publications, dictionary, reference books, cookbooks & guidebooks.
ISBN Prefix(es): 978-0-89919; 978-0-395; 978-1-85697; 978-0-7534; 978-0-618; 978-1-88152
Number of titles published annually: 400 Print; 1 CD-ROM; 1 Online; 14 Audio
Total Titles: 3,300 Print; 2 CD-ROM; 2 Online; 110 Audio
Imprints: The American Heritage® Dictionaries; Betty Crocker®; Clarion Books; CliffsNotes™; Etch; Graphia; Harcourt Children's Books; HMH Audio; HMH Franchise; Houghton Mifflin Harcourt; Houghton Mifflin Harcourt Books for Young Readers; Mariner Books; Rux Martin Books; Sandpiper; Versify; Webster's New World® College Dictionary
Editorial Office(s): 3 Park Ave, New York, NY 10016
Distributed by Hachette Book Group
Distributor for Larousse; Old Farmer's Almanac
Orders to: Houghton Mifflin Harcourt Trade Customer Service, 9205 Southpark Center Loop, 3rd fl, Orlando, FL 32819 *Toll Free Tel:* 800-225-3362 *Toll Free Fax:* 800-634-7568 *E-mail:* tradecustomerservice@hmhpub.com
Returns: Houghton Mifflin Harcourt, Trade Returns Dept, 2700 N Richardt Ave, Indianapolis, IN 46219
Distribution Center: Raincoast Books, 2440 Viking Way, Richmond, BC V6V 1N2, Canada *Tel:* 604-448-7100 *Fax:* 604-270-7161 *E-mail:* customerservice@raincoast.com

House of Collectibles
Imprint of Penguin Random House LLC
1745 Broadway, New York, NY 10019
Tel: 212-782-9000
Web Site: www.penguinrandomhouse.com
Publisher that collectors, dealers & investors around the world turn to for detailed reference information & current market values on all antiques & collectibles. The House of Collectibles books are compiled by experts, renowned for accuracy & completeness & profusely illustrated, many with full color. Accept unsol proposals & mss from authors who are experts in the antiques & collectibles areas, also accept mss & proposals from agents.
Total Titles: 4 Print

House to House Publications
Division of DOVE International
11 Toll Gate Rd, Lititz, PA 17543
Tel: 717-627-1996 *Toll Free Tel:* 800-848-5892 *Fax:* 717-627-4004
E-mail: h2hp@dcfi.org
Web Site: www.h2hp.com
Key Personnel
Pubns Ed: Lou Anne Good
Founded: 1997
Provide resources for the body of Christ worldwide.
ISBN Prefix(es): 978-1-886973
Number of titles published annually: 4 Print; 15 E-Book; 1 Audio
Total Titles: 50 Print; 5 Audio
Imprints: Partnership Publications

Housing Assistance Council
1025 Vermont Ave NW, Suite 606, Washington, DC 20005
Tel: 202-842-8600 *Fax:* 202-347-3441
E-mail: hac@ruralhome.org
Web Site: www.ruralhome.org
Key Personnel
Sr Policy Analyst: Leslie R Strauss
  E-mail: leslie@ruralhome.org
Founded: 1971
Provides technical housing services, loans, program & policy assistance, training, research & information. Specialize in research reports, technical manuals & information pieces, all exclusively about low-income rural housing in the US.
ISBN Prefix(es): 978-1-58064
Number of titles published annually: 8 Print; 8 Online
Total Titles: 80 Print; 50 Online
Branch Office(s)
55 Marietta St, Suite 1350, Atlanta, GA 30303
  Tel: 404-892-4824 *Fax:* 404-892-1204
  E-mail: southeast@ruralhome.org
10100 NW Ambassador Dr, Suite 310, Kansas City, MO 64153-1362 *Tel:* 816-880-0400 *Fax:* 816-880-0500 *E-mail:* midwest@ruralhome.org

§HRD Press
22 Amherst Rd, Amherst, MA 01002-9709
SAN: 201-9213
Tel: 413-253-3488 *Toll Free Tel:* 800-822-2801 *Fax:* 413-253-3490
E-mail: info@hrdpress.com; customerservice@hrdpress.com
Web Site: www.hrdpress.com
Key Personnel
Publr: Robert W Carkhuff
Cust Rel Mgr: Sam MacLeod
Founded: 1972
Textbooks & off-the-shelf workshops on human resource development, management & training. Packaged training materials & assessments.
ISBN Prefix(es): 978-0-914234; 978-0-87425
Number of titles published annually: 25 Print
Total Titles: 600 Print; 200 E-Book
Distributed by Training & Development Materials of Canada (Canada)
Foreign Rep(s): Eurospan Ltd (Europe); HRD Central (Australia); Human Capital Partners (Nigeria); Management Learning Resources (UK); Multimedia HRD Pvt Ltd (India); Trainco (South Africa); Training & Development Materials of Canada (Canada)

Hudson Institute
1201 Pennsylvania Ave NW, Suite 400, Washington, DC 20004
Tel: 202-974-2400 *Fax:* 202-974-2410
E-mail: info@hudson.org
Web Site: www.hudson.org
Key Personnel
Pres & CEO: Kenneth R Weinstein
COO: John P Walters
SVP: Lewis Libby
Sr Fellow & Dir, Pub Aff & Spec Projs: David Tell
Founded: 1961
Books, monographs, briefing papers, newsletters.
ISBN Prefix(es): 978-1-55813
Number of titles published annually: 20 Print; 500 Online
Total Titles: 60 Print; 60 E-Book

§Human Kinetics Inc
1607 N Market St, Champaign, IL 61820
Mailing Address: PO Box 5076, Champaign, IL 61825-5076 SAN: 211-7088
Tel: 217-351-5076 *Toll Free Tel:* 800-747-4457 *Fax:* 217-351-1549 (orders/cust serv)
E-mail: info@hkusa.com
Web Site: www.humankinetics.com

Key Personnel
Founder & Pres: Rainer Martens
CEO: Skip Maier
CFO: Tina Daniel
VP & Coach Educ Dir: Ted Miller
VP & HR Dir: Holly Gilly
VP, Trade & Prof Div Dir: Jason Muzinic
VP & Dir, Sales & Mktg: Steve Ruhlig
Academic Div Dir: Ray Vallese
Journals Div Dir: Kathleen Burgener
Founded: 1974
Scholarly books, college textbooks, continuing education courses & trade books in physical education, sports medicine & science, coaching, sport technique & fitness, courses, CDs & DVDs.
ISBN Prefix(es): 978-0-931250; 978-0-87322; 978-0-88011; 978-0-918438; 978-0-7360; 978-0-912781; 978-1-4504; 978-1-4925
Number of titles published annually: 200 Print
Total Titles: 1,165 Print; 804 E-Book
Branch Office(s)
Human Kinetics Canada, 475 Devonshire Rd, Unit 100, Windsor, ON N8Y 2L5, Canada *Tel:* 519-971-9500 *Toll Free Tel:* 800-465-7301 (CN) *Fax:* 519-971-9797 *E-mail:* info@hkcanada.com
Foreign Office(s): Human Kinetics UK, Europe & Middle East, 107 Bradford Rd, Stanningley, Leeds LS28 6AT, United Kingdom *Tel:* (0113) 255 5665 *Fax:* (0113) 255 5885 *E-mail:* hk@hkeurope.com
Foreign Rep(s): Aditya Books (India); Africa Connection, Old School House (Angola, Benin, Cameroon, Cape Verde, Cote d'Ivoire (Ivory Coast), Gabon, The Gambia, Ghana, Liberia, Mali, Mozambique, Niger, Sao Tome and Principe, Senegal, Uganda, Zambia, Zimbabwe); Alkem Co (Bangladesh, Brunei, Indonesia, Laos, Malaysia, Philippines, Singapore, Thailand); Asian Books (Sri Lanka); Atlantic Publishers & Distributors (India); Bookport (trade) (Croatia, Gibraltar, Greece, Italy, Malta, Montenegro, Portugal, Serbia, Slovenia, Spain); CBS Publishers & Distributors (India); Charran Publishing House (Trinidad and Tobago); Comprajato (Brazil); Cranbury International LLC (Caribbean, Latin America); CRW Marketing Services for Publishers Inc (Philippines, Saipan); Dasansogo Co Ltd (Korea); Disvan Enterprises (India); Eureka Press (Japan); Laszlo Horvath (Austria, Czechia, Hungary, Montenegro, North Macedonia, Poland, Romania, Russia, Slovakia); Icon Books (Malaysia, Singapore, Vietnam); IPR (Middle East, North Africa); Kemper Conseil (Belgium, France, Germany, Switzerland); Kinemed Technologies (Chile); KinesWorld (China, Hong Kong); Libreria Medica (Colombia); Flavio Marcello (academic) (Italy, Portugal, Spain); Research Periodicals & Book Services (Tanzania); Saras Books (India); Unifacmanu Trading Co Ltd (Taiwan)

§Human Rights Watch
350 Fifth Ave, 34th fl, New York, NY 10118-3299
Tel: 212-290-4700 *Fax:* 212-736-1300
E-mail: hrwpress@hrw.org
Web Site: www.hrw.org
Key Personnel
Commns Dir: Emma Daly *Tel:* 212-216-1835
Sr Media Offr: Philippa Stewart
Founded: 1978
Nonprofit human rights organization publishing books & newsletters on human rights practices in more than 80 countries worldwide; documents arbitrary imprisonment, censorship, disappearances, due process of law, murder, prison conditions, torture, violations of laws of war & other abuses of internationally recognized human rights.

ISBN Prefix(es): 978-0-938579; 978-0-929692; 978-1-56432
Number of titles published annually: 67 Print
Total Titles: 1,000 Print; 60 E-Book
Imprints: Human Rights Watch Books

§Humanix Books LLC
Division of Newsmax Media
8 W 40 St, 20th fl, New York, NY 10804
Toll Free Tel: 855-371-7810
E-mail: info@humanixbooks.com
Web Site: www.humanixbooks.com
Key Personnel
Publr: Mary Glenn *E-mail:* maryg@humanixbooks.com
Founded: 2012
Trade paperbacks, hardcover & ebooks in the following areas: finance, investing, health, wellness, lifestyle, business, leadership, management, politics, current events, success, motivation, history & military.
ISBN Prefix(es): 978-1-63006
Number of titles published annually: 8 Print; 8 Online; 8 E-Book
Total Titles: 15 Print; 15 Online; 15 E-Book; 1 Audio
Orders to: Perseus Distribution *Toll Free Tel:* 800-343-4499 *E-mail:* orderentry@perseusbooks.com
Distribution Center: Perseus Distribution *Toll Free Tel:* 800-343-4499 *E-mail:* orderentry@perseusbooks.com
Membership(s): Association of American Publishers (AAP)

Huntington Press Publishing
3665 Procyon St, Las Vegas, NV 89103-1907
Tel: 702-252-0655 *Toll Free Tel:* 800-244-2224 *Fax:* 702-252-0675
E-mail: editor@huntingtonpress.com
Web Site: www.huntingtonpress.com
Key Personnel
Publr: Anthony Curtis *E-mail:* publisher@huntingtonpress.com
Founded: 1983
Books relating to gambling & Las Vegas.
ISBN Prefix(es): 978-0-929712; 978-1-935396; 978-1-944877
Number of titles published annually: 5 Print
Total Titles: 140 Print; 200 Online; 66 E-Book

Hutton Publishing
140D Heritage Village, Southbury, CT 06488
Tel: 203-405-6227
E-mail: huttonbooks@hotmail.com
Key Personnel
Ed-in-Chief: Caroline DuBois Hutton
Founded: 2004
Digital publishing for Kindle, Nook, etc; print-on-demand. All books receive personal attention & are professionally designed & listed for distribution in the Ingram catalog, available through Amazon, B&N Online & local bookstores. Promotion notes available for all Huttonelectronicpublishing.com authors. All royalties are split 50-50, author & publisher. Some books paid 100% by authors, others, by special arrangement with the publisher, at varying percentages subsidized by the publisher. Please inquire by e-mail for further information. Prize-winning illustrators available as needed.
This publisher has indicated that 100% of their product line is author subsidized.
ISBN Prefix(es): 978-0-9742894; 978-0-9785171
Number of titles published annually: 10 Print; 10 E-Book
Total Titles: 40 Print; 20 E-Book
Distribution Center: Lightning Source Inc, 1246 Heil Quaker Blvd, La Vergne, TN 37086

Ibex Publishers
PO Box 30087, Bethesda, MD 20824

SAN: 696-866X
Tel: 301-718-8188 *Toll Free Tel:* 888-718-8188 *Fax:* 301-907-8707
E-mail: info@ibexpub.com
Web Site: ibexpub.com
Key Personnel
Publr: Mr Farhad Shirzad *E-mail:* fs@ibex.net
Founded: 1979
English & Persian language books about Iran.
ISBN Prefix(es): 978-0-936347; 978-1-58814
Number of titles published annually: 30 Print
Total Titles: 600 Print; 3 CD-ROM; 5 Audio
Imprints: Ibex Press; Iranbooks Press
Distributor for Farhang Moaser

IBFD North America Inc (International Bureau of Fiscal Documentation)
Division of IBFD Foundation
8300 Boone Blvd, Suite 380, Vienna, VA 22182
Tel: 703-442-7757
E-mail: info@ibfd.org
Web Site: www.ibfd.org
Key Personnel
Regl Acct Mgr: Horacio Jarquin *E-mail:* h.jarquin@ibfd.org
Founded: 1938
International taxation & investment & tax law.
Number of titles published annually: 30 Print
Total Titles: 30 Print; 1 CD-ROM; 42 Online
Foreign Office(s): Reitlandpark 301, 1019 DW Amsterdam, Netherlands (headquarters) *Tel:* (020) 554 0100

ICMA, see International City/County Management Association (ICMA)

Idyll Arbor Inc
39129 264 Ave SE, Enumclaw, WA 98022
Tel: 360-825-7797 *Fax:* 360-825-5670
E-mail: sales@idyllarbor.com
Web Site: www.idyllarbor.com
Key Personnel
Pres & Intl Rts: Tom Blaschko *E-mail:* tom@idyllarbor.com
Founded: 1984
Publish health care books, information for recreational therapists & activity directors & books on social issues. The Issues Press imprint covers important social issues such as addictions & health care for returning military personnel. Titles published under the Pine Winds Press imprint relate to discussions of the life force, including spiritual reality, Bigfoot, fairies & other strange phenomena.
ISBN Prefix(es): 978-1-882883; 978-0-937663; 978-1-930461; 978-1-61158
Number of titles published annually: 8 Print; 8 E-Book
Total Titles: 100 Print; 50 E-Book; 1 Audio
Imprints: Issues Press; Pine Winds Press
Foreign Rights: Columbine Communications (worldwide exc Canada & USA)
Membership(s): Book Publishers of the Northwest (BPNW); Independent Book Publishers Association (IBPA); Pacific Northwest Booksellers Association (PNBA)

§IEEE Computer Society
2001 "L" St NW, Suite 700, Washington, DC 20036-4928
SAN: 264-620X
Tel: 202-371-0101 *Toll Free Tel:* 800-678-4333 (memb info) *Fax:* 202-728-9614
E-mail: help@computer.org
Web Site: www.computer.org
Key Personnel
Publr: Robin Baldwin *E-mail:* rbaldwin@computer.org
Mgr, Mktg & Communs: Katherine Mansfield *E-mail:* k.mansfield@computer.org
Founded: 1980

Tutorials, reports, reprint collections, conference proceedings, textbooks & CD-ROMs.
ISBN Prefix(es): 978-0-8186; 978-0-7695
Number of titles published annually: 155 Print
Total Titles: 1,000 Print; 5 CD-ROM
Branch Office(s)
10662 Los Vaqueros Circle, Los Alamitos, CA 90720-1314 *Tel:* 714-821-8380 *Fax:* 714-821-4010
Foreign Office(s): KFK Bldg, 2-14-14 Minami-Aoyama, Minato-ku, Tokyo 107-0062, Japan *Tel:* (03) 3408 3118 *Fax:* (03) 3408 3553 *E-mail:* tokyo.ofc@computer.org

§IEEE Press
Division of Institute of Electrical & Electronics Engineers Inc (IEEE)
445 Hoes Lane, Piscataway, NJ 08854
Tel: 732-981-0060 *Fax:* 732-867-9946
E-mail: pressbooks@ieee.org (proposals & info)
Web Site: www.ieee.org/press
Key Personnel
Mng Ed: Vaishali Damle *Tel:* 732-465-6655 *E-mail:* v.damle@ieee.org
Founded: 1971
Professional books & texts in electrical & computer engineering, computer science, electrotechnology, general engineering, applied mathematics. Tutorials in technical subjects.
ISBN Prefix(es): 978-0-87942; 978-0-7803; 978-0-471
Number of titles published annually: 40 Print
Total Titles: 900 Print; 800 E-Book
Imprints: Wiley-IEEE Press
Distributed by John Wiley & Sons Inc
Foreign Rep(s): John Wiley & Sons Inc
Foreign Rights: John Wiley & Sons Inc
Membership(s): Association of American Publishers (AAP)

IET USA Inc
379 Thornall St, Edison, NJ 08837
Tel: 732-321-5575 *Fax:* 732-321-5702
E-mail: ietusa@theiet.org
Web Site: www.theiet.org
Key Personnel
VP & Gen Mgr: Michael Ornstein
Founded: 1871
Professional books, journals, magazines & conference proceedings in many areas of electrical & electronic engineering, including telecommunications, computing, power, control, radar, circuits, materials & more.
ISBN Prefix(es): 978-0-85296; 978-0-906048; 978-0-86341
Number of titles published annually: 30 Print
Total Titles: 500 Print; 300 E-Book
Imprints: IEE; Inspec; Peter Peregrinus Ltd
Foreign Office(s): The IET, Suite G, 10F, China Merchants Tower, No 118 Jianguo Rd, Chaoyang District, Beijing 100022, China *Tel:* (010) 6566 4687 *E-mail:* china@theiet.org *Web Site:* www.theiet.org.cn
IET Hong Kong, 4412-4413 Cosco Tower, 183 Queen's Rd Central, Hong Kong, Hong Kong *Tel:* 2778 1611 *Fax:* 2778 1711 *E-mail:* admin@theiet.org.hk
IET India, Unit No 405 & 406, 4th fl, West Wing, Raheja Towers, MG Rd, Bangalore 560 001, India *Tel:* (080) 4089 2222 *E-mail:* india@theiet.in *Web Site:* theiet.in
The Institution of Engineering & Technology, Michael Faraday House, 6 Hills Way, Stevenage, Herts SG1 2AY, United Kingdom (journal & magazine sales), Contact: Neil Dennis *Tel:* (01438) 313 311 *E-mail:* postmaster@theiet.org
Foreign Rep(s): Cranbury International LLC (Latin America, Mexico, South America)
Orders to: c/o Books International Inc, PO Box 605, Herndon, VA 20172 *Tel:* 703-661-1573 *Toll Free Tel:* 800-230-7286 (US &

CN) *Fax:* 703-661-1501 *E-mail:* ieemail@presswarehouse.com
Distribution Center: c/o Books International Inc, PO Box 605, Herndon, VA 20172 *Tel:* 703-661-1500 *Fax:* 703-661-1501
Membership(s): Association of Learned & Professional Society Publishers (ALPSP); STM

IFPRI, see International Food Policy Research Institute

§Ignatius Press
Division of Guadalupe Associates Inc
1348 Tenth Ave, San Francisco, CA 94122-2304
SAN: 214-3887
Toll Free Tel: 800-651-1531 (orders); 888-615-3186 (cust serv) *Fax:* 415-387-0896
E-mail: info@ignatius.com
Web Site: www.ignatius.com
Key Personnel
Pres: Mark Brumley *E-mail:* mark@ignatius.com
Art Dir: Roxanne Lum *E-mail:* roxanne@ignatius.com
Mktg Dir: Anthony J Ryan *E-mail:* tony@ignatius.com
Ed: Fr Joseph Fessio SJ
Prodn Ed: Carolyn Lemon
Mktg Mgr: Eva Mutean *E-mail:* eva@ignatius.com
Foreign Rts: Penelope Boldrick *E-mail:* penelope@ignatius.com
Founded: 1978
ISBN Prefix(es): 978-0-89870; 978-1-58617; 978-1-62164; 978-1-68149
Number of titles published annually: 60 Print
Total Titles: 750 Print; 25 Audio
Distributor for Bethlehem Books; Veritas
Foreign Rep(s): Ancoh Enterprises (Nigeria); B Broughton Co Ltd (Canada); Freedom Publishing (Australia, New Zealand); Gracewing Publishing (Europe, UK); John XXIII Fellowship Co-op Ltd (Australia, New Zealand); St Andrew's Church Supply (Canada); Sunrise Marian Distribution (Canada); Veritas Publications (Ireland)

IHS Press, see Indiana Historical Society Press

IHS Press
222 W 21 St, Suite F-122, Norfolk, VA 23517
Toll Free Tel: 877-447-7737 *Toll Free Fax:* 877-447-7737
E-mail: info@ihspress.com; tradesales@ihspress.com (wholesale sales); order@ihspress.com
Web Site: www.ihspress.com
Founded: 2001
ISBN Prefix(es): 978-0-9714894; 978-0-9718286; 978-1-932528; 978-1-60570
Number of titles published annually: 12 Print; 12 E-Book
Total Titles: 42 Print; 42 E-Book
Distribution Center: Independent Publishers Group (IPG), 814 N Franklin St, Chicago, IL 60610

§Illinois State Museum Society
Affiliate of Illinois State Museum
502 S Spring St, Springfield, IL 62706-5000
Tel: 217-782-7386 *Fax:* 217-782-1254
E-mail: subscriptions@museum.state.il.us
Web Site: www.illinoisstatemuseum.org
Key Personnel
Museum Dir: Cinnamon Catlin-Legutko
Mng Ed: Andy Hanson *Tel:* 217-782-6700 *E-mail:* andrew.hanson@illinois.gov
Founded: 1877
Softcover texts, quarterly magazines, quarterly newsletters, quarterly calendars of events & activities brochures, educational posters & CD-ROM.
ISBN Prefix(es): 978-0-89792

Number of titles published annually: 4 Print
Total Titles: 1 CD-ROM

§Illuminating Engineering Society of North America (IES)
120 Wall St, 17th fl, New York, NY 10005-4001
Tel: 212-248-5000 *Fax:* 212-248-5017; 212-248-5018
E-mail: ies@ies.org
Web Site: www.ies.org
Key Personnel
Mktg Mgr: Clayton Gordon *Tel:* 212-248-5000 ext 110 *E-mail:* cgordon@ies.org
Founded: 1906
ISBN Prefix(es): 978-0-87995
Number of titles published annually: 10 Print; 1 E-Book
Total Titles: 90 Print; 2 E-Book
Distributor for Taylor & Francis; Techstreet

Imagination Publishing Group
PO Box 1304, Dunedin, FL 34697
Toll Free Tel: 888-701-6481 *Fax:* 727-361-0584
E-mail: info@imaginationpublishinggroup.com
Web Site: www.imaginationpublishinggroup.com
Key Personnel
Pres: Alan Wayne
Asst: Miranda Jade
Founded: 2008
Publisher of fine quality printed products & educational apps for mobile devices.
ISBN Prefix(es): 978-0-9800
Number of titles published annually: 5 Print; 2 Audio
Total Titles: 3 Print; 1 Audio
Membership(s): American Booksellers Association (ABA); Association of Booksellers for Children; Florida Association for Media in Education (FAME); Florida Association for Partners in Education; Florida Authors & Publishers Association Inc (FAPA); Society of Children's Book Writers & Illustrators (SCBWI); Southern Independent Booksellers for Children

§Imago Press
3710 E Edison St, Tucson, AZ 85716
Tel: 520-444-2265
Web Site: www.oasisjournal.org
Key Personnel
Publr: Leila Joiner *E-mail:* ljoiner@dakotacom.net
Founded: 2002
Provide a place for older authors to present their work to appreciative audiences. Our flagship offering is the *OASIS Journal*, an annual anthology of short fiction, short nonfiction & poetry by writers over fifty, which originated with the OASIS Institute, a national nonprofit organization that promotes ongoing education for seniors.
ISBN Prefix(es): 978-0-9725303; 978-0-9799341; 978-1-935437; 978-0-9981791
Number of titles published annually: 2 Print; 2 E-Book
Total Titles: 54 Print; 24 E-Book
Imprints: As Sabr; Pennywyse Press
Membership(s): Independent Book Publishers Association (IBPA)

§ImaJinn Books
Imprint of BelleBooks
PO Box 300921, Memphis, TN 38130
Tel: 901-344-9024 *Fax:* 901-344-9068
E-mail: bellebooks@bellebooks.com
Web Site: www.imajinnbooks.com
Founded: 1998
Specialize in publishing & selling paranormal romance, urban fantasy, regency romance & erotica.
ISBN Prefix(es): 978-1-893896; 978-0-9759653; 978-1-933417; 978-1-61026
Number of titles published annually: 25 Print

Total Titles: 150 Print
Membership(s): The Association of Publishers for Special Sales (APSS); Independent Book Publishers Association (IBPA)

Immedium
Imprint of Immedium Inc
535 Rockdale Dr, San Francisco, CA 94127
Mailing Address: PO Box 31846, San Francisco, CA 94131
Tel: 415-452-8546 *Fax:* 360-937-6272
E-mail: orders@immedium.com; sales@immedium.com
Web Site: www.immedium.com
Key Personnel
Publr: Oliver Chin *E-mail:* o.chin@comcast.net
Ed: Don Menn
Acqs Ed: Amy Ma
Graphic Design: Elaine Chu
Founded: 2005
Publish wonderfully illustrated children's picture books, Asian American topics & contemporary arts & culture.
ISBN Prefix(es): 978-1-59702
Number of titles published annually: 3 Print; 3 Online; 3 E-Book
Total Titles: 50 Print; 50 Online; 50 E-Book
Foreign Rights: HarperCollins UK (UK & Commonwealth)
Orders to: Consortium Book Sales & Distribution, The Keg House, Suite 101, 34 13 Ave NE, Minneapolis, MN 55413-1007 *Tel:* 612-746-2600 *Toll Free Tel:* 800-283-3572 (cust serv, Jackson, TN) *Fax:* 612-746-2606 *E-mail:* info@cbsd.com *Web Site:* www.cbsd.com SAN: 200-6049
Returns: Consortium Book Sales & Distribution, The Keg House, Suite 101, 34 13 Ave NE, Minneapolis, MN 55413-1007 *Tel:* 612-746-2600 *Toll Free Tel:* 800-283-3572 (cust serv, Jackson, TN) *Fax:* 612-746-2606 *E-mail:* info@cbsd.com *Web Site:* www.cbsd.com SAN: 200-6049
Shipping Address: Consortium Book Sales & Distribution, The Keg House, Suite 101, 34 13 Ave NE, Minneapolis, MN 55413-1007 *Tel:* 612-746-2600 *Toll Free Tel:* 800-283-3572 (cust serv, Jackson, TN) *Fax:* 612-746-2606 *E-mail:* info@cbsd.com *Web Site:* www.cbsd.com SAN: 200-6049
Warehouse: Consortium Book Sales & Distribution, The Keg House, Suite 101, 34 13 Ave NE, Minneapolis, MN 55413-1007 *Tel:* 612-746-2600 *Toll Free Tel:* 800-283-3572 (cust serv, Jackson, TN) *Fax:* 612-746-2606 *E-mail:* info@cbsd.com *Web Site:* www.cbsd.com SAN: 200-6049
Distribution Center: Consortium Book Sales & Distribution, The Keg House, Suite 101, 34 13 Ave NE, Minneapolis, MN 55413-1007 *Tel:* 612-746-2600 *Toll Free Tel:* 800-283-3572 (cust serv, Jackson, TN) *Fax:* 612-746-2606 *E-mail:* info@cbsd.com *Web Site:* www.cbsd.com SAN: 200-6049

§Impact Publications/Development Concepts Inc
7820 Sudley Rd, Suite 100, Manassas, VA 20109
Tel: 703-361-7300 *Toll Free Tel:* 800-361-1055 (cust serv) *Fax:* 703-335-9486
E-mail: query@impactpublications.com
Web Site: www.impactpublications.com; www.veteransworld.com
Key Personnel
Pres: Ronald Krannich, PhD
Founded: 1982
Career & travel publications.
ISBN Prefix(es): 978-1-57023; 978-0-942710
Number of titles published annually: 18 Print
Total Titles: 167 Print
Distributed by National Book Network

In the Garden Publishing
Division of What Would Love Do International Ltd
7525 Paragon Rd, No 752252, Dayton, OH 45459
Mailing Address: PO Box 752252, Dayton, OH 45475 SAN: 920-3389
Tel: 937-317-0859
E-mail: editor@inthegardenpublishing.com
Web Site: www.inthegardenpublishing.com
Key Personnel
Publr: Christine Horner *E-mail:* admin@inthegardenpublishing.com
Founded: 2012
Discover your inner guru. Conscious community & brilliant minds unite. Together, what can we create?
ISBN Prefix(es): 978-0-9855314; 978-0-9888333
Number of titles published annually: 5 Print; 5 Online; 5 E-Book
Total Titles: 9 Print; 15 Online; 8 E-Book
Imprints: Yugen Press (fiction)

§Incentive Publications by World Book
180 N LaSalle St, Suite 900, Chicago, IL 60101
Toll Free Tel: 800-967-5325; 800-975-3250; 888-482-9764 (trade dept) *Toll Free Fax:* 888-922-3766
E-mail: tradeorders@worldbook.com
Web Site: www.incentivepublications.com
Founded: 1968 (acquired by World Book 2013)
Preschool through high school supplementary educational materials for students, parents & teachers.
ISBN Prefix(es): 978-0-913916; 978-0-86530
Number of titles published annually: 25 Print
Total Titles: 425 Print; 1 CD-ROM

§Independent Information Publications
Division of Computing!
3357 21 St, San Francisco, CA 94110
Tel: 415-643-8600
E-mail: sharisteiner@gmail.com
Web Site: www.movedoc.com
Founded: 1982
ISBN Prefix(es): 978-0-913733
Number of titles published annually: 4 Print; 1 CD-ROM; 6 Online; 2 E-Book
Total Titles: 5 Print; 1 CD-ROM; 4 Online; 2 E-Book
Imprints: IIP Consumers Series
Branch Office(s)
IIP, 500 Kentucky Ave, Savannah, GA 31404, Contact: Cima Star *Tel:* 912-233-8873
Shipping Address: Pathway Book Service, PO Box 89, Gilsum, NH 03448 *Tel:* 603-357-0236 *E-mail:* pbs@pathwaybook.com *Web Site:* www.pathwaybook.com
Distribution Center: Pathway Book Service, PO Box 89, Gilsum, NH 03448 *Tel:* 603-357-0236 *E-mail:* pbs@pathwaybook.com *Web Site:* www.pathwaybook.com
Membership(s): Bay Area Independent Publishers Association (BAIPA); Independent Book Publishers Association (IBPA)

§Independent Institute
100 Swan Way, Suite 200, Oakland, CA 94621-1428
Tel: 510-632-1366 *Toll Free Tel:* 800-927-8733 *Fax:* 510-568-6040
E-mail: orders@independent.org
Web Site: www.independent.org
Key Personnel
Founder & CEO: David J Theroux *Tel:* 510-632-1366 ext 104 *E-mail:* dtheroux@independent.org
CFO: Martin Buerger *Tel:* 510-632-1366 ext 110 *E-mail:* mbuerger@independent.org
Exec Dir: Graham Walker *Tel:* 510-632-1366 ext 151 *E-mail:* gwalker@independent.org
Pubns Dir: Christopher Briggs *Tel:* 510-632-1366 ext 16 *E-mail:* cbriggs@independent.org

Res Dir: William Shughart, II *E-mail:* william.shughart@usu.edu
Exec Ed, Books: Roy M Carlisle *Tel:* 510-568-6049 *E-mail:* rcarlisle@independent.org
Soc Media Mgr: Shurti Kothiwal *Tel:* 510-632-1366 ext 181 *E-mail:* skothiwal@independent.org
Founded: 1986
Nonprofit research & publication. Branch office in Washington, DC.
ISBN Prefix(es): 978-0-945999; 978-1-59813
Number of titles published annually: 6 Print; 1 CD-ROM; 2 Online; 6 E-Book; 1 Audio
Total Titles: 109 Print; 90 E-Book
Branch Office(s)
1455 Pennsylvania Ave NW, Suite 400, Washington, DC 20004, Dir, Center on Peace & Liberty: Ivan Eland *Tel:* 202-249-7806 *E-mail:* ieland@independent.org
Distribution Center: Independent Publishers Group, 814 N Franklin St, Chicago, IL 60610 *Toll Free Tel:* 800-888-4741 *Web Site:* www.ipgbook.com
Membership(s): Association of American Publishers (AAP); Independent Book Publishers Association (IBPA)

Indiana Historical Society Press
450 W Ohio St, Indianapolis, IN 46202-3269
SAN: 201-5234
Tel: 317-232-1882; 317-234-0026 (orders); 317-234-2716 (edit) *Toll Free Tel:* 800-447-1830 (orders) *Fax:* 317-234-0562 (orders); 317-233-0857 (edit)
E-mail: ihspress@indianahistory.org; orders@indianahistory.org
Web Site: www.indianahistory.org; shop.indianahistory.org (orders)
Key Personnel
Pres & CEO: Jody Blankenship
Sr Ed: Ray Boomhower *E-mail:* rboomhower@indianahistory.og
Natl Sales Coord: Becke Bolinger *Tel:* 317-234-3683 *E-mail:* bbolinger@indianahistory.org
Founded: 1886
Books, journals & newsletters on Indiana history, including an illustrated history magazine & a family history magazine. Also offers videos, recordings, prints, note cards & other gift items.
ISBN Prefix(es): 978-0-87195
Number of titles published annually: 4 Print; 1 Online; 4 E-Book
Total Titles: 100 Print; 1 Online; 3 Audio

Indiana University African Studies Program
Indiana University, 355 N Jordan, Rm GA 3072, Bloomington, IN 47405
Tel: 812-855-8284 *Fax:* 812-855-6734
E-mail: afrist@indiana.edu
Web Site: www.indiana.edu/~afrist; www.go.iu.edu/afrist
Key Personnel
Dir: John Hanson
Assoc Dir: Tavy Aherne *Tel:* 812-855-5081
Founded: 1965
Monograph & working papers, humanities, interdisciplinary study of Africa.
ISBN Prefix(es): 978-0-941934
Number of titles published annually: 50 Print
Total Titles: 52 Print

§Indiana University Press
Herman B Wells Library 350, 1320 E Tenth St, Bloomington, IN 47405-3907
SAN: 202-5647
Tel: 812-855-8817 *Toll Free Tel:* 800-842-6796 (orders only) *Fax:* 812-855-7931; 812-855-8507
E-mail: iupress@indiana.edu; iuporder@indiana.edu (orders)
Web Site: www.iupress.indiana.edu

Key Personnel
Dir: Gary Dunham
Assoc Dir: Dave Hulsey *Tel:* 812-855-6553
  E-mail: hulseyd@indiana.edu
Dir, Acqs: Dee Mortensen *Tel:* 812-855-0268
  E-mail: mortense@indiana.edu
Dir, Opers & Electronic Publg: Michael Regoli
  Tel: 812-855-3830 *E-mail:* regoli@indiana.edu
Technol Dir: Ted Boardman *Tel:* 812-855-6468
  E-mail: tboardma@indiana.edu
Acq Ed: Jennika Baines *Tel:* 812-855-2756
  E-mail: bainesj@indiana.edu; Janice Frisch
  Tel: 812-856-5810 *E-mail:* frischj@indiana.edu
Mgr, Accts Receivable: Kimberly Bower
  Tel: 812-855-4134 *E-mail:* kchilder@indiana.
  edu
Mktg Mgr: Julie Davis *Tel:* 812-855-3113
  E-mail: julmsmit@indiana.edu; Michelle Sybert
  Tel: 812-855-5031 *E-mail:* msybert@indiana.
  edu
Mktg Mgr, Journals: Jacklyn Lord *Tel:* 812-855-
  4522 *E-mail:* jvfarris@indiana.edu
Rts & Perms Mgr: Stephen Williams *Tel:* 812-
  855-6314 *E-mail:* smw9@indiana.edu
Acctg Asst: Brent Starr *Tel:* 812-855-5366
  E-mail: brstarr@indiana.edu
Founded: 1950
Trade & scholarly nonfiction; film & media stud-
  ies, literature & music, African studies, back-
  list, classical studies, contemporary issues, cul-
  tural studies, folklore, international studies,
  Jewish studies, journals, Middle East studies,
  paleontology, philanthropy, politics/political
  science, railroads & transportation, Russian
  studies.
ISBN Prefix(es): 978-0-253
Number of titles published annually: 150 Print; 2
  CD-ROM; 145 E-Book; 5 Audio
Total Titles: 3,672 Print; 8 CD-ROM; 1,548 E-
  Book
Imprints: Quarry Books (regional imprint for
  Midwest)
Foreign Rights: Agencia Literaria Carmen Bal-
  cells SA (Maribel Luque) (Spain); Book-
  man Literary Agency (Ib H Lauritzen) (Den-
  mark); The English Agency (Tsutomu Yawata)
  (Japan); The Deborah Harris Agency (Efrat
  Lev) (Israel); The Italian Literary Agency
  srl (Maria Stefania Fietta) (Italy); Liepman
  AG (Marc Koralnik) (Germany); La Nouvelle
  Agence (Anne Maizeret) (France); O A Liter-
  ary Agency (Michael Avramides) (Greece)
Orders to: Ingram Publisher Services, 1210 In-
  gram Dr, Chambersburg, PA 17202 *Tel:* 717-
  262-4860 *Toll Free Tel:* 800-648-3013
  E-mail: pubsupport@ingramcontent.com *Web
  Site:* ipage.ingramcontent.com
Shipping Address: Ingram Publisher Services,
  1210 Ingram Dr, Chambersburg, PA 17202
  Tel: 717-262-4860 *Toll Free Tel:* 800-648-3013
  E-mail: pubsupport@ingramcontent.com *Web
  Site:* ipage.ingramcontent.com
Distribution Center: Ingram Publisher Services,
  1210 Ingram Dr, Chambersburg, PA 17202
  Tel: 717-262-4860 *Toll Free Tel:* 800-648-3013
  E-mail: pubsupport@ingramcontent.com *Web
  Site:* ipage.ingramcontent.com

§Industrial Press Inc
32 Haviland St, Suite 3, Norwalk, CT 06854
SAN: 202-6945
Tel: 203-956-5593 ext 0 (cust serv)
  Toll Free Tel: 888-528-7852 ext 0 (cust serv)
  Fax: 203-354-9391 (cust serv)
E-mail: info@industrialpress.com (cust serv)
Web Site: books.industrialpress.com; ebooks.
  industrialpress.com
Key Personnel
Owner & Pres: Alex Luchars *E-mail:* aluchars@
  industrialpress.com
Cont: Vanisse Mascia *E-mail:* vmascia@
  industrialpress.com

Publr: Judy Bass *E-mail:* jbass@industrialpress.
  com
Mng Ed & Ed, Machinery's Handbook:
  Laura Brengelman *E-mail:* lbrengelman@
  industrialpress.com
Sales Assoc: Jana Rahrig *E-mail:* jrahrig@
  industrialpress.com
Founded: 1883
Scientific & technical handbooks, professional &
  reference books for engineering, technology,
  manufacturing & education.
ISBN Prefix(es): 978-0-8311
Number of titles published annually: 28 Print; 5
  CD-ROM; 28 E-Book
Total Titles: 320 Print; 30 CD-ROM; 120 E-Book
Foreign Rep(s): Academic Marketing Services
  (Botswana, Lesotho, Namibia, South Africa,
  Swaziland); China Publishing Services Ltd
  (China); Co Info Pty Ltd (Australia, Fiji, New
  Zealand, Papua New Guinea); Cranbury In-
  ternational LLC (Central America, Mexico,
  Puerto Rico, South America, West Indies); Dis-
  van Enterprises (India); Nelson Education Ltd
  (Canada); Transatlantic Publishers Group Ltd
  (Europe, Middle East); The White Partnership
  (Indonesia, Malaysia, Philippines, Singapore,
  South Korea, Sri Lanka, Thailand)
Membership(s): Association of American Publish-
  ers (AAP)

Information Age Publishing Inc
PO Box 79049, Charlotte, NC 28271-7047
Tel: 704-752-9125 *Fax:* 704-752-9113
E-mail: infoage@infoagepub.com
Web Site: www.infoagepub.com
Key Personnel
Pres & Publr: George F Johnson
  E-mail: george@infoagepub.com
Founded: 1999
Social science publisher of academic & schol-
  arly book series & journals. Specialties include
  black studies, educational technology & leader-
  ship titles.
Information Age is a no returns publisher.
ISBN Prefix(es): 978-1-930608; 978-1-931576;
  978-1-59311; 978-1-60752; 978-1-61735; 978-
  1-62396; 978-1-68123
Number of titles published annually: 240 Print;
  120 E-Book
Total Titles: 3,500 Print; 1,500 E-Book
Foreign Rep(s): Co Info Pty Ltd (Australia);
  Cranbury International LLC (Caribbean, Puerto
  Rico, South America); The Eurospan Group
  (Europe); Mohamed Feroz (Indonesia); Jeffrey
  Lim (Indochina, Philippines, Vietnam); Login
  Canada (Canada); Maruzen Co Ltd (Japan);
  Mercury Retail Pty Ltd (Australia); Sara Books
  Pvt Ltd (India); Taylor & Francis Asia Pacific
  (China, Hong Kong, Korea, Singapore, Taiwan,
  Thailand); Taylor & Francis Publishing Ser-
  vices (Brunei, Malaysia)
Foreign Rights: International Publishers Represen-
  tatives (IPR) (worldwide)

§Information Gatekeepers Inc (IGI)
Division of IGI Group Inc
PO Box 606, Winchester, MA 01890
Tel: 617-782-5033 *Fax:* 617-507-8338
E-mail: info@igigroup.com
Web Site: www.igigroup.com
Key Personnel
Chief Analyst & Ed-in-Chief: Dr Hui Pan
  E-mail: hpan@igigroup.com
Mng Ed: Bev Wilson *E-mail:* editor@igigroup.
  com
Founded: 1977
Fiber optics, optical networks, wireless, ATM,
  XDSL & telecommunications, trade shows,
  conferences, newsletters, market studies & con-
  sulting.
ISBN Prefix(es): 978-0-918435; 978-1-56851
Number of titles published annually: 35 Print;
  100 CD-ROM; 20 E-Book

Total Titles: 540 Print; 100 CD-ROM; 50 E-Book
Foreign Rep(s): Children Magazine Services
  (England); Global Information Inc (Japan);
  Investment Publications Information Service
  (Australia); Overseas Information Center (OIC)
  (Korea)
Membership(s): Institute of Electrical and Elec-
  tronics Engineers Inc (IEEE); The Optical So-
  ciety (OSA); Plastic Optical Fiber Trade Orga-
  nization (POFTO)

§Information Today, Inc
143 Old Marlton Pike, Medford, NJ 08055-8750
Tel: 609-654-6266 *Toll Free Tel:* 800-300-9868
  (cust serv) *Fax:* 609-654-4309
E-mail: custserv@infotoday.com
Web Site: www.infotoday.com
Key Personnel
Pres & CEO: Thomas H Hogan
VP, Admin: John Yersak
VP, Mktg & Busn Devt: Thomas Hogan, Jr
VP, IT: Bill Spence *E-mail:* spence@infotoday.
  com
Dir of Sales, Lib & Info Div: Lauri Rimler
  E-mail: lwrimler@infotoday.com
Prodn Mgr: Tiffany Chamenko
  E-mail: tchamenko@infotoday.com
Mktg & Exhibits Mgr: Robert Colding
  E-mail: rcolding@infotoday.com
Founded: 1980
Publisher specializing in: Books, directories,
  newspapers, journals, newsletters, conferences
  & information services for users & producers of digital information content & technologies, including professionals in the library,
  publishing, online information, K-12 education, business research & IT, knowledge management, customer relationship management,
  speech technology & streaming media industries. ITI's reference division is the publisher
  of *LMP, ILMP, American Book Trade Directory, Library and Book Trade Almanac* & other
  professional reference titles.
ISBN Prefix(es): 978-0-938734; 978-0-904933;
  978-1-57387; 978-0-910965
Number of titles published annually: 28 Print; 15
  E-Book
Total Titles: 460 Print; 230 E-Book
Imprints: ASI Books (books for indexing professionals from the American Society for Indexing); ASIS&T Monograph Series (scholarly
  monographs from the American Society for
  Information Science & Technology); Cyber-
  Age Books (books for tech-savvy consumers
  & business information users; nationally dis-
  tributed to the book trade by IPG); Information
  Today Books (practical books for library & in-
  formation professionals)
Membership(s): Association for Independent Information Professionals; Mystery Writers of
  America (MWA); Special Libraries Association
  (SLA)

Infosources Publishing
140 Norma Rd, Teaneck, NJ 07666
Tel: 201-836-7072
Web Site: www.infosourcespub.com
Key Personnel
Publr & Ed: Arlene L Eis
Founded: 1981
Legal reference books, newsletters, online
  databases. Publisher of *The Informed Librar-
  ian Online.*

ISBN Prefix(es): 978-0-939486; 978-0-9842928;
978-0-9842214
Number of titles published annually: 3 Print; 1
Online
Total Titles: 6 Print

Inkwater Press
Imprint of Firstbooks.com Inc
6750 SW Franklin St, Suite A, Portland, OR
97223
Tel: 503-968-6777 *Fax:* 503-968-6779
E-mail: orders@inkwaterbooks.com
Web Site: www.inkwater.com
Key Personnel
Pres: Jeremy Solomon *E-mail:* jeremy@inkwater.
com
Founded: 2002
Publishing services to individuals & corporations
as well as author subsidized publishing.
This publisher has indicated that 95% of their
product line is author subsidized.
ISBN Prefix(es): 978-0-9719414; 978-1-59299;
978-1-62901
Number of titles published annually: 70 Print; 70
E-Book
Total Titles: 430 Print; 115 E-Book; 2 Audio
Imprints: Franklin Street Books

Inner Traditions International Ltd
One Park St, Rochester, VT 05767
Mailing Address: PO Box 388, Rochester, VT
05767
Tel: 802-767-3174 *Toll Free Tel:* 800-246-8648
Fax: 802-767-3726
E-mail: customerservice@InnerTraditions.com
Web Site: www.InnerTraditions.com
Key Personnel
Pres: Ehud C Sperling *E-mail:* prez@
InnerTraditions.com
VP, Opers: Diane Shepard *E-mail:* dianes@
InnerTraditions.com
Dir, Sales & Mktg: John Hays *E-mail:* johnh@
InnerTraditions.com
Ed-in-Chief: Jeanie Levitan *E-mail:* jeaniel@
InnerTraditions.com
Acqs Ed: Jon Graham *E-mail:* jong@
InnerTraditions.com
Curator, Sacred Planet Books: Richard Grossinger
Audiobook Mgr: Megan Rule *E-mail:* meganr@
InnerTraditions.com
Print Mgr: Jon Desautels *E-mail:* jond@
InnerTraditions.com
Foreign Rts & Perms: Maria Loftus
E-mail: marial@InnerTraditions.com
Publicity: Manzanita Carpenter
E-mail: manzanitac@InnerTraditions.com
Sales & Mktg: Andrea Raymond *E-mail:* andyr@
InnerTraditions.com
Spec Sales: Jessica Arsenault *E-mail:* jessa@
InnerTraditions.com
Founded: 1975
Nonfiction cloth & quality trade paperbacks; au-
dio cassettes & CDs (ethnic music & medita-
tion aids).
ISBN Prefix(es): 978-0-89281; 978-1-899171;
978-1-84409; 978-1-59477; 978-1-62055; 978-
0-905249; 978-1-64411
Number of titles published annually: 82 Print; 82
E-Book; 60 Audio
Total Titles: 1,545 Print; 1,159 E-Book; 86 Audio
Imprints: Bear & Co Inc; Bear Cub Books; Bindu
Books; Destiny Books; Destiny Recordings;
Earthdancer Books; Findhorn Press; Healing
Arts Press; Inner Traditions; Inner Traditions
Audio; Inner Traditions en Espanol; Inner Tra-
ditions India; Park Street Press; Sacred Planet
Books
Foreign Rights: Akcali Copyright Agency
(Turkey); Big Apple Agency Inc (China, Tai-
wan); Blackbird Literary Agency (Netherlands);
The Book Publishers' Association of Israel, In-
ternational Promotion & Literary Rights Dept
(Israel); Graal Literary Agency (Poland); Ilidio

Matos Agency (Portugal); International Editors'
Co SA (Spain); The Italian Literary Agency
(Italy); Simona Kessler International Copy-
right Agency Ltd (Romania); Alexander Ko-
rzhenevski Agency (Russia); Montreal Con-
tacts/The Rights Agency (Canada); Andrew
Nurnberg Associates (Baltic States, Bulgaria,
Czechia, Hungary); Plima doo (Croatia); Read
n Right Agency (Greece); Schindler's Liter-
ary Agency (Brazil); Thomas Schlueck GmbH
(Germany); Agence Schweiger (France); Tuttle-
Mori Agency Inc (Indonesia, Japan, Thailand);
Eric Yang Agency (Korea)
Orders to: Inner Traditions International - Bear
& Co, c/o Simon & Schuster, 100 Front
St, Riverside, NJ 08075 *Toll Free Tel:* 800-
223-2336 *Toll Free Fax:* 800-943-9831
E-mail: purchaseorders@simonandschuster.com
Returns: Simon & Schuster, c/o Jacobson Logis-
tics, 4406 Industrial Park Rd, Bldg 7, Camp
Hill, PA 17011 (truckload shipments must call
for an appt: 800-967-3914 ext 5318)
Warehouse: Inner Traditions International -
Bear & Co, c/o Simon & Schuster, 100
Front St, Riverside, NJ 08075 *Toll Free
Tel:* 800-943-9831 *E-mail:* purchaseorders@
simonandschuster.com
See separate listing for:
Bear & Co Inc

The Innovation Press
1001 Fourth Ave, Suite 3200, Seattle, WA 98154
Tel: 360-870-9988
E-mail: info@theinnovationpress.com
Web Site: www.theinnovationpress.com
Key Personnel
Publr: Asia Citro *E-mail:* acitro@
theinnovationpress.com
Founded: 2015
We publish quirky, creative books (often with a
STEM-focus) for kids PreK-grade 6.
ISBN Prefix(es): 978-1-943147
Number of titles published annually: 5 Print; 3 E-
Book
Total Titles: 14 Print; 7 E-Book
Foreign Rep(s): Michael Abbott (Africa, Europe,
Middle East); Jason Howell (Canada); Suk Lee
(Asia); Nella Soeterboek (Australia); James
Wickham (UK)
Foreign Rights: Kaplan/DeFiore Rights (Linda
Kaplan) (worldwide)
Warehouse: Baker & Taylor Publisher Services
(BTPS), 30 Amberwood Pkwy, Ashland, OH
44805 *Toll Free Tel:* 888-814-0208
Distribution Center: Baker & Taylor Publisher
Services (BTPS), 30 Amberwood Pkwy, Ash-
land, OH 44805 *Toll Free Tel:* 888-814-0208
Web Site: www.btpubservices.com
Membership(s): American Booksellers Associ-
ation (ABA); The Children's Book Council
(CBC); Pacific Northwest Booksellers Asso-
ciation (PNBA); Publishers Association of the
West (PubWest)

Insight Editions
800 "A" St, San Rafael, CA 94901
Tel: 415-526-1370 *Toll Free Tel:* 800-809-3792
Toll Free Fax: 866-509-0515
E-mail: info@insighteditions.com; marketing@
insighteditions.com
Web Site: insighteditions.com
Key Personnel
Pres & Publr: Raoul Goff
Assoc Publr: Vanessa Lopez
VP, Sales: Julie Hamilton *Tel:* 415-526-1370 ext
223 *E-mail:* jhamilton@insighteditions.com
Head, Sales & Mktg: Terry Newell
PR Dir: Darcy Cohan
Exec Ed: Mark Irwin
Assoc Mng Ed: Lauren LePera
Asst Ed: Tessa Murphy
Publicity Mgr: Lauren Kretzschmar

Sales Mgr: Jacqui Goff *E-mail:* j.goff@
insighteditions.com; Jennifer Metzger
Asst Design Mgr: Alison Corn
Proj Coord: Colton Long
Founded: 2000
Renowned for creating beautiful, innovative books
that excel in the marketplace. Insight Editions
brings the vision & style of high-end illustrated
books to the realm of the arts & entertainment.
ISBN Prefix(es): 978-1-933784
Number of titles published annually: 75 Print
Total Titles: 300 Print
Imprints: Mandala Earth
Subsidiaries: Weldon Owen International
Distributed by Simon & Schuster
See separate listing for:
Mandala Earth

Institute of Continuing Legal Education
1020 Greene St, Ann Arbor, MI 48109-1444
Tel: 734-764-0533 *Toll Free Tel:* 877-229-4350
Fax: 734-763-2412 *Toll Free Fax:* 877-229-
4351
E-mail: icle@umich.edu
Web Site: www.icle.org
Key Personnel
Dir: David R Watson
Educ Dir: Jeffrey E Kirkey
Founded: 1959
Michigan law books in print & online.
ISBN Prefix(es): 978-0-88288
Number of titles published annually: 33 Print
Total Titles: 58 Print; 55 Online
Imprints: ICLE

**§Institute of Environmental Sciences &
Technology - IEST**
1827 Walden Office Sq, Suite 400, Schaumburg,
IL 60173
Tel: 847-981-0100 *Fax:* 847-981-4130
E-mail: information@iest.org
Web Site: www.iest.org
Key Personnel
Exec Dir: Angela McKay *Tel:* 847-981-0100 ext
6010 *E-mail:* executive@iest.org
Mgr, Tech Progs: Jennifer Sklena *Tel:* 847-981-
0100 ext 6011 *E-mail:* technicaldept@iest.org
Coord, Membership & Acctg: Mara
Douvris *Tel:* 847-981-0100 ext 6109
E-mail: membershipdept@iest.org
Coord, Educ & Meetings: Heather
Wooden *Tel:* 847-981-0100 ext 6014
E-mail: education@iest.org
Asst, Memb & Corp Rel: Susan Sta-
matkin *Tel:* 847-981-0100 ext 6015
E-mail: customerservice@iest.org
Commns & Mktg: Heather Swink
E-mail: communications@iest.org
Corp Growth & Devt: Christine Davis *Tel:* 224-
875-6112 *E-mail:* marketing@iest.org
Founded: 1953
A multidisciplinary, international society whose
members are recognized worldwide for their
contributions to the environmental sciences
in the area of contamination control & clean-
rooms; environmental testing; or nanotechnol-
ogy facilities.
ISBN Prefix(es): 978-0-915414; 978-1-877862;
978-0-9747313; 978-0-9787868; 978-0-
9841330; 978-1-937280
Number of titles published annually: 3 Print; 1
CD-ROM; 3 Online
Total Titles: 75 Print; 26 CD-ROM; 48 Online

Institute of Governmental Studies
Subsidiary of University of California, Berkeley
109 Moses Hall, No 2370, Berkeley, CA 94720-
2370
Tel: 510-642-1428
E-mail: igspress@berkeley.edu
Web Site: www.igs.berkeley.edu

Key Personnel
Dir, Pubns: Ethan Rarick *E-mail:* erarick@
berkeley.edu
Pubns Ed: Maria Wolf *E-mail:* mariaw@berkeley.
edu
Public policy issues.
ISBN Prefix(es): 978-0-87772
Number of titles published annually: 6 Print
Total Titles: 54 Print

§**Institute of Jesuit Sources (IJS)**
Boston College, Institute for Advanced Jesuit
Studies, 140 Commonwealth Ave, Chestnut,
MA 02467
Tel: 617-552-2568 *Fax:* 617-552-2575
E-mail: jesuitsources@bc.edu
Web Site: jesuitsources.bc.edu
Key Personnel
Dir: Fr Casey Beaumier
Founded: 1961
Books on history & spirituality of the society
of Jesus (Jesuits) translated from non-English
sources & originally in English.
ISBN Prefix(es): 978-0-912422; 978-1-880810
Number of titles published annually: 8 Print
Total Titles: 150 Print; 1 CD-ROM

§**Institute of Mathematical Geography**
Division of Arlinghaus Enterprises LLC
1964 Boulder Dr, Ann Arbor, MI 48104
Tel: 734-975-0246
E-mail: image@imagenet.org
Web Site: www.imagenet.org
Key Personnel
Founding Dir: Sandra Lach Arlinghaus
Founded: 1986
Publish scholarly books & college textbooks,
electronic journals & books.
ISBN Prefix(es): 978-1-877751
Number of titles published annually: 3 Print
Total Titles: 39 Print; 13 E-Book

Institute of Police Technology & Management
Division of University of North Florida
12000 Alumni Dr, Jacksonville, FL 32224-2678
Tel: 904-620-4786 *Fax:* 904-620-2453
E-mail: info@iptm.org
Web Site: www.iptm.org
Key Personnel
Dir: Cameron Pucci *E-mail:* cpucci@unf.edu
Founded: 1980
In-service training for law enforcement, civilian
personnel; marketing of publications, templates
& videos. Specialize in traffic crash investiga-
tion & reconstruction; law enforcement man-
agement & supervision; criminal investigation;
forensic technology; DUI & drug law enforce-
ment; radar/laser speed enforcement; gangs &
other specialized subjects.
ISBN Prefix(es): 978-1-884566
Number of titles published annually: 7 Print; 2
CD-ROM
Total Titles: 65 Print; 6 CD-ROM
Foreign Rep(s): Paul Feenan (Australia, South
Pacific)
Foreign Rights: Pacific Traffic Education Centre
(Canada)

The Institutes™
720 Providence Rd, Suite 100, Malvern, PA
19355-3433
Tel: 610-644-2100 *Toll Free Tel:* 800-644-2101
Fax: 610-640-9576
E-mail: customerservice@theinstitutes.org
Web Site: www.theinstitutes.org
Key Personnel
Pres & CEO: Peter Miller
Property-casualty continuing insurance education.
ISBN Prefix(es): 978-0-89463; 978-0-89462
Number of titles published annually: 12 Print
Total Titles: 120 Print

The Institution of Engineering & Technology,
see IET USA Inc

Inter-American Development Bank
Division of Multilateral Development Bank
1300 New York Ave NW, Washington, DC 20577
Tel: 202-623-1000 *Fax:* 202-623-3096
E-mail: pic@iadb.org
Web Site: publications.iadb.org
Key Personnel
Pres: Luis Alberto Moreno
EVP: Julie T Katzman
Founded: 1959
Economic development in Latin America & the
Caribbean.
ISBN Prefix(es): 978-0-940602; 978-1-886938;
978-1-931003; 978-1-59782
Number of titles published annually: 30 Print
Total Titles: 160 Print
Distributed by Johns Hopkins University Press

§**Inter-University Consortium for Political &
Social Research (ICPSR)**
Affiliate of University of Michigan Institute for
Social Research
330 Packard St, Ann Arbor, MI 48104
Mailing Address: PO Box 1248, Ann Arbor, MI
48106-1248
Tel: 734-647-5000 *Fax:* 734-647-8200
E-mail: help@icpsr.umich.edu
Web Site: www.icpsr.umich.edu
Key Personnel
Dir: Maggie Levenstein *Tel:* 734-615-8400
E-mail: maggiel@umich.edu
Asst Dir: J Trent Alexander *Tel:* 734-647-7736
E-mail: jtalex@umich.edu
Founded: 1962
Provides access to social science data collec-
tions & documentation. Training on quantita-
tive methods & data management, data sharing
services.
ISBN Prefix(es): 978-0-89138
Number of titles published annually: 300 Online
Total Titles: 7,500 Online

**Intercultural Development Research
Association (IDRA)**
5815 Callaghan Rd, Suite 101, San Antonio, TX
78228
Tel: 210-444-1710 *Fax:* 210-444-1714
E-mail: contact@idra.org
Web Site: www.idra.org
Key Personnel
Pres & CEO: Celina Moreno
Dir, Communs: Christie Goodman
Founded: 1973
Independent, nonprofit organization. Our mis-
sion is to achieve equal educational opportunity
for every child through strong public schools
that prepare all students to access & succeed in
college. IDRA strengthens & transforms pub-
lic education by providing dynamic training;
useful research, evaluation & frameworks for
action; timely policy analyses; & innovative
materials & programs.
ISBN Prefix(es): 978-1-878550; 978-1-935737
Number of titles published annually: 10 Print
Total Titles: 50 Print

Intercultural Press Inc
Imprint of Nicholas Brealey Publishing
53 State St, Boston, MA 02109
Tel: 617-523-3801
E-mail: info@nicholasbrealey.com
Web Site: nbuspublishing.com
Key Personnel
Sales Mgr: Melissa Carl
Founded: 1980
Books, training & educational materials on in-
ternational, cross-cultural & diversity subjects,
including reference books, bibliographies, man-
uals, handbooks, nonfiction.

ISBN Prefix(es): 978-0-933662; 978-1-877864;
978-1-931930; 978-0-9842471
Number of titles published annually: 20 Print
Total Titles: 300 Print
Distribution Center: Hachette Book Group, New
York, NY

Interlink Publishing Group Inc
46 Crosby St, Northampton, MA 01060
SAN: 664-8908
Tel: 413-582-7054 *Toll Free Tel:* 800-238-LINK
(238-5465) *Fax:* 413-582-7057
E-mail: info@interlinkbooks.com
Web Site: www.interlinkbooks.com
Key Personnel
VP: Ruth Lane Moushabeck
Publr & Edit Dir: Michel Moushabeck
Tel: 413-582-7054 ext 204 *E-mail:* michel@
interlinkbooks.com
Assoc Publr: Leyla Moushabeck
Dir, Opers: Brenda Eaton
Ed: John Fiscella
Publicist: Whitney Sanderson
Founded: 1987
World travel, world literature, world his-
tory/politics/current affairs, art, ethnic cooking
& illustrated children's books.
ISBN Prefix(es): 978-0-940793; 978-1-56656
Number of titles published annually: 55 Print; 40
E-Book
Total Titles: 996 Print; 500 E-Book
Imprints: Cadogan Guides; Clockroot Books;
Crocodile Books; Interlink Books; Olive
Branch Press
Distributor for Banipal Books; Barzan Publish-
ing; Camerapix Publishers; Geddes & Gros-
set; Georgina Campbell Guides; Good Hotel
Guides; Macmillan Caribbean; Rucksack Read-
ers; Serif Publishing; Sheldrake Press; Signal
Books; Sunflower Books; The Urban Explorer
- "Only In" Guides; Waverley Books; Neil Wil-
son Publishing
Foreign Rep(s): Network Book Distribution
Ltd (Europe, UK); Peter Ward Book Exports
(Richard Ward) (Middle East)
Distribution Center: Ingram Content Group, One
Ingram Blvd, La Vergne, TN 37086 *Tel:* 615-
793-5000

International Book Centre Inc
2391 Auburn Rd, Shelby Township, MI 48317
SAN: 208-7022
Tel: 586-254-7230 *Fax:* 586-254-7230
E-mail: ibc@ibcbooks.com
Web Site: www.ibcbooks.com
Key Personnel
Owner: Doris Mukalla
Founded: 1974
Publisher of foreign language books. Specialize in
the language & culture of the Middle East.
ISBN Prefix(es): 978-0-86685
Number of titles published annually: 2 Print; 2
Audio
Total Titles: 28 Print; 5 Audio
Distributor for Compass Publications; Library
du Liban (Lebanon); New Readers Press; Ox-
ford University Press; Pro Lingua Associates;
Stacey International Ltd (London); University
of Michigan

§**International City/County Management
Association (ICMA)**
777 N Capitol St NE, Suite 500, Washington, DC
20002-4201
Tel: 202-289-4262 *Toll Free Tel:* 800-745-8780
Fax: 202-962-3500
E-mail: customerservices@icma.org
Web Site: icma.org
Founded: 1914
Local government leadership & management or-
ganization that provides member support; pub-
lications, data & information; peer & results-
oriented assistance; training & professional de-

velopment to more than 11,000 city, town & county experts throughout the world.
ISBN Prefix(es): 978-0-87326
Number of titles published annually: 10 Print; 2 CD-ROM; 25 Online
Total Titles: 200 Print; 7 CD-ROM; 85 Online
Warehouse: PBD, 1650 Bluegrass Lakes Pkwy, Alpharetta, GA 30004 *Tel:* 770-442-8633
Distribution Center: PBD, 1650 Bluegrass Lakes Pkwy, Alpharetta, GA 30004 *Tel:* 770-442-8633

International Code Council Inc
3060 Saturn St, Suite 100, Brea, CA 92821
Tel: 562-699-0541 *Toll Free Tel:* 888-422-7233 *Fax:* 562-908-5524 *Toll Free Fax:* 866-891-1695
E-mail: order@icc-es.org
Web Site: www.iccsafe.org
Key Personnel
EVP & Dir, Busn Devt: Mark Johnson *Tel:* 562-699-0541 ext 3248 *E-mail:* mjohnson@icc-es.org
Founded: 1922
Publisher of construction codes & regulations used in US & abroad.
ISBN Prefix(es): 978-1-58001; 978-1-884590; 978-1-892395; 978-1-60983
Number of titles published annually: 60 Print; 10 CD-ROM
Total Titles: 300 Print; 20 CD-ROM

§International Council of Shopping Centers (ICSC)
1221 Avenue of the Americas, 41st fl, New York, NY 10020-1099
Web Site: www.icsc.org
Key Personnel
VP, Communs & Publg: Dana Muldrow *Tel:* 646-728-3571 *E-mail:* dmuldrow@icsc.com
Founded: 1957
ISBN Prefix(es): 978-0-927547; 978-0-913598; 978-1-58268
Number of titles published annually: 20 E-Book
Total Titles: 2 CD-ROM; 60 E-Book
Branch Office(s)
120 Eglinton Ave E, Suite 605, Toronto, ON M4P 1E2, Canada *Tel:* 416-486-4511 *Fax:* 416-486-3280 *E-mail:* bcarter@icsc.org
Foreign Office(s): 29 Queen Anne's Gate, London SW1H 9BU, United Kingdom *Tel:* (020) 7976 3102 *Fax:* (020) 7976 3101 *E-mail:* info.europe@icsc.org
Distribution Center: BrightKey, 9050 Junction Dr, Annapolis Junction, MD 20701 *Tel:* 301-362-6900

International Food Policy Research Institute
Member of Consultative Group on International Agricultural Research (CGIAR)
1201 Eye St NW, Washington, DC 20005-3915
Tel: 202-862-5600 *Fax:* 202-862-5606
E-mail: ifpri@cgiar.org
Web Site: www.ifpri.org
Key Personnel
Dir Gen: Shenggen Fan
Dir, Communs & Pub Aff: Rajul Pandya-Lorch *Tel:* 202-862-8185 *E-mail:* r.pandya-lorch@cgiar.org
Founded: 1975
Research reports, occasional papers & newsletter series, books, briefs, abstracts.
ISBN Prefix(es): 978-0-89629
Number of titles published annually: 270 Print; 2 CD-ROM; 270 Online
Total Titles: 3,980 Print; 21 CD-ROM; 3,634 Online
Distributed by Johns Hopkins University Press

International Foundation of Employee Benefit Plans
18700 W Bluemound Rd, Brookfield, WI 53045

Mailing Address: PO Box 69, Brookfield, WI 53008-0069
Tel: 262-786-6700 *Toll Free Tel:* 888-334-3327 *Fax:* 262-786-8780
E-mail: editor@ifebp.org
Web Site: www.ifebp.org
Key Personnel
Dir, Res & Pubns: Kelli Kolsrud *E-mail:* kellik@ifebp.org
Founded: 1954
ISBN Prefix(es): 978-0-89154
Number of titles published annually: 2 Print; 5 E-Book
Total Titles: 30 Print; 20 E-Book
Membership(s): Association Media & Publishing; Independent Book Publishers Association (IBPA)

The International Institute of Islamic Thought
500 Grove St, Suite 200, Herndon, VA 20170
Tel: 703-471-1133 *Fax:* 703-471-3922
E-mail: iiit@iiit.org
Web Site: www.iiit.org
Founded: 1981
Books, audiobooks & videos.
ISBN Prefix(es): 978-0-912463; 978-1-56564
Number of titles published annually: 40 Print
Total Titles: 500 Print

§International Linguistics Corp
12220 Blue Ridge Blvd, Suite G, Kansas City, MO 64030
Tel: 816-765-8855 *Toll Free Tel:* 800-237-1830 (orders)
E-mail: learnables@sbcglobal.net
Web Site: www.learnables.com
Key Personnel
Gen Mgr: Jennifer Elliott
Founded: 1976
Foreign & English language materials, language teaching materials.
ISBN Prefix(es): 978-0-939990; 978-1-887371; 978-0-9814540
Number of titles published annually: 3 Print; 3 CD-ROM; 1 Online; 3 Audio
Total Titles: 52 Print; 10 CD-ROM; 1 Online; 50 Audio

International Literacy Association (ILA)
258 Chapman Rd, Suite 203, Newark, DE 19702
Mailing Address: PO Box 8139, Newark, DE 19714-8139
Tel: 302-731-1600 *Toll Free Tel:* 800-336-7323 (US & CN) *Fax:* 302-731-1057
E-mail: customerservice@reading.org
Web Site: www.literacyworldwide.org; www.reading.org
Key Personnel
Exec Dir: Marcie Craig Post
Founded: 1956
Books & journals related to reading instruction & literary education.
ISBN Prefix(es): 978-0-87207
Number of titles published annually: 10 Print; 5 E-Book
Total Titles: 150 Print; 15 E-Book
Foreign Rights: Academics Plus (Andrea Permel) (UK); Eurospan Group (Catherine Lawn) (Trinidad and Tobago)

§International Monetary Fund (IMF), Editorial & Publications Division
700 19 St NW, HQ1-5-355, Washington, DC 20431
SAN: 203-8188
Tel: 202-623-7430 *Fax:* 202-623-7201
E-mail: publications@imf.org
Web Site: bookstore.imf.org; elibrary.imf.org (online collection)
Key Personnel
Publr: Jeffrey Hayden
Assoc Publr: Jim Beardow

Founded: 1946
Publishes a wide variety of books, periodicals, multimedia & digital products covering global economics, international finance, monetary policy, statistics, exchange rates & general macroeconomic issues.
ISBN Prefix(es): 978-0-939934; 978-1-55775; 978-1-58906; 978-1-61635
Number of titles published annually: 120 Print; 12 CD-ROM; 120 Online; 200 E-Book
Total Titles: 1,200 Print
Orders to: IMF Publications, PO Box 92780, Washington, DC 20090
Membership(s): Association of American Publishers (AAP); Association of Learned & Professional Society Publishers (ALPSP); Association of University Presses (AUPresses); Crossref

§International Press of Boston Inc
387 Somerville Ave, Somerville, MA 02143
Mailing Address: PO Box 502, Somerville, MA 02143
Tel: 617-623-3016 *Fax:* 617-623-3101
E-mail: ipb-orders@intlpress.com
Web Site: www.intlpress.com
Founded: 1992
Publish books, monographs, conference proceedings in advanced mathematics.
ISBN Prefix(es): 978-1-57146
Number of titles published annually: 5 Print
Total Titles: 125 Print; 3 CD-ROM
Distributed by AMS

International Publishers Co Inc
235 W 23 St, New York, NY 10011
SAN: 202-5655
Tel: 212-366-9816 *Fax:* 212-366-9820
E-mail: service@intpubnyc.com
Web Site: www.intpubnyc.com
Key Personnel
Pres & Ed: Betty Smith
Founded: 1924
Short discount titles & Marxist classics. Trade in cloth & paperback, general nonfiction, social sciences, classic & contemporary Marxism-Leninism, literature, poetry & biography, labor, women's studies.
ISBN Prefix(es): 978-0-7178
Number of titles published annually: 4 Print
Total Titles: 160 Print
Imprints: New World Paperbacks
Foreign Rep(s): Global Book Marketing (London, UK)
Returns: Whitehurst & Clark, 1200 County Rd, Rte 523, Flemington, NJ 08822
Warehouse: Whitehurst & Clark, 1200 County Rd, Rte 523, Flemington, NJ 08822, Contact: Brad Searles *Tel:* 908-782-2323 *Fax:* 908-237-2407
Membership(s): American Booksellers Association (ABA); The Association of Publishers for Special Sales (APSS); Independent Book Publishers Association (IBPA); National Association of College Stores (NACS)

§International Risk Management Institute Inc
12222 Merit Dr, Suite 1600, Dallas, TX 75251-2266
Tel: 972-960-7693 *Fax:* 972-371-5120
E-mail: info27@irmi.com
Web Site: www.irmi.com
Key Personnel
CFO: Ron Allen
Pres: Jack Gibson
Founded: 1978
Publish both print & online books on commercial & personal lines of insurance.
ISBN Prefix(es): 978-1-886813; 978-0-938358; 978-1-933686
Number of titles published annually: 20 Print; 36 Online
Total Titles: 35 Print

International Society for Technology in Education
1530 Wilson Blvd, Suite 730, Arlington, VA 22209
Tel: 503-342-2848 (intl) *Toll Free Tel:* 800-336-5191 (US & CN)
E-mail: iste@iste.org
Web Site: www.iste.org; www.isteconference.org
Key Personnel
CEO: Richard Culatta
Chief Mktg Offr: Tracee Aliotti
Chief Membership Offr: Jessica Medaille
Founded: 1979
Work with experienced educators to develop & produce practical resources for classroom teachers, teacher educators & technology leaders. Home of the National Educational Technology Standards (NETS), ISTE is the trusted source for educational technology books & courseware.
ISBN Prefix(es): 978-1-56484
Number of titles published annually: 12 Print
Total Titles: 60 Print
Branch Office(s)
621 SW Morrison St, Suite 800, Portland, OR 97205 *Fax:* 503-882-0813
Distribution Center: Ingram Publisher Services, One Ingram Blvd, La Vergne, TN 37086 *Tel:* 615-793-5000 *Toll Free Tel:* 866-400-5351 (orders) *E-mail:* ips@ingramcontent.com *Web Site:* www.ingramcontent.com

§International Society of Automation (ISA)
67 T W Alexander Dr, Research Triangle Park, NC 27709-0185
Mailing Address: PO Box 12277, Research Triangle Park, NC 27709-2277
Tel: 919-549-8411 *Fax:* 919-549-8288
E-mail: info@isa.org
Web Site: www.isa.org
Key Personnel
Exec Dir: Mary Ramsey
Dir, Mktg & Corp Partnerships: Jennifer Halsey *Tel:* 919-990-9287 *E-mail:* jhalsey@isa.org
Founded: 1945
Technical books, references, journals, video-based training programs, directories, software, standards, proceedings, CD-ROM, electronic references.
ISBN Prefix(es): 978-1-55617; 978-1-939660; 978-0-87664; 978-0-9791330; 978-1-936007; 978-1-941546; 978-0-9792343; 978-1-934394; 978-1-937560
Number of titles published annually: 20 Print
Total Titles: 139 Print; 10 CD-ROM; 20 E-Book
Foreign Rep(s): Eurospan (Europe)

§International Wealth Success Inc
PO Box 186, Merrick, NY 11566-0186
Tel: 516-766-5850 *Toll Free Tel:* 800-323-0548 *Fax:* 516-766-5919
E-mail: admin@iwsmoney.com
Web Site: www.iwsmoney.com
Key Personnel
Pres & Ed: David Hicks
Founded: 1966
Publish a variety of business & financial titles in the fields of small business, real estate, mail order, import-export & financing.
ISBN Prefix(es): 978-0-934311; 978-0-914306; 978-1-56150
Number of titles published annually: 6 Print; 6 CD-ROM; 4 Online; 70 E-Book; 4 Audio
Total Titles: 120 Print; 120 CD-ROM; 70 Online; 100 E-Book; 12 Audio

InterVarsity Press
Division of InterVarsity Christian Fellowship/USA
430 Plaza Dr, Westmont, IL 60559-1234
SAN: 202-7089
Mailing Address: PO Box 1400, Downers Grove, IL 60515
Tel: 630-734-4000 *Toll Free Tel:* 800-843-9487 *Fax:* 630-734-4200
E-mail: email@ivpress.com
Web Site: www.ivpress.com
Key Personnel
Publr: Jeff Crosby *Tel:* 630-734-4017 *E-mail:* jcrosby@ivpress.com
Assoc Publr & Dir, Edit: Cindy Bunch *Tel:* 630-734-4078 *E-mail:* cbunch@ivpress.com
Edit Dir, Academic: Jon Boyd *E-mail:* jboyd@ivpress.com
Art Dir: David Fassett *E-mail:* dfassett@ivpress.com
Dir, Mktg: Helen Lee *Tel:* 630-734-4038 *E-mail:* hlee@ivpress.com
Dir, Sales: Justin Paul Lawrence *Tel:* 630-734-4124 *E-mail:* jplawrence@ivpress.com
Sr Rts & Contracts Mgr: Ellen Hsu *Tel:* 630-734-4034 *E-mail:* ehsu@ivpress.com
Founded: 1947
Religion (interdenominational); textbooks.
ISBN Prefix(es): 978-0-87784; 978-0-8308
Number of titles published annually: 130 Print; 130 E-Book; 10 Audio
Total Titles: 2,000 Print; 1,200 E-Book; 50 Audio
Imprints: IVP Academic (publishing to facilitate broader conversations in the academy & the church); IVP Books (thoughtful books on church, culture & mission); IVP Connect (resources for Bible study & small groups); IVP Praxis (bringing together theory & practice for the advancement of ministry); LifeGuide Bible Studies (studies on books of the Bible & key Biblical topics)
Membership(s): Evangelical Christian Publishers Association (ECPA)

§Interweave Press LLC
Imprint of Golden Peak Media
4868 Innovation Dr, Fort Collins, CO 80525
Web Site: www.interweave.com
Founded: 1975
ISBN Prefix(es): 978-0-934026; 978-1-883010; 978-1-931499; 978-0-9796073; 978-1-4402; 978-1-63250; 978-1-59668; 978-1-62033
Number of titles published annually: 9 Print
Total Titles: 350 Print

Iris Press
Imprint of The Iris Publishing Group Inc
969 Oak Ridge Tpke, No 328, Oak Ridge, TN 37830
Web Site: www.irisbooks.com
Key Personnel
Publr: Robert Cumming *E-mail:* rcumming@irisbooks.com
Ed & Designer: Beto Cumming *E-mail:* bcumming@irisbooks.com
Audio Pubns: Willie Cumming *E-mail:* wcumming@irisbooks.com
Founded: 1975
Publisher of print editions of high quality poetry & literary prose.
ISBN Prefix(es): 978-0-916078; 978-1-60454
Number of titles published annually: 10 Print
Total Titles: 180 Print

Iron Gate Publishing
PO Box 999, Niwot, CO 80544
Tel: 303-530-2551 *Fax:* 303-530-5273
E-mail: editor@irongate.com
Web Site: www.irongate.com
Key Personnel
Publr & Ed: Dina C Carson
Founded: 1990
Genealogy, family history, Colorado local history, self-publishing, reference.
ISBN Prefix(es): 978-1-879579; 978-0-9724975; 978-1-68224

Number of titles published annually: 15 Print; 25 E-Book
Total Titles: 120 Print; 25 E-Book
Membership(s): The Association of Publishers for Special Sales (APSS); Colorado Independent Publishers Association (CIPA); Independent Book Publishers Association (IBPA); Publishers Association of the West (PubWest)

ISI Books
Imprint of Intercollegiate Studies Institute Inc
3901 Centerville Rd, Wilmington, DE 19807-1938
Tel: 302-652-4600 *Toll Free Tel:* 800-526-7022 *Fax:* 302-652-1760
E-mail: info@isi.org; isibooks@isi.org
Web Site: www.isibooks.org
Key Personnel
Pres: Charley Copeland
VP & Ed-in-Chief: Jed Donahue *E-mail:* jdonahue@isi.org
Founded: 1993
Publisher of serious but accessible nonfiction titles. ISI also publishes the esteemed quarterly journal *Modern Age* (founded in 1957 by Russell Kirk).
ISBN Prefix(es): 978-1-882926; 978-1-932236
Number of titles published annually: 4 Print; 4 E-Book
Total Titles: 50 Print; 100 E-Book

Island Press
2000 "M" St NW, Suite 650, Washington, DC 20036
SAN: 212-5129
Tel: 202-232-7933 *Toll Free Tel:* 800-828-1302 *Fax:* 202-234-1328
E-mail: info@islandpress.org
Web Site: www.islandpress.org
Key Personnel
Pres: David Miller
VP & Dir, Sales & Mktg: Julie Marshall
Exec Ed: Heather Boyer
Founded: 1984
Books about the environment for professionals, students & general readers, autobiography-scientific; land use planning; environmental economics; nature essays; "green" architecture.
ISBN Prefix(es): 978-0-933280; 978-1-55963; 978-1-59726; 978-1-61091
Number of titles published annually: 40 Print; 40 E-Book
Total Titles: 1,000 Print; 800 E-Book
Imprints: Shearwater Books
Distributor for Techne Press
Shipping Address: University of Chicago Distribution Center, 11030 S Langley Ave, Chicago, IL 60628 *Tel:* 773-702-7000 *Toll Free Tel:* 800-621-2736 *Fax:* 773-702-7212 *Toll Free Fax:* 800-621-8476 *E-mail:* custserv@press.uchicago.edu

Islandport Press
247 Portland St, Bldg C, Yarmouth, ME 04096
Mailing Address: PO Box 10, Yarmouth, ME 04096
Tel: 207-846-3344 *Fax:* 207-619-9975
E-mail: info@islandportpress.com
Web Site: www.islandportpress.com
Key Personnel
Publr: Dean Lunt
Edit Dir: Melissa Kim
Art Dir: Teresa Lagrange
Ed-at-Large: Genevieve Morgan
Sales Rep: Holly Eddy
Opers Mgr: Shannon Butler
Sales & Mktg Asst: Taylor McCafferty
Founded: 1999
Islandport is a dynamic, award-winning publisher dedicated to stories rooted in the essence & sensibilities of New England.

ISBN Prefix(es): 978-0-9671662; 978-0-9763231; 978-1-934031; 978-1-939017; 978-1-944762
Number of titles published annually: 15 Print; 5 E-Book
Total Titles: 120 Print; 30 E-Book
Foreign Rights: Transatlantic Literary Agency (worldwide exc USA)
Distribution Center: Baker & Taylor Publisher Services, 30 Amberwood Pkwy, Ashland, OH 44805, Dir of Mktg & PR: Kristen Steele
E-mail: ksteele@btpubservices.com *Web Site:* www.btpubservices.com

ISTE, see International Society for Technology in Education

§Italica Press
99 Wall St, Suite 650, New York, NY 10005
SAN: 695-1805
Tel: 917-371-0563
E-mail: inquiries@italicapress.com
Web Site: www.italicapress.com
Key Personnel
Pres & Publr, Electronic Publg: Eileen Gardiner
 E-mail: egardiner@italicapress.com
Secy & Publr, Electronic Publg: Ronald G Musto
 E-mail: rgmusto@italicapress.com
Founded: 1985
English translations of Latin & Italian works from the Middle Ages to the present.
ISBN Prefix(es): 978-0-934977; 978-1-59910
Number of titles published annually: 6 Print; 6 E-Book
Total Titles: 220 Print; 160 E-Book
Imprints: Pierrepont Street Press

§Italics Publishing
100 Northcliffe Dr, No 223, Gulf Breeze, FL 32561
E-mail: submissions@italicspublishing.com (submissions)
Web Site: italicspublishing.com
Founded: 2016
Italics Publishing is a traditional (non-subsidy) publisher specializing in small press, POD, & digital publishing. Combining cutting edge, best-in-class publishing practices with selective criteria for signing up new authors, Italics caters to the new generations of readers, keen on technology & with little time to spare. Our imprint welcomes submissions from young-at-heart, bright authors who deliver intriguing, mold-breaking work in adult genre fiction, contemporary fiction, commercial fiction, & short stories collections. Through the voices of our avant-garde authors, we invite readers to embark on an entertaining, yet intellectually stimulating adventure, inspired by the challenging realm of our modern social, technological, & business environment.
ISBN Prefix(es): 978-0-9843846; 978-0-945302
Number of titles published annually: 6 Print; 8 E-Book; 4 Audio
Total Titles: 12 Print; 12 E-Book; 6 Audio

iUniverse
Division of Author Solutions LLC
1663 Liberty Dr, Bloomington, IN 47403
Toll Free Tel: 800-AUTHORS (288-4677)
Web Site: www.iuniverse.com
Key Personnel
COO, Author Solutions: Bill Becher
Pres, Author Solutions: Bill Elliott
Founded: 1999
iUniverse is the industry's leading book marketing, editorial services & supported self-publishing company. The iUniverse management team has extensive editorial & managerial experience with traditional publishers such as Random House, Wiley, Macmillan, Chronicle Books & Addison-Wesley. iUniverse maintains a strategic alliance with Chapters Indigo

in Canada & titles accepted into the iUniverse Rising Star program are featured in a special collection on www.barnesandnoble.com.
This publisher has indicated that 100% of their product line is author subsidized.
ISBN Prefix(es): 978-0-9665514; 978-1-58348; 978-0-9668591; 978-1-893652; 978-0-595
Number of titles published annually: 2,500 Print
Total Titles: 40,000 Print
Distribution Center: Baker & Taylor LLC
Ingram Book Group

Jade Rabbit, see Quite Specific Media Group Ltd

§Jain Publishing Co
PO Box 3523, Fremont, CA 94539
SAN: 213-6503
Tel: 510-659-8272 *Fax:* 510-659-0501
E-mail: mail@jainpub.com
Web Site: www.jainpub.com
Key Personnel
Pres & Publr: Mukesh Jain
Founded: 1989
A humanities & social sciences publisher that publishes academic & scholarly references, as well as books for the general reader in both print & electronic formats.
ISBN Prefix(es): 978-0-89581; 978-0-87573
Number of titles published annually: 8 Print; 6 E-Book
Total Titles: 200 Print; 40 E-Book
Imprints: Asian Humanities Press

Jeter Publishing, see Gallery Books

Jewish Lights
Imprint of Turner Publishing Co
4507 Charlotte Ave, Suite 100, Nashville, TN 37209
SAN: 134-5621
Tel: 615-255-BOOK (255-2665) *Fax:* 615-255-5081
E-mail: marketing@turnerpublishing.com
Web Site: jewishlights.com; www.turnerpublishing.com
Key Personnel
Pres & Publr, Turner Publishing Co: Todd Bottorff
Founded: 1990
General trade adult & children's books on spirituality, theology, philosophy, mysticism, women's studies, recovery/self-help/healing & history for people of all faiths & backgrounds.
ISBN Prefix(es): 978-1-879045; 978-1-58023
Number of titles published annually: 5 Print; 5 E-Book
Total Titles: 500 Print; 450 E-Book

Jewish Publication Society
2100 Arch St, Philadelphia, PA 19103
SAN: 201-0240
Tel: 215-832-0600 *Toll Free Tel:* 800-234-3151
 Fax: 215-568-2017
Web Site: www.jps.org
Key Personnel
Dir & Acqs Ed: Barry L Schwartz
 E-mail: bschwartz@jps.org
Mng Ed: Joy Weinberg *Tel:* 917-363-9056
 E-mail: jweinberg@jps.org
Off Mgr: Rachna Khanna *Tel:* 215-832-0612
 E-mail: rkhanna@jps.org
Founded: 1888
Books of Jewish interest.
ISBN Prefix(es): 978-0-8276
Number of titles published annually: 8 Print; 8 E-Book
Total Titles: 250 Print
Distributed by University of Nebraska Press

Foreign Rep(s): Eurospan (Europe, Latin America, Middle East, UK & Commonwealth); Scholarly Book Service (Canada)
Membership(s): Association of University Presses (AUPresses)

§Jhpiego
Affiliate of Johns Hopkins University
1615 Thames St, Baltimore, MD 21231-3492
Tel: 410-537-1800 *Fax:* 410-537-1473
E-mail: info@jhpiego.net
Web Site: www.jhpiego.org
Key Personnel
Pres & CEO: Leslie D Mancuso, PhD
COO: Edwin J Judd
CIO: Glenn R Strachan
VP, Global Engagement & Communs: Melody McCoy
Founded: 1973
Reproductive health, medical texts, family planning, maternal health, HIV/AIDS & cervical cancer prevention & treatment, infection prevention.
ISBN Prefix(es): 978-0-929817; 978-1-943408
Number of titles published annually: 20 Print
Total Titles: 80 Print; 4 CD-ROM

JHU Press, see Johns Hopkins University Press

§JIST Publishing
Division of EMC Publishing LLC
875 Montreal Way, St Paul, MN 55102
SAN: 240-2351
Toll Free Tel: 800-328-1452 *Toll Free Fax:* 800-328-4564
E-mail: educate@emcp.com
Web Site: jist.emcp.com
Key Personnel
Sr Acct Mgr: Bob Grilliot *Tel:* 855-213-0737
Founded: 1981
Job search (resumes, cover letters, interviewing), career planning, job retention, occupational reference, assessment, self-help, career exploration, occupational information, character education, life skills, CD-ROMs & reference books, videos & software.
ISBN Prefix(es): 978-0-942784; 978-1-56370; 978-1-57112; 978-1-930780; 978-1-55864; 978-1-59357; 978-1-63332
Number of titles published annually: 50 Print; 2 CD-ROM; 20 E-Book; 1 Audio
Total Titles: 350 Print; 6 CD-ROM; 250 E-Book; 1 Audio
Imprints: JIST Career Solutions
Membership(s): Independent Book Publishers Association (IBPA)

John Deere Publishing
Division of Deere & Co
5440 Corporate Park Dr, Davenport, IA 52807
Toll Free Tel: 800-522-7448 (orders) *Fax:* 563-355-3690
E-mail: deere_bookstore_support@midlandcorp.com
Web Site: techpubs.deere.com
Founded: 1967
ISBN Prefix(es): 978-0-86691
Number of titles published annually: 8 Print
Total Titles: 27 Print
Distribution Center: Midland Elanders, Davenport, IA 52807

§Johns Hopkins University Press
Affiliate of Johns Hopkins University
2715 N Charles St, Baltimore, MD 21218-4363
SAN: 202-7348
Tel: 410-516-6900; 410-516-6987 (journal orders outside US & CN) *Toll Free Tel:* 800-537-5487 (book orders & cust serv); 800-548-1784 (journal orders) *Fax:* 410-516-6968; 410-516-3866 (journal orders); 410-516-6998 (orders)

E-mail: hfscustserv@press.jhu.edu (cust serv); jrnlcirc@press.jhu.edu (journal orders)
Web Site: www.press.jhu.edu; muse.jhu.edu
Key Personnel
Dir: Barbara Kline Pope E-mail: bkp@press.jhu.edu
Edit Dir: Gregory M Britton E-mail: gb@press.jhu.edu
Assoc Dir & Sr Dir, Fin & Admin: Erik A Smist E-mail: eas@press.jhu.edu
Co-Mktg & Sales Dir: Davida Breier E-mail: dgb@press.jhu.edu; Heidi M Vincent E-mail: hmv@press.jhu.edu
Dir, Journals Sales & Mktg: Lisa Klose E-mail: llk@press.jhu.edu
Assoc Mktg Dir: Claire McCabe Tamberino E-mail: cmt@press.jhu.edu
Journals Publr: William M Breichner E-mail: wmb@press.jhu.edu
Mng Ed: Juliana M McCarthy E-mail: jmm@press.jhu.edu
Sr Acqs Ed: Tiffany Gasbarrini E-mail: tg@press.jhu.edu; Matthew McAdam E-mail: mxm@press.jhu.edu; Joe Rusko E-mail: jr@press.jhu.edu
Acqs Ed: Robin W Coleman E-mail: rwc@press.jhu.edu; Laura Davulis E-mail: lbd@press.jhu.edu
Assoc Ed: Catherine L Goldstead E-mail: cg@press.jhu.edu
Asst Ed: Kyle Gipson
Fulfillment Systems Proj Mgr: Matt Brook E-mail: mb@press.jhu.edu
Journals Opers Mgr: Shannon T Fortner E-mail: stf@press.jhu.edu
Journals Prodn Mgr: Carol Hamblen E-mail: crh@press.jhu.edu
Prod Mgr: Claire McCabe Tamberino E-mail: cmt@press.jhu.edu
Publicity Mgr: Kathryn Marguy E-mail: krm@press.jhu.edu
Publicity Offr: Jack Holmes E-mail: jmh@press.jhu.edu
Publicist: John D Moore E-mail: jdm@press.jhu.edu; Rebecca Rozenberg E-mail: rer@press.jhu.edu
Rts Mgr: Kelly Rogers E-mail: klr@press.jhu.edu
Mktg & Sales Coord: Catherine Bergeron E-mail: cab@press.jhu.edu
Promos Coord: Kristina Lykke E-mail: kkl@press.jhu.edu
Sr Graphic Artist: Susan Ventura E-mail: sjv@press.jhu.edu
Sales & Metadata Specialist: Devon Renwick E-mail: dbr@press.jhu.edu
Founded: 1878
Scholarly books, nonfiction of general interest, paperbacks, scholarly journals.
ISBN Prefix(es): 978-0-8018; 978-1-4214
Number of titles published annually: 175 Print
Total Titles: 4,200 Print; 5 Online; 3,200 E-Book
Divisions: HFS (Hopkins Fulfillment Services)
Sales Office(s): Terry & Read LLC, 2031 N Craig St, Altadena, CA 91001, Contact: Alan Read Fax: 626-356-4630 E-mail: alanread@earthlink.net
Terry & Read LLC, 247 Fourth St, Loft 402, Oakland, CA, Contact: David Terry Tel: 510-813-9854 Fax: 510-465-7668 E-mail: dmterry@aol.com
Miller Trade Book Marketing, 363 W Erie St, Suite 7-E, Chicago, IL 60654, Contact: Bruce Miller Tel: 312-423-7880 Fax: 312-276-8109 E-mail: orders@millertrade.com
Terry & Read LLC, 19216 SE 46 Place, Issaquah, WA 98027, Contact: Ted H Terry Tel: 425-747-3411 Fax: 425-747-0366 E-mail: colterryassoc@aol.com
Foreign Rep(s): Academic Book Promotion (Fred Hermans) (Benelux, Denmark, France, Iceland, Scandinavia); Apex Knowledge Sdn Bhd (Simon Tay) (Brunei, Malaysia); Aromix Books Co Ltd (Jane Lam) (Hong Kong); Avicenna Partnership Ltd (Bill Kennedy) (Bahrain,

Egypt, Iran, Iraq, Kuwait, Lebanon, Libya, Oman, Qatar, Saudi Arabia, Sudan, Syria, United Arab Emirates, Yemen); Avicenna Partnership Ltd (Claire de Gruchy) (Algeria, Cyprus, Greece, Jordan, Malta, Morocco, Palestine, Tunisia, Turkey); CRW Books (Tony Sagun) (Philippines); Everest International Publishing Services (Wei Zhao) (China); Footprint Books Pty Ltd (Kate O'Reilly) (Australia, Fiji, New Zealand, Papua New Guinea); ICK-Information & Culture Korea (Mr Se-Yung Jun) (Korea); Ewa Ledochowicz (Eastern Europe); Lexa Publishers' Representatives (Mical Moser) (Canada); Uwe Luedemann (Austria, Germany, Italy, Portugal, Spain, Switzerland); Mirjam Mayenburg (Benelux); B K Norton Ltd (Ms Meihua Sun) (Taiwan); Provider of Contents & Information (Mr P C Tham) (Singapore); Rockbook Inc (Japan); Robert Towers (Ireland, Northern Ireland); Kevin van Hasselt (Africa, Caribbean); The White Partnership (Andrew White) (India); World Press (Saleem Malik) (Pakistan); Yale Representation Ltd (Andrew Jarmain) (UK)
Foreign Rights: The Chinese Connection Agency (China); Du Ran Kim Agency (Korea); The English Agency (Japan); Graal Literary Agency (Poland); The Deborah Harris Agency (Israel); International Editors' Co (Spain); The Italian Literary Agency srl (Italy); Japan UNI Agency (Japan); The Kalem Literary Agency (Turkey); La Nouvelle Agence (France); Tuttle-Mori Agency Inc (Japan)
Advertising Agency: Welch, Mirabile & Co Inc
Orders to: HFS, PO Box 50370, Baltimore, MD 21211-4370 Toll Free Tel: 800-537-5487 Fax: 410-516-6998 E-mail: hfscustserv@press.jhu.edu
Returns: HFS, c/o Maple Logistics Solutions, Lebanon Distribution Ctr, PO Box 1287, Lebanon, PA 17042
Warehouse: Maple Logistics Solutions, Lebanon Distribution Ctr, 704 Legionaire Dr, Fredricksburg, PA 17026
Membership(s): Association of American Publishers (AAP); Book Industry Study Group (BISG)

Lyndon B Johnson School of Public Affairs
University of Texas at Austin, 2315 Red River St, Austin, TX 78712-1536
Mailing Address: University of Texas at Austin, PO Box Y E 2700, Austin, TX 78713-8925
Tel: 512-471-3200 Fax: 512-471-4697
E-mail: lbjdeansoffice@austin.utexas.edu
Web Site: www.utexas.edu/lbj
Key Personnel
Asst Dean, Communs: Susan Binford E-mail: susan.binford@austin.utexas.edu
Founded: 1972
Working papers; public service monographs; policy research projects; conference proceedings.
Return policy: No refunds; replace damaged books only. All sales are final. Prepayment usually required.
ISBN Prefix(es): 978-0-89940
Number of titles published annually: 8 Print
Total Titles: 300 Print

§Jones & Bartlett Learning LLC
Division of Ascend Learning
5 Wall St, Burlington, MA 01803
Tel: 978-443-5000 Toll Free Tel: 800-832-0034 Fax: 978-443-8000
E-mail: info@jblearning.com
Web Site: www.jblearning.com
Key Personnel
VP: Dave Cella Tel: 978-639-3482 E-mail: dcella@jblearning.com
Founded: 1983
Academic & professional publisher.
ISBN Prefix(es): 978-0-86720; 978-0-7637; 978-1-4496; 978-1-284
Number of titles published annually: 300 Print

Total Titles: 2,500 Print; 100 CD-ROM
Foreign Rep(s): Advanced Marketing Associates (Kevin Fong) (Malaysia, Singapore); Jones & Bartlett India Pvt Ltd (Vinod Vasishtha) (Bangladesh, India, Nepal, Sri Lanka); Cengage Australia & New Zealand (Australia, Fiji, New Zealand); Merry Chang (Taiwan); China Publishers Services Ltd (Helwis Tjhai) (China); Class Publishing (Lorna Downing) (Europe, UK); Cranbury International LLC (Caribbean, South America); IGroup (Asia Pacific) Ltd (Indonesia); IGroup Asia Pacific Ltd (Marivel Cornita) (Guam, Philippines); IGroup Press Co Ltd (Vitit Lim) (Cambodia, Laos, Myanmar, Thailand, Vietnam); Impact Korea (ChongHo Ra) (South Korea); IPR (International Publishers Representatives) (Middle East); Jones & Bartlett India Pvt Ltd (Vinod Vasishtha) (Bangladesh, India, Nepal, Sri Lanka); Guy Simpson (East Africa); Watson Marketing (Jill Watson) (South Africa); The White Partnership (Andrew White) (Ethiopia, Japan); World Press (Saleem Malik) (Pakistan)
Returns: 905 Carlow Dr, Unit 5, Bolingbrook, IL 60490
Warehouse: 905 Carlow Dr, Unit 5, Bolingbrook, IL 60490

§Joshua Tree Publishing
3 Golf Ctr, Suite 201, Hoffman Estates, IL 60169
Tel: 312-893-7525
E-mail: info@joshuatreepublishing.com
Web Site: www.joshuatreepublishing.com; www.centaurbooks.com (imprint); www.chiralhouse.com (imprint)
Key Personnel
Pres & Publr: John Paul Owles E-mail: jpo@joshuatreepublishing.com
Founded: 1977
Believe in authors & dedicated to making the dream of being a published author a reality. Specialize in works that uplift the human spirit, inspire people to reach for higher goals & touch the hearts of readers.
ISBN Prefix(es): 978-0-9710954; 978-0-9778311; 978-0-9768677; 978-0-9845904; 978-0-9823703; 978-0-9829803; 978-1-941049
Number of titles published annually: 25 Print; 25 E-Book
Total Titles: 101 Print; 75 E-Book
Imprints: Centaur Books; Chiral House
Membership(s): Book Publicists of Southern California (BPSC); Independent Book Publishers Association (IBPA)

Judaica Press Inc
123 Ditmas Ave, Brooklyn, NY 11218
SAN: 204-9856
Tel: 718-972-6200 Toll Free Tel: 800-972-6201 Fax: 718-972-6204
E-mail: info@judaicapress.com; orders@judaicapress.com; submissions@judaicapress.com
Web Site: www.judaicapress.com
Key Personnel
Pres: Gloria Goldman
Mng Ed: Nachum Shapiro
Founded: 1963
Classic & contemporary Jewish literature in Hebrew & English.
ISBN Prefix(es): 978-0-910818; 978-1-880582; 978-1-932443; 978-1-60763
Number of titles published annually: 25 Print; 6 E-Book
Total Titles: 400 Print; 19 E-Book
Imprints: Zahava Publications
Foreign Rep(s): Kulmus (Israel); Lehmanns (Europe, UK)

Judson Press
Division of American Baptist Churches in the USA
1075 First Ave, King of Prussia, PA 19406

SAN: 201-0348
Toll Free Tel: 800-458-3766 *Fax:* 610-768-2107
Web Site: www.judsonpress.com
Key Personnel
Publr: Laura Alden *E-mail:* laura.alden@abhms.
org
Mktg Dir: Linda Johnson-LeBlanc *Tel:* 610-768-
2458 *E-mail:* linda.johnson-leblanc@abhms.org
Busn Mgr: Alma Hazboun
Ed: Rebecca Irwin-Diehl *Tel:* 610-768-2109
E-mail: rebecca.irwin-diehl@abhms.org
Founded: 1824
Religion (Baptist & nondenominational Chris-
tian), African American, women & multicul-
tural; cloth & paperback.
ISBN Prefix(es): 978-0-8170
Number of titles published annually: 12 Print; 2
Audio
Total Titles: 350 Print; 1 CD-ROM; 2 Audio

Jump!
5357 Penn Ave, Minneapolis, MN 55419
Toll Free Tel: 888-799-1860 *Toll Free Fax:* 800-
675-6679
E-mail: customercare@jumplibrary.com
Web Site: www.jumplibrary.com
Key Personnel
Pres: Gabe Kaufman *E-mail:* gabe@jumplibrary.
com
Founded: 2012
Publish children's nonfiction with a focus on
high-interest subjects for beginning & emergent
readers. Books combine vibrant colors with
captivating photography & corresponding text
to draw readers into the subject & encourage
reading success.
ISBN Prefix(es): 978-1-62031; 978-1-62496; 978-
1-645276; 978-1-641289; 978-1-645270
Number of titles published annually: 175 Print;
175 E-Book; 30 Audio
Total Titles: 900 Print; 900 E-Book
Imprints: Blue Owl Books (social & emotional
learning, health & wellness); Bullfrog Books;
Pogo; Tadpole Books (preK)
Foreign Rep(s): Saunders Book Co (Canada)
Returns: 2150 Howard Dr W, North Mankato,
MN 56003
Shipping Address: 2150 Howard Dr W, North
Mankato, MN 56003
Warehouse: 2150 Howard Dr W, North Mankato,
MN 56003
Distribution Center: 2150 Howard Dr W, North
Mankato, MN 56003
Membership(s): Educational Book & Media Asso-
ciation (EBMA)

Jump at the Sun
Imprint of Disney-Hyperion Books
125 West End Ave, 3rd fl, New York, NY 10023
Web Site: books.disney.com
Founded: 1998
Books celebrating the African-American experi-
ence & culture.
ISBN Prefix(es): 978-0-7868
Number of titles published annually: 2 Print; 2 E-
Book
Total Titles: 100 Print; 100 E-Book

§Just World Books LLC
PO Box 5484, Charlottesville, VA 22905
Toll Free Tel: 888-506-3769
E-mail: sales@justworldbooks.com
Web Site: justworldbooks.com
Key Personnel
Owner: Helena Cobban
Founded: 2010
ISBN Prefix(es): 978-0-9845056; 978-1-935982
Number of titles published annually: 8 Print
Total Titles: 41 Print; 30 E-Book
Distribution Center: Independent Publishers
Group (IPG), 814 N Franklin St, Chicago, IL
60610 *Toll Free Tel:* 800-888-4741

§Kabbalah Publishing
Division of Kabbalah Centre International
1062 S Robertson Blvd, Los Angeles, CA 90035
Tel: 310-657-5404
E-mail: kcla@kabbalah.com; losangeles@
kabbalah.com
Web Site: www.kabbalah.com
Founded: 2002
Dedicated to bringing the world's oldest & deep-
est treasury of spiritual wisdom.
ISBN Prefix(es): 978-1-57189; 978-0-943688;
978-0-924457
Number of titles published annually: 15 Print; 2
CD-ROM; 2 Online; 2 E-Book; 2 Audio
Total Titles: 35 Print; 3 CD-ROM; 2 Online; 4 E-
Book; 4 Audio
Foreign Rights: Kabbalah Agency (worldwide)
Distribution Center: Publishers Group West, 1700
Fourth St, Berkeley, CA 94710 *Tel:* 510-809-
3700 *Fax:* 510-809-3777

Kaeden Corp
PO Box 16190, Rocky River, OH 44116-0190
Tel: 440-617-1400 *Toll Free Tel:* 800-890-7323
Fax: 440-617-1403
E-mail: info@kaeden.com
Web Site: www.kaeden.com
Key Personnel
Pres: Craig Urmston *E-mail:* curmston@kaeden.
com
Founded: 1986
Books for emergent, early & fluent readers,
grades K-3, reading recovery & guided read-
ing programs.
ISBN Prefix(es): 978-1-879835; 978-1-57874;
978-1-61181; 978-1-61181
Number of titles published annually: 16 Print
Total Titles: 300 Print; 7 CD-ROM; 72 E-Book; 7
Audio
Imprints: Kaeden Books
Membership(s): American Educational Publishers;
Association of American Publishers (AAP);
International Literacy Association (ILA); Na-
tional Council of Teachers of English (NCTE);
Reading Recovery Council of North America

Kalaniot Books
Imprint of Endless Mountains Publishing Co
72 Glenmaura National Blvd, Suite 104B,
Moosic, PA 18507
Tel: 862-251-2296; 570-878-7960
E-mail: info@endlessmountainspublishing.com
Web Site: www.endlessmountainspublishing.com
Key Personnel
Publr & Creative Dir: Lilian Rosenstreich
E-mail: lili@endlessmountainspublishing.com
Publr & Busn Mgr: Mitchel Weiss
E-mail: mitchel@endlessmountainspublishing.
com
Founded: 2018
Focuses on publishing books of interest to Jewish
children.
ISBN Prefix(es): 978-0-9988527
Number of titles published annually: 8 Print

Kalmbach Publishing Co
21027 Crossroads Circle, Waukesha, WI 53186
Mailing Address: PO Box 1612, Waukesha, WI
53187-1612
Tel: 262-796-8776 *Toll Free Tel:* 800-533-6644
(cust serv & orders); 800-558-1544 *Fax:* 262-
798-6592
E-mail: customerservice@kalmbach.com
Web Site: www.kalmbach.com
Key Personnel
SVP, Sales & Mktg: Dan Lance *E-mail:* dlance@
kalmbach.com
Edit Dir: Diane M Bacha *E-mail:* dbacha@
kalmbach.com
Books Ed-in-Chief: Diane Wheeler
E-mail: dwheeler@kalmbach.com
Founded: 1934

Special interest books, calendars & magazines in
the astronomy, jewelry making, crafts, hobby &
collectibles market.
ISBN Prefix(es): 978-0-89024; 978-0-913135;
978-0-89778; 978-0-8238; 978-0-87116; 978-0-
933168; 978-1-62700
Number of titles published annually: 35 Print
Total Titles: 135 Print
Imprints: Greenberg Books; Kalmbach Books
Distributed by Publishers Group West (PGW)

§Kamehameha Publishing
Division of Kamehameha Schools
1887 Makukone St, Pauahi Admin Bldg, Suite
211, Honolulu, HI 96817
E-mail: publishing@ksbe.edu
Web Site: kamehamehapublishing.org
Key Personnel
Dir: Ron Cox
Founded: 1933
Book, journal & poster publishing in the areas of
Hawaiian history, studies, language & culture.
ISBN Prefix(es): 978-0-87336
Number of titles published annually: 12 Print
Total Titles: 100 Print; 7 E-Book
Imprints: Kamehameha Schools Press
Distributed by Islander Group
Membership(s): The Association of Publishers
for Special Sales (APSS); Hawaii Book Pub-
lishers Association (HBPA); Independent Book
Publishers Association (IBPA)

Kane Miller Books
Imprint of EDC Publishing
4901 Morena Blvd, Suite 213, San Diego, CA
92117
SAN: 295-8945
E-mail: submissions@kanemiller.com; info@
kanemiller.com
Web Site: www.kanemiller.com
Key Personnel
Publr: Kira Lynn
Edit/Mktg: Lynn Kelley; Sarah Trenholme
Mktg/Soc Media: Kayla VernonClark
Founded: 1984
Juvenile board, novelty & picture books & middle
grade fiction from around the world.
ISBN Prefix(es): 978-0-916291; 978-1-929132;
978-1-933605; 978-1-61067; 978-1-68464
Number of titles published annually: 125 Print
Total Titles: 450 Print
Warehouse: Educational Development Corp, 5402
S 122 E Ave, Tulsa, OK 74146
Distribution Center: Publishers Group Canada,
300-76 Stafford St, Toronto, ON M6J 2S1,
Canada *Tel:* 416-934-9900 *E-mail:* info@
pgcbooks.ca *Web Site:* www.pgcbooks.ca
Membership(s): American Booksellers Associ-
ation (ABA); American Library Association
(ALA); Association of Booksellers for Chil-
dren; United States Board on Books for Young
People (USBBY)

Kapp Books LLC
3602 Rocky Meadow Ct, Fairfax, VA 22033
Tel: 703-261-9171 *Fax:* 703-621-7162
E-mail: info@kappbooks.com
Web Site: www.kappbooks.com
Key Personnel
Principal: Parveen Ahuja
Founded: 2006
ISBN Prefix(es): 978-1-60346
Number of titles published annually: 100 Print
Total Titles: 350 Print; 10 CD-ROM

Kar-Ben Publishing
Imprint of Lerner Publishing Group Inc
241 First Ave N, Minneapolis, MN 55401
Tel: 612-332-3344 *Toll Free Tel:* 800-4-
KARBEN (452-7236) *Fax:* 612-332-7615
Toll Free Fax: 800-332-1132
Web Site: www.karben.com

Key Personnel
Chmn: Harry J Lerner
Pres: Adam Lerner
Publr: Joni Sussman *E-mail:* jsussman@karben.
 com
Dir of Rts, Spec Sales & Intl Dist: Maria Kjoller
Founded: 1974
Jewish-themed picture books, calendars; preschool
 & primary, holiday books, folktales, bible sto-
 ries.
ISBN Prefix(es): 978-1-58013
Number of titles published annually: 25 Print; 25
 E-Book
Total Titles: 300 Print; 195 E-Book; 15 Audio
Foreign Rep(s): Thomas Allen (Canada); Bravo
 (UK)
Membership(s): Association of Jewish Libraries

Kazi Publications Inc
3023 W Belmont Ave, Chicago, IL 60618
Tel: 773-267-7001 *Fax:* 773-267-7002
E-mail: info@kazi.org
Web Site: www.kazi.org
Key Personnel
Pres: Liaquat Ali
Mktg Dir: Mary Bakhtiar
Founded: 1972
Nonprofit organization; print, publish & dis-
 tribute; Islamic books in Arabic, English &
 Urdu.
ISBN Prefix(es): 978-0-935782; 978-1-56744;
 978-0-933511; 978-1-871031; 978-1-930637
Number of titles published annually: 30 Print; 6
 E-Book
Total Titles: 401 Print; 150 E-Book
Imprints: ABC International Group Inc; Abjad
 Books; Great Books of the Islamic World; Li-
 brary of Islam

§J J Keller & Associates, Inc
3003 Breezewood Lane, Neenah, WI 54957
Mailing Address: PO Box 368, Neenah, WI
 54957-0368
Tel: 920-722-2848 *Toll Free Tel:* 877-564-2333
 Toll Free Fax: 800-727-7516
E-mail: contactus@jjkeller.com;
 customerservice@jjkeller.com
Web Site: www.jjkeller.com
Key Personnel
Chmn: Robert L Keller
VChmn & Treas: Jim Keller
Pres & CEO: Marne Keller-Krikava
EVP & COO: Rustin R Keller
CFO: Dana S Gilman
Dir, Creative & Promos: Tom Hines
Sr Admin Asst: Michele Davis
Founded: 1953
Publish regulatory compliance, "best practices"
 & training products dealing with occupational
 safety, job safety, environment & industry &
 motor-carrier (trucking) operations. On de-
 mand, print, CD-ROM, intranet & Internet for-
 mats.
ISBN Prefix(es): 978-1-57943; 978-0-934674;
 978-1-877798; 978-1-59042; 978-9789130;
 978-1-60287; 978-1-61099; 978-1-68008
Number of titles published annually: 4 Print; 12
 E-Book
Total Titles: 300 Print; 100 CD-ROM
Branch Office(s)
7273 State Rd 76, Neenah, WI 54956-9614
Sales Office(s): 1315 Gillingham Rd, Neenah, WI
 54956-4503
600 S Nicolet Rd, Appleton, WI 54914-8285
700 N Lynndale Dr, Appleton, WI 54914-3019
Distributor for Chilton Book Co; International
 Air Transport Association; National Archives
 & Records Administration; National Institute
 of Occupational Safety & Health; Office of the
 Federal Register; Research & Special Programs
 Administration of the US Department of Trans-
 portation; John Wiley & Sons Inc

Kelsey Street Press
2824 Kelsey St, Berkeley, CA 94705
E-mail: info@kelseyst.com
Web Site: www.kelseyst.com
Key Personnel
Founding Ed: Patricia Dienstfrey; Rena Rosen-
 wasser
Ed & Publr: Ramsay Breslin
Founded: 1974
Nonprofit press, publish experimental poetry &
 short fiction by women & collaborations be-
 tween poets & artists.
ISBN Prefix(es): 978-0-932716
Number of titles published annually: 3 Print
Total Titles: 45 Print
Orders to: Small Press Distribution, 1341 Sev-
 enth St, Berkeley, CA 94710 *Tel:* 510-524-1668
 Toll Free Tel: 800-869-7553 *E-mail:* orders@
 spdbooks.org *Web Site:* www.spdbooks.org
Membership(s): Community of Literary Maga-
 zines & Presses (CLMP)

Kendall Hunt Publishing Co
4050 Westmark Dr, Dubuque, IA 52002-2624
SAN: 203-9184
Mailing Address: PO Box 1840, Dubuque, IA
 52004-1840
Tel: 563-589-1000 *Toll Free Tel:* 800-228-0810
 (orders) *Fax:* 563-589-1046 *Toll Free Fax:* 800-
 772-9165
E-mail: orders@kendallhunt.com
Web Site: www.kendallhunt.com
Key Personnel
Chmn & CEO: Mark C Falb
Pres & COO: Chad M Chandlee
VP, Opers: Tim Beitzel
VP, Higher Educ Div: David Tart
VP, K-12 Div: Charles Cook
Founded: 1969
Higher education custom publishing, K-12 math
 & science.
ISBN Prefix(es): 978-0-8403; 978-0-7872; 978-0-
 7575; 978-1-4652; 978-1-5249
Number of titles published annually: 1,500 Print;
 200 Online
Total Titles: 6,500 Print; 10 CD-ROM; 5,500 On-
 line; 6,500 E-Book
Membership(s): National Council of Supervisors
 of Mathematics (NCSM); National Council of
 Teachers of Mathematics (NCTM); National
 Science Teachers Association (NSTA)

Kennedy Information Inc
Division of Bloomberg BNA
24 Railroad St, Keene, NH 03431
Tel: 603-357-8103 *Toll Free Tel:* 800-531-0140
Key Personnel
COO: Daniel Houder
Founded: 1970
Newsletters, special reports, books, directories of
 management consultants, executive recruiters &
 outplacement consultants.
ISBN Prefix(es): 978-0-916654; 978-1-885922;
 978-1-58673; 978-1-932079; 978-1-934717
Number of titles published annually: 15 Print; 1
 CD-ROM; 3 Online
Total Titles: 50 Print; 1 CD-ROM

Kensington Books, see Kensington Publishing
Corp

Kensington Publishing Corp
119 W 40 St, New York, NY 10018
SAN: 207-9860
Tel: 212-407-1500 *Toll Free Tel:* 800-221-2647
 Fax: 212-935-0699
Web Site: www.kensingtonbooks.com
Key Personnel
Chmn, Pres & CEO: Steven Zacharius
 E-mail: szacharius@kensingtonbooks.com
SVP & CFO: Michael Rosamilia
VP & Publr: Lynn Cully

VP & Gen Mgr: Adam Zacharius
Gen Coun: Barbara Bennett
Assoc Publr: Jackie Dinas
Creative Dir: Janice Rossi
Dir, Communs: Vida Engstrand
 E-mail: vengstrand@kensingtonbooks.com
Dir, Opers: Angela Tucker
Dir, Soc Media & Digital Sales: Alex Nicolajsen
Edit Dir: Alicia Condon; Gary Goldstein; Wendy
 McCurdy
IT Dir: Jonathan Cohen
Prodn Dir: Joyce Kaplan
Assoc Dir, Sales: Darla Freeman
Ed-in-Chief, Citadel Press: Michaela Hamilton
Ed-in-Chief, Kensington: John Scognamiglio
Exec Ed, Citadel Press: Denise Silvestro
Exec Ed: Esi Sogah
Asst Ed: Norma Perez-Hernandez
Sr Communs Mgr: Ann Pryor *E-mail:* apryor@
 kensingtonbooks.com
Communs Mgr: Larissa Ackerman
 E-mail: lackerman@kensingtonbooks.
 com; Michelle Addo *E-mail:* maddo@
 kensingtonbooks.com
Subs Rts Mgr: Susanna Gruninger
Founded: 1974
Independent commercial publisher of popular fic-
 tion & nonfiction across all formats.
ISBN Prefix(es): 978-0-8065; 978-0-7860; 978-1-
 4967; 978-1-4201; 978-1-5161
Number of titles published annually: 500 Print
Imprints: Brava; Citadel Press (nonfiction); Da-
 fina (commercial fiction & nonfiction centered
 on race & cultural identity); Kensington Hard-
 cover; Kensington Mass-Market; Kensington
 Trade Paperback; KTeen; Lyrical Press; Lyri-
 cal Shine (digital first contemporary romance);
 Lyrical Underground (digital first thriller, mys-
 tery, suspense & horror); Pinnacle Books (mass
 market westerns, thrillers, crime); Rebel Base
 Books; John Scognamiglio Books; Lyle Stuart
 Books; Urban Books; Urban Christian; Urban
 Renaissance; Zebra Books
Distributed by Penguin Group USA, A Penguin
 Random House Company
Distributor for Urban Books
Foreign Rights: ANA Sofia (Anna Droumeva,
 Mira Droumeva, Kamelia Emilova) (Bulgaria);
 Big Apple Agency Inc (China, Taiwan, Thai-
 land, Vietnam); The Book Publishers' Associa-
 tion of Israel, International Promotion & Liter-
 ary Rights Dept (Beverly Levit) (Israel); Sandra
 Bruna Agency (Brazil, South America, Spain);
 Donzelli, Fietta Agency Srls (Stephania Fietta)
 (Italy); The English Agency Ltd (Corinne Sh-
 ioji) (Japan); Graal Literary Agency (Poland);
 Imprima Korea Agency (Terry Kim) (Korea);
 Nurcihan Kesim Literary Agency (Turkey);
 Maxima Creative Agency (Santo Manurung)
 (Indonesia); La Nouvelle Agence (France); An-
 drew Nurnberg Associates (Tatjana Zoldnere)
 (Baltic States); Andrew Nurnberg Associates
 (Judit Hermann) (Croatia, Hungary); Andrew
 Nurnberg Literary Agency (Ludmilla Sushkova)
 (Russia); Kristin Olson Literary Agency SRO
 (Czechia, Slovakia); Read n Right Agency
 (Nike Davarinou) (Greece); Thomas Schlueck
 GmbH (Germany); Sebes & Bisseling Liter-
 ary Agency (Netherlands, Scandinavia); Dorie
 Simmonds Agency (Australia, British Com-
 monwealth, UK & Commonwealth, UK Com-
 monwealth); Tuttle-Mori Agency Inc (Misa
 Morikawa) (Japan, Thailand)
Warehouse: Penguin Group USA, A Penguin
 Random House Company, Pittston, PA
Distribution Center: Penguin Random House
 Publisher Services, 400 Hahn Rd, West-
 minster, MD 21157 *Toll Free Tel:* 800-
 733-3000 *Toll Free Fax:* 800-659-2436
 E-mail: customerservice@randomhouse.com

Kent State University Press
1118 University Library Bldg, 1125 Risman Dr,
 Kent, OH 44242

SAN: 201-0437
Mailing Address: PO Box 5190, Kent, OH 44242-0001
Tel: 330-672-7913 *Fax:* 330-672-3104
E-mail: ksupress@kent.edu
Web Site: www.kentstateuniversitypress.com
Key Personnel
Dir: Susan Wadsworth-Booth
Mng Ed: Mary Young *Tel:* 330-672-8101
  E-mail: mdyoung@kent.edu
Acquiring Ed: Will Underwood *Tel:* 330-672-8094 *E-mail:* wunderwo@kent.edu
Founded: 1965
Scholarly nonfiction, with emphasis on Civil War history, literary studies (Tolkien, C S Lewis, Hemingway), biography & Midwest regional.
ISBN Prefix(es): 978-0-87338; 978-1-60635
Number of titles published annually: 30 Print; 35 E-Book; 5 Audio
Total Titles: 850 Print; 1,250 E-Book; 20 Audio
Imprints: Black Squirrel Books
Foreign Rep(s): Eurospan Ltd (Africa, Europe, Middle East, UK); Scholarly Book Services Inc (Canada)
Orders to: Baker & Taylor Publisher Services, 30 Amberwood Pkwy, Ashland, OH 44805, Contact: Elaine Lattanzi *Tel:* 567-215-0030 *Toll Free Tel:* 888-814-0208 *E-mail:* info@btpubservices.com *Web Site:* www.btpubservices.com
Returns: Baker & Taylor Publisher Services, 30 Amberwood Pkwy, Ashland, OH 44805, Contact: Elaine Lattanzi *Tel:* 567-215-0030 *Toll Free Tel:* 888-814-0208 *E-mail:* info@btpubservices.com *Web Site:* www.btpubservices.com
Warehouse: Baker & Taylor Publisher Services, 30 Amberwood Pkwy, Ashland, OH 44805, Contact: Elaine Lattanzi *Tel:* 567-215-0030 *Toll Free Tel:* 888-814-0208 *E-mail:* info@btpubservices.com *Web Site:* www.btpubservices.com
Distribution Center: Baker & Taylor Publisher Services, 30 Amberwood Pkwy, Ashland, OH 44805, Contact: Elaine Lattanzi *Tel:* 567-215-0030 *Toll Free Tel:* 888-814-0208 *E-mail:* info@btpubservices.com *Web Site:* www.btpubservices.com
Membership(s): American Booksellers Association (ABA); Association of University Presses (AUPresses)

Kessinger Publishing LLC
PO Box 1404, Whitefish, MT 59937
Web Site: www.kessinger.net
Key Personnel
Pres: Roger A Kessinger
Founded: 1988
On demand publisher. Specialize in rare, scarce & out of print books.
ISBN Prefix(es): 978-0-922802; 978-1-56459; 978-0-7661; 978-1-4191; 978-1-161; 978-0-548; 978-1-104; 978-1-120; 978-1-160; 978-1-162; 978-1-163; 978-1-164; 978-1-165; 978-1-166; 978-1-167; 978-1-168; 978-1-169; 978-1-4179; 978-1-4253; 978-1-4254; 978-1-4286; 978-1-4304; 978-1-4325; 978-1-4326; 978-1-4367; 978-1-4370; 978-1-4373; 978-1-4365; 978-1-4368; 978-1-4371; 978-1-4374; 978-1-4366; 978-1-4369; 978-1-4372
Number of titles published annually: 5,000 Print; 5,000 E-Book
Imprints: Kessinger Publishing®

Kidsbooks LLC
3535 W Peterson Ave, Chicago, IL 60659
SAN: 666-3729
Tel: 773-509-0707 *Fax:* 773-509-0404
E-mail: customerservice@kidsbooks.com
Web Site: www.kidsbooks.com
Key Personnel
CEO & Foreign Rts Agent: Dan Blau
Founded: 1987

Promotional book publishers of children, juvenile & hardcover, Search & Find®, board books, cloth books & other novelty books.
ISBN Prefix(es): 978-0-942025; 978-1-56156; 978-1-58865; 978-1-62885
Number of titles published annually: 100 Print
Total Titles: 3,000 Print
Imprints: Fun For All; KidsBooks; Learning Challenge

Jessica Kingsley Publishers Inc
400 Market St, Suite 400, Philadelphia, PA 19106
SAN: 256-2391
Tel: 215-922-1161 *Toll Free Tel:* 866-416-1078 (cust serv) *Fax:* 215-922-1474
E-mail: hello.usa@jkp.com
Web Site: www.jkp.com
Key Personnel
Chmn: Jessica Kingsley
VP, Sales & Mktg: David Corey
Mktg Mgr: Yojaira Cordero
Mktg Assoc: Katelynn Bartleson
Sales & Mktg Coord: Stephanie DeMuzio
Relationship Coord: Julia Zullo
Founded: 1987 (US office opened 2004)
Publish books for the consumer on autism spectrum disorders & related developmental disorders; books for professionals in expressive arts therapies: art, music, drama & dance & social work; books on Tai Chi & Quigong.
ISBN Prefix(es): 978-1-85302; 978-1-84310; 978-1-84819; 978-1-874579; 978-1-900990; 978-0-902817; 978-1-904787; 978-1-905818; 978-1-84642; 978-1-84905; 978-1-84985; 978-0-85701; 978-0-85700; 978-1-78450
Number of titles published annually: 250 Print
Total Titles: 1,800 Print
Imprints: Singing Dragon
Foreign Office(s): 73 Collier St, London N1 9BE, United Kingdom, Sales Dir: Mark Scott *Tel:* (020) 7833 2307 *E-mail:* hello@jkp.com
Foreign Rep(s): Avicenna Partnership Ltd (Bill Kennedy) (Bahrain, Egypt, Iran, Iraq, Kuwait, Lebanon, Libya, Oman, Qatar, Saudi Arabia, Sudan, United Arab Emirates, Yemen); Avicenna Partnership Ltd (Claire de Gruchy) (Algeria, Jordan, Morocco, Palestine, Tunisia, Turkey); Brookside Publishing Services (Ireland); Compass Academic (UK); Durnell Marketing Ltd (Europe); Footprint Books Pty Ltd (Australia, New Zealand); Taylor & Francis Asia Pacific (Brunei, China, Hong Kong, Indonesia, Japan, Macau, Malaysia, Philippines, Singapore, Taiwan, Thailand, Vietnam); UBC Press (Canada); United Publishers Services Ltd (Japan)
Distribution Center: Books International, PO Box 960, Herndon, VA 20172 *Toll Free Tel:* 866-416-1078 *Fax:* 703-611-1501 *E-mail:* jkpmail@presswarehouse.com

Kinship Books
305 Cedar Heights Rd, Rhinebeck, NY 12572
Tel: 845-876-4592 (orders)
E-mail: kinship@hvc.rr.com
Web Site: www.kinshipny.com
Key Personnel
Owner: Nancy V Kelly
Founded: 1967
Books of genealogical source information, histories, directory & journals.
ISBN Prefix(es): 978-1-56012
Number of titles published annually: 5 Print
Total Titles: 330 Print

§Kirkbride Bible Co Inc
1102 Deloss St, Indianapolis, IN 46203
Mailing Address: PO Box 606, Indianapolis, IN 46206-0606
Tel: 317-633-1900 *Toll Free Tel:* 800-428-4385 *Fax:* 317-633-1444

E-mail: sales@kirkbride.com; info@kirkbride.com
Web Site: www.kirkbride.com
Key Personnel
Pres: Michael Gage
Founded: 1915
Bible publisher, adult & children.
ISBN Prefix(es): 978-0-88707; 978-0-934854
Number of titles published annually: 5 Print
Total Titles: 7 Print; 3 CD-ROM
Advertising Agency: Canal Advertising

Kiva Publishing Inc
10 Bella Loma, Santa Fe, NM 87506
Tel: 909-896-0518
E-mail: kivapub@aol.com
Web Site: www.kivapub.com
Key Personnel
Publr: Stephen W Hill
Founded: 1993
Publish Native American & Southwest regional books & cards.
ISBN Prefix(es): 978-1-885772
Number of titles published annually: 3 Print
Total Titles: 40 Print
Membership(s): The Association of Publishers for Special Sales (APSS); Independent Book Publishers Association (IBPA); New Mexico Publishers Association; Publishers Association of the West (PubWest)

Klutz
Imprint of Scholastic Trade Division
524 Broadway, 5th fl, New York, NY 10012
Tel: 212-343-6360 *Toll Free Tel:* 800-737-4123 (cust serv)
E-mail: sales@klutz.com (all sales inquires); marketing@klutz.com (all mktg inquiries); publicity@klutz.com (all publicity inquires)
Web Site: www.klutz.com; store.scholastic.com
Key Personnel
SVP & Gen Mgr: Stacy Lellos
Founded: 1977
Premium brand of book-based activity kits, committed to inspiring creativity in every kid with a unique combination of crystal clear instructions, custom tools & materials & a hearty helping of humor.
ISBN Prefix(es): 978-0-932592; 978-1-57054; 978-1-878257; 978-1-59174; 978-0-545
Number of titles published annually: 30 Print
Total Titles: 140 Print
Foreign Rep(s): Scholastic Asia (Selina Lee) (Asia); Scholastic Australia Ltd (Australia); Scholastic Canada Ltd (Canada); Scholastic Ltd (UK); Scholastic New Zealand Ltd (New Zealand)
Orders to: 2931 E McCarty St, Jefferson City, MO 65101 *Toll Free Tel:* 888-724-1872 *Toll Free Fax:* 877-724-1872 *E-mail:* orders@klutz.com
Membership(s): American Specialty Toy Retailing Association (ASTRA)

Kluwer Law International (KLI), see Wolters Kluwer Law & Business

§Alfred A Knopf
Imprint of Knopf Doubleday Publishing Group
c/o Penguin Random House Inc, 1745 Broadway, New York, NY 10019
Tel: 212-751-2600 *Fax:* 212-572-2662 (foreign rts)
Web Site: knopfdoubleday.com
Key Personnel
EVP & Publr: Reagan Arthur
SVP & Assoc Publr: Christine Gillespie
SVP & Edit Dir: Jordan Pavlin
VP & Exec Dir, Sales Mgmt & Planning: Beth Meister
VP & Group Sales Dir: Christopher Dufault
VP & Creative Dir: John Gall

VP & Dir, Promo: Gabrielle Brooks
VP & Dir, Publicity: Nicholas Latimer
VP & Sr Ed: Victoria Wilson; Jonathan Segal
Deputy Publr & Exec Dir, Mktg & Publicity: Paul Bogaards
Mng Ed: Katherine Hourigan
Sr Ed: Lexy Bloom; Ann Close; Jennifer Jackson; Andrew Miller; Tim O'Connell
Poetry Ed: Deborah Garrison
Ed-at-Large: Carole Baron
Dir, Publicity: Erinn Hartman
Dir, Translation Rts: Suzanne Smith
Rts Dir: Sean Yule
Deputy Dir, Publicity & Promo: Kathy Zuckerman
Assoc Dir, Publicity: Josie Kals
Asst Dir, Mktg: Julianne Clancy; Sara Eagle
Asst Dir, Publicity: Jessica Purcell
Mktg Mgr: Emily Murphy
Publicity Mgr: Jordan Rodman
Publicist: Abby Endler; Elizabeth Lindsay; Sarah New; Katie Schoder
Assoc Publicist: Emily Reardon
Founded: 1915
Penguin Random House & its publishing entities are not accepting unsol submissions, proposals, mss, or submission queries via e-mail at this time.
Foreign Rights: ALS-Agenzia Letteraria Santachiara (Roberto Santachiara) (Italy); Anthea Agency (Katalina Sabeva) (Bulgaria); Bardon-Chinese Media Agency (Xu Weiguang) (China); Bardon-Chinese Media Agency (Yu-Shiuan Chen) (Taiwan); The English Agency (Junzo Sawa) (Japan); Graal Literary Agency (Maria Strarz-Kanska) (Poland); The Deborah Harris Agency (Ilana Kurshan) (Israel); JLM Literary Agency (Nelly Moukakos) (Greece); Katai & Bolza Literary (Peter Bolza) (Croatia, Hungary); KCC (MiSook Hong) (Korea); Simona Kessler International (Simona Kessler) (Romania); Licht & Burr Literary Agency (Trine Licht) (Scandinavia); La Nouvelle Agence (Vanessa Kling) (France); Kristin Olson Literary Agency (Kristin Olson) (Czechia); Sebes & Bisseling Literary Agency (Paul Sebes) (Netherlands)

Kodansha USA Inc
Subsidiary of Kodansha Ltd (Japan)
451 Park Ave S, 7th fl, New York, NY 10016
SAN: 201-0526
Tel: 917-322-6200 *Fax:* 212-935-6929
E-mail: info@kodansha-usa.com
Web Site: www.kodanshausa.com
Key Personnel
COO: Takashi Sakuda
Founded: 2008
Publishes hardcover & paperback books in English on Japanese cultures, history, art, architecture, design, craft, gardening, literature, material arts, language, cookbooks, travel & memoirs.
ISBN Prefix(es): 978-0-87011; 978-1-56836; 978-1-935429; 978-1-61262; 978-1-63236
Number of titles published annually: 4 Print
Total Titles: 270 Print
Imprints: Kodansha America; Kodansha Globe; Kodansha International
Distributor for Japan Publications Inc; Japan Publications Trading Co Inc
Foreign Rep(s): Bill Bailey Publishers' Representatives (Baltic States, Hungary, Southeast Europe, Western Europe); InterMedia Americana Ltd (Eastern Europe); Turnaround Publisher Services Ltd (Ireland, UK)
Distribution Center: Penguin Random House Publisher Services, 451 Park Ave S, New York, NY 10016 (worldwide exc Continental Europe, Ireland & UK) *Tel:* 917-322-6200 *Fax:* 212-935-6929 *E-mail:* info@kodansha-usa.com

Penguin Random House Canada, 320 Front St W, Suite 1400, Toronto, ON M5V 3B6, Canada *Toll Free Tel:* 888-523-9292 *Toll Free Fax:* 888-562-9924

§Kogan Page
c/o Martin P Hill Consulting, 122 W 27 St, 10th fl, New York, NY 10001
Tel: 929-362-7262
E-mail: info@koganpage.com
Web Site: www.koganpage.com
Key Personnel
Contact: Courtney Dramis
Founded: 1967
Books, ebooks & digital solutions.
ISBN Prefix(es): 978-0-7494
Number of titles published annually: 120 Print; 120 E-Book
Total Titles: 900 Print; 500 E-Book
Editorial Office(s): 45 Gee St, London EC1V 3RS, United Kingdom *Tel:* (020) 7278 0433 *E-mail:* kpinfo@koganpage.com
Foreign Office(s): Kogan Page Ltd, 45 Gee St, London EC1V 3RS, United Kingdom *Tel:* (020) 7278 0433
Foreign Rep(s): Kogan Page Ltd (London) (worldwide exc USA)
Foreign Rights: Kogan Page Ltd (London) (worldwide exc USA)
Billing Address: Ingram Publisher Services, One Ingram Blvd, La Vergne, TN 37086
Orders to: Ingram Publisher Services, One Ingram Blvd, La Vergne, TN 37086 *Toll Free Tel:* 800-961-2026 *Toll Free Fax:* 800-838-1149 *E-mail:* customer.service@ingrampublisherservices.com
Returns: Ingram Publisher Services, 1210 Ingram Dr, Chambersburg, PA 17201
Distribution Center: Ingram Publisher Services, One Ingram Blvd, La Vergne, TN 37086

§Koho Pono LLC
15024 SE Pinegrove Loop, Clackamas, OR 97015
Tel: 503-723-7392
E-mail: info@kohopono.com; orders@ingrambook.com
Web Site: kohopono.com
Key Personnel
Publr: Scott Burr *Tel:* 408-689-0888; Dayna Hubenthal
Founded: 2010
Multimedia publishing company that is passionate about growth & improvement for all aspects of life: business, career, relationships & personal. Specialize in innovation, awareness, process improvement, change management & strengthening relationships for business & individuals. Support the evolution of consciousness, self-exploration & the pursuit of increasing relevance in life.
ISBN Prefix(es): 978-0-984554
Number of titles published annually: 3 Print; 3 Online; 3 E-Book; 3 Audio
Total Titles: 6 Print; 6 Online; 2 E-Book; 3 Audio
Shipping Address: Lightning Source Inc, 1246 Heil Quaker Blvd, La Vergne, TN 37086, Contact: Amy Waugh *Tel:* 615-213-5815 *Fax:* 615-213-4725 *E-mail:* inquiry@lightningsource.com
Warehouse: Lightning Source Inc, 1246 Heil Quaker Blvd, La Vergne, TN 37086, Contact: Amy Waugh *Tel:* 615-213-5815 *Fax:* 615-213-4725 *E-mail:* inquiry@lightningsource.com
Distribution Center: Ingram Book Co, One Ingram Blvd, La Vergne, TN 37086 *Tel:* 615-793-5000 *Toll Free Tel:* 800-937-8200 *E-mail:* customer.service@ingrambook.com
Lightning Source Inc, 1246 Heil Quaker Blvd, La Vergne, TN 37086, Contact: Amy Waugh *Tel:* 615-213-5815 *Fax:* 615-213-4725 *E-mail:* inquiry@lightningsource.com

Konecky & Konecky LLC
72 Ayers Point Rd, Old Saybrook, CT 06475

Tel: 860-388-0878
E-mail: sean.konecky@gmail.com
Web Site: www.koneckyandkonecky.com
Key Personnel
Publr: Sean Konecky *E-mail:* sean.konecky@gmail.com
Founded: 1982
Hardcover art books & Civil War history, military history, biography, religion & spirituality.
ISBN Prefix(es): 978-1-56852; 978-0-914427
Number of titles published annually: 10 Print
Total Titles: 250 Print
Imprints: Konecky & Konecky (K&K); Tabard Press
Distributor for Octavo Editions

HJ Kramer Inc
Division of New World Library
PO Box 1082, Tiburon, CA 94920
Tel: 415-884-2100 (ext 10) *Toll Free Tel:* 800-972-6657 *Fax:* 415-435-5364
E-mail: hjkramer@jps.net
Web Site: www.hjkramer.com; www.newworldlibrary.com
Key Personnel
Intl Rts: Suezen Stone *Tel:* 415-499-1622 *Fax:* 415-499-1654 *E-mail:* Suezenstone@msn.com
Mktg & Publicity: Monique Muhlenkamp *E-mail:* monique@newworldlibrary.com
Founded: 1984
Personal growth, self-help, spiritual growth, trade paperbacks & hardcovers. Any correspondence regarding mss must be accompanied by an appropriately sized SASE.
ISBN Prefix(es): 978-0-915811; 978-1-932073
Number of titles published annually: 3 Print; 3 E-Book
Total Titles: 85 Print
Foreign Rep(s): Akasha Books Ltd (New Zealand); Brumby Books (Australia); Publishers Group Canada (Canada); Publishers Group UK (UK); Real Books (South Africa)
Orders to: Publisher Group West, 1700 Fourth St, Berkeley, CA 94710 *Toll Free Tel:* 800-788-3123 *Fax:* 510-528-3444

§Krause Publications Inc
Imprint of Penguin Random House LLC
1745 Broadway, New York, NY 10019
Tel: 212-782-9000
Web Site: www.penguinrandomhouse.com
Founded: 1952
Penguin Random House & its publishing entities are not accepting unsol submissions, proposals, mss, or submission queries via e-mail at this time.
Number of titles published annually: 150 Print
Total Titles: 1,000 Print

Kregel Publications
Division of Kregel Inc
2450 Oak Industrial Dr NE, Grand Rapids, MI 49505
SAN: 298-9115
Tel: 616-451-4775 *Toll Free Tel:* 800-733-2607 *Fax:* 616-451-9330
E-mail: kregelbooks@kregel.com
Web Site: www.kregel.com
Key Personnel
Pres: Jerold W Kregel
Exec Dir, Sales & Mktg: David Hill *Tel:* 616-451-4775 ext 235 *E-mail:* dave@kregel.com
Publr & Rts & Perms: Dennis Hillman
Founded: 1949
Evangelical Christian publications including devotionals, Bible study & reference.
ISBN Prefix(es): 978-0-8254
Number of titles published annually: 75 Print
Total Titles: 1,500 Print
Imprints: Editorial Portavoz; Kregel Academic & Professional; Kregel Classics; Kregel Kidzone

Distributor for Candle Books; Monarch Books
Foreign Rep(s): Christian Art Wholesale (South
Africa); Christian Literature Crusade (Japan);
David C Cook (Canada); Omega Distribution
(New Zealand); STL Distribution (UK); Word
of Life Press (Korea)
Membership(s): Evangelical Christian Publishers
Association (ECPA)
See separate listing for:
Editorial Portavoz

Krieger Publishing Co
1725 Krieger Lane, Malabar, FL 32950
SAN: 202-6562
Tel: 321-724-9542 *Fax:* 321-951-3671
E-mail: info@krieger-publishing.com
Web Site: www.krieger-publishing.com
Key Personnel
Pres: Donald E Krieger
Cust Serv: Ann Krieger
Founded: 1969
A scientific-technical publisher serving the col-
lege textbook market. Reprints & new titles:
technical, science, psychology, geology, human-
ities, ecology, history, social sciences, engineer-
ing, mathematics, chemistry, adult educational,
herpetology, space science.
ISBN Prefix(es): 978-0-88275; 978-0-89464; 978-
0-89874; 978-1-57524
Number of titles published annually: 5 Print
Total Titles: 800 Print
Imprints: Anvil Series; Orbit Series; Professional
Practices
Foreign Rep(s): Eurospan (Middle East, UK)
Advertising Agency: Krieger Enterprises Inc

KTAV Publishing House Inc
527 Empire Blvd, Brooklyn, NY 11225
Tel: 201-963-9524; 718-972-5449 *Fax:* 718-972-
6307
E-mail: orders@ktav.com
Web Site: www.ktav.com
Key Personnel
Founder: Bernie Scharfstein *E-mail:* bernie@ktav.
com
Owner & CEO: Moshe Heller *E-mail:* moshe@
ktav.com
VP, Busn Devt: Raphael Freeman
E-mail: raphael@ktav.com
Publr: Tzvi Mauer *E-mail:* tzvi@ktav.com
Publr, Targum Publishers: Akiva Atwood
E-mail: akiva@ktav.com
Mgr: Levi Rodal *E-mail:* levi@ktav.com
Founded: 1921
Books of Jewish interest; juvenile, textbooks;
scholarly Judaica & interfaith issues.
ISBN Prefix(es): 978-0-87068; 978-0-88125; 978-
1-60280
Number of titles published annually: 20 Print
Total Titles: 840 Print
Distributor for Yeshiva University Press

Kumarian Press
Division of Lynne Rienner Publishers Inc
1800 30 St, Suite 314, Boulder, CO 80301
Tel: 303-444-6684 *Fax:* 303-444-0824
E-mail: questions@rienner.com
Web Site: www.rienner.com
Key Personnel
CEO: Lynne Rienner
Founded: 1977
Academic, professional books, college textbooks
in social sciences: international development,
international relations, political science, politi-
cal economy, economics, globalization, women
& gender studies, conflict resolution, environ-
ment, sustainability, civil society & NGOs.
ISBN Prefix(es): 978-0-931816; 978-1-56549;
978-1-887208
Number of titles published annually: 3 Print; 3 E-
Book
Total Titles: 300 Print; 300 E-Book

Foreign Rep(s): Catamount (Latin America);
China Publishers Marketing (China, Hong
Kong, Taiwan); Eurospan (Australia, Europe,
New Zealand, UK); MHM Ltd (Japan); Tay-
lor & Francis (Asia-Pacific, Korea, Southeast
Asia); Viva Books (India)
Membership(s): Association of American Publish-
ers (AAP)

Kumon Publishing North America
300 Frank Burr Blvd, Suite 6, Teaneck, NJ 07666
Tel: 201-836-2105 *Fax:* 201-836-1559
E-mail: books@kumon.com
Web Site: www.kumonbooks.com
Key Personnel
SVP: Brian Klingborg
Founded: 2004
Publisher of children's educational books & toys.
ISBN Prefix(es): 978-4-7743; 978-1-933241
Number of titles published annually: 30 Print
Total Titles: 160 Print

L & R Publishing, see Hellgate Press

Lake Superior Publishing LLC
109 W Superior St, Suite 200, Duluth, MN 55802
Mailing Address: PO Box 16417, Duluth, MN
55816-0417
Tel: 218-722-5002 *Toll Free Tel:* 888-BIG-LAKE
(244-5253) *Fax:* 218-722-4096
E-mail: edit@lakesuperior.com
Web Site: www.lakesuperior.com
Key Personnel
Publr: Beth Bily *E-mail:* beth@lakesuperior.com;
Ron Brochu *E-mail:* rb@lakesuperior.com
Ed: Konnie Le May *E-mail:* kon@lakesuperior.
com
Founded: 1979
Began as regional magazine publisher & ex-
panded services to include books, travel guides,
calendars, maps & merchandise.
ISBN Prefix(es): 978-0-942235
Number of titles published annually: 2 Print
Total Titles: 32 Print
Membership(s): Content Delivery & Storage As-
sociation (CDSA); Midwest Independent Book-
sellers Association (MIBA); Midwest Indepen-
dent Publishing Association (MIPA); Minnesota
Magazine & Publications Association (MMPA)

LAMA Books
2381 Sleepy Hollow Ave, Hayward, CA 94545-
3429
Tel: 510-785-1091 *Toll Free Tel:* 888-452-6244
Fax: 510-785-1099
Web Site: www.lamabooks.com
Key Personnel
Pres, Sales & Mktg Dir: Steve Meyer
E-mail: steve@lamabooks.com
Founded: 1970
Develop & publish books for heating, ventilating
& air conditioning (HVAC) field; occupational
trades, reading development, teacher prepa-
ration; directories-occupational programs in
California community colleges.
ISBN Prefix(es): 978-0-88069
Number of titles published annually: 5 Print
Total Titles: 50 Print

Lanahan Publishers Inc
324 Hawthorne Rd, Baltimore, MD 21210-2303
SAN: 859-1288
Tel: 410-366-2434 *Toll Free Tel:* 866-345-1949
Fax: 410-366-8798
E-mail: lanahan@aol.com
Web Site: www.lanahanpublishers.com
Key Personnel
Pres: Donald W Fusting
Founded: 1995
College textbook publisher.
ISBN Prefix(es): 978-0-9652687; 978-1-930398

Number of titles published annually: 4 Print
Total Titles: 20 Print

Landauer Publishing
Imprint of Fox Chapel Publishing Co Inc
1970 Broad St, East Petersburg, PA 17520
Tel: 717-560-4703 *Toll Free Tel:* 800-457-9112
Fax: 717-560-4702
E-mail: customerservice@foxchapelpublishing.
com
Web Site: landauerpub.com
Key Personnel
Pres & Publr: Jeramy Landauer
Founded: 1991
Publishing & licensing for the home arts working
with leading designers & artists.
ISBN Prefix(es): 978-1-890621; 978-0-9646870;
978-0-9793711; 978-0-9770166; 978-1-935726;
978-0-9825586; 978-0-9818040
Number of titles published annually: 12 Print
Total Titles: 114 Print
Foreign Rep(s): A Great Notion (Canada); Alba
Patchwork (Spain); N Jefferson (Canada); Quilt
Source (Canada); John Reed Book Distribution
(Australia); RJR Fabrics (Europe); Roundhouse
Group (England); Stallion Press (Singapore);
Virka (Iceland)
Membership(s): American Booksellers Associa-
tion (ABA); Independent Book Publishers As-
sociation (IBPA)

Landisfarne Books, see SteinerBooks Inc

§Peter Lang Publishing Inc
Subsidiary of Peter Lang AG (Switzerland)
80 Broadway, 5th fl, New York, NY 10004
SAN: 241-5534
Tel: 703-661-1584 *Toll Free Tel:* 800-770-5264
(cust serv) *Fax:* 703-996-1010
E-mail: newyork.editorial@peterlang.com;
customerservice@plang.com
Web Site: www.peterlang.com
Key Personnel
SVP & Global Head, Edit: Dr Farideh Koohi-
Kamali *E-mail:* f.koohi@peterlang.com
Publr & Exec Ed: Patricia Mulrane Clayton
E-mail: p.mulrane@peterlang.com
Acqs Ed: Dr Erika Hendrix *E-mail:* e.hendrix@
peterlang.com; Dr Meagan Simpson *E-mail:* m.
simpson@peterlang.com; Michelle Smith
E-mail: m.smith@peterlang.com
Founded: 1982
Scholarly monographs & textbooks in the hu-
manities, social sciences, media studies,
Festschriften & conference proceedings.
ISBN Prefix(es): 978-0-8204; 978-1-4331; 978-1-
4539 (ebooks)
Number of titles published annually: 240 Print
Total Titles: 2,500 Print
Foreign Office(s): PIE Peter Lang SA Editions
Scientifiques Internationales, One Ave Maurice,
6e etage, 1050 Brussels, Belgium *Tel:* (02) 347
72 36 *Fax:* (02) 347 72 37 *E-mail:* brussels@
peterlang.com
Peter Lang GmbH Internationaler Verlag der
Wissenschaften, Fehlerstr 8, 12161 Berlin,
Germany *Tel:* (030) 232567900 *Fax:* (030)
232567902 *E-mail:* berlin@peterlang.com
Peter Lang GmbH Wydawnictwo Naukowe, ul
Zimorowica 2 m 11, 02-062 Warsaw, Poland,
Contact: Lukasz Galecki *Tel:* (66) 0759467
E-mail: l.galecki@peterlang.com
Peter Lang AG, Wabernstr 40, 3007 Bern,
Switzerland *Tel:* (031) 306 17 17 *Fax:* (031)
306 17 27 *E-mail:* bern@peterlang.com
Peter Lang GmbH Uluslararasi Bilimsel Yayinevi,
3 Cadde, Sardalya Sokak No 7, 34450
Sariyer, Istanbul, Turkey, Contact: Esra Bahsi
Tel: (0212) 271 7755; (0541) 541 12 33 (cell)
E-mail: e.bahsi@peterlang.com
Peter Lang Ltd International Academic Publish-
ers, 52 St Giles, Oxford OX1 3LU, United
Kingdom (Ireland & UK) *Tel:* (01865) 514160

Fax: (01865) 604028 *E-mail:* oxford@
peterlang.com
Distribution Center: IBI, PO Box 960, Herndon, VA 20172 (US only) *Tel:* 703-661-1584 *Fax:* 703-996-1010 *E-mail:* peterlang@
presswarehouse.com
University of Toronto Press, 5201 Dufferin St,
Toronto, ON M3H 5T8, Canada *Tel:* 416-667-7791 *Toll Free Tel:* 800-565-9523
(North America) *Fax:* 416-667-7832 *Toll
Free Fax:* 800-221-9985 (North America)
E-mail: utpress@utpress.utoronto.ca
Hachette Livre, One Ave Gutenberg, 78316 Maurepas Cedex, France (French-language titles
in French-speaking Europe exc Switzerland
& including French CN) *Tel:* 01 30 66 20 66
E-mail: webmaster-saisie@hachette-livre.fr *Web
Site:* www.hachette-diffusion.fr
NBN, 10 Thornbury Rd, Plymouth PL6 7PP,
United Kingdom (worldwide exc CN,
French-speaking Europe, Switzerland & US)
Tel: (01752) 202301 *Fax:* (01752) 202333
E-mail: orders@nbninternational.com

§Langmarc Publishing
7500 Shadowridge Run, No 28, Austin, TX
78749
Mailing Address: PO Box 90488, Austin, TX
78709-0488
Tel: 512-394-0989 *Toll Free Tel:* 800-864-1648
(orders)
E-mail: langmarc@booksails.com
Web Site: www.langmarc.com
Key Personnel
Pres & Lib Sales Dir: Lois Qualben
Founded: 1991
Publisher of inspirational titles.
ISBN Prefix(es): 978-1-880292
Number of titles published annually: 3 Print; 20
E-Book
Total Titles: 75 Print
Imprints: Harbor Lights

Lantern Books
Division of Lantern Publishing & Media
128 Second Place, Garden Suite, Brooklyn, NY
11231
Tel: 212-414-2275
E-mail: editorial@lanternbooks.com; info@
lanternmedia.net
Web Site: lanternbooks.presswarehouse.com/
home/home.aspx
Key Personnel
Pres: Gene Gollogly *E-mail:* gene@lanternbooks.
com
Dir, Publg: Martin Rowe *E-mail:* martin@
lanternbooks.com
Founded: 1999
Publishers of books on veganism, social justice,
family therapy & non-violence issues.
ISBN Prefix(es): 978-1-59056; 978-1-930051
Number of titles published annually: 10 Print
Total Titles: 250 Print; 200 Online; 200 E-Book;
50 Audio
Distributed by Red Wheel/Weiser
Foreign Rep(s): Deep Books (Europe, UK); Footprint Books (Australia)
Foreign Rights: Findhorn Press (Sabine Weeke)
(worldwide exc USA)
Membership(s): American Booksellers Association (ABA)

LARB Books
Division of Los Angeles Review of Books
6671 Sunset Blvd, Suite 1521, Los Angeles, CA
90028
Tel: 323-952-3950
E-mail: larbbooks@lareviewofbooks.org
Web Site: larbbooks.org
Key Personnel
Ed-in-Chief/Dir: Tom Lutz *E-mail:* tom@
lareviewofbooks.org

Exec Ed: Boris Dralyuk *E-mail:* boris@
lareviewofbooks.org
Asst Dir: Stephanie Malak *E-mail:* smalak@
lareviewofbooks.org
Publicity & Mktg: Nanda Dyssou
E-mail: nanda@lareviewofbooks.org
Mng Dir: Jessica Kubinec *E-mail:* jessica@
lareviewofbooks.org
Founded: 2013
ISBN Prefix(es): 978-1-940660; 978-1-942904
Number of titles published annually: 5 Print; 5 E-Book
Total Titles: 7 Print; 5 E-Book
Imprints: Les Figues Press; Outcaste Press
Foreign Rights: Agencia Literaria Carmen Balcells SA (Anna Bofill) (Spanish-speaking countries)
Distribution Center: Publishers Group West
(PGW), 1700 Fourth St, Berkeley, CA 94710
Tel: 510-809-3700 *Toll Free Tel:* 866-400-5351
(cust serv) *Fax:* 510-809-3777 *E-mail:* info@
pgw.com *Web Site:* www.pgw.com SAN: 202-8522

Laredo Publishing Co
465 Westview Ave, Englewood, NJ 07631
Tel: 201-408-4048
E-mail: info@laredopublishing.com
Web Site: www.laredopublishing.com
Key Personnel
Pres: Sam Laredo *E-mail:* laredo@
laredopublishing.com
VP & Exec Ed: Raquel Benatar *E-mail:* raquel@
laredopublishing.com
Founded: 1991
ISBN Prefix(es): 978-1-56492
Number of titles published annually: 25 Print
Total Titles: 150 Print
Imprints: Renaissance House
See separate listing for:
Renaissance House

Lark Crafts
Imprint of Sterling Publishing Co Inc
1166 Avenue of the Americas, 17th fl, New York,
NY 10036
Tel: 212-532-7160
E-mail: editorial@sterlingpub.com;
customerservice@sterlingpublishing.com
Web Site: larkcrafts.com; www.facebook.com/
LarkCrafts; www.sterlingpublishing.com
Key Personnel
Ed: Elysia Liang
Founded: 1979
How-to books in crafts & photography.
ISBN Prefix(es): 978-0-937274; 978-1-887374;
978-1-57990; 978-1-60059; 978-1-4547
Number of titles published annually: 120 Print
Total Titles: 400 Print
Foreign Rights: Sterling Publishing Co Inc
Shipping Address: Sterling Publishing Co Inc, 40
Saw Mill Pond Rd, Edison, NJ 08837 *Toll Free
Tel:* 800-367-9692 *Toll Free Fax:* 800-542-7567

Larson Publications
4936 State Rte 414, Burdett, NY 14818
Tel: 607-546-9342 *Toll Free Tel:* 800-828-2197
Fax: 607-546-9344
E-mail: custserv@larsonpublications.com
Web Site: www.larsonpublications.com
Key Personnel
Mktg Dir & Publr: Amy Opperman Cash
E-mail: amy@larsonpublications.com
Founded: 1982
Resources for spiritual independence & social
relevance.
ISBN Prefix(es): 978-0-943914; 978-1-936012
Number of titles published annually: 6 Print; 1
CD-ROM; 1 Online; 5 E-Book
Total Titles: 96 Print; 1 CD-ROM; 25 E-Book; 3
Audio

Foreign Rep(s): Gazelle Book Services Ltd (Europe, UK); Bokforlaget Robert Larson (Scandinavia)
Foreign Rights: Literaryventuresfund (Mary
Bisbee-Beek)
Distribution Center: New Leaf Distributing Co, 401 Thornton Rd, Lithia Springs,
GA 30122-1557 *Tel:* 770-948-7845 *Toll
Free Tel:* 800-326-2665 *Fax:* 770-944-2313
E-mail: newleaf@newleaf-dist.com *Web
Site:* newleafdist.com
National Book Network, 15200 NBN Way,
Blue Ridge Summit, PA 17214 *Toll Free
Tel:* 800-462-6420 *Toll Free Fax:* 800-338-4550 *E-mail:* custserv@nbnbooks.com *Web
Site:* www.nbnbooks.com

§Lasaria Creative Publishing
4094 Majestic Lane, Suite 352, Fairfax, VA
22033
E-mail: info@lasariacreative.com
Web Site: www.lasariacreative.com
Key Personnel
Publg Analyst: Adam Lee
Founded: 2003
Author-owned independent publishing company
looking for nonfiction, general fiction, short
stories & juvenile fiction books. We encourage
first time authors & are willing to help get your
work into mainstream distribution channels.
Also offer editing services for new authors.
ISBN Prefix(es): 978-0-9818367; 978-0-9836671
Number of titles published annually: 10 Print; 10
Online; 10 E-Book
Total Titles: 14 Print; 12 Online; 12 E-Book

Laughing Elephant Books
3645 Interlake N, Seattle, WA 98103
Tel: 206-447-9229 *Toll Free Tel:* 800-354-0400
Fax: 206-447-9189
E-mail: support@laughingelephant.com
Web Site: www.laughingelephant.com
Key Personnel
Pres: Benjamin Darling
Founded: 1986
Publish books, cards & printed gifts with an emphasis on imagery, especially from antique
children's books, self-generating content.
ISBN Prefix(es): 978-1-883211; 978-0-9621131;
978-1-59583
Number of titles published annually: 5 Print
Total Titles: 80 Print

§Law School Admission Council
662 Penn St, Newtown, PA 18940
Mailing Address: PO Box 40, Newtown, PA
18940
Tel: 215-968-1101
E-mail: lsacaccounts@lsac.org
Web Site: www.lsac.org
Key Personnel
Dir, Communs: Wendy Margolis *Tel:* 215-968-1219 *E-mail:* wmargolis@lsac.org
Founded: 1947
Standardized testing, legal education & law
school admission activities, law school admission test preparation.
ISBN Prefix(es): 978-0-9846360
Number of titles published annually: 4 Print; 2
Online; 3 E-Book
Total Titles: 30 Print; 2 Online; 8 E-Book
Sales Office(s): Ingram Publisher Services,
One Ingram Blvd, La Vergne, TN 37086
Toll Free Tel: 866-400-5351 *Toll Free
Fax:* 800-838-1149 *E-mail:* customer.service@
ingrampublisherservices.com *Web Site:* ipage.
ingramcontent.com SAN: 631-8630
Orders to: Ingram Publisher Services, One
Ingram Blvd, La Vergne, TN 37086 *Toll
Free Tel:* 866-400-5351 *Toll Free Fax:* 800-838-1149 *E-mail:* customer.service@

ingrampublisherservices.com *Web Site:* ipage. ingramcontent.com SAN: 631-8630
Distribution Center: Ingram Publisher Services, One Ingram Blvd, La Vergne, TN 37086 *Toll Free Tel:* 866-400-5351 *Toll Free Fax:* 800-838-1149 *E-mail:* customer.service@ingrampublisherservices.com *Web Site:* ipage. ingramcontent.com SAN: 631-8630

The Lawbook Exchange Ltd
33 Terminal Ave, Clark, NJ 07066-1321
Tel: 732-382-1800 *Toll Free Tel:* 800-422-6686
Fax: 732-382-1887
E-mail: law@lawbookexchange.com
Web Site: www.lawbookexchange.com
Key Personnel
Pres: Greg Talbot
Mng Ed, Talbot Publishing: Valerie L Horowitz
E-mail: vhorowitz@lawbookexchange.com
Founded: 1981
Publisher of books on legal history & political science. Publisher of reprints of legal classics, many with new scholarly introductions.
ISBN Prefix(es): 978-1-886363; 978-1-58477; 978-0-9630106
Number of titles published annually: 20 Print
Total Titles: 1,300 Print; 9 E-Book
Imprints: Talbot Publishing
Membership(s): Antiquarian Booksellers Association of America (ABAA); International League of Antiquarian Booksellers

Merloyd Lawrence Inc
102 Chestnut St, Boston, MA 02108
SAN: 658-4012
Tel: 617-523-5895 *Fax:* 617-263-2749
Key Personnel
Pres & Ed: Merloyd Ludington Lawrence
Founded: 1982
Number of titles published annually: 5 Print; 4 E-Book
Total Titles: 80 Print; 42 E-Book

§Lawyers & Judges Publishing Co Inc
917 N Swan Rd, Suite 300, Tucson, AZ 85711
Mailing Address: PO Box 30040, Tucson, AZ 85751-0040
Tel: 520-323-1500 *Fax:* 520-323-0055
E-mail: sales@lawyersandjudges.com
Web Site: www.lawyersandjudges.com
Key Personnel
Pres & Publr: Steve Weintraub
Founded: 1963
Professional, text & reference materials in law, accident reconstruction, legal economics & taxation, forensics, medicine.
ISBN Prefix(es): 978-0-88450; 978-0-913875; 978-1-930056
Number of titles published annually: 20 Print; 8 CD-ROM; 10 E-Book
Total Titles: 200 Print; 16 CD-ROM; 50 E-Book

Leadership Connect
1407 Broadway, Suite 318, New York, NY 10018
Tel: 212-627-4140 *Toll Free Tel:* 800-627-0311
Fax: 212-645-0931
E-mail: info@leadershipconnect.io
Web Site: www.leadershipconnect.io
Key Personnel
CEO: Michael Crosby *E-mail:* mcrosby@leadershipconnect.io
CTO: Stefan Chopin *E-mail:* schopin@leadershipconnect.io
VP, Admin & Treas: Jim Gee *E-mail:* jgee@leadershipconnect.io
VP, Content: Tom Zurla *E-mail:* tzurla@leadershipconnect.io
VP, Sales: Hugh Murphy *E-mail:* hmurphy@leadershipconnect.io
Founded: 1969
Operates at the intersection of government, business & media. We are a people intelligence ser-

vice for over 4,000 clients seeking to develop business or influence senior & mid-level decision makers. We use a mix of advanced technology & old-fashioned proprietary research to provide the highest quality data via the web, mobile devices & CRM systems.
Number of titles published annually: 16 Print
Total Titles: 16 Print; 3 Online
Imprints: Yellow Books
Branch Office(s)
1667 "K" St NW, Suite 801, Washington, DC 20006, VP, Content: Tom Zurla *Tel:* 202-347-7757 *Fax:* 202-628-3430 *E-mail:* tzurla@leadershipconnect.io

Leadership Directories, see Leadership Connect

Leadership Ministries Worldwide
1928 Central Ave, Chattanooga, TN 37408
Tel: 423-855-2181 *Toll Free Tel:* 800-987-8790
E-mail: info@lmw.org
Web Site: lmw.org; store.lmw.org
Key Personnel
Interim Pres: Noah Craig
Commentaries.
ISBN Prefix(es): 978-1-57407; 978-0-945863
Number of titles published annually: 12 Print
Total Titles: 275 Print
Membership(s): Evangelical Christian Publishers Association (ECPA)

Leaf Storm Press
PO Box 4670, Santa Fe, NM 87502-4670
Tel: 505-216-6155
E-mail: leafstormpress@gmail.com
Web Site: leafstormpress.com
Key Personnel
Publr: Andy Dudzik *E-mail:* publisher@leafstormpress.com
Founded: 2014
ISBN Prefix(es): 978-0-9914105; 978-0-9970207
Number of titles published annually: 8 Print; 8 E-Book; 4 Audio
Total Titles: 8 Print; 6 E-Book
Distribution Center: Publishers Group West, 1700 Fourth St, Berkeley, CA 94710 *Tel:* 510-809-3700 *Toll Free Tel:* 866-400-5351 (cust serv) *Fax:* 510-809-3777 *Web Site:* www.pgw.com
Membership(s): American Booksellers Association (ABA); Association of American Publishers (AAP); Independent Book Publishers Association (IBPA)

Learnables Foreign Language Courses, see International Linguistics Corp

§THE Learning Connection®
4100 Silverstar Rd, Suite D, Orlando, FL 32808
Toll Free Tel: 800-218-8489 *Fax:* 407-292-2123
E-mail: tlc@tlconnection.com
Web Site: www.tlconnection.com
Key Personnel
Gen Mgr: Ryan Handberg *E-mail:* ryan@tlconnection.com
Founded: 1991
Thematic literacy centers & teacher's guides for early childhood & middle school; parent involvement & family literacy; bilingual, math, science, multicultural, manipulatives, technology.
ISBN Prefix(es): 978-1-56831
Number of titles published annually: 15 Print; 15 CD-ROM; 5 Audio
Total Titles: 1,000 Print; 15 CD-ROM; 50 Audio
Imprints: PAKS-Parents & Kids
Branch Office(s)
300 E 93 St, Suite 29C, New York, NY 10128, VP, NJ Accts: Timothy Sasman
Membership(s): International Literacy Association (ILA)

Learning Links Inc
26 Haypress Rd, Cranbury, NJ 08512
SAN: 175-081X
Mailing Address: PO Box 326, Cranbury, NJ 08512 SAN: 175-081X
Tel: 516-437-9071 *Toll Free Tel:* 800-724-2616
Fax: 516-437-5392 *Toll Free Fax:* 888-960-2508
E-mail: info@learninglinks.com
Web Site: www.learninglinks.com
Founded: 1976
Publish study guides for novels for school use, grades 1-12. Distribute paperback books, audios, videos, craft kits & book-related toys.
ISBN Prefix(es): 978-0-88122; 978-1-56982; 978-0-7675
Number of titles published annually: 25 Print
Total Titles: 850 Print
Imprints: Novel-Ties Study Guides
Divisions: Swan Books
Distributor for Harcourt; HarperCollins; Houghton Mifflin Harcourt Publishing Company; Penguin Group USA, A Penguin Random House Company; Penguin Random House Inc
Membership(s): International Literacy Association (ILA); National Council of Teachers of English (NCTE)

LearningExpress
Unit of EBSCO Information Services
224 W 29 St, 3rd fl, New York, NY 10001
Toll Free Tel: 800-295-9556 (ext 2)
Web Site: learningexpresshub.com
Key Personnel
Chief Revenue Offr: Kheil McIntyre
CTO: Tammy Cunningham
SVP, Content: Ilsa Halpern, PhD
Dir, Cust Serv: Shana Ashwood-Viala
Dir, Mktg: Janine Y Swenson *E-mail:* jswenson@ebsco.com
Founded: 1995
Publishes print & online test-preparation resources, skill building tools, study guides & career guidance materials for the trade, library, school & consumer markets.
ISBN Prefix(es): 978-1-57685; 978-1-61103
Number of titles published annually: 32 Print; 15 E-Book
Sales Office(s): National Book Network, 4501 Forbes Blvd, Suite 200, Lanham, MD 20706 *Tel:* 301-459-3366 *Fax:* 301-429-5746
Orders to: National Book Network, 15200 NBN Way, Blue Ridge Summit, PA 17214 *Tel:* 717-794-3800 *Toll Free Tel:* 800-462-6420 *Fax:* 717-794-3828 *Toll Free Fax:* 800-338-4550 *E-mail:* customercare@nbnbooks.com
Returns: National Book Network, 15200 NBN Way, Blue Ridge Summit, PA 17214 *Tel:* 717-794-3800 *Toll Free Tel:* 800-462-6420 *Fax:* 717-794-3828 *Toll Free Fax:* 800-338-4550 *E-mail:* customercare@nbnbooks.com
Warehouse: National Book Network, 15200 NBN Way, Blue Ridge Summit, PA 17214

Lectorum Publications Inc
205 Chubb Ave, Lyndhurst, NJ 07071
Toll Free Tel: 800-345-5946 *Fax:* 201-559-2201
Toll Free Fax: 877-532-8676
E-mail: lectorum@lectorum.com
Web Site: www.lectorum.com
Key Personnel
Pres & CEO: Alex Correa *E-mail:* acorrea@lectorum.com
Cust Serv Mgr: Gladys Ochoa *E-mail:* gochoa@lectorum.com
Lib & Trade Sales Mgr: Ingeborg Portales *E-mail:* iportales@lectorum.com
Opers Mgr: Fernando Febus *E-mail:* ffebus@lectorum.com
Educ Sales: Hilda Viskovic *E-mail:* hviskovic@lectorum.com
Founded: 1960

Distribute children & adult books in Spanish, with over 25,000 titles from more than 500 domestic & foreign publishers. Serves schools & libraries, as well as the trade & various specialized markets, with children's books in Spanish, including works originally written in Spanish, translations from other languages & the Spanish language editions of many popular children's books.
ISBN Prefix(es): 978-1-880507; 978-1-930332; 978-0-9625162; 978-1-933032; 978-1-941802; 978-1-63245
Number of titles published annually: 10 Print
Total Titles: 300 Print

Lederer Books
Division of Messianic Jewish Publishers
6120 Day Long Lane, Clarksville, MD 21029
Tel: 410-531-6644 *Toll Free Tel:* 800-410-7367 (orders) *Fax:* 410-531-9440 *Toll Free Fax:* 800-327-0048
E-mail: customerservice@messianicjewish.net
Web Site: www.messianicjewish.net
Key Personnel
Pres: Barry Rubin *E-mail:* president@messianicjewish.net
Founded: 1949
Publish & distribute Messianic Jewish books, bibles & other resources.
ISBN Prefix(es): 978-1-880226; 978-1-936716
Number of titles published annually: 6 Print
Total Titles: 137 Print; 30 E-Book
Distributor for Chosen People Ministries; First Fruits of Zion; Jewish New Testament Publications
Foreign Rep(s): Winfried Bluth (Europe)
Foreign Rights: Winfried Bluth (Europe)
Membership(s): Evangelical Christian Publishers Association (ECPA)

Lee & Low Books Inc
95 Madison Ave, Suite 1205, New York, NY 10016
Tel: 212-779-4400 *Toll Free Tel:* 888-320-3190 (ext 28, orders only) *Fax:* 212-683-1894 (orders only); 212-532-6035
E-mail: general@leeandlow.com
Web Site: www.leeandlow.com
Key Personnel
Pres: Craig Low *E-mail:* clow@leeandlow.com
Publr: Jason Low
Edit Dir: Cheryl Klein
Ed-at-Large: Louise May
Founded: 1991
Publisher of high quality multicultural children's books. We provide for the school, library & bookstore market.
ISBN Prefix(es): 978-1-880000; 978-1-885008; 978-1-58430; 978-1-60060; 978-0-89239; 978-1-62014
Number of titles published annually: 15 Print; 15 E-Book
Total Titles: 650 Print; 50 E-Book; 50 Audio
Imprints: Bebop Books; Children's Book Press; Dive Into Reading; Lee & Low Games; Shen's Books; Tu Books
See separate listing for:
Children's Book Press
Shen's Books

Legacy Bound
Formerly Curious Cat Books
Division of Legacy Toys
5 N Central Ave, Ely, MN 55731
Tel: *Toll Free Tel:* 800-909-9698
E-mail: orders@legacybound.net
Web Site: www.legacybound.net
Key Personnel
Mktg: Laura Moberly *E-mail:* laura@legacybound.net
Founded: 1999

ISBN Prefix(es): 978-0-9677057; 978-0-9766264; 978-0-9794202; 978-0-9801045; 978-0-9819307; 978-0-9883508; 978-0-9835189
Number of titles published annually: 3 Print
Total Titles: 25 Print
Imprints: Rosebud Books
Warehouse: Legacy Toys, 3 Chapman St, Ely, MN 55731
Distribution Center: Baker & Taylor, 501 S Gladiolus St, Momence, IL 60954-1799, Mdse Admin: Ms Robin Bright *Tel:* 908-541-7425 *Toll Free Tel:* 800-775-2300 *Fax:* 815-802-2444 *Toll Free Fax:* 800-411-8433 *E-mail:* pc@baker-taylor.com *Web Site:* www.baker-taylor.com
North Country Books, 220 Lafayette St, Utica, NY 13502 *Tel:* 315-735-4877 *Toll Free Tel:* 800-342-7409 *Fax:* 315-738-4342 *E-mail:* ncbooks@verizon.net *Web Site:* www.northcountrybooks.com
Membership(s): Independent Book Publishers Association (IBPA); Midwest Independent Publishing Association (MIPA)

Lehigh University Press
Affiliate of Rowman & Littlefield Publishing Group
B-040 Christmas-Saucon Hall, 14 E Packer Ave, Bethlehem, PA 18015
Tel: 610-758-3933 *Fax:* 610-758-6331
E-mail: inlup@lehigh.edu
Web Site: lupress.cas2.lehigh.edu
Key Personnel
Dir: Kate Crassons
Mng Ed: Tricia J Moore
Founded: 1985
18th century American studies, East Asian studies, literary theory & criticism, history & technology, science, sociology, biography & the arts. Submissions welcome on any topic that is intellectually substantive.
ISBN Prefix(es): 978-1-61146
Number of titles published annually: 10 Print
Total Titles: 149 Print
Distributed by Rowman & Littlefield

§Leisure Arts Inc
Division of Liberty Media
104 Champs Blvd, Suite 100, Maumelle, AR 72113
SAN: 666-9565
Tel: 501-868-8800 *Toll Free Tel:* 800-643-8030 *Toll Free Fax:* 877-710-5603 (catalog)
E-mail: customer_service@leisurearts.com
Web Site: www.leisurearts.com
Key Personnel
SVP, Sales & Mktg: Ray Wolf
VP, Publg: Peg Couch
VP, Retail Sales: Martha Adams
Founded: 1971
Hard & soft cover books featuring instructions for needlework, crafts, cooking & gardening.
ISBN Prefix(es): 978-0-942237; 978-1-57486; 978-1-60140; 978-1-60900; 978-1-4647
Number of titles published annually: 200 Print
Total Titles: 2,000 Print

§The Lentz Leadership Institute LLC
540 Arlington Lane, Grayslake, IL 60030
SAN: 857-7994
Tel: 702-719-9214
E-mail: orders@lentzleadership.com
Web Site: www.lentzleadership.com; www.refractivethinker.com; www.pensieropress.com; www.narratorepress.com
Key Personnel
The Academic Entrepreneur: Dr Cheryl Lentz *E-mail:* drcheryllentz@gmail.com
Founded: 2008
Publishes scholarly materials as part of The Anthology Series: The Refractive Thinker Series, to include the educational seminar series for public speaking. Individual books & individ-

ual doctoral or graduate level publications by participating authors are also published. Offer APA doctoral & graduate editing services.
This publisher has indicated that 85% of their product line is author subsidized.
ISBN Prefix(es): 978-0-9823036; 978-0-9828740; 978-0-9840054
Number of titles published annually: 18 Print; 8 Online; 25 E-Book; 1 Audio
Total Titles: 31 Print; 31 Online; 200 E-Book; 2 Audio
Imprints: Narratore Press; Pensiero Press; The Refractive Thinker® Press
Distribution Center: Ingram/Lightning Source Inc, 1246 Heil Quaker Blvd, La Vergne, TN 37086 *Tel:* 615-213-5815 *Fax:* 615-213-4725 *E-mail:* inquiry@lightningsource.com *Web Site:* www.lightningsource.com
Membership(s): The Association of Publishers for Special Sales (APSS); Independent Book Publishers Association (IBPA)

Lerner Publications
Imprint of Lerner Publishing Group Inc
241 First Ave N, Minneapolis, MN 55401
SAN: 201-0828
Tel: 612-332-3344 *Toll Free Tel:* 800-328-4929 *Fax:* 612-332-7615 *Toll Free Fax:* 800-332-1132
E-mail: info@lernerbooks.com; custserve@lernerbooks.com
Web Site: www.lernerbooks.com; www.facebook.com/lernerbooks
Key Personnel
Chmn: Harry J Lerner
Pres & Publr: Adam Lerner
EVP & COO: Mark Budde
EVP & CFO: Margaret Thomas
EVP, Sales: David Wexler
VP, Ed-in-Chief: Andy Cummings
VP, Mktg: Rachel Zugschwert
Publg Dir, School & Lib: Jenny Krueger
Dir, HR: Cyndi Radant
Dir, Rts, Spec Sales & Intl Dist: Maria Kjoller
School & Lib Mktg Dir: Lois Wallentine
Founded: 1959
Juveniles: science, history, sports, fiction, art, geography, aviation, environment, ethnic, multicultural issues & activity books.
Number of titles published annually: 225 Print; 225 E-Book
Total Titles: 1,680 Print; 920 E-Book
Foreign Rep(s): Thomas Allen & Son (trade) (Canada); Bounce Sales & Marketing Ltd (UK); INT Books (Australia); Phambili (Southern Africa); Publishers Marketing Service (Malaysia, Singapore); Saunders Book Co (education) (Canada); South Pacific Books (New Zealand)
Foreign Rights: Japan Foreign-Rights Centre (Japan); Korea Copyright Center (KCC) (Korea); Agence Michelle Lapautre (France); Literarische Agentur Silke Weniger (Germany)
Warehouse: Lerner Publishing Group Inc, 1251 Washington Ave N, Minneapolis, MN 55401, Mgr: Ken Rued

Lerner Publishing Group Inc
Division of Lerner Universal Corp
241 First Ave N, Minneapolis, MN 55401
SAN: 201-0828
Tel: 612-332-3344 *Toll Free Tel:* 800-328-4929 *Fax:* 612-332-7615 *Toll Free Fax:* 800-332-1132
E-mail: info@lernerbooks.com; custserve@lernerbooks.com
Web Site: www.lernerbooks.com; www.facebook.com/lernerbooks
Key Personnel
Chmn: Harry J Lerner
Publr & CEO: Adam Lerner
EVP & COO: Mark Budde
EVP & CFO: Margaret Thomas

EVP, Sales: David Wexler
VP & Ed-in-Chief: Andy Cummings
VP, Mktg: Rachel Zugschwert
Edit Dir, Graphic Universe: Greg Hunter
Publg Dir, School & Lib: Jenny Krueger
Dir, HR: Cyndi Radant
Dir of Rts, Spec Sales & Intl Dist: Maria Kjoller
School & Lib Mktg Dir: Lois Wallentine
School & Lib Sales Mgr: Brad Richason
Founded: 1959
ISBN Prefix(es): 978-0-87614; 978-1-58013; 978-0-8225; 978-0-7613; 978-1-57505; 978-0-92937; 978-0-93049; 978-1-58196
Number of titles published annually: 450 Print
Total Titles: 4,800 Print; 3,800 E-Book
Imprints: Bumba Books; Carolrhoda Books Inc; Carolrhoda Lab™; Darby Creek Publishing; ediciones Lerner; First Avenue Editions; Graphic Universe™; Hungry Tomato; Kar-Ben Publishing; Lerner Digital; Lerner Publications; LernerClassroom; Millbrook Press; Twenty-First Century Books; Zest Books
Divisions: Lerner Publisher Services
Distributor for Andersen Press; Big & Small; Creston Books; Walter Foster Publishing; Full Tilt; Gecko Press; Lantana Publishing; Maverick Arts Publishing; One Elm Press; Quarto Library; Red Chair Press; Starberry Books; We Do Listen Foundation
Foreign Rep(s): Thomas Allen & Son (trade) (Canada); Bravo (Kar-Ben) (UK & the continent); INT Books (Australia); J Appleseed, A Division of Saunders (Canada); Mazeltov Books (Kar-Ben) (Australia); Phambili Agencies (Botswana, Lesotho, Namibia, South Africa, Swaziland, Zimbabwe); Publishers Marketing Services (Brunei, Malaysia, Singapore); Saunders Book Co (education) (Canada); South Pacific Books (New Zealand)
Foreign Rights: Japan Foreign-Rights Centre (Japan); Korea Copyright Center (KCC) (Korea); Agence Michelle Lapautre (France); Literarische Agentur Silke Weniger (Germany)
Warehouse: 1251 Washington Ave N, Minneapolis, MN 55401, Mgr: Ken Rued
See separate listing for:
Carolrhoda Books Inc
Carolrhoda Lab™
ediciones Lerner
First Avenue Editions
Graphic Universe™
Kar-Ben Publishing
Lerner Publications
LernerClassroom
Millbrook Press
Twenty-First Century Books
Zest Books

LernerClassroom
Imprint of Lerner Publishing Group Inc
241 First Ave N, Minneapolis, MN 55401
Tel: 612-332-3344 *Toll Free Tel:* 800-328-4929 *Fax:* 612-332-7615 *Toll Free Fax:* 800-332-1132
E-mail: info@lernerbooks.com; custserve@lernerbooks.com
Web Site: www.lernerbooks.com; www.facebook.com/lernerbooks
Key Personnel
Chmn: Harry J Lerner
Pres & Publr: Adam Lerner
EVP & COO: Mark Budde
EVP & CFO: Margaret Thomas
EVP, Sales: David Wexler
VP & Ed-in-Chief: Andy Cummings
VP, Mktg: Rachel Zugschwert
Publg Dir, School & Lib: Jenny Krueger
Dir, HR: Cyndi Radant
Dir, Rts, Spec Sales & Intl Dist: Maria Kjoller
School & Lib Mktg Dir: Lois Wallentine
Nonfiction children's publications.
Number of titles published annually: 50 Print
Total Titles: 860 Print; 55 E-Book

Foreign Rep(s): Thomas Allen & Son (trade) (Canada); Bounce Sales & Marketing Ltd (UK); INT Books (Australia); J Appleseed, A Division of Saunders (Canada); Phambili Agencies (Botswana, Lesotho, Namibia, Southern Africa); Publishers Marketing Services (Brunei, Malaysia, Singapore); Saunders Book Co (education) (Canada); South Pacific Books (New Zealand)
Foreign Rights: Japan Foreign-Rights Centre (Japan); Korea Copyright Center (KCC) (Korea); Agence Michelle Lapautre (France); Literarische Agentur Silke Weniger (Germany)
Warehouse: 1251 Washington Ave N, Minneapolis, MN 55401, Mgr: Ken Rued

Letterbox/Papyrus of London Publishers USA
10501 Broom Hill Dr, Suite 1-F, Las Vegas, NV 89134-7339
Tel: 702-256-3838
E-mail: lb27383@cox.net
Key Personnel
Mng Dir: Anthony Wade
Ed-in-Chief: Geoffrey Hutchison-Cleaves, MA
Fin Offr: Josef Kase *Tel:* 702-256-3838 ext 2
Spec Orders Mgr: Erica Neubauer *Tel:* 702-256-3838 ext 1
Rts & Perms: Mrs H Neubauer *Tel:* 702-256-3838 ext 8
Founded: 1946 (in London)
No submissions accepted.
ISBN Prefix(es): 978-0-943698
Number of titles published annually: 4 Print
Total Titles: 138 Print
Imprints: Challenges of Aging (instruction booklets); Difficult Subjects Made Easy (instruction booklets)
Advertising Agency: ShowKase Advertising & Public Relations, 3250 S Fort Apache Rd, Suite 217, Las Vegas, NV 89117, Acct Exec: Ms Robin Lindsay
Distribution Center: Amazon.com
Baker & Taylor Books, PO Box 8888, Momence, IL 60954 *Tel:* 908-541-7459
Barnes & Noble

Letterbox Service, see Letterbox/Papyrus of London Publishers USA

Lexington Books
Imprint of Rowman & Littlefield Publishing Group
4501 Forbes Blvd, Suite 200, Lanham, MD 20706
Tel: 301-459-3366
Web Site: rowman.com/page/lexington
Key Personnel
Dir, Edit: Nicolette Amstutz *Tel:* 301-459-3366 ext 5514 *E-mail:* namstutz@rowman.com
Premier publisher of scholarly monographs in the social sciences & humanities. Subjects include political science, political theory, philosophy, history, international relations, literary studies, sociology, anthropology, religion, communications, cultural studies, education, psychology, linguistics & area studies.
ISBN Prefix(es): 978-0-7391; 978-1-4985; 978-1-7936
Number of titles published annually: 600 Print; 600 E-Book
Total Titles: 6,000 Print; 5,000 E-Book
Orders to: Rowman & Littlefield Publishing Group, 15200 NBN Way, Blue Ridge Summit, PA 17214 *Tel:* 717-794-3800 *Toll Free Tel:* 800-462-6420 *Fax:* 717-794-3803 *E-mail:* customercare@rowman.com
Membership(s): Association of American Publishers (AAP)

§LexisNexis®
Division of RELX Group PLC
230 Park Ave, Suite 7, New York, NY 10169

SAN: 202-6317
Tel: 212-309-8100 *Toll Free Fax:* 800-437-8674
Web Site: www.lexisnexis.com
Key Personnel
CEO: Mike Walsh
Founded: 1897
Multivolume legal reference works, state codes & single-volume legal texts, treatises & casebooks. Most material also in online versions.
ISBN Prefix(es): 978-0-409; 978-0-87215; 978-0-672; 978-0-87473; 978-0-406; 978-0-327; 978-0-88063; 978-0-930273; 978-1-55834; 978-1-56257
Imprints: Michie
Shipping Address: Broome Corp Park, 136 Carlin Rd, Conklin, NY 13748 *Tel:* 607-772-2600 *Toll Free Fax:* 800-323-9608

§LexisNexis® Matthew Bender®
Member of The LexisNexis® Group
701 E Water St, Charlottesville, VA 22902
Tel: 434-972-7600
Web Site: www.lexisnexis.com
Founded: 1887
Treatises, text & form books, newsletters, periodicals & manuals for the legal, accounting, insurance, banking & related professions, selected libraries on CD-ROM.
Branch locations also in New York City & Dayton, OH.
ISBN Prefix(es): 978-0-8205; 978-1-4224
Total Titles: 577 Print; 277 CD-ROM; 27 Online; 277 E-Book
Branch Office(s)
Immaculata Hall, 32 S Ewing St, Helena, MT 59601 *Toll Free Tel:* 800-227-9597

Liberty Fund Inc
11301 N Meridian St, Carmel, IN 46032-4564
Tel: 317-842-0880 *Toll Free Tel:* 800-955-8335; 800-866-3520 *Fax:* 317-579-6060 (cust serv); 708-534-7803
E-mail: books@libertyfund.org; info@libertyfund.org
Web Site: www.libertyfund.org
Key Personnel
Mng Ed: Patti Ordower
Mktg & Fulfillment Coord: Michele Roberts *Tel:* 317-842-0880 ext 4920 *E-mail:* mroberts@libertyfund.org
Founded: 1960
A publisher of print & electronic scholarly resources including new editions of classic works in American constitutional history, European history, natural law, law, modern political thought, economics & education.
ISBN Prefix(es): 978-0-913966; 978-0-86597; 978-1-61487
Number of titles published annually: 10 Print; 3 Online
Total Titles: 425 Print; 150 Online; 1 Audio
Foreign Rep(s): Academic Sales & Marketing (Andrew Jones) (Midlands, Northern England); Chris Ashdown (Asia); Mara Cheli (Italy); Leonidas Diamantopoulos (Cyprus, Greece); Everybodys Book's (Warren Halford) (Southern Africa); Export Sales Agency (Ted Dougherty) (Austria, Germany, Switzerland); Four Corners Sales Agency (Michael Darcy) (Ireland, London, Scotland, Southern England, Wales); Gazelle Academic (Mark Trotter) (London); Iberian Book Services (Peter & Charlotte Prout) (Gibraltar, Portugal, Spain); Flavio Marcello (Italy); Marketing Solutions LLP (Andrew Wallace) (Central London, UK, East Anglia, England); Maya Publishers Pvt Ltd (India); David Towle (Baltic States, Northern Europe, Scandinavia)
Returns: c/o Ware-Pak, Returns Dept, 2427 Bond St, University Park, IL 60484
Distribution Center: Ingram Publisher Services, One Ingram Blvd, La Vergne, TN 37086 (US & CN) *Tel:* 615-793-5000 *Toll Free Tel:* 866-

400-5351 *E-mail:* ips@ingramcontent.com *Web Site:* www.ingramcontent.com

Scholarly Book Services Inc, 289 Ridgeland Ave, Unit 105, Toronto, ON M6A 1Z6, Canada *Toll Free Tel:* 800-847-9736 *Toll Free Fax:* 800-220-9895

Membership(s): American Library Association (ALA); Association of American Publishers (AAP)

Libraries Unlimited
Imprint of ABC-CLIO
147 Castilian Dr, Santa Barbara, CA 93117
Mailing Address: PO Box 1911, Santa Barbara, CA 93116-1911
Tel: 805-968-1911 *Toll Free Tel:* 800-368-6868 *Toll Free Fax:* 888-873-7017
E-mail: customerservice@abc-clio.com
Web Site: www.abc-clio.com
Founded: 1964
Library science textbooks, annotated bibliographies, reference books, professional books for school media specialists as well as resource & activity books for librarians & teachers; storytelling resources & collections.
ISBN Prefix(es): 978-0-313; 978-0-87287; 978-1-56308; 978-1-59158
Number of titles published annually: 80 Print
Total Titles: 600 Print; 5 Audio

The Library of America
14 E 60 St, New York, NY 10022-1006
SAN: 286-9918
Tel: 212-308-3360 *Fax:* 212-750-8352
E-mail: info@loa.org
Web Site: www.loa.org
Key Personnel
Pres & Publr: Max Rudin
COO: Daniel W Baker
Assoc Publr: Brian McCarthy
Edit Dir: John Kulka
Dir, Mktg: David Cloyce Smith
Mng Ed: Trish Hoard
Cust Serv Mgr: Laura Gazlay
Publicity Mgr: Leslie Schwartz
Founded: 1979
Collected editions of classic American authors; literature, history, philosophy, drama, poetry & journalism.
ISBN Prefix(es): 978-0-940450; 978-1-883011; 978-1-931082; 978-1-59853
Number of titles published annually: 16 Print
Total Titles: 500 Print
Distributed by Penguin Random House Inc
Foreign Rep(s): Penguin Random House Canada (Canada); United Publishers Service (Japan)
Warehouse: Penguin Random House Inc, One Grosset Dr, Kirkwood, NY 13795

Mary Ann Liebert Inc
140 Huguenot St, 3rd fl, New Rochelle, NY 10801-5215
Tel: 914-740-2100 *Toll Free Tel:* 800-654-3237 *Fax:* 914-740-2101
E-mail: info@liebertpub.com
Web Site: www.liebertonline.com
Key Personnel
Publr & CEO: Mary Ann Liebert
  E-mail: mliebert@liebertpub.com
SVP: Harriet I Matysko
Ad Prodn Mgr: Kathleen De Souza
Founded: 1980
Medical & sci-tech journals, books & newspapers. Additional subjects include: biomedical research, integrative medicine (CAM), public policy, public health/policy, gender & population studies, regenerative medicine, clinical medicine, biotechnology, environmental studies, humanities, life sciences, allied health & surgery.
ISBN Prefix(es): 978-0-913113; 978-1-934854

Number of titles published annually: 3 Print; 3 Online
Total Titles: 65 Print; 70 Online
Divisions: Genetic Engineering & Biotechnology News
Foreign Office(s): Impress Media, Carrington Kirk, Carrington, Midlothian EH23 4LR, United Kingdom, Contact: Hilary Turnbull *Tel:* (01875) 825700 *Fax:* (01875) 825701 *E-mail:* hturnbull@genengnews.com

Life Cycle Books
Division of Life Cycle Books Ltd (Canada)
PO Box 799, Fort Collins, CO 80522
SAN: 692-7173
Toll Free Tel: 800-214-5849
E-mail: orders@lifecyclebooks.com
Web Site: www.lifecyclebooks.com
Key Personnel
Founder & Pres: Paul Broughton *E-mail:* paulb@lifecyclebooks.com
Founded: 1973
Books, pamphlets, brochures & audiovisuals on human life issues.
ISBN Prefix(es): 978-0-919225
Number of titles published annually: 6 Print
Total Titles: 41 Print

Light-Beams Publishing
36 Blandings Way, Biddeford, ME 04005
Tel: 603-659-1300
E-mail: info@light-beams.com
Web Site: www.light-beams.com
Key Personnel
Mktg Mgr & Trade Contact: Barry Kane
  E-mail: bkane@light-beams.com
Founded: 2000
Specialize in & publishes award-winning children's books & videos for children ages 3 & up.
ISBN Prefix(es): 978-0-9708104; 978-0-9766289
Number of titles published annually: 8 Print

Light Publications
Hope Artiste Village, 1005 Main St, Suite 1212, Pawtucket, RI 02806
Mailing Address: PO Box 2462, Providence, RI 02906
Tel: 401-484-0228
E-mail: info@lightpublications.com
Web Site: lightpublications.com
Key Personnel
Pres: Stephen Brendan *E-mail:* stephen@lightpublications.com
Founded: 1999
ISBN Prefix(es): 978-0-9702642; 978-0-9824707; 978-1-940060
Number of titles published annually: 2 Print; 5 Online; 3 E-Book; 1 Audio
Total Titles: 20 Print; 25 Online; 20 E-Book; 8 Audio
Membership(s): Independent Book Publishers Association (IBPA)

Light Technology Publishing LLC
4030 E Huntington Dr, Flagstaff, AZ 86004
Mailing Address: PO Box 3540, Flagstaff, AZ 86003-3540
Tel: 928-526-1345 *Toll Free Tel:* 800-450-0985 *Fax:* 928-714-1132
E-mail: publishing@lighttechnology.net
Web Site: www.lighttechnology.com
Key Personnel
Owner & Publr: O'Ryin Swanson
Sidona Journal, metaphysical publications, mostly channelled.
ISBN Prefix(es): 978-1-891824; 978-1-929385
Number of titles published annually: 10 Print; 1 Online; 10 E-Book; 10 Audio

Total Titles: 200 Print; 1 Online; 200 E-Book; 10 Audio
Membership(s): Association of American Publishers (AAP)

Lighthouse Publishing of the Carolinas
Division of Iron Stream Media
Affiliate of Christian Devotions Ministries
2333 Barton Oaks Dr, Raleigh, NC 27614-7940
E-mail: lighthousepublishingcarolinas@gmail.com
Web Site: lpcbooks.com
Key Personnel
Founder & CEO: Eddie Jones
ISBN Prefix(es): 978-0-9833196; 978-0-9822065; 978-0-9847655; 978-1-938499
Number of titles published annually: 40 Print; 40 E-Book; 30 Audio
Total Titles: 210 Print; 210 Online; 210 E-Book; 90 Audio
Imprints: BLING! Romance (clean contemporary romance with an edge); Candlelight Romance (inspirational contemporary romance); Firefly Southern Fiction (Southern characters & tradition, historical & contemporary); Guiding Light Women's Fiction (contemporary & historical); Harambee Press (writers of color); Heritage Beacon Fiction (historical fiction); IlluminateYA Fiction (fiction & nonfiction that reflect today's authentic youth culture, morals & values); Lamplighter Mysteries & Suspense (cozy murder mysteries, thrillers & suspense); Smitten Historical Romance (stories from Regency era through 1970s); Sonrise Devotionals (Christian devotionals); Straight Street Books (Christian living nonfiction); Trailblazer Western Fiction (tales of the American West)
Distribution Center: Amazon
Ingram
Spring Arbor
Membership(s): Independent Book Publishers Association (IBPA)

Liguori Publications
One Liguori Dr, Liguori, MO 63057-1000
Tel: 636-464-2500 *Toll Free Tel:* 800-325-9521 *Toll Free Fax:* 800-325-9526 (sales)
E-mail: liguori@liguori.org (sales & cust serv)
Web Site: www.liguori.org
Key Personnel
Pres & Publr: Fr Byron Miller
Dir, Fin & Busn Opers: Tracey Kane
Dir, Sales, Mktg & Prod Devt: Mary Wuertz von Holt
Sales & Cust Serv Mgr: Chuck Healy
Founded: 1947 (by Redemptorist priests & brothers)
Roman Catholic publisher & nonprofit ministry of the Catholic Redemptorist congregation of fathers & brothers. Our mission is to spread the Word of God & the gospel of Jesus Christ through print & electronic media. We publish inspirational books & pamphlets, parish bulletins, newsletters & other religious education materials, along with our flagship product, *Liguorian* magazine.
ISBN Prefix(es): 978-0-89243; 978-0-7648
Number of titles published annually: 20 Print
Total Titles: 2,000 Print; 40 CD-ROM; 2,000 Online; 600 E-Book
Imprints: Liguori; Libros Liguori (Spanish language titles)
Distributor for Redemptorist Publications
Foreign Rep(s): Garratt (Australia); Majellan (Australia); Redemptorist Publications (England)
Membership(s): Association of Catholic Publishers Inc; Catholic Press Association (CPA)

Limelight Editions
Imprint of Rowman & Littlefield Publishing Group
PO Box 1520, Wayne, NJ 07470-1520

Tel: 973-987-5363
Web Site: limelighteditions.com
Key Personnel
Sr Exec Ed: John Cerullo
Full service educational & professional training publisher that produces books, book/media on the performing arts including cinema, dance & theater.
ISBN Prefix(es): 978-0-87910
Number of titles published annually: 20 Print; 10 Audio
Total Titles: 400 Print; 50 Audio
Foreign Rep(s): Publishers Group UK (UK); Rowman & Littlefield International (worldwide exc Canada, Ireland, UK & USA)
Orders to: National Book Network, 15200 NBN Way, Blue Ridge Summit, PA 17214 *Toll Free Tel:* 800-462-6420 *Toll Free Fax:* 800-338-4550
Returns: National Book Network, Returns Dept, 15200 NBN Way, Bldg B, Blue Ridge Summit, PA 17214
Warehouse: National Book Network, 15200 NBN Way, Blue Ridge Summit, PA 17214 *Tel:* 717-794-3800
Distribution Center: National Book Network, 15200 NBN Way, Blue Ridge Summit, PA 17214 *Tel:* 717-794-3800

Linden Publishing Co Inc

2006 S Mary St, Fresno, CA 93721
Tel: 559-233-6633 *Toll Free Tel:* 800-345-4447 (orders) *Fax:* 559-233-6933
Web Site: lindenpub.com
Key Personnel
Pres & Publr: Richard Sorsky *E-mail:* richard@lindenpub.com
Founded: 1977
ISBN Prefix(es): 978-0-941936; 978-1-933502; 978-1-884956; 978-1-884995
Number of titles published annually: 12 Print; 5 E-Book
Total Titles: 230 Print; 112 E-Book
Imprints: Craven Street Books; Pace Press; Quill Driver Books
Foreign Rights: Books Crossing Borders (worldwide)
Distribution Center: Ingram Publisher Services, One Ingram Blvd, La Vergne, TN 37086
Membership(s): Independent Book Publishers Association (IBPA)

LinguaText LLC

103 Walker Way, Newark, DE 19711
SAN: 238-0307
Tel: 302-453-8695
E-mail: text@linguatextbooks.com
Web Site: www.linguatextbooks.com
Key Personnel
Owner & Publr: Michael Bolan
Founded: 1978
Publish foreign language textbooks, Hispanic monographs & classics of Spanish & French literature designed for the English-speaking college student.
ISBN Prefix(es): 978-0-936388; 978-0-942566; 978-1-58871; 978-1-58977
Number of titles published annually: 15 Print
Total Titles: 400 Print; 3 CD-ROM; 2 E-Book
Imprints: Cervantes & Co (Spanish classics series); Juan de la Cuesta Hispanic Monographs (literary criticism, monographs, critical editions); Moliere & Co (French classics series)
Distribution Center: GOBI® Library Solutions from EBSCO, 999 Maple St, Contoocook, NH 03229 *Tel:* 603-746-3102 *Toll Free Tel:* 800-258-3774 *Fax:* 603-746-5628 *Web Site:* gobi.ebsco.com
Baker & Taylor, 2550 W Tyvola Rd, Suite 300, Charlotte, NC 28217 *Toll Free Tel:* 800-775-1800 *E-mail:* btinfo@baker-taylor.com

Ingram, One Ingram Blvd, La Vergne, TN 37086 *Toll Free Tel:* 866-400-5351 *E-mail:* ips@ingramcontent.com
Membership(s): Textbook & Academic Authors Association (TAA)

§Lippincott Williams & Wilkins

Unit of Wolters Kluwer Health
333 Seventh Ave, New York, NY 10001
Toll Free Tel: 800-933-6525
E-mail: orders@lww.com
Web Site: www.lww.com
Key Personnel
Dir, Corp Communs, Health Learning, Res & Practice: Connie Hughes *Tel:* 646-674-6348 *E-mail:* connie.hughes@wolterskluwer.com
Founded: 1792
Medicine, dentistry life sciences, nursing, allied health, veterinary medicine books, journals, textbooks, looseleaf, newsletters & media.
ISBN Prefix(es): 978-0-8021; 978-0-397; 978-0-316; 978-0-683; 978-0-7817; 978-1-4698; 978-1-60929; 978-1-60831; 978-8067; 978-1-60547; 978-1-881063; 978-0-88167; 978-0-89004; 978-0-89313; 978-0-89640; 978-0-911216
Total Titles: 4,000 E-Book
Branch Office(s)
351 W Camden St, Baltimore, MD 21201 *Tel:* 410-528-4000
2 Commerce Sq, 2001 Market St, Philadelphia, PA 19103 *Tel:* 215-521-8300 *Fax:* 215-521-8902
Foreign Office(s): Lippincott Williams & Wilkins Pty Ltd, 66 Talavera Rd, Macquarie Park, NSW 2113, Australia *Tel:* (02) 9857 1313
Lippincott Williams & Wilkins Asia Ltd, 15/F, W Sq, 314-324 Hennessy Rd, Wan Chai, Hong Kong *Tel:* 2610 7000 *Fax:* 2610 7098
25 Canada Sq, Canary Wharf, 41st fl, London E14 5LQ, United Kingdom *Tel:* (020) 3197 6500 *Fax:* (020) 3197 6501
Warehouse: 16522 Hunters Green Pkwy, Hagerstown, MD 21740 *Tel:* 301-223-2300 *Fax:* 301-223-2400
Distribution Center: 16522 Hunters Green Pkwy, Hagerstown, MD 21740 *Tel:* 301-223-2300 *Fax:* 301-223-2400

Listen & Live Audio Inc

803 13 St, Union City, NJ 07087
Tel: 201-558-9000 *Toll Free Tel:* 800-653-9400 (orders) *Fax:* 201-558-9800
Web Site: www.listenandlive.com
Key Personnel
Pres: Alfred C Martino *E-mail:* alfred@listenandlive.com
Publr: Alisa Weberman *E-mail:* alisa@listenandlive.com
Founded: 1995
Strictly audiobooks, self-help, fiction, motivational & men's adventure.
ISBN Prefix(es): 978-1-885408; 978-1-931953; 978-1-59316
Number of titles published annually: 10 Audio
Total Titles: 600 Audio
Membership(s): Audio Publishers Association; Independent Book Publishers Association (IBPA)

little bee books

251 Park Ave S, 12th fl, New York, NY 10010
Toll Free Tel: 844-321-0237
E-mail: info@littlebeebooks.com
Web Site: littlebeebooks.com
Key Personnel
Founder & CEO: Shimul Tolia
Founder & CFO: Thomas Morgan
VP, Sales: Tim Murray
Art Dir: Rob Wall
Mng Ed: Dave Barrett
Sr Ed: Brett Duquette
Sr Ed, BuzzPop: Rebecca Webster

Assoc Ed, Little Bee Books & Yellow Jacket: Charlie Ilgunas
Designer: David DeWitt
Prodn Mgr: Terence Campo; Barbara Cho; Elizabeth Peskin
Mktg Coord: Matthew Sciarappa
Prodn Coord: Melissa Pangaro
Mktg & Publicity Asst: Tristan Lueck; Jordan Mondell; Samantha Sacks
Sales Asst: Josie Dallam
Founded: 2014
Creative & fun books for busy little bees ages 0-12 designed to entertain, inspire & educate.
Agented submissions only. No unsol mss accepted.
ISBN Prefix(es): 978-1-4998
Number of titles published annually: 150 Print
Total Titles: 46 Print
Imprints: BuzzPop; Yellow Jacket (middle grade readers 8-14)
Distributed by Simon & Schuster, Inc
Foreign Rep(s): Bonnier Publishing (James Tavendale) (worldwide)
Foreign Rights: Bonnier Publishing (Nick Franklin) (worldwide)
Billing Address: Simon & Schuster, Inc, 100 Front St, Riverside, NJ 08075
Orders to: Simon & Schuster, Inc, 100 Front St, Riverside, NJ 08075 *Toll Free Tel:* 800-223-2336
Returns: Simon & Schuster, Inc, c/o Jacobson Logistics, 4406 Industrial Park Rd, Bldg 7, Camp Hill, PA 17011
Shipping Address: Simon & Schuster, Inc, 100 Front St, Riverside, NJ 08075
Warehouse: Simon & Schuster, Inc, 100 Front St, Riverside, NJ 08075
Distribution Center: Simon & Schuster, Inc, 100 Front St, Riverside, NJ 08075
Membership(s): Association of American Publishers (AAP)

§Little, Brown and Company

Division of Hachette Book Group
1290 Avenue of the Americas, New York, NY 10104
Tel: 212-364-1100 *Fax:* 212-364-0952
E-mail: firstname.lastname@hbgusa.com
Web Site: www.littlebrown.com; www.hachettebookgroup.com
Key Personnel
SVP & Publr: Bruce Nichols
VP, Deputy Publr: Craig Young
VP, Ed-in-Chief: Judy Clain
VP, Publr, Digital & Pbk: Terry Adams
VP, Edit Dir, Mulholland Books & Exec Ed, Little, Brown and Company: Josh Kendall
VP, Subs Rts, HBG: Nancy Wiese
VP, Patterson Publg Dir: Ned Rust
VP, Publr & Ed-in-Chief, Little, Brown Spark: Tracy Behar
VP, Creative Dir: Mario Pulice
VP & Exec Dir, Publicity: Sabrina Callahan
VP, Exec Ed: Asya Muchnick
VP, Edit Dir, Voracious: Michael Szczerban
Dir, Intl Rts: Tracy Williams
Fin Dir: Paul Boccardi
Dir of Mng Edit: Mary Tondorf-Dick
Exec Ed: Vanessa Mobley
Sr Ed: Marisa Vigilante; Philip Marino
Mktg Dir, Little, Brown & Mulholland Books: Pamela Brown
Mktg Dir, Little, Brown Spark: Jessica Chun
Dir, Mktg & Publicity, JIMMY Patterson Books: Erinn McGrath
Assoc Dir, Mktg: Kimberly Sheu
Sr Mktg Mgr: Ashley Marudas
Mktg Mgr: Ira Boudah
Soc Media Dir: Lauren Hesse
Dir, Publicity: Katharine Meyers; Elizabeth Garriga
Asst Dir, Publicity, Little, Brown Spark & Voracious: Jules Horbachevsky

Assoc Dir, Publicity: Lena Little
Mktg & Publicity Assoc, JIMMY Patterson Books: Julie Guacci
Digital Engagement Mgr, JIMMY Patterson Books: Joshua Johns
Exec Art Dir, JIMMY Patterson Books: Tracy Shaw
Sr Art Dir: Gregg Kulick
Sr Art Dir, Little, Brown Ad: Timothy Harrington
Exec Ed, JIMMY Patterson Books: Denise Roy
Ed, JIMMY Patterson Books: Shannon Jamieson Vazquez
Dir, Brand Devt, JIMMY Patterson Books: Bill Robinson
Sales Mgr, JIMMY Patterson Books: Elizabeth Guess
Exec Dir of Publicity: Nicole Dewey
Founded: 1837
Little, Brown and Company, the adult trade division of Hachette Book Group, is one of the country's oldest & most distinguished publishing houses. Unsol/unagented mss not accepted.
ISBN Prefix(es): 978-0-316
Number of titles published annually: 279 Print
Total Titles: 2,023 Print
Imprints: Back Bay Books; Little, Brown Spark; Mulholland Books; JIMMY Patterson Books; Voracious
Sales Office(s): Hachette Book Group, 1290 Avenue of the Americas, New York, NY 10104 (spec mkts) *Toll Free Tel:* 800-222-6747 *Toll Free Fax:* 800-477-5925
Foreign Rights: Agencia Literaria Carmen Balcells SA (Portugal, Spain); Bardon-Chinese Media Agency (China, Taiwan); BMSR Ag Literaria (Brazil); The Italian Literary Agency srl (Italy); JLM Literary Agency (Greece); Nurcihan Kesim Literary Agency (Turkey); The KM Agency (Netherlands); Agence Michelle Lapautre (France); Mohrbooks AG Literary Agency (Germany); Andrew Nurnberg Associates Ltd (Baltic States, Bulgaria, Croatia, Czechia, Hungary, Poland, Romania, Russia & former USSR); I Pitarski Ltd Literary Agency (Israel); Sane Toregard Agency (Scandinavia); Tuttle-Mori Agency Inc (Japan); Eric Yang Agency (Korea)
Orders to: Hachette Book Group, 53 State St, Boston, MA 02109 *Toll Free Tel:* 800-759-0190 *Toll Free Fax:* 800-286-9471
Returns: Hachette Book Group, 322 S Enterprise Blvd, Lebanon, IN 46052
Shipping Address: Hachette Book Group, 121 N Enterprise Blvd, Lebanon, IN 46052

Little, Brown Books for Young Readers
Division of Hachette Book Group
1290 Avenue of the Americas, New York, NY 10104
SAN: 200-2205
Tel: 212-364-1100 *Toll Free Tel:* 800-759-0190 (cust serv)
Web Site: www.hachettebookgroup.com
Key Personnel
EVP, HBG & Publr, Little, Brown Books for Young Readers: Megan Tingley
VP, Edit Dir, Picture Books: Andrea Spooner
VP, Assoc Publr: Jackie Engel
VP & Ed-in-Chief: Alvina Ling
VP, Creative Dir: David Caplan
Dir, Brand Publg, Licensing & Media Tie-in: Samantha Schutz
Edit Dir, Poppy & Nonfiction: Farrin Jacobs
Exec Dir, School & Lib Mktg: Victoria Stapleton
Exec Dir, Mktg: Emilie Polster
Dir, Subs Rts: Janelle DeLuise
Busn Mgr: Tom Guerin
Dir, Licensing & Mgmt: Sandra Cohen
Sr Mgr, School & Lib Mtkg Dir: Michelle Campbell
Assoc Dir, Creative Opers: Nisha Panchal-Terhune
Assoc Art Dir, Mktg & Communs: Becky Munich

Graphic Designer: Jessica Mercado
Digital Mktg Assoc: Valerie Wong
Mktg Coord: Bill Grace
Sr Mktg Mgr (YA): Stefanie Hoffman
Exec Dir, Publicity: Marisa Russell
Edit Dir, Graphic Publg: Andrea Colvin
Assoc Publicity Dir: Siena Koncsol
Sr Publicity Mgr: Katharine McAnarney
Founded: 1837
Specializes in board books, novelty items, picture books, middle reader, young adult fiction & nonfiction & selected media tie-ins.
ISBN Prefix(es): 978-0-316
Number of titles published annually: 284 Print
Total Titles: 1,845 Print
Imprints: LB Kids; Poppy
Orders to: Hachette Book Group, 53 State St, Boston, MA 02109 *Toll Free Tel:* 800-759-0190 *Toll Free Fax:* 800-286-9471
Shipping Address: Hachette Book Group Distribution Center, 121 N Enterprise Blvd, Lebanon, IN 46052 *Tel:* 765-483-9900 *Fax:* 765-483-0706
Membership(s): American Library Association (ALA); Association of American Publishers (AAP); The Children's Book Council (CBC); Women's National Book Association (WNBA)

The Little Entrepreneur
Imprint of Harper Arrington Publishing & Media
c/o Harper Arrington Media, 18701 Grand River, Suite 105, Detroit, MI 48223
Toll Free Tel: 888-435-9234 *Fax:* 248-281-0373
E-mail: info@startingaclothingline.com
Web Site: www.thelittlee.com
Key Personnel
Co-Founder & Publr: Jay Arrington; Michael Harper
Media Rel: John Thomas
Media Contact: Lance Smith
Founded: 2004
ISBN Prefix(es): 978-0-9764161
Number of titles published annually: 3 Print; 1 CD-ROM
Total Titles: 4 Print; 2 CD-ROM; 1 Online
Distributed by Harper Arrington Publishing

Little Simon, see Simon & Schuster Children's Publishing

§Liturgical Press
Division of The Order of St Benedict Inc
PO Box 7500, St John's Abbey, Collegeville, MN 56321-7500
SAN: 202-2494
Tel: 320-363-2213 *Toll Free Tel:* 800-858-5450 *Fax:* 320-363-3299 *Toll Free Fax:* 800-445-5899
E-mail: sales@litpress.org
Web Site: www.litpress.org
Key Personnel
Dir: Peter Dwyer *Tel:* 320-363-2533 *E-mail:* pdwyer@litpress.org
Fin Dir: Sandra Eiynck *Tel:* 320-363-2225 *E-mail:* seiynck@litpress.org
Sales & Mktg Mgr: Brian Woods *Tel:* 320-363-3953 *E-mail:* bwoods@litpress.org
Founded: 1926
Began publishing for the church in 1926 & continues to sustain the original mission of proclaiming the good news of Jesus Christ. Liturgical Press is a trusted publisher of liturgy, scripture, theology & spirituality evolving to serve the changing needs of the church.
ISBN Prefix(es): 978-0-87907; 978-0-8146
Number of titles published annually: 80 Print; 50 E-Book
Total Titles: 2,500 Print; 950 E-Book; 20 Audio
Imprints: Cistercian Publications; Michael Glazier Books; Liturgical Press Academic; Liturgical Press Books; Pueblo Books

Foreign Rep(s): B Broughton Co Ltd (Canada); The Catholic Bookshop (South Africa); Claretian Publications (Philippines); John Garratt Publishing (Australia); Katong Catholic Book Centre Pte Ltd (Malaysia, Singapore); Norwich Books & Music (European Union, Ireland, UK); Pleroma Christian Supplies (New Zealand); Spring Arbor/Ingram (Tennessee)
See separate listing for:
Cistercian Publications

Liturgy Training Publications
Subsidiary of Archdiocese of Chicago
3949 S Racine Ave, Chicago, IL 60609-2523
SAN: 670-9052
Tel: 773-579-4900 *Toll Free Tel:* 800-933-1800 (US & CN only orders) *Fax:* 773-579-4929
E-mail: orders@ltp.org
Web Site: www.ltp.org
Key Personnel
Dir: Deanna M Keefe *Tel:* 773-579-4900 ext 3570 *E-mail:* dkeefe@ltp.org
Mng Ed: Michael A Dodd *Tel:* 773-579-4900 ext 3586
Mktg & Sales Mgr: Melissa Budak *Tel:* 773-579-4900 ext 3591
Sales Supv & Trade Rep: Irene Sanchez *Tel:* 773-579-4900 ext 3566 *E-mail:* isanchez@ltp.org
Founded: 1964
Books & periodicals on Roman Catholic liturgy, worship & prayer in the home & church.
ISBN Prefix(es): 978-0-929650; 978-1-56854; 978-1-59525
Number of titles published annually: 30 Print; 2 CD-ROM; 20 E-Book; 2 Audio
Total Titles: 500 Print; 6 CD-ROM; 80 E-Book; 7 Audio
Imprints: Catechesis of the Good Shepherd Publications; Hillenbrand Books
Distributor for United States Catholic Conference Publications (select titles)
Foreign Rep(s): The Catholic Bookshop (South Africa); Garrett Publishing (Australia); Katong Catholic Book Centre (Malaysia, Philippines); McCrimmons Bookstore/Publisher (UK exc Ireland); Pleroma Christian Supplies (New Zealand)
Membership(s): Association of Catholic Publishers Inc

Living Language
Imprint of Penguin Random House LLC
c/o Penguin Random House, 1745 Broadway, New York, NY 10019
Tel: 212-782-9000 *Toll Free Tel:* 800-733-3000 (orders)
E-mail: support@livinglanguage.com
Web Site: www.livinglanguage.com
Key Personnel
Pres & Publr, Penguin Random House Audio Group: Amanda D'Acierno
VP, Content Prodn: Daniel Zitt
VP, Mktg: Heather Dalton
VP, Publicity: Katherine Fleming Punia
Assoc Dir, Digital Content: Alison Skrabek
Ed: Suzanne McQuade
Founded: 1946
Self-study foreign language & ESL. Online courses & digital content; Sign Language & dictionaries. Penguin Random House & its publishing entities are not accepting unsol submissions, proposals, mss, or submission queries via e-mail at this time.
Total Titles: 15 Print; 83 Online; 140 E-Book; 62 Audio
Returns: Penguin Random House LLC, 1019 N State Rd 47, Crawfordsville, IN 47933
Distribution Center: Penguin Random House LLC, 400 Hahn Rd, Westminster, MD 21157 *Toll Free Tel:* 800-940-7046

§Living Stream Ministry (LSM)
2431 W La Palma Ave, Anaheim, CA 92801

Mailing Address: PO Box 2121, Anaheim, CA
92814-0121
Tel: 714-991-4681 Toll Free Tel: 800-549-5164
Fax: 714-236-6005
E-mail: books@lsm.org
Web Site: www.lsm.org
Key Personnel
Intl Rts Contact: Yorke Warden E-mail: yorke@
lsm.org
Lib Sales Dir: John Pester
Founded: 1963
Religious publications.
ISBN Prefix(es): 978-0-87083; 978-1-57593; 978-
0-7363
Number of titles published annually: 100 Print
Total Titles: 2,000 Print

Livingston Press
Division of University of West Alabama
University of West Alabama, Sta 22, Livingston,
AL 35470
SAN: 851-917X
Tel: 205-652-3470
Web Site: www.livingstonpress.uwa.edu
Key Personnel
Dir: Joe Taylor E-mail: jwt@uwa.edu
Founded: 1984
ISBN Prefix(es): 978-0-942979; 978-0-930501;
978-1-931982; 978-1-60489
Number of titles published annually: 8 Print; 8 E-
Book; 2 Audio
Total Titles: 140 Print; 90 E-Book; 2 Audio
Imprints: Swallow's Tale Press
Distributor for Swallow's Tale Press
Distribution Center: Small Press Distribution,
1341 Seventh St, Berkeley, CA 94710-1409
Tel: 510-524-1668 Toll Free Tel: 800-869-7553
E-mail: spd@spdbooks.org Web Site: www.
spdbooks.org
Membership(s): Community of Literary Maga-
zines & Presses (CLMP); Independent Book
Publishers Association (IBPA)

Llewellyn Publications
Division of Llewellyn Worldwide Ltd
2143 Wooddale Dr, Woodbury, MN 55125
SAN: 201-100X
Tel: 651-291-1970 Toll Free Tel: 800-843-6666
Fax: 651-291-1908
E-mail: publicity@llewellyn.com;
customerservice@llewellyn.com
Web Site: www.llewellyn.com
Key Personnel
Publr: Bill Krause
Dir, Sales & Mktg: Tom Lund E-mail: toml@
llewellyn.com
Sr Publicist: Kat Sanborn Tel: 651-312-8452
E-mail: kats@llewellyn.com
Publicist: Jake-Ryan Kent
Founded: 1901
Body, mind, spirit. Trade publisher.
ISBN Prefix(es): 978-0-87542; 978-1-56718; 978-
0-7387
Number of titles published annually: 110 Print;
10 CD-ROM
Total Titles: 900 Print
Imprints: Llewellyn; Midnight Ink
Distributor for Blue Angel; Lo Scarabeo
Foreign Rep(s): PGUK (Ireland, UK)
Foreign Rights: Oxana Schroeder (worldwide)
Distribution Center: Thomas Allen & Son Lim-
ited, 195 Allstate Pkwy, Markham, ON L3R
4T8, Canada Toll Free Tel: 800-387-4333
E-mail: orders@t-allen.com Web Site: www.
thomasallen.ca SAN: 115-1762

The Local History Co
112 N Woodland Rd, Pittsburgh, PA 15232-2849
Tel: 412-362-2294 Toll Free Tel: 866-362-0789
(orders) Fax: 412-362-8192

E-mail: info@thelocalhistorycompany.com;
sales@thelocalhistorycompany.com; editor@
thelocalhistorycompany.com
Web Site: www.thelocalhistorycompany.com
Founded: 2001
Publishers of history & heritage.
ISBN Prefix(es): 978-0-9711835; 978-0-9744715;
978-0-9770429
Number of titles published annually: 10 Print
Total Titles: 25 Print
Imprints: Towers Maguire Publishing
Membership(s): Independent Book Publishers As-
sociation (IBPA)

Locks Art Publications/Locks Gallery
Division of Locks Gallery
600 Washington Sq S, Philadelphia, PA 19106
Tel: 215-629-1000
E-mail: info@locksgallery.com
Web Site: www.locksgallery.com
Key Personnel
Dir: Sueyun Locks
Founded: 1968
Exhibition catalogue, monographs on contempo-
rary art.
ISBN Prefix(es): 978-1-879173; 978-0-9623799
Number of titles published annually: 8 Print
Total Titles: 45 Print

Loft Press Inc
9293 Fort Valley Rd, Fort Valley, VA 22652
Tel: 540-933-6210 Fax: 540-933-6523
E-mail: Books@LoftPress.com
Web Site: www.loftpress.com
Key Personnel
Pres & Publr: Stephen R Hunter
Ed-in-Chief: Ann A Hunter
Founded: 1987
ISBN Prefix(es): 978-0-9630797; 978-1-893846
Number of titles published annually: 3 Print; 2
CD-ROM
Total Titles: 139 Print; 2 CD-ROM; 1 E-Book
Imprints: Eschat Press (religion); Far Muse Press;
Merry Muse Press; Punch Press
Subsidiaries: AAH Graphics Inc
Advertising Agency: AAH Advertising Tel: 540-
933-6211
Membership(s): Washington Publishers (WP)

Logos Press
Imprint of thinkBiotech LLC
3909 Witmer Rd, Suite 416, Niagara Falls, NY
14305
Fax: 815-346-3514
E-mail: info@logos-press.com
Web Site: www.logos-press.com
Key Personnel
Ed: Yali Friedman
Founded: 2003
Specialize in reference & textbooks addressing
the use of knowledge to make intelligent strate-
gic decisions. Target audiences include college
& advanced courses, business managers, di-
rectors & C-level executives. The objective is
to help advanced students & decision makers
implement their ideas based on solid funda-
mentals.
ISBN Prefix(es): 978-0-9734676; 978-1-934899
Number of titles published annually: 4 Print; 4
Online
Total Titles: 12 Print; 4 Online

Lonely Planet
124 Linden St, Oakland, CA 94607
Tel: 510-250-6400 Toll Free Tel: 800-275-8555
(orders)
E-mail: info@lonelyplanet.com
Web Site: www.lonelyplanet.com
Key Personnel
Pres & CEO: Luis Cabrera
COO: Theo Sathanantha
Publr, Lonely Planet Kids: Hanna Otero

VP, Client Solutions: Jennifer Pentes
Dir, Sales (Americas) & Gen Mgr: Patricia Kelly
Sr Design Mgr: Gerilyn Attebery
Sr Sales Mgr & Children's Specialist: Peg
O'Donnell
Prodn Mgr, Lonely Planet Kids: Lisa Ford
Publicist, Trade Titles: Mariko Conner
Founded: 1973
Create & deliver the most compelling & compre-
hensive travel content in the world, giving trav-
ellers trustworthy information, engaging opin-
ions, powerful images & informed perspectives
on destinations around the globe. While known
primarily for its 600+ travel guidebooks, we
also offer an award-winning web site, photo-
graphic image library, television production,
distribution & digital travel content licensing.
ISBN Prefix(es): 978-0-908086; 978-0-86442
Number of titles published annually: 100 Print
Total Titles: 600 Print
Imprints: Lonely Planet Kids
Branch Office(s)
315 W 36 St, 10th fl, New York, NY 10018
230 Franklin Rd, Bldg 2B, Franklin, TN 37064
Foreign Office(s): 551 Swanston St, Carlon 3053,
Australia Tel: (03) 8379 8000
302 DLF City Ct, Sikanderpurj Gurgaon 122 002,
India
240 Blackfriars Rd, London SE1 8NW, United
Kingdom
Distributed by Hachette Book Group
Foreign Rep(s): A B E Marketing (Poland); Al-
tair (Spain); Asia Books Co Ltd (Thailand);
Asia Publishers' Services Ltd (China, Hong
Kong, Taiwan); David Bateman Ltd (New
Zealand); The Book Centre (Pakistan); Book-
traders Ltd (Cyprus, Czechia, Greece, Israel,
Malta, Middle East, Turkey); Brettschneider
(Germany); CDE (sales: English & French edi-
tions) (France); Centralivros (Portugal); TB
Clarke (Overseas Pty Ltd) (Fiji); CLB Market-
ing Services (Croatia, Hungary, Montenegro,
Romania, Serbia, Slovenia); CV Java Books
(Indonesia); Dinternal (Russia); Electra Me-
dia Group Pty Ltd (Guam, Micronesia, Philip-
pines); Eleftheroudakis SA (Greece); Faradawn
(South Africa); Freytag & Berndt U Artaria
KG (Austria); Geocentre ILH (Germany); Geo-
graphical Tours Ltd (Israel); IMA Distribution
(East Asia); India Book Distributors (Bombay)
Ltd (India, Nepal); Intercontinental Marketing
Corp (Japan); International Educational Library
(Greece); Kartbutiken (Sweden); Lannoo Pub-
lishers (Belgium); Logos Arri Srl (Italy); MPH
Distributors (Malaysia, Singapore); Nilsson &
Lamm Bv (Netherlands); Olf SA (Switzerland);
Raincoast Books (Canada); Cav Giovanni Rus-
sano SAS (Italy); Scanvik ApS (Denmark, Fin-
land, Iceland, Norway); Jana Seta (Latvia);
Shoestring International (Korea); Sklep Po-
droznika (Poland); Sodis (dist) (France); Text
Book Centre Ltd (Kenya); Trak Trade Centre
(Estonia); The Travel Bookshop (Switzerland);
Vijitha Yapa Bookshop (Pvt) Ltd (Sri Lanka);
Westland Sundries Ltd (Kenya); Yab Yay Yay-
imcilik Sanayi (Turkey)

§Long River Press
Imprint of Sinomedia International Group
360 Swift Ave, Suite 48, South San Francisco,
CA 94080
Tel: 650-872-7718 (ext 312) Fax: 650-872-7808
E-mail: editor@sinomediausa.com
Key Personnel
Sr Ed: Chris Robyn
Founded: 2002
Independent small press publishing trade titles in
Asian history, philosophy, culture, mind-body-
spirit. Unsol proposals are accepted but cannot
be returned without SASE.
ISBN Prefix(es): 978-1-59265
Number of titles published annually: 10 Print; 5
E-Book
Total Titles: 120 Print; 20 E-Book

Looseleaf Law Publications Inc
Division of Warodean Corp
43-08 162 St, Flushing, NY 11358
Mailing Address: PO Box 650042, Fresh Meadows, NY 11365-0042
Tel: 718-359-5559 *Toll Free Tel:* 800-647-5547
Fax: 718-539-0941
E-mail: info@looseleaflaw.com
Web Site: www.looseleaflaw.com
Key Personnel
Owner: Michael L Loughrey
VP & Edit: Mary Loughrey
Sales Dir: Hilary McKeon
Founded: 1967
Law books; study aids for law enforcement, students, attorneys & court personnel.
ISBN Prefix(es): 978-0-930137; 978-1-889031; 978-1-932777
Number of titles published annually: 200 Print
Total Titles: 25 CD-ROM

§Lorenz Educational Press
Division of The Lorenz Corp
501 E Third St, Dayton, OH 45402
Mailing Address: PO Box 802, Dayton, OH 45401-0802
Tel: 937-228-6118 *Toll Free Tel:* 800-444-1144
Fax: 937-223-2042
E-mail: order@lorenz.com
Web Site: www.lorenzeducationalpress.com
Key Personnel
VP: Debra Kaiser *E-mail:* debk@lorenz.com
Founded: 2008
Educational publishing division includes visual resources, instructional guides & reproducibles, elementary supplementals.
ISBN Prefix(es): 978-1-42911
Number of titles published annually: 10 Print
Total Titles: 75 Print; 75 E-Book; 7 Audio
Membership(s): Education Market Association

Lost Classics Book Company LLC
411 N Wales Dr, Lake Wales, FL 33853-3881
Tel: 863-632-1981 (edit off)
E-mail: mgeditor@lostclassicsbooks.com
Web Site: www.lostclassicsbooks.com
Key Personnel
Owner: Michael Alan Fitterling
Founded: 1996
Republish late 19th & early 20th century literature & textbooks to aid parents & teachers in educating children.
ISBN Prefix(es): 978-0-9652735; 978-1-890623
Number of titles published annually: 8 Print
Total Titles: 43 Print
Imprints: Road Dog Publications (motorcycle & adventure travel)
Distribution Center: National Book Network, 15200 NBN Way, Blue Ridge Summit, PA 17214 *Tel:* 717-794-3800 *Fax:* 717-794-3828
E-mail: customercare@nbnbooks.com *Web Site:* www.nbnbooks.com

Lost Horse Press
105 Lost Horse Lane, Sandpoint, ID 83864
Tel: 208-255-4410
E-mail: losthorsepress@mindspring.com
Web Site: www.losthorsepress.org
Key Personnel
Publr: Christine Holbert
Founded: 1998
Nonprofit independent press that publishes poetry titles of emerging as well as published poets & makes available fine contemporary literature through cultural, educational & publishing programs & activities.
ISBN Prefix(es): 978-0-9668612; 978-0-9717265; 978-0-9762114; 978-0-9800289
Number of titles published annually: 10 Print; 1 Audio
Total Titles: 126 Print; 2 CD-ROM; 1 Audio
Distributed by University of Washington Press

Distribution Center: University of Washington Press, 4333 Brooklyn Ave NE, Seattle, WA 98195 *Tel:* 410-516-6956 *Toll Free Tel:* 800-537-5487 *Fax:* 410-516-6998
E-mail: hfscustserv@press.jhu.edu *Web Site:* www.washington.edu/uwpress
Membership(s): Community of Literary Magazines & Presses (CLMP)

Lotus Light Publications, see Lotus Press

Lotus Press
Division of Lotus Brands Inc
PO Box 325, Twin Lakes, WI 53181-0325
Tel: 262-889-8561 *Toll Free Tel:* 800-824-6396 (orders) *Fax:* 262-889-2461; 262-889-8591
E-mail: lotuspress@lotuspress.com
Web Site: www.lotuspress.com
Key Personnel
Pres: Santosh Krinsky *E-mail:* santosh@lotuspress.com
Founded: 1981
Health, yoga, Native American & New Age metaphysics, Vedic astrology.
ISBN Prefix(es): 978-0-941524; 978-0-910261; 978-0-914955; 978-0-940985; 978-0-940676; 978-1-60869
Number of titles published annually: 6 Print; 2 CD-ROM; 2 Online; 15 E-Book; 3 Audio
Total Titles: 325 Print; 5 CD-ROM; 10 Online; 175 E-Book; 42 Audio
Imprints: Arcana Publishing; Dipti; Shangri-La; Specialized Software
Distributor for Back to Eden Books; Dipti; East West Cultural Center; Les Editions ETC; Inner Worlds Music; November Moon; SABDA; Sadhana Publications; Samata Books; Sri Aurobindo Ashram; Star Sounds
Warehouse: 1100 Lotus Dr, Bldg 3, Silver Lake, WI 53170

Louisiana State University Press
338 Johnston Hall, Baton Rouge, LA 70803
Tel: 225-578-6294
E-mail: lsupress@lsu.edu
Web Site: lsupress.org
Key Personnel
Dir: MaryKatherine Callaway *Tel:* 225-578-6144 *E-mail:* mkc@lsu.edu
Assoc Dir & Design & Prodn Mgr: Laura Gleason *Tel:* 225-578-6469 *E-mail:* lgleasn@lsu.edu
Mng Ed: Lee Sioles *Tel:* 225-578-6467 *E-mail:* lsioles@lsu.edu
Fin Opers Mgr: Becky Brown *Tel:* 225-578-6415 *E-mail:* rbrown1@lsu.edu
Founded: 1935
Scholarly, regional, general; humanities & social sciences; southern history & literature; poetry; government & political science; music; paperbacks; fiction.
ISBN Prefix(es): 978-0-8071
Number of titles published annually: 85 Print
Total Titles: 1,000 Print; 4 CD-ROM
Foreign Rep(s): Scholarly Book Services Inc (Canada)
Foreign Rights: McIntosh & Otis
Orders to: Longleaf Services Inc, 116 S Boundary St, Chapel Hill, NC 27514-3808 *Tel:* 919-966-7449 *Toll Free Tel:* 800-848-6224 *Fax:* 919-962-2704 *Toll Free Fax:* 800-272-6817 *E-mail:* customerservice@longleafservices.org *Web Site:* www.longleafservices.org
Returns: Longleaf Services Inc, c/o Ingram Publisher Services, 1250 Ingram Dr, Chambersburg, PA 17202
Warehouse: Longleaf Services Inc, c/o Ingram Publisher Services, 1250 Ingram Dr, Chambersburg, PA 17202
Membership(s): American Association of University Presses (AAUP)

Love Inspired Books
Imprint of Harlequin Enterprises Ltd
233 Broadway, Suite 1001, New York, NY 10279
SAN: 200-2450
Tel: 212-553-4200 *Toll Free Tel:* 888-432-4879 *Fax:* 212-227-8969
E-mail: customerservice@harlequin.ca
Web Site: www.harlequin.com
Key Personnel
Publr & CEO: Craig Swinwood
Exec Ed: Tina James
Ed: Emily Rodmell
Founded: 1997
Inspirational romance novels, romantic suspense & women's fiction.
ISBN Prefix(es): 978-0-373
Number of titles published annually: 192 Print
Imprints: Love Inspired®; Love Inspired® Historical; Love Inspired® Suspense
Distribution Center: 3010 Walden Ave, Depew, NY 14043

§Loving Healing Press Inc
5145 Pontiac Trail, Ann Arbor, MI 48105
SAN: 255-7770
Tel: 734-417-4266 *Toll Free Tel:* 888-761-6268 (US & CN) *Fax:* 734-663-6861
E-mail: info@lovinghealing.com; info@lhpress.com
Web Site: www.lovinghealing.com; www.modernhistorypress.com (imprint)
Key Personnel
Pres: Prof Victor R Volkman *E-mail:* victor@lhpress.com
Founded: 2003
Dedicated to producing books about innovative & rapid therapies to empower authors in redefining what is possible for healing the mind & spirit.
ISBN Prefix(es): 978-1-932690
Number of titles published annually: 15 Print; 15 E-Book
Total Titles: 250 Print; 250 E-Book
Imprints: AMI Press (official press of Applied Metapsychology International); Future Psychiatry Press (rethinking psychiatry & pharmacology); Marvelous Spirit Press (dedicated to helping your spiritual transformation & growth); Modern History Press (memoirs of people who have lived through significant events); Rocky Mountain Region Disaster Mental Health Institute Press (leading the way for strategic management of crisis response, first responders & rural responders); Victorian Heritage Press (showcasing the best of 19th century contemporary histories)
Foreign Rep(s): Ingram International (Australia, Europe, UK & Commonwealth)
Foreign Rights: IPR Licensing (worldwide exc USA)
Membership(s): Independent Book Publishers Association (IBPA)

Loyola Press
3441 N Ashland Ave, Chicago, IL 60657
SAN: 211-6537
Tel: 773-281-1818 *Toll Free Tel:* 800-621-1008 *Fax:* 773-281-0555 (cust serv); 773-281-4129 (edit)
E-mail: customerservice@loyolapress.com
Web Site: www.loyolapress.com
Key Personnel
Pres & Publr: Joellyn Cicciarelli
Exec Ed, Acqs: Gary Jansen
Busn Dev & Mktg Mgr: Andrew Yankech
Founded: 1912
Catholic publisher of books for elementary schools, parishes & the general trade.
ISBN Prefix(es): 978-0-8294
Number of titles published annually: 25 Print; 5 Audio

Total Titles: 350 Print
Returns: 677 Brighton Beach Rd, Menasha, WI
54952

LPC Books, see Lighthouse Publishing of the
Carolinas

LPD Press/Rio Grande Books
925 Salamanca NW, Los Ranchos de Albu-
querque, NM 87107-5647
Tel: 505-344-9382
E-mail: lpdpress@q.com
Web Site: nmsantos.com
Key Personnel
Publr: Paul Rhetts
Founded: 1984
Publisher of books on the American Southwest
& a quarterly magazine on the art & culture of
the American Southwest.
ISBN Prefix(es): 978-0-9641542; 978-1-890689;
978-1-943681
Number of titles published annually: 10 Print; 10
E-Book
Total Titles: 350 Print; 1 CD-ROM; 50 E-Book
Imprints: Rio Grande Books
Membership(s): Independent Book Publishers As-
sociation (IBPA); New Mexico Book Associa-
tion; New Mexico Book Co-op

§LRP Publications
360 Hiatt Dr, Palm Beach Gardens, FL 33418
Mailing Address: PO Box 24668, West Palm
Beach, FL 33416-4668
Tel: 561-622-6520 *Toll Free Tel:* 800-341-7874
Fax: 561-622-2423
E-mail: custserve@lrp.com
Web Site: www.lrp.com; www.shoplrp.com
Key Personnel
Pres: Kenneth F Kahn
Founded: 1977
Legal & general nonfiction in the areas of educa-
tion, bankruptcy, employment, disability, work-
ers compensation, personal injury & human
resources.
ISBN Prefix(es): 978-0-934753
Number of titles published annually: 500 Print;
10 CD-ROM; 95 Online; 5 Audio
Total Titles: 9,000 Print; 10 CD-ROM; 95 Online;
8 Audio
Subsidiaries: LRP Magazine Group
Divisions: Jury Verdict Research
Branch Office(s)
1350 Market St, Suite 202, Tallahassee, FL 32312
Tel: 850-219-9600
747 Dresher Rd, Suite 500, Horsham, PA 19044
Tel: 215-784-0941 *Fax:* 215-784-9639

LRS
Division of Library Reproduction Service
19146 Van Ness Ave, Torrance, CA 90501
Tel: 310-354-2610 *Toll Free Tel:* 800-255-5002
Fax: 310-354-2601
E-mail: largeprintsb@aol.com
Web Site: lrs-largeprint.com
Key Personnel
Pres: Peter Jones
Founded: 1946
Large print books for adults & children including
classics & fiction.
ISBN Prefix(es): 978-1-58118
Number of titles published annually: 10 Print
Total Titles: 150 Print

Lucent Press
Imprint of The Rosen Publishing Group Inc
29 E 21 St, New York, NY 10010
Toll Free Tel: 800-237-9932 *Toll Free Fax:* 888-
436-4643
Web Site: rosenpublishing.com
Founded: 1988

Curriculum-related nonfiction books aimed at the
junior high level that explore current issues,
historical topics, health, science/technology
& biography. Active series include: *Diseases
& Disorders, Hot Topics, People in the News,
Technology 360 & World History.*
ISBN Prefix(es): 978-1-56006; 978-1-59018
Number of titles published annually: 85 Print; 60
E-Book
Distributor for Greenhaven Press; KidHaven Press

§Lucky Marble Books
Imprint of PageSpring Publishing
2671 Bristol Rd, Columbus, OH 43221
Mailing Address: PO Box 21133, Columbus, OH
43221
Tel: 614-264-5588
E-mail: sales@pagespringpublishing.com
Web Site: www.luckymarblebooks.com
Key Personnel
Ed: Katherine Matthews *Tel:* 614-327-3676
E-mail: yaeditor@pagespringpublishing.com
Sales & Mktg Dir: Lynn Bartels
Founded: 2012
Independent publisher. Specialize in high quality
fiction for young adult & middle grade readers.
ISBN Prefix(es): 978-1-939403
Number of titles published annually: 3 Print; 3 E-
Book

Luna Bisonte Prods
137 Leland Ave, Columbus, OH 43214
Tel: 614-846-4126
Web Site: www.johnmbennett.net; www.lulu.com/
spotlight/lunabisonteprods
Key Personnel
Head & Intl Rts: John M Bennett
E-mail: bennettjohnm@gmail.com
Founded: 1974
Avant-garde to experimental literature & poetry.
ISBN Prefix(es): 978-0-935350; 978-1-892280;
978-1-938521
Number of titles published annually: 25 Print; 2
Audio
Total Titles: 400 Print; 53 Audio

Lutheran Braille Workers Inc
13471 California St, Yucaipa, CA 92399
Mailing Address: PO Box 5000, Yucaipa, CA
92399-1450
Tel: 909-795-8977 *Toll Free Tel:* 800-925-6092
Fax: 909-795-8970
E-mail: lbw@lbwinc.org
Web Site: www.lbwinc.org
Key Personnel
Pres: Rev Dennis Stueve
Founded: 1943
Produce & distribute free braille & large print
biblical & Christian literature in more than 30
languages for the blind & visually impaired in
over 120 countries.
Number of titles published annually: 5 Print
Total Titles: 200 Print

Lynx House Press
420 W 24 St, Spokane, WA 99203
Tel: 509-624-4894
E-mail: lynxhousepress@gmail.com
Web Site: www.lynxhousepress.org
Key Personnel
Dir & Ed-in-Chief: Christopher Howell
E-mail: cnhowell@ewu.edu
Assoc Ed: Kristina Morgan
Intl Rts: John Orr
Founded: 1972
Fiction & poetry.
ISBN Prefix(es): 978-0-89924
Number of titles published annually: 4 Print
Total Titles: 160 Print
Distributed by University of Washington Press

The Lyons Press
Imprint of The Globe Pequot Press
246 Goose Lane, Guilford, CT 06437
Tel: 203-458-4500 *Fax:* 201-458-4601
E-mail: info@rowman.com
Web Site: rowman.com/page/lyonspress
Key Personnel
Subs Rts Dir: Clare Cox *E-mail:* ccox@rowman.
com
Founded: 1978
Outdoors, natural history, sports, fitness, cooking,
military history, fishing, hunting, equine, non-
fiction, fiction, practical, Americana, outdoor
skills, pets, nautical, survival & adventure.
ISBN Prefix(es): 978-1-55821; 978-0-8329; 978-
1-58574; 978-1-59228; 978-0-936644; 978-0-
941130
Number of titles published annually: 180 Print
Total Titles: 1,500 Print
Distribution Center: National Book Network,
4501 Forbes Blvd, Suite 200, Lantham, MD
20706 *Tel:* 301-459-3366 *Web Site:* nbnbooks.
com

M U Press, see Marquette University Press

MAA Press, see The Mathematical Association
of America

Pat MacKay Projects, see Quite Specific Media
Group Ltd

§Macmillan
Subsidiary of Verlagsgruppe Georg von
Holtzbrinck GmbH
120 Broadway, 22nd fl, New York, NY 10271
Tel: 646-307-5151
E-mail: press.inquiries@macmillan.com
Web Site: www.macmillan.com
Key Personnel
COO: Andrew Weber
Pres, Macmillan Publishers US: Don Weisberg
Pres & Publr, Macmillan Children's Publishing
Group: Jon Yaged
Pres & Publr, Macmillan Audio: Mary Beth
Roche
Pres & Publr, Farrar, Straus & Giroux: Mitzi An-
gel
Pres & Publr, St Martin's Press: Sally Richardson
Pres & Publr, Tom Doherty Associates: Thomas
Doherty
Pres, Sales: Jennifer Gonzalez
EVP, Edit Devt & Content Innovation: Will
Schwalbe
EVP, Fin, Strategy & Analytics: Dan Schwartz
EVP, Mktg & Consumer Strategy: Jeff Carroll
SVP & Gen Coun: Paul Sleven
SVP, Communs & Events: Erin Coffey
SVP, Fin: Edward Garrett
SVP, Fulfillment: Guy Browning
SVP, Group Strategy & M&A: Kenneth Eng
SVP, Online & Digital Sales Opers & Analy-
sis/Mgr, Amazon, E-Book Sales & Sales &
Opers Teams: Tom Stouras
SVP, Publg Opers & Technol: Leslie Padgett
SVP, Strategic Publg Devt: Cristina Gilbert
VP & Dir, Academic & Lib Mktg: Peter Janssen
VP & Global HR Dir: Helaine Ohl
VP, Academic, Lib, Wholesale & Intl Sales:
Brian Heller
VP, Adult Mass Mdse Sales/Mgr, Dist Sales
Team: Laura Pennock
VP, Children's Sales Reporting: Jennifer Edwards
VP, Client Publr Sales & Dist: Nora Flaherty
VP, Client Publr Servs: Liz Tzetzo
VP, Field Sales & Publr Liaison: Tim Greco
VP, Intl Sales & Mktg: Devin Luna
VP, Sales Opers: Brian McSharry
VP, Spec Mkts, Premium Retail, Retail & Whole-
sale: Alice Baker
VP, Trade & CN Sales: John Edwards
Sr Dir, Busn Planning: Esther Kim

Sr Dir, Lib Mktg & Natl Accts Mgr: Talia Sherer
Sr Dir, Trade & Inside Sales: Christine Jaeger
Sr Natl Accts Mgr: Cristina Cushing
Dir, Communs: Catherine Marvin
Dir, Field Sales Team: Holly Ruck
Dir, Intl Rts: Marta Fleming
Dir, Natl Specialty Retail: Jackie Waggner
Dir, Talent & Devt: Sonali Goel
Ebook Channel Dir: Jonathan Hollingsworth
Sr Ebook Acct Mgr: Leigh George
Sr Natl Acct Mgr: Patricia Doherty
Sr Natl Accts Mgr: Jeanette Zwart
Sr Mgr, Sales Opers: Joseph O'Leary
Sr Mgr, Talent Acq: Natasha Taylor
Edelweiss Mgr: Daniela Plunkett
Intl Sales Mgr: Filipe Silva
Mgr, Global Trade Div: John Sargent
Natl Accts Mgr: Jaime Bode
Assoc Mktg Mgr: Kara Warschausky
Assoc Natl Accts Mgr: Susan Carner
Asst Client Acct Mgr: Vanessa Torres
Asst Mgr & Publr Liaison: Gretchen Fredericksen
Lib Mktg Coord, Young Adult: Emily Day
Natl Accts Sales Coord: Kristen Bonanno; Eunice Pak
Sales Coord: Jake Swirsky
Sales Coord, Adult Mdse: Kathleen McCutcheon
Sr Sales Analyst: Anthony Jimenez
Founded: 1986
Macmillan is the administrative, sales, distribution & information technology arm of the Macmillan group in the US, which includes Bedford, Freeman & Worth Publishing Group, LLC (W H Freeman, Worth Publishers & Bedford/St Martin's); Tom Doherty Associates, LLC (Tor & Forge Books); Faber & Faber Inc; Farrar, Straus & Giroux, LLC; Feiwel & Friends; First Second; Hayden McNeil; Henry Holt and Company, LLC; Macmillan Audio; Nature America Inc; Palgrave Macmillan; Picador; Roaring Brook Press; St Martin's Press, LLC; Scientific American Inc; Square Fish.
Distribution Center: MPS Distribution Center, 16365 James Madison Hwy, Gordonsville, VA 22942 *Toll Free Tel:* 888-330-8477 *Fax:* 540-672-7540 (cust serv) *Toll Free Fax:* 800-672-2054 (orders) *E-mail:* orders@mpsvirginia.com
See separate listing for:
Tom Doherty Associates, LLC
Farrar, Straus & Giroux, LLC
Henry Holt and Company, LLC
Macmillan Audio
Macmillan Learning
St Martin's Press, LLC

Macmillan Audio
Division of Macmillan
120 Broadway, 22nd fl, New York, NY 10271
Tel: 646-307-5151 *Toll Free Tel:* 888-330-8477 (cust serv)
Web Site: www.macmillanaudio.com
Key Personnel
Pres, Macmillan Publishers US: Don Weisberg
Pres & Publr: Mary Beth Roche
  E-mail: marybeth.roche@macmillan.com
VP & Assoc Publr: Robert Allen
VP & Mktg Dir: Samantha Edelson
Sr Art Dir: Margo Goody
Dir, Prodn: Guy Oldfield
Founded: 1987
ISBN Prefix(es): 978-1-55927; 978-0-7927; 978-0-940687; 978-1-59397; 978-1-4272
Number of titles published annually: 500 Audio
Orders to: MPS Order Dept, 16365 James Madison Hwy, Gordonsville, VA 22942-8501 *Toll Free Tel:* 888-330-8477 *Fax:* 540-672-7540 *Toll Free Fax:* 800-672-2054
Membership(s): Audio Publishers Association; Publishers' Publicity Association

§Macmillan Learning
Subsidiary of Macmillan
41 Madison Ave, New York, NY 10010

Tel: 212-576-9400 *Fax:* 212-689-2383
Web Site: www.macmillanlearning.com
Key Personnel
CTO: Chelsea Valentine
Chief Learning Offr: Dr Adam Black
SVP, Fin: Simon Horrer
SVP, Sales: Craig Bleyer
VP, Communs: Kate Geraghty
VP, Content Mgmt: Catherine Woods
VP, Strategy: Elizabeth Widdicombe
VP, Supply Chain: Bill Gadoury
Sr Dir, Content Standards & Accessibility: Rachel Comerford
Dir, Content Mgmt Solutions: Susan Brown
Gen Mgr: Susan Winslow
Founded: 1999
Imprints: Bedford, Freeman & Worth High School Publishers; Bedford/St Martin's; W H Freeman; Hayden-McNeil; Worth Publishers
See separate listing for:
Bedford/St Martin's
W H Freeman
Worth Publishers

§Macmillan Reference USA™
Imprint of Gale
27500 Drake Rd, Farmington Hills, MI 48331-3535
Tel: 248-699-4253 *Toll Free Tel:* 800-877-4253 *Toll Free Fax:* 877-363-4253
E-mail: gale.customercare@cengage.com
Web Site: www.gale.cengage.com/macmillan
Key Personnel
SVP, Gen Mgr: Paul Gazzolo
SVP, Mng Dir, Intl: Terry Robinson
SVP, Sales North America: Brian McDonough
VP, Mktg & Communs: Harmony Faust
ISBN Prefix(es): 978-0-02
Number of titles published annually: 22 E-Book
Total Titles: 92 E-Book

Mage Publishers Inc
4601 N Park Ave, No 1616, Chevy Chase, MD 20815
Web Site: www.mage.com
Key Personnel
Art Dir: Najmieh Batmanglij *E-mail:* nb@mage.com
Publr & Ed: Mohammad Batmanglij
  E-mail: mb@mage.com
Asst to Publr & Rts Contact: Amin Sepehri
  E-mail: as@mage.com
Founded: 1985
Persian literature, art & culture in English; poetry, fiction, art & history.
ISBN Prefix(es): 978-0-934211; 978-1-933823; 978-1-949445
Number of titles published annually: 4 Print
Total Titles: 75 Print
Imprints: Mage Persian Editions
Returns: 1708A Crossroads Dr, Odenton, MD 21113
Warehouse: BrightKey, 1780A Crossroads Dr, Odenton, MD 21113, Mgr: Sally Jack *Tel:* 301-604-3305 *E-mail:* sjack@brightkey.net
Membership(s): Association of American Publishers (AAP)

The Magni Co
Subsidiary of The Magni Group Inc
7106 Wellington Point Rd, McKinney, TX 75070
Tel: 972-540-2050 *Fax:* 972-540-1057
E-mail: sales@magnico.com; info@magnico.com
Web Site: www.magnico.com
Key Personnel
CEO: Evan B Reynolds *E-mail:* ereynolds@magnico.com
Co-CEO: Darlene Reynolds
Founded: 1982
Health & beauty, weight loss, informative & organizer books.
ISBN Prefix(es): 978-1-882330

Number of titles published annually: 5 Print; 1 CD-ROM; 3 Online; 50 E-Book; 2 Audio
Total Titles: 65 Print; 2 CD-ROM; 50 Online; 52 E-Book; 9 Audio
Imprints: MAGNI
Membership(s): American Booksellers Association (ABA)

Maharishi University of Management Press
Subsidiary of Maharishi University of Management
1000 N Fourth St, Dept 1155, Fairfield, IA 52557-1155
Tel: 641-472-1101 *Toll Free Tel:* 800-831-6523 *Fax:* 641-472-1122
E-mail: mumpress@mum.edu
Web Site: www.mumpress.com
Key Personnel
Dir: Harry Bright
Founded: 1974
Specialize in books about transcendental meditation.
ISBN Prefix(es): 978-0-9616944; 978-0-923569
Number of titles published annually: 5 Print
Total Titles: 50 Print
Distributed by Penguin Group USA, A Penguin Random House Company (select titles)

Management Advisory Services & Publications (MASP)
PO Box 81151, Wellesley Hills, MA 02481-0001
SAN: 203-8692
Tel: 781-235-2895 *Fax:* 781-235-5446
E-mail: info@masp.com
Web Site: www.masp.com
Key Personnel
Principal & Ed: Jay Kuong *E-mail:* jaykmasp@aol.com
Founded: 1972
A well established publications & advisory & training services company with a concentration in enterprise governance, internal controls, information technology security, auditing & contingency planning & business continuity fields. This includes reference books, journals & practitioners' manuals. Under the enterprise governance field, MASP publishes books on Sarbanes-Oxley compliance. Additionally, as part of the diversification efforts, we publish a few literary fiction books.
ISBN Prefix(es): 978-0-940706
Number of titles published annually: 3 Print
Total Titles: 75 Print
Foreign Office(s): Santa Fe Ave, Buenos Aires, Argentina, Contact: D Ramos
  E-mail: dramos@satlink.com

§Management Sciences for Health
200 Rivers Edge Dr, Medford, MA 02155
Tel: 617-250-9500 *Fax:* 617-250-9090
E-mail: bookstore@msh.org
Web Site: www.msh.org
Key Personnel
Deputy Dir, Pubns: Barbara K Timmons *Tel:* 617-250-9291 *E-mail:* btimmons@msh.org
Procurement Offr: Natasha Mahoney *Tel:* 617-250-9262
Founded: 1971
Established to assist, promote, evaluate, manage & perform research on the delivery of health care, establish methods & procedures leading to the improvement of health & social services & conduct education & publishing in these areas. MSH's publications unit develops & distributes books & a quarterly periodical to further MSH's mission, which is to help close the gap between knowledge about public health problems & action to solve them.
MSH currently stocks about 3 dozen products, most of which are books (including monographs, manuals & handbooks, some are available on CD-ROM). Many are available in lan-

guages other than English. Major products are The Manager continuing education quarterly; Managing Drug Supply (first published in 1981); instructional manuals (CORE, MOST, HOSPICAL, FIMAT); the Lessons from MSH & Stubbs monograph series; the series of success stories (20-page color booklets that present the highlights of successful programs) & books ranging from textbooks to syntheses of research.

MHS has offices in Afghanistan, Angola, Guinea, Haiti, Indonesia, Malawi, Philippines & Senegal.

ISBN Prefix(es): 978-0-913723

Number of titles published annually: 2 Print; 1 CD-ROM

Total Titles: 39 Print; 4 CD-ROM

Branch Office(s)

45 Broadway, Suite 320, New York, NY 10006

4301 N Fairfax Dr, Suite 400, Arlington, VA 22203-1627 *Tel:* 703-524-6575 *Fax:* 703-524-7898

Distributed by Kumarian Press

Membership(s): Independent Book Publishers Association (IBPA)

Mandala Earth

Imprint of Insight Editions

800 "A" St, San Rafael, CA 94901

Tel: 415-526-1370 *Toll Free Fax:* 866-509-0515

E-mail: info@mandalapublishing.com

Web Site: www.mandalaeartheditions.com

Key Personnel

Publr & CEO: Raoul Goff *E-mail:* raoul@insighteditions.com

Sales Dir: Julie Hamilton *E-mail:* j.hamilton@insighteditions.com

Sales Mgr: Jacqui Goff *E-mail:* j.goff@insighteditions.com

Full color coffee table books & minibooks, as well as decks, calendars, journals, greeting cards, art prints & incense. Topics include: environmental issues, women's studies, Asian art, music, philosophy, cross-cultural issues & Hinduism. Cutting-edge environmental & cultural topics that feature the unique voices & new concepts of leading thinkers, environmentalists, photojournalists, cultural commentators & artists.

ISBN Prefix(es): 978-1-886069; 978-1-932771; 978-1-60109; 978-0-945475

Number of titles published annually: 15 Print; 2 Audio

Total Titles: 300 Print; 200 Online; 10 Audio

Distributed by Simon & Schuster

Foreign Rep(s): Bill Bailey Publishers Representatives (Europe); Book Promotions (Jonathan Ball) (South Africa); Gilles Fauveau (Japan, Korea); Jaime Gregorio (Philippines); NewSouth Books (Australia, New Zealand); Penguin Books India (Bangladesh, India, Maldives, Nepal, Pakistan, Sri Lanka); Perseus International (Suk Lee) (Malaysia, Singapore); Perseus International (Edison Garcia) (Caribbean, Latin America, Middle East, North Africa); June Poonpanich (Cambodia, Indonesia, Laos, Thailand, Vietnam); Publishers Group UK (UK); Wei Zhao (China, Hong Kong, Taiwan)

Mandel Vilar Press

Affiliate of Americas for Conservation + the Arts

19 Oxford Ct, Simsbury, CT 06070

Tel: 806-790-4731

E-mail: info@mvpress.org

Web Site: mvpress.org

Key Personnel

Co-Publr & Press Dir: Dr Robert A Mandel *E-mail:* robert@mvpress.org

Co-Publr & Ed: Irene Vilar *Tel:* 303-330-6597 *E-mail:* irenevilar@gmail.com

Co-Founder & Ed: Dr Dena Mandel *Tel:* 806-790-4874 *E-mail:* mvpdmandel@gmail.com

Edit Admin: Lhotse Springer *E-mail:* lhotse@americasforconservation.org

Ms & Prodn Ed: Mary Beth Hinton *E-mail:* mbhinton2@gmail.com

Prodn & Design Mgr: Barbara Werden *E-mail:* barbarawerden@gmail.com

Founded: 2014

Nonprofit publishing arm of Americas for Conservation + the Arts (a 501(c)(3) organization) dedicated to connecting the literature of the Americas by uniting the works of the best writers of Latin & Latino America with the leading ethnic & minority writers of North America.

ISBN Prefix(es): 978-1-942134

Number of titles published annually: 5 Print; 5 E-Book

Total Titles: 15 Print; 12 E-Book

Distributor for Dryad Press

Orders to: Ingram Publisher Services, 210 American Dr, Jackson, TN 38301-5037 *Toll Free Tel:* 800-343-4499 *Toll Free Fax:* 800-351-5073 *E-mail:* ipsjacksonorders@ingrampublishers.com

Returns: Ingram Publisher Services, 193 Edwards Dr, Jackson, TN 38301-5070 *Toll Free Tel:* 800-343-4499

Warehouse: Ingram Publisher Services, 210 American Dr, Jackson, TN 38301-5037 *Toll Free Tel:* 800-343-4499 *Toll Free Fax:* 800-351-5073 *E-mail:* ipsjacksonorders@ingrampublishers.com

Distribution Center: Consortium Book Sales & Distribution, The Keg Housem Suite 101, 34 13 Ave NE, Minneapolis, MN 55413-1007 (an Ingram brand) *Tel:* 612-746-2600 *Toll Free Tel:* 800-283-3572 (cust serv, Jackson, TN) *Fax:* 612-746-2606 *E-mail:* info@cbsd.com *Web Site:* www.cbsd.com SAN: 200-6049

Manic D Press Inc

250 Banks St, San Francisco, CA 94110-0804

Mailing Address: PO Box 410804, San Francisco, CA 94141

Tel: 415-648-8288

E-mail: info@manicdpress.com

Web Site: www.manicdpress.com

Key Personnel

Publr & Intl Rts: Jennifer Joseph

Founded: 1984

Poetry & unusual fiction & alternative travel books, emphasis on innovative, new & established styles, writers & artists, paperbacks, general adult books.

ISBN Prefix(es): 978-0-916397; 978-1-933149

Number of titles published annually: 6 Print

Total Titles: 200 Print

Foreign Rep(s): Ingram Group; Publishers Group Canada (Canada); Turnaround Distribution (Europe)

Distribution Center: Consortium Book Sales & Distribution, The Keg House, 34 13 Ave NE, Suite 101, Minneapolis, MN 55413-1007 *Tel:* 612-746-2600 *Toll Free Tel:* 800-283-3572 (cust serv) *Fax:* 612-746-2606 *Web Site:* www.cbsd.com

Manning Publications Co

20 Baldwin Rd, PO Box 761, Shelter Island, NY 11964

Mailing Address: 5260 Mac Dr, Grand Forks, ND 58201

Tel: 203-626-1510

E-mail: sales@manning.com; support@manning.com (cust serv)

Web Site: www.manning.com

Key Personnel

Publr: Marjan Bace *E-mail:* maba@manning.com

Assoc Publr: Michael Stephens

Founded: 1990

Full-scale company whose titles are distributed in the US, Europe & Asia.

ISBN Prefix(es): 978-1-884777; 978-1-930110; 978-1-932394; 978-1-933988; 978-1-61729; 978-1-935182; 978-1-63343

Number of titles published annually: 25 Print; 10 E-Book

Total Titles: 300 Print; 20 CD-ROM; 200 E-Book

Distributed by Dreamtech Press; Pearson Education; Simon & Schuster, Inc (US & CN)

Distribution Center: O'Reilly Media Inc, 1005 Granvenstein Hwy N, Sebastopol, CA 95472 (US & CN) *Tel:* 707-829-0515 *Toll Free Tel:* 800-998-9939 *Toll Free Fax:* 800-997-9901 *E-mail:* retailcs@oreilly.com *Web Site:* www.oreilly.com

Woodslane Pty Ltd, Unit 7/5 Vuko Place, Warriewood, NSW 2102, Australia (Australia, New Zealand, Pacific Islands) *Tel:* (02) 9970 5111 *Fax:* (02) 9970 5002 *E-mail:* info@woodslane.com.au *Web Site:* www.woodslane.com.au

Dreamtech Press, 19-A, Ansari Rd, Darya Ganj, New Delhi 110 002, India (Bangladesh, Bhutan, India, Maldives, Nepal, Pakistan, Sri Lanka) *Tel:* (011) 43551180 *E-mail:* info@dreamtechpress.com *Web Site:* dreamtechpress.com

Pansing Distribution Pte Ltd, 438 Ang Mo Kio Industrial Park 1, off Ang Mo Kio Ave 10, Singapore, Singapore (Hong Kong, Malaysia, Singapore, South Korea, Taiwan, Thailand) *Tel:* 6319 9939 *Fax:* 6459 4931 *E-mail:* infobooks@pansing.com

Pearson Education, Edinburgh Gate, Harlow, Essex CM20 2JE, United Kingdom (Africa, Europe, UK) *Tel:* (01279) 623928 *Fax:* (01279) 414130 *E-mail:* enq.orders@pearsoned-ema.com *Web Site:* www.pearson-books.com

MapEasy Inc

PO Box 80, Wainscott, NY 11975-0080

Tel: 631-537-6213 *Fax:* 631-537-4541

E-mail: info@mapeasy.com

Web Site: www.mapeasy.com

Founded: 1990

Guidemaps & location guides to cities in North America, Western Europe & Asia.

ISBN Prefix(es): 978-1-878979; 978-1-929038

Number of titles published annually: 4 Print

Total Titles: 72 Print

MAR*CO Products Inc

PO Box 686, Hatfield, PA 19440

Tel: 215-956-0313 *Toll Free Tel:* 800-448-2197 *Fax:* 215-956-9041

E-mail: help@marcoproducts.com; sales@marcoproducts.com

Web Site: www.marcoproducts.com

Key Personnel

Founder & Dir: Arden Martenz

Pres: Cameon Funk

VP: Warren Funk

Founded: 1977

Educational guidance materials for elementary & secondary counselors, psychologists & social workers.

ISBN Prefix(es): 978-1-884063; 978-1-57543

Number of titles published annually: 12 Print; 20 Online; 25 E-Book

Total Titles: 300 Print; 400 Online

Distributed by ASCA; Boulden Publishing; Burnell Books; Calloway House; Career Kids FYI; CFKR Career; Character Development; Community Intervention; Courage to Change; Cress Productions Co; EDU Reference; Educational Media Corp; Incentive Plus; Jist; Mental Health Resources; National Center for Youth Issues/STARS; National Professional Resources; National Resource Center for Youth Services; Paperbacks for Educators; School Speciality; SourceResource; WRS Group; YouthLight Inc

Distributor for Boulden; Educational Media; HarperCollins; National Center for Youth Issues/STARS

Returns: 214 Kale Rd, New Bern, NC 28562
Distribution Center: NIMCO Bookstore

Marathon Press
1500 Square Turn Blvd, Norfolk, NE 68701
Mailing Address: PO Box 407, Norfolk, NE
68702-0407
Tel: 402-371-5040 *Toll Free Tel:* 800-228-0629
Fax: 402-371-9382
E-mail: info@marathonpress.net
Web Site: www.marathonpress.com
Key Personnel
Owner: Rex Alewel
Pres: Bruce Price
Founded: 1974
Books on professional photography.
This publisher has indicated that 90% of their
product line is author subsidized.
ISBN Prefix(es): 978-0-934420
Number of titles published annually: 5 Print
Total Titles: 650 Print

Maren Green Publishing Inc
5630 Memorial Ave N, Suite 3, Oak Park
Heights, MN 55082
Tel: 651-439-4500 *Toll Free Tel:* 800-287-1512
Fax: 651-439-4532
E-mail: info@marengreen.com
Web Site: www.marengreen.com
Key Personnel
Owner & Pres: Todd Snow *E-mail:* toddsnow@
marengreen.com
Founded: 2006
Fiction & nonfiction books for children newborn
to age 9.
This publisher has indicated that 100% of their
product line is author subsidized.
ISBN Prefix(es): 978-1-934277
Number of titles published annually: 5 Print
Total Titles: 25 Print
Imprints: Books Good For Young Children™
Distributed by Crabtree Publishing Co
Foreign Rights: Sylvia Hayse Literary Agency
(worldwide)

Marick Press
PO Box 36253, Grosse Pointe Farms, MI 48236
Tel: 313-407-9236
E-mail: orders@marickpress.com
Web Site: www.marickpress.com
Key Personnel
Founding Publr: Mariela Griffor
E-mail: mgriffor@marickpress.com
Assoc Ed: Christine Howson; Scott Minar
A not-for-profit literary publisher founded to pre-
serve the best work by poets around the world
including many under published women poets.
We seek out & publish the best new work from
an eclectic range of aesthetics - work that is
technically accomplished, distinctive in style &
thematically fresh.
ISBN Prefix(es): 978-0-9779703; 978-1-934851
Number of titles published annually: 8 Print
Total Titles: 70 Print

Marine Education Textbooks
124 N Van Ave, Houma, LA 70363-5895
SAN: 215-9651
Tel: 985-879-3866 *Fax:* 985-879-3911
E-mail: email@marineeducationtextbooks.com
Web Site: www.marineeducationtextbooks.com
Key Personnel
Opers Mgr: Gwen M Block *E-mail:* gwen@
ourmet.com
Ed: Richard A Block
Founded: 1970
Training & educational books for preparation of
USCG Exams. Marine safety signs, nautical
charts.
ISBN Prefix(es): 978-0-934114; 978-1-879778
Number of titles published annually: 6 Print

Total Titles: 40 Print
Imprints: Marine Survey Press

Marine Techniques Publishing
311 W River Rd, Augusta, ME 04330-3991
SAN: 298-7805
Tel: 207-622-7984
E-mail: promariner@roadrunner.com
Web Site: marinetechpublishing.com;
www.groups.yahoo.com/group/
marinetechniquespublishing
Key Personnel
Owner & Pres: James L Pelletier
Founded: 1983
Industry specific directories; maritime/worldwide
merchant marine; naval architecture; marine
biology, chemistry, geology; civil, marine en-
gineering; electrical, electronic marine engi-
neering; energy, oil & gas offshore; mechani-
cal marine engineering; transportation, marine.
Commercial merchant marine - worldwide di-
rectories, *Mariner's Employment Guide* & mar-
itime autobiographies (true maritime stories).
This publisher has indicated that 25% of their
product line is author subsidized.
ISBN Prefix(es): 978-0-9644915; 978-0-9798008
Number of titles published annually: 5 Print; 10
Online; 2 E-Book; 2 Audio
Total Titles: 25 Print; 8 CD-ROM; 10 Online; 2
E-Book; 2 Audio
Distributed by Elsevier Science, Technology &
Business Books; PennWell Business & Indus-
trial Division
Distributor for Academic Press; Best Publish-
ing Co; Butterworth-Heinemann; Clarkson
Research Services Ltd; Elsevier, Science &
Technology Books; Focal Press; Gulf Profes-
sional Publishers; PennWell Business & Indus-
trial Division; W B Saunders Co; Waterfront
Soundings Productions; Witherby Seamanship
International Ltd
Foreign Rep(s): Chapters Inc (Canada); W H
Everett & Sons Ltd (England, London, UK);
Lavoisier (France)
Distribution Center: Follett School Solu-
tions Inc, 1340 Ridgeview Dr, McHenry,
IL 60050 *Tel:* 815-759-1700 *Toll Free
Tel:* 888-511-5114 (cust serv) *Fax:* 815-
759-9831 *Toll Free Fax:* 800-852-5458
E-mail: info@follettlearning.com *Web
Site:* www.follettlearning.com SAN: 169-1902
Baker, Lyman & Co Inc, 5250 Veterans Memorial
Blvd, Metairie, LA 70006 *Toll Free Tel:* 800-
535-6956 *E-mail:* sales@bakerlyman.com *Web
Site:* www.bakerlyman.com
Emery-Pratt Co, 1966 W Main St, Owosso, MI
48867 *Toll Free Tel:* 800-248-3887 *Toll Free
Fax:* 800-523-6379 *Web Site:* www.emery-
pratt.com
Membership(s): American Maritime Association;
American Society of Naval Engineers; Asso-
ciation of Marine Engineers; The Association
of Publishers for Special Sales (APSS); Inde-
pendent Book Publishers Association (IBPA);
Independent Publishers of New England
(IPNE); Lloyd's Maritime Information Regis-
ter; Women's Maritime Association (WMA)

Markowski International Publishers
One Oakglade Circle, Hummelstown, PA 17036-
9525
Tel: 717-566-0468
E-mail: info@possibilitypress.com
Web Site: www.possibilitypress.com; www.
aeronauticalpublishers.com
Key Personnel
Publr: Mike Markowski
Founded: 1981
Books on personal development, business, suc-
cess, motivation, aviation & model aviation.
ISBN Prefix(es): 978-0-938716
Number of titles published annually: 6 Print
Total Titles: 40 Print

Imprints: Aeronautical Publishers; Possibility
Press
Membership(s): Independent Book Publishers As-
sociation (IBPA)

Marquette University Press
Division of Marquette University
1415 W Wisconsin Ave, Milwaukee, WI 53233
Mailing Address: PO Box 3141, Milwaukee, WI
53201-3141
Tel: 414-288-1564 *Fax:* 414-288-7813
Web Site: www.marquette.edu/mupress
Key Personnel
Dir: Dr Andrew Tallon *E-mail:* andrew.tallon@
marquette.edu
Mgr: Maureen Kondrick *E-mail:* maureen.
kondrick@marquette.edu
Founded: 1916
Publications in the humanities by scholars of in-
ternational reputation. Specialize in philosophy,
theology, humanities & history in addition to
regional studies relating to the city of Milwau-
kee & the state of Wisconsin.
ISBN Prefix(es): 978-0-87462; 978-1-62600
Number of titles published annually: 12 Print; 10
E-Book
Total Titles: 500 Print; 275 E-Book
Foreign Rep(s): Eurospan (Africa, Europe, Middle
East); Scholarly Book Services Inc (Canada)
Orders to: Baker & Taylor Publisher Ser-
vices, 30 Amberwood Pkwy, Ashland, OH
44805, Contact: Elaine Lattanzi *Tel:* 567-
215-0030 *Toll Free Tel:* 888-814-0208
E-mail: info@btpubservices.com *Web
Site:* www.btpubservices.com
Returns: Baker & Taylor Publisher Ser-
vices, 30 Amberwood Pkwy, Ashland, OH
44805, Contact: Elaine Lattanzi *Tel:* 567-
215-0030 *Toll Free Tel:* 888-814-0208
E-mail: info@btpubservices.com *Web
Site:* www.btpubservices.com
Distribution Center: Baker & Taylor Publisher Services, 30 Amberwood Pkwy, Ash-
land, OH 44805, Contact: Elaine Lattanzi
Tel: 567-215-0030 *Toll Free Tel:* 888-814-
0208 *E-mail:* info@btpubservices.com *Web
Site:* www.btpubservices.com
Membership(s): American Association of University Presses (AAUP); Association of Jesuit
University Presses

Marquis Who's Who
Imprint of Marquis Who's Who Ventures LLC
100 Connell Dr, Suite 2300, Berkeley Heights, NJ
07922
Tel: 908-673-0100 *Toll Free Tel:* 844-394-6946
Fax: 908-356-0184
E-mail: info@marquisww.com; customerservice@
marquisww.com (cust serv, sales)
Web Site: www.marquiswhoswho.com
Founded: 1899
Publisher of comprehensive biographical refer-
ences available in print, online & mailing list.
Major Marquis Who's Who publications in-
clude *Who's Who in America*, *Who's Who in
the World* & *Who's Who of American Women*.
ISBN Prefix(es): 978-0-8379
Number of titles published annually: 8 Print
Total Titles: 12 Print; 1 Online

Marriage Transformation LLC
PO Box 249, Harrison, TN 37341
Tel: 423-599-0153
Web Site: www.marriagetransformation.com;
www.transformationlearningcenter.com
Key Personnel
Pres: Susanne M Alexander *E-mail:* susanne@
marriagetransformation.com
Relationship & marriage education.
This publisher has indicated that 90% of their
product line is author subsidized.
ISBN Prefix(es): 978-0-9726893

Number of titles published annually: 3 Print
Total Titles: 8 Print; 20 E-Book
Distributed by Longman
Distribution Center: Ingram Content Group-Lightning Source, One Ingram Blvd, La Vergne, TN 37086 (US, Australia & UK)
Tel: 615-793-5000
Membership(s): National Association for Relationship & Marriage Education (NARME)

Marshall Cavendish Education
Member of Times International Publishing Group
99 White Plains Rd, Tarrytown, NY 10591-9001
Tel: 914-332-8888 *Toll Free Tel:* 800-821-9881
  Fax: 914-332-1082
E-mail: mce@marshallcavendish.com;
  customerservice@marshallcavendish.com
Web Site: www.mceducation.us
Key Personnel
Dir, US: Vivian Cheng
Accts Payable/Accts Receivable Assoc: Imelda Guarin
Sr Educ Consultant: Christopher Coyne
Educ/Sales Consultant: Thomas Corbia; Ellen Lauterbach
Founded: 1970
International publisher of books, directories, magazines & digital platforms. Products reach across the globe in 13 languages & our publishing network spans Asia & the US. Dedicated to the promotion of lifelong learning & self-development.
ISBN Prefix(es): 978-1-85435; 978-0-7614
Number of titles published annually: 320 Print; 10 Online; 300 E-Book
Total Titles: 1,200 Print; 57 Online; 590 E-Book
Imprints: Marshall Cavendish Adult Trade; Marshall Cavendish Benchmark; Marshall Cavendish Digital; Marshall Cavendish Education; Marshall Cavendish Reference
Distributed by Marshall Cavendish Ltd (UK)
Foreign Rep(s): Peter Pal Library Suppliers (Australia)
Warehouse: Swan Packaging, 415 Hamburg Tpke, Wayne, NJ 07470
Distribution Center: Baker & Taylor Publisher Services, 30 Amberwood Pkwy, Ashland, OH 44805 *Tel:* 567-215-0030 *Toll Free Tel:* 888-814-0208 *E-mail:* orders@btpubservices.com
  Web Site: www.btpubservices.com
Membership(s): American Library Association (ALA); The Children's Book Council (CBC)

Martindale-Hubbell, see Martindale LLC

§Martindale LLC
121 Chanlon Rd, Suite 110, New Providence, NJ 07974
SAN: 205-8863
Mailing Address: PO Box 1001, Summit, NJ 07902-1001
Tel: 908-464-6800; 908-771-7777 (intl)
  Toll Free Tel: 800-526-4902 *Fax:* 908-771-8704
E-mail: info@martindale.com
Web Site: www.martindale.com
Founded: 1868
Publisher of the *Martindale-Hubbell Law Directory* in hard copy, on CD-ROM & available online; containing listings of over 1 million lawyers & law firms worldwide. Other publications include *Law Digest*, a summary of laws from each of the 50 states & 80 countries; *Martindale-Hubbell International Law Directory*, designed for the international legal community & *Martindale-Hubbell Bar Register of Preeminent Lawyers*, listing of over 8,900 law practices designated as outstanding by members of the legal community.
ISBN Prefix(es): 978-1-56160; 978-1-934528; 978-1-60366
Number of titles published annually: 5 Print; 1 CD-ROM; 1 Online

Total Titles: 5 Print; 1 CD-ROM; 1 Online
Imprints: Martindale-Hubbell®

Martingale®
19021 120 Ave NE, Suite 102, Bothell, WA 98011
Tel: 425-483-3313 *Toll Free Tel:* 800-426-3126
  Fax: 425-486-7596
E-mail: info@martingale-pub.com
Web Site: www.martingale-pub.com
Key Personnel
CFO: Keith Brants
Publr: Jennifer Keltner
Dir, Mktg: Karen Johnson *Tel:* 425-368-1387
  E-mail: kjohnson@martingale-pub.com
Dir, Sales: Wendy Jacobson *E-mail:* wjacobson@martingale-pub.com
Founded: 1976
Quilting, knitting & crafting.
ISBN Prefix(es): 978-1-56477; 978-0-943574; 978-1-60468
Number of titles published annually: 55 Print; 55 E-Book
Total Titles: 250 Print; 300 E-Book
Imprints: That Patchwork Place
Returns: Returns Dept, Bldg A, Suite 500, 15100 Woodinville-Redmond Rd NE, Woodinville, WA 98072

Maryland Historical Society
201 W Monument St, Baltimore, MD 21201
Tel: 410-685-3750 *Fax:* 410-385-2105
Web Site: www.mdhs.org
Key Personnel
Dir, Pubns: Martina Kado, PhD *Tel:* 410-685-3750 ext 335 *E-mail:* mkado@mdhs.org
Founded: 1844
Publish historical books.
ISBN Prefix(es): 978-0-938420; 978-0-9842135; 978-0-9965944
Number of titles published annually: 5 Print
Total Titles: 45 Print
Distribution Center: HFS (Hopkins Fulfillment Services), 2715 N Charles St, Baltimore, MD 21218 *Tel:* 410-516-6965 *Toll Free Tel:* 800-537-5487 (US & CN) *Fax:* 410-516-6998 *E-mail:* hfscustserv@press.jhu.edu *Web Site:* hfs.jhu.edu

Maryland History Press
PO Box 206, Fruitland, MD 21826-0206
Tel: 443-397-0912
E-mail: ehpatterson@earthlink.net
Web Site: www.marylandhistorypress.com
Key Personnel
Pres: Elaine Patterson *Tel:* 443-397-0912
Founded: 1999
Editing, proofreading for almost any topic/web site. Publish books on diversified topics by various authors to help celebrate America's uniqueness...people, events, culture & environs. Services provided are publishing services, author-subsidy program, consignments, distribution services via national company, book searches & web site exposure through major online booksellers.
This publisher has indicated that 85% of their product line is author subsidized.
ISBN Prefix(es): 978-0-9703802
Number of titles published annually: 3 Print
Total Titles: 12 Print; 11 Online
Distributor for Tapestry Press Ltd
Warehouse: 109 Clyde Ave, Fruitland, MD 21826

Mason Crest Publishers
Imprint of National Highlights
450 Parkway Dr, Suite D, Broomall, PA 19008
SAN: 990-6800
Tel: 610-543-6200 *Toll Free Tel:* 866-MCP-BOOK (627-2665) *Fax:* 610-543-3878
Web Site: www.masoncrest.com

Key Personnel
CEO: Dan Hilferty *Tel:* 610-543-6200 ext 104
  E-mail: dhilferty@nationalhighlights.com
Pres: Louis Cohen *Tel:* 917-763-7760
  E-mail: lcohen@nationalhighlights.com
Cont: Diana Daniels *Tel:* 610-543-6200 ext 109
  E-mail: ddaniels@nationalhighlights.com
Intl Rts & Mktg Dir: Michelle Luke *Tel:* 812-604-1603 *E-mail:* mluke@nationalhighlights.com
Busn Devt: Becki Stewart *Tel:* 954-243-7180
  E-mail: bstewart@nationalhighlights.com
Cust Serv: Grace Baffa *Tel:* 610-543-6200 ext 113 *E-mail:* gbaffa@nationalhighlights.com
Founded: 2001
Mason Crest Publishers is committed to publishing the finest nonfiction school, library & curriculum products available today. Our titles are full-color & include a glossary, index, further reading section, Internet resources & are library bound. Subjects include reality shows.
ISBN Prefix(es): 978-1-59084; 978-1-4222; 978-1-59482
Number of titles published annually: 300 Print; 1,500 E-Book
Total Titles: 2,000 Print; 2,500 E-Book
Foreign Rep(s): Mare Nostrum Distributors (Maura Brescia) (Argentina, Chile, Uruguay); Missing Link Education CC (Farida Adam & Moreblessing Ngwenya) (South Africa); PSI/Publishers' Services International Inc (James Schmelzer) (worldwide); Saunders Book Company (James Saunders) (Canada); Target Book Sales (Jonathan Brooks) (UK)
Returns: 701 Ashland Ave, Bays 1 & 2, Folcroft, PA 19032, Opers Mgr: Lee Wark *Tel:* 610-583-0211 *Fax:* 610-583-0212
Shipping Address: 701 Ashland Ave, Bays 1 & 2, Folcroft, PA 19032, Opers Mgr: Lee Wark *Tel:* 610-583-0211 *Fax:* 610-583-0212
Warehouse: 701 Ashland Ave, Bays 1 & 2, Folcroft, PA 19032, Opers Mgr: Lee Wark *Tel:* 610-583-0211 *Fax:* 610-583-0212
Distribution Center: 701 Ashland Ave, Bays 1 & 2, Folcroft, PA 19032, Opers Mgr: Lee Wark *Tel:* 610-583-0211 *Fax:* 610-583-0212
Membership(s): Friends of Libraries of USA (FOLUSA); Independent Book Publishers Association (IBPA)

The Massachusetts Historical Society
1154 Boylston St, Boston, MA 02215-3695
Tel: 617-536-1608 *Fax:* 617-859-0074
E-mail: publications@masshist.org
Web Site: www.masshist.org
Key Personnel
Chief Technol & Media Offr: Chris Coveney *Tel:* 617-646-0539 *E-mail:* ccoveney@masshist.org
Dir, Communs: Carol Knauff *Tel:* 617-646-0554 *E-mail:* cknauff@masshist.org
Dir, Pubns: Ondine E Le Blanc *Tel:* 617-646-0524 *E-mail:* oleblanc@masshist.org
Worthington C Ford Ed of Pubns: Ondine E Le Blanc *Tel:* 617-646-0524 *E-mail:* oleblanc@masshist.org
Assoc Ed: Jim Connolly *Tel:* 617-646-0513 *E-mail:* jconnolly@masshist.org
Robert Treat Paine Papers Asst Ed: Christina Carrick *Tel:* 617-646-0576 *E-mail:* ccarrick@masshist.org
Founded: 1792
Scholarly historical regional publications.
ISBN Prefix(es): 978-0-934909; 978-0-9652584; 978-1-936520
Number of titles published annually: 3 Print
Total Titles: 500 Print
Distributed by University of Virginia Press

Massachusetts Institute of Technology Libraries
77 Massachusetts Ave, Bldg 14, Rm 0551, Cambridge, MA 02139-4307

E-mail: docs@mit.edu
Web Site: libraries.mit.edu/docs
Key Personnel
Dir, Libs: Chris Bourg *Tel:* 617-253-5297
   E-mail: cbourg@mit.edu
Assoc Dir, Admin: Keith Glavash *Tel:* 617-253-7059 *E-mail:* kglavash@mit.edu
Founded: 1863
MIT theses, dissertations, technical reports & working papers.
ISBN Prefix(es): 978-0-911379
Number of titles published annually: 2,000 Print
Total Titles: 15,000 Print

§Master Books®
Imprint of New Leaf Publishing Group Inc
3142 Hwy 103 N, Green Forest, AR 72638
Mailing Address: PO Box 726, Green Forest, AR 72638
Tel: 870-438-5288 *Toll Free Tel:* 800-999-3777
E-mail: sales@masterbooks.com; nlp@nlpg.com; submissions@newleafpress.net
Web Site: www.masterbooks.com; www.nlpg.com/imprint/master-books
Key Personnel
Pres, New Leaf Publishing Group: Tim Dudley
Ed-in-Chief: Laura Welch
Edit Asst: Craig Froman
Founded: 1976
Publish Biblically-based, scientifically sound creation materials & curriculum.
ISBN Prefix(es): 978-0-89051
Number of titles published annually: 25 Print; 20 E-Book
Total Titles: 425 Print; 3 CD-ROM; 70 E-Book; 2 Audio

Mastery Education
Subsidiary of Peoples Educational Holdings Inc
PO Box 513, Saddle Brook, NJ 07663-0513
Tel: 201-712-0090 *Toll Free Tel:* 800-822-1080
   Fax: 201-712-0045
E-mail: cs@masteryeducation.com
Web Site: masteryeducation.com; www.measuringuplive2.com
Founded: 1990
Publisher & marketer of print & electronic educational materials for the K-12 school market. We focus our efforts in test preparation, assessment & instruction & college preparation.
ISBN Prefix(es): 978-1-61526; 978-1-61527; 978-1-936025; 978-1-936027; 978-1-936028; 978-1-936029; 978-1-936030; 978-1-61602; 978-1-61734; 978-1-60979; 978-1-936026; 978-1-936031; 978-1-56256; 978-1-58984; 978-1-4138
Number of titles published annually: 50 Print
Total Titles: 2,000 Print
Imprints: Asante®; Measuring Up®
Membership(s): International Society for Technology in Education (ISTE®)

Materials Research Society
506 Keystone Dr, Warrendale, PA 15086-7537
SAN: 686-0125
Tel: 724-779-3003 *Fax:* 724-779-8313
E-mail: info@mrs.org
Web Site: www.mrs.org
Key Personnel
Dir, Communs: Eileen Kiley
Founded: 1973
Scientific reports on leading edge topics in materials research.
ISBN Prefix(es): 978-0-931837; 978-1-55899
Number of titles published annually: 30 Print
Total Titles: 1,100 Print

Math Solutions®
Unit of Houghton Mifflin Harcourt
One Harbor Dr, Suite 101, Sausalito, CA 94965
Toll Free Tel: 877-234-7323 *Toll Free Fax:* 800-724-4716

E-mail: info@mathsolutions.com; orders@mathsolutions.com
Web Site: www.mathsolutions.com; store.mathsolutions.com
Key Personnel
Founder: Marilyn Burns
VP & Gen Mgr: Patricio Dujan
Sr Dir, Mktg: Mary Garrison
Dir, Content Devt: Patty Clark
Dir, Prof Learning: Lisa Bush
Assoc Dir, Fin: John Fortune
Assoc Dir, Opers: Taber Auren
Assoc Dir, Opers & Busn Systems: Taeyana Kamir
Exec Ed: Jamie Cross *E-mail:* jcross@mathsolutions.com
Sr Mktg Mgr: Kelli Cook
Founded: 1994
Dedicated to improving the teaching of mathematics by providing professional development of the highest quality to teachers & administrators.
ISBN Prefix(es): 978-0-941355; 978-1-935099
Number of titles published annually: 10 Print
Total Titles: 80 Print
Returns: Houghton Mifflin Harcourt, Intervention Services Group Book Returns, 1900 S Batavia Ave, Geneva, IL 60134
Shipping Address: 1805 S McDowell Blvd, Petaluma, CA 94954, Contact: Taber Auren *Tel:* 707-769-0722
Warehouse: 1805 S McDowell Blvd, Petaluma, CA 94954, Contact: Taber Auren *Tel:* 707-769-0722
Membership(s): ASCD; National Council of Teachers of Mathematics (NCTM)

Math Teachers Press Inc
4850 Park Glen Rd, Minneapolis, MN 55416
Tel: 952-545-6535 *Toll Free Tel:* 800-852-2435
   Fax: 952-546-7502
E-mail: info@movingwithmath.com
Web Site: www.movingwithmath.com
Key Personnel
Founder & Pres: Caryl K Pierson
   E-mail: cpierson@movingwithmath.com
Founded: 1980
PreK-12 manipulative-based math curriculum.
ISBN Prefix(es): 978-0-933383; 978-1-891192; 978-1-931106; 978-1-59167
Number of titles published annually: 3 Print
Total Titles: 70 Print

The Mathematical Association of America
1529 18 St NW, Washington, DC 20036-1358
SAN: 203-9737
Tel: 202-387-5200 *Toll Free Tel:* 800-741-9415
   Fax: 202-265-2384
E-mail: maahq@maa.org; advertising@maa.org (pubns)
Web Site: www.maa.org
Key Personnel
Chief Busn Offr: Ben Spaisman
Exec Dir: Michael Pearson *E-mail:* mpearson@maa.org
Dir, Fin: Kimberly Rutland-Starks
Dir, Pubns Opers: Carol Baxter *E-mail:* cbaxter@maa.org
Sr Acqs Ed: Stephen Kennedy *E-mail:* kennedy@maa.org
Founded: 1915
Membership organization comprised of college mathematics educators, high school teachers & others interested in mathematics.
ISBN Prefix(es): 978-0-88385; 978-0-9835005; 978-1-939512; 978-1-61444
Number of titles published annually: 3 Online; 2 E-Book
Orders to: MAA Service Center, PO Box 91112, Washington, DC 20090-1112 *Tel:* 301-617-7800 *Toll Free Tel:* 800-331-1622 *Fax:* 240-396-5647 *E-mail:* maaservice@maa.org

§Maven House Press
4 Snead Ct, Palmyra, VA 22963
Tel: 610-883-7988
E-mail: info@mavenhousepress.com
Web Site: mavenhousepress.com
Key Personnel
Publr & Ed-in-Chief: Jim Pennypacker
   E-mail: jim@mavenhousepress.com
Desktop Publr, Ed & Indexer: Deborah Weiss
Founded: 2012
Publisher of nonfiction books (business, personal success, other).
ISBN Prefix(es): 978-1-938548
Number of titles published annually: 4 Print; 4 E-Book
Total Titles: 20 Print; 20 E-Book; 2 Audio
Foreign Rights: Russo Rights (worldwide)
Distribution Center: Publishers Group West, 1700 Fourth St, Berkeley, CA 94710 *Tel:* 510-809-3700 *Toll Free Tel:* 866-400-5351 *Toll Free Fax:* 800-838-1149 *E-mail:* ips@ingramcontent.com *Web Site:* www.pgw.com
Membership(s): The Association of Publishers for Special Sales (APSS); Independent Book Publishers Association (IBPA)

§Mazda Publishers Inc
PO Box 2603, Costa Mesa, CA 92628
SAN: 658-120X
Tel: 714-751-5252 *Fax:* 714-751-4805
E-mail: mazdapub@aol.com
Web Site: www.mazdapublishers.com
Key Personnel
Publr & CEO: Dr A Kamron Jabbari
VP: Fay Zamani
Ed-at-Large: Noel Silver; Ann West; Diane L Wilcox
Acqs Ed: Hilary Eastwood
Founded: 1980
Publishes scholarly books dealing with the Middle East, Central Asia & North Africa; critical reviews of poetry; Central Asia including art & architecture.
ISBN Prefix(es): 978-1-56859
Number of titles published annually: 32 Print
Total Titles: 634 Print
Imprints: Blind Owl Press

McBooks Press
Imprint of Rowman & Littlefield Publishing Group
246 Goose Lane, Guildord, CT 06357
Tel: 203-458-4500
E-mail: info@rowman.com
Web Site: www.mcbooks.com
Founded: 1979
Trade books. Specialize in historical fiction, vegetarianism, New York State regional books, period nautical, military fiction, sports including boxing.
ISBN Prefix(es): 978-1-59013
Number of titles published annually: 6 Print; 6 E-Book
Total Titles: 185 Print; 145 E-Book
Foreign Rep(s): Gazelle Book Services Ltd (Europe, UK)
Orders to: National Book Network *Toll Free Tel:* 800-462-6420 *Toll Free Fax:* 800-338-4550 *E-mail:* customercare@nbnbooks.com *Web Site:* www.nbnbooks.com
Distribution Center: National Book Network *Toll Free Tel:* 800-462-6420 *Toll Free Fax:* 800-338-4550 *E-mail:* customercare@nbnbooks.com *Web Site:* www.nbnbooks.com
Membership(s): Association of American Publishers (AAP)

Lisa McConnell Inc, see Big Guy Books

The McDonald & Woodward Publishing Co
695 Tall Oaks Dr, Newark, OH 43055

Tel: 740-641-2691 *Toll Free Tel:* 800-233-8787
Fax: 740-641-2692
E-mail: mwpubco@mwpubco.com
Web Site: www.mwpubco.com
Key Personnel
Publr & Intl Rts Mgr: Jerry N McDonald
E-mail: jmcd@mwpubco.com
Mktg Mgr: Trish Newcomb *E-mail:* tnewcomb@
mwpubco.com
Founded: 1986
Books (primarily adult) in natural history & cultural history; co-publish with educational & governmental entities.
ISBN Prefix(es): 978-0-939923
Number of titles published annually: 8 Print
Total Titles: 80 Print

Margaret K McElderry Books, see Simon & Schuster Children's Publishing

McFarland
960 NC Hwy 88 W, Jefferson, NC 28640
Mailing Address: Box 611, Jefferson, NC 28640-0611
Tel: 336-246-4460 *Toll Free Tel:* 800-253-2187 (orders) *Fax:* 336-246-5018; 336-246-4403 (orders)
E-mail: info@mcfarlandpub.com
Web Site: mcfarlandbooks.com
Key Personnel
Founder & Ed-in-Chief: Robert Franklin
E-mail: rfranklin@mcfarlandpub.com
Pres: Rhonda Herman *E-mail:* rherman@
mcfarlandpub.com
VP & Edit Dir: Steve Wilson *E-mail:* swilson@
mcfarlandpub.com
VP, Sales & Mktg: Karl-Heinz Roseman
E-mail: kroseman@mcfarlandpub.com
Sr Acqs Ed: Gary Mitchem *E-mail:* gmitchem@
mcfarlandpub.com
Acqs Ed: Charles Perdue *E-mail:* cperdue@
mcfarlandpub.com
Subs & Intl Rts: Adam Phillips
E-mail: aphillips@mcfarlandpub.com
Founded: 1979
A leading independent publisher of academic & nonfiction books, known for covering popular topics in a serious fashion & for manufacturing books to meet high library standards.
ISBN Prefix(es): 978-0-89950; 978-0-7864
Number of titles published annually: 385 Print; 380 E-Book; 3 Audio
Total Titles: 6,400 Print; 4,500 E-Book; 20 Audio
Imprints: Exposit Books; Toplight Books
Subsidiaries: McFarland & Co Ltd Publishers (London, UK)
Foreign Rep(s): Eurospan (Africa, Asia-Pacific, Australia, Europe, India, Middle East)
Returns: 961 NC Hwy 88 W, Jefferson, NC 28640
Shipping Address: 961 NC Hwy 88 W, Jefferson, NC 28640

§McGraw-Hill Career Education
Division of McGraw-Hill Higher Education
1333 Burr Ridge Pkwy, Burr Ridge, IL 60527
Tel: 630-789-4000 *Toll Free Tel:* 800-338-3987 (cust serv) *Fax:* 630-789-5523; 614-755-5645 (cust serv)
Web Site: www.mhhe.com
Key Personnel
VP & Natl Sales Mgr: Alan Hensley
E-mail: alan.hensley@mheducation.com
Mng Dir: Scott Davidson *Tel:* 314-439-6862
E-mail: scott.davidson@mheducation.com
Founded: 2001
Provides textbooks & educational materials to post-secondary, trade & career schools.
ISBN Prefix(es): 978-0-697; 978-0-256; 978-0-07
Number of titles published annually: 100 Print; 7 CD-ROM; 50 Online; 75 E-Book
Total Titles: 2,315 Print; 250 Online; 350 E-Book

Branch Office(s)
McGraw-Hill Learning Solutions, 8900 Keystone at the Crossing, Suite 950, Indianapolis, IN 46240
Returns: 860 Taylor Station Rd, Blacklick, OH 43004-0539
Distribution Center: 860 Taylor Station Rd, Blacklick, OH 43004-0539

McGraw-Hill Contemporary Learning Series
Division of McGraw-Hill Higher Education
501 Bell St, Dubuque, IA 52001
SAN: 201-3460
Toll Free Tel: 800-243-6532
Web Site: www.mhcls.com
Key Personnel
Pres, Sci, Engg & Mathematics: Kurt Strand
Tel: 563-584-6633 *Fax:* 563-584-6600
E-mail: kurt_strand@mcgraw-hill.com
SVP, Sales MHHE: Doug Hughes
Tel: 630-789-5121 *Fax:* 630-789-6944
E-mail: doug_hughes@mcgraw-hill.com
VP, Creative Solutions: Mr Christian Perlee
Tel: 732-275-1251 *E-mail:* christian.perlee@
mheducation.com
Founded: 1971
Thought-provoking series of supplements & online web sites appropriate for college-level courses or for library purchase. Materials span over 20 disciplines & cover compelling, current topics & issues. The publications include annual discipline readers, debate style readers, online readers, geographic/atlas readers & college textbooks.
ISBN Prefix(es): 978-0-07; 978-0-697; 978-0-87967; 978-1-56134; 978-0-7024; 978-0-7235; 978-1-25
Number of titles published annually: 50 Print; 50 Online; 125 E-Book
Total Titles: 350 Print; 350 Online; 246 E-Book

McGraw-Hill Create
Division of McGraw-Hill Higher Education
2 Penn Plaza, New York, NY 10121
Toll Free Tel: 800-962-9342
E-mail: mhhe.create@mheducation.com
Web Site: create.mheducation.com; shop.mheducation.com
Key Personnel
Dir, Content & Opers: Cat Mattura *Tel:* 201-618-2497 *E-mail:* cat.mattura@mheducation.com
Dir, Print Solutions, The McGraw Hill Cos: Beth Kundert
Custom products derived from McGraw-Hill copyrighted material; college textbook & ebook adaptations; supplemental materials.
ISBN Prefix(es): 978-1-308; 978-1-309
Number of titles published annually: 20 Print
Distribution Center: The McGraw-Hill Companies Distribution Center, 860 Taylor Station Rd, Blacklick, OH 43004-0504

McGraw-Hill/Dushkin, see McGraw-Hill Contemporary Learning Series

§McGraw-Hill Education
2 Penn Plaza, New York, NY 10121-2298
Tel: 212-904-2000
E-mail: international_cs@mheducation.com; seg_customerservice@mheducation.com (PreK-12); hep_customerservice@mheducation.com (higher education)
Web Site: www.mheducation.com
Key Personnel
Pres & CEO: Simon Allen
Chief Communs Offr: Catherine J Mathis
Chief Digital Offr: Stephen Laster
CIO: Angelo T DeGenaro
Pres, McGraw-Hill Education Higher Educ: William Okun
Pres, McGraw-Hill & Profl: Scott Grillo
SVP & Gen Coun: David Stafford

Pres, School Group: Heath Morrison
Founded: 1989
McGraw-Hill Education, a division of The McGraw-Hill Companies (NYSE: MHP), is a leading global provider of instructional, assessment & reference solutions that empower professionals & students of all ages. McGraw-Hill Education has offices in numerous countries & publishes in more than 40 languages.
ISBN Prefix(es): 978-1-259; 978-1-260; 978-1-264; 978-1-265; 978-1-266
Imprints: Glencoe/McGraw-Hill; The Grow Network/McGraw-Hill; Macmillan/McGraw-Hill; McGraw-Hill Contemporary; McGraw-Hill Create; McGraw-Hill Education Australia, New Zealand & South Africa; McGraw-Hill Education Europe, Middle East and Africa; McGraw-Hill Education Latin America; McGraw-Hill Education Mexico; McGraw-Hill Education Spain; McGraw-Hill Humanities, Social Sciences, Languages; McGraw-Hill/Irwin; McGraw-Hill Professional; McGraw-Hill Professional Development; McGraw-Hill Ryerson; McGraw-Hill School Education Group; McGraw-Hill Science, Engineering, Mathematics; SRA/McGraw-Hill; Tata/McGraw-Hill
Distribution Center: The McGraw-Hill Companies Distribution Center, 2460 Kerper Blvd, Dubuque, IA 52001-0545
The McGraw-Hill Companies Distribution Center, 860 Taylor Station Rd, Blacklick, OH 43004-0504
Membership(s): Association of American Publishers (AAP)
See separate listing for:
McGraw-Hill Higher Education
McGraw-Hill Professional Publishing Group
McGraw-Hill School Education Group

§McGraw-Hill Higher Education
Division of McGraw-Hill Education
1333 Burr Ridge Pkwy, Burr Ridge, IL 60527
Tel: 630-789-4000 *Toll Free Tel:* 800-338-3987 (cust serv) *Fax:* 614-755-5645 (cust serv)
Web Site: www.mhhe.com
Key Personnel
Group Pres, US Educ: Peter Cohen
SVP, MHHE Fin: Mona Leung *E-mail:* mona.leung@mheducation.com
SVP, Prods & Mkts: Kurt Strand *Tel:* 563-584-6633 *Fax:* 563-584-6600 *E-mail:* kurt.strand@
mheducation.com
SVP, Sales: Doug Hughes *Tel:* 630-789-5121
E-mail: doug.hughes@mheducation.com
VP, Content Prodn & Tech Servs: Kim David
Tel: 563-584-6650 *Fax:* 563-584-6701
E-mail: kim.david@mheducation.com
VP, MHHE Global Publg: Michael Hays
Tel: 212-904-5979 *Fax:* 212-904-5974
E-mail: michael.hays@mheducation.com
Founded: 1996
College texts.
ISBN Prefix(es): 978-0-07; 978-0-697; 978-0-256; 978-0-87; 978-1-25
Number of titles published annually: 1,100 Print; 50 CD-ROM; 750 Online; 800 E-Book; 5 Audio
Total Titles: 12,000 Print; 1,600 CD-ROM; 6,000 Online; 6,000 E-Book; 120 Audio
Imprints: McGraw-Hill/Irwin; McGraw-Hill Learning Solutions; McGraw-Hill Science, Engineering, Mathematics
Divisions: McGraw-Hill Contemporary Learning Series; McGraw-Hill Create; McGraw-Hill Humanities, Social Sciences, Languages
Orders to: The McGraw-Hill Companies, Distribution Center, 860 Taylor Station Rd, Blacklick, OH 43004-0539 *Toll Free Tel:* 800-338-3987 *Fax:* 614-755-5654
Returns: The McGraw-Hill Companies, Distribution Center, 860 Taylor Station Rd, Blacklick, OH 43004-0539 *Toll Free Tel:* 800-338-3987 *Fax:* 614-755-5654

Shipping Address: The McGraw-Hill Companies, Distribution Center, 860 Taylor Station Rd, Blacklick, OH 43004-0539 *Toll Free Tel:* 800-338-3987 *Fax:* 614-755-5654

Warehouse: The McGraw-Hill Companies, Distribution Center, 860 Taylor Station Rd, Blacklick, OH 43004-0539 *Toll Free Tel:* 800-338-3987 *Fax:* 614-755-5654

Distribution Center: The McGraw-Hill Companies, Distribution Center, 860 Taylor Station Rd, Blacklick, OH 43004-0539 *Toll Free Tel:* 800-338-3987 *Fax:* 614-755-5654

See separate listing for:
McGraw-Hill Career Education
McGraw-Hill Contemporary Learning Series
McGraw-Hill Create
McGraw-Hill Humanities, Social Sciences, Languages
McGraw-Hill/Irwin
McGraw-Hill Science, Engineering, Mathematics

McGraw-Hill Humanities, Social Sciences, Languages
Division of McGraw-Hill Higher Education
2 Penn Plaza, 21st fl, New York, NY 10121
Tel: 212-904-2000 *Toll Free Tel:* 800-338-3987 (cust serv) *Fax:* 614-755-5645 (cust serv)
Web Site: www.mhhe.com
Key Personnel
SVP, Prods & Mkts: Kurt Strand *Tel:* 563-584-6633 *Fax:* 563-584-6600 *E-mail:* kurt.strand@mheducation.com
SVP, Sales: Doug Hughes *Tel:* 630-789-5121 *Fax:* 630-789-6944 *E-mail:* doug.hughes@mheducation.com
VP & Ed-in-Chief: Mike Ryan *Tel:* 212-904-3044 *Fax:* 212-904-3813 *E-mail:* michael.ryan@mheducation.com
VP, Content Prodn & Tech Servs: Kim David *Tel:* 563-584-6650 *Fax:* 563-584-6701 *E-mail:* kim.david@mheducation.com
Founded: 1944
Publishes college textbooks & numerous ebooks.
ISBN Prefix(es): 978-0-07; 978-0-697; 978-0-87; 978-1-25
Number of titles published annually: 300 Print; 11 CD-ROM; 225 Online; 275 E-Book; 15 Audio
Total Titles: 3,500 Print; 150 CD-ROM; 2,500 Online; 2,500 E-Book; 225 Audio
Returns: 860 Taylor Station Rd, Blacklick, OH 43004-0539
Distribution Center: 860 Taylor Station Rd, Blacklick, OH 43004-0539

§McGraw-Hill/Irwin
Division of McGraw-Hill Higher Education
1333 Burr Ridge Pkwy, Burr Ridge, IL 60527
Tel: 630-789-4000 *Toll Free Tel:* 800-338-3987 (cust serv) *Fax:* 630-789-6942; 614-755-5645 (cust serv)
Web Site: www.mhhe.com
Key Personnel
SVP, Prods & Mkts: Kurt Strand *Tel:* 563-584-6633 *E-mail:* kurt.strand@mheducation.com
VP & Natl Sales Mgr: Doug Hughes *Tel:* 630-789-5121 *E-mail:* doug_hughes@mcgraw-hill.com
VP, Content Prodn & Tech Servs: Kim David *Tel:* 563-584-6650 *E-mail:* kim_david@mcgraw-hill.com
Founded: 1933
College textbooks & numerous ebook titles.
ISBN Prefix(es): 978-0-07; 978-0-697; 978-0-256
Number of titles published annually: 230 Print; 57 CD-ROM; 200 Online; 200 E-Book
Total Titles: 2,100 Print; 630 CD-ROM; 1,500 Online; 1,500 E-Book; 1 Audio
Returns: 860 Taylor Station Rd, Blacklick, OH 43004-0539
Distribution Center: 860 Taylor Station Rd, Blacklick, OH 43004-0539

§McGraw-Hill Professional Publishing Group
Division of McGraw-Hill Education
2 Penn Plaza, New York, NY 10121
Tel: 646-766-2000
Web Site: www.mhprofessional.com; www.mheducation.com
Key Personnel
CFO: J Garrett Henn
Pres: Scott Grillo
VP: James Shanahan
ISBN Prefix(es): 978-1-260

McGraw-Hill School Education Group
Division of McGraw-Hill Education
8787 Orion Place, Columbus, OH 43240
Tel: 614-430-4000 *Toll Free Tel:* 800-848-1567
Web Site: www.mheducation.com
Key Personnel
Chief Sales Offr: Pete Silva
Pres, School: Heath Morrison
Founded: 1971
Educational materials for elementary, middle school & high school.
ISBN Prefix(es): 978-0-02; 978-0-07; 978-0-31; 978-0-39; 978-0-53; 978-0-65; 978-0-67; 978-0-80; 978-0-84; 978-0-89; 978-0-93; 978-0-96; 978-1-57; 978-1-58; 978-1-88
Branch Office(s)
303 E Wacker Dr, Chicago, IL 60601 *Tel:* 312-233-6500
2 Penn Plaza, New York, NY 10121 *Tel:* 212-904-2000
Foreign Rep(s): The McGraw-Hill Companies (worldwide); McGraw-Hill Ryerson Limited (Canada)
Orders to: 860 Taylor Station Rd, Blacklick, OH 43004-0543 *Tel:* 614-759-3825 ext 3825 *Toll Free Tel:* 800-334-7344 *Fax:* 614-759-3670
Returns: 6405 Commerce Ct, Groveport, OH 43125
Shipping Address: 6405 Commerce Ct, Groveport, OH 43125 *Tel:* 614-835-2302 *Fax:* 614-835-2303
Distribution Center: 6405 Commerce Ct, Groveport, OH 43125 *Toll Free Tel:* 800-334-7344

§McGraw-Hill Science, Engineering, Mathematics
Division of McGraw-Hill Higher Education
501 Bell St, Dubuque, IA 52001
Tel: 563-584-6000 *Toll Free Tel:* 800-338-3987 (cust serv) *Fax:* 614-755-5645 (cust serv)
Web Site: www.mhhe.com
Key Personnel
SVP, Prods & Mkts: Kurt Strand *Tel:* 563-584-6633 *Fax:* 563-584-6600 *E-mail:* kurt.strand@mheducation.com
SVP, Sales: Doug Hughes *Tel:* 630-789-5121 *Fax:* 630-789-6944 *E-mail:* doug.hughes@mheducation.com
VP & Gen Mgr: Marty Lange *Tel:* 563-584-6648 *Fax:* 563-584-6601 *E-mail:* marty.lange@mheducation.com
VP, Content Prodn & Tech Servs: Kim David *Tel:* 563-584-6650 *Fax:* 563-584-6701 *E-mail:* kim.david@mheducation.com
Founded: 1944
College textbook publisher.
ISBN Prefix(es): 978-0-07; 978-0-697; 978-1-25
Number of titles published annually: 260 Print; 8 CD-ROM; 240 Online; 240 E-Book
Total Titles: 1,790 Print; 337 CD-ROM; 2,000 Online; 2,000 E-Book
Imprints: McGraw-Hill
Branch Office(s)
1333 Burr Ridge Pkwy, Burr Ridge, IL 60527 *Tel:* 630-789-4000 *Fax:* 630-789-5030
Returns: 860 Taylor Station Rd, Blacklick, OH 43004-0539
Distribution Center: 860 Taylor Station Rd, Blacklick, OH 43004-0539

McPherson & Co
148 Smith Ave, Kingston, NY 12401
SAN: 203-0632
Mailing Address: PO Box 1126, Kingston, NY 12402-1126
Tel: 845-331-5807
E-mail: bmcphersonco@gmail.com
Web Site: www.mcphersonco.com
Key Personnel
Publr & Ed-in-Chief: Bruce R McPherson
Founded: 1973
ISBN Prefix(es): 978-0-914232; 978-0-929701; 978-1-878352 (Saroff Editions); 978-1-62054
Number of titles published annually: 5 Print; 5 E-Book
Total Titles: 150 Print; 15 E-Book
Imprints: Documentext; Recovered Classics; Saroff Editions; Treacle Press
Subsidiaries: Waverley West
Foreign Rights: Kerigan-Moro Literary (Portugal, Spain); La Nouvelle Agence (France); Prava i prevodi (Bulgaria, Czechia, Hungary, Poland, Serbia, Slovenia); Literarische Agentur Simon (Germany); Rita Vivian Literary (Italy)
Orders to: PO Box 1126, Kingston, NY 12402-1126
Distribution Center: Central Books Ltd, 50 Freshwater Rd, Chadwell Heath RM8 1RX, United Kingdom (UK only) *Tel:* (020) 8525 8800 *Fax:* (020) 8599 2694 *E-mail:* contactus@centralbooks.com *Web Site:* www.centralbooks.com
Membership(s): Community of Literary Magazines & Presses (CLMP)

McSweeney's Publishing
849 Valencia St, San Francisco, CA 94110
Tel: 415-642-5609 (cust serv)
E-mail: custserv@mcsweeneys.net
Web Site: www.mcsweeneys.net
Key Personnel
Publr & Ed: Kristina Kerns
Publicity Dir: Eric Cromie *E-mail:* eric@mcsweeneys.net
Ed: Claire Eoyle
Founded: 1998
ISBN Prefix(es): 978-1-936365
Number of titles published annually: 25 Print
Total Titles: 150 Print
Foreign Rights: The Wylie Agency (worldwide)
Distribution Center: Baker & Taylor Publisher Services, 30 Amberwood Pkwy, Ashland, OH 44805 *Tel:* 567-215-0030 *Toll Free Tel:* 888-814-0208 *E-mail:* orders@btpubservices.com
Web Site: www.btpubservices.com

MDR, A D&B Co
6 Armstrong Rd, Suite 301, Shelton, CT 06484
Tel: 203-926-4800 *Toll Free Tel:* 800-333-8802 *Fax:* 203-225-4603 *Toll Free Fax:* 866-532-7097
E-mail: mdrinfo@dnb.com
Web Site: mdreducation.com
Key Personnel
Gen Mgr: Aaron Stibel *Tel:* 203-225-4827
VP, Mktg: Kristina James *Tel:* 312-345-4356
Founded: 1969
First choice for marketing information & services for the K-12, higher education, library, early childhood & related education markets. Powered by the most complete, current & accurate education databases available in the industry, MDR provides e-mail contacts & deployment, direct mail lists, sales contact & lead solutions, along with web & social media marketing services.
ISBN Prefix(es): 978-1-57953; 978-1-943664
Number of titles published annually: 53 Print
Branch Office(s)
20 S Clark St, Suite 2100, Chicago, IL 60603, VP, Clients: Steve Gatland *Tel:* 312-263-4169 *Fax:* 312-345-4360

me+mi publishing inc
2600 Beverly Dr, Unit 113, Aurora, IL 60502
Tel: 630-588-9801 *Toll Free Tel:* 888-251-1444
Web Site: www.memima.com
Key Personnel
Principal & Publr: Gladys Rosa-Mendoza; Mark
Wesley
Founded: 2002
Independent publisher dedicated to creating the
highest quality books available in 2 or more
languages for infants & toddlers.
ISBN Prefix(es): 978-0-9679748; 978-1-931398
Total Titles: 33 Print
Imprints: The English Spanish Foundation Series
Membership(s): Independent Book Publishers As-
sociation (IBPA)

§R S Means from The Gordian Group
1099 Hingham St, Suite 201, Rockland, MA
02370
Toll Free Tel: 800-448-8182 (cust serv); 800-334-
3509 (sales) *Toll Free Fax:* 800-632-6732
Web Site: www.rsmeans.com
Founded: 1942
A leader in construction cost estimating data, an-
alytics & life cycle cost analysis available in 4
convenient formats: online, books, ebooks +/or
CDs.
ISBN Prefix(es): 978-0-911950; 978-0-87629;
978-1-936335
Number of titles published annually: 25 Print
Total Titles: 150 Print
Divisions: Cost Annuals
Distributed by John Wiley & Sons Inc
Advertising Agency: The Stancliff Agency

Medals of America Press
Division of Medals of America
114 Southchase Blvd, Fountain Inn, SC 29644
Toll Free Tel: 800-605-4001 *Toll Free Fax:* 800-
407-8640
Web Site: moapress.com
Key Personnel
Publr: Frank Foster *Tel:* 864-275-1527 *Fax:* 864-
601-1108 *E-mail:* ffoster@moapress.com
Wholesale Mgr: Steve Heckenthorn
E-mail: sheck@usmedals.com
Founded: 1992
Offer complete illustrated guides to United States
military medals, decorations & insignia of the
Army, Navy, Marines, Air Force, Coast Guard
& Merchant Marines, United Nations & Viet-
nam.
ISBN Prefix(es): 978-1-884452
Number of titles published annually: 6 Print; 1
CD-ROM; 18 Online; 8 E-Book
Total Titles: 16 Print; 1 CD-ROM; 18 Online; 12
E-Book
Imprints: Military Medals of America
Distributed by Medals of America

MedBooks Inc
Division of Professional Education Workshops &
Seminars
PO Box 12805, Dallas, TX 75225
Tel: 972-643-1809; 972-643-1802 *Fax:* 972-643-
1859
E-mail: medbooks@medbooks.com;
customerservice@medbooks.com; sales@
medbooks.com
Web Site: www.medbooks.com
Key Personnel
Owner & Pres: Patrice Morin-Spatz *Tel:* 972-955-
4855 (cell) *E-mail:* A81056@hotmail.com
Founded: 1985
Specialize in books on health insurance coding &
processing for medical offices, insurance com-
panies & other health professions.
ISBN Prefix(es): 978-0-923369; 978-0-9762699;
978-0-9822597; 978-0-9773154; 978-0-
9831904; 978-0-9790318; 978-0-9797234; 978-
0-9800627; 978-1-937816

Number of titles published annually: 5 Print
Total Titles: 25 Print
Distributed by JA Majors
Membership(s): Independent Book Publishers As-
sociation (IBPA); Textbook & Academic Au-
thors Association (TAA)

**Medical Group Management Association
(MGMA)**
104 Inverness Terr E, Englewood, CO 80112-
5306
Tel: 303-799-1111; 303-799-1111 (ext 1888, book
orders) *Toll Free Tel:* 877-275-6462
E-mail: support@mgma.com; infocenter@mgma.
com
Web Site: www.mgma.com
Founded: 1926
Specialize in medical practice management.
ISBN Prefix(es): 978-1-56829; 978-0-933948
Number of titles published annually: 8 Print; 4
CD-ROM; 1 E-Book
Total Titles: 150 Print; 15 CD-ROM; 1 E-Book; 2
Audio
Branch Office(s)
Government Affairs, 1717 Pennsylvania Ave
NW, No 600, Washington, DC 20006, Con-
tact: Anders Gilberg *Tel:* 202-293-3450
E-mail: govaff@mgma.org
Distributor for American Medical Association;
Aspen Publishers; Greenbranch; HAP (Health
Adminstration Press); Jones & Bartlett Learn-
ing; J Wiley & Sons

Medical Physics Publishing Corp (MPP)
4555 Helgesen Dr, Madison, WI 53718
Tel: 608-262-4021; 608-224-4508
Toll Free Tel: 800-442-5778 (cust serv)
Fax: 608-224-5016
E-mail: mpp@medicalphysics.org
Web Site: www.medicalphysics.org
Key Personnel
Gen Mgr & Intl Rts: Ms Bobbett Shaub *Tel:* 608-
224-4508 *E-mail:* bobbett@medicalphysics.org
Ed: Todd Hanson *E-mail:* todd@medicalphysics.
org
Founded: 1985
Publish & distribute books in medical physics &
related fields.
ISBN Prefix(es): 978-0-944838; 978-1-930524
Number of titles published annually: 6 Print; 6 E-
Book
Total Titles: 100 Print; 8 CD-ROM; 35 Online;
35 E-Book

Medieval Institute Publications
Division of Medieval Institute of Western Michi-
gan University
WMU East Campus, 100-E Walwood Hall, Kala-
mazoo, MI 49008
Mailing Address: 1903 W Michigan Ave, Kala-
mazoo, MI 49008-5432
Tel: 269-387-8754 *Fax:* 269-387-8750
Web Site: www.wmich.edu/medievalpublications
Key Personnel
Dir: Jana K Schulman *Tel:* 269-387-8745
Ed-in-Chief: Theresa Whitaker *Tel:* 269-387-8747
Founded: 1978
Academic publications on late antique & me-
dieval studies.
ISBN Prefix(es): 978-1-918720; 978-1-879288;
978-1-58044
Number of titles published annually: 14 Print
Total Titles: 215 Print
Membership(s): Association of University Presses
(AUPresses)

§MedMaster Inc
3337 Hollywood Oaks Dr, Fort Lauderdale, FL
33312
Mailing Address: PO Box 640028, Miami, FL
33164-0028

Tel: 954-962-8414 *Toll Free Tel:* 800-335-3480
Fax: 954-962-4508
E-mail: mmbks@aol.com
Web Site: www.medmaster.net
Key Personnel
Founder & Pres: Stephen Goldberg
E-mail: stgoldberg@aol.com
VP & Secy: Michael Goldberg
Founded: 1979
Medical book & software publishers; medical
subjects for education of medical students &
other health professionals.
This publisher has indicated that 100% of their
product line is author subsidized.
ISBN Prefix(es): 978-0-940780; 978-1-935660
Number of titles published annually: 6 Print; 1
CD-ROM; 1 E-Book
Total Titles: 31 Print; 8 CD-ROM
Warehouse: 360 NE 191 St, Miami, FL 33179

Mel Bay Publications Inc
1734 Gilsinn Lane, Fenton, MO 63026
Tel: 636-257-3970 *Toll Free Tel:* 800-863-5229
Fax: 636-257-5062 *Toll Free Fax:* 800-660-
9818
E-mail: email@melbay.com
Web Site: www.melbay.com
Key Personnel
Pres: Bill Bay
Acct Mgr: Julie Wakefield *E-mail:* julie@melbay.
com
Info Systems Mgr: Sharon Feldmann
E-mail: sharon@melbay.com
Founded: 1947
Innovative instructional & performance material
for most instruments.
ISBN Prefix(es): 978-0-7866; 978-0-87166; 978-
1-56222; 978-1-60974; 978-1-61065; 978-1-
61911; 978-1-5134
Number of titles published annually: 60 Print; 60
E-Book
Total Titles: 4,000 Print; 2,600 E-Book
Imprints: Mel Bay
Distributor for AMA; William Bay Music; Danc-
ing Hands; Stefan Grossman's Guitar Work-
shop

The Edwin Mellen Press
240 Portage Rd, Lewiston, NY 14092
Mailing Address: PO Box 450, Lewiston, NY
14092-0450 SAN: 207-110X
Tel: 716-754-2266; 716-754-2788 (order fulfill-
ment) *Fax:* 716-754-4056
E-mail: editor@mellenpress.com
Web Site: www.mellenpress.com
Key Personnel
Founder & Publr: Herbert Richardson
Dir & Acqs: Dr John Rupnow *E-mail:* jrupnow@
mellenpress.com
Fulfillment Dir: Irene Miller *E-mail:* imiller@
mellenpress.com
Prodn Mgr & Perms Ed: Patricia Schultz
E-mail: pschultz@mellenpress.com
Founded: 1974
Non-subsidy academic publisher of books in the
humanities of social sciences. Publish mono-
graphs, critical editions, collections, transla-
tions, revisionist studies, constructive essays,
bibliographies, dictionaries, reference guides &
dissertations.
ISBN Prefix(es): 978-0-88946; 978-0-7734; 978-
0-935106; 978-0-7799; 978-1-4955
Number of titles published annually: 200 Print
Total Titles: 8,000 Print
Foreign Office(s): The Edwin Mellen Press
Ltd, 16 College St, Lampeter, Ceredigion
SA48 7DY, United Kingdom, Mgr, Wales/
UK Off: Iona Williams *Tel:* (01570) 423
356 *Fax:* (01570) 423 775 *E-mail:* emp@
mellenpress.co.uk *Web Site:* www.mellenpress.
co.uk
Advertising Agency: Lewiston Business Services

137

Menasha Ridge Press
Imprint of AdventureKEEN
2204 First Ave S, Suite 102, Birmingham, AL
35233
Toll Free Tel: 888-604-4537 *Fax:* 205-326-1012
E-mail: info@adventurewithkeen.com
Web Site: www.menasharidge.com; www.
adventurewithkeen.com
Key Personnel
COO: Molly B Merkle *Tel:* 205-443-7993
Publr: Robert W Sehlinger
Mktg & Publicity: Tanya Sylvan *E-mail:* tanya@
adventurewithkeen.com
Founded: 1982
Outdoor recreation, travel, nature & reference
guides.
ISBN Prefix(es): 978-0-89732; 978-1-63404
Number of titles published annually: 35 Print; 35
E-Book
Total Titles: 226 Print; 200 E-Book
Orders to: Publishers Group West, 1700 Fourth
St, Berkeley, CA 94710 *Tel:* 510-809-3700 *Toll
Free Tel:* 800-788-3123 *Fax:* 510-809-3733
E-mail: tom.lupoff@pgw.com *Web Site:* www.
pgw.com
Returns: Keen Communications, Returns Dept,
1700 Madison Rd, Cincinnati, OH 45206
E-mail: info@keencommunication.com *Web
Site:* keencommunication.com
Membership(s): American Booksellers Associa-
tion (ABA); Southern Independent Booksellers
Alliance (SIBA)

§MennoMedia
100 S Mason St, Suite B, Harrisonburg, VA
22801
Mailing Address: PO Box 866, Harrisonburg, VA
22803
Toll Free Tel: 800-245-7894 (orders & cust serv
US) *Toll Free Fax:* 877-271-0760
E-mail: info@mennomedia.org
Web Site: www.mennomedia.org
Key Personnel
Exec Dir & Publr: Amy Gingerich
E-mail: amyg@mennomedia.org
Mng Ed: Melodie Davis
Founded: 1878
An agency of Mennonite Church USA & Men-
nonite Church Canada. Small denominational
publisher. Specialize in the production of inno-
vative Christian education resources for chil-
dren, youth, young adults, adults & intergener-
ational groups. Topics of interest include mate-
rials on peace & justice, evangelism, Christian
service & radical Christian discipleship.
ISBN Prefix(es): 978-0-8361 (Herald Press); 978-
1-5138
Number of titles published annually: 10 Print
Imprints: Herald Press
Branch Office(s)
718 N Main St, Newton, KS 67114 *Tel:* 316-281-
4412 *Toll Free Tel:* 800-245-7894 *Fax:* 540-
242-4476
See separate listing for:
Herald Press

Mercer University Press
368 Orange St, Macon, GA 31201
Mailing Address: 1501 Mercer University Dr,
Macon, GA 31207 SAN: 220-0716
Tel: 478-301-2880 *Toll Free Tel:* 866-895-1472
Fax: 478-301-2585
E-mail: mupressorders@mercer.edu
Web Site: www.mupress.org
Key Personnel
Dir: Marc Jolley *Tel:* 478-301-2880
E-mail: jolley_ma@mercer.edu
Publg Asst: Marsha Luttrell *Tel:* 478-301-4266
E-mail: luttrell_mm@mercer.edu
Mktg Dir: Mary Beth Kosowski *Tel:* 478-301-
4262 *E-mail:* kosowski_mb@mercer.edu
Cust Serv Assoc: Heather Comer *Tel:* 478-301-
4261 *E-mail:* comer_hm@mercer.edu

Busn Off: Jenny Toole *Tel:* 478-301-4267
E-mail: toole_rw@mercer.edu
Founded: 1979
History, philosophy, religion, Southern studies,
Southern literature, literary studies, regional
interest.
ISBN Prefix(es): 978-0-86554; 978-0-88146
Number of titles published annually: 40 Print
Total Titles: 1,500 Print
Foreign Rep(s): The Eurospan Group (Africa,
Central Asia, Europe, Middle East, UK)
Warehouse: 1701 Seventh St, Macon, GA 31206
Membership(s): American Association of Univer-
sity Presses (AAUP)

Meriwether Publishing
Division of Pioneer Drama Service Inc
c/o Pioneer Drama Service, 9707-A E Easter
Lane, Englewood, CO 80112
Mailing Address: PO Box 4267, Englewood, CO
80155-4267
Tel: 303-779-4035 *Toll Free Tel:* 800-333-7262
Fax: 303-779-4315
E-mail: books@pioneerdrama.com
Web Site: www.pioneerdrama.com
Key Personnel
Publr: Steven Fendrich *E-mail:* steve@
pioneerdrama.com
Exec Ed: Debra Fendrich *E-mail:* debra@
pioneerdrama.com
Book Dept Mgr: Lori Conary
Founded: 1960
Books on theater, drama, performing arts, cos-
tuming, stagecraft, theatre games, play antholo-
gies, improvisation, plays, musicals, theatre arts
DVDs, theatre/drama education.
ISBN Prefix(es): 978-0-916260; 978-1-56608
Number of titles published annually: 4 Print
Total Titles: 200 Print
Foreign Rep(s): Gazelle Book Services Ltd (Eu-
rope, UK)
Membership(s): Publishers Association of the
West (PubWest)

§Merriam Press
489 South St, Hoosick Falls, NY 12090
Tel: 518-949-0882
E-mail: merriampress@gmail.com
Web Site: www.merriam-press.com
Key Personnel
Owner: Ray Merriam *E-mail:* ray@merriam-
press.com
Founded: 1988
Primarily World War II/military history, memoirs
& some fiction.
This publisher has indicated that 90% of their
product line is author subsidized.
ISBN Prefix(es): 978-1-57638
Number of titles published annually: 50 Print; 75
E-Book
Total Titles: 300 Print; 300 E-Book

§Merriam-Webster Inc
Subsidiary of Encyclopaedia Britannica Inc
47 Federal St, Springfield, MA 01102
Mailing Address: PO Box 281, Springfield, MA
01102-0281
Tel: 413-734-3134 *Toll Free Tel:* 800-828-1880
(orders & cust serv) *Fax:* 413-731-5979 (sales)
E-mail: support@merriam-webster.com
Web Site: www.merriam-webster.com
Key Personnel
VP & Dir, Sales: Jed Santoro *E-mail:* jsantoro@
m-w.com
VP, Busn Devt: Matthew Dube
Dir, Mktg: Meghan Lunghi *E-mail:* mlunghi@m-
w.com
Founded: 1828
Dictionaries & language reference products.
ISBN Prefix(es): 978-0-87779; 978-1-68150
Number of titles published annually: 4 Print

Total Titles: 102 Print; 7 CD-ROM; 2 Online; 2
E-Book
Divisions: Federal Street Press
See separate listing for:
Federal Street Press

Mesorah Publications Ltd
4401 Second Ave, Brooklyn, NY 11232
SAN: 213-1269
Tel: 718-921-9000 *Toll Free Tel:* 800-637-6724
Fax: 718-680-1875
E-mail: info@artscroll.com; orders@artscroll.com
Web Site: www.artscroll.com
Key Personnel
Publr: Nosson Scherman
Contact: Jacob Brander
Founded: 1976
Judaica, Bible study, liturgical materials, juvenile,
history, Holocaust, Talmud, novels.
ISBN Prefix(es): 978-0-89906; 978-1-57819; 978-
1-4226
Number of titles published annually: 50 Print
Total Titles: 850 Print
Imprints: Art Scroll Series; Shaar Press; Tamar
Books
Distributor for NCSY Publications
Foreign Rep(s): Stephen Blitz (Israel)
Returns: 222 44 St, Brooklyn, NY 11232

§Messianic Jewish Publishers
Division of Messianic Jewish Communications
6120 Day Long Lane, Clarksville, MD 21029
Tel: 410-531-6644; 616-970-2449
Toll Free Tel: 800-410-7367 (orders)
Fax: 410-531-9440; 717-761-7273 (orders)
Toll Free Fax: 800-327-0048 (orders)
E-mail: editor@messianicjewish.net;
customerservice@messianicjewish.net
Web Site: messianicjewish.net/publish
Key Personnel
Pres & Publr: Barry Rubin
Founded: 1949
Publish & distribute Messianic Jewish books &
other products.
ISBN Prefix(es): 978-1-880226; 978-1-936716
Number of titles published annually: 12 Print; 6
E-Book
Total Titles: 82 Print; 40 E-Book
Divisions: Lederer Books
Distributor for Chosen People Ministries; First
Fruits of Zion; Jewish New Testament Publica-
tions
Foreign Rep(s): Winfried Bluth (Europe)
Foreign Rights: Winfried Bluth (Europe)
Distribution Center: Baker & Taylor Pub-
lisher Services, 30 Amberwood Pkwy, Ash-
land, OH 44805 (worldwide) *Tel:* 567-
215-0030 *Toll Free Tel:* 888-814-0208
E-mail: orders@btpubservices.com *Web
Site:* www.btpubservices.com
Membership(s): Evangelical Christian Publishers
Association (ECPA)
See separate listing for:
Lederer Books

Metropolitan Classics
Division of Fort Ross Inc
26 Arthur Place, Yonkers, NY 10701
Tel: 914-375-6448
Web Site: www.fortrossinc.com
Key Personnel
Pres & Exec Dir: Dr Vladimir Kartsev
E-mail: vkartsev2000@yahoo.com
Founded: 1992
Books in Russian. Russia, Ukraine, Kazakhstan-
related books in English, co-publishing.
ISBN Prefix(es): 978-1-57480
Number of titles published annually: 4 Print; 4
Online; 4 E-Book
Total Titles: 50 Print; 4 Online; 4 E-Book
Foreign Rep(s): Nova Littera (Baltic States, Be-
larus, Eastern Europe, Russia, Ukraine)

§The Metropolitan Museum of Art
1000 Fifth Ave, New York, NY 10028
SAN: 202-6279
Tel: 212-535-7710
E-mail: editorial@metmuseum.org
Web Site: www.metmuseum.org
Key Personnel
Pres & CEO: Daniel Weiss
Chief of Staff: Laurel Britton
Dir: Max Hollein
Publr & Ed-in-Chief: Mark Polizzotti
SVP, Secy & Gen Counsel: Sharon Cott
Deputy Dir, Exhibitions: Quincy Houghton
Assoc Publr & Gen Mgr, Pubns: Gwen Roginsky
Chief Prodn Mgr: Peter Antony
Founded: 1870
Art books, exhibition catalogs, quarterly bulletin, annual journal.
ISBN Prefix(es): 978-0-87099; 978-1-58839
Number of titles published annually: 30 Print
Total Titles: 300 Print; 5 CD-ROM
Distributed by Yale University Press
Foreign Rep(s): Yale University Press
Warehouse: Middle Village, Queens, NY 11381-0001

MFA Publications
Imprint of Museum of Fine Arts Boston
465 Huntington Ave, Boston, MA 02115
Tel: 617-369-4233
E-mail: publications@mfa.org
Web Site: www.mfa.org/publications
Key Personnel
Head, Prodn & Design: Terry McAweeney
Pubns Coord: Hope Stockton *E-mail:* hstockton@mfa.org
Founded: 1877
Exhibition & collection catalogues; general interest & trade arts publications, children's books. No returns accepted.
ISBN Prefix(es): 978-0-87846
Number of titles published annually: 12 Print
Total Titles: 80 Print
Imprints: ArtWorks
Distributed by Thames & Hudson (outside of North America)
Warehouse: c/o PSSC, 46 Development Rd, Fitchburg, MA 01420
Distribution Center: Distributed Art Publishers (DAP), 155 Sixth Ave, 2nd fl, New York, NY 10013 (North America)

Michelin Maps & Guides
Division of Michelin North America Inc
One Parkway S, Greenville, SC 29615-5022
E-mail: michelin.guides@michelin.com
Web Site: guide.michelin.com; michelinmedia.com
Key Personnel
Consumer PR: Lauren McClure *Tel:* 864-458-6871 *E-mail:* lauren.mcclure@michelin.com
Founded: 1900
Specialize in travel publications; hotel & restaurant guides.
ISBN Prefix(es): 978-2-06
Number of titles published annually: 50 Print
Total Titles: 175 Print
Distributed by Editions du Renouveau Pedagogique (French titles in Canada); Langenscheidt Publishing Group; MAPART Publishing (CN only); NBN (guides for North America); Penguin Canada (English titles in Canada)
Orders to: PO Box 19001, Greenville, SC 29615 *Toll Free Tel:* 800-423-0485 *Toll Free Fax:* 800-378-7471

Michigan Municipal League
Affiliate of National League of Cities
1675 Green Rd, Ann Arbor, MI 48105
Mailing Address: PO Box 1487, Ann Arbor, MI 48106-1487
Tel: 734-662-3246 *Toll Free Tel:* 800-653-2483
E-mail: contact@mml.org

Web Site: www.mml.org
Key Personnel
Communs Specialist & Ed: Lisa Donavan *Tel:* 734-669-6318 *E-mail:* ldonavan@mml.org
Ed: Tawny Pearson *Tel:* 734-669-6301 *E-mail:* tpearson@mml.org
Founded: 1899
Municipal topics & newsletters, services & publications for local governments in Michigan.
ISBN Prefix(es): 978-1-929923
Number of titles published annually: 6 Print
Distributor for Crisp Books

§Michigan State University Press (MSU Press)
Division of Michigan State University
Manly Miles Bldg, Suite 25, 1405 S Harrison Rd, East Lansing, MI 48823-5245
SAN: 202-6295
Tel: 517-355-9543 *Fax:* 517-432-2611
Web Site: msupress.org
Key Personnel
Dir: Gabriel Dotto *Tel:* 517-884-6900 *E-mail:* dotto@msu.edu
Asst Dir & Ed-in-Chief: Julie L Loehr *Tel:* 517-884-6905 *E-mail:* loehr@msu.edu
Mktg & Sales Mgr: Julie K Reaume *Tel:* 517-884-6920 *E-mail:* reaumej@msu.edu
Mng Ed: Kristine M Blakeslee *Tel:* 517-884-6912 *E-mail:* blakes17@msu.edu
Digital Prodn Specialist: Annette K Tanner *Tel:* 517-884-6910 *E-mail:* tanneran@msu.edu
Busn & Fin Offr: Julie Wrzesinski *Tel:* 517-884-6922 *E-mail:* wrzesin2@msu.edu
Founded: 1947
Scholarly works & general nonfiction trade books.
ISBN Prefix(es): 978-0-944311; 978-0-937191; 978-0-87013; 978-1-62896; 978-1-62895; 978-1-60917; 978-1-61186; 978-1-938065; 978-1-941258; 978-0-9967252
Number of titles published annually: 40 Print; 2 CD-ROM; 10 E-Book
Total Titles: 650 Print; 4 CD-ROM; 59 E-Book
Distributed by UBC Press, Canada
Distributor for Aquatic Ecosystem Health & Management Society Books; MSU Museum; University of Manitoba Press
Foreign Rep(s): Eurospan (Europe); Raincoast Books-University of British Columbia Press (Canada)
Orders to: Chicago Distribution Center, 11030 S Langley Ave, Chicago, IL 60628 *Tel:* 773-702-7000 *Toll Free Tel:* 800-621-2736 *Fax:* 773-702-7212 *Toll Free Fax:* 800-621-8476 *E-mail:* orders@press.uchicago.edu *Web Site:* www.press.uchicago.edu
Returns: Chicago Distribution Center, 11030 S Langley Ave, Chicago, IL 60628 *Tel:* 773-702-7000 *Toll Free Tel:* 800-621-2736 *Fax:* 773-702-7212 *Toll Free Fax:* 800-621-8476 *E-mail:* orders@press.uchicago.edu *Web Site:* www.press.uchicago.edu
Distribution Center: Chicago Distribution Center, 11030 S Langley Ave, Chicago, IL 60628 *Tel:* 773-702-7000 *Toll Free Tel:* 800-621-2736 *Fax:* 773-702-7212 *Toll Free Fax:* 800-621-8476 *E-mail:* orders@press.uchicago.edu *Web Site:* www.press.uchicago.edu
Membership(s): American Association of University Presses (AAUP); Society for Scholarly Publishing (SSP)

Midnight Marquee Press Inc
9721 Britinay Lane, Baltimore, MD 21234
Tel: 410-665-1198
E-mail: mmarquee@aol.com
Web Site: www.midmar.com
Key Personnel
Pres: Gary Svehla
VP & Lib Sales Dir: Susan Svehla
Founded: 1995

Publisher of books, two magazines, graphic novels with the main focus on film history, biographies & mysteries.
ISBN Prefix(es): 978-1-887664; 978-1-936168
Number of titles published annually: 4 Print
Total Titles: 150 Print

§Mighty Media Press
Division of Mighty Media Inc
1201 Currie Ave, Minneapolis, MN 55403
Tel: 612-455-0252; 612-399-1969 *Fax:* 612-338-4817
E-mail: info@mightymedia.com
Web Site: www.mightymediapress.com
Key Personnel
Publr & Creative Dir: Nancy Tuminelly *E-mail:* nancy@mightymedia.com
Mktg Dir & Publicity: Sammy Bosch *E-mail:* sammy@mightymedia.com
Publg Dir: Lauren Kukla *E-mail:* lauren@mightymedia.com
Founded: 2005
Delivers captivating books & media that ignite a child's curiosity, imagination, social awareness & sense of adventure.
ISBN Prefix(es): 978-0-9765201; 978-0-9798249; 978-0-9824584; 978-0-9830219; 978-1-938063
Number of titles published annually: 6 Print; 6 E-Book
Total Titles: 36 Print; 40 E-Book
Imprints: Mighty Media Junior Readers (middle grade literature); Mighty Media Kids (picture books & first reader/beginner books); Red Portal Press
Foreign Rights: Letter Soup Rights Agency (Allison Olson) (worldwide)
Returns: Publishers Group West, Returns Dept, 193 Edwards Dr, Jackson, TN 38301
Distribution Center: Publishers Group West, 1700 Fourth St, Berkeley, CA 94710 *Tel:* 510-809-3700 *Toll Free Tel:* 866-400-5351 *Fax:* 510-809-3777
Membership(s): American Booksellers Association (ABA); The Children's Book Council (CBC); Midwest Independent Booksellers Association (MIBA); Midwest Independent Publishing Association (MIPA); Minnesota Book Publishers Roundtable; Minnesota Bookbuilders; Society of Children's Book Writers & Illustrators (SCBWI)

Mike Murach & Associates Inc
4340 N Knoll Ave, Fresno, CA 93722
SAN: 264-2255
Tel: 559-440-9071 *Toll Free Tel:* 800-221-5528 *Fax:* 559-440-0963
E-mail: murachbooks@murach.com
Web Site: www.murach.com
Key Personnel
Pres: Ben Murach
Founded: 1974
Computer books.
ISBN Prefix(es): 978-0-911625; 978-1-890774; 978-1-943872; 978-1-943873
Number of titles published annually: 5 Print
Total Titles: 50 Print
Distributed by Shroff Publishers (reprints)
Foreign Rep(s): BPB Publications Ltd (India); Gazelle Book Services Ltd (Continental Europe, UK); Woodslane Pty Ltd (Australia, New Zealand)

§Milady
Division of Cengage Learning
Executive Woods, 5 Maxwell Dr, Clifton Park, NY 12065-2919
Tel: 518-348-2300 *Toll Free Tel:* 800-998-7498 *Fax:* 518-373-6309
E-mail: info@milady.com
Web Site: milady.cengage.com
Key Personnel
Exec Dir: Sandra Bruce

E-Commerce Dir: Slavik Volinsky
Prod Dir: Kara Melillo
Founded: 1928
Textbooks, workbooks, exam reviews, digital so-
lutions & instructional videos, newsletters, cos-
metology & beauty education.
ISBN Prefix(es): 978-0-8273; 978-0-7668; 978-0-
87350; 978-1-4018; 978-1-4180; 978-1-28576
Number of titles published annually: 20 Print
Total Titles: 50 Print
Foreign Office(s): Cengage Learning-Australia, 80
Dorcas St, Level 7, South Melbourne, Victoria
3205, Australia *Tel:* (03) 9685 4111 *Fax:* (03)
9685 4199
Cengage Learning-Latin America, Av Santa Fe
505 piso 12, Colonia Cruz Manca Sante Fe,
Cuajimalpa, 05349 Mexico, CDMX, Mexico
Tel: (0155) 1500 6000
Cengage Learning-EMEA, Cheriton House, North
Way, Andover, Hants SP10 5BE, United King-
dom *Tel:* (01264) 332424 *Fax:* (01264) 342763
Distribution Center: 10650 Toebben Dr, Indepen-
dence, KY 41051
Membership(s): American Association of Cosme-
tology Schools (AACS); National Association
of Barber Boards of America (NABBA); The
National-Interstate Council of State Boards of
Cosmetology Inc (NIC); Professional Beauty
Association (PBA)

Military Info Publishing
PO Box 41211, Plymouth, MN 55442
Tel: 763-533-8627
E-mail: publisher@military-info.com
Web Site: www.military-info.com
Key Personnel
Publr: Bruce A Hanesalo
Founded: 1987
Reprint historical military technology, includ-
ing 34 books, 11,000 photocopies & 400 other
items.
ISBN Prefix(es): 978-1-886848
Number of titles published annually: 4 Print
Total Titles: 41 Print

Military Living Publications
Division of Military Marketing Services Inc
333 Maple Ave E, Suite 3130, Vienna, VA
22180-4717
Tel: 703-237-0203 *Fax:* 703-552-8855
E-mail: customerservice@militaryliving.
com; sales@militaryliving.com; editor@
militaryliving.com
Web Site: www.militaryliving.com
Key Personnel
CEO: William R Crawford, Sr
Founded: 1969
Publisher of military travel atlases, maps & direc-
tories; for military only.
ISBN Prefix(es): 978-0-914862; 978-1-931424
Number of titles published annually: 8 Print
Total Titles: 12 Print
Foreign Rep(s): US Forces Exchanges

Milkweed Editions
1011 Washington Ave S, Suite 300, Minneapolis,
MN 55415-1246
Tel: 612-332-3192 *Toll Free Tel:* 800-520-6455
Fax: 612-215-2550
Web Site: milkweed.org
Key Personnel
Publr & CEO: Daniel Slager
Mng Dir: Patrick Thomas
E-mail: patrick_thomas@milkweed.org
Mktg Dir: Joanna R Demkiewicz *Tel:* 612-215-
2556 *E-mail:* joanna_demkiewicz@milkweed.
org
Ed: Joey McGarvey
Warehouse Mgr: Celia Mattison
Engagement Coord: Abby Travis
Publicist: Jordan Bascom
Founded: 1980

Literary, nonprofit, independent press.
ISBN Prefix(es): 978-0-915943; 978-1-57131
Number of titles published annually: 18 Print; 18
E-Book; 1 Audio
Total Titles: 250 Print; 10 E-Book; 5 Audio
Distribution Center: Publishers Group West, 1700
Fourth St, Berkeley, CA 94710 *Tel:* 510-809-
3700 *Toll Free Tel:* 800-788-3123 *Fax:* 510-
528-3444
Membership(s): American Booksellers Associ-
ation (ABA); The Children's Book Council
(CBC); Community of Literary Magazines &
Presses (CLMP); Independent Book Publish-
ers Association (IBPA); Midwest Independent
Booksellers Association (MIBA); Southern In-
dependent Booksellers Alliance (SIBA)

Millbrook Press
Imprint of Lerner Publishing Group Inc
241 First Ave N, Minneapolis, MN 55401
Tel: 612-332-3344 *Toll Free Tel:* 800-328-4929
Fax: 612-332-7615 *Toll Free Fax:* 800-332-
1132
E-mail: info@lernerbooks.com; custserve@
lernerbooks.com
Web Site: www.lernerbooks.com; www.facebook.
com/millbrookpress
Key Personnel
Chmn: Harry J Lerner
Pres & Publr: Adam Lerner
EVP & COO: Mark Budde
EVP & CFO: Margaret Thomas
EVP, Sales: David Wexler
VP & Ed-in-Chief: Andy Cummings
VP, Mktg: Rachel Zugschwert
Publg Dir, School & Lib: Jenny Krueger
Dir, HR: Cyndi Radant
Dir, Rts, Spec Sales & Intl Dist: Maria Kjoller
Edit Dir: Carol Hinz
School & Lib Mktg Dir: Lois Wallentine
Founded: 1989
ISBN Prefix(es): 978-1-56294; 978-1-878841;
978-0-7613; 978-1-878137
Total Titles: 630 Print; 775 E-Book
Foreign Rep(s): Thomas Allen & Son (Canada);
Bounce Sales & Marketing Ltd (UK); INT
Books (Australia); J Appleseed, A Divi-
sion of Saunders (Canada); Phambili Agen-
cies (Botswana, Lesotho, Namibia, South-
ern Africa); Publishers Marketing Services
(Brunei, Malaysia, Singapore); Saunders Book
Co (educ) (Canada); South Pacific Books (New
Zealand)
Foreign Rights: Japan Foreign-Rights Centre
(Japan); Korea Copyright Center (KCC) (Ko-
rea); Agence Michelle Lapautre (France); Liter-
arische Agentur Silke Weniger (Germany)
Warehouse: 1251 Washington Ave N, Minneapo-
lis, MN 55401, Mgr: Ken Rued

Richard K Miller Associates
2413 Main St, Suite 331, Miramar, FL 33025
Toll Free Tel: 888-928-RKMA (928-7562)
Toll Free Fax: 877-928-7562
Web Site: rkma.com
Key Personnel
Pres: Richard K Miller *E-mail:* richard.miller@
rkma.com
Founded: 1972
Market research reference handbooks for col-
lege & corporate libraries. Subjects include
consumer behavior, marketing, retail, travel,
healthcare, entertainment & restaurants.
ISBN Prefix(es): 978-1-57783
Number of titles published annually: 6 Print; 6
Online; 1 E-Book
Total Titles: 12 Print; 12 Online; 12 E-Book

§Milliken Publishing Co
Division of The Lorenz Corp
501 E Third St, Dayton, OH 45402

Mailing Address: PO Box 802, Dayton, OH
45401-0802
Tel: 937-228-6118 *Toll Free Tel:* 800-444-1144
Fax: 937-223-2042
E-mail: order@lorenz.com
Web Site: www.lorenzeducationalpress.com
Key Personnel
VP, Mktg: Debra Kaiser *E-mail:* debk@lorenz.
com
Founded: 1960
Educational publishing division includes visual
resources, instructional guides & reproducibles;
elementary supplementals.
ISBN Prefix(es): 978-0-88335; 978-1-55863; 978-
1-4291; 978-0-7877
Number of titles published annually: 20 Print
Total Titles: 400 Print; 20 CD-ROM; 400 E-
Book; 6 Audio
Membership(s): Education Market Association

Denene Millner Books, see Simon & Schuster
Children's Publishing

§The Minerals, Metals & Materials Society (TMS)
Affiliate of AIME
5700 Corporate Dr, Suite 750, Pittsburgh, PA
15237
Tel: 724-776-9000 *Toll Free Tel:* 800-759-4867
Fax: 724-776-3770
E-mail: publications@tms.org (orders)
Web Site: www.tms.org/bookstore (orders); www.
tms.org
Key Personnel
Exec Dir: James J Robinson *E-mail:* robinson@
tms.org
Dept Head, Content: Matt Baker
E-mail: mbaker@tms.org
Founded: 1871
Leading professional society dedicated to the de-
velopment & dissemination of scientific & en-
gineering knowledge for materials-centered
technology. The society is the only professional
organization that encompasses the entire spec-
trum of materials & engineering, from minerals
processing through the advanced applications
of materials.
ISBN Prefix(es): 978-0-87339
Number of titles published annually: 20 Print
Total Titles: 200 Print; 20 E-Book
Distributed by Springer

Minnesota Historical Society Press
Division of Minnesota Historical Society
345 Kellogg Blvd W, St Paul, MN 55102-1906
SAN: 202-6384
Tel: 651-259-3205 *Fax:* 651-297-1345
E-mail: info-mnhspress@mnhs.org
Web Site: www.mnhs.org/mnhspress
Key Personnel
Dir & Acqs Ed: Josh Leventhal *Tel:* 651-259-
3218 *E-mail:* josh.leventhal@mnhs.org
Ed-in-Chief: Ann Regan *Tel:* 651-259-3206
E-mail: ann.regan@mnhs.org
Mng Ed: Shannon M Pennefeather *Tel:* 651-259-
3212 *E-mail:* shannon.pennefeather@mnhs.org
Mktg & Sales Mgr: Mary Poggione *Tel:* 651-259-
3204 *E-mail:* mary.poggione@mnhs.org
Sales Mgr: Serenity Shanklin *Tel:* 651-259-3202
E-mail: serenity.shanklin@mnhs.org
Founded: 1849
Scholarly & trade books on Upper Midwest his-
tory & prehistory.
ISBN Prefix(es): 978-0-87351; 978-1-68134
Number of titles published annually: 20 Print; 10
E-Book
Total Titles: 430 Print; 140 E-Book; 6 Audio
Warehouse: Ingram Publisher Services, La
Vergne, TN *Toll Free Tel:* 844-841-0257 (or-
ders) *E-mail:* ips@ingramcontent.com
Membership(s): American Association of Univer-
sity Presses (AAUP)

MIT List Visual Arts Center
MIT E 15-109, 20 Ames St, Cambridge, MA 02139
Tel: 617-253-4400; 617-253-4680
E-mail: listinfo@mit.edu
Web Site: listart.mit.edu
Key Personnel
Dir: Paul C Ha
Founded: 1966
Contemporary art.
ISBN Prefix(es): 978-0-938437
Number of titles published annually: 6 Print
Distribution Center: Distributed Art Publishers (DAP), 155 Sixth Ave, 2nd fl, New York, NY 10013 *Tel:* 212-627-1999 *Fax:* 212-627-9484
E-mail: orders@artbook.com

§The MIT Press
One Rogers St, Cambridge, MA 02142
SAN: 202-6414
Tel: 617-253-5255 *Toll Free Tel:* 800-405-1619 (orders) *Fax:* 617-258-6779; 617-577-1545 (orders)
Web Site: mitpress.mit.edu
Key Personnel
Cont: Charles Hale *Tel:* 617-258-0577 *E-mail:* chale@mit.edu
Dir: Amy Brand *E-mail:* amybrand@mit.edu
Dir, Fin & Opers & Assoc Dir: Brent Oberlin *Tel:* 617-253-5250 *E-mail:* brento@mit.edu
Dir, Intl Property Licensing: William Smith
Dir, Journals & Open Access: Nick Lindsay *Tel:* 617-258-0594 *E-mail:* nlindsay@mit.edu
Dir, Sales: David Goldberg *Tel:* 617-253-8838 *E-mail:* davidgol@mit.edu
Edit Dir: Gita Manaktala *Tel:* 617-253-3172 *E-mail:* manak@mit.edu
Exec Ed: Marie Lee *Tel:* 617-253-1558 *E-mail:* marielee@mit.edu
Mng Ed: Michael Sims *Tel:* 617-253-2080 *E-mail:* msims@mit.edu
Exec Ed: Robert Prior *Tel:* 617-253-1584 *E-mail:* prior@mit.edu
Sr Acqs Ed: Phil Laughlin *Tel:* 617-252-1636 *E-mail:* laughlin@mit.edu; Douglas Sery *Tel:* 617-253-5187 *E-mail:* dsery@mit.edu
Sr Acqs Ed, Art & Architecture: Thomas Weaver
Acqs Ed: Beth Clevenger *Tel:* 617-253-4113 *E-mail:* eclev@mit.edu
Acqs Ed, Physical Sciences, Engg & Math: Jermey Matthews
Asst Acqs Ed: Laura Keeler *Tel:* 617-253-3757 *E-mail:* lkeeler@mit.edu
Sr Mgr, Digital Prods: Gabe Harp
Design Mgr: Yasuyo Iguchi *Tel:* 617-253-8034 *E-mail:* iguchi@mit.edu
Exhibits Mgr: John Costello *Tel:* 617-258-5764 *E-mail:* jcostell@mit.edu
Prodn Mgr: Janet Rossi *Tel:* 617-253-2882 *E-mail:* janett@mit.edu
Exec Publicist: Colleen Lanick *Tel:* 617-253-2874 *E-mail:* colleenl@mit.edu
Textbook Promos Mgr: Michelle Pullano *Tel:* 617-253-3620 *E-mail:* mpullano@mit.edu
Bookstore Mgr: John Jenkins *Tel:* 617-253-5249 *E-mail:* jjenkins@mit.edu
Founded: 1962
Scholarly & professional books, advanced textbooks, nonfiction trade books & reference books; architecture & design, cognitive sciences & linguistics, computer science & artificial intelligence, economics & management sciences, environmental studies; philosophy, neuroscience; technology studies; new media; paperbacks, journals.
ISBN Prefix(es): 978-0-262; 978-0-89706
Number of titles published annually: 250 Print
Total Titles: 8,000 Print; 5 CD-ROM; 2 Online; 1 E-Book
Imprints: Bradford Books
Foreign Office(s): The MIT Press Ltd, One Duchess St, Suite 2, London W1W 6AN, United Kingdom *Tel:* (020) 7306 0603

Fax: (020) 7306 0604 *E-mail:* info@mitpress.org.uk
Distributor for AAAI Press; Afterall Books; Canadian Centre for Architecture; no place press; Semiotext(e)
Foreign Rep(s): APD Singapore Pte Ltd (Ian Pringle) (Brunei, Cambodia, Indonesia, Laos, Malaysia, Myanmar, Philippines, Singapore, Thailand, Vietnam); Aromix Books Company Ltd (Jane Lam & Nick Wonn) (Hong Kong); Avicenna Partnership Ltd (Claire de Gruchy) (Algeria, Cyprus, Israel, Jordan, Malta, Morocco, Palestine, Tunisia, Turkey); Avicenna Partnership Ltd (Bill Kennedy) (Bahrain, Egypt, Iran, Iraq, Kuwait, Lebanon, Libya, Oman, Qatar, Saudi Arabia, Syria, United Arab Emirates); Everest International Publishing Services (Wei Zhao) (China); Footprint Books Pty Ltd (Australia, New Zealand); Information & Culture Korea (ICK) (Se-Yung Jun & Min-Hwa Yoo) (South Korea); Itsabook (James Papworth) (Caribbean, Latin America); BK Norton (Chiafeng Peng) (Taiwan); Penguin Random House India Pvt Ltd (Bangladesh, Bhutan, India, Nepal, Pakistan, Sri Lanka); Rockbook Inc (Akiko Iwamoto & Gilles Fauveau) (Japan); University Press Group (Dominique Bartshukoff) (Austria, Croatia, Czechia, Germany, Greece, Hungary, Netherlands, Portugal, Slovenia, Spain); University Press Group (Peter Jacques) (Belgium, Europe, France, Italy, Poland, Scandinavia, Switzerland); University Press Group (Ben Mitchell) (Europe, Ireland, UK)
Foreign Rights: Agencia Literaria Carmen Balcells SA (Maribel Luque) (Spain); Bardon-Chinese Media Agency (Joanne Yang) (Taiwan); The Berlin Agency (Frauke Jung-Lindemann) (Germany); The English Agency (Tsutomu Yawata) (Japan); Graal Literary Agency (Lukasz Wrobel) (Poland); The Deborah Harris Agency (Ilana Kurshan) (Israel); The Kayi Agency (Dilek Kayi) (Turkey); KCC (Sageun Lee) (Korea); Alexander Korzheneveski Agency (Alexander Korzheneveski) (Russia); OA Literary Agency (Michael Avramides) (Greece); Reiser Literary Agency (Roberto Gilodi) (Italy); Agencia Riff (Joao Riff) (Brazil)
Distribution Center: Penguin Random House Publisher Services, 400 Hahn Rd, Westminster, MD 21157 *Tel:* 410-848-1900 *Toll Free Tel:* 800-726-0600
Membership(s): Association of American Publishers (AAP); Association of University Presses (AUPresses)

Mitchell Lane Publishers Inc
2001 SW 31 Ave, Hallandale, FL 33009
SAN: 858-3749
Tel: 954-985-9400 *Toll Free Tel:* 800-223-3251 *Fax:* 954-987-2200
E-mail: customerservice@mitchelllane.com
Web Site: www.mitchelllane.com
Key Personnel
Sales Mgr, Mktg Mgr & Prod Content: Rachel Collin *E-mail:* rachel@mitchelllane.com
Founded: 1993
Nonfiction for children & young adults.
ISBN Prefix(es): 978-1-883845; 978-1-58415; 978-1-61228; 978-1-68020
Number of titles published annually: 100 Print; 100 E-Book
Total Titles: 1,500 Print; 650 E-Book
Foreign Rep(s): CrossCan Educational (Canada); Edu-Reference (Canada); David Hall (Africa, Australia, Continental Europe, Ireland, Malaysia, Singapore, South Africa)
Membership(s): Educational Book & Media Association (EBMA)

MOA Press, see Medals of America Press

§Modern Language Association of America (MLA)
85 Broad St, Suite 500, New York, NY 10004-2434
SAN: 202-6422
Tel: 646-576-5000 *Fax:* 646-458-0030
Web Site: www.mla.org
Key Personnel
Exec Dir: Paula Krebs
Head, Mktg & Sales: Kathleen M Hansen *E-mail:* khansen@mla.org
Head, Publg Opers: Angela Gibson *E-mail:* agibson@mla.org
Founded: 1883
Research & teaching tools in languages & literature; professional publications for college teachers.
ISBN Prefix(es): 978-0-87352; 978-1-60329
Number of titles published annually: 12 Print
Total Titles: 300 Print; 1 CD-ROM; 1 Online
Distribution Center: HFS (Hopkins Fulfillment Services), 2715 N Charles St, Baltimore, MD 21218 *Tel:* 410-516-6965 *Toll Free Tel:* 800-537-5487 (US & CN) *Fax:* 410-516-6998 *E-mail:* hfscustserv@press.jhu.edu *Web Site:* hfs.jhu.edu

§Modern Memoirs
34 Main St, No 6, Amherst, MA 01002-2367
Tel: 413-253-2353
Web Site: www.modernmemoirs.com; www.whitepoppypress.com
Key Personnel
Founder & Pres: Kitty Axelson-Berry *E-mail:* kitty@modernmemoirs.com
Assoc Publr: Vinsula Hastings *E-mail:* vinsula@modernmemoirs.com
Founded: 1994
Private publishing services for discerning clients. This publisher has indicated that 100% of their product line is author subsidized.
ISBN Prefix(es): 978-0-9662602; 978-0-9772337; 978-0-9856595; 978-0-9834752; 978-0-9905709
Number of titles published annually: 15 Print
Total Titles: 225 Print
Imprints: White Poppy Press
Membership(s): Association of Personal Historians; Independent Book Publishers Association (IBPA)

Modern Publishing
Division of Kappa Books Publishers LLC
6198 Butler Pike, Suite 200, Blue Bell, PA 19422
Tel: 215-643-6385 *Fax:* 215-628-3571
Web Site: kappabooks.com
Key Personnel
Pres: Andrew Steinberg *E-mail:* asteinberg@kappabooks.com
Founded: 1969
Juvenile, reference books; general nonfiction, humor, puzzle books.
This publisher has indicated that 25% of their product line is author subsidized.
ISBN Prefix(es): 978-0-7666

MoMA, see The Museum of Modern Art (MoMA)

The Monacelli Press
Imprint of Phaidon Press Ltd
65 Bleecker St, 8th fl, New York, NY 10012
Tel: 212-229-9925
E-mail: contact@monacellipress.com
Web Site: www.monacellipress.com
Key Personnel
Pres & Publr: Gianfranco Monacelli
Assoc Publr: Victoria Craven
VP, Prodn: Michael Vagnetti
Edit Dir: Alan Rapp
Mktg & Publicity Dir: Jessica A Gilo
Mng Ed: Elizabeth White

Ed (design, fine art, gardening, interior design, lifestyle): Jenny Florence
Founded: 1994
High-quality, illustrated, hardcover & paperback books on art, architecture, decorative arts, interior design, fashion, photography, landscape, urbanism & graphic design.
ISBN Prefix(es): 978-1-58093; 978-1-885254
Number of titles published annually: 24 Print; 1 E-Book
Total Titles: 400 Print; 10 E-Book
Imprints: Monacelli Studio (applied arts)
Foreign Rep(s): Penguin Random House Canada (Canada); Publishers Group UK (Ireland, UK)
Orders to: Penguin Random House Publisher Services (PRHPS), 400 Hahn Rd, Westminster, MD 21157 Toll Free Tel: 800-733-3000 Toll Free Fax: 800-659-2436 E-mail: customerservice@penguinrandomhouse.com

Mondial
203 W 107 St, Suite 6-C, New York, NY 10025
Tel: 646-807-8031 Fax: 208-361-2863
E-mail: contact@mondialbooks.com
Web Site: www.mondialbooks.com
Key Personnel
Owner: Uday K Dhar
Publr: Ulrich Becker
Founded: 2004
Specialize in fiction & nonfiction translated into English from other languages or originally written in English or German. All kinds of publications (fiction & nonfiction) in the international language Esperanto.
ISBN Prefix(es): 978-1-59569
Number of titles published annually: 15 Print; 15 E-Book
Total Titles: 220 Print; 1 CD-ROM; 110 E-Book

Mondo Publishing
980 Avenue of the Americas, New York, NY 10018
Tel: 212-268-3560 Toll Free Tel: 888-88-MONDO (886-6636) Toll Free Fax: 888-532-4492
E-mail: info@mondopub.com
Web Site: www.mondopub.com
Key Personnel
Pres: Mark Vineis
Edit Dir: Megan Linke
Mktg: Sonya Fleming
Founded: 1986
K-5 literacy materials & professional development services.
ISBN Prefix(es): 978-1-879531; 978-1-57255; 978-1-58653; 978-1-59034; 978-1-59336; 978-1-60201; 978-1-60715; 978-1-61736; 978-1-62889; 978-1-63060; 978-1-63061; 978-1-68156
Number of titles published annually: 200 Print
Total Titles: 500 Print
Imprints: Mondo
Warehouse: 200 Sherwood Ave, Farmingdale, NY 11735
Membership(s): The Children's Book Council (CBC)

The Mongolia Society Inc
Indiana University, 703 Eigenmann Hall, 1900 E Tenth St, Bloomington, IN 47406-7512
Tel: 812-855-4078 Fax: 812-855-4078
E-mail: monsoc@indiana.edu
Web Site: mongoliasociety.org
Key Personnel
VP & Chmn of the Bd: Dr Christopher Atwood
Pres: Dr Alicia Campi
Exec Dir: Susie Drost
Co-Mng Ed: Dr Timothy May; Dr Peter Marsh
Treas: Tserenchunt Ledges
Secy: Dr Melissa Chakars
Founded: 1961
Interests, culture & language of Mongolia.

ISBN Prefix(es): 978-0-910980
Number of titles published annually: 4 Print
Total Titles: 60 Print

Monkfish Book Publishing Co
22 E Market St, Suite 304, Rhinebeck, NY 12572
Tel: 845-876-4861
E-mail: monkfish@monkfishpublishing.com
Web Site: www.monkfishpublishing.com
Key Personnel
Publr: Paul Cohen E-mail: paul@monkfishpublishing.com
Founded: 2002
Publisher of spirituality & religion titles. Also operates a self-publishing company.
ISBN Prefix(es): 978-0-9823246; 978-0-9766843; 978-0-9726357; 978-0-9798828; 978-0-9749359; 978-0-9789427; 978-0-9824530; 978-0-9825255; 978-0-9826441; 978-0-9830517; 978-0-9833589; 978-1-936940; 978-1-939681; 978-1-944037
Number of titles published annually: 12 Print; 4 Online; 12 E-Book
Total Titles: 66 Print; 32 Online; 66 E-Book
Divisions: Epigraph Publishing Service (subsidy publishers)
Orders to: Consortium Book Sales & Distribution, The Keg House, Suite 101, 34 13 Ave NE, Minneapolis, MN 55413-1007 Tel: 612-746-2600 Toll Free Tel: 800-283-3572 (cust serv, Jackson, TN) Fax: 612-746-2606 E-mail: info@cbsd.com Web Site: www.cbsd.com SAN: 200-6049
Distribution Center: Consortium Book Sales & Distribution, The Keg House, Suite 101, 34 13 Ave NE, Minneapolis, MN 55413-1007 Tel: 612-746-2600 Toll Free Tel: 800-283-3572 (cust serv, Jackson, TN) Fax: 612-746-2606 E-mail: info@cbsd.com Web Site: www.cbsd.com SAN: 200-6049

Montemayor Press
663 Hyland Hill Rd, Washington, VT 05675
Mailing Address: PO Box 546, Montpelier, VT 05601
Tel: 802-552-0750
E-mail: mail@montemayorpress.com
Web Site: www.montemayorpress.com
Key Personnel
Publr: Edward Myers
Exec Ed: Edith Poor
Founded: 1999
Independent publisher whose mission is to print & distribute quality fiction & nonfiction to adult, young adult & juvenile audiences.
ISBN Prefix(es): 978-0-9674477; 978-1-932727
Number of titles published annually: 5 Print; 2 E-Book
Total Titles: 36 Print; 4 E-Book
Membership(s): Community of Literary Magazines & Presses (CLMP); Independent Book Publishers Association (IBPA)

Monthly Review Press
Division of Monthly Review Foundation Inc
134 W 29 St, Suite 706, New York, NY 10001
SAN: 202-6481
Tel: 212-691-2555
E-mail: mreview@igc.org
Web Site: monthlyreview.org
Key Personnel
Mng Dir: Martin Paddio
Edit Dir: Michael D Yates
Mktg Publicity Mgr: Susie Day
Founded: 1949
Economics, politics, history, sociology & world affairs.
ISBN Prefix(es): 978-0-85345; 978-1-58367
Number of titles published annually: 15 Print
Total Titles: 550 Print
Distributed by New York University Press

Billing Address: New York University Press, 838 Broadway, 3rd fl, New York, NY 10003
Orders to: New York University Press, 838 Broadway, 3rd fl, New York, NY 10003 Toll Free Tel: 800-996-6987 Fax: 212-995-3833 E-mail: orders@nyupress.org
Returns: Ingram Publisher Services, One Ingram Blvd, La Vergne, TN 37086 SAN: 631-8630
Warehouse: Ingram Publisher Services, One Ingram Blvd, La Vergne, TN 37086 SAN: 631-8630

Moody Publishers
Affiliate of The Moody Bible Institute
820 N La Salle Blvd, Chicago, IL 60610
SAN: 202-5604
Tel: 312-329-2101 Toll Free Tel: 800-678-8812 Fax: 312-329-2144 Toll Free Fax: 800-678-3329
E-mail: mpcustomerservice@moody.edu; mporders@moody.edu; publicity@moody.edu
Web Site: www.moodypublishers.com
Key Personnel
VP: Paul Santhouse
Assoc Publr: John Hinkley
Founded: 1894
Religion (interdenominational).
ISBN Prefix(es): 978-0-8024; 978-1-881273 (Northfield Publishing)
Number of titles published annually: 75 Print
Total Titles: 1,000 Print; 10 Audio
Imprints: Northfield Publishing; River North Fiction; WingSpread Publishers
Foreign Rep(s): Biblicum AS (Norway); Bookhouse Australia Ltd (Australia); Challenge Bookshops (Nigeria); Christian Art Wholesale (South Africa); Christian Literature Crusade (Hong Kong); David C Cook Distribution (Canada); Editeurs de Litterature Biblique (Germany); Euro-Outreach Ministries (East Africa, Kenya, Nairobi); Hong Kong Tien Dao Publishing House Ltd (Belgium); Kesho Publications (Zimbabwe); Matopo Book Room (Philippines); Overseas Missionary Fellowship (Canada); Rhema Boekimport (Singapore); S & U Book Centre (New Zealand); S-U Wholesale
Shipping Address: 215 W Locust St, Chicago, IL 60610

Moonshine Cove Publishing LLC
150 Willow Point, Abbeville, SC 29620
E-mail: publisher@moonshinecovepublishing.com
Web Site: moonshinecovepublishing.com
Key Personnel
Publr: Gene D Robinson
Founded: 2011
Independently owned small publisher currently accepting queries. Do not send anything by regular mail, electronic submission only. Submit your query to publisher@moonshinecovepublishing.com. Do not send anything except a query letter with the first 5 pages of your ms pasted into the body of the e-mail (pasted, not attached). We will not open attachments or click on embedded links. If we ask to see your ms, send it only if it's your final edit. If you're still thinking of making changes, make them before sending your ms.
ISBN Prefix(es): 978-1-937327; 978-1-945181; 978-1-952439
Number of titles published annually: 23 Print; 23 E-Book
Total Titles: 225 Print; 225 E-Book; 1 Audio

Morehouse Publishing
Imprint of Church Publishing Inc
19 E 34 St, New York, NY 10016
SAN: 202-6511
Tel: 212-592-1800 Toll Free Tel: 800-242-1918 (retail orders only)
E-mail: churchpublishingorders@pbd.com
Web Site: www.churchpublishing.org

Key Personnel
VP, Prodn: Lorraine Simonello
  E-mail: churchpublishingorders@pbd.com
Founded: 1884
Spirituality, religious, lay ministry, liturgy, church supplies, music CDs, all from an Episcopal/Anglican perspective. No illustrated children's books.
ISBN Prefix(es): 978-0-8192
Number of titles published annually: 40 Print; 35 E-Book
Total Titles: 800 Print; 650 E-Book
Foreign Rep(s): Norwich Books & Music (Europe)
Warehouse: PBD Worldwide, Alpharetta, GA

Morgan James Publishing
5 Penn Plaza, 23rd fl, New York, NY 10001
Tel: 212-655-5470 *Fax:* 516-908-4496
E-mail: support@morganjamespublishing.com
Web Site: www.morganjamespublishing.com
Key Personnel
Founder: David L Hancock *E-mail:* david@morganjamespublishing.com
Founded: 2003
Provides entrepreneurs with the vital information, inspiration & guidance they need to be successful.
ISBN Prefix(es): 978-0-9746133; 978-0-9758570; 978-0-9760901; 978-0-9768491; 978-1-933596; 978-1-60037; 978-0-9815058; 978-0-9817906; 978-0-9820750; 978-0-9823793; 978-0-9835013; 978-0-9840316; 978-1-938467; 978-0-9846170; 978-0-9828590; 978-0-9833715; 978-1-61448; 978-0-9837125; 978-1-63047; 978-1-63195
Number of titles published annually: 285 Print; 285 E-Book
Total Titles: 3,000 Print; 3,000 E-Book
Imprints: Guerrilla Marketing Press; Morgan James Faith; Morgan James Fiction; Morgan James Kids
Returns: IPS Warehouse, 1280 Ingram Dr, Chambersburg, PA 17201
Membership(s): Association of American Publishers (AAP)

Morgan Kaufmann
Imprint of Elsevier Inc
50 & 60 Hampshire St, 5th fl, Cambridge, MA 02139
Web Site: www.elsevier.com/books-and-journals/morgan-kaufmann
Founded: 1984
Computer science book publishers including database, networking, architecture, engineering, graphics & artificial intelligence.
ISBN Prefix(es): 978-0-12; 978-1-55860
Number of titles published annually: 65 Print
Total Titles: 552 Print; 606 E-Book
Orders to: 3251 Riverport Lane, Maryland Heights, MO 63043
Returns: 3251 Riverport Lane, Maryland Heights, MO 63043
Warehouse: 3251 Riverport Lane, Maryland Heights, MO 63043

Moriah Books
PO Box 1094, Casper, WY 82602
Web Site: moriahbook.com
Founded: 2014
Independent publisher of Rocky Mountain regional, history, historical fiction & religious titles.
ISBN Prefix(es): 978-0-9970417
Number of titles published annually: 6 Print
Total Titles: 3 Print

§Morning Sun Books Inc
1200 County Rd 523, Flemington, NJ 08822
Tel: 908-806-6216 *Fax:* 908-237-2407
E-mail: sales@morningsunbooks.com

Web Site: morningsunbooks.com
Key Personnel
Pres: Robert J Yanosey
Founded: 1986
Vintage railroad photography.
ISBN Prefix(es): 978-1-878887; 978-1-58248
Number of titles published annually: 36 Print
Total Titles: 500 Print
Editorial Office(s): 9 Pheasant Lane, Scotch Plains, NJ 07076

Morton Publishing Co
925 W Kenyon Ave, Unit 12, Englewood, CO 80110
SAN: 210-9174
Tel: 303-761-4805 *Fax:* 303-762-9923
E-mail: contact@morton-pub.com; returns@morton-pub.com
Web Site: www.morton-pub.com
Key Personnel
Pres: David Ferguson *E-mail:* davidf@morton-pub.com
VP, Opers: Chrissy DeMier *E-mail:* chrissyd@morton-pub.com
VP, Sales & Mktg: Carter Fenton
  E-mail: carterf@morton-pub.com
Returns: Heather Herman *E-mail:* heatherh@morton-pub.com
Founded: 1977
Allied health, biology, chemistry, pharmacy, physical science.
ISBN Prefix(es): 978-0-89582; 978-1-61731; 978-1-64043
Number of titles published annually: 10 Print
Total Titles: 50 Print
Foreign Rep(s): Northrose Associates (Canada)

Mountain n' Air Books
2947-A Honolulu Ave, La Crescenta, CA 91214
Mailing Address: PO Box 12540, La Crescenta, CA 91224-5540
Tel: 818-248-9345 *Toll Free Tel:* 800-446-9696
  Toll Free Fax: 800-303-5578
E-mail: contact@mountain-n-air.com
Web Site: www.mountain-n-air.com
Key Personnel
Pres: Gilberto d'Urso *E-mail:* gilberto@mountain-n-air.com
Publr & Ed: Mary K d'Urso
Off Mgr: Elvira Sakalenka *E-mail:* elvira@mountain-n-air.com
Founded: 1985
Outdoor guides, nonfiction, cookbooks & travel adventures, maps.
ISBN Prefix(es): 978-1-879415
Number of titles published annually: 6 Print
Total Titles: 99 Print
Imprints: Mountain Air Books
Distributor for Tom Harrison Cartography

Mountain Press Publishing Co
1301 S Third W, Missoula, MT 59801
SAN: 202-8832
Mailing Address: PO Box 2399, Missoula, MT 59806-2399
Tel: 406-728-1900 *Toll Free Tel:* 800-234-5308
  Fax: 406-728-1635
E-mail: info@mtnpress.com
Web Site: www.mountain-press.com
Key Personnel
History Ed: Gwen McKenna
Natural History & Roadside Geology Series Ed: Jennifer Carey
Gen Mgr: John Rimel *E-mail:* johnargyle@aol.com
Busn Mgr: Rob Williams
Mktg Mgr: Anne Iverson *Tel:* 406-728-1900 ext 131 *E-mail:* anne@mtnpress.com
Graphic Design: Jeannie Painter
Founded: 1948
ISBN Prefix(es): 978-0-87842; 978-0-9632562; 978-0-9626999; 978-1-886370; 978-1-889921;

978-1-892784; 978-0-9676747; 978-0-9717748; 978-0-9724827
Number of titles published annually: 20 Print
Total Titles: 150 Print
Imprints: Geology Underfoot Series; Mountain Sports Press Series; Roadside Geology Series; Roadside History Series; Tumbleweed Series
Distributor for Bucking Horse Books; Clark City Press; Hops Press; Npustin Press; RainStone Press; Western Edge Press

The Mountaineers Books
Division of The Mountaineers
1001 SW Klickitat Way, Suite 201, Seattle, WA 98134
Tel: 206-223-6303 *Fax:* 206-223-6306
E-mail: mbooks@mountaineersbooks.org; customerservice@mountaineersbooks.org
Web Site: www.mountaineersbooks.org
Key Personnel
Publr: Tom Helleberg
Dir, Conservation & Advancement: Helen Cherullo *Tel:* 206-223-6303 ext 122
Dir, Mktg & Innovation: Doug Canfield *Tel:* 206-223-6303 ext 114
Dir, Sales & Mktg: Darryl Booker
Ed-in-Chief: Kate Rogers *Tel:* 206-223-6303 ext 109
Sr Ed: Mary Metz *Tel:* 206-223-6303 ext 119
Publicist: Marissa Litak *Tel:* 206-223-6303 ext 110
Founded: 1961
Mountaineering, backpacking, hiking, cross-country skiing, bicycling, canoeing, kayaking, trekking, nature, conservation, green living & sustainability; outdoor how-to, guidebooks & maps; nonfiction adventure-travel accounts; biographies of outdoor people; reprint editions of mountaineering classics; adventure narratives.
ISBN Prefix(es): 978-0-89886; 978-0-916890; 978-0-938567; 978-1-59485; 978-1-63374; 978-1-68051
Number of titles published annually: 30 Print
Total Titles: 550 Print
Imprints: Braided River; Skipstone
Distributor for Adventure Cycling Association; The American Alpine Club Press; Appalachian Trail Conservancy (ATC); Colorado Mountain Club Press; Green Trails Maps
Foreign Rep(s): Cordee Publishing (UK)

§De Gruyter Mouton
Imprint of Walter de Gruyter GmbH
125 Pearl St, Boston, MA 02110
Mailing Address: 121 High St, 3rd fl, Boston, MA 02110
Tel: 857-284-7073 *Fax:* 857-284-7358
E-mail: service@degruyter.com
Web Site: www.degruyter.com
Founded: 1956
Scholarly books & journals.
ISBN Prefix(es): 978-0-311; 978-90-279
Number of titles published annually: 100 Print; 2 Online
Total Titles: 2,500 Print; 3 CD-ROM; 10 Online
Foreign Office(s): Walter de Gruyter GmbH, Genthinerstr 13, 10728 Berlin, Germany *Tel:* (030) 260 05-0 *Fax:* (030) 260 05-251
Distributed by Walter de Gruyter Inc
Foreign Rep(s): Allied Publishers Ltd (India, Nepal, Sri Lanka); Book Club International (Bangladesh); Combined Representatives Worldwide Inc (Philippines); D A Books & Journals (Australia, New Zealand); Walter de Gruyter Inc (Canada, Mexico); Verlags und Kommissionsbuchhandlung Dr Franz Hain (Austria); Kumi Trading (South Korea); Kweilin Bookstore (Taiwan); Maruzen Co Ltd (Japan); Pak Book Corp (Pakistan); Parry's Book Center (Sendjrjan Berhad) (Brunei, Malaysia, Singapore); Swinden Book Co Ltd (Hong Kong)

Distribution Center: PO Box 361, Birmingham, AL 35242 (journals & yearbooks) *Tel:* 205-995-1567 *Toll Free Tel:* 800-633-4931 *Fax:* 205-995-1588 *E-mail:* degruyterus@subscriptionoffice.com

TriLiteral LLC, 100 Maple Ridge Dr, Cumberland, RI 02864 (books, ebooks & bundles, databases) *Tel:* 401-531-2800 *Toll Free Tel:* 800-405-1619 *E-mail:* orders@triliteral.org

HGV Hanseatische Gesellschaft fuer Verlagsservice mbH, Holzwiesenstr 2, 72127 Kusterdingen, Germany (worldwide exc the Americas) *Tel:* (07071) 9353-55 *Fax:* (07071) 9353-93 *E-mail:* orders@degruyter.com

Moznaim Publishing Corp
4304 12 Ave, Brooklyn, NY 11219
SAN: 214-4123
Tel: 718-438-7680 *Fax:* 718-438-1305
E-mail: sales@moznaim.com
Web Site: www.moznaim.com
Key Personnel
Pres: Menachem Wagshal
VP: Moshe Sternlicht
Founded: 1981
Judaica books in Hebrew, English & Spanish.
ISBN Prefix(es): 978-0-940118; 978-1-885220
Number of titles published annually: 7 Print
Total Titles: 200 Print
Foreign Office(s): 10 Telmie Yosef St, Mishor Adumim, Israel *Tel:* (02) 5333441 *Fax:* (02) 5354345
Distributor for Avamra Institute; Breslov Research Institute; Red Wheel/Weiser/Conari

MRTS
Imprint of Arizona Center for Medieval & Renaissance Studies (ACMRS)
PO Box 874402, Tempe, AZ 85287-4402
Tel: 480-727-6503 *Toll Free Tel:* 800-621-2736 (orders) *Fax:* 480-965-1681 *Toll Free Fax:* 800-621-8476 (orders)
E-mail: mrts@asu.edu
Web Site: acmrspress.com
Key Personnel
Mng Ed: Roy Rukkila *E-mail:* roy.rukkila@asu.edu
Scholarly/academic press. Specialize in medieval & Renaissance texts & studies.
ISBN Prefix(es): 978-0-86698
Number of titles published annually: 10 Print
Total Titles: 492 Print
Sales Office(s): Chicago Distribution Center, 11030 S Langley Ave, Chicago, IL 60628 *Tel:* 773-702-7000 *Toll Free Tel:* 800-621-2736 *Fax:* 773-702-7212 *Toll Free Fax:* 800-621-8476 *E-mail:* orders@press.uchicago.edu *Web Site:* www.press.uchicago.edu
Billing Address: Chicago Distribution Center, 11030 S Langley Ave, Chicago, IL 60628 *Tel:* 773-702-7000 *Toll Free Tel:* 800-621-2736 *Fax:* 773-702-7212 *Toll Free Fax:* 800-621-8476 *E-mail:* orders@press.uchicago.edu *Web Site:* www.press.uchicago.edu
Orders to: Chicago Distribution Center, 11030 S Langley Ave, Chicago, IL 60628 *Tel:* 773-702-7000 *Toll Free Tel:* 800-621-2736 *Fax:* 773-702-7212 *Toll Free Fax:* 800-621-8476 *E-mail:* orders@press.uchicago.edu *Web Site:* www.press.uchicago.edu
Returns: Chicago Distribution Center, 11030 S Langley Ave, Chicago, IL 60628 *Tel:* 773-702-7000 *Toll Free Tel:* 800-621-2736 *Fax:* 773-702-7212 *Toll Free Fax:* 800-621-8476 *E-mail:* orders@press.uchicago.edu *Web Site:* www.press.uchicago.edu
Distribution Center: Chicago Distribution Center, 11030 S Langley Ave, Chicago, IL 60628 *Tel:* 773-702-7000 *Toll Free Tel:* 800-621-2736 *Fax:* 773-702-7212 *Toll Free Fax:* 800-621-8476 *E-mail:* orders@press.uchicago.edu *Web Site:* www.press.uchicago.edu

MTV Books, see Gallery Books

§Multicultural Publications Inc
1939 Manchester Rd, Akron, OH 44314
Mailing Address: PO Box 8001, Akron, OH 44320-0001
Tel: 330-865-9578 *Fax:* 330-865-9578
E-mail: multiculturalpub@prodigy.net
Web Site: www.multiculturalpub.net
Key Personnel
Pres & CEO: Bobby L Jackson
Dir, Mktg & Promos & Intl Rts: James Lynell
Lib Sales Dir: Rae Neal
Founded: 1992
Books, greeting cards, dolls & stuffed toys, multimedia.
ISBN Prefix(es): 978-0-9634932; 978-1-884242
Number of titles published annually: 1 Print; 1 CD-ROM; 1 Online
Total Titles: 28 Print; 2 CD-ROM; 28 Online; 4 Audio

Multnomah
Imprint of Crown Publishing Group
10807 New Allegiance Dr, Suite 500, Colorado Springs, CO 80921
Tel: 719-590-4999 *Toll Free Tel:* 800-603-7051 (orders) *Fax:* 719-590-8977 *Toll Free Fax:* 800-294-5686 (orders)
E-mail: info@waterbrookmultnomah.com
Web Site: waterbrookmultnomah.com
Founded: 2006
Publishes Christian books that proclaim the Gospel & equip followers of Jesus to make disciples. Seek timeless messages from trusted Christian voices that challenge readers to approach life from a Biblical perspective.
ISBN Prefix(es): 978-1-59052; 978-1-60142
Number of titles published annually: 19 Print
Membership(s): Evangelical Christian Publishers Association (ECPA)

Municipal Analysis Services Inc
PO Box 13453, Austin, TX 78711-3453
Tel: 512-704-7194
E-mail: munilysis@gmail.com
Web Site: sites.google.com/site/gregmichels/home
Key Personnel
Pres: Greg Michels
Founded: 1983
Analysis of local governments.
ISBN Prefix(es): 978-1-55507; 978-0-31738
Number of titles published annually: 82 Print; 40 CD-ROM; 80 E-Book
Total Titles: 2,200 Print; 200 CD-ROM; 540 E-Book

The Museum of Modern Art (MoMA)
Publications Dept, 11 W 53 St, New York, NY 10019
SAN: 202-5809
Tel: 212-708-9443
E-mail: moma_publications@moma.org
Web Site: www.moma.org
Key Personnel
Publr: Christopher Hudson
Edit Dir: Don McMahon
Prodn Dir: Marc Sapir *Tel:* 212-708-9745 *E-mail:* marc_sapir@moma.org
Mktg & Book Devt Coord: Hannah Kim *Tel:* 212-708-9449 *E-mail:* hannah_kim@moma.org
Founded: 1929
Art, architecture, design, photography, film.
ISBN Prefix(es): 978-0-87070; 978-1-63345
Number of titles published annually: 18 Print
Total Titles: 1,250 Print
Distributed by Distributed Art Publishers (DAP) (US & CN only)
Foreign Rep(s): Thames & Hudson Ltd (worldwide exc Canada & USA)

Warehouse: South River Distribution, South River, NJ 08882
Membership(s): American Alliance of Museums (AAM); American Association of University Presses (AAUP); CAA

§Museum of New Mexico Press
Unit of New Mexico State Department of Cultural Affairs
725 Camino Lejo, Suite C, Santa Fe, NM 87505
SAN: 202-2575
Mailing Address: PO Box 2087, Santa Fe, NM 87504-2087
Tel: 505-476-1155; 505-272-7777 (orders) *Toll Free Tel:* 800-249-7737 (orders) *Fax:* 505-476-1156 *Toll Free Fax:* 800-622-8667 (orders)
Web Site: www.mnmpress.org
Key Personnel
Dir: Anna Gallegos *Tel:* 505-476-1154 *E-mail:* anna.gallegos@state.nm.us
Art Dir & Prodn Mgr: David Skolkin *Tel:* 505-476-1159 *E-mail:* david.skolkin@state.nm.us
Edit Dir: Lisa Pachaco *Tel:* 505-476-1157 *E-mail:* lisa.pachaco@state.nm.us
Mktg & Sales Dir: Janet L Dick *Tel:* 504-476-1158 *E-mail:* janetldick@state.nm.us
Founded: 1951
Publications related to Native America, Hispanic Southwest, 20th century art, photography, folk art & folklore, nature & gardening, architecture & the Americas.
ISBN Prefix(es): 978-0-89013
Number of titles published annually: 15 Print
Total Titles: 140 Print
Distributed by University of New Mexico Press
Foreign Rep(s): Gazelle Book Services Ltd (Europe)
Orders to: University of New Mexico Press, 1312 Basehart Rd SE, Albuquerque, NM 87106-4363 *E-mail:* custserv@upress.unm.edu
Warehouse: University of New Mexico Press, 1312 Basehart Rd SE, Albuquerque, NM 87106-4363 *E-mail:* custserv@upress.unm.edu

Mutual Publishing LLC
1215 Center St, Suite 210, Honolulu, HI 96816
Tel: 808-732-1709 *Fax:* 808-734-4094
E-mail: info@mutualpublishing.com
Web Site: www.mutualpublishing.com
Key Personnel
Publr: Bennett Hymer
Founded: 1974
Publishing, print brokering & packaging. Editorial & design services; trade, mass market paperback, coffee table & souvenir books.
ISBN Prefix(es): 978-1-56647; 978-0-935180
Number of titles published annually: 30 Print
Total Titles: 330 Print
Imprints: Scripta
Membership(s): Hawaii Book Publishers Association (HBPA)

NAB, see National Association of Broadcasters (NAB)

NACE International
15835 Park Ten Place, Houston, TX 77084
Tel: 281-228-6200; 281-228-6223 *Toll Free Tel:* 800-797-NACE (797-6223) *Fax:* 281-228-6300
E-mail: firstservice@nace.org
Web Site: www.nace.org
Key Personnel
CEO: Bob Chalker *Tel:* 281-228-6250
Pubns Activities Dir: Bernardo Duran
Founded: 1943
Publishes technical books on corrosion control & prevention & materials selection, design & degradation issues. Books are developed by individual authors/editors utilizing corrosion experts to contribute text. Compilations of technical papers from NACE conferences & symposia are also issued on an annual basis.

ISBN Prefix(es): 978-1-877914; 978-0-915567; 978-1-57590
Number of titles published annually: 7 Print; 1 E-Book
Distributed by Australasian Corrosion Association Inc
Distributor for ASM International; ASTM; AWS; Butterworth-Heinemann; Cambridge University Press; CASTI Publishing; Compass Publications; CRC Press; Marcel Dekker Inc; E&FN Spon; Elsevier Science Publishers; Gulf Publishing; Industrial Press; Institute of Materials; ISO; McGraw-Hill; MTI; Prentice Hall; Professional Publications; SSPC; Swedish Corrosion Institute; John Wiley & Sons Inc
Foreign Rep(s): ABI (India); ATP (Europe); BI Publications (Asia); IBS (India)

NASW Press
Division of National Association of Social Workers (NASW)
750 First St NE, Suite 800, Washington, DC 20002
SAN: 202-893X
Tel: 202-408-8600 Fax: 203-336-8312
E-mail: press@naswdc.org
Web Site: www.naswpress.org
Key Personnel
Publr: Cheryl Bradley Tel: 202-336-8214
 E-mail: cbradley.nasw@socialworkers.org
Mng Ed, Journals & Books: Julie Gutin Tel: 202-408-8600 ext 281 E-mail: jgutin.nasw@socialworkers.org
Sr Ed: Sarah Lowman Tel: 202-408-8600 ext 398 E-mail: slowman.nasw@socialworkers.org
Founded: 1955
Professional & scholarly books & journals in the social sciences.
ISBN Prefix(es): 978-0-87101
Number of titles published annually: 6 Print; 2 CD-ROM; 6 E-Book
Total Titles: 120 Print; 70 E-Book
Billing Address: PBD Worldwide Fulfillment Services, 1650 Bluegrass Lakes Pkwy, Alpharetta, GA 30004 Tel: 770-238-0450 Toll Free Tel: 800-227-3590 Fax: 770-442-9742 Toll Free Fax: 866-494-1499
Orders to: PBD Worldwide Fulfillment Services, 1650 Bluegrass Lakes Pkwy, Alpharetta, GA 30004 Tel: 770-238-0450 Toll Free Tel: 800-227-3590 Fax: 770-442-9742 Toll Free Fax: 866-494-1499
Returns: PBD Worldwide Fulfillment Services, 1650 Bluegrass Lakes Pkwy, Alpharetta, GA 30004 Tel: 770-238-0450 Toll Free Tel: 800-227-3590 Fax: 770-442-9742 Toll Free Fax: 866-494-1499
Distribution Center: PBD Worldwide Fulfillment Services, 1650 Bluegrass Lakes Pkwy, Alpharetta, GA 30004 Tel: 770-238-0450 Toll Free Tel: 800-227-3590 Fax: 770-442-9742 Toll Free Fax: 866-494-1499

Nataraj Books
7967 Twist Lane, Springfield, VA 22153
Tel: 703-455-4996 Fax: 703-455-4001
E-mail: nataraj@erols.com; orders@natarajbooks.com; natarajbooks@gmail.com
Web Site: www.natarajbooks.com
Key Personnel
Pres: Vinod Mahajan
Founded: 1986
Books from South Asia.
ISBN Prefix(es): 978-1-881338
Number of titles published annually: 7 Print
Total Titles: 70 Print
Orders to: 7073 Brookfield Plaza, Springfield, VA 22150

§National Academies Press (NAP)
Division of National Academies

Lockbox 285, 500 Fifth St NW, Washington, DC 20001
SAN: 202-8891
Toll Free Tel: 800-624-6242 Fax: 202-334-2451 (cust serv); 202-334-2793 (mktg dept)
E-mail: customer_service@nap.edu
Web Site: www.nap.edu
Key Personnel
Dir, Publg Opers: Alphonse MacDonald Tel: 202-334-3625 E-mail: amacdonald@nas.edu
Dir, Publg Servs: Dottie Lewis Tel: 202-334-2409 E-mail: dlewis@nas.edu
Art Dir: Holly Sten Tel: 202-334-2601 E-mail: hsten@nas.edu
Founded: 1863
Science, technology & health, scholarly & trade books.
ISBN Prefix(es): 978-0-309
Number of titles published annually: 200 Print
Total Titles: 5,000 Print; 6,000 E-Book
Foreign Rep(s): Kinokuniya (Japan); Marston Book Services Ltd (Africa, Middle East, UK, Western Europe); Maruzen Co Ltd (Japan); World Scientific Publishing Co Pte Ltd (Brunei, China, Hong Kong, India, Indonesia, Korea, Malaysia, Philippines, Singapore, Taiwan, Thailand)
Foreign Rights: Amelie Cherlin (Arab Middle East); Tuttle-Mori (Japan); Andrew Nurnberg Associates (China); Eric Yang Agency
Orders to: Marston Book Service Ltd, PO Box 269, Abingdon, Oxon OX14 4YN, United Kingdom (for UK & Europe) Tel: (01235) 465500 Fax: (01235) 465555 Web Site: www.marston.co.uk
Returns: 22883 Quicksilver Dr, Dulles, VA 20166
Membership(s): Association of American Publishers (AAP)

National Association of Broadcasters (NAB)
1771 "N" St NW, Washington, DC 20036
Tel: 202-429-5300
E-mail: nab@nab.org
Web Site: www.nab.org
Key Personnel
Pres & CEO: Gordon H Smith
EVP, Conventions & Busn Opers: Mr Chris Brown Tel: 202-429-5335
EVP, Mktg: Michelle Lehman E-mail: mlehman@nab.org
Trade association representing radio & television stations & companies that serve the broadcasting industry.
ISBN Prefix(es): 978-0-89324
Number of titles published annually: 15 Print
Total Titles: 71 Print
Distributed by Allyn & Bacon; Lawrence Erlbaum Associates; Focal Press; Macmillan; Tab Books

§National Association of Insurance Commissioners
1100 Walnut St, Suite 1500, Kansas City, MO 64106-2197
Tel: 816-842-3600 Fax: 816-783-8175
E-mail: prodserv@naic.org
Web Site: www.naic.org
Key Personnel
Mgr, Implementation: Renee Brownfield E-mail: rbrownfield@naic.org
Founded: 1871
ISBN Prefix(es): 978-0-89382; 978-1-59917
Number of titles published annually: 110 Print
Total Titles: 356 Print; 110 Online; 110 E-Book
Branch Office(s)
NAIC Government Relations, Hall of the States, Suite 700, 4444 N Capitol St NW, Washington, DC 20001, Dir: Ethan Sonnichsen Tel: 202-471-3990 Fax: 816-460-7493
Capital Markets & Investment Analysis Office, One New York Plaza, Suite 4210, New York, NY 10004, Dir: Chris Evangel Tel: 212-398-9000 Fax: 212-382-4207

National Association of Secondary School Principals (NASSP)
1904 Association Dr, Reston, VA 20191-1537
Tel: 703-860-0200 Toll Free Tel: 800-253-7746; 866-647-7253 (sales)
E-mail: membership@nassp.org
Web Site: www.nassp.org
Key Personnel
Dir, Pub Aff: Bob Farrace Tel: 703-909-4661 E-mail: farraceb@nassp.org
Founded: 1916
Journals, magazines, monographs, newsletters, videos & software.
ISBN Prefix(es): 978-0-88210
Number of titles published annually: 6 Print
Total Titles: 74 Print
Imprints: NASSP
Advertising Agency: YGS Group

National Book Co
Division of Educational Research Associates
PO Box 8795, Portland, OR 97280-8795
SAN: 212-4661
Tel: 503-228-6345 Fax: 810-885-5811
E-mail: info@eralearning.com
Web Site: www.eralearning.com
Key Personnel
Dir, Spec Materials: Mark R Salser
Founded: 1965
Individualized mastery learning programs for elementary, secondary & college levels, consisting of multimedia materials in business education, home economics, language skills, mathematics, science, shorthand skills, social studies, general & vocational education; special trade publications, particularly in subjects relating to education. Computer software, reference books, Black/Afro-American history, ESL.
ISBN Prefix(es): 978-0-89420
Number of titles published annually: 25 Print
Total Titles: 175 Print; 100 Audio
Imprints: Halcyon House

National Braille Press
88 Saint Stephen St, Boston, MA 02115-4312
Tel: 617-266-6160 Toll Free Tel: 800-548-7323 (cust serv); 888-965-8965 Fax: 617-437-0456
E-mail: contact@nbp.org
Web Site: www.nbp.org
Key Personnel
Pres: Brian A MacDonald E-mail: bmacdonald@nbp.org
VP, Braille Pubns: Tony Grima Tel: 617-266-6160 ext 429 E-mail: agrima@nbp.org
VP, Devt & Major Gifts: Joseph Quintanilla
VP, Prodn: Jackie Sheridan-Witterschein
Dir, Sales: Nicole Noble
Founded: 1929
Braille books & magazines.
ISBN Prefix(es): 978-0-939173
Number of titles published annually: 40 Print; 20 E-Book
Total Titles: 65 Print; 40 E-Book

National Catholic Educational Association
1005 N Glebe Rd, Suite 525, Arlington, VA 22201
Tel: 571-257-0010 Toll Free Tel: 800-711-6232 Fax: 703-243-0025
E-mail: nceaadmin@ncea.org
Web Site: www.ncea.org
Key Personnel
PR Mgr: Margaret Kaplow E-mail: mkaplow@ncea.org
Mktg Communs Mgr: Kisha Bricsoe E-mail: kbriscoe@ncea.org
Graphic Design & Prodn Mgr: Bea Ruiz E-mail: ruiz@ncea.org
Founded: 1904
Professional development organization that also produces publications in the area of nonfiction: educational trends, methodology, innovative programs, teacher education & in-service, re-

search, technology, financial & public relations programs, management systems all applicable to nonpublic education.
ISBN Prefix(es): 978-1-55833
Number of titles published annually: 25 Print; 25 E-Book
Total Titles: 450 Print; 250 E-Book

§National Center for Children in Poverty

Division of Mailman School of Public Health at Columbia University
722 W 168 St, New York, NY 10032
Tel: 646-284-9600; 212-304-6073
E-mail: info@nccp.org
Web Site: www.nccp.org
Key Personnel
Dir: Heather Koball, PhD
Founded: 1989
Nonprofit publisher of monographs, reports, statistical updates, working papers & issue briefs concerning children under 6 who live in poverty in the US. Topics cover impact of poverty on child health & development; statistical profiles of poor children & their families; research programs on the effects of poverty; research on policies that could reduce the young child poverty rate; integrated social & human services (private & public) for low-income families. Welfare reform & children, research forum on children, families & the new federalism.
ISBN Prefix(es): 978-0-926582
Number of titles published annually: 24 Print
Total Titles: 40 Print; 20 E-Book

National Center For Employee Ownership (NCEO)

1629 Telegraph Ave, Suite 200, Oakland, CA 94612
Tel: 510-208-1300 *Fax:* 510-272-9510
E-mail: customerservice@nceo.org
Web Site: www.nceo.org
Key Personnel
Exec Dir: Loren Rodgers *Tel:* 510-208-1307
  E-mail: lrodgers@nceo.org
Dir, Publg & Info Technol: Scott Rodrick
  Tel: 510-208-1315 *E-mail:* srodrick@nceo.org
Founded: 1981
Employee ownership books, pamphlets & newsletter.
ISBN Prefix(es): 978-0-926902; 978-1-932924; 978-1-938220
Number of titles published annually: 8 Print; 8 E-Book
Total Titles: 60 Print

National Conference of State Legislatures (NCSL)

7700 E First Place, Denver, CO 80230
Tel: 303-364-7700 *Fax:* 303-364-7800
E-mail: books@ncsl.org
Web Site: www.ncsl.org
Key Personnel
Exec Dir: William T Pound
Founded: 1975
Books, magazines, series of papers & issue briefs on state public policy issues.
ISBN Prefix(es): 978-1-55516; 978-1-58024; 978-0-941336
Number of titles published annually: 100 Print
Total Titles: 200 Print
Branch Office(s)
444 N Capitol St NW, Suite 515, Washington, DC 20001 *Tel:* 202-624-5400 *Fax:* 202-737-1069

National Council of Teachers of English (NCTE)

340 N Neil St, Suite 104, Champaign, IL 61820
Tel: 217-328-3870 *Toll Free Tel:* 877-369-6283 (cust serv) *Fax:* 217-328-9645
E-mail: customerservice@ncte.org

Web Site: www.ncte.org
Key Personnel
Exec Dir: Emily Kirkpatrick *Tel:* 217-278-3601
  E-mail: ekirkpatrick@ncte.org
Div Dir, Pubns & Perms Coord: Kurt Austin
  Tel: 217-278-3619
Sr Ed: Bonny Graham *Tel:* 217-278-3618
Purch & Prodn Mgr: Charles Hartman *Tel:* 217-278-3664
Founded: 1911
Nonprofit professional association of educators in English studies, literacy & language arts. Specialize in the teaching of English & the language arts at all grade levels; research reports; guidelines & position statements; journals; professional development books.
ISBN Prefix(es): 978-0-8141
Number of titles published annually: 15 Print; 10 E-Book
Total Titles: 300 Print; 2 CD-ROM; 45 E-Book
Imprints: Principles in Practice

§National Council of Teachers of Mathematics (NCTM)

1906 Association Dr, Reston, VA 20191-1502
SAN: 202-9057
Tel: 703-620-9840 *Toll Free Tel:* 800-235-7566
  Fax: 703-476-2970
E-mail: nctm@nctm.org
Web Site: www.nctm.org
Key Personnel
Exec Dir: Ken Krehbiel
Dir, Pubns: Eleanore Tapscott *Tel:* 703-620-9840 ext 2129
Founded: 1920
Professional publications, including books (printed & online), monographs & yearbooks. Members include individuals, institutions, students, teachers & educators. Multiyear plans available to individual & institutional members.
ISBN Prefix(es): 978-0-87353; 978-1-68054
Number of titles published annually: 15 Print; 3 Online
Total Titles: 175 Print; 15 E-Book
Distributed by Eric Armin Inc Education Ctr; Delta Education; Didax Educational Resources; Educators Outlet; ETA Cuisenaire; Lakeshore Learning Materials; NASCO; Spectrum
Distribution Center: Copyright Clearance Center Inc, 222 Rosewood Dr, Danvers, MA 01923
  Tel: 978-750-8400

National Education Association (NEA)

1201 16 St NW, Washington, DC 20036-3290
Tel: 202-833-4000 *Fax:* 202-822-7974
Web Site: www.nea.org
Key Personnel
Pres: Lily Eskelsen Garcia
VP: Becky Pringle
Secy/Treas: Princess R Moss
Exec Dir: John C Stocks
Sr Dir, Communs: Ramona Oliver
Founded: 1857
Professional development publications for K-12 & higher education & AV materials for educators. Web site with resources & general information for educators & the general public.
ISBN Prefix(es): 978-0-8106
Number of titles published annually: 7 Print; 2 CD-ROM; 2 Online
Total Titles: 189 Print; 2 CD-ROM; 9 Online
Imprints: NEA Professional Library

§National Gallery of Art

Sixth & Constitution Ave NW, Washington, DC 20565
Mailing Address: 2000 B South Club Dr, Landover, MD 20785
Tel: 202-842-6200 *Fax:* 202-408-8530
E-mail: publishingoffice@nga.gov
Web Site: www.nga.gov

Key Personnel
Deputy Publr & Prodn Mgr: Chris Vogel
Ed-in-Chief: Emiko K Usui
Founded: 1941
Exhibition catalogues, catalogues of the collection & scholarly monographs.
ISBN Prefix(es): 978-0-89468
Number of titles published annually: 15 Print; 3 Online
Total Titles: 112 Print; 2 CD-ROM; 3 Online
Divisions: Department of Education Resources
Distributed by Abrams; DAP; Lund Humphries/Ashgate; Princeton University Press; Thames & Hudson; University of Chicago Press; Yale University Press

National Geographic Books

Division of National Geographic Partners
1145 17 St NW, Washington, DC 20036-4688
SAN: 202-8956
Tel: 202-857-7000 *Toll Free Tel:* 877-866-6486
E-mail: ngbooks@cdsfulfillment.com
Web Site: www.nationalgeographic.com/books/; ngbooks.buysub.com
Key Personnel
SVP & Gen Mgr, Books: Hector Sierra
  E-mail: hector.sierra@natgeo.com
SVP, Kids Content: Jennifer Emmett
  E-mail: jennifer.emmett@natgeo.com
VP & Edit Dir, Kids Books: Rebecca Baines
  E-mail: rebecca.baines@natgeo.com
Publr & Edit Dir, Adult Books: Lisa Thomas
  E-mail: lisa.thomas@natgeo.com
Sr Dir, Digital Book Publg: Rachel Graham
  E-mail: rachel.graham@natgeo.com
Sr Dir Mktg, Books: Daneen Goodwin
  E-mail: daneen.goodwin@natgeo.com
Dir, Kids Mktg: Ruth Chamblee *E-mail:* ruth.chamblee@natgeo.com
Deputy Ed, Adult Books: Hilary Black
  E-mail: hilary.black@natgeo.com
Edit Mgr: Bridget Hamilton *E-mail:* bridget.hamilton@natgeo.com
Founded: 1888
Nonfiction general illustrated reference, travel, photography, history, science. Children's nonfiction with emphasis on school & library markets.
ISBN Prefix(es): 978-0-7922; 978-0-87044; 978-1-4262; 978-1-4263
Number of titles published annually: 140 Print
Total Titles: 2,500 Print; 500 E-Book
Imprints: National Geographic Kids Books; National Geographic Under the Stars (kids fiction)
Distributed by HarperCollins UK (Australia, New Zealand & UK-kids books); Penguin Random House (worldwide exc UK); Simon & Schuster UK (UK-adult books)
Foreign Rights: Gordon Fournier (worldwide); Andrea Wollitz (USA)
Membership(s): Association of American Publishers (AAP); The Children's Book Council (CBC)

National Geographic Learning

Unit of Cengage Learning
20 Channel Center St, Boston, MA 02210
Tel: 617-289-7796
E-mail: schoolcustomerservice@cengage.com
Web Site: www.ngl.cengage.com/school
Founded: 1980
Provides quality PreK-12, academic & adult education instructional solutions for reading, science, social studies, mathematics, world languages, ESL/ELD, advanced, honors & electives, career & technical education & professional development. Catalog available online at ngl.cengage.com/assets/html/catalogs.
ISBN Prefix(es): 978-0-917837; 978-1-56334
Number of titles published annually: 10 CD-ROM; 10 Online
Membership(s): Association of American Publishers (AAP)

§**National Golf Foundation**
501 N Hwy A1A, Jupiter, FL 33477-4577
Tel: 561-744-6006 *Toll Free Tel:* 888-275-4643
Fax: 561-744-6107
E-mail: general@ngf.org
Web Site: www.ngf.org
Key Personnel
Pres & CEO: Dr Joseph Beditz
Founded: 1936
Premier publisher of research & information for the business of golf. Over 200 publications are offered on golf consumer research, industry & market trends, golf facility development & operations, golf range development, instruction & player development.
ISBN Prefix(es): 978-0-9638647; 978-1-57701
Number of titles published annually: 4 Print
Total Titles: 100 Print; 1 CD-ROM; 2 Online; 1 Audio

National Information Standards Organization (NISO)
3600 Clipper Mill Rd, Suite 302, Baltimore, MD 21211-1948
Tel: 301-654-2512 *Fax:* 410-685-5278
E-mail: nisohq@niso.org
Web Site: www.niso.org
Key Personnel
Exec Dir: Todd Carpenter *E-mail:* tcarpenter@niso.org
Dir, Community Engagement: Alice Meadows
Dir, Content: Jill O'Neill *E-mail:* joneill@niso.org
Dir, Strategic Initiatives: Jason Griffey
Assoc Dir, Progs: Nettie Lagace
  E-mail: nlagace@niso.org
Off Mgr: Kimberly Graham *E-mail:* kgraham@niso.org
Founded: 1939 (incorporated as US 501(c)(3) in 1982)
Maintain & develop technical standards for libraries, publishers & information services.
ISBN Prefix(es): 978-1-880124; 978-1-937522
Number of titles published annually: 6 Print; 10 E-Book
Total Titles: 70 Print; 70 Online; 70 E-Book
Imprints: NISO Press

National Institute for Trial Advocacy (NITA)
1685 38 St, Suite 200, Boulder, CO 80301-2735
Tel: 720-890-4860 *Toll Free Tel:* 877-648-2632; 800-225-6482 (orders & returns) *Fax:* 720-890-7069
E-mail: customerservice@nita.org; sales@nita.org
Web Site: www.nita.org
Key Personnel
Exec Dir: Wendy McCormack
  E-mail: wmccormack@nita.org
Dir, Mktg: Daniel McHugh *E-mail:* dmchugh@nita.org
Assoc Exec Dir, Opers: Jennifer Schneider
  E-mail: jschneider@nita.org
Dir, Pubns: Eric Sorensen *E-mail:* esorensen@nita.org
Founded: 1970
Legal & litigation training.
ISBN Prefix(es): 978-1-55681; 978-1-60156
Number of titles published annually: 20 Print; 1 CD-ROM
Total Titles: 350 Print; 2 CD-ROM; 12 Audio

National Learning Corp
212 Michael Dr, Syosset, NY 11791
Tel: 516-921-8888 *Toll Free Tel:* 800-632-8888
  Fax: 516-921-8743
E-mail: info@passbooks.com
Web Site: www.passbooks.com
Key Personnel
Pres & CEO: Michael P Rudman
Founded: 1967
Basic competency tests for college, high school & occupations; functional literacy; career, general,

vocational & technical, adult & continuing, special, cooperative & community education; professional licensure; test preparation books for civil service, postal service, government careers, armed forces, high school & college equivalency; college, graduate & professional school enhancement; certification & licensing in engineering & technical careers, teaching, law, dentistry, medicine & allied health professions.
ISBN Prefix(es): 978-0-8373; 978-0-8293
Number of titles published annually: 7 Print
Total Titles: 6,000 Print
Imprints: Career Examination Passbooks®
Subsidiaries: Delaney Books Inc; Frank Merriwell Inc
Membership(s): Association of American Publishers (AAP)

National Notary Association (NNA)
9350 De Soto Ave, Chatsworth, CA 91311-4926
Mailing Address: PO Box 2402, Chatsworth, CA 91313-2402
Tel: 818-739-4000 *Toll Free Tel:* 800-876-6827
  Toll Free Fax: 800-833-1211
E-mail: services@nationalnotary.org
Web Site: www.nationalnotary.org
Key Personnel
Pres & CEO: Thomas A Heymann
CFO: Rob Clark
VP & CIO/CTO: Dave Stephenson
EVP: Deborah M Thaw
VP, Busn Devt: Chris Sturdivant
VP, Mktg: Thomas K Hayden
Founded: 1957
Publish books, periodical, videos, seminars.
ISBN Prefix(es): 978-0-9600158; 978-0-933134; 978-1-891133; 978-1-59767
Number of titles published annually: 15 Print
Total Titles: 40 Print

National Resource Center for Youth Services
Division of University of Oklahoma Outreach
Schusterman Ctr, Bldg 4W, 4502 E 41 St, Tulsa, OK 74135-2512
Tel: 918-660-3700 *Toll Free Tel:* 800-274-2687
  Fax: 918-660-3737
Web Site: www.nrcys.ou.edu
Key Personnel
Dir: Kristi Charles *E-mail:* klcharles@ou.edu
Founded: 1985
Curricula & resource manuals for professionals & volunteers who work with foster care & at-risk teenagers.
ISBN Prefix(es): 978-1-878848
Number of titles published annually: 3 Print
Total Titles: 20 Print

National Science Teachers Association (NSTA)
1840 Wilson Blvd, Arlington, VA 22201-3000
Tel: 703-312-9205 *Toll Free Tel:* 800-277-5300
  (orders) *Toll Free Fax:* 888-433-0526 (orders)
E-mail: publisher@nsta.org (gen info); orders@nsta.org
Web Site: www.nsta.org/publications/press/; www.nsta.org/store
Founded: 1944
Books & periodicals.
ISBN Prefix(es): 978-0-87355; 978-1-93353; 978-1-936137; 978-1-935155; 978-1-936959; 978-1-938946; 978-1-941316
Number of titles published annually: 25 Print; 25 E-Book
Total Titles: 350 Print; 350 E-Book
Imprints: NSTA Ebooks+; NSTA Kids; NSTA Press®
Foreign Rep(s): Alkem (Southeast Asia); Eurospan (worldwide exc Canada & Southeast Asia); University of Toronto Press (Canada)
Foreign Rights: Cat Russo (worldwide)
Orders to: PO Box 90214, Washington, DC 20090-5300

Returns: 3280 Summit Ridge Pkwy, Duluth, GA 30096
Membership(s): Association Media & Publishing; Association of American Publishers (AAP); Association of American Publishers PreK-12 Learning Group; Independent Book Publishing Professionals Group (IBPPG)

The National Underwriter Co
Division of ALM Media LLC
4157 Olympic Blvd, Suite 225, Erlanger, KY 41018
Tel: 859-692-2100 *Toll Free Tel:* 800-543-0874
  Toll Free Fax: 800-874-1916
E-mail: customerservice@nuco.com
Web Site: www.nationalunderwriter.com
Founded: 1897
ISBN Prefix(es): 978-0-87218; 978-1-936362; 978-1-938130; 978-1-939829; 978-1-941627
Number of titles published annually: 11 Print
Total Titles: 216 Print; 46 E-Book

National Wildlife Federation
11100 Wildlife Center Dr, Reston, VA 20190-5362
Toll Free Tel: 800-477-5034
Web Site: www.zoobooks.com
Key Personnel
Sales Mgr: Kurt Von Hertsenberg *E-mail:* kurt@zoobooks.com
Founded: 1980
Books on wildlife & animals. Publisher of *Zoobooks* magazine.
ISBN Prefix(es): 978-0-937934; 978-1-888153
Number of titles published annually: 27 Print; 27 E-Book
Total Titles: 200 Print; 200 E-Book
Membership(s): Association of American Publishers PreK-12 Learning Group

§**Naval Institute Press**
Division of US Naval Institute
291 Wood Rd, Annapolis, MD 21402-5034
SAN: 202-9006
Tel: 410-268-6110 *Toll Free Tel:* 800-233-8764
  Fax: 410-295-1084; 410-571-1703 (cust serv)
E-mail: webmaster@navalinstitute.org; customer@navalinstitute.org (cust serv)
Web Site: www.nip.org; www.usni.org
Key Personnel
CEO: Peter H Daly
Dir: Adam Kane
Dir, Sales & Mktg: Claire Noble *Tel:* 410-295-1039 *E-mail:* cnoble@usni.org; Robin Noonan
Dir, Dead Reckoning: Gary Thompson
Press Dir: Rick Russell *E-mail:* rrussell@usni.org
Mng Ed: Susan Corrado *Tel:* 410-295-1032
  E-mail: scorrado@usni.org
Sr Acqs Ed: Thomas Cutler *E-mail:* tcutler@usni.org
Prodn Ed: Rachel Crawford
Subs Rts Ed: Susan Todd Brook *E-mail:* sbrook@usni.org
Digital Mktg & Database Mgr: Meagan Szekely
Publicity Mgr: Jacqline Barnes *Tel:* 410-295-1028
  E-mail: jbarnes@usni.org
Cust Serv: Jaemellah Kemp
Founded: 1873
Naval & maritime subjects: professional, biography, science, history, ship & aviation references, US Naval Institute magazines; literature.
ISBN Prefix(es): 978-0-87021; 978-1-55750; 978-1-59114; 978-1-61251; 978-1-68247
Number of titles published annually: 65 Print
Total Titles: 800 Print
Imprints: Dead Reckoning
Distributed by Publishers Group West (PGW) (digital only)
Foreign Rep(s): Eurospan Group (Africa, Asia, Australia, Europe, India, Middle East, Oceania, UK); Scholarly Book Services Inc (Canada)

Warehouse: US Naval Institute, 2427 Bond St, University Park, IL 60466
Membership(s): Association of University Presses (AUPresses)

NavPress Publishing Group
Division of The Navigators
3820 N 30 St, Colorado Springs, CO 80904
SAN: 211-5352
Tel: 719-598-1212 *Toll Free Tel:* 800-323-9400; 855-277-9400 (cust serv) *Toll Free Fax:* 800-684-0247
Web Site: www.navpress.com
Key Personnel
Publr: Don Pape
Founded: 1975
Paperbacks, mass market & trade, hardcovers, periodicals; religious (Protestant) materials.
ISBN Prefix(es): 978-0-89109; 978-1-57683; 978-1-60006; 978-1-61521; 978-1-61747; 978-1-61291; 978-1-63146; 978-1-64158
Number of titles published annually: 15 Print
Total Titles: 600 Print; 2 Audio
Imprints: NavPress
Distributed by Tyndale House Publishers Inc
Orders to: Tyndale House Publishers Inc, 351 Executive Dr, Carol Stream, IL 60188

NBM Publishing Inc
160 Broadway, E Wing, Suite 700, New York, NY 10038
SAN: 210-0835
Tel: 646-559-4681 *Toll Free Tel:* 800-886-1223
Fax: 212-643-1545
E-mail: admin@nbmpub.com
Web Site: www.nbmpub.com
Key Personnel
Pres & Publr: Terry Nantier
Off Mgr: May Wong *E-mail:* mayw@nbmpub.com
Founded: 1976
Graphic novels.
ISBN Prefix(es): 978-0-918348; 978-1-56163; 978-1-68112
Number of titles published annually: 20 Print; 20 E-Book
Total Titles: 250 Print; 100 E-Book
Imprints: Eurotica (erotic graphic novels from European authors)
Foreign Rep(s): IPG (Canada); Turnaround (Europe, UK)
Orders to: IPG Distribution Center, 600 N Pulaski Rd, Chicago, IL 60624 *Toll Free Tel:* 800-888-IPG1 (888-4741)
Returns: IPG Distribution Center, 600 N Pulaski Rd, Chicago, IL 60624
Warehouse: IPG Distribution Center, 600 N Pulaski Rd, Chicago, IL 60624
Distribution Center: IPG Distribution Center, 600 N Pulaski Rd, Chicago, IL 60624
Membership(s): Association of American Publishers (AAP); The Children's Book Council (CBC); Independent Book Publishers Association (IBPA)

Neibauer Press
Division of Louis Neibauer Co Inc
20 Industrial Dr, Warminster, PA 18974
Tel: 215-322-6200 *Toll Free Tel:* 800-322-6203 (orders) *Fax:* 215-322-2495
E-mail: info@neibauer.com
Web Site: www.neibauer.com; www.churchsupplier.com (orders)
Key Personnel
Pres: Nathan Neibauer *E-mail:* nathan@neibauer.com
Founded: 1967
ISBN Prefix(es): 978-1-878259
Number of titles published annually: 5 Print
Total Titles: 30 Print
Divisions: ChurchSupplier.com

§New City Press
Division of Focolare Movement
202 Comforter Blvd, Hyde Park, NY 12538
SAN: 203-7335
Tel: 845-229-0335 *Toll Free Tel:* 800-462-5980 (orders only) *Fax:* 845-229-0351
E-mail: info@newcitypress.com; orders@newcitypress.com
Web Site: www.newcitypress.com
Key Personnel
Publr & Gen Mgr: Claude Blanc
Accts Payable: Manuel Salazar *E-mail:* manuel.salazar@newcitypress.com
Cust Serv: Mike Lyons *Tel:* 845-229-0335 ext 1
Founded: 1964
Publishes spiritual works of all Christian eras, including the Church Fathers, the spiritual masters of the middle-ages, as well as publications of contemporary spirituality & theology.
ISBN Prefix(es): 978-0-911782; 978-1-56548
Number of titles published annually: 15 Print
Total Titles: 300 Print
Imprints: NCP
Distributor for Ciudad Nueva (Argentina, Spain); New City (Great Britain)
Foreign Rep(s): Enderle Book Co (Japan); John Garratt Publishing (Australia); Jerome's Specialist Booksellers (New Zealand); Joseph's Inspirational (Canada); New City (China, England, Ireland, Philippines); Preca Bookshop (Malta)

§New Concepts Publishing
5265 Humphreys Rd, Lake Park, GA 31636
E-mail: newconcepts@newconceptspublishing.com
Web Site: www.newconceptspublishing.com
Key Personnel
Pres & PR: Madris De Pasture *E-mail:* madris@newconceptspublishing.com
Founded: 1996
ISBN Prefix(es): 978-1-58608; 978-1-891020; 978-1-60394
Number of titles published annually: 50 Print; 192 Online; 144 E-Book
Total Titles: 200 Print; 700 Online; 700 E-Book

New Directions Publishing Corp
80 Eighth Ave, 19th fl, New York, NY 10011
SAN: 202-9081
Tel: 212-255-0230
E-mail: editorial@ndbooks.com; publicity@ndbooks.com
Web Site: ndbooks.com
Key Personnel
Pres & Publr: Barbara Epler
EVP: Laurie Callahan
Art Dir & Prodn Mgr: Erik Rieselbach
Foreign Rts Dir: Declan Spring *E-mail:* dspring@ndbooks.com
Publicity Dir: Mieke Chew; Brittany Dennison
Founded: 1936
Modern literature, poetry, criticism & belles lettres.
ISBN Prefix(es): 978-0-8112
Number of titles published annually: 30 Print
Total Titles: 930 Print
Distributed by W W Norton & Company Inc
Foreign Rep(s): Everest International Publishing Services (Wei Zhao) (China); B K Norton Ltd (Korea, Taiwan); W W Norton & Co Ltd (Africa, Europe, Ireland, Middle East, UK); Pansing Distribution Pte Ltd (Brunei, Malaysia, Singapore); Publishers Group Canada (Canada); Rockbook (Gilles Fauveau) (Japan); Transglobal Publishers Services Ltd (Hong Kong, Macau); US PubRep Inc (Caribbean, Central America, Mexico, South America); John Wiley & Sons Australia Ltd (Australia, New Zealand)
Foreign Rights: Agencia Literaria Carmen Balcells SA (Anna Bofill) (Spain); The Deborah Harris Agency (Deborah Harris) (Israel); Agence Hoffman (Luisa Straub) (Germany);

The Italian Literary Agency SRL (Beatrice Beraldo) (Italy); Agence Michelle Lapautre (Catherine Lapoutre) (France); Orion Literary Agency (Harumi Sakai) (Japan); Peters, Fraser & Dunlop Literary Agents (Laura McNeill) (British Commonwealth); Agencia Riff (Lucia Riff) (Brazil)

§New Forums Press Inc
1018 S Lewis St, Stillwater, OK 74074
Mailing Address: PO Box 876, Stillwater, OK 74076-0876
Tel: 405-372-6158 *Toll Free Tel:* 800-606-3766
Fax: 405-377-2237
E-mail: submissions@newforums.com
Web Site: www.newforums.com
Key Personnel
Pres: Douglas Dollar *E-mail:* ddollar@newforums.com
Founded: 1981
Practical & innovative academic journals, newsletters & books for educators in colleges & universities. Textbooks are also a primary interest.
ISBN Prefix(es): 978-0-913507; 978-1-58107
Number of titles published annually: 25 Print; 1 Online; 3 E-Book
Total Titles: 250 Print; 1 Online; 5 E-Book
Advertising Agency: Copy & Art, 219 E Greenvale Ct, Stillwater, OK 74075 *Tel:* 405-377-8224
Membership(s): The Association of Publishers for Special Sales (APSS)

New Harbinger Publications Inc
5674 Shattuck Ave, Oakland, CA 94609
Tel: 510-652-0215 *Toll Free Tel:* 800-748-6273 (orders only) *Fax:* 510-652-5472
Toll Free Fax: 800-652-1613
E-mail: nhhelp@newharbinger.com; customerservice@newharbinger.com
Web Site: www.newharbinger.com
Key Personnel
Publr: Matthew (Matt) McKay, PhD *E-mail:* matt.mckay@newharbinger.com
Assoc Publr: Catharine A Meyers *E-mail:* catharine@newharbinger.com
Prodn Mgr: Michele Waters *E-mail:* michele@newharbinger.com
Intl Rts: Dorothy Smyk *E-mail:* dorothy@newharbinger.com
Founded: 1973
We offer the best in self-help psychology; real tools for real change. Now offering spirituality titles from our Non-Duality Press & Reveal Press imprints, which offer new wisdom for living consciously in our modern world.
ISBN Prefix(es): 978-1-57224; 978-0-934986; 978-1-879237; 978-1-60882; 978-1-62625
Number of titles published annually: 60 Print; 60 E-Book
Total Titles: 800 Print; 450 E-Book; 20 Audio
Imprints: Context Press; Impact; Instant Help; Noetic Books; Non-Duality Press; Reveal Press
Foreign Rights: Bookreps NZ Ltd (New Zealand); Little, Brown Book Group (Europe, UK); Raincoast Books (Canada, UK); Real Books (South Africa); John Reed Book Distributors (Australia); Southern Publishers Group (New Zealand)
Returns: 660 S Mansfield St, Ypsilanti, MI 48197

New Horizon Press
PO Box 669, Far Hills, NJ 07931-0669
SAN: 677-119X
Tel: 908-604-6311
E-mail: nhp@newhorizonpressbooks.com
Web Site: www.newhorizonpressbooks.com
Key Personnel
VP, Fin & Mktg: JoAnne C Thomas *E-mail:* jct@newhorizonpressbooks.com
Founded: 1982

True stories of uncommon heroes, true crime, social issues, behavioral, political science & psychologically-oriented nonfiction, trade paper, children's self-help, helping children deal with crisis.
ISBN Prefix(es): 978-0-88282; 978-1-933893
Number of titles published annually: 12 Print; 12 E-Book
Total Titles: 340 Print; 62 Online
Imprints: Small Horizons
Foreign Rights: Books Crossing Borders (Betty Ann Crawford) (worldwide)
Orders to: Publishers Group West (Perseus Distribution), 1700 Fourth St, Berkeley, CA 94710 *Toll Free Tel:* 800-788-3123 *Fax:* 510-809-3777 *Toll Free Fax:* 800-351-5073 *Web Site:* www. pgw.com
Returns: Perseus Distribution Returns Dept, 1700 Fourth St, Berkeley, CA 94710 *Toll Free Tel:* 800-788-3123 *Toll Free Fax:* 800-351-5073
Distribution Center: Publishers Group West (Perseus Distribution), 1700 Fourth St, Berkeley, CA 94710 *Tel:* 510-809-3700 *Toll Free Tel:* 800-788-3123 *Fax:* 510-809-3777 *Toll Free Fax:* 800-351-5073 *E-mail:* info@pgw.com *Web Site:* www.pgw.com

New Issues Poetry & Prose
Affiliate of Western Michigan University
c/o Western Michigan University, 1903 W Michigan Ave, Kalamazoo, MI 49008-5463
Tel: 269-387-8185
E-mail: new-issues@wmich.edu
Web Site: www.wmich.edu/newissues
Key Personnel
Mng Ed: Kimberly Kolbe
Ed-in-Chief: William Olsen
Founded: 1996
ISBN Prefix(es): 978-1-930974; 978-0-932826; 978-1-936970
Number of titles published annually: 6 Print
Total Titles: 180 Print
Distribution Center: Chicago Distribution Center (CDC), 11030 S Langley Ave, Chicago, IL 60628 *Tel:* 773-702-7010 *Toll Free Fax:* 800-621-8476

New Leaf Press
Imprint of New Leaf Publishing Group Inc
3142 Hwy 103 N, Green Forest, AR 72638-2233
Mailing Address: PO Box 726, Green Forest, AR 72638-0726
Tel: 870-438-5288 *Toll Free Tel:* 800-999-3777 *Fax:* 870-438-5120
E-mail: nlp@newleafpress.net; submissions@newleafpress.net
Web Site: www.nlpg.com
Key Personnel
Pres, New Leaf Publishing Group: Tim Dudley
VP, Mktg & Sales, New Leaf Publishing Group: Randy Pratt
Asst Ed: Craig Froman
Founded: 1975
Christian living & creation books; evangelical, devotionals.
ISBN Prefix(es): 978-0-89221
Number of titles published annually: 35 Print; 35 E-Book
Total Titles: 425 Print; 200 E-Book

New Poets Series, see BrickHouse Books Inc

The New Press
120 Wall St, 31st fl, New York, NY 10005
Tel: 212-629-8802 *Toll Free Tel:* 800-343-4489 (orders) *Fax:* 212-629-8617 *Toll Free Fax:* 800-351-5073 (orders)
E-mail: newpress@thenewpress.com
Web Site: www.thenewpress.com
Key Personnel
Exec Dir: Diane Wachtell
Publr: Ellen Adler

Edit Dir: Carl Bromley
Fin Dir: Carline Yup
Prodn Dir: Fran Forte
Assoc Edit Dir: Tara Grove
Exec Ed: Marc Favreau
Sr Mng Ed: Maury Botton
Ed: Zakia Henderson-Brown
Publicity Mgr: Derek Warker
Sr Publicist: Jessica Yu
Founded: 1990
Nonprofit publisher in the public interest; politics, education, current affairs, history, biography, economics, international fiction in translation.
ISBN Prefix(es): 978-1-56584; 978-1-59558; 978-1-62097
Number of titles published annually: 50 Print
Total Titles: 1,200 Print; 200 E-Book
Foreign Rep(s): MK International Ltd (Japan); I B Taurus & Co Ltd (worldwide); Two Rivers Distribution (USA); University of Toronto Press (Canada)
Foreign Rights: Agencia Literaria Carmen Balcells SA (Spain); Ursula Bender (Germany); Ann Christine Danielsson (Scandinavia); Cristina de Mello e Souza; Beth Elon (Israel); Mary Kling (France); William Miller (Japan); Susanna Zevi (Italy)

New Readers Press
Division of ProLiteracy
104 Marcellus, Syracuse, NY 13204
SAN: 202-1064
Tel: 315-422-9121 *Toll Free Tel:* 800-448-8878 *Toll Free Fax:* 866-894-2100
E-mail: nrp@proliteracy.org
Web Site: www.newreaderspress.com
Key Personnel
Sales & Busn Dir: Susan Willey *Tel:* 315-422-9121 ext 2470
Founded: 1965
Books & periodicals for adults & young adult reading at a 0-8 reading level, basic reading & writing materials, ESL, mathematics & GED prep.
ISBN Prefix(es): 978-0-88336; 978-1-56420; 978-1-56853; 978-0-929631; 978-1-944057
Number of titles published annually: 20 Print
Total Titles: 400 Print; 41 Audio
Foreign Rights: Laubach Literacy Ontario (Canada)

New Rivers Press
c/o Minnesota State University Moorhead, 1104 Seventh Ave S, Moorhead, MN 56563
Tel: 218-477-5870 *Fax:* 218-477-2236
E-mail: nrp@mnstate.edu
Web Site: www.newriverspress.com; www.mnstate.edu/newriverspress
Key Personnel
Dir: Travis Dolence *Tel:* 218-477-2358 *E-mail:* travis.dolence@mnstate.edu
Mng Ed: Nathan Rundquist *E-mail:* rundquisna@mnstate.edu
Sr Ed: Dr Kevin Carollo *Tel:* 218-477-2939 *E-mail:* carollo@mnstate.edu
Founded: 1968
Books of poetry, short stories & novellas, creative nonfiction, memoir.
ISBN Prefix(es): 978-0-912284; 978-0-89823
Number of titles published annually: 8 Print; 6 E-Book
Total Titles: 375 Print
Distribution Center: Small Press Distribution, 1341 Seventh St, Berkeley, CA 94710 *Toll Free Tel:* 800-869-7553 *E-mail:* spd@spdbooks.org *Web Site:* www.spdbooks.org
Membership(s): Association of Writers & Writing Programs (AWP); Community of Literary Magazines & Presses (CLMP)

New Win Publishing
Division of Academic Learning Co LLC

9682 Telstar Ave, Suite 110, El Monte, CA 91731
SAN: 217-1201
Tel: 626-448-3448 *Fax:* 626-602-3817
E-mail: info@academiclearningcompany.com
Web Site: newwinpublishing.com; wbusinessbooks.com
Key Personnel
Publr: Arthur Chou
Founded: 1988
General nonfiction: business books for sales, marketing & entrepreneurship, crafts, reference, health & nutrition, healthy gourmet cooking, career development, outdoor sports, hunting, shooting, fishing, decoys & dogs.
ISBN Prefix(es): 978-0-8329; 978-0-87691
Number of titles published annually: 25 Print
Total Titles: 70 Print
Imprints: WBusiness Books; Winchester Press; ZHealth Books

New World Library
Division of Whatever Publishing Inc
14 Pamaron Way, Novato, CA 94949
SAN: 211-8777
Tel: 415-884-2100 *Toll Free Tel:* 800-227-3900 (ext 52, retail orders); 800-972-6657 *Fax:* 415-884-2199
E-mail: escort@newworldlibrary.com
Web Site: www.newworldlibrary.com
Key Personnel
Pres: Marc Allen *E-mail:* marc@newworldlibrary.com
Edit Dir: Georgia Hughes *E-mail:* georgia@newworldlibrary.com
Mktg Dir & Assoc Publr: Munro Magruder *E-mail:* munro@newworldlibrary.com
Prodn Dir: Tona Pearce Meyers *E-mail:* tona@newworldlibrary.com
Publicity Dir: Monique Muhlenkamp *E-mail:* monique@newworldlibrary.com
Exec Ed: Jason Gardner *E-mail:* jason@newworldlibrary.com
Submissions Ed: Joel Prin *E-mail:* joel@newworldlibrary.com
Foreign Rts Mgr: Danielle Galat *E-mail:* danielle@newworldlibrary.com
Soc Media Mgr & Sr Publicist: Kim Corbin *E-mail:* kim@newworldlibrary.com
Spec Sales Mgr: Ami Parkerson *E-mail:* ami@newworldlibrary.com
Founded: 1977
Publisher of books on self-improvement, personal growth & spirituality, health & wellness, pets & animals, psychology & women's interest.
ISBN Prefix(es): 978-0-915811; 978-0-931432; 978-1-880032; 978-0-945934; 978-1-57731; 978-1-882591; 978-1-930722; 978-1-932073; 978-1-60868
Number of titles published annually: 35 Print; 35 E-Book; 1 Audio
Total Titles: 600 Print; 500 E-Book; 48 Audio
Imprints: Amber-Allen Publishing; Nataraj; Eckhart Tolle Editions
Divisions: HJ Kramer Inc
Foreign Rep(s): Akasha Books (New Zealand); Brumby Books (Australia); Dempsey-Your Distributor (Canada); Ingram International (Continental Europe, India, Japan, Korea, Latin America, Middle East, Philippines, South America, Southeast Asia, Taiwan); Publishers Group Canada (Canada); Publishers Group UK (UK); SG Distribution (South Africa)
Distribution Center: Publishers Group West, 193 Edwards Dr, Jackson, TN 38301-7795 *Toll Free Tel:* 800-788-3123 *Web Site:* www.pgw.com
Membership(s): Association of American Publishers (AAP); Publishers Association of the West (PubWest); Publishing Professionals Network (PPN)
See separate listing for:
HJ Kramer Inc

New York Academy of Sciences (NYAS)

7 World Trade Center, 40th fl, 250 Greenwich St, New York, NY 10007-2157
SAN: 203-753X
Tel: 212-298-8600 *Toll Free Tel:* 800-843-6927
Fax: 212-298-3650
E-mail: nyas@nyas.org; annals@nyas.org; customerservice@nyas.org
Web Site: www.nyas.org
Key Personnel
Pres & CEO: Ellis Rubenstein *Tel:* 212-298-8686
E-mail: erubenstein@nyas.org
EVP & COO: T C Wescott *Tel:* 212-298-8695
E-mail: tcwescott@nyas.org
SVP & Chief Admin Offr: Wendy Caruso Schneider *Tel:* 212-298-8680 *E-mail:* wschneider@nyas.org
SVP, Opers: Erica Cullmann *Tel:* 212-298-8619
E-mail: ecullman@nyas.org
Exec Dir, Sci Pubns & Ed-in-Chief, Annals of the NYAS: Douglas Braaten, PhD *Tel:* 212-298-8634 *E-mail:* dbraaten@nyas.org
Founded: 1817
Annals & transactions of the New York Academy of Sciences; also publish *Update Magazine.*
ISBN Prefix(es): 978-0-89072; 978-0-89766; 978-1-57331
Number of titles published annually: 28 Print
Total Titles: 333 Print
Distributed by Wiley Blackwell Publishers

The New York Botanical Garden Press

Division of New York Botanical Garden
2900 Southern Blvd, Bronx, NY 10458-5126
Tel: 718-817-8721 *Fax:* 718-817-8842
E-mail: nybgpress@nybg.org
Web Site: www.nybgpress.org
Founded: 1896
Dissemination of information on the scientific study of plants.
ISBN Prefix(es): 978-0-89327
Number of titles published annually: 10 Print
Total Titles: 244 Print
Warehouse: Maple Logistics Solutions, York Distribution Center, PO Box 15100, York, PA 17405
Distribution Center: Maple Logistics Solutions, York Distribution Center, PO Box 15100, York, PA 17405
Membership(s): Association of American Publishers (AAP)

§New York State Bar Association

One Elk St, Albany, NY 12207
SAN: 226-1952
Tel: 518-463-3200 *Toll Free Tel:* 800-582-2452
Fax: 518-463-5993
E-mail: mrc@nysba.org
Web Site: www.nysba.org
Key Personnel
Pubns Dir: Daniel J McMahon
E-mail: dmcmahon@nysba.org
Pubns Coord: Naomi Pitts *E-mail:* npitts@nysba.org
Founded: 1985
Legal publications, including hardbound, looseleaf, softbound & ebooks.
ISBN Prefix(es): 978-0-942954; 978-1-57969
Number of titles published annually: 110 Print; 6 CD-ROM
Total Titles: 600 Print; 500 Online

New York University Press

838 Broadway, 3rd fl, New York, NY 10003-4812
SAN: 658-1293
Tel: 212-998-2575 (edit) *Toll Free Tel:* 800-996-6987 (orders) *Fax:* 212-995-4798 (orders)
E-mail: nyupressinfo@nyu.edu; orders@nyupress.org
Web Site: www.nyupress.org

Key Personnel
Dir: Ellen Chodosh *E-mail:* ellen.chodosh@nyu.edu
Mktg & Sales Dir: Mary Beth Jarrad
E-mail: mary.jarrad@nyu.edu
Assoc Dir & Ed-in-Chief: Eric Zinner
E-mail: eric.zinner@nyu.edu
Exec Ed: Ilene Kalish *E-mail:* ilene.kalish@nyu.edu
Sr Ed: Jennifer Hammer *E-mail:* jennifer.hammer@nyu.edu
Ed: Clara Platter *E-mail:* clara.platter@nyu.edu
Design & Prodn Mgr: Charles Hames
E-mail: charles.hames@nyu.edu
Publicity Mgr: Betsy Steve *E-mail:* betsy.steve@nyu.edu
Sr Opers Supv: Kevin Cooper *E-mail:* kevin.cooper@nyu.edu
Founded: 1916
Publish a wide array of provocative & compelling titles, as well as works of lasting scholarly & reference value.
ISBN Prefix(es): 978-0-8147; 978-1-4798
Number of titles published annually: 125 Print
Total Titles: 2,000 Print
Distributor for Monthly Review Press; New Village Press
Returns: Ingram Publisher Services, 1210 Ingram Dr, Chambersburg, PA 17202
Membership(s): Association of American Publishers (AAP); Association of University Presses (AUPresses)

Newbury Street Press

Imprint of New England Historic Genealogical Society
99-101 Newbury St, Boston, MA 02116
Tel: 617-226-1206 *Toll Free Tel:* 888-296-3447 (NEHGS membership) *Fax:* 617-536-7307
E-mail: sales@nehgs.org
Web Site: www.americanancestors.org
Key Personnel
Pres & CEO: D Brenton Simons
SVP & COO: Ryan Woods *Tel:* 617-226-1205
E-mail: rwoods@nehgs.org
VP, Advancement: Susan Fugliese *Tel:* 617-226-1218 *E-mail:* susan.fugliese@nehgs.org
Publg Dir: Sharon Inglis *Tel:* 617-226-1210
E-mail: sharon.inglis@nehgs.org
Ed-in-Chief: Scott C Steward *Tel:* 617-226-1208
E-mail: scott.steward@nehgs.org
Sales Coord: Rick Park *Tel:* 617-226-1212
E-mail: rpark@nehgs.org
Founded: 1996
A special publications division of the New England Historic Genealogical Society which publishes compiled genealogies.
ISBN Prefix(es): 978-0-88082
Number of titles published annually: 20 Print; 5 E-Book
Total Titles: 150 Print; 5 E-Book

NewSouth Books

Imprint of NewSouth Inc
105 S Court St, Montgomery, AL 36104
Tel: 334-834-3556
E-mail: info@newsouthbooks.com
Web Site: www.newsouthbooks.com
Key Personnel
Co-Founder & Publr: Suzanne La Rosa
E-mail: suzanne@newsouthbooks.com
Co-Founder & Ed-in-Chief: Randall Williams
Founded: 2000
Premier independent publisher based in the South. Books include literary fiction & nonfiction, with a special emphasis on books about the history & culture of the South. Selective acquisitions with the goal of publishing works that help develop understanding of racial, ethnic, religious & political identities.
ISBN Prefix(es): 978-1-58838; 978-1-60306
Number of titles published annually: 20 Print; 15 Online; 15 E-Book

Total Titles: 800 Print; 450 Online; 450 E-Book
Billing Address: Ingram Publisher Services (IPS), One Ingram Blvd, La Vergne, TN 37016
Returns: Ingram Publisher Services (IPS), One Ingram Blvd, La Vergne, TN 37016
E-mail: ips@ingramcontent.com
Shipping Address: Ingram Publisher Services (IPS), One Ingram Blvd, La Vergne, TN 37016
E-mail: ips@ingramcontent.com
Warehouse: Ingram Publisher Services (IPS), One Ingram Blvd, La Vergne, TN 37016
E-mail: ips@ingramcontent.com
Distribution Center: Ingram Publisher Services (IPS), One Ingram Blvd, La Vergne, TN 37016
E-mail: ips@ingramcontent.com
Membership(s): Southern Independent Booksellers Alliance (SIBA)

NFB Publishing

119 Dorchester Rd, Buffalo, NY 14213
Tel: 716-510-0520
E-mail: submissions@nfbpublishing.com
Web Site: www.nfbpublishing.com
Key Personnel
Founder: Mark Pogodzinski
Founded: 2009
Publishing new & engaging authors. Provides editorial services, interior & cover design, publicity & a chance to succeed. Accepting submissions in all genres, fiction, nonfiction, poetry, short stories, children's books.
ISBN Prefix(es): 978-0-9978317; 978-0-9984018
Number of titles published annually: 10 Print; 10 E-Book
Total Titles: 85 Print; 75 E-Book
Imprints: Amelia Press (children's books); NFB
Membership(s): Association of American Publishers (AAP); Better Business Bureau (BBB)

§Nilgiri Press

Division of Blue Mountain Center of Meditation
3600 Tomales Rd, Tomales, CA 94971
Mailing Address: PO Box 256, Tomales, CA 94971
Tel: 707-878-2369
E-mail: info@easwaran.org
Web Site: www.easwaran.org
Key Personnel
Press Coord: Debbie McMurray *E-mail:* debbie.mcmurray@nilgiripress.org
Intl Rts: Jennifer Jones *E-mail:* jennifer.jones@nilgiripress.org
Founded: 1972
Timeless wisdom for daily living books, videos, audios & online courses.
ISBN Prefix(es): 978-0-915132; 978-1-888314; 978-1-58638
Number of titles published annually: 3 Print; 10 E-Book; 10 Audio
Total Titles: 28 Print
Foreign Rep(s): Publishers Group West
Foreign Rights: Publishers Group West (Canada)

No Frills Buffalo, see NFB Publishing

§No Starch Press

245 Eighth St, San Francisco, CA 94103
Tel: 415-863-9900 *Toll Free Tel:* 800-420-7240
Fax: 415-863-9950
E-mail: info@nostarch.com; sales@nostarch.com
Web Site: www.nostarch.com
Key Personnel
Founder: William Pollock
Sales Dir: Sean Concannon
Sales Mgr: Julia Borden
Ed: Tyler Ortman
Founded: 1994
Carefully crafts the finest in geek entertainment. The growing list of award-winning No Starch Press best sellers covers topics like LEGO, hacking, STEM, programming, science, & math. Our titles have personality, our authors

are passionate & our books tackle topics that people care about.
ISBN Prefix(es): 978-1-886411; 978-1-59627
Number of titles published annually: 30 Print; 30 E-Book
Total Titles: 250 Print; 300 E-Book
Distributed by O'Reilly Media Inc
Distribution Center: Penguin Random House Publisher Services, 400 Hahn Rd, Westminster, MD 21157 *E-mail:* distribution@penguinrandomhouse.com *Web Site:* www.penguinrandomhouse.com
Membership(s): Association of American Publishers (AAP); Independent Book Publishers Association (IBPA)

§NOLO
Subsidiary of Internet Brands Inc
7031 Koll Center Pkwy, Suite 100, Pleasanton, CA 94566
SAN: 206-7935
Web Site: www.nolo.com
Founded: 1971
Leading provider of plain-English legal & business books, software, online forms & information for consumers & businesses. Founded by 2 legal aid attorneys, Nolo products help you handle many legal matters yourself. All books are written in concise, conversational English by Nolo's team of lawyer editors & regularly revised & updated to comply with changes in the law & technology. With over 50 web properties, the Nolo Network is one of the Web's largest libraries of free consumer-friendly legal information. Nolo also offers a Lawyer Directory for consumers & small businesses that want to find a local lawyer to handle or consult on a particular legal problem.
This publisher has indicated that 100% of their product line is author subsidized.
ISBN Prefix(es): 978-0-87337; 978-1-41330
Number of titles published annually: 60 Print; 200 Online; 140 E-Book
Total Titles: 140 Print; 200 Online; 140 E-Book
Distribution Center: Ingram Publisher Services, One Ingram Blvd, La Vergne, TN 37086 *Toll Free Tel:* 855-802-8230 *Toll Free Fax:* 800-838-1149 *E-mail:* customerservice@ingrampublisherservices.com *Web Site:* www.ingrampublisherservices.com
Membership(s): American Library Association (ALA); Independent Book Publishers Association (IBPA)

Norilana Books
PO Box 209, Highgate Center, VT 05459-0209
SAN: 851-8556
E-mail: service@norilana.com
Web Site: www.norilana.com
Key Personnel
Owner & Publr: Vera Nazarian
Founded: 2006
Beautifully produced & packaged editions, primarily classics of world literature & quality originals.
ISBN Prefix(es): 978-1-934169; 978-1-934648; 978-1-60762
Number of titles published annually: 3 Print
Total Titles: 300 Print
Imprints: Curiosities; Leda; Spirit; The Sword of Norilana; TaLeKa; YA Angst

§North Atlantic Books
Division of Society for the Study of Native Arts & Sciences
2526 Martin Luther King Jr Way, Berkeley, CA 94704
SAN: 203-1655
Tel: 510-549-4270 *Fax:* 510-549-4276
Web Site: www.northatlanticbooks.com

Key Personnel
Publr: Tim McKee *E-mail:* tmckee@northatlanticbooks.com
Sr Dir, Sales & Dist: Janet Levin *Tel:* 510-549-4270 ext 35 *E-mail:* jlevin@northatlanticbooks.com
Art Dir: Jasmine Hromjak *E-mail:* jhromjak@northatlanticbooks.com
Contracts Mgr: Susan Bumps *Tel:* 510-549-4270 ext 13 *E-mail:* sbumps@northatlanticbooks.com
Foreign Rts & Perms Mgr: Sarah Serafimidis *Tel:* 510-549-4270 ext 16 *E-mail:* sserafimidis@northatlanticbooks.com
Mktg Mgr: Bevin Donahue *E-mail:* bdonahue@northatlanticbooks.com
Publicity Mgr: Julia Sadowski *E-mail:* jsadowski@northatlanticbooks.com
Founded: 1974
North Atlantic Books has been located in Berkeley, California since 1977. Over this period, North Atlantic has become a leading publisher of alternative health, nutrition, bodywork, martial arts & spiritual titles.
ISBN Prefix(es): 978-1-883319; 978-0-913028; 978-0-938190; 978-1-55643; 978-1-58394 (Frog Ltd Books); 978-0-942941
Number of titles published annually: 50 Print; 50 E-Book; 10 Audio
Total Titles: 1,000 Print; 600 E-Book; 10 Audio
Imprints: Blue Snake Books; Evolver Editions; Frog Books
Distributor for DharmaCafe; Energy Arts; Ergos Institute; Heaven & Earth Publications; New Pacific Press
Foreign Rep(s): Faradawn (South Africa); Penguin Random House Canada (Canada); Penguin Random House Inc International Sales Div (worldwide); Publishers Group UK (UK)
Orders to: Penguin Random House Publisher Services (PRHPS), 400 Hahn Rd, Westminster, MD 21157 (bookstore orders) *Toll Free Tel:* 800-733-3000 *Toll Free Fax:* 800-659-2436 *E-mail:* customerservice@penguinrandomhouse.com *Web Site:* www.penguinrandomhouse.com
Returns: Penguin Random House Returns Dept, 1019 N State Rd 47, Crawfordsville, IN 47933
Distribution Center: Penguin Random House Publisher Services (PRHPS), 400 Hahn Rd, Westminster, MD 21157
Membership(s): Book Promotion Forum

North Carolina Office of Archives & History
Historical Publications Branch, 4610 Mail Service Ctr, Raleigh, NC 27699-4610
Tel: 919-807-7290
E-mail: historical.publications@ncdcr.gov
Web Site: www.ncdcr.gov
Key Personnel
Admin: Michael Ray Hill *Tel:* 919-807-7288 *E-mail:* michael.hill@ncdcr.gov
Founded: 1903
State government agency that publishes nonfiction hardcover & trade paperback books relating to North Carolina as well as the *North Carolina Historical Review*, a quarterly scholarly journal of history.
ISBN Prefix(es): 978-0-86526
Number of titles published annually: 8 Print
Total Titles: 152 Print
Distribution Center: University of North Carolina Press, 116 S Boundary St, Chapel Hill, NC 27514-3808 *Toll Free Tel:* 800-848-6224 *Toll Free Fax:* 800-272-6817 *Web Site:* www.uncpress.org

North Country Books Inc
220 Lafayette St, Utica, NY 13502-4312
Tel: 315-735-4877 *Toll Free Tel:* 800-342-7409 (orders) *Fax:* 315-738-4342
E-mail: ncbooks@verizon.net
Web Site: www.northcountrybooks.com

Key Personnel
Owner & Pres: Robert B Igoe, Jr *E-mail:* rbigoe@verizon.net
Gen Mgr: Zach Steffen
Founded: 1965
Book publisher & distributor of New York State regional titles to bookstores, schools & libraries, booksellers & non-traditional outlets.
ISBN Prefix(es): 978-0-932052; 978-0-925168; 978-0-9601158; 978-1-59531
Number of titles published annually: 5 Print
Total Titles: 140 Print
Imprints: North Country Books
Membership(s): Independent Book Publishers Association (IBPA)

North Country Press
126 Main St, Unity, ME 04988
SAN: 247-9680
Tel: 207-948-2208
E-mail: info@northcountrypress.com
Web Site: www.northcountrypress.com
Key Personnel
Publr: Patricia Newell
Founded: 1977
Regional press dealing with New England subjects (specialize in Maine). Three lines: outdoor (hunting, fishing, etc); humor, lore; literature (mysteries, essays, poetry).
ISBN Prefix(es): 978-0-945980; 978-1-943424
Number of titles published annually: 9 Print
Total Titles: 60 Print

North Point Press
Imprint of Farrar, Straus & Giroux, LLC
18 W 18 St, 8th fl, New York, NY 10011
Tel: 212-741-6900 *Toll Free Tel:* 888-330-8477 *Fax:* 212-633-9385
Web Site: www.fsgbooks.com
Key Personnel
VP & Dir, Publicity: Sarita Varma
VP, Contracts & Perms: Erika Seidman
Founded: 1981
Nonfiction, environment, nature, design, food, spirituality.
ISBN Prefix(es): 978-0-86547
Number of titles published annually: 10 Print
Foreign Rep(s): HarperCollins Publishers (Canada); Jacaranda Wiley Ltd (Australia); Orion Ltd (worldwide)
Foreign Rights: ANA Baltic (Tatjana Zoldnere) (Estonia, Latvia, Lithuania); AnatoliaLit Agency (Amy Spangler & Eda Caca) (Turkey); Anthea Agency (Katalina Sabeva) (Bulgaria); L'Autre Agence (Corinne Marotte & Marie Lannurien) (France); Bardon-Chinese Media Agency (David Tsai) (China, Taiwan); Anoukh Foerg Agency (Germany); Deborah Harris Agency (Geula Geurts) (Israel); International Copyright Agency (Simon Kessler & Marina Adriana) (Romania); The Italian Literary Agency srl (Claire Sabatie-Garat) (Italy); Anna Jarota Agency (Dominika Bojanowska) (Poland); Katai & Bolza (Peter Bolza) (Hungary); KCC (Kyung Kang) (Korea); MB Agencia Literaria (Monica Martin & Ines Planells) (Latin America, Spain); Kristin Olson Literary Agency sro (Czechia); Plima Literary Agency (Vuk Perisic) (Albania, Croatia, Serbia, Slovenia); Read 'n Right Agency (Nike Davarinou) (Greece); Riff Agency (Laura & Joao Paulo Riff) (Brazil); Sebes & Bisseling Literary Agency (Paul Sebes) (Netherlands); Synopsis Literary Agency (Olga Zasetskaya) (Russia); Tuttle-Mori Agency Inc (Asako Kawachi) (Japan)

North River Press Publishing Corp
27 Rosseter St, Great Barrington, MA 01230
SAN: 202-1048
Mailing Address: PO Box 567, Great Barrington, MA 01230-0567

Tel: 413-528-0034 *Toll Free Tel:* 800-486-2665
Fax: 413-528-3163 *Toll Free Fax:* 800-BOOK-FAX (266-5329)
E-mail: info@northriverpress.com
Web Site: www.northriverpress.com
Key Personnel
Pres: Laurence Gadd
VP: Amy Gallagher
Founded: 1971
General nonfiction, business books, hardcovers &
paperback.
ISBN Prefix(es): 978-0-88427
Number of titles published annually: 6 Print; 6 E-Book
Total Titles: 40 Print; 40 E-Book; 20 Audio

North Star Editions Inc
2297 Waters Dr, Mendota Heights, MN 55120
SAN: 990-2325
Tel: 651-204-3515 *Toll Free Tel:* 888-417-0195
Fax: 952-582-1000
E-mail: sales@northstareditions.com
Web Site: www.northstareditions.com
Key Personnel
Mktg Communs Mgr: Megan Naidl *Tel:* 952-446-7239 *E-mail:* mnaidl@northstareditions.com
Sales Coord: Sam Temple *E-mail:* stemple@northstareditions.com
Founded: 2016
ISBN Prefix(es): 978-0-7387; 978-0-9848801;
978-0-9886491; 978-1-939967; 978-1-63163;
978-1-63517; 978-1-63583
Number of titles published annually: 125 Print;
125 E-Book; 4 Audio
Total Titles: 222 Print; 240 E-Book; 4 Audio
Imprints: Flux (young adult fiction); Focus Readers (juvenile nonfiction); Jolly Fish Press (hybrid)
Foreign Rep(s): INT Books (Australia, New Zealand); Roundhouse Group (Europe, Ireland, UK); Saunders Book Co (Canada)

North Star Press of Saint Cloud Inc
19485 Estes Rd, Clearwater, MN 55320
Tel: 320-558-9062
E-mail: info@northstarpress.com
Web Site: www.northstarpress.com
Key Personnel
Owner: Corinne A Dwyer
Busn Mgr: Curtis Weinrich
Founded: 1969
Regional, Minnesota history & fiction, general
fiction, poetry.
ISBN Prefix(es): 978-0-87839
Number of titles published annually: 15 Print; 15 E-Book
Total Titles: 1,000 Print; 150 E-Book
Membership(s): Midwest Independent Publishing Association (MIPA); Minnesota Library Association (MLA)

Northern Illinois University Press
Imprint of Cornell University Press
2280 Bethany Rd, DeKalb, IL 60115
SAN: 202-8875
Tel: 815-753-1075 *Fax:* 815-753-1631
Web Site: cornellpress.cornell.edu/imprints/northern-illinois-university-press
Key Personnel
Acqs Ed: Amy Farranto *E-mail:* afarranto@niu.edu
Founded: 1965
Publishes scholarly & trade books on a variety of topics in the humanities & social sciences. In fulfilling its educational mission, the Press publishes books for both specialists & general readers.
ISBN Prefix(es): 978-0-87580; 978-1-60909
Number of titles published annually: 25 Print
Total Titles: 600 Print
Imprints: Switchgrass Books (literary fiction)

Distribution Center: Longleaf Services (US)
Toll Free Tel: 800-848-6224 *E-mail:* orders@longleafservices.org
Ampersand (CN) *Toll Free Tel:* 866-849-3819 (Toronto); 888-323-7118 (Vancouver) *Web Site:* ampersandinc.ca
Combined Academic Publishers (CAP) (Africa, Asia, Middle East, Oceania & UK) *Tel:* (01423) 526350 *Web Site:* combinedacademic.co.uk
Membership(s): American Association for the Advancement of Slavic Studies (AAASS); American Association of University Presses (AAUP); American Historical Association; Organization of American Historians (OAH)

Northwestern University Press
629 Noyes St, Evanston, IL 60208-4210
SAN: 202-5787
Tel: 847-491-2046 *Toll Free Tel:* 800-621-2736 (orders only) *Fax:* 847-491-8150
E-mail: nupress@northwestern.edu
Web Site: www.nupress.northwestern.edu
Key Personnel
Interim Co-Dir/Mng Ed: Anne Gendler *Tel:* 847-491-3844 *E-mail:* a-gendler@northwestern.edu
Interim Co-Dir/Busn Analyst: Amy Schultz *Tel:* 847-491-8310 *E-mail:* amy.schultz@northwestern.edu
Edit Dir: Parneshia Jones *E-mail:* p-jones3@northwestern.edu
Acqs Ed: Trevor Perri *E-mail:* trevor.perri@northwestern.edu
Prodn Mgr: Morris (Dino) Robinson *Tel:* 847-467-3392 *E-mail:* morris-robinson@northwestern.edu
Acqs Coord: Patrick Samuel *E-mail:* patrick.samuel2@northwestern.edu
Digital Content & Systems Coord: Emily Dalton *Tel:* 847-476-2434 *E-mail:* emily.dalton@northwestern.edu
Intellectual Property Specialist: Liz Hamilton *Tel:* 847-491-2458 *E-mail:* emhamilton@northwestern.edu
Founded: 1958
Part of Northwestern University, the Press publishes mostly scholarly books, with an emphasis on literature & language, philosophy, works in translation & theater, as well as trade books in the areas of fiction, poetry & play scripts.
ISBN Prefix(es): 978-0-8101
Number of titles published annually: 65 Print
Imprints: Curbstone Books; TriQuarterly Books (contemporary American fiction & poetry)
Distributor for Lake Forest College Press (Chicago area studies); Tia Chucha Press
Orders to: Chicago Distribution Center, 11030 S Langley, Chicago, IL 60628 *Toll Free Tel:* 800-621-2736 *Toll Free Fax:* 800-621-8476
Distribution Center: Chicago Distribution Center, 11030 S Langley, Chicago, IL 60628 *Toll Free Tel:* 800-621-2736 *Toll Free Fax:* 800-621-8476
Membership(s): Association of University Presses (AUPresses)
See separate listing for:
TriQuarterly Books

§W W Norton & Company Inc
500 Fifth Ave, New York, NY 10110-0017
SAN: 202-5795
Tel: 212-354-5500 *Toll Free Tel:* 800-233-4830 (orders & cust serv) *Fax:* 212-869-0856
Toll Free Fax: 800-458-6515
E-mail: orders@wwnorton.com
Web Site: wwnorton.com
Key Personnel
Chmn: W Drake McFeely
VChmn: Roby Harrington
VChmn & Publg Dir: Jeannie Luciano
Pres: Julia Reidhead
COO: Jorie Krumpfer
CFO: Stephen King
VP & Exec Art Dir: Ingsu Liu

VP & Sr Publicity Dir: Elizabeth Riley
VP & Dir, Coll Dept: Michael Wright
VP & Dir, Intl Sales: Dorothy M Cook
VP & Dir, Mktg: Meredith McGinnis
VP & Dir, Prof Books Div: Deborah A Malmud
VP & Dir, Subs Rts: Elisabeth Kerr
VP & Dir, Trade Prodn: Julia Druskin
VP & Edit Dir, Digital Media: Karl Bakeman
VP & Exec Ed: Alane Mason
VP & Exec Ed, Trade Dept: Jill Bialosky
VP & Ed-in-Chief: John Glusman
VP & Mng Ed: Nancy K Palmquist
VP & Sr Ed: Amy Cherry; Tom Mayer; Matt Weiland
VP & Ed: Jon Durbin; Erik Fahlgren; Peter J Simon; Sheri Snavely; Betsy Twitchell
VP & Ed, Digital Media: Steve Hoge
VP & Music Ed: Maribeth Payne
VP & Sr Proj Mgr: April Lange
VP & HR Mgr: Jamie Finkelman
VP, Opers: Nomi Victor
VP, Prodn: Tim McGuire
VP, Spec Accts: Rick Raeber
Publg Dir & Ed-in-Chief, Liveright: Robert Weil
Dir, Coll Dept: Stephen P Dunn
Dir, Mktg & Publicity: Kevin Olsen
Dir, Trade Sales: Steven Pace
Publicity Dir: Rachel Salzman
Publicity Dir, Trade: Erin Lovett
Publg Dir, Norton Young Readers: Simon Boughton
Sr Ed: Brendan Curry; Melanie Tortoroli
Sr Ed, Liveright: Katie Henderson Adams; Dan Gerstle
Ed: Marilyn Moller; Jack Repcheck
Trade Ed: Quynh Do
Assoc Ed, Liveright: Gina Iaquinta
Metadata Opers Mgr: Caroline A Hayes
Sr Publicist: Kyle Radler
Sr Publicist, Liveright: Cordelia Calvert
Founded: 1923
General nonfiction & fiction; trade paperbacks; college texts, professional books, architecture & interior design.
No unsol mss accepted.
ISBN Prefix(es): 978-0-393; 978-0-87140 (Liveright & Co); 978-1-324
Number of titles published annually: 400 Print; 110 E-Book
Total Titles: 4,800 Print; 75 CD-ROM; 600 E-Book
Imprints: Liveright; Norton Young Readers
Divisions: The Countryman Press
Foreign Office(s): W W Norton & Company Ltd, 15 Carlisle St, London W1D 3BS, United Kingdom *Tel:* (020) 7323 1579
E-mail: academic@wwnorton.co.uk *Web Site:* www.wwnorton.com
Distributor for Abbeville Press; Blue Guides; George Braziller Inc; The Countryman Press; Fantagraphics Books; Kales Press; Liveright; New Directions Publishing Corp; The Overlook Press; Pegasus Books; Persea Books; Pushcart Press; Quantuck Lane Press; Thames & Hudson; Tilbury House Publishers; Tin House Books; Well-Trained Mind Press
Foreign Rep(s): Everest International Publishing Services (Wei Zhao) (China); Hardy Bigfoss International Co Ltd (Cambodia, Laos, Myanmar, Thailand, Vietnam); B K Norton Ltd (Korea, Taiwan); W W Norton & Company Ltd (UK) (Africa, Europe, India, Ireland, Middle East, UK); Pansing Distribution Pte Ltd (Brunei, Malaysia, Singapore); Penguin Random House Canada (Canada); Rockbook (Gilles Fauveau) (Japan); Transglobal Publishers Services Ltd (Hong Kong, Macau); US PubRep Inc (Caribbean, Central America, Mexico, South America); John Wiley & Sons Australia Ltd (Australia, New Zealand)
Foreign Rights: Akcali Copyright Agency (Turkey); L'Autre Agence (France); Bardon-Chinese Media Agency (China, Taiwan); Casanovas & Lynch (Portugal, Spain); Graal

Literary Agency (Poland); The Deborah Harris Agency (Israel); International Copyright Agency (Romania); Japan UNI Agency (Japan); Katai & Bolza (Hungary); Duran Kim Agency (Korea); Mohrbooks AG Literary Agency (Germany); Nordin Agency (Scandinavia); Andrew Nurnberg Associates (Baltic States, Bulgaria, Russia); Kristin Olson Literary Agency sro (Czechia); The Riff Agency (Brazil); Roberto Santachiara Literary Agency (Italy); Marianne Schoenbach Literary Agency BV (Netherlands)
Advertising Agency: Verso Advertising
Shipping Address: National Book Co Inc, Keystone Industrial Park, Scranton, PA 18512
See separate listing for:
The Countryman Press

Norwood House Press
PO Box 1306, Fairport, NY 14450
Tel: 773-467-0837 *Toll Free Tel:* 866-565-2900 *Fax:* 773-467-9686 *Toll Free Fax:* 866-565-2901
E-mail: customerservice@norwoodhousepress.com
Web Site: www.norwoodhousepress.com
Founded: 2005
Specialize in children's books for the school & library.
ISBN Prefix(es): 978-1-59953; 978-1-60357; 978-1-68404; 978-1-68450
Number of titles published annually: 100 Print; 100 E-Book; 25 Audio
Total Titles: 1,000 Print; 500 E-Book
Warehouse: Corporate Graphics, 150 Kingswood Dr, Mankato, MN 56001

Nova Press
PO Box 692023, West Hollywood, CA 90069
Tel: 310-601-8551
E-mail: novapress@aol.com
Web Site: www.novapress.net
Key Personnel
Pres & Electronic Publg: Jeff Kolby
Founded: 1993
Publishes test prep books, software, phone apps & online courses for the SAT, ACT, GRE, LSAT, GMAT, MCAT & TOEFL.
ISBN Prefix(es): 978-1-889057; 978-1-944595
Number of titles published annually: 6 Print; 6 Online
Total Titles: 40 Print; 6 CD-ROM; 40 Online; 40 E-Book

Nova Science Publishers Inc
400 Oser Ave, Suite 1600, Hauppauge, NY 11788-3619
Tel: 631-231-7269 *Fax:* 631-231-8175
E-mail: nova.main@novapublishers.com
Web Site: www.novapublishers.com
Key Personnel
Pres: Nadya Columbus
Founded: 1985
Scientific, technical, medical & social sciences publishing. Trade books, hardcover & softcover.
ISBN Prefix(es): 978-0-941743; 978-1-56072; 978-1-59033; 978-1-59454; 978-1-60021; 978-1-60456; 978-1-60692; 978-1-60741; 978-1-60876; 978-1-61668; 978-1-61728; 978-1-61761; 978-1-61122; 978-1-61209; 978-1-61324; 978-1-61470; 978-1-62100; 978-1-61942; 978-1-62081; 978-1-62257; 978-1-62417; 978-1-62618; 978-1-62808; 978-1-62948; 978-1-63117; 978-1-63321; 978-1-63463; 978-1-63482; 978-1-63483; 978-1-63484; 978-1-63485; 978-1-5361
Number of titles published annually: 2,000 Print; 10 CD-ROM
Total Titles: 25,000 Print
Imprints: Kroshka Publications; Noel; Nova Biomedical Publications; Nova Business &

Management Publications; Nova ESL Publications; Nova Global Affairs Publications; Nova History Publications; Nova Music Publications; Nova Publications; Nova Video Productions; Novinka Publications; Snova; Troitsa Publications

NPS, see BrickHouse Books Inc

NRCYS, see National Resource Center for Youth Services

NRP Direct
430 Mountain Ave, Suite 403, New Providence, NJ 07974
Tel: 908-517-0780 *Toll Free Tel:* 844-592-4197 *Fax:* 908-608-3012 (cust serv)
E-mail: info@nrpdirect.com
Web Site: www.nrpdirect.com
Founded: 1915
Publisher of business information directories available in print, online & mailing list for commercial & reference use.
ISBN Prefix(es): 978-0-87217
Number of titles published annually: 5 Print
Total Titles: 5 Print; 1 Online

Nursesbooks.org, The Publishing Program of ANA
Division of American Nurses Association
8515 Georgia Ave, Suite 400, Silver Spring, MD 20910-3492
SAN: 851-3481
Tel: 301-628-5000 *Toll Free Tel:* 800-274-4262; 800-637-0323 (orders) *Fax:* 301-628-5342
E-mail: anp@ana.org
Web Site: www.Nursesbooks.org; www.NursingWorld.org
Key Personnel
Publr: Joe Vallina *Tel:* 301-628-5118 *E-mail:* joseph.vallina@ana.org
Ed & Proj Mgr: Erin Walpole *E-mail:* erin.walpole@ana.org
Sr Mktg Specialist: Novella Green *Tel:* 301-628-5072 *E-mail:* novella.green@ana.org
Publishes books on ANA core issues & programs, including ethics, leadership, quality, specialty practice, advanced practice & the profession's enduring legacy. Best known for the foundational documents of the profession on nursing ethics, scope & standards of practice & social policy, Nursesbooks.org is the publisher for the professional, career-oriented nurse, reaching & serving nurse educators, administrators, managers & researchers as well as staff nurses in the course of their professional development.
ISBN Prefix(es): 978-1-55810
Number of titles published annually: 14 Print; 10 E-Book
Total Titles: 95 Print; 60 E-Book
Imprints: ANCC Magnet Recognition Program; Nursing Knowledge Center
Sales Office(s): American Nurses Association (ebook site license sales), Busn Opers Specialist, Publg: Tony Ward *Tel:* 301-628-5194 *E-mail:* tony.ward@ana.org
ANA Nursing Knowledge Center (pubn sales integrated with other prods & servs), Specialist, Prod Sales & Servs: Mary Louise Cobb *Tel:* 301-628-5274 *E-mail:* marylouise.cobb@ana.org
Distribution Center: PBD Worldwide Inc, 1650 Bluegrass Lakes Pkwy, Alpharetta, GA 30004, Acct Coord: Lisa Johansen *Tel:* 770-280-0105 *E-mail:* lisa.johansen@pbd.com *Web Site:* www.pbd.com
Membership(s): Association Media & Publishing

NYBG Press, see The New York Botanical Garden Press

§Nystrom Education
Division of Social Studies School Service
10200 Jefferson Blvd, Culver City, CA 90232
Mailing Address: PO Box 802, Culver City, CA 90232
Tel: 310-839-2436 *Toll Free Tel:* 800-421-4246 *Fax:* 310-839-2249 *Toll Free Fax:* 800-944-5432
E-mail: access@nystromeducation.com; customerservice@nystromeducation.com
Web Site: www.nystromeducation.com
Key Personnel
Natl Sales Dir: Jennifer Carlson *E-mail:* jcarlson@nystromeducation.com
Founded: 1903
Social studies, history & geography programs, maps, globes, atlases & multimedia.
ISBN Prefix(es): 978-0-7825; 978-0-88463
Number of titles published annually: 3 Print
Total Titles: 50 Print; 5 CD-ROM; 1 E-Book

NYU Press, see New York University Press

§OAG Worldwide
801 Warrenville Rd, Suite 555, Lisle, IL 60532
Tel: 630-515-5300 *Toll Free Tel:* 800-342-5624 (cust serv)
E-mail: contactus@oag.com
Web Site: www.oag.com
Key Personnel
CEO: Phil Callow
CFO: Matt Plose
Founded: 1929
Supplier of independent travel info.
ISBN Prefix(es): 978-0-9776295
Number of titles published annually: 7 Print; 5 CD-ROM; 5 Online
Total Titles: 11 Print; 5 CD-ROM; 5 Online
Branch Office(s)
9130 S Dadeland Blvd, Suite 1620, Miami, FL 33156
55 Chapel St, Suite 103, Newton, MA 02458
Foreign Office(s): No 3710B Jingguang Bldg, Hujialou, Chaoyang District, Beijing 100020, China *Tel:* 5095 5965 *Fax:* 5095 5961
701 Cross Office, 1-18-6 Nishi Shinbashi, Minato-ku, Tokyo 105-0003, Japan *Tel:* 36402 7301 *Fax:* 36402 7306 *E-mail:* acustsvcjpn@oag.com
6 Shenton Way, OUE Downtown 2, No 24-08A, Singapore 068809, Singapore *Tel:* 6395-5888 *Fax:* 6395-5866
One Capability Green, Luton, Beds LU1 3LU, United Kingdom (headquarters) *Tel:* (01582) 695050 *Fax:* (01582) 695230 *E-mail:* customers@oag.com

Oak Knoll Press
310 Delaware St, New Castle, DE 19720
Tel: 302-328-7232 *Toll Free Tel:* 800-996-2556 *Fax:* 302-328-7274
E-mail: oakknoll@oakknoll.com; publishing@oakknoll.com
Web Site: www.oakknoll.com
Key Personnel
Pres: Robert D Fleck, III *E-mail:* rob@oakknoll.com
Mng Ed: Matthew Young
Antiquarian & Lib Sales: Robert Fleck, III *E-mail:* rob@oakknoll.com
Founded: 1976
Publish scholarly books (books about books), bibliographies, book arts & book history.
ISBN Prefix(es): 978-1-884718; 978-1-58456; 978-1-872116; 978-0-938768
Number of titles published annually: 25 Print
Total Titles: 1,100 Print; 1 CD-ROM
Distributor for American Antiquarian Society; Bibliographical Society of America; Bibliographical Society of University of Virginia; The Bibliographical Society (UK); Block Museum; Boston College; John Carter Brown Library;

Bryn Mawr College; Catalpa Press; Caxton Club; Center for Book Arts; Chapin Library; Cotsen Children's Library (Princeton); Fondation Custodia; The Grolier Club; Hes & De Graaf; Historic New Orleans Collection; Library of Congress-Center for the Book; The Manuscript Society; New England Bibliographies; Providence Athenaeum; Rivendale Press; Tate Galleries; Texas State Historical Association; Typophiles; Winterthur Museum; Yushodo Press

Membership(s): Antiquarian Booksellers Association of America (ABAA); Association of American Publishers (AAP); International League of Antiquarian Booksellers

The Oaklea Press
41 Old Mill Rd, Richmond, VA 23226-3111
Tel: 804-218-2394
Web Site: oakleapress.com
Founded: 1995
Trade book publisher. Fees charged for ghostwriting & proofing. Send message via web site.
ISBN Prefix(es): 978-1-892538; 978-0-9646601; 978-0-9664098
Number of titles published annually: 6 Print; 8 E-Book; 6 Audio
Total Titles: 45 Print; 8 E-Book; 6 Audio
Membership(s): Independent Book Publishers Association (IBPA)

Oberlin College Press
Subsidiary of Oberlin College
50 N Professor St, Oberlin, OH 44074-1091
SAN: 212-1883
Tel: 440-775-8408 *Fax:* 440-775-8124
E-mail: oc.press@oberlin.edu
Web Site: www.oberlin.edu/ocpress
Key Personnel
Mng Ed & Intl Rts Contact: Marco Wilkinson
Ed: David Walker; David Young
Assoc Ed: Pamela Alexander; Kazim Ali; DeSales Harrison; Lynn Powell
Ed-at-Large: Martha Collins
Founded: 1969
Poetry in translation; contemporary American poetry.
ISBN Prefix(es): 978-0-932440
Number of titles published annually: 3 Print
Total Titles: 55 Print
Distribution Center: Chicago Distribution Center (CDC), 11030 S Langley Ave, Chicago, IL 60628 *Tel:* 773-702-7010 *Toll Free Fax:* 800-621-8476
Membership(s): Community of Literary Magazines & Presses (CLMP)

Ocean Tree Books
1325 Cerro Gordo Rd, Santa Fe, NM 87501
Mailing Address: PO Box 1295, Santa Fe, NM 87504 SAN: 241-0478
Tel: 505-983-1412 *Fax:* 505-983-0899
E-mail: richard@oceantree.com
Web Site: www.oceantree.com
Key Personnel
Dir: Richard Polese
Publicity & Mktg: Hudson White
Off Mgr: Martin Burch
Founded: 1983
General trade with emphasis on southwestern & southern travel, faith & spirit & peacemaking.
ISBN Prefix(es): 978-0-943734; 978-0-9712548
Number of titles published annually: 4 Print
Total Titles: 30 Print
Imprints: Adventure Roads Travel; OTB Legacy Editions; Peacewatch Editions
Distributed by Treasure Chest Books
Foreign Rep(s): Blessingway Author Services (worldwide)
Foreign Rights: Blessingway Author Services
Distribution Center: Baker & Taylor
Books West LLC

New Leaf Distributing Co
Membership(s): Independent Book Publishers Association (IBPA); New Mexico Book Association; Publishers Association of the West (PubWest)

Oceanview Publishing Inc
1620 Main St, Suite 11, Sarasota, FL 34236
Tel: 941-387-8500
Web Site: oceanviewpub.com
Key Personnel
Dir, Mktg & Publicity: Autumn Beckett
E-mail: autumnb@oceanviewpub.com
Publg Mgr: Lee Randall
Edit Asst: Emily Baar *E-mail:* emilyb@oceanviewpub.com
Founded: 2006
ISBN Prefix(es): 978-1-933515; 978-1-60809
Number of titles published annually: 13 Print
Total Titles: 52 Print
Distribution Center: Midpoint Trade Books, 814 N Franklin St, Suite 100, Chicago, IL 60610 *Tel:* 312-337-0747 *Toll Free Tel:* 800-888-4741 *Fax:* 312-337-5985 *E-mail:* orders@ipgbook.com *Web Site:* www.midpointtrade.com
Membership(s): International Thriller Writers Inc (ITW); Mystery Writers of America (MWA)

§OCP
5536 NE Hassalo St, Portland, OR 97213
Tel: 503-281-1191 *Toll Free Tel:* 800-548-8749 *Fax:* 503-282-3486 *Toll Free Fax:* 800-843-8181
E-mail: liturgy@ocp.org
Web Site: www.ocp.org
Key Personnel
Publr: Wade Wisler
Chief Prod Offr: Jim Wasko
Cust Serv Mgr: Tim Dooley *Tel:* 503-460-5329
E-mail: timd@ocp.org
Founded: 1922
Books of music & liturgy.
ISBN Prefix(es): 978-0-915531; 978-0-9602378; 978-0-912405; 978-1-56929; 978-0-915903; 978-1-57992
Number of titles published annually: 25 Print; 25 Audio
Total Titles: 500 Print; 1 CD-ROM; 1 Online; 2,500 Audio
Imprints: Pastoral Press
Foreign Rights: Decani Music; Rainbow Book Agencies (Australia); Universal Songs (England, Europe, Ireland, UK)
Membership(s): Church Music Publishers Association (CMPA)

Octane Press
815A Brazos St, No 658, Austin, TX 78701
Tel: 512-334-9441; 512-761-4555 (sales)
Fax: 512-430-5343
E-mail: info@octanepress.com; sales@octanepress.com
Web Site: octanepress.com/content/submissions
Key Personnel
Founder & Publr: Lee Klancher *Tel:* 512-430-1940 *E-mail:* lee@octanepress.com
Graphic Designer: Tom Heffron *E-mail:* tom@octanepress.com
Founded: 2010
Niche book publisher.
ISBN Prefix(es): 978-0-9821733; 978-0-9829131; 978-1-937747
Number of titles published annually: 10 Print; 5 E-Book
Total Titles: 60 Print; 25 E-Book
Editorial Office(s): 201 W Fifth St, Suite 1100, Austin, TX 78701 (no unscheduled walk-in visits) *Tel:* 512-430-1943
Foreign Rep(s): Publishers Group UK (Continental Europe)
Returns: LSC Communication, Attn: Returns, 677 Brighton Beach Rd, Menasha, WI 54952

Shipping Address: LSC Communications, 675 Brighton Beach Rd, Menasha, WI 54952
Warehouse: LSC Communication, Attn: Receiving, 675 Brighton Beach Rd, Menasha, WI 54952
Membership(s): Independent Book Publishers Association (IBPA)

Odyssey Books
Division of The Ciletti Publishing Group Inc
2421 Redwood Ct, Longmont, CO 80503-8155
Tel: 720-494-1473 *Fax:* 720-494-1471
E-mail: books@odysseybooks.net
Key Personnel
Pres & Publr: Barbara Ciletti
Promo: Erin Jones
Founded: 1995
Provides fiction & nonfiction for the retail trade, library, education & consumer markets.
ISBN Prefix(es): 978-0-9768655
Number of titles published annually: 20 Print
Membership(s): American Booksellers Association (ABA); American Library Association (ALA); CMN; Independent Book Publishers Association (IBPA); International Literacy Association (ILA); National Council of Teachers of English (NCTE); National Science Teachers Association (NSTA)

§OECD Washington Center
Division of Organization for Economic Cooperation & Development (France)
1776 "I" St NW, Suite 450, Washington, DC 20006
Tel: 202-785-6323 *Toll Free Tel:* 800-456-6323 (dist ctr/pubns orders) *Fax:* 202-785-0350
E-mail: washington.contact@oecd.org; oecdilibrary@oecd.org (sales)
Web Site: www.oecd-ilibrary.org
Key Personnel
Sales & Mktg Mgr: Iain Williamson *Tel:* 202-822-3870 *E-mail:* iain.williamson@oecd.org
Founded: 1961
Periodicals, books, online services & statistical data.
ISBN Prefix(es): 978-92-64; 978-92-821; 978-92-65; 978-0-9501741
Number of titles published annually: 450 Online; 450 E-Book
Total Titles: 15,600 Online; 15,600 E-Book
Foreign Office(s): 2 rue Andre-Pascal, 75775 Paris Cedex 16, France *Tel:* 01 45 24 82 00 *Fax:* 01 45 24 85 00
Distributor for International Energy Agency; International Transportation Forum; Nuclear Energy Agency
Orders to: Turpin Distribution Services Ltd, The Bleachery, 143 West St, New Milford, CT 06776 *Toll Free Tel:* 800-456-6323 *Fax:* 860-350-0039 *E-mail:* oecdma@turpin-distribution.com
Distribution Center: Turpin Distribution Services Ltd, The Bleachery, 143 West St, New Milford, CT 06776 *Toll Free Tel:* 800-456-6323 *Fax:* 860-350-0039

Ohio Genealogical Society
611 State Rte 97 W, Bellville, OH 44813-8813
Tel: 419-886-1903 *Fax:* 419-886-0092
E-mail: ogs@ogs.org
Web Site: www.ogs.org
Key Personnel
Pres: Margaret Cheney *E-mail:* president@ogs.org
Lib Dir: Thomas Stephen Neel *E-mail:* tneel@ogs.org
Founded: 1959
Family history library & society.
ISBN Prefix(es): 978-0-935057
Number of titles published annually: 3 Print
Total Titles: 25 Print

Ohio State University Foreign Language Publications

Division of Ohio State University Foreign Language Center

198 Hagerty Hall, 1775 College Rd, Columbus, OH 43210-1309

Tel: 614-292-3838 *Toll Free Tel:* 800-678-6999

E-mail: flpubs@osu.edu

Web Site: flpubs.osu.edu

Key Personnel

Pubns Mgr: Lauren Barrett

Founded: 1972

Foreign language individualized instruction materials for less commonly taught languages.

ISBN Prefix(es): 978-0-87415

Number of titles published annually: 3 Print

Total Titles: 280 Print

The Ohio State University Press

180 Pressey Hall, 1070 Carmack Rd, Columbus, OH 43210-1002

Tel: 614-292-6930 *Fax:* 614-292-2065

Toll Free Fax: 800-621-8476

E-mail: info@osupress.org

Web Site: ohiostatepress.org

Key Personnel

Dir: Tony Sanfilippo *Tel:* 614-292-7818

E-mail: tony@osupress.org

Asst Dir: Kathy Edwards *Tel:* 614-292-3692

E-mail: kathy@osupress.org

Mktg Dir: Laurie Avery *Tel:* 614-292-1462

E-mail: laurie@osupress.org

Mng Ed: Tara Cyphers *Tel:* 614-292-3667

E-mail: tara@osupress.org

Founded: 1957

General scholarly & trade nonfiction & fiction; classics.

ISBN Prefix(es): 978-0-8142

Number of titles published annually: 40 Print

Total Titles: 300 Print

Imprints: Mad Creek Books

Distribution Center: University of Chicago Distribution Center, 11030 S Langley Ave, Chicago, IL 60628 *Tel:* 773-568-1550 *Toll Free Tel:* 800-621-2736 *Fax:* 773-702-7212

Ohio University Press

Alden Library, Suite 101, 30 Park Place, Athens, OH 45701-2901

Tel: 740-593-1154

Web Site: www.ohioswallow.com

Key Personnel

Interim Dir & Prodn Mgr: Beth Pratt *Tel:* 740-593-1162 *E-mail:* prattb@ohio.edu

Edit Coord: Tyler Balli *E-mail:* tylerballi@ohio.edu

Acqs Ed: Ricky S Huard *Tel:* 740-593-1157

E-mail: huard@ohio.edu

Acqs Admin, Rts & Perms: Sally R Welch

E-mail: welchs@ohio.edu

Sales Mgr: Jeff Kallet *Tel:* 740-593-1158

E-mail: kallet@ohio.edu

Publicity Coord: Laura Andre *Tel:* 740-593-1153

E-mail: andrel@ohio.edu

Founded: 1964

Publisher of scholarly & trade books.

ISBN Prefix(es): 978-0-8214; 978-0-8040; 978-0-89680; 978-0-940717

Number of titles published annually: 50 Print

Total Titles: 600 Print

Imprints: Swallow Press

Foreign Rep(s): Combined Academic Publishers Ltd (UK); Scholarly Book Services Inc (Canada)

Orders to: Chicago Distribution Center, 11030 S Langley Ave, Chicago, IL 60628 *Tel:* 773-702-7212 *Toll Free Tel:* 800-621-2736 *Fax:* 773-702-7212 *Toll Free Fax:* 800-621-8476

Warehouse: Chicago Distribution Center, 11030 S Langley Ave, Chicago, IL 60628 *Tel:* 773-702-7212 *Toll Free Tel:* 800-621-2736 *Toll Free Fax:* 800-621-8476

Membership(s): American Association of University Presses (AAUP)

See separate listing for:

Swallow Press

§Olde & Oppenheim Publishers

3219 N Margate Place, Chandler, AZ 85224

E-mail: olde_oppenheim@hotmail.com

Key Personnel

Dir, Mktg: Mike Gratz

Animation, satire, slice-of-life.

ISBN Prefix(es): 978-0-944861

Number of titles published annually: 3 Print; 5 Online; 2 E-Book

Total Titles: 13 Print

Omnibus Press

Imprint of Music Sales Group

180 Madison Ave, 24th fl, New York, NY 10016

Tel: 212-254-2100 *Toll Free Tel:* 800-431-7187

Fax: 212-254-2013 *Toll Free Fax:* 800-345-6842

E-mail: info@omnibuspress.com

Web Site: www.omnibuspress.com; www.musicsales.com

Key Personnel

Off Mgr: Kari Shannon

Founded: 1976

Pop culture, music & film books.

ISBN Prefix(es): 978-0-8256; 978-0-7119; 978-0-86001; 978-1-84449

Number of titles published annually: 40 Print

Total Titles: 500 Print

Distributor for Big Meteor Publishing; Gramophone

Distribution Center: Music Sales Distribution Center, 445 Bellvale Rd, Chester, NY 10918 *Tel:* 845-469-4699 *Toll Free Tel:* 800-431-7187 *Fax:* 845-469-7544 *Toll Free Fax:* 800-345-6842 *E-mail:* info@musicsales.com *Web Site:* www.musicsales.com

Independent Publishers Group (IPG), 814 N Franklin St, Chicago, IL 60610 *Toll Free Tel:* 800-888-4741 *E-mail:* orders@ipgbook.com *Web Site:* www.ipgbook.com

Omnidawn Publishing

2200 Adeline St, Suite 150, Oakland, CA 94607

SAN: 299-3236

Tel: 510-237-5472 *Toll Free Tel:* 800-792-4957

Fax: 510-232-8525

E-mail: manager@omnidawn.com

Web Site: www.omnidawn.com

Key Personnel

Founder & Publr: Kenneth Keegan

E-mail: kkeegan@omnidawn.com; Rusty Morrison *E-mail:* rusty@omnidawn.com

Mng Ed: Gillian Hamel *E-mail:* ghamel@omnidawn.com

Founded: 1996

Publishers of poetry, fabulist & new wave fabulist fiction.

ISBN Prefix(es): 978-1-890650

Number of titles published annually: 26 Print

Total Titles: 131 Print

Distribution Center: Chicago Distribution Center (CDC), 11030 S Langley Ave, Chicago, IL 60628 *Tel:* 773-702-7010 *Toll Free Fax:* 800-621-8476

§Omnigraphics Inc

615 Griswold, Suite 520, Detroit, MI 48226

SAN: 249-2520

Tel: 610-461-3548 *Toll Free Tel:* 800-234-1340 (cust serv) *Fax:* 610-532-9001

Toll Free Fax: 800-875-1340 (cust serv)

E-mail: contact@omnigraphics.com; customerservice@omnigraphics.com

Web Site: omnigraphics.com

Key Personnel

Publr: Peter E Ruffner

VP: Kevin Hayes

Founded: 1985

Reference books, directories, periodicals & journals for libraries & schools.

ISBN Prefix(es): 978-1-55888; 978-0-7808

Number of titles published annually: 40 Print; 1 Online

Total Titles: 400 Print; 1 Online

Advertising Agency: Marley & Cratchit

Orders to: PO Box 8002, Aston, PA 19014-8002

Returns: 105 Commerce Dr, Aston, PA 19014

Omohundro Institute of Early American History & Culture

Swem Library, Ground fl, 400 Landrum Dr, Williamsburg, VA 23185

Mailing Address: PO Box 8781, Williamsburg, VA 23187-8781 SAN: 201-5161

Tel: 757-221-1110 *Fax:* 757-221-1047

E-mail: ieahc1@wm.edu

Web Site: oieahc.wm.edu

Key Personnel

Exec Dir: Karin A Wulf *Tel:* 757-221-1133

E-mail: kawulf@wm.edu

Books Ed: Catherine E Kelly *Tel:* 757-221-1118

E-mail: cekelly01@wm.edu

Founded: 1943

Scholarly books on the histories & cultures of North America circa 1450-1820, including related developments in the British Isles, Europe, West Africa & the Caribbean. Founded & still sponsored by the College of William & Mary.

ISBN Prefix(es): 978-0-910776

Number of titles published annually: 6 Print

Total Titles: 247 Print

Distributed by The University of North Carolina Press

One On One Book Publishing/Film-Video Publications

7944 Capistrano Ave, West Hills, CA 91304

SAN: 211-1527

Tel: 818-340-6620; 818-340-0175 *Fax:* 818-340-6620

E-mail: onebookpro@aol.com

Key Personnel

Pres & Publr: Alan Gadney

VP & Exec Ed: Carolyn Porter

Ed: Nancy Gadney

Founded: 1974

Reference books, directories & audio/video cassettes on film, video, photography, TV/radio broadcasting, writing, theater, business & finance, performing arts, publishing.

ISBN Prefix(es): 978-0-930828

Number of titles published annually: 20 Print; 4 E-Book; 10 Audio

Total Titles: 25 Print; 4 E-Book; 16 Audio

Foreign Rep(s): Australia & New Zealand Book Co (Australia); Fitzhenry & Whiteside (Canada); Reed Methuen Publishers (New Zealand)

Advertising Agency: Carolyn Chadwick Advertising

Membership(s): The Association of Publishers for Special Sales (APSS); Book Publicists of Southern California (BPSC); BookWorks; Independent Book Publishers Association (IBPA); Publishing Professionals Network (PPN)

§Ooligan Press

Portland State University, PO Box 751, Portland, OR 97207

Tel: 503-725-9748 *Fax:* 503-725-3561

E-mail: ooligan@ooliganpress.pdx.edu

Web Site: ooligan.pdx.edu

Key Personnel

Publr: Abbey Gaterud

Founded: 2001

ISBN Prefix(es): 978-1-932010; 978-1-947845

Number of titles published annually: 4 Print; 4 E-Book; 4 Audio

Total Titles: 30 Print

Orders to: Ingram Publisher Services, One Ingram Blvd, La Vergne, TN 37086-1986 *Toll Free Tel:* 866-400-5351
Distribution Center: Ingram Publisher Services, One Ingram Blvd, La Vergne, TN 37086-1986 *Toll Free Tel:* 866-400-5351
Membership(s): Association of Writers & Writing Programs (AWP); Publishers Association of the West (PubWest)

§Open Books Press
Imprint of Pen & Publish Inc
4735 S State Rd 446, Bloomington, IN 47401
Tel: 314-827-6567; 812-837-9226
E-mail: info@openbookspress.com
Web Site: openbookspress.com
Key Personnel
Publr: Jennifer Geist *E-mail:* jennifer@openbookspress.com
Co-Founder & Pres: Paul Burt *E-mail:* paul@penandpublish.com
Co-Founder: Dee Burt *E-mail:* dee@penandpublish.com
Founded: 2010
Publish quality trade paperbacks & ebooks worldwide, including adult nonfiction & fiction for all ages.
Number of titles published annually: 4 Print; 4 E-Book
Total Titles: 24 Print; 14 E-Book
Membership(s): Independent Book Publishers Association (IBPA)

Open Court Publishing Co
Division of Cricket Media
70 E Lake St, Suite 800, Chicago, IL 60601
Tel: 312-701-1720 *Toll Free Tel:* 800-815-2280
Fax: 312-701-1728
E-mail: opencourt@cricketmedia.com
Web Site: www.opencourtbooks.com
Key Personnel
Edit Dir: David Ramsay Steele
Ed: Kerri Mommer
Founded: 1887
Publisher of academic philosophy, popular culture & philosophy books.
ISBN Prefix(es): 978-0-87548; 978-0-912050; 978-0-89688; 978-0-8126
Number of titles published annually: 12 Print
Total Titles: 350 Print

Open Horizons Publishing Co
PO Box 2887, Taos, NM 87571
Tel: 575-751-3398
E-mail: books@bookmarketingbestsellers.com
Web Site: bookmarketingbestsellers.com
Key Personnel
Owner & Publr: John Kremer *E-mail:* johnkremer@bookmarket.com
Founded: 1982
Books for publishers & direct marketers.
ISBN Prefix(es): 978-0-912411
Number of titles published annually: 3 Print; 3 CD-ROM; 3 Online; 40 E-Book; 3 Audio
Total Titles: 21 Print; 16 CD-ROM; 6 Online; 43 E-Book; 12 Audio
Distribution Center: National Book Network, 4720 Boston Way, No A, Lanham, MD 20706-4310, Pres: Jed Lyons *Tel:* 301-459-3366 *Fax:* 301-459-2118
Membership(s): The Association of Publishers for Special Sales (APSS); Independent Book Publishers Association (IBPA)

The Optical Society (OSA)
2010 Massachusetts Ave NW, Washington, DC 20036-1023
Tel: 202-223-8130 *Toll Free Tel:* 800-766-4672
E-mail: custserv@osa.org
Web Site: www.osa.org

Key Personnel
Chief Publg Offr: Elizabeth Nolan *Tel:* 202-416-1949 *E-mail:* enolan@osa.org
CIO: Sean Bagshaw *Tel:* 202-416-1905 *E-mail:* sbagsh@osa.org
Sr Publr: Kelly Cohen *Tel:* 202-416-1917 *E-mail:* kcohen@osa.org
Sr Dir, Publg Sales & Mktg: Daphne Greenwood *Tel:* 202-416-1405 *E-mail:* dgreen@osa.org
Dir, Sales Americas: Alan N Tourtlotte *Tel:* 202-416-1908 *Fax:* 202-416-1408 *E-mail:* atourt@osa.org
Intl Subn Agents Contact: Rosita Banks-Taylor *Tel:* 202-416-1433 *E-mail:* rtaylo@osa.org
Rts & Perms: Susannah Lehman *Tel:* 202-416-1901 *E-mail:* slehman@osa.org
Founded: 1916
Journal publishing, meetings & technical membership.
ISBN Prefix(es): 978-1-55752
Number of titles published annually: 20 Online
Total Titles: 230 Online
Foreign Rep(s): Globe Publication Pvt Ltd (India); iGroup (Asia exc India, Japan & South Korea, Australia, New Zealand); Kinokuniya (Japan); Shinwon Datanet (South Korea)
Membership(s): American Institute of Physics

Optometric Extension Program Foundation (OEP)
2300 York Rd, Suite 113, Timonium, MD 21093
Tel: 410-561-3791
E-mail: admin@oepf.org
Web Site: www.oepf.org
Key Personnel
Exec Dir: Line Vreven *E-mail:* line.vreven@oepf.org
Clinical Curriculum Coord: Karen Ruder *E-mail:* karen.ruder@oepf.org
Founded: 1928
Optometric postgraduate education. Books, journals, pamphlets, catalogs & directories.
ISBN Prefix(es): 978-0-943599; 978-0-929780
Number of titles published annually: 10 Print; 1 CD-ROM
Total Titles: 150 Print; 3 CD-ROM

§OptumInsight™
11000 Optum Circle, Eden Prairie, MN 55344
Tel: 952-833-7100 *Toll Free Tel:* 888-445-8745
Web Site: www.optum.com
Key Personnel
CEO: Robert Musslewhite
Founded: 1983
Books & software for health care professionals.
ISBN Prefix(es): 978-1-56337; 978-1-56329
Number of titles published annually: 90 Print; 5 Online
Total Titles: 90 Print; 8 CD-ROM; 5 Online
Distributed by American Medical Association; Mosby
Distributor for American Medical Association; Medical Economics; Mosby

Orange Frazer Press Inc
37 1/2 W Main St, Wilmington, OH 45177
Mailing Address: PO Box 214, Wilmington, OH 45177-0214
Tel: 937-382-3196 *Fax:* 937-383-3159
E-mail: ofrazer@erinet.com
Web Site: www.orangefrazer.com
Key Personnel
Publr: Marcy Hawley
Ed: John Baskin
Proj Mgr: Sarah Hawley
Founded: 1987
Regional book publisher specializing in Ohio nonfiction (reference, sports, commentary, travel, nature, etc). Production & design is considered "high-end".
This publisher has indicated that 80% of their product line is author subsidized.

ISBN Prefix(es): 978-1-882203; 978-0-9619637; 978-1-933197
Number of titles published annually: 25 Print
Total Titles: 200 Print

Orbis Books
Division of Maryknoll Fathers & Brothers
PO Box 302, Maryknoll, NY 10545-0302
SAN: 202-828X
Tel: 914-941-7636 *Toll Free Tel:* 800-258-5838 (orders, Mon-Fri 8AM-4PM EST) *Fax:* 914-941-7005
E-mail: orbisbooks@maryknoll.org
Web Site: orbisbooks.com
Key Personnel
Publr & Ed-in-Chief: Robert Ellsberg *E-mail:* rellsberg@maryknoll.org
Assoc Publr & Mktg Mgr: Bernadette B Price *E-mail:* bprice@maryknoll.org
Busn Mgr: William Medeot *E-mail:* bmedeot@maryknoll.org
Sales Mgr: Michael Lawrence *E-mail:* mlawrence@maryknoll.org
Acqs Ed: Paul McMahon *E-mail:* pmcmahon@maryknoll.org; Jill O'Brien *E-mail:* jobrien@maryknoll.org
Rts & Perms: Doris Goodnough *E-mail:* dgoodnough@maryknoll.org
Founded: 1970
Offering a wide range of books on prayer, spirituality, Catholic life, theology, mission & current affairs.
ISBN Prefix(es): 978-0-88344; 978-1-57075; 978-1-60833; 978-1-62698
Number of titles published annually: 50 Print; 50 E-Book
Total Titles: 900 Print; 615 E-Book
Foreign Rep(s): Bayard/Novalis Distribution (Canada); Catholic Book Shop (South Africa); Garratt Publishing (Australia)
Advertising Agency: Roth Advertising, PO Box 96, Sea Cliff, NY 11579-0096, Pres: Daniel Roth *Tel:* 516-674-8603 *Fax:* 516-368-3885 *E-mail:* dan@rothadvertising.com
Warehouse: Maryknoll Center Warehouse, 79 Ryder Rd, Ossining, NY 10562, Mgr: Al Sanders *Tel:* 914-941-7636 ext 2458
Membership(s): American Booksellers Association (ABA); Association of Catholic Publishers Inc

Orbit
Division of Hachette Book Group
1290 Avenue of the Americas, New York, NY 10104
Tel: 212-364-1100 *Toll Free Tel:* 800-759-0190
Web Site: www.orbitbooks.net
Key Personnel
SVP, HBG & Publr, Orbit: Tim Holman
VP, Assoc Publr: Alex Lencicki
VP, Creative Dir: Lauren Panepinto
Sr Ed: Brit Hvide; Bradley Englert; Priyanka Krishnan
Ed: Nivia Evans
Sr Publicist: Ellen Wright
Assoc Publicist: Angela Man
Sr Online Mktg Mgr: Laura Fitzgerald
Mktg Mgr: Paola Crespo
Busn Mgr: May Choy
Sr Designer: Lisa Marie Pompilio
Designer: Crystal Ben
Graphic Designer: Stephanie Hess
Founded: 2008
Orbit is a leading publisher of science fiction & fantasy with imprints in the UK, US & Australia. We publish across the spectrum of science fiction & fantasy—from action-packed urban fantasy to widescreen space opera; from sweeping epic adventures to near-future thrillers.
Number of titles published annually: 80 Print
Total Titles: 400 Print
Imprints: Redhook

Orders to: Hachette Book Group, 53 State St, Boston, MA 02109 *Toll Free Tel:* 800-759-0190 *Toll Free Fax:* 800-286-9471
Shipping Address: Hachette Book Group Distribution Center, 121 N Enterprise Blvd, Lebanon, IN 46052 *Tel:* 765-483-9900 *Fax:* 765-483-0706

Oregon Catholic Press, see OCP

Oregon State University Press
121 The Valley Library, Corvallis, OR 97331-4501
SAN: 202-8328
Tel: 541-737-3166
Key Personnel
Dir: Tom Booth *E-mail:* thomas.booth@oregonstate.edu
EDP Mgr: Micki Reaman *E-mail:* micki.reaman@oregonstate.edu
Acqs Ed: Kim Hogeland *E-mail:* kim.hogeland@oregonstate.edu
Mktg Mgr: Marty Brown *E-mail:* marty.brown@oregonstate.edu
Founded: 1961
ISBN Prefix(es): 978-0-87071
Number of titles published annually: 20 Print
Total Titles: 350 Print
Distribution Center: Chicago Distribution Center, 11030 S Langley Ave, Chicago, IL 60628 *Toll Free Tel:* 800-621-2736
Membership(s): Association of University Presses (AUPresses); Pacific Northwest Booksellers Association (PNBA); Publishers Association of the West (PubWest)

O'Reilly Media Inc
1005 Gravenstein Hwy N, Sebastopol, CA 95472
Tel: 707-827-7000; 707-827-7019 (cust support) *Toll Free Tel:* 800-998-9938; 800-889-8969 *Fax:* 707-829-0104; 707-824-8268
E-mail: orders@oreilly.com; support@oreilly.com
Web Site: www.oreilly.com
Key Personnel
Founder & CEO: Tim O'Reilly
Founded: 1978
Technology & business learning solutions provider.
ISBN Prefix(es): 978-0-937175; 978-1-56592; 978-0-596
Number of titles published annually: 140 Print; 65 E-Book
Total Titles: 800 Print
Branch Office(s)
2 Ave de Lafayette, 6th fl, Boston, MA 02111 *Tel:* 617-354-5800 *Fax:* 617-661-1116
Foreign Office(s): O'Reilly Beijing, Cheng Ming Mansion, Bldg C, Suite 807, No 2 Xizhimen South St, Xicheng District, Beijing 100035, China, Contact: Michelle Chen *Tel:* (010) 88097475 *Fax:* (010) 88097463 *E-mail:* orb@oreilly.com *Web Site:* www.oreilly.com.cn
Intelligent Plaza, Bldg 1-F, 12-22, Yotsuyasaka-machi, Shinjuku-ku, Tokyo 160-0002, Japan, General Dept Section, Sales: Kenji Watari *E-mail:* japan@oreilly.co.jp *Web Site:* www.oreilly.co.jp
5 St George's Yard, Farnham, Surrey GU9 7LW, United Kingdom *Tel:* (01252) 721284 *Fax:* (01252) 722337 *E-mail:* information@oreilly.co.uk
Distributor for Packt Publishing (technol ebook prog)
Foreign Rep(s): WoodsLane (Australia, New Zealand)

Organization for Economic Cooperation & Development (OECD), see OECD Washington Center

Oriental Institute Publications
Division of University of Chicago

1155 E 58 St, Chicago, IL 60637
Tel: 773-702-5967 *Fax:* 773-702-9853
E-mail: oi-publications@uchicago.edu
Web Site: oi.uchicago.edu
Key Personnel
Mng Ed, Pubns: Thomas Urban *E-mail:* turban@uchicago.edu
Founded: 1919
Academic publications.
ISBN Prefix(es): 978-0-918986; 978-1-885923
Number of titles published annually: 10 Print; 10 Online
Total Titles: 250 Print; 1,000 Online
Orders to: Casemate | academic, 1950 Lawrence Rd, Havertown, PA 19083 *Tel:* 610-853-9131 *Fax:* 610-853-9146 *E-mail:* info@casemateacademic.com *Web Site:* www.oxbowbooks.com/dbbc
Distribution Center: Casemate | academic, 1950 Lawrence Rd, Havertown, PA 19083 *Tel:* 610-853-9131 *Fax:* 610-853-9146 *E-mail:* info@casemateacademic.com *Web Site:* www.oxbowbooks.com/dbbc

The Original Falcon Press
1753 E Broadway Rd, No 101-277, Tempe, AZ 85282
Tel: 602-708-1409
E-mail: info@originalfalcon.com
Web Site: www.originalfalcon.com
Key Personnel
Pres: Nicholas Tharcher *E-mail:* nick@originalfalcon.com
Founded: 1982
Books, audios & videos.
ISBN Prefix(es): 978-1-935150; 978-1-61869
Number of titles published annually: 10 Print; 10 E-Book; 10 Audio
Total Titles: 50 Print; 40 E-Book; 30 Audio
Imprints: Falcon Press; Golden Dawn Publications; New Falcon Publications
Distribution Center: New Leaf Distributing Co, 401 Thornton Rd, Lithia Springs, GA 30122-1557 *Tel:* 770-948-7845 *Fax:* 770-944-2313 *E-mail:* newleaf@newleaf-dist.com *Web Site:* newleafdist.com
Gazelle Book Services Ltd, White Cross Mills, Hightown, Lancaster, Lancs LA1 4XS, United Kingdom *Tel:* (0152) 528500 *Fax:* (0152) 528510 *E-mail:* sales@gazellebookservices.co.uk *Web Site:* www.gazellebookservices.co.uk

ORO editions
31 Commercial Blvd, Suite F, Novato, CA 94949
Mailing Address: 1705 Clark Lane, Suite 2, Redondo Beach, CA 90278
Tel: 415-883-3300 *Fax:* 415-883-3309
E-mail: info@oroeditions.com
Web Site: www.oroeditions.com
Key Personnel
Contact: Gordon Goff *E-mail:* gordon@oroeditions.com
Founded: 2003
ISBN Prefix(es): 978-0-9746800; 978-0-9774672; 978-0-9793801; 978-0-9795395; 978-0-9814628; 978-0-9820607; 978-0-9819857; 978-0-9826226; 978-0-935935
Number of titles published annually: 100 Print; 4 E-Book
Total Titles: 1 E-Book
Imprints: Applied Research + Design Publishing; Goff Books
Foreign Rep(s): Antique Collectors Club (ACC) (Africa, Europe, Middle East); APD Singapore Pte Ltd (Singapore); Asia Publishers Services Ltd (China, Hong Kong, Korea, Taiwan); NewSouth Books (Australia, New Zealand)
Distribution Center: Ingram Publisher Services (IPS), 1210 Ingram Dr, Chambersburg, PA 17202

Membership(s): Independent Book Publishers Association (IBPA); Independent Publishers Association; Publishing Professionals Network (PPN)

Other Press
267 Fifth Ave, 6th fl, New York, NY 10016
Tel: 212-414-0054 *Toll Free Tel:* 877-843-6843 *Fax:* 212-414-0939
E-mail: editor@otherpress.com; marketing@otherpress.com; publicity@otherpress.com
Web Site: www.otherpress.com
Key Personnel
Publr: Judith Gurewich
CFO: Bill Foo
Edit Dir: Janice Goldklang
Dir, Mktg: Terrie Akers
Dir, Subs Rts: Lauren Shekari
Publicity Dir: Jessica Greer
Opers Mgr: Iisha Stevens
Assoc Ed: Alexandra Poreda
Prodn Ed: Yvonne Cardenas
Assoc Publicist: Esther Kim
Mktg Asst: Christie Michel
Founded: 1998
Publish literary fiction, literature in translation, trade nonfiction, memoirs, cultural studies, biographies & other subjects.
ISBN Prefix(es): 978-1-892746; 978-1-59051
Number of titles published annually: 25 Print; 25 E-Book
Foreign Rep(s): AnatoliaLit Agency (Amy Marie Spangler) (Turkey); Donatella D'Ormesson (France); The English Agency Ltd (Hamish Macaskill) (Japan); The Deborah Harris Agency (Rena Rossner) (Israel); Danny Hong Agency (Danny Hong) (Korea); Iris Literary Agency (Catherine Fragou) (Greece); Marc Koralnik Liepman AG (Germany); Prava i prevodi (Milena Kaplarevic) (Baltic States, Eastern Europe); Vicki Satlow Literary Agency (Vicki Satlow) (Italy)
Foreign Rights: MB Agencia Literaria (Monica Martin) (Brazil, Catalonia, Portugal, Spain); Peony Literary Agency (Marysia Juszczakiewicz & Tina Chou) (China, Taiwan)
Distribution Center: Penguin Random House Inc, Customer Service, 400 Hahn Rd, Westminster, MD 21157 *Toll Free Tel:* 800-733-3000 *Toll Free Fax:* 800-659-2436 *E-mail:* csorders@penguinrandomhouse.com *Web Site:* www.penguinrandomhouse.biz
Penguin Random House Inc, International Sales, 1745 Broadway, New York, NY 10019 *Fax:* 212-572-6045 *E-mail:* international@penguinrandomhouse.com
Penguin Random House Canada, Customer Service, 320 Front St W, Suite 1400, Toronto, ON M5V 3B6, Canada *Toll Free Tel:* 888-523-9292 *Toll Free Fax:* 888-562-9924 *E-mail:* csorders@penguinrandomhouse.com *Web Site:* www.penguinrandomhouse.biz
Membership(s): American Booksellers Association (ABA); Community of Literary Magazines & Presses (CLMP); Independent Book Publishers Association (IBPA)

§Our Sunday Visitor Publishing
Division of Our Sunday Visitor Inc
200 Noll Plaza, Huntington, IN 46750
SAN: 202-8344
Tel: 260-356-8400 *Toll Free Tel:* 800-348-2440 (orders) *Fax:* 260-356-8472 *Toll Free Fax:* 800-498-6709
E-mail: osvbooks@osv.com (book orders)
Web Site: www.osv.com
Key Personnel
Chmn of the Bd: Bishop Kevin C Rhoades
Assoc Publr & Ed: Owen Campion *E-mail:* ocampion@osv.com
Exec Asst: Michelle Hogan *E-mail:* mhogan@osv.com
Founded: 1912

Religious books: trade, adult & juvenile general interest & reference, hardcover & paperback, early childhood school; newsweekly, religious magazines & newspapers, CD-ROM.
ISBN Prefix(es): 978-0-87973; 978-1-931709; 978-0-9707756; 978-1-59276; 978-1-61278; 978-1-68192
Number of titles published annually: 60 Print
Total Titles: 600 Print; 6 CD-ROM; 8 Audio
Foreign Rep(s): Baker & Taylor (worldwide exc Canada, France, Malta, New Zealand, South Africa & UK); B Broughton (Canada); Catholic Supplies (New Zealand); Preca (Malta); Veritas (UK); Veritas Co Ltd (Ireland); Grace Wing (worldwide exc Australia); Word of Life (Australia)

The Overlook Press
Imprint of Harry N Abrams Inc
195 Broadway, 9th fl, New York, NY 10007
SAN: 200-2434
Tel: 212-673-2210; 845-679-6838 (orders & dist)
E-mail: abrams@abramsbooks.com; sales@abramsbooks.com (orders)
Web Site: www.abramsbooks.com/imprints/overlookpress/; www.abramsbooks.com/overlooksales/
Founded: 1971
Fiction, general nonfiction, theatre, biography, art, architecture, history, design, film, popular culture, hardcover reprints & trade paperbacks.
ISBN Prefix(es): 978-0-87951; 978-1-58567; 978-1-59020; 978-1-4683
Number of titles published annually: 40 Print
Total Titles: 1,000 Print
Imprints: Ardis Russian Literature; Elephant's Eye; Tusk Ivory; Tusk Paperbacks
Foreign Rights: Akcali Copyright Agency (Atilla Izgi Turgut) (Turkey); Agencia Literaria Carmen Balcells SA (Anna Bofill) (Portugal, South America, Spain); Book/Lab Literary Agency (Agata Zabowska) (Poland); The Deborah Harris Agency (Geula Gerts) (Israel); The Italian Literary Agency (Maria Vittoria Puccetti) (Italy); JLM Literary Agency (John L Moukakos) (Greece); Agence Michelle Lapautre (Catherine Lapautre) (Belgium, France); Licht & Burr Literary Agency ApS (Trine Licht) (Scandinavia); Liepman AG Literary Agency (Marc Koralnik) (Austria, Germany, Switzerland); Andrew Nurnberg Associates (Anna Droumeva) (Bulgaria, Romania, Serbia); Andrew Nurnberg Associates Agency Moscow (Ludmilla Suskova); Andrew Nurnberg Associates Baltic (Tatjana Zoldnere) (Estonia, Latvia, Lithuania); Andrew Nurnberg Associates Budapest (Judit Hermann) (Croatia, Hungary); Andrew Nurnberg Associates International Ltd (Nina Yang) (China); Andrew Nurnberg Associates International Ltd (Whitney Hsu) (Taiwan); Agencia Riff (Roberto Matos) (Brazil); Sebes & Bisseling Literary Agency (Paul Sebes) (Netherlands); Tuttle-Mori Agency Inc (Asako Kawachi & Misa Morikawa) (Japan); Eric Yang Agency (Sue Yang) (Korea)
Membership(s): Association of American Publishers (AAP); National Book Foundation

Richard C Owen Publishers Inc
PO Box 585, Katonah, NY 10536-0585
Tel: 914-232-3903 *Toll Free Tel:* 800-336-5588
Fax: 914-232-3977
Web Site: www.rcowen.com
Key Personnel
Pres & Publr: Richard C Owen
E-mail: richardowen@rcowen.com
Founded: 1982
Education, language arts & literacy.
ISBN Prefix(es): 978-0-913461; 978-1-878450; 978-1-57274
Number of titles published annually: 5 Print

Total Titles: 378 Print
Warehouse: 247 Rte 100, Somers, NY 10589

Owl About Books Publisher Inc
1632 Royalwood Circle, Joshua, TX 76058
Mailing Address: PO Box 867, Joshua, TX 76058
Tel: 682-553-9078 *Fax:* 817-558-8983
E-mail: owlaboutbooks@gmail.com
Web Site: www.owlaboutbooks.com
Key Personnel
Pres: Dorota Harrington
Founded: 2011
Privately owned & devoted to publishing literature for children. Educational series philosophy is best described by the company's motto "Children's learning has no limits." Specialize in beautifully illustrated reading resources for parents & children with special needs. Well-placed fun facts accompany most of the stories & provide educational benefit.
ISBN Prefix(es): 978-1-937752
Number of titles published annually: 7 Print; 7 Online
Total Titles: 14 Print; 14 Online
Membership(s): Independent Book Publishers Association (IBPA)

§Oxford University Press USA
Division of University of Oxford
198 Madison Ave, New York, NY 10016
SAN: 202-5892
Toll Free Tel: 800-451-7556 (orders); 800-445-9714 (cust serv) *Fax:* 919-677-1303
E-mail: custserv.us@oup.com
Web Site: global.oup.com
Key Personnel
Pres & Academic Publr: Niko Pfund
VP, Higher Educ: John Challice
VP, Transformation & Delivery: Laurea Salvatore
Publr, Scholarly & Online Ref: Damon Zucca
Head, US Content Opers: Deborah Shor
Academic Prod Dir: Casper Grathwohl
Edit Dir, Higher Educ: Patrick Lynch
Ed-in-Chief, Humanities: Suzanne Ryan Melamed
Ed, Academic & Trade: Theo Calderara; David McBride
Facilities Supv: Lorraine Betancourt
Founded: 1896
Scholarly, professional & reference books in the humanities, science, medicine & social studies; nonfiction trade, Bibles, college textbooks, music, ESL, paperbacks, children's books, journals, online reference & online scholarly. Prospective authors should consult the Oxford University Press web site for submission guidelines & proposal submission policy.
ISBN Prefix(es): 978-0-19
Number of titles published annually: 3,000 Print; 6 CD-ROM; 200 Online; 500 E-Book; 30 Audio
Total Titles: 26,000 Print; 27 CD-ROM; 400 Online; 700 E-Book; 250 Audio
Imprints: Clarendon Press; Sinauer Associates
Foreign Office(s): Great Clarendon St, Oxford OX2 6DP, United Kingdom (worldwide headquarters) *Tel:* (018165) 556767 *Fax:* (018165) 556646 *E-mail:* onlinequeries.uk@oup.com
Distributor for The American Chemical Society; American University in Cairo; Arnold Clarendon; Cold Spring Harbor Laboratory Press; Engineering Press; Getty; Greenwich Medical Media; Grove Dictionaries; Hurst; IRL; Kodansha; Roxbury Publishing; Saunders; Stamford University Press; Thomson Publishing
Foreign Rights: Gersh Agency
Returns: 2001 Evans Rd, Cary, NC 27513 *Toll Free Tel:* 800-280-0280
Warehouse: 2001 Evans Rd, Cary, NC 27513 *Toll Free Tel:* 800-280-0280
Distribution Center: 2001 Evans Rd, Cary, NC 27513 *Toll Free Tel:* 800-280-0280

Membership(s): American Association of University Presses (AAUP); Association of American Publishers (AAP); Book Industry Study Group (BISG)

Ozark Mountain Publishing Inc
PO Box 754, Huntsville, AR 72740-0754
Tel: 479-738-2348 *Toll Free Tel:* 800-935-0045
Fax: 479-738-2448
E-mail: info@ozarkmt.com
Web Site: www.ozarkmt.com
Key Personnel
Gen Mgr: Nancy Vernon *E-mail:* nancy@ozarkmt.com
Gen Mgr Asst: Brandy McDonald
E-mail: brandy@ozarkmt.com
Founded: 1992
Publish nonfiction, New Age/metaphysical & spiritual type books. No poetry.
ISBN Prefix(es): 978-0-9632776; 978-1-886940; 978-1-940265; 978-1-950639 (Big Sandy Press); 978-1-950608
Number of titles published annually: 10 Print; 10 E-Book; 5 Audio
Total Titles: 126 Print; 111 E-Book; 14 Audio
Imprints: Big Sandy Press
Distributed by Red Wheel/Weiser/Conari

P & R Publishing Co
1102 Marble Hill Rd, Phillipsburg, NJ 08865
SAN: 205-3918
Mailing Address: PO Box 817, Phillipsburg, NJ 08865
Tel: 908-454-0505 *Toll Free Tel:* 800-631-0094
Fax: 908-859-2390
E-mail: sales@prpbooks.com; info@prpbooks.com
Web Site: www.prpbooks.com
Key Personnel
Pres: Bryce H Craig *E-mail:* bryce@prpbooks.com
VP: Ian M Thompson *E-mail:* ian@prpbooks.com
Sr Proj Mgr: Aaron Gottier *E-mail:* aarong@prpbooks.com
Founded: 1930
Christian books for all ages (Reformed Theology).
ISBN Prefix(es): 978-0-87552; 978-1-59638
Number of titles published annually: 60 Print; 100 E-Book
Total Titles: 750 Print; 1 CD-ROM; 200 E-Book
Foreign Rights: F J Rudy & Associates (Fred Rudy) (worldwide)
Membership(s): Evangelical Christian Publishers Association (ECPA)

Pace University Press
Unit of Pace University
MS in Publishing, 8th fl, 551 Fifth Ave, New York, NY 10176
Tel: 212-346-1417 *Fax:* 212-346-1165
Web Site: www.pace.edu/press
Key Personnel
Dir: Manuela Soares *E-mail:* msoares@pace.edu
Assoc Dir: Stephanie Hsu *E-mail:* shsu@pace.edu
Founded: 1988
Academic books in the humanities.
ISBN Prefix(es): 978-0-944473
Number of titles published annually: 6 Print
Total Titles: 55 Print

Pacific Press® Publishing Association
Division of Seventh-Day Adventist Church
1350 N Kings Rd, Nampa, ID 83687-3193
Mailing Address: PO Box 5353, Nampa, ID 83653-5353
Tel: 208-465-2500 *Toll Free Tel:* 800-447-7377
Fax: 208-465-2531
Web Site: www.pacificpress.com
Key Personnel
CIO: Ed Bahr *Tel:* 208-465-2630 *E-mail:* ed.bahr@pacificpress.com

Pres & Gen Mgr: Dale Galusha *Tel:* 208-465-2501 *E-mail:* dale.galusha@pacificpress.com
VP, Fin: Robert Hastings *Tel:* 208-465-2536 *E-mail:* robert.hastings@pacificpress.com
VP, Mktg & Sales: Doug Church *Tel:* 208-465-2505 *E-mail:* doug.church@pacificpress.com
VP, Prod Devt: Miguel Valdivia *Tel:* 208-465-2595 *E-mail:* miguel.valdivia@pacificpress.com
VP, Prodn: Robert Congleton *Tel:* 208-465-2611 *E-mail:* robert.congleton@pacificpress.com
Magazine Sr Ed: Marvin Moore *Tel:* 208-465-2577 *E-mail:* marvin.moore@pacificpress.com
Magazine Juv Ed: Kathy Beagles Coneff *Tel:* 208-465-2580 *E-mail:* kathy.coneff@pacificpress.com
Sales Mgr: Dave Gatton *Tel:* 208-465-2618 *E-mail:* dave.gatton@pacificpress.com
Ad: Bonnie Laing *Tel:* 208-465-2524 *E-mail:* bonnie.laing@pacificpress.com
Intl Rts: Carolyn Curtis *Tel:* 208-465-2511 *E-mail:* carolyn.curtis@pacificpress.com
Founded: 1874
Religion (Seventh-day Adventist).
ISBN Prefix(es): 978-0-8163; 978-1-5180
Number of titles published annually: 39 Print
Total Titles: 350 Print; 2 CD-ROM; 675 Online; 2 Audio

Pact Press
Imprint of Regal House Publishing
c/o Regal House Publishing, 806 Oberlin Rd, No 12094, Raleigh, NC 27605
E-mail: info@regalhousepublishing.com
Web Site: pactpress.com
Founded: 2016
Pact Press is dedicated to the publication & promotion of high-quality literature that speaks to topical social issues such as religious tolerance, gender equality, immigration, discrimination, racism, poverty, addiction, & LGBTQIA concerns. Pact Press publishes poetry, full-length fiction, memoirs & through the auspices of our nonprofit, The Regal House Initiative, an anthology series that benefits reputable nonprofits. We provide extensive editorial support to our authors & strong pre- & post-release digital marketing campaigns to further amplify our authors' outreach efforts. We seek authors with whom we can form meaningful partnerships, working together in a collaborative fashion to best polish & promote their work. We are delighted to accept submissions directly from authors at: regalhousepublishing.submittable.com/submit.
ISBN Prefix(es): 978-0-9912612; 978-0-9988398; 978-1-947548
Number of titles published annually: 5 Print; 5 E-Book
Orders to: Independent Publishers Group, 814 N Franklin St, Chicago, IL 60610 *Toll Free Tel:* 800-888-4741 *Web Site:* www.ipgbook.com
Distribution Center: Independent Publishers Group, 814 N Franklin St, Chicago, IL 60610 *Tel:* 312-337-0747 *Fax:* 312-337-5985 *Web Site:* www.ipgbook.com
Membership(s): American Booksellers Association (ABA); The Children's Book Council (CBC); Community of Literary Magazines & Presses (CLMP); Independent Book Publishers Association (IBPA); Southern Independent Booksellers Alliance (SIBA)

Paintbox Press
275 Madison Ave, Suite 600, New York, NY 10016
Tel: 212-878-6610
E-mail: info@paintboxpress.com
Web Site: www.paintboxpress.com
Key Personnel
Owner: Pamela Pease
PR: Kelly Crawford
Founded: 1998
Pop-ups & books on art & design.

ISBN Prefix(es): 978-0-966943; 978-0-977790
Number of titles published annually: 4 Print
Total Titles: 10 Print
Membership(s): AIGA, the professional association for design; The Children's Book Council (CBC); Society of Illustrators

§Palgrave Macmillan
Imprint of Springer Nature
One New York Plaza, Suite 4500, New York, NY 10004-1562
Tel: 212-726-9200
E-mail: sales-ny@springernature.com
Web Site: www.palgrave.com; www.springernature.com
Key Personnel
Trade Sales Dir, Americas: Marit Vagstad
Founded: 1952
Scholarly & trade publisher - cross market publisher.
ISBN Prefix(es): 978-0-312; 978-0-333; 978-1-4039; 978-0-230
Number of titles published annually: 3,200 Print; 2 Online; 850 E-Book
Total Titles: 28,000 Print
Distributor for Berg Publishers; British Film Institute; Manchester University Press; Pluto Press; I B Tauris & Co Ltd; Zed Books
Membership(s): Association of American Publishers Professional & Scholarly Publishing Division

Palladium Books Inc
39074 Webb Ct, Westland, MI 48185
SAN: 294-9504
Tel: 734-721-2903 (orders)
Web Site: www.palladiumbooks.com
Key Personnel
Pres: Kevin Siembieda *E-mail:* ksiembieda@palladiumbooks.com
Sr Ed: Alex Marciniszyn *E-mail:* alex@palladiumbooks.com
Founded: 1981
Role-playing game books & supplements.
ISBN Prefix(es): 978-0-916211; 978-1-57457
Number of titles published annually: 12 Print
Total Titles: 200 Print

§Palm Island Press
3607 Maine Ave, Sebring, FL 33870
SAN: 298-4024
Tel: 305-296-3102
E-mail: pipress2@gmail.com
Key Personnel
Gen Mgr: Donald Langille
Founded: 1994
ISBN Prefix(es): 978-0-9643434; 978-0-9743524
Number of titles published annually: 3 Print; 2 E-Book
Total Titles: 15 Print; 2 E-Book
Membership(s): Florida Authors & Publishers Association Inc (FAPA); Independent Book Publishers Association (IBPA)

Palmetto Bug Books
1345 NE 105 St, No 2, Miami Shores, FL 33138
Tel: 305-531-9813
E-mail: palmettobugbooks@gmail.com
Key Personnel
Pres: Reginald Roach
Founded: 1992
Small publisher of fiction with a slant toward South Florida.
ISBN Prefix(es): 978-0-9634499
Number of titles published annually: 4 Print; 1 Online; 1 E-Book
Total Titles: 4 Print; 4 Online; 4 E-Book

Pangaea Publications
402 Church St, Wisconsin Dells, WI 53965
Tel: 651-226-2032 *Fax:* 651-226-2032

E-mail: info@pangaea.org
Web Site: pangaea.org
Key Personnel
Publr & Ed: Bonnie Hayskar *E-mail:* bonzi@pangaea.org
Founded: 1991
Publisher for nature & peoples of the earth.
ISBN Prefix(es): 978-0-9630180; 978-1-929165
Number of titles published annually: 4 Print
Total Titles: 32 Print

§Pantheon Books
Imprint of Knopf Doubleday Publishing Group
c/o Penguin Random House Inc, 1745 Broadway, New York, NY 10019
Tel: 212-751-2600 *Fax:* 212-572-2662 (foreign rts)
Web Site: knopfdoubleday.com
Key Personnel
EVP & Publr: Reagan Arthur
SVP & Assoc Publr: Christine Gillespie
VP & Exec Dir, Sales Mgmt & Planning: Beth Meister
VP & Exec Ed: Erroll McDonald
Deputy Publr & Exec Dir, Mktg & Publicity: Paul Bogaards
Mng Ed: Altie Karper
Dir, Ad: Katie Burns
Dir, Publicity: Michiko Clark
Assoc Dir, Publicity: Josie Kals
Asst Dir, Mktg: Sara Eagle
Sr Ed: Deborah Garrison; Shelley Wanger
Mktg Mgr: Julianne Clancy; Dani Toth
Founded: 1942
Penguin Random House & its publishing entities are not accepting proposals, mss or submission queries via e-mail at this time.
Foreign Rep(s): Century Hutchinson Group (South America); Colt Associates (Africa exc South Africa); Steve Franklin (Israel); India Book Distributors (India); International Publishers Representatives (Middle East exc Israel); Pandemic Ltd (Continental Europe exc Scandinavia); Penguin Random House Canada (Canada); Penguin Random House New Zealand (New Zealand); Penguin Random House UK (UK); Periodical Management Group Inc (Mexico); Random Century (Australia); Saga Books ApS (Scandinavia); Sonrisa Book Service (Latin America exc Mexico); Yohan (Japan)
Foreign Rights: Arts & Licensing International (China); Agencia Literaria Carmen Balcells SA (Spain); Agencia Literaria BMSR (Brazil); DRT International (Korea); The English Agency (Japan); Graal Literary Agency (Poland); JLM Literary Agency (Greece); Katai & Bolza (Hungary); Agence Michelle Lapautre (France); Licht & Licht Agency (Scandinavia); Literarni Agentura (Czechia); Roberto Santachiara (Italy); Sebes & Bisseling Literary Agency (Netherlands)

§Pants On Fire Press
2062 Harbor Cove Way, Winter Garden, FL 34787
Tel: 863-546-0760
E-mail: submission@pantsonfirepress.com
Web Site: www.pantsonfirepress.com
Key Personnel
Publr: David Powers *E-mail:* david@pantsonfirepress.com
Dir, Mktg: Cris Francet *E-mail:* cris@pantsonfirepress.com
Founded: 2007
Award-winning book publisher of middle grade, young adult, new adult, travel & tourism books.
ISBN Prefix(es): 978-0-9827271
Number of titles published annually: 12 Print; 8 E-Book; 1 Audio
Total Titles: 62 Print; 62 E-Book; 2 Audio

Foreign Rights: The Gersh Agency (Joe Veltre)
(worldwide)
Distribution Center: Independent Publishers
Group (IPG), 814 N Franklin St, Chicago, IL
60610 *Tel:* 415-489-7000 *Fax:* 415-489-7049
Membership(s): Independent Book Publishers Association (IBPA)

Papercutz
160 Broadway, E Wing, Suite 700, New York,
NY 10038
Tel: 646-559-4681 *Toll Free Tel:* 800-886-1223
Fax: 212-643-1545
E-mail: papercutz@papercutz.com
Web Site: www.papercutz.com
Key Personnel
Pres & CEO: Terry Nantier
Ed-in-Chief: Jim Salicup
Founded: 2005
Graphic novels for ages 7-14.
ISBN Prefix(es): 978-1-59707; 978-1-62991
Number of titles published annually: 50 Print; 50
E-Book
Total Titles: 350 Print; 200 E-Book
Imprints: Charmz (early crush comics for girls
ages 10-14); SuperGenius (graphic novels for
teens & older)
Distributed by Macmillan
Orders to: MPS Distribution Center, 16365 James
Madison Hwy, Gordonsville, VA 22942 *Toll
Free Tel:* 888-330-8477 *Toll Free Fax:* 800-
672-2054
Warehouse: MPS Distribution Center, 16365
James Madison Hwy, Gordonsville, VA
22942 *Toll Free Tel:* 888-330-8477 *Toll Free
Fax:* 800-672-2054
Distribution Center: MPS Distribution Center,
16365 James Madison Hwy, Gordonsville, VA
22942 *Toll Free Tel:* 888-330-8477 *Toll Free
Fax:* 800-672-2054
Membership(s): Association of American Pub-
lishers (AAP); The Children's Book Council
(CBC)

Papyrus Publishers, see Letterbox/Papyrus of
London Publishers USA

Parachute Publishing LLC
Division of Parachute Properties LLC
157 Columbus Ave, Suite 518, New York, NY
10023
Tel: 212-691-1422
Key Personnel
Chmn & CEO: Joan Waricha *E-mail:* jwaricha@
parachuteproperties.com
Chair: Jane Stine *E-mail:* jstine@
parachuteproperties.com
Founded: 1983
Children's & adult fiction & nonfiction: original
books & series, books from licensed properties.
ISBN Prefix(es): 978-0-938753
Number of titles published annually: 100 Print
Total Titles: 1,000 Print
Distributed by Bantam; Bendon; Berkley; Dor-
ling Kindersley; Grosset; Harcourt; Harper-
Collins; HarperEntertainment; Kensington;
Little, Brown; Penguin Random House Inc;
Pocket Books; Running Press; Scholastic; Si-
mon & Schuster, Inc
Membership(s): American Book Producers Asso-
ciation (ABPA); The Children's Book Council
(CBC)

Paraclete Press Inc
36 Southern Eagle Cartway, Brewster, MA 02631
SAN: 282-1508
Mailing Address: PO Box 1568, Orleans, MA
02653-1568
Tel: 508-255-4685 *Toll Free Tel:* 800-451-5006
Fax: 508-255-5705
E-mail: mail@paracletepress.com;
customerservice@paracletepress.com

Web Site: www.paracletepress.com
Founded: 1981
Spirituality, personal testimonies, devotionals, lit-
erary fiction, new editions of classics & CDs.
ISBN Prefix(es): 978-1-55725; 978-0-941478
Number of titles published annually: 38 Print; 3
Audio
Total Titles: 145 Print; 90 Audio
Distributor for Abbey of Saint Peter of Solesmes;
Gloriae Dei Cantores
Distribution Center: Baker & Taylor Publisher
Services, 30 Amberwood Pkwy, Ashland, OH
44805 (US & CN) *Tel:* 567-215-0030 *Toll Free
Tel:* 888-814-0208 *E-mail:* info@btpubservices.
com *Web Site:* www.btpubservices.com
Membership(s): Association of Catholic Publish-
ers Inc; Evangelical Christian Publishers Asso-
ciation (ECPA)

§Paradigm Publications
Division of Redwing Book Co
202 Bendix Dr, Taos, NM 87571
Tel: 575-758-7758 *Toll Free Tel:* 800-873-3946
(US); 888-873-3947 (CN) *Fax:* 575-758-7768
E-mail: info@paradigm-pubs.com
Web Site: www.paradigm-pubs.com; www.
redwingbooks.com
Key Personnel
Publr: Robert L Felt *E-mail:* bob@paradigm-
pubs.com
Founded: 1980
Scholarly books on traditional Chinese medicine
& acupuncture.
ISBN Prefix(es): 978-0-912111; 978-0-9908698
Number of titles published annually: 2 Print
Total Titles: 60 Print; 40 E-Book

Paradise Cay Publications Inc
120 Monda Way, Blue Lake, CA 95525
Mailing Address: PO Box 29, Arcata, CA 95518-
0029
Tel: 707-822-9063 *Toll Free Tel:* 800-736-4509
Fax: 707-822-9163
E-mail: info@paracay.com; orders@paracay.com
Web Site: www.paracay.com
Key Personnel
Owner & Dir: Jim Morehouse *E-mail:* james@
paracay.com
Founded: 1977
Nautical books, videos, art prints, cruising guides
& software.
ISBN Prefix(es): 978-0-939837; 978-0-9646036;
978-1-937196; 978-1-929214
Number of titles published annually: 6 Print
Total Titles: 82 Print; 4 Audio
Imprints: Pardey Publications
Foreign Rep(s): Boat Books (Australia); Islam-
orado Internacional (Panama); The Nautical
Mind (Canada); Transpacific Marine (New
Zealand)

Paragon House
3600 Labore Rd, Suite 1, St Paul, MN 55110-
4144
Tel: 651-644-3087 *Toll Free Tel:* 800-447-3709
Fax: 651-644-0997
E-mail: paragon@paragonhouse.com
Web Site: www.paragonhouse.com
Key Personnel
Pres: Dr Gordon L Anderson
Founded: 1963
Nonfiction; academic/scholarly monographs, trade
& college paperbacks. History, philosophy, cul-
ture, governance, economy.
ISBN Prefix(es): 978-1-55778; 978-0-913729;
978-0-913757; 978-0-89226; 978-0-943852;
978-0-88702; 978-1-885118; 978-1-61083
(ebooks)
Number of titles published annually: 4 Print
Total Titles: 400 Print
Foreign Rep(s): Roundhouse Publishing (Europe,
UK)

Orders to: Baker & Taylor Publisher Services,
30 Amberwood Pkwy, Ashland, OH 44805
Tel: 567-215-0030 *Toll Free Tel:* 888-814-
0208 *E-mail:* orders@btpubservices.com *Web
Site:* www.btpubservices.com
Distribution Center: Baker & Taylor Publisher
Services, 30 Amberwood Pkwy, Ashland, OH
44805 *Tel:* 567-215-0030 *Toll Free Tel:* 888-
814-0208 *E-mail:* orders@btpubservices.com
Web Site: www.btpubservices.com

§Parallax Press
Division of Unified Buddhist Church
2236B Sixth St, Berkeley, CA 94710
Mailing Address: PO Box 7355, Berkeley, CA
94707-0355
Tel: 510-540-6411 *Toll Free Tel:* 800-863-5290
(orders) *Fax:* 510-981-1157
Web Site: www.parallax.org
Key Personnel
Publr: Hisae Matsuda *E-mail:* hisae@parallax.org
Art & Prodn Dir: Terri Saul *E-mail:* terri@
parallax.org
Digital Mktg Dir: Stephen Houghton
E-mail: stephen.houghton@parallax.org
Media & Opers Dir: Steven D Low
E-mail: steven@parallax.org
Sales & Inventory Dir: Heather Harrison
E-mail: heather@parallax.org
Edit Dir, Palm Leaves Press: Terry Barber
E-mail: terry@parallax.org
Publicity Dir: Earlita Chenault *Tel:* 510-944-9032
E-mail: earlita@parallax.org
Mktg Mgr: Katie Eberle *E-mail:* katie@parallax.
org
Sr Ed: Jacob Surpin *E-mail:* jacob@parallax.org
Founded: 1986
Nonprofit organization publishing books about
mindfulness, justice & joy.
ISBN Prefix(es): 978-0-938077; 978-1-888375;
978-1-935209; 978-0-9846271; 978-1-937006;
978-1-941529
Number of titles published annually: 24 Print
Total Titles: 200 Print; 7 Audio
Imprints: Palm Leaves Press (scholarly Buddhist
titles); Plum Blossom Books (mindfulness
books for children)
Foreign Rights: Cecile Barendsma (worldwide
exc Germany, India, Thailand & Vietnam);
Brother Phap Kham (Vietnam); Literaturmanu-
faktur (Ursula Richard) (Germany); Plum Village Foundation (Thailand); Shantum Seth (In-
dia)
Distribution Center: Penguin Random House
Publisher Services (PRHPS), 400 Hahn
Rd, Westminster, MD 21157 *Toll Free
Tel:* 800-659-2436 *E-mail:* distribution@
penguinrandomhouse.com *Web Site:* www.
penguinrandomhouse.biz/publisherservices
Penguin Random House Publisher Ser-
vices (PRHPS), 1745 Broadway, New
York, NY 10019 *Fax:* 212-572-4961
E-mail: distribution@penguinrandomhouse.
com *Web Site:* www.penguinrandomhouse.
biz/publisherservices
Penguin Random House Canada, 320 Front
St W, Suite 1400, Toronto, ON M5V 3B6,
Canada *Web Site:* www.penguinrandomhouse.ca
SAN: 201-3975

Paramount Market Publishing Inc
274 N Goodman St, Suite D214, Rochester, NY
14607
Tel: 607-275-8100
E-mail: editors@paramountbooks.com
Web Site: www.paramountbooks.com
Founded: 1999
Marketing, market research, market segments &
brand management.
ISBN Prefix(es): 978-0-9571439; 978-0-9725290;
978-0-9766973; 978-0-9786602; 978-0-
9801745; 978-0-9819869; 978-0-9830436

Number of titles published annually: 6 Print; 6 E-Book
Total Titles: 110 Print; 80 E-Book
Imprints: PMP

Parenting Press
Imprint of Chicago Review Press
13751 Lake City Way NE, Suite 110, Seattle, WA 98125
Mailing Address: PO Box 75267, Seattle, WA 98175-0267
Tel: 206-364-2900 *Toll Free Tel:* 800-99-BOOKS (992-6657) *Fax:* 206-364-0702
E-mail: office@parentingpress.com; marketing@ parentingpress.com
Web Site: www.parentingpress.com
Founded: 1979
Parenting, social skill building, personal safety for children, discipline, feelings, temperament, development, boundaries, problem solving, social relations.
ISBN Prefix(es): 978-0-943990; 978-0-9602862 (co-published with Raefield-Roberts); 978-1-884734; 978-1-936903
Number of titles published annually: 6 Print; 26 Online; 2 E-Book
Total Titles: 85 Print; 5 Online; 44 E-Book
Distribution Center: Independent Publishers Group (IPG), 814 N Franklin St, Chicago, IL 60610 *Tel:* 312-337-0747 *Toll Free Tel:* 800-888-4741 *Fax:* 312-337-5985 *Web Site:* www. ipgbook.com
Membership(s): Book Publishers of the Northwest (BPNW); Independent Book Publishers Association (IBPA); Publishers Association of the West (PubWest)

Park Place Publications
591 Lighthouse Ave, Suite 10, Pacific Grove, CA 93950
SAN: 297-5238
Mailing Address: PO Box 722, Pacific Grove, CA 93950-0722
Tel: 831-649-6640
E-mail: publishingbiz@sbcglobal.net
Web Site: www.parkplacepublications.com
Key Personnel
Owner & Publr: Patricia Hamilton
Founded: 1991
Provides book publishing, graphic design & prepress services. Founded on the premise that "Books make a world of difference" (the company slogan).
This publisher has indicated that 90% of their product line is author subsidized.
ISBN Prefix(es): 978-1-935530; 978-1-943887
Number of titles published annually: 15 Print; 15 Online; 10 E-Book
Total Titles: 75 Print; 15 Online; 10 E-Book
Imprints: Alamos Press (American & Mexican culture & bilingual); At Home on the Road (travel); Keepers of Our Culture (personal & historical stories, memoirs); Pacific Grove Books (city related content)
Distribution Center: Ingram Content Group, One Ingram Blvd, La Vergne, TN 37086 *Tel:* 615-793-5000 *Web Site:* www.ingramcontent.com
Membership(s): Association of Personal Historians; The Association of Publishers for Special Sales (APSS); Independent Book Publishers Association (IBPA); Small Publishers, Artists & Writers Network (SPAWN)

§Parmenides Publishing
3753 Howard Hughes Pkwy, Suite 200, Las Vegas, NV 89169
SAN: 254-4342
Tel: 702-892-3934 *Fax:* 702-892-3939
E-mail: info@parmenides.com
Web Site: www.parmenides.com

Key Personnel
Publr & CEO: Sara Hermann *E-mail:* sherman@ parmenides.com
VP & Sales Dir: Gale Carr *E-mail:* gcarr@ parmenides.com
Founded: 2000
Independent publishing house. Specialize in literature on philosophy, especially ancient Greek philosophy for the academic & trade markets.
ISBN Prefix(es): 978-1-930972
Number of titles published annually: 4 Print; 4 Online; 4 E-Book; 4 Audio
Total Titles: 49 Print; 49 Online; 45 E-Book; 4 Audio
Divisions: ParmenidesAudio™; ParmenidesFiction™
Foreign Rep(s): APAC (Tom Cassidy) (Brunei, Cambodia, China, Hong Kong, Indonesia, Malaysia, Myanmar, Singapore, Taiwan, Thailand, Vietnam)
Orders to: The University of Chicago Press Distribution Center, 1427 E 60 St, Chicago, IL 60637 *Toll Free Tel:* 800-621-2736 *Fax:* 773-702-9756 *E-mail:* orders@press.uchicago.edu
Returns: The University of Chicago Press Distribution Center, 11030 S Langley, Chicago, IL 60628 *Tel:* 773-702-7700 *Fax:* 773-702-9756 *Toll Free Fax:* 800-621-8476 *E-mail:* orders@ press.uchicago.edu
Shipping Address: The University of Chicago Press Distribution Center, 11030 S Langley, Chicago, IL 60628 *Tel:* 773-702-7700 *Fax:* 773-702-9756 *Toll Free Fax:* 800-621-8476 *E-mail:* orders@press.uchicago.edu
Warehouse: The University of Chicago Press Distribution Center, 11030 S Langley, Chicago, IL 60628 *Tel:* 773-702-7700 *Fax:* 773-702-9756 *Toll Free Fax:* 800-621-8476 *E-mail:* orders@ press.uchicago.edu
Distribution Center: The University of Chicago Press Distribution Center, 11030 S Langley, Chicago, IL 60628 *Tel:* 773-702-7700 *Toll Free Tel:* 800-621-8476 (orders) *Fax:* 773-702-9756 *Toll Free Fax:* 800-621-8476 *E-mail:* orders@ press.uchicago.edu
Membership(s): Association of American Publishers (AAP)

Path Press Inc
708 Washington St, Evanston, IL 60202
SAN: 630-2041
Tel: 847-492-0177
E-mail: pathpressinc@aol.com
Key Personnel
Pres: Bennett J Johnson
Founded: 1962
Books for African-American & Third World people.
This publisher has indicated that 25% of their product line is author subsidized.
ISBN Prefix(es): 978-0-910671
Number of titles published annually: 6 Print
Total Titles: 51 Print
Subsidiaries: African-American Book Distributors Inc
Membership(s): Independent Book Publishers Association (IBPA)

Pathfinder Publishing Inc
120 S Houghton Rd, Suite 138, Tucson, AZ 85748
SAN: 694-2571
Tel: 520-647-0158
Web Site: www.pathfinderpublishing.com
Key Personnel
Pres & CEO: Bill Mosbrook
Founded: 1985
Books & audiobooks. Specialize in music, psychology, nautical & military history.
ISBN Prefix(es): 978-0-934793
Number of titles published annually: 3 Print; 1 Audio

Total Titles: 50 Print; 3 Audio
Membership(s): Independent Book Publishers Association (IBPA)

Paul Dry Books
1700 Sansom St, Suite 700, Philadelphia, PA 19103
Tel: 215-231-9939
E-mail: editor@pauldrybooks.com
Web Site: www.pauldrybooks.com
Key Personnel
Owner & Publr: Paul Dry *E-mail:* pdry@ pauldrybooks.com
Mng Ed: John Corenswet *E-mail:* jcorenswet@ pauldrybooks.com; William Schofield
Philosophy, fiction, history, essays, young adult fiction & nonfiction.
ISBN Prefix(es): 978-0-9664913; 978-0-9679675; 978-1-58988
Number of titles published annually: 8 Print
Total Titles: 125 Print; 50 E-Book

Pauline Books & Media
Division of Daughters of St Paul
50 Saint Paul's Ave, Boston, MA 02130
SAN: 203-8900
Tel: 617-522-8911 *Toll Free Tel:* 800-876-4463 (orders); 800-836-9723 (cust serv) *Fax:* 617-541-9805
E-mail: editorial@paulinemedia.com (ms submissions); orderentry@pauline.org (cust serv)
Web Site: www.pauline.org/pbmpublishing
Key Personnel
Publr: Sr Marie James Hunt
Digital Mgr: Sr Kathryn James Hermes
Edit Mgr: Sr Mary Leonora Wilson
Promo Mgr: Sr Maria Kim-Ngan Bui
Adult Acqs Ed: Sr Maria Grace Denato; Sr Christina Wegendt
Book Center Acqs: Anthony Ruggiero
Children's & Teen Ed: Sr Marlyn Evangelina Monge; Troy Norman
Edit Asst, Acqs: Courtney Ward
Intl Rts & Perms: Nicole Anzuoni
Founded: 1932
Spirituality, prayer books, teachers' resources for religious education, liturgical books, church documents, adult religious instruction, saints lives, faith & culture, music & music CDs.
ISBN Prefix(es): 978-0-8198
Number of titles published annually: 50 Print; 30 E-Book; 1 Audio
Total Titles: 600 Print; 72 Audio
Imprints: Catholic Approach Series; Encounter the Saints Series (children); Faith & Culture; Pauline Comics & Graphic Novels (children & teens); Pauline Teen; The Saints Series; Theology of the Body Series
Membership(s): Association of Catholic Publishers Inc; Catholic Press Association (CPA); Society of Children's Book Writers & Illustrators (SCBWI)

§Paulist Press
997 Macarthur Blvd, Mahwah, NJ 07430-9990
SAN: 202-5159
Tel: 201-825-7300 *Toll Free Tel:* 800-218-1903 *Fax:* 201-825-6921 *Toll Free Fax:* 800-836-3161
E-mail: info@paulistpress.com; publicity@ paulistpress.com
Web Site: www.paulistpress.com
Key Personnel
Pres & Publr: Mark-David Janus, CSP
Edit Dir: Trace Murphy
Dir, Mktg: Gloria Capik
Dir, Mktg & Sales: Bob Byrns *E-mail:* bbyrns@ paulistpress.com
Sr Academic Ed: Donna Crilly
Founded: 1865

Resources with emphasis on biblical studies, Christian, Catholic & ecumenical formation & education, ethics & social issues, pastoral ministry, personal growth, spirituality, philosophy, theology.
ISBN Prefix(es): 978-0-8091
Number of titles published annually: 60 Print
Total Titles: 1,650 Print; 1,000 E-Book; 3 Audio
Imprints: The Newman Press; Stimulus Books
Foreign Rep(s): Bayard Novalis Distribution (Canada); Brumby Sunstate (Australia); Katong Catholic Book Center (Singapore); KCBS Inc (Korea); Norwich Books & Music (Europe); Pleroma Christian Supplies (New Zealand); St Pauls-India (India)
Returns: 39 Ramapo Valley Rd, Mahwah, NJ 07430
Warehouse: 39 Ramapo Valley Rd, Mahwah, NJ 07430
Membership(s): Association of Catholic Publishers Inc

Peabody Museum Press
Unit of Peabody Museum of Archaeology & Ethnology, Harvard University
11 Divinity Ave, Cambridge, MA 02138
Tel: 617-495-4255; 617-495-3938 (edit)
E-mail: peapub@fas.harvard.edu
Web Site: www.peabody.harvard.edu/publications
Key Personnel
Dir, Pubns: Joan O'Donnell
Founded: 1888
ISBN Prefix(es): 978-0-87365
Number of titles published annually: 6 Print
Total Titles: 140 Print
Distributed by Harvard University Press
Orders to: Harvard University Press, c/o TriLiteral LLC, 100 Maple Ridge Dr, Cumberland, RI 02864-1769 *Tel:* 401-531-2300 *Toll Free Tel:* 800-405-1619 *Fax:* 401-531-2801 *Toll Free Fax:* 800-406-9145 *E-mail:* customer.care@triliteral.org

§Peachpit Press
Imprint of Pearson Education Ltd
1301 Sansome St, San Francisco, CA 94111
Toll Free Tel: 800-283-9444
E-mail: info@peachpit.com; ask@peachpit.com
Web Site: www.peachpit.com
Founded: 1986
ISBN Prefix(es): 978-0-201; 978-1-56609; 978-0-321; 978-0-938151
Number of titles published annually: 180 Print
Total Titles: 400 Print
Imprints: New Riders

Peachtree Publishing Co Inc
1700 Chattahoochee Ave, Atlanta, GA 30318-2112
SAN: 212-1999
Tel: 404-876-8761 *Toll Free Tel:* 800-241-0113 *Fax:* 404-875-2578 *Toll Free Fax:* 800-875-8909
E-mail: hello@peachtree-online.com; orders@peachtree-online.com; sales@peachtree-online.com
Web Site: www.peachtree-online.com
Key Personnel
Pres & Publr: Margaret Quinlin
VP & Assoc Publr: Kathy Landwehr
Sales: Laura Palermo *Tel:* 404-876-8761 ext 114
Subs Rts: Farah Gehy *E-mail:* gehy@peachtree-online.com
Founded: 1977
Children's fiction & nonfiction, self-help & health/parenting & regional guides.
ISBN Prefix(es): 978-0-931948; 978-0-934601; 978-1-56145; 978-1-68263; 978-99927-862
Number of titles published annually: 40 Print
Total Titles: 400 Print

Imprints: Freestone; Peachtree Jr
Foreign Rep(s): Fitzhenry & Whiteside Publishers (Canada)

Pearson Allyn & Bacon
Imprint of Pearson Higher Education
501 Boylston St, Boston, MA 02116
Tel: 617-848-6000 *Toll Free Tel:* 800-428-4466 *Fax:* 617-848-6016
Web Site: home.pearsonhighered.com
Founded: 1868
College textbook publisher focusing on a select number of social science, education & humanities disciplines.
ISBN Prefix(es): 978-0-205; 978-0-321
Number of titles published annually: 310 Print
Total Titles: 2,300 Print

Pearson Arts & Sciences
Division of Pearson Education Ltd
221 River St, Hoboken, NJ 07030
Tel: 917-981-2200
Web Site: www.pearsonhighered.com
Number of titles published annually: 200 Print

Pearson Benjamin Cummings
Imprint of Pearson Higher Education
1301 Sansome St, San Francisco, CA 94111-1122
Tel: 415-402-2500 *Toll Free Tel:* 800-922-0579 (orders) *Toll Free Fax:* 800-445-6991 (orders)
Web Site: home.pearsonhighered.com
Key Personnel
VP & Dir, Media Strategy: Stacy Treco
Specialize in anatomy & physiology, biology, health & kinesiology, microbiology.
ISBN Prefix(es): 978-0-201; 978-0-582; 978-0-8053; 978-0-321; 978-0-8465

§Pearson Business Publishing
Unit of Pearson Higher Education
221 River St, Hoboken, NJ 07030-4772
Tel: 201-236-7000
Web Site: www.pearsonhighered.com
Key Personnel
Mgr, Content Prodn: Melissa Feimer

Pearson Education Ltd
225 River St, Hoboken, NJ 07030-4772
Tel: 201-236-7000 *Fax:* 201-236-6549
Web Site: www.pearsoned.com
Key Personnel
Chief Corp Aff Offr: Deirdre Latour
Chief Mktg Offr: Alexa Christon
ISBN Prefix(es): 978-0-582
See separate listing for:
Pearson Arts & Sciences
Pearson ELT
Pearson Higher Education

Pearson ELT
Division of Pearson Education Ltd
221 River St, Hoboken, NJ 07030
Toll Free Tel: 877-202-4572 *Toll Free Fax:* 800-445-6991
E-mail: english@pearson.com
Web Site: www.pearsonelt.com
Number of titles published annually: 100 Print
Foreign Office(s): Edinburgh Gate, Harlow, Essex CM20 2JE, United Kingdom *Tel:* (01279) 623623 *Fax:* (01279) 621330 *E-mail:* eltinquiries@pearson.com

Pearson Higher Education
Division of Pearson Education Ltd
225 River St, Hoboken, NJ 07030-4772
Tel: 201-236-7000
Web Site: www.pearson.com/us/higher-education.html
Key Personnel
EVP: Logan Campbell

ISBN Prefix(es): 978-0-13; 978-0-205; 978-0-8428; 978-0-87618; 978-0-87619; 978-0-87628; 978-0-89303
Imprints: Pearson Allyn & Bacon; Pearson Benjamin Cummings
See separate listing for:
Pearson Allyn & Bacon
Pearson Benjamin Cummings
Pearson Business Publishing
Pearson Learning Solutions

Pearson® K12 Learning LLC, see Savvas Learning Co LLC

Pearson Learning Solutions
Unit of Pearson Higher Education
501 Boyleston St, Suite 900, Boston, MA 02116
SAN: 214-0225
Tel: 617-671-3300 *Toll Free Tel:* 800-428-4466 (orders); 800-635-1579
E-mail: pcp@pearson.com
Web Site: www.pearsoned.com
ISBN Prefix(es): 978-0-8087; 978-0-536; 978-1-4386; 978-0-555; 978-0-558; 978-1-256; 978-1-269; 978-1-323
Branch Office(s)
Pearson Custom Publishing, 7110 Ohms Lane, Edina, MN 55439-2143 *Tel:* 952-831-1881 *Toll Free Tel:* 800-922-2579 *Fax:* 952-831-3167

T H Peek Publisher
Division of Clearweave Corp
PO Box 7406, Ann Arbor, MI 48107
SAN: 693-9708
Tel: 734-222-8205 *Fax:* 734-661-0136
E-mail: info@thpeekpublisher.com
Web Site: www.thpeekpublisher.com
Key Personnel
Owner: Colin D O'Brien
Founded: 1966
Ms acquisition, editorial, art, design, distribution, advertising & promotion.
ISBN Prefix(es): 978-0-917962; 978-1-935770
Number of titles published annually: 3 Print
Total Titles: 10 Print
Imprints: Alice Greene & Co

Pelican Publishing Co
Imprint of Arcadia Publishing
400 Poydras St, Suite 900, New Orleans, LA 70130
Tel: 504-368-1175 *Toll Free Tel:* 800-843-1724 *Fax:* 504-368-1195
E-mail: sales@pelicanpub.com (sales); office@pelicanpub.com (permission); promo@pelicanpub.com (publicity)
Web Site: www.pelicanpub.com
Key Personnel
Pres & Publr: Kathleen Calhoun Nettleton *Tel:* 504-368-1175 ext 312
Promo Dir: Antoinette de Alteriis
Dir, Sales: Don Anderson
Ed & ISBN Contact: Nina Kooij *E-mail:* editorial@pelicanpub.com
Rts & Perms: Sally Boitnott *Tel:* 504-368-1175 ext 310
Founded: 1926
General, motivational, inspirational, nostalgia, note cards, almanacs, business & children's.
ISBN Prefix(es): 978-0-911116; 978-0-88289; 978-1-56554; 978-1-58980; 978-1-4556
Number of titles published annually: 50 Print; 25 E-Book
Total Titles: 2,600 Print; 12 CD-ROM; 1,100 E-Book; 35 Audio
Imprints: Dove Inspirational Press
Subsidiaries: Pelican International Corp
Distributor for Hope Publishing House; Marmac Publishing Co; SelfHelp Success Books

Foreign Rights: Everybody's Books CC (South Africa); Gazelle Agency (Europe, Ireland, UK); John M Reed (Australia, New Zealand)
Membership(s): Museum Store Association (MSA); Southern Independent Booksellers Alliance (SIBA)

§Pen & Publish LLC
4719 Holly Hills Ave, St Louis, MO 63116
Tel: 314-827-6567
E-mail: info@penandpublish.com
Web Site: www.penandpublish.com
Key Personnel
Owner & Publr: Jennifer Geist *E-mail:* jennifer@penandpublish.com
Founded: 2004
Publishes books by & for schools & nonprofits. Also offers author services to help writers with self-publishing, editing, design & more. Its traditional imprints include Brick Mantel Books, Open Books Press & Transformation Media Books.
This publisher has indicated that 50% of their product line is author subsidized.
ISBN Prefix(es): 978-1-941799; 978-0-9768391; 978-0-9779530; 978-0-9790446; 978-0-9800429; 978-0-9817264; 978-0-9823850; 978-0-9842258; 978-0-9844600; 978-0-9845751; 978-0-9846359; 978-0-9852737; 978-0-9859367
Number of titles published annually: 3 Print; 3 E-Book
Total Titles: 100 Print; 14 E-Book
Imprints: Brick Mantel Books (literary fiction & poetry); Open Books Press (fiction for all ages & nonfiction for adults); Transformation Media Books (body/mind/spirit)
Membership(s): Independent Book Publishers Association (IBPA); Midwest Independent Booksellers Association (MIBA); St Louis Publishers Association
See separate listing for:
Brick Mantel Books
Open Books Press

Pen-L Publishing
12 W Dickson St, No 4455, Fayetteville, AR 72702
Web Site: www.pen-l.com
Key Personnel
Publr: Kimberly Pennell *E-mail:* kimberly@pen-l.com
Founded: 2012
ISBN Prefix(es): 978-1-942428; 978-1-942428; 978-1-68313
Number of titles published annually: 24 Print; 24 E-Book; 4 Audio
Total Titles: 91 Print; 91 E-Book; 6 Audio
Membership(s): International Thriller Writers Inc (ITW); Society of Children's Book Writers & Illustrators (SCBWI); Western Writers of America (WWA)

Pendragon Press
Subsidiary of Camelot Publishing Co Inc
52 White Hill Rd, Hillsdale, NY 12529-5839
Mailing Address: PO Box 190, Hillsdale, NY 12529
Tel: 518-325-6100 *Toll Free Tel:* 877-656-6381 (orders)
E-mail: editor@pendragonpress.com; orders@pendragonpress.com
Web Site: www.pendragonpress.com
Key Personnel
Mng Ed: Robert J Kessler
Founded: 1972
Reference works on books & musicology including music/aesthetics, biographies, music theory, organ, harpsichord, historic brass, 20th century music, French opera, music & religion.
ISBN Prefix(es): 978-0-918728; 978-0-945193; 978-1-57647

Number of titles published annually: 10 Print
Total Titles: 400 Print
Distributed by LIM Editrice SRL (Italy); G Ricordi (Italy)
Foreign Rep(s): Eurospan Ltd (Europe)

Penfield Books
215 Brown St, Iowa City, IA 52245
SAN: 221-6671
Tel: 319-337-9998 *Toll Free Tel:* 800-728-9998
  Fax: 319-351-6846
E-mail: penfield@penfieldbooks.com; orders@penfieldbooks.com
Web Site: www.penfieldbooks.com
Key Personnel
Publr: Joan Liffring-Zug Bourret
Founded: 1979 (as Penfield Press)
Ethnic titles including Czech, Danish, Dutch, Finnish, French, German, Irish, Italian, Mexican, Norwegian, Polish, Scandinavian, Scottish, Slovak, Swedish & Ukrainian; cookbooks; crafts & folk art; history; ethnic cultural cookbooks, cookbooks of the states. No unsol mss.
ISBN Prefix(es): 978-0-941016; 978-1-932043; 978-1-57216
Number of titles published annually: 6 Print; 6 CD-ROM; 20 E-Book
Total Titles: 174 Print; 268 Online; 75 E-Book

Penguin Books
Imprint of Penguin Group USA, A Penguin Random House Company
375 Hudson St, New York, NY 10014
Tel: 212-366-2000
E-mail: penguinpublicity@us.penguingroup.com
Web Site: www.penguinclassics.com; www.penguin.com
Key Personnel
Pres & Publr: Brian Tart
VP & Deputy Publr: Patrick Nolan
VP & Publr, Penguin Classics: Elda Rotor
Exec Mng Ed: Matt Giarratano
Exec Ed: Meg Leder
Exec Ed, Penguin Classics & Penguin Books: John Siciliano
Assoc Ed: Matt Klise; Victoria Savanh
Asst Ed: Gretchen Schmid; Elizabeth Vogt
Assoc Dir, Publicity: Shannon Twomey
Assoc Dir, Publicity, Viking/Penguin: Rebecca Marsh
Publicity Mgr: Maya Baran
Exec Publicist, Viking/Penguin: Shelby Meizlik
Sr Publicist: Alison Klooster; Brianna Linden; Chris Smith
Sr Publicist, Viking/Penguin: Kristina Fazzalaro
Publicist: Sara DeLozier
Assoc Publicist: Sara Chuirazzi; Jessica Fitzpatrick; Theresa Gaffney; Sara Leonard
Digital Mktg Mgr: Ryan Murphy
Founded: 1935
Penguin Random House & its publishing entities are not accepting unsol submissions, proposals, mss, or submission queries via e-mail at this time.
Number of titles published annually: 244 Print
Total Titles: 4,425 Print
Imprints: Penguin; Penguin Classics; Penguin Compass; Penguin 20th Century Classics
Advertising Agency: Spier NY

Penguin Group USA, A Penguin Random House Company
375 Hudson St, New York, NY 10014
Tel: 212-366-2000 *Toll Free Tel:* 800-847-5515 (inside sales); 800-631-8571 (cust serv)
  Fax: 212-366-2666; 607-775-4829 (inside sales)
E-mail: online@us.penguingroup.com
Web Site: www.penguin.com
Key Personnel
Pres, Penguin Publishing Group: Allison Dobson
Pres & Publr, Penguin Press: Ann Godoff

Pres & Publr, Portfolio & Sentinel Books: Adrian Zackheim
Pres & Publr, Viking: Brian Tart
Pres, Penguin Young Readers: Jen Loja
Pres, Putnam & Dutton: Ivan Held
EVP & Dir, HR: Paige McInerney
SVP & Dir, Sales for Penguin Young Readers Group: Felicia Frazier
SVP & Dir, Subs Rts: Leigh Butler
SVP & Group Sales Dir: Lauren Monaco
SVP, Dist: James C Clark
SVP, Strategy & Fin: Katie Ziga
VP & Assoc Publr, Pbks (Putnam/Dutton): Benjamin Lee
VP & Corp Dir, HR: Carol Peterson
VP & Dir, Bldg Admin: Heidi Kagan
VP & Dir, Mktg & Publicity, Portfolio/Sentinel: Tara Gilbride
VP & Dir, Opers: Yvette Dano
VP & Print Prodn Dir: Vincenzo Ruggiero
VP, Busn Mgmt: Tina McCormick
VP, Educ Sales & Mktg: Michael Gentile
VP, Global Talent Mgmt: Jo Mallia
VP, Order Fulfillment: Linda Bay
Sr Exec Dir, Nonfiction Backlist: Carrie Swetonic
Edit Dir, Plume: Philip Budnick
Dir, Ad: Ashley Fisher-Tranese
Dir, Consumer Onsights, Penguin Publishing Group: Anuja Palkar
Dir, Mfg Procurement: Mike Gallagher
Dir, Intellectual Property Group: Peter Harris
Dir, Publicity, Portfolio/Sentinel: Margot Stamas
Dir, Strategy & Fin: Liz Ichniowski
Mktg Dir, Dutton/Plume: Stephanie Cooper
Assoc Art Dir, Ad: Vi-An Nguyen
Assoc Dir, Publicity: Shannon Twomey
Assoc Dir, Publicity, Viking/Penguin: Rebecca Marsh
Ed-in-Chief, Avery: Caroline Sutton
Ed-in-Chief, Viking: Andrea Schulz
Exec Ed, Portfolio & Edit Dir, Sentinel: Bria Sanford
Exec Ed, Portfolio, Sentinel & Current: Eric Nelson
Exec Ed, Putnam: Margo Lipschultz
Ed, Penguin: Margaux Weisman
Ed, Portfolio/Sentinel: Leah Trouwborst
Assoc Ed, Avery: Gigi Campo
Assoc Ed, Dutton: Stephanie Kelly
Assoc Ed, Portfolio/Sentinel: Merry Sun
Assoc Ed, Putnam: Danielle Dieterich
Asst Ed, Dutton: Cassidy Sachs
Asst Ed, Pam Dorman Books & Viking: Jeramie Orton
Asst Ed, Portfolio/Sentinel: Helen Healey; Vivian Roberson
Asst Ed, Putnam: Sofie Brooks
Exec Publicity Mgr, Putnam: Katie McKee
Mgr, Busn Devt: Casey Blue James
Media Rel Mgr: Erica Glass
Asst Mktg Mgr, Dutton/Plume: Natalie Church
Asst Mktg Mgr, Portfolio/Sentinel: Mary Kate Skehan
Exec Publicist, Viking/Penguin: Shelby Meizlik
Sr Publicist: Tony Forde
Sr Publicist, Portfolio/Sentinel: Alison Coolidge
Sr Publicist, Viking/Penguin: Kristina Fazzalaro
Publicist, Portfolio/Sentinel: Alyssa Adler; Marisol Salaman
Publicist, Viking/Penguin: Sara DeLozier
Founded: 1996
Publisher of consumer books in both hardcover & paperback for adults & children. Also produces maps, calendars, audiobooks & mass merchandise products.
Adult: hardcover, trade paperbacks & mass market paperbacks (originals & reprints)
Children: hardcover picture books, paperback picture books, board & novelty books
Young Adult: hardcover & trade paperback
Mass merchandise products.
Penguin Random House & its publishing entities are not accepting unsol submissions, proposals,

mss, or submission queries via e-mail at this time.

Imprints: Ace (pbk); Ace/Putnam (hardcover); Avery; Current; DAW (hardcover & pbk); Dial Books for Young Readers (children's); Pamela Dorman Books; Dutton (hardcover); Dutton Children's Books (children's); Grosset & Dunlap (children's); Grosset/Putnam (hardcover); InterMix; Jove (pbk); Onyx (pbk); PaperStar (children's); Penguin (pbk); Penguin Classics (pbk); Penguin Life; The Penguin Press; Penguin Workshop; Philomel Books (children's); Plume (pbk); Portfolio; Price Stern Sloan (children's, hardcover & pbk); Puffin (children's); Putnam (hardcover); Razorbill; Riverhead Books (hardcover & pbk); ROC (pbk); Sentinel; Signet (pbk); Signet Classics (pbk); Studio; Tarcher Perigee; Topaz (pbk); Viking (hardcover); Viking Children's Books (children's); Viking Compass (hardcover); Viking Life; Frederick Warne (children's); Wee Sing (children's)

Divisions: Berkley Publishing Group

Distributor for Arkangel; Bibli O'Phile; Consumer Guide/PIL; DAW Books Inc; Dream Works; Granta; HighBridge Audio; Kensington Publishing Corp; The Library of America; The Monacelli Press

Foreign Rights: Penguin (Australia, Canada, India, New Zealand, South Africa, UK); Penguin Putnam International Sales

Advertising Agency: Mesa Group; Spier NY

Membership(s): Association of American Publishers (AAP)

See separate listing for:

Avery
Berkley Publishing Group
Celebra
DAW Books Inc
DK Publishing
Dutton
Penguin Books
The Penguin Press
Penguin Workshop
Penguin Young Readers Group
Philomel
Plume
Portfolio
Puffin Books
GP Putnam's Sons (Hardcover)
Riverhead Books
TarcherPerigee
Viking
Viking Children's Books
Viking Studio

The Penguin Press

Imprint of Penguin Group USA, A Penguin Random House Company
375 Hudson St, New York, NY 10014
Web Site: thepenguinpress.com
Key Personnel
Pres & Ed-in-Chief: Ann Godoff
VP & Publr: Scott Moyers
VP & Exec Dir, Copyediting: Tory Klose
VP, Art Dir: Darren Haggar
Assoc Publr & Dir, Mktg: Matt Boyd
Publicity Dir: Sarah Hutson
Assoc Mktg Dir: Danielle Plafsky
Assoc Publicity Dir: Juliana Kiyan
Asst Publicity Dir: Gail Brussel
Exec Mng Ed, Penguin Group USA: Tricia Conley
Exec Ed: Ed Park; Virginia Smith Younce
Sr Ed: William Heyward; Christopher Richards
Ed: Emily Cunningham; Lindsay Whalen
Assoc Ed: Casey Denis
Mktg Mgr: Lauren Lauzon
Publicity Mgr: Colleen Boyle
Mktg Coord: Shina Patel
Founded: 2003
Publishers of literary fiction & select nonfiction.

Penguin Random House & its publishing entities are not accepting unsol submissions, proposals, mss, or submission queries via e-mail at this time.
Number of titles published annually: 38 Print
Total Titles: 127 Print

Penguin Random House Audio Publishing

Subsidiary of Penguin Random House LLC
1745 Broadway, New York, NY 10019
E-mail: audio@penguinrandomhouse.com
Web Site: www.penguinrandomhouseaudio.com
Key Personnel
Pres & Publr: Amanda D'Acierno
SVP, Content Prodn: Dan Zitt
SVP, Mktg & Publicity: Donna Passannante
SVP, Opers: Sue Daulton
VP, Audio Fin & Strategy: Len Wiggins
VP, Content & Busn Devt: Lance Fitzgerald
VP, Mktg: Heather Dalton
VP, Publicity: Katie Punia
Dir, Acqs & Edit Opers: Catherine Bucaria
Dir, Audio Prodn: Karen Dzienkonski
Dir, Post-Prodn & Technol: Ok Hee Kolwitz
Assoc Dir, Creative Mktg: Jennifer Rubins
Assoc Dir, Digital Prods: Dennis Tyrrell
Assoc Dir, Mktg Strategy: Victoria Tomao
Assoc Dir, Strategic Mktg: Taraneh Djangi
Exec Prodr: Sarah Jaffe; Linda Korn
Prodr: Nick Martorelli
Mng Ed: Kelly Atkinson
Ed: Jennifer Donovan
Sr Mgr, Creative Partnership Devt: Kelly Gildea
Sr Mgr, Digital Prodn Platforms: Julie Wilson
Sr Mgr, Mktg Strategy: Robert Guzman
Sr Publicity Mgr: Nicole Morano
Sr Soc Media Mgr: Juliette Koronkiewicz
Assoc Mgr, Post-Prodn: Simon Katz
Asst Mgr, Rts & Perms: Tara Hart
Assoc Publicist: Heather Job
Proj Mgmt Coord: Ruby Liu
Penguin Random House & its publishing entities are not accepting unsol submissions, proposals, mss, or submission queries via e-mail at this time.
Number of titles published annually: 500 Print; 300 Audio
Total Titles: 2,000 Print; 894 Audio
Imprints: Books on Tape™ (includes Listening Library®)
See separate listing for:
Books on Tape™
Random House Reference/Random House Puzzles & Games

Penguin Random House Large Print

Imprint of Penguin Random House LLC
1745 Broadway, New York, NY 10019
Tel: 212-782-9000
Web Site: www.penguinrandomhouse.com
Founded: 1990
Acquires & publishes general interest fiction & nonfiction in large print editions.
Penguin Random House & its publishing entities are not accepting unsol submissions, proposals, mss, or submission queries via e-mail at this time.
Number of titles published annually: 40 Print
Total Titles: 300 Print

§Penguin Random House LLC

1745 Broadway, New York, NY 10019
SAN: 202-5507
Tel: 212-782-9000 *Toll Free Tel:* 800-726-0600
Web Site: www.penguinrandomhouse.com
Key Personnel
Chmn: Philip Hoffman
CEO: Madeline McIntosh
CFO: James Johnston
Pres & Publr, Knopf Doubleday Publishing Group: Maya Mavjee

Pres & Publr, Random House Children's Books: Barbara Marcus
Pres & Publr, Random House Publishing Group: Gina Centrello
Pres & Dir, Strategic Devt: Nina von Moltke
Pres, US Sales: Jaci Updike
EVP & Deputy Publr: David Drake
EVP & Chief Legal Offr: Anke Steinecke
EVP & Dir, Corp Communs: Claire von Schilling
EVP & Dir, Mktg Strategy & Consumer Engagement: Sanyu Dillon
EVP & Publr, Ballantine Bantam Dell: Kara Welsh
EVP & Publr, Digital Content: Scott Shannon
EVP & Publr, Knopf, Pantheon & Schocken: Reagan Arthur
EVP, Supply Chain: Annette Danek
SVP & Deputy Gen Coun: Matthew Martin
SVP, Digital Strategy: Matt Schwartz
SVP, Lib Sales & Digital Strategy/SVP & Dir, Sales Opers: Skip Dye
SVP, Mass Mdse & Dist Sales: Tom Cox
SVP, Online & Digital Sales: Jeff Weber
SVP, Publg Devt & Author Platforms: Alison Rich
SVP, Retail Sales: Kim Shannon
SVP, Sales Devt: Randi Rosenkranz
SVP, Sales Strategic Planning: Julie Black
SVP, Strategic Busn Planning, US Digital Prod Devt, Audio & Fodor's: Susan Livingston
SVP, Strategic Opers & Projs: Alyssa Awe
VP & Publr, Knopf Books for Young Readers: Melanie Nolan
VP & Dir, Consumer Engagement: Suzie Sisoler
VP & Dir, Digital Video: John Clinton
VP & Dir, Mktg Strategy & Campaigns & Analytics: Erica Curtis
VP & Dir, Strategy & Devt, Spec Mkts: Sarah Williams
VP & Imprint Sales Dir, Crown Trade, Crown Forum, Currency, WaterBrook, Multnomah, Image & Convergent: Todd Berman
VP & Group Sales Dir, Knopf Doubleday: Christopher Dufault
VP, Edit Dir (Digital) & Assoc Publr (Romance): Gina Wachtel
VP, Backlist Sales: Candice Chaplin
VP, Educ Dist Sales: Cletus Durkin
VP, Educ Sales & Mktg: Michael Gentile
VP, Global Mergers & Acqs: Manuel Sangrise
VP, Lib Mktg, Adult Lib Group: Jennifer Childs
VP, PRH Labs: Brendan Cahill
VP, Strategy & Corp Devt: Divya Sawhney
Sr Dir, Cust Opers: Jessica Wells
Dir, Global Strategy & Corp Devt: Iria Alvarez
Dir, Licensing & Busn Devt: Rachael Perriello
Publg Dir, Vintage Espanol: Cristobal Pera
Edit Dir, Picture Books, Knopf Books for Young Readers: Rotem Moscovich
Sales Dir, Higher Educ: Kimberly Woods
Sales Dir, K-12 School Educ: Travis Temple
Assoc Dir, Consumer Shows & Conferences: Lindsey Elias
Assoc, Global Strategy & Corp Devt: Lea Stoeger
Sr Mgr, Publg Devt & Author Platforms: Stephanie Bowen
Sr Mktg Mgr, Convergent Books: Jessalyn Foggy
Publg Mgr, Vintage Espanol: Ingrid Paredes
Mng Ed, Knopf Books for Young Readers: Jake Eldred
Assoc Mng Ed, The Princeton Review: Amanda Yee
Assoc Mng Ed, Random House Children's Books: Megan Williams
Sr Ed, Del Rey: Sarah Peed
Ed, Del Rey: Tom Hoeler
Assoc Ed, Del Rey: Alex Larned
Asst Ed, Knopf Books for Young Readers: Karen Greenberg
Penguin Random House & its publishing entities are not accepting unsol submissions, proposals, mss, or submission queries via e-mail at this time.

Imprints: Alibi (mystery, thriller, suspense); Amphoto Books; Anchor Books; Shaye Areheart Books; Ballantine Books; Ballantine Wellspring; Bantam Books; Books on Tape™; Broadway Books; Clarkson Potter; Convergent Books; Crescent Books; Crimeline; Currency; Del Rey; Delacorte Books for Young Readers; Delacorte Press; Dell; Dell Laurel Leaf; Dell Yearling; Delta; Derrydale; The Dial Press; Disney Books for Young Readers; Domain; Doubleday; Doubleday Books for Young Readers; Doubleday/Galilee; Doubleday/Image; Doubleday Religious Publishing; Dragonfly Books; DTP; Tim Duggan Books; Ember; Everyman's Library; Fanfare; Fawcett; David Fickling Books; Flirt (new adult); Golden Books; Gramercy Books; Harmony Books; Hogarth; House of Collectibles; Hydra (science fiction & fantasy); Image Catholic Books; Island; Ivy Books; Alfred A Knopf; Knopf Books for Young Readers; Knopf Guides; Wendy Lamb Books; Laurel Leaf Books; Listening Library®; Living Language; Loveswept (digital only romance); Lucas Books; Main Street Books; Modern Library; The New Jerusalem Bible; Now I'm Reading!™; One World; Pantheon Books; Penguin Random House Audio; Potter Craft; Potter Style; The Princeton Review; Quickie Books; Random House; Random House Books for Young Readers; Random House Children's Publishing; Random House Digital; Random House Large Print Publishing; Random House Puzzles & Games; Random House Reference & Information Publishing; Razorbill; Rodale Books; Schocken Books; Schwartz & Wade Books; SJP; Skylark; Spectra; Sylvan Learning; Nan A Talese; Ten Speed Press; Three Rivers Press; Villard Books; Vintage Books; Vintage Children's Classics; Vintage Espanol; WaterBrook Multnomah; Watson-Guptill; Wings Books; Yearling Books; Zinc Ink
Branch Office(s)
Ten Speed Press/Crown Publishing Group, 6001 Shellmound St, Suite 600, Emeryville, CA 94608 *Tel:* 510-285-3000
Books on Tape Studios, 20970-B Warner Center Lane, Woodland Hills, CA 91367 *Tel:* 818-676-0969
WaterBrook Multnomah, 10807 New Allegiance Dr, Suite 500, Colorado Springs, CO 80921 *Tel:* 719-590-4999
Penguin Random House Grupo Editorial, 8950 SW 74 Ct, Suite 2010, Miami, FL 33156 *Tel:* 786-509-8730
Appetite by Random House, 55 Water St, Suite 512, Vancouver, BC V6B 1A1, Canada *Tel:* 604-566-9806
Penguin Random House Canada, 320 Front St W, Suite 1400, Toronto, ON M5V 2B6, Canada, CEO: Kristin Cochrane *Tel:* 416-364-4449 *Toll Free Tel:* 888-523-9292 (orders) *Fax:* 416-598-7764 *Web Site:* penguinrandomhouse.ca
Foreign Office(s): Penguin Random House Grupo Editorial, Humberto Primo 555, C1103ACK Buenos Aires, Argentina *Tel:* (011) 5235-4400
Penguin Random House Australia, 100 Pacific Hwy, Level 3, North Sydney, NSW 2060, Australia, CEO: Julie Burland *Tel:* (02) 9954 9966
Penguin Random House Australia, 707 Collins St, Melbourne, Victoria 3008, Australia *Tel:* (03) 9811 2400
United Book Distributors, 30 Centre Rd, Scoresby, Victoria 3179, Australia *Tel:* (03) 8537 4599
Penguin Random House Grupo Editorial/Editorial Sudamericana Chilena SA, Merced 280, Piso 6, Santiago, Chile *Tel:* (02) 27828200
Penguin Random House China, B-7 Jiaming Ctr, 27 E Third Ring Rd N, Chaoyang District, Beijing 100020, China *Tel:* (010) 8587 7777
Penguin Random House China, Suite 2001-02, 20/F Central Plaza, No 227 Huangpi Rd N, Shanghai 200003, China *Tel:* (010) 8587 7711

Penguin Random House Grupo Editorial, Carrera 5A, No 34A-09, Bogota, Cundinamarca, Colombia *Tel:* (01) 743-0700
DK Verlag GmbH, Arnulfstr 124, Munich 80636, Germany *Tel:* (089) 44 23 26 0
Penguin Random House India, Penguin Offices, 7th fl, Infinity Tower C, DLF Cyber City, Gurgaon, Haryana 122 002, India *Tel:* (0124) 478-5600
DK, DKMindmill Corporate Tower, 3rd fl, Plot No 24A, Sector 16A, Film City, Noida, UP 201 301, India *Tel:* (0120) 468-9600
Penguin Random House Malaysia, Level 1, Tower 2A, Ave 5 Bangsar S, No 8 Jl Kerinchi, 59200 Kuala Lumpur, Malaysia *Tel:* (03) 2247-3800
Penguin Random House Grupo Editorial, Miguel de Cervantes Saavedra, 301, piso 1, Colonia Granada, Delegacion Miguel Hidalgo, 11520 Mexico, CDMX, Mexico *Tel:* (0155) 30678400
Penguin Random House New Zealand, 67 Apollo Dr, Rosedale, Auckland 0632, New Zealand, CEO: Julie Burland *Tel:* (09) 442-7400
Penguin Random House Grupo Editorial, Av Ricardo Palma 341, Oficina 504 Miraflores, Lima, Peru *Tel:* (01) 206 3260
Penguin Random House Singapore, 9 N Buona Vista Dr, No 13-01, The Metropolis Tower One, Singapore 138588, Singapore *Tel:* 6715 8989
Penguin Random House South Africa, The Estuaries No 4, Oxbow Crescent, Century Way, Century City, Cape Town 7441, South Africa, CEO: Steve Connolly *Tel:* (021) 460-5400
Penguin Random House South Africa, Rose Bank Office Park, Block D, 181 Jan Smuts Ave, Parktown N, Johannesburg 2193, South Africa *Tel:* (011) 327-3550
Penguin Random House Korea, 373 Gangnamdaero, 15F, Seocho-gu, Seoul 06621, South Korea
Penguin Random House Grupo Editorial, Travessera de Gracia 47-49, 08021 Barcelona, Spain *Tel:* 93 366 03 00
Penguin Random House Grupo Editorial, Luchana, 23 1a Planta, 28010 Madrid, Spain *Tel:* 91 535 81 90
The Book Service Distribution Center, Colchester Rd, Frating Green, Colchester, Essex C07 7DW, United Kingdom *Tel:* (01206) 256000
Grantham Book Services, Trent Rd, Grantham, Lincs NG31 7XQ, United Kingdom *Tel:* (01476) 541000 *Fax:* (01476) 541060
Random House Children's, 61-63 Uxbridge Rd, Ealing, London W5 5SA, United Kingdom *Tel:* (020) 8231 6800
Random House UK Ltd, 20 Vauxhall Bridge Rd, London SW1V 2SA, United Kingdom, CEO: Tom Weldon *Tel:* (020) 7840 8400 *Fax:* (020) 7233 8791
Transworld Publishers, 61-63 Uxbridge Rd, Ealing, London W5 5SA, United Kingdom *Tel:* (020) 8579 2652
Penguin Random House Grupo Editorial/Editorial Sudamericana Uruguaya SA, Colonia 950 Piso 6, 11100 Montevideo, Uruguay *Tel:* 29013668
Distribution Center: Crawfordsville Distribution Center, 1021 N State Rd 47, Crawfordsville, IN 47933, SVP: Lori de Reza *Tel:* 765-362-5125
Westminster Distribution Center, 400 Bennett Cerf Dr, Westminster, MD 21157 *Tel:* 410-848-1900
Reno Distribution Center, 1160 Trademark Dr, Suite 111, Reno, NV 89521, SVP: Lori de Reza
Mississauga Distribution Centre, 6971 Columbus Rd, Mississauga, ON L5T 1K1, Canada *Tel:* 416-364-4449
Rugby Distribution Center, Warwicks CV23 0WB, United Kingdom *Tel:* (01788) 514300
Membership(s): Association of American Publishers (AAP); Book Industry Study Group (BISG)
See separate listing for:
Betterway Books
House of Collectibles

Krause Publications Inc
Living Language
Penguin Random House Audio Publishing
Penguin Random House Large Print
Random House Children's Books
Random House Publishing Group
Razorbill
Writer's Digest Books

Penguin Workshop
Imprint of Penguin Group USA, A Penguin Random House Company
1745 Broadway, New York, NY 10019
Tel: 212-366-2000
Web Site: www.penguin.com/publishers/penguinworkshop/
Key Personnel
Pres & Publr: Francesco Sedita
VP & Assoc Publr: Daniel Moreton
Edit Dir: Rob Valois
Dir of Preschool Publg: Cecily Kaiser
Founded: 2017
Penguin Random House & its publishing entities are not accepting unsol submissions, proposals, mss, or submission queries via e-mail at this time.
Number of titles published annually: 170 Print

Penguin Young Readers Group
Division of Penguin Group USA, A Penguin Random House Company
345 Hudson St, New York, NY 10014
Tel: 212-366-2000; 212-414-3553 *Fax:* 212-414-3340
Web Site: www.penguin.com/children
Key Personnel
Pres: Jen Loja
Pres & Publr, Nancy Paulsen Books: Nancy Rose Paulsen
Pres & Publr, Putnam Books for Young Readers & Razorbill: Jennifer Klonsky
Publr, Penguin Workshop & World of Eric Carle: Francesco Sedita
EVP & Assoc Publr: Jocelyn Schmidt
SVP & Dir, Sales: Felicia Frazier
SVP, Busn Opers & Strategy: Robyn Bender
VP & Publr, Kathy Dawson Books: Kathy Dawson
VP & Assoc Publr: Jennifer Haller
VP & Exec Dir, Prodn: Nadine Britt
VP & Exec Dir, Publicity & Corp Communs: Shanta Newlin
VP & Exec Dir, School & Lib Mktg/Creative Mktg Dir: Carmela Iaria
VP & Dir, Contracts & Busn Aff: George Schumacher
VP & Dir, Subs Rts: Helen Boomer
VP & Dir, Trade Sales: Debra Polansky
VP, Busn Devt: Stephanie Sabol
VP, Digital Content Devt: Adam Royce
VP, Educ Sales & Mktg: Michael Gentile
VP, Mktg: Emily Romero
Exec Dir, Publicity: Elyse Marshall
Sr Dir, Publicity: Olivia Russo
Creative Dir: Mary Mekarnom
Dir, Natl Accts: Cristi Navarro
Dir, Preschool & Young Readers Mktg: Jed Bennett
Dir, Preschool Publg, Penguin Workshop: Cecily Kaiser
Exec Ed, Kokila: Zareen Jaffery
Mgr, Trade Mktg: Brianna Lockhart
Digital Mktg Coord: James Akinaka
Mktg Coord: Lyana Salcedo
Sr Publicist: Tessa Meischeid
Founded: 1997
Children's hardcover picture books; fiction & nonfiction; trade paperbacks; picture book paperbacks; board & novelty books; calendars.
Penguin Random House & its publishing entities are not accepting unsol submissions, proposals, mss, or submission queries via e-mail at this time.

Imprints: Kathy Dawson Books; Dial Books for Young Readers; Dutton Children's Books; Firebird; Grosset & Dunlap; Kokila Books; Nancy Paulsen Books; Penguin Workshop; Philomel; Price Stern Sloan; PSS; Puffin Books; GP Putnam's Sons; Razorbill; Speak; Viking Children's Books; Frederick Warne; World of Eric Carle

Distribution Center: Penguin Group Distribution Center, One Grosset Dr, Kirkwood, NY 13795 *Tel:* 607-775-1740

See separate listing for:
Dial Books for Young Readers
Dutton Children's Books
GP Putnam's Sons (Children's)

Penn State University Press
University Support Bldg 1, Suite C, 820 N University Dr, University Park, PA 16802-1003
SAN: 213-5760
Tel: 814-865-1327 *Toll Free Tel:* 800-326-9180 *Fax:* 814-863-1408 *Toll Free Fax:* 877-778-2665
E-mail: orders@psupress.org; orders@eisenbrauns.org
Web Site: www.psupress.org; www.eisenbrauns.org
Key Personnel
Dir: Patrick Alexander *Tel:* 814-867-2209
  E-mail: pha3@psu.edu
Sales & Mktg Dir: Brendan Coyne *Tel:* 814-863-5994 *E-mail:* bbc5228@psu.edu
Assoc Press Dir, Design & Prodn Mgr: Jennifer Norton *Tel:* 814-863-8061 *E-mail:* jsn4@psu.edu
Ed-in-Chief: Kendra Boileau *Tel:* 814-863-0524
  E-mail: klb60@psu.edu
Exec Ed: Eleanor Goodman *E-mail:* ehg11@psu.edu
Mng Ed: Laura Reed-Morrisson *Tel:* 814-865-1606 *E-mail:* lxr168@psu.edu
Acquiring Ed, Eisenbrauns: Jennifer Singletary
IT Mgr: Ed Spicer *E-mail:* res122@psu.edu
Journals Mgr: Diana Pesek *Tel:* 814-867-2223
  E-mail: dlp28@psu.edu
Sr Designer: Regina Starace *E-mail:* ras35@psu.edu
Founded: 1956
Scholarly books & journals; art & architectural history; literature & literary criticism, philosophy, religion, archaeology, biblical studies, languages of the ancient Near East, social sciences, law, history, Latin American studies, regional books on Mid-Atlantic area. Special Series: Literature & Philosophy; Penn State Series in the History of the Book; Re-Reading the Canon; Keystone Books (regional); American & European Philosophy; Magic in History; Rural Studies; Refiguring Modernism; Buildings, Landscapes & Societies.
ISBN Prefix(es): 978-0-271; 978-1-575; 978-1-883 (formerly CDL); 978-0-962 (formerly CDL); 978-0-966 (formerly CDL); 978-0-873 (formerly CDL)
Number of titles published annually: 100 Print; 45 E-Book
Total Titles: 2,200 Print; 55 Online; 400 E-Book; 2 Audio
Imprints: Eisenbrauns (specialize in ancient Near East); Keystone Books (regional titles); Metalmark (reprints of public domain books on Pennsylvania)
Distributor for Abo Akademi University (specialize in ancient Near East); American Oriental Society; Deo Publishing; National Gallery of Singapore; Neo-Assyrian Text Corpus (FFAR, Helsinki, Finland)
Foreign Rep(s): Footprint Books Pty Ltd (Australia, Fiji, New Zealand, Papua New Guinea); Lexa Publishers (Mical Moser) (Canada); Oxford Publicity Group (Continental Europe, Ireland, UK); Ian Taylor Associates Ltd (China); US PubRep (Craig Falk) (Caribbean, Central

Africa, Mexico); Kelvin van Hasselt (Africa); The White Partnership (Hong Kong, India, Indonesia, Pakistan, Philippines, Singapore, South Korea, Taiwan, Thailand)
Orders to: Parson Weems' Publisher Services LLC, 310 N Front St, Suite 4-10, Wilmington, NC 28401, Mgr: Causten Stehle *Tel:* 914-948-4259 *Toll Free Fax:* 866-651-0337 *E-mail:* office@parsonweems.com *Web Site:* www.parsonweems.com
Membership(s): American Academy of Religion (AAR); American Council of Learned Societies (ACLS); Art Libraries Society (ARLIS); Association of American Publishers (AAP); Association of University Presses (AUPresses); Book Industry Study Group (BISG); Modern Language Association (MLA); Organization of American Historians (OAH); Society for Scholarly Publishing (SSP); Society of Bible Literature (SBL)
See separate listing for:
Eisenbrauns

Pennsylvania Historical & Museum Commission
Subsidiary of The Commonwealth of Pennsylvania
State Museum Bldg, 300 North St, Harrisburg, PA 17120-0053
SAN: 282-1532
Tel: 717-787-3362; 717-787-5526 (orders)
E-mail: ra-shoppaheritage@pa.gov
Web Site: www.phmc.pa.gov; www.shoppaheritage.com
Key Personnel
Exec Dir: Andrea Bakewell Lowery
  E-mail: alowery@pa.gov
Founded: 1945
Books, booklets & references on Pennsylvania prehistory, history, culture & natural history, both scholarly & popular.
ISBN Prefix(es): 978-0-911124; 978-0-89271
Number of titles published annually: 5 Print
Total Titles: 145 Print

§Pennsylvania State Data Center
Subsidiary of Institute of State & Regional Affairs
Penn State Harrisburg, 777 W Harrisburg Pike, Middletown, PA 17057-4898
Tel: 717-948-6336 *Fax:* 717-948-6754
E-mail: pasdc@psu.edu
Web Site: pasdc.hbg.psu.edu
Key Personnel
Dir: Susan Copella *Tel:* 717-948-6427
  E-mail: sdc3@psu.edu
Founded: 1981
Policy, demographical analytical reports, hard copy & computer discs.
ISBN Prefix(es): 978-0-939667; 978-1-58036
Number of titles published annually: 5 Print; 5 CD-ROM
Total Titles: 130 Print; 130 CD-ROM; 1 E-Book

Pennsylvania State University Press, see Penn State University Press

PennWell Books
Division of PennWell Corp
1421 S Sheridan Rd, Tulsa, OK 74112
Mailing Address: PO Box 21288, Tulsa, OK 74121-1288
Tel: 918-831-9421 *Toll Free Tel:* 800-752-9764 *Fax:* 918-831-9555
E-mail: sales@pennwell.com
Web Site: www.pennwellbooks.com
Key Personnel
CEO: Mark Wilmoth
EVP: Jayne Gilsinger
Sr Acqs Mgr & Video Prodr: Mark Haugh
  E-mail: mhaugh@pennwell.com

Sales & Mktg Coord: Holly Fournier
  E-mail: hollyf@pennwell.com
Acqs Ed, Petroleum & Power Books: Steve Hill
  E-mail: steveh@pennwell.com
Founded: 1973
Publish both technical & nontechnical books for petroleum, power & fire services industries. Written by selected industry experts, our books will help you broaden your expertise in your current field, understand other related disciplines & provide quick-glance references as a topic arrives in your daily routine. Our products make excellent classroom, seminar & in-house training texts.
ISBN Prefix(es): 978-0-912212; 978-0-87814; 978-1-59370; 978-0-9795633
Number of titles published annually: 8 Print
Total Titles: 400 Print; 5 Audio
Divisions: Fire Engineering Books & Videos; PennWell Petroleum Books; PennWell Power Books
Foreign Rep(s): Cranbury International LLC (Ethan Atkin) (Caribbean, Central America, South America); Disvan Enterprises (Ish Dawar) (India); Eurospan (Africa, Asia, Australasia, Europe, Middle East); Tahir M Lodhi (Pakistan); Tony Poh (Southeast Asia)
See separate listing for:
Fire Engineering Books & Videos

Penny-Farthing Productions
Imprint of Penny-Farthing Productions Inc
One Sugar Creek Center Blvd, Suite 820, Sugar Land, TX 77478
Tel: 713-780-0300 *Toll Free Tel:* 800-926-2669 *Fax:* 713-780-4004
E-mail: corp@pfproductions.com
Web Site: www.pfproductions.com
Key Personnel
Mktg Coord: Julia Ahadi *E-mail:* julia@pfproductions.com
Proj Dir: Courtney Huddleston
  E-mail: courtney@pfproductions.com
Graphic Designer: Andre McBride
  E-mail: design@pfproductions.com
Corp Off Mgr: Pam Johnston
Founded: 1998
Penny-Farthing Productions Inc officially opened its doors in 1998 as Penny-Farthing Press Inc with a small staff & a plan to create comic books & children's books exemplifying quality storytelling, artwork, & printing. Starting with *The Victorian*, PFP expanded its line to 10 titles, keeping output small enough to maintain the highest quality. PFP has won numerous awards including the Gutenberg D'Argent Medal & several Spectrum Awards & was also featured in the Dec 24, 2001 issue of Publisher's Weekly. PFP & President Ken White strive to work with talented & energetic individuals in order to put exquisite pieces of art into the hands of readers everywhere.
ISBN Prefix(es): 978-0-9673683; 978-0-9719012; 978-0-9842143; 978-0-9991709
Number of titles published annually: 4 Print
Total Titles: 24 Print; 3 Online; 3 E-Book
Distribution Center: Amazon
Bookazine
Brodart
Children's Plus Inc
Follett School Solutions
Membership(s): American Booksellers Association (ABA); Independent Book Publishers Association (IBPA); Publishers Association of the West (PubWest)

§Pentecostal Publishing House
Subsidiary of United Pentecostal Church International
36 Research Park Ct, Weldon Spring, MO 63304
SAN: 219-3817
Tel: 314-837-7300 *Toll Free Tel:* 866-819-7667 *Fax:* 314-837-6574 (orders)

Web Site: www.pentecostalpublishing.com; wordaflamepress.com

Key Personnel
Ed-in-Chief & Publr: Mr Robin Johnston
 E-mail: rjohnston@upci.org
Assoc Ed: Lee Ann Alexander
 E-mail: lalexander@upci.org
Founded: 1945
Trade paperbacks, periodicals, bibliographies; religion (Protestant), Bibles, foreign languages, crafts, self-help.
ISBN Prefix(es): 978-0-912315; 978-0-932581; 978-1-56722; 978-0-7577
Number of titles published annually: 10 Print; 10 CD-ROM; 10 E-Book
Total Titles: 400 Print; 35 CD-ROM; 200 E-Book; 1 Audio
Imprints: WAP Academic; WAP Children; Word Aflame Press
Distributed by Christian Network International; Innovative Marketing
Distribution Center: Anchor Distributors, 1030 Hunt Valley Circle, New Kensington, PA 15068 *Toll Free Tel:* 800-444-4484 *Toll Free Fax:* 800-765-1960 *E-mail:* anchor. customerservice@anchordistributors.com
Spring Arbor Distributors Inc, One Ingram Blvd, La Vergne, TN 37086 *Toll Free Tel:* 800-395-4340 *Toll Free Fax:* 800-876-0186 *E-mail:* customerservice@ingramcontent.com

Peradam Press
Subsidiary of The Center for Cultural & Naturalist Studies
PO Box 6, North San Juan, CA 95960-0006
Tel: 530-277-9324 *Fax:* 530-559-0754
E-mail: peradam@earthlink.net
Key Personnel
Pres & Sr Ed: Linda Birkholz
Exec Ed: Corinne Boyle
Ed: Patricia Hicks
Founded: 1993
General trade books hardcover & paperbacks.
ISBN Prefix(es): 978-1-885420
Number of titles published annually: 10 Print
Total Titles: 81 Print
Shipping Address: 19074 Oak Tree Rd, Nevada City, CA 95959

Perfection Learning
1000 N Second Ave, Logan, IA 51546
Mailing Address: PO Box 500, Logan, IA 51546-0500
Tel: 712-644-2831 *Toll Free Tel:* 800-831-4190 *Toll Free Fax:* 800-543-2745
E-mail: orders@perfectionlearning.com
Web Site: perfectionlearning.com
Key Personnel
Design Dir: Randy Messer *E-mail:* rmesser@ perfectionlearning.com
Edit Dir, Elem: Sue Thies *E-mail:* sthies@ perfectionlearning.com
Mktg Opers Dir: Mark Hagenberg
 E-mail: mhagenberg@perfectionlearning.com
Founded: 1926
Elementary & secondary product line covers such content areas as reading, literature, language arts, math, test preparation, social studies, world languages, science & more.
ISBN Prefix(es): 978-0-89598; 978-0-7807; 978-0-7891; 978-0-8124; 978-1-56312; 978-0-7569; 978-1-60686; 978-1-63419; 978-1-62974; 978-1-62766; 978-1-61563; 978-1-61383; 978-1-61384; 978-1-62299; 978-1-62359; 978-1-62765; 978-1-68064; 978-1-68065; 978-1-68240
Number of titles published annually: 30 Print
Total Titles: 500 Print
Imprints: Cover Craft; Cover-to-Cover; Literature & Thought; Passages; Retold Classics; Summit Books; Tale Blazers
Divisions: Turtleback Books

Distributor for Abrams; Ace Books; Airmont; Annick Press; Archway; Atheneum; Baker Books; Ballantine; Bantam; Barrons; Berkley; Blake Books; Candlewick Press; Charlesbridge Press; Chelsea House; Children's Press; Chronicle Books; Crabtree Publishing Co; Crown; Disney Press; Distri Books; DK; Doubleday; Dutton; F+W Media Inc; Farrar, Straus & Giroux Inc; Fawcett; Firefly; First Avenue; Free Spirit; Fulcrum; Golden Books; Greenhaven Press Inc; Hammond; Hayes; Gareth Stevens; Frederick Warne
Foreign Rep(s): School Book Fairs Ltd (Ron Grant) (Canada)

The Permanent Press
4170 Noyac Rd, Sag Harbor, NY 11963
Tel: 631-725-1101
Web Site: www.thepermanentpress.com
Key Personnel
Co-Publr: Judith Shepard *E-mail:* judith@ thepermanentpress.com; Martin Shepard
 E-mail: shepard@thepermanentpress.com
Mng Ed: Nick Collins *E-mail:* nick@ thepermanentpress.com
ISBN Prefix(es): 978-1-877946; 978-0-932966; 978-1-57962
Number of titles published annually: 16 Print
Total Titles: 600 Print
Imprints: Second Chance Press
Foreign Rights: AnatoliaLit Agency (Amy Marie Spangler) (Turkey); The English Agency (Atsushi Hori) (Japan); Lora Fountain Agency (Lora Fountain) (France); Jill Hughes (Eastern Europe); Jane Judd Literary Agency (Jane Judd) (UK); Andrew Nurnberg Associates International Ltd (Jackie Huang) (China); Andrew Nurnberg Associates International Ltd (Whitney Hsu) (Taiwan); Thomas Schlueck Agency GmbH (Franka Zastrow) (Germany); R Vivian Literary Agency (Rita Vivian) (Italy); Eric Yang Agency (Sue Yang) (Korea); Zarana Agencia Literaria Republica Argentina (Marta Sevilla) (Brazil, Portugal, Spain)
See separate listing for:
Second Chance Press

Persea Books
90 Broad St, Suite 2100, New York, NY 10004
SAN: 212-8233
Tel: 212-260-9256
E-mail: info@perseabooks.com; poetry@ perseabooks.com; publicity@perseabooks.com
Web Site: www.perseabooks.com
Key Personnel
Pres & Publr: Michael Braziller
VP & Edit Dir: Karen Braziller
Poetry Ed: Gabriel Fried
Publicity: Jonah Fried
Founded: 1975
ISBN Prefix(es): 978-0-89255
Number of titles published annually: 12 Print; 10 E-Book
Total Titles: 500 Print; 40 E-Book
Imprints: A Karen & Michael Braziller Book
Distributed by W W Norton & Company Inc (worldwide exc Canada); Penguin Random House Canada (CN only)
Orders to: W W Norton & Company Inc, 500 Fifth Ave, New York, NY 10110 *Toll Free Tel:* 800-233-4830
Distribution Center: W W Norton & Company Inc c/o National Book Co, Keystone Industrial Park, Scranton, PA 18512 *Toll Free Fax:* 800-233-4830

§Perseus Books
Division of Hachette Book Group
1290 Avenue of the Americas, New York, NY 10104
Tel: 212-340-8100 *Toll Free Tel:* 800-343-4499 (cust serv) *Fax:* 212-340-8105

Web Site: www.perseusbooks.com
Key Personnel
SVP, Publr: Susan Weinberg
VP, Publr, Avalon Travel: Bill Newlin
VP, Publr, Basic Books: Lara Heimert
VP, Publr, Hachette Books: Mary Ann Naples
VP, Publr, PublicAffairs: Clive Priddle
VP, Publr, Running Press: Kristin Kiser
VP, Assoc Publr, Avalon Travel: Jaimee Callaway
VP, Assoc Publr, Basic Books: TJ Kelleher
VP, Assoc Publr, Hachette Books: Michelle Aielli
VP, Assoc Publr & Publicity Dir, PublicAffairs: Jaime Leifer
VP, Assoc Publr, Running Press (Adult): Jessica Schmidt
VP, Acqs, Avalon Travel: Grace Fujimoto
VP, Edit Dir, Avalon Travel: Kevin McLain
VP, Prodn, Avalon Travel: Jane Musser
Publg Dir, Black Dog & Leventhal: Becky Koh
Gen Asst to the SVP, Perseus Books, Admin Support, PublicAffairs: Iris Torres
Asst to the Publr, Running Press: Tina Camma
Edit Dir, Hachette Books/Da Capo Lifelong: Renee Sedliar
Edit Dir, Running Press: Jennifer Kasius
Edit Dir, Running Press Kids: Julie Matysik
Edit Dir, History & Social Sciences, Basic Books: Brian Distelberg
Exec Ed, Da Capo Press: Bob Pigeon
Exec Ed, Hachette Books: Krishan Trotman
Exec Ed, Hachette Books (focusing on commercial nonfiction): Brant Rumble
Exec Ed, Hachette Books/Da Capo Press: Ben Schafer
Exec Ed, PublicAffairs: Benjamin Adams; Colleen Lawrie
Group Mng Ed, Basic Books & PublicAffairs: Melissa Raymond
Mng Ed, Da Capo Press: Fred Francis
Asst Mng Ed, PublicAffairs: Olivia Loperfido
Sr Ed, Basic Books & Seal Press: Claire Potter
Sr Ed, Black Dog & Leventhal: Lisa Tenaglia
Sr Ed, Da Capo Lifelong: Dan Ambrosio
Sr Ed, Moon: Sabrina Young; Kathryn Ettinger; Leah Gordon
Sr Ed, Rick Steves: Madhu Prasher
Sr Ed, Running Press: Kristen Wiewora; Jordana Tusman; Shannon Connors Fabricant
Ed, Basic Books: Connor Guy; Eric Henney
Ed, Rick Steves: Jamie Andrade
Assoc Ed, Avalon Travel: Kristi Mitsuda
Assoc Ed, Moon: Kimberly Ehart
Assoc Ed, Rick Steves: Sierra Machado
Asst Ed, Basic Books: Carrie Napolitano; Katie Lambright
Asst Ed, Da Capo Lifelong: Miriam Riad
Asst Ed, Hachette Books: David Lamb
Acqs Ed, Avalon Travel: Megan Anderluh
Acqs Assoc, Avalon: Kathryn Roque
Sr Dir, Mktg, Hachette Books: Michael Barrs; Odette Fleming
Mktg Dir, Black Dog & Leventhal/Dir, Ad & Sales Promo, Running Press & Black Dog & Leventhal: Betsy Hulsebosch
Mktg Dir, Basic Books: Nancy Sheppard; Jessica Breen
Mktg Dir, PublicAffairs: Lindsay Fradkoff
Sr Mktg Designer, Digital Brand Mgr, Running Press: Daniel Cantada
Sr Mktg Mgr, Basic Books: Allison Finkel
Mktg Mgr, Hachette Book/Da Capo Press: Quinn Fariel
Digital Mktg Mgr, Avalon Travel: Kimi Owens
Assoc Mgr, Digital Mktg & Soc Media, Running Press: Cassie Drumm
Asst Mktg Mgr, PublicAffairs: Miguel Cervantes
Sr Mktg Assoc, Avalon Travel: Clare Haugh
Assoc Mktg Ed, Avalon Travel: Hannah Brezack
Online Mktg Coord, Avalon Travel: Crystal Turnau
Sr Publicity & Mktg Mgr, Running Press Kids: Valerie Howlett
Publicity & Mktg Mgr, Running Press: Amy Cianfrone

Publicity & Mktg Assoc, Avalon Travel: Erika Lara

Publicity & Mktg Assoc, Hachette Books: Anna Hall

Publicity Dir, Basic Books: Liz Wetzel

Publicity Mgr, Black Dog & Leventhal: Kara Thornton

Publicity Mgr, Hachette Books: Michael Giarratano

Publicity Mgr, PublicAffairs: Josie Urwin

Publicity Mgr, Running Press: Seta Zink

Sr Publicist, Basic Books: Kait Howard; Kelsey Odorczyk

Sr Publicist, Hachette Books: Sarah Falter

Publicist, Basic Books: Jenny Lee

Publg Technologies Mgr, Avalon Travel: Darren Alessi

Creative Dir, Basic Books: Chin-Yee Lai

Creative Dir, Hachette Book/Black Dog & Leventhal: Amanda Kain

Creative Dir, Running Press: Frances Soo Ping Chow

Dir, Miniature Editions & Licensing, Running Press: Jennifer Leczkowski

Assoc Design Dir, Running Press: Joshua McDonnell

Art Dir, PublicAffairs: Peter Garceau

Sr Prodn Mgr & Mgr, Prod Devt, Running Press: Frank Sipala

Sr Prodn Designer, Avalon Travel: Rue Flaherty

Dim Designer/Sampler, Running Press: Mark Governa

Sr Designer, Basic Books: Ann Kirchner

Sr Designer, Running Press: Susan Van Horn; Amanda Richmond

Cartography Dir, Avalon Travel: Michael Morgenfeld

Sr Cartography Ed, Avalon Travel: Albert Angulo

Sr Cartographer, Avalon Travel: Katherine Bennett

Founded: 1997

ISBN Prefix(es): 978-0-465 (Basic Books); 978-1-884822 (Black Dog & Leventhal); 978-1-57912 (Black Dog & Leventhal); 978-0-306 (Da Capo Press); 978-1-56282 (Hachette Books); 978-0-7868 (Hachette Books); 978-0-316 (Black Dog & Leventhal); 978-1-4013 (Hachette Books); 978-1-60376 (Black Dog & Leventhal); 978-1-63191 (Black Dog & Leventhal); 978-1-161 (PublicAffairs); 978-0-762 (Running Press); 978-1-580 (Seal Press); 978-1-631 (Avalon Travel)

Number of titles published annually: 50 Print

Total Titles: 530 Print

Imprints: Avalon Travel (includes Moon & Rick Steves); Basic Books (includes Seal Press); Hachette Books (includes Da Capo Press, Da Capo Lifelong & Hachette Go); PublicAffairs (includes Bold Type Books); Running Press (includes Black Dog & Leventhal, RP Studio, Running Press Kids & Running Press Miniatures)

Orders to: 1094 Flex Dr, Jackson, TN 38301 Toll Free Tel: 800-343-4499 Toll Free Fax: 800-351-5073

Membership(s): Association of American Publishers (AAP); National Book Foundation

Peter Pauper Press, Inc

202 Mamaroneck Ave, Suite 400, White Plains, NY 10601-5376

SAN: 204-9449

Tel: 914-681-0144 Fax: 914-681-0389

E-mail: customerservice@peterpauper.com; orders@peterpauper.com; marketing@peterpauper.com

Web Site: www.peterpauper.com

Key Personnel

CEO: Laurence Beilenson E-mail: lbeilenson@peterpauper.com

VP: John Hartley E-mail: jhartley@peterpauper.com

Creative Dir: Heather Zschock
 E-mail: hzschock@peterpauper.com

Dir, Spec Sales: Esther Beilenson

Founded: 1928

Decorated hardcover gift, inspirational; quotations, miniatures, journals, photo albums, children's picture books, children's activity books, travel guides.

ISBN Prefix(es): 978-0-88088; 978-1-59359; 978-1-44130; 978-1-44131; 978-1-44132

Number of titles published annually: 150 Print; 5 E-Book

Total Titles: 1,300 Print; 270 E-Book

Foreign Rep(s): Alejandra Garza (Mexico); Saskia Knobbe (Netherlands); Bara Kristinsdottir (Iceland); Peter Pauper Press Pty (Australia); Peter Pauper Press UK (UK); Phambili (Southern Africa); Israel Ring (Brazil)

Returns: Conri Services Inc, 5 Skyline Dr, Hawthorne, NY 10532

Shipping Address: Conri Services Inc, 5 Skyline Dr, Hawthorne, NY 10532, Contact: Connie Levene Tel: 914-592-2300 Fax: 914-592-2174

Warehouse: Conri Services Inc, 5 Skyline Dr, Hawthorne, NY 10532, Contact: Connie Levene Tel: 914-592-2300 Fax: 914-592-2174

§Peterson Institute for International Economics (PIIE)

1750 Massachusetts Ave NW, Washington, DC 20036-1903

SAN: 293-2865

Tel: 202-328-9000 Fax: 202-328-5432

E-mail: media@piie.com

Web Site: piie.com

Key Personnel

Pres: Adam S Posen E-mail: apoffice@piie.com

VP, Pubns & Communs: Steven R Weisman Tel: 202-454-1331

Founded: 1981

International economic policy publications.

ISBN Prefix(es): 978-0-88132

Number of titles published annually: 15 Print; 8 Online; 8 E-Book

Total Titles: 300 Print; 35 E-Book

Foreign Rep(s): Columbia University Press (Africa, Eastern Europe, Iran, Israel, Russia, Turkey, Western Europe)

Returns: Columbia University Press, 61 W 62 St, New York, NY 10023

Distribution Center: Columbia University Press, 61 W 62 St, New York, NY 10023

Membership(s): Association of American Publishers (AAP); Society for Scholarly Publishing (SSP); Washington Publishers (WP)

§Peterson's

8740 Lucent Blvd, Suite 400, Highlands Ranch, CO 80129

Tel: 609-896-1800 Toll Free Tel: 800-338-3282

E-mail: pubmarketing@petersons.com

Web Site: www.petersons.com

Key Personnel

Publg Dir: Bernadette Webster

Founded: 1966

Education, career books, software & CD-ROM, data licensing, test preparation, financial aid & adult education, online lead generation.

ISBN Prefix(es): 978-0-87866; 978-1-56079; 978-0-7689

Number of titles published annually: 50 Print; 10 E-Book

Total Titles: 120 Print; 10 E-Book

Imprints: B.E.S. (children's, lifestyle & hobby); Peterson's/Pacesetter Books

Foreign Rights: Ann-Christine Daniellsson Agency (Scandinavia); International Editors' Co (Latin America, Spain); Frederique Parretta Agency (Canada (French-speaking), France); Pikarski (Israel); Tuttle-Mori Agency Inc (Japan, Thailand)

Orders to: Hachettte Book Group, 53 State St, Boston, MA 02109 (US & CN) Toll Free

Tel: 800-759-0190 Toll Free Fax: 800-286-9471; Hachette Book Group, 1290 Avenue of the Americas, New York, NY 10104 (intl orders) Tel: 212-364-1325 Fax: 212-364-0933 E-mail: international@hbgusa.com

Distribution Center: Two Rivers Distribution, an Ingram brand, 1400 Broadway, Suite 520, New York, NY 10018 Toll Free Tel: 866-400-5351 E-mail: ips@ingramcontent.com Web Site: tworiversdistribution.com

Membership(s): Book Industry Study Group (BISG)

§Petroleum Extension Service (PETEX)

Unit of The University of Texas at Austin, Cockrell School of Engineering

JJ Pickle Research Campus, 10100 Burnet Rd, Bldg 2, Austin, TX 78758-4445

Tel: 512-471-5940 Toll Free Tel: 800-687-4132 Fax: 512-471-9410 Toll Free Fax: 800-687-7839

E-mail: info@petex.utexas.edu

Web Site: cee.utexas.edu/ce/petex

Key Personnel

Dir, Publg, Communs & Branding: Debby Denehy

Founded: 1944

Develops, produces & delivers technical & non-technical training courses, publications & e-product solutions for employees in various sectors of the petroleum industry.

ISBN Prefix(es): 978-0-88698

Number of titles published annually: 10 Print

Total Titles: 400 Print

Branch Office(s)

4702 N Sam Houston Pkwy W, Suite 800, Houston, TX 77086

§Pflaum Publishing Group

Division of Bayard Inc

3055 Kettering Blvd, Suite 100, Dayton, OH 45439

Toll Free Tel: 800-523-4625; 800-543-4383 (ext 1136, cust serv) Toll Free Fax: 800-370-4450

E-mail: service@pflaum.com

Web Site: www.pflaum.com

Key Personnel

VP & Dir, Sales: Michael Raffio

Edit Dir: David Dziena

Founded: 1885

Weekly liturgical magazines for PreK-8. Sacramental preparation for children & teens, catechetical resources for PreK-12, religious educators & youth ministers.

ISBN Prefix(es): 978-0-937997; 978-0-89837; 978-1-933178; 978-1-935042; 978-1-939105

Number of titles published annually: 20 Print

Total Titles: 75 Print

Membership(s): Association of Catholic Publishers Inc; National Catholic Education Association (NCEA); National Catholic Educational Exhibitors (NCEE)

Phaidon

65 Bleecker St, 8th fl, New York, NY 10012

Tel: 212-652-5400 Toll Free Tel: 800-759-0190 (cust serv) Fax: 212-652-5410

Toll Free Fax: 800-286-9471 (cust serv)

E-mail: enquiries@phaidon.com

Web Site: www.phaidon.com

Key Personnel

CEO: Keith Fox

COO: Philip Ruppel

VP & Group Publr: Deborah Aaronson

VP, Global Mktg & Communs: Linda Brennan

Publr: Emilia Terragni

Art Dir, Children's Books: Meagan Bennett

Dir of Sales, North America: Amy Hordes Tel: 646-400-4584 E-mail: ahordes@phaidon.com

Exec Commissioning Ed, Food: Emily Takoudes

Proj Ed, Food: Anne Goldberg

Founded: 1923

Premier global publisher of the creative arts with over 1,500 titles in print. We work with the world's most influential artists, chefs, writers & thinkers to produce innovative books on art, photography, design, architecture, fashion, food & travel & illustrated books for children. Head-quartered in London & New York City.

ISBN Prefix(es): 978-0-7148

Number of titles published annually: 80 Print

Total Titles: 1,500 Print

Foreign Office(s): Phaidon Sarl, 55 rue Traver-siere, 75012 Paris, France *Tel:* 01 55 28 38 38 *Fax:* 01 55 28 38 39

Phaidon Verlag, Innstr 30, 10243 Berlin, Germany *Tel:* (030) 28 04 08 35 *Fax:* (030) 28 04 48 79

Phaidon Press Ltd, 18 Regents Wharf, All Saints St, London N1 9PA, United Kingdom *Tel:* (020) 7843 1000 *Fax:* (020) 7843 1010

Phi Delta Kappa International®

1820 N Fort Myer Dr, Suite 320, Arlington, VA 22209

Mailing Address: PO Box 13090, Arlington, VA 22219

Tel: 812-339-1156 *Toll Free Tel:* 800-766-1156 *Fax:* 812-339-0018

E-mail: memberservices@pdkintl.org

Web Site: www.pdkintl.org

Key Personnel

CEO: Josh Starr

Founded: 1906

International professional association of educators.

ISBN Prefix(es): 978-0-87367

Number of titles published annually: 8 Print

Total Titles: 12 Print

Foreign Rep(s): Unifacmann Trading Co (Taiwan)

Philadelphia Museum of Art

PO Box 7646, Philadelphia, PA 19101-7646

Tel: 215-763-8100 *Fax:* 215-236-4465

Web Site: www.philamuseum.org

Key Personnel

Prodn Mgr: Rich Bonk

Ed: Mary Cason; Kathleen Krattenmaker; David Updike

Founded: 1901

Illustrated scholarly works on the permanent collection & exhibitions at the museum.

ISBN Prefix(es): 978-0-87633

Number of titles published annually: 5 Print

Total Titles: 114 Print

Distributed by Yale University Press

Philomel

Imprint of Penguin Group USA, A Penguin Random House Company

345 Hudson St, New York, NY 10014

Tel: 212-366-2000

Web Site: www.penguin.com/publishers/philomel

Key Personnel

Pres & Publr: Ken Wright

Assoc Publr: Jill Santopolo

Art Dir: Ellice Lee

Sr Ed: Liza Kaplan

Ed: Kelsey Murphy

Assoc Ed: Talia Benamy; Cheryl Eissing

Sr Designer: Monique Sterling

Founded: 1980

Penguin Random House & its publishing entities are not accepting unsol submissions, proposals, mss, or submission queries via e-mail at this time.

Number of titles published annually: 41 Print

Total Titles: 367 Print

Philosophical Library Inc

275 Central Park W, Suite 12D, New York, NY 10024

Tel: 212-873-6070 *Fax:* 212-873-6070

E-mail: editors@philosophicallibrary.com

Web Site: philosophicallibrary.com

Key Personnel

Dir: Regeen Runes Kiernan-najar

Founded: 1941

Comprehensive collection of mid-level reference books. A consistent source for serious readers, libraries, academic institutions & booksellers worldwide. Also have a program for print on demand.

ISBN Prefix(es): 978-0-8022

Number of titles published annually: 125 Print; 170 E-Book; 75 Audio

Total Titles: 2,500 Print; 300 E-Book

Distributed by Open Road Integrated Media

Philosophy Documentation Center

PO Box 7147, Charlottesville, VA 22906-7147

Tel: 434-220-3300 *Toll Free Tel:* 800-444-2419 *Fax:* 434-220-3301

E-mail: order@pdcnet.org

Web Site: www.pdcnet.org

Key Personnel

Dir: George Leaman *E-mail:* leaman@pdcnet.org

Assoc Dir: Pamela K Swope *E-mail:* pkswope@pdcnet.org

Electronic Publg & Mktg: Susanne Mueller-Grote *E-mail:* smg@pdcnet.org

Founded: 1966

Scholarly, nonprofit publisher of peer-reviewed journals, book series, conference proceedings & specialized reference materials. Provides a range of publishing services, including on-line hosting of full-text content, secure access solutions, membership management, order fulfillment for print or electronic publications & rights management.

ISBN Prefix(es): 978-0-912632; 978-1-889680; 978-1-63435

Number of titles published annually: 15 Print; 30 Online; 10 E-Book

Total Titles: 150 Print; 200 Online; 30 E-Book

Distributor for Zeta Books (online access)

Membership(s): Society for Scholarly Publishing (SSP)

Piano Press

1425 Ocean Ave, Suite 5, Del Mar, CA 92014

Mailing Address: PO Box 85, Del Mar, CA 92014-0085

Tel: 619-884-1401 *Fax:* 858-755-1104

E-mail: pianopress@pianopress.com

Web Site: www.pianopress.com

Key Personnel

Owner & Ed: Elizabeth C Axford *E-mail:* lizaxford@pianopress.com

Music Typesetter: David Murray; Mark So

Audio Engr: John Dawes; Denny Martin; Matthew Dela Pola; Peter Sprague; Kris Stone

Webmaster & Mktg: Frank Tranfaglia

Edit Asst: Kathy Alward; Carol Buckley; Katie Cook; Dee Rome; Gay Salo

Founded: 1998

Publishes songbooks & CDs as well as music-related coloring books & poetry for the educational & family markets.

ISBN Prefix(es): 978-0-9673325; 978-1-931844

Number of titles published annually: 6 Print; 1 Audio

Total Titles: 100 Print

Membership(s): The American Society of Composers, Authors and Publishers (ASCAP); The Recording Academy (NARAS); Society of Children's Book Writers & Illustrators (SCBWI)

Picador

Imprint of Farrar, Straus & Giroux, LLC

120 Broadway, New York, NY 10271

Tel: 646-307-5151 *Fax:* 212-253-9627

E-mail: publicity@picadorusa.com

Web Site: us.macmillan.com/picador

Key Personnel

VP & Assoc Publr: Hank Cochrane

VP, Sales & Mktg: Darin Keesler *E-mail:* darin.keesler@picadorusa.com

Exec Ed: Anna deVries *E-mail:* anna.devries@picadorusa.com

Sr Natl Accts Mgr: Cristina Cushing

Sr Publicist: Marlena Brown *E-mail:* marlena.brown@picadorusa.com

Founded: 1995

ISBN Prefix(es): 978-0-312

Number of titles published annually: 90 Print

Total Titles: 7,000 Print

Distribution Center: MPS Distribution Center, 16365 James Madison Hwy, Gordonsville, VA 22942-8501 *Toll Free Tel:* 888-330-8477 *Fax:* 540-672-7540 (cust serv) *Toll Free Fax:* 800-672-2054 (orders)

The Picasso Project

Imprint of Alan Wofsy Fine Arts

1109 Geary Blvd, San Francisco, CA 94109

Tel: 415-292-6500 *Fax:* 415-292-6594

E-mail: editeur@earthlink.net (edit); picasso@art-books.com (orders)

Web Site: www.art-books.com

Key Personnel

Mgr: Adios Butler

Ed: Alan Hyman

Founded: 1990

Publish & distribute comprehensive catalogues on the works of Pablo Picasso. Distribution center located in Ashland, OH.

ISBN Prefix(es): 978-0-915346; 978-1-55660

Number of titles published annually: 6 Print; 4 CD-ROM

Total Titles: 100 Print; 12 CD-ROM

Imprints: Beauxarts; Collegium Graphicum

Distributed by Alan Wofsy Fine Arts

Distributor for Cramer (Switzerland); Kornfeld (Switzerland); Ramie (France)

Billing Address: PO Box 2210, San Francisco, CA 94126-2110

Membership(s): Association of American Publishers (AAP)

Piccadilly Books Ltd

PO Box 25203, Colorado Springs, CO 80936-5203

SAN: 665-9969

Tel: 719-550-9887

E-mail: orders@piccadillybooks.com

Web Site: www.piccadillybooks.com

Key Personnel

Publr: Bruce Fife *E-mail:* bruce@piccadillybooks.com

Founded: 1985

Health & nutrition, entertainment, performing arts, humorous skits & sketches, writing.

ISBN Prefix(es): 978-0-941599; 978-1-936709

Number of titles published annually: 3 Print

Total Titles: 85 Print; 51 E-Book; 2 Audio

Foreign Rep(s): Gazelle Book Services Ltd (Europe)

Foreign Rights: ST&A Agency (Europe, Latin America)

Membership(s): Independent Book Publishers Association (IBPA)

Pieces of Learning Inc

1112 N Carbon St, Suite A, Marion, IL 62959-8976

SAN: 298-461X

Tel: 618-964-9426 *Toll Free Tel:* 800-729-5137 *Toll Free Fax:* 800-844-0455

E-mail: info@piecesoflearning.com

Web Site: piecesoflearning.com

Key Personnel

Pres: Tyler Young

Founded: 1989

Teacher supplementary educational books; mail order.

ISBN Prefix(es): 978-1-880505; 978-0-9623835; 978-1-931334; 978-1-934358; 978-1-937113
Number of titles published annually: 16 Print
Total Titles: 350 Print; 50 E-Book
Distributed by A W Peller & Associates; Prufrock Press
Membership(s): Education Market Association

The Pilgrim Press/United Church Press
700 Prospect Ave, Cleveland, OH 44115-1100
Tel: 216-736-2100 *Toll Free Tel:* 800-537-3394 (orders)
E-mail: permissions@thepilgrimpress.com; store@ucc.org (orders)
Web Site: www.thepilgrimpress.com
Key Personnel
Publr: Rev Rachel Hackenberg
Dir, Sales & Dist: Marie Tyson *E-mail:* tysonm@ucc.org
Founded: 1617
Diverse spiritualities; peace & justice; world religions; contemporary ministry.
ISBN Prefix(es): 978-0-8298
Number of titles published annually: 10 Print
Total Titles: 500 Print

Pineapple Press
Imprint of The Globe Pequot Press
203 Royal Poinciana Way, Suite E, Palm Beach, FL 33480
Web Site: www.pineapplepress.com
Founded: 1982
ISBN Prefix(es): 978-0-910923; 978-1-56164; 978-1-68334
Number of titles published annually: 20 Print
Total Titles: 365 Print
Distribution Center: National Book Network (NBN), 15200 NBN Way, Blue Ridge Summit, PA 17214 *Tel:* 717-794-3800 *Toll Free Tel:* 800-462-6420 *Toll Free Fax:* 800-338-4550 *E-mail:* customercare@nbnbooks.com
Web Site: www.nbnbooks.com

Pinnacle Books, see Kensington Publishing Corp

Pippin Press
229 E 85 St, New York, NY 10028
Mailing Address: PO Box 1347, Gracie Sta, New York, NY 10028
Tel: 212-288-4920 *Fax:* 908-237-2407
Key Personnel
Pres, Publr & Ed-in-Chief: Barbara Francis
Mng Ed & Rts Dir: Gregory Filling
Sr Ed: Joyce Segal
Sales Mgr & Lib Sales Dir: Alan Frese
Founded: 1987
Small chapter books for ages 7-10, humorous fiction for all ages, novels for ages 8-12 & unusual nonfiction for ages 6-12.
ISBN Prefix(es): 978-0-945912
Number of titles published annually: 4 Print
Total Titles: 55 Print
Foreign Rep(s): Baker & Taylor Books (Canada); Baker & Taylor International (worldwide exc Canada)
Orders to: Whitehurst & Clark Book Fulfillment Inc, 1200 County Rd, Rte 523, Flemington, NJ 08822 *Tel:* 908-782-2323 *Toll Free Tel:* 800-488-8040
Returns: Whitehurst & Clark Book Fulfillment Inc, 1200 County Rd, Rte 523, Flemington, NJ 08822 *Tel:* 908-782-2323 *Toll Free Tel:* 800-488-8040
Shipping Address: Whitehurst & Clark Book Fulfillment Inc, 1200 County Rd, Rte 523, Flemington, NJ 08822 *Tel:* 908-782-2323 *Toll Free Tel:* 800-488-8040
Warehouse: Whitehurst & Clark Book Fulfillment Inc, 1200 County Rd, Rte 523, Flemington, NJ 08822 *Tel:* 908-782-2323 *Toll Free Tel:* 800-488-8040

Distribution Center: Whitehurst & Clark Book Fulfillment Inc, 1200 County Rd, Rte 523, Flemington, NJ 08822 *Tel:* 908-782-2323 *Toll Free Tel:* 800-488-8040
Membership(s): American Library Association (ALA)

Planert Creek Press
E4843 395 Ave, Menomonie, WI 54751
SAN: 855-7454
Tel: 715-235-4110
E-mail: publisher@planertcreekpress.com
Web Site: www.planertcreekpress.com
Key Personnel
Publr: David Tank
Founded: 2008
Specialize in 3D books & topics related to West Central Wisconsin.
This publisher has indicated that 100% of their product line is author subsidized.
ISBN Prefix(es): 978-0-9815064; 978-0-9962218
Number of titles published annually: 3 Print; 3 Online
Total Titles: 13 Print; 3 Online; 1 Audio
Membership(s): National Stereoscopic Association (NSA); Society of Children's Book Writers & Illustrators (SCBWI)

Planners Press
Imprint of Routledge
205 N Michigan Ave, Suite 1200, Chicago, IL 60601
Tel: 312-431-9100 *Fax:* 312-786-6700
E-mail: customerservice@planning.org
Web Site: www.planning.org
Key Personnel
Sr Ed: Kate Schell *E-mail:* kathryn.schell@taylorandfrancis.com
Founded: 1978
Books on planning.
ISBN Prefix(es): 978-0-918286; 978-1-884829; 978-1-932364
Number of titles published annually: 5 Print
Total Titles: 120 Print; 15 E-Book
Warehouse: LSC North, 7539-7621 Zionsville Rd, Indianapolis, IN 46268 *Toll Free Tel:* 800-634-7064

Platinum Press LLC
281 Hicks St, Brooklyn, NY 11201
Tel: 718-875-4092 *Fax:* 718-875-5065
Key Personnel
Pres: Herbert J Cohen *E-mail:* herbertjcohen@aol.com
Founded: 1990
Publish nonfiction; book producer & packager; appointment books, diaries, date books, journals, blankbooks & joke books.
ISBN Prefix(es): 978-1-879582
Number of titles published annually: 12 Print
Total Titles: 145 Print; 2 E-Book

Platypus Media LLC
725 Eighth St SE, Washington, DC 20003
Tel: 202-546-1674 *Toll Free Tel:* 877-PLATYPS (752-8977) *Fax:* 202-546-2356
E-mail: info@platypusmedia.com
Web Site: www.platypusmedia.com
Key Personnel
Pres & Dir: Dia L Michels
Founded: 2000
An independent publisher creating books for families, teachers & parenting professionals.
ISBN Prefix(es): 978-1-930775
Number of titles published annually: 7 Print
Total Titles: 32 Print; 1 Audio
Distribution Center: National Book Network, 4501 Forbes Blvd, Suite 200, Lanham, MD 20706 *Tel:* 301-459-3366 *Toll Free Tel:* 800-464-6420 *Fax:* 301-459-5746 *Toll Free Fax:* 800-338-4550 *Web Site:* www.nbnbooks.com

Membership(s): The Association of Publishers for Special Sales (APSS); The Children's Book Council (CBC); Independent Book Publishers Association (IBPA); Washington Publishers (WP); Women's National Book Association (WNBA)

Pleasure Boat Studio: A Literary Press
3710 SW Barton St, Seattle, WA 98126
Tel: 206-962-0460
E-mail: pleasboatpublishing@gmail.com
Web Site: www.pleasureboatstudio.com
Key Personnel
Publr: Lauren Grosskopf
Founded: 1996
Fiction, nonfiction & poetry.
ISBN Prefix(es): 978-0-9651413; 978-1-929355; 978-0-912887
Number of titles published annually: 10 Print; 5 E-Book
Total Titles: 120 Print; 20 E-Book
Imprints: Aequitas Books (nonfiction only); Caravel Books (mysteries only)
Foreign Rights: Books Crossing Borders (worldwide)
Membership(s): Community of Literary Magazines & Presses (CLMP); Independent Book Publishers Association (IBPA)

Plexus Publishing, Inc.

§Plexus Publishing, Inc
Affiliate of Information Today, Inc
143 Old Marlton Pike, Medford, NJ 08055
Tel: 609-654-6500 *Fax:* 609-654-4309
E-mail: info@plexuspublishing.com
Web Site: www.plexuspublishing.com
Key Personnel
Pres & CEO: Thomas H Hogan
VP, Mktg & Busn Devt: Thomas Hogan, Jr
Mktg & Exhibits Mgr: Robert Colding *Tel:* 609-654-6500 ext 330 *E-mail:* rcolding@plexuspublishing.com
Sales & Admin: Deb Kranz *Tel:* 609-654-6500 ext 117 *E-mail:* dkranz@plexuspublishing.com
HR Dir: Mary S Hogan *E-mail:* shogan@plexuspublishing.com
Founded: 1977
Regional book publisher specializing in nature, history & fiction for readers interested in the NJ Pinelands, Atlantic City/Jersey shore, Philadelphia & surrounds. No children's books, poetry, religion, or calendars.
ISBN Prefix(es): 978-0-937548; 978-0-9666748
Number of titles published annually: 3 Print
Total Titles: 52 Print; 25 E-Book; 2 Audio
Imprints: Medford Press (trade book titles, nationally dist by IPG); Plexus Books (regional titles/NJ topics especially Southern NJ history, nature/Pinelands, fiction)
Membership(s): Independent Book Publishing Professionals Group (IBPPG); Mystery Writers of America (MWA)

§Plough Publishing House
151 Bowne Dr, Walden, NY 12586-2832
SAN: 202-0092
Mailing Address: PO Box 398, Walden, NY 12586-0398
Tel: 845-572-3455 *Toll Free Tel:* 800-521-8011
E-mail: info@plough.com; editor@plough.com
Web Site: www.plough.com
Key Personnel
Mgr: Sam Hine
Founded: 1920

Religion (Anabaptist), church history, children's education, Christian communal living; music; social justice, radical Christianity; social issues.
ISBN Prefix(es): 978-0-87486
Number of titles published annually: 10 Print; 10 Online; 10 E-Book; 1 Audio
Total Titles: 150 Print; 150 Online; 150 E-Book; 5 Audio
Foreign Office(s): 4188 Gwydir Hwy, Elsmore, NSW 2360, Australia
Brightling Rd, Robertsbridge, East Sussex TN32 5DR, United Kingdom *E-mail:* contact@ploughbooks.co.uk
Distribution Center: Ingram Publisher Services, One Ingram Blvd, La Vergne, TN 37086
Toll Free Tel: 866-400-5351 *E-mail:* ips@ingramcontent.com *Web Site:* www.ingramcontent.com

Ploughshares
Subsidiary of Ploughshares Inc
Emerson College, 120 Boylston St, Boston, MA 02116
Tel: 617-824-3757
E-mail: pshares@pshares.org
Web Site: www.pshares.org
Key Personnel
Exec Dir & Ed-in-Chief: Ladette Randolph
Founded: 1971
Journal publishing.
ISBN Prefix(es): 978-0-933277; 978-1-933058; 978-1-62608
Number of titles published annually: 4 Print
Total Titles: 118 Print; 9 E-Book
Membership(s): Combined Book Exhibit (CBE)

§Plowshare Media
405 Vincente Way, La Jolla, CA 92037
SAN: 857-2933
Mailing Address: PO Box 278, La Jolla, CA 92038
Tel: 858-454-5446
E-mail: sales@plowsharemedia.com
Web Site: plowsharemedia.com
Key Personnel
Mng Partner: Maryann Callery *E-mail:* mc@plowsharemedia.com; Thomas P Tweed *E-mail:* tt@plowsharemedia.com
Founded: 2008
Handle all aspects of book publishing including acquisition, editing, typesetting, cover design, printing, marketing & promotion.
ISBN Prefix(es): 978-0-9860428; 978-0-9821145
Number of titles published annually: 2 Print; 2 E-Book
Total Titles: 12 Print; 10 E-Book
Imprints: RELS Press (nonprofit)
Membership(s): Independent Book Publishers Association (IBPA)

§Plum Tree Books
Imprint of Classical Academic Press
2151 Market St, Camp Hill, PA 17011
Tel: 717-730-0711
E-mail: info@classicalsubjects.com
Web Site: www.plumtreebooks.com
Key Personnel
Publr: Christopher Perrin *E-mail:* cperrin@classicalsubjects.com
Founded: 2012
Old Virtues, New Stories™ - children's stories presented entirely through digital formats.
ISBN Prefix(es): 978-1-60051
Number of titles published annually: 10 E-Book

§Plume
Division of Penguin Group USA, A Penguin Random House Company
375 Hudson St, New York, NY 10014
Tel: 212-366-2000 *Fax:* 212-243-6002
Web Site: www.penguin.com/publishers/plume

Key Personnel
SVP & Publr, Dutton, Plume & Tiny Reparations Books: Christine Ball
VP, Assoc Publr & Dir, Mktg & Publicity: Aileen Boyle
Exec Dir, Ad & Promo: Jaime Mendola-Hobbie
Edit Dir: Jill Schwartzman
Mktg Dir: Stephanie Cooper
Assoc Dir, Publg, Putnam/Dutton/Berkley: Liza Cassity
Exec Mng Ed: Matt Giarratano
Exec Ed: Becky Cole
Ed: Amber Oliver
Exec Publicist: Marian Brown
Asst Mktg Mgr: Natalie Church
Mktg Coord: Molly Pieper
Founded: 1970
Penguin Random House & its publishing entities are not accepting unsol submissions, proposals, mss, or submission queries via e-mail at this time.
Number of titles published annually: 100 Print
Total Titles: 700 Print
Imprints: Tiny Reparations Books

Plunkett Research Ltd
PO Drawer 541737, Houston, TX 77254-1737
Tel: 713-932-0000 *Fax:* 713-932-7080
E-mail: customersupport@plunkettresearch.com
Web Site: www.plunkettresearch.com
Key Personnel
Publr & CEO: Jack W Plunkett
  E-mail: jack_plunkett@plunkettresearch.com
Founded: 1985
A leading provider of global business & industry information to corporate, library, academic & government markets. Plunkett's unique reference books & online service offer comprehensive market research, industry statistics & trends analysis covering all of the world's vital industries.
ISBN Prefix(es): 978-0-9638268; 978-1-891775; 978-1-59392; 978-1-60879; 978-1-62831
Number of titles published annually: 40 Print; 29 CD-ROM; 40 Online; 40 E-Book
Total Titles: 40 Print; 40 Online; 40 E-Book

Pocket Books, see Gallery Books

§Pocket Press Inc
PO Box 25124, Portland, OR 97298-0124
Toll Free Tel: 888-237-2110 *Toll Free Fax:* 877-643-3732
E-mail: sales@pocketpressinc.com
Web Site: www.pocketpressinc.com
Key Personnel
Pres: Bruce Coorpender
Sales & Mktg: Bob Born
Founded: 1992
Reference books for law enforcement.
ISBN Prefix(es): 978-1-884493; 978-1-61371
Number of titles published annually: 120 Print
Total Titles: 120 Print

Pocol Press
320 Sutton St, Punxsutawney, PA 15767
SAN: 253-6021
Tel: 703-870-9611
E-mail: info@pocolpress.com
Web Site: www.pocolpress.com
Key Personnel
Owner & Publr: J Thomas Hetrick
Founded: 1999
Leaders in short fiction & baseball history from first time non-agented authors. Several books used as college textbooks. All titles also ebooks available from Amazon for Kindle.
ISBN Prefix(es): 978-1-929763
Number of titles published annually: 4 Print; 4 E-Book

Total Titles: 86 Print; 86 E-Book
Membership(s): The Association of Publishers for Special Sales (APSS)

Pointed Leaf Press
136 Baxter St, New York, NY 10013
Tel: 212-941-1800 *Fax:* 212-941-1822
E-mail: info@pointedleafpress.com
Web Site: www.pointedleafpress.com
Key Personnel
Publr & Edit Dir: Suzanne Slesin
Founded: 2002
This publisher has indicated that 50% of their product line is author subsidized.
ISBN Prefix(es): 978-0-9727661; 978-0-9777875; 978-0-9823585; 978-0-9833889; 978-1-938461
Number of titles published annually: 9 Print

Poisoned Pen Press
Imprint of Sourcebooks Inc
4014 N Goldwater Blvd, Suite 201, Scottsdale, AZ 85251
Tel: 480-945-3375 *Toll Free Tel:* 800-421-3976 *Fax:* 480-949-1707
E-mail: info@poisonedpenpress.com
Web Site: www.poisonedpenpress.com
Key Personnel
Ed Dir, Sourcebooks & Poisoned Pen Press: Anna Michels *E-mail:* anna.michels@sourcebooks.com
Dir, Devt: Robert Rosenwald *E-mail:* robert@poisonedpenpress.com
Dir, Mktg: Molly Waxman *E-mail:* molly.waxman@sourcebooks.com
Mng Ed: Diane DiBiase *E-mail:* diane.dibiase@sourcebooks.com
Data Entry Specialist: Kacie Blackburn
  E-mail: kacie@poisonedpenpress.com
Founded: 1997
Publishing high quality works in the field of mystery. Interested in publishing books that we think booksellers everywhere & especially independent mystery booksellers would want to have available to sell. Electronic submissions only. Visit www.poisonedpenpress.com, click on Submission for guidelines & information.
ISBN Prefix(es): 978-1-890208; 978-1-929345 (The Poisoned Pencil); 978-1-59058; 978-1-46420; 978-1-61595 (ebooks)
Number of titles published annually: 60 Print; 60 E-Book
Total Titles: 800 Print; 500 E-Book
Distribution Center: Sourcebooks Inc, 1935 Brookdale Rd, Suite 139, Naperville, IL 60563
Tel: 630-961-3900 *E-mail:* customerservice@sourcebooks.com *Web Site:* www.sourcebooks.com
Membership(s): Association of American Publishers (AAP); Independent Book Publishers Association (IBPA); Publishers Association of the West (PubWest)

§Polar Bear & Company
Imprint of Solon Center for Research & Publishing
8 Brook St, Solon, ME 04979
Mailing Address: PO Box 311, Solon, ME 04979-0311 SAN: 858-8902
Tel: 207-319-4727
Web Site: polarbearandco.com
Key Personnel
Exec Dir: Paul du Houx
Founded: 1998
To help build community with quality books & art.
ISBN Prefix(es): 978-1-882190
Number of titles published annually: 6 Print; 6 E-Book
Total Titles: 60 Print; 8 E-Book
Orders to: Ingram Lightning Source Inc, 1246 Heil Quaker Blvd, La Vergne, TN 37086

E-mail: inquiry@lightningsource.com Web
Site: www.lightningsource.com
Distribution Center: Ingram Lightning Source
Inc, 1246 Heil Quaker Blvd, La Vergne,
TN 37086 Toll Free Tel: 800-509-4156
E-mail: inquiry@lightningsource.com Web
Site: www.lightningsource.com
Membership(s): Independent Publishers of New
England (IPNE); Maine Writers & Publishers
Alliance (MWPA)

Polebridge Press
Division of Westar Institute
PO Box 346, Farmington, MN 55024
Tel: 651-200-2372
E-mail: orders@westarinstitute.org
Web Site: www.westarinstitute.org
Key Personnel
Publr: Arthur J Dewey
Art Dir & Prodn Mgr: Robaire Ream
E-mail: robaire.ream@westarinstitute.org
Opers Dir & Dist Mgr: Bill Lehto E-mail: bill.
lehto@westarinstitute.org
Mng Ed: Char Matejovsky E-mail: char@
westarinstitute.org
Acqs Ed: David Galston Tel: 905-577-5726
E-mail: dgalston@westarinstitute.org
Developmental Ed: Cassandra Farrin Tel: 208-
954-6848 E-mail: cfarrin@westarinstitute.org
Founded: 1981
Publishes up-to-date reference works for biblical
scholars, primarily in support of research on
the historical Jesus & the origins of Christian-
ity as well as philosophical theology; scholarly
books produced by Westar seminars, research
projects & by individual scholars; books & pe-
riodicals that disseminate the results of critical
scholarship on religion to the public.
ISBN Prefix(es): 978-1-59815; 978-0-944344
Number of titles published annually: 10 Print; 6
E-Book; 3 Audio
Total Titles: 110 Print; 30 E-Book; 93 Audio
Returns: 660 S Mansfield, Ypsilanti, MI 48197
Tel: 651-605-5275

Police Executive Research Forum
1120 Connecticut Ave NW, Suite 930, Washing-
ton, DC 20036
Tel: 202-466-7820
Web Site: www.policeforum.org
Key Personnel
Exec Dir: Chuck Wexler Tel: 202-454-8326
E-mail: cwexler@policeforum.org
Dir, Communs: Craig Fischer Tel: 202-454-8332
E-mail: cfischer@policeforum.org
Chief of Staff: Andrea Luna Tel: 202-454-8346
E-mail: aluna@policeforum.org
Communs Coord: James McGinty Tel: 202-454-
8310 E-mail: jmcginty@policeforum.org
Founded: 1977
Community policing, POP, police research &
management, police & criminal justice.
ISBN Prefix(es): 978-1-878734; 978-1-934485
Number of titles published annually: 7 Print
Total Titles: 70 Print
Distribution Center: Whitehurst & Clark, 1200
Rte 523, Flemington, NJ 08822, Contact: Brad
Searles Toll Free Tel: 888-202-4563 Fax: 908-
237-2407 E-mail: wcbooks@aol.com

Polis Books
1201 Hudson St, No 211S, Hoboken, NJ 07030
E-mail: info@polisbooks.com; submissions@
polisbooks.com
Web Site: www.polisbooks.com; facebook.com/
PolisBooks; twitter.com/PolisBooks
Key Personnel
Publr: Jason Pinter E-mail: jpinter@polisbooks.
com
Ed, Agora: Chantelle Aimee Osman
E-mail: cosman@polisbooks.com
Founded: 2013

Publishing primarily commercial fiction in adult,
young adult & middle grade.
ISBN Prefix(es): 978-1-940610
Number of titles published annually: 30 Print; 50
E-Book; 40 Audio
Imprints: Agora
Foreign Rights: Biagi Literary Management
(worldwide)
Distribution Center: Publishers Group West,
1700 Fourth St, Berkeley, CA 94710 Toll Free
Tel: 800-788-3123 SAN: 202-8522
Membership(s): International Thriller Writers Inc
(ITW); Mystery Writers of America (MWA);
Society of Children's Book Writers & Illustra-
tors (SCBWI)

Pomegranate Communications Inc
19018 NE Portal Way, Portland, OR 97230
Tel: 503-328-6500 Toll Free Tel: 800-227-1428
Fax: 503-328-9330 Toll Free Fax: 800-848-
4376
E-mail: contactus@pomegranate.com
Web Site: www.pomegranate.com
Key Personnel
Pres & Intl Rts: Thomas F Burke
Publr: Katie Burke
Exec Dir: Darius Burke
Founded: 1968
Fine arts publisher of books, calendars, puzzles,
stationery & children's products.
ISBN Prefix(es): 978-0-87654; 978-1-56640; 978-
0-7649
Number of titles published annually: 12 Print
Total Titles: 120 Print
Imprints: PomegranateKids
Foreign Rep(s): Ashton International Market-
ing Services (Julian Ashton) (Far East, Mid-
dle East); Canadian Manda Group (Canada);
Pomegranate Europe Ltd (Europe, UK)
Membership(s): American Specialty Toy Retailing
Association (ASTRA); MSA

Portfolio
Subsidiary of Penguin Group USA, A Penguin
Random House Company
375 Hudson St, New York, NY 10014
Web Site: www.penguin.com/meet/publishers/
portfolio
Key Personnel
Pres & Publr: Adrian Zackheim
VP & Exec Dir, Copyediting: Tory Klose
VP & Dir, Mktg & Publicity: Tara Gilbride
Dir, Publicity, Portfolio/Sentinel: Margot Stamas
Edit Dir: Niki Papadopoulos
Exec Mng Ed, Penguin Group USA: Tricia Con-
ley
Exec Ed, Portfolio & Edit Dir, Sentinel: Bria
Sandford
Sr Ed: Trish Daly; Noah Schwartzberg
Ed: Natalie Horbachevsky
Ed, Portfolio/Sentinel: Leah Trouwborst
Assoc Ed: Jesse Maeshiro; Merry Sun
Asst Ed: Vivian Roberson
Asst Ed, Portfolio/Sentinel: Helen Healey
Publicity Mgr: Stefanie Rosenblum
Sr Publicist, Portfolio/Sentinel: Alison Coolidge
Publicist, Portfolio/Sentinel: Alyssa Adler;
Marisol Salaman
Asst Mktg & Soc Media Mgr: Katherine
Valentino
Mktg Coord: Madeline Montgomery
Founded: 2001
Specialize in management, leadership, marketing,
business narrative, investing, personal finance,
economics, technology, sales, entrepreneurship
& career advice.
Penguin Random House & its publishing entities
are not accepting unsol submissions, proposals,
mss, or submission queries via e-mail at this
time.
Number of titles published annually: 78 Print
Total Titles: 286 Print
Imprints: Optimism Press

Potomac Books
Imprint of University of Nebraska Press
University of Nebraska-Lincoln, 1111 Lincoln
Mall, Suite 400, Lincoln, NE 68508
Mailing Address: PO Box 880630, Lincoln, NE
68588-0630
Tel: 402-472-3581 Fax: 402-472-6214
E-mail: pressmail@unl.edu
Web Site: www.nebraskapress.unl.edu/potomac/
Founded: 1984 (as Brassey's Inc until 2005)
ISBN Prefix(es): 978-1-57488; 978-1-59797; 978-
1-61234
Number of titles published annually: 80 Print; 50
E-Book
Total Titles: 550 Print; 400 E-Book
Foreign Rep(s): Casemate UK Ltd (Andrew Tar-
ring) (Europe, UK); Peribo (Australia, New
Zealand)
Foreign Rights: The Asano Agency Inc (Japan);
CA-LINK International LLC (China); Julio F-
Yanez Agencia Literaria SL (Spanish-speaking
countries); Graal Literary Agency (Eastern Eu-
rope, Poland); Natoli, Stefan & Oliva (Italy);
La Nouvelle Agence (France)
Orders to: Longleaf Services Inc, 116 S
Boundary St, Chapel Hill, NC 27514-
3808 Tel: 919-966-7449 Toll Free Tel: 800-
848-6224 Fax: 919-962-2704 Toll Free
Fax: 800-272-6817 E-mail: customerservice@
longleafservices.org
Membership(s): Association of University Presses
(AUPresses)

Clarkson Potter Publishers
Imprint of Crown Publishing Group
1745 Broadway, New York, NY 10019
Tel: 212-782-9000
Web Site: crownpublishing.com/imprint/clarkson-
potter
Founded: 1959
Dedicated lifestyle group within Penguin Random
House, home to a community of award-winning
& bestselling chefs, cooks, designers, arts &
writers-visionaries who see to entertain, engage
& teach. Commercial & literary diverse list,
including cookbooks, illustrated gift books &
a growing line of paper products such as jour-
nals, postcards, stationery & games.
Penguin Random House & its publishing entities
are not accepting unsol submissions, proposals,
mss, or submission queries via e-mail at this
time.
Number of titles published annually: 145 Print
Total Titles: 1,000 Print
Imprints: Clarkson Potter
Foreign Rep(s): Penguin Random House Inc
(worldwide)
Orders to: Penguin Random House Inc, 400
Hahn Rd, Westminster, MD 21157 Toll
Free Tel: 800-733-3000 E-mail: csorders@
randomhouse.com; Penguin Random House of
Canada Inc, Diversified Sales, 2775 Matheson
Blvd E, Mississauga, ON L4W 4P4, Canada
Toll Free Tel: 800-668-4247 Fax: 905-624-8091

powerHouse Books
Imprint of powerHouse Cultural Entertainment
Inc
32 Adams St, Brooklyn, NY 11201
Tel: 212-604-9074
E-mail: info@powerhousebooks.com
Web Site: www.powerhousebooks.com
Key Personnel
CEO: Daniel Power
Publr: Craig Cohen E-mail: craig@
powerhousebooks.com
Founded: 1995
Contemporary art, photography & image-based
cultural books.
ISBN Prefix(es): 978-1-57687
Number of titles published annually: 35 Print
Total Titles: 700 Print

Distributor for Antinous Press; Juno Books; MTV Press; Throckmorton Press; VH1 Press; Vice Books
Foreign Rep(s): Penguin Random House (worldwide)
Foreign Rights: Bookwise International Pty Ltd (Australia); Critiques Livres (France); Turnaround (UK)
Warehouse: Random House
Distribution Center: Penguin Random House Publisher Services (PRHPS)

§PPI, A Kaplan Company
332 Front St, Suite 501, La Crosse, WI 54601
SAN: 264-6315
Tel: 650-593-9119 *Fax:* 650-592-4519
E-mail: info@ppi2pass.com
Web Site: ppi2pass.com
Key Personnel
Prod Mktg Mgr: Jared Schulze
Founded: 1975
Provider of exam review books, online products & live & online classes in the fields of engineering, land surveying, LEED, architecture, interior design & landscape architecture. Specialty engineering areas include civil, structural, seismic, mechanical, electrical, environmental, chemical, nuclear, geotechnical & industrial engineering fields.
ISBN Prefix(es): 978-0-932276; 978-0-912045; 978-1-888577; 978-1-59126
Number of titles published annually: 10 Print; 1 CD-ROM; 2 Online; 5 E-Book
Total Titles: 120 Print; 20 Online; 20 E-Book
Distributor for American Association of State Highway & Transportation Officials; American Wood Council (American Forest & Paper Association) (National Design Specification for Wood Construction (NDS) & others); International Code Council; McGraw-Hill Professional (green building, design & construction titles, LEED titles); National Council of Examiners for Engineering & Surveying; SmartPros; Transportation Research Board Code; US Green Building Council (LEED reference guides)
Membership(s): American Society of Civil Engineers; American Society of Engineering Educators; American Society of Mechanical Engineers (ASME); National Society of Professional Engineers; US Green Building Council (USGBC)

§Practice Management Information Corp (PMIC)
4727 Wilshire Blvd, Suite 302, Los Angeles, CA 90010
SAN: 139-438X
Tel: 323-954-0224 *Fax:* 323-954-0253
E-mail: customer.service@pmiconline.com
Web Site: pmiconline.stores.yahoo.net
Key Personnel
Pres & Publr: James B Davis
Founded: 1986
Books & software for physicians, hospitals, insurance companies & other healthcare professionals on medical coding, reimbursement, practice management, financial management & medical risk management.
ISBN Prefix(es): 978-1-878487 (Health Information Press); 978-1-57066; 978-1-885987; 978-1-936977; 978-1-939852; 978-1-943009
Number of titles published annually: 35 Print
Total Titles: 35 Print
Imprints: Health Information Press (HIP)
Sales Office(s): 200 W 22 St, Suite 253, Lombard, IL 60148 *Toll Free Tel:* 800-633-4215; 800-MEDSHOP (orders) *Toll Free Fax:* 800-633-6556 (orders)

§Practising Law Institute
1177 Avenue of the Americas, New York, NY 10036

SAN: 203-0136
Tel: 212-824-5700 *Toll Free Tel:* 800-260-4PLI (260-4754, cust serv) *Toll Free Fax:* 800-321-0093 (local)
E-mail: info@pli.edu (cust serv)
Web Site: www.pli.edu
Key Personnel
CFO & Treas: Frank De Vivo *Tel:* 212-824-5709 *E-mail:* fdevivo@pli.edu
CIO: Christopher Rousseau *Tel:* 212-824-5878 *E-mail:* crousseau@pli.edu
Pres: Anita C Shapiro *Tel:* 212-824-5701 *E-mail:* ashapiro@pli.edu
EVP: Sandra R Geller *Tel:* 212-824-5796 *E-mail:* sgeller@pli.edu
VP, HR: Joan Sternberg *Tel:* 212-824-5764 *E-mail:* jsternberg@pli.edu
VP, Mktg & Communs: David Smith *Tel:* 212-590-8838 *E-mail:* dsmith@pli.edu
VP, Progs: Kara L O'Brien, Esq *Tel:* 212-824-5852 *E-mail:* kobrien@pli.edu
VP, Publg: Ellen Siegel *Tel:* 212-824-5761 *E-mail:* esiegel@pli.edu
Founded: 1933
Professional books for lawyers; CDs, DVDs, CD-ROMs, programs.
ISBN Prefix(es): 978-0-87224; 978-1-4024
Number of titles published annually: 210 Print
Total Titles: 330 Print; 4 CD-ROM; 330 Online
Imprints: PLI
Branch Office(s)
685 Market St, Suite 100, San Francisco, CA 94105-4202 *Tel:* 415-498-3800
Shipping Address: PMDS, 1780A Crossroads Dr, Odenton, MD 21113 *Tel:* 301-604-3305

PRB Productions
963 Peralta Ave, Albany, CA 94706-2144
Tel: 510-526-0722
E-mail: prbprdns@aol.com
Web Site: www.prbmusic.com
Key Personnel
Prop & Publr: Peter R Ballinger; Leslie J Gold
Founded: 1989
Specialize in publishing high-quality performing editions of instrumental & vocal music from the Baroque & Classical eras, along with original contemporary works for early & contemporary instruments & voices. Customized music typesetting services available by special arrangement.
ISBN Prefix(es): 978-1-56571
Number of titles published annually: 10 Print
Total Titles: 300 Print

PREP Publishing
Subsidiary of PREP Inc
3528 Turnberry Circle, Fayetteville, NC 28303
Tel: 910-483-6611 *Toll Free Tel:* 800-533-2814
E-mail: preppub@aol.com
Web Site: www.prep-pub.com
Key Personnel
Publr: Anne McKinney
Lib Sales Dir: Frances Sweeney
Founded: 1994
Books designed to enrich people's lives & help optimize the human experience. Publisher of general trade books, fiction & nonfiction, especially books related to careers, job hunting, government jobs & business planning, marketing & entrepreneurship. Fiction titles include mysteries, Christian fiction & romance.
ISBN Prefix(es): 978-1-885288
Number of titles published annually: 8 Print
Total Titles: 52 Print
Imprints: Business Success Series; Government Jobs Series; Judeo Christian Ethics Series; Anne McKinney Career Series
Advertising Agency: McKinney Communications, PO Box 66, Fayetteville, NC 28302-0066, Contact: Pat Mack
Warehouse: 435 W Russell St, Fayetteville, NC 28301

Membership(s): Community of Literary Magazines & Presses (CLMP); Independent Book Publishers Association (IBPA); Southern Independent Booksellers Alliance (SIBA)

Presbyterian Publishing Corp (PPC)
100 Witherspoon St, Louisville, KY 40202
Tel: 502-569-5000 *Toll Free Tel:* 800-523-1631 (US only) *Fax:* 502-569-5113
E-mail: customerservice@presbypub.com
Web Site: www.wjkbooks.com
Key Personnel
Pres & Publr: Marc Lewis
VP & COO: Monty Anderson *E-mail:* manderson@wjkbooks.com
Assoc Publr: David Dobson *E-mail:* ddobson@wjkbooks.com
VP, Mktg & eCommerce: Alicia Samuels *E-mail:* asamuels@wjkbooks.com
Founded: 1838
Academic & scholarly books, general trade religious books & children's picture books.
ISBN Prefix(es): 978-0-664; 978-0-8042
Number of titles published annually: 60 Print; 2 CD-ROM; 60 E-Book; 10 Audio
Total Titles: 2,100 Print; 5 CD-ROM; 1,000 E-Book
Imprints: Flyaway Books (children's picture books); Westminster John Knox Press (WJK) (adult academic & trade)
Distributor for Epworth; SCM
Foreign Rep(s): Parasource (Canada); SCM Press (Europe, UK)
Foreign Rights: Mosaic Rights Services (worldwide exc North America & UK)
Warehouse: Ingram Publisher Services, 14 Ingram Blvd, La Vergne, TN 37086 *Toll Free Tel:* 866-400-5351 *E-mail:* ips@ingramcontent.com
Distribution Center: Spring Arbor Distributors *Toll Free Tel:* 800-395-4340 *Toll Free Fax:* 800-876-0186 *E-mail:* orders@springarbor.com
Membership(s): Association of American Publishers (AAP); The Children's Book Council (CBC); Society of Children's Book Writers & Illustrators (SCBWI)
See separate listing for:
Westminster John Knox Press (WJK)

The Press at California State University, Fresno
Unit of California State University, Fresno
2380 E Keats, M/S MB 99, Fresno, CA 93740-8024
Tel: 559-278-4103 *Fax:* 559-278-6758
E-mail: press@csufresno.edu
Web Site: shop.thepressatcsufresno.com; thepressatcsufresno.com
Key Personnel
Gen Mgr: Gail Freeman
Founded: 1982
Art, architecture, drama, music, film & the media, photography, New Age politics, business, autobiography, Armenian history, Fresno history & literary magazine. Peer-reviewed multidisciplinary victimology journal.
ISBN Prefix(es): 978-0-912201
Number of titles published annually: 4 Print; 1 Online; 1 E-Book
Total Titles: 30 Print; 1 E-Book

Prevention Products & Services Inc, see The Bureau for At-Risk Youth

Mathew Price International Inc
2404 W Main St, Wailuku, HI 96793
Tel: 808-244-9585
E-mail: info@mathewprice.com
Web Site: www.mathewprice.com
Key Personnel
Pres: Mathew Price *E-mail:* mathewp@mathewprice.com

Founded: 1983
ISBN Prefix(es): 978-1-84248; 978-0-9516844
Number of titles published annually: 15 Print
Total Titles: 300 Print

§Price World Publishing
3971 Hoover Rd, Suite 77, Columbus, OH 43123-2839
Toll Free Tel: 888-234-6896 *Fax:* 216-803-0350
E-mail: info@priceworldpublishing.com
Web Site: www.priceworldpublishing.com
Key Personnel
Pres & Exec Ed: Robert Price, Esq *Tel:* 888-234-6896 ext 713 *E-mail:* rprice@priceworldpublishing.com
Founded: 2001
Bringing books & ebooks to global markets.
ISBN Prefix(es): 978-1-932549; 978-0-9724102; 978-1-61984; 978-1-93691
Number of titles published annually: 3 Print; 3 E-Book
Total Titles: 81 Print; 2 CD-ROM; 387 E-Book
Distributed by David Bateman Ltd (New Zealand); Cardinal Publishers Group (US)
Foreign Rep(s): Gazelle Book Services Ltd (UK); Monarch Books of Canada (Canada); John Reed Books (Australia); Rights & Distribution Inc (Brunei, Hong Kong, Malaysia, New Zealand, Philippines, Singapore, South Africa, Thailand)
Foreign Rights: Rights & Distribution Inc
Orders to: Cardinal Publishers Group, 2402 Shadeland Ave, Suite A, Indianapolis, IN 46219, Pres: Tom Doherty *Tel:* 317-352-8200 *Fax:* 317-352-8202 *E-mail:* tdoherty@cardinalpub.com *Web Site:* www.cardinalpub.com
Membership(s): American Bar Association (ABA); Independent Book Publishers Association (IBPA)

Primary Research Group Inc
2585 Broadway, Suite 156, New York, NY 10025
Tel: 212-736-2316 *Fax:* 212-412-9097
E-mail: primaryresearchgroup@gmail.com
Web Site: www.primaryresearch.com
Key Personnel
Pres: James Moses
Founded: 1989
Monographs, books, surveys & research reports on library science industry, economics, publishing (book, electronic & magazine), telecommunication, entertainment & higher education.
ISBN Prefix(es): 978-0-9626749; 978-1-57440
Number of titles published annually: 65 Print
Total Titles: 425 Print
Distributed by Academic Book Center; Ambassador Books; Coutts Library Service; Croft House Books; Eastern Book Company; Ebsco; MarketResearch.com; Midwest Library Service; OPAMP Technical Books; Emory Pratt; ProQuest LLC; Research & Markets; Rittenhouse Book Distributors; Total Information; Yankee Book Peddler

Princeton Architectural Press
202 Warren St, Hudson, NY 12534
Tel: 518-671-6100 *Toll Free Tel:* 800-722-6657 (dist); 800-759-0190 (sales)
E-mail: sales@papress.com
Web Site: www.papress.com
Key Personnel
Founder: Kevin C Lippert *Tel:* 518-671-6100 ext 301 *E-mail:* lippert@papress.com
Owner: Jack Jensen
Publr: Lynn Grady
Edit Dir: Jennifer Lippert *Tel:* 518-671-6100 ext 302 *E-mail:* jennifer@papress.com
Design Dir: Paul Wagner *E-mail:* paul@papress.com
Prodn Dir: Janet Behning *E-mail:* behning@papress.com

Prog Dir, Children's: Rob Shaeffer *E-mail:* rob@papress.com
Prog Dir, Paper & Goods: Sara McKay *E-mail:* mckay@papress.com
Sales & Mktg Dir: Lia Hunt *E-mail:* lia@papress.com
Prodn Ed: Parker Menzimer
Assoc Ed: Stephanie Holstein
Mktg Mgr: Jessica Tackett
Prodn Coord: Marisa Tesoro
Founded: 1981
Publisher of high quality books in architecture, graphic design & visual culture, arts & photography, children's & stationery.
ISBN Prefix(es): 978-0-910413; 978-1-878271; 978-1-56898; 978-1-61689
Number of titles published annually: 75 Print; 50 E-Book
Total Titles: 1,000 Print
Distributed by Chronicle Books
Distributor for Moleskine Books
Foreign Rep(s): Abrams & Chronicle UK (Europe, Ireland, UK); Hachette Book Group (Central America, Latin America, Middle East, South America, USA); Sonya Jeffery (Australia); Raincoast Books (Canada)

§Princeton Book Co Publishers
15 West Front St, Trenton, NJ 08608
Tel: 609-426-0602 *Toll Free Tel:* 800-220-7149 *Fax:* 609-426-1344
E-mail: pbc@dancehorizons.com
Web Site: www.dancehorizons.com
Key Personnel
Pres & Rts & Perms: Charles Woodford
Ed-in-Chief: Connie Woodford
Founded: 1975
Specialize in dance.
ISBN Prefix(es): 978-0-916622; 978-0-87127; 978-0-903102; 978-0-85418; 978-0-932582; 978-0-7121; 978-0-8463; 978-0-340
Number of titles published annually: 6 Print; 3 E-Book
Total Titles: 150 Print; 14 E-Book
Imprints: Dance Horizons; Dance Horizons Video; Elysian Editions (adult nonfiction)
Distributed by Dance Books Ltd
Distributor for Dance Books Ltd; Dance Notation Bureau
Foreign Rep(s): Dance Books Ltd (UK); John Reed Book Distribution (Australia)

§The Princeton Review
Imprint of Random House Children's Books
c/o Penguin Random House Inc, 1745 Broadway, MD 16-1, New York, NY 10019
Toll Free Tel: 800-273-8439 (orders only)
Web Site: www.princetonreview.com
Key Personnel
VP & Publr: Tom Russell
Publg Dir: Alison Stoltzfus
Founded: 1981
Test preparation, college & graduate school guides, career guides & general study aids.
Penguin Random House & its publishing entities are not accepting unsol submissions, proposals, mss, or submission queries via e-mail at this time.
Number of titles published annually: 75 Print; 12 CD-ROM
Total Titles: 230 Print; 15 CD-ROM

Princeton University Press
41 William St, Princeton, NJ 08540-5237
Tel: 609-258-4900 *Fax:* 609-258-6305
Web Site: press.princeton.edu
Key Personnel
CIO: Dennis Langlois *Tel:* 609-258-3083 *E-mail:* dennis_langlois@press.princeton.edu
Chief Digital Mktg Strategist: Colleen Suljic
Dir: Christie Henry *E-mail:* christie_henry@press.princeton.edu

Exec Asst to Dir: Martha Camp *Tel:* 609-258-4953 *E-mail:* martha_camp@press.princeton.edu
Assoc Dir & CFO: Scot Kuehm *Tel:* 609-258-3083 *E-mail:* scot_kuehm@press.princeton.edu
Asst Dir/Global Devt Dir/Publr (history): Brigitta van Rheinberg *Tel:* 609-258-4935 *E-mail:* brigitta_vanrheinberg@press.princeton.edu
Ad & Mktg Art Dir: Heather Hansen *E-mail:* heather_hansen@press.princeton.edu
Dir, Ad & Soc Media: Donna Liese *Tel:* 609-258-4924 *E-mail:* donna_liese@press.princeton.edu
Dir, Sales: Timothy Wilkins *Tel:* 609-258-4877 *E-mail:* timothy_wilkins@press.princeton.edu
Dir, Web Technol & Servs: Ann Ambrose *E-mail:* ann_ambrose@press.princeton.edu
Global Promos Dir: Julia Haav *Tel:* 609-258-2831 *E-mail:* julia_haav@press.princeton.edu
Intl Sales Dir: Andrew Brewer *E-mail:* andrew_brewer@press.princeton.edu
Mktg Dir: Katie Hope
UK Intl Rts Dir/Digital & Audio Publr: Kim Williams *E-mail:* kimberley_williams@press.princeton.edu
Assoc Dir, Mktg Opers: Leslie Nangle *Tel:* 609-258-5881 *E-mail:* leslie_nangle@press.princeton.edu
Assoc Dir, Sales & Mktg: Laurie Schlesinger *Tel:* 609-258-4898 *E-mail:* laurie_schlesinger@press.princeton.edu
Asst Dir & Dir, Editing, Design & Prodn: Neil Litt *Tel:* 609-258-5066 *E-mail:* neil_litt@press.princeton.edu
Publr (anthropology, religion): Fred Appel *Tel:* 609-258-2484 *E-mail:* fred_appel@press.princeton.edu
Publr (architecture, art): Michelle Komie *Tel:* 609-258-4569 *E-mail:* michelle_komie@press.princeton.edu
Publr (field guides) & Exec Ed (biology, natural history, ornithology): Robert Kirk *Tel:* 609-258-4884 *E-mail:* robert_kirk@press.princeton.edu
Publr (humanities) & Asst Ed-in-Chief (ancient history, archaeology, classics, philosophy, political theory): Robert Tempio *Tel:* 609-258-0843 *E-mail:* robert_tempio@press.princeton.edu
Edit Dir (humanities): Eric Crahan *Tel:* 609-258-4922 *E-mail:* eric_crahan@press.princeton.edu
Edit Dir (sciences): Alison Kalett *Tel:* 609-258-9232 *E-mail:* alison_kalett@press.princeton.edu
Head, Paperback Publg & Exec Ed (sociology): Meagan Levinson *Tel:* 609-258-4908 *E-mail:* meagan_levinson@press.princeton.edu
Exec Ed (literature): Anne Savarese *Tel:* 609-258-4937 *E-mail:* anne_savarese@press.princeton.edu
Exec Ed (mathematics): Vickie Kearn *Tel:* 609-258-2321 *E-mail:* vickie_kearn@press.princeton.edu
Mng Ed: Elizabeth Byrd *Tel:* 609-258-2589 *E-mail:* elizabeth_byrd@press.princeton.edu
Sr Ed (history): Priya Nelson
Sr Ed (humanities): Ben Tate
Sr Ed (economics, finance): Joe Jackson *Tel:* 609-258-9428 *E-mail:* joe_jackson@press.princeton.edu
Sr Ed (political science): Bridget Flannery-McCoy
Ed (computer science, neuroscience): Hallie Stebbins
Ed (engineering, mathematics): Susannah Shoemaker
Assoc Ed (ancient world, philosophy, political theory): Matt Rohal
Assoc Ed (economics, political science): Hannah Paul *E-mail:* hannah_paul@press.princeton.edu
Assoc Ed (history): Amanda Peery *Tel:* 609-258-4920 *E-mail:* amanda_peery@press.princeton.edu
Assoc Ed (physical sciences): Jessica Yao
Asst Ed (history): Thalia Leaf *E-mail:* thalia_leaf@press.princeton.edu

Edit Assoc: Charlie Allen; Lauren Bucca
E-mail: lauren_bucca@press.princeton.
edu; Jacqueline Delaney; Pamela Weidman
E-mail: pamela_weidman@press.princeton.edu;
Kristin Zodrow *E-mail:* kristin_zodrow@press.
princeton.edu
Ed-at-Large (higher education): Peter Daugherty
Tel: 609-258-6778 *E-mail:* peter_daugherty@
press.princeton.edu
Design Mgr: Jessica Massabrook
E-mail: jessica_massabrook@press.princeton.
edu
Mgr, Sciences: Sara Henning-Stout
Perms Mgr: Lisa Black
Promos Mgr: James Schneider; Maria Whelan
Curator, Ideas & Partnerships: Debra Liese
E-mail: debra_liese@press.princeton.edu
Sr Publicist: Katie Lewis *E-mail:* katie_lewis@
press.princeton.edu; Jodi Price
Publicist: Kate Hensley; Tayler Lord
E-mail: tayler_lord@press.princeton.edu
Digital Promos Specialist: Stephanie Rojas
E-mail: stephanie_rojas@press.princeton.edu
Promos Assoc: Nathalie Levine; Alyssa Sanford
Promos Assoc, Sciences: Matt Taylor
E-mail: matt_taylor@press.princeton.edu
Academic Spec Sales & Mktg Assoc: Barbara
Tonetti
Spec Sales & Mktg Assoc: Jennifer Zuccaro
Ad Coord: Meredith McMahon
E-mail: meredith_mcmahon@press.princeton.
edu
Sr Designer: Chris Ferrante
E-mail: chris_ferrante@press.princeton.edu
Exhibits: Melissa Burton *Tel:* 609-258-4915
E-mail: melissa_burton@press.princeton.edu
Founded: 1905
Scholarly, scientific & trade books on all subjects.
ISBN Prefix(es): 978-0-691
Number of titles published annually: 250 Print;
125 E-Book
Total Titles: 4,000 Print; 2,000 E-Book
Imprints: Bollingen Series; PUP Audio
Foreign Office(s): 6 Oxford St, Woodstock, Oxon
OX20 1TR, United Kingdom, Global Pro-
mos Dir: Caroline Priday *Tel:* (01993) 814500
Fax: (01993) 814504 *E-mail:* caroline_priday@
press.princeton.edu
Distributor for Zone Books
Foreign Rep(s): ADP Singapore Pte Ltd (Lilian
Koe) (Malaysia); ADP Singapore Pte Ltd (Ian
Pringle) (Singapore, Southeast Asia); Avicenna
Partnership Ltd (Claire de Gruchy) (Algeria,
Cyprus, Israel, Jordan, Libya, Malta, Morocco,
Palestine, Tunisia, Turkey); Avicenna Partner-
ship Ltd (Bill Kennedy) (Bahrain, Egypt, Iran,
Iraq, Kuwait, Lebanon, Libya, Oman, Qatar,
Saudi Arabia, Syria, United Arab Emirates);
Dominique Bartshukoff (Europe); Book Mar-
keting Services (S Janakiraman) (Bangladesh,
India, Sri Lanka); Craig Faulk (Caribbean,
Central America, South America); Footprint
Books Pty Ltd (Australia, New Zealand); ICK
(Information & Culture Korea) (Se-Yung Jun)
(Korea); Peter Jacques (Europe); Lexa Publish-
ers Representatives (Mical Moser) (Canada);
MHM Ltd (Japan); B K Norton Ltd (Lillian
Hsiao) (Taiwan); Princeton Asia (Beijing) Con-
sulting Co Ltd (Lingxi Li) (China); Rockbook
(Gilles Fauveau) (Japan); University Press
Group (Europe, South Africa, UK); Kelvin van
Hasselt Publishing Services (Africa exc North
& South Africa); World Press (Saleem Malik)
(Pakistan)
Foreign Rights: Akcali Copyright (Mustafa
Urgen) (Turkey); ANA Sofia Ltd (Mira
Droumeva) (Bulgaria, Romania); L'Autre
Agency (Corinne Marotte) (France); Agencia
Literaria Carmen Balcells SA (Maribel Luque)
(Latin America, Spain); Bardon-Chinese Me-
dia Agency (David Tsai) (China); Book/Lab
Literary Agency (Agata Zabowska) (Poland);
Bookman Literary Agency (Mr Ib H Lau-
ritzen) (Denmark, Finland, Iceland, Norway,

Sweden); Dar Cherlin (Amelie Cherlin) (Arab
Middle East); The English Agency (Tsutomu
Yawata) (Japan); Paul & Peter Fritz AG (Chris-
tian Dittus) (Germany); The Deborah Harris
Agency (Geula Geurts) (Israel); JLM Literary
Agency (John L Moukakos) (Greece); Ilidio
Matos Agencia Literaria Lda (Goncalo Gama
Pinto) (Portugal); Andrew Nurnberg Asso-
ciates (Judit Hermann) (Croatia, Hungary);
Andrew Nurnberg Associates (Lucie Polakova)
(Czechia, Slovakia, Slovenia); Andrew Nurn-
berg Associates Baltic (Tatjana Zoldnere) (Es-
tonia, Latvia, Lithuania); Prava i prevodi (Nada
Cipranic) (Montenegro, Serbia); Reiser Literary
Agency (Roberto Gilodi) (Italy); Agencia RIFF
(Joao Paulo Riff) (Brazil); Marianne Schoen-
bach Literary Agency (Marianne Schoenbach)
(Netherlands); Synopsis Literary Agency (Olga
Zasetskaya) (Russia); Eric Yang Agency (Sue
& Jackie Yang) (Korea)
Orders to: Ingram Publisher Services (US,
CN, Asia (except Japan), Australia & Latin
America) *Toll Free Tel:* 866-400-5351
E-mail: ordersupport@ingramcontent.com;
The University Press Group Ltd, New Era Es-
tate, Oldlands Way, Bognor Regis, West Sus-
sex PO22 9NQ, United Kingdom (UK, Eu-
rope & South Africa), Off Mgr: Lois Edwards
Tel: (01243) 842165 *Fax:* (01243) 842167
E-mail: lois@upguk.com
Distribution Center: NewSouth Books, UNSW
Randwick Campus, Bldg R1F, 22-32 King St,
Randwick, NSW 2031, Australia (Australia &
New Zealand) *Tel:* (02) 8936 1400 *Fax:* (02)
8936 1440 *Web Site:* www.newsouthbooks.com.
au
Membership(s): American Association of Univer-
sity Presses (AAUP); Association of American
Publishers (AAP); Book Industry Study Group
(BISG)

Printing Industries of America (PIA), see
PRINTING United Alliance

§PRINTING United Alliance
Formerly Printing Industries of America (PIA);
Specialty Graphic Imaging Association (SGIA)
10015 Main St, Fairfax, VA 22031-3489
Tel: 703-385-1335 *Toll Free Tel:* 888-385-3588
Fax: 703-273-0456
E-mail: assist@printing.org; info@printing.org
Web Site: www.printing.org
Key Personnel
Mgr, Pubn (PA Off): Samuel G Shea
E-mail: sshea@printing.org
Mng Ed: Lauren Searson *E-mail:* lsearson@
printing.org
Founded: 2020 (thru the merger of Printing In-
dustries of America & Specialty Graphic Imag-
ing Association)
Textbooks & reference books on graphic commu-
nications techniques & technology.
ISBN Prefix(es): 978-0-88362
Number of titles published annually: 3 Print; 2 E-
Book
Total Titles: 200 Print; 10 E-Book
Branch Office(s)
1325 "G" St NW, Suite 500, Washington, DC
20005
2000 Corporate Dr, Suite 205, Wexford, PA
15090 *Tel:* 412-741-6860 *Toll Free Tel:* 800-
910-4283 *Fax:* 412-741-2311

PRO-ED Inc
8700 Shoal Creek Blvd, Austin, TX 78757-6897
SAN: 222-1349
Tel: 512-451-3246 *Toll Free Tel:* 800-897-3202
Fax: 512-451-8542 *Toll Free Fax:* 800-397-
7633
E-mail: info@proedinc.com
Web Site: www.proedinc.com

Key Personnel
COO & Gen Coun: Robert Lum *Tel:* 512-451-
3246 ext 664 *E-mail:* blum@proedinc.com
Exec Ed: Kathy Synatschk *E-mail:* ksynatschk@
proedinc.com
Founded: 1977
College & professional reference books, tests,
student materials, journals in education & psy-
chology.
ISBN Prefix(es): 978-0-936104; 978-0-89079;
978-0-88744; 978-1-933014; 978-1-944480;
978-1-4164
Number of titles published annually: 50 Print
Total Titles: 1,500 Print

Pro Lingua Associates Inc
74 Cotton Mill Hill, Suite A-315, Brattleboro, VT
05301
SAN: 216-0579
Tel: 802-257-7779 *Toll Free Tel:* 800-366-4775
Fax: 802-257-5117
E-mail: info@prolinguaassociates.com
Web Site: www.prolinguaassociates.com
Key Personnel
Pres & Publr: Arthur A Burrows *E-mail:* andy@
prolinguaassociates.com
VP & Ed: Raymond C Clark
Treas & Lib Sales Dir: Elise C Burrows
Secy: Mike Jerald
Founded: 1980
Teacher resource handbooks, language teacher
training handbooks, English language & for-
eign language texts.
ISBN Prefix(es): 978-0-86647
Number of titles published annually: 7 Print
Total Titles: 120 Print; 44 Audio
Foreign Rep(s): English Central (Canada); En-
glish Language Bookshop (England); Foreign
Language Bookshop (Australia); Foreign Lan-
guage Ltd (Korea); Independent Publishers In-
ternational (Japan); Nellie's Group Ltd (Japan)
Membership(s): The Children's Book Council
(CBC); TESOL International Association

§Productivity Press
Imprint of CRC Press
711 Third Ave, 8th fl, New York, NY 10017
Tel: 212-216-7800 *Toll Free Tel:* 800-634-7064
(orders); 800-797-3803
E-mail: orders@taylorandfrancis.com
Web Site: www.crcpress.com
Key Personnel
Sr Acqs Ed: Kristine Mednansky *Tel:* 630-
482-9886 *E-mail:* kristine.mednansky@
taylorandfrancis.com; Michael Sinocchi
Tel: 212-216-7867 *E-mail:* michael.sinocchi@
taylorandfrancis.com
Founded: 1983
Books & AV programs. Publishes & distributes
materials on productivity, quality improvement,
product development, corporate management,
profit management & employee involvement
for business & industry. Many products are di-
rect source materials from Japan that have been
translated into English for the first time.
ISBN Prefix(es): 978-0-915299; 978-1-56327;
978-0-527
Number of titles published annually: 12 Print
Total Titles: 200 Print; 4 CD-ROM
Imprints: Healthcare Performance Press; Productivity Press Spanish Imprint
Foreign Rep(s): Asia Pacific Research Center
(Singapore); Books Aplenty (South Africa);
Learning & Productivity (Australia); Prism
Books Private Ltd (India); Productivity Edi-
torial Consultores SPD CV (Mexico)

Professional Communications Inc
1223 W Main, Suite 1427, Durant, OK 74702-
1427
Tel: 580-745-9838 *Toll Free Tel:* 800-337-9838
Fax: 580-745-9837

E-mail: info@pcibooks.com
Web Site: www.pcibooks.com
Key Personnel
Pres & Publr: J Malcolm Beasley *Tel:* 631-661-2852 *Fax:* 631-661-2167 *E-mail:* jmbpci@earthlink.net
VP: Phyllis Jones Freeny
Founded: 1992
Medical publishing & communications company.
ISBN Prefix(es): 978-1-884735; 978-0-9632400; 978-0-932610; 978-1-943236
Number of titles published annually: 5 Print
Total Titles: 55 Print
Branch Office(s)
400 Center Bay Dr, West Islip, NY 11795 (bulk sales only)

§The Professional Education Group LLC (PEG)
700 Twelve Oaks Center Dr, Suite 104, Wayzata, MN 55391
Tel: 952-933-9990 *Toll Free Tel:* 800-229-2531
E-mail: orders@proedgroup.com
Web Site: www.proedgroup.com
Key Personnel
Pres: Henry Lake *E-mail:* henry@proedgroup.com
Founded: 1981
Continuing legal education materials; audio & video programs & books.
ISBN Prefix(es): 978-0-943380; 978-1-932831
Number of titles published annually: 6 Print; 1 CD-ROM; 6 Online
Total Titles: 43 Print; 40 CD-ROM; 40 Online
Distributor for American Bar Association; American Law Institute; Chicago Review Press; Penguin Random House; Wolters Kluwer
Membership(s): Association for Continuing Legal Education (ACLEA)

Professional Publications Inc, see PPI, A Kaplan Company

Professional Resource Press
Imprint of Professional Resource Exchange Inc
3251 New England St, Sarasota, FL 34231
SAN: 240-1223
Mailing Address: PO Box 3197, Sarasota, FL 34230-3197
Tel: 941-343-9601 *Toll Free Tel:* 800-443-3364 (orders & cust serv) *Fax:* 941-343-9201
Toll Free Fax: 866-804-4843 (orders only)
E-mail: cs@prpress.com
Web Site: www.prpress.com
Key Personnel
Pres: Jeffrey D Klosterman *E-mail:* jdk@prpress.com
Mng Ed: Laurie Y Girsch *E-mail:* lyg@prpress.com
Founded: 1980
Books on clinical & forensic psychology, CD-ROMs, DVDs, continuing education programs & texts for mental health & health care professionals. Includes medicine & nursing.
ISBN Prefix(es): 978-0-943158; 978-1-56887
Number of titles published annually: 3 Print; 1 CD-ROM; 4 E-Book; 3 Audio
Total Titles: 230 Print; 10 CD-ROM; 4 E-Book; 17 Audio
Membership(s): The Association of Publishers for Special Sales (APSS)

Progressive Press
3716 37 St, San Diego, CA 92105-2409
SAN: 222-5395
Tel: 619-892-7781 *Fax:* 619-892-7781
E-mail: info@progressivepress.com
Web Site: www.progressivepress.com
Key Personnel
Owner: John-Paul Leonard
Founded: 1973
Small publisher of political trade paperbacks. Also provides distribution for one Canadian

publisher & several self-published authors. Frontlist: politics, backlist: New Age.
ISBN Prefix(es): 978-0-930852; 978-1-61577
Number of titles published annually: 6 Print
Total Titles: 60 Print
Imprints: Arthritis Research; Banned Books; Collections Livrier; Leaves of Healing; Prensa Pensar; Progressive Press; Tree of Life Books
Distributor for Global Research
Foreign Rep(s): Gazelle Book Services Ltd (UK); New Horizons (South Africa); Woodslane (Australia)
Foreign Rights: Beniamino Soressi (Italy); Thinkers Library (Malaysia); Gerhard Wisnewski (Germany)
Membership(s): The Imaging Alliance; Independent Book Publishers Association (IBPA)

Prometheus Books
Imprint of The Globe Pequot Press
59 John Glenn Dr, Amherst, NY 14228-2119
SAN: 202-0289
Tel: 716-691-0133 *Fax:* 716-691-0137
E-mail: marketing@prometheusbooks.com; editorial@prometheusbooks.com; rights@prometheusbooks.com
Web Site: www.prometheusbooks.com
Key Personnel
Publr: Jonathan Kurtz *E-mail:* jkurtz@prometheusbooks.com
VP, Busn & Admin Dir: Lynette Nisbet *E-mail:* lnisbet@prometheusbooks.com
VP, Mktg: Jill Maxick *Tel:* 716-691-0133 ext 219 *E-mail:* jmaxick@prometheusbooks.com
Dir, Rts: Gretchen Kurtz *E-mail:* gkurtz@prometheusbooks.com
Edit Dir, Pyr: Rene Sears *E-mail:* rsears@prometheusbooks.com
Edit Dir, Seventh Street Books: Dan Mayer *E-mail:* dmayer@prometheusbooks.com
Ed-in-Chief: Steven L Mitchell *E-mail:* smitchell@prometheusbooks.com
Ed: Jake Bonar
Mgr, Print-on-Demand Div: Patrick Martin *E-mail:* pmartin@prometheusbooks.com
Founded: 1969
Provocative, progressive & independent nonfiction press publishing under 4 imprints, including 2 genre fiction imprints.
ISBN Prefix(es): 978-0-87975; 978-1-57392; 978-1-59102; 978-1-61614
Number of titles published annually: 85 Print; 85 E-Book
Total Titles: 2,800 Print; 1,800 E-Book
Imprints: Humanity Books (scholarly/academic)
Distribution Center: National Book Network (NBN), 4501 Forbes Blvd, Suite 200, Lanham, MD 20706 *Toll Free Tel:* 800-462-6420 *Toll Free Fax:* 800-338-4550 *E-mail:* customercare@nbnbooks.com *Web Site:* www.nbnbooks.com

§ProQuest LLC
Subsidiary of Cambridge Information Group Inc
789 E Eisenhower Pkwy, Ann Arbor, MI 48108
Mailing Address: PO Box 1346, Ann Arbor, MI 48106-1346
Tel: 734-761-4700 *Toll Free Tel:* 800-521-0600; 877-779-6768 (sales)
E-mail: sales@proquest.com
Web Site: www.proquest.com
Key Personnel
Chmn: Andy Snyder
CEO: Matti Shem Tov
Pres & CFO: Robert VanHees
COO: Yair Amsterdam
CTO: Roger Valade
Pres, ProQuest Books & Chief Strategy Offr: Oren Beit-Arie
Gen Coun: Kevin A Noms
SVP & Gen Mgr, ProQuest Information Solutions: Rafael Sidi

SVP, Global Content Alliances: Julie Carroll-Davis
SVP, Global HR: Marian Roberge
SVP, Global Sales & Mktg: James Holmes
Founded: 1872
Publisher, distributor & aggregator of value-added information to libraries, government, universities & schools in over 160 countries. Access to information in periodicals, newspapers, doctoral dissertations & out of print books (retrospective scholarly works). Produce & publish Dissertation Abstracts International.
ISBN Prefix(es): 978-0-912380; 978-0-88692; 978-0-89093; 978-1-55655; 978-0-8357; 978-0-608; 978-0-7837; 978-0-591; 978-0-9702937; 978-0-599; 978-1-931694; 978-1-59399; 978-0-496; 978-0-542; 978-1-4247; 978-0-9778091; 978-1-4345; 978-0-549; 978-1-60205; 978-1-109; 978-1-124; 978-1-267; 978-1-303; 978-1-321; 978-1-339
Number of titles published annually: 56 Print
Total Titles: 56 Print
Subsidiaries: R R Bowker LLC
Branch Office(s)
699 James L Hart Pkwy, Ypsilanti, MI 48197 *Tel:* 734-879-5300 *Fax:* 734-879-5301
6413 Congress Ave, Suite 260, Boca Raton, FL 33487
620 S Third St, Suite 500, Louisville, KY 40202 *Tel:* 502-583-4111
7500 Old Georgetown Rd, Suite 1400, Bethesda, MD 20814
630 Central Ave, New Providence, NJ 07974 *Tel:* 908-795-3500
888 Seventh Ave, 17th fl, New York, NY 10019 *Tel:* 212-331-7700
3 Ingram Blvd, La Vergne, TN 37086 *Tel:* 615-793-5000
5252 N Edgewood Dr, Suite 125, Provo, UT 84604 *Tel:* 801-765-1737
99 Canal Center Plaza, Suite 200, Alexandria, VA 22314 *Tel:* 703-212-8520
1501 First Ave S, Suite 400, Seattle, WA 98134 *Tel:* 206-336-7510
Foreign Office(s): 607 St Kilda Rd, 1st fl, Melbourne, Victoria 3004, Australia *Tel:* (03) 8517 8333 *Fax:* (03) 8517 8399
Unit 804, Tower E1, Beijing Oriental Plaza, No 1 E Chang An Ave, Dong Cheng District, Beijing 100738, China *Tel:* (010) 5977 6010 *Fax:* (010) 8460 8669
Taskoepruestr 1, 22761 Hamburg, Germany *Tel:* (040) 89 809 0 *Fax:* (040) 89 809 250
16A W Sq, 318 Hennessy Rd, Wanchai, Hong Kong *Tel:* 2836 5636 *Fax:* 2834 7133
315, AKD Tower, Near HUDA Off, Sector 14, Gurgaon 122 001, India *Tel:* (0124) 4100615
Mitsubishi Juko Yokohama Bldg, 3-3-1, Minatomirai, Nishi-ku, Yokohama-shi, Kanagawa 220-8401, Japan *Tel:* (045) 342 4780 *Fax:* (045) 342 4784
B909, Phileo Damansara 1, No 9 Jl 16/11, 46350 Petaling Jaya, Selangor, Malaysia *Tel:* (03) 7954 2880 *Fax:* (03) 7958 3446
Regus Kraanspoor, Kraanspoor 50, 1033 SE Amsterdam, Netherlands *Tel:* (020) 6353190 *Fax:* (020) 6337765
Sungil Bldg, 4th fl, 584 Gangnam-daego, Gangnam-gu, Seoul 06043, South Korea *Tel:* (02) 733-5119 *Fax:* (02) 734-5120
Velazquez 100-5º D, 28006 Madrid, Spain *Tel:* 91 575 5597 *Fax:* 91 575 5585
Al-Thurayya II, Off 1304, PO Box 502568, Dubai, United Arab Emirates *Tel:* (04) 4331810 *Fax:* (04) 3697646
The Quorum, Barnwell Rd, Cambridge CB5 8SW, United Kingdom *Tel:* (01223) 215 512 *Fax:* (01223) 215 513
3 Dorset Rise, 5th fl, London EC4Y 8EN, United Kingdom *Tel:* (020) 7832 1700 *Fax:* (020) 7832 1710

Avon House, Headlands Business Park, Salisbury Rd, Ringwood, Hants BH24 3PB, United Kingdom *Tel:* (01425) 471160
See separate listing for:
R R Bowker LLC

§Prospect Park Books
2359 Lincoln Ave, Altadena, CA 91001
Tel: 626-793-9796
E-mail: info@prospectparkbooks.com
Web Site: www.prospectparkbooks.com
Key Personnel
Publr & Founding Partner: Colleen Dunn Bates
Founded: 2006
Trade publisher.
ISBN Prefix(es): 978-0-9753939; 978-0-9844102; 978-0-9834594; 978-1-938849; 978-1-945551
Number of titles published annually: 10 Print; 8 E-Book
Total Titles: 50 Print; 40 E-Book
Imprints: Raymond Press
Foreign Rights: Kaplan/DeFiore Rights (worldwide)
Warehouse: Ingram Publisher Services, 210 American Dr, Jackson, TN 38301 *Toll Free Tel:* 800-343-4499
Distribution Center: Consortium Book Sales & Distribution, The Keg House, Suite 101, 34 13 Ave NE, Minneapolis, MN 55413-1007 *Tel:* 612-746-2600 *Toll Free Tel:* 800-283-3572 (cust serv, Jackson, TN) *Fax:* 612-746-2606 *E-mail:* info@cbsd.com *Web Site:* www.cbsd.com SAN: 200-6049
Membership(s): Association of American Publishers (AAP); Community of Literary Magazines & Presses (CLMP); International Association of Culinary Professionals (IACP); Publishers Association of the West (PubWest)

ProStar Publications Inc
226 W Florence Ave, Inglewood, CA 90301
SAN: 210-525X
Toll Free Tel: 800-481-6277
E-mail: editor@prostarpublications.com
Web Site: www.prostarpublications.com
Key Personnel
Pres & Publr: Peter L Griffes *E-mail:* peter@prostarpublications.com
Founded: 1965
Books about boating: regional guides, planning, navigation data, nautical charts, marine fauna, how-to, travel, technical, general fiction & music.
ISBN Prefix(es): 978-0-930030; 978-1-57785; 978-1-942388
Number of titles published annually: 145 Print
Total Titles: 440 Print; 30 CD-ROM
Imprints: Atlantic Boating Almanac; Lighthouse Press; Pacific Boating Almanac; US Coast Pilot

§The PRS Group Inc
5800 Heritage Landing Dr, Suite E, East Syracuse, NY 13057-9358
Tel: 315-431-0511 *Fax:* 315-431-0200
E-mail: custserv@prsgroup.com
Web Site: www.prsgroup.com
Key Personnel
Pres & CEO: Christopher McKee
Exec Dir: Dianna Spinner *E-mail:* dspinner@prsgroup.com
Circ Mgr: Patti Davis
Founded: 1979
Over 100 reports, newsletters, journals & volumes per year for international business. No returns without prior approval.
ISBN Prefix(es): 978-1-933539; 978-1-931077; 978-1-941119; 978-1-936241
Number of titles published annually: 3 Print
Total Titles: 20 Print; 100 CD-ROM; 100 Online; 100 E-Book
Imprints: International Country Risk Guide; Political Risk Services

Prufrock Press
PO Box 8813, Waco, TX 76714-8813
SAN: 851-9188
Tel: 254-756-3337 *Toll Free Tel:* 800-998-2208 *Fax:* 254-756-3339 *Toll Free Fax:* 800-240-0333
E-mail: info@prufrock.com
Web Site: www.prufrock.com
Key Personnel
Publr & Mktg Dir: Joel McIntosh *E-mail:* jmcintosh@prufrock.com
Ed & Perms Coord: Katy McDowall *E-mail:* kmcdowall@prufrock.com
Founded: 1977
Publish supplementary text books & teacher guides for grades K-12, including gifted educational materials.
ISBN Prefix(es): 978-1-883055; 978-1-882664; 978-0-931724; 978-1-59363; 978-1-61821
Number of titles published annually: 20 Print
Total Titles: 566 Print
Editorial Office(s): 5926 Balcones Dr, Suite 220, Austin, TX 78731 *Tel:* 512-300-2220 *Fax:* 512-300-2221
Membership(s): Independent Book Publishers Association (IBPA)

PSMJ Resources Inc
10 Midland Ave, Newton, MA 02458
Tel: 617-965-0055 *Toll Free Tel:* 800-537-PSMJ (537-7765) *Fax:* 617-965-5152
Web Site: www.psmj.com
Founded: 1980
Books, survey reports & digital toolbox programs for architects, engineers, interior designers, urban designers, planners, landscape architects on business & financial management; marketing; time & personnel management; legal topics; project management; human resources; newsletters; consulting & educational seminars.
ISBN Prefix(es): 978-1-55538
Number of titles published annually: 15 Print; 12 E-Book
Total Titles: 50 Print; 25 E-Book
Branch Office(s)
2746 Rangewood Dr, Atlanta, GA 30345 *Tel:* 770-723-9651 *Fax:* 815-461-7478
Foreign Office(s): PO Box 773, Artarmon, NSW 2064, Australia *Tel:* (02) 9411 4819 *Fax:* (02) 9419 6044
419 City Rd, South Melbourne, Victoria 3205, Australia *Tel:* (03) 9686-3846 *Fax:* (03) 9686-1958

§Psychological Assessment Resources Inc (PAR)
16204 N Florida Ave, Lutz, FL 33549
Tel: 813-449-4065 *Toll Free Tel:* 800-331-8378 *Fax:* 813-961-2196 *Toll Free Fax:* 800-727-9329
Web Site: www.parinc.com
Key Personnel
Exec Chmn & Founder: R Bob Smith, III *E-mail:* bsmith@parinc.com
CEO: Kristin Greco
Pres & COO: Travis White *E-mail:* twhite@parinc.com
Exec VP & CIO: Jim Eddy
Exec VP & CFO: Donna Drackett
VP, Mktg: Eric Jessen *E-mail:* ejessen@parinc.com
VP, Dist: Greg Presson
Dir, Sales: David Houser
Dir, Prod Devt: Melissa A Messer
Dir, Cust Support: Daniel McFadden *E-mail:* dmcfadden@parinc.com
Founded: 1978
Career, psychological, neuropsychology, educational & clinical assessments products; software.
ISBN Prefix(es): 978-0-911907
Number of titles published annually: 10 Print; 2 CD-ROM; 1 Online

Total Titles: 150 Print; 20 CD-ROM; 3 Online; 5 Audio
Distributed by ACER; Pro-Ed; Western Psychological Service
Distributor for American Guidance Service; Pro-Ed; Rorschach Workshops
Foreign Rep(s): ACER (Australia); Tea Ediciones (Spain); Testzentrale (Germany)
Returns: 16130 N Florida Ave, Lutz, FL 33549 *E-mail:* gpresson@parinc.com
Warehouse: 16130 N Florida Ave, Lutz, FL 33549 *E-mail:* gpresson@parinc.com

Public Citizen
1600 20 St NW, Washington, DC 20009
Tel: 202-588-1000
Web Site: www.citizen.org
Key Personnel
CFO: Joe Stoshak
Pres: Robert Weissman
Founded: 1971
Books & reports; consumer advocacy organization.
ISBN Prefix(es): 978-0-937188; 978-1-58231
Number of titles published annually: 47 Print
Total Titles: 48 Print
Divisions: Congress Watch; Democracy Is For People; Energy Program; Global Trade Watch; Health Research Group; Litigation Group
Branch Office(s)
215 Pennsylvania Ave SE, Washington, DC 20003 *Tel:* 202-546-4996
309 E 11 St, Suite 2, Austin, TX 78701 *Tel:* 512-477-1155
Distributed by Addison-Wesley; Simon & Schuster Pocket Books
Foreign Rights: Random House-Pantheon

§Publication Consultants
8370 Eleusis Dr, Anchorage, AK 99502
Tel: 907-349-2424 *Fax:* 907-349-2426
E-mail: books@publicationconsultants.com
Web Site: www.publicationconsultants.com
Key Personnel
Owner & Publr: Evan Swensen *E-mail:* evan@publicationconsultants.com
Founded: 1978
ISBN Prefix(es): 978-0-9644809; 978-1-888125; 978-1-59433
Number of titles published annually: 50 Print; 50 E-Book
Total Titles: 460 Print; 330 E-Book
Membership(s): Alaska Writers Guild; Better Business Bureau (BBB)

Publications International Ltd (PIL)
8140 N Lehigh Ave, Morton Grove, IL 60053
Tel: 847-676-3470 *Fax:* 847-676-3671
E-mail: customer_service@pubint.com
Web Site: pilbooks.com
Key Personnel
CEO: Louis Weber
VP, Acqs & Proj Mgmt: Jenny Barney
Dir, Natl Accts: Scott Cox
Founded: 1967
ISBN Prefix(es): 978-0-88176; 978-1-56173; 978-1-68022
Number of titles published annually: 400 Print

§Puffin Books
Imprint of Penguin Group USA, A Penguin Random House Company
345 Hudson St, New York, NY 10014
Tel: 212-366-2000
Web Site: www.penguin.com/publishers/puffin
Key Personnel
Pres & Publr: Eileen Bishop Kreit
Assoc Publr & Mng Ed: Gerard Mancini
VP & Exec Art Dir, Penguin Young Readers Design Group: Deborah Kaplan
Penguin Random House & its publishing entities are not accepting unsol submissions, proposals,

mss, or submission queries via e-mail at this time.
Number of titles published annually: 150 Print
Membership(s): The Children's Book Council (CBC)

Purdue University Press
Stewart Ctr 190, 504 W State St, West Lafayette, IN 47907-2058
SAN: 203-4026
Tel: 765-494-2038 *Fax:* 765-496-2442
E-mail: pupress@purdue.edu
Web Site: www.thepress.purdue.edu
Key Personnel
Dir: Justin Race *Tel:* 765-494-8251
    E-mail: racej@purdue.edu
Edit, Design & Prodn Mgr: Katherine Purple
    E-mail: kpurple@purdue.edu
Sales & Mktg Mgr: Bryan Shaffer
    E-mail: bshaffer@purdue.edu
Founded: 1960
Publisher of scholarly titles with emphasis on business, veterinary medicine, health issues & the humanities.
ISBN Prefix(es): 978-0-911198; 978-1-55753
Number of titles published annually: 25 Print; 25 E-Book
Total Titles: 350 Print; 50 E-Book
Foreign Rep(s): The Eurospan Group (Continental Europe, Israel, Middle East, UK)
Orders to: Longleaf Services, 116 S Boundary St, Chapel Hill, NC 27514 *Toll Free Tel:* 800-627-7377 *E-mail:* orders@longleafservices.org *Web Site:* www.longleafservices.org
Distribution Center: Longleaf Services, 116 S Boundary St, Chapel Hill, NC 27514 *Toll Free Tel:* 800-627-7377 *E-mail:* orders@longleafservices.org *Web Site:* www.longleafservices.org
UTP Distribution, 5201 Dufferin St, Toronto, ON M3H 5T8, Canada *Toll Free Tel:* 800-565-9523 *E-mail:* utpbooks@utpress.utoronto.ca *Web Site:* www.utpdistribution.com
Eurospan Group, Gray's Inn House, 127 Clerkenwell Rd, London EC1R 5DB, United Kingdom (worldwide exc CN & US) *Tel:* (01767) 604972 *E-mail:* info@eurospangroup.com *Web Site:* www.eurospanbookstore.com/purdue
Membership(s): American Association of University Presses (AAUP)

Purple House Press
Imprint of Purple House Inc
8100 US Hwy 62 E, Cynthiana, KY 41031
Mailing Address: PO Box 787, Cynthiana, KY 41031
Tel: 859-235-9970
Web Site: www.purplehousepress.com
Key Personnel
Publr: Jill Morgan *E-mail:* jill@purplehousepress.com
Dir, Cust Fulfillment, Managed Info Servs: Ray Sanders *E-mail:* ray@purplehousepress.com
Prepress & Clerical: Hayley Morgan-Sanders
    E-mail: hayley@purplehousepress.com
Founded: 2000
Reissue of children's classics from the 1920s-1990s.
ISBN Prefix(es): 978-1-930900
Number of titles published annually: 8 Print; 2 E-Book
Total Titles: 75 Print; 20 E-Book
Foreign Rights: McIntosh & Otis (worldwide)

Purple Mountain Press Ltd
1064 Main St, Fleischmanns, NY 12430
Mailing Address: PO Box 309, Fleischmanns, NY 12430-0309 SAN: 222-3716
Tel: 845-254-4062 *Toll Free Tel:* 800-325-2665 (orders) *Fax:* 845-254-4476
E-mail: purple@catskill.net
Web Site: www.catskill.net/purple

Key Personnel
Pres & Publr: Wray Rominger
Founded: 1973
Publish adult nonfiction books about colonial history & New York State; history, natural history, folklore, the arts, outdoor recreation, a few regional mysteries, also maritime books.
ISBN Prefix(es): 978-0-935796; 978-0-916346; 978-1-930098
Number of titles published annually: 6 Print
Total Titles: 150 Print
Divisions: Harbor Hill Books
Distributor for Carmania Press London (North America only)

Pushcart Press
PO Box 380, Wainscott, NY 11975-0380
SAN: 202-9871
Tel: 631-324-9300
Web Site: www.pushcartprize.com/pushcartpress
Key Personnel
Pres: Bill Henderson
Founded: 1972
Trade books, literary anthologies.
ISBN Prefix(es): 978-0-916366; 978-1-888889
Number of titles published annually: 6 Print
Total Titles: 65 Print
Distributed by W W Norton & Company Inc
Distribution Center: 500 Fifth Ave, New York, NY 10110

GP Putnam's Sons (Children's)
Member of Penguin Young Readers Group
345 Hudson St, New York, NY 10014
Tel: 212-366-2000 *Fax:* 212-414-3393
Web Site: www.penguin.com/publishers/gpputnamssonsbooksforyoungread
Key Personnel
Pres & Publr, Nancy Paulsen Books: Nancy Paulsen
Pres & Publr, Putnam Books for Young Readers & Razorbill: Jennifer Klonsky
VP & Art Dir: Cecilia Yung
Assoc Dir, Publg, Putnam/Dutton/Berkley: Liza Cassity
Assoc Edit Dir: Susan Kochan
Exec Ed: Arianne Lewin
Sr Ed: Stacey Barney
Ed, Nancy Paulsen Books: Sara LaFleur
Assoc Ed: Katherine Perkins
Asst Ed: Kate Meltzer
Edit Asst: Amalia Frick
Founded: 1838
Penguin Random House & its publishing entities are not accepting unsol submissions, proposals, mss, or submission queries via e-mail at this time.
Number of titles published annually: 51 Print
Total Titles: 386 Print
Membership(s): The Children's Book Council (CBC)

GP Putnam's Sons (Hardcover)
Imprint of Penguin Group USA, A Penguin Random House Company
375 Hudson St, New York, NY 10014
Tel: 212-366-2000 *Fax:* 212-366-2643
E-mail: online@penguinputnam.com
Web Site: www.penguin.com/publishers/gpputnamssons
Key Personnel
Pres: Ivan Held
SVP & Publr, Putnam: Sally Kim
SVP & Dir, Publg Mgmt: Catharine Lynch
VP & Assoc Publr, Paperbacks: Benjamin Lee
VP & Dir, Publicity: Alexis Welby
VP & Prodn Dir: William Peabody
VP & Exec Ed: Christine Pepe; Mark Tavani
Assoc Publr & Mktg Dir, Putnam: Ashley Pattison McClay
Exec Dir, Ad & Promo: Jaime Mendola-Hobbie
Art Dir: Claire Vaccaro

Dir, Copy Editing: Linda Rosenberg
Assoc Dir, Publg, Putnam/Dutton/Berkley: Liza Cassity
Exec Ed: Tara Singh Carlson; Michelle Howry
Sr Ed: Sara Minnich
Assoc Ed: Danielle Dieterich; Gabriella Mongelli
Asst Ed: Danielle Springer
Sr Publicity Mgr: Ashley Hewlett
Mktg Mgr, Putnam/Dutton: Katie Parry
Asst Mktg Mgr, Putnam: Brennin Cummings; Anna Romig
Publicist: Kristen Bianco; Elora Weil
Assoc Publicist: Carolyn Darr; Bonnie Rice; Madeline Schmitz
Founded: 1838
Fiction & general nonfiction.
Penguin Random House & its publishing entities are not accepting unsol submissions, proposals, mss, or submission queries via e-mail at this time.
Number of titles published annually: 65 Print
Total Titles: 208 Print
Imprints: Putnam; Marian Wood Books
Advertising Agency: Mesa Group

Pyncheon House
6 University Dr, Suite 105, Amherst, MA 01002
SAN: 297-6269
Key Personnel
Ed-in-Chief: David R Rhodes
Founded: 1991
Fine editions & trade books; contemporary poetry, short fiction, novels & essays; member of Library of Congress CIP Program.
ISBN Prefix(es): 978-1-881119
Number of titles published annually: 5 Print
Total Titles: 17 Print

Quail Ridge Press (QRP)
Imprint of Southwestern Publishing House Inc
2451 Atrium Way, Nashville, TN 37214
Toll Free Tel: 800-358-0560 *Fax:* 615-391-2815
Web Site: www.swphbooks.com/quail-ridge-press.html
Key Personnel
Publr: Sheila Thomas *E-mail:* sthomas@swpublishinggroup.com
Founded: 1978
Cookbook publisher.
ISBN Prefix(es): 978-0-937552; 978-1-893062; 978-1-938879; 978-1-934193
Number of titles published annually: 4 Print
Total Titles: 150 Print

§Quality Medical Publishing Inc
11802 Borman Dr, St Louis, MO 63146
Tel: 314-878-7808
E-mail: customerservice@qmp.com
Web Site: www.qmp.com
Key Personnel
Pres & CEO: Andrew Berger *E-mail:* aberger@qmp.com
Founded: 1986
Medical books (especially surgery); plastic, neurological, spine & orthopaedics.
ISBN Prefix(es): 978-0-942219; 978-1-57626
Number of titles published annually: 16 Print
Total Titles: 145 Print; 2 CD-ROM
Imprints: QMP

Quarto Publishing Group USA Inc
Division of Quarto Group Inc (London, UK)
100 Cummings Ctr, Suite 265D, Beverly, MA 01915
Tel: 978-282-9590 *Toll Free Tel:* 800-328-0590 (sales) *Fax:* 978-283-2742
E-mail: sales@quartous.com
Web Site: www.quartoknows.com
Key Personnel
CEO: Ken Fund
Dir, New Busn Devt: Scott Sheppard *Tel:* 978-282-3581 *E-mail:* scott.sheppard@quarto.com

Mktg Dir: Kristine Anderson *E-mail:* kristine.anderson@quarto.com

Sales Opers Mgr: Deb Moreau *Tel:* 978-272-3510 *E-mail:* deb.moreau@quarto.com

Founded: 2004

Represents a dynamic group of imprints dedicated to providing quality & excellence to its readers. Each imprint embodies the breadth & scope of its specialty topics.

ISBN Prefix(es): 978-0-86573; 978-0-7603; 978-1-59253; 978-0-929261; 978-1-56010; 978-1-59233; 978-1-58923; 978-1-59186; 978-1-61673; 978-1-61058; 978-1-61059; 978-1-61060; 978-1-62788; 978-0-89738; 978-0-912612; 978-1-63159; 978-0-9640392; 978-1-888608; 978-1-930604; 978-1-936309; 978-1-60058; 978-1-937994; 978-1-939581; 978-1-63106; 978-1-63322; 978-1-942875

Number of titles published annually: 300 Print

Total Titles: 4,000 Print

Imprints: becker&mayer!; Book Sales; Burgess Lea Press; Cool Springs Press; Creative Publishing International; Fair Winds Press; Walter Foster Jr; Walter Foster Publishing; Harvard Common Press; MoonDance Press; Motorbooks; Quarry Books; QDS; Race Point Publishing; Rock Point Gift & Stationery; Rockport Publishers; Seagrass Press; SmartLab Toys; Voyager Press; Wellfleet Press

Branch Office(s)

26391 Crown Valley Pkwy, Suite 220, Mission Viejo, CA 92691 *Tel:* 949-380-7510 *Fax:* 949-380-7575

142 W 36 St, 4th fl, New York, NY 10018 *Tel:* 212-779-4972 *Fax:* 212-779-6058

11120 NE 33 Place, Suite 201, Bellevue, WA 98004 *Tel:* 425-827-7120 *Fax:* 425-828-9659

Distributed by Allen & Unwin (Australia & New Zealand); Hachette Book Group (North America)

Distributor for CLEVER Publishing

See separate listing for:

Book Sales

Fair Winds Press

Walter Foster Publishing Inc

Harvard Common Press

Quincannon Publishing Group

PO Box 8100, Glen Ridge, NJ 07028-8100

Tel: 973-380-9942

E-mail: editors@quincannongroup.com (query first via e-mail)

Web Site: www.quincannongroup.com

Key Personnel

Ed-in-Chief: Alan Quincannon

Ed: Holly Benedict

Trade Sales/Consulting Ed: Jeanne Wilcox

Lib Sales/Admin Asst: Patricia McCauley

Publicity: Nora Dempsey

Founded: 1990

Regional mystery novels made unique by involving some element of a region's history (i.e. the story's setting & time frame or the mystery's origin). Custom tailored history books for local or regional museums, municipalities & organizations. May consider historical fiction tied to a local or regional museum.

ISBN Prefix(es): 978-1-878452

Number of titles published annually: 3 Print

Total Titles: 24 Print

Imprints: Compass Point Mysteries; Jersey Yarns; Learning & Coloring Books; Quincannon; Rune-Tales; Tory Corner Editions

§Quintessence Publishing Co Inc

411 N Raddant Rd, Batavia, IL 60510

SAN: 215-9783

Tel: 630-736-3600 *Toll Free Tel:* 800-621-0387 *Fax:* 630-736-3633

E-mail: contact@quintbook.com; service@quintbook.com

Web Site: www.quintpub.com

Key Personnel

Pres: H W Haase

EVP: William Hartman *Tel:* 630-736-3600 ext 413 *E-mail:* whartman@quintbook.com

Founded: 1950

Professional & scholarly books, journals, medicine, dentistry, health & nutrition, medical history.

ISBN Prefix(es): 978-0-931386; 978-0-86715; 978-1-85097; 978-1-883695

Number of titles published annually: 20 Print; 2 CD-ROM

Total Titles: 410 Print; 80 CD-ROM; 250 Audio

Imprints: Quintessence Books; Quintessence of Dental Technology; Quintessence Pockets

Foreign Office(s): 2-4 Ifenpfad, 12107 Berlin, Germany *Tel:* (030) 761-805 *Fax:* (030) 761-80693 *E-mail:* info@quintessenz.de *Web Site:* www.quintessenz.de

Quint House Bldg, 326 Hongo, Bunkyo-ku Tokyo, Japan *Tel:* (03) 5842-2270 *Fax:* (03) 5800-7598 *E-mail:* info@quint-j.co.jp *Web Site:* www.quint-j.co.jp

2 Graston Rd, New Malden, Surrey KT3 3AB, United Kingdom *Tel:* (020) 8949-6087 *Fax:* (020) 8336-1484 *E-mail:* info@quintpub.co.uk *Web Site:* www.quintpub.co.uk

Distributor for Quintessence Publishing Co Ltd (Japan); Quintessence Publishing Ltd (London); Quintessence Verlags GmbH

Advertising Agency: QPC Advertising Inc

Quirk Books

215 Church St, Philadelphia, PA 19106

Tel: 215-627-3581 *Fax:* 215-627-5220

E-mail: general@quirkbooks.com

Web Site: www.quirkbooks.com

Key Personnel

Owner & CEO, Quirk Productions: David Borgenicht

Pres & Publr: Brett Cohen

VP, Digital & Print Prodn: John McGurk

VP, Publicity & Mktg: Nicole De Jackmo

VP, Sales: Moneka Hewlett

Edit Dir: Jhanteigh Kupihea *E-mail:* jhanleigh@quirkbooks.com

Exec Mng Ed: Mary Ellen Wilson

Sr Ed: Rick Chillot *E-mail:* rick@quirkbooks.com

Proj Ed: Jane Morley

Asst Ed: Rebecca Gyllenhaal

Sr Contracts Mgr: Shaquona Crews

Mktg Mgr & Publicist: Jennifer Murphy

Assoc Sales Mgr: Kate Brown

Media Coord: Christina Schillaci

Founded: 2002

Publishing list focuses on irreverent pop-culture, humor, gift, self-help & "impractical" reference books. The actual subject matter of our books is quite diverse. Publish everything from childcare tips & magic tricks to advice on stain removal. All of our books have a distinct sense of style, a refreshing sense of humor & innovative production values.

ISBN Prefix(es): 978-1-931686; 978-1-59474

Number of titles published annually: 25 Print

Total Titles: 150 Print

Distribution Center: Penguin Random House Publisher Services, 1745 Broadway, New York, NY 10019 *Toll Free Tel:* 800-733-3000 *Toll Free Fax:* 800-659-2436 *E-mail:* distribution@penguinrandomhouse.com

Quite Specific Media Group Ltd

Division of Silman-James Press Inc

141 N Clark Dr, Unit 1, West Hollywood, CA 90048

Tel: 310-205-0665

E-mail: info@silmanjamespress.com

Web Site: www.quitespecificmedia.com; www.silmanjamespress.com

Key Personnel

Publr: Ralph Pine

Founded: 1967

Publish original books as well as co-publish with foreign publishers. Specialize in costumes, fashion & theatre.

ISBN Prefix(es): 978-0-89676

Number of titles published annually: 8 Print

Total Titles: 380 Print

Imprints: By Design Press; Costume & Fashion Press; Drama Publishers; EntertainmentPro; Jade Rabbit; Pat MacKay Projects

Foreign Rep(s): Nick Hern Books (UK)

Orders to: Silman-James Press Inc *Tel:* 323-661-9922 *Toll Free Tel:* 877-SJP-BOOK (757-2665) *Fax:* 323-661-9933 *E-mail:* info@silmanjamespress.com

Distribution Center: Silman-James Press Inc *Fax:* 323-214-7943 *E-mail:* info@silmanjamespress.com

Quixote Press

3544 Blakslee St, Wever, IA 52658

Tel: 319-372-7480 *Toll Free Tel:* 800-571-2665 *Fax:* 319-372-7485

E-mail: heartsntummies@gmail.com

Key Personnel

Pres: Bruce Carlson

Founded: 1985

Regional paperback books of humor or folklore & cookbooks. Consulting work for self-publishers.

ISBN Prefix(es): 978-1-878488; 978-1-57166

Number of titles published annually: 30 Print

Total Titles: 350 Print

Divisions: Black Iron Cookin' Co; Hearts 'n Tummies Cookbook Co; Kid Help Publishing Co; PYO (Publish Your Own Co); Raise the Dough in 30 Days Co

See separate listing for:

Hearts 'n Tummies Cookbook Co

§Radix Press

Subsidiary of UGF/OR

11715 Bandlon Dr, Houston, TX 77072

Tel: 281-879-5688

Web Site: www.vvfh.org; www.specialforcesbooks.com

Key Personnel

Dir: Stephen Sherman *E-mail:* sherman1@flash.net

Founded: 1983

Directories, reference books. All unsol mss sent will be discarded.

ISBN Prefix(es): 978-0-9624009; 978-0-9623992; 978-1-929932

Number of titles published annually: 3 Print; 1 CD-ROM; 2 E-Book

Total Titles: 60 Print; 14 CD-ROM; 9 E-Book

Imprints: Electric Strawberry Press

§Rainbow Books Inc

PO Box 430, Highland City, FL 33846-0430

SAN: 221-9859

Tel: 863-648-4420 *Fax:* 863-647-5951

E-mail: rbibooks@aol.com

Web Site: www.rainbowbooksinc.com

Key Personnel

Pres: Betsy A Lampe

VP: Charles M Lampe

Founded: 1978

How-to & self-help for both the adult lay & the juvenile markets; mystery & women's fiction titles for adults.

ISBN Prefix(es): 978-0-935834; 978-1-56825

Number of titles published annually: 10 Print; 10 E-Book

Total Titles: 120 Print; 23 E-Book

Foreign Rep(s): Hagenbach & Bender (worldwide exc USA)

Foreign Rights: HBG Productions & International Publishers Alliance (worldwide exc USA)

Returns: 5435 Highlands Vue Lane, Lakeland, FL 33812 (must get prior authorization. Location is residential)

Warehouse: Publishers Storage & Shipping Corp, 660 S Mansfield St, Ypsilanti, MI 48197-5167, Contact: Donna Moore *Tel:* 734-487-9720 *Fax:* 734-487-1890 *E-mail:* dmoore@psscmi.com *Web Site:* www.pssc.com

Membership(s): Association of American Publishers (AAP); Florida Authors & Publishers Association Inc (FAPA)

§RAND Corp
1776 Main St, Santa Monica, CA 90407-2138
Mailing Address: PO Box 2138, Santa Monica, CA 90407-2138
Tel: 310-393-0411 *Fax:* 310-393-4818
Web Site: www.rand.org
Key Personnel
Mng Dir, Off External Aff: Jeremy Rawitch
  E-mail: jrawitch@rand.org
Dir, Publg: Paul Murphy *E-mail:* murphy@rand.org
Assoc Dir, Communs: Steve Kistler
Mng Ed: Erin-Elizabeth Johnson
  E-mail: ejohnson@rand.org
Mgr, Busn: Laura Shaw *E-mail:* lshaw@rand.org
Mgr, Prodn: Todd Duft *E-mail:* duft@rand.org
Print & Dist Mgr: Tim Erickson *Tel:* 310-393-0411 ext 6141 *E-mail:* tim@rand.org
Cust Serv Supv: Amy Majczyk *Tel:* 412-683-2300 ext 4929 *E-mail:* amajczyk@rand.org
Founded: 1948
Public policy research.
ISBN Prefix(es): 978-0-8330
Number of titles published annually: 400 Print; 100 Online; 50 E-Book
Total Titles: 30,000 Print; 24,000 Online; 1,800 E-Book
Divisions: Office of External Affairs
Foreign Rep(s): NBN Canada (Canada); NBN/DA Trade (Australia, New Zealand); NBN International (Europe, Middle East, UK)
Orders to: RAND Distribution Services, 4570 Fifth Ave, Pittsburgh, PA 15213, Cust Serv Mgr: Amy Majczyk *Tel:* 310-451-7002 *Toll Free Tel:* 877-584-8642 *Fax:* 412-683-2800 *E-mail:* order@rand.org
Distribution Center: National Book Network, 15200 NBN Way, Blue Ridge Summit, PA 17214 *Tel:* 717-794-3800 *Toll Free Tel:* 800-462-6420 *Toll Free Fax:* 800-338-4550 *E-mail:* vfunk@nbnbooks.com *Web Site:* www.nbnbooks.com
Membership(s): AIGA, the professional association for design; American Association of University Presses (AAUP); Public Relations Society of America Inc (PRSA); Society for Scholarly Publishing (SSP)

§Rand McNally
9855 Woods Dr, Skokie, IL 60077
SAN: 203-3917
Mailing Address: PO Box 7600, Chicago, IL 60680-7600
Tel: 847-329-8100 *Toll Free Tel:* 877-446-4863 *Toll Free Fax:* 877-469-1298
E-mail: mediarelations@randmcnally.com; tndsupport@randmcnally.com
Web Site: www.randmcnally.com
Key Personnel
CEO: Stephen Fletcher
CTO: Yusuf Ozturk
VP, Mktg: Kendra Ensor
Design Dir: Joerg Metzner
Prod Mgr: Mastan Holtzer
Founded: 1856
Road atlases & maps; world atlases; mileage & routing publications & software; educational maps, atlases; children's atlases, maps, books; electronic multimedia products; retail & online stores; online travel services, travel software.
Publisher of the *Thomas Guide* atlas series.
ISBN Prefix(es): 978-0-528
Number of titles published annually: 20 Print
Total Titles: 100 Print; 5 CD-ROM

Imprints: Rand McNally for Kids
Warehouse: 106 Hi-Lane, Richmond, KY 40475

Rand Smith LLC, see Rand-Smith Publishing

Rand-Smith Publishing
204 College Ave, Ashland, VA 23005
Tel: 804-874-6012
E-mail: randsmithllc@gmail.com
Web Site: www.rand-smith.com
Key Personnel
Publr: David Smitherman
Acqs: Jeff Howard
Founded: 2019
ISBN Prefix(es): 978-1-950544
Number of titles published annually: 15 Print; 15 E-Book
Total Titles: 4 Print; 4 E-Book
Distribution Center: Ingram

Peter E Randall Publisher
5 Greenleaf Woods Dr, Suite 102, Portsmouth, NH 03801
Mailing Address: PO Box 4726, Portsmouth, NH 03802-4726
Tel: 603-431-5667 *Fax:* 603-431-3566
E-mail: media@perpublisher.com
Web Site: www.perpublisher.com
Key Personnel
Owner & CEO: Deidre C Randall
  E-mail: deidre@perpublisher.com
Founded: 1970
This publisher has indicated that 100% of their product line is author subsidized.
ISBN Prefix(es): 978-0-914339; 978-1-931807; 978-0-9817898; 978-0-9828236; 978-1-937721
Number of titles published annually: 20 Print; 5 E-Book

Random House Children's Books
Division of Penguin Random House LLC
1745 Broadway, 10th fl, New York, NY 10019
Tel: 212-782-9000
Web Site: www.randomhousekids.com
Key Personnel
Pres & Publr: Barbara Marcus
Pres & Publr, Beginner Books & Dr Seuss Publg Prog: Cathy Goldsmith
EVP, Publg Opers: Rich Romano
EVP & Deputy Publr: Judith Haut
SVP & Publr, Delacorte Press: Beverly Horowitz
SVP & Publr, Random House/Golden Books, Doubleday & Crown Books for Young Readers Group: Mallory Loehr
SVP & Dir, Prodn: Linda Palladino
SVP, Mktg: John Adamo
VP & Publr, Crown Books for Young Readers: Emily Easton; Phoebe Yeh
VP & Publg Dir, Classic Brands & PreK: Sonali Fry
VP & Publg Dir, Schwartz & Wade Books: Anne Schwartz; Lee Wade
VP & Exec Dir, Publicity & Corp Communs: Dominique Cimina
VP & Dir, Brand/Category Mgmt: Enid Chaban
VP, Retail & Dist Sales: Becky Green
VP & Dir, Natl Accts, Mass Mdse Sales: Christina Jeffries
VP & Assoc Publg Dir: Michelle Nagler
VP & Exec Mng Ed: Denise DeGennaro
VP, Group Sales Dir & Dir, Mass Mdse Sales: Mark Santella
VP, Mktg, Licensed & Proprietary Brands: Kerri Benvenuto
VP, Subs Rts Mkts: Pam White
Sr Exec Art Dir: Tracy Tyler; Roberta Ludlow
Exec Dir, Copy-Editing: Alison Kolani
Exec Dir, Mktg Prodn & Opers: Beth Conte
Exec Dir, Publicity: Noreen Herits
Exec Dir, School & Lib Mktg: Adrienne Waintraub
Exec Edit Dir: Maria Modugno

Edit Dir: Caroline Abbey
Sr Dir, Digital Mktg: Kate Keating
Dir, Category Mktg: Diana Blough
Dir, Intl Rts & Proprietary Publg: Jocelyn Lange
Dir, Mng Edit: Janet Foley
Dir, Publicity: Mary McCue
Dir, Publicity Events: Casey Ward
Publg Dir, Random House Graphic: Gina Gagliano
Assoc Publg Dir & Exec Ed, Knopf/Crown: Nancy Siscoe
Sr Art Dir: Sharon Burkle; Nicole de las Heras; Alison Impey; Maureen McLaughlin; April Ward
Art Dir, Random House Books for Young Readers: Jan Gerardi
Art Dir, Random House/Golden Books for Young Readers: Jason Zamajtuk
Art Dir, Visual Mdsg: So Lin Wong
Assoc Art Dir, KDD Art Group: Stephanie Moss
Assoc Art Dir: Sarah Hokanson
Assoc Dir, Copyediting: Melinda Ackell
Assoc Dir, Publicity: Jillian Vandall
Assoc Dir, Publg Opers Busn Process & Support: Hanna Glidden
Asst Art Dir: Katrina Damkoehler; Catherine Mucciardi; Jinna Shin
Sr Exec Ed: Sara Sargent
Sr Exec Ed, Delacorte Press: Wendy Loggia; Krista Marino
Exec Ed: Alice Jonaitis
Mng Ed: Jennifer Baker
Sr Mktg Mgr: Stephanie O'Cain
Sr Mktg Mgr, Digital: Cayla Rasi
Sr Prodn Mgr: Tracy Heydweiller; Mary Ellen Owens
Assoc, Publicity & Corp Communs: Elena Meuse
Sr Publicist: Kristopher Kam; Josh Redlich
Publicist: Lili Feinberg
Assoc Publicist: Emma Benshoff
Edit Dir, Knopf Children's: Erin Clarke
Edit Dir, Little Golden Books & Sesame Street: Andrea Posner-Sanchez
Edit Dir, Sesame Workshop, Random House Books for Young Readers: Naomi Kleinberg
Ed-in-Chief & Exec Dir, Licensed Publg, Golden Books: Chris Angelilli
Ed-in-Chief, Doubleday/Golden Books: Frances Gilbert
Exec Ed, Random House Books for Young Readers: Heidi Kilgras
Exec Ed, Random House Books for Young Readers/Golden Books Group: Mary Man-Kong
Exec Creative Dir: Martha Rago
Edit Dir, Novelty, Random House/Golden Books Young Readers Group: Dennis Shealy
Dir, Digital Mktg & Strategy: Elizabeth Ward
Dir, Licensing: Rachel Bader
Dir, Mktg, Licensed & Proprietary Brands: Derek Elmer
Dir, Trade Mktg: Kelly McGauley
Assoc Publg Dir, Knopf Children's: Melanie Nolan
Asst Art Dir: Regina Flath
Asst Dir, Licensed & Proprietary Brands: Krister Engstrom
Mng Ed, Opers: Megan Williams
Sr Ed, Knopf Books for Young Readers: Michele Burke
Sr Ed, Knopf Children's: Katherine Harrison
Sr Ed, Random House/Golden Books Young Readers Group: Diane Landolf
Sr Ed, Random House Graphic: Whitney Leopard
Sr Ed, Schwartz & Wade Books: Annie Kelley
Ed: Kristen Depken; Meika Hashimoto
Ed, Delacorte Press: Kelsey Horton
Ed, Knopf Children's: Kelly Delaney
Ed, Rodale Kids: Dani Valladares
Assoc Ed: Rachel Chlebowski; Lauren Clauss; Sasha Henriques; Michael Joosten; Jenna Lettice; Tricia Lin
Assoc Ed, Classic Brand Team: Maria Correa
Assoc Ed, Delacorte Press: Audrey Ingerson; Monica Jean

Assoc Ed, Golden Books: Courtney Carbone
Assoc Ed, Knopf Children's: Marisa Dinovis; Karen Greenberg
Assoc Ed, Wendy Lamb Books: Dana Carey
Asst Ed: Polo Orozco
Asst Ed, Knopf Books for Young Readers: Stephen Brown
Asst Ed, Schwartz & Wade: Stephanie Pitts
Copy Ed: Stephanie Bay
Assoc Copy Ed: Bess Schelper; Madelin Stone
Sr Mgr, Digital Mktg: Jenn Inzetta; Hanna Lee
Sr Mktg Mgr: Kristin Schulz
Sr Mktg Mgr, Licensed & Proprietary Brands Mktg: Lauren Adams
Sr Prodn Mgr: Jennifer Moreno
Sr Prod Mgr, Digital Mktg: Whitney Aaronson
Mgr, Lib Mktg: Emily Duval
Mktg & Publicity Mgr, Random House Graphic: Nicole Valdez
Mktg Mgr: Hannah Black; Tara Greico; Jules Kelly
Mktg Mgr, Licensed & Proprietary Brands: Danielle Klimashousky
Prodn Mgr: Thomas Marshall
Assoc E-Mail Mktg Mgr: Annie Gardner
Assoc Mgr, Digital Mktg: Laura Hernandez
Assoc Mgr, Prod Devt: Kate Glider
Assoc Mgr, Subs Rts Dept: Mariana Ramos
Assoc Prodn Mgr: Natalia Dextre
Asst Mgr, Prodn: Claribel Vasquez
Asst Mgr, School & Lib Mktg: Emily Petrick
Asst Mgr, School Mktg: Natalie Capogrossi
Asst Mgr, Subs Rts: Kristina Forest; Lauren Diaz Morgan
Mktg Assoc: Jena DeBois
Mktg Coord: Anika Bates; David Gilmore; Megan Mitchell
Exec Mng Prodr: Alison Folino
Prodn Supv: Maggie Gibson; Elizabeth Peskin; Alice Rahaeuser; Erika Schwartz
Prodn Assoc: Lauren Diethelm; Luke McCord
Publg Consultant: Robin Corey
Sr Designer: Melanie Bermudez; Bob Bianchini; Xiomara Nieves; Ray Shappel
Sr Designer, Interior Design Team: Andrea Lau
Sr Designer, Middle Grade: Carol Ly
Sr Mktg Designer: Michael Caiati
Designer: Cathy Bobak; Michelle Cunningham; Casey Moses
Designer, Brand Mktg Design Team: Allyssa Price
Designer, Brands & Licensing Team: Michelle Kim
Designer, Interior Design Team: Jen Valero
Designer, Trade Mktg Design Team: Michael Caiati
Jr Designer: Monique Razzouk
Sr Developer, Digital Mktg: Rob Roglev
Creative Servs Admin: Stacey Sundar
Penguin Random House & its publishing entities are not accepting unsol submissions, proposals, mss, or submission queries via e-mail at this time.
Imprints: Bluefire; Crown Books for Young Readers; Delacorte Press; Dragonfly Books; Ember; Golden Books; Alfred A Knopf Books for Young Readers; Laurel-Leaf; Make Me A World; The Princeton Review; Random House Books for Young Readers; Random House Graphic; Rodale Kids; Schwartz & Wade Books; Sylvan Learning; Underlined; Wendy Lamb Books; Yearling Books
Warehouse: Crawfordsville Distribution Center, 1019 N State Rd 47, Crawfordsville, IN 47933
Distribution Center: Crawfordsville Distribution Center, 1019 N State Rd 47, Crawfordsville, IN 47933
See separate listing for:
The Princeton Review

Random House Publishing Group
Division of Penguin Random House LLC
1745 Broadway, New York, NY 10019

SAN: 202-5507
Toll Free Tel: 800-200-3552
Web Site: www.randomhousebooks.com
Key Personnel
Pres & Publr: Gina Centrello
Pres & COO: Nihar Malaviya
Pres & Dir, Strategic Devt: Nina von Moltke
Group EVP & Dir, Busn & Publg Opers: Bill Takes
CFO, Penguin Random House: James Johnston
EVP & Publr, Ballantine Bantam Dell: Kara Welsh
EVP & Publr, Digital Content: Scott Shannon
EVP, Assoc Publr & Exec Edit Dir: Kate Medina
EVP, Exec Creative Dir, Mktg & PR: Theresa Zoro
EVP, Corp Communs: Claire von Schilling
Group SVP & Creative Dir: Paolo Pepe
SVP & Deputy Publr, Random House/Spiegel & Grau/One World; Publr, The Modern Library: Tom Perry
SVP & Exec Dir, Publg Opers: Lisa Feuer
SVP & Exec Dir, Subs Rts: Denise Cronin
SVP & Dir, Mktg & Busn Devt: Leigh Marchant
SVP & Dir, Penguin Random House Intl Sales & Mktg: Cyrus Kheradi
SVP & Dir, Publicity: Susan Corcoran
SVP & Edit Dir: Linda Marrow
SVP & Ed-in-Chief: Robin Desser
SVP & Ed-in-Chief, Ballantine Bantam Dell: Jennifer Hershey
SVP, Backlist Strategy & Devt: Hannah Rahill; Matt Schwartz
SVP, Digital Marketplace Devt: Amanda Close
SVP, Global Mergers & Acqs: Manuel Sansigre
SVP, Group Sales Dir: Cynthia Lasky
VP & Deputy Publr, Del Rey/VP & Dir, Licensing, Random House Group: Keith Clayton
VP & Deputy Publr, Fiction: Avideh Bashirrad
VP & Assoc Publr: Gina Wachtel
VP & Exec Ed, Random House: Andrea Walker
VP & Exec Ed: Mark Warren
VP & Exec Ed, One World: Elizabeth Mendez Berry
VP & Dir, Mktg, Media Coaching, Random House: Barbara Fillon
VP & Dir, Natl Accts: Lynn Kovach
VP & Dir, Sales Mktg: Stacey Witcraft
VP & Edit Dir, Ballantine Bantam Dell: Kara Cesare; Kate Miciak
VP & Edit Dir, The Dial Press: Whitney Frick
VP & Exec Ed, Ballantine: Susanna Porter
VP & Imprint Sales Dir: Allyson Pearl
VP, Exec Mng Ed & Copy Chief, Random House: Benjamin Dreyer
VP, Copy: Grant Neumann
Publr & Ed-in-Chief, One World: Christopher Jackson
Publr, Random House: Andy Ward
Exec Dir, Art/Design: Robbin Schiff
Sr Art Dir: Joe Perez; Beck Stvan
Sr Dir, Creative Servs: Annette Melvin
Creative Dir, Del Ray: Elizabeth Schaefer
Dir, Content Servs: Erika Seyfried
Dir, Foreign Rts: Rachel Kind
Dir, Mktg, Ballantine Bantam Dell: Quinne Rogers
Dir, Online Copy Strategy & Optimization: Daniel Christensen
Dir, Publicity, Ballantine Bantam Dell: Jennifer Garza
Dir, Publicity, Del Rey: David Moench
Deputy Dir, Publicity: London King; Cindy Murray
Assoc Dir, Publicity: Melanie DeNardo; Greg Kubie
Assoc Dir, Publicity, Random House: Michelle Jasmine
Assoc Dir, Lib Mktg: Elizabeth Fabian
Exec Ed: Shauna Summers
Exec Ed, Ballantine Bantam Dell: Tracy Devine; Andra Miller; Mary Reynics; Brendan Vaughan; Sara Weiss

Exec Ed, Random House: Ben Greenberg; Hilary Redmon
Sr Ed: Caitlin McKenna; Anna Pitoniak
Sr Ed, Ballantine Bantam Dell: Anne Speyer
Sr Ed, One World: Nicole Counts
Sr Ed, The Dial Press: Annie Chagnot; Katy Nishimoto
Ed: Kate Collins Curnin; Anne Groell; Sam Nicholson; Marie Pantojan; Clio Seraphim
Ed, Ballantine Bantam Dell: Emily Hartley; Elana Seplow-Jolley
Ed, One World: Victory Matsui
Ed, Random House: Molly Turpin
Assoc Ed: Emma Caruso
Assoc Ed, One World: Erica Min
Ed-at-Large: Susan Mercandetti
Sr Mgr, Consumer Insights: Kesley Tiffey
Sr Mktg Mgr, Ballantine Bantam Dell: Allison Schuster
Sr Publg Mgr: Mika Kasuga
Sr Soc Media Mgr: Sophie Vershbow
Mgr, Creative Content: Danielle Siess
Mgr, Events: Kaitlin Darcy Russolese
Partnerships Mgr: Stacy Horowitz
Publg Mgr: Erica Gonzalez
Sr Mktg Mgr, Random House: Jess Bonet
Sr Publicist: Isabella Biedenharn
Asst Mktg Mgr, Ballantine Bantam Dell & Del Rey: Ashleigh Heaton
Asst Mktg Mgr, Ballantine Bantam Dell: Colleen Nuccio
Asst Mktg Mgr, Random House, Dial, Modern Library & One World: Katie Tull
Publg Mgr: Bridget Kearney
Sr Analyst, Busn Insights: Thomas Yuhas
Sr Publicist: Emily Isayeff; Dhara Parikh
Assoc Publicist: Ella Maslin; Melissa Sanford
Founded: 1925
General fiction & nonfiction hardcover, trade & mass market paperbacks.
Penguin Random House & its publishing entities are not accepting unsol submissions, proposals, mss, or submission queries via e-mail at this time.
ISBN Prefix(es): 978-0-307; 978-1-101; 978-0-89141; 978-0-345; 978-0-449; 978-0-8129; 978-0-307; 978-1-4000; 978-1-58836; 978-0-8041
Number of titles published annually: 700 Print; 150 E-Book
Total Titles: 5,900 Print; 1,100 E-Book
Imprints: Alibi (mystery, thriller, suspense); Ballantine Books; Bantam Books; Crown Publishing Group; Del Rey; Delacorte Press; Dell; The Dial Press; Flirt (new adult); Hydra (science fiction & fantasy); LENNY; Loveswept (digital only romance); Lucas Books; Modern Library; One World; Presidio Press; Random House; Villard; Zinc Ink
Warehouse: 400 Hahn Rd, Westminster, MD 21157
See separate listing for:
Crown Publishing Group

Random House Reference/Random House Puzzles & Games
Imprint of Penguin Random House Audio Publishing
c/o Penguin Random House Inc, 1745 Broadway, New York, NY 10019
Tel: 212-782-9000
Web Site: www.penguinrandomhouse.com
Key Personnel
Pres & Publr: Amanda D'Acierno
Publishes reference, crossword puzzle books & chess books & price guides for collectibles.
Penguin Random House & its publishing entities are not accepting unsol submissions, proposals, mss, or submission queries via e-mail at this time.
Total Titles: 215 Print
Imprints: Boston Globe Puzzle Books; Chicago Tribune Crosswords; House of Collectibles;

Los Angeles Times Crosswords; New York Times Crosswords; Random House Webster's; Washington Post Crosswords

Rational Island Publishers
Division of The Re-evaluation Counseling Communities
719 Second Ave N, Seattle, WA 98109
Tel: 206-284-0311
E-mail: ircc@rc.org
Web Site: www.rc.org
Key Personnel
Ed: Lisa Kauffman
Founded: 1954
Articles about Re-evaluation Counseling (Co-Counseling) - the theory, the practice, the applications & implications.
ISBN Prefix(es): 978-0-911214; 978-0-913937; 978-1-885357; 978-1-58429; 978-1-893165
Number of titles published annually: 6 Print
Total Titles: 263 Print

§Rattapallax Press
532 La Guadia Place, Suite 353, New York, NY 10012
Web Site: www.rattapallax.com
Key Personnel
Founder & Pres: Ram Devineni
Ed-in-Chief: Flavia Rocha
Founded: 2000
ISBN Prefix(es): 978-1-892494
Number of titles published annually: 4 Print; 1 CD-ROM; 15 Online; 15 E-Book; 15 Audio
Total Titles: 15 Print; 1 CD-ROM; 15 Online; 15 E-Book; 15 Audio
Distribution Center: Small Press Distribution, 1341 Seventh St, Berkeley, CA 94710-1409 *Tel:* 510-524-1668 *Toll Free Tel:* 800-869-7553 *E-mail:* spd@spdbooks.org *Web Site:* www.spdbooks.org
Membership(s): Community of Literary Magazines & Presses (CLMP)

§Raven Publishing Inc
125 Cherry Creek Rd, Norris, MT 59745
SAN: 254-5861
Mailing Address: PO Box 2866, Norris, MT 59745
Tel: 406-685-3545 *Toll Free Tel:* 866-685-3545
E-mail: info@ravenpublishing.net
Web Site: www.ravenpublishing.net
Key Personnel
Founder & Pres: Janet Muirhead Hill *E-mail:* janet@ravenpublishing.net
Founded: 2001
ISBN Prefix(es): 978-0-9714161; 978-0-9772525; 978-0-9820893; 978-0-9827377; 978-1-937849
Number of titles published annually: 4 Print; 4 E-Book
Total Titles: 42 Print; 2 CD-ROM; 39 E-Book; 2 Audio
Billing Address: PO Box 2866, Norris, MT 59745
Membership(s): Independent Book Publishers Association (IBPA)

§Ravenhawk™ Books
Division of The 6DOF Group
311 E Drowsey Circle, Payson, AZ 85541
Tel: 520-402-9033 *Fax:* 520-402-9033
Web Site: www.facebook.com/6DOFRavenhawk
Key Personnel
Publr: Karl Lasky
Founded: 1998
Royalty publisher. Specialize in general trade, hard/softcover, fiction, nonfiction, self-help, teaching texts for professionals, crime, mystery & suspense fiction. Ebooks, CD/DVD audiobooks. Ms submissions are by invitation only through acknowledged literary agents.
ISBN Prefix(es): 978-1-893660
Number of titles published annually: 6 Print; 4 CD-ROM; 4 Online; 12 E-Book; 4 Audio

Total Titles: 44 Print; 4 Online; 4 E-Book
Distribution Center: Baker & Taylor LLC, 2550 W Tyvola Rd, Suite 300, Charlotte, NC 28217 *Tel:* 704-998-3100 *Fax:* 704-998-3319 *E-mail:* btinfo@baker-taylor.com *Web Site:* www.baker-taylor.com
Ingram Content Group Inc, One Ingram Blvd, La Vergne, TN 37086-1986 *Tel:* 615-793-5000 *Web Site:* www.ingramcontent.com
Membership(s): Interactive Creative Artists Network (ICAN); National Writers Association (NWA); Society of Southwestern Authors

Razorbill
Imprint of Penguin Random House LLC
345 Hudson St, New York, NY 10014
Tel: 212-366-2000
Web Site: www.penguin.com/meet/publishers/razorbill
Key Personnel
Pres & Publr: Jennifer Klonsky
Founded: 2004
Penguin Random House & its publishing entities are not accepting unsol submissions, proposals, mss, or submission queries via e-mail at this time.
Number of titles published annually: 42 Print
Total Titles: 159 Print

Reader's Digest Select Editions
Division of Trusted Media Brands Inc
44 S Broadway, White Plains, NY 10601
Tel: 914-238-1000 *Toll Free Tel:* 877-732-4438 (cust serv)
Web Site: www.facebook.com/selecteditions
Key Personnel
Exec Ed: Jim Menick
Sr Ed: Amy Reilly
Founded: 1950
Publishers of hardcover fiction anthology books in condensed form. Selections are licensed from original publisher.
ISBN Prefix(es): 978-0-89577

Reader's Digest Trade Publishing
Division of Trusted Media Brands Inc
44 S Broadway, White Plains, NY 10601
SAN: 240-9720
Tel: 914-238-1000
Web Site: rdtradepublishing.com
Key Personnel
Chief Content Offr: Bruce Kelley
Founded: 1971
Illustrated trade (retail) reference books on home maintenance & repair, gardening, home decorating, crafts, art instruction, cooking, health & fitness, pet care, music, family reference, religion & inspiration, science & nature, travel & atlases, humor.
ISBN Prefix(es): 978-0-7621; 978-1-61765; 978-1-62145
Number of titles published annually: 100 Print
Total Titles: 350 Print
Distributed by Simon & Schuster, Inc
Orders to: Simon & Schuster, Inc, 100 Front St, Riverside, NJ 08075 *Toll Free Tel:* 800-223-2336 (US); 800-268-3216 (CN) *Toll Free Fax:* 800-943-9831 (US); 888-849-8151 (CN)

Recorded Books Inc, an RBmedia company
270 Skipjack Rd, Prince Frederick, MD 20678
SAN: 677-8887
Tel: 410-535-5590 *Toll Free Tel:* 877-732-2898 *Fax:* 410-535-5499
E-mail: customerservice@recordedbooks.com
Web Site: www.recordedbooks.com
Key Personnel
Pres & CEO: Tom MacIsaac
COO: Edward Longo *E-mail:* elongo@recordedbooks.com
Chief Content Offr: Troy Juliar

CFO: Neil Tress *E-mail:* ntress@recordedbooks.com
CIO & CTO: Mike Pyland
Dir, Acqs: Brian Sweany *E-mail:* bsweany@recordedbooks.com
Founded: 1979
Independent publisher of unabridged audiobooks & distributor of films & other media content delivered in CD & downloadable formats, to consumers, libraries & schools.
ISBN Prefix(es): 978-0-7887; 978-1-4025; 978-1-55690; 978-1-84197; 978-1-4193; 978-1-84505; 978-1-4281; 978-1-4361; 978-1-4407; 978-1-4498; 978-1-4561; 978-1-4618; 978-1-4640; 978-1-4703; 978-1-4906; 978-1-5019
Number of titles published annually: 700 Print; 250 CD-ROM; 100 Online; 50 E-Book; 787 Audio
Total Titles: 8,000 Print; 1,000 CD-ROM; 100 Online; 50 E-Book; 5,808 Audio
Imprints: Classics Library; Clipper Audio (UK); Film Movement; The Great Courses; Griot Audio; Harlequin Romance Library™; ITK (In the Know) Audio; Lone Star Audio; Maple Leaf Audio; Mystery Library; RB Shorts; Recorded Books Audiolibros; Recorded Books Development; Recorded Books Inspirational; Romantic Sounds Audio; Sci-Fi Audio; Southern Voices Audio; Western Library; Your Coach in a Box
Foreign Office(s): WF Howes Ltd, Unit 4, Rearsby Business Park, Gaddesby Lane, Rearsby, Leics LE7 4YH, United Kingdom (recorded books) *Tel:* (01664) 423000 *Fax:* (01664) 423005 *E-mail:* info@wfhowes.co.uk *Web Site:* www.wfhowes.co.uk
Membership(s): Audio Publishers Association

Red Chair Press
PO Box 333, South Egremont, MA 01258-0333
Tel: 413-528-2398 (edit off) *Toll Free Tel:* 800-328-4929 (orders & cust serv)
E-mail: info@redchairpress.com
Web Site: www.redchairpress.com
Key Personnel
CFO: David P Sheehan *Tel:* 917-608-6198 *E-mail:* david@redchairpress.com
Pres & Publr: Keith Garton *E-mail:* keith@redchairpress.com
Art Dir: Jeff Dinardo *Tel:* 978-371-0111 ext 1 *E-mail:* jeff@redchairpress.com
Founded: 2009
Fiction & nonfiction learning books & ebooks; social & emotional learning with an emphasis on good decision-making for ages 3-10. No unsol mss.
ISBN Prefix(es): 978-1-936163; 978-1-937529; 978-1-63440; 978-1-947159 (One Elm Books)
Number of titles published annually: 30 Print; 24 E-Book
Total Titles: 150 Print; 32 CD-ROM; 120 E-Book
Imprints: One Elm Books (middle grade novels); Rocking Chair Kids (picture books ages 5 & under)
Foreign Rep(s): Lerner Publishing Group Inc (Maria Kjoller) (worldwide exc Canada & USA)
Distribution Center: Lerner Publisher Services, 1251 Washington Ave N, Minneapolis, MN 55401 *Toll Free Tel:* 800-328-4929 *Web Site:* www.lernerbooks.com
Membership(s): American Booksellers Association (ABA); Association of American Publishers PreK-12 Learning Group; The Children's Book Council (CBC); Independent Book Publishers Association (IBPA); Independent Publishers of New England (IPNE); Society of Children's Book Writers & Illustrators (SCBWI)

Red Hen Press
PO Box 40820, Pasadena, CA 91114
Tel: 626-356-4760 *Fax:* 626-356-9974
Web Site: www.redhen.org

Key Personnel
Publr: Mark E Cull *E-mail:* mark@redhen.org
Mng Ed: Kate Gale *E-mail:* kategale@verizon.net
Founded: 1994
Publish perfect bound collections of poetry, short stories & books of a literary nature. Also sponsor several literary awards, along with the literary journal *The Los Angeles Review.*
ISBN Prefix(es): 978-0-9890361; 978-1-888996; 978-1-59709
Number of titles published annually: 22 Print
Total Titles: 350 Print
Imprints: Arktoi Books; Boreal Books; Hybrid Nation; Pighog Books; Story Line Press; Xeno Books
Distribution Center: Chicago Distribution Center, 11030 S Langley, Chicago, IL 60628 *Toll Free Tel:* 800-621-2736 *Toll Free Fax:* 800-621-8476 *E-mail:* orders@press.uchicago.edu
Membership(s): Association of Writers & Writing Programs (AWP); Community of Literary Magazines & Presses (CLMP)

Red Moon Press
PO Box 2461, Winchester, VA 22604-1661
Tel: 540-722-2156
Web Site: www.redmoonpress.com
Key Personnel
Owner: Jim Kacian *E-mail:* jim.kacian@redmoonpress.com
Founded: 1993
Largest & most prestigious publisher of English-language haiku & related forms in the world.
ISBN Prefix(es): 978-1-9657818; 978-1-893959; 978-1-936848; 978-1-947271
Number of titles published annually: 15 Print
Total Titles: 350 Print
Imprints: Pond Frog Editions; Soffietto Editions

The Red Sea Press Inc
541 W Ingham Ave, Suite B, Trenton, NJ 08638
Tel: 609-695-3200 *Fax:* 609-695-6466
E-mail: customerservice@africaworldpressbooks.com
Web Site: www.africaworldpressbooks.com
Key Personnel
Fin Cont: Senait Kassahun Checole
Founded: 1983
Publisher of books on the Horn of Africa, Latin America; distributor of books on the Third World.
ISBN Prefix(es): 978-0-932415; 978-1-56902
Number of titles published annually: 100 Print
Total Titles: 1,200 Print
Imprints: Karnak House
Foreign Rights: Turnaround Publisher Services (Europe, London)

Red Wheel/Weiser
65 Parker St, Suite 7, Newburyport, MA 01950
Tel: 978-465-0504 *Toll Free Tel:* 800-423-7087 (orders) *Fax:* 978-465-0243
E-mail: info@rwwbooks.com
Web Site: www.redwheelweiser.com
Key Personnel
Pres & CEO: Michael Kerber *Tel:* 978-465-0504 ext 1115 *E-mail:* mkerber@rwwbooks.com
Assoc Publr: Greg Brandenburgh; Peter Turner
Assoc Publr, Career Press: Michael Pye
Creative Dir: Kathryn Sky-Peck
Publicity Dir: Bonni Hamilton
Sales Dir, Natl Accts: Laurie Kelly-Pye
Publicist: Eryn Eaton
Mng Ed: Jane Hagaman
Sr Acqs Ed: Christine LeBlond
Prodn Mgr: Michael Conlon
Founded: 1957
Self-help, spirituality, inspiration, women's interest & esoteric subjects from many traditions.
ISBN Prefix(es): 978-0-943233 (Conari); 978-0-87728 (Weiser); 978-1-57863 (Weiser); 978-1-59003 (Red Wheel); 978-1-57324 (Conari)

Number of titles published annually: 50 Print
Total Titles: 1,200 Print
Imprints: Career Press; Dharma Spring; Disinformation Books; Hampton Roads Publishing
Distributor for Cleis Press; Nicolas Hays Inc; Lantern Publishing & Media; Ozark Mountain Publishing Inc; Viva Editions
Foreign Rep(s): Brumby Books (Australia); Deep Books (UK); Georgetown Publications (Canada)
Foreign Rights: Linda Biagi (translation)
Warehouse: Books International Inc, 22883 Quicksilver Dr, Dulles, VA 20166
Membership(s): American Booksellers Association (ABA)
See separate listing for:
Hampton Roads Publishing

Redleaf Press
Division of Think Small
10 Yorkton Ct, St Paul, MN 55117
SAN: 212-8691
Tel: 651-641-0508 *Toll Free Tel:* 800-423-8309 *Toll Free Fax:* 800-641-0115
E-mail: customerservice@redleafpress.org; sales@redleafpress.org
Web Site: www.redleafpress.org
Key Personnel
Dir, Mktg: Eric Johnson *E-mail:* ejohnson@redleafpress.org
Acqs & Devt Ed: Lindsey Smith *E-mail:* lsmith@redleafpress.org
Founded: 1973
Resources for early childhood professionals including. early childhood curriculum, professional development, family child care business, record keeping & parenting.
ISBN Prefix(es): 978-0-934140; 978-1-884834; 978-1-929610; 978-1-933653; 978-1-60554
Number of titles published annually: 30 Print; 1 CD-ROM; 2 Online; 27 E-Book
Total Titles: 350 Print; 15 CD-ROM; 10 Online; 300 E-Book; 1 Audio
Distributor for New Shoots Publishing (New Zealand)
Foreign Rights: Nordlyset Literary Agency (worldwide)
Distribution Center: Consortium Book Sales & Distribution, The Keg House, Suite 101, 34 13 Ave NE, Minneapolis, MN 55413-1007 (US book trade & libs) *Tel:* 612-746-2600 *Toll Free Tel:* 800-283-3572 (cust serv, Jackson, TN) *Fax:* 612-746-2606 *E-mail:* info@cbsd.com *Web Site:* www.cbsd.com SAN: 200-6049
Login Canada, 300 Saulteaux Crescent, Winnipeg, MB R3J 3T2, Canada, Mktg Mgr: Melanie Lauze *Tel:* 204-831-3832 *Toll Free Tel:* 800-665-1148 *Toll Free Fax:* 800-665-0103 *Web Site:* www.lb.ca
Pademelon Press, PO Box 41, Jamberoo, NSW 2533, Australia (Australia & New Zealand), Publg Dir: Alison Moodie *Tel:* (02) 4236 1881 *Fax:* (02) 9680 4634 *E-mail:* enquiry@pademelonpress.com.au *Web Site:* www.pademelonpress.com.au
Eurospan Group, Gray's Inn House, 127 Clerkenwell Rd, London EC1R 5DB, United Kingdom (UK, Continental Europe, Africa, Asia & Middle East), Mktg Exec: Siobhan Peters *Tel:* (0845) 474 4572 *E-mail:* info@eurospanbookstore.com *Web Site:* www.eurospanbookstore.com
Membership(s): Education Market Association

Robert D Reed Publishers
PO Box 1992, Bandon, OR 97411-1192
Tel: 541-347-9882 *Fax:* 541-347-9883
E-mail: 4bobreed@msn.com
Web Site: rdrpublishers.com
Key Personnel
Publr: Robert D Reed
Founded: 1977

All types of publications for trade, educational institutions, individuals & corporations.
ISBN Prefix(es): 978-1-889710; 978-1-885003; 978-1-931741
Number of titles published annually: 25 Print
Total Titles: 225 Print
Foreign Rep(s): Sylvia Hayse Literary Agency

Reedswain Inc
88 Wells Rd, Spring City, PA 19475
Tel: 610-495-9578 *Toll Free Tel:* 800-331-5191 *Fax:* 610-495-6632
E-mail: orders@reedswain.com
Web Site: www.reedswain.com
Key Personnel
Pres & Foreign Rts: Richard Kentwell
Founded: 1987
Soccer coaching books.
ISBN Prefix(es): 978-1-59164; 978-0-9651020; 978-1-890946
Number of titles published annually: 10 Print
Total Titles: 190 Print

Referee Books
Imprint of Referee Enterprises Inc
2017 Lathrop Ave, Racine, WI 53405
Tel: 262-632-8855 *Toll Free Tel:* 800-733-6100 *Fax:* 262-632-5460
E-mail: customerservice@referee.com
Web Site: www.referee.com
Key Personnel
Pres: Barry Mano *E-mail:* bmano@naso.org
Dir, Admin: Corey Ludwin
Founded: 1976
Publish sports officiating publications; magazines, books, manuals & booklets on officiating, umpiring, baseball, basketball, football, soccer, softball & athletics referee books.
ISBN Prefix(es): 978-1-58208; 978-0-9660209
Number of titles published annually: 30 Print
Total Titles: 75 Print

Reference Publications Inc
218 Saint Clair River Dr, Algonac, MI 48001
SAN: 208-4392
Mailing Address: PO Box 344, Algonac, MI 48001-0344
Tel: 810-794-5722
E-mail: referencepub@sbcglobal.net
Key Personnel
Pres & Ed: Marie Aline Irvine
Founded: 1975
Mail order & reference books. Specialize in botanical & medicinal plants, Americana, Amerindian & African reference books & botanical works.
ISBN Prefix(es): 978-0-917256
Number of titles published annually: 2 Print
Total Titles: 24 Print
Imprints: Encyclopaedia Africana
Sales Office(s): PO Box 344, Algonac, MI 48001-0344

ReferencePoint Press Inc
17150 Via del Campo, Suite 205, San Diego, CA 92127
Mailing Address: PO Box 27779, San Diego, CA 92198
Tel: 858-618-1314 *Toll Free Tel:* 888-479-6436 *Fax:* 858-618-1730
E-mail: info@referencepointpress.com
Web Site: www.referencepointpress.com
Key Personnel
Pres & Publr: Dan Leone *Tel:* 858-618-1314 ext 102 *E-mail:* dan@referencepointpress.com
Founded: 2006
Publish series nonfiction for young adults: current issues, health, science & paranormal.
ISBN Prefix(es): 978-1-60152; 978-1-68282
Number of titles published annually: 100 Print; 100 E-Book
Total Titles: 700 Print; 700 E-Book
Foreign Rep(s): Saunders Book Co (Canada)

Returns: Bang Fulfillment, 217 Etak Dr, Brainerd, MN 56401
Warehouse: Bang Fulfillment, 217 Etak Dr, Brainerd, MN 56401, Contact: Perry Gienger *Toll Free Tel:* 800-328-0450 *Fax:* 218-829-7145 *E-mail:* perryg@bangprinting.com

Reformation Heritage Books
2965 Leonard St NE, Grand Rapids, MI 49525
Tel: 616-977-0889 *Fax:* 616-285-3246
E-mail: orders@heritagebooks.org
Web Site: www.heritagebooks.org
Key Personnel
Chmn: Joel R Beeke
Contact: Jonathan Engelsma
Founded: 1994
Sell new & used religious books with emphasis on experiential religion. Also republish out-of-print Puritan works.
ISBN Prefix(es): 978-1-892777; 978-1-60178
Number of titles published annually: 40 Print
Total Titles: 250 Print; 70 E-Book

§Regal Crest Enterprises
2028 E Ben White Blvd, No 240-1113, Austin, TX 78741
Tel: 409-527-1188 *Toll Free Fax:* 866-294-9628
E-mail: info@regalcrestbooks.biz
Web Site: www.regalcrest.biz
Key Personnel
Owner: Cathy C Bryerose
Founded: 2003
Traditional royalty publisher using innovative print technology.
ISBN Prefix(es): 978-1-932300; 978-1-935053; 978-1-61929
Number of titles published annually: 25 Print; 25 E-Book
Imprints: Blue Beacon Books (nonfiction); Mystic Books (paranormal); Quest Books (action, adventure, mystery, police procedure, detective); Regal Crest (drama & general fiction); Silver Dragon Books (science fiction/fantasy); Troubadour Books (poetry, short story, anthology); YA Books (young adult); Yellow Rose Books (romance)
Foreign Rep(s): Bella Distribution Inc (worldwide); Ingram (worldwide)
Distribution Center: Bella Distribution Inc, 1041 Aenon Church Rd, Tallahassee, FL 32302 *Toll Free Tel:* 800-533-1973
Ingram, One Ingram Blvd, La Vergne, TN 17202

Regal House Publishing
806 Oberlin Rd, No 12094, Raleigh, NC 27605
E-mail: info@regalhousepublishing.com
Web Site: regalhousepublishing.com
Key Personnel
Founder, Publr & Ed-in-Chief: Jaynie Royal
Mng Ed: Pam Van Dyk
Sr Ed: Ruth Feiertag
Founded: 2014
Passionately dedicated to the furtherance of exquisitely written literary works & the writers who pen them. Traditional publishing house accepting submissions directly from writers. Provide extensive editorial support for writers & formulate a marketing partnership pre- & post-publication.
ISBN Prefix(es): 978-0-9912612; 978-0-9988398; 978-1-947548
Number of titles published annually: 20 Print; 20 E-Book
Imprints: Fitzroy Books (middle grade, new adult & young adult fiction); Pact Press (anthologies, poetry & short story collections, full-length & literary fiction)
Distribution Center: Independent Publishers Group, 814 N Franklin St, Chicago, IL 60610 *Tel:* 312-337-0747 *Fax:* 312-337-5985 *Web Site:* www.ipgbook.com

Membership(s): American Booksellers Association (ABA); The Children's Book Council (CBC); Community of Literary Magazines & Presses (CLMP); Independent Book Publishers Association (IBPA); Poets & Writers; Southern Independent Booksellers Alliance (SIBA)
See separate listing for:
Fitzroy Books
Pact Press

Regent Press Publishers & Printers
2747 Regent St, Berkeley, CA 94705
Tel: 510-845-1196
E-mail: regentpress@mindspring.com
Web Site: www.regentpress.net
Key Personnel
Owner, Publr & Mng Ed: Mark Weiman
Founded: 1978
This publisher has indicated that 50% of their product line is author subsidized.
Number of titles published annually: 20 Print; 1 CD-ROM; 15 E-Book
Total Titles: 250 Print; 30 CD-ROM; 30 E-Book

Regnery Publishing
Subsidiary of Salem Media Group
300 New Jersey Ave NW, Washington, DC 20001
Tel: 202-216-0600 *Toll Free Tel:* 888-219-4747 *Fax:* 202-393-1795
Web Site: www.regnery.com
Key Personnel
Pres & Publr: Thomas Spence
Dir, Publg Opers: Matt Maschino *E-mail:* matthew.maschino@regnery.com
Dir, Publicity: Alyssa Cordova *E-mail:* alyssa.cordova@regnery.com
Dir, Sales: Mark Bloomfield
Mng Ed: Kathleen Curran
Asst Mng Ed: Kathryn Riggs
Exec Ed: Harry W Crocker, III
Principal Ed: Paul Choix
Perms: Will Hudson *E-mail:* william.hudson@regnery.com
Founded: 1947
Trade book publisher.
ISBN Prefix(es): 978-0-89526; 978-1-59698; 978-1-62157
Number of titles published annually: 50 Print; 50 E-Book
Total Titles: 1,000 Print; 800 E-Book
Imprints: Gateway Editions; Regnery; Regnery Faith; Regnery Fiction (thrillers); Regnery History; Regnery Kids
Distribution Center: Simon & Schuster Inc *E-mail:* purchaseorders@simonandschuster.com

Regular Baptist Press
Division of General Association of Regular Baptist Churches
3715 N Ventura Dr, Arlington Heights, IL 60004
Tel: 847-843-1600 *Toll Free Tel:* 800-727-4440 (cust serv) *Fax:* 847-843-3757
E-mail: orders@rbpstore.org
Web Site: regularbaptistpress.org
Key Personnel
Dir: David Gunn
Busn Dir: Tony Randolph
Founded: 1952
Curriculum & Christian books.
ISBN Prefix(es): 978-0-87227; 978-1-59402; 978-1-60776; 978-1-62940
Number of titles published annually: 6 Print
Imprints: Regular Baptist Books (trade books)

§Remember Point Inc
PO Box 1448, Pacific Palisades, CA 90272
Tel: 310-896-8716
E-mail: info@rememberpoint.com
Web Site: www.rememberpoint.com; www.longfellowfindsahome.com
Key Personnel
Pres & Publr: Linda Sue Miller

Mktg Dir: Terry Megan
Founded: 2010
ISBN Prefix(es): 978-0-9988351
Number of titles published annually: 4 Print; 4 E-Book; 1 Audio
Total Titles: 7 Print; 1 Online; 5 E-Book

Renaissance House
Imprint of Laredo Publishing Co
465 Westview Ave, Englewood, NJ 07631
Tel: 201-408-4048
Web Site: www.renaissancehouse.net
Key Personnel
Pres: Sam Laredo *E-mail:* laredo@renaissancehouse.net
VP & Exec Ed: Raquel Benatar *E-mail:* raquel@renaissancehouse.net
Founded: 1991
Specialize in the creation, development & management of educational & multicultural publishing projects for the Latino Market, young readers. Manage editorial & art projects. Work with more than 60 illustrators & offer editorial services, translations English to Spanish, illustrations & art project management. See web site to view our publishing projects & available publishing rights.
ISBN Prefix(es): 978-1-56492
Number of titles published annually: 30 Print
Total Titles: 150 Print

Research & Education Association (REA)
258 Prospect Plains Rd, Cranbury, NJ 08512
Tel: 732-819-8880 *Fax:* 732-819-8808 (orders)
E-mail: info@rea.com
Web Site: www.rea.com
Key Personnel
Publr: Pamela Weston *E-mail:* pweston@rea.com
Founded: 1959
Professional books, secondary & college study guides & test preparation books, biology, business, engineering, mathematics, general science, history, social sciences, accounting & computer science.
ISBN Prefix(es): 978-0-87891; 978-0-7386
Number of titles published annually: 50 Print
Total Titles: 1,200 Print; 10 CD-ROM; 3 Audio

Research Press
2612 N Mattis Ave, Champaign, IL 61822
SAN: 203-381X
Mailing Address: PO Box 7886, Champaign, IL 61826
Tel: 217-352-3273 *Toll Free Tel:* 800-519-2707 *Fax:* 217-352-1221
E-mail: rp@researchpress.com; orders@researchpress.com
Web Site: www.researchpress.com
Key Personnel
Chmn of the Bd: David Parkinson
Pres: Judy Parkinson
Busn Mgr: Deborah Wilcoxon
Prodn Mgr: Jeff Helgesen
Founded: 1968
ISBN Prefix(es): 978-0-87822
Number of titles published annually: 4 Print
Total Titles: 400 Print
Foreign Rep(s): Eurospan (Africa, Asia-Pacific, Caribbean, Europe, Latin America, Middle East, UK)
Foreign Rights: Books Crossing Borders

Resilient Publishing
406 S Third St, Boise, ID 83702
Tel: 208-258-9544
E-mail: submissions@resilientpublishing.com
Web Site: www.resilientpublishing.com; www.facebook.com/ResilientPub
Key Personnel
CEO: Lynn Hardy
Mktg & PR Support: Kate Delano-Condax Decker
Tech Ed: Phil Athens; Angela Gaudioso

Graphic Designer & Tech Support: Robert Morrissey
Cover Artist: Jeff Sharpton
Founded: 2009
Commitment fee $299. Authors receive 75% of income from bound book sales & 65% of income from ebook sales.
ISBN Prefix(es): 978-1-936408; 978-0-9841902; 978-1-937703; 978-0-9843669; 978-0-9845045
Number of titles published annually: 15 Print; 15 Online; 15 E-Book; 2 Audio
Total Titles: 40 Print; 40 Online; 40 E-Book
Distributor for Anderson Design; Brynwood Publishing
Membership(s): Idaho Writers Guild

§Revell

Division of Baker Publishing Group
PO Box 6287, Grand Rapids, MI 49516-6287
SAN: 203-3801
Tel: 616-676-9185 *Toll Free Tel:* 800-877-2665; 800-679-1957 *Fax:* 616-676-9573
Web Site: www.bakerpublishinggroup.com
Key Personnel
Pres: Dwight Baker
Edit Dir: Jennifer Leep
Mng Ed: Kristin Kornoelje
Prodn & ISBN Contact: Robert Bol
Rts & Perms & Intl Rts: Marilyn Gordon
Founded: 1870
Religious publisher.
ISBN Prefix(es): 978-0-8007
Number of titles published annually: 100 Print
Total Titles: 5 Audio
Imprints: Spire Books
Foreign Rep(s): Christian Art (South Africa); David C Cook Distribution (Canada); Marston Book Services Ltd (Europe, UK); Soul Distributors Ltd (New Zealand)
Shipping Address: 6030 E Fulton Rd, Ada, MI 49301

Lynne Rienner Publishers Inc

1800 30 St, Suite 314, Boulder, CO 80301
SAN: 683-1869
Tel: 303-444-6684 *Fax:* 303-444-0824
E-mail: questions@rienner.com; cservice@rienner.com
Web Site: www.rienner.com
Key Personnel
Pres & CEO: Lynne C Rienner
Dir, Mktg & Sales: Sally Glover
  E-mail: sglover@rienner.com
Sr Acqs Ed, Political Sci & Intl Rel: Marie-Claire Antoine
Cust Serv Mgr: Patty Troiano
Founded: 1984
Scholarly & reference books & journals, college textbooks; comparative politics, US politics, international relations, sociology, Third World literature & literary criticism.
ISBN Prefix(es): 978-1-56549; 978-0-931477; 978-1-55587; 978-0-89410; 978-1-58826; 978-1-935049 (FirstForumPress); 978-1-62637
Number of titles published annually: 70 Print
Total Titles: 1,050 Print
Divisions: FirstForumPress (scholarly monographs); Kumarian Press
Distributor for Center for US-Mexican Studies; Ayebia Clarke Publishing Ltd (African lit); St Andrews Center for Syrian Studies
Foreign Rep(s): China Publishers Marketing (China, Hong Kong, Taiwan); Co Info Pty Ltd (Australia); Cranbury International LLC (Caribbean, Latin America); Far Eastern Booksellers (Japan); Kinokuniya Co Ltd (Japan); KL Book Distributors (Malaysia); Maruzen Co Ltd (Japan); PMS Publishers Services Pte Ltd (Brunei, Indonesia, Malaysia, Singapore); Turpin Distribution (Europe); Viva (India)
Warehouse: 22883 Quicksilver Dr, Dulles, VA 20166, Contact: Vartan Ajamian

Membership(s): Association of American Publishers (AAP)
See separate listing for:
Kumarian Press

Rio Nuevo Publishers

451 N Bonita Ave, Tucson, AZ 85745
Mailing Address: PO Box 5250, Tucson, AZ 85703
Tel: 520-623-9558 *Toll Free Tel:* 800-969-9558 *Fax:* 520-624-5888 *Toll Free Fax:* 800-715-5888
E-mail: info@rionuevo.com (cust serv)
Web Site: www.rionuevo.com
Founded: 1999
Publisher of fine regional southwestern & western photographic, cooking, art, culture & historical books & quality Native American books.
ISBN Prefix(es): 978-1-887896; 978-1-933855; 978-0-918080; 978-1-940322; 978-0-9700750
Number of titles published annually: 12 Print
Total Titles: 125 Print
Imprints: Rio Chico (educ & children's books)

Rising Sun Publishing

PO Box 70906, Marietta, GA 30007-0906
Tel: 770-518-0369 *Toll Free Tel:* 800-524-2813 *Fax:* 770-587-0862
E-mail: info@rspublishing.com
Web Site: www.rspublishing.com
Key Personnel
CFO: Mychal Wynn
Founded: 1982
Primary focus is educational training & materials.
ISBN Prefix(es): 978-1-880463
Number of titles published annually: 5 Print
Total Titles: 32 Print; 4 Audio

River City Publishing LLC

1719 Mulberry St, Montgomery, AL 36106
Tel: 334-265-6753
Key Personnel
Publr: Carolyn Newman
Ed: Fran Norris
Founded: 1989
Acquisition, editing, design, composition, marketing & sales of new books. Regional fiction & narrative nonfiction, especially books about the South, civil rights, folk art, contemporary fiction, regionally related travel history.
ISBN Prefix(es): 978-1-881320; 978-0-9622815; 978-1-57966; 978-0-913515; 978-1-880216
Number of titles published annually: 4 Print; 4 E-Book
Total Titles: 200 Print
Imprints: Elliott & Clark Publishing; River City Kids; Starrhill Press
Membership(s): Southern Independent Booksellers Alliance (SIBA)

§Riverdale Avenue Books (RAB)

5676 Riverdale Ave, Bronx, NY 10471
Tel: 212-279-6418
E-mail: customerservice@riverdaleavebooks.com
Web Site: www.riverdaleavebooks.com
Key Personnel
Publr: Lori Perkins *E-mail:* lori@riverdaleavebooks.com
Founded: 2012
Hybrid publisher of fiction & nonfiction, digital & print.
ISBN Prefix(es): 978-1-936833 (Magnus); 978-1-62601 (RAB)
Number of titles published annually: 60 Print; 60 E-Book
Total Titles: 450 Print; 450 E-Book
Imprints: Binge Watcher's Guide (TV/movie pop culture); Circlet (erotic sci-fi/fantasy); Dagger (mystery/thriller); Hera (fiction & nonfiction for women of a certain age); 120 Days (reprints of LGBTQ pulp fiction); RAB Afraid (horror); RAB Desire (erotica & romance); RAB Gam-

ing; RAB Pop (pop culture); RAB SFF (science fiction/fantasy); RAB Sports; RAB Truth (memoir & biography); RAB Verve (lifestyle); Riverdale/Magnus (LGBTQ titles)
Foreign Rights: Linda Biagli (worldwide)
Distribution Center: OverDrive, One OverDrive Way, Cleveland, OH 44125 *Tel:* 216-573-6886 *Fax:* 216-573-6888 *Web Site:* company.overdrive.com
Ingram Content Group Inc, One Ingram Blvd, La Vergne, TN 37086-1986 *Tel:* 615-793-5000
Membership(s): Association of American Publishers (AAP)
See separate listing for:
Circlet Press

§Riverhead Books

Imprint of Penguin Group USA, A Penguin Random House Company
375 Hudson St, New York, NY 10014
Tel: 212-366-2000
Web Site: www.penguin.com/publishers/riverhead
Key Personnel
Pres & Publr: Geoffrey Kloske
VP & Edit Dir: Rebecca Saletan
VP & Ed-in-Chief: Sarah McGrath
VP & Exec Ed: Cal Morgan
Exec Ed: Jake Morrissey; Courtney Young
VP, Assoc Publr & Dir, Mktg: Kate Stark
VP, Assoc Publr & Dir, Publicity: Jynne Dilling Martin
Art Dir: Helen Yentus
Assoc Dir, Publicity: Katharine Freeman; Claire McGinnis
Publicist: Glory Plata
Ed: Laura Perciasepe
Founded: 1994
Penguin Random House & its publishing entities are not accepting unsol submissions, proposals, mss, or submission queries via e-mail at this time.
Number of titles published annually: 40 Print
Total Titles: 115 Print
Advertising Agency: Mesa Group

Riverside Publishing, see Houghton Mifflin Harcourt Assessments

Rizzoli International Publications Inc

Subsidiary of RCS Rizzoli Corp New York
300 Park Ave S, 4th fl, New York, NY 10010-5399
Tel: 212-387-3400 *Toll Free Tel:* 800-522-6657 (orders only) *Fax:* 212-387-3535
E-mail: publicity@rizzoliusa.com
Web Site: www.rizzoliusa.com
Key Personnel
VP & Publr: Charles Miers
VP, Sales & Mktg Opers: Jennifer deForest Pierson
Assoc Publr: David Morton
Assoc Publr, HLLA, Universe & Welcome Books: Jim Muschett
Exec Dir, Publicity: Pam Sommers
Dir, Spec Sales & Fulfillment: Tracey Petitt
Assoc Dir, Prodn: Kaija Markoe
Assoc Dir, Publicity: Jessica Napp
Client Publr Sales Mgr: Sarah Carstens
Foreign Sales Mgr: Jerry Hoffnagle
Mktg Mgr, Creative Servs & Soc/New Media: Linda Pricci
Sales Mgr: John Deen
Founded: 1974
Fine arts, architecture, photography, decorative arts, cookbooks, gardening & landscape design, fashion & sports.
ISBN Prefix(es): 978-0-8478; 978-0-941807; 978-1-932183; 978-1-59962
Number of titles published annually: 100 Print
Imprints: Ex Libris; Flammarion; Hardie Grant; Marsilio; RCS Libri; Rizzoli Electa; Rizzoli, New York; Universe; Welcome Enterprises Inc
Distributed by Penguin Random House

Distributor for Editions Flammarion; National Trust; Pavilion Books; Pavilion Children's; Pitkin; Portico; Skira Editore; Smith Street Books
Advertising Agency: Rizzoli Graphic Studios
Orders to: Penguin Random House Publisher Services, 400 Hahn Rd, Westminster, MD 21157 *Toll Free Tel:* 800-733-3000 *Toll Free Fax:* 800-659-2436; Penguin Random House of Canada Ltd, 2775 Mattheson Blvd E, Mississauga, ON L4W 4P7, Canada *Toll Free Tel:* 800-733-3000 *Toll Free Fax:* 800-659-2436
Returns: Penguin Random House, 1019 N State Rd 47, Crawfordsville, IN 47933; Penguin Random House of Canada Ltd, 2775 Mattheson Blvd E, Mississauga, ON L4W 4P7, Canada *Toll Free Tel:* 800-733-3000 *Toll Free Fax:* 800-659-2436
See separate listing for:
Universe Publishing
Welcome Enterprises Inc

The RoadRunner Press
Subsidiary of RoadRunner Press LLC
124 NW 32 St, Oklahoma City, OK 73118
Mailing Address: PO Box 2564, Oklahoma City, OK 73101
Tel: 405-524-6205 *Fax:* 405-524-6312
E-mail: info@theroadrunnerpress.com; orders@ theroadrunnerpress.com
Web Site: www.theroadrunnerpress.com
Key Personnel
Publr & Ed: Jeanne Devlin *Tel:* 405-615-8293 *E-mail:* jeanne@theroadrunnerpress.com
Founded: 2011
Small indie publishing house specializing in quality young adult fiction & regional nonfiction as well as select nonfiction & literary fiction with an emphasis on Native American voices from the American West.
ISBN Prefix(es): 978-1-937054
Number of titles published annually: 10 Print; 6 E-Book; 1 Audio
Total Titles: 30 Print; 8 E-Book
Foreign Rep(s): Fitzhenry & Whiteside (Canada)
Billing Address: The RoadRunner Press, PO Box 2564, Oklahoma City, OK 73101
Membership(s): The Children's Book Council (CBC); Independent Book Publishers Association (IBPA); Midwest Independent Publishing Association (MIPA); Mountains & Plains Independent Publishers Association; New Mexico Book Association; New Mexico Book Co-op; Publishers Association of the West (PubWest); Western Writers of America (WWA)

Roaring Brook Press
Member of Macmillan Children's Publishing Group
120 Broadway, New York, NY 10271
Tel: 646-307-5151
Web Site: us.macmillan.com/publishers/roaring-brook-press
Key Personnel
Pres & Publr, Macmillan Children's Publishing Group: Jon Yaged
SVP & Publg Dir: Jennifer Besser
SVP & Deputy Publr: Allison Verost
VP & Assoc Publr: Angus Killick
VP & Sr Creative Dir: Beth Clark
VP, Subs Rts: Kristin Dulaney
Exec Dir, Ad & Promo: Mariel Dawson
Exec Dir, Publicity: Molly Ellis
Sr Art Dir: Sharismar Rodriguez
Art Dir, First Second Books: Kirk Benshoff
Dir, Mktg: Kathryn Little
Dir, School & Lib Mktg: Lucy Del Priore
Edit & Creative Dir, First Second Books: Mark Siegel
Edit Dir, First Second Books: Calista Brill
Asst Dir, Publicity: Morgan Kane
Exec Ed: Connie Hsu
Sr Mng Ed: Hayley Jozwiak

Sr Prodn Ed: Ilana Worrell
Sr Ed: Katherine Jacobs
Ed: Emily Feinberg; Kate Meltzer
Ed, First Second Books: Robyn Chapman
Sr Assoc Ed: Mekisha Telfer
Asst Ed: Megan Abbate; Luisa Beguiristain
Asst Ed, First Second Books: Kiara Valdez
Mktg Mgr: Katie Quinn
Studio Mgr: Ginny Dominguez
Designer: Cassie Gonzales
Publicist: Morgan Rath
Assoc Publicist: Madison Furr
Sr Coord: Debbie Cobb
Founded: 2002
ISBN Prefix(es): 978-0-7613; 978-1-59643
Number of titles published annually: 50 Print
Imprints: First Second Books

Roaring Forties Press
1053 Santa Fe Ave, Berkeley, CA 94706
Tel: 510-527-5461
E-mail: info@roaringfortiespress.com
Web Site: www.roaringfortiespress.com
Key Personnel
Founder & Publr: Deirdre Greene *E-mail:* dmg@ roaringfortiespress.com; Nigel Quinney *E-mail:* nq@roaringfortiespress.com
Founded: 2005
Publisher of nonfiction books & travel books with a twist.
ISBN Prefix(es): 978-0-9766706; 978-0-9777429; 978-0-9823410; 978-1-938901; 978-0-9843165
Number of titles published annually: 4 Print; 4 E-Book
Total Titles: 21 Print; 70 E-Book
Distribution Center: Publishers Group West, 1700 Fourth St, Berkeley, CA 94710 *Tel:* 510-809-3700 *Toll Free Tel:* 800-788-3123 *Fax:* 510-809-3777 *Web Site:* www.pgw.com
Perseus Books Group UK, 69-70 Temple Chambers, 3-7 Temple Ave, London EC4Y 0HP, United Kingdom *Tel:* (020) 7353 7771 *Fax:* (020) 7353 7786 *E-mail:* enquiries@ perseusbooks.co.uk *Web Site:* www. perseusbooksgroup.com
Membership(s): Independent Book Publishers Association (IBPA)

The Rockefeller University Press
Unit of Rockefeller University
950 Third Ave, 2nd fl, New York, NY 10022
Tel: 212-327-7938
E-mail: rupress@rockefeller.edu
Web Site: www.rupress.org
Key Personnel
Fin Dir: Ray Fastiggi *Tel:* 212-327-8567 *E-mail:* fastigg@rockefeller.edu
Prodn Dir: Robert J O'Donnell *Tel:* 212-327-8545 *E-mail:* odonner@rockefeller.edu
Mktg Assoc: Laraine Karl *E-mail:* lkarl@ rockefeller.edu
Founded: 1906
Currently publishes biomedical journals & books.
ISBN Prefix(es): 978-0-87470
Number of titles published annually: 3 Print
Total Titles: 36 Print; 3 Online
Foreign Rep(s): iGroup Asia Pacific Ltd (Asia-Pacific)
Membership(s): Association of American Publishers Professional & Scholarly Publishing Division; Association of Learned & Professional Society Publishers (ALPSP); Association of University Presses (AUPresses); Society for Scholarly Publishing (SSP)

RockHill Publishing LLC
PO Box 62241, Virginia Beach, VA 23466-2241
Tel: 757-692-2021
E-mail: jlh@rockhillpublishing.com
Web Site: rockhillpublishing.com

Key Personnel
Publr: James L Hill *E-mail:* jlhill@ rockhillpublishing.com
Founded: 2013
Independent publishing house.
ISBN Prefix(es): 978-1-945286
Number of titles published annually: 3 Print; 3 Online; 3 E-Book
Total Titles: 8 Print; 8 Online; 8 E-Book
Distributed by The Ishmael Tree (titles in Arabic)
Foreign Rights: ARC Mohammed International LLC (Gigi Ishmael) (worldwide)
Membership(s): Independent Book Publishers Association (IBPA)

Rocky Mountain Mineral Law Foundation
9191 Sheridan Blvd, Suite 203, Westminster, CO 80031
Tel: 303-321-8100 *Fax:* 303-321-7657
E-mail: info@rmmlf.org
Web Site: www.rmmlf.org
Key Personnel
Exec Dir: Alex Ritchie *Tel:* 303-321-8100 ext 101
Dir, Pubns: Margo MacDonnell *Tel:* 303-321-8100 ext 116
Assoc Dir: Frances Hartogh *Tel:* 303-321-8100 ext 107; Mark Holland *Tel:* 303-321-8100 ext 106 *E-mail:* mholland@rmmlf.org
Founded: 1955
Natural resources & legal education.
ISBN Prefix(es): 978-0-929047; 978-1-882047; 978-1-943497
Number of titles published annually: 6 Print
Total Titles: 81 Print; 1 CD-ROM

Rod & Staff Publishers Inc
14193 Hwy 172, Crockett, KY 41413
Mailing Address: PO Box 3, Crockett, KY 41413-0003
Tel: 606-522-4348 *Fax:* 606-522-4896
Key Personnel
Mgr: John D Martin
Founded: 1958
Religious storybooks; church, Sunday & Christian school materials & tracts.
ISBN Prefix(es): 978-0-7399
Number of titles published annually: 20 Print
Total Titles: 700 Print

Roman Catholic Books
Division of Catholic Media Apostolate Inc
PO Box 2286, Fort Collins, CO 80522-2286
Tel: 970-490-2735 *Fax:* 904-493-8781
Web Site: www.booksforcatholics.com
Key Personnel
Pres: Roger A McCaffrey *E-mail:* cxpeditor@ gmail.com
Founded: 1981
Traditional Catholic books.
ISBN Prefix(es): 978-0-912141; 978-1-929291; 978-0-9793540; 978-1-934888
Number of titles published annually: 10 Print
Total Titles: 270 Print

Roncorp Music
Division of Northeastern Music Publications Inc
PO Box 1210, Coatesville, PA 19320
Tel: 610-679-5400
E-mail: info@nemusicpub.com
Web Site: www.nemusicpub.com
Key Personnel
Pres: Randy Navarre
Founded: 1978
Music & music texts.
ISBN Prefix(es): 978-0-939103
Number of titles published annually: 15 Print
Total Titles: 300 Print
Distributed by Carl Fischer/Theodore Presser

Ronin Publishing Inc
PO Box 3436, Oakland, CA 94609

Tel: 510-420-3669 *Fax:* 510-420-3672
E-mail: ronin@roninpub.com
Web Site: www.roninpub.com
Key Personnel
Publr: Dr Beverly Potter *E-mail:* beverly@
roninpub.com
Founded: 1983
Small, independent publisher in San Francisco
Bay Area.
ISBN Prefix(es): 978-0-914171; 978-1-57951
Number of titles published annually: 4 Print; 4 E-
Book
Total Titles: 125 Print; 100 E-Book; 2 Audio
Imprints: And/Or Press; Books for Independent
Minds
Foreign Rep(s): Ingram (worldwide); Ingram/
PGW (worldwide)
Foreign Rights: Interlicense LLC (worldwide)
Distribution Center: Ingram/Publishers Group
West, 1700 Fourth St, Berkeley, CA 94710
Tel: 510-809-3700 *Fax:* 510-809-3777
E-mail: info@pgw.com *Web Site:* www.pgw.
com

§Rootstock Publishing
Imprint of Multicultural Media Inc
27 Main St, Suite 6, Montpelier, VT 05602
SAN: 299-1543
Tel: 802-839-0371
E-mail: info@rootstockpublishing.com
Web Site: www.rootstockpublishing.com
Key Personnel
Pres: Stephen McArthur *E-mail:* stephen@
rootstockpublishing.com
Founded: 1994 (as Multicultural Media Inc)
Fiction & nonfiction book publisher.
This publisher has indicated that 80% of their
product line is author subsidized.
ISBN Prefix(es): 978-1-57869
Number of titles published annually: 6 Print
Total Titles: 8 Print
Membership(s): Independent Book Publishers As-
sociation (IBPA); Independent Publishers of
New England (IPNE); New England Indepen-
dent Booksellers Association (NEIBA); New
England Library Association (NELA)

The Rosen Publishing Group Inc
29 E 21 St, New York, NY 10010
SAN: 203-3720
Toll Free Tel: 800-237-9932 *Toll Free Fax:* 888-
436-4643
E-mail: info@rosenpub.com
Web Site: www.rosenpublishing.com
Key Personnel
Pres: Roger Rosen
Founded: 1950
Hardcover, library editions, vocational guidance;
personal guidance; music & art catalogs; drug
abuse prevention, self-esteem development, values & ethics, new international writing, multicultural, African heritage, graphic nonfiction,
curriculum related nonfiction. Grades PreK-12.
ISBN Prefix(es): 978-0-8239; 978-1-4042; 978-1-
4358; 978-1-60851; 978-1-60852; 978-1-60853;
978-1-60854; 978-1-61511; 978-1-61512; 978-
1-61513; 978-1-61514; 978-1-61530; 978-1-
61531; 978-1-61532; 978-1-61533; 978-1-4488;
978-1-4777; 978-1-4824; 978-1-4994; 978-1-
68048; 978-1-5081
Number of titles published annually: 200 Print
Total Titles: 2,000 Print
Imprints: Britannica Educational Publishing; Editorial Buenas Letras; Gareth Stevens Publishing; Greenhaven Press®; KidHaven Publishing; Lucent Press; The New York Times Educational Publishing; PowerKids Press; Rosen
Central; Rosen Digital; Rosen Young Adult;
Windmill Books
Divisions: Rosen Classroom Books & Materials
Warehouse: Maple Logistics Solutions, York Distribution Ctr, 60 Grumbacher Rd, York, PA
17406

See separate listing for:
Gareth Stevens Publishing
Greenhaven Press®
Lucent Press

§RosettaBooks
125 Park Ave, 25th fl, New York, NY 10017
Tel: 646-274-1970 *Fax:* 212-977-5997 (e-fax)
E-mail: rights@rosettabooks.com; production@
rosettabooks.com
Web Site: www.rosettabooks.com
Key Personnel
CEO: Arthur Klebanoff
Founded: 2001
ISBN Prefix(es): 978-0-7953
Number of titles published annually: 10 Print; 25
E-Book; 10 Audio
Total Titles: 50 Print; 800 E-Book; 40 Audio
Distributed by Simon & Schuster
Distribution Center: Simon & Schuster, New
York, NY (trade print titles) *Toll Free Tel:* 800-
223-2336

§Ross Books
PO Box 4340, Berkeley, CA 94704-0340
Tel: 510-841-2474 *Fax:* 510-295-2531
E-mail: sales@rossbooks.com
Web Site: www.rossbooks.com
Key Personnel
Owner & Pres: Franz H Ross *E-mail:* franz@
rossbooks.com
Sales: Benny Juarez
Founded: 1977
General trade books & ebooks.
ISBN Prefix(es): 978-0-89496
Number of titles published annually: 4 Print; 1
CD-ROM; 3 E-Book; 1 Audio
Total Titles: 26 Print; 2 CD-ROM; 2 Online; 6 E-
Book; 2 Audio
Imprints: Baldar
Membership(s): Book Promotion Forum

§Rothstein Associates Inc
4 Arapaho Rd, Brookfield, CT 06804-3104
Tel: 203-740-7400 *Toll Free Tel:* 888-768-4783
Fax: 203-740-7401
E-mail: info@rothstein.com
Web Site: www.rothstein.com; www.
rothsteinpublishing.com
Key Personnel
Pres & CEO: Philip Jan Rothstein *E-mail:* pjr@
rothstein.com
Chief Mktg Offr: Mr Glyn Davies *Tel:* 415-259-
9137 *E-mail:* glyndavies@rothstein.com
Exec Ed: Kristen Noakes-Fry *Tel:* 727-258-8389
E-mail: knfwriter@rothstein.com
Founded: 1985
Publisher of digital & print content in business
continuity, risk management, crisis communica-
tions, crisis management & emergency manage-
ment for professionals & students.
ISBN Prefix(es): 978-0-9641648; 978-1-931332;
978-1-944480
Number of titles published annually: 15 Print; 9
CD-ROM; 25 E-Book
Total Titles: 80 Print; 36 CD-ROM; 30 E-Book
Divisions: NDY Publishing; Rothstein Publishing
Foreign Rep(s): iGroup.net (Asia-Pacific, Aus-
tralasia)

§The Rough Notes Co Inc
Subsidiary of Insurance Publishing Plus Corp
11690 Technology Dr, Carmel, IN 46032-5600
Tel: 317-582-1600 *Toll Free Tel:* 800-428-
4384 (cust serv) *Fax:* 317-816-1000
Toll Free Fax: 800-321-1909
E-mail: rnc@roughnotes.com
Web Site: www.roughnotes.com
Key Personnel
EVP & COO: Sam Berman
Ad & Natl Sales Dir: Eric Hall *E-mail:* ehall@
roughnotes.com

Founded: 1878
Technical/educational reference material specific
to the property/casualty insurance industry.
ISBN Prefix(es): 978-1-56461; 978-0-942326;
978-1-877723
Number of titles published annually: 13 Print
Total Titles: 38 Print; 4 Online
Advertising Agency: AdCom Group

Round Table Companies
Subsidiary of Writers of the Round Table Press
Inc
1027 Kenton Rd, Deerfield, IL 60015
Mailing Address: PO Box 511, Highland Park, IL
60035
Tel: 949-375-1006 *Fax:* 815-346-2398
Web Site: www.roundtablecompanies.com
Key Personnel
CEO: Corey Michael Blake *Tel:* 847-682-3493
E-mail: corey@roundtablecompanies.com
Dir, Client Experience: Yolanda Knight
E-mail: yolanda@roundtablecompanies.com
Founded: 1996
Round Table Companies (RTC) support leaders
interested in changing the world. Clients see
their purpose brought to life while their thought
leadership brand infrastructure is executed &
their community built. Core values are bril-
liance, love, joy, courage, momentum, honesty,
community & growth which create an atmo-
sphere where transformation occurs through the
magic of storytelling & the impact of human
connection.
This publisher has indicated that 90% of their
product line is author subsidized.
ISBN Prefix(es): 978-0-61066; 978-0-9814545;
978-0-9822206; 978-1-939418
Number of titles published annually: 6 Print; 6 E-
Book
Total Titles: 99 Print; 66 E-Book
Imprints: Round Table Comics
Foreign Rights: Graal Literary Agency (Albania,
Bulgaria, Croatia, Czechia, Estonia, Hungary,
Latvia, Lithuania, Poland, Romania, Serbia,
Slovakia, Slovenia); Grayhawk Agency (China,
Indonesia, Taiwan, Thailand, Vietnam); Danny
Hong Agency (Korea); International Editors'
Co (Argentina, Brazil, Portugal, Spain); Tuttle-
Mori Agency Inc (Japan)
Shipping Address: Lightning Source Inc, 1246
Heil Quaker Blvd, La Vergne, TN 37086, Con-
tent Acq Publr Sales Rep: Pam Dover *Tel:* 615-
213-4437 *Fax:* 615-213-4735 *E-mail:* pam.
dover@ingramcontent.com
Distribution Center: Lightning Source Inc, 14
Ingram Blvd, PO Box 3006, La Vergne, TN
37086-1986, Content Acq Publr Sales Rep:
Pam Dover *Tel:* 615-213-4437 *Fax:* 615-213-
4735 *E-mail:* pam.dover@ingramcontent.com
Membership(s): Independent Book Publishers As-
sociation (IBPA)

Routledge
Member of Taylor & Francis Group, an Informa
Business
711 Third Ave, New York, NY 10017
SAN: 213-196X
Tel: 212-216-7800 *Toll Free Tel:* 800-634-7064
(order enquiries, cust serv) *Fax:* 212-564-7854
Web Site: www.routledge.com
Founded: 1836
Academic books in the humanities, social & behavioral sciences. Academic reference. Professional titles in architecture, education & the
behavioral sciences.
ISBN Prefix(es): 978-0-915202 (formerly Accelerated Development); 978-1-55959 (formerly
Accelerated Development); 978-0-87630 (formerly Brunner-Routledge); 978-1-57958 (formerly Fitzroy Dearborn); 978-0-8240 (formerly
Garland); 978-0-8153 (formerly Garland); 978-
0-415; 978-0-87830 (Theatre Arts); 978-1-
85000 (formerly RoutledgeFalmer); 978-0-7007

(formerly Routledge Curzon); 978-0-419 (formerly Spon); 978-0-946653 (formerly Europa); 978-1-85743 (formerly Europa); 978-0-7494 (formerly Kogan Page); 978-90-5701 (formerly Gordon & Breach); 978-1-58391 (formerly Brunner-Routledge); 978-1-88496 (formerly Fitzroy Dearborn); 978-90-5702 (formerly Harwood Academic); 978-3-7186 (formerly Harwood Academic); 978-90-5823 (formerly Harwood Academic); 978-0-19713 (formerly Routledge Curzon); 978-0-72860 (formerly Routledge Curzon); 978-0-75070 (formerly RoutledgeFalmer)

Number of titles published annually: 2,000 Print; 2,000 Online; 2,000 E-Book

Total Titles: 33,000 Print; 21,000 Online; 21,000 E-Book

Imprints: CRC Press; Planners Press

Sales Office(s): Taylor & Francis, 6000 Broken Sound Pkwy, Suite 300, Boca Raton, FL 33487 *Tel:* 561-994-0555 *Toll Free Tel:* 800-272-7737 *Fax:* 561-989-8732 *Toll Free Fax:* 800-374-3401

Foreign Office(s): 2 Park Sq, Milton Park, Abingdon Oxon OX14 4RN, United Kingdom, Group Sales Dir: Christoph Chesher *Tel:* (020) 7017 6000 *Fax:* (020) 7017 6699 *E-mail:* book.orders@tandf.co.uk

Warehouse: Taylor & Francis, 7625 Empire Dr, Florence, KY 41042-2919 *Toll Free Tel:* 800-634-7064 *Toll Free Fax:* 800-248-4724 *E-mail:* orders@taylorandfrancis.com

See separate listing for:
Planners Press

Rowe Publishing LLC
655 Old Lifsey Springs Rd, Molena, GA 30258
Tel: 785-302-0451
E-mail: info@rowepub.com
Web Site: www.rowepub.com
Founded: 2010
Publisher of education, fiction, nonfiction, & children books.
ISBN Prefix(es): 978-0-9833971; 978-0-9851196; 978-1-939054; 978-1-64446
Number of titles published annually: 10 Print; 5 E-Book
Total Titles: 125 Print; 41 E-Book
Imprints: Rowe Publishing; Rowe Publishing & Design

Rowman & Littlefield
4501 Forbes Blvd, Suite 200, Lanham, MD 20706
SAN: 208-5143
Tel: 301-459-3366 *Toll Free Tel:* 800-462-6420 (ext 3024, cust serv) *Fax:* 301-429-5748
Web Site: rowman.com
Key Personnel
Group CEO: Jed Lyons
COO: Robert Marsh
CFO: Michael Lippenholz
SVP & Publr: Julie Kirsch
VP & Sr Exec Acqs Ed: Jonathan Sisk
 E-mail: jsisk@rowman.com
VP, Sales & Mktg: Karen Allman
 E-mail: kallman@rowman.com
Dir, Rts & Perms: Clare Cox *E-mail:* ccox@rowman.com
Sr Exec Ed: John Cerullo
Sr Acq Ed: Carol Flannery
Sr Prodn Ed: Clare Cerullo
Busn Devt Mgr: Michael Lyons
Founded: 1949
Nonfiction publishing in the humanities & social sciences.
ISBN Prefix(es): 978-0-8476; 978-1-56699; 978-0-7425; 978-1-4422; 978-0-87471; 978-0-9632098; 978-1-888051; 978-1-931890; 978-1-933494; 978-1-936283; 978-1-61281; 978-1-4616; 978-1-4617; 978-1-62093; 978-1-4758
Number of titles published annually: 600 Print; 600 E-Book; 50 Audio

Total Titles: 20,000 Print; 12,000 E-Book
Foreign Office(s): 10 Thornbury Rd, Plymouth, Devon PL6 7PP, United Kingdom, Contact: Ben Glover *Tel:* (020) 3111 1080 *Fax:* (020) 3111 1091 *E-mail:* bglover@rowman.com
Foreign Rep(s): APD Singapore Pte Ltd (Brunei, Cambodia, Indonesia, Laos, Malaysia, Singapore, Thailand, Vietnam); Aristotle House (Simons Watts) (Cameroon, Ethiopia, The Gambia, Ghana, Kenya, Malawi, Mauritius, Nigeria, Tanzania, Uganda); Asia Publishers Service Ltd (China, Hong Kong, Philippines, Taiwan); Avicenna Partnership Ltd (Middle East, North Africa); Co Info Pty Ltd (Australia, New Zealand, Papua New Guinea); Cranbury International LLC (Caribbean, Central America, Mexico, Puerto Rico, South America); Durnell Marketing Ltd (Andrew Durnell) (Europe); Juta & Co Ltd (Botswana, Lesotho, Namibia, South Africa, Swaziland, Zimbabwe); Overleaf (Bangladesh, Bhutan, India, Nepal, Sri Lanka); Publishers Representatives (Tahir Lodhi) (Pakistan); Quantum Publishing Solutions Ltd (Jim Chalmers) (UK); United Publishers Services Ltd (Japan); Wise Book Solutions (Korea)
Warehouse: 15200 NBN Way, Warehouse C, Blue Ridge Summit, PA 17214 *Tel:* 717-794-3800 *Fax:* 717-794-3803

Royal Fireworks Press
PO Box 399, Unionville, NY 10988
Tel: 845-726-4444 *Fax:* 845-726-3824
E-mail: mail@rfwp.com
Web Site: www.rfwp.com
Key Personnel
Dir, Order Dept & Cust Rel: Margaret Foley
Founded: 1977
Educational materials for gifted children, their parents & teachers; reading materials; adult literacy/education materials; fiction series for middle school: mystery & adventure; novels of growing up; young adult science fiction; youth against violence early childhood program (K-3).
ISBN Prefix(es): 978-0-89824; 978-0-88092
Number of titles published annually: 80 Print
Total Titles: 1,000 Print; 120 E-Book
Distributor for KAV Books; Silk Label Books; Trillium Press

Russell Sage Foundation
112 E 64 St, New York, NY 10065
SAN: 201-4521
Tel: 212-750-6000 *Toll Free Tel:* 800-524-6401 *Fax:* 212-371-4761
E-mail: info@rsage.org
Web Site: www.russellsage.org
Key Personnel
Pres: Sheldon Danzinger
Dir, Communs: David Haproff *Tel:* 212-750-6037
Dir, Pubns: Suzanne Nichols
Founded: 1907
Sociology, economics, political science.
ISBN Prefix(es): 978-0-87154; 978-1-61044
Number of titles published annually: 20 Print
Total Titles: 1,000 Print
Shipping Address: Chicago Distribution Center, 11030 S Langley Ave, Chicago, IL 60628 *Tel:* 773-702-7010 *Toll Free Fax:* 800-621-8476 *Web Site:* press.uchicago.edu

§Russian Information Services Inc
PO Box 567, Montpelier, VT 05601
Tel: 802-223-4955 *Toll Free Tel:* 800-639-4301
E-mail: orders@russianlife.com
Web Site: www.russianlife.com
Key Personnel
Pres & Publr: Paul E Richardson *E-mail:* paulr@russianlife.com
Founded: 1990

Publish magazines (including *Russian Life*), books, info, maps for business & independent travel to Russia.
ISBN Prefix(es): 978-1-880100
Number of titles published annually: 3 Print; 3 E-Book
Total Titles: 30 Print; 30 E-Book
Imprints: Edward & Dee

Rutgers University Press
Division of Rutgers, The State University of New Jersey
106 Somerset St, 3rd fl, New Brunswick, NJ 08901
SAN: 203-364X
Tel: 848-445-7762; 848-445-7761 (sales) *Fax:* 732-745-4935
E-mail: sales@rutgersuniversitypress.org
Web Site: www.rutgersuniversitypress.org
Key Personnel
Dir: Micah Kleit *Tel:* 848-445-7784
 E-mail: mbk82@press.rutgers.edu
Asst to the Dir & Assoc Ed: Elisabeth Maselli *Tel:* 848-445-7785 *E-mail:* esm102@press.rutgers.edu
Edit Dir: Kimberly Guinta *Tel:* 848-445-7786
 E-mail: kimberly.guinta@rutgers.edu
Fin Dir: David Flum *Tel:* 848-445-7763
 E-mail: dflum@press.rutgers.edu
Prodn & Art Dir: Jennifer Blanc-Tal *Tel:* 848-445-7764 *E-mail:* jfb131@press.rutgers.edu
Sales & Mktg Dir: Jeremy Grainger *Tel:* 848-445-7781 *E-mail:* jg1160@press.rutgers.edu
Exec Ed: Peter Mickulas *Tel:* 848-445-7752 *E-mail:* mickulas@press.rutgers.edu; Nicole Solano *Tel:* 848-445-7787 *E-mail:* nicole.solano@rutgers.edu
Prodn Ed: Daryl Browler *Tel:* 848-445-7761 *E-mail:* djb147@press.rutgers.edu; Vincent Nordhaus *Tel:* 848-445-7797 *E-mail:* vincent.nordhaus@press.rutgers.edu; Alissa Zarro *Tel:* 848-445-7756 *E-mail:* ajz45@press.rutgers.edu
Ed: Lisa Banning *Tel:* 848-445-7791
 E-mail: lmb333@press.rutgers.edu
Sr Promo Mgr: Brice Hammack *Tel:* 848-445-7765 *E-mail:* bhammack@press.rutgers.edu
IT Mgr: Penny Burke *E-mail:* pborden@press.rutgers.edu
Publicity Mgr: Courtney Brach *Tel:* 848-445-7775 *E-mail:* clb301@press.rutgers.edu
Founded: 1936
Since its founding as a nonprofit publisher, Rutgers University Press has been dedicated to the advancement & dissemination of knowledge to scholars, students & the general reading public. An integral part of one of the leading public research & teaching universities in the US, the Press reflects & is essential to the University's missions of research, instruction & service. To carry out these goals, books are published in electronic & print format in a broad array of disciplines across the humanities, social sciences & sciences. Fulfilling its mandate to serve the people of New Jersey, books of scholarly & popular interest on the state & surrounding region are also published. Working with authors throughout the world, the Press seeks books that meet high editorial standards, facilitate the exchange of ideas, enhance teaching & make scholarship accessible to a wide range of readers. It celebrates & affirms its role as a major cultural institution that contributes significantly to the ideas that shape the critical issues of our day.
ISBN Prefix(es): 978-0-8135; 978-1-9788
Number of titles published annually: 90 Print; 80 Online; 80 E-Book
Total Titles: 3,500 Print; 1,600 Online; 1,600 E-Book
Foreign Rep(s): Eurospan (worldwide exc Canada & USA); University of British Columbia Press (Canada)

Foreign Rights: McIntosh & Otis Inc (worldwide)
Returns: Chicago Distribution Center (CDC),
11030 S Langley Ave, Chicago, IL 60628
SAN: 202-5280
Distribution Center: Chicago Distribution Cen-
ter (CDC), 11030 S Langley Ave, Chicago, IL
60628 *Tel:* 773-702-7000 *Toll Free Tel:* 800-
621-2736 *Fax:* 773-702-7212 *Toll Free
Fax:* 800-621-8476 *E-mail:* orders@press.
uchicago.edu *Web Site:* press.uchicago.edu/cdc
SAN: 202-5280
Membership(s): American Association of Uni-
versity Presses (AAUP); American Booksellers
Association (ABA); New Atlantic Indepen-
dent Booksellers Association (NAIBA); New
England Independent Booksellers Association
(NEIBA)

§Saddleback Educational Publishing
151 Kalmus Dr, Suite J-1, Costa Mesa, CA 92626
SAN: 860-0902
Tel: 714-640-5200 *Toll Free Tel:* 888-SDLBACK
(735-2225); 800-637-8715 *Fax:* 714-640-5297
Toll Free Fax: 888-734-4010
E-mail: contact@sdlback.com
Web Site: www.sdlback.com
Key Personnel
Pres: Arianne McHugh
Founded: 1982
Publish high-interest, low-readabilty material for
middle school & high school. Solutions for
struggling learners.
ISBN Prefix(es): 978-1-56254; 978-1-59905; 978-
1-61651; 978-1-60291; 978-1-62250; 978-1-
62670; 978-1-63078; 978-1-68021
Number of titles published annually: 200 Print;
10 CD-ROM; 20 E-Book; 10 Audio
Total Titles: 2,000 Print; 150 CD-ROM; 400 E-
Book; 150 Audio
Distributed by Children's Plus; Delaney
Distribution Center: Follett School Solu-
tions Inc, 1340 Ridgeview Dr, McHenry,
IL 60050 *Tel:* 815-759-1700 *Toll Free
Tel:* 888-511-5114 (cust serv) *Fax:* 815-
759-9831 *Toll Free Fax:* 800-852-5458
E-mail: info@follettlearning.com *Web
Site:* www.follettlearning.com SAN: 169-1902
Saunders Book Co, PO Box 308, Collingwood,
ON L9Y 3Z7, Canada *Tel:* 705-445-4777 *Toll
Free Tel:* 800-461-9120 *Fax:* 705-445-9569
Toll Free Fax: 800-561-1763 *E-mail:* info@
saundersbooks.ca
Membership(s): American Educational Publish-
ers; Educational Book & Media Association
(EBMA)

§William H Sadlier Inc
9 Pine St, New York, NY 10005
SAN: 204-0948
Tel: 212-227-2120 *Toll Free Tel:* 800-221-5175
(cust serv) *Fax:* 212-312-6080
E-mail: customerservice@sadlier.com
Web Site: www.sadlier.com
Key Personnel
Chmn of the Bd: Frank S Dinger
Pres & CEO: Raymond Fagan
VP & Dir, Mktg: Alexandra Rivas-Smith
VP & Natl Field Sales Mgr: Dan McElhinny
VP & Natl Sales Admin: Kevin O'Donnell
Creative Dir: Vincent Gallo
Gen Coun: Angela Dinger
Cust Serv: Melissa Gibbons
Founded: 1832
Preschool, elementary & secondary textbooks on
catechetics, sacraments, reading/language arts,
mathematics; adult catechetical programs.
ISBN Prefix(es): 978-0-87105; 978-0-8215; 978-
1-4217
Number of titles published annually: 4 Print

**§SAE (Society of Automotive Engineers
International)**
400 Commonwealth Dr, Warrendale, PA 15096-
0001
SAN: 216-0811
Tel: 724-776-4841; 724-776-4970 (outside US &
CN) *Toll Free Tel:* 877-606-7323 (cust serv)
Fax: 724-776-0790 (cust serv)
E-mail: publications@sae.org; customerservice@
sae.org
Web Site: www.sae.org
Key Personnel
CEO: David L Schutt
Founded: 1905
Scientific & technical publications.
ISBN Prefix(es): 978-0-89883; 978-1-56091; 978-
0-7680; 978-1-4686
Number of titles published annually: 150 Print
Total Titles: 650 Print; 23 CD-ROM; 1 Online;
15 E-Book; 1 Audio
Branch Office(s)
1200 "G" St NW, Suite 800, Washington, DC
20005 *Tel:* 202-434-8943 *Fax:* 202-463-7319
Effective Training Inc (ETI), 14143 Farmington
Rd, Livonia, MI 48154 *Tel:* 734-744-5940 *Toll
Free Tel:* 800-886-0909 *Fax:* 734-744-5979
Automotive Headquarters, 755 W Big Beaver Rd,
Suite 1600, Troy, MI 48084 *Tel:* 248-273-2455
Fax: 248-273-2494
Foreign Office(s): 280 Blvd du Souverain,
1160 Brussels, Belgium *Tel:* (02) 789-23-44
E-mail: info-sae-europe@associationhq.com
SAE International China Off, Rm 2503, Litong
Plaza, No 1350 N Sichuan Rd, Hongkou Dis-
trict, Shanghai 200080, China *Tel:* (021) 6140
8900 *Fax:* (021) 6140 8901
SAE Aerospace Standards, One York St, London
W1U 6PA, United Kingdom *Tel:* (020) 7034
1250 *Fax:* (020) 7034 1257
Distributor for Coordinating Research Council Inc
Foreign Rep(s): Aeromarine Vehicles (Singapore);
Allied Publishers Pvt Ltd (India); Booknet Co
Ltd (Thailand); Catarac (China); China Na-
tional Publications (China); China Publishers
Marketing (China); EBSCO Korea (Korea);
Eurospan (Marc Bedwell) (Asia-Pacific exc
China); Eurospan Group (Africa, Asia-Pacific,
Australasia, Brazil, Europe, Middle East, Ocea-
nia); Eurospan India (India); GDI Co Ltd (Ko-
rea); IHS de Mexico (Latin America, Mex-
ico); Kinokuniya Co Ltd (Japan); Maruzen
Co Book Division (Japan); Normdocs (Rus-
sia); Pak Book Corp (Pakistan); PB for Books
(Pathumthani) Co Ltd (Thailand); SAE Aus-
tralasia (Australasia, Oceania); SAE Brasil
(Brazil); SAE of Japan (Japan); Ta Tong Book
Co Ltd (Taiwan); UBS Library Services Pte
Ltd (Singapore); UBSD Distribution Sdn Bhd
(Malaysia); Unifacamanu Trading Co Ltd (Tai-
wan); YPJ Publications & Distributors Sdn Bhd
(Malaysia)

Safari Press
15621 Chemical Lane, Bldg B, Huntington
Beach, CA 92649
Tel: 714-894-9080 *Toll Free Tel:* 800-451-4788
Fax: 714-894-4949
E-mail: info@safaripress.com
Web Site: www.safaripress.com
Key Personnel
CEO: Ludo J Wurfbain
Chief Ed: Jacque Neufeld
Founded: 1984
Specialize in big-game hunting, firearms, wing-
shooting, Africana & sporting; hardcover trade
& limited editions.
ISBN Prefix(es): 978-0-940143; 978-1-57157
Number of titles published annually: 10 Print
Total Titles: 340 Print
Distributor for Quiller

Safer Society Foundation Inc
33 Park St, Brandon, VT 05733

Mailing Address: PO Box 340, Brandon, VT
05733-0340
Tel: 802-247-3132 *Fax:* 802-247-4233
E-mail: info@safersociety.org
Web Site: www.safersociety.org
Founded: 1985
Specialize in titles relating to the prevention &
treatment of sexual abuse.
ISBN Prefix(es): 978-1-884444
Number of titles published annually: 4 Print
Total Titles: 80 Print
Imprints: Safer Society Press
Foreign Rep(s): Open Leaves Books (Australia);
Visions Book Store Ltd (Canada)

Saga Press, see Gallery Books

Sagamore Publishing LLC
3611 N Staley Rd, Suite B, Champaign, IL 61822
SAN: 292-5788
Tel: 217-359-5940 *Toll Free Tel:* 800-327-5557
(orders) *Fax:* 217-359-5975
E-mail: web@sagamorepub.com
Web Site: www.sagamorepub.com
Key Personnel
Publr: Dr Joseph J Bannon, Sr
Pres: Peter L Bannon
Dir, Prodn & Devt: Susan M Davis
Sales & Mktg Mgr: Misti Gilles
E-mail: mgilles@sagamorepub.com
Founded: 1974
ISBN Prefix(es): 978-0-915611; 978-1-57167;
978-1-58382
Number of titles published annually: 13 Print
Total Titles: 210 Print; 6 Online
Distributor for American Academy for Park &
Recreation Administration
Foreign Rep(s): Gazelle Book Services Ltd (Con-
tinental Europe, Ireland, UK); HM Leisure
Planning (Australia, New Zealand)

SAGE Publishing
2455 Teller Rd, Thousand Oaks, CA 91320
Toll Free Tel: 800-818-7243 *Toll Free Fax:* 800-
583-2665
E-mail: info@sagepub.com; orders@sagepub.com
Web Site: www.sagepublishing.com
Key Personnel
Founder & Exec Chmn: Sara Miller McCune
Pres & CEO: Blaise R Simqu
Founded: 1965
SAGE Publishing is an independent company that
disseminates journals, books & library products
for the educational, scholarly & professional
markets.
ISBN Prefix(es): 978-0-8039
Number of titles published annually: 800 Print
Imprints: CQ Press; Learning Matters; Adam
Matthew
Divisions: Corwin
Branch Office(s)
2600 Virginia Ave NW, Suite 600, Washington,
DC 20037
Foreign Office(s): SAGE Publishing Australia,
114 William St, Level 20, Melbourne, Victoria
3000, Australia *Web Site:* au.sagepub.com
SAGE Publications India Pvt Ltd, B1/I-1 Mohan
Cooperative Industrial Area, Mathura Rd, New
Delhi 110 044, India *Tel:* (011) 4053 9222
Fax: (011) 4053 9234 *Web Site:* in.sagepub.
com
18 Cross St, No 10-10/11/12, China Sq Central,
Singapore 048423, Singapore
SAGE Publications Ltd, One Oliver's Yard, 55
City Rd, London EC1Y 1SP, United Kingdom
Tel: (020) 7324 8500 *Fax:* (020) 7324 8600
E-mail: market@sagepub.co.uk *Web Site:* uk.
sagepub.com
Foreign Rep(s): Sage Publications India Pvt Ltd
(India, South Asia); Sage Publications Ltd
(Africa, Asia-Pacific, Europe, Middle East,

UK); United Publishers Services Ltd (Japan, Korea)
See separate listing for:
Corwin
CQ Press

St Andrews University Press
Subsidiary of St Andrews University
1700 Dogwood Mile, Laurinburg, NC 28352-5598
Tel: 910-277-5555 *Toll Free Tel:* 800-763-0198
 Fax: 910-277-5020
Web Site: www.sa.edu/st-andrews-university-press
Key Personnel
Asst Ed: Madge McKeithen
Founded: 1969
ISBN Prefix(es): 978-0-932662; 978-1-879934
Number of titles published annually: 5 Print
Total Titles: 82 Print

St Augustine's Press Inc
PO Box 2285, South Bend, IN 46680-2285
Tel: 574-291-3500 *Fax:* 574-291-3700
E-mail: bruce@staugustine.net
Web Site: www.staugustine.net
Key Personnel
Pres & Publr: Bruce Fingerhut *E-mail:* bruce@staugustine.net
Prodn: Benjamin Fingerhut *Tel:* 773-983-8471
 E-mail: benjaminfingerhut@yahoo.com
Founded: 1996
Scholarly & trade publishing in humanities.
ISBN Prefix(es): 978-1-890318; 978-1-883357; 978-1-58731
Number of titles published annually: 35 Print
Total Titles: 600 Print; 4 E-Book
Imprints: Carthage Reprints
Editorial Office(s): 17917 Killington Way, South Bend, IN 46614-9773, Contact: Bruce Fingerhut *Tel:* 574-291-3500 *E-mail:* bruce@staugustine.net
Sales Office(s): University of Chicago Press, Sales Dept, 1429 E 60 St, Chicago, IL 60637-2954, Sales Dir: John Kessler *Tel:* 773-702-7248 *Fax:* 773-702-9756 *E-mail:* jkessler@press.uchicago.edu
Distributed by University of Chicago Press
Distributor for Dumb Ox Books (publishes the Aristotelian Commentaries of Thomas Aquinas & like works); Hardwood Press (trade books, mostly in sports & regional works); New Criterion Books (poetry prize)
Foreign Rights: Jeremy Beer (worldwide exc USA)
Advertising Agency: Design Promotion
Billing Address: Chicago Distribution Center, 11030 S Langley Ave, Chicago, IL 60628-3893
Orders to: Chicago Distribution Center, 11030 S Langley Ave, Chicago, IL 60628-3893, Karen Hyzy *Tel:* 773-702-7000 *Toll Free Tel:* 800-621-2736 *Fax:* 773-702-7212 *Toll Free Fax:* 800-621-8476 *E-mail:* kh@press.uchicago.edu
Returns: Chicago Distribution Center, 11030 S Langley Ave, Chicago, IL 60628-3893
Shipping Address: Chicago Distribution Center, 11030 S Langley Ave, Chicago, IL 60628-3893, Contact: Karen Hyzy *Tel:* 773-702-7000 *Toll Free Tel:* 800-621-2736 *Fax:* 773-702-7212 *Toll Free Fax:* 800-621-8476 *E-mail:* kh@press.uchicago.edu
Warehouse: Chicago Distribution Center, 11030 S Langley Ave, Chicago, IL 60628-3893
Distribution Center: Chicago Distribution Center, 11030 S Langley Ave, Chicago, IL 60628-3893 *Toll Free Tel:* 800-621-8471 *Toll Free Fax:* 800-621-8471 *E-mail:* kh@press.uchicago.edu

Saint Herman Press
Subsidiary of Brotherhood of Saint Herman of Alaska

4430 Mushroom Lane, Platina, CA 96076
SAN: 661-583X
Mailing Address: PO Box 70, Platina, CA 96076-0070
Tel: 530-352-4430 *Fax:* 530-352-4432
E-mail: stherman@stherman.com
Web Site: www.sainthermanmonastery.com
Key Personnel
CFO: Nicholas Liebmann
Pres: Abbott Damascene
Secy: Paisius Bjerke
Founded: 1963
Publisher of books about the Orthodox Christian faith & Orthodox monasticism. Special emphasis on recent saints & spirituality, curriculum & textbooks.
ISBN Prefix(es): 978-0-938635; 978-1-887904
Number of titles published annually: 3 Print
Total Titles: 77 Print
Imprints: Brotherhood of Saint Herman of Alaska; Fr Seraphim Rose Foundation; St Herman Press; St Xenia Skete
Distributed by Light & Life Publishing Co
Foreign Rep(s): Vladimir Ivlenkov (Australia); Orthodox Christian Books Ltd (Nicholas Chapman) (England)

§St James Press®
Imprint of Gale
27500 Drake Rd, Farmington Hills, MI 48331-3535
Tel: 248-699-4253 *Toll Free Tel:* 800-877-4253 (orders) *Toll Free Fax:* 877-363-4253
E-mail: gale.customerservice@cengage.com
Web Site: www.gale.com
Founded: 1968
ISBN Prefix(es): 978-1-55862; 978-0-912289; 978-1-4103
Number of titles published annually: 8 E-Book
Total Titles: 303 Print

Saint Johann Press
315 Schraalenburgh Rd, Haworth, NJ 07641
Tel: 201-387-1529 *Fax:* 201-501-0698
Web Site: www.stjohannpress.com
Key Personnel
Pres: David Biesel *E-mail:* d.biesel@verizon.net
VP: Diane Biesel
Dir, Sales & Promos: Deborah Brugger
Founded: 1990
Started as a book packager & consultant. Began publishing in 1998.
ISBN Prefix(es): 978-1-878282; 978-1-937943
Number of titles published annually: 12 Print
Total Titles: 170 Print
Membership(s): American Academy of Religion (AAR); American Library Association (ALA); Combined Book Exhibit (CBE); Independent Book Publishers Association (IBPA); Society for American Baseball Research; USMC Combat Correspondents Association (USMCCCA)

St Joseph's University Press
5600 City Ave, Philadelphia, PA 19131-1395
SAN: 240-8368
Tel: 610-660-3402 *Fax:* 610-660-3412
E-mail: sjupress@sju.edu
Web Site: www.sjupress.com
Key Personnel
Dir: Mr Carmen R Croce *E-mail:* ccroce@sju.edu
Edit Dir: Rev Joseph F Chorpenning *Tel:* 610-660-1214 *E-mail:* jchorpen@sju.edu
Founded: 1971
Scholarly books on early modern Catholicism & the visual arts, regional studies (Philadelphia & environs), Jesuit studies (history, visual arts).
ISBN Prefix(es): 978-0-916101
Number of titles published annually: 5 Print
Total Titles: 78 Print
Membership(s): American Association of University Presses (AAUP); Association of Jesuit University Presses

St Martin's Press, LLC
Subsidiary of Macmillan
120 Broadway, New York, NY 10271
Tel: 646-307-5151
Web Site: us.macmillan.com/smp
Key Personnel
Chmn: Sally Richardson
Pres: Jennifer Enderlin
EVP & COO, Macmillan Trade Publg: Steve Cohen
EVP, Mktg & Digital Media Strategy: Jeff Dodes
SVP & Exec Publg Dir/Publr, Minotaur Books: Andrew Martin
SVP & Ed-in-Chief: George Witte
VP & Assoc Publr: Lisa Senz
VP & Assoc Publr, Nonfiction: Laura Clark
VP & Exec Dir, Publicity: Tracey Guest
VP & Publg Dir, St Martin's Paperbacks & Griffin: Anne Marie Tallberg
VP & Edit Dir, St Martin's Essentials: Joel Fotinos
VP, Edit Dir & Assoc Publr, Minotaur Books: Kelley Ragland
VP & Creative Dir, Pbks: Michael Storrings
VP & Exec Ed: Peter Wolverton
VP, Creative Servs & Ad: Tom Thompson
VP, Fin & Acctg: John Cusack
VP, Mktg: Paul Hochman
VP, Mktg & Sales Opers: Joe Goldschein
VP, Mktg, Communs & Audience Devt: Brant Janeway
VP, Publicity & Independent Bookseller Liaison: Dori Weintraub
VP, Rts: Kerry Nordling
Div VP, Publg Opers: Sidney Conde
Div VP, Dir of Publicity: John Murphy
Div VP, Creative Dir, Trade: Stephen Snider
Assoc Publr, Wednesday Books & Exec Ed, St Martin's: Eileen Rothschild
Exec Art Dir, SMP/Minotaur: David Rotstein
Dir, Creative Services: Kim Ludlam
Dir, Intl Rts: Marta Fleming
Edit Dir, Paperbacks: Monique Patterson
Edit Dir, Wednesday Books: Sara Goodman
Assoc Dir, Mktg: Erica Martirano; Martin Quinn
Assoc Dir, Publicity: Gabrielle Gantz
Assoc Publicity Dir, Pbk/Ref Group: John Karle
Asst Dir, Publicity: Rebecca Lang; Jessica Zimmerman
Asst Dir, Publicity, St Martin's/Minotaur: Sarah Melnyk
Asst Mktg Dir: Marissa Sangiacomo
Sr Exec Mng Ed, Trade: Amelie Littell
Exec Mng Ed, Pbk/Ref Group: John Rounds
Exec Ed: Elizabeth Beier; Sarah Cantin; Elisabeth Dyssegaard; Michael Flamini; Keith Kahla; Marcia Markland; Marc Resnick; Charles Spicer; Karen Wolny
Exec Ed, Minotaur Books: Catherine Richards
Exec Ed-at-Large: Leslie Gelbman
Sr Ed: Michael Homler; Daniela Rapp
Sr Ed, Castle Point Books: Courtney Littler
Sr Ed, Nonfiction: Kara Rota
Sr Ed, St Martin's & Wednesday Books: Vicki Lame
Ed: Pronoy Sarkar; Alexandra Sehulster
Assoc Ed: Laura Apperson; Sylvan Creekmore; Lauren Jablonski; Hannah O'Grady
Assoc Ed, St Martin's Press/Wednesday Books: Jennie Conway; Tiffany Shelton
Asst Ed: Rachel Diebel; Sarah Grill; Gwen Hawkes; Alice Pfeifer; Kevin Reilly
Asst Ed, St Martin's Press/Minotaur: Nettie Finn
Asst Ed, Thomas Dunne Books: Janine Barlow; Samantha Zukergood
Sr Mgr, Digital Ad Opers: Erik Platt
Sr Mktg Mgr: Joe Brosnan; Michelle Cashman; Danielle Prielipp; DJ DeSmyter; Allison Ziegler
Sr Mktg Opers Mgr: Meaghan Leahy
Sr Natl Accts Mgr: Jeanette Zwart
Sr Publg Mgr: Nichole Argyres
Mktg Mgr: Sara Beth Haring; Karen Masnica; John Nicholas

Assoc Mktg Mgr: Beatrice Jason; Kim Lew
Asst Mktg Mgr: Stephen Erickson; Titi Oluwo
Sr Publicity Mgr: Katie Bassel; Jessica Lawrence
Publicity Mgr: Kathryn Hough Boutross; Mary
   Moates
Asst Mgr, Ad Opers: Dylan Helstien
Sr Publicist: Justin Velella
Publicist: Meghan Harrington; Kayla Janus
Assoc Publicist: Clare Mauer
Edit Dept Coord: Sara Thwaite
Founded: 1952
General nonfiction, fiction, reference, scholarly,
   mass market, travel, children's books.
ISBN Prefix(es): 978-0-312; 978-1-4039; 978-0-
   230; 978-1-4272; 978-1-250; 978-1-1370; 978-
   1-4299; 978-1-4668
Number of titles published annually: 1,000 Print
Imprints: All Points Books; Thomas Dunne
   Books; Golden Books Adult Publishing;
   Golden Guides; LA Weekly Books; Minotaur
   Books; Priddy Books; Renaissance Books; St
   Martin's Castle Point; St Martin's Dead Let-
   ter; St Martin's Essentials; St Martin's Griffin;
   St Martin's Paperbacks; St Martin's Press; St
   Martin's True Crime; St Martin's True Crime
   Classics; Stonewall Inn Editions; Swerve; Tru-
   man Talley Books; Wednesday Books
Foreign Rep(s): H B Fenn & Co Ltd (Canada);
   Macmillan India (India); Macmillan New
   Zealand (New Zealand); Melia UK (Ireland,
   UK); Pan Macmillan Australia (Australia); Pan
   Macmillan-Hong Kong (Asia, Middle East);
   Pan Macmillan South Africa (South Africa);
   Pan Macmillan UK (Caribbean, Europe, Israel,
   Latin America)
Foreign Rights: Big Apple Agency Inc (China,
   Taiwan); The Book Publishers Association of
   Israel (Israel); Eliane Benisti (France); Inter-
   national Editors' Co (Portugal, South Amer-
   ica, Spain); Nurcihan Kesim Literary Agency
   Inc (Turkey); Lex Copyright Office (Hungary);
   Literary Services (Italy); Prava i prevodi (East-
   ern Europe, Greece); Sane Toregard Agency
   (Denmark, Finland, Iceland, Norway, Sweden);
   Thomas Schlueck GmbH (Germany); Tuttle-
   Mori Agency Inc (Thailand)
Distribution Center: MPS Distribution Center,
   16365 James Madison Hwy, Gordonsville, VA
   22942-8501 Toll Free Tel: 888-330-8477 Toll
   Free Fax: 800-672-2054
Membership(s): Association of American Publish-
   ers (AAP)

Saint Mary's Press
Subsidiary of Christian Brothers Publications
702 Terrace Heights, Winona, MN 55987-1320
SAN: 203-073X
Tel: 507-457-7900 Toll Free Tel: 800-533-8095
   Toll Free Fax: 800-344-9225
E-mail: smpress@smp.org
Web Site: www.smp.org
Key Personnel
Pres & CEO: John M Vitek
Exec Dir, Delivery: Caren Yang
Libn & ISBN Contact: Connie Jensen
   E-mail: cjensen@smp.org
Founded: 1943
High school curriculum, paperbound & digital;
   religion (Catholic); Bibles, youth ministry re-
   sources.
ISBN Prefix(es): 978-0-88489; 978-1-59982
Number of titles published annually: 25 Print; 8
   E-Book
Total Titles: 500 Print; 30 E-Book
Distributor for Group Publishing
Foreign Rep(s): The Bible Society (New
   Zealand); B Broughton Ltd (Canada); Catholic
   News, Books & Media (Singapore); John Gar-
   ratt Publishing (Australia); Herald Publications
   Sdn Bhd (Malaysia); Pleroma Christian Sup-
   plies (New Zealand); Redemptorist Publications
   (UK)

Saint Nectarios Press
10300 Ashworth Ave N, Seattle, WA 98133-9410
SAN: 159-0170
Tel: 206-522-4471 Toll Free Tel: 800-643-4233
E-mail: orders@stnectariospress.com
Web Site: www.stnectariospress.com
Founded: 1977
Traditional Eastern Orthodox books.
ISBN Prefix(es): 978-0-913026
Number of titles published annually: 3 Print
Total Titles: 70 Print

St Pauls
Division of The Society of Saint Paul
2187 Victory Blvd, Staten Island, NY 10314-6603
SAN: 201-2405
Tel: 718-761-0047 (edit & prodn); 718-698-2759
   (mktg & billing) Toll Free Tel: 800-343-2522
   Fax: 718-761-0057
E-mail: sales@stpauls.us; marketing@stpauls.us
Web Site: www.stpauls.us
Key Personnel
Ed-in-Chief & Contact, ISBN & Rts & Perms: Br
   Zbigniew Gawron E-mail: editor@stpauls.us
Treas: Br Marco Bulgarelli
Prodn Mgr & Art Dir: Br Edward Donaher
   E-mail: edonaher@aol.com
Copy Ed: Br Frank Sadowski
Mktg: Fr Tony Bautista Tel: 718-698-2759
Founded: 1961
Religion (Catholic), bible, education, pastoral
   care, prayer books, biography, spirituality,
   psychology, philosophy, theology, Spanish ti-
   tles (Roman Catholic), bereavement, church,
   ethics, homilies, liturgy, marriage & family life,
   prayer, religious education, saints' lives, scrip-
   ture, cassettes & videos.
ISBN Prefix(es): 978-0-8189
Number of titles published annually: 24 Print; 10
   CD-ROM; 20 Online; 20 E-Book
Total Titles: 425 Print; 85 CD-ROM; 105 Online;
   105 E-Book
Foreign Office(s): Edizioni Paoline, Piazza Soncino 5, 520092 Cinisello Balsamo MI, Italy

Salaam Reads, see Simon & Schuster Children's
Publishing

Salem Press
Imprint of Grey House Publishing Inc™
2 University Plaza, Suite 310, Hackensack, NJ
07601
SAN: 208-838X
Tel: 201-968-0500 Toll Free Tel: 800-221-1592
   Fax: 201-968-0511
E-mail: csr@salempress.com
Web Site: salempress.com
Key Personnel
Gen Mgr: Jim Wright E-mail: jwright@
   salempress.com
Founded: 1949
Reference books & online products for middle
   school, secondary school, colleges & public
   libraries.
ISBN Prefix(es): 978-0-89356; 978-1-58765
Number of titles published annually: 50 Print; 50
   Online; 50 E-Book
Total Titles: 460 Print; 425 Online; 460 E-Book
Imprints: Magill's Choice
Foreign Rep(s): Aditya Books Pvt Ltd
   (Bangladesh, India, Nepal, Pakistan, Sri
   Lanka); Alkem Co (S) Pte Ltd (Brunei, Hong
   Kong, Indonesia, Korea, Malaysia, Philip-
   pines, Singapore, Taiwan, Thailand, Vietnam);
   Eurospan Ltd (Africa, Europe, Middle East,
   UK); Grey House Publishing Canada (Canada);
   Yushodo Co Ltd (Japan)

Salina Bookshelf Inc
1120 W University Ave, Suite 102, Flagstaff, AZ
86001
SAN: 253-0503

Toll Free Tel: 877-527-0070 Fax: 928-526-0386
Web Site: www.salinabookshelf.com
Key Personnel
Pres: Eric Lockard Tel: 877-527-0700 ext 425
   E-mail: elockard@salinabookshelf.com
Art Dir: Corey Begay Tel: 877-527-0700 ext 202
Founded: 1994
Publisher of multicultural books with a strong fo-
   cus on the stories of the Navajo people. Our
   textbooks, children's picture books & elec-
   tronic media in Navajo & English are resources
   for the home, library & classroom. We recog-
   nize the importance of portraying traditional
   language & culture & of making this knowl-
   edge accessible to a broad spectrum of curious
   minds.
ISBN Prefix(es): 978-1-893354; 978-0-9644189
Number of titles published annually: 10 Print; 3
   Audio
Total Titles: 100 Print; 1 CD-ROM; 20 Audio
Membership(s): American Indian Library Association; The Children's Book Council (CBC); Independent Book Publishers Association (IBPA);
   Publishers Association of the West (PubWest)

SAMS Technical Publishing LLC
Division of AGS Capital Inc
9850 E 30 St, Indianapolis, IN 46229
Toll Free Tel: 800-428-7267
E-mail: customercare@samswebsite.com
Web Site: www.samswebsite.com
Key Personnel
COO: Alan McFarland
Journalist Publr: Alan Symons
Founded: 1946
Publisher of Quickfact & Photofact® service
   manuals.
ISBN Prefix(es): 978-0-7906
Number of titles published annually: 150 Print
Total Titles: 4,800 Print
Imprints: Indy-Tech Publishing; Photofact®;
   Quickfact®
Distributor for Butterworth-Heinemann; McGraw-
   Hill; Prompt Publications

San Diego State University Press
Division of San Diego State University Founda-
tion
Arts & Letters 283/MC 6020, 5500 Campanile
Dr, San Diego, CA 92182-6020
Tel: 619-594-6220 (orders); 619-594-1524 (re-
   turns) Fax: 619-594-4998 (returns)
E-mail: memo@sdsu.edu
Web Site: sdsupress.sdsu.edu
Key Personnel
Ed/Dir: Dr Bill Nericcio Tel: 619-594-1524
   E-mail: bnericci@mail.sdsu.edu
Ed: Prof Harry Polkinhorn E-mail: hpolkinh@
   mail.sdsu.edu
Founded: 1959
Scholarly & trade, monographs.
ISBN Prefix(es): 978-0-916304; 978-1-879691
Number of titles published annually: 5 Print; 2
   Online
Imprints: Amatl Comix; Binational Press; Hyper-
   bole
Distributor for Institute for Regional Studies of
   the Californias

§Santa Monica Press LLC
16236 San Dieguito Rd, Suite 1-28, Rancho Santa
Fe, CA 92067
SAN: 298-1459
Mailing Address: PO Box 850, Solana Beach, CA
92075
Tel: 858-793-1890 Toll Free Tel: 800-784-9553
E-mail: books@santamonicapress.com
Web Site: www.santamonicapress.com
Key Personnel
Publr: Jeffrey Goldman E-mail: jgoldman@
   santamonicapress.com
Founded: 1994

Publish an eclectic line of books. Our critically acclaimed titles are sold in retail outlets around the world. Our authors are recognized experts who receive coverage both nationally & internationally. We're not afraid to cast a wide editorial net. Our list of lively & modern nonfiction titles includes books in such categories as popular culture, film history, photography, humor, biography, travel & reference.
ISBN Prefix(es): 978-0-9639946; 978-1-891661; 978-1-59580
Number of titles published annually: 12 Print; 12 E-Book
Total Titles: 150 Print; 100 E-Book
Foreign Rep(s): Ingram Publisher Services (worldwide exc North America); Ingram Publisher Services/Publishers Group West (North America)
Foreign Rights: Nordlyset Literary Agency (worldwide)
Orders to: Ingram Publisher Services, 1200 Ingram Dr, Chambersburg, PA 17202 *Toll Free Tel:* 800-400-5351 *Toll Free Fax:* 800-838-1149 *E-mail:* ips@ingramcontent.com *Web Site:* www.ingramcontent.com
Returns: Ingram Publisher Services, 1200 Ingram Dr, Chambersburg, PA 17202 *Toll Free Tel:* 800-400-5351 *Toll Free Fax:* 800-838-1149 *E-mail:* ips@ingramcontent.com *Web Site:* www.ingramcontent.com
Warehouse: Ingram Publisher Services, 193 Edwards Dr, Jackson, TN 38301 *Toll Free Tel:* 800-343-4499 *Toll Free Fax:* 800-351-5073 *Web Site:* www.ingramcontent.com/publishers/publisher-services
Distribution Center: Publishers Group West (PGW), an Ingram brand, 1700 Fourth St, Berkeley, CA 94710 *Toll Free Tel:* 800-343-4499 *Toll Free Fax:* 800-351-5073 *E-mail:* info@pgw.com *Web Site:* www.pgw.com

Santillana USA Publishing Co
Subsidiary of Grupo Santillana
2023 NW 84 Ave, Doral, FL 33122
SAN: 205-1133
Tel: 305-591-9522 *Toll Free Tel:* 800-245-8584
E-mail: customerservice@santillanausa.com
Web Site: www.santillanausa.com
Key Personnel
Pres & CEO: Miguel A Tapia *E-mail:* mtapia@santillanausa.com
COO: Marta Moldes Gomez *E-mail:* mmoldes@santillanausa.com
CTO: Javier Cabrera *E-mail:* jcabrera@santillanausa.com
Dir, Children's Books Div: Isabel Mendoza *E-mail:* imendoza@santillanausa.com
Natl Sales Dir: Arturo Castillon *E-mail:* acastillon@santillanausa.com
Mktg Dir: Kathy Jimenez *Tel:* 305-591-9522 ext 247 *E-mail:* kjimenez@santillanausa.com
Prodn Mgr: Jacqueline Rivera *E-mail:* jrivera@santillanausa.com
Founded: 1972
Educational & Spanish language trade books; ESL & bilingual textbooks; Spanish as a foreign language.
ISBN Prefix(es): 978-0-88272; 978-1-56014; 978-1-58105; 978-1-58986; 978-1-59437; 978-1-59820; 978-1-60396; 978-1-61605; 978-1-61435; 978-1-62263; 978-1-63113
Number of titles published annually: 50 Print; 3 CD-ROM; 5 Audio
Total Titles: 1,200 Print; 3 CD-ROM; 15 Audio
Membership(s): Association of American Publishers (AAP)

SAR Press, see School for Advanced Research Press

Sarabande Books Inc
822 E Market St, Louisville, KY 40206

Tel: 502-458-4028 *Fax:* 502-458-4065
E-mail: info@sarabandebooks.org
Web Site: www.sarabandebooks.org
Key Personnel
Pres: Sarah Gorham *E-mail:* sgorham@sarabandebooks.org
Dir, Mktg & Publicity: Joanna Englert *E-mail:* joanna@sarabandebooks.org
Mng Ed: Kristen Miller *E-mail:* kmiller@sarabandebooks.org
Prodn Mgr: Danika Isdahl *E-mail:* danika@sarabandebooks.org
Founded: 1994
Short fiction, poetry & literary nonfiction collections.
ISBN Prefix(es): 978-1-889330; 978-1-932511; 978-0-9641151; 978-1-936747; 978-1-941411
Number of titles published annually: 10 Print; 1 E-Book
Total Titles: 220 Print; 1 E-Book
Distribution Center: Consortium/Perseus Distribution, 1094 Flex Dr, Jackson, TN 38301-5070 *Toll Free Tel:* 800-283-3572 *Toll Free Fax:* 800-351-5073
Membership(s): Academy of American Poets; American Booksellers Association (ABA); Association of Writers & Writing Programs (AWP); Community of Literary Magazines & Presses (CLMP); PEN Center USA

§SAS Press
Imprint of SAS Institute Inc
100 SAS Campus Dr, Cary, NC 27513-2414
Tel: 919-677-8000 *Toll Free Tel:* 800-727-0025 *Fax:* 919-677-4444
E-mail: saspress@sas.com
Web Site: support.sas.com/en/books.html
Key Personnel
Publisher: Sian Roberts *Tel:* 919-531-2548 *E-mail:* sian.roberts@sas.com
Founded: 1990
Books about SAS or JMP software.
ISBN Prefix(es): 978-1-55544; 978-1-58025; 978-1-59047; 978-1-61290; 978-1-59994; 978-1-60764; 978-1-62959; 978-1-62960; 978-1-63526; 978-1-64295; 978-1-951684; 978-1-951685
Number of titles published annually: 20 Print
Total Titles: 125 Print; 120 Online; 120 E-Book
Distributor for John Wiley & Sons Inc (ebook formats only)

SAS Publishing, see SAS Press

Sasquatch Books
1904 S Third Ave, Suite 710, Seattle, WA 98101
SAN: 289-0208
Tel: 206-467-4300 *Toll Free Tel:* 800-775-0817 *Fax:* 206-467-4301
E-mail: custserv@sasquatchbooks.com
Web Site: sasquatchbooks.com
Key Personnel
VP, Sales & Strategy: Jenny Abrami *Tel:* 510-749-9838 *E-mail:* jabrami@sasquatchbooks.com
Publr, Spruce Books: Sharyn Rosart
Dir, Mktg: Nicole Sprinkle *Tel:* 206-826-4318 *E-mail:* nsprinkle@sasquatchbooks.com
Edit Dir: Jennifer Worick
Assoc Mgr, Mktg & Publicity, Little Bigfoot: Whitney Berger *Tel:* 206-826-4321 *E-mail:* wberger@sasquatchbooks.com
Sr Ed: Hannah Elnan
Publicist: Molly Woolbright *Tel:* 206-826-4326 *E-mail:* mwoolbright@sasquatchbooks.com
Founded: 1986
Nonfiction of & from the West Coast.
ISBN Prefix(es): 978-0-934007; 978-0-912365; 978-1-57061; 978-1-63217
Number of titles published annually: 40 Print
Total Titles: 390 Print; 3 Audio
Imprints: Little Bigfoot; Spruce Books

Foreign Rep(s): Random House of Canada Inc (Canada)
Foreign Rights: Park Literary & Media
Orders to: Penguin Random House Inc, 400 Hahn Rd, Westminster, MD 21157 (Attn: order entry) *Toll Free Tel:* 800-733-3000 *Toll Free Fax:* 800-659-2436 *E-mail:* customerservice@penguinrandomhouse.com; Random House of Canada Inc, Diversified Sales, 2775 Matheson Blvd E, Mississauga, ON L4W 4P4, Canada *Toll Free Tel:* 800-668-4247 *Fax:* 905-624-6217 *E-mail:* canadaspecialmarkets@penguinrandomhouse.com

§Satya House Publications
22 Turkey St, Hardwick, MA 01037
Mailing Address: PO Box 122, Hardwick, MA 01037
Tel: 413-477-8743
E-mail: info@satyahouse.com; orders@satyahouse.com
Web Site: www.satyahouse.com
Key Personnel
Publr: Julie Murkette *E-mail:* julie@satyahouse.com
Founded: 2003
Independent publishing company.
This publisher has indicated that 25% of their product line is author subsidized.
ISBN Prefix(es): 978-0-9729191; 978-0-9818720; 978-1-9358740
Number of titles published annually: 4 Print; 4 E-Book
Total Titles: 20 Print; 1 CD-ROM; 9 E-Book
Foreign Rep(s): Gazelle Book Services Ltd (UK)
Foreign Rights: Sylvia Hayse Literary Agency LLC (worldwide exc USA)
Distribution Center: Independent Publishers Group (IPG), 814 N Franklin St, Chicago, IL 60610 *Tel:* 312-337-0747 *Web Site:* www.ipgbook.com
Membership(s): Independent Book Publishers Association (IBPA); Independent Publishers of New England (IPNE)

Savant Books & Publications LLC
2630 Kapiolani Blvd, Suite 1601, Honolulu, HI 96826
Tel: 808-941-3927 (9AM-noon HST)
E-mail: savantbooks@gmail.com; savantdistribution@gmail.com
Web Site: www.savantbooksandpublications.com; www.savantdistribution.com
Key Personnel
Owner: Daniel S Janik
Ed-in-Chief: David Shinsato
Founded: 2007
Publishes unpublished, post-modern works of enduring value "with a twist" for English readers throughout the world. Special interest areas include: fiction (novels - all genres), nonfiction (transformative education, memoirs, academic theses & dissertations of note, single-author textbooks & workbooks). Under the Aignos Publishing imprint publishes avant garde, experimental & innovative works that "push the leading edge" of all genres of fiction & nonfiction.
ISBN Prefix(es): 978-0-9841175; 978-0-9845552; 978-0-9829987; 978-0-9832861; 978-0-9852506; 978-0-9886640; 978-0-9915622; 978-0-9963255; 978-0-9972472; 978-0-9860233 (Aignos); 978-0-9895191 (Aignos); 978-0-9904322 (Aignos); 978-0-9970020 (Aignos)
Number of titles published annually: 15 Print; 1 CD-ROM; 15 Online; 15 E-Book; 1 Audio
Total Titles: 140 Print; 1 CD-ROM; 110 Online; 140 E-Book; 5 Audio
Imprints: Aignos Publishing (avant garde)
Membership(s): Independent Book Publishers Association (IBPA)

§Savvas Learning Co LLC
Formerly Pearson® K12 Learning LLC
15 E Midland Ave, Suite 502, Paramus, NJ 07652
Toll Free Tel: 800-848-9500
Web Site: www.savvas.com
Key Personnel
CEO: Bethlam Forsa
SVP & CFO: Paul Fletcher
SVP & CIO: Bryan Smith
SVP & Gen Coun: Andy Yoo
SVP & Head, Sales & Sales Opers: James Lippe
SVP, Prod Technol: Michael Chai
SVP, Prodn & Opers: Paul Despins
VP, HR: Melissa Schwartzmann
VP, Mktg & Communs: Maureen Link
ISBN Prefix(es): 978-0-13; 978-0-328; 978-1-4183
Branch Office(s)
3075 W Ray Rd, Chandler, AZ 85226
3088 Sanders Rd, Northbrook, IL 60062
501 Boylston St, Boston, MA 02116

SBL Press
Unit of Society of Biblical Literature
The Luce Ctr, Suite 350, 825 Houston Mill Rd, Atlanta, GA 30329
Tel: 404-727-3100 *Fax:* 404-727-3101 (corp)
E-mail: sbl@sbl-site.org
Web Site: www.sbl-site.org
Key Personnel
Dir: Bob Buller *E-mail:* bob.buller@sbl-site.org
Mktg Mgr: Kathie Klein *Tel:* 404-727-2325
E-mail: kathie.klein@sbl-site.org
Sales Mgr: Heather McMurray *Tel:* 404-727-3096
E-mail: heather.mcmurray@sbl-site.org
Founded: 1880
Publishing program of the Society of Biblical Literature, a learned society whose purpose is to stimulate the critical investigation of Biblical literature.
ISBN Prefix(es): 978-0-89130; 978-0-7885; 978-0-88414; 978-1-58983
Number of titles published annually: 43 Print; 43 Online; 43 E-Book
Total Titles: 850 Print; 200 Online; 200 E-Book
Distributor for Brown Judaic Studies; Sheffield Phoenix Press
Orders to: PO Box 2243, Williston, VT 05495-2243 *Tel:* 802-864-6185 *Toll Free Tel:* 877-725-3334 *Fax:* 802-864-7626
Returns: 82 Winter Sport Lane, Williston, VT 05495 *Tel:* 802-864-6185 *Toll Free Tel:* 877-725-3334 *Fax:* 802-864-7626
Warehouse: 82 Winter Sport Lane, Williston, VT 05495 *Tel:* 802-864-6185 *Toll Free Tel:* 877-725-3334 *Fax:* 802-864-7626

SBPRA, see Strategic Book Publishing & Rights Agency (SBPRA)

Scarsdale Publishing Ltd
333 Mamaroneck Ave, White Plains, NY 10607
E-mail: scarsdale@scarsdalepublishing.com
Web Site: scarsdalepublishing.com
Key Personnel
Publr & CEO: Sharona Wilhelm *Tel:* 914-302-2625
Mng Dir: Joseph Moore
Mng Ed: Kimberly Comeau
Founded: 2014
ISBN Prefix(es): 978-0-9972146; 978-0-9980815
Number of titles published annually: 40 Print; 10 Audio
Total Titles: 20 Print; 50 E-Book
Imprints: Blue Vista (women's fiction); Clairmont House (historical romance); Darklake (paranormal/fantasy); East Point (contemporary romance); Half Hour Reads; Scarsdale Voices

Scepter Publishers
PO Box 360694, Strongsville, OH 44149
Tel: 212-354-0670 *Toll Free Tel:* 800-322-8773
Fax: 646-417-7707
E-mail: info@scepterpublishers.org
Web Site: www.scepterpublishers.org
Key Personnel
Assoc Publr: Robert Singerline *E-mail:* robert@scepterpublishers.org
Orders & Cust Serv: Kevin Lay *E-mail:* kevin@scepterpublishers.org
Founded: 1954
Catholic book publishing including doctrinal works, theology & liturgy.
ISBN Prefix(es): 978-0-933932; 978-0-1889334; 978-1-594170
Number of titles published annually: 10 Print
Total Titles: 170 Print

Schaffner Press
PO Box 41567, Tucson, AZ 85717
Web Site: www.schaffnerpress.com
Key Personnel
Publr: Tim Schaffner *E-mail:* tim@schaffnerpress.com
Ed: Sean Murphy *Tel:* 520-869-7632
E-mail: sean@schaffnerpress.com
Founded: 2001
Independent publisher of books of social relevance for the discerning reader.
ISBN Prefix(es): 978-0-9710598; 978-0-9801394; 978-0-9824332; 978-1-936182; 978-1-943156
Number of titles published annually: 8 Print; 8 E-Book
Total Titles: 60 Print; 60 E-Book
Foreign Rights: Susan Schulman Literary Agency LLC
Distribution Center: Independent Publishers Group, 814 N Franklin St, Chicago, IL 60610 *Tel:* 312-337-0747 *Toll Free Tel:* 800-888-4741 *Fax:* 312-337-5985 *Web Site:* www.ipgbook.com

Schiffer Publishing Ltd
4880 Lower Valley Rd, Atglen, PA 19310
SAN: 208-8428
Tel: 610-593-1777 *Fax:* 610-593-2002
E-mail: info@schifferbooks.com; customercare@schifferbooks.com; sales@schifferbooks.com; marketing@schifferbooks.com
Web Site: www.schifferbooks.com
Key Personnel
Pres & Ed-in-Chief: Pete Schiffer
Founded: 1974
Collecting, art books, antiques, architecture, toys, woodcarving, hobbies, weaving, color, metaphysics, aviation, military books, automotive books, design & fashion.
ISBN Prefix(es): 978-0-87033; 978-0-916838; 978-0-88740; 978-0-7643; 978-0-89538; 978-0-978278; 978-1-5073
Number of titles published annually: 300 Print
Total Titles: 5,000 Print
Imprints: Cornell Maritime Press; Geared Up Publications; LW Books; Red Feather; Schiffer; Schiffer Fashion Press; Schiffer Kids; Schiffer LTD; Schiffer Military History; Tidewater Publishers; Whitford Press
Distributor for The Donning Company Publishers
Foreign Rep(s): Thomas Allen & Son Ltd (Canada); Gazelle Book Services Ltd (Europe, UK); Peter Hyde Associates (South Africa); JCC Enterprises Inc (Caribbean, Central America, Mexico, South America); Nationwide Book Distributors (New Zealand); Peribo Pty Ltd (Australia); Publishers International Marketing Ltd (Asia); Sara Books Pvt Ltd (India)
Foreign Rights: Bushwood Books (Europe)
See separate listing for:
Cornell Maritime Press

G Schirmer Inc/Associated Music Publishers Inc
Unit of Wise Music Group
180 Madison Ave, 24th fl, New York, NY 10016
Tel: 212-254-2100 *Fax:* 212-254-2013
E-mail: schirmer@schirmer.com
Web Site: www.musicsalesclassical.com
Key Personnel
CEO: Tomas Wise *E-mail:* tomas.wise@wisemusic.com
EVP & CFO: John Castaldo *E-mail:* john.castaldo@wisemusic.com
Pres: Robert Thompson *E-mail:* robert.thompson@wisemusic.com
Dir, Prodn: Peter Stanley Martin *E-mail:* peter.martin@schirmer.com
Dir, Publg Admin: David Flachs *E-mail:* david.flachs@schirmer.com
Committed to intelligent, educational & entertaining books about all aspects of music, especially the recording arts, music business, genre histories & musician biographies.
ISBN Prefix(es): 978-0-8256; 978-0-7119
Number of titles published annually: 25 Print
Total Titles: 300 Print
Membership(s): American Booksellers Association (ABA); American Society of Journalists & Authors (ASJA); Independent Book Publishers Association (IBPA); Women's National Book Association (WNBA)

§Schlager Group Inc
1111 W Mockingbird Lane, Suite 735, Dallas, TX 75247
Toll Free Tel: 888-416-5727 *Fax:* 469-325-3700
E-mail: info@schlagergroup.com; sales@schlagergroup.com
Web Site: www.schlagergroup.com
Key Personnel
Pres: Neil Schlager *Tel:* 888-416-5727 ext 801
E-mail: neil@schlagergroup.com
VP: Benjamin Painter *Tel:* 888-416-5727 ext 802 *E-mail:* benjamin@schlagergroup.com; Sarah Robertson *Tel:* 888-416-5727 ext 804
E-mail: sarah@schlagergroup.com
Founded: 1997
Publisher of books & Internet materials for libraries as well as higher education & K-12 courses in history & related subjects.
ISBN Prefix(es): 978-1-935306; 978-0-9797758
Number of titles published annually: 2 Print; 1 Online; 2 E-Book
Total Titles: 5 Print; 1 Online; 5 E-Book
Imprints: Milestone Documents; Schlager Reference

§Schocken Books
Imprint of Knopf Doubleday Publishing Group
c/o Penguin Random House Inc, 1745 Broadway, New York, NY 10019
Tel: 212-751-2600 *Fax:* 212-572-2662 (foreign rts)
Web Site: knopfdoubleday.com
Key Personnel
EVP & Publr: Reagan Arthur
VP & Exec Dir, Sales Mgmt & Planning: Beth Meister
Edit Dir & Mng Ed: Altie Karper
Dir, Ad: Katie Burns
Dir, Publicity: Michiko Clark
Asst Dir, Mktg: Sara Eagle
Mktg Mgr: Julianne Clancy; Dani Toth
Founded: 1931
Penguin Random House & its publishing entities are not accepting unsol submissions, proposals, mss, or submission queries via e-mail at this time.
Foreign Rep(s): Century Hutchinson Group (South America); Colt Associates (Africa exc South Africa); Steve Franklin (Israel); India Book Distributors (India); International Publishers Representatives (Middle East exc Israel); Pandemic Ltd (Continental Europe exc Scandinavia); Penguin Random House Canada (Canada); Penguin Random House New Zealand (New Zealand); Penguin Ran-

dom House UK (UK); Periodical Management Group Inc (Mexico); Random Century (Australia); Saga Books ApS (Scandinavia); Sonrisa Book Service (Latin America exc Mexico); Yohan (Japan)

Foreign Rights: Arts & Licensing International (China); Agencia Literaria Carmen Balcells SA (Spain); Agencia Literaria BMSR (Brazil); DRT International (Korea); The English Agency (Japan); Graal Literary Agency (Poland); JLM Literary Agency (Greece); Katai & Bolza (Hungary); Agence Michelle Lapautre (France); Licht & Licht Agency (Scandinavia); Literarni Agentura (Czechia); Roberto Santachiara (Italy); Sebes & Bisseling Literary Agency (Netherlands)

Scholastic Education
Division of Scholastic Inc
557 Broadway, New York, NY 10012
Tel: 212-343-6100 *Fax:* 212-343-6189
Web Site: www.scholastic.com
Key Personnel
Pres: Greg Worrell
EVP & Pres, Scholastic Magazines Group: Beth Polcari
Chief Academic Offr: Michael Haggen
SVP, Strategy & Solution Devt: Harold Edwards
SVP, Innovation & Devt: Pam Allyn
SVP, Natl Sales Mgr: Chris Hedrick
SVP, Prof Learning Servs: Dr Carol Chanter
SVP & Publr: Janelle Cherrington
VP, Curriculum Mktg: Richard Bourque
VP, Integrated Mktg: Jennifer Wishna
VP & Publr: Lois Bridges
VP, Data Analysis & Academic Planning: Karen Burke
VP, Publr, Integrated Prod Devt: Adam Berkin
Scholastic Education is a leading provider of literacy curriculum & a responsive partner of schools & districts. Through print & technology-based learning programs for Pre-K to grade 12, expert professional development, family & community engagement, & learning supports, Scholastic Education provides teachers, families, & communities with the tools they need to support each & every child.
ISBN Prefix(es): 978-0-516; 978-0-590; 978-0-531; 978-0-7172; 978-0-439; 978-0-926891; 978-1-55998; 978-1-57809; 978-1-59009; 978-0-545
Divisions: Assessment; Curriculum Solutions; Early Childhood Education; Professional Development; Publishing Services; Research; Sales & Marketing; Technology

Scholastic Inc
557 Broadway, New York, NY 10012
Tel: 212-343-6100 *Toll Free Tel:* 800-SCHOLASTIC (724-6527)
Web Site: www.scholastic.com
Key Personnel
Chmn, Pres & CEO: Richard Robinson
CFO: Kenneth Cleary
EVP, Gen Coun: Andrew Hedden
EVP, Pres, Trade Publg: Ellie Berger
EVP, Pres, Book Clubs & e-Commerce: Judy A Newman
EVP & Pres, Scholastic Book Fairs: Sasha Quinton
EVP, Corp Devt: Hugh Roome
Pres, Scholastic Education: Greg Worrell
EVP & Pres, Intl: Nelson Hitchcock
EVP, Global Corp Communs: Stephanie Smirnov
EVP & CTO: Satbir Bedi
Chief Strategy Offr: Iole Lucchese
EVP & Pres, Scholastic Magazines Group: Beth Polcari
Founded: 1920
Scholastic Corporation (NASDAQ: SCHL) is the world's largest publisher & distributor of children's books, a leading provider of print & digital instructional materials for grades Pre-

K to grade 12 & a producer of educational & entertaining children's media. The company creates quality books & ebooks, print & technology-based learning programs, classroom magazines & other products & services that support children's learning both in school & at home. With operations in 14 international offices & exports to 135 countries, Scholastic makes quality, affordable books available to all children around the world through school-based book clubs & book fairs, classroom collections, school & public libraries, retail & online. True to its mission of over 99 years to encourage the personal & intellectual growth of all children beginning with literacy, the company has earned a reputation as a trusted partner to educators & families. Learn more at www.scholastic.com.
ISBN Prefix(es): 978-0-590; 978-0-439
Distribution Center: 2931 E McCarty St, Jefferson City, MO 65101
100 Plaza Drive W, Secaucus, NJ 07094
Membership(s): American Library Association (ALA); Association of American Publishers (AAP); Association of National Advertisers Inc (ANA); The Children's Book Council (CBC); The Council of Chief State School Officers (CCSSO); Council of Great City Schools; Education Commission of the States; International Literacy Association (ILA); National Governor's Association (NGA); New York Women in Communications Inc (NYWICI); SocialMedia.org; Software & Information Industry Association (SIIA)
See separate listing for:
Scholastic Education
Scholastic International
Scholastic Trade Division

§Scholastic International
Division of Scholastic Inc
557 Broadway, New York, NY 10012
Tel: 212-343-6100; 646-330-5288 (intl cust serv)
Toll Free Tel: 800-SCHOLASTIC (724-6527)
Fax: 646-837-7878
E-mail: international@scholastic.com
Key Personnel
EVP & Pres, Intl: Nelson Hitchcock
SVP & Publr, Intl Educ: Duriva Aziz
VP, Intl Fin: Joe Macca
VP, Export Sales & Mktg: Anne Boynton-Trigg
Scholastic International includes the publication & distribution of products & services outside the US by the company's international operations & its export sales business. Scholastic has operations in Canada, the UK, Australia, New Zealand & Asia, & export sales representatives in the rest of the world.
ISBN Prefix(es): 978-0-590; 978-0-439; 978-0-545
Subsidiaries: Scholastic Asia (with cos in China, India, Malaysia & Singapore & sales offs in Indonesia, Philippines, Taiwan & Thailand); Scholastic Australia Pty Ltd; Scholastic Canada Ltd; Scholastic Ltd UK; Scholastic New Zealand Ltd

Scholastic Trade Division
Division of Scholastic Inc
557 Broadway, New York, NY 10012
Tel: 212-343-6100; 212-343-4685 (export sales)
Fax: 212-343-4714 (export sales)
Web Site: www.scholastic.com
Key Personnel
Pres, Trade Publg: Ellie Berger
SVP, Gen Mgr, Klutz: Stacy Lellos
SVP, Fin & Strategic Initiatives: David Ascher
SVP, Mktg: Erin M Berger
SVP, Film, TV Devt, Scholastic Entertainment: Caitlin Friedman
VP, Digital Publr & Pres of Weston Woods & Scholastic Audio: Lori Benton
VP, Publr & Edit Dir, Scholastic Press: David Levithan
VP, Publr: Liza Baker
VP, Publr-at-Large: Ken Geist
VP, Publr, Licensing: Debra Dorfman
VP, Ed-at-Large: Andrea Pinkney
VP, Creative Dir & Edit Dir, Graphix: David Saylor
VP, Trade Sales: Alan Smagler
VP, Fin: Ken Yamamoto
VP, Publg Opers: JoAnne Mojica
VP & Mng Ed: Leslie Garych
VP, Global Brand Publicity: Charisse Meloto
Exec Ed & Mgr, Scholastic en espanol: Maria Dominguez
Sr Dir, Publicity: Lauren Donovan
Dir, Busn Devt, Scholastic Entertainment: Anthony Kosiewska
Scholastic Trade Books is an award-winning publisher of original children's books. Scholastic publishes more than 600 new hardcover, paperback & novelty books each year & brings beloved stories & characters to life beyond the printed page via virtually every platform or screen kids access.
ISBN Prefix(es): 978-0-590; 978-0-439; 978-0-545
Number of titles published annually: 600 Print
Total Titles: 6,000 Print
Imprints: The Blue Sky Press; Cartwheel Books; Chicken House; David Fickling Books; Graphix; Klutz; Little Shepherd; Orchard Books; Point; PUSH; Scholastic Audio; Scholastic en Espanol; Scholastic Focus; Scholastic Inc; Scholastic Licensed Publishing; Scholastic Nonfiction; Scholastic Paperbacks; Scholastic Press; Scholastic Reference; Weston Woods
Distribution Center: 2931 E McCarty St, Jefferson City, MO 65102 *Tel:* 573-635-5881
See separate listing for:
Klutz

Schonfeld & Associates Inc
1932 Terramar Lane, Virginia Beach, VA 23456
SAN: 255-2361
Toll Free Tel: 800-205-0030
E-mail: saiinfo@saibooks.com
Web Site: www.saibooks.com
Key Personnel
Pres: Carol Greenhut *E-mail:* cgreenhut@saibooks.com
Founded: 1977
Author statistical reference works.
ISBN Prefix(es): 978-1-878339; 978-1-932024; 978-0-989055; 978-0-996048; 978-0-996248; 978-1-945225
Number of titles published annually: 9 E-Book
Total Titles: 9 E-Book

School for Advanced Research Press
660 Garcia St, Santa Fe, NM 87505
Mailing Address: PO Box 2188, Santa Fe, NM 87504-2188
E-mail: press@sarsf.org
Web Site: sarweb.org
Key Personnel
Acqs Ed: Sarah Soliz *E-mail:* soliz@sarsf.org
Founded: 1907
Scholarly & general-interest books on anthropology, archaeology, Native American art & the American Southwest.
ISBN Prefix(es): 978-1-930618; 978-0-933452; 978-1-934691; 978-1-938645
Number of titles published annually: 5 Print
Total Titles: 150 Print
Distributed by University of New Mexico Press
Orders to: University of New Mexico Press
Tel: 919-966-7449 *Toll Free Tel:* 800-848-6224
Web Site: www.unmpress.com

School Guide Publications
420 Railroad Way, Mamaroneck, NY 10543

Tel: 914-632-1220 *Toll Free Tel:* 800-433-7771
E-mail: info@schoolguides.com
Web Site: www.graduateguide.com; www.
schoolguides.com; www.religiousministries.com
Key Personnel
Pres & Publr: Myles Ridder *E-mail:* mridder@
schoolguides.com
Founded: 1886
Directories for colleges, institutions & religious
communities.
Number of titles published annually: 5 Print; 3
Online
Total Titles: 15 Print; 3 Online
Membership(s): National Association of College
Admission Counseling (NACAC)

School of Government
Division of The University of North Carolina at
Chapel Hill
University of North Carolina, CB 3330, Chapel
Hill, NC 27599-3330
Tel: 919-966-4119 *Fax:* 919-962-2709
Web Site: www.sog.unc.edu
Key Personnel
Sales & Mktg Mgr: Mary Judge *E-mail:* judge@
sog.unc.edu
Founded: 1931
Textbooks, casebooks, manuals & guidebooks,
monographs, reports, ebooks & bulletins.
ISBN Prefix(es): 978-1-56011
Number of titles published annually: 20 Print; 1
CD-ROM; 5 Online; 1 E-Book
Total Titles: 200 Print

§School Zone Publishing Co
1819 Industrial Dr, Grand Haven, MI 49417
Tel: 616-846-5030 *Toll Free Tel:* 800-253-0564
Fax: 616-846-6181
Web Site: www.schoolzone.com
Key Personnel
Pres: Jonathan Hoffman
VP, Sales & Mktg: Sharon Winningham
Tel: 616-846-5030 ext 217 *E-mail:* sharonw@
schoolzone.com
Founded: 1979
Instructional materials for early childhood, PreK
to 6th grade; educational workbooks, flashcards
& software.
ISBN Prefix(es): 978-0-88743; 978-0-938256;
978-1-58947; 978-1-60041; 978-1-68147; 978-
1-60159
Number of titles published annually: 12 Print; 12
CD-ROM
Total Titles: 350 Print; 50 CD-ROM

Schreiber Publishing Inc
PO Box 4193, Rockville, MD 20849
SAN: 203-2465
Tel: 301-589-5831 *Toll Free Tel:* 800-296-1961
(sales) *Fax:* 443-920-3540
E-mail: language@schreiberpublishing.net
Web Site: schreiberlanguage.com; shengold.com
Founded: 1954 (as Shengold Publishers)
Books on language & translation, Judaica history,
Holocaust memoirs, juveniles, reference books,
fiction, art books.
ISBN Prefix(es): 978-0-88400; 978-1-887563
Number of titles published annually: 10 Print; 7
E-Book; 1 Audio
Total Titles: 145 Print; 32 E-Book; 1 Audio
Foreign Rights: Bet Alim (Israel); Gazelle Book
Services Ltd (Europe, UK); Importadora Agri-
men (Latin America)
Shipping Address: Casemate | IPM, 1950
Lawrence Rd, Havertown, PA 19083
Tel: 610-853-9131 *E-mail:* casemate@
casematepublishers.com *Web Site:* www.
casemateipm.com
Distribution Center: Casemate | IPM, 1950
Lawrence Rd, Havertown, PA 19083

Tel: 610-853-9131 *E-mail:* casemate@
casematepublishers.com *Web Site:* www.
casemateipm.com

§Science & Humanities Press
Subsidiary of Banis & Associates
63 Summit Point, St Charles, MO 63301-0571
Tel: 636-394-4950
Web Site: sciencehumanitiespress.com;
beachhousebooks.com; macroprintbooks.com;
earlyeditionsbooks.com; heuristicsbooks.com
Key Personnel
Publr & CEO: Robert J Banis *E-mail:* banis@
sciencehumanitiespress.com
Founded: 1994
Publish books with a mission. Titles include
adapting to living with a disability, computer
capabilities, education & specialized medi-
cal/wellness topics. Most interested in books
that have enduring human value, promoting the
kind of world we all want to live in. Prefer inquiries by e-mail. No unsol mss; author guide-
lines on web site (sciencehumanitiespress.com).
ISBN Prefix(es): 978-1-888725; 978-1-59630
Number of titles published annually: 20 Print; 20
E-Book; 1 Audio
Total Titles: 110 Print; 10 Online; 60 E-Book; 4
Audio
Imprints: BeachHouse Books; Early Editions
Books; Heuristic Books; MacroPrintBooks
Membership(s): Independent Book Publishers As-
sociation (IBPA); St Louis Publishers Associa-
tion

Science, Naturally
Affiliate of Platypus Media
725 Eighth St SE, Washington, DC 20003
Tel: 202-465-4798 *Toll Free Tel:* 866-724-9876
Fax: 202-558-2132
E-mail: info@sciencenaturally.com
Web Site: www.sciencenaturally.com
Key Personnel
Pres: Dia L Michels
Founded: 2001
Committed to creating & distributing engaging &
educational STEM books for kids.
ISBN Prefix(es): 978-0-9678020; 978-0-9700106;
978-1-938492
Number of titles published annually: 5 Print; 5 E-
Book
Total Titles: 11 Print; 7 E-Book
Distribution Center: National Book Network,
4501 Forbes Blvd, Lanham, MD 20706
Tel: 301-459-3366 *Fax:* 301-429-5746
E-mail: customercare@nbnbooks.com

ScienceThrillers Media
PO Box 601392, Sacramento, CA 95860-1392
Tel: 916-712-3334
E-mail: query@sciencethrillersmedia.com
Web Site: www.sciencethrillersmedia.com
Key Personnel
Publr: Dr Amy Rogers *E-mail:* publisher@
sciencethrillersmedia.com
Founded: 2014
Specialize in page-turning stories (fiction or non-
fiction) that feature science, technology, en-
gineering, math, or medicine in the plot, or a
protagonist in one of those fields.
ISBN Prefix(es): 978-1-940419
Number of titles published annually: 3 Print; 3 E-
Book; 1 Audio
Membership(s): California Writers Club (CWC);
Independent Book Publishers Association
(IBPA); International Thriller Writers Inc
(ITW); Northern California Publishers & Au-
thors Association (NCPA)

Scobre Press Corp
2255 Calle Clara, La Jolla, CA 92037
Fax: 858-551-1232
E-mail: info@scobre.com

Web Site: www.scobre.com; scobre.
bookbuddyaudio.com
Key Personnel
Owner & Pres: Scott Blumenthal
Owner: Brett Hodus
Founded: 1999
ISBN Prefix(es): 978-0-9741695; 978-1-933423;
978-0-9708992; 978-0-9741997; 978-0-
9766240; 978-1-934713; 978-1-61570; 978-
1-62920; 978-1-93471
Number of titles published annually: 6 Print
Total Titles: 32 Print
Imprints: Scobre Educational
Distribution Center: Lerner Publishing Group Inc,
1251 Washington Ave N, Minneapolis, MN
55401 *Toll Free Tel:* 800-328-4929 *Toll Free
Fax:* 800-332-1132 *Web Site:* www.lernerbooks.
com

Scout Press, see Gallery Books

Scribner
Imprint of Scribner Publishing Group
1230 Avenue of the Americas, New York, NY
10020
Key Personnel
SVP, Publr: Nan Graham *Tel:* 212-632-4930
E-mail: nan.graham@simonandschuster.com
VP, Assoc Publr: Roz Lippel *Tel:* 212-698-7666
E-mail: roz.lippel@simonandschuster.com
VP, Ed-in-Chief: Colin Harrison *Tel:* 212-632-
4942 *E-mail:* colin.harrison@simonandschuster.
com
VP, Dir of Subs Rts: Paul O'Halloran
Tel: 212-698-7367 *E-mail:* paul.o'halloran@
simonandschuster.com
VP, Dir of Publicity & Mktg: Brian Belfiglio
Tel: 212-632-4945 *E-mail:* brian.belfiglio@
simonandschuster.com
Art Dir: Jaya Miceli *Tel:* 212-632-4959
E-mail: jaya.miceli@simonandschuster.com
Deputy Dir of Publicity: Katie Monaghan
Tel: 212-632-4950 *E-mail:* katie.monaghan@
simonandschuster.com; Kate Lloyd
Tel: 212-632-4951 *E-mail:* kate.lloyd@
simonandschuster.com
VP, Exec Ed: Rick Horgan *Tel:* 212-698-1129
E-mail: rick.horgan@simonandschuster.
com; Kathryn Belden *Tel:* 212-632-4932
E-mail: kathryn.belden@simonandschuster.com
Exec Ed: Valerie Steiker *Tel:* 212-698-7652
E-mail: valerie.steiker@simonandschuster.com;
Kara Watson *Tel:* 212-632-4936 *E-mail:* kara.
watson@simonandschuster.com
Assoc Ed: Sarah Goldberg *Tel:* 212-632-4903
E-mail: sarah.goldberg@simonandschuster.com;
Sally Howe *Tel:* 212-698-2445 *E-mail:* sally.
howe@simonandschuster.com
Asst Ed: Tamar McCollom *Tel:* 212-632-4920
E-mail: tamar.mccollom@simonandschuster.
com
Edit Asst: Emily Greenwald *Tel:* 212-632-4921
E-mail: emily.greenwald@simonandschuster.
com
Sr Mktg Mgr: Ashley Gilliam *Tel:* 212-698-2889
E-mail: ashley.gilliam@simonandschuster.com
Publg Mgr: Julia Lee McGill *Tel:* 212-698-2286
E-mail: julia.lee.mcgill@simonandschuster.com
ISBN Prefix(es): 978-0-684; 978-0-7432
Number of titles published annually: 70 Print
Imprints: Scribner Classics; Scribner Poetry

Scripta Humanistica Publishing International
Subsidiary of Brumar Communications
1383 Kersey Lane, Potomac, MD 20854
Tel: 301-294-7949 *Fax:* 301-424-9584
E-mail: info@scriptahumanistica.com
Web Site: www.scriptahumanistica.com
Founded: 1984
Publish reference books in the humanities.
ISBN Prefix(es): 978-0-916379; 978-1-882528
Number of titles published annually: 5 Print

Total Titles: 175 Print; 175 Online
Editorial Office(s): Dept of Romance Languages, 512 Williams Hall, Philadelphia, PA 19104-6305, Gen Ed: Jose M Regueiro *Tel:* 215-898-5124 *Fax:* 215-898-0933 *E-mail:* jregueir@sas.upenn.edu
Foreign Rep(s): Grant & Cutler Ltd (Northern Europe, UK); Leader Books SA (Greece, Middle East); Portico (Africa, Southern Europe, Spain); Scripta Humanistica (Caribbean, Latin America); Spain Shobo Co Inc (Asia, Australia, New Zealand)
Distribution Center: Baker & Taylor, 501 S Gladiolus Ave, Momence, IL 60954-1799 *Tel:* 815-472-2444
Ingram/Lightning Source, 7315 Innovation Blvd, Fort Wayne, IN 46818-1371 *E-mail:* csacademic@ingramcontent.com *Web Site:* www.ingramcontent.com
Midwest Library Service, 11443 Saint Charles Rock Rd, Bridgeton, MO 63044-2789 *Tel:* 314-739-3100 *Fax:* 314-739-1326 *E-mail:* madden@midwestls.com *Web Site:* www.midwestls.com
Yankee Book Peddler Inc, 999 Maple St, Contoocook, NH 03229-3374 *Tel:* 603-746-3102 *Fax:* 603-746-5628
Scripta Humanistica, Calle Union 657, Miramar 00907, Puerto Rico *Tel:* 809-723-2445
Leader Books SA, 62 Koniaristr, 115 21 Ampelokipi, Greece *Tel:* 210 6452825 *Fax:* 210 6449924
Spain Shobo Co Ltd, Yamoto, PO Box 12, Miyagui 981-0503, Japan *Tel:* (0225) 84-1280 *Fax:* (0225) 84-1283 *E-mail:* info@spainshobo.co.jp
Portico Librerias SA, Calle Munoz Seca 6, 50005 Zaragoza, Spain *Tel:* 976 55 70 39 *Fax:* 976 35 32 26 *E-mail:* jalcrudo@porticolibrerias.es
Grant & Cutler Ltd, 55-57 Great Marlborough St, London W1V 1DD, United Kingdom *Tel:* (0171) 734-2012

Search Institute Press®
Division of Search Institute
The Banks Bldg, Suite 125, 615 First Ave NE, Minneapolis, MN 55413
Tel: 612-376-8955; 612-692-5520
Toll Free Tel: 800-888-7828 *Fax:* 612-692-5553
E-mail: si@search-institute.org
Web Site: www.search-institute.org
Key Personnel
Co-Chair: Jeff Peterson; Ann Curme Shaw
Contracts & Proj Mgr: Jan DeWall
E-mail: jand@search-institute.org
Provide practical, hope-filled books to create a world in which young people are valued & thrive. Content is based on Search Institute's 50 years of research & focuses on the 40 Developmental Assets®, a framework of qualities, experiences & relationships youth need to succeed. Publishes resources for adults & youth that help strengthen communities by nurturing parents, concerned & caring adults, young people, educators & youth, family & community service professionals.
ISBN Prefix(es): 978-1-57482
Number of titles published annually: 4 Print; 4 E-Book
Total Titles: 110 Print; 50 E-Book
Distribution Center: Independent Publishers Group (IPG), 814 N Franklin St, Chicago, IL 60610 *Tel:* 312-337-0747 *Toll Free Tel:* 800-888-4741 (orders) *Fax:* 312-337-5985 *E-mail:* orders@ipgbook.com *Web Site:* www.ipgbook.com
Membership(s): ABC

Second Chance Press
Imprint of The Permanent Press
4170 Noyac Rd, Sag Harbor, NY 11963
SAN: 213-1633
Tel: 631-725-1101

E-mail: info@thepermanentpress.com
Web Site: www.thepermanentpress.com
Key Personnel
Co-Publr: Chris Knopf *E-mail:* chris@thepermanentpress.com; Judith Shepard *E-mail:* judith@thepermanentpress.com; Martin Shepard *E-mail:* shepard@thepermanentpress.com
Mng Ed: Nick Collins *E-mail:* nick@thepermanentpress.com
Typesetting, Design & Prodn: Susan Ahlquist *E-mail:* susan@thepermanentpress.com
Founded: 1977
Originals & reprints of literary works in hardcover & paperback.
ISBN Prefix(es): 978-0-933256
Number of titles published annually: 16 Print
Total Titles: 600 Print
Foreign Rights: Nike Davarinou (Greece); Kira Dominguez (Australia); Lora Fountain Agency (France); Jill Hughes (Eastern Europe); International Editors (Jennifer Houge) (Portugal, Spain); Jane Judd (UK); Andrew Nurnberg Associates (China); ONK Agency Ltd (Turkey); Thomas Schlueck GmbH (Germany); Rita Vivian (Italy); Eric Yang (Korea)

Seedling Publications Inc
Imprint of Continental Press Inc
520 E Bainbridge St, Elizabethtown, PA 17022
Toll Free Tel: 800-233-0759 *Toll Free Fax:* 888-834-1303
E-mail: edcsr@continentalpress.com
Web Site: www.continentalpress.com
Key Personnel
CEO: Daniel Raffensperger
Pres: Eric Beck
VP & Publr: Megan Bergonzi
VP, Mktg: Robyn Matus
Founded: 1992
Books for beginning readers grades K-2, leveled readers-parental involvement materials.
ISBN Prefix(es): 978-0-8454
Number of titles published annually: 15 Print
Total Titles: 275 Print
Distributed by Kendall Hunt Publishing
Foreign Rep(s): PSI

SelectBooks Inc
325 W 38 St, Suite 306, New York, NY 10018
Tel: 212-206-1997 *Fax:* 212-206-3815
E-mail: info@selectbooks.com
Web Site: www.selectbooks.com
Key Personnel
Founder & Publr: Kenzi Sugihara *E-mail:* kenzi@selectbooks.com
Dir, Mktg: Kenichi Sugihara *E-mail:* kenichi@selectbooks.com
Founded: 2001
ISBN Prefix(es): 978-1-59079
Number of titles published annually: 21 Print; 23 E-Book; 2 Audio
Total Titles: 100 Print; 3 Audio
Foreign Rights: Waterside Productions (worldwide)
Orders to: Midpoint Trade Books, 814 N Franklin St, Suite 100, Chicago, IL 60610 *Tel:* 312-337-0747 *Toll Free Tel:* 800-888-4741 *Fax:* 312-337-5985 *E-mail:* orders@ipgbook.com *Web Site:* www.midpointtrade.com
Returns: Midpoint Trade Books, 814 N Franklin St, Suite 100, Chicago, IL 60610 *Tel:* 312-337-0747 *Toll Free Tel:* 800-888-4741 *Fax:* 312-337-5985 *E-mail:* orders@ipgbook.com *Web Site:* www.midpointtrade.com
Distribution Center: Midpoint Trade Books, 814 N Franklin St, Suite 100, Chicago, IL 60610 *Tel:* 312-337-0747 *Toll Free Tel:* 800-888-4741 *Fax:* 312-337-5985 *E-mail:* orders@ipgbook.com *Web Site:* www.midpointtrade.com
Baker & Taylor, 2550 W Tyvola Rd, Suite 300, Charlotte, NC 28217 *Tel:* 704-998-3100 *Toll*

Free Tel: 800-775-1800 *Web Site:* www.baker-taylor.com
Ingram Content Group Inc, One Ingram Blvd, La Vergne, TN 37086 *Tel:* 615-793-5000 *E-mail:* inquiry@ingramcontent.com *Web Site:* www.ingramcontent.com
Membership(s): Independent Book Publishers Association (IBPA)

Self-Realization Fellowship Publishers
3208 Humboldt St, Los Angeles, CA 90031
SAN: 204-5788
Tel: 323-276-6002 *Toll Free Tel:* 888-773-8680 *Fax:* 323-927-1624
E-mail: sales@yogananda-srf.org
Web Site: www.yogananda-srf.org; bookstore.yogananda-srf.org/ (orders)
Key Personnel
Sales Mgr: Phil Gray
Mktg: Mike Baake *E-mail:* mikeb@yogananda-srf.org
Founded: 1920 (by Paramahansa Yogananda)
Publisher for the complete works of Paramahansa Yogananda.
ISBN Prefix(es): 978-0-87612
Number of titles published annually: 10 Print; 7 Audio
Returns: 3233 N San Fernando Rd, Unit 2, Los Angeles, CA 90065, Contact: Mark Russell *Tel:* 323-276-6000 *E-mail:* markr@yogananda-srf.org SAN: 204-5688
Membership(s): Independent Book Publishers Association (IBPA)

Sentient Publications LLC
PO Box 1851, Boulder, CO 80306
Tel: 303-443-2188
E-mail: contact@sentientpublications.com
Web Site: www.sentientpublications.com
Key Personnel
Publr: Connie Shaw *E-mail:* cshaw@sentientpublications.com
Founded: 2001
Publish quality nonfiction books with cutting edge perspectives.
ISBN Prefix(es): 978-0-9710786; 978-1-59181
Number of titles published annually: 5 E-Book
Total Titles: 115 Print; 130 E-Book; 10 Audio
Foreign Rights: ANA Sofia Ltd (Bulgaria, Romania); Asli Karasuil Telif Haklari Ajansi (Turkey); Book Publishers Association of Israel (Israel); Giro di Parole (Italy); The English Agency (Japan); International Editors' Co (Spain); JLM Literary Agency (Greece); Agence Michelle Lapautre (France); Maxima Creative Agency (Indonesia); Andrew Nurnberg (China); Piper & Poppenhusen (Germany); H Katia Schumer (Brazil); Silkroad Publishers Agency (Thailand)
Orders to: National Book Network, 4720 Boston Way, Lanham, MD 20706 *Tel:* 301-459-3366 *Toll Free Tel:* 800-462-6420 *Fax:* 301-459-1705 *Web Site:* www.nbnbooks.com
Shipping Address: National Book Network, 4720 Boston Way, Lanham, MD 20706 *Tel:* 301-459-3366 *Toll Free Tel:* 800-462-6420 *Fax:* 301-459-1705 *Web Site:* www.nbnbooks.com
Distribution Center: National Book Network, 4720 Boston Way, Lanham, MD 20706 *Tel:* 301-459-3366 *Toll Free Tel:* 800-462-6420 *Fax:* 301-459-1705 *Web Site:* www.nbnbooks.com

Serindia Publications
PO Box 10335, Chicago, IL 60610-0335
Fax: 312-664-4389
E-mail: info@serindia.com
Web Site: www.serindia.com
Key Personnel
Publr: Shane Suvikapakornkul
Founded: 1976 (in London)
ISBN Prefix(es): 978-1-932476

Number of titles published annually: 11 Print
Total Titles: 60 Print
Distributed by Art Media Resources Inc (US & CN)
Foreign Rep(s): Kodansha Europe (Europe, UK); Paragon Asia Co Ltd (Singapore, Southeast Asia, Thailand); United Century Book Service (Hong Kong, Mainland China); The Variety Book Depot (Bhutan, India, Nepal, South Asia)

Seven Stories Press
140 Watts St, New York, NY 10013
Tel: 212-226-8760 *Toll Free Tel:* 800-733-3000 (orders) *Fax:* 212-226-1411
E-mail: sevenstories@sevenstories.com
Web Site: www.sevenstories.com
Key Personnel
Publr: Daniel Simon
Dir, Mktg & Publicity, Triangle Square Books: Ruth Weiner *E-mail:* ruth@sevenstories.com
Opers Dir: Jon Gilbert *E-mail:* jon@sevenstories.com
Rts Dir: Silvia Stramenga
Sr Ed: Lauren Hooker
Founded: 1995
Publish original hardcover & paperback books for the general reader in the area of literature, literature in translation, popular culture, politics, media studies, health & nutrition & sports. No unsol mss.
ISBN Prefix(es): 978-1-58322; 978-1-888363; 978-1-60980
Number of titles published annually: 50 Print; 15 E-Book; 2 Audio
Total Titles: 560 Print; 370 E-Book
Imprints: Siete Cuentos Editorial (Spanish lang); Triangle Square Books for Young Readers
Foreign Rep(s): Penguin Random House (all other territories); Turnaround Distribution (UK)
Foreign Rights: AnatoliaLit Agency (Turkey); Big Apple Agency (China, Taiwan); Paul & Peter Fritz Agency (Germany); Deborah Harris Literary Agency (Israel); Japan Uni Agency Inc (Japan); Katai & Bolza Agency (Hungary); Duran Kim Agency (Korea); MB Agencia Literaria (Spain, Spanish Latin America); Piergiorgio Nicolazzini Literary Agency (Italy); Sandorf Literary Agency (Croatia, Serbia, Slovenia); Ludmilla Shuskova (Russia); Villas-Boas & Moss Agencia Literaria (Brazil, Portugal)
Distribution Center: Penguin Random House, 400 Hahn Rd, Westminster, MD 21157 *Tel:* 612-746-2600 *Toll Free Tel:* 800-283-3572 (cust serv) *Fax:* 612-746-2606 *Web Site:* www.penguinrandomhouse.com

1765 Productions
PO Box 4151, Oakton, VA 22124-8151
Tel: 202-813-9421
E-mail: 1765productions@gmail.com
Key Personnel
Publr & Prodr: Patrick G Finegan, Jr
Founded: 1990
Subject specialties include finance, film scripts & screenplays.
ISBN Prefix(es): 978-1-878905
Number of titles published annually: 4 Print
Total Titles: 6 Print

§Shadow Mountain
PO Box 30178, Salt Lake City, UT 84130-0178
Tel: 801-534-1515 *Toll Free Tel:* 800-453-3876
E-mail: submissions@shadowmountain.com; info@shadowmountain.com
Web Site: shadowmountain.com
Key Personnel
Edit Mgr & Acqs Ed: Lisa Mangum
Subs Rts Mgr: Dave Brown
Founded: 1985
US-based publisher committed to providing books (print, electronic & audio) that offer value-based messages for readers of all ages. Pub-

lish quality children's fantasy & numerous bestsellers in the inspiration, fiction, history & business genres.
ISBN Prefix(es): 978-0-88494; 978-0-87747; 978-1-59038; 978-1-57345; 978-1-57008; 978-0-87579; 978-1-60908; 978-1-60641; 978-1-60907; 978-1-62972; 978-1-62973
Number of titles published annually: 25 Print; 2 Online; 25 E-Book; 10 Audio
Total Titles: 200 Print; 2 Online; 70 E-Book; 80 Audio
Imprints: Proper Romance
Distribution Center: Baker & Taylor, 2550 W Tyvola Rd, Suite 300, Charlotte, NC 28217 *Tel:* 704-998-3100 *Web Site:* btol.com
Ingram Content Group, One Ingram Blvd, La Vergne, TN 37086 *Tel:* 615-793-5000 *Web Site:* www.ingramcontent.com
Membership(s): ABC; The Children's Book Council (CBC); Independent Book Publishers Association (IBPA); Mountains & Plains Independent Publishers Association; Romance Writers of America (RWA)

§Shambhala Publications Inc
4720 Walnut St, Boulder, CO 80301
SAN: 203-2481
Tel: 303-222-9598 *Toll Free Tel:* 866-424-0030 (off); 888-424-2329 (cust serv)
E-mail: customercare@shambhala.com
Web Site: www.shambhala.com
Key Personnel
Founder & Ed-in-Chief: Samuel Bercholz
Owner, EVP, Publr of Roost Books: Sara Bercholz
Owner, EVP, Publr of Bala Kids & Course Prodn Mgr: Ivan Bercholz
Pres: Nikko Odiseos
Publr: KJ Grow
Sr Advisor: Jonathan Green
Sr Dir, Prodn & Design/Creative Dir, Bala Kids & Roost Books: Kara Plikaitis
Edit Dir, Bala Kids: Juree Sondker
Mktg & Publicity Dir, Roost Books: Claire Kelley
Prodn & Design Dir: Lora Zorian
Sales & Mktg Dir: Elina Vaysbeyn
Mng Ed: Liz Shaw
Asst Mng Ed: John Golebiewski
Sr Ed: David O'Neal
Ed: Beth Frankl; Sarah Stanton
Ed, Roost Books: Jennifer Urban-Brown
Rts Mgr: Oliver Glosband
Sr Designer: Jim Zaccaria
Sr Designer, Roost Books: Daniel Urban-Brown
Publicist: Katelin Ross
Mktg Assoc: Adria Batt
Founded: 1969
Trade books; art, literature, comparative religion, philosophy, science, psychology & related subjects.
ISBN Prefix(es): 978-0-307; 978-0-87773; 978-1-56957; 978-1-57062; 978-1-59030; 978-1-61180
Number of titles published annually: 85 Print; 50 Online
Total Titles: 1,050 Print; 50 Online
Imprints: Bala Kids; Prajna Studios; Roost Books; Snow Lion
Distributed by Penguin Random House Inc
Foreign Rep(s): Airlift Books (UK); Penguin Random House Australia Ltd (Australia); Penguin Random House of Canada Ltd (Canada); Penguin Random House of New Zealand (New Zealand)
Foreign Rights: ACER (Elizabeth Atkins) (Brazil, Portugal, Spain); Alcali Copyright Agency (Atilla Izgi Turgut) (Turkey); Anthea Agency (Katalina Sabeva) (Bulgaria); Bardon-Chinese Media Agency (Chang-Chih Tsai) (China); The English Agency Ltd (Junzo Sawa) (Japan); Ersilia Literary Agency (Evangelia Avloniti) (Greece); Anoukh Foerg (Germany); The Deb-

orah Harris Agency (Ms Efrat Lev) (Israel); International Copyright Agency Ltd (Simona Kessler) (Romania); Katai & Bolza Literary Agents (Peter Bolza) (Croatia, Hungary, Slovenia); Alexander Korzhenevski Agency (Alexander Korzhenevski) (Russia); Macadamia Literary Agency (Poland); Maxima Creative Agency (Santo Manurung) (Indonesia); La Nouvelle Agence (Vanessa Kling) (France); Andrew Nurnberg Associates Baltic (Tatjana Zoldnere) (Estonia, Latvia, Lithuania); Kristin Olson Literary Agency (Kristin Olson) (Czechia, Slovakia); Marianne Schonbach Literary Agency (Marianne Schoenbach) (Netherlands); Alexander Schwarz Literary Agency (Alexander Schwarz) (Denmark, Finland, Norway, Sweden); Sibylle Books Literary Agency (Ms Young-Sun Choi) (Korea); Tuttle-Mori Agency (Ms Pimolporn Yutisri) (Thailand, Vietnam); Susanna Zevi Agenzia Letteraria (Susanna Zevi) (Italy)
Advertising Agency: Vermillion Graphics, Boulder, CO 80302
Returns: Penguin Random House, Returns Dept, 400 Bennett Dr, Westminster, MD 21157
Shipping Address: Penguin Random House Distribution Center, 400 Hahn Rd, Westminster, MD 21157
See separate listing for:
Snow Lion

Shen's Books
Imprint of Lee & Low Books Inc
95 Madison Ave, Suite 1205, New York, NY 10016
Tel: 212-779-4400 *Fax:* 212-683-1894
E-mail: general@leeandlow.com
Web Site: www.leeandlow.com
Founded: 1985
Children's books.
ISBN Prefix(es): 978-1-885008
Number of titles published annually: 3 Print
Total Titles: 27 Print
Membership(s): American Booksellers Association (ABA); Independent Book Publishers Association (IBPA)

Shepard Publications
1117 N Garden St, Apt 302, Bellingham, WA 98225
Web Site: www.shepardpub.com
Key Personnel
Owner & Pres: Aaron Shepard
ISBN Prefix(es): 978-0-938497; 978-1-62035; 978-0-9849616
Number of titles published annually: 4 Print; 10 E-Book
Total Titles: 50 Print; 54 E-Book
Imprints: Islander Images (photography); Islander Press; Shepard & Piper (literary fiction & nonfiction); Simple Productions (nonviolence, lifestyle alternatives, music); Skyhook Press (children's)

Sherman Asher Publishing
126 Candelario St, Santa Fe, NM 87501
Tel: 505-988-7214
E-mail: westernedge@santa-fe.net
Web Site: www.shermanasher.com; www.westernedgepress.com
Key Personnel
Owner & Publr: James Mafchir
Founded: 1995
Literary books that include Spanish, English & bilingual memoirs & Judaica.
ISBN Prefix(es): 978-0-9644196; 978-1-890932
Number of titles published annually: 3 Print
Total Titles: 35 Print
Imprints: Western Edge Press
Distribution Center: SCB Distributors, 15608 S New Century Dr, Gardena, CA 90248

Tel: 310-532-9400 *Toll Free Tel:* 800-729-6423
Fax: 310-532-7001
See separate listing for:
Western Edge Press

SIAM, see Society for Industrial & Applied Mathematics

Side Street, see BrickHouse Books Inc

Siglio
PO Box 111, Catskill, NY 12414
Tel: 310-857-6935
E-mail: publisher@sigliopress.com
Web Site: sigliopress.com
Key Personnel
Publr: Lisa Pearson
Founded: 2008
Dedicated to publishing uncommon books that live at the intersection of art & literature.
ISBN Prefix(es): 978-0-9799562; 978-1-938221
Number of titles published annually: 4 Print
Total Titles: 38 Print
Distribution Center: Distributed Art Publishers (DAP), 75 Broad St, Suite 630, New York, NY 10004 *Tel:* 212-627-1999 *Toll Free Tel:* 800-338-2665 *Fax:* 212-627-9484 *Toll Free Fax:* 800-478-3128 *E-mail:* orders@dapinc.com

Signalman Publishing
3700 Commerce Blvd, Kissimmee, FL 34741
Tel: 407-504-4103 *Toll Free Tel:* 888-907-4423
E-mail: info@signalmanpublishing.com
Web Site: www.signalmanpublishing.com
Key Personnel
Pres: John McClure
Founded: 2008
Specialize in bringing nonfiction works to the Kindle format. Have also branched out into trade paper with both nonfiction & fiction works.
This publisher has indicated that 45% of their product line is author subsidized.
ISBN Prefix(es): 978-0-9840614; 978-1-935991; 978-1-940145
Number of titles published annually: 12 Print; 14 E-Book
Total Titles: 56 Print; 76 E-Book
Imprints: Trinity Grace Press
Orders to: Lightning Source, 1246 Heil Quaker Blvd, La Vergne, TN 37086, Contact: Justine Bylo *Tel:* 212-714-9000 *Fax:* 615-213-4725 *E-mail:* justine.bylo@ingramcontent.com
Shipping Address: Lightning Source, 1246 Heil Quaker Blvd, La Vergne, TN 37086, Contact: Justine Bylo *Tel:* 212-714-9000 *Fax:* 615-213-4725 *E-mail:* justine.bylo@ingramcontent.com
Membership(s): The Association of Publishers for Special Sales (APSS); Christian Small Publishers Association

Signature Books Publishing LLC
564 W 400 N, Salt Lake City, UT 84116-3411
SAN: 217-4391
Toll Free Tel: 800-356-5687
E-mail: people@signaturebooks.com
Web Site: www.signaturebooks.com; www.signaturebookslibrary.org
Key Personnel
Pres & Co-Founder: George D Smith
Dir: Gary James Bergera
Ed: John Hatch
Busn Mgr: Keiko Jones
Edit Mgr: Ronald L Priddis
Mktg Mgr: Devery S Anderson
Prodn Mgr: Jason Francis
Prodn Asst: Greg Jones
Founded: 1981
Specialize in the promotion of the study of Mormonism.
ISBN Prefix(es): 978-0-941214; 978-1-56085

Number of titles published annually: 7 Print; 4 E-Book
Distribution Center: Chicago Distribution Center, 11030 S Langley Ave, Chicago, IL 60628 *Tel:* 773-702-7010 *Toll Free Tel:* 800-621-2736 *Toll Free Fax:* 800-621-8476 *E-mail:* orders@press.uchicago.edu *Web Site:* www.press.uchicago.edu

SIL International
7500 W Camp Wisdom Rd, Dallas, TX 75236-5629
Fax: 972-708-7363
E-mail: publications_intl@sil.org
Web Site: www.sil.org; www.ethnologue.com
Key Personnel
Dir, Busn Servs: Gayle Sheehan
E-mail: gpsbusinessmgr_intl@sil.org
Founded: 1934
Academic organization.
ISBN Prefix(es): 978-0-88312; 978-1-55671
Number of titles published annually: 5 Print; 2 E-Book
Total Titles: 230 Print; 945 Online; 12 E-Book
Subsidiaries: Summer Institute of Linguistics
Foreign Rights: Global Rights Management (worldwide)

Silman-James Press Inc
141 N Clark Dr, Unit 1, West Hollywood, CA 90048
Tel: 310-205-0665 *Fax:* 323-214-7943
E-mail: info@silmanjamespress.com
Web Site: www.silmanjamespress.com
Key Personnel
Publr: Gwen Feldman *E-mail:* gwen@silmanjamespress.com; Jim Fox *E-mail:* jim@silmanjamespress.com
Founded: 1990
Publisher of books on film, filmmaking, the motion picture industry & the performing arts.
ISBN Prefix(es): 978-1-879505; 978-1-935247
Number of titles published annually: 5 Print
Total Titles: 150 Print; 45 E-Book
Divisions: Quite Specific Media; Siles Press (chess & nonfiction titles)
Foreign Rep(s): Gazelle Book Services Ltd (Continental Europe, UK)
Returns: 660 S Mansfield, Ypsilanti, MI 48197
See separate listing for:
Quite Specific Media Group Ltd

Silver Leaf Books LLC
13 Temi Rd, Holliston, MA 01746
Mailing Address: PO Box 6460, Holliston, MA 01746
E-mail: sales@silverleafbooks.com; editor@silverleafbooks.com; customerservice@silverleafbooks.com
Web Site: www.silverleafbooks.com
Key Personnel
Mng Dir & Dir, Fin: Clifford B Bowyer
E-mail: cbbowyer@silverleafbooks.com
Edit Mgr: Brett Fried
Sales Mgr: Marilyn Fried
Founded: 2003
ISBN Prefix(es): 978-0-9744354; 978-0-9787782; 978-1-60975
Number of titles published annually: 16 Print; 25 E-Book
Total Titles: 130 Print; 129 E-Book

Simcha Press
Imprint of Health Communications Inc
3201 SW 15 St, Deerfield Beach, FL 33442-8190
Tel: 954-360-0909 ext 212 *Toll Free Tel:* 800-851-9100 *Toll Free Fax:* 800-424-7652
E-mail: simchapress@hcibooks.com
Web Site: www.hcibooks.com
Key Personnel
Dir, Communs & Mgr: Kim Weiss
E-mail: kimw@hcibooks.com

Founded: 1999
Nonfiction titles for those on the path of Jewish enrichment. Jewish interest, spirituality, inspirational, mysticism & recovery.
ISBN Prefix(es): 978-0-932194; 978-1-55874; 978-0-7573
Number of titles published annually: 4 Print; 4 Online; 4 E-Book
Total Titles: 13 Print; 13 Online; 8 E-Book

Simon & Schuster
Imprint of Simon & Schuster Publishing Group
1230 Avenue of the Americas, New York, NY 10020
Tel: 212-698-7000 *Toll Free Tel:* 800-223-2348 (cust serv); 800-223-2336 (orders) *Toll Free Fax:* 800-943-9831 (orders)
Web Site: www.simonandschuster.com
Key Personnel
SVP, Publr: Dana Canedy
VP & Assoc Publr: Richard Rhorer
VP & Ed-in-Chief: Marysue Rucci
VP & Exec Ed: Priscilla Painton; Robert Bender; Eamon Dolan; Justin Schwartz
VP & Exec Art Dir, Trade Art: Jackie Seow
VP & Publr, 37 INK: Dawn Davis
VP & Dir, Publicity: Julia Prosser
Dir of Subs Rts: Marie Florio
Subs Rts Mgr: Sandy Hill
Subs Rights Coord: Mabel Marte Taveras
Exec Ed: Stephanie Frerich; Sean Manning
Sr Ed: Stuart Roberts
Ed: Emily Graff; Carina Guiterman
Assoc Ed: Johanna Li; Megan Hogan; Zach Knoll
Asst Ed: Emily Simonson
Asst Ed, 37 INK: Chelcee Johns
Edit Asst: Lashanda Anakwah; Maria Mendez; Hana Park; Tzipora Baitch
Dir Mng Edit: Kimberly Goldstein
Mng Edit Asst: Maxwell Smith; Rafael Taveras
Exec Publicist: Anne Pearce
Sr Publicist: Elizabeth Gay; Caitlyn Reuss; Cat Boyd; Brianna Scharfenberg
Publicist: Kirstin Berndt
Assoc Publicist: Christine Calella; Heidi Meier
Assoc Dir, Publicity: Larry Hughes
Asst Dir, Publicity: Margaret Southard
Mgr, Publicity: Elizabeth Gay
Publicity Asst: Chonise Bass; Angela Ching; Kassandra Rhoads
Mktg Dir: Stephen Bedford
Sr Mktg Mgr: Elizabeth Breeden
Mktg Mgr: Leila Siddiqui
Assoc Mktg Mgr: Elise Ringo
Mktg Asst: Francesca Carlos
Art Dir: Alison Forner
Asst Dir, Art: David Litman
ISBN Prefix(es): 978-0-684
Number of titles published annually: 125 Print
Imprints: Adams Media; Folger Shakespeare Library; Free Press; 37 INK
Foreign Rights: Ackali Copyright Agency (Turkey); Antonella Antonelli Agenzia (Italy); Book Publishers Association of Israel (Israel); Japan UNI Agency (Japan); JLM Literary Agency (Greece); KCC (Korea Copyright Center) (Korea); Mohrbooks AG Literary Agency (Germany); La Nouvelle Agence (France); Andrew Nurnberg Associates (Bulgaria, Croatia, Czechia, Estonia, Hungary, Latvia, Lithuania, Montenegro, Poland, Romania, Serbia, Slovakia, Slovenia); Sane Toregard Agency (Denmark, Finland, Iceland, Norway); Sebes & Bisseling Literary Agency (Netherlands); Tuttle-Mori Agency Inc (Thailand)
See separate listing for:
Adams Media

Simon & Schuster Audio
Division of Simon & Schuster, Inc
1230 Avenue of the Americas, New York, NY 10020
Web Site: audio.simonandschuster.com

Key Personnel
Pres & Publr: Chris Lynch
VP & Exec Prodr: Elisa Shokoff
VP & Edit Dir: Tom Spain
VP, Pimsleur Language Programs: Tom McLean
VP & Assoc Publr: Sarah Lieberman
Asst Dir, Mktg & Publicity: Lauren Pires
Audiobooks & Pimsleur Language Programs.
ISBN Prefix(es): 978-0-684; 978-0-7435; 978-0-671; 978-1-4423
Number of titles published annually: 500 Audio
Imprints: Audioworks; Beyond Words; Encore; Pimsleur; Sound Ideas
Distributor for Monostereo
Shipping Address: Total Warehouse Services, 2207 Radcliffe St, Bristol, PA 19007

Simon & Schuster Books for Young Readers, see Simon & Schuster Children's Publishing

§Simon & Schuster Children's Publishing
Division of Simon & Schuster, Inc
1230 Avenue of the Americas, New York, NY 10020
Tel: 212-698-7000
Web Site: www.simonandschuster.com/kids; www.simonandschuster.com/teen; simonandschuster.net; simonandschuster.biz
Key Personnel
Pres & Publr: Jon Anderson
SVP & Publr, S&S Books for Young Readers, Atheneum, McElderry, Salaam Reads, Denene Millner Books: Justin Chanda
VP & Publr, Simon Spotlight, Little Simon, Aladdin Books: Valerie Garfield
VP & Publr, Paula Wiseman Books: Paula Wiseman
VP & Publr, Beach Lane Books: Allyn Johnston
VP & Publr, Caitlyn Dlouhy Books: Caitlyn Dlouhy
VP & Deputy Publr, S&S Books for Young Readers, Atheneum, McElderry, Paula Wiseman, Beach Lane, Caitlyn Dlouhy, Salaam Reads, Denene Millner: Anne Zafian
VP, Exec Ed, Aladdin: Liesa Abrams
Publr-at-Large, Denene Millner Books: Denene Millner
VP, Edit Dir, McElderry: Karen Wojtyla
Edit Dir, S&S Books for Young Readers: Kendra Levin
Edit Dir, Atheneum: Reka Simonsen
Edit Dir, Little Simon: Jeffrey Salane
Edit Dir, Simon Spotlight: Siobhan Ciminera
Edit Dir, Aladdin: Kristin Gilson
Exec Ed, Aladdin: Karen Nagel
Exec Ed, Simon Spotlight: Lisa Rao
Sr Ed, Beach Lane: Andrea Welch
Sr Ed, S&S Books for Young Readers: Krista Vitola; Jennifer Ung; Nicole Ellul
Sr Ed, Aladdin: Allyson Heller
Sr Ed, Paula Wiseman Books: Sylvie Frank
Sr Ed, Little Simon: Hannah Lambert
Sr Ed, Simon Spotlight: Beth Barton
Ed, Atheneum: Alexa Pastor
Ed, McElderry: Kate Prosswimmer; Sarah McCabe
Ed, S&S Books for Young Readers, Salaam Reads: Deeba Zargarpur
Ed, Simon Spotlight: Lisa Lauria
VP & Creative Dir: Dan Potash
Exec Art Dir, Atheneum, McElderry, Beach Lane: Sonya Chaghatzbanian
Exec Art Dir, Little Simon, Simon Spotlight: Laura Roode
Exec Art Dir, S&S Books for Young Readers, Paula Wiseman Books, Denene Millner Books: Lucy Cummins
Exec Art Dir, Aladdin: Karin Paprocki
VP, Subs Rts: Stephanie Voros
VP, Dir of Mktg & Publicity: Lauren Hoffman
VP, Dir of Educ & Lib Mktg: Michelle Leo

Sr Mktg Dir, S&S Books for Young Readers, Atheneum, McElderry, Beach Lane, Salaam Reads, Denene Millner Books: Chrissy Noh
Dir, Mktg, Aladdin, Simon Spotlight, Little Simon: Caitlin Sweeny
Sr Dir, Publicity, Aladdin, Little Simon, Simon Spotlight, Paula Wiseman Books: Nicole Russo
Sr Dir, Publicity, S&S Children's, McElderry, Atheneum, Beach Lane, Salaam Reads, Denene Millner Books: Lisa Moraleda
Dir, Digital Mktg: Anna Jarzab
Sr Ed, McElderry: Ruta Rimas
Preschool through young adult, hardcover & paperback fiction, nonfiction, trade, library, mass market titles & novelty books.
ISBN Prefix(es): 978-0-02; 978-0-609; 978-0-689; 978-0-7434; 978-1-4169
Number of titles published annually: 750 Print
Total Titles: 4,329 Print
Imprints: Aladdin Books (includes Caitlyn Dlouhy Books; chapter books, middle grade fiction, series, graphic novels); Atheneum Books for Young Readers (picture books, middle grade & teen fiction & nonfiction); Beach Lane Books (picture books); Little Simon (preschool & novelty); Margaret K McElderry Books (picture books, middle grade, teen & fantasy fiction); Denene Millner Books (books for all ages on the Black American experience); Salaam Reads (books for all ages on the Muslim experience); Simon & Schuster Books for Young Readers (picture & chapter books, middle grade & teen fiction & nonfiction); Simon Spotlight (beginning readers, licensed publishing); Paula Wiseman Books (picture books, middle grade & teen fiction & nonfiction)

§Simon & Schuster, Inc
Division of ViacomCBS Inc
1230 Avenue of the Americas, New York, NY 10020
SAN: 200-2450
Tel: 212-698-7000 *Toll Free Tel:* 800-223-2336 (orders) *Fax:* 212-698-7007 *Toll Free Fax:* 800-943-9831 (orders)
E-mail: firstname.lastname@simonandschuster.com; purchaseorders@simonandschuster.com (orders)
Web Site: www.simonandschuster.com
Key Personnel
Pres & CEO: Jonathan Karp
EVP, COO & CFO: Dennis Eulau
EVP & Gen Coun: Veronica Jordan
SVP & Deputy Gen Coun: Jennifer Weidman
Pres & Publr, Simon & Schuster Audio: Chris Lynch
Pres & Publr, Simon & Schuster Children's Publishing: Jon Anderson
Pres & Publr, Simon & Schuster Canada: Kevin Hanson
SVP, Publr, Simon & Schuster: Dana Canedy
SVP, Publr, Scribner: Nan Graham
SVP, Publr, Atria Publishing Group: Libby McGuire
SVP, Publr, Gallery Publishing Group: Jennifer Bergstrom
VP, Publr, Avid Reader Press: Jofie Ferrari-Adler
VP, Publr, Adams Media: Karen Cooper
VP, Publr, Tiller Press: Theresa DiMasi
Chief Exec & Publr, Simon & Schuster UK Ltd: Ian Chapman
Mng Dir, Simon & Schuster (Australia) Pty Ltd: Dan Ruffino
Mng Dir, Simon & Schuster India: Rahul Srivastava
EVP, Chief Mktg Offr: Liz Perl
SVP, Sales: Gary Urda
SVP, Corp Communs: Adam Rothberg
VP, HR: David Snow
VP, Dir, Strategic Opers & Busn Devt: Doug Stambaugh
VP, Group Cont: Deepak Daswani

VP, Gen Mgr, Adult, Children's & Audio: Craig Mandeville
VP, Gen Mgr, Simon & Schuster Publisher Services: Michael Perlman *Tel:* 212-698-7061 *E-mail:* michael.perlman@simonandschuster.com
VP, Client Publr Servs: Stephen Black
VP, Busn Devt: Joe Bulger
VP, Exec Mng Ed, Prodn & Copy Editing: Irene Kheradi
VP, Design & Digital Content Devt: Samantha Cohen
VP, Opers & Dist Servs: Chris Wagner
VP, Dir of Educ & Lib Mktg: Michelle Leo
VP, Contracts & Perms: Jeff Wilson
VP, Exec Dir, Corp Mktg: Sue Fleming
VP, Digital Mktg: Sienna Farris
VP, Digital Technol: Stephen Morgan
Founded: 1924
ISBN Prefix(es): 978-1-55850; 978-0-02; 978-0-941831; 978-1-885223; 978-0-7867; 978-0-13; 978-1-878990; 978-0-07; 978-0-7318; 978-0-669; 978-0-86417; 978-1-58062; 978-1-58180; 978-0-88708; 978-0-7434; 978-1-58270; 978-1-86842; 978-0-7435; 978-1-4169; 978-1-4165; 978-1-59337; 978-0-89256; 978-0-9674601; 978-0-9711953; 978-1-58229; 978-1-59309; 978-1-60061; 978-1-84737; 978-1-84738; 978-1-84739; 978-0-684; 978-0-7432; 978-0-689; 978-0-671; 978-1-4391; 978-1-903650; 978-1-4423; 978-1-4424; 978-1-4516; 978-1-84983; 978-0-9870685; 978-1-921462; 978-1-84970; 978-1-921470; 978-0-85720; 978-0-85707; 978-1-62266; 978-1-4711; 978-1-4767; 978-1-4814; 978-1-922052; 978-1-925030; 978-0-85783; 978-0-85941; 978-0-87605; 978-1-5011; 978-1-925184; 978-1-59869; 978-1-60550; 978-1-4405; 978-1-939867; 978-1-925310; 978-1-5082; 978-1-925368; 978-1-925456; 978-1-5072; 978-0-932102; 978-0-9714010; 978-1-4403; 978-1-5344; 978-1-936399; 978-1-4972; 978-1-925533; 978-1-925596; 978-1-925640; 978-1-935562; 978-1-935562; 978-81-933552; 978-81-933552; 978-1-925750; 978-1-925791; 978-1-9821; 978-93-86797; 978-0-9874196; 978-1-76085; 978-1-925048; 978-1-925685; 978-1-4178; 978-1-902421; 978-1-7971; 978-0-6481008; 978-0-6482267
Branch Office(s)
Beach Lane Books, 5666 La Jolla Blvd, No 154, La Jolla, CA 92037 *Tel:* 858-551-0860 *Fax:* 858-551-0492
Pimsleur Language Programs, Damonmill Sq, 9 Pond Lane, Suite 6B, Concord, MA 01742 *Tel:* 978-369-7525
Adams Media, 57 Littlefield St, Avon, MA 02322 *Tel:* 508-427-7100 *Fax:* 508-427-6790
Simon & Schuster, 1639 Rte 10 E, Parsippany, NJ 07054 (royalties, accts payable, fin) *Tel:* 973-656-6000 *Fax:* 973-656-6070
Simon & Schuster Canada, 116 King St E, Suite 300, Toronto, ON M5A 1J3, Canada *Tel:* 647-427-8882 *Fax:* 647-430-9446
Foreign Office(s): Simon & Schuster Australia Pty Ltd, 450 Miller St, Suite 19a, Level 1, Bldg C, Cammeray, NSW 2062, Australia *Tel:* (02) 9983 6600 *Fax:* (02) 9988 4232 (sales & mktg) *E-mail:* cservice@simonandschuster.com.au *Web Site:* www.simonandschuster.com.au/
Simon & Schuster Publishers India Pvt Ltd, 2316, Tower-A, The Corenthum A -41, Sector -62, Noida, Uttar Pradesh 201301, India
Simon & Schuster UK Ltd, 222 Gray's Inn Rd, 1st fl, London WC1X 8HB, United Kingdom *Tel:* (020) 7316-1900 *Fax:* (020) 7316-0333 *E-mail:* enquiries@simonandschuster.co.uk *Web Site:* www.simonandschuster.co.uk
Distributor for Aconyte; Andrews McMeel Publishing LLC; Artics; Baen Books; Baseball America; Beyond Words; BL Publishing (div of Games Workshop); Boom! Studios; Canterbury Classics (part of Printer's Row); Cardoza Publishing; Centennial Media; Chicken Soup

for the Soul Publishing; Cider Mill Press Book Publishers LLC (including Applesauce Press imprint); City Point Press; Downtown Bookworks; Fantoons; Flame Tree Publishing; Forefront; Frederator Books LLC; Gakken; Gallup (worldwide); Galvanized Media; Games Workshop; Hazelden; Health Communications Inc; Hispanic Info & Telecommunications Newtork; Hooked on Phonics (Sandviks HOP Inc/Sandvik Publishing); Humanoids Inc; Igloo Books; Indigo River; Inner Traditions/Bear & Company; Insight Editions; Juniper Publishing; Kaplan Publishing (including Manhattan Prep); Katalitix Media; Keenspot; Kinfolk; Law & Crime Books; Legendary Comics; little bee books; Manhattan Prep Publishing; Manning Publications; Manuscript; Mayo Clinic; Merck Publishing; Moll Anderson Productions; Mrs Wordsmith; NorthSouth Books (div of Nord-Sued Verlag); Oneworld Publications; Oni Press; Open Road Publishing; Pegasus; Permuted Press LLC; Petzel; Piggyback Interactive; Pikachu Press (Pokemon Company International); Pike & Powder; The Pokemon Company International; Post Hill Press LLC; Printer's Row; Reader's Digest Books (div of Trusted Media Brands Inc); Rebellion; Regan Arts; Regnery Publishing; Ripley Entertainment Inc (Ripley's Believe it or Not); Rosetta Books; Ryland Peters & Small (including CICO Books); Silver Dolphin Books (part of Printer's Row); Skyhorse; Start Publishing LLC; Studio Fun International (part of Printer's Row); Tanglewood; Thunder Bay Press (part of Printer's Row); Timbuktu; To The Stars Inc; Tra Publishing; Ubisoft; Ulysses Press; Victory Belt Publishing; VIZ Media; Waterhouse; Weldon Owen Publishing; Wisdom Publications; World Almanac (div of Facts on File); Yilin Press (Mandarin ebooks); Zaffre; Z2 Comics; Zuiker Press; David Zwirner Books
Returns: Simon & Schuster, c/o Jacobson Companies, 4406 Industrial Park Rd, Bldg 7, Camp Hill, PA 17011 (by appt; to schedule call 717-730-5212 ext 5316)
Shipping Address: Riverside Distribution Center, 100 Front St, Riverside, NJ 08075 (trade, children's, audio, mass-market & dist clients) *Tel:* 856-461-6500 *Fax:* 856-824-2402; Milan Distribution Center, 4071 Denton Fly Rd, Milan, TN 38358, VP, Gen Mgr, Warehouse Opers: Chris Wagner *Tel:* 731-562-2665 *Fax:* 731-562-2500
Membership(s): Association of American Publishers (AAP); Book Industry Study Group (BISG)
See separate listing for:
Avid Reader Press
Simon & Schuster Audio
Simon & Schuster Children's Publishing
Simon & Schuster Sales Division
Tiller Press

Simon & Schuster Sales Division
Division of Simon & Schuster, Inc
1230 Avenue of the Americas, New York, NY 10020
Tel: 212-698-7000
Key Personnel
SVP, Sales: Gary Urda *Tel:* 212-698-7389 *E-mail:* gary.urda@simonandschuster.com
VP & Dir, Natl Accts: Paula Amendolara *Tel:* 212-698-7069 *E-mail:* paula.amendolara@simonandschuster.com
VP & Exec Dir, Global Digital & Intl Sales: Colin Shields *Tel:* 212-698-7536 *E-mail:* colin.shields@simonandschuster.com
VP, Independent Retail Sales: Wendy Sheanin *Tel:* 212-698-7359 *E-mail:* wendy.sheanin@simonandschuster.com
VP & Dir, Children's Sales: Christina Pecorale *Tel:* 212-698-1126 *E-mail:* christina.pecorale@simonandschuster.com

VP, Spec Sales: Nicole Verlin Vines *Tel:* 212-698-7409 *E-mail:* nicole.vinesverlin@simonandschuster.com
VP, Dist Client Sales: Kim Gray *Tel:* 212-698-2192 *E-mail:* kim.gray@simonandschuster.com
VP & Dir, Sales Opers: Eileen Gentillo *Tel:* 212-698-7470 *E-mail:* eileen.gentillo@simonandschuster.com
Distributor for Andrews McMeel Publishing LLC; Applesauce Press (children's); Baen Books; Baseball America; Boom! Studios; Cardoza Publishing; Cernunnos; Chicken Soup for the Soul Publishing; Cider Mill Press Book Publishers LLC; Downtown Bookworks; Frederator Books LLC; Gallup (worldwide); Galvanized Media; Games Workshop; Hazelden; Health Communications Inc; Hooked On Phonics; Insight Editions; Juniper Publishing; Kaplan Publishing; Katalitix; Kinfolk; little bee books; Manhattan Prep; Manning Publications Co; Merck Publishing; NorthSouth Books; Omnific; Oni Press; Open Road; Permuted Press LLC; Piggyback Interactive; Post Hill Press LLC; Reader's Digest Children's Books; Rebellion; Regan Arts; Ripley Entertainment Inc; To the Stars Inc; Uncrate LLC; VIZ Media; Waterhouse Press; Weldon Owen; World Almanac (div of Facts on File)

Simon Spotlight, see Simon & Schuster Children's Publishing

§Sinauer Associates
Imprint of Oxford University Press (OUP)
Oxford University Press Higher Education, 2001 Evans Rd, Cary, NC 27513
Toll Free Tel: 800-280-0280 *Fax:* 919-678-1435
E-mail: highered.us@oup.com; custserv.us@oup.com
Web Site: sinauer.com
Founded: 1969
College textbooks & reference works in the biological & behavioral sciences.
ISBN Prefix(es): 978-0-87893; 978-1-60535
Number of titles published annually: 10 Print
Total Titles: 100 Print; 10 CD-ROM; 7 Online
Foreign Rep(s): Oxford University Press ANZ (Australia, New Zealand); Oxford University Press Canada (Canada); Oxford University Press Hong Kong (Hong Kong); Oxford University Press India (India); Oxford University Press Japan (Japan); Oxford University Press Malaysia (Malaysia, Singapore); Oxford University Press UK (Africa exc South Africa, Europe, Middle East, UK); Oxford University Press USA (worldwide exc Africa, Australia, Canada, Europe, Hong Kong, India, Japan, Korea, Malaysia, New Zealand, Singapore & UK); Shinil Books Co Ltd (Korea); World Science Publishing Co (Korea)

§SkillPath Publications
Division of The Graceland University Center for Professional Development & Lifelong Learning Inc
6900 Squibb Rd, Mission, KS 66202
Mailing Address: PO Box 2768, Mission, KS 66201-2768
Tel: 913-362-3900 *Toll Free Tel:* 800-873-7545 *Fax:* 913-362-4241
E-mail: customercare@skillpath.com; products@skillpath.com
Web Site: www.skillpath.com
Founded: 1989
Books, audio programs, computer based training.
ISBN Prefix(es): 978-1-878542; 978-1-57294; 978-1-929874; 978-1-934589; 978-1-60811
Number of titles published annually: 4 Print
Total Titles: 124 Print; 26 Audio
Divisions: CompuMaster

Branch Office(s)
8300 Lawson Rd, Milton, ON L9T 0A4, Canada
Web Site: www.skillpath.ca
Distributor for Franklin Covey; Pearson Technology; Thomson Publishing; John Wiley & Sons Inc

Skinner House Books
Imprint of Unitarian Universalist Association
c/o Unitarian Universalist Assn, 24 Farnsworth St, Boston, MA 02210-1409
Tel: 617-742-2100 *Fax:* 617-948-6466
E-mail: skinnerhouse@uua.org
Web Site: www.skinnerhouse.org
Key Personnel
Edit Dir: Mary Benard
Edit Asst: Betsy Martin *Tel:* 617-948-4644 *E-mail:* betsymartin@uua.org
Founded: 1975
Specialize in spirituality, inspirational literature, books on church resources for religious liberals.
ISBN Prefix(es): 978-0-933840; 978-1-55896
Number of titles published annually: 15 Print; 15 E-Book
Total Titles: 265 Print
Sales Office(s): Red Wheel/Weiser/Conari, 65 Parker St, Suite 7, Newburyport, MA 01950 *Tel:* 978-465-0504 *Toll Free Tel:* 800-423-7087 *Fax:* 978-465-0243 *E-mail:* orders@redwheelweiser.com *Web Site:* redwheelweiser.com
Returns: Red Wheel/Weiser/Conari, 65 Parker St, Suite 7, Newburyport, MA 01950 *Tel:* 978-465-0504 *Toll Free Tel:* 800-423-7087 *Fax:* 978-465-0243 *E-mail:* orders@redwheelweiser.com *Web Site:* redwheelweiser.com
Distribution Center: Red Wheel/Weiser/Conari, 65 Parker St, Suite 7, Newburyport, MA 01950 *Tel:* 978-465-0504 *Toll Free Tel:* 800-423-7087 *Fax:* 978-465-0243 *E-mail:* info@redwheelweiser.com *Web Site:* redwheelweiser.com

Sky Pony Press
Imprint of Skyhorse Publishing Inc
307 W 36 St, 11th fl, New York, NY 10018
Tel: 212-643-6816 *Fax:* 212-643-6819
E-mail: skypony@skyhorsepublishing.com; info@skyhorsepublishing.com; submissions@skyhorsepublishing.com
Web Site: www.skyponypress.com
Key Personnel
Ed-in-Chief: Alison Weiss *Tel:* 212-643-6816 ext 229 *E-mail:* aweiss@skyhorsepublishing.com
Ed: Becky Herrick *Tel:* 212-643-6816 ext 238 *E-mail:* bherrick@skyhorsepublishing.com; Rachel Stark *Tel:* 212-643-6816 ext 235 *E-mail:* rstark@skyhorsepublishing.com
Edit Asst: Katrina Enright *Tel:* 212-643-6816 ext 253 *E-mail:* kenright@skyhorsepublishing.com
Founded: 2011
ISBN Prefix(es): 978-1-61145; 978-1-60239; 978-1-61608; 978-1-62087; 978-1-62636; 978-1-63220; 978-1-62914; 978-1-62873; 978-1-5107; 978-1-63158; 978-1-63450
Number of titles published annually: 100 Print
Total Titles: 800 Print
Foreign Rights: Biagi Literary Management (Linda Biagi) (worldwide)
Orders to: Two Rivers Distribution, 1400 Broadway, Suite 520, New York, NY 10018
Warehouse: 210 American Dr, Jackson, TN 38301
Distribution Center: Two Rivers Distribution, 1400 Broadway, Suite 520, New York, NY 10018

SkyLight Paths
Imprint of Turner Publishing Co
4507 Charlotte Ave, Suite 100, Nashville, TN 37209
SAN: 134-5621

Tel: 615-255-BOOK (255-2665) *Fax:* 615-255-5081
E-mail: marketing@turnerpublishing.com
Web Site: www.skylightpaths.com; www.turnerpublishing.com
Key Personnel
Pres & Publr, Turner Publishing Co: Todd Bottorff
Founded: 1999
General trade books for seekers & believers of all faith traditions. Subject areas include spirituality, children's, self-help, crafts, interfaith, spiritual living, eastern & western religion.
ISBN Prefix(es): 978-1-893361; 978-1-59473
Number of titles published annually: 5 Print; 5 E-Book
Total Titles: 350 Print; 350 E-Book

§SLACK® Incorporated, A Wyanoke Group Company
6900 Grove Rd, Thorofare, NJ 08086-9447
SAN: 201-8632
Tel: 856-848-1000 *Toll Free Tel:* 800-257-8290 *Fax:* 856-848-6091
E-mail: sales@slackinc.com; editor@slackinc.com; customerservice@slackinc.com
Web Site: www.healio.com/books
Key Personnel
Chief Prod Offr: April Underwood
Chief Sales Offr: Mike Graziani
VP, Digital Innovation & Busn Devt: Christine Martynick
VP, Mktg & Audience Devt: Lee Gaymon
VP, Mktg, Health Care Books & Journals: Michelle Gatt
Edit Dir: Katrina Altersitz Wells
Edit Dir, Health Care Books & Journals: Karen G Stanwood
Head, Global Mktg: Kelly Watkins
Exec Ed: John Schoen
Mng Ed: Gina Brockenbrough
Founded: 1960
Academic textbooks & professional reference books: medicine, occupational therapy, physical therapy, ophthalmology, gastroenterology, orthopedics, athletic training, pediatrics, nursing & other areas.
ISBN Prefix(es): 978-1-55642
Number of titles published annually: 35 Print; 35 E-Book
Total Titles: 250 Print; 250 E-Book
Foreign Rep(s): EuroSpan (Europe); Login Canada (Canada)
Foreign Rights: John Scott Co
Advertising Agency: Alcyon Advertising
Distribution Center: 200 Richardson Ave, Bldg B, Swedesboro, NJ 08085

Sleeping Bear Press™
2395 S Huron Pkwy, Suite 200, Ann Arbor, MI 48104
Toll Free Tel: 800-487-2323 *Fax:* 734-794-0004
E-mail: customerservice@sleepingbearpress.com
Web Site: www.sleepingbearpress.com
Key Personnel
Publr: Heather Hughes
Mgr, Publicity: Julia Hlavac *E-mail:* julia.hlavac@sleepingbearpress.com
Sales & Mktg: Amy Patrick *E-mail:* amy.patrick@sleepingbearpress.com
Founded: 1998
Publisher of children's books infants to young adults.
ISBN Prefix(es): 978-1-57504; 978-1-886947; 978-1-58536
Number of titles published annually: 40 Print
Total Titles: 500 Print
Membership(s): American Library Association (ALA); Association of Children's Booksellers; International Literacy Association (ILA)

§Small Beer Press
150 Pleasant St, No 306, Easthampton, MA 01027
Tel: 413-203-1636 *Fax:* 413-203-1636
E-mail: info@smallbeerpress.com
Web Site: smallbeerpress.com
Key Personnel
Founder & Publr: Gavin J Grant
Founder: Kelly Link
CTO: Michael J Deluca
Founded: 2000
ISBN Prefix(es): 978-1-931520; 978-1-61873
Number of titles published annually: 8 Print; 10 E-Book
Total Titles: 100 Print; 150 E-Book
Sales Office(s): Consortium Book Sales & Distribution, The Keg House, Suite 101, 34 13 Ave N, Minneapolis, MN 55413-1007 *Tel:* 612-746-2600 *Toll Free Tel:* 800-283-3572 (cust serv, Jackson, TN) *Fax:* 612-746-2606 *E-mail:* info@cbsd.com *Web Site:* www.cbsd.com SAN: 200-6049
Foreign Rep(s): Cooke International (Ron Eckel) (worldwide)
Foreign Rights: Cooke Agency International (worldwide)
Billing Address: Consortium Book Sales & Distribution, The Keg House, Suite 101, 34 13 Ave N, Minneapolis, MN 55413-1007 *Tel:* 612-746-2600 *Toll Free Tel:* 800-283-3572 (cust serv, Jackson, TN) *Fax:* 612-746-2606 *E-mail:* info@cbsd.com *Web Site:* www.cbsd.com SAN: 200-6049
Orders to: Consortium Book Sales & Distribution, The Keg House, Suite 101, 34 13 Ave N, Minneapolis, MN 55413-1007 *Tel:* 612-746-2600 *Toll Free Tel:* 800-283-3572 (cust serv, Jackson, TN) *Fax:* 612-746-2606 *E-mail:* info@cbsd.com *Web Site:* www.cbsd.com SAN: 200-6049
Returns: Consortium Book Sales & Distribution, The Keg House, Suite 101, 34 13 Ave N, Minneapolis, MN 55413-1007 *Tel:* 612-746-2600 *Toll Free Tel:* 800-283-3572 (cust serv, Jackson, TN) *Fax:* 612-746-2606 *E-mail:* info@cbsd.com *Web Site:* www.cbsd.com SAN: 200-6049
Shipping Address: Consortium Book Sales & Distribution, The Keg House, Suite 101, 34 13 Ave N, Minneapolis, MN 55413-1007 *Tel:* 612-746-2600 *Toll Free Tel:* 800-283-3572 (cust serv, Jackson, TN) *Fax:* 612-746-2606 *E-mail:* info@cbsd.com *Web Site:* www.cbsd.com SAN: 200-6049
Warehouse: Consortium Book Sales & Distribution, The Keg House, Suite 101, 34 13 Ave N, Minneapolis, MN 55413-1007 *Tel:* 612-746-2600 *Toll Free Tel:* 800-283-3572 (cust serv, Jackson, TN) *Fax:* 612-746-2606 *E-mail:* info@cbsd.com *Web Site:* www.cbsd.com SAN: 200-6049
Distribution Center: Consortium Book Sales & Distribution, The Keg House, Suite 101, 34 13 Ave N, Minneapolis, MN 55413-1007 *Tel:* 612-746-2600 *Toll Free Tel:* 800-283-3572 (cust serv, Jackson, TN) *Fax:* 612-746-2606 *E-mail:* info@cbsd.com *Web Site:* www.cbsd.com SAN: 200-6049
Membership(s): Community of Literary Magazines & Presses (CLMP); PEN American Center; Science Fiction & Fantasy Writers of America (SFWA)

Small Business Advisors Inc
2005 Park St, Atlantic Beach, NY 11509
Tel: 516-374-1387 *Fax:* 516-374-1175
E-mail: info@smallbusinessadvice.com
Web Site: www.smallbusinessadvice.com
Key Personnel
CEO & Founder: Joe Gelb *E-mail:* joe@smallbusinessadvice.com
VP, Admin: Arthur VanDam
E-mail: arthurvandam1@gmail.com

Contact: Barbara Goetz *E-mail:* barbara@smallbusinessadvice.com
Founded: 1991
Publisher of books, ebooks & blogs on small business, finance & marketing/copyrighting.
ISBN Prefix(es): 978-1-890158
Number of titles published annually: 4 Print
Total Titles: 20 Print; 1 Audio
Membership(s): American Library Association (ALA); Association of Accredited Small Business Consultants (AASBC); Independent Book Publishers Association (IBPA)

§SME (Society of Manufacturing Engineers)
1000 Town Ctr, Suite 1910, Southfield, MI 48075
SAN: 203-2376
Tel: 313-425-3000 *Toll Free Tel:* 800-733-4763 (cust serv) *Fax:* 313-425-3400
E-mail: publications@sme.org
Web Site: www.sme.org
Key Personnel
Exec Dir & CEO: Sandi Bouckley *Tel:* 313-425-3100 *E-mail:* sbouckley@sme.org
Dir, Prof Devt: Jeannine Kunz
Books & TU Billing Serv: Maria Mukavitz *Tel:* 313-425-3028
E-Libn: Carol Tower *Tel:* 313-425-3288 *E-mail:* ctower@sme.org
Founded: 1932
Professional engineering association.
ISBN Prefix(es): 978-0-87263; 978-1-62104
Number of titles published annually: 3 Print
Total Titles: 150 Print; 21 CD-ROM
Branch Office(s)
7100 Woodbine Ave, Suite 312, Markham, ON L3R 5J2, Canada *Tel:* 905-752-4415 *Toll Free Tel:* 888-322-7333 *Fax:* 905-479-0113 *E-mail:* canadasales@sme.org
Distributed by American Technical Publishers Inc; McGraw-Hill; Productivity Press
Distributor for Industrial Press; McGraw-Hill; Prentice Hall; John Wiley & Sons Inc
Foreign Rights: American Technical Publishers (UK); DA Books Pty Ltd (Australia); Elsevier Science Publishers (Netherlands)

Smith & Kraus Publishers Inc
177 Lyme Rd, Hanover, NH 03755
Mailing Address: PO Box 32, Newton, IL 62448
Tel: 618-783-0519 *Toll Free Tel:* 877-668-8680 *Fax:* 618-783-0520
E-mail: editor@smithandkraus.com; info@smithandkraus.com; customerservice@smithandkraus.com
Web Site: www.smithandkraus.com
Key Personnel
Co-Founder: Eric Kraus
Co-Founder & Publr: Marisa Smith
Founded: 1990
Drama books, monologues, books of interest to our theatrical community, play anthologies.
ISBN Prefix(es): 978-0-9622722; 978-1-880399; 978-1-57525
Number of titles published annually: 84 Print
Total Titles: 500 Print
Imprints: In an Hour Books LLC (playwrights); Smith & Kraus Books For Kids (young adult fiction)
Subsidiaries: Smith & Kraus Global (world affairs)

§M Lee Smith Publishers
Division of BLR®—Business & Legal Resources
100 Winners Circle, Suite 300, Brentwood, TN 37027
Mailing Address: PO Box 5094, Brentwood, TN 37024-5094
Tel: 615-373-7517 *Toll Free Tel:* 800-274-6774; 800-727-5257
E-mail: custserv@mleesmith.com; service@blr.com
Web Site: www.mleesmith.com; www.blr.com

Key Personnel
CFO: Lawton Miller
VP, Legal: Brad Forrister
Founded: 1975
Legal newsletters/legal book related titles.
ISBN Prefix(es): 978-0-925773; 978-1-60029;
978-0-9605796
Number of titles published annually: 130 Print
Total Titles: 2 CD-ROM; 60 Online

Steve Smith Autosports
PO Box 11631, Santa Ana, CA 92711-1631
Tel: 714-639-7681 *Fax:* 714-639-9741
Web Site: www.stevesmithautosports.com
Key Personnel
Pres & Publr: Steve Smith *E-mail:* steve@
ssapubl.com
Founded: 1971
Specialize in auto racing technical books.
ISBN Prefix(es): 978-0-936834
Number of titles published annually: 5 Print
Total Titles: 200 Print

Smithsonian Institution Scholarly Press
Division of Smithsonian Institution
Aerospace Bldg, 704-A, MRC 957, Washington,
DC 20013
Mailing Address: PO Box 37012, Washington
DC, DC 20013-7012
Tel: 202-633-3017 *Fax:* 202-633-6877
E-mail: schol_press@si.edu
Web Site: scholarlypress.si.edu
Key Personnel
Prog Asst: Stephanie Summerhays
Founded: 1966
General trade & adult nonfiction.
ISBN Prefix(es): 978-0-87474; 978-1-56098; 978-
1-58834
Number of titles published annually: 8 Print
Total Titles: 800 Print
Distributed by Penguin Random House Inc

§Smyth & Helwys Publishing Inc
6316 Peake Rd, Macon, GA 31210-3960
Tel: 478-757-0564 *Toll Free Tel:* 800-747-3016
(orders only) *Fax:* 478-757-1305
E-mail: information@helwys.com
Web Site: www.helwys.com
Key Personnel
Pres & CEO: Cecil P Staton, Jr
Publr & EVP: Keith Gammons *E-mail:* keith@
helwys.com
Ed, Adult Formations: Darrell Pursiful
E-mail: darrell@helwys.com
Ed, Connection Series: Michael L Ruffin
E-mail: michael@helwys.com
Ed, Reflections: Carol Younger *E-mail:* carol@
helwys.com
Founded: 1990
Christian books, literature, Sunday school books
(curriculum).
ISBN Prefix(es): 978-1-880837; 978-0-9628455;
978-1-57312
Number of titles published annually: 30 Print
Total Titles: 330 Print
Foreign Rep(s): Grace Wing Publishers (England)

Snow Lion
Imprint of Shambhala Publications Inc
4720 Walnut St, Boulder, CO 80301
E-mail: customercare@shambhala.com
Web Site: www.shambhala.com/snowlion
Key Personnel
Pres: Nikko Odiseos *E-mail:* nodiseos@
shambhala.com
Founded: 1980
Trade & scholarly books on Tibetan Buddhism &
Tibet.
ISBN Prefix(es): 978-0-937938; 978-1-55939
Number of titles published annually: 20 Print; 20
E-Book
Total Titles: 350 Print; 250 E-Book; 1 Audio

**Society for Human Resource Management
(SHRM)**
1800 Duke St, Alexandria, VA 22314
Tel: 703-548-3440 *Toll Free Tel:* 800-283-7476
(orders)
E-mail: books@shrm.org
Web Site: www.shrm.org
Key Personnel
Mgr, Book Publg: Matthew Davis
Founded: 1948
Professional association with more than 275,000
members in over 160 countries.
ISBN Prefix(es): 978-1-58644
Number of titles published annually: 12 Print; 12
E-Book
Total Titles: 134 Print; 71 E-Book; 1 Audio
Foreign Rights: Russo Rights (worldwide exc
USA)

§Society for Industrial & Applied Mathematics
3600 Market St, 6th fl, Philadelphia, PA 19104-
2688
Tel: 215-382-9800 *Toll Free Tel:* 800-447-7426
Fax: 215-386-7999
E-mail: siambooks@siam.org
Web Site: www.siam.org
Key Personnel
Publr: David K Marshall *E-mail:* marshall@siam.
org
Prodn Mgr: Donna Witzleben *E-mail:* witzleben@
siam.org
Pubns Mgr: Mitch Chernoff *E-mail:* chernoff@
siam.org
Exec Ed: Elizabeth Greenspan
E-mail: greenspan@siam.org
Mng Ed: Kelly Thomas *E-mail:* thomas@siam.
org
Sr Pubns Coord: Heather Blythe *E-mail:* blythe@
siam.org
Prodn Coord: Cally Shrader *E-mail:* shrader@
siam.org
Founded: 1952
Journals, books, conferences & reprints in math-
ematics/computer science/statistics/physical
science.
ISBN Prefix(es): 978-0-89871; 978-1-61197
Number of titles published annually: 20 Print
Total Titles: 450 Print; 400 E-Book

§Society for Mining, Metallurgy & Exploration
12999 E Adam Aircraft Circle, Englewood, CO
80112
Tel: 303-948-4200 *Toll Free Tel:* 800-763-3132
Fax: 303-973-3845
E-mail: cs@smenet.org; books@smenet.org
Web Site: www.smenet.org
Key Personnel
Exec Dr: Dave Kanagy
Sr Ed: Bill Gleason *Tel:* 303-948-4234
E-mail: gleason@smenet.org; Georgene Renner
Tel: 303-948-4254 *E-mail:* renner@smenet.org
Pubns Ed: Steve Kral *Tel:* 303-948-4245
E-mail: kral@smenet.org
Founded: 1871
Publish mining related monthly magazine, quar-
terly journal, trade books, hardbound & paper-
back.
ISBN Prefix(es): 978-0-87335
Number of titles published annually: 3 Print; 5 E-
Book
Total Titles: 80 Print; 15 CD-ROM
Foreign Rep(s): Affiliated East-West Press (India);
Australian Mineral Foundation (Australia)

The Society for Protective Coatings, see SSPC:
The Society for Protective Coatings

Society of American Archivists
17 N State St, Suite 1425, Chicago, IL 60602-
4061
SAN: 211-7614

Tel: 312-606-0722 *Toll Free Tel:* 866-722-7858
Fax: 312-606-0728
Web Site: www.archivists.org
Key Personnel
Dir, Publg: Teresa Brinati *E-mail:* tbrinati@
archivists.org
Edit & Prodn: Abigail Christian
E-mail: achristian@archivists.org
Founded: 1936
Archival literature; preservation.
ISBN Prefix(es): 978-0-931828; 978-1-931666
Number of titles published annually: 5 Print
Total Titles: 72 Print

Society of Automotive Engineers International,
see SAE (Society of Automotive Engineers
International)

Society of Biblical Literature, see SBL Press

**Society of Environmental Toxicology &
Chemistry (SETAC)**
229 S Baylen St, 2nd fl, Pensacola, FL 32502
Tel: 850-469-1500 *Toll Free Fax:* 888-296-4136
E-mail: setac@setac.org
Web Site: www.setac.org
Key Personnel
Pubns Mgr: Jennifer Lynch *Tel:* 850-469-1500 ext
109 *E-mail:* jen.lynch@setac.org
Founded: 1979
Supports publications of scientific value relating
to environmental topics. Proceedings of techni-
cal workshops that explore current & prospec-
tive environmental issues are published as peer-
reviewed technical documents. Publications are
used by scientists, engineers & managers be-
cause of their technical basis & comprehensive,
state-of-the-science reviews; association press;
nonprofit, professional society.
Journal publications co-published with John Wi-
ley & Sons. Some books jointly published with
CRC Press or John Wiley & Sons.
ISBN Prefix(es): 978-1-880611
Number of titles published annually: 2 Print; 1
CD-ROM; 2 Online; 2 E-Book
Total Titles: 105 Print; 5 CD-ROM; 3 Online; 2
E-Book
Imprints: SETAC Press
Foreign Office(s): Av de la Toison d'Or 67 b 6,
1060 Brussels, Belgium *Tel:* (02) 772 72 81
Fax: (02) 770 53 86 *E-mail:* setaceu@setac.org

§Society of Exploration Geophysicists
8801 S Yale Ave, Suite 500, Tulsa, OK 74137
Tel: 918-497-5500 *Fax:* 918-497-5557
E-mail: web@seg.org
Web Site: www.seg.org
Key Personnel
Assoc Exec Dir, Knowledge Mgmt:
Ted Bakamjian *Tel:* 918-497-5506
E-mail: tbakamjian@seg.org
Dir, Journals & Books: Jennifer Cobb *Tel:* 918-
497-5537 *E-mail:* jcobb@seg.org
Founded: 1930
Textbooks, videos, technical journals, magazines
& meeting papers.
ISBN Prefix(es): 978-1-56080; 978-0-931830
Number of titles published annually: 5 Print; 5
Online; 5 E-Book
Total Titles: 87 Print; 9 CD-ROM; 141 Online;
141 E-Book
Shipping Address: 8801 S Yale Ave, Suite 110,
Tulsa, OK 74137
Distribution Center: Eurospan, Gray's Inn House,
127 Clerkenwell Rd, London EC1R 5DB,
United Kingdom *Tel:* (020) 3286 2420

Society of Manufacturing Engineers, see SME
(Society of Manufacturing Engineers)

The Society of Naval Architects & Marine Engineers (SNAME)
99 Canal Center Plaza, Suite 310, Alexandria, VA 22314
SAN: 202-0572
Tel: 703-997-6701 *Toll Free Tel:* 800-798-2188
Fax: 703-997-6702
Web Site: www.sname.org
Key Personnel
Exec Dir: Gene Sanders *Tel:* 703-997-6704
  E-mail: gsanders@sname.org
Dir, Mktg & Communs: Val Hutnan *Tel:* 703-997-6709 *E-mail:* vhutnan@sname.org
Mktg & Communs Coord: Deryck White
  Tel: 703-997-6711 *E-mail:* dwhite@sname.org
Reference books, directories, periodicals, technical research reports & bulletins on naval architecture, marine engineering & ocean engineering.
ISBN Prefix(es): 978-0-9603048; 978-0-939773; 978-1-941762
Number of titles published annually: 4 Print
Total Titles: 29 Print
Foreign Office(s): c/o ELKCO Marine Consultants, 61, Poseidonos Ave, Paleo Faliro, 175 62 Attica, Greece *Tel:* 210 452 8205 *Fax:* 210 452 8202

Soho Press Inc
853 Broadway, New York, NY 10003
SAN: 202-5531
Tel: 212-260-1900
E-mail: soho@sohopress.com; publicity@sohopress.com
Web Site: sohopress.com
Key Personnel
Publr: Bronwen Hruska *E-mail:* bhruska@sohopress.com
Assoc Publr: Juliet Grames
VP & Dir, Mktg & Publicity: Paul Oliver
  E-mail: poliver@sohopress.com
VP & Exec Ed: Mark Doten *E-mail:* mdoten@sohopress.com
VP & Dir, Mktg: Rudy Martinez
  E-mail: rmartinez@sohopress.com
Art Dir: Janine Agro
Mng Ed: Rachel Kowal
Ed & Rts Mgr: Amara Hoshijo
Digital Mktg Mgr: Kevin Murphy
  E-mail: kmurphy@sohopress.com
Sales Mgr: Steven Tran
Sr Publicist: Abby Koski
Founded: 1986 (first books published in 1987)
Hard & softcover trade books: fiction, mysteries, general nonfiction, history & social history.
ISBN Prefix(es): 978-0-939149; 978-1-56947; 978-1-61695
Number of titles published annually: 90 Print; 68 E-Book
Total Titles: 350 Print
Imprints: Soho Crime; Soho Press; Soho Teen
Foreign Rights: ACER Agencia Literaria (Elizabeth Atkins) (Spain); AnatoliaLit Agency (Amy Spangler) (Turkey); English Agency (Corinne Shioji) (Japan); Grayhawk Agency (Gray Tan) (Taiwan); Deborah Harris Agency (Ilana Kurshan) (Israel); International Editors Co (Flavia Sala) (Brazil); Leonardt & Hoier Literary Agency (Anneli Hoier) (Denmark, Finland, Norway, Sweden); Michael Meller Literary Agency (Franka Zastrow) (Germany); Jan Michael (Belgium, Netherlands); Daniela Micura Literary Services (Italy); PLS (Publishing Language Service) (Yang Young Chul) (Korea); Prava i prevodi (Nada Popovic) (Bulgaria, Croatia, Czechia, Estonia, Hungary, Latvia, Lithuania, Poland, Romania, Russia, Serbia, Slovakia, Slovenia); Read N' Right Agency (Nike Davarinou) (Greece)
Orders to: Penguin Random House Publisher Services (PRHPS), 400 Hahn Rd, Westminster, MD 21157 *Toll Free Tel:* 800-733-3000; 800-669-1536 (electronic orders) *Toll*

Free Fax: 800-659-2436 *Web Site:* www.penguinrandomhouse.biz SAN: 631-760X; Penguin Random House Canada, 2775 Matheson Blvd E, Mississauga, ON L4W 4P7, Canada *Toll Free Tel:* 888-523-9292; 800-258-4233 (electronic orders) *Toll Free Fax:* 888-562-9924
Distribution Center: Penguin Random House Publisher Services (PRHPS), 400 Hahn Rd, Westminster, MD 21157 *Toll Free Tel:* 800-733-3000; 800-669-1536 (electronic orders) *Toll Free Fax:* 800-659-2436 *Web Site:* www.penguinrandomhouse.biz SAN: 631-760X
Penguin Random House Canada, 2775 Matheson Blvd E, Mississauga, ON L4W 4P7, Canada *Toll Free Tel:* 888-523-9292; 800-258-4233 (electronic orders) *Toll Free Fax:* 888-562-9924

Soil Science Society of America (SSSA)
5585 Guilford Rd, Madison, WI 53711-5801
Tel: 608-273-8080 *Fax:* 608-273-2021
Web Site: www.soils.org
Key Personnel
CEO: Nicholas J Goeser, PhD *Tel:* 608-327-9034
CFO: Wes Meixelsperger *Tel:* 608-268-4958
Dir of Publns: Matt Wascavage *Tel:* 608-819-3916
Mng Ed, Books, Monographs, Spec Pubns, Methods of Soil Sciences: Danielle Lynch
  Tel: 608-268-4976
Founded: 1936
Technical books for professionals in soil science.
ISBN Prefix(es): 978-0-89118
Number of titles published annually: 6 E-Book
Total Titles: 90 Print

Solano Press Books
PO Box 773, Point Arena, CA 95468
Tel: 707-884-4508 *Toll Free Tel:* 800-931-9373
  Fax: 707-884-4109
E-mail: spbooks@solano.com
Web Site: www.solano.com
Key Personnel
Publr: Ling-Yen Jones
Acqs Ed: Natalie Macris
Asst to Publr: Nancy McLaughlin
Founded: 1984
Professional books: law, public administration, real estate, land use, environment, urban planning, environmental analysis & management.
ISBN Prefix(es): 978-0-9614657; 978-0-923956; 978-1-938166
Number of titles published annually: 4 Print
Total Titles: 25 Print; 8 E-Book

Solution Tree
555 N Morton St, Bloomington, IN 47404
Tel: 812-336-7700 *Toll Free Tel:* 800-733-6786
  Fax: 812-336-7790
E-mail: pubs@solutiontree.com; orders@solutiontree.com
Web Site: www.solutiontree.com
Key Personnel
Chief Mktg Offr: Erica Dooley-Dorocke
  E-mail: erica.dooley-dorocke@solutiontree.com
VP, Sales: Joan Brooks *Tel:* 800-733-6786 ext 472 *E-mail:* joan.brooks@solutiontree.com
Founded: 1998
Works to transform education worldwide by empowering educators to raise student achievement. With more than 48,962 educators attending professional learning events & more than 5,500 professional development days in schools each year, Solution Tree helps teachers & administrators confront essential challenges. Solution Tree has a catalog of more than 500 titles, hundreds of videos & online courses & is the creator of Global PD, an online tool that facilitates the work of professional learning communities for more than 20,000 educators.
ISBN Prefix(es): 978-1-879639; 978-1-932127
Number of titles published annually: 45 Print; 45 E-Book

Total Titles: 500 Print; 420 E-Book; 4 Audio
Imprints: Solution Tree Press
Branch Office(s)
Solution Tree Education Canada, PO Box 3250, Mission, BC V2V 4J4, Canada, Exec Dir, Busn Devt & Opers: Chris Allen *Toll Free Tel:* 800-733-6786 ext 023 *E-mail:* chris.allen@solutiontree.com

Somerset Hall Press
416 Commonwealth Ave, Suite 612, Boston, MA 02215
Tel: 617-236-5126
E-mail: info@somersethallpress.com
Web Site: www.somersethallpress.com
Key Personnel
Publr: Dean Papademetriou
Founded: 2001
Independent press specializing in literary & scholarly titles with a special interest in Greek studies.
ISBN Prefix(es): 978-0-9724661; 978-0-9774610; 978-1-935244
Number of titles published annually: 3 Print
Total Titles: 20 Print

Soncino Press Ltd
123 Ditmas Ave, Brooklyn, NY 11218
Tel: 718-972-6200 *Toll Free Tel:* 800-972-6201
  Fax: 718-972-6204
E-mail: info@soncino.com
Web Site: www.soncino.com
Key Personnel
Pres: Gloria Goldman
Mng Ed: Norman Shapiro
Bible, Talmud & Judaism.
ISBN Prefix(es): 978-1-871055; 978-0-900689
Number of titles published annually: 20 Print
Total Titles: 100 Print

Sophia Institute Press®
18 Celina Ave, Unit 1, Nashua, NH 03063
Mailing Address: PO Box 5284, Manchester, NH 03108 SAN: 657-7172
Tel: 603-641-9344 *Toll Free Tel:* 800-888-9344
  Fax: 603-641-8108 *Toll Free Fax:* 888-288-2259
E-mail: orders@sophiainstitute.com
Web Site: www.sophiainstitute.com
Key Personnel
Pres: Charlie McKinney
VP, Mktg: Tom Allen
Dir, Sales: Michael DeMonico
Dir, Prodn: Sheila M Perry
Founded: 1983
Books on religion (Roman Catholicism).
ISBN Prefix(es): 978-0-918477; 978-1-928832; 978-1-933184
Number of titles published annually: 60 Print
Total Titles: 300 Print
Foreign Rep(s): Cenacle House Ltd (UK); Family Life International (New Zealand); John XXIII Fellowship (Australia); Redemptorist Publications (UK); St Joseph's Workshops (Canada); Sunrise Marion Center (Canada)

§Soul Mate Publishing
3210 Sherwood Dr, Walworth, NY 14568
Web Site: www.soulmatepublishing.com
Key Personnel
Founder & Sr Ed: Deborah Gilbert
  E-mail: debby@soulmatepublishing.com
Founded: 2011
ISBN Prefix(es): 978-1-61935
Number of titles published annually: 100 E-Book
Total Titles: 15 Print; 120 E-Book
Membership(s): Romance Writers of America (RWA)

§Sound Feelings Publishing
18375 Ventura Blvd, No 8000, Tarzana, CA 91356
Tel: 818-757-0600

E-mail: information@soundfeelings.com
Web Site: www.soundfeelings.com
Key Personnel
Founder & Pres: Howard Richman
This publisher has indicated that 80% of their product line is author subsidized.
ISBN Prefix(es): 978-0-9615963; 978-1-882060
Number of titles published annually: 3 Print; 3 E-Book; 2 Audio
Total Titles: 15 Print; 10 E-Book; 11 Audio
Foreign Rep(s): Gazelle Book Services Ltd (Europe)

Sounds True Inc

413 S Arthur Ave, Louisville, CO 80027
Tel: 303-665-3151 *Toll Free Tel:* 800-333-9185 (US); 888-303-9185 (US & CN)
E-mail: customerservice@soundstrue.com; stpublicity@soundstrue.com
Web Site: www.soundstrue.com
Key Personnel
Founder & Publr: Tami Simon
Assoc Publr: Jaime Schwalb
VP, Opers: Wendy Pardo
Sr Art Dir: Rachael Murray
Edit Dir: Haven Iverson
Exec Ed: Jennifer Brown
Sr Ed: Diana Ventimiglia
Acqs Ed: Melissa Valentine
Children's Acq Ed: Jen Adams
Freelance Ed-at-Large: Caroline Pincus
Opers Mgr: April Sargent
Prod Mktg Mgr: Jaclyn Hawkins; Chloe Prusiewicz
Publicity Mgr: Nick Small
Founded: 1985
ISBN Prefix(es): 978-1-56455; 978-1-59179; 978-1-60407; 978-1-62203
Number of titles published annually: 30 Print; 30 E-Book; 40 Audio
Total Titles: 200 Print; 150 E-Book; 800 Audio
Distributed by Macmillan

§Sourcebooks LLC

1935 Brookdale Rd, Suite 139, Naperville, IL 60563
SAN: 666-7864
Mailing Address: PO Box 4410, Naperville, IL 60567-4410
Tel: 630-961-3900 *Toll Free Tel:* 800-432-7444 *Fax:* 630-961-2168
E-mail: info@sourcebooks.com; customersupport@sourcebooks.com
Web Site: www.sourcebooks.com
Key Personnel
Publr & CEO: Dominique Raccah
SVP & COO: Barbara Briel
SVP & Dir, Technol & Content Delivery: Lynn Dilger
SVP & Edit Dir: Todd Stocke *Tel:* 630-536-0543 *E-mail:* todd.stocke@sourcebooks.com
VP & Dir, Sales & Mktg: Chris Bauerle *E-mail:* chris.bauerle@sourcebooks.com
Exec Dir, Sales: Sean Murray
Sr Art Dir: Brittany Vibbert
Art Dir: Heather VenHuizen
Art Dir, Children's: John Aardema; Maryn Arreguin
Edit Dir, Sourcebooks & Poisoned Pen Press: Anna Michels
Edit Dir, Sourcebooks Casablanca: Deb Werksman *Tel:* 203-876-9790 *E-mail:* deb.werksman@sourcebooks.com
Edit Dir, Sourcebooks Jabberwocky & Sourcebooks Young Readers: Steve Geck *Tel:* 212-414-1701 ext 2226 *E-mail:* steve.geck@sourcebooks.com
Edit Dir, Sourcebooks Jabberwocky Nonfiction & Sourcebooks eXplore: Kelly Barrales-Saylor
Edit Dir, Sourcebooks Landmark: Shana Drehs *Tel:* 630-536-0535 *E-mail:* shana.drehs@sourcebooks.com
Sr Dir, Mktg, Fiction: Molly Waxman

Dir, Mktg, Nonfiction & Mystery: Liz Kelsch
Dir, Mktg, Retail & Creative Servs: Valerie Pierce *Tel:* 630-961-3900 ext 233 *E-mail:* valerie.pierce@sourcebooks.com
Dir, Mktg, Sourcebooks Jabberwocky: Heather Moore *E-mail:* heather.moore@sourcebooks.com
Dir, Publg Opers: Sarah Cardillo
Dir, Sales, Custom & Proprietary: Alexis Banyon
Dir, Sales, Schools, Libs & Independent Bookstores: Margaret Coffee
Creative Dir, Children's: Jordan Kost
Sales Dir: Chuck Deane
Assoc Art Dir, Adult Nonfiction: Heather Morris
Assoc Art Dir, Children's: Allison Sundstrom
Assoc Creative Dir: Kelly Lawler
Mng Ed: Bret Kehoe
Mng Ed, Children's & Young Adult: April Wills
Assoc Mng Ed: Heather Hall
Sr Ed, Simple Truths: Meg Gibbons
Sr Ed, Sourcebooks Casablanca: Mary Altman
Sr Ed, Sourcebooks Fire: Annie Berger
Sr Ed, Sourcebooks Jabberwocky & Fire: Eliza Swift
Sr Prodn Ed: Cassie Gutman; Jessica Thelander
Ed, Sourcebooks Jabberwocky, Young Readers & Fire: Molly Cusick
Assoc Prodn Ed: Jessica Smith
Assoc Ed: Christa Desir; Taylor Maccoux; Erin McClary
Assoc Ed, Sourcebooks & Sourcebooks Landmark: MJ Johnston
Asst Content Ed: Rachel Gilmer
Asst Ed: Kate Roddy
Asst Ed, Sourcebooks eXplore: Emma Hintzen; Julie Larson
Sr Mktg Mgr, Casablanca & Fire: Beth Sochacki
Cust Serv Mgr: Margaret Kelly; Suzanne Walker
Data & Analytics Dept Mgr: Christy Droege
Busn Data & Analytics Mgr: Stephanie Lewis
E-Commerce Opers Mgr: Brad Hentz
Mktg Mgr, Libs: Beth Oleniczak
Natl Accts Mgr, Gift & Regl: Liz Otte
Natl Sales Acct Mgr: Tim Golden
Publg Mgr, Entertainment Group: Karen Shapiro
Purch Mgr: Deve McLemore
Rts & Export Mgr: Sierra Stovall
Sales Acct Mgr: Stephanie Levasseur
Assoc Impact Mktg Mgr, Sourcebooks Landmark: Cristina Arreola
Asst Mktg Mgr, Sourcebooks Casablanca: Stefani Sloma
Ebook Prodn Coord: Jessica Zulli
Sales Coord: Carrie Conlisk
Digital Mktg Specialist: Molly Fletcher
Mktg Assoc: Ashlyn Keil; Caitlin Lawler; Shauneice Robinson; Morgan Vogt
Mktg Specialist: Michael Leali; Allison Lewis
Mktg Specialist, Children's Books: Mallory Hyde
Metadata Strategy Specialist: Jennifer Sterkowitz
Sr Designer: Stephanie Gafron; Stephanie Rocha; Amanda Skolek
Sr Graphic Design Mgr: Jenna Quatraro
Print Buyer: Cristina Wilson
Digital Content Specialist: Katie Cooper
Events Mktg Specialist: Lizzie Lewandowski
Accts Payable Assoc: Claudette Soriano
Author Rel Assoc: Katie Stutz
Royalty Assoc, Acctg: Lauren McClearn
Subs Rts & Intl Sales Assoc: Sophia Ramos
Founded: 1987
Nonfiction, fiction, romance novels, children's books, young adult, gift books & calendars.
ISBN Prefix(es): 978-0-942061; 978-1-57071; 978-1-57248; 978-0-913825; 978-1-883518; 978-0-9629162; 978-1-887166; 978-1-4022; 978-1-4926; 978-1-7282
Number of titles published annually: 400 Print; 270 E-Book
Total Titles: 3,000 Print; 1,700 E-Book
Imprints: Dawn Publications; Little Pickle Press (children's nonfiction); Poisoned Pen Press (mystery, thriller, horror); Simple Truths (busn & personal devt); Sourcebooks (adult non-

fiction & ref); Sourcebooks Casablanca (romance fiction); Sourcebooks eXplore (children's nonfiction); Sourcebooks Fire (young adult); Sourcebooks Jabberwocky (children's books); Sourcebooks Landmark (adult fiction); Sourcebooks Wonderland; Sourcebooks Young Readers
Branch Office(s)
18 Cherry St, Suite 1W, Milford, CT 06460
Tel: 203-876-9790
Sourcebooks New York, 232 Madison Ave, Suite 805, New York, NY 10018 *Tel:* 212-414-1701
Distributed by Penguin Random House India (India & subcontinent)
Distributor for Prufrock Press
Foreign Rights: Eliane Benisti Literary Agency (Eliane Benisti) (France); The Deborah Harris Agency (Israel); Inter-Ko (Korea); Nurcihan Kesim Literary Agency Inc (Turkey); Maxima Creative Agency (Indonesia); Piergiorgio Nicolazzini (Italy); Nova Littera Ltd (Russia); Prava i prevodi (Eastern Block, Slovakia); Schindler's Literary Agency (Brazil); Tuttle-Mori Agency Inc (Japan, Thailand); Yanez Agencia Literaria (Spain)
Returns: RR Donnelley, 677 Brighton Beach Rd, Menasha, WI 54952
Warehouse: RR Donnelley, N9234 Lake Park Rd, Appleton, WI 54915 *Tel:* 920-969-6400 *Fax:* 920-969-6441
Distribution Center: Baker & Taylor Global Publishers Services (GPS), 2550 W Tyvola Rd, Chicago, IL 28217 *E-mail:* gps@baker-taylor.com
Raincoast Books, 2440 Viking Way, Richmond, BC V6V 1N2, Canada *Toll Free Tel:* 800-663-5714 *Toll Free Fax:* 800-565-3770 *E-mail:* info@raincoast.com
Melia Publishing Services, One St Peter's Rd, Maidenhead, Berks SL6 7QU, United Kingdom
See separate listing for:
Dawn Publications Inc
Poisoned Pen Press

Sourced Media Books

15 Via Picato, San Clemente, CA 92673
Tel: 949-813-0182
E-mail: editor@sourcedmediabooks.com
Web Site: sourcedmediabooks.com
Key Personnel
Publr: Amy Cook, PhD; Jennifer Durrant
Sr Ed: J'Nel Wright
Founded: 2009
ISBN Prefix(es): 978-0-9841068; 978-1-937458
Number of titles published annually: 10 Print; 15 Online; 15 E-Book
Total Titles: 45 Print; 18 Online; 18 E-Book
Distributed by Gibbs-Smith; Many Hats Media
Distribution Center: Brigham Distributing, 110 S 800 W, Brigham City, UT 84302

South Carolina Bar

Continuing Legal Education Div, 950 Taylor St, Columbia, SC 29201
Mailing Address: PO Box 608, Columbia, SC 29202-0608
Tel: 803-799-6653 *Toll Free Tel:* 800-768-7787
E-mail: scbar-info@scbar.org
Web Site: www.scbar.org
Key Personnel
Continuing Legal Educ Dir: Terry Burnett *Tel:* 803-799-6653 ext 152 *E-mail:* tburnett@scbar.org
Pubns Dir: Alicia Chandler Hutto *Tel:* 803-799-6653 ext 119 *E-mail:* ahutto@scbar.org
Founded: 1979
Law materials, legal treatises, manuals & software.
ISBN Prefix(es): 978-0-943856
Number of titles published annually: 10 Print
Total Titles: 100 Print

South Dakota Historical Society Press
900 Governors Dr, Pierre, SD 57501
Tel: 605-773-6009 *Fax:* 605-773-6041
E-mail: info@sdshspress.com; orders@sdshspress.com
Web Site: sdshspress.com
Key Personnel
Dir & Ed-in-Chief: Nancy Tystad Koupal
   Tel: 605-773-4371 *E-mail:* Nancy.Koupal@state.sd.us
Mktg Dir & Assoc Ed: Jennifer McIntyre
   Tel: 605-773-8161 *E-mail:* Jennifer.McIntyre@state.sd.us
Mng Ed: Jeanne Ode *Tel:* 605-773-6008
   E-mail: Jeanne.Ode@state.sd.us
Founded: 1997
The South Dakota Historical Society Press is committed to producing books that reflect the rich & varied history of South Dakota & the region.
ISBN Prefix(es): 978-0-9622621; 978-0-9715171; 978-0-9749195; 978-0-9777955; 978-0-9798940; 978-0-9845041; 978-0-9846505; 978-0-9852905; 978-0-9860355; 978-1-941813; 978-0-9822749; 978-0-9852817
Number of titles published annually: 7 Print
Total Titles: 55 Print
Foreign Rep(s): Eurospan Group (worldwide exc North America)

South Platte Press
PO Box 163, David City, NE 68632-0163
Tel: 402-367-3554
E-mail: railroads@windstream.net
Web Site: www.southplattepress.net
Key Personnel
Publr: James J Reisdorff
Founded: 1982
Railroad related titles.
ISBN Prefix(es): 978-0-942035
Number of titles published annually: 5 Print
Total Titles: 25 Print

Southern Historical Press Inc
375 W Broad St, Greenville, SC 29601
Mailing Address: PO Box 1267, Greenville, SC 29602-1267
Tel: 864-233-2346 *Toll Free Tel:* 800-233-0152
E-mail: southernhistoricalpress@gmail.com
Web Site: www.southernhistoricalpress.com
Key Personnel
Pres: LaBruce M S Lucas
Founded: 1967
Historical & genealogical books.
ISBN Prefix(es): 978-0-89308
Number of titles published annually: 20 Print
Total Titles: 370 Print

Southern Illinois University Press
Division of Southern Illinois University
1915 University Press Dr, SIUC Mail Code 6806, Carbondale, IL 62901-4323
SAN: 203-3623
Tel: 618-453-2281 *Fax:* 618-453-1221
Web Site: www.siupress.com
Key Personnel
Mktg & Sales Mgr: Amy Etcheson *Tel:* 618-453-6623 *E-mail:* aetcheson@siu.edu
Rts & Perms Mgr: Angela Moore-Swafford
   Tel: 618-453-6617 *E-mail:* rights@siu.edu
Acqs Ed: Kristine Priddy *Tel:* 618-453-6631
   E-mail: mkpriddy@siu.edu
Founded: 1956
Scholarly nonfiction, educational material, rhetoric & composition, aviation, history, theatre, regional history & poetry.
ISBN Prefix(es): 978-0-8093
Number of titles published annually: 30 Print; 30 E-Book
Total Titles: 1,400 Print; 2 CD-ROM; 400 E-Book; 17 Audio

Foreign Rep(s): Eurospan (Andrew Wong) (Europe, Middle East); Scholarly Book Services Inc (Laura Rust) (Canada)
Distribution Center: Chicago Distribution Center, 11030 S Langley Ave, Chicago, IL 60628-3830 *Toll Free Tel:* 800-621-2736 *Toll Free Fax:* 800-621-8476
Membership(s): Association of University Presses (AUPresses)

Soyinfo Center
1021 Dolores Dr, Lafayette, CA 94549-0234
SAN: 212-8411
Tel: 925-283-2991
Web Site: www.soyinfocenter.com
Key Personnel
Pres & Ed-in-Chief: William Shurtleff
Founded: 1976
Books & bibliographies on all aspects of soybeans & soyfoods; industry & marketing studies. 90 books since 2008 published in PDF format on the web free of charge.
ISBN Prefix(es): 978-0-933332; 978-1-928914; 978-1-948436
Number of titles published annually: 10 Print; 10 Online
Total Titles: 162 Print; 60 Online

Sparkhouse, see Augsburg Fortress Publishers, Publishing House of the Evangelical Lutheran Church in America

Sparkhouse Family, see Augsburg Fortress Publishers, Publishing House of the Evangelical Lutheran Church in America

Specialty Graphic Imaging Association (SGIA), see PRINTING United Alliance

SPIE
1000 20 St, Bellingham, WA 98225-6705
Mailing Address: PO Box 10, Bellingham, WA 98227-0010
Tel: 360-676-3290 *Toll Free Tel:* 888-504-8171 (orders) *Fax:* 360-647-1445
E-mail: help@spie.org; customerservice@spie.org (orders)
Web Site: www.spie.org
Key Personnel
Pubns Dir: Eric Pepper *Tel:* 360-685-5473
   E-mail: eric@spie.org
Pubns Busn Devt Mgr: Mary Summerfield
   Tel: 360-685-5588 *E-mail:* marysu@spie.org
SPIE Press Mgr: Tim Lamkins *Tel:* 360-685-5475
   E-mail: timl@spie.org
Journals Mgr: Karolyn Labes *Tel:* 360-685-5421
   E-mail: karolyn@spie.org
Founded: 1955
Scientific, technical books & journals, proceedings of symposia.
ISBN Prefix(es): 978-0-8194
Number of titles published annually: 30 Print; 400 Online; 30 E-Book
Total Titles: 400 Print; 407 E-Book
Imprints: Proceedings of SPIE (spie.org/publications/conference-proceedings); SPIE Digital Library (www.spiedigitallibrary.org); SPIE Journals (spie.org/publications/spie-journals); SPIE Press (spie.org/publications/books)
Foreign Rep(s): Applied Media (India); Eurospan (Europe, Middle East, North Africa); Princeton Selling Group (Canada, USA)
Foreign Rights: Applied Media (India)
Membership(s): Copyright Clearance Center (CCC); Crossref; Society for Scholarly Publishing (SSP)

SPIE, The international society for optics and photonics, see SPIE

Spinsters Ink
Imprint of Bella Books
PO Box 10543, Tallahassee, FL 32302
Tel: 850-576-2370 *Toll Free Tel:* 800-729-4992
E-mail: info@bellabooks.com
Web Site: www.bellabooks.com/Publisher-spinsters-ink-cat.html
Key Personnel
Publr: Linda Hill
Founded: 1978
Novels & nonfiction by women about LGBT lives & issues, including social justice.
ISBN Prefix(es): 978-1-935226; 978-1-883523
Number of titles published annually: 8 Print; 12 E-Book
Total Titles: 100 Print; 24 E-Book
Imprints: Grave Issues
Foreign Rep(s): Airlift Book Co (Europe); Bulldog Distribution (Australia)
Distribution Center: Bella Distribution

Spizzirri Publishing Inc
PO Box 9397, Rapid City, SD 57709-9397
Tel: 605-348-2749 *Toll Free Tel:* 800-325-9819
   Fax: 605-348-6251 *Toll Free Fax:* 800-322-9819
E-mail: spizzpub@aol.com
Web Site: www.spizzirri.com
Key Personnel
Pres: Linda Spizzirri
Founded: 1978
Educational coloring books, book-CD packages, activity books, workbooks & how-to-draw books. PreK-5th grade featuring realistic illustrations & museum curator approved texts on topics, including everything from dinosaurs to space.
ISBN Prefix(es): 978-0-86545
Number of titles published annually: 3 Print
Total Titles: 200 Print

§Springer
Subsidiary of Springer Science+Business Media
233 Spring St, New York, NY 10013-1578
Tel: 212-460-1500 *Toll Free Tel:* 800-SPRINGER (777-4643) *Fax:* 212-460-1700
E-mail: customerservice@springer.com
Web Site: www.springer.com
Key Personnel
Cont: Ned Woods
VP, Applied Sci: Dieter Merkle
VP, HR: Eileen Purelis *E-mail:* eileen.purelis@springer.com
VP, Prodn: Henry Krell
VP, Publg Devt & Head, Edit Dept, Astronomy: Harry Blom
Edit Dir: Antoinette Cimino *E-mail:* antoinette.cimino@springer.com
Edit Dir, Biomedicine: Carolyn Honour
Edit Dir, Clinical Medicine: Richard Lansing
   E-mail: richard.lansing@springer.com
Edit Dir, Computer Sci & Engg: Jennifer Evans
Founded: 1842 (1964 NY off)
Scientific, medical, technical, research, reference books & periodicals.
ISBN Prefix(es): 978-0-387
Number of titles published annually: 6,500 Print; 6,000 E-Book
Total Titles: 70,000 Print; 36,000 Online; 38,000 E-Book
Imprints: Apress; BioMed Central; Birkhauser Science; Copernicus; Current Medicine Group; Humana Press; Springer Healthcare
Foreign Office(s): Heidelberger Platz 3, 14197 Berlin, Germany
Tiergartenstr 17, 69121 Heidelberg, Germany
Van Godewijckstr 30, 3311 GX Dordrecht, Netherlands
Membership(s): International Association of Scientific, Technical & Medical Publishers (ISTM)

§Springer Publishing Co
11 W 42 St, 15th fl, New York, NY 10036-8002

SAN: 203-2236
Tel: 212-431-4370 *Toll Free Tel:* 877-687-7476
E-mail: marketing@springerpub.com; cs@
springerpub.com (orders); textbook@
springerpub.com; specialsales@springerpub.
com
Web Site: www.springerpub.com
Key Personnel
CEO: Mary E Gatsch *E-mail:* mgatsch@
springerpub.com
Publr, Med, Health & Behaviorial Sci: Beth Kaufman Barry *E-mail:* bbarry@springerpub.com
Publr, Nursing: Elizabeth Nieginski
E-mail: enieginski@springerpub.com
Sr Sales Dir, Higher Educ: Gary Darlington; Jill Ferguson
Dir, Behavioral Sciences: Kate Dimock
E-mail: kdimock@springerpub.com
Dir, Digital Devt: Suzanne Toppy
E-mail: stoppy@springerpub.com
Dir, Licensing & Busn Devt: Mindy Anderson
Dir, Nurse Educ: Adrianne Brigido
E-mail: abrigido@springerpub.com
Sales Dir, Trade, Pharma & Rts: Reina Santana
E-mail: rsantana@springerpub.com
Sr Acqs Ed, Healthcare Admin & Oncology: David D'Addona *E-mail:* ddaddona@
springerpub.com
Sr Acqs Ed, Textbooks: Rhonda Dearborn
E-mail: rdearborn@springerpub.com
Sr Ed, Nursing: Joe Morita *E-mail:* jmorita@
springerpub.com
Assoc Acqs Ed, Nursing: Rachel Landes
E-mail: rlandes@springerpub.com
Founded: 1950 (Feb 2004, acquired by Mannheim Holdings, LLC, subsidiary of Mannheim Trust)
Professional books, encyclopedias, college textbooks & journals; nursing, psychology, gerontology/geriatrics, medical education, public health, rehabilitation, social work & scholarly health sciences.
ISBN Prefix(es): 978-0-8261
Number of titles published annually: 100 Print
Total Titles: 700 Print
Imprints: Demos Medical Publishing
Foreign Rep(s): Avicenna Partnership Ltd (Middle East); Cranbury International (Ethan Atkin) (Latin America); The Eurospan Group (Africa, Europe, UK); Footprint Books Pty Ltd (Australia, New Zealand); Login Canada (Canada); Nankodo Co Ltd (Japan); Taylor & Francis Asia Pacific (Brunei, China, Hong Kong, Indonesia, Korea, Malaysia, Philippines, Singapore, Taiwan, Thailand, Vietnam); Viva Books Pvt Ltd (Vinod Vasishtha & Pradeep Kumar) (India)
Membership(s): American Medical Publishers Association; Association of American Publishers (AAP); STM
See separate listing for:
Demos Medical Publishing

Square One Publishers Inc
115 Herricks Rd, Garden City Park, NY 11040
Tel: 516-535-2010 *Toll Free Tel:* 877-900-BOOK (900-2665) *Fax:* 516-535-2014
E-mail: sq1publish@aol.com
Web Site: www.squareonepublishers.com
Key Personnel
Pres & Publr: Rudy Shur
Art Dir: Jeannie Tudor
VP, Mktg, PR & Rts: Anthony Pomes
Sales Dir: Ken Kaiman
Mgr, Opers: Robert Love
Exec Ed: Joanne Abrams
Sr Ed: Marie Caratozzolo
Ed: Michael Weatherhead
Founded: 2000
Specialize in adult nonfiction books. Topics covered include collectibles, cooking, general interest, history, how-to, parenting, self-help & health.
ISBN Prefix(es): 978-0-7570

Number of titles published annually: 25 Print
Total Titles: 500 Print; 1 Audio
Imprints: Ocean Publishing
Distributed by Thomas Allen & Son
Distributor for InnoVision Health Media; Rainbow Ridge Books
Foreign Rep(s): Thomas Allen & Son (Canada); Brumby Sunstate (Australia, New Zealand); G D Daby (Southeast Asia); Deep Books Ltd (Europe, UK); Phambili Agencies (South Africa)
Membership(s): American Booksellers Association (ABA); American Library Association (ALA); The Association of Publishers for Special Sales (APSS); Independent Book Publishers Association (IBPA)

§SSPC: The Society for Protective Coatings
800 Trumbull Dr, Pittsburgh, PA 15205-4365
Tel: 412-281-2331 *Toll Free Tel:* 877-281-7772 (US only) *Fax:* 412-444-3591
E-mail: info@sspc.org
Web Site: www.sspc.org
Key Personnel
Exec Dir: William Worms *Tel:* 412-281-2331 ext 2230 *E-mail:* worms@sspc.org
Dir, Technol & Communs: Michael Kline
Tel: 412-281-2331 ext 2207 *E-mail:* kline@
sspc.org
Memb Servs Asst/Pubns Coord: Cara Blyzwick *Tel:* 412-281-2331 ext 2232
E-mail: blyzwick@sspc.org
Founded: 1950
Technical publications; CD-ROMs, standards for industry.
This publisher has indicated that 50% of their product line is author subsidized.
ISBN Prefix(es): 978-0-938477; 978-1-889060
Number of titles published annually: 12 Print
Total Titles: 80 Print
Distributed by Technology Publishing Co
Membership(s): ASAE

§Stackpole Books
Imprint of Rowman & Littlefield Publishing Group
31 E Main St, New Kingstown, PA 17072
Mailing Address: PO Box 90, New Kingstown, PA 17072
Tel: 717-590-8974
Web Site: www.stackpolebooks.com
Key Personnel
Publr: Judith Schnell *E-mail:* jschnell@rowman.com
Founded: 1933
Trade book publisher in the categories of outdoor sports, nature, crafts, history, military reference & regional. Strong in fly fishing, nature guides, military history & military reference, we publish deep in our niche areas. Presently expanding into the fast-growing world of ebooks while continuing to produce alternative, high-quality hardcovers & trade paperbacks.
ISBN Prefix(es): 978-0-8117
Number of titles published annually: 60 Print
Total Titles: 1,500 Print
Distribution Center: National Book Network, 15200 NBN Way, Blue Ridge Summit, PA 17214 *Tel:* 717-794-3800 *Fax:* 717-794-3828

§Standard Publishing
Imprint of David C Cook
4050 Lee Vance Dr, Colorado Springs, CO 80918
SAN: 110-5515
Toll Free Tel: 800-323-7543 *Toll Free Fax:* 800-430-0726
Web Site: www.standardpub.com
Founded: 1866
Religious children's books, Sunday school literature & supplies, youth & adult trade books.
ISBN Prefix(es): 978-0-87239; 978-0-87403; 978-0-7847

Number of titles published annually: 75 Print
Total Titles: 700 Print; 30 CD-ROM
Imprints: HeartShaper®; Standard Lesson Commentary®; Standard Lesson Quarterly®; Standard Lesson Resources®

§Standard Publishing Corp
10 High St, Boston, MA 02110
Tel: 617-457-0600 *Toll Free Tel:* 800-682-5759
Fax: 617-457-0608
Web Site: www.spcpub.com
Key Personnel
Pres & Publr: John C Cross, Esq *E-mail:* j.cross@spcpub.com
Edit: Deborah Dukeshire
Mktg Mgr: Susanne Edes Dillman *Tel:* 617-457-0611 ext 77 *E-mail:* s.dillman@spcpub.com
Founded: 1865
Information for insurance professionals.
ISBN Prefix(es): 978-0-923240
Number of titles published annually: 10 Print
Total Titles: 10 Print; 3 CD-ROM
Subsidiaries: John Liner Organization
Branch Office(s)
Insurance Record, 9601 White Rock Trail, Suite 213, Dallas, TX 75238
Distributed by LexisNexis®; Silverplume, a Vertafore Co

Stanford University Press
425 Broadway St, Redwood City, CA 94063-3126
SAN: 203-3526
Tel: 650-723-9434 *Fax:* 650-725-3457
E-mail: info@www.sup.org; publicity@www.sup.org; sales@www.sup.org
Web Site: www.sup.org
Key Personnel
Publr: Michael Keller
Publg Dir & Ed-in-Chief: Kate Wahl *Tel:* 650-498-9420 *E-mail:* kwahl@stanford.edu
Dir: Dr Alan Harvey *Tel:* 650-723-6375
E-mail: aharvey@stanford.edu
Dir, Edit, Design & Prodn: David Zielonka
Tel: 650-724-5365 *E-mail:* zielonka@stanford.edu
Dir, Fin & Opers: Jean H Kim *Tel:* 650-725-0838
E-mail: plcmnkim@stanford.edu
Art Dir: Robert Ehle *E-mail:* ehle@stanford.edu
Exec Ed: Erica Wetter *Tel:* 650-725-7717
E-mail: ewetter@stanford.edu
Sr Ed: Steve Catalano *Tel:* 650-724-7079
E-mail: catalan@stanford.edu; Marcela Maxfield *Tel:* 650-498-3396 *E-mail:* mmaxfiel@
stanford.edu; Friederike Sundaram *Tel:* 650-736-8207 *E-mail:* fsundara@stanford.edu
Acqs Ed: Jenny Gavacs *E-mail:* jgavacs@
stanford.edu; Margo Irvin *Tel:* 650-498-9023
E-mail: mcirvin@stanford.edu
Assoc Ed: Faith Wilson Stein *Tel:* 650-497-4991
E-mail: fwstein@stanford.edu
Asst Ed: Caroline McKusick *Tel:* 650-498-9420
E-mail: cmck@stanford.edu
Contracts & Rts Mgr: Greta Lindquist *Tel:* 650-725-0815
Mktg Mgr: Stephanie Adams *Tel:* 650-736-1782
E-mail: stephanie.adams@stanford.edu
Prodn Mgr: Mike Sagara *Tel:* 650-725-0839
E-mail: msagara@stanford.edu
Sales & Exhibits Mgr: Kate Templar *Tel:* 650-725-0820
Publicist: Bridget Kinsella *Tel:* 510-465-3853
E-mail: bridgetkinsella@stanford.edu
Founded: 1925
ISBN Prefix(es): 978-0-8047; 978-1-5036
Number of titles published annually: 130 Print; 40 E-Book
Total Titles: 3,000 Print; 400 E-Book
Imprints: Redwood Press; Stanford Briefs; Stanford Business Books
Foreign Rep(s): Canadian Manga Group (Canada); Combined Academic Publishers Ltd (Africa, Asia-Pacific, Europe, Middle East); In-

gram UK (Matthew Dickie) (Caribbean, Latin America)

Distribution Center: Ingram Content Group LLC, One Ingram Blvd, La Vergne, TN 37086 *Toll Free Tel:* 866-400-5351 *E-mail:* ordersupport@ingramcontent.com

Membership(s): Association of American Publishers (AAP); Association of University Presses (AUPresses)

Star Bright Books Inc
13 Landsdowne St, Cambridge, MA 02139
Tel: 617-354-1300 *Fax:* 617-354-1399
E-mail: info@starbrightbooks.com; orders@starbrightbooks.com
Web Site: www.starbrightbooks.org
Key Personnel
Publr: Deborah Shine
Founded: 1994
Independent children's book publisher focused on diversity & inclusion. Star Bright Books is committed to producing high quality board books, picture books & chapter books that meet the needs of all children. Books are available in 26 languages.
ISBN Prefix(es): 978-1-887734; 978-1-932065; 978-1-59572
Number of titles published annually: 16 Print
Total Titles: 400 Print; 80 E-Book
Foreign Rep(s): Fitzhenry & Whiteside (Canada); Roundhouse Group (Europe, UK)
Membership(s): American Booksellers Association (ABA); American Library Association (ALA); Association of Children's Booksellers; National Association for the Education of Young Children (NAEYC); Society of Children's Book Writers & Illustrators (SCBWI); Women's Business Enterprise National Council; Women's Business Enterprise Network (WBENC)

Star Publishing Co Inc
PO Box 5165, Belmont, CA 94002-5165
SAN: 212-6958
Tel: 650-591-3505
E-mail: starpublishing@gmail.com
Web Site: www.starpublishing.com
Key Personnel
Publr: Stuart A Hoffman
Founded: 1978
College/university textbooks, laboratory manuals; reference books; professional books; California history/local history.
ISBN Prefix(es): 978-0-89863
Number of titles published annually: 14 Print
Total Titles: 450 Print
Imprints: Encore Editions

Star Trek®, see Gallery Books

§STARbooks Press
PO Box 711612, Herndon, VA 20171
E-mail: publish@starbookspress.com; contact@starbookspress.com
Web Site: www.starbookspress.com
Key Personnel
Sr Edit Dir: Eric Summers
Founded: 1989
ISBN Prefix(es): 978-1-877978; 978-1-891855
Number of titles published annually: 8 Print
Total Titles: 30 Print; 1 Audio

§Starcrafts LLC
68A Fogg Rd, Epping, NH 03042
SAN: 208-5380
Tel: 603-734-4300 *Toll Free Tel:* 866-953-8458 (24/7 message ctr) *Fax:* 603-734-4311
E-mail: astrosales@astrocom.com
Web Site: acspublications.com; www.astrocom.com

Key Personnel
Owner & Publr: Maria K Simms *E-mail:* maria@astrocom.com
Cust Serv: Thomas Canfield *E-mail:* tom@astrocom.com
Founded: 1973
Astrology: ephemerides, chart interpretation.
ISBN Prefix(es): 978-0-935127; 978-0-917086; 978-0-9762422; 978-1-934976
Number of titles published annually: 4 Print; 1 CD-ROM
Total Titles: 60 Print; 5 CD-ROM; 1 Audio
Imprints: ACS Publications; Starcrafts Publishing
Foreign Rep(s): The Rights Agency (Canada)
Distribution Center: New Leaf Distributing Co, 401 Thornton Rd, Lithia Springs, GA 30122-1557 *Tel:* 770-948-7845 *Fax:* 770-944-2313 *E-mail:* newleaf@newleaf-dist.com *Web Site:* newleafdist.com

Stargazer Publishing Co
958 Stanislaus Dr, Corona, CA 92881
Mailing Address: PO Box 77002, Corona, CA 92877-0100
Tel: 951-898-4619 *Toll Free Tel:* 800-606-7895 (orders) *Fax:* 951-898-4633
E-mail: stargazer@stargazerpub.com; orders@stargazerpub.com
Web Site: www.stargazerpub.com
Founded: 1995
Publisher of educational & business books.
ISBN Prefix(es): 978-0-9643853; 978-1-933277; 978-0-9713756
Number of titles published annually: 10 Print; 5 E-Book
Total Titles: 48 Print; 5 CD-ROM; 5 E-Book
Warehouse: Publishers Storage & Shipping Corp, 660 S Mansfield, Ypsilanti, MI 48197
Membership(s): Independent Book Publishers Association (IBPA); National Association of College Stores (NACS); Publishers Association of Los Angeles

StarGroup International Inc
1194 Old Dixie Hwy, Suite 201, West Palm Beach, FL 33413
Tel: 561-547-0667 *Fax:* 561-843-8530
E-mail: info@stargroupinternational.com
Web Site: stargroupinternational.com
Key Personnel
Pres & CEO: Brenda Star *E-mail:* brenda@stargroupinternational.com
Creative Dir: Mel Abfier
Head Writer & Film/Video Prodr: Gwen Carden; Linda Haas
Internet Mktg Coord: Butch Butler
Mktg, Media & Website Devt: Rusty Durham
Media Specialist: Sam Smyth
Founded: 1983
Create books to be used as marketing & media tools. For over 2 decades have maintained access to the best researchers, writers, editors, proofreaders, designers & printers in the industry, while offering public relations & marketing services. Specialize in creating books for clients to enhance their credibility & position them as experts in their field.
This publisher has indicated that 75% of their product line is author subsidized.
ISBN Prefix(es): 978-1-884886
Number of titles published annually: 25 Print
Total Titles: 150 Print
Membership(s): Florida Authors & Publishers Association Inc (FAPA); Independent Book Publishers Association (IBPA)

State University of New York Press
10 N Pearl St, 4th fl, Albany, NY 12207
SAN: 760-7261
Tel: 518-944-2800 *Toll Free Tel:* 877-204-6073 (orders) *Fax:* 518-320-1592 *Toll Free Fax:* 877-204-6074 (orders)

E-mail: info@sunypress.edu (edit off); suny@presswarehouse.com (orders)
Web Site: www.sunypress.edu
Key Personnel
Dir: Tim Stookesberry
Co-Dir & Acqs: James Peltz *Tel:* 518-944-2815 *E-mail:* james.peltz@sunypress.edu
Dir, Mktg & Publicity: Fran Keneston *Tel:* 518-944-2807 *E-mail:* fran.keneston@sunypress.edu
Rts & Perms: Sharla Clute *Tel:* 518-944-2803 *E-mail:* sharla.clute@sunypress.edu
Founded: 1966
Scholarly nonfiction, especially works in philosophy, psychology, African American studies, gender/sexuality studies, American Indian studies, museum/archival science, Asian studies & religious studies.
ISBN Prefix(es): 978-0-87395; 978-0-88706; 978-0-7914; 978-1-4384
Number of titles published annually: 150 Print; 140 Online; 140 E-Book
Total Titles: 6,140 Print; 4,000 Online; 6,040 E-Book; 2 Audio
Imprints: Excelsior Editions
Distributor for Albany Institute of History & Art; Codhill Press; Samuel Dorsky Museum of Art; Mount Ida Press; Muswell Hill Press; New Netherland Institute; Rockefeller Institute Press; Uncrowned Queens
Foreign Rep(s): Cassidy & Associates Inc (China, Hong Kong, Taiwan); Lexa Publishers' Representatives (Canada); MHM Ltd (Japan); US PubRep (Caribbean, Central America, Mexico, Puerto Rico, South America)
Billing Address: PO Box 960, Herndon, VA 20172-0960, Cust Serv *Tel:* 703-661-1575 *Fax:* 703-996-1010
Orders to: PO Box 960, Herndon, VA 20172-0960, Cust Serv *Tel:* 703-661-1575 *Fax:* 703-996-1010
Returns: 22883 Quicksilver Dr, Dulles, VA 20166, Cust Serv *Tel:* 703-661-1575 *Fax:* 703-996-1010
Shipping Address: 22835 Quicksilver Dr, Dulles, VA 20166 *Tel:* 703-661-1575 *Fax:* 703-996-1010
Warehouse: PO Box 960, Herndon, VA 20172-0960, Cust Serv *Tel:* 703-661-1575 *Fax:* 703-996-1010
Distribution Center: NBN International, Estover Rd, Plymouth PL6 7PY, United Kingdom *Tel:* (01752) 202-301 *Fax:* (01752) 202-233 *E-mail:* orders@nbninternational.com
Membership(s): American Booksellers Association (ABA); Association of University Presses (AUPresses)
See separate listing for:
Excelsior Editions

Steerforth Press
31 Hanover St, Suite 1, Lebanon, NH 03766
Tel: 603-643-4787 *Fax:* 603-643-4788
E-mail: info@steerforth.com
Web Site: www.steerforth.com
Key Personnel
Founder & Publr: Chip Fleischer *E-mail:* chip@steerforth.com
Assoc Publr, Publicity & Digital Media: Devin Wilkie *E-mail:* devin@steerforth.com
Dir, Publg Opers & Foreign Rts: Helga Schmidt *E-mail:* helga@steerforth.com
Founded: 1993
ISBN Prefix(es): 978-1-883642; 978-0-944072; 978-1-58195; 978-1-58642
Number of titles published annually: 10 Print
Total Titles: 300 Print
Imprints: Truth to Power Books (T2P)
Foreign Rights: Big Apple Agency Inc (Taiwan); Agence Bookman (Scandinavia); The English Agency (Japan); Anouk H Foerg; Harris-Elon Agency (Israel); International Editors' Co SA (Argentina, Brazil, Latin America, Portugal, Spain); Katai & Bolza (Hungary); David Mar-

shall; Daniela Micura Literary Services (Italy); Onk Agency (Turkey)

Distribution Center: Penguin Random House Distribution Center, 400 Hahn Rd, Westminster, MD 21157 *Toll Free Tel:* 800-733-3000 *Toll Free Fax:* 800-659-2436

Membership(s): American Booksellers Association (ABA); Independent Book Publishers Association (IBPA); New England Independent Booksellers Association (NEIBA)

§SteinerBooks Inc
Imprint of Anthroposophic Press Inc
610 Main St, Suite 1, Great Barrington, MA 01230
Tel: 413-528-8233
E-mail: service@steinerbooks.org; friends@steinerbooks.org
Web Site: steiner.presswarehouse.com
Key Personnel
Pres & CEO: Gene Gollogly *E-mail:* gene@steinerbooks.org
Edit & Artistic Dir: Mary Giddens *E-mail:* mary@steinerbooks.org
Ed-in-Chief: Christopher Bamford *E-mail:* cbamford@cbamford.cnc.net
Sr Ed & Translator: Marsha Post *E-mail:* marsha@steinerbooks.org
Prodn Mgr: Stephan O'Reilly *E-mail:* stephan@steinerbooks.org
Founded: 1928
American & English editions of works by Rudolf Steiner & related authors.
ISBN Prefix(es): 978-0-910142; 978-0-88010; 978-0-89345; 978-0-9674562; 978-0-9779825; 978-0-9804044; 978-0-9831984; 978-0-9832261; 978-0-9853658; 978-1-62148
Number of titles published annually: 15 Print
Distributed by Rudolf Steiner Press UK
Distributor for Chiron Publications; Clairview Books; Floris Books; Hawthorn Press; Lantern Books; Rudolph Steiner Press; Temple Lodge Publishing
Foreign Rep(s): Ceres (New Zealand); Peter Hyde & Associates (South Africa); Rudolf Steiner Press (UK)
Orders to: PO Box 960, Herndon, VA 20172-0960 *Tel:* 703-661-1594 *Fax:* 703-661-1501
SAN: 201-1824

Stellar Publishing
2114 S Live Oak Pkwy, Wilmington, NC 28403
SAN: 860-2298
Tel: 910-269-7444
Web Site: www.stellar-publishing.com
Key Personnel
Publr: Jasper Williams *E-mail:* publisher@stellar-publishing.com
Founded: 2000
This publisher has indicated that 50% of their product line is author subsidized.
ISBN Prefix(es): 978-0-970341
Number of titles published annually: 3 Print
Total Titles: 9 Print

§Stenhouse Publishers
Division of Highlights for Children Education Group
One Monument Way, Portland, ME 04101-3400
Tel: 207-253-1600 *Toll Free Tel:* 888-363-0566 *Fax:* 207-253-5121 *Toll Free Fax:* 800-833-9164
E-mail: customerservice@stenhouse.com
Web Site: www.stenhouse.com
Key Personnel
Mng Ed: William Varner *E-mail:* wvarner@stenhouse.com
Founded: 1993
Professional books for teachers.
ISBN Prefix(es): 978-1-57110
Number of titles published annually: 25 Print; 3 Online; 15 E-Book

Total Titles: 400 Print; 275 E-Book; 3 Audio
Distributor for Pembroke Publishers
Foreign Rep(s): Eurospan (Africa, Central America, China, Europe, Hong Kong, India, Japan, Korea, South America, Taiwan, UK); Hawker Brownlow (Australia, New Zealand); Pembroke Publishers (Canada); Publishers Marketing Services (Southeast Asia)
Billing Address: PO Box 11020, Portland, ME 04104-7020, Opers Mgr: Elaine Cyr *E-mail:* ecyr@stenhouse.com
Warehouse: 4200 Parkway Ct, Hilliard, OH 43026, Contact: Vicki Woolwhine *Tel:* 614-487-2883 *Fax:* 614-529-0670

Sterling Publishing Co Inc
Subsidiary of Barnes & Noble Inc
1166 Avenue of the Americas, 17th fl, New York, NY 10036-2715
SAN: 211-6324
Mailing Address: PO Box 5078, New York, NY 10087-5078
Tel: 212-532-7160 *Toll Free Tel:* 800-367-9692 *Fax:* 212-213-2495 *Toll Free Fax:* 800-542-7567
E-mail: custservice@sterlingpublishing.com; customerservice@sterlingpublishing.com; editorial@sterlingpublishing.com; tradesales@sterlingpublishing.com
Web Site: www.sterlingpublishing.com
Key Personnel
Pres: Theresa Thompson
VP, Fin: Thomas M Allen
VP, Sales Opers & Inventory Planning: Adria Dougherty
Dir, HR: Kerri Cuocci
Exec Ed, Children's: Eve Adler; Suzy Capozzi
Sr Mgr, Foreign & Subs Rts: Toula Ballas *E-mail:* tballas@sterlingpublishing.com
Founded: 1949
Publisher of quality nonfiction & fiction books for adults & children. Subject categories include art & photography, cookbooks, wine, self-improvement, mind/body/spirit, business, history, reference, science & nature, home reference, gardening, music, sports, lifestyle & design, hobbies, crafts, classics, study guides, puzzles & games, children's nonfiction, picture, board & humor books.
This publisher has indicated that 50% of their product line is author subsidized.
ISBN Prefix(es): 978-0-7607; 978-0-937274 (Lark Books); 978-1-887374 (Lark Books); 978-1-57990 (Lark Books); 978-0-8069; 978-1-895569 (Sterling/Tamos); 978-1-4027; 978-1-58816 (Hearst); 978-1-58663 (SparkNotes); 978-1-59308 (Barnes & Noble Classics); 978-1-60059 (Lark Books); 978-1-4114 (SparkNotes); 978-1-934618 (Begin Smart); 978-1-4351 (Fall River Press); 978-1-4547 (Lark Books); 978-1-4549; 978-1-60736 (Ecosystem); 978-1-61837 (Hearst)
Number of titles published annually: 800 Print
Total Titles: 5,000 Print
Imprints: Flashkids; Hearst Books; Lark; Puzzlewright Press; Sterling; Sterling Children's Books; Sterling Epicure; Sterling Ethos; Sterling Signature
Distributor for Against All Odds Productions; Amber Books Ltd; Boxer Books; Brooklyn Botanic Garden; Enchanted World; Liminal 11; Sally Milner Publishing; Pavilion; Salaryia; Sixth&Spring Books; White Star Publishers
Foreign Rep(s): David Bateman Ltd (New Zealand); Canadian Manda Group (Canada); GMC Distribution (Asia, Europe, Middle East, UK); NewSouth Books (Australia)
Foreign Rights: ANA Sofia Ltd (Bulgaria, Romania, Southeast Europe); Guiliana Bernardi (Italy); Agence Litteraire Lora Fountain (Lora Fountain) (France); Graal Literary Agency (Tomasz Berezinski) (Poland); Katai & Bolza Literary Agents (Peter Bolza) (Hungary); KCC

(Seong-ah Bak) (Korea); Ute Korner Literary Agent SL (Sandra Rodericks) (Portugal, Spain); Alexander Korzhenevski (Russia); Andrew Nurnberg Associates International Ltd (Whitney Hsu) (Taiwan); Andrew Nurnberg Associates International Ltd (Jackie Huang) (China); Kristin Olson Literary Agency SRO (Czechia); Literarische Agentur Silke Weniger (Silke Weniger) (Germany)
Returns: LSC Communications, Attn: Returns, 677 Brighton Beach Rd, Menasha, WI 54952
Warehouse: LSC Communications-Lake Park, N9234 Lake Park Rd, Appleton, WI 54915
See separate listing for:
Lark Crafts

§Stewart, Tabori & Chang
Imprint of Harry N Abrams Inc
195 Broadway, 9th fl, New York, NY 10007
SAN: 239-0361
Tel: 212-206-7715 *Fax:* 212-519-1210
E-mail: abrams@abramsbooks.com
Web Site: www.abramsbooks.com/imprints/stc
Key Personnel
Pres & CEO: Michael Jacobs *E-mail:* mjacobs@abramsbooks.com
SVP & Publr, Adult Trade: Michael Sand *E-mail:* msand@abramsbooks.com
SVP, Intl Trade Sales: Mary Wowk *E-mail:* mwowk@abramsbooks.com
SVP, Mktg & Publicity: Melanie Chang *E-mail:* mchang@abramsbooks.com
Founded: 1981
Art, illustrated gift books, gardening, cookbooks, African American history, interior design, New Age, photography, popular culture, humor, weddings.
ISBN Prefix(es): 978-1-55670; 978-0-941434; 978-1-58479; 978-1-61769
Number of titles published annually: 80 Print
Total Titles: 350 Print
Foreign Rights: General Publishing (Canada); HI Marketing Ltd (Europe, UK); Korea Copyright Center (Korea); New Holland (Australia); Onslow Books Ltd (Europe); Sigma Literary Agency (Korea); Southern Publishers Group (New Zealand); Tuttle-Mori Agency Inc (Japan); David Williams (South America)

§Stipes Publishing LLC
204 W University Ave, Champaign, IL 61820
Mailing Address: PO Box 526, Champaign, IL 61824-0526
Tel: 217-356-8391 *Fax:* 217-356-5753
E-mail: stipes01@sbcglobal.net
Web Site: www.stipes.com
Key Personnel
Partner: J L Hecker
Founded: 1927
Primarily educational, some overlap trade publishing in music & horticulture.
ISBN Prefix(es): 978-0-87563; 978-1-58874
Number of titles published annually: 15 Print
Total Titles: 550 Print; 2 CD-ROM; 1 Online; 1 E-Book; 2 Audio

STM Learning Inc
1220 Paddock Dr, Florissant, MO 63033
Tel: 314-434-2424
E-mail: info@stmlearning.com; orders@stmlearning.com
Web Site: www.stmlearning.com
Key Personnel
Pres: Marianne Whaley *E-mail:* marianne@stmlearning.com
VP: Glenn Whaley *E-mail:* glenn@stmlearning.com
Founded: 1993
STM Learning is the expert in publishing leading clinical research for professionals who are in positions to serve & protect victims of abuse. Our customers consider STM Learning prod-

ucts to be the most trusted scientific, technical & medical resources available to aid in their efforts to identify, report, treat & prevent child maltreatment & domestic violence.
ISBN Prefix(es): 978-1-878060; 978-1-936590
Number of titles published annually: 8 Print; 8 E-Book
Total Titles: 60 Print; 60 E-Book
Foreign Rep(s): CoreSource (worldwide); Eurospan (worldwide)
Advertising Agency: GW Graphics & Publishing
Distribution Center: Amazon.com
Barnes & Noble
Rittenhouse Book Distributors Inc, 511 Feheley Dr, King of Prussia, PA 19406 *Toll Free Tel:* 800-345-6425 *Toll Free Fax:* 800-223-7488
Web Site: www.rittenhouse.com

STOCKCERO Inc
3785 NW 82 Ave, Suite 302, Doral, FL 33166
Tel: 305-722-7628 *Fax:* 305-722-7628
E-mail: academicservices@stockcero.com; sales@stockcero.com
Web Site: www.stockcero.com
Key Personnel
CEO: Pablo Agrest Berge *E-mail:* pagrest@stockcero.com
Founded: 2000
Committed to building an ever expanding collection of significant books, comprising Spanish literature, both Peninsular & Latin American. Our editions are conceived with modern non-native Spanish-speaking readers & students in mind, so they include updated & sharply focused footnotes, prefaces & bibliographies written by scholarly literary editors.
ISBN Prefix(es): 978-1-934768
Number of titles published annually: 14 Print
Total Titles: 181 Print; 157 Online

§Stone Bridge Press Inc
1393 Solano Ave, Suite C, Albany, CA 94706
Mailing Address: PO Box 8208, Berkeley, CA 94706
Tel: 510-524-8732
E-mail: sbp@stonebridge.com; sbpedit@stonebridge.com
Web Site: www.stonebridge.com
Key Personnel
Founder & Publr: Peter Goodman
Founded: 1989
Books on Japan & Asia.
ISBN Prefix(es): 978-0-89346 (Heian International); 978-1-880656; 978-0-9628137; 978-1-933330; 978-1-61172
Number of titles published annually: 6 Print; 10 Online; 10 E-Book
Total Titles: 120 Print; 15 Online; 75 E-Book
Imprints: Three L Media
Foreign Rep(s): Perseus International (Australia)
Distribution Center: Consortium Book Sales & Distribution, The Keg House, 34 13 Ave NE, Suite 101, Minneapolis, MN 55413-1007 (US & CN) *Tel:* 612-746-2600 *Toll Free Tel:* 800-283-3572 (cust serv, Jackson, TN) *Fax:* 612-746-2606 *E-mail:* info@cbsd.com *Web Site:* www.cbsd.com SAN: 200-6049
Membership(s): Independent Book Publishers Association (IBPA)

Stone Pier Press
PO Box 170572, San Francisco, CA 94117
Tel: 415-484-2821
E-mail: hello@stonepierpress.org
Web Site: www.stonepierpress.org
Key Personnel
Publr: Clare Ellis *E-mail:* clare@stonepierpress.org
Dir, Partnerships & Devt: Faith Lemon *E-mail:* faith@stonepierpress.org
Founded: 2017

Environmental publisher with a food focus producing books & news that highlight how to eat, grow & dispose of our food in a way that builds a cooler, kinder & healthier world. Our thinking is that by focusing on solutions, we make it easier for any one of us to act on them.
ISBN Prefix(es): 978-0-9988623
Number of titles published annually: 8 Print; 8 E-Book
Distributed by Chelsea Green Publishing Co

Stonewall, see BrickHouse Books Inc

Stoneydale Press Publishing Co
523 Main St, Stevensville, MT 59870-2839
Mailing Address: PO Box 188, Stevensville, MT 59870-0188
Tel: 406-777-2729 *Toll Free Tel:* 800-735-7006 *Fax:* 406-777-2521
E-mail: stoneydale@stoneydale.com
Web Site: www.stoneydale.com
Key Personnel
Publr: Dale A Burk
Founded: 1976
Outdoor recreation, regional history & reminisces of Northern Rockies region.
ISBN Prefix(es): 978-0-912299; 978-1-931291; 978-1-938707
Number of titles published annually: 8 Print
Total Titles: 190 Print
Membership(s): Mountains & Plains Booksellers Association (MPBA); Pacific Northwest Booksellers Association (PNBA)

Storey Publishing LLC
Division of Workman Publishing Co Inc
210 MASS MoCA Way, North Adams, MA 01247
SAN: 203-4158
Tel: 413-346-2100 *Toll Free Tel:* 800-441-5700 (orders); 800-827-7444 (cust serv) *Fax:* 413-346-2199 *Toll Free Fax:* 800-865-3429 (cust serv)
E-mail: sales@storey.com; feedback@storey.com
Web Site: www.storey.com
Key Personnel
Publr & Edit Dir: Deborah Balmuth *E-mail:* deborah.balmuth@storey.com
Mng Ed & Dir, Contracts: Jennifer Travis
Rts Dir: Maribeth Casey *Tel:* 413-346-2135 *E-mail:* maribeth.casey@storey.com
Proj Ed: Michal Lumsden
HR & Opers Mgr: Marci Saunders *E-mail:* marci.saunders@storey.com
Trade & Spec Sales Mgr: Janea Brachfeld *E-mail:* janea.brachfeld@storey.com
Founded: 1983
How-to books on country living, gardening, cooking, natural health, home building, country business, crafts, small-scale livestock, pets, beer & wine, children's nonfiction.
ISBN Prefix(es): 978-0-945352; 978-0-88266; 978-1-58017; 978-0-9727925; 978-1-60342; 978-1-61212; 978-1-63586
Number of titles published annually: 50 Print
Total Titles: 600 Print
Foreign Rep(s): Thomas Allen & Sons Ltd (Canada); Bill Bailey Publishers' Representatives (Europe); Bookreps NZ Ltd (Susan Holmes) (New Zealand); Michelle Morrow Curreri (Asia, Middle East); IMA/Intermediaamericana Ltd (David Williams) (Caribbean, Latin America); Melia Publishing Services (UK); Peribo Pty Ltd (Michael Coffey) (Australia); Real Books (South Africa)

Story Monsters LLC
4696 W Tyson St, Chandler, AZ 85226-2903
Tel: 480-940-8182 *Fax:* 480-940-8787
Web Site: www.StoryMonsters.com; www.DragonflyBookAwards.com; www.AuthorBookings.com; www.

StoryMonstersApproved.com; www.storymonstersink.com
Key Personnel
Pres: Linda F Radke *E-mail:* Linda@StoryMonsters.com
Founded: 1985
Dedicated to helping authors of all genres strive for excellence with book production, marketing & promotion. Publish the award-winning *Story Monsters Ink®* magazine. Provide publishers support services in areas such as editing, cover design & publicity. Sponsor of the Dragonfly Book Awards.
ISBN Prefix(es): 978-0-9619853; 978-1-877749; 978-1-58985
Number of titles published annually: 10 Print
Total Titles: 36 Print; 12 E-Book
Imprints: School Express Press (publishing plan for schools, teachers & librarians); Story Monsters Press (children's books)
Divisions: AuthorBookings.com (connecting authors, artists, schools & libraries); SchoolBookings.com
Membership(s): Arizona Professional Writers (APW); The Children's Book Council (CBC); Independent Book Publishers Association (IBPA); National Federation of Press Women; New Mexico Publishers Association; Small Publishers, Artists & Writers Network (SPAWN)

§The Story Plant
Division of Studio Digital CT LLC
PO Box 4331, Stamford, CT 06907
Tel: 203-722-7920
E-mail: thestoryplant@thestoryplant.com
Web Site: www.thestoryplant.com
Key Personnel
Publr: Lou Aronica *E-mail:* lou.aronica@thestoryplant.com
Assoc Publr: Mitchell Maxwell *E-mail:* mitchell.maxwell@thestoryplant.com
Founded: 2008
Independent publisher of commercial fiction. The focus is on author development & building publishing programs for each author.
ISBN Prefix(es): 978-1-61188; 978-1-945839
Number of titles published annually: 25 Print; 25 E-Book; 5 Audio
Total Titles: 175 Print; 175 E-Book; 15 Audio
Distribution Center: National Book Network, 4501 Forbes Blvd, Lanham, MD 20706 *Tel:* 301-459-3366
Membership(s): American Booksellers Association (ABA); Association of American Publishers (AAP)

Strategic Book Publishing & Rights Agency (SBPRA)
12620 FM W 1960, Suite A-4507, Houston, TX 77065
SAN: 853-8492
Tel: 703-637-6006
Web Site: sbpra.net; www.facebook.com/sbpra.us
Founded: 2007
Provides book publishing, marketing & ebook services to writers around the world. Catalog of more than 5,000 authors. Books are available through Ingram as well as in bookstores such as Barnes & Noble & all online channels. Attends & exhibits at the major book expositions in London, New York, China & Germany each year.
This publisher has indicated that 50% of their product line is author subsidized.
ISBN Prefix(es): 978-1-61204
Number of titles published annually: 475 Print; 85 E-Book
Total Titles: 2,786 Print; 3,062 Online; 336 E-Book

§Strategic Media Books LLC
782 Wofford St, Rock Hill, SC 29730

Tel: 803-366-5440
E-mail: contact@strategicmediabooks.com
Web Site: strategicmediabooks.com
Key Personnel
Pres: Ron Chepesiuk
Partner: Barbara Casey
Founded: 2010
Publisher of crime, true crime & southern interest books.
ISBN Prefix(es): 978-0-9852440; 978-1-939521
Number of titles published annually: 8 Print; 8 Online; 8 E-Book; 3 Audio
Total Titles: 28 Print; 25 Online; 25 E-Book; 3 Audio
Foreign Rep(s): Cardinal Publishers Group (UK)
Membership(s): Independent Book Publishers Association (IBPA)

Stress Free Kids®
2561 Chimney Springs Dr, Marietta, GA 30062
Tel: 678-642-9555 *Toll Free Fax:* 866-302-2759
E-mail: media@stressfreekids.com
Web Site: www.stressfreekids.com
Key Personnel
Founder: Lori Lite; Rick Lite
Founded: 1996
Books, CDs (physical & digital formats), lesson plans to help children & teens manage stress, lower anxiety & decrease anger, while improving self-esteem.
ISBN Prefix(es): 978-0-9708633; 978-0-9787781; 978-0-9800328
Number of titles published annually: 2 Print; 5 Online; 4 E-Book; 4 Audio
Total Titles: 35 Print; 12 Audio

The Jesse Stuart Foundation (JSF)
4440 13 St, Ashland, KY 41102
SAN: 245-8837
Mailing Address: PO Box 669, Ashland, KY 41105-0669
Tel: 606-326-1667 *Fax:* 606-325-2519
E-mail: jsf@jsfbooks.com
Web Site: www.jsfbooks.com
Key Personnel
CEO & Sr Ed: James M Gifford, PhD
Founded: 1979
Publisher of Appalachia-Kentuckiana. Not accepting unsol mss at this time.
ISBN Prefix(es): 978-0-945084
Number of titles published annually: 4 Print
Total Titles: 75 Print

Stylus Publishing LLC
22883 Quicksilver Dr, Sterling, VA 20166-2019
SAN: 299-1853
Mailing Address: PO Box 605, Herndon, VA 20172-0605
Tel: 703-661-1504 (edit & sales)
  Toll Free Tel: 800-232-0223 (orders & cust serv) *Fax:* 703-661-1547
E-mail: stylusmail@styluspub.com (orders & cust serv); stylusinfo@styluspub.com
Web Site: styluspub.presswarehouse.com
Key Personnel
Pres & Publr: John von Knorring *E-mail:* jvk@styluspub.com
VP, Mktg & Publicity Mgr: Andrea Ciecierski *Tel:* 703-996-1036 *E-mail:* andrea@styluspub.com
Sales Mgr: Jean Westcott *Tel:* 703-661-1541 *E-mail:* jean.westcott@styluspub.com
Founded: 1996
Publish books for faculty & administrators in higher education. Distributes books in the areas of art, business, training, psychology & psychotherapy as well as educational & scholarly titles & books on Third World development & the environment.
ISBN Prefix(es): 978-1-57922; 978-1-62036
Number of titles published annually: 30 Print; 30 E-Book

Total Titles: 400 Print; 2 CD-ROM; 150 E-Book
Distributor for Baseball Prospectus; Cabi Books; Campus Compact; Commonwealth Scientific & Industrial Research Organization (CSIRO); CSREA; Mercury Learning & Information; Myers Education Press; National Resource Center for The First-Year Experience & Students in Transition; River Publishers; Thorogood Publishing; Trentham Books Ltd; UCL IOE Press; World Health Organization (WHO)
Foreign Rep(s): Cranbury International (Central America, South America); Eurospan (Asia, Australia, Europe, Middle East, UK)
Distribution Center: Books International Inc, 22883 Quicksilver Dr, Dulles, VA 20166

Success Advertising & Publishing
Division of The Success Group
3419 Dunham Rd, Warsaw, NY 14569
SAN: 678-9501
Tel: 585-786-5663
Key Personnel
Pres & Publr: Allan H Smith
  E-mail: allan33001@aol.com
VP: Ginger B Smith
Book Ed: Robin Garretson
Founded: 1978
How-to, self-help, crafts, business, home-based business.
ISBN Prefix(es): 978-0-931113
Number of titles published annually: 7 Print
Total Titles: 58 Print
Divisions: Academy of Continuing Education; National Doll Society of America; Success Advertising

Summer Institute of Linguistics Inc, see SIL International

§Summertime Publications Inc
4115 E Palo Verde Dr, Phoenix, AZ 85018
E-mail: summertime.publications@gmail.com
Web Site: www.summertimepublications.com
Key Personnel
Dir, Pubns & CEO: Laurel Leffmann
Founded: 2009
Small press. Quality books about France; also memoirs, history, science fiction, short story, literary fiction & nonfiction.
ISBN Prefix(es): 978-0-9823698; 978-1-940333
Number of titles published annually: 3 Print; 4 E-Book
Total Titles: 9 Print; 14 E-Book
Imprints: PWN; Summertime
Distributor for ACHCBYZ (Paris academic press specializing in Byzantine history)
Foreign Rights: IPR License Ltd (worldwide exc China); Rightol Media (China)
Membership(s): Independent Book Publishers Association (IBPA)

§Summit University Press
63 Summit Way, Gardiner, MT 59030-9314
Tel: 406-848-9292; 406-848-9500 (retail orders)
  Fax: 406-848-9555
E-mail: info@summituniversitypress.com; rights@summituniversitypress.com
Web Site: www.summituniversitypress.com
Key Personnel
Publg Dir: Steven Webb *E-mail:* swebb@summituniversitypress.com
Founded: 1975
Global publisher of fine books, ebooks, audiobooks & DVDs on spirituality. Very active foreign rights sales. Specialize in New Age & mind, body & spirit.
ISBN Prefix(es): 978-0-916766; 978-0-922729; 978-1-932890; 978-1-60988
Number of titles published annually: 4 Print; 45 Online; 45 E-Book
Total Titles: 100 Print; 20 CD-ROM; 45 Online; 47 E-Book; 70 Audio

Distribution Center: National Book Network, 15200 NBN Way, Blue Ridge Summit, PA 17214 *Tel:* 717-794-3800 *Toll Free Tel:* 800-462-6420 *Toll Free Fax:* 800-338-4550 *E-mail:* customercare@nbnbooks.com *Web Site:* www.nbnbooks.com
NBN Canada/Rowman & Littlefield Publishing Group, 67 Mowat Ave, Suite 241, Toronto, ON M6K 3E3, Canada *Tel:* 416-534-1660 *Toll Free Tel:* 877-626-2665 *Fax:* 416-534-3699 *Web Site:* www.nbnbooks.com
NBN International, Plymbridge House, Estover Rd, Plymouth, Devon PL6 7PY, United Kingdom *Tel:* (01752) 202300 *Fax:* (01752) 202330 *E-mail:* enquiries@nbninternational.com
Membership(s): Independent Book Publishers Association (IBPA)

Sun Books, see Sun Publishing Company

Sun Publishing Company
Division of The Sun Companies
PO Box 5588, Santa Fe, NM 87502-5588
SAN: 206-1325
Tel: 505-471-5177; 505-660-0704
  Toll Free Tel: 877-849-0051
E-mail: info@sunbooks.com
Web Site: www.sunbooks.com; abooksource.com
Key Personnel
Pres & Rts/Perms: Skip Whitson
Founded: 1973
Motivational, success, business, recovery, inspirational, history, self-help, new thought, philosophy, western mysticism, scholarly; oriental philosophy & studies. No unsol mss. Query first by e-mail.
ISBN Prefix(es): 978-0-89540
Number of titles published annually: 10 Print
Total Titles: 400 Print
Imprints: Far West Publishing; Sun Books
Advertising Agency: Sun Agency

§Sunbelt Publications Inc
1250 Fayette St, El Cajon, CA 92020-1511
SAN: 630-0790
Tel: 619-258-4911 *Toll Free Tel:* 800-626-6579 (cust serv) *Fax:* 619-258-4916
E-mail: service@sunbeltpub.com; info@sunbeltpub.com
Web Site: sunbeltpublications.com
Key Personnel
CEO: Lowell Lindsay *E-mail:* llindsay@sunbeltpub.com
Pres: Diana Lindsay *Tel:* 619-258-4911 ext 104 *E-mail:* dlindsay@sunbeltpub.com
Pubns Mgr: Debi Young *Tel:* 619-258-4905 ext 103 *E-mail:* dyoung@sunbeltpub.com
Sales Mgr: Lisa Gulick *Tel:* 619-258-4911 ext 112
Acctg Coord: Maria Groschup-Black *Tel:* 619-258-4905 ext 108 *E-mail:* maria@sunbeltpub.com
Mktg Coord: Rebecca Kriz *Tel:* 619-258-4911 ext 114
Founded: 1984
Publisher & distributor of natural history, citizen science, pictorial & travel specializing in Southwest US & Baja, California.
ISBN Prefix(es): 978-0-932653; 978-0-916251
Number of titles published annually: 10 Print
Total Titles: 75 Print
Membership(s): Association of Earth Science Editors (AESE); Independent Book Publishers Association (IBPA); Outdoor Writers Association of America (OWAA); Publishers Association of the West (PubWest)

Sundance/Newbridge Publishing
Division of Rowman & Littlefield Publishing Group
33 Boston Post Rd W, Suite 440, Marlborough, MA 01752

Toll Free Tel: 888-200-2720; 800-343-8204 (Sundance cust serv & orders); 800-867-0307 (Newbridge cust serv & orders) *Toll Free Fax:* 800-456-2419 (orders)
E-mail: info@sundancepub.com; info@ newbridgeonline.com
Web Site: www.sundancepub.com; www. newbridgeonline.com
Key Personnel
Pres: Paul Konowitch *E-mail:* pkonowitch@ sundancepub.com
SVP, Sales: John Atkocaitis *E-mail:* jatkocaitis@ sundancepub.com
Founded: 1981
Supplemental educational publisher for PreK-8 that creates standards-based classroom materials for reading in the content areas.
ISBN Prefix(es): 978-1-56784; 978-1-58273; 978-1-4007
Number of titles published annually: 150 Print; 36 Audio
Total Titles: 680 Print; 118 Audio
Imprints: Early Math; Early Science; Early Social Studies; GoFacts Guided Writing; Kids Corner; Newbridge Discovery Links; Ranger Rick Science Program; Thinking Like a Scientist
Foreign Rep(s): Schmelzer PSI
Membership(s): Association of American Publishers (AAP); International Literacy Association (ILA); National Science Teachers Association (NSTA)

§Sunrise River Press
Affiliate of Cartech Books/Specialty Press
838 Lake St S, Forrest Lake, MN 55025
Tel: 651-277-1400 *Toll Free Tel:* 800-895-4585
E-mail: info@sunriseriverpress.com; sales@ sunriseriverpress.com
Web Site: www.sunriseriverpress.com
Key Personnel
Sales & Mktg: Bob Wilson
Publisher of consumer books & books for the professional healthcare market with an emphasis on self-help, weight loss, nutrition, diet, food & recipes with additional focus on family health, fitness & specific diseases such as cancer, anorexia, Alzheimer's, autism & depression.
ISBN Prefix(es): 978-0-9624814; 978-1-934716
Number of titles published annually: 10 Print

Sunstone Press
PO Box 2321, Santa Fe, NM 87504-2321
SAN: 214-2090
Tel: 505-988-4418 *Toll Free Tel:* 800-243-5644 *Fax:* 505-988-1025 (orders only)
Web Site: www.sunstonepress.com
Key Personnel
Pres & Treas: James Clois Smith, Jr
Dir, Opers & Sales: Carl Daniel Condit
Founded: 1971
Mainstream & Southwestern US titles, general nonfiction, fiction & how-to craft books.
ISBN Prefix(es): 978-0-913270; 978-0-86534; 978-1-61139 (ebooks); 978-1-63293
Number of titles published annually: 100 Print; 300 E-Book
Total Titles: 1,600 Print; 1,500 E-Book
Foreign Rights: Daniel Bial Literary Agency
Membership(s): New Mexico Book Association

SUNY Press, see State University of New York Press

Superintendent of Documents, see US Government Publishing Office (GPO)

Surrey Books
Imprint of Agate Publishing
1328 Greenleaf St, Evanston, IL 60202
SAN: 275-8857

Tel: 847-475-4457 *Toll Free Tel:* 800-326-4430
Web Site: agatepublishing.com/surrey
Key Personnel
Pres & Publr: Doug Seibold *E-mail:* seibold@ agatepublishing.com
Founded: 1982
Trade books. Specialize in nonfiction: cooking, health & lifestyle.
ISBN Prefix(es): 978-0-940625; 978-1-57284
Number of titles published annually: 20 Print
Total Titles: 120 Print
Distribution Center: Publishers Group West, 1700 Fourth St, Berkeley, CA 94710 *Tel:* 510-809-3700 *Toll Free Tel:* 800-788-3123 (cust serv) *Fax:* 510-809-3777 *E-mail:* info@pgw.com *Web Site:* www.pgw.com
Membership(s): International Association of Culinary Professionals (IACP)

§Swallow Press
Imprint of Ohio University Press
Alden Library, Suite 101, 30 Park Place, Athens, OH 45701-2909
Tel: 740-593-1154
Web Site: www.ohioswallow.com
Key Personnel
Acqs Ed: Ricky S Huard *Tel:* 740-593-1157 *E-mail:* huard@ohio.edu
Acqs Admin, Rts & Perms: Sally R Welch *E-mail:* welchs@ohio.edu
Founded: 1940
Publisher of scholarly & trade books.
ISBN Prefix(es): 978-0-8214; 978-0-8040
Number of titles published annually: 45 Print
Foreign Rep(s): Combined Academic Publishers (Africa, Europe, Middle East, Pacific Rim)
Orders to: Chicago Distribution Center, 11030 S Langley Ave, Chicago, IL 60628 *Toll Free Tel:* 800-621-2736 *Toll Free Fax:* 800-621-8476
Warehouse: Chicago Distribution Center, 11030 S Langley Ave, Chicago, IL 60628 *Toll Free Tel:* 800-621-2736 *Toll Free Fax:* 800-621-8476

Swan Isle Press
11030 S Langley Ave, Chicago, IL 60628
Tel: 773-728-3780 (edit); 773-702-7000 (cust serv) *Toll Free Tel:* 800-621-2736 (cust serv) *Fax:* 773-702-7212 (cust serv) *Toll Free Fax:* 800-621-8476 (cust serv)
E-mail: info@swanislepress.com
Web Site: www.swanislepress.com
Key Personnel
Founder, Dir & Ed: David Rade
Founded: 1999
Not-for-profit, 501(c)(3) literary publisher, dedicated to publishing fiction, nonfiction & poetry in translation.
ISBN Prefix(es): 978-0-9678808; 978-0-9748881
Number of titles published annually: 4 Print; 2 E-Book
Total Titles: 30 Print; 3 E-Book
Distributed by University of Chicago Press
Foreign Rep(s): University of Chicago Press (worldwide)
Orders to: Baker & Taylor, 2550 W Tyvola Rd, Suite 300, Charlotte, NC 28217 *Tel:* 704-998-3100 *Toll Free Tel:* 800-775-1800 *E-mail:* btinfo@baker-taylor.com *Web Site:* www.baker-taylor.com; Ingram Book Co, One Ingram Blvd, La Vergne, TN 37086 *Tel:* 615-793-5000 *Toll Free Tel:* 800-937-8200 *E-mail:* customer.service@ingrambook.com *Web Site:* www.ingrambook.com
Membership(s): Association of American Publishers (AAP)

Swedenborg Foundation
320 N Church St, West Chester, PA 19380
SAN: 202-5280
Tel: 610-430-3222 *Toll Free Tel:* 800-355-3222 (cust serv) *Fax:* 610-430-7982
E-mail: info@swedenborg.com

Web Site: swedenborg.com
Key Personnel
Exec Dir: Morgan Beard *Tel:* 610-430-3222 ext 102 *E-mail:* mbeard@swedenborg.com
Ed: John Connolly *Tel:* 610-430-3222 ext 101 *E-mail:* jconnolly@swedenborg.com
Mktg Coord: Amy Acquarola *Tel:* 610-430-3222 ext 103 *E-mail:* aacquarola@swedenborg.com
Founded: 1849
Books & DVDs by, or relating to, the theological works & spiritual insights of Emanuel Swedenborg & related literature.
ISBN Prefix(es): 978-0-87785
Number of titles published annually: 10 Print
Total Titles: 200 Print
Orders to: Continental Sales Inc (CSI), 213 W Main St, Barrington, IL 60010 *Tel:* 847-381-6530 *Fax:* 847-382-0419 *E-mail:* bookreps@ wybel.com; Wybel Marketing Group Inc, 213 W Main St, Barrington, IL 60010 *Tel:* 847-382-0384 *Fax:* 847-382-0385 *E-mail:* bookreps@wybel.com; Melman-Moster Associates Inc, 43 Yawpo Ave, Suite 6, Oakland, NJ 07436 *Tel:* 201-651-9400 *Fax:* 201-651-9440 *E-mail:* books@melman-moster.com; Faherty & Associates, 6665 SW Hampton St, Suite 100, Portland, OR 97223 *Tel:* 503-639-3113 *Fax:* 503-598-9850 *E-mail:* faherty@fahertybooks.com; Southern Territory Associates, 4508 64 St, Lubbock, TX 79414 *Tel:* 806-799-9997 *Fax:* 806-799-9777 *E-mail:* sta77@suddenlink.net; Rainbow Book Agencies, 303 Arthur St, Fairfield 3078, Australia *Tel:* (0613) 9481 6611 *Fax:* (0613) 9481 2371 *E-mail:* rba@rainbowbooks.com.au *Web Site:* www.rainbowbooks.com.au
Returns: University of Chicago Press/The Chicago Distribution Center, 11030 S Langley Ave, Chicago, IL 60628
Distribution Center: University of Chicago Press/The Chicago Distribution Center, 11030 S Langley Ave, Chicago, IL 60628

§SYBEX Inc
Division of John Wiley & Sons Inc
111 River St, Hoboken, NJ 07030-5774
SAN: 211-1667
Tel: 201-748-6000 *Fax:* 201-748-6088
Web Site: www.sybex.com; www.wiley.com
Founded: 1976
For beginning, intermediate & advanced users of all types of software & hardware, including how-to books on various networking, word processing, database, graphics & spreadsheet software, certification, as well as computer games & Internet books, graphics & programming.
ISBN Prefix(es): 978-0-89588; 978-0-7821; 978-0-47028
Number of titles published annually: 150 Print
Total Titles: 601 Print; 2 CD-ROM
Branch Office(s)
One Montgomery St, Suite 1200, San Francisco, CA 94104 *Tel:* 415-433-1740 *Fax:* 415-433-0499
10475 Crosspoint Blvd, Indianapolis, IN 46256 *Tel:* 317-572-3000
Foreign Rep(s): Robert Blake (Central America, Mexico); Phillip Bowie (Caribbean); Computercollectief (Netherlands); Lidel Edicoes Tecnicas Lda (Portugal); Ledy Martinez (Brazil, South America); John Wiley & Sons Canada Ltd (Canada); John Wiley & Sons Ltd (Natalie Lord) (Europe exc Austria, Germany & Switzerland, UK); John Wiley & Sons Singapore Pte Ltd (Singapore); Wiley-VCH Verlag GmbH (Austria, Germany, Switzerland)

§SynergEbooks
948 New Hwy 7, Columbia, TN 38401
SAN: 254-4962
Tel: 931-223-8290 (9AM-9PM CST)
E-mail: synergebooks@aol.com
Web Site: www.synergebooks.com

Key Personnel
Publr & Exec Ed: Debra Staples
Founded: 1999
Electronic publishing house & bookstore that also include CD-ROMs, audiobooks & trade paperbacks. Genres include fiction, nonfiction, romance, young adults fantasy, science fiction, poetry, humor, mystery/suspense, inspiration, cookbooks, self-help/reference, business, true crime, New Age, Native American & a children's section.
ISBN Prefix(es): 978-0-9702; 978-0-7443; 978-1-931540
Number of titles published annually: 35 Print; 24 E-Book
Total Titles: 250 Print; 360 Online; 360 E-Book
Imprints: YourSpecs (self-publishing ebook conversion service)
Membership(s): Electronically Published Internet Connection (EPIC); Independent Book Publishers Association (IBPA)

Syracuse University Press
621 Skytop Rd, Suite 110, Syracuse, NY 13244-5290
SAN: 206-9776
Tel: 315-443-5534 *Toll Free Tel:* 800-365-8929 (cust serv) *Fax:* 315-443-5545
E-mail: supress@syr.edu
Web Site: press.syr.edu
Key Personnel
Dir: Alice Randal Pfeiffer *Tel:* 315-443-5535 *E-mail:* arpfeiff@syr.edu
Acqs Ed: Deborah Manion *Tel:* 315-443-5647 *E-mail:* dmmanion@syr.edu; Peggy Solic *Tel:* 315-443-5543 *E-mail:* masolic@syr.edu
Sr Busn Mgr: Karen Lockwood *Tel:* 315-443-5536 *E-mail:* kflockwo@syr.edu
Edit & Prodn Mgr: Kay Steinmetz *Tel:* 315-443-9155 *E-mail:* kasteinm@syr.edu
Sr Designer: Lynn Wilcox *Tel:* 315-443-1975 *E-mail:* lphoppel@syr.edu
Mktg Coord: Lisa Kuerbis *Tel:* 315-443-5546 *E-mail:* lkuerbis@syr.edu
Acctg Asst: Bobbi Clapps *Tel:* 315-443-5538 *E-mail:* baclaps@syr.edu
Founded: 1943
Scholarly, general & regional nonfiction; Middle East, Irish studies, medieval, women's studies, Iroquois studies, television, religion & politics, geography, sports & leisure, space, place & society, literature, Jewish studies (fiction & nonfiction).
ISBN Prefix(es): 978-0-8156
Number of titles published annually: 50 Print; 50 E-Book
Total Titles: 1,800 Print; 400 E-Book
Distributed by Arlen House; Dedalus Press
Distributor for Arlen House; Pucker Gallery; Sheep Meadow Press (poetry)
Foreign Rep(s): Eurospan University Press Group Ltd (Africa, Asia, Continental Europe, Middle East, UK); Rob Igoe Jr (New York State); Miller Trade Book Marketing (Midwestern States); Bob Rosenberg Group (13 Western States); UMG Publishers Representatives (David K Brown) (Eastern States); UTP Distribution (Canada)
Orders to: Longleaf Services Inc, 116 S Boundary St, Chapel Hill, NC 27514-8895 *Tel:* 919-966-7449 *Toll Free Tel:* 800-848-6224 *Fax:* 919-962-2704 *Toll Free Fax:* 800-272-6817 *E-mail:* customerservice@longleafservices.org *Web Site:* www.longleafservices.org
Returns: Longleaf Services Inc, c/o Ingram Publisher Services, 1550 Heil Quaker Blvd, Suite 200, La Vergne, TN 37086 *Tel:* 919-966-7449 *Toll Free Tel:* 866-400-5351 *Fax:* 919-962-2704 *Toll Free Fax:* 800-272-6817 *E-mail:* credit@longleafservices.org
Distribution Center: Longleaf Services Inc, 116 S Boundary St, Chapel Hill, NC 27514-

8895 *Tel:* 919-966-7449 *Toll Free Tel:* 800-848-6224 *Fax:* 919-962-2704 *Toll Free Fax:* 800-272-6817 *E-mail:* customerservice@longleafservices.org *Web Site:* www.longleafservices.org
Membership(s): American Association of University Presses (AAUP)

Tachyon Publications LLC
1459 18 St, No 139, San Francisco, CA 94107
Tel: 415-285-5615
E-mail: tachyon@tachyonpublications.com
Web Site: www.tachyonpublications.com
Key Personnel
Publr & Ed: Jacob Weisman *E-mail:* jw@tachyonpublications.com
Mng Ed: Jill Roberts *E-mail:* jill@tachyonpublications.com
Ed: Jaymee Goh *E-mail:* jaymee.goh@tachyonpublications.com
Lead Designer: Elizabeth Story *E-mail:* elizabeth@tachyonpublications.com
Publicist: James DeMaiolo *E-mail:* jim@tachyonpublications.com
Soc Media Strategist: Rick Klaw *Tel:* 512-777-9036 *E-mail:* rick@tachyonpublications.com
Founded: 1995
Science fiction, fantasy & genre publishing.
ISBN Prefix(es): 978-0-9648320; 978-1-892391; 978-1-61696
Number of titles published annually: 10 Print; 12 E-Book
Total Titles: 173 Print; 80 E-Book
Foreign Rep(s): Andi Richman (worldwide)
Foreign Rights: JABberwocky Literary Agency (Joshua Bilmes) (worldwide)
Orders to: Baker & Taylor Publisher Services, 30 Amberwood Pkwy, Ashland, OH 44805 *Tel:* 567-215-0030 *Toll Free Tel:* 888-814-0208 *E-mail:* info@btpubservices.com *Web Site:* www.btpubservices.com
Distribution Center: Baker & Taylor Publisher Services, 30 Amberwood Pkwy, Ashland, OH 44805 *Tel:* 567-215-0030 *Toll Free Tel:* 888-814-0208 *E-mail:* info@btpubservices.com *Web Site:* www.btpubservices.com
Membership(s): Science Fiction & Fantasy Writers of America (SFWA)

§Tahrike Tarsile Qur'an Inc
80-08 51 Ave, Elmhurst, NY 11373
Tel: 718-446-6472 *Fax:* 718-446-4370
E-mail: read@koranusa.org
Web Site: www.koranusa.org
Key Personnel
Pres: Aun Ali Khalfan
Publishers & distributors of the Holy Quran & other Islamic books, videos & CDs.
ISBN Prefix(es): 978-0-940368; 978-1-879402
Number of titles published annually: 125 Print
Total Titles: 150 Print

§Nan A Talese
Imprint of Knopf Doubleday Publishing Group
c/o Penguin Random House Inc, 1745 Broadway, New York, NY 10019
Tel: 212-751-2600 *Fax:* 212-572-2662 (foreign rts)
E-mail: ddaypub@randomhouse.com
Web Site: knopfdoubleday.com
Key Personnel
Assoc Ed: Dan Meyer
Founded: 1990
Penguin Random House & its publishing entities are not accepting unsol submissions, proposals, mss or submission queries via e-mail at this time.
Foreign Rights: ALS-Agenzia Letteraria Santachiara (Roberto Santachiara) (Italy); Anthea Agency (Katalina Sabeva) (Bulgaria); Bardon-Chinese Media Agency (Xu-Weiguang) (China); Bardon-Chinese Media Agency (Yu-

Shiuan Chen) (Taiwan); The English Agency (Junzo Sawa) (Japan); Graal Literary Agency (Maria Strarz-Kanska) (Poland); The Deborah Harris Agency (Ilana Kurshan) (Israel); JLM Literary Agency (Nelly Moukakos) (Greece); Katai & Bolza Literary (Peter Bolza) (Croatia, Hungary); KCC (MiSook Hong) (Korea); Simona Kessler International (Simona Kessler) (Romania); Licht & Burr Literary Agency (Trine Licht) (Scandinavia); La Nouvelle Agency (Vanessa Kling) (France); Kristin Olson Literary Agency (Kristin Olson) (Czechia); Sebes & Bisseling Literary Agency (Paul Sebes) (Netherlands)

§TAN Books
Imprint of Saint Benedict Press LLC
PO Box 269, Gastonia, NC 28053
Tel: 704-731-0651 *Toll Free Tel:* 800-437-5876 *Fax:* 815-226-7770
E-mail: customerservice@tanbooks.com
Web Site: www.tanbooks.com
Key Personnel
Chmn & CEO: Robert Gallagher
Publr: Conor Gallagher
Dir: Brian Kennelly
Dir, Mktg: Christian Tappe
Founded: 1967
Publish traditional Catholic books, especially reprint classic works.
ISBN Prefix(es): 978-0-89555
Number of titles published annually: 15 Print
Total Titles: 550 Print

T&T Clark International
Imprint of Bloomsbury Publishing PLC
1385 Broadway, 5th fl, New York, NY 10018
E-mail: askacademic@bloomsbury.com
Web Site: www.bloomsbury.com/us/academic/academic-subjects/theology/t-t-clark
Founded: 1821
Biblical studies, theology & church history.
ISBN Prefix(es): 978-0-8264; 978-1-56338; 978-0-334; 978-0-7162; 978-0-567
Number of titles published annually: 100 Print
Total Titles: 2,200 Print
Orders to: Bloomsbury USA, MPS/BUSA Orders, 16365 James Madison Hwy, Gordonsville, VA 22942 *Toll Free Tel:* 888-330-8477 *Toll Free Fax:* 800-672-2054 *E-mail:* orders@mpsvirginia.com

Tanglewood Publishing
1060 N Capitol Ave, Suite E-395, Indianapolis, IN 46204
Tel: 812-877-9488 *Toll Free Tel:* 800-788-3123 (orders)
E-mail: info@tanglewoodbooks.com; orders@tanglewoodbooks.com
Web Site: www.tanglewoodbooks.com
Key Personnel
Publr: Peggy Tierney *E-mail:* ptierney@tanglewoodbooks.com
Publg Mgr: Matt Buchanan *E-mail:* matt@tanglewoodbooks.com
Acqs Ed: Kairi Hamlin *E-mail:* khamlin@tanglewoodbooks.com
Founded: 2003
ISBN Prefix(es): 978-0-9749303; 978-1-933718
Number of titles published annually: 5 Print; 1 Audio
Total Titles: 37 Print; 2 Audio
Distributed by Simon & Schuster, Inc

Tantor Media Inc
Division of Recorded Books
6 Business Park, Old Saybrook, CT 06475
Toll Free Tel: 877-782-6867 *Toll Free Fax:* 888-782-7821
Web Site: www.tantor.com

Key Personnel
Dir, Acqs: Ron Formica *Tel:* 877-782-6867 ext 31
  E-mail: ron@tantor.com
Founded: 2001
Independent publisher & producer of audiobooks.
Number of titles published annually: 1,000 Online; 1,000 Audio
Total Titles: 7,000 Online; 7,000 Audio
Imprints: Tantor Audio; Tantor Media
Foreign Rep(s): IPS (worldwide)
Membership(s): American Library Association (ALA); Audio Publishers Association; Public Library Association (PLA)

Tapestry Press Ltd
19 Nashoba Rd; Littleton, MA 01460
Tel: 978-486-0200 *Toll Free Tel:* 800-535-2007
E-mail: publish@tapestrypress.com
Web Site: www.tapestrypress.com
Key Personnel
Co-Owner: Michael J Miskin
Publr: Elizabeth A Larsen
Pres: Sara E Hofeldt
Founded: 1988
College textbooks & journals; custom textbooks & anthologies.
ISBN Prefix(es): 978-0-924234; 978-1-56888; 978-1-59830
Number of titles published annually: 70 Print
Total Titles: 75 Print

Taplinger Publishing Co Inc
PO Box 175, Marlboro, NJ 07746-0175
SAN: 213-6821
Tel: 305-256-7880 *Fax:* 305-256-7816
E-mail: taplingerpub@yahoo.com (rts & perms, edit, corp only)
Key Personnel
CEO: Theodore D Rosenfeld
Founded: 1955
General nonfiction, including art, biography, calligraphy, graphic arts, history, music.
ISBN Prefix(es): 978-0-8008
Number of titles published annually: 4 Print
Total Titles: 100 Print
Imprints: Crescendo
Foreign Rep(s): Baker & Taylor International (Africa, Asia, Europe, South Africa, South America)
Orders to: Parkwest Publications LLC, PO Box 310251, Miami, FL 33231-0251, Dir: Brian Squire *Tel:* 305-256-7880 *E-mail:* mail@parkwestpubs.com *Web Site:* www.parkwestpubs.com
Returns: Parkwest Publications LLC, 14332 SW 142 Ave, Miami, FL 33186, Dir: Brian Squire *Tel:* 305-256-7880
Warehouse: Parkwest Publications LLC, 14332 SW 142 Ave, Miami, FL 33186, Dir: Brian Squire *Tel:* 305-256-7880
Distribution Center: Parkwest Publications LLC, PO Box 310251, Miami, FL 33231-0251, Dir: Brian Squire *Tel:* 305-256-7880 *E-mail:* mail@parkwestpubs.com *Web Site:* www.parkwestpubs.com

TarcherPerigee
Imprint of Penguin Group USA, A Penguin Random House Company
375 Hudson St, New York, NY 10014
Tel: 212-366-2000 *Fax:* 212-366-2643
E-mail: customerservice@penguinrandomhouse.com (cust serv); TarcherPerigeePublicity@penguinrandomhouse.com (media queries)
Web Site: www.tarcherbooks.com; www.facebook.com/TarcherPerigee; www.penguin.com/publishers/tarcherperigee
Key Personnel
Publr: Megan Newman
Assoc Publr: Lindsay Gordon
VP & Ed-in-Chief: Marian Lizzi

VP, Exec Ed & Dir, Backlist & Reissues: Mitch Horowitz
Edit Dir: Sara Carder
Publicity Dir: Anne Kosmoski
Assoc Publicity Dir: Casey Maloney
Asst Mktg Dir: Farin Schlussel
Sr Ed: Stephanie Bowen; Nina Shield
Ed: Joanna Ng
Assoc Ed: Lauren Appleton
Asst Mktg Mgr: Roshe Anderson
Mktg & Publicity Coord: Tyler Fields
Publicist: Alexandra Bruschi
Founded: 2015
Core publishing areas include self-improvement, creativity, parenting, spirituality & gift/inspiration.
Penguin Random House & its publishing entities are not accepting unsol submissions, proposals, mss, or submission queries via e-mail at this time.
Number of titles published annually: 73 Print
Total Titles: 517 Print
Advertising Agency: Spier NY

Taschen America
NeueHouse, 6121 Sunset Blvd, Los Angeles, CA 90028
Tel: 323-463-4441 *Toll Free Tel:* 888-TASCHEN (827-2436)
E-mail: contact-us@taschen.com
Web Site: www.taschen.com
Key Personnel
Busn Mgr: Meghan Clarke *E-mail:* m.clarke@taschen.com
Founded: 1996
Publishers of high-quality, reasonably priced illustrated books on the subjects of art, architecture, design, photography, erotica, gay interest & popular culture.
ISBN Prefix(es): 978-3-8228; 978-3-8365
Number of titles published annually: 120 Print
Total Titles: 500 Print
Imprints: Taschen GmbH
Distribution Center: Ingram, One Ingram Blvd, La Vergne, TN 37086 *Toll Free Tel:* 888-558-2624

§The Taunton Press Inc
63 S Main St, Newtown, CT 06470
SAN: 210-5144
Mailing Address: PO Box 5506, Newtown, CT 06470-5506
Tel: 203-426-8171 *Toll Free Tel:* 800-477-8727 (cust serv); 800-888-8286 (orders) *Fax:* 203-426-3434
E-mail: booksales@taunton.com
Web Site: www.taunton.com
Key Personnel
CEO: Dan McCarthy
Dir, Book Sales: John Bacigalupi
Founded: 1975
Woodworking, home building, fiber arts, cooking & gardening books, magazines, DVDs & web sites.
ISBN Prefix(es): 978-0-918804; 978-0-942391; 978-1-56158; 978-1-60085; 978-1-63186
Number of titles published annually: 25 Print; 10 CD-ROM; 25 E-Book; 1 Audio
Total Titles: 525 Print; 100 CD-ROM; 10 Online; 300 E-Book; 1 Audio
Distributor for Guild of Master Craftsman (North America); Lucky Spool (North America & Australia)
Foreign Rep(s): Thomas Allen & Sons; Guild of Master Craftsman
Warehouse: 141 Sheridan Dr, Naugatuck, CT 06770
Distribution Center: Ingram Publisher Services, One Ingram Blvd, La Vergne, TN 37086 *Tel:* 615-793-5000

Taylor & Francis Inc
530 Walnut St, Suite 850, Philadelphia, PA 19106

Tel: 215-625-8900 *Toll Free Tel:* 800-354-1420
  Fax: 215-207-0050; 215-207-0046 (cust serv)
E-mail: support@tandfonline.com
Web Site: www.taylorandfrancis.com
Key Personnel
CEO: Annie Callanan
Pres: Kevin J Bradley
VP, Prodn: Ed Cilurso *E-mail:* ed.cilurso@taylorandfrancis.com
Global Publg Dir, Journals: Leon Heward-Mills
Journals Mktg Dir: Deborah Lovell
  E-mail: deborah.lovell@taylorandfrancis.com
Founded: 1974
Journals in engineering, physical science, psychology, sociology, physics, chemistry, mathematics, environmental science, business, public health, marketing, arts, anthropology, political science, library science & LGBT studies.
ISBN Prefix(es): 978-1-56032; 978-0-87630; 978-0-86377; 978-0-8448; 978-0-85066; 978-0-85109; 978-0-905273; 978-1-85000
Number of titles published annually: 585 Print
Total Titles: 1,500 Print
Imprints: Cogent OA; CRC Press; Garland Science; Routledge; Taylor & Francis Asia Pacific; Taylor & Francis Books
Foreign Office(s): Taylor & Francis Group, Milton Park, 2 & 4 Park Sq, Abingdon, Oxon OX14 4RN, United Kingdom *Tel:* (020) 7017 6000 *Fax:* (020) 7017 6699 *E-mail:* enquiries@taylorandfrancis.com
Orders to: 7625 Empire Dr, Florence, KY 41042-2929 *Tel:* 859-727-5000 *Toll Free Tel:* 800-634-7064 *Fax:* 859-647-4029 *Toll Free Fax:* 800-248-4724 *E-mail:* orders@taylorandfrancis.com; Bookpoint, 130 Milton Park, Abingdon, Oxon OX14 4SB, United Kingdom (Africa, Asia, Australia, Europe) *Tel:* (01235) 400 400 *Web Site:* bookpoint.wp.hachette.co.uk
Distribution Center: 7625 Empire Dr, Florence, KY 41042 *Tel:* 859-727-5000 *Toll Free Tel:* 800-634-7064 *Fax:* 859-647-4029 *Toll Free Fax:* 800-248-4724 *E-mail:* orders@taylorandfrancis.com

TCU Press
3000 Sandage Ave, Fort Worth, TX 76109
Mailing Address: TCU Box 298300, Fort Worth, TX 76129
Tel: 817-257-7822 *Toll Free Tel:* 800-826-8911 (orders) *Fax:* 817-257-5075
Web Site: www.prs.tcu.edu
Key Personnel
Dir: Dan Williams *Tel:* 817-257-5907 *E-mail:* d.e.williams@tcu.edu
Prodn Mgr: Melinda Esco *Tel:* 817-257-6874 *E-mail:* m.esco@tcu.edu
Mktg Coord: Rebecca Allen *Tel:* 817-257-6872 *E-mail:* rebecca.a.allen@tcu.edu
Ed: Kathy S Walton *Tel:* 817-257-5074 *E-mail:* k.s.walton@tcu.edu
Off Mgr: Molly Spain *E-mail:* molly.spain@tcu.edu
Founded: 1947
History & literature of Texas & the American West.
ISBN Prefix(es): 978-0-912646; 978-0-87565
Number of titles published annually: 15 Print; 20 Online
Total Titles: 492 Print; 20 Online; 100 E-Book; 1 Audio
Distributed by Texas A&M University Press
Foreign Rep(s): Texas A&M University Press
Shipping Address: Texas A&M University Press, Lewis St, Lindsy Bldg, College Station, TX 77843-4354, Mgr, Cust Rel: Wynona McCormick
Warehouse: Texas A&M University Press, Lewis St, Lindsy Bldg, College Station, TX 77843-4354, Mgr, Cust Rel: Wynona McCormick
Membership(s): Association of University Presses (AUPresses)

Teach Me Tapes Inc

10400 N Enterprise Dr, Mequon, WI 53092
Mailing Address: PO Box 698, Mequon, WI 53092
Toll Free Tel: 800-456-4656
E-mail: marie@teachmetapes.com
Web Site: www.teachmetapes.com
Key Personnel
Owner & Pres: Judy Mahoney *E-mail:* judy@teachmetapes.com
Founded: 1985
Offers a series of books with CDs that introduce children to new languages using familiar songs & stories.
ISBN Prefix(es): 978-0-934633; 978-1-59972
Number of titles published annually: 3 Print
Total Titles: 100 Print; 37 Audio
Distribution Center: Amazon.com
Follett School Solutions Inc, 1340 Ridgeview Dr, McHenry, IL 60050 *Tel:* 815-759-1700 *Toll Free Tel:* 888-511-5114 (cust serv) *Fax:* 815-759-9831 *Toll Free Fax:* 800-852-5458 *E-mail:* info@follettlearning.com *Web Site:* www.follettlearning.com SAN: 169-1902

Teacher Created Resources Inc

12621 Western Ave, Garden Grove, CA 92481
Tel: 714-891-7895 *Toll Free Tel:* 800-662-4321; 888-343-4335 *Toll Free Fax:* 800-525-1254
E-mail: custserv@teachercreated.com
Web Site: www.teachercreated.com
Key Personnel
Founder & Pres: Mary Dupuy Smith
Founded: 1977
Publishes PreK-12 curriculum programs, supplemental resource materials & technology products. Also provides professional staff development for teachers.
ISBN Prefix(es): 978-1-55734; 978-1-57690; 978-1-4206; 978-1-4570
Number of titles published annually: 250 Print
Total Titles: 1,500 Print
Divisions: Edupress Inc
See separate listing for:
Edupress Inc

§Teachers College Press

Affiliate of Teachers College, Columbia University
1234 Amsterdam Ave, New York, NY 10027
SAN: 213-263X
Tel: 212-678-3929 *Fax:* 212-678-4149
E-mail: tcpress@tc.edu
Web Site: www.tcpress.com
Key Personnel
Dir: Jennifer Feldman
Creative Dir: Dave Strauss
Prodn Dir: Michael Weinstein
Mng Prodn Ed: Karl Nyberg
Exec Acqs Ed: Brian Ellerbeck *E-mail:* ellerbeck@tc.edu
Sr Acqs Ed: Sarah J Biondello *E-mail:* biondello@tc.edu
Sr Prodn Ed: Lori Tate
Acqs Ed: Emily Spangler *E-mail:* spangler@tc.edu
Prodn Ed & Electronic Publg Specialist: John Bylander
Busn Mgr: Monica Carrera
Digital Mktg Mgr: Emily Freyer
Mktg Mgr: Nancy Power
Reprint Mgr: Debra Jackson Whyte
Sales & New Busn Devt Mgr: Sally Kling
Subs Rts & Perms Mgr: Christina Brianik
Outreach Coord: Michael McGann
Founded: 1904
Professional books & textbooks in education; tests, classroom materials & reference works.
ISBN Prefix(es): 978-0-8077
Number of titles published annually: 60 Print; 1 CD-ROM
Total Titles: 1,123 Print; 1 CD-ROM

Foreign Rep(s): Eurospan Ltd (worldwide exc Canada & USA); Guidance Center (Canada)
Orders to: Hawker Brownlow Education, 2/47 Wangara Rd, Cheltenham, Victoria 3192, Australia (select Australia editions) *Tel:* (03) 8558 2444 *Fax:* (03) 8558 2400 *E-mail:* tdupay@hbe.com.au *Web Site:* www.hbe.com.au; University of Toronto Press-Guidance Centre, 5201 Dufferin St, Toronto, ON M3H 5T8, Canada (CN) *Toll Free Tel:* 800-565-9523 *Toll Free Fax:* 800-221-9985 *E-mail:* utpbooks@utpress.utoronto.ca *Web Site:* www.utpguidancecentre.com; Eurospan Group, c/o Turpin Distribution, Stratton Business Park, Pegasus Dr Biggleswade, Beds SG18 8TQ, United Kingdom (Africa, Asia-Pacific, Australia, Caribbean, Europe, Latin America, Middle East, New Zealand & UK) *Tel:* (01767) 604972 *Fax:* (01767) 601640 *E-mail:* eurospan@turpin-distribution.com *Web Site:* www.eurospanbookstore.com/tcp
Returns: Attn: Returns Dept, 30 Amberwood Pkwy, Ashland, OH 44805
Distribution Center: Baker & Taylor Publisher Services, 30 Amberwood Pkwy, Ashland, OH 44805 *Toll Free Tel:* 800-575-6566 *Toll Free Fax:* 866-406-1274 *E-mail:* tcp.orders@btpubservices.com
Membership(s): American Association of University Presses (AAUP); Association of American Publishers (AAP); Book Industry Study Group (BISG)

§Teacher's Discovery

Division of American Eagle Co Inc
2741 Paldan Dr, Auburn Hills, MI 48326
Toll Free Tel: 800-832-2437 *Toll Free Fax:* 800-287-4509
E-mail: help@teachersdiscovery.com
Web Site: www.teachersdiscovery.com
Key Personnel
Owner: Skip McWilliams
Dir, Mktg: Steve Giroux
Founded: 1968
Sell supplemental classroom teaching materials for Spanish, French, German, English & Social Studies. See www.vocesdigital.com for prize-winning digital courseware (e-textbooks).
ISBN Prefix(es): 978-1-884473; 978-0-7560
Number of titles published annually: 200 Print

§Teaching & Learning Co

501 E Third St, Dayton, OH 45402
Mailing Address: PO Box 802, Dayton, OH 45401-0802
Tel: 937-228-6118 *Toll Free Tel:* 800-444-1144 *Fax:* 937-223-2042
E-mail: info@lorenz.com
Web Site: www.lorenzeducationalpress.com
Key Personnel
VP, Mktg: Debra Kaiser *E-mail:* debk@lorenz.com
Founded: 1994
Educational publishing division includes visual resources, instructional guides & reproducibles, elementary supplementals.
ISBN Prefix(es): 978-1-57310
Number of titles published annually: 35 Print
Total Titles: 400 Print; 325 E-Book; 10 Audio
Membership(s): Education Market Association

§Teaching Strategies LLC

4500 East-West Hwy, Suite 300, Bethesda, MD 20814
Tel: 301-634-0818 *Toll Free Tel:* 800-637-3652 *Fax:* 301-657-0250; 301-634-0833
E-mail: info@teachingstrategies.com
Web Site: www.teachingstrategies.com
Founded: 1988
Curriculum, assessment & training materials for early childhood education (birth-age 8) & parent's guides; web subscription service.

ISBN Prefix(es): 978-1-879537; 978-0-9602892; 978-1-60617
Number of titles published annually: 5 Print
Total Titles: 66 Print
Distributor for Gryphon House
Orders to: PO Box 42243, Washington, DC 20015
Returns: Teaching Strategies Inc, c/o RRD P & F, 1077 Prospect Lane, Kaukauna, WI 54130

§Temple University Press

Division of Temple University of the Commonwealth System of Higher Education
1852 N Tenth St, Philadelphia, PA 19122-6099
SAN: 202-7666
Tel: 215-926-2140 *Toll Free Tel:* 800-621-2736 *Fax:* 215-926-2141
E-mail: tempress@temple.edu
Web Site: tupress.temple.edu
Key Personnel
Dir: Mary Rose Muccie *E-mail:* maryrose.muccie@temple.edu
Asst Dir & Mktg Dir: Ann-Marie Anderson *E-mail:* anderson@temple.edu
Ed-in-Chief: Aaron Javsicas *E-mail:* aaron.javsicas@temple.edu
Ad & Promo Mgr: Irene Imperio Kull *E-mail:* irene.imperio@temple.edu
Busn Mgr: Karen Baker *E-mail:* karen.baker@temple.edu
Publicity Mgr: Gary Kramer *E-mail:* gkramer@temple.edu
Rts & Perms & Intl Rts: Ashley Petrucci *E-mail:* ashley.petrucci@temple.edu
Founded: 1969
Scholarly books; all regional interests.
ISBN Prefix(es): 978-0-87722; 978-1-56639; 978-1-59213; 978-1-4399
Number of titles published annually: 45 Print
Total Titles: 1,450 Print
Foreign Rep(s): Baker & Taylor Ltd (Asia, The Pacific, worldwide exc Canada); Combined Academic Publishing (CAP) (Europe); Lynn McClory (Canada)
Returns: Temple University Press Chicago Distribution Center, 11030 S Langley, Chicago, IL 60628 *Tel:* 773-702-7000 *Fax:* 773-702-7000 *Toll Free Fax:* 800-621-8476
Warehouse: Temple University Press Chicago Distribution Center, 11030 S Langley, Chicago, IL 60628, Contact: Karen Hyzy *Tel:* 773-702-7000 *Fax:* 773-702-7000 *Toll Free Fax:* 800-621-8476
Membership(s): Association of University Presses (AUPresses); Society for Scholarly Publishing (SSP)

Templegate Publishers

302 E Adams St, Springfield, IL 62701
SAN: 123-0115
Mailing Address: PO Box 5152, Springfield, IL 62705-5152
Tel: 217-522-3353 (edit & sales)
Toll Free Tel: 800-367-4844 (orders only)
E-mail: wisdom@templegate.com; orders@templegate.com (sales)
Web Site: www.templegate.com
Key Personnel
Dir & Owner: Thomas M Garvey *E-mail:* tmg@templegate.com
Exec Ed, Rts & Perms & Publicity: John Fisher
Sales & Ad Mgr, ISBN & Lib Sales Dir: Elaine Garvey
Founded: 1947
Nonfiction.
ISBN Prefix(es): 978-0-87243
Number of titles published annually: 4 Print
Total Titles: 225 Print
Imprints: Octavo Press
Foreign Rep(s): Gracewing (Europe)

Templeton Press

Subsidiary of John Templeton Foundation

300 Conshohocken State Rd, Suite 550, West Conshohocken, PA 19428
Tel: 484-531-8380 *Fax:* 484-531-8382
E-mail: tpinfo@templetonpress.org
Web Site: www.templetonpress.org
Key Personnel
Publr: Susan Arellano *E-mail:* sarellano@templetonpress.org
Sr Publg Coord: Angelina Horst
Mktg & Publicity Coord: Dan Reilly
Edit/Prodn & Cust Serv Mgr: Trish Vergilio
Founded: 1997
Focus on science & religion, spirituality & health, character development & business.
ISBN Prefix(es): 978-1-890151; 978-1-932031; 978-1-59947
Number of titles published annually: 8 Print; 8 E-Book
Total Titles: 173 Print; 173 E-Book
Foreign Rights: Kaplan/Defiore (worldwide)
Billing Address: Chicago Distribution Center, 11030 S Langley Ave, Chicago, IL 60628 *Tel:* 773-702-7000 *Toll Free Tel:* 800-621-2736 *Fax:* 773-702-7212 *Toll Free Fax:* 800-621-8476 *Web Site:* press.uchicago.edu/cdc
Orders to: Chicago Distribution Center, 11030 S Langley Ave, Chicago, IL 60628 *Tel:* 773-702-7000 *Toll Free Tel:* 800-621-2736 *Fax:* 773-702-7212 *Toll Free Fax:* 800-621-8476 *Web Site:* press.uchicago.edu/cdc
Returns: Chicago Distribution Center, 11030 S Langley Ave, Chicago, IL 60628 *Tel:* 773-702-7000 *Toll Free Tel:* 800-621-2736 *Fax:* 773-702-7212 *Toll Free Fax:* 800-621-8476 *Web Site:* press.uchicago.edu/cdc
Shipping Address: Chicago Distribution Center, 11030 S Langley Ave, Chicago, IL 60628 *Tel:* 773-702-7000 *Toll Free Tel:* 800-621-2736 *Fax:* 773-702-7212 *Toll Free Fax:* 800-621-8476 *Web Site:* press.uchicago.edu/cdc
Warehouse: Chicago Distribution Center, 11030 S Langley Ave, Chicago, IL 60628 *Tel:* 773-702-7000 *Toll Free Tel:* 800-621-2736 *Fax:* 773-702-7212 *Toll Free Fax:* 800-621-8476 *Web Site:* press.uchicago.edu/cdc
Distribution Center: Chicago Distribution Center, 11030 S Langley Ave, Chicago, IL 60628 *Tel:* 773-702-7000 *Toll Free Tel:* 800-621-2736 *Fax:* 773-702-7212 *Toll Free Fax:* 800-621-8476 *Web Site:* press.uchicago.edu/cdc
Membership(s): Independent Book Publishers Association (IBPA)

Temporal Mechanical Press
Division of Enos Mills Cabin Museum
6760 Hwy 7, Estes Park, CO 80517-6404
Tel: 970-586-4706
E-mail: info@enosmills.com
Web Site: www.enosmills.com
Key Personnel
Owner: Elizabeth M Mills; Eryn Mills
ISBN Prefix(es): 978-1-928878
Number of titles published annually: 3 Print
Total Titles: 32 Print

Ten Speed Press
Imprint of Crown Publishing Group
6001 Shellmound St, Suite 600, Emeryville, CA 94608
Tel: 510-285-3000 *Toll Free Tel:* 800-841-BOOK (841-2665)
Web Site: crownpublishing.com/imprint/ten-speed-press
Founded: 1971
Illustrated books. Actively seeks out new & established authors who are authorities & tastemakers in the world of food, drink, design, reference & humor. Create cookbooks, illustrated gift titles, popular business titles & groundbreaking self-help titles.
Penguin Random House & its publishing entities are not accepting unsol submissions, proposals,

mss, or submission queries via e-mail at this time.
Number of titles published annually: 100 Print
Total Titles: 587 Print
Imprints: Food52 Works; Lorena Jones Books (cooking & lifestyle)
Foreign Rep(s): Penguin Random House Inc (worldwide)
Orders to: Penguin Random House Inc, 400 Hahn Rd, Westminster, MD 21157 *Toll Free Tel:* 800-733-3000 *E-mail:* csorders@randomhouse.com; Penguin Random House of Canada Inc, Diversified Sales, 2775 Matheson Blvd E, Mississauga, ON L4W 4P4, Canada *Toll Free Tel:* 800-668-4247 *Fax:* 905-624-8091

Teora USA LLC
9443 Rosehill Dr, Bethesda, MD 20817
SAN: 256-1220
Tel: 301-986-6990
E-mail: teorausa@gmail.com
Web Site: www.teora.com
Key Personnel
Busn Mgr: Teodor Raducanu
Founded: 2003
ISBN Prefix(es): 978-1-59496
Number of titles published annually: 6 Print
Total Titles: 60 Print
Imprints: Teora
Membership(s): Independent Book Publishers Association (IBPA)

Terra Nova Books
33 Alondra Rd, Santa Fe, NM 87508
Tel: 505-670-9319 *Fax:* 509-461-9333
E-mail: publisher@terranovabooks.com; marketing@terranovabooks.com
Web Site: www.terranovabooks.com
Key Personnel
Co-Owner & Publr: Scott Gerber
Co-Owner & Ed: Marty Gerber *Tel:* 505-470-6797 *E-mail:* editor@terranovabooks.com
VP, Mktg: Joanna V Hill *Tel:* 267-304-8521
Founded: 2012
Innovative independent book publisher actively developing fresh new titles & authors titles across a wide range of genres.
ISBN Prefix(es): 978-1-938288; 978-1-948749
Number of titles published annually: 8 Print; 8 E-Book
Total Titles: 72 Print; 40 E-Book
Sales Office(s): SCB Distributors, 15608 S New Century Dr, Gardena, CA 90248, Sales & Mktg Mgr: Gabriel Wilmoth *Tel:* 310-532-9400 *Toll Free Tel:* 800-729-6423 *E-mail:* gabriel@scbdistributors.com *Web Site:* scbdistributors.com
Foreign Rep(s): SCB Distributors (Steve Paton) (Western Canada); SCB Distributors (Terry Fernihough) (New Brunswick, CN, Nova Scotia, CN, Ontario, CN, Prince Edward Island, CN); SCB Distributors (Karen Stacey) (Quebec, CN)
Orders to: SCB Distributors, 15608 S New Century Dr, Gardena, CA 90248, Sales & Mktg Mgr: Gabriel Wilmoth *Tel:* 310-532-9400 *Toll Free Tel:* 800-729-6423 *E-mail:* gabriel@scbdistributors.com *Web Site:* scbdistributors.com
Returns: SCB Distributors, 15608 S New Century Dr, Gardena, CA 90248, Sales & Mktg Mgr: Gabriel Wilmoth *Tel:* 310-532-9400 *Toll Free Tel:* 800-729-6423 *E-mail:* gabriel@scbdistributors.com *Web Site:* scbdistributors.com
Distribution Center: SCB Distributors, 15608 S New Century Dr, Gardena, CA 90248, Sales & Mktg Mgr: Gabriel Wilmoth *Tel:* 310-532-9400 *Toll Free Tel:* 800-729-6423 *E-mail:* gabriel@scbdistributors.com *Web Site:* scbdistributors.com

TESOL International Association
1925 Ballenger Ave, Alexandria, VA 22314-6820

Tel: 703-836-0774 *Fax:* 703-836-7864; 703-836-6447
E-mail: publications@tesol.org; info@tesol.org; members@tesol.org
Web Site: www.tesol.org
Key Personnel
Exec Dir & CEO: Rosa Aronson, PhD *Tel:* 703-836-0774 ext 505 *E-mail:* raronson@tesol.org
Founded: 1966
Education association & publisher of professional education books & products for the ESL teaching profession.
ISBN Prefix(es): 978-0-939791; 978-1-1931; 978-1-931185; 978-1-942223; 978-1-942799; 978-1-945351
Number of titles published annually: 6 Print
Total Titles: 90 Print; 1 CD-ROM
Distributed by Alta Book Center Publishers; New Readers Press; Saddleback Educational
Foreign Rep(s): Eurospan Group (worldwide)
Orders to: PO Box 79283, Baltimore, MD 21279 *Tel:* 240-646-7037 *Toll Free Tel:* 888-891-0041 *Fax:* 301-206-9789 *E-mail:* tesolpubs@brightkey.net
Distribution Center: BrightKey Inc, 9050 Junction Dr, Annapolis Junction, MD 20701 *E-mail:* tesolpubs@brightkey.net

Teton NewMedia Inc
90 E Simpson, Suite 110, Jackson, WY 83001
Mailing Address: PO Box 4833, Jackson, WY 83001
Tel: 307-732-0028 *Toll Free Tel:* 877-306-9793 *Fax:* 307-734-0841
E-mail: sales@tetonnm.com
Web Site: www.tetonnm.com
Key Personnel
Owner: John F Spahr *Tel:* 877-306-9793 ext 103 *E-mail:* lodgepole@tetonnm.com
Pres & Ed-in-Chief: Carroll C Cann *Tel:* 610-594-7634 *E-mail:* ccann@tetonnm.com
Creative Dir: Sue Haun *Tel:* 307-883-5640 *E-mail:* sue@fiftysixforty.com
Mktg Mgr: Sara Scartz-Montesano *Tel:* 307-732-0028 ext 101 *E-mail:* sara@tetonnm.com
Prod Mgr: Mike Albiniak *Tel:* 307-883-5640 *E-mail:* mike@fiftysixforty.com
Founded: 1999 (by John Sphar & Carroll Cann)
Health science publisher that focuses on producing high quality, affordable veterinary text & reference books.
ISBN Prefix(es): 978-1-893441; 978-1-59161
Number of titles published annually: 6 Print; 2 CD-ROM
Total Titles: 25 Print; 18 CD-ROM
Distributed by Blackwells; LifeLearn; Logan Brothers; Rittenhouse; Yankee
Distributor for LifeLearn

Texas A&M University Press
Division of Texas A&M University
John H Lindsey Bldg, Lewis St, 4354 TAMU, College Station, TX 77843-4354
SAN: 207-5237
Tel: 979-845-1436 *Toll Free Tel:* 800-826-8911 (orders) *Fax:* 979-847-8752 *Toll Free Fax:* 888-617-2421 (orders)
E-mail: bookorders@tamu.edu
Web Site: www.tamupress.com
Key Personnel
Dir: Dr Jay Dew *Tel:* 979-458-3980 *E-mail:* jaydew@tamu.edu
Lib Sales Dir & Mktg Mgr: Kyle Littlefield *Tel:* 979-458-3983 *E-mail:* k-littlefield@tamu.edu
Ed-in-Chief: Dr Thom Lemmons *Tel:* 979-845-0758 *E-mail:* thom.lemmons@tamu.edu
Design Mgr: Mary Ann Jacob *Tel:* 979-845-3694 *E-mail:* m-jacob@tamu.edu
Fin Mgr: Dianna Sells *Tel:* 979-845-0146 *E-mail:* d-sells@tamu.edu
Mgr, Cust Rel: Wynona McCormick *Tel:* 979-458-3994 *E-mail:* wynona@tamu.edu

Publicity & Ad Mgr: Christine Brown *Tel:* 979-458-3982 *E-mail:* christinebrown@tamu.edu
Trade Sales: Kathryn Lloyd *Tel:* 979-458-3981 *E-mail:* k-lloyd@tamu.edu
Founded: 1974
Scholarly nonfiction, regional studies, economics, history, natural history, presidential studies, anthropology, US-Mexican borderlands studies, women's studies, nautical archaeology, military studies, agriculture, Texas history & archaeology.
ISBN Prefix(es): 978-0-89096; 978-1-58544; 978-1-60344; 978-1-60344
Number of titles published annually: 60 Print; 1 CD-ROM
Total Titles: 1,500 Print; 2 CD-ROM; 1,450 E-Book; 45 Audio
Distributor for Stephen F Austin State University Press; McWhiney Foundation Press/State House Press; Texas Christian University Press; Texas Review Press; Texas State Historical Association; University of North Texas Press
Foreign Rep(s): Eurospan Group (Europe, UK); Scholarly Book Services Inc (Laura Rust) (Canada); US PubRep (Craig Falk) (Latin America)
Foreign Rights: Tamu Press
Membership(s): Association of University Presses (AUPresses)

Texas Christian University Press, see TCU Press

Texas State Historical Association
3001 Lake Austin Blvd, Suite 3.116, Austin, TX 78703
Tel: 512-471-2600 *Fax:* 512-473-8691
Web Site: www.tshaonline.org
Key Personnel
Mng Ed: Ryan R Schumacher *Tel:* 512-471-5862 *E-mail:* ryan.schumacher@tshaonline.org
Founded: 1897
Books & articles related to Texas history.
ISBN Prefix(es): 978-0-87611; 978-1-62511
Number of titles published annually: 4 Print; 4 E-Book
Total Titles: 100 Print; 33 E-Book
Distributed by Texas A&M University Press

Texas Tech University Press
1120 Main St, 2nd fl, Lubbock, TX 79401
SAN: 218-5989
Mailing Address: PO Box 41037, Lubbock, TX 79409-1037 SAN: 218-5989
Tel: 806-742-2982 *Toll Free Tel:* 800-832-4042
E-mail: ttup@ttu.edu
Web Site: www.ttupress.org
Key Personnel
Dir: Brian L Ott
Mng Ed: Joanna Conrad *E-mail:* joanna.conrad@ttu.edu
Sr Acqs Ed: Travis Snyder *E-mail:* travis.snyder@ttu.edu
Ed: Christie Perlmutter *E-mail:* christie.perlmutter@ttu.edu
Sales & Mktg Mgr: John Brock *E-mail:* john.brock@ttu.edu
Sr Designer: Hannah Gaskamp *E-mail:* hannah.gaskamp@ttu.edu
Founded: 1971
Scholarly books & journals: History, culture & natural history of Texas, the Southwest & the Great Plains; photography; military history; sports history; American roots music; memoirs, especially of the American West; sustainability studies; gender in the American West.
ISBN Prefix(es): 978-0-89672; 978-1-68283; 978-1-945797 (Texas Tech University Libraries)
Number of titles published annually: 20 Print; 15 E-Book
Total Titles: 450 Print; 100 E-Book
Distributor for National Ranching Heritage Center

Foreign Rep(s): Eurospan Group (Africa, Asia, Europe, Middle East, The Pacific, UK)
Distribution Center: Longleaf Services Inc, 116 S Boundary St, Chapel Hill, NC 27514-3808 *Toll Free Tel:* 800-848-6224 ext 1 *Fax:* 919-962-2704 *E-mail:* orders@longleafservices.org
Membership(s): Association of University Presses (AUPresses); Publishers Association of the West (PubWest)

§University of Texas Press
Division of University of Texas
3001 Lake Austin Blvd, 2.200, Austin, TX 78703
SAN: 212-9876
Mailing Address: PO Box 7819, Austin, TX 78713-7819
Tel: 512-471-7233 *Fax:* 512-232-7178
E-mail: utpress@uts.cc.utexas.edu; info@utpress.utexas.edu
Web Site: utpress.utexas.edu
Key Personnel
CFO: Joyce Lewandoski
Dir: Robert Devens
Dir, Press: Dave Hamrick
Asst Dir, Sales & Mktg Mgr: Gianna La Norte
Ed-in-Chief: Dawn Durante
Acq Ed: Jim Burr
Mgr & Intl Rts Contact: Ines ter Horst
Ad, Exhibits Mgr: Chris Farmer
Credit Mgr & Cust Serv: Brenda Jo Hoggutt
Natl Sales Mgr: Bob Barnett
Prodn Mgr: Ellen McKie
Asst Mktg Mgr: Nancy Bryan
Founded: 1950
General scholarly nonfiction, Latin America, Middle Eastern studies, Southwest regional, social sciences, humanities & science, linguistics, architecture, classics, natural history, Latin American literature in translation.
ISBN Prefix(es): 978-0-292
Number of titles published annually: 100 Print
Total Titles: 2,200 Print; 1 CD-ROM; 1 Online
Distributor for Bat Conservation International; Institute for Mesoamerican Studies; Menil Foundation; Rothko Chapel; Texas Parks & Wildlife Department
Foreign Rep(s): Codash (Canada); Combined Academic Publisher (Australia, New Zealand); Nicholas Esson (Europe, UK); Marketing Dept, University of Texas (Caribbean)
Membership(s): Association of American Publishers (AAP); Association of University Presses (AUPresses)

Texas Western Press
Affiliate of University of Texas at El Paso
c/o University of Texas at El Paso, 500 W University Ave, El Paso, TX 79968-0633
SAN: 202-7712
Tel: 915-747-5688 *Toll Free Tel:* 800-488-3798 (orders only) *Fax:* 915-747-5345
E-mail: twpress@utep.edu
Web Site: twp.utep.edu
Key Personnel
Dir: Robert Stakes
Founded: 1952
Scholarly books on the history, art, photography & culture of the American Southwest.
ISBN Prefix(es): 978-0-87404
Number of titles published annually: 2 Print
Total Titles: 63 Print; 1 Audio
Imprints: Southwestern Studies
Distributed by University of Texas Press

TFH Publications Inc
Subsidiary of Central Garden & Pet Corp
PO Box 427, Neptune, NJ 07754
SAN: 202-7720
Toll Free Tel: 855-273-7527 (cust serv) *Fax:* 732-988-5466 (cust serv); 732-776-8763 (sales)
E-mail: info@tfh.com (cust serv); sales@tfh.com

Web Site: www.tfhpublications.com; www.tfh.com; www.facebook.com/TfhPetBooks
Key Personnel
Pres & CEO: Glen Axelrod
Founded: 1952
Pet care reference books & specialty magazines.
ISBN Prefix(es): 978-0-87666; 978-0-86622; 978-0-7938; 978-1-890087 (Microcosm Books); 978-0-9820262 (Microcosm Books)
Number of titles published annually: 40 Print; 40 E-Book
Total Titles: 1,200 Print; 200 E-Book
Imprints: Microcosm Books
Divisions: Nylabone Products
Foreign Rep(s): Brooklands Aquarium Ltd (New Zealand); Fitzhenry & Whiteside (Canada); Rolf C Hagen Ltd (Canada); Interpet Publishing (England); TFH Pty Ltd (Australia); Trinity Books (South Africa)
Foreign Rights: R&G Media (Richard Gay) (worldwide)

Thames & Hudson
500 Fifth Ave, New York, NY 10110
SAN: 202-5795
Tel: 212-354-3763 *Toll Free Tel:* 800-233-4830 *Fax:* 212-398-1252
E-mail: bookinfo@thames.wwnorton.com
Web Site: www.thamesandhudsonusa.com
Key Personnel
Publr & CEO: Sophy Thompson
Publr & Pres: Will Balliett
Assoc Edit Dir: Elizabeth Keene
Assoc Mktg Dir: Lauren Miller
Publicity: Harry Burton
Mktg Assoc: Anna Skrabacz
Founded: 1977
Nonfiction trade, quality paperbacks & college texts on art, archaeology, architecture, crafts, history & photography.
ISBN Prefix(es): 978-0-500
Number of titles published annually: 150 Print
Total Titles: 1,000 Print
Distributed by W W Norton & Company Inc
Advertising Agency: Verso
Shipping Address: National Book Co Inc, Keystone Industrial Park, Scranton, PA 18512
Membership(s): Association of American Publishers (AAP)

Theatre Communications Group
520 Eighth Ave, 24th fl, New York, NY 10018-4156
Tel: 212-609-5900 *Fax:* 212-609-5901
E-mail: info@tcg.org
Web Site: www.tcg.org
Key Personnel
Exec Dir & CEO: Teresa Eyring
Deputy Dir & COO: Adrian Budhu
Publr: Terence Nemeth *Tel:* 212-609-5900 ext 239 *E-mail:* tnemeth@tcg.org
Dir, Ad: Carol Van Keuren *Tel:* 212-609-5900 ext 240 *E-mail:* cvankeuren@tcg.org
Edit Dir: Kathy Sova *Tel:* 212-609-5900 ext 243 *E-mail:* ksova@tcg.org
Assoc Art Dir: Monet Cogbill *Tel:* 212-609-5900 ext 221 *E-mail:* mcogbill@tcg.org
Pubns Mgr: Erin Salvi *Tel:* 212-609-5900 ext 246 *E-mail:* esalvi@tcg.org
Founded: 1961
Performing arts, dramatic literature.
ISBN Prefix(es): 978-0-930452; 978-1-55936
Number of titles published annually: 24 Print; 20 E-Book
Total Titles: 450 Print; 200 E-Book
Distributor for Chance Magazine; 53rd State Press; Nick Hern Books; League of Professional Theatre Women; Padua Playwrights Press; PAJ Publications; Playscripts Inc; Playwrights Canada Press; Martin E Segal Theatre

Center Publications; Ubu Repertory Theatre Publications
Foreign Rep(s): Nick Hern Books (UK); Playwrights Canada Press (Canada)

§Theosophical University Press
Affiliate of Theosophical Society (Pasadena)
PO Box C, Pasadena, CA 91109-7107
SAN: 205-4299
Tel: 626-798-3378
E-mail: tupress@theosociety.org
Web Site: www.theosociety.org
Key Personnel
Dir: Randell C Grubb
Mgr & Intl Rts: Will Thackara
Cust Serv: Ina Belderis
Founded: 1886
Quality theosophical literature.
ISBN Prefix(es): 978-0-911500; 978-1-55700
Number of titles published annually: 2 Print; 5 Online; 2 E-Book
Total Titles: 86 Print; 1 CD-ROM; 115 Online; 84 E-Book; 7 Audio
Imprints: Sunrise Library
Foreign Office(s): Theosophischer Verlag GmbH, Brunnenstr 11, 56414 Hundsangen, Germany, Contact: Jochen Hannappel *Tel:* (06435) 96033 *Fax:* (06435) 96053 *E-mail:* info@theosophischer-verlag.de *Web Site:* www.theosophischer-verlag.de
Theosophical University Press Agency, Daal en Bergselaan 68, 2565 AG The Hague, Netherlands, Contact: Coen Vonk *Tel:* (070) 323 1776 *Fax:* (070) 325 7275 *E-mail:* tupa@theosofie.net *Web Site:* www.theosofie.net
Theosophical University Press South African Agency, PO Box 504, Constantia 7848, South Africa, Contact: Dewald Bester *Tel:* (021) 4342281 *E-mail:* besterdewald@gmail.com
The Theosophical Society, 43 Stephenson Grove, Rainhill, Merseyside L35 9AB, United Kingdom, Contact: Patrick Powell *E-mail:* ts-uk@talktalk.net *Web Site:* www.theosophical.org.uk
Warehouse: 2416 N Lake Ave, Altadena, CA 91001

§Thieme Medical Publishers Inc
Subsidiary of Georg Thieme Verlag KG
333 Seventh Ave, 18th fl, New York, NY 10001
SAN: 202-7399
Tel: 212-760-0888 *Toll Free Tel:* 800-782-3488 *Fax:* 212-947-1112
E-mail: customerservice@thieme.com
Web Site: www.thieme.com
Key Personnel
SVP: Dr Cathrin Weinstein
Founded: 1979
Electronic products, apps, books, journals, textbooks in clinical medicine, dentistry, speech & hearing, allied health, audiology, organic chemistry plus electronic products, medical education & databases.
ISBN Prefix(es): 978-0-913258; 978-0-86577; 978-1-58890; 978-1-60406; 978-1-62623
Number of titles published annually: 50 Print; 3 CD-ROM; 50 Online
Total Titles: 605 Print; 50 Online; 605 E-Book
Foreign Office(s): Thieme Publishers Rio, Argentina Bldg, 16th fl, Ala A, 228, Praia do Botafogo, 22250-040 Rio de Janeiro-RJ, Brazil, VP: Daniel Schiff *Tel:* (021) 3736-3631
Georg Thieme Verlag, PO Box 30 11 20, 70451 Stuttgart, Germany *Tel:* (0711) 89310 *Fax:* (0711) 8931410 *E-mail:* customerservice@thieme.de *Web Site:* www.thieme.de
Thieme Medical & Scientific Publishers Pvt Ltd, A-12, Sector 2, 2nd fl, Noida, Uttar Pradesh 201 301, India *Tel:* (0120) 427 4461 *Fax:* (0120) 427 4465 *E-mail:* customerservice@thieme.in
Distributor for AO Foundation

Foreign Rep(s): Login Canada (Canada); Woodslane (Australia)
Foreign Rights: Heike Schwabenthan (worldwide)
Warehouse: Mount Joy Distribution Center, 1000 Strickler Rd, Mount Joy, PA 17552
Membership(s): Association of American Publishers (AAP); Independent Publishers Association; STM

Third World Press
7822 S Dobson Ave, Chicago, IL 60619
Mailing Address: PO Box 19730, Chicago, IL 60619
Tel: 773-651-0700 *Fax:* 773-651-7286
E-mail: twpbooks@thirdworldpressfoundation.org
Web Site: thirdworldpressfoundation.org
Key Personnel
Publr: Haki R Madhubuti
Ed: Gwendolyn Mitchell
Founded: 1967
Publishers of quality Black fiction, nonfiction, poetry, drama, young adult & children literature; primarily adult literature.
ISBN Prefix(es): 978-0-88378
Number of titles published annually: 10 Print
Total Titles: 140 Print
Distribution Center: Ingram Publisher Services, One Ingram Blvd, La Vergne, TN 37086 *Toll Free Tel:* 866-400-5351

Charles C Thomas Publisher Ltd
2600 S First St, Springfield, IL 62704
SAN: 201-9485
Tel: 217-789-8980 *Toll Free Tel:* 800-258-8980 *Fax:* 217-789-9130
E-mail: books@ccthomas.com
Web Site: www.ccthomas.com
Key Personnel
Pres: Michael Payne Thomas
Founded: 1927
Medicine, allied health sciences, science, technology, education, public administration, law enforcement, behavioral & social sciences, special education.
ISBN Prefix(es): 978-0-398
Number of titles published annually: 60 Print
Total Titles: 905 Print
Advertising Agency: Thomas Advertising Agency

§Thomas Nelson
Imprint of HarperCollins Christian Publishing
501 Nelson Place, Nashville, TN 37214
SAN: 209-3820
Mailing Address: PO Box 141000, Nashville, TN 37214-1000
Tel: 615-889-9000 *Toll Free Tel:* 800-251-4000 *Fax:* 615-902-1548
Web Site: www.thomasnelson.com
Key Personnel
Pres & CEO, Christian Publg Div: Mark Schoenwald
SVP, Author & Partnership Devt: Matt Baugher
SVP & Group Publr, Bibles: John Kramp
SVP, Bible Mktg & New Initiatives: Doug Lockhart
SVP, Children's & Gift Group Publr: Laura Minchew
SVP, Sales: Tom Knight
VP & Publr, Nelson Books: Timothy Paulson
VP & Publr, Thomas Nelson Bibles: Philip Nation
VP & Publr, Tommy Nelson®: Shannon Marchese
VP & Publr, W Publishing: Damon Reiss
VP, Mktg, W Publishing Group: Denise George
Publr, Emanate Books: Joel Kneedler
Publr, Fiction: Amanda Bostic
Publr, Harper Christian Specialty Div: LeeEric Fesko
Assoc Publr, Gift Books: MacKenzie Howard
Assoc Publr, Nelson Books: Jessica Wong
Sr Mktg Dir: Tim Marshall

Dir, Corp Communs: Casey Harrell
Mktg Dir: Mark Glesne
Mktg Dir, Nelson Books: Karen Jackson
Mktg Dir, W Publishing Group: Kristi Smith
Publicity Dir, Thomas Nelson Gift: Stefanie Schroeder
Publicity Dir, W Publishing Group: Sara Broun; Becky Melvin
Sr Acqs Ed, W Publishing: Kyle Olund
Acqs Ed: Jocelyn Bailey
Founded: 1798
Bibles & Testaments, trade, Christian & inspirational books, gift books, children's books & videos.
ISBN Prefix(es): 978-0-8407; 978-1-4047
Number of titles published annually: 600 Print
Total Titles: 3,500 Print; 6 CD-ROM; 30 Audio
Imprints: Emanate Books; Nelson Books; Grupo Nelson (Spanish-language); Tommy Nelson®; W Publishing Group
Distributed by Winston-Derek
See separate listing for:
Tommy Nelson®

§Thomson West
Imprint of Thomson Reuters Legal Solutions
610 Opperman Dr, Eagan, MN 55123
Tel: 651-687-7000 *Toll Free Tel:* 844-209-1086 (sales); 800-328-4880 (cust serv)
Web Site: legalsolutions.thomsonreuters.com
Founded: 1804
Publisher of state statutes, attorney general opinions & practice manuals for the US & international.
ISBN Prefix(es): 978-0-314; 978-0-8322; 978-0-7620; 978-0-8366; 978-0-87632; 978-1-5392
Returns: 525 Wescott Rd, Eagan, MN 55123

Thorndike Press®
Imprint of Gale
10 Water St, Suite 310, Waterville, ME 04901
Toll Free Tel: 800-223-1244 (ext 4, cust serv/orders) *Toll Free Fax:* 800-558-4676 (orders)
E-mail: gale.printorders@cengage.com; international@cengage.com (cust orders outside US & CN)
Web Site: www.gale.com/thorndike
Key Personnel
Publr: Jamie Knobloch *E-mail:* jamie.knobloch@cengage.com
Edit Dir: Mary P Smith *Tel:* 207-861-7517 *E-mail:* mary.p.smith@cengage.com
Assoc Mktg Mgr: Barb Littlefield *Tel:* 207-861-7532 *E-mail:* barb.littlefield@cengage.com
Founded: 1980
Large print titles for the public library market.
ISBN Prefix(es): 978-0-7862; 978-1-4104; 978-1-58724; 978-1-59414; 978-1-59413; 978-1-59415
Number of titles published annually: 1,500 Print
Total Titles: 4,000 Print
Distributor for Grand Central/Hachette Large Print; HarperLuxe; Mills & Boon Large Print; Random House Large Print

ThunderStone Books
6575 Horse Dr, Las Vegas, NV 89131
E-mail: info@thunderstonebooks.com
Web Site: www.thunderstonebooks.com
Key Personnel
Mng Dir: Robert Noorda *E-mail:* robert.noorda@thunderstonebooks.com
Edit Dir: Rachel Noorda *E-mail:* rachel.noorda@thunderstonebooks.com
Founded: 2014
Specialize in children's books that have an educational aspect. We are not looking for curriculum for learning certain subjects, but rather stories that encourage learning for children, whether that be learning about a new language/culture or learning more about science & math in a fun, fictional format. We want to

help children to gain a love for other languages & subjects so that they are curious about the world around them. We are currently accepting fiction & nonfiction submissions. In the area of language, our expertise lies in stories concerning Mandarin Chinese (language, culture, setting +/or mythology), but we are open to other languages as well. For submissions concerning other subjects, we are quite open to anything which creatively teaches & inspires, particularly in areas such as math or science. Fiction submissions that have an educational element are encouraged & welcome.
ISBN Prefix(es): 978-1-63411
Number of titles published annually: 6 Print; 6 E-Book
Total Titles: 5 Print; 5 E-Book
Foreign Office(s): 3B Bow St, Stirling FK8 1BS, United Kingdom *Tel:* (07825) 483348
Orders to: Ingram Content Group LLC, One Ingram Blvd, La Vergne, TN 37086, Contact: Ron Smithson *Tel:* 615-793-5000 *Toll Free Tel:* 800-937-8222 ext 35176 *E-mail:* ron. smithson@ingramcontent.com
Returns: Ingram Content Group LLC, One Ingram Blvd, La Vergne, TN 37086, Contact: Ron Smithson *Tel:* 615-793-5000 *Toll Free Tel:* 800-937-8222 ext 35176 *E-mail:* ron. smithson@ingramcontent.com
Shipping Address: Ingram Content Group LLC, One Ingram Blvd, La Vergne, TN 37086, Contact: Ron Smithson *Tel:* 615-793-5000 *Toll Free Tel:* 800-937-8222 ext 35176 *E-mail:* ron. smithson@ingramcontent.com
Warehouse: Ingram Content Group LLC, One Ingram Blvd, La Vergne, TN 37086, Contact: Ron Smithson *Tel:* 615-793-5000 *Toll Free Tel:* 800-937-8222 ext 35176 *E-mail:* ron. smithson@ingramcontent.com
Distribution Center: Ingram Content Group LLC, One Ingram Blvd, La Vergne, TN 37086, Contact: Ron Smithson *Tel:* 615-793-5000 *Toll Free Tel:* 800-937-8222 ext 35176 *E-mail:* ron. smithson@ingramcontent.com
Membership(s): Publishers Association of the West (PubWest)

Tide-mark Press
207 Oakwood Ave, West Hartford, CT 06119
SAN: 222-1802
Tel: 860-310-3370 *Toll Free Tel:* 800-338-2508 *Fax:* 860-310-3654
E-mail: customerservice@tide-mark.com
Key Personnel
Publr: Scott Kaeser *Tel:* 860-310-3370 ext 108 *E-mail:* scott@tide-mark.com
ISBN Prefix(es): 978-1-63114
Number of titles published annually: 4 Print
Total Titles: 48 Print
Foreign Rep(s): Gazelle Book Services Ltd (Europe)
Billing Address: PO Box 4047, Hartford, CT 06147
Membership(s): American Booksellers Association (ABA); Museum Store Association (MSA)

Tiger Tales
5 River Rd, Suite 128, Wilton, CT 06897-4069
SAN: 253-6382
Tel: 920-387-2333 *Fax:* 920-387-9994
Web Site: www.tigertalesbooks.com
Key Personnel
Art Dir: Michelle Martinez
Sales Dir: Barb Knight *E-mail:* barbknight@ tigertalesbooks.com
Opers Mgr: Jeannie Rubsam *Tel:* 203-834-0005 *Fax:* 203-834-0004 *E-mail:* jrubsam@ tigertalesbooks.com
Ed: Tammi Salzano
Founded: 2000
Publishes imaginative & entertaining hardcover picture books as well as board books for children ages 2-7. For ages 6-10, Tiger Tales pub-

lishes fiction series: *Pet Rescue Adventures & There's a Dragon....* Middle-grade nonfiction imprint *360 Degrees* is dedicated to building a broader view of our world. Tiger Tales remains steadfast in its commitment to publishing children's books that will capture the imagination of children.
ISBN Prefix(es): 978-1-58925; 978-1-68010; 978-1-944530 (360 Degrees)
Number of titles published annually: 100 Print
Total Titles: 650 Print
Imprints: 360 Degrees
Sales Office(s): PO Box 70, Iron Ridge, WI 53035
Orders to: 1263 Southwest Blvd, Kansas City, KS 66103, Contact: Vanessa Ottens *Tel:* 913-362-7400 *Fax:* 913-362-7401 *E-mail:* vanessa@ midpt.com
Returns: 1263 Southwest Blvd, Kansas City, KS 66103 *Tel:* 913-362-7400 *Fax:* 913-362-7401 *E-mail:* lreeder@tigertalesbooks.com
Shipping Address: 1263 Southwest Blvd, Kansas City, KS 66103, Contact: Vanessa Ottens *Tel:* 913-362-7400 *Toll Free Tel:* 888-454-0097 *Fax:* 913-362-7401 *E-mail:* vanessa@midpt. com
Warehouse: 1263 Southwest Blvd, Kansas City, KS 66103, Contact: Vanessa Ottens *Tel:* 913-362-7400 *Toll Free Tel:* 888-454-0097 *Fax:* 913-362-7401 *E-mail:* vanessa@midpt. com
Membership(s): American Booksellers Association (ABA)

Tilbury House Publishers
Imprint of WordSplice Studio LLC
12 Starr St, Thomaston, ME 04861
Tel: 207-582-1899 *Toll Free Tel:* 800-582-1899 (orders) *Fax:* 207-582-8227
E-mail: tilbury@tilburyhouse.com
Web Site: www.tilburyhouse.com
Key Personnel
Publr: Tristram Coburn; Jonathan Eaton
Founded: 1990
ISBN Prefix(es): 978-0-88448
Number of titles published annually: 25 Print
Total Titles: 175 Print
Distributed by W W Norton & Company Inc
Distributor for Marshall Wilkes Publishing
Membership(s): American Booksellers Association (ABA); Independent Book Publishers Association (IBPA)

Tiller Press
Imprint of Simon & Schuster, Inc
1230 Avenue of the Americas, New York, NY 10020
Key Personnel
VP, Publr: Theresa DiMasi
Dir of Cultural Intelligence: Sam Ford
Art Dir: Patrick Sullivan
Assoc Dir of Mktg: Laura Flavin
Exec Ed: Anja Schmidt
Sr Ed: Emily Carleton
Ed: Hannah Robinson
Assoc Ed: Lauren Hummel; Veronica Alvarado
Publicity Mgr: Marlena Brown
Founded: 2019
Number of titles published annually: 60 Print

Timber Press Inc
Division of Workman Publishing Co Inc
133 SW Second Ave, Suite 450, Portland, OR 97204
SAN: 216-082X
Tel: 503-227-2878 *Toll Free Tel:* 800-327-5680 *Fax:* 503-227-3070
E-mail: info@timberpress.com
Web Site: www.timberpress.com
Key Personnel
Publr: Andrew Beckman
Ed-in-Chief: Tom Fischer

Founded: 1976
Gardening, horticulture, botany, natural history, Pacific Northwest regional.
ISBN Prefix(es): 978-0-88192
Number of titles published annually: 40 Print
Total Titles: 300 Print
Distributed by Thomas Allen & Son

TLC, see THE Learning Connection®

The Toby Press LLC
PO Box 8531, New Milford, CT 06776-8531
SAN: 253-9985
Tel: 203-830-8508 *Fax:* 203-830-8512
E-mail: toby@tobypress.com; sales@korenpub. com
Web Site: www.tobypress.com; www.korenpub. com
Key Personnel
Publr: Matthew Miller *E-mail:* publisher@ tobypress.com
Sales Dir: Shlomo Peterseil *Tel:* 203-830-8509
Founded: 1999
Publish Jewish religious texts, Jewish philosophy, Holocaust memoirs.
ISBN Prefix(es): 978-1-902881; 978-1-59264
Number of titles published annually: 50 Print
Total Titles: 800 Print
Imprints: Koren Publishers (Hebrew Bibles & other Jewish religious texts); Maggid (contemporary Jewish thought); Steinsaltz (Talmud, Bible with commentary, Hassidism)
Distributor for Ofeq Books; Steinsaltz
Shipping Address: Focus Mailing, One Prindle Lane, Danbury, CT 06811 *Tel:* 203-830-8500 *Fax:* 203-830-2516 *Web Site:* www. focusmailing.com
Warehouse: Focus Mailing, One Prindle Lane, Danbury, CT 06811 *Tel:* 203-830-8500 *Fax:* 203-830-2516 *Web Site:* www. focusmailing.com
Distribution Center: Focus Mailing, One Prindle Lane, Danbury, CT 06811 *Tel:* 203-830-8500 *Fax:* 203-830-2516 *Web Site:* www. focusmailing.com
Baker & Taylor, 2550 W Tyvola Rd, Suite 300, Charlotte, NC 28217 *Tel:* 714-998-3100 *Toll Free Tel:* 800-775-1800 *Fax:* 704-998-3319
Brodart, 500 Arch St, Williamsport, PA 17701 *Tel:* 570-326-2461 *Toll Free Tel:* 800-999-6799 *Fax:* 570-326-1479
Ingram, One Ingram Blvd, La Vergne, TN 37086 *Toll Free Tel:* 800-400-5351

§Todd Publications
15494 Fiorenza Circle, Delray Beach, FL 33446
SAN: 207-0804
Tel: 561-910-0440 *Fax:* 561-910-0440
E-mail: toddpub@yahoo.com
Key Personnel
Ed/Publr: Barry Klein
Founded: 1973
Directories & reference books to the trade. Returns accepted within 30 days when in resalable condition.
This publisher has indicated that 50% of their product line is author subsidized.
ISBN Prefix(es): 978-0-87340; 978-0-915344; 978-0-873400
Number of titles published annually: 3 Print; 3 E-Book

Tommy Nelson®
Imprint of Thomas Nelson
501 Nelson Place, Nashville, TN 37214
Mailing Address: PO Box 141000, Nashville, TN 37214-1000
Tel: 615-889-9000; 615-902-1485 (cust serv) *Toll Free Tel:* 800-251-4000
Web Site: www.tommynelson.com
Key Personnel
Pres & CEO: Mark Schoenwald
VP & Publr: Shannon Marchese

Publr, Harper Christian Specialty Div: MacKenzie Howard
Sr Dir, Mktg: Robin Richardson
Founded: 1984
Inspirational children's books for evangelical & secular marketplace & other products.
ISBN Prefix(es): 978-0-8499; 978-1-4003
Number of titles published annually: 75 Print; 10 Audio
Total Titles: 400 Print; 8 E-Book; 50 Audio

§Top of the Mountain Publishing

Division of Powell Productions
4837 62 St N, St Petersburg, FL 33709
SAN: 287-590X
Tel: 727-391-3958
Key Personnel
Dir: Judith Powell; Tag Powell
Intl Rts & Lib Sales Dir: Sharon Boulder
PR: Lance Wilson
Founded: 1979
Exhibits at international, national bookfairs, BFA, Frankfurt Book Fairs; no unsol mss.
ISBN Prefix(es): 978-1-56087
Number of titles published annually: 30 Print; 100 Audio
Total Titles: 100 Print; 12 CD-ROM
Advertising Agency: Powell Productions
Distribution Center: New Leaf Distributing Co, 401 Thornton Rd, Lithia Springs, GA 30122-1557 *Tel:* 770-948-7845 *Fax:* 770-944-2313 *E-mail:* domestic@newleaf-dist.com *Web Site:* www.newleaf-dist.com

§Top Publications Ltd

2745 Dallas Pkwy, Suite 420, Plano, TX 75093
Tel: 972-628-6414 *Fax:* 972-233-0713
E-mail: bill@toppub.com
Web Site: toppub.com
Key Personnel
Mgr: Bill Manchee *E-mail:* wm.manchee@gmail.com
Founded: 1999
ISBN Prefix(es): 978-0-9666366; 978-1-929976; 978-1-935722; 978-1-7333283
Number of titles published annually: 3 Print; 2 CD-ROM; 3 E-Book
Total Titles: 58 Print; 19 CD-ROM; 58 E-Book; 19 Audio
Imprints: TOP
Orders to: IngramSpark, La Vergne, TN 37086-3650 *Web Site:* ingramspark.com
Membership(s): Independent Book Publishers Association (IBPA)

Tor/Forge Books, see Tom Doherty Associates, LLC

Torah Umesorah Publications

Division of Torah Umesorah-National Society for Hebrew Day Schools
620 Foster Ave, Brooklyn, NY 11230
Tel: 718-259-1223 *Fax:* 718-259-1795
E-mail: publications@torah-umesorah.org
Key Personnel
Dir, Pubns: Shmuel Yaakov Klein
Founded: 1946
Text teaching aids & visual aids for Yeshiva-day schools & Hebrew schools, students & teachers; posters & workbooks.
ISBN Prefix(es): 978-0-914131; 978-1-878895
Number of titles published annually: 5 Print
Total Titles: 82 Print

Tortuga Press

2777 Yulupa Ave, PMB 181, Santa Rosa, CA 95405
SAN: 299-1756
Tel: 707-544-4720 *Fax:* 707-595-5331
E-mail: info@tortugapress.com
Web Site: www.tortugapress.com

Key Personnel
Publr: Matthew Gollub *E-mail:* mg@tortugapress.com
Off Mgr: Simone Peters
Founded: 1997
Creator of award-winning children's literature & multimedia products to delight & open young people's minds.
ISBN Prefix(es): 978-1-889910
Number of titles published annually: 4 Print; 2 Audio
Total Titles: 28 Print; 8 Audio
Warehouse: CubeSmart, 220 Business Park Dr, Rohnert Park, CA 94928
Membership(s): California Association of Bilingual Education; California School Library Association (CSLA); Independent Book Publishers Association (IBPA); Texas Library Association

§TotalRecall Publications Inc

1103 Middlecreek, Friendswood, TX 77546
Tel: 281-992-3131
E-mail: sales@totalrecallpress.com
Web Site: www.totalrecallpress.com
Key Personnel
Pres: Bruce Moran *E-mail:* bruce@totalrecallpress.com
Founded: 1998
Publish nonfiction books in a variety of professional fields, including library science & library assistant/technician education (Learn Library Skills Series) & financial certification exam preparation, with many titles adopted as college texts. The exam preparation study guides offer free downloads of a proprietary interactive test engine that generates randomized mock exams designed to identify a candidate's strengths & weaknesses & determine where to allocate study time. These titles are also distributed electronically to libraries, corporations & government agencies via EBSCOHost, ebrary & Books24x7.com. The company has expanded into fiction, especially mystery/thrillers, along with self-help, travel & religion.
ISBN Prefix(es): 978-1-59095
Number of titles published annually: 50 Print; 10 Online; 50 E-Book
Total Titles: 400 Print; 120 Online; 250 E-Book

§Tower Publishing Co

650 Cape Rd, Standish, ME 04084
Tel: 207-642-5400 *Toll Free Tel:* 800-969-8693
E-mail: info@towerpub.com
Web Site: www.towerpub.com
Key Personnel
Publr: Michael Lyons
Mng Ed: Mary Anne Hildreth
Business & manufacturing directories, law publications, business databases.
ISBN Prefix(es): 978-0-89442
Number of titles published annually: 20 Print

Tracks Publishing

458 Dorothy Ave, Ventura, CA 93003
Tel: 805-754-0248
E-mail: tracks@cox.net
Web Site: www.startupsports.com
Key Personnel
Owner: Doug Werner
Founded: 1993
ISBN Prefix(es): 978-1-884654; 978-1-935937
Number of titles published annually: 2 Print; 6 E-Book
Total Titles: 45 Print; 135 E-Book
Distribution Center: Independent Publishers Group (IPG), 814 N Franklin St, Chicago, IL 60610 *Tel:* 312-337-0747 *Fax:* 312-337-5985 *E-mail:* frontdesk@ipgbook.com *Web Site:* www.ipgbook.com
Membership(s): Independent Book Publishers Association (IBPA)

Trafalgar Square Books

388 Howe Hill Rd, North Pomfret, VT 05053
SAN: 213-8859
Mailing Address: PO Box 257, North Pomfret, VT 05053-0257
Tel: 802-457-1911 *Toll Free Tel:* 800-423-4525 *Fax:* 802-457-1913
E-mail: contact@trafalgarbooks.com
Web Site: www.trafalgarbooks.com; www.horseandriderbooks.com
Key Personnel
Pres & Publr: Caroline Robbins
Mng Dir: Martha Cook *E-mail:* mcook@trafalgarbooks.com
Dir, Mktg & Promo: Kim Cook *E-mail:* kcook@trafalgarbooks.com
Mng Ed: Rebecca Didier *E-mail:* rdidier@trafalgarbooks.com
Founded: 1972
ISBN Prefix(es): 978-0-943955; 978-1-57076; 978-1-64601
Number of titles published annually: 25 Print
Total Titles: 300 Print
Distributor for J A Allen; Kenilworth Press; Pferdia TV
Distribution Center: Ingram Publisher Services, One Ingram Blvd, La Vergne, TN 37086 *Tel:* 615-793-5000 *Toll Free Tel:* 855-867-1920 *Web Site:* www.ingramcontent.com

Trafford

Division of Author Solutions LLC
1663 Liberty Dr, Bloomington, IN 47403
Toll Free Tel: 888-232-4444
E-mail: customersupport@trafford.com; sales@trafford.com
Web Site: www.trafford.com
Key Personnel
COO, Author Solutions: Bill Becher
Pres, Author Solutions: Bill Elliott
Founded: 1995
The first company in the world to offer an "on-demand publishing service" & led the independent publishing revolution since its establishment. One of the earliest publishers to utilize the Internet for selling books. More than 16,000 authors from over 120 countries have utilized Trafford's experience for self-publishing their books.
This publisher has indicated that 100% of their product line is author subsidized.
ISBN Prefix(es): 978-1-55369; 978-1-55212; 978-1-55395; 978-1-4120; 978-1-4122; 978-1-4251
Number of titles published annually: 800 Print
Total Titles: 2,243 Print
Distribution Center: Baker & Taylor LLC, 2550 W Tyvola Rd, Suite 300, Charlotte, NC 28217 *Tel:* 704-998-3100 *Toll Free Tel:* 800-775-1800 *E-mail:* btinfo@baker-taylor.com *Web Site:* www.baker-taylor.com
Ingram Book Group, One Ingram Blvd, La Vergne, TN 37086 *Tel:* 615-793-5000 *Toll Free Tel:* 800-937-8200 *E-mail:* customer.service@ingrambook.com *Web Site:* www.ingrambook.com
Membership(s): American Booksellers Association (ABA)

Trans-Atlantic Publications Inc

33 Ashley Dr, Schwenksville, PA 19473
SAN: 694-0234
Tel: 215-925-2762 *Fax:* 215-925-1912
Web Site: www.transatlanticpub.com; www.businesstitles.com
Key Personnel
Pres & Intl Rts: Ronald Smolin
Mgr: Jeff Goldstein *E-mail:* jeffgolds@comcast.net
Founded: 1984
Popular culture.
ISBN Prefix(es): 978-1-891696
Number of titles published annually: 200 Print
Total Titles: 2,500 Print

Imprints: BainBridgeBooks
Distributor for Book Guild; Financial Times Publishing; Hodder Education; IndieBooks; Instituto Monsa de Ediciones SA (art books from Spain); Longman; Arnoldo Mondadori Electa; Nexus Special Interests; Pearson Education; Nelson Thornes

Transcontinental Music Publications (TMP)
Division of American Conference of Cantors (ACC)
1375 Remington Rd, Suite M, Schaumburg, IL 60173-4844
Tel: 847-781-7800 *Fax:* 847-781-7801
E-mail: tmp@accantors.org
Web Site: www.transcontinentalmusic.com
Key Personnel
COO: Rachel Roth
Founded: 1938
Publishers of Jewish music.
ISBN Prefix(es): 978-1-8074
Number of titles published annually: 50 Print; 5 Audio
Total Titles: 1,000 Print; 75 Audio
Imprints: Hazamir; Theophilis
Membership(s): MPA - The Association of Magazine Media; National Music Publishers' Association (NMPA)

§Transportation Research Board (TRB)
Division of The National Academies of Sciences, Engineering & Medicine
500 Fifth St NW, Washington, DC 20001
Tel: 202-334-3213 (orders); 202-334-3072 (subns) *Fax:* 202-334-2519
E-mail: trbsales@nas.edu
Web Site: trb.org
Key Personnel
Mgr, Pubn Sales & Affiliate Servs: Andrea Kisiner *Tel:* 202-334-3214
Founded: 1920
Research results, TRR (online journal), bibliographies & abstracts on books pertaining to civil engineering, public transit, aviation, freight, transportation administration & economics & transportation law.
ISBN Prefix(es): 978-0-309
Number of titles published annually: 150 Print; 5 CD-ROM; 100 Online
Total Titles: 2,600 Print; 40 CD-ROM; 1,000 Online
Orders to: Lockbox 936135, 3585 Atlanta Ave, Hapeville, GA 30354

Travel Keys
PO Box 160691, Sacramento, CA 95816-0691
SAN: 682-2452
Mailing Address: PO Box 162266, Sacramento, CA 95816-2266
Tel: 916-452-5200 *Fax:* 916-452-5200
Key Personnel
Publr & Ed: Peter B Manston
Ed: Robert C Bynum
Founded: 1984
How-to travel books & antique guides; travel books worldwide; newsletter about travel books.
ISBN Prefix(es): 978-0-931367
Number of titles published annually: 7 Print
Total Titles: 20 Print
Editorial Office(s): PO Box 160691, Sacramento, CA 95816-0691 SAN: 682-2452
Advertising Agency: Travel Key Media, 2510 "S" St, Sacramento, CA 95816-7307
Billing Address: PO Box 160691, Sacramento, CA 95816-0691 SAN: 682-2452
Orders to: PO Box 162266, Sacramento, CA 95816-2266
Returns: PO Box 162266, Sacramento, CA 95816-2266
Shipping Address: Travel Key Media, 2510 "S" St, Sacramento, CA 95816-7307, Contact: P Manuski

Travelers' Tales
Subsidiary of Solas House Inc
2320 Bowdoin St, Palo Alto, CA 94306
Tel: 650-462-2110
E-mail: ttales@travelerstales.com
Web Site: travelerstales.com
Key Personnel
Publr: James O'Reilly
Exec Ed: Larry Habegger
Ed-at-Large: Sean O'Reilly
Founded: 1992
Sponsors annual Solas Awards for Best Travel Writing. For more information see www.besttravelwriting.com.
ISBN Prefix(es): 978-1-885211; 978-1-932361
Number of titles published annually: 5 Print; 5 E-Book; 1 Audio
Total Titles: 160 Print; 1 Audio
Sales Office(s): Publishers Group West, 1700 Fourth St, Berkeley, CA 94710 *Tel:* 510-528-1444 *Fax:* 510-528-3444
Billing Address: Publishers Group West, 1700 Fourth St, Berkeley, CA 94710 *Tel:* 510-528-1444 *Fax:* 510-528-3444
Orders to: Publishers Group West, 1700 Fourth St, Berkeley, CA 94710 *Tel:* 510-528-1444 *Fax:* 510-528-3444
Shipping Address: Ingram Publisher Services, 210 American Dr, Jackson, TN 38301 *Tel:* 615-213-7412 *Toll Free Tel:* 800-343-4499
Warehouse: Ingram Publisher Services, 210 American Dr, Jackson, TN 38301 *Tel:* 615-213-7412
Distribution Center: Publishers Group West, 1700 Fourth St, Berkeley, CA 94710 *Tel:* 510-528-1444 *Fax:* 510-528-3444

Treasure Bay Inc
PO Box 119, Novato, CA 94948
Tel: 415-884-2888 *Fax:* 415-884-2840
E-mail: customerservice@treasurebaybooks.com
Web Site: www.treasurebaybooks.com
Key Personnel
Pres: Don Panec
Founded: 1997
Publishes educational children's books, specializing in books for parent involvement in reading.
ISBN Prefix(es): 978-1-891327; 978-1-60115
Number of titles published annually: 10 Print
Total Titles: 100 Print

Treehaus Communications Inc
PO Box 249, Loveland, OH 45140-0249
Tel: 513-683-5716 *Toll Free Tel:* 800-638-4287 (orders) *Fax:* 513-683-2882 (orders)
E-mail: treehaus@treehaus1.com
Web Site: www.treehaus1.com
Key Personnel
Publr & Owner: Gerard A Pottebaum
Founded: 1972
Children's books, liturgical & catechetical material for children & adults.
ISBN Prefix(es): 978-0-929496; 978-1-886510
Number of titles published annually: 6 Print
Total Titles: 55 Print

Triad Publishing Co
Imprint of Triad Communications Inc
PO Box 13355, Gainesville, FL 32604
Fax: 304-727-9345 *Toll Free Fax:* 800-854-4947
E-mail: orders@triadpublishing.com
Web Site: www.triadpublishing.com
Key Personnel
Pres & Dir: Lorna Rubin *E-mail:* lorna@triadpublishing.com
Order Dept & Cust Rel: Donna L Hamon *E-mail:* donna@triadpublishing.com
Founded: 1971
Consumer health & medical education for professionals.
ISBN Prefix(es): 978-0-937404
Total Titles: 18 Print; 2 CD-ROM; 2 E-Book

Returns: IFM Services, 2302 Kanawha Terr, St Albans, WV 25177
Shipping Address: IFM Services, 2302 Kanawha Terr, St Albans, WV 25177
Membership(s): The Association of Publishers for Special Sales (APSS); Independent Book Publishers Association (IBPA); National Association of Science Writers

The Trinity Foundation
PO Box 68, Unicoi, TN 37692-0068
Tel: 423-743-0199 *Fax:* 423-743-2005
Web Site: www.trinityfoundation.org
Key Personnel
Pres & Dir: Thomas W Juodaitis *E-mail:* tjtrinityfound@aol.com
Founded: 1977
Scholarly Christian books.
ISBN Prefix(es): 978-0-940931; 978-1-891777
Number of titles published annually: 5 Print; 5 E-Book; 1 Audio
Total Titles: 85 Print; 1 CD-ROM; 27 E-Book; 2 Audio

Trinity University Press
Unit of Trinity University
One Trinity Place, San Antonio, TX 78212-7200
Tel: 210-999-8884 *Fax:* 210-999-8838
E-mail: books@trinity.edu
Web Site: www.tupress.org
Key Personnel
Dir: Thomas Payton
Mng Ed: Sarah Nawrocki
Busn Mgr: Lee Ann Sparks
Mktg Mgr: Ms Burgin Streetman
Sr Acqs Ed: Marguerite Avery
Asst Ed: Steffanie Mortis
Founded: 2002 (after 14 years of inoperation)
Publish titles for the general trade & academic markets.
ISBN Prefix(es): 978-1-59534; 978-0-911536
Number of titles published annually: 12 Print; 12 E-Book
Total Titles: 150 Print; 100 E-Book
Distribution Center: Publishers Group West, 1700 Fourth St, Berkeley, CA 94710 (booksellers & libraries) *Toll Free Tel:* 800-788-3123 *Fax:* 510-528-3614

TripBuilder Media Inc
180 Post Rd E, Suite 200, Westport, CT 06880
SAN: 297-7893
Tel: 203-227-1255 *Toll Free Tel:* 800-525-9745 *Fax:* 203-227-1257
E-mail: info@tripbuildermedia.com
Web Site: www.tripbuildermedia.com
Key Personnel
Pres: Nancy Judson *E-mail:* njudson@tripbuilder.com
EVP: Steven Tanzer
Founded: 1989
Travel guides.
ISBN Prefix(es): 978-1-56621
Number of titles published annually: 20 Print

TriQuarterly Books
Imprint of Northwestern University Press
629 Noyes St, Evanston, IL 60208
Tel: 847-491-7420 *Toll Free Tel:* 800-621-2736 (orders only) *Fax:* 847-491-8150
E-mail: nupress@northwestern.edu
Web Site: www.nupress.northwestern.edu
Founded: 1989
Special attention to new writing talent, the non-commercial work of established writers & writing in translation. Special emphasis on poetry.
ISBN Prefix(es): 978-0-8101
Number of titles published annually: 8 Print
Total Titles: 75 Print
Imprints: Curbstone

TRISTAN Publishing
2355 Louisiana Ave N, Minneapolis, MN 55427
Tel: 763-545-1383 *Toll Free Tel:* 866-545-1383
Fax: 763-545-1387
E-mail: info@tristanpublishing.com
Web Site: www.tristanpublishing.com
Key Personnel
Owner & Publr: Brett Waldman
  E-mail: bwaldman@tristanpublishing.com
Owner & VP Sales, Mktg & Relationships: Sheila
  Waldman *E-mail:* swaldman@tristanpublishing.
  com
Founded: 2002
Exquisite gift books that inspire, uplift & touch
  lives.
ISBN Prefix(es): 978-0-931674
Number of titles published annually: 6 Print
Total Titles: 60 Print; 2 Audio
Imprints: Have a Little Faith; TRISTAN OUT-
  DOORS; Waldman House Press

Triumph Books
814 N Franklin St, Chicago, IL 60610
Tel: 312-337-0747 *Toll Free Tel:* 800-888-4741
  (cust serv) *Fax:* 312-280-5470; 312-337-5985
Web Site: www.triumphbooks.com
Key Personnel
Group Publr: Cynthia Sherry
Publr: Noah Amstadter
Edit Dir: Tom Bast
Dir, Mktg: Andrea Baird
Dir, Prodn: Allison Felus
Mktg Mgr: Tom Galvin
Publicist: Samantha Frontera
Founded: 1989
Leading publisher of sports titles & official rule
  books of NFL, NHL, MLB, NCAA, among
  others.
ISBN Prefix(es): 978-0-9624436; 978-1-880141;
  978-1-57243; 978-1-892049 (Benchmark
  Press); 978-1-60078; 978-1-62368; 978-1-
  61749; 978-1-62937
Number of titles published annually: 95 Print; 75
  E-Book
Total Titles: 600 Print; 450 E-Book
Imprints: Benchmark Press; Triumph Entertain-
  ment
Foreign Rep(s): Monarch Books of Canada
  (Canada); Peribo Pty Ltd (Australia, New
  Zealand)
Foreign Rights: RoundHouse Publishing Ltd (Eu-
  rope, UK)
Returns: Independent Publishers Group (IPG),
  600 N Pulaski Rd, Chicago, IL 60624
Distribution Center: Independent Publishers
  Group (IPG), 600 N Pulaski Rd, Chicago,
  IL 60624 *E-mail:* orders@ipgbook.com *Web
  Site:* www.ipgbook.com
Membership(s): American Booksellers Associa-
  tion (ABA)

§Triumph Learning LLC
Affiliate of School Specialty Inc
80 Northwest Blvd, Nashua, NH 03063
Toll Free Tel: 800-225-5700 (cust serv)
E-mail: customerservice.eps@schoolspecialty.com
Web Site: eps.schoolspecialty.com/coach
Key Personnel
CFO & COO: Manish Mohta
Exec Ed, Sci: Marilyn Locker
Exec Ed, Math: Amy Goodale
Founded: 1964
Print & digital K-12 Common Core resources,
  standards-aligned instructional materials & ef-
  fective literacy programs.
ISBN Prefix(es): 978-0-87694; 978-1-58620; 978-
  1-59823; 978-1-60471; 978-1-60824; 978-1-
  61997; 978-1-62362; 978-1-62928
Number of titles published annually: 150 Print;
  40 CD-ROM
Total Titles: 1,000 Print; 40 CD-ROM

Imprints: Buckle Down; Coach; Jumpstart; Ladders; Options; Plugged-in to Reading; Waggle;
  Workout
Warehouse: One Beeman Rd, Northborough, MA
  01532
Membership(s): Association of American Publishers (AAP)

Truman State University Press
Unit of Truman State University
100 E Normal Ave, Kirksville, MO 63501-4221
Tel: 660-785-7336 *Toll Free Tel:* 800-916-6802
  Fax: 660-785-4480
E-mail: tsup@truman.edu
Web Site: tsup.truman.edu
Key Personnel
Dir & Ed-in-Chief: Barbara Smith-Mandell
  E-mail: bsm@truman.edu
Founded: 1986
University Press, scholarly, early modern stud-
  ies, American studies, regional & general titles,
  contemporary nonfiction & poetry.
ISBN Prefix(es): 978-0-940474; 978-0-943549;
  978-1-931112; 978-1-935503
Number of titles published annually: 14 Print; 14
  E-Book
Total Titles: 200 Print; 80 E-Book
Foreign Rep(s): Gazelle Book Services Ltd (Eu-
  rope)
Distribution Center: Longleaf Services Inc, 116 S
  Boundary St, Chapel Hill, NC 27514-3808 *Toll
  Free Tel:* 800-848-6224 *Toll Free Fax:* 800-
  272-6817 *E-mail:* orders@longleafservices.org
Web Site: www.longleafservices.org

Trusted Media Brands Inc
750 Third Ave, 3rd fl, New York, NY 10017
SAN: 212-4416
Tel: 646-293-6299 *Toll Free Tel:* 877-732-4438
  (cust serv) *Fax:* 646-293-6251
E-mail: customercare@trustedmediabrands.com;
  press@trustedmediabrands.com
Web Site: www.trustedmediabrands.com; www.rd.
  com
Key Personnel
Pres & CEO: Bonnie Kintzer
Chief Content Offr: Beth Tomkiw
Chief Content Offr, Reader's Digest: Bruce Kel-
  ley
Chief Digital Offr: Vincent Errico
Chief People Offr: Jen Tyrrell
CTO: Nick Contardo
CFO: Dean Durbin
Chief Mktg Offr: Alec Casey
Chief Revenue Offr: John Boland
SVP, HR: Phyllis Gebhardt
SVP, Sales: Lora Gier *E-mail:* lora.gier@
  trustedmediabrands.com
VP, Gen Coun & Secy: Mark Sirota
Divisions: Reader's Digest Trade Publishing
Branch Office(s)
44 S Broadway, White Plains, NY 10601
  Tel: 914-238-1000
1610 N Second St, Suite 102, Milwaukee, WI
  53212
Membership(s): Association of American Publish-
  ers (AAP)
See separate listing for:
Reader's Digest Trade Publishing

TSG Foundation, see TSG Publishing
  Foundation Inc

§TSG Publishing Foundation Inc
28641 N 63 Place, Cave Creek, AZ 85331
SAN: 250-6726
Mailing Address: PO Box 7068, Cave Creek, AZ
  85327-7068
Tel: 480-502-1909 *Fax:* 480-502-0713
E-mail: info@tsgfoundation.org
Web Site: www.tsgfoundation.org

Key Personnel
Pres & Intl Rts: Gita Saraydarian
Founded: 1987
Publish & sell books by Torkom Saraydarian,
  spiritual training center.
ISBN Prefix(es): 978-0-929874; 978-0-911794;
  978-0-9656203
Number of titles published annually: 3 Print
Total Titles: 120 Print; 1 CD-ROM
Foreign Rep(s): TSG (UK) Ltd (Europe, UK)

Tudor Publishers Inc
Subsidiary of Cornwallis Press (young adult fic-
  tion & nonfiction)
3109 Shady Lawn Dr, Greensboro, NC 27408
Tel: 336-288-5395
E-mail: tudorpublishers@triad.rr.com
Key Personnel
Pres: Eugene E Pfaff, Jr
Sr Publr: Pamela Cocks
Assoc Ed: Nancy Strange
Founded: 1985
Specialize in adult fiction & nonfiction.
ISBN Prefix(es): 978-0-936389
Number of titles published annually: 12 Print
Total Titles: 80 Print

Tughra Books
Imprint of Blue Dome Inc
335 Clifton Ave, Clifton, NJ 07011
Tel: 646-415-9331 *Fax:* 646-827-6228
E-mail: info@tughrabooks.com
Web Site: www.tughrabooks.com
Key Personnel
Dir, Pubns: Huseyin Senturk *E-mail:* senturk@
  tughrabooks.com
Dir, Mktg: Ahmet Idil *E-mail:* agi@tughrabooks.
  com
Sr Ed: Hakan Yesilova *E-mail:* yesilova@
  tughrabooks.com
Founded: 2001
Publishing, design & printing.
ISBN Prefix(es): 978-975-7388; 978-0-9704370;
  978-1-59784; 978-1-68236
Number of titles published annually: 15 Print
Total Titles: 185 Print
Imprints: The Fountain; The Light
Foreign Rep(s): Gazelle Book Services Ltd (Eu-
  rope, UK)
Distribution Center: National Book Network
  (NBN), 4501 Forbes Blvd, Suite 200, Lanham,
  MD 20706 *Tel:* 301-459-3366 *Fax:* 301-429-
  5746 *Web Site:* www.nbnbooks.com
Membership(s): American Booksellers Associa-
  tion (ABA); Association of American Pub-
  lishers (AAP); Independent Book Publishers
  Association (IBPA)

Tumblehome Learning Inc
201 Newbury St, Suite 201, Boston, MA 02116
E-mail: info@tumblehomelearning.com
Web Site: www.tumblehomelearning.com
Key Personnel
Chair: Penny Noyce *E-mail:* penny@
  tumblehomelearning.com
Pres: Barnas Monteith *E-mail:* barnas@
  tumblehomelearning.com
Opers: Yuyi Ling *E-mail:* yuyi@
  tumblehomelearning.com
Founded: 2010
Helps kids imagine themselves as young scientists
  & engineers & encourages them to experience
  science through adventure & discovery. Publish
  science & adventure mystery stories, picture
  books & occasional nonfiction.
ISBN Prefix(es): 978-0-9850008; 978-0-9897924;
  978-0-9907829; 978-1-943431
Number of titles published annually: 6 Print; 4
  Online; 4 E-Book
Total Titles: 18 Print; 6 E-Book
Membership(s): The Children's Book Council
  (CBC); National Science Teachers Association
  (NSTA)

Tupelo Press Inc
60 Roberts Dr, Suite 308, North Adams, MA 01247
SAN: 254-3281
Tel: 413-664-9611 *Fax:* 413-664-9711
E-mail: info@tupelopress.org
Web Site: www.tupelopress.org
Key Personnel
Publr: Jeffrey Levine *E-mail:* publisher@tupelopress.org
Ed-in-Chief: Kristina Marie Darling
E-mail: kdarling@tupelopress.org
Founded: 1999
Independent, nonprofit literary press.
ISBN Prefix(es): 978-1-932195; 978-1-936797
Number of titles published annually: 16 Print; 7 E-Book
Total Titles: 223 Print; 17 E-Book; 12 Audio
Membership(s): Association of Writers & Writing Programs (AWP); Community of Literary Magazines & Presses (CLMP)

Turner Publishing Co
4507 Charlotte Ave, Suite 100, Nashville, TN 37209
Tel: 615-255-BOOK (255-2665) *Fax:* 615-255-5081
E-mail: marketing@turnerpublishing.com; submissions@turnerpublishing.com; editorial@turnerpublishing.com
Web Site: www.turnerpublishing.com; www.facebook.com/turner.publishing
Key Personnel
Pres & Publr: Todd Bottorff
CFO: Angie Lithgow
Rts Dir & Exec Ed: Stephanie Beard
Tel: 615-255-2665 ext 105 *E-mail:* sbeard@turnerpublishing.com
Mng Ed: Heather Howell
Founded: 1984
Trade publisher.
ISBN Prefix(es): 978-0-943763 (GemStone Press); 978-1-879045 (Jewish Lights); 978-1-58023 (Jewish Lights); 978-1-893361 (SkyLight Paths); 978-1-59120 (Basic Health Publications); 978-1-59473 (SkyLight Paths); 978-1-56311
Number of titles published annually: 36 Print
Total Titles: 3,000 Print
Imprints: Ancestry; Basic Health Publications; Christian Journeys; Fieldstone Alliance; GemStone Press; Hunter House; Iroquois Press (fiction); Jewish Lights; Keylight Books; Ramsey & Todd; SkyLight Paths; Turner; Wiley
Branch Office(s)
445 Park Ave, 9th fl, New York, NY 10022
Tel: 646-291-8961 *Fax:* 646-291-8962
Warehouse: c/o IPS, 1210 Ingram Dr, Chambersburg, PA 17202
Membership(s): American Booksellers Association (ABA); Association of American Publishers (AAP); Independent Book Publishers Association (IBPA)
See separate listing for:
Basic Health Publications
GemStone Press
Jewish Lights
SkyLight Paths

Turtle Point Press
208 Java St, 5th fl, Brooklyn, NY 11222-5748
Tel: 212-741-1393
E-mail: info@turtlepointpress.com
Web Site: www.turtlepointpress.com
Key Personnel
Publr & Edit Dir: Ruth Greenstein
Publg Assoc & Proj Ed: Jeffrey Peer
Founded: 1990
Contemporary & rediscovered fiction, poetry, literary nonfiction.
ISBN Prefix(es): 978-0-9627987; 978-1-885983; 978-1-885583; 978-1-933527
Number of titles published annually: 10 Print

Total Titles: 120 Print
Imprints: Books & Co/Turtle Point; Helen Marx/Turtle Point; Turtle Point
Foreign Rep(s): Turnaround (UK)
Distribution Center: Consortium Book Sales & Distribution, The Keg House, 34 13 Ave NE, Suite 101, Minneapolis, MN 55413-1007
Tel: 612-746-2600 *Toll Free Tel:* 866-400-5351
Fax: 612-746-2606 *E-mail:* info@cbsd.com
Web Site: www.cbsd.com SAN: 200-6049

§Tuttle Publishing
Member of Periplus Publishing Group
Airport Business Park, 364 Innovation Dr, North Clarendon, VT 05759-9436
SAN: 213-2621
Tel: 802-773-8930 *Toll Free Tel:* 800-526-2778
Fax: 802-773-6993 *Toll Free Fax:* 800-FAX-TUTL (329-8885)
E-mail: info@tuttlepublishing.com; orders@tuttlepublishing.com
Web Site: www.tuttlepublishing.com
Key Personnel
Secy & Owner: Michael Sargent
Pres & CEO: Eric Oey
Publg Dir: Ed Walters
Sales & Mktg Dir: Christopher Johns
E-mail: cjohns@tuttlepublishing.com
Founded: 1948
Founded by Charles E Tuttle in Tokyo, Tuttle Publishing publishes books to span the East & West, publisher of high quality books & book kits on a wide range of topics including Asian culture, cooking, martial arts, spirituality, philosophy, travel, language, art, architecture & design.
ISBN Prefix(es): 978-0-8048; 978-4-333 (Kosei Publishing Co); 978-1-85391 (Merehurst Ltd); 978-0-460 (Everyman Paperbacks); 978-4-07 (Shufunotomo Co); 978-4-900737; 978-962-593 (Periplus Editions); 978-0-945971 (Periplus Editions); 978-0-935621 (Healing Tao Books); 978-0-933756 (Paperweight Press); 978-0-7946 (Periplus Editions); 978-0-970171 (Kotan); 978-1-840590 (Milet); 978-4-8053
Number of titles published annually: 152 Print
Total Titles: 2,000 Print; 20 Audio
Imprints: Everyman's Classic Library in Paperback; Kosei Publishing Co; Kotan Publishing Inc; Merehurst Ltd; Milet Publishing Ltd; Periplus Editions
Foreign Office(s): Yaekari Bldg, 3rd fl, 5-4-12 Osaki, 141-0032 Shinagawa-ku, Tokyo 141-0032, Japan *Tel:* (03) 5437 0171 *Fax:* (03) 5437 0755 *E-mail:* sales@tuttle.co.jp *Web Site:* www.tuttle.co.jp
Distributor for Healing Tao Books; Kosei Publishing Co; Kotan Publishing Inc; Milet Publishing Ltd; Paperweight Press; Periplus Editions; Shanghai Press; Shufunotomo Co; Tai Chi Foundation
Foreign Rep(s): Bill Bailey Publishers Representatives (Europe); Berkeley Books Pte Ltd (Southeast Asia); Humphrys Roberts Associates (Caribbean, Central America, Mexico); IMA/Intermediaamericana Ltd (David Williams) (South America); Publishers Group Canada (Canada); Publishers Group UK (UK); Trinity Books (South Africa); Van Ditmar Boekenimport BV (Netherlands); Ward Intl (Book Exports) Ltd (Richard Ward) (Middle East)
Distribution Center: Publishers Group West (PGW), 1700 Fourth St, Berkeley, CA 94710 (print books, ebooks & gift sales) *Tel:* 510-809-3700 *Toll Free Tel:* 800-788-3123 *Fax:* 510-809-3777 *E-mail:* info@pgw.com *Web Site:* www.pgw.com SAN: 202-8522

Tuxedo Press
546 E Springville Rd, Carlisle, PA 17015
Tel: 717-258-9733 *Fax:* 717-243-0074
E-mail: info@tuxedo-press.com

Web Site: tuxedo-press.com
Key Personnel
Publr: Thomas R Benjey *E-mail:* tom@tuxedo-press.com
Assoc Ed: Ann Fitch *E-mail:* ann@tuxedo-press.com
Founded: 2005
Small press of nonfiction books. Titles released to date have been historical in nature. Future releases may also include political topics. New releases are offset print; reprints are POD. Considering expansion to audiobooks. Titles are of US interest only.
ISBN Prefix(es): 978-0-9774486; 978-1-936161
Number of titles published annually: 3 Print
Total Titles: 15 Print; 3 E-Book
Advertising Agency: Anne Dozier & Associates, 313 E 84 St, Suite 1-B, New York, NY 10028, Contact: Anne Dozier *Tel:* 212-717-0276
E-mail: annedozier@aol.com
Orders to: Ingram Book Co, 14 Ingram Blvd, La Vergne, TN 37086 *Tel:* 615-213-5335
Fax: 615-213-5430
Distribution Center: Ingram Book Co, 14 Ingram Blvd, La Vergne, TN 37086 *Tel:* 615-213-5335
Fax: 615-213-5430
Membership(s): Independent Book Publishers Association (IBPA)

Twenty-First Century Books
Imprint of Lerner Publishing Group Inc
241 First Ave N, Minneapolis, MN 55401
Tel: 612-332-3344 *Toll Free Tel:* 800-328-4929
Fax: 612-332-7615 *Toll Free Fax:* 800-332-1132
E-mail: info@lernerbooks.com; custserve@lernerbooks.com
Web Site: www.lernerbooks.com; www.facebook.com/lernerbooks
Key Personnel
Chmn: Harry J Lerner
Pres & Publr: Adam Lerner
EVP & COO: Mark Budde
EVP & CFO: Margaret Thomas
EVP, Sales: David Wexler
VP & Ed-in-Chief: Andy Cummings
VP, Mktg: Rachel Zugschwert
Publg Dir, School & Lib: Jenny Krueger
Dir, HR: Cyndi Radant
Dir, Rts, Spec Sales & Intl Dist: Maria Kjoller
School & Lib Mktg Dir: Lois Wallentine
Assoc Edit Dir: Shaina Olmanson
Publisher of nonfiction books for the upper grades & young adults.
ISBN Prefix(es): 978-0-8050; 978-1-56294; 978-0-7613; 978-0-941477
Number of titles published annually: 15 Print; 30 E-Book
Total Titles: 480 Print; 255 E-Book
Foreign Rep(s): Thomas Allen & Son (trade) (Canada); Bravo (UK); INT Books (Australia); J Appleseed, A Division of Saunders (Canada); Phambili Agencies (Botswana, Lesotho, Namibia, Southern Africa); Publishers Marketing Services (Brunei, Malaysia, Singapore); Saunders Book Co (education) (Canada); South Pacific Books (New Zealand, South Pacific)
Foreign Rights: Japan Foreign-Rights Centre (Japan); Korea Copyright Center (KCC) (Korea); Agence Michelle Lapautre (France); Literarische Agentur Silke Weniger (Germany)
Warehouse: 1251 Washington Ave N, Minneapolis, MN 55401, Mgr: Ken Rued

§Twenty-Third Publications
Division of Bayard Inc
One Montauk Ave, Suite 200, New London, CT 06320
Tel: 860-437-3012 *Toll Free Tel:* 800-321-0411 (orders) *Toll Free Fax:* 800-572-0788
E-mail: resources@twentythirdpublications.com
Web Site: www.twentythirdpublications.com

Key Personnel
VP & Edit Dir: Dan Connors *E-mail:* dan.
   connors@bayard-inc.com
Publr: Therese Ratliff *E-mail:* tratliff@
   twentythirdpublications.com
Art Dir: Jeff McCall *E-mail:* jeff.mccall@bayard-
   inc.com
Mktg Dir: Dan Smart *E-mail:* dsmart@
   twentythirdpublications.com
Assoc Dir, Sales & Mktg: Kerry Moriarty
Founded: 1967
ISBN Prefix(es): 978-0-89622; 978-1-58595
Number of titles published annually: 45 Print; 6
   CD-ROM
Total Titles: 450 Print; 24 CD-ROM
Distributed by Columba (UK); John Garrett (Aus-
   tralia); Novalis (Canada)
Distributor for Novalis (Canada)
Foreign Rights: Bayard Presse International (Asia,
   Central Europe, Eastern Europe)
Membership(s): Association of Catholic Publish-
   ers Inc; Catholic Press Association (CPA)

§Twilight Times Books
PO Box 3340, Kingsport, TN 37664-0340
Tel: 423-323-0183 *Fax:* 423-323-0183
E-mail: publisher@twilighttimes.com
Web Site: www.twilighttimesbooks.com
Key Personnel
Publr: Lida E Quillen
Mng Ed: Ardy M Scott
Ed: Eric Olsen
Tech Support: Michael D Bobbitt
Founded: 1999
Royalty paying small press trade publisher of
   speculative fiction. Our mission is to promote
   excellence in writing & great literature. Cur-
   rently publishing limited edition hardcover, first
   edition trade paperback books & ebooks as
   downloads in various formats.
ISBN Prefix(es): 978-1-931201; 978-1-933353;
   978-1-60619
Number of titles published annually: 14 Print; 14
   E-Book
Total Titles: 125 Print; 175 E-Book
Imprints: Paladin Timeless Books; Twilight Vi-
   sions
Distribution Center: Follett Library Resources,
   1340 Ridgeview Dr, McHenry, IL 60050-7048
Brodart Co, 50 Arch St, Williamsport, PA 17701
   Tel: 570-326-2461 *Toll Free Tel:* 800-474-9816
   Toll Free Fax: 800-999-6799 *E-mail:* support@
   brodart.com *Web Site:* www.brodart.com
Membership(s): Association of American Pub-
   lishers (AAP); The Association of Publish-
   ers for Special Sales (APSS); Electronically
   Published Internet Connection (EPIC); Inde-
   pendent Book Publishers Association (IBPA);
   Small Publishers, Artists & Writers Network
   (SPAWN); Speculative Literature Foundation

Two Thousand Three Associates
135 Chilean Ave, Palm Beach, FL 33480
Tel: 386-690-2503
E-mail: ttta1@att.net
Web Site: www.twothousandthree.com
Key Personnel
Intl Rts & Lib Sales Dir: Frederick B Smith
Mktg Dir: Hank Hankshaw
Publicity Dir: Barbara Brent
Asst to Pres: Geoffery Crawford Tell
Founded: 1995
Nonfiction including memoirs, humor, sports &
   travel.
ISBN Prefix(es): 978-0-9639905; 978-1-892285
Number of titles published annually: 4 Print
Total Titles: 16 Print
Membership(s): Independent Publishers Associa-
   tion

§Tyndale House Publishers Inc
351 Executive Dr, Carol Stream, IL 60188

SAN: 206-7749
Tel: 630-668-8300 *Toll Free Tel:* 800-323-9400;
   855-277-9400 *Toll Free Fax:* 866-622-9474
Web Site: www.tyndale.com
Key Personnel
Pres & CEO: Mark Taylor
SVP & Group Publr: Ron Beers
Sr Dir, Corp Media: Alan Huizenga
Dir, Intl Publg: James Elwell
PR Dir: Katie Dodillet
Founded: 1962
Religion: hardcover & paperback originals &
   reprints, ebooks, Bibles, reference, DVDs, au-
   dio CDs & software.
ISBN Prefix(es): 978-0-8423; 978-1-4143
Number of titles published annually: 125 Print; 1
   CD-ROM; 73 Online; 75 E-Book; 25 Audio
Total Titles: 1,000 Print; 5 CD-ROM; 300 E-
   Book; 225 Audio
Imprints: BarnaBooks (George Barna titles);
   Living Books (mass mkt pbk); Resurgence
   (Mars Hill Church); SaltRiver (deeper Christian
   thought); Tyndale Audio (adult audiobooks);
   Tyndale Entertainment (kids' audio/video prod-
   ucts); Tyndale Kids (children's); Tyndale Mo-
   mentum; Tyndale Ninos (Spanish children's)
Distributor for Focus on the Family; NavPress
Advertising Agency: Design Promotion
Membership(s): Evangelical Christian Publishers
   Association (ECPA)

UCLA Latin American Center Publications
Unit of University of California, Los Angeles
UCLA Latin American Institute, 10343 Bunche
   Hall, Los Angeles, CA 90095
Mailing Address: PO Box 951447, Los Angeles,
   CA 90095-1447
Tel: 310-825-4571 *Fax:* 310-206-6859
E-mail: latinamctr@international.ucla.edu
Web Site: www.international.ucla.edu/lai
Key Personnel
Dir: Kevin Terraciano *E-mail:* terraciano@
   international.ucla.edu
Dir, Pubns: Orchid Mazurkiewicz
   E-mail: orchidm@ucla.edu
Asst Dir: Bryan Pitts *E-mail:* bpitts@
   international.ucla.edu
Pubns Mgr: Marcelo Jatoba *Tel:* 310-825-6634
   E-mail: mjatoba@international.ucla.edu
Founded: 1959
Publish scholarly books & journals in Latin
   American studies & the *Hispanic American
   Periodicals Index (HAPI).*
ISBN Prefix(es): 978-0-87903
Number of titles published annually: 6 Print; 1
   CD-ROM; 1 Online
Total Titles: 124 Print; 1 CD-ROM; 1 Online

Ugly Duckling Presse
The Old American Can Factory, 232 Third St,
   Suite E303, Brooklyn, NY 11215
Tel: 347-948-5170
E-mail: office@uglyducklingpresse.
   org; orders@uglyducklingpresse.org;
   publicity@uglyducklingpresse.org; rights@
   uglyducklingpresse.org
Web Site: uglyducklingpresse.org
Key Personnel
Mng Ed: Matvei Yankelevich *E-mail:* matvei@
   uglyducklingpresse.org
Ed: Anna Moschovakis *E-mail:* anna@
   uglyducklingpresse.org; Rebekah Smith
   E-mail: rebekah@uglyducklingpresse.org
Founded: 1993
A nonprofit arts & publishing collective.
ISBN Prefix(es): 978-0-9727684; 978-1-946433
Number of titles published annually: 24 Print; 2
   Audio
Total Titles: 200 Print
Distributor for United Artists
Distribution Center: Distributed Art Publishers
   (DAP), 75 Broad St, Suite 630, New York, NY
   10004 (art-related titles) *Tel:* 212-627-1999

Fax: 212-627-9484 *E-mail:* orders@artbook.
   com *Web Site:* www.artbook.com
Small Press Distribution (SPD), 1341 Seventh St,
   Berkeley, CA 94710-1409 *Tel:* 510-524-1668
   Toll Free Tel: 800-869-7553 (US) *Fax:* 510-
   524-0852 *E-mail:* spd@spdbooks.org *Web
   Site:* www.spdbooks.org
Raincoast Books Distribution Ltd, 2440 Viking
   Way, Richmond, BC V6V 1N2, Canada
   Tel: 604-448-7100 *Toll Free Tel:* 800-663-
   5714 (cust serv) *Toll Free Fax:* 800-565-3770
   (orders) *E-mail:* info@raincoast.com *Web
   Site:* www.raincoast.com
Antenne Books, The Sunroom, Hackney Downs
   Studios, 17 Amhurst Terr, London E8 2BT,
   United Kingdom (UK art-related titles)
   Tel: (020) 3582 8257
Inpress Books, Milburn House, Dean St, New-
   castle upon Tyne NE1 1LF, United Kingdom
   Tel: (0191) 230 8104 *E-mail:* enquiries@
   inpressbooks.co.uk *Web Site:* inpressbooks.co.
   uk
Membership(s): Community of Literary Maga-
   zines & Presses (CLMP)

UL Press, see University of Louisiana at
Lafayette Press

Ulysses Press
195 Montague St, 14th fl, Brooklyn, NY 11201
Mailing Address: PO Box 3440, Berkeley, CA
   94703
Tel: 510-601-8301 *Toll Free Tel:* 800-377-2542
   Fax: 510-601-8307
E-mail: ulysses@ulyssespress.com
Web Site: www.ulyssespress.com
Key Personnel
CEO: Ray Riegert *E-mail:* rayriegert@
   ulyssespress.com
EVP & Publr: Keith Riegert
   E-mail: keithriegert@ulyssespress.com
Dir, Edit & Acqs: Casie Vogel
   E-mail: casievogel@ulyssespress.com
Dir, Mktg & Opers: Bridget Thoreson
   E-mail: bridgetthoreson@ulyssespress.com
Acqs Ed: Claire Sielaff *E-mail:* clairesielaff@
   ulyssespress.com
Asst Ed: Ashten Evans *E-mail:* ashtenevans@
   ulyssespress.com
Founded: 1983
Health & fitness books, cookbooks, pop culture
   & trivia, lifestyle, crafts & hobbies titles, mind,
   body & spirit.
ISBN Prefix(es): 978-0-915233; 978-1-56975
Number of titles published annually: 60 Print; 50
   E-Book
Total Titles: 600 Print
Imprints: Amorata Press; Hidden Travel Series;
   Seastone
Distributed by Simon & Schuster, Inc
Foreign Rep(s): Hi Marketing (Central America,
   Continental Europe, Far East, South Africa,
   South America, UK); Raincoast Book Distribu-
   tion Ltd (Canada)
Foreign Rights: Linda Biagi (worldwide)
Orders to: Simon & Schuster, Inc, Order Process-
   ing Dept, 100 Front St, Riverside, NJ 08075
   E-mail: purchaseorders@simonandschuster.com
Shipping Address: 3286 Adeline St, Suite 1,
   Berkeley, CA 94703 *Toll Free Tel:* 800-377-
   2542
Membership(s): Independent Book Publishers As-
   sociation (IBPA); Society of American Travel
   Writers (SATW)

Unarius Academy of Science Publications
Division of Unarius Educational Foundation
145 S Magnolia Ave, El Cajon, CA 92020-4522
SAN: 168-9614
Tel: 619-444-7062 *Toll Free Tel:* 800-475-7062
   Fax: 619-444-9637
E-mail: uriel@unarius.org
Web Site: www.unarius.org

Key Personnel
Ed: Celeste Appel
Founded: 1954
Books, CDs/MP3s & DVDs/MP4s describing a new science of life, past life therapy, extraterrestrial civilizations, the prehistory of earth, the psychology of consciousness: a course in self-mastery. Unarius provides the foundation for personal growth that will lead to the development of self-mastery & the clairvoyant aptitudes of the mind. Classes in past-life therapy are webcast on Sunday & Wednesday 7pm PT.
ISBN Prefix(es): 978-0-932642; 978-0-935097
Number of titles published annually: 4 Print
Total Titles: 90 Print; 70 Audio
Divisions: Audio Books; Unarius Video Productions; Visionary Art

Editorial Unilit
Division of Spanish House Inc
8167 NW 84 St, Medley, FL 33166
Tel: 305-592-6136 *Toll Free Tel:* 800-767-7726
Fax: 305-592-0087
E-mail: info@editorialunilit.com; customerservice@editorialunilit.com
Web Site: www.editorialunilit.com
Key Personnel
Pres: David Ecklebarger
Sales Dir: Mariana Tafura *E-mail:* mariana@editorialunilit.com
Sales Mgr: Carlos Hernandez *E-mail:* carlos@editorialunilit.com
Founded: 1989
Publishing for the Spanish family.
ISBN Prefix(es): 978-1-56063; 978-0-7899; 978-0-945792
Number of titles published annually: 40 Print
Total Titles: 900 Print

§United Nations Publications
300 E 42 St, 9th fl, New York, NY 10017
SAN: 206-6718
Tel: 703-661-1571 *Fax:* 703-996-1010
E-mail: publications@un.org
Web Site: shop.un.org
Key Personnel
Chief: Sherri Aldis *E-mail:* aldis@un.org
Acqs Offr: Nicolas Bovay *E-mail:* bovay@un.org
Sales & Mktg Offr: Irina Lumelsky *E-mail:* lumelsky@un.org
Founded: 1946
Promotes the knowledge & work of the UN to scholars, information specialists, policy-makers & influencers. We publish approximately 500 new titles per year in economic & social development, international law & justice, peacekeeping & security, human rights & refugees, natural resources & more.
ISBN Prefix(es): 978-92-1 (United Nations Publications); 978-92-807 (UNEP); 978-92-808 (United Nations University); 978-92-806 (UNICEF); 978-88-000 (UNICEF); 978-184-966 (DESA); 978-1-849 (UNEP); 978-1-618 (UNFPA); 978-92-9137 (ITC)
Number of titles published annually: 500 Print; 60 Online
Total Titles: 2,300 Print; 35 CD-ROM; 160 E-Book
Sales Office(s): Books International, PO Box 960, Herndon, VA 20172
Distributor for Food & Agriculture Organization of the United Nations (FAO); International Atomic Energy Agency (IAEA); International Criminal Tribunal for Rwanda (UNICTR); International Criminal Tribunal for the former Yugoslavia (ICTY); International Organization for Migration (IOM); International Trade Centre (ITC); Office of the United Nations High Commissioner for Human Rights (OHCHR); United Nations Children's Fund (UNICEF); United Nations Development Programme (UNDP); United Nations Economic & Social Commission for Asia & the Pacific (ESCAP); United Nations Economic & Social Commission for Western Asia (ESCWA); United Nations Economic Commission for Africa (ECA); United Nations Economic Commission for Europe (ECE); United Nations Economic Commission for Latin America & the Caribbean (ECLAC); United Nations High Commissioner for Refugees (UNHCR); United Nations Human Settlements Programme (UN-HABITAT); United Nations Industrial Development Organization (UNIDO); United Nations Institute for Disarmament Research (UNIDIR); United Nations Institute for Training & Research (UNITAR); United Nations International Research & Training Institute for the Advancement of Women (INSTRAW); United Nations Interregional Crime & Justice Research Institute (UNICRI); United Nations Office for Project Services (UNOPS); United Nations Office for the Coordination of Humanitarian Affairs (OCHA); United Nations Office on Drugs & Crime (UNODC); United Nations Population Fund (UNFPA); United Nations Research Institute for Social Development (UNRISD); United Nations University (UNU)
Foreign Rep(s): Eurospan Group (Africa, Asia, China, Europe, Hong Kong, Middle East, Taiwan)
Returns: Books International, 22883 Quicksilver Dr, Dulles, VA 20166
Shipping Address: Books International, PO Box 960, Herndon, VA 20172
Warehouse: Books International, 22883 Quicksilver Dr, Dulles, VA 20166

§United States Holocaust Memorial Museum
100 Raoul Wallenberg Place SW, Washington, DC 20024-2126
Tel: 202-488-0400; 202-314-7837; 202-488-6144 (orders) *Toll Free Tel:* 800-259-9998 (orders) *Fax:* 202-479-9726; 202-488-0438 (orders)
E-mail: cahs_publications@ushmm.org
Web Site: www.ushmm.org
Key Personnel
Busn Devt Mgr, Museum Bookstore & Holocaust Lib Sales Opers: Paul Messersmith
Emerging Scholars Prog Offr: Steven Feldman
Pubns Offr, Mandel Ctr Staff Applied Res Projs: Mel Hecker
Assoc Creative Dir: Amy Donovan
Perms: Karen Coe
Sr Ed: Brabara Martinez
Ed: Clare Rosenson
Founded: 1993
Co-publish original monographs, translations, classic reprints, testimonial materials & a scholarly journal; publish memoirs & related titles of Holocaust Publications' Holocaust Library imprint (assets acquired in 1993) as well as occasional papers, exhibition catalogues & related works.
ISBN Prefix(es): 978-0-89604
Number of titles published annually: 12 Print
Total Titles: 160 Print
Imprints: Holocaust Library
Foreign Rights: Goldfarb & Associates (selected titles)

United States Institute of Peace Press
2301 Constitution Ave NW, Washington, DC 20037
Tel: 703-661-1590 (cust serv) *Toll Free Tel:* 800-868-8064 (cust serv)
E-mail: usipmail@presswarehouse.com (orders)
Web Site: bookstore.usip.org
Key Personnel
Dir: Jake Harris
Mng Ed: Richard Walker
Founded: 1989
Publisher of influential books, reports & briefs on the prevention, management & peaceful resolution of international conflicts. All books & reports arise from research & fieldwork sponsored by the Institute's many programs & the Press is committed to extending the reach of the Institute's work by continuing to publish significant & sustainable publications for practitioners, scholars, diplomats & students. In keeping with the best traditions of scholarly publishing, each work undergoes thorough peer review by external subject experts to ensure that the research & conclusions are balanced, relevant & sound.
ISBN Prefix(es): 978-1-878379; 978-1-929223; 978-1-601270
Number of titles published annually: 10 Print
Total Titles: 250 Print
Orders to: PO Box 605, Herndon, VA 20172-0605 (sales & returns/bookseller, wholesaler & instl) *E-mail:* usipmail@presswarehouse.com
SAN: 254-6965
Shipping Address: 22883 Quicksilver Dr, Dulles, VA 20166 (indiv returns)

United States Pharmacopeia
12601 Twinbrook Pkwy, Rockville, MD 20852-1790
Tel: 301-881-0666 *Toll Free Tel:* 800-227-8772
Fax: 301-816-8237 (mktg)
E-mail: marketing@usp.org
Web Site: www.usp.org
Key Personnel
CEO: Ronald T Piervincenzi, PhD
Founded: 1820
Reference books & directories; Databases in print & electronic formats.
ISBN Prefix(es): 978-0-913595
Number of titles published annually: 5 Print
Total Titles: 25 Print; 2 CD-ROM
Distributed by Consumer Reports
Foreign Rep(s): Deutscher Apotheker Verlag (Austria, Germany, Switzerland); Login Canada (Canada); Maruzen Co Ltd (Japan); Pharmaceutical Society of Australia (Australia); Pharmasystems (Canada); Ernesto Reichmann Distribuidora de Livros Ltda (Brazil)
Distribution Center: Matthews Book Co, 11559 Rock Island Ct, Maryland Heights, MO 63043 *Tel:* 314-432-1400 *Toll Free Fax:* 800-421-8816
Rittenhouse Book Distributors, Inc, 522 Feheley Dr, King of Prussia, PA 19406 *Toll Free Tel:* 800-345-6425 *Toll Free Fax:* 800-223-7488
National Technical Information Service, 5285 Port Royal Rd, Springfield, VA 22161 *Tel:* 703-487-4825 *Fax:* 703-487-4098
Promachem LLC, PO Box 1126, 2931 Soldier Springs Rd, Laramie, WY 82070 *Tel:* 307-742-6343 *Fax:* 307-745-7936
Login Canada, 300 Saulteaux Crescent, Winnipeg, MB R3J 3T2, Canada *Tel:* 204-837-2987 (cust serv) *Toll Free Tel:* 800-665-1148 (cust serv) *Web Site:* lb.ca

United States Tennis Association
70 W Red Oak Lane, White Plains, NY 10604
Tel: 914-696-7000 *Fax:* 914-696-7027
Web Site: www.usta.com
Key Personnel
Dir, Publg: Richard S Rennert *E-mail:* rennert@usta.com
Founded: 1881
Tennis materials; books, magazines & souvenir programs.
ISBN Prefix(es): 978-0-938822
Number of titles published annually: 5 Print
Total Titles: 25 Print
Distributed by Triumph Books; Universe Publishing; H O Zimman Inc

Univelt Inc
Affiliate of American Astronautical Society
740 Metcalf St, No 13, Escondido, CA 92025
Mailing Address: PO Box 28130, San Diego, CA 92198-0130
Tel: 760-746-4005 *Fax:* 760-746-3139

E-mail: sales@univelt.com
Web Site: www.univelt.com; www.astronautical.org
Key Personnel
Pres & Publr: Robert H Jacobs
Founded: 1970
Publisher for American Astronautical Society, International Academy of Astronautics, Lunar & Planetary Society, National Space Society. Specialize in astronautics & aerospace engineering.
ISBN Prefix(es): 978-0-912183; 978-0-87703
Number of titles published annually: 10 Print; 6 CD-ROM
Total Titles: 363 Print
Distributor for Astronautical Society of Western Australia; US Space Foundation

Universal-Publishers Inc
200 Spectrum Center Dr, 3rd fl, Irvine, CA 92618-5004
SAN: 299-3635
Tel: 561-750-4344 *Toll Free Tel:* 800-636-8329 (US only) *Fax:* 561-750-6797
Web Site: www.universal-publishers.com
Key Personnel
Publr & CEO: Jeffrey R Young
Artistic & Edit Dir: Shereen Siddiqui, PhD
Founded: 1997
Dictionaries, encyclopedias, textbooks-all, university presses. Scholarly books, reprints, professional books, paperbacks, directories & reference books.
ISBN Prefix(es): 978-1-58112; 978-1-59942; 978-1-61233; 978-1-62734
Number of titles published annually: 60 Print; 50 E-Book
Total Titles: 1,500 Print; 1,000 E-Book
Imprints: Brown Walker Press; Dissertation.com
Distribution Center: Ingram Book Group, One Ingram Blvd, La Vergne, TN 37086 *Tel:* 615-793-5000 *Web Site:* www.ingramcontent.com
Bertrams, One Broadland Business Park, Norwich NR7 0WF, United Kingdom *E-mail:* books@bertrams.com *Web Site:* www.bertrams.com
See separate listing for:
Dissertation.com

Universe Publishing
Imprint of Rizzoli International Publications Inc
300 Park Ave S, 4th fl, New York, NY 10010
Tel: 212-387-3400 *Fax:* 212-387-3535
Web Site: www.rizzoliusa.com
Founded: 1990
Architecture, fine art, photography, illustrated gift books, fashion, culinary, popular culture, children's, design, style & calendars.
ISBN Prefix(es): 978-0-87663; 978-1-55550; 978-0-7893
Number of titles published annually: 60 Print
Imprints: Universe; Universe Calendars
Distributed by Random House
Foreign Rep(s): Angell Eurosales (Gill Angell & Stewart Siddall) (Scandinavia); Bill Bailey Publishers' Representatives (Austria, Benelux, France, Germany, Switzerland); David Bateman Ltd (New Zealand); Bookport Associates (Greece, Italy, Malta, Portugal, Spain); Michelle Curreri (Far East, Indian subcontinent, Southeast Asia); Hardie Grant Books (Australia); Marston Book Services Ltd (Europe, UK); Penguin Random House of Canada (Canada); Publishers Group UK (UK); Rizzoli International Publications (Jerry Hoffnagle) (Eastern Europe, Sub-Saharan Africa); SG Distributors (Giulietta Campanelli) (Botswana, Mozambique, Namibia, South Africa, Zimbabwe); Peter Ward Book Exports (Richard Ward) (Middle East, North Africa); Cynthia Zimpfer (Caribbean, Latin America)

University Council for Educational Administration (UCEA)
Michigan State University, College of Education, 620 Farm Lane, 432 Erickson Hall, East Lansing, MI 48824
Tel: 434-243-1041
E-mail: ucea@msu.edu
Web Site: www.ucea.org
Key Personnel
Exec Dir: Monica Byrne-Jimenez
    E-mail: mcbyrnej@iu.edu
Founded: 1947
Books, journals, monographs, newsletters.
ISBN Prefix(es): 978-1-55996
Number of titles published annually: 5 Print
Total Titles: 23 Print

University of Alabama Press
200 Hackberry Lane, 2nd fl, Tuscaloosa, AL 35487
Mailing Address: PO Box 870380, Tuscaloosa, AL 35487-0380
Tel: 205-348-5180 *Fax:* 205-348-9201
Web Site: www.uapress.ua.edu
Key Personnel
Dir: Linda Manning *Tel:* 205-348-1560
    E-mail: lmanning@uapress.ua.edu
Mktg Dir: Clint Kimberling *Tel:* 205-348-1566
    E-mail: ckimberling@uapress.ua.edu
Ed-in-Chief: Daniel Waterman *Tel:* 205-348-5538
    E-mail: dwaterman@uapress.ua.edu
Mng Ed: Vanessa Rusch *Tel:* 205-348-9708
    E-mail: vrusch@uapress.ua.edu
Busn Mgr: Rosalyn Carr *Tel:* 205-348-1567
    E-mail: rcarr@uapress.ua.edu
Prodn Mgr: W Richard Cook *Tel:* 205-348-1571
    E-mail: rcook@uapress.ua.edu
Rts & Perms Mgr: Claire Lewis Evans *Tel:* 205-348-1561 *E-mail:* levans@uapress.ua.edu
Sales Mgr: Kristi Henson *Tel:* 205-348-9534
    E-mail: khenson@uapress.ua.edu
Mktg Coord: Blanche Sarratt *Tel:* 205-348-3476
    E-mail: bsarratt@uapress.ua.edu
Founded: 1945
American & Latin American history & culture, religious & ethnohistory, rhetoric & communications, African American & Native American studies, Judaic studies, Southern regional studies, theatre & regional trade titles.
ISBN Prefix(es): 978-0-8173; 978-0-914590; 978-0-932511; 978-1-57366
Number of titles published annually: 70 Print; 25 E-Book
Total Titles: 1,200 Print; 100 E-Book
Imprints: Fiction Collective 2 (FC2)
Foreign Rep(s): Eurospan (Europe)
Orders to: Chicago Distribution Center, 11030 S Langley Ave, Chicago, IL 60628 *Tel:* 773-702-7000 *Toll Free Tel:* 800-621-2736 *Fax:* 773-702-7212 *Toll Free Fax:* 800-621-8476 SAN: 630-6047
Distribution Center: Chicago Distribution Center, 11030 S Langley Ave, Chicago, IL 60628 *Tel:* 773-702-7000 (orders) *Toll Free Tel:* 800-621-2736 (orders) *Fax:* 773-702-7212 *Toll Free Fax:* 800-621-8476 SAN: 630-6047
See separate listing for:
Fiction Collective Two Inc (FC2)

§University of Alaska Press
Elmer E Rasmuson Library, 1732 Tanana Loop, Suite 402, Fairbanks, AK 99775
Mailing Address: PO Box 756240, Fairbanks, AK 99775-6240 SAN: 203-3011
Tel: 907-474-5831 *Toll Free Tel:* 888-252-6657 (US only) *Fax:* 907-474-5502
Web Site: www.alaska.edu/uapress
Key Personnel
Dir & Acqs Ed: Nate Bauer *Tel:* 907-687-4453
    E-mail: nate.bauer@alaska.edu
Sales & Mktg Mgr: Laura Walker *E-mail:* laura.walker@alaska.edu

Prodn Ed: Krista West *Tel:* 907-474-6413
    E-mail: krista.west@alaska.edu
Founded: 1967
Emphasis on scholarly & nonfiction works related to Alaska, the circumpolar regions & the North Pacific rim.
ISBN Prefix(es): 978-0-912006; 978-1-889963; 978-1-60223
Number of titles published annually: 24 Print
Total Titles: 220 Print
Imprints: Alaska Literary Series; Alaska Writer Laureate Series; Classic Reprint Series; Geology & Geography of Alaska Series; Great Explorer Series; LanternLight Library; Literary Reprint Series; Oral Biography Series; Rasmuson Library Historical Translation Series; Snowy Owl Books
Distributor for Alaska Native Language Center; Alaska Quarterly Review; Alaska Sea Grant; Alutiiq Museum; Anchorage Museum Association; Anchorage Museum of Art History; Arctic Studies Center of the Smithsonian Museum; Far to the North Press; Geophysical Institute; Limestone Press; Spirit Mountain Press; UA Museum; Vanessapress
Distribution Center: Chicago Distribution Center, 11030 S Langley Ave, Chicago, IL 60628 *Toll Free Tel:* 800-621-2736 *Toll Free Fax:* 800-621-8476
Membership(s): Alaska History Association; Alaska Library Association; Association of University Presses (AUPresses); Independent Book Publishers Association (IBPA); Pacific Northwest Booksellers Association (PNBA)

The University of Arizona Press
1510 E University Blvd, Tucson, AZ 85721
SAN: 205-468X
Mailing Address: PO Box 210055, Tucson, AZ 85721-0055
Tel: 520-621-1441 *Toll Free Tel:* 800-426-3797 (orders) *Fax:* 520-621-8899 *Toll Free Fax:* 800-426-3797
E-mail: uap@uapress.arizona.edu
Web Site: www.uapress.arizona.edu
Key Personnel
Dir: Kathryn Conrad *E-mail:* kconrad@uapress.arizona.edu
Ed-in-Chief: Kristen Buckles *E-mail:* kbuckles@uapress.arizona.edu
Sr Ed: Dr Allyson Carter *E-mail:* allysonc@uapress.arizona.edu
Editing & Prodn Mgr: Amanda Krause
    E-mail: akrause@uapress.arizona.edu
Publicity Mgr: Rosemary Brandt *Tel:* 520-621-3920 *E-mail:* rbrandt@uapress.arizona.edu
Founded: 1959
Scholarly & regional nonfiction about Arizona, the American West & Mexico, Latino studies, Latin American studies, Native American studies, anthropology & environmental studies.
ISBN Prefix(es): 978-0-8165
Number of titles published annually: 55 Print
Total Titles: 783 Print
Foreign Rep(s): William Gills (Africa, Europe, Middle East); University of British Columbia Press (Canada)
Membership(s): American Association of University Presses (AAUP); Arizona Book Publishing Association; Publishers Association of the West (PubWest)

The University of Arkansas Press
Division of The University of Arkansas
McIlroy House, 105 N McIlroy Ave, Fayetteville, AR 72701
Tel: 479-575-7544
E-mail: info@uapress.com
Web Site: www.uapress.com
Key Personnel
Dir & Publr: Mike Bieker *Tel:* 479-575-3859
    E-mail: mbieker@uark.edu

Editor-in-Chief: David Scott Cunningham *Tel:* 479-575-5767 *E-mail:* dscunnin@uark.edu

Mng Ed: Janet Foxman *Tel:* 479-575-5295 *E-mail:* foxman@uark.edu

Ad & Communs Mgr: Charlie Shields *Tel:* 479-575-7258 *E-mail:* cmoss@uark.edu

Busn & Dist Servs Mgr: Sam Ridge *Tel:* 479-575-3858 *E-mail:* sridge@uark.edu

Mktg & Sales Mgr: Melissa King *Tel:* 479-575-7715 *E-mail:* mak001@uark.edu

Prodn Mgr: Liz Lester *Tel:* 479-575-6780 *E-mail:* lizl@uark.edu

Founded: 1980

General humanities: civil rights, poetry, sports, food, regional.

ISBN Prefix(es): 978-0-938626; 978-1-55728; 978-0-912456; 978-1-68226; 978-1-61075

Number of titles published annually: 20 Print

Total Titles: 620 Print; 150 E-Book

Distributor for Butler Center for Arkansas Studies; Moon City Press; Ozark Society

Foreign Rep(s): Eurospan Group (Africa, Asia-Pacific, Continental Europe, Middle East, UK); Scholarly Book Services (Bev Calder) (Canada)

Foreign Rights: Eurospan (Africa, Europe, Middle East, UK)

Distribution Center: Chicago Distribution Center, 11030 S Langley Ave, Chicago, IL 60628 *Tel:* 773-702-7000 *Toll Free Tel:* 800-621-2736 *Fax:* 773-702-7212 *E-mail:* orders@press.uchicago.edu

Membership(s): American Association of University Presses (AAUP)

University of California, ANR Publications, see ANR Publications University of California

§University of California Institute on Global Conflict & Cooperation

Subsidiary of University of California

9500 Gilman Dr, MC 0518, La Jolla, CA 92093-0518

Tel: 858-534-6106 *Fax:* 858-534-7655

E-mail: igcc-communications@ucsd.edu

Web Site: igcc.ucsd.edu

Key Personnel

Mng Ed: Lindsay Morgan *E-mail:* l2morgan@ucsd.edu

Founded: 1983

Policy briefs & newsletters, policy papers & books authored by members of the University of California faculty & other participants in sponsored research programs.

ISBN Prefix(es): 978-0-934637

Number of titles published annually: 2 Print

Total Titles: 74 Print; 60 E-Book

Distributed by The Brookings Institution Press; Columbia International Affairs Online (CIAO); Cornell University Press; Garland Publishers; Lynn-Reinner Publishing; Penn State University Press; Princeton University Press; Transaction Publishers Inc; University of Michigan Press; Westview Press

§University of California Press

155 Grand Ave, Suite 400, Oakland, CA 94612-3758

Tel: 510-883-8232 *Fax:* 510-836-8910

E-mail: generalmailbox@ucpress.edu

Web Site: www.ucpress.edu

Key Personnel

Exec Dir: Tim Sullivan *E-mail:* tsullivan@ucpress.edu

Art Dir: Lia Tjandra

Dir, Intellectual Property & Subs Rts: Clare Wellnitz *E-mail:* cwellnitz@ucpress.edu

Dir, Mktg & Sales: Elena McAnespia *E-mail:* emcanespie@ucpress.edu

Edit Dir: Kim Robinson *E-mail:* krobinson@ucpress.edu

Sr Acqs Ed: Michelle Lipinski *E-mail:* mlipinski@ucpress.edu

Acqs Ed: Stacy Eisenstark *E-mail:* seisenstark@ucpress.edu; Niels Hooper *E-mail:* nhooper@ucpress.edu; Reed Malcolm *E-mail:* rmalcolm@ucpress.edu; Kate Marshall *E-mail:* kmarshall@ucpress.edu; Archna Patel *E-mail:* apatel@ucpress.edu; Raina Polivka *E-mail:* rpolivka@ucpress.edu; Maura Roessner *E-mail:* mroessner@ucpress.edu; Eric A Schmidt *E-mail:* eschmidt@ucpress.edu; Naomi Schneider *E-mail:* nschneider@ucpress.edu

Founded: 1893

Trade nonfiction, scholarly & scientific nonfiction, translations & journals; paperbacks, limited fiction (reprints).

ISBN Prefix(es): 978-0-520

Number of titles published annually: 260 Print; 10 Online; 10 E-Book

Total Titles: 4,200 Print; 60 Online; 60 E-Book

Imprints: Ahmanson-Murphy (fine arts); The Atkinson Family Foundation (higher educ); The George Gund Foundation (African American studies); The Fletcher Jones Foundation (humanities); Philip E Lilienthal (Asian studies); Joan Palevsky (classical lit); Roth Family Foundation (music); A Naomi Schneider Book; Simpson (humanities); The S Mark Taper Foundation (Jewish studies)

Distributor for art-SITES; British Film Institute; Sierra Club Books (adult trade)

Foreign Rep(s): Avicenna Partnership Ltd (Claire De Gruchy) (Algeria, Cyprus, Israel, Jordan, Malta, Middle East, Morocco, North Africa, Palestine, Southeast Europe, Tunisia, Turkey); Avicenna Partnership Ltd (Bill Kennedy) (Bahrain, Egypt, Iran, Iraq, Kuwait, Lebanon, Libya, Oman, Qatar, Saudi Arabia, Syria, United Arab Emirates, Yemen); B K Agency Ltd (Chiafeng Peng) (Brunei, Cambodia, Indonesia, Laos, Malaysia, Myanmar, Philippines, Singapore, Taiwan, Thailand, Vietnam); Everest International Publishing Service (Wei Zhao) (China); ICK (Information & Culture Korea) (Se-Yung Jun) (South Korea); Penguin Random House India Pvt Ltd (Rajeev Das) (Bangladesh, Bhutan, India, Nepal, Pakistan, Sri Lanka); Rockbook (Gilles Fauveau & Ayako Owada) (Hong Kong, Japan); US PubRep (Craig Falk) (Caribbean, Central America, Mexico, South America); Kelvin Van Hasselt (Africa exc North & South Africa)

Advertising Agency: Fiat Lux

Orders to: Ingram Publisher Services, One Ingram Blvd, La Vergne, TN 37086 (CN & US) *Toll Free Tel:* 866-400-5351 *E-mail:* ips@ingramcontent.com *Web Site:* www.ingramcontent.com; Wiley Australia, PO Box 1226, Milton, Qld 4064, Australia (Australia & New Zealand) *Tel:* (07) 3859 9611 *Fax:* (07) 3859 9626 *E-mail:* custservice@wiley.com *Web Site:* www.wiley.com/en-au/contactus; John Wiley & Sons Ltd, LEC-1 New Era Estates, Oldlands Way, Bognor Regis, West Sussex PO22 9NQ (Africa, Europe, India & Middle East) *Tel:* (01243) 843291 *Fax:* (01243) 843302 *E-mail:* customer@wiley.co.uk *Web Site:* www.upguk.com

Returns: Ingram Customer Returns Center, 1210 Ingram Dr, Chambersburg, PA 17202

Membership(s): Association of American Publishers (AAP)

University of Chicago Press

1427 E 60 St, Chicago, IL 60637-2954

SAN: 202-5280

Tel: 773-702-7700; 773-702-7600

Toll Free Tel: 800-621-2736 (orders) *Fax:* 773-702-9756; 773-660-2235 (orders); 773-702-2708

E-mail: custserv@press.uchicago.edu; marketing@press.uchicago.edu

Web Site: www.press.uchicago.edu

Key Personnel

Dir: Garrett P Kiely *Tel:* 773-702-8878 *E-mail:* gkiely@uchicago.edu

Deputy Dir: Christopher Heiser *Tel:* 773-702-2998 *E-mail:* cheiser@uchicago.edu

Edit Dir, Humanities & Sci: Alan G Thomas *Tel:* 773-702-7644 *E-mail:* athomas2@uchicago.edu

Dir, Intellectual Property: Laura Leichum *Tel:* 773-702-6096 *E-mail:* lleichum@uchicago.edu

Dir, IT: Patti O'Shea *Tel:* 773-702-8521 *E-mail:* poshea@uchicago.edu

Dir, Journals: Ashley Towne *Tel:* 773-753-4241 *E-mail:* atowne@uchicago.edu

Mktg Dir, Books Div: Levi Stahl

Promos & Mktg Communs Dir, Books Div: Carrie Olivia Adams

Asst Edit Dir: Charles Myers *Tel:* 773-702-7648 *E-mail:* myersc@uchicago.edu

Exec Ed: Susan Bielstein *Tel:* 773-702-7633 *E-mail:* smb1@uchicago.edu

Exec Ed, American History, Urban Studies & Regl Titles: Timothy Mennel *Tel:* 773-702-0158 *E-mail:* tmennel@uchicago.edu

Exec Ed, Economics, Busn & Public Policy: Chad Zimmerman

Exec Ed, Sci Studies: Karen Merikangas Darling *Tel:* 773-702-7641 *E-mail:* darling@uchicago.edu

Sr Ed, Educ, Jazz & Sociology: Elizabeth Branch Dyson *Tel:* 773-702-7637 *E-mail:* ebd@uchicago.edu

Sr Ed, Ref & Writing Guides: Mary Laur *Tel:* 773-702-7326 *E-mail:* mlaur@uchicago.edu

Sr Ed, Sciences: Joseph Calamia

Ed: Marta Tonegutti *Tel:* 773-702-0427 *E-mail:* mtonegut@uchicago.edu

Ed, Economics, Busn & Fin: Jane Macdonald *Tel:* 773-702-7638 *E-mail:* janem@uchicago.edu

Ed, Life Sciences: Scott Gast *Tel:* 773-702-2705 *E-mail:* sgast@uchicago.edu

Pbk Ed: Maggie Hivnor *Tel:* 773-702-7649 *E-mail:* mhivnorl@uchicago.edu

Assoc Ed, Cartography, Geography & Life Sciences: Rachel Kelly Unger

Assoc Ed, Philosophy, Religious Studies & Rhetoric: Kyle Wagner

Asst Ed: Randolph Petilos *Tel:* 773-702-7647 *E-mail:* rpetilos@uchicago.edu

UK Ed-at-Large: James Attlee

Intl Rts Mgr, Books: Beatrice Bourgogne *Tel:* 773-702-7741 *E-mail:* bbourgogne@uchicago.edu

Asst to Dir: Ellen Zalewski *Tel:* 773-702-8879 *E-mail:* emz1@uchicago.edu

Founded: 1891

Scholarly, nonfiction, advanced texts, monographs, clothbound & paperback, scholarly & professional journals, reference books & atlases.

ISBN Prefix(es): 978-0-226

Number of titles published annually: 250 Print

Total Titles: 5,400 Print; 1 E-Book

Foreign Rep(s): Academic Book Promotions (Benelux, France, Scandinavia); The American University Press Group (Hong Kong, Japan, Korea, Taiwan); Thomas Cassidy (China); Ewa Ledochowicz (Eastern Europe); Uwe Ludemann (Austria, Germany, Italy, Switzerland); Mediamatics (India); Publishers Marketing & Research Associates (Caribbean, Latin America); Arie Ruitenbeek (Portugal, Spain); The University Press Group (Australia, Canada, New Zealand); University Presses Marketing (Greece, Ireland, Israel, UK); Yale Representation Ltd (UK)

Distribution Center: Chicago Distribution Center (CDC), 11030 S Langley Ave, Chicago, IL 60628 *Toll Free Fax:* 800-621-8476 (US & CN)

John Wiley & Sons Ltd, European Dist Ctr, New Era Estate, Oldlands Way, Bognor Regis, West Sussex PO22 9NQ, United Kingdom *Tel:* (01243) 779777 *Fax:* (01243) 820250 *E-mail:* cs-books@wiley.co.uk
Membership(s): American Association of University Presses (AAUP); Association of American Publishers (AAP)

University of Delaware Press
200A Morris Library, 181 S College Ave, Newark, DE 19717-5267
Tel: 302-831-1149 *Fax:* 302-831-6549
E-mail: ud-press@udel.edu
Web Site: library.udel.edu/udpress
Key Personnel
Dir: Julia Oestreich *E-mail:* joestrei@udel.edu
Founded: 1922
Literary studies, especially Shakespeare, Renaissance & early modern literature; 18th century studies, French literature, art history & history & cultural studies of Delaware & the Eastern Shore.
Ms editorial, design & production services are provided by the University of Virginia Press.
ISBN Prefix(es): 978-0-87413; 978-1-61149
Number of titles published annually: 37 Print
Total Titles: 1,053 Print
Distribution Center: Longleaf Services, 116 S Boundary St, Chapel Hill, NC 27514-3808 *Toll Free Tel:* 800-848-6224 *E-mail:* orders@longleafservices.org *Web Site:* www.longleafservices.org
Quantum Publishing Solutions Ltd, 2 Cheviot Rd, Paisley PA2 8AN, United Kingdom *Tel:* (07702) 831967
Durnell Marketing Ltd, 2 Linden Close, Tunbridge Wells TN4 8HH, United Kingdom (Europe including Ireland) *Tel:* (01892) 544272 *Fax:* (01892) 511152 *E-mail:* orders@durnell.co.uk

University of Georgia Press
Main Library, 3rd fl, 320 S Jackson St, Athens, GA 30602
Fax: 706-542-2558; 706-542-6770
Web Site: www.ugapress.org
Key Personnel
Dir: Lisa Bayer *Tel:* 706-542-0027 *E-mail:* lbayer@uga.edu
Dir, Mktg & Digital Initiatives: David E Des Jardines *Tel:* 706-542-9758 *E-mail:* ddesjard@uga.edu
Dir, Mktg & Sales: Steven Wallace
Asst Dir for Acqs & Ed-in-Chief: Mick Gusinde-Duffy *Tel:* 706-542-9907 *E-mail:* mickgd@uga.edu
Asst Dir for Edit, Design & Prodn: Jon Davies *Tel:* 706-542-2101 *E-mail:* jdavies@uga.edu
Busn Mgr: Phyllis Wells *Tel:* 706-542-7250 *E-mail:* pwells@uga.edu
Asst Edit, Design & Prodn Mgr: Melissa Buchanan *Tel:* 706-542-4488 *E-mail:* melissa.buchanan@uga.edu
Founded: 1938
Publisher of scholarly works, creative & literary works, regional works & digital projects.
ISBN Prefix(es): 978-0-8203
Number of titles published annually: 70 Print; 60 E-Book
Total Titles: 2,000 Print; 600 E-Book
Imprints: Milestone Press
Foreign Rep(s): Eurospan Group (worldwide exc Canada & USA)
Orders to: Longleaf Services Inc, 116 S Boundary St, Chapel Hill, NC 27514-3808 *Tel:* 919-966-7449 *Toll Free Tel:* 800-848-6224 *Fax:* 919-962-2704 *Toll Free Fax:* 800-272-6817 *E-mail:* orders@longleafservices.org *Web Site:* www.longleafservices.org
Returns: Longleaf Services - Returns, c/o Ingram Publisher Services, 1250 Ingram Dr,

Chambersburg, PA 17202 *E-mail:* credit@longleafservices.org
Shipping Address: Longleaf Services Inc, 116 S Boundary St, Chapel Hill, NC 27514-3808 *Tel:* 919-966-7449 *Toll Free Tel:* 800-848-6224 *Fax:* 919-962-2704 *Toll Free Fax:* 800-272-6817 *E-mail:* customerservice@longleafservices.org *Web Site:* www.longleafservices.org
Warehouse: Longleaf Services Inc, 116 S Boundary St, Chapel Hill, NC 27514-3808 *Tel:* 919-966-7449 *Toll Free Tel:* 800-848-6224 *Fax:* 919-962-2704 *Toll Free Fax:* 800-272-6817 *E-mail:* customerservice@longleafservices.org *Web Site:* www.longleafservices.org
Membership(s): Association of University Presses (AUPresses)

University of Hawaii Press
2840 Kolowalu St, Honolulu, HI 96822-1888
SAN: 202-5353
Tel: 808-956-8255 *Toll Free Tel:* 888-UHPRESS (847-7377) *Fax:* 808-988-6052 *Toll Free Fax:* 800-650-7811
E-mail: uhpbooks@hawaii.edu
Web Site: www.uhpress.hawaii.edu
Key Personnel
Interim Dir, Publr & CFO: Joel Cosseboom *E-mail:* cosseboo@hawaii.edu
Exec Ed: Pamela Kelley *Tel:* 808-956-6207 *E-mail:* pkelley@hawaii.edu
Mng Ed: Cheryl Loe *Tel:* 808-956-8276 *E-mail:* cheryl.loe@hawaii.edu; Grace Wen *Tel:* 808-956-8834 *E-mail:* gracewen@hawaii.edu
Acqs Ed: Stephanie Chun *Tel:* 808-956-8695 *E-mail:* chuns@hawaii.edu; Masako Ikeda *Tel:* 808-956-8696 *E-mail:* masakoi@hawaii.edu
Design & Prodn Mgr: Santos Barbasa *Tel:* 808-956-8277 *E-mail:* barbasa@hawaii.edu
Digital Mktg Mgr: Blaine Tolentino *Tel:* 808-956-4262 *E-mail:* blainemt@hawaii.edu
Digital Publg Mgr: Trond Knutsen *Tel:* 808-956-6227 *E-mail:* tknutsen@hawaii.edu
Journals Mgr: Pamela Wilson *Tel:* 808-956-6790 *E-mail:* pwilson6@hawaii.edu
Prod Mgr: Steve Hirashima *Tel:* 808-956-8698 *E-mail:* stevehir@hawaii.edu
Promo Mgr: Carol Abe *Tel:* 808-956-8697 *E-mail:* abec@hawaii.edu
Sales, E-Web & Prod Mgr: Royden Muranaka *Tel:* 808-956-6214 *E-mail:* royden@hawaii.edu
IT Specialist: Collin Wong *Tel:* 808-956-6209 *E-mail:* cwong808@hawaii.edu
Founded: 1947
Scholarly & general books & monographs, particularly those dealing with the Pacific & Asia; regional books; journals.
ISBN Prefix(es): 978-0-8248; 978-0-87022
Number of titles published annually: 70 Print; 100 E-Book
Total Titles: 1,500 Print; 1,500 E-Book
Imprints: Kolowalu Books; Latitude 20
Distributor for Ai Pohaku Press; Asian Civilisations Museum; Ateneo De Manila University Press; BDK America; College of Tropical Agriculture & Human Resources; Denby Fawcett; Hawaii Nikkei; Hawaiian Mission Children's Society; Hui Hanai; Huia Publishers; Institute of Buddhist Studies; iPRECIATION; Island Research & Education Initiative; Isle Botanica; Japan Playwrights Association; Kailua Historical Society; Kalamaku Press; Kanji Press; Korea Institute, Harvard University; Levesque Publications; Little Island Press; The Lontar Foundation; Manoa Heritage Center; MerwinAsia; The Mozhai Foundation; Jonathan Napela Center, Brigham Young University-Hawaii; Native Books; NIAS Press; North Beach-West Maui Benefit Fund Inc; Ocarina Books; Permanent Agriculture Re-

sources; Punahou School; Renaissance Books; Seoul Selection; Shanghai Press & Publishing Development Co; Richard F Taitano Micronesia Area Research Center; Three Pines Press; University of the Philippines Press
Foreign Rep(s): The Eurospan Group (Africa, Continental Europe, Middle East, UK); Scholarly Book Services Inc (Canada)
Membership(s): American Association of University Presses (AAUP)

University of Illinois Press
Unit of University of Illinois
1325 S Oak St, MC-566, Champaign, IL 61820-6903
SAN: 202-5310
Tel: 217-333-0950 *Fax:* 217-244-8082
E-mail: uipress@uillinois.edu; journals@uillinois.edu
Web Site: www.press.uillinois.edu
Key Personnel
Dir & Ed-in-Chief: Laurie Matheson *Tel:* 217-244-4685 *E-mail:* lmatheso@uillinois.edu
Art Dir: Dustin Hubbart *Tel:* 217-333-9227 *E-mail:* dhubbart@uillinois.edu
Direct Mktg & Ad Mgr: Denise Peeler *Tel:* 217-244-4690 *E-mail:* dpeeler@uillinois.edu
Edit Design & Prodn Mgr: Jennifer Comeau *Tel:* 217-244-3279 *E-mail:* jlcomeau@uillinois.edu
Exhibits Mgr: Margo Chaney *Tel:* 217-244-6491 *E-mail:* mechaney@uillinois.edu
Journals Mgr: Clydette Wantland *Tel:* 217-244-6496 *E-mail:* cwantland@uillinois.edu
Mktg & Sales Mgr: Michael Roux *Tel:* 217-244-4683 *E-mail:* mroux@uillinois.edu
Prodn Mgr: Kristine Ding *Tel:* 217-244-4701 *E-mail:* kding@uillinois.edu
Publicity Mgr: Heather Gernenz *Tel:* 217-244-4689 *E-mail:* gernenz2@illinois.edu
Founded: 1918
Working-class & ethnic studies, religion, architecture, film studies, communication & media studies, political science, folklore, Chicago, food studies, immigration studies, American history, women's history, music history, regional history, sport history, gender & sexuality studies.
ISBN Prefix(es): 978-0-252
Number of titles published annually: 90 Print
Total Titles: 2,400 Print; 10 Online; 1,100 E-Book
Foreign Rep(s): B K Norton Ltd (Canada); Combined Academic Publishers Ltd (Africa, China, Europe, Middle East, UK); Footprint (Australia); B K Norton Ltd (Hong Kong, Korea, Taiwan); US PubRep (Caribbean including Puerto Rico, Mexico, South America)
Orders to: Chicago Distribution Center, 11030 S Langley Ave, Chicago, IL 60628 *Tel:* 773-702-7000 *Toll Free Tel:* 800-621-2736 *Fax:* 773-702-7212 *Toll Free Fax:* 800-621-8476 *E-mail:* orders@press.uchicago.edu
Returns: Chicago Distribution Center, 11030 S Langley Ave, Chicago, IL 60628 *Tel:* 773-702-7000 *Toll Free Tel:* 800-621-2736 *Fax:* 773-702-7212 *Toll Free Fax:* 800-621-8476 *E-mail:* orders@press.uchicago.edu
Warehouse: Chicago Distribution Center, 11030 S Langley Ave, Chicago, IL 60628 *Tel:* 773-702-7000 *Toll Free Tel:* 800-621-2736 *Fax:* 773-702-7212 *Toll Free Fax:* 800-621-8476 *E-mail:* orders@press.uchicago.edu
Membership(s): Association of American Publishers (AAP); Association of University Presses (AUPresses)

University of Iowa Press
119 W Park Rd, 100 Kuhl House, Iowa City, IA 52242-1000
SAN: 282-4868

Tel: 319-335-2000 *Toll Free Tel:* 800-621-2736 (orders only) *Fax:* 319-335-2055 *Toll Free Fax:* 800-621-8476 (orders only)
E-mail: uipress@uiowa.edu
Web Site: www.uipress.uiowa.edu
Key Personnel
Dir: James McCoy *Tel:* 319-335-2013 *E-mail:* james-mccoy@uiowa.edu
Assoc Dir/Design & Prodn Mgr: Karen Copp *Tel:* 319-335-2014 *E-mail:* karen-copp@uiowa.edu
Mktg Dir: Allison T Means *Tel:* 319-335-3440 *E-mail:* allison-means@uiowa.edu
Mng Ed: Susan Hill Newton *Tel:* 319-335-2011 *E-mail:* susan-hillnewton@uiowa.edu
Acqs Ed: Meredith Stabel *Tel:* 319-335-2012 *E-mail:* meredith-stabel@uiowa.edu
Off Mgr: Angie Dickey *Tel:* 319-335-3424 *E-mail:* angela-dickey@uiowa.edu
Rts & Perms Mgr: Suzanne Glemot *Tel:* 319-335-2008
Founded: 1969
Poetry, short fiction & creative nonfiction. As the only university press in the state, Iowa is also dedicated to preserving the literature, history, culture, wildlife & natural areas of the Midwest.
ISBN Prefix(es): 978-0-87745; 978-1-58729; 978-1-60938
Number of titles published annually: 35 Print; 35 E-Book
Total Titles: 800 Print
Foreign Rep(s): Eurospan Group (Africa, Asia, Australia, Europe, Middle East, UK)
Orders to: Chicago Distribution Center, 11030 S Langley Ave, Chicago, IL 60628 *Tel:* 773-702-7010 *Toll Free Tel:* 800-621-2736 *Fax:* 773-660-2235 *Toll Free Fax:* 800-621-8476 *E-mail:* orders@press.uchicago.edu
Returns: Chicago Distribution Center, 11030 S Langley Ave, Chicago, IL 60628 *Tel:* 773-702-7010 *Toll Free Tel:* 800-621-2736 *Fax:* 773-660-2235 *Toll Free Fax:* 800-621-8476 *E-mail:* orders@press.uchicago.edu
Distribution Center: Chicago Distribution Center, 11030 S Langley Ave, Chicago, IL 60628 *Tel:* 773-702-7010 *Toll Free Tel:* 800-621-2736 *Fax:* 773-660-2235 *Toll Free Fax:* 800-621-8476 *E-mail:* orders@press.uchicago.edu
Membership(s): American Association of University Presses (AAUP)

University of Louisiana at Lafayette Press
PO Box 43558, Lafayette, LA 70504-3558
Tel: 337-482-6027
E-mail: press.submissions@louisiana.edu
Web Site: ulpress.org
Key Personnel
Publr & Dir: Dr Joshua Caffery
Mng Ed: Devon Lord
Prodn Mgr: Mary Duhe
Sales & Mktg Mgr: Somer Greer
Founded: 1973
Publish titles on Louisiana culture & history.
ISBN Prefix(es): 978-0-940984; 978-1-887366; 978-1-935754; 978-1-946160
Number of titles published annually: 12 Print; 5 E-Book
Total Titles: 200 Print; 25 E-Book
Shipping Address: 302 E Saint Mary Blvd, Lafayette, LA 70504

University of Massachusetts Press
East Experiment Station, 671 N Pleasant St, Amherst, MA 01003
Tel: 413-545-2217 *Fax:* 413-545-1226
E-mail: info@umpress.umass.edu
Web Site: www.umass.edu/umpress
Key Personnel
Dir: Mary V Dougherty *Tel:* 413-545-4990 *E-mail:* mvd@umpress.umass.edu
Busn Mgr: Yvonne Crevier *Tel:* 413-545-4994 *E-mail:* ycrevier@umpress.umass.edu

Exec Ed: Matt Becker *Tel:* 413-545-4989 *E-mail:* mbecker@umpress.umass.edu
Sr Ed: Brian Halley *Tel:* 617-287-5610 *E-mail:* brian.halley@umb.edu
Mktg Mgr: Courtney J Andree *E-mail:* cjandree@umpress.umass.edu
Assoc Prodn Mgr & Design: Sally Nichols *Tel:* 413-545-4997 *E-mail:* snichols@umpress.umass.edu
Founded: 1963
Scholarly works & serious nonfiction, including African American studies, American history, American studies, architecture & landscape design, disability studies, environmental studies, gender studies, history of the book, journalism & media studies, literary & cultural studies, Native American studies, technology studies, urban studies & books of regional interest.
ISBN Prefix(es): 978-0-87023; 978-1-55849; 978-1-62534
Number of titles published annually: 40 Print; 35 E-Book
Total Titles: 1,000 Print; 400 E-Book
Foreign Rep(s): Eurospan (Africa, Europe, Middle East, UK)
Distribution Center: HFS, PO Box 50370, Baltimore, MD 21211-4370 *Tel:* 410-516-6965 *Toll Free Tel:* 800-537-5487 (US & CN) *Fax:* 410-516-6998 *E-mail:* hfscustserv@press.jhu.edu *Web Site:* hfs.jhu.edu
Brunswick Books, 20 Maud St, Suite 303, Toronto, ON M5V 2M5, Canada *Tel:* 416-703-3598 *Fax:* 416-703-6561 *E-mail:* orders@brunswickbooks.ca *Web Site:* www.brunswickbooks.ca
Membership(s): Association of University Presses (AUPresses)

University of Michigan Press
Unit of University of Michigan
839 Greene St, Ann Arbor, MI 48104-3209
SAN: 202-5329
Tel: 734-764-4388 *Fax:* 734-615-1540
E-mail: um.press@umich.edu
Web Site: www.press.umich.edu
Key Personnel
Dir: Charles Watkinson
Founded: 1930
Aims for diversity in its books & in its audiences.
ISBN Prefix(es): 978-0-472
Number of titles published annually: 110 Print; 100 E-Book
Total Titles: 3,500 Print
Distributor for Center for Chinese Studies, University of Michigan; Center for Japanese Studies, University of Michigan; Center for South & Southeast Asian Studies, University of Michigan
Foreign Rep(s): Eurospan (Europe)
Foreign Rights: University of Chicago Press
Returns: Chicago Distribution Center (CDC), 11030 S Langley Ave, Chicago, IL 60628 *Toll Free Tel:* 800-621-2736 *Toll Free Fax:* 800-621-8476 *E-mail:* orders@press.uchicago.edu
Distribution Center: Chicago Distribution Center (CDC), 11030 S Langley Ave, Chicago, IL 60628 *Toll Free Tel:* 800-621-2736 *Toll Free Fax:* 800-621-8476 *E-mail:* orders@press.uchicago.edu

University of Minnesota Press
Unit of University of Minnesota
111 Third Ave S, Suite 290, Minneapolis, MN 55401-2520
SAN: 213-2648
Tel: 612-301-1990 *Fax:* 612-301-1980
E-mail: ump@umn.edu
Web Site: www.upress.umn.edu
Key Personnel
Dir: Doug Armato
Edit Dir: Jason Weidemann
Assoc Dir: Susan Doerr
Asst Dir, Book Div & Mktg Dir: Emily Hamilton

Mng Ed: Laura Westlund
Regl Ed: Erik Anderson
Prodn Mgr: Daniel Ochsner
Sales Mgr: Matt Smiley
Direct Mail: Maggie Sattler
Intl Rts & Perms: Jeff Moen
Publicist: Heather Skinner
Founded: 1925
Recognized internationally for its innovative, boundary-breaking editorial program in the humanities & social sciences & as publisher of the Minnesota Multiphasic Personality Inventory (MMPI), the most widely used objective tests of personality in the world. Minnesota also maintains as part of its mission a strong commitment to publishing books on the people, history & natural environment of Minnesota & the upper Midwest.
Among the founding members of the Association of University Presses (AUPresses).
ISBN Prefix(es): 978-0-8166; 978-1-4529
Number of titles published annually: 110 Print; 95 E-Book
Total Titles: 3,360 Print; 2,899 E-Book
Distributor for Univocal Publishing
Foreign Rep(s): Combined Academic Publishers (Africa, Asia exc Japan, Europe, Middle East, UK); Lexa Publishers (Canada); NewSouth Books (Australia, New Zealand); United Publishers Services Ltd (Japan)
Returns: Chicago Distribution Center, 11030 S Langley Ave, Chicago, IL 60628
Shipping Address: Chicago Distribution Center, 11030 S Langley Ave, Chicago, IL 60628 *Tel:* 773-568-1550 *Toll Free Tel:* 800-621-2736 (orders only) *Toll Free Fax:* 800-621-8476 (orders only)
Warehouse: Chicago Distribution Center, 11030 S Langley Ave, Chicago, IL 60628 *Tel:* 773-702-7000 *Toll Free Tel:* 800-621-2736 *Fax:* 773-702-7212 *Toll Free Fax:* 800-621-8476
Membership(s): Association of American Publishers (AAP); Association of University Presses (AUPresses); Crossref; Minnesota Book Publishers Roundtable

University of Missouri Press
113 Heinkel Bldg, 201 S Seventh St, Columbia, MO 65211
SAN: 203-3143
Tel: 573-882-7641; 573-882-3000 (publicity & sales enquiries) *Toll Free Tel:* 800-621-2736 (orders) *Fax:* 573-884-4498 *Toll Free Fax:* 800-621-8476 (orders)
E-mail: upress@missouri.edu; umpmarketing@missouri.edu (publicity & sales enquiries)
Web Site: upress.missouri.edu
Key Personnel
Dir: David M Rosenbaum *Tel:* 573-882-9478 *E-mail:* rosenbaumd@missouri.edu
Ed-in-Chief: Andrew J Davidson *Tel:* 573-882-9997 *E-mail:* davidsonaj@missouri.edu
Acqs Ed: Gary Kass *Tel:* 573-823-0813 *E-mail:* kassg@missouri.edu
Assoc Acqs Ed: Mary Conley *Tel:* 602-430-7802 *E-mail:* conleyms@missouri.edu
Busn Mgr: Tracy Tritschler *Tel:* 573-882-9459 *E-mail:* tritschlert@missouri.edu
Sales & Mktg Mgr: Ms Robin Rennison *Tel:* 573-882-9672 *E-mail:* rennisonr@missouri.edu
EDP Coord: Drew Griffith *Tel:* 573-882-3044 *E-mail:* griffithd@missouri.edu
Mktg Coord: Deanna Davis *E-mail:* davisdea@missouri.edu
Mktg Asst: Megan Casey *E-mail:* caseymg@missouri.edu
Founded: 1958
Scholarly books, general trade, art, regional, intellectual thought, history, literary criticism, African-American, journalism, political science, sports & women's studies. Also publishes original works by, for & about Missourians.
ISBN Prefix(es): 978-0-8262
Number of titles published annually: 14 Print

Total Titles: 900 Print
Distributor for Missouri History Museum; Missouri Life Magazine; St Louis Mercantile Library
Foreign Rep(s): The Eurospan Group (Africa, Europe, Middle East); RTM Asia-Pacific Book Marketing (Asia, Australia, New Zealand, Pacific Islands)
Orders to: Chicago Distribution Center, 11030 S Langley Ave, Chicago, IL 60628
E-mail: orders@press.uchicago.edu

University of Nebraska Press
Division of University of Nebraska at Lincoln
1111 Lincoln Mall, Lincoln, NE 68588-0630
Tel: 402-472-3581; 919-966-7449 (cust serv & foreign orders) *Toll Free Tel:* 800-848-6224 (cust serv & US orders) *Fax:* 402-472-6214; 919-962-2704 (cust serv & foreign orders) *Toll Free Fax:* 800-526-2617 (cust serv & US orders)
E-mail: pressmail@unl.edu
Web Site: www.nebraskapress.unl.edu
Key Personnel
Dir: Donna Shear *Tel:* 402-472-2861
E-mail: dshear2@unl.edu
Ed-in-Chief: Bridget Barry *E-mail:* bbarry2@unl.edu
Publicity Mgr: Rosemary Vestal *Tel:* 402-472-7710 *E-mail:* rvestal2@unl.edu
Rts & Perms, Intl Rts: Leif Milliken *Tel:* 402-472-7702 *E-mail:* lmilliken2@unl.edu
Founded: 1941
General scholarly nonfiction, including anthropology, sports history, literature & criticism, history of the Trans-Mississippi West.
ISBN Prefix(es): 978-0-8032
Number of titles published annually: 150 Print; 150 E-Book
Total Titles: 4,000 Print; 1,000 E-Book
Imprints: Bison Books; Potomac Books
Distributor for Buros Institute; Society for American Baseball Research
Foreign Rep(s): Ampersand (Canada); Combined Academic Publishers Ltd (Europe)
Advertising Agency: Scholarly Press Advertising Services
Warehouse: Longleaf Services Inc, c/o Ingram Publisher Services, 1250 Ingram Dr, Chambersburg, PA 17202
Distribution Center: Longleaf Services Inc, 116 S Boundary St, Chapel Hill, NC 27514-3808 *Tel:* 919-966-7449 *Toll Free Tel:* 800-848-6224 *Fax:* 919-962-2704 *Toll Free Fax:* 800-272-6817 *E-mail:* customerservice@longleafservices.org *Web Site:* www.longleafservices.org
Membership(s): American Association of University Presses (AAUP)
See separate listing for:
Potomac Books

University of Nevada Press
c/o University of Nevada, Continuing Educ Bldg, MS 0166, Reno, NV 89557-0166
SAN: 203-316X
Tel: 775-784-6573 *Fax:* 775-784-6200
Web Site: www.unpress.nevada.edu
Key Personnel
Mktg & Sales Mgr: Sara Hendricksen *Tel:* 775-682-7395 *E-mail:* shendricksen@unpress.nevada.edu
Edit, Design & Prodn Mgr: Alrica Goldstein *Tel:* 775-682-7390 *E-mail:* alricag@unpress.nevada.edu
Busn Mgr: JoAnne Banducci *Tel:* 775-682-7387 *E-mail:* jbanducci@unpress.nevada.edu
Mktg Asst: Iris Saltus *Tel:* 775-682-7394 *E-mail:* isaltus@unpress.nevada.edu
Founded: 1961
ISBN Prefix(es): 978-0-87417; 978-1-948908; 978-1-943859

Number of titles published annually: 20 Print; 20 E-Book
Total Titles: 400 Print
Foreign Rep(s): Eurospan University Press Group (Africa, Central America, Europe, Middle East, South America, UK)
Orders to: Chicago Distribution Center, 11030 S Langley Ave, Chicago, IL 60628 *Toll Free Tel:* 800-621-2736 *Toll Free Fax:* 800-621-8476 *E-mail:* custserv@press.uchicago.edu
Warehouse: Chicago Distribution Center, 11030 S Langley Ave, Chicago, IL 60628 *Toll Free Tel:* 800-621-2736 *Toll Free Fax:* 800-621-8476 *E-mail:* custserv@press.uchicago.edu
Membership(s): American Association of University Presses (AAUP); Publishers Association of the West (PubWest)

University of New Mexico Press
One University of New Mexico, Albuquerque, NM 87131-0001
SAN: 213-9588
Mailing Address: MSC05 3185, One University of New Mexico, Albuquerque, NM 87131-0001
Tel: 505-272-7777 *Fax:* 505-277-3343
E-mail: custserv@unm.edu (order dept)
Web Site: unmpress.com
Key Personnel
Dir: Stephen Hull *Tel:* 505-277-3280
E-mail: sphull@unm.edu
Sr Acqs Ed: Elise M McHugh *Tel:* 505-277-3327 *E-mail:* elisemc@unm.edu; Michael Millman *Tel:* 505-277-3284 *E-mail:* mmillman@unm.edu
Sr Ed: Alexandra Hoff *Tel:* 505-277-3436
E-mail: aewhoff@unm.edu
Edit, Design & Prodn Mgr: James Ayers *Tel:* 505-277-3324 *E-mail:* ayers@unm.edu
Mktg & Sales Mgr: Katherine White *Tel:* 505-277-3294 *E-mail:* kwhite03@unm.edu
Sr Book Designer: Felicia Cedillos *Tel:* 505-277-3322 *E-mail:* fcedillo@unm.edu; Mindy Hill *Tel:* 505-277-3333 *E-mail:* mindybasingerhill@unm.edu
Acqs Coord & Ebook Prodn Ed: Sonia Dickey *Tel:* 505-277-3297 *E-mail:* soniad@unm.edu
Founded: 1929
General, scholarly & regional books, Latin American studies & native studies.
ISBN Prefix(es): 978-0-8263
Number of titles published annually: 75 Print
Total Titles: 1,750 Print
Foreign Rep(s): Eurospan Ltd (Africa, Asia, Australia, Europe, Middle East, New Zealand, UK); UBC Press (Canada); US PubRep (Craig Falk) (Caribbean, Latin America, Mexico, Puerto Rico)
Distribution Center: Longleaf Services Inc, 116 S Boundary St, Chapel Hill, NC 27514-3808 *Tel:* 919-966-7449 *Toll Free Tel:* 800-848-6224 *Fax:* 919-962-2704 *Toll Free Fax:* 800-272-6817 *E-mail:* orders@longleafservices.org *Web Site:* www.longleafservices.org
Membership(s): Association of University Presses (AUPresses)

University of New Orleans Press
Division of University of New Orleans
2000 Lakeshore Dr, New Orleans, LA 70148
Tel: 504-280-7457
E-mail: unopress@uno.edu
Web Site: www.uno.edu/unopress
Key Personnel
Ed-in-Chief: Abram Shalom Himelstein
Mng Ed: George Darby
Ed: Chelsey Shannon
Book Designer: Alex Dimeff
Sales: Ann Hackett
Founded: 2003
ISBN Prefix(es): 978-0-9728143; 978-0-9706190; 978-1-60801
Number of titles published annually: 4 Print; 3 E-Book

Total Titles: 40 Print; 3 E-Book
Distribution Center: Hopkins Fulfillment Services (HFS), PO Box 50370, Baltimore, MD 21211-4370 *Tel:* 410-516-6965 *Toll Free Tel:* 800-537-5487 *Fax:* 410-516-6998 *E-mail:* hfscustserv@press.jhu.edu *Web Site:* hfs.jhu.edu
Brunswick Books, 14 Afton Ave, Toronto, ON M6J 1R7, Canada *Tel:* 416-703-3598 *Fax:* 416-703-6561 *E-mail:* orders@brunswickbooks.ca *Web Site:* www.brunswickbooks.ca
Membership(s): Independent Book Publishers Association (IBPA)

§The University of North Carolina Press
116 S Boundary St, Chapel Hill, NC 27514-3808
SAN: 203-3151
Tel: 919-966-3561
E-mail: uncpress@unc.edu
Web Site: www.uncpress.org
Key Personnel
Dir: John Sherer
Sr Dir, Mktg & Digital Busn Devt: Dino Battista *Tel:* 919-962-0579 *E-mail:* dino_battista@unc.edu
Edit Dir: Mark Simpson-Vos *Tel:* 919-962-0535
Asst Dir & Sr Ed: Charles Grench *Tel:* 919-962-0481 *E-mail:* charles_grench@unc.edu
Exec Ed: Deborah Gershenowitz
Sr Ed: Brandon Proia
Sales Mgr: Susan Garrett *Tel:* 919-962-0475 *E-mail:* susan_garrett@unc.edu
Publicist: Alison Shay
Founded: 1922
General, scholarly, regional.
ISBN Prefix(es): 978-1-8078
Number of titles published annually: 100 Print
Total Titles: 776 E-Book
Imprints: Ferris & Ferris Books
Distributor for Museum of Early Southern Decorative Arts; North Carolina Museum of Art; Southeastern Center for Contemporary Art; Valentine Museum
Foreign Rep(s): EDIREP (Caribbean, Central America, Mexico, South America); Eurospan University Press Group (Africa, Continental Europe, Middle East, UK); Scholarly Book Services Inc (Canada)
Advertising Agency: Brimley Agency
Orders to: Long Leaf Services Inc, 116 S Boundary St, Chapel Hill, NC 27514-3808 *Toll Free Tel:* 800-848-6224 *E-mail:* customerservice@longleafservices.org *Web Site:* www.longleafservices.org
Returns: Longleaf Returns, c/o Ingram Publisher Services, 1210 Ingram Dr, Chambersburg, PA 17202
Membership(s): Association of American Publishers (AAP); Book Industry Study Group (BISG)

§University of North Texas Press
Willis Library, Rm 251P, 1506 Highland St, Denton, TX 76201
SAN: 249-4280
Mailing Address: 1155 Union Circle, No 311336, Denton, TX 76203-5017
Tel: 940-565-2142 *Fax:* 940-369-8760
Web Site: untpress.unt.edu
Key Personnel
Dir: Ronald Chrisman *E-mail:* ronald.chrisman@unt.edu
Asst Dir: Karen DeVinney *E-mail:* karen.devinney@unt.edu
Mktg Mgr: Bess Whitby *E-mail:* elizabeth.whitby@unt.edu
Founded: 1987
ISBN Prefix(es): 978-0-929398; 978-1-57441
Number of titles published annually: 16 Print; 5 Online; 16 E-Book
Total Titles: 300 Print; 75 Online; 100 E-Book
Foreign Rep(s): East-West Export Books (Asia, Australia, Hawaii, New Zealand, Pacific Islands); Eurospan Group (Europe); Scholarly

Book Services Inc (Canada); US PubRep (Latin America)
Distribution Center: Texas A&M University Press Consortium, John H Lindsey Bldg, Lewis St, 4354 TAMU, College Station, TX 77843-4354 *Toll Free Tel:* 800-826-8911 *Toll Free Fax:* 888-617-2421
Membership(s): American Association of University Presses (AAUP)

University of Notre Dame Press
310 Flanner Hall, Notre Dame, IN 46556
SAN: 203-3178
Tel: 574-631-6346 *Fax:* 574-631-8148
E-mail: undpress@nd.edu
Web Site: www.undpress.nd.edu
Key Personnel
Dir: Stephen M Wrinn *Tel:* 574-631-3265
   E-mail: swrinn@nd.edu
Sr Acqs Ed: Eli Bortz *Tel:* 574-631-4912
   E-mail: ebortz@nd.edu
Acqs Ed: Stephen Little *Tel:* 574-631-4906
   E-mail: slittle2@nd.edu
Mng Ed: Rebecca De Boer *Tel:* 574-631-4908
   E-mail: rdeboer@nd.edu
Busn Mgr: Diane Schaut *Tel:* 574-631-4904
   E-mail: dschaut@nd.edu
Mktg Mgr: Kathryn D Pitts *Tel:* 574-631-3267
   Fax: 574631-4410 *E-mail:* pitts.5@nd.edu
Prodn & Design Mgr: Wendy McMillen *Tel:* 574-631-4907 *E-mail:* wmcmill@nd.edu
Coord, Off Servs: Gina Bixler *Tel:* 574-631-4915
   E-mail: gbixler@nd.edu
Founded: 1949
Academic books, hardcover & paperback; philosophy, Irish studies, literature, theology, international relations, sociology & general interest.
ISBN Prefix(es): 978-0-268
Number of titles published annually: 50 Print
Total Titles: 1,200 Print
Foreign Rep(s): Eurospan
Returns: Chicago Distribution Center, 11030 S Langley, Chicago, IL 60628 *Tel:* 773-702-7000 (rest of world) *Toll Free Tel:* 800-621-2736 (US & CN) *Fax:* 773-702-7212 (rest of world) *Toll Free Fax:* 800-621-8476 (US & CN)
Distribution Center: Chicago Distribution Center, 11030 S Langley Ave, Chicago, IL 60628 *Tel:* 773-702-7000 (rest of world) *Toll Free Tel:* 800-621-2736 (US & CN) *Fax:* 773-702-7212 (rest of world) *Toll Free Fax:* 800-621-8476 (US & CN)
Membership(s): Association of University Presses (AUPresses)

University of Oklahoma Press
2800 Venture Dr, Norman, OK 73069-8216
SAN: 203-3194
Tel: 405-325-2000
Web Site: www.oupress.com
Key Personnel
Dir, Fin & Opers & Dir, Sales & Mktg: Dale Bennie *Tel:* 405-325-3207 *E-mail:* dbennie@ou.edu
Mng Ed: Steven Baker *Tel:* 405-325-1325
   E-mail: steven.b.baker@ou.edu
EDP Mgr: Tony Roberts *Tel:* 405-325-3186
   E-mail: tonyroberts@ou.edu
Publicity Mgr: Katie Baker *Tel:* 405-325-3200
   E-mail: katie-baker@ou.edu
Founded: 1928
Scholarly & general interest books on Americana, Native American studies, Western history, regional interest, natural history, anthropology, archaeology, military history, literature, classical studies, women's studies & political science.
ISBN Prefix(es): 978-0-8061; 978-0-87062 (Arthur H Clark Co)
Number of titles published annually: 90 Print; 80 E-Book
Total Titles: 2,059 Print; 5 CD-ROM; 1,961 E-Book

Imprints: Arthur H Clark Co
Distributor for Cherokee Heritage Press; Denver Art Museum; Gilcrease Museum
Distribution Center: Longleaf Services, 116 S Boundary St, Chapel Hill, NC 27514-3808 *Toll Free Tel:* 800-848-6224 ext 1 *Fax:* 919-962-2704 *Toll Free Fax:* 800-272-6817
   E-mail: customerservice@longleafservices.org
   Web Site: www.longleafservices.org SAN: 203-3151
Membership(s): Association of University Presses (AUPresses)

§University of Pennsylvania Museum of Archaeology & Anthropology
Division of University of Pennsylvania
3260 South St, Philadelphia, PA 19104-6324
Tel: 215-898-4119; 215-898-4000
E-mail: publications@pennmuseum.org
Web Site: www.penn.museum
Key Personnel
Dir, Pubns: Page Selinsky, PhD
Founded: 1887
ISBN Prefix(es): 978-0-934718; 978-0-924171; 978-1-931707; 978-1-949057; 978-1-934536
Number of titles published annually: 4 Print; 4 E-Book
Total Titles: 210 Print; 18 CD-ROM
Distributed by University of Pennsylvania Press
Billing Address: Ingram Publisher Services, Box 631, 14 Ingram Blvd, La Vergne, TN 37086 *Toll Free Tel:* 866-400-5351 *E-mail:* ips@ingramcontent.com
Orders to: Ingram Publisher Services, Box 631, 14 Ingram Blvd, La Vergne, TN 37086 *Toll Free Tel:* 866-400-5351 *Toll Free Fax:* 800-838-1149 *E-mail:* ips@ingramcontent.com
Returns: Ingram Publisher Services, 193 Edwards Dr, Jackson, TN 38301 *Tel:* 731-988-4440 ext 1230 *Toll Free Tel:* 866-400-5351 *E-mail:* ips@ingramcontent.com
Shipping Address: Ingram Publisher Services, Box 631, 14 Ingram Blvd, La Vergne, TN 37086 *Toll Free Tel:* 866-400-5351 *E-mail:* ips@ingramcontent.com

University of Pennsylvania Press
3905 Spruce St, Philadelphia, PA 19104
SAN: 202-5345
Tel: 215-898-6261 *Fax:* 215-898-0404
E-mail: custserv@pobox.upenn.edu
Web Site: www.pennpress.org
Key Personnel
Dir: Mary C Francis
Mktg Dir: Laura Waldron *Tel:* 215-898-1673
   E-mail: lwaldron@upenn.edu
Busn Mgr: Joseph Guttman *Tel:* 215-898-1670
   E-mail: josephgg@upenn.edu
Editing & Prodn Mgr: Elizabeth Glover *Tel:* 215-898-1675 *E-mail:* gloverel@upenn.edu
Publicity & PR Mgr: Gigi Lamm *Tel:* 215-898-1674 *E-mail:* glamm@upenn.edu
Ed-in-Chief: Peter A Agree *Tel:* 215-573-3816
   E-mail: agree@upenn.edu
Mng Ed: Lily Palladino *Tel:* 215-898-1678
   E-mail: lilypall@upenn.edu
History Ed: Robert Lockhart *Tel:* 215-898-1677
   E-mail: rlockhar@upenn.edu
Humanities Ed: Jerome E Singerman *Tel:* 215-898-1681 *E-mail:* singerma@upenn.edu
Consulting Ed: Damon Linker *Tel:* 610-613-4546
   E-mail: linkerpennpress@gmail.com
Consulting Ed (UK): Deborah Blake
   E-mail: dcblake.pennpress@virginmedia.com
Founded: 1890
Scholarly & semipopular nonfiction, especially in history, literature & criticism, social sciences & human rights.
ISBN Prefix(es): 978-0-8122; 978-1-5128
Number of titles published annually: 120 Print; 120 Online
Total Titles: 3,250 Print; 2,650 E-Book

Foreign Rep(s): Combined Academic Publishers (Africa, Arab Middle East, Asia, Austria, China, UK); Durnell Marketing Ltd (Continental Europe); Scholarly Book Services Inc (Canada)
Returns: Penn Press, c/o Maple Logistics Solutions, Lebanon Distribution Ctr, 704 Legionaire Dr, Fredericksburg, PA 17026
Warehouse: Maple Logistics Solutions, Lebanon Distribution Ctr, PO Box 1287, 704 Legionaire Dr, Lebanon, PA 17042 *Tel:* 717-865-7600 *Web Site:* www.maplelogisticsssolutions.com
Marston Book Services Ltd, 160 Eastern Ave, Milton Park, Oxon OX14 4SB, United Kingdom, Asst Cust Servs & Trade Mgr: Donna Green *Tel:* (01235) 465630 *Fax:* (01235) 465555 *E-mail:* donna.green@marston.co.uk *Web Site:* www.marston.co.uk/home.htm
Membership(s): American Association of University Presses (AAUP); Association of American Publishers Professional & Scholarly Publishing Division

University of Pittsburgh Press
7500 Thomas Blvd, Pittsburgh, PA 15260
Tel: 412-383-2456 *Fax:* 412-383-2466
E-mail: info@upress.pitt.edu
Web Site: www.upress.pitt.edu
Key Personnel
Dir: Peter W Kracht *E-mail:* pkracht@upress.pitt.edu
Dir, Mktg & Sales: John Fagan *E-mail:* jfagan@upress.pitt.edu
Dir, Opers: David Baumann *E-mail:* dbaumann@upress.pitt.edu
Opers Admin: Eileen O'Malley
   E-mail: eomalley@upress.pitt.edu
Edit Dir: Sandy Crooms *E-mail:* scrooms@upress.pitt.edu
Edit & Prodn Dir: Alexander Wolfe
   E-mail: awolfe@upress.pitt.edu
Mng Ed: Amy Sherman *E-mail:* asherman@upress.pitt.edu
Sr Acqs Ed: Abby Collier *E-mail:* acollier@upress.pitt.edu; Joshua Shanholtzer *E-mail:* jshanholtzer@upress.pitt.edu
Prodn Ed: Melissa Dias-Mandoly
   E-mail: mdiasmandoly@upress.pitt.edu
Design & Prodn Mgr: Joel Coggins
   E-mail: jcoggins@upress.pitt.edu
Mktg Coord: Kelly Thomas *E-mail:* kthomas@upress.pitt.edu
Mktg Asst: Sheena Carroll *E-mail:* scarroll@upress.pitt.edu
Publicist: Chloe Wertz *E-mail:* cwertz@upress.pitt.edu
Founded: 1936
Scholarly nonfiction, poetry, regional books, short fiction, Russian & East European studies, composition & rhetoric, Latin American studies, environmental history, urban studies, philosophy of science, political science.
ISBN Prefix(es): 978-0-8229
Number of titles published annually: 65 Print
Total Titles: 1,700 Print; 1,300 E-Book
Sales Office(s): Chicago Distribution Center, 11030 S Langley Ave, Chicago, IL 60628
Foreign Rep(s): Casemate UK (Africa, Europe, Middle East, UK); Oxbow Books (Africa, Europe, Middle East, UK)
Billing Address: Chicago Distribution Center, 11030 S Langley Ave, Chicago, IL 60628
Returns: Chicago Distribution Center, 11030 S Langley Ave, Chicago, IL 60628
Warehouse: Chicago Distribution Center, 11030 S Langley Ave, Chicago, IL 60628 *Tel:* 773-702-7000 *Toll Free Tel:* 800-621-2736 *Fax:* 773-702-7212 *Toll Free Fax:* 800-621-8471
Distribution Center: Chicago Distribution Center, 11030 S Langley Ave, Chicago, IL 60628
Membership(s): Association of University Presses (AUPresses)

University of Puerto Rico Press

Subsidiary of University of Puerto Rico
Edificio La Editorial (level 2), Carr No 1, KM
12.0, Jardin Botanico Norte, San Juan, PR
00927
Mailing Address: PO Box 23322, Rio Pedras, PR
00931-3322 SAN: 208-1245
Tel: 787-250-0435; 787-250-0550
  Toll Free Tel: 877-338-7788 *Fax:* 787-753-9116
E-mail: info@laeditorialupr.com
Web Site: www.laeditorialupr.com
Key Personnel
Admin Offr: Ruth Morales *E-mail:* ruth.
  morales3@upr.edu
Ed: Rosa Vanessa Otero *E-mail:* rosa.otero1@upr.
  edu
Sales: Jose Burgos *E-mail:* joseburgos73@gmail.
  com; Ramon Lugo
Founded: 1947
General fiction & nonfiction, reference books,
  college texts; Latin America.
ISBN Prefix(es): 978-0-8477
Number of titles published annually: 10 Print; 10
  E-Book
Total Titles: 1,047 Print; 50 E-Book
Imprints: Coleccion Antologia Personal; Colec-
  cion Aqui y Ahora; Coleccion Caribena; Colec-
  cion Ciencias Naturales; Coleccion Clasicos No
  Tan Clasicos; Coleccion Cuadernos La Torre;
  Coleccion Cuentos de un Mundo Perdido;
  Coleccion Cultura Basica; Coleccion Obras
  Completas Eugenio Maria de Hostos (edi-
  cion critica); Coleccion Dos Lenguas; Colec-
  cion Mujeres de Palabra; Coleccion Nueve
  Pececitos; Coleccion Puertorriquena; Coleccion
  San Pedrito
Foreign Rep(s): Baker & Taylor/Libros Sin Fron-
  teras (USA); DESA (Latin America); Lectorum
  Publications (USA); Libreria La Trinitaria (Do-
  minican Republic)
Membership(s): American Association of Univer-
  sity Presses (AAUP)

University of Rochester Press

Affiliate of Boydell & Brewer Inc
668 Mount Hope Ave, Rochester, NY 14620-2731
Tel: 585-275-0419 *Fax:* 585-271-8778
E-mail: boydell@boydellusa.net
Web Site: www.urpress.com
Key Personnel
Edit Dir: Sonia Kane *E-mail:* sonia.kane@
  rochester.edu
Prodn Dir: Sue Smith *E-mail:* smith@boydellusa.
  net
Founded: 1989
ISBN Prefix(es): 978-1-878822; 978-1-58046
Number of titles published annually: 27 Print
Total Titles: 650 Print
Foreign Office(s): PO Box 9, Woodbridge, Suf-
  folk IP12 3DF, United Kingdom
Foreign Rep(s): Boydell & Brewer (Europe,
  Japan)
Warehouse: Publishers Storage & Shipping Corp,
  231 Industrial Park, 46 Development Rd, Fitch-
  burg, MA 01420-6019, Contact: John Salvey
  Tel: 978-345-2121 *Fax:* 978-348-1233

§University of South Carolina Press

Affiliate of University of South Carolina
1600 Hampton St, Suite 544, Columbia, SC
  29208
SAN: 203-3224
Tel: 803-777-5245 *Toll Free Tel:* 800-768-2500
  (orders) *Fax:* 803-777-0160 *Toll Free Fax:* 800-
  868-0740 (orders)
Web Site: www.sc.edu/uscpress
Key Personnel
Dir: Richard Brown
Asst Dir, Opers: Linda Haines Fogle *Tel:* 803-
  777-4848 *E-mail:* lfogle@mailbox.sc.edu
Busn Mgr: Vicki Sewell *Tel:* 803-777-7754
  E-mail: sewellv@mailbox.sc.edu

Design & Prodn Mgr: Pat Callahan *Tel:* 803-777-
  2449 *E-mail:* mpccallah@mailbox.sc.edu
Mng Ed: William Adams *Tel:* 803-777-5075
  E-mail: adamswb@mailbox.sc.edu
Acqs Ed, African American Studies, Civil Rights
  & Southern History: Ehren Foley
Acqs Ed, Regional Books: Aurora Bell
Publicity Mgr: MacKenzie Fraser-Bub Collier
Asst to Dir: Vicki Bates *Tel:* 803-777-5245
  E-mail: batesvc@mailbox.sc.edu
Founded: 1944
American history/studies, Southern studies, mil-
  itary history, maritime history, literary studies
  including contemporary American & British
  literature & modern world literature, religious
  studies, speech/communication, social work.
ISBN Prefix(es): 978-0-87249; 978-1-57003
Number of titles published annually: 50 Print
Total Titles: 1,300 Print; 2 CD-ROM; 2 Audio
Imprints: Story River Books (Southern fiction)
Distributor for McKissick Museum; Saraland
  Press; South Carolina Bar Association; South
  Carolina Historical Society
Foreign Rep(s): Eurospan University Press Group
  (Europe, UK); Scholarly Book Services Inc
  (Canada)
Warehouse: 718 Devine St, Columbia, SC 29208,
  Orders: Ms Lee Heckle *Tel:* 803-777-1774
  Fax: 803-777-0026
Distribution Center: HFS, PO Box 50370, Bal-
  timore, MD 21211-4370 *Tel:* 410-516-6965
  Toll Free Tel: 800-537-5487 *Fax:* 410-516-
  6998 *E-mail:* hfscustserv@press.jhu.edu *Web
  Site:* hfs.jhu.edu
Membership(s): American Association of Uni-
  versity Presses (AAUP); Southern Independent
  Booksellers Alliance (SIBA)

University of Tennessee Press

Division of University of Tennessee
110 Conference Center Bldg, 600 Henley St,
  Knoxville, TN 37996-4108
SAN: 212-9930
Tel: 865-974-3321 *Toll Free Tel:* 800-621-2736
  (orders) *Fax:* 865-974-3724 *Toll Free Fax:* 800-
  621-8476 (orders)
E-mail: custserv@utpress.org
Web Site: www.utpress.org
Key Personnel
Dir: Scott Danforth *E-mail:* danforth@utk.edu
Acqs Ed: Thomas Wells *E-mail:* twells@utk.edu
Busn Mgr: Lisa Davis *E-mail:* ldavis49@utk.edu
Mktg Mgr: Tom Post *Tel:* 865-974-5466
  E-mail: tpost@utk.edu
Mktg Asst: Linsey Sims *Tel:* 865-974-4444
  E-mail: lsims9@utk.edu
Founded: 1940
Scholarly & regional nonfiction.
ISBN Prefix(es): 978-0-87049; 978-1-57233; 978-
  1-62190
Number of titles published annually: 40 Print
Total Titles: 1,200 Print
Foreign Rep(s): East-West Export Books Inc
  (Asia, The Pacific); Eurospan Group (Africa,
  Central Asia, Europe, Middle East, UK)
Distribution Center: Chicago Distribution Center,
  11030 S Langley, Chicago, IL 60628 *Toll Free
  Tel:* 800-621-2736 *Fax:* 773-702-7212
Membership(s): Association of American Publish-
  ers (AAP); Association of University Presses
  (AUPresses)

University of Texas at Arlington College of Architecture, Planning & Public Affairs

601 S Nedderman Dr, Suite 203, Arlington, TX
  76019
E-mail: cappa@uta.edu
Web Site: www.uta.edu/cappa
Newsletter, working papers, books, reports on
  community revitalization, population projection,
  charter school evaluation, strategic planning,
  land use planning, transportation planning, social welfare policy, urban politics, social plan-

ning, urban public finance, consensus, building
  & dispute resolution, group facilitation, urban
  management, environmental planning & analysis.
ISBN Prefix(es): 978-0-936440
Number of titles published annually: 15 Print
Total Titles: 40 Print

§The University of Utah Press

Subsidiary of University of Utah
J Willard Marriott Library, Suite 5400, 295 S
  1500 E, Salt Lake City, UT 84112-0860
SAN: 220-0023
Tel: 801-585-9786 *Fax:* 801-581-3365
E-mail: hannah.new@utah.edu
Web Site: www.uofupress.com
Key Personnel
Dir & Mng Ed: Glenda Cotter *E-mail:* glenda.
  cotter@utah.edu
Prodn Mgr: Jessica Booth *E-mail:* jessica.booth@
  utah.edu
Busn Mgr & Perms: Janalyn Guo
  E-mail: janalyn.guo@utah.edu
Founded: 1949
Scholarly books, regional studies, anthropology,
  archaeology, linguistics, Mesoamerican stud-
  ies, natural history, Western history, outdoor
  recreation.
ISBN Prefix(es): 978-0-87480; 978-1-60781; 978-
  1-67469
Number of titles published annually: 32 Print; 30
  E-Book
Total Titles: 600 Print
Imprints: Bonneville Books (trade); Boxelder
  Books
Distributor for BYU Museum of Peoples & Cul-
  tures; BYU Studies; KUED (Utah PBS affili-
  ate); Western Epics Publications
Foreign Rep(s): Eurospan (Africa, Europe)
Orders to: The Chicago Distribution Center,
  11030 S Langley Ave, Chicago, IL 60628
  Tel: 773-702-7000 *Toll Free Tel:* 800-621-2736
  Fax: 773-702-7212 *Toll Free Fax:* 800-621-
  8741 *Web Site:* www.uofupress.com
Returns: The Chicago Distribution Center, 11030
  S Langley Ave, Chicago, IL 60628

The University of Virginia Press

Affiliate of University of Virginia
PO Box 400318, Charlottesville, VA 22904-4318
Tel: 434-924-3468 (cust serv); 434-924-3469
  (cust serv) *Toll Free Tel:* 800-831-3406 (orders)
  Fax: 434-982-2655 *Toll Free Fax:* 877-288-
  6400
E-mail: vapress@virginia.edu
Web Site: www.upress.virginia.edu
Key Personnel
Dir: Suzanne Morse Moomaw
Asst Dir/Ed-in-Chief & Humanities Ed: Eric
  Brandt
Dir, Mktg & Sales: Jason Coleman *Tel:* 434-924-
  1450 *E-mail:* jgc3h@virginia.edu
Publicity Dir: Emily Grandstaff *Tel:* 434-982-
  2932 *E-mail:* ekg4a@virginia.edu
Mng Ed, Ms Edit/Design & Prodn: Ellen Satrom
  Tel: 434-924-6065 *E-mail:* esatrom@virginia.
  edu
Acqs Ed, Architecture & Environmental: Boyd
  Zenner *Tel:* 434-924-1373 *E-mail:* bz2v@
  virginia.edu
Acqs Ed, Soc Sci & History: Richard Holway
  Tel: 434-924-7301 *E-mail:* rkh2a@virginia.edu
Cust Serv Mgr: Brenda Fitzgerald *E-mail:* bwf@
  virginia.edu
Database Mgr: Mary MacNeil *E-mail:* mmm5w@
  virginia.edu
Founded: 1963
General scholarly nonfiction with emphasis on
  history, literature & regional books.
UVA Press provides ms editorial, design & pro-
  duction services for the University of Delaware
  Press.
ISBN Prefix(es): 978-0-8139; 978-978-0

Number of titles published annually: 65 Print; 60 E-Book

Total Titles: 1,350 Print

Distributor for Colonial Society of Massachusetts; Mount Vernon Ladies Association

Foreign Rep(s): Eurospan (Europe); Scholarly Book Services Inc (Canada)

Shipping Address: Longleaf Services, 116 S Boundary St, Chapel Hill, NC 27514-3808 *Toll Free Tel:* 800-848-6224 *Toll Free Fax:* 800-272-6817 *E-mail:* orders@longleafservices.org SAN: 203-3151

Membership(s): American Association of University Presses (AAUP)

§University of Washington Press

Unit of University of Washington Libraries

4333 Brooklyn Ave NE, Seattle, WA 98105-9570

SAN: 212-2502

Mailing Address: PO Box 359570, Seattle, WA 98195-9570

Tel: 206-543-4050 *Toll Free Tel:* 800-537-5487 (orders) *Fax:* 206-543-3932; 410-516-6998 (orders)

E-mail: uwapress@uw.edu

Web Site: uwapress.uw.edu

Key Personnel

Dir: Nicole Mitchell *Tel:* 206-685-9373 *E-mail:* nfmm@uw.edu

Art Dir: Katrina Noble

Dir, Mktg & Sales: Julie Fergus *E-mail:* jaf88@uw.edu

Exec Ed: Lorri Hagman *E-mail:* lhagman@uw.edu

Ed-in-Chief: Larin McLaughlin *Tel:* 206-221-4995 *E-mail:* lmclaugh@uw.edu

Edit, Design & Prodn Mgr: Margaret Sullivan

Publicity Mgr: Kait Heacock

Founded: 1920

General scholarly nonfiction, reprints, imports.

ISBN Prefix(es): 978-0-295

Number of titles published annually: 68 Print

Total Titles: 1,500 Print; 1 CD-ROM

Foreign Rep(s): Combined Academic Publisher Ltd (UK); Douglas & McIntyre (Canada); University of British Columbia Press (Canada)

Distribution Center: c/o HFS (Hopkins Fulfillment Services), PO Box 50370, Baltimore, MD 21211-4370 (US) *Tel:* 410-516-6965 *Toll Free Tel:* 800-537-5487 *Fax:* 410-516-6998 *E-mail:* hfscustserv@press.jhu.edu *Web Site:* hfs.jhu.edu

Membership(s): Association of University Presses (AUPresses)

University of Wisconsin Press

Unit of University of Wisconsin-Madison

728 State St, Suite 443, Madison, WI 53706-1418

SAN: 501-0039

Tel: 608-263-1110; 608-263-0668 (journal orders) *Toll Free Tel:* 800-621-2736 (book orders) *Fax:* 608-263-1173 *Toll Free Fax:* 800-621-2736 (book orders)

E-mail: uwiscpress@uwpress.wisc.edu

Web Site: uwpress.wisc.edu

Key Personnel

Dir: Dennis Lloyd *E-mail:* dlloyd2@wisc.edu

Ed-in-Chief: Nathan Macbrien *E-mail:* macbrien@wisc.edu

Journals Mgr: Toni Gunnison *Tel:* 608-263-0667 *E-mail:* gunnison@wisc.edu

Prodn Mgr & ISBN Contact: Terry Emmrich *Tel:* 608-263-0731 *E-mail:* temmrich@wisc.edu

Publicity Mgr: Kaitlin Svabek *Tel:* 608-263-0734 *E-mail:* svabek@wisc.edu

Rights & Permissions Mgr: Anne McKenna *Tel:* 608-263-1131 *E-mail:* rights@uwpress.wisc.edu

Sales & Mktg Mgr: Casey LaVela *Tel:* 608-263-0814 *E-mail:* casey.lavela@wisc.edu

Founded: 1936

Academic press, including regional Midwest titles & trade titles.

ISBN Prefix(es): 978-0-87972; 978-0-299; 978-1-928755; 978-0-9671787; 978-8-158; 978-0-9682722; 978-0-924119; 978-0-9655464; 978-0-9718963; 978-0-9624369; 978-0-932900; 978-1-931569; 978-0-9623206; 978-0-9653519; 978-0-9700602; 978-0-9789590; 978-0-9817723

Number of titles published annually: 60 Print; 60 E-Book

Total Titles: 1,480 Print; 1,100 E-Book

Distributor for The Center for the Study of Upper Midwestern Culture; Wisconsin Veterans Museum

Foreign Rep(s): Eurospan Ltd (Africa, Asia, Australia, Continental Europe, Iceland, Ireland, Middle East, New Zealand, The Pacific, UK)

Advertising Agency: Ad Vantage *E-mail:* advertising@uwpress.wisc.edu

Orders to: Chicago Distribution Center, 11030 S Langley Ave, Chicago, IL 60628-3892 *Tel:* 773-702-7000 *Toll Free Tel:* 800-621-2736 *Fax:* 773-702-7212 *Toll Free Fax:* 800-621-8476 *E-mail:* custserv@press.uchicago.edu SAN: 202-5280

Returns: Chicago Distribution Center, 11030 S Langley Ave, Chicago, IL 60628-3892 SAN: 202-5280

Shipping Address: Chicago Distribution Center, 11030 S Langley Ave, Chicago, IL 60628-3892 *E-mail:* custserv@press.uchicago.edu SAN: 202-5280

Warehouse: Chicago Distribution Center, 11030 S Langley Ave, Chicago, IL 60628-3892 *E-mail:* custserv@press.uchicago.edu SAN: 202-5280

Distribution Center: Chicago Distribution Center, 11030 S Langley Ave, Chicago, IL 60628-3892 *Tel:* 773-568-1550 *Toll Free Tel:* 800-621-2736 *Fax:* 773-660-2235 *Toll Free Fax:* 800-621-8476 SAN: 202-5280

Eurospan Group, c/o Turpin Distribution, Stratton Business Park, Pegasus Dr, Biggleswade, Beds SG18 8TQ, United Kingdom (Africa, Asia, Australia, Europe, Middle East, New Zealand, the Pacific, Russia & UK) *Tel:* (01767) 604972 *Fax:* (01767) 601640 *E-mail:* eurospan@turpin-distribution.com

Membership(s): Association of University Presses (AUPresses); Great Lakes Independent Booksellers Association (GLIBA); Midwest Independent Booksellers Association (MIBA); Wisconsin Library Association

University Press of America Inc

4501 Forbes Blvd, Suite 200, Lanham, MD 20706

SAN: 200-2256

Tel: 301-459-3366 *Toll Free Tel:* 800-462-6420 *Fax:* 301-429-5748 *Toll Free Fax:* 800-338-4550

Web Site: www.univpress.com

Key Personnel

VP & Publr: Julie Kirsch *E-mail:* jkirsch@rowman.com

VP, Mfg & Prodn: Stephen Driver

Dir, Mktg: Dave Horvath *E-mail:* dhorvath@rowman.com

Mgr, Rts & Perms & Intl Rts Contact: Clare Cox *E-mail:* ccox@rowman.com

Acqs Ed: Holly Buchanan *E-mail:* hbuchanan@univpress.com

Founded: 1975

Scholarly monographs, college texts, conference proceedings, professional books & reprints in the social sciences & the humanities.

ISBN Prefix(es): 978-0-8191; 978-0-7618

Number of titles published annually: 100 Print; 100 E-Book

Total Titles: 10,000 Print; 2,000 E-Book

Branch Office(s)

67 Mowat Ave, Suite 241, Toronto, ON M6K 3E3, Canada, Contact: Les Petriw *Tel:* 416-534-1660 *Toll Free Tel:* 877-626-2665

Fax: 416-534-3699 *E-mail:* kstinson@rowmanlittlefield.com

Distributor for Atlantic Council; Center for National Policy Press; Harvard Center for International Affairs; International Law Institute; Joint Center for Political & Economic Studies Press; White Burkett Miller Center; Society of the Cincinnati

Foreign Rep(s): NBN Plymbridge (Europe, UK); United Publishers Services (Japan)

Foreign Rights: United Publishers Service (Japan)

Shipping Address: 15200 NBN Way, Blue Ridge Summit, PA 17214-0191 *Toll Free Tel:* 800-462-6420 *Fax:* 717-794-3812 *Toll Free Fax:* 800-338-4550

Membership(s): Association of American Publishers (AAP)

University Press of Colorado

245 Century Circle, Suite 202, Louisville, CO 80027

SAN: 202-1749

Tel: 720-406-8849 *Toll Free Tel:* 800-621-2736 (orders) *Fax:* 720-406-3443

Web Site: www.upcolorado.com

Key Personnel

Dir: Darrin Pratt *E-mail:* darrin@upcolorado.com

Acqs Ed: Charlotte Steinhardt *E-mail:* charlotte@upcolorado.com

Founded: 1965

Scholarly & regional nonfiction.

ISBN Prefix(es): 978-0-87081; 978-1-60732

Number of titles published annually: 30 Print; 30 E-Book

Total Titles: 340 Print; 3 CD-ROM; 334 E-Book

Imprints: Utah State University Press

Distributor for Center for Literary Publishing; History Colorado; Western Press Books

Foreign Rep(s): NBN International (Asia, Australia, UK & the continent)

Orders to: Chicago Distribution Center, 11030 S Langley, Chicago, IL 60628 *Toll Free Tel:* 800-621-2736 *E-mail:* custserv@press.uchicago.edu

Returns: Chicago Distribution Center, Returns Processing Ctr, 11030 S Langley, Chicago, IL 60628 *Toll Free Tel:* 800-621-2736

Distribution Center: Chicago Distribution Center, 11030 S Langley, Chicago, IL 60628 *Toll Free Tel:* 800-621-2736

Membership(s): Association of University Presses (AUPresses)

See separate listing for:

Utah State University Press

University Press of Florida

Affiliate of State University System of Florida

2046 NE Waldo Rd, Suite 2100, Gainesville, FL 32609

SAN: 207-9275

Tel: 352-392-1351 *Toll Free Tel:* 800-226-3822 (orders only) *Fax:* 352-392-0590 *Toll Free Fax:* 800-680-1955 (orders only)

E-mail: press@upress.ufl.edu; orders@upress.ufl.edu

Web Site: www.upf.com

Key Personnel

Dir & Dir, Sales & Mktg: Romi Gutierrez *E-mail:* romi@upress.ufl.edu

Assoc Dir & EDP Mgr: Michele Fiyak-Burkley *E-mail:* mf@upress.ufl.edu

Assoc Dir & IT Dir: Bryan Lutz *E-mail:* bryan@upress.ufl.edu

Asst Dir & Opers Mgr: Jackie Panetta *E-mail:* jackie@upress.ufl.edu

Mng Ed: Marthe Walters *E-mail:* marthe@upress.ufl.edu

Founded: 1945

Scholarly & regional nonfiction.

ISBN Prefix(es): 978-0-8130

Number of titles published annually: 100 Print; 100 E-Book

Total Titles: 2,830 Print; 1,850 E-Book

Foreign Rights: Codasat Canada (Canada); Eurospan Group (Africa, Asia, Europe, Middle East, The Pacific, UK)
Membership(s): American Association of University Presses (AAUP)

§University Press of Kansas
2502 Westbrooke Circle, Lawrence, KS 66045-4444
SAN: 203-3267
Tel: 785-864-4154; 785-864-4155 (orders) *Fax:* 785-864-4586
E-mail: upress@ku.edu; upkorders@ku.edu (orders)
Web Site: www.kansaspress.ku.edu
Key Personnel
Dir: Conrad Roberts *Tel:* 785-864-9158 *E-mail:* ceroberts@ku.edu
Ed-in-Chief: Joyce Harrison *Tel:* 785-864-9162 *E-mail:* joyce@ku.edu
Mktg & Sales Dir: Mike Kehoe *Tel:* 785-864-9165 *E-mail:* mkehoe@ku.edu
Mng Ed: Kelly Chrisman Jacques *Tel:* 785-864-9186 *E-mail:* kcj@ku.edu
Art Dir & Webmaster: Karl Janssen *Tel:* 785-864-9164 *E-mail:* kjanssen@ku.edu
Acqs Ed: David Congdon *Tel:* 785-864-6059 *E-mail:* dcongdon@ku.edu; Bethany Mowry *Tel:* 785-864-1459 *E-mail:* brmowry@ku.edu
Direct Mail & Exhibits Mgr: Debra Diehl *Tel:* 785-864-9166 *E-mail:* ddiehl@ku.edu
Publicity Mgr: Derek Helms *Tel:* 785-864-9170 *E-mail:* helms@ku.edu
Founded: 1946
Represents the six state universities: Emporia State University, Fort Hays State University, Kansas State University, Pittsburg State University, the University of Kansas & Wichita State University. Established as a consortium by the Board of Regents, the press is governed by a Board of Trustees, who are the chief academic officers of the six universities & who appoint faculty members from each institution to serve on the advisory Editorial Committee. The press is located on the west campus of the University of Kansas. The press publishes work on American politics (including the presidency, American political thought & public policy), military history & intelligence studies, American history (especially political, cultural, intellectual & western), environmental policy & history, American studies, film studies, law & legal history, Native American studies & books about Kansas & the Midwest. Our books have reached a wide audience both inside & outside the academy & have been recognized for their contributions to important scholarly & public debates.
ISBN Prefix(es): 978-978-07006
Number of titles published annually: 47 Print
Total Titles: 1,612 Print; 1 CD-ROM
Foreign Rep(s): Eurospan Ltd (Africa, Europe, Middle East, UK); Scholarly Book Services Inc (Canada)
Returns: University Press of Kansas Warehouse, 2445 Westbrooke Circle, Lawrence, KS 66045-4440, Dist & Cust Serv Coord: Ralph Machado *Tel:* 785-864-4156 *E-mail:* upkwarehouse@ku.edu
Warehouse: University Press of Kansas Warehouse, 2445 Westbrooke Circle, Lawrence, KS 66045-4440, Dist & Cust Serv Coord: Ralph Machado *Tel:* 785-864-4156 *E-mail:* upkwarehouse@ku.edu
Membership(s): Association of University Presses (AUPresses)

The University Press of Kentucky
663 S Limestone St, Lexington, KY 40508-4008
SAN: 203-3275
Tel: 859-257-8400 *Fax:* 859-257-8481
Web Site: www.kentuckypress.com

Key Personnel
Dir, Editing, Design & Prodn: David Cobb *Tel:* 859-257-4252 *Fax:* 859-257-2984 *E-mail:* dlcobb2@email.uky.edu
Dir, Fin & Admin: Craig Wilkie *Tel:* 859-257-8436 *Fax:* 859-257-7975 *E-mail:* crwilk00@email.uky.edu
Asst Dir, Fin & Admin: Teresa Wells Collins *Tel:* 859-257-8405 *E-mail:* twell1@email.uky.edu
Sr Acqs Ed: Anne Dean Dotson *Tel:* 859-257-8434 *Fax:* 859-323-1873 *E-mail:* adwatk0@email.uky.edu
Dir: Ashley Runyon
Founded: 1943
ISBN Prefix(es): 978-0-8131
Number of titles published annually: 60 Print; 70 E-Book
Total Titles: 1,200 Print; 550 E-Book
Distributor for Kentucky Historical Society
Foreign Rep(s): Eurospan (UK & the continent); Scholarly Book Services Inc (Canada)
Orders to: HFS, PO Box 50370, Baltimore, MD 21211-4370 *Tel:* 410-516-6956 *Toll Free Tel:* 800-537-5487 *Fax:* 410-516-6998 *E-mail:* hfscustserv@press.jhu.edu
Returns: HFS, c/o Maple Logistics Solutions, Lebanon Distribution Ctr, 704 Legionaire Dr, Fredericksburg, PA 17026 *Toll Free Tel:* 800-537-5487 *Fax:* 410-516-6998 *E-mail:* hfscustserv@press.jhu.edu
Membership(s): Association of American Publishers (AAP); Association of University Presses (AUPresses)

University Press of Mississippi
3825 Ridgewood Rd, Jackson, MS 39211-6492
SAN: 203-1914
Tel: 601-432-6205 *Toll Free Tel:* 800-737-7788 (orders & cust serv) *Fax:* 601-432-6217
E-mail: press@mississippi.edu
Web Site: www.upress.state.ms.us
Key Personnel
Dir: Craig Gill *E-mail:* cgill@mississippi.edu
Assoc Dir/Mktg Dir: Steve Yates *E-mail:* syates@mississippi.edu
Asst to the Dir: Carlton McGrone *E-mail:* cmcgrone@mississippi.edu
Sr Acqs Ed: Katie Keene *E-mail:* kkeene@mississippi.edu
Proj Ed: Valerie Jones *E-mail:* vjones@mississippi.edu
Assoc Proj Ed: Laura Strong *E-mail:* lstrong@mississippi.edu
Assoc Ed: Emily Snyder Bandy *E-mail:* ebandy@mississippi.edu; Lisa McMurtray *E-mail:* lmcmurtray@mississippi.edu
Edit Assoc: Mary Heath *E-mail:* mheath@mississippi.edu
Busn Mgr: Tonia Lonie *E-mail:* tlonie@mississippi.edu
Data Servs & Course Adoptions Mgr: Kathy Burgess *E-mail:* kburgess@mississippi.edu
Electronic, Exhibits & Direct-to-Consumer Sales Mgr: Kristin Kirkpatrick *E-mail:* kkirkpatrick@mississippi.edu
Prodn & Design Mgr: Todd Lape *E-mail:* tlape@mississippi.edu
Proj Mgr: Mrs Shane Gong Stewart *E-mail:* sgong@mississippi.edu
Publicity & Promos Mgr: Courtney McCreary *E-mail:* cmccreary@mississippi.edu
Rts & Contracts Mgr: Cynthia Foster *E-mail:* cfoster@mississippi.edu
Mktg Asst & Digital Publg Coord: Ms Jordan Nettles *E-mail:* jnettles@mississippi.edu
Cust Serv & Order Supv: Ms Sandy Alexander *E-mail:* salexander@mississippi.edu
Sr Book Designer: Pete Halverson *E-mail:* phalverson@mississippi.edu
Book Designer: Jennifer Mixon *E-mail:* jmixon@mississippi.edu
Founded: 1970

Publisher of trade & scholarly books, nonfiction, fiction & regional.
ISBN Prefix(es): 978-0-87805; 978-1-57806; 978-1-934110; 978-1-60473; 978-1-61703; 978-1-62103; 978-1-62846; 978-1-62674; 978-1-4968
Number of titles published annually: 80 Print; 80 E-Book
Total Titles: 2,500 Print; 2,000 E-Book
Foreign Rep(s): Eurospan (Africa, Asia-Pacific, Caribbean, Continental Europe, Indian subcontinent, Ireland, Latin America, Middle East, UK); University of British Columbia Press (Canada)
Returns: Maple Logistics Solutions, Lebanon Distribution Ctr, 704 Legionaire Dr, Fredericksburg, PA 17026 (non-USPS deliveries); Maple Logistics Solutions, Lebanon Distribution Ctr, PO Box 1287, Lebanon, PA 17042 (all USPS deliveries)
Warehouse: Maple Logistics Solutions, Lebanon Distribution Ctr, 704 Legionaire Dr, Fredericksburg, PA 17026
Membership(s): Association of University Presses (AUPresses)

University Publishing House
PO Box 1664, Mannford, OK 74044
Tel: 918-865-4726
E-mail: upub5@outlook.com
Web Site: www.universitypublishinghouse.net
Key Personnel
Owner & Pres: Randell Nyborg
Founded: 1987
Industrial & automotive, classic fiction reprints, mail order books & industrial processes.
ISBN Prefix(es): 978-1-877767; 978-1-57002
Number of titles published annually: 5 Print
Total Titles: 140 Print

University Science Books
20 Edgehill Rd, Mill Valley, CA 94941
SAN: 213-8085
Tel: 703-661-1572 (cust serv, orders) *Fax:* 703-661-1572 (cust serv, orders)
E-mail: usbmail@presswarehouse.com (cust serv, orders)
Web Site: www.uscibooks.com
Key Personnel
Pres: Bruce Armbruster
VP & Intl Rts Contact: Kathy Armbruster
Assoc Publr/Edit: Jane Ellis *Tel:* 973-378-3900 *Fax:* 973-378-3925 *E-mail:* bjellis@igc.org
Founded: 1978
Intermediate level college textbooks & monographs in astronomy, chemistry, biochemistry & physics, environmental science, technical writing, biology, reference books, children's books.
ISBN Prefix(es): 978-0-935702; 978-1-891389; 978-1-938787; 978-1-940380
Number of titles published annually: 8 Print; 8 E-Book
Total Titles: 200 Print; 200 E-Book
Foreign Rep(s): Scion Publishing Ltd (British Commonwealth, Central Europe, Continental Europe, Europe)
Foreign Rights: SBS Livraria Internacional (Brazil); Sci-Tech Publishing Co Ltd (Taiwan); UBS Library Services Pte Ltd (Singapore); Viva Books (India)
Orders to: Books International Inc, PO Box 605, Herndon, VA 20172, Contact: Todd Riggleman *Tel:* 703-661-1572 *Fax:* 703-661-1501
Returns: Books International Inc, 22883 Quicksilver Dr, Dulles, VA 20166 (15% restocking fee, damaged books not accepted, books must be in original shrinkwrap for credit) *Tel:* 703-661-1572 *Fax:* 703-661-1501
Distribution Center: Books International Inc, 22883 Quicksilver Dr, Dulles, VA 20166 (15% discount on all web site orders) *Tel:* 703-661-1572 *Fax:* 703-661-1501 *E-mail:* usbmail@presswarehouse.com

UnKnownTruths.com Publishing Co
8815 Conroy Windermere Rd, Suite 190, Orlando, FL 32835
SAN: 255-6375
Tel: 407-929-9207
E-mail: info@unknowntruths.com
Web Site: unknowntruths.com
Key Personnel
Pres: Walter Parks *E-mail:* hparks@cfl.rr.com
Founded: 2002
Formed to publish true stories of the unusual or of the previously unexplained. Stories typically provide radically different views from those that have shaped the understandings of our natural world, our religions, our science, our history & even the foundations of our civilizations. Also include stories of the very important life-extending medical breakthroughs: stem cell therapies, genetic therapies, cloning & other emerging findings that promise to change the very meaning of life.
ISBN Prefix(es): 978-0-9745393
Number of titles published annually: 12 Print; 4 Online
Advertising Agency: James Brooke & Associates, 2660 Second St, Suite 1, Santa Monica, CA 90405, PR: Cherie Carter *Tel:* 310-396-8070 *Fax:* 310-396-8071 *E-mail:* cherie@unknowntruths.com
Distribution Center: New Leaf Distributing Co, 401 Thornton Rd, Lithia Springs, GA 30122-1557 *Tel:* 770-948-7845 *Fax:* 770-944-2313 *Web Site:* newleafdist.com
Quality Books Inc, 1003 W Pines Rd, Oregon, IL 61061 *Toll Free Tel:* 800-323-4241 *Fax:* 815-732-4499
Membership(s): The Association of Publishers for Special Sales (APSS); Independent Book Publishers Association (IBPA)

§Unlimited Publishing LLC
PO Box 99, Nashville, IN 47448
Founded: 2000
Bringing back out of print books & new nonfiction by professional writers. Agented submissions only. No simultaneous submissions. Send proposal & first 10 pages by post.
ISBN Prefix(es): 978-1-58832
Number of titles published annually: 1 Print; 1 Online; 1 E-Book
Total Titles: 250 Print
Membership(s): Independent Book Publishers Association (IBPA)

UNO Press, see University of New Orleans Press

W E Upjohn Institute for Employment Research
300 S Westnedge Ave, Kalamazoo, MI 49007-4686
Tel: 269-343-5541; 269-343-4330 (pubns) *Toll Free Tel:* 888-227-8569 *Fax:* 269-343-7310
E-mail: publications@upjohn.org; communications@upjohn.org
Web Site: www.upjohn.org
Key Personnel
Mgr, Pubns: Richard Wyrwa
Founded: 1959
Labor economics & industrial relations.
ISBN Prefix(es): 978-0-88099; 978-0-911558
Number of titles published annually: 6 Print; 6 E-Book
Total Titles: 225 Print; 200 E-Book
Imprints: Upjohn Press
Membership(s): Association of University Presses (AUPresses)

§Upper Access Inc
87 Upper Access Rd, Hinesburg, VT 05461
SAN: 667-1195
Tel: 802-482-2988
E-mail: upperaccessbooks@gmail.com

Web Site: www.upperaccess.com
Key Personnel
VP & Publr: Stephen T Carlson *E-mail:* steve@upperaccess.com
Assoc Publr: Thomas Gray
Sales Dir: Kristen Lewis
Founded: 1986
Publisher of nonfiction books to improve the quality of life.
ISBN Prefix(es): 978-0-942679
Number of titles published annually: 3 Print; 2 E-Book
Total Titles: 57 Print; 8 E-Book
Imprints: Upper Access Books
Orders to: Midpoint National, 1263 Southwest Blvd, Kansas City, KS 66103 (trade sales & returns) *Tel:* 913-362-7400 *E-mail:* info@midpt.com *Web Site:* www.midpt.com
Returns: Midpoint National, 1263 Southwest Blvd, Kansas City, KS 66103 (trade sales & returns) *Tel:* 913-362-7400 *E-mail:* info@midpt.com *Web Site:* www.midpt.com
Shipping Address: Midpoint Trade Books, 814 N Franklin St, Suite 100, Chicago, IL 60610 (trade sales & returns) *Tel:* 312-337-0747 *Toll Free Tel:* 800-888-4741 *Fax:* 312-337-5985 *Web Site:* www.midpointtrade.com
Warehouse: Midpoint Trade Books, 814 N Franklin St, Suite 100, Chicago, IL 60610 (trade sales & returns) *Tel:* 312-337-0747 *Toll Free Tel:* 800-888-4741 *Fax:* 312-337-5985 *Web Site:* www.midpointtrade.com
Distribution Center: Midpoint National, 1263 Southwest Blvd, Kansas City, KS 66103 (trade sales & returns) *Tel:* 913-362-7400 *E-mail:* info@midpt.com *Web Site:* www.midpt.com
Membership(s): The Association of Publishers for Special Sales (APSS); Independent Book Publishers Association (IBPA); Independent Publishers of New England (IPNE); Publishers North (PubNorth)

§Upper Room Books
Division of The Upper Room
1908 Grand Ave, Nashville, TN 37212
SAN: 203-3364
Tel: 615-340-7200 *Toll Free Tel:* 800-972-0433
Web Site: books.upperroom.org
Key Personnel
Acqs Ed: Joanna Bradley *E-mail:* jbradley@upperroom.org
Dir, Prodn & Scheduling: Debbie Gregory *Tel:* 615-340-7224
Founded: 1935
Prayer & devotional life publications. No fiction or poetry accepted.
ISBN Prefix(es): 978-0-8358
Number of titles published annually: 20 Print; 20 E-Book
Imprints: Fresh Air Books
Foreign Rights: Mosaic Rights Management (Cindy Riggins)
Warehouse: PBD Inc, 1650 Bluegrass Pkwy, Alpharetta, GA 30201
Membership(s): American Booksellers Association (ABA); Evangelical Christian Publishers Association (ECPA); Protestant Church-Owned Publishers Association (PCPA)
See separate listing for:
Fresh Air Books

Upstart Books™
Division of Demco Inc
PO Box 7488, Madison, WI 53707
Tel: 608-241-1201 *Toll Free Tel:* 800-356-1200 (orders); 800-962-4463 (cust serv) *Toll Free Fax:* 800-245-1329 (orders)
E-mail: custserv@demco.com; order@demco.com
Web Site: www.demco.com/upstart
Key Personnel
Prod Devt Mgr, Lib Mkts: Heidi Green
Founded: 1990

Reading activities & library skills for teachers & children's librarians; storytelling activity books & Internet resources.
ISBN Prefix(es): 978-0-917846; 978-0-913853; 978-1-57950; 978-1-932146
Number of titles published annually: 12 Print
Total Titles: 100 Print

Urim Publications
527 Empire Blvd, Brooklyn, NY 11225-3121
Tel: 718-972-5449 *Fax:* 718-972-6307
E-mail: urimpublisher@gmail.com
Web Site: www.urimpublications.com
Key Personnel
Publr: Tzvi Mauer
Children's Book Ed: Shari Dash Greenspan *E-mail:* children@urimpublications.com
Founded: 1997
Publisher & worldwide distributor of new & classic books with Jewish content.
ISBN Prefix(es): 978-965-7108
Number of titles published annually: 8 Print
Total Titles: 35 Print
Editorial Office(s): HaUman, 9 HaUman St, 2nd fl, PO Box 52287, Jerusalem 91521, Israel *Tel:* (02) 679-7633 *Fax:* (02) 679-7634
Distribution Center: Independent Publishers Group (IPG), 814 N Franklin St, Chicago, IL 60610 *Toll Free Tel:* 800-888-4741

Urzone Inc, see Zone Books

US Conference of Catholic Bishops
USCCB Publishing, 3211 Fourth St NE, Washington, DC 20017
Toll Free Tel: 800-235-8722 *Fax:* 301-779-8596 (orders)
E-mail: css@usccb.org
Web Site: store.usccb.org
Founded: 1938
The official publisher for the US Catholic Bishop & Vatican documents; English & Spanish.
ISBN Prefix(es): 978-1-55586; 978-1-57455; 978-1-60137
Number of titles published annually: 15 Print
Total Titles: 550 Print
Returns: USCCB Returns, 3570 Bladensburg Rd, Brentwood, MD 20722
Membership(s): Association of Catholic Publishers Inc

US Games Systems Inc
179 Ludlow St, Stamford, CT 06902
SAN: 206-1368
Tel: 203-353-8400 *Toll Free Tel:* 800-54-GAMES (544-2637) *Fax:* 203-353-8431
E-mail: info@usgamesinc.com
Web Site: www.usgamesinc.com
Key Personnel
Founder & Chmn: Stuart R Kaplan *Tel:* 203-353-8400 ext 301
Pres: Ricky Cruz
VP, Export Sales: Barbara Bensaid
Creative Dir: Paula Palmer
Founded: 1968
Popular & scholarly works in the field of tarot, wellness, inspiration, spirituality, educational games & the history of symbolism of playing cards; reprints of historical tarot decks & playing cards from the past five centuries.
ISBN Prefix(es): 978-0-913866; 978-0-88079; 978-1-57281
Number of titles published annually: 20 Print
Total Titles: 400 Print; 5 E-Book
Imprints: Cove Press
Distributor for Blue Angel Publishing; KonigsFurt
Foreign Rep(s): Avvalon-Lo Scarabeo (Russia); Fonix Musik (Denmark); KonigsFurt (Germany); Publishers Group (UK); Stjarn Distribution (Sweden); Vykintasd Urniezius (Lithuania)

§US Government Publishing Office (GPO)
Division of US Government
Superintendent of Documents, 732 N Capitol St
NW, Washington, DC 20401
Tel: 202-512-1800 *Toll Free Tel:* 866-512-1800
(orders) *Fax:* 202-512-1998
E-mail: contactcenter@gpo.gov
Web Site: www.gpo.gov; bookstore.gpo.gov
(sales)
Key Personnel
Dir & CEO: Hugh Nathanial Halpern
CFO: William Boesch
CIO: Sam Musa
Chief PR Offr: Gary Somerset
Inspector Gen: Michael Leary
Superintendent, Documents: Laurie Hall
Dir, Sales & Mktg: Lisa Williams
Founded: 1861
Distributor & printer of federal government publi-
cations & public documents in various formats
including ebooks; military, space exploration,
political science.
ISBN Prefix(es): 978-0-16
Number of titles published annually: 250 Print;
15 Online
Total Titles: 2,500 Print; 140 CD-ROM
Orders to: PO Box 979050, St Louis, MO 63197-
9000

Utah Geological Survey
Division of Utah Department of Natural Re-
sources
1594 W North Temple, Suite 3110, Salt Lake
City, UT 84116-3154
Mailing Address: PO Box 146100, Salt Lake
City, UT 84114-6100
Tel: 801-537-3300 *Toll Free Tel:* 888-UTAH-
MAP (882-4627, bookstore) *Fax:* 801-537-
3400
E-mail: geostore@utah.gov
Web Site: geology.utah.gov
Key Personnel
Pubns Mgr: Jennifer Miller *Tel:* 801-537-3318
E-mail: jlmiller@utah.gov
Founded: 1949
ISBN Prefix(es): 978-1-55791
Number of titles published annually: 30 Print; 15
CD-ROM; 5 Online
Total Titles: 702 Print

Utah State University Press
Imprint of University Press of Colorado
3078 Old Main Hill, Logan, UT 84322-3078
Tel: 435-797-1362
Web Site: www.usupress.com
Key Personnel
Dir: Darrin Pratt *E-mail:* darrin@upcolorado.com
Founded: 1972
ISBN Prefix(es): 978-0-87421; 978-1-60732
Number of titles published annually: 20 Print
Total Titles: 250 Print
Membership(s): Association of University Presses
(AUPresses)

UVA Press, see The University of Virginia Press

VanDam Inc
The VanDam Bldg, 121 W 27 St, New York, NY
10001
Tel: 212-929-0416 *Toll Free Tel:* 800-UNFOLDS
(863-6537) *Fax:* 212-929-0426
E-mail: info@vandam.com
Web Site: www.vandam.com
Key Personnel
Pres/Creative Dir: Stephan Van Dam *Tel:* 212-
929-0416 ext 10 *E-mail:* stephan@vandam.com
Dir, Opers: Jessy Cerda *Tel:* 212-929-0416 ext 16
E-mail: jessy@vandam.com
Founded: 1984
Publisher of UNFOLDS®, StreetSmart & Pop-
Up maps; Urban@tlas city atlases. Licensor of

patented folding technology used to produce
UNFOLDS® products.
ISBN Prefix(es): 978-0-931141; 978-1-932527;
978-1-934395
Number of titles published annually: 50 Print
Total Titles: 250 Print
Divisions: VanDam Publishing
Foreign Rep(s): LAC (Italy); RV Verlag (Ger-
many)

Vandamere Press
3580 Morris St N, St Petersburg, FL 33713
SAN: 657-3088
Mailing Address: PO Box 149, St Petersburg, FL
33731
Tel: 727-556-0950 *Toll Free Tel:* 800-551-7776
Fax: 727-556-2560
E-mail: orders@vandamere.com
Web Site: www.vandamere.com
Key Personnel
Publr & Ed-in-Chief: Arthur Brown
E-mail: abrown@vandamere.com
Dir, Spec Sales: Stephanie Brown
Sr Book Ed & Acq Ed: Jerry Frank
Wholesale Sales: John Cabin
Founded: 1984
ISBN Prefix(es): 978-0-918339
Number of titles published annually: 8 Print
Total Titles: 70 Print
Distributor for ABI Professional Publications
(non-exclusive); JMC Press (exclusive to trade);
NRH Press (non-exclusive); Quodlibetal Fea-
tures

Vanderbilt University Press
Division of Vanderbilt University
2301 Vanderbilt Place, PMB 401813, Nashville,
TN 37240-1813
SAN: 202-9308
Tel: 615-322-3585 *Toll Free Tel:* 800-848-6224
(orders only) *Fax:* 615-343-0308
E-mail: vupress@vanderbilt.edu
Web Site: www.vanderbiltuniversitypress.com
Key Personnel
Dir: Gianna Mosser
Mng Ed: Joell Smith Borne
Busn Mgr & Rts & Perms: Cynthia Yeager
Design & Prodn Mgr: Drohan DiSanto
Sales & Mktg Mgr: Betsy Phillips *E-mail:* betsy.
phillips@vanderbilt.edu
Mktg & New Media Assoc: Jenna Phillips
Founded: 1940
Scholarly nonfiction, humanities, social sciences,
literary criticism, history, regional studies.
ISBN Prefix(es): 978-0-8265
Number of titles published annually: 25 Print
Total Titles: 600 Print; 400 E-Book
Distributor for Country Music Foundation Press
Foreign Rep(s): Ampersand (Canada); Eurospan
(all other territories)
Distribution Center: Longleaf Services Inc,
116 S Boundary St, Chapel Hill, NC 27514-
3808 *Tel:* 919-966-7449 *Toll Free Tel:* 800-
848-6224 (US) *Fax:* 919-962-2704 *Toll Free
Fax:* 800-272-6817 (US) *E-mail:* orders@
longleafservices.org
Membership(s): Association of University Presses
(AUPresses)

Vault.com Inc
132 W 31 St, 16th fl, New York, NY 10001
Tel: 212-366-4212 *Toll Free Tel:* 800-535-2074
Fax: 212-366-6117 (cust serv)
E-mail: editors@vault.com; customerservice@
vault.com
Web Site: www.vault.com
Key Personnel
Sr Fin Ed: Derek Loosvelt
Founded: 1997
"Insider" career development for professionals.
ISBN Prefix(es): 978-1-58131

Number of titles published annually: 4 Print; 10
Online
Total Titles: 61 Print; 124 Online

Vedanta Press
Subsidiary of Vedanta Society of Southern Cali-
fornia
1946 Vedanta Place, Hollywood, CA 90068
Tel: 323-960-1728; 323-960-1736 (catalog)
Fax: 323-465-9568
E-mail: vpress@vedanta.com
Web Site: www.vedanta.com
Key Personnel
Mgr: Robert Adjemian *E-mail:* bob@vedanta.com
Founded: 1945
ISBN Prefix(es): 978-81-85301 (Advaita
Ashrama); 978-0-87481; 978-81-8172 (Ramakr-
ishna Math); 978-81-7505
Number of titles published annually: 1 CD-ROM;
15 Online
Total Titles: 17 CD-ROM; 25 Online
Distributor for Advaita Ashrama; Ananda
Ashrama; Ramakrishna Math; Ramakrishna-
Vivekananda Center of New York
Membership(s): Independent Book Publishers As-
sociation (IBPA)

Velazquez Press
Division of Academic Learning Co LLC
9682 Telstar Ave, Suite 110, El Monte, CA 91731
Tel: 626-448-3448 *Fax:* 626-602-3817
E-mail: info@academiclearningcompany.com
Web Site: www.velazquezpress.com
Key Personnel
Mng Dir: Arthur Chou
Dir, Busn Devt: Jonathan Ruiz *E-mail:* jruiz@
academiclearningcompany.com
Founded: 2003
Publisher of bilingual dictionaries.
ISBN Prefix(es): 978-1-59495
Number of titles published annually: 4 Print
Total Titles: 10 Print

The Vendome Press
244 Fifth Ave, Suite 2043, New York, NY 10001
Tel: 212-737-1857
E-mail: info@vendomepress.com
Web Site: www.vendomepress.com
Key Personnel
Pres & Publr: Mark Magowan
Prodn Dir: Jim Spivey
Publicity Dir: Meghan Phillips
Ed: Jackuelen Decter
Founded: 1981
Illustrated art, architecture & lifestyle books.
ISBN Prefix(es): 978-0-86565
Number of titles published annually: 10 Print
Total Titles: 100 Print
Distributed by Abrams Books; Thames & Hudson

Vernon Press
Imprint of Vernon Art & Science Inc
1000 N West St, Suite 1200, Wilmington, DE
19801
Tel: 302-250-4440
E-mail: info@vernonpress.com
Web Site: www.vernonpress.com
Key Personnel
Dir: Rosario Batana
ISBN Prefix(es): 978-1-62273
Number of titles published annually: 60 Print

Verso
20 Jay St, Suite 1010, Brooklyn, NY 11201
Tel: 718-246-8160 *Fax:* 718-246-8165
E-mail: verso@versobooks.com
Web Site: www.versobooks.com
Key Personnel
Mng Dir: Jacob Stevens
Mktg Mgr: Anne Rumberger
Ed: Jessie Kindig

Founded: 1970
Nonfiction, progressive studies on politics, history, society & culture.
ISBN Prefix(es): 978-0-86091; 978-0-85984; 978-0-84467
Number of titles published annually: 80 Print
Total Titles: 2,000 Print
Imprints: Verso Fiction
Foreign Office(s): 6 Meard St, London W1F OE6, United Kingdom
Distributed by Penguin (Canada)
Foreign Rep(s): Verso (England)
Foreign Rights: Verso (worldwide)
Shipping Address: Marston Book Services, Kemp Hall Bindery, Osney Mead, Oxford, United Kingdom

Vesuvian Books
Division of Vesuvian Media Group Inc
2817 West End Ave, No 126-283, Nashville, TN 37203
Mailing Address: 711 Dolly Parton Pkwy, No 4313, Sevierville, TN 37864
E-mail: info@vesuvianmedia.com
Web Site: www.vesuvianbooks.com
Key Personnel
Founder & CEO: Italia Gandolfo *Tel:* 615-447-8444 *E-mail:* italia@vesuvianmedia.com
Exec Chmn: Thomas N Ellsworth
Art Dir: Sam Shearon
Creative Dir: Michael J Canales
Dir, Acqs: Beth Isaacs
Dir, Busn Devt: Gareth Worthington *Tel:* (079) 929 15 67 *E-mail:* gareth@vesuvianmedia.com
Dir, Opers: LK Griffie *Tel:* 714-243-8723 *E-mail:* lk@vesuvianmedia.com
Founded: 2015
A multimedia corporation dedicated to creating quality entertainment across literary & visual arts. Vesuvian Books does not accept unsol submissions. Prospective authors & illustrators must submit their work through an agent.
ISBN Prefix(es): 978-1-944109
Number of titles published annually: 15 Print; 15 Online; 15 E-Book
Total Titles: 48 Print; 51 E-Book; 3 Audio
Imprints: Black Spot Books; Rosewind Romance
Foreign Rights: Books Crossing Borders (Betty Anne Crawford) (worldwide exc USA)
Billing Address: 711 Dolly Parton Pkwy, No 4313, Sevierville, TN 37864 *Tel:* 502-836-1201
Distribution Center: Independent Publishers Group (IPG), 814 N Franklin St, Chicago, IL 60610, VP, Publr Devt: Richard T Williams *Tel:* 312-337-0747 *Toll Free Tel:* 800-888-4741 *Fax:* 312-337-5985 *E-mail:* rwilliams@ipgbook.com *Web Site:* www.ipgbook.com
Membership(s): American Booksellers Association (ABA); Horror Writers Association (HWA); Independent Book Publishers Association (IBPA); International Thriller Writers Inc (ITW)

VH-1, see Gallery Books

Viking
Imprint of Penguin Group USA, A Penguin Random House Company
375 Hudson St, New York, NY 10014
Tel: 212-366-2000 *Fax:* 212-243-6002
Web Site: www.penguin.com/publishers/vikingbooks
Key Personnel
Pres & Publr: Brian Tart
SVP & Creative Art Dir: Paul Buckley
VP & Publr, Pamela Dorman Books: Pamela Dorman
VP, Assoc Publr & Dir, Mktg: Kate Stark
VP, Assoc Publr & Edit Dir (Nonfiction): Wendy Wolf
VP & Exec Dir, Copyediting: Tory Klose
VP & Exec Ed: Paul Slovak

VP & Exec Publicist: Carolyn Coleburn
Exec Dir, Ad & Promo: Dennis Swaim
Exec Publicity Dir: Lindsay Prevette
Assoc Dir, Publicity: Shannon Twomey
Assoc Dir, Publicity, Viking/Penguin: Rebecca Marsh
Publicity Mgr: Maya Baran
Exec Publicist, Viking/Penguin: Shelby Meizlik
Sr Publicist: Kristina Fazzalaro; Tony Forde; Alison Klooster; Brianna Linden; Chris Smith; Olivia Taussig
Publicist: Sara DeLozier
Assoc Publicist: Sara Chuirazzi; Jessica Fitzpatrick; Theresa Gaffney; Andrea Lam; Sara Leonard
Ed-in-Chief: Andrea Schulz
Exec Mng Ed: Tricia Conley
Exec Ed: Carolyn Carlson; Rick Kot; Allison Lorentzen; Laura Tisdel
Sr Ed: Lindsey Schwoeri
Ed: Georgia Bodnar; Emily Wunderlich
Assoc Ed: Terezia Cicel; Amy Sun
Assoc Ed, Pamela Dorman Books: Jeramie Orton
Asst Ed: Diego Nunez
Founded: 1925
Penguin Random House & its publishing entities are not accepting unsol submissions, proposals, mss, or submission queries via e-mail at this time.
Number of titles published annually: 75 Print
Total Titles: 250 Print
Imprints: Pamela Dorman Books; Viking Compass
Advertising Agency: Spier NY

Viking Children's Books
Imprint of Penguin Group USA, A Penguin Random House Company
345 Hudson St, New York, NY 10014
Fax: 212-414-3393
E-mail: youngreaderspublicity@us.penguingroup.com
Web Site: www.penguin.com/publishers/vikingchildrensbooks
Key Personnel
Pres & Publr: Ken Wright
Assoc Publr & Mng Ed: Gerard Mancini
Edit Dir, Picture Books: Tamar Brazis; Tracy Gates
Exec Ed: Jenny Bak
Assoc Ed: Maggie Rosenthal
Ed-at-Large: Regina Hayes
Founded: 1933
Penguin Random House & its publishing entities are not accepting unsol submissions, proposals, mss, or submission queries via e-mail at this time.
Number of titles published annually: 60 Print
Membership(s): The Children's Book Council (CBC)

Viking Studio
Imprint of Penguin Group USA, A Penguin Random House Company
375 Hudson St, New York, NY 10014
Tel: 212-366-2000 *Fax:* 212-366-2636
E-mail: averystudiopublicity@us.penguingroup.com
Web Site: www.penguin.com
Key Personnel
Pres & Publr: Brian Tart
Founded: 1988
Penguin Random House & its publishing entities are not accepting unsol submissions, proposals, mss, or submission queries via e-mail at this time.
Number of titles published annually: 4 Print
Total Titles: 40 Print
Advertising Agency: Spier NY

Carl Vinson Institute of Government
University of Georgia, 201 N Milledge Ave, Athens, GA 30602

Tel: 706-542-2736 *Fax:* 706-542-9301
Web Site: www.cviog.uga.edu
Key Personnel
Dir: Laura Meadows *Tel:* 706-542-6192 *E-mail:* lmeadows@uga.edu
Founded: 1927
Instruction, technical assistance, research & publications for state & local governments & communities.
ISBN Prefix(es): 978-0-89854
Number of titles published annually: 10 Print; 2 CD-ROM
Total Titles: 70 Print; 3 CD-ROM

Vintage Books
Imprint of Knopf Doubleday Publishing Group c/o Penguin Random House Inc, 1745 Broadway, New York, NY 10019
Tel: 212-572-2420
E-mail: vintageanchorpublicity@randomhouse.com
Web Site: knopfdoubleday.com/imprint/vintage
Key Personnel
Publr: Suzanne Herz
SVP & Edit Dir: Luann Walther
VP & Assoc Publr: Beth Lamb
VP & Exec Ed: Edward Kastenmeier
Exec Dir, Publicity & Soc Media: James Meader
Sr Dir, Sales Mktg & Busn Devt: Laura Crisp
Design Dir: Claudia Martinez
Dir, Ad & Promo: Irena Vukov-Kendes
Dir, Digital Mktg: Paige Smith
Assoc Dir, Publicity: Angie Venezia
Mng Ed: Barbara Richard
Mktg Mgr: Laura Chamberlain; Jessica Deitcher
Publicity Mgr: Julie Ertl
Founded: 1954
Penguin Random House & its publishing entities are not accepting unsol submissions, proposals, mss, or submission queries via e-mail at this time.
Number of titles published annually: 175 Print; 190 E-Book
Total Titles: 2,650 Print; 1,750 E-Book
Imprints: Vintage Shorts (ebooks)
Foreign Rights: Anthea Agency (Katalina Sabeva) (Bulgaria); Bardon-Chinese Media Agency (Xu Weiguang) (China); Bardon-Chinese Media Agency (Yu Shiuan Chen & David Tsai) (Taiwan); The English Agency (Hamish Macaskill & Junzo Sawa) (Japan); Graal Literary Agency (Maria Strarz-Kanska) (Poland); The Deborah Harris Agency (Ilana Kurshan) (Israel); JLM Literary Agency (Nelly Moukakou) (Greece); Katai & Bolza Literary (Peter Bolza) (Croatia, Hungary, Serbia); Simona Kessler Agency (Simona Kessler) (Romania); Korea Copyright Center (MiSook Hong) (Korea); Licht & Burr Literary Agency (Trine Licht) (Scandinavia); La Nouvelle Agence (Vanessa Kling) (France); Kristin Olson Literary Agency (Kristin Olson) (Czechia); Agenzia Letteraria Santachiara (Roberto Santachiara) (Italy); Sebes & Bisseling Literary Agency (Holland)

Visible Ink Press®
43311 Joy Rd, Suite 414, Canton, MI 48187-2075
Tel: 734-667-3211 *Fax:* 734-667-4311
E-mail: info@visibleinkpress.com
Web Site: www.visibleinkpress.com
Key Personnel
Publr: Roger Janecke
Founded: 1989
Popular reference publisher specializing in handy answer books, spiritual phenomena & multicultural history.
ISBN Prefix(es): 978-0-8103; 978-0-7876; 978-1-57859
Number of titles published annually: 10 Print; 10 E-Book
Total Titles: 200 Print; 300 E-Book

Distribution Center: Publishers Group West, 210 America Dr, Jackson, TN 38301 *Toll Free Tel:* 800-343-4499; 866-400-5351 (cust serv) *E-mail:* ipsjacksonorders@ingramcontent.com

§Visual Profile Books Inc
389 Fifth Ave, Suite 1105, New York, NY 10016
SAN: 213-1552
Tel: 516-445-0116
Web Site: www.visualprofilebooks.com
Key Personnel
Publr: Larry Fuersich *E-mail:* larry@visualprofilebooks.com
Edit Dir: Roger Yee *E-mail:* rhtyee@gmail.com
Founded: 1931
Architecture, interior & graphic design.
ISBN Prefix(es): 978-0-9825989
Number of titles published annually: 15 Print
Total Titles: 568 Print
Distribution Center: National Book Network, 15200 NBN Way, Blue Ridge Summit, PA 17214 *Tel:* 717-794-3800 *Fax:* 717-794-3828 *E-mail:* customercare@nbnbooks.com *Web Site:* nbnbooks.com

Viva Editions, see Cleis Press

Ludwig von Mises Institute
518 W Magnolia Ave, Auburn, AL 36832
Tel: 334-321-2100 *Fax:* 334-321-2119
E-mail: info@mises.org
Web Site: www.mises.org
Key Personnel
CEO: Jeff Deist
Bookstore Mgr: Brandon Hill *E-mail:* brandon@mises.org
Founded: 1982
Nonprofit educational organization devoted to the Austrian School of Economics.
ISBN Prefix(es): 978-0-945466; 978-1-933550; 978-1-61016
Number of titles published annually: 5 Print; 5 Audio
Total Titles: 60 Print

§Voyager Sopris Learning Inc
Imprint of Cambium Learning Inc
17855 Dallas Pkwy, Suite 400, Dallas, TX 75287
Tel: 303-651-2829 *Toll Free Tel:* 800-547-6747 *Fax:* 303-776-5934 *Toll Free Fax:* 888-819-7767
E-mail: customerservice@voyagersopris.com
Web Site: www.voyagersopris.com
Founded: 1978
Training, development materials for educators.
ISBN Prefix(es): 978-0-944584; 978-1-57035; 978-1-59318
Number of titles published annually: 100 Print
Total Titles: 350 Print

§Wake Forest University Press
2518 Reynolda Rd, Winston-Salem, NC 27106
Mailing Address: PO Box 7333, Winston-Salem, NC 27109-7333
Tel: 336-758-5448 *Fax:* 336-842-3853
E-mail: wfupress@wfu.edu
Web Site: wfupress.wfu.edu
Key Personnel
Founder & Advising Ed: Dillon Johnston
Dir & Ed: Jefferson Holdridge
Advising Asst Dir: Candide Jones
Mgr: Amanda Keith
Founded: 1975
Contemporary Irish poetry.
ISBN Prefix(es): 978-0-916390; 978-1-930630
Number of titles published annually: 5 Print
Total Titles: 100 Print
Distribution Center: Independent Publishers Group (IPG), 814 N Franklin St, Chicago, IL 60610 *Toll Free Tel:* 800-888-4741 *Fax:* 312-337-5985 *E-mail:* orders@ipgbook.com

Walch Education
40 Walch Dr, Portland, ME 04103-1286
SAN: 203-0268
Tel: 207-772-2846 *Toll Free Tel:* 800-558-2846 *Fax:* 207-772-3105 *Toll Free Fax:* 888-991-5755
E-mail: customerservice@walch.com
Web Site: www.walch.com
Key Personnel
Pres: Al Noyes *E-mail:* anoyes@walch.com
Founded: 1927
Educational books & supplementary materials for middle school through adult.
ISBN Prefix(es): 978-0-8251
Number of titles published annually: 100 Print; 75 Online
Total Titles: 1,700 Print; 850 Online
Membership(s): ASCD; International Literacy Association (ILA); National Council for the Social Studies (NCSS); National Council of Teachers of English (NCTE); National Council of Teachers of Mathematics (NCTM); National Science Teachers Association (NSTA)

Walch Publishing, see Walch Education

Waldorf Publishing
2140 Hall Johnson Rd, No 102-345, Grapevine, TX 76051
Tel: 972-674-3131
E-mail: info@waldorfpublishing.com
Web Site: www.waldorfpublishing.com
Key Personnel
Owner & Publr: Barbara Terry
Founded: 2014
ISBN Prefix(es): 978-1-68419; 978-1-943275; 978-1-943277; 978-1-944245; 978-1-945173
Number of titles published annually: 55 Print; 55 CD-ROM; 55 Online; 55 E-Book; 55 Audio
Total Titles: 200 Print; 200 CD-ROM; 200 Online; 200 E-Book; 200 Audio
Foreign Rights: Susan Schulman Literary Agency (worldwide)

Warner Press
Affiliate of Church of God
2902 Enterprise Dr, Anderson, IN 46013
Tel: 765-644-7721 *Toll Free Tel:* 800-741-7721 (orders) *Fax:* 765-640-8005
E-mail: wporders@warnerpress.org
Web Site: www.warnerpress.org
Key Personnel
Pres: Eric King
VP, Sales: Connie Crist
VP, Prod Mktg: Regina Jackson
Founded: 1881
Specialize in religious books, activity books, coloring books & greeting cards.
ISBN Prefix(es): 978-0-87162; 978-1-59317
Number of titles published annually: 6 Print

§Washington State University Press
Division of Washington State University
Cooper Publications Bldg, 2300 Grimes Way, Pullman, WA 99164-5910
SAN: 206-6688
Mailing Address: PO Box 645910, Pullman, WA 99164-5910
Tel: 509-335-7880 *Toll Free Tel:* 800-354-7360 (orders)
E-mail: wsupress@wsu.edu
Web Site: wsupress.wsu.edu
Key Personnel
Dir: Edward Sala *E-mail:* sala@wsu.edu
Asst Dir & Ed-in-Chief: Linda Bathgate *Tel:* 509-335-7630 *E-mail:* linda.bathgate@wsu.edu
Busn Opers Mgr: Kerry Darnall *E-mail:* kdarnall@wsu.edu
Mktg Mgr: Caryn Lawton *Tel:* 509-335-7877 *E-mail:* lawton@wsu.edu
Founded: 1928

Trade & scholarly books focusing on the history, natural history, military history, culture & politics of the greater Pacific Northwest region (Washington, Idaho, Oregon, Western Montana, British Columbia & Alaska). Refer to web site for submission guidelines.
ISBN Prefix(es): 978-0-87422
Number of titles published annually: 8 Print
Total Titles: 182 Print
Sales Office(s): Book Travelers West, 3614A California Ave SW, No 228, Seattle, WA 98116, Kurtis Lowe *Tel:* 206-932-7865 *E-mail:* kurtis@booktravelerswest.com
Book Travelers West, 1026 Florin Rd, No 164, Sacramento, CA 95831, Kevin Peters *Tel:* 310-710-1306 *E-mail:* kevin@booktravelerswest.com
Book Travelers West, 2921 W 38 Ave, No 335, Denver, CO 80211, Phoebe Gaston *Tel:* 513-886-1130 *E-mail:* phoebe@booktravelerswest.com
Distributor for Oregon California Trails Assn; Oregon Writers Colony (single title); Pacific Institute (single title); Washington State Historical Society (single title); WSU Museum of Art
Distribution Center: Baker & Taylor Books, PO Box 8888, Momence, IL 60954 (US & CN) *Toll Free Tel:* 800-775-1100 *Toll Free Fax:* 800-775-7480
Ingram Book Co, One Ingram Blvd, La Vergne, TN 37086 (US & CN) *Toll Free Tel:* 800-937-8000
Membership(s): Association of University Presses (AUPresses)

Water Environment Federation
601 Wythe St, Alexandria, VA 22314-1994
Tel: 703-684-2400 *Toll Free Tel:* 800-666-0206 (cust serv) *Fax:* 703-684-2492
E-mail: inquiry@wef.org
Web Site: www.wef.org
Key Personnel
Pubns: Karah DeMarco *Tel:* 703-684-2400 ext 7211 *E-mail:* kdemarco@wef.org
Founded: 1928
Scientific publisher of environmental titles. Seeks authors of sound, state-of-the-art environmental material.
ISBN Prefix(es): 978-0-943244; 978-1-881369; 978-1-572783
Number of titles published annually: 15 Print
Total Titles: 220 Print

§Water Resources Publications LLC
PO Box 630026, Highlands Ranch, CO 80163-0026
SAN: 209-9136
Tel: 720-873-0171 *Toll Free Tel:* 800-736-2405 *Fax:* 720-873-0173 *Toll Free Fax:* 800-616-1971
E-mail: info@wrpllc.com
Web Site: www.wrpllc.com
Founded: 1971
Publishing & distributing books & computer software on water resources & related fields.
ISBN Prefix(es): 978-0-918334; 978-1-887201
Number of titles published annually: 10 Print
Total Titles: 220 Print; 35 CD-ROM
Distributor for ASAE
Shipping Address: 10607 Flatiron Rd, Littleton, CO 80124 *Toll Free Fax:* 844-270-6832
Warehouse: 10607 Flatiron Rd, Littleton, CO 80124 *Toll Free Fax:* 844-270-6832

WaterBrook
Imprint of Crown Publishing Group
10807 New Allegiance Dr, Suite 500, Colorado Springs, CO 80921
Tel: 719-590-4999 *Toll Free Tel:* 800-603-7051 (orders) *Fax:* 719-590-8977 *Toll Free Fax:* 800-294-5686 (orders)
E-mail: info@waterbrookmultnomah.com

Web Site: waterbrookmultnomah.com
Founded: 1996
Publishes Christian books that seek to intensify & satisfy a reader's elemental thirst for a deeper relationship with God. Seek messages that draw on the Bible, experiential learning, story, practical guidance & inspiration to help readers thrive in their faith.
Penguin Random House & its publishing entities are not accepting unsol submissions, proposals, mss, or submission queries via e-mail at this time.
Number of titles published annually: 41 Print
Imprints: Shaw Books
Membership(s): Evangelical Christian Publishers Association (ECPA)

Watermark Publishing
1000 Bishop St, Suite 806, Honolulu, HI 96813
Tel: 808-587-7766 *Toll Free Tel:* 866-900-BOOK (900-2665) *Fax:* 808-521-3461
E-mail: info@bookshawaii.net
Web Site: www.bookshawaii.net
Key Personnel
Dir, Sales & Mktg: Dawn Sakamoto *Tel:* 808-534-7170 *E-mail:* dawn@bookshawaii.net
ISBN Prefix(es): 978-0-9720932; 978-0-9705787; 978-0-9631154; 978-0-9753740; 978-0-9779143; 978-0-9790647; 978-0-9796769; 978-0-9815086
Number of titles published annually: 8 Print
Total Titles: 55 Print

Watson-Guptill Publications
Imprint of Crown Publishing Group
c/o Ten Speed Press, 6001 Shellmount St, Suite 600, Emeryville, CA 94608
Web Site: crownpublishing.com/imprint/watson-guptill
Founded: 1937
Hard-working & influential illustrated art books. Seeks out respected authorities who instruct & inspire artists in a wide range of art & craft. List covers both fine art & practical art instruction in traditional disciplines such as drawing, painting, sculpture & printmaking. Also publish modern books focused on artistic pursuits such as craft, collage, mixed media, comics, sequential art, cartooning, manga & animation.
Number of titles published annually: 60 Print
Total Titles: 800 Print
Orders to: Penguin Random House Inc, 400 Hahn Rd, Westminster, MD 21157 *Toll Free Tel:* 800-733-3000 *E-mail:* csorders@randomhouse.com; Penguin Random House of Canada Inc, Diversified Sales, 2775 Mattheson Blvd E, Mississauga, ON L4W 4P4, Canada *Toll Free Tel:* 800-668-4247 *Fax:* 905-624-8091

Watson Publishing International LLC
349 Old Plymouth Rd, Sagamore Beach, MA 02562
Mailing Address: PO Box 1480, Sagamore Beach, MA 02562
E-mail: orders@shpusa.com
Web Site: www.shpusa.com; www.watsonpublishing.com
Key Personnel
Mgr: Laura Bergeron
Founded: 1971
Scholarly books on the history, philosophy & sociology of science, technology & medicine.
ISBN Prefix(es): 978-0-88135
Number of titles published annually: 5 Print
Total Titles: 120 Print
Imprints: Prodist; Science History Publications USA; Neale Watson Academic Publications

Waveland Press Inc
4180 IL Rte 83, Suite 101, Long Grove, IL 60047-9580
SAN: 209-0961

Tel: 847-634-0081 *Fax:* 847-634-9501
E-mail: info@waveland.com
Web Site: www.waveland.com
Key Personnel
Pres & Publr: Neil Rowe
Ed: Carol Rowe
Ed & Mktg Mgr: Thomas Curtin
Ed, Prodn Mgr & Intl Rts: Don Rosso
Founded: 1975
College textbooks & supplements.
ISBN Prefix(es): 978-0-88133; 978-0-917974; 978-1-57766; 978-1-4786
Number of titles published annually: 40 Print
Total Titles: 700 Print
Subsidiaries: Sheffield Publishing Co
Warehouse: 9009 Antioch Rd, Salem, WI 53168, Gen Mgr: Steve Nelson

Wayne State University Press
Leonard N Simons Bldg, 4809 Woodward Ave, Detroit, MI 48201-1309
SAN: 202-5221
Tel: 313-577-6120 *Toll Free Tel:* 800-978-7323 *Fax:* 313-577-6131
E-mail: bookorders@wayne.edu
Web Site: www.wsupress.wayne.edu
Key Personnel
Dir: Stephanie Williams *Tel:* 313-577-4607
Ed-in-Chief: Annie Martin *Tel:* 313-577-8335 *E-mail:* annie.martin@wayne.edu
Acqs Ed: Marie Sweetman *Tel:* 313-577-4220 *E-mail:* marie.sweetman@wayne.edu
Design & Prodn Mgr: Kristin Harpster *Tel:* 313-577-4604 *E-mail:* kmharpster@wayne.edu
Mktg & Sales Mgr: Emily Nowak *Tel:* 313-577-6128 *E-mail:* enowak@wayne.edu
Order Fulfillment Mgr: Theresa Martinelli *Tel:* 313-577-6126 *E-mail:* theresa.martinelli@wayne.edu
Founded: 1941
Scholarly & trade books in African American studies, film & television, women's studies, Jewish studies, poetry, speech & language pathology, fairy tales & folklore, regional studies & urban studies.
ISBN Prefix(es): 978-0-8143
Number of titles published annually: 40 Print
Total Titles: 2,500 Print; 2 CD-ROM
Imprints: Great Lakes Books; Painted Turtle Books (general interest trade)
Foreign Rep(s): Eurospan (Africa, Europe, Middle East, UK)
Warehouse: 40 W Hancock St, Detroit, MI 48201
Membership(s): Association of University Presses (AUPresses)

Wayside Publishing
2 Stonewood Dr, Freeport, ME 04032
Toll Free Tel: 888-302-2519
E-mail: info@waysidepublishing.com; support@waysidepublishing.com
Web Site: waysidepublishing.com
Key Personnel
Pres: Greg Greuel
Mgr, Opers: Nicole Lyons
Founded: 1988
Humanities, English & foreign language textbooks & history.
ISBN Prefix(es): 978-1-877653
Number of titles published annually: 5 Print
Total Titles: 54 Print

Welcome Enterprises Inc
Imprint of Rizzoli International Publications Inc
300 Park Ave S, New York, NY 10010
Tel: 212-387-3400
Web Site: www.rizzoliusa.com
Founded: 1980
Illustrated books for adult trade & gift market.
ISBN Prefix(es): 978-0-941807
Number of titles published annually: 8 Print
Total Titles: 100 Print

Distributed by Random House
Distributor for AAP; Cerf & Peterson; Music Sales; Zeke Holdings Ltd
Distribution Center: Random House, 400 Hahn Rd, Westminster, MD 21157 *Toll Free Tel:* 800-733-3000 *Toll Free Fax:* 800-659-2436
Membership(s): American Book Producers Association (ABPA)

Welcome Rain Publishers LLC
217 Thompson St, Suite 473, New York, NY 10012
Tel: 212-686-1909
Web Site: welcomerain.com
Key Personnel
Publr: John Weber
Founded: 1997
General trade publisher.
ISBN Prefix(es): 978-1-56649
Number of titles published annually: 21 Print
Total Titles: 95 Print
Distribution Center: National Book Network (NBN), 15200 NBN Way, Blue Ridge Summit, PA 17214 *Tel:* 717-794-3800 *Fax:* 717-794-3828

Welcome to My Worlds
1630 W Gail Dr, Chandler, AZ 85224-4045
Tel: 480-773-8958
Web Site: kbshawauthor.com
Key Personnel
Publr: Keith Shaw
Founded: 2010
ISBN Prefix(es): 978-0-9828090
Number of titles published annually: 3 Print; 3 E-Book
Total Titles: 13 Print; 1 Online; 21 E-Book
Membership(s): Society of Children's Book Writers & Illustrators (SCBWI); Society of Southwestern Authors

Well-Trained Mind Press
18021 The Glebe Lane, Charles City, VA 23030
Tel: 804-829-5043 *Toll Free Tel:* 877-322-3445 (orders) *Fax:* 804-829-5704
E-mail: support@welltrainedmind.com
Web Site: welltrainedmind.com
Key Personnel
CEO & Ed-in-Chief: Susan Wise Bauer
Exec Admin: Kim Norton
Founded: 2001
Publish educational books for home school families & schools & books for the well-trained mind.
ISBN Prefix(es): 978-0-9714129; 978-1-933339; 978-0-9728603; 978-1-942968
Number of titles published annually: 5 Print
Total Titles: 29 Print
Distributed by W W Norton & Company Inc
Foreign Rights: Richard Henshaw (Central America, South America)

Wellington Press
Division of BooksUPrint.com Inc
9601-30 Miccosukee Rd, Tallahassee, FL 32309
E-mail: peacegames@aol.com
Web Site: www.peacegames.com
Key Personnel
Pres & Intl Rts: David W Felder, PhD
Founded: 1982
Publish philosophy books, including texts, & role play peacegames that examine conflicts of all types.
ISBN Prefix(es): 978-0-910959; 978-1-57501
Number of titles published annually: 10 Print; 10 E-Book
Total Titles: 85 Print; 90 Online; 100 E-Book

Eliot Werner Publications Inc
31 Willow Lane, Clinton Corners, NY 12514
Mailing Address: PO Box 268, Clinton Corners, NY 12514
Tel: 845-266-4241 *Fax:* 845-266-3317

E-mail: eliotwerner217@gmail.com
Web Site: www.eliotwerner.com
Founded: 2001
Academic & scholarly books in anthropology, archaeology, psychology, sociology & related fields; writing, editing & contract publishing.
ISBN Prefix(es): 978-0-9712427; 978-0-9719587; 978-0-9752738; 978-0-9797731; 978-0-9898249
Number of titles published annually: 4 Print
Total Titles: 56 Print
Imprints: Percheron Press
Distribution Center: Ian Stevens Distribution, 70 Enterprise Dr, No 2, Bristol, CT 06010, Fin & Off Mgr: Melanie Palleria *Tel:* 860-584-6546 *Fax:* 860-516-4873 *E-mail:* melanie@isdistribution.com *Web Site:* www.isdistribution.com

Wesleyan Publishing House
Division of The Wesleyan Church
13300 Olio Rd, Fishers, IN 46037
Mailing Address: PO Box 50434, Indianapolis, IN 46250
Tel: 317-774-3853 *Toll Free Tel:* 800-493-7539 *Fax:* 317-774-3865 *Toll Free Fax:* 800-788-3535
E-mail: wph@wesleyan.org
Web Site: www.wesleyan.org/books
Key Personnel
Proj Communs Mgr: Susan LeBaron
   E-mail: lebarons@wesleyan.org
Founded: 1968
ISBN Prefix(es): 978-0-89827
Number of titles published annually: 40 Print
Total Titles: 60 Print
Membership(s): Christian Holiness Partnership (CHP); Evangelical Christian Publishers Association (ECPA); Holiness Publisher's Association (HPA); Protestant Church-Owned Publishers Association (PCPA)

Wesleyan University Press
215 Long Lane, Middletown, CT 06459-0433
Tel: 860-685-7712 *Fax:* 860-685-7712
Web Site: www.wesleyan.edu/wespress
Key Personnel
Dir & Ed-in-Chief: Suzanna L Tamminen
   Tel: 860-685-7727 *E-mail:* stamminen@wesleyan.edu
Mktg Mgr: Jaclyn Wilson *Tel:* 860-685-7725
   E-mail: jwilson05@wesleyan.edu
Publicist & Web Mgr: Stephanie Elliott *Tel:* 860-685-7723 *E-mail:* selliott@wesleyan.edu
Founded: 1957
Editorial program which has been awarded 6 Pulitzer Prizes; distinguished history of publishing scholarly & trade books that have influenced American poetry & critical thought over the last four decades.
ISBN Prefix(es): 978-0-8195
Number of titles published annually: 25 Print
Total Titles: 425 Print
Distribution Center: Hopkins Fulfillment Services (HFS), PO Box 50370, Baltimore, MD 21211-4370 (CN & US) *Tel:* 410-516-6965 *Toll Free Tel:* 800-537-5487 *Fax:* 410-516-6998 *E-mail:* hfcustserv@press.jhu.edu *Web Site:* www.hfsbooks.com
Oxbow Books Ltd, c/o Orca Book Services, 160 Eastern Ave, Milton Park, Abingdon, Oxon OX14 4SB, United Kingdom (Europe, Middle East & UK) *Tel:* (01235) 465500 *Fax:* (01235) 465555 *E-mail:* tradeorders@orcabookservices.co.uk
Membership(s): Association of American Publishers (AAP); Association of University Presses (AUPresses); NEBA

§West Academic
444 Cedar St, Suite 700, St Paul, MN 55101
Toll Free Tel: 877-888-1330

E-mail: customerservice@westacademic.com; support@westacademic.com; media@westacademic.com
Web Site: www.westacademic.com
Key Personnel
Sr Natl & Intl Acct Mgr: Scott Duckson
   Tel: 651-202-4764 *E-mail:* scott.duckson@westacademic.com
Founded: 1953
Law school casebook, statute, study aid & career success publisher.
ISBN Prefix(es): 978-0-1590; 978-0-3141
Number of titles published annually: 50 Print; 2 CD-ROM
Total Titles: 375 Print; 10 CD-ROM; 60 Audio
Imprints: Foundation Press; Gilbert
Returns: West Academic Distribution Center, 10650 Toebben Dr, Independence, KY 41051
See separate listing for:
Foundation Press

West Margin Press®
Unit of Ingram Content Group LLC
1700 Fourth St, Berkeley, CA 94710
Tel: 510-809-3761
E-mail: info-ga@westmarginpress.com
Web Site: www.westmarginpress.com
Key Personnel
Publg Dir: Jennifer Newens
Mktg Mgr: Angela Zbornik *E-mail:* angela.zbornik@westmarginpress.com
Founded: 1967
ISBN Prefix(es): 978-1-55868; 978-0-88240; 978-0-8108; 978-1-94182; 978-0-78108
Number of titles published annually: 35 Print; 30 E-Book
Total Titles: 300 Print; 125 E-Book
Imprints: Alaska Northwest Books®; Graphic Arts Books®
Distribution Center: Ingram Publisher Services, One Ingram Blvd, La Vergne, TN 37086 *Toll Free Tel:* 866-400-5351 *Toll Free Fax:* 800-838-1149 *E-mail:* ips@ingramcontent.com
Membership(s): Publishers Association of the West (PubWest)

West Virginia University Press
West Virginia University, PO Box 6295, Morgantown, WV 26506-6295
Tel: 304-293-8400
Web Site: www.wvupress.com
Key Personnel
Dir/Acqs Ed (Nonfiction): Derek Krissoff
   E-mail: derek.krissoff@mail.wvu.edu
Acqs Ed & Mktg Opers Mgr: Sarah Munroe
   E-mail: semunroe@mail.wvu.edu
Founded: 1965
ISBN Prefix(es): 978-1-933202; 978-0-937058
Number of titles published annually: 12 Print; 1 CD-ROM; 1 Audio
Total Titles: 75 Print; 8 CD-ROM; 2 Audio
Orders to: Chicago Distribution Center, 11030 S Langley Ave, Chicago, IL 60628 *Toll Free Tel:* 800-621-2736 *Toll Free Fax:* 800-621-8476 *E-mail:* orders@press.chicago.edu
Distribution Center: Chicago Distribution Center, 11030 S Langley Ave, Chicago, IL 60628 *Tel:* 773-702-7000 (intl) *Toll Free Tel:* 800-621-2736 *Fax:* 773-702-7212 (intl) *Toll Free Fax:* 800-621-8476
Membership(s): Association of University Presses (AUPresses)

Western Edge Press
Imprint of Sherman Asher Publishing
126 Candelario St, Santa Fe, NM 87501
Tel: 505-988-7214
E-mail: westernedge@santa-fe.net
Web Site: www.westernedgepress.com; www.shermanasher.com
Key Personnel
Owner & Publr: James Mafchir

Founded: 1995
Western nonfiction, art, cooking, history, archaeology & Spanish/English bilingual oral history.
ISBN Prefix(es): 978-1-890932
Number of titles published annually: 3 Print
Total Titles: 35 Print
Distribution Center: Mountain Press, Missoula, MT 59806 *Toll Free Tel:* 800-234-5308 *Fax:* 310-532-7001 *E-mail:* mtnpress@montana.com *Web Site:* www.mountainpresspublish.com

Western Pennsylvania Genealogical Society
4400 Forbes Ave, Pittsburgh, PA 15213-4007
Tel: 412-687-6811 (answering machine)
E-mail: info@wpgs.org
Web Site: www.wpgs.org
Founded: 1974
ISBN Prefix(es): 978-0-9745162
Number of titles published annually: 6 Print; 50 Online
Total Titles: 6 Print; 50 Online
Membership(s): National Genealogical Society

Western Reflections Publishing Co
951B N Hwy 149, Lake City, CO 81235
Mailing Address: PO Box 1149, Lake City, CO 81235-1149
Tel: 970-944-0110
E-mail: publisher@westernreflectionspublishing.com
Web Site: www.westernreflectionspublishing.com
Key Personnel
Pres: P David Smith
Founded: 1996
History & culture of the western US with an emphasis on Colorado.
ISBN Prefix(es): 978-1-890437; 978-1-932738
Number of titles published annually: 6 Print
Total Titles: 210 Print

Westernlore Press
PO Box 35305, Tucson, AZ 85740-5305
SAN: 202-9650
Tel: 520-297-5491
Key Personnel
Pres & Ed: Lynn R Bailey
Treas & ISBN Contact: Anne G Bailey
Founded: 1941
History & biography, anthropology, historic archaeology & historic sites & ethnohistory pertaining to the greater American West.
ISBN Prefix(es): 978-0-87026
Number of titles published annually: 4 Print
Total Titles: 65 Print

§Westminster John Knox Press (WJK)
Imprint of Presbyterian Publishing Corp (PPC)
100 Witherspoon St, Louisville, KY 40202-1396
SAN: 202-9669
Tel: 502-569-5052 *Toll Free Tel:* 800-523-1631 (US & CN) *Fax:* 502-569-8308
   Toll Free Fax: 800-541-5113 (US & CN)
E-mail: customer_service@wjkbooks.com; orders@wjkbooks.com
Web Site: www.wjkbooks.com
Key Personnel
Pres & Publr: David Dobson *E-mail:* ddobson@wjkbooks.com
VP, Treas & COO: Monty Anderson
   E-mail: manderson@wjkbooks.com
VP, Mktg: Alicia Samuels *E-mail:* asamuels@wjkbooks.com
Ed-in-Chief: Robert A Ratcliff *E-mail:* rratcliff@wjkbooks.com
Rts & Perms: Michele Blum *E-mail:* mblum@wjkbooks.com
Founded: 1838
With a publishing heritage that dates back more than 160 years, WJK Press publishes religious & theological books & resources for scholars, clergy, laity & general readers. The publisher

employs the motto "Challenging the Mind, Nourishing the Soul".
ISBN Prefix(es): 978-0-664; 978-0-8042
Number of titles published annually: 150 Print
Total Titles: 1,100 Print; 2 CD-ROM; 2 Audio
Distributor for Canterbury Press; Church House Publishing; St Andrews Press; SCM Press; Woodlake Publishing Inc
Foreign Rep(s): Africa Christian Textbooks (ACT) (Nigeria); Canaanland Distributors Sdn Bhd (Malaysia); Chinese Christian Literacy Mission (Rocky C L Chen) (Taiwan); Christian Book Discounters (South Africa); Claretian Communications Foundation Inc (Philippines); Cross Communications Ltd (Alexander Y C Lee) (Hong Kong); John Garratt Publishing (Australia); Korea Christian Book Service Inc (South Korea); MediaCom Education Inc (Australia); Methodist Publishing House (South Africa); Norwich Books & Music (Europe, UK); Omega Distributors (New Zealand); Parasource (Canada); Pustaka SUFES Sdn Bhd (Malaysia); St Pauls India (India); SCM Press (Europe, UK); SKS Books Warehouse (Lek Eng Khiang) (Singapore)
Returns: 3904 Produce Rd, Suite 104, Louisville, KY 40218

Wheatherstone Press
Subsidiary of Dickinson Consulting Group
11595 SW Butner Rd, No 22, Portland, OR 97225
Tel: 503-244-8929
E-mail: relocntr@nwlink.com
Web Site: www.wheatherstonepress.com
Key Personnel
Pres & CEO: Jan Dickinson
Founded: 1983
Publishes handbooks & step-by-step guides covering all phases of relocation, including internationally.
ISBN Prefix(es): 978-0-9613011
Number of titles published annually: 3 Print
Total Titles: 49 Print

§Whiskey Creek Press
Imprint of Start Publishing LLC
221 River St, 9th fl, Suite 9137, Hoboken, NJ 07030
Tel: 212-431-5455
E-mail: publisher@whiskeycreekpress.com
Web Site: whiskeycreekpress.com
Founded: 2003
Traditional royalty-paying small press, publishing fiction in ebook & print formats. Titles can be purchased through Amazon Kindle, Barnes & Noble Nook & Apple ITunes.
ISBN Prefix(es): 978-1-60313; 978-1-61160
Number of titles published annually: 50 Print; 200 E-Book
Total Titles: 500 Print; 1,350 E-Book
Imprints: Torrid Books (sensual & erotic romances)

§Whitaker House
1030 Hunt Valley Circle, New Kensington, PA 15068
Tel: 724-334-7000 Toll Free Tel: 800-444-4484 (sales) Fax: 724-334-1200
E-mail: publisher@whitakerhouse.com; sales@whitakerhouse.com
Web Site: www.whitakerhouse.com
Key Personnel
Mng Dir: Tom Cox
Founded: 1970
ISBN Prefix(es): 978-0-88368; 978-1-60374; 978-1-62911
Number of titles published annually: 70 Print; 1 CD-ROM; 70 E-Book; 8 Audio
Total Titles: 500 Print; 20 CD-ROM; 400 E-Book; 40 Audio

Imprints: Banner Publishing; Smart Kidz; Whitaker Espanol
Warehouse: Anchor Distributors, 1030 Hunt Valley Circle, New Kensington, PA 15068, Mgr: Jimmy Luther
Membership(s): American Christian Fiction Writers (ACFW); Evangelical Christian Publishers Association (ECPA)

White Cloud Press
300 E Hersey St, Suite 11, Ashland, OR 97520
Mailing Address: PO Box 3400, Ashland, OR 97520
Tel: 541-488-6415 Fax: 541-482-7708
E-mail: info@whitecloudpress.com
Web Site: www.whitecloudpress.com
Key Personnel
Publr: Steve Scholl E-mail: scholl@whitecloudpress.com
Prodn Mgr: Christy Collins E-mail: christy@whitecloudpress.com
Founded: 1993
General trade, emphasis on religion & fiction.
ISBN Prefix(es): 978-1-883991; 978-0-9745245
Number of titles published annually: 6 Print
Total Titles: 60 Print; 40 E-Book; 4 Audio
Imprints: Caveat Press; Confluence Books; River-Wood Books
Subsidiaries: Confluence Book Services
Foreign Rights: Danny Baror; Nigel Yorwerth
Distribution Center: Publishers Group West, 1700 Fourth St, Berkeley, CA 94710 Toll Free Tel: 800-788-3123 Toll Free Fax: 800-351-5073 E-mail: orderentry@perseusbooks.com Web Site: www.pgw.com
Publishers Group Canada, 300-76 Stafford St, Toronto, ON M6J 2S1, Canada Toll Free Tel: 800-747-8147 Fax: 416-934-1410 E-mail: info@pgcbooks.ca Web Site: pgcbooks.ca
Membership(s): Independent Book Publishers Association (IBPA)

White Pine Press
PO Box 236, Buffalo, NY 14201
Tel: 716-627-4665 Fax: 716-627-4665
E-mail: wpine@whitepine.org
Web Site: www.whitepine.org
Key Personnel
Mng Dir: Elaine La Mattina
Publr & Ed: Dennis Maloney E-mail: dennismaloney@yahoo.com
Founded: 1973
Specialize in poetry & literature in translation.
ISBN Prefix(es): 978-0-934834; 978-1-877727; 978-1-877800; 978-1-893996
Number of titles published annually: 10 Print
Total Titles: 160 Print
Subsidiaries: Springhouse Editions
Distributor for Springhouse Editions
Distribution Center: Consortium Book Sales & Distribution, The Keg House, Suite 101, 34 13 Ave NE, Minneapolis, MN 55413-1007 Tel: 612-746-2600 Toll Free Tel: 800-283-3572 (cust serv, Jackson, TN) Fax: 612-746-2606 E-mail: info@cbsd.com Web Site: www.cbsd.com SAN: 200-6049

Whitman, Albert & Co, see Albert Whitman & Co

§Whittier Publications Inc
3115 Long Beach Rd, Oceanside, NY 11572
Tel: 516-432-8120 Toll Free Tel: 800-897-TEXT (897-8398) Fax: 516-889-0341
E-mail: info@whitbooks.com
Web Site: www.whitbooks.com
Key Personnel
Pres: Judith Etra
Founded: 1990
Textbooks, trade, self-help.

ISBN Prefix(es): 978-1-878045; 978-1-57604
Number of titles published annually: 200 Print

§Whole Person Associates Inc
101 W Second St, Suite 203, Duluth, MN 55802
Tel: 218-727-0500 Toll Free Tel: 800-247-6789 Fax: 218-727-0505
E-mail: books@wholeperson.com
Web Site: www.wholeperson.com
Key Personnel
Owner & Publr: Jack Kosmach
Founded: 1980
Stress management & wellness promotion.
ISBN Prefix(es): 978-0-938586; 978-1-57025
Number of titles published annually: 8 Print
Total Titles: 218 Print; 29 CD-ROM; 38 Audio
Membership(s): Independent Book Publishing Professionals Group (IBPPG)

§Wide World of Maps Inc
2133 E Indian School Rd, Phoenix, AZ 85016
Tel: 602-279-2323 Toll Free Tel: 800-279-7654
Web Site: www.maps4u.com
Key Personnel
Pres & CEO: James L Willinger
Founded: 1975
Atlases, charts, guide books, maps, map software, map accessories & more.
ISBN Prefix(es): 978-0-938448; 978-1-887749
Number of titles published annually: 6 Print; 2 CD-ROM
Total Titles: 20 Print; 2 CD-ROM
Imprints: Yellow 1
Divisions: Desert Charts; Metro Maps; Phoenix Mapping Service
Branch Office(s)
17232 N Cave Creek Rd, Phoenix, AZ 85032 Tel: 602-279-2323 ext 3 Fax: 602-368-1412
2155 E University Dr, Tempe, AZ 85281 Tel: 602-279-2323 ext 4
Distributed by Rand McNally
Distributor for Benchmark Maps; Big Sky Maps; Franko Maps; MacVan Maps (Colorado Springs); Metro Maps; Rand McNally

Wide World Publishing
PO Box 476, San Carlos, CA 94070-0476
SAN: 211-1462
Tel: 650-593-2839
E-mail: wwpbl@aol.com
Web Site: wideworldpublishing.com
Key Personnel
Partner & Intl Rts: Elvira Monroe
Founded: 1976
Trade paperbacks, cookbooks, mathematics books/calendars, travel books & guides.
ISBN Prefix(es): 978-0-933174; 978-1-884550
Number of titles published annually: 4 Print
Total Titles: 146 Print; 21 E-Book
Foreign Rep(s): Ingram/Publishers Group West (Asia, Canada, Europe)
Orders to: Publishers Group West, 1700 Fourth St, Berkeley, CA 94710 Tel: 510-809-3700 Toll Free Tel: 866-400-4351 Fax: 510-809-3777 SAN: 202-8522; Ingram Content Group, One Ingram Blvd, La Vergne, TN 37086 Tel: 615-795-5000 Web Site: www.ingramcontent.com
Distribution Center: Publishers Group West, 1700 Fourth St, Berkeley, CA 94710 Tel: (510) 809-3700 Toll Free Tel: 866-400-5351 Fax: (510) 809-3777 Web Site: www.pgw.com SAN: 202-8522
Ingram Publisher Services, 12101 Ingram Dr, Chambersburg, PA 17202 E-mail: iqsupport@ingramcontent.com Web Site: www.ingrampublisherservices.com/contact
Ingram Content Group, One Ingram Blvd, La Vergne, TN 37086 Tel: 615-793-5000 Web Site: www.ingramcontent.com

Markus Wiener Publishers Inc
231 Nassau St, Princeton, NJ 08542

SAN: 282-5465
Tel: 609-921-1141 *Fax:* 609-921-1140
E-mail: publisher@markuswiener.com
Web Site: www.markuswiener.com
Key Personnel
Pres: M Markus Wiener
VP: Shelley Frisch
Founded: 1981
Independent publisher of academic & trade books
& journals in the areas of world history, Latin
American & Caribbean history, Middle Eastern
& African history & culture. Its publications
also include related topics in music, religion,
women's history, Jewish history, western civi-
lization & slavery.
ISBN Prefix(es): 978-0-910129; 978-0-945179;
978-1-55876
Number of titles published annually: 25 Print
Total Titles: 300 Print
Foreign Rep(s): Eurospan (Europe)

Michael Wiese Productions
12400 Ventura Blvd, No 1111, Studio City, CA
91604
Tel: 818-379-8799 *Toll Free Tel:* 800-833-5738
(orders) *Fax:* 818-986-3408
E-mail: mwpsales@earthlink.net; fulfillment@
portcity.com
Web Site: www.mwp.com
Key Personnel
Founder & Publr: Michael Wiese
VP: Ken Lee *Tel:* 206-271-0287 *E-mail:* kenlee@
earthlink.net
Spec Sales: Michele Chong *Tel:* 818-841-4123
Founded: 1981
Publisher of books on screenwriting & filmmak-
ing.
ISBN Prefix(es): 978-0-941188
Number of titles published annually: 15 Print
Total Titles: 300 Print
Imprints: Divine Arts
Distribution Center: Ingram Publisher Ser-
vices, One Ingram Blvd, La Vergne,
TN 37086 *Toll Free Tel:* 866-400-
5351 *E-mail:* customerservice@
ingrampublisherservices.com *Web Site:* www.
ingrampublisherservices.com

Wilderness Adventures Press Inc
45 Buckskin Rd, Belgrade, MT 59714
Tel: 406-388-0112 *Toll Free Tel:* 866-400-2012
E-mail: books@wildadvpress.com
Web Site: store.wildadvpress.com
Key Personnel
Pres & Prodn Ed: Chuck Johnson *Tel:* 406-
388-0112 ext 12 *Fax:* 406-388-0120
E-mail: chuck@wildadvpress.com
Secy & Treas: Blanche Johnson *Tel:* 406-
388-0112 ext 14 *Fax:* 406-388-0120
E-mail: blanche@wildadvpress.com
Founded: 1994
Outdoor guidebooks, sporting books & cook-
books, fly fishing, dog training & big game
hunting, plus maps.
ISBN Prefix(es): 978-1-885106; 978-1-932098;
978-1-940239
Number of titles published annually: 6 Print
Total Titles: 90 Print
Distributed by American West Books; Angler's
Book Supply; Raymond C Rumpf & Son Inc
Distribution Center: Baker & Taylor, 2550 W
Tyvola Rd, Suite 300, Charlotte, NC 28217
Tel: 704-998-3100 *Toll Free Tel:* 800-775-1800
Web Site: www.baker-taylor.com
Ingram Publisher Services, One Ingram Blvd,
La Vergne, TN 37086 *Toll Free Tel:* 866-
400-5351 *E-mail:* customerservice@
ingrampublisherservices.com *Web Site:* www.
ingrampublisherservices.com
Barnes & Noble *Tel:* 516-338-8000 *Web Site:* bn.
com

Wildflower Press
Affiliate of Oakbrook Press
c/o Oakbrook Press, 3301 S Valley Dr, Rapid
City, SD 57703
Mailing Address: PO Box 3362, Rapid City, SD
57709
Tel: 605-381-6385
E-mail: info@wildflowerpress.org
Web Site: www.wildflowerpress.org
Key Personnel
Pres: L J Bryant *E-mail:* wildflowerpress@live.
com
Publicity Dir: Robert E Fuchs *E-mail:* pr@
wildflowerpress.org
Literary Agent: Charlene Caulfield
Sales: Jordan Dadah
Edit: Leisette Fox
Billing: Christina MacLachlan
Founded: 2010
Small press specializing in publishing works of
fiction with a significant message. Not a vanity
press; no funds required to publish.
ISBN Prefix(es): 978-0-9835332
Number of titles published annually: 5 Print; 5 E-
Book
Total Titles: 12 Print; 13 E-Book
Membership(s): Independent Book Publishers As-
sociation (IBPA)

Wildlife Education Ltd, see National Wildlife
Federation

Wildside Press LLC
7945 MacArthur Blvd, Suite 215, Cabin John,
MD 20818
Tel: 301-762-1305 *Fax:* 301-762-1306
E-mail: wildside@wildsidepress.com;
wildsidepress@yahoo.com
Web Site: wildsidepress.com
Key Personnel
Publr: John Betancourt
Dir, Publg Opers: Carla Coupe
Founded: 1989
Reprints of classic science fiction, fantasy, mys-
tery, reference & mainstream.
ISBN Prefix(es): 978-1-880448; 978-1-58715;
978-1-59224
Number of titles published annually: 1,500 Print;
400 E-Book; 100 Audio
Total Titles: 16,000 Print; 1,400 E-Book; 800 Au-
dio
Imprints: Borgo Press; Owlswick Press
Foreign Rights: Virginia Kidd Literary Agency
(worldwide)

§Wiley-Blackwell
Imprint of John Wiley & Sons Inc
111 River St, Hoboken, NJ 07030-5774
Tel: 201-748-6000 *Fax:* 201-748-6088
E-mail: info@wiley.com
Web Site: www.wiley.com
Founded: 1984
General, scholarly, reference & college texts, with
an emphasis on the humanities, social sciences
& business. Also medical allied health, vet-
erinary, earth & life sciences, environment &
engineering.
ISBN Prefix(es): 978-0-631; 978-0-85520; 978-0-
86216; 978-1-55786; 978-1-57718
Number of titles published annually: 500 Print
Total Titles: 4,500 Print

§John Wiley & Sons Inc
111 River St, Hoboken, NJ 07030-5774
SAN: 202-5183
Tel: 201-748-6000 *Toll Free Tel:* 800-225-5945
(cust serv) *Fax:* 201-748-6088
E-mail: info@wiley.com
Web Site: www.wiley.com
Key Personnel
Chmn: Jesse C Wiley
Pres & CEO: Brian Napack

EVP & Group Exec: Matthew S Kissner
Corp Secy: Joanna Jia
CFO & EVP, Technol & Opers: John Kritzmacher
Chief People Offr: Danielle McMahan
Chief Prod Offr, Res Busn: Jay Flynn
CTO: Aref Matin
EVP & Chief HR Offr: Archana Singh
EVP & Chief Mktg Offr: Clay Stobaugh
EVP & Chief Strategy Offr: Taneli Ruda
EVP & Gen Coun: Gary M Rinck
EVP & Gen Mgr, Res: Judy Verses
EVP, Knowledge & Learning: Ella Balagula
SVP & Corp Cont: Christopher Caridi
SVP & Treas: Vincent Marzano
Sr Acqs Ed: Zachary Schisgal
Sr Advisor: Mark Allin
Founded: 1807
Global publisher of print & electronic products
specializing in professional & consumer books
& subscription services; scientific, technical,
medical books & journals; textbooks & educa-
tional materials for undergraduate & graduate
students as well as lifelong learners. Wiley has
publishing, marketing & distribution centers in
the US, Canada, Europe, Asia & Australia.
ISBN Prefix(es): 978-0-470; 978-0-471; 978-0-
442; 978-0-8436; 978-0-87055
Number of titles published annually: 1,500 Print
Total Titles: 15,000 Print
Imprints: American Geophysical Union; Architec-
tural Graphic Standards; Capstone; Cochrane
Library; CrossKnowledge; Culinary Institute of
America; Current Protocols; Ernst & Sohn; Es-
sential Evidence Plus; Everything DiSC®; For
Dummies®; GIT Verlag; Jacaranda; Jossey-
Bass; JK Lasser; The Leadership Challenge®;
Merck; MOAC; RSMeans; Spectroscopy
Now; Sybex; Teach Yourself Visually; Wiley-
Blackwell; Wiley Custom Select; Wiley Global
Education; Wiley-IEEE Press; Wiley Online Li-
brary; Wiley Science Solutions; Wiley-VCH;
Wiley Visualizing; WileyPLUS; Workplace
Learning Solutions; Wrightbooks; Wrox™
Branch Office(s)
One Montgomery St, Suite 1000, San Francisco,
CA 94104 *Tel:* 415-433-1740 *Fax:* 415-433-
0499
Union Sta, 1550 Wewatta St, Denver, CO 80202
851 Trafalgar Ct, Suite 420, Maitland, FL 32751
1415 W 22 St, Suite 800, Oak Brook, IL 60523
Tel: 630-366-2900 *Fax:* 630-528-3101
10475 Crosspoint Blvd, Indianapolis, IN 46256
(cust care ctr/consumer accts) *Tel:* 317-572-
3000; 317-572-3994 (consumer tech support)
Fax: 317-572-4000
101 Station Landing, Suite 300, Medford, MA
02155 *Tel:* 781-388-8200 *Fax:* 781-388-8210
400 Hwy 169, Suite 300, Minneapolis, MN
55426 *Tel:* 763-765-2222 *Fax:* 763-765-2276
5205 Lake Shore Dr, Waco, TX 76710 *Tel:* 254-
751-1644
90 Eglington Ave E, Suite 300, Toronto, ON
M4P 2Y3, Canada *Tel:* 416-236-4433 *Toll Free
Tel:* 800-567-4797 *Fax:* 416-236-8743 *Toll Free
Fax:* 800-565-6802 *E-mail:* canada@wiley.com
Distribution Center: One Wiley Dr, Som-
erset, NJ 08875-1272 (US cust care op-
ers/trade & wholesale) *Fax:* 732-302-2300
E-mail: custserv@wiley.com
Membership(s): Association of American Publish-
ers (AAP)
See separate listing for:
SYBEX Inc
Wiley-Blackwell
John Wiley & Sons Inc Global Education
**John Wiley & Sons Inc Professional Develop-
ment**

§John Wiley & Sons Inc Global Education
Division of John Wiley & Sons Inc
111 River St, Hoboken, NJ 07030-5774
Tel: 201-748-6000 *Toll Free Tel:* 800-225-5945
(cust serv) *Fax:* 201-748-6008

E-mail: info@wiley.com
Web Site: www.wiley.com
Key Personnel
VP, Cust Engagement: Susan Elbe
Total Titles: 615 Print

**§John Wiley & Sons Inc Professional
   Development**
Division of John Wiley & Sons Inc
111 River St, Hoboken, NJ 07030-5774
Tel: 201-748-6000 *Toll Free Tel:* 800-225-5945
   (cust serv) *Fax:* 201-748-6088
E-mail: info@wiley.com
Web Site: www.wiley.com
Global brands include For Dummies, Jossey-
   Bass, Bloomberg Press, Sybex, Wrox, Pfeiffer,
   Fisher Investments Press, J K Lasser, Lead-
   ership Challenge, Wiley Learning Institute,
   Therascribe & Wiley CPA Exam Review.

**John Wiley & Sons Inc Scientific, Technical,
   Medical & Scholarly (STMS)**, see
   Wiley-Blackwell

William Carey Library Publishers, see William
   Carey Publishing

William Carey Publishing
Formerly William Carey Library Publishers
Division of Frontier Ventures
10 W Dry Creek Circle, Littleton, CO 80120
Tel: 720-372-7036
E-mail: publishing@wclbooks.org
Web Site: www.missionbooks.org
Key Personnel
Dir, Publg: Denise Wynn
Founded: 1969
Christian publisher. Specialize in cross-cultural
   Christian mission work & experiences in fron-
   tier countries. Publishing practical, tactical,
   theoretical, or narrative Christian missiology.
ISBN Prefix(es): 978-0-87808
Number of titles published annually: 15 Print; 15
   E-Book
Total Titles: 250 Print
Imprints: William Carey Library; William Carey
   Press
Orders to: Anchor Distributors, 1030 Hunt Valley
   Circle, New Kensington, PA 15068
Membership(s): Evangelical Christian Publishers
   Association (ECPA); Independent Book Pub-
   lishers Association (IBPA)

§Williams & Company Book Publishers
1317 Pine Ridge Dr, Savannah, GA 31406
Tel: 912-352-0404
E-mail: bookpub@comcast.net
Web Site: www.pubmart.com
Key Personnel
Publr & Ed-in-Chief: Thomas A Williams, PhD
Founded: 1989
Niche market nonfiction.
ISBN Prefix(es): 978-1-878853
Number of titles published annually: 15 Print
Total Titles: 50 Print
Imprints: Venture Press; Williams & Co Publish-
   ers
Warehouse: Juliana Group, 1110 Staley Ave, Sa-
   vannah, GA 31405
Membership(s): Independent Publishers Associa-
   tion

Willow Creek Press
9931 Hwy 70 W, Minocqua, WI 54548
Mailing Address: PO Box 147, Minocqua, WI
   54548 SAN: 991-5117
Tel: 715-358-7010 *Toll Free Tel:* 800-850-9453
   Fax: 715-358-2807
E-mail: info@willowcreekpress.com
Web Site: www.willowcreekpress.com

Key Personnel
Publr & Ed-in-Chief: Tom Petrie
VP, Sales: Jeremy Petrie *E-mail:* jpetrie@
   willowcreekpress.com
Founded: 1986
Publish high quality books most specifically related to nature, animals, wildlife, hunting, fishing & gardening. The company also offers a
   unique line of cookbooks & has established a
   niche in the pet book market. The company
   also publishes high quality nature, wild life,
   fishing, pet & sporting calendars.
ISBN Prefix(es): 978-1-57223
Number of titles published annually: 24 Print
Total Titles: 130 Print; 3 Audio
Membership(s): Association of American Publishers (AAP)

Wilshire Book Co
22647 Ventura Blvd, No 314, Woodland Hills,
   CA 91364-1416
SAN: 205-5368
Tel: 818-700-1522
E-mail: sales@mpowers.com
Web Site: www.mpowers.com
Key Personnel
Pres & Rts & Perms: Marcia Powers
Founded: 1967 (by Melvin Powers)
Psychological, self-help, motivational & inspira-
   tional books, adult fables; mail order, business,
   advertising & marketing; horse, bridge; origi-
   nals & reprints.
ISBN Prefix(es): 978-0-87980
Number of titles published annually: 3 Print
Total Titles: 23 Print

Wimmer Cookbooks
Division of Mercury Printing, an RR Donnelley
   Co
4650 Shelby Air Dr, Memphis, TN 38118
Toll Free Tel: 800-548-2537 *Fax:* 901-363-1771
E-mail: info@wimmerco.com
Web Site: www.wimmerco.com
Key Personnel
Acct Coord: Robyn Hite
Sales & Mktg: Terry Rayner *Tel:* 214-676-2444
Founded: 1946
Development, publishing, manufacturing, mar-
   keting & distribution of community & self-
   published cookbooks.
ISBN Prefix(es): 978-1-879958
Number of titles published annually: 50 Print
Total Titles: 300 Print
Imprints: Tradery House

Windsor Books
Division of Windsor Marketing Corp
260 W Main St, Suite 5, Bayshore, NY 11706
SAN: 203-2945
Mailing Address: PO Box 280, Brightwaters, NY
   11718
Tel: 631-665-6688 *Toll Free Tel:* 800-321-5934
E-mail: windsor.books@att.net
Web Site: www.windsorpublishing.com
Key Personnel
Founder: Alfred Schmidt
Mng Ed: Jeff Schmidt
Founded: 1968
Business, economics & investment.
ISBN Prefix(es): 978-0-930233
Number of titles published annually: 5 Print
Advertising Agency: A Schmidt Agency

§Wings Press
PO Box 591176, San Antonio, TX 78259
E-mail: wingspresspublishing@gmail.com
Web Site: www.wingspress.com
Key Personnel
Publr & Ed: M Milligan
Founded: 1975
Literary book publishing.
ISBN Prefix(es): 978-0-916727; 978-0-930324

Number of titles published annually: 3 Print; 3 E-
   Book
Total Titles: 230 Print; 4 CD-ROM; 200 E-Book;
   4 Audio
Foreign Rights: Independent Publisher's Group
   (Susan M Sewall)
Orders to: Independent Publisher's Group
   (IPG), 814 N Franklin St, Chicago, IL 60624
   Tel: 312-337-0747 *Toll Free Tel:* 800-888-0747
   Fax: 312-337-5985 *E-mail:* orders@ipgbook.
   com
Returns: Independent Publisher's Group Distri-
   bution Center, 600 N Pulaski Rd, Chicago,
   IL 60624 *Tel:* 312-337-0747 *Fax:* 312-
   337-5985 *Toll Free Fax:* 800-888-0747
   E-mail: frontdesk@ipgbook.com
Shipping Address: Independent Publisher's
   Group Distribution Center, 600 N Pulaski
   Rd, Chicago, IL 60624 *Tel:* 312-337-0747
   Fax: 312-337-5985 *E-mail:* orders@ipgbook.
   com
Warehouse: Independent Publisher's Group Distri-
   bution Center, 600 N Pulaski Rd, Chicago, IL
   60624 *Tel:* 312-337-0747 *Fax:* 312-337-5985
   E-mail: orders@ipgbook.com
Distribution Center: Independent Publisher's
   Group Distribution Center, 600 N Pulaski Rd,
   Chicago, IL 60624 *Tel:* 312-337-0747 *Toll
   Free Tel:* 800-888-0747 *Fax:* 312-337-5985
   E-mail: orders@ipgbook.com
Membership(s): Association of Writers & Writ-
   ing Programs (AWP); Community of Literary
   Magazines & Presses (CLMP)

Winters Publishing
705 E Washington St, Greensburg, IN 47240
SAN: 298-1645
Mailing Address: PO Box 501, Greensburg, IN
   47240
Tel: 812-663-4948 *Toll Free Tel:* 800-457-3230
   Fax: 812-663-4948
E-mail: winterspublishing@gmail.com
Web Site: www.winterspublishing.com
Key Personnel
Owner & Publr: Mr Tracy Winters
Founded: 1988
Produces high-quality, custom books for individ-
   uals & groups. We publish community & cor-
   porate history books for cities & organizations
   celebrating centennials, bicentennials & other
   milestone events. We also work with individual
   authors & publish children's books, books for
   the Christian market, cookbooks for the bed &
   breakfast industry & a variety of other fiction
   & nonfiction books.
ISBN Prefix(es): 978-0-9625329; 978-1-883651
Number of titles published annually: 15 Print; 2
   E-Book
Total Titles: 105 Print; 5 E-Book
Imprints: Faith Press
Distribution Center: Ingram Book Co, One Ingram Blvd, La Vergne, TN 37086 *Tel:* 615-
   793-5000

Winterthur Museum, Garden & Library
5105 Kennett Pike, Winterthur, DE 19735
Tel: 302-888-4663 *Toll Free Tel:* 800-448-3883
   Fax: 302-888-4950
Web Site: www.winterthur.org
Key Personnel
Contact: Onie Rollins
ISBN Prefix(es): 978-0-912724
Number of titles published annually: 4 Print
Total Titles: 80 Print
Distributed by ACC Art Books; Monacelli Press;
   W W Norton & Company Inc; University of
   Pennsylvania Press
Membership(s): American Alliance of Museums
   (AAM); American Booksellers Association
   (ABA); Art Libraries Society (ARLIS)

Winterwolf Press
1810 E Sahara Ave, Suite 737, Las Vegas, NV 89014
Toll Free Tel: 855-ICE-WOLF (423-9653)
E-mail: info@winterwolfpress.com; questions@winterwolfpress.com; admin@winterwolfpress.com (orders)
Web Site: winterwolfpress.com
Key Personnel
Owner & Founder: Laura Cantu
Dir, Opers & Acqs: Arleen Barreiros
Dir, Busn Devt & Submissions Liaison: Wendy Scott
Sr Ed: Teresa Kennedy
ISBN Prefix(es): 978-0-9885851
Number of titles published annually: 6 Print; 6 Online; 6 E-Book; 6 Audio
Imprints: Shadow Wolf Press
Distributor for Shadow Wolf Press
Billing Address: 8635 W Sahara Ave, No 425, Las Vegas, NV 89117
Returns: 8635 W Sahara Ave, No 425, Las Vegas, NV 89117
Membership(s): Independent Book Publishers Association (IBPA)

§Wisconsin Department of Public Instruction
125 S Webster St, Madison, WI 53703
Mailing Address: PO Box 7841, Madison, WI 53707-7841
Tel: 608-266-2188 *Toll Free Tel:* 800-441-4563 (US only); 800-243-8782 (US only)
E-mail: pubsales@dpi.wi.gov
Web Site: pubsales.dpi.wi.gov
Key Personnel
State Superintendent of Public Instruction: Carolyn Stanford Taylor *Tel:* 608-266-8687 *E-mail:* carolyn.stanford.taylor@dpi.wi.gov
Specialize in English, math, science & social studies, character education, driver education & traffic safety, career & technical education, world languages & teaching strategies.
ISBN Prefix(es): 978-1-57337
Number of titles published annually: 8 Print; 4 CD-ROM
Total Titles: 120 Print; 10 CD-ROM

Wisdom Publications Inc
199 Elm St, Somerville, MA 02144
Tel: 617-776-7416 *Toll Free Tel:* 800-272-4050 (orders) *Fax:* 617-776-7841
E-mail: info@wisdompubs.org; submission@wisdompubs.org
Web Site: www.wisdompubs.org
Key Personnel
Pres: Timothy J McNeill
CEO/Publr: Daniel T Aitken
Sr Ed: David Kittelstrom
Exec Ed: Josh Bartok
Sr Ed: Laura Cunningham
Ed: Mary Petrusewicz
Prodn Ed: Ben Gleason
Brand & Mktg Mgr: Kestrel Slocombe
Content Ed: Brianna Quick
Prodn Specialist: Lindsay D'Andrea
Founded: 1976
Books on Buddhism published in various series encompassing theory & practice, biography, history, art & culture.
ISBN Prefix(es): 978-0-86171
Number of titles published annually: 30 Print
Total Titles: 300 Print
Imprints: Pali Text Society
Distributed by Simon & Schuster
Foreign Rep(s): PPUK (England)
Foreign Rights: ACER (Spain); Eliane Benisti (France); Chinese Connection Agency (China); Fritz Literary Agency (Germany); Eric Yang Agency (Korea)
Orders to: Simon & Schuster, 100 Front St, Riverside, NJ 08075 *Toll Free Tel:* 800-223-2336 *Toll Free Fax:* 800-943-9831

Paula Wiseman Books, see Simon & Schuster Children's Publishing

Wizards of the Coast LLC
Subsidiary of Hasbro Inc
1600 Lind Ave SW, Suite 400, Renton, WA 98057-3305
Mailing Address: PO Box 707, Renton, WA 98057-0707
Tel: 425-226-6500
E-mail: press@wizards.com
Web Site: company.wizards.com; www.wizards.com
Founded: 1975 (as TSR Inc)
Publisher of fantasy, science fiction & horror novels. Young adult game material; role-playing games, trading card games, board games & books, makers of Dungeons & Dragons. Not seeking proposals for our shared world lines at this time.
ISBN Prefix(es): 978-0-88038; 978-1-56076; 978-0-7869
Number of titles published annually: 50 Print; 60 E-Book
Total Titles: 300 Print
Distributed by Penguin Random House

Alan Wofsy Fine Arts
1109 Geary Blvd, San Francisco, CA 94109
SAN: 207-6438
Mailing Address: PO Box 2210, San Francisco, CA 94126-2210
Tel: 415-292-6500 *Toll Free Tel:* 800-660-6403 *Fax:* 415-292-6594 (off & cust serv); 510-251-1840 (acctg)
E-mail: order@art-books.com (orders); editeur@earthlink.net (edit); beauxarts@earthlink.net (cust serv)
Web Site: www.art-books.com
Key Personnel
Chmn of the Bd: Lord Cohen
CEO: Alan Wofsy
Art Dir: Zeke Greenberg
Ed, French Books: Charles DuPont
Ed, German Books: Willi Rahm
PR Mgr: Milton J Goldbaum
Website Mgr: Steven Barich
Website & Imaging: Matt Novack
Mktg: Andy Redkin
Libn: Adios Butler
Coun: Judith Mazia
Rts: Elizabeth Regina Snowden
Founded: 1969
Art reference books, bibliographies, art books, iconographies, prints, posters & note cards.
ISBN Prefix(es): 978-0-915346; 978-1-55660; 978-0-8150; 978-0-89648
Number of titles published annually: 20 Print; 5 CD-ROM; 60 Online
Total Titles: 350 Print; 10 CD-ROM; 500 Online
Imprints: Beauxarts; Collegium Graphicum; The Picasso Project
Divisions: Wittenborn Art Books
Branch Office(s)
401 Terry Francois St, Suite 202, San Francisco, CA 94126-2133 (sales & cust serv) *Tel:* 415-872-9711 *E-mail:* emgoodman@mindspring.com
Distributor for Bora; Brusberg (Berlin); Cramer (Geneva); Huber; Ides et Calendes; Kornfeld & Co (Bern); Welz; Wittenborn Art Books
Warehouse: Ashland, OH 44805
Distribution Center: Ashland, OH 44805
Membership(s): Association of American Publishers (AAP)
See separate listing for:
The Picasso Project

Wolfman Books
410 13 St, Oakland, CA 94612
Tel: 510-679-4650
E-mail: hello@wolfmanhomerepair.com

Web Site: wolfmanhomerepair.com
Key Personnel
Founder/Dir: Justin Carder
Founded: 2014
Wolfman Books is a bookstore, small press, artist residency program, & community arts hub in downtown Oakland. As a small press, we are dedicated to hybrid & experimental nonfiction, poetry, & artist books, as well as a quarterly magazine, New Life Quarterly, largely but not exclusively focused on Bay Area writers & artists.
ISBN Prefix(es): 978-0-9983461
Number of titles published annually: 3 Print
Total Titles: 10 Print
Distribution Center: Small Press Distribution, 1341 Seventh St, Berkeley, CA 94710-1409 *Tel:* 510-524-1668 *Toll Free Tel:* 800-869-7553 *Fax:* 510-524-0852 *E-mail:* spd@spdbooks.org *Web Site:* www.spdbooks.org SAN: 204-5826

§Wolters Kluwer Law & Business
Subsidiary of Wolters Kluwer
76 Ninth Ave, 7th fl, New York, NY 10011-5201
SAN: 203-4999
Tel: 212-771-0600; 301-698-7100 (cust serv outside US) *Toll Free Tel:* 800-234-1660 (cust serv)
E-mail: customer.service@wolterskluwer.com; lrusmedia@wolterskluwer.com
Web Site: lrus.wolterskluwer.com
Key Personnel
VP & Chief Content Offr: Gustavo Dobles
Dir, Mktg & Communs: Linda Gharib
Founded: 1959
Publisher of legal, business & health care titles for professionals. Publishes more than 500 journals, newsletters, electronic products & loose-leaf manuals & has more than 1,000 active professional & textbook titles.
ISBN Prefix(es): 978-0-89443; 978-0-912862; 978-0-8342; 978-1-56706; 978-0-87189; 978-0-8080; 978-0-444; 978-1-56542; 978-1-878375; 978-0-9625969; 978-1-56759; 978-0-7355; 978-0-7896; 978-0-87457; 978-0-87622; 978-0-916592; 978-1-4548
Number of titles published annually: 100 Print; 16 CD-ROM; 55 Online
Total Titles: 1,500 Print; 107 CD-ROM; 55 Online; 1 Audio
Foreign Rep(s): David Bartolone
Distribution Center: 7201 McKinney Circle, Frederick, MD 21704 *Tel:* 301-698-7100 *Fax:* 301-695-7931

Wolters Kluwer US Corp
Subsidiary of Wolters Kluwer NV (The Netherlands)
2700 Lake Cook Rd, Riverwoods, IL 60015
Tel: 847-267-7000 *Fax:* 847-580-5192
E-mail: info@wolterskluwer.com
Web Site: www.wolterskluwer.com
Key Personnel
CEO & Chmn of the Bd: Nancy McKinstry
CFO: Kevin Entricken
Dir, Mktg Communs: Linda Gharib *E-mail:* linda.gharib@wolterskluwer.com
Medical books & journals, law books, business & tax publications.
Total Titles: 5,000 Print
Imprints: Adis International; Aspen Publishers Incorporated; CCH Incorporated; CT Corporation; Lippincott, Williams & Wilkins
Foreign Office(s): Zuidpoolsingel 2, PO Box 1030, 2400 BA Alphen aan den Rijn, Netherlands (headquarters) *Tel:* (0172) 641 400 *Fax:* (0172) 474 889

Woodbine House
6510 Bells Mill Rd, Bethesda, MD 20817
SAN: 692-3445
Tel: 301-897-3570 *Toll Free Tel:* 800-843-7323 *Fax:* 301-897-5838

E-mail: info@woodbinehouse.com
Web Site: www.woodbinehouse.com
Key Personnel
Publr: Fran Marinaccio
Mktg Mgr & Intl Rts: Fran M Marinaccio
  E-mail: fmarinaccio@woodbinehouse.com
Mktg & Sales Mgr: Beth Binns *E-mail:* bbinns@
  woodbinehouse.com
Ed, Acqs Ed & Perms: Susan S Stokes
  E-mail: sstokes@woodbinehouse.com
Founded: 1985
Trade nonfiction, hardcover & paperback.
ISBN Prefix(es): 978-0-933149; 978-1-890627;
  978-1-60613
Number of titles published annually: 5 Print; 5 E-
  Book
Total Titles: 125 Print; 60 E-Book
Foreign Rep(s): Gazelle Book Services Ltd (Eu-
  rope); Silvereye Education Publications (Aus-
  tralia, Pacific Rim); University of Toronto Press
  (Canada)
Foreign Rights: Writer's House
Returns: IFC, 3570 Bladensburg Rd, Brentwood,
  MD 20722 *Tel:* 301-779-4660
Warehouse: Woodbine House, c/o IFC, 3570
  Bladensburg Rd, Brentwood, MD 20722

Woodrow Wilson Center Press
Division of The Woodrow Wilson International
  Center for Scholars
One Woodrow Wilson Plaza, 1300 Pennsylvania
  Ave NW, Washington, DC 20004-3027
Tel: 202-691-4122
Web Site: wilsoncenter.org/woodrow-wilson-
  center-press
Founded: 1988
Humanities & social sciences; policy studies.
ISBN Prefix(es): 978-0-943875; 978-1-930365
Number of titles published annually: 8 Print; 8 E-
  Book
Total Titles: 200 Print
Imprints: Wilson Center Press; Woodrow Wil-
  son Center Press/Johns Hopkins University
  Press; Woodrow Wilson Center Press/Stan-
  ford University Press; Woodrow Wilson Center
  Press/Columbia University Press
Distributed by Columbia University Press; Johns
  Hopkins University Press; Stanford University
  Press; University of California Press
Membership(s): Association of American Publish-
  ers (AAP); Association of University Presses
  (AUPresses)

WoodstockArts
PO Box 1342, Woodstock, NY 12498
Tel: 845-679-8111; 845-679-8555 *Fax:* 419-793-
  3452
E-mail: info@woodstockarts.com
Web Site: woodstockarts.com
Key Personnel
Founder: Julia Blelock *E-mail:* jblelock@
  woodstockarts.com; Weston Blelock
  E-mail: wblelock@woodstockarts.com
Founded: 1999
All the arts of Woodstock including the art of liv-
  ing.
ISBN Prefix(es): 978-0-9679268; 978-0-9977164
Number of titles published annually: 3 Print; 3 E-
  Book
Total Titles: 10 Print
Distributor for Bushwhack Press; Opus 40;
  Woodstock Artists Association & Museum;
  Woodstock Byrdcliffe Guild
Distribution Center: BCH Fulfillment & Distri-
  bution, 33 Oakland Ave, Harrison, NY 10528
  Tel: 914-835-0015 *Toll Free Tel:* 800-431-1579
  Fax: 914-835-0398 *E-mail:* orders@bookch.
  com
Membership(s): Independent Book Publishers As-
  sociation (IBPA)

Workers Compensation Research Institute
955 Massachusetts Ave, Cambridge, MA 02139

Tel: 617-661-9274 *Fax:* 617-661-9284
E-mail: wcri@wcrinet.org
Web Site: www.wcrinet.org
Key Personnel
Pubns Specialist: Sarah Solorzano
Founded: 1983
Workers compensation public policy research.
ISBN Prefix(es): 978-0-935149
Number of titles published annually: 40 Print
Total Titles: 500 Print

§Workman Publishing Co Inc
225 Varick St, 9th fl, New York, NY 10014-4381
SAN: 203-2821
Tel: 212-254-5900 *Toll Free Tel:* 800-722-7202
  Fax: 212-254-8098
E-mail: info@workman.com; orders@workman.
  com
Web Site: www.workman.com
Key Personnel
Exec Chair of the Bd & Pres: Carolan Workman
CEO: Dan Reynolds
COO: Glenn D'Agnes *E-mail:* glenn@workman.
  com
Cont: William Jackson *E-mail:* bill@workman.
  com
Publr & Edit Dir: Susan Bolotin *E-mail:* susan@
  workman.com
Publr, Workman Audio: Ana Maria Allessi
  E-mail: anamaria@workman.com
Exec Assoc Publr: Page Edmunds *E-mail:* page@
  workman.com
Exec Dir, Digital Opers: Kate Travers
  E-mail: kate@workman.com
Exec Dir, Gift & Mass Merchant Sales: Jodi
  Weiss *E-mail:* jodiw@workman.com
Exec Dir, Natl Sales: James Wehrle
  E-mail: james@workman.com
Exec Dir, New Busn Devt: Jenny Mandel
  E-mail: jenny@workman.com
Exec Dir, Publicity & Mktg: Rebecca Carlisle
  E-mail: rcarlisle@workman.com
Group Creative Dir: David Schiller
  E-mail: david@workman.com
Art Dir, Children's Publg: Sara Corbett
  E-mail: scorbett@workman.com
Creative Dir: Vaughn Andrews *E-mail:* vaughn@
  workman.com
Creative Dir, Calendars: Kelly Lynch
  E-mail: kelly@workman.com
Dir & Mng Ed: Claire McKean *E-mail:* claire@
  workman.com
Dir, Children's Publg: Traci Todd *E-mail:* traci@
  workman.com
Dir, Contracts: Ian Gross *E-mail:* ian@workman.
  com
Dir, Credit & Collections: Margaret Gerak
  E-mail: peggy@workman.com
Dir, Cust Serv & Fulfillment: Shirley Ortiz
  E-mail: shirley@workman.com
Dir, Gift Sales: Adelia Kalyvas *E-mail:* adelia@
  workman.com
Dir, Intl Sales: Sara High *E-mail:* sara@
  workman.com
Dir, Mktg: Moira Kerrigan *E-mail:* moira@
  workman.com
Dir, Photo Dept: Anne Kerman *E-mail:* annek@
  workman.com
Dir, Prodn: Doug Wolff *E-mail:* doug@workman.
  com
Dir, Sales Opers: Angela Campbell
  E-mail: angela@workman.com
Dir, Speakers Bureau: Carol Schneider
  E-mail: carol@workman.com
Dir, Spec Mkts & Custom Publg: Emily Krasner
  E-mail: emily@workman.com
Rights Dir: Kendra Poster *E-mail:* kendra@
  workman.com
Assoc Dir, Field Sales: Liz Hunter *E-mail:* lizh@
  workman.com
Sr Prodn Ed: Hillary Leary
Assoc Prodn Ed: Samantha Gil

Sr Mgr, Foreign Rts & Co-Editions: Allison Hug-
  gins
Gen Mgr, Opers & HR: Jill Salayi *E-mail:* jill@
  workman.com
Digital Sales Mgr: Gabrielle Greco
Natl Acct Mgr, Online & Digital Sales: Katharina
  Gadow *E-mail:* katharina@workman.com
Natl Accts Mgr: Caitlin Kleinschmidt
  E-mail: caitlin@workman.com
Asst Gift Sales Mgr: Amanda German
Founded: 1967
General nonfiction, calendars.
ISBN Prefix(es): 978-0-89480; 978-1-56305; 978-
  0-7611
Number of titles published annually: 345 Print
Divisions: Algonquin Books of Chapel Hill; Ar-
  tisan; Storey Publishing LLC; Timber Press;
  Workman Speakers Bureau
Distributor for Duo Press; Erewhon Books; The
  Experiment; Familius
Foreign Rep(s): Thomas Allen & Son Ltd
  (Canada); Bookreps New Zealand (New
  Zealand); Hardie Grant Books (Australia);
  Melia Publishing Services (Ireland, UK)
Foreign Rights: Big Apple Agency Inc (China,
  Taiwan); Julio F-Yanez Agencia Literaria SL
  (Latin America, Portugal, Spain); Graal Lit-
  erary Agency (Poland); Japan UNI Agency
  (Japan); JLM Literary Agency (Greece); Katai
  & Bolza Literary Agency (Hungary); KCC
  (Korea); Alexander Korahenevski Agency (Rus-
  sia); Kristin Olson Literary Agency (Czechia);
  Mickey Pikarski (Israel); Sebes & Bisseling
  Literary Agency (Netherlands)
Returns: LSC Communications, Brighton Beach
  Rd, Menasha, WI 54952
Warehouse: LSC Communications, Book Fulfill-
  ment Serv, N9234 Lake Park Rd, Appleton, WI
  54915
Membership(s): Association of American Publish-
  ers (AAP)
See separate listing for:
Algonquin Books
Artisan
Storey Publishing LLC
Timber Press Inc

World Almanac®
Imprint of Skyhorse Publishing Inc
307 W 36 St, 11 fl, New York, NY 10018
SAN: 211-6944
Tel: 212-643-6816 *Toll Free Tel:* 800-322-8755
  Fax: 212-643-6819
E-mail: info@skyhorsepublishing.com
Web Site: www.skyhorsepublishing.com
Key Personnel
Exec Ed: Sarah Janssen
Founded: 1868
Annual juvenile & adult reference books.
ISBN Prefix(es): 978-1-60057
Number of titles published annually: 6 Print
Total Titles: 9 Print; 3 E-Book
Foreign Rep(s): Adnkronos Libri SRL (Italy)

§World Bank Publications
Member of The World Bank Group
Office of the Publisher, 1818 "H" St NW, U-11-
  1104, Washington, DC 20433
Tel: 202-458-4497; 202-473-1000
  Toll Free Tel: 800-645-7247 (cust serv)
  Fax: 202-522-2631
E-mail: books@worldbank.org; pubrights@
  worldbank.org (foreign rts)
Web Site: www.worldbank.org/en/research
Key Personnel
Pres, World Bank Group & Chmn of the Bd of
  Dirs: Dr Jim Yong Kim
Founded: 1944
Publish over 200 new titles annually in support
  of the World Bank's mission to fight poverty &
  distributes them globally in both print & elec-
  tronic formats; electronic online subscription
  database; international affairs.

ISBN Prefix(es): 978-0-8213
Number of titles published annually: 200 Print;
10 CD-ROM; 3 Online; 30 E-Book
Total Titles: 2,000 Print; 50 CD-ROM; 3 Online;
50 E-Book
Imprints: World Bank
Foreign Rep(s): Africa Connection (Guy Simpson) (Sub-Saharan Africa); African Moon Press (Chris Reinders) (Southern Africa); Co Info Pty Ltd (Australia, New Zealand); Eurospan Group (Africa, Central Asia, East Asia, Europe, Ireland, Middle East, UK); Far Eastern Booksellers (East Asia, Japan); International Publishers Representatives (Middle East, North Africa); Viva Books Pvt Ltd (South Asia)
Membership(s): Association of American Publishers (AAP)

§World Book Inc
Subsidiary of The Scott Fetzer Co
180 N LaSalle, Suite 900, Chicago, IL 60601
SAN: 201-4815
Tel: 312-729-5800 *Toll Free Tel:* 800-967-5325 (consumer sales, US); 800-463-8845 (consumer sales, CN); 800-975-3250 (school & lib sales, US); 800-837-5365 (school & lib sales, CN); 866-866-5200 (web sales) *Fax:* 312-729-5600; 312-729-5606 *Toll Free Fax:* 800-433-9330 (school & lib sales, US); 888-690-4002 (school & lib sales, CN)
E-mail: customercare@worldbook.com
Web Site: www.worldbook.com
Key Personnel
Pres: Jim O'Rourke
VP, Edit & Ed-in-Chief: Paul A Kobasa
Founded: 1917
Publisher of high-quality, award-winning, educational reference & nonfiction publications for the school & library market & home market, in print & online formats.
ISBN Prefix(es): 978-0-7166
Number of titles published annually: 40 Print
Total Titles: 350 Print; 10 Online
Imprints: Bright Connections Media, A World Book Encyclopedia Company
See separate listing for:
Bright Connections Media, A World Book Encyclopedia Company

World Citizens
Affiliate of Cinema Investments Co Inc
PO Box 131, Mill Valley, CA 94942-0131
Tel: 415-380-8020; 415-233-2822 (direct)
Toll Free Tel: 800-247-6553 (orders only)
Key Personnel
Ed-in-Chief: Joan Ellen
Ed: John Ballard
Assoc Ed: Jack Henry
Sales Mgr & Intl Rts: Steve Ames
Founded: 1984
Cross cultural & multicultural novels & texts. Adult, educational, trade & young adult divisions.
ISBN Prefix(es): 978-0-932279
Number of titles published annually: 6 Print; 4 CD-ROM; 6 E-Book; 4 Audio
Total Titles: 18 Print
Imprints: Classroom Classics; New Horizons Book Publishing Co; Skateman Publications
Distributed by Inland
Distribution Center: Baker & Taylor Publisher Services, 30 Amberwood Pkwy, Ashland, OH 44805 *Tel:* 567-215-0030 *Toll Free Tel:* 888-814-0208 *E-mail:* info@btpubservices.com *Web Site:* www.btpubservices.com

§World Resources Institute
10 "G" St NE, Suite 800, Washington, DC 20002
Tel: 202-729-7600 *Fax:* 202-729-7610
Web Site: www.wri.org
Founded: 1982

Professional, scholarly & general interest publications, including energy, the environment, agriculture, forestry, natural resources, economics, geography, climate, biotechnology & development. Some titles co-published with university presses & commercial publishers.
ISBN Prefix(es): 978-0-915825; 978-1-56973
Number of titles published annually: 10 Print
Total Titles: 420 Print; 2 CD-ROM

§World Scientific Publishing Co Inc
27 Warren St, Suite 401-402, Hackensack, NJ 07601
Tel: 201-487-9655 *Fax:* 201-487-9656
E-mail: wspc_us@wspc.com; sales@wspc.com; mkt@wspc.com; editor@wspc.com
Web Site: www.worldscientific.com
Key Personnel
Chmn & Ed-in-Chief: K K Phuna
Group Mng Dir: Doreen Kiu
Mng Dir: Max Phua
Founded: 1981
ISBN Prefix(es): 978-1-944659
Number of titles published annually: 400 Print
Total Titles: 5,000 Print
Subsidiaries: Imperial College Press
Foreign Office(s): World Scientific Publishing (Beijing), B1505, Caizhi International Bldg, No 18 Zhongguancun E Rd, Haidan District, Beijing 100083, China *Tel:* (010) 82601201 *E-mail:* wspbj@wspc.com
Global Consultancy (Shanghai) Pte Ltd, Shanghai Bund International Tower, Rm 2003, No 99, Huangpu Rd, Shanghai 200080, China *Tel:* (021) 63254982 *Fax:* (021) 63254985 *E-mail:* shanghai@worldscientific.com.cn
World Scientific Publishing Co Pte Ltd, Theresienstr 66, 80333 Munich, Germany *Tel:* (089) 12414-770 *Fax:* (089) 12414-7710 *E-mail:* munich@wspc.com
World Scientific Publishing (HK) Co Ltd, PO Box 72482, Kowloon Central Post Office, Hong Kong, Hong Kong *Tel:* 2771 8791 *Fax:* 2771 8155 *E-mail:* hongkong@worldscientific.com.hk
World Scientific Publishing Co Pte Ltd, No 16 SW Boag Rd, T Nagar, Chennai 600 017, India *Tel:* (044) 52065464 *Fax:* (044) 52065464
World Scientific Publishing Co, Kiriat Hatikshoret-Neve Ilan, Suite 226, Harei, 90805 Yehuda, Israel *Tel:* (054) 4403728 *Fax:* (02) 5791532; (02) 5791533 *E-mail:* rspindel@wspc.com
World Scientific Publishing Co, c/o Science Press Tokyo, 2F, No 3 Katou Bldg, 23-2 Yushima 2-chome, Bunkyo-ku, Tokyo 113-0034, Japan *Tel:* (080) 81080-6881 *E-mail:* wspc_japan@wspc.com
World Scientific Publishing Co Pte Ltd, 5 Toh Tuck Link, Singapore 596224, Singapore *Tel:* 6466 5775 *Fax:* 6467 7667 *E-mail:* wspc@wspc.com.sg
World Scientific Publishing Co Pte Ltd, 8F, No 162, Sec 4, Roosevelt Rd, Taipei 10091, Taiwan *Tel:* (02) 2369-1366 *Fax:* (02) 2366-0460 *E-mail:* wsptw@ms13.hinet.net
World Scientific Publishing (UK) Ltd, 57 Shelton St, London WC2H 9HE, United Kingdom *Tel:* (020) 7836 0888 *Fax:* (020) 7836 2020 *E-mail:* sales@wspc.co.uk
Warehouse: 46 Development Rd, Fitchburg, MA 01420

§World Trade Press LLC
616 E Eighth St, Suite 7, Traverse City, MI 49686
Tel: 707-778-1124 *Toll Free Tel:* 800-833-8586 *Fax:* 231-642-5300
Web Site: www.worldtradepress.com
Key Personnel
Publr & CEO: Edward G Hinkelman
Tel: 707-778-1124 ext 204 *E-mail:* egh@worldtradepress.com

Founded: 1992
The Global Knowledge Company. Large-scale databases of country information for culture, business, travel, local living & food.
ISBN Prefix(es): 978-0-9631864; 978-1-885073
Number of titles published annually: 8 Print; 240 Online; 26 E-Book
Total Titles: 118 Print; 240 Online; 126 E-Book

WorldTariff
Division of FedEx Corp
220 Montgomery St, Suite 448, San Francisco, CA 94104-3410
Tel: 415-391-7501 *Toll Free Tel:* 866-268-7602
Web Site: ftn.fedex.com/wtonline
Founded: 1961
Publish customs duty & tax information.
ISBN Prefix(es): 978-1-56745
Number of titles published annually: 100 Print
Total Titles: 22 Online
Foreign Office(s): Eurotariff, National House, 60-66 Wardour St, 6th fl, London W1V 3HP, United Kingdom

§Worth Publishers
Imprint of Macmillan Learning
One New York Plaza, 46th fl, New York, NY 10004
Tel: 212-576-9400; 212-375-7000
E-mail: press.inquiries@macmillan.com
Web Site: www.macmillanlearning.com/college/us
Founded: 1966
Social science texts for the higher education market & advanced high school courses.
ISBN Prefix(es): 978-1-57259; 978-1-4292; 978-0-7167
Number of titles published annually: 10 E-Book
Total Titles: 300 Print
Foreign Rep(s): Macmillan East Asia (China, Hong Kong, Indonesia, Korea, Philippines, Singapore, Thailand, Vietnam); Macmillan Publishers (Taiwan); Palgrave Macmillan (Australia, New Zealand); Palgrave Macmillan UK (Africa, Caribbean, Europe, India, Japan, Latin America, Middle East, Pakistan, UK); USBD Distribution Sdn Bhd (Malaysia)
Orders to: MPS Distribution Center, 16365 James Madison Hwy (US Rte 15), Gordonsville, VA 22942 *Toll Free Tel:* 888-330-8477 *Toll Free Fax:* 800-672-2054 *E-mail:* orders@mpsvirginia.com
Returns: MPS Returns Center, 14301 Litchfield Dr, Orange, VA 22960
Warehouse: MPS Distribution Center, 16365 James Madison Hwy (US Rte 15), Gordonsville, VA 22942 *Toll Free Tel:* 888-330-8477 *Toll Free Fax:* 800-672-2054 (orders) *E-mail:* orders@mpsvirginia.com

§Write Stuff Enterprises LLC
1001 S Andrews Ave, Suite 200, Fort Lauderdale, FL 33316
Tel: 954-462-6657 *Fax:* 954-462-6023
E-mail: info@writestuffbooks.com
Web Site: www.writestuffbooks.com
Key Personnel
Founder, Chmn & CEO: Jeffrey L Rodengen
Pres, Publr & CFO: Marianne Roberts
Founded: 1986
Leading publisher of historical works focusing on industry & technology.
ISBN Prefix(es): 978-0-945903; 978-1-932022
Number of titles published annually: 4 Print; 4 E-Book
Imprints: Write Stuff®
Membership(s): American Booksellers Association (ABA); Independent Book Publishers Association (IBPA)

WriteLife Publishing
Imprint of Boutique of Quality Books Publishing
960 Oaktree Blvd, Christianburg, VA 24073
E-mail: writelife@boutiqueofqualitybooks.com

Web Site: www.writelife.com; www.facebook.
com/writelife
Key Personnel
Pres & Publr: Terri Leidich *E-mail:* terri@
bqnpublishing.com
Soc Media/IT Mgr: John Daly
E-mail: johndailybooks@hotmail.com
Acqs Ed: Allison Itterly
Founded: 2008
ISBN Prefix(es): 978-1-60808
Number of titles published annually: 12 Print; 12
E-Book
Total Titles: 90 Print; 90 E-Book
Membership(s): Independent Book Publishers
Association (IBPA); Midwest Independent
Booksellers Association (MIBA); Mountains
& Plains Independent Booksellers Association
(MPIBA)

Writer's AudioShop
1316 Overland Stage Rd, Dripping Springs, TX
78620
Tel: 512-476-1616
E-mail: wrtaudshop@aol.com
Web Site: www.writersaudio.com
Key Personnel
Publr: Elaine Davenport
Founded: 1985
Audio publisher.
ISBN Prefix(es): 978-1-880717
Number of titles published annually: 4 Audio
Total Titles: 35 Audio
Membership(s): Audio Publishers Association

Writer's Digest Books
Imprint of Penguin Random House LLC
1745 Broadway, New York, NY 10019
Top-quality instructional & reference books to
help creative people find personal satisfaction
& professional success. Topics covered include
writing, publishing, songwriting & personal
growth.
Penguin Random House & its publishing entities
are not accepting unsol submissions, proposals,
mss, or submission queries via e-mail at this
time.
Number of titles published annually: 28 Print
Total Titles: 150 Print
Distribution Center: Two Rivers Distribution, 1400 Broadway, Suite 520, New
York, NY 10018 *Toll Free Tel:* 866-400-
5351 *E-mail:* ips@ingramcontent.com *Web
Site:* www.tworiversdistribution.com

WRP, see Water Resources Publications LLC

§Wyndham Hall Press
10372 W Munro Lake Dr, Levering, MI 49755
SAN: 686-6743
Tel: 419-648-9124
E-mail: orders@wyndhamhallpress.com
Web Site: www.wyndhamhallpress.com
Key Personnel
Mng Ed: Mark S McCullough *E-mail:* mark@
wyndhamhallpress.com
Founded: 1982
Scholarly monographs & textbooks.
ISBN Prefix(es): 978-1-55605; 978-0-932269
Number of titles published annually: 8 Print
Total Titles: 240 Print

§Xist Publishing
PO Box 61593, Irvine, CA 92602
Tel: 949-478-2568
E-mail: info@xistpublishing.com
Web Site: www.xistpublishing.com
Key Personnel
COO: Jacob Lee
Pres: Calee Lee
Founded: 2010

Digital-first publisher. Specialize in children's
ebooks for every major device.
ISBN Prefix(es): 978-1-62395; 978-1-5324
Number of titles published annually: 50 Print;
200 E-Book; 30 Audio
Total Titles: 300 Print; 1,000 E-Book; 60 Audio
Foreign Rep(s): Sylvia Hayse (worldwide)
Membership(s): Society of Children's Book Writ-
ers & Illustrators (SCBWI)

Xlibris Corp
Imprint of Author Solutions LLC
1663 Liberty Dr, Suite 200, Bloomington, IN
47403
Toll Free Tel: 844-714-8691; 888-795-4274
Fax: 610-915-0294
E-mail: info@xlibris.com; media@xlibris.com
Web Site: www.xlibris.com; www.authorsolutions.
com/our-imprints/xlibris
Key Personnel
COO: Bill Becher
CIO: Joe Steinbach
Pres: Bill Elliott
Founded: 1997
One of the leading publishing services providers
for authors, Xlibris provides authors with a
broad set of publishing options including hard-
cover, trade paperback, custom leather bound
& full-color formats. In addition, Xlibris of-
fers its authors the widest selection of profes-
sional, marketing & bookselling services. Since
its founding, Xlibris has published more than
25,000 titles.
This publisher has indicated that 100% of their
product line is author subsidized.
ISBN Prefix(es): 978-0-7388; 978-0-9663501;
978-1-4010; 978-1-4134; 978-1-59926; 978-1-
4257; 978-1-4363; 978-1-4415
Number of titles published annually: 5,100 Print
Total Titles: 25,000 Print
Distribution Center: Baker & Taylor LLC, 2550
W Tyvola Rd, Suite 300, Charlotte, NC 28217
Tel: 704-998-3100 *Toll Free Tel:* 800-775-1800
Web Site: www.baker-taylor.com
Ingram Book Group, One Ingram Blvd, La
Vergne, TN 37086 *Tel:* 615-793-5000 *Web
Site:* www.ingramcontent.com
Membership(s): American Booksellers Associa-
tion (ABA)

§XML Press
Subsidiary of R L Hamilton & Associates LLC
24310 Moulton Pkwy, Suite O-175, Laguna Hills,
CA 92637
SAN: 920-7481
Tel: 970-231-3624
E-mail: publisher@xmlpress.net
Web Site: xmlpress.net
Key Personnel
Publr: Richard Hamilton *E-mail:* hamilton@
xmlpress.net
Founded: 2008
Specialize in publications for technical commu-
nicators, content strategists, managers & mar-
keters, with an emphasis on XML technology,
social media & management. Also provides
publication services to corporations that want
to make their technical documentation available
in print form through retail channels.
ISBN Prefix(es): 978-0-9822191; 978-1-937434
Number of titles published annually: 12 Print; 12
E-Book
Total Titles: 35 Print; 33 E-Book
Distribution Center: Ingram, One Ingram Blvd,
La Vergne, TN 37086
Membership(s): Organization of Advancement
of Structured Information Standards (OASIS);
Society for Technical Communication (STC)

Yale Center for British Art
1080 Chapel St, New Haven, CT 06510-2302

Mailing Address: PO Box 208280, New Haven,
CT 06520-8280
Tel: 203-432-8929 *Fax:* 203-432-1626
E-mail: ycba.publications@yale.edu
Web Site: britishart.yale.edu
Key Personnel
Dir: Courtney J Martin *E-mail:* ycba.director@
yale.edu
Deputy Dir, Res, Exhibitions & Pubns: Martina
Droth *Tel:* 203-432-2545 *E-mail:* martina.
droth@yale.edu
Head, Exhibitions & Pubns: Nathan Flis *Tel:* 203-
432-6774 *E-mail:* nathan.flis@yale.edu
Devt Ed & Pubns Mgr: Deborah Cannarella
Tel: 203-432-2141 *E-mail:* deborah.
cannarella@yale.edu
Ed: Christopher Lotis
Founded: 1977
Exhibition catalogues.
ISBN Prefix(es): 978-0-930606
Number of titles published annually: 4 Print
Total Titles: 61 Print

§Yale University Press
Division of Yale University
302 Temple St, New Haven, CT 06511-8909
SAN: 203-2740
Mailing Address: PO Box 209040, New Haven,
CT 06520-9040
Tel: 203-432-0960; 203-432-0966 (sales); 401-
531-2800 (cust serv) *Toll Free Tel:* 800-405-
1619 (cust serv) *Fax:* 203-432-0948; 203-
432-8485 (sales); 401-531-2801 (cust serv)
Toll Free Fax: 800-406-9145 (cust serv)
E-mail: sales.press@yale.edu (sales); customer.
care@triliteral.org (cust serv)
Web Site: www.yalebooks.com; yalepress.yale.
edu/yupbooks
Key Personnel
COO: Kate Brown
Publr, Art & Architecture/Exec Dir, E-Portal: Pa-
tricia Fidler
Dir: John Donatich
Art Dir: Nancy Ovedovitz
Dir, Edit, Design & Prodn Opers: Jenya Weinreb
Dir, Ms Editing, Design & Prodn, Art Books:
Kate Zanzucchi
Dir, Mktg & Promo: Heather D'Auria
Edit Dir: Seth Ditchik
Publicity Dir: Brenda King
Sales Dir: Jay Cosgrove
Deputy Dir, Fin: Timothy Haire
Asst Sales Dir, Head of Digital & Art Sales:
Stephen Cebik
Sr Exec Ed, Sci & Medicine: Jean E Thomson
Black
Mng Ed: Dorothea Halliday
Exec Ed: Jennifer Banks
Sr Ed: Adina Popescu Berk
Sr Ed, Art & Architecture: Katherine Boller
Ed: Jaya Aninda Chatterjee
Ed, Classics & Ancient World: Heather Gold
Ed, Lang, Lit & Performing Arts: Sarah Miller
Assoc Ed, Art & Architecture: Amy Canonico
Asst Ed & Mktg Mgr: Travis Kimbel
Educ Mktg Mgr: Debra Bozzi
Mgr, Ad & Exhibits: Ellen Freiler
Mktg Mgr, Art & Architecture: Jessica Holahan
Online Mktg Mgr: Michael Hoak
Sr Publicist: Jennifer Doerr; Liz Pelton; Robert
Pranzatelli
Publicist: Roland Coffey; Caitlin Gallagher
Art Book Dist Partner Coord: Nick Geller
Founded: 1908
Scholarly publications.
ISBN Prefix(es): 978-0-300
Number of titles published annually: 350 Print
Total Titles: 5,000 Print
Imprints: Yale Press Audio
Foreign Office(s): 47 Bedford Sq, London WC1B
3DP, United Kingdom, Head, Rts: Olivia Willis
Tel: (020) 7079-4900 *Fax:* (020) 7079-4901

E-mail: sales@yaleup.co.uk *Web Site:* www.
yalebooks.co.uk
Distributor for The Art Institute of Chicago; The
Bard Graduate Center; Beinecke Rare Book &
Manuscript Library; Dallas Museum of Art;
Harvard University Art Museums; The Jew-
ish Museum; Kimbell Art Museum; Paul Mel-
lon Centre; The Menil Collection; Mercator-
fonds; The Metropolitan Museum of Art; Na-
tional Gallery, London; National Gallery of Art
(Washington, DC); Philadelphia Museum of
Art; Princeton University Art Museum; Sterling
& Francine Clark Art Institute; Whitney Mu-
seum of American Art; Yale Center for British
Art; Yale University Art Gallery
Foreign Rep(s): Craig Falk (Latin America); Mi-
cal Moser (Canada)
Shipping Address: TriLiteral LLC, 100 Maple
Ridge Dr, Cumberland, RI 02864-1769
Tel: 401-658-4226
Membership(s): Association of American Publish-
ers (AAP); Association of University Presses
(AUPresses)

§Yard Dog Press
710 W Redbud Lane, Alma, AR 72921-7247
Tel: 479-632-4693 *Fax:* 479-632-4693
Web Site: www.yarddogpress.com
Key Personnel
Owner & Ed-in-Chief: Selina Rosen
E-mail: selinarosen@cox.net
Tech Ed & Orders Contact: Lynn Rosen
E-mail: lynnstran@cox.net
Founded: 1995
Micro press specializing in science fiction, fan-
tasy & horror. Closed to unsol submissions.
Special pricing for bulk orders.
ISBN Prefix(es): 978-1-893687; 978-0-9824704;
978-1-937105; 978-1-945941
Number of titles published annually: 4 Print; 4 E-
Book
Total Titles: 130 Print; 130 E-Book
Imprints: Double Dog (flip books - two short
novels); Fantasy Writers' Asylum; Just Cause
(non-genre books)
Membership(s): Science Fiction & Fantasy Writ-
ers of America (SFWA)

YBK Publishers Inc
39 Crosby St, New York, NY 10013
Tel: 212-219-0135
E-mail: readmybook@ybkpublishers.com; info@
ybkpublishers.com
Web Site: www.ybkpublishers.com
Key Personnel
Pres: Otto Barz *E-mail:* obarz@ybkpublishers.
com
Founded: 2001
General trade & nonfiction.
ISBN Prefix(es): 978-0-9703923; 978-0-9764359;
978-1-936411; 978-0-9790972; 978-0-9800508;
978-0-9824012
Number of titles published annually: 7 Print
Total Titles: 90 Print; 5 E-Book
Distribution Center: Lightning Source, 1246 Heil
Quaker Blvd, La Vergne, TN 37086 *Tel:* 615-
213-5815 *Fax:* 615-213-4426 *E-mail:* info@
ybkpublishers.com
Membership(s): Association of American Publish-
ers (AAP); PEN American Center

Yeshiva University Press
500 W 185 St, New York, NY 10033
Tel: 212-960-5400
Web Site: www.yu.edu/books
Key Personnel
Pres: Ari Berman *Tel:* 646-592-4300
E-mail: president@yu.edu
ISBN Prefix(es): 978-0-87068; 978-0-88125; 978-
1-60280
Number of titles published annually: 10 Print
Total Titles: 71 Print

YMAA Publication Center Inc
PO Box 480, Wolfeboro, NH 03894
SAN: 665-2077
Tel: 603-569-7988 *Toll Free Tel:* 800-669-8892
Fax: 603-569-1889
E-mail: info@ymaa.com
Web Site: www.ymaa.com
Key Personnel
Publr: David Ripianzi
Prodn Mgr: Tim Comrie
Sales Rep: David Silver
Founded: 1984
Publisher of in-depth books, videos & DVDs on
martial arts, meditation, traditional Chinese
medicine & alternative health therapies.
ISBN Prefix(es): 978-0-940871; 978-1-886969;
978-1-59439
Number of titles published annually: 10 Print; 10
E-Book
Total Titles: 90 Print; 70 E-Book; 4 Audio
Distributor for Wind Records (Chinese healing
music)
Foreign Rep(s): Big Apple Agency (Maggie Han)
(China, Taiwan); The Book Publishers Asso-
ciation of Israel (Shoshi Grajower) (Israel);
Julio F-Yanez Agencia Literaria SL (Montse
Yanez) (Mexico, Spain); Graal Literary Agency
(Madga Cabajewska) (Poland); Imprima Ko-
rea Agency (Joseph Lee) (Korea); International
Copyright Agency (Simona Kessler) (Roma-
nia); Japan UNI Agency (Taeko Nagatsuka)
(Japan); JS Literary & Media Agency (Somjai
Raksasee) (Thailand); Nurcihan Kesim Literary
Agency Inc (Filiz Karaman) (Turkey); Maxima
Creative Agency (Santo Manurung) (Indone-
sia); Nova Littera SL (Konstantin Paltchikov)
(Russia); Andrew Nurnberg Associates (Tat-
jana Zoldnere) (Latvia, Lithuania, Ukraine);
Andrew Nurnberg Associates (Anna Droumeva)
(Bulgaria); Andrew Nurnberg Associates (Pe-
tra Tobiskova) (Czechia); OA Literary Agency
(Michael Avramides) (Greece); Plima Literary
Agency (Mila Perisic) (Croatia, Serbia, Slove-
nia); Schindler's Literary Agency (Suely Pedro
Dos Santos) (Brazil); Ralph & Sheila Summers
(Hong Kong, Korea, Malaysia, Philippines, Sin-
gapore, Taiwan, Thailand); Tuttle-Mori Agency
Inc (Fumi Nishijima) (Japan)
Foreign Rights: Agencia Literaria (Brazil, Portu-
gal); Big Apple Agency Inc (China, Taiwan);
Bookman (Denmark, Finland, Iceland, Nor-
way, Sweden); Julio F-Yanez Agencia Literaria
SL (Mexico, Spain, Spanish Latin America,
Spanish-speaking countries); Imprima Korea
Agency (Korea); Jarir Bookstore (Egypt, Mid-
dle East, Saudi Arabia); JS Literary & Media
Agency (Thailand); La Nouvelle Agency (Bel-
gium, Switzerland); Nova Littera Ltd (Russia);
Andrew Nurnberg Associates (Baltic States);
Andrew Nurnberg Associates Sofia (Bulgaria);
OA Literary Agency (Greece); Permissions &
Rights (Albania, Croatia, Montenegro, Serbia,
Slovenia); Tuttle-Mori Agency Inc (Japan)
Orders to: New Leaf Distributing Co, 401
Thornton Rd, Lithia Springs, GA 30122-
1557 *Tel:* 770-948-7845 *Fax:* 770-994-
2313 *E-mail:* newleaf@newleaf-dist.com
Web Site: newleafdist.com; Baker & Taylor,
2550 W Tyvola Rd, Charlotte, NC *Toll Free
Tel:* 800-775-1800 *Fax:* 704-998-3100 *Web
Site:* www.baker-taylor.com; National Book
Network, 15200 NBN Way, Blue Ridge Sum-
mit, PA 17214 *Tel:* 717-794-3800 *Toll Free
Tel:* 800-462-6420 *Toll Free Fax:* 800-338-
4550 *E-mail:* custserv@nbnbooks.com *Web
Site:* www.nbnbooks.com; Ingram Book Co,
One Ingram Blvd, La Vergne, TN *Tel:* (615)
793-5000 *Toll Free Tel:* 800-937-8200 *Web
Site:* www.ingrambook.com
Distribution Center: National Book Net-
work, 15200 NBN Way, Blue Ridge Sum-
mit, PA 07214 *Tel:* 717-794-3800 *Toll Free
Tel:* 800-338-4550 *Toll Free Fax:* 800-338-

4550 *E-mail:* custserv@nbnbooks.com *Web
Site:* www.nbnbooks.com
Membership(s): American Booksellers Association (ABA); Independent Book Publishers Association (IBPA)

§Yotzeret Publishing
PO Box 18662, St Paul, MN 55118-0662
Tel: 651-470-3853 *Fax:* 651-224-7447
E-mail: info@yotzeretpublishing.com; orders@
yotzeretpublishing.com
Web Site: yotzeretpublishing.com
Key Personnel
Publr: Sheyna Galyan
Founded: 2002
Adult & children's books & ebooks from a Jew-
ish perspective.
ISBN Prefix(es): 978-1-59287
Number of titles published annually: 2 Print; 2 E-
Book; 1 Audio
Total Titles: 10 Print; 7 E-Book
Orders to: Itasca Books, 5120 Cedar Lake Rd,
Minneapolis, MN 55416, Dist Mgr: Mark
Jung *Tel:* 952-345-4488 *Toll Free Tel:* 800-
901-3480 *Fax:* 952-920-0541 *E-mail:* orders@
itascabooks.com *Web Site:* www.itascabooks.
com
Distribution Center: Itasca Books, 5120 Cedar
Lake Rd, Minneapolis, MN 55416, Dist Mgr:
Mark Jung *Tel:* 952-342-4888 ext 118 *Toll
Free Tel:* 800-901-3480 ext 118 *Fax:* 952-920-
0541 *E-mail:* orders@itascabooks.com *Web
Site:* www.itascabooks.com
Membership(s): Independent Book Publishers As-
sociation (IBPA); Midwest Independent Pub-
lishing Association (MIPA); Minnesota Book
Publishers Roundtable

YWAM Publishing
Division of Youth With A Mission
PO Box 55787, Seattle, WA 98155-0787
Tel: 425-771-1153 *Toll Free Tel:* 800-922-2143
Fax: 425-775-2383
E-mail: books@ywampublishing.com
Web Site: www.ywampublishing.com
Key Personnel
Mktg Dir: Wenche Warren *E-mail:* marketing@
ywampublishing.com
Founded: 1960
Books on missions, evangelism, discipleship &
homeschooling.
ISBN Prefix(es): 978-0-927545
Number of titles published annually: 10 Print; 2
CD-ROM
Total Titles: 260 Print; 15 CD-ROM; 10 Audio
Distributor for Emerald Books
Shipping Address: 7825 230 St SW, Edmonds,
WA 98026
Warehouse: 7825 230 St SW, Edmonds, WA
98026

§Zagat Inc
424 Broadway, 5th fl, New York, NY 10013
SAN: 289-4777
Toll Free Tel: 800-540-9609
E-mail: feedback@zagat.com; press@zagat.com
Web Site: www.zagat.com
Key Personnel
Co-Founder, Co-Chair & CEO: Tim Zagat
Co-Founder & Co-Chair: Nina S Zagat
E-mail: nina@zagat.com
Founded: 1979
Provider of consumer survey-based information
on where to eat, drink, stay & play worldwide.
ISBN Prefix(es): 978-1-57006; 978-1-60478
Number of titles published annually: 49 Online

Zaner-Bloser Inc
Subsidiary of Highlights for Children Inc
1400 Goodale Blvd, Suite 200, Grandview
Heights, OH 43212
Mailing Address: PO Box 16764, Columbus, OH
43216-6764

Toll Free Tel: 800-421-3018 (cust serv)
   Toll Free Fax: 800-992-6087 (orders)
E-mail: customerexperience@zaner-bloser.com
Web Site: www.zaner-bloser.com
Key Personnel
Pres: Lisa Carmona
Founded: 1888
Elementary textbooks for critical thinking, whole
   language, substance abuse prevention, spelling
   & handwriting; modality (learning styles) kit,
   professional education books, storytelling kits
   & early childhood education.
ISBN Prefix(es): 978-0-88309; 978-0-88085
Number of titles published annually: 200 Print
Foreign Rep(s): Children's Press
Advertising Agency: EDPUB
Orders to: PO Box 16764, Columbus, OH 43216-
   6764
Returns: 10650 Toebben Dr, Independence, KY
   41051
Warehouse: 4200 Parkway Ct, Hilliard, OH
   43026

Zebra Books, see Kensington Publishing Corp

§Zeig, Tucker & Theisen Inc
2632 E Thomas Rd, Suite 201, Phoenix, AZ
   85016
Tel: 480-389-4342
Web Site: www.zeigtucker.com
Key Personnel
Pres: Jeffrey K Zeig, PhD *E-mail:* jeff@erickson-
   foundation.org
Busn Mgr: Stacey Moore *E-mail:* stacey@
   erickson-foundation.org
Mng Ed: Chuck Lakin *E-mail:* chuck@zeigtucker.
   com
Edit: Suzi Tucker
Founded: 1998
Independent publisher in the behavioral sciences.
ISBN Prefix(es): 978-1-891944; 978-1-932462;
   978-1-934442
Number of titles published annually: 10 Print
Total Titles: 45 Print; 8 Audio
Orders to: AIDCVT *Toll Free Tel:* 855-446-1222
   Fax: 802-864-7626 *E-mail:* ztt.orders@aidcvt.
   com

Zest Books
Imprint of Lerner Publishing Group Inc
241 First Ave N, Minneapolis, MN 55401
Tel: 612-332-3344 *Toll Free Tel:* 800-328-4929
   Toll Free Fax: 800-332-1132
E-mail: info@lernerbooks.com; publicity@
   lernerbooks.com; custserve@lernerbooks.com
   (orders)
Web Site: lernerbooks.com
Key Personnel
Chmn: Harry J Lerner
Pres & Publr: Adam Lerner
EVP & COO: Mark Budde
EVP & CFO: Margaret Thomas
EVP, Edit: Andy Cummings
EVP, Mktg: Rachel Zugschwert
EVP, Sales: David Wexler
Dir, Rts, Spec Sales & Intl Dist: Maria Kjoller
Edit Dir: Ashley Kuehl
Publg Dir, School & Lib: Jenny Krueger
School & Lib Mktg Dir: Lois Wallentine
Assoc Edit Dir: Shaina Olmanson
Founded: 2006
ISBN Prefix(es): 978-0-9772660
Number of titles published annually: 5 Print; 20
   E-Book
Total Titles: 125 Print; 275 E-Book
Foreign Rep(s): Thomas Allen & Son Ltd (trade)
   (Canada); Bounce Sales & Marketing Ltd
   (UK); Phambili Agencies (Botswana, Lesotho,
   Namibia, South Africa); Publishers Marketing
   Services (Brunei, Malaysia, Singapore); Saun-
   ders Book Co (school & lib) (Canada)

Foreign Rights: Japan Foreign-Rights Centre
   (Japan); Korea Copyright Center (KCC) (Korea); Agence Michelle Lapautre (France); Literarische Agentur Silke Weniger (Germany)
Warehouse: 1251 Washington Ave N, Minneapolis, MN 55401, Mgr: Ken Rued

§Zondervan
Subsidiary of HarperCollins Christian Publishing
3900 Sparks Dr, Grand Rapids, MI 49546
SAN: 203-2694
Tel: 616-698-6900 *Toll Free Tel:* 800-226-1122;
   800-727-1309 (retail orders) *Fax:* 616-698-
   3350 *Toll Free Fax:* 800-698-3256 (retail or-
   ders)
Web Site: www.zondervan.com
Key Personnel
Pres & CEO: Mark Schoenwald
SVP & Publr, Zondervan Reflective & Zondervan
   Academic: Stanley N Gundry
SVP, Children's & Gift Group Publr: Laura
   Minchew
SVP, Sales: Tom Knight
VP & Publr, Fiction: Amanda Bostic
VP & Publr, Zonderkidz: Megan Dobson
VP & Publr, Zondervan Bible Group: Melinda
   Bouma
VP & Publr, Zondervan Books & Zondervan
   Thrive: Webster Younce
VP of Mktg, Children's & Gift: Michael Aulisio
VP of Mktg, Zondervan Books & Zondervan
   Thrive: Paul Fisher
VP of Mktg, Zondervan Reflective & Zondervan
   Academic: Jesse Hillman
Assoc Publr, Zondervan Books & Zondervan
   Thrive: Stephanie Smith
Assoc Publr, Zondervan Reflective: Ryan Pazdur
Sr Mktg Dir, ZonderKidz Bibles: Kevin Traub
Mktg Dir of Online Learning, Academic Div:
   Kent Hendricks
PR Dir, Zondervan Books & Zondervan Thrive:
   Robin Barnett
Publicity Dir, Zonderkidz: Jessica Westra
Exec Ed, Zondervan Academic: Katya Covrett
Sr Acqs Ed, Zondervan Books & Zondervan
   Thrive: Mick Silva
Acqs Ed, Fiction: Jocelyn Bailey
Acqs Ed, Nonfiction: Andy Rogers
Sr Mgr of PR, Zondervan Academic, Zonder-
   van Reflective & Thomas Nelson & Zondervan
   Bibles: Amy Bigler
Sr Publicity Mgr, Zondervan Books & Zondervan
   Thrive: Trinity McFadden
Founded: 1931
A world leader in Christian communications &
   the leading Christian publishing brand. For
   more than 75 years, Zondervan has delivered
   transformational Christian experiences through
   general & academic resources authored by influential leaders & emerging voices & been
   honored with more Christian Book Awards
   than any other publisher. Headquartered in
   Grand Rapids, MI, with offices in San Diego &
   Miami, Zondervan conducts events & publishes
   its bestselling Bibles, books, audio, video, curriculum, software & digital products through
   its Zondervan, eZondervan, Zonderkidz, Youth
   Specialties, Editorial Vida & National Pastors
   Convention brands. Zondervan resources are
   sold worldwide through retail stores, online
   & by Zondervan ChurchSource & are translated into nearly 200 languages in more than
   60 countries.
ISBN Prefix(es): 978-0-310
Number of titles published annually: 200 Print; 4
   CD-ROM; 30 Online; 50 E-Book; 50 Audio
Total Titles: 5,000 Print; 30 CD-ROM; 300 On-
   line; 300 E-Book; 400 Audio
Imprints: Zondervan Academic; Zondervan Re-
   flective; Zondervan Thrive
Divisions: Zonderkidz

Returns: 2205 E Lincoln Way, La Porte, IN
   46350
Membership(s): American Booksellers Associ-
   ation (ABA); Association of American Pub-
   lishers (AAP); Audio Publishers Association;
   Better Business Bureau (BBB); Book Industry
   Study Group (BISG); Chamber of Commerce;
   Evangelical Christian Publishers Association
   (ECPA); Evangelical Press Association (EPA);
   International Christian Visual Media Asso-
   ciation (ICVM); Society of Bible Literature
   (SBL); Society of Children's Book Writers &
   Illustrators (SCBWI); Software & Information
   Industry Association (SIIA)

Zone Books
633 Vanderbilt St, Brooklyn, NY 11218
Tel: 718-686-0048 *Fax:* 718-686-9045
E-mail: info@zonebooks.org
Web Site: www.zonebooks.org
Key Personnel
Dir: Meighan Gale *E-mail:* mgale@zonebooks.org
Assoc Ed: Kyra Simone *E-mail:* ksimone@
   zonebooks.org
Founded: 1985
Publish books in the arts, humanities & social
   sciences.
ISBN Prefix(es): 978-0-942299; 978-1-890951
Number of titles published annually: 6 Print
Total Titles: 100 Print
Foreign Rights: Casanovas & Lynch Agencia Lit-
   eraria (Maria Lynch) (Brazil, France, Greece,
   Netherlands, Portugal, Spain); English Agency
   (Kohei Hattori) (Japan); Paul & Peter Fritz
   Agency (Antonia Fritz) (Germany); Graal Lit-
   erary Agency (Paulina Machnik) (Eastern Eu-
   rope); Imprima Agency (Jehee Yun) (South
   Korea); Reiser Agency (Roberto Gilodi) (Italy);
   Rightol Media Ltd (Alice Sun) (China, South-
   east Asia)
Distribution Center: Princeton University Press,
   41 William St, Princeton, NJ 08540 *Tel:* 609-
   258-4900 *Web Site:* www.press.princeton.edu

Zoobooks, see National Wildlife Federation

Zumaya Publications LLC
3209 S Interstate 35, Suite 1086, Austin, TX
   78741
Tel: 512-333-4055 *Fax:* 512-276-6745
E-mail: publisher@zumayapublications.com;
   acquisitions@zumayapublications.com
Web Site: www.zumayapublications.com
Key Personnel
Publr & Exec Ed: Elizabeth K Burton
Founded: 2001
Trade paperback & ebook formats offering full-
   length works of fiction & nonfiction.
ISBN Prefix(es): 978-1-934135; 978-1-934841;
   978-1-61271
Number of titles published annually: 20 Print; 20
   E-Book
Total Titles: 200 Print; 200 E-Book
Imprints: Zumaya Arcane (true ghost stories,
   magic-based fiction); Zumaya Boundless
   (LGBTQA); Zumaya Embraces (romance,
   women's fiction); Zumaya Enigma (mystery,
   thriller); Zumaya Fabled Ink (graphic novels);
   Zumaya Otherworlds (science fiction, fantasy,
   dark fantasy/horror, paranormal mystery &
   suspense); Zumaya Thresholds (young adult,
   middle grade); Zumaya Yesterdays (historical
   fiction & mysteries)
Distribution Center: Ingram/Lightning Source,
   One Ingram Blvd, La Vergne, TN 37086 *Toll
   Free Tel:* 800-509-4156
Membership(s): Independent Book Publishers Association (IBPA)

U.S. Publishers — Geographic Index

U.S. Publishers — Type of Publication Index

CHILDREN'S BOOKS

COMPUTER SOFTWARE

DATABASES

DICTIONARIES, ENCYCLOPEDIAS

DIRECTORIES, REFERENCE BOOKS

FINE EDITIONS, ILLUSTRATED BOOKS

FOREIGN LANGUAGE & BILINGUAL BOOKS

GENERAL TRADE BOOKS - HARDCOVER

JUVENILE & YOUNG ADULT BOOKS

PAPERBACK BOOKS - MASS MARKET

PAPERBACK BOOKS - TRADE

PERIODICALS, JOURNALS

PROFESSIONAL BOOKS

REPRINTS

SCHOLARLY BOOKS

TRANSLATIONS

U.S. Publishers — Subject Index

ANIMALS, PETS

ANTHROPOLOGY

ANTIQUES

ARCHAEOLOGY

ARCHITECTURE & INTERIOR DESIGN

ASIAN STUDIES

ASTROLOGY, OCCULT

ASTRONOMY

AUTOMOTIVE

BEHAVIORAL SCIENCES

BIBLICAL STUDIES

BIOGRAPHY, MEMOIRS

BIOLOGICAL SCIENCES

CAREER DEVELOPMENT

CHEMISTRY, CHEMICAL ENGINEERING

CHILD CARE & DEVELOPMENT

CIVIL ENGINEERING

COMMUNICATIONS

CRAFTS, GAMES, HOBBIES

CRIMINOLOGY

DEVELOPING COUNTRIES

DISABILITY, SPECIAL NEEDS

DRAMA, THEATER

ELECTRONICS, ELECTRICAL ENGINEERING

ENERGY

ENGINEERING (GENERAL)

ENGLISH AS A SECOND LANGUAGE

ENVIRONMENTAL STUDIES

FASHION

FICTION

FILM, VIDEO

FINANCE

HEALTH, NUTRITION

HISTORY

HOUSE & HOME

HUMOR

INSPIRATIONAL, SPIRITUALITY

JOURNALISM

LABOR, INDUSTRIAL RELATIONS

LANGUAGE ARTS, LINGUISTICS

LAW

MANAGEMENT

MILITARY SCIENCE

MUSIC, DANCE

MYSTERIES, SUSPENSE

NATIVE AMERICAN STUDIES

OUTDOOR RECREATION

PSYCHOLOGY, PSYCHIATRY

PUBLIC ADMINISTRATION

PUBLISHING & BOOK TRADE REFERENCE

RADIO, TV

REAL ESTATE

REGIONAL INTERESTS

SCIENCE (GENERAL)

SCIENCE FICTION, FANTASY

SECURITIES

SELF-HELP

SOCIAL SCIENCES, SOCIOLOGY

SPORTS, ATHLETICS

TECHNOLOGY

VETERINARY SCIENCE

WESTERN FICTION

WINE & SPIRITS

WOMEN'S STUDIES

Imprints, Subsidiaries & Distributors

A G Fiction™, *imprint of* American Girl Publishing

A-R Editions Inc, *distributor for* AIM (American Institute of Musicology)

AAAI Press, *imprint of* Association for the Advancement of Artificial Intelligence, *distributed by* The MIT Press

AAH Graphics Inc, *subsidiary of* Loft Press Inc

A&D Xtreme, *imprint of* ABDO Publishing Co Inc

AAP, *distributed by* Welcome Enterprises Inc

AAPG (American Association of Petroleum Geologists), *distributor for* Geological Society of London, *distributed by* Affiliated East-West Press Private Ltd, Canadian Society of Petroleum Geologists, Geological Society of London

AATEC Publications, *distributed by* Chelsea Green Publishing Co

Abaris Books, *division of* Opal Publishing Corp

Abbeville Kids, *imprint of* Abbeville Publishing Group

Abbeville Press, *imprint of* Abbeville Publishing Group, *distributed by* W W Norton & Company Inc

Abbey of Saint Peter of Solesmes, *distributed by* Paraclete Press Inc

ABC International Group Inc, *imprint of* Kazi Publications Inc

Abdo & Daughters, *imprint of* ABDO Publishing Co Inc

Abdo Digital, *imprint of* ABDO Publishing Co Inc

Abdo Kids, *imprint of* ABDO Publishing Co Inc

Abdo Kids Jumbo, *imprint of* ABDO Publishing Co Inc

Abdo Kids Junior, *imprint of* ABDO Publishing Co Inc

Abdo Publishing, *imprint of* ABDO Publishing Co Inc

ABDO Publishing Co Inc, *subsidiary of* Abdo Consulting Group Inc (ACGI), Abdo Consulting Group Inc (ACGI), *distributed by* Rockbottom Book Co

Abdo Zoom, *imprint of* ABDO Publishing Co Inc

Abedus Press, *distributed by* Gem Guides Book Co

The Aberdeen Group, *distributor for* Craftsman Book Co

ABI Professional Publications, *distributed by* Vandamere Press

Abingdon Press, *imprint of* The United Methodist Publishing House, *distributor for* Church Publishing Inc, Judson Press, Upper Room Books

Abjad Books, *imprint of* Kazi Publications Inc

Ableton, *distributed by* Hal Leonard Corp

Abo Akademi University, *distributed by* Penn State University Press

Abrams, *distributor for* National Gallery of Art, *distributed by* Perfection Learning

Abrams & Chronicle Books, *distributor for* Harry N Abrams Inc

Abrams Appleseed, *imprint of* Harry N Abrams Inc

Abrams Books, *imprint of* Harry N Abrams Inc, *distributor for* The Vendome Press

Abrams Books for Young Readers, *imprint of* Harry N Abrams Inc

Abrams ComicArts, *imprint of* Harry N Abrams Inc

Harry N Abrams Inc, *distributed by* Hachette Book Group

Harry N Abrams Inc, *subsidiary of* La Martiniere Groupe, *distributor for* American Federation of Arts, Booth-Clibborn Editions, Cameron + Company Inc, Cernunnos, The Colonial Williamsburg Foundation, Editions Alain Ducasse, 5 Continents Editions, Getty Publications, Lucky Spool Media (Australia, New Zealand & North America), Museum of Modern Art Children's Books, SelfMadeHero, Tate Publishing, V&A Publishing, The Vendome Press, *distributed by* Abrams & Chronicle Books (Great Britain), Editions Alain

Abrams Image, *imprint of* Harry N Abrams Inc

Abrams Learning Trends, *subsidiary of* Learning Trends LLC, *distributor for* General Education Services (New Zealand)

Abrams Noterie, *imprint of* Harry N Abrams Inc

Abrams Plus, *imprint of* Harry N Abrams Inc

Abrams Press, *imprint of* Harry N Abrams Inc

The ABS Group, *distributed by* American Academy of Environmental Engineers & Scientists®

ACA, *imprint of* American Counseling Association

Academic Book Center, *distributor for* Primary Research Group Inc

Academic Press, *imprint of* Elsevier BV, *distributed by* Marine Techniques Publishing

Academy Chicago, *imprint of* Chicago Review Press

The Academy of American Franciscan History, *distributed by* The Catholic University of America Press

Academy of Continuing Education, *division of* Success Advertising & Publishing

Academy of Nutrition & Dietetics, *distributed by* Small Press United (Eat Right Press)

ACC Art Books, *division of* ACC Art Books (England), ACC Art Books (England), *distributor for* George Braziller Inc, Winterthur Museum, Garden & Library

ACC Distribution, *division of* ACC Art Books

ACC Editions, *imprint of* ACC Art Books

Accord Publishing, *imprint of* Andrews McMeel Publishing LLC

Accuity, *division of* Reed Business Information Ltd

Ace, *imprint of* Penguin Group USA, A Penguin Random House Company

Ace Books, *imprint of* Berkley Publishing Group, *distributed by* Perfection Learning

Ace/Putnam, *imprint of* Penguin Group USA, A Penguin Random House Company

ACER, *distributor for* Psychological Assessment Resources Inc (PAR)

ACHCBYZ, *distributed by* Summertime Publications Inc

Aconyte, *distributed by* Simon & Schuster, Inc

Acoustica, *distributed by* Hal Leonard Corp

Acres USA, *division of* Acres USA Inc, Acres USA Inc

Acropolis Books, *distributed by* DeVorss & Co

ACS Publications, *imprint of* Starcrafts LLC

ACTA Publications, *distributor for* Grief Watch, Pilgrim's Guide Books, Veritas

ACTA Sports, *imprint of* ACTA Publications

Action Language Learning, *distributed by* Cheng & Tsui Co Inc

ACU Press, *affiliate of* Abilene Christian University

Ad Infinitum Books, *distributor for* Cross-Cultural Communications

Ad Infinitum Press, *distributed by* Cross-Cultural Communications

Adams Business, *imprint of* Adams Media

Adams Media, *imprint of* Simon & Schuster

Adapted Classics, *imprint of* ArtWrite Productions

ADC the Map People, *subsidiary of* American Map Corp, *distributed by* Hagstrom Map

Addison & Highsmith Publishers, *imprint of* Histria Books

Addison-Wesley, *distributor for* Public Citizen

Adir Press, *distributed by* Feldheim Publishers

Adis International, *imprint of* Wolters Kluwer US Corp

Advaita Ashrama, *distributed by* Vedanta Press

Adventure Cycling Association, *distributed by* The Mountaineers Books

Adventure Publications, *imprint of* AdventureKEEN

Adventure Roads Travel, *imprint of* Ocean Tree Books

AdventureKEEN, *distributor for* Blacklock Nature Photography, Kollath-Stensaas, Nodin Press, Pocket Guides Publishing, *distributed by* Gem Guides Book Co

Adventures in Odyssey, *imprint of* Focus on the Family

Adventures Unlimited Press (AUP), *distributor for* Eagle Wing Books, EDFU Books, Yelsraek Publishing

The AEI Press, *division of* American Enterprise Institute, *distributed by* MIT (selected titles)

Aequitas Books, *imprint of* Pleasure Boat Studio: A Literary Press

Aerie Books, *imprint of* Tom Doherty Associates, LLC

Aerolite Meteorites LLC, *distributed by* Gem Guides Book Co

Aeronautical Publishers, *imprint of* Markowski International Publishers

AF Editions, *distributed by* Casemate | publishers

AFB Press, *imprint of* American Foundation for the Blind (AFB)

Affiliated East-West Press Private Ltd, *distributor for* AAPG (American Association of Petroleum Geologists)

African-American Book Distributors Inc, *subsidiary of* Path Press Inc

African American Islamic Institute, *distributed by* Fons Vitae

Editions d'Afrique du Nord, *distributed by* Edgewise Press Inc

Afterall Books, *distributed by* The MIT Press

Aftershocks Media, *division of* Epicenter Press Inc

Against All Odds Productions, *distributed by* Sterling Publishing Co Inc

Agape, *division of* Hope Publishing Co

Agathon Press, *imprint of* Algora Publishing

The Agency at Brown Books, *division of* Brown Books Publishing Group

Agenda Publishing, *distributed by* Columbia University Press

Agora, *imprint of* Polis Books

AHA (American Hospital Association), *imprint of* Health Forum Inc

aha! Chinese, *distributed by* Cheng & Tsui Co Inc

Aha Communications, *distributed by* Gryphon House Inc

Ahhh Muse, *distributed by* Gem Guides Book Co

Ahmanson-Murphy, *imprint of* University of California Press

Ai Pohaku Press, *distributed by* University of Hawaii Press

AICPA Professional Publications, *subsidiary of* American Institute of Certified Public Accountants, *distributor for* Wiley, *distributed by* Practitioners Publishing Co, Thomson Reuters

Aignos Publishing, *imprint of* Savant Books & Publications LLC

AIM (American Institute of Musicology), *distributed by* A-R Editions Inc

Air Sea Media, *distributed by* Casemate | publishers

Air War Publications, *distributed by* Casemate | publishers

Airfile Publications, *distributed by* Casemate | publishers

Airmont, *distributed by* Perfection Learning

AirTurn, *distributed by* Hal Leonard Corp

AK Press Distribution, *subsidiary of* AK Press Inc, AK Press Inc, *distributor for* Arbeiter Ring, Autonomedia, Crimethinc, Freedom Press, Charles H Kerr, Kersplebedelo

ALA Neal-Schuman, *imprint of* The American Library Association (ALA)

Aladdin Books, *imprint of* Simon & Schuster Children's Publishing

Editions Alain, *distributor for* Harry N Abrams Inc

Alamos Press, *imprint of* Park Place Publications

Alan Wofsy Fine Arts, *distributor for* Bora, Brusberg (Berlin), Cramer (Geneva), Huber, Ides et Calendes, Kornfeld & Co (Bern), The Picasso Project, Welz, Wittenborn Art Books

Alaska Literary Series, *imprint of* University of Alaska Press

Alaska Native Language Center, *division of* University of Alaska Fairbanks, *distributed by* University of Alaska Press

Alaska Northwest Books®, *imprint of* West Margin Press®

Alaska Quarterly Review, *distributed by* University of Alaska Press

Alaska Sea Grant, *distributed by* University of Alaska Press

Alaska Writer Laureate Series, *imprint of* University of Alaska Press

Albany Institute of History & Art, *distributed by* Excelsior Editions, State University of New York Press

Alchemical Press, *imprint of* Holmes Publishing Group LLC

Alexandrian Press, *imprint of* Holmes Publishing Group LLC

Alfred Music, *distributor for* Daisy Rock Girl Guitars, Dover Publications Inc, Drum Channel, Faber Music Ltd, MakeMusic Inc, Penguin, WEA

Algonquin Books, *division of* Workman Publishing Co Inc, *distributor for* Fearless Critic Media, Greenwich Workshop Press, HighBridge Audio, *distributed by* Workman Publishing Co Inc

Algonquin Books of Chapel Hill, *division of* Workman Publishing Co Inc

Algonquin Young Readers, *imprint of* Algonquin Books

Alibi, *imprint of* Penguin Random House LLC, Random House Publishing Group

Alice James Books, *division of* Alice James Poetry Cooperative Inc

All Points Books, *imprint of* St Martin's Press, LLC

All Rights Reserved Ltd, *distributed by* Gingko Press Inc

Allen & Unwin, *distributor for* Quarto Publishing Group USA Inc

J A Allen, *distributed by* Trafalgar Square Books

Thomas Allen & Son, *distributor for* Square One Publishers Inc, Timber Press Inc

Alloy Entertainment LLC, *member of* Warner Bros Entertainment Group, *distributed by* Avon Books, HarperCollins, Hyperion, Little, Brown & Company, Penguin Group USA, A Penguin Random House Company, Penguin Random House Inc, Scholastic Books, Simon & Schuster

Allworth Press, *imprint of* Skyhorse Publishing Inc

Allyn & Bacon, *distributor for* National Association of Broadcasters (NAB)

Alma Little, *imprint of* Elva Resa Publishing

Alpha Books, *subsidiary of* DK Publishing

Alpine Views Publishing Co, *distributed by* Gem Guides Book Co

Alta Book Center Publishers, *distributor for* TESOL International Association

Alutiiq Museum, *distributed by* University of Alaska Press

AMA, *distributed by* Mel Bay Publications Inc

AMA Research, *distributed by* FurnitureCore

Amadeus Press, *imprint of* Rowman & Littlefield Publishing Group, *distributed by* Hal Leonard Corp

Amara, *imprint of* Entangled Publishing LLC

Amatl Comix, *imprint of* San Diego State University Press

Frank Amato Publications Inc, *distributor for* Haugen Enterprises (cooking & hunting titles)

Ambassador Books, *distributor for* Primary Research Group Inc

Ambassador International, *division of* Emerald House Inc

Amber-Allen Publishing, *imprint of* New World Library

Amber Books Ltd, *distributed by* Sterling Publishing Co Inc

Amberjack Publishing, *imprint of* Chicago Review Press

Amble Press, *imprint of* Bywater Books Inc

Amelia Press, *imprint of* NFB Publishing

America West Publishers, *subsidiary of* Global Insights Inc

American Academy for Park & Recreation Administration, *distributed by* Sagamore Publishing LLC

American Academy of Environmental Engineers & Scientists®, *distributor for* The ABS Group, CRC Press, McGraw-Hill, Pearson Education, Prentice Hall, John Wiley & Sons Inc

The American Alpine Club Press, *division of* The American Alpine Club, *distributed by* The Mountaineers Books

American Anthropological Association (AAA), *distributed by* Wiley-Blackwell

American Antiquarian Society, *distributed by* Oak Knoll Press

American Association for Vocational Instructional Materials, *distributor for* Southeastern Cooperative Wildlife Disease Study

American Association of State Highway & Transportation Officials, *distributed by* PPI, A Kaplan Company

American Bar Association, *distributed by* The Professional Education Group LLC (PEG)

American Carriage House Publishing, *distributed by* Faith Works Books

American Ceramic Society (ACerS), *distributor for* American Society for Nondestructive Testing

The American Chemical Society, *distributor for* Royal Society of Chemistry, *distributed by* Oxford University Press USA

American College of Healthcare Executives Management Series, *imprint of* Health Administration Press

American College of Surgeons, *distributed by* Cine-Med Inc, Scientific American Medicine

American Council for an Energy Efficient Economy (ACEEE), *distributed by* Chelsea Green Publishing Co

American Council on Education, *distributed by* Rowman & Littlefield

American Dust Publications, *distributed by* Dustbooks

American Federation of Arts, *distributed by* Harry N Abrams Inc, Distributed Art Publishers, D Giles Ltd, Hudson Hills Press Inc, Scala Publishers, University of Washington Press, Yale University Press

American Geophysical Union, *imprint of* John Wiley & Sons Inc

American Geosciences Institute (AGI), *distributed by* W H Freeman, It's About Time Inc, Prentice Hall

American Girl Library®, *imprint of* American Girl Publishing

American Girl Publishing, *subsidiary of* Mattel

The American Girls Collection®, *imprint of* American Girl Publishing

American Guidance Service, *distributed by* Psychological Assessment Resources Inc (PAR)

The American Heritage® Dictionaries, *imprint of* Houghton Mifflin Harcourt Trade & Reference Division

American Institute of Buddhist Studies, *distributed by* Columbia University Press

American Institute of Chemical Engineers (AIChE), *distributor for* ASM International (selected titles), Dechema (selected titles), Engineering Foundation, IchemE (selected titles), *distributed by* Dechema (selected titles)

American Institute of Physics, *distributed by* Springer-Verlag

American Law Institute, *distributed by* The Professional Education Group LLC (PEG)

American Law Institute Continuing Legal Education (ALI CLE), *affiliate of* American Law Institute

American Literatures Initiative, *imprint of* Fordham University Press

American Map Corp, *member of* Kappa Map Group LLC, *distributor for* De Lorme Atlas, Kappa Map Group LLC, RV Guides, Stubs Magazine, *distributed by* Arrow Maps Inc, Creative Sales Corp, Hagstrom Map

American Maritain Association, *distributed by* The Catholic University of America Press

American Mathematical Society, *distributor for* Annales de la faculte des sciences de Toulouse mathematiques, Bar-Ilan University, Brown University, European Mathematical Society, Hindustan Book Agency, Independent University of Moscow, International Press, Mathematica Josephina, Mathematical Society of Japan, Narosa Publishing House, Ramanujan Mathematical Society, Science Press USA Inc, Societe Mathematique de France, Tata Institute of Fundamental Research, Theta Foundation of Bucharest, University Press, Vieweg Verlag Publications

American Medical Association, *distributor for* OptumInsight™, *distributed by* Medical Group Management Association (MGMA), OptumInsight™

American Milestones, *imprint of* Gallopade International Inc

American Oriental Society, *distributed by* Penn State University Press

American Philosophical Society, *distributed by* Diane Publishing Co

American Poetry Review/Honickman, *distributed by* Copper Canyon Press

American Psychiatric Association (APA), *distributed by* American Psychiatric Association Publishing

American Psychiatric Association Publishing, *division of* American Psychiatric Association (APA), *distributor for* American Psychiatric Association (APA), Group for the Advancement of Psychiatry

American School of Classical Studies at Athens, *imprint of* ASCSA Publications

American Society for Mechanical Engineers (ASME), *distributor for* American Society for Nondestructive Testing

American Society for Metals (ASM), *distributor for* American Society for Nondestructive Testing

American Society for Nondestructive Testing, *distributed by* American Ceramic Society (ACerS), American Society for Mechanical Engineers (ASME), American Society for Metals (ASM), The American Welding Society (AWS), ASTM, Edison Welding Institute, Mean Free Path

American Society for Quality (ASQ), *distributed by* GOAL/QPC, IEEE Computer Society Press, McGraw-Hill Professional Publishing, Productivity Press

American Technical Publishers Inc, *distributor for* Craftsman Book Co, SME (Society of Manufacturing Engineers)

American Travelers Press, *distributed by* Gem Guides Book Co

American University in Cairo, *distributed by* Oxford University Press USA

American Water Works Association (AWWA), *distributor for* CRC Press, McGraw-Hill, John Wiley & Sons

The American Welding Society (AWS), *distributor for* American Society for Nondestructive Testing

American West Books, *distributor for* Wilderness Adventures Press Inc

American Wood Council (American Forest & Paper Association), *distributed by* PPI, A Kaplan Company

The Americas Review, *subsidiary of* Arte Publico Press

AMI-Ascension Mastery, *distributed by* Gem Guides Book Co

AMI Press, *imprint of* Loving Healing Press Inc

Amicus Ink, *imprint of* Amicus, *distributed by* Chronicle Books

Amistad, *imprint of* HarperCollins General Books Group

Amorata Press, *imprint of* Ulysses Press

Amphoto Books, *imprint of* Crown Publishing Group, Penguin Random House LLC

AMS, *distributor for* International Press of Boston Inc

Amulet Books, *imprint of* Harry N Abrams Inc

An Inc Original, *imprint of* Greenleaf Book Group LLC

Ananda Ashrama, *distributed by* Vedanta Press

ANCC Magnet Recognition Program, *imprint of* Nursesbooks.org, The Publishing Program of ANA

Ancestry, *imprint of* Turner Publishing Co

Anchor Books, *imprint of* Knopf Doubleday Publishing Group, Penguin Random House LLC

Anchorage Museum Association, *distributed by* University of Alaska Press

Anchorage Museum of Art History, *distributed by* University of Alaska Press

Ancient City Press, *imprint of* Gibbs Smith Publisher

Ancient Faith Publishing, *division of* Ancient Faith Ministries, *distributed by* St Tikhon's, St Vladimir's

And/Or Press, *imprint of* Ronin Publishing Inc

Andersen Press, *distributed by* Lerner Publishing Group Inc

Anderson Design, *distributed by* Resilient Publishing

Andrea Press, *distributed by* Casemate | publishers

Andrews McMeel Publishing LLC, *division of* Andrews McMeel Universal, *distributor for* Gooseberry Patch (North America), Signatures Network, Sporting News, Universe Publishing Calendars, Vegan Heritage Press, *distributed by* Simon & Schuster, Inc, Simon & Schuster Sales Division

Andrews University Press, *division of* Andrews University

Andy Cohen Books, *imprint of* Henry Holt and Company, LLC

Angel City Press, *distributed by* Gibbs Smith Publisher, Gibbs Smith Publisher

Angelus Press, *subsidiary of* The Society of Saint Pius X, Southwest District, *distributed by* Fatima Crusader

Angler's Book Supply, *distributor for* Wilderness Adventures Press Inc

Anglican Book Centre, *distributed by* Forward Movement

Animal Media Group LLC, *subsidiary of* Animal Inc

Annales de la faculte des sciences de Toulouse mathematiques, *distributed by* American Mathematical Society

Annick Press, *distributed by* Perfection Learning

Anomaly Press, *distributed by* Chelsea Green Publishing Co

Another Great Achiever Series, *imprint of* Advance Publishing Inc

Anqa Press, *distributed by* Fons Vitae

ANR Publications University of California, *division of* Agriculture & Natural Resources, University of California

Antares, *distributed by* Hal Leonard Corp

Antient Press, *imprint of* Heritage Books Inc

Antinous Press, *distributed by* powerHouse Books

Coleccion Antologia Personal, *imprint of* University of Puerto Rico Press

Anvil Series, *imprint of* Krieger Publishing Co

AO Foundation, *distributed by* Thieme Medical Publishers Inc

AOCS Press, *division of* American Oil Chemists' Society

AOTA Press, *imprint of* The American Occupational Therapy Association Inc (AOTA)

APA Books®, *imprint of* American Psychological Association

APA Style, *imprint of* American Psychological Association

APA Video®, *imprint of* American Psychological Association

APC Enterprise LLC, *distributed by* Gem Guides Book Co

Aperture, *distributed by* Fons Vitae

Aperture Books, *division of* Aperture Foundation Inc

Aperture Monographs, *imprint of* Aperture Books

Apogee, *distributed by* Hal Leonard Corp

Appalachian Mountain Club Books, *division of* Appalachian Mountain Club

Appalachian Trail Conservancy (ATC), *distributor for* Appalachian Trail Museum Society, Keystone Trails Association, Maine Appalachian Trail Club, Potomac Appalachian Trail Club, *distributed by* Mountaineers Books, The Mountaineers Books

Appalachian Trail Museum Society, *distributed by* Appalachian Trail Conservancy (ATC)

Applause Theatre & Cinema Books, *imprint of* The Globe Pequot Press, *distributor for* The Working Arts Library, Glenn Young Books

Apples & Honey Press, *imprint of* Behrman House Inc

Applesauce Press, *imprint of* Cider Mill Press Book Publishers LLC, *distributed by* Simon & Schuster Sales Division

Applied Research + Design Publishing, *imprint of* ORO editions

Appraisal Institute, *distributed by* Dearborn Trade

Apress, *imprint of* Springer

Apress Media LLC, *division of* Springer Nature

APS PRESS, *imprint of* The American Phytopathological Society (APS)

Aquarius, *distributed by* Hal Leonard Corp

Aquatic Ecosystem Health & Management Society Books, *distributed by* Michigan State University Press (MSU Press)

Coleccion Aqui y Ahora, *imprint of* University of Puerto Rico Press

Arba Sicula, *distributed by* Cross-Cultural Communications

Arbeiter Ring, *distributed by* AK Press Distribution

Arbordale Publishing, *distributed by* Gem Guides Book Co

ARC (Magazine & Press), *imprint of* Cross-Cultural Communications

Arcade Publishing Inc, *imprint of* Skyhorse Publishing Inc

Arcadia Children's Books, *imprint of* Arcadia Publishing Inc

Arcana Publishing, *imprint of* Lotus Press

Archetype, *distributed by* Fons Vitae

Archimap, *distributed by* Gingko Press Inc

Architectural Graphic Standards, *imprint of* John Wiley & Sons Inc

Archival, *distributed by* Donald M Grant Publisher Inc

Archway, *distributed by* Perfection Learning

Arctic Studies Center of the Smithsonian Museum, *distributed by* University of Alaska Press

Arcus, *distributed by* Franklin, Beedle & Associates Inc

Ardis Russian Literature, *imprint of* The Overlook Press

ARE Press, *division of* The Association for Research & Enlightenment Inc (ARE), The Association for Research & Enlightenment Inc (ARE)

Shaye Areheart Books, *imprint of* Penguin Random House LLC

Ariel Press, *subsidiary of* Light, *distributor for* Enthea Press, Kudzu House

The Arion Press, *division of* Lyra Corp

Arkangel, *distributed by* Penguin Group USA, A Penguin Random House Company

Arktoi Books, *imprint of* Red Hen Press

Arlen House, *distributor for* Syracuse University Press, *distributed by* Syracuse University Press

Eric Armin Inc Education Ctr, *distributor for* National Council of Teachers of Mathematics (NCTM)

Jason Aronson Inc, *imprint of* Rowman & Littlefield Publishing Group

Arrangers Publishing LLC, *distributed by* Hal Leonard Corp

Arrow Maps Inc, *subsidiary of* American Map Corp, *distributor for* American Map Corp, *distributed by* Hagstrom Map

ARSIS Audio, *imprint of* ECS Publishing Group

Arsis Press, *imprint of* Empire Publishing Service, *distributed by* Empire Publishing Service

Art Image Publications, *division of* GB Publishing Inc

The Art Institute of Chicago, *distributed by* Yale University Press

Art Media Resources Inc, *distributor for* Serindia Publications

Art Power, *distributed by* Gingko Press Inc

Art Scroll Series, *imprint of* Mesorah Publications Ltd

art-SITES, *distributed by* University of California Press

Art String Publishing, *distributed by* Hal Leonard Corp

Artabras, *imprint of* Abbeville Publishing Group

Arte Publico Press, *affiliate of* University of Houston, *distributor for* Bilingual Review Press, Latin American Review Press, *distributed by* Empire Publishing Service

Artech House®, *subsidiary of* Horizon House Publications Inc, Horizon House Publications Inc

Artemis Books, *imprint of* Gateways Books & Tapes

Arthritis Research, *imprint of* Progressive Press

Artics, *distributed by* Simon & Schuster, Inc

Artisan, *division of* Workman Publishing Co Inc, *distributor for* Greenwich Workshop Press

ArtWorks, *imprint of* MFA Publications

As Sabr, *imprint of* Imago Press

ASAE, *distributed by* Water Resources Publications LLC

Asante®, *imprint of* Mastery Education

ASCA, *distributor for* MAR*CO Products Inc

ASCD, *distributor for* Council for Exceptional Children (CEC)

ASCE Press, *imprint of* American Society of Civil Engineers (ASCE)

ASCP Press, *subsidiary of* American Society for Clinical Pathology

Ash Tree Publishing, *distributed by* Brumby Sunstate, Dempsey Your Distributor, Nutri-Books

Ashgate, *distributed by* William S Hein & Co Inc

Ashland Poetry Press, *affiliate of* Ashland University

Ashley Music, *distributed by* Hal Leonard Corp

ASI Books, *imprint of* Information Today, Inc

Asian Civilisations Museum, *distributed by* University of Hawaii Press

Asian Humanities Press, *imprint of* Jain Publishing Co

ASIS&T Monograph Series, *imprint of* Information Today, Inc

ASM International, *distributed by* American Institute of Chemical Engineers (AIChE), NACE International

ASM Press, *division of* American Society for Microbiology

ASME Press, *imprint of* American Society of Mechanical Engineers (ASME)

Aspatore Books, *division of* Thomson Reuters

Aspen, *distributed by* William S Hein & Co Inc

Aspen Publishers, *distributed by* Medical Group Management Association (MGMA)

Aspen Publishers Incorporated, *imprint of* Wolters Kluwer US Corp

Aspire Press, *imprint of* Hendrickson Publishers Inc

Assessment, *division of* Scholastic Education

Association for Information Science & Technology (ASIS&T), *distributed by* Information Today, Inc, John Wiley & Sons Inc

Association for Talent Development (ATD) Press, *distributed by* Cengage Learning Asia Pte Ltd (Asia), Eurospan Group (Europe, Middle East & the former Soviet Bloc), Knowledge Resources (South Africa), National Book Network (NBN) (US, CN, Australia & New Zealand)

Association of College & Research Libraries (ACRL), *division of* The American Library Association (ALA)

ASTM, *distributor for* American Society for Nondestructive Testing, *distributed by* NACE International

Astragal Press, *imprint of* Rowman & Littlefield Publishing Group

Astronautical Society of Western Australia, *distributed by* Univelt Inc

At Home on the Road, *imprint of* Park Place Publications

Ateneo De Manila University Press, *distributed by* University of Hawaii Press

Atheneum, *distributed by* Perfection Learning

Atheneum Books for Young Readers, *imprint of* Simon & Schuster Children's Publishing

The Atkinson Family Foundation, *imprint of* University of California Press

Atlantic Boating Almanac, *imprint of* ProStar Publications Inc

Atlantic Council, *distributed by* University Press of America Inc

Atlantic Law Book Co, *division of* Peter Kelsey Publishing Inc, Peter Kelsey Publishing Inc

Atlantic Monthly Press, *imprint of* Grove Atlantic Inc

Atria Books, *imprint of* Atria Publishing Group

Atria Trade Paperback, *imprint of* Atria Books

Attara, *distributed by* Hachai Publishing

Audio Books, *division of* Unarius Academy of Science Publications

Audioworks, *imprint of* Simon & Schuster Audio

Augsburg Fortress, *imprint of* Augsburg Fortress Publishers, Publishing House of the Evangelical Lutheran Church in America

August House Audio, *imprint of* August House Inc

August House Little Folk, *imprint of* August House Inc

August House Story Cove, *imprint of* August House Inc

AUPHA Press/Health Administration Press, *imprint of* Health Administration Press

Aureole Editions, *imprint of* ECS Publishing Group

Aurora Press, *distributed by* Gem Guides Book Co

Stephen F Austin State University Press, *distributed by* Texas A&M University Press

Australasian Corrosion Association Inc, *distributor for* NACE International

Austrian Film Museum Books, *distributed by* Columbia University Press

Auteur Publishing, *distributed by* Columbia University Press

AuthorBookings.com, *division of* Story Monsters LLC

AuthorHouse, *division of* Author Solutions LLC

Authorlink® Press, *imprint of* Authorlink®

Autonomedia, *distributed by* AK Press Distribution

Avalon House, *distributed by* Chelsea Green Publishing Co

Avalon Travel, *imprint of* Perseus Books

Avamra Institute, *distributed by* Moznaim Publishing Corp

Avant-Guide, *unit of* Empire Press Media Inc

Avery, *imprint of* Penguin Group USA, A Penguin Random House Company, Penguin Group USA, A Penguin Random House Company

AVF Modeller, *distributed by* Casemate | publishers

Aviaeology, *distributed by* Casemate | publishers

Avid, *distributed by* Hal Leonard Corp

Avid Reader Press, *imprint of* Simon & Schuster, Inc

Avon, *imprint of* HarperCollins General Books Group

Avon Books, *distributor for* Alloy Entertainment LLC

Avon Impulse, *imprint of* HarperCollins General Books Group

AWS, *distributed by* NACE International

AWWA, *imprint of* American Water Works Association (AWWA)

Axe Heauen, *distributed by* Hal Leonard Corp

Ayal Press, *imprint of* Feldheim Publishers

Artes Monte Azul, *imprint of* Blue Mountain Arts Inc

Back Bay Books, *imprint of* Little, Brown and Company

Back to Eden Books, *distributed by* Lotus Press

Backbeat Books, *imprint of* The Globe Pequot Press

BADM Books, *distributed by* Father & Son Publishing Inc

Baen Books, *distributed by* Simon & Schuster, Inc, Simon & Schuster Sales Division

Baen Publishing Enterprises, *distributed by* Simon & Schuster

Baha'i Publishing, *subsidiary of* The National Spiritual Assembly of the Baha'is of the United States, The National Spiritual Assembly of the Baha'is of the United States

BainBridgeBooks, *imprint of* Trans-Atlantic Publications Inc

Baker Books, *division of* Baker Publishing Group, *distributor for* Focus on the Family, *distributed by* Perfection Learning

Baker's Plays, *distributor for* Samuel French Inc, *distributed by* Samuel French Inc

Bala Kids, *imprint of* Shambhala Publications Inc

Balboa Press, *division of* Hay House Inc

Baldar, *imprint of* Ross Books

Jonathan Ball Publishers, *distributor for* Europa Editions

Ball Publishing, *imprint of* Chicago Review Press

Ballantine, *distributed by* Perfection Learning

Ballantine Books, *imprint of* Penguin Random House LLC, Random House Publishing Group

Ballantine Wellspring, *imprint of* Penguin Random House LLC

Balzer + Bray, *imprint of* HarperCollins Children's Books

B&H Academic, *imprint of* B&H Publishing Group

B&H Espanol, *imprint of* B&H Publishing Group

B&H kids, *imprint of* B&H Publishing Group

B&H Publishing, *imprint of* B&H Publishing Group

B&H Publishing Group, *imprint of* LifeWay Christian Resources

Banipal Books, *distributed by* Interlink Publishing Group Inc

Banned Books, *imprint of* Progressive Press

Banner Publishing, *imprint of* Whitaker House

Bantam, *distributor for* Parachute Publishing LLC, *distributed by* Perfection Learning

Bantam Books, *imprint of* Penguin Random House LLC, Random House Publishing Group

Bar Ilan, *distributed by* Gefen Books

Bar-Ilan University, *distributed by* American Mathematical Society

Barbour Books, *imprint of* Barbour Publishing Inc

The Bard Graduate Center, *distributed by* Yale University Press

BarnaBooks, *imprint of* Tyndale House Publishers Inc

Barnes & Noble Classics, *imprint of* Fine Creative Media, Inc

Barricade Books, *imprint of* Barricade Books Inc

Barringer Publishing, *division of* Schlesinger Advertising & Marketing

Barrons, *distributed by* Perfection Learning

Bartleby Press, *subsidiary of* Jackson Westgate Publishing Group

Barzan Publishing, *distributed by* Interlink Publishing Group Inc

Baseball America, *distributed by* Simon & Schuster, Inc, Simon & Schuster Sales Division

Baseball Prospectus, *distributed by* Stylus Publishing LLC

Basheer, *distributed by* Gingko Press Inc

Bashu Publishing, *distributed by* CN Times Books

Basic Books, *imprint of* Perseus Books

Basic Health Guides, *imprint of* Basic Health Publications

Basic Health Publications, *imprint of* Turner Publishing Co

Randol Bass Music, *distributed by* ECS Publishing Group

Bat Conservation International, *distributed by* University of Texas Press

David Bateman Ltd, *distributor for* Price World Publishing

Battlebridge, *distributed by* Franklin, Beedle & Associates Inc

William Bay Music, *distributed by* Mel Bay Publications Inc

Bayard, *distributed by* Crabtree Publishing Co

Bazic Products, *distributed by* Gem Guides Book Co

BDK America, *distributed by* University of Hawaii Press

Beach Lane Books, *imprint of* Simon & Schuster Children's Publishing

Beach Lloyd Publishers LLC, *distributor for* Le Chambon-sur-Lignon, CIDEB (Italy), Fondation pour la Memoire de la Shoah (Paris), Kar-Ben Publishing, Kiron Editions du Felin (Paris), JP Lattes (Paris), Le Manuscrit (Paris), Oxford University Press (NYC), *distributed by* Tralco (CN)

BeachHouse Books, *imprint of* Science & Humanities Press

Beacon Hill Press of Kansas City, *subsidiary of* The Foundry Publishing

Beaming Books, *imprint of* Augsburg Fortress Publishers, Publishing House of the Evangelical Lutheran Church in America

Bear & Bobcat Books, *imprint of* Hameray Publishing Group Inc, *distributed by* Hameray Publishing Group Inc

Bear & Co Inc, *imprint of* Inner Traditions International Ltd

Bear Cub Books, *imprint of* Inner Traditions International Ltd

BearManor Bare, *imprint of* BearManor Media

BearManor Fiction, *imprint of* BearManor Media

Bearport Publishing Co Inc, *distributor for* Ruby Tuesday Books

Beauxarts, *imprint of* The Picasso Project, Alan Wofsy Fine Arts

Bebop Books, *imprint of* Lee & Low Books Inc

becker&mayer!, *imprint of* Quarto Publishing Group USA Inc

Bedford, Freeman & Worth High School Publishers, *imprint of* Macmillan Learning

Bedford/St Martin's, *imprint of* Macmillan Learning

Beekman Books Inc, *distributor for* C W Daniel, Gomer Press, Music Sales Corp, Kogan Page

Begell-Atom LLC, *subsidiary of* Begell House Inc Publishers

Beginning Readers, *imprint of* ABDO Publishing Co Inc

Behemoth Publishing, *distributed by* CarTech Inc

Behrman House Inc, *distributor for* Rossel Books

Beignet Books, *imprint of* BrickHouse Books Inc

Beinecke Rare Book & Manuscript Library, *distributed by* Yale University Press

Belknap Press, *imprint of* Harvard University Press

Bell Bridge Books, *imprint of* BelleBooks

Bella Books, *distributed by* Turnaround (London)

Belle Isle Books, *imprint of* Brandylane Publishers Inc

Bellerophon Books, *distributed by* Gem Guides Book Co

Belwin, *imprint of* Alfred Music

BenBella Vegan, *imprint of* BenBella Books Inc

Benchmark Maps, *distributed by* Gem Guides Book Co, Wide World of Maps Inc

Benchmark Press, *imprint of* Triumph Books

Bendon, *distributor for* Parachute Publishing LLC

John Benjamins North America Inc, *subsidiary of* John Benjamins Publishing Co

Bentley Publishers, *division of* Robert Bentley Inc, Robert Bentley Inc

BePuzzled, *division of* University Games

Berg Publishers, *distributed by* Palgrave Macmillan

Berger Books, *imprint of* Dark Horse Comics

Berghahn Books Ltd (UK), *division of* Berghahn Books

Berklee Press, *imprint of* Hal Leonard Corp, *distributed by* Hal Leonard Corp

Berkley, *distributor for* Parachute Publishing LLC, *distributed by* Perfection Learning

Berkley Books, *imprint of* Berkley Publishing Group

Berkley Publishing Group, *division of* Penguin Group USA, A Penguin Random House Company, Penguin Group USA, A Penguin Random House Company

Bernan, *imprint of* Rowman & Littlefield Publishing Group

Leonard Bernstein, *distributed by* Hal Leonard Corp

Berrett-Koehler Publishers, *distributed by* Dreamscape Media LLC

Berry Street Books, *imprint of* Eifrig Publishing LLC

Bertrams UK, *distributor for* Dissertation.com

B.E.S., *imprint of* Peterson's

Bess Press, *distributed by* The Islander Group (TIG) (Hawaii wholesaler/book dist)

Best Books International, *subsidiary of* Empire Publishing Service

Best Publishing Co, *distributed by* Marine Techniques Publishing

Emily Bestler Books, *imprint of* Atria Books

Beta Books, *imprint of* Bandanna Books

Bethany House Publishers, *division of* Baker Publishing Group

Bethlehem Books, *affiliate of* Bethlehem Community, *distributed by* Ignatius Press

Betterway Books, *imprint of* Penguin Random House LLC

Betty Crocker®, *imprint of* Houghton Mifflin Harcourt Trade & Reference Division

Beyond Words, *imprint of* Atria Books, Simon & Schuster Audio, *distributed by* Simon & Schuster, Inc

Bibli O'Phile, *distributed by* Penguin Group USA, A Penguin Random House Company

Bibliographical Society of America, *distributed by* Oak Knoll Press

Bibliographical Society of University of Virginia, *distributed by* Oak Knoll Press

The Bibliographical Society (UK), *distributed by* Oak Knoll Press

Bider Technology, *distributed by* Cheng & Tsui Co Inc

Big & Small, *distributed by* Lerner Publishing Group Inc

Big Buddy Books, *imprint of* ABDO Publishing Co Inc

Big Meteor Publishing, *distributed by* Omnibus Press

Big Picture Press, *imprint of* Candlewick Press

Big Sandy Press, *imprint of* Ozark Mountain Publishing Inc

Big Sky Maps, *distributed by* Wide World of Maps Inc

Big Sky Publishing, *distributed by* Casemate | publishers

Big Tree Books, *imprint of* Easy Money Press

Bilingual Review Press, *distributed by* Arte Publico Press

Binational Press, *imprint of* San Diego State University Press

Bindu Books, *imprint of* Inner Traditions International Ltd

Binge Watcher's Guide, *imprint of* Riverdale Avenue Books (RAB)

Biographical Publishing Co, *distributor for* Eagles Landing Publishing, Spyglass Books LLC

BioMed Central, *imprint of* Springer

Bird Dog Publishing, *imprint of* Bottom Dog Press

Birkhauser Science, *imprint of* Springer

Birlinn, *distributed by* Casemate | publishers

Bison Books, *imprint of* University of Nebraska Press

BJU Press, *unit of* BJU Education Group

BL Publishing, *distributed by* Simon & Schuster, Inc

Black Cat, *imprint of* Grove Atlantic Inc

Black Classic Press, *distributed by* Publishers Group West (PGW)

Black Coral, *imprint of* Genesis Press Inc

Black Heritage: Celebrating Culture, *imprint of* Gallopade International Inc

Black Iron Cookin' Co, *division of* Quixote Press

Black Sheep Books for Young Readers, *imprint of* Akashic Books

Black Sparrow, *imprint of* David R Godine Inc

Black Spot Books, *imprint of* Vesuvian Books

Black Squirrel Books, *imprint of* Kent State University Press

Blacklock Nature Photography, *distributed by* AdventureKEEN

Blackwells, *distributor for* Teton NewMedia Inc

John F Blair Publisher, *distributor for* The Colonial Williamsburg Foundation

Blake Books, *distributed by* Perfection Learning

Blind Owl Press, *imprint of* Mazda Publishers Inc

BLING! Romance, *imprint of* Lighthouse Publishing of the Carolinas

Bliss, *imprint of* Entangled Publishing LLC

Block Museum, *distributed by* Oak Knoll Press

Bloody Brits Press, *imprint of* Bywater Books Inc

Bloomberg Law Book Division, *division of* Bloomberg BNA

Bloom's Literary Criticism, *imprint of* Infobase Learning

Bloomsbury, *imprint of* Bloomsbury Publishing Inc

Bloomsbury Academic, *distributor for* Paragon House, Spring Publications

Bloomsbury Press, *imprint of* Bloomsbury Publishing Inc

Bloomsbury Publishing Inc, *distributed by* Macmillan

Bloomsbury USA, *imprint of* Bloomsbury Publishing Inc

Blossom Hill Books, *distributed by* Gem Guides Book Co

BLR®—Business & Legal Resources, *division of* Simplify Compliance LLC

Blue & Gray, *imprint of* Book Sales

Blue Angel, *distributed by* Llewellyn Publications

Blue Angel Publishing, *distributed by* US Games Systems Inc

Blue Apple Books, *distributed by* Chronicle Books

Blue Beacon Books, *imprint of* Regal Crest Enterprises

Blue Guides, *distributed by* W W Norton & Company Inc

Blue Microphones, *distributed by* Hal Leonard Corp

Blue Mountain Press®, *imprint of* Blue Mountain Arts Inc

Blue Note, *imprint of* Blue Note Publications Inc

Blue Note Books, *imprint of* Blue Note Publications Inc

Blue Owl Books, *imprint of* Jump!

Blue Poppy Press, *division of* Blue Poppy Enterprises Inc, *distributed by* China Books, New Leaf Books, Partner's Book Distributing Inc, Partner's/West Book Distributing Inc, Redwing Book Co, Satas

Blue Sky Gallery, *distributed by* Franklin, Beedle & Associates Inc

The Blue Sky Press, *imprint of* Scholastic Trade Division

Blue Snake Books, *imprint of* North Atlantic Books

Blue Vista, *imprint of* Scarsdale Publishing Ltd

BlueBridge, *imprint of* United Tribes Media Inc

Bluefire, *imprint of* Random House Children's Books

BNI Publications, *distributor for* Craftsman Book Co, *distributed by* Craftsman Book Co

Bobolink Media Inc, *distributed by* Gem Guides Book Co

Fred Bock Music Company, *distributed by* Hal Leonard Corp

Bollingen Series, *imprint of* Princeton University Press

Bolt, *imprint of* Black Rabbit Books

Bolt!, *imprint of* ABDO Publishing Co Inc

Bonneville Books, *imprint of* Cedar Fort Inc, The University of Utah Press

Book Guild, *distributed by* Trans-Atlantic Publications Inc

Book House, *imprint of* Black Rabbit Books

Book Marketing Works, *subsidiary of* Book Marketing Works LLC

Book Peddlers, *distributed by* Gryphon House Inc

Book Publishing Co, *distributed by* Gem Guides Book Co

Book Sales, *imprint of* Quarto Publishing Group USA Inc

Books Alive, *imprint of* BPC

Books & Co/Turtle Point, *imprint of* Turtle Point Press

Books for Independent Minds, *imprint of* Ronin Publishing Inc

Books Good For Young Children™, *imprint of* Maren Green Publishing Inc

Books In Motion, *division of* Classic Ventures Ltd, Classic Ventures Ltd

Books on Tape™, *imprint of* Penguin Random House Audio Publishing, Penguin Random House LLC, *distributor for* Listening Library®

Boom! Studios, *distributed by* Simon & Schuster, Inc, Simon & Schuster Sales Division

Boosey & Hawkes, *distributed by* Hal Leonard Corp

Booth-Clibborn Editions, *distributed by* Harry N Abrams Inc

Bora, *distributed by* Alan Wofsy Fine Arts

Borden Publishing, *distributed by* Gem Guides Book Co

Boreal Books, *imprint of* Red Hen Press

Borgo Press, *imprint of* Wildside Press LLC

Boson Books™, *imprint of* Bitingduck Press LLC

Boston College, *distributed by* Oak Knoll Press

Boston Globe Puzzle Books, *imprint of* Random House Reference/Random House Puzzles & Games

Botanica Press, *imprint of* BPC

Boulden, *distributed by* MAR*CO Products Inc

Boulden Publishing, *distributor for* MAR*CO Products Inc

Bourget Bros, *distributed by* Gem Guides Book Co

R R Bowker LLC, *subsidiary of* ProQuest LLC

R R Bowker's Books in Print Series, *imprint of* Grey House Publishing Inc™

Boxelder Books, *imprint of* The University of Utah Press

Boxer Books, *distributed by* Sterling Publishing Co Inc

Boydell & Brewer Inc, *affiliate of* Boydell & Brewer Ltd (UK), *distributor for* Pendragon Press, *distributed by* Casemate | publishers (North & South America), Casemate | publishers

Boydell Press, *imprint of* Boydell & Brewer Inc

Boyds Mills Press, *imprint of* Boyds Mills & Kane

Boye Knives Press, *distributed by* Chelsea Green Publishing Co

Boys Town Press, *division of* Father Flanagan's Boys' Home, *distributed by* CSH Educational Resources Pte Ltd (Singapore), Deep Books Ltd (Europe & UK), Silvereye Learning Resources (NSW, Australia), University of Toronto Press (Canada)

BPC, *distributor for* Cherokee Publications, Crazy Crow, CRCS Publications, Critical Path, Gentle World, Hippocrates Publications, Magni Co, Moon River Publishing, Second Nature, Sproutman Publications, Uproar Books

BPI Records, *imprint of* Bridge Publications Inc

Bradford Books, *imprint of* The MIT Press

Brady, *distributed by* Fire Engineering Books & Videos

Braided River, *imprint of* The Mountaineers Books

Deya Brashears, *distributed by* Gryphon House Inc

Brava, *imprint of* Kensington Publishing Corp

Brazen, *imprint of* Entangled Publishing LLC

George Braziller Inc, *distributed by* ACC Art Books, W W Norton & Company Inc

A Karen & Michael Braziller Book, *imprint of* Persea Books

Breakthrough Publications, *imprint of* Breakthrough Publications Inc

Nicholas Brealey Publishing, *imprint of* John Murray (Publishers) Ltd (UK), John Murray Press, *distributed by* Hachette Book Group

Breslov Research Institute, *distributed by* Moznaim Publishing Corp

Brethren Press, *division of* Church of the Brethren

DS Brewer, *imprint of* Boydell & Brewer Inc

Brewers Publications, *division of* Brewers Association

Brick Mantel Books, *imprint of* Pen & Publish LLC, Pen & Publish LLC

Brick Tower Press, *subsidiary of* J T Colby & Co Inc

Bridge, *imprint of* Bridge-Logos

Bridge Audio, *imprint of* Bridge Publications Inc

Bridge-Logos, *distributor for* Warboys LLC

Bright Connections Media, A World Book Encyclopedia Company, *imprint of* World Book Inc

Bright Ring, *imprint of* Chicago Review Press

Bright Ring Publishing, *distributed by* Gryphon House Inc

Brill Inc, *subsidiary of* Koninklijke Brill NV

Brilliance Audio, *subsidiary of* Amazon Publishing

Britannica Educational Publishing, *imprint of* The Rosen Publishing Group Inc

British Film Institute, *distributed by* Palgrave Macmillan, University of California Press

Broadside Books, *imprint of* HarperCollins General Books Group

Broadstone Books, *distributed by* Fons Vitae

Broadway Books, *imprint of* Crown Publishing Group, Penguin Random House LLC

The Brookings Institution Press, *division of* The Brookings Institution, *distributor for* University of California Institute on Global Conflict & Cooperation

Brooklands Books Ltd, *distributed by* CarTech Inc

Brooklyn Botanic Garden, *distributed by* Sterling Publishing Co Inc

Brookes, *distributed by* Council for Exceptional Children (CEC)

Brotherhood of Saint Herman of Alaska, *imprint of* Saint Herman Press

Brown Bear Books, *imprint of* Black Rabbit Books

Brown Books Kids, *division of* Brown Books Publishing Group

Brown Books Publishing Group, *distributor for* Finding My Way Books

John Carter Brown Library, *distributed by* Oak Knoll Press

Brown Judaic Studies, *distributed by* SBL Press

Brown University, *distributed by* American Mathematical Society

Brown Walker Press, *imprint of* Universal-Publishers Inc

Brumby Sunstate, *distributor for* Ash Tree Publishing

Brusberg (Berlin), *distributed by* Alan Wofsy Fine Arts

Bryn Mawr College, *distributed by* Oak Knoll Press

Bryn Mawr Commentaries, *distributed by* Hackett Publishing Co Inc

Brynmorgen Press, *distributed by* Gem Guides Book Co

Brynwood Publishing, *distributed by* Resilient Publishing

Bucking Horse Books, *distributed by* Mountain Press Publishing Co

Buckle Down, *imprint of* Triumph Learning LLC

Bucknell University Press, *distributed by* Rutgers University Press

Buddy Books, *imprint of* ABDO Publishing Co Inc

Barbara Budrich Publishers, *distributed by* Columbia University Press

Editorial Buenas Letras, *imprint of* The Rosen Publishing Group Inc

Bufflehead Books, *imprint of* Down The Shore Publishing Corp

BuilderBooks, *division of* National Association of Home Builders (NAHB)

Builders Book Inc, *distributor for* Craftsman Book Co, *distributed by* Craftsman Book Co

Building Blocks, *distributed by* Gryphon House Inc

Building News Inc, *distributed by* Craftsman Book Co

Bulgarian-American Cultural Society ALEKO, *subsidiary of* Cross-Cultural Communications

Bullfrog Books, *imprint of* Jump!

Bumba Books, *imprint of* Lerner Publishing Group Inc

Bureau of Economic Geology, *unit of* University of Texas at Austin, Jackson School of Geosciences, *distributor for* Gulf Coast Association of Geological Societies, Gulf Coast Section SEPM, Texas Memorial Museum (selected titles)

Burgess Lea Press, *imprint of* Quarto Publishing Group USA Inc

Burnell Books, *distributor for* MAR*CO Products Inc

Burns Archive Press, *imprint of* Burns Archive Photographic Distributors Ltd

Jasper Burns, *distributed by* Gem Guides Book Co

Buros Institute, *distributed by* University of Nebraska Press

Bushwhack Press, *distributed by* WoodstockArts

Business & Research Associates, *distributed by* FurnitureCore

Business Expert Press, *subsidiary of* IGroup

Business Research Services Inc, *distributor for* Riley & Johnson

Business Success Series, *imprint of* PREP Publishing

Butler Center for Arkansas Studies, *distributed by* The University of Arkansas Press

Butterworth-Heinemann, *distributed by* Marine Techniques Publishing, NACE International, SAMS Technical Publishing LLC

Butterworths, *distributed by* William S Hein & Co Inc

BuzzPop, *imprint of* little bee books

By Design Press, *imprint of* Quite Specific Media Group Ltd

Byte Level Books, *imprint of* Ashland Creek Press

BYU Museum of Peoples & Cultures, *distributed by* The University of Utah Press

BYU Studies, *distributed by* The University of Utah Press

Cabi Books, *distributed by* Stylus Publishing LLC

Cadogan Guides, *imprint of* Interlink Publishing Group Inc

Caissa Editions, *affiliate of* Dale A Brandreth Books

Cakewalk, *distributed by* Hal Leonard Corp

Cal-Earth, *distributed by* Chelsea Green Publishing Co

Calico, *imprint of* ABDO Publishing Co Inc

Calico Kid, *imprint of* ABDO Publishing Co Inc

California Bill's, *distributed by* CarTech Inc

Calkins Creek, *imprint of* Boyds Mills & Kane

Calloway House, *distributor for* MAR*CO Products Inc

Cambridge University Press, *division of* University of Cambridge, *distributed by* NACE International

Camden House, *imprint of* Boydell & Brewer Inc

Camel Press, *imprint of* Epicenter Press Inc

Camerapix Publishers, *distributed by* Interlink Publishing Group Inc

Cameron + Company Inc, *distributed by* Harry N Abrams Inc

Georgina Campbell Guides, *distributed by* Interlink Publishing Group Inc

Campus Compact, *distributed by* Stylus Publishing LLC

Canadian Centre for Architecture, *distributed by* The MIT Press

Canadian Society of Petroleum Geologists, *distributor for* AAPG (American Association of Petroleum Geologists)

Candied Plums, *imprint of* Paper Republic LLC

Candle Books, *distributed by* Kregel Publications

Candlelight Romance, *imprint of* Lighthouse Publishing of the Carolinas

Candlewick Entertainment, *imprint of* Candlewick Press

Candlewick Press, *subsidiary of* Trustbridge Global Media, *distributed by* Perfection Learning

Candlewick Studio, *imprint of* Candlewick Press

C&T Publishing Inc, *distributed by* National Book Network

Canterbury Classics, *distributed by* Simon & Schuster, Inc

Canterbury Press, *distributed by* Westminster John Knox Press (WJK)

Gloriae Dei Cantores, *distributed by* Paraclete Press Inc

Capitol Enquiry Inc, *distributor for* Center for Investigative Reporting

Capstone, *imprint of* John Wiley & Sons Inc

Capstone Press, *imprint of* Capstone Publishers™

Capstone Young Readers, *imprint of* Capstone Publishers™

Caravel Books, *imprint of* Pleasure Boat Studio: A Literary Press

Cardinal Publishers Group, *distributor for* Price World Publishing

Cardoza Publishing, *distributed by* Simon & Schuster, Inc, Simon & Schuster Sales Division

Career Examination Passbooks®, *imprint of* National Learning Corp

Career Kids FYI, *distributor for* MAR*CO Products Inc

Career Press, *imprint of* Red Wheel/Weiser

Coleccion Caribena, *imprint of* University of Puerto Rico Press

Carina Press, *imprint of* Harlequin Enterprises Ltd

Carmania Press London, *distributed by* Purple Mountain Press Ltd

Carolrhoda Books Inc, *imprint of* Lerner Publishing Group Inc

Carolrhoda Lab™, *imprint of* Lerner Publishing Group Inc

Carson Dellosa Publishing LLC, *distributor for* Key Education, Mark Twain Media

CarTech Inc, *distributor for* Behemoth Publishing, Brooklands Books Ltd, California Bill's, Wolfgang Publications

Carthage Reprints, *imprint of* St Augustine's Press Inc

Cartwheel Books, *imprint of* Scholastic Trade Division

Casa Bautista, *distributed by* Editorial Bautista Independiente

Casa Bautista de Publicaciones, *affiliate of* Southern Baptist Convention, *distributed by* LifeWay Christian Resources

Casa Creation, *imprint of* Charisma Media

Casemate, *distributed by* Casemate | publishers

Casemate | publishers, *division of* Casemate Group, *distributor for* AF Editions, Air Sea Media, Air War Publications, Airfile Publications, Andrea Press, AVF Modeller, Aviaeology, Big Sky Publishing, Birlinn (UK), Boydell & Brewer Inc, Casemate (USA), Chipotle Publishing, Claymore Press, Clear Vue Publishing, Colourpoint, Compendium (UK), Compendium Films, D-Day Publishing (Belgium), Fighting High Publishing, Fonthill Media, Formac (Canada), Foundry, Front Street Press (USA), Frontline Books, Greenhill Books, Grub Street Publishing (UK), Harpia Publishing, Heimdal, Helion & Co Ltd (UK), Editions Charles Herissey (France), Histoire & Collections (France), Historical Indexes (USA), History Facts, Histria Books, Kagero, De Krijger (Belgium), Lombardy Studios, Lorimer, LRT Editions, Military History Press, MMP-Books (UK/Poland), Model Centrum Progres, Mortons Media Group, Moselle River, Panzerwrecks, PeKo Publishing, PelikaanPers, Pen & Sword (UK), Pen & Sword Digital, Philedition, Pool of London Press, Pritzker Military Museum & Library, Riebel-Roque, RN Publishing (USA), S I Publicaties BV, Sabrestorm Publishing, Savas Beatie (USA), Savas Publishing, Scarab Miniatures, Seaforth Publishing, Tattered Flag, 30 Degrees South Publishers, WAG Books, Warlord Games

CASTI Publishing, *distributed by* NACE International

Castle Books, *imprint of* Book Sales

Catalpa Press, *distributed by* Oak Knoll Press

Catapult, *imprint of* Counterpoint Press LLC

Catechesis of the Good Shepherd Publications, *imprint of* Liturgy Training Publications

Catholic Approach Series, *imprint of* Pauline Books & Media

The Catholic University of America Press, *division of* The Catholic University of America, *distributor for* The Academy of American Franciscan History, American Maritain Association, Franciscan University Press, Humanum Academic Press, Institute for the Psychological Sciences Press (IPS), Sapientia Press

Caveat Press, *imprint of* White Cloud Press

Caxton Club, *distributed by* Oak Knoll Press

Caxton Press, *division of* The Caxton Printers Ltd, The Caxton Printers Ltd, *distributor for* Hambleton Publishing, Historic Idaho Series, Photosmith Books, Snake Country Publishing, University of Idaho Asian American Comparative Collection, University of Idaho Press

CBP/EMH, *imprint of* Casa Bautista de Publicaciones

CCH, a Wolters Kluwer business, *subsidiary of* Wolters Kluwer

CCH Incorporated, *imprint of* Wolters Kluwer US Corp

CCH Peterson, *subsidiary of* CCH, a Wolters Kluwer business

CCH Riverwoods, *subsidiary of* CCH, a Wolters Kluwer business

CCH St Petersburg, *subsidiary of* CCH, a Wolters Kluwer business

CCH Tax Compliance, *subsidiary of* CCH, a Wolters Kluwer business

CCH Washington DC, *subsidiary of* CCH, a Wolters Kluwer business

CD Sheet Music, *distributed by* Hal Leonard Corp

Cedar Fort Inc, *distributor for* Horizon Publishers & Distributors Inc

Cedar Grove Publishing, *subsidiary of* WRTB LLC

CEF Press, *subsidiary of* Child Evangelism Fellowship Inc, Child Evangelism Fellowship Inc

Celebra, *imprint of* Penguin Group USA, A Penguin Random House Company, Penguin Group USA, A Penguin Random House Company

Cengage Learning Asia Pte Ltd, *distributor for* Association for Talent Development (ATD) Press

Cengage Learning Australia, *distributed by* Cheng & Tsui Co Inc

Centaur Books, *imprint of* Joshua Tree Publishing

Centennial Media, *distributed by* Simon & Schuster, Inc

Center for Book Arts, *distributed by* Oak Knoll Press

Center for Chinese Studies, University of Michigan, *distributed by* University of Michigan Press

Center for Creative Leadership LLC, *affiliate of* Smith Richardson Foundation, *distributor for* Free Press, Harvard Business School Press, Jossey-Bass, Lominger Inc, John Wiley & Sons Inc, *distributed by* Jossey-Bass, John Wiley & Sons Inc

Center for East Asian Studies (CEAS), *subsidiary of* Western Washington University

Center for Investigative Reporting, *distributed by* Capitol Enquiry Inc

Center for Japanese Studies, University of Michigan, *distributed by* University of Michigan Press

The Center for Learning, *division of* Social Studies School Service

Center for Literary Publishing, *distributed by* University Press of Colorado

Center for National Policy Press, *distributed by* University Press of America Inc

Center for Romanian Studies, *imprint of* Histria Books

Center for South & Southeast Asian Studies, University of Michigan, *distributed by* University of Michigan Press

Center for the Child Care Workforce, *distributed by* Gryphon House Inc

The Center for the Study of Upper Midwestern Culture, *distributed by* University of Wisconsin Press

Center for US-Mexican Studies, *distributed by* Lynne Rienner Publishers Inc

Center of Emigrants from Serbia, *distributed by* Cross-Cultural Communications

Center Street, *imprint of* Hachette Nashville

Centerbrook Publishing, *subsidiary of* Centerstream Publishing LLC

Centerstream Publishing LLC, *distributed by* Hal Leonard Corp, Hal Leonard Corp

Central Recovery Press (CRP), *unit of* Central Recovery Treatment

Cerf & Peterson, *distributed by* Welcome Enterprises Inc

Cernunnos, *distributed by* Harry N Abrams Inc, Simon & Schuster Sales Division

Cervantes & Co, *imprint of* LinguaText LLC

CFI, *imprint of* Cedar Fort Inc

CFKR Career, *distributor for* MAR*CO Products Inc

Chalice Press, *division of* Christian Board of Publications

Challenges of Aging, *imprint of* Letterbox/Papyrus of London Publishers USA

Le Chambon-sur-Lignon, *distributed by* Beach Lloyd Publishers LLC

Chance Magazine, *distributed by* Theatre Communications Group

Chapin Library, *distributed by* Oak Knoll Press

Chapter Books, *imprint of* ABDO Publishing Co Inc

Character Development, *distributor for* MAR*CO Products Inc

Charles Press Publishers, *subsidiary of* Oxbridge Corporation

Charles River Media, *imprint of* Cengage Learning

Charles Scribner's Sons®, *imprint of* Gale

Charlesbridge Press, *distributed by* Perfection Learning

CharlesbridgeTEEN, *imprint of* Charlesbridge Publishing Inc

Charmz, *imprint of* Papercutz

Chartwell Books, *imprint of* Book Sales

Chatterbox Press, *distributed by* Gryphon House Inc

Cheap Bastards, *imprint of* The Globe Pequot Press

Checkerboard Library, *imprint of* ABDO Publishing Co Inc

Chelsea Clubhouse, *imprint of* Chelsea House

Chelsea Green Publishing Co, *distributor for* AATEC Publications, American Council for an Energy Efficient Economy (ACEEE), Anomaly Press, Avalon House, Boye Knives Press, Cal-Earth, Earth Pledge, Eco Logic Books, Ecological Design Institute, Ecological Design Press, Empowerment Institute, Filaree Productions, Flower Press, Foundation for Deep Ecology, Fox Maple Press, Green Books, Green Building Press, Green Man Publishing, Groundworks, Hand Print Press, Holmgren Design Services, Jenkins Publishing, Knossus Project, Left To Write Press, Madison Area Community Supported Agriculture Coalition, Marion Institute, marketumbrella.org, Metamorphic Press, Moneta Publications, Ottographics, Peregrinzilla, Permanent Publications, Daniela Piazza Editore, Polyface, Propriometrics Press, Rainsource Press, Raven Press, Anita Roddick Publications, Rural Science Foundation, Seed Savers, Service Employees International Union, Slow Food Editore, Solar Design Associa-

tion, Stone Pier Press, Stonefield Publishing, Sun Plans Inc, Sustainability Press, Trailblazer Press, Trust for Public Land, Yes Books

Chelsea House, *imprint of* Infobase Learning, *distributed by* Perfection Learning

Chelsea Publishing Co Inc, *imprint of* American Mathematical Society

Cheng & Tsui Co Inc, *distributor for* Action Language Learning, aha! Chinese, Bider Technology, Cengage Learning Australia, China International Book Trading Co (Beijing, selected titles only), China Soft, China Sprout, Crabtree Publishing Co, Curriculum Corp, Facets Video, Ilchokak Publishers, Italian School of East Asian Studies, JPT America Inc, Oxford University Press, Pan Asian Publications, Panmun Academic Services, Panpac Education, Paradigm Busters, Pearson Education Australia, Royal Asiatic Society (Korea Branch), SMC Publishing, Sogang University Institute, SUP Publishing Logistics, US International Publishing, White Rabbit Press, Zeitgeist Films

Cherokee Heritage Press, *distributed by* University of Oklahoma Press

Cherokee Publications, *distributed by* BPC

Cherry Lane Music Co, *imprint of* Hal Leonard Corp, *distributed by* Hal Leonard Corp

Chesapeake Bay Maritime Museum, *distributed by* Cornell Maritime Press

Chestnut Hills Press, *imprint of* BrickHouse Books Inc

Chicago Review Press, *distributed by* Gryphon House Inc, The Professional Education Group LLC (PEG)

Chicago Tribune Crosswords, *imprint of* Random House Reference/Random House Puzzles & Games

Chicken House, *imprint of* Scholastic Trade Division

Chicken Soup for the Soul Publishing, *distributed by* Simon & Schuster, Inc, Simon & Schuster Sales Division

Children's Book Press, *imprint of* Lee & Low Books, Lee & Low Books Inc

Children's Plus, *distributor for* Saddleback Educational Publishing

Children's Press, *distributed by* Perfection Learning

Children's Resources International, *distributed by* Gryphon House Inc

Child's Play®, *affiliate of* Child's Play (International) Ltd

Child's Play International, *distributed by* Heimburger House Publishing Co

The Child's World Inc, *distributor for* Tradition Books

Chilton Book Co, *distributed by* J J Keller & Associates, Inc

China Books, *division of* Sinomedia International Group, *distributor for* Blue Poppy Press

China Encyclopedia Publishing House, *distributed by* Homa & Sekey Books

China Intercontinental Press, *distributed by* Homa & Sekey Books

China International Book Trading Co, *distributed by* Cheng & Tsui Co Inc

China Soft, *distributed by* Cheng & Tsui Co Inc

China Sprout, *distributed by* Cheng & Tsui Co Inc

China Zhejiang Publishing United Group, *distributed by* Homa & Sekey Books

Chinese University Press, *distributed by* Columbia University Press

Chipotle Publishing, *distributed by* Casemate | publishers

Chiral House, *imprint of* Joshua Tree Publishing

Chiron Publications, *distributed by* SteinerBooks Inc

Choi's Gallery, *distributed by* Gingko Press Inc

ChordBuddy, *distributed by* Hal Leonard Corp

Chosen Books, *division of* Baker Publishing Group

Chosen People Ministries, *distributed by* Lederer Books, Messianic Jewish Publishers

Christian Classics, *imprint of* Ave Maria Press

Christian Journeys, *imprint of* Turner Publishing Co

Christian Large Print, *imprint of* Gale

Christian Network International, *distributor for* Pentecostal Publishing House

Christian Press, *division of* Brown Books Publishing Group

The Christian Science Publishing Society, *division of* The First Church of Christ, Scientist

Chronicle, *distributor for* Country Music Foundation Press

Chronicle Books, *distributor for* Amicus Ink, Blue Apple Books, Handprint Books Inc, Hardie Grant Books, Laurence King Publishing, Levine Querido, Moleskine, Princeton Architectural Press, Quadrille Publishing, SmartLab, SmartsCo, *distributed by* Gem Guides Book Co, Hachette Book Group, Perfection Learning

Chronicle Bridge, *imprint of* Chronicle Books

Chronicle Chroma, *imprint of* Chronicle Books

Chronicle Prism, *imprint of* Chronicle Books

Chronology Books, *imprint of* History Publishing Co LLC

Church House Publishing, *distributed by* Westminster John Knox Press (WJK)

Church Publishing Inc, *distributed by* Abingdon Press

Churchill Livingstone, *imprint of* Elsevier, Health Sciences Division

ChurchSupplier.com, *division of* Neibauer Press

CIDEB, *distributed by* Beach Lloyd Publishers LLC

Cider Mill Press, *imprint of* Cider Mill Press Book Publishers LLC

Cider Mill Press Book Publishers LLC, *distributed by* Simon & Schuster, Inc, Simon & Schuster Sales Division

Coleccion Ciencias Naturales, *imprint of* University of Puerto Rico Press

Cine-Med Inc, *distributor for* American College of Surgeons

Circle Time Publishers, *distributed by* Gryphon House Inc

Circlet, *imprint of* Riverdale Avenue Books (RAB)

Circlet Press, *imprint of* Riverdale Avenue Books, Riverdale Avenue Books (RAB)

Cistercian Publications, *imprint of* Liturgical Press, *distributed by* Liturgical Press

Citadel Press, *imprint of* Kensington Publishing Corp

City Point Press, *distributed by* Simon & Schuster, Inc

Ciudad Nueva, *distributed by* New City Press

Clairmont House, *imprint of* Scarsdale Publishing Ltd

Clairview Books, *distributed by* SteinerBooks Inc

Arnold Clarendon, *distributed by* Oxford University Press USA

Clarendon Press, *imprint of* Oxford University Press USA

Clarion Books, *imprint of* Houghton Mifflin Harcourt, Houghton Mifflin Harcourt Trade & Reference Division, *distributed by* Houghton Mifflin Harcourt

Clarity Sound & Light, *imprint of* Crystal Clarity Publishers

Arthur H Clark Co, *imprint of* University of Oklahoma Press

Clark City Press, *distributed by* Mountain Press Publishing Co

Ayebia Clarke Publishing Ltd, *distributed by* Lynne Rienner Publishers Inc

Clarkson Potter, *imprint of* Crown Publishing Group, Penguin Random House LLC, Clarkson Potter Publishers

Clarkson Potter Publishers, *imprint of* Crown Publishing Group, *distributor for* The Colonial Williamsburg Foundation

Clarkson Research Services Ltd, *distributed by* Marine Techniques Publishing

Coleccion Clasicos No Tan Clasicos, *imprint of* University of Puerto Rico Press

Classic Reprint Series, *imprint of* University of Alaska Press

Classics, *imprint of* ABDO Publishing Co Inc

Classics Library, *imprint of* Recorded Books Inc, an RBmedia company

Classics With a Twist, *imprint of* Empire Publishing Service

Classroom Classics, *imprint of* World Citizens

Claymore Press, *distributed by* Casemate | publishers

Clear Creek Publisher, *distributed by* Gem Guides Book Co

Clear Day Books, *imprint of* Clarity Press Inc

Clear Vue Publishing, *distributed by* Casemate | publishers

Clearfield Co Inc, *subsidiary of* Genealogical Publishing Co

Cleartype American Map Corp, *imprint of* American Map Corp

Cleis Press, *imprint of* Start Publishing LLC, *distributed by* Red Wheel/Weiser

Sydney Gurewitz Clemens, *distributed by* Gryphon House Inc

Clerc Books, *imprint of* Gallaudet University Press

Clerisy Press, *imprint of* AdventureKEEN

CLEVER Publishing, *distributed by* Quarto Publishing Group USA Inc

CLIE, *distributed by* Editorial Bautista Independiente

CliffsNotes™, *imprint of* Houghton Mifflin Harcourt Trade & Reference Division

Clipper Audio (UK), *imprint of* Recorded Books Inc, an RBmedia company

Clockroot Books, *imprint of* Interlink Publishing Group Inc

Cloister Recordings, *distributed by* Gateways Books & Tapes

Close Up Publishing, *division of* Close Up Foundation

Closson Press, *distributor for* Hearthside Books, Darvin Martin CDs, Retrospect Publishing, *distributed by* Janaway Publishing, Masthof Press

CMC, *distributor for* dbS Productions

CN Times Books, *imprint of* CN Times Inc, *distributor for* Bashu Publishing, Foreign Language Press, Intercontinental Press, Phoenix Publishing

Coach, *imprint of* Triumph Learning LLC

Coastal Publishing, *distributed by* Epicenter Press Inc

Cochrane Library, *imprint of* John Wiley & Sons Inc

Codhill Press, *distributed by* State University of New York Press

Coffeetown Press, *imprint of* Epicenter Press Inc

Cogent OA, *imprint of* Taylor & Francis Inc

Cold Spring Harbor Laboratory Press, *division of* Cold Spring Harbor Laboratory, *distributed by* Oxford University Press USA

Collections Livrier, *imprint of* Progressive Press

The College Board, *distributed by* Macmillan

College of Tropical Agriculture & Human Resources, *distributed by* University of Hawaii Press

Collegium Graphicum, *imprint of* The Picasso Project, Alan Wofsy Fine Arts

Colonial Roots, *imprint of* Heritage Books Inc

Colonial Society of Massachusetts, *distributed by* The University of Virginia Press

Colonial Williamsburg, *imprint of* The Colonial Williamsburg Foundation

The Colonial Williamsburg Foundation, *distributed by* Harry N Abrams Inc, John F Blair Publisher, Clarkson Potter Publishers, Lexington Books, National Geographic, Ohio University Press, Quite Specific Media Group Ltd, Rowman & Littlefield, Scholastic Inc, Stackpole Books, Texas Tech University Press, The University of Virginia Press, Yale University Press

Colorado Mountain Club Press, *distributed by* The Mountaineers Books

Colorprint American Map Corp, *imprint of* American Map Corp

Colourpoint, *distributed by* Casemate | publishers

Columba, *distributor for* Twenty-Third Publications

Columbia Books on Architecture & the City, *distributed by* Columbia University Press

Columbia Business School Publishing, *imprint of* Columbia University Press

Columbia International Affairs Online (CIAO), *distributor for* University of California Institute on Global Conflict & Cooperation

Columbia University Press, *distributor for* Agenda Publishing, American Institute of Buddhist Studies, Austrian Film Museum Books, Auteur Publishing, Barbara Budrich Publishers, Chinese University Press, Columbia Books on Architecture & the City, Maria Curie-Sklodowska University Press, Harrington Park Press, Harrington Park Press (frontlist titles), ibidem Press (English language titles exc China & India), Jagiellonian University Press, Peterson Institute for International Economics, Slovenian Cinematheque, Transcript Verlag, Tulika Books, University of Tokyo Press, Woodrow Wilson Center Press

Commonwealth Editions, *imprint of* Applewood Books Inc

Commonwealth Scientific & Industrial Research Organization (CSIRO), *distributed by* Stylus Publishing LLC

Community Intervention, *distributor for* MAR*CO Products Inc

Companion Guides, *imprint of* Boydell & Brewer Inc

CompanionHouse Books, *imprint of* Fox Chapel Publishing Co Inc

Compass, *imprint of* Brigantine Media

Compass American Guides, *imprint of* Fodor's Travel

Compass Point Books, *imprint of* Capstone Publishers™

Compass Point Mysteries, *imprint of* Quincannon Publishing Group

Compass Publications, *distributed by* International Book Centre Inc, NACE International

Compendium, *distributed by* Casemate | publishers

Compendium Films, *distributed by* Casemate | publishers

CompuMaster, *division of* SkillPath Publications

Comstock Publishing Associates, *imprint of* Cornell University Press

Conari Press, *distributed by* Gryphon House Inc

Concord Library, *imprint of* Beacon Press

Concordia Gospel Outreach, *division of* Concordia Publishing House

Concordia Publishing House, *subsidiary of* The Lutheran Church, Missouri Synod, The Luthern Church, Missouri Synod

Concordia Technology Solutions, *division of* Concordia Publishing House

Confluence Book Services, *subsidiary of* White Cloud Press

Confluence Books, *imprint of* White Cloud Press

Congress Watch, *division of* Public Citizen

The Connecticut Law Tribune, *division of* ALM Media LLC

Consciousness Classics, *imprint of* Gateways Books & Tapes

Consort Press, *distributed by* ECS Publishing Group

Consortium, *distributor for* Enchanted Lion Books

Conspire Creative, *division of* Everything Goes Media LLC

Consumer Guide/PIL, *distributed by* Penguin Group USA, A Penguin Random House Company

Consumer Reports, *distributor for* United States Pharmacopeia

Context Press, *imprint of* New Harbinger Publications Inc

Continental AfrikaPublishers, *division of* Afrikamawu Miracle Mission, AMI Inc

Contra/Thought, *imprint of* Holmes Publishing Group LLC

Convergent Books, *imprint of* Crown Publishing Group, Penguin Random House LLC

Cool Springs Press, *imprint of* Quarto Publishing Group USA Inc

Coordinating Research Council Inc, *distributed by* SAE (Society of Automotive Engineers International)

Copernicus, *imprint of* Springer

Copper Canyon Press, *distributor for* American Poetry Review/Honickman

Core Library, *imprint of* ABDO Publishing Co Inc

Cormorant Books, *imprint of* Down The Shore Publishing Corp

Cormorant Calendars, *imprint of* Down The Shore Publishing Corp

Cornell East Asia Series, *imprint of* Cornell University Press

Cornell Maritime Press, *imprint of* Schiffer Publishing Ltd, *distributor for* Chesapeake Bay Maritime Museum, Independent Seaport Museum, Literary House Press, Maryland Historical Trust Press, Maryland Sea Grant Program

Cornell University Press, *division of* Cornell University, *distributor for* Leuven University Press, University of California Institute on Global Conflict & Cooperation

Corwin, *division of* SAGE Publishing, *distributor for* SAGE UK Resources for Educators

Cosimo Books, *imprint of* Cosimo Inc

Cosimo Classics, *imprint of* Cosimo Inc

Cosimo Reports, *imprint of* Cosimo Inc

Cost Annuals, *division of* R S Means from The Gordian Group

Costume & Fashion Press, *imprint of* Quite Specific Media Group Ltd

Cotsen Children's Library (Princeton), *distributed by* Oak Knoll Press

Cotsen Institute of Archaeology Press, *division of* University of California, Los Angeles

Council for Exceptional Children (CEC), *distributor for* Brookes (selected titles), Free Spirit (selected titles), Guilford (selected titles), National Professional Resources (selected titles), *distributed by* ASCD, National Professional Resources (selected titles)

Council Oak Books, *imprint of* Chicago Review Press, *distributed by* Gryphon House Inc

Council on Foreign Relations Press, *division of* Council on Foreign Relations

Counterpoint, *imprint of* Counterpoint Press LLC

Country Music Foundation Press, *division of* Country Music Hall of Fame® & Museum, *distributed by* Chronicle, Oxford University Press USA, Providence Publishing, Universe, Vanderbilt University Press

The Countryman Press, *division of* W W Norton & Company Inc, *distributed by* W W Norton & Company Inc, Penguin Books (CN only)

Courage to Change, *distributor for* MAR*CO Products Inc

Coutts Library Service, *distributor for* Primary Research Group Inc

Cove Press, *imprint of* US Games Systems Inc

Cover Craft, *imprint of* Perfection Learning

Cover-to-Cover, *imprint of* Perfection Learning

Covet, *imprint of* Entangled Publishing LLC

Franklin Covey, *distributed by* SkillPath Publications

Coyote Press, *affiliate of* Archaeological Consulting

CPFS CA Princeton Fulfillment Service, *distributed by* Gem Guides Book Co

CQ Press, *imprint of* SAGE Publishing

Crabtree Publishing Co, *distributor for* Bayard, Maren Green Publishing Inc, *distributed by* Cheng & Tsui Co Inc, Gem Guides Book Co, Perfection Learning

Crabtree Publishing Co Ltd, *subsidiary of* Crabtree Publishing Co

Craftsman Book Co, *distributor for* BNI Publications, Builders Book Inc, Building News Inc, Home Builders Press, *distributed by* The Aberdeen Group, American Technical Publishers Inc, BNI Publications, Builders Book Inc

Cramer (Geneva), *distributed by* Alan Wofsy Fine Arts

Cramer (Switzerland), *distributed by* The Picasso Project

Craven Street Books, *imprint of* Linden Publishing Co Inc

Crazy Crow, *distributed by* BPC

CRC Press, *imprint of* Routledge, Taylor & Francis Group, an Informa Business, Taylor & Francis Inc, *distributed by* American Academy of Environmental Engineers & Scientists®, American Water Works Association (AWWA), NACE International

CRCS Publications, *distributed by* BPC

Creation House, *imprint of* Charisma Media

Creative Digital, *imprint of* Creative Editions

Creative Editions, *imprint of* The Creative Co

Creative Education, *imprint of* Creative Editions

Creative Homeowner, *imprint of* Fox Chapel Publishing Co Inc

Creative Paperbacks, *imprint of* Creative Editions

Creative Publishing International, *imprint of* Quarto Publishing Group USA Inc

Creative Sales Corp, *subsidiary of* American Map Corp, *distributor for* American Map Corp, *distributed by* Hagstrom Map

Creighton University Press, *distributed by* Fordham University Press

Crescendo, *imprint of* Taplinger Publishing Co Inc

Crescent Books, *imprint of* Penguin Random House LLC

Cress Productions Co, *distributor for* MAR*CO Products Inc

Crestline, *imprint of* Book Sales

Creston Books, *distributed by* Lerner Publishing Group Inc

Cricket Cottage Publishing LLC, *unit of* Justice & Chaos Entertainment LLC

Crimeline, *imprint of* Penguin Random House LLC

Crimethinc, *distributed by* AK Press Distribution

Crisp Books, *distributed by* Michigan Municipal League

Critical Path, *distributed by* BPC

Crocodile Books, *imprint of* Interlink Publishing Group Inc

Croft House Books, *distributor for* Primary Research Group Inc

Cross-Cultural Communications, *division of* Cross-Cultural Literary Editions Inc, *distributor for* Ad Infinitum Press, Arba Sicula (Magazine, US), Center of Emigrants from Serbia (Serbia), Decalogue Books (US), The Feral Press (US), Greenfield Review Press (US), Hochelaga (Canada), Immagine&Poesia (Italy), Legas Publishers (CN), Lips (Magazine & Press) (US), Pholiota Press Inc (England), The Seventh Quarry Press (Wales), Shabdaguchha (Magazine & Press) (Bangladesh & US), Sicilia Parra (Magazine, US), Word & Quill Press (US), *distributed by* Ad Infinitum Books, Hochelaga (Canada)

Cross-Cultural Prototypes, *imprint of* Cross-Cultural Communications

CrossKnowledge, *imprint of* John Wiley & Sons Inc

Crossquarter Breeze, *imprint of* Crossquarter Publishing Group

Crossroad, *imprint of* The Crossroad Publishing Co

CrossTIME, *imprint of* Crossquarter Publishing Group

Crossway, *division of* Good News Publishers

Crown, *distributed by* Perfection Learning

Crown Archetype, *imprint of* Crown Publishing Group

Crown Books for Young Readers, *imprint of* Random House Children's Books

Crown Business, *imprint of* Crown Publishing Group

Crown Forum, *imprint of* Crown Publishing Group

Crown House Publishing Co LLC, *division of* Crown House Publishing Ltd, Crown House Publishing Ltd (UK Co), *distributor for* Developing Press Co, Human Alchemy Publications, Institute Press, Transforming Press

Crown Publishers, *imprint of* Crown Publishing Group

Crown Publishing Group, *imprint of* Random House Publishing Group

Crystal Lotus, *distributed by* Gem Guides Book Co

Crystalis Institute Press, *distributed by* Gem Guides Book Co

CSH Educational Resources Pte Ltd, *distributor for* Boys Town Press

CSI Publications, *imprint of* Christian Schools International

The CSIS Press, *division of* Center for Strategic & International Studies, *distributed by* Rowman & Littlefield

CSLI Publications, *distributed by* University of Chicago Press

CSREA, *distributed by* Stylus Publishing LLC

CSWE Press, *division of* Council on Social Work Education

CT Corporation, *imprint of* Wolters Kluwer US Corp

Coleccion Cuadernos La Torre, *imprint of* University of Puerto Rico Press

Coleccion Cuentos de un Mundo Perdido, *imprint of* University of Puerto Rico Press

Culinary Institute of America, *imprint of* John Wiley & Sons Inc

Coleccion Cultura Basica, *imprint of* University of Puerto Rico Press

Cup of Tea Books, *imprint of* PageSpring Publishing

Curbstone, *imprint of* TriQuarterly Books

Curbstone Books, *imprint of* Northwestern University Press

Maria Curie-Sklodowska University Press, *distributed by* Columbia University Press

Curiosities, *imprint of* Norilana Books

Curnow Music, *distributed by* Hal Leonard Corp

Currency, *imprint of* Crown Publishing Group, Penguin Random House LLC

Current, *imprint of* Penguin Group USA, A Penguin Random House Company

Current Medicine Group, *imprint of* Springer

Current Protocols, *imprint of* John Wiley & Sons Inc

Curriculum Corp, *distributed by* Cheng & Tsui Co Inc

Curriculum Solutions, *division of* Scholastic Education

James Curry Ltd, *imprint of* Boydell & Brewer Inc

Custom House, *imprint of* HarperCollins General Books Group

CWLA Press, *imprint of* Child Welfare League of America (CWLA)

CyberAge Books, *imprint of* Information Today, Inc

Cycle Publishing, *imprint of* Cycle Publishing LLC

CYPI, *distributed by* Gingko Press Inc

Cypress House, *imprint of* Comp-Type Inc, *affiliate of* QED Press

D-Day Publishing, *distributed by* Casemate | publishers

Dafina, *imprint of* Kensington Publishing Corp

Dagger, *imprint of* Riverdale Avenue Books (RAB)

Daisy Rock Girl Guitars, *distributed by* Alfred Music

Dallas Museum of Art, *distributed by* Yale University Press

Dance Books Ltd, *distributor for* Princeton Book Co Publishers, *distributed by* Princeton Book Co Publishers

Dance Horizons, *imprint of* Princeton Book Co Publishers

Dance Horizons Video, *imprint of* Princeton Book Co Publishers

Dance Notation Bureau, *distributed by* Princeton Book Co Publishers

Dancing Ants Press, *imprint of* Dancing Dakini Press

Dancing Hands, *distributed by* Mel Bay Publications Inc

C W Daniel, *distributed by* Beekman Books Inc

John Daniel & Co, *division of* Daniel & Daniel Publishers Inc, Daniel & Daniel Publishers Inc, *distributor for* Fithian Press, Perseverance Press

DAP, *distributor for* National Gallery of Art

Dar Nun, *distributed by* Fons Vitae

Darby Creek Publishing, *imprint of* Lerner Publishing Group Inc

Dark Horse Books, *imprint of* Dark Horse Comics

Dark Horse Comics, *affiliate of* Dark Horse Entertainment, *distributed by* LPC Group Inc

Darklake, *imprint of* Scarsdale Publishing Ltd

The Dartnell Corporation, *subsidiary of* Eli Research Inc

Dash!, *imprint of* ABDO Publishing Co Inc

David Fickling Books, *imprint of* Penguin Random House LLC, Scholastic Trade Division

David Publishing, *distributor for* Fire Engineering Books & Videos

Davies-Black, *imprint of* Nicholas Brealey Publishing

DAW, *imprint of* Penguin Group USA, A Penguin Random House Company

DAW Books Inc, *imprint of* Penguin Group USA, A Penguin Random House Company, Penguin Group USA, A Penguin Random House Company, *distributed by* Penguin Group USA, A Penguin Random House Company, Penguin Group USA, A Penguin Random House Company

DAW/Fantasy, *imprint of* DAW Books Inc

DAW/Fiction, *imprint of* DAW Books Inc

DAW/Science Fiction, *imprint of* DAW Books Inc

The Dawn Horse Press, *division of* The Adidam Holy Institution

Dawn Publications, *imprint of* Sourcebooks LLC

Dawn Publications Inc, *imprint of* Sourcebooks Inc, Sourcebooks LLC

DawnSignPress, *distributor for* Gallaudet University Press, MIT Press, Penguin Random House Inc, *distributed by* Gryphon House, Gryphon House Inc

Kathy Dawson Books, *imprint of* Penguin Young Readers Group

The Day That Was Different, *imprint of* Gallopade International Inc

dbS Productions, *distributed by* CMC

DC, *imprint of* DC Comics Inc

DC Black Label, *imprint of* DC Comics Inc

DC Comics, *imprint of* DC Comics Inc

DC Comics Inc, *unit of* DC Entertainment

DC Kids, *imprint of* DC Comics Inc

Walter De Gruyter Inc, *division of* Walter de Gruyter GmbH, Walter de Gruyter GmbH, *distributor for* De Gruyter Mouton

De Haske Publications, *distributed by* Hal Leonard Corp

Coleccion Obras Completas Eugenio Maria de Hostos, *imprint of* University of Puerto Rico Press

Juan de la Cuesta Hispanic Monographs, *imprint of* LinguaText LLC

De Lorme Atlas, *distributed by* American Map Corp, Hagstrom Map

Dead Reckoning, *imprint of* Naval Institute Press

Dearborn Trade, *distributor for* Appraisal Institute

Decalogue Books, *distributed by* Cross-Cultural Communications

Dechema, *distributor for* American Institute of Chemical Engineers (AIChE), *distributed by* American Institute of Chemical Engineers (AIChE)

Dedalus Press, *distributor for* Syracuse University Press

Deep Books Ltd, *distributor for* Boys Town Press

Deep River Books, *imprint of* Deep River Books LLC

Marcel Dekker Inc, *distributed by* NACE International

Del Rey, *imprint of* Penguin Random House LLC, Random House Publishing Group

Delacorte Books for Young Readers, *imprint of* Penguin Random House LLC

Delacorte Press, *imprint of* Penguin Random House LLC, Random House Children's Books, Random House Publishing Group

Delaney, *distributor for* Saddleback Educational Publishing

Delaney Books Inc, *subsidiary of* National Learning Corp

Dell, *imprint of* Penguin Random House LLC, Random House Publishing Group

Dell Laurel Leaf, *imprint of* Penguin Random House LLC

Dell Yearling, *imprint of* Penguin Random House LLC

Delmar Publishers Inc, *distributed by* Gryphon House Inc

Delmarva Roots, *imprint of* Heritage Books Inc

Delphinium Books, *distributed by* HarperCollins

Delta, *imprint of* Penguin Random House LLC

Delta Education, *distributor for* National Council of Teachers of Mathematics (NCTM)

Democracy Is For People, *division of* Public Citizen

Demos Health, *imprint of* Demos Medical Publishing

Demos Medical Publishing, *imprint of* Springer Publishing Co

Dempsey Your Distributor, *distributor for* Ash Tree Publishing

Denby Fawcett, *distributed by* University of Hawaii Press

Denver Art Museum, *distributed by* University of Oklahoma Press

Deo Publishing, *distributed by* Penn State University Press

Department of Education Resources, *division of* National Gallery of Art

Derrydale, *imprint of* Penguin Random House LLC

Deseret Book, *imprint of* Deseret Book Co

Deseret Book Co, *subsidiary of* Deseret Management Corp, Deseret Management Corp

Desert Charts, *division of* Wide World of Maps Inc

Design Originals, *imprint of* Fox Chapel Publishing Co Inc

Destiny Books, *imprint of* Inner Traditions International Ltd

Destiny Image Inc, *subsidiary of* Nori Media Group

Destiny Recordings, *imprint of* Inner Traditions International Ltd

Developing Press Co, *distributed by* Crown House Publishing Co LLC

DeVorss & Co, *distributor for* Acropolis Books (Joel S Goldsmith titles), Touch for Health, White Eagle Publishing Trust (England)

DeVorss Publications, *imprint of* DeVorss & Co

Dey Street Books, *imprint of* HarperCollins General Books Group

Dharma Spring, *imprint of* Red Wheel/Weiser

DharmaCafe, *distributed by* North Atlantic Books

Michael di Capua Books, *imprint of* Disney-Hyperion Books

Dial Books for Young Readers, *imprint of* Penguin Group USA, A Penguin Random House Company, Penguin Young Readers Group

The Dial Press, *imprint of* Penguin Random House LLC, Random House Publishing Group

Diamond Dan Publications, *distributed by* Gem Guides Book Co

Diane Publishing Co, *distributor for* American Philosophical Society

Dictionary Series, *imprint of* Bandanna Books

Didax Educational Resources, *distributor for* National Council of Teachers of Mathematics (NCTM)

Difficult Subjects Made Easy, *imprint of* Letterbox/Papyrus of London Publishers USA

Dipti, *imprint of* Lotus Press, *distributed by* Lotus Press

DiscoverNet Publishing, *division of* DiscoverNet

Discovery House Publishers, *division of* Our Daily Bread Ministries

Disinformation Books, *imprint of* Red Wheel/Weiser

Disney Book Group, *distributed by* Hachette Book Group

Disney Books for Young Readers, *imprint of* Penguin Random House LLC

Disney Children's Book Group, *division of* Disney Publishing Worldwide

Disney Editions, *imprint of* Disney Publishing Worldwide

Disney-Hyperion, *imprint of* Disney Publishing Worldwide

Disney-Hyperion Books, *imprint of* Disney Book Group

Disney Lucasfilm Press, *imprint of* Disney Publishing Worldwide

Disney Press, *division of* The Walt Disney Co, The Walt Disney Co, *imprint of* Disney Publishing Worldwide, *distributed by* Hachette Book Group (USA), Perfection Learning

Disney Publishing Worldwide, *subsidiary of* The Walt Disney Co, The Walt Disney Co

Dissertation.com, *imprint of* Universal-Publishers Inc, *distributed by* Bertrams UK

Distri Books, *distributed by* Perfection Learning

Distributed Art Publishers, *distributor for* American Federation of Arts

Distributed Art Publishers (DAP), *distributor for* The Museum of Modern Art (MoMA)

Dive Into Reading, *imprint of* Lee & Low Books Inc

Diversion Books, *division of* Diversion Publishing Corp, *distributor for* Zubaan Books

Divine Arts, *imprint of* Michael Wiese Productions

DJ Inkers, *imprint of* Carson Dellosa Publishing LLC

DK, *distributed by* Perfection Learning

DK/Penguin, *distributed by* Gem Guides Book Co

DK Publishing, *division of* Penguin Group USA, A Penguin Random House Company, Penguin Group USA, A Penguin Random House Company

Documentary Media, *distributed by* Epicenter Press Inc

Documentext, *imprint of* McPherson & Co

Dogwise Publishing, *division of* Direct Book Service Inc

Tom Doherty Associates, LLC, *subsidiary of* Macmillan, *distributed by* Macmillan

Domain, *imprint of* Penguin Random House LLC

Domus Latina Publishing, *distributed by* Focus

The Donning Company Publishers, *subsidiary of* Walsworth, *distributed by* Schiffer Publishing Ltd

Dordt Press, *affiliate of* Dordt University

Dorling Kindersley, *distributor for* Parachute Publishing LLC

Pamela Dorman Books, *imprint of* Penguin Group USA, A Penguin Random House Company, Viking

Samuel Dorsky Museum of Art, *distributed by* State University of New York Press

Coleccion Dos Lenguas, *imprint of* University of Puerto Rico Press

Dots & Lines Inc, *distributed by* Hal Leonard Corp

Double Dog, *imprint of* Yard Dog Press

Doubleday, *imprint of* Knopf Doubleday Publishing Group, Penguin Random House LLC, *distributed by* Perfection Learning

Doubleday Books for Young Readers, *imprint of* Penguin Random House LLC

Doubleday/Galilee, *imprint of* Penguin Random House LLC

Doubleday/Image, *imprint of* Penguin Random House LLC

Doubleday Religious Publishing, *imprint of* Penguin Random House LLC

Dove Inspirational Press, *imprint of* Pelican Publishing Co

Dover Publications Inc, *distributed by* Alfred Music, Gem Guides Book Co

Down East Books, *imprint of* The Globe Pequot Press, Rowman & Littlefield Publishing Group, *distributor for* Nimbus Publishing Ltd (selected titles, CN sales only)

Downtown Bookworks, *distributed by* Simon & Schuster, Inc, Simon & Schuster Sales Division

Downtown Press, *imprint of* Gallery Books

DragonFish Comics, *imprint of* Gauthier Publications Inc

Dragonfly Books, *imprint of* Penguin Random House LLC, Random House Children's Books

Drama Publishers, *imprint of* Quite Specific Media Group Ltd

Drawn & Quarterly, *distributed by* Farrar, Straus & Giroux, LLC

Dream Works, *distributed by* Penguin Group USA, A Penguin Random House Company

Dreaming Robot Press, *imprint of* Studio Weaver

Dreamscape Media LLC, *division of* Midwest Tapes, *distributor for* Berrett-Koehler Publishers, Gildan Media, Hallmark Publishing, HarperCollins, Ideal Audiobooks, Penguin Random House Inc, Radio Archives

Dreamtech Press, *distributor for* Manning Publications Co

Drum Channel, *distributed by* Alfred Music

Dryad Press, *distributed by* Mandel Vilar Press

DTP, *imprint of* Penguin Random House LLC

Editions Alain Ducasse, *distributed by* Harry N Abrams Inc

Tim Duggan Books, *imprint of* Penguin Random House LLC

Duke University Press, *distributor for* Forest History Society

Dumb Ox Books, *distributed by* St Augustine's Press Inc

Dumbarton Oaks, *distributed by* Harvard University Press

Thomas Dunne Books, *imprint of* St Martin's Press, LLC

Dunstan House, *distributed by* ECS Publishing Group

Duo Press, *distributed by* Workman Publishing Co Inc

Dustbooks, *distributor for* American Dust Publications

Dutton, *division of* Penguin Group USA, A Penguin Random House Company, Penguin Group USA, A Penguin Random House Company, *imprint of* Penguin Group USA, A Penguin Random House Company, *distributed by* Perfection Learning

Dutton Children's Books, *imprint of* Penguin Group USA, A Penguin Random House Company, Penguin Young Readers Group

Eagle Editions, *imprint of* Heritage Books Inc

Eagle Wing Books, *distributed by* Adventures Unlimited Press (AUP)

Eagles Landing Publishing, *distributed by* Biographical Publishing Co

Eakin Press, *imprint of* Wild Horse Media Group

E&FN Spon, *distributed by* NACE International

Early Childhood Education, *division of* Scholastic Education

Early Editions Books, *imprint of* Science & Humanities Press

Early Educator's Press, *distributed by* Gryphon House Inc

Early English Text Society, *imprint of* Boydell & Brewer Inc

Early Math, *imprint of* Sundance/Newbridge Publishing

Early Science, *imprint of* Sundance/Newbridge Publishing

Early Social Studies, *imprint of* Sundance/Newbridge Publishing

Earth Pledge, *distributed by* Chelsea Green Publishing Co

Earthdancer Books, *imprint of* Inner Traditions International Ltd

East Asian Legal Studies Program (EALSP), *division of* University of Maryland School of Law

East Point, *imprint of* Scarsdale Publishing Ltd

East West Cultural Center, *distributed by* Lotus Press

Eastern Book Company, *distributor for* Primary Research Group Inc

Eastland Press, *imprint of* Terence Dalton Ltd, *distributor for* Journal of Chinese Medicine Publications

Easy Money Press, *subsidiary of* Wolford & Associates

Ebsco, *distributor for* Primary Research Group Inc

Ecco, *imprint of* HarperCollins General Books Group

Eclectic Book Press, *imprint of* Endless Mountains Publishing Co

Eco Logic Books, *distributed by* Chelsea Green Publishing Co

Ecological Design Institute, *distributed by* Chelsea Green Publishing Co

Ecological Design Press, *distributed by* Chelsea Green Publishing Co

ECS Publishing Group, *distributor for* Randol Bass Music, Consort Press, Dunstan House, Edition Delrieu, Gaudia Music & Arts, Laurendale Associates, Layali Music Publishing, Prime Music, Evelyn Simpson-Curenton, Stainer & Bell Ltd, Vireo Press

EDC Publishing, *division of* Educational Development Corp, Educational Development Corp, *distributor for* Usborne Publishing Ltd

EDFU Books, *distributed by* Adventures Unlimited Press (AUP)

Edge of Sports, *imprint of* Akashic Books

Edgewise Press Inc, *distributor for* Editions d'Afrique du Nord, Libri Canali Bassi, Paolo Torti degli Alberti

ediciones Lerner, *imprint of* Lerner Publishing Group Inc

Edison Welding Institute, *distributor for* American Society for Nondestructive Testing

Edition Delrieu, *distributed by* ECS Publishing Group

Editions Durand, *distributed by* Hal Leonard Corp

Les Editions ETC, *distributed by* Lotus Press

Editions Flammarion, *distributed by* Rizzoli International Publications Inc

Editions Max Eschig, *distributed by* Hal Leonard Corp

Editions Salabert, *distributed by* Hal Leonard Corp

Editions Technip, *distributed by* Gulf Energy Information

Editorial Bautista Independiente, *division of* Baptist Mid-Missions, *distributor for* Casa Bautista, CLIE, Portavoz

Editorial Concordia, *division of* Concordia Publishing House

Editorial Portavoz, *division of* Kregel Publications, *imprint of* Kregel Publications

EDU Reference, *distributor for* MAR*CO Products Inc

Educational Development, *distributed by* Gem Guides Book Co

Educational Insights, *subsidiary of* Learning Resources

Educational Media, *distributed by* MAR*CO Products Inc

Educational Media Corp, *distributor for* MAR*CO Products Inc

Educators for Social Responsibility, *distributed by* Gryphon House Inc

Educators Outlet, *distributor for* National Council of Teachers of Mathematics (NCTM)

Edupress Inc, *division of* Teacher Created Resources Inc

Edward & Dee, *imprint of* Russian Information Services Inc

Eerdmans Books for Young Readers, *imprint of* Wm B Eerdmans Publishing Co

Wm B Eerdmans Publishing Co, *distributed by* Fitzhenry & Whiteside

Eifrig Publishing, *imprint of* Eifrig Publishing LLC

Eisenbrauns, *imprint of* Penn State University Press, The Pennsylvania State University Press

Electric Strawberry Press, *imprint of* Radix Press

The Electrochemical Society (ECS), *distributed by* John Wiley & Sons (monographs)

Elephant's Eye, *imprint of* The Overlook Press

Elliott & Clark Publishing, *imprint of* River City Publishing LLC

Elsevier, *distributed by* Gulf Energy Information

Elsevier Engineering Information (Ei), *subsidiary of* Elsevier Inc

Elsevier, Health Sciences Division, *division of* RELX Group PLC, *distributor for* G W Medical Publisher

Elsevier Inc, *subsidiary of* RELX Group PLC

Elsevier, Science & Technology Books, *distributed by* Marine Techniques Publishing

Elsevier Science Publishers, *distributed by* NACE International

Elsevier Science, Technology & Business Books, *distributor for* Marine Techniques Publishing

Elstreet Educational, *imprint of* Bartleby Press

Elva Resa, *imprint of* Elva Resa Publishing

Elysian Editions, *imprint of* Princeton Book Co Publishers

EM Books, *distributed by* Hal Leonard Corp

Emanate Books, *imprint of* Thomas Nelson

EMB Fulfillment/Consignment, *distributed by* Gem Guides Book Co

Ember, *imprint of* Penguin Random House LLC, Random House Children's Books

Embrace, *imprint of* Entangled Publishing LLC

EMC Publishing LLC, *division of* Carnegie Learning Inc, *distributor for* Sybex Inc

Emerald Books, *affiliate of* YWAM Publishing, *distributed by* YWAM Publishing

Emerald Point Press, *imprint of* Epicenter Press Inc

EMI Christian, *distributed by* Hal Leonard Corp

Emmaus Road Publishing Inc, *division of* St Paul Center for Biblical Theology

EMP, *imprint of* Easy Money Press

Empire, *imprint of* Avant-Guide

Empire Publishing Service, *distributor for* Arsis Press, Arte Publico Press, Ian Henry Publications, ISH Group (worldwide exc Australia), Paul Mould Publishing

Empire State Editions, *imprint of* Fordham University Press

Empowerment Institute, *distributed by* Chelsea Green Publishing Co

Enchanted Lion Books, *distributed by* Consortium, Farrar, Straus & Giroux, LLC

Enchanted World, *distributed by* Sterling Publishing Co Inc

Encore, *imprint of* Simon & Schuster Audio

Encore Editions, *imprint of* Star Publishing Co Inc

Encounter the Saints Series, *imprint of* Pauline Books & Media

Encyclopaedia Africana, *imprint of* Reference Publications Inc

Energy Arts, *distributed by* North Atlantic Books

Energy Program, *division of* Public Citizen

Energy Psychology Press, *division of* Energy Psychology Group

Engineering Foundation, *distributed by* American Institute of Chemical Engineers (AIChE)

Engineering Press, *distributed by* Oxford University Press USA

The English Spanish Foundation Series, *imprint of* me+mi publishing inc

Ensign Peak, *imprint of* Deseret Book Co

Enslow, *imprint of* Enslow Publishing LLC

Enslow Elementary, *imprint of* Enslow Publishing LLC

Entangled Publishing LLC, *distributed by* Macmillan

Entangled Select, *imprint of* Entangled Publishing LLC

Entangled Teen, *imprint of* Entangled Publishing LLC

EntertainmentPro, *imprint of* Quite Specific Media Group Ltd

Enthea Press, *imprint of* Ariel Press, *distributed by* Ariel Press

Entomological Society of America, *distributed by* Oxford University Press

Environmental Law Institute, *distributed by* Island Press

EPIC Edge, *imprint of* ABDO Publishing Co Inc

EPIC Escape, *imprint of* ABDO Publishing Co Inc

EPIC Extreme, *imprint of* ABDO Publishing Co Inc

EPIC Press, *imprint of* ABDO Publishing Co Inc

Epicenter Press Inc, *distributor for* Coastal Publishing, Documentary Media

Epigraph Publishing Service, *division of* Monkfish Book Publishing Co

EPS/School Specialty Literacy & Intervention, *division of* School Specialty Inc

Epworth, *distributed by* Presbyterian Publishing Corp (PPC)

Erewhon Books, *distributed by* Workman Publishing Co Inc

Ergos Institute, *distributed by* North Atlantic Books

Lawrence Erlbaum Associates, *distributor for* National Association of Broadcasters (NAB)

Ernst & Sohn, *imprint of* John Wiley & Sons Inc

Eschat Press, *imprint of* Loft Press Inc

Eshel Books, *imprint of* Bartleby Press

Essential Evidence Plus, *imprint of* John Wiley & Sons Inc

Essential Library, *imprint of* ABDO Publishing Co Inc

ETA Cuisenaire, *distributor for* National Council of Teachers of Mathematics (NCTM)

Etch, *imprint of* Houghton Mifflin Harcourt Trade & Reference Division

LJ Ettinger, *distributed by* Gem Guides Book Co

Europa Compass, *imprint of* Europa Editions

Europa Editions, *subsidiary of* E/O Edizioni SRL, E/O Edizioni SRL, *distributed by* Jonathan Ball Publishers, NewSouth Books

European Mathematical Society, *distributed by* American Mathematical Society

Eurospan Group, *distributor for* Association for Talent Development (ATD) Press

Eurotica, *imprint of* NBM Publishing Inc

M Evans & Company, *imprint of* Rowman & Littlefield Publishing Group

Evergreen Pacific Publishing, *imprint of* Evergreen Pacific Publishing Ltd

Evergreen Press, *distributed by* Heimburger House Publishing Co

Everyman's Classic Library in Paperback, *imprint of* Tuttle Publishing

Everyman's Library, *imprint of* Knopf Doubleday Publishing Group, Penguin Random House LLC

Everything, *imprint of* Adams Media

Everything DiSC®, *imprint of* John Wiley & Sons Inc

Everything Goes Media, *imprint of* Everything Goes Media LLC

Evolver Editions, *imprint of* North Atlantic Books

Ex Libris, *imprint of* Rizzoli International Publications Inc

Excelsior Editions, *imprint of* State University of New York Press, *distributor for* Albany Institute of History & Art, Uncrowned Queens

Executive Essentials, *imprint of* Health Administration Press

The Experiment, *distributed by* Workman Publishing Co Inc

Exposit Books, *imprint of* McFarland

Expressive Editions, *imprint of* Cross-Cultural Communications

Faber Music Ltd, *distributed by* Alfred Music, Hal Leonard Corp

FACETS, *distributed by* Gem Guides Book Co

Facets Video, *distributed by* Cheng & Tsui Co Inc

Fact Publishers, *imprint of* Cross-Cultural Communications

Facts On File, *imprint of* Infobase Learning

Fair Winds Press, *imprint of* Quarto Publishing Group USA Inc

Fairchild Books, *division of* Bloomsbury Publishing PLC

Fairfax Genealogical Society, *distributed by* Heritage Books Inc

The Fairmont Press Inc, *distributed by* Taylor & Francis

Faith & Culture, *imprint of* Pauline Books & Media

Faith & Fellowship Publishing, *subsidiary of* Church of the Lutheran Brethren

Faith Library Publications, *subsidiary of* RHEMA Bible Church, *distributed by* Harrison House, Whitaker

Faith Press, *imprint of* Winters Publishing

Faith Works Books, *distributor for* American Carriage House Publishing

faithQuest, *imprint of* Brethren Press

FaithWalk Publishing, *imprint of* CSS Publishing Co Inc

FaithWords, *imprint of* Hachette Nashville

Falcon®, *imprint of* The Globe Pequot Press

Falcon Press, *imprint of* The Original Falcon Press

Familius, *distributed by* Workman Publishing (worldwide exc CN), Workman Publishing Co Inc

Family Center of Nova University, *distributed by* Gryphon House Inc

Family Communications, *distributed by* Hal Leonard Corp

F+W Media Inc, *distributed by* Gem Guides Book Co, Perfection Learning

Fanfare, *imprint of* Penguin Random House LLC

Fanny Press, *imprint of* Epicenter Press Inc

Fantagraphics Books, *distributed by* W W Norton & Company Inc

Fantasy Writers' Asylum, *imprint of* Yard Dog Press

Fantoons, *distributed by* Simon & Schuster, Inc

Far Muse Press, *imprint of* Loft Press Inc

Far to the North Press, *distributed by* University of Alaska Press

Far West Publishing, *imprint of* Sun Publishing Company

Farrar, Straus & Giroux Books for Young Readers, *imprint of* Farrar, Straus & Giroux, LLC, Macmillan Children's Publishing Group

Farrar, Straus & Giroux Inc, *distributed by* Perfection Learning

Farrar, Straus & Giroux, LLC, *subsidiary of* Macmillan, *distributor for* Drawn & Quarterly, Enchanted Lion Books, Gray Wolf Books

Father & Son Publishing Inc, *distributor for* BADM Books

Fatima Crusader, *distributor for* Angelus Press

Fawcett, *imprint of* Penguin Random House LLC, *distributed by* Perfection Learning

Fearless Critic Media, *distributed by* Algonquin Books

Federal Street Press, *division of* Merriam-Webster Inc

Feldheim Publishers, *distributor for* Adir Press, Jerusalem Publications, Mosaica Press

Jean Feldman, *distributed by* Gryphon House Inc

Fence Books, *imprint of* Fence Magazine Inc

Fence Digital, *imprint of* Fence Books

Fenris Brothers, *imprint of* Crossquarter Publishing Group

The Feral Press, *distributed by* Cross-Cultural Communications

Margaret Ferguson Books, *imprint of* Holiday House Publishing Inc

Ferguson Publishing, *imprint of* Infobase Learning

Ferris & Ferris Books, *imprint of* The University of North Carolina Press

David Fickling Books, *imprint of* Penguin Random House LLC, Scholastic Trade Division

Fiction Collective 2 (FC2), *imprint of* University of Alabama Press

Fiction Collective Two Inc (FC2), *imprint of* University of Alabama Press, *distributed by* University of Alabama Press

Fieldstone Alliance, *imprint of* Turner Publishing Co

53rd State Press, *distributed by* Theatre Communications Group

Fighting High Publishing, *distributed by* Casemate | publishers

Les Figues Press, *imprint of* LARB Books

Filaree Productions, *distributed by* Chelsea Green Publishing Co

Film Movement, *imprint of* Recorded Books Inc, an RBmedia company

Filmakers Library, *imprint of* Alexander Street, a ProQuest Company

Financial Executives Research Foundation Inc (FERF), *affiliate of* Financial Executives International (FEI)

Financial Ratings Series, *imprint of* Grey House Publishing Inc™

Financial Times Press, *imprint of* Pearson Education Ltd

Financial Times Publishing, *distributed by* Trans-Atlantic Publications Inc

Findhorn Press, *imprint of* Inner Traditions International Ltd

Finding My Way Books, *distributed by* Brown Books Publishing Group

FineEdge.com LLC, *distributed by* Heritage House, Sunbelt Publications Inc

Fire Engineering Books & Videos, *division of* PennWell Books, *distributor for* Brady, Idea Bank, IFSTA, Mosby, *distributed by* David Publishing, Fire Protection Publications

Fire Protection Publications, *distributor for* Fire Engineering Books & Videos

Firebird, *imprint of* Penguin Young Readers Group

Firefall Editions, *imprint of* Firefallmedia

Firefall Originals, *imprint of* Firefall Editions

Firefly, *distributed by* Perfection Learning

Firefly Books, *distributed by* Gem Guides Book Co

Firefly Books Ltd, *distributed by* Heimburger House Publishing Co

Firefly Southern Fiction, *imprint of* Lighthouse Publishing of the Carolinas

Fireside Fiction, *imprint of* Heritage Books Inc

First Avenue, *distributed by* Perfection Learning

First Avenue Editions, *imprint of* Lerner Publishing Group Inc

First Fruits of Zion, *distributed by* Lederer Books, Messianic Jewish Publishers

First Second Books, *imprint of* Roaring Brook Press

FirstForumPress, *division of* Lynne Rienner Publishers Inc

Carl Fischer/Theodore Presser, *distributor for* Roncorp Music

Fish Pond, *imprint of* Deep River Books LLC

Fisher Productions, *imprint of* Franciscan Media

Fithian Press, *distributed by* John Daniel & Co

Fitzhenry & Whiteside, *distributor for* Wm B Eerdmans Publishing Co

Fitzroy Books, *imprint of* Regal House Publishing

5 Continents Editions, *distributed by* Harry N Abrams Inc

Five Star™, *imprint of* Gale

Flame Tree Publishing, *distributed by* Simon & Schuster, Inc

Flammarion, *imprint of* Rizzoli International Publications Inc

Flashkids, *imprint of* Sterling Publishing Co Inc

Fleamarket Music, *distributed by* Hal Leonard Corp

Flirt, *imprint of* Penguin Random House LLC, Random House Publishing Group

Floris Books, *distributed by* Gryphon House Inc, SteinerBooks Inc

Flower Press, *distributed by* Chelsea Green Publishing Co

Flux, *imprint of* North Star Editions Inc

Flyaway Books, *imprint of* Presbyterian Publishing Corp (PPC)

FMP, *imprint of* Forward Movement

Focal Press, *distributor for* National Association of Broadcasters (NAB), *distributed by* Marine Techniques Publishing

Focus, *imprint of* Hackett Publishing Co Inc, *distributor for* Domus Latina Publishing

Focus on the Family, *distributed by* Baker Books, Moody Press, Tyndale House Publishers Inc, Zondervan

Focus Readers, *imprint of* North Star Editions Inc

Fodor's, *imprint of* Fodor's Travel

Fodor's Travel, *division of* Internet Brands Inc

Folger Shakespeare Library, *imprint of* Simon & Schuster

Fondation Custodia, *distributed by* Oak Knoll Press

Fondation pour la Memoire de la Shoah, *distributed by* Beach Lloyd Publishers LLC

Fons Vitae, *distributor for* African American Islamic Institute, Anqa Press (UK), Aperture (NY), Archetype (UK), Broadstone Books, Dar Nun, Golganooza Press (UK), Islamic Texts Society (UK), Matheson Trust, Parabola, Paragon, Parvardigar Press, Sophia Perennis, Pir Press (NY), Qiblah Books, Quilliam Press (UK), Sandala Productions, Sri Lanka Institute of Traditional Studies, Thesaurus Islamicus Foundation, Tradigital, White Thread Press (US), Wisdom Foundation, World Wisdom (US), Zaytuna Institute Press (US)

Fonthill Media, *distributed by* Casemate | publishers

Food & Agriculture Organization of the United Nations (FAO), *distributed by* United Nations Publications

Food52 Works, *imprint of* Ten Speed Press

For Dummies®, *imprint of* John Wiley & Sons Inc

Fordham University Press, *distributor for* Creighton University Press, Institute for Advanced Study in the Theatre Arts (IASTA), Little Room Press, Rockhurst University Press, St Bede's Publications, University of San Francisco Press, *distributed by* Heimburger House Publishing Co, Oxford University Press (US & CN)

Forefront, *distributed by* Simon & Schuster, Inc

Foreign Language Press, *distributed by* CN Times Books

Forest History Society, *distributed by* Duke University Press

Forest of Peace, *imprint of* Ave Maria Press

Forever, *imprint of* Grand Central Publishing

Forever Yours, *imprint of* Grand Central Publishing

Forge Books, *imprint of* Tom Doherty Associates, LLC

Formac, *distributed by* Casemate | publishers

Fortress Press, *imprint of* Augsburg Fortress Publishers, Publishing House of the Evangelical Lutheran Church in America

Forward Movement, *affiliate of* The Episcopal Church, *distributor for* Anglican Book Centre

Fossil News, *distributed by* Gem Guides Book Co

Frances Foster Books, *imprint of* Farrar, Straus & Giroux Books for Young Readers

Walter Foster Jr, *imprint of* Quarto Publishing Group USA Inc

Walter Foster Publishing, *imprint of* Quarto Publishing Group USA Inc, *distributed by* Lerner Publishing Group Inc

Walter Foster Publishing Inc, *imprint of* Quarto Publishing Group USA Inc

G T Foulis, *distributed by* Haynes North America Inc

Foundation for Deep Ecology, *distributed by* Chelsea Green Publishing Co

Foundation Press, *imprint of* West Academic

Foundry, *distributed by* Casemate | publishers

The Fountain, *imprint of* Tughra Books

4th Dimension Press, *imprint of* ARE Press

Fowler Museum at UCLA, *distributed by* University of Washington Press

Fox Chapel Publishing Co Inc, *distributor for* Reader's Digest, Taunton Sterling Dover

Fox Maple Press, *distributed by* Chelsea Green Publishing Co

Franciscan Communications, *imprint of* Franciscan Media

Franciscan University Press, *distributed by* The Catholic University of America Press

Franklin, Beedle & Associates Inc, *distributor for* Arcus, Battlebridge, Blue Sky Gallery, Photolucida Book, Ringing Bell Press, Tayo Press, Wordstock

Franklin Street Books, *imprint of* Inkwater Press

Franko Maps, *distributed by* Wide World of Maps Inc

Frederator Books LLC, *distributed by* Simon & Schuster, Inc, Simon & Schuster Sales Division

Free Press, *imprint of* Simon & Schuster, *distributed by* Center for Creative Leadership LLC

Free Spirit, *distributed by* Council for Exceptional Children (CEC), Perfection Learning

Free Wheel Publications, *distributed by* Gem Guides Book Co

Freedom Fox Press, *imprint of* Dancing Lemur Press LLC

Freedom Press, *distributed by* AK Press Distribution

Freeform, *imprint of* Disney Publishing Worldwide

W H Freeman, *imprint of* Macmillan Learning, *distributor for* American Geosciences Institute (AGI)

Freestone, *imprint of* Peachtree Publishing Co Inc

Samuel French Inc, *distributor for* Baker's Plays, Samuel French Ltd (UK), *distributed by* Baker's Plays, Samuel French Ltd (UK)

Samuel French Ltd, *distributor for* Samuel French Inc, *distributed by* Samuel French Inc

Fresh Air Books, *imprint of* Upper Room Books

Friends United Press, *subsidiary of* Friends United Meeting

Frog Books, *imprint of* North Atlantic Books

Frog Legs Ink, *imprint of* Gauthier Publications Inc

Front Street Press, *distributed by* Casemate | publishers

Front Table Books, *imprint of* Cedar Fort Inc

Frontline Books, *distributed by* Casemate | publishers

FT Press, *imprint of* Financial Times Press

Fulcrum, *distributed by* Perfection Learning

Full Tilt, *distributed by* Lerner Publishing Group Inc

Fun For All, *imprint of* Kidsbooks LLC

FunTreks Inc, *distributed by* Gem Guides Book Co

FurnitureCore, *distributor for* AMA Research, Business & Research Associates

Future Psychiatry Press, *imprint of* Loving Healing Press Inc

G W Medical Publisher, *distributed by* Elsevier, Health Sciences Division

Gakken, *distributed by* Simon & Schuster, Inc

Galaxy Audio, *imprint of* Galaxy Press

Galaxy Music Corp, *imprint of* ECS Publishing Group

Gale, *division of* Cengage Learning, *subsidiary of* Cengage Learning

Gallaudet University Press, *distributed by* DawnSignPress

Gallery Books, *imprint of* Gallery Publishing Group

Gallery 13, *imprint of* Gallery Books

Gallup, *distributed by* Simon & Schuster, Inc, Simon & Schuster Sales Division

Galvanized Media, *distributed by* Simon & Schuster, Inc, Simon & Schuster Sales Division

Games Workshop, *distributed by* Simon & Schuster, Inc, Simon & Schuster Sales Division

Garden Art Press, *imprint of* ACC Art Books

GardenGuy.Com, *distributed by* Gem Guides Book Co

Gareth Stevens Publishing, *imprint of* The Rosen Publishing Group Inc

Garland Publishers, *distributor for* University of California Institute on Global Conflict & Cooperation

Garland Science, *imprint of* Taylor & Francis Inc

Garret Metal Detectors, *distributed by* Gem Guides Book Co

John Garrett, *distributor for* Twenty-Third Publications

Gaslight Publications, *imprint of* Empire Publishing Service

Gateway Editions, *imprint of* Regnery Publishing

Gateway to Healthcare Management, *imprint of* Health Administration Press

Gateways Books & Tapes, *division of* Institute for the Development of the Harmonious Human Being Inc, Institute for the Development of the Harmonious Human Being Inc, *distributor for* Cloister Recordings (audio & video tapes)

Gateways Fine Art Series, *imprint of* Gateways Books & Tapes

Gaudia Music & Arts, *distributed by* ECS Publishing Group

Gaudium Publishing, *imprint of* Histria Books

Geared Up Publications, *imprint of* Schiffer Publishing Ltd

Gecko Press, *distributed by* Lerner Publishing Group Inc

Geddes & Grosset, *distributed by* Interlink Publishing Group Inc

Gefen Books, *distributor for* Bar Ilan, Magnes Press

Gem Book Publishers, *distributed by* Gem Guides Book Co

Gem Guides Book Co, *distributor for* Abedus Press, AdventureKEEN, Aerolite Meteorites LLC, Ahhh Muse, Alpine Views Publishing Co, American Travelers Press, AMI-Ascension Mastery, APC Enterprise LLC, Arbordale Publishing, Aurora Press, Bazic Products, Bellerophon Books, Benchmark Maps, Blossom Hill Books, Bobolink Media Inc, Book Publishing Co, Borden Publishing, Bourget Bros, Brynmorgen Press, Jasper Burns, Chron-

icle Books, Clear Creek Publisher, CPFS CA Princeton Fulfillment Service, Crabtree Publishing Co, Crystal Lotus, Crystalis Institute Press, Diamond Dan Publications, DK/Penguin, Dover Publications Inc, Educational Development, EMB Fulfillment/Consignment, LJ Ettinger, FACETS, F+W Media Inc, Firefly Books, Fossil News, Free Wheel Publications, FunTreks Inc, GardenGuy.Com, Garret Metal Detectors, Gem Book Publishers, The Gem Shop, Gitche Gumee Agate & History Museum, Global Graphics, Golden West Books, Good Karma Factory, Grand Canyon Association, Hachette Book Group, Hancock House, HarperCollins Publishers, Tom Harrison Maps, Hay House, Le Hayes, Heaven & Earth LLC, Heyday, Houghton Mifflin, Impactika, Independent Publishers Group, Infobase Publishing, Ingram Publisher Services, Ingram Publisher Services/Two Rivers, Inner Traditions, International Jewelry Publications, Journal Publications, Shelley Kaehr, KC Publications, Keene Engineering, Konecky & Konecky, Leaning Tree Tales LLC, Light Technology Publishing, Llewellyn Worldwide, Majestic Press, Maturango Museum, Mineral Land Publications, Mojave River Valley Museum, Mountain Press Publishing, The Mountaineers Books, MPS, Museon Publishing, National Book Network, National Historic Route 66 Federation, Natural Inspirations/Brush Creek, Nature Trails Press, Naturegraph, Nevada Publications, New Era Productions, Northwest Distributors LLC, W W Norton & Company Inc, Park Partners Inc, Penguin Random House, Pentrex, Pinyon Publishing, Quarto Publishing Group/Hachette Book Group, Quest Publishing, Quick Reference Publishing Inc, Chris Ralph, Katrina Raphaell, Reading With Peaches LLC, Real Adventure Publishing, Red Wheel/Weiser/Conari, Ronald Ringsrud Co, Riverbend Publishing, Ryland Peters & Small, San Gabriel Mountains Regional Conservancy, Schiffer Publishing Ltd, Scholastic, Scholastic Library Publishing, Sierra Outdoor Products, Edition du Signe, Mark Silva, Simon & Schuster, Gibbs Smith, Sounds True Inc, Spotted Dog Press, Sterling Publishing Co Inc, Leighton Stone, Storey Publishing LLC, Delos Toole Gold Books, Track & Trail Publications, Treasure Chest Books, Trees Company Press, TVL VIDEO, University of Nebraska, Waterford Press, Wesanne Publications, Ronald S Wielgus, WolfWalker Collection, *distributed by* Nevada Publications

The Gem Shop, *distributed by* Gem Guides Book Co

Gembooks, *imprint of* Gem Guides Book Co

GemStone Press, *imprint of* Turner Publishing Co

Gender Genre, *imprint of* Bandanna Books

Genealogical Publishing Co, *subsidiary of* Genealogical.com

General Education Services (New Zealand), *distributed by* Abrams Learning Trends

Genetic Engineering & Biotechnology News, *division of* Mary Ann Liebert Inc

Gennadeion Monographs, *imprint of* ASCSA Publications

Gentle World, *distributed by* BPC

Geological Society of London, *distributor for* AAPG (American Association of Petroleum Geologists), *distributed by* AAPG (American Association of Petroleum Geologists)

Geology & Geography of Alaska Series, *imprint of* University of Alaska Press

Geology Underfoot Series, *imprint of* Mountain Press Publishing Co

Geophysical Institute, *distributed by* University of Alaska Press

GetFitNow.com Books, *imprint of* Hatherleigh Press Ltd

Getting Smart, *imprint of* Eifrig Publishing LLC

Getty, *distributed by* Oxford University Press USA

Getty Publications, *distributed by* Harry N Abrams Inc, University of Chicago Press (US only)

Gibbs-Smith, *distributor for* Sourced Media Books

Gibbs Smith Publisher, *distributor for* Angel City Press

Gilbert, *imprint of* West Academic

Gilcrease Museum, *distributed by* University of Oklahoma Press

Gildan Media, *distributed by* Dreamscape Media LLC, Hachette Book Group

D Giles Ltd, *distributor for* American Federation of Arts

Gingko Press, *distributed by* Gingko Press Inc

Gingko Press Inc, *distributor for* All Rights Reserved Ltd, Archimap, Art Power, Basheer, Choi's Gallery, CYPI, Gingko Press, Rebel Arts, Sandu Publications, Sendpoints Books Co Ltd, Upper Playground, Victionary, Wax Facts Press, Zero+ Publishing

GIT Verlag, *imprint of* John Wiley & Sons Inc

Gitche Gumee Agate & History Museum, *distributed by* Gem Guides Book Co

Gival Press, *imprint of* Gival Press LLC

Michael Glazier Books, *imprint of* Liturgical Press

Glencoe/McGraw-Hill, *imprint of* McGraw-Hill Education

Peter Glenn Publications, *division of* Blount Communications Corp

Global Graphics, *distributed by* Gem Guides Book Co

Global Research, *distributed by* Progressive Press

Global Trade Watch, *division of* Public Citizen

Globe Pequot, *imprint of* The Globe Pequot Press

Globe Pequot Press, *distributed by* Heimburger House Publishing Co

The Globe Pequot Press, *division of* Rowman & Littlefield Publishing Group

GOAL/QPC, *distributor for* American Society for Quality (ASQ)

David R Godine, Publisher, *imprint of* David R Godine Inc

Godwin Books, *imprint of* Henry Holt and Company, LLC

GoFacts Guided Writing, *imprint of* Sundance/ Newbridge Publishing

Goff Books, *imprint of* ORO editions

Golden Books, *imprint of* Penguin Random House LLC, Random House Children's Books, *distributed by* Perfection Learning

Golden Books Adult Publishing, *imprint of* St Martin's Press, LLC

Golden Dawn Publications, *imprint of* The Original Falcon Press

Golden Egg Press, *imprint of* Goosebottom Books

Golden Guides, *imprint of* St Martin's Press, LLC

Golden West Books, *distributed by* Gem Guides Book Co

Golden West Cookbooks, *division of* American Traveler Press

Golganooza Press, *distributed by* Fons Vitae

Gomer Press, *distributed by* Beekman Books Inc

Good Hotel Guides, *distributed by* Interlink Publishing Group Inc

Good Karma Factory, *distributed by* Gem Guides Book Co

goop press, *imprint of* Grand Central Publishing

Gooseberry Patch, *imprint of* The Globe Pequot Press, *distributed by* Andrews McMeel Publishing LLC

Goosebottom Books, *imprint of* Goosebottom Books LLC

Gorgias Press LLC, *distributor for* Yeshiva University Museum Press

Gosling Press, *imprint of* Goosebottom Books

Gospel Publishing House, *division of* General Council of the Assemblies of God

Government Jobs Series, *imprint of* PREP Publishing

GPP® Travel, *imprint of* The Globe Pequot Press

Grab a Pencil Press, *imprint of* Applewood Books Inc

Gracie Belle, *imprint of* Akashic Books

Gramercy Books, *imprint of* Penguin Random House LLC

Gramophone, *distributed by* Omnibus Press

Grand Canyon Association, *distributed by* Gem Guides Book Co

Grand Central/Hachette Large Print, *distributed by* Thorndike Press®

Grand Central Publishing, *division of* Hachette Book Group

Grand Harbor Press, *imprint of* Brilliance Audio

Donald M Grant Publisher Inc, *distributor for* Archival, Oswald Train

Granta, *distributed by* Penguin Group USA, A Penguin Random House Company

Graphia, *imprint of* Houghton Mifflin Harcourt Trade & Reference Division

Graphic Arts Books®, *imprint of* West Margin Press®

Graphic Novels, *imprint of* ABDO Publishing Co Inc

Graphic Planet, *imprint of* ABDO Publishing Co Inc

Graphic Universe™, *imprint of* Lerner Publishing Group Inc

Graphix, *imprint of* Scholastic Trade Division

Grave Issues, *imprint of* Spinsters Ink

Gray Wolf Books, *distributed by* Farrar, Straus & Giroux, LLC

Graydon House Books, *imprint of* Harlequin Enterprises Ltd

Great Books of the Islamic World, *imprint of* Kazi Publications Inc

The Great Courses, *imprint of* Recorded Books Inc, an RBmedia company

Great Explorer Series, *imprint of* University of Alaska Press

Great Lakes Books, *imprint of* Wayne State University Press

The Greeley Co, *subsidiary of* HCPro

Green Books, *distributed by* Chelsea Green Publishing Co

Green Building Press, *distributed by* Chelsea Green Publishing Co

Green Knees, *imprint of* Azro Press

Green Man Publishing, *distributed by* Chelsea Green Publishing Co

Green Trails Maps, *distributed by* The Mountaineers Books

Greenberg Books, *imprint of* Kalmbach Publishing Co

Greenbranch, *distributed by* Medical Group Management Association (MGMA)

Alice Greene & Co, *imprint of* T H Peek Publisher

Greenfield Review Press, *distributed by* Cross-Cultural Communications

Greenhaven Press, *distributed by* Lucent Press

Greenhaven Press®, *imprint of* The Rosen Publishing Group Inc

Greenhaven Press Inc, *distributed by* Perfection Learning

Greenhill Books, *distributed by* Casemate | publishers

Greenleaf Book Group Press, *imprint of* Greenleaf Book Group LLC

Greenway Music Press, *imprint of* A-R Editions Inc

Greenwich Medical Media, *distributed by* Oxford University Press USA

Greenwich Workshop Press, *distributed by* Algonquin Books, Artisan

Greenwillow Books, *imprint of* HarperCollins Children's Books

Greenwood Publishing Group, *imprint of* ABC-CLIO

Grey House, *imprint of* Grey House Publishing Inc™

Grey House Publishing Canada, *division of* Grey House Publishing Inc™

Grief Watch, *distributed by* ACTA Publications

Griffin Technology, *distributed by* Hal Leonard Corp

Griot Audio, *imprint of* Recorded Books Inc, an RBmedia company

The Grolier Club, *distributed by* Oak Knoll Press

Grosset, *distributor for* Parachute Publishing LLC

Grosset & Dunlap, *imprint of* Penguin Group USA, A Penguin Random House Company, Penguin Young Readers Group

Grosset/Putnam, *imprint of* Penguin Group USA, A Penguin Random House Company

Stefan Grossman's Guitar Workshop, *distributed by* Mel Bay Publications Inc

GroundSwell, *imprint of* BPC

Groundworks, *distributed by* Chelsea Green Publishing Co

Group for the Advancement of Psychiatry, *distributed by* American Psychiatric Association Publishing

Group Publishing, *distributed by* Saint Mary's Press

Grove Dictionaries, *distributed by* Oxford University Press USA

Grove Press, *imprint of* Grove Atlantic Inc

Grove Press UK, *imprint of* Grove Atlantic Inc

The Grow Network/McGraw-Hill, *imprint of* McGraw-Hill Education

Grub Street Publishing, *distributed by* Casemate | publishers

B R Gruener Publishing Co, *imprint of* John Benjamins Publishing Co

Gryphon House, *distributor for* DawnSignPress, *distributed by* Teaching Strategies LLC

Gryphon House Inc, *subsidiary of* Kaplan Early Learning Co, *distributor for* Aha Communications, Book Peddlers, Deya Brashears, Bright Ring Publishing, Building Blocks, Center for the Child Care Workforce, Chatterbox Press, Chicago Review Press, Children's Resources International, Circle Time Publishers, Sydney Gurewitz Clemens, Conari Press, Council Oak Books, DawnSignPress, Delmar Publishers Inc, Early Educator's Press, Educators for Social Responsibility, Family Center of Nova University, Jean Feldman, Floris Books, Hawthorne Press, Hunter House Publishers, Kaplan Press, Miss Jackie Inc, Monjeu Press, National Center Early Childhood Workforce, New England AEYC, Nova Southeastern University, Pademelon Press, Partner Press, Pollyanna Productions, Robins Lane Press, School Renaissance, Southern Early Childhood Association, Steam Press, Syracuse University Press, Teaching Strategies LLC, Telshare Publishing

Guerrilla Marketing Press, *imprint of* Morgan James Publishing

Guiding Light Women's Fiction, *imprint of* Lighthouse Publishing of the Carolinas

Guild of Master Craftsman, *distributed by* The Taunton Press Inc

Guilford, *distributed by* Council for Exceptional Children (CEC)

Guitar World, *distributed by* Hal Leonard Corp

Gulf Coast Association of Geological Societies, *distributed by* Bureau of Economic Geology

Gulf Coast Section SEPM, *distributed by* Bureau of Economic Geology

Gulf Energy Information, *distributor for* Editions Technip, Elsevier, Pennwell, Simon & Schuster, Wiley

Gulf Professional Publishers, *distributed by* Marine Techniques Publishing

Gulf Publishing, *distributed by* NACE International

The George Gund Foundation, *imprint of* University of California Press

Haase House, *imprint of* Easy Money Press

Hachai Publishing, *distributor for* Attara, Kerem, Living Lessons

Hachette Audio, *division of* Hachette Book Group

Hachette Book Group, *division of* Hachette Livre, *distributor for* Harry N Abrams Inc, Nicholas Brealey Publishing, Chronicle Books, Disney Book Group, Disney Press, Gildan Media, Hachette UK, Houghton Mifflin Harcourt, Houghton Mifflin Harcourt Trade & Reference Division, Kids Can Press, Lonely Planet, Marvel Worldwide Inc, Moleskine, Octopus Books, Peterson's, Phaidon Press, Phoenix International Publications (PiKids), Quarto Publishing Group, Quarto Publishing Group USA Inc, Quercus Books, Sheldon Press (all print & digital), Time Inc Books, Yen Press, *distributed by* Gem Guides Book Co

Hachette Books, *imprint of* Perseus Books

Hachette Nashville, *division of* Hachette Book Group

Hachette UK, *distributed by* Hachette Book Group

Hackett Publishing Co Inc, *distributor for* Bryn Mawr Commentaries

Hagstrom Map, *subsidiary of* American Map Corp, *distributor for* ADC The Map People, American Map Corp, Arrow Maps Inc, Creative Sales Corp, De Lorme Atlas, Hammond World Atlas Corp, RV International Maps & Atlases, Stubs Guides, Trakker Maps Inc

Hagstrom Map Co Inc, *subsidiary of* American Map Corp

Hal Leonard Corp, *distributor for* Ableton, Acoustica, AirTurn, Amadeus Press, Antares, Apogee, Aquarius, Arrangers Publishing LLC, Art String Publishing, Ashley Music, Avid, Axe Heauen, Berklee Press, Leonard Bernstein, Blue Microphones, Fred Bock Music Company, Boosey & Hawkes, Cakewalk, CD Sheet Music, Centerstream Publishing LLC, Cherry Lane Music Co, ChordBuddy, Curnow Music, De Haske Publications, Dots & Lines Inc, Editions Durand, Editions Max Eschig, Editions Salabert, EM Books, EMI Christian, Faber Music Ltd, Family Communications, Fleamarket Music, Griffin Technology, Guitar World, Hamilton Stands, Hartke, G Henle Verlag, Homespun Tapes, Hudson Music, IK Multimedia, Lauren Keiser Music, Lorie Lane, Line 6, M-Audio, Ashley Mark Publishing Co, Edward B Marks Music, Meredith Music, Mighty Bright, Modern Drummer Publications, Music Minus One, Music Sales America, Musicians Institute Press, Noteflight, Peermusic Classical, PreSonus, Professional Music Institute, Propellerhead, PWM Editions, QSC, Ricordi, Lee Roberts Publications, Rock House, Rubank Publications, St Nicolas Music Inc, Samson Audio, G Schirmer Inc/Associated Music Publishers Ltd, Schott Music, Shawnee Press, Sibelius, Sikorski, Sony, Steinberg, Sterling Publishing Co Inc, String Letter Publishing, Tara Publications, Tycoon Percussion, Vintage Guitar, Voyageur Press, Waltons Irish Music, Willis Music, XLN Audio, Yamaha

Hal Leonard Performing Arts Publishing Group, *division of* Hal Leonard Corp

Halcyon House, *imprint of* National Book Co

Half Hour Reads, *imprint of* Scarsdale Publishing Ltd

Hallmark Publishing, *distributed by* Dreamscape Media LLC

Hambleton Publishing, *distributed by* Caxton Press

Hameray Publishing Group Inc, *distributor for* Bear & Bobcat Books

Hamewith, *imprint of* Baker Books

Hamilton Books, *imprint of* Rowman & Littlefield Publishing Group

Hamilton Stands, *distributed by* Hal Leonard Corp

Hammond, *distributed by* Perfection Learning

Hammond World Atlas Corp, *subsidiary of* American Map Corp, *distributed by* Hagstrom Map

Hampton Roads Publishing, *imprint of* Red Wheel/Weiser, *distributed by* Red Wheel/Weiser

Hancock House, *distributed by* Gem Guides Book Co

Hand Print Press, *distributed by* Chelsea Green Publishing Co

Handprint Books Inc, *imprint of* Chronicle Books, *distributed by* Chronicle Books

Hanover Square Press, *imprint of* Harlequin Enterprises Ltd

Hanser Publications LLC, *subsidiary of* Carl Hanser Verlag GmbH & Co KG

HAP (Health Adminstration Press), *distributed by* Medical Group Management Association (MGMA)

Happy Fox, *imprint of* Fox Chapel Publishing Co Inc

Harambee Press, *imprint of* Lighthouse Publishing of the Carolinas

Harbor Hill Books, *division of* Purple Mountain Press Ltd

Harbor Lights, *imprint of* Langmarc Publishing

Harcourt, *distributor for* Parachute Publishing LLC, *distributed by* Learning Links Inc

Harcourt Children's Books, *imprint of* Houghton Mifflin Harcourt Trade & Reference Division

Hardie Grant, *imprint of* Rizzoli International Publications Inc

Hardie Grant Books, *distributed by* Chronicle Books

Hardwood Press, *distributed by* St Augustine's Press Inc

Harlequin, *imprint of* Harlequin Enterprises Ltd

Harlequin Audio, *imprint of* Harlequin Enterprises Ltd

Harlequin Enterprises Ltd, *division of* Harper-Collins, *distributed by* Simon & Schuster

Harlequin Romance Library™, *imprint of* Recorded Books Inc, an RBmedia company

Harmony Books, *imprint of* Crown Publishing Group, Penguin Random House LLC

Harper, *imprint of* HarperCollins General Books Group

Harper Arrington Publishing, *distributor for* The Little Entrepreneur

Harper Business, *imprint of* HarperCollins General Books Group

Harper Design, *imprint of* HarperCollins General Books Group

Harper Luxe, *imprint of* HarperCollins General Books Group

Harper Perennial, *imprint of* HarperCollins General Books Group

Harper Voyager, *imprint of* HarperCollins General Books Group

Harper Wave, *imprint of* HarperCollins General Books Group

HarperAlley, *imprint of* HarperCollins Children's Books

HarperAudio, *imprint of* HarperCollins Children's Books, HarperCollins General Books Group

HarperCollins, *imprint of* HarperCollins Children's Books, *distributor for* Alloy Entertainment LLC, Delphinium Books, Parachute Publishing LLC, *distributed by* Dreamscape Media LLC, Heimburger House Publishing Co, Learning Links Inc, MAR*CO Products Inc

HarperCollins Children's Books, *division of* HarperCollins Subsidiaries

HarperCollins e-books, *imprint of* HarperCollins Children's Books

HarperCollins Espanol, *imprint of* HarperCollins General Books Group

HarperCollins General Books Group, *division of* HarperCollins Publishers

HarperCollins Publishers, *subsidiary of* News Corp, *distributed by* Gem Guides Book Co

HarperCollins Publishers India Ltd, *distributor for* Harvard University Press

HarperCollins UK, *distributor for* National Geographic Books

HarperEntertainment, *distributor for* Parachute Publishing LLC

HarperLegend, *imprint of* HarperCollins General Books Group

HarperLuxe, *distributed by* Thorndike Press®

HarperOne, *imprint of* HarperCollins General Books Group

HarperVia, *imprint of* HarperCollins General Books Group

Harpia Publishing, *distributed by* Casemate | publishers

Harrington Park Press, *distributed by* Columbia University Press

Harrison House, *distributor for* Faith Library Publications

Harrison House Publishers, *subsidiary of* Nori Media Group

Tom Harrison Cartography, *distributed by* Mountain n' Air Books

Tom Harrison Maps, *distributed by* Gem Guides Book Co

Hartke, *distributed by* Hal Leonard Corp

Harvard Art Museums, *distributed by* Yale University Press

Harvard Business Reference, *imprint of* Harvard Business Review Press

Harvard Business Review Press, *division of* Harvard Business Publishing

Harvard Business School Press, *distributed by* Center for Creative Leadership LLC

Harvard Center for International Affairs, *distributed by* University Press of America Inc

Harvard Center for Middle Eastern Studies, *distributed by* Harvard University Press

Harvard Center for Population Studies, *distributed by* Harvard University Press

Harvard Center for the Study of World Religions, *distributed by* Harvard University Press

Harvard College Library, *distributed by* Harvard University Press

Harvard Common Press, *imprint of* Quarto Publishing Group USA Inc

Harvard Department of Sanskrit & Indian Studies, *distributed by* Harvard University Press

Harvard Department of the Classics, *distributed by* Harvard University Press

Harvard Education Press, *imprint of* Harvard Education Publishing Group

Harvard Education Publishing Group, *division of* Harvard Graduate School of Education

Harvard Educational Review, *imprint of* Harvard Education Publishing Group

Harvard Ukrainian Research Institute, *subsidiary of* Harvard University, *distributed by* Harvard University Press

Harvard University Art Museums, *distributed by* Yale University Press

Harvard University Asia Center, *distributed by* Harvard University Press

Harvard University David Rockefeller Center for Latin American Studies, *distributed by* Harvard University Press

Harvard University Press, *distributor for* Dumbarton Oaks, Harvard Center for Middle Eastern Studies, Harvard Center for Population Studies, Harvard Center for the Study of World Religions, Harvard College Library (including Houghton Library Judaica div), Harvard Department of Sanskrit & Indian Studies, Harvard Department of the Classics, Harvard Ukrainian Research Institute, Harvard University Asia Center, Harvard University David Rockefeller Center for Latin American Studies, Harvard-Yenching Institute, Peabody Museum of Archaeology & Ethnology, Peabody Museum Press, *distributed by* HarperCollins Publishers India Ltd (Indian subcontinent)

Harvard-Yenching Institute, *distributed by* Harvard University Press

Hatherleigh Press Ltd, *distributed by* Penguin Random House Inc

Haugen Enterprises, *distributed by* Frank Amato Publications Inc

Have a Little Faith, *imprint of* TRISTAN Publishing

Haven, *imprint of* Bridge-Logos

Hawaii Nikkei, *distributed by* University of Hawaii Press

Hawaiian Mission Children's Society, *distributed by* University of Hawaii Press

Hawthorn Press, *distributed by* SteinerBooks Inc

Hawthorne Press, *distributed by* Gryphon House Inc

Hay House, *distributed by* Gem Guides Book Co

Hay House Business, *imprint of* Hay House Inc

Hayden-McNeil, *imprint of* Macmillan Learning

Hayes, *distributed by* Perfection Learning

Le Hayes, *distributed by* Gem Guides Book Co

Haynes North America Inc, *division of* The Haynes Publishing Group, *distributor for* G T Foulis, Haynes Owners Workshop Manuals, Oxford Illustrated Press, *distributed by* Motorbooks

Haynes Owners Workshop Manuals, *distributed by* Haynes North America Inc

Nicolas Hays Inc, *distributed by* Red Wheel/Weiser

Hazamir, *imprint of* Transcontinental Music Publications (TMP)

Hazelden, *distributed by* Simon & Schuster, Inc, Simon & Schuster Sales Division

Hazelden/Johnson Institute, *imprint of* Hazelden Publishing

Hazelden/Keep Coming Back, *imprint of* Hazelden Publishing

Hazelden-Pittman Archives Press, *imprint of* Hazelden Publishing

Hazelden Publishing, *division of* The Hazelden Betty Ford Foundation, *distributor for* Obsessive Anonymous, *distributed by* Health Communications Inc (trade), Simon & Schuster

HCI Books, *imprint of* Health Communications Inc

HCI Printing & Publishing, *division of* Health Communications Inc

HCI Teens, *imprint of* Health Communications Inc

HCPro, *division of* BLR®—Business & Legal Resources

Healing Arts Press, *imprint of* Inner Traditions International Ltd

Healing Tao Books, *distributed by* Tuttle Publishing

Health Administration Press, *division of* Foundation of the American College of Healthcare Executives

Health Communications Inc, *distributor for* Hazelden Publishing, *distributed by* Simon & Schuster Inc, Simon & Schuster, Inc, Simon & Schuster Sales Division

Health Forum Inc, *subsidiary of* American Hospital Association

Health Information Press (HIP), *imprint of* Practice Management Information Corp (PMIC)

Health Professions Press, *subsidiary of* Paul H Brookes Publishing Co Inc

Health Research Group, *division of* Public Citizen

Healthcare Performance Press, *imprint of* Productivity Press

HealthLeaders Media, *division of* BLR®—Business & Legal Resources

Healthy Living, *imprint of* BPC

Healthy Living Books, *imprint of* Hatherleigh Press Ltd

Hearst Books, *imprint of* Sterling Publishing Co Inc

Heartdrum Books, *imprint of* HarperCollins Children's Books

Hearthside Books, *distributed by* Closson Press

Hearts 'n Tummies Cookbook Co, *division of* Quixote Press

HeartShaper®, *imprint of* Standard Publishing

Heaven & Earth LLC, *distributed by* Gem Guides Book Co

Heaven & Earth Publications, *distributed by* North Atlantic Books

Hebrew Union College Press, *division of* Hebrew Union College

Heimburger House Publishing Co, *distributor for* Child's Play International, Evergreen Press, Firefly Books Ltd, Fordham University Press, Globe Pequot Press, HarperCollins, Johns Hopkins University Press, Houghton Mifflin Harcourt, Iconografix, Indiana University Press, Kalmbach Publishing Co, Krause Publications, Motorbooks, National Book Network, New York University Press, W W Norton & Company Inc, Penguin Putnam Inc, Pictorial Histories Publishing Co, Steam Passages Publishing, Sterling Publishing Co Inc, Sugar Cane Press, Syracuse University Press, Thunder Bay Press, University of Minnesota Press, John Wiley & Sons

Heimdal, *distributed by* Casemate | publishers

William S Hein & Co Inc, *distributor for* Ashgate, Aspen, Butterworths, Sweet & Maxwell, John Wiley & Sons Inc

Heinemann, *division of* Houghton Mifflin Harcourt, *distributed by* Pearson (Canada, Australia & New Zealand)

Heinemann Raintree, *division of* Capstone Publishers™, *imprint of* Capstone Publishers™

Heliconia Press, *imprint of* Fox Chapel Publishing Co Inc

Helion & Co Ltd, *distributed by* Casemate | publishers

Hellgate Press, *imprint of* L & R Publishing

G Henle Verlag, *distributed by* Hal Leonard Corp

Henry Holt, *imprint of* Henry Holt and Company, LLC

Henry Holt Books for Younger Readers, *imprint of* Henry Holt and Company, LLC

Ian Henry Publications, *distributed by* Empire Publishing Service

Her Own Words, *imprint of* Her Own Words LLC

Hera, *imprint of* Riverdale Avenue Books (RAB)

Herald Press, *imprint of* MennoMedia

Herald Publishing House, *division of* Community of Christ

Herb & Spice, *imprint of* Crossquarter Publishing Group

Herder & Herder, *imprint of* The Crossroad Publishing Co

Here & Now, *imprint of* Gallopade International Inc

Editions Charles Herissey, *distributed by* Casemate | publishers

Heritage Beacon Fiction, *imprint of* Lighthouse Publishing of the Carolinas

Heritage Books, *imprint of* Heritage Books Inc

Heritage Books Inc, *distributor for* Fairfax Genealogical Society, National Genealogical Society, Virginia Genealogical Society

Heritage Builders, *imprint of* Focus on the Family

Heritage House, *distributor for* FineEdge.com LLC

Nick Hern Books, *distributed by* Theatre Communications Group

Heroes & Helpers, *imprint of* Gallopade International Inc

Hes & De Graaf, *distributed by* Oak Knoll Press

Hesperia, *imprint of* ASCSA Publications

Heuristic Books, *imprint of* Science & Humanities Press

Hewitt Homeschooling Resources, *division of* Hewitt Research Foundation

Heyday, *distributed by* Gem Guides Book Co

HFS, *division of* Johns Hopkins University Press

Hi Jinx, *imprint of* Black Rabbit Books

Hidden Travel Series, *imprint of* Ulysses Press

High Tide Monograph Series, *imprint of* High Tide Press

High Tide Press, *subsidiary of* The Trinity Foundation

HighBridge Audio, *distributed by* Algonquin Books, Penguin Group USA, A Penguin Random House Company

Highgate Press, *imprint of* ECS Publishing Group

Highland/Etling, *imprint of* Alfred Music

Highlights Learning, *imprint of* Highlights for Children Inc

Highlights Press, *imprint of* Highlights for Children Inc

Hill & Wang, *division of* Farrar, Straus & Giroux, LLC, *imprint of* Farrar, Straus & Giroux, LLC

Lawrence Hill Books, *imprint of* Chicago Review Press

Hillenbrand Books, *imprint of* Liturgy Training Publications

Hillsdale College Press, *division of* Hillsdale College

Hilton Publishing Co, *division of* HPC

Himalayan Institute Press, *division of* Himalayan International Institute of Yoga Science & Philosophy

Hindustan Book Agency, *distributed by* American Mathematical Society

Hippocrates Publications, *distributed by* BPC

Hispanic Info & Telecommunications Newtork, *distributed by* Simon & Schuster, Inc

Histoire & Collections, *distributed by* Casemate | publishers

Historic Idaho Series, *distributed by* Caxton Press

Historic New Orleans Collection, *distributed by* Oak Knoll Press

Historical Indexes, *distributed by* Casemate | publishers

History Colorado, *distributed by* University Press of Colorado

History Facts, *distributed by* Casemate | publishers

History Press, *imprint of* Arcadia Publishing Inc

History Publishing Company, *imprint of* History Publishing Co LLC

Histria Books, *division of* Histria LLC, *distributed by* Casemate | publishers

Histria Kids, *imprint of* Histria Books

HMH Audio, *imprint of* Houghton Mifflin Harcourt Trade & Reference Division

HMH Franchise, *imprint of* Houghton Mifflin Harcourt Trade & Reference Division

Hoard's Dairyman Magazine, *imprint of* W D Hoard & Sons Co

Hobble Creek Press, *imprint of* Cedar Fort Inc

Hochelaga, *distributor for* Cross-Cultural Communications, *distributed by* Cross-Cultural Communications

Hodder Education, *distributed by* Trans-Atlantic Publications Inc

Hogarth, *imprint of* Crown Publishing Group, Penguin Random House LLC

Hogrefe AG, *distributed by* Hogrefe Publishing Corp

Hogrefe Publishing Corp, *subsidiary of* Hogrefe Verlag GmbH & Co Kg, *distributor for* Hogrefe AG (Switzerland), Hogrefe Verlag (Germany)

Hogrefe Verlag, *distributed by* Hogrefe Publishing Corp

Hohm Press, *subsidiary of* HSM LLC

Holiday House Publishing Inc, *distributed by* Pengin Random House

Holman Bibles, *imprint of* B&H Publishing Group

Holmes Publishing Group, *imprint of* Holmes Publishing Group LLC

Holmes Publishing Group LLC, *distributor for* Jerusalem Press (UK), Starfire Publishing (UK), Theion Publishing (Germany), Three Hands Press (US), Von Zos Publishing, Xoanon Publishing (US)

Holmgren Design Services, *distributed by* Chelsea Green Publishing Co

Holocaust Library, *imprint of* United States Holocaust Memorial Museum

Henry Holt and Company, LLC, *division of* Macmillan, Macmillan

Matt Holt Books, *imprint of* BenBella Books Inc

Holt Paperbacks, *imprint of* Henry Holt and Company, LLC

Holy Cross Orthodox Press, *division of* Hellenic College Holy Cross

Homa & Sekey Books, *distributor for* China Encyclopedia Publishing House, China Intercontinental Press, China Zhejiang Publishing United Group

Home Builders Press, *distributed by* Craftsman Book Co

Homespun Tapes, *distributed by* Hal Leonard Corp

Homestead Publishing, *affiliate of* Book Design Ltd

Hooked On Phonics, *distributed by* Simon & Schuster, Inc, Simon & Schuster Sales Division

Hoover Institution Press, *subsidiary of* Hoover Institution on War, Revolution & Peace

Hoover's Business Press, *imprint of* Hoover's Inc

Hoover's Handbooks, *imprint of* Hoover's Inc

Hoover's Inc, *subsidiary of* Dun & Bradstreet

Hope Publishing House, *distributed by* Pelican Publishing Co

Johns Hopkins University Press, *affiliate of* Johns Hopkins University, *distributor for* Inter-American Development Bank, International Food Policy Research Institute, Woodrow Wilson Center Press, *distributed by* Heimburger House Publishing Co

Hops Press, *distributed by* Mountain Press Publishing Co

Horizon Publishers, *imprint of* Cedar Fort Inc

Horizon Publishers & Distributors Inc, *distributed by* Cedar Fort Inc

Hospital & Healthcare Compensation Service, *subsidiary of* John R Zabka Associates Inc, John R Zabka Associates Inc

Houghton Mifflin, *distributed by* Gem Guides Book Co

Houghton Mifflin Harcourt, *imprint of* Houghton Mifflin Harcourt Trade & Reference Division, *distributor for* Clarion Books, Old Farmer's Almanac, *distributed by* Hachette Book Group, Heimburger House Publishing Co

Houghton Mifflin Harcourt Assessments, *subsidiary of* Houghton Mifflin Harcourt

Houghton Mifflin Harcourt Books for Young Readers, *imprint of* Houghton Mifflin Harcourt Trade & Reference Division

Houghton Mifflin Harcourt K-12 Publishers, *division of* Houghton Mifflin Harcourt

Houghton Mifflin Harcourt Publishing Company, *distributed by* Learning Links Inc

Houghton Mifflin Harcourt Trade & Reference Division, *division of* Houghton Mifflin Harcourt, *distributor for* Larousse, Old Farmer's Almanac, *distributed by* Hachette Book Group

Hourglass, *imprint of* Baker Books

House of Collectibles, *imprint of* Penguin Random House LLC, Random House Reference/Random House Puzzles & Games

House to House Publications, *division of* DOVE International

Howard Books, *imprint of* Atria Books

HQ, *imprint of* Harlequin Enterprises Ltd

HQN Books, *imprint of* Harlequin Enterprises Ltd

HRD Press, *distributed by* Training & Development Materials of Canada (Canada)

Huber, *distributed by* Alan Wofsy Fine Arts

Hudson Hills Press Inc, *distributor for* American Federation of Arts

Hudson Music, *distributed by* Hal Leonard Corp

Hui Hanai, *distributed by* University of Hawaii Press

Huia Publishers, *distributed by* University of Hawaii Press

Human Alchemy Publications, *distributed by* Crown House Publishing Co LLC

Human Rights Watch Books, *imprint of* Human Rights Watch

Humana Press, *imprint of* Springer

Humanity Books, *imprint of* Prometheus Books

Humanix Books LLC, *division of* Newsmax Media

Humanoids Inc, *distributed by* Simon & Schuster, Inc

Humanum Academic Press, *distributed by* The Catholic University of America Press

Hungry Goat Press, *imprint of* Gauthier Publications Inc

Hungry Tomato, *imprint of* Lerner Publishing Group Inc

Hunter House, *imprint of* Turner Publishing Co

Hunter House Publishers, *distributed by* Gryphon House Inc

Hurst, *distributed by* Oxford University Press USA

Hybrid Nation, *imprint of* Red Hen Press

Hydra, *imprint of* Penguin Random House LLC, Random House Publishing Group

Hyperbole, *imprint of* San Diego State University Press

Hyperion, *distributor for* Alloy Entertainment LLC

Hyperion Books for Children, *imprint of* Disney Publishing Worldwide

Hypermedia Inc, *imprint of* Frederic C Beil Publisher Inc

Ibex Press, *imprint of* Ibex Publishers

Ibex Publishers, *distributor for* Farhang Moaser

IBFD North America Inc (International Bureau of Fiscal Documentation), *division of* IBFD Foundation

ibidem Press, *distributed by* Columbia University Press

IchemE, *distributed by* American Institute of Chemical Engineers (AIChE)

ICLE, *imprint of* Institute of Continuing Legal Education

Iconografix, *distributed by* Heimburger House Publishing Co

Idea Bank, *distributed by* Fire Engineering Books & Videos

Ideal Audiobooks, *distributed by* Dreamscape Media LLC

Ides et Calendes, *distributed by* Alan Wofsy Fine Arts

IEE, *imprint of* IET USA Inc

IEEE Computer Society Press, *distributor for* American Society for Quality (ASQ)

IEEE Press, *division of* Institute of Electrical & Electronics Engineers Inc (IEEE), Institute of Electrical and Electronics Engineers Inc (IEEE), *distributed by* John Wiley & Sons Inc

IFSTA, *distributed by* Fire Engineering Books & Videos

Igloo Books, *distributed by* Simon & Schuster, Inc

Ignatius Press, *division of* Guadalupe Associates Inc, Guadalupe Associates Inc, *distributor for* Bethlehem Books, Veritas

Ignite, *imprint of* Entangled Publishing LLC

IIP Consumers Series, *imprint of* Independent Information Publications

IK Multimedia, *distributed by* Hal Leonard Corp

Ikonographics, *imprint of* Franciscan Media

Ilchokak Publishers, *distributed by* Cheng & Tsui Co Inc

Illinois State Museum Society, *affiliate of* Illinois State Museum

IlluminateYA Fiction, *imprint of* Lighthouse Publishing of the Carolinas

Illuminating Engineering Society of North America (IES), *distributor for* Taylor & Francis, Techstreet

ILR Press, *imprint of* Cornell University Press

Image Books, *imprint of* Crown Publishing Group

Image Catholic Books, *imprint of* Penguin Random House LLC

Imagine Publishing, *imprint of* Charlesbridge Publishing Inc

Imago Mundi, *imprint of* David R Godine Inc

ImaJinn Books, *imprint of* BelleBooks

IMM Lifestyle Books, *imprint of* Fox Chapel Publishing Co Inc

Immagine&Poesia, *distributed by* Cross-Cultural Communications

Immedium, *imprint of* Immedium Inc

Impact, *imprint of* New Harbinger Publications Inc

Impact Publications/Development Concepts Inc, *distributed by* National Book Network

Impactika, *distributed by* Gem Guides Book Co

Imperial College Press, *subsidiary of* World Scientific Publishing Co Inc

In an Hour Books LLC, *imprint of* Smith & Kraus Publishers Inc

In Extenso Press, *imprint of* ACTA Publications

In the Garden Publishing, *division of* What Would Love Do International Ltd

Incentive Plus, *distributor for* MAR*CO Products Inc

Independence Press, *imprint of* Herald Publishing House

Independent Information Publications, *division of* Computing!

Independent Publishers Group, *division of* Chicago Review Press, *distributed by* Gem Guides Book Co

Independent Seaport Museum, *distributed by* Cornell Maritime Press

Independent University of Moscow, *distributed by* American Mathematical Society

Indiana University Press, *distributed by* Heimburger House Publishing Co

IndieBooks, *distributed by* Trans-Atlantic Publications Inc

Indigo, *imprint of* Genesis Press Inc

Indigo Love Spectrum, *imprint of* Genesis Press Inc

Indigo River, *distributed by* Simon & Schuster, Inc

Indigo Vibe, *imprint of* Genesis Press Inc

Indulgence, *imprint of* Entangled Publishing LLC

Industrial Press, *distributed by* NACE International, SME (Society of Manufacturing Engineers)

Indy-Tech Publishing, *imprint of* SAMS Technical Publishing LLC

Infobase Publishing, *distributed by* Gem Guides Book Co

Information Gatekeepers Inc (IGI), *division of* IGI Group Inc

Information Today Books, *imprint of* Information Today, Inc

Information Today, Inc, *distributor for* Association for Information Science & Technology (ASIS&T)

Ingram Publisher Services, *distributed by* Gem Guides Book Co

Ingram Publisher Services/Two Rivers, *distributed by* Gem Guides Book Co

Inkwater Press, *imprint of* Firstbooks.com Inc, Firstbooks.com Inc

Inkyard Press, *imprint of* Harlequin Enterprises Ltd

Inland, *distributor for* World Citizens

Inner Traditions, *imprint of* Inner Traditions International Ltd, *distributed by* Gem Guides Book Co

Inner Traditions Audio, *imprint of* Inner Traditions International Ltd

Inner Traditions/Bear & Company, *distributed by* Simon & Schuster, Inc

Inner Traditions en Espanol, *imprint of* Inner Traditions International Ltd

Inner Traditions India, *imprint of* Inner Traditions International Ltd

Inner Worlds Music, *distributed by* Lotus Press

Innovation & Tourisms (INTO), *imprint of* Cognizant Communication Corp

Innovative Marketing, *distributor for* Pentecostal Publishing House

InnoVision Health Media, *distributed by* Square One Publishers Inc

Inprint Editions, *imprint of* Black Classic Press

Insight Editions, *distributed by* Simon & Schuster, Simon & Schuster, Inc, Simon & Schuster Sales Division

Insight Media, *imprint of* Alexander Street, a ProQuest Company

Inspec, *imprint of* IET USA Inc

Instant Help, *imprint of* New Harbinger Publications Inc

Institute for Advanced Study in the Theatre Arts (IASTA), *distributed by* Fordham University Press

Institute for Mesoamerican Studies, *distributed by* University of Texas Press

Institute for Regional Studies of the Californias, *distributed by* San Diego State University Press

Institute for the Psychological Sciences Press (IPS), *distributed by* The Catholic University of America Press

Institute of Buddhist Studies, *distributed by* University of Hawaii Press

Institute of Governmental Studies, *subsidiary of* University of California, Berkeley

Institute of Materials, *distributed by* NACE International

Institute of Mathematical Geography, *division of* Arlinghaus Enterprises LLC

Institute of Police Technology & Management, *division of* University of North Florida

Institute Press, *distributed by* Crown House Publishing Co LLC

Instituto Monsa de Ediciones SA, *distributed by* Trans-Atlantic Publications Inc

Integrity Music, *division of* David C Cook

Inter-American Development Bank, *division of* Multilateral Development Bank, *distributed by* Johns Hopkins University Press

Inter-University Consortium for Political & Social Research (ICPSR), *affiliate of* University of Michigan Institute for Social Research

Intercontinental Press, *distributed by* CN Times Books

Intercultural Press, *imprint of* Nicholas Brealey Publishing

Intercultural Press Inc, *division of* Nicholas Brealey Publishing, *imprint of* Nicholas Brealey Publishing

Interlink Books, *imprint of* Interlink Publishing Group Inc

Interlink Publishing Group Inc, *distributor for* Banipal Books, Barzan Publishing, Camerapix Publishers, Georgina Campbell Guides, Geddes & Grosset, Good Hotel Guides, Macmillan Caribbean, Rucksack Readers, Serif Publishing, Sheldrake Press, Signal Books, Sunflower Books, The Urban Explorer - "Only In" Guides, Waverley Books, Neil Wilson Publishing

InterMix, *imprint of* Penguin Group USA, A Penguin Random House Company

International Air Transport Association, *distributed by* J J Keller & Associates, Inc

International Atomic Energy Agency (IAEA), *distributed by* United Nations Publications

International Book Centre Inc, *distributor for* Compass Publications, Library du Liban (Lebanon), New Readers Press, Oxford University Press, Pro Lingua Associates, Stacey International Ltd (London), University of Michigan

International Code Council, *distributed by* PPI, A Kaplan Company

International Country Risk Guide, *imprint of* The PRS Group Inc

International Criminal Tribunal for Rwanda (UNICTR), *distributed by* United Nations Publications

International Criminal Tribunal for the former Yugoslavia (ICTY), *distributed by* United Nations Publications

International Energy Agency, *distributed by* OECD Washington Center

International Food Policy Research Institute, *member of* Consultative Group on International Agricultural Research (CGIAR), *distributed by* Johns Hopkins University Press

International Jewelry Publications, *distributed by* Gem Guides Book Co

International Law Institute, *distributed by* University Press of America Inc

International Organization for Migration (IOM), *distributed by* United Nations Publications

International Press, *distributed by* American Mathematical Society

International Press of Boston Inc, *distributed by* AMS

International Trade Centre (ITC), *distributed by* United Nations Publications

International Transportation Forum, *distributed by* OECD Washington Center

InterVarsity Press, *division of* InterVarsity Christian Fellowship/USA

Interweave Press LLC, *imprint of* Golden Peak Media

Ione Press, *imprint of* ECS Publishing Group

iPRECIATION, *distributed by* University of Hawaii Press

Iranbooks Press, *imprint of* Ibex Publishers

Iris Press, *imprint of* The Iris Publishing Group Inc

IRL, *distributed by* Oxford University Press USA

Iroquois Press, *imprint of* Turner Publishing Co

ISH Group, *distributed by* Empire Publishing Service

The Ishmael Tree, *distributor for* RockHill Publishing LLC

ISI Books, *imprint of* Intercollegiate Studies Institute Inc

Islamic Texts Society, *distributed by* Fons Vitae

Island, *imprint of* Penguin Random House LLC

Island Press, *distributor for* Environmental Law Institute, Techne Press

Island Research & Education Initiative, *distributed by* University of Hawaii Press

Islander Group, *distributor for* Kamehameha Publishing

The Islander Group (TIG), *distributor for* Bess Press

Islander Images, *imprint of* Shepard Publications

Islander Press, *imprint of* Shepard Publications

Isle Botanica, *distributed by* University of Hawaii Press

ISO, *distributed by* NACE International

IsraBook, *subsidiary of* Gefen Books

Issues Press, *imprint of* Idyll Arbor Inc

Italian School of East Asian Studies, *distributed by* Cheng & Tsui Co Inc

ITK (In the Know) Audio, *imprint of* Recorded Books Inc, an RBmedia company

It's About Time Inc, *distributor for* American Geosciences Institute (AGI)

iUniverse, *division of* Author Solutions LLC

IVP Academic, *imprint of* InterVarsity Press

IVP Books, *imprint of* InterVarsity Press

IVP Connect, *imprint of* InterVarsity Press

IVP Praxis, *imprint of* InterVarsity Press

Ivy Books, *imprint of* Penguin Random House LLC

Jacaranda, *imprint of* John Wiley & Sons Inc

Jade Rabbit, *imprint of* Quite Specific Media Group Ltd

Jagiellonian University Press, *distributed by* Columbia University Press

Janaway Publishing, *distributor for* Closson Press

Japan Playwrights Association, *distributed by* University of Hawaii Press

Japan Publications Inc, *distributed by* Kodansha USA Inc

Japan Publications Trading Co Inc, *distributed by* Kodansha USA Inc

Jenkins Publishing, *distributed by* Chelsea Green Publishing Co

Jersey Yarns, *imprint of* Quincannon Publishing Group

Jerusalem Press, *distributed by* Holmes Publishing Group LLC

Jerusalem Publications, *distributed by* Feldheim Publishers

Jeter Publishing, *imprint of* Gallery Books

Jewish Lights, *imprint of* Turner Publishing Co

The Jewish Museum, *distributed by* Yale University Press

Jewish New Testament Publications, *distributed by* Lederer Books, Messianic Jewish Publishers

Jewish Publication Society, *distributed by* University of Nebraska Press

Jhpiego, *affiliate of* Johns Hopkins University

Jist, *distributor for* MAR*CO Products Inc

JIST Career Solutions, *imprint of* JIST Publishing

JIST Publishing, *division of* EMC Publishing LLC

JMC Press, *distributed by* Vandamere Press

John Deere Publishing, *division of* Deere & Co

John Macrae Books, *imprint of* Henry Holt and Company, LLC

Johns Hopkins University Press, *affiliate of* Johns Hopkins University, *distributor for* Inter-American Development Bank, International Food Policy Research Institute, Woodrow Wilson Center Press, *distributed by* Heimburger House Publishing Co

Joint Center for Political & Economic Studies Press, *distributed by* University Press of America Inc

Jolly Fish Press, *imprint of* North Star Editions Inc

Jones & Bartlett Learning, *distributed by* Medical Group Management Association (MGMA)

Jones & Bartlett Learning LLC, *division of* Ascend Learning

The Fletcher Jones Foundation, *imprint of* University of California Press

Kaylie Jones Books, *imprint of* Akashic Books

Lorena Jones Books, *imprint of* Ten Speed Press

Jossey-Bass, *imprint of* John Wiley & Sons Inc, *distributor for* Center for Creative Leadership LLC, *distributed by* Center for Creative Leadership LLC

Journal of Chinese Medicine Publications, *distributed by* Eastland Press

Journal Publications, *distributed by* Gem Guides Book Co

JourneyForth Books, *division of* BJU Press, *imprint of* BJU Press

Jove, *imprint of* Berkley Publishing Group, Penguin Group USA, A Penguin Random House Company

JPT America Inc, *distributed by* Cheng & Tsui Co Inc

Judeo Christian Ethics Series, *imprint of* PREP Publishing

Judson Press, *division of* American Baptist Churches in the USA, *distributed by* Abingdon Press

Juloya, *imprint of* Elva Resa Publishing

Jump at the Sun, *imprint of* Disney-Hyperion Books, Disney Publishing Worldwide

Jumpstart, *imprint of* Triumph Learning LLC

Juniper Publishing, *distributed by* Simon & Schuster, Inc, Simon & Schuster Sales Division

Juno Books, *distributed by* powerHouse Books

Jury Verdict Research, *division of* LRP Publications

Just Cause, *imprint of* Yard Dog Press

Kabbalah Publishing, *division of* Kabbalah Centre International

Kaeden Books, *imprint of* Kaeden Corp

Shelley Kaehr, *distributed by* Gem Guides Book Co

Kagero, *distributed by* Casemate | publishers

Kailua Historical Society, *distributed by* University of Hawaii Press

Kalamaku Press, *distributed by* University of Hawaii Press

Kalaniot Books, *imprint of* Endless Mountains Publishing Co

Kales Press, *distributed by* W W Norton & Company Inc

Kalindi Press, *imprint of* Hohm Press

Kalmbach Books, *imprint of* Kalmbach Publishing Co

Kalmbach Publishing Co, *distributed by* Heimburger House Publishing Co, Publishers Group West (PGW)

Kalmus, *imprint of* Alfred Music

Kamehameha Publishing, *division of* Kamehameha Schools, *distributed by* Islander Group

Kamehameha Schools Press, *imprint of* Kamehameha Publishing

Kane Miller Books, *imprint of* EDC Publishing

Kane Press, *imprint of* Boyds Mills & Kane

Kanji Press, *distributed by* University of Hawaii Press

Kaplan Press, *distributed by* Gryphon House Inc

Kaplan Publishing, *distributed by* Simon & Schuster, Inc, Simon & Schuster Sales Division

Kappa Map Group LLC, *distributed by* American Map Corp

Kar-Ben Publishing, *imprint of* Lerner Publishing Group Inc, *distributed by* Beach Lloyd Publishers LLC

Karnak House, *imprint of* The Red Sea Press Inc

Katalitix, *distributed by* Simon & Schuster Sales Division

Katalitix Media, *distributed by* Simon & Schuster, Inc

KAV Books, *distributed by* Royal Fireworks Press

KC Publications, *distributed by* Gem Guides Book Co

Keene Engineering, *distributed by* Gem Guides Book Co

Keenspot, *distributed by* Simon & Schuster, Inc

Keepers of Our Culture, *imprint of* Park Place Publications

Lauren Keiser Music, *distributed by* Hal Leonard Corp

J J Keller & Associates, Inc, *distributor for* Chilton Book Co, International Air Transport Association, National Archives & Records Administration, National Institute of Occupational Safety & Health, Office of the Federal Register, Research & Special Programs Administration of the US Department of Transportation, John Wiley & Sons Inc

Kendall Green, *imprint of* Gallaudet University Press

Kendall Hunt Publishing, *distributor for* Seedling Publications Inc

Kenilworth Press, *distributed by* Trafalgar Square Books

Kennedy Information Inc, *division of* Bloomberg BNA

Kensington, *distributor for* Parachute Publishing LLC

Kensington Hardcover, *imprint of* Kensington Publishing Corp

Kensington Mass-Market, *imprint of* Kensington Publishing Corp

Kensington Publishing Corp, *distributor for* Urban Books, *distributed by* Penguin Group USA, A Penguin Random House Company, Penguin Group USA, A Penguin Random House Company

Kensington Trade Paperback, *imprint of* Kensington Publishing Corp

Kentucky Historical Society, *distributed by* The University Press of Kentucky

Kerem, *distributed by* Hachai Publishing

Charles H Kerr, *distributed by* AK Press Distribution

Kersplebedelo, *distributed by* AK Press Distribution

Kessinger Publishing®, *imprint of* Kessinger Publishing LLC

Key Education, *distributed by* Carson Dellosa Publishing LLC

Keylight Books, *imprint of* Turner Publishing Co

Keynote Speakers Today, *imprint of* Avant-Guide

Keystone Books, *imprint of* Penn State University Press

Keystone Trails Association, *distributed by* Appalachian Trail Conservancy (ATC)

Keywords Press, *imprint of* Atria Books

Kid Help Publishing Co, *division of* Quixote Press

KidHaven Press, *distributed by* Lucent Press

KidHaven Publishing, *imprint of* The Rosen Publishing Group Inc

Kids Can Press, *distributed by* Hachette Book Group

Kids Corner, *imprint of* Sundance/Newbridge Publishing

KidsBooks, *imprint of* Kidsbooks LLC

Kimbell Art Museum, *distributed by* Yale University Press

Kinfolk, *distributed by* Simon & Schuster, Inc, Simon & Schuster Sales Division

Laurence King Publishing, *distributed by* Chronicle Books

The King Legacy, *imprint of* Beacon Press

Kingswell, *imprint of* Disney Publishing Worldwide

Kiron Editions du Felin, *distributed by* Beach Lloyd Publishers LLC

Klutz, *imprint of* Scholastic Trade Division

Alfred A Knopf, *imprint of* Knopf Doubleday Publishing Group, Penguin Random House LLC

Alfred A Knopf Books for Young Readers, *imprint of* Random House Children's Books

Knopf Books for Young Readers, *imprint of* Penguin Random House LLC

Knopf Guides, *imprint of* Penguin Random House LLC

Knossus Project, *distributed by* Chelsea Green Publishing Co

Knowledge Resources, *distributor for* Association for Talent Development (ATD) Press

Kodansha, *distributed by* Oxford University Press USA

Kodansha America, *imprint of* Kodansha USA Inc

Kodansha Globe, *imprint of* Kodansha USA Inc

Kodansha International, *imprint of* Kodansha USA Inc

Kodansha USA Inc, *subsidiary of* Kodansha Ltd (Japan), Kodansha Ltd (Japan), *distributor for* Japan Publications Inc, Japan Publications Trading Co Inc

Kokila Books, *imprint of* Penguin Young Readers Group

Kollath-Stensaas, *distributed by* AdventureKEEN

Kolowalu Books, *imprint of* University of Hawaii Press

Konecky & Konecky, *distributed by* Gem Guides Book Co

Konecky & Konecky (K&K), *imprint of* Konecky & Konecky LLC

Konecky & Konecky LLC, *distributor for* Octavo Editions

KonigsFurt, *distributed by* US Games Systems Inc

Korea Institute, Harvard University, *distributed by* University of Hawaii Press

Koren Publishers, *imprint of* The Toby Press LLC

Kornfeld (Switzerland), *distributed by* The Picasso Project

Kornfeld & Co (Bern), *distributed by* Alan Wofsy Fine Arts

Kosei Publishing Co, *imprint of* Tuttle Publishing, *distributed by* Tuttle Publishing

Kotan Publishing Inc, *imprint of* Tuttle Publishing, *distributed by* Tuttle Publishing

HJ Kramer Inc, *division of* New World Library

Krause Publications, *distributed by* Heimburger House Publishing Co

Krause Publications Inc, *imprint of* Penguin Random House LLC

Pam Krauss Books, *imprint of* Avery

Kregel Academic & Professional, *imprint of* Kregel Publications

Kregel Classics, *imprint of* Kregel Publications

Kregel Kidzone, *imprint of* Kregel Publications

Kregel Publications, *division of* Kregel Inc, Kregel Inc, *distributor for* Candle Books, Monarch Books

De Krijger, *distributed by* Casemate | publishers

Kroshka Publications, *imprint of* Nova Science Publishers Inc

KTAV Publishing House Inc, *distributor for* Yeshiva University Press

KTeen, *imprint of* Kensington Publishing Corp

Kudzu House, *imprint of* Ariel Press, *distributed by* Ariel Press

KUED, *distributed by* The University of Utah Press

Kumarian Press, *division of* Lynne Rienner Publishers Inc, *distributor for* Management Sciences for Health

LA Weekly Books, *imprint of* St Martin's Press, LLC

Ladders, *imprint of* Triumph Learning LLC

Lake Claremont Press, *imprint of* Everything Goes Media LLC

Lake Forest College Press, *distributed by* Northwestern University Press

Lakeshore Learning Materials, *distributor for* National Council of Teachers of Mathematics (NCTM)

Wendy Lamb Books, *imprint of* Penguin Random House LLC, Random House Children's Books

Lamplighter Mysteries & Suspense, *imprint of* Lighthouse Publishing of the Carolinas

Landauer Publishing, *imprint of* Fox Chapel Publishing Co Inc

Lorie Lane, *distributed by* Hal Leonard Corp

Peter Lang Publishing Inc, *subsidiary of* Peter Lang AG (Switzerland), Peter Lang AG (Switzerland)

Langenscheidt Publishing Group, *distributor for* Michelin Maps & Guides

Lantana Publishing, *distributed by* Lerner Publishing Group Inc

Lantern Books, *division of* Lantern Publishing & Media, *distributed by* Red Wheel/Weiser, SteinerBooks Inc

Lantern Publishing & Media, *distributed by* Red Wheel/Weiser

LanternLight Library, *imprint of* University of Alaska Press

LARB Books, *division of* Los Angeles Review of Books

Large Print Press™, *imprint of* Gale

Lark, *imprint of* Sterling Publishing Co Inc

Lark Crafts, *imprint of* Sterling Publishing Co Inc

Larousse, *distributed by* Houghton Mifflin Harcourt Trade & Reference Division

JK Lasser, *imprint of* John Wiley & Sons Inc

Latin American Review Press, *distributed by* Arte Publico Press

Latitude 20, *imprint of* University of Hawaii Press

JP Lattes, *distributed by* Beach Lloyd Publishers LLC

Launch!, *imprint of* ABDO Publishing Co Inc

Laurel-Leaf, *imprint of* Random House Children's Books

Laurel Leaf Books, *imprint of* Penguin Random House LLC

Laurendale Associates, *distributed by* ECS Publishing Group

Law & Crime Books, *distributed by* Simon & Schuster, Inc

Layali Music Publishing, *distributed by* ECS Publishing Group

LB Kids, *imprint of* Little, Brown Books for Young Readers

The Leadership Challenge®, *imprint of* John Wiley & Sons Inc

Leafwood Publishers, *imprint of* ACU Press

League of Professional Theatre Women, *distributed by* Theatre Communications Group

Leaning Tree Tales LLC, *distributed by* Gem Guides Book Co

Learning & Coloring Books, *imprint of* Quincannon Publishing Group

Learning Challenge, *imprint of* Kidsbooks LLC

The Learning Company, *division of* Houghton Mifflin Harcourt

Learning Links Inc, *distributor for* Harcourt, HarperCollins, Houghton Mifflin Harcourt Publishing Company, Penguin Group USA, A Penguin Random House Company, Penguin Random House Inc

Learning Matters, *imprint of* SAGE Publishing

LearningExpress, *unit of* EBSCO Information Services

Leaves of Healing, *imprint of* Progressive Press

Leda, *imprint of* Norilana Books

Lederer Books, *division of* Messianic Jewish Publishers, *distributor for* Chosen People Ministries, First Fruits of Zion, Jewish New Testament Publications

Lee & Low Games, *imprint of* Lee & Low Books Inc

Left To Write Press, *distributed by* Chelsea Green Publishing Co

Legacy Bound, *division of* Legacy Toys

Legas Publishers, *distributed by* Cross-Cultural Communications

Legendary Comics, *distributed by* Simon & Schuster, Inc

Legendary Locals, *imprint of* Arcadia Publishing Inc

Lehigh University Press, *affiliate of* Rowman & Littlefield Publishing Group, *distributed by* Rowman & Littlefield

Leisure Arts Inc, *division of* Liberty Media

LENNY, *imprint of* Random House Publishing Group

Hal Leonard Corp, *distributor for* Ableton, Acoustica, AirTurn, Amadeus Press, Antares, Apogee, Aquarius, Arrangers Publishing LLC, Art String Publishing, Ashley Music, Avid, Axe Heauen, Berklee Press, Leonard Bernstein, Blue Microphones, Fred Bock Music Company, Boosey & Hawkes, Cakewalk, CD Sheet Music, Centerstream Publishing LLC, Cherry Lane Music Co, ChordBuddy, Curnow Music, De Haske Publications, Dots & Lines Inc, Editions Durand, Editions Max Eschig, Editions Salabert, EM Books, EMI Christian, Faber Music Ltd, Family Communications, Fleamarket Music, Griffin Technology, Guitar World, Hamilton Stands, Hartke, G Henle Verlag, Homespun Tapes, Hudson Music, IK Multimedia, Lauren Keiser Music, Lorie Lane, Line 6, M-Audio, Ashley Mark Publishing Co, Edward B Marks Music, Meredith Music, Mighty Bright, Modern Drummer Publications, Music Minus One, Music Sales America, Musicians Institute Press, Noteflight, Peermusic Classical, PreSonus, Professional Music Institute, Propellerhead, PWM Editions, QSC, Ricordi, Lee Roberts Publications, Rock House, Rubank Publications, St Nicolas Music Inc, Samson Audio, G Schirmer Inc/Associated Music Publishers Ltd, Schott Music, Shawnee Press, Sibelius, Sikorski, Sony, Steinberg, Sterling Publishing Co Inc, String Letter Publishing, Tara Publications, Tycoon Percussion, Vintage Guitar, Voyageur Press, Waltons Irish Music, Willis Music, XLN Audio, Yamaha

Lerner Digital, *imprint of* Lerner Publishing Group Inc

Lerner Publications, *imprint of* Lerner Publishing Group Inc

Lerner Publisher Services, *division of* Lerner Publishing Group Inc

Lerner Publishing Group Inc, *division of* Lerner Universal Corp, *distributor for* Andersen Press, Big & Small, Creston Books, Walter Foster Publishing, Full Tilt, Gecko Press, Lantana Publishing, Maverick Arts Publishing, One Elm Press, Quarto Library, Red Chair Press, Starberry Books, We Do Listen Foundation

LernerClassroom, *imprint of* Lerner Publishing Group Inc

The Letter People®, *imprint of* Abrams Learning Trends

Leuven University Press, *distributed by* Cornell University Press

Leveled Readers, *imprint of* ABDO Publishing Co Inc

Levesque Publications, *distributed by* University of Hawaii Press

Levine Querido, *distributed by* Chronicle Books

Lexington Books, *imprint of* Rowman & Littlefield Publishing Group, *distributor for* The Colonial Williamsburg Foundation

LexisNexis®, *division of* RELX Group PLC, *distributor for* Standard Publishing Corp

LexisNexis® Matthew Bender®, *member of* The LexisNexis® Group

Libraries Unlimited, *imprint of* ABC-CLIO

Library du Liban (Lebanon), *distributed by* International Book Centre Inc

The Library of America, *distributed by* Penguin Group USA, A Penguin Random House Company, Penguin Random House Inc

Library of Congress-Center for the Book, *distributed by* Oak Knoll Press

Library of Islam, *imprint of* Kazi Publications Inc

Libri Canali Bassi, *distributed by* Edgewise Press Inc

Life Cycle Books, *division of* Life Cycle Books Ltd (Canada)

Life on the Edge, *imprint of* Focus on the Family

LifeGuide Bible Studies, *imprint of* InterVarsity Press

LifeLearn, *distributor for* Teton NewMedia Inc, *distributed by* Teton NewMedia Inc

LifeTools, *imprint of* American Psychological Association

LifeWay Christian Resources, *distributor for* Casa Bautista de Publicaciones

The Light, *imprint of* Tughra Books

Light & Life Publishing Co, *distributor for* Saint Herman Press

Light Technology Publishing, *distributed by* Gem Guides Book Co

Lighthouse Press, *imprint of* ProStar Publications Inc

Lighthouse Publishing of the Carolinas, *division of* Iron Stream Media, *affiliate of* Christian Devotions Ministries

Lightning Rod Press, *imprint of* American Philosophical Society

Liguori, *imprint of* Liguori Publications

Libros Liguori, *imprint of* Liguori Publications

Liguori Publications, *distributor for* Redemptorist Publications

Philip E Lilienthal, *imprint of* University of California Press

LIM Editrice SRL (Italy), *distributor for* Pendragon Press

Limelight Editions, *imprint of* Rowman & Littlefield Publishing Group

Limestone Press, *distributed by* University of Alaska Press

Liminal 11, *distributed by* Sterling Publishing Co Inc

Line 6, *distributed by* Hal Leonard Corp

John Liner Organization, *subsidiary of* Standard Publishing Corp

Linnaean Press, *imprint of* Bentley Publishers

Lippincott Williams & Wilkins, *unit of* Wolters Kluwer Health

Lippincott, Williams & Wilkins, *imprint of* Wolters Kluwer US Corp

Lips (Magazine & Press), *distributed by* Cross-Cultural Communications

LIS (Legal Information Services), *subsidiary of* CCH, a Wolters Kluwer business

Listening Library®, *imprint of* Books on Tape™, Penguin Random House LLC, *distributed by* Books on Tape™

Literary House Press, *distributed by* Cornell Maritime Press

Literary Reprint Series, *imprint of* University of Alaska Press

Literature & Arts, *imprint of* Her Own Words LLC

Literature & Thought, *imprint of* Perfection Learning

Litigation Group, *division of* Public Citizen

little bee books, *distributed by* Simon & Schuster, Inc, Simon & Schuster Sales Division

Little Bigfoot, *imprint of* Sasquatch Books

Little, Brown, *distributor for* Parachute Publishing LLC

Little, Brown & Company, *distributor for* Alloy Entertainment LLC

Little, Brown and Company, *division of* Hachette Book Group

Little, Brown Books for Young Readers, *division of* Hachette Book Group

Little, Brown Spark, *imprint of* Little, Brown and Company

The Little Entrepreneur, *imprint of* Harper Arrington Publishing & Media, *distributed by* Harper Arrington Publishing

Little Island Press, *distributed by* University of Hawaii Press

Little Pickle Press, *imprint of* Sourcebooks LLC

Little Room Press, *distributed by* Fordham University Press

Little Shepherd, *imprint of* Scholastic Trade Division

Little Simon, *imprint of* Simon & Schuster Children's Publishing

Liturgical Press, *division of* The Order of St Benedict Inc, *distributor for* Cistercian Publications

Liturgical Press Academic, *imprint of* Liturgical Press

Liturgical Press Books, *imprint of* Liturgical Press

Liturgy Training Publications, *subsidiary of* Archdiocese of Chicago, *distributor for* United States Catholic Conference Publications (select titles)

Liveright, *imprint of* W W Norton & Company Inc, *distributed by* W W Norton & Company Inc

Living Books, *imprint of* Tyndale House Publishers Inc

Living Language, *imprint of* Penguin Random House LLC

Living Lessons, *distributed by* Hachai Publishing

Livingston Press, *division of* University of West Alabama, *distributor for* Swallow's Tale Press

Llewellyn, *imprint of* Llewellyn Publications

Llewellyn Publications, *division of* Llewellyn Worldwide Ltd, *distributor for* Blue Angel, Lo Scarabeo

Llewellyn Worldwide, *distributed by* Gem Guides Book Co

Locks Art Publications/Locks Gallery, *division of* Locks Gallery

Logan Brothers, *distributor for* Teton NewMedia Inc

Logion Press, *imprint of* Gospel Publishing House

Logos, *imprint of* Bridge-Logos

Logos Press, *imprint of* thinkBiotech LLC

Lombardy Studios, *distributed by* Casemate | publishers

Lominger Inc, *distributed by* Center for Creative Leadership LLC

Lone Star Audio, *imprint of* Recorded Books Inc, an RBmedia company

Lonely Planet, *distributed by* Hachette Book Group

Lonely Planet Kids, *imprint of* Lonely Planet

Long River Press, *imprint of* Sinomedia International Group

Longman, *distributor for* Marriage Transformation LLC, *distributed by* Trans-Atlantic Publications Inc

The Lontar Foundation, *distributed by* University of Hawaii Press

Looking Glass Library, *imprint of* ABDO Publishing Co Inc

Looseleaf Law Publications Inc, *division of* Warodean Corp

Lorenz Educational Press, *division of* The Lorenz Corp

Lorimer, *distributed by* Casemate | publishers

Los Angeles Times Crosswords, *imprint of* Random House Reference/Random House Puzzles & Games

Lost Coast Press, *imprint of* Cypress House

Lost Horse Press, *distributed by* University of Washington Press

Lotus Press, *division of* Lotus Brands Inc, Lotus Brands Inc, *distributor for* Back to Eden Books, Dipti, East West Cultural Center, Les Editions ETC, Inner Worlds Music, November Moon, SABDA, Sadhana Publications, Samata Books, Sri Aurobindo Ashram, Star Sounds

Love Inspired®, *imprint of* Harlequin Enterprises Ltd, Love Inspired Books

Love Inspired Books, *imprint of* Harlequin Enterprises Ltd

Love Inspired® Historical, *imprint of* Love Inspired Books

Love Inspired® Suspense, *imprint of* Love Inspired Books

Lovestruck, *imprint of* Entangled Publishing LLC

Loveswept, *imprint of* Penguin Random House LLC, Random House Publishing Group

LPC Group Inc, *distributor for* Dark Horse Comics

LRP Magazine Group, *subsidiary of* LRP Publications

LRS, *division of* Library Reproduction Service

LRT Editions, *distributed by* Casemate | publishers

Lucas Books, *imprint of* Penguin Random House LLC, Random House Publishing Group

Lucent Press, *imprint of* The Rosen Publishing Group Inc, *distributor for* Greenhaven Press, KidHaven Press

Lucky Marble Books, *imprint of* PageSpring Publishing

Lucky Spool, *distributed by* The Taunton Press Inc

Lucky Spool Media, *distributed by* Harry N Abrams Inc

Luna Books, *imprint of* Harlequin Enterprises Ltd

Lund Humphries/Ashgate, *distributor for* National Gallery of Art

LW Books, *imprint of* Schiffer Publishing Ltd

Lynn-Reinner Publishing, *distributor for* University of California Institute on Global Conflict & Cooperation

Lynx House Press, *distributed by* University of Washington Press

The Lyons Press, *imprint of* The Globe Pequot Press

Lyrical Press, *imprint of* Kensington Publishing Corp

Lyrical Shine, *imprint of* Kensington Publishing Corp

Lyrical Underground, *imprint of* Kensington Publishing Corp

M & H Type, *division of* The Arion Press

M-Audio, *distributed by* Hal Leonard Corp

The M Press, *imprint of* Dark Horse Comics

Pat MacKay Projects, *imprint of* Quite Specific Media Group Ltd

Macmillan, *subsidiary of* Verlagsgruppe Georg von Holtzbrinck GmbH, Verlagsgruppe Georg von Holtzbrinck GmbH, *distributor for* Bloomsbury Publishing Inc, The College Board, Tom Doherty Associates, LLC, Entangled Publishing LLC, National Association of Broadcasters (NAB), Papercutz, Sounds True Inc

Macmillan Audio, *division of* Macmillan

Macmillan Caribbean, *distributed by* Interlink Publishing Group Inc

Macmillan Learning, *subsidiary of* Macmillan

Macmillan/McGraw-Hill, *imprint of* McGraw-Hill Education

Macmillan Reference USA™, *imprint of* Gale

MacroPrintBooks, *imprint of* Science & Humanities Press

MacVan Maps, *distributed by* Wide World of Maps Inc

MAD Books, *imprint of* DC Comics Inc

Mad Creek Books, *imprint of* The Ohio State University Press

Madison Area Community Supported Agriculture Coalition, *distributed by* Chelsea Green Publishing Co

Mage Persian Editions, *imprint of* Mage Publishers Inc

Maggid, *imprint of* The Toby Press LLC

Magic Readers, *imprint of* ABDO Publishing Co Inc

Magic Wagon, *imprint of* ABDO Publishing Co Inc

Magill's Choice, *imprint of* Salem Press

Magination Press®, *imprint of* American Psychological Association

Magnes Press, *distributed by* Gefen Books

MAGNI, *imprint of* The Magni Co

Magni Co, *distributed by* BPC

The Magni Co, *subsidiary of* The Magni Group Inc

Maharishi University of Management Press, *subsidiary of* Maharishi University of Management, *distributed by* Penguin Group USA, A Penguin Random House Company (select titles)

Main Street Books, *imprint of* Penguin Random House LLC

Maine Appalachian Trail Club, *distributed by* Appalachian Trail Conservancy (ATC)

Majestic Press, *distributed by* Gem Guides Book Co

JA Majors, *distributor for* MedBooks Inc

Make Me A World, *imprint of* Random House Children's Books

MakeMusic Inc, *distributed by* Alfred Music

Management Sciences for Health, *distributed by* Kumarian Press

Manchester University Press, *distributed by* Palgrave Macmillan

Mandala Earth, *imprint of* Insight Editions, *distributed by* Simon & Schuster

Mandel Vilar Press, *affiliate of* Americas for Conservation + the Arts, *distributor for* Dryad Press

Manhattan Prep, *distributed by* Simon & Schuster Sales Division

Manhattan Prep Publishing, *distributed by* Simon & Schuster, Inc

Manning Publications, *distributed by* Simon & Schuster, Inc

Manning Publications Co, *distributed by* Dreamtech Press, Pearson Education, Simon & Schuster, Inc (US & CN), Simon & Schuster Sales Division

Manoa Heritage Center, *distributed by* University of Hawaii Press

Manuscript, *distributed by* Simon & Schuster, Inc

The Manuscript Society, *distributed by* Oak Knoll Press

Le Manuscrit, *distributed by* Beach Lloyd Publishers LLC

Many Hats Media, *distributor for* Sourced Media Books

MAPART Publishing, *distributor for* Michelin Maps & Guides

Maple Leaf Audio, *imprint of* Recorded Books Inc, an RBmedia company

MAR*CO Products Inc, *distributor for* Boulden, Educational Media, HarperCollins, National Center for Youth Issues/STARS, *distributed by* ASCA, Boulden Publishing, Burnell Books, Calloway House, Career Kids FYI, CFKR Career, Character Development, Community Intervention, Courage to Change, Cress Productions Co, EDU Reference, Educational Media Corp, Incentive Plus, Jist, Mental Health Resources, National Center for Youth Issues/STARS, National Professional Resources, National Resource Center for Youth Services, Paperbacks for Educators, School Speciality, SourceResource, WRS Group, YouthLight Inc

Marble Arch, *imprint of* Atria Books

Maren Green Publishing Inc, *distributed by* Crabtree Publishing Co

Marine Survey Press, *imprint of* Marine Education Textbooks

Marine Techniques Publishing, *distributor for* Academic Press, Best Publishing Co, Butterworth-Heinemann, Clarkson Research Services Ltd, Elsevier, Science & Technology Books, Focal Press, Gulf Professional Publishers, PennWell Business & Industrial Division, W B Saunders Co, Waterfront Soundings Productions, Witherby Seamanship International Ltd, *distributed by* Elsevier Science, Technology & Business Books, PennWell Business & Industrial Division

Mariner Books, *imprint of* Houghton Mifflin Harcourt Trade & Reference Division

Marion Institute, *distributed by* Chelsea Green Publishing Co

Ashley Mark Publishing Co, *imprint of* Hal Leonard Corp, *distributed by* Hal Leonard Corp

marketumbrella.org, *distributed by* Chelsea Green Publishing Co

MarketResearch.com, *distributor for* Primary Research Group Inc

Edward B Marks Music, *distributed by* Hal Leonard Corp

Marmac Publishing Co, *distributed by* Pelican Publishing Co

Marquette University Press, *division of* Marquette University

Marquis Who's Who, *imprint of* Marquis Who's Who Ventures LLC

Marriage Transformation LLC, *distributed by* Longman

Carole Marsh Books, *imprint of* Gallopade International Inc

Carole Marsh Mysteries, *imprint of* Gallopade International Inc

Marshall Cavendish Adult Trade, *imprint of* Marshall Cavendish Education

Marshall Cavendish Benchmark, *imprint of* Marshall Cavendish Education

Marshall Cavendish Digital, *imprint of* Marshall Cavendish Education

Marshall Cavendish Education, *member of* Times International Publishing Group, *imprint of* Marshall Cavendish Education, *distributed by* Marshall Cavendish Ltd (UK)

Marshall Cavendish Ltd, *distributor for* Marshall Cavendish Education

Marshall Cavendish Reference, *imprint of* Marshall Cavendish Education

Marsilio, *imprint of* Rizzoli International Publications Inc

Darvin Martin CDs, *distributed by* Closson Press

Rux Martin Books, *imprint of* Houghton Mifflin Harcourt Trade & Reference Division

Martindale-Hubbell®, *imprint of* Martindale LLC

Marvel, *imprint of* Disney Publishing Worldwide

Marvel Illustrated, *imprint of* ABDO Publishing Co Inc

Marvel Picture Books, *imprint of* ABDO Publishing Co Inc

Marvel Worldwide Inc, *distributed by* Hachette Book Group

Marvelous Spirit Press, *imprint of* Loving Healing Press Inc

Helen Marx/Turtle Point, *imprint of* Turtle Point Press

Maryland Historical Trust Press, *distributed by* Cornell Maritime Press

Maryland History Press, *distributor for* Tapestry Press Ltd

Maryland Sea Grant Program, *distributed by* Cornell Maritime Press

Mason Crest Publishers, *imprint of* National Highlights

The Massachusetts Historical Society, *distributed by* University of Virginia Press

Master Books®, *imprint of* New Leaf Publishing Group Inc

Masters of Photography, *imprint of* Aperture Books

Mastery Education, *subsidiary of* Peoples Educational Holdings Inc

Masthof Press, *distributor for* Closson Press

Math Solutions®, *unit of* Houghton Mifflin Harcourt

Mathematica Josephina, *distributed by* American Mathematical Society

Mathematical Society of Japan, *distributed by* American Mathematical Society

Matheson Trust, *distributed by* Fons Vitae

Adam Matthew, *imprint of* SAGE Publishing

Maturango Museum, *distributed by* Gem Guides Book Co

Maunsel & Co Publishers, *imprint of* Academica Press

Maverick Arts Publishing, *distributed by* Lerner Publishing Group Inc

Mayo Clinic, *distributed by* Simon & Schuster, Inc

McBooks Press, *imprint of* Rowman & Littlefield Publishing Group

MCD/FSG, *imprint of* Farrar, Straus & Giroux, LLC

Margaret K McElderry Books, *imprint of* Simon & Schuster Children's Publishing

McFarland & Co Ltd Publishers, *subsidiary of* McFarland

McGraw-Hill, *imprint of* McGraw-Hill Science, Engineering, Mathematics, *distributor for* SME (Society of Manufacturing Engineers), *distributed by* American Academy of Environmental Engineers & Scientists®, American Water Works Association (AWWA), NACE International, SAMS Technical Publishing LLC, SME (Society of Manufacturing Engineers)

McGraw-Hill Career Education, *division of* McGraw-Hill Higher Education

McGraw-Hill Contemporary, *imprint of* McGraw-Hill Education

McGraw-Hill Contemporary Learning Series, *division of* McGraw-Hill Higher Education

McGraw-Hill Create, *division of* McGraw-Hill Higher Education, *imprint of* McGraw-Hill Education

McGraw-Hill Education Australia, New Zealand & South Africa, *imprint of* McGraw-Hill Education

McGraw-Hill Education Europe, Middle East and Africa, *imprint of* McGraw-Hill Education

McGraw-Hill Education Latin America, *imprint of* McGraw-Hill Education

McGraw-Hill Education Mexico, *imprint of* McGraw-Hill Education

McGraw-Hill Education Spain, *imprint of* McGraw-Hill Education

McGraw-Hill Higher Education, *division of* McGraw-Hill Education

McGraw-Hill Humanities, Social Sciences, Languages, *division of* McGraw-Hill Higher Education, *imprint of* McGraw-Hill Education

McGraw-Hill/Irwin, *division of* McGraw-Hill Higher Education, *imprint of* McGraw-Hill Education, McGraw-Hill Higher Education

McGraw-Hill Learning Solutions, *imprint of* McGraw-Hill Higher Education

McGraw-Hill Professional, *imprint of* McGraw-Hill Education, *distributed by* PPI, A Kaplan Company

McGraw-Hill Professional Publishing, *distributor for* American Society for Quality (ASQ)

McGraw-Hill Professional Publishing Group, *division of* McGraw-Hill Education

McGraw-Hill Ryerson, *imprint of* McGraw-Hill Education

McGraw-Hill School Education Group, *division of* McGraw-Hill Education, *imprint of* McGraw-Hill Education

McGraw-Hill Science, Engineering, Mathematics, *division of* McGraw-Hill Higher Education, *imprint of* McGraw-Hill Education, McGraw-Hill Higher Education

McGraw-Hill Professional Development, *imprint of* McGraw-Hill Education

Anne McKinney Career Series, *imprint of* PREP Publishing

McKissick Museum, *distributed by* University of South Carolina Press

McWhiney Foundation Press/State House Press, *distributed by* Texas A&M University Press

Md Books, *imprint of* May Davenport Publishers

MDR, A D&B Co, *division of* Dun & Bradstreet Corp

Mean Free Path, *distributor for* American Society for Nondestructive Testing

R S Means from The Gordian Group, *distributed by* John Wiley & Sons Inc

Measuring Up®, *imprint of* Mastery Education

Medals of America, *distributor for* Medals of America Press

Medals of America Press, *division of* Medals of America, *distributed by* Medals of America

MedBooks Inc, *division of* Professional Education Workshops & Seminars, *distributed by* JA Majors

Medford Press, *imprint of* Plexus Publishing, Inc

Medical Economics, *distributed by* OptumInsight™

Medical Group Management Association (MGMA), *distributor for* American Medical Association, Aspen Publishers, Greenbranch, HAP (Health Adminstration Press), Jones & Bartlett Learning, J Wiley & Sons

Medical Publishing (Gefen), *division of* Gefen Books

Medieval Institute Publications, *division of* Medieval Institute of Western Michigan University

Mel Bay, *imprint of* Mel Bay Publications Inc

Mel Bay Publications Inc, *distributor for* AMA, William Bay Music, Dancing Hands, Stefan Grossman's Guitar Workshop

Paul Mellon Centre, *distributed by* Yale University Press

Memoirs, *imprint of* American Philosophical Society

Menasha Ridge Press, *division of* Keen Communications, *imprint of* AdventureKEEN

The Menil Collection, *distributed by* Yale University Press

Menil Foundation, *distributed by* University of Texas Press

Mental Health Resources, *distributor for* MAR*CO Products Inc

Mercatorfonds, *distributed by* Yale University Press

Merck, *imprint of* John Wiley & Sons Inc

Merck Publishing, *distributed by* Simon & Schuster, Inc, Simon & Schuster Sales Division

Mercury Learning & Information, *distributed by* Stylus Publishing LLC

Meredith Music, *distributed by* Hal Leonard Corp

Merehurst Ltd, *imprint of* Tuttle Publishing

Meriwether Publishing, *division of* Pioneer Drama Service Inc

Merriam-Webster Inc, *subsidiary of* Encyclopaedia Britannica Inc

Frank Merriwell Inc, *subsidiary of* National Learning Corp

Merry Muse Press, *imprint of* Loft Press Inc

MerwinAsia, *distributed by* University of Hawaii Press

Mesorah Publications Ltd, *distributor for* NCSY Publications

Messianic Jewish Publishers, *division of* Messianic Jewish Communications, *distributor for* Chosen People Ministries, First Fruits of Zion, Jewish New Testament Publications

Metalmark, *imprint of* Penn State University Press

Metamorphic Press, *distributed by* Chelsea Green Publishing Co

Metro Maps, *division of* Wide World of Maps Inc, *distributed by* Wide World of Maps Inc

Metropolitan Books, *imprint of* Henry Holt and Company, LLC

Metropolitan Classics, *division of* Fort Ross Inc

The Metropolitan Museum of Art, *distributed by* Yale University Press

MFA Publications, *imprint of* Museum of Fine Arts Boston, *distributed by* Thames & Hudson (outside of North America)

Michelin Maps & Guides, *division of* Michelin North America Inc, *distributed by* Langenscheidt Publishing Group, MAPART Publishing (CN only), NBN (guides for North America), Editions du Renouveau Pedagogique (French titles in Canada), Penguin Canada (English titles in Canada)

Michie, *imprint of* LexisNexis®

Michigan Municipal League, *affiliate of* National League of Cities, *distributor for* Crisp Books

Michigan State University Press (MSU Press), *division of* Michigan State University, *distributor for* Aquatic Ecosystem Health & Management Society Books, MSU Museum, University of Manitoba Press, *distributed by* UBC Press, Canada

Microcosm Books, *imprint of* TFH Publications Inc

Microtraining Associates, *imprint of* Alexander Street, a ProQuest Company

Midewin Series, *imprint of* High Tide Press

Midnight Ink, *imprint of* Llewellyn Publications

Midnight Marquee Press Inc, *affiliate of* Luminary Press

Midrashic Editions, *imprint of* Cross-Cultural Communications

Midwest Library Service, *distributor for* Primary Research Group Inc

Mighty Bright, *distributed by* Hal Leonard Corp

Mighty Media Junior Readers, *imprint of* Mighty Media Press

Mighty Media Kids, *imprint of* Mighty Media Press

Mighty Media Press, *division of* Mighty Media Inc

Mike Murach & Associates Inc, *distributed by* Shroff Publishers (reprints)

Milady, *division of* Cengage Learning

Milestone Documents, *imprint of* Schlager Group Inc

Milestone Press, *imprint of* University of Georgia Press

Milet Publishing Ltd, *imprint of* Tuttle Publishing, *distributed by* Tuttle Publishing

Military History Press, *distributed by* Casemate | publishers

Military Living Publications, *division of* Military Marketing Services Inc, Military Marketing Services Inc

Military Medals of America, *imprint of* Medals of America Press

Millbrook Press, *imprint of* Lerner Publishing Group Inc

Kane Miller Books, *imprint of* EDC Publishing

White Burkett Miller Center, *distributed by* University Press of America Inc

Milliken Publishing Co, *division of* The Lorenz Corp, The Lorenz Corp

Denene Millner Books, *imprint of* Simon & Schuster Children's Publishing

Mills & Boon Large Print, *distributed by* Thorndike Press®

Sally Milner Publishing, *distributed by* Sterling Publishing Co Inc

minedition, *imprint of* Boyds Mills & Kane

Mineral Land Publications, *distributed by* Gem Guides Book Co

The Minerals, Metals & Materials Society (TMS), *affiliate of* AIME, *distributed by* Springer

Minnesota Historical Society Press, *division of* Minnesota Historical Society

Minotaur Books, *imprint of* St Martin's Press, LLC

MIRA, *imprint of* Harlequin Enterprises Ltd

Miranda Press Trade Division, *imprint of* Cognizant Communication Corp

Miss Jackie Inc, *distributed by* Gryphon House Inc

Missouri History Museum, *distributed by* University of Missouri Press

Missouri Life Magazine, *distributed by* University of Missouri Press

MIT, *distributor for* The AEI Press

MIT Kids Press, *imprint of* Candlewick Press

MIT Press, *distributed by* DawnSignPress

The MIT Press, *distributor for* AAAI Press, Afterall Books, Canadian Centre for Architecture, no place press, Semiotext(e)

MITeen Press, *imprint of* Candlewick Press

MJF Books, *imprint of* Fine Creative Media, Inc

MMPBooks, *distributed by* Casemate | publishers

MOAC, *imprint of* John Wiley & Sons Inc

Farhang Moaser, *distributed by* Ibex Publishers

Model Centrum Progres, *distributed by* Casemate | publishers

Modern Drummer Publications, *distributed by* Hal Leonard Corp

Modern History Press, *imprint of* Loving Healing Press Inc

The Modern Language Initiative, *imprint of* Fordham University Press

Modern Learning Press, *imprint of* EPS/School Specialty Literacy & Intervention

Modern Library, *imprint of* Penguin Random House LLC, Random House Publishing Group

Modern Masters, *imprint of* Abbeville Publishing Group

Modern Publishing, *division of* Kappa Books Publishers LLC

Mojave River Valley Museum, *distributed by* Gem Guides Book Co

Moleskine, *distributed by* Chronicle Books, Hachette Book Group

Moleskine Books, *distributed by* Princeton Architectural Press

Moliere & Co, *imprint of* LinguaText LLC

Moll Anderson Productions, *distributed by* Simon & Schuster, Inc

Monacelli Press, *distributor for* Winterthur Museum, Garden & Library

The Monacelli Press, *imprint of* Phaidon Press Ltd, *distributed by* Penguin Group USA, A Penguin Random House Company

Monacelli Studio, *imprint of* The Monacelli Press

Monarch Books, *distributed by* Kregel Publications

Arnoldo Mondadori Electa, *distributed by* Trans-Atlantic Publications Inc

Mondo, *imprint of* Mondo Publishing

Moneta Publications, *distributed by* Chelsea Green Publishing Co

Monjeu Press, *distributed by* Gryphon House Inc

Monostereo, *distributed by* Simon & Schuster Audio

Monthly Review Press, *division of* Monthly Review Foundation Inc, Monthly Review Foundation Inc, *distributed by* New York University Press

Moody Press, *distributor for* Focus on the Family

Moody Publishers, *affiliate of* Ministry of Moody Bible Institute, The Moody Bible Institute

Moon City Press, *distributed by* The University of Arkansas Press

Moon River Publishing, *distributed by* BPC

MoonDance Press, *imprint of* Quarto Publishing Group USA Inc

Morehouse Publishing, *imprint of* Church Publishing Inc

Morgan James Faith, *imprint of* Morgan James Publishing

Morgan James Fiction, *imprint of* Morgan James Publishing

Morgan James Kids, *imprint of* Morgan James Publishing

Morgan Kaufmann, *imprint of* Elsevier Inc

MorningStar Music Publishers, *imprint of* ECS Publishing Group

Morrow Gift, *imprint of* HarperCollins General Books Group

William Morrow, *imprint of* HarperCollins General Books Group

William Morrow Paperbacks, *imprint of* HarperCollins General Books Group

Mortons Media Group, *distributed by* Casemate | publishers

Mosaica Press, *distributed by* Feldheim Publishers

Mosby, *imprint of* Elsevier, Health Sciences Division, *distributor for* OptumInsight™, *distributed by* Fire Engineering Books & Videos, OptumInsight™

Moselle River, *distributed by* Casemate | publishers

Motorbooks, *imprint of* Quarto Publishing Group USA Inc, *distributor for* Haynes North America Inc, *distributed by* Heimburger House Publishing Co

Paul Mould Publishing, *imprint of* Empire Publishing Service, *distributed by* Empire Publishing Service

Mount Blue, *imprint of* Genesis Press Inc

Mount Ida Press, *distributed by* State University of New York Press

Mt Nittany Press, *imprint of* Eifrig Publishing LLC

Mount Vernon Ladies Association, *distributed by* The University of Virginia Press

Mountain Air Books, *imprint of* Mountain n' Air Books

Mountain n' Air Books, *distributor for* Tom Harrison Cartography

Mountain Press Publishing, *distributed by* Gem Guides Book Co

Mountain Press Publishing Co, *distributor for* Bucking Horse Books, Clark City Press, Hops Press, Npustin Press, RainStone Press, Western Edge Press

Mountain Sports Press Series, *imprint of* Mountain Press Publishing Co

Mountaineers Books, *distributor for* Appalachian Trail Conservancy (ATC)

The Mountaineers Books, *division of* The Mountaineers, *distributor for* Adventure Cycling Association, The American Alpine Club Press, Appalachian Trail Conservancy (ATC), Colorado Mountain Club Press, Green Trails Maps, *distributed by* Gem Guides Book Co

De Gruyter Mouton, *imprint of* Walter de Gruyter GmbH, Walter de Gruyter GmbH, *distributed by* Walter de Gruyter Inc

The Mozhai Foundation, *distributed by* University of Hawaii Press

Moznaim Publishing Corp, *distributor for* Avamra Institute, Breslov Research Institute, Red Wheel/Weiser/Conari

MPS, *distributed by* Gem Guides Book Co

Mrs Wordsmith, *distributed by* Simon & Schuster, Inc

MRTS, *imprint of* Arizona Center for Medieval & Renaissance Studies (ACMRS), Arizona Center for Medieval & Renaissance Studies (ACMRS)

MSU Museum, *distributed by* Michigan State University Press (MSU Press)

MTI, *distributed by* NACE International

MTV Books, *imprint of* Gallery Books

MTV Press, *distributed by* powerHouse Books

Mudborn Press, *imprint of* Bandanna Books

Coleccion Mujeres de Palabra, *imprint of* University of Puerto Rico Press

Mulholland Books, *imprint of* Little, Brown and Company

Multnomah, *imprint of* Crown Publishing Group

Museon Publishing, *distributed by* Gem Guides Book Co

Museum of Early Southern Decorative Arts, *distributed by* The University of North Carolina Press

The Museum of Modern Art (MoMA), *distributed by* Distributed Art Publishers (DAP) (US & CN only)

Museum of Modern Art Children's Books, *distributed by* Harry N Abrams Inc

Museum of New Mexico Press, *unit of* New Mexico State Department of Cultural Affairs, *distributed by* University of New Mexico Press

Music Inc, *imprint of* Alfred Music

Music Minus One, *distributed by* Hal Leonard Corp

Music Sales, *distributed by* Welcome Enterprises Inc

Music Sales America, *distributed by* Hal Leonard Corp

Music Sales Corp, *distributed by* Beekman Books Inc

Musicians Institute Press, *imprint of* Hal Leonard Corp, *distributed by* Hal Leonard Corp

Muswell Hill Press, *distributed by* State University of New York Press

My Healthy Church, *imprint of* Gospel Publishing House

Mycroft & Moran, *imprint of* Arkham House Publishers Inc

Myers Education Press, *distributed by* Stylus Publishing LLC

MyReportLinks.com Books, *imprint of* Enslow Publishing LLC

Mystery Library, *imprint of* Recorded Books Inc, an RBmedia company

Mystic Books, *imprint of* Regal Crest Enterprises

NACE International, *distributor for* ASM International, ASTM, AWS, Butterworth-Heinemann, Cambridge University Press, CASTI Publishing, Compass Publications, CRC Press, Marcel Dekker Inc, E&FN Spon, Elsevier Science Publishers, Gulf Publishing, Industrial Press, Institute of Materials, ISO, McGraw-Hill, MTI, Prentice Hall, Professional Publications, SSPC, Swedish Corrosion Institute, John Wiley & Sons Inc, *distributed by* Australasian Corrosion Association Inc

Jonathan Napela Center, Brigham Young University-Hawaii, *distributed by* University of Hawaii Press

Narosa Publishing House, *distributed by* American Mathematical Society

Narratore Press, *imprint of* The Lentz Leadership Institute LLC

NASCO, *distributor for* National Council of Teachers of Mathematics (NCTM)

NASSP, *imprint of* National Association of Secondary School Principals (NASSP)

NASW Press, *division of* National Association of Social Workers (NASW)

Nataraj, *imprint of* New World Library

National Academies Press (NAP), *division of* National Academies

National Archives & Records Administration, *distributed by* J J Keller & Associates, Inc

National Association of Broadcasters (NAB), *distributed by* Allyn & Bacon, Lawrence Erlbaum Associates, Focal Press, Macmillan, Tab Books

National Book Co, *division of* Educational Research Associates

National Book Network, *distributor for* C&T Publishing Inc, Impact Publications/Development Concepts Inc, *distributed by* Gem Guides Book Co, Heimburger House Publishing Co

National Book Network (NBN), *distributor for* Association for Talent Development (ATD) Press

National Center Early Childhood Workforce, *distributed by* Gryphon House Inc

National Center for Children in Poverty, *division of* Mailman School of Public Health at Columbia University

National Center for Youth Issues/STARS, *distributor for* MAR*CO Products Inc, *distributed by* MAR*CO Products Inc

National Council of Examiners for Engineering & Surveying, *distributed by* PPI, A Kaplan Company

National Council of Teachers of Mathematics (NCTM), *distributed by* Eric Armin Inc Education Ctr, Delta Education, Didax Educational Resources, Educators Outlet, ETA Cuisenaire, Lakeshore Learning Materials, NASCO, Spectrum

National Doll Society of America, *division of* Success Advertising & Publishing

National Gallery, London, *distributed by* Yale University Press

National Gallery of Art, *distributed by* Abrams, DAP, Lund Humphries/Ashgate, Princeton University Press, Thames & Hudson, University of Chicago Press, Yale University Press

National Gallery of Singapore, *distributed by* Penn State University Press

National Genealogical Society, *distributed by* Heritage Books Inc

National Geographic, *distributor for* The Colonial Williamsburg Foundation

National Geographic Books, *division of* National Geographic Partners, *distributed by* HarperCollins UK (Australia, New Zealand & UK-kids books), Penguin Random House (worldwide exc UK), Simon & Schuster UK (UK-adult books)

National Geographic Kids Books, *imprint of* National Geographic Books

National Geographic Learning, *unit of* Cengage Learning

National Geographic Under the Stars, *imprint of* National Geographic Books

National Historic Route 66 Federation, *distributed by* Gem Guides Book Co

National Institute of Occupational Safety & Health, *distributed by* J J Keller & Associates, Inc

National Professional Resources, *distributor for* Council for Exceptional Children (CEC), MAR*CO Products Inc, *distributed by* Council for Exceptional Children (CEC)

National Ranching Heritage Center, *distributed by* Texas Tech University Press

National Resource Center for The First-Year Experience & Students in Transition, *distributed by* Stylus Publishing LLC

National Resource Center for Youth Services, *division of* University of Oklahoma Outreach, *distributor for* MAR*CO Products Inc

National Trust, *distributed by* Rizzoli International Publications Inc

The National Underwriter Co, *division of* ALM Media LLC

Native Books, *distributed by* University of Hawaii Press

Native Voices, *imprint of* BPC

Natural Inspirations/Brush Creek, *distributed by* Gem Guides Book Co

Nature Study Guides, *imprint of* AdventureKEEN

Nature Trails Press, *distributed by* Gem Guides Book Co

Naturegraph, *distributed by* Gem Guides Book Co

Naval Institute Press, *division of* US Naval Institute, *distributed by* Publishers Group West (PGW) (digital only)

NavPress, *imprint of* NavPress Publishing Group, *distributed by* Tyndale House Publishers Inc

NavPress Publishing Group, *division of* The Navigators, *distributed by* Tyndale House Publishers Inc

NBN, *distributor for* Michelin Maps & Guides

NCP, *imprint of* New City Press

NCSY Publications, *distributed by* Mesorah Publications Ltd

NDY Publishing, *division of* Rothstein Associates Inc

NEA Professional Library, *imprint of* National Education Association (NEA)

Near Eastern Press, *imprint of* Holmes Publishing Group LLC

Neibauer Press, *division of* Louis Neibauer Co Inc, Louis Neibauer Co Inc

Nelson Books, *imprint of* Thomas Nelson

Grupo Nelson, *imprint of* Thomas Nelson

Neo-Assyrian Text Corpus, *distributed by* Penn State University Press

Nevada Publications, *distributor for* Gem Guides Book Co, *distributed by* Gem Guides Book Co

New American Fiction Series, *imprint of* Green Integer

New American Poetry Series, *imprint of* Green Integer

New City, *distributed by* New City Press

New City Press, *division of* Focolare Movement, *distributor for* Ciudad Nueva (Argentina, Spain), New City (Great Britain)

New Criterion Books, *distributed by* St Augustine's Press Inc

New Directions Publishing Corp, *distributed by* W W Norton & Company Inc

New England AEYC, *distributed by* Gryphon House Inc

New England Bibliographies, *distributed by* Oak Knoll Press

New Era Productions, *distributed by* Gem Guides Book Co

New Falcon Publications, *imprint of* The Original Falcon Press

New Horizons Book Publishing Co, *imprint of* World Citizens

New Issues Poetry & Prose, *affiliate of* Western Michigan University

The New Jerusalem Bible, *imprint of* Penguin Random House LLC

New Leaf Books, *distributor for* Blue Poppy Press

New Leaf Press, *imprint of* New Leaf Publishing Group Inc

New Netherland Institute, *distributed by* State University of New York Press

New Pacific Press, *distributed by* North Atlantic Books

New Poets Series, *imprint of* BrickHouse Books Inc

New Readers Press, *division of* ProLiteracy, ProLiteracy, *distributor for* TESOL International Association, *distributed by* International Book Centre Inc

New Riders, *imprint of* Peachpit Press

New Shoots Publishing, *distributed by* Redleaf Press

New Traditions, *imprint of* Gallopade International Inc

New Village Press, *distributed by* New York University Press

New Win Publishing, *division of* Academic Learning Co LLC

New World Library, *division of* Whatever Publishing Inc, Whatever Publishing Inc

New World Paperbacks, *imprint of* International Publishers Co Inc

New York Academy of Sciences (NYAS), *distributed by* Wiley Blackwell Publishers

The New York Botanical Garden Press, *division of* New York Botanical Garden

New York Times Crosswords, *imprint of* Random House Reference/Random House Puzzles & Games

The New York Times Educational Publishing, *imprint of* The Rosen Publishing Group Inc

New York University Press, *distributor for* Monthly Review Press, New Village Press, *distributed by* Heimburger House Publishing Co

Newbridge Discovery Links, *imprint of* Sundance/Newbridge Publishing

Newbury Street Press, *imprint of* New England Historic Genealogical Society

The Newman Press, *imprint of* Paulist Press

NewSouth Books, *imprint of* NewSouth Inc, *distributor for* Europa Editions

Nexus Special Interests, *distributed by* TransAtlantic Publications Inc

NFB, *imprint of* NFB Publishing

NIAS Press, *distributed by* University of Hawaii Press

Nightfire, *imprint of* Tom Doherty Associates, LLC

Nightingale Editions, *imprint of* Cross-Cultural Communications

Nilgiri Press, *division of* Blue Mountain Center of Meditation

Nimbus Publishing Ltd, *distributed by* Down East Books

NISO Press, *imprint of* National Information Standards Organization (NISO)

no place press, *distributed by* The MIT Press

No Starch Press, *distributed by* O'Reilly Media Inc

Nodin Press, *distributed by* AdventureKEEN

Noel, *imprint of* Nova Science Publishers Inc

Noesis Press, *imprint of* The Davies Group Publishers

Noetic Books, *imprint of* New Harbinger Publications Inc

NOLO, *subsidiary of* Internet Brands Inc

Non-Duality Press, *imprint of* New Harbinger Publications Inc

Nonpareil Books, *imprint of* David R Godine Inc

North Atlantic Books, *division of* Society for the Study of Native Arts & Sciences, *distributor for* DharmaCafe, Energy Arts, Ergos Institute, Heaven & Earth Publications, New Pacific Press

North Beach-West Maui Benefit Fund Inc, *distributed by* University of Hawaii Press

North Carolina Museum of Art, *distributed by* The University of North Carolina Press

North Country Books, *imprint of* North Country Books Inc

North Point Press, *imprint of* Farrar, Straus & Giroux, LLC

Northern Illinois University Press, *imprint of* Cornell University Press

Northfield Publishing, *imprint of* Moody Publishers

NorthSouth Books, *distributed by* Simon & Schuster, Inc, Simon & Schuster Sales Division

Northwest Corner Books, *imprint of* Epicenter Press Inc

Northwest Distributors LLC, *distributed by* Gem Guides Book Co

Northwestern University Press, *distributor for* Lake Forest College Press (Chicago area studies), Tia Chucha Press

W W Norton & Company Inc, *distributor for* Abbeville Press, Blue Guides, George Braziller Inc, The Countryman Press, Fantagraphics Books, Kales Press, Liveright, New Directions Publishing Corp, The Overlook Press, Pegasus Books, Persea Books, Pushcart Press, Quantuck Lane Press, Thames & Hudson, Tilbury House Publishers, Tin House Books, Well-Trained Mind Press, Winterthur Museum, Garden & Library, *distributed by* Gem Guides Book Co, Heimburger House Publishing Co

Norton Young Readers, *imprint of* W W Norton & Company Inc

Norwalk Press, *imprint of* BPC

Nosy Crow, *imprint of* Candlewick Press

Noteflight, *distributed by* Hal Leonard Corp

Nova Biomedical Publications, *imprint of* Nova Science Publishers Inc

Nova Business & Management Publications, *imprint of* Nova Science Publishers Inc

Nova ESL Publications, *imprint of* Nova Science Publishers Inc

Nova Global Affairs Publications, *imprint of* Nova Science Publishers Inc

Nova History Publications, *imprint of* Nova Science Publishers Inc

Nova Music Publications, *imprint of* Nova Science Publishers Inc

Nova Publications, *imprint of* Nova Science Publishers Inc

Nova Southeastern University, *distributed by* Gryphon House Inc

Nova Video Productions, *imprint of* Nova Science Publishers Inc

Novalis, *distributor for* Twenty-Third Publications, *distributed by* Twenty-Third Publications

Novel-Ties Study Guides, *imprint of* Learning Links Inc

November Moon, *distributed by* Lotus Press

Novinka Publications, *imprint of* Nova Science Publishers Inc

Now I'm Reading!™, *imprint of* Penguin Random House LLC

Npustin Press, *distributed by* Mountain Press Publishing Co

NRH Press, *distributed by* Vandamere Press

NSTA Ebooks+, *imprint of* National Science Teachers Association (NSTA)

NSTA Kids, *imprint of* National Science Teachers Association (NSTA)

NSTA Press®, *imprint of* National Science Teachers Association (NSTA)

Nuclear Energy Agency, *distributed by* OECD Washington Center

Coleccion Nueve Pececitos, *imprint of* University of Puerto Rico Press

Number Success, *imprint of* Advance Publishing Inc

Nursesbooks.org, The Publishing Program of ANA, *division of* American Nurses Association

Nursing Knowledge Center, *imprint of* Nursesbooks.org, The Publishing Program of ANA

Nutri-Books, *distributor for* Ash Tree Publishing

Nylabone Products, *division of* TFH Publications Inc

Nystrom Education, *division of* Social Studies School Service

Oak Knoll Press, *distributor for* American Antiquarian Society, Bibliographical Society of America, Bibliographical Society of University of Virginia, The Bibliographical Society (UK), Block Museum, Boston College, John Carter Brown Library, Bryn Mawr College, Catalpa Press, Caxton Club, Center for Book Arts, Chapin Library, Cotsen Children's Library (Princeton), Fondation Custodia, The Grolier Club, Hes & De Graaf, Historic New Orleans Collection, Library of Congress-Center for the Book, The Manuscript Society, New England Bibliographies, Providence Athenaeum, Riven-

dale Press, Tate Galleries, Texas State Historical Association, Typophiles, Winterthur Museum, Yushodo Press

Oberlin College Press, *subsidiary of* Oberlin College

Obsessive Anonymous, *distributed by* Hazelden Publishing

Obsidian, *imprint of* Genesis Press Inc

Ocarina Books, *distributed by* University of Hawaii Press

Ocean Publishing, *imprint of* Square One Publishers Inc

Ocean Tree Books, *distributed by* Treasure Chest Books

Octavo Editions, *distributed by* Konecky & Konecky LLC

Octavo Press, *imprint of* Templegate Publishers

Octopus Books, *distributed by* Hachette Book Group

Odyssey Books, *division of* The Ciletti Publishing Group Inc

OECD Washington Center, *division of* Organization for Economic Cooperation & Development (France), *distributor for* International Energy Agency, International Transportation Forum, Nuclear Energy Agency

Ofeq Books, *distributed by* The Toby Press LLC

Office of External Affairs, *division of* RAND Corp

Office of the Federal Register, *distributed by* J J Keller & Associates, Inc

Office of the United Nations High Commissioner for Human Rights (OHCHR), *distributed by* United Nations Publications

Ohio State University Foreign Language Publications, *division of* Ohio State University Foreign Language Center

Ohio University Press, *distributor for* The Colonial Williamsburg Foundation

Old Farmer's Almanac, *distributed by* Houghton Mifflin Harcourt, Houghton Mifflin Harcourt Trade & Reference Division

Old Pond, *imprint of* Fox Chapel Publishing Co Inc

Olive Branch Press, *imprint of* Interlink Publishing Group Inc

Omnibus Press, *imprint of* Music Sales Group, *distributor for* Big Meteor Publishing, Gramophone

Omnific, *distributed by* Simon & Schuster Sales Division

Omohundro Institute of Early American History & Culture, *distributed by* The University of North Carolina Press

One Elm Books, *imprint of* Red Chair Press

One Elm Press, *distributed by* Lerner Publishing Group Inc

120 Days, *imprint of* Riverdale Avenue Books (RAB)

One Signal Publishers, *imprint of* Atria Books

1000 Readers, *imprint of* Gallopade International Inc

One World, *imprint of* Penguin Random House LLC, Random House Publishing Group

Oneworld Publications, *distributed by* Simon & Schuster, Inc

Oni Press, *distributed by* Simon & Schuster, Inc, Simon & Schuster Sales Division

Onyx, *imprint of* Penguin Group USA, A Penguin Random House Company

OPAMP Technical Books, *distributor for* Primary Research Group Inc

Open Books Press, *imprint of* Pen & Publish Inc, Pen & Publish LLC

Open Court Publishing Co, *division of* Cricket Media

Open Lens, *imprint of* Akashic Books

Open Road, *distributed by* Simon & Schuster Sales Division

Open Road Integrated Media, *distributor for* Philosophical Library Inc

Open Road Publishing, *distributed by* Simon & Schuster, Inc

Open Scroll, *imprint of* Bridge-Logos

Optimism Press, *imprint of* Portfolio

Options, *imprint of* Triumph Learning LLC

OptumInsight™, *distributor for* American Medical Association, Medical Economics, Mosby, *distributed by* American Medical Association, Mosby

Opus Communications, *imprint of* HCPro

Opus 40, *distributed by* WoodstockArts

Oral Biography Series, *imprint of* University of Alaska Press

Orb Books, *imprint of* Tom Doherty Associates, LLC

Orbis Books, *division of* Maryknoll Fathers & Brothers

Orbit, *division of* Hachette Book Group

Orbit Series, *imprint of* Krieger Publishing Co

Orchard Books, *imprint of* Scholastic Trade Division

Oregon California Trails Assn, *distributed by* Washington State University Press

Oregon Writers Colony, *distributed by* Washington State University Press

O'Reilly Media Inc, *distributor for* No Starch Press, Packt Publishing (technol ebook prog)

Oriental Institute Publications, *division of* University of Chicago

Orphiflamme Press™, *imprint of* Blue Mountain Arts Inc

Osprey Publishing, *imprint of* Bloomsbury Publishing Inc

Ostrich Editions, *imprint of* Cross-Cultural Communications

OTB Legacy Editions, *imprint of* Ocean Tree Books

Christy Ottaviano Books, *imprint of* Henry Holt and Company, LLC

Ottographics, *distributed by* Chelsea Green Publishing Co

Our Sunday Visitor Publishing, *division of* Our Sunday Visitor Inc

Outcaste Press, *imprint of* LARB Books

Outdoor Books & Maps, *imprint of* APC Publishing

The Overlook Press, *imprint of* Harry N Abrams Inc, *distributed by* W W Norton & Company Inc

Owlswick Press, *imprint of* Wildside Press LLC

Oxford Illustrated Press, *distributed by* Haynes North America Inc

Oxford University Press, *distributor for* Entomological Society of America, Fordham University, *distributed by* Beach Lloyd Publishers LLC, Cheng & Tsui Co Inc, International Book Centre Inc

Oxford University Press USA, *division of* University of Oxford, *distributor for* The American Chemical Society, American University in Cairo, Arnold Clarendon, Cold Spring Harbor Laboratory Press, Country Music Foundation Press, Engineering Press, Getty, Greenwich Medical Media, Grove Dictionaries, Hurst, IRL, Kodansha, Roxbury Publishing, Saunders, Stamford University Press, Thomson Publishing

Ozark Mountain Publishing Inc, *distributed by* Red Wheel/Weiser, Red Wheel/Weiser/Conari

Ozark Society, *distributed by* The University of Arkansas Press

Pace Press, *imprint of* Linden Publishing Co Inc

Pace University Press, *unit of* Pace University

Pacific Boating Almanac, *imprint of* ProStar Publications Inc

Pacific Grove Books, *imprint of* Park Place Publications

Pacific Institute, *distributed by* Washington State University Press

Pacific Press® Publishing Association, *division of* Seventh-Day Adventist Church

Packt Publishing, *distributed by* O'Reilly Media Inc

Pact Press, *imprint of* Regal House Publishing

Pademelon Press, *distributed by* Gryphon House Inc

Padua Playwrights Press, *distributed by* Theatre Communications Group

Kogan Page, *distributed by* Beekman Books Inc

Painted Turtle Books, *imprint of* Wayne State University Press

PAJ Publications, *distributed by* Theatre Communications Group

PAKS-Parents & Kids, *imprint of* THE Learning Connection®

Paladin Timeless Books, *imprint of* Twilight Times Books

Joan Palevsky, *imprint of* University of California Press

Palgrave Macmillan, *imprint of* Springer Nature, *distributor for* Berg Publishers, British Film Institute, Manchester University Press, Pluto Press, I B Tauris & Co Ltd, Zed Books

Pali Text Society, *imprint of* Wisdom Publications Inc

Palm Leaves Press, *imprint of* Parallax Press

Pan Asian Publications, *distributed by* Cheng & Tsui Co Inc

Panmun Academic Services, *distributed by* Cheng & Tsui Co Inc

Panpac Education, *distributed by* Cheng & Tsui Co Inc

Pantheon Books, *imprint of* Knopf Doubleday Publishing Group, Penguin Random House LLC

Panzerwrecks, *distributed by* Casemate | publishers

Paolo Torti degli Alberti, *distributed by* Edgewise Press Inc

Paperbacks for Educators, *distributor for* MAR*CO Products Inc

Papercutz, *distributed by* Macmillan

PaperStar, *imprint of* Penguin Group USA, A Penguin Random House Company

Paperweight Press, *distributed by* Tuttle Publishing

Parabola, *distributed by* Fons Vitae

Parachute Publishing LLC, *division of* Parachute Properties LLC, *distributed by* Bantam, Bendon, Berkley, Dorling Kindersley, Grosset, Harcourt, HarperCollins, HarperEntertainment, Kensington, Little, Brown, Penguin Random House Inc, Pocket Books, Running Press, Scholastic, Simon & Schuster, Inc

Paraclete Press Inc, *division of* Creative Joys Inc, *distributor for* Abbey of Saint Peter of Solesmes, Gloriae Dei Cantores

Paradigm Busters, *distributed by* Cheng & Tsui Co Inc

Paradigm Education Solutions, *division of* EMC Publishing LLC

Paradigm Publications, *division of* Redwing Book Co

Paragon, *distributed by* Fons Vitae

Paragon House, *distributed by* Bloomsbury Academic

Parallax Press, *division of* Unified Buddhist Church

Paraview Pocket Books, *imprint of* Cosimo Inc

Paraview Press, *division of* Cosimo Inc

Paraview Special Editions, *imprint of* Cosimo Inc

Pardey Publications, *imprint of* Paradise Cay Publications Inc

Parenting Press, *imprint of* Chicago Review Press

Park Partners Inc, *distributed by* Gem Guides Book Co

Park Row Books, *imprint of* Harlequin Enterprises Ltd

Park Street Press, *imprint of* Inner Traditions International Ltd

ParmenidesAudio™, *division of* Parmenides Publishing

ParmenidesFiction™, *division of* Parmenides Publishing

Partner Press, *distributed by* Gryphon House Inc

Partner's Book Distributing Inc, *distributor for* Blue Poppy Press

Partner's/West Book Distributing Inc, *distributor for* Blue Poppy Press

Partnership Publications, *imprint of* House to House Publications

Parvardigar Press, *distributed by* Fons Vitae

Passages, *imprint of* Perfection Learning

Pastoral Press, *imprint of* OCP

JIMMY Patterson Books, *imprint of* Little, Brown and Company

Pauline Books & Media, *division of* Daughters of St Paul

Pauline Comics & Graphic Novels, *imprint of* Pauline Books & Media

Pauline Teen, *imprint of* Pauline Books & Media

Nancy Paulsen Books, *imprint of* Penguin Young Readers Group

Pavilion, *distributed by* Sterling Publishing Co Inc

Pavilion Books, *distributed by* Rizzoli International Publications Inc

Pavilion Children's, *distributed by* Rizzoli International Publications Inc

Peabody Museum of Archaeology & Ethnology, *distributed by* Harvard University Press

Peabody Museum Press, *unit of* Peabody Museum of Archaeology & Ethnology, Peabody Museum of Archaeology & Ethnology, Harvard University, *distributed by* Harvard University Press

Peacewatch Editions, *imprint of* Ocean Tree Books

Peachpit Press, *imprint of* Pearson Education Ltd

Peachtree Jr, *imprint of* Peachtree Publishing Co Inc

Pearson, *distributor for* Heinemann

Pearson Allyn & Bacon, *imprint of* Pearson Higher Education

Pearson Arts & Sciences, *division of* Pearson Education Ltd

Pearson Benjamin Cummings, *imprint of* Pearson Higher Education

Pearson Business Publishing, *unit of* Pearson Higher Education

Pearson Education, *distributor for* Manning Publications Co, *distributed by* American Academy of Environmental Engineers & Scientists®, Trans-Atlantic Publications Inc

Pearson Education Australia, *distributed by* Cheng & Tsui Co Inc

Pearson ELT, *division of* Pearson Education Ltd

Pearson Higher Education, *division of* Pearson Education Ltd

Pearson Learning Solutions, *unit of* Pearson Higher Education

Pearson Technology, *distributed by* SkillPath Publications

Editions du Renouveau Pedagogique, *distributor for* Michelin Maps & Guides

T H Peek Publisher, *division of* Clearweave Corp

Peermusic Classical, *distributed by* Hal Leonard Corp

Pegasus, *distributed by* Simon & Schuster, Inc

Pegasus Books, *distributed by* W W Norton & Company Inc

PeKo Publishing, *distributed by* Casemate | publishers

Pelican International Corp, *subsidiary of* Pelican Publishing Co

Pelican Publishing Co, *imprint of* Arcadia Publishing, Arcadia Publishing Inc, *distributor for* Hope Publishing House, Marmac Publishing Co, SelfHelp Success Books

PelikaanPers, *distributed by* Casemate | publishers

A W Peller & Associates, *distributor for* Pieces of Learning Inc

Pembroke Publishers, *distributed by* Stenhouse Publishers

Pen & Sword, *distributed by* Casemate | publishers

Pen & Sword Digital, *distributed by* Casemate | publishers

Pendragon Press, *subsidiary of* Camelot Publishing Co Inc, Camelot Publishing Co Inc, *distributed by* Boydell & Brewer Inc, LIM Editrice SRL (Italy), G Ricordi (Italy)

Pengin Random House, *distributor for* Holiday House Publishing Inc

Penguin, *imprint of* Penguin Books, Penguin Group USA, A Penguin Random House Company, *distributor for* Verso, *distributed by* Alfred Music

Penguin Books, *imprint of* Penguin Group USA, A Penguin Random House Company, Penguin Group USA, A Penguin Random House Company, *distributor for* The Countryman Press

Penguin Canada, *distributor for* Michelin Maps & Guides

Penguin Classics, *imprint of* Penguin Books, Penguin Group USA, A Penguin Random House Company

Penguin Compass, *imprint of* Penguin Books

Penguin Group USA, A Penguin Random House Company, *distributor for* Alloy Entertainment LLC, Arkangel, Bibli O'Phile, Consumer Guide/PIL, DAW Books Inc, Dream Works, Granta, HighBridge Audio, Kensington Publishing Corp, The Library of America, Maharishi University of Management Press, The Monacelli Press, *distributed by* Learning Links Inc

Penguin Life, *imprint of* Penguin Group USA, A Penguin Random House Company

The Penguin Press, *imprint of* Penguin Group USA, A Penguin Random House Company, Penguin Group USA, A Penguin Random House Company

Penguin Putnam Inc, *distributed by* Heimburger House Publishing Co

Penguin Random House, *distributor for* National Geographic Books, Rizzoli International Publications Inc, Wizards of the Coast LLC, *distributed by* Gem Guides Book Co, The Professional Education Group LLC (PEG)

Penguin Random House Audio, *imprint of* Penguin Random House LLC

Penguin Random House Audio Publishing, *subsidiary of* Penguin Random House LLC

Penguin Random House Canada, *distributor for* Persea Books

Penguin Random House Inc, *distributor for* Alloy Entertainment LLC, Hatherleigh Press Ltd, The Library of America, Parachute Publishing LLC, Shambhala Publications Inc, Smithsonian Institution Scholarly Press, *distributed by* DawnSignPress, Dreamscape Media LLC, Learning Links Inc

Penguin Random House India, *distributor for* Sourcebooks LLC

Penguin Random House Large Print, *imprint of* Penguin Random House LLC

Penguin 20th Century Classics, *imprint of* Penguin Books

Penguin Workshop, *imprint of* Penguin Group USA, A Penguin Random House Company, Penguin Group USA, A Penguin Random House Company, Penguin Young Readers Group

Penguin Young Readers Group, *division of* Penguin Group USA, A Penguin Random House Company, Penguin Group USA, A Penguin Random House Company

PenMark Press, *imprint of* The Davies Group Publishers

Penn State University Press, *distributor for* Abo Akademi University (specialize in ancient Near East), American Oriental Society, Deo Publishing, National Gallery of Singapore, Neo-Assyrian Text Corpus (FFAR, Helsinki, Finland), University of California Institute on Global Conflict & Cooperation

Pennsylvania Historical & Museum Commission, *subsidiary of* The Commonwealth of Pennsylvania

Pennsylvania State Data Center, *subsidiary of* Institute of State & Regional Affairs

Pennwell, *distributed by* Gulf Energy Information

PennWell Books, *division of* PennWell Corp, PennWell Corp

PennWell Business & Industrial Division, *distributor for* Marine Techniques Publishing, *distributed by* Marine Techniques Publishing

PennWell Petroleum Books, *division of* PennWell Books

PennWell Power Books, *division of* PennWell Books

Penny-Farthing Productions, *imprint of* Penny-Farthing Productions Inc

Pennywyse Press, *imprint of* Imago Press

Pensiero Press, *imprint of* The Lentz Leadership Institute LLC

Pentecostal Publishing House, *subsidiary of* United Pentecostal Church International, *distributed by* Christian Network International, Innovative Marketing

Pentrex, *distributed by* Gem Guides Book Co

Peradam Press, *subsidiary of* The Center for Cultural & Naturalist Studies

Percheron Press, *imprint of* Eliot Werner Publications Inc

Peter Peregrinus Ltd, *imprint of* IET USA Inc

Peregrinzilla, *distributed by* Chelsea Green Publishing Co

Sophia Perennis, *distributed by* Fons Vitae

Perfection Learning, *distributor for* Abrams, Ace Books, Airmont, Annick Press, Archway, Atheneum, Baker Books, Ballantine, Bantam, Barrons, Berkley, Blake Books, Candlewick Press, Charlesbridge Press, Chelsea House, Children's Press, Chronicle Books, Crabtree Publishing Co, Crown, Disney Press, Distri Books, DK, Doubleday, Dutton, F+W Media Inc, Farrar, Straus & Giroux Inc, Fawcett, Firefly, First Avenue, Free Spirit, Fulcrum, Golden Books, Greenhaven Press Inc, Hammond, Hayes, Gareth Stevens, Frederick Warne

Periplus Editions, *imprint of* Tuttle Publishing, *distributed by* Tuttle Publishing

Permanent Agriculture Resources, *distributed by* University of Hawaii Press

Permanent Publications, *distributed by* Chelsea Green Publishing Co

Permuted Press LLC, *distributed by* Simon & Schuster, Inc, Simon & Schuster Sales Division

Persea Books, *distributed by* W W Norton & Company Inc, W W Norton & Company Inc (worldwide exc Canada), Penguin Random House Canada (CN only)

Perseus Books, *division of* Hachette Book Group

Perseverance Press, *distributed by* John Daniel & Co

Personal Profiles, *division of* Brown Books Publishing Group

Peterson Institute for International Economics, *distributed by* Columbia University Press

Peterson's, *distributed by* Hachette Book Group

Peterson's/Pacesetter Books, *imprint of* Peterson's

Petroleum Extension Service (PETEX), *unit of* The University of Texas at Austin, Cockrell School of Engineering

Petzel, *distributed by* Simon & Schuster, Inc

Pferdia TV, *distributed by* Trafalgar Square Books

Pflaum Publishing Group, *division of* Bayard Inc

Phaidon Press, *distributed by* Hachette Book Group

Phantom Books & Music, *imprint of* Empire Publishing Service

Philadelphia Museum of Art, *distributed by* Yale University Press

Philedition, *distributed by* Casemate | publishers

Philomel, *imprint of* Penguin Group USA, A Penguin Random House Company, Penguin Group USA, A Penguin Random House Company, Penguin Young Readers Group

Philomel Books, *imprint of* Penguin Group USA, A Penguin Random House Company

Philosophical Library Inc, *distributed by* Open Road Integrated Media

Philosophy Documentation Center, *distributor for* Zeta Books (online access)

Phoenix International Publications, *distributed by* Hachette Book Group

Phoenix Mapping Service, *division of* Wide World of Maps Inc

Phoenix Publishing, *distributed by* CN Times Books

Pholiota Press Inc, *distributed by* Cross-Cultural Communications

Phonics Adventure, *imprint of* Advance Publishing Inc

Photofact®, *imprint of* SAMS Technical Publishing LLC

Photolucida Book, *distributed by* Franklin, Beedle & Associates Inc

Photosmith Books, *distributed by* Caxton Press

Daniela Piazza Editore, *distributed by* Chelsea Green Publishing Co

Picador, *imprint of* Farrar, Straus & Giroux, LLC

The Picasso Project, *imprint of* Alan Wofsy Fine Arts, Alan Wofsy Fine Arts, *distributor for* Cramer (Switzerland), Kornfeld (Switzerland), Ramie (France), *distributed by* Alan Wofsy Fine Arts

Pictorial Histories Publishing Co, *distributed by* Heimburger House Publishing Co

Picture Books, *imprint of* ABDO Publishing Co Inc

Picture Window Books, *imprint of* Capstone Publishers™

Pieces of Learning Inc, *distributed by* A W Peller & Associates, Prufrock Press

Pierrepont Street Press, *imprint of* Italica Press

Piggyback Interactive, *distributed by* Simon & Schuster, Inc, Simon & Schuster Sales Division

Pighog Books, *imprint of* Red Hen Press

Pikachu Press, *distributed by* Simon & Schuster, Inc

Pike & Powder, *distributed by* Simon & Schuster, Inc

Pilgrim's Guide Books, *distributed by* ACTA Publications

Pimsleur, *imprint of* Simon & Schuster Audio

Pinata Books, *imprint of* Arte Publico Press

Pine Winds Press, *imprint of* Idyll Arbor Inc

Pineapple Press, *imprint of* The Globe Pequot Press

Pinnacle Books, *imprint of* Kensington Publishing Corp

Pinyon Publishing, *distributed by* Gem Guides Book Co

Pioneer Press, *imprint of* Cedar Fort Inc

Pir Press, *distributed by* Fons Vitae

Pitkin, *distributed by* Rizzoli International Publications Inc

Plain Sight Publishing, *imprint of* Cedar Fort Inc

Planners Press, *imprint of* Routledge

Playscripts Inc, *distributed by* Theatre Communications Group

Playwrights Canada Press, *distributed by* Theatre Communications Group

Plexus Books, *imprint of* Plexus Publishing, Inc

Plexus Publishing, Inc, *affiliate of* Information Today, Inc

PLI, *imprint of* Practising Law Institute

Ploughshares, *subsidiary of* Ploughshares Inc

Plugged-in to Reading, *imprint of* Triumph Learning LLC

Plum Blossom Books, *imprint of* Parallax Press

Plum Tree Books, *imprint of* Classical Academic Press

Plumbago Books, *imprint of* Boydell & Brewer Inc

Plume, *division of* Penguin Group USA, A Penguin Random House Company, Penguin Group USA, A Penguin Random House Company, *imprint of* Penguin Group USA, A Penguin Random House Company

Pluto Press, *distributed by* Palgrave Macmillan

PMP, *imprint of* Paramount Market Publishing Inc

Pocket Books, *imprint of* Gallery Books, *distributor for* Parachute Publishing LLC

Pocket Guides Publishing, *distributed by* AdventureKEEN

Pocket Paragons, *imprint of* David R Godine Inc

Pogo, *imprint of* Jump!

Point, *imprint of* Scholastic Trade Division

Poisoned Pen Press, *imprint of* Sourcebooks Inc, Sourcebooks LLC

The Pokemon Company International, *distributed by* Simon & Schuster, Inc

Polar Bear & Company, *imprint of* Solon Center for Research & Publishing

Polebridge Press, *division of* Westar Institute

Political Risk Services, *imprint of* The PRS Group Inc

Pollyanna Productions, *distributed by* Gryphon House Inc

Polyface, *distributed by* Chelsea Green Publishing Co

PomegranateKids, *imprint of* Pomegranate Communications Inc

Pond Frog Editions, *imprint of* Red Moon Press

Pool of London Press, *distributed by* Casemate | publishers

Poplar Books, *imprint of* Book Sales

Poppy, *imprint of* Little, Brown Books for Young Readers

Portavoz, *distributed by* Editorial Bautista Independiente

Neal Porter Books, *imprint of* Holiday House Publishing Inc

Portfolio, *subsidiary of* Penguin Group USA, A Penguin Random House Company, Penguin Group USA, A Penguin Random House Company, *imprint of* Penguin Group USA, A Penguin Random House Company

Portico, *distributed by* Rizzoli International Publications Inc

Portraits of America, *imprint of* The Donning Company Publishers

Possibility Press, *imprint of* Markowski International Publishers

Post Hill Press LLC, *distributed by* Simon & Schuster, Inc, Simon & Schuster Sales Division

Potomac Appalachian Trail Club, *distributed by* Appalachian Trail Conservancy (ATC)

Potomac Books, *imprint of* University of Nebraska Press

Clarkson Potter Publishers, *imprint of* Crown Publishing Group, *distributor for* The Colonial Williamsburg Foundation

Potter Craft, *imprint of* Penguin Random House LLC

Potter Style, *imprint of* Penguin Random House LLC

powerHouse Books, *division of* PowerHouse Cultural Entertainment Inc, *imprint of* power-House Cultural Entertainment Inc, *distributor for* Antinous Press, Juno Books, MTV Press, Throckmorton Press, VH1 Press, Vice Books

PowerKids Press, *imprint of* The Rosen Publishing Group Inc

PPI, A Kaplan Company, *distributor for* American Association of State Highway & Transportation Officials, American Wood Council (American Forest & Paper Association) (National Design Specification for Wood Construction (NDS) & others), International Code Council, McGraw-Hill Professional (green building, design & construction titles, LEED titles), National Council of Examiners for En-

gineering & Surveying, SmartPros, Transportation Research Board Code, US Green Building Council (LEED reference guides)

Practitioners Publishing Co, *distributor for* AICPA Professional Publications

Praeger, *imprint of* ABC-CLIO

Prajna Studios, *imprint of* Shambhala Publications Inc

Emory Pratt, *distributor for* Primary Research Group Inc

Prensa Pensar, *imprint of* Progressive Press

Prentice Hall, *distributor for* American Geosciences Institute (AGI), *distributed by* American Academy of Environmental Engineers & Scientists®, NACE International, SME (Society of Manufacturing Engineers)

PREP Publishing, *subsidiary of* PREP Inc, PREP Inc

Presbyterian Publishing Corp (PPC), *distributor for* Epworth, SCM

Presidio Press, *imprint of* Random House Publishing Group

PreSonus, *distributed by* Hal Leonard Corp

The Press at California State University, Fresno, *unit of* California State University, Fresno

La Presse, *imprint of* Fence Books

Price Stern Sloan, *imprint of* Penguin Group USA, A Penguin Random House Company, Penguin Young Readers Group

Price World Publishing, *distributed by* David Bateman Ltd (New Zealand), Cardinal Publishers Group (US)

Priddy Books, *imprint of* St Martin's Press, LLC

Primary Research Group Inc, *distributed by* Academic Book Center, Ambassador Books, Coutts Library Service, Croft House Books, Eastern Book Company, Ebsco, MarketResearch.com, Midwest Library Service, OPAMP Technical Books, Emory Pratt, ProQuest LLC, Research & Markets, Rittenhouse Book Distributors, Total Information, Yankee Book Peddler

Primary Source Media™, *imprint of* Gale

Prime Crime, *imprint of* Berkley Publishing Group

Prime Music, *distributed by* ECS Publishing Group

Princeton Architectural Press, *distributor for* Moleskine Books, *distributed by* Chronicle Books

Princeton Book Co Publishers, *distributor for* Dance Books Ltd, Dance Notation Bureau, *distributed by* Dance Books Ltd

The Princeton Review, *imprint of* Penguin Random House LLC, Random House Children's Books

Princeton University Art Museum, *distributed by* Yale University Press

Princeton University Press, *distributor for* National Gallery of Art, University of California Institute on Global Conflict & Cooperation, Zone Books

Principles in Practice, *imprint of* National Council of Teachers of English (NCTE)

Printer's Row, *distributed by* Simon & Schuster, Inc

Pritzker Military Museum & Library, *distributed by* Casemate | publishers

Pro-Ed, *distributor for* Psychological Assessment Resources Inc (PAR), *distributed by* Psychological Assessment Resources Inc (PAR)

Pro Lingua Associates, *distributed by* International Book Centre Inc

Proceedings, *imprint of* American Philosophical Society

Proceedings of SPIE, *imprint of* SPIE

Process Media Inc, *imprint of* Feral House

Prodist, *imprint of* Watson Publishing International LLC

Productivity Press, *imprint of* CRC Press, *distributor for* American Society for Quality (ASQ), SME (Society of Manufacturing Engineers)

Productivity Press Spanish Imprint, *imprint of* Productivity Press

Professional Development, *division of* Scholastic Education

The Professional Education Group LLC (PEG), *distributor for* American Bar Association, American Law Institute, Chicago Review Press, Penguin Random House, Wolters Kluwer

Professional Music Institute, *distributed by* Hal Leonard Corp

Professional Practices, *imprint of* Krieger Publishing Co

Professional Publications, *distributed by* NACE International

Professional Resource Press, *imprint of* Professional Resource Exchange Inc

Progressive Press, *imprint of* Progressive Press, *distributor for* Global Research

Prometheus Books, *imprint of* The Globe Pequot Press

Prompt Publications, *distributed by* SAMS Technical Publishing LLC

Propellerhead, *distributed by* Hal Leonard Corp

Proper Romance, *imprint of* Shadow Mountain

Propriometrics Press, *distributed by* Chelsea Green Publishing Co

ProQuest LLC, *subsidiary of* Cambridge Information Group Inc, *distributor for* Primary Research Group Inc

Providence Athenaeum, *distributed by* Oak Knoll Press

Providence Press, *division of* Hope Publishing Co

Providence Publishing, *distributor for* Country Music Foundation Press

Prufrock Press, *distributor for* Pieces of Learning Inc, *distributed by* Sourcebooks LLC

PS&E Publications, *imprint of* Bartleby Press

PSS, *imprint of* Penguin Young Readers Group

Psychological Assessment Resources Inc (PAR), *distributor for* American Guidance Service, Pro-Ed, Rorschach Workshops, *distributed by* ACER, Pro-Ed, Western Psychological Service

Public Citizen, *distributed by* Addison-Wesley, Simon & Schuster Pocket Books

PublicAffairs, *imprint of* Perseus Books

Publishers Group West (PGW), *distributor for* Black Classic Press, Kalmbach Publishing Co, Naval Institute Press

Publishing Services, *division of* Scholastic Education

Pucker Gallery, *distributed by* Syracuse University Press

Pueblo Books, *imprint of* Liturgical Press

Coleccion Puertorriquena, *imprint of* University of Puerto Rico Press

Puffin, *imprint of* Penguin Group USA, A Penguin Random House Company

Puffin Books, *imprint of* Penguin Group USA, A Penguin Random House Company, Penguin Group USA, A Penguin Random House Company, Penguin Young Readers Group

Punahou School, *distributed by* University of Hawaii Press

Punch Press, *imprint of* Loft Press Inc

PUP Audio, *imprint of* Princeton University Press

Purple House Press, *imprint of* Purple House Inc

Purple Mountain Press Ltd, *distributor for* Carmania Press London (North America only)

PUSH, *imprint of* Scholastic Trade Division

Pushcart Press, *distributed by* W W Norton & Company Inc

Putnam, *imprint of* Penguin Group USA, A Penguin Random House Company, GP Putnam's Sons (Hardcover)

GP Putnam's Sons, *imprint of* Penguin Young Readers Group

GP Putnam's Sons (Children's), *member of* Penguin Young Readers Group

GP Putnam's Sons (Hardcover), *imprint of* Penguin Group USA, A Penguin Random House Company, Penguin Group USA, A Penguin Random House Company

Puzzlewright Press, *imprint of* Sterling Publishing Co Inc

PWM Editions, *distributed by* Hal Leonard Corp

PWN, *imprint of* Summertime Publications Inc

PYO (Publish Your Own Co), *division of* Quixote Press

QDS, *imprint of* Quarto Publishing Group USA Inc

QED Press, *imprint of* Cypress House

Qiblah Books, *distributed by* Fons Vitae

QMP, *imprint of* Quality Medical Publishing Inc

QSC, *distributed by* Hal Leonard Corp

Quadrille Publishing, *distributed by* Chronicle Books

Quail Ridge Press (QRP), *imprint of* Southwestern Publishing House Inc

Quantuck Lane Press, *distributed by* W W Norton & Company Inc

Quarry Books, *imprint of* Indiana University Press, Quarto Publishing Group USA Inc

Quarto Library, *distributed by* Lerner Publishing Group Inc

Quarto Publishing Group, *distributed by* Hachette Book Group

Quarto Publishing Group/Hachette Book Group, *distributed by* Gem Guides Book Co

Quarto Publishing Group USA Inc, *division of* Quarto Group Inc, Quarto Group Inc (London, UK), *distributor for* CLEVER Publishing, *distributed by* Allen & Unwin (Australia & New Zealand), Hachette Book Group (North America)

Quercus Books, *distributed by* Hachette Book Group

Quest Books, *imprint of* Regal Crest Enterprises

Quest for Success, *imprint of* Advance Publishing Inc

Quest Publishing, *distributed by* Gem Guides Book Co

Quick Reference Publishing Inc, *distributed by* Gem Guides Book Co

Quickfact®, *imprint of* SAMS Technical Publishing LLC

Quickie Books, *imprint of* Penguin Random House LLC

Quiet Fox, *imprint of* Fox Chapel Publishing Co Inc

Quill Driver Books, *imprint of* Linden Publishing Co Inc

Quill Tree Books, *imprint of* HarperCollins Children's Books

Quiller, *distributed by* Safari Press

Quilliam Press, *distributed by* Fons Vitae

Quincannon, *imprint of* Quincannon Publishing Group

Quintessence Books, *imprint of* Quintessence Publishing Co Inc

Quintessence of Dental Technology, *imprint of* Quintessence Publishing Co Inc

Quintessence Pockets, *imprint of* Quintessence Publishing Co Inc

Quintessence Publishing Co Inc, *distributor for* Quintessence Publishing Co Ltd (Japan), Quintessence Publishing Ltd (London), Quintessence Verlags GmbH

Quintessence Publishing Co Ltd (Japan), *distributed by* Quintessence Publishing Co Inc

Quintessence Publishing Ltd (London), *distributed by* Quintessence Publishing Co Inc

Quintessence Verlags GmbH, *distributed by* Quintessence Publishing Co Inc

Quite Specific Media, *division of* Silman-James Press Inc

Quite Specific Media Group Ltd, *division of* Silman-James Press Inc, *distributor for* The Colonial Williamsburg Foundation

Quodlibetal Features, *distributed by* Vandamere Press

RAB Afraid, *imprint of* Riverdale Avenue Books (RAB)

RAB Desire, *imprint of* Riverdale Avenue Books (RAB)

RAB Gaming, *imprint of* Riverdale Avenue Books (RAB)

RAB Pop, *imprint of* Riverdale Avenue Books (RAB)

RAB SFF, *imprint of* Riverdale Avenue Books (RAB)

RAB Sports, *imprint of* Riverdale Avenue Books (RAB)

RAB Truth, *imprint of* Riverdale Avenue Books (RAB)

RAB Verve, *imprint of* Riverdale Avenue Books (RAB)

Rabbit's Foot Press™, *imprint of* Blue Mountain Arts Inc

Race Point Publishing, *imprint of* Quarto Publishing Group USA Inc

Radiant Life Curriculum, *imprint of* Gospel Publishing House

Radio Archives, *distributed by* Dreamscape Media LLC

Radio Theatre, *imprint of* Focus on the Family

Radix Press, *subsidiary of* UGF/OR

Rainbow Bridge Publishing, *imprint of* Carson Dellosa Publishing LLC

Rainbow Ridge Books, *distributed by* Square One Publishers Inc

Rainsource Press, *distributed by* Chelsea Green Publishing Co

RainStone Press, *distributed by* Mountain Press Publishing Co

Raise the Dough in 30 Days Co, *division of* Quixote Press

Chris Ralph, *distributed by* Gem Guides Book Co

Ramakrishna Math, *distributed by* Vedanta Press

Ramakrishna-Vivekananda Center of New York, *distributed by* Vedanta Press

Ramanujan Mathematical Society, *distributed by* American Mathematical Society

Ramie (France), *distributed by* The Picasso Project

Ramsey & Todd, *imprint of* Turner Publishing Co

Rand McNally, *distributor for* Wide World of Maps Inc, *distributed by* Wide World of Maps Inc

Rand McNally for Kids, *imprint of* Rand McNally

Random House, *imprint of* Penguin Random House LLC, Random House Publishing Group, *distributor for* Universe Publishing, Welcome Enterprises Inc

Random House Books for Young Readers, *imprint of* Penguin Random House LLC, Random House Children's Books

Random House Children's Books, *division of* Penguin Random House LLC

Random House Children's Publishing, *imprint of* Penguin Random House LLC

Random House Digital, *imprint of* Penguin Random House LLC

Random House Graphic, *imprint of* Random House Children's Books

Random House Large Print, *distributed by* Thorndike Press®

Random House Large Print Publishing, *imprint of* Penguin Random House LLC

Random House Publishing Group, *division of* Penguin Random House LLC

Random House Puzzles & Games, *imprint of* Penguin Random House LLC

Random House Reference & Information Publishing, *imprint of* Penguin Random House LLC

Random House Reference/Random House Puzzles & Games, *imprint of* Penguin Random House Audio Publishing

Random House Webster's, *imprint of* Random House Reference/Random House Puzzles & Games

Ranger Rick Science Program, *imprint of* Sundance/Newbridge Publishing

Katrina Raphaell, *distributed by* Gem Guides Book Co

Rasmuson Library Historical Translation Series, *imprint of* University of Alaska Press

Rational Island Publishers, *division of* The Re-evaluation Counseling Communities

Raven Press, *distributed by* Chelsea Green Publishing Co

Ravenhawk™ Books, *division of* The 6DOF Group, The 6DOF Group

Raymond Press, *imprint of* Prospect Park Books

Rayo, *imprint of* HarperCollins General Books Group

Razorbill, *imprint of* Penguin Group USA, A Penguin Random House Company, Penguin Random House LLC, Penguin Young Readers Group

RB Shorts, *imprint of* Recorded Books Inc, an RBmedia company

RCS Libri, *imprint of* Rizzoli International Publications Inc

Reader's Digest, *distributed by* Fox Chapel Publishing Co Inc

Reader's Digest Books, *distributed by* Simon & Schuster, Inc

Reader's Digest Children's Books, *distributed by* Simon & Schuster Sales Division

Reader's Digest Select Editions, *division of* Trusted Media Brands Inc

Reader's Digest Trade Publishing, *division of* Trusted Media Brands Inc, *distributed by* Simon & Schuster, Inc

Reading Success, *imprint of* Advance Publishing Inc

Reading With Peaches LLC, *distributed by* Gem Guides Book Co

Real Adventure Publishing, *distributed by* Gem Guides Book Co

REAL Phonics™, *imprint of* Broden Books LLC

Rebel Arts, *imprint of* Gingko Press Inc, *distributed by* Gingko Press Inc

Rebel Base Books, *imprint of* Kensington Publishing Corp

Rebellion, *distributed by* Simon & Schuster, Inc, Simon & Schuster Sales Division

Recorded Books Audiolibros, *imprint of* Recorded Books Inc, an RBmedia company

Recorded Books Development, *imprint of* Recorded Books Inc, an RBmedia company

Recorded Books Inspirational, *imprint of* Recorded Books Inc, an RBmedia company

Recovered Classics, *imprint of* McPherson & Co

Red Chair Press, *distributed by* Lerner Publishing Group Inc

Red Dress Ink, *imprint of* Harlequin Enterprises Ltd

Red Feather, *imprint of* Schiffer Publishing Ltd

Red Portal Press, *imprint of* Mighty Media Press

Red Wheel/Weiser, *distributor for* Cleis Press, Hampton Roads Publishing, Nicolas Hays Inc, Lantern Books, Lantern Publishing & Media, Ozark Mountain Publishing Inc, Viva Editions

Red Wheel/Weiser/Conari, *distributor for* Ozark Mountain Publishing Inc, *distributed by* Gem Guides Book Co, Moznaim Publishing Corp

Redemptorist Publications, *distributed by* Liguori Publications

Redhook, *imprint of* Orbit

Redleaf Press, *division of* Think Small, *distributor for* New Shoots Publishing (New Zealand)

Redwing Book Co, *distributor for* Blue Poppy Press

Redwood Press, *imprint of* Stanford University Press

Referee Books, *imprint of* Referee Enterprises Inc

Reform Judaism Publishing, *imprint of* Central Conference of American Rabbis/CCAR Press

The Refractive Thinker® Press, *imprint of* The Lentz Leadership Institute LLC

Regal Crest, *imprint of* Regal Crest Enterprises

Regan Arts, *distributed by* Simon & Schuster, Inc, Simon & Schuster Sales Division

Regina Press, *imprint of* Catholic Book Publishing Corp

Regnery, *imprint of* Regnery Publishing

Regnery Faith, *imprint of* Regnery Publishing

Regnery Fiction, *imprint of* Regnery Publishing

Regnery History, *imprint of* Regnery Publishing

Regnery Kids, *imprint of* Regnery Publishing

Regnery Publishing, *subsidiary of* Salem Media Group, *distributed by* Simon & Schuster, Inc

Regular Baptist Books, *imprint of* Regular Baptist Press

Regular Baptist Press, *division of* General Association of Regular Baptist Churches

RELS Press, *imprint of* Plowshare Media

Renaissance Books, *imprint of* St Martin's Press, LLC, *distributed by* University of Hawaii Press

Renaissance House, *imprint of* Laredo Publishing Co

Research, *division of* Scholastic Education

Research & Markets, *distributor for* Primary Research Group Inc

Research & Special Programs Administration of the US Department of Transportation, *distributed by* J J Keller & Associates, Inc

Resilient Publishing, *distributor for* Anderson Design, Brynwood Publishing

Resurgence, *imprint of* Tyndale House Publishers Inc

Resurrection Press, *imprint of* Catholic Book Publishing Corp

Retold Classics, *imprint of* Perfection Learning

Retro Science Fiction, *imprint of* Gateways Books & Tapes

Retrospect Publishing, *distributed by* Closson Press

Reveal Press, *imprint of* New Harbinger Publications Inc

Revell, *division of* Baker Publishing Group

Ribbits, *imprint of* Focus on the Family

Ricordi, *distributed by* Hal Leonard Corp

G Ricordi (Italy), *distributor for* Pendragon Press

Riebel-Roque, *distributed by* Casemate | publishers

Lynne Rienner Publishers Inc, *distributor for* Center for US-Mexican Studies, Ayebia Clarke Publishing Ltd (African lit), St Andrews Center for Syrian Studies

Rigby, *imprint of* Houghton Mifflin Harcourt K-12 Publishers

Riley & Johnson, *distributed by* Business Research Services Inc

Ringing Bell Press, *distributed by* Franklin, Beedle & Associates Inc

Ronald Ringsrud Co, *distributed by* Gem Guides Book Co

Rio Chico, *imprint of* Rio Nuevo Publishers

Rio Grande Books, *imprint of* LPD Press/Rio Grande Books

Rick Riordan Presents, *imprint of* Disney-Hyperion Books

Ripley Entertainment Inc, *distributed by* Simon & Schuster, Inc, Simon & Schuster Sales Division

Rittenhouse, *distributor for* Teton NewMedia Inc

Rittenhouse Book Distributors, *distributor for* Primary Research Group Inc

Rivendale Press, *distributed by* Oak Knoll Press

River City Kids, *imprint of* River City Publishing LLC

River Grove Books, *imprint of* Greenleaf Book Group LLC

River North Fiction, *imprint of* Moody Publishers

River Publishers, *distributed by* Stylus Publishing LLC

Riverbend Publishing, *distributed by* Gem Guides Book Co

Riverdale/Magnus, *imprint of* Riverdale Avenue Books (RAB)

Riverhead Books, *imprint of* Penguin Group USA, A Penguin Random House Company, Penguin Group USA, A Penguin Random House Company

RiverWood Books, *imprint of* White Cloud Press

Rizzoli Electa, *imprint of* Rizzoli International Publications Inc

Rizzoli International Publications Inc, *subsidiary of* RCS Rizzoli Corp New York, RCS Rizzoli Corp New York, *distributor for* Editions Flammarion, National Trust, Pavilion Books, Pavilion Children's, Pitkin, Portico, Skira Editore, Smith Street Books, *distributed by* Penguin Random House

Rizzoli, New York, *imprint of* Rizzoli International Publications Inc

RN Publishing, *distributed by* Casemate | publishers

Road Dog Publications, *imprint of* Lost Classics Book Company LLC

The RoadRunner Press, *subsidiary of* RoadRunner Press LLC

Roadside Geology Series, *imprint of* Mountain Press Publishing Co

Roadside History Series, *imprint of* Mountain Press Publishing Co

Roaring Brook Press, *member of* Macmillan Children's Publishing Group

Lee Roberts Publications, *distributed by* Hal Leonard Corp

Robins Lane Press, *distributed by* Gryphon House Inc

ROC, *imprint of* Penguin Group USA, A Penguin Random House Company

Rock House, *distributed by* Hal Leonard Corp

Rock Point Gift & Stationery, *imprint of* Quarto Publishing Group USA Inc

Rockbottom Book Co, *distributor for* ABDO Publishing Co Inc

Rockefeller Institute Press, *distributed by* State University of New York Press

The Rockefeller University Press, *unit of* Rockefeller University

RockHill Publishing LLC, *distributed by* The Ishmael Tree (titles in Arabic)

Rockhurst University Press, *distributed by* Fordham University Press

Rocking Chair Kids, *imprint of* Red Chair Press

Rockport Publishers, *imprint of* Quarto Publishing Group USA Inc

Rocky Mountain Region Disaster Mental Health Institute Press, *imprint of* Loving Healing Press Inc

Rodale Books, *imprint of* Crown Publishing Group, Penguin Random House LLC

Rodale Kids, *imprint of* Random House Children's Books

Anita Roddick Publications, *distributed by* Chelsea Green Publishing Co

Roman Catholic Books, *division of* Catholic Media Apostolate Inc

Romantic Sounds Audio, *imprint of* Recorded Books Inc, an RBmedia company

Roncorp Music, *division of* Northeastern Music Publications Inc, *distributed by* Carl Fischer/Theodore Presser

Roost Books, *imprint of* Shambhala Publications Inc

Rootstock Publishing, *imprint of* Multicultural Media Inc

Rorschach Workshops, *distributed by* Psychological Assessment Resources Inc (PAR)

Rose Dog Books, *imprint of* Dorrance Publishing Co Inc

Fr Seraphim Rose Foundation, *imprint of* Saint Herman Press

Rose Kidz, *imprint of* Hendrickson Publishers Inc

Rose Publishing, *imprint of* Hendrickson Publishers Inc

Rosebud Books, *imprint of* Legacy Bound

Rosen Central, *imprint of* The Rosen Publishing Group Inc

Rosen Classroom Books & Materials, *division of* The Rosen Publishing Group Inc

Rosen Digital, *imprint of* The Rosen Publishing Group Inc

Rosen Young Adult, *imprint of* The Rosen Publishing Group Inc

Rosetta Books, *distributed by* Simon & Schuster, Inc

RosettaBooks, *distributed by* Simon & Schuster

Rosewind Romance, *imprint of* Vesuvian Books

Rossel Books, *distributed by* Behrman House Inc

Roth Family Foundation, *imprint of* University of California Press

Rothko Chapel, *distributed by* University of Texas Press

Rothstein Publishing, *division of* Rothstein Associates Inc

The Rough Notes Co Inc, *subsidiary of* Insurance Publishing Plus Corp, Insurance Publishing Plus Corp

Round Table Comics, *imprint of* Round Table Companies

Round Table Companies, *subsidiary of* Writers of the Round Table Press Inc

Routledge, *member of* Taylor & Francis Group, an Informa Business, *imprint of* Taylor & Francis Inc

Rowe Publishing, *imprint of* Rowe Publishing LLC

Rowe Publishing & Design, *imprint of* Rowe Publishing LLC

Rowman & Littlefield, *imprint of* Rowman & Littlefield Publishing Group, *distributor for* American Council on Education, The Colonial Williamsburg Foundation, The CSIS Press, Lehigh University Press

Roxbury Publishing, *distributed by* Oxford University Press USA

Royal Asiatic Society (Korea Branch), *distributed by* Cheng & Tsui Co Inc

Royal Fireworks Press, *distributor for* KAV Books, Silk Label Books, Trillium Press

Royal Historical Society, *imprint of* Boydell & Brewer Inc

Royal Society of Chemistry, *distributed by* The American Chemical Society

RSMeans, *imprint of* John Wiley & Sons Inc

Rubank Publications, *distributed by* Hal Leonard Corp

Ruby Tuesday Books, *distributed by* Bearport Publishing Co Inc

Rucksack Readers, *distributed by* Interlink Publishing Group Inc

Raymond C Rumpf & Son Inc, *distributor for* Wilderness Adventures Press Inc

Rune-Tales, *imprint of* Quincannon Publishing Group

Running Press, *imprint of* Perseus Books, *distributor for* Parachute Publishing LLC

Rural Science Institute, *distributed by* Chelsea Green Publishing Co

Rutgers University Press, *division of* Rutgers, The State University of New Jersey, *distributor for* Bucknell University Press

RV Guides, *distributed by* American Map Corp

RV International Maps & Atlases, *distributed by* Hagstrom Map

Ryland Peters & Small, *distributed by* Gem Guides Book Co, Simon & Schuster, Inc

S-A Design Books, *imprint of* CarTech Inc

S I Publicaties BV, *distributed by* Casemate | publishers

SABDA, *distributed by* Lotus Press

Sabrestorm Publishing, *distributed by* Casemate | publishers

Sacred Planet Books, *imprint of* Inner Traditions International Ltd

Saddleback Educational, *distributor for* TESOL International Association

Saddleback Educational Publishing, *distributed by* Children's Plus, Delaney

Sadhana Publications, *distributed by* Lotus Press

SAE (Society of Automotive Engineers International), *distributor for* Coordinating Research Council Inc

Safari Press, *distributor for* Quiller

Safer Society Press, *imprint of* Safer Society Foundation Inc

Saga Press, *imprint of* Gallery Books

Sagamore Publishing LLC, *distributor for* American Academy for Park & Recreation Administration

Sage, *imprint of* Genesis Press Inc

SAGE UK Resources for Educators, *distributed by* Corwin

St Andrews Center for Syrian Studies, *distributed by* Lynne Rienner Publishers Inc

St Andrews Press, *distributed by* Westminster John Knox Press (WJK)

St Andrews University Press, *subsidiary of* St Andrews University

St Augustine's Press Inc, *distributor for* Dumb Ox Books (publishes the Aristotelian Commentaries of Thomas Aquinas & like works), Hardwood Press (trade books, mostly in sports & regional works), New Criterion Books (poetry prize), *distributed by* University of Chicago Press

St Bede's Publications, *distributed by* Fordham University Press

Saint Herman Press, *subsidiary of* Brotherhood of Saint Herman of Alaska, *distributed by* Light & Life Publishing Co

St Herman Press, *imprint of* Saint Herman Press

St James Press®, *imprint of* Gale

St Louis Mercantile Library, *distributed by* University of Missouri Press

St Martin's Castle Point, *imprint of* St Martin's Press, LLC

St Martin's Dead Letter, *imprint of* St Martin's Press, LLC

St Martin's Essentials, *imprint of* St Martin's Press, LLC

St Martin's Griffin, *imprint of* St Martin's Press, LLC

St Martin's Paperbacks, *imprint of* St Martin's Press, LLC

St Martin's Press, *imprint of* St Martin's Press, LLC

St Martin's Press, LLC, *subsidiary of* Macmillan

St Martin's True Crime, *imprint of* St Martin's Press, LLC

St Martin's True Crime Classics, *imprint of* St Martin's Press, LLC

Saint Mary's Press, *subsidiary of* Christian Brothers Publications, *distributor for* Group Publishing

St Nicolas Music Inc, *distributed by* Hal Leonard Corp

St Pauls, *division of* The Society of Saint Paul

St Tikhon's, *distributor for* Ancient Faith Publishing

St Vladimir's, *distributor for* Ancient Faith Publishing

St Xenia Skete, *imprint of* Saint Herman Press

The Saints Series, *imprint of* Pauline Books & Media

Salaam Reads, *imprint of* Simon & Schuster Children's Publishing

Salaryia, *distributed by* Sterling Publishing Co Inc

Salem Press, *imprint of* Grey House Publishing Inc™

Sales & Marketing, *division of* Scholastic Education

SaltRiver, *imprint of* Tyndale House Publishers Inc

Samata Books, *distributed by* Lotus Press

SAMS Technical Publishing LLC, *division of* AGS Capital Inc, *distributor for* Butterworth-Heinemann, McGraw-Hill, Prompt Publications

Samson Audio, *distributed by* Hal Leonard Corp

San Diego State University Press, *division of* San Diego State University Foundation, *distributor for* Institute for Regional Studies of the Californias

San Gabriel Mountains Regional Conservancy, *distributed by* Gem Guides Book Co

Coleccion San Pedrito, *imprint of* University of Puerto Rico Press

Sandala Productions, *distributed by* Fons Vitae

Sandcastle, *imprint of* ABDO Publishing Co Inc

Sandpiper, *imprint of* Houghton Mifflin Harcourt Trade & Reference Division

The Sandstone Press, *imprint of* Frederic C Beil Publisher Inc

Sandu Publications, *distributed by* Gingko Press Inc

Santillana USA Publishing Co, *subsidiary of* Grupo Santillana

Sapientia Press, *distributed by* The Catholic University of America Press

Saraland Press, *distributed by* University of South Carolina Press

Saroff Editions, *imprint of* McPherson & Co

Sarto House, *imprint of* Angelus Press

SAS Press, *imprint of* SAS Institute Inc, *distributor for* John Wiley & Sons Inc (ebook formats only)

Satas, *distributor for* Blue Poppy Press

Saunders, *distributed by* Oxford University Press USA

W B Saunders Co, *distributed by* Marine Techniques Publishing

WB Saunders Co, *imprint of* Elsevier, Health Sciences Division

Savas Beatie, *distributed by* Casemate | publishers

Savas Publishing, *distributed by* Casemate | publishers

Saxon, *imprint of* Houghton Mifflin Harcourt K-12 Publishers

SBL Press, *unit of* Society of Biblical Literature, *distributor for* Brown Judaic Studies, Sheffield Phoenix Press

Scala Publishers, *distributor for* American Federation of Arts

Scandalous, *imprint of* Entangled Publishing LLC

Scarab Miniatures, *distributed by* Casemate | publishers

Lo Scarabeo, *distributed by* Llewellyn Publications

Scarsdale Voices, *imprint of* Scarsdale Publishing Ltd

Schiffer, *imprint of* Schiffer Publishing Ltd

Schiffer Fashion Press, *imprint of* Schiffer Publishing Ltd

Schiffer Kids, *imprint of* Schiffer Publishing Ltd

Schiffer LTD, *imprint of* Schiffer Publishing Ltd

Schiffer Military History, *imprint of* Schiffer Publishing Ltd

Schiffer Publishing Ltd, *distributor for* The Donning Company Publishers, *distributed by* Gem Guides Book Co

E C Schirmer Music Co, *imprint of* ECS Publishing Group

G Schirmer Inc/Associated Music Publishers Inc, *unit of* Wise Music Group

G Schirmer Inc/Associated Music Publishers Ltd, *distributed by* Hal Leonard Corp

Schirmer Reference™, *imprint of* Gale

Schlager Reference, *imprint of* Schlager Group Inc

A Naomi Schneider Book, *imprint of* University of California Press

Schocken Books, *imprint of* Knopf Doubleday Publishing Group, Penguin Random House LLC

Scholarly Digital Editions, *imprint of* Boydell & Brewer Inc

Scholarly Resources Inc, *imprint of* Gale

Scholastic, *distributor for* Parachute Publishing LLC, *distributed by* Gem Guides Book Co

Scholastic Asia, *subsidiary of* Scholastic International

Scholastic Audio, *imprint of* Scholastic Trade Division

Scholastic Australia Pty Ltd, *subsidiary of* Scholastic International

Scholastic Books, *distributor for* Alloy Entertainment LLC

Scholastic Canada Ltd, *subsidiary of* Scholastic International

Scholastic Education, *division of* Scholastic Inc

Scholastic en Espanol, *imprint of* Scholastic Trade Division

Scholastic Focus, *imprint of* Scholastic Trade Division

Scholastic Inc, *imprint of* Scholastic Trade Division, *distributor for* The Colonial Williamsburg Foundation

Scholastic International, *division of* Scholastic Inc

Scholastic Library Publishing, *distributed by* Gem Guides Book Co

Scholastic Licensed Publishing, *imprint of* Scholastic Trade Division

Scholastic Ltd UK, *subsidiary of* Scholastic International

Scholastic New Zealand Ltd, *subsidiary of* Scholastic International

Scholastic Nonfiction, *imprint of* Scholastic Trade Division

Scholastic Paperbacks, *imprint of* Scholastic Trade Division

Scholastic Press, *imprint of* Scholastic Trade Division

Scholastic Reference, *imprint of* Scholastic Trade Division

Scholastic Trade Division, *division of* Scholastic Inc

School Express Press, *imprint of* Story Monsters LLC

School for Advanced Research Press, *distributed by* University of New Mexico Press

School of Government, *division of* The University of North Carolina at Chapel Hill, The University of North Caroline at Chapel Hill

School Renaissance, *distributed by* Gryphon House Inc

School Speciality, *distributor for* MAR*CO Products Inc

SchoolBookings.com, *division of* Story Monsters LLC

Schott Music, *distributed by* Hal Leonard Corp

Schwartz & Wade Books, *imprint of* Penguin Random House LLC, Random House Children's Books

Sci-Fi Audio, *imprint of* Recorded Books Inc, an RBmedia company

Science & Humanities Press, *subsidiary of* Banis & Associates

Science History Publications USA, *imprint of* Watson Publishing International LLC

Science, Naturally, *affiliate of* Platypus Media

Science Press USA Inc, *distributed by* American Mathematical Society

Scientific American, *imprint of* Farrar, Straus & Giroux, LLC

Scientific American Medicine, *distributor for* American College of Surgeons

SCM, *distributed by* Presbyterian Publishing Corp (PPC)

SCM Press, *distributed by* Westminster John Knox Press (WJK)

Scobre Educational, *imprint of* Scobre Press Corp

John Scognamiglio Books, *imprint of* Kensington Publishing Corp

Scorched, *imprint of* Entangled Publishing LLC

Scottish Text Society, *imprint of* Boydell & Brewer Inc

Scout Press, *imprint of* Gallery Books

Scribner, *imprint of* Scribner Publishing Group

Scribner Classics, *imprint of* Scribner

Scribner Poetry, *imprint of* Scribner

Scripta, *imprint of* Mutual Publishing LLC

Scripta Humanistica Publishing International, *subsidiary of* Brumar Communications

Seaforth Publishing, *distributed by* Casemate | publishers

Seagrass Press, *imprint of* Quarto Publishing Group USA Inc

Search Institute Press®, *division of* Search Institute

Seastone, *imprint of* Ulysses Press

Second Chance Press, *imprint of* The Permanent Press

Second Nature, *distributed by* BPC

Seed Savers, *distributed by* Chelsea Green Publishing Co

Seedling Publications Inc, *imprint of* Continental Press Inc, *distributed by* Kendall Hunt Publishing

Martin E Segal Theatre Center Publications, *distributed by* Theatre Communications Group

SelfHelp Success Books, *distributed by* Pelican Publishing Co

SelfMadeHero, *distributed by* Harry N Abrams Inc

Semiotext(e), *distributed by* The MIT Press

Sendpoints Books Co Ltd, *distributed by* Gingko Press Inc

Sentinel, *imprint of* Penguin Group USA, A Penguin Random House Company

Seoul Selection, *distributed by* University of Hawaii Press

Serif Publishing, *distributed by* Interlink Publishing Group Inc

Serindia Publications, *distributed by* Art Media Resources Inc (US & CN)

Servant Books, *imprint of* Franciscan Media

Service Employees International Union, *distributed by* Chelsea Green Publishing Co

SETAC Press, *imprint of* Society of Environmental Toxicology & Chemistry (SETAC)

7th Generation, *imprint of* BPC

The Seventh Quarry, *imprint of* Cross-Cultural Communications

The Seventh Quarry Press, *imprint of* Cross-Cultural Communications, *distributed by* Cross-Cultural Communications

Shaar Press, *imprint of* Mesorah Publications Ltd

Shabdaguchha (Magazine & Press), *distributed by* Cross-Cultural Communications

Shadow Mountain, *imprint of* Deseret Book Co

Shadow Wolf Press, *imprint of* Winterwolf Press, *distributed by* Winterwolf Press

Shakespeare Playbooks, *imprint of* Bandanna Books

Shambhala Publications Inc, *distributed by* Penguin Random House Inc

Shanghai Press, *distributed by* Tuttle Publishing

Shanghai Press & Publishing Development Co, *distributed by* University of Hawaii Press

Shangri-La, *imprint of* Lotus Press

Shaw Books, *imprint of* WaterBrook

Shawnee Press, *distributed by* Hal Leonard Corp

Shearwater Books, *imprint of* Island Press

Sheep Meadow Press, *distributed by* Syracuse University Press

Sheffield Phoenix Press, *distributed by* SBL Press

Sheffield Publishing Co, *subsidiary of* Waveland Press Inc

Sheldon Press, *distributed by* Hachette Book Group

Sheldrake Press, *distributed by* Interlink Publishing Group Inc

Shen's Books, *imprint of* Lee & Low Books Inc

Shepard & Piper, *imprint of* Shepard Publications

W B Sheridan, *imprint of* Academica Press

Shiloh Kidz, *imprint of* Barbour Publishing Inc

Shiloh Run Press, *imprint of* Barbour Publishing Inc

G Shirmer, *imprint of* Hal Leonard Corp

Short Tales, *imprint of* ABDO Publishing Co Inc

ShowForth Videos, *division of* BJU Press, *imprint of* BJU Press

Shroff Publishers, *distributor for* Mike Murach & Associates Inc

Shufunotomo Co, *distributed by* Tuttle Publishing

Sibelius, *distributed by* Hal Leonard Corp

Sicilia Parra, *distributed by* Cross-Cultural Communications

Side Street, *imprint of* BrickHouse Books Inc

Sierra Club Books, *imprint of* Counterpoint Press LLC, *distributed by* University of California Press

Sierra College Press, *imprint of* Heyday

Sierra Outdoor Products, *distributed by* Gem Guides Book Co

Siete Cuentos Editorial, *imprint of* Seven Stories Press

Signal Books, *distributed by* Interlink Publishing Group Inc

Signatures Network, *distributed by* Andrews McMeel Publishing LLC

Edition du Signe, *distributed by* Gem Guides Book Co

Signet, *imprint of* Berkley Publishing Group, Penguin Group USA, A Penguin Random House Company

Signet Classics, *imprint of* Penguin Group USA, A Penguin Random House Company

Sikorski, *distributed by* Hal Leonard Corp

Siles Press, *division of* Silman-James Press Inc

Silhouette, *imprint of* Harlequin Enterprises Ltd

Silk Label Books, *distributed by* Royal Fireworks Press

Siloam Press, *imprint of* Charisma Media

Mark Silva, *distributed by* Gem Guides Book Co

Silver Dolphin Books, *distributed by* Simon & Schuster, Inc

Silver Dragon Books, *imprint of* Regal Crest Enterprises

Silvereye Learning Resources, *distributor for* Boys Town Press

Silverplume, a Vertafore Co, *distributor for* Standard Publishing Corp

Simcha Press, *imprint of* Health Communications Inc

Simon & Schuster, *imprint of* Simon & Schuster Publishing Group, *distributor for* Alloy Entertainment LLC, Baen Publishing Enterprises, Harlequin Enterprises Ltd, Hazelden Publishing, Insight Editions, Mandala Earth, RosettaBooks, Wisdom Publications Inc, *distributed by* Gem Guides Book Co, Gulf Energy Information

Simon & Schuster Audio, *division of* Simon & Schuster, Inc, *distributor for* Monostereo

Simon & Schuster Books for Young Readers, *imprint of* Simon & Schuster Children's Publishing

Simon & Schuster Children's Publishing, *division of* Simon & Schuster, Inc

Simon & Schuster Inc, *distributor for* Health Communications Inc

Simon & Schuster, Inc, *division of* ViacomCBS Inc, *distributor for* Aconyte, Andrews McMeel Publishing LLC, Artics, Baen Books, Baseball America, Beyond Words, BL Publishing (div of Games Workshop), Boom! Studios, Canterbury Classics (part of Printer's Row), Cardoza Publishing, Centennial Media, Chicken Soup for the Soul Publishing, Cider Mill Press Book Publishers LLC, Cider Mill Press Book Publishers LLC (including Applesauce Press imprint), City Point Press, Downtown Bookworks, Fantoons, Flame Tree Publishing, Forefront, Frederator Books LLC, Gakken, Gallup (worldwide), Galvanized Media, Games Workshop, Hazelden, Health Communications Inc, Hispanic Info & Telecommunications Newtork, Hooked on Phonics (Sandviks HOP Inc/Sandvik Publishing), Humanoids Inc, Igloo Books, Indigo River, Inner Traditions/Bear & Company, Insight Editions, Juniper Publishing, Kaplan Publishing (including Manhattan Prep), Katalitix Media, Keenspot, Kinfolk, Law & Crime Books, Legendary Comics, little bee books, Manhattan Prep Publishing, Manning Publications, Manning Publications Co, Manuscript, Mayo Clinic, Merck Publishing, Moll Anderson Productions, Mrs Wordsmith, NorthSouth Books (div of NordSued Verlag), Oneworld Publications, Oni Press, Open Road Publishing, Parachute Publishing LLC, Pegasus, Permuted Press LLC, Petzel, Piggyback Interactive, Pikachu Press (Pokemon Company International), Pike & Powder, The Pokemon Company International, Post Hill Press LLC, Printer's Row, Reader's Digest Books (div of Trusted Media Brands Inc), Reader's Digest Trade Publishing, Rebellion, Regan Arts, Regnery Publishing, Ripley Entertainment Inc (Ripley's Believe it or Not), Rosetta Books, Ryland Peters & Small (including CICO Books), Silver Dolphin Books (part of Printer's Row), Skyhorse, Start Publishing LLC, Studio Fun International (part of Printer's Row), Tanglewood, Tanglewood Publishing, Thunder Bay Press (part of Printer's Row), Timbuktu, To The Stars Inc, Tra Publishing, Ubisoft, Ulysses Press, Victory Belt Publishing, VIZ Media, Waterhouse, Weldon Owen Publishing, Wisdom Publications, World Almanac (div of Facts on File), Yilin Press (Mandarin ebooks), Zaffre, Z2 Comics, Zuiker Press, David Zwirner Books

Simon & Schuster Pocket Books, *distributor for* Public Citizen

Simon & Schuster Sales Division, *division of* Simon & Schuster, Inc, *distributor for* Andrews McMeel Publishing LLC, Applesauce Press (children's), Baen Books, Baseball America, Boom! Studios, Cardoza Publishing, Cernunnos, Chicken Soup for the Soul Publishing, Cider Mill Press Book Publishers LLC, Downtown Bookworks, Frederator Books LLC, Gallup (worldwide), Galvanized Media, Games Workshop, Hazelden, Health Communications Inc, Hooked On Phonics, Insight Editions, Juniper Publishing, Kaplan Publishing, Katalitix, Kinfolk, little bee books, Manhattan Prep, Manning Publications Co, Merck Publishing, NorthSouth Books, Omnific, Oni Press, Open Road, Permuted Press LLC, Piggyback Interactive, Post Hill Press LLC, Reader's Digest Children's Books, Rebellion, Regan Arts, Ripley Entertainment Inc, To the Stars Inc, Uncrate LLC, VIZ Media, Waterhouse Press, Weldon Owen, World Almanac (div of Facts on File)

Simon & Schuster UK, *distributor for* National Geographic Books

Simon Spotlight, *imprint of* Simon & Schuster Children's Publishing

Simple Productions, *imprint of* Shepard Publications

Simple Truths, *imprint of* Sourcebooks LLC

Simpson, *imprint of* University of California Press

Evelyn Simpson-Curenton, *distributed by* ECS Publishing Group

Sinauer Associates, *imprint of* Oxford University Press (OUP), Oxford University Press USA

Singing Dragon, *imprint of* Jessica Kingsley Publishers Inc

Sisra Music Publishing, *imprint of* Empire Publishing Service

Six House, *subsidiary of* Gallopade International Inc

Sixth&Spring Books, *distributed by* Sterling Publishing Co Inc

SJP, *imprint of* Penguin Random House LLC

Skateman Publications, *imprint of* World Citizens

SkillPath Publications, *division of* The Graceland University Center for Professional Development & Lifelong Learning Inc, *distributor for* Franklin Covey, Pearson Technology, Thomson Publishing, John Wiley & Sons Inc

SkillsTutor, *division of* Houghton Mifflin Harcourt

Skinner House Books, *imprint of* Unitarian Universalist Association

Skipstone, *imprint of* The Mountaineers Books

Skira Editore, *distributed by* Rizzoli International Publications Inc

Sky Pony Press, *imprint of* Skyhorse Publishing Inc

Skyhook Press, *imprint of* Shepard Publications

Skyhorse, *distributed by* Simon & Schuster, Inc

Skylark, *imprint of* Penguin Random House LLC

SkyLight Paths, *imprint of* Turner Publishing Co

Slovenian Cinematheque, *distributed by* Columbia University Press

Slow Food Editore, *distributed by* Chelsea Green Publishing Co

Small Horizons, *imprint of* New Horizon Press

Small Press United, *distributor for* Academy of Nutrition & Dietetics

Smart Apple Media, *imprint of* Black Rabbit Books

Smart Kidz, *imprint of* Whitaker House

Smart Pop, *imprint of* BenBella Books Inc

Smart Sex Stuff for Kids, *imprint of* Gallopade International Inc

SmartLab, *distributed by* Chronicle Books

SmartLab Toys, *imprint of* Quarto Publishing Group USA Inc

SmartPros, *distributed by* PPI, A Kaplan Company

SmartsCo, *distributed by* Chronicle Books

SMC Publishing, *distributed by* Cheng & Tsui Co Inc

SME (Society of Manufacturing Engineers), *distributor for* Industrial Press, McGraw-Hill, Prentice Hall, John Wiley & Sons Inc, *distributed by* American Technical Publishers Inc, McGraw-Hill, Productivity Press

Smith & Kraus Books For Kids, *imprint of* Smith & Kraus Publishers Inc

Smith & Kraus Global, *subsidiary of* Smith & Kraus Publishers Inc

Gibbs Smith, *distributed by* Gem Guides Book Co

Gibbs Smith Publisher, *distributor for* Angel City Press

M Lee Smith Publishers, *division of* BLR®—Business & Legal Resources

Smith Street Books, *distributed by* Rizzoli International Publications Inc

Smithsonian Institution Scholarly Press, *division of* Smithsonian Institution, *distributed by* Penguin Random House Inc

Smitten Historical Romance, *imprint of* Lighthouse Publishing of the Carolinas

Snake Country Publishing, *distributed by* Caxton Press

Snova, *imprint of* Nova Science Publishers Inc

Snow Lion, *imprint of* Shambhala Publications Inc

Snowy Owl Books, *imprint of* University of Alaska Press

Societe Mathematique de France, *distributed by* American Mathematical Society

Society for American Baseball Research, *distributed by* University of Nebraska Press

Society of the Cincinnati, *distributed by* University Press of America Inc

Soffietto Editions, *imprint of* Red Moon Press

Soft Skull Press, *imprint of* Counterpoint Press LLC

Sogang University Institute, *distributed by* Cheng & Tsui Co Inc

Soho Crime, *imprint of* Soho Press Inc

Soho Press, *imprint of* Soho Press Inc

Soho Teen, *imprint of* Soho Press Inc

Solar Design Association, *distributed by* Chelsea Green Publishing Co

Solution Tree Press, *imprint of* Solution Tree

Somerset Press, *division of* Hope Publishing Co

Sommer-Time Story Classics Series, *imprint of* Advance Publishing Inc

Sommer-Time Story Series, *imprint of* Advance Publishing Inc

Sonrise Devotionals, *imprint of* Lighthouse Publishing of the Carolinas

Sony, *distributed by* Hal Leonard Corp

Sorin Books, *imprint of* Ave Maria Press

Sound Ideas, *imprint of* Simon & Schuster Audio

Sounds True Inc, *distributed by* Gem Guides Book Co, Macmillan

Sourcebooks, *imprint of* Sourcebooks LLC

Sourcebooks Casablanca, *imprint of* Sourcebooks LLC

Sourcebooks eXplore, *imprint of* Sourcebooks LLC

Sourcebooks Fire, *imprint of* Sourcebooks LLC

Sourcebooks Jabberwocky, *imprint of* Sourcebooks LLC

Sourcebooks Landmark, *imprint of* Sourcebooks LLC

Sourcebooks LLC, *distributor for* Prufrock Press, *distributed by* Penguin Random House India (India & subcontinent)

Sourcebooks Wonderland, *imprint of* Sourcebooks LLC

Sourcebooks Young Readers, *imprint of* Sourcebooks LLC

Sourced Media Books, *distributed by* Gibbs-Smith, Many Hats Media

SourceResource, *distributor for* MAR*CO Products Inc

South Carolina Bar Association, *distributed by* University of South Carolina Press

South Carolina Historical Society, *distributed by* University of South Carolina Press

Southeast Asia Program Publications, *imprint of* Cornell University Press

Southeastern Center for Contemporary Art, *distributed by* The University of North Carolina Press

Southeastern Cooperative Wildlife Disease Study, *distributed by* American Association for Vocational Instructional Materials

Southern Early Childhood Association, *distributed by* Gryphon House Inc

Southern Illinois University Press, *division of* Southern Illinois University

Southern Voices Audio, *imprint of* Recorded Books Inc, an RBmedia company

Southwestern Studies, *imprint of* Texas Western Press

Sparkhouse, *imprint of* Augsburg Fortress Publishers, Publishing House of the Evangelical Lutheran Church in America

Speak, *imprint of* Penguin Young Readers Group

Specialized Software, *imprint of* Lotus Press

Spectra, *imprint of* Penguin Random House LLC

Spectroscopy Now, *imprint of* John Wiley & Sons Inc

Spectrum, *distributor for* National Council of Teachers of Mathematics (NCTM)

Spellbound, *imprint of* ABDO Publishing Co Inc

SPIE Digital Library, *imprint of* SPIE

SPIE Journals, *imprint of* SPIE

SPIE Press, *imprint of* SPIE

Spinsters Ink, *imprint of* Bella Books

Spire Books, *imprint of* Revell

Spirit, *imprint of* Norilana Books

Spirit Mountain Press, *distributed by* University of Alaska Press

Sporting News, *distributed by* Andrews McMeel Publishing LLC

SportsZone, *imprint of* ABDO Publishing Co Inc

Spotlight, *imprint of* ABDO Publishing Co Inc

Spotlight Books, *imprint of* Empire Publishing Service

Spotted Dog Press, *distributed by* Gem Guides Book Co

Jack Spratt Choral Music, *imprint of* Empire Publishing Service

Spring Publications, *distributed by* Bloomsbury Academic

Springer, *subsidiary of* Springer Science+Business Media, *distributor for* The Minerals, Metals & Materials Society (TMS)

Springer Healthcare, *imprint of* Springer

Springer-Verlag, *distributor for* American Institute of Physics

Springhouse Editions, *subsidiary of* White Pine Press, *distributed by* White Pine Press

Sproutman Publications, *distributed by* BPC

Spruce Books, *imprint of* Sasquatch Books

Spyglass Books LLC, *distributed by* Biographical Publishing Co

Square One Publishers Inc, *distributor for* Inno-Vision Health Media, Rainbow Ridge Books, *distributed by* Thomas Allen & Son

SRA/McGraw-Hill, *imprint of* McGraw-Hill Education

Sri Aurobindo Ashram, *distributed by* Lotus Press

Sri Lanka Institute of Traditional Studies, *distributed by* Fons Vitae

SSPC, *distributed by* NACE International

SSPC: The Society for Protective Coatings, *distributed by* Technology Publishing Co

Stacey International Ltd (London), *distributed by* International Book Centre Inc

Stackpole Books, *imprint of* Rowman & Littlefield Publishing Group, *distributor for* The Colonial Williamsburg Foundation

Stainer & Bell Ltd, *distributed by* ECS Publishing Group

Stamford University Press, *distributed by* Oxford University Press USA

Standard Lesson Commentary®, *imprint of* Standard Publishing

Standard Lesson Quarterly®, *imprint of* Standard Publishing

Standard Lesson Resources®, *imprint of* Standard Publishing

Standard Publishing, *imprint of* David C Cook

Standard Publishing Corp, *distributed by* Lexis-Nexis®, Silverplume, a Vertafore Co

Stanford Briefs, *imprint of* Stanford University Press

Stanford Business Books, *imprint of* Stanford University Press

Stanford University Press, *distributor for* Woodrow Wilson Center Press

Star Sounds, *distributed by* Lotus Press

Star Trek®, *imprint of* Gallery Books

Starberry Books, *imprint of* Boyds Mills & Kane, *distributed by* Lerner Publishing Group Inc

Starcrafts Publishing, *imprint of* Starcrafts LLC

Starfire Publishing, *distributed by* Holmes Publishing Group LLC

Starrhill Press, *imprint of* River City Publishing LLC

Starscape, *imprint of* Tom Doherty Associates, LLC

Start Publishing LLC, *distributed by* Simon & Schuster, Inc

State Experience, *imprint of* Gallopade International Inc

State Stuff, *imprint of* Gallopade International Inc

State University of New York Press, *distributor for* Albany Institute of History & Art, Codhill Press, Samuel Dorsky Museum of Art, Mount

Ida Press, Muswell Hill Press, New Netherland Institute, Rockefeller Institute Press, Uncrowned Queens

Steam Passages Publishing, *distributed by* Heimburger House Publishing Co

Steam Press, *distributed by* Gryphon House Inc

Steeple Hill, *imprint of* Harlequin Enterprises Ltd

Steinberg, *distributed by* Hal Leonard Corp

Rudolf Steiner Press UK, *distributor for* SteinerBooks Inc

Rudolph Steiner Press, *distributed by* SteinerBooks Inc

SteinerBooks Inc, *imprint of* Anthroposophic Press Inc, *distributor for* Chiron Publications, Clairview Books, Floris Books, Hawthorn Press, Lantern Books, Rudolph Steiner Press, Temple Lodge Publishing, *distributed by* Rudolf Steiner Press UK

Steinsaltz, *imprint of* The Toby Press LLC, *distributed by* The Toby Press LLC

Stenhouse Publishers, *division of* Highlights for Children Education Group, *distributor for* Pembroke Publishers

Sterling, *imprint of* Sterling Publishing Co Inc

Sterling & Francine Clark Art Institute, *distributed by* Yale University Press

Sterling Children's Books, *imprint of* Sterling Publishing Co Inc

Sterling Epicure, *imprint of* Sterling Publishing Co Inc

Sterling Ethos, *imprint of* Sterling Publishing Co Inc

Sterling Publishing Co Inc, *subsidiary of* Barnes & Noble Inc, *distributor for* Against All Odds Productions, Amber Books Ltd, Boxer Books, Brooklyn Botanic Garden, Enchanted World, Liminal 11, Sally Milner Publishing, Pavilion, Salaryia, Sixth&Spring Books, White Star Publishers, *distributed by* Gem Guides Book Co, Hal Leonard Corp, Heimburger House Publishing Co

Sterling Signature, *imprint of* Sterling Publishing Co Inc

Gareth Stevens, *distributed by* Perfection Learning

Stewart, Tabori & Chang, *imprint of* Harry N Abrams Inc

Stimulus Books, *imprint of* Paulist Press

Stone Arch Books, *imprint of* Capstone Publishers™

Leighton Stone, *distributed by* Gem Guides Book Co

Stone Pier Press, *distributed by* Chelsea Green Publishing Co

Stonefield Publishing, *distributed by* Chelsea Green Publishing Co

Stonewall, *imprint of* BrickHouse Books Inc

Stonewall Inn Editions, *imprint of* St Martin's Press, LLC

Storey Publishing LLC, *division of* Workman Publishing Co Inc, *distributed by* Gem Guides Book Co

Story Line Press, *imprint of* Red Hen Press

Story Monsters Press, *imprint of* Story Monsters LLC

The Story Plant, *division of* Studio Digital CT LLC

Story River Books, *imprint of* University of South Carolina Press

Straight Street Books, *imprint of* Lighthouse Publishing of the Carolinas

String Letter Publishing, *distributed by* Hal Leonard Corp

Strong Books, *imprint of* Book Marketing Works LLC

Lyle Stuart Books, *imprint of* Kensington Publishing Corp

Stubs Guides, *distributed by* Hagstrom Map

Stubs Magazine, *distributed by* American Map Corp

Studio, *imprint of* Penguin Group USA, A Penguin Random House Company

Studio Fun International, *distributed by* Simon & Schuster, Inc

Stylus Publishing LLC, *distributor for* Baseball Prospectus, Cabi Books, Campus Compact, Commonwealth Scientific & Industrial Research Organization (CSIRO), CSREA, Mercury Learning & Information, Myers Education Press, National Resource Center for The First-Year Experience & Students in Transition, River Publishers, Thorogood Publishing, Trentham Books Ltd, UCL IOE Press, World Health Organization (WHO)

Success Advertising, *division of* Success Advertising & Publishing

Success Advertising & Publishing, *division of* The Success Group

Suffolk Records Society, *imprint of* Boydell & Brewer Inc

Sugar Cane Press, *distributed by* Heimburger House Publishing Co

Summer Institute of Linguistics, *subsidiary of* SIL International

Summertime, *imprint of* Summertime Publications Inc

Summertime Publications Inc, *distributor for* ACHCBYZ (Paris academic press specializing in Byzantine history)

Summit Books, *imprint of* Perfection Learning

Sun & Moon Classics, *imprint of* Green Integer

Sun Books, *imprint of* Sun Publishing Company

Sun Plans Inc, *distributed by* Chelsea Green Publishing Co

Sun Publishing Company, *division of* The Sun Companies

Sunbelt Publications Inc, *distributor for* FineEdge.com LLC

Sundance/Newbridge Publishing, *division of* Rowman & Littlefield Publishing Group

Sunflower Books, *distributed by* Interlink Publishing Group Inc

Sunrise Library, *imprint of* Theosophical University Press

Sunrise River Press, *affiliate of* Cartech Books/Specialty Press

SUP Publishing Logistics, *distributed by* Cheng & Tsui Co Inc

Super Sandcastle, *imprint of* ABDO Publishing Co Inc

SuperGenius, *imprint of* Papercutz

Supplement Editions, *imprint of* Bandanna Books

Sure Fire Press, *imprint of* Holmes Publishing Group LLC

Surrey Books, *imprint of* Agate Publishing

Sustainability Press, *distributed by* Chelsea Green Publishing Co

Swallow Press, *imprint of* Ohio University Press

Swallow's Tale Press, *imprint of* Livingston Press, *distributed by* Livingston Press

Swan Books, *division of* Learning Links Inc

Swan Isle Press, *distributed by* University of Chicago Press

Swedish Corrosion Institute, *distributed by* NACE International

Sweet & Maxwell, *distributed by* William S Hein & Co Inc

Sweetwater Books, *imprint of* Cedar Fort Inc

Swerve, *imprint of* St Martin's Press, LLC

Switchgrass Books, *imprint of* Northern Illinois University Press

The Sword of Norilana, *imprint of* Norilana Books

Sybex, *imprint of* John Wiley & Sons Inc

Sybex Inc, *division of* John Wiley & Sons Inc, *distributed by* EMC Publishing LLC

Sylvan Learning, *imprint of* Penguin Random House LLC, Random House Children's Books

Synergy, *imprint of* Bridge-Logos

Syracuse University Press, *distributor for* Arlen House, Pucker Gallery, Sheep Meadow Press (poetry), *distributed by* Arlen House, Dedalus Press, Gryphon House Inc, Heimburger House Publishing Co

Tab Books, *distributor for* National Association of Broadcasters (NAB)

Tabard Press, *imprint of* Konecky & Konecky LLC

Tabernacle Publishing, *division of* Hope Publishing Co

Tadpole Books, *imprint of* Jump!

The TAFT Group®, *imprint of* Gale

Tai Chi Foundation, *distributed by* Tuttle Publishing

Richard F Taitano Micronesia Area Research Center, *distributed by* University of Hawaii Press

Talbot Publishing, *imprint of* The Lawbook Exchange Ltd

Tale Blazers, *imprint of* Perfection Learning

TaLeKa, *imprint of* Norilana Books

Nan A Talese, *imprint of* Knopf Doubleday Publishing Group, Penguin Random House LLC

Talking Donkey Press, *imprint of* All About Kids Publishing

Tamar Books, *imprint of* Mesorah Publications Ltd

Tamesis Books, *imprint of* Boydell & Brewer Inc

TAN Books, *imprint of* Saint Benedict Press LLC

T&T Clark International, *imprint of* Bloomsbury Publishing PLC

Tanglewood, *distributed by* Simon & Schuster, Inc

Tanglewood Publishing, *distributed by* Simon & Schuster, Inc

Tantor Audio, *imprint of* Tantor Media Inc

Tantor Media, *imprint of* Tantor Media Inc

Tantor Media Inc, *division of* Recorded Books

The S Mark Taper Foundation, *imprint of* University of California Press

Tapestry Press Ltd, *distributed by* Maryland History Press

Tara Publications, *distributed by* Hal Leonard Corp

Tarcher Perigee, *imprint of* Penguin Group USA, A Penguin Random House Company

TarcherPerigee, *imprint of* Penguin Group USA, A Penguin Random House Company, Penguin Group USA, A Penguin Random House Company

Taschen GmbH, *imprint of* Taschen America

Tata Institute of Fundamental Research, *distributed by* American Mathematical Society

Tata/McGraw-Hill, *imprint of* McGraw-Hill Education

Tate Galleries, *distributed by* Oak Knoll Press

Tate Publishing, *distributed by* Harry N Abrams Inc

Tattered Flag, *distributed by* Casemate | publishers

The Taunton Press Inc, *distributor for* Guild of Master Craftsman (North America), Lucky Spool (North America & Australia)

Taunton Sterling Dover, *distributed by* Fox Chapel Publishing Co Inc

I B Tauris & Co Ltd, *distributed by* Palgrave Macmillan

Taylor & Francis, *distributor for* The Fairmont Press Inc, *distributed by* Illuminating Engineering Society of North America (IES)

Taylor & Francis Asia Pacific, *imprint of* Taylor & Francis Inc

Taylor & Francis Books, *imprint of* Taylor & Francis Inc

Taylor Trade, *imprint of* The Globe Pequot Press

Tayo Press, *distributed by* Franklin, Beedle & Associates Inc

TCU Press, *distributed by* Texas A&M University Press

Teach Yourself Visually, *imprint of* John Wiley & Sons Inc

Teachers College Press, *affiliate of* Teachers College, Columbia University

Teacher's Discovery, *division of* American Eagle Co Inc

Teaching Strategies LLC, *distributor for* Gryphon House, *distributed by* Gryphon House Inc

Techne Press, *distributed by* Island Press

Technology, *division of* Scholastic Education

Technology Publishing Co, *distributor for* SSPC: The Society for Protective Coatings

Techstreet, *distributed by* Illuminating Engineering Society of North America (IES)

TEEN Crave, *imprint of* Entangled Publishing LLC

TEEN Crush, *imprint of* Entangled Publishing LLC

Katherine Tegen Books, *imprint of* HarperCollins Children's Books

Telshare Publishing, *distributed by* Gryphon House Inc

Templar Books, *imprint of* Candlewick Press

Temple Lodge Publishing, *distributed by* Steiner-Books Inc

Temple University Press, *division of* Temple University of the Commonwealth System of Higher Education

Templeton Press, *subsidiary of* John Templeton Foundation

Temporal Mechanical Press, *division of* Enos Mills Cabin Museum

Ten Speed Press, *imprint of* Crown Publishing Group, Penguin Random House LLC

Teora, *imprint of* Teora USA LLC

Terrapin Greetings, *imprint of* Down The Shore Publishing Corp

TESOL International Association, *distributed by* Alta Book Center Publishers, New Readers Press, Saddleback Educational

Teton NewMedia Inc, *distributor for* LifeLearn, *distributed by* Blackwells, LifeLearn, Logan Brothers, Rittenhouse, Yankee

Texas A&M University Press, *division of* Texas A&M University, Texas A&M University, *distributor for* Stephen F Austin State University Press, McWhiney Foundation Press/State House Press, TCU Press, Texas Christian University Press, Texas Review Press, Texas State Historical Association, University of North Texas Press

Texas Christian University Press, *distributed by* Texas A&M University Press

Texas Memorial Museum, *distributed by* Bureau of Economic Geology

Texas Parks & Wildlife Department, *distributed by* University of Texas Press

Texas Review Press, *distributed by* Texas A&M University Press

Texas State Historical Association, *distributed by* Oak Knoll Press, Texas A&M University Press

Texas Tech University Press, *distributor for* The Colonial Williamsburg Foundation, National Ranching Heritage Center

University of Texas Press, *division of* University of Texas, *distributor for* Bat Conservation International, Institute for Mesoamerican Studies, Menil Foundation, Rothko Chapel, Texas Parks & Wildlife Department, Texas Western Press

Texas Western Press, *affiliate of* University of Texas at El Paso, *distributed by* University of Texas Press

TFH Publications Inc, *subsidiary of* Central Garden & Pet Corp

Thames & Hudson, *distributor for* MFA Publications, National Gallery of Art, The Vendome Press, *distributed by* W W Norton & Company Inc

That Patchwork Place, *imprint of* Martingale®

That the World May Know, *imprint of* Focus on the Family

Theatre Communications Group, *distributor for* Chance Magazine, 53rd State Press, Nick Hern Books, League of Professional Theatre Women, Padua Playwrights Press, PAJ Publications, Playscripts Inc, Playwrights Canada Press, Martin E Segal Theatre Center Publications, Ubu Repertory Theatre Publications

Theion Publishing, *distributed by* Holmes Publishing Group LLC

Theology of the Body Series, *imprint of* Pauline Books & Media

Theophilis, *imprint of* Transcontinental Music Publications (TMP)

Theosophical University Press, *affiliate of* Theosophical Society (Pasadena)

Thesaurus Islamicus Foundation, *distributed by* Fons Vitae

Theta Books, *imprint of* Bridge Publications Inc

Theta Foundation of Bucharest, *distributed by* American Mathematical Society

Thieme Medical Publishers Inc, *subsidiary of* Georg Thieme Verlag KG, *distributor for* AO Foundation

Thinking Like a Scientist, *imprint of* Sundance/Newbridge Publishing

30 Degrees South Publishers, *distributed by* Casemate | publishers

37 INK, *imprint of* Simon & Schuster

Thomas Nelson, *imprint of* HarperCollins Christian Publishing, *distributed by* Winston-Derek

Thomson Publishing, *distributed by* Oxford University Press USA, SkillPath Publications

Thomson Reuters, *distributor for* AICPA Professional Publications

Thomson West, *imprint of* Thomson Reuters Legal Solutions

Thorndike Press, *subsidiary of* Cengage Learning

Thorndike Press®, *imprint of* Gale, *distributor for* Grand Central/Hachette Large Print, HarperLuxe, Mills & Boon Large Print, Random House Large Print

Nelson Thornes, *distributed by* Trans-Atlantic Publications Inc

Thorogood Publishing, *distributed by* Stylus Publishing LLC

Three Hands Press, *distributed by* Holmes Publishing Group LLC

Three Hills, *imprint of* Cornell University Press

360 Degrees, *imprint of* Tiger Tales

Three L Media, *imprint of* Stone Bridge Press Inc

Three Pines Press, *distributed by* University of Hawaii Press

Three Rivers Press, *imprint of* Crown Publishing Group, Penguin Random House LLC

Throckmorton Press, *distributed by* powerHouse Books

Thunder Bay Press, *distributed by* Heimburger House Publishing Co, Simon & Schuster, Inc

Tia Chucha Press, *distributed by* Northwestern University Press

Tidewater Publishers, *imprint of* Cornell Maritime Press, Schiffer Publishing Ltd

Tilbury House Publishers, *imprint of* WordSplice Studio LLC, *distributor for* Marshall Wilkes Publishing, *distributed by* W W Norton & Company Inc

Tiller Press, *imprint of* Simon & Schuster, Inc

Timber Press, *division of* Workman Publishing Co Inc

Timber Press Inc, *division of* Workman Publishing Co Inc, *distributed by* Thomas Allen & Son

Timbuktu, *distributed by* Simon & Schuster, Inc

Time Inc Books, *distributed by* Hachette Book Group

Times Books, *imprint of* Henry Holt and Company, LLC

Tin House Books, *distributed by* W W Norton & Company Inc

Tiny Golem Press, *subsidiary of* Everything Goes Media LLC

Tiny Reparations Books, *imprint of* Plume

To the Stars Inc, *distributed by* Simon & Schuster, Inc, Simon & Schuster Sales Division

The Toby Press LLC, *distributor for* Ofeq Books, Steinsaltz

Toccata Press, *imprint of* Boydell & Brewer Inc

Today's Books, *imprint of* History Publishing Co LLC

Today's Titles, *imprint of* History Publishing Co LLC

Eckhart Tolle Editions, *imprint of* New World Library

Tommy Nelson®, *imprint of* Thomas Nelson

Tonga Books, *imprint of* Europa Editions

Delos Toole Gold Books, *distributed by* Gem Guides Book Co

TOP, *imprint of* Top Publications Ltd

Top Keynote Speakers, *imprint of* Avant-Guide

Top of the Mountain Publishing, *division of* Powell Productions

Topaz, *imprint of* Penguin Group USA, A Penguin Random House Company

Toplight Books, *imprint of* McFarland

Tor, *imprint of* Tom Doherty Associates, LLC

Tor Classics, *imprint of* Tom Doherty Associates, LLC

Tor Teen, *imprint of* Tom Doherty Associates, LLC

Torah Umesorah Publications, *division of* Torah Umesorah-National Society for Hebrew Day Schools

Torrid Books, *imprint of* Whiskey Creek Press

Tory Corner Editions, *imprint of* Quincannon Publishing Group

Total Information, *distributor for* Primary Research Group Inc

Touch for Health, *distributed by* DeVorss & Co

Tourism Dynamic, *imprint of* Cognizant Communication Corp

Towers Maguire Publishing, *imprint of* The Local History Co

Tra Publishing, *distributed by* Simon & Schuster, Inc

Track & Trail Publications, *distributed by* Gem Guides Book Co

Tradery House, *imprint of* Wimmer Cookbooks

Tradigital, *distributed by* Fons Vitae

Tradition Books, *imprint of* The Child's World Inc, *distributed by* The Child's World Inc

Trafalgar Square Books, *distributor for* J A Allen, Kenilworth Press, Pferdia TV

Trafford, *division of* Author Solutions LLC

Trailblazer Press, *distributed by* Chelsea Green Publishing Co

Trailblazer Western Fiction, *imprint of* Lighthouse Publishing of the Carolinas

Oswald Train, *distributed by* Donald M Grant Publisher Inc

Training & Development Materials of Canada, *distributor for* HRD Press

Trakker Maps Inc, *subsidiary of* American Map Corp, *distributed by* Hagstrom Map

Tralco, *distributor for* Beach Lloyd Publishers LLC

Trans-Atlantic Publications Inc, *distributor for* Book Guild, Financial Times Publishing, Hodder Education, IndieBooks, Instituto Monsa de Ediciones SA (art books from Spain), Longman, Arnoldo Mondadori Electa, Nexus Special Interests, Pearson Education, Nelson Thornes

Transaction Publishers Inc, *distributor for* University of California Institute on Global Conflict & Cooperation

Transactions, *imprint of* American Philosophical Society

Transcontinental Music Publications (TMP), *division of* American Conference of Cantors (ACC)

Transcript Verlag, *distributed by* Columbia University Press

Transformation Media Books, *imprint of* Pen & Publish LLC

Transforming Press, *distributed by* Crown House Publishing Co LLC

Transportation Research Board (TRB), *division of* The National Academies of Sciences, Engineering & Medicine

Transportation Research Board Code, *distributed by* PPI, A Kaplan Company

Travelers' Tales, *subsidiary of* Solas House Inc

Treacle Press, *imprint of* McPherson & Co

Treasure Chest Books, *distributor for* Ocean Tree Books, *distributed by* Gem Guides Book Co

Tree of Life Books, *imprint of* Progressive Press

Trees Company Press, *distributed by* Gem Guides Book Co

Trends Experts, *imprint of* Avant-Guide

Trentham Books Ltd, *distributed by* Stylus Publishing LLC

Triad Publishing Co, *imprint of* Triad Communications Inc

Triangle Square Books for Young Readers, *imprint of* Seven Stories Press

Trillium Press, *distributed by* Royal Fireworks Press

Trinity Grace Press, *imprint of* Signalman Publishing

Trinity University Press, *unit of* Trinity University

TriQuarterly Books, *imprint of* Northwestern University Press

TRISTAN OUTDOORS, *imprint of* TRISTAN Publishing

Triumph Books, *distributor for* United States Tennis Association

Triumph Entertainment, *imprint of* Triumph Books

Triumph Learning LLC, *affiliate of* School Specialty Inc

Troitsa Publications, *imprint of* Nova Science Publishers Inc

Troubadour Books, *imprint of* Regal Crest Enterprises

Truman State University Press, *unit of* Truman State University

Truman Talley Books, *imprint of* St Martin's Press, LLC

Trust for Public Land, *distributed by* Chelsea Green Publishing Co

Trusted Books, *imprint of* Deep River Books LLC

Truth to Power Books (T2P), *imprint of* Steerforth Press

Tu Books, *imprint of* Lee & Low Books Inc

Tudor Publishers Inc, *subsidiary of* Cornwallis Press, Cornwallis Press (young adult fiction & nonfiction)

Tughra Books, *imprint of* Blue Dome Inc

Tulika Books, *distributed by* Columbia University Press

Tumbleweed Series, *imprint of* Mountain Press Publishing Co

Turnaround (London), *distributor for* Bella Books

Turner, *imprint of* Turner Publishing Co

Turtle Point, *imprint of* Turtle Point Press

Turtleback Books, *division of* Perfection Learning

Tusk Ivory, *imprint of* The Overlook Press

Tusk Paperbacks, *imprint of* The Overlook Press

Tuttle Publishing, *member of* Periplus Publishing Group, *distributor for* Healing Tao Books, Kosei Publishing Co, Kotan Publishing Inc, Milet Publishing Ltd, Paperweight Press, Periplus Editions, Shanghai Press, Shufunotomo Co, Tai Chi Foundation

TVL VIDEO, *distributed by* Gem Guides Book Co

Mark Twain Media, *distributed by* Carson Dellosa Publishing LLC

Twelve, *imprint of* Grand Central Publishing

Twenty-First Century Books, *imprint of* Lerner Publishing Group Inc

Twenty-Third Publications, *division of* Bayard Inc, *distributor for* Novalis (Canada), *distributed by* Columba (UK), John Garrett (Australia), Novalis (Canada)

Twilight Visions, *imprint of* Twilight Times Books

TwoDot®, *imprint of* The Globe Pequot Press

Tycoon Percussion, *distributed by* Hal Leonard Corp

Tyndale Audio, *imprint of* Tyndale House Publishers Inc

Tyndale Entertainment, *imprint of* Tyndale House Publishers Inc

Tyndale House Publishers Inc, *distributor for* Focus on the Family, NavPress, NavPress Publishing Group

Tyndale Kids, *imprint of* Tyndale House Publishers Inc

Tyndale Momentum, *imprint of* Tyndale House Publishers Inc

Tyndale Ninos, *imprint of* Tyndale House Publishers Inc

Typophiles, *distributed by* Oak Knoll Press

U X L™, *imprint of* Gale

UA Museum, *distributed by* University of Alaska Press

UBC Press, Canada, *distributor for* Michigan State University Press (MSU Press)

Ubisoft, *distributed by* Simon & Schuster, Inc

Ubu Repertory Theatre Publications, *distributed by* Theatre Communications Group

UCL IOE Press, *distributed by* Stylus Publishing LLC

UCLA Latin American Center Publications, *unit of* University of California, Los Angeles

Udig, *imprint of* Andrews McMeel Publishing LLC

Ugly Duckling Presse, *distributor for* United Artists

Ulysses Press, *distributed by* Simon & Schuster, Inc

Unarius Academy of Science Publications, *division of* Unarius Educational Foundation

Unarius Video Productions, *division of* Unarius Academy of Science Publications

Uncrate LLC, *distributed by* Simon & Schuster Sales Division

Uncrowned Queens, *distributed by* Excelsior Editions, State University of New York Press

Underlined, *imprint of* Random House Children's Books

Editorial Unilit, *division of* Spanish House Inc

United Artists, *distributed by* Ugly Duckling Presse

United Nations Children's Fund (UNICEF), *distributed by* United Nations Publications

United Nations Development Programme (UNDP), *distributed by* United Nations Publications

United Nations Economic & Social Commission for Asia & the Pacific (ESCAP), *distributed by* United Nations Publications

United Nations Economic & Social Commission for Western Asia (ESCWA), *distributed by* United Nations Publications

United Nations Economic Commission for Africa (ECA), *distributed by* United Nations Publications

United Nations Economic Commission for Europe (ECE), *distributed by* United Nations Publications

United Nations Economic Commission for Latin America & the Caribbean (ECLAC), *distributed by* United Nations Publications

United Nations High Commissioner for Refugees (UNHCR), *distributed by* United Nations Publications

United Nations Human Settlements Programme (UN-HABITAT), *distributed by* United Nations Publications

United Nations Industrial Development Organization (UNIDO), *distributed by* United Nations Publications

United Nations Institute for Disarmament Research (UNIDIR), *distributed by* United Nations Publications

United Nations Institute for Training & Research (UNITAR), *distributed by* United Nations Publications

United Nations International Research & Training Institute for the Advancement of Women (INSTRAW), *distributed by* United Nations Publications

United Nations Interregional Crime & Justice Research Institute (UNICRI), *distributed by* United Nations Publications

United Nations Office for Project Services (UNOPS), *distributed by* United Nations Publications

United Nations Office for the Coordination of Humanitarian Affairs (OCHA), *distributed by* United Nations Publications

United Nations Office on Drugs & Crime (UNODC), *distributed by* United Nations Publications

United Nations Population Fund (UNFPA), *distributed by* United Nations Publications

United Nations Publications, *distributor for* Food & Agriculture Organization of the United Nations (FAO), International Atomic Energy Agency (IAEA), International Criminal Tribunal for Rwanda (UNICTR), International Criminal Tribunal for the former Yugoslavia (ICTY), International Organization for Migration (IOM), International Trade Centre (ITC), Office of the United Nations High Commissioner for Human Rights (OHCHR), United Nations Children's Fund (UNICEF), United Nations Development Programme (UNDP), United Nations Economic & Social Commission for Asia & the Pacific (ESCAP), United Nations Economic & Social Commission for Western Asia (ESCWA), United Nations Economic Commission for Africa (ECA), United Nations Economic Commission for Europe (ECE), United Nations Economic Commission for Latin America & the Caribbean (ECLAC), United Nations High Commissioner for Refugees (UNHCR), United Nations Human Settlements Programme (UN-HABITAT), United Nations Industrial Development Organization (UNIDO), United Nations Institute for Disarmament Research (UNIDIR), United Nations Institute for Training & Research (UNITAR), United Nations International Research & Training Institute for the Advancement of Women (INSTRAW), United Nations Interregional Crime & Justice Research Institute (UNICRI), United Nations Office for Project Services (UNOPS), United Nations Office for the Coordination of Humanitarian Affairs (OCHA), United Nations Office on Drugs &

Crime (UNODC), United Nations Population Fund (UNFPA), United Nations Research Institute for Social Development (UNRISD), United Nations University (UNU)

United Nations Research Institute for Social Development (UNRISD), *distributed by* United Nations Publications

United Nations University (UNU), *distributed by* United Nations Publications

United States Catholic Conference Publications, *distributed by* Liturgy Training Publications

United States Pharmacopeia, *distributed by* Consumer Reports

United States Tennis Association, *distributed by* Triumph Books, Universe Publishing, H O Zimman Inc

Univelt Inc, *affiliate of* American Astronautical Society, *distributor for* Astronautical Society of Western Australia, US Space Foundation

Universe, *imprint of* Rizzoli International Publications Inc, Universe Publishing, *distributor for* Country Music Foundation Press

Universe Calendars, *imprint of* Universe Publishing

Universe Publishing, *imprint of* Rizzoli International Publications Inc, *distributor for* United States Tennis Association, *distributed by* Random House

Universe Publishing Calendars, *distributed by* Andrews McMeel Publishing LLC

University of Alabama Press, *distributor for* Fiction Collective Two Inc (FC2)

University of Alaska Press, *distributor for* Alaska Native Language Center, Alaska Quarterly Review, Alaska Sea Grant, Alutiiq Museum, Anchorage Museum Association, Anchorage Museum of Art History, Arctic Studies Center of the Smithsonian Museum, Far to the North Press, Geophysical Institute, Limestone Press, Spirit Mountain Press, UA Museum, Vanessapress

The University of Arkansas Press, *division of* The University of Arkansas, *distributor for* Butler Center for Arkansas Studies, Moon City Press, Ozark Society

University of California Institute on Global Conflict & Cooperation, *subsidiary of* University of California, *distributed by* The Brookings Institution Press, Columbia International Affairs Online (CIAO), Cornell University Press, Garland Publishers, Lynn-Reinner Publishing, Penn State University Press, Princeton University Press, Transaction Publishers Inc, University of Michigan Press, Westview Press

University of California Press, *distributor for* artSITES, British Film Institute, Sierra Club Books (adult trade), Woodrow Wilson Center Press

University of Chicago Press, *distributor for* CSLI Publications, Getty Publications, National Gallery of Art, St Augustine's Press Inc, Swan Isle Press

University of Hawaii Press, *distributor for* Ai Pohaku Press, Asian Civilisations Museum, Ateneo De Manila University Press, BDK America, College of Tropical Agriculture & Human Resources, Denby Fawcett, Hawaii Nikkei, Hawaiian Mission Children's Society, Hui Hanai, Huia Publishers, Institute of Buddhist Studies, iPRECIATION, Island Research & Education Initiative, Isle Botanica, Japan Playwrights Association, Kailua Historical Society, Kalamaku Press, Kanji Press, Korea Institute, Harvard University, Levesque Publications, Little Island Press, The Lontar Foundation, Manoa Heritage Center, MerwinAsia, The Mozhai Foundation, Jonathan Napela Center, Brigham Young University-Hawaii, Native Books, NIAS Press, North Beach-West Maui Benefit Fund Inc, Ocarina Books, Permanent Agriculture Resources, Punahou School, Renaissance Books, Seoul Selection, Shanghai Press & Publishing Development Co, Richard F Taitano Micronesia Area Research Center, Three Pines Press, University of the Philippines Press

University of Idaho Asian American Comparative Collection, *distributed by* Caxton Press

University of Idaho Press, *distributed by* Caxton Press

University of Illinois Press, *unit of* University of Illinois

University of Manitoba Press, *distributed by* Michigan State University Press (MSU Press)

University of Michigan, *distributed by* International Book Centre Inc

University of Michigan Press, *unit of* University of Michigan, *distributor for* Center for Chinese Studies, University of Michigan, Center for Japanese Studies, University of Michigan, Center for South & Southeast Asian Studies, University of Michigan, University of California Institute on Global Conflict & Cooperation

University of Minnesota Press, *unit of* University of Minnesota, *distributor for* Univocal Publishing, *distributed by* Heimburger House Publishing Co

University of Missouri Press, *distributor for* Missouri History Museum, Missouri Life Magazine, St Louis Mercantile Library

University of Nebraska, *distributed by* Gem Guides Book Co

University of Nebraska Press, *division of* University of Nebraska at Lincoln, *distributor for* Buros Institute, Jewish Publication Society, Society for American Baseball Research

University of New Mexico Press, *distributor for* Museum of New Mexico Press, School for Advanced Research Press

University of New Orleans Press, *division of* University of New Orleans

The University of North Carolina Press, *distributor for* Museum of Early Southern Decorative Arts, North Carolina Museum of Art, Omohundro Institute of Early American History & Culture, Southeastern Center for Contemporary Art, Valentine Museum

University of North Texas Press, *distributed by* Texas A&M University Press

University of Oklahoma Press, *distributor for* Cherokee Heritage Press, Denver Art Museum, Gilcrease Museum

University of Pennsylvania Museum of Archaeology & Anthropology, *division of* University of Pennsylvania, *distributed by* University of Pennsylvania Press

University of Pennsylvania Press, *distributor for* University of Pennsylvania Museum of Archaeology & Anthropology, Winterthur Museum, Garden & Library

University of Puerto Rico Press, *subsidiary of* University of Puerto Rico

University of Rochester Press, *imprint of* Boydell & Brewer Inc, *affiliate of* Boydell & Brewer Inc

University of San Francisco Press, *distributed by* Fordham University Press

University of South Carolina Press, *affiliate of* University of South Carolina, *distributor for* McKissick Museum, Saraland Press, South Carolina Bar Association, South Carolina Historical Society

University of Tennessee Press, *division of* University of Tennessee

University of Texas Press, *division of* University of Texas, *distributor for* Bat Conservation International, Institute for Mesoamerican Studies, Menil Foundation, Rothko Chapel, Texas Parks & Wildlife Department, Texas Western Press

University of the Philippines Press, *distributed by* University of Hawaii Press

University of Tokyo Press, *distributed by* Columbia University Press

University of Toronto Press, *distributor for* Boys Town Press

The University of Utah Press, *subsidiary of* University of Utah, *distributor for* BYU Museum of Peoples & Cultures, BYU Studies, KUED (Utah PBS affiliate), Western Epics Publications

The University of Virginia Press, *affiliate of* University of Virginia, *distributor for* Colonial Society of Massachusetts, The Colonial Williamsburg Foundation, Mount Vernon Ladies Association

University of Virginia Press, *distributor for* The Massachusetts Historical Society

University of Washington Press, *unit of* University of Washington Libraries, *distributor for* American Federation of Arts, Fowler Museum at UCLA, Lost Horse Press, Lynx House Press

University of Wisconsin Press, *unit of* University of Wisconsin-Madison, *distributor for* The Center for the Study of Upper Midwestern Culture, Wisconsin Veterans Museum

University Press, *distributed by* American Mathematical Society

University Press of America Inc, *distributor for* Atlantic Council, Center for National Policy Press, Harvard Center for International Affairs, International Law Institute, Joint Center for Political & Economic Studies Press, White Burkett Miller Center, Society of the Cincinnati

University Press of Colorado, *distributor for* Center for Literary Publishing, History Colorado, Western Press Books

University Press of Florida, *affiliate of* State University System of Florida

The University Press of Kentucky, *distributor for* Kentucky Historical Society

Univocal Publishing, *distributed by* University of Minnesota Press

Unofficial Guides, *imprint of* AdventureKEEN

Upjohn Press, *imprint of* W E Upjohn Institute for Employment Research

Upper Access Books, *imprint of* Upper Access Inc

Upper Playground, *distributed by* Gingko Press Inc

Upper Room Books, *division of* The Upper Room, *imprint of* Abingdon Press, *distributed by* Abingdon Press

Uproar Books, *distributed by* BPC

Upstart Books™, *division of* Demco Inc

Urban Books, *imprint of* Kensington Publishing Corp, *distributed by* Kensington Publishing Corp

Urban Christian, *imprint of* Kensington Publishing Corp

The Urban Explorer - "Only In" Guides, *distributed by* Interlink Publishing Group Inc

Urban Renaissance, *imprint of* Kensington Publishing Corp

US Coast Pilot, *imprint of* ProStar Publications Inc

US Games Systems Inc, *distributor for* Blue Angel Publishing, KonigsFurt

US Government Publishing Office (GPO), *division of* US Government

US Green Building Council, *distributed by* PPI, A Kaplan Company

US International Publishing, *distributed by* Cheng & Tsui Co Inc

US Space Foundation, *distributed by* Univelt Inc

Usborne Books, *imprint of* EDC Publishing

Usborne Publishing Ltd, *distributed by* EDC Publishing

User's Guides, *imprint of* Basic Health Publications

Utah Geological Survey, *division of* Utah Department of Natural Resources

Utah State University Press, *imprint of* University Press of Colorado

Valentine Museum, *distributed by* The University of North Carolina Press

Van der Plas Publications, *imprint of* Cycle Publishing LLC

V&A Publishing, *distributed by* Harry N Abrams Inc

VanDam Publishing, *division of* VanDam Inc

Vandamere Press, *distributor for* ABI Professional Publications (non-exclusive), JMC Press (exclusive to trade), NRH Press (non-exclusive), Quodlibetal Features

Vanderbilt University Press, *division of* Vanderbilt University, *distributor for* Country Music Foundation Press

Vanessapress, *distributed by* University of Alaska Press

Varlik, *subsidiary of* Cross-Cultural Communications

Vedanta Press, *subsidiary of* Vedanta Society of Southern California, *distributor for* Advaita Ashrama, Ananda Ashrama, Ramakrishna Math, Ramakrishna-Vivekananda Center of New York

Vegan Heritage Press, *distributed by* Andrews McMeel Publishing LLC

Velazquez Press, *division of* Academic Learning Co LLC

The Vendome Press, *distributed by* Abrams Books, Harry N Abrams Inc, Thames & Hudson

Venture Press, *imprint of* Williams & Company Book Publishers

Verba Mundi, *imprint of* David R Godine Inc

Veritas, *distributed by* ACTA Publications, Ignatius Press

Vernon Press, *imprint of* Vernon Art & Science Inc

Versify, *imprint of* Houghton Mifflin Harcourt Trade & Reference Division

Verso, *distributed by* Penguin (Canada)

Verso Fiction, *imprint of* Verso

Vesuvian Books, *division of* Vesuvian Media Group Inc

VH1 Books, *imprint of* Gallery Books

VH1 Press, *distributed by* powerHouse Books

Vice Books, *distributed by* powerHouse Books

Victionary, *distributed by* Gingko Press Inc

Victorian Heritage Press, *imprint of* Loving Healing Press Inc

Victory Belt Publishing, *distributed by* Simon & Schuster, Inc

Victory History of the Counties of England, *imprint of* Boydell & Brewer Inc

Vieweg Verlag Publications, *distributed by* American Mathematical Society

Viking, *imprint of* Penguin Group USA, A Penguin Random House Company, Penguin Group USA, A Penguin Random House Company

Viking Children's Books, *imprint of* Penguin Group USA, A Penguin Random House Company, Penguin Group USA, A Penguin Random House Company, Penguin Young Readers Group

Viking Compass, *imprint of* Penguin Group USA, A Penguin Random House Company, Viking

Viking Life, *imprint of* Penguin Group USA, A Penguin Random House Company

Viking Studio, *imprint of* Penguin Group USA, A Penguin Random House Company, Penguin Group USA, A Penguin Random House Company

Villard, *imprint of* Random House Publishing Group

Villard Books, *imprint of* Penguin Random House LLC

Vintage Books, *imprint of* Knopf Doubleday Publishing Group, Penguin Random House LLC

Vintage Children's Classics, *imprint of* Penguin Random House LLC

Vintage Espanol, *imprint of* Penguin Random House LLC

Vintage Guitar, *imprint of* Hal Leonard Corp, *distributed by* Hal Leonard Corp

Vintage Shorts, *imprint of* Vintage Books

Vireo Press, *distributed by* ECS Publishing Group

Virginia Genealogical Society, *distributed by* Heritage Books Inc

Vision, *imprint of* Grand Central Publishing

Visionary Art, *division of* Unarius Academy of Science Publications

Vita Histria, *imprint of* Histria Books

Viva Editions, *distributed by* Red Wheel/Weiser

VIZ Media, *distributed by* Simon & Schuster, Inc, Simon & Schuster Sales Division

Volo, *imprint of* Disney-Hyperion Books

Von Zos Publishing, *distributed by* Holmes Publishing Group LLC

Voracious, *imprint of* Little, Brown and Company

Voyage, *imprint of* Brigantine Media

Voyager Press, *imprint of* Quarto Publishing Group USA Inc

Voyager Sopris Learning Inc, *imprint of* Cambium Learning Inc

Voyageur Press, *distributed by* Hal Leonard Corp

W Publishing Group, *imprint of* Thomas Nelson

WAG Books, *distributed by* Casemate | publishers

Waggle, *imprint of* Triumph Learning LLC

Walden Pond Press, *imprint of* HarperCollins Children's Books

Waldman House Press, *imprint of* TRISTAN Publishing

Wallflower Press, *imprint of* Columbia University Press

Waltons Irish Music, *distributed by* Hal Leonard Corp

WAP Academic, *imprint of* Pentecostal Publishing House

WAP Children, *imprint of* Pentecostal Publishing House

Warboys LLC, *distributed by* Bridge-Logos

Warlord Games, *distributed by* Casemate | publishers

Frederick Warne, *imprint of* Penguin Group USA, A Penguin Random House Company, Penguin Young Readers Group, *distributed by* Perfection Learning

Warner/Chappell Music Inc, *imprint of* Alfred Music

Warner Press, *affiliate of* Church of God

Washington Post Crosswords, *imprint of* Random House Reference/Random House Puzzles & Games

Washington Service Bureau, *subsidiary of* CCH, a Wolters Kluwer business

Washington Square Press, *imprint of* Atria Books

Washington State Historical Society, *distributed by* Washington State University Press

Washington State University Press, *division of* Washington State University, *distributor for* Oregon California Trails Assn, Oregon Writers Colony (single title), Pacific Institute (single title), Washington State Historical Society (single title), WSU Museum of Art

Water Resources Publications LLC, *distributor for* ASAE

WaterBrook, *imprint of* Crown Publishing Group

WaterBrook Multnomah, *imprint of* Penguin Random House LLC

Waterfall Press, *imprint of* Brilliance Audio

Waterford Press, *distributed by* Gem Guides Book Co

Waterfront Soundings Productions, *distributed by* Marine Techniques Publishing

Waterhouse, *distributed by* Simon & Schuster, Inc

Waterhouse Press, *distributed by* Simon & Schuster Sales Division

WaterLife Books, *imprint of* Deep River Books LLC

Watson-Guptill, *imprint of* Crown Publishing Group, Penguin Random House LLC

Watson-Guptill Publications, *imprint of* Crown Publishing Group

Neale Watson Academic Publications, *imprint of* Watson Publishing International LLC

Waverley Books, *distributed by* Interlink Publishing Group Inc

Waverley West, *subsidiary of* McPherson & Co

Wax Facts Press, *distributed by* Gingko Press Inc

WBusiness Books, *imprint of* New Win Publishing

We Do Listen Foundation, *distributed by* Lerner Publishing Group Inc

WEA, *distributed by* Alfred Music

Webster's New World® College Dictionary, *imprint of* Houghton Mifflin Harcourt Trade & Reference Division

Wednesday Books, *imprint of* St Martin's Press, LLC

Wee Sing, *imprint of* Penguin Group USA, A Penguin Random House Company

Irene Weinberger Books, *imprint of* Hamilton Stone Editions

Welcome Enterprises Inc, *imprint of* Rizzoli International Publications Inc, *distributor for* AAP, Cerf & Peterson, Music Sales, Zeke Holdings Ltd, *distributed by* Random House

Weldon Owen, *distributed by* Simon & Schuster Sales Division

Weldon Owen International, *subsidiary of* Insight Editions

Weldon Owen Publishing, *distributed by* Simon & Schuster, Inc

Well-Trained Mind Press, *distributed by* W W Norton & Company Inc

Wellfleet Press, *imprint of* Quarto Publishing Group USA Inc

Wellington Press, *division of* BooksUPrint.com Inc

Welz, *distributed by* Alan Wofsy Fine Arts

Wendy Lamb Books, *imprint of* Penguin Random House LLC, Random House Children's Books

Wesanne Publications, *distributed by* Gem Guides Book Co

Wesleyan Publishing House, *division of* The Wesleyan Church

West 44 Books, *imprint of* Enslow Publishing LLC

West Margin Press®, *unit of* Ingram Content Group LLC

Western Edge Press, *imprint of* Sherman Asher Publishing, Sherman Asher Publishing, *distributed by* Mountain Press Publishing Co

Western Epics Publications, *distributed by* The University of Utah Press

Western Horseman, *imprint of* The Globe Pequot Press

Western Library, *imprint of* Recorded Books Inc, an RBmedia company

Western Press Books, *distributed by* University Press of Colorado

Western Psychological Service, *distributor for* Psychological Assessment Resources Inc (PAR)

Westminster John Knox Press (WJK), *imprint of* Presbyterian Publishing Corp (PPC), *distributor for* Canterbury Press, Church House Publishing, St Andrews Press, SCM Press, Woodlake Publishing Inc

Weston Woods, *imprint of* Scholastic Trade Division

Westview Press, *distributor for* University of California Institute on Global Conflict & Cooperation

Wheatherstone Press, *subsidiary of* Dickinson Consulting Group

Wheeler Publishing™, *imprint of* Gale

Whiskey Creek Press, *imprint of* Start Publishing LLC

Whitaker, *distributor for* Faith Library Publications

Whitaker Espanol, *imprint of* Whitaker House

White Eagle Publishing Trust (England), *distributed by* DeVorss & Co

White Pine Press, *distributor for* Springhouse Editions

White Poppy Press, *imprint of* Modern Memoirs

White Rabbit Press, *distributed by* Cheng & Tsui Co Inc

White Star Publishers, *distributed by* Sterling Publishing Co Inc

White Thread Press, *distributed by* Fons Vitae

Whitford Press, *imprint of* Schiffer Publishing Ltd

Whitney Museum of American Art, *distributed by* Yale University Press

Wide World of Maps Inc, *distributor for* Benchmark Maps, Big Sky Maps, Franko Maps, MacVan Maps (Colorado Springs), Metro Maps, Rand McNally, *distributed by* Rand McNally

Ronald S Wielgus, *distributed by* Gem Guides Book Co

Wilderness Adventures Press Inc, *distributed by* American West Books, Angler's Book Supply, Raymond C Rumpf & Son Inc

Wilderness Press, *imprint of* AdventureKEEN

Wildflower Press, *affiliate of* Oakbrook Press

Wildsam, *imprint of* Arcadia Publishing Inc

Wiley, *imprint of* Turner Publishing Co, *distributed by* AICPA Professional Publications, Gulf Energy Information

Wiley-Blackwell, *imprint of* John Wiley & Sons Inc, *distributor for* American Anthropological Association (AAA)

Wiley Blackwell Publishers, *distributor for* New York Academy of Sciences (NYAS)

Wiley Custom Select, *imprint of* John Wiley & Sons Inc

Wiley Global Education, *imprint of* John Wiley & Sons Inc

Wiley-IEEE Press, *imprint of* IEEE Press, John Wiley & Sons Inc

J Wiley & Sons, *distributed by* Medical Group Management Association (MGMA)

John Wiley & Sons, *distributor for* The Electrochemical Society (ECS), *distributed by* American Water Works Association (AWWA), Heimburger House Publishing Co

John Wiley & Sons Inc, *distributor for* Association for Information Science & Technology (ASIS&T), Center for Creative Leadership LLC, IEEE Press, R S Means from The Gordian Group, *distributed by* American Academy of Environmental Engineers & Scientists®, Center for Creative Leadership LLC, William S Hein & Co Inc, J J Keller & Associates, Inc, NACE International, SAS Press, SkillPath Publications, SME (Society of Manufacturing Engineers)

John Wiley & Sons Inc Global Education, *division of* John Wiley & Sons Inc, John Wiley & Sons Inc

John Wiley & Sons Inc Professional Development, *division of* John Wiley & Sons Inc

Wiley Online Library, *imprint of* John Wiley & Sons Inc

Wiley Science Solutions, *imprint of* John Wiley & Sons Inc

Wiley-VCH, *imprint of* John Wiley & Sons Inc

Wiley Visualizing, *imprint of* John Wiley & Sons Inc

WileyPLUS, *imprint of* John Wiley & Sons Inc

Marshall Wilkes Publishing, *distributed by* Tilbury House Publishers

William Carey Library, *imprint of* William Carey Publishing

William Carey Press, *imprint of* William Carey Publishing

William Carey Publishing, *division of* Frontier Ventures

William, James & Co, *imprint of* Franklin, Beedle & Associates Inc

Williams & Co Publishers, *imprint of* Williams & Company Book Publishers

Willis Music, *distributed by* Hal Leonard Corp

Willow Bend Books, *imprint of* Heritage Books Inc

Wilson Center Press, *imprint of* Woodrow Wilson Center Press

H W Wilson, *imprint of* Grey House Publishing Inc™

Neil Wilson Publishing, *distributed by* Interlink Publishing Group Inc

Wimmer Cookbooks, *division of* Mercury Printing, an RR Donnelley Co

Winchester Press, *imprint of* New Win Publishing

Wind Records, *distributed by* YMAA Publication Center Inc

Windmill Books, *imprint of* The Rosen Publishing Group Inc

Windsor Books, *division of* Windsor Marketing Corp, Windsor Marketing Corp

Kelley Wingate Publications, *imprint of* Carson Dellosa Publishing LLC

Wings Books, *imprint of* Penguin Random House LLC

WingSpread Publishers, *imprint of* Moody Publishers

Winston-Derek, *distributor for* Thomas Nelson

Winterthur Museum, *distributed by* Oak Knoll Press

Winterthur Museum, Garden & Library, *distributed by* ACC Art Books, Monacelli Press, W W Norton & Company Inc, University of Pennsylvania Press

Winterwolf Press, *distributor for* Shadow Wolf Press

Wisconsin Veterans Museum, *distributed by* University of Wisconsin Press

Wisdom Foundation, *distributed by* Fons Vitae

Wisdom Publications, *distributed by* Simon & Schuster, Inc

Wisdom Publications Inc, *distributed by* Simon & Schuster

Paula Wiseman Books, *imprint of* Simon & Schuster Children's Publishing

Witherby Seamanship International Ltd, *distributed by* Marine Techniques Publishing

Witness Impulse, *imprint of* HarperCollins General Books Group

Wittenborn Art Books, *division of* Alan Wofsy Fine Arts, *distributed by* Alan Wofsy Fine Arts

Wizards of the Coast LLC, *subsidiary of* Hasbro Inc, *distributed by* Penguin Random House

Alan Wofsy Fine Arts, *distributor for* Bora, Brusberg (Berlin), Cramer (Geneva), Huber, Ides et Calendes, Kornfeld & Co (Bern), The Picasso Project, Welz, Wittenborn Art Books

Wolfgang Publications, *distributed by* CarTech Inc

WolfWalker Collection, *distributed by* Gem Guides Book Co

Wolters Kluwer, *distributed by* The Professional Education Group LLC (PEG)

Wolters Kluwer Law & Business, *subsidiary of* Wolters Kluwer, Wolters Kluwer

Wolters Kluwer US Corp, *subsidiary of* Wolters Kluwer NV (The Netherlands)

Women In Nontraditional Careers, *imprint of* Her Own Words LLC

Women's History, *imprint of* Her Own Words LLC

Women's Publications, *imprint of* Consumer Press

Marian Wood Books, *imprint of* GP Putnam's Sons (Hardcover)

S Woodhouse Books, *imprint of* Everything Goes Media LLC

Woodlake Publishing Inc, *distributed by* Westminster John Knox Press (WJK)

Woodrow Wilson Center Press, *division of* The Woodrow Wilson International Center for Scholars, Woodrow Wilson International Center for Scholars, *distributed by* Columbia University Press, Johns Hopkins University Press, Stanford University Press, University of California Press

Woodrow Wilson Center Press/Columbia University Press, *imprint of* Woodrow Wilson Center Press

Woodrow Wilson Center Press/Johns Hopkins University Press, *imprint of* Woodrow Wilson Center Press

Woodrow Wilson Center Press/Stanford University Press, *imprint of* Woodrow Wilson Center Press

Woodstock Artists Association & Museum, *distributed by* WoodstockArts

Woodstock Byrdcliffe Guild, *distributed by* WoodstockArts

WoodstockArts, *distributor for* Bushwhack Press, Opus 40, Woodstock Artists Association & Museum, Woodstock Byrdcliffe Guild

Word Aflame Press, *imprint of* Pentecostal Publishing House

Word & Quill Press, *distributed by* Cross-Cultural Communications

WordSong, *imprint of* Boyds Mills & Kane

Wordstock, *distributed by* Franklin, Beedle & Associates Inc

The Working Arts Library, *distributed by* Applause Theatre & Cinema Books

Workman Publishing, *distributor for* Familius

Workman Publishing Co Inc, *distributor for* Algonquin Books, Duo Press, Erewhon Books, The Experiment, Familius

Workman Speakers Bureau, *division of* Workman Publishing Co Inc

Workout, *imprint of* Triumph Learning LLC

Workplace Learning Solutions, *imprint of* John Wiley & Sons Inc

World Almanac, *distributed by* Simon & Schuster, Inc, Simon & Schuster Sales Division

World Almanac®, *imprint of* Skyhorse Publishing Inc

World Bank, *imprint of* World Bank Publications

World Bank Publications, *member of* The World Bank Group

World Book Inc, *subsidiary of* The Scott Fetzer Co

World Catholic Press, *imprint of* Catholic Book Publishing Corp

World Citizens, *affiliate of* Cinema Investments Co Inc, *distributed by* Inland

World Health Organization (WHO), *distributed by* Stylus Publishing LLC

World Noir, *imprint of* Europa Editions

World of Eric Carle, *imprint of* Penguin Young Readers Group

World Wisdom, *distributed by* Fons Vitae

The World's Largest Publishing Co, *subsidiary of* Gallopade International Inc

WorldTariff, *division of* FedEx Corp

Worldwide Mystery, *imprint of* Harlequin Enterprises Ltd

Worth Publishers, *imprint of* Macmillan Learning

Worthy Publishing, *imprint of* Hachette Nashville

Wrightbooks, *imprint of* John Wiley & Sons Inc

Write Stuff®, *imprint of* Write Stuff Enterprises LLC

WriteLife Publishing, *imprint of* Boutique of Quality Books Publishing

Writers & Artists on Photography Series, *imprint of* Aperture Books

Writer's Digest Books, *imprint of* Penguin Random House LLC

Wrox™, *imprint of* John Wiley & Sons Inc

WRS Group, *distributor for* MAR*CO Products Inc

WSU Museum of Art, *distributed by* Washington State University Press

Wyrick & Co, *imprint of* Gibbs Smith Publisher

Xemplar, *imprint of* Crossquarter Publishing Group

Xeno Books, *imprint of* Red Hen Press

Xlibris Corp, *imprint of* Author Solutions LLC

XLN Audio, *distributed by* Hal Leonard Corp

XML Press, *subsidiary of* R L Hamilton & Associates LLC

Xoanon Publishing, *distributed by* Holmes Publishing Group LLC

Xpat Fiction, *imprint of* Franklin, Beedle & Associates Inc

YA Angst, *imprint of* Norilana Books

YA Books, *imprint of* Regal Crest Enterprises

YACK!, *imprint of* Eifrig Publishing LLC

Yale Center for British Art, *distributed by* Yale University Press

Yale Press Audio, *imprint of* Yale University Press

Yale University Art Gallery, *distributed by* Yale University Press

Yale University Press, *division of* Yale University, *distributor for* American Federation of Arts, The Art Institute of Chicago, The Bard Graduate Center, Beinecke Rare Book & Manuscript Library, The Colonial Williamsburg Foundation, Dallas Museum of Art, Harvard Art Museums, Harvard University Art Museums, The Jewish Museum, Kimbell Art Museum, Paul Mellon Centre, The Menil Collection, Mercatorfonds, The Metropolitan Museum of Art, National Gallery, London, National Gallery of Art, National Gallery of Art (Washington, DC), Philadelphia Museum of Art, Princeton University Art Museum, Sterling & Francine Clark Art Institute, Whitney Museum of American Art, Yale Center for British Art, Yale University Art Gallery

Yamaha, *distributed by* Hal Leonard Corp

Yankee, *distributor for* Teton NewMedia Inc

Yankee Book Peddler, *distributor for* Primary Research Group Inc

Yearling Books, *imprint of* Penguin Random House LLC, Random House Children's Books

Yellow Books, *imprint of* Leadership Connect

Yellow Jacket, *imprint of* little bee books

Yellow 1, *imprint of* Wide World of Maps Inc

Yellow Rose Books, *imprint of* Regal Crest Enterprises

Yelsraek Publishing, *distributed by* Adventures Unlimited Press (AUP)

Yen Press, *distributed by* Hachette Book Group

Yes Books, *distributed by* Chelsea Green Publishing Co

Yeshiva University Museum Press, *distributed by* Gorgias Press LLC

Yeshiva University Press, *distributed by* KTAV Publishing House Inc

Yilin Press, *distributed by* Simon & Schuster, Inc

YMAA Publication Center Inc, *distributor for* Wind Records (Chinese healing music)

York Medieval Press, *imprint of* Boydell & Brewer Inc

Glenn Young Books, *distributed by* Applause Theatre & Cinema Books

Your Coach in a Box, *imprint of* Recorded Books Inc, an RBmedia company

YourSpecs, *imprint of* SynergEbooks

YouthLight Inc, *distributor for* MAR*CO Products Inc

Yugen Press, *imprint of* In the Garden Publishing

Yushodo Press, *distributed by* Oak Knoll Press

YWAM Publishing, *division of* Youth With A Mission, *distributor for* Emerald Books

Zaffre, *distributed by* Simon & Schuster, Inc

Zahava Publications, *imprint of* Judaica Press Inc

Zaner-Bloser Inc, *subsidiary of* Highlights for Children Inc

Zaytuna Institute Press, *distributed by* Fons Vitae

Zebra Books, *imprint of* Kensington Publishing Corp

Zed Books, *distributed by* Palgrave Macmillan

Zeitgeist Films, *distributed by* Cheng & Tsui Co Inc

Zeke Holdings Ltd, *distributed by* Welcome Enterprises Inc

Zephyr Press, *imprint of* Chicago Review Press

Zerogram Press, *imprint of* Green Integer

Zero+ Publishing, *distributed by* Gingko Press Inc

Zest Books, *imprint of* Lerner Publishing Group Inc

Zeta Books, *distributed by* Philosophy Documentation Center

ZHealth Books, *imprint of* New Win Publishing

H O Zimman Inc, *distributor for* United States Tennis Association

Zinc Ink, *imprint of* Penguin Random House LLC, Random House Publishing Group

Zonderkidz, *division of* Zondervan

Zondervan, *subsidiary of* HarperCollins Christian Publishing, *distributor for* Focus on the Family

Zondervan Academic, *imprint of* Zondervan

Zondervan Reflective, *imprint of* Zondervan

Zondervan Thrive, *imprint of* Zondervan

Zone Books, *distributed by* Princeton University Press

Z2 Comics, *distributed by* Simon & Schuster, Inc

Zubaan Books, *distributed by* Diversion Books

Zuiker Press, *distributed by* Simon & Schuster, Inc

Zumaya Arcane, *imprint of* Zumaya Publications LLC

Zumaya Boundless, *imprint of* Zumaya Publications LLC

Zumaya Embraces, *imprint of* Zumaya Publications LLC

Zumaya Enigma, *imprint of* Zumaya Publications LLC

Zumaya Fabled Ink, *imprint of* Zumaya Publications LLC

Zumaya Otherworlds, *imprint of* Zumaya Publications LLC

Zumaya Thresholds, *imprint of* Zumaya Publications LLC

Zumaya Yesterdays, *imprint of* Zumaya Publications LLC

David Zwirner Books, *distributed by* Simon & Schuster, Inc

Canadian Publishers

Listed in alphabetical order are those Canadian publishers that have reported to *LMP* that they produce an average of three or more books annually. Publishers that have appeared in a previous edition of *LMP*, but whose output currently does not meet our defined rate of activity, will be reinstated when their annual production reaches the required level. It should be noted that this rule of publishing activity does not apply to publishers of dictionaries, encyclopedias, atlases or Braille books or to university presses.

The definition of a book excludes charts, pamphlets, folding maps, sheet music and material with stapled bindings. Publishers that make their titles available only in electronic or audio format are included if they meet the stated criteria. In the case of packages, the book must be of equal or greater importance than the accompanying piece. With few exceptions, new publishers are not listed prior to having published at least three titles within a year.

§ before the company name indicates those publishers involved in electronic publishing.

ACTA Press
200-4040 Bowness Rd NW, Calgary, AB T3B 3R7
Tel: 403-288-1195 *Fax:* 403-247-6851
E-mail: journals@actapress.com; publish@ actapress.com; sales@actapress.com
Web Site: www.actapress.com
Key Personnel
Owner & Mng Dir: Dr Mohamed H Hamza
Founded: 1972
Scientific & technical conference proceedings & journals; computers, control & power systems, information technology, robotics, signal & image processing. Publishes the proceedings from all of the IASTED conferences & the 12 journals that IASTED generates.
Publishes in English.
ISBN Prefix(es): 978-0-88986
Number of titles published annually: 5 Print; 5 Online
Total Titles: 900 Print

Annick Press Ltd
15 Patricia Ave, Toronto, ON M2M 1H9
SAN: 115-0065
Tel: 416-221-4802 *Fax:* 416-221-8400
E-mail: annickpress@annickpress.com
Web Site: www.annickpress.com
Key Personnel
Dir: Rick Wilks
Sales & Rts Dir: Gayna Theophilus
  E-mail: gaynat@annickpress.com
Mktg Mgr: Amanda Olson
Assoc Ed: Claire Caldwell
Founded: 1975
Fiction & nonfiction for children & young adults.
Publishes in English, French.
ISBN Prefix(es): 978-0-920236; 978-0-920303; 978-1-55037; 978-1-55451
Number of titles published annually: 24 Print
Total Titles: 425 Print
U.S. Rep(s): Ian Booth; Nicholas Booth; Bob Ditter; Rachel Ginsburg; Tom Hamburg; Larry Hollern; David Lewis; Ted Lucia; Thomas Martin; Thomas J McFadden Associates; McLemore/Hollern & Associates Inc; Parisa Michailidis (spec sales); Kevin T Monahan; Frank Porter; Ann Quinn; Sirak & Sirak; Jennifer Sorensen (spec sales); Michael R Watson; Karen Winters; Debra Woodward; Karen Woodward
Foreign Rep(s): CSH Educational Resources Pte Ltd (Singapore); Jay Books (New Zealand); Lexsys Ltd (Caribbean); John Reed Book Distribution (Australia); Ediciones Samara (Mexico)
Foreign Rights: Bardon-Chinese Media Agency (Jian-Mei Wang) (China); Bardon-Chinese Media Agency (Cynthia Chang) (Hong Kong, Taiwan); The Deborah Harris Agency (Efrat Lev) (Israel); International Editors' Co (Flavia Sala) (Brazil); International Editors' Co (Liliana Costa) (Latin America); International Editors' Co (Jennifer Hoge) (Portugal, Spain);

Japan UNI Agency Inc (May Fujinaga) (Japan); Simona Kessler Agency (Romania); Agence Michelle Lapautre (Catherine Lapautre) (France); Literarische Agentur & Medienservice (Barbara Kuper) (Germany); Servizi Editoriali Guido Lagomarsino (Anna Spadolini) (Italy)
Distribution Center: University of Toronto Press, 5201 Dufferin St, Toronto, ON M3H 5T8
  Tel: 416-667-7791 *Toll Free Tel:* 800-565-9523
  Fax: 416-667-7832 *Toll Free Fax:* 800-221-9885 *E-mail:* utpbooks@utpress.utoronto.ca
  Web Site: www.utpress.utoronto.ca
Membership(s): Association of Canadian Publishers (ACP); Ontario Arts Council; Organization of Book Publishers of Ontario (OBPO)

Anvil Press Publishers
278 E First Ave, Vancouver, BC V5T 1A6
Mailing Address: PO Box 3008, MPO, Vancouver, BC V6B 3X5
Tel: 604-876-8710 *Fax:* 604-879-2667
E-mail: info@anvilpress.com
Web Site: www.anvilpress.com
Key Personnel
Publr: Brian Kaufman
Asst Publr & Mktg Coord: Karen Green
Publg Asst: Kara Lang
Founded: 1988
Literary, all genres; theatre & modern contemporary literature. Mostly Canadian authored titles only.
Publishes in English.
ISBN Prefix(es): 978-1-895636; 978-1-897535; 978-1-927380
Number of titles published annually: 12 Print
Total Titles: 90 Print
Distribution Center: Raincoast Books, 2440 Viking Way, Richmond, BC V6V 1N3 *Toll Free Tel:* 800-663-5714 *Fax:* 604-270-7161 *Toll Free Fax:* 800-565-3770 *E-mail:* orders@ raincoast.com
Small Press Distribution, 1341 Seventh St, Berkeley, CA 94710-1409, United States *Tel:* 510-524-1668 *Toll Free Tel:* 800-869-7553 (US) *Fax:* 510-524-0852 *E-mail:* spd@spdbooks.org
Membership(s): Association of Book Publishers of British Columbia; Association of Canadian Publishers (ACP); Literary Press Group

§Aquila Communications Inc
281 rue Alice-Carriere St, Beaconsville, QC H9W 6E6
Toll Free Tel: 800-667-7071 *Fax:* 514-505-4579
  Toll Free Fax: 866-338-1948
Web Site: www.aquilacommunications.com
Key Personnel
Founder & Pres: Sami Kelada
Contact: Mike Kelada *E-mail:* mike@ aquilacommunications.com
Founded: 1970
High-interest/low-vocabulary readers for learners of French as a second language, grades 4

through college. Also, short humorous situational dialogues in comic book format for kids & teens. Funny episodes of daily life of North American kids & teens (home & school).
Publishes in French.
ISBN Prefix(es): 978-0-88510; 978-2-89054
Number of titles published annually: 15 Print
Total Titles: 500 Print; 100 Audio
Imprints: Scaramouche
Distributed by Aquila Communications Ltd

Arsenal Pulp Press
211 E Georgia St, No 202, Vancouver, BC V6A 1Z6
Tel: 604-687-4233 *Toll Free Tel:* 888-600-PULP (600-7857) *Fax:* 604-687-4283
E-mail: info@arsenalpulp.com
Web Site: www.arsenalpulp.com
Key Personnel
Publr: Brian Lam
Assoc Publr: Robert Ballantyne *E-mail:* robert@ arsenalpulp.com
Dir, Mktg & Publicity: Cynara Geissler
Prodn Mgr: Oliver McPartlin
Designer & Prodn Mgr: Jazmin Welch
Assoc Ed: Susan Safyan
Founded: 1982 (as Pulp Press Book Publishers)
Literary press.
Publishes in English.
ISBN Prefix(es): 978-0-88978; 978-1-55152
Number of titles published annually: 20 Print
Total Titles: 360 Print
Imprints: Advance Editions; Little Sister's Classics; Pulp Press; Robin's Egg Books; Tillacum Library
U.S. Rep(s): Consortium Book Sales & Distribution
Foreign Rep(s): NewSouth Books (Australia, New Zealand); Turnaround Publisher Services (Europe, UK)
Distribution Center: University of Toronto Press Distribution, 5201 Dufferin St, Toronto, ON M3H 5T8 *Toll Free Tel:* 800-565-9523 *Toll Free Fax:* 800-221-9985 *E-mail:* utpbooks@ utpress.utoronto.ca *Web Site:* www.utpress. utoronto.ca
Consortium Book Sales & Distribution, c/o Perseus Distribution, 1094 Flex Dr, Jackson, TN 38301-5070, United States *Toll Free Tel:* 800-283-3572 *Toll Free Fax:* 800-351-5073 *E-mail:* orderentry@perseusbooks.com *Web Site:* www.cbsd.com

Athabasca University Press
Edmonton Learning Ctr, Peace Hills Trust Tower, 1200, 10011-109 St, Edmonton, AB T5J 3S8
Tel: 780-497-3412 *Fax:* 780-421-3298
E-mail: aupress@athabascau.ca
Web Site: www.aupress.ca
Key Personnel
Dir & Mktg/Prodn Coord: Megan Hall *Tel:* 780-428-2067 *E-mail:* director.aupress@athabascau. ca

Sr Aqs Ed: Pamela Holway *Tel:* 780-428-7278
E-mail: editor.aupress@athabascau.ca
Founded: 2008
This publisher has indicated that 25% of their
product line is author subsidized.
Publishes in English, French.
ISBN Prefix(es): 978-0-919737; 978-0-920982;
978-1-897425; 978-1-926836; 978-1-927356
Number of titles published annually: 20 Print
Distribution Center: UBC Press, c/o UTP Distri-
bution, 5201 Dufferin St, Toronto, ON M3H
5T8 *Tel:* 416-667-7791 *Toll Free Tel:* 800-565-
9523 *Fax:* 416-667-7832 *Toll Free Fax:* 800-
221-9985 *E-mail:* utpbooks@utpress.utoronto.
ca
Chicago Distribution Center, 11030 S Langley Ave, Chicago, IL 60628, United States
Tel: 773-702-7000 *Toll Free Tel:* 800-621-
2736 *E-mail:* orders@press.uchicago.edu *Web
Site:* press.uchicago.edu/cdc
Combined Academic Publishers, Windsor House,
Cornwall Rd, Harrogate, N Yorks HG1 2PW,
United Kingdom (UK, Africa, China, Europe, Hong Kong, Middle East & Taiwan)
Tel: (01423) 526350 *E-mail:* enquiries@
combinedacademic.co.uk *Web Site:* www.
combinedacademic.co.uk

B & B Publishing
4823 Sherbrooke St W, Off 275, Westmount, QC
H3Z 1G7
Tel: 514-932-9466 *Fax:* 514-932-5929
E-mail: editions@ebbp.ca
Key Personnel
Publr: Paul Beullac
Founded: 1996
Publisher of educational materials; books & wall
maps for schools across Canada.
Publishes in English, French.
ISBN Prefix(es): 978-0-88537; 978-2-7615
Number of titles published annually: 10 Print
Total Titles: 400 Print
Distributed by Brault & Bouthillier Ltee; Brault
& Bouthillier School Supplies
Foreign Rep(s): Bricolux (Belgium); Canada Or-
tho (France); Intelligence Insight LLP (Singa-
pore); Wesco (France)
Distribution Center: 700, ave Beaumont, Mon-
treal, QC H3N 1V5 *Tel:* 514-273-9186
Fax: 514-273-8627

§Bayeux Arts Inc
2403, 510-Sixth Ave SE, Calgary, AB T2G 1L7
E-mail: mail@bayeux.com
Web Site: bayeux.com
Key Personnel
Co-Publr & Dir: Swapna Gupta
Co-Publr: Ashis Gupta *E-mail:* agupta@bayeux.
com
Ed, Children's Lit: Judd Palmer
E-mail: jpalmer@bayeux.com
Ed, Fiction/Nonfiction/Poetry: Mercedes Batiz-
Benet *E-mail:* mercedes@bayeux.com
Founded: 1994
Committed to producing books of beauty that
build bridges across cultures.
Publishes in English.
ISBN Prefix(es): 978-1-896209; 978-1-897411;
978-1-988440
Number of titles published annually: 10 Print
Imprints: Odd Little Books; Rosencrantz Comics
Distribution Center: LitDistCo, 8300 Law-
son Rd, Milton, ON L9T 0A4 *Toll Free
Tel:* 800-591-6250 *Toll Free Fax:* 800-591-6251
E-mail: ordering@litdistco.ca *Web Site:* www.
litdistco.ca
Chicago Distribution Center, 11030 S Lang-
ley Ave, Chicago, IL 60628, United States
Tel: 773-702-7010 *Toll Free Fax:* 800-621-8476
Membership(s): Literary Press Group of Canada

Beliveau Editeur
567 rue Bienville, Boucherville, QC J4B 2Z5

Tel: 450-679-1933
Web Site: www.beliveauediteur.com
Key Personnel
Pres & CEO: Mathieu Beliveau
E-mail: mbeliveau@beliveauediteur.com
Asst Ed: Diane Perreault *E-mail:* dperreault@
beliveauediteur.com
Founded: 1975
Specialize in recovery, geopolitics & self-help,
medicine, taxation & motivation.
Publishes in French.
ISBN Prefix(es): 978-2-89092
Number of titles published annually: 30 Print
Total Titles: 250 Print
Foreign Rep(s): DG Diffusion (France); Servidis
(Switzerland)
Distribution Center: Prologue Inc, 1650, Lionel-
Bertrand, Boisbriand, QC J7H 1N7 *Toll Free
Tel:* 800-363-2864

Between the Lines
401 Richmond St W, No 277, Toronto, ON M5V
3A8
SAN: 115-0189
Tel: 416-535-9914 *Toll Free Tel:* 800-718-7201
Fax: 416-535-1484
E-mail: info@btlbooks.com
Web Site: btlbooks.com
Key Personnel
Art Dir & Prodn Mgr: Jennifer Tiberio
Accts Mgr: Paula Brill
Mktg & Sales Mgr: Renee Knapp
Mng Ed: Amanda Crocker
Publicist: Matthew Adams *E-mail:* publicity@
btlbooks.com
Founded: 1977
Nonfiction, social, economic & political works
dealing with international development issues
& Canadian social issues.
Publishes in English.
ISBN Prefix(es): 978-0-919946; 978-0-921284;
978-1-896357; 978-1-897071; 978-1-926662;
978-1-77113
Number of titles published annually: 16 Print
Total Titles: 263 Print
U.S. Rep(s): Brunswick Books
Foreign Rep(s): Brunswick Books (Canada)
Orders to: Brunswick Books, 20 Maud St, Suite
303, Toronto, ON M5V 2M5 *Tel:* 416-703-
3598; Central Books Ltd, 50 Freshwater Rd,
Chadwell Heath RM8 1RX, United Kingdom
Tel: (020) 8525 8800 *Fax:* (020) 8599 2694
E-mail: contactus@centralbooks.com *Web
Site:* www.centralbooks.com
Membership(s): Canada Council for the Arts; On-
tario Arts Council

Black Rose Books Ltd
CP 35788 Succ Leo-Pariseau, Montreal, QC H2X
0A4
SAN: 115-2653
Tel: 514-844-4076
E-mail: info@blackrosebooks.com
Web Site: blackrosebooks.com
Key Personnel
Coord: Dimitrios Roussopoulos *E-mail:* mavros@
blackrosebooks.com
Admin: Clara-Swan Kennedy *Tel:* 514-969-2589
E-mail: swan@blackrosebooks.com
Founded: 1969
Publishing in the social sciences & humanities.
Publishes in English.
ISBN Prefix(es): 978-0-919618; 978-0-919619;
978-0-920057; 978-0-921689; 978-1-55164;
978-1-895431
Number of titles published annually: 15 Print; 15
E-Book
Total Titles: 600 Print; 75 E-Book
Sales Office(s): University of Chicago Press/
Chicago Distribution Center, 11030 S Lan-
gley Ave, Chicago, IL 60628, United States
Tel: 773-702-7000 *Toll Free Tel:* 800-621-2736
(USA) *E-mail:* orders@press.uchicago.edu

Global Book Marketing, 50 Freshwater Rd,
Chadwell Heath RM8 1RX, United King-
dom *Tel:* (020) 8590 9700 *E-mail:* tz@
globalbookmarketing.co.uk *Web Site:* www.
globalbookmarketing.co.uk *Web Site:* www.
globalbookmarketing.co.uk
Distributed by University of Chicago Press (USA
& International); University of Toronto Press
(Canada)
Foreign Rep(s): Rightol (China)
Orders to: University of Toronto Press, 5201
Dufferin Street, Toronto, ON M3H 5T8 *Toll
Free Tel:* 800-565-9523 *E-mail:* utpbooks@
utpress.utoronto.ca; University of Chicago
Press/Chicago Distribution Center, 11030 S
Langley Ave, Chicago, IL 60628, United States
Tel: 773-702-7000 *Toll Free Tel:* 800-621-2736
(USA) *E-mail:* orders@press.uchicago.edu *Web
Site:* press.uchicago.edu/index.html; Central
Books Ltd, 50 Freshwater Rd, Chadwell Heath
RM8 1RX, United Kingdom *Tel:* (020) 8525
8800 *E-mail:* contactus@centralbooks.com
Returns: University of Toronto Press, 5201 Duf-
ferin St, Toronto, ON M3H 5T8; University
of Chicago Press/Chicago Distribution Cen-
ter, 11030 S Langley Ave, Chicago, IL 60628,
United States; Central Books Ltd, 50 Fresh-
water Rd, Chadwell Heath RM8 1RX, United
Kingdom
Membership(s): Association of Canadian Pub-
lishers (ACP); Association of English-language
Publishers of Quebec (AELAQ)

Blue Bike Books
4811-51 Ave, Stony Plain, AB T7Z 1C4
Mailing Address: 11414-119 St NW, Edmonton,
AB T5G 2X6
Tel: 780-435-2376
Web Site: www.bluebikebooks.com
Key Personnel
Publr: Peter J Boer *E-mail:* peterb@
bluebikebooks.com
Founded: 2005
Publish humor, trivia books & children's nonfic-
tion. Large number of regional trivia titles as
well as national ones.
Publishes in English.
ISBN Prefix(es): 978-1-897278; 978-0-9739116;
978-1-926700
Number of titles published annually: 5 Print; 10
E-Book
Total Titles: 93 Print; 42 E-Book
Imprints: Mega Machines; Super Explorers
U.S. Rep(s): Lone Pine Publishing
Foreign Rep(s): Gazelle Book Services Ltd
(Africa, Asia-Pacific exc China, Central South-
ern England, Continental Europe, Eastern Eu-
rope, UK, UK & the continent)
Orders to: Canadian Book Distributors Ltd,
11414 119 St, Edmonton, AB T5G 2X6
Tel: 780-433-9333 *Toll Free Tel:* 800-661-9017
Fax: 780-433-9646 *Toll Free Fax:* 800-424-
7173 *E-mail:* accounts@lonepinepublishing.
com *Web Site:* www.lonepinepublishing.com
Shipping Address: Canadian Book Distributors
Ltd, 11414 119 St, Edmonton, AB T5G 2X6
Tel: 780-433-9333 *Toll Free Tel:* 800-661-9017
Fax: 780-433-9646 *Toll Free Fax:* 800-424-
7173 *E-mail:* accounts@lonepinepublishing.
com *Web Site:* www.lonepinepublishing.com
Distribution Center: Canadian Book Distributors
Ltd, 11414 119 St, Edmonton, AB T5G 2X6
Tel: 780-433-9333 *Toll Free Tel:* 800-661-9017
Fax: 780-433-9646 *Toll Free Fax:* 800-424-
7173 *E-mail:* accounts@lonepinepublishing.
com *Web Site:* www.lonepinepublishing.com
Membership(s): Book Publishers Association of
Alberta

Editions du Bois-de-Coulonge
1140 Ave de Montigny, Sillery, QC G1S 3T7
Tel: 418-683-6332
Web Site: www.ebc.qc.ca

Key Personnel
Owner & Pres: Dr Richard Leclerc, PhD
 E-mail: rleclerc@ebc.qc.ca
Founded: 1995
Publish & distribute books about music, multimedia, television & movies.
Publishes in French.
ISBN Prefix(es): 978-2-9801397
Number of titles published annually: 1 Print
Total Titles: 7 Print
Membership(s): Association for the Export of Canadian Books

Books We Love Ltd, see BWL Publishing Inc

§Borealis Press Ltd
8 Mohawk Crescent, Nepean, ON K2H 7G6
Tel: 613-829-0150 *Toll Free Tel:* 877-696-2585
 Fax: 613-829-7783
E-mail: drt@borealispress.com
Web Site: www.borealispress.com
Founded: 1972
Canadian-oriented general titles of most types. No unsol mss, query first. Include synopsis +/or outline & sample chapter with SASE.
Publishes in English, French.
ISBN Prefix(es): 978-0-88887; 978-1-896133 (Tecumseh Press); 978-0-919594; 978-0-919662 (Tecumseh Press)
Number of titles published annually: 24 Print
Subsidiaries: Tecumseh Press
Distributed by Blackwell; EBSCO; Ex Libris; Hein

The Boston Mills Press
Division of Firefly Books Ltd
50 Staples Ave, Unit 1, Richmond Hill, ON L4B 0A7
Tel: 416-499-8412 *Toll Free Tel:* 800-387-6192
 Fax: 416-499-8313 *Toll Free Fax:* 800-450-0391
E-mail: service@fireflybooks.com
Web Site: www.fireflybooks.com
Key Personnel
Dir, Prodn & Co-Editions: Jacqueline Hope Raynor
Founded: 1974
Canadian & American history, guide books, large format colour photograph books.
Publishes in English.
ISBN Prefix(es): 978-0-919822; 978-0-919783; 978-1-55046
Number of titles published annually: 20 Print
Total Titles: 200 Print
Distributed by Firefly Books Ltd

BPS Books
Division of Bastian Publishing Services Ltd
47 Anderson Ave, Toronto, ON M5P 1H6
Tel: 416-609-2004
Web Site: www.bpsbooks.com
Key Personnel
Publr & Ed-in-Chief: Donald G Bastian
Founded: 2007
Print-on-demand publisher of original & reprint trade paperbacks for the US, Canadian & UK markets via bookstore web sites such as the Amazon sites in all 3 countries. No unsol mss, query first using online form.
This publisher has indicated that 90% of their product is author subsidized.
Publishes in English, French.
ISBN Prefix(es): 978-1-926645; 978-0-9784402; 978-0-9809231; 978-1-927483; 978-0-9783286
Number of titles published annually: 5 Print; 5 E-Book
Total Titles: 75 Print; 26 E-Book
Membership(s): Word Guild

Brault & Bouthillier
Division of B & B School Supplies

700 ave Beaumont, Montreal, QC H3N 1V5
Tel: 514-273-9186 *Toll Free Tel:* 800-361-0378
 Fax: 514-273-8627 *Toll Free Fax:* 800-361-0378
E-mail: ventes@bb.ca
Web Site: bb.ca
Key Personnel
Pres: Paul LeBrun *E-mail:* paullebrun@bb.ca
VP, Busn Devt: Yves Brault *Tel:* 514-273-9186 ext 219 *E-mail:* yvesbrault@bb.ca
Sales Dir: Claude Vaillancourt *Tel:* 514-273-9186 ext 227 *E-mail:* cvaillancourt@bb.ca
Founded: 1944
Pedagogical & scientific.
Publishes in English, French.
ISBN Prefix(es): 978-0-88537; 978-2-7615
Number of titles published annually: 100 Print
Branch Office(s)
150 Brittania Rd E, Unit 7, Mississauga, ON L4Z 2A4 *Tel:* 905-890-0404 *Toll Free Tel:* 800-668-1108 *Fax:* 905-890-7999 *Toll Free Fax:* 800-839-7718
Distributed by DPLU Inc (Montreal); B B Jocus (Toronto)

Breakwater Books Ltd
One Stamp's Lane, St John's, NL A1C 6E6
Mailing Address: PO Box 2188, St John's, NL A1C 6E6
Tel: 709-722-6680 *Toll Free Tel:* 800-563-3333 (orders) *Fax:* 709-753-0708
E-mail: info@breakwaterbooks.com; orders@breakwaterbooks.com
Web Site: www.breakwaterbooks.com
Key Personnel
Owner & Pres: Rebecca Rose
Founded: 1973
Books primarily about education & trade books.
Publishes in English, French.
ISBN Prefix(es): 978-0-919519; 978-0-919948; 978-0-920911; 978-1-55081
Number of titles published annually: 16 Print
Total Titles: 600 Print

Brick Books
22 Spencer Ave, Toronto, ON M6K 2J6
Tel: 416-455-8385
E-mail: brenda@brickbooks.ca
Web Site: www.brickbooks.ca
Key Personnel
Publr: Alayna Munce
Gen Mgr: Kitty Lewis
Founded: 1975
Publish poetry collections by Canadian authors.
Publishes in English.
ISBN Prefix(es): 978-0-919626; 978-1-894078; 978-1-77131
Number of titles published annually: 7 Print
Total Titles: 224 Print; 201 E-Book
Distribution Center: LitDistCo, 8300 Lawson Rd, Milton, ON L9T 0A4 *Toll Free Tel:* 800-591-6250 *Toll Free Fax:* 800-591-6251 *E-mail:* orders@litdistco.ca *Web Site:* www.litdistco.ca
Membership(s): Association of Canadian Publishers (ACP); Literary Press Group of Canada; Organization of Book Publishers of Ontario (OBPO)

Brindle & Glass Publishing Ltd
Imprint of TouchWood Editions
1075 Pendergast St, Suite 103, Victoria, BC V8V 0A1
Tel: 250-360-0829 *Fax:* 250-386-0829
E-mail: info@touchwoodeditions.com
Web Site: www.touchwoodeditions.com
Key Personnel
Publr: Taryn Boyd
Founded: 2001
Literary press.
Publishes in English.

ISBN Prefix(es): 978-1-897142; 978-0-9732481; 978-1-926972; 978-1-927366
Number of titles published annually: 4 Print
Total Titles: 110 Print
Foreign Rep(s): Heritage Group (Canada); Publishers Group West (PGW) (USA)
Distribution Center: Heritage Group Distribution, 19272 96 Ave, Suite 8, Surrey, BC V4N 4C1 *Tel:* 604-881-7067 *Toll Free Tel:* 800-665-3302 *Fax:* 604-881-7068 *Toll Free Fax:* 800-566-3336 *E-mail:* orders@hgdistribution.com *Web Site:* www.hgdistribution.com
Membership(s): Canada Council for the Arts

§Broadview Press
280 Perry St, Unit 5, Peterborough, ON K9J 2J4
SAN: 115-6772
Mailing Address: PO Box 1243, Peterborough, ON K9J 7H5
Tel: 705-743-8990 *Fax:* 705-743-8353
E-mail: customerservice@broadviewpress.com
Web Site: www.broadviewpress.com
Key Personnel
Founder & CEO: Don Le Pan *Tel:* 250-824-5015 *Fax:* 250-824-5001 *E-mail:* don.lepan@broadviewpress.com
Pres: Leslie Dema *Tel:* 519-821-0706 *Fax:* 519-265-6544 *E-mail:* dema@broadviewpress.com
Mng Ed: Tara Lowes *E-mail:* taralowes@broadviewpress.com
Accts Mgr: LeeAnna Dykstra *E-mail:* ldykstra@broadviewpress.com
Exam Copies Coord: Lisa Reid
 E-mail: examcopies@broadviewpress.com
Founded: 1985
The word "broadview" expresses a great deal about the approach that guides our publishing program. Our focus is very much on English studies & philosophy, but within those two core subject areas we are open to a broad range of academic approaches & political viewpoints. We are proud to publish pedagogically valuable books that make a real contribution to scholarship. We welcome feminist perspectives & we have a strong commitment to the environment. Our publishing program is internationally oriented & our individual titles often appeal to a broad readership; we publish many titles that are of as much interest to the general reader as they are to academics & students.
Publishes in English.
ISBN Prefix(es): 978-0-921149; 978-1-55111; 978-1-55481
Number of titles published annually: 45 Print; 40 E-Book
Total Titles: 600 Print; 425 E-Book
Branch Office(s)
10 Douglas St, Suite B, Guelph, ON N1H 2S9 *Tel:* 519-821-2171 *Fax:* 519-265-6544
515-815 First St SW, Calgary, AB T2P 1N3 *Tel:* 403-232-1443 *Fax:* 403-233-0001 *E-mail:* broadview@broadviewpress.com
555 Riverwalk Pkwy, Tonawanda, NY 14150, United States
U.S. Rep(s): Brad DeVetten
Returns: 555 Riverwalk Pkwy, Tonawanda, NY 14150, United States

Broquet Inc
97-B, Montee des Bouleaux, St-Constant, QC J5A 1A9
Tel: 450-638-3338 *Fax:* 450-638-4338
E-mail: info@broquet.qc.ca
Web Site: www.broquet.qc.ca
Key Personnel
Pres & Ed: Antoine Broquet
Artistic Dir: Brigit Levesque
Prodn Dir: Ms Josee Fortin
Founded: 1979
Nature books & astronomy.
Publishes in French.
ISBN Prefix(es): 978-2-89000; 978-2-89654

Number of titles published annually: 100 Print;
12 E-Book
Total Titles: 800 Print; 40 E-Book
Foreign Rep(s): Dilisco (Benelux, France); Servidis (Switzerland)
Distribution Center: Prologue Inc, 1650, blvd
Lionel-Bertrand, Boisbriand, QC J7H 1N7
Tel: 450-434-0306 *Toll Free Tel:* 800-363-2864
Fax: 450-434-2627 *Toll Free Fax:* 800-361-
8088

Brush Education Inc
6531-111 St, Edmonton, AB T6H 4R5
SAN: 115-0324
Tel: 780-989-0910 *Toll Free Tel:* 855-283-0900
Fax: 780-989-0930 *Toll Free Fax:* 855-283-
6947
E-mail: contact@brusheducation.ca
Web Site: www.brusheducation.ca
Key Personnel
Partner: Glenn Rollans *E-mail:* glenn.rollans@
brusheducation.ca
Mng Ed: Lauri Seidlitz *E-mail:* lauri.seidlitz@
brusheducation.ca
Founded: 1975
Independent publisher of books for college, university & professional audiences. Our publishing program includes medial & health sciences, education & K9 training.
Publishes in English.
ISBN Prefix(es): 978-0-920490; 978-1-55059
Number of titles published annually: 17 Print; 15
E-Book
Total Titles: 120 Print; 50 E-Book
Distributed by University of Toronto Press
Orders to: University of Toronto Press, 5201 Dufferin St, Toronto, ON M3H 5T8 (CN & US)
Tel: 416-667-7791 *Toll Free Tel:* 800-565-9523
Fax: 416-667-7832 *Toll Free Fax:* 800-221-
9985 *E-mail:* utpbooks@utpress.utoronto.ca
Membership(s): Association of Canadian Publishers (ACP); Book Publishers Association of
Alberta

§BWL Publishing Inc
Formerly Books We Love Ltd
100 Chinook Winds Place SW, Unit 4105, Airdrie, AB T4B-4B4
Tel: 403-710-4869
E-mail: bwlgeneral@telus.net
Web Site: bookswelove.net; www.facebook.com/
groups/153824114796417
Key Personnel
Pres: Brian Roberts
VP & Publr: Judith Pittman
E-mail: judepittman@telus.net
Founded: 2010
Publisher of genre fiction written by Canadian,
American & international authors, including
historical fiction, romance (in all forms), mystery, suspense, thrillers, fantasy, paranormal,
young adult, science fiction, western & more.
Publishes in English.
ISBN Prefix(es): 978-1-927476; 978-1-927476;
978-1-927111; 978-0-9867433; 978-1-77145;
978-0-9867514; 978-1-926965; 978-1-77362;
978-1-77299
Number of titles published annually: 60 Print;
600 E-Book; 20 Audio
Total Titles: 400 Print; 800 E-Book; 20 Audio
Membership(s): Romance Writers of America
(RWA)

Callawind Publications Inc
3551 St Charles Blvd, Suite 179, Kirkland, QC
H9H 3C4
Tel: 514-685-9109
E-mail: info@callawind.com
Web Site: www.callawind.com
Key Personnel
Mktg: Pamela Carmen *E-mail:* pamela@
callawind.com

Founded: 1995
Custom book publisher. Specialize in children's
picture books, board books, coffee table books
& cookbooks.
This publisher has indicated that 100% of their
product line is author subsidized.
Publishes in English.
ISBN Prefix(es): 978-1-896511
Number of titles published annually: 15 Print
Total Titles: 100 Print
Membership(s): The Association of Publishers
for Special Sales (APSS); Independent Book
Publishers Association (IBPA)

§Canada Law Book®
Division of Thomson Reuters Canada Ltd
One Corporate Plaza, 2075 Kennedy Rd, Toronto,
ON M1T 3V4
Tel: 416-609-3800 (cust rel & orders)
Toll Free Tel: 800-387-5351 (cust rel, CN &
US only); 800-347-5164 (cust rel & orders, CN
& US) *Fax:* 416-298-5082 (cust rel & orders,
Toronto) *Toll Free Fax:* 877-750-9041 (cust rel
& orders, CN only)
E-mail: customersupport.legaltaxcanada@tr.com
Web Site: www.carswell.com
Founded: 1855 (as Upper Canada Law Journal)
Law books.
Publishes in English.
ISBN Prefix(es): 978-0-88804
Number of titles published annually: 50 Print; 3
CD-ROM; 3 E-Book
Total Titles: 480 Print; 25 CD-ROM; 40 Online;
9 E-Book
Subsidiaries: Canadian Lawyer/Law Times Media,
a Thomson Reuters business
Returns: 245 Bartley Dr, Toronto, ON M4A 2V8
Distribution Center: 245 Bartley Dr, Toronto, ON
M4A 2V8

Canadian Bible Society
10 Carnforth Rd, Toronto, ON M4A 2S4
SAN: 112-5559
Tel: 416-757-4171 *Toll Free Tel:* 800-465-2425
Fax: 416-757-3376
E-mail: custserv@biblesociety.ca
Web Site: www.biblescanada.com; www.
biblesociety.ca
Founded: 1904
Bibles, new testaments, scripture portions, selections; scriptures in foreign languages.
Publishes in English, French.
ISBN Prefix(es): 978-0-88834
Number of titles published annually: 20 Print; 5
Audio
Total Titles: 2,500 Print; 50 Audio
U.S. Publishers Represented: American Bible Society
Foreign Rep(s): United Bible Societies (worldwide)
Membership(s): United Bible Societies

Canadian Circumpolar Institute (CCI) Press
Imprint of University of Alberta Press
1-16 Rutherford Library South, 11204 89 Ave
NW, Edmonton, AB T6G-2J4
Tel: 780-492-3662 *Fax:* 780-492-0719
Web Site: www.uap.ualberta.ca
Founded: 1960 (as Boreal Institute for Northern
Studies; reconfigured & renamed 1990 as CCI;
acquired 2013 by University of Alberta Press)
Publishes in English.
ISBN Prefix(es): 978-1-896445; 978-0-919058
Number of titles published annually: 2 Print; 2 E-
Book
Total Titles: 140 Print
Sales Office(s): Ampersand Canada's Book &
Gift Agency Inc, 321 Carlaw Ave, Suite 213,
Toronto, ON M4M 2S1, Contact: Saffron
Beckwith *Tel:* 416-703-0666 ext 124 *Fax:* 416-
703-4745 *E-mail:* saffronb@ampersandinc.ca
Web Site: www.ampersandinc.ca

U.S. Rep(s): Johns Hopkins University Press
Billing Address: University of Toronto Press,
5201 Dufferin St, Toronto, ON M3H 5T8
Tel: 416-667-7841 *Toll Free Tel:* 800-565-9523
Fax: 416-667-7832 *Toll Free Fax:* 800-221-
9985 *E-mail:* utpbooks@utpress.utoronto.ca
Web Site: www.utpress.utoronto.ca
Orders to: University of Toronto Press, 5201 Dufferin St, Toronto, ON M3H 5T8 *Tel:* 416-667-
7841 *Toll Free Tel:* 800-565-9523 *Fax:* 416-
667-7832 *Toll Free Fax:* 800-221-9985 *E-mail:* utpbooks@utpress.utoronto.ca *Web
Site:* www.utpress.utoronto.ca
Returns: University of Toronto Press, 5201 Dufferin St, Toronto, ON M3H 5T8 *Tel:* 416-667-
7841 *Toll Free Tel:* 800-565-9523 *Fax:* 416-
667-7832 *Toll Free Fax:* 800-221-9985
E-mail: utpbooks@utpress.utoronto.ca *Web
Site:* www.utpress.utoronto.ca
Shipping Address: University of Toronto Press,
5201 Dufferin St, Toronto, ON M3H 5T8
Tel: 416-667-7841 *Toll Free Tel:* 800-565-9523
Fax: 416-667-7832 *Toll Free Fax:* 800-221-
9985 *E-mail:* utpbooks@utpress.utoronto.ca
Web Site: www.utpress.utoronto.ca
Distribution Center: University of Toronto Press,
5201 Dufferin St, Toronto, ON M3H-5T8,
Client Serv Rep: Jackie Courtney *Tel:* 416-667-
7841 *Toll Free Tel:* 800-565-9523 *Fax:* 416-
667-7832 *Toll Free Fax:* 800-221-9985
E-mail: utpbooks@utpress.utoronto.ca *Web
Site:* www.utpress.utoronto.ca
Johns Hopkins University Press, 2715 N Charles
St, Baltimore, MD 21218, United States (does
not carry all CCI Press titles), Dir, HFS/Co-
Dir, Mktg & Sales: Davida Breier *Tel:* 410-
516-6961 *Fax:* 410-516-6998 *E-mail:* dgb@
press.jhu.edu *Web Site:* www.press.jhu.edu
Gazelle Book Services Ltd, White Cross Mills,
Hightown, Lancaster, Lancs LA1 4XS, United
Kingdom *Tel:* (01524) 528500 *Fax:* (01524)
528510 *E-mail:* sales@gazellebookservices.co.
uk *Web Site:* www.gazellebookservices.co.uk

Canadian Council on Social Development
(Conseil canadien de developpement social)
190 O'Connor St, Suite 100, Ottawa, ON K2P
2R3
Mailing Address: PO Box 13713, Kanata, ON
K2K 1X6
Tel: 613-236-8977 *Fax:* 613-236-2750
E-mail: info@ccsd.ca
Web Site: www.ccsd.ca
Key Personnel
Pres & CEO: Peggy Taillon *Tel:* 613-236-8977
ext 22 *E-mail:* taillon@ccsd.ca
VP, Res & Policy: Katherine Scott *Tel:* 613-236-
8977 ext 21 *E-mail:* scott@ccsd.ca
Founded: 1920
Social policy, poverty, retirement, income security, economics, sustainable development self-
help & aboriginal peoples.
Publishes in English, French.
ISBN Prefix(es): 978-0-88810
Number of titles published annually: 12 Print
Total Titles: 100 Print
Distributed by Renouf Publishing Ltd

Canadian Energy Research Institute
3512 33 St NW, Suite 150, Calgary, AB T2L 2A6
Tel: 403-282-1231 *Fax:* 403-290-2251
E-mail: info@ceri.ca
Web Site: www.ceri.ca
Key Personnel
Pres & CEO: Allan Fogwill
Founded: 1975
Energy research, conferences.
Publishes in English.
ISBN Prefix(es): 978-0-920522; 978-1-896091
Number of titles published annually: 8 Print
Total Titles: 156 Print

Canadian Institute of Resources Law
(L'Institut canadien du droit des ressources)
Faculty of Law, University of Calgary, 2500 University Dr NW, MFH 3353, Calgary, AB T2N 1N4
Tel: 403-220-3200 *Fax:* 403-282-6182
E-mail: cirl@ucalgary.ca
Web Site: www.cirl.ca
Founded: 1979
Leading national centre of expertise on legal & policy issues relating to Canada's natural resources.
Publishes in English.
ISBN Prefix(es): 978-0-919269
Number of titles published annually: 4 Print; 3 Online
Total Titles: 96 Print; 64 Online

Canadian Institute of Ukrainian Studies Press
Division of Canadian Institute of Ukrainian Studies
University of Toronto, 256 McCaul St, Rm 308, Toronto, ON M5T 1W5
Tel: 416-946-7326 *Fax:* 416-978-2672
E-mail: cius@ualberta.ca
Web Site: www.ciuspress.com
Key Personnel
Exec Dir: Marko R Stech *E-mail:* m.stech@utoronto.ca
Founded: 1976
Publisher of scholarly works in Ukranian studies & Ukrainian Canadian studies.
Publishes in English, French.
ISBN Prefix(es): 978-0-920862; 978-1-895571; 978-1-894865; 978-1-894301
Number of titles published annually: 5 Print
Total Titles: 180 Print
U.S. Rep(s): Baker & Taylor Books
Orders to: University of Alberta, 4-30 Pembina Hall, Edmonton, AB T6G 2H8 *Tel:* 780-492-2973 *Fax:* 780-492-4967 *E-mail:* cius@ualberta.ca
Returns: University of Alberta, 4-30 Pembina Hall, Edmonton, AB T6G 2H8 *Tel:* 780-492-2973 *Fax:* 780-492-4967 *E-mail:* cius@ualberta.ca

Canadian Museum of History (Musee canadien de l'histoire)
100 Laurier St, Gatineau, QC K1A 0M8
Tel: 819-776-7000 *Toll Free Tel:* 800-555-5621 (North American orders only) *Fax:* 819-776-7187
Web Site: www.historymuseum.ca
Key Personnel
Mgr, Publg & Corp Prods: Pascal Laplante *E-mail:* pascal.laplante@historymuseum.ca
Coord, Corp Prods & Eng Lang Ed: Lee Wyndham *Tel:* 819-776-8385 *E-mail:* lee.wyndham@historymuseum.ca
Founded: 1968 (as the National Museum of Man)
Publications in the subject areas of museology, anthropology, archaeology, ethnology, folk culture, history, contemporary Native & Inuit art, native studies.
Publishes in English, French.
ISBN Prefix(es): 978-1-988282
Number of titles published annually: 15 Print
Total Titles: 400 Print; 8 CD-ROM
Distribution Center: University of Toronto Press, 5201 Dufferin St, Toronto, ON M3H 5T8 *Toll Free Tel:* 800-565-9523 *E-mail:* utpbooks@utpress.utoronto.ca SAN: 115-1134
Membership(s): Association for the Export of Canadian Books; Association of Canadian Publishers (ACP)

§Canadian Scholars' Press Inc
425 Adelaide St W, Suite 200, Toronto, ON M5V 3C1
SAN: 118-9484

Tel: 416-929-2774 *Toll Free Tel:* 800-463-1998 *Fax:* 416-929-1926
E-mail: info@cspi.org; info@canadianscholars.ca; editorial@canadianscholars.ca; orders@canadianscholars.ca
Web Site: www.canadianscholars.ca; www.womenspress.ca
Key Personnel
Pres: Andrew Wayne *Tel:* 416-929-2774 ext 220 *E-mail:* awayne@canadianscholars.ca
VP: Drew Hawkins *Tel:* 416-929-2774 ext 225 *E-mail:* dhawkins@canadianscholars.ca
Dir, Publg: Lily Bergh *Tel:* 416-929-2774 ext 218 *E-mail:* lily.bergh@canadianscholars.ca
Mktg Mgr: Emma Melnyk *Tel:* 416-929-2774 ext 232 *E-mail:* emma.melnyk@canadianscholars.ca
Prodn Mgr: Caley Clements *Tel:* 416-929-2774 ext 222 *E-mail:* caley.clements@canadianscholars.ca
Founded: 1986
Scholarly books & texts for post-secondary education. Trade books-feminist orientation.
Publishes in English, French.
ISBN Prefix(es): 978-0-921627; 978-1-55130; 978-0-921881; 978-0-88961 (Women's Press); 978-1-89418
Number of titles published annually: 24 Print; 10 E-Book
Total Titles: 400 Print; 6 CD-ROM; 80 E-Book
Divisions: Women's Press
Distribution Center: Eurospan Group, 3 Henrietta St, London WC2E 8LU, United Kingdom (Africa, Asia Pacific, Caribbean, Europe, Latin America, Middle East & UK) *Tel:* (01767) 604972 *Fax:* (01767) 601640 *E-mail:* eurospan@turpin-distribution.com
Membership(s): Association of Canadian Publishers (ACP); Canada Council for the Arts; Ontario Arts Council; Organization of Book Publishers of Ontario (OBPO)

Captus Press Inc
1600 Steeles Ave W, Units 14 & 15, Concord, ON L4K 4M2
Tel: 416-736-5537 *Fax:* 416-736-5793
E-mail: info@captus.com
Web Site: www.captus.com
Key Personnel
Pres: Randy Hoffman *E-mail:* randy@captus.com
Mgr: Pauline Lai *E-mail:* pauline@captus.com
Accts Admin & Intl Rts: Lily Chu *E-mail:* lily@captus.com
Founded: 1987
Publication of textbooks, scholarly books, professional books, nonfiction trade books & multimedia Internet courses. Publishes in Spanish also.
Publishes in English, French.
ISBN Prefix(es): 978-0-921801; 978-1-896691; 978-1-895712; 978-1-55322
Number of titles published annually: 28 Print; 2 Online; 1 E-Book
Total Titles: 163 Print; 10 Online; 10 E-Book
Imprints: Captus Press; Captus University Publications; University Press of Canada

§Carswell
Imprint of Thomson Reuters Canada Ltd
One Corporate Plaza, 2075 Kennedy Rd, Toronto, ON M1T 3V4
Tel: 416-609-5811 (sales); 416-609-3800 *Toll Free Tel:* 800-387-5164 (CN & US) *Fax:* 416-298-5094 (sales); 416-298-5082 *Toll Free Fax:* 877-750-9041 (CN only)
E-mail: customersupport.legaltaxcanada@tr.com
Web Site: store.thomsonreuters.ca
Founded: 1864
Canada's leading provider of specialized information & electronic research solutions to the legal, tax, accounting & human resources markets. Carswell provides integrated information in a range of formats, including books, loose-

leaf services, journals, newsletters, CD-ROMs & online.
Publishes in English, French.
ISBN Prefix(es): 978-0-459; 978-0-88820; 978-0-7798
Number of titles published annually: 100 Print
Total Titles: 1,113 Print; 10 Online
Returns: 245 Bartley Dr, Toronto, ON M4A 2V8
Distribution Center: 245 Bartley Dr, Toronto, ON M4A 2V8

CCI Press, see Canadian Circumpolar Institute (CCI) Press

Centre for Reformation & Renaissance Studies (CRRS)
71 Queen's Park Crescent E, Toronto, ON M5S 1K7
Tel: 416-585-4465 *Fax:* 416-585-4430 (attn: CRRS)
E-mail: crrs.publications@utoronto.ca
Web Site: crrs.ca
Key Personnel
Dir: Ethan Matt Kavaler *E-mail:* crrs.director@utoronto.ca
Graduate Fellow, Pubns & Promos: Leslie Wexler
Founded: 1965
Specialty library & academic publisher.
Publishes in English, French.
ISBN Prefix(es): 978-0-7727; 978-0-9697512
Number of titles published annually: 10 Print
Total Titles: 102 Print
Imprints: Dovehouse Press

Centre Franco-Ontarien de Ressources en Alphabetisation (Centre FORA)
PO Box 56, Hanmer, ON P3P 1S9
Tel: 705-524-3672 *Toll Free Tel:* 888-814-4422 (orders, CN only) *Fax:* 705-524-8535
E-mail: info@centrefora.on.ca
Web Site: www.centrefora.on.ca
Founded: 1989
Nonprofit organization that publishes learning materials for adult literacy & distribute education materials for all ages.
Publishes in French.
ISBN Prefix(es): 978-2-921706; 978-1-895336; 978-2-89567
Number of titles published annually: 20 Print
Total Titles: 150 Print

The Charlton Press Corp
Division of Charlton International Inc
991 Victoria St N, Kitchener, ON N2B 3C7
Tel: 416-962-2665 *Toll Free Tel:* 866-663-8827 *Fax:* 519-579-0532
E-mail: chpress@charltonpress.com
Web Site: www.charltonpress.com
Key Personnel
Owner: Marc Drake *Tel:* 416-964-1632
Founded: 1952
Specialize in 20th century numismatics.
Publishes in English.
ISBN Prefix(es): 978-0-88968; 978-2-9800475
Number of titles published annually: 4 Print
Total Titles: 12 Print

Chartered Professional Accountants of Canada (CPA Canada)
277 Wellington St W, Toronto, ON M5V 3H2
Tel: 416-977-3222 *Toll Free Tel:* 800-268-3793 *Fax:* 416-977-8585
E-mail: member.services@cpacanada.ca
Web Site: www.cpacanada.ca; www.facebook.com/CPACanada/
Key Personnel
Pres & CEO: Joy Thomas
Dir, Pubns: Liz Cram *Tel:* 416-204-3433
Founded: 1917
Taxation, accounting, auditing, financial.
Publishes in English, French.

ISBN Prefix(es): 978-0-88800; 978-1-55385
Number of titles published annually: 15 Print
Total Titles: 200 Print
Branch Office(s)
100-4200 N Fraser Way, Burnaby, BC V5J 5K7
  Tel: 604-669-3555 *Toll Free Tel:* 800-663-1529
  Fax: 604-689-5845
1201-350 Sparks St, Ottawa, ON K1R 7S8
  Tel: 613-789-7771 *Fax:* 613-789-7772
680, rue Sherbrooke W, 17th fl, Montreal, QC
  H3A 2M7

§ChemTec Publishing
38 Earswick Dr, Toronto, ON M1E 1C6
Tel: 416-265-2603 *Fax:* 416-265-1399
E-mail: orderdesk@chemtec.org
Web Site: www.chemtec.org
Key Personnel
CEO: Anna Wypych
Circ Mgr: Anna Fox
Founded: 1988
Additives, blends, polymers, recycling & rheol-
  ogy.
Publishes in English.
ISBN Prefix(es): 978-1-895198
Number of titles published annually: 7 Print
Total Titles: 80 Print; 10 CD-ROM

Cheneliere Education Inc
Division of TC Media
5800, rue St Denis, bureau 900, Montreal, QC
  H2S 3L5
Tel: 514-273-1066 *Toll Free Tel:* 800-565-5531
  Fax: 514-276-0324 *Toll Free Fax:* 800-814-
  0324
E-mail: info@cheneliere.ca
Web Site: www.cheneliere.ca
Key Personnel
Gen Mgr: Patrick Lutzy *E-mail:* patrick.lutzy@tc.
  tc
Founded: 1971
School, college & university textbooks; voca-
  tional; French Immersion; teaching skills &
  book packaging (French & English languages).
Publishes in French.
ISBN Prefix(es): 978-2-89310; 978-2-89461; 978-
  2-7650
Number of titles published annually: 200 Print
Imprints: Beauchemin; Gaetan Morin Editeur;
  Graficor
U.S. Publishers Represented: McGraw-Hill Inc
Warehouse: McGraw-Hill Ryerson Limited, 300
  Water St, Whitby, ON L1N 9B6
See separate listing for:
Gaetan Morin Editeur

CIUS Press, see Canadian Institute of Ukrainian
Studies Press

Coach House Books
80 bpNichol Lane, Toronto, ON M5S 3J4
Tel: 416-979-2217 *Toll Free Tel:* 800-367-6360
  (outside Toronto) *Fax:* 416-977-1158
E-mail: mail@chbooks.com
Web Site: www.chbooks.com
Key Personnel
Founder & Publr: Stan Bevington *E-mail:* stan@
  chbooks.com
Edit Dir: Alana Wilcox *E-mail:* alana@chbooks.
  com
Managing Ed: Crystal Sikma *E-mail:* crystal@
  chbooks.com
Publicist: Jessica Rattray *E-mail:* jessica@
  chbooks.com
Founded: 1965
Literary small press specializing in experimental
  fiction & poetry.
Publishes in English.
ISBN Prefix(es): 978-1-55245
Number of titles published annually: 16 Print; 5
  Online
Total Titles: 140 Print; 60 Online

Foreign Rights: Amo Agency (Amo Noh) (South
  Korea); AnatoliaLit Agency (Amy Spangler)
  (Turkey); Sandra Bruna Agencia Literaria SL
  (Natalia Berenguer) (Portugal, Spain); English
  Agency Japan (Hamish Macaskill) (Japan); The
  Grayhawk Agency (Lora Fountain) (China, Tai-
  wan); Mohr Books Literary Agency (Annelie
  Geissler) (Germany); Piergiorgio Nicolazzini
  Literary Agency (Maura Solinas) (Italy); San-
  drine Paccher (France)
Distribution Center: Publishers Group Canada,
  76 Stafford St, Suite 300, Toronto, ON M6J
  2S1 (CN orders), Sales Dir: Lori Richard-
  son *Tel:* 416-934-9900 *Fax:* 416-934-1410
  E-mail: info@pgcbooks.ca *Web Site:* www.
  pgcbooks.ca
Consortium Book Sales & Distribution, The Keg
  House, Suite 101, 34 13 Ave NE, Minneapolis, MN 55413-1007, United States (US orders)
  Tel: 612-746-2600 *Toll Free Tel:* 800-283-3572
  (cust serv, Jackson, TN) *Fax:* 612-746-2606
  E-mail: info@cbsd.com *Web Site:* www.cbsd.
  com SAN: 200-6049
Membership(s): Association of Canadian Publish-
  ers (ACP); Community of Literary Magazines
  & Presses (CLMP); Literary Press Group

Collector Grade Publications Inc
PO Box 1046, Cobourg, ON K9A 4W5
Tel: 905-342-3434 *Fax:* 905-342-3688
E-mail: info@collectorgrade.com
Web Site: www.collectorgrade.com
Key Personnel
Pres: R Blake Stevens
Founded: 1979
Accurate, in-depth studies of modern small arms.
  Technical reference books.
Publishes in English.
ISBN Prefix(es): 978-0-88935
Number of titles published annually: 3 Print
Total Titles: 60 Print

Company's Coming Publishing Ltd
87 E Pender St, Vancouver, BC V6A 1S9
Tel: 780-450-6223 (orders & inquiries)
  Toll Free Tel: 800-661-9017 (CN); 800-518-
  3541 (US) *Fax:* 780-450-1857
E-mail: info@companyscoming.com
Web Site: www.companyscoming.com
Key Personnel
Pres: Grant Lovig
Founded: 1981
Publish cookbooks, craft books & stationery
  products.
Publishes in English.
ISBN Prefix(es): 978-0-9690695; 978-0-9693322;
  978-1-895455; 978-1-896891; 978-1-897069;
  978-1-897477; 978-1-927126
Number of titles published annually: 25 Print
Total Titles: 200 Print
Distribution Center: Booklogic, 2311 96 St, Ed-
  monton, AB T6N 1G3

Comptables professionnels agrees du Canada,
  see Chartered Professional Accountants of
  Canada (CPA Canada)

Conseil canadien de developpement social, see
  Canadian Council on Social Development
  (Conseil canadien de developpement social)

**The Continuing Legal Education Society of
British Columbia (CLEBC)**
500-1155 W Pender St, Vancouver, BC V6E 2P4
Tel: 604-669-3544; 604-893-2121 (cust serv)
  Toll Free Tel: 800-663-0437 (CN) *Fax:* 604-
  669-9260
E-mail: custserv@cle.bc.ca
Web Site: www.cle.bc.ca
Key Personnel
CEO: Ron Friesen *Tel:* 604-893-2114
  E-mail: rfriesen@cle.bc.ca

Dir, Pubns: Susan Munro *Tel:* 604-893-2106
  E-mail: smunro@cle.bc.ca
Mktg Mgr: Adam Simpkins *Tel:* 604-893-2168
  E-mail: adams@cle.bc.ca
Founded: 1976
Publish course materials, practice manuals & case
  digests.
Publishes in English.
ISBN Prefix(es): 978-0-86504; 978-1-55258
Number of titles published annually: 35 Print; 35
  Online
Total Titles: 50 Print; 1 CD-ROM; 48 Online
Imprints: CLEBC

Cormorant Books Inc
260 Spadina Ave, Suite 502, Toronto, ON M4Y
  1P9
Tel: 416-925-8887
E-mail: info@cormorantbooks.com
Web Site: www.cormorantbooks.com
Key Personnel
Pres & Publr, Cormorant Books: Marc Cote
  E-mail: m.cote@cormorantbooks.com
Mng Dir: Sarah Cooper *E-mail:* s.cooper@
  cormorantbooks.com
Founded: 1986
Independent literary publisher of Canadian au-
  thors.
Publishes in English.
ISBN Prefix(es): 978-0-920953; 978-1-896951;
  978-1-896332; 978-1-897151; 978-1-77086
Number of titles published annually: 20 Print; 16
  E-Book
Total Titles: 150 Print; 100 E-Book
Imprints: DCB; The Riverbank Press
Distribution Center: University of Toronto Press,
  5201 Dufferin St, Toronto, ON M3H 5T8
  Tel: 416-667-7791 *Toll Free Tel:* 800-565-9523
  Fax: 416-667-7832 *Toll Free Fax:* 800-221-
  9985 *E-mail:* utpbooks@utpress.utoronto.ca
  Web Site: www.utpress.utoronto.ca

La Courte Echelle
4388, rue Saint-Denis, Suite 315, Montreal, QC
  H2J 2L1
Tel: 514-312-6950
E-mail: info@courteechelle.com
Web Site: courteechelle.groupecourteechelle.com
Key Personnel
Gen Dir: Marieve Talbot
Artistic Dir: Julie Massy
Literary Dir & Children's Ed: Carole Tremblay
Edit Asst: Celine Comtois
Communs Coord: Melina Schoenborn
Sales Coord: Marianne Dalpe
Graphic Designer: Catherine Charbonneau
Founded: 1978
Children's, young adult & adult fiction. No unsol
  mss accepted.
Publishes in French.
ISBN Prefix(es): 978-2-89021; 978-1-894731;
  978-2-89651; 978-2-89695
Number of titles published annually: 50 Print
Total Titles: 545 Print
Distribution Center: Hachette Canada, 9001 de
  l'Acadie, bureau 1002, Montreal, QC H4N 3H5
  Tel: 514-382-3034 *Toll Free Tel:* 888-422-4388
  Fax: 514-381-5088 *E-mail:* info@hachette.qc.
  ca *Web Site:* www.hachette.qc.ca
Socadis Inc, 420 rue Stinson, Montreal, QC H4N
  3L7 *Tel:* 514-331-3300 *Toll Free Tel:* 800-361-
  2847 *Fax:* 514-745-3282
Librairie du Quebec a Paris, Diffusion du Nou-
  veau Monde (DNM), 30, rue Gay-Lussac,
  75005 Paris, France (France & Europe)
  Tel: 01 43 54 49 02 *Fax:* 01 43 54 39 15
  E-mail: dnm@librairieduquebec.fr *Web
  Site:* www.librairieduquebec.fr

§Crabtree Publishing Co Ltd
Subsidiary of Crabtree Publishing Co (USA)
616 Welland Ave, St Catharines, ON L2M 5V6
SAN: 115-1436

Tel: 905-682-5221 *Toll Free Tel:* 800-387-7650
  Fax: 905-682-7166 *Toll Free Fax:* 800-355-
  7166
E-mail: custserv@crabtreebooks.com; sales@
  crabtreebooks.com; orders@crabtreebooks.com
Web Site: www.crabtreebooks.com
Key Personnel
Pres: Peter A Crabtree *E-mail:* peter_c@
  crabtreebooks.com
Publr: Bobbie Kalman *E-mail:* bobbiek@
  crabtreebooks.com
VP, Edit: Kathy Middleton *E-mail:* kathy_m@
  crabtreebooks.com
VP, Mktg: Julie Alguire *E-mail:* julie_a@
  crabtreebooks.com
VP, Opers: Craig Culliford *E-mail:* craig_c@
  crabtreebooks.com
Dir, New Media: Rob MacGregor
  E-mail: rob_m@crabtreebooks.com
Dir, Sales: Andrea Crabtree *E-mail:* andrea_c@
  crabtreebooks.com
Warehouse Mgr: Karl Kasper
  E-mail: warehouse@crabtreebooks.com
Cust Serv: Candice Pinkerton
  E-mail: candice_c@crabtreebooks.com
Founded: 1978
Children's nonfiction & fiction, library binding &
  paperback for school & trade.
Publishes in English, French.
ISBN Prefix(es): 978-0-86505; 978-0-7787; 978-
  1-4271
Number of titles published annually: 524 Print;
  262 E-Book
Total Titles: 5,964 Print; 2,276 E-Book; 105 Au-
  dio
Imprints: Look, Listen & Learn Audio Books
Distributor for Bayard; Maren Green Publishing
  Inc
Foreign Rep(s): Everybody's Books (Namibia,
  South Africa); Novella (Australia, New
  Zealand); Roundhouse Group (European Union,
  UK)
Membership(s): American Alliance of Museums
  (AAM); American Booksellers Association
  (ABA); American Library Association (ALA);
  American Marketing Association; Educational
  Book & Media Association (EBMA); National
  Science Teachers Association (NSTA); Ontario
  Library Association

CRRS, see Centre for Reformation &
  Renaissance Studies (CRRS)

§Database Directories
588 Dufferin Ave, London, ON N6B 2A4
Tel: 519-433-1666 *Fax:* 519-430-1131
E-mail: mail@databasedirectory.com
Web Site: www.databasedirectory.com
Key Personnel
CEO: Lesley Classic *E-mail:* lclassic@
  databasedirectory.com
Founded: 1995
Directories & e-files on libraries, schools, col-
  leges, universities, academic retailers & munici-
  palities.
Publishes in English.
ISBN Prefix(es): 978-1-896537
Number of titles published annually: 3 Print; 4
  CD-ROM; 4 Online
Total Titles: 10 Print; 10 CD-ROM; 4 Online

§DC Canada Education Publishing (DCCED)
180 Metcalfe St, Suite 204, Ottawa, ON K2P 1P5
Tel: 613-565-8885 *Toll Free Tel:* 888-565-0262
  Fax: 613-565-8881
E-mail: info@dc-canada.ca
Web Site: www.dc-canada.ca
Key Personnel
Publg Dir: Mei Dang
Founded: 1995
Publishes in English.

ISBN Prefix(es): 978-0-9738439; 978-0-9738440;
  978-0-9808816; 978-0-9810549; 978-1-926776
Number of titles published annually: 6 Print

§Double Dragon Publishing Inc
1-5762 Hwy 7 E, Markham, ON L3P 7Y4
Mailing Address: PO Box 54016, Markham, ON
  L3P 7Y4
E-mail: sales@double-dragon-ebooks.com
Web Site: www.double-dragon-ebooks.com
Key Personnel
Publr & CEO: Deron Douglas
Founded: 2001
Publishes ebooks & trade paperbacks in the fantasy, science fiction, speculative fiction, horror
  & suspense genres. Established with the goal
  of building a Canadian-based publishing venue
  for the growing number of good but unpub-
  lished fiction writers around the world. Dedi-
  cated to publishing quality works of fiction &
  nonfiction & will continue to publish works in
  various genres in both the ebook & traditional
  paper book formats. Make special efforts to
  publish a specific number of works written by
  North American Aboriginal authors each year.
Publishes in English.
ISBN Prefix(es): 978-1-894841; 978-1-55404
Number of titles published annually: 40 Print;
  100 E-Book
Total Titles: 40 Print; 125 E-Book
Imprints: Blood Moon Publishing; Carnal De-
  sires Publishing; DDP Literary Press; Double
  Dragon eBooks; Double Dragon Press; Dragon
  Dance; Dragon Tooth Fantasy; Dragon's Heart
  Romance

Doubleday Canada
Imprint of Penguin Random House Canada
320 Front St W, Suite 1400, Toronto, ON M5V
  3B6
SAN: 115-0340
Tel: 416-364-4449 *Fax:* 416-598-7764
Web Site: www.penguinrandomhouse.ca
Key Personnel
CEO, PRHC: Kristin Cochrane
CFO, PRHC: Barry Gallant
Chief Strategy & Opers Offr, PRHC: Robert
  Wheaton
SVP & Dir, Prodn: Janine Laporte
Publr: Amy Black
Sr Mng Ed: Susan Burns
Ed-in-Chief: Martha Kanya-Forstner
Sr Ed: Bhavna Chauhan
Ed: Kiara Kent; Zoe Maslow
Founded: 1937
General trade nonfiction (current affairs, politics,
  business, sports); fiction, children's illustrated.
Penguin Random House Canada & its publishing
  entities are not accepting unsol submissions,
  proposals, mss, or submission queries via e-
  mail at this time.
Publishes in English.
Number of titles published annually: 60 Print; 5
  E-Book
Total Titles: 1,172 Print; 41 E-Book
Imprints: Anchor Canada; Bond Street Books;
  Seal Books
Membership(s): Canadian Publishers' Council

Douglas & McIntyre (2013) Ltd
4437 Rondeview Rd, Madeira Park, BC V0N 2H1
Mailing Address: PO Box 219, Madeira Park, BC
  V0N 2H0
Toll Free Tel: 800-667-2988
E-mail: info@douglas-mcintyre.com
Web Site: www.douglas-mcintyre.com
Key Personnel
Interim Publr: Howard White
Founded: 1970
Focus on biographies, native art & history, archi-
  tecture, literary fiction & cookbooks.
Publishes in English.

ISBN Prefix(es): 978-0-88894; 978-1-55054; 978-
  1-55365; 978-1-77100; 978-0-920841; 978-1-
  55051; 978-1-926812; 978-1-926685; 978-1-
  926706
Number of titles published annually: 90 Print
Total Titles: 1,500 Print
Distributed by University of Toronto Press
Membership(s): Association for the Export of
  Canadian Books; Association of American Pub-
  lishers (AAP); Association of Book Publishers
  of British Columbia; Association of Canadian
  Publishers (ACP)

Dundurn Press Ltd
3 Church St, Suite 500, Toronto, ON M5E 1M2
SAN: 115-0359
Tel: 416-214-5544
E-mail: info@dundurn.com; publicity@dundurn.
  com; sales@dundurn.com
Web Site: www.dundurn.com
Key Personnel
Pres & Publr: Kirk Howard *E-mail:* khoward@
  dundurn.com
Founded: 1972
Specialize in Canadian history, social sciences,
  some biography & art, fiction & mysteries.
Publishes in English.
ISBN Prefix(es): 978-0-919670; 978-0-9690454;
  978-0-88924; 978-0-88882; 978-1-55488; 978-
  1-4597
Number of titles published annually: 100 Print
Total Titles: 2,500 Print; 1,800 E-Book
Distribution Center: University of Toronto
  Press Distribution, 5201 Dufferin St, Toronto,
  ON M3H 5T8 *Tel:* 416-667-7791 *Toll Free
  Tel:* 800-565-9523 *Fax:* 416-667-7832 *Toll Free
  Fax:* 800-221-9985 *Web Site:* www.utpress.
  utoronto.ca
Ingram Publisher Services, One Ingram Blvd,
  La Vergne, TN 37086-1986, United States
  Toll Free Tel: 855-802-8228 *Toll Free
  Fax:* 800-838-1149 *E-mail:* customer.service@
  ingrampublisherservices.com *Web Site:* www.
  ingrampublisherservices.com
Lightning Source UK Ltd, Chapter House,
  Pitfield, Kiln Farm, Milton Keynes MK11
  3LW, United Kingdom *Tel:* 0800 136-
  0600 *E-mail:* ukips_customer_service@
  ingramcontent.com
Membership(s): Association of Canadian Publishers (ACP)

Ecrits des Forges
992-A rue Royale, Trois-Rivieres, QC G9A 4H9
Tel: 819-840-8492
E-mail: ecritsdesforges@gmail.com
Web Site: www.ecritsdesforges.com
Key Personnel
Admin Dir: Etienne Poirier
Literary Dir: Bernard Pozier
Founded: 1971
Publish poetry.
Publishes in French.
ISBN Prefix(es): 978-2-89046
Number of titles published annually: 50 Print
Total Titles: 1,125 Print
Distributed by DCR; Prologue
Membership(s): Association nationale des editeurs
  de livres (ANEL)

ECW Press
665 Gerrard St E, Toronto, ON M4M 1Y2
SAN: 115-1274
Tel: 416-694-3348
E-mail: info@ecwpress.com
Web Site: www.ecwpress.com
Key Personnel
Co-Publr: Jack David *E-mail:* jack@ecwpress.
  com
Founded: 1974
Publishes in English.

ISBN Prefix(es): 978-0-920763; 978-1-55022;
978-0-920802; 978-1-77041
Number of titles published annually: 50 Print
Total Titles: 1,200 Print; 400 E-Book
Imprints: misFit
Foreign Rights: David Caron (worldwide exc
Canada & USA)
Distribution Center: Baker & Taylor Pub-
lisher Services, 30 Amberwood Pkwy, Ash-
land, OH 44805, United States *Tel:* 567-
215-0030 *Toll Free Tel:* 888-814-0208
E-mail: info@btpubservices.com *Web
Site:* www.btpubservices.com
Membership(s): Association of Canadian Publish-
ers (ACP); Literary Press Group

**EDGE Science Fiction & Fantasy Publishing
Inc**
Imprint of Hades Publications Inc
PO Box 1714, Calgary, AB T2P 2L7
Tel: 403-254-0160 *Fax:* 403-254-0456
E-mail: admin@hadespublications.com
Web Site: www.edgewebsite.com
Key Personnel
Pres & Publr: Brian Hades *E-mail:* publisher@
hadespublications.com
Mktg: Janice Shoults
Founded: 1996
Encourage, produce & promote thought-provoking
science fiction & fantasy & horror literature by
"bringing the magic alive-one world at a time"
with each new book released. Independent pub-
lisher of science fiction & fantasy novels in
hardcover or trade paperback format. Produce
high-quality books with lots of attention to de-
tail & lots of marketing effort.
Publishes in English.
ISBN Prefix(es): 978-1-894063; 978-1-896944;
978-1-77053
Number of titles published annually: 8 Print
Total Titles: 87 Print; 1 Audio
Imprints: Absolute XPress; Tesseract Books
U.S. Rep(s): Baker & Taylor; Fitzhenry & White-
side; Ingram Book Co
Distribution Center: Fitzhenry & Whiteside,
195 Allstate Pkwy, Markham, ON L3R 4T8
(CN & US) *Toll Free Tel:* 800-387-9776 *Toll
Free Fax:* 800-260-9777 *E-mail:* bookinfo@
fitzhenry.ca
Membership(s): Book Publishers Association of
Alberta; The Imaging Alliance; Independent
Book Publishers Association (IBPA); IPAC

Les Editions Alire
120 cote du Passage, Levis, QC G6V 5S9
Tel: 418-835-4441 *Fax:* 418-838-4443
E-mail: info@alire.com
Web Site: www.alire.com
Key Personnel
Admin Dir: Melanie Bissonnette *E-mail:* melanie.
bissonnette@alire.com
Edit Dir: Jean Pettigrew *E-mail:* jean.pettigrew@
alire.com
Dir, Sales: Louise Alain *E-mail:* louise.alain@
alire.com
Founded: 1996
Publish French Canadian popular genre fiction.
Publishes in French.
ISBN Prefix(es): 978-2-922145; 978-2-89615;
978-2-9801068
Number of titles published annually: 10 Print
Total Titles: 131 Print
Distribution Center: Messageries ADP, 2315, rue
de la Province, Longueuil, QC J4G 1G4 (CN
& US) *Tel:* 450-640-1237 *Fax:* 450-674-6237
Interforum Editis, Immeuble Paryseine, 3,
allee de la Seine, 94854 Ivry Cedex, France
Tel: 02 38 32 71 00 *Fax:* 02 28 32 71 28
E-mail: cdes-export@interforum.fr *Web
Site:* www.interforum.fr
Membership(s): Association nationale des editeurs
de livres (ANEL)

Editions ASTED
Subsidiary of Association pour l' Avancement des
Sciences et des Techniques de la Documenta-
tion
2065 rue Parthenais, Bureau 387, Montreal, QC
H2K 3T1
Tel: 514-281-5012 *Fax:* 514-281-8219
E-mail: editions@asted.org; info@asted.org
Web Site: www.asted.org
Key Personnel
Exec Dir: Lionel Villalonga *E-mail:* lvillalonga@
asted.org
Founded: 1973
Publishes in French.
ISBN Prefix(es): 978-2-921548; 978-2-89055;
978-2-923563; 978-2-89123; 978-2-89224
Number of titles published annually: 3 Print

Les Editions Caractere
Division of TC Media Livres
5800, rue St-Denis, bureau 900, Montreal, QC
H2S 3L5
Tel: 450-461-2782 *Toll Free Tel:* 855-861-2782
E-mail: caractere@tc.tc
Web Site: www.tcmedialivres.com
Founded: 2004
Publishes in French.
ISBN Prefix(es): 978-2-923351; 978-2-89642;
978-2-89643
Number of titles published annually: 130 Print
Distribution Center: Prologue Inc, 1650, Li-
onel Bertrand, Boisbriand, QC J7H 1N7
Tel: 450-434-0306 *Toll Free Tel:* 800-363-2864
Fax: 450-434-4135 *Toll Free Fax:* 800-361-
8088

Les Editions Chouette
1001 Lenoir St, Suite B-238, Montreal, QC H4C
2Z6
Tel: 514-925-3325 *Fax:* 514-925-3323
E-mail: info@editions-chouette.com
Web Site: www.chouette-publishing.com
Key Personnel
Publr & Ed: Anne Paradis
Founded: 1987
Produce children's books adapted to each age
group from birth to age six, with the well-
known Caillou character.
Publishes in English, French.
ISBN Prefix(es): 978-2-9800909; 978-2-921198;
978-2-89450; 978-2-89718
Number of titles published annually: 30 Print
U.S. Rep(s): Client Distribution Services
Foreign Rep(s): Simon Payette
Warehouse: Publishers Group West, 1700
Fourth St, Berkeley, CA 94710, United States
Tel: 510-809-3700 *Toll Free Tel:* 866-400-5351
(cust serv) *Fax:* 510-809-3777 *Web Site:* www.
pgw.com
Distribution Center: Canadian Manda Group,
165 Dufferin St, Toronto, ON M6K 3H6
Tel: 416-516-0911 *Fax:* 416-516-0917
E-mail: info@mandagroup.com *Web
Site:* www.canadianmandagroup.ca
Publishers Group West, 1700 Fourth St, Berke-
ley, CA 94710, United States *Tel:* 510-809-
3700 *Toll Free Tel:* 866-400-5351 (cust serv)
Fax: 510-809-3777 *Web Site:* www.pgw.com

Editions de la Pleine Lune
223 34 Ave, Lachine, QC H8T 1Z4
Tel: 514-634-7954
E-mail: editpllune@videotron.ca
Web Site: www.pleinelune.qc.ca
Key Personnel
Literary Dir: Marie-Madeleine Raoult
Founded: 1975
Publishes in French.
ISBN Prefix(es): 978-2-89024
Number of titles published annually: 8 Print
Total Titles: 250 Print

Distribution Center: Diffusion Dimedia,
539, Lebau Blvd, St-Laurent, QC H4N
1S2 *Tel:* 514-336-3941 *Fax:* 514-331-
3916 *E-mail:* general@dimedia.qc.ca *Web
Site:* www.dimedia.com
La Librairie du Quebec a Paris et DNM, 30, rue
Gay Lussac, 75005 Paris, France *Tel:* 01 43 54
49 02 *Fax:* 01 43 54 39 15 *Web Site:* www.
librairieduquebec.fr
Membership(s): Association nationale des editeurs
de livres (ANEL)

Les Editions de l'Hexagone
Division of Groupe Ville-Marie Litterature
4545, rue Frontenac, 3rd fl, Montreal, QC H2H
2R7
Tel: 514-849-5259
Web Site: www.edhexagone.com
Key Personnel
VP, Edit: Martin Balthazar
Edit Dir: Alain-Nicolas Renaud
Ed: Melikah Abdelmoumen; Ariane Caron-
Lacoste
Prodn Mgr: Sophie Deschenes
Founded: 1953
Publishes in French.
ISBN Prefix(es): 978-2-89006; 978-2-89295; 978-
2-89648; 978-0-88508
Number of titles published annually: 30 Print
Total Titles: 35 Print
Foreign Office(s): Immeuble Paryseine, 3, Allee
de la Seine, 94854 Ivry Cedex, France *Tel:* 01
49 59 12 40 *Fax:* 06 16 94 14 38
Orders to: Messageries ADP, 2315 rue de la
Province, Longueuil, QC J4G 1G4 *Tel:* 450-
640-1234 *Toll Free Tel:* 800-771-3022
Fax: 450-640-1251 *Toll Free Fax:* 800-603-
0433 *E-mail:* adpcommandes@messageries-
adp.com *Web Site:* www.messageries-adp.com
Warehouse: Messageries ADP, 2315 rue de la
Province, Longueuil, QC J4G 1G4 *Tel:* 450-
640-1234 *Toll Free Tel:* 800-771-3022
Fax: 450-640-1251 *Toll Free Fax:* 800-603-
0433 *Web Site:* www.messageries-adp.com

Les Editions de Mortagne
CP 116, Boucherville, QC J4B 5E6
Tel: 450-641-2387 *Fax:* 450-655-6092
E-mail: info@editionsdemortagne.com
Web Site: www.editionsdemortagne.com
Key Personnel
Founder & Pres: Max Permingeat
VP, Admin & Prodn: Alexandra Pellerin
VP, Editions & Promo: Sandy Pellerin
Founded: 1978
Novels.
Publishes in French.
ISBN Prefix(es): 978-2-89074
Number of titles published annually: 15 Print
Total Titles: 15 Print
Foreign Office(s): BP 13, 16700 Ruffec, France
Tel: 05 45 85 79 00
Distribution Center: Prologue, 1650 blvd
Lionel-Bertrand, Broisbriand, QC J7N 1N7
Tel: 450-434-0306 *Toll Free Tel:* 800-363-
2864 *Fax:* 450-434-2627 *Toll Free Fax:* 800-
361-8088 *E-mail:* prologue@prologue.ca *Web
Site:* www.prologue.ca
DG Diffusion, Zl de Bogues, 31750 Escalquens,
France *Tel:* 05 55 51 80 00 *Fax:* 05 55 62 17
39
Distribution Servidis, Chemin des Chalets
7, 1279 Chavannes-de-Bogis, Switzerland
Tel: (022) 960 95 23 *Fax:* (022) 960 95 77
Web Site: www.servidis.ch
Membership(s): Association nationale des editeurs
de livres (ANEL)

Les Editions du Ble
340, blvd Provencher, St Boniface, MB R2H 0G7
Tel: 204-237-8200 *Fax:* 204-233-8182
E-mail: direction@editionsduble.ca
Web Site: ble.avoslivres.ca

Key Personnel
Dir Gen: Emmanuelle Rigaud
Founded: 1974
Publish books in French (novels, essays, poetry) pertaining mainly to the Canadian West (but not exclusively).
Publishes in French.
ISBN Prefix(es): 978-2-921347; 978-2-923673
Number of titles published annually: 6 Print
Total Titles: 100 Print
Distribution Center: Diffusion Dimedia Inc, 539 Blvd Lebeau, Saint-Laurent, QC H4N 1S2 *Tel:* 514-336-3941 *Web Site:* www.dimedia.com

Les Editions du Boreal
4447, rue St-Denis, Montreal, QC H2J 2L2
Tel: 514-287-7401 *Fax:* 514-287-7664
E-mail: boreal@editionsboreal.qc.ca
Web Site: www.editionsboreal.qc.ca
Key Personnel
Dir Gen: Pascal Assathiany
Dir: Jean Bernier
Founded: 1963
General literature, essays, history, translations, children's & philosophy.
Publishes in French.
ISBN Prefix(es): 978-2-89052; 978-2-7646; 978-0-88503
Number of titles published annually: 70 Print
Total Titles: 1,700 Print
Distributed by Editions Du Seuil (Europe)
Foreign Rights: AMV Agencia Literaria (Eduardo Melon Vallat) (Portugal, Spain); AnatoliaLit Literary & Copyright Agency (Amy Spangler) (Turkey); Balla & Co Literary Agents (Catherine Balla) (Hungary); Berla & Griffini Rights Agency (Erica Berla) (Italy); Bureau des Copyrights Francais (Corinne Quentin) (Japan); The Grayhawk Agency (Nicolas Wu) (Taiwan); Anastasia Lester (Belarus, Bosnia and Herzegovina, Bulgaria, Croatia, Czechia, Estonia, Kosovo, Latvia, Lithuania, Montenegro, North Macedonia, Poland, Russia, Serbia, Slovakia, Slovenia, Ukraine); Liepman AG Literary Agency (Marc Koralnik) (Germany); Rightol Media Ltd (Zoe Luo) (China); 2 Seas Agency (Marleen Seegers) (Iceland, Netherlands, Scandinavia, USA)
Distribution Center: Diffusion Dimedia, 539, blvd Lebeau, Ville St-Laurent, QC H4N 1S2 *Tel:* 514-336-3941 *Fax:* 514-331-3916 *E-mail:* info@dimedia.qc.ca *Web Site:* www.dimedia.com
Volumen, 25, blvd Romain Rolland, CS 21418, 75993 Paris Cedex 14, France (Europe) *Tel:* 01 41 48 84 60 *Fax:* 01 64 48 49 63 *E-mail:* volumen@volumen.fr

Editions du CHU Sainte-Justine
Unit of Direction de l'enseignement
3175, chemin de la Cote-Sainte-Catherine, Montreal, QC H3T 1C5
Tel: 514-345-4671 *Fax:* 514-345-4631
E-mail: edition.hsj@ssss.gouv.qc.ca
Web Site: www.editions-chu-sainte-justine.org
Key Personnel
Publg Dir: Marise Labrecque *Tel:* 514-345-7743 *E-mail:* marise.labrecque.hsj@ssss.gouv.qc.ca
Sales Dir: Jean-Francois Hebert *Tel:* 514-345-4931 ext 5541 *E-mail:* jean-francois.hebert.hsj@ssss.gouv.qc.ca
Ed: Marie-Eve Lefebvre *Tel:* 514-345-2350 *E-mail:* marie-eve.lefebvre.hsj@ssss.gouv.qc.ca
ISBN Prefix(es): 978-2-921215; 978-2-921858; 978-2-922770; 978-2-89619
Number of titles published annually: 20 Print
Distribution Center: Prologue, 1650 blvd Lionel-Bertrand, Boisbriand, QC J7H 1N7 *Tel:* 450-434-0306 *Toll Free Tel:* 800-363-2864 *Fax:* 450-434-2627 *Toll Free Fax:* 800-361-8088 *E-mail:* prologue@prologue.ca *Web Site:* www.prologue.ca

SDL La Caravelle, Rue du Pre-aux-oies, 303, 1130 Brussels, Belgium (Belgium & Luxembourg) *Tel:* (02) 240 93 08 *Fax:* (02) 216 35 98 *E-mail:* info@sdlcaravelle.com
Daudin Distribution, One, rue Guynemer, 78114 Magny-les Hameaux, France *Tel:* 01 30 48 74 74 *Fax:* 01 34 98 02 44 *E-mail:* commandes@daudin.fr
Servidis, Chemin des chalets, 1279 Chavannes-de-Bogis, Switzerland *Tel:* (022) 960 95 32 *Fax:* (022) 960 95 77 *E-mail:* commande@servidis.ch

§Les Editions du Noroit
4609, rue D'Iberville, espace 202, Montreal, QC H2H 2L9
Tel: 514-727-0005
E-mail: lenoroit@lenoroit.com
Web Site: www.lenoroit.com
Key Personnel
Literary Dir: Paul Belanger
Founded: 1971
Poetry.
Publishes in French.
ISBN Prefix(es): 978-2-89018; 978-0-88524
Number of titles published annually: 25 Print
Total Titles: 730 Print; 1 CD-ROM; 10 Audio
Distribution Center: Diffusion Dimedia Inc, 539 blvd Lebeau, Montreal, QC H4N 1S2 *Tel:* 514-336-3941 *Fax:* 514-331-3916 *E-mail:* general@dimedia.qc.ca *Web Site:* www.dimedia.com

Les Editions du Remue-Menage
La Maison Parent-Roback, 110 rue Sainte-Therese, bureau 303, Montreal, QC H2Y 1E6
Tel: 514-876-0097 *Fax:* 514-876-7951
E-mail: info@editions-rm.ca
Web Site: www.editions-rm.ca
Key Personnel
Ed: Rachel Bedard; Valerie Lefebvre-Faucher *E-mail:* vlf@editions-rm.ca; Anne Migner-Laurin *E-mail:* amlaurin@editions-rm.ca
Edit Asst: Camille Simard *E-mail:* camille.simard@editions-rm.ca
Founded: 1976
Specialize in feminist books.
Publishes in English, French.
ISBN Prefix(es): 978-2-89091
Number of titles published annually: 15 Print
Total Titles: 170 Print
Distributed by Export Livre (Europe, US); Hushion House Publishing Ltd (CN, US); Librairie du Quebec (France)
Foreign Rep(s): Library Plaisir (Egypt); S A Vander (Belgium)
Distribution Center: Diffusion Dimedia, 539 blvd Lebeau, St-Laurent, QC H4N 1S2 *Tel:* 514-336-3941 *Fax:* 514-331-3916 *Toll Free Fax:* 800-667-3941 *E-mail:* commandes@dimedia.qc.ca
Membership(s): Association nationale des editeurs de livres (ANEL)

Les Editions du Septentrion
835 Turnbull Ave, Quebec City, QC G1R 2X4
Tel: 418-688-3556 *Fax:* 418-527-4978
E-mail: info@septentrion.qc.ca
Web Site: www.septentrion.qc.ca
Key Personnel
Pres & Publr: Denis Vaugeois
Dir Gen & Ed: Gilles Herman
Founded: 1988
Full service publisher.
Publishes in English, French.
ISBN Prefix(es): 978-2-89448; 978-0-89664; 978-0-88514; 978-0-921114; 978-0-89011
Number of titles published annually: 30 Print
Total Titles: 700 Print
Divisions: Hamac
Distributed by Baraka Books
Distribution Center: Dimedia, 539 blvd Lebeau, St-Laurent, QC H4N 1S2

Les Editions du Vermillon
305, rue St-Patrick, Ottawa, ON K1N 5K4
Tel: 613-241-4032 *Fax:* 613-241-3109
E-mail: leseditionsduvermillon@rogers.com
Web Site: www.leseditionsduvermillon.ca
Key Personnel
Founder & Edit Dir: Jacques Flamand
CEO: Monique Bertoli
Founded: 1982
Poetry, novels, children's books, textbooks, essays.
Publishes in English, French.
ISBN Prefix(es): 978-0-919925; 978-1-895873; 978-1-894547; 978-1-897058; 978-1-926628; 978-2-89040; 978-1-77120
Number of titles published annually: 12 Print
Total Titles: 400 Print
Foreign Rep(s): Diffusion Albert-le-Grand (Switzerland); Librairie du Quebec (France)
Foreign Rights: Montreal-Contacts (worldwide)
Distribution Center: Librairie du Quebec, 300, rue Gay Lussac, 75005 Paris, France *Tel:* 01 43 54 49 02 *Fax:* 01 43 54 39 15 *E-mail:* liquebec@noos.fr
Diffusion Albert le Grand SA, 20, rue de Beaumont, 1701 Fribourg, Switzerland *Tel:* (026) 425 85 95 *Fax:* (026) 425 85 90 *E-mail:* diffusion@albert-le-grand.ch
Membership(s): Canada Council for the Arts; Ontario Arts Council

Les Editions Fides
Subsidiary of Coopsco
7333 place des Roseraies, bureau 100, Anjou, QC H1M 2X6
Tel: 514-745-4290 *Fax:* 514-745-4299
E-mail: editions@groupefides.com
Web Site: www.editionsfides.com
Key Personnel
CEO: Claude Rheaume
Edit Dir: Michel Maille *Tel:* 514-745-4290 ext 355
Edit Dir, Fides Educ: M Jean-Pierre Albert *Tel:* 514-745-4290 ext 352 *E-mail:* jean-pierre.albert@groupefides.com
Dir, Fin & Admin: Michel Perreault
Mktg: David Senechal
Founded: 1937
Publishes in French.
ISBN Prefix(es): 978-0-7755; 978-2-7621; 978-2-87374; 978-2-89007; 978-2-923989
Number of titles published annually: 60 Print
Total Titles: 2,000 Print
Distribution Center: Socadis, 420 rue Stinson, Ville St-Laurent, QC H4N 3L7 *Tel:* 514-331-3300 *Toll Free Tel:* 800-361-2847 *Fax:* 514-745-3282 *Toll Free Fax:* 866-803-5422 *E-mail:* socinfo@socadis.com
Sofedis, 11, rue Soufflot, 75005 Paris, France (Europe) *Tel:* 01 53 10 25 25 *Fax:* 01 53 10 25 26 *E-mail:* info@sofedis.fr

Editions FouLire
4339, rue des Becassines, Quebec, QC G1G 1V5
Tel: 418-628-4029 *Toll Free Tel:* 877-628-4029 (CN & US) *Fax:* 418-628-4801
E-mail: info@foulire.com; edition@foulire.com
Web Site: www.foulire.com
Key Personnel
Ed: Yvon Brochu
Head, Communs & Soc Media: Marc Proulx
Prodn & Mktg: Danielle Lajeunesse
Founded: 2002
Publishers of books for children.
Publishes in French.
ISBN Prefix(es): 978-2-89591
Number of titles published annually: 30 Print
Total Titles: 3,500 Print
Foreign Rights: Ambre Communication (Pascale Patte-Wilbert) (France)
Distribution Center: Prologue Inc, 1650, blvd Lionel-Bertrand, Boisbriand, QC J7H 1N7 *Tel:* 450-434-0306 *Toll Free Tel:* 800-363-2864

Fax: 450-434-2627 *Toll Free Fax:* 800-361-8088 *E-mail:* prologue@prologue.ca
Librairie du Quebec, 30, rue Gay-Lussac, 75005 Paris, France *Tel:* 01 43 54 49 02 *Fax:* 01 43 54 39 15 *E-mail:* liquebec@noos.fr

Les Editions Ganesha Inc
CP 484, succursale d'Youville, Montreal, QC H2P 2W1
Tel: 450-641-2395
E-mail: courriel@editions-ganesha.qc.ca
Web Site: www.editions-ganesha.qc.ca
Key Personnel
Publr: Andre Beaudoin
Founded: 1978
Publishes in French.
ISBN Prefix(es): 978-2-89145
Number of titles published annually: 3 Print
Total Titles: 68 Print

Les Editions Goelette Inc
1350 Marie-Victorin, St-Bruno-de-Montarville, Quebec, QC J3V 6B9
Tel: 450-653-1337 *Toll Free Tel:* 800-463-4961
Fax: 450-653-9924
E-mail: info@boutiquegoelette.com
Web Site: www.boutiquegeolette.com
Key Personnel
Pres: Alain Delorme
Publr: Ingrid Remazeilles
Dir, Prodn: Chantel Morisset
Founded: 1997
Publishes in English, French.
ISBN Prefix(es): 978-2-9804941; 978-2-9806291; 978-2-922983; 978-2-89638; 978-2-89690
Number of titles published annually: 200 Print
Total Titles: 2,000 Print
Distribution Center: Les Messageries ADP, 2315, rue de la Province, Longueuil, QC J4G 1G4 *Tel:* 450-640-1234 *Toll Free Tel:* 800-771-3022 *Fax:* 450-640-1251 *Toll Free Fax:* 800-603-0433

Les Editions Heritage Inc
1101, ave Victoria, St-Lambert, QC J4R 1P8
Tel: 514-875-0327
Key Personnel
CEO & Pres of the Council: Jacques Payette
Pres: Sylvie Payette
Founded: 1968
Juvenile, adult & French language.
Publishes in French.
ISBN Prefix(es): 978-0-7773; 978-2-7625
Number of titles published annually: 250 Print
Total Titles: 2,000 Print
Foreign Rights: Barbara Creary
Membership(s): Association for Canadian Publishers in the US

Editions Hurtubise
Division of Groupe HMH
1815, ave De Lorimier, Montreal, QC H2K 3W6
Tel: 514-523-1523 *Toll Free Tel:* 800-361-1664
Fax: 514-523-9969
Web Site: www.editionshurtubise.com
Key Personnel
Pres: Herve Foulon
VP, Publg & Opers: Arnaud Foulon
E-mail: arnaud.foulon@groupehmh.com
VP, Sales & Mktg: Alexandrine Foulon
E-mail: alexandrine.foulon@groupehmh.com
Prodn Mgr: Dominique Lemay
E-mail: dominique.lemay@editionshurtubise.com
Publg Mgr: Andre Gagnon *E-mail:* andre.gagnon@editionshurtubise.com
Rts Mgr: Sandra Felteau *E-mail:* sandra.felteau@groupehmh.com
Sr Ed: Sandrine Lazure *E-mail:* sandrine.lazure@editionshurtubise.com
Founded: 1960

French Canadian publishing house. Fiction & nonfiction, adult & young adult.
Publishes in French.
ISBN Prefix(es): 978-2-89045; 978-2-89428; 978-2-89647; 978-0-7758; 978-2-89723; 978-2-89781
Number of titles published annually: 80 Print; 60 E-Book; 10 Audio
Total Titles: 1,200 Print; 700 E-Book; 10 Audio
Imprints: Bibliotheque Quebecoise (BQ)
Distributor for Bibliotheque Quebecoise: Marcel Didier; Editions MultiMondes; Editions XYZ
Warehouse: Distribution HMH, 1815, ave De Lorimier, Montreal, QC H2K 3W6, Head of Dist: Guylaine Halle *E-mail:* guylaine.halle@distributionhmh.com *Web Site:* www.distributionhmh.com
Distribution Center: Distribution HMH, 1815, ave De Lorimier, Montreal, QC H2K 3W6, Head of Dist: Guylaine Halle *E-mail:* guylaine.halle@distributionhmh.com *Web Site:* www.distributionhmh.com

Les Editions JCL
688, rue St-Joseph, Marieville, QC J3M 1H1
Tel: 450-460-4438
E-mail: info@jcl.qc.ca
Web Site: www.jcl.qc.ca
Key Personnel
Pres & Intl Rts: Daniel Bertrand
Dir Gen: Elsa Galardo
Founded: 1977
Novels, nonfiction & youth literature.
Publishes in French.
ISBN Prefix(es): 978-2-920176; 978-2-89431; 978-2-89432
Number of titles published annually: 26 Print
Total Titles: 521 Print
Foreign Rights: Gregory Messina (European Union exc France)
Distribution Center: Messageries ADP, 2315, rue de la Province, Longueuil, QC J4G 1G4 *Tel:* 450-640-1234 *Toll Free Tel:* 800-771-3022 *Fax:* 450-640-1251 *Toll Free Fax:* 800-603-0433
Librairie du Quebec, 30, rue Gay Lussac, 75005 Paris, France (France & Europe) *Tel:* 01 45 54 49 02 *Fax:* 01 43 54 39 15 *E-mail:* libraires@librairieduquebec.fr *Web Site:* www.librairieduquebec.fr
Servidis/Transat, Chemin des Chalets 7, 1279 Chavannes-de-Bogis, Switzerland *Tel:* (022) 960 95 10 *Fax:* (022) 776 63 64 *E-mail:* admin@servidis.ch *Web Site:* www.servidis.ch

Editions Le Dauphin Blanc Inc
825, blvd Lebourgneuf, Suite 125, Quebec, QC G2J 0B9
Tel: 418-845-4045 *Fax:* 418-845-1933
E-mail: info@dauphinblanc.com
Web Site: www.dauphinblanc.com
Key Personnel
CEO: Alain Williamson
E-mail: alainwilliamson@dauphinblanc.com
Asst Dir & Prodn Mgr: Annie Sauvgeau
Founded: 1991
Publishes in French.
ISBN Prefix(es): 978-2-89436
Number of titles published annually: 50 Print
Distribution Center: Prologue Inc, 1650, blvd Lionel-Bertrand, Boisbriand, QC J7H 1N7 *Tel:* 450-434-0306 *Toll Free Tel:* 800-363-2864 *Fax:* 450-434-2627 *Web Site:* www.prologue.ca
DG Diffusion, Zl de Bogues, 31750 Escalquens, France (Belgium & France) *Tel:* 05 61 00 09 99 *Fax:* 05 61 00 23 12 *E-mail:* adv@dgdiffusion.com *Web Site:* www.dgdiffusion.com
Diffusion Transat/Servidis, Chemin des Chalets 7, 1279 Chavannes-de-Bogis, Switzerland *Tel:* (022) 42 77 40 *Fax:* (022) 43 46 46 *E-mail:* transat@transatdiffusion.ch

Editions Marie-France
CP 32263 BP Waverly, Montreal, QC H3L 3X1
Tel: 514-329-3700 *Toll Free Tel:* 800-563-6644 (CN) *Fax:* 514-329-0630
E-mail: editions@marie-france.qc.ca
Web Site: www.marie-france.qc.ca
Key Personnel
Pres: Jean Lachapelle
VP: Joanne Lacombe
Founded: 1977
School, kindergarten, elementary & secondary adult & university in French, natural sciences, human sciences, music, economic education & physics. Some titles in both French & English.
Publishes in English, French.
ISBN Prefix(es): 978-2-89168
Number of titles published annually: 25 Print
Total Titles: 1,001 Print
Membership(s): Association nationale des editeurs de livres (ANEL)

§Editions Mediaspaul
3965, blvd Henri-Bourassa E, Montreal, QC H1H 1L1
Tel: 514-322-7341 *Fax:* 514-322-4281
E-mail: editeur@mediaspaul.ca
Web Site: mediaspaul.ca
Key Personnel
Exec Dir: Joseph Sciortino *E-mail:* jsciortino@mediaspaul.ca
Publr: Gilles Collicelli
Founded: 1975
Religious & photographic books.
Publishes in French.
ISBN Prefix(es): 978-2-7122; 978-0-88840; 978-2-89039; 978-2-89420
Number of titles published annually: 20 Print
Total Titles: 300 Print
Foreign Rep(s): Paul Johnston
Distribution Center: Sodis, 128 Ave du Marechal de Lattre de Tassigny, 77400 Lagny-sur-Marne, France *Web Site:* www.sodis.fr

Editions Michel Quintin
2259 Papineau Ave, Suite 104, Montreal, QC H2K 4J5
SAN: 116-5356
Tel: 514-379-3774
E-mail: info@editionsmichelquintin.ca
Web Site: www.editionsmichelquintin.ca
Key Personnel
Pres: Michel Quintin
VP: Collette Dufresne
Founded: 1982
Nonfiction on fauna, nature, environment.
Publishes in French.
ISBN Prefix(es): 978-2-920438; 978-2-89435
Number of titles published annually: 60 Print
Total Titles: 700 Print
Branch Office(s)
4770 rue Foster, Waterloo, QC J0E 2N0 *Tel:* 450-539-3774
Editorial Office(s): PO Box 340, Waterloo, QC J0E 2N0
Foreign Rep(s): Bacon & Hughes (Canada); Interforum Editis
Distribution Center: Les Messageries ADP, 1261-A rue Shearer, Montreal, QC H3K 3G4 *Tel:* 514-523-1182 *Fax:* 514-939-0705

Editions MultiMondes
Affiliate of Groupe HMH
1815, Avenue de Lorimier, Montreal, QC H2K 3W6
Tel: 514-523-1523 *Toll Free Tel:* 800-361-1664 *Fax:* 514-523-9969
Web Site: www.multim.com
Key Personnel
Exec Dir: Dominique Lemay *E-mail:* dominique.lemay@editionsmultimondes.com
Edit Dir: Raymond Lemieux *E-mail:* raymond.lemieux@editionsmultimondes.com

Edit Asst: Sarah Jalbert *E-mail:* jalbert@
editionsmultimondes.com
Founded: 1988
Books on science & the environment.
Publishes in English, French.
ISBN Prefix(es): 978-2-921146; 978-2-89544
Number of titles published annually: 20 Print
Total Titles: 200 Print
Distribution Center: GEODIF, One, rue Thenard,
Paris 75005, France (Europe) *E-mail:* geodif@
eyolles.com

Les Editions Phidal Inc
5740 Ferrier, Montreal, QC H4P 1M7
Tel: 514-738-0202 *Toll Free Tel:* 800-738-7349
Fax: 514-738-5102
E-mail: info@phidal.com; customer@phidal.com
(sales & export)
Web Site: www.phidal.com
Key Personnel
Publr: Lionel Soussan
Founded: 1979
Full service publisher.
Publishes in English, French.
ISBN Prefix(es): 978-2-89393; 978-2-7643; 978-
2-920129
Number of titles published annually: 55 Print

Les Editions Pierre Tisseyre
155, rue Maurice, Rosemere, QC J7A 2S8
Tel: 514-335-0777 *Fax:* 514-335-6723
E-mail: info@edtisseyre.ca
Web Site: www.tisseyre.ca
Key Personnel
Pres: Charles Tisseyre
Mng Ed: Michelle Tisseyre *E-mail:* mtisseyre@
edtisseyre.ca
Sr Ed: Genevieve Mativat; Melanie Perreault
Founded: 1947
Primarily publish novels, novellas, essays, mem-
oirs, novels for young people & children's liter-
ature.
Publishes in French.
ISBN Prefix(es): 978-2-89051; 978-2-89633; 978-
0-7753
Number of titles published annually: 55 Print
Total Titles: 800 Print
Distribution Center: Prologue, 1650, Blvd
Lionel-Bertrand, Boisbriand, QC J7H 1N7
Tel: 450-434-0306 *Toll Free Tel:* 800-363-2864
E-mail: prologue@prologue.ca

Editions Trecarre
Imprint of Groupe Librex
La Tourelle, 1055, blvd Rene-Levesque E, Bureau
300, Montreal, QC H2L 4S5
Tel: 514-849-5259 *Fax:* 514-849-1388
Web Site: www.editions-trecarre.com
Key Personnel
Rts Mgr: Carole Boutin *Tel:* 514-373-2743
E-mail: carol.boutin@groupelibrex.com
Founded: 1982
How-to books, cookbooks, practical books, health
& lifestyle.
Publishes in French.
ISBN Prefix(es): 978-2-89249; 978-2-89568
Number of titles published annually: 15 Print
Total Titles: 700 Print; 100 E-Book
Warehouse: Les Messageries ADP, 2315, de la
province, Longueuil, QC J4G 1G4 *Tel:* 450-
640-1234 *Toll Free Tel:* 800-361-4806

§Les Editions Un Monde Different
3905 Isabelle, bureau 101, Brossard, QC J4Y 2R2
Mailing Address: CP 51546, Greenfield Park, QC
J4V 3N8
Tel: 450-656-2660 *Toll Free Tel:* 800-443-2582
Fax: 450-659-9328
E-mail: info@umd.ca
Web Site: www.umd.ca
Key Personnel
Owner & Ed: Michel Ferron

Asst Ed: Manon Martel
Cust Serv/Promo & Mktg: Monique Duchesneau
E-mail: mduchesneau@umd.ca
Founded: 1977
Motivational & inspirational books.
Publishes in French.
ISBN Prefix(es): 978-2-89225; 978-2-920000
Number of titles published annually: 25 Print
Total Titles: 750 Print
Distribution Center: Messageries ADP, 2315,
rue de la Province, Longueuil, QC J4G 1G4
Tel: 450-640-1234 *Fax:* 450-640-1251
Interforum Editis, Immeuble Paryseine, 3, alle de
la Seine, 94854 Ivry, Cedex, France (Europe)
Tel: 01 49 59 11 56 *Fax:* 01 49 59 11 91

Les Editions Vents d'Ouest
109, rue Wright, bureau 202, Gatineau, QC J8X
2G7
Tel: 819-770-6377
E-mail: info@ventsdouest.ca
Web Site: www.ventsdouest.ca
Key Personnel
Pres: Michel Tessier
VP: Gilles Parent
Dir, Gen Lit: Jeanne Duhaime; Pierre Gregoire;
Jacques Michaud
Coord & Dir, Young Adult Lit: Michel Lavoie
Founded: 1993
Novels, short stories, history.
Publishes in French.
ISBN Prefix(es): 978-2-921603; 978-2-89537
Number of titles published annually: 18 Print
Total Titles: 220 Print
Distribution Center: Prologue Inc, 1650 Blvd
Lionel-Bertrand, Boisbriand, QC J7H 1N7
Tel: 450-434-0306 *Toll Free Tel:* 800-363-2864
Fax: 450-434-2627 *Toll Free Fax:* 800-361-
8088
Librairie du Quebec a Paris, 30, rue Gay-Lussac,
750005 Paris, France *Tel:* 01 43 54 49 02
Fax: 01 43 54 39 15

Les Editions XYZ inc
Affiliate of Groupe HMH
1815, ave De Lorimier, Montreal, QC H2K 3W6
Tel: 514-525-2170 *Fax:* 514-525-7537
E-mail: info@editionsxyz.com
Web Site: www.editionsxyz.com
Key Personnel
Dir Gen & Publr: Pascal Genet *Tel:* 514-
525-2170 ext 260 *E-mail:* pascal.genet@
editionsxyz.com
Prodn Mgr: Nathalie Tasse *Tel:* 514-525-2170 ext
255 *E-mail:* nathalie.tasse@editionsxyz.com
Ed: Marie-Pierre Barathon *Tel:* 514-525-2170
ext 270 *E-mail:* marie-pierre.barathon@
editionsxyz.com
Founded: 1985
Novels, short stories & essays on literature.
Publishes in French.
ISBN Prefix(es): 978-2-89261; 978-2-89772
Number of titles published annually: 20 Print; 20
E-Book
Total Titles: 457 Print; 175 Online; 145 E-Book
Distribution Center: Distribution HMH, 1815,
Ave de Lorimier, Montreal, QC H2K 3W6
Tel: 514-523-1523 *Toll Free Tel:* 800-361-
1664 *Fax:* 514-523-9969 *Web Site:* www.
distributionhmh.com
Distribution du Nouveau Monde (DNM), 30, rue
Gay Lussac, 75005 Paris, France *Tel:* 01 43 54
50 24 *Fax:* 01 43 54 39 15
Membership(s): Association nationale des editeurs
de livres (ANEL)

§Editions Yvon Blais
Imprint of Thomson Reuters Canada Ltd
75-4700 rue Queen, Montreal, QC H3C 2N6
Tel: 514-842-3937 *Toll Free Tel:* 800-363-3047
Fax: 450-263-9256

E-mail: editionsyvonblais.commandes@
thomsonreuters.com (cust serv)
Web Site: www.editionsyvonblais.com
Key Personnel
Dir, Pubns: Marie-Noelle Guay
Founded: 1978
Legal publishing.
Publishes in French.
ISBN Prefix(es): 978-2-89073; 978-2-89451; 978-
2-89635; 978-2-89730
Number of titles published annually: 30 Print
Total Titles: 800 Print
Returns: 245 Bartley Dr, Toronto, ON M4A 2V8

Emond Montgomery Publications Ltd
60 Shaftesbury Ave, Toronto, ON M4T 1A3
Tel: 416-975-3925 *Toll Free Tel:* 888-837-0815
Fax: 416-975-3924
E-mail: orders@emp.ca
Web Site: www.emp.ca
Key Personnel
Pres: D Paul Emond *Tel:* 416-975-3925 ext 233
E-mail: pemond@emp.ca
VP, Educ Div: Anthony Rezek *Tel:* 416-975-3925
ext 229 *E-mail:* arezek@emp.ca
VP, Prodn & Admin: Paula Pike *Tel:* 416-975-
3925 ext 223 *E-mail:* ppike@emp.ca
Mktg Mgr: Holly Penick *Tel:* 416-975-3925 ext
246 *E-mail:* hpenick@emp.ca
Founded: 1978
Academic publisher.
Publishes in English.
ISBN Prefix(es): 978-0-920722; 978-1-55239
Number of titles published annually: 30 Print; 40
E-Book
Total Titles: 200 Print; 40 E-Book
Returns: 240 Industrial Pkwy S, Unit 4, Door 1,
Aurora, ON L4G 3V6, Contact: Judith Lynn
E-mail: jlynn@emp.ca
Warehouse: 240 Industrial Pkwy S, Unit 4, Door
1, Aurora, ON L4G 3V6, Contact: Judith Lynn
E-mail: jlynn@emp.ca

ERPI, see Pearson ERPI

Fairleigh Dickinson University Press
Affiliate of Rowman & Littlefield
842 Cambie St, Vancouver, BC V6B 2P6
Tel: 604-648-4476 *Fax:* 604-648-4489
E-mail: fdupress@fdu.edu
Web Site: www.fdupress.org
Key Personnel
Dir: James Gifford
Founded: 1967 (in Madison, NJ)
Publishes books in the humanities & social sci-
ences, with special strengths in history & liter-
ature. FDU Press relocated to the Vancouver,
BC campus in 2017.
Publishes in English.
ISBN Prefix(es): 978-0-8386; 978-1-61147
Number of titles published annually: 30 Print; 30
E-Book
Total Titles: 1,500 Print; 280 E-Book
Distributed by Rowman & Littlefield
Foreign Rep(s): Eurospan (Europe, UK); Schol-
arly Book Services (Canada); United Publishers
Services (Japan)

§Fairwinds Press
PO Box 668, Lions Bay, BC V0N 2E0
Tel: 604-913-0649
E-mail: orders@fairwinds-press.com
Web Site: www.fairwinds-press.com
Key Personnel
Publr & Intl Rts: Leslie Nolin *E-mail:* leslie@
fairwinds-press.com
Founded: 1997
Publishes in English.
ISBN Prefix(es): 978-0-9682149; 978-0-9780974;
978-0-9881081
Number of titles published annually: 3 Print; 2 E-
Book

Total Titles: 17 Print; 6 E-Book
Membership(s): Independent Publishers Association

Fernwood Publishing
32 Oceanvista Lane, Black Point, NS B0J 1B0
Tel: 902-857-1388 *Fax:* 902-857-1328
E-mail: info@fernpub.ca; roseway@fernpub.ca
Web Site: fernwoodpublishing.ca
Key Personnel
Co-Publr: Wayne Antony *E-mail:* wayne@
fernpub.ca; Errol Sharpe *E-mail:* errol@
fernpub.ca
Prodn Coord & Publr/Mng Ed, Roseway: Beverly
Rach *E-mail:* bev@fernpub.ca
Mktg Mgr, Academic Titles: Nancy Malek
Mktg Mgr, Trade Titles: Curran Faris
Mng Ed: Candida Hadley *E-mail:* candida@
fernpub.ca
Fin, Perms & Rts: James Patterson
Founded: 1991
Social sciences & humanities, emphasizing labour
studies, women's studies, gender studies, criti-
cal theory & research, political economy, cul-
tural studies & social work for use in under-
graduate courses in colleges & universities.
Publishes in English.
ISBN Prefix(es): 978-1-895686; 978-1-55266
Number of titles published annually: 30 Print
Total Titles: 500 Print
Imprints: Roseway Publishing
Branch Office(s)
748 Broadway Ave, Winnipeg, MB R3G 0X3
Tel: 204-474-2958 *Fax:* 204-475-2813
U.S. Rep(s): Brunswick Books
Foreign Rep(s): Central Books Ltd (UK)
Orders to: Brunswick Books, 20 Maud St, Suite
303, Toronto, ON M5V 2M5 (North Amer-
ica & Australia) *Tel:* 416-703-3598 *Fax:* 416-
703-6561 *E-mail:* orders@brunswickbooks.
ca *Web Site:* www.brunswickbooks.ca; Cen-
tral Books Ltd, 50 Freshwater Rd, Chadwell
Heath RM8 1RX, United Kingdom (UK & Europe) *Tel:* (020) 8525 8800 *Fax:* (020) 8599
2694 *E-mail:* contactus@centralbooks.com *Web
Site:* www.centralbooks.com
Returns: Brunswick Books, c/o TTS Distributing,
155 Edward St, Aurora, ON L4G IW3

Fifth House Publishers
Division of Fitzhenry & Whiteside Limited
195 Allstate Pkwy, Markham, ON L3R 4T8
Tel: 905-477-9700 *Toll Free Tel:* 800-387-9776
E-mail: godwit@fitzhenry.ca; bookinfo@fitzhenry.
ca (cust serv)
Web Site: www.fifthhousepublishers.ca
Key Personnel
Publr: Tracey Dettman *E-mail:* tdettman@
fitzhenry.ca
Founded: 1982
Trade publisher focusing on Western Canadian
interest books & First Nations titles.
Publishes in English, French.
ISBN Prefix(es): 978-0-920079; 978-1-895618;
978-1-894004; 978-1-894856; 978-1-897252;
978-1-927083
Number of titles published annually: 18 Print
Total Titles: 211 Print; 1 CD-ROM; 5 E-Book; 1
Audio
Distributed by Fitzhenry & Whiteside Limited
Orders to: Firefly Books, 50 Staples Ave, Unit
1, Richmond Hill, ON L4B 0A7 (US only)
E-mail: service@fireflybooks.com
Returns: Firefly Books, c/o Frontier Distribut-
ing, 145 Gruner Rd, Cheektowaga, NY 14227,
United States (US only)
Membership(s): Book Publishers Association of
Alberta

Firefly Books Ltd
50 Staples Ave, Unit 1, Richmond Hill, ON L4B
0A7

Tel: 416-499-8412 *Toll Free Tel:* 800-387-6192
(CN); 800-387-5085 (US) *Fax:* 416-499-8313
Toll Free Fax: 800-450-0391 (CN); 800-565-
6034 (US)
E-mail: service@fireflybooks.com
Web Site: www.fireflybooks.com
Key Personnel
Pres: Lionel Koffler
VP: Leon Gouzoules
Mgr, Foreign Rts, Licensing & Contracts:
Parisa Michailidis *Tel:* 416-499-8412 ext 157
E-mail: parisa.fireflybooks@gmail.com
Founded: 1977
North American publisher & distributor of nonfic-
tion adult & children's books.
Publishes in English.
ISBN Prefix(es): 978-0-920668; 978-1-895565;
978-1-896284; 978-1-55209; 978-1-55297; 978-
1-55407; 978-1-77085
Number of titles published annually: 220 Print
Total Titles: 2,000 Print; 25 Online
Divisions: The Boston Mills Press
Branch Office(s)
8514 Long Canyon Dr, Austin, TX 78730-2183,
United States *Tel:* 512-372-8500 *Fax:* 512-372-
2499
Distributor for Boston Mills Press; Cottage Life;
Firefly Books; Fitzhenry & Whiteside; Kiddy
Chronicles Publishing; Mikaya Press; Robert
Rose Inc
Foreign Rep(s): Angell Eurosales (Gill Angell &
Stewart Siddall) (Denmark, Finland, Iceland,
Norway, Scandinavia, Sweden); Ashton Inter-
national Marketing Services (Julian Ashton)
(Asia); Baccus Books (Owen Early) (South
Africa, Sub-Saharan Africa); Bookport As-
sociates (Joe Portelli) (Greece, Italy, Malta,
Portugal, Southern Europe, Spain); Cranbury
International LLC (Ethan Atkin) (Caribbean,
Latin America); European Marketing Services
(Anselm Robinson) (Austria, Belgium, France,
Germany, Switzerland, Western Europe); Chris
Lloyd Sales & Marketing Services (Northern
Europe, UK); Peribo Pty Ltd (Australia); Butler
Sims Ltd (Ireland)
Returns: c/o Frontier Distributing, 145 Gruner
Rd, Cheektowaga, NY 14227, United States
Membership(s): American Booksellers Associa-
tion (ABA); Association of Canadian Publish-
ers (ACP)
See separate listing for:
The Boston Mills Press

Fitzhenry & Whiteside Limited
195 Allstate Pkwy, Markham, ON L3R 4T8
SAN: 115-1444
Tel: 905-477-9700 *Toll Free Tel:* 800-387-9776
Fax: 905-477-2834 *Toll Free Fax:* 800-260-
9777
E-mail: bookinfo@fitzhenry.ca; godwit@fitzhenry.
ca
Web Site: www.fitzhenry.ca
Key Personnel
COO: Holly Doll *E-mail:* hdoll@fitzhenry.ca
CFO: Peter Stubbs
Pres: Sharon Fitzhenry *Tel:* 905-477-9700 ext 228
E-mail: sfitz@fitzhenry.ca
Compt: Earl Leibovitch *E-mail:* earll@fitzhenry.
ca
Mgr, Cust Serv: Judy Ghoura *E-mail:* jghoura@
fitzhenry.ca
Publr Rel: Sonya Gilliss *E-mail:* sonya.gilliss@
fitzhenry.ca
Founded: 1966
Trade, reference & children's books, educational
material for elementary, high school & college.
Publishes in English.
ISBN Prefix(es): 978-0-88902; 978-1-55005; 978-
1-55041; 978-1-55285; 978-1-894004 (Fifth
House); 978-1-894856 (Fifth House); 978-0-
88995; 978-1-55455; 978-1-77050
Number of titles published annually: 70 Print
Total Titles: 1,100 Print

Divisions: Fifth House Publishers; Red Deer
Press Inc; Whitecap Books
Distributor for Black Moss Press; Boulder Publi-
cations; ChiZine Publications; Clockwise Press;
DC Books; Wm B Eerdmans Publishing Co;
The Glenbow Museum; Grub Street Publish-
ing; Hades - Edge Science Fiction & Fantasy
Publishing; Icon Empire Press; Inhabit Media
Inc; Veronica Lane Books; Lee & Low Books;
Manor House Publishing; Mosaic Press; New
Internationalist Publications; Nunavut Arctic
College; Annika Parance Publishing; Peachtree
Publishers; Pemmican Publications; Railfare
DC Books; Royal British Columbia Museum
Press; Sands Press; Thirty Six Peonies Pub-
lishing; Tilbury House Publishers; Tradewind
Books; Tree House Press Inc; Whitecap Books
U.S. Publishers Represented: Arbordale Publish-
ing; ArtScroll Mesorah; Dawn Publications;
Epicenter Press; Lee & Low Books; McDonald
& Woodward; MVP Kids; Peachtree Publish-
ers; Road Runner Press; Star Bright Books;
teNeues; Tilbury House Publishers; Tundra
Books
U.S. Rep(s): Firefly Books
Returns: Firefly Books Ltd, c/o Frontier Distribut-
ing, 145 Gruner Rd, Cheektowaga, NY 14227,
United States
See separate listing for:
Fifth House Publishers
Red Deer Press Inc
Whitecap Books

Flammarion Quebec
375 Ave Laurier W, Montreal, QC H2V 2K3
Tel: 514-277-8807 *Fax:* 514-278-2085
E-mail: info@flammarion.qc.ca
Web Site: www.flammarion.qc.ca
Key Personnel
Publr: Louise Loiselle *E-mail:* lloiselle@
flammarion.qc.ca
Gen Dir, Dist: Guy Gougeon
Founded: 1974
Best sellers, translations, Quebec literature, nov-
els.
Publishes in French.
ISBN Prefix(es): 978-2-89077
Number of titles published annually: 20 Print
Total Titles: 325 Print
Imprints: Advenir; Bis (Pocket Book)
Distributor for AB Ludis; Alibi; Ambre SA;
Amethis-Grenouille; Ariane; Arola; Art Global;
Art Lys; Art Lys Jeunesse; Atelier 10; Artemis;
Aubier; Auzou; Autrement; Beaux-Arts mag;
Belize; Des Bulles dans l'Ocean; Casterman;
Centre Georges Pompidou; Centre Pompi-
dou Jeunesse; Champs; Chariot d'or; Climats;
Contre-dires; De Courberon; Courrier du Livre;
Dangles; Dervy; DG Duffuseur; Le Dilettante;
Documents; Editions Retrouvees; Editions So-
ciete du Figaro; Ego Comme X; Ensba; Es-
prit du livre; Exergue; Eveil et Decouvertes;
Eyrolles; Fablus; Flammarion; Fluide Glacial;
Genex Editions; GF; Grancher; Viviane Hamy;
Harlequin; Hoebeke; Horay; J'ai lu; Jouvence
Bussiere; Jungle; Lacroix; Nicole Lambert;
Lerelie; De L'Herne; Librio; Lux; Josette
Lyon; McGray; Medicis; Mic Mac; MK2 Edi-
tions; Musee du quai Branly; Neige-Galerie;
Neopol; Nouveau Projet; Nova; Organisation-
Management; Paquet; La Pasteque; Le Petit
Fute; Pierre de soleil; Piktos; La Presse; Profil
Sante; Pygmalion; Rizzoli International Publi-
cations; RMN Adulte; RMN Jeunesse; Rogers;
Rue de Sevre; Sarbacane; Sarbacane BD; Sassi;
Leo Scheer; Septembre Inc; Septembre Je-
unesse; Skira Editore; Somogy; Sophia Pub-
lications; Spice Box; Steinkis; La Tengo; 13e
Note Editions; Tom'poche; Trajectoire; Guy
Tredaniel; Ullman; VDB; Vega; Vox Populi;
Warum-Vraoum; Zeste
Warehouse: 420 Stinson, St-Laurent, QC H4N
2E9

Flanker Press Ltd

1243 Kenmount Rd, Unit 1, Paradise, NL A1L 0V8
Mailing Address: PO Box 2522, Sta C, St John's, NL A1C 6K1
Tel: 709-739-4477 *Toll Free Tel:* 866-739-4420 *Fax:* 709-739-4420
E-mail: info@flankerpress.com; sales@ flankerpress.com
Web Site: www.flankerpress.com
Key Personnel
Pres: Garry Cranford *Tel:* 709-739-4477 ext 23
Mgr: Bob Woodworth *Tel:* 709-739-4477 ext 21
Prodn Mgr: Jerry Cranford *Tel:* 709-739-4477 ext 30
Digital Coord: Peter Hanes *Tel:* 709-739-4477 ext 29
Mktg & Publicity Coord: Cassandra Aucoin *Tel:* 709-739-4477 ext 24
Sales Rep: Ed Oldford *Tel:* 709-739-4477 ext 22
Founded: 1994
Wholly Canadian-owned trade book publisher.
Publishes in English.
ISBN Prefix(es): 978-0-9698767; 978-1-894463; 978-1-897317; 978-1-926881; 978-1-77117
Number of titles published annually: 20 Print; 20 E-Book
Imprints: Brazen Books; Flanker Press; Pennywell Books
Membership(s): Association of Canadian Publishers (ACP); Atlantic Publishers Marketing Association

Flowerpot Press

2160 S Service Rd W, Oakville, ON L6L 5N1
Tel: 416-479-0695 *Toll Free Tel:* 866-927-5001
E-mail: info@flowerpotpress.com; order@ flowerpotpress.com
Web Site: www.flowerpotpress.com
Founded: 2005
Publish titles for young readers ages 4-12.
Publishes in English.
ISBN Prefix(es): 978-1-77093; 978-1-4867; 978-1-926988
Number of titles published annually: 60 Print; 60 E-Book
Total Titles: 200 Print; 350 E-Book
Editorial Office(s): 142 Second Ave N, Franklin, TN 37064, United States
Distribution Center: Baker & Taylor Publisher Services, 30 Amberwood Pkwy, Ashland, OH 44805, United States *Tel:* 567-215-0030 *Toll Free Tel:* 888-814-0208 *E-mail:* info@btpubservices.com *Web Site:* www.btpubservices.com

Folklore Publishing

11717-9B Ave NW, Unit 2, Edmonton, AB T6J 7B7
Tel: 780-435-2376
Web Site: www.folklorepublishing.com
Key Personnel
Pres & Publr: Faye Boer *E-mail:* fboer@ folklorepublishing.com
Founded: 2001
Publisher of popular history of North America, humor & children's nonfiction.
Publishes in English.
ISBN Prefix(es): 978-1-894864; 978-1-897206 (iThink Books); 978-1-926677; 978-1-77311
Number of titles published annually: 5 Print; 5 E-Book; 5 Audio
Total Titles: 112 Print; 55 E-Book; 5 Audio
Imprints: Full Court Press (sports history); ICON Press (celebrity bios); iThink Books (children's educ titles)
Sales Office(s): Canada Book Distributors/Book-Logic, 11414 119 St NW, Edmonton, AB T5G 2X6 *Tel:* 780-433-9333 *Toll Free Tel:* 800-661-9017 *Fax:* 780-433-9646 *Toll Free Fax:* 800-424-7173 *E-mail:* info@lonepinepublishing. com *Web Site:* www.lonepinepublishing.com
U.S. Rep(s): Lone Pine Publishing

Foreign Rep(s): Canada Book Distributors/Book-Logic (Canada (English-speaking)); Gazelle Book Services Ltd (UK & the continent)
Billing Address: Canada Book Distributors/ BookLogic, 11414 119 St NW, Edmonton, AB T5G 2X6 *Tel:* 780-433-9333 *Toll Free Tel:* 800-661-9017 *Fax:* 780-433-9646 *Toll Free Fax:* 800-424-7173 *E-mail:* accounts@ lonepinepublishing.com *Web Site:* www. lonepinepublishing.com
Orders to: Canada Book Distributors/BookLogic, 11414 119 St NW, Edmonton, AB T5G 2X6 *Tel:* 780-433-9333 *Toll Free Tel:* 800-661-9017 *Fax:* 780-433-9646 *Toll Free Fax:* 800-424-7173 *E-mail:* accounts@lonepinepublishing. com *Web Site:* www.lonepinepublishing.com
Returns: Canada Book Distributors/BookLogic, 11414 119 St NW, Edmonton, AB T5G 2X6 *Tel:* 780-433-9333 *Toll Free Tel:* 800-661-9017 *Fax:* 780-433-9646 *Toll Free Fax:* 800-424-7173 *E-mail:* info@lonepinepublishing.com *Web Site:* www.lonepinepublishing.com
Distribution Center: Canada Book Distributors/BookLogic, 11414 119 St NW, Edmonton, AB T5G 2X6 *Tel:* 780-433-9333 *Toll Free Tel:* 800-661-9017 *Fax:* 780-433-9646 *Toll Free Fax:* 800-424-7173 *E-mail:* accounts@ lonepinepublishing.com *Web Site:* www. lonepinepublishing.com
Membership(s): Book Publishers Association of Alberta

Gaetan Morin Editeur

Imprint of Cheneliere Education Inc
5800, rue St-Denis, bureau 900, Montreal, QC H2S 3L5
Tel: 514-273-1066 *Toll Free Tel:* 800-565-5531 *Fax:* 514-276-0324 *Toll Free Fax:* 800-814-0324
E-mail: info@cheneliere.ca
Web Site: www.cheneliere.ca
Key Personnel
Gen Mgr: Patrick Lutzy *E-mail:* patrick.lutzy@tc. tc
Founded: 1977
Textbooks, college, university & professional books.
Publishes in French.
ISBN Prefix(es): 978-2-89105; 978-0-88612; 978-2-910749; 978-2-89632
Number of titles published annually: 20 Print; 1 CD-ROM
Total Titles: 300 Print; 2 CD-ROM

Golden Meteorite Press

Subsidiary of Golden Meteorite Press Ltd
11919 82 St NW, Suite 103, Edmonton, AB T5B 2W4
Tel: 780-378-0063 *Fax:* 780-378-0063
Key Personnel
Ed & Lib Sales Dir: Austin Mardon *E-mail:* aamardon@yahoo.ca
Intl Rts: C Curry
Founded: 1989
Preferred submission is outline. Canadian SASE or IRC is required or else material is recycled. Accept fiction & nonfiction mss in all categories & genres. Submit to editor. Response in 12 weeks on all complete ms submissions. No phone calls please.
Publishes in English, French.
ISBN Prefix(es): 978-1-895385; 978-1-897; 978-1-894573; 978-0-929024; 978-1-897480
Number of titles published annually: 11 Print
Total Titles: 85 Print

Goose Lane Editions

500 Beaverbrook Ct, Suite 330, Fredericton, NB E3B 5X4
SAN: 115-3420
Tel: 506-450-4251 *Toll Free Tel:* 888-926-8377 *Fax:* 506-459-4991

E-mail: info@gooselane.com; customerservice@ gooselane.com
Web Site: www.gooselane.com
Key Personnel
Publr: Susanne Alexander *Tel:* 506-450-4251 ext 222 *E-mail:* s.alexander@gooselane.com
Creative Dir: Julie Scriver *Tel:* 506-450-4251 ext 223 *E-mail:* jscriver@gooselane.com
Publicity Mgr: Kathleen Peacock *Tel:* 506-450-4251 ext 230 *E-mail:* publicity@gooselane.com
Fiction Ed: Bethany Gibson *E-mail:* bgibson@ gooselane.com
Poetry Ed: Ross Leckie *E-mail:* rleckie@ gooselane.com
Prodn Ed: Martin Ainsley *Tel:* 506-450-4251 ext 226 *E-mail:* mainsley@gooselane.com
Publg Asst: Angela Williams *Tel:* 506-450-4251 ext 225 *E-mail:* awilliams@gooselane.com
Founded: 1954
Primarily deal with Canadian authors. Submissions not accepted from outside of Canada.
Publishes in English.
ISBN Prefix(es): 978-0-920110; 978-0-919197; 978-0-86492
Number of titles published annually: 20 Print; 20 E-Book
Total Titles: 310 Print; 20 E-Book
Distributed by University of Toronto Press
Distribution Center: University of Toronto Press Distribution, 5201 Dufferin St, Toronto, ON M3H 5T8 *Tel:* 416-667-7791 *Fax:* 416-667-7832 *E-mail:* utpbooks@utpress.utoronto.ca
University of Toronto Press Distribution, 2250 Military Rd, Tonawanda, NY 14150, United States *Toll Free Tel:* 800-221-9523 *Toll Free Fax:* 800-221-9985
Membership(s): American Audiobook Publishers Association; Association of Canadian Publishers (ACP); Atlantic Publishers Marketing Association; Literary Press Group of Canada

Greystone Books Ltd

Affiliate of The Heritage Group
343 Railway St, Suite 201, Vancouver, BC V6A 1A4
Tel: 604-875-1550 *Fax:* 604-875-1556
E-mail: info@greystonebooks.com
Web Site: www.greystonebooks.com
Key Personnel
Publr: Rob Sanders *Tel:* 604-875-1550 ext 205 *E-mail:* rob.sanders@greystonebooks.com
Publr, Aldana Libros: Patricia Aldana
Edit Dir: Jennifer Croll
Sales & Mktg Dir: Jen Gauthier *Tel:* 604-875-1550 ext 202 *E-mail:* jenniferg@ greystonebooks.com
Consulting Creative Dir, Greystone Kids: Sara Gillingham
Ed: Paula Ayer; Lucy Kenward
Ed, Picture Books, Greystone Kids: Kallie George
Mktg Mgr: Megan Jones
Digital Mktg Coord: Josh Oliveira
Founded: 1993
Publishes in English.
ISBN Prefix(es): 978-0-88894; 978-1-55054; 978-1-55365; 978-0-88833; 978-1-77100; 978-1-927435; 978-1-77164
Number of titles published annually: 30 Print
Total Titles: 400 Print
Imprints: Aldana Libros; Greystone Kids
Distributed by University of Toronto Press
U.S. Rep(s): Publishers Group West
Foreign Rights: Eliane Benisti (France); Silvia Brunelli (Italy); Marysia Juszczakiewicz (China); Yukiko Kurioka (Japan); Angela Reynolds (Portugal, Spain)
Orders to: University of Toronto Press Distribution, 5201 Dufferin St, Toronto, ON M3H 5T8 (through Pubnet) *Tel:* 416-667-7791 *Toll Free Tel:* 800-565-9523 *Fax:* 416-667-7832 *Toll Free Fax:* 800-221-9985 *E-mail:* utpbooks@utpress. utoronto.ca SAN: 115-1134; Publishers Group West/Ingram Publisher Services, 210 Amer-

ican Dr, Jackson, TN 38301, United States (submit orders to sales rep via IPS Cart on iPage) *Toll Free Tel:* 866-400-5351 *Toll Free Fax:* 800-838-1149 *E-mail:* ips@ingramcontent. com *Web Site:* www.ingramcontent.com; Publishers Group West/Perseus International, 250 W 57 St, 15th fl, New York, NY 10107, United States (intl orders) *Tel:* 212-581-7839 *E-mail:* intlorders@perseusbooks.com
Membership(s): Association for the Export of Canadian Books; Association of American Publishers (AAP); Association of Book Publishers of British Columbia; Association of Canadian Publishers (ACP)

Groundwood Books
Subsidiary of House of Anansi Press Inc
128 Sterling Rd, Lower Level, Toronto, ON M6R 2B7
Tel: 416-363-4343 *Fax:* 416-363-1017
E-mail: genmail@groundwoodbooks.com
Web Site: www.houseofanansi.com
Key Personnel
Owner & Chmn of the Bd: Scott Griffin
Pres: Semareh Al-Hillal
VP, Fin: Allan Ibarra
VP, Publg Opers: Matt Williams
VP, Sales & Licensing: Barbara Howson
Dir, Cross-Media Dept: Erin Mallory
Edit Dir: Janie Yoon
Mktg Mgr: Laura Chapnick *E-mail:* lchapnick@ anansi.ca
Publicity Dir: Laura Meyer
Mktg Mgr: Fred Horler
Mng Ed: Maria Golikova
Publr: Karen Li
Founded: 1978
Publish children's books, picture books, novels, nonfiction & folktales; publishes in Spanish also.
Publishes in English.
ISBN Prefix(es): 978-0-88899; 978-1-55498
Number of titles published annually: 25 Print
Total Titles: 500 Print
Sales Office(s): Martin & Associates Sales Agency, 594 Windermere Ave, Toronto, ON M6S 3L8 (Atlantic, ON & QC), Contact: Michael Martin *Tel:* 416-769-3947 *Toll Free Tel:* 866-225-3439 *Fax:* 416-769-5967 *E-mail:* memartin@interlog.com
Foreign Rights: Bardon Media Agency (Jianmei Wang & Cynthia Chang) (China); Casanovas & Lynch Literary Agency (Brazil, Latin America, Portugal, Spain); Japan UNI Agency Inc (Maiko Fujinaga) (Japan)
Distribution Center: University of Toronto Press Distribution Division, 5201 Dufferin St, Toronto, ON M3H 5T8 *Tel:* 416-667-7791 *Toll Free Tel:* 800-565-9523 *Fax:* 416-667-7832 *Toll Free Fax:* 800-221-9985 SAN: 115-1134
Publishers Group West/Ingram, 1700 Fourth St, Berkeley, CA 94710, United States *Toll Free Tel:* 800-343-4499 *Toll Free Fax:* 800-351-5073 *E-mail:* orderentry@ingram.com *Web Site:* www.perseusdistribution.com
Membership(s): Association of Canadian Publishers (ACP); International Board on Books for Young People (IBBY); Organization of Book Publishers of Ontario (OBPO)

§Groupe Educalivres Inc
1699, blvd le Corbusier, bureau 350, Laval, QC H7S 1Z3
Tel: 514-334-8466 *Toll Free Tel:* 800-567-3671 (info serv) *Fax:* 514-334-8387
Toll Free Fax: 800-267-4387
E-mail: infoservice@grandduc.com
Web Site: www.educalivres.com
Key Personnel
VP, Fin & Admin: Joe Cristofaro
School & professional textbooks.
Publishes in English, French.

ISBN Prefix(es): 978-2-7607; 978-0-03; 978-2-7655
Number of titles published annually: 12 Print
Divisions: Editions Grand Duc; Grand Duc en ligne

Groupe Modulo
Imprint of TC Media Books Inc
c/o TC Media Books Inc, 5800 St Denis St, Suite 900, Montreal, QC H2S 3L5
Tel: 514-273-1066 *Toll Free Tel:* 800-565-5531 *Fax:* 514-276-0234 *Toll Free Fax:* 800-814-0324
Web Site: www.groupemodulo.com
Founded: 1975
School books, dictionaries, children's books, professional & technical textbooks.
Publishes in English, French.
ISBN Prefix(es): 978-2-920922; 978-2-89443; 978-2-89113; 978-2-920210; 978-2-89593; 978-0-88560
Number of titles published annually: 100 Print
Total Titles: 2,000 Print

Groupe Sogides Inc
Division of Groupe Livre Quebecor Media Inc
955 rue Amherst, Montreal, QC H2L 3K4
Tel: 514-523-1182 *Fax:* 514-597-0370
Web Site: sogides.com
Key Personnel
Pres, Sogides: Celine Massicotte
Rts Dir, Groupe Homme: Florence Bisch
Founded: 1967
Practical books, cookbooks, biographies, general interest books, popular psychology, art books, poetry, diaries, art calendars & stationery, novels, drama.
Publishes in French.
ISBN Prefix(es): 978-2-7619; 978-0-7760; 978-2-89026; 978-2-89194; 978-2-89044; 978-2-89043; 978-2-89347
Number of titles published annually: 150 Print
Total Titles: 2,000 Print
Imprints: Les Editions de l'Homme; La Griffe; Le Jour Editeur; Juniper Publishing; Petit Homme; Utilis
Subsidiaries: Le Groupe Ville-Marie Litterature
Branch Office(s)
Les Editions de l'Homme, Immeuble Paryseine, 3 Allee de la Seine, 94854 Ivry Cedex, France, Contact: Anne Da Cunha-Guillegault *Tel:* 01 49 59 11 56 *Fax:* 01 49 59 11 33
Distributed by Vivendi Universal Publishing
Distributor for Actif; Atlas; Berlitz Fixot; Chouette; Le Cri; Edimag; Fleuve Noir; Gault & Millau; Heritage; De L'Homme; Hors Collection; JCL; Albin Michel Jeunesse; Julliard; Robert Laffont; Langues pour tous; Albin Michel; Albin Michel Education; Editions Modus Vivendi; Nathan; Nathan Education; Option Sante; Olivier Orban; Perrin; Plon; Pocket; La Presse; Presses de la Cite (Poche); Presses de la Cite Litterature; Presses Libres; Michel Quintin; Quinze; Du Rocher; Rouge & Or; Seghers; Selection du Reader's Digest; Solar; Time-Life; Trapeze; Usborne; Claire Vigne; VLB; XYZ (Typo Seulement)
U.S. Publishers Represented: Reader's Digest
Distribution Center: Messageries ADP, 2315, rue de la Province, Longuevil, QC J4G 1G4 *Tel:* 450-640-1237 *Web Site:* www.messageriesadp.com

Guerin Editeur Ltee
800, Blvd Industriel, bureau 200, St-Jean-sur-Richelieu, QC J3B 8G4
Tel: 514-842-3481 *Fax:* 514-842-4923
Web Site: www.guerin-editeur.qc.ca
Key Personnel
Pres: France Larochelle *E-mail:* france. larochelle@guerin-editeur.qc.ca
VP: Claude Legault

Secy: Ginette Laperriere
Founded: 1970
Publisher of books for schools from kindergarten to university.
Publishes in English, French.
ISBN Prefix(es): 978-2-7601
Number of titles published annually: 80 Print; 2 Audio
Total Titles: 2,300 Print; 43 Audio
Foreign Rep(s): Librairie du Quebec (France); Librairie Pelagie (Eastern Canada); Patrimoine SPRL (Belgium); Servidis SA (Switzerland); Sopodriff Sarl (Africa); Pierre Carme Yves Levy (Haiti)

§Guernica Editions Inc
1569 Heritage Way, Oakville, ON L6M 2Z7
Tel: 905-599-5304
E-mail: info@guernicaeditions.com
Web Site: www.guernicaeditions.com; www. facebook.com/guernicaed
Key Personnel
Publr & Chief Admin Offr: Connie McParland *E-mail:* conniemcparland@guernicaeditions. com
Publr & Ed-in-Chief: Michael Mirolla *E-mail:* michaelmirolla@guernicaeditions.com
Admin Asst/Publicist: Anna Geisler *E-mail:* annageisler@guernicaeditions.com
Founded: 1978
Literary press specializing in Canadian writing (prose, poetry, literary criticism, drama & social studies), translation into English, some foreign publications in the English language.
Publishes in English.
ISBN Prefix(es): 978-0-919349; 978-0-920717; 978-2-89135; 978-1-55071; 978-1-77183
Number of titles published annually: 25 Print
Total Titles: 450 Print
Sales Office(s): Literary Press Group, 425 Adelaide St W, Suite 700, Toronto, ON M5V 3C1, Sales Mgr & US Rep: Tan Light *Tel:* 416-483-1321 *Fax:* 416-483-2510 *E-mail:* sales@lpg.ca *Web Site:* www.lpg.ca
Distribution Center: University of Toronto Press, 5201 Dufferin St, Toronto, ON M3H 5T8 *Toll Free Tel:* 800-565-9523 *Toll Free Fax:* 800-221-9985
Gazelle Book Services Ltd, White Cross Mills, Hightown, Lancaster, Lancs LA1 1XS, United Kingdom *Tel:* (01524) 528500 *Fax:* (01524) 528510 *E-mail:* sales@gazellebookservices.co. uk *Web Site:* www.gazellebookservices.co.uk
Midpoint Trade Books, 814 N Franklin St, Suite 100, Chicago, IL 60610, United States *Tel:* 312-337-0747 *Toll Free Tel:* 800-888-4741 *Fax:* 312-337-5985 *E-mail:* orders@ipgbook. com *Web Site:* www.midpointtrade.com

Hancock House Publishers Ltd
19313 Zero Ave, Surrey, BC V3S 9R9
Mailing Address: 1431 Harrison Ave, Blaine, WA 98230-5005, United States
Tel: 604-538-1114 *Toll Free Tel:* 800-938-1114 *Fax:* 604-538-2262 *Toll Free Fax:* 800-983-2262
E-mail: sales@hancockhouse.com; info@ hancockhouse.com
Web Site: www.hancockhouse.com
Key Personnel
Pres: David Hancock
Founded: 1975
Biographical nature guide books.
Publishes in English.
ISBN Prefix(es): 978-0-88839; 978-0-919654; 978-1-55205
Number of titles published annually: 20 Print
Total Titles: 450 Print
Foreign Rep(s): Gazelle Book Services Ltd (UK)
Distribution Center: Ampersand Inc, 321 Carlaw Ave, Suite 213, Toronto, ON M4M 2S1

Tel: 416-703-0666 *Toll Free Tel:* 866-849-3819
Fax: 416-703-4745 *Toll Free Fax:* 866-849-3819

Harbour Publishing Co Ltd
4437 Rondeview Rd, Madeira Park, BC V0N 2H0
Mailing Address: PO Box 219, Madeira Park, BC V0N 2H0
Tel: 604-883-2730 *Toll Free Tel:* 800-667-2988
Fax: 604-883-9451
E-mail: info@harbourpublishing.com
Web Site: www.harbourpublishing.com
Key Personnel
Publr: Howard White
Mktg Mgr: Marisa Alps
Prodn Coord: Anna Comfort
Founded: 1972
History & culture of British Columbia & West Coast, including fiction, nonfiction & poetry by Canadian authors.
Publishes in English.
ISBN Prefix(es): 978-0-920080; 978-1-55017
Number of titles published annually: 20 Print; 1 CD-ROM; 1 Audio
Total Titles: 600 Print; 1 CD-ROM; 5 Audio
Imprints: Lost Moose Books
Distributor for Nightwood Editions
Foreign Rep(s): Ampersand Inc (Canada); Gazelle Book Services Ltd (Eastern Europe, Ireland, UK, Western Europe)
Orders to: 12672 Lagoon Rd, Madeira Park, BC V0N 2H0 *E-mail:* orders@harbourpublishing.com
Warehouse: 12672 Lagoon Rd, Madeira Park, BC V0N 2H0 *Tel:* 604-883-2460
Distribution Center: 12672 Lagoon Rd, Madeira Park, BC V0N 2H0

§Harlequin Enterprises Ltd
Division of HarperCollins
Bay Adelaide Centre, East Tower, 22 Adelaide St W, 41st fl, Toronto, ON M5H 4E3
SAN: 115-3749
Tel: 416-445-5860 *Toll Free Tel:* 888-432-4879; 800-370-5838 (ebook inquiries)
E-mail: customerservice@harlequin.com
Web Site: www.harlequin.com
Key Personnel
Publr & CEO: Craig Swinwood
CFO: Andrew Wright
EVP & Publr, Harlequin Brand Group: Brent Lewis
EVP & Publr, Harlequin Trade Publishing: Loriana Sacilotto *E-mail:* loriana.sacilotto@harpercollins.com
EVP, Direct to Consumer: Christina Clifford
VP, Edit, Harlequin Brand Group: Dianne Moggy *E-mail:* diane.moggy@harpercollins.com
VP, Mktg, Harlequin Brand Group: Merjane Schoueri
VP, Sales: Alex Osuszek
VP & CIO: Margaret Morrison
VP, Gen Coun & Secy: Karen Louie
Acting VP, Mktg: Amy Jones
Sr Dir, Direct-to-Consumer: Heather Allen
Sr Dir, Global Series Mktg: Farah Mullick
Dir, Digital Sales: Marianna Ricciuto
Dir, Overseas Publg Strategy: Emily Martin
Dir, Romance Publicity: Michelle Renaud *E-mail:* public-relations@harlequin.ca
Dir, Subs Rts & Harlequin Audio: Reka Rubin
Edit Dir, Carina Press: Angela James
Edit Dir, Inkyard Press: Natashya Wilson
Edit Dir, HQN Books & Graydon House Books: Susan Swinwood
Edit Dir, MIRA: Nicole Brebner
Edit Dir, Park Row Books: Erika Imranyi
Exec Ed: Kathleen Scheibling
Global Mng Ed: Roxanne Finkelstein
Mng Ed: Punam Patel
Ed: Adrienne Macintosh
Ed, Graydon House Books: Melanie Fried
Assoc Ed, Carina Press: Stephanie Doig

Assoc Ed: Dana Grimaldi
Assoc Ed, MIRA: Michelle Meade
Asst Ed, HQN: Brittany Lavery
Asst Ed, MIRA: Margot Mallinson
Mgr, Author Engagement: Miranda Indrigo
Founded: 1949 (in Winnipeg, MB, CN)
Publishes in more than 30 languages in 150 international markets on 6 continents.
Publishes in English, French.
ISBN Prefix(es): 978-0-373; 978-1-55166; 978-0-7783; 978-1-58314; 978-1-55254; 978-1-4268; 978-1-4603; 978-1-4592
Number of titles published annually: 1,320 Print; 30 Online; 1,530 E-Book; 75 Audio
Total Titles: 30 Online; 1,850 E-Book; 95 Audio
Imprints: Avon; Carina Press (digital-first); Graydon House Books (commercial women's fiction); Hanover Square Press; Harlequin Dare; Harlequin Desire; Harlequin Heartwarming; Harlequin Historical; Harlequin Intrigue; Harlequin Kimani Arabesque; Harlequin Kimani Press (African-American); Harlequin Kimani Romance; Harlequin Kimani TRU; Harlequin LUNA (fantasy/paranormal); Harlequin Medical Romance; Harlequin MIRA; Harlequin Nocturne; Harlequin Presents; Harlequin Romance; Harlequin Romantic Suspense; Harlequin Special Edition; HQN™; Inkyard Press (young adult fiction); Love Inspired® (inspirational romance); Love Inspired® Suspense; Park Row Books; Silhouette Intimate Moments (series romance); Spice (erotic fiction); Worldwide Mystery
Branch Office(s)
195 Broadway, 24th fl, New York, NY 10007, United States *Tel:* 212-207-7000 SAN: 200-2450
Foreign Office(s): Harlequin Mills & Boon, Westerhill Rd, Bishopbriggs, Glasgow G64 2QT, United Kingdom *E-mail:* csmillsandboon@harpercollins.co.uk *Web Site:* www.millsandboon.co.uk
Advertising Agency: Vickers & Benson-Direct
Distribution Center: Harlequin Fulfillment Services, 3010 Walden Ave, Depew, NY 14043, United States *Tel:* 716-686-1800 *Web Site:* harlequinfulfillmentservices.com
Membership(s): Association of American Publishers (AAP); Association of Canadian Publishers (ACP); Book Industry Study Group (BISG)
See separate listing for:
Worldwide Library

§HarperCollins Canada Ltd
Division of HarperCollins Publishers
2 Bloor St E, 20th fl, Toronto, ON M4W 1A8
Tel: 416-975-9334 *Fax:* 416-975-5223
E-mail: hcorder@harpercollins.com
Web Site: www.harpercollins.ca
Key Personnel
SVP & Exec Publr: Iris Tupholme *Tel:* 416-975-9334 ext 123 *E-mail:* Iris.Tupholme@HarperCollins.com
VP, Mktg & Sales: Leo MacDonald
Publr, Patrick Crean Editions: Patrick Crean
Sr Coun & Dir, Legal Aff: Jeremy Rawlings
Dir, Subs Rts & Publg Opers: Lisa Rundle
Exec Ed: Kate Cassaday
Founded: 1989
Literary & commercial fiction, nonfiction, children's books, cookbooks, reference & spiritual books. Distribute for all HarperCollins companies in the US, UK & Australia.
Publishes in English.
ISBN Prefix(es): 978-1-4434
Number of titles published annually: 100 Print
Total Titles: 1,500 Print
Imprints: Collins; Patrick Crean Editions; Harper Avenue; HarperCollins Canada; Harper Perennial; HarperWeekend

Heritage House Publishing Co Ltd
Member of The Heritage Group

1075 Pendergast St, No 103, Victoria, BC V8V 0A1
Tel: 250-360-0829 *Fax:* 250-386-0829
E-mail: heritage@heritagehouse.ca
Web Site: www.heritagehouse.ca
Key Personnel
Publr: Rodger Touchie
Sr Ed: Lara Kordic
Publicity: Leslie Kenny
Founded: 1969
Publishes in English.
ISBN Prefix(es): 978-1-895811; 978-1-894384; 978-1-894974; 978-0-919214; 978-0-9690546; 978-1-926613; 978-1-926936; 978-1-927051; 978-1-927527
Number of titles published annually: 30 Print
Total Titles: 175 Print
Orders to: Heritage Group Distribution, 19272 96 Ave, Suite 8, Surrey, BC V4N 4C1 *Tel:* 604-881-7067 *Toll Free Tel:* 800-665-3302 *Fax:* 604-881-7068 *Toll Free Fax:* 800-566-3336 *E-mail:* orders@hgdistribution.com
Distribution Center: Heritage Group Distribution, 19272 96 Ave, Suite 8, Surrey, BC V4N 4C1 *Tel:* 604-881-7067 *Toll Free Tel:* 800-665-3302 *Fax:* 604-881-7068 *Toll Free Fax:* 800-566-3336 *E-mail:* orders@hgdistribution.com
Membership(s): Association of Book Publishers of British Columbia; Association of Canadian Publishers (ACP)

Les Heures bleues
4455 Coolbrook Ave, No 2, Montreal, QC H4A 3G1
Tel: 438-399-2077 *Fax:* 450-671-7718
E-mail: editions.lesheuresbleues@gmail.com
Web Site: www.heuresbleues.com
Founded: 1996
Publishes in French.
ISBN Prefix(es): 978-2-922265
Number of titles published annually: 8 Print
Total Titles: 90 Print; 40 E-Book
Distribution Center: Diffusion Dimedia, 539, blvd Lebeau, Montreal, QC H4N 1S2 *Tel:* 515-336-3941 *E-mail:* info@dimedia.qc.ca *Web Site:* www.dimedia.com
La Librarie du Quebec a Paris, 30, rue Gay-Lussac, 75005 Paris, France *Tel:* 01 43 54 49 02 *E-mail:* libraires@librairieduquebec.fr *Web Site:* www.librairieduquebec.fr
Membership(s): Association nationale des editeurs de livres (ANEL)

§House of Anansi Press Inc
128 Sterling Rd, Lower Level, Toronto, ON M6R 2B7
Tel: 416-363-4343 *Fax:* 416-363-1017
E-mail: customerservice@houseofanansi.com
Web Site: www.houseofanansi.com
Key Personnel
Owner & Chmn of the Bd: Scott Griffin
Publr: Bruce Walsh
VP, Publg Opers: Matt Williams
VP, Sales & Licensing: Barbara Howson
VP, Sales & Mktg: Karen Brochu
Assoc Publr: Janie Yoon
Dir, Cross-Media Group: Erin Mallory
Dir, Cross-Media Dept: Laura Brady
Mktg Dir: Carolyn McNeillie
Publicity Dir: Laura Meyer
Ed: Michelle MacAleese; Douglas Richmond
Sr Designer: Alysia Shewchuk
Sr Publicist: Cindy Ma
Publicist: Lindsay Holung
Intl Sales Assoc: Caryn Cathcart
Rts Assoc: Erica Mojzes
Founded: 1967
Literary publishing; fiction, poetry, criticism & belles lettres.
Publishes in English.
ISBN Prefix(es): 978-0-88784; 978-1-77089; 978-1-48700
Number of titles published annually: 30 Print

Total Titles: 200 Print
Imprints: Ambrosia; Anansi International; Arachnide Editions; Astoria; Spiderline (crime fiction)
Subsidiaries: Groundwood Books
Foreign Rights: Akcali Copyright Agency (Atilla Turgut) (Turkey); Anthea Agency (Zlatka Paskaleva) (Bulgaria); Bestun Agency (Yumi Chun) (Korea); Big Apple Agency (Amanda Chen) (Mainland China); Big Apple Agency (Chris Lin) (Taiwan); Casanovas & Lynch Literary Agency (Brazil, Latin America, Portugal, Spain); Paul & Peter Fritz Agency (Antonia Fritz) (Germany); Japan UNI Agency Inc (Yukiko Kurioka) (Japan); Antonia Kerrigan Agency (Antonia Kerrigan) (Latin America, Spain); Simona Kessler Agency (Simona Kessler) (Romania)
Distribution Center: Publishers Group West, 1700 Fourth St, Berkeley, CA 94710, United States (US orders) Tel: 510-809-3700 Toll Free Tel: 800-343-4499 Fax: 510-809-3777 Toll Free Fax: 800-351-5073 Web Site: www.pgw.com
See separate listing for:
Groundwood Books

C D Howe Institute
67 Yonge St, Suite 300, Toronto, ON M5E 1J8
Tel: 416-865-1904 Fax: 416-865-1866
E-mail: cdhowe@cdhowe.org
Web Site: www.cdhowe.org
Key Personnel
Pres & CEO: William B P Robson
    E-mail: bill_robson@cdhowe.org
SVP & COO: Duncan Munn E-mail: dmunn@cdhowe.org
VP, Media & Ed: James Fleming Tel: 416-865-1904 ext 9216 E-mail: jfleming@cdhowe.org
Founded: 1958
Economics & social policy studies.
Publishes in English, French.
ISBN Prefix(es): 978-0-88806
Number of titles published annually: 48 Print
Total Titles: 150 Print
Distributed by Renouf Publishing Co (Ottawa)

Inclusion Press International
47 Indian Trail, Toronto, ON M6R 1Z8
Tel: 416-658-5363 Fax: 416-658-5067
E-mail: inclusionpress@inclusion.com
Web Site: www.inclusion.com
Key Personnel
Founding Publr: Marsha Forest; Jack Pearpoint
    E-mail: jack@inclusion.com
Founded: 1989
Inclusion, change, diversity & community.
Publishes in English.
ISBN Prefix(es): 978-1-895418
Number of titles published annually: 5 Print; 2 CD-ROM; 2 E-Book
Total Titles: 100 Print; 10 CD-ROM; 4 E-Book
Distribution Center: Inclusion Distribution, United Kingdom

Insomniac Press
520 Princess Ave, London, ON N6B 2B8
Tel: 519-266-3556
Web Site: www.insomniacpress.com
Key Personnel
Publr: Mike O'Connor E-mail: mike@insomniacpress.com
Mng Ed: Dan Varrette E-mail: dan@insomniacpress.com
Founded: 1992
General trade publisher of fiction, nonfiction & poetry.
Publishes in English.
ISBN Prefix(es): 978-1-895837; 978-1-894663; 978-1-897178; 978-1-897414; 978-1-897415; 978-1-926582; 978-1-55483
Number of titles published annually: 16 Print
Total Titles: 235 Print

Orders to: LitDistCo, 8300 Lawson Rd, Milton, ON L9T 0A4 (CN & US) Toll Free Tel: 800-591-6250 Toll Free Fax: 800-591-6251 E-mail: ordering@litdistco.ca Web Site: www.litdistco.ca; The Literary Press Group of Canada, 425 Adelaide St W, Suite 700, Toronto, ON M5V 3C1 (CN & US) Tel: 416-483-1321 Fax: 416-483-2510 Web Site: www.lpg.ca; Wakefield Press, One The Parade West, Kent Town, SA 5067, Australia (Australia) Tel: (08) 8362 8800 Fax: (08) 8362 7592 Web Site: www.wakefieldpress.com.au; BookWise Asia Pte Ltd, D'Centennial, Suite 03-02, 100 Lorong 23 Geylang, Singapore 388398, Singapore (Southeast Asia) Tel: 6743 2815 Fax: 6743 2817 Web Site: www.bookwise.com.au/publishers; Gazelle Book Services Ltd, White Cross Mills, Hightown, Lancaster, Lancs LA1 4XS, United Kingdom (UK & Europe) Tel: (01524) 528500 Fax: (01524) 528510 E-mail: sales@gazellebookservices.co.uk Web Site: www.gazellebookservices.co.uk
Membership(s): Literary Press Group of Canada

L'Institut canadien du droit des ressources, see Canadian Institute of Resources Law (L'Institut canadien du droit des ressources)

Institute for Research on Public Policy (IRPP)
1470 Peel St, No 200, Montreal, QC H3A 1T1
Tel: 514-985-2461 Fax: 514-985-2559
E-mail: irpp@irpp.org
Web Site: irpp.org
Key Personnel
Pres & CEO: Graham Fox E-mail: gfox@irpp.org
VP, Opers: Suzanne Ostiguy McIntyre Tel: 514-787-0740 E-mail: smcintyre@irpp.org
VP, Res: France St-Hilaire E-mail: fsthilaire@irpp.org
Res Dir: Joanne Castonguay
    E-mail: jcastonguay@irpp.org; Stephen Tapp
    E-mail: stapp@irpp.org
Edit Coord: Francesca Worrall E-mail: fworrall@irpp.org
Founded: 1972
Research on public policy.
Publishes in English, French.
ISBN Prefix(es): 978-0-88645; 978-0-920380
Number of titles published annually: 200 Online
Total Titles: 500 Print

Institute of Intergovernmental Relations
Queen's University, Robert Sutherland Hall, Rm 412, Kingston, ON K7L 3N6
Tel: 613-533-2080 Fax: 613-533-6868
E-mail: iigr@queensu.ca
Web Site: www.queensu.ca/iigr
Key Personnel
Dir: Dr Christian Leurpecht
Pubns Coord & Admin Secy: Mary Kennedy
Founded: 1965
Publish research & other scholarly work on Canadian federalism & intergovernmental relations; ethnicity, government & political science.
Publishes in English, French.
ISBN Prefix(es): 978-1-55339
Number of titles published annually: 2 Print; 69 E-Book
Total Titles: 106 Print; 85 Online; 69 E-Book
Distributed by McGill-Queen's University Press (Canada)

Institute of Psychological Research, Inc.
76 Ave, Mozart W, Montreal, QC H2S 1C4
Tel: 514-382-3000 Toll Free Tel: 800-363-7800 Fax: 514-382-3007 Toll Free Fax: 888-382-3007
E-mail: info@irpcanada.com
Web Site: www.irpcanada.com
Founded: 1958 (incorporated in 1964)
Psychological tests & materials.
Publishes in English, French.

ISBN Prefix(es): 978-0-88509; 978-2-89109
Number of titles published annually: 10 Print
Imprints: IPR; IRP
Distributed by Editions Editest (Belgium); Librairie du Quebec a Paris (France)
Distributor for Aseba (CN); Hogrefe France (CN); Hans Huber (Rorschach only)
U.S. Publishers Represented: Academic Therapy Publications; American Orthopsychiatric; Behavior Sciences Systems; Editions Behaviora; Martin M Bruce; Cardall Associates; Center for Psychological Services; Clinical Psychology Publishing; Nigel Cox; Educational & Clinical Publications; Educational Industrial Testing Service; Educators Publishing Services; Granada Learning; Guidance Associates of Delaware; Harvard University Press; Hogrefe UK; Industrial Psychology; Institute for Personality & Ability Testing; International Tests; Lafayette Instrument; Language Research Associates; Multi Health Systems; National Foundation for Educational Research; Pacific Book; Pro Ed; Psychological Assessment Resources; Psychological Test Specialists; Psychologists & Educators; Research Psychologist Press; Sheridan Psychological Services; Stoelting; Western Psychological Services

Institute of Public Administration of Canada
1075 Bay St, Suite 401, Toronto, ON M5S 2B1
Tel: 416-924-8787 Fax: 416-924-4992
E-mail: ntl@ipac.ca
Web Site: www.ipac.ca
Key Personnel
CEO: Robert Taylor, PhD Tel: 416-924-8787 ext 230 E-mail: rtaylor@ipac.ca
Mng Ed: Christy Paddick Tel: 905-447-6351 (cell) E-mail: cpaddick@ipac.ca
Ed: Evert A Lindquist
Founded: 1947
National bilingual English/French nonprofit organization, concerned with the theory & practice of public management, with 20 regional groups across Canada. Provide networks & forums regionally, nationally & internationally. Specialize in political science, Canadian history & Canadian law.
Publishes in English, French.
ISBN Prefix(es): 978-0-919400; 978-0-920715; 978-0-919696; 978-1-55061
Number of titles published annually: 10 Print; 5 E-Book
Total Titles: 600 Print; 50 Online; 10 E-Book; 5 Audio

§International Self-Counsel Press Ltd
1481 Charlotte Rd, North Vancouver, BC V7J 1H1
SAN: 115-0545
Tel: 604-986-3366 Toll Free Tel: 800-663-3007
E-mail: orders@self-counsel.com; sales@self-counsel.com
Web Site: www.self-counsel.com
Founded: 1971
Legal, business & reference books.
Publishes in English, French.
ISBN Prefix(es): 978-1-55180; 978-1-77040
Number of titles published annually: 24 Print; 5 CD-ROM
Total Titles: 230 Print
Branch Office(s)
Self Counsel Press Inc, 4152 Meridian St, Suite 105-471, Bellingham, WA 98226, United States
Foreign Rights: Atmarr Agency Services (China, France, Germany, Japan, Korea, Philippines, Taiwan, Thailand)
Distribution Center: University of Toronto Press, 10 St Mary St, Suite 700, Toronto, ON M4Y 2W8 Tel: 416-978-2239 Toll Free Tel: 800-565-9523 (orders) Fax: 416-978-4738 E-mail: utpbooks@utpress.utoronto.ca
Independent Publishers Group (IPG), 814 N Franklin St, Chicago, IL 60610, United States

Toll Free Tel: 800-888-4741 Fax: 312-337-5985 E-mail: orders@ipgbook.com Web Site: www. ipgbook.com

Membership(s): American Library Association (ALA)

International Travel Maps & Books, see ITMB Publishing Ltd

Irwin Law Inc
14 Duncan St, Suite 206, Toronto, ON M5H 3G8
SAN: 810-0144
Tel: 416-862-7690 Toll Free Tel: 888-314-9014
Fax: 416-862-9236
E-mail: info@irwinlaw.com; contact@irwinlaw.com
Web Site: www.irwinlaw.com
Key Personnel
Pres & Publr: Jeffrey Miller Tel: 416-862-7690 ext 223 E-mail: jmiller@irwinlaw.com
VP & Ed-in-Chief: Lesley Steeve Tel: 416-862-7690 ext 229 E-mail: lsteeve@irwinlaw.com
Founded: 1996
Publisher of books & other material for lawyers & law students.
Publishes in English.
ISBN Prefix(es): 978-1-55221
Number of titles published annually: 20 Print; 20 E-Book
Total Titles: 200 Print; 100 E-Book
Distributor for The Federation Press (North America only)
Foreign Rep(s): The Federation Press (Australia, New Zealand)
Returns: c/o JAG Business Services, 1675 Sismet Rd, Unit 1, Mississauga, ON L4W 4K8
Membership(s): Association of Canadian Publishers (ACP); Organization of Book Publishers of Ontario (OBPO)

ITMB Publishing Ltd
12300 Bridgeport Rd, Richmond, BC V6V 1J5
Tel: 604-273-1400 Fax: 604-273-1488
E-mail: itmb@itmb.com
Web Site: www.itmb.com
Key Personnel
Pres: Jack Joyce
Founded: 1983
Publisher/distributor of international travel maps & atlases.
Publishes in English.
ISBN Prefix(es): 978-1-55341; 978-0-921463; 978-1-895907
Number of titles published annually: 30 Print
Total Titles: 425 Print
Distributor for Borch; Freytag & Bernot; Gizi; National Geographic; Nelles; Rand McNally
Membership(s): International Map Industry Association (IMIA)

Ivey Publishing, see Richard Ivey School of Business

Richard Ivey School of Business
Division of Ivey Management Services
Ivey Business School at Western University, 1255 Western Rd, London, ON N6G 0N1
Tel: 519-661-3206; 519-661-3208
Toll Free Tel: 800-649-6355 Fax: 519-661-3485; 519-661-3882
E-mail: cases@ivey.uwo.ca
Web Site: www.iveycases.com; www.ivey.uwo.ca
Founded: 1923
Publish business case studies for university business courses.
Publishes in English, French.
ISBN Prefix(es): 978-0-919534
Number of titles published annually: 200 Print
Total Titles: 3,500 Print
Distributed by Caseplace (The Aspen Institute's Centre for Business Education); Cengage

Learning (USA); Centrale de Cas et de Medias Pedagogiques (CCMP) (Paris, France); College of Commerce (National Chengchi University, Taiwan); European Case Clearing House (ECCH) (UK); IESE Publishing (Spain); Institute for International Studies and Training (IIST) (Japan); LAD Publishing (USA); McGraw-Hill (USA); National Archive Publishing (USA); Pearson Custom Publishing (USA); Study.Net (USA); University Readers Inc (USA)
Distributor for Asian Business Case Center/ Nanyang Business School at Nanyang Technological University; China-Europe International Business School (CEIBS); China Management Case Sharing Centre; China University of Hong Kong; College of Commerce (National Chengchi University, Taiwan); Darden Business School; Gordon Institute of Business Science (University of Pretoria, South Africa); Harvard Business Review; Harvard Business School Publishing; Indian Institute of Management Bangalore; Indian School of Business (India); Ivey Business Journal (reprints); National University of Singapore; Northeastern University; Peking University (China); Thunderbird School of Global Management; Tsinghua University (China); University of Regina-Paul J Hill School of Business; University of West Indies; Yonsei University (Korea; Harvard Business School cases & Harvard Business Review reprints)
U.S. Rep(s): Harvard Business School Publishing (case studies & HBR reprints)
Foreign Rep(s): European Case Clearing House (Europe)

Kids Can Press Ltd
Division of Corus Entertainment Inc
25 Dockside Dr, Toronto, ON M5A 0B5
Tel: 416-479-7000 Toll Free Tel: 800-265-0884 Fax: 416-960-5437
E-mail: info@kidscan.com; customerservice@kidscan.com
Web Site: www.kidscanpress.com; www.kidscanpress.ca
Key Personnel
Pres & Publr: Lisa Lyons Johnston
Assoc Publr, Creative: Naseem Hrab
Assoc Publr, Opers & Busn Devt: Lara Caplan
Cont, Corus Entertainment: June Samms
Art Dir: Marie Bartholomew
Edit Dir: Yvette Ghione
Rts Dir: Adrienne Tang
Sales Dir: Molly Helferty
Mng Ed: Jennifer Grimbleby
Ed: Kathleen Keenan; Katie Scott
Mgr, Opers: Amelie Roberge
Intl Sales Mgr & Brand Mgr: Alison Van Ginkel
Mktg Assoc: Kate Patrick
Sales Assoc: Alison Lapp
Founded: 1973
Books for children exclusively.
Publishes in English.
ISBN Prefix(es): 978-0-919964; 978-1-55074; 978-1-55337; 978-0-921103; 978-1-55453; 978-1-77138
Number of titles published annually: 75 Print
Total Titles: 500 Print
Imprints: CitizenKid™; Franklin the Turtle; KCP Loft; Kids Can Do It; Scaredy Squirrel
Distributed by Hachette Book Group
Orders to: Hachette Book Group, Order Dept, 185 N Mount Zion Rd, Lebanon, IN 46052, United States Toll Free Tel: 800-759-0190 Toll Free Fax: 800-286-9471 E-mail: order.desk@hbgusa.com Web Site: www.hachettebookgroup.com
Returns: Hachette Book Group, Attn Returns Dept, 322 S Enterprise Blvd, Lebanon, IN 46052, United States Toll Free Tel: 800-759-0190 Web Site: www.hachettebookgroup.com

Shipping Address: Hachette Book Group, Lebanon, IN, United States Toll Free Tel: 800-759-0190 Toll Free Fax: 800-286-9471 Web Site: www.hachettebookgroup.com

Kindred Productions
Division of Mennonite Brethren Church
1310 Taylor Ave, Winnipeg, MB R3M 3Z6
Tel: 204-669-6575 Toll Free Tel: 800-545-7322 Fax: 204-654-1865
E-mail: kindred@mbchurches.ca
Web Site: www.kindredproductions.com
Key Personnel
Cust Serv Rep: Helga Kasdorf
Founded: 1982
Denominational material, Low German Bible, trade books & church resources.
Publishes in English, French.
ISBN Prefix(es): 978-0-919797; 978-0-921788; 978-1-894791
Number of titles published annually: 15 Print
Total Titles: 250 Print

Kinesiology Books Publisher
Subsidiary of Sport Books Publisher
212 Robert St (side basement door), Toronto, ON M5S 2K7
Tel: 416-323-9438 Fax: 416-966-9022
E-mail: sbp@sportbookspub.com; kbp@kinesiology101.com
Web Site: www.sportbookspub.com
Key Personnel
Pres: Dr Peter Klavora E-mail: peter.klavora@utoronto.ca
Exec Dir: Tania Klavora
Founded: 1983
Activity books, sports books & DVDs; subjects include physical education, exercise science textbooks & kinesiology. Orders accepted by mail, fax or online. Returns accepted if in mint condition.
Publishes in English, French.
ISBN Prefix(es): 978-0-920905
Number of titles published annually: 5 Print; 1 CD-ROM
Total Titles: 48 Print; 3 CD-ROM
Branch Office(s)
PO Box 2583, Niagara Falls, NY 14302, United States

§Knopf Canada
Imprint of Penguin Random House Canada
320 Front St W, Suite 1400, Toronto, ON M5V 3B6
SAN: 201-3975
Tel: 416-364-4449 Toll Free Tel: 888-523-9292 Fax: 416-598-7764
Web Site: www.penguinrandomhouse.ca
Key Personnel
CEO, PRHC: Kristin Cochrane
CFO, PRHC: Barry Gallant
Chief Strategy & Opers Offr, PRHC: Robert Wheaton
Exec Publr & EVP, PRHC: Louise Dennys
SVP & Dir, Prodn: Janine Laporte
Publr, KRC: Anne Collins
Publg Dir, KC: Lynn Henry
Founded: 1991
Penguin Random House Canada & its publishing entities are not accepting unsol submissions, proposals, mss, or submission queries via e-mail at this time.
Publishes in English.
Number of titles published annually: 40 Print
Imprints: Vintage Canada
Distributed by Penguin Random House Canada
Shipping Address: Penguin Random House Canada, 6971 Columbus Rd, Mississauga, ON L5T 1K1
Membership(s): Canadian Publishers' Council

Laurier Books Ltd
PO Box 8493, Ottawa, ON K1G 3H9
SAN: 168-2806
Tel: 613-738-2163 *Toll Free Fax:* 855-736-9160
E-mail: laurierbooks@yahoo.com
Key Personnel
Pres: L Marthe
Lib Sales Dir: R Lalwani
Founded: 1975
All foreign language dictionaries, Native American publications, annuals, bibliographic products, business directories, distribution, publishing, mail orders.
Publishes in English.
ISBN Prefix(es): 978-1-895959; 978-1-55394
Number of titles published annually: 15 Print
Total Titles: 3,000 Print
U.S. Rep(s): IBD Ltd

§LexisNexis® Canada Inc
Member of The LexisNexis® Group
111 Gordon Baker Rd, Suite 900, Toronto, ON M2H 3R1
Tel: 905-479-2665 *Toll Free Tel:* 800-668-6481; 800-387-0899 (cust care); 800-255-5174 (sales)
E-mail: service@lexisnexis.ca (cust serv); sales@lexisnexis.ca
Web Site: www.lexisnexis.ca
Key Personnel
Dir, Training & Cust Care: Jeff Morrison
 E-mail: jeff.morrison@lexisnexis.ca
Cust Serv Mgr, Print & CD-ROM Div: Barbara Brumwell *Tel:* 905-415-5816 *E-mail:* barbara.brumwell@lexisnexis.ca
Prog Coord: Luc Meloche *E-mail:* luc.meloche@lexisnexis.ca
Founded: 1912
Books, looseleaf services, newsletters, journals, legal publishing & online services.
Publishes in English, French.
ISBN Prefix(es): 978-0-409; 978-0-433
Number of titles published annually: 80 Print; 20 CD-ROM
Branch Office(s)
112 Kent St, Suite 700, Ottawa, ON K1P 5P2
 Tel: 613-238-3499 *Toll Free Tel:* 800-387-0899
1200 Ave McGill College, Suite 1100, Montreal, QC H3B 4G7 *Tel:* 514-287-0339

Lidec Inc
800, blvd Industriel, bureau 202, Saint-Jean-sur-Richlieu, QC J3B 8G4
Tel: 514-843-5991 *Toll Free Tel:* 800-350-5991 (CN only) *Fax:* 514-843-5252
E-mail: lidec@lidec.qc.ca
Web Site: www.lidec.qc.ca
Founded: 1965
Publisher of school books.
Publishes in English, French.
ISBN Prefix(es): 978-2-7608
Number of titles published annually: 30 Print
Total Titles: 1,500 Print

Life Cycle Books Ltd
11 Progress Ave, Unit 6, Toronto, ON M1P 4S7
SAN: 110-8417
Toll Free Tel: 866-880-5860 *Toll Free Fax:* 866-260-8172
E-mail: orders@lifecyclebooks.ca; billing@lifecyclebooks.ca; support@lifecyclebooks.ca
Web Site: www.lifecyclebooks.com
Key Personnel
Founder & Pres: Paul Broughton *E-mail:* paulb@lifecyclebooks.com
Founded: 1973
Human life issues.
Publishes in English, French.
ISBN Prefix(es): 978-0-919225
Number of titles published annually: 3 Print
Total Titles: 41 Print

Lone Pine Publishing
87 E Pender, Vancouver, BC V6A 1S9
SAN: 115-4125
Mailing Address: 11414 119 St NW, Edmonton, AB T5G 2X6
Tel: 780-433-9333 *Toll Free Tel:* 800-661-9017 *Fax:* 780-433-9646 *Toll Free Fax:* 800-424-7173
E-mail: info@lonepinepublishing.com
Web Site: www.lonepinepublishing.com
Key Personnel
Pres: Shane Kennedy
Founded: 1980
Natural history, travel, recreation, popular history, bird guides & gardening.
Publishes in English.
ISBN Prefix(es): 978-1-55105; 978-1-894877 (Ghost House Books); 978-0-919433
Number of titles published annually: 5 Print
Total Titles: 800 Print; 50 E-Book
Imprints: Ghost House Books
Branch Office(s)
1808 "B" St NW, Suite 140, Auburn, WA 98001, United States, Sales Mgr: Desiree Levings *Tel:* 253-394-0400 *Toll Free Tel:* 800-518-3541 *Fax:* 253-394-0405 *Toll Free Fax:* 800-548-1169 *E-mail:* order@lonepinepublishing.com
Distributor for Blue Bike Books; Dragon Hill Publishing; Eschia Books; Folklore Publishing; Editions de la Montagne Verte; Partners Publishing; Quagmire Press; Red Deer College Press
U.S. Rep(s): Baker & Taylor; Benjamin News; Book People; Ingram Book Co; Sunbelt

James Lorimer & Co Ltd, Publishers
117 Peter St, Suite 304, Toronto, ON M5V 0M3
Tel: 416-362-4762 *Fax:* 416-362-3939
Web Site: www.lorimer.ca
Key Personnel
Pres & Publr: James Lorimer
Promos: Jess Morgan
Founded: 1970
Hardcover & paperback trade; business, economics, finance, history, politics; children's books; social sciences & sociology; cookbooks; illustrated history.
Publishes in English.
ISBN Prefix(es): 978-1-55028; 978-0-88862; 978-1-55277; 978-1-4594
Number of titles published annually: 12 Print
Total Titles: 600 Print
Orders to: Formac Distributing, 5502 Atlantic St, Halifax, NS B3H 1G4 *Toll Free Tel:* 800-565-1975 *Fax:* 902-425-0166 *E-mail:* orderdesk@formac.ca
Warehouse: Formac Distributing, 5502 Atlantic St, Halifax, NS B3H 1G4 *Tel:* 902-421-7022 *Toll Free Tel:* 800-565-1975 *Fax:* 902-425-0166 *E-mail:* orderdesk@formac.ca *Web Site:* www.formac.ca

Madonna House Publications
2888 Dafoe Rd, Combermere, ON K0J 1L0
Tel: 613-756-3728 *Toll Free Tel:* 888-703-7110 *Fax:* 613-756-0103 *Toll Free Fax:* 877-717-2888
E-mail: publications@madonnahouse.org
Web Site: www.madonnahouse.org/publications
Founded: 1988
Publishes in English, French.
ISBN Prefix(es): 978-0-921440; 978-1-897145
Number of titles published annually: 4 Print; 2 Audio
Total Titles: 68 Print; 68 Online; 15 Audio
Branch Office(s)
879-431 State St, Ogdensburg, NY 13669, United States
Membership(s): Catholic Publishers Association; CMN

§Master Point Press
214 Merton St, Suite 205, Toronto, ON M4S 1A6
Tel: 647-956-4933
E-mail: info@masterpointpress.com
Web Site: www.masterpointpress.com; www.ebooksbridge.com (ebook sales)
Key Personnel
Founder & Co-Owner: Ray Lee
Co-Owner: Linda Lee
Founded: 1994
Books on contract bridge.
Publishes in English.
ISBN Prefix(es): 978-0-9698461; 978-1-894154; 978-1-897106; 978-1-55494; 978-1-77140
Number of titles published annually: 20 Print; 20 E-Book
Total Titles: 250 Print; 10 CD-ROM; 300 E-Book
Distributor for Better Bridge Now
U.S. Rep(s): Strauss Consultants, 45 Main St, Brooklyn, NY 11201, United States
Foreign Rep(s): The Bridge Shop (Australia); Orca Book Services (UK)
Orders to: Georgetown Terminal Warehouses Ltd, 34 Armstrong Ave, Georgetown, ON L7G 4R9 *Tel:* 905-873-2750 *Fax:* 905-873-6170 *E-mail:* orders@gtwcanada.com *Web Site:* www.gtwcanada.com; Baker & Taylor, 2550 W Tyvola Rd, Suite 300, Charlotte, NC 28217, United States *Tel:* 704-998-3100 *Toll Free Tel:* 800-775-1800 *E-mail:* btinfo@btol.com *Web Site:* www.baker-taylor.com; Ingram Book Group, One Ingram Blvd, La Vergne, TN 37086, United States *Tel:* 615-793-5000 *Toll Free Tel:* 800-937-8200 *E-mail:* customer.service@ingramcontent.com; Orca Book Services, 160 Eastern Ave, Milton Park, Abingdon, Oxon OX14 4SB, United Kingdom *Tel:* (01235) 465500 *E-mail:* tradeorders@orcabookservices.co.uk *Web Site:* www.orcabookservices.co.uk
Shipping Address: Georgetown Terminal Warehouses Ltd, 34 Armstrong Ave, Georgetown, ON L7G 4R9

§Mawenzi House Publishers Ltd
39 Woburn Ave (B), Toronto, ON M5W 1K5
Tel: 416-483-7191
E-mail: info@mawenzihouse.com
Web Site: www.mawenzihouse.com
Key Personnel
Publr: Ms Nurjehan Aziz
Founded: 1985 (as TSAR Publications)
Canadian literature, multicultural & international literature. No unsol mss, query first.
Publishes in English.
ISBN Prefix(es): 978-0-920661; 978-1-894770
Number of titles published annually: 8 Print
Total Titles: 101 Print
U.S. Rep(s): Small Press Distribution Inc, 1341 Seventh St, Berkeley, CA 94710, United States
Distribution Center: University of Toronto Press Inc, 5201 Dufferin St, Toronto, ON M3H 5T8 (CN & US) *Tel:* 416-667-7791 *Toll Free Tel:* 800-565-9523 *Fax:* 416-667-7832 *Toll Free Fax:* 800-221-9985 *E-mail:* utpbooks@utpress.utoronto.ca
Small Press Distribution Inc, 1341 Seventh St, Berkeley, CA 94710, United States *Tel:* 510-524-1668 *Toll Free Tel:* 800-869-7553 *Fax:* 510-524-0852
Membership(s): Literary Press Group

McClelland & Stewart Ltd
Imprint of Penguin Random House Canada
320 Front St W, Suite 1400, Toronto, ON M5V 3B6
Tel: 416-364-4449 *Fax:* 416-598-7764
E-mail: customerservicescanada@penguinrandomhouse.com; publicity@ca.penguingroup.com
Web Site: penguinrandomhouse.ca/imprints/mcclelland-stewart
Key Personnel
Publr: Jared Bland
Publr, Signal: Douglas Pepper

Publg Mgr: Kelly Joseph
Ed-in-Chief: Martha Kanya-Forstner
Sr Ed: Jenny Bradshaw
Sr Ed & Assoc Publr, Emblem Editions: Anita Chong
Poetry Ed: Dionne Brand
Ed-at-Large: Haley Cullingham; Jordan Ginsberg
Asst Ed: Joe Lee
Founded: 1906
Penguin Random House Canada & its publishing entities are not accepting unsol submissions, proposals, mss, or submission queries via e-mail at this time.
Publishes in English.
Number of titles published annually: 70 Print
Total Titles: 2,000 Print
Imprints: Signal (nonfiction)
Divisions: Tundra Books

McGill-Queen's University Press
1010 Sherbrooke W, Suite 1720, Montreal, QC H3A 2R7
Tel: 514-398-3750 *Fax:* 514-398-4333
E-mail: mqup@mqup.ca
Web Site: www.mqup.ca
Key Personnel
Exec Dir: Philip Cercone *Tel:* 514-398-2910
   E-mail: philip.cercone@mcgill.ca
Mktg Dir: Erin Rolfs
Ed-in-Chief: Jonathan Crago *Tel:* 514-398-7480
   E-mail: jonathan.crago@mcgill.ca
Mng Ed: Ryan Van Huijstee *Tel:* 514-398-3922
   E-mail: ryan.vanhuijstee@mcgill.ca
Asst Mng Ed: Kathleen Fraser *Tel:* 514-398-2068
   E-mail: kathleen.fraser@mcgill.ca
Sr Ed: Kyla Madden *Tel:* 514-398-2056
   E-mail: kyla.madden@mcgill.ca
Acqs Ed: Khadija Coxon *Tel:* 613-533-2155
   E-mail: khadija.coxon@queensu.ca
Prodn Mgr: Elena Goranescu McAdam *Tel:* 514-398-7395 *E-mail:* elena.goranescu@mcgill.ca
Rts & Projs Mgr: Natalie Blachere *Tel:* 514-398-2121 *E-mail:* natalie.blachere@mcgill.ca
Sales Mgr: Jack Hannan *Tel:* 514-398-5165
   E-mail: jack.hannan@mcgill.ca; Linda Iarrera
Founded: 1970
Original peer-reviewed, high-quality books in all areas of social sciences & humanities. Our emphasis is on providing an outlet for Canadian authors & scholarship. Publish authors from around the world.
Publishes in English, French.
ISBN Prefix(es): 978-0-88629; 978-0-88911; 978-0-7735; 978-0-7709; 978-1-55240; 978-0-9690334
Number of titles published annually: 120 Print
Total Titles: 3,000 Print; 5 CD-ROM
Branch Office(s)
Douglas Library Bldg, 93 University Ave, Kingston, ON K7L 5C4 *Tel:* 613-533-2155 *Fax:* 613-533-6822 *E-mail:* mqup@queensu.ca
Distributor for CIGI Press; John Deutsch Institute for the Study of Economic Policy; Fontanus Monograph Series; Institute for Research on Public Policy; McCord Museum; Queen's Policy Studies Series; Les Editions du Septentrion (English titles)
Foreign Rep(s): The African Moon Press (Chris Reinders) (South Africa); Avicenna Partnership Ltd (Bill Kennedy) (Middle East); Colin Flint Ltd (Ben Greig, Steven Haslemere & Wilf Jones) (Denmark, Finland, Iceland, Norway, Sweden); Claire De Gruchy (Middle East); Charles Gibbes (Cyprus, Greece); Mare Nostrum (Katie Machin) (Belgium, France, Luxembourg, Netherlands); Mare Nostrum (Frauke Feldmann) (Austria, Germany, Switzerland); Mare Nostrum (Francesca Pollard & David Pickering) (Italy); Mare Nostrum (Cristina De Lara Ruiz) (Portugal, Spain); Quantum Publishing Solutions Ltd (Jim Chalmers) (England, Ireland, Scotland, Wales); Research Press (India, Indian subcontinent)

Distribution Center: c/o Georgetown Terminal Warehouses, 34 Armstrong Ave, Georgetown, ON L7G 4R9 *Tel:* 905-873-9781 *Toll Free Tel:* 877-864-8477 *Fax:* 905-873-6170 *Toll Free Fax:* 877-864-4272 *E-mail:* orders@gtwcanada.com
Chicago Distribution Center, 11030 S Langley Ave, Chicago, IL 60628, United States *Tel:* 773-702-7000 *Toll Free Tel:* 800-621-2736 *Fax:* 773-702-7212 *Toll Free Fax:* 800-621-8476 *E-mail:* orders@press.uchicago.edu SAN: 202-5280
Research Press, FF21 Megacity Mall, M G Rd, Gurgaon, Haryana 122 011, India *Tel:* (0124) 4040017 *Fax:* (011) 23281819 *E-mail:* marketing@researchpress.co.in
Marston Book Services Ltd, 160 Eastern Ave, Milton Park, Abingdon, Oxon OX14 4SB, United Kingdom *Tel:* (01235) 465500 *Fax:* (01235) 465555 *E-mail:* trade.orders@marston.co.uk *Web Site:* www.pubeasy.com
Membership(s): American Association of University Presses (AAUP); Association of Canadian Publishers (ACP); Association of Canadian University Presses (ACUP)

§McGraw-Hill Ryerson
Division of McGraw-Hill Education
300 Water St, Whitby, ON L1N 9B6
SAN: 115-060X
Tel: 905-430-5000 *Toll Free Tel:* 800-565-5758 (cust serv) *Fax:* 905-430-5020
   Toll Free Fax: 800-463-5885
Web Site: www.mheducation.ca
Publishes & distributes higher educational & professional products in both print & non-print media.
Publishes in English.
ISBN Prefix(es): 978-0-07; 978-0-7700
Number of titles published annually: 70 Print; 40 CD-ROM; 30 Online
Total Titles: 1,300 Print; 150 CD-ROM; 200 Online; 50 E-Book
Distributed by McGraw-Hill Publishing Cos
Distributor for Glencoe/McGraw-Hill; Jamestown Education; McGraw-Hill; McGraw-Hill/Irwin; MedMaster Inc; Open Court; Osborne; Schaum's; SRA; Wright Group
U.S. Publishers Represented: The McGraw-Hill Cos
Membership(s): Canadian Educational Resources Council; Canadian Publishers' Council

Modus Vivendi Publishing Inc
55, rue Jean-Talon Ouest, Montreal, QC H2R-2W8
Tel: 514-272-0433 *Fax:* 514-272-7234
E-mail: info@groupemodus.com
Web Site: www.groupemodus.com
Key Personnel
Founder & CEO: Marc Alain
VP, Publg & Opers: Isabelle Jodoin
Founded: 1992
General trade publishing.
Publishes in French.
ISBN Prefix(es): 978-2-921556; 978-2-89523; 978-2-89543 (Presses Aventure); 978-2-923720 (Editions Bravo!); 978-2-89670 (Editions Bravo!)
Number of titles published annually: 200 Print
Divisions: Editions Bravo!; Presses Aventure
Distribution Center: Les Messageries ADP, 2315, rue de la Province, Longueuil, QC J4G 1G4 (French) *Tel:* 450-640-1237 *Toll Free Tel:* 866-874-1237 *Fax:* 450-674-6237 *Toll Free Fax:* 866-874-6237 *E-mail:* adpcommandes@sogides.com
Georgetown Publications, 34 Armstrong Ave, Georgetown, ON L7G 4R9 (English) *Tel:* 905-702-7093

Moose Hide Books
Imprint of Moose Enterprise Book & Theatre Play Publishing
684 Walls Rd, Prince Township, ON P6A 6K4
Tel: 705-779-3331 *Fax:* 705-779-3331
E-mail: mooseenterprises@on.aibn.com
Web Site: www.moosehidebooks.com
Key Personnel
Owner & Publr: Richard Mousseau
   E-mail: rmousseau@moosehidebooks.com
Ed: Edmond Alcid *E-mail:* ealcid@moosehidebooks.com
Book & theatre play publishing. Full author royalties paid. 90% of authors are new. House assists new first time authors.
This publisher has indicated that 50% of their product line is author subsidized.
Publishes in English.
ISBN Prefix(es): 978-1-894650; 978-1-927393
Number of titles published annually: 7 Print; 7 E-Book; 1 Audio
Total Titles: 200 Print; 100 Online; 25 E-Book; 1 Audio

§Mosaic Press
1252 Speers Rd, Units 1 & 2, Oakville, ON L6L 5N9
Tel: 905-825-2130 *Fax:* 905-825-2130
E-mail: info@mosaic-press.com
Web Site: www.mosaic-press.com
Key Personnel
Publr: Howard Aster
Founded: 1975
Literary scholarly books. No unsol mss.
ISBN Prefix(es): 978-0-88962; 978-1-77161
Number of titles published annually: 20 Print
Total Titles: 502 Print
Distribution Center: Independent Publishers Group (IPG), 814 N Franklin St, Chicago, IL 60610, United States (US, CN, Australia & New Zealand) *Tel:* 312-337-0747 *Toll Free Tel:* 800-888-4741 *Fax:* 312-337-5985 *E-mail:* orders@ipgbook.com *Web Site:* www.ipgbook.com
Orca Book Services, 160 Eastern Ave, Milton Park, Abingdon, Oxon OX14 4SB, United Kingdom *Tel:* (01235) 465 521 *Fax:* (01235) 465 521 *E-mail:* tradeorders@orcabookservices.co.uk *Web Site:* www.orcabookservices.co.uk

Musee canadien de l'histoire, see Canadian Museum of History (Musee canadien de l'histoire)

Narada Press
3165-133 Weber St N, Waterloo, ON N2J 3G9
Tel: 519-886-1969
Founded: 1993
General books on economics, development studies, Asian studies, Vietnamese studies. Directories, reference books, foreign language, scholarly books, college textbooks.
Publishes in English.
ISBN Prefix(es): 978-1-895938
Number of titles published annually: 5 Print

National Gallery of Canada Boutique
380 Sussex Dr, Ottawa, ON K1N 9N4
Mailing Address: PO Box 427, Sta A, Ottawa, ON K1N 9N4
Tel: 613-990-0962 (mail order sales)
E-mail: ngcbook@gallery.ca
Web Site: www.gallery.ca
Founded: 1980
Exhibition catalogues, monographs, permanent collection series, books on photography, posters.
Publishes in English, French.
ISBN Prefix(es): 978-0-88884
Number of titles published annually: 4 Print

Nelson Education Ltd
Affiliate of Cengage Learning

1120 Birchmount Rd, Scarborough, ON M1K 5G4
Tel: 416-752-9100 *Toll Free Tel:* 800-268-2222 (cust serv) *Fax:* 416-752-8101
Toll Free Fax: 800-430-4445
E-mail: peopleandengagement@nelson.com
Web Site: www.nelson.com
Key Personnel
Pres & CEO: Steven Brown
CFO: Stephen Aubert
SVP, Media & Prodn Servs: Susan Cline
SVP & Mng Dir, K-20: Jessica Mosher
VP, People & Engagement: Jessica Phinn
Founded: 1914
School, college, test, professional & reference. Publishes in English.
ISBN Prefix(es): 978-0-919913; 978-1-896081; 978-0-7705; 978-0-17; 978-0-7725; 978-1-85032
Number of titles published annually: 700 Print
Total Titles: 11,864 Print; 30 CD-ROM; 30 E-Book; 100 Audio
U.S. Publishers Represented: American Technical Publishers Inc (ATP); Aseba; Brooks-Cole Publishing; Canada Housing & Mortgage Corp (CMHC); Centennial Press; Course Technology Inc; Craftsman; DC Heath Canada Ltd (school & coll); Delmar Publishers Inc; Douglas & McIntyre; Duxbury Press; Exclusive; Goodheart Willcox; Great Source Educational; Groupe Beauchemin; HarperCollins; Heinemann; Heinle & Heinle Publishers Inc; Houghton Mifflin Harcourt Publishing Company (school, coll & trade); Indigo Instrument; Industrial Press; International Thomson Publishing Services; Irwin Publishing; Learning Media Co; McDougall Littell & Co; Mondo; Nelson Thomson Learning; Nelson Thomson Learning Australia; Norbry; Peterson's; Phoenix Learning Resources; PWS Publishing; Reidmore Publishing; The Riverside Publishing Co; William H Sadlier; Scott Jones; South Western Education & College Publishing; Texere; Thomas Learning Asia; VideoActive Production; Wadsworth Publishers; West Publishing (educ prods only); West Virginia University (FIT)
Membership(s): Canadian Educational Resources Council; Canadian Publishers' Council

§New Author Publishing
4 E Fulford Place, Brockville, ON K6V 2Z8
Tel: 613-865-7471
Web Site: www.newauthorpublishing.com
Key Personnel
Owner: Gary Wolfe *E-mail:* gary@newauthorpublishing.com
Founded: 2013
Print on demand & ebook publishing.
Publishes in English.
ISBN Prefix(es): 978-1-928045
Number of titles published annually: 8 Print; 8 Online; 8 E-Book
Total Titles: 30 Print; 30 Online; 30 E-Book

New Star Books Ltd
107-3477 Commercial St, Vancouver, BC V5N 4E8
SAN: 115-1908
Tel: 604-738-9429
E-mail: info@newstarbooks.com
Web Site: www.newstarbooks.com
Key Personnel
Pres & Publr: Rolf Maurer
Founded: 1970
Publishers of contemporary prose literature including fiction, criticism & memoir, poetry, nonfiction on social issues & current affairs, politics, labor, feminism, sexuality/gender. Emphasis on British Columbia & Western Canada.
Publishes in English.
ISBN Prefix(es): 978-0-919888; 978-0-919573; 978-0-921586; 978-1-55420
Number of titles published annually: 10 Print

Total Titles: 110 Print
Branch Office(s)
1574 Gulf Rd, No 1517, Point Roberts, WA 98281, United States
Foreign Rights: Acacia House Publishing (worldwide exc Canada)
Distribution Center: Brunswick Books, 14 Afton Ave, Toronto, ON M6J 1R7 *Tel:* 416-703-3598 *Fax:* 416-703-6561 *E-mail:* info@brunswickbooks.ca
Membership(s): Literary Press Group

§New World Publishing (Canada)
PO Box 36075, Halifax, NS B3J 3S9
Tel: 902-576-2055 (inquiries) *Toll Free Tel:* 877-211-3334 (orders) *Fax:* 902-576-2095
Web Site: www.newworldpublishing.com
Key Personnel
Owner & Mng Ed: Dr Francis Mitchell *E-mail:* francis@newworldpublishing.com
Founded: 1995
Publishes in English.
ISBN Prefix(es): 978-1-895814
Number of titles published annually: 4 Print; 1 E-Book; 1 Audio
Total Titles: 53 Print; 7 CD-ROM; 5 Online; 5 E-Book; 5 Audio
Distributed by Glen Margaret Publishing (most independent & gift stores in Maritimes)
Returns: 19 Frenchman's Rd, Oakfield, NS B2T-1A9 *E-mail:* nwp1@eastlink.ca
Warehouse: JEM Enterprises, 79 Jackson Rd, Apt 3, Dartmouth, NS B3A 4A7, Shipper: Ms Jacqui E Mitchell *Tel:* 902-449-7552 *E-mail:* nwp1@eastlink.ca
Membership(s): Atlantic Publishers Marketing Association

NeWest Press
8540 109 St, No 201, Edmonton, AB T6G 1E6
Tel: 780-432-9427 *Fax:* 780-433-3179
E-mail: info@newestpress.com; orders@newestpress.com
Web Site: www.newestpress.com
Key Personnel
Gen Mgr: Matt Bowes
Mktg & Prodn Coord: Claire Kelly
Founded: 1977
Committed to developing & publishing first-time writers, as well as ensuring the availability of Canadian classics.
Publishes in English.
ISBN Prefix(es): 978-0-920316; 978-0-920897; 978-1-896300; 978-1-897126; 978-1-927063
Number of titles published annually: 12 Print
Total Titles: 140 Print
Sales Office(s): Literary Press Group, 425 Adelaide St W, Suite 700, Toronto, ON M5V 3C1, Sales Mgr: Tan Light *Tel:* 416-483-1321 *Fax:* 416-483-2510 *E-mail:* sales@lpg.ca
Foreign Rep(s): Gazelle Book Services Ltd (Europe, UK)
Distribution Center: LitDistCo, 8300 Lawson Rd, Milton, ON L9T 0A4 *Toll Free Tel:* 800-591-6250 *Toll Free Fax:* 800-591-6251 *E-mail:* ordering@litdistco.ca *Web Site:* www.litdistco.ca
Membership(s): Association of Canadian Publishers (ACP); Book Publishers Association of Alberta; Crime Writers of Canada; Literary Press Group of Canada

Nimbus Publishing Ltd
3731 Mackintosh St, Halifax, NS B3K 5A5
SAN: 115-0685
Mailing Address: PO Box 9166, Halifax, NS B3K 5M8
Tel: 902-455-4286 *Toll Free Tel:* 800-NIMBUS9 (646-2879) *Fax:* 902-455-5440
Toll Free Fax: 888-253-3133
E-mail: customerservice@nimbus.ca
Web Site: www.nimbus.ca

Key Personnel
Sr Ed: Whitney Moran *E-mail:* editorial@nimbus.ca
Prodn Mgr: Heather Bryan *E-mail:* hbryan@nimbus.ca
Sales Mgr & Foreign Rts: Terrilee Bulger *Tel:* 902-455-4286 ext 223 *E-mail:* tbulger@nimbus.ca
Mktg Coord: Matt McNeill *Tel:* 902-455-4286 ext 226 *E-mail:* mmcneill@nimbus.ca
Billing: Phyllis Murray
Founded: 1978
Regional nonfiction books, relevant to the Atlantic-Canadian experience, social & natural history, children's books, cookbooks, travel, biography, photography & nautical.
Publishes in English, French.
ISBN Prefix(es): 978-0-920852; 978-0-919380; 978-0-921054; 978-0-921128; 978-1-55109; 978-1-77108
Number of titles published annually: 45 Print
Total Titles: 1,000 Print
Imprints: Nimbus; Vagrant Press (fiction)
Distributor for Acadiensis Press; Acorn Press; Bouton D'or Acadie; Breton Books; Bunim & Bannigan; Cape Breton University Press; Down East; Heritage House; Maritime Lines; Pottersfield Press
U.S. Publishers Represented: Down East; Flat Hammock Press; Mystic Seaport Museum Inc; Sheridan House; Wooden Boat
U.S. Rep(s): Downeast Books
Distribution Center: Baker & Taylor Distribution Services, 30 Amberwood Pkwy, Ashland, OH 44805, United States (US only) *Tel:* 567-215-0030 *Toll Free Tel:* 888-814-0208 *E-mail:* info@btpubservices.com *Web Site:* www.btpubservices.com
Membership(s): Association for the Export of Canadian Books; Association of Canadian Publishers (ACP); Atlantic Publishers Marketing Association; NEBA

Novalis Publishing
Division of Bayard Canada
10 Lower Spadina Ave, Suite 400, Toronto, ON M5V 2Z2
Tel: 416-363-3303 *Toll Free Tel:* 877-702-7773 *Fax:* 416-363-9409 *Toll Free Fax:* 877-702-7775
E-mail: books@novalis.ca
Web Site: www.novalis.ca
Key Personnel
Edit Dir: Simon Appolloni *E-mail:* simon.appolloni@novalis.ca
Publg Dir: Joseph Sinasac *E-mail:* joseph.sinasac@novalis.ca
Mktg Mgr: Matthew Sottile
Sales Mgr: Maria Medeiros
Founded: 1936
Religious children's & adult books, periodicals & religious books (Catholic/Christian).
Publishes in English, French.
ISBN Prefix(es): 978-2-89088; 978-2-89507; 978-2-89646; 978-0-88587; 978-1-895195
Number of titles published annually: 30 Print
Total Titles: 360 Print
Distributor for Canterbury Press; Catholic Health Alliance of Canada (CHAC); Church House Publishing; Columba Press; Creative Communications for the Parish; Crossroad Publishing; Jewish Lights Publishing/Skylight Paths; Liguori Publications; Loyola Press; Morehouse Publishing/Church Publishing/Seabury; Orbis Books; Paulist Press; Penguin Random House; Pflaum Publishing Group; Printery House; Saint Mary's Press; St Vladimir Seminary Press; SCM Press; Editions du Signe; Twenty Third Publications; Wild Goose Publications
U.S. Publishers Represented: Creative Communications for the Parish; Jewish Lights Publishing; Orbis Books; Paulist Press; Pflaum Gospel Weeklies; Saint Mary's Press; Twenty-Third Publications

Billing Address: BND Distribution, 4475 Frontenac St, Montreal, QC H2H 2S2 *Tel:* 514-278-3020 *Toll Free Tel:* 800-387-7164 *Fax:* 514-278-3030 *Toll Free Fax:* 800-204-4140 *Web Site:* www.novalis.com
Orders to: BND Distribution, 4475 Frontenac St, Montreal, QC H2H 2S2 *Tel:* 514-278-3020 *Toll Free Tel:* 800-387-7164 *Fax:* 514-278-3030 *Toll Free Fax:* 800-204-4140 *Web Site:* www.novalis.com
Returns: BND Distribution, 4475 Frontenac St, Montreal, QC H2H 2S2 *Tel:* 514-278-3020 *Toll Free Tel:* 800-387-7164 *Fax:* 514-278-3030 *Toll Free Fax:* 800-204-4140 *Web Site:* www.novalis.com
Shipping Address: BND Distribution, 4475 Frontenac St, Montreal, QC H2H 2S2 *Tel:* 514-278-3020 *Toll Free Tel:* 800-387-7164 *Fax:* 514-278-3030 *Toll Free Fax:* 800-204-4140 *Web Site:* www.novalis.com
Warehouse: BND Distribution, 4475 Frontenac St, Montreal, QC H2H 2S2 *Tel:* 514-278-3020 *Toll Free Tel:* 800-387-7164 *Fax:* 514-278-3030 *Toll Free Fax:* 800-204-4140 *Web Site:* www.novalis.com

Oberon Press
145 Spruce St, Suite 205, Ottawa, ON K1R 6P1
SAN: 115-0723
Tel: 613-238-3275 *Fax:* 613-238-3275
E-mail: oberon@sympatico.ca
Web Site: www.oberonpress.ca
Key Personnel
Pres: Michael Macklem
VP & Gen Mgr: Nicholas Macklem
Founded: 1966
Canadiana, fiction, history, biography, poetry & travel.
Publishes in English.
ISBN Prefix(es): 978-0-88750; 978-0-7780
Number of titles published annually: 7 Print
Total Titles: 671 Print

One Act Play Depot
618 Memorial Dr, PO Box 335, Spiritwood, SK S0J 2M0
E-mail: plays@oneactplays.net; orders@oneactplays.net
Web Site: oneactplays.net
Key Personnel
Mng Ed: Fraser MacFarlane
Ed: K Balvenie
Founded: 2002
Publication, sale & distribution of one-act plays. Orders ship within 24 hours. Accept submissions only in February of each year.
Publishes in English.
ISBN Prefix(es): 978-1-894910; 978-1-926849
Number of titles published annually: 10 Print; 10 E-Book
Total Titles: 170 Print; 110 E-Book

Oolichan Books
PO Box 2278, Fernie, BC V0B 1M0
SAN: 115-4680
Tel: 250-423-6113
E-mail: info@oolichan.com
Web Site: www.oolichan.com
Key Personnel
Founder & Ed: Ronald Smith
Publr: Randal Macnair
Consulting Ed: Pat Smith
Asst to the Publr: Carolyn Nikodym
Founded: 1974
Publishers of literary fiction, poetry & literary nonfiction. Publish only Canadian authors.
Publishes in English.
ISBN Prefix(es): 978-0-88982
Number of titles published annually: 10 Print
Total Titles: 160 Print
Shipping Address: 542 B Second Ave, Fernie, BC V0B 1M0

Distribution Center: University of Toronto Press, 5201 Dufferin St, Toronto, ON M3H 5T8 *Toll Free Tel:* 800-565-9523 *E-mail:* utpbooks@utpress.utoronto.ca
Membership(s): Association of Book Publishers of British Columbia; Association of Canadian Publishers (ACP); Literary Press Group

Orca Book Publishers
1016 Balmoral Rd, Victoria, BC V8T 1A8
Toll Free Tel: 800-210-5277 *Toll Free Fax:* 877-408-1551
E-mail: orca@orcabook.com
Web Site: www.orcabook.com
Key Personnel
Founder & Pres: Bob Tyrrell
Publr: Andrew Wooldridge *E-mail:* andrew@orcabook.com
Founded: 1984
Children & young adult literature.
Publishes in English, French.
ISBN Prefix(es): 978-1-55143; 978-0-920501; 978-1-4598; 978-1-55469
Number of titles published annually: 80 Print
Total Titles: 1,000 Print
Branch Office(s)
PO Box 468, Custer, WA 98240-0468, United States
Distributor for The Book Publishing Co; Creative Book Publishing; Formac Publishing; Lobster Press; James Lorimer & Co; Nimbus Publishing; Polestar Calendars; Second Story Press; 7th Generation; Sono Nis Press; Sumach Press; Tradewind Books; Tuckamore Books; Tudor House
Foreign Rights: Transatlantic Literary Agency (Amy Tompkins)
Returns: 7056 Portal Way, Suite 110, Ferndale, WA 98248, United States (US returns via courier)
Membership(s): American Booksellers Association (ABA); American Library Association (ALA); Association of Book Publishers of British Columbia; Association of Canadian Publishers (ACP); Educational Book & Media Association (EBMA)

Owlkids Books Inc
Division of Bayard Canada
10 Lower Spadina Ave, Suite 400, Toronto, ON M5V 2Z2
Tel: 416-340-2700 *Fax:* 416-340-9769
E-mail: owlkids@owlkids.com
Web Site: www.owlkidsbooks.com
Key Personnel
Publr: Karen Boersma
Dir, Sales & Mktg: Judy Brunsek
Founded: 1976
Award-winning publisher of books for children ages 3-13.
Publishes in English.
ISBN Prefix(es): 978-0-920775; 978-1-895688; 978-1-894379; 978-1-897066; 978-1-897349; 978-1-926973; 978-0-919872; 978-1-926818
Number of titles published annually: 25 Print
Total Titles: 150 Print; 50 E-Book
Orders to: University of Toronto Press, 5201 Dufferin St, Toronto, ON M3H 5T8 *Tel:* 416-667-7791 *Toll Free Tel:* 800-565-9523 *Fax:* 416-667-7832 *Toll Free Fax:* 800-221-9985 *E-mail:* utpbooks@utpress.utoronto.ca *Web Site:* www.utpress.utoronto.ca; Publishers Group West, 1700 Fourth St, Berkeley, CA 94710, United States *Toll Free Tel:* 866-400-5351 *Toll Free Fax:* 800-838-1149 *E-mail:* ips@ingramcontent.com *Web Site:* www.pgw.com
Membership(s): Association of Canadian Publishers (ACP); Educational Book & Media Association (EBMA); Organization of Book Publishers of Ontario (OBPO)

Pacific Educational Press
Imprint of University of British Columbia Press c/o UBC Press, 2029 West Mall, Vancouver, BC V6T 1Z2
Tel: 604-822-5959; 604-827-2232 (cust serv) *Toll Free Tel:* 855-827-2232
E-mail: pep.admin@ubc.ca; pep.sales@ubc.ca
Web Site: pacificedpress.ca
Founded: 1971
Textbooks for teacher education programs, education materials, materials which are generally used in classrooms or educational institutes, books on education topics & issues for a general readership.
Publishes in English.
ISBN Prefix(es): 978-0-88865; 978-1-895766
Number of titles published annually: 6 Print
Total Titles: 104 Print; 16 E-Book
Distributor for Critical Thinking Consortium (TC2)
Distribution Center: Georgetown Terminal Warehouse, 34 Armstrong Ave, Georgetown, ON L7G 4R9 *Tel:* 905-873-9781 *Toll Free Tel:* 877-864-8477 (CN only) *Fax:* 905-873-6170 *Toll Free Fax:* 877-864-4272 (CN only) *E-mail:* orders@gtwcanada.com
Membership(s): Association of Book Publishers of British Columbia; Association of Canadian Publishers (ACP)

Palimpsest Press
1171 Eastlawn Ave, Windsor, ON N8S 3J1
Tel: 519-259-2112
E-mail: publicity@palimpsestpress.ca
Web Site: www.palimpsestpress.ca
Key Personnel
Publr: Aimee Parent Dunn *E-mail:* aimee@palimpsestpress.ca
Manager: Shaun Dunn
Publicity Manager: Abigail Roelens
Fiction Ed/Copy-Editor: Ginger Pharand
Poetry Ed: Jim Johnstone; Dawn Kresan *E-mail:* dawnkresan@palimpsestpress.ca
Founded: 2000
Publish poetry collections, nonfiction, essays, literary fiction.
Publishes in English.
ISBN Prefix(es): 978-0-9733952; 978-1-926794; 978-0-9784917
Number of titles published annually: 6 Print
Total Titles: 30 Print
Imprints: Anstruther Books
Sales Office(s): The Literary Press Group of Canada, 234 Eglinton Ave E, Suite 401, Toronto, ON M4P 1K5 *Tel:* 416-483-1321 *Fax:* 416-483-2510 *E-mail:* sales@lpg.ca *Web Site:* lpg.ca
Orders to: LitDistCo, 8300 Lawson Rd, Milton, ON L9T 0A4 *Toll Free Tel:* 800-591-6250 *Toll Free Fax:* 800-591-6251 *E-mail:* ordering@litdistco.ca *Web Site:* www.litdistco.ca
Shipping Address: LitDistCo, 8300 Lawson Rd, Milton, ON L9T 0A4 *Toll Free Tel:* 800-581-6250 *Toll Free Fax:* 800-581-6251 *Web Site:* www.litdistco.ca
Warehouse: LitDistCo, 8300 Lawson Rd, Milton, ON L9T 0A4 *Toll Free Tel:* 800-581-6250 *Toll Free Fax:* 800-581-6251 *Web Site:* www.litdistco.ca
Distribution Center: LitDistCo, 8300 Lawson Rd, Milton, ON L9T 0A4 *Toll Free Tel:* 800-591-6250 *Toll Free Fax:* 800-591-6251 *E-mail:* ordering@litdistco.ca *Web Site:* www.litdistco.ca
Membership(s): Association of Canadian Publishers (ACP); Literary Press Group of Canada

§Paulines Editions
5610 rue Beaubien est, Montreal, QC H1T 1X5
Tel: 514-253-5610 *Fax:* 514-253-1907
E-mail: fsp-paulines@videotron.ca
Web Site: www.editions.paulines.qc.ca

Key Personnel
Dir & Intl Rts Contact: Vanda Salvador
Lib Sales Dir: Lucille Paradis
Founded: 1956
Religious books.
Publishes in English, French.
ISBN Prefix(es): 978-2-920912
Number of titles published annually: 4 Print
Total Titles: 60 Print
Distributed by Mediaspaul (Montreal)

§Pearson Education Canada
Division of Pearson Canada Inc
26 Prince Andrew Place, North York, ON M3C 2H4
SAN: 115-0022
Toll Free Tel: 800-567-3800 *Fax:* 416-447-7755
Toll Free Fax: 800-263-7733
E-mail: cdn.ordr@pearsoned.com
Web Site: www.pearson.com/ca; www. mypearsonstore.ca
Founded: 1966
Educational textbooks, trade, reference.
Publishes in English, French.
ISBN Prefix(es): 978-0-201
Total Titles: 5,700 Print
Imprints: Addison Wesley; Allyn & Bacon; Benjamin Cummings; Longman; Prentice Hall
Orders to: Pearson Canada Operations Centre, 195 Harry Walker Pkwy N, Newmarket, ON L3Y 7B4
Returns: Pearson Canada Operations Centre, Consumer Returns Dept, 195 Harry Walker Pkwy N, Ontario L3Y 7B4
Distribution Center: Pearson Canada Operations Centre, 195 Harry Walker Pkwy N, Newmarket, ON L3Y 7B4 *Tel:* 905-853-7888 *Fax:* 905-853-7865

Pearson ERPI
Division of Pearson PLC
1611 Cremazie Blvd E, 10th fl, Montreal, QC H2M 2P2
Tel: 514-334-2690 *Toll Free Tel:* 800-263-3678 *Fax:* 514-334-4720 *Toll Free Fax:* 800-643-4720
E-mail: bienvenue@pearsonerpi.com
Web Site: pearsonerpi.com; pearsonplc.ca
Key Personnel
Artistic Dir: Helene Cousineau *E-mail:* helene.cousineau@pearsonerpi.com
Intl Rts: Lise Barras *Tel:* 514-334-2690 ext 2445 *E-mail:* lise.barras@pearsonerpi.com
Founded: 1965
Textbooks.
Publishes in English, French.
ISBN Prefix(es): 978-2-7613
Number of titles published annually: 50 Print; 12 CD-ROM; 50 Online
Total Titles: 950 Print; 15 CD-ROM; 50 Online
Distributed by De Boeck; Pearson Education France
Distributor for Campus Press France; Duculot; Pearson Canada (ESL series); Prentice-Hall
Membership(s): Association nationale des editeurs de livres (ANEL)

Pembroke Publishers Ltd
538 Hood Rd, Markham, ON L3R 3K9
Tel: 905-477-0650 *Toll Free Tel:* 800-997-9807 *Fax:* 905-477-3691 *Toll Free Fax:* 800-339-5568
Web Site: www.pembrokepublishers.com
Key Personnel
Pres & Intl Rts: Mary Macchiusi *E-mail:* mary@pembrokepublishers.com
Mng Dir: Claudia Connolly
Founded: 1985
Educational books.
Publishes in English.
ISBN Prefix(es): 978-0-921217; 978-1-55138
Number of titles published annually: 10 Print

Total Titles: 300 Print; 100 E-Book
Distributor for Stenhouse Publishers
U.S. Publishers Represented: Stenhouse Publishers
U.S. Rep(s): Stenhouse Publishers
Foreign Rep(s): Eurospan (UK); Hawker Brownlow Education (Australia, New Zealand); PMS (Singapore); Stenhouse Publishers (USA)
Distribution Center: Eurospan, 3 Henrietta St, Covent Garden, London WC2E 8LU, United Kingdom
Membership(s): Organization of Book Publishers of Ontario (OBPO)

Penguin Books Canada Limited, see Penguin Group (Canada)

§Penguin Group (Canada)
Imprint of Penguin Random House Canada
320 Front St W, Suite 1400, Toronto, ON M5V 3B6
Tel: 416-364-4449 *Fax:* 416-598-7764
E-mail: customerservicescanada@penguinrandomhouse.com; publicity@ca.penguingroup.com
Web Site: penguinrandomhouse.ca/imprints/penguin-canada
Key Personnel
Chmn: Rob Prichard
COO: Barry Gallant
Pres & Publr: Nicole Winstanley
VP, Fin: Helena Hung
VP, HR: Ann Wood
Dir, Prodn: Janette Lush
Rts & Contracts Mgr: David Whiteside
Founded: 1974
General trade & paperback books, hardcover & classics.
Penguin Random House Canada & its publishing entities are not accepting unsol submissions, proposals, mss, or submission queries via e-mail at this time.
Publishes in English.
Number of titles published annually: 3,280 Print
Total Titles: 76,500 Print
Imprints: A&C Black UK; Ace; Albatross; Alpha Books; Arden; Arkana; Atlantic Books; Avery; BBC Children's Books; Berkley; Berkshire House; Bibli O'Phile; Bloomberg Press; Bloomsbury UK; Bloomsbury USA; Blue Hen; Boulevard; Callaway; Canongate; Celebra; Chamberlain Brothers; Children's High Level Group; Corinthian Books; The Countryman Press; Current; Dalkey Archive Press; DAW; Dial Books for Young Readers; Dutton; Dutton Children's Books; Europa Editions; Faber & Faber Ltd; Fig Tree; Firebird; Foul Play Press; Gotham Books; GP Putnam & Sons; Grosset & Dunlap; Hamish Hamilton; Hamish Hamilton Canada; Hamish Hamilton Juvenile; Heat; Hippocrene Books; Home; HP Books; Hudson Street Press; Humanity Books; Icon Books; Michael Joseph; Michael Joseph Juvenile; Jove; Kales Press; Ladybird; Allen Lane; Library of America; Liveright; Meridian; Methuen Canadian List; Minedition; Modern Gems; New Directions; Noah Publications; W W Norton & Company Inc; Onyx; Overlook Press; Peace Hill Press; Pegasus Books; Penguin Audio UK; Penguin Australia; Penguin Canada; Penguin Classics; Penguin Compass; Penguin 007; Penguin India; Penguin Ireland; Penguin New Zealand; Penguin Paperbacks; Penguin Press; Penguin South Africa; Penguin UK; Perigee; Persea Books; Philomel Books; Pi Press; Planet Dexter; Plume; Portfolio; Prentice Hall Cda; Prentice Hall Press; Price Stern Sloan; Price Stern Sloan Merchandise; Prime Crime; Profile Books; Prometheus Books; Puffin Canada; Puffin UK; Puffin USA; Pushcart Press; Putnam Audio; PYR Books; Quantuck Lane; Razorbill; Rose Reisman; Riverhead; Roadside Amusements; Roc; Screen Press Books; Sen-

tinel; Short Books; Signet; Smithsonian; Speak; Tarcher; Thames & Hudson; Time Out Guides Ltd; Tusk/Ivories; Verso Press Canada; Verso Press UK; Verso Press USA; Viking Canada; Viking Children's Books; Viking Penguin Audio; Viking Studio; Viking UK; Viking UK Juvenile; Viking USA; Walting Street; Frederick Warne; Wee Sing; Which Books; Wizard Books
Distributor for Alpha Books; Arkangel; Atlantic Books; Avery; BBC Children's Books; Berkley Publishing; Bibli O'Phile; Bloomsbury Press; Callaway; Canongate; DAW; Dutton; Europa Editions; Faber & Faber Ltd; Fig Tree; Gotham Books; Hamish Hamilton; Hamish Hamilton Canada; Hippocrene Books; Hudson Street Press; Icon Books; Michael Joseph; Ladybird; Allen Lane; Library of America; Michelin North America (Canada) (English titles in Canada); New American Library; W W Norton & Company Inc; Overlook Press; Penguin Audio UK; Penguin Australia; Penguin Books USA; Penguin Canada; Penguin India; Penguin New Zealand; Penguin Press; Penguin Random House Audio Publishing; Penguin South Africa; Penguin UK; Penguin Young Readers; Plume; Portfolio; Prometheus Books; Puffin Canada; Putnam; Rose Reisman; Verso Press USA; Viking Canada; Viking Penguin Audio; Viking USA; Frederick Warne; Which Book
Distribution Center: Pearson Canada Distribution Centre, 195 Harry Walker Pkwy, Newmarket, ON L3Y 7B4 *Tel:* 905-713-3852 *Toll Free Tel:* 800-399-6858 *Toll Free Fax:* 800-363-2665
Web Site: www.pearsoned.ca

Penguin Random House Canada
Division of Penguin Random House LLC
320 Front St W, Suite 1400, Toronto, ON M5V 3B6
SAN: 201-3975
Tel: 416-364-4449 *Toll Free Tel:* 888-523-9292 (cust serv) *Fax:* 416-598-7764
Web Site: www.penguinrandomhouse.ca
Key Personnel
CEO: Kristin Cochrane
CFO: Barry Gallant
COO: Robert Wheaton
Exec Publr & EVP: Louise Dennys
SVP & Dir, Prodn: Janine Laporte
VP, PRHC & Publr, Penguin Canada: Nicole Winstanley
VP & Publr, Appetite by Random House: Robert McCullough
VP & Deputy Publr: Marion Garner
VP, Mktg & Communs: Beth Lockley
VP, Sales: Charidy Johnston
Prodn Dir: Carla Kean
Dir, Communs: Katie Saunoris
Publicity Dir: Josh Glover
Founded: 1944
Penguin Random House Canada & its publishing entities are not accepting unsol submissions, proposals, mss, or submission queries via e-mail at this time.
Publishes in English.
Imprints: Anchor Canada; Appetite by Random House; Bond Street Books; Doubleday Canada; Emblem Editions; Fenn-M&S; Douglas Gibson Books; Hamish Hamilton Canada; Knopf Canada; Allen Lane Canada; McClelland & Stewart; Penguin Canada; Penguin Teen; Portfolio Canada; Puffin Canada; Random House Canada; Razorbill Canada; Seal Books; Signal; Strange Light; Tundra Books; Viking Canada; Vintage Canada
Warehouse: 6971 Columbus Rd, Mississauga, ON L5T 1K1
Membership(s): Canadian Publishers' Council
See separate listing for:
Doubleday Canada
Knopf Canada
McClelland & Stewart Ltd
Penguin Group (Canada)

Seal Books
Tundra Books

Pontifical Institute of Mediaeval Studies, Department of Publications
59 Queen's Park Crescent E, Toronto, ON M5S 2C4
SAN: 115-0804
Tel: 416-926-7142 *Fax:* 416-926-7258
Web Site: www.pims.ca
Key Personnel
Ed-in-Chief: Fred R Unwalla *E-mail:* unwalla@chass.utoronto.ca
Founded: 1936
Scholarly publishing on the Middle Ages.
Publishes in English, French.
ISBN Prefix(es): 978-0-88844
Number of titles published annually: 10 Print
Total Titles: 350 Print
Orders to: University of Toronto Press, 5201 Dufferin St, Toronto, ON M3H 5T8 *Tel:* 416-667-7791 *Toll Free Tel:* 800-565-9523 *Fax:* 416-667-7832 *Toll Free Fax:* 800-221-9985 *E-mail:* orders@utpress.utoronto.ca *Web Site:* www.utpress.utoronto.ca
Distribution Center: University of Toronto Press, 5201 Dufferin St, Toronto, ON M3H 5T8 *Tel:* 416-667-7791 *Toll Free Tel:* 800-565-9523 *Fax:* 416-667-7832 *Toll Free Fax:* 800-221-9985 *E-mail:* orders@utpress.utoronto.ca *Web Site:* www.utpress.utoronto.ca

§Porcupine's Quill Inc
68 Main St, Erin, ON N0B 1T0
Mailing Address: PO Box 160, Erin, ON N0B 1T0
Tel: 519-833-9158
E-mail: pql@sentex.net
Web Site: porcupinesquill.ca; www.facebook.com/theporcupinesquill
Key Personnel
Publr: Tim Inkster
Founded: 1974
Modern Canadian literature, poetry & art.
Publishes in English.
ISBN Prefix(es): 978-0-88984
Number of titles published annually: 10 Print
Total Titles: 100 Print
U.S. Rep(s): University of Toronto Press
Membership(s): Association of Canadian Publishers (ACP); Canada Council for the Arts; Literary Press Group; Ontario Arts Council

Portage & Main Press
318 McDermot, Suite 100, Winnipeg, MB R3A 0A2
Tel: 204-987-3500 *Toll Free Tel:* 800-667-9673 *Fax:* 204-947-0080 *Toll Free Fax:* 866-734-8477
E-mail: customerservice@portageandmainpress.com
Web Site: www.portageandmainpress.com
Key Personnel
Owner, Publr, Rts & Perms: Catherine Gerbasi
Edit Dir: Annalee Greenberg
Dir, Mktg: Kirsten Phillips
Founded: 1967 (as Peguis Publishers)
Educational resource (K-12).
Publishes in English.
ISBN Prefix(es): 978-0-919566; 978-0-920541; 978-1-895411; 978-1-894110; 978-1-55379; 978-0-9699032; 978-0-9694264
Number of titles published annually: 14 Print; 14 E-Book
Total Titles: 200 Print; 200 E-Book
Imprints: HighWater Press

Pottersfield Press
248 Leslie Rd, East Lawrencetown, NS B2Z 1T4
SAN: 115-0790
Toll Free Tel: 800-646-2879 (orders only)
E-mail: pottersfieldcreative@gmail.com

Web Site: www.pottersfieldpress.com
Key Personnel
Pres & Publr: Lesley Choyce
Founded: 1979
Fiction, books about the sea, books of Atlantic & Canada; nonfiction, books of literary travel.
Publishes in English.
ISBN Prefix(es): 978-0-919001; 978-1-895900; 978-1-897426; 978-1-988286
Number of titles published annually: 16 Print; 16 E-Book
Total Titles: 170 Print; 2 CD-ROM; 16 E-Book; 4 Audio
Imprints: Atlantic Classics Series
Distributed by Nimbus Publishing
U.S. Rep(s): Nimbus Publishing
Orders to: c/o Nimbus Publishing, 3660 Strawberry Hill St, Halifax, NS B3K 5A9 *Toll Free Tel:* 800-646-2879 *Toll Free Fax:* 888-253-3133 *E-mail:* customerservice@nimbus.ca *Web Site:* www.nimbus.ca
Shipping Address: c/o Nimbus Publishing, 3731 MacIntosh St, Halifax, NS B3K 5A5 *Tel:* 904-455-4286-orders only *Toll Free Tel:* 800-646-2879 *Toll Free Fax:* 888-253-3133 *E-mail:* customerservice@nimbus.ca *Web Site:* www.nimbus.ca
Membership(s): Atlantic Publishers Marketing Association

PrairieView Press
625 Seventh St, Gretna, MB R0G 0V0
Mailing Address: PO Box 460, Gretna, MB R0G 0V0
Tel: 204-327-6543 *Toll Free Tel:* 800-477-7377 *Toll Free Fax:* 866-480-0253
Web Site: prairieviewpress.com
Key Personnel
Owner & Pres: Chester Goossen
Secy: Darleen Loewen
Contact: Chad Goossen
Founded: 1968
Quality reading material for children & adults; songbooks. Over 2,000 titles in distribution, listed in catalog.
Publishes in English.
ISBN Prefix(es): 978-0-920035; 978-1-896199; 978-1-897080
Number of titles published annually: 36 Print
Total Titles: 1,450 Print
Branch Office(s)
PO Box 88, Neche, ND 58265-0088, United States

Les Presses de l'Université d'Ottawa, see University of Ottawa Press (Presses de l'Université d'Ottawa)

§Les Presses de l'Universite de Montreal
5450, chemin de la Cote-des-Neiges, bureau 100, Montreal, QC H3T 1Y6
Mailing Address: CP 6128, Centre-ville, Montreal, QC H3C 3J7
Tel: 514-343-6933 *Fax:* 514-343-2232
E-mail: pum@umontreal.ca
Web Site: www.pum.umontreal.ca
Key Personnel
Dir Gen: Patrick Poirier *E-mail:* poirierp@editionspum.ca
Founded: 1962
ISBN Prefix(es): 978-2-7606
Number of titles published annually: 40 Print; 80 E-Book
Foreign Rep(s): Patrimoine SPRL (Belgium, Luxembourg); Servidis SA (Switzerland); SODIS (France)
Distribution Center: Socadis, 420, rue Stinson, St-Laurent, QC *Tel:* 514-331-3300 *Toll Free Tel:* 800-361-2847 *Fax:* 514-745-3282 *Toll Free Fax:* 866-803-5422 *E-mail:* socinfo@socadis.com

Les Presses de l'Universite du Quebec
Division of Universite du Quebec
2875 blvd Laurier, Suite 450, Quebec, QC G1V 2M2
Tel: 418-657-4399 *Fax:* 418-657-2096
E-mail: puq@puq.ca
Web Site: www.puq.ca
Founded: 1969
University press.
Publishes in English, French.
ISBN Prefix(es): 978-2-7605; 978-0-7770; 978-2-920073
Number of titles published annually: 80 Print
Total Titles: 1,300 Print
Distributor for Figura; Imaginaire du Nord; Tele-Universite
Distribution Center: Prologue Inc, 1650, blvd Lionel-Bertrand, Boisbriand, QC J7H 1N7 *Toll Free Tel:* 800-363-2864 *Toll Free Fax:* 800-361-8088 *E-mail:* sac@prologue.ca *Web Site:* www.prologue.ca
Independent Publishers Group, 814 N Franklin St, Chicago, IL 60610, United States (English titles only) *Toll Free Tel:* 800-888-4741 *Fax:* 312-337-5985 *E-mail:* frontdesk@ipgbook.com *Web Site:* www.ipgbook.com
Patrimoine SPRL, Milcamps Ave 119 B, 1030 Brussels, Belgium *Tel:* (02) 7366847 *Fax:* (02) 7366847 *E-mail:* patrimoine@telenet.be
Sodis SARL, 128 Ave du Marechal de Lattre de Tassigny, 77400 Lagny-sur-Marne, France *Tel:* 01 60 07 82 99 *Fax:* 01 64 30 32 27 *E-mail:* portail@sodis.fr *Web Site:* www.sodis.fr
Servidis SA, Chemin des Chalets 7, 1279 Chavannes-de-Bogis, Switzerland *Tel:* (022) 940 95 32 *Fax:* (022) 960 95 77 *E-mail:* pgavillet@servidis.ch *Web Site:* www.servidis.ch

§Les Presses de l'Universite Laval
Division of Universite du Quebec
2180, Chemin Sainte-Foy, 1st fl, Quebec, QC G1V 0A6
Tel: 418-656-2803 *Fax:* 418-656-3305
E-mail: presses@pul.ulaval.ca
Web Site: www.pulaval.com
Key Personnel
Gen Dir & Ed: Denis Dion *E-mail:* denis.dion@pul.ulaval.ca
Gen Ed: Andre Baril *E-mail:* andr.baril@sympatico.ca
Ed: Andre Baril *E-mail:* andr.baril@sympatico.ca; Helene Cormier *E-mail:* helene.cormier@pul.ulaval.ca
Admin: Sylvie Hudon *E-mail:* sylvie.hudon@pul.ulaval.ca
Communs: Sylvie Servant *E-mail:* sylvie.servant@pul.ulaval.ca
Prodn: Jocelyne Naud *E-mail:* jocelyne.naud@pul.ulaval.ca
Dir Asst: Dominique Gingras *E-mail:* dominique.gingras@pul.ulaval.ca
Founded: 1950
Books in the humanities & social sciences with an emphasis on subjects of interest in Quebec & Canada, administration, economy.
Publishes in French.
ISBN Prefix(es): 978-2-7637; 978-0-7746
Number of titles published annually: 120 Print
Foreign Rights: Librairie du Quebec (France); Patrimoine SPRL (Belgium); Servidis (Switzerland)
Distribution Center: Prologue Inc, 1650, blvd Lionel-Bertrand, Boisbriand, QC J7H 1N7 (CN & US) *Tel:* 450-434-0306 *Toll Free Tel:* 800-363-2864 *E-mail:* prologue@prologue.ca *Web Site:* www.prologue.ca

Editions Prise de parole
109 Elm St, Suite 205, Sudbury, ON P3C 1T4
Mailing Address: CP 550, Sudbury, ON P3E 4R2
Tel: 705-675-6491 *Fax:* 705-673-1817

E-mail: info@prisedeparole.ca
Web Site: www.prisedeparole.ca
Key Personnel
Co-Exec Dir & Dir, Publg: Denise Truax
E-mail: dtruax@prisedeparole.ca
Co-Exec Dir & Dir, Mktg: Stephane Cormier
E-mail: scormier@prisedeparole.ca
Cont: Alain Mayotte E-mail: amayotte@
prisedeparole.ca
Founded: 1973
Poetry, novels, drama, textbooks, essays.
Publishes in French.
ISBN Prefix(es): 978-2-89423; 978-2-89744; 978-2-921573; 978-2-920814
Number of titles published annually: 18 Print
Total Titles: 386 Print; 545 Online; 211 E-Book
Distribution Center: Diffusion Dimedia, 1650, blvd Lionel-Bertrand, Boisbriand, QC J7H 1N7 Tel: 450-434-0306
Membership(s): Association nationale des editeurs de livres (ANEL); Regroupement des Editeurs Canadiens-Francais (RECF)

Productive Publications
380 Brooke Ave, Lower Level, North York, ON M5M 2L6
SAN: 117-1712
Tel: 416-483-0634 Toll Free Tel: 877-879-2669 (orders) Fax: 416-322-7434
E-mail: productivepublications@rogers.com
Web Site: www.productivepublications.ca
Key Personnel
Owner & Pres: Iain Williamson
Founded: 1985
Trade paperback books; business, finance, communications, finance, computers, management, marketing, taxation, personal finance, entrepreneurship, self-help.
Publishes in English.
ISBN Prefix(es): 978-0-920847; 978-1-896210; 978-1-55270
Number of titles published annually: 28 Print
Total Titles: 180 Print

§Les Publications du Quebec
1000, rte de l'Eqalise, Bureau 500, Quebec, QC G1V 3V9
Tel: 418-643-5150 Toll Free Tel: 800-463-2100 (Quebec province only) Fax: 418-643-6177 Toll Free Fax: 800-561-3479
E-mail: publicationsduquebec@cspq.gouv.qc.ca
Web Site: www.publicationsduquebec.gouv.qc.ca
Key Personnel
Dir: Sylvie Ferland
Founded: 1982
Government publications.
Publishes in English, French.
ISBN Prefix(es): 978-2-550; 978-2-551; 978-0-7754
Number of titles published annually: 200 Print; 20 Online
Total Titles: 4,000 Print; 100 Online

§QA International (QAI)
Division of Groupe Quebec Amerique
329 De la Commune W, 3rd fl, Montreal, QC H2Y 2E1
Tel: 514-499-3000 Fax: 514-499-3010
Web Site: www.qa-international.com
Key Personnel
Founder & CEO: Jacques Fortin
Dir, Busn Devt: Rossana Sommaruga
Founded: 1989
Create, develop & produce editorial content built around state-of-the-art computer images for publication in print & electronic media throughout the world.
Publishes in French.
ISBN Prefix(es): 978-2-7644
Number of titles published annually: 60 Print
Total Titles: 770 Print

Quattro Books Inc
12 Concord Ave, 2nd fl, Toronto, ON M6H 2P1
Tel: 647-748-7484
E-mail: info@quattrobooks.ca
Web Site: www.quattrobooks.ca
Key Personnel
Exec Dir & Publr: Luciano Iacobelli
E-mail: luciano@quattrobooks.ca
Assoc Publr: Sonia D'Agostino
Publishes in English.
ISBN Prefix(es): 978-0-9782806; 978-0-9810186; 978-1-926802
Number of titles published annually: 16 Print; 16 E-Book
Imprints: Fourfront Editions
Distribution Center: LitDistCo, 8300 Lawson Rd, Milton, ON L9T 0A4 E-mail: ordering@ litdistco.ca Web Site: www.litdistco.ca
Membership(s): Literary Press Group of Canada

Reader's Digest Association Canada ULC (Selection du Reader's Digest Canada SRI)
1100 Rene Levesque Blvd W, 8th fl, Suite 822, Montreal, QC H3B 5H5
Tel: 514-940-0751 Toll Free Tel: 888-459-3333 (cust serv) Fax: 514-940-3637
E-mail: erdcustserv@cdsfulfillment.com
Web Site: www.readersdigest.ca
Founded: 1943
Magazine subscriptions, fiction & general nonfiction books in condensed form.
Publishes in English, French.
ISBN Prefix(es): 978-0-89577; 978-0-88850; 978-0-276; 978-2-7098; 978-0-7621; 978-1-55475
Number of titles published annually: 12 Print
Total Titles: 12 Print
Warehouse: 3010 Walden Ave, Depew, NY 14043, United States
Membership(s): Canadian Marketing Association (CMA)

Red Deer Press Inc
Division of Fitzhenry & Whiteside Limited
195 Allstate Pkwy, Markham, ON L3R 4T8
Tel: 905-477-9700 Toll Free Tel: 800-387-9776 (orders)
E-mail: rdp@reddeerpress.com; bookinfo@ fitzhenry.ca
Web Site: www.reddeerpress.com
Key Personnel
Publr: Richard Dionne Tel: 800-387-9776 ext 248 E-mail: dionne@reddeerpress.com
Dir, Sales: Sonya Gilliss Tel: 800-387-9776 ext 250 E-mail: sonya.gilliss@fitzhenry.ca
Children's Ed: Peter Carver
Cust Serv: Judy Ghoura Tel: 800-387-9776 ext 225
Founded: 1975
Publishes in English.
ISBN Prefix(es): 978-0-88995
Number of titles published annually: 15 Print
Total Titles: 400 Print
Imprints: Robert J Sawyer Books
Distribution Center: Firefly Books Ltd, 50 Staples Ave, Unit 1, Richmond Hill, ON L4B 0A7 Tel: 416-499-8412 Toll Free Tel: 800-387-6192 Fax: 416-499-8313 Toll Free Fax: 800-450-0391 E-mail: service@fireflybooks.com Web Site: www.fireflybooks.com

Rocky Mountain Books Ltd (RMB)
Member of The Heritage Group
103-1075 Pendergast St, Victoria, BC V8V 0A1
Tel: 250-360-0829 Fax: 250-386-0829
Web Site: www.rmbooks.com
Key Personnel
Publr, Acqs, Foreign Rts, Sales & Mktg: Don Gorman E-mail: don@rmbooks.com
Art Dir: Chyla Cardinal E-mail: chyla@rmbooks.com
Sr Ed: Joe Wilderson E-mail: joe@rmbooks.com

Publr Asst, Admin & Publicity: Rick Wood
E-mail: rick@rmbooks.com
Founded: 1979
Regional publisher of books on outdoor activities, mountain literature & mountain biographies.
Publishes in English.
ISBN Prefix(es): 978-0-9690038; 978-0-921102; 978-1-894765; 978-1-897522; 978-1-926855; 978-1-927330; 978-1-77160
Number of titles published annually: 30 Print
Total Titles: 188 Print
Branch Office(s)
414 13 Ave NE, Calgary, AB T2E 1C2 (design & edit) Tel: 403-271-3145 Fax: 403-249-2968
Orders to: Heritage Group Distribution, 19272 96 Ave, Suite 8, Surrey, BC V4N 4C1 Tel: 604-881-7067 Toll Free Tel: 800-665-3302 Fax: 604-881-7068 Toll Free Fax: 800-566-3336 E-mail: orders@hgdistribution.com Web Site: www.hgdistribution.com
Distribution Center: Heritage Group Distribution, 19272 96 Ave, Suite 8, Surrey, BC V4N 4C1 Tel: 604-881-7067 Toll Free Tel: 800-665-3302 Fax: 604-881-7068 Toll Free Fax: 800-566-3336 E-mail: orders@hgdistribution.com Web Site: www.hgdistribution.com
Membership(s): Book Publishers Association of Alberta

Ronsdale Press Ltd
3350 W 21 Ave, Vancouver, BC V6S 1G7
SAN: 116-2454
Tel: 604-738-4688 Fax: 604-731-4548
E-mail: ronsdale@shaw.ca
Web Site: ronsdalepress.com
Key Personnel
Dir & Intl Rts: Ronald Hatch
Lib Sales Dir: Veronica Hatch
Founded: 1988
Literary press, children's, history, literary & regional. Specialize in Canadian authors.
Publishes in English.
ISBN Prefix(es): 978-0-921870; 978-1-55380
Number of titles published annually: 12 Print; 12 E-Book
Total Titles: 265 Print
Distribution Center: LitDistCo, 8300 Lawson Rd, Milton, ON L9T 0A4 (US only) Toll Free Tel: 800-591-6250 Toll Free Fax: 800-591-6251 Web Site: www.litdistco.ca
Raincoast Books, 2440 Viking Way, Richmond, BC V6V 1N2 Toll Free Tel: 800-663-5714 Toll Free Fax: 800-565-3770 E-mail: customerservice@raincoast.com Web Site: www.raincoast.com
Small Press Distribution, 1341 Seventh St, Berkeley, CA 94710-1409, United States Tel: 510-524-1668 Toll Free Tel: 800-869-7553 Fax: 510-524-0852 E-mail: spd@spdbooks.org Web Site: www.spdbooks.org
Baker & Taylor, 2550 W Tyvola Rd, Suite 300, Charlotte, NC 28217, United States Tel: 704-998-3100 Toll Free Tel: 800-775-1800 E-mail: btinfo@baker-taylor.com Web Site: www.baker-taylor.com
Ingram Content Group, One Ingram Blvd, La Vergne, TN 37086, United States Tel: 615-793-5000 E-mail: inquiry@ingramcontent.com Web Site: www.ingramcontent.com
Gazelle Book Services Ltd, White Cross Mills, Hightown, Lancaster, Lancs LA1 4XS, United Kingdom (UK & Europe) Tel: (01524) 528500 Fax: (01524) 528510 E-mail: sales@ gazellebookservices.co.uk Web Site: www. gazellebookservices.co.uk
Membership(s): Association of Book Publishers of British Columbia; Association of Canadian Publishers (ACP); Literary Press Group of Canada

Robert Rose Inc
120 Eglinton Ave E, Suite 800, Toronto, ON M4P 1E2

Tel: 416-322-6552 *Fax:* 416-322-6936
Web Site: www.robertrose.ca
Founded: 1995
Publishes in English.
ISBN Prefix(es): 978-1-896503; 978-0-7788
Number of titles published annually: 25 Print
Total Titles: 285 Print
Distributed by Firefly Books Ltd

§Royal Ontario Museum Press
100 Queen's Park, Toronto, ON M5S 2C6
Tel: 416-586-8000 *Fax:* 416-586-5642
E-mail: info@rom.on.ca
Web Site: www.rom.on.ca
Key Personnel
Dir & CEO: John Basseches
Founded: 1912
Scholarly & general books on art, archaeology &
sciences.
Publishes in English, French.
ISBN Prefix(es): 978-0-88854
Number of titles published annually: 8 Print
Total Titles: 100 Print
U.S. Rep(s): University of Toronto Press (NY)
Warehouse: University of Toronto Press, 5201
Dufferin St, Toronto, ON M3H 5T8, Con-
tact: Carol Trainor *Tel:* 416-667-7791 *Toll
Free Tel:* 800-565-9523 *Fax:* 416-667-7832
E-mail: utpbooks@utpress.utoronto.ca *Web
Site:* www.utpress.utoronto.ca
Distribution Center: University of Toronto Press,
5201 Dufferin St, Toronto, ON M3H 5T8, Con-
tact: Carol Trainor *Tel:* 416-667-7791 *Toll
Free Tel:* 800-565-9523 *Fax:* 416-667-7832
E-mail: utpbooks@utpress.utoronto.ca *Web
Site:* www.utpress.utoronto.ca

Guy Saint-Jean Editeur Inc
4490, rue Garand, Laval, QC H7L 5Z6
Tel: 450-663-1777
E-mail: info@saint-jeanediteur.com
Web Site: saint-jeanediteur.com
Key Personnel
Pres: Nicole Saint-Jean *E-mail:* nicole@saint-
jeanediteur.com
VP, Publg: Marie-Claire Saint-Jean
E-mail: mclaire@saint-jeanediteur.com
Mng Dir: Jean Pare *E-mail:* jean.pare@saint-
jeanediteur.com
Prodn/Opers Dir: Jacques Frechette
E-mail: jacques@saint-jeanediteur.com
Founded: 1981
Publishes in English, French.
ISBN Prefix(es): 978-2-920340; 978-2-89455
Number of titles published annually: 30 Print; 10
E-Book
Total Titles: 550 Print
Imprints: Green Frog Publishing
Foreign Office(s): Saint-Jean Editeur (France), 30-
32 rue de Lappe, 75011 Paris, France, Contact:
Christian Richard *Tel:* 01 39 76 99 43 *Fax:* 01
39 76 21 78 *E-mail:* gsj.editeur@free.fr
U.S. Publishers Represented: CDS
Foreign Rep(s): INT Press (Australia, New
Zealand); Christian Richard (Europe)
Foreign Rights: Elizabeth Brayne (Europe)
Distribution Center: Prologue, 1650, blvd Lionel-
Bertrand, Boisbriand, QC J7H 1N7 *Tel:* 450-
434-0306 *Toll Free Tel:* 800-363-2864 *Web
Site:* www.prologue.ca
Librairie du Quebec, 30, rue Gay Lussac, 75005
Paris, France *Tel:* 01 43 54 49 02 *Fax:* 01 43
54 39 15 *E-mail:* libraires@librairieduquebec.fr
Servidis SA, Chemin des Chalets 7, 1279
Chavannes-de-Bogis, Switzerland *Tel:* (022)
960 95 23 *Fax:* (022) 960 95 77 *Web
Site:* www.servidis.ch
Membership(s): Association nationale des editeurs
de livres (ANEL)

§Sara Jordan Publishing
Division of Jordan Music Productions Inc

RPO Lakeport Box 28105, St Catharines, ON
L2N 7P8
Tel: 905-938-5050 *Toll Free Tel:* 800-567-7733
Fax: 905-938-9970 *Toll Free Fax:* 800-229-
3855
Web Site: www.sara-jordan.com
Key Personnel
Pres: Sara Jordan
Founded: 1990
Publish educational resources.
Publishes in English, French.
ISBN Prefix(es): 978-1-895523; 978-1-894262;
978-1-55386
Number of titles published annually: 6 Print; 2
Audio
Total Titles: 100 Print; 60 Audio
Distribution Center: Gazelle Book Services
Ltd, White Cross Mills, Hightown, Lancaster,
Lancs LA1 4XS, United Kingdom *Tel:* (01524)
528500 *Fax:* (01524) 528510 *E-mail:* sales@
gazellebookservices.co.uk *Web Site:* www.
gazellebookservices.co.uk
Membership(s): Association of Canadian Publish-
ers (ACP)

Scholastic Canada Ltd
Subsidiary of Scholastic Inc
604 King St W, Toronto, ON M5V 1E1
SAN: 115-5164
Tel: 905-887-7323 *Toll Free Tel:* 800-268-3860
(CN) *Toll Free Fax:* 866-387-4944
E-mail: custserve@scholastic.ca
Web Site: www.scholastic.ca
Key Personnel
Pres, Fin, Opers & Admin: Anne Browne
Tel: 905-887-7323 ext 4396 *E-mail:* abrowne@
scholastic.ca
Pres, Mktg & Publg: Nancy Pearson *Tel:* 416-
915-3515 *E-mail:* npearson@scholastic.ca
VP, French Div: Chantale Gravel Lalonde
Tel: 416-915-3510 *E-mail:* clalonde@
scholastic.ca
VP, Publg: Diane Kerner *Tel:* 416-915-3523
E-mail: dkerner@scholastic.ca
VP, Reading Clubs: Vicki Pasternak *Tel:* 416-915-
3516 *E-mail:* vpasternak@scholastic.ca
VP, Trade: Kathy Goncharenko *Tel:* 416-915-3517
E-mail: kgoncharenko@scholastic.ca
Rts & Contracts: Maral Maclagan *Tel:* 416-915-
3524 *E-mail:* mmaclagan@scholastic.ca
Founded: 1957
Publish & distribute children's books & educa-
tional materials in both official languages.
Publishes in English, French.
ISBN Prefix(es): 978-0-590; 978-0-439; 978-0-
7791; 978-1-55268; 978-0-545; 978-1-4431;
978-1-338
Imprints: Les Editions Scholastic; North Winds
Press; Scholastic Canada
Divisions: Scholastic Book Fairs Canada Inc
Branch Office(s)
175 Hillmount Rd, Markham, ON L6C 1Z7
Distributor for Blue Sky Press (exclusive in CN);
Cartwheel Books (exclusive in CN); Chicken
House (exclusive in CN); Children's Press (ex-
clusive in CN); Franklin Watts (US) (exclusive
in CN); Grolier (exclusive in CN); Klutz (ex-
clusive in CN); Arthur A Levine Books (ex-
clusive in CN); Orchard Books (exclusive in
CN); Scholastic en Espanol (exclusive in CN);
Scholastic Graphix (exclusive in CN); Scholas-
tic Nonfiction (exclusive in CN); Scholastic
Paperbacks (exclusive in CN); Scholastic Press
(exclusive in CN); Scholastic Reference (exclusive in CN)
U.S. Publishers Represented: Scholastic Inc
U.S. Rep(s): Scholastic Inc
Foreign Rights: Akcali Copyright Agency (Begum Ayfer) (Turkey); Bardon-Chinese Media Agency (Electra Chang & Shirley Vivi
Chang) (Mainland China); Bardon-Chinese
Media Agency (Cynthia Chang) (Taiwan); San-
dra Bruna Agencia Literaria (Sandra Bruna)

(Spain); Graal Sp zoo (Tomasz Berezinski)
(Poland); JLM Literary Agency (Nelly, Tatiana & John Moukakos) (Greece); Simona
Kessler Agency (Adriana Marina) (Romania); Maxima Creative Agency (Santo Manurung) (Indonesia); Nika Literary Agency (Vania Kadiyska) (Bulgaria); Andrew Nurnberg
Agency (Olga Lutova) (Russia); Seibel Publishing Services Ltd (Patricia Seibel) (Brazil);
Shinwon Agency Co (Jihyun Hwang) (Korea); Tuttle-Mori Agency Inc (Solan Natsume)
(Japan)

§Seal Books
Imprint of Penguin Random House Canada
320 Front St W, Suite 1400, Toronto, ON M5V
3B6
SAN: 201-3975
Tel: 416-364-4449 *Toll Free Tel:* 888-523-9292
(order desk) *Fax:* 416-598-7764
Web Site: www.penguinrandomhouse.ca
Key Personnel
CEO, PRHC: Kristin Cochrane
CFO, PRHC: Barry Gallant
Chief Strategy & Opers Offr, PRHC: Robert
Wheaton
VP & Dir, Mktg Strategy & Assoc Publr, PRHC:
Scott Sellers
SVP & Dir, Prodn: Janine Laporte
Deputy Dir, Prodn: Carla Kean
Founded: 1977
No unsol mss; prefer queries in advance from po-
tential authors.
Publishes in English.
Number of titles published annually: 18 Print
Membership(s): Canadian Publishers' Council

§Second Story Press
20 Maud St, Suite 401, Toronto, ON M5V 2M5
Tel: 416-537-7850 *Fax:* 416-537-0588
E-mail: info@secondstorypress.ca
Web Site: secondstorypress.ca
Key Personnel
Publr, Owner & Pres: Margie Wolfe
Gen Mgr: Phuong Truong
Prodn Mgr: Melissa Kaita
Mktg & Promos Mgr: Emma Rodgers
Mktg & Promos Coord: Allie Chenoweth
Founded: 1988
Feminist-inspired books for adults & young read-
ers.
Publishes in English.
ISBN Prefix(es): 978-0-929005; 978-1-896764;
978-1-897187; 978-0-921299
Number of titles published annually: 14 Print
Total Titles: 108 Print
Distributor for The Azrieli Foundation; The Book
Publishing Co; Desputeaux & Aubin (aka The
Caillou Books) (English-speaking CN)
U.S. Rep(s): Orca Books (children's books)
Orders to: University of Toronto Press, 5201
Dufferin St, North York, ON M3H 5T8
Tel: 416-667-7791 *Toll Free Tel:* 800-565-
9523 *Fax:* 416-667-7832 *Toll Free Fax:* 800-
221-9985; Orca Book Publishers, PO Box
468, Custer, WA 98240-0468, United States
(US, children's books) *Toll Free Tel:* 800-210-
5277 *Fax:* 250-380-1892 *Web Site:* www.us.
orcabook.com; Gazelle Book Services Ltd,
White Cross Mills, Hightown, Lancaster,
Lancs LA1 4XS, United Kingdom *Tel:* (01524)
528500 *Fax:* (01524) 528510 *E-mail:* sales@
gazellebookservices.co.uk *Web Site:* www.
gazellebookservices.co.uk
Shipping Address: University of Toronto Press,
5201 Dufferin St, North York, ON M3H 5T8
Tel: 416-667-7791 *Toll Free Tel:* 800-565-9523
Fax: 416-667-7832 *Toll Free Fax:* 800-221-
9985
Distribution Center: University of Toronto Press,
5201 Dufferin St, North York, ON M3H 5T8

Tel: 416-667-7791 *Toll Free Tel:* 800-565-9523
Fax: 416-667-7832 *Toll Free Fax:* 800-221-9985

Selection du Reader's Digest Canada SRI, see
Reader's Digest Association Canada ULC
(Selection du Reader's Digest Canada SRI)

Self-Counsel Press, see International
Self-Counsel Press Ltd

J Gordon Shillingford Publishing Inc
PO Box 86, RPO Corydon Ave, Winnipeg, MB
R3M 3S3
Tel: 204-779-6967
E-mail: jgshill2@mymts.net
Web Site: www.jgshillingford.com
Key Personnel
Pres & Publr: Gordon Shillingford
Founded: 1992
Primarily a literary publisher of nonfiction, the-
ater, poetry & social history. Publish works of
Canadian citizens only.
Publishes in English.
ISBN Prefix(es): 978-0-9689709; 978-0-920486;
978-1-896239; 978-0-9697261; 978-1-897289;
978-1-927922
Number of titles published annually: 14 Print
Total Titles: 272 Print
Imprints: The Muses' Co; Scirocco Drama; Wat-
son & Dwyer
Distribution Center: University of Toronto Press,
5210 Dufferin St, Toronto, ON M3H 5T8
Tel: 416-667-7791 *Toll Free Tel:* 800-565-9523
Fax: 416-667-7856 *Toll Free Fax:* 800-221-
9985 *E-mail:* utpbooks@utpress.utoronto.ca
University of Toronto Press, 2250 Military
Rd, Tonawanda, NY 14150, United States
Tel: 416-667-7791 *Toll Free Tel:* 800-565-9523
Fax: 416-667-7832 *Toll Free Fax:* 800-221-
9985 *E-mail:* utpbooks@utpress.utoronto.ca
Membership(s): Association of Canadian Pub-
lishers (ACP); Association of Manitoba Book
Publishers (AMBP); Literary Press Group

Signature Editions
PO Box 206, RPO Corydon, Winnipeg, MB R3M
3S7
Tel: 204-779-7803
E-mail: submissions@signature-editions.com;
orders@signature-editions.com
Web Site: www.signature-editions.com
Key Personnel
Publr: Karen Haughian *E-mail:* khaughian@
signature-editions.com
Mystery Ed: Doug Whiteway
Poetry Ed: Garry Thomas Morse
Founded: 1986 (as Nuage Editions)
Literary publisher which publishes Canadian au-
thors in the genres of fiction, nonfiction, poetry
& drama.
Publishes in English.
ISBN Prefix(es): 978-0-921833; 978-1-897109;
978-1-927426; 978-1-773240
Number of titles published annually: 10 Print; 5
E-Book
Total Titles: 170 Print; 65 E-Book; 10 Audio
Distributor for Cyclops Press
Foreign Rep(s): The Literary Press Group of
Canada (Tan Light) (USA)
Orders to: University of Toronto Press (UTP),
5201 Dufferin St, North York, ON M3H 5T8
Tel: 416-667-7791 *Toll Free Tel:* 800-565-9523
Fax: 416-667-7832 *Toll Free Fax:* 800-221-
9985 *E-mail:* utpbooks@utpress.utoronto.ca;
University of Toronto Press (UTP), 2250 Mili-
tary Rd, Tonawanda, NY 14150, United States
Tel: 416-667-7791 *Toll Free Tel:* 800-565-9523
Fax: 416-667-7832 *Toll Free Fax:* 800-221-
9985 *E-mail:* utpbooks@utpress.utoronto.ca
Returns: University of Toronto Press (UTP),
5201 Dufferin St, North York, ON M3H 5T8

Tel: 416-667-7791 *Toll Free Tel:* 800-565-9523
Fax: 416-667-7832 *Toll Free Fax:* 800-221-
9985 *E-mail:* utpbooks@utpress.utoronto.ca
Shipping Address: University of Toronto Press
(UTP), 5201 Dufferin St, North York, ON
M3H 5T8 *Tel:* 416-667-7791 *Toll Free
Tel:* 800-565-9523 *Fax:* 416-667-7832 *Toll Free
Fax:* 800-221-9985 *E-mail:* utpbooks@utpress.
utoronto.ca
Distribution Center: University of Toronto
Press (UTP), 5201 Dufferin St, North York,
ON M3H 5T8 *Tel:* 416-667-7791 *Toll Free
Tel:* 800-565-9523 *Fax:* 416-667-7832 *Toll Free
Fax:* 800-221-9985 *E-mail:* utpbooks@utpress.
utoronto.ca
University of Toronto Press (UTP), 2250 Mili-
tary Rd, Tonawanda, NY 14150, United States
Tel: 416-667-7791 *Toll Free Tel:* 800-565-9523
Fax: 416-667-7832 *Toll Free Fax:* 800-221-
9985 *E-mail:* utpbooks@utpress.utoronto.ca
Membership(s): Association of Canadian Pub-
lishers (ACP); Association of Manitoba Book
Publishers (AMBP); Literary Press Group of
Canada

Simon & Pierre Publishing Co Ltd
Imprint of The Dundurn Group
3 Church St, Suite 500, Toronto, ON M5E 1M2
Tel: 416-214-5544
E-mail: info@dundurn.com
Web Site: www.dundurn.com
Key Personnel
Pres & Publr: J Kirk Howard *E-mail:* khoward@
dundurn.com
Founded: 1991
Fiction.
Publishes in English.
ISBN Prefix(es): 978-0-9690454; 978-0-88924
Number of titles published annually: 80 Print
Total Titles: 133 Print
Distributed by Dundurn Press
Distribution Center: University of Toronto Press,
5201 Dufferin St, Toronto, ON M3H 5T8
Tel: 416-667-7791 *Toll Free Tel:* 800-565-9523
Fax: 416-667-7832 *Toll Free Fax:* 800-221-
9985 *E-mail:* utpbooks@utpress.utoronto.ca
Web Site: www.utpress.utoronto.ca
Ingram Publisher Services, PO Box 3006,
La Vergne, TN 37086-1986, United States
Toll Free Tel: 855-802-8228 *Toll Free
Fax:* 800-838-1149 *E-mail:* customer.service@
ingrampublisherservices.com *Web Site:* www.
ingrampublisherservices.com
Ingram Publisher Services, Chapter House,
Pitfield, Kiln Farm, Milton Keynes MK11
3LW, United Kingdom (UK & Europe)
Tel: 0800 136-0600 *E-mail:* ipsuksupport@
ingramcontent.com

Simon & Schuster Canada
Subsidiary of Simon & Schuster, Inc
166 King St E, Suite 300, Toronto, ON M5A 1J3
Tel: 647-427-8882 *Toll Free Tel:* 800-387-0446;
800-268-3216 (orders) *Fax:* 647-430-9446
Toll Free Tel: 888-849-8151 (orders)
E-mail: info@simonandschuster.ca
Web Site: www.simonandschuster.ca
Key Personnel
Pres & Publr: Kevin Hanson *E-mail:* kevin.
hanson@simonandschuster.ca
VP, Sales & Mktg: David Millar *E-mail:* david.
millar@simonandschuster.ca
VP, Mktg & Publicity: Felicia Quon
E-mail: felicia.quon@simonandschuster.ca
VP, Edit Dir: Nita Pronovost *E-mail:* nita.
pronovost@simonandschuster.ca
Dir, Busn Aff: Kien Vuong *E-mail:* kien.vuong@
simonandschuster.ca
Dir, Publicity & Canadian Sales: Adria Iwasutiak
E-mail: adria.iwasutiak@simonandschuster.ca
Assoc Dir, Publicity: Rita Silva *E-mail:* rita.
silva@simonandschuster.ca

Sr Ed: Laurie Grassi *E-mail:* laurie.grassi@
simonandschuster.ca; Sarah St Pierre
E-mail: sarah.stpierre@simonandschuster.
ca; Justin Stoller *E-mail:* justin.stoller@
simonandschuster.ca
Publishes in English.
Distributor for Andrews McMeel Publishing LLC;
Baen Books; Baseball America; Black Library;
Blue Heeler Books; BOOM! Studios; Cardoza
Publishing; Cernunnos Publishing; Chicken
Soup for the Soul; Cider Mill Press Book Pub-
lishers LLC; Downtown Books; Gallup Press;
Galvanized Media; Games Workshop; Good
Books; Hazelden Publishing; Hooked on Phon-
ics; Insight Editions; Juniper Press; Kaplan
Publishing; KinFolk; John Locke Publishing;
Merck; NorthSouth Books; Oni Press; Open
Road Press; Permuted Press; Piggyback Press;
Pikachu Press; Post Hill Press; Printer's Row
Publishing Group; Reader's Digest; Rebellion;
Regnery Publishing; Restless Books; Ripley's
Publishing; Simon & Schuster; SimonUK; Sky-
horse Publishing; Studio Fun International; To
the Stars; Ubisoft Entertainment; Uncrate; Vic-
tory Belt Publishing; Viz; Weldon Owen Pub-
lishing; Wisdom Publications; World Almanac;
Zaffre Books

Simply Read Books
501-5525 West Blvd, Vancouver, BC V6M 3W6
Tel: 604-727-2960
E-mail: go@simplyreadbooks.com
Web Site: www.simplyreadbooks.com
Founded: 2001
Our approach to illustrated children's books follows the finest publishing tradition & spirit
with inspired content, extraordinary artwork,
outstanding graphic design form & quality production. We introduce contemporary books
with a modern appeal & fresh outlook & offer a careful selection of timeless stories that
link the past with the present. We specialize
in high-quality, unique picture books & fiction. Before submitting, please browse our web
site, bookstores & libraries to look at & read
what we publish. This will give you an idea of
whether or not your story or illustrations would
fit with our list.
Publishes in English, French.
ISBN Prefix(es): 978-1-894965; 978-0-9688768;
978-1-897476; 978-1-927018
Number of titles published annually: 20 Print
Total Titles: 200 Print
Sales Office(s): Ingram Content Group, One Ingram Blvd, La Vergne, TN 37086, United
States *Tel:* 615-793-5000 *E-mail:* inquiry@
ingramcontent.com *Web Site:* www.
ingramcontent.com
Orders to: Ingram Content Group, One In-
gram Blvd, La Vergne, TN 37086, United
States *Tel:* 615-793-5000 *E-mail:* inquiry@
ingramcontent.com *Web Site:* www.
ingramcontent.com
Returns: Ingram Publisher Services, 1210 Ingram
Dr, Chambersburg, PA 17202, United States
Tel: 717-262-4860 *E-mail:* customerservice@
ingrampublisherservices.com
Warehouse: Ingram Content Group, One In-
gram Blvd, La Vergne, TN 37086, United
States *Tel:* 615-793-5000 *E-mail:* inquiry@
ingramcontent.com *Web Site:* www.
ingramcontent.com
Distribution Center: Ingram Content Group, One
Ingram Blvd, La Vergne, TN 37086, United
States *Tel:* 615-793-5000 *E-mail:* inquiry@
ingramcontent.com *Web Site:* www.
ingramcontent.com
Membership(s): Association for Canadian Pub-
lishers in the US; Independent Book Publishers
Association (IBPA)

Gordon Soules Book Publishers Ltd
2372 Haywood Ave, West Vancouver, BC V7V
1X7
SAN: 115-0987
Tel: 604-922-6588 *Fax:* 604-922-6574
E-mail: books@gordonsoules.com
Web Site: www.gordonsoules.com
Key Personnel
Pres: Gordon Soules
Founded: 1965
Publishers & distributors of high quality trade
books.
Publishes in English.
ISBN Prefix(es): 978-0-919574; 978-1-894661;
978-0-920045
Number of titles published annually: 4 Print
Total Titles: 65 Print

Summerthought Publishing
PO Box 2309, Banff, AB T1L 1C1
Tel: 403-762-0535 *Fax:* 403-762-3095
Toll Free Fax: 800-762-3095 (orders)
E-mail: info@summerthought.com; sales@
summerthought.com
Web Site: summerthought.com
Key Personnel
Co-Owner & Publr: Andrew Hempstead
Sales, Mktg & Opers: Dianne Melton
E-mail: dianne@summerthought.com
Founded: 1971
Publisher of Canadian Rockies nonfiction books.
Publishes in English.
ISBN Prefix(es): 978-0-9782375; 978-0-9699732;
978-0-9811491; 978-0-919934; 978-1-926983
Number of titles published annually: 3 Print; 3 E-
Book
Total Titles: 30 Print; 9 E-Book
Imprints: EJH Literary Enterprises
Foreign Rep(s): Cordee (UK); Freytag & Berndt
(Europe)

Synaxis Press
37323 Hawkins Rd, Dewdney, BC V0M 1H0
Tel: 604-826-9336
E-mail: synaxis@new-ostrog.org
Web Site: synaxispress.ca
Key Personnel
Illus: Vasili Novakshonoff
Ed: Archbishop Lazar Puhalo
Founded: 1972
Theology for the Orthodox church & children's
books.
Publishes in English, French.
ISBN Prefix(es): 978-0-919672
Number of titles published annually: 6 Print
Total Titles: 90 Print
Distributed by Light & Life Publishing Co

TCP Press
Imprint of The Communication Project
20200 Marsh Hill Rd, Uxbridge, ON L9P 1R3
Tel: 905-852-3777 *Toll Free Tel:* 800-772-7765
E-mail: tcp@tcpnow.com
Web Site: www.tcppress.com
Key Personnel
Dir, Publg: Brian Puppa
Founded: 1984
Trade & educational books for both children &
adults.
Publishes in English, French.
ISBN Prefix(es): 978-1-896232
Number of titles published annually: 4 Print; 1
CD-ROM; 5 E-Book; 1 Audio
Total Titles: 26 Print; 3 CD-ROM; 6 E-Book; 3
Audio
Membership(s): Independent Publishers Associa-
tion

Tecumseh Press, see Borealis Press Ltd

Theytus Books Ltd
Subsidiary of Okanagan Indian Educational Re-
sources Society
154 Enowkin Trail, RR 2, Site 50, Comp 8, Pen-
ticton, BC V2A 6J7
SAN: 115-1517
Tel: 250-493-7181 *Fax:* 250-493-5302
E-mail: order@theytus.com; marketing@theytus.
com
Web Site: www.theytus.com
Key Personnel
Publr: Greg Younging *Tel:* 250-493-7181 ext 201
Sales & Mktg: Ann Doyon
Founded: 1980
Native history, culture, politics, education & liter-
ature.
Publishes in English, French.
ISBN Prefix(es): 978-0-919441; 978-1-894778
Number of titles published annually: 4 Print
Total Titles: 83 Print; 4 CD-ROM
Distribution Center: Sandhill Book Marketing,
Mill Crook Industrial Park, Unit 4, 3308 Ap-
paloosa Rd, Kelowna, BC V1V 2G9 (AB &
BC), Contact: Nancy Wise *Tel:* 250-491-1446
Toll Free Tel: 800-667-3848 *Fax:* 250-491-4066
E-mail: info@sandhillbooks.com
University of Toronto Press, 5201 Dufferin St,
North York, ON M3H 5T8 (CN exc AB & BC)
Tel: 416-667-7791 *Toll Free Tel:* 800-565-9523
Fax: 416-667-7832 *Web Site:* www.utpress.
utoronto.ca
Membership(s): Association of Canadian Publish-
ers (ACP)

Thistledown Press
410 Second Ave, Saskatoon, SK S7K 2C3
SAN: 115-1061
Tel: 306-244-1722 *Fax:* 306-244-1762
E-mail: tdpress@thistledownpress.com;
editorial@thistledownpress.com; marketing@
thistledownpress.com
Web Site: www.thistledownpress.com
Key Personnel
Owner & Publr: Allan Forrie
Publg & Prodn Mgr: Jackie Forrie
Sales, Fulfillment, Promos & Edit: Nicole Hal-
doupis
Founded: 1975
Poetry, fiction & nonfiction by Canadian authors;
Irish poetry; fiction for young adults.
Publishes in English.
ISBN Prefix(es): 978-0-920066; 978-0-920633;
978-1-895449; 978-1-894345; 978-1-897235
Number of titles published annually: 14 Print
Total Titles: 250 Print
U.S. Rep(s): Amazon.com; University of Toronto
Press
Distribution Center: University of Toronto
Press, 5201 Dufferin St, Toronto, ON M3H
5T8 *Tel:* 416-667-7791 *Toll Free Tel:* 800-
565-9523 (CN & US) *Fax:* 416-667-7832
Toll Free Fax: 800-221-9985 (CN & US)
E-mail: utpbooks@utpress.utoronto.ca *Web
Site:* www.utpress.utoronto.ca

Thompson Educational Publishing Inc
20 Ripley Ave, Toronto, ON M6S 3N9
Tel: 416-766-2763 (admin & orders)
Toll Free Tel: 877-366-2763 *Fax:* 416-766-0398
(admin & orders)
E-mail: info@thompsonbooks.com
Web Site: www.thompsonbooks.com
Key Personnel
Pres: Keith Thompson
VP, Teacher & Student Success: Faye Thompson
Busn Dir: Rowan Thompson
Founded: 1989
High school, college & university textbooks.
Publishes in English.
ISBN Prefix(es): 978-1-55077; 978-0-921332
Number of titles published annually: 6 Print
Total Titles: 170 Print

Distribution Center: University of Toronto Press
Distribution, 5201 Dufferin St, Toronto, ON
M3H 5T8 (CN orders, higher educ) *Toll Free
Tel:* 800-565-9523 *Toll Free Fax:* 800-221-
9985 *E-mail:* utpbooks@utpress.utoronto.ca
Web Site: www.utpress.utoronto.ca
University of Toronto Press Distribution, 2250
Military Rd, Tonawanda, NY 14150, United
States (US orders, higher educ) *Toll Free
Tel:* 800-565-9523 *Toll Free Fax:* 800-221-
9985 *E-mail:* utpbooks@utpress.utoronto.ca
Web Site: utpress.utoronto.ca
Membership(s): Association of Canadian Pub-
lishers (ACP); Ontario Business Educator's
Association (OBEA); Organization of Book
Publishers of Ontario (OBPO)

TouchWood Editions
Member of The Heritage Group
103-1075 Pendergast St, Victoria, BC V8V 0A1
Tel: 250-360-0829 *Fax:* 250-386-0829
E-mail: info@touchwoodeditions.com
Web Site: www.touchwoodeditions.com
Key Personnel
Publr: Taryn Boyd *E-mail:* taryn@
touchwoodeditions.com
Founded: 1985
Publishes in English.
ISBN Prefix(es): 978-1-894898; 978-1-926741;
978-1-926971; 978-0-920663; 978-1-927129;
978-1-77151
Number of titles published annually: 12 Print; 18
E-Book
Total Titles: 224 Print; 170 E-Book
Imprints: Brindle & Glass
Orders to: Heritage Group Distribution, 19272-
96 Ave, Suite 8, Surrey, BC V4N 4C1
Tel: 604-881-7067 *Toll Free Tel:* 800-665-3302
Fax: 604-881-7068 *Toll Free Fax:* 800-566-
3336 *E-mail:* orders@hgdistribution.com *Web
Site:* www.hgdistribution.com
Returns: Heritage Group Distribution, 19272-
96 Ave, Suite 8, Surrey, BC V4N 4C1
Tel: 604-881-7067 *Toll Free Tel:* 800-665-3302
Fax: 604-881-7068 *Toll Free Fax:* 800-566-
3336 *E-mail:* orders@hgdistribution.com *Web
Site:* www.hgdistribution.com
Shipping Address: Heritage Group Distribution,
19272-96 Ave, Suite 8, Surrey, BC V4N 4C1
Tel: 604-881-7067 *Toll Free Tel:* 800-665-3302
Fax: 604-881-7068 *Toll Free Fax:* 800-566-
3336 *E-mail:* orders@hgdistribution.com *Web
Site:* www.hgdistribution.com
Warehouse: Heritage Group Distribution,
19272-96 Ave, Suite 8, Surrey, BC V4N 4C1
Tel: 604-881-7067 *Toll Free Tel:* 800-665-3302
Fax: 604-881-7068 *Toll Free Fax:* 800-566-
3336 *E-mail:* orders@hgdistribution.com *Web
Site:* www.hgdistribution.com
Distribution Center: Heritage Group Distribution,
19272-96 Ave, Suite 8, Surrey, BC V4N 4C1
Tel: 604-881-7067 *Toll Free Tel:* 800-665-3302
Fax: 604-881-7068 *Toll Free Fax:* 800-566-
3336 *E-mail:* orders@hgdistribution.com *Web
Site:* www.hgdistribution.com
Membership(s): Association of Book Publishers
of British Columbia; Association of Canadian
Publishers (ACP)
See separate listing for:
Brindle & Glass Publishing Ltd

Townson Publishing Co Ltd
PO Box 1404, Sta A, Vancouver, BC V6C 2P7
Tel: 604-886-0594
E-mail: admin@gpub.com; rights@gpub.ca
Web Site: generalpublishing.com
Key Personnel
Chmn: Donald Townson
Ed & Rts: Jack House
Founded: 1977
Publisher of general trade books.
Publishes in English, French.
ISBN Prefix(es): 978-0-920822

Number of titles published annually: 6 Print; 6 E-Book

Total Titles: 16 Print; 6 E-Book

Imprints: Townson Publishing

Subsidiaries: Associated Merchandisers Inc (USA)

Branch Office(s)

700 Harrison Ave, Unit 129, Blaine, WA 98231-0129, United States

U.S. Rep(s): K E Russell

Foreign Rep(s): General Merchandisers Inc (UK, USA); Wah K Lee (China, Singapore, Taiwan)

Tradewind Books
202-1807 Maritime Mews, Vancouver, BC V6H 3W7

Tel: 604-662-4405

E-mail: tradewindbooks@yahoo.com; tradewindbooks@gmail.com

Web Site: www.tradewindbooks.com

Key Personnel

Owner & Publr: Michael Katz

Art Dir & Co-Publr: Carol Frank

Ed: Kim Aippersbach

Copy-Ed: Viktoria Cseh

Founded: 1996

Children's picture books, chapter books & young adults novels.

Publishes in English.

ISBN Prefix(es): 978-1-896580; 978-1-926890

Number of titles published annually: 8 Print

Total Titles: 112 Print

Distributed by Fitzhenry & Whiteside (CN); Orca Book Publishers (US)

U.S. Rep(s): Orca Books

Foreign Rep(s): Turnaround Publisher Services Ltd (UK)

Distribution Center: Turnaround Publisher Services Ltd, Olympia Trading Estate, Unit 3, Coburg Rd, Wood Green, London N22 6TZ, United Kingdom *Tel:* (020) 8829 3000 *Fax:* (020) 8881 5088 *E-mail:* enquirie@turnaround-uk.com

Membership(s): Association of Book Publishers of British Columbia; Association of Canadian Publishers (ACP)

§Tralco-Lingo Fun
PO Box 79008, RPO Garth, Hamilton, ON L9C 7N6

Tel: 905-575-5717 *Toll Free Tel:* 888-487-2526

E-mail: sales@tralco.com

Web Site: www.tralco.com

Key Personnel

Owner & Pres: Karen Traynor *E-mail:* karen@tralco.com

Founded: 1982

Publisher & distributor of second language educational materials.

Publishes in French.

ISBN Prefix(es): 978-0-921376; 978-1-55409

Number of titles published annually: 10 Print; 12 CD-ROM

Total Titles: 300 Print

Branch Office(s)

3909 Witmer Rd, No 856, Niagara Falls, NY 14305, United States

Distributor for Languages for Kids

Membership(s): Education Market Association

Tundra Books
Imprint of Penguin Random House Canada

320 Front St W, Suite 1400, Toronto, ON M5V 3B6

SAN: 115-5415

Tel: 416-364-4449 *Toll Free Tel:* 888-523-9292 (orders); 800-588-1074 *Fax:* 416-598-7764 *Toll Free Fax:* 888-562-9924 (orders)

E-mail: tundra@mcclelland.com

Web Site: tundrabooks.wordpress.com

Key Personnel

Publr: Tara Walker *Tel:* 416-364-4449 ext 813951

Founded: 1967

Children's books/

Penguin Random House Canada & its publishing entities are not accepting unsol submissions, proposals, mss, or submission queries via e-mail at this time.

Publishes in English, French.

Number of titles published annually: 50 Print

Total Titles: 350 Print

Branch Office(s)

Tundra Books of Northern New York, PO Box 1030, Plattsburgh, NY 12901, United States

Distributed by Everybody's Books CC (South Africa); Forrester Books NZ Ltd (New Zealand); El Hombre de la Mancha (Costa Rica & Panama); El Hormiguero (Guatemala)

U.S. Publishers Represented: Tundra Books of Northern New York

U.S. Rep(s): Jack Eichkorn & Associates Inc; R&R Book Co; Southern Territory Associates Inc

Foreign Rights: Cooke Agency International

Orders to: Penguin Random House Canada, 6971 Columbus Rd, Mississauga, ON L5T 1K1; Random House Inc - Distribution Center, 400 Hahn Rd, Westminster, MD 21157, United States *Toll Free Tel:* 800-726-0600; 800-733-3000 *Toll Free Fax:* 800-659-2436

Returns: Random House Inc, 1019 N State Rd 47, Crawfordsville, IN 47933, United States

Warehouse: Random House Inc - Distribution Center, 400 Hahn Rd, Westminster, MD 21157, United States *Toll Free Tel:* 800-726-0600 *Toll Free Fax:* 800-659-2436

Membership(s): American Booksellers Association (ABA); American Library Association (ALA); Association of Booksellers for Children; International Board on Books for Young People (IBBY)

Turnstone Press
Artspace Bldg, 206-100 Arthur St, Winnipeg, MB R3B 1H3

SAN: 115-1096

Tel: 204-947-1555 *Toll Free Tel:* 888-363-7718 *Fax:* 204-942-1556

E-mail: info@turnstonepress.com

Web Site: www.turnstonepress.com

Key Personnel

Assoc Publr & Intl Rts: Jamis Paulson

Founded: 1976

Literary press including fiction, nonfiction, poetry, literary criticism, biography, travel fiction & adventure all with a strong Canadian focus.

Publishes in English.

ISBN Prefix(es): 978-0-88801

Number of titles published annually: 10 Print

Total Titles: 300 Print

Imprints: Ravenstone Books

Returns: LitDistCo, 8300 Lawson Rd, Milton, ON L9T 0A4 *Toll Free Tel:* 800-591-6250 *Toll Free Fax:* 800-591-6251 *E-mail:* orders@litdistco.ca *Web Site:* www.litdistco.ca

Distribution Center: LitDistCo, 8300 Lawson Rd, Milton, ON L9T 0A4 *Toll Free Tel:* 800-591-6250 *Toll Free Fax:* 800-591-6251 *E-mail:* orders@litdistco.ca *Web Site:* www.litdistco.ca

Membership(s): Literary Press Group of Canada

UBC Press, see University of British Columbia Press

Ulysses Travel Guides
4176, rue Saint-Denis, Montreal, QC H2W 2M5

Tel: 514-843-9882 (ext 2232); 514-843-9447 (bookstore) *Toll Free Tel:* 800-748-9171 *Fax:* 514-843-9448

E-mail: info@ulysses.ca; st-denis@ulysses.ca

Web Site: www.ulyssesguides.com

Key Personnel

Pres: Daniel Desjardins *Tel:* 514-843-9447 ext 2224 *E-mail:* daniel@ulysses.ca

VP, Publg: Claude Morneau *E-mail:* claude@ulysses.ca

Founded: 1980

Travel books.

Publishes in English, French.

ISBN Prefix(es): 978-2-921444; 978-2-89464; 978-2-9801872; 978-1-894676

Number of titles published annually: 25 Print; 25 E-Book; 2 Audio

Total Titles: 175 Print; 175 E-Book; 2 Audio

Imprints: Guides de Voyage Ulysses

Branch Office(s)

560, Ave du President-Kennedy, Montreal, QC H3A 1J9 *Tel:* 514-843-7222 *E-mail:* pk@ulysse.ca *Web Site:* www.guidesulysse.com

Distributor for A A Publications; Dakota; Footprint Handbooks; Editions Sylvain Harvey; ITMB Publishing Ltd; Odyssey Publications; PassPorter Travel Press; Rother Walking Guides; Trans Canada Trail Foundation; Vacation Works Publications

University of Alberta Press
Ring House 2, Edmonton, AB T6G 2E1

SAN: 118-9794

Tel: 780-492-3662 *Fax:* 780-492-0719

Web Site: www.uap.ualberta.ca

Key Personnel

Dir & Publr: Douglas Hildebrand *Tel:* 780-492-0717 *E-mail:* dhildebr@ualberta.ca

Assoc Dir: Cathie Crooks *Tel:* 780-492-5820 *E-mail:* ccrooks@ualberta.ca

Mng Ed: Mary Lou Roy *Tel:* 780-492-9488 *E-mail:* marylou.roy@ualberta.ca

Acq Ed: Peter Midgley *Tel:* 780-492-7714 *E-mail:* pmidgley@ualberta.ca

Busn Admin: Basia Kowal *E-mail:* bkowal@ualberta.ca

Prodn & Designer: Alan Brownoff *Tel:* 780-492-8285 *E-mail:* abrownof@ualberta.ca

Founded: 1969

Contemporary publisher of scholarly & creative books distinguished by their editorial care, exceptional design & global reach.

Publishes in English.

ISBN Prefix(es): 978-0-88864; 978-1-77212

Number of titles published annually: 22 Print; 15 E-Book

Total Titles: 400 Print; 450 E-Book; 2 Audio

Imprints: CCI Press; Gutteridge Books; Pica Pica Books; Polynya Press

Sales Office(s): Ampersand Canada's Book & Gift Agency Inc, 321 Carlaw Ave, Suite 213, Toronto, ON M4M 2S1, Contact: Saffron Beckwith *Tel:* 416-703-0666 ext 124 *Fax:* 416-703-4745 *E-mail:* saffronb@ampersandinc.ca *Web Site:* www.ampersand.ca

U.S. Rep(s): Wayne State University Press

Foreign Rep(s): Gazelle Academic (Albania, Andorra, Armenia, Austria, Bahrain, Belarus, Belgium, Bosnia and Herzegovina, Botswana, Bulgaria, Cambodia, China, Continental Europe, Croatia, Cyprus, Czechia, Denmark, Egypt, Ethiopia, Europe, Finland, France, Georgia, Germany, Gibraltar, Greece, Hungary, Iceland, India, Indonesia, Iran, Iraq, Ireland, Israel, Italy, Japan, Jordan, Kenya, Laos, Latvia, Liechtenstein, Lithuania, Luxembourg, Malaysia, Malta, Moldova, Monaco, Montenegro, Mozambique, Myanmar, Namibia, Netherlands, North Macedonia, Norway, Oman, Poland, Portugal, Qatar, Romania, Russia, Serbia, Slovakia, Slovenia, South Africa, Spain, Sweden, Switzerland, Taiwan, Turkey, Uganda, Ukraine, United Arab Emirates, UK, UK & the continent, UK Commonwealth)

Orders to: University of Toronto Press, 5201 Dufferin St, Toronto, ON M3H 5T8 *Tel:* 416-667-7841 *Toll Free Tel:* 800-565-9523 *Fax:* 416-667-7832 *Toll Free Fax:* 800-221-9985

E-mail: utpbooks@utpress.utoronto.ca *Web Site:* www.utpress.utoronto.ca

Returns: University of Toronto Press, 5201 Dufferin St, Toronto, ON M3H 5T8 *Tel:* 416-667-7841 *Toll Free Tel:* 800-565-9523 *Fax:* 416-667-7832 *Toll Free Fax:* 800-221-9985 *E-mail:* utpbooks@utpress.utoronto.ca *Web Site:* www.utpress.utoronto.ca

Shipping Address: University of Toronto Press, 5201 Dufferin St, Toronto, ON M3H 5T8 *Tel:* 416-667-7841 *Toll Free Tel:* 800-565-9523 *Fax:* 416-667-7832 *Toll Free Fax:* 800-221-9985 *E-mail:* utpbooks@utpress.utoronto.ca *Web Site:* www.utpress.utoronto.ca

Warehouse: University of Toronto Press, 5201 Dufferin St, Toronto, ON M3H 5T8 *Tel:* 416-667-7841 *Toll Free Tel:* 800-565-9523 *Fax:* 416-667-7832 *Toll Free Fax:* 800-221-9985 *E-mail:* utpbooks@utpress.utoronto.ca *Web Site:* www.utpress.utoronto.ca

Distribution Center: University of Toronto Press, 5201 Dufferin St, Toronto, ON M3H 5T8 *Tel:* 416-667-7841 *Toll Free Tel:* 800-565-9523 *Fax:* 416-667-7832 *Toll Free Fax:* 800-221-9985 *E-mail:* utpbooks@utpress.utoronto.ca *Web Site:* www.utpress.utoronto.ca

HFS (Hopkins Fulfillment Services), 2715 N Charles St, Baltimore, MD 21218, United States *Toll Free Tel:* 800-537-5487 *E-mail:* hfscustserv@press.jhu.edu *Web Site:* hfs.jhu.edu

Gazelle Book Services Ltd, White Cross Mills, Hightown, Lancaster, Lancs LA1 4XS, United Kingdom *Tel:* (01524) 528500 *Fax:* (01524) 528510 *E-mail:* sales@gazellebookservices.co.uk *Web Site:* www.gazellebookservices.co.uk

Membership(s): Association of Canadian Publishers (ACP); Association of Canadian University Presses (ACUP); Association of University Presses (AUPresses); Book Publishers Association of Alberta

See separate listing for:
Canadian Circumpolar Institute (CCI) Press

University of British Columbia Press

2029 West Mall, Vancouver, BC V6T 1Z2
SAN: 115-1118
Tel: 604-822-5959 *Toll Free Tel:* 877-377-9378 *Fax:* 604-822-6083 *Toll Free Fax:* 800-668-0821
E-mail: frontdesk@ubcpress.ca
Web Site: www.ubcpress.ca
Key Personnel
Dir: Melissa Pitts *Tel:* 604-822-6376 *E-mail:* pitts@ubcpress.ca
Asst Dir, Prodn & Edit Servs: Holly Keller *Tel:* 604-822-4545 *E-mail:* keller@ubcpress.ca
Sr Ed (Kelowna): Randy Schmidt *Tel:* 250-764-4761 *Fax:* 250-764-4709 *E-mail:* schmidt@ubcpress.ca
Sr Ed (Toronto): James MacNevin *Tel:* 289-779-2414 *E-mail:* macnevin@ubcpress.ca
Publicity & Events Mgr: Kerry Kilmartin *Tel:* 604-822-8244 *E-mail:* kilmartin@ubcpress.ca
Edit Coord: Nadine Pedersen *Tel:* 604-827-1795 *E-mail:* pedersen@ubcpress.ca
Ed: Megan Brand *Tel:* 604-822-5885 *E-mail:* brand@ubcpress.ca; Leslie Erickson *Tel:* 604-822-4548 *E-mail:* erickson@ubcpress.ca; Ann Macklem *Tel:* 604-822-0093 *E-mail:* macklem@ubcpress.ca
Academic Mktg Mgr: Harmony Johnson *Tel:* 604-822-1978 *E-mail:* johnson@ubcpress.ca
Mktg Mgr: Laraine Coates *Tel:* 604-822-6486 *E-mail:* coates@ubcpress.ca
Founded: 1971
Academic & scholarly publications; native studies, law & society, military history, northern studies, sexuality, political science & forestry.
Publishes in English.
ISBN Prefix(es): 978-0-88865; 978-0-7748
Number of titles published annually: 70 Print

Total Titles: 900 Print; 2 CD-ROM; 1 E-Book
Imprints: On Campus; On Point Press; Pacific Education Press; Purich Books; UBC Press
Branch Office(s)
587 Markham St, 2nd fl, Toronto, ON M6G 2L7 *Fax:* 416-535-9677
Distributed by University of Washington Press
Distributor for Art Gallery of New South Wales; Athabasca University Press (worldwide); Canadian Forest Service (worldwide); Editors Canada (worldwide); Fowler Museum at UCLA; International Sculpture Center; Island Press; Jessica Kingsley Publishers; Laval University Press (worldwide, English language books); Lost Horse Press; Lynx House Press; Museum for African Art; National Gallery of Australia; Oregon State University Press; Power Publications; Silkworm Books; UCLA Chicano Studies Research Center Press; University of Arizona Press; University of Washington Press; Western Geographical Press (worldwide)
U.S. Publishers Represented: Island Press; Last Horse Press; Lynx House Press; Oregon State University Press; University of Arizona Press; University of Washington Press; Western Geographical Press (worldwide)
U.S. Rep(s): University of Washington Press
Foreign Rep(s): Combined Academic Publishers (Africa, Europe, Middle East, UK); Special Book Services Ltd (South America)
Orders to: University of Toronto Press Distribution, 5201 Dufferin St, Toronto, ON M3H 5T8 *Tel:* 416-667-7791 *Toll Free Tel:* 800-565-9523 *Fax:* 416-667-7832 *Toll Free Fax:* 800-221-9985 *E-mail:* utpbooks@utpress.utoronto.ca; University of Washington Press, c/o HFS, PO Box 50370, Baltimore, MD 21211-4370, United States *Tel:* 410-516-6956 *Toll Free Tel:* 800-537-5487 (US) *Fax:* 410-516-6998 *E-mail:* hfscustserv@press.jhu.edu
Distribution Center: University of Toronto Press Distribution, 5201 Dufferin St, Toronto, ON M3H 5T8 *Tel:* 416-667-7791 *Toll Free Tel:* 800-565-9523 *Fax:* 416-667-7832 *Toll Free Fax:* 800-221-9985 *E-mail:* utpbooks@utpress.utoronto.ca
Chicago Distribution Center (CDC), 11030 S Langley Ave, Chicago, IL 60628, United States *Tel:* 773-702-7010 *Toll Free Tel:* 800-621-8476 *Web Site:* press.uchicago.edu/cdc
Membership(s): Association of Book Publishers of British Columbia; Association of Canadian Publishers (ACP); Association of Canadian University Presses (ACUP); Association of University Presses (AUPresses); International Association of Scholarly Publishers (IASP)
See separate listing for:
Pacific Educational Press

University of Calgary Press

2500 University Dr NW, Calgary, AB T2N 1N4
Tel: 403-220-7578 *Fax:* 403-282-0085
E-mail: ucpress@ucalgary.ca
Web Site: press.ucalgary.ca
Key Personnel
Dir: Brian Scivener *Tel:* 403-220-3511 *E-mail:* brian.scivener@ucalgary.ca
Edit & Mktg Coord: Helen Hajnoczky *Tel:* 403-220-4208 *E-mail:* helen.hajnoczky@ucalgary.ca
Mktg Specialist: Alison Cobra *Tel:* 403-220-3979 *E-mail:* alison.cobra@ucalgary.ca
Founded: 1981
Specialize in scholarly books that make a difference. Series subjects include history, parks & protected areas, regional history, Northern studies, Africa, cinema studies, cultural studies, Canadian military & military history & communications studies.
Publishes in English, French.
ISBN Prefix(es): 978-0-919813; 978-1-895176; 978-1-55238

Number of titles published annually: 20 Print; 2 CD-ROM; 10 Online; 20 E-Book
Total Titles: 400 Print; 5 CD-ROM; 25 Online; 150 E-Book
U.S. Rep(s): Michigan State University Press
Foreign Rep(s): Gazelle Book Services Ltd (Europe, UK)
Foreign Rights: Roli Books (New Delhi)
Distribution Center: Georgetown Terminal Warehouses, 34 Armstrong Ave, Georgetown, ON L7G 4R9 *Toll Free Tel:* 877-864-8477 *Toll Free Fax:* 877-864-4272 *E-mail:* orders@gtwcanada.com *Web Site:* www.gtwcanada.com
Longleaf Services Inc, 116 S Boundary St, Chapel Hill, NC 27514-3808, United States *Tel:* 919-966-7449 *Toll Free Tel:* 800-848-6224 *Fax:* 919-962-2704 *Toll Free Fax:* 800-272-6817 *E-mail:* customerservice@longleafservices.org *Web Site:* www.longleafservices.org
Gazelle Book Services Ltd, White Cross Mills, Hightown, Lancaster, Lancs LA1 4XS, United Kingdom (Asia, Europe, Middle East, South Africa & UK) *Tel:* (01524) 528500 *Fax:* (01524) 528510 *E-mail:* sales@gazellebookservices.co.uk *Web Site:* www.gazellebookservices.co.uk
Membership(s): Association for Canadian Publishers in the US; Association of Canadian Publishers (ACP); Book Publishers Association of Alberta

University of Manitoba Press

University of Manitoba, 301 St Johns College, 92 Dysart Rd, Winnipeg, MB R3T 2M5
SAN: 115-5474
Tel: 204-474-9495 *Fax:* 204-474-7566
E-mail: uofmpress@umanitoba.ca
Web Site: uofmpress.ca
Key Personnel
Dir: David Carr *Tel:* 204-474-9242 *E-mail:* carr@cc.umanitoba.ca
Mng Ed: Glenn Bergen *Tel:* 204-474-7338 *E-mail:* d.bergen@umanitoba.ca
Acqs Ed: Jill McConkey *Tel:* 204-474-8804 *E-mail:* jill.mcconkey@umanitoba.ca
Sales & Mktg Supv: David Larsen *Tel:* 204-474-9998 *E-mail:* david.larsen@umanitoba.ca
Promos & Publicity Coord: Ariel Gordon *Tel:* 204-474-8408 *E-mail:* ariel.gordon@umanitoba.ca
Founded: 1967
Scholarly & general titles in humanities & social sciences; western Canadian history & native studies.
Publishes in English.
ISBN Prefix(es): 978-0-88755
Number of titles published annually: 14 Print
Total Titles: 120 Print
Distributed by University of Toronto Press (Canadian sales); Michigan State University Press (US sales)
Distribution Center: University of Toronto Press, 5201 Dufferin St, Toronto, ON M3H 5T8 *Tel:* 416-667-7791 *Toll Free Tel:* 800-565-9523 *Fax:* 416-667-7856 *Toll Free Fax:* 800-221-9985 *E-mail:* utpbooks@utpress.utoronto.ca
Michigan State University Press, c/o Chicago Distribution Center, 11030 S Langley Ave, Chicago, IL 60628, United States *Toll Free Tel:* 800-621-2736 *Toll Free Fax:* 800-621-8476 *E-mail:* orders@press.chicago.edu *Web Site:* www.msupress.org

University of Ottawa Press (Presses de l'Université d'Ottawa)

Affiliate of University of Ottawa
542 King Edward Ave, Ottawa, ON K1N 6N5
Tel: 613-562-5246 *Fax:* 613-562-5247
E-mail: puo-uop@uottawa.ca; acquisitions@uottawa.ca
Web Site: press.uottawa.ca

Key Personnel
Dir: Lara Mainville, MA *Tel:* 613-562-5663
  E-mail: lara.mainville@uottawa.ca
Acqs Ed: Veronica Omana *Tel:* 613-562-5800 ext
  3065
Prodn Mgr: Suzanne Cloutier *Tel:* 613-562-5800
  ext 2853 *E-mail:* scloutier@uottawa.ca; Eliz-
  abeth Schwaiger *Tel:* 613-562-5800 ext 3064
  E-mail: eschwaig@uottawa.ca
Digital Prodn & Mktg Coord: Mireille Piche
  Tel: 613-562-5800 ext 2853 *E-mail:* mireille.
  piche@uottawa.ca
Prodn Coord: Annie-Pier Charbonneau *Tel:* 613-
  562-5800 ext 4922 *E-mail:* annie-pier.
  charbonneau@uottawa.ca
Admin Asst: Sonia Rheault
Founded: 1936
Scholarly & trade books. The oldest francophone
  university press & only fully bilingual univer-
  sity press in North America.
Publishes in English, French.
ISBN Prefix(es): 978-0-7766; 978-2-7603
Number of titles published annually: 22 Print; 22
  E-Book
Total Titles: 450 Print; 400 E-Book
Foreign Rep(s): Ampersand Inc (Canada (English-
  speaking)); CEDIF (France); Durnell Marketing
  (Europe exc UK); Oxford Publicity Partner-
  ship (UK); Patrimoine Diffusion SPRL (Bel-
  gium, Luxembourg, Netherlands); Prologue Inc
  (Canada (French-speaking)); Servidis (Switzer-
  land)
Distribution Center: University of Toronto Press
  (UTP), 5201 Dufferin St, North York, ON
  M3H 5T8 (English titles to CN) *Tel:* 416-667-
  7791 *Toll Free Tel:* 800-565-9523 *Fax:* 416-
  667-7832 *Toll Free Fax:* 800-221-9985
  E-mail: utpbooks@utpress.utoronto.ca *Web
  Site:* www.utpress.utoronto.ca
Prologue Inc, 1650 Lionel-Bertrand Blvd,
  Boisbriand, QC J7H 1N7 (French titles to
  CN) *Tel:* 450-434-0306 *Toll Free Tel:* 800-
  363-2864 *Toll Free Fax:* 800-361-8088
  E-mail: prologue@prologue.ca *Web Site:* www.
  prologue.ca
Patrimoine Diffusion SPRL, 119 Milcamps
  Ave, 1030 Brussels, Belgium, Contact: Eric
  Durigneux *Tel:* (02) 736 68 47 *Fax:* (02) 736
  68 47 *E-mail:* patrimoine@telenet.be
Distribution du Nouveau Monde, 30 rue Guy
  Lussac, 75005 Paris, France (French titles to
  France) *Tel:* 01 43 54 49 02 *Fax:* 01 43 54
  39 15 *E-mail:* dnm@librairieduquebec.fr *Web
  Site:* www.librairieduquebec.fr
Servidis SA, Chemin des Chalets 7, 1279
  Chavannes-de-Bogis, Switzerland (French
  titles to Switzerland) *Tel:* (022) 960 95 25
  Fax: (022) 776 63 64 *E-mail:* commande@
  servidis.ch *Web Site:* www.servidis.ch
Marston Book Services Ltd, 160 Milton Park,
  PO Box 269, Abingdon, Oxon OX14 4YN,
  United Kingdom (English titles to Europe
  & UK) *Tel:* (01235) 465521 *Fax:* (01235)
  465555 *E-mail:* direct.orders@marston.co.uk
  Web Site: www.marston.co.uk
Membership(s): American Association of Uni-
  versity Presses (AAUP); Association nationale
  des editeurs de livres (ANEL); Association of
  Canadian Publishers (ACP); Association of
  Canadian University Presses (ACUP)

University of Regina Press
2 Research Dr, Suite 246, Regina, SK S4S 7H9
SAN: 115-0278
Mailing Address: University of Regina, 3737
  Wascana Pkwy, Regina, SK S4S 0A2
Tel: 306-585-4758 *Fax:* 306-585-4699
E-mail: uofrpress@uregina.ca
Web Site: uofrpress.ca
Key Personnel
Sr Ed: Donna Grant *Tel:* 306-585-4787
  E-mail: donna.grant@uregina.ca

Ed: David McLennan *Tel:* 306-585-4789
  E-mail: david.mclennan@uregina.ca
Media & Publicity: Melissa Shirley *Tel:* 647-389-
  9510 *E-mail:* melissa.shirley@uregina.ca
Founded: 1973
Scholarly paperbacks & hardcovers on cultural &
  economic development & history of Canadian
  Plains & western Canada.
Publishes in English, French.
ISBN Prefix(es): 978-0-88977
Number of titles published annually: 15 Print
Total Titles: 90 Print; 1 CD-ROM
Distribution Center: University of Toronto
  Press Distribution, 5201 Dufferin St, Toronto,
  ON M3H 5T8 *Tel:* 416-667-7791 *Toll Free
  Tel:* 800-565-9523 (CN & US) *Fax:* 416-667-
  7832 *Toll Free Fax:* 800-221-9985 (CN & US)
  E-mail: utpbooks@utpress.utoronto.ca *Web
  Site:* www.utpress.utoronto.ca
Ingram Publisher Services, c/o Customer
  Service, 14 Ingram Blvd, Box 631, La
  Vergne, TN 37086, United States *Toll Free
  Tel:* 866-400-5351 *Toll Free Fax:* 800-838-
  1149 *E-mail:* ips@ingramcontent.com *Web
  Site:* www.ipage.ingramcontent.com
Gazelle Book Services Ltd, White Cross Mills,
  Hightown, Lancaster, Lancs LA1 4XS, United
  Kingdom *Tel:* (01524) 528500 *Fax:* (01524)
  528510 *E-mail:* sales@gazellebookservices.co.
  uk *Web Site:* www.gazellebookservices.co.uk
Membership(s): Association of Canadian Publish-
  ers (ACP); Association of Canadian Univer-
  sity Presses (ACUP); Saskatchewan Publishers
  Group

§University of Toronto Press
Division of Multicultural History Society of
  Canada
10 St Mary St, Suite 700, Toronto, ON M4Y
  2W8
Tel: 416-978-2239 *Fax:* 416-978-4738
E-mail: info@utpress.utoronto.ca
Web Site: www.utpress.utoronto.ca; www.
  utppublishing.com
Key Personnel
Pres, CEO & Publr: John Yates *Tel:* 416-978-
  2239 ext 2222 *E-mail:* jyates@utpress.utoronto.
  ca
VP, Dist & MIS: Hamish Cameron *Tel:* 416-667-
  7773 *E-mail:* hcameron@utpress.utoronto.ca
VP, Scholarly Publg: Lynn Fisher *Tel:* 416-
  978-2239 ext 2243 *E-mail:* lfisher@utpress.
  utoronto.ca
Founded: 1901
Publisher, distributor & university bookstore.
Publishes in English.
ISBN Prefix(es): 978-0-8020; 978-0-7727; 978-1-
  4426
Number of titles published annually: 200 Print;
  100 E-Book
Total Titles: 3,500 Print; 500 E-Book
Imprints: Rotman-UTP Publishing; University of
  Toronto
Divisions: Pippin Publishing; University of
  Toronto Press Guidance Centre; University of
  Toronto Press Journals Division
Branch Office(s)
2250 Military Rd, Tonawanda, NY 14150, United
  States *Tel:* 716-693-2768 *Fax:* 716-693-2167
Distributor for Aga Khan Museum; Alberta En-
  vironment Protection; Thomas Allen Books;
  Annick Press; Arlifice Books; Arsenal Pulp
  Press; Aspasia Books; Athabasca University;
  Azriel Foundation; Beach Holme Publishing;
  Biblioasis; Black Dog Publishing; Black Rose
  Books; Blue Butterfly Books; Boardwalk; Book
  Publishing Co; Breakwater Books; Brush Ed-
  ucation; Canadian Forest Service; Canadian
  Museum of History; Canadian Museum of Na-
  ture; Canadian War Museum; Career Press/New
  Page Books; Caslon Inc; CAW/TCA Canada;
  Central European University Press; Chair of
  Ukranian Studies; Child's Play Publishing; Cor-

morant Books; Cornell University Press; Dance
Collection Danse; Douglas & McIntyre; The
Dundurn Group; Durvile Publications; Every-
where Now; Eyewear Publishing; Fulchrum;
Golden Dog; Goose Lane Editions; Chelsea
Green Publishing; Greystone Books; Ground-
wood Books; Gryphon House; Guernica Edi-
tions; Guidance Centre; Harvest House; Nick
Hearn; Heritage House Publishing; The History
Press; Hounslow; House of Anansi Press; Inte-
grative Leadership International Ltd; Interlink
Publishing Group; International Self-Counsel
Press Ltd; Island Press; ISSI; Journal of Prison-
ers on Prisons; Jump Math; Edgar Kent; Jessica
Kingsley Publishers; Knowledge Bureau; Peter
Lang Publishing Group; Wilfrid Laurier Uni-
versity Press; Legas Publishing; Mage Publish-
ers; Mawenzi House; McGilligan Books; Me
to We Books; Museum of New Mexico; Na-
tional Museum of Science & Technology; NC
Press; The New Press; New Society Publish-
ers; NewBridge Press; No Exit Press; OISE
Press; Oolichan Books; Oregon State Uni-
versity; Owlkids Books; Pajama Press; Penn
State University Press; Playwrights Canada;
Pontifical Institute of Medieval Studies; Por-
cupine's Quill; Les Presses de L'Universite
Laval; Princess Margaret Hospital Foundation;
Rocky Mountain Books; Royal Ontario Mu-
seum; Science for Peace; Second Story Press;
Seraphim Editions; J Gordon Shillingford Pub-
lishing Inc; Signature Editions; Silman-James
Press; Simon & Pierre Publishing; Sister Vi-
sion Press; Kathy Smart; Smith Bonappetit &
Son; Subway Books; Teachers College Press;
Theatre Communication Group; Theatre Mu-
seum; Theytus Books Ltd; Thistledown Press;
Thompson Educational Publishing Inc; Toronto
Alliance; Toronto Heschel School; TouchWood
Editions; Transaction Publishers; Twin Guinep
Ltd; University of Alberta Press; University of
Arizona Press; University of British Columbia
Press; University of Georgia Press; Univer-
sity of Manitoba Press; University of Nebraska
Press; University of New Mexico Press; Uni-
versity of Ottawa Press; University of Regina,
Canadian Plains Research Centre; University
of Texas Press; University of Toronto Centre
for Public Management; University of Toronto
Centre for Urban & Community Studies; Uni-
versity of Toronto Press Higher Education;
University of Toronto Press Scholarly Publish-
ing Division; University of Washington Press;
University Press of Colorado; Utah State Uni-
versity Press; UTP Journals - Canadian The-
atre Review; Wall & Emerson Inc; Washington
State University; Western Geographical Press;
Wolsak & Wynn Publishers; Woodbine House;
Word of Mouth Production; XYZ Editeur
U.S. Rep(s): Terry & Read LLC (Southwest
  coast); Ben Schrager (Northeast); Trim Asso-
  ciates (Gary Trim) (Midwest)
Foreign Rep(s): Cranbury International LLC
  (Ethan Atkin) (Caribbean, Central America,
  South America); Durnell Marketing Ltd (An-
  drew Durnell) (Europe, Iceland, Ireland, Is-
  rael, Northern Ireland, Russia); Everest Interna-
  tional Publishing Services (Wei Zhao) (China);
  Oxford Publicity Partnership Ltd (Gary Hall)
  (UK); Viva Books Pvt Ltd (India)
Returns: 5201 Dufferin St, North York, ON M3H
  5T8 (worldwide exc CN, India, Japan, UK/Eu-
  rope & US)
Warehouse: 2250 Military Rd, Tonawanda, NY
  14150, United States
5201 Dufferin St, North York, ON M3H 5T8
  (worldwide exc CN, India, Japan, UK/Europe
  & US)
Distribution Center: 5201 Dufferin St, North
  York, ON M3H 5T8 (worldwide exc CN, India, Japan, UK/Europe & US) *Tel:* 416-667-
  7791 *Toll Free Tel:* 800-565-9523 *Fax:* 416-
  667-7832 *Toll Free Fax:* 800-221-9985
  E-mail: utpbooks@utpress.utoronto.ca

2250 Military Rd, Tonawanda, NY 14150, United States *Tel:* 716-693-2768

Viva Books Pvt Ltd, 4737/23 Ansari Rd, Darya Ganj, New Delhi 110 002, India *Tel:* (011) 42242200 *Fax:* (011) 42242240 *E-mail:* viva@vivagroupindia.net

MHM Ltd, 1-1-13-4F Kanda Jimbocho, Chiyoda-ku, Tokyo 101-0051, Japan *Tel:* (03) 3518-9181 *Fax:* (03) 3518-9523 *E-mail:* sales@mhmlimited.co.jp

NBN International, Airport Business Ctr, 10 Thornbury Rd, Plymouth, Devon PL6 7PP, United Kingdom (UK & Europe) *Tel:* (01752) 202301 *Fax:* (01752) 202333 *E-mail:* orders@nbninternational.com *Web Site:* distribution.nbni.co.uk

Membership(s): American Association of University Presses (AAUP); Association of Canadian Publishers (ACP); Association of Canadian University Presses (ACUP); Organization of Book Publishers of Ontario (OBPO)

Vehicule Press

PO Box 42094, CP Roy, Montreal, QC H2W-2T3
Tel: 514-844-6073
E-mail: vp@vehiculepress.com; admin@vehiculepress.com
Web Site: www.vehiculepress.com
Key Personnel
Publr & Gen Ed: Simon Dardick; Nancy Marrelli
Mng Ed: Vicki Marcok
Ed, Esplanade Books: Dimitri Nasrallah
Ed, Signal Editions: Carmine Starnino
Mktg & Promos Mgr: Maya Assouad
Founded: 1973
Paperback trade; fiction, jazz, biography, literature, poetry, translation.
Publishes in English.
ISBN Prefix(es): 978-0-919890; 978-1-55065
Number of titles published annually: 14 Print
Total Titles: 530 Print
Imprints: Esplanade Books (fiction); Signal Editions (poetry)
U.S. Rep(s): IPG (Independent Publishers Group)
Returns: LitDistCo, 8300 Lawson Rd, Milton, ON L9T 0A4 *Tel:* 905-877-4411 *Toll Free Tel:* 800-591-6250 *Fax:* 905-877-4410 *Toll Free Fax:* 800-591-6251
Shipping Address: LitDistCo, 8300 Lawson Rd, Milton, ON L9T 0A4 *Tel:* 905-877-4411 *Toll Free Tel:* 800-591-6250 *Fax:* 905-877-4410 *Toll Free Fax:* 800-591-6251
Distribution Center: LitDistCo, 8300 Lawson Rd, Milton, ON L9T 0A4 *Tel:* 905-877-4411 *Toll Free Tel:* 800-591-6250 *Fax:* 905-877-4410 *Toll Free Fax:* 800-591-6251
Membership(s): Association of Canadian Publishers (ACP); Literary Press Group

VLB editeur

Division of Groupe Ville-Marie Litterature
4545, rue Frontenac, 3rd fl, Montreal, QC H2H 2R7
Tel: 514-849-5259
Web Site: www.edvlb.com
Key Personnel
VP, Edit: Martin Balthazar
Edit Dir: Alain-Nicolas Renaud
Ed: Melikah Abdelmoumen; Ariane Caron-Lacoste
Prodn Mgr: Sophie Deschenes
Founded: 1976
Publishes in French.
ISBN Prefix(es): 978-2-89005
Number of titles published annually: 20 Print; 18 E-Book
Total Titles: 600 Print; 250 E-Book
Foreign Office(s): Immeuble Paryseine, 3, Allee de la Seine, 94854 Ivry Cedex, France *Tel:* 01 49 59 12 40 *Fax:* 06 16 94 14 38
Distribution Center: Messageries ADP, 2315 Rue de la Province, Longueuil, QC J4G 1G4

Weigl Educational Publishers Ltd

6325 Tenth St SE, Calgary, AB T2H 2Z9
SAN: 115-1312
Tel: 403-233-7747 *Toll Free Tel:* 800-668-0766 *Fax:* 403-233-7769 *Toll Free Fax:* 866-449-3445
E-mail: orders@weigl.ca
Web Site: www.weigl.ca; av2books.com
Key Personnel
Pres & Publr: Linda Weigl *E-mail:* linda@weigl.com
Founded: 1979
School library resources & textbooks for grades K-12 in English & French. Emphasis on: Canadian history, social studies & public affairs; science; multiculturalism; career/vocational/life management; distance education; books & guides for teachers.
Publishes in English.
ISBN Prefix(es): 978-0-919879; 978-1-896990; 978-1-55388
Number of titles published annually: 40 Print
Total Titles: 200 Print
Branch Office(s)
350 Fifth Ave, 59th fl, New York, NY 10118, United States *Toll Free Tel:* 866-649-3445 *E-mail:* av2books@weigl.com
Distributed by The Creative Co (US); Rourke Publishing; Saunders Book Co (CN); Smart Apple Media (US)

Whitecap Books

Division of Fitzhenry & Whiteside Limited
314 W Cordova St, Suite 209, Vancouver, BC V6B 1E8
Tel: 604-681-6181 *Toll Free Tel:* 800-387-9776 *Toll Free Fax:* 800-260-9777
Web Site: www.whitecap.ca
Key Personnel
Publr: Nick Rundall *Tel:* 905-477-9700 ext 244 *E-mail:* nickr@whitecap.ca
Ed: Patrick Geraghty *E-mail:* patrickg@whitecap.ca
Designer: Andrew Bagatella *E-mail:* andrewb@whitecap.ca
Founded: 1977
Trade books, photography, cookery, regional, gardening, outdoor guide books, natural history, juvenile nonfiction & illustrated children's books, juvenile fiction.
Publishes in English.
ISBN Prefix(es): 978-1-55110; 978-1-55285; 978-1-77050
Number of titles published annually: 85 Print
Total Titles: 480 Print
Imprints: Walrus Books
U.S. Rep(s): Firefly Books
Returns: Fitzhenry & Whiteside, 195 Allstate Pkwy, Markham, ON L3R 4T8

John Wiley & Sons Canada Ltd

Subsidiary of John Wiley & Sons Inc
90 Eglinton Ave E, Suite 300, Toronto, ON M4P 2Y3
Tel: 416-236-4433 *Toll Free Tel:* 800-225-5945 (orders only) *Fax:* 416-236-8743 (cust serv); 416-236-4447 *Toll Free Fax:* 800-565-6802 (orders)
E-mail: canada@wiley.com
Web Site: www.wiley.ca
Founded: 1968
Textbooks for colleges & universities; trade, professional & reference.
Publishes in English, French.
ISBN Prefix(es): 978-0-470; 978-0-471
Number of titles published annually: 50 Print
Total Titles: 600 Print
Distributor for John Wiley & Sons Inc
Distribution Center: 6045 Freemont Blvd, Mississauga, ON L5R 4J3 *Tel:* 416-236-4433 *Fax:* 416-236-8743

Wilfrid Laurier University Press

75 University Ave W, Waterloo, ON N2L 3C5
Tel: 519-884-0710 *Toll Free Tel:* 866-836-5551 (CN & US) *Fax:* 519-725-1399
E-mail: press@wlu.ca
Web Site: www.wlupress.wlu.ca
Key Personnel
Dir: Lisa Quinn *Tel:* 519-884-0710 ext 2843 *E-mail:* lquinn@wlu.ca
Mng Ed: Rob Kohlmeier *Tel:* 519-884-0710 ext 6119 *E-mail:* rkohlmeier@wlu.ca
Sr Ed: Siobhan McMenemy *Tel:* 519-884-0710 ext 3782 *E-mail:* smcmenemy@wlu.ca
Sales & Mktg Coord: Clare Hitchens *Tel:* 519-884-0710 ext 2665 *E-mail:* chitchens@wlu.ca
Digital Projs Coord: Murray Tong *Tel:* 519-884-0710 ext 3029 *E-mail:* mtong@wlu.ca
Prodn Coord: Mike Bechthold *Tel:* 519-884-0710 ext 6122 *E-mail:* mbechthold@wlu.ca
Founded: 1974
Publish scholarly & general interest books in the social sciences & humanities.
Publishes in English.
ISBN Prefix(es): 978-0-88920; 978-1-55458; 978-0-921821
Number of titles published annually: 30 Print; 30 Online
Total Titles: 416 Print; 400 Online
Imprints: Laurier Digital
Distributor for Laurier Centre for Military Strategic & Disarmament Studies; Toronto International Film Festival
Foreign Rep(s): Blue4Books Inc (Midwest USA, Southeast USA, Southwest USA); CRW Marketing Services for Publishers (Tony Sagun) (Philippines, Thailand); Terry Fernihough (Ontario, CN); Gazelle Book Services Ltd (Caribbean, Continental Europe, India, Ireland, Israel, Japan, Latin America, Middle East, South Africa, Southeast Asia, Sub-Saharan Africa, UK); Bob Rosenberg Group (Western USA); Ben Schrager (Northeast USA); Karen Stacey (Quebec, CN); Leona & Jerry Trainer (Eastern Canada)
Orders to: University of Toronto Press Distribution, 5201 Dufferin St, Toronto, ON M3H 5T8 *Toll Free Tel:* 800-565-9523 *Toll Free Fax:* 800-221-9985 *E-mail:* utpbooks@utpress.utoronto.ca; Ingram Publisher Services, 14 Ingram Blvd, La Vergne, TN 37086, United States *Toll Free Tel:* 866-400-5351; Gazelle Book Services Ltd, White Cross Mills, Hightown, Lancaster, Lancs LA1 4XS, United Kingdom (outside North America) *Tel:* (01524) 528500 *Fax:* (01524) 528510 *E-mail:* sales@gazellebookservices.co.uk *Web Site:* www.gazellebookservices.co.uk
Membership(s): Association of Canadian Publishers (ACP); Association of Canadian University Presses (ACUP); Association of University Presses (AUPresses); Organization of Book Publishers of Ontario (OBPO)

WLU Press, see Wilfrid Laurier University Press

Wood Lake Publishing Inc

485 Beaver Lake Rd, Kelowna, BC V4V 1S5
Tel: 250-766-2778 *Toll Free Tel:* 800-663-2775 (orders & cust serv) *Fax:* 250-766-2736 *Toll Free Fax:* 888-841-9991 (orders & cust serv)
E-mail: info@woodlake.com; customerservice@woodlake.com
Web Site: www.woodlakebooks.com
Key Personnel
Pres & Publr: Patty Berube
Mktg Promos & Sales: Samantha Michaels *E-mail:* samantham@woodlake.com
Founded: 1980
Books, church curriculum & periodicals.
Publishes in English.
ISBN Prefix(es): 978-1-55145; 978-0-919599; 978-0-929032

Number of titles published annually: 8 Print.
Total Titles: 135 Print
Imprints: CopperHouse; Seasons of the Spirit;
  Whole People of God Online; Wood Lake
Distributed by Augsburg Canada; Presbyterian
  Church of Canada; United Church of Canada
Distributor for Northstone

§Worldwide Library
Imprint of Harlequin Enterprises Ltd

225 Duncan Mill Rd, Don Mills, ON M3B 3K9
Mailing Address: PO Box 603, Fort Erie, ON
  L2A 5X3
Tel: 416-445-5860 *Toll Free Tel:* 888-432-4879
E-mail: customerservice@harlequin.com
Web Site: www.harlequin.com
Founded: 1982
Mass market fiction.
Publishes in English.
ISBN Prefix(es): 978-0-373

Number of titles published annually: 5 Print; 9 E-
  Book
Imprints: Worldwide Mystery
Branch Office(s)
PO Box 9049, Buffalo, NY 14269-9049, United
  States
Foreign Rights: Booklink (Europe)
Warehouse: 3010 Walden Ave, Depew, NY
  14043, United States

Small Presses

Listed here, in alphabetical order, are U.S. & Canadian publishers who were not eligible to be listed in the sections covering U.S. Publishers or Canadian Publishers. Many of these publishers are new or offer distinctive titles they wish to make known to the users of *Literary Market Place*. Entries in this section are paid listings.

Publishers interested in participating in this section in future editions of LMP are invited to contact **Lauri Rimler, Advertising Sales** by e-mail at lwrimler@infotoday.com, by phone at 800-409-4929 (press 1) or 908-219-0088, or by mail at Information Today, Inc., 121 Chanlon Road, Suite G-20, New Providence, NJ 07974-2195.

Acroterion Books
5305 Harvard Rd, Lawrence, KS 66049-4781
Tel: 785-917-0773
E-mail: info@acroterionbooks.com
Web Site: www.acroterionbooks.com
Key Personnel
Edit Dir: Charles Anthony Silvestri
Artistic Dir: Anne Horjus *Tel:* 608-355-0481
Founded: 2013
Our mission is to offer picture books of the highest quality, combining words with music & illustrations & create powerful connections between these different forms of art.
Titles include *Leonardo Dreams of His Flying Machine (ISBN: 978-1-5400-6880-4); SLEEP (ISBN: 978-1-4803-5402-9)*
Distributed by Amazon.com; Barnes & Noble; Hal Leonard; J W Pepper; Sheet Music Plus

Adams-Pomeroy Press
103 N Jackson St, Albany, WI 53502
Mailing Address: PO Box 189, Albany, WI 53502
Tel: 608-862-3645 *Toll Free Tel:* 877-862-3645
Fax: 608-862-3647
E-mail: adamspomeroy@tds.net
Founded: 1996
Adams-Pomeroy Press publishes books in the areas of education, multicultural nonfiction, juvenile fiction & fiction.
Titles include *Americans of Different Faiths; Basic Level Literacy Programs for English-Speaking and Non-English-Speaking Adults: A Variety of Options; Haunted Hill (A Sam & Stephanie Mystery); How Big Is Your Class? Practical Tips for Teaching Small and Large Primary Grade Classes; Missing What's-Her-Name; Mixed Heritage: Your Source for Books for Children and Teens about Persons and Families of Mixed Racial, Ethnic, and/or Religious Heritage; My Reading Buddy Is a Dog!: Your Resource for Creating and Running a Canine Reading Buddy Program; Unconquered Territory*
ISBN Prefix(es): 978-0-9661009; 978-0-9667921
Membership(s): The Association of Publishers for Special Sales (APSS); Independent Book Publishers Association (IBPA)

Alazar Press
Imprint of Royal Swan Enterprises Inc
201 Orchard Lane, Carrboro, NC 27510
SAN: 853-0521
Tel: 919-274-0653
E-mail: alazar.press@gmail.com
Web Site: www.alazar-press.com
Key Personnel
Publr: Rosemarie Gulla *E-mail:* rgulla@nc.rr.com
Gen Mgr: Joseph Gulla
Founded: 2007
Focused on engaging young people with ideas, Alazar Press is dedicated to producing quality books for children of all ages & is aligned with the mission of Royal Swan Enterprises.
Royal Swan Enterprises offers high quality literature & accompanying ideas in a vital & relevant manner in order to best serve the developing minds of young people. Royal Swan acknowledges the inherent worth & dignity of all

children & works to equip them with the tools of a literate & reflective society. Asserting the primacy of building true emotional engagement to learning, Royal Swan develops books, story frameworks, methods, products & services for young learners & their families.
Titles include *The Artist and the King; By Trolley Past Trimbledon Bridge; I'm Going to Sing, Black American Spirituals Volume Two; On the Wings of the Swan; PAR-TAY: Dance of the Veggies (And Their Friends); The Thumbtack Dancer; Walk Together Children, Black American Spirituals Volume One; The Women Who Caught The Babies*
ISBN Prefix(es): 978-0-9793000; 978-0-9977720
Distributed by Independent Publishers Group (IPG)
Membership(s): American Library Association (ALA); International Literacy Association (ILA); North Carolina Reading Association (NCRA); Triangle Reading Council

Filsinger & Company Ltd
288 W 12 St, Suite 2R, New York, NY 10014
Tel: 212-243-7421 (by appt)
E-mail: filsingercompany@gmail.com
Web Site: www.filsingerco.com
Key Personnel
Pres: Cheryl Filsinger
Founded: 1974 (reinstated 2010)
Publisher of museum-quality children's books including the NEIGHBORS series.
Retail availability: *Bummer* at Sustenance Books, Murphys, CA; *NEIGHBORS* series at Canio's (Sag Harbor, NY) & The South Fork Natural History Museum (Bridgehampton, NY); *Philippe The Black Sheep* at Albertine (NYC), McNally Jackson (NYC), & Book Hampton (East Hampton, NY).
Forthcoming title: *JJ amid the hedges.*
Titles include *Bummer (print & ebook); The Children's Pack of Frames; NEIGHBORS The Water Critters; NEIGHBORS The Yard Critters Book I; NEIGHBORS The Yard Critters TOO; Philippe The Black Sheep (print ed in English, ebooks in English & French); Under the Escalator (print & video)*
ISBN Prefix(es): 978-0-916754
Distributed by Amazon.com (print & ebooks); Baker & Taylor (print); Follett School Solutions (print); kobo.com (ebooks)

Moonstone Press LLC
4816 Carrington Circle, Sarasota, FL 34243
SAN: 852-5625
Tel: 301-765-1081 *Fax:* 301-765-0510
E-mail: mazeprod@erols.com
Web Site: www.moonstonepress.net
Key Personnel
Publr: Stephanie Maze
Founded: 2001
Publishes quality photography-based books in English & Spanish for ages 3 & up. Award-winning book titles include: *Healthy Foods from A to Z/Comida sana de la A a la Z; Keeping Fit from A to Z/Mantente en forma de la A a la Z; Breastfeeding Around the World/Amamantar alrededor del mundo; Mo-*

ments in the Wild/Momentos en el reino animal (4 title series); *With Ballet in My Soul: Adventures of a Globetrotting Impresario* (ISBN: 978-0-9834983-8-4); *Famous Dishes from Around the World/Platos famosos de todo el mundo.*
ISBN Prefix(es): 978-0-9707768; 978-0-9769542; 978-0-9834983
Distributed by IPG/Small Press United
Membership(s): Independent Book Publishers Association (IBPA); White House Press Photographers Association

Omniscient Publishing
Imprint of Peak Performance Publishing
14728 Shirley St, Omaha, NE 68144
Tel: 402-334-1676 *Fax:* 402-334-4437
Web Site: www.thevaticanfiles.com
Key Personnel
Pres: Stephen J Brennan, PhD
  E-mail: brennan160@cox.net
Founded: 2015
Omniscient Publishing was created to house the fiction literature produced by Peak Performance Publishing authors.
For information about *The Vatican Files*, or to order a copy, go to www.thevaticanfiles.com.
Titles include *The Vatican Files*
ISBN Prefix(es): 978-1-893353
Distributed by Kindle Direct Publishing; Smashwords

Painted Hills Publishing
16500 Dakota Ridge Rd, Longmont, CO 80503
Tel: 303-823-6642
E-mail: cw@livingimagescjw.com
Web Site: www.wildhoofbeats.com; www.livingimagescjw.com
Key Personnel
Owner: Carol Walker
Founded: 2008
Publishes photography books on wild horses with the purpose of educating the public about the wild horse situation in the US. Also publishes books on the techniques of photographing domestic & wild horses.
Titles include *Galloping to Freedom: Saving the Adobe Town Appaloosas; Horse Photography: The Dynamic Guide for Horse Lovers; Wild Hoofbeats: America's Vanishing Wild Horses*
ISBN Prefix(es): 978-0-9817936
Distributed by Baker & Taylor; Gazelle International; Greenleaf Book Group
Membership(s): Independent Book Publishers Association (IBPA); Professional Photographers of America (PPA)

Pragma Media
Imprint of Pragma Design Inc
PO Box 413, Bertam, TX 78605
SAN: 991-1200
Tel: 512-436-0606
E-mail: soicandfriends@pragma.media
Web Site: soicnsot.pragma.media
Key Personnel
Pres: Jeff Dunnihoo *Tel:* 512-965-0071
  E-mail: jeffhoo.pm@pragma-design.com

Founded: 2018

In the course of Pragma Design's engineering business, the increasing amount of multimedia resources required for the communication & distribution of leading edge technological & educational multimedia necessitated the launch of Pragma Media in 2018. Additionally, Pragma Media focuses on the educational pipeline entry of Pre-K & entry-level teaching materials, curricula & instructional electronic systems worldwide, especially targeted at technologically developing areas.

Titles include *MSOP and DPAK: One Hot Day (ISBN: 978-1-7322836-5-7 softcover, 978-1-7322836-6-4 hardcover)*; *SOIC and SOT: The Microchips (ISBN: 978-1-7322836-1-9 softcover, 978-1-7322836-2-6 hardcover)*; *TSSOP Gets Zapped: with Static Electricity (ISBN: 978-1-7322836-3-3 softcover, 978-1-7322836-4-0 hardcover)*; *y SOT: los Microchips (ISBN: 978-1-7322836-7-1 hardcover, Spanish)*

ISBN Prefix(es): 978-1-7322836

Distributed by ESD Association; Ingram; Mouser Inc; SMTA International

Membership(s): American Library Association (ALA); Society of Children's Book Writers & Illustrators (SCBWI); Writer's League of Texas

Three Wishes Publishing Company
26500 W Agoura Rd, Suite 102-754, Calabasas, CA 91302
Tel: 818-878-0902 *Fax:* 818-878-1805

E-mail: Alva710@aol.com
Web Site: www.threewishespublishing.com
Founded: 2007

Children's book publisher.

Titles include *Circus Fever*; *Dancing Dreidels*; *Dear Master Dragon*; *I'm 5*; *On Your Mark, Get Set, Go!*; *The Pirate Princess*

ISBN Prefix(es): 978-0-9796380

Distributed by Amazon.com; Baker & Taylor; Barnes & Noble; Follett School Solutions Inc

Membership(s): American Library Association (ALA); Angels of the Arts; Association of Jewish Libraries of Southern California (AJLSC); California Library Association; Children's Book Writers of Los Angeles (CBW-LA); Children's Literature Council of Southern California; Independent Book Publishers Association (IBPA); Reading Is Fundamental of Southern California; Society of Children's Book Writers & Illustrators (SCBWI)

TJ Publishers Inc
PO Box 702701, Dallas, TX 75370
Toll Free Tel: 800-999-1168 *Fax:* 972-416-0944
E-mail: TJPubinc@aol.com
Key Personnel
Pres: T Patrick O'Rourke
Founded: 1978

Publisher & distributor of quality books, DVDs & other materials related to sign language & deafness including several best sellers.

Titles include *A Basic Course in American Sign Language (2nd ed)*; *Student Study Guide to A Basic Course in American Sign Language*

ISBN Prefix(es): 978-0-932666

Worthy & James Publishing
PO Box 362015, Milpitas, CA 95036
SAN: 852-5765
Tel: 408-945-3963
E-mail: worthy1234@sbcglobal.net; mail@worthyjames.com
Web Site: www.worthyjames.com
Key Personnel
Mgr: Diane James
Mgr/Author: Greg Mostyn
Founded: 2006

Publications in basic accounting, payroll, & finance.

Titles include *Basic Accounting Concepts, Principles, and Procedures (vol 1, ISBN: 978-0-9914231-0-1)*; *Basic Accounting Concepts, Principles, and Procedures (vol 2, ISBN: 978-0-9914231-1-8)*; *The Payroll Process, A Basic Guide to U.S. Payroll Procedures and Requirements (ISBN: 978-0-9914231-9-4)*

ISBN Prefix(es): 978-0-9914231

Distributed by Itasca Books; Amazon; Baker & Taylor; Ingram

Membership(s): Independent Book Publishers Association (IBPA)

Editorial Services & Agents

Editorial Services — Activity Index

FACT CHECKING

GHOSTWRITING

SPECIAL ASSIGNMENT WRITING

STATISTICS

TECHNICAL WRITING

TRANSCRIPTION EDITING

Editorial Services

For information on other companies who provide services to the book industry, see **Consultants, Book Producers, Typing & Word Processing Services** and **Artists & Art Services**.

A+ English LLC/Book-Editing.com/Book Editing Associates
PO Box 1369, Mansfield, TX 76063
Tel: 469-789-3030
E-mail: editingnetwork@gmail.com
Web Site: www.editing-writing.com; www.book-editing.com; www.helpwithstatistics.com; www.apawriting.com; childrensbookeditors.com; www.christianeditorsnetwork.com; dissertationwriting.com; statisticstutors.com
Key Personnel
Freelance Network Coord: Lynda Lotman
Founded: 1976
Serving writers (unpublished, published), publishers (mainstream, genre, trade, academic), agents, researchers & businesses. Ms evaluations, copy-editing, developmental editing, submission materials (query letters, book proposals), mentoring & ghostwriting. We work with fiction, nonfiction, medical/scientific/technical material, business documents & textbooks.
Membership(s): Science Fiction & Fantasy Writers of America (SFWA)

A Westport Wordsmith
101 Winfield St, Norwalk, CT 06855
Tel: 203-939-9484
E-mail: pj104daily@aol.com
Key Personnel
Prop: Peggy Daily
Founded: 1999
Proofreading (nonfiction & fiction) & indexing of trade books. Americanization.
Membership(s): American Society for Indexing (ASI); Editorial Freelancers Association (EFA)

AAH Graphics Inc
Subsidiary of Loft Press Inc
9293 Fort Valley Rd, Fort Valley, VA 22652
Tel: 540-933-6210 *Fax:* 540-933-6523
E-mail: aah@aahgraphics.com
Web Site: www.aahgraphics.com
Key Personnel
Pres: Ann A Hunter
Founded: 1973
Complete editorial through production serving publishers & individuals. Design of text, jackets & covers, composition & production management through manufacturing.
Membership(s): National Press Club

Aaron-Spear
PO Box 42, Brooksville, ME 04617
Tel: 207-326-8764
Key Personnel
Prop: Jody Spear
Developmental editing & copy-editing of scholarly mss in the humanities. Rewriting for style & sensibility as well as clarity, consistency & accuracy. Specialize in art history & environmental studies.

About Books Inc
1001 Taurus Dr, Colorado Springs, CO 80906
Tel: 719-440-8932 *Fax:* 719-213-2602
Web Site: www.about-books.com
Key Personnel
Owner & Pres: Debi Flora *E-mail:* debiflora@about-books.com
Owner & VP: Scott Flora *E-mail:* scott@about-books.com

Founded: 1977
Complete writing, editorial & book development services: editing; cover & interior design; ebooks & print books; specialize in nonfiction books on all subjects.
Membership(s): The Association of Publishers for Special Sales (APSS)

Accurate Writing & More
16 Barstow Lane, Hadley, MA 01035
Tel: 413-586-2388
Web Site: www.accuratewriting.com; www.frugalmarketing.com; www.goingbeyondsustainability.com; www.transformpreneur.com; www.greenandprofitable.com; www.twitter.com/shelhorowitz
Key Personnel
Owner & Dir: Shel Horowitz *E-mail:* shel@principledprofit.com
Dir: Dina Friedman
Founded: 1981
Advertising & promotion copywriting, ghostwriting, editing, publishing consulting, interviewing, ms analysis, research, rewriting, special assignment writing & publishing consulting for authors, publishers & green/social change businesses.
Membership(s): Connecticut Authors & Publishers Association; Independent Book Publishers Association (IBPA); Independent Publishers of New England (IPNE); National Writers Union (NWU); Western New England Editorial Freelancers Network

J Adel Art & Design
586 Ramapo Rd, Teaneck, NJ 07666
Tel: 201-836-2606
E-mail: jadelnj@aol.com
Key Personnel
Creative Dir: Judith Adel
Founded: 1985
Freelance copy, illustration & design services for publishers.
Membership(s): Middletown Art Group; New Jersey Water Color Society

AEIOU Inc
894 Piermont Ave, Piermont, NY 10968
Tel: 845-359-1911
Key Personnel
Pres: Cynthia Crippen *E-mail:* ccrippen@verizon.net
Founded: 1976

Rodelinde Albrecht
PO Box 444, Lenox Dale, MA 01242-0444
Tel: 413-243-4350
E-mail: rodelinde@gmail.com
Founded: 1979
Full editorial services; scanning; copy/line editing (hard copy/electronic); rewriting; castoff, typemarking; proofreading; proof-checking & consulting.

AllWrite Advertising & Publishing
3300 Buckeye Rd, Suite 264, Atlanta, GA 30341
Mailing Address: PO Box 1071, Atlanta, GA 30301
Tel: 770-284-8983 *Fax:* 770-284-8986
E-mail: questions@allwritepublishing.com

Web Site: allwritepublishing.com
Key Personnel
Pres & Publr: Annette R Johnson
E-mail: annette@allwritepublishing.com
Founded: 1996
A conventional publisher that also offers editorial services for self-publishers & those who need promotional documents or materials, including booklets & brochures. Provides comprehensive editing & proofreading services: checking syntax, grammar, punctuation & style; & offering substantive/line editing, developmental editing & production editing. Get a free online quote at www.e-allwrite.com.
Membership(s): Writers Guild of America, East (WGAE)

Jeanette Almada
452 W Aldine, Unit 215, Chicago, IL 60657
Tel: 773-404-9350
E-mail: jmalmada@sbcglobal.net
Founded: 1981
As a writer, reporter & editor, I can cover or even rewrite almost any story. Areas of interest historically have included urban lifestyle issues from neighborhoods to hobbies, corporate histories, cultures & communications & newsletters. More recent interests are politics of food & water (particularly the Great Lakes), seed saving & seed savers, heirloom crops, growing food, some farm & organic topics.

Ampersand Group
1136 Maritime Way, Suite 717, Kanata, ON K2K 0M1, Canada
Tel: 613-435-5066
Key Personnel
Pres: Ed Matheson *E-mail:* ematheson@bell.net
Founded: 2002
Book publishing consultants for publishers, business, government & individuals with publishing problems. Specialize in project management, general book design & production.

Barbara S Anderson
706 W Davis Ave, Ann Arbor, MI 48103-4855
Tel: 734-995-0125
E-mail: bsa@watercolorbarbara.com
Rewriting, proofreading, ms analysis & line editing. For related services, see listing in Artists & Art Services.

Denice A Anderson
210 E Church St, Clinton, MI 49236
Tel: 517-456-4990 *Fax:* 517-456-4990
E-mail: deniceanderson@frontier.com
Founded: 1984
Copy-editing, line editing & proofreading; fiction & nonfiction; art, history, medical, legal, business, newspapers, journals & directories.
Membership(s): Editorial Freelancers Association (EFA)

Jim Anderson
77 S Second St, Brooklyn, NY 11249
Tel: 718-388-1083
E-mail: jim.and@att.net

Angel Editing Services
PO Box 752, Mountain Ranch, CA 95246

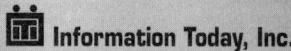
Tel: 209-728-8364
E-mail: info@stephaniemarohn.com
Web Site: www.stephaniemarohn.com
Key Personnel
Owner & Ed: Stephanie Marohn
Founded: 1993
Full range of editorial services, from developmental editing through copy-editing. Specialize in nonfiction trade books, particularly psychospiritual topics, metaphysics, natural medicine & other alternative thought.

Angels Editorial Services
1630 Main St, No 41, Coventry, CT 06238
Tel: 860-742-5279
E-mail: angelsus@aol.com
Key Personnel
Pres: Prof Claire Connelly, PhD
Founded: 1969
Ms or disk: counseling & psychotherapy, science & computers, textbooks, GLBT, fiction & nonfiction, animals.
Membership(s): American Copy Editors Society (ACES); Society for Technical Communication (STC)

Aptara Inc
Subsidiary of iEnergizer
2901 Telestar Ct, Suite 522, Falls Church, VA 22042
Tel: 703-352-0001
E-mail: moreinfo@aptaracorp.com
Web Site: www.aptaracorp.com
Key Personnel
Pres: Samir Kakar
EVP, Fin & Cont: Prashant Kapoor
SVP, Busn & Contact Ctr Opers: Ashish Madan
Busn Devt: Michael Scott *E-mail:* michael.scott@aptaracorp.com
Founded: 1988
Liaison for complete or any combination of production services, ranging from simple 1-color to complex 4-color projects & copy-editing. Offer ebook conversions & end-to-end solutions publishing services in print & digital.
Branch Office(s)
150 California St, Suite 301, Newton, MA 02458 *Tel:* 617-423-7755
11009 Metric Blvd, Bldg J, Suite 150, Austin, TX 78758 *Tel:* 512-876-5997
299 Elizabeth St, Level 1, Sydney 2000, Australia *Tel:* (02) 8251 0070
Tower 1 & 2, 8/100, Acharya Thulasi Rd (Shandy Rd), Pallavaram, Chennai 600 043, India *Tel:* (044) 22640676
No 2310, Doon Express Business Park, Saharanpur Rd, Bldg 2000, Dehradun 248 002, India *Tel:* (0135) 2644055
7B, Leela Infopark, Technopark, Trivandrum, Kerala 695 581, India *Tel:* (047) 14063370
A-37, Sector-60, Noida 201 301, India *Tel:* (0120) 7182424
D-10, Sector-2, Noida 201 301, India *Tel:* (0120) 24423678
SEZ Bldg 4A, 1st fl, S P Infocity, Pune Saswad Rd, Phursungi, Pune 412 308, India *Tel:* (020) 66728000

Archon Editorial LLC
815 King St, Suite 204, Alexandria, VA 22314
Tel: 703-838-1650
E-mail: stoddardbc@gmail.com
Web Site: www.archoneditorial.com
Key Personnel
Owner: Brooke C Stoddard *E-mail:* brooke@archoneditorial.com
Founded: 1983
Magazine & book writing & editing. Can handle design & production.
Membership(s): American Society of Journalists & Authors (ASJA); The Authors Guild; Editorial Freelancers Association (EFA); National Press Club

ASJA Freelance Writer Search
Affiliate of American Society of Journalists & Authors Inc
355 Lexington Ave, 15th fl, New York, NY 10017
Tel: 212-997-0947
E-mail: asjaoffice@asja.org
Web Site: www.freelancewritersearch.com
Key Personnel
Exec Dir: Alexandra Owens
Founded: 1948
Vital resource for anyone seeking the services of professional writers for articles, books, book proposals, brochures, annual reports, speeches, TV & film scripts, advertising copy, publicity campaigns, corporate communications & more. Free, private listing service goes only to the 1,300 professional members of ASJA.

Associated Editors
27 W 96 St, New York, NY 10025
Tel: 212-662-9703 *Fax:* 212-662-9703
Key Personnel
Contact: Lynne Glasner *E-mail:* lyngla1@gmail.com
Copy-editing, rewriting, proofreading, research, developmental editing. Specialize in elementary & secondary textbooks; nonfiction trade books.
Membership(s): Editorial Freelancers Association (EFA)

Astor Indexers
22 S Commons, Kent, CT 06757
Tel: 860-592-0225; 570-534-8951 (cell)
Key Personnel
Owner: Jane Farnol *E-mail:* bjfarnol@snet.net
Founded: 1970
Indexing is our only business. Staff handles all subjects; hard copy, e-mail or disk. Quality, speed & accuracy are our trademarks.

Audrey Owen
494 Eaglecrest Dr, Gibsons, BC V0N 1V8, Canada
E-mail: editor@writershelper.com
Web Site: www.writershelper.com
Founded: 2002
Besides the editing services offered by other agencies, I also specialize in educative editing that becomes a mini tutorial designed for, but is not restricted to, self-publishing writers. Also offer substantive editing.
Membership(s): Editors' Association of Canada/Association canadienne des reviseurs (EAC); Federation of British Columbia Writers

The Author's Friend
548 Ocean Blvd, No 12, Long Branch, NJ 07740
Tel: 732-571-8051
Key Personnel
Prop: Judith Stein *E-mail:* jstein@panix.com
Founded: 1976
Copy & line editing, proofreading & transcription editing. Specialize in religion & spirituality, psychology, medicine, self-help, bibliographies & esoterica.

Backman Writing & Communications
32 Hillview Ave, Rensselaer, NY 12144
Tel: 518-449-4985
Web Site: www.backwrite.com
Key Personnel
Principal: John Backman *E-mail:* johnb@backwrite.com
Founded: 1986
Articles, blogs, advertising & marketing copy. Areas of focus: Spirituality, higher education, engineering, financial services & generally making the complex simple.

Kathleen Barnes
238 W Fourth St, Suite 3-C, New York, NY
10014
Tel: 212-924-8084
E-mail: kbarnes@compasscommunications.org
Writing, rewriting, line editing, copy-editing &
proofreading.

Diana Barth
535 W 51 St, Suite 3-A, New York, NY 10019
Tel: 212-307-5465
E-mail: diabarth@juno.com
Founded: 1970
All subjects; specialize in performing arts, health,
psychology, education & travel. Feature &
ghostwriter.

Anita Bartholomew
16650 SE Sunridge Lane, Portland, OR 97267
Tel: 774-264-8205
E-mail: anita@anitabartholomew.com
Web Site: www.anitabartholomew.com
Founded: 1993
Developmental editor. Specialize in fiction &
narrative nonfiction. Have ghosted fiction
& nonfiction. Co-authored a leading OB-
GYN's award-winning memoir. Clients in-
clude authors (typically referred by their lit-
erary agents), publishers & nonprofits. En-
dorsements/testimonials available on web site
& LinkedIn profile.

Mark E Battersby
PO Box 527, Ardmore, PA 19003-0527
Tel: 610-924-9157 *Fax:* 610-924-9159
E-mail: mebatt12@earthlink.net
Web Site: www.thetaxscribe.com
Founded: 1971
Freelance writer. Specialize in tax & financial
features, columns, web content & white papers.

Beaver Wood Associates
655 Alstead Center Rd, Alstead, NH 03602
Mailing Address: PO Box 717, Alstead, NH
03602
Tel: 603-835-7900
Web Site: www.beaverwood.com
Key Personnel
Owner: Jeanne C Moody *E-mail:* jcmoody@
beaverwood.com
Founded: 1985
Indexing, copy-editing & proofreading.
Membership(s): American Society for Indexing
(ASI)

Barbara Bergstrom MA LLC
13 Stockton Way, Howell, NJ 07731
Tel: 732-363-8372
Offers complete editorial services: copy-editing,
ms analysis, critique, development of mss,
proofreading, research, revision, rewriting,
condensations, copyfitting, writing, ghostwriting, transcription editing, project development
& management, production services & editing for publishers, authors, academics, medical professionals, psychologists, businesses,
public figures, associations & organizations.
Act as publisher-author liaison, or as author's
agent, full project management for publishers with mss needing copy-editing, revision
+/or editor to work with author, or for self-
publishing authors. Will travel to meet with
authors to develop & edit mss. Meticulous editor (former university faculty) will copy-edit
Masters Thesis & Doctoral Dissertation, or
we can help you to prepare your ms for publication. Business, medical, psychological &
technical writing, editing of user manuals into
clearly understood English, project management & editing of in-house publications. Tran-
scribe & edit books to tape. Special expertise

in psychology, comparative literature, fiction,
nonfiction, autobiography & memoirs, biography, art, art history, history, East Asian culture
(China, Korea, Japan), Eastern philosophy &
religions (Buddhism, Taoism, Confucianism,
Shinto), T'ai Ch'i, martial arts, women's stud-
ies, natural healing, New Age, Native American, alternative healing sciences, meditation,
"how-to", health & fitness, self-help, English,
ESL & more. ESL authors welcome. We are
the editing/contracting agency for Dr Fred Pen-
zel whose books include the award-winning
*Obsessive-Compulsive Disorders: A Complete
Guide to Getting Well and Staying Well* & *The
Hair-Pulling Problem: A Complete Guide to
Trichotillomania.* We also edited Jae Woong
Kim's *Polishing the Diamond Enlightening the
Mind.* Call before submitting mss. Leave your
name, number & brief message about your
project. Ask about our specials. Also see listing
under Consultants.

BiblioGenesis
152 Coddington Rd, Ithaca, NY 14850
Tel: 607-277-9660
Web Site: www.bibliogenesis.com
Key Personnel
Owner: Marian Hartman Rogers
  E-mail: mrogers@lightlink.com
Founded: 1987
Full editorial services encompassing all aspects
of ms development: analysis, writing, rewriting, content editing, copy-editing, line editing,
proofreading, fact checking, research & special assignment writing. Specialize in scholarly
works (classical & medieval studies, European
history & literature, anthropology & gender
studies, Middle Eastern studies, geography &
travel); languages (French, German, Greek,
Latin).

Bloom Ink
6437 Maple Hills Dr, Bloomfield Hills, MI 48301
Tel: 248-291-0370
E-mail: info@bloomwriting.com
Web Site: www.bloomwriting.com
Key Personnel
Founder & Principal: Barbara Bloom
Founded: 2008
Provides a range of editing & publishing services
including copy-editing, developmental editing,
audio abridgements (fiction, nonfiction), book
proposals, query letters & ghostwriting as well
as assistance with self-publishing, book layout
& design.
Membership(s): Editorial Freelancers Association
(EFA)

Heidi Blough, Book Indexer
3784 Fairway Park Dr, Apt 108, Copley, OH
44321
Tel: 330-666-1157
E-mail: indexing@heidiblough.com
Web Site: www.heidiblough.com
Key Personnel
Owner: Heidi Blough
Founded: 2001
Indexing diverse topics that include: aerospace;
biography; business, cooking, food & nutrition;
engineering; general trade subjects; health &
hospital administration; history, government
& politics; how-to; maritime & transportation
subjects.
Membership(s): American Society for Indexing
(ASI)

Blue & Ude Writers' Services
4249 Nuthatch Way, Clinton, WA 98236
Mailing Address: PO Box 145, Clinton, WA
98236-0145
Tel: 360-341-1630
E-mail: blue@whidbey.com

Web Site: www.blueudewritersservices.com; www.
sunbreakpress.com
Key Personnel
Partner: Marian Blue; Wayne Ude
Founded: 1991
Provides all aspects of creative & technical writ-
ing & editing, including critiques, revisions &
promotional copy.

Book Editing Associates, see A+ English
LLC/Book-Editing.com/Book Editing
Associates

Book-Editing.com, see A+ English
LLC/Book-Editing.com/Book Editing
Associates

BookCrafters LLC
Box C, Convent Station, NJ 07961
Web Site: bookcraftersllc.com
Key Personnel
Founder, Pres & Ed: Elizabeth Zack
  E-mail: ezack@bookcraftersllc.com
Founded: 2003
Specialize in ms development & content editing.
Editor with over 25 years of publishing experi-
ence assists published authors & first-time writ-
ers in developing & polishing mss, proposals &
query letters.

The Bookmill
501 Palisades Dr, No 315, Pacific Palisades, CA
90272-2848
Tel: 310-459-0190
E-mail: thebookmill1@verizon.net
Web Site: www.thebookmill.us
Key Personnel
Dir & Ed: Barbara Marinacci
Founded: 1982
Ms critiques; developmental editing for books,
articles; preparing queries & proposals; word
processing; contacts with agents, editors &
publishers; blurb writing, book doctoring, pro-
posals, restructuring & revising, transcribing.

Boston Informatics
35 Byard Lane, Westborough, MA 01581
Tel: 508-366-8176
Web Site: www.bostoninformatics.com
Key Personnel
Principal: M (May) H Hasso *E-mail:* mhsh2009@
verizon.net
Founded: 2002
Provides indexing services for ebooks, databases,
web & back of the book. Subjects covered include: business, finance & management, nutrition, health & allied sciences, social sciences,
technology & engineering. Other services include taxonomy development, fact checking,
information searching & word processing.
Membership(s): American Society for Indexing
(ASI)

Boston Road Communications
227 Boston Rd, Groton, MA 01450-1959
Tel: 978-448-8133
Key Personnel
Owner: Christine R Lindemer
  E-mail: crlindemer@verizon.net
Founded: 2002
Indexing business, computer technology, quality
management, project management, health care,
history, agriculture, cookbooks, how-to, liter-
ary criticism & other subjects. Over 400 books
indexed.

Brady Literary Management
PO Box 64, Hartland Four Corners, VT 05049
Tel: 802-436-2455
Key Personnel
Owner: Sally R Brady *E-mail:* bradylit@
vermontel.net

Founded: 1988

Ms analysis, conceptual, developmental & line editing, book doctoring, rewriting; trade fiction & nonfiction; contacts with agents, editors & publishers. Work on a fee basis.

Hilary R Burke
59 Sparks St, Ottawa, ON K1P 6C3, Canada
Mailing Address: Box 133, Sta B, Ottawa, ON K1P 6C3, Canada
Tel: 613-237-4658
E-mail: hburke99@yahoo.com
Promotional writing of fiction & nonfiction.

BZ/Rights & Permissions Inc
145 W 86 St, New York, NY 10024
Tel: 212-924-3000 *Fax:* 212-924-2525
E-mail: info@bzrights.com
Web Site: www.bzrights.com
Key Personnel
Pres: Barbara Zimmerman *E-mail:* bz@bzrights.com
Founded: 1980
Clears rights for literary materials, music, film & TV clips, photos, art, celebrities for educational projects - printed textbooks, spoken word recordings, new electronic media, DVDs/videocassettes. Work with film & TV producers & ad agencies. Publisher of *The Mini-Encyclopedia of Public Domain Songs & They Never Renewed: Songs You Never Dreamed Were in the Public Domain.*
Membership(s): Association of Independent Music Publishers (AIMP); The Copyright Society of the USA (CSUSA); Independent Book Publishers Association (IBPA)

Carpe Indexum
1960 Deer Run Rd, LaFayette, NY 13084
Tel: 315-677-3030
E-mail: info@carpeindexum.com
Web Site: www.carpeindexum.com
Key Personnel
Owner: Michele Combs *E-mail:* mrothen2@twcny.rr.com
Founded: 2004
Services include back-of-book & XML indexing services; research & fact checking; editing at various levels; copywriting & work-for-hire; XML/XSLT consulting.
Membership(s): American Society for Indexing (ASI); Editorial Freelancers Association (EFA); Society of American Archivists (SAA)

R E Carsch, MS-Consultant
1453 Rhode Island St, San Francisco, CA 94107-3248
Tel: 415-533-8356
E-mail: recarsch@mzinfo.com
Founded: 1973
Full-range, custom information editorial services including, fact checking, interviewing, ms analysis, proofreading, research & industry overviews.
Membership(s): Art Libraries Society of North America (ARLIS/NA)

Carol Cartaino
2000 Flat Run Rd, Seaman, OH 45679
Tel: 937-764-1303 *Fax:* 937-764-1303
E-mail: cartaino@aol.com
Founded: 1986
Content, developmental & line editing; ms analysis; rewriting & collaboration; development & packaging of book ideas & book programs. Nonfiction & fiction. Also expert assistance of all kinds for self-publishers & solutions for problem mss.

Claudia Caruana
PO Box 654, Murray Hill Sta, New York, NY 10016
Tel: 516-488-5815
E-mail: ccaruana29@hotmail.com
Copy-editing, ms analysis, rights & permissions, picture search, proofreading, research, rewriting, special assignment writing, magazine photography.

Catalyst Communication Arts
94 Chuparrosa Dr, San Luis Obispo, CA 93401
Tel: 805-235-2351 *Fax:* 805-543-7140
Web Site: www.sonsieconroy.com
Key Personnel
Owner: Sonsie Carbonara Conroy *E-mail:* sconroy@slonet.org
Founded: 1980
Specialize in indexing college textbooks, cookbooks, self-help, trade nonfiction.

Catalyst Creative Services
619 Marion Plaza, Palo Alto, CA 94301-4251
Tel: 650-325-1500
E-mail: afriendlyghostwriter@gmail.com
Web Site: www.catalystcreative.us
Key Personnel
Owner & Chief Catalyst: Dennis Alan Briskin *E-mail:* chief@catalystcreative.us
Founded: 1975
Our clients get published. We offer complete editorial services (fiction & nonfiction), from intelligent strategy (you must aim at the right target) to the structure, composition, revisions & final polish. We help companies & non-professional writers clarify, craft & publish their work for educated adult readers. We also ghostwrite for well-funded individuals with a story to tell or a cause to promote. (We respect academic integrity.) Writing contains both art & technique. We can show you the art & teach you the technique. We accept debit/credit cards.
Membership(s): Association of Ghostwriters; National Writers Union (NWU)

Jeanne Cavelos Editorial Services
PO Box 75, Mont Vernon, NH 03057
Tel: 603-673-6234
Web Site: jeannecavelos.com
Key Personnel
Owner: Jeanne Cavelos *E-mail:* jcavelos@comcast.net
Founded: 1994
Published, best-selling writer & former senior editor at major publishing house. Full editorial services for publishers, book packagers, businesses, agents & authors. From line edit to thorough edit, to heavy edit. Detailed reader's reports. Book proposal doctoring. Editorial consulting, creative development. Newsletters, magazine articles, novelizations. Handle the full range of fiction & nonfiction. Specialize in thrillers, literary fiction, fantasy, science fiction, horror, popular culture, self-help, health & science.
Membership(s): Horror Writers Association (HWA); Science Fiction & Fantasy Writers of America (SFWA)

CeciBooks Editorial & Publishing Consultation
7057 26 Ave NW, Seattle, WA 98117
Mailing Address: PO Box 17229, Seattle, WA 98127
E-mail: ceci@cecibooks.com
Web Site: www.cecibooks.com
Key Personnel
Owner: Ceci Miller
Founded: 1988
Provide complete book development & production from concept & content to finished book. Innovative in assembling teams of experts to develop, write, edit, design & produce su-

perior products. Specialty is kids nonfiction (both trade & curriculum), but we also do adult books on topics such as history, biography, science, how-to & business. We do education (textbooks, teacher resources, reference), focusing on social sciences, literacy & soft science. Produce publisher-initiated titles as well as original books. Will work with other packagers to co-produce books.
Membership(s): Independent Book Publishers Association (IBPA); Society of Children's Book Writers & Illustrators (SCBWI); Women's Business Exchange

Cenveo Publisher Services
555 Virginia Dr, Fort Washington, PA 19034
Tel: 267-470-1590 *Fax:* 215-591-9093
E-mail: info.psg@cenveo.com
Web Site: www.cenveopublisherservices.com
Key Personnel
CFO: John Pennie
Pres: Atul Goel
VP, Journal Publg Servs: Debbie McClanahan
VP, Learning Solutions: Waseem Andrabi
VP, Media & Intl Delivery Ctr: Dwayne Reed
Dir, Mktg: Mike Groth *E-mail:* mike.groth@cenveo.com
Founded: 1998
Our school division offers complete PreK-12 educational publishing services including product planning & development, editorial development, correlations & customizations, management & production. Editorial expertise includes mathematics, science, reading/language arts & social studies/humanities. Extensive experience creating student & teacher's editions. Our higher education division provides full service development for higher education products. Services include editorial project management, content creation, developmental editing, production, supplemental creation & management.
Branch Office(s)
3575 Hempland Rd, Lancaster, PA 17601
Tel: 717-285-9095
5457 Twin Knolls Rd, Suite 200, Columbia, MD 21045 *Tel:* 410-850-0500 *Toll Free Tel:* 800-257-5529
2905 Byrdhill Rd, Richmond, VA 23228
No 31 Kempapura, Hebbal, Bangalore 560 024, India *Tel:* (080) 4000 4888
36 Barnaby Rd, Kilpauk, Chennai, Tamil Nadu 600 010, India *Tel:* (044) 4205 8888
Marwah Ctr, 5th fl, Krishanlal Marwah Marg, Andheri East, Mumbai 400 072, India *Tel:* (022) 4098 5200
Steller IT Park, Tower I, 3rd fl, C 25, Sector 62, Noida 201 301, India *Tel:* (0120) 461 3700
One Mulgrave Chambers, 26-28 Mulgrave Rd, Sutton, Surrey SM2 6LE, United Kingdom

Margaret Cheasebro
5709 Holmes Dr, Farmington, NM 87402
Tel: 505-325-1557
E-mail: mwriter4571@yahoo.com
Web Site: www.margaretcheasebro.com
Founded: 1986
Freelance writer. Specialize in articles about people, places & issues of the Four Corners area, nonfiction books about alternative healing & related subjects.
Membership(s): The Authors Guild; National Federation of Press Women; New Mexico Press Women

Ruth Chernia
198 Victor Ave, Toronto, ON M4K 1B2, Canada
Tel: 416-466-0164
E-mail: rchernia@editors.ca; rchernia@sympatico.ca
Web Site: www.editors.ca/profile/444/ruth-chernia
Founded: 1983

Provides professional editorial & publishing consultation to companies & individuals.

Membership(s): Editors' Association of Canada/Association canadienne des reviseurs (EAC)

Clear Concepts
1329 Federal Ave, Suite 6, Los Angeles, CA 90025
Tel: 323-285-0325
Key Personnel
Owner: Karen Kleiner
Founded: 1986
Provides writing, substantive editing & research. Specializes in holistic health, fiction, children's books, technology & business. Owner holds BA from UCLA in Communications.
Membership(s): Society for Technical Communication (STC)

Clerical Plus
97 Blueberry Lane, Shelton, CT 06484
Tel: 203-225-0879 *Fax:* 203-225-0879
E-mail: clericalplus@aol.com
Web Site: www.clericalplus.net
Key Personnel
Pres: Rose Brown
Founded: 1990
Transcription/office support service company.

Clotilde's Secretarial & Management Services
PO Box 871926, New Orleans, LA 70187
Tel: 504-242-2912
E-mail: elcsy58@att.net
Key Personnel
Pres & Admin Mgr: Elvira C Sylve
Asst: Lillian Gail Tillman
Founded: 1989
Proofread & edit journals, newsletters, mss, research papers & medical documents. Specialize in preparing & typing research papers, grant proposals, medical & legal documents. Legal course work—Louisiana laws: briefs, business law, computer research & software, family law, interviewing, legal writing, litigation & researching in Westlaw.
Membership(s): National Association of Legal Assistants

Dwight Clough
W7502 County Rd "G", Pardeeville, WI 53954
Tel: 608-429-1440
E-mail: lmp@dwightclough.com
Web Site: dwightclough.com
Founded: 1983
Serving authors & publishers, helping them to write & self-publish their books on Amazon.

Coastside Editorial
PO Box 181, Moss Beach, CA 94038
E-mail: bevjoe@pacific.net
Key Personnel
Contact: Beverly McGuire
Membership(s): Editcetera

Robert L Cohen
182-12 Horace Harding Expwy, Suite 2M, Fresh Meadows, NY 11365
Tel: 718-762-1195 *Toll Free Tel:* 866-EDITING (334-8464) *Fax:* 917-781-0703
E-mail: wordsmith@sterlingmp.com
Web Site: www.rlcwordsandmusic.com; www.linkedin.com/in/robertcohen17
Copy, line (substantive) & developmental editing of academic, trade & reference books; editing & rewriting of books/policy briefs/working papers for think tanks & nonprofits; lexicography; radio & AV scriptwriting; speechwriting & other contract writing. Specialize in international relations (especially Middle East & related countries & regions), history (including military history), social sci-

ences, urban affairs & public policy, politics & government, psychology & education, media & communications, Judaica & religion, music, sports. Writing teacher for businesses/nonprofits/individuals.
Membership(s): American Society for Jewish Music; Cambridge Academic Editors Network; Editorial Freelancers Association (EFA)

Cohesion®
511 W Bay St, Suite 480, Tampa, FL 33606
Tel: 813-999-3111 *Toll Free Tel:* 866-727-6800
Web Site: www.cohesion.com
Key Personnel
CEO: John Owens
Chief Strategy Offr: John Larson
Founded: 1982
Complete book & journal content development & production services: writing, copy-editing, developmental editing, indexing, proofreading; project management; abstracting, advertising & promotion copywriting, bibliographies, fact checking, interviewing, developmental editing, ms analysis, rewriting, special assignment writing, transcription editing; design, art rendering, photo research, covers & jackets; permissions; in-house composition as well as development of electronic publishing products, including HTML & XML coding & supervising printing. Online editing experts (visit EditExpress.com). Specialize in technical subject areas: college, medical & allied health, computer science, law, physical & life sciences & engineering.
Branch Office(s)
6760 Alexander Bell Dr, Suite 120, Columbia, MD 21046 *Toll Free Tel:* 800-560-0630
5151 Pfeiffer Rd, Suite 105, Cincinnati, OH 45242 *Tel:* 513-587-7700

Copywriters' Council of America™ (CCA)
Division of The Linick Group Inc
CCA Bldg, 7 Putter Lane, Middle Island, NY 11953-1920
Mailing Address: PO Box 102, Middle Island, NY 11953-0102
Tel: 631-924-3888; 631-775-6075 *Fax:* 631-924-8555
Key Personnel
Chmn, Consulting Group: Andrew S Linick, PhD
  E-mail: cca4dmcopy@gmail.com
EVP: Roger Dextor
Dir, Spec Projs: Barbara Deal
Edit Advisor: Shane Clarke
Over 35,000 freelance advertising copywriters, editors, communication specialists & journalists; covering publishing, Internet direct response/direct mail field for health, physical fitness, gourmet, how-to, martial arts, self improvement, travel & tourism, photography, sports & recreation, business communications & high tech for books, magazines, manuals, newsletters, in-house organs & courses. Marketing, research, rewriting, special assignment writing, copy-editing, indexing, proofreading, ms analysis; video production, audio-video news releases; interviews & profiles; rights & permissions. Also offer annual seminars, workshops & trade show to writers/editors who would like to increase their income. Phone consultation available. Provide comprehensive graphic redesign/new web site content development, interactive services with web site marketing makeover advice for first-time authors, self-publishers, professionals & entrepreneurs. Specializes in online advertising/PR, links to top search engines, consulting on a 100% satisfaction guarantee. Free site evaluation marketing checklist (a $250 value) for LMP readers.
Branch Office(s)
7 Lincoln Ave, Smithtown, NY 11787

Course Crafters Inc
243 Greenleaf Rd, Anson, ME 04911

Mailing Address: PO Box 100, Amesbury, MA 01913
Tel: 207-696-4050
E-mail: info@coursecrafters.com
Web Site: www.coursecrafters.com
Key Personnel
Publr & CEO: Lise B Ragan
Founded: 1993
Author & packager of educational materials, K-adult, with a unique focus in the growing English Language Learner (ELL) market. Specialize in ESL, bilingual education & literacy material for English language learners, their teachers & parents. Provide services to publishers in market research, consulting, conceptualizing, writing/editing & developing marketing/sales plans. Also can develop customized materials for schools. Print, audio, video & multimedia in ESL & Spanish; professional development, instructional materials & assessment.
Membership(s): TESOL International Association

Creative Freelancers Inc
PO Box 366, Tallevast, FL 34270
Toll Free Tel: 800-398-9544
Web Site: www.freelancers1.com
Key Personnel
Pres: Marilyn Howard
Freelance copy & art services for publishing & advertising. Designers, artists, copy-editors, all creative areas, translations.

CS International Literary Agency
43 W 39 St, New York, NY 10018
Tel: 212-921-1610; 212-391-9208
E-mail: query@csliterary.com; csliterary08@gmail.com
Web Site: www.csliterary.com
Key Personnel
Literary Agent: Cynthia Neesemann
Ms analysis, evaluation & agent representation available for nonfiction, fiction & screenplays. We assist writers in developing strategies to achieve ms publication or film production & to find the writing niche that suits their talents & personality in general or specialized markets. We are particularly responsive to helping beginning writers to improve their writing skills & style with suggestions for better plotting, characterization, dialogue & structure. Fees are very reasonable. Interests extend to full range of topics whether fact or fantasy, including international, occult, ethnic, political, historical & religious subjects, mysteries & comedies. Query with short synopsis of project.

Cultural Studies & Analysis
1123 Montrose St, Philadelphia, PA 19147-3721
Tel: 215-592-8544
E-mail: info@culturalanalysis.com
Web Site: www.culturalanalysis.com
Key Personnel
Dir: Margaret J King, PhD *E-mail:* mjking9@comcast.net
Sr Analyst: Jamie O'Boyle
Founded: 1994
Specialize in cultural analysis; identify consumer values & decision making. We do not provide novel writing.

Cypress House
155 Cypress St, Fort Bragg, CA 95437
Tel: 707-964-9520 *Toll Free Tel:* 800-773-7782 *Fax:* 707-964-7531
Web Site: www.cypresshouse.com
Key Personnel
Pres: Cynthia Frank *E-mail:* cynthia@cypresshouse.com
Mng Ed: Joe Shaw *E-mail:* joeshaw@cypresshouse.com
Complete editorial, design, production, marketing & promotion services to independent publish-

ers. Editorial services include ms evaluation, editing, rewriting, copymarking & proofing. Production services include book, cover & page design & make-up to camera-ready. Marketing & promotion services for selected titles.

Membership(s): American Booksellers Association (ABA); Bay Area Independent Publishers Association (BAIPA); California Independent Booksellers Alliance (CALIBA); Independent Book Publishers Association (IBPA); Pacific Northwest Booksellers Association (PNBA)

John M Daniel Literary Services
PO Box 2790, McKinleyville, CA 95519
Tel: 707-839-3495
E-mail: jmd@danielpublishing.com
Web Site: www.danielpublishing.com/litserv.htm
Key Personnel
Ed: John M Daniel
Specialize in fiction & memoir.

Darla Bruno Writing Coach, Developmental Editor
42 Trenton Ave, Frenchtown, NJ 08825
E-mail: editor@darlabruno.com
Web Site: www.darlabruno.com
Developmental editing, rewriting, critiques, marketing, coaching. Specialize in memoir & literary fiction, as well as self-help, personal development, spiritual, health & wellness.

Mari Lynch Dehmler, see Fine Wordworking

Christina Di Martino Literary Services
87 Hamilton Place, No 7G, New York, NY 10031
Tel: 212-996-9086; 561-283-1549
E-mail: writealotmail@gmail.com
Key Personnel
Owner: Christina Di Martino
Full book line services, collaboration of book projects, freelance writing for national magazines & teaching of writing.

diacriTech Inc
4 S Market St, 4th fl, Boston, MA 02109
Tel: 617-600-3366 *Fax:* 617-848-2938
Web Site: www.diacritech.com
Key Personnel
EVP: Madhu Rajamani *E-mail:* madhu@diacritech.com
Dir, Prodn & Edit Servs: Maureen Ross
E-mail: m.ross@diacritech.com
Founded: 1997
Specialize in meeting educational publishing needs. Full service development includes project management, editorial & content development services, print & digital production, art & prepress services. In-house staff of over 800 are experienced with all phases & disciplines of K-12, college & STM. Facilities in Boston, MA, Manchester, NH & in Chennai, Madurai & Kottayam in India.

DK Research Inc
9 Wicks Dr, Commack, NY 11725-3921
Tel: 631-543-5537 *Fax:* 631-543-5549
E-mail: dkresearch@optimum.net
Web Site: www.dkresearchinc.com
Key Personnel
Owner & Pres: Diane Kraut
Founded: 1993
Handle all phases of text & photo permission clearance. Also available for ms assessments for items requiring permission.
Membership(s): Editorial Freelancers Association (EFA)

Double Play
303 Hillcrest Rd, Belton, MO 64012-1852
Tel: 816-651-7118

Key Personnel
Pres: Lloyd Johnson *E-mail:* wlloydj@yahoo.com
VP: Connie Johnson
Writing & research about baseball; sports, baseball museum consultant, exhibits; working on database of professional baseball.
Membership(s): Society for American Baseball Research

Drennan Communications
6 Robin Lane, East Kingston, NH 03827
Tel: 603-642-8002 *Fax:* 603-642-8002
Key Personnel
Pres & Edit Dir: William D Drennan
VP & Sr Ed: Christina L Drennan
Founded: 1980
Line editing, copy-editing, ms analysis, proofreading, rewriting, ghostwriting, special assignment writing, condensations, typemarking, abstracting, fact checking, interviewing, research, advertising & promotion copywriting.

Drummond Books
2111 Cleveland St, Evanston, IL 60202
Tel: 847-302-2534
E-mail: drummondbooks@gmail.com
Key Personnel
Owner: Siobhan Drummond
Editorial & production services for web, print & ebooks, editorial management, project management from raw ms to finished book, copy-editing, substantive editing, proofreading & indexing.

DWJ BOOKS LLC
14 Hill Side Lane, East Hampton, NY 11937
Tel: 631-267-8270
E-mail: info@dwjbooks.com
Web Site: www.dwjbooks.com
Key Personnel
EVP: Lauren Fedorko *E-mail:* lfedorko@dwjbooks.com
Edit Dir: Darrell Kozlowski
Founded: 2005 (developing & packaging original content since 1988)
Full service book & electronic development of large scale nonfiction projects & single titles for library & general reference publishing, test prep publishing, & curriculum-aligned publishing. Editorial services include: proposals, consulting, hiring of freelance staffs, writing, research, line & content editing, copy-editing, proofreading, indexing, fact checking, translating, special assignment writing, preparing files for print & online products.
Membership(s): American Book Producers Association (ABPA); American Library Association (ALA)

Earth Edit
PO Box 114, Maiden Rock, WI 54750
Tel: 715-448-3009
Key Personnel
Contact: George Dyke *E-mail:* gmdyke@gmail.com
Copy-editing & proofreading of college-level texts in geography, environmental science, oceanography, astronomy & cosmology, computer science.

East Mountain Editing Services
PO Box 1895, Tijeras, NM 87059-1895
Tel: 505-281-8422
Web Site: www.spanishindexing.com
Key Personnel
Mgr: Francine Cronshaw *E-mail:* cronshaw@nmia.com
Founded: 1992
Indexing (back-of-the-book) in Spanish or English. Also French, Italian & Portuguese. Expert witness on Spanish surnames. Special at-

tention to Canadian editions. Consulting on bilingual or Spanish language editions. For experience, see web site.
Membership(s): American Society for Indexing (ASI)

Edit Etc
26 Country Lane, Brunswick, ME 04011
Tel: 914-715-5849
E-mail: atkedit@cs.com
Web Site: www.anntkeene.com
Key Personnel
Pres: Ann T Keene
Founded: 1985
Editing, writing, copywriting, research, photo research.
Membership(s): The Authors Guild

Edit Resource LLC
Division of Stanford Creative Services LLC
19265 Lincoln Green Lane, Monument, CO 80132
Tel: 719-290-0757
E-mail: info@editresource.com
Web Site: www.editresource.com
Key Personnel
Owner: Elisa Stanford *E-mail:* elisa@editresource.com; Eric Stanford *E-mail:* eric@editresource.com
Founded: 1998
A writing & editing services provider.

EditAmerica
115 Jacobs Creek Rd, Ewing, NJ 08628-1014
Tel: 609-882-5852
Web Site: www.EditAmerica.com; www.linkedin.com/in/PaulaPlantier
Key Personnel
Owner/Founder/Editor/Proofer/Fact Checker: Paula Plantier *E-mail:* paulaplantier@yahoo.com
Founded: 1979
Expert copy editing, line editing, ms editing, rewriting/revising/repurposing, fact checking & proofreading of written communications in the areas of accounting, advertising, business, college application essays, company annual reports, cover letters, curricula vitae, dissertations, education, executive biographies, fiction, finance, Forms 10-K & 10-Q, marketing, medicine, newsletters, news releases, nonfiction, peer-reviewed & refereed medical/scientific journal articles, pharmaceutics, pharmacology, press releases, religious treatises, resumes, theses, user's manuals & web site content. Strict adherence to client-set deadlines. Satisfaction guaranteed for editorial services performed.
Membership(s): American Copy Editors Society (ACES); Editorial Freelancers Association (EFA); Society for Advancing Business Editing and Writing (SABEW)

Editcetera
2034 Blake St, Suite 5, Berkeley, CA 94704
Tel: 510-849-1110
E-mail: info@editcetera.com
Web Site: www.editcetera.com
Key Personnel
Dir: Barbara Fuller *E-mail:* barbara@editcetera.com
Founded: 1971
Association of freelance publishing professionals. Clients include trade publishers, el-hi & college textbook publishers, self-publishers, authors, scholars, packagers, computer companies (software & hardware), universities & corporations. Services available include production management from mss through bound books as well as writing, rewriting, developmental editing, copy-editing, coaching of writers, proofreading, indexing & web editing. Rigorous testing &

review of all members. Educational programs available to the public include live workshops, webinars, flex training & customized training.

EditCraft Editorial Services
422 Pine St, Grass Valley, CA 95945
Tel: 530-273-3934
Web Site: www.editcraft.com
Key Personnel
Prop: Eric W Engles, PhD *E-mail:* eric@editcraft. com
Founded: 1986
Editorial services for publishers, independent authors, scholars & technology companies.
Membership(s): Bay Area Editors' Forum

The Editorial Department LLC
8476 E Speedway Blvd, Suite 202, Tucson, AZ 85710
Tel: 520-546-9992
E-mail: admin@editorialdepartment.com
Web Site: www.editorialdepartment.com
Key Personnel
Founder: Renni Browne
Pres & Dir, Edit Servs: Ross Browne
    E-mail: rsb@editorialdepartment.com
Lead Ed, Romance & Women's Fiction: Lindsay Guzzardo
Founded: 1980
Ms critique & evaluation, line & copy-editing, novelizations & adaptations, book proposals, agent referral service, book cover design, book illustration, interior layout, ebook formatting, book/author marketing, publishing consultation, screenplay critique & consultation.

The Editors Circle
24 Holly Circle, Easthampton, MA 01027
Tel: 862-596-9709
E-mail: query@theeditorscircle.com
Web Site: www.theeditorscircle.com
Key Personnel
Ed: Bonny Fetterman *Tel:* 718-739-1057
    E-mail: bvfetterman@aol.com; Beth Lieberman
    Tel: 310-403-1602 *E-mail:* liebermanedit@
    socal.rr.com; John Paine *E-mail:* jpaine@
    johnpaine.com; Susan Schwartz *Tel:* 212-877-
    3211 *E-mail:* susan.sas22@gmail.com
Founded: 2005
A group of independent editors & publishing consultants with many years of in-house & freelance experience providing a wide range of editorial services for both fiction & nonfiction books, including: evaluating & critiquing book proposals & partial or complete mss; developing & editing book proposals, query letters & mss; ghostwriting, rewriting, or collaborating on book proposals & mss; consulting on self-publishing & digital publishing opportunities; providing referrals to suitable agents & publishers.

Diane Eickhoff
3808 Genessee St, Kansas City, MO 64111
Tel: 816-561-6693
E-mail: diane.eickhoff@gmail.com
Founded: 2000

Irene Elmer
2806 Cherry St, Berkeley, CA 94705-2310
Tel: 510-883-1265
E-mail: ielmer@lmi.net
Founded: 1969
Rewriting, line editing & copy-editing of trade fiction & nonfiction, textbooks & scholarly works. Specialize in difficult rewrites, dialogue & lively presentation of difficult material. Special assignment writing of adult texts; trade nonfiction; high-interest, low-readability el-hi texts (fiction, drama, nonfiction).
Membership(s): Editcetera

Catherine C Elverston ELS
3242 NW 5 St, Gainesville, FL 32609
Tel: 352-222-0625 (cell)
E-mail: celverston@gmail.com
All aspects of editing, preparing mss for publication, information research & retrieval. Also an agent.
Membership(s): American Medical Writers Association (AMWA); Board of Editors in the Life Sciences

R Elwell Indexing
193 Main St, Cold Spring, NY 10516
Tel: 845-667-1036
E-mail: r.elwell.indexing@gmail.com
Founded: 1975
Indexing.

Enough Said
3959 NW 29 Lane, Gainesville, FL 32606
Tel: 352-262-2971
E-mail: enoughsaid@cox.net
Key Personnel
Owner/Ed: Ms Heath Lynn Silberfeld
Founded: 1984
Full range of hard copy & electronic editorial services for nonfiction trade, mass market, textbook & self-publishing projects.

Farrar Writing & Editing
4638 Manchester Rd, Mound, MN 55364
Tel: 952-451-5982 *Fax:* 952-472-6874 (call first)
Web Site: www.writeandedit.net
Key Personnel
Freelance Writer & Ed: Amy E Farrar
    E-mail: amyfarrar@mchsi.com
Founded: 1999
Published book author; book editor. Clients include book publishers, individuals, nonprofits, magazines, newspapers & general businesses. Subjects include fiction & nonfiction, environmental, social, travel & health/medical. Interested parties with book projects in need of editing, send e-mail with synopsis of book, type of editorial service being sought, budget & deadline.
Membership(s): Professional Editors Network (PEN)

Betsy Feist Resources
140 E 81 St, Unit 7-E, New York, NY 10028-1875
Tel: 212-861-2014
E-mail: bfresources@rcn.com
Key Personnel
Pres: Betsy Feist
Complete editorial services, including development, writing, project management & editorial/production coordination. Specialize in instructional & informational materials.

Jerry Felsen
3960 NW 196 St, Miami Gardens, FL 33055-1869
Tel: 305-625-5012
E-mail: jfelsen0@att.net
Computer science, artificial intelligence, information systems & computer applications in business & investing; professional papers & business reports.

Fine Wordworking
PO Box 3041, Monterey, CA 93942-3041
Tel: 831-375-6278
E-mail: info@finewordworking.com
Web Site: marilynch.com
Key Personnel
Owner: Mari Lynch Dehmler
Founded: 1981
Writing, editing & proofreading of literary, business, personal & other material. Ghostwriting,

collaborative writing & editing of adult, young adult & children's nonfiction books. Editing & proofreading of fiction. Well versed in Chicago style. Web content development & design collaboration. Interviewing, research & other support. Phone calls welcome.

Richard A Flom, see Lynn C Kronzek, Richard A Flom & Robert Flom

Robert Flom, see Lynn C Kronzek, Richard A Flom & Robert Flom

Focus Strategic Communications Inc
2474 Waterford St, Oakville, ON L6L 5E6, Canada
Tel: 905-825-8757
E-mail: info@focussc.com
Web Site: www.focussc.com
Key Personnel
Dir: Adrianna Edwards *E-mail:* aedwards@ focussc.com; Ron Edwards *E-mail:* redwards@ focussc.com
Founded: 1988
Provide complete book development & production from concept & content to finished book. Innovative in assembling teams of experts to develop, write, edit, design & produce superior products. Specialty is children's nonfiction (both trade & curriculum) but also do adult books on topics such as history, biography, science, how-to & business. Also education (textbooks, teacher resources, reference), focusing on social sciences, literacy & soft science. Produce publisher-initiated titles as well as original books. Will work with other packagers to co-produce books.

Foster Travel Publishing
1623 Martin Luther King Jr Way, Berkeley, CA 94709
Tel: 510-549-2202
Web Site: www.fostertravel.com
Key Personnel
Owner & Pres: Lee Foster *E-mail:* lee@ fostertravel.com
Founded: 1972
Picture search, research, writing; travel (emphasizing locations, history, wine, nature). Specialize in Northern California, the West, Mexico-Baja, Europe, the Orient. Writing & photography available on web site. Provides travel writing/photography services for print & web editorial markets.
Membership(s): American Society of Media Photographers (ASMP); Bay Area Independent Publishers Association (BAIPA); Bay Area Travel Writers; Society of American Travel Writers (SATW)

Sandi Frank
8 Fieldcrest Ct, Cortlandt Manor, NY 10567
Tel: 914-739-7088
E-mail: sfrankmail@aol.com
Specialize in nonfiction in many disciplines, including textbooks, bibliographies, medical texts & journals, social sciences, scholarly material & cookbooks.
Membership(s): American Society for Indexing (ASI)

Fromer
1606 Noyes Dr, Silver Spring, MD 20910-2224
Tel: 301-585-8827
Key Personnel
Pres: Margot J Fromer *E-mail:* margotfromer@ erols.com
Founded: 1980

Writing, rewriting & consultation in all aspects of health care & medicine; ms analysis, special assignment writing.
Membership(s): American Medical Writers Association (AMWA); Science Writers' Association

Diane Gallo
49 Hilton St, Gilbertsville, NY 13776
Mailing Address: PO Box 106, Gilbertsville, NY 13776
Tel: 607-783-2386 *Fax:* 607-783-2386
E-mail: dgallo@stny.rr.com
Web Site: www.dianegallo.com
Interviewing & video scripts.

Michael Garrett, see ManuscriptCritique.com

The Gary-Paul Agency
1549 Main St, Stratford, CT 06615
Tel: 203-345-6167
Web Site: www.thegarypaulagency.com; www.nutmegpictures.com
Key Personnel
Owner: Gary Maynard *E-mail:* garret@thegarypaulagency.com
Founded: 1994
Literary agency that represents & promotes screenplays. Specialize in script development. WGAe Signatory.
Branch Office(s)
127 Horseshoe Rd, Fayston, VT 05660 *Tel:* 203-556-8671
Membership(s): Writers Guild of America, East (WGAE)

Fred Gebhart
PO Box 111, Gold Hill, OR 97525
Tel: 541-855-8975
E-mail: fgebhart@pobox.com
Web Site: www.fredgebhart.com
Founded: 1981
Editorial, whitepaper & advertorial writing in medical, pharmaceutical, medical device & healthcare topics.
Membership(s): American Medical Writers Association (AMWA); American Society of Journalists & Authors (ASJA); International Society of Travel Medicine; National Association of Science Writers

Gelles-Cole Literary Enterprises
2163 Lima Loop, PMB 01-408, Laredo, TX 78045-9452
Tel: 845-810-0029
Web Site: www.literaryenterprises.com
Key Personnel
Founder & Pres: Sandi Gelles-Cole *E-mail:* sandigc@gmail.com
Founded: 1983
Editorial consultant (book doctor). Specialize in commercial fiction & nonfiction serving authors, publishers & literary agents; writing coach; consultant for self-publishing authors, collaboration. Editorial specialty is development of concept & character development. Provide an intense word by word tutorial focusing on concept, style, voice, pace & characterization & for nonfiction, structure. Offers help to experts & other authors developing their material for the general public. Also have small publishing arm. Soft spot for first novels.

Nancy C Gerth PhD
1431 Harlan's Trail, Sagle, ID 83860
Tel: 208-304-9066
E-mail: docnangee@nancygerth.com
Web Site: www.nancygerth.com
Founded: 2005
Freelance indexing & related services. Index focus: Scholarly, specialize in American history, indigenous studies, postmodernism. PhD in

philosophy (Cornell University). Providing information services since 1988.
Membership(s): American Society for Indexing (ASI); Pacific Northwest Chapter of American Society for Indexing

GGP Publishing Inc
105 Calvert St, Suite 201, Harrison, NY 10528-3138
Tel: 914-834-8896 *Fax:* 914-834-7566
Web Site: www.GGPPublishing.com
Key Personnel
Pres & Publg Dir: Generosa Gina Protano *E-mail:* GGProtano@GGPPublishing.com
Founded: 1991
Packager for trade & educational publishers. All editorial, art & design, production & printing services—from concept to bound books or any segment(s) of this publishing process. Trade (fiction & nonfiction) & children's books, textbooks (el-hi, college & adult education), professional, reference & how-to books, cookbooks, audiotapes, videotapes & CDs. Specialize in the development of materials for the study of foreign languages (such as French, German, Italian, Japanese, Latin, Portuguese, Russian & Spanish) & ESL, as well as in the development of materials for bilingual education & language arts. In addition, we translate complete or partial programs from & into the various languages & act as literary agents & foreign publisher representatives.
Membership(s): American Book Producers Association (ABPA)

Cathe Giffuni, see Research Research

Sheri Gilbert
123 Van Voorhis Ave, Rochester, NY 14617
Tel: 585-342-0331
E-mail: shergilb@aol.com
Web Site: www.permissionseditor.com
Reviews mss for permissions identification; preparing permissions reports; obtaining permissions for text, art, photographs & song lyrics. Creating credit lines & source notes.

Donald Goldstein
1500 E 17 St, Brooklyn, NY 11230
Tel: 718-375-9346
E-mail: dgoldsbkyn@aol.com
Founded: 1988
Sports, sociology, American politics, the labor movement, Israel, Jewish related subjects; research, interviewing, copy-editing, rewriting, special assignment writing & proofreading.

Robert M Goodman
140 West End Ave, Unit 11-J, New York, NY 10023
Tel: 917-439-1097
E-mail: bobbybgood@gmail.com
Membership(s): Editorial Freelancers Association (EFA)

P M Gordon Associates Inc
Affiliate of New Door Books
2115 Wallace St, Philadelphia, PA 19130
Tel: 215-769-2525
Web Site: www.pmgordonassociates.com
Key Personnel
Pres: Peggy M Gordon
VP: Douglas C Gordon *E-mail:* doug@newdoorbooks.com
Founded: 1982
Developmental editing, rewriting & copy-editing for trade, text & corporate books; indexing. Complete design & production services.

Sherry Gottlieb
Unit of wordservices.com

300 W Ninth St, No 126, Oxnard, CA 93030-7098
Tel: 805-382-3425
E-mail: writer@wordservices.com
Web Site: www.wordservices.com
Founded: 1991
Private editorial service that specializes in fiction & screenplays. Edited over 450 book mss, mostly fiction. Several clients have sold their books to major publishers.

Graphic World Publishing Services
Division of Graphic World Inc
11687 Adie Rd, St Louis, MO 63043
Tel: 314-567-9854 *Fax:* 314-567-7178
E-mail: quote@gwinc.com
Web Site: www.gwinc.com
Key Personnel
Pres & CEO: Kevin P Arrow
EVP, Opers: Michael J Loomis *E-mail:* mike.loomis@gwinc.com
EVP, Technol: Andrew R Vosburgh *E-mail:* a.vosburgh@gwinc.com
Dir, Publg & Media Servs: Suzanne Kastner
Complete editorial & project management services from ms through final files, including interior & cover design, composition services, electronic publishing services & art rendering.

Paul Greenland Communications Inc
9184 Longfellow Lane, Machesney Park, IL 61115
Tel: 815-240-4108 *Toll Free Tel:* 888-798-7786
Web Site: www.paulgreenland.com
Key Personnel
Owner: Paul R Greenland
Services include writing, ghostwriting & collaboration, research, editing & proofreading. Published nonfiction author, marketing/communications professional & former senior editor of national business magazine. Contributor to many leading reference books (Cengage Learning, University of Chicago Press, Facts on File). Interview subjects include celebrities, athletes & leading business executives. Specialize in reference, business, biography & history. References available upon request.
Membership(s): Editorial Freelancers Association (EFA)

Joan K Griffitts Indexing
3909 W 71 St, Indianapolis, IN 46268-2257
Tel: 317-297-7312
E-mail: jkgriffitts@gmail.com
Web Site: www.joankgriffittsindexing.com
Founded: 1989
Indexing & proofreading of textbooks, trade books, reference books, technical documentation, catalogs & newspapers by former librarian. Most subjects; specialize in business, science, sports, gardening, computer science, library science, education, taxation & social science. Various computer formats & e-mail delivery. Technical editing of various types of books & magazines including crochet, knit, weaving, etc.
Membership(s): American Society for Indexing (ASI)

Anne Hebenstreit
20 Tip Top Way, Berkeley Heights, NJ 07922
Tel: 908-665-0536
Copy-editing & proofreading of el-hi & college texts & trade books.

Helm Editorial Services
300 Canopy Walk Lane, Unit 325, Palm Coast, FL 33237
Tel: 954-525-5626

E-mail: lynnehelm12@aol.com
Freelance writing, line editing & publishing for executives & authors.

Herr's Indexing Service
76-340 Kealoha St, Kailua Kona, HI 96740
Tel: 808-365-4348
E-mail: linda@herrsindexing.com
Web Site: www.herrsindexing.com
Key Personnel
Owner: Linda Herr Hallinger
 E-mail: lindahallinger@gmail.com
Founded: 1944
Provide quality & affordable indexes for a variety of topics. Specialize in medical books.
Membership(s): American Society for Indexing (ASI); Editorial Freelancers Association (EFA)

L Anne Hirschel DDS
5990 Highgate Ave, East Lansing, MI 48823
Tel: 517-333-1748
E-mail: alicerichard@comcast.net
Medicine & dentistry, consumer/patient information, continuing education & editing for foreign speaking scientists.
Membership(s): American Dental Association; Medical Writers Association

Burnham Holmes
182 Lakeview Hill Rd, Poultney, VT 05764-9179
Tel: 802-287-9707 *Fax:* 802-287-9707 (computer fax/modem)
E-mail: burnham.holmes@castleton.edu
Founded: 1990
Write textbooks, fiction & general nonfiction, juvenile, young adult, plays & children's books.
Membership(s): The Authors Guild; League of Vermont Writers

Henry Holmes Literary Agent/Book Publicist/Marketing Consultant
Mitchell Heights, Apt 205, 2100 S Main St, Fall River, MA 02724
Tel: 508-672-2258; 508-415-4062 (cell)
Key Personnel
Pres & Literary Agent: Henry Holmes
Founded: 1997
Nonfiction: biography, business, education, law, health, history, sports, etc. Exclusive literary agent/book publicist for authors. Authors must present complete book proposal with SASE when submitting. Impeccable presentation is a must. Prefer books targeted at general audiences rather than an exclusive or limited market. Send letter with a good hook & a list of publishers you have contacted in the past. Do not send any spiral bound proposals; word count must be stated. Include past publicity & endorsement(s). Commission 15%. Contract must be signed. Upon receipt of signed contract, author will be sent a media portfolio with marketing data, tip sheet & full compliment of media contact listings. Professional consultation related to all media, freelance assignments, interviewing celebrities, professional athletes, musicians, political figures & other famous people.

IndexEmpire Indexing Services
16740 Orville Wright Dr, Riverside, CA 92518
Tel: 951-697-2819
E-mail: indexempire@gmail.com
Key Personnel
Indexer: Jean F Middleton
Founded: 1999
Provides back-of-the-book indexes for nonfiction books of all types.
Membership(s): American Society for Indexing (ASI)

Indexing by the Book
PO Box 12513, Tucson, AZ 85732-2513
Tel: 520-750-8439
E-mail: indextran@cox.net
Web Site: www.indexingbythebook.com
Key Personnel
Indexer: Cynthia J Coan
Founded: 2003
Index books & serials. Specialize in health/medicine, history (especially Arizona/Southwest), education, language studies, library science, social sciences & psychology. Index adult, children's & Spanish language titles. Also translate print materials from Spanish & Swedish into English. Specialties in the translation field include medicine & law/patents.
Membership(s): American Society for Indexing (ASI); American Translators Association (ATA); National Council on Interpreting in Health Care (NCIHC)

Integra Software Services Inc
Division of Integra Software Services Pvt Ltd
1110 Jorie Blvd, Suite 200, Oak Brook, IL 60523
Tel: 630-586-2579 *Fax:* 630-586-2599
E-mail: marketing@integra.co.in
Web Site: www.integra.co.in
Key Personnel
Dir, Edit Devt: Ingrid Benson *E-mail:* ingrid.benson@integra.co.in
Design Mgr: Emily Friel *E-mail:* emily.friel@integra.co.in
Founded: 1991
Project management, development & production support for book publishers. Full range of publishing services, including developmental editing, design, rights & permissions, photo research, copy-editing & indexing, proofreading, language polishing, typesetting, XML & conversion, illustrations & artwork, ebooks & digital services. Specialty areas are business & economics, computer science, mathematics, science, history, English, medical & education texts.

Iridescent Orange Press, see Wambtac Communications

Jan Williams Indexing Services
300 Dartmouth College Hwy, Lyme, NH 03768-3207
Tel: 603-795-4924
Web Site: www.janwilliamsindexing.com
Key Personnel
Prop: Jan Williams
Founded: 1998
Back-of-book indexes for trade, scholarly, reference & textbooks; database/online indexes for journals.
Membership(s): American Society for Indexing (ASI)

Jenkins Group Inc
1129 Woodmere Ave, Suite B, Traverse City, MI 49686
Tel: 231-933-0445 *Toll Free Tel:* 800-706-4636
 Fax: 231-933-0448
E-mail: info@bookpublishing.com
Web Site: www.bookpublishing.com
Key Personnel
CEO: Jerrold R Jenkins *Tel:* 231-933-0445 ext 1008 *E-mail:* jrj@bookpublishing.com
Pres & COO: James Kalajian *Tel:* 231-933-0445 ext 1006 *E-mail:* jjk@bookpublishing.com
Dir, Consulting & Mktg Servs: Kim Hornyak *Tel:* 231-933-0445 ext 1013
 E-mail: khornyak@bookpublishing.com
Mng Ed, Independent Publisher Online: Jim Barnes *E-mail:* jimb@bookpublishing.com

Book Prodn Mgr: Leah Nicholson *Tel:* 231-933-0445 ext 1015 *E-mail:* lnicholson@bookpublishing.com
Founded: 1990
Full service custom book publishing services for corporations, independent authors, organizations & small press publishers. Services include registrations, typesetting, cover design, color separations, ghostwriting, illustration & photo placement, galley preparation & print management.

JFE Editorial
190 Ocean Dr, Gun Barrel City, TX 75156
Tel: 817-560-7018
E-mail: jford@jfe-editorial.com; juneford1@gmail.com
Founded: 1987
Founded by Ms Ford, a nationally published author, ghostwriter, project manager, editor & proofreader. Developmental editor of children's & juvenile mss. Focus includes: writing, ghostwriting, rewriting, special assignment writing; developmental, copy, line, style & content editing; proofreading; ms analysis; permissions, interviewing; fact checking; database management, research & input, coding, editing. Published in genres ranging from children's, trade & true crime to scholastic, self-help & sports books; also a variety of magazine articles. Coordinator of many high-dollar projects & extremely successful at transforming complex material into easily understood information. Ms Ford is a speaker for grades 3-12, universities & conferences.

JL Communications
10205 Green Holly Terr, Silver Spring, MD 20902
Tel: 301-593-0640
Key Personnel
Writer, Ed & Poet: Joyce Eileen Latham
Founded: 1996

Just Creative Writing & Indexing Services (JCR)
301 Wood Duck Dr, Greensboro, MD 21639
Tel: 443-262-2136
E-mail: judy@justcreativewriting.com
Web Site: www.justcreativewriting.com
Key Personnel
Sole Prop: Judith Reveal *E-mail:* 19editor45@gmail.com
Founded: 2005
Provides editorial services for fiction & nonfiction; professional back-of-the-book indexing; autoethnographic dissertation editing; book reviews.
Membership(s): Eastern Shore Writers' Association (ESWA); Editorial Freelancers Association (EFA); Maryland Writers' Association; National Association of Independent Writers & Editors (NAIWE); National Book Critics Circle (NBCC)

Ann T Keene, see Edit Etc

Keim Publishing
66 Main St, Suite 807, Yonkers, NY 10701
Tel: 917-655-7190
Key Personnel
Owner & Pres: Betty Keim *E-mail:* mieklb@gmail.com
Founded: 1985
Editorial, permissions, production, photo editing, research; fact checking; writing, rewriting. Editorial, production & development of promotional materials, corporate reports, newsletters, brochures & pamphlets; development of web sites & other electronic materials. Development & production of program books & other materials for conferences & conventions.

Jascha Kessler
218 16 St, Santa Monica, CA 90402-2216
Tel: 310-393-7968 *Fax:* 310-393-7968 (by request only)
E-mail: urim.urim@gmail.com
Web Site: www.jfkessler.com; www.xlibris.com
Freelance reviews of poetry, fiction, history, philosophy, current affairs. Criticism as well as "cultural commentary" on the arts, theater & dance.
Membership(s): The American Society of Composers, Authors and Publishers (ASCAP)

Bill Koehnlein
236 E Fifth St, New York, NY 10003-8545
Tel: 212-674-9145
E-mail: koehnlein.bill@gmail.com
Founded: 1982
Indexing & editing: all subjects, especially current affairs, social science, American labor & radical history, radical political movements & theory: socialism, Marxism, anarchism. Also food & nutrition issues, especially vegetarianism & veganism.

Barry R Koffler
Featherside, 14 Ginger Rd, High Falls, NY 12440
Tel: 845-687-9851
E-mail: barkof@feathersite.com
Founded: 1979
Indexing, proofreading, editing. Writing most subjects (including encyclopedic). Specialize in popular & scientific works on animals & natural history.

KOK Edit
15 Hare Lane, East Setauket, NY 11733-3606
Tel: 631-997-8191 *Fax:* 631-474-9849
E-mail: editor@kokedit.com
Web Site: www.kokedit.com; twitter.com/kokedit; www.facebook.com/K.OmooreKlopf; www.linkedin.com/in/kokedit; www.editor-mom.blogspot.com
Key Personnel
Owner: Katharine O'Moore-Klopf
Founded: 1995
Medical editor providing copy-editing & substantive editing to publishers of medical textbooks, professional books & journal articles & providing English language editing to researcher-authors who are non-native English speakers. Certified by the Board of Editors in the Life Sciences.
Membership(s): American Medical Writers Association (AMWA); Board of Editors in the Life Sciences; Council of Science Editors (CSE); Editorial Freelancers Association (EFA); World Association of Medical Editors (WAME)

Eileen Kramer
336 Great Rd, Stow, MA 01775
Tel: 978-897-4121
E-mail: kramer@tiac.net
Copy-editor/proofreader/ESL teacher/curriculum developer. Specialize in academic journals & textbooks for STEM.

Lynn C Kronzek, Richard A Flom & Robert Flom
Affiliate of Lynn C Kronzek & Associates
145 S Glenoaks Blvd, Suite 240, Burbank, CA 91502
Tel: 818-768-7688
Key Personnel
Principal: Lynn C Kronzek *E-mail:* lckronzek@sbcglobal.net
Founded: 1989
Nonfiction writing & editorial services, with particular expertise in history, multicultural & Judaic studies, government/public affairs & religion. Also, sports writing & analysis, with a focus on basketball. Professional associations include: Editorial Board, The Public Historian, National Council on Public History; American Association for State & Local History; Immigration & Ethnic History Society; the Rabbinical Assembly.

Polly Kummel LLC
624 Boardman Rd, Aiken, SC 29803
Tel: 803-641-6831
E-mail: editor@amazinphrasin.com; pollyk1@msn.com
Web Site: www.amazinphrasin.com
Founded: 1990
Nonfiction (all subjects; trade & academic): copy-editing; proofreading; substantive/developmental editing; coaching. Specialties: journalism, history, political science, memoir, equestrian subjects. Dissertation/thesis help for humanities grad students; electronic editing. More than 30 years of experience.
Membership(s): Editorial Freelancers Association (EFA); Professional Editors Network (PEN)

Lachina Creative Inc
3791 S Green Rd, Cleveland, OH 44122
Tel: 216-292-7959
E-mail: info@lachina.com
Web Site: www.lachina.com
Key Personnel
Founder & Pres: Jeffrey A Lachina
Founded: 1989
Project management, editorial development, copy-editing, biomedical illustration, indexing, page composition, book & jacket design, proofreading, technical illustration.

Lynne Lackenbach Editorial Services
31 Pillsbury Rd, East Hampstead, NH 03826
Tel: 603-329-8133
E-mail: lynnelack@gmail.com
Full line of editorial services to college & professional publishers. Specialize in scientific & technical material.

Bob Land, see Land on Demand

Land on Demand
20 Long Crescent Dr, Bristol, VA 24201
Tel: 423-366-0513
E-mail: landondemand@gmail.com
Web Site: boblandedits.blogspot.com
Key Personnel
Prop & Ed: Bob Land
Founded: 1994
Editing, indexing, proofreading. Full-time freelancer since 1994; freelancer since 1986; full-time editor, writer, proofreader 1981-1994.

The Learning Source Ltd
644 Tenth St, Brooklyn, NY 11215
E-mail: info@learningsourceltd.com
Web Site: www.learningsourceltd.com
Key Personnel
Dir: Gary Davis; Wendy Davis
Mng Ed: Brian Ableman
Provides a full range of editorial & book-producing services from concept through ms & design to film & bound book. Specialty areas include children's fiction & nonfiction, adult reference & nonfiction series & classroom materials. Sister company to Ivy Gate Books.
Membership(s): ASCD; International Literacy Association (ILA); National Council for the Social Studies (NCSS); National Council of Teachers of English (NCTE); National Council of Teachers of Mathematics (NCTM)

Debra Lemonds
PO Box 5516, Pasadena, CA 91117-0516
Tel: 626-844-9363
E-mail: dlemonds@zoho.com
Founded: 1984
Photo editing. Graphic design.
Membership(s): American Society of Picture Professionals (ASPP)

Andrew S Linick PhD, The Copyologist®
Subsidiary of The Linick Group Inc
Linick Bldg, 7 Putter Lane, Middle Island, NY 11953
Mailing Address: PO Box 102, Middle Island, NY 11953-0102
Tel: 631-924-3888; 631-775-6075 *Fax:* 631-924-8555
E-mail: linickgroup@gmail.com
Web Site: topmarketingadvisor.com
Key Personnel
CEO & Creative Dir: Andrew S Linick, PhD
  E-mail: topmarketingadvisor@gmail.com
EVP: Roger Dextor
Founded: 1968
Complete editorial & copywriting services: copy analysis & line editing, research, rewriting for direct response, direct mail, mail order, sales promotions; specialize in newsletters, newspapers, magazines, house organs & seminars; catalog writing, business & consumer launch packages & in-house seminars on how to sell what you write; articles, nonfiction books & manuals. Phone consultation available; consumer, trade, business to business, all markets, media & subjects; ms analysis & development, proofreading, special assignment writing, ghostwriting, e-mail marketing campaigns for publishers. Provide comprehensive graphic redesign/new web site content development, interactive services with web site marketing makeover advice for first-time authors, self-publishers, professionals & entrepreneurs. Specializes in flash, animation, merchant accounts, online advertising/PR, links to top search engines, consulting on a 100% satisfaction guarantee. Free site evaluation marketing checklist (a $250 value) for LMP readers. For over 50 years we have helped first-time authors & best-selling authors/publishers/entrepreneurs successfully promote books. Call for help today.
Membership(s): Independent Book Publishers Association (IBPA)

Elliot Linzer
126-10 Powells Cove Blvd, College Point, NY 11356
Tel: 718-353-1261
E-mail: elinzer@juno.com
Founded: 1971
Indexing of trade books, textbooks, reference books & scholarly books. Fifty years experience.
Membership(s): American Society for Indexing (ASI); Editorial Freelancers Association (EFA)

Little Chicago Editorial Services
154 Natural Tpke, Ripton, VT 05766
Mailing Address: PO Box 185, Ripton, VT 05766
Tel: 802-388-9782
Web Site: andreachesman.com
Key Personnel
Writer & Ed: Andrea Chesman
  E-mail: andreachesman@gmail.com
Membership(s): International Association of Culinary Professionals (IACP)

Lumina Datamatics Inc
Affiliate of Datamatics Global Services (Mumbai)
4 Collins Ave, Plymouth, MA 02360
Tel: 508-746-0300 *Fax:* 508-746-3233
Web Site: luminadatamatics.com
Key Personnel
SVP: Jack Mitchell *Tel:* 508-746-0300 ext 203
  E-mail: jack.mitchell@luminad.com
SVP, Content Technol: John Wheeler
  E-mail: john.wheeler@luminad.com

SVP, Prod Devt: Gordon Laws *E-mail:* gordon. laws@luminad.com

SVP, Sales: Prashant Prabhu *E-mail:* prashant. prabhu@luminad.com

VP, Fin & Acctg: John Chappell *E-mail:* john. chappell@luminad.com

Founded: 2005

Content & solutions provider that specializes in partnering with publishers, learning companies, assessment providers & others to automate & produce results-driven learning solutions. Offers a full service solution, or can partner with you & your most valued resources to help you achieve game-changing advantages over your closest competitors. Beyond the traditional production & delivery services that include everything from authoring & development to the complete production process, specializes in assessment authoring, AIG (automatic item generation), adaptive assessment, analytics, instructional design, simulation-based learning (with reporting engine), print & digital permissions (enterprise platform & service), audio/video & more. Employs over 1,800 US & offshore resources. Areas of specialization include K-12, higher education, professional & scholarly publishing, as well as accessibility & ADA compliance. All disciplines served including, but not limited to, mathematics, history, social studies, reading, social sciences, political science, humanities, hard sciences, computer science, business, engineering, world languages, English language teaching, ESL & technical trades & workforce readiness.

Branch Office(s)

31572 Industrial Rd, Suite 400, Livonia, MI 48150 *Toll Free Tel:* 800-717-9153 *Fax:* 734-525-4455

510 Thornall St Metropark, Suite 100, Edison, NJ 08837 (sales) *Toll Free Tel:* 888-772-5532 *Fax:* 732-635-0600

345 Seventh Ave, 4th fl, New York, NY 10001 *Tel:* 646-453-1000 *Fax:* 212-564-8285

1797 Seddon Ct, Ashland, OH 44805 *Tel:* 419-289-0558 *Fax:* 418-289-8923

3265 Farmtrail Rd, York, PA 17406 *Tel:* 717-764-4000

Datamatics Global Services GmbH doo, Gunduliceva br 33, 78000 Banja Luka, Bosnia and Herzegovina *Tel:* 51304120

Im Leuschner, Park 3, 64347 Griesheim, Germany *Tel:* (06155) 862 99-0 *Fax:* (06155) 862 99-19

Ascendas International Tech Park, Taramani Rd, 12th fl, Phase II, Chennai 600 113, India *Tel:* (044) 6604 6000; (044) 6604 6001; (044) 6604 6002 *Fax:* (044) 6604 6098

Knowledge Ctr, St No 17, MIDC, Andheri (E), Mumbai 400 093, India *Tel:* (022) 6102 0000 *Fax:* (022) 2834 3669

Suyojit Datamatics Knowledge Center, Suyojit IT Park, Survey No 804, Unit No S1-S3, Nashik-Mumbai Hwy, Nashik 422 002, India *Tel:* (0253) 610 2222 *Fax:* (0253) 610 2271

Off No 5, 2nd fl, Tower 1, Stellar IT Park, C-25, Sector 62, Noida 201 301, India *Tel:* (0120) 494 0999

Plot No 29-34, East Coast Rd, Saram Revenue Village, Oulgaret Municipality, Lawspet Post, Puducherry 605 008, India *Tel:* (0413) 660 4500; (0413) 660 4501

Mari Lynch, see Fine Wordworking

Elizabeth Lyon
1980 Cleveland St, Eugene, OR 97405
Tel: 541-357-4181
E-mail: elyon123@comcast.net
Web Site: www.elizabethlyon.com
Founded: 1988
Full-time independent editor. Specializes in novels, memoirs, nonfiction books & proposals. Advises writers how to write & connect with literary agents. Coaches how to self-publish. Over 60 writers have found publication with large publishers & small presses, while dozens have "gone indie," some to great success & acclaim. Elizabeth has written 6 books on writing & 2 booklets, including best-selling *Nonfiction Book Proposals Anybody Can Write* & *Manuscript Makeover* on revising novels.
Membership(s): Northwest Editors Guild; Oregon Writers Colony; Willamette Writers Association

Phyllis Manner
17 Springdale Rd, New Rochelle, NY 10804
Tel: 914-834-4707 *Fax:* 914-834-4707
E-mail: pmanner@aol.com; manneredit@gmail. com
Specialize in medicine, biochemistry & archeology.
Membership(s): American Society for Indexing (ASI); Archeological Institute of America (AIA)

ManuscriptCritique.com
PO Box 362, Clay, AL 35048
Web Site: www.manuscriptcritique.com
Key Personnel
Pres: Michael Garrett *E-mail:* mike@ manuscriptcritique.com
Founded: 1995
Editorial services for aspiring authors, including line edit & content evaluation.

Danny Marcus Word Worker
Division of D M Enterprises
62 Washington St, Suite 2, Marblehead, MA 01945-3553
Tel: 781-631-3886; 781-290-9174 (cell) *Fax:* 781-631-3886
E-mail: emildanelle@yahoo.com
Founded: 1984
Proofreading, line editing & copy-editing. Specialize in politics, income taxes, government, history, current events, all kinds of fiction & general nonfiction.
Membership(s): Cambridge Academic Editors Network

Joy Matkowski
212 Ridge Hill Rd, Mechanicsburg, PA 17050
Tel: 717-620-8490
E-mail: jmatkowski1@comcast.net
Copy-editing & proofreading.

Peter Mayeux
8148 Regent Dr, Lincoln, NE 68507-3366
Tel: 402-466-8547
E-mail: pm41923@windstream.net
Resumes, original research, writing papers & projects, Power Point presentations, broadcast commercial writing, textbooks & media scripts.

Anita D McClellan Associates
464 Common St, Suite 142, Belmont, MA 02478-2704
Tel: 617-575-9203
E-mail: adm@anitamcclellan.com
Web Site: www.anitamcclellan.com
Key Personnel
Mng Dir: Anita D McClellan
Founded: 1988
Developmental editing, nonfiction proposal development, revising, restructuring, book doctoring, fiction & nonfiction.
Membership(s): The Authors Guild; Bay Area Editors' Forum; Cape Cod Writers Center; Editorial Freelancers Association (EFA); Independent Book Publishers Association (IBPA); Independent Publishers of New England (IPNE); International Women's Writing Guild (IWWG); National Book Critics Circle (NBCC); Sisters in Crime; Society of Children's Book Writers & Illustrators (SCBWI); Women's National Book Association (WNBA)

Pamela Dittmer McKuen
87 Tanglewood Dr, Glen Ellyn, IL 60137
Tel: 630-545-0867
E-mail: pmckuen@gmail.com
Web Site: www.pamelamckuen.com; www. allthewriteplaces.com
Special assignment writing, editorial & corporate projects, periodicals, copy-editing, interviewing & research.
Membership(s): Association of Women in Journalism; National Association of Real Estate Editors

Pat McNees
10643 Weymouth St, Suite 204, Bethesda, MD 20814
Tel: 301-897-8557
E-mail: patmcnees@gmail.com
Web Site: www.patmcnees.com; www. writersandeditors.com
Founded: 1971
Articles, books, photohistories. Specialize in memoirs, personal histories, biographies & organizational histories. Teach memoir writing & do substantial editing, rewriting & book doctoring. Theme anthologies & stories about food, dancing & travel.
Membership(s): American Society of Journalists & Authors (ASJA); Association of Health Care Journalists; Association of Personal Historians; The Authors Guild; Biographers International Organization (BIO); Editorial Freelancers Association (EFA); Independent Book Publishers Association (IBPA); National Association of Science Writers; PEN American Center

MC2 Solutions LLC
5101 Violet Lane, Madison, WI 53714
Tel: 608-240-4959
Key Personnel
Writer/Ed: Mark Crawford *E-mail:* mark. crawford@charter.net
Founded: 1995
Servicing all audiences including academic, technical, science, corporate & public relations. Additional services include: substantive editing, promotional writing & writing of corporate histories, business writing, marketing & communications, feature writing, editing & proofreading.

Tom Mellers Publishing Services (TMPS)
60 Second Ave, Suite 8, New York, NY 10003
Tel: 212-254-4958
E-mail: tmps71@yahoo.com
Comprehensive rights & permissions administration, acquiring & granting rights for text of all kinds, photos, art, video, film, music, spoken word. Acquiring services range from consulting with rightseekers, to evaluating permissionable material, setting up projects, sending & tracking requests, negotiating fees, preparing acknowledgments, administering payment & righting contracts. Granting services include drafting contracts, negotiating & collecting fees & preparing records (edit-in). Copyright registration. Specialize in literary estates. All subjects & media. Extensive editing & editorial services, from author consultation to ms analysis, fact checking & rewriting to project supervision (including typemarking, book design, line editing, copy-editing, proofreading). Ghostwriting & special assignment writing, author representation & photo research, drafting contracts, image research & international work with museums.
Branch Office(s)
4629 Vestal Pkwy E, Vestal, NY 13850 *Tel:* 607-798-7994

Fred C Mench Professor of Classics Emeritus
207 Saint Martins Lane, Smyrna, TN 37167
Tel: 615-459-0765
E-mail: fmench@earthlink.net
Text editing, especially classical antiquity or English literature. Past projects included reading drafts of Roman historical novels for content & form, writing reviews of scholarly & fictional works (especially on ancient Rome). Book review editor of the journal *Classical World* for 15 years, involving extensive condensing of submitted texts. Special areas: Julius Caesar, Roman republic, Latin texts, the Bible, Greek mythology & G B Shaw. Also available for general editing.
Membership(s): Society for Classical Studies (SCS)

Metropolitan Editorial & Writing Service
Subsidiary of Metropolitan Research Co
4455 Douglas Ave, Riverdale, NY 10471
Tel: 718-549-5518
Key Personnel
Pres: Chauncey G Olinger, Jr *E-mail:* cgolinger@verizon.net
Founded: 1982
Editing, ms analysis, rewriting & restyling of general, professional & scholarly writing, especially in economics, business, social sciences, humanities, medicine & pharmacy. Specialize in editorial collaboration with authors; oral history interviewing.

Susan T Middleton
366A Norton Hill Rd, Ashfield, MA 01330-9601
Tel: 413-628-4039
E-mail: smiddle@crocker.com
Founded: 1985
Book revision & collaboration; substantive editing, line editing & copy-editing for individuals (all subjects & genres) & for trade & college markets (especially sciences & engineering).
Membership(s): Western New England Editorial Freelancers Network

Stephen M Miller Inc
15727 S Madison Dr, Olathe, KS 66062
Tel: 913-768-7997
Web Site: www.stephenmillerbooks.com
Key Personnel
Pres: Stephen M Miller *E-mail:* steve@stephenmillerbooks.com
Founded: 1994
Writing, editing; bible specialty & health subspecialty. Full-time freelance writer & former editor, books, magazines & newspaper. Seminary & journalism school graduate, Kansas City area. Clientele of top national book publishers & magazines.
Membership(s): Evangelical Christian Publishers Association (ECPA); Society of Bible Literature (SBL); Wesleyan Theological Society

Kathleen Mills Editorial Services
327 E King St, Chardon, OH 44024
Tel: 440-285-4347
E-mail: mills_edit@yahoo.com
Key Personnel
Edit Dir: Kathleen Mills
Founded: 1990
More than 30 years of publishing experience. Editing, writing, author liaison & project management. Arts & humanities, social sciences, reference, medical, college, business, general nonfiction & web sites. Clients include the Cleveland Museum of Art, Akron Art Museum, Western Reserve Historical Society, Case Western Reserve University, UCLA & many others.

Sondra Mochson
18 Overlook Dr, Port Washington, NY 11050

Tel: 516-883-0961
All subjects, text & trade.

Mary Mueller
516 Bartram Rd, Moorestown, NJ 08057
Tel: 856-778-4769
E-mail: mamam49@aol.com
Abstracting, copy-editing, ghostwriting, indexing, proofreading, rewriting & book reviewing-publicity. Specialize in consumer education, gardening, health, nutrition, house & home organizing, science & technology, hobby art & craft books & how-to-books.

Nina Neimark Editorial Services
543 Third St, Brooklyn, NY 11215
Tel: 718-499-6804
E-mail: pneimark@hotmail.com
Key Personnel
Pres: Nina Neimark
Founded: 1965
Specialize in scholarly books & college texts on environmental issues, history, art, music, social sciences; also general nonfiction. Mss analysis & development, content & photo research, rewriting, copy-editing, proofreading, production editing & complete book packaging services.

Newgen North America Inc
Subsidiary of Newgen KnowledgeWorks
2714 Bee Cave Rd, Suite 201, Austin, TX 78746
Tel: 512-478-5341 *Fax:* 512-476-4756
E-mail: sales@newgen.co
Web Site: www.newgen.co
Key Personnel
Pres: Maran Elancheran *E-mail:* maran@newgen.co
EVP: Tej PS Sood *E-mail:* tej@newgen.co
Founded: 1955
Prepares project material for copy-editor, supervises the copy-editing, serves as liaison with the author, reviews the final ms & makes sure that all elements of the project are complete & ready to be turned over to a designer. Ensures that file conversions, coding & cleanup properly prepare book material for each stage in the process. Convert files to ebook formats. Scan printed books to prepare new print file & ebook files.

Sue Newton
1385 Cypress Point Lane, Suite 202, Ventura, CA 93003
Tel: 805-765-4412; 805-827-1961
E-mail: sue.edit@gmail.com
Ms & line editing services including the correction of spelling errors, grammar, punctuation, syntax & consistency. Minor rewrites. 20 years experience in the publishing industry including fiction, nonfiction, autobiographies, textbooks, medical records & advertising.
Membership(s): Small Publishers, Artists & Writers Network (SPAWN); Ventura County Writers Club

Donald Nicholson-Smith
50 Plaza St E, Apt 1D, Brooklyn, NY 11238
Tel: 718-636-4732
E-mail: mnr.dns@verizon.net
French-English literary translation.
Membership(s): Translators Association (London)

Veronica Oliva
304 Lily St, San Francisco, CA 94102-5608
Tel: 415-337-7707
E-mail: veronicaoliva@sbcglobal.net
Founded: 1994

Permissions editor: Trade & educational publishers. Specialty: French, Spanish & Italian college level textbooks.
Membership(s): Bay Area Editors' Forum

Oyster River Press
36 Oyster River Rd, Durham, NH 03824-3029
Tel: 603-868-5006
E-mail: oysterriverpress@comcast.net
Web Site: www.oysterriverbooks.com; www.facebook.com/OysterRiverPress
Key Personnel
Publr & Ed: Cicely Buckley
Founded: 1987
Interviewing, special assignment writing, translating services to/from French, Spanish, Russian.

Pacific Publishing Services
PO Box 1150, Capitola, CA 95010-1150
Tel: 831-476-8284 *Fax:* 831-476-8294
E-mail: pacpubs@attglobal.net
Key Personnel
Pres: Albert Lee Strickland
Assoc: Lynne Ann De Spelder
Research, editorial & writing services for trade, text & corporate publications.

Karen L Pangallo
27 Buffum St, Salem, MA 01970
Tel: 978-744-8796
E-mail: pangallo@noblenet.org; kpangallo@gmail.com

Diane Patrick
140 Carver Loop, No 21A, Bronx, NY 10475-2954
E-mail: dpatrickediting@aol.com
Web Site: www.dianepatrick.net
Expert who creates & polishes written materials for publishers, editors, agents, academics, legal professionals, entertainers & business owners.
Membership(s): American Library Association (ALA); International Women's Writing Guild (IWWG); New York Association of Black Journalists

PeopleSpeak
25401 Alicia Pkwy, Suite L-512, Laguna Hills, CA 92653
Tel: 949-581-6190 *Fax:* 949-581-4958
E-mail: pplspeak@att.net
Web Site: www.detailsplease.com/peoplespeak
Key Personnel
Sr Ed: Sharon Goldinger
Founded: 1985
An eye for details. Copy-editing; specialize in nonfiction mss, marketing materials, newsletters, directories.
Membership(s): Independent Book Publishers Association (IBPA); Publishers Association of Los Angeles; San Diego Professional Editors Network

Rebecca Pepper
434 NE Floral Place, Portland, OR 97232
Tel: 503-236-5802
E-mail: rpepper@rpepper.net
Founded: 1986
Membership(s): Editcetera; Editorial Freelancers Association (EFA); Northwest Editors Guild

The Permissions Group Inc
401 S Milwaukee Ave, Suite 180, Wheeling, IL 60090
Tel: 847-635-6550 *Toll Free Tel:* 800-374-7985 *Fax:* 847-635-6968
E-mail: info@permissionsgroup.com
Web Site: www.permissionsgroup.com
Key Personnel
Dir: Sherry Hoesly *E-mail:* sherry_hoesly@permissionsgroup.com

Founded: 1990
Full service copyright & permissions consulting company. Specialize in ms review & analysis, rights negotiation, individualized consulting.

Elsa Peterson Ltd
41 East Ave, Norwalk, CT 06851-3919
Tel: 203-846-8331
E-mail: epltd@earthlink.net
Founded: 1984
Offer a full range of editorial services personalized to your project: developmental editing, substantive editing, writing, rights clearance, picture research, translation (Spanish to English).
Membership(s): Association for Psychological Science (APS); Editorial Freelancers Association (EFA); Textbook & Academic Authors Association (TAA)

Evelyn Walters Pettit
114 S Park Ave, Suite E, Winter Park, FL 32789-7012
Tel: 407-620-0131 (cell); 407-644-1711 *Fax:* 407-644-1711
E-mail: bookseller@brandywinebooks.com
Copy & line editing, rewriting & proofreading. Specialize in professional & reference books, journal articles & magazines & books in general. Experience in subjects ranging from social & biological sciences to engineering & mathematics to business.

Meredith Phillips
4127 Old Adobe Rd, Palo Alto, CA 94306
Tel: 650-857-9555
E-mail: mphillips0743@comcast.net
Former author & award-nominated mystery publisher (Perseverance Press). Editing (developmental, line, copy), researching, fact checking, proofreading of trade books (fiction or nonfiction).

PhotoEdit Inc
3505 Cadillac Ave, Suite P-101, Costa Mesa, CA 92626
Toll Free Tel: 888-450-0946 *Fax:* 714-434-5937
Toll Free Fax: 800-804-3707
Web Site: www.photoeditinc.com
Key Personnel
Photo Edit Dir: Tashauna Johnson *Tel:* 714-434-5935 *E-mail:* tashauna.johnson@photoeditinc.com
Founded: 1987
Photographers; large stock on hand.

Pictures & Words Editorial Services
3100 "B" Ave, Anacortes, WA 98221
Tel: 360-293-8476
E-mail: editor@picturesandwords.com
Web Site: www.picturesandwords.com/words
Key Personnel
Owner: Kristi Hein
Founded: 1995
Versatile generalist serving trade publishers & authors. Cookbooks, health & well-being, gardening (including New York Times best seller *A Year in Flowers*), nature & environment, education, consumer interest & activism, business & fiction.
Membership(s): American Copy Editors Society (ACES); Bay Area Editors' Forum; Northwest Editors Guild

Caroline Pincus Book Midwife
101 Wool St, San Francisco, CA 94110
Tel: 415-516-6206
E-mail: cpincus1958@gmail.com
Web Site: www.carolinepincus.com
Key Personnel
Book Midwife: Caroline Pincus

Founded: 1998
Nonfiction proposal & ms development & book doctoring for the general trade. Specialize in health, personal growth, women's issues.

J P Pochron Writer for Hire
830 Lake Orchid Circle, No 203, Vero Beach, FL 32962
Tel: 772-569-2967
E-mail: hotwriter15@hotmail.com
Key Personnel
Owner & Writer: J P Pochron
Former editor, reporter & freelance writer, with marketing, advertising & public relations experience. Press releases, promotional copy, commercials, personal & business letter writing are services offered. Eight years library reference experience to assist with research.

Wendy Polhemus-Annibell
PO Box 464, Peconic, NY 11958
Tel: 631-833-6942
E-mail: wannibell@gmail.com
Founded: 1987
Freelance copy-editing, line editing, developmental editing, proofreading, project management. Specialize in college textbooks (particularly English/grammar/writing/rhetoric texts) & fiction/nonfiction trade books, with an emphasis on editorial excellence.

The Professional Writer
175 W 12 St, Suite 6D, New York, NY 10011
Tel: 212-414-0188; 917-658-1946 (cell)
E-mail: paul@theprofessionalwriter.com
Key Personnel
Owner: Paul Wisenthal *E-mail:* paulwisenthal@gmail.com
Founded: 1989
Book networking to the industry, book development—includes creative writing/editing, writer's block, project preparation. Copywriting for brochures, media kits, newsletters, business & investment proposals, writers coach & grants. Script writing, script doctor for TV/film/radio. Speech writing. Youth market specialists. Story development workshops.
Membership(s): The Authors Guild; National Writers Union (NWU)

Pronk Media Inc
PO Box 340, Beaverton, ON L0K 1A0, Canada
Tel: 416-441-3760
E-mail: info@pronk.com
Web Site: www.pronk.com
Key Personnel
Pres: Gord Pronk *Tel:* 416-441-3760 ext 203 *E-mail:* gord@pronk.com
Founded: 1981 (as Pronk & Associates Inc)
Print design & production, including product conceptualization & prototypes, design & art direction, photo research & licensing, infographics, charts, graphs, technical art, page design, layout & production.

Proofed to Perfection Editing Services
6519 Sherrill Baggett Rd, Godwin, NC 28344
Tel: 910-980-0832
E-mail: inquiries@proofedtoperfection.com
Web Site: www.proofedtoperfection.com
Key Personnel
Sr Ed & Proj Coord: Pamela Cangioli *E-mail:* pamg@proofedtoperfection.com
Founded: 2006
Full service editing company. Specialize in comprehensive, professional book editing. We offer proofreading, copy-editing, developmental editing, book evaluations & book proposals at competitive rates. Our editors have traditional publishing experience & offer personal, quality

service. All new clients get a free sample edit & book critique.
Membership(s): American Christian Fiction Writers (ACFW); Editorial Freelancers Association (EFA); Evangelical Christian Publishers Association (ECPA)

Generosa Gina Protano Publishing, see GGP Publishing Inc

Publishing Resources Inc
425 Carr 693, PMB 160, Dorado, PR 00646
Tel: 787-647-9342
E-mail: pri@chevako.net
Web Site: www.publishingresources.net
Key Personnel
Pres: Ronald J Chevako
EVP & Ed: Anne W Chevako
Prodn: Jay A Chevako
Founded: 1982
Complete services including ms development, research, writing, translation (Spanish-English; English-Spanish), indexing, content editing & line editing by US trained professionals & full production services.

Publishing Synthesis Ltd
39 Crosby St, New York, NY 10013
Tel: 212-219-0135
E-mail: mainmail@pubsyn.com
Web Site: www.pubsyn.com
Key Personnel
Pres: Otto H Barz *E-mail:* obarz@pubsyn.com
VP & Spec Projs Coord: Ellen Small *E-mail:* esmall@pubsyn.com
Founded: 1975
Editing, design, typesetting & prepress production of trade, college text & highly technical books.
Membership(s): Book Industry Guild of New York; Independent Book Publishers Association (IBPA)

Jerry Ralya
7909 Vt Rte 14, Craftsbury Common, VT 05827
Tel: 802-586-7514
E-mail: jerryralya@gmail.com
Founded: 1980
Editing, indexing & preparing online test materials for college textbooks in medicine, science, nursing & the behavioral sciences.
Membership(s): Editorial Freelancers Association (EFA)

The Reading Component
3900 Parkview Lane, 3B, Irvine, CA 92612-2003
Mailing Address: 2155 N Bellflower Blvd, PMB 169, Long Beach, CA 90815
Tel: 949-387-6330
Key Personnel
Owner: Helen M Winton *E-mail:* hmwinton@outlook.com
Founded: 1994

Research Research
240 E 27 St, Suite 20-K, New York, NY 10016-9238
Tel: 212-779-9540 *Fax:* 212-779-9540
E-mail: ehtac@msn.com
Key Personnel
Pres: Cathe Giffuni
Founded: 1987

Judith Riven Literary Agent LLC
250 W 16 St, Suite 4F, New York, NY 10011
Tel: 212-255-1009 *Fax:* 212-255-8547
E-mail: rivenlitqueries@gmail.com
Web Site: rivenlit.com
Key Personnel
Owner & Pres: Judith Riven
Founded: 1993
Editorial consultation, developmental & structural editing, line editing, ms analysis.

The Roberts Group
12803 Eastview Curve, Apple Valley, MN 55124
Tel: 952-322-4005
E-mail: info@editorialservice.com
Web Site: www.editorialservice.com
Key Personnel
Owner: Sherry Roberts; Tony Roberts
Founded: 1990
Book design, production, editorial services & web
development. A one-stop creative resource for
quality interior book design, typesetting, editing, proofreading, indexing, Kindle & e-pub
formatting. Serving established presses & self-
publishers. Competitive prices. We pay attention to details & will work to meet your deadlines. See web site for more info & samples.
Membership(s): Independent Book Publishers Association (IBPA); Midwest Independent Publishing Association (MIPA); Professional Editors Network (PEN)

Peter Rooney
332 Bleecker St, PMB X-6, New York, NY
10014-2980
Tel: 917-376-1792 *Fax:* 212-226-8047
E-mail: magneticreports@gmail.com
Web Site: www.magneticreports.xyz
Indexer, programmer/consultant for indexes,
databases, directories, catalogues raisonnes.
Large & small projects.
Membership(s): American Society for Indexing
(ASI)

Dick Rowson
4701 Connecticut Ave NW, Suite 503, Washington, DC 20008
Tel: 202-244-8104
E-mail: rcrowson2@aol.com
Helps authors find good publishers & appraise
mss.
Membership(s): Association for Slavic, East European & Eurasian Studies (ASEEES); Overseas Press Club

Sachem Publishing Associates Inc
402 W Lyon Farm Dr, Greenwich, CT 06831
Tel: 203-813-3077
E-mail: sachempub@optonline.net
Key Personnel
Pres & Ed: Stephen P Elliott
Founded: 1974
Complete trade & mail order book preparation
& packaging; editorial services, from concept
to finished books. Specialize in consumer &
educational reference books, including encyclo-
pedias & dictionaries.

Salmon Bay Indexing
PO Box 2362, Vashon, WA 98070
Tel: 206-612-3993
Web Site: salmonbayindexing.com
Key Personnel
Indexer: Beth Nauman-Montana *E-mail:* beth@
salmonbayindexing.com
Founded: 2002
Professional indexer. Provides indexes for books
& ebooks in all subject areas. Every project is
delivered on time & according to client guide-
lines.

Barbara S Salz LLC Photo Research
127 Prospect Place, South Orange, NJ 07079
Tel: 646-734-5949
E-mail: bsalz.photo@gmail.com
Image research & permissions for books, maga-
zines, exhibitions & advertising.
Membership(s): American Society of Picture Pro-
fessionals (ASPP)

Paul Samuelson
117 Oak Dr, San Rafael, CA 94901

Tel: 415-517-0700 (cell)
E-mail: paul@storywrangler.com
Web Site: www.storywrangler.com
Also consults on narrative material & screenplays.

C J Scheiner Books
PO Box 96, Brooklyn, NY 11226-0096
Tel: 718-469-1089
Key Personnel
Owner: C J Scheiner
Literature searches, special assignment writing,
fact checking, research, photo research illustra-
tions provided, bibliographies & source lists,
text & introduction writing. Specialize in erot-
ica, curiosa & sexology.

Schoolhouse Indexing
10-B Parade Ground Rd, Etna, NH 03750
Tel: 603-643-1617
Web Site: schoolhouseindexing.com
Key Personnel
Owner & Indexer: Christine Hoskin
    E-mail: christine@schoolhousefarm.net
Freelance indexing business. Professional indexing services offered include the fields of law
& legal issues, education (in both English &
French), business & economics, children's elementary education/nonfiction, travel, hospitality
& tourism, social sciences & culture, health &
psychology, history & biography, environmental
sciences, geology, engineering, construction &
architecture. Indexing queries regarding general
indexing information, rates & availability are
welcome.
Membership(s): American Society for Indexing
(ASI)

Schoolhouse Network
PO Box 1518, Northampton, MA 01061
Tel: 480-427-4836
E-mail: schoolhousenetwork@gmail.com
Key Personnel
Pres: Marilyn Greco
Dir, Curriculum: Mary K Messick
Founded: 1998
Provides a comprehensive range of editorial service & products to educational publishers,
development groups, schools & other educational institutions for PreK, K-12 & college
in both print & electronic media in the areas
of reading/language arts, ESL, literature, social studies, health & science. Develop student
& teacher editions, leveled readers, children's
books, graphic novels, fiction & nonfiction,
trade book publications which include memoir,
poetry, travel with accompanying art & photography.
Membership(s): Editorial Freelancers Association (EFA); International Literacy Association
(ILA); National Association for the Education
of Young Children (NAEYC); TESOL International Association

Schroeder Indexing Services
23 Camilla Pink Ct, Bluffton, SC 29909
Tel: 843-705-9779
E-mail: sanindex@schroederindexing.com
Web Site: www.schroederindexing.com
Key Personnel
Owner & CEO: Sandi Schroeder
Produce custom indexes using CINDEX, a ded-
icated indexing software. Company web site
includes current information on clients & ti-
tles indexed, information on planning an index,
downloadable Project Information Sheet & re-
quest for an estimate.
Membership(s): American Society for Indexing
(ASI)

Franklin L Schulaner
PO Box 507, Kealakekua, HI 96750-0507

Tel: 808-322-3785
E-mail: fschulaner@hawaii.rr.com

Sherri Schultz/Words with Grace
1810 Alder St, No 105, Eugene, OR 97401
Tel: 206-928-2015
E-mail: WordsWithGraceEditorial@gmail.com
Founded: 1992
Experienced copy-editor & proofreader of fic-
tion & nonfiction books, web content & more.
Works with clients around the country. Spe-
cial expertise in politics, environment, travel,
literary nonfiction & art.
Membership(s): Northwest Editors Guild; Spring-
field/Eugene-area Editors (SEE)

Sciendex
1388 Leisure Dr, Summerville, SC 29486
Tel: 843-693-6689
Web Site: www.sciendex.com
Key Personnel
Owner/Indexer: Samantha Miller
    E-mail: samanthamiller@mindspring.com
Founded: 2004
Index preparation for topics including the sci-
ences (environmental science, biology, chem-
istry, geology, medicine), biographies, cooking,
nutrition, & general trade subjects.

Scribendi Inc
405 Riverview Dr, Chatham, ON N7M 0N3,
Canada
Tel: 519-351-1626 (cust serv) *Fax:* 519-354-0192
E-mail: customerservice@scribendi.com
Web Site: www.scribendi.com
Key Personnel
CEO: Enrico Magnani, MA *E-mail:* enrico.
magnani@scribendi.com
Pres: Patrica Riopel *E-mail:* patricia.riopel@
scribendi.com
Founded: 1997
On demand proofreading & editing services avail-
able 24/7. Web site offers instant quotes on
all standard services; call or e-mail for special
project quotes or long-term arrangements.

SDP Publishing Solutions LLC
36 Captain's Way, East Bridgewater, MA 02333
Tel: 617-775-0656
Web Site: www.sdppublishingsolutions.com
Key Personnel
Publr & Consultant: Lisa Akoury-Ross
    E-mail: lross@sdppublishing.com
Ghostwriter, Developmental Ed & Copy-Ed:
Kathleen A Tracy
Developmental Ed & Copy-Ed: Lisa Schleipfer;
Susan Strecker
Ed: Beth Raps
Prof Proofreader/Proofchecker: Karen Grennan
Artist: Randy Jennings
Cover & Interior Designer: Howard Johnson
Admin Asst: Kim Sexton
Publisher's Asst: Samantha Eldredge
Founded: 2009
Specialize in editorial services for all genres in-
cluding fiction, nonfiction, memoirs, business
books, children's books & more. Our business
is designed to review mss & determine the best
editorial approach for each author. From ghostwriting, developmental editing, copy-editing &
proofreading, we help our authors become better writers! We also write effective marketing
kits, query letters, analysis of the competitive
marketplace, along with the marketing & media
landscape for those who wish to pitch to literary agents & traditional publishers. We offer
optimal publishing solutions for authors worldwide from literary agency representation, to
worldwide marketing, including international
rights & independent publishing.

Alexa Selph
4300 McClatchey Circle, Atlanta, GA 30342

Tel: 404-256-3717
E-mail: lexa101@aol.com

Barry Sheinkopf
c/o The Writing Ctr, 601 Palisade Ave, Englewood Cliffs, NJ 07632
Tel: 201-567-4017 *Fax:* 201-567-7202
E-mail: bsheinkopf@optonline.net
Founded: 1977
Trade, scholarly & professional publications, book design & self-publishing.
Membership(s): The Authors Guild; Mystery Writers of America (MWA)

Monika Shoffman-Graves
70 Transylvania Ave, Key Largo, FL 33037
Tel: 305-451-1462 *Fax:* 305-451-1462
E-mail: mograv@gmail.com
Indexing, ms analysis, proofreading & research.

Roger W Smith
59-67 58 Rd, Maspeth, NY 11378-3211
Tel: 718-416-1334
E-mail: brandeis106@gmail.com
Founded: 1982
Membership(s): Editorial Freelancers Association (EFA)

Stackler Editorial Agency
200 Woodland Ave, Summit, NJ 07901
Tel: 510-912-9187
E-mail: ed.stackler@gmail.com
Web Site: www.fictioneditor.com
Key Personnel
Owner: Ed Stackler
Founded: 1996
Editorial services for novelists of crime, thriller & suspense fiction.

Nancy Steele
2210 Pine St, Philadelphia, PA 19103-6516
Tel: 215-732-5175
E-mail: Nancy.Steele.Edits@gmail.com
Founded: 1999
Versatile, intuitive editor with more than 20 years of experience in editing nonfiction. Expertise in American art & antiques, anthologies, biographies & memoirs, business & technology, psychology, reference & illustrated books. Special interest in the arts of Japan.
Membership(s): National Association of Science Writers

Sterling Media Productions LLC, see Robert L Cohen

Jeri L Stolk
8 Rush Vine Ct, Owings Mills, MD 21117
Tel: 410-864-8109
E-mail: jeristolk@gmail.com
Edit journals & books, especially academic.

Vivian Sudhalter
1202 Loma Dr, No 117, Ojai, CA 93023
Tel: 805-640-9737
E-mail: vivians09@att.net
Freelance editor. Specialize in fiction & nonfiction books on women's studies, holistic health, memoirs & other genres. I improve finished mss by copy-editing for good grammar, flow, punctuation, usage & consistency, while maintaining the author's authentic voice. I also help shape books from inception by working with authors to create the structure that will best serve their vision. Having been in the book publishing industry for more than 4 decades, I provide insights into the publication process, whether conventional or POD. Contact by e-mail preferred.

Fraser Sutherland
39 Helena Ave, Toronto, ON M6G 2H3, Canada
Tel: 416-652-5735
E-mail: rodfrasers@gmail.com
Founded: 1970
General editorial services. Specialize in dictionaries & reference books (lexicography), ms analysis & rewriting.
Membership(s): Dictionary Society of North America; Editors' Association of Canada/Association canadienne des reviseurs (EAC); PEN Canada

Thodestool Fiction Editing
40 McDougall Rd, Waterloo, ON N2L 2W5, Canada
Web Site: www.thodestool.ca
Key Personnel
Owner: Vanessa Ricci-Thode
E-mail: vanessariccithode@gmail.com
Founded: 2010
Focus on providing editing services for speculative fiction (science fiction, fantasy, horror) of varying lengths, with a focus on structural/developmental editing & ms evaluations.
Membership(s): Canadian Author's Association; Editors' Association of Canada/Association canadienne des reviseurs (EAC)

Susan Thornton
6090 Liberty Ave, Vermilion, OH 44089
Tel: 440-967-1757
E-mail: allenthornton@earthlink.net
Key Personnel
Freelance Copy Ed: Allen Thornton; Susan Thornton
Medical, technical, mathematics, university press, college text, reference, trade nonfiction & journals on hard copy & on disk.

Twin Oaks Indexing
Division of Twin Oaks Community
138 Twin Oaks Rd, Suite W, Louisa, VA 23093
Tel: 540-894-5126
Web Site: www.twinoakscommunity.org
Key Personnel
Mgr: Rachel Nishan
Founded: 1981

Wambtac Communications
1512 E Santa Clara Ave, Santa Ana, CA 92705
Tel: 714-954-0580 *Toll Free Tel:* 800-641-3936
E-mail: wambtac@wambtac.com
Web Site: www.wambtac.com; claudiasuzanne.com (prof servs)
Key Personnel
Owner, Founder & Creative Partner: Claudia Suzanne *E-mail:* claudiasuzanne@gmail.com
Founded: 1995
Ghostwriting services & training.
Membership(s): Independent Book Publishers Association (IBPA)

WC Publishing, see Wambtac Communications

Toby Wertheim
240 E 76 St, New York, NY 10021
Tel: 212-472-8587
E-mail: tobywertheim@yahoo.com
Research/editor.

Rosemary Wetherold
4507 Cliffstone Cove, Austin, TX 78735
Tel: 512-892-1606
E-mail: roses@ix.netcom.com
Founded: 1985
Copy-editing, substantive editing, desktop publishing. Varied subjects, including biological sciences & natural history.

WFS, see Write for Success Editing Services

Barbara Mlotek Whelehan
7064 SE Cricket Ct, Stuart, FL 34997
Tel: 954-554-0765 (cell); 772-463-0818 (home)
E-mail: barbarawhelehan@bellsouth.net
More than 30 years of publishing experience. All subjects; specialize in personal finance, investments, mutual funds, business & consumer topics. Also copy-edit fiction.

White Oak Editions, see Carol Cartaino

Eleanor B Widdoes
417 W 120 St, New York, NY 10027
Tel: 917-886-6401 (cell)
E-mail: widdoese@aa.org
Indexing, proofreading, research, bibliographies & newsletters.

Windhaven®
466 Rte 10, Orford, NH 03777
Tel: 603-512-9251 (cell)
Web Site: www.windhavenpress.com
Key Personnel
Dir & Ed: Nancy C Hanger *E-mail:* nhanger@windhavenpress.com
Ed & Consultant: Andrew V Phillips
E-mail: andrew@windhavenpress.com
Founded: 1985
Consulting & developmental editing, line editing, copy-editing, proofreading.
Membership(s): Editorial Freelancers Association (EFA); National Writers Union (NWU)

WordCo Indexing Services Inc
49 Church St, Norwich, CT 06360
Tel: 860-886-2532 *Toll Free Tel:* 877-WORDCO-3 (967-3263) *Fax:* 860-886-1155
E-mail: office@wordco.com
Web Site: www.wordco.com
Key Personnel
Founder & CEO: Stephen Ingle *E-mail:* sringle@wordco.com
Proj Coord: Amy Moriarty *E-mail:* amoriarty@wordco.com
Founded: 1988
Since 1988, WordCo has completed thousands of thorough & accurate indexes in hundreds of subject areas for many major publishers. WordCo's in-house team of professionally trained indexers has the experience & capability to complete your indexing projects professionally & on time. Rush service & ebook indexing available.
Membership(s): American Society for Indexing (ASI)

Words into Print
208 Java St, 5th fl, Brooklyn, NY 11222
E-mail: query@wordsintoprint.org
Web Site: wordsintoprint.org
Key Personnel
Ed: Jeff Alexander *E-mail:* jeffale73@gmail.com; Becky Cabaza *E-mail:* rtcbooks@gmail.com; Jane Fleming Fransson *E-mail:* janef13@gmail.com; Ruth Greenstein *E-mail:* rg@greenlinepublishing.com; Emily Loose *E-mail:* emilylooselit@gmail.com; Julie Miesionczek *E-mail:* julie@writewithjulie.com; Anne Cole Norman *E-mail:* acole157@gmail.com
Founded: 1998
An alliance of top New York publishing professionals who offer a broad range of editorial services to authors, publishers, literary agents, book packagers & content providers.

Words with Grace, see Sherri Schultz/Words with Grace

Working With Words
5320 SW Mayfair Ct, Beaverton, OR 97005
Tel: 503-644-4317
E-mail: editor@zzz.com
Key Personnel
Owner: Sue Mann
Founded: 1985
Freelance editorial services. General trade, non-fiction. Subjects include children's, cookbooks, creativity, historical, inspirational, memoirs, self-help, spiritual, training. Substantive editing. Online & hard copy.
Membership(s): Northwest Editors Guild

Wright Information Indexing Services
PO Box 658, Sandia Park, NM 87047
Tel: 505-281-2600
Web Site: www.wrightinformation.com
Key Personnel
Owner & Pres: Jan C Wright *E-mail:* jancw@wrightinformation.com
Founded: 1991
Book, ebook & online indexing services. Specialize in single-source publications; 2009 winner of H W Wilson Award for Excellence in Indexing.
Membership(s): American Society for Indexing (ASI)

Write for Success Editing Services
PO Box 292153, Los Angeles, CA 90029-8653
Tel: 323-356-8833
E-mail: writeforsuccessediting@gmail.com
Web Site: www.write-for-success.com
Key Personnel
Owner/Ed: Christine Van Zandt
  E-mail: christine@write-for-success.com
Founded: 2009
Full service professional editor & writer. Helping writers from creation to publication. Knowledgeable, experienced, thorough, kind, responsive, timely feedback. Industry & current marketplace insight. Education includes master's degree in English literature. Freelance writing or ghostwriting assistance. Based in Los Angeles. For writers seeking traditional or self-publication in fiction, nonfiction, or memoir, adult or children's considered (picture book, chapter book, middle grade, young adult). Query letters, synopses, proposals, author bios, book blurbs. Mastery of current reference guides.

Membership(s): Bay Area Editors' Forum; Editorial Freelancers Association (EFA); Independent Book Publishers Association (IBPA); Society of Children's Book Writers & Illustrators (SCBWI)

The Write Way
3048 Horizon Lane, Suite 1102, Naples, FL 34109
Tel: 239-273-9145
E-mail: darekane@gmail.com
Key Personnel
Pres: Roberta Kane
Also handle advertising & marketing.

The Writer's Lifeline Inc
400 S Burnside Ave, Suite 11B, Los Angeles, CA 90036
Tel: 323-932-1685
Web Site: www.thewriterslifeline.com
Key Personnel
CEO: Kenneth Atchity, PhD *E-mail:* kja@thewriterslifeline.com
EVP: Chris Kuhne *E-mail:* chris@storymerchant.com
Founded: 1996
A full service editorial company, providing non-fiction book writers, novelists, business, professional, technical & screenwriters with assistance in storytelling, mentoring, perfecting their style & craft, style-structure-concept-line editing, ghostwriting, publishing consulting, development, translation, advertising & promotion, printing & self-publishing, distribution & research.
Sister companies: Atchity Productions; Story Merchant; Story Merchant Books.
Membership(s): American Comparative Literature Association; The Authors Guild; National Academy of Television Arts & Sciences (NATAS); PEN American Center; Women in Film (WIF)

Writer's Relief, Inc
18766 John J Williams Hwy, Unit 4, Box 335, Rehoboth Beach, DE 19971
Toll Free Tel: 866-405-3003 *Fax:* 201-641-1253
E-mail: info@writersrelief.com
Web Site: www.WritersRelief.com
Key Personnel
Pres: Ronnie L Smith *E-mail:* ronnie@wrelief.com

Founded: 1994
Don't have time to submit your writing? We can help. Submission leads & cover/query letter guidelines. Join the 60,000+ writers who subscribe to *Submit Write Now!*, our free e-publication.

Wyman Indexing
1311 Delaware Ave SW, No S332, Washington, DC 20024
Tel: 443-336-5497
Web Site: www.wymanindexing.com
Key Personnel
Owner & Chief Indexer: Pilar Wyman
  E-mail: pilarw@wymanindexing.com
Founded: 1990
Freelance indexing & consulting. Specialize in medicine, technology & current events. Also provide Spanish-to-English translation services.
Membership(s): American Medical Writers Association (AMWA); American Society for Indexing (ASI)

Zebra Communications
230 Deerchase Dr, Woodstock, GA 30188-4438
Tel: 770-924-0528
E-mail: bobbie@zebraeditor.com
Web Site: www.zebraeditor.com
Key Personnel
Owner: Bobbie Christmas *E-mail:* bzebra@aol.com
Founded: 1992
Editorial services that specialize in fiction & nonfiction books as well as magazines.
Membership(s): Atlanta Writers Club; Florida Writers Association; Georgia Writers Association; International Guild of Professional Business Consultants; Society for the Preservation of English Language Literature (SPELL); South Carolina Writers Workshop; Southeastern Writers Association; The Writers' Network

Robert Zolnerzak
101 Clark St, Unit 20-K, Brooklyn, NY 11201
Tel: 718-522-0591
E-mail: rzolnerzak@gmail.com
Computer-assisted indexing for medical, scientific & computer science textbooks & journals since 1973.
Membership(s): American Society for Indexing (ASI); Editorial Freelancers Association (EFA)

Literary Agents

The agents listed here are among the most active in the field. Prior to obtaining a listing in *LMP*, potential entrants are required to submit verifiable references from publishers with whom they have placed titles. Letters in parentheses following the agency name indicate fields of activity:

(L)–Literary Agent   (D)–Dramatic Agent   (L-D)–Literary & Dramatic Agent

Those individuals who are members of the Association of Authors' Representatives are identified by the presence of (AAR) after their name.

Authors seeking literary representation are advised that some agents request a nominal reading fee that may be applied to the agent's commission upon representation. Other agencies may charge substantially higher fees which may not be applicable to a future commission and which are not refundable. The recommended course is to first send a query letter with an outline, sample chapter, and a self-addressed stamped envelope (SASE). Should an agent express interest in handling the manuscript, full details of fees and commissions should be obtained in writing before the complete manuscript is sent. Should an agency require significant advance payment from an author, the author is cautioned to make a careful investigation to determine the agency's standing in the industry before entering an agreement. The author should always retain a copy of the manuscript in his or her possession.

AAA Books Unlimited (L)
3060 Blackthorn Rd, Riverwoods, IL 60015
Tel: 847-444-1220 *Fax:* 847-607-8335
Web Site: www.aaabooksunlimited.com
Key Personnel
Principal: Nancy Rosenfeld *E-mail:* nancy@aaabooksunlimited.com
Founded: 1993
Full service literary agency to provide clients with first class service "over & above" what normally is handled by a literary agency. We offer content-copy-line editing services. No unsol mss, query first.
Titles recently placed: *A Mother's Grace: Healing the World, One Woman at a Time*, Michelle Moore; *An Introduction to Mozart: "The Music, The Man, The Myths"*, Roye E Wates, PhD; *Anatomy of a False Confession: The Interrogation and Conviction of Brendan Dassey*, Michael Cicchini; *Baseball and American Culture*, John Rossi; *Beautiful Smile, Healthy Body: Your Guide to Authentic Holistic Dental Care, Optimal Health, and Natural Vitality*, Rev Dr Stephen A Lawrence, David Tabatsky; *Belief To Die For*, James Alcock, PhD; *Breaking the Cycle: Free Yourself from Sex Addiction, Porn Obsession, and Shame*, George N Collins, MA, Andrew Adleman, MA; *Circus Lab*, Jackie Leigh Davis; *Demystifying Hospice: Stories of Caregivers and Patients Partnering with Hospice*, Karen J Clayton; *Erotic Marriage: Break Free from the Negative Sexual Script and Improve the Sexual and Emotional Quality of Your Relationship*, Dr Frederick D Mondin; *Forget Dieting: "It's All About Data Fueling"*, Candice P Rosen, RN, MSW; *Hidden: The Mysteries of Nature and Secrets of Cheats*, Loren Pankratz, PhD; *How Surviving the Second World War Taught Me How to Live*, Sgt Daniel Altman, Fawn Zwickel; *I Hate the Man I Love*, Joan E Childs, LCSW; *I've Gotta Get Out of My Own Way*, Abraham J Twerski; *In Search of a Theory of Everything: The Philosophy Behind Physics*, Demetris Nicolaides, PhD; *Into The Rabbit Hole (6 book series)*, Micah T Dank; *Laughing at Myself: My Education in Congress, on the Farm, and at the Movies*, Secretary/Congressman Dan Glickman; *Make Your Own Damn Cheese*, John A Chuback, MD; *Mindfulness for Borderline Personality Disorder*, Blaise Aguirre, MD, Dr Gillian Galen; *Minyan: Ten Overlapping Stories*, John J Clayton; *Mood: The Key to Understanding Ourselves and Others*, Patrick M Burke, PhD; *Negroes with Guns: The Black Tradition of Arms*, Nicholas Johnson; *Overcoming Destructive Anger*, Bernard Golden, PhD; *Parenting Your Child with Autism: Practical Solutions, Strategies, and Advice for Helping Your Family*, M Anjali Sastry, PhD, Blaise Aguirre, MD; *Pitchfork Populism: The Trump*

Effect on Ten American Dynamics, Brad Kane; *Quantum Leaps in the Wrong Direction*, Arthur W Wiggins, Charles M Wynn, PhD, Sidney Harris; *Reimagining Men's Cancers*, Mark Boguski, MD, Michelle Berman, MD, David Tabatsky; *Reimagining Women's Cancers*, Mark Boguski, MD, Michelle Berman, MD, David Tabatsky; *Rx for Hope: A Cancer Care Model to Optimize the Immune System Integrating Low Dose Chemotherapy and Complementary Medicine*, Nick Chen, MD, PhD, David Tabatsky; *Teshuvah and Recovery*, Abraham J Twerski, MD; *The Human Side of Science*, Arthur W Wiggins, Charles M Wynn, PhD, Sidney Harris; *The Nun's Rabbi: The Rabbi-Psychiatrist and the Sisters of St Francis*, Abraham J Twerski, MD; *The Parkinson's Blues*, John J Clayton; *The Truth About Cardiovascular Health*, Jay N Cohn, MD; *The Unlikeliest of Places: How Nachman Libeskind Survived the Nazis, the Gulags and Soviet Communism*, Annette Libeskind Berkovits; *Transparency in Government: What it Means and How You Can Make it Happen*, Donald Gordon; *Under a Dark Eye: A Family Story*, Sharon Dunn; *With Friends Like These (The Joth Proctor Fixer series)*, James V Irving; *Wrestling with Angels: New & Collected Stories*, John J Clayton

The Aaland Agency (L)
PO Box 849, Inyokern, CA 93527-0849
Tel: 760-384-3910
E-mail: anniejo41@gmail.com
Web Site: www.the-aaland-agency.com
Key Personnel
Dir & Fiction/Nonfiction: Jo Ann Krueger
Foreign Rep, CN & Europe: Richard Allan
Romance/Adventure: Mitzi Rhone
Founded: 1991
Adult fiction & nonfiction. One-inch margins & space & a half. Any format, e-mail file attachment, hard copy or CD is acceptable (e-mail file preferred). Crime drama, romance/adventure, children's stories, biographies & textbooks gladly accepted. No fees for ms review/evaluation. Complete ms or first 3 chapters. No unsol mss, query first.
Titles recently placed: *Cypher*, T R Dawson; *The Hydra Brief*, William Davison; *USS Kitty Hawk: The Last Warrior*, Marty S Bourdon

Dominick Abel Literary Agency Inc (L)
146 W 82 St, Suite 1-A, New York, NY 10024
Tel: 212-877-0710 *Fax:* 212-595-3133
E-mail: agency@dalainc.com
Web Site: www.dalainc.com
Key Personnel
Pres: Dominick Abel *E-mail:* dominick@dalainc.com
Founded: 1975

Adult fiction & nonfiction. Handle film & TV rights. No unsol mss, query first by e-mail; no reading fee. Representatives in Hollywood & all major foreign countries.
Foreign Rep(s): Akcali Agency (Turkey); Big Apple Agency Inc (China, Indonesia, Malaysia, Taiwan, Vietnam); The Buckman Agency (Germany, Israel, Scandinavia); The English Agency (Japan); David Grossman Literary Agency (UK Commonwealth); The Italian Literary Agency (Italy); Korean Copyright Center (Korea); Lex Copyright Agency (Hungary); La Nouvelle Agence (France); Prava i prevodi (Eastern Europe, Greece, Russia, Ukraine); Lennart Sane Agency (Brazil, Central America, Netherlands, Portugal, South America, Spain); Tuttle-Mori Agency Inc (Thailand)
Membership(s): The Authors Guild; Authors Registry; Copyright Clearance Center (CCC); Mystery Writers of America (MWA)

Abrams Artists Agency (L-D)
275 Seventh Ave, 26th fl, New York, NY 10001
Tel: 646-486-4600 *Fax:* 646-486-0100
E-mail: literary@abramsartny.com
Web Site: www.abramsartists.com
Key Personnel
Dir, Foreign Rts: David Doerrer
Agent, Book & Publg Div: Simon Green
Literary Agent: Sarah L Douglas; Katie Gamelli; Max Grossman; Ron Gwiazda; Ben Izzo; Charles Kopelman; Amy Wagner
Founded: 1977
Plays, screenplays, film & TV rights. No unsol mss, query first. Submit synopsis. No reading fee.
Branch Office(s)
9200 Sunset Blvd, 11th fl, Los Angeles, CA 90069, Contact: Norma Robbins *Tel:* 310-859-0625 *E-mail:* contactla@abramsartists.com

Acacia House Publishing Services Ltd (L)
51 Chestnut Ave, Brantford, ON N3T 4C3, Canada
Tel: 519-752-0978 *Fax:* 519-752-0978
Key Personnel
Mng Dir: Bill Hanna *E-mail:* bhanna.acacia@rogers.com
Founded: 1985
Adult fiction; no science fiction, occult, horror; most nonfiction. Handle film & TV rights for authors. Handle foreign rights for 4 client publishers. Territories handled directly by Acacia include Australia, Bulgaria, Canada (English-speaking), Czechia, Estonia, Latvia, Lithuania, Slovakia, UK, USA. No unsol mss, query first; submit outline & first 50 pages. Only typed, double-spaced mss may be submitted with return postage. No reading fee. Fee charged for photocopying & postage or courier.

Foreign Rights: Akcali (Turkey); Agencia Literaria Carmen Balcells SA (Portugal, Spain); Big Apple Agency Inc (China, Hong Kong, Malaysia, Taiwan, Vietnam); Paul & Peter Fritz AG (Austria, Germany); Graal Literary Agency (Poland); Harris-Elon Agency (Ilana Kurshan) (Israel); International Literatuur Bureau BV (Netherlands); International Press Agency (South Africa); Japan UNI Agency Inc (Japan); Katai & Bolza (Bosnia and Herzegovina, Croatia, Hungary, Montenegro, Serbia, Slovenia); Simona Kessler (Romania); Duran Kim Agency (Korea); Alexander Korzhenevski (Russia); Maxima Creative Agency (Santo Manarung) (Indonesia); Daniela Micura Literary Services (nonfiction only) (Italy); Montreal-Contact (French-speaking countries); A Nicolaissen Agency (Scandinavia); Read n' Right (Greece); Silk Road Agency (Thailand)

Aevitas Creative Management (L-D)
19 W 21 St, Suite 501, New York, NY 10010
Tel: 212-765-6900
Web Site: aevitascreative.com
Key Personnel
Co-CEO: David Kuhn (AAR); Todd Shuster
Pres: Esmond Harmsworth
Sr Partner: Jennifer Gates; Laura Nolan (AAR); Janet Silver; Lane Zachary
Partner: Michelle Brower; Bridget Wagner Matzie; Rick Richter; Jane von Mehren
Agent: Erica Bauman; Sarah Bowlin; Justin Brouckaert; Chris Bucci; Nick Chiles; Maggie Cooper; Jon Michael Darga; Ariel Foxman; Lori Galvin; David Granger; Chelsey Heller; Jim Kelly; Georgia Frances King; Danya Kukafka; Sarah Lazin; Sarah Levitt; Will Lippincott; Jen Marshall; Penny Moore; Lauren Sharp; Michael Signorelli; Becky Sweren; Nan Thornton; Susan Zanger
Consulting Agent: Rob Arnold; Karen Brailsford
Dir, Book Packaging & Story Devt: Rex Ogle
Foreign Rts Dir: Erin Files
Literary, commercial & genre fiction & nonfiction, mystery, thriller, non-category romance, science fiction, biography, current affairs, business, psychology, memoir, science & history, young adult, children's. No unsol mss, e-mail only query letters, full plot; synopsis or detailed chapters summary plus 3 sample chapters up to 50 pages. No mss returned without SASE. No reading fee.
Branch Office(s)
3532 Hayden Ave, Culver Sity, CA 90232
Tel: 310-270-9096
601 "I" St NW, Washington, DC 20001 *Tel:* 202-836-8923
545 Boylston St, 11th fl, Boston, MA 02116
Tel: 617-262-2400
Foreign Office(s): ACM UK Ltd, London, United Kingdom, Chmn & CEO: Toby Mundy
Foreign Rights: Agencia Riff (Laura & Joao Paulo Riff) (Brazil); ELST Literary Agency (Kalina Stefanova) (Bulgaria); Ersilia Literary Agency (Greece); Grayhawk Agency (China, Indonesia, Taiwan, Thailand, Vietnam); Literarische Agentur Hoffman GmbH (Andrea Wildgruber); Agence Michelle Lapautre (France); Susanna Lea Associates (translation rights) (UK); Prava i prevodi (Eastern Europe); Sebes & Bisseling Literary Agency (Netherlands)

Agency Chicago (L-D)
7000 Phoenix Ave NE, Suite 202, Albuquerque, NM 87110
E-mail: agency.chicago@usa.com
Key Personnel
Owner: Ernest Santucci
Assoc: Shelly Chou
Founded: 1988
Professional & cross-over writers. No unsol mss, query letter first; handle film, stage & TV

rights; no reading fee. True crime & police procedural, historical fiction, humor, politics, Southwest & general wellness.

Agency for the Performing Arts Inc, see APA Talent & Literary Agency

The Ahearn Agency Inc (L)
2021 Pine St, New Orleans, LA 70118
Tel: 504-861-8395 *Fax:* 504-866-6434
Web Site: www.ahearnagency.com
Key Personnel
Pres: Pamela G Ahearn *E-mail:* pahearn@aol.com
Founded: 1992
General fiction, adult; no poetry, plays, young adult, articles or autobiographies. Specialize in women's fiction & suspense. No unsol mss, query first with SASE. No reading fee. Do not send attachments with e-mail queries unless requested.
Titles recently placed: *A Mortal Likeness*, Laura Joh Rowland; *A Season to Lie*, Emily Littlejohn; *Just a Breath Away*, Carlene Thompson; *Married at Midnight*, Gerri Russell; *Mister Tender's Girl*, Carter Wilson; *The Pleasures of Passion*, Sabrina Jeffries; *Washington Power Play*, Allan Topol
Foreign Rights: Lorella Belli Agency (Lorella Belli) (UK); Agence Eliane Benisti (Eliane Benisti) (France); Prava i prevodi (Eastern Europe); Thomas Schluek GmbH (Germany)
Membership(s): International Thriller Writers Inc (ITW); Mystery Writers of America (MWA); Romance Writers of America (RWA)

Betsy Amster Literary Enterprises (L)
607 Foothill Blvd, No 1061, La Canada Flintridge, CA 91012
Tel: 626-529-5667
E-mail: rights@amsterlit.com (rts inquiries); b.amster.assistant@gmail.com (adult book queries); b.amster.kidsbooks@gmail.com (children & young adult book queries)
Web Site: www.amsterlit.com
Key Personnel
Pres: Betsy Amster (AAR)
Agent, Children's & Young Adult: Mary Cummings
Founded: 1992
Adult areas of interest: literary fiction, upscale commercial women's fiction, voice-driven mysteries & thrillers, narrative nonfiction (especially by journalists), travelogues, memoirs (including graphic memoirs), social issues & trends, psychology, self-help, popular culture, women's issues, history & biography, lifestyle, careers, health & medicine, parenting, cooking & nutrition, gardening & quirky gift books. Children's & young adult: fiction (from picture books to middle grade & young adult novels, including contemporary & historical, humor, mystery, fantasy & multi-cultural), literary nonfiction (picture book biographies, science, nature, mindfulness & social awareness issues) & poetry. No unsol mss. Handle film & TV rights for client book properties via co-agents; no reading fee. Address queries for adult books to b.amster.assistant@gmail.com & for children's & young adult titles to b.amster.kidsbooks@gmail.com. For fiction or memoirs, embed the first 3 pages in the body of your e-mail; for nonfiction, embed the overview of your proposal. For children's picture books, embed the entire text. Do not represent screenplays, poetry, western, fantasy, science fiction, action adventure, techno thrillers, spy capers, apocalyptic scenarios or political or religious arguments. We do not open attachments unless we have requested them; no phone, fax or snail mail queries.
Foreign Rights: Big Apple Agency Inc (China); Donatella d'Ormesson (France); The En-

glish Agency (Japan) Ltd (Japan); Japan UNI Agency Inc (Japan); Korea Copyright Center (KCC) (MiSook Hong) (Korea); Mohrbooks AG Literary Agency (Germany); Prava i prevodi (Bulgaria, Croatia, Czechia, Estonia, Greece, Hungary, Latvia, Lithuania, North Macedonia, Poland, Romania, Russia, Serbia, Slovakia, Slovenia, Turkey); Lennart Sane Agency AB (Philip Sane) (Brazil, Holland, Portugal, Scandinavia, Spain, Spanish Latin America); Vicki Satlow (Italy); Abner Stein Agency (UK)
Membership(s): PEN Center USA

Anderson Literary Management LLC (L)
244 Fifth Ave, 11th fl, New York, NY 10001
Tel: 212-645-6045 *Fax:* 212-741-1936
E-mail: info@andersonliterary.com
Web Site: www.andersonliterary.com
Key Personnel
Pres: Kathleen Anderson (AAR)
 E-mail: kathleen@andersonliterary.com
Represents quality fiction & nonfiction (adult, young adult & middle grade) for print, electronic, film & television.
Membership(s): PEN American Center

Andy Ross Literary Agency (L)
767 Santa Ray Ave, Oakland, CA 94610
Tel: 510-238-8965
E-mail: andyrossagency@hotmail.com
Web Site: www.andyrossagency.com
Key Personnel
Agent: Andy Ross (AAR)
Founded: 2008
Specialize in narrative nonfiction, journalism, history, current events, literary, commercial & young adult fiction.
Queries: send by e-mail only including "query" in the title header. Letters should be kept to a half page. State the project category in the first sentence & provide a very brief description. Proposals: submit by e-mail only. See web site for additional query & proposal guidelines. No fees.
Titles recently placed: *Beauty of the Broken*, Tawni Waters; *Not Your Mothers Slow Cooker Book*, Beth Hensperger; *Snowball in a Blizzard*, Steven Hatch; *The Arab of Warsaw*, Randall Platt; *The Tango War*, Mary Jo McConahay; *To the Secretary: Leaked Embassy Cables and America's Foreign Policy Disconnect*, Mary Thompson-Jones; *You Don't Own Me: The Life and Times of Lesley Gore*, Trevor Tolliver; *Zionism: The Birth and Transformation of an Ideal*, Milton Viorst

APA Talent & Literary Agency (L-D)
405 S Beverly Dr, Beverly Hills, CA 90212
Tel: 310-888-4200
Web Site: www.apa-agency.com
Key Personnel
Owner: Lee Dinstman
SVP (Nashville): Steve Lassiter
Founded: 1962
Handle film & TV rights. No unsol mss; query first. Submit outline & sample chapters & SASE. No reading fee; 10% commission. Represent writers & producers.
Branch Office(s)
3060 Peachtree Rd NW, Suite 1480, Atlanta, GA 30305 *Tel:* 404-254-5876
135 W 50 St, 17th fl, New York, NY 10020
Tel: 212-205-4320
150 Fourth Ave N, Penthouse, Nashville, TN 37219 *Tel:* 615-297-0100
151 Yonge St, Suite 1100, Toronto, ON M5C 2W7, Canada *Tel:* 416-646-7373
Foreign Office(s): 222 Soho Sq, London W1D 4NS, United Kingdom *Tel:* (020) 3871 0520

Arcadia (L)
159 Lake Place S, Danbury, CT 06810-7261
Tel: 203-797-0993
E-mail: arcadialit@gmail.com
Key Personnel
Pres: Victoria Gould Pryor (AAR)
Founded: 1986
Not seeking new clients.
Foreign Rights: Japan UNI Agency Inc (Japan);
Barbara Levy Agency (UK); The Marsh
Agency (translation)
Membership(s): The Authors Guild

Arthur Pine Associates Inc, see InkWell
Management

Aurous Inc (L)
PO Box 20490, New York, NY 10017
Tel: 212-628-9729 *Fax:* 212-535-7861
Key Personnel
Pres: Kay McCauley *E-mail:* kaymcc25@aol.com
Busn Mgr: Christopher Shepard
Agent: Kirby McCauley
Founded: 1974
Adult fiction & nonfiction. Motion picture & TV
rights from book properties only. No unsol
mss. Projects by referral only. No reading fee.
Agents in all principal foreign countries.
Foreign Rights: ZENO Agency

The Axelrod Agency (L)
55 Main St, Chatham, NY 12037
Mailing Address: PO Box 357, Chatham, NY
12037
Tel: 518-392-2100
Key Personnel
Pres: Steven Axelrod (AAR) *E-mail:* steve@
axelrodagency.com
Foreign Rts Dir: Lori Antonson *E-mail:* lori@
axelrodagency.com
Founded: 1983
Fiction & nonfiction, film & TV rights. No unsol
mss, query first. No reading fee. E-mail queries
receive attention first.

Elizabeth H Backman (L)
86 Johnnycake Hollow Rd, Pine Plains, NY
12567
Mailing Address: PO Box 762, Pine Plains, NY
12567-0762
Tel: 518-398-9344 *Fax:* 518-398-6368
E-mail: bethcountry@fairpoint.net
Key Personnel
Owner: Elizabeth H Backman
Ad Serv: Donn King Potter
Founded: 1981
Literary & commercial fiction; nonfiction; current
events, politics, business, biography, the arts,
cooking, diet, health, sports, gardening, history,
science, self-help & psychology; audio & video
cassettes. Author representatives, consulting
editors, advertising & promotion copywriters.
No unsol mss, query first with SASE; submit
introduction, cover letter, chapter by chapter
outline or table of contents, 3 sample chapters
& author's bio or complete ms with cover letter
& author's bio. Reading fees: $100 for propos-
als, $500 for complete mss; 15% agency fee
plus expenses (phone, mail, photocopying, etc).
Handle film & TV rights.
Foreign Rights: Lennart Sane (Netherlands, Portugal, Scandinavia, Spain); Thomas Schlueck
GmbH (Germany); Tuttle-Mori Agency Inc
(Japan)

Malaga Baldi Literary Agency (L-D)
233 W 99, Suite 19C, New York, NY 10025
Tel: 212-222-3213
E-mail: baldibooks@gmail.com
Web Site: www.baldibooks.com

Key Personnel
Pres: Malaga Baldi
Founded: 1986
Cultural history, nonfiction & literary-edgy fic-
tion. No unsol mss, query first with SASE; no
reading fee.
Titles recently placed: *Dancing Man*, Bob Avian,
Tom Santopietro; *Furry Nation*, Joe Strike;
May We Suggest, Alison Pearlman; *One Step
for Mankind*, Charles Pappas; *The Contender*,
William J Mann; *Three Sheets to the Wind*,
Cynthia Barrett; *Tomb of the Unknown Racist*,
Blanche McCrary Boyd; *Urban Tantra (2nd
ed)*, Barbara Carrellas
Foreign Rep(s): Abner Stein (UK)
Foreign Rights: Eliane Benisti (France); Marsh
Agency (Europe); Owls Agency Inc (Japan)

**A Richard Barber/Peter Berinstein &
Associates** (L)
60 E Eighth St, Suite 21-N, New York, NY
10003
Tel: 212-737-7266 *Fax:* 860-927-3942
E-mail: barberrich@aol.com
Key Personnel
Pres: A Richard Barber
Sr Assoc: Peter Berinstein
Handle software, film & TV rights. Specialize in
fiction & nonfiction. No fees. No unsol mss,
query first by mail (include SASE). No fax or
e-mail submissions.
Branch Office(s)
80 N Main St, Kent, CT 06757-0887 *Tel:* 860-
927-4911

Baror International Inc (L)
PO Box 868, Armonk, NY 10504-0868
Tel: 914-273-9199 *Fax:* 914-273-5058
Web Site: www.barorint.com
Key Personnel
Pres: Danny Baror *E-mail:* danny@barorint.com
Literary Agent: Heather Baror-Shapiro
E-mail: heather@barorint.com
Specialize in international & domestic represen-
tation of literary works in both fiction & non-
fiction ranging in genre including commercial
fiction, literary titles, science fiction, fantasy,
young adult & more. No unsol mss.

Loretta Barrett Books Inc (L)
101 Fifth Ave, 11th fl, New York, NY 10003
Tel: 212-242-3420
E-mail: lbbagencymail@gmail.com
Web Site: www.lorettabarrettbooks.com
Key Personnel
Pres: Nick Mullendore
Founded: 1990
Fiction & nonfiction. No poetry or children's lit-
erature, no screenplays; no unsol mss, query
first by e-mail only. Submit outlines, sample
chapters & bio (nonfiction); synopsis & bio
(fiction). Representatives on the West Coast &
in all major foreign countries. No reading fee.
Foreign Rights: Akcali Copyright Agency
(Turkey); Eliane Benisti Agency (France);
Capel & Land Ltd (Australia, UK); Andrew
Nurnberg Associates International Ltd (Main-
land China, Taiwan); Prava i prevodi (Baltic
States, Czechia, Eastern Europe, Slovakia,
Ukraine); Lennart Sane Agency AB (Scandi-
navia); Thomas Schlueck GmbH (Germany);
Synopsis Literary Agency (Russia); Tuttle-Mori
Agency Inc (Japan); Eric Yang Agency (Korea)

Meredith Bernstein Literary Agency Inc (L)
2095 Broadway, Suite 505, New York, NY 10023
Tel: 212-799-1007 *Fax:* 212-799-1145
E-mail: MGoodBern@aol.com
Web Site: www.meredithbernsteinliteraryagency.
com
Key Personnel
Agent: Meredith Bernstein (AAR)

Adult fiction (commercial & literary) & nonfiction; memoirs, current events, biography, health
& fitness, women's issues, mysteries & special
projects; crafts & creative endeavors. No poetry
or screenplays. No unsol mss, query first online
(no attachments) or by mail (include SASE).
For fiction, submit a 1-page query letter; nonfiction send 1-page query letter, table of contents & information on why you are an expert
in this field. Handle film & TV rights only for
books represented. Representatives in foreign
countries & on the West Coast. No reading fee.
Membership(s): The Authors Guild; Sisters in
Crime; Women's Media Group

The Bethel Agency (L-D)
PO Box 21043, Park West Sta, New York, NY
10025
Tel: 212-864-4510
E-mail: bethelagcy@aol.com
Key Personnel
Pres: Lewis R Chambers
Founded: 1967
Books & articles, fiction & nonfiction; stage
plays, motion picture & TV properties; for-
eign & domestic. Represents photojournalists.
Handles film & TV rights. No unsol mss, query
first. No initial reading fee. Submissions of
proposals are accepted via "snail mail" ONLY.

Vicky Bijur Literary Agency (L)
27 W 20 St, Suite 1003, New York, NY 10011
Tel: 212-580-4108
E-mail: queries@vickybijuragency.com
Web Site: www.vickybijuragency.com
Key Personnel
Agent: Vicky Bijur (AAR)
Assoc Agent: Alexandra Franklin
Founded: 1988
Adult fiction & nonfiction. No poetry, science fic-
tion, fantasy or horror. No unsol mss. Fiction:
query first; paste first chapter in body of e-
mail. Nonfiction: query first. No phone queries.
We respond only to queries sent via e-mail.
No reading fee. Agents in all principal foreign
countries. Handle film & TV rights.
Titles recently placed: *Beaten Down, Worked
Up*, Steven Greenhouse; *Difficult Lives, Hitch-
ing Rides*, James Sallis; *Every Night Is Pizza
Night*, Kenji Lopez-Alt; *Let Justice Descend*,
Lisa Black; *Louise's Crossing*, Sarah Shaber;
My Life as a Villainess, Laura Lippman; *Or-
pheus Girl*, Brynne Rebele-Henry; *Sarah Jane*,
James Sallis; *Tangled Roots*, Marcia Talley;
The Cartoon Guide to Biology, Larry Gonick,
David Wessner; *The Satapur Moonstone*, Sujata
Massey; *Wild at Heart*, Alice Outwater
Foreign Rights: AnatoliaLit Agency (Turkey);
The English Agency Japan (Japan); The Gray-
hawk Agency (China, Taiwan); The Deborah
Harris Agency (Israel); The Italian Literary
Agency SRL (Italy); Agence Michelle Lapautre
(France); Liepman Agency AG (Germany);
Maxima Creative Agency (Indonesia); Prava
i prevodi (Bulgaria, Czechia, Estonia, Greece,
Hungary, Poland, Russia, Serbia, Slovakia);
Lennart Sane Agency (Argentina, Brazil, Den-
mark, Finland, Holland, Norway, Portugal,
Spain, Sweden); Abner Stein Agency (Eng-
land); Tuttle-Mori Agency Inc (Thailand); Eric
Yang Agency (Korea)

David Black Agency (L-D)
Subsidiary of Black Inc
335 Adams St, 27th fl, Suite 2707, Brooklyn, NY
11201
Tel: 718-852-5500 *Fax:* 718-852-5539
Web Site: www.davidblackagency.com
Key Personnel
Pres: David Black (AAR) *E-mail:* dblack@
dblackagency.com

Agent: Rica Allannic *E-mail:* rallannic@
dblackagency.com; Jennifer Herrera
E-mail: jherrera@dblackagency.com; Deborah Hofmann; Gary Morris *Tel:* 718-852-5518 *E-mail:* gmorris@dblackagency.
com; Susan Raihofer *Tel:* 718-852-5542
E-mail: sraihofer@dblackagency.com;
Sarah Smith *E-mail:* ssmith@dblackagency.
com; Joy Tutela (AAR) *Tel:* 718-852-5533
E-mail: jtutela@dblackagency.com
Founded: 1990
Literary & commercial fiction & nonfiction, especially sports, politics, business, health, fitness, romance, parenting, psychology & social issues. No poetry. No unsol mss, query first with SASE. No reading fee. Agents in all principal foreign countries. Handle film & TV rights. No mysteries or thrillers.
Foreign Rights: Bardon-Chinese Media Agency (Ming-Ming Liu) (China); Eliane Benisti Agent Litteraire (Eliane Benisti & Noemi Rollet) (France); The Deborah Harris Agency (Efrat Lev) (Israel); International Editors' Co (Spanish) (Latin America, Spain); The Italian Literary Agency srl (Italy); Katai & Bolza Literary Agents (Peter Bolza) (Hungary); Maxima Creative Agency (Santo Manurung) (Indonesia); Mohrbooks AG Literary Agency (Sabine Ibach, Bettina Kaufmann, Sebastian Ritscher & Cristina Uytiepo) (Germany); Prava i prevodi (Milena Lukic, Ana Milenkovic & Jelena Todosijevic) (Bulgaria, Croatia, Czechia, Estonia, Greece, Latvia, Lithuania, Poland, Russia, Serbia, Slovenia); Agencia Riff (JP, Laura & Lucia Riff) (Brazil, Portugal); Sebes & Bisseling Literary Agency (Paul Sebes) (Netherlands); Abner Stein Agency (Caspian Dennis) (Australia, UK); Tuttle-Mori Agency Inc (Japan, Thailand); Eric Yang Agency (Sue Yang) (Korea)

Bleecker Street Associates Inc (L)
215 Thompson St, Suite 519, New York, NY 10012
Tel: 212-677-4492 *Fax:* 212-388-0001
Key Personnel
Pres: Agnes Birnbaum
Founded: 1984
No unsol mss, query first about book project & author with SASE (cannot respond nor return materials without SASE). Do not query via e-mail, phone or fax. Handle film & TV rights for clients' own work only. Fiction & nonfiction; no poetry, plays or screenplays; handle magazine articles by book clients only. No reading fee.
Titles recently placed: *Handy Forensics Answer Book*, Patricia Barnes-Svarney, Thomas V Svarney; *Harlen Ellison Biography*, Nat Segaloff; *Haunted: Malevolent Ghosts, Threatening Phantoms*, Brad Steiger, Sherry Steiger; *Jimmy & Fay*, Michael W Mayo; *St Catherine of Sienna*, Shelley Emling; *Under a Flaming Sky*, Daniel James Brown
Foreign Rights: Bookman (Netherlands, Scandinavia); The English Agency (Japan) Ltd (Japan); International Editors' Co (Portugal, South America, Spain); The Italian Literary Agency srl (Italy); Thomas Schlueck GmbH (Germany); Abner Stein Agency (British Commonwealth)

Reid Boates Literary Agency (L-D)
69 Cooks Crossroad, Pittstown, NJ 08867-0328
Mailing Address: PO Box 328, Pittstown, NJ 08867-0328
Tel: 908-797-8087
E-mail: reid.boates@gmail.com
Key Personnel
Sole Prop: Reid Boates
Founded: 1985
Narrative +/or how-to nonfiction, health, spirituality, wellness, business & sports. Handle film & TV rights. No fiction. Most new clients by

referral. No reading fee. Agents in all major foreign markets. No unsol mss, submit written query with SASE.
Titles recently placed: *A Year Without Mary*, Coleman Barks; *Mindfulness*, Joseph Goldstein; *The Illuminated Hafiz*, Michael Green
Foreign Rep(s): Eliane Benisti (France); Raquel de la Concha (Spain); EYA (Korea); Michael Meller (Eastern Europe, Germany, UK); Owl's Agency (Japan) Ltd (Japan)

Alison Bond Literary Agency (L)
171 W 79 St, No 143, New York, NY 10024
Key Personnel
Principal: Alison M Bond *E-mail:* alison@
bondlit.com
Founded: 1982
Literary fiction, memoir/biography, women's issues & narrative nonfiction. Not accepting new writers at present. Agents in most European/Asian countries. No genre categories.
Membership(s): Women's Media Group

Bond Literary Agency (L)
201 Milwaukee St, Suite 200, Denver, CO 80206
Tel: 303-781-9305
E-mail: queries@bondliteraryagency.com
Web Site: bondliteraryagency.com
Key Personnel
Owner & Agent: Sandra Bond *E-mail:* sandra@
bondliteraryagency.com
Assoc Agent: Becky LeJeune *E-mail:* becky@
bondliteraryagency.com; Patrick Munnelly
E-mail: patrick@bondliteraryagency.com
Founded: 1998
Sandra represents adult literary & commercial fiction including mystery/crime fiction & women's fiction (no memoir, romance, children's picture books, health, poetry or screenplays); juvenile fiction; narrative nonfiction, science for a general audience, business. Nonfiction authors must have excellent credentials & a strong platform. Becky is looking for adult & young adult horror, fantasy, science fiction. Patrick is looking for adult & young adult fantasy, science fiction & LGBTQ fiction.
Talented, previously unpublished writers will be considered. No unsol mss, query by e-mail first to queries@bondliteraryagency.com (letter in the body of the e-mail, no attachments). No snail mail. No phone calls please. Full mss submissions by request only. Sell foreign & film/TV rights through subagents. No fees charged.
Titles recently placed: *CLIMB: Leaving Safe and Finding Strength on 100 Summits in Japan*, Susan Spann; *Cold Case: The Assassination of Pat Garrett*, W C Jameson; *Cold Case: The Tombstone Mysteries*, W C Jameson; *Edo Burning: A Hiro Hattori Mystery*, Susan Spann; *Hollywood Her Story: An Illustrated History of Women and the Movies*, Jill Tietjen, Barbara Bridges; *Lost In a Place So Small*, Rick Collignon; *Once Again*, Catherine Wallace Hope; *Rocky Mountains Train Robberies*, W C Jameson; *The Age of Agile*, Stephen Denning; *The Girl on the Ferris Wheel*, Len Vlahos, Julie Halpern; *The Last Train Robber*, W C Jameson; *These Wicked Waters*, Emily Layne; *Victorio Peak*, W C Jameson
Foreign Rights: Kleinworks Agency (Judy Klein) (worldwide exc USA)

BookEnds Literary Agency (L)
136 Long Hill Rd, Gillette, NJ 07933
Web Site: www.bookendsliterary.com
Key Personnel
Pres & Literary Agent: Jessica H Faust (AAR)
E-mail: jfaust@bookendsliterary.com
Sr Literary Agent: Kim Lionetti (AAR)
E-mail: klsubmissions@bookendsliterary.com;

Jessica Alvarez (AAR) *E-mail:* jalvarez@
bookendsliterary.com
Literary Agent: Rachel Brooks *E-mail:* rbrooks@
bookendsliterary.com; Naomi Davis
E-mail: ndavis@bookendsliterary.com; Moe
Ferrara *E-mail:* mferrara@bookendsliterary.
com; Amanda Jain *E-mail:* ajain@
bookendsliterary.com; Tracy Marchini
E-mail: tmsubmissions@bookendsliterary.
com; Natascha Morris *E-mail:* nmorris@
bookendsliterary.com
Assoc Literary Agent: Emily Forney; James McGowan *E-mail:* jmcgowan@bookendsliterary.
com
Literary Asst: Umaima Saleem
Founded: 1999
Represents fiction & nonfiction in all genres for adults & children alike. Mission is to advocate for authors while helping them achieve their dreams.
All queries should be made through Query Manager.
Titles recently placed: *A Deadly Inside Scoop*, Abby Collette; *Belle Revolte*, Linsey Miller; *Bennie's True Colors*, Norene Paulson; *Boston Billionaires (series)*, Naima Simone; *Conan the Librarian*, Tara Luebbe, Becky Cattie; *Final Catcall*, Sofie Kelly; *Fox and the Box*, Yvonne Ivinson; *Goodbye, Mr Spalding*, Jennifer Robin Barr; *Heads or Tails*, Mona D Shroff; *How to Catch a Wicked Viscount*, Amy Rose Bennett; *Hug*, Charlene Chua; *Ice Cube Tray Recipes*, Jen Karetnick; *My Rainbow*, DeShanna Neal, Trinity Neal; *Never Entice an Earl*, Lily Dalton; *Newly(un)wed*, Erica Slotter, PhD, Patrick Markey, PhD; *Only Mostly Devastated*, S Gonzales; *Project AIDEN*, Lindsey Frydman; *Reborn (Shadow Falls: After Dark)*, C C Hunter; *Refraction*, Naomi Hughes; *Relative Fortunes*, Marlowe Benn; *Sealand: The Astonishing True Story of the World's Foremost Micronation and the Family Who Founded It*, Dylan Taylor-Lehman; *Six Cloves Under*, Gin Jones; *Sleep Over*, Heidi Bleackley; *Some Enchanted Eclair*, Bailey Cates; *Swords & Fire Trilogy 2*, Melissa Caruso; *Take it Back*, Kia Abdullah; *The Chai Factor*, Farah Heron; *The Coffin Maker*, Breeann Allison; *The Creator Mindset*, Nir Bashan; *The Key to Happily Ever After*, Tif Marcelo; *The October Girl*, Matthew Dow Smith; *The Secret, Book & Scone Society (4th & 5th in series)*, Ellery Adams; *The Shadows Between Us*, Tricia Levenseller; *The Spinster's Guide to Romance*, Jennifer Delamere; *Threadbare*, Lisa Iriarte; *Too Sticky*, Jen Malia; *Unbreak Me*, Michelle Hazen; *Warrior of the Wild*, Tricia Levenseller; *We Could Be Heroes*, Margaret Finnegan; *Webb Glass Shop Mysteries (4th-6th in series)*, Cheryl Hollon; *Young Captain Nemo*, Jason Henderson
Foreign Rep(s): The Book Project Agency (non-exclusive) (Greece); Book/lab (Poland); The English Agency (Japan); Julio F-Yanez Agencia Literaria SL (Portugal, Spain); Deborah Harris Agency (Israel); Imprima Korea Agency (Korea); Kayi Literary Agency (Turkey); Agence Michelle Lapautre (France); Andrew Nurnberg (China, Czechia, Slovakia, Slovenia, Taiwan); Tuttle-Mori Agency Inc (Japan)
Membership(s): Mystery Writers of America (MWA); Romance Writers of America (RWA); Science Fiction & Fantasy Writers of America (SFWA); Society of Children's Book Writers & Illustrators (SCBWI)

Books & Such (L)
52 Mission Circle, Suite 122, PMB 170, Santa Rosa, CA 95409-5370
Tel: 707-538-4184
Web Site: booksandsuch.com
Key Personnel
Founder & Pres: Janet Kobobel Grant
E-mail: janet@booksandsuch.com

VP: Wendy Lawton *E-mail:* wendy@
booksandsuch.com
Sr Literary Agent, Adult Fiction, Nonfiction &
Teen: Rachelle Gardner *E-mail:* rachelle@
booksandsuch.com
Literary Agent: Cynthia Ruchti
Literary Agent, Teens, Twenties & Thirties:
Rachel Kent *E-mail:* rachel@booksandsuch.
com
Founded: 1996
Handles fiction & nonfiction. Submission by e-
mail (no attachments). No phone calls. No un-
sol mss, query first. No fees.
Titles recently placed: *Marriage Triggers*, Guy
Lia, Amber Lia; *Prepared for Anything*, Kathi
Lipp; *Ten Little Stars*, Deb Gruelle; *The
Grumble-Free Year*, Tricia Goyer; *The Santa
Claus Chronicles*, Dan Short, Rene Gutteridge;
Wholehearted Faith, Rachel Held Evans
Branch Office(s)
PO Box 1227, Hilmar, CA 95324-1227 *Tel:* 209-
634-1913
Membership(s): Advanced Writers & Speakers
Association (AWSA); American Christian Fic-
tion Writers (ACFW); Romance Writers of
America (RWA)

BookStop Literary Agency LLC (L)
67 Meadow View Rd, Orinda, CA 94563
E-mail: info@bookstopliterary.com
Web Site: www.bookstopliterary.com
Key Personnel
Pres & CEO: Kendra Marcus
Literary Agent: Ms Minju Chang
Founded: 1984
Juvenile & young adult mss only (fiction & non-
fiction) & illustration for children's books, es-
pecially diverse perspectives, humorous voices,
intense young adult fiction, clever middle grade
& topics & mss for the Hispanic, African-
American, Asian-American juvenile markets
in the US. Accept unsol mss. Submit full mss
for picture books; first 10 pages for fiction;
sample chapters & outline for nonfiction. See
web site for additional submission information.
No reading fee.
Titles recently placed: *Echo*, Pam Munoz Ryan;
Hensel and Gretel: Ninja Chicks, Corey
Schwartz, Rebecca Gomez; *My New Mom &
Me*, Renata Galindo; *This is Not a Werewolf
Story*, Sandra Evans

Georges Borchardt Inc (L-D)
136 E 57 St, New York, NY 10022
Tel: 212-753-5785
E-mail: georges@gbagency.com
Web Site: www.gbagency.com
Key Personnel
Founder & Pres: Georges Borchardt (AAR)
Founder: Anne Borchardt (AAR)
VP & Foreign Rts Dir: Valerie Borchardt (AAR)
E-mail: valerie@gbagency.com
Agent: Samantha Shea *E-mail:* samantha@
gbagency.com
Foreign Rts Asst: Rachel Ludwig
E-mail: rachell@gbagency.com
Asst: Cora Markowitz *E-mail:* cora@gbagency.
com
Founded: 1967
Fiction & nonfiction. No unsol mss; handle film
& TV rights & software. No fees charged.
Titles recently placed: *American Breakdown*,
David Bromwich; *Eliot Among the Women*,
Lyndall Gordon; *Godshot*, Chelsea Bieker;
Grand, Charles Johnson; *Kill List*, Amit Ma-
jmudar; *Killer's Choice*, Louis Begley; *Ma-
chines Like Me*, Ian McEwan; *Mothertrucker*,
Amy Butcher; *My Baby First Birthday*, Jenny
Zhang; *Once Upon A River*, Diane Setterfield;
Ordinary Hazards, Anna Bruno; *Outside Look-
ing In*, TC Boyle; *Talking With Bears*, Gay
Bradshaw; *The Future of Israel*, Omri Boehm;
The Hotel Neversink, Adam O'Fallon Price;

The Seductive Lure of the Authoritarian State,
Anne Applebaum; *Valentine*, Beth Wetmore;
Who Killed Jane Stanford?, Richard White
Foreign Rights: Agencia Literaria Carmen Bal-
cells (Maribel Luque) (Spain); Bardon-Chinese
Media Agency (Ming-Ming Lui) (Chinese);
Tassy Barham Associates (Brazil); English
Agency (Junzo Sawa) (Japanese); Graal Lit-
erary Agency (Marcin Biegaj) (Polish); Deb-
orah Harris Agency (Efrat Lev) (Israel); The
Italian Literary Agency SRL; Japan UNI
Agency (Miko Yamanouchi) (Japanese); JLM
Agency (Nelly & John Moukakou) (Greek);
Asli Karasuil Literary Agency (Turkish); Katai
& Bolza (Peter Bolza) (Hungarian); Korean
Copyright Center (Misook Hong) (Korean);
Agence Michelle Lapautre (Catherine Lapautre)
(France); Mohrbooks AG Literary Agency (Se-
bastian Ritscher) (German); Andrew Nurnberg
Associates (Kristine Shatrovska) (Baltic States);
Andrew Nurnburg Associates (Anna Droumeva)
(Bulgarian & Romanian); Andrew Nurnberg
Associates (Ludmilla Sushkova) (Russian);
Kristin Olson Literary Agency sro (Kristin Ol-
son) (Czech); RDC Agencia Literaria (Raquel
de la Concha) (Portuguese) (Portugal); Mari-
anne Schoenbach Literary Agency BV (Mar-
ianne Schoenbach) (Dutch); Sheil Land As-
sociates (Vivien Green) (British); Abner Stein
(Caspian Dennis) (UK); Sane Toregard Agency
(Ulf Toregard) (Scandinavia); Tuttle-Mori
Agency Inc (Asako Kawachi) (Japanese)

Bradford Literary Agency (L)
5694 Mission Center Rd, Suite 347, San Diego,
CA 92108
Tel: 619-521-1201
E-mail: queries@bradfordlit.com
Web Site: www.bradfordlit.com
Key Personnel
Agent: Laura Bradford (AAR) *E-mail:* laura@
bradfordlit.com; Natalie Lakosil
E-mail: natalie@bradfordlit.com; Kari Sutherland *E-mail:* kari@bradfordlit.com; Jennifer
Chen Tran *E-mail:* jen@bradfordlit.com;
Katherine Wessbecher *E-mail:* katherine@
bradfordlit.com
Founded: 2001
A boutique agency offering a full range of representation services to authors, both published
& pre-published. We are an editorial-focused
agency & prefer to work closely with our authors in helping to build strong, sustainable careers. We believe the best author-agent relationships extend beyond making sales. In order to
best serve our client's needs, we must also be a
partner, advisor, careful listener, troubleshooter
& advocate.
We are currently acquiring fiction: romance (historical, romantic suspense, paranormal, category, contemporary, erotic); urban fantasy,
women's fiction (contemporary, upmarket, literary), mystery, thrillers, young adult, middle
grade, chapter books, picture books (Natalie &
Kari only), graphic novels & visually driven
projects (Jennifer only). Also nonfiction: business, relationships, biography/memoir, self-
help, parenting, narrative humor, pop culture,
illustrated/graphic design, food & cooking,
history & social issues. We are not currently
acquiring: poetry, screenplays, short stories,
westerns, horror, New Age, religion, crafts.
We accept unsol mss. Queries are accepted by e-
mail only to queries@bradfordlit.com. We do
not open e-mail attachments, unless specifically
requested by an agent. Your entire submission
must appear in the body of the e-mail & not as
an attachment. The subject line should begin as
follows: QUERY: (The title of the ms or any
short message you would like us to see should
follow). For fiction: Please e-mail a query letter along with the first chapter of your ms & a
synopsis. Please be sure to include the genre &

word count in your cover letter. For nonfiction:
submit a book proposal including an outline,
sample material, author bio & competitive survey. No fees.
Titles recently placed: *A Place at the Table*, Saa-
dia Faruqi; *Beneath the Ashes*, Dea Poirier;
Boats Will Float, Andria Rosenbaum; *Dancing
at the Pity Party*, Tyler Feder; *Emblem Isle:
Curse of the Night Witch*, Alex Aster; *Grave-
maidens*, Kelly Coon; *Hearts, Strings, and
Other Breakable Things*, Jacqueline Firkins;
Honor Lost, Ann Aguirre; *Jingle Bells and
Wedding Vows*, Barbara Dunlop; *Just Make Be-
lieve*, Maggie Robinson; *King of Manhattan*,
Joanna Shupe; *Let Me Hear a Rhyme*, Tiffany
Jackson; *Let's Call It Doomsday*, Katie Henry;
Love Her or Lose Her, Tessa Bailey; *Master
Class*, Christina Dalcher; *Modern Caravan*,
Kate Oliver; *Molten Mud Murder*, Sara John-
son; *Once Upon a Cowboy Christmas*, Soraya
Lane; *Popularity Code*, Stephanie Faris; *Temp-
tation at His Door*, Joss Wood; *The First 7*,
Laura Pohl; *The Lady Rogue*, Jenn Bennett;
The Secret She Keeps, HelenKay Dimon; *To-
day, Tonight, Tomorrow*, Rachel Solomon; *Two
Dogs on a Trike*, Gabi Snyder; *Who Do You
Think You Are?*, Siobhan Gallagher; *Wings of
Ebony*, J Elle; *Yasmin the Soccer Star*, Saadia
Faruqi
Foreign Rights: Taryn Fagerness Agency (Taryn
Fagerness) (Albania, Argentina, Australia,
Brazil, Bulgaria, Canada, China, Croatia,
Czechia, Denmark, Estonia, Finland, France,
Germany, Greece, Hungary, Iceland, India,
Indonesia, Israel, Italy, Japan, Korea, Latvia,
Lithuania, Mexico, Netherlands, Norway,
Poland, Portugal, Romania, Russia, Serbia,
Slovakia, Spain, Sweden, Taiwan, Thailand,
Turkey, Ukraine, UK, Vietnam)
Membership(s): American Library Association
(ALA); Romance Writers of America (RWA);
Society of Children's Book Writers & Illustra-
tors (SCBWI)

Brandt & Hochman Literary Agents Inc (L)
1501 Broadway, Suite 2310, New York, NY
10036
Tel: 212-840-5760 *Fax:* 212-840-5776
Web Site: brandthochman.com
Key Personnel
Pres: Gail Hochman (AAR) *E-mail:* ghochman@
bromasite.com
Sr Agent: Mitchell Waters (AAR)
Agent & Foreign Rts: Marianne Merola (AAR)
E-mail: mmerola@bromasite.com
Agent: Emily Forland (AAR) *E-mail:* eforland@
bromasite.com; Emma Patterson (AAR)
E-mail: epatterson@bromasite.com; Jody Kahn
(AAR) *E-mail:* jkahn@bromasite.com; Henry
Thayer (AAR) *E-mail:* hthayer@bromasite.com
Audio Rts & Perms Contact: Lina Granada
(AAR) *E-mail:* lgranada@bromasite.com
Represents fiction & nonfiction, including liter-
ary, mystery/thriller, memoir, narrative nonfiction, journalism, history, current affairs, health,
science, pop culture, lifestyle, art history &
children's books. No screenplays or textbooks.
No unsol mss, query first by e-mail or regular mail. Responses to e-mailed queries not
guaranteed. Queries limited to 2 pages. Include
SASE if sending by regular mail. See web site
for specific submission preferences for each
agent. No reading fee. Fee charged for making
copies & book/galley purchases. Co-agents in
most foreign countries.

The Joan Brandt Agency (L)
788 Wesley Dr NW, Atlanta, GA 30305
Tel: 404-351-8877 *Fax:* 404-351-0068
Key Personnel
Pres: Joan Brandt
Founded: 1990

Fiction & nonfiction (no science fiction, horror, fantasy, historical or romance). No unsol mss, query first with SASE; submit letter plus brief synopsis. Agents present in all principal countries.

Barbara Braun Associates Inc (L)
7 E 14 St, Suite 19F, New York, NY 10003
Tel: 917-414-3022
Web Site: www.barbarabraunagency.com
Key Personnel
Pres: Barbara Braun (AAR) *E-mail:* barbara@barbarabraunagency.com
Assoc: John F Baker
Founded: 1994
Represents both literary & commercial fiction as well as serious nonfiction, including memoir, biography, cultural history, women's issues, pop culture, art & architecture. Fiction is strong on stories for women, art-related fiction, historical & multicultural stories & mysteries & thrillers. Interested in narrative nonfiction & current affairs. No unsol mss, query by referral only, by e-mail to bbasubmissions@gmail.com. Include brief summary of book, word count, genre, any relevant publishing experience & first 5 pages of ms pasted into the body of the e-mail. No reading or other fees.
Foreign Rights: Jean V Naggar Literary Agency (Jennifer Weltz) (worldwide)
Membership(s): The Authors Guild; PEN American Center

M Courtney Briggs Esq, Authors Representative (L)
Chase Tower, 28th fl, 100 N Broadway Ave, Oklahoma City, OK 73102
Key Personnel
Author's Rep: M Courtney Briggs
Founded: 1994
Fiction & nonfiction, adult & juvenile with emphasis on children's books, including picture books, middle grade & young adult books. Represent authors & illustrators of trade books of all types. Handle film & TV rights. No unsol mss, query first by regular mail with SASE, include publishing history; published authors only; no reading fees.
Membership(s): Society of Children's Book Writers & Illustrators (SCBWI)

Brockman Inc (L)
260 Fifth Ave, 10th fl, New York, NY 10001
Tel: 212-935-8900 *Fax:* 212-935-5535
E-mail: rights@brockman.com
Web Site: www.brockman.com
Key Personnel
Chmn: John Brockman
CEO: Max Brockman
Pres: Katinka Matson
VP: Russell Weinberger
Literary & software agency. No unsol mss. Deal direct in all foreign markets. No fees charged.

Curtis Brown Ltd (L-D)
228 E 45 St, 3rd fl, New York, NY 10017
Tel: 212-473-5400
Web Site: www.curtisbrown.com
Key Personnel
CEO: Timothy F Knowlton (AAR)
Pres: Peter L Ginsberg (AAR)
EVP & Book Agent: Ginger Knowlton (AAR)
VP & Book Agent: Ginger Clark (AAR); Elizabeth Harding (AAR); Jonathan Lyons (AAR); Laura Blake Peterson (AAR)
Dir, Foreign Rts: Sarah Perillo (AAR)
Book Agent: Noah Ballard (AAR); Katherine Fausset (AAR)
Assoc Book Agent: Kerry D'Agostino (AAR); Steven Salpeter (AAR)
Film & TV Rts: Holly Frederick (AAR)

Dir of Foreign Rts & Book Agent: Jonathan Lyons
Founded: 1914
Handle general trade fiction & nonfiction, juvenile. No unsol mss, query first with SASE. Submit outline or sample chapters. Please refer to Agents page on web site for specific submission policies per agent. Most agents do not reply to queries unless interested. No reading fee. Other fees charged (for photocopies, express mail, etc). Handle film & TV rights & merchandising & multimedia. No playwrights. Representatives in all major foreign countries.
Branch Office(s)
1750 Montgomery St, San Francisco, CA 94111
Tel: 415-954-8566

Marie Brown Associates (L)
412 W 154 St, New York, NY 10032
Tel: 212-939-9725
E-mail: submissions.mbrownlit@gmail.com
Key Personnel
Owner & Pres: Marie D Brown
Founded: 1984
Adult & juvenile fiction & nonfiction. Handle film & TV rights through representatives in Hollywood. No unsol mss, query first; submit outline & sample chapters or full ms on request, 12 point, double-spaced, 1-sided only, typed, white paper & unbound. Include SASE. E-mail queries accepted. No reading fee.

Browne & Miller Literary Associates (L)
52 Village Place, Hinsdale, IL 60521
Tel: 312-922-3063
E-mail: mail@browneandmiller.com
Web Site: www.browneandmiller.com
Key Personnel
Pres: Danielle Egan-Miller (AAR)
E-mail: danielle@browneandmiller.com
Founded: 1971
General adult trade fiction & nonfiction. No horror, sci-fi, young adult or children's books. No unsol mss, query first by e-mail. No reading fee.
Foreign Rep(s): Agence Eliane Benisti (Eliane Benisti) (France); Big Apple Agency Inc (China, Taiwan); Book Publishers Association of Israel (Israel); The English Agency (Japan) Ltd (Japan); Julio F-Yanez Agencia Literaria (Montse Yanez) (Mexico, South America, Spain); International Copyright Agency Ltd (Simona Kessler) (Romania); Japan UNI Agency Inc (Japan); KCBS Literary Agency (Hosung Maeng) (Korea); Nurcihan Kesim Literary Agency (Turkey); Macadamia Agency (Poland); Natoli, Stefan & Oliva (Roberta Oliva) (Italy); Andrew Nurnberg Associates Baltic (Tatjana Zoldnere) (Estonia, Latvia, Lithuania); Andrew Nurnberg Associates Hungary (Croatia, Hungary); Andrew Nurnberg Associates Prague (Czechia, Slovakia); Andrew Nurnberg Associates Sofia (Albania, Bulgaria, North Macedonia, Serbia); Riff Agency (Brazil); Thomas Schluck Agency (Germany); Synopsis Agency (Russia); Tuttle-Mori Agency Inc (Japan); Eric Yang Agency (Korea)
Membership(s): The Authors Guild; Mystery Writers of America (MWA); Romance Writers of America (RWA)

J B Bryans Literary (L)
7 Meetinghouse Ct, Indian Mills, NJ 08088
Tel: 609-922-0369
E-mail: info@brylit.com
Web Site: brylit.com
Key Personnel
Pres: John B Bryans *E-mail:* john@brylit.com
Founded: 2017
Literary agency & consultancy founded to provide close personal attention to the needs of a small stable of established & emerging authors.

Adult commercial & literary fiction & nonfiction. No children's books. Fiction: historical, adventure, mystery & culturally relevant novels distinguished by quirky, relatable characters caught up in strange, challenging & funny situations. Nonfiction: history, politics, environment, true crime, regional (NJ), business, cyberculture, library & information science, education, biography, music & humor. No unsol mss, query first. Send e-mail with working title in the subject line & short description of the work in the message body. We will reply to request ms or sample chapters if interested.

Don Buchwald & Associates Inc (L)
10 E 44 St, New York, NY 10017
Tel: 212-867-1200 *Fax:* 212-867-2434
E-mail: info@buchwald.com
Web Site: www.buchwald.com
Key Personnel
Pres & CEO (NY): Don Buchwald *E-mail:* don@buchwald.com
VP & CFO: Stephen Fisher *E-mail:* steve@buchwald.com
EVP, Legal & Admin Aff: Richard Basch *E-mail:* richard@buchwald.com
Agent (NY): David Lewis *E-mail:* davidl@buchwald.com; Jonathan Mason *E-mail:* jmason@buchwald.com; Joanne Nici *E-mail:* jonici@buchwald.com
Talent representatives & literary agency: TV, film, commercial, theatre & broadcasting. No unsol mss, query first. No reading fee.
Branch Office(s)
6500 Wilshire Blvd, Suite 2200, Los Angeles, CA 90048 *Tel:* 323-665-7400 *Fax:* 323-665-7470

Judith Buckner Literary Agency (L-D)
12721 Hart St, North Hollywood, CA 91605
Tel: 818-982-8202 *Fax:* 818-764-6844
Key Personnel
Pres: Judith Buckner *E-mail:* jbuckner@pacbell.net
Founded: 1970
Handle commercial & literary fiction & nonfiction, some film & TV scripts. No children's, young adult, romance, science fiction or horror. No unsol mss; query first by letter or e-mail. No reading fee. Commission 15% domestic, 20% foreign. Handle film & TV rights. If invited to submit, for fiction send first fifty pages & brief synopsis of remainder. For nonfiction, send proposal including overview, target market, outline or table of contents, sample chapter, author's bio, survey of competition & reasons why your book is superior & marketing plan.

The Bukowski Agency Ltd (L)
14 Prince Arthur Ave, Suite 202, Toronto, ON M5R 1A9, Canada
Tel: 416-928-6728 *Fax:* 416-963-9978
E-mail: info@bukowskiagency.com
Web Site: www.bukowskiagency.com
Key Personnel
Pres & Primary Agent: Denise Bukowski
Founded: 1986
Adult trade except genre fiction by Canadian authors. No unsol mss, query first by regular mail. Submit proposal & sample for nonfiction; query & sample for fiction. No reading fees. Commission plus disbursements.
Foreign Rights: AJA Literary Agency (Anna Jarota) (France); Akcali Copyright Agency (Atilla Izgi Turgut) (Istanbul); Big Apple Agency (Vincent Lin) (China, Taiwan); The Foreign Office (Teresa Vilarrubla) (Latin America, Portugal, Spain); Graal Literary Agency (Filip Wojciechowski) (Eastern Europe, Poland); Grandi & Associati (Alessandra Mele) (Italy); The Deborah Harris Agency (Ilana Kurshan) (Israel); A M Heath & Co Ltd

(Bill Hamilton) (UK); Japan UNI Agency Inc
(Cecilia Kashiwamura) (Japan); JLM Liter-
ary Agency (John Moukakou) (Greece); Katai
& Bolza Literary Agents (Peter Bolza) (Hun-
gary); Duran Kim Agency (Duran Kim) (Ko-
rea); Licht & Burr (Trine Licht) (Scandinavia);
Mohrbooks AG Literary Agency (Annelie
Geissler) (Germany); Marianne Schoenbach
Literary Agency (Marianne Schoenbach) (Hol-
land); The Van Lear Agency (Elizabeth Van
Lear) (Russia)

Sheree Bykofsky Associates Inc (L)
PO Box 706, Brigantine, NJ 08203
E-mail: submitbee@aol.com
Web Site: www.shereebee.com
Key Personnel
Pres & Agent: Sheree Bykofsky (AAR)
Founded: 1991
Adult trade & mass market nonfiction & fiction.
No unsol mss, send e-query in body of e-mail
to submitbee@aol.com. Handle film & TV
rights through subagents. No fees.
Foreign Rights: Bardon-Chinese Media Agency
(China, Taiwan); Eliane Benisti Agency
(France); Book/lab Literary Agency (Poland);
Dalia Ever Hadani (Israel); Japan UNI Agency
Inc (Japan); Alexander Korzhenevski (Rus-
sia); Piergiorgio Nicolazzini (Italy); OA Liter-
ary Agency (Greece); Kristin Olson Literary
Agency (Czechia, Slovakia); ONK Agency Ltd
(Eastern Europe, Greece, Turkey); Plima Liter-
ary Agency (Croatia, Serbia, Slovenia); RDC
Agencia Literaria SL (Latin America, Portugal,
Spain); Thomas Schlueck Literarische Agen-
tur (Germany); Marianne Schoenbach Literary
Agency (Netherlands); Abner Stein Agency
(UK); Eric Yang (Korea); Pimolporn Yutsiri
(Indonesia, Thailand, Vietnam)
Membership(s): Atlantic City Chamber of Com-
merce; PR Council

Kimberley Cameron & Associates LLC (L)
1550 Tiburon Blvd, Suite 704, Tiburon, CA
94920
Tel: 415-789-9191 *Fax:* 415-789-9177
Web Site: www.kimberleycameron.com
Key Personnel
Pres & Literary Agent: Kimberley Cameron
(AAR) *E-mail:* kimberley@kimberleycameron.
com
Literary Agent: Lisa Abellera *E-mail:* lisa@
kimberleycameron.com; Amy Cloughly
E-mail: amy@kimberleycameron.com;
Elizabeth Kracht *E-mail:* elizabeth@
kimberleycameron.com; Ms Dorian Maffei *E-mail:* dorian@kimberleycameron.
com; Mary Moore (AAR) *E-mail:* mary@
kimberleycameron.com
Founded: 1957 (as Reece Halsey Agency)
Represent quality writing in book-length fiction &
nonfiction, including memoirs, biographies,
literary fiction, mainstream fiction, science
fiction, mysteries & thrillers. Do not handle
screenplays, poetry or children's literature.
Handle film & TV rights. E-mail all queries.
For fiction, include 1-page synopsis & first 50
pages as separate attachments. For nonfiction,
send complete proposal including sample chapters. No fees charged Please submit through the
individual agent's page at our web site.
Titles recently placed: *24 Life Lessons and Stories from the Say Hey Kid*, Willie Mays, John
Shea
Foreign Rights: The Fielding Agency (Whitney
Lee) (worldwide)
Membership(s): Sisters in Crime

Carlisle & Co LLC, see InkWell Management

Maria Carvainis Agency Inc (L)
Rockefeller Center, 1270 Avenue of the Ameri-
cas, Suite 2320, New York, NY 10020
Tel: 212-245-6365 *Fax:* 212-245-7196
E-mail: mca@mariacarvainisagency.com
Web Site: mariacarvainisagency.com
Key Personnel
Pres: Maria Carvainis (AAR)
Contracts & Subs Rts Mgr: Martha Guzman
(AAR)
Assoc Agent: Elizabeth Copps (AAR)
Literary Asst: Samantha Brody
Founded: 1977
Represents a wide range of fiction & nonfiction
with special interest in literary & mainstream
fiction, mystery & suspense, thrillers, historicals, contemporary women's fiction, young
adult & middle grade, memoir, biography, history, business, psychology, pop culture & popular science. We do not represent screenplays,
children's picture books, science fiction, or poetry. If you would like to query the agency,
please send a query letter, a synopsis of the
work, first 5-10 pages & note of any writing credentials. The agency prefers e-mailed
queries: mca@mariacarvainisagency.com.
Titles recently placed: *Anything for You*, Kristan
Higgins; *Blue for the Water*, Sonja Yoerg; *Fric-
tion*, Sandra Brown; *If You Only Knew*, Kristan
Higgins; *Palindrome*, Ephraim Rinsky; *Ruby
Clyde*, Corabel Shofner; *The Infinite*, Nicholas
Mainieri; *The Survivor's Club*, Mary Balogh
Membership(s): American Booksellers Associa-
tion (ABA); The Authors Guild; International
Thriller Writers Inc (ITW); Mystery Writers of
America (MWA); Romance Writers of America
(RWA); Society of Children's Book Writers &
Illustrators (SCBWI)

Linda Chester Literary Agency (L-D)
630 Fifth Ave, Suite 2000, New York, NY 10111
Tel: 212-218-3350
E-mail: submissions@lindachester.com
Web Site: www.lindachester.com
Key Personnel
Principal: Linda Chester (AAR)
Exec Mgr: Gary Jaffe *E-mail:* gjaffe@
lindachester.com
Literary Agent: Laurie Fox *Tel:* 510-435-3635
E-mail: laurie@lindachester.com
Quality adult fiction & nonfiction. Handle film &
TV rights. No reading fes; no unsol mss, query
first.
Branch office in California.
Foreign Rights: The Fielding Agency LLC (Whit-
ney Lee)

Faith Childs Literary Agency Inc (L)
915 Broadway, Suite 1009, New York, NY 10010
Tel: 212-995-9600
Web Site: faithchildsliteraryagency.com
Key Personnel
Pres: Faith Hampton Childs (AAR)
E-mail: faith@faithchildsliteraryagency.com
Subs Rts Assoc: Diana Lachatanere
E-mail: dianalachatanere@
faithchildsliteraryagency.com
Founded: 1990
Specialize in fiction & nonfiction film & TV
rights. No unsol mss, queries or unreferred
clients accepted. Agents in all principal coun-
tries.
Foreign Rep(s): The English Agency (Japan) Ltd
(Japan)

Cine/Lit Representation (L-D)
PO Box 802918, Santa Clarita, CA 91380-2918
Tel: 661-513-0268
E-mail: cinelit@att.net
Key Personnel
Partner: Anna Cottle; Mary Alice Kier (AAR)
Founded: 1991

Not accepting submissions at this time. No reading fee. Representatives in all major foreign
markets. Handle film & TV rights.
Membership(s): British Academy of Film & Television Arts/Los Angeles (BAFTA/LA); Film
Independent

Wm Clark Associates (L)
54 W 21 St, Suite 809, New York, NY 10010
Tel: 212-675-2784
E-mail: general@wmclark.com
Web Site: www.wmclark.com
Key Personnel
Principal: William Clark (AAR)
E-mail: wmclark@wmclark.com
Founded: 1999
Represents mainstream & literary fiction & quality nonfiction to the book publishing, mo-
tion picture, television & new media fields.
No reading fees; handle film & TV rights for
books written by clients only; does not represent screenplays. In addition to selling directly in the global English language markets,
translation rights are sold directly in the German, Italian, Spanish, Portuguese, Latin American, French, Dutch & Scandinavian territories; through corresponding agents in China,
Bulgaria, Czechia, Latvia, Poland & Hungary,
Russia, Ukraine, Japan, Greece, Israel, Turkey,
Korea, Taiwan & Thailand. Other network partners provide services including editorial consultation, media training, lecture booking, marketing support & public relations. Queries sent by
any method other than through web site query
page will be discarded unread.
Titles recently placed: *Marilyn: The Passion and
the Paradox*, Lois Banner; *Modern Monopo-
lies: What It Takes to Dominate the 21st Cen-
tury Economy*, Alex Moazed, Nicholas John-
son; *Nothing's Bad Luck: The Life and Work of
Warren Zevon*, Chad Kushins; *The Buried: An
Archaeology of the Egyptian Revolution*, Peter
Hessler; *The Louvre: A History*, James Gardner
Foreign Rights: Book/lab (Poland); Kalem
Agency (Turkey); Andrew Nurnberg Associates
Ltd (China, Taiwan); Synopsis Literary Agency
(Russia & former USSR); Tuttle-Mori Agency
Inc (Japan); Eric Yang Agency (Taiwan)
Membership(s): The Authors Guild; PEN Interna-
tional

Collier Associates (L)
309 Kelsey Park Circle, Palm Beach Gardens, FL
33410
Mailing Address: PO Box 15759, West Palm
Beach, FL 33416
Tel: 561-514-6548
E-mail: dmccabooks@gmail.com
Key Personnel
Pres & Agent: Dianna Collier
Agent: Charles Todd *E-mail:* charles@
charlestodd.com
Founded: 1976
Fiction & nonfiction adult books. Fiction: war
novels, mysteries, true crime, romance, contemporary & historical. Nonfiction: biographies
& autobiographies of well-known people, popular works of political subjects & history, ex-
poses, popular works on medical & scientific
subjects, finance, popular reference & how-
to books, health, beauty & motherhood. Also
handle film & TV rights for adult books only
with co-agents. No unsol mss, query first with
SASE; submit outline, sample chapters & bio;
no reading fee for published authors of trade
books, may charge fee for full-length book mss
for unpublished authors; charge cost of copying
ms; submission postage; books ordered for subsidiary rights. When ms is submitted it should
meet the Chicago Manual of Style Guidelines,
along with a sample chapter by chapter outline
& SASE. Submissions must be in Microsoft
Word format, 1 sided pages, all pages num-

bered at bottom center, header with author &
title right justified, double spaced, Courier font,
12 point. All others submissions may be discarded. Include cover proposal letter & chapter-
by-chapter outline. Co-agents on West Coast &
in many foreign countries.
Foreign Rep(s): Big Apple Agency Inc (China,
Japan, Taiwan); Julio F-Yanez Agencia Lit-
eraria SL (Portugal, South America, Spain);
International Literature Bureau BV (Nether-
lands); Johnson & Alcock Ltd (British Com-
monwealth); Mohrbooks AG Literary Agency
(Austria, Germany, Switzerland); Tuttle-Mori
Agency Inc (Japan)
Foreign Rights: Agence Michelle Lapautre
(France); Light & Burr (Denmark, Finland,
Iceland, Norway, Sweden)
Membership(s): Mystery Writers of America
(MWA)

Frances Collin Literary Agency (L)
PO Box 33, Wayne, PA 19087
E-mail: queries@francescollin.com
Web Site: www.francescollin.com
Key Personnel
Owner: Frances Collin (AAR)
Literary Agent: Sarah Yake (AAR)
  E-mail: sarah@francescollin.com
Founded: 1948
Successor to Marie Rodell-Frances Collin Literary
Agency (1975).
Trade fiction & nonfiction; no original screen-
plays. Special interest in the following areas:
literary fiction, biography, history, travel, en-
vironmental, nature, memoir, fantasy/science
fiction. No unsol mss, query via e-mail to
queries@francescollin.com. Send query letter describing your project (text in the body
of the e-mail only, e-mails with unsol attachments will be deleted unread). Handle film &
TV rights through sub-agents; representatives
in all foreign markets. No fees.

Don Congdon Associates Inc (L)
110 William St, Suite 2202, New York, NY
10038-3914
Tel: 212-645-1229 *Fax:* 212-727-2688
E-mail: dca@doncongdon.com
Web Site: www.doncongdon.com
Key Personnel
Agent: Cristina Concepcion (AAR); Michael
Congdon (AAR); Katie Grimm (AAR); Katie
Kotchman (AAR); Maura Kye-Casella (AAR);
Susan Ramer (AAR)
Founded: 1983
Handle any & all trade books. Handle film & TV
rights for regular clients. No unsol mss, query
first with a 1-page synopsis of your work &
relevant background & SASE or e-mail with-
out attachments. In heading include "Query"
& agent's full name. Include a sample chap-
ter in body of e-mail. Now accepting new &
professional authors. No reading fee.
Foreign Rep(s): AnatoliaLit Agency (Amy Span-
gler) (Turkey); Big Apple Agency Inc (Chris
Lin) (Taiwan); Big Apple Agency Inc (Lily
Chen, Luc Kwanten, Erica Zhou & Wendy
King) (China, Thailand, Vietnam); Casanovas
& Lynch Agencia Literaria (Marina Penalva)
(Portugal, South America, Spain); Nurichan
Kesim Literary Agency (Filiz Karaman)
(Turkey); Agence Michelle Lapautre (Catherine
Lapautre) (France); Maxima Creative Agency
(Santo Manurung) (Indonesia); Andrew Nurn-
berg Associates Baltic (Tatjana Zoldnere) (Es-
tonia, Latvia, Lithuania); Andrew Nurnberg
Associates Budapest (Judit Hermann) (Croa-
tia, Hungary); Andrew Nurnberg Associates
International (Marei Pittner) (Denmark, Fin-
land, Iceland, Netherlands, Norway, Sweden);
Andrew Nurnberg Associates International (An-
drew Nurnberg & Sabine Pfannenstiel) (Germany); Andrew Nurnberg Associates Prague

(Petra Tobiskova) (Czechia, Slovakia, Slove-
nia); Andrew Nurnberg Associates Sofia (Anna
Droumeva) (Bulgaria, Romania, Serbia); An-
drew Nurnberg Associates Warsaw (Marcin
Biegaj) (Poland); Andrew Nurnberg Literary
Agency Moscow (Ludmilla Sushkova) (Russia);
Owls Agency (Monika Taga) (Japan); Read
n' Right Agency (Nike Davarinou) (Greece);
Vicki Satlow Literary Agency (Vicki Satlow)
(Italy); Abner Stein Agency (Caspian Den-
nis & Anna Carmichael) (UK); Tuttle-Mori
Agency Inc (Asako Kawachi, Ken Mori &
Misa Morikawa) (Japan); Eric Yang Agency
(Henry Shin) (Korea)

The Doe Coover Agency (L)
PO Box 668, Winchester, MA 01890
Tel: 781-721-6000 *Fax:* 781-721-6727
E-mail: info@doecooveragency.com
Web Site: www.doecooveragency.com
Key Personnel
Pres: Doe Coover
Agent: Colleen Mohyde
Founded: 1986
Nonfiction & fiction. Specialize in literary fiction,
business, history & biography, psychology, sci-
ence & health, cooking & food writing, garden-
ing, humor, sports & music. No poetry, fantasy,
science fiction or screenplays. E-mail queries
only; see web site for submission guidelines.
Handle film & TV rights on agency projects only.
15% commission.
Titles recently placed: *A Girl's Guide to Missiles*,
Karen Piper; *Biography of Garry Trudeau*,
Steve Weinberg; *Canal House Kitchen Basics*,
Christopher Hirsheimer, Melissa Hamilton;
Lessons from a Grandfather, Jacques Pepin;
*Living with Cancer: A Step-by-Step Guide for
Coping Medically and Emotionally with your
Diagnosis*, Dr Vicki Jackson, Dr Patrick Ryan,
Michelle Seaton; *The Life She Wished to Live:
Biography of Marjorie Kinnan Rawlings*, Ann
McCutchan; *Where the Wild Coffee Grows*, Jeff
Koehler
Foreign Rights: The English Agency (Japan) Ltd
(Japan); The Marsh Agency (Europe); Abner
Stein Agency (UK)

CreativeWell Inc (L)
PO Box 3130, Memorial Sta, Upper Montclair,
NJ 07043
Tel: 973-783-7575
E-mail: info@creativewell.com
Web Site: www.creativewell.com
Key Personnel
Pres: George M Greenfield *E-mail:* george@
creativewell.com
Founded: 2003
Primarily nonfiction, film & TV rights. No unsol
mss. No reading fee; other fees charged (for
photocopies, express mail, etc). Representa-
tives in principal foreign countries. Also offers full
service lecture representation.
Titles recently placed: *52 Reasons to Vote for
Hillary*, Bernard Whitman, Brittany L Stals-
burg, PhD; *Finding Calm Clarity*, Due Quach;
*First They Killed My Father: A Daughter of
Cambodia Remembers*, Loung Ung; *Lincoln's
Gamble: The Tumultuous Six Months That
Gave America the Emancipation Proclama-
tion and Changed the Course of the Civil War*,
Todd Brewster; *Metaphors Be With You*, Dr
Mardy Grothe; *Nobody: Casualties of Amer-
ica's War on the Vulnerable from Ferguson to
Flint and Beyond*, Marc Lamont Hill; *The Art
of Movement*, Ken Browar, Deborah Ory; *To
Hell and Back: The Last Train from Hiroshima*,
Charles Pellegrino

Crichton & Associates Inc (L)
6940 Carroll Ave, Takoma Park, MD 20912
Tel: 301-495-9663

E-mail: cricht1@aol.com
Web Site: www.crichton-associates.com
Key Personnel
Pres: Sha-Shana Crichton
Founded: 2002
For fiction, submit first 3 chapters with synop-
sis & bio. For nonfiction, submit proposal
with bio. No fees charged. Send queries to
query@crichton-associates.com.
Membership(s): Romance Writers of America
(RWA)

Richard Curtis Associates Inc (L)
200 E 72 St, Suite 28J, New York, NY 10021
Tel: 212-772-7363
E-mail: info@curtisagency.com
Web Site: www.curtisagency.com
Key Personnel
Pres: Richard Curtis (AAR)
  E-mail: rcurtisagency@gmail.com
Founded: 1979
No stage plays or screenplays, short fiction, ar-
ticles or poetry. Handle film & TV rights. No
unsol mss, query first via US mail with SASE
or via submission form on the web site.
Foreign Rights: Baror International Inc (world-
wide exc USA)
Membership(s): Mystery Writers of America
(MWA); Romance Writers of America (RWA);
Science Fiction & Fantasy Writers of America
(SFWA)

Darhansoff & Verrill (L)
133 W 72 St, Rm 304, New York, NY 10023
Tel: 917-305-1300
E-mail: permissions@dvagency.com
Web Site: www.dvagency.com
Key Personnel
Agent: Liz Darhansoff
Agent & Rights Dir: Michele Mortimer
Agent: Chuck Verrill
Off Mgr: Eric Amling
Founded: 1975
Fiction & nonfiction, literary fiction, young adult,
memoirs, sophisticated suspense, history, sci-
ence, biography, pop culture & current af-
fairs. No theatrical plays or film scripts. No
unsol mss, query first with SASE or by e-mail
via submissions@dvagency.com. Film & TV
rights handled by Los Angeles associates, Lynn
Pleshette, Richard Green & UTA. Agents in
many foreign countries. No fees charged.
Foreign Rights: Alkcali Copyright Agency (Ozgur
Emir) (Turkey); Bardon-Chinese Media Agency
(Joanne Yang) (China); Eliane Benisti Agency
(France); The Book Publishers Association of
Israel (Dalia Ever Hadani) (Israel); The English
Agency (Hamish Macaskill) (Japan); Julio F-
Yanez Agencia Literaria SL (Montse Yanez)
(Spain); Graal Literary Agency (Maria Strarz-
Kanska) (Poland); International Copyrights
Agency (Simona Kessler) (Romania); Inter-
rights (Svetlana Stefanova) (Bulgaria); The Ital-
ian Literary Agency srl (Italy); JLM Literarary
Angency (John Moukakis) (Greece); Katai &
Bolza (Peter Bolza) (Hungary); Licht & Burr
(Trine Licht) (Scandinavia); Zvonimir Majdak
(Croatia); Mohrbooks AG Literary Agency (Se-
bastian Ritscher) (Germany); Andrew Nurnberg
Agency (Lumilla Shushkova) (Russia); Andrew
Nurnberg Association Baltic (Tatjana Zold-
nere) (Latvia); Kristin Olson Literary Agency
(Kristin Olson) (Czechia); Agencia Riff (Laura
Riff & Joao Paulo Riff) (Brazil, Portugal); The
Sayle Agency (Rachel Calder) (UK); Sebes &
Bisseling Literary Agency (Paul Sebes) (Hol-
land); Shin Won Agency (Tae Kim) (Korea)

Liza Dawson Associates (L)
121 W 27 St, Suite 1201, New York, NY 10001
Tel: 212-465-9071
Web Site: www.lizadawsonassociates.com

Key Personnel
CFO & Foreign Rts Mgr: Havis Dawson
   E-mail: hdawson@lizadawsonassociates.com
Pres: Liza Dawson (AAR) *E-mail:* queryliza@
   lizadawsonassociates.com
Sr Literary Agent: Tom Miller
Literary Agent: Rachel Beck; Caitlin Blasdell
   E-mail: querycaitlin@lizadawsonassociates.
   com; Hannah Bowman *E-mail:* queryhannah@
   lizadawsonassociates.com
Assoc Literary Agent: Caitie Flum
   E-mail: querycaitie@lizadawson.com
Founded: 1996
Agents are supported by a strong team that sells audio, foreign, licensing & television & film rights. Represent commercial fiction & literary fiction. In nonfiction, we are drawn to narratives that explore life's complexities. We represent books for most ages, some of which are award-winners & New York Times bestsellers. We work with both debut novelists as well as published writers, helping them craft their proposals.
Foreign Rights: Akcali Copyright Agency (Atilla Izgi Turgut) (Turkey); Eliane Benisti Agency (Leon de la Menadiere, sci-fi/fantasy only) (France); Graal Literary Agency (Marcin Biegaj) (Albania, Baltic States, Bulgaria, Greece, Hungary, Iceland, North Macedonia, Poland, Romania, Serbia, Slovenia); The Grayhawk Agency (Gray Tan) (China, Taiwan, Thailand, Vietnam); Danny Hong Agency (Danny Hong) (Korea); Alexander Korzhenevski Agency (Alexander Korzhenevski) (Russia); Piergiorgio Nicollazzini Agency (Maura Solinas, sci-fi/fantasy only) (Italy); Kristin Olson Literary Agency (Kristin Olson) (Czechia); Thomas Schlueck GmbH (Bastian Schlueck, sci-fi/fantasy only) (Germany); Tuttle-Mori Agency Inc (Misa Morikawa, fiction; Manami Tamaoki, nonfiction) (Japan)
Membership(s): Women's Media Group

J de S Associates Inc (L)
9 Shagbark Rd, South Norwalk, CT 06854
Tel: 203-838-7571 *Fax:* 203-866-2713
Web Site: www.jdesassociates.com
Key Personnel
Pres: Jacques de Spoelberch *E-mail:* jdespoel@
   aol.com
Founded: 1975
Fiction & nonfiction. No unsol mss, query first. Send outline & 2 sample chapters; no reading fee. Agents & film representatives in major foreign countries.

The Jennifer DeChiara Literary Agency (L)
245 Park Ave, 39th fl, New York, NY 10167
Tel: 212-372-8989
Web Site: www.jdlit.com
Key Personnel
Owner, Pres & Agent: Jennifer DeChiara
   E-mail: jenndec@aol.com
Sr Agent: Stephen Fraser
   E-mail: fraserstephena@gmail.com
Agent: Marie Lamba *E-mail:* marie.
   jdlit@gmail.com; Roseanne Wells
   E-mail: roseannelitagent@gmail.com
Assoc Agent: Whitley Abell *E-mail:* whitley.
   jdlit@gmail.com; Alex Barba *E-mail:* alex.
   jdlit@gmail.com; Megan Barnard; Tara
   Gilbert; Amy Giuffrida; Cari Lamba
   E-mail: cari.jdlit@gmail.com; David Laurell
   E-mail: dlaurell@aol.com; Damian McNicholl
   E-mail: damianmcnichollvarney@gmail.
   com; Colleen Oefelein *E-mail:* colleen@
   adventurewrite.com; Tori Sharp; Alexandra
   Weiss *E-mail:* alexweiss.jdlit@gmail.com
Film/TV Mgr: Kimberly Guidone
Founded: 2001
Accepting queries in the following areas: children's books for every age (picture books, middle grade & young adult), adult fiction & nonfiction in a wide range of genres. Accept e-mail queries only, with "Query" in the subject line; no attachments. Co-agents in every country. No fees.
Titles recently placed: *Bees In The Trees*, Ruth Horowitz; *Daughter of Australia*, Harmony Verna; *Eliza Bing Is (Not) A Big, Fat Quitter*, Carmella Van Vleet; *Fannie Never Flinches*, Mary Cronk Farrell; *Girl*, M-E Girard; *Guts For Glory*, JoAnna Lapati; *Hazy Bloom*, Jennifer Hamburg; *Honestly, Ben*, Bill Konigsberg; *I Only Know Who I Am When I Am Somebody Else*, Danny Aiello; *I'll Be Damned*, Eric Braeden; *Irena's Children*, Mary Cronk Farrell; *Izzy Barr, Running Star*, Claudia Mills; *Luke Veracruz Saves The Day*, Jeff Anderson; *My Days...Happy and Otherwise*, Marion Ross; *My Girls: A Lifetime with Carrie and Debbie*, Todd Fisher; *Not Young, Still Restless: My Life So Far*, Jeanne Cooper; *Omega Days*, John L Campbell; *Openly Straight*, Bill Konigsberg; *Peanut Butter and Brains*, Joe McGee; *Quack*, Jennifer Hamburg; *Sitting Next to Jesus*, Carol Lynch Williams; *Skynned Alive: Keeping the Best in Lynyrd Skynyrd, America's Greatest Rock 'n' Roll Band*, Artimus Pyle; *Stuck In My Sister's Fat*, Carol Lynch Williams; *The Ed Lucas Story*, Ed Lucas, Christopher Lucas; *The Hole Story of the Doughnut*, Pat Miller; *The Jumbie Seed*, Tracey Baptiste; *The Jumbies*, Tracey Baptiste; *The Nora Notebooks*, Claudia Mills; *The One-Way Bridge*, Cathie Pelletier; *The Porcupine of Truth*, Bill Konigsberg; *The Quantum League*, Matthew Kirby; *The Summer Experiment*, Cathie Pelletier; *The Write-Brain Workbook (10th anniversary ed)*, Bonnie Neubauer; *The Year After Henry*, Cathie Pelletier; *Three Truths and a Lie*, Brent Hartinger; *Tippi*, Tippi Hedren; *To The Stars! The Story of Kathy Sullivan, First American Woman to Walk in Space*, Carmella Van Vleet, Kathy Sullivan; *Toni Tennille, A Memoir*, Toni Tennille; *Waggers*, Stacy A Nyikos; *Whistle Root*, Christopher Pennell
Foreign Rights: Books Crossing Borders (Betty Anne Crawford) (USA)

DeFiore and Company Literary Management Inc (L)
47 E 19 St, 3rd fl, New York, NY 10003
Tel: 212-925-7744 *Fax:* 212-925-9803
E-mail: info@defliterary.com; submissions@
   defliterary.com
Web Site: www.defliterary.com
Key Personnel
Founder & Pres: Brian DeFiore (AAR)
   E-mail: querybrian@defliterary.com
Dir, Busn Aff: Adam Schear (AAR)
   E-mail: adam@defliterary.com
Dir, Foreign Rts: Linda Kaplan
Literary Agent & UK Rts Dir: Meredith Kaffel Simonoff (AAR) *E-mail:* meredith@defliterary.com
Literary Agent: Laurie Abkemeier (AAR)
   E-mail: laurie@defliterary.com; Miriam
   Altschuler (AAR) *E-mail:* querymiriam@
   defliterary.com; Reiko Davis *E-mail:* reiko@
   defliterary.com; Matthew Elblonk
   E-mail: matthew@defliterary.com; Lisa Gallagher *E-mail:* lgsubmissions@defliterary.com;
   Cassie Hanjian; Caryn Karmatz Rudy (AAR)
   E-mail: caryn@defliterary.com; Rebecca
   Strauss (AAR) *E-mail:* rebecca@defliterary.
   com; Nicole Tourtelot *E-mail:* nicole@
   defliterary.com
Founded: 1999
Handles mainstream fiction, suspense fiction, business, self-help, narrative nonfiction, cookbooks & memoirs.
Titles recently placed: *Digital Minimalism*, Cal Newport; *Dining In*, Alison Roman; *Friday Black*, Nana Kwame Adjei-Brenyah; *Hidden Hormones*, Neal Barnard; *More Than Words*,

Jill Santopolo; *The Dumb Things Smart People Do With Their Money*, Jill Schlesinger
Foreign Rep(s): Meredith Kaffel Simonoff (UK)
Foreign Rights: The Book Publishers Association of Israel (Delia Ever Hadani) (Israel); JLM Literary Agency (John Moukakos) (Greece); Kayi Agency (Dilek Kayi) (Turkey); Andrew Nurnberg Associates (Sabine Pfannenstiel, London) (Germany); Andrew Nurnberg Associates (Claire Anouchian, London) (France, Quebec, CN); Andrew Nurnberg Associates (Lucy Flynn) (Latin America exc Brazil, Portugal, Spain); Andrew Nurnberg Associates (Barbara Barbieri) (Brazil, Italy); Andrew Nurnberg Associates (Marei Pittner, London) (Netherlands, Scandinavia); Andrew Nurnberg Associates (Anna & Mira Droumeva, Sofia) (Bulgaria, Romania, Serbia); Andrew Nurnberg Associates (Petra Tobiskova & Jana Borovanova, Prague) (Czechia, Slovakia, Slovenia); Andrew Nurnberg Associates (Aleksandra Lapinska & Renata Paczewska, Warsaw) (Poland); Andrew Nurnberg Associates (Judit Hermann, Budapest) (Croatia, Hungary); Andrew Nurnberg Associates (Ludmila Sushkova, Moscow) (Russia); Andrew Nurnberg Associates (Tatjana Zoldnere, Latvia) (Estonia, Latvia, Lithuania, Ukraine); Andrew Nurnberg Associates (Jackie Huang, Beijing) (China); Andrew Nurnberg Associates (Whitney Hsu, Taipei) (Taiwan); Tuttle-Mori Agency Inc (Ken Mori & Manami Tamaoki) (Japan); Tuttle-Mori Agency Inc (Thananchai Pandey, Bangkok) (Thailand); Eric Yang Agency (Henry Shin) (Korea)

Joelle Delbourgo Associates Inc (L)
101 Park St, Montclair, NJ 07042
Tel: 973-773-0836 (call only during standard business hours)
Web Site: www.delbourgo.com
Key Personnel
Founder & Pres, Agent & Consultant: Joelle Delbourgo (AAR) *E-mail:* joelle@delbourgo.com
Agent: Jacqueline Flynn *Tel:* 201-981-4181
   E-mail: jacquie@delbourgo.com
Edit Consultant: Carrie Cantor *Tel:* 973-783-1005
   E-mail: cantor.carrie@gmail.com; John Paine
   E-mail: jpaine@johnpaine.com
Founded: 2000
Boutique firm handling a wide range of adult fiction (literary & commercial) & nonfiction (narrative, prescriptive, reference). Young adult & middle grade fiction. E-mail queries only accepted, but check submission guidelines on web site. Materials will not be returned.
Titles recently placed: *An Afterlife*, Fran Bartkowski; *Beyond the Call*, Eileen Rivers; *Cold Hard Truth About You and Me*, Anne Greenwood Brown; *Golden State*, Ben H Winters; *Hot White Grief Parade*, Alexandra Silber; *How to Think About God(s)*, Philip Freeman; *Husbands and Other Sharp Objects*, Marilyn Simon Rothstein; *Prisoner 865*, Debbie Cenziper; *The Inspiration Code*, Kristi Hedges; *The Mindful Woman*, Caroline S Welch; *The Secret Letters Project*, Julie Merrick; *The Winged Herds of Anok*, Jennifer Alvarez; *Witness: Lessons from Elie Wiesel's Classroom*, Ariel Burger
Foreign Rights: Duran Kim Agency (Korea); Maxima Agency (Indonesia); Jenny Meyer Literary Agency (worldwide exc Asia); Andrew Nurnberg Associates Inc (China); Tuttle-Mori Agency Inc (Japan)
Membership(s): Women's Media Group

D4EO Literary Agency (L-D)
7 Indian Valley Rd, Weston, CT 06883
Tel: 203-544-7180 *Fax:* 203-544-7160
Web Site: www.d4eoliteraryagency.com; www.
   publishersmarketplace.com/members/d4eo;
   twitter.com/d4eo

Key Personnel
Principal: Robert (Bob) G Diforio *E-mail:* bob@
d4eo.com
Founded: 1991
Represent trade books of all types, fiction, non-fiction, business. No unsol mss, query first with SASE. Submit outline & sample chapters, if requested. No reading fee. Handle film & TV rights. Prefer recommendation from client or publisher. For middle grade & young adult: query with query letter & first 5 pages of your project in the body of the e-mail, no attachments.
Foreign Rep(s): Agence Litteraire Eliane Benisti (France); Nabu International Literary & Film Agency (Italy)
Foreign Rights: Anthea Agency (Katalena Sabeva) (Bulgaria); Agence Litteraire Eliane Benisti (Eliane Benisti) (France); Michael Meller Literary Agency GmbH (Michael Meller) (Germany); Nabu International Literary & Film Agency (Silvia Brunelli) (Italy); Tuttle-Mori Agency Inc (Ken Mori) (Japan)

Sandra Dijkstra Literary Agency (L)
1155 Camino del Mar, PMB 515, Del Mar, CA 92014-2605
Web Site: dijkstraagency.com
Key Personnel
Pres & Agent: Sandra Dijkstra
Agency Mgr & Agent: Elise Capron
Tel: 858-755-3115 ext 100 *E-mail:* elise@
dijkstraagency.com
Agent: Suzy Evans *E-mail:* suzy@dijkstraagency.
com; Thao Le *Tel:* 858-755-3115 ext 105
E-mail: thao@dijkstraagency.com; Jill Marr
Tel: 858-755-3115 ext 108 *E-mail:* jill@
dijkstraagency.com; Jessica Watterson
E-mail: jessica@dijkstraagency.com
Fin Mgr: Jennifer Kim *Tel:* 858-755-3115 ext 106
E-mail: jennifer@dijkstraagency.com
Subrights Mgr: Andrea Cavallaro
E-mail: andrea@dijkstraagency.com
Founded: 1981
Fiction: contemporary, women's, literary, suspense, thrillers, science fiction & fantasy. Nonfiction: narrative, history, business, psychology, self-help, science & memoir/biography. Works in conjunction with foreign & film agents. E-mail submissions only. See web site for most up-to-date guidelines. No reading fee.
Foreign Rights: Bardon-Chinese Media Agency (China, Taiwan); Sandra Bruna Agencia Literaria (Portugal, Spain); The English Agency (Japan) Ltd (Japan); Graal Literary Agency (Poland); The Italian Literary Agency srl (Italy); Katai & Bolza (Hungary); Licht & Burr (Scandinavia); Maxima Creative Agency (Indonesia); La Nouvelle Agence (France); ONK Agency (Turkey); Prava i prevodi (Eastern Europe); Sebes & Bisseling Literary Agency (Netherlands); Abner Stein Agency (UK); Synopsis Agency (Baltic States, Russia); TBPAI (Israel); Tuttle-Mori Agency Inc (Thailand); Eric Yang Agency (Korea)
Membership(s): The Authors Guild

Janis A Donnaud & Associates Inc (L)
77 Bleecker St, No C1-25, New York, NY 10012
Tel: 212-431-2663 *Fax:* 212-431-2667
E-mail: jdonnaud@aol.com
Key Personnel
Pres: Janis A Donnaud (AAR)
Founded: 1993
Nonfiction by experts in their fields: biography, business, history, mind/body/spirit, health, lifestyle, cookbooks/food writing, African-American, popular science, memoir, narrative nonfiction, cultural subjects, animal books, contemporary social issues, "Big Think" Books, women's issues. Does not handle fiction. Query letter by e-mail – sample material only on re-quest. Handle film, TV & international rights. No phone calls.
Titles recently placed: *Arthritis: Taming the Flame*, Susan Blum, MD; *Dinner*, Melissa Clark; *Forks Over Knives Global Flavors*, Brian Wendel, Darshana Ghacker; *Skinnytaste Fast and Slow*, Gina Homolka; *The Blue Apron Cookbook*, Blue Apron; *The Little Dogist*, Elias Weiss Friedman
Foreign Rights: Agence Litteraire Eliane Benisti (France); Berla & Griffini (Italy); Big Apple Agency Inc (China, Taiwan); Graal Literary Agency (Eastern Europe); Kalem Agency (Turkey); Liepman Agency (Germany); Lennart Sane Agency (Scandinavia, Spanish- & Portuguese-speaking countries); Sebes & Bisseling (Netherlands); Shinwon Agency (Korea); Abner Stein Agency (UK & Commonwealth); Tuttle-Mori Agency Inc (Japan)
Membership(s): The Authors Guild

Jim Donovan Literary (L)
5635 SMU Blvd, Suite 201, Dallas, TX 75206
Tel: 214-696-9411
E-mail: jdlqueries@sbcglobal.net
Key Personnel
Owner & Pres: Jim Donovan
Agent: Melissa Shultz
Founded: 1993
Literary & commercial fiction & nonfiction, especially biography, history, popular culture & sports. No poetry, short stories, science fiction/fantasy or children's. Accept unsol mss only with SASE. For nonfiction, query first with letter & SASE. For fiction, submit first 30-40 pages & synopsis with SASE. May query with e-mail, no attachments, response only if interested. No online submissions accepted. Handle film & TV rights for clients only. Agents in Hollywood & major foreign countries. No fees, 15% commission on monies earned.
Titles recently placed: *Crossing the Bloody Line*, Jeff Guinn; *Devils on Their Trail*, W K Stratton; *Four Days in Gettysburg*, Tim McGrath; *Merry Christmas from the Fam-O-Lee*, Robert Earl Keen; *Only the Brave*, Don Keith; *Perfectly Hidden Depression*, Dr Margaret Rutherford; *Rogues' Gallery*, John Oller; *The Earth Is All That Lasts*, Mark Gardner; *The Hamilton Affair*, Elizabeth Cobbs

Drennan Literary Agency (L)
6 Robin Lane, East Kingston, NH 03827
Tel: 603-642-8002 *Fax:* 603-642-8002
Key Personnel
Pres: William D Drennan
Contact: Christina L Drennan
Founded: 1980
Scholarly only. No unsol mss, query first with outline & SASE. No reading fee.

Dunham Literary Inc (L)
110 William St, Suite 2202, New York, NY 10038
Tel: 212-929-0994
Web Site: dunhamlit.com
Key Personnel
Founder, Pres & Agent: Jennie Dunham (AAR)
Agent: Leslie Zampetti (AAR)
Founded: 2000
Literary fiction & nonfiction, children's book writers & illustrators. No plays or screenplays. Handle film & TV rights for books represented. No unsol mss, query letter first with SASE. No fax or e-mail queries. No reading fee.
Foreign Rights: Taryn Fagerness Agency (worldwide exc USA)
Membership(s): Society of Children's Book Writers & Illustrators (SCBWI)

Dunow, Carlson & Lerner Literary Agency Inc (L)
27 W 20 St, Suite 1107, New York, NY 10011
Tel: 212-645-7606
E-mail: mail@dclagency.com
Web Site: www.dclagency.com
Key Personnel
Literary Agent: Jennifer Carlson (AAR); Arielle Datz (AAR); Stacia Decker (AAR); Henry Dunow (AAR); Erin Hosier; Amy Hughes; Eleanor Jackson; Julia Kenny (AAR); Betsy Lerner; Edward Necarsulmer, IV (AAR); Chris Rogers; Yishai Seidman (AAR); Rachel Vogel
Founded: 2005
Query first, fiction & nonfiction. Handle film & TV rights. Agents in all foreign territories. Submit outlines & sample chapters with SASE. No reading fee.
Foreign Rights: Akcali Copyright Agency (Turkey); Big Apple Agency Inc (China, Taiwan); The English Agency (Japan); Grayhawk Agency (China, Taiwan); The Deborah Harris Agency (Israel); David Higham Associates (UK); JLM Literary Agency (Greece); Andrew Nurnberg Associates (Eastern Europe, Europe, Russia, South America); Owls Agency Inc (Japan); Abner Stein Agency (UK); Tuttle-Mori Agency Inc (Japan); Eric Yang (Korea)

Dupree, Miller & Associates Inc (L)
4311 Oak Lawn Ave, Suite 650, Dallas, TX 75219
Tel: 214-559-2665 *Fax:* 214-559-7243
E-mail: editorial@dupreemiller.com
Web Site: www.dupreemiller.com
Key Personnel
Founder & CEO: Jan Miller *E-mail:* jmr@
dupreemiller.com
Pres: Shannon Marven
Sr Agent: Nena Madonia
Fiction & nonfiction. No children's, science fiction, fantasy, horror, short stories, poetry or screenplays. No unsol mss; accept query letter only, with SASE enclosed for reply. No fees. Market & promote own books both regionally & nationally.

Dystel, Goderich & Bourret LLC (L-D)
One Union Sq W, Suite 904, New York, NY 10003
Tel: 212-627-9100 *Fax:* 212-627-9313
Web Site: www.dystel.com
Key Personnel
Pres & Partner: Jane Dystel (AAR)
Agent & Partner: Michael Bourret (AAR)
E-mail: mbourret@dystel.com; Miriam Goderich *Tel:* 212-627-9100 ext 16
E-mail: miriam@dystel.com
VP, Subs Rts Dir & Agent: Lauren E Abramo
Tel: 212-627-9100 ext 13 *E-mail:* labramo@
dystel.com
VP, Sr Agent: Jim McCarthy (AAR) *Tel:* 212-627-9100 ext 15 *E-mail:* jmccarthy@dystel.
com
VP & Agent: Stacey Kendall Glick
E-mail: sglick@dystel.com
Proj Mgr, Ebook Prog & Agent: Sharon Pelletier
Tel: 212-627-9100 ext 25 *E-mail:* spelletier@
dystel.com
Royalties Mgr & Agent: Michael Hoogland
Tel: 212-627-9100 ext 14 *E-mail:* mhoogland@
dystel.com
Agent: Jessica Papin *E-mail:* jpapin@dystel.com;
John Rudolph *E-mail:* jrudolph@dystel.com;
Ann Leslie Tuttle
Asst & Agent: Erin Young *E-mail:* eyoung@
dystel.com
Asst: Amy Elizabeth Bishop *Tel:* 212-627-9100
ext 10 *E-mail:* abishop@dystel.com
Subs Rts & Royalties Asst: Kemi Faderin
Tel: 212-627-9100 ext 11 *E-mail:* kfaderin@
dystel.com

Founded: 1994 (as Jane Dystel Literary Management)

General fiction & nonfiction, also cookbooks & children's books. No unsol mss, query letter or e-mail query with outline & first 50 pages. No reading fee. Handle film & TV rights. Firm also has a West Coast office staffed by Michael Bourret & Erin Young (e-mail queries only).

Titles recently placed: *100 Days*, Nicole McInnes; *Adnan's Story*, Rabia Chaudry; *All Better Now*, Emily Wing Smith; *As I Descended*, Robin Talley; *Bad Boy*, Elliot Wake; *Cooking Solo*, Klancy Miller; *Epitaph*, Mary Doria Russell; *Essential Oils for Healing*, Vannoy Gentles Fite; *Fat Boy vs the Cheerleaders*, Geoff Herbach; *Filthy Rich*, Raine Miller; *Good as Gone*, Amy Gentry; *If I Stay*, Gayle Forman; *In a French Kitchen*, Susan Loomis; *Inspector of the Dead*, David Morrell; *Invisible Man, Got the Whole World Watching*, Mychal Denzel Smith; *Irena's Children*, Tilar Mazzeo; *It Ends With Us*, Colleen Hoover; *Junk*, Allison Stewart; *Making It Right*, Catherine Bybee; *Miranda and Caliban*, Jacqueline Carey; *My Sweet Angel*, John Glatt; *Smashed, Mashed, Boiled & Baked*, Raghavan Iyer; *Strange Glow*, Timothy J Jorgensen; *The All-Star Antes Up*, Nancy Herkness; *The Duration*, Dave Fromm; *The Glittering Court*, Richelle Mead; *The Leper Spy*, Ben Montgomery; *The One Real Thing*, Samantha Young; *The Remedy*, Suzanne Young; *The Remember Balloons*, Jessie Oliveros; *The Seasoned Life*, Ayesha Curry; *The Storyteller*, Aaron Starmer; *The Thunder Beneath Us*, Nicole Blades; *The Ugly Dumpling*, Stephanie Campisi; *The Valley*, Helen Bryan; *The Vanilla Bean Baking Book*, Sarah Kieffer; *The World From Up Here*, Cecilia Galante; *Trusting You and Other Lies*, Nicole Williams; *Until Friday Night*, Abbi Glines; *Up in Flames*, Abbi Glines; *Vegetarian India*, Madhur Jaffrey; *Zeroboxer*, Fonda Lee

Foreign Rep(s): Ali (Italy); ANAW (Poland); Agence Litteraire Eliane Benisti (France); Big Apple Agency Inc (China); EAJ (Japan); International Editors' Co (Latin America, Spain); Kayi Literary (Turkey); Mohrbooks AG Literary Agency (Germany); Andrew Nurnberg (Eastern Europe); Read 'n' Right (Greece); Agencia Riff (Brazil); Sebes & Bisseling Literary Agency (Netherlands); Abner Stein Agency (UK); TBPAI (Israel); Ulf Toregard Agency (Scandinavia); Tuttle-Mori Agency Inc (Thailand); Eric Yang Agency (Korea)

Anne Edelstein Literary Agency LLC (L)
404 Riverside Dr, New York, NY 10025
Tel: 212-414-4923
E-mail: info@aeliterary.com; rights@aeliterary.com
Web Site: www.aeliterary.com
Key Personnel
Pres: Anne Edelstein (AAR)
Founded: 1990
Literary fiction & narrative nonfiction (including memoir, history, psychology, religion & culinary); handle film & TV rights; agents in all principal foreign countries.
No unsol mss.
Foreign Rights: AM Heath (Victoria Hobbs) (UK); AnatoliaLit Agency (Turkey); L'Autre Agence (Corinne Marotte) (France); Silvia Bastos Agencia Literaria SL (Pau Centellas) (Spain); Petra Eggers Agency (Petra Eggers) (Germany); The English Agency (Japan); The Grayhawk Agency (China, Taiwan); The Harris Agency (Efrat Lev) (Israel); Danny Hong Agency (Danny Hong) (Korea); The Italian Literary Agency srl (Italy); Prava i prevodi (Eastern Europe); Sebes & Bisseling (Holland, Scandinavia); The Van Lear Agency (Russia); Villas-Boas & Moss Literary Agency (Brazil)
Membership(s): The Authors Guild

The Lisa Ekus Group LLC (L)
57 North St, Hatfield, MA 01038
Tel: 413-247-9325 *Fax:* 413-247-9873
E-mail: info@lisaekus.com
Web Site: lisaekus.com
Key Personnel
Principal & Pres: Lisa Ekus (AAR)
    E-mail: lisaekus@lisaekus.com
Mgr & Literary Assoc: Sally Ekus
    E-mail: sally@lisaekus.com
Founded: 1982
Since our inception in 1982, we have been helping both new & established authors & chefs make their mark on the culinary landscape. All of our nationally recognized culinary promotions are built on the same foundation: to create innovative strategies, pay meticulous attention to client needs & effectively & productively network across the culinary, media & publishing industries.
In 2000 we expanded our award-winning expertise to include author representation & literary agent services. Within 8 years, our literary agency facilitated more than 150 book deals, representing over 90 authors & numerous leading publishers internationally.
We offer comprehensive media training programs designed for authors, chefs, spokespeople, show hosts & food professionals & orchestrate creative partnerships between individuals & corporations in the culinary industry. Specialty areas include: food, nutrition, health & wine & spirit.
Accept unsol mss. Submissions should be in the form of a complete proposal & we provide detailed guidelines on our web site. No fees, clients are billed for expenses.
Titles recently placed: *Coconuts and Collards: Recipes and Stories from Puerto Rico to the Deep South*, Von Diaz; *Food Is the Solution: What to Eat to Save the World - 80+ Recipes for a Greener Planet and a Healthier You*, Matthew Prescott; *Hot for Food Vegan Comfort Classics: 101 Recipes to Feed Your Face*, Lauren Toyota; *Secrets of the Southern Table: A Food Lover's Tour of the Global South*, Virginia Willis; *Smart Meal Prep for Beginners: Recipes and Weekly Plans for Healthy, Ready-to-Go Meals*, Toby Amidor; *SOUL: A Chef's Culinary Evolution in 150 Recipes*, Todd Richards; *Sous Vide Made Simple: 60 Everyday Recipes for Perfectly Cooked Meals*, Lisa Q Fetterman; *Tex-Mex Cookbook: Traditions, Innovations, and Comfort Foods from Both Sides of the Border*, Ford Fry, Jessica Dupuy; *The Comfort Food Mash-Up Cookbook: 80 Delicious Recipes for Reimagining Your Favorite Dishes*, Dan Whalen; *The Wicked Healthy Cookbook: Free. From. Animals.*, Chad Sarno, Derek Sarno
Foreign Rights: The Jean V Naggar Literary Agency
Membership(s): International Association of Culinary Professionals (IACP); Women Presidents' Organization

Ethan Ellenberg Literary Agency (L)
155 Suffolk St, Suite 2R, New York, NY 10002
Tel: 212-431-4554
E-mail: agent@ethanellenberg.com
Web Site: www.ethanellenberg.com
Key Personnel
Pres & Agent: Ethan Ellenberg (AAR)
Agent: Evan Gregory (AAR)
Assoc Agent & Off Mgr: BiBi Lewis
Founded: 1984
Commercial & literary fiction & nonfiction. Fiction: specialize in science fiction, fantasy, romance & all women's fiction. Suspense, thriller, mystery, first novels, all children's books including new adult & middle grade. Nonfiction: narrative nonfiction, history, adventure, science. Accepting new clients, both published & unpublished. No reading fees; accept

unsol submissions with SASE. E-mail submissions without attachments accepted, but prefer submissions by mail. For fiction: first 3 chapters, synopsis & SASE. For nonfiction: proposal, including outline & author bio, sample chapters, if available. Co-agents in Hollywood & all principal foreign countries.
Titles recently placed: *Adrift*, Tony Peak; *Arkads World*, James Cambias; *Ben Franklin's in My Kitchen*, Candace Fleming; *Best Friend's Forever*, Margot Hunt; *Bulldozer 3*, Candace Fleming, Eric Rohmann; *Echo in Onyx (3 book series)*, Sharon Shinn; *Flames of Rebellion (3 books)*, Jay Allan; *Frontlines (series)*, Marko Kloos; *Hot and Badgered (3 book series)*, Shelly Laurenston; *Java Jive (series)*, Caroline Fardig; *Nest of the Monarch*, Kay Kenyon; *Persistence*, Marc Costanzo; *Shadow Hunt*, Melissa F Olson; *Solar Warden (3 book series)*, Ian Douglas; *The Body Under the Piano*, Marthe Jocelyn; *The Farmer's Daughter*, Shelly Laurenston; *The Singularity Trap*, Dennis E Taylor; *Twelve Book Deal with Tor*, John Scalzi; *Twilight's Desires*, Amanda Ashley; *We Are Legion (Bobiverse Series)*, Dennis E Taylor
Foreign Rights: Eliane Benisti (France); Berla & Griffini (Italy); Big Apple Agency (China); Book Publishers Association of Israel (Israel); BookCosmos Agency (Korea); The English Agency (Japan); Alexander Korzhenevski Agency (Russia); Mo Literary Agency (Holland); Prava i prevodi (Eastern Europe); RDC Agencia Literaria SL (Spain); Thomas Schlueck Agency (Germany)
Membership(s): The Authors Guild; Authors Registry; Mystery Writers of America (MWA); Romance Writers of America (RWA); Science Fiction & Fantasy Writers of America (SFWA); Society of Children's Book Writers & Illustrators (SCBWI)

Nicholas Ellison Agency (L)
3 Tara Dr, Brookfield, CT 06804-2324
Web Site: www.thenicholasellisonagency.com
Key Personnel
Pres: Nicholas Ellison
Founded: 1932
Fiction & narrative nonfiction (all subjects). No children's or science fiction. No unsol mss, query first. Submit sample chapters. Include a cover letter & brief synopsis of first 20 pages of mss. Handle film & TV rights. Fees charged for photocopying & books ordered. Agents in principal foreign countries.

Felicia Eth Literary Representation (L)
555 Bryant St, Suite 350, Palo Alto, CA 94301
Tel: 415-970-9717
E-mail: feliciaeth.literary@gmail.com
Web Site: www.ethliterary.com
Key Personnel
Pres: Felicia Eth (AAR)
Founded: 1989
Diverse nonfiction including narrative, psychology, health & popular science; including women's issues, investigative journalism & biography. Selective mainstream literary fiction. No unsol mss, query first for fiction, proposal for nonfiction. No discs, no files by e-mail. Handle film & TV rights for clients, books only through sub-agents in LA. No reading fee. Xeroxing costs & overseas mail, FedEx charged to client, $75 for full-length ms to cover mailing. Commission is 15% domestic & 20% foreign. Foreign rights agents in all major territories.
Titles recently placed: *A Place Outside the Law*, Peter Jan Honigsberg; *Fastest Things on Wings*, Terry Masear; *The Collapse of Parenting*, Leonard Sax; *The Devil's Cup: A History of the World According to Coffee*, Stewart Lee Allen; *The Memory Thief*, Emily Coin

Mary Evans Inc (L)
242 E Fifth St, New York, NY 10003-8501
Tel: 212-979-0880 *Fax:* 212-979-5344
E-mail: info@maryevansinc.com
Web Site: www.maryevansinc.com
Key Personnel
Pres: Mary Evans (AAR)
Agent: Leslie Meredith
Literary fiction, narrative nonfiction, commercial fiction, self-help, science & history, graphic novels & memoirs. Nonfiction should be submitted in proposal form & fiction with a query letter, a synopsis & 3 sample chapters, SASE required. Accept unsol mss. Handle film & TV rights, no reading fee.
Foreign Rights: Akcali Copyright Agency (Ozgur Emir) (Turkey); Berla and Griffini Rights Agency (Erica Berla) (Italy); The Book Publishers Association of Israel (Dalia Ever-Hadani) (Israel); Chandler Crawford Agency (Holland); The Grayhawk Agency (Gray Tan) (China, Taiwan); International Editors (Maru de Montserrat) (Portugal, Spain); LEX Copyright Office (Norbert Uzseka) (Hungary); Licht & Burr (Trine Licht) (Scandinavia); Liepman Agency (Mark Koralnik) (Germany); La Nouvelle Agence (Michele Kanonidis) (France); Andrew Nurnberg Associates (Ludmila Sushkova) (Russia); Owls Agency Inc (Mario Tauchi) (Japan); Prava i prevodi (Ana Milenkovic) (Eastern Europe, Greece); Riff Agency (Lauri Riff) (Brazil); Eric Yang Agency (Henry Shin) (Korea)

Feigenbaum Publishing Consultants Inc (L)
61 Bounty Lane, Jericho, NY 11753
Tel: 516-647-8314 (cell)
Key Personnel
Pres: Laurie Feigenbaum
  E-mail: lauriefeigenbaum@gmail.com
Founded: 1991
Contract negotiations & review, agenting, trademark & copyright registration, permissions clearance & general publishing advice. Expertise in book publishing & electronic publishing. No unsol mss, query first. Hourly fee or commission. Contracts negotiation, $95 per hour for contracts review, negotiation, trademark & copyright registration & permissions.

FinePrint Literary Management (L)
207 W 106 St, Suite 1D, New York, NY 10025
Tel: 212-279-6214
E-mail: assist@fineprint.com
Web Site: www.fineprintlit.com
Key Personnel
CEO: Peter Rubie (AAR) *E-mail:* peter@fineprintlit.com
In-House Subs Rts Dir: Jacqueline Murphy
  E-mail: jacqueline@fineprintlit.com
Agent: Lauren Bieker *Tel:* 212-279-1412
  E-mail: lauren@fineprintlit.com; June Clark
  E-mail: june@fineprintlit.com; Laura Wood
  E-mail: laura@fineprintlit.com
Founded: 2007 (formed by the merger of the Peter Rubie Agency & the Imprint Agency)
High quality fiction & nonfiction. Handle film, TV & foreign rights through sub-agents. No unsol mss, query first. Submit outline & first two chapters with one page query letter & proposal. No reading fees. Photocopying fees. Some foreign mailing charges. Please send queries to the appropriate e-mail for the agent you wish to query.
Titles recently placed: *30 Days a Black Man*, Bill Steigerwald; *A Secret History of Witches*, Louisa Morgan (aka Louise Marley); *Ants Among Elephants*, Sujatha Gidla; *Apprenticed to Venus*, Tristine Rainer; *August Snow*, Stephen M Jones; *Ayurveda Lifestyle Medicine*, Acharya Shunya; *Charlie Henry: Rob Thy Neighbor*, David Thurlo; *Chest of Bone*, Vicki Stiefel; *Dangers of Dating a Rebound Vam-*

pire, Molly Harper White; *Death is a Bargain*, Noreen Smith; *Donny's Inferno*, P W Catanese; *Dreamland*, Sam Quinones; *Eccentrics, Mavericks, and Outsiders at War*, Jason Ridler; *Evolution Underground*, Anthony J Martin; *Fizzopolis*, Patrick Carman; *Floors*, Patrick Carman; *Graphene*, Les Johnson; *Grim Expectations*, K W Jeter; *Hummus and Homicide*, Tina Kashian; *Jane on the Brain*, Wendy S Jones; *Mask of the Sun*, John Dvorak; *Napoleon III: The Last Emperor of France*, Alan Strauss-Schom; *Red Sky*, Chris Goff; *Signal*, Patrick Lee; *The Divided City*, Luke McCallin; *The End of Breast Cancer*, Kathleen Ruddy; *The Equity Culture*, B Mark Smith; *The First Circumnavigators: Unsung Heroes of the Age of Discovery*, Harry Kelsey; *The Invasive*, Michael Hodges; *The Runner Up Presidency*, Mark Weston; *Undercover Warrior*, Aimee Thurlo, David Thurlo; *Wonderlandscape*, John Clayton
Foreign Rep(s): Lorella Belli (UK); The Book Publishers' Association of Israel (Israel); Donatella d'Ormesson (France); The English Agency (Japan); Grayhawk Agency (China, Taiwan); International Editors (Latin America, Spain); Japan UNI Agency Inc (Japan); Nurcihan Kesim (Turkey); Lennart Sane Agency AB (Scandinavia); Lex Copywright Agency (Hungary); Maxima Creative Agency (Indonesia); PNLA (Italy); Prava i prevodi (Eastern Europe); Agencia Literaria Riff (Brazil); Thomas Schlueck GmbH (Germany); Tuttle-Mori Agency Inc (Malaysia, Thailand, Vietnam); Eric Yang Agency (Korea)

The Fischer-Harbage Agency Inc (L)
540 President St, 3rd fl, Brooklyn, NY 11215
Tel: 212-695-7105
E-mail: info@fischerharbage.com
Web Site: www.fischerharbage.com
Key Personnel
Pres: Ryan Fischer-Harbage
Assoc Agent: Christopher Hermelin
Founded: 2007
Full service boutique literary agency specializing in fiction, memoir, narrative nonfiction & current events. No unsol mss, query first with a short description, bio & first chapter of your book in the body of an e-mail to submissions@fischerharbage.com. No fees, standard commission paid.
Titles recently placed: *A Crash of Rhinos: and other wild animal groups*, Greg Danylyshyn, Stephan Lomp; *American Spies: Modern Surveillance, Why You Should Care, and What to Do About It*, Jennifer Granick; *Contrary Motion: A Novel*, Andy Mozina; *Forever Painless: End Chronic Pain and Reclaim Your Life in 30 Minutes a Day*, Miranda Esmonde-White; *Liar: A Memoir*, Rob Roberge; *Literary Starbucks: Fresh-Brewed, Half-Caf, No-Whip Bookish Humor*, Nora Katz, Wilson Josephson, Jill Poskanzer; *Lord of the Swallows: A Malko Linge Novel*, Gérard de Villiers; *Raising an Entrepreneur: 10 Rules for Nurturing Risk Takers, Problem Solvers, and Changemakers*, Margot Machol Bisnow; *Surface to Air: A Malko Linge Novel*, Gérard de Villiers; *Surpassing Certainty: What My Twenties Taught Me*, Janet Mock; *Testimony*, Robbie Robertson
Foreign Rights: Linda Biagi Rights Management (worldwide)

Flannery Literary (L)
1140 Wickfield Ct, Naperville, IL 60563
Web Site: flanneryliterary.com
Key Personnel
Owner: Jennifer Flannery *E-mail:* jennifer@flanneryliterary.com
Founded: 1992
Represents authors of books written for children & young adults. No unsol mss, query first via

e-mail. No snail mail or phone queries. No fees.
Membership(s): American Booksellers Association (ABA); American Library Association (ALA); Chicago Women in Publishing; International Literacy Association (ILA); National Council of Teachers of English (NCTE); Society of Children's Book Writers & Illustrators (SCBWI)

Peter Fleming Agency (L)
PO Box 458, Pacific Palisades, CA 90272
Tel: 310-454-1373
E-mail: peterfleming408@gmail.com
Key Personnel
Pres: Peter Fleming
Nonfiction: that rare expertise so vital in America that nonbook readers will buy it, read it! Includes populist, contrarian, dissent, suppressed information overlooked or avoided by mainstream media (ex: corporate/political crimes). Interested in authors with strong platforms, web sites, blogs & seminar experience. No unsol mss, query first with SASE. Submit outline. No reading fee. Clients billed for major postage, FedEx, foreign communication & other pre-approved expenses.

Sheldon Fogelman Agency Inc (L)
420 E 72 St, New York, NY 10021
Tel: 212-532-7250 *Fax:* 212-685-8939
E-mail: info@sheldonfogelmanagency.com
Web Site: sheldonfogelmanagency.com
Key Personnel
Pres & Literary Agent: Sheldon Fogelman
Asst Agent/Foreign Rts Mgr: Janine Hauber
Asst Agent: Amy Stern
Founded: 1975
Juvenile trade books of all types. Handle all rights, including film, TV, & foreign. Query with full picture book mss or first chapters & synopsis of novel. E-mail only. Include publishing history. No reading fee.

Folio Literary Management (L)
The Film Center Bldg, 630 Ninth Ave, Suite 1101, New York, NY 10036
Tel: 212-400-1494 *Fax:* 212-967-0977
Web Site: www.foliolit.com
Key Personnel
Founding Partner: Scott Hoffman; Jeff Kleinman (AAR)
Partner: Claudia Cross (AAR); Steve Troha (AAR); Emily van Beek
SVP, Dir, Opers & Agent: Frank Weimann
SVP & Agent: Erin Niumata; Marcy Posner (AAR)
VP: Erin Harris
Dir, Intl Rts & Agent: Melissa White
Contracts Mgr & Agent: Michael Harriot
Agent: Jan Baumer; Jamie Chambliss; Rachel Ekstrom Courage; John Cusick; Dado Derviskadic; Katherine Latshaw; Don Laventhall; Jeff Silberman (AAR)
Literary & Dramatic Rts Agent: Ruth Pomerance
Founded: 2006
A full service literary agency with co-agents around the world. No unsol mss, query first via e-mail. No fees.
Titles recently placed: *10-Day Green Smoothie Cleanse*, J J Smith; *Anchor & Sophia*, Tommy Wallach; *But Enough About Me*, Burt Reynolds; *Deep Nutrition*, Dr Cate Shanahan; *Ginny Moon*, Benjamin Ludwig; *Girls on the Verge*, Sharon Biggs Waller; *Hustle*, Neal Patel, Patrick Vlaskovits, Jonas Koffler; *I Killed Zoe Spanos*, Kit Frick; *I'm Judging You*, Luvvie Ajay; *Jackie's Girl*, Kathy McKeon; *Maybe a Mermaid*, Josephine Cameron; *Only Child*, Rhiannon Navin; *Saints and Misfits*, S K Ali; *Seven Deadly Shadows*, Courtney Alameda, Valynne Maetani; *The Ballerina Body*, Misty

Copeland; *The Better Liar*, Tanen Jones; *The Grown-Up's Guide to Teenage Humans*, Josh Shipp; *The Marsh King's Daughter*, Karen Dionne; *The Pieces of Piper Perish*, Kayla Cagan; *The Reminders*, Val Emmich; *The Seven Torments of Amy and Craig*, Don Zolidis; *The Wellness Mama Cookbook*, Katie Spears; *Tia and Tamera Mowry*, Twintuition; *Wallis in Love*, Andrew Morton; *Warren Buffett's Ground Rules*, Jeremy Miller; *Where the Light Gets In*, Kimberly Williams-Paisley

Foreign Rights: Berla & Griffini (Italy); The Book Publishers Association of Israel (Israel); Catherine Fragou (Greece); Graal Literary Agency (Poland); The Grayhawk Agency (China, Taiwan); Danny Hong Agency (Korea); IECO (Portugal); Asli Karasuil Telif Haklari (Turkey); Agence Michelle Lapautre (France); Maxima Creative Agency (Indonesia); Prava i prevodi (Czechia, Russia, Serbia); Riff Agency (Brazil); Thomas Schlueck GmbH (Germany); Marianne Schoenbach Literary Agency (Netherlands); Livia Stoia Literary Agency (Romania); Ulf Toregard Agency (Scandinavia); Tuttle-Mori Agency Inc (Japan, Thailand, Vietnam); Susanna Zevi Agenzia Letteraria (Italy)

Fort Ross Inc - International Representation for Artists (L)
Division of Fort Ross Inc
26 Arthur Place, Yonkers, NY 10701
Tel: 914-375-6448
Key Personnel
Pres & Exec Dir: Dr Vladimir P Kartsev
E-mail: vkartsev2000@gmail.com
Founded: 1992
Fiction: American, Kazakh & Russian classics, romance, mysteries, science fiction, fantasy, adventure. Provide publishers with texts & illustrations. Publishing books in English & Russian ("Metropolitan Classics").
Titles recently placed: *End of the Legend*, Abish Kekilbaev; *Lonely Yurt*, Smagul Yelubay; *The Code of the Word*, Olzhas Suleimenov
Foreign Rep(s): Nova Littera (Baltic States, Belarus, Russia, Ukraine)

Lynn C Franklin Associates Ltd (L)
1350 Broadway, Suite 2015, New York, NY 10018
Tel: 212-868-6311 *Fax:* 212-868-6312
E-mail: agency@franklinandsiegal.com
Key Personnel
Pres & Agent: Lynn C Franklin (AAR)
Rts Mgr: Claudia Nys
Adult commercial & literary fiction; middle grade & young adult fiction; & general nonfiction with special interest in self-help, health, psychology, personal growth & biographies, as well as current international affairs. No unsol mss, query e-mail (no attachments). No reading fee. Representatives in Hollywood & in all major foreign countries. Handle film & TV rights.
Titles recently placed: *The Book of Forgiving: The Four-Fold Path of Healing for Ourselves and Our World*, Desmond M Tutu, Mpho A Tutu; *The Customer Rules: The 39 Essential Rules for Delivering Sensational Service*, Lee Cockerell; *The Wahls Protocol*, Terry Wahls, MD, Eve Adamson
Foreign Rights: ACER Agencia Literaria (Elizabeth Atkins) (Portugal, Spain, Spanish Latin America); Eliane Benisti Literary Agency (France); Book Publishers Association of Israel (Israel); Chinese Connection Agency (China, Taiwan); Mary Clemmey Literary Agency (Mary Clemmey) (Australia, New Zealand, UK); The English Agency (Japan) Ltd (Japan); Fritz Agency (Germany); Graal Literary Agency (Poland); Berla e Griffini (Erica Berla) (Italy); Katai & Bolza (Hungary); Simona Kessler International Copyright Agency

(Romania); Maxima Creative (Indonesia); Andrew Nurnberg Associates (Russia); Kristin Olson (Czechia); Prava i prevodi (Bulgaria, Croatia, Montenegro, Serbia, Slovenia); Read n' Right Agency (Greece); Agencia Riff (Brazil); Lennart Sane Agency (Netherlands, Scandinavia); Eric Yang Agency (Korea)

Jeanne Fredericks Literary Agency Inc (L)
221 Benedict Hill Rd, New Canaan, CT 06840
Tel: 203-972-3011 *Fax:* 203-972-3011
E-mail: jeanne.fredericks@gmail.com (no unsol attachments)
Web Site: jeannefredericks.com
Key Personnel
Pres: Jeanne Fredericks (AAR)
Founded: 1997 (purchased assets of Susan P Urstadt Inc in May 1997)
Adult nonfiction only, especially practical popular reference, health & medical, gardening, practical how-to, biography, antiques & decorative arts, natural history, cookbooks, women's issues, history. No unsol mss, query first by e-mail or by mail with SASE. If requested, submit proposal, author biography (including previous publishing history), detailed outline & sample chapters by e-mail or by mail with SASE. Do not require signature for delivery. Handle film & TV rights with co-agent. No reading fee.
Titles recently placed: *Between Grit and Grace*, Sasha Shillcutt, MD; *Chefs & Company*, Maria Isabella; *Coming to Our Senses About Concussion*, Elizabeth Sandel, MD; *Hangovers to Hangnails: Tips, Tricks & Treatments Every College Student Needs to Know*, Jill Grimes, MD; *How to Build Your Own Tiny House*, Roger Marshall; *Storm of the Century*, Willie Drye; *The Autoimmune Disease Handbook*, Julius Birnbaum, MD; *The Colorful Dry Garden*, Maureen Gilmer; *The Secret Language of Cells*, Jonathan Lieff, MD; *Yoga Nidra for Stress Relief*, Julie Lusk
Foreign Rep(s): Books Crossing Borders (worldwide)
Membership(s): The Authors Guild

Robert A Freedman Dramatic Agency Inc (D)
1501 Broadway, Suite 2310, New York, NY 10036
Tel: 212-840-5760 *Fax:* 212-840-5776
Key Personnel
Pres: Robert A Freedman (AAR)
E-mail: rfreedmanagent@aol.com
SVP: Marta Praeger (AAR)
Agent: Samara Anderson
Founded: 1928 (as Harold Freedman Brandt & Brandt Dramatic Department Inc, until 1981)
Dramatic scripts for stage, motion picture & TV. No unsol mss, query first. No reading fee. Material placed for production/publication is subject to 10% commission. Agents in all European countries. Will co-agent with literary agents to handle film rights & books.

Sarah Jane Freymann Literary Agency LLC (L)
59 W 71 St, Suite 9-B, New York, NY 10023
Tel: 212-362-9277
E-mail: submissions@sarahjanefreymann.com
Web Site: www.sarahjanefreymann.com
Key Personnel
Owner & Agent: Sarah Jane Freymann
E-mail: sarah@sarahjanefreymann.com
Assoc: Katharine Sands *Tel:* 212-751-8892; Steven Schwartz *Tel:* 212-362-1998
E-mail: steve@sarahjanefreymann.com
Founded: 1974
Represents book-length fiction & general nonfiction. Fiction: popular fiction plus quality mainstream, literary fiction & young adult. Nonfiction: spiritual/inspirational, psychology,

self-help; women's/men's issues; health (conventional & alternative); cookbooks; narrative nonfiction, natural science, nature, memoirs, biography; current events, multicultural issues, popular culture; illustrated books, lifestyle, garden, design, architecture, humor, sports, travel & business. No unsol mss, query first with SASE. Handle film & TV rights with subagents. Representation in all foreign markets. No reading fee.

Fredrica S Friedman & Co Inc (L)
857 Fifth Ave, New York, NY 10065
Tel: 212-639-9455
E-mail: info@fredricafriedman.com
Web Site: www.fredricafriedman.com
Key Personnel
Pres: Fredrica S Friedman
Founded: 2000
Literary management firm that represents best selling & award-winning authors. General nonfiction & fiction. No poetry, plays, screenplays, children's picture books, science fiction/fantasy or horror. No unsol mss-query first. Send all queries by e-mail, no attachments. See web site for detailed submission information. Hard copy materials will not be returned; no fees.

Candice Fuhrman Literary Agency (L)
10 Cypress Hollow Dr, Tiburon, CA 94920
Tel: 415-383-1014
E-mail: fuhrmancandice@gmail.com
Key Personnel
Pres & Owner: Candice Fuhrman
Nonfiction: health, memoir, psychology, women's issues, how-to & self-help; literary & commercial fiction. No unsol mss.
Currently not accepting new clients.
Foreign Rights: Jenny Meyer Literary Agency

The Garamond Agency Inc (L)
12 Horton St, Newburyport, MA 01950
E-mail: query@garamondagency.com
Web Site: www.garamondagency.com
Key Personnel
Dir: Lisa Adams; David Miller
Adult nonfiction, all subjects. No unsol mss, query by e-mail first. Submit cover letter, outline, synopsis, author bio & SASE. No reading fees. Handle TV & movie rights.
Foreign Rights: AnatoliaLit Agency (Turkey); Bardon-Chinese Media Agency (China, Taiwan); Berla & Griffini Rights Agency (Italy); Raquel de la Concha Agencia Literaria (Portugal, Spain); Corto Literary (Croatia, Montenegro, North Macedonia, Romania, Serbia, Slovenia); Anna Jarota Agency (France, Poland); Katai & Bolza Literary Agents (Hungary); Duran Kim Agency (Korea); Mo Literary Services (Netherlands, Scandinavia); Mohrbooks AG Literary Agency (Germany); Andrew Nurnberg Association Sofia (Bulgaria); Andrew Nurnberg Literary Agency (Russia & former USSR); The Riff Agency (Brazil); Tuttle-Mori Agency Inc (Japan)
Membership(s): The Authors Guild

Max Gartenberg Literary Agency (L)
912 N Pennsylvania Ave, Yardley, PA 19067
Tel: 215-295-9230
Web Site: www.maxgartenberg.com
Key Personnel
Agent: Anne G Devlin *E-mail:* agdevlin@aol.com
Founded: 1954
Children & adult nonfiction books. No unsol mss, query first. Submit formal book proposal, outline & sample as requested. No reading fee. Handle film & TV rights. Agents in all principal foreign markets.
Titles recently placed: *Baby Panda Goes Wild!*, David Salomon; *Beyond Your Baby's Checkup*, Luke Voytas, MD; *Cured*, Anne McTiernan; *Everything a New Elementary School Teacher*

REALLY Needs to Know, Otis Kreigel; *Snow: A History of the World's Most Fascinating Flake*, Anthony R Wood; *The Enlightened College Applicant*, Andrew Belasco, Dave Bergman; *The New Senior Man*, Thelma Reese, Barbara Fleisher; *What to Believe When You're Expecting*, Jonathan Schaffir
Foreign Rights: International Editors' Co (Argentina); Mohrbooks AG Literary Agency (Switzerland); La Nouvelle Agence (France); Lennart Sane (Sweden); Tuttle-Mori Agency Inc (Japan)

Gelfman Schneider/ICM Partners (L)
Affiliate of John Farquharson Ltd
850 Seventh Ave, Suite 903, New York, NY 10019
Tel: 212-245-1993 *Fax:* 212-245-8678
E-mail: mail@gelfmanschneider.com
Web Site: gelfmanschneider.com
Key Personnel
Agent: Jane Gelfman (AAR); Deborah Schneider (AAR)
Assoc Agent: Penelope Burns (AAR)
General trade fiction & nonfiction. Queries by mail only, no e-mail queries will be considered. No unsol mss, query first with SASE. Submit sample chapters & outline. Handle film & TV rights. No reading fee.
Foreign Rights: Curtis Brown Ltd (translation, UK)
Membership(s): The Authors Guild; Authors Registry

The Gersh Agency (TGA) (L-D)
41 Madison Ave, 33rd fl, New York, NY 10010
Tel: 212-997-1818
Web Site: gershbooks.com
Key Personnel
Partner & Head of Books Dept: J Joseph Veltre, III
Books & IP Agent: Hannah Vaughn
Books Dept Coord: Alice Lawson
Founded: 2007 (1949 as talent agency)
Fiction, nonfiction, adult & juvenile, film & TV rights & plays. No unsol mss. Unsol materials will not be accepted or considered. No online submission unless requested. No reading fee.
Branch Office(s)
9465 Wilshire Blvd, Suite 600, Beverly Hills, CA 90212 (talent div) *Tel:* 310-274-6611

GGP Publishing Inc (L)
105 Calvert St, Suite 201, Harrison, NY 10528-3138
Tel: 914-834-8896 *Fax:* 914-834-7566
Web Site: www.GGPPublishing.com
Key Personnel
Pres & Publg Dir: Generosa Gina Protano
E-mail: GGProtano@GGPPublishing.com
Founded: 1991
Fiction & nonfiction; educational materials, English & foreign languages. Handle film & TV rights. No unsol mss, query first. Reading fees on all submissions, refundable from commission; fee charged for photocopying & postage or courier. Editorial & translation services also available.
Membership(s): American Book Producers Association (ABPA)

Susan Gleason (L)
325 Riverside Dr, Suite 41, New York, NY 10025
Tel: 212-662-3876
E-mail: sgleasonliteraryagent@gmail.com
Founded: 1992
Adult trade & mass market, fiction & nonfiction. No unsol mss, query first with SASE.
Handle film & TV rights, foreign rights. No reading fees.

Global Lion Intellectual Property Management Inc (L-D)
Affiliate of Millennium Lion Inc
PO Box 669238, Pompano Beach, FL 33066
Tel: 754-222-6948 *Fax:* 754-222-6948
E-mail: queriesgloballionmgt@gmail.com
Web Site: www.globallionmanagement.com
Key Personnel
Pres: Peter Miller *E-mail:* peter@globallionmgt.com
Assoc: Charlie Serabian *E-mail:* charlie@globallionmgt.com
Represents transformational & spiritual nonfiction, young adult, commercial fiction, nonfiction, true crime & celebrity books. Also handles film & TV rights for original properties. Represents literary & film properties internationally. See web site for additional submission guidelines. Works with co-agents in select foreign territories & deals directly with foreign publishers. No fees charged.
Titles recently placed: *Helter Skelter*, Vincent Bugliosi, Curt Gentry; *History of the World*, Jean-Pierre Isbouts; *Manifesto*, Sir Ken Robinson
Foreign Rep(s): Big Apple Agency Inc (China); Peter Bolza (Hungary); Tuttle-Mori Agency Inc (Japan)

Globo Libros Literary Management (L)
450 E 63 St, New York, NY 10065
Web Site: www.globo-libros.com; www.publishersmarketplace.com/members/dstockwell
Key Personnel
Literary Agent: Diane Stockwell *E-mail:* diane.stockwell@gmail.com
Founded: 2006
Specialize in nonfiction authors from the US & abroad. Looking for compelling narrative nonfiction, current events, history, cookbooks, memoir, biography, parenting & self-help by authors of any background. We also offer book length & short translations from Spanish into English. Query by e-mail only with a detailed summary of the project & author bio in the body of the message. No attachments. No fees charged.
Titles recently placed: *Cocina Ligera*, Johana Clavel; *Democracy Under Threat*, Jake Braun; *Hipster Death Rattle*, Richie Narvaez; *Killing the Story: The War on Journalists in Mexico*, Temoris Grecko; *Why Don't They Want Us Here? Stories of Resistance and Resilience from Mexicans Living in the United States*, Eileen Truax
Membership(s): The Authors Guild

Goldfarb & Associates (L-D)
721 Gibbon St, Alexandria, VA 22314
Tel: 202-466-3030 *Fax:* 703-836-5644
E-mail: rlglawlit@gmail.com
Web Site: www.ronaldgoldfarb.com
Key Personnel
Founder & Owner: Ronald L Goldfarb
Literary Agent: Ms Gerrie Lipson Sturman; Robbie Anna Hare
Off Mgr: Steven Seigart
Founded: 1966
Only select new clients accepted. Fiction & serious nonfiction; no romance or science fiction. No unsol mss, query first with e-mail/letter, outline or synopsis, sample of best chapter, bio & SASE. No reading fee.
Branch Office(s)
177 Ocean Lane Dr, Suite 1101, Key Biscayne, FL 33149

Frances Goldin Literary Agency, Inc (L-D)
214 W 29 St, Suite 410, New York, NY 10001
Tel: 212-777-0047 *Fax:* 212-228-1660
E-mail: agency@goldinlit.com
Web Site: www.goldinlit.com

Key Personnel
VP & Sr Agent: Ellen Geiger (AAR); Sam Stoloff (AAR)
Sr Agent & Rts Dir: Matt McGowan (AAR)
E-mail: mm@goldinlit.com
Agent: Caroline Eisenmann (AAR); Roz Foster; Ria Julien
Founded: 1977
No unsol mss or work previously submitted to publishers, query first with letter & SASE. No racist, sexist, agist, homophobic or pornographic material considered. Adult literary fiction & serious progressive nonfiction. Agents in Hollywood & all major foreign countries. No software. Handle film & TV rights. No reading fee.
Foreign Rep(s): Anthea Agency (Bulgaria); Eliane Benisti (France); Berla & Griffini Rights Agency (Italy); Corto Literary Agency (Diana Matulic) (Bosnia and Herzegovina, Croatia, Montenegro, North Macedonia, Serbia); Graal Literary Agency (Maria Starz-Kanska) (Poland); The Grayhawk Agency (Gray Tan) (China, Taiwan); David Grossman Literary Agency Ltd (David Grossman) (England, UK); The Deborah Harris Agency (Israel); International Editors' Co (Nicholas Costa) (Argentina); International Editors' Co (Flavia Sala) (Brazil); International Editors' Co (Isabel Monteagudo) (Spain); Japan UNI Agency Inc (Japan); JLM Literary Agency (John L Moukakos) (Greece); Simona Kessler International (Romania); Lex Copyright Office (Hungary); Liepman AG Literary Agency (Germany); Kristin Olson Literary Agency (Kristin Olson) (Czechia); Lennart Sane Agency (Lennart Sane) (Iceland, Netherlands, Scandinavia, Sweden); Synopsis Literary Agency (Natalia Sanina) (Russia); Asli Karasuil Telif Literary Agency (Turkey); Tuttle-Mori Agency Inc (Indonesia, Malaysia, Thailand, Vietnam); The Eric Yang Agency (Sue Yang) (Korea)

Irene Goodman Literary Agency (L)
27 W 24 St, Suite 700B, New York, NY 10010
Tel: 212-604-0330
E-mail: queries@irenegoodman.com
Web Site: www.irenegoodman.com
Key Personnel
Pres: Irene Goodman (AAR) *E-mail:* irene.queries@irenegoodman.com
VP: Miriam Kriss *E-mail:* miriam.queries@irenegoodman.com; Barbara Poelle *E-mail:* barbara.queries@irenegoodman.com
Agent: Pam Gruber; Victoria Marini (AAR) *E-mail:* victoria.queries@irenegoodman.com; Kim Perel *E-mail:* kim.queries@irenegoodman.com; Whitney Ross *E-mail:* whitney.queries@irenegoodman.com
Founded: 1978
Commercial & literary fiction & nonfiction including mysteries, romance, women's fiction, thrillers & suspense. No poetry, inspirational fiction, screenplays or children's picture books. Handle film & TV rights through Steven Fisher in Los Angeles. No unsol mss, query first with first 10 pages & synopsis via e-mail. No snail mail. See web site under submission guidelines for each agent's preferences. No reading fee.
Foreign Rep(s): Danny Baror
Foreign Rights: Baror International Agency

Doug Grad Literary Agency Inc (L)
68 Jay St, Suite W11, Brooklyn, NY 11201-1189
Tel: 718-788-6067
E-mail: query@dgliterary.com
Web Site: www.dgliterary.com
Key Personnel
Pres: Doug Grad *E-mail:* doug.grad@dgliterary.com
Founded: 2008
Commercial fiction & nonfiction in a wide variety of genres & subjects. See web site for

additional information. Send cover letter only with brief description of book. Will ask to see more material if interested, via e-mail only to query@dgliterary.com. Do not send hard copies of proposals or mss. No fees.

Titles recently placed: *A Vision of Ice: Book Two of the EarthEnd Saga*, Gillian Anderson, Jeff Rovin; *Abandoned in Hell: The Fight for Vietnam's Fire Base Kate*, William Albracht, Marvin J Wolf; *Arch Enemy*, Leo Maloney; *Bounty*, Michael Byrnes; *Breaking the Ice: My Journey and Evolution through Hockey*, Pat LaFontaine, Allan Kreda; *El Guettar: America's First Victory Against the Nazi War Machine*, Leo Barron; *Igniting the American Revolution: 1773-1775*, Derek W Beck; *Lords of an Empty Land*, Randy Denmon; *Pet Friendly*, Sue Pethick; *Plantation Shudders*, Ellen Byron; *Storm's Thunder*, Brandon Boyce; *Totally Scripted: The Guide to Hollywood Idioms, Phrases, Quotes and Words That Have Changed the English Language*, Josh Chetwynd; *Where Divers Dare: The Hunt for the Last U-Boat*, Randall Peffer

Foreign Rep(s): Alice Bauer (worldwide)

Foreign Rights: Alice Bauer (worldwide)

Graham Agency (D)
115 W 45 St, Suite 505, New York, NY 10036
Tel: 212-489-7730
Key Personnel
Prop: Earl Graham
Founded: 1971
Full-length stage plays & musicals only. No unsol mss, query by mail first. Submit brief description. No reading fee, 10% commission.

Sanford J Greenburger Associates Inc (L)
55 Fifth Ave, New York, NY 10003
Tel: 212-206-5600 *Fax:* 212-463-8718
Web Site: greenburger.com; www.sjga.com
Key Personnel
Pres: Heide Lange (AAR) *E-mail:* queryhl@sjga.com
Dir, Intl Rts: Stefanie Diaz *Tel:* 221-206-5628 *E-mail:* sdiaz@greenburger.com
Dir, Intl Scouting Dept: Agnes Krup *E-mail:* akrup@sjga.com
Sr Agent: Stephanie Delman (AAR) *E-mail:* sdelman@sjga.com
Agent: Matt Bialer *E-mail:* querymb@sjga.com; Faith Hamlin (AAR) *E-mail:* fhamlin@sjga.com; Daniel Mandel *E-mail:* querydm@sjga.com; Rachel Dillon-Fried *E-mail:* rfried@sjga.com; Wendi Gu; Edward Maxwell *E-mail:* emaxwell@sjga.com; Sarah Phair
Sr Scout, Adult Fiction & Nonfiction: Megan Reid *E-mail:* mreid@sjga.com
Sr Scout, Children's & Young Adult: Hanna Masaryk *E-mail:* hmasaryk@sjga.com
Scout: John Bowers; Kirsten Kim
Founded: 1932
Fiction, nonfiction, young adult & children's. No unsol mss, physical or phone queries. Query e-mail first. Submit outline or synopsis & sample chapter. No reading fee. Copying fee. Agents in all principal foreign countries.
Foreign Rights: Graal Literary Agency (Poland); Deborah Harris Agency (Israel); The Italian Literary Agency SRL (Italy); Licht & Burr (Scandinavia); MB Agencia Literaria (Brazil, Catalonia, Galicia, Portugal, Spain); Mohrbooks AG Literary Agency (Germany); La Nouvelle Agence (France, Quebec, CN); Andrew Nurnberg Associates (Netherlands); Andrew Nurnberg Associates (Baltic) (Estonia, Latvia, Lithuania, Ukraine); Andrew Nurnberg Associates (Bucharest) (Romania); Andrew Nurnberg Associates (Budapest) (Croatia, Hungary); Andrew Nurnberg Associates International Ltd (China, Taiwan); Andrew Nurnberg Associates (Prague) (Czechia, Slovakia, Slovenia); Andrew Nurnberg Associates (Sofia) (Albania, Bulgaria, North Macedonia, Serbia);

Andrew Nurnberg Literary Agency (Russia); Read n Right Agency (Greece); Abner Stein Agency (UK); Tuttle-Mori Agency Inc (Indonesia, Japan, Thailand, Vietnam); Eric Yang Agency (Korea)

Jill Grinberg Literary Management LLC (L)
392 Vanderbilt Ave, Brooklyn, NY 11238
Tel: 212-620-5883
E-mail: info@jillgrinbergliterary.com
Web Site: www.jillgrinbergliterary.com
Key Personnel
Pres & Literary Agent: Jill Grinberg (AAR) *E-mail:* jill@jillgrinbergliterary.com
Head, Rts, Contracts & Legal/Literary Agent: Sophia Seidner (AAR) *E-mail:* sophia@jillgrinbergliterary.com
Literary Agent: Katelyn Detweiler (AAR) *E-mail:* katelyn@jillgrinbergliterary.com; Larissa Melo Pienkowski *E-mail:* larissa@jillgrinbergliterary.com
Literary Agent & Foreign Rts Assoc: Sam Farkas (AAR) *E-mail:* sam@jillgrinbergliterary.com
Founded: 1999
Hands-on, full service agency whose mission is helping authors to launch, develop & sustain successful careers. Please submit to info@jillgrinbergliterary.com. We are accepting submissions in all categories for adult fiction & nonfiction, children's fiction & nonfiction. Paste your query letter in the body of your e-mail & attach your first 50 pages as a docx file. See web site for more specific guidelines.

Jill Grosjean Literary Agency (L)
1390 Millstone Rd, Sag Harbor, NY 11963
Tel: 631-725-7419 *Fax:* 631-725-8632
E-mail: JillLit310@aol.com
Key Personnel
Owner & Literary Agent: Jill Grosjean
Founded: 1999
Literary fiction, mystery/suspense, women's fiction. No unsol mss, query first; e-mail queries preferred, no downloads or attachments. No fees charged. Foreign rights in UK, France, Italy, Spain, Netherlands, South America.
Titles recently placed: *A Spark of Death*, Bernadette Pajer; *A Thread So Thin*, Marie Bostwick; *Beating the Babushka*, Tim Maleeny; *Betrayal in Time*, Julie McElwain; *Caught in Time*, Julie McElwain; *Comfort and Joy*, Marie Bostwick; *Emma and the Vampires*, Wayne Josephson; *Fatal Induction*, Bernadette Pajer; *House of Ashes*, Loretta Marion; *Jump*, Tim Maleeny; *Murder in Time*, Julie McElwain; *Nectar*, David Fickett; *Shadows in Time*, Julie McElwain; *Snow Angels*, Marie Bostwick; *Spectres in the Smoke*, Tony Broadbent; *Stealing the Dragon*, Tim Maleeny; *Storm of Secrets*, Loretta Marion; *The Black Widow Agency*, Felicia Donovan; *The Edison Effect*, Bernadette Pajer; *The Gold Pawn*, L A Chandlar; *The Lighterman's Curse*, Loretta Marion; *The Pearl Dagger*, L A Chandlar; *The Silver Gun*, L A Chandlar; *The Smoke*, Tony Broadbent; *Thread of Truth*, Marie Bostwick; *Threading the Needle*, Marie Bostwick; *Tim Cratchit's Christmas Carol*, Jim Piecuch; *Twist in Time*, Julie McElwain

Laura Gross Literary Agency Ltd (L)
PO Box 610326, Newton Highlands, MA 02461
Tel: 617-964-2977 *Fax:* 617-964-3023
E-mail: query@lg-la.com
Web Site: www.lg-la.com
Key Personnel
Pres: Laura Gross (AAR)
Jr Agent: Lauren Scovel
Founded: 1988
No unsol mss, query or e-mail first. On web site, submit query using form: lg-la.com/contact. Fiction, commercial & literary; nonfiction, se-

rious topics, social, political, cultural issues & psychology. Include list of previous publications & bio. No reading fee.
Foreign Rights: Teri Tobias Agency LLC (worldwide exc UK)

The Charlotte Gusay Literary Agency (L-D)
10532 Blythe Ave, Los Angeles, CA 90064
Tel: 310-559-0831 *Fax:* 310-559-2639
E-mail: gusayagency1@gmail.com
Web Site: www.gusay.com
Founded: 1988
Fiction & nonfiction, screenplay, children & adult, humor, parenting; crossover literary/commercial fiction; gardening, women's & men's issues, feminism, psychology, memoir, biography, travel. Handle film & TV rights. Represent selected illustrators, especially children's. No unsol mss, query first with SASE by snail mail or by e-mail; ONLY when agency requests, submit one-page synopsis & first 3 chapters or first 50 pages (for fiction); proposal (for nonfiction). Include SASE. No reading fee. For borderline queries we sometimes give prospective clients the benefit of the doubt & impose a nominal processing fee allowing the prospective clients to decide whether to submit their material or not. Once client is signed, client is responsible for providing agency hard copies of mss (as necessary) & shipping expenses (as necessary).
Titles recently placed: *Afropessimism*, Frank B Wilderson III; *Everything I Need to Know I Learned in the Twilight Zone*, Mark Dawidziak (ed); *Osawatomie*, Randy Michael Signor; *Outrageous Fortune: Growing Up at Leeds Castle*, Anthony Russell; *Rod Serling: His Life, Work and Imagination*, Nicholas Parisi; *Sensing the Rhythm: Finding My Voice in a World Without Sound*, Mandy Harvey, Mark Atteberry; *The Burma Spring: Aung San Suu Kyi and the Struggle for the Soul of Burma*, Rena Pederson; *The Reputation Economy*, Michael Fertik, David Thompson; *Theodore Roosevelt for Nature Lovers*, Mark Dawidziak; *Waco: A Survivor's Story*, David Thibodeau, Leon Whiteson, Aviva Layton; *Working Actor: Breaking in, Making a Living and Making a Life in the Fabulous Trenches of Show Business*, David Bottrell
Foreign Rep(s): The Fielding Agency (Whitney Lee) (worldwide)
Membership(s): The Authors Guild; PEN American Center; PEN Center USA West

Lisa Hagan Literary (L)
110 Martin Dr, Bracey, VA 23919
Tel: 434-636-4138
E-mail: LisaHaganLiterary@yahoo.com
Web Site: www.publishersmarketplace.com/members/LisaHagan
Key Personnel
Owner, Pres & Agent: Lisa Hagan
Founded: 1995
Business/investing/finance, health, mind/body/spirit, science & self-help. No unsol mss, query first with letter. Handles film & TV rights for books only. No fee charged.
Titles recently placed: *100 Days to Calm*, Amy Leigh Mercree; *Astrology Guide: Unveil Your Unique Gifts*, Claudia Trivelas; *From Footprints to Handprints: Creating Sustainability to Grow and Heal the Planet*, Jon Biemer; *Healing Depression Without Medication: A Psychiatrist's Guide to Balancing Mind, Body, and Soul*, Dr Jodie Skillicorn; *Never Trust a Sneaky Pony: And Other Things They Did Not Teach Me in Vet School*, Dr Madison Seaman; *Our Own Forever: A Mother, A Son, and the Unthinkable*, Patti Hall; *Oxalate Overload: Skip Toxic Superfoods and Reclaim a Vibrant Life*, Sally K Norton; *The Documentary Filmmaking Guide: Tell Your Story from Concept to Distribution*,

Betsy Chasse; *The Mars Egnima*, Nick Redfern; *The Soul of Purpose: A Step-by-Step Approach to a Purpose-Filled, Healthy Life*, Jaya Jaya Myra; *Toxin Conspiracies: The Systematic Poisoning of Our Air, Water, Food and Bodies*, Marie D Jones; *Turbo Metabolism: Preventing and Reversing Diabetes and Other Metabolic Diseases by Treating the Causes*, Pankaj Vij, MD; *Understanding is the New Healing*, Dr Mary Helen Hensley; *Way Out There: Adventures of a Wilderness Trekker*, J Robert Harris; *Your Whole Heart Solution: What You Can Do to Prevent and Reverse Heart Disease Now*, Joel K Kahn, MD; *Zen Camera: Creative Awakening with a Daily Practice in Photography*, David Ulrich

The Joy Harris Literary Agency Inc (L)
1501 Broadway, Suite 2310, New York, NY 10036
Tel: 212-924-6269 *Fax:* 212-840-5776
E-mail: contact@joyharrisliterary.com
Web Site: www.joyharrisliterary.com
Key Personnel
Pres: Joy Harris (AAR) *E-mail:* joy@ joyharrisliterary.com
Agent & Subs Rts: Adam Reed (AAR) *E-mail:* adam@joyharrisliterary.com
No unsol mss, query first. No poetry, screenplays or self-help.

Hartline Literary Agency LLC (L)
123 Queenston Dr, Pittsburgh, PA 15235
Tel: 412-829-2483 *Toll Free Fax:* 888-279-6007
Web Site: www.hartlineliterary.com
Key Personnel
Founder: Joyce Hart *E-mail:* joyce@ hartlineliterary.com
Pres: Jim Hart *E-mail:* jim@hartlineliterary.com
Agent: Diana Flegal *E-mail:* diana@ hartlineliterary.com; Linda Glaz *E-mail:* linda@ hartlineliterary.com; Cyle Young *E-mail:* cyle@ hartlineliterary.com
Founded: 1992
Advise clients on how to prepare proposals & advise them concerning what various publishers are looking for. Also help clients plan their literary careers. Our expertise is in the Christian market & we also work in the general market. Looking for clean, wholesome fiction for adults & inspiring nonfiction. Mss reflecting a Christian worldview preferred, even for the general market. Fiction: romance, romantic suspense, women's fiction, mystery/suspense, humor, chick/mom lit & general fiction. Nonfiction: self-help, Christian living, prayer, health, humor & business.
Accepts unsol mss. Submit cover letter, author bio, marketing analysis, summary & 3 sample chapters. If submitting via e-mail, send as an attachment & send the entire submission in one file. We do not accept submissions in multiple files. We accept e-mail, US mail, UPS & FedEx submissions. See web site for complete submission details. No fees.
Titles recently placed: *21 Days of Grace*, Kathy Ide; *A Pair of Miracles: A Story of Autism, Faith, and Determined Parenting*, Karla Akins; *A Secret to Die For*, Lisa Harris; *All She Left Behind*, Jane Kirkpatrick; *Among the Poppies*, J'nell Ciesielski; *Anchored*, Deborah Bailey; *Anna's Crossing*, Suzanne Woods Fisher; *Assassination Generation*, Adam Davis; *At First Glance*, Susan Tuttle; *Barefoot Revolution: Biblical Spirituality for Finding God*, Paul Marshall; *Behind the Badge*, Adam Davis; *Beneath a Michigan Moon*, Candice Patterson; *Blow Out the Candles and Say Goodbye*, Linda Glaz; *C is for Christmas*, Michelle Medlock Adams; *Coffee Shop Devotions*, Tessa Emily Hall; *Confessions of an Adoptive Parent*, Mike Berry; *Coral*, Sara Ella; *Cowboys and Angels*, David Stearman; *Deadly Exchange*, Lisa Har-

ris; *Desert Secrets*, Lisa Harris; *Everything She Didn't Say*, Jane Kirkpatrick; *Fabulous & Focused*, Michelle Medlock Adams, Gena Maselli; *Fallen Leaves*, Tessa Emily Hall; *Fatal Cover-Up*, Lisa Harris; *Finding Jesus in Israel: Through the Holy Land on the Road Less Traveled*, Buck Storm; *Fire Paste, Fast Freeze*, Tim Shoemaker; *God Needed a Puppy*, John Gray, Shanna Brickell; *Her Deadly Reunion*, Beth Ann Ziarnik; *Hidden Treasures: Finding Hope at the End of Life's Journey*, Robin Bertram; *High as the Heavens*, Kate Breslin; *In the Grip of God*, George Cargil; *Jeremy Winters (series)*, Tom Threadgill; *Jessie's Hope*, Jennifer Hallmark; *Journey Into Silence*, Chaim Bentorah; *Learning God's Love Language: A Guide to Personal Hebrew Word Study*, Chaim Bentorah; *Liar's Winter*, Cindy Sproles; *Like Me or Not*, Dawn Owens; *Lydia*, Diana Wallis Taylor; *Making God Smile*, Kim Henry; *Mary, Mother of God*, Diana Wallis Taylor; *Minding the Light*, Suzanne Woods Fisher; *Missing*, Lisa Harris; *Mountain Hideaway*, Christy Barritt; *Multiple Choice: Finding the Best Answer for Your Child's Education*, Martha Singleton; *My Heart Belongs on Mackinac Island*, Carrie Fancett Pagels; *On Command*, Adam Davis; *Operation Moonbeam*, Michelle Medlock Adams; *Overcoming Shame*, Dr Mark W Baker; *Phoebe's Light*, Suzanne Woods Fisher; *Police Marriage Devotion*, Adam Davis; *Reclaiming Sanity*, Dr Laurel Shaler; *Relational Reset*, Dr Laurel Shaler; *Renewed: A 40-Day Devotional for Healing from Church Hurt and for Loving Well in Ministry*, Leigh Powers; *Rescued Hearts*, Hope Toler Dougherty; *Resenting God*, John Snyder; *Ruffling Society*, Kay Moser; *Secrets and Wishes*, Kathleen Rouser; *Shadow of Suspicion*, Christy Barritt; *She Who Went First*, Jane Kirkpatrick; *Silent Noisy Night*, Jill Roman Lord; *Skirting Convention*, Kay Moser; *Spiritual Prepper*, Jake McCandless; *Spiritual Wisdom for a Happier Life*, Dr Mark W Baker; *Stand In Brides (No 1)*, Dorothy Clark; *That Grand Easter Day*, Jill Roman Lord; *The Baby Assignment*, Christy Barritt; *The Bravest You*, Adam Smith; *The Children of Main Street*, Merilyn Howton; *The Devil's Daughter*, Cindy Sproles; *The Light Before Day*, Suzanne Woods Fisher; *The Nanny's Secret Child*, Lorraine Beatty; *The Newcomer*, Suzanne Woods Fisher; *The Quieting*, Suzanne Woods Fisher; *The Return*, Suzanne Woods Fisher; *The Very Best Story Ever Told*, Robin Currie; *The View Through Your Window*, Greg Singleton, Martha Singleton; *Though This Be Madness (Lilly Long Mysteries)*, Penny Richards; *To Claim Her Heart*, Jodie Wolfe; *Touched by God*, Andrew Gabriel; *Unbreakable (Unblemished Trilogy)*, Sara Ella; *Unearthed: Discover Life as God's Masterpiece*, Raj Pillai; *Unraveling (Unblemished Trilogy)*, Sara Ella; *Vanishing Point*, Lisa Harris; *What Ever Happened to Happily Ever After?*, David Clarke; *What Is a Family?*, Annette Griffin; *What the Moon Saw*, D L Koontz; *Whiskey Burning*, John Turney; *Winning the Heart of Your Child*, Mike Berry; *With This Peace*, Karen Campbell Prough; *Working Women Devotionals*, Gena Maselli
Membership(s): American Christian Fiction Writers (ACFW)

John Hawkins and Associates Inc (L)
80 Maiden Lane, Suite 1503, New York, NY 10038
Tel: 212-807-7040
E-mail: jha@jhalit.com
Web Site: jhalit.com
Key Personnel
Pres & Foreign Rts Dir: Moses Cardona (AAR) *E-mail:* moses@jhalit.com

Agent: Warren Frazier (AAR) *E-mail:* frazier@ jhalit.com; Anne Hawkins (AAR) *E-mail:* ahawkins@jhalit.com; William Reiss (AAR) *E-mail:* reiss@jhalit.com
Perms & Rts: Annie Kronenberg *E-mail:* annie@ jhalit.com
Founded: 1893 (by Paul R Reynolds)
No unsol mss, query first. Submit 1-page bio & 1- to 3-page outline with SASE. No reading fee. Photocopy charges & fees for other services. Handle film & TV rights, software.
Titles recently placed: *A Book of American Martyrs*, Joyce Carol Oates; *Fortune Smiles*, Adam Johnson; *Friendly Fire*, John Gilstrap; *Grief Cottage*, Gail Godwin; *Perfume River*, Robert Olen Butler; *The Mask*, Taylor Stevens; *The Moth Catcher*, Ann Cleeves
Foreign Rep(s): Sara Menguc Inc (UK)

The Jeff Herman Agency LLC (L)
29 Park St, Stockbridge, MA 01262
Mailing Address: PO Box 1522, Stockbridge, MA 01262
Tel: 413-298-0077
E-mail: submissions@jeffherman.com
Web Site: www.jeffherman.com
Key Personnel
Pres: Jeffrey H Herman *E-mail:* jeff@jeffherman.com
VP: Deborah Levine
Founded: 1985
Nonfiction, reference, health, self-help, how-to, business, technology, spirituality & textbooks. No unsol mss, query first with letter & SASE. No reading fee. Handle software, film & TV rights. Agents in all principal foreign countries.
Foreign Rep(s): Asano (Japan); De la Concha (Portugal, Spain)

Hill Nadell Literary Agency (L)
6442 Santa Monica Blvd, Suite 201, Los Angeles, CA 90038
Tel: 310-860-9605 *Fax:* 323-380-5206
E-mail: queries@hillnadell.com; rights@ hillnadell.com (rts & perms)
Web Site: www.hillnadell.com
Key Personnel
Pres: Bonnie Nadell
Sr Agent: Dara Hyde
Founded: 1979
Literary & commercial fiction, narrative nonfiction, current affairs, memoirs & pop culture; film & TV rights only if handling the book. No unsol mss, query first with SASE. No reading fee. Co-agents in all foreign countries.
Titles recently placed: *Barely Missing Everything*, Matt Mendez; *Dominicana*, Angie Cruz; *On Trails: An Exploration*, Robert Moor; *The Deer Camp*, Dean Kuipers; *The Lightest Object in the Universe*, Kimi Eisele; *The Only Living Girl*, David Gallaher, Steve Ellis; *The Sun Is a Compass*, Caroline Van Hemert; *The Tenth Island*, Diana Marcum; *The Worst Kind of Want*, Liska Jacobs
Foreign Rights: ANA Baltic (Baltic States); ANA Prague (Czechia, Slovakia, Slovenia); ANA Sofia (Albania, Bulgaria, North Macedonia, Romania, Serbia); AnatoliaLit (Turkey); Berla & Griffini Rights Agency (Italy); Big Apple Agency Shanghai (China); Big Apple Agency Taiwan (Taiwan); Ersilia Literary (Greece); Anoukh Foerg Literary Agency (Germany); The Foreign Office (Brazil, Latin America, Portugal, Spain); Anna Jarota Agency (France, Poland, Russia); KCC (Korea); Schoenbach Literary Agency (Netherlands); Ulf Toregard Agency (Scandinavia)

The Barbara Hogenson Agency Inc (L-D)
165 West End Ave, Suite 19-C, New York, NY 10023
Tel: 212-874-8084 *Fax:* 212-595-6748

E-mail: bhogenson@aol.com
Key Personnel
Pres: Barbara Hogenson (AAR)
Contract Mgr: Lori Styler
Founded: 1994
Recommendation by clients only. Literary fiction, nonfiction, full-length plays, consider some illustrated books. No screenplays or teleplays. No fees.
Membership(s): The Authors Guild; Authors Registry; The Dramatists Guild of America; Society of Stage Directors & Choreographers (SSDC); Writers Guild of America (WGA)

Henry Holmes Literary Agent/Book Publicist/Marketing Consultant (L)
Mitchell Heights, Apt 205, 2100 S Main St, Fall River, MA 02724
Tel: 508-672-2258; 508-415-4062 (cell)
Key Personnel
Pres & Literary Agent: Henry Holmes
Founded: 1997
Nonfiction, no unsol mss, query first. Send query letter with chapters 1 & 2. If published, include past publicity, endorsement(s) etc. SASE. Ten mailings sent to preferred publishers via mss/CDs (this includes publisher research, query letter, packing, mailing, etc, at competitive rates. Independent of my representation, professional consultation via freelance assignments/project work would be based on involvement & duration of project based on competitive fees. Specialize in consulting, marketing, media publicity, talk show placement, etc. 15% standard commission. No reading fee. Retainer fee charged if ms is acceptable.

Hornfischer Literary Management LP (L)
PO Box 50544, Austin, TX 78763
Tel: 512-472-0011
E-mail: queries@hornfischerlit.com
Web Site: www.hornfischerlit.com
Key Personnel
Pres: Jim Hornfischer
Founded: 2001
Quality narrative nonfiction, biography & autobiography, current events, US history, military history & world history, political & cultural subjects science, medicine/health, business/management/finance, academic writing & research that has a general-interest audience. No unsol mss; query first through e-mail, no longer accept queries through mail. No fees.
Titles recently placed: *A Darker Sea*, James L Haley; *Army of None: Autonomous Weapons and the Future of War*, Paul Scharre; *Beirut Rules: The Murder of a CIA Station Chief and Hezbollah's War Against America*, Fred Burton, Samuel M Katz; *Bringing Columbia Home: The Untold Story of a Lost Space Shuttle and Her Crew*, Michael D Leinbach, Jonathan H Ward; *Captive Paradise: A History of Hawaii*, James L Haley; *Crashback: The Power Clash Between the US and China in the Pacific*, Michael Fabey; *Destination Casablanca: Exile, Espionage, and the Battle for North Africa in World War II*, Meredith Hindley; *Giant: Elizabeth Taylor, Rock Hudson, James Dean, Edna Ferber, and the Making of a Legendary American Film*, Don Graham; *Harpoon: Inside the Covert War Against Terrorism's Money Masters*, Nitsana Darshan-Leitner, Samuel M Katz; *Harvey Penick: The Life and Wisdom of the Man Who Wrote the Book on Golf*, Kevin Robbins; *Hurricane Season: The Unforgettable Story of the 2017 Houston Astros and the Resilience of a City*, Joe Holley; *In the Arena: Good Citizens, a Great Republic, and How One Speech Can Reinvigorate America*, Pete Hegseth; *Indestructible: One Man's Rescue Mission That Changed the Course of WWII*, John R Bruning; *Necessary Evil: How to Fix Finance by Saving Human Rights*, David Kin-

ley; *Never Call Me a Hero*, N Jack "Dusty" Kleiss, Timothy Orr, Laura Orr; *No One Cares About Crazy People: My Family and the Heartbreak of Mental Illness in America*, Ron Powers; *Phenomena: The Secret History of the US Government's Investigations Into Extrasensory Perception and Psychokinesis*, Annie Jacobsen; *Reviving America: How Repealing Obamacare, Replacing the Tax Code and Reforming The Fed will Restore Hope and Prosperity*, Steve Forbes, Elizabeth Ames; *The Cloudbuster Nine: The Untold Story of Ted Williams and the Baseball Team That Helped Win World War II*, Anne R Keene; *The Last Republicans: Inside the Extraordinary Relationship Between George H W Bush and George W Bush*, Mark K Updegrove; *The Possibility Dogs: What I Learned from Second-Chance Rescues About Service, Hope, and Healing*, Susannah Charleson

ICM Partners (L-D)
65 E 55 St, New York, NY 10022
Tel: 212-556-5600
Web Site: www.icmtalent.com
Key Personnel
Mng Dir: Chris Silbermann
Co-Pres: Kevin Crotty; Sloan Harris
Co-Head, Publg Dept: Jennifer Joel; Esther Newberg
Head, Media Rts Dept: Alexandra Machinist
Partner: Kristine Dahl; Raphael Sagalyn; Amanda Urban
Literary Agent: Amelia "Molly" Atlas; Hillary Jacobson; Heather Karpas; Kristyn Keene; Dan Kirschen; Zoe Sandler; Anna Stein; Kari Stuart; Tina Wexler
Founded: 1975
Handle film & TV rights. No unsol mss, query first. No reading fee.
Branch Office(s)
10250 Constellation Blvd, Los Angeles, CA 90067 *Tel:* 310-550-4000

InkWell Management (L)
521 Fifth Ave, 26th fl, New York, NY 10175
Tel: 212-922-3500 *Fax:* 212-922-0535
E-mail: info@inkwellmanagement.com
Web Site: inkwellmanagement.com
Key Personnel
Founder & Pres: Michael Carlisle; Richard S Pine; Kim Witherspoon *E-mail:* kim@inkwellmanagement.com
Dir, Subs Rts: Alexis Hurley *E-mail:* alexis@inkwellmanagement.com
Agent: David Forrer; George Lucas; Kristin van Ogtrop
Busn Mgr: Jennifer Witherell *E-mail:* jwitherell@inkwellmanagement.com
Founded: 2004 (created through the merger of Arthur Pine Associates Inc, Carlisle & Co LLC & Witherspoon Associates Inc)
General nonfiction & fiction books. No screenplays, plays, poetry. Motion picture, TV & foreign rights. No unsol mss, query first with SASE; submissions must be on an exclusive basis. No fees.
Titles recently placed: *Antony & Cleopatra*, Colleen McCullough; *Knockemstiff*, Donald Ray Pollock; *Mister Pip*, Lloyd Jones; *Right is Wrong*, Arianna Huffington; *Sepulchre*, Kate Mosse; *The Ghost*, Robert Harris

InterLicense Ltd (L)
110 Country Club Dr, Suite A, Mill Valley, CA 94941
Tel: 415-381-9780 *Fax:* 415-381-6485
E-mail: foreignrights@interlicense.net
Web Site: interlicense.net
Key Personnel
VP: Juliette Mroczkowski
Exec Dir: Manfred Mroczkowski

Founded: 1981
Foreign & subsidiary rights agency. No unsol mss, query first.

International Titles (L)
931 E 56 St, Austin, TX 78751-1724
Tel: 512-909-2447
Web Site: www.internationaltitles.com
Key Personnel
Dir: Loris Essary *E-mail:* loris@internationaltitles.com
Represent all genres; primary emphasis on sales of foreign rights. No fees charged, no submission policy.

International Transactions Inc (L)
28 Alope Way, Gila, NM 88038
Mailing Address: PO Box 97, Gila, NM 88038
Tel: 845-373-9696 *Fax:* 480-393-5162
E-mail: info@internationaltransactions.us
Web Site: www.intltrans.com
Key Personnel
Pres: Peter Riva *E-mail:* priva@intltrans.com
VP & Dir: Sandra Anne Riva *E-mail:* sriva@intltrans.com
Founded: 1975
International literary & licensing agency. Specialize in nonfiction (including large projects), fiction, illustrated & children's. We cannot help every prospective author nor can we review every ms. Send a submission query (only) via e-mail. If, within 3 weeks, we are interested, we will call for more material. Also handles film & TV rights only based on books represented. No fees.
Titles recently placed: *Absinthe*, Guido Eekhaut; *An Independent Empire*, Michael Kochin, Michael Taylor; *Angelina Ballerina (series)*, Katharine Holabird, Helen Craig; *Dragon Walk*, Robert Wintner; *Freedom Trail*, Robert Wheeler; *Hemingway's Cuba*, Robert Wheeler; *Kidnapped On Safari*, Peter Riva; *Marlene Dietrich*, Maria Riva; *Normandy*, Niklas Zetterling; *Purgatory*, Guido Eekhaut; *Radical Virus*, Azeem Ibrahim; *Santini's Hero*, Bernie Schein; *The Depression Scam*, Allan Leventhal, PhD; *The Preserve*, Steve Anderson; *The Wine Table*, Vickie Reh; *Twinkle (series)*, Katharine Holabird, Sarah Warburton; *Within Our Grasp*, Sharman Apt Russell; *You Were There Before My Eyes*, Maria Riva; *Yuma (This Is Cuba)*, David Ariosto
Foreign Office(s): Rechtsanwalt Roth, Gewurzmuhlstr 5, 80538 Munich, Germany *Tel:* (089) 55 26 26 55

JABberwocky Literary Agency Inc (L)
49 W 45 St, 12th fl, New York, NY 10036
Tel: 917-388-3010 *Fax:* 917-388-2998
Web Site: www.awfulagent.com
Founded: 1994
Full line of fiction & nonfiction trade books, particularly genre fiction (science fiction, fantasy, mystery, horror), literary fiction, young adult & middle grade & serious nonfiction (biography, science, history). No unsol mss, query first with biographical information & SASE. Will request mss after reviewing query if interested. Handle film & TV rights for regular clients. No reading fee. No fax or phone queries & always check the web site to see which agents are currently accepting e-mail queries.
Titles recently placed: *Final Girls Support Group*, Grady Hendrix; *Girly Drinks*, Mallory O'Meara; *Not Dead Enough*, Tyffany Neiheiser; *Prom Theory*, Ann Russek; *Rusted Magic*, Justina Ireland; *The Devil and the Rose*, Allison Epstein
Foreign Rep(s): AnatoliaLit Agency (Turkey); Anthea Agency (Albania, Bulgaria); Tassy Barham Associates (Brazil); Agence Eliane Benisti (France); Book Publishers Association

(Israel); Book/lab Literary Agency (Poland); Bookman (Scandinavia); The English Agency (Japan) Ltd (Japan); Julio F-Yanez Agencia Literaria SL (Portugal, Spain); Paul & Peter Fritz AG (Germany); The Grayhawk Agency (China, Indonesia, Taiwan, Thailand, Vietnam); Danny Hong Agency (Korea); Katai & Bolza (Croatia, Hungary, Serbia, Slovenia); Simona Kessler (Romania); Alexander Korzhenevski (Russia); Piergiorgio Nicolazzini (Italy); Andrew Nurnberg (Baltic States); Kristin Olson (Czechia); Read N Right (Greece); Zeno Agency Ltd (UK)

Membership(s): Science Fiction & Fantasy Writers of America (SFWA)

Melanie Jackson Agency LLC (L)
41 W 72 St, Suite 3F, New York, NY 10023
Tel: 212-873-3373
Key Personnel
Owner & Agent: Melanie Jackson
Perms: Matthew Dissen
No unsol mss, query first.
Foreign Rep(s): Liepman Agency (Germany); Rogers, Coleridge & White (UK); Roberto Santachiara (Italy)

Janklow & Nesbit Associates (L)
285 Madison Ave, 21st fl, New York, NY 10017
Tel: 212-421-1700 *Fax:* 212-355-1403
E-mail: info@janklow.com
Web Site: www.janklowandnesbit.com
Key Personnel
Sr Partner: Morton L Janklow
Partner: Lynn Nesbit
SVP: Anne Sibbald
Agent: Chris Clemans; Melissa Flashman; Allison Hunter; Lucas W Janklow; Kirby Kim; Stefanie Lieberman; Paul Lucas; P J Mark; Richard Morris; Emma Parry; Brooks Sherman; Marya Spence
Founded: 1989 (successor to Morton L Janklow Assoc Inc founded in 1975)
General fiction & nonfiction. Handle film & TV rights for book represented; no reading fee.
Foreign Office(s): Janklow & Nesbit (UK) Ltd, 13-A Hillgate St, London W87SP, United Kingdom, Contact: Rachel Balcombe *Tel:* (020) 7243 2975 *Fax:* (020) 7243 4339 *E-mail:* queries@janklow.co.uk *Web Site:* www.janklowandnesbit.co.uk

Janus Literary Agency (L)
PO Box 837, Methuen, MA 01844
Tel: 978-273-4227
E-mail: janusliteraryagency@gmail.com
Web Site: janusliteraryagency.com
Key Personnel
Owner: Lenny Cavallaro
Founded: 1980
No new clients at this time. No reading fee. Possible handling fees if agency represents author & deals with editors via hard copy; none for electronic submissions. Provide editing, ghostwriting services +/or rewrites for a fee; also consultation on digital publication & POD/self-publication. No unsol mss, query first by e-mail only without attachments unless requested. Nonfiction: prospectus, outline, sample chapter. No longer handling fiction. Will reply only if interested.

Jellinek & Murray Literary Agency (L-D)
47-231 Kamakoi Rd, Kaneohe, HI 96744
Tel: 808-239-8451
Key Personnel
Pres: Roger Jellinek *E-mail:* rgr.jellinek@gmail.com
Founded: 1995
General adult fiction & nonfiction. No genre fiction. No unsol mss, query first with an e-mail.

Submit proposal, outline, 2 sample chapters, author bio & credentials & platform, by e-mail. No reading fees. Handle film & TV rights.

Carolyn Jenks Agency (L-D)
30 Cambridge Park Dr, Suite 3140, Cambridge, MA 02140
Tel: 617-233-9130
E-mail: queries@carolynjenksagency.com (submissions)
Web Site: www.carolynjenksagency.com
Key Personnel
Owner, CEO & Dir: Carolyn Jenks
  E-mail: carolynjenks@comcast.net
Founded: 1979
Literary & commercial fiction & nonfiction. All genres. Theatre, film & screenwriters represented. Signatory to Writers Guild of America. Contact by e-mail or via web site. Electronic submissions only; prefer query via web site. No fees charged.
Titles recently placed: *Adrift in a Vanishing City*, Vincent Czyz; *Esther*, Rebecca Kanner; *Snafu*, Miryam Sifan; *The Christos Mosaic*, Vincent Czyz; *The Red Tent (20th anniversary ed)*, Anita Diamant; *True Surrealism*, Christopher Klim; *Two Maidens of the Sword*, Anne Echols
Membership(s): Writers Guild of America (WGA)

JET Literary Associates Inc (L)
941 Calle Mejia, Suite 507, Santa Fe, NM 87501
Tel: 505-780-0721
Web Site: www.jetliterary.wordpress.com
Key Personnel
Pres (Austria off): Jim Trupin
  E-mail: jetliterary@gmail.com
VP: Elizabeth Trupin-Pulli *E-mail:* etp@jetliterary.com
Founded: 1975
General book-length fiction & nonfiction. Specialize in adult fiction & commercial nonfiction; no memoirs, plays, poetry, how-to, business/finance, science fiction/fantasy, young adult or books for young children. No unsol mss, e-mail query first. No reading fees. Full representation in all foreign markets.
Foreign Office(s): Esterhazygasse 9A/26, 1060 Vienna, Austria *Tel:* (01) 587 0077 *Fax:* (01) 587 0077
Foreign Rep(s): Eliane Benisti (France); Big Apple Agency Inc (China); Educational Materials Enterprises (Greece); Julio F-Yanez Agencia Literaria SL (Brazil, Spain); Fritz Agency (Germany); Nurcihan Kesim Literary Agency Inc (Turkey); Kohn (Netherlands); Lennart Sane (Sweden); Living Literary Agency (Italy); Tuttle-Mori Agency Inc (Japan)
Foreign Rights: Abner Stein Agency (UK)

JMW Group Inc (L)
347 Rte 6, No 867, Mahopac, NY 10541
Tel: 914-841-7105 *Fax:* 914-248-8861
E-mail: jmwgroup@jmwgroup.net
Web Site: jmwgroup.net
Key Personnel
Dir of Licensing: Sara Castle
VP, Rts: Pete Allen
Founded: 1949
Publisher, Rights agency; no fees charged.

Jody Rein Books Inc (L)
7741 S Ash Ct, Centennial, CO 80122
Tel: 303-694-9386
Web Site: www.jodyreinbooks.com
Key Personnel
Pres: Jody Rein (AAR) *E-mail:* jodyrein@jodyreinbooks.com
Founded: 1994
Specialize in adult narrative & commercial nonfiction. Some literary fiction. Handle film & TV rights through agents. Send query to assistant@jodyreinbooks.com. Agency responds

if interested in project. See also Author Planet Publishing Services listing.
Titles recently placed: *Anzio: Desperate Valour*, Flint Whitlock; *Crazy Horse Weeps*, Joseph Marshall III; *You Can Draw It in Just 30 Minutes*, Mark Kistler
Foreign Rep(s): The English Agency (Japan); Grayhawk Agency (China, Taiwan); Japan UNI Agency Inc (Japan); Eric Yang Agency (Korea)
Foreign Rights: Judy Klein (worldwide exc China, Japan, Korea, Thailand & USA)
Membership(s): The Authors Guild

Jones Hutton Literary Associates (L)
140D Heritage Village, Southbury, CT 06488
Tel: 203-558-4478
E-mail: huttonbooks@hotmail.com
Key Personnel
Mng Ed: Caroline DuBois Hutton
Sr Ed: Arthur B Layton
Founded: 1994
We welcome both new & established writers & work closely with our authors to put all material in the best possible shape for submission to publishing houses. We handle both fiction & nonfiction but no sci-fi, juvenile or short story collections. We take only a few authors at a time & give to each the utmost personal attention.
To access our web site, giving editor bios & submission requirements, please send an e-mail to the address above for a link. We look forward to seeing your work &, hopefully, working with you.

The Karpfinger Agency (L)
357 W 20 St, New York, NY 10011-3379
Tel: 212-691-2690 *Fax:* 212-691-7129
E-mail: info@karpfinger.com (no queries or submissions)
Web Site: karpfinger.com
Key Personnel
Owner: Barney M Karpfinger
Foreign Rts Mgr: Cathy Jaque
Agent: Kate Garrick
Contact: Sam Chidley
Founded: 1985
Quality fiction & nonfiction. No unsol mss. See web site for specific instructions for queries. No reading fee. Direct representation in foreign markets.

Keller Media Inc (L)
578 Washington Blvd, No 745, Marina del Rey, CA 90292
Toll Free Tel: 800-278-8706
E-mail: query@kellermedia.com
Web Site: kellermedia.com/query
Key Personnel
CEO & Sr Agent: Wendy Keller
Literary Agent: Megan Close Zavala
Edit Dir: Alex Schnitzler
Founded: 1989
Represent nonfiction in the following categories: business (sales, management, marketing); finance; self-help (parenting, women's issues, relationships, pop psychology, etc); health (alternative & allopathic); metaphysical/spiritual/inspirational (never religious); nature, science, archaeology, reference, how-to (do anything). Do not send poetry, scripts, your memoir unless you are a celebrity, religious or juvenile books or first person accounts of overcoming some medical or mental condition. Most of agency's authors are either experts in their field, successful professional speakers, have their own radio, infomercial or television program, or are a household name. For best results, fill in the simple form on the web site. Please do not mail your self-published book unless requested.

Titles recently placed: *Podcasting for Profit*, Stephen Woessner; *Relentless*, Mick Dawson; *Serve Up, Coach Down*, Nathan Jamail; *Spend It All, Leave It All*, Josh Jalinski; *The Close Encounters Man*, Mark O'Connell; *The Honest Body Project*, Natalie McCain

Membership(s): National Association for Female Executives; National Speakers Association (NSA); United States Women's Chamber of Commerce

Natasha Kern Literary Agency Inc (L)
PO Box 1069, White Salmon, WA 98672
Tel: 509-493-3803
Web Site: www.natashakernliterary.com
Key Personnel
Pres: Natasha Kern
Founded: 1986
Currently closed to queries from unpublished writers.
Represent commercial adult fiction, inspirational fiction & young adult fiction. Actively represent all women's fiction; multicultural fiction; mainstream fiction; inspirational, historical & contemporary romance; romantic suspense, thrillers, & all subgenres of mysteries from cozies to PIs. DO NOT represent children's, horror, science fiction, short stories, poetry, sports, scholarly or coffee-table books. Handle film & TV rights only on represented books. Represented in all principal foreign countries as well as in Hollywood.
Titles recently placed: *Castles in the Clouds*, Myra Johnson; *Keeper of the Stars*, Robin Lee Hatcher
Foreign Rep(s): Agencia Literaria Carmen Balcells SA (Spain); Agence Eliane Benisti (France); Phillip Chen (China, Taiwan); The Italian Literary Agency srl (Italy); Prava i prevodi (Eastern Europe); Lucia Riff (Brazil); Lennart Sane (Scandinavia); Junzo Sawa (Japan); Tom Schlueck (Germany); Lorna Soifer (Israel)

Louise B Ketz Agency (L)
414 E 78 St, Suite 1-B, New York, NY 10075
Tel: 212-249-0668
E-mail: ketzagency@aol.com
Key Personnel
Pres: Louise B Ketz
Founded: 1986
Nonfiction only: science, business, sports, reference, history. No unsol mss, query letter, chapter outline, table of contents, sample chapter, author biography. No reading fee.
Titles recently placed: *The Traveler's Guide to Space: For One-Way Settlers and Round-Trip Tourists*, Neil F Comins
Membership(s): Editorial Freelancers Association (EFA); National Association of Professional & Executive Women (NAPEW); United States Commission on Military History

Virginia Kidd Agency Inc (L)
538 E Harford St, PO Box 278, Milford, PA 18337
Tel: 570-296-6205
Web Site: vk-agency.com
Key Personnel
Literary Agent, Foreign & Translation Rts, Film Queries: Christine M Cohen *E-mail:* chrisco@ptd.net
Literary Agent, Ebooks, Contracts & Royalties: Vaughne L Hansen *E-mail:* vaughne@ptd.net
Literary Agent, Submission Queries & Perms: William D Reeve *E-mail:* wmreeve@ptd.net
Founded: 1965
We are seeking quality, marketable fiction with an eye toward strong character development & fresh storytelling. While our focus remains on speculative fiction, we will consider works beyond that if the story is compelling. We repre-

sent science fiction/fantasy, dark fantasy, historical fiction, popular fiction & adventures. Cozy mystery & romance too. Overall, the characters & their story are more important than the genre.
Titles recently placed: *Hollywood North*, Michael Libling; *Reign of the Favored Women (series)*, Ann Chamberlin; *Relic*, Alan Dean Foster; *Strange Music*, Alan Dean Foster; *The Compleat Mad Amos*, Alan Dean Foster; *The Very Best of the Best*, Gardner Dozois; *The Year's Best Science Fiction 36*, Gardner Dozois
Foreign Rep(s): Bardon Chinese Media Agency (China); Bridge Communications Co (Thailand); Paul & Peter Fritz AG (Germany); International Editors' Co (Portugal, South America, Spain); The Italian Literary Agency SRL (Italy); Alexander Korzhenevski (Estonia, Latvia, Lithuania, Russia); Agence Litteraire Lenclud (France); Prava i prevodi (Central Europe, Eastern Europe, Greece, Turkey); Lennart Sane (Netherlands, Scandinavia); Tuttle-Mori Agency Inc (Japan); Eric Yang Agency Inc (Korea)
Foreign Rights: LEX Copyright Office (Hungary)

Kirchoff/Wohlberg Inc (L)
897 Boston Post Rd, Madison, CT 06443
Tel: 203-245-7308 *Fax:* 203-245-3218
E-mail: info@kirchoffwohlberg.com
Web Site: www.kirchoffwohlberg.com
Key Personnel
Pres: Morris A Kirchoff
VP: Ronald P Zollshan
Founded: 1974
Children & young adult fiction & nonfiction trade books only. Representing author & author/illustrators. Agency does not handle adult titles. No fees.
Membership(s): AIGA, the professional association for design; American Library Association (ALA); Book Industry Guild of New York; Bookbuilders of Boston; International Literacy Association (ILA); Society of Children's Book Writers & Illustrators (SCBWI); Society of Illustrators

Harvey Klinger Inc (L)
300 W 55 St, Suite 11V, New York, NY 10019
Tel: 212-581-7068 *Fax:* 212-315-3823
E-mail: queries@harveyklinger.com
Web Site: www.harveyklinger.com
Key Personnel
Pres: Harvey Klinger (AAR) *E-mail:* harvey@harveyklinger.com
Dir, Devt: Wendy Levinson *E-mail:* wendy@harveyklinger.com
Agent: David Dunton *E-mail:* david@harveyklinger.com; Andrea Somberg *E-mail:* andrea@harveyklinger.com; Rachel Ridout *E-mail:* rachel@harveyklinger.com; Cate Hart
Assoc Agent: Analieze Cervantes; Jennifer Herrington
Founded: 1977
Mainstream adult & children's fiction & nonfiction. Handle film & TV rights. No unsol full mss or faxes; do not phone or fax; no reading fee. E-mail query with brief synopsis. First 5 pages ms pasted into body of e-mail also allowed. Representatives in Hollywood & all principal foreign countries.
Foreign Rights: Eliane Benisti (France); David Grossman Literary Agency Ltd (David Grossman) (UK); Daniela Micura Literary Services (Daniela Micura) (Italy); Prava i prevodi (Ana Milenkovic) (Eastern Europe, Russia); Lennart Sane (Philip Sane) (Brazil, Holland, Latin America, Portugal, Scandinavia, Spain); Thomas Schlueck GmbH (Thomas Schlueck) (Germany); Tuttle-Mori Agency Inc (Ken

Mori) (Japan); Eric Yang Agency (Sue Yang) (Korea)
Membership(s): PEN Center USA

Kneerim & Williams Agency (L-D)
90 Canal St, Boston, MA 02114
Tel: 617-303-1650
Web Site: www.kwlit.com
Key Personnel
Agency Admin: Hope Denekamp *Tel:* 617-303-1651 *E-mail:* hope@kwlit.com
Partner: John Taylor "Ike" Williams *E-mail:* ike@kwlit.com
Mng Partner: Jill Kneerim *E-mail:* jill@kwlit.com
Agent: Lucy Cleland *Tel:* 617-303-1654 *E-mail:* lucy@kwlit.com; Katherine Flynn *E-mail:* kflynn@kwlit.com; Carol Franco *E-mail:* carolfranco@comcast.net
Affiliated Agent: Carolyn Savarese
Founded: 1990
Handles books, film & television rights. Does not handle children's picture books & genre fiction; no romance, western or science fiction & fantasy. No unsol mss, query first. Send query via e-mail to agent. Query should contain a cover letter explaining your book & why you are qualified to write it. You may include a two-page synopsis, one sample chapter, a curriculum vitae or history of your publications.
For dramatic rights inquiries, contact Lucy Cleland & Katherine Flynn. For other inquiries, contact Lucy Cleland & Hope Denekamp.
Titles recently placed: *Approaching Ali*, Davis Miller; *Brain Storms*, Jon Palfreman; *Breed of Heroes*, Julie Flavell; *Department of Experiments*, Amanda Claybaugh; *Do Your Om Thing*, Rebecca Pacheo; *Eat Drink and Remarry*, Margo Howard; *Evicted*, Matthew Desmond; *Existential Prescriptions*, Gordon Marino; *Extreme You*, Sarah Robb O'Hagan; *Formerly Known as Food*, Kristin Wartman Lawless; *Four Strong*, Rosann Sdoia; *Great Fire*, Lou Ureneck; *Honeydew*, Edith Pearlman; *How Did We Miss That?*, Amy Webb; *How Star Wars Conquered the Universe*, Chris Taylor; *More Than a Scarecrow: The Life of Ray Bolger*, Holly Van Leuven; *New World Inc*, John Butman, Simon Targett; *Self-Reg*, Stuart Shanker, Teresa Barker; *The Arsonist*, Sue Miller; *The Bettencourt Affair*, Tom Sancton; *The Feather Underground*, Kirk Johnson; *The Gates of Europe*, Serhii Plokhii; *The Last Great Day*, Jerald Walker; *The Mantle of Command, Commander in Chief*, Nigel Hamilton; *The Meaning of Human Existence*, E O Wilson; *The Power of Little Ideas*, David Robertson; *The President's Shadow*, Brad Meltzer; *The Quartet*, Joe Ellis; *The Shift*, Theresa Brown; *The Sirens of Mars*, Sarah Stewart Johnson; *The Story of Literature*, Martin Puchner; *The Virgin Vote*, Jon Grinspan; *The Worm at the Core*, Sheldon Solomon, Tom Pyszczynski, Jeff Greenberg
Foreign Rep(s): Baror International Inc (translation); Zoe Pagnamenta Agency (UK & Commonwealth)
Foreign Rights: Baror International Inc (translation); Zoe Pagnamenta Agency (UK & Commonwealth)

The Knight Agency Inc (L)
232 W Washington St, Madison, GA 30650
E-mail: admin@knightagency.net
Web Site: www.knightagency.net
Key Personnel
Owner & Pres: Deidre Knight
VP: Judson Knight
VP, Sales & Agent: Pamela Harty
VP, Opers & Agent: Elaine Spencer (AAR)
Agent: Melissa Jeglinski
Agent, FL Office: Lucienne Diver
Agent, CA Office: Nephele Tempest

Assoc Agent: Janna Bonikowski; Kristy Hunter; Travis Pennington; Jackie Williams
Bookkeeper, Off Admin: Jamie Pritchett
Founded: 1996
Fiction: commercial fiction, women's fiction, literary & multicultural fiction, historical fiction, young adult, middle grade, romance, LGBQT, science fiction & fantasy. In nonfiction: business, self-help, finance, true crime, memoir, music/entertainment, media-related, pop culture, how-to, psychology, travel, health, inspirational/religious, reference & holiday books. No anthology collections, short stories or poetry. No unsol mss, query first by sending a brief summary or proposal, author info & first 5 pages by e-mail (no attachments). Allow a 2- to 4-week response time for queries. Upon request only submit the following:
For fiction: first 3 chapters, synopsis or outline & copy of original query.
Nonfiction: proposal or outline, first 1-3 chapters, summary of author's qualifications, unique marketing opportunities & copy of original query.
Allow 8-12 weeks for ms review. No reading fee. 15% commission on domestic sales, 15-25% on foreign. May use sub-agent for sale or film & foreign rights. Screenplays not accepted. See web site for submission details. All queries managed through querymanager.com.
Titles recently placed: *A Man to Hold on To*, Marilyn Pappano; *Archangel's Legion*, Nalini Singh; *Burning Dawn*, Gena Showalter; *Cal Leandros (series)*, Rob Thurman; *Chicagoland Vampire*, Chloe Neill; *Eversea*, Natasha Boyd; *Ghost Seer*, Robin Owens; *Ink*, Amanda Sun; *Linger*, Lauren Hawkeye; *Nexus*, Ramez Naam; *Risky Game*, Tracy Solheim; *Sanctuary Island*, Lily Everett; *Stupid Girl*, Cindy Miles; *Talk Dirty to Me*, Dakota Cassidy; *Teach Me a Lesson*, Jasmine Haynes; *The Deamon Prism*, Carol Berg; *The Duke Can Go to the Devil*, Erin Knightley; *The Golden City*, J Kathleen Cheney; *The Great Library*, Rachel Caine; *The Last Monster*, Ginger Garrett; *The Memory Child*, Steena Holmes; *Wickedly Powerful*, Deborah Blake
Branch Office(s)
14622 Ventura Blvd, No 785, Sherman Oaks, CA 91403
PO Box 2659, Land O Lakes, FL 34639
Foreign Rights: ANA Sofia Ltd (Bulgaria); Julio F-Yanez Agencia Literaria SL (Montse Yanez) (Brazil, Portugal, Spain); The Fielding Agency (Whitney Lee) (Brazil, Bulgaria, China, Croatia, Czechia, Estonia, Greece, Hungary, Israel, Korea, Latvia, Lithuania, Poland, Portugal, Romania, Russia, Serbia, Slovakia, Slovenia, Taiwan, UK); Graal Literary Agency (Poland); Katai & Bolza Literary Agents (Hungary); Kayi Literary Agency Ltd (Turkey); The Lenclud Agency (France); Nova Littera (Russia); Kristin Olson Literary Agency (Czechia); PNLA / Piergiorgio Nicolazzini Literary Agency (Maura Solinas) (Italy); Read N Right Agency (Greece); Lennart Sane Agency (Scandinavia); Thomas Schlueck GmbH (Germany)
Membership(s): The Authors Guild; Mystery Writers of America (MWA); Romance Writers of America (RWA); Science Fiction & Fantasy Writers of America (SFWA); Society of Children's Book Writers & Illustrators (SCBWI); Women's Fiction Writers Association (WFWA)

Paul Kohner Agency (L-D)
9300 Wilshire Blvd, Suite 555, Beverly Hills, CA 90212
Tel: 310-550-1060 *Fax:* 310-276-1083
Key Personnel
Pres & Owner: Pearl Wexler
Literary Agent: Stephen Moore

Founded: 1938
Film & TV rights. No unsol mss, query first. No reading fee; fees for extensive copying or binding charges.

Linda Konner Literary Agency (L)
10 W 15 St, Suite 1918, New York, NY 10011
Tel: 212-691-3419 *Fax:* 212-691-0935
Web Site: www.lindakonnerliteraryagency.com
Key Personnel
Pres: Linda Konner (AAR) *E-mail:* ldkonner@cs.com
Founded: 1996
Health, nutrition, diet, relationships, sex, pop psychology, self-help, parenting, cookbooks, business & career/personal finance, celebrity/pop culture. No fiction, children's or memoir. No unsol mss, query first with one-page query & SASE or via e-mail. Submit outline & one to two sample chapters. No reading fee. 15% fee on US sales & up to 25% on foreign sales. One-time expense fee of $65, deducted from publisher's advance payment.
Titles recently placed: *80/20 Triathlon*, Matt Fitzgerald, David Warden; *Get Money: Learn How to Live the Life You Want, Not Just the Life You Can Afford*, Kristin Wong; *The Reducetarian Solution*, Brian Kateman; *Tiny Buddha's Gratitude Journal*, Lori Deschene
Foreign Rights: Books Crossing Borders (Betty Anne Crawford) (worldwide exc USA)
Membership(s): American Society of Journalists & Authors (ASJA); The Authors Guild

Barbara S Kouts Literary Agency LLC (L)
PO Box 560, Bellport, NY 11713
Tel: 631-286-1278 *Fax:* 631-286-1538
E-mail: bkouts@aol.com
Key Personnel
Owner: Barbara S Kouts
Founded: 1980
Specialize in children's fiction & nonfiction. No unsol mss, query first. Submit synopsis or outline & sample chapters. No reading fee, but copy fees would apply, no software. Handle film & TV rights from sale of books. Agents in all principal foreign countries.
Membership(s): Society of Children's Book Writers & Illustrators (SCBWI)

Stuart Krichevsky Literary Agency Inc (L)
6 E 39 St, Suite 500, New York, NY 10016
Tel: 212-725-5288 *Fax:* 212-725-5275
E-mail: query@skagency.com
Web Site: skagency.com
Key Personnel
Pres: Stuart Krichevsky (AAR)
Literary Agent & Rts Dir: Ross Harris (AAR)
Literary Agent & Busn Mgr: Hannah Schwartz (AAR)
Literary Agent: Melissa Danaczko; David Patterson; Laura Usselman (AAR); Mackenzie Brady Watson (AAR)
Assoc Literary Agent: Aemilia Phillips
Founded: 1995
Fiction & nonfiction. No reading fee. No unsol mss, query first; prefer e-mail queries (no attachments) to query@skagency.com. Include query letter & synopsis. To submit to Shana Cohen include letter, synopsis & first 2 pages to SQquery@skagency.com.
Foreign Rights: Akcali Copyright Trade & Tourism Co Ltd (Turkey); The Deborah Harris Agency (Israel); Andrew Nurnberg Associates (China, Europe, South Africa); Tuttle-Mori Agency Inc (Japan); Eric Yang (Korea)

The LA Literary Agency (L)
1264 N Hayworth Ave, Los Angeles, CA 90046
Tel: 323-654-5288
E-mail: laliteraryagency@mac.com
Web Site: www.laliteraryagency.com

Key Personnel
Literary Agent: Ann Cashman *E-mail:* ann@laliteraryagency.com; Eric Lasher *E-mail:* eric.laliterary@mac.com; Maureen Lasher *E-mail:* maureen.laliterary@mac.com
Founded: 1980
Specialize in narrative nonfiction, commercial & literary fiction. Nonfiction: query, qualifications & proposal; Fiction: query & ms. See web site for books, clients & submission information.

Ladderbird Literary Agency (L-D)
45 Midland St, Worcester, MA 01602
Tel: 508-459-9590
Web Site: www.ladderbird.com
Key Personnel
Agent/Owner: Beth Marshea *Tel:* 617-276-2406 *E-mail:* bethmarshea@ladderbird.com
Film/Television Agent: Heather Sparks *Tel:* 415-217-9067
Agent: Trevor Ketner *E-mail:* trevorketner@ladderbird.com; Elle McKenzie *E-mail:* ellemckenzie@ladderbird.com; Em Lysaght *E-mail:* emlysaght@ladderbird.com; Kianna Shore *E-mail:* kiannashore@ladderbird.com; Leah Pierre *E-mail:* leahpierre@ladderbird.com
Foreign Rts Agent: Katelin Spector
Founded: 2017
Full service literary agency offering editorial services, rights & subsidiary rights sales & royalty management. Sales commission only. No fees.
Titles recently placed: *Everyman*, M Shelly Conner; *Midnight at the Oasis*, Martin Padgett; *Ration*, Cody T Luff; *Saving Ruby King*, Cathy West

Peter Lampack Agency Inc (L)
350 Fifth Ave, Suite 5300, New York, NY 10118
Tel: 212-687-9106 *Fax:* 212-687-9109
Web Site: www.peterlampackagency.com
Key Personnel
Pres: Peter A Lampack
Agent & Foreign Rts: Rema Dilanyan *E-mail:* rema@peterlampackagency.com
Agent: Andrew Lampack *E-mail:* andrew@peterlampackagency.com
Off Mgr: Tatiana Dossov *E-mail:* bookkeeping@peterlampackagency.com
Founded: 1977
Commercial & literary fiction; nonfiction by recognized experts in a given field (especially autobiography, biography, law, finance, politics, history). Handle motion picture & TV rights from book properties only. No stageplays, teleplays or screenplays. No unsol mss. Query with letter which describes the nature of the ms plus author's credentials if any, sample chapter & synopsis by e-mail only.
Titles recently placed: *Final Option*, Clive Cussler, Boyd Morrison; *Journey of the Pharaohs*, Clive Cussler, Graham Brown; *The Death of Jesus*, J M Coetzee; *The Martyrdom of Collins Catch the Bear*, Gerry Spence; *The Titanic Secret*, Clive Cussler, Justin Scott
Foreign Rep(s): Big Apple Agency Inc (China, Taiwan); Prava i prevodi (Eastern Europe, Greece); Tuttle-Mori Agency Inc (Japan, Thailand); Eric Yang Agency (Korea)

The Ned Leavitt Agency (L)
752 Creeklocks Rd, Rosendale, NY 12472
Tel: 845-658-3333
Web Site: www.nedleavittagency.com
Key Personnel
Pres: Ned Leavitt (AAR) *E-mail:* nedleavitt@aol.com
Agent: Jillian Sweeney *E-mail:* jsweeney@nedleavittgency.com
Literary & commercial fiction & nonfiction, books on spirituality & psychology. No unsol mss. Submissions by recommendation only. Rejections not returned, no reading fee.

Levine|Greenberg|Rostan Literary Agency (L)
307 Seventh Ave, Suite 2407, New York, NY 10001
Tel: 212-337-0934 *Fax:* 212-337-0948
Web Site: lgrliterary.com
Key Personnel
Principal: Daniel Greenberg (AAR) *E-mail:* dgreenberg@lgrliterary.com; James Levine (AAR) *E-mail:* jlevine@lgrliterary.com; Stephanie Rostan (AAR) *E-mail:* srostan@lgrliterary.com
Agent & Rts Dir: Mike Nardullo
Busn Mgr: Melissa Rowland *E-mail:* mrowland@lgrliterary.com
Agent & Digital Rts Mgr: Kerry Sparks (AAR) *E-mail:* ksparks@lgrliterary.com
Agent: Sarah Bedingfield *E-mail:* sbedingfield@lgrliterary.com; Lindsay Edgecombe (AAR) *E-mail:* ledgecombe@lgrliterary.com; Victoria Skurnick (AAR) *E-mail:* vskurnick@lgrliterary.com; Danielle Svetcov (AAR) *E-mail:* dsvetcov@lgrliterary.com; Monika Verma (AAR) *E-mail:* mverma@lgrliterary.com
Assoc Agent: Courtney Paganelli
Assoc Agent & Rts Mgr: Tim Wojcik *E-mail:* twojcik@lgrliterary.com
Agent-at-Large: Arielle Eckstut
Founded: 1989
Narrative nonfiction, business, technology, psychology, parenting, health, humor, women's, men's, sexuality, education & social issues, popular culture, narrative nonfiction, fiction, cookbooks, sports. Online queries via the How To Submit page on web site or e-mail queries to submit@levinegreenberg.com. Attachments limited to 50 pages. Handle software, film & TV rights. No reading fee.
Foreign Rights: AnatoliaLit Agency (Turkey); Bardon-Chinese Media Agency (China, Taiwan); Eliane Benisti Agence Litteraire (France); The Book Publishers Association of Israel (Israel); Bridge Communications; The English Agency (Japan); Ersilia Literary Agency (Greece); The Foreign Office (Latin America, Portugal, Spain); Graal Literary Agency (Czechia, Eastern Europe, Poland); Literarische Agentur Hoffman GmbH (Germany); Internationaal Literatuur Bureau (Netherlands); Korea Copyright Center (KCC) (Korea); Maxima Creative Agency (Indonesia, Malaysia); Agencia Riff (Brazil); Vicki Satlow Agency (Italy); Abner Stein Agency (UK); Synopsis Literary Agency (Baltic States, Estonia, Russia); Ulf Toregard Agency (Scandinavia)

Robert Lieberman Agency (L)
Subsidiary of Ithaca Film & Writing Works
475 Nelson Rd, Ithaca, NY 14850
Tel: 607-273-8801
Web Site: www.kewgardensmovie.com/CUPeople/users/rhl10
Key Personnel
Pres: Robert H Lieberman *E-mail:* RHL10@cornell.edu
Founded: 1994
ABSOLUTELY NONFICTION ONLY! WILL NOT RESPOND TO FICTION QUERIES. Specialize in college level textbooks by established & recognized academics in all fields, as well as trade books in science, math, economics, engineering, medicine, psychology, computers & other academic areas that would be of general or popular interest. Represent producers of CD-ROM/multimedia/software, film & videos that fall into these categories. Submissions can be proposals +/or sample chapters, resume & table of contents. No unsol mss, query first (prefer e-mail query); will give quick response by e-mail but will accept mail query with SASE; handle software; no reading fees.

Literary & Creative Artists Inc (L)
3543 Albemarle St NW, Washington, DC 20008-4213
Tel: 202-362-4688 *Fax:* 202-362-8875
E-mail: lcadc@earthlink.net (queries, no attachments)
Web Site: www.lcadc.com
Key Personnel
Founder & Pres: Muriel G Nellis
VP: Jane F Roberts
Founded: 1981
Specialize in adult trade fiction & nonfiction credentialed authors only. No poetry or academic/technical work. No unsol mss, query first by mail addressed to Muriel Nellis with SASE or by e-mail (no attachments). Require exclusive review period of 2-3 weeks. No reading fee. Visit the submission page on our web site for more information.
Membership(s): American Bar Association (ABA); American Booksellers Association (ABA); The Authors Guild

Literary Artists Representatives (L)
575 West End Ave, Suite GRC, New York, NY 10024-2711
Tel: 212-679-7788
E-mail: litartists@aol.com
Key Personnel
Pres: Madeline Perrone
VP: Samuel Fleishman
Founded: 1993
Emphasizes adult trade, nonfiction (narrative, biography, memoir, current affairs, business, culture, history, how-to, film/TV, personal finance, sciences, sports, motivational). Handle film, TV electronic rights. Co-agents in Hollywood & other selected cities. No unsol mss, query first via e-mail. No fiction or poetry. No fees.
Titles recently placed: *Alley-Oop to Aliyah: African American Hoopsters in the Holy Land*, David A Goldstein; *Disney U: How Disney University Develops the World's Most Engaged, Loyal, and Customer-Centric Employees*, Doug Lipp; *First Over There: America's First Battle of World War I: The Attack on Cantigny May 28-31, 1918*, Matthew James Davenport; *Investment Mistakes Even Smart Investors Make and How to Avoid Them*, Larry E Swedroe, RC Balaban; *JFK in the Senate: Pathway to the Presidency*, John T Shaw; *King of the Dinosaur Hunters*, Lowell Dingus; *Lady in the Dark: Iris Barry and the Art of Film*, Robert Sitton; *Millionaire Expat: How to Build Wealth Living Overseas*, Andrew Hallam; *Political Mercenaries: How Fundraisers Allowed Billionaires to Take Over Politics*, Lindsay Mark Lewis, Jim Arkedis; *The $1,000 Challenge: How One Family Slashed Its Budget Without Moving Under a Bridge or Living on Government Cheese*, Brian J O'Connor; *The Intelligent Option Investor: Applying Value Investing to the World of Options*, Erik Kobayashi-Solomon; *The Women's Guide to Successful Investing: Achieving Financial Security and Realizing Your Goals*, Nancy Tengler; *Think, Act, and Invest Like Warren Buffett: The Winning Strategy to Help You Achieve Your Financial and Life Goals*, Larry Swedroe

Literary Management Group LLC (L)
521 Oakley Dr, Nashville, TN 37220
Tel: 615-812-4445
Web Site: www.literarymanagementgroup.com
Key Personnel
Pres & CEO: Bruce R Barbour *E-mail:* brucebarbour@literarymanagementgroup.com
VP, Prod Devt: Karen Moore *Tel:* 614-266-2876 *E-mail:* karenmoorebarbour@gmail.com
Founded: 1997
Nonfiction: Christian, motivational & inspirational. No unsol mss, query first with letter prior to submission of ms for review. E-mail proposal, outline, sample chapters. We do not represent fiction, screenplays, children's, poetry, text or reference.
Membership(s): Evangelical Christian Publishers Association (ECPA)

Lowenstein Associates Inc (L-D)
115 E 23 St, 4th fl, New York, NY 10010
Tel: 212-206-1630
E-mail: assistant@bookhaven.com (queries, no attachments)
Web Site: www.lowensteinassociates.com
Key Personnel
Pres: Barbara Lowenstein (AAR)
Founded: 1976
Electronic queries (no attachments). No westerns, textbooks, children's picture books or books needing translation. Fiction: submit via authors.me or send a one-page query with first 10 pages in the body of the e-mail; nonfiction: submit via authors.me or send a one-page query, table of contents & a proposal (if available) in the body of the e-mail to assistant@bookhaven.com. Include the word QUERY & the project name in the subject line. Address the e-mail to the agent you want to consider your work. Visit our web site to find more information about each agent's interests. No reading fee.
Membership(s): Romance Writers of America (RWA)

Donald Maass Literary Agency (L)
1000 Dean St, Suite 252, Brooklyn, NY 11238
Tel: 212-727-8383
E-mail: info@maassagency.com
Web Site: www.maassagency.com
Key Personnel
Pres: Donald Maass (AAR) *E-mail:* dmaass@maassagency.com
VP & Agent: Jennifer Jackson (AAR) *E-mail:* jjackson@maassagency.com
Rts Dir & Agent: Katie Shea Boutillier (AAR) *E-mail:* ksboutillier@maassagency.com
Agent: Michael Curry (AAR) *E-mail:* mcurry@maassagency.com; Kat Kerr; Cameron McClure (AAR) *E-mail:* cmcclure@maassagency.com; Caitlin McDonald (AAR); Jennifer Goloboy (AAR); Paul Stevens (AAR)
Founded: 1980
Literary agency for professional novelists, representing more than 100 authors & selling more than 150 novels every year to major publishers in the US & overseas. Also handles book-to-film & TV rights. Leading clients include Anne Bishop, Jim Butcher, Diane Duane, Nnedi Okorafor, Anne Perry, Cherie Priest & Brent Weeks. See web site for submission guidelines. Query via e-mail with 1-page letter, first 5 pages of novel & 1- to 2-page synopsis, pasted into e-mail; no attachments.
Titles recently placed: *Beneath the Rising*, Premee Mohamed; *Black Jewels: The Queen's Bargain*, Anne Bishop; *Dresden Files: Peace Talks*, Jim Butcher; *Escaping Exodus: Symbiosis*, Nicky Drayden; *Fate of the Fallen*, Kel Kade; *For the Sake of the Game*, Leslie S Klinger; *Ikenga*, Nnedi Okorafor; *Machine (2nd in The White Space series)*, Elizabeth Bear; *Network Effect, A Murderbot Novel*, Martha Wells; *One Fatal Flaw (3rd in The Daniel Pitt series)*, Anne Perry; *Phoenix Extravagant*, Yoon Ha Lee; *Shadows of the Short Days*, Alexander Dan Vilhjalmsson; *Stormsong*, C L Polk; *The Burning White*, Brent Weeks; *The Past and Other Things That Should Stay Buried*, Shaun David Hutchinson; *The Space Between Worlds*, Micaiah Johnson
Foreign Rights: Book Publishers Association of Israel (Israel); Donzelli Fietta Agency (Italy); The English Agency (Japan) (Japan); Grayhawk Agency (China, Indonesia, Taiwan,

Thailand, Vietnam); International Editors Co (Brazil, South America, Spain); Anna Jarota Agency (France); A Korzhenevski Agency (Russia, Ukraine); MBA Literary Agents Ltd (UK); ONK Agency Ltd (Turkey); Prava i prevodi (Bulgaria, Czechia, Montenegro, Poland, Romania, Serbia); Lennart Sane Agency AB (Denmark, Finland, Netherlands, Norway, Sweden); Thomas Schlueck GmbH (Germany); Eric Yang Agency (Korea)

Membership(s): Mystery Writers of America (MWA); Romance Writers of America (RWA); Science Fiction & Fantasy Writers of America (SFWA)

Gina Maccoby Literary Agency (L)
PO Box 60, Chappaqua, NY 10514-0060
Tel: 914-238-5630
E-mail: query@maccobylit.com
Web Site: www.publishersmarketplace.com/members/GinaMaccoby
Key Personnel
Principal: Gina Maccoby (AAR)
Founded: 1986
High quality fiction & nonficton for adults & children. Handle film & TV rights for clients' work only. No screenplays. No unsol mss; query first. E-mail queries preferred. Include SASE if querying by regular mail. Owing to the volume of queries received, we will only respond if interested. No reading fee. May recover the cost of books purchased for submissions; airmail shipping of books overseas; overnight shipping domestically if requested by client; bank fees incurred related to transfers of payments; legal fees incurred with prior client approval. Co-agents in Hollywood & overseas.
Foreign Rep(s): AnatoliaLit Agency (Turkey); Big Apple Agency Inc (China); Graal Literary Agency (Poland); Mohrbooks AG Literary Agency (Germany); Andrew Nurnberg Associates (Bulgaria, Estonia, Latvia, Lithuania, Russia, Ukraine); Lennart Sane Agency (Brazil, Portugal, Scandinavia, Spain, Spanish Latin America)
Membership(s): The Authors Guild; Society of Children's Book Writers & Illustrators (SCBWI)

Ricia Mainhardt Agency, see RMA

Carol Mann Agency (L)
55 Fifth Ave, 18th fl, New York, NY 10003
Tel: 212-206-5635 *Fax:* 212-675-4809
E-mail: submissions@carolmannagency.com
Web Site: www.carolmannagency.com
Key Personnel
Pres: Carol Mann (AAR)
Agent: Iris Blasi; Gareth Esersky; Myrsini Stephanides; Joanne Wyckoff; Laura Yorke
Founded: 1977
Literary & commercial fiction, no genre fiction, general nonfiction & memoir. Subs-agents in Los Angeles & for all foreign languages. No unsol mss, query first. E-mail queries only (no attachments). Mailed queries no longer accepted. For fiction & memoir, send a synopsis, brief bio & first 25 pages of ms. All other nonfiction, submit synopsis & brief bio. No reading fee. Handle film & TV rights for book clients only.
Foreign Rights: Akcali Copyright Agency (Turkey); Am Oved (Dalia Ever-Hadani) (Israel); Anthea Agency (Bulgaria); Eliane Benisti Agency (France); Big Apple Agency Inc (China, Indonesia, Taiwan); Graal Literary Agency (Poland); The Italian Literary Agency srl (Italy); JLM Literary Agency (Greece); Katai & Bolza Literary Agents (Hungary); Simona Kessler International Copyright Agency (Romania); Licht & Burr Literary Agency (Trine Licht) (Denmark, Iceland, Norway, Swe-

den); Mohrbooks AG Literary Agency (Germany); Andrew Nurnberg Associates Baltic (Kristine Supe) (Latvia); Andrew Nurnberg Literary Agency (Ludmilla Sushkova) (Russia); Kristin Olson Literary Agency (Czechia); Prava i prevodi (Ana Milenkovic) (Serbia); Guillermo Schavelzon & Associados (Jacoba Casier) (Spain); Schindler's Literary Agency (Brazil); Sebes & Bisseling Literary Agency (Paul Sebes) (Netherlands); Abner Stein Associates (Arabella Stein) (England); Tuttle-Mori Agency Inc (Manami Tamaoki) (Japan); Tuttle-Mori Agency Inc (Pimolporn Yutisri) (Thailand); Shin Won Agency (Tae Eun Kim) (Korea)

Freya Manston Associates Inc (L)
145 W 58 St, New York, NY 10019
Tel: 212-247-3075
Key Personnel
Pres: Freya Manston
Fiction & nonfiction. No unsol mss; not accepting new queries at this time. Agents in all principal countries. No fees charged.

March Tenth Inc (L)
24 Hillside Terr, Montvale, NJ 07645
Tel: 201-387-6551 *Fax:* 201-387-6552
Web Site: www.march10th.com
Key Personnel
Pres: Sandra Choron *E-mail:* schoron@aol.com
VP: Harry Choron *E-mail:* hchoron@aol.com
Founded: 1980
General nonfiction & fiction; specialize in popular culture. No children's or young adult novels, plays, screenplays or poetry. No unsol mss, query first. E-mail queries accepted. If mailing hard copy, include a SASE for materials you want returned. See web site for additional information. No reading fee. Book production services available. Handle film & TV rights. 15% commission.
Titles recently placed: *It's Not About the Shark*, David Niven; *Shakespeare Saved My Life*, Laura Bates

Denise Marcil Literary Agency LLC (L)
Affiliate of Marcil-O'Farrell Literary LLC
483 Westover Rd, Stamford, CT 06902
Tel: 203-327-9970 *Fax:* 203-327-9970
Web Site: www.marcilofarrellagency.com
Key Personnel
Mgr & Agent: Denise Marcil (AAR)
  E-mail: denise@marcilofarrellagency.com
Agent: Anne Marie O'Farrell (AAR)
  Tel: 516-365-6029 *E-mail:* annemarie@marcilofarrellagency.com
Founded: 1977
Denise Marcil no longer accepts new authors. Do not query. Send nonfiction e-mail queries to Anne Marie O'Farrell at annemarie@marcilofarrellagency.com, who represents personal growth, self-help including mind, body, spirit, alternative health, spirituality, business, careers, sports, travel, cookbooks, gift books & quirky books. No unsol mss, query first via e-mail. Sub-agents in all major countries.
Titles recently placed: *Dr Knox*, Peter Spiegelman; *For Every Little Thing*, June Cotner, Nancy Tupper-Ling; *Glad to Be Human*, Irene O'Garden; *Healing the Thyroid with Ayurveda*, Dr Marianne Teitelbaum; *Herons Landing, Snowfall on Lighthouse Lane, Summer on Mirror Lake*, JoAnn Ross; *Lilac Lane*, Sherryl Woods; *Magic Lantern*, Peter Spiegelman; *The Healthy Brain Book*, Dr William Sears, Dr Vincent Fortanasce; *The Healthy Motherhood Journal*, Martha Sears, RN, Hayden Livesday Sears; *The Warrior Heart Practice*, HeatherAsh

Amara; *Titanic Sisters*, Patricia Falvey; *Willow Brook Road*, Sherryl Woods
Membership(s): The Authors Guild; Women's Media Group

Mildred Marmur Associates Ltd (L)
2005 Palmer Ave, PMB 127, Larchmont, NY 10538
Tel: 914-834-1170 *Fax:* 914-833-1175
E-mail: marmur@westnet.com
Key Personnel
Pres: Mildred Marmur (AAR)
Founded: 1987
Nonfiction only. No unsol mss; referrals only. Represented in Hollywood & foreign markets. Does not charge fees.
Membership(s): The Authors Guild

Marsal Lyon Literary Agency LLC (L)
665 San Rodolfo Dr, Suite 124, PMB 121, Solana Beach, CA 92075
Tel: 760-814-8507
Web Site: www.marsallyonliteraryagency.com
Key Personnel
Owner & Literary Agent: Kevan Lyon
  E-mail: kevan@marsallyonliteraryagency.com; Jill Marsal *E-mail:* jill@marsallyonliteraryagency.com
Literary Agent: Jolene Haley *E-mail:* jolene@marsallyonliteraryagency.com; Shannon Hassan *E-mail:* shannon@marsallyonliteraryagency.com; Patricia Nelson *E-mail:* patricia@marsallyonliteraryagency.com; Deborah Ritchken *E-mail:* deborah@marsallyonliteraryagency.com
Founded: 2009
Dedicated to helping authors successfully place their work. Members have many years of experience in the publishing industry & possess a diverse & unique skill set. Have worked with many bestselling & award-winning authors, as well as first-time authors.
Fiction genres & categories represented: commercial, mainstream, multicultural, mystery, suspense, thriller, women's fiction, romance (all genres), young adult & middle grade. Non-fiction represented: biography, business/economics/investing/finance, diet, fitness & health, history/politics/current events, investigative journalism, lifestyle, memoirs, narrative nonfiction, parenting, pets/animals, pop culture & music, psychology, relationships/advice, science & nature, self-help, sports, women's issues. No unsol ms, query first. Writers are encouraged to visit the web site to determine who might be the best fit for your work. For electronic submissions (preferred), send query letter & write QUERY in the subject line of the e-mail. Hard copy submissions: for fiction, send cover letter, one-page synopsis of work & first 10 pages of ms; for nonfiction, include either cover letter or cover letter & complete proposal. No fees.
The Taryn Fagerness Agency represents foreign, audio & film subsidiary rights.
Titles recently placed: *$6 Million in Cash*, Anthony M DeStefano; *A Better Man*, Candis Terry; *A Brazen Bargain*, Laura Trentham; *A Covert Affair*, Katie Reus; *A Father's Desperate Rescue*, Amelia Autin; *A License to Wed*, Diana Quincy; *A Peach of a Pair*, Kim Boykin; *A Perfect Plan*, Anna Sugden; *A Pressing Engagement*, Anna Lee Huber; *A Promise of Fire*, Amanda Bouchet; *A Second Chance at Murder*, Diana Orgain; *A Wild Highland Heart*, Kathleen Bittner Roth; *All the Good Parts*, Loretta Nyhan; *All There Is*, Violet Duke; *Almost Anywhere*, Krista Schlyer; *An Indecent Invitation*, Laura Trentham; *At the Edge*, Laura Griffin; *Beach House Brunch: 100 Delicious Ways to Start Your Long Summer Days*, Lei Shishak; *Beauty and the Highland Beast*, Lecia Cornwall; *Black Rose*, Jenna Ryan; *Bleeding Pixels*, Patrick Markey, Chris Ferguson;

Blind Spot, Katana Collins; *Bound by Duty*, Cat Schield; *Breaking the Rules*, Katie McGarry; *Broken*, Candace Havens; *Bulletproof Badge*, Angi Morgan; *Camp So and So*, Mary McCoy; *Cat Got Your Diamonds*, Julie Chase; *Caught Up in the Touch*, Laura Trentham; *China's New Red Guard*, Jude Blanchette; *Christmas Joy*, Nancy Naigle; *Cliteracy*, Laurie Mintz; *Come on Closer*, Kendra Leigh Castle; *Counting Stars*, Kathleen Long; *Crude Nation*, Raul Gallegos; *Demon of Mine*, Rayna Vause; *Dial Em for Murder*, Marni Bates; *Die Young with Me*, Robert Rufus; *Dirtiest Secret*, J Kenner; *Ernesto: Hemingway's Years in Cuba*, Andrew Feldman; *Eternal Sonata*, Jamie Metzl; *Evenings in Paris*, Jeanne Mackin; *Every Yesterday*, Nancy Naigle; *Everywhere and Every Way*, Jennifer Probst; *Fatal Identity*, Marie Force; *Flawless*, Stefanie Little; *Flirting with Scandal*, Chanel Cleeton; *Fly with Me*, Chanel Cleeton; *Follow Me*, Tiffany Snow; *Forbidden Fling*, Skye Jordan; *Forever Beach*, Shelley Noble; *Forgetting August*, J L Berg; *Forgotten Secrets*, Robin Perini; *From Duke 'Til Dawn*, Eva Leigh; *Haunted Vintage Mystery*, Rose Pressey; *Haven*, A R Ivanovich; *Heart & Sell*, Shari Levitin; *Her Highland Rogue*, Violetta Rand; *Hide from Me*, Mary Lindsey; *Highland Vixen*, Mary Wine; *His Deception*, Patricia Rosemoor; *Hostage Rescue Hero*, Elizabeth Heiter; *House Trained*, Jackie Bouchard; *I See You*, Molly McAdams; *In Another Life*, Julie Christine Johnson; *In His Shadow*, Tiffany Snow; *It Had to Be Fate*, Tamra Baumann; *It Started with Goodbye*, Christina June; *It's in His Smile*, Shelly Alexander; *Karma Khullar's Mustache*, Kristi Wientge; *Last Call*, Kristen Lepionka; *Last Kiss of Summer*, Marina Adair; *Le French Oven*, Hillary Davis; *Leaving Amarillo*, Caisey Quinn; *Les Desserts*, Hillary Davis; *Let the Good Prevail*, Logan Miller, Noah Miller; *Listen to Me*, Kristen Proby; *Listen to the Moon*, Rose Lerner; *Little House in the Hollywood Hills*, Charlotte Stewart, Andy Demsky; *Monet's Palate Cookbook: The Artist and His Kitchen Garden at Giverny*, Aileen Bordman, Derek Fell; *Moonlight Over Paris*, Jennifer Robson; *My Dear Hamilton*, Laura Kamoie, Stephanie Dray; *My Paris Market Cookbook: A Culinary Tour of Flavors and Seasonal Recipes*, Emily Dilling; *Nanny Makes Three*, Cat Schield; *Oblivion*, Jennifer L Armentrout; *Pill City*, Kevin Deutsch; *Ping Pong Heart*, Martin Limon; *Pippa's Magical Garden*, Pippa Rossi; *Portrait of a Conspiracy* (book 1 of the Da Vinci's Disciples trilogy), Donna Russo Morin; *Power Play*, Tiffany Snow; *Rebels Like Us*, Liz Reinhardt; *Redeeming the Billionaire Seal*, Lauren Canan; *Relentless Protector*, Hope White; *Return to Marker Ranch*, Claire McEwen; *Ride Hard*, Laura Kaye; *Salem's Cipher*, Jess Lourey; *Seconds to Live*, Melinda Leigh; *Secrets of Nanreath Hall*, Alix Rickloff; *Seized*, Elizabeth Heiter; *Serving Trouble*, Sara Jane Stone; *Smart Girl*, Rachel Hollis; *Surviving Cancer*, David Palma; *Sweet Madness*, Trisha Leaver, Lindsay Currie; *Take Me Home Tonight*, Erika Kelly; *Terror in Taffeta*, Marla Cooper; *Texan's Baby*, Barb Han; *The Accidental Scot*, Patience Griffin; *The Betrayal of the Bonfire of the Vanities* (book 3 of the Da Vinci's Disciples trilogy), Donna Russo Morin; *The Competition* (book 2 of the Da Vinci's Disciples trilogy), Donna Russo Morin; *The Crows of Beara*, Julie Christine Johnson; *The Empress of Bright Moon* (book 2 of The Moon in the Palace duology), Weina Dai Randel; *The Good Daughter*, Alexandra Burt; *The Heir Hunter*, Diane Capri; *The Invisible Shore*, Jacquelyn McShulskis; *The Irresistible Rogue*, Valerie Bowman; *The Kiss on Castle Road*, Lauren Christopher; *The Last August Rose*, Tessa Arlen; *The Memory Diet*, Judi Zucker, Shari Zucker; *The Moon in the Palace* (book 1 of The Moon in the Palace duology), Weina Dai Randel; *The New Way We Make War*, Louis Del Monte; *The Other Mythology*, Bill Hansen; *The Perfectly Proper Paranormal Museum*, Kirsten Weiss; *The Portable Feast: Creative Meals for Work and Play*, Jeanne Kelley; *The Possibility of Somewhere*, Julia Day; *The Problem with Forever*, Jennifer L Armentrout; *The Puppy Proposal*, Katie Meyer; *The Secret Ingredient of Wishes*, Susan Bishop Crispell; *The Secret of Us*, Camille Di Maio; *The Sweetheart Racket*, Cheryl Ann Smith; *The Tao of Running*, Gary Dudney; *The World's Greatest Adventure Machine*, Frank L Cole; *Then He Kissed Me*, Laura Trentham; *This Loving Feeling*, Miranda Liasson; *This Victorian Life*, Sarah Chrisman; *To Kiss a Thief*, Susanna Craig; *To Steal a Heart*, K C Bateman; *Trail of Echoes*, Rachel Howzell Hall; *Trick or Deceit*, Shelley Freydont; *Turn Me Loose*, Rosalind James; *Unthinkable*, Nina Croft; *Upscale Downhome: Family Recipes, All Gussied Up*, Rachel Hollis; *Visibility Marketing*, David Avrin; *What the Waves Know*, Tamara Valentine; *Whispers in the Mist*, Lisa Alber; *Windy City Blues*, Renee Rosen; *With Love from the Inside*, Angela Pisel; *Worth the Trouble*, Jamie Beck; *Write Naked*, Jennifer Probst

Foreign Rights: Taryn Fagerness Agency LLC (Albania, Argentina, Australia, Brazil, Bulgaria, Canada, China, Croatia, Czechia, Denmark, Estonia, Finland, France, Germany, Greece, Hungary, Iceland, India, Indonesia, Israel, Italy, Japan, Korea, Latvia, Lithuania, Mexico, Netherlands, Norway, Poland, Portugal, Romania, Russia, Serbia, Slovakia, Slovenia, Spain, Sweden, Taiwan, Thailand, Turkey, Ukraine, UK, Vietnam)

Membership(s): Romance Writers of America (RWA)

The Evan Marshall Agency (L)
One Pacio Ct, Roseland, NJ 07068-1121
Tel: 973-287-6216
Web Site: www.evanmarshallagency.com
Key Personnel
Pres: Evan S Marshall (AAR) *E-mail:* evan@evanmarshallagency.com
Founded: 1987
Considers new clients by referral only. Represents all genres of adult & young adult full-length fiction.
Titles recently placed: *A Catered New Year's Eve*, Isis Crawford; *A Man for Honor*, Emma Miller; *All About Evie*, Cathy Lamb; *Mrs Morris and the Ghost*, Traci Wilton; *Murder in an Irish Churchyard*, Carlene O'Connor; *The Devil's Wind*, Steve Goble; *The Intended Victim*, Alexandra Ivy; *The Irishman's Daughter*, V S Alexander; *The Scotsman Who Swept Me Away*, Hannah Howell; *Too Sweet to Be Good*, K M Jackson

The Martell Agency (L)
1350 Avenue of the Americas, Suite 1205, New York, NY 10019
Tel: 212-317-2672
Web Site: www.themartellagency.com
Key Personnel
Owner: Alice Fried Martell
Contact: Stephanie Finman
Founded: 1985
Fiction & nonfiction. Handle film & TV rights. No unsol mss, query first. Submit query letters by e-mail, sample material only on request. Include market analysis for nonfiction & author biography. No reading fee. Represented in foreign markets.
Titles recently placed: *Accountable*, Michael O'Leary, Warren Valdmanis; *Blood Relations*, Jonathan Moore; *FOMO: Fear of Missing Out*, Patrick McGinnis; *Sounds Wild and Broken*, David George Haskell; *The Genius of Women*, Janice Kaplan
Foreign Rep(s): Eliane Benisti (France); Julio F- Yanez Agencia Literaria SL (Montse Yanez) (Brazil, Portugal, Spain, Spanish Latin America); Deborah Harris Agency (Efrat Lev) (Israel); Jill Hughes Agent (Eastern Europe, Greece, Middle East); Nurchian Kesim (Filiz Karaman) (Turkey); Liepman Agency (Germany, Switzerland); Maxima Creative Agency (Indonesia, Malaysia); Natoli Stefan & Oliva SA (Italy); Andrew Nurnberg Associates International (Whitney Hsu) (Taiwan); Andrew Nurnberg Associates International (Jackie Huang) (China); Sebes & Bisseling (Netherlands, Scandinavia); Abner Stein (Australia, UK & Commonwealth); Tuttle-Mori Agency Inc (Japan); Tuttle-Mori Agency Inc (Thananchai Pandey) (Thailand); Eric Yang Agency (Henry Shin) (Korea)

Martin Literary Management (L)
15601 32 Ave SE, Mill Creek, WA 98012
Tel: 206-466-1773 (no phone queries) *Fax:* 206-466-1774
Web Site: www.martinliterarymanagement.com
Key Personnel
Literary Mgr & Agent: Sharlene Martin *E-mail:* sharlene@martinlit.com
Literary Mgr: Adria Goetz *E-mail:* adria@martinlit.com
Assoc Literary Mgr: Natalie Grazian *E-mail:* natalie@martinlit.com
Agent: Clelia Gore *E-mail:* clelia@martinlit.com
Founded: 2003
Nonfiction, picture books, middle grade, young adult, adult nonfiction, adult fiction, lifestyle, gift books. Query in accordance with submission guidelines & agents' preferences on web site. Now a "green agency," only e-mail queries will be accepted. No fees charged.
Titles recently placed: *Angels All Around Us*, Rebekah Gregory, Anthony Flacco; *Band Geeks*, Amy Cobb; *Breakthrough*, Jack Andraka, Matthew Lysiak; *Chasing Portraits*, Elizabeth Rynecki; *Dario and the Whale*, Cheryl Lawton; *Finding My Shine*, Nastia Liukin; *Geoengineering a New Climate*, Jennifer Swanson; *Horace J Edwards and the Time Keepers: Secret of the Scarab Beetle*, William Meyer; *Maximum Harm*, Michele McPhee; *The Art of the Con*, Anthony Amore; *Too Pretty to Live*, Dennis Brooks; *Wisteria Jane Hummel*, Amber Harris
Foreign Rights: Taryn Fagerness Agency (worldwide exc Canada & US Territories)

Martin-McLean Literary Associates LLC (L)
5023 W 120 Ave, Suite 228, Broomfield, CO 80020
Tel: 303-465-2056 *Fax:* 303-465-2056
E-mail: martinmcleanlit@aol.com
Web Site: www.martinmcleanlit.com
Key Personnel
Agent & CEO: Lisa Ann Martin, PhD
Founded: 1986
Literary fiction, nonfiction, health issues, psychology, how-to, self-help, sports, new thought, critical thinking, scholarly, biographies, memoirs, autobiographies & murder mystery. No unsol mss. Query first with letter, synopsis, total word count of ms & e-mail address to the agency's street address or by e-mail. Requirements: send proposal with SASE, follow submission directions on web site, or call for agency brochure. No evaluation or reading fee; work at $60/hour. New writers welcome.
Services: editing, proposal development & critique. Book development available. Ghostwriters can be matched to author. Agents worldwide with Internet access.
Titles recently placed: *A Bird in the Hand*, Jerry Banks; *Angel Kisses: Kildare Beginnings*, Karen K Hoiland; *Angel Kisses: The Gift of In-*

firmity, Karen K Hoiland; *Constellation Draco*, J R Bacon; *Diary of a Mad Seducer*, Paul de Vito; *How to Avoid the Over-diagnosis and Over-treatment of Prostate Cancer*, Anthony H Horan, MD; *In God's Sunshine*, Weldon Schenck; *Indian Zero to American Hero: An Incredible Story of a Slumdog Scientist*, Dr B Vithal Shetty; *Intimate Voyages*, Cynthia Wasieczko; *Lighter Than Air: Painting with the Colors of the Wind*, Paul de Vito; *Mandy and Thelma*, Billie Thomas; *Mountains of Poetry: Colorado Poems by Colorado Kids*, Coyote Authors Club; *Reflections on Hidden Faces*, Paul de Vito; *Tears of Laughter*, Paul de Vito; *The Elements of Selling: Everyone Has Something to Sell*, Alan Zell; *The End of Days*, J R Bacon; *The Feral Pistillate*, Warner Bair II; *The Magic Law of Increase: Tithing Your Way to Prosperity*, Lisa Ann Martin, PhD; *The Rise and Fall of the Prostate Cancer Scam*, Anthony H Horan, MD; *The Sacred Agreements: Purpose. Passion. And the Power to Lead.*, Marsh Engle; *The Second District*, Jerry Banks; *The Three R's Make the World Go Around!*, Jade Martin, Dylan George, Kyra Mowry, Valerie Ulsh; *The Uncertain Believer*, Edward Correia; *Vulture Culture*, Eric Gerst

Margret McBride Literary Agency (L)
PO Box 9128, La Jolla, CA 92038
Tel: 858-454-1550
E-mail: staff@mcbridelit.com
Web Site: www.mcbrideliterary.com
Key Personnel
Owner & Pres: Margret McBride (AAR)
Agent: Faye Atchison
Founded: 1981
Specialize in fiction, nonfiction & business. See submission guidelines on web site. E-mail submissions preferred. No snail mail. No poetry, romance, children's or screenplays. Foreign rights sub-agents in all major countries.
Titles recently placed: *According to Audrey*, Happy LaShelle; *Cheech Is Not My Real Name*, Richard "Cheech" Marin; *Financial Freedom*, Grant Sabatier; *The Go-Giver Influencer*, Bob Burg, John David Mann; *The Go-Giver Leader*, Bob Burg, John David Mann
Foreign Rights: Akcali Copyright (Turkey); The Asano Agency (Kiyoshi Asano) (Japan); Bardon Chinese Media Agency (David Tsai) (China); Eliane Benisti Agency (France); Raquel De La Concha Agencia Literaria (Portugal, Spain, Spanish- & Portuguese-speaking countries, Spanish Latin America, Spanish-speaking countries); Caroline van Gelderen Literary Agency (Netherlands); KCC (Korea Copyright Center) (Korea); Licht & Burr (Scandinavia); Maxima Creative Agency (Santo Manarung) (Indonesia); I Pikarski (Israel); Pravi i prevodi (Eastern Europe)
Membership(s): The Authors Guild; Society of Children's Book Writers & Illustrators (SCBWI); Writers Guild of America (WGA)

E J McCarthy Agency (L)
405 Maple St, Suite H, Mill Valley, CA 94941
Tel: 415-383-6639
E-mail: ejmagency@gmail.com
Web Site: www.publishersmarketplace.com/ members/ejmccarthy
Key Personnel
Owner: E J McCarthy
Founded: 2003
Independent literary agency from former executive editor (Bantam Doubleday Dell, Ballentine/Random House). Subject specialties: history, military history, politics, sports, biography, media, memoir, thrillers & other nonfiction. No reading fee. Query first by e-mail.
Titles recently placed: *8 Seconds of Courage*, Flo Groberg, Tom Sileo; *Air Apaches*, Jay A Stout; *Fire and Forget: Short Stories from the Long War*, Roy Scranton (ed), Matt Gallagher (ed); *Fire in My Eyes*, Brad Snyder, Tom Sileo; *Hell's Angels*, Jay A Stout; *One Bullet Away*, Nathaniel Fick; *Our Year of War*, Daniel P Bolger; *The Sling & the Stone*, Thomas X Hammes; *The Unforgiving Minute*, Craig M Mullaney; *Wanted Dead or Alive*, Benjamin Runkle; *War Play*, Corey Mead; *When Books Went to War*, Molly Guptill Manning; *Why We Lost*, Daniel P Bolger

Gerard McCauley Agency Inc (L)
PO Box 844, Katonah, NY 10536-0844
Tel: 914-232-5700
Key Personnel
Pres: Gerard McCauley
E-mail: gerrymccauley44@gmail.com
Founded: 1970
Nonfiction; educational materials. No unsol mss. Representatives in all major foreign countries. Not currently considering new mss. Does not charge fees.

Anita D McClellan Associates (L)
464 Common St, Suite 142, Belmont, MA 02478-2704
Tel: 617-575-9203
E-mail: adm@anitamcclellan.com
Web Site: www.anitamcclellan.com
Key Personnel
Agent: Anita McClellan (AAR)
Founded: 1988
General fiction & nonfiction, including feminism. No unsol mss, query first by e-mail without attachments, no work previously submitted to publishers. Submit outline or synopsis & first 2,500 words. No software. No reading fees charged.
Membership(s): The Authors Guild; Bay Area Editors' Forum; Cape Cod Writers Center; Editorial Freelancers Association (EFA); Grub Street; Independent Book Publishing Professionals Group (IBPPG); International Women's Writing Guild (IWWG); National Book Critics Circle (NBCC); Sisters in Crime; Society of Children's Book Writers & Illustrators (SCBWI); Women's National Book Association (WNBA)

McIntosh and Otis Inc (L)
207 E 37 St, Suite BG, New York, NY 10016
Tel: 212-687-7400 *Fax:* 212-687-6894
E-mail: info@mcintoshandotis.com
Web Site: www.mcintoshandotis.com
Key Personnel
Owner & CEO: Eugene H Winick
Pres & Sr Adult Agent: Elizabeth Winick Rubinstein (AAR)
Agent, Children's Dept: Christa Heschke (AAR)
Agent: Adam Muhlig
Royalty Admin: Alecia Douglas
Founded: 1928
Represent adult & juvenile fiction & nonfiction books. No unsol mss, query first via e-mail. See web site for instructions. No reading fees. Handle film & TV rights for represented clients only. Agents in most major foreign countries.
Foreign Rep(s): AnatoliaLit Agency (adult) (Turkey); Bardon-Chinese Media Agency (Mainland China, Taiwan); Book/lab Literary Agency (Poland); Julio F-Yanez Agencia Literaria SL (Latin America, Portugal, Spain); The Deborah Harris Agency (Israel); The Italian Literary Agency SRL (Italy); Japan UNI Agency Inc (Japan); KCC-Korea Copyright Center, Inc (Korea); Simona Kessler International Copyright Agency Ltd (Romania); Agence Michelle Lapautre (juvenile) (France); Mohrbooks AG Literary Agency (Germany); La Nouvelle Agence (adult) (France); Andrew Nurnburg Associates (Bulgaria, Czechia, Hungary, Latvia, Lithuania, Russia); Prava i prevodi (Croatia, Georgia, Serbia, Slovakia, Slovenia, Ukraine); Read n Right Agency (Greece); Sebes & Bisseling Literary Agency (Denmark, Finland, Netherlands, Norway, Scandinavia, Sweden); Abner Stein Agency (UK)

McLean Literary Associates, see Martin-McLean Literary Associates LLC

Sally Hill McMillan LLC (L)
429 E Kingston Ave, Charlotte, NC 28203
Tel: 704-334-0897
E-mail: mcmagency@aol.com
Key Personnel
Pres: Sally Hill McMillan
Founded: 1990 (converted to LLC 2011)
Southern fiction & adult trade nonfiction; no unsol mss, query first & await further instructions. No science fiction, military, horror, fantasy/adventure children's books or cookbooks. No reading fee. Handle film, TV, foreign & electronic rights through sub-agents.
Titles recently placed: *Art of Arranging Flowers*, Lynne Hinton Branard; *Coastal Birds*, John Yow; *Traveling Light*, Lynne Hinton Branard
Foreign Rights: The Fielding Agency (all other territories); Thomas Schlueck GmbH (Germany)
Membership(s): Women's National Book Association (WNBA)

Mendel Media Group LLC (L)
115 W 30 St, Suite 209, New York, NY 10001
Tel: 646-239-9896
Web Site: www.mendelmedia.com
Key Personnel
Mng Partner: Scott Mendel (AAR)
E-mail: scott@mendelmedia.com
Founded: 2002
Represent nonfiction writers in most subject areas, from biography & serious history to health & relationships. Nonfiction clientele includes individual authors & institutions whose works, collections, archives, researchers +/or policy experts contribute to important public discussions & debates. Also represent more lighthearted nonfiction projects, when they suit the market particularly well. The agency's fiction writers principally write historical & contemporary multicultural fiction, contemporary thrillers & mainstream women's fiction.
E-mail submissions
only to query@mendelmedia.com (do not use attachments). No longer accept or read submissions sent by mail. No fees. If we want to read more or discuss your work, we will respond to you by e-mail or phone within a few weeks. In any case, do not call or e-mail to inquire about your query.
Fiction queries: If you have a novel you would like to submit, please paste a synopsis & first 20 pages into the body of your e-mail, below a detailed letter about your publication history & the history of the project, if it has been submitted previously to publishers or other agents.
Nonfiction queries: If you have a completed nonfiction book proposal & sample chapters, you should paste those into the body of an e-mail, below a detailed letter about your publication history & the history of the project, if it has been submitted previously to any publishers or other agents.
Membership(s): American Association of University Professors; The Authors Guild; Modern Language Association (MLA); Mystery Writers of America (MWA); Romance Writers of America (RWA); Society of Children's Book Writers & Illustrators (SCBWI)

Scott Meredith Literary Agency LP (L)
125 Park Ave, 25th fl, New York, NY 10017
Tel: 646-218-9240 *Fax:* 212-977-5997
E-mail: info@scottmeredith.com

Web Site: www.scottmeredith.com
Key Personnel
Pres: Arthur M Klebanoff *E-mail:* aklebanoff@
rosettabooks.com
VP, Fin: Maxine Schweitzer
E-mail: mschweitzer@scottmeredith.com
Dir, Subs Rts: Mary Jo Anne Valko-Warner
E-mail: mjaz@ptd.net
Founded: 1946
More than 1,500 titles in print. No unsol mss,
query first. No fees charged.

Metamorphosis Literary Agency (L)
12837 S Seminole Dr, Olathe, KS 66062
Tel: 646-397-1640
E-mail: info@metamorphosisliteraryagency.com
Web Site: www.metamorphosisliteraryagency.com
Key Personnel
Owner & Sr Agent: Stephanie Hansen *Tel:* 913-
530-3304
Literary Agent: Amy Brewer *E-mail:* abrewer@
metamorphosisliteraryagency.com;
Patty Carothers *E-mail:* pcarothers@
metamorphosisliteraryagency.com
Founded: 2016
Our mission is to help authors become traditionally published. We represent commercial fiction
that is well-crafted, including fantasy, mystery,
romance, science fiction & young adult. The
agency works closely with authors to ensure
their book is in the best presentable form. Our
publishing connections come from numerous
conferences, luck & genuine care. We do not
charge reading fees.
No unsol mss, query first. Please only query unpublished projects. Format the ms in a word
document to size 12 either Times Roman or
Arial font, justified align, no manual tabs,
header top left (title & your name), page numbers beginning on page 2 bottom right & a
cover page with just the title & your name.
Titles recently placed: *Aslan: Running Joy*,
Kristin Kaldahl; *Cookie & Milk!*, Michele
McAvoy; *Dancing With Daddy*, Anitra Schulte;
ETA, Ibrahim Ashmawey; *Goodwill*, Tiffany
Killoren; *I Love Me!*, LaRonda Gardner Mid-
dlemiss; *Keeping Score*, Shannon Stults; *Prima
Gina, Ballerina*, Kelly Mangan; *Proximity*,
Joel Lawrence; *Pups, Cakes & Wedding Dates*,
Caroline Flynn; *Relentless*, Karen Lynch; *The
Ghost and the Wolf*, Shelly X Leonn; *The Guy
He Was Supposed To Be*, Larissa Lopes; *The
Noisy Classroom*, Angela Johnson; *When My
Cousins Come To Town*, Angela Shante; *Witch-
ery*, Dana Swift
Foreign Rep(s): AnatoliaLit Agency (Amy Marie
Spangler) (Turkey); Book/lab Literary Agency
(Poland); Lora Fountain Literary Agency (Lora
Fountain) (Belgium (French-speaking), Brazil,
Canada, France, Holland, Italy, Portugal, Spain,
Switzerland)

The Miller Agency Inc (L)
630 Ninth Ave, Suite 1102, New York, NY 10036
Tel: 212-206-0913 *Fax:* 212-206-1473
Key Personnel
Contact: Sharon Bowers *E-mail:* sharon@
mbgliterary.com; Angela Miller
E-mail: angela@mbgliterary.com
Fiction & nonfiction. No unsol mss. Handle soft-
ware, film & TV rights. No reading fee. Sub-
agents in all principle foreign countries.

Montreal-Contacts/The Rights Agency (L)
1350 Sherbrooke St E, Suite 1, Montreal, QC
H2L 1M4, Canada
Tel: 514-400-7075 *Fax:* 514-400-1045
Web Site: www.montreal-contacts.com/?lang=en
Key Personnel
Owner: Jean-Sebastien Dufresne
E-mail: jsdufresne@montreal-contacts.com
Founded: 1981

Represents publishers +/or literary agents exclusively for foreign rights. No author representation. Does not handle original mss. Representation in all principal countries through 20
corresponding agents covering 50 languages.
Representing full catalogues or selected titles
with new online promotional platform eMedi-
aRights.

Howard Morhaim Literary Agency Inc (L)
30 Pierrepont St, Brooklyn, NY 11201-3371
Tel: 718-222-8400
E-mail: info@morhaimliterary.com
Web Site: www.morhaimliterary.com
Key Personnel
Pres: Howard Morhaim (AAR) *E-mail:* howard@
morhaimliterary.com
Agent: Patrice Caldwell; Kim-Mei Kirtland
E-mail: kimmei@morhaimliterary.com; Kate
McKean (AAR) *E-mail:* kate@morhaimliterary.
com; DongWon Song *E-mail:* dongwon@
morhaimliterary.com
General adult & young adult fiction & nonfiction.
Howard Morhaim is not accepting unsol mss.
Kate McKean is open to submissions. E-mail
your query letter along with 3 sample chapters
(for fiction) or full proposal (for nonfiction).
No reading fee. Handle film & TV rights. Representatives in all principal foreign markets.
Foreign Rep(s): Baror International (worldwide
exc Portugal, Spain & UK); Rain Management Group (Michael Prevett, film & TV);
RDC Agencia Literaria (Portugal, Spain); Abner Stein Agency (UK)

Henry Morrison Inc (L)
PO Box 235, Bedford Hills, NY 10507-0235
Tel: 914-666-3500
E-mail: hmorrison1@aol.com
Key Personnel
Pres: Henry Morrison
Founded: 1965
Fiction & nonfiction. Handle film & TV rights.
No unsol mss, query first with outline &
SASE. No reading fee. Fee for ms copies, gal-
leys, bound books for foreign & movie sales &
ordering books for subsidiary rights.
Titles recently placed: *Barely Legal*, Parnell Hall,
Stuart Woods; *The Bourne Initiative*, Eric Van
Lustbader; *The Money Shot*, Parnell Hall, Stu-
art Woods

Movable Type Management (L)
244 Madison Ave, Suite 334, New York, NY
10016
Web Site: www.movabletm.com
Founded: 2002
Full service literary agency representing writers
of adult trade fiction & nonfiction.
After a brief stint at a renowned literary agency,
Adam Chromy went out on his own to represent a novel written by a close friend. The
gamble paid off & the book was sold on a pre-
emptive offer. Since that auspicious start in
2002, Adam's fresh, rule-breaking approach has
led to dozens of book deals at major publishing
houses, a national & New York Times Bestseller & a number of film deals for his clients'
projects.
No unsol mss, e-mail query first. Send e-mail
with "query" in subject line & description of
project & brief author bio. See web site for
submission policies; no fees charged.
Titles recently placed: *Dead in the Water*, Annelise Ryan; *Glow Kids*, Dr Nicholas Kardaras;
Never Quit, Jimmy Settle, Don Rearden; *Rage*,
Zygmunt Miloszewski; *Sex in the Museum*,
Sarah Forbes; *The Forever Summer*, Jamie
Brenner; *The Last Days of Cafe Leila*, Donia
Bijan

Bonnie Nadell Literary Agency, see Hill Nadell
Literary Agency

Jean V Naggar Literary Agency Inc (JVNLA)
(L)
216 E 75 St, Suite 1-E, New York, NY 10021
Tel: 212-794-1082
E-mail: jvnla@jvnla.com
Web Site: www.jvnla.com
Key Personnel
Pres & Agent: Jennifer Weltz (AAR)
E-mail: jweltz@jvnla.com
Agent: Alicia Brooks *E-mail:* abrooks@jvnla.
com; Ariana Philips (AAR) *E-mail:* aphilips@
jvnla.com; Alice Tasman *E-mail:* atasman@
jvnla.com
Founded: 1978
Represents a wide range of fiction, nonfiction &
children's books. International rights, film &
TV rights for the books represented. No un-
sol mss, query first (see web site for complete,
up-to-date submission guidelines). No reading
fee. Commissions: 15% domestic, 20% foreign
translation & film.
Titles recently placed: *Big Foot and Little Foot*,
Ellen Potter; *Daughters of the Lake*, Wendy
Webb; *Don't Make Me Pull Over*, Richard
Ratay; *Eating the Sun*, Ella Frances Sanders;
House on Fire, Bonnie Kistler; *Quick Prep
Cooking with Your Instant Pot*, Stefanie Bun-
dalo; *The Perfect Alibi*, Phillip Margolin; *The
Romanov Empress*, C W Gortner
Foreign Rep(s): Akcali Copyright Agency
(Turkey); Big Apple Agency (Mainland China,
Taiwan); Graal Literary Agency (Poland);
Greene & Heaton (UK); Deborah Harris
Agency (Israel); Danny Hong Agency (Korea);
International Editors Co (Brazil, Latin America,
Portugal, Spain); The Italian Literary Agency
SRL (Italy); JLM Agency (Greece); Katai &
Bolza Literary Agency (Hungary); Simona
Kessler International Copyright Agency (Ro-
mania); Agence Michelle Lapautre (France);
Licht & Burr Literary Agency (Scandinavia);
Liepman Agency (Germany); Maxima Cre-
ative Agency (Indonesia); Mo Literary Ser-
vices (Netherlands); Andrew Nurnberg Literary
Agency (Baltic States, Bulgaria, Czechia, Rus-
sia); PLIMA (Montenegro, Serbia); Silkroad
Publishers Agency (Thailand); Tuttle-Mori
Agency Inc (Japan)

Nelson Literary Agency LLC (L)
1732 Wazee St, Suite 207, Denver, CO 80202-
1284
Tel: 303-292-2805
E-mail: info@nelsonagency.com
Web Site: www.nelsonagency.com
Key Personnel
COO/CFO: Brian Nelson
Pres & Founding Agent: Kristin Nelson (AAR)
Literary Agent: Danielle Burby; Joanna MacKen-
zie (AAR); Quressa Robinson
Dir, Literary Devt: Angie Hodapp
Contracts Mgr & Royalty Auditor: Sam Cronin
Literary Asst: Tallahj Curry; Maria Heater
Founded: 2002
Accept queries solely through QueryManager.
Four agents represent a wide span of genres in
the adult & children's market. See web site for
submission guidelines.
Titles recently placed: *A Psalm of Storms and
Silence*, Roseanne A Brown; *Etta Invincible*,
Reese Eschmann; *Lady Sherlock Series (books
6 & 7)*, Sherry Thomas; *Malorie & Musical
Chairs*, Josh Malerman; *Minor Catastrophes*,
Kathleen West; *My Kind of People*, Lisa Duffy;
Prime Deception, Valerie Valdes; *Seasons of
Terror*, Richard Chizmar; *Skyhunter*, Marie Lu;
Talespinners Series (book 3), Scott Reintgen;
The Cost of Knowing, Brittney Morris; *The
Elephant's Girl*, Celesta Rimington; *The Pa-
per Girl of Paris*, Jordyn Taylor; *The Prison*

Healer, Lynette Noni; *What Kind of Woman?*, Kate Baer; *You & Me & Us*, Alison Hammer
Foreign Rights: Jenny Meyer Literary Agency (worldwide exc Asia); Nelson Literary Agency (Asia)
Membership(s): Romance Writers of America (RWA); Science Fiction & Fantasy Writers of America (SFWA); Society of Children's Book Writers & Illustrators (SCBWI)

Regula Noetzli Literary Agent (L)
Affiliate of Charlotte Sheedy Literary Agency Inc
2344 County Rte 83, Pine Plains, NY 12567
Tel: 518-398-6260
E-mail: regula@taconic.net; regula@sheedylit.com
Adult fiction & nonfiction only with special interest in mysteries, biographies, psychology, popular science, sociology & environmental issues. Query first with outline & sample chapter. Representatives in Hollywood & most major foreign countries. No reading fees, no software.

The Betsy Nolan Literary Agency (L)
Division of The Nolan/Lehr Group Inc
112 E 17 St, Suite 1W, New York, NY 10003
Tel: 212-967-8200 *Fax:* 212-967-7292
E-mail: dblehr@cs.com
Key Personnel
Founding Partner: Betsy Nolan
Pres: Donald Lehr
Agent: Carla Glasser
Off Mgr: Jennifer Alperen
Nonfiction, popular culture, child care, psychology, cookbooks, how-to, biography, African-American & Judaica. No poetry. No unsol mss, query first; submit outline, no more than three sample chapters & author background; no reading fee; SASE.
Titles recently placed: *Celebrate Everything*, Darcy Miller; *Seaside Houses*, Nick Voulgaris; *Simple Matters*, Erin Boyle; *Urban Farm Store's Guide for the Perplexed Chicken Keeper*, Robert & Hannah Litt

Objective Entertainment (L-D)
609 Greenwich St, 6th fl, New York, NY 10014
Tel: 212-431-5454 *Fax:* 917-464-6394
Web Site: www.objectiveent.com
Key Personnel
COO: Jarred Weisfeld *E-mail:* Jarred@objectiveent.com
Pres: Ian Kleinert *E-mail:* IK@objectiveent.com
Founded: 2007
Full service management company specializing in book publishing, dramatic writing, talent & television packaging. Handles literary, dramatic & film rights, all commerical & adult trade publishing. No unsol mss. Submit query letter. No fees charged.

Fifi Oscard Agency Inc (L-D)
1440 Broadway, 23rd fl, New York, NY 10018
Tel: 212-764-1100
E-mail: agency@fifioscard.com
Web Site: fifioscard.com
Key Personnel
Pres & Literary Agent: Peter Sawyer *Tel:* 212-764-1100 ext 3 *E-mail:* psawyer@fifioscard.com
VP & Literary Agent: Carmen La Via *Tel:* 212-764-1100 ext 2 *E-mail:* laviagent@fifioscard.com
Founded: 1955
General fiction & nonfiction, all areas; film & TV rights; scripts for stage, motion picture & TV. Have always represented talent as well. No fees charged. No unsol mss, query first; submit outline & sample chapter if requested. See web site for more instruction.
Foreign Rep(s): Bardon-Chinese Media Agency (China); Julio F-Yanez Agencia Literaria SL

(Spain); Caroline Van Gelderan (Netherlands); Imprima Korea (Korea); The Italian Literary Agency srl (Italy); Agence Michelle Lapautre (France); Thomas Schlueck GmbH (Germany); Abner Stein Agency (England)

Kathi J Paton Literary Agency (L)
Box 2044, Radio City Sta, New York, NY 10101-2044
Tel: 212-265-6586
E-mail: kjplitbiz@optonline.net
Web Site: www.patonliterary.com
Key Personnel
Owner: Kathi J Paton
Founded: 1987
Interested in biography, computers/technology, business/investing/finance, history, health, sports, science, literary fiction, parenting, Christian life & issues, popular culture, humor, investigative journalism & progressive politics/current affairs. No unsol mss; e-mail queries only with a brief description. If requested, e-mail proposal (nonfiction) or synopsis (fiction) & sample chapter. Sorry, no science fiction, horror, poetry, juvenile or self-published books. No reading fee. Subs-agents in all major foreign markets & Hollywood.
Titles recently placed: *Bureau of Spies: The Secret Connections between Espionage and Journalism in Washington*, Steven T Usdin; *Catholic Women Confront Their Church: Stories of Hurt and Hope*, Celia V Wexler
Membership(s): The Authors Guild

PearlCo Literary Agency, LLC (L)
6596 Heronswood Cove, Memphis, TN 38119
Tel: 901-754-5276
Web Site: www.pearlcoliteraryagency.com
Key Personnel
Owner & Agent: Susan Perlman Cohen
E-mail: susanperlmancohen@gmail.com
Founded: 2015
No unsol mss. Query first by mail or e-mail. No fees.

Dan Peragine Literary Agency (L)
227 Beechwood Ave, Bogota, NJ 07603
Tel: 201-390-0468 *Fax:* 201-390-0468
E-mail: dpliterary@aol.com
Key Personnel
Owner & Pres: Dan Peragine
E-mail: dannyperagine@aol.com
Founded: 1991
Specialize in behavioral sciences, biography, environment, history, Christian, inspirational, nonfiction, self-help, computers, sports, photography, all high school & college textbooks, advanced placement & testing, musical groups, World War I, World War II. Handle software, film & TV rights. Represent photographic archives & books of all types. No unsol mss, query first with a complete proposal; if sending fiction, include any type of readers report or outside review with the submission; submit sample chapters single page, double-spaced, or on disk (do not send by e-mail if it needs to be downloaded). No reading fees, fees charged for editorial development, re-writes, ghostwriters, publishing consulting, full book packaging & book marketing.
Membership(s): American Booksellers Association (ABA); American Society of Picture Professionals (ASPP); National Press Photographers Association (NPPA); Professional Photographers of America (PPA)

Alison Picard Literary Agent (L-D)
PO Box 2000, Cotuit, MA 02635
Tel: 508-477-7192 *Fax:* 508-477-7192 (call first)
E-mail: ajpicard@aol.com
Founded: 1985

Representing adult & juvenile/young adult fiction & nonfiction. Beginners welcome. No unsol mss, query first with letter & SASE; no phone or fax queries. Upon positive response, submit double-spaced complete ms. No fees charged.
Titles recently placed: *365 Days of Slow Cooker Recipes*, Stephanie O'Dea; *Curse of the Jade Lily*, David Housewright; *Decided on the Battlefield*, David Johnson; *Fear of Beauty*, Susan Froetschel; *Not Your Mother's Freezer Cookbook*, Jessica Fisher; *Seconds (new ed)*, David Ely; *The Efficiency Trap: Finding a Better Way to Achieve a Sustainable Energy Future*, Steve Hallett; *The Finest Hours (middle grade ed)*, Michael Tougias, Casey Sherman; *Three Cheers for Girls*, Sara Hunt; *Torn*, Stephanie Guerra; *Totally Together: Shortcuts to an Organized Life*, Stephanie O'Dea
Foreign Rights: John Pawsey (Europe)

Pimlico Agency, see Aurous Inc

Pinder Lane & Garon-Brooke Associates Ltd (L)
159 W 53 St, New York, NY 10019
Tel: 212-489-0880 *Fax:* 212-489-7104
E-mail: pinderlanegaronbrooke@gmail.com
Web Site: www.pinderlaneandgaronbrooke.com
Key Personnel
Owner & Agent: Dick Duane (AAR); Robert Thixton (AAR)
Founded: 1996
Fiction & nonfiction, film & TV rights. No unsol mss, query first. No reading fee. Submit short synopsis, double-spaced & unbound. Representatives in Hollywood & all foreign markets.
Titles recently placed: *War and Craft*, Tom Doyle
Foreign Rep(s): Abner Stein Agency (UK)

Pippin Properties Inc (L)
110 W 40 St, Suite 1704, New York, NY 10018
Tel: 212-338-9310
E-mail: info@pippinproperties.com
Web Site: www.pippinproperties.com; www.facebook.com/pippinproperties
Key Personnel
Founder, Pres & Creative Dir: Holly M McGhee
VP & Sr Agent: Elena Giovinazzo
Sr Agent: Sara Crowe
Mgr, Subs Rts: Cameron Chase
Art Mgr: Ashley Valentine
Founded: 1998
Represent authors & artists for children's picture books, middle grade novels, chapter books & young adult novels. To submit, e-mail query & first chapter. Handle film, TV & foreign rights.
Foreign Rep(s): Rights People (worldwide exc USA)

Pom Inc (L-D)
18-15 215 St, Bayside, NY 11360
Tel: 516-487-3441
Key Personnel
Pres: Dan Green *E-mail:* dangreen@pomlit.com
Founded: 1990
Fiction & general nonfiction. No unsol mss. Please do not fax or e-mail. Handle electronic, film & TV rights. No reading fee.
Titles recently placed: *Inventing Equality*, Michael Bellesile; *Juice*, Robert Bryce; *Napoleonic Wars*, Alex Mikaberidze; *Thaddeus Stevens*, Bruce Levine; *The Republic in Peril*, Carol Berkin; *Thunder at the Gates*, Douglas Egerton

The Aaron M Priest Literary Agency Inc (L)
200 W 41 St, 21st fl, New York, NY 10036
Tel: 212-818-0344 *Fax:* 212-573-9417
E-mail: info@aaronpriest.com
Web Site: www.aaronpriest.com
Key Personnel
Pres & Agent: Aaron M Priest (AAR)
E-mail: querypriest@aaronpriest.com

Agent: Lucy Childs Baker (AAR)
  E-mail: querychilds@aaronpriest.com;
  Mitch Hoffman *E-mail:* queryhoffman@
  aaronpriest.com; Lisa Erbach Vance (AAR)
  E-mail: queryvance@aaronpriest.com
Founded: 1974
Our agents are interested in the following:
Aaron Priest: thrillers, general fiction
Lisa Erbach Vance: general fiction, mystery,
  thrillers, upmarket women's fiction, historical
  fiction, narrative nonfiction, memoir
Lucy Childs Baker: literary & commercial fiction,
  historical fiction, memoir, edgy women's fiction
Mitch Hoffman: thrillers, suspense, crime fiction, literary fiction, narrative nonfiction, politics, popular science, history, memoir, current
  events, pop culture
For all agents: no poetry, no screenplays. The
  best way to query all agents is to submit a
  query letter via e-mail. The query should be
  about one page long describing your work as
  well as your background. No attachments, however a first chapter pasted into the body of an
  e-mail query is acceptable. Do not submit to
  more than one agent at a time at this agency
  (we urge you to consider each agent's emphasis before submitting). We will get back to you
  within 4 weeks, but only if interested. No fees
  are charged.

Prospect Agency (L)
285 Fifth Ave, PMB 445, Brooklyn, NY 11215
Tel: 718-788-3217 *Fax:* 718-360-9582
Web Site: www.prospectagency.com
Key Personnel
Founder, Pres & Literary Agent (NJ Off):
  Emily Sylvan Kim (AAR) *E-mail:* esk@
  prospectagency.com
Literary Agent (NJ Off): Rachel Orr
  E-mail: rko@prospectagency.com
Literary Agent: Ann Rose; Emma Sector
Foreign Rts: Tina Shen
Founded: 2005
Full service literary agency representing a range
  of fiction, nonfiction, illustrators, romance, lit-
  erary fiction, middle grade fiction & picture
  books, adult commercial fiction, women's fic-
  tion & young adult titles. No unsol mss, query
  first via web. Only queries submitted through
  our web site are accepted. Queries sent by e-
  mail or regular mail not accepted. Send query
  letter, 3 chapters & a brief synopsis via submission form on web site. No fees charged.
  Full guidelines on web site.
Titles recently placed: *A Trapezoid Is Not a Dinosaur*, Suzanne Morris; *Bayou Bachelors
  (books 1-3)*, Geri Krotow; *Do You Feel It Too?*,
  Nicola Rendell; *Going Deep*, Tracy Wolff;
  Honey Series (books 1-3), Kristen Ashley;
  Make Me, Tracy Wolff; *Pirate Kids (books 1-
  4)*, Johanna Gohmann; *Shimmy Bang Sparkle*,
  Nicola Rendell; *The Black Door*, AdriAnne
  Strickland; *The Night We Met*, Katherine Fleet;
  The Stray, Molly Ruttan; *Transference*, Ava
  Harrison; *Ursula Funland (books 1-4)*, Johanna
  Gohmann; *Wake*, Samantha Clark; *Where the
  Sun Shines Out*, Kevin Catalano; *Wild Baby*,
  Cori Doerrfeld; *Worth the Wait*, Claudia Con-
  nor
Branch Office(s)
551 Valley Rd, PMB 377, Upper Montclair, NJ
  07043 *Tel:* 201-669-2620
Foreign Rights: The Fielding Agency (Whitney
  Lee) (worldwide)

Generosa Gina Protano Publishing, see GGP
  Publishing Inc

Puddingstone Literary, Authors' Agents (L-D)
Subsidiary of Cohen Group LLC
11 Mabro Dr, Denville, NJ 07834-9607
Tel: 973-366-3622

Key Personnel
Dir: Alec Bernard
Memb: Michael R Cohen
Founded: 1972
General trade & mass market fiction & nonfiction; motion picture scripts & teleplays. Handle
  film & TV rights. No unsol mss, query first
  with SASE. Submit outline & sample chapters.
  No reading fee. Representatives in Hollywood
  & foreign countries. Fee for ms copies, galleys
  & bound books for foreign & domestic submissions.

Raines & Raines (L-D)
103 Kenyon Rd, Medusa, NY 12120
Tel: 518-239-8311 *Fax:* 518-239-6029
Key Personnel
Partner: Joan Raines (AAR); Keith Korman
Founded: 1961
Handle film & TV rights. No unsol mss, query
  first; submit one page; no reading fee. Agents
  in all principal countries.
Foreign Rep(s): Agencia Literaria Carmen Bal-
  cells SA; Big Apple Agency Inc; Bookman;
  Campbell Thomson & McLaughlin; Fritz; The
  Italian Literary Agency srl; Agence Michelle
  Lapautre; Nurnberg; Tuttle-Mori Agency Inc

Charlotte Cecil Raymond, Literary Agent (L)
32 Bradlee Rd, Marblehead, MA 01945
Tel: 781-631-6722 *Fax:* 781-631-6722
E-mail: raymondliterary@gmail.com
Adult nonfiction & literary fiction; no juvenile,
  young adult, poetry, short stories, fantasy, science fiction or screenplays. No unsol mss,
  query first with SASE; submit outline & sample chapters. No reading fee.

Rees Literary Agency (L)
14 Beacon St, Suite 710, Boston, MA 02108
Tel: 617-227-9014 *Fax:* 617-227-8762
Web Site: www.reesagency.com
Key Personnel
Agent: Mr Lorin Rees (AAR) *E-mail:* lorin@
  reesagency.com; Ashley Herring Blake; Ann
  Collette *E-mail:* agent10702@aol.com; Rebecca Podos *E-mail:* rebecca@reesagency.com
Founded: 1983
Literary fiction, nonfiction, young adult, business,
  biography, health, history, self-help, psychol-
  ogy, current affairs, humor, mystery, thrillers,
  etc. For fiction, include query letter +/or syn-
  opsis & the first 3 chapters. For nonfiction,
  enclose a complete book proposal or substantial
  treatment. See web site for complete book list.
Foreign Rights: Taryn Fagerness (Albania, Ar-
  gentina, Australia, Brazil, Bulgaria, Canada,
  China, Croatia, Czechia, Denmark, Estonia,
  Finland, France, Germany, Greece, Hungary,
  Iceland, India, Indonesia, Israel, Italy, Japan,
  Korea, Latvia, Lithuania, Mexico, Netherlands,
  Norway, Poland, Portugal, Romania, Russia,
  Serbia, Slovakia, Slovenia, Spain, Sweden, Tai-
  wan, Thailand, Turkey, UK, Vietnam)
Membership(s): PEN American Center

Renaissance Literary & Talent (L-D)
PO Box 17379, Beverly Hills, CA 90209
Tel: 323-848-8305
E-mail: query@renaissancemgmt.net
Web Site: renaissancemgmt.net
Key Personnel
Pres: Alan Nevins *E-mail:* alan@
  renaissancemgmt.net
Agent: Berta Treitl
Founded: 1993
Commercial fiction & nonfiction. Handle film &
  TV rights; novels. No unsol mss. Query first.
  Handle highly recommended mss. Submit out-
  lines & sample chapters. No reading fee, 15%
  commission.

The Amy Rennert Agency Inc (L)
1550 Tiburon Blvd, Suite 302, Tiburon, CA
  94920
Tel: 415-789-8955
E-mail: queries@amyrennert.com (no unsol
  queries)
Web Site: amyrennert.com
Key Personnel
Pres: Amy Rennert
Busn Mgr: Joanna Waintraub
  E-mail: jwaintraub@grfllp.com
Founded: 1999
Specialize in books that matter. Amy has spent
  more than 25 years in the publishing business,
  pursuing her passion for the written word. The
  agency represents a select group of quality
  fiction & nonfiction writers - many of them
  award-winners & dozens of agency books have
  been New York Times & national bestsellers.
  We provide career management for established
  & first time authors & our breadth of experience in many genres enables us to meet the
  needs of a diverse clientele. The agency has
  developed a reputation since its inception for a
  passionate commitment to agency writers. We
  are purposely a small organization to facilitate
  hands-on personalized service & attention to
  our authors & their books.
We are not currently accepting unsol submissions.
Foreign Rights: Taryn Fagerness (worldwide)
Membership(s): The Authors Guild

Ann Rittenberg Literary Agency Inc (L)
15 Maiden Lane, Suite 206, New York, NY
  10038
Tel: 212-684-6936 *Fax:* 212-684-6929
E-mail: info@rittlit.com
Web Site: www.rittlit.com
Key Personnel
Pres: Ann Rittenberg (AAR)
Assoc Agent: Rosie Jonker *E-mail:* rosie@rittlit.
  com
Founded: 1992
Literary fiction & nonfiction; no genre fiction, no
  screenplays. Co-agents in all principal foreign
  countries as well as Hollywood. Query letter
  & first 3 chapters of double-spaced ms with
  SASE; no queries by fax.
Titles recently placed: *Safe Houses*, Dan Fesper-
  man; *The Blue Kingfisher*, Erica Wright; *The
  Coronation*, Boris Akunin; *The Disappeared*,
  Paul Doiron; *The Doctor and the Dreamer*,
  Jack Nisbet; *The Field Guide to Dumb Birds of
  North America*, Matt Kracht; *When You Can't
  Stop*, James W Hall; *Wolf Pack*, C J Box; *Your
  First Novel (revised & expanded ed)*, Laura
  Whitcomb, Ann Rittenberg, Camille Goldin
Foreign Rights: Akcali Copyright Agency
  (Turkey); The Grayhawk Agency (China, In-
  donesia, Taiwan, Thailand); The Deborah
  Harris Agency (Israel); Japan UNI Agency
  Incorporated (Japan); JLM Literary Agency
  (Greece); Korea Copyright Center (South Ko-
  rea); La Nouvelle Agence (France); Andrew
  Nurnberg Associates (Brazil, Bulgaria, Croatia,
  Czechia, Germany, Hungary, Italy, Netherlands,
  Poland, Portugal, Romania, Russia, Serbia,
  Slovakia, Slovenia, Spain, UK); Ulf Toregard
  Agency (Denmark, Finland, Norway, Sweden)
Membership(s): The Authors Guild

Judith Riven Literary Agent LLC (L)
250 W 16 St, Suite 4F, New York, NY 10011
Tel: 212-255-1009 *Fax:* 212-255-8547
E-mail: rivenlitqueries@gmail.com
Web Site: rivenlit.com
Key Personnel
Owner & Pres: Judith Riven
Founded: 1993
Fiction & nonfiction. Handle film & TV rights
  for book clients only. One page query letter de-
  scribing material with SASE. Unless requested,
  no mss accepted. E-mail queries are accepted

but no attachments. We are not currently accepting science fiction, fantasy, or horror submissions.

Titles recently placed: *Over There: America in The Great War, 1917-1918*, Lisa Davis

Riverside Literary Agency (L)
41 Simon Keets Rd, Leyden, MA 01337
Tel: 413-772-0067 *Fax:* 413-772-0969
E-mail: rivlit@sover.net
Web Site: www.riversideliteraryagency.com
Key Personnel
Pres: Susan Lee Cohen
Founded: 1990
Adult fiction & nonfiction. No unsol mss, query first with SASE. No reading fees. Handle film & TV rights & foreign rights with co-agents.

RMA (L)
85 Lincoln St, 1st fl, Meriden, CT 06451
Tel: 718-434-1893 *Fax:* 203-440-1013
Web Site: www.ricia.com
Key Personnel
Owner: Ricia Mainhardt *E-mail:* riciarma@gmail.com
Founded: 1987
Popular fiction, especially science fiction, fantasy, mystery, thriller, romance; nonfiction, especially pop culture, history & science. Do not accept poetry. Online submissions preferred. For fiction, submit query letter, brief one paragraph pitch & 1-2 page synopsis in body of the e-mail. Attach ms. For nonfiction, in the body of the e-mail with the cover letter, include a high concept pitch & a detailed table of contents. Include sample chapters or ms as an attachment. Handle audio & drama rights for client's books only. Affiliates handle translation, film & TV rights for client's books. No reading fee. Branch office in Hollywood, CA.
Membership(s): Mystery Writers of America (MWA); Romance Writers of America (RWA); Science Fiction & Fantasy Writers of America (SFWA)

Roam Agency (L)
45 Main St, Suite 727, Brooklyn, NY 11201-1076
E-mail: roam@roamagency.com
Web Site: www.roamagency.com
Key Personnel
Founder, Agent & Dir: Anthony Arnove
Founded: 2002
Adult nonfiction & fiction, handles all subsidiary rights. No unsol mss, query first by e-mail. No reading fee.
Titles recently placed: *The Ministry of Utmost Happiness*, Arundhati Roy; *What I Learned in a Thousand Towns*, Dar Williams; *Who Rules the World?*, Noam Chomsky
Foreign Rights: AnatoliaLit Agency (Turkey); BC Agency (Mr Mihai Taru) (Korea); Best Literary & Rights Agency (Korea); Big Apple Agency (Lily Chen & Dr Luc Kwanten) (China, Indonesia, Malaysia, Taiwan, Vietnam); Brandt New Agency (Carina Brandt) (Finland, Iceland, Netherlands, Norway, Sweden); The English Agency (Japan) Ltd (Tsutomu Yawata) (Japan); Paul & Peter Fritz AG Literatur Agentur (Christian Dittus) (Germany, Switzerland); David Grossman Literary Agency (David Grossman) (English-speaking countries outside North America); The Deborah Harris Agency (Rena Rossner) (Israel); International Editors' Co SA (Isabel Monteagudo) (Spanish-speaking countries); Korea Copyright Center Inc (Korea); Nabu International Literary Agency (Silvia Brunelli) (Italy); Prava i prevodi (Nada Popovic) (Albania, Bosnia and Herzegovina, Bulgaria, Croatia, Czechia, Estonia, Hungary, Latvia, Lithuania, North Macedonia, Poland, Romania, Russia, Serbia, Slovakia,

Slovenia, Ukraine); Read n' Right Agency (Nike Davarinou) (Greece); Riff Agency (Laura & Joao Paulo Riff) (Brazil, Portugal)

B J Robbins Literary Agency (L)
5130 Bellaire Ave, North Hollywood, CA 91607
E-mail: robbinsliterary@gmail.com
Key Personnel
Owner & Pres: B J Robbins (AAR)
Founded: 1992
Literary & commercial fiction, general nonfiction. Handle film & TV rights for agency clients only. E-mail queries only. No unsol attachments.
Titles recently placed: *Blood Brothers*, Deanne Stillman; *Elk Head Woman*, Stephen Graham Jones; *Little Bighorn*, John Hough, Jr; *Mapping the Interior*, Stephen Graham Jones; *Shoot for the Moon*, James Donovan; *The Sixth Conspirator*, Max Byrd
Foreign Rights: The Marsh Agency (worldwide exc UK); Abner Stein Agency (UK)
Membership(s): PEN American Center

Roger Williams Agency (L-D)
Division of New England Publishing Associates Inc
17 Paddock Dr, Lawrence Twp, NJ 08648
Mailing Address: PO Box 66066, Lawrenceville, NJ 08648-6066
Tel: 860-973-2439
E-mail: roger@rogerwilliamsagency.com
Web Site: www.rogerwilliamsagency.com
Key Personnel
Agent & Mng Dir: Roger S Williams (AAR)
Founded: 1983
No unsol mss, query first. See web site for submission details.
Foreign Rights: Books Crossing Borders (worldwide)
Membership(s): American Booksellers Association (ABA); The Authors Guild; Organization of American Historians (OAH)

Linda Roghaar Literary Agency LLC (L)
133 High Point Dr, Amherst, MA 01002
Tel: 413-256-1921
E-mail: contact@lindaroghaar.com
Web Site: www.lindaroghaar.com
Key Personnel
Owner & Pres: Linda L Roghaar (AAR)
E-mail: linda@lindaroghaar.com
Founded: 1996
Full service agency handling mainly nonfiction; lifestyle, crafts, religion & spirituality, history, self-help. No romance, horror or science fiction. Manage comprehensive rights. No unsol mss, query with SASE first. No reading fee. Domestic sales commission: 15%.
Titles recently placed: *CatWise*, Pam Johnson-Bennett; *Complete Crochet Course*, Shannon Mullet-Bowlsby; *Cornell '77*, Peter Conners; *East-Meets-West Quilts*, Patricia Belyea; *Home Spa Lab*, Maya Pagan; *Little Book of Celtic Wisdom*, Carl McColman; *Sweaters Every Day*, Amy Herzog; *The Mitten Handbook*, Mary Scott Huff; *The Patterned Home*, Kristin Nicholas

The Roistacher Literary Agency (L)
545 W 111 St, Suite 7J, New York, NY 10025-1965
Tel: 212-222-1405
Key Personnel
Pres: Robert E Roistacher *E-mail:* rer41@columbia.edu
Founded: 1978
General nonfiction, especially journalism, social science & public policy. Literary fiction only from published writers. No unsol mss, query first. For nonfiction, submit prospectus, curricu-

lum vitae, 2 sample chapters, chapter outline & table of contents. No reading fee.
Titles recently placed: *Climate, Clothing, and Agriculture in Prehistory*, Ian Gilligan, Cambridge University Press

The Rosenberg Group (L)
23 Lincoln Ave, Marblehead, MA 01945
Tel: 781-990-1341 *Fax:* 781-990-1344
E-mail: rosenberglitsubmit@icloud.com
Web Site: www.rosenberggroup.com
Key Personnel
Agent: Barbara Collins Rosenberg (AAR)
Founded: 1998
Representing romance & women's fiction; trade nonfiction (check web site for areas of nonfiction interest); college level textbooks for the first & second year courses. No unsol mss, query first via e-mail. Representatives in all foreign markets.
Membership(s): Romance Writers of America (RWA)

Rita Rosenkranz Literary Agency (L)
440 West End Ave, Suite 15D, New York, NY 10024-5358
Tel: 212-873-6333 *Fax:* 212-873-5225
Web Site: www.ritarosenkranzliteraryagency.com
Key Personnel
Agent: Rita Rosenkranz (AAR)
E-mail: rrosenkranz@mindspring.com
Founded: 1990
Nonfiction, adult; no unsol mss, query first with SASE or via e-mail; no fees.
Membership(s): The Authors Guild; Women's Media Group

Jane Rotrosen Agency LLC (L)
85 Broad St, 28th fl, New York, NY 10004
Tel: 212-593-4330 *Fax:* 212-935-6985
Web Site: janerotrosen.com
Key Personnel
Founder: Jane Rotrosen Berkey (AAR)
Agent: Andrea Cirillo *E-mail:* acirillo@janerotrosen.com; Christina Hogrebe *E-mail:* chogrebe@janerotrosen.com; Annelise Robey *E-mail:* arobey@janerotrosen.com; Meg Ruley *E-mail:* mruley@janerotrosen.com; Kathy Schneider; Amy Tannenbaum *E-mail:* atannenbaum@janerotrosen.com
Subs Rts Dir: Sabrina Prestia
Subs Rts Assoc: Hannah Rody-Wright
Global Rts Mgr: Danielle Sickles
E-mail: dsickles@janerotrosen.com
Edit Asst: Rebecca Scherer (AAR)
E-mail: rscherer@janerotrosen.com
Founded: 1974
Fiction & nonfiction. No unsol mss or queries. Query by referral only. Handle film & TV rights. No reading fee. 15% commission in US & CN co-represented abroad & on the West Coast.
Membership(s): The Authors Guild

Regina Ryan Books (L)
251 Central Park W, Suite 7-D, New York, NY 10024
Tel: 212-787-5589
E-mail: queries@reginaryanbooks.com
Web Site: www.reginaryanbooks.com
Key Personnel
Pres: Regina Ryan (AAR) *E-mail:* reginaryan@reginaryanbooks.com
Founded: 1976
Book-length works of nonfiction for adult & juvenile markets. Specialize in narrative nonfiction, journalism, natural history, science (especially the brain), psychology, history, business, popular culture, cooking & food (especially in relation to travel), non-religious contemporary spirituality, wellness, diet & fitness, self-help, parenting, nature, gardening, pets, architecture,

biography, women's issues. No poetry, screenplays or software. To send a proposal, please read the guidelines on the web site & submit via e-mail to queries@reginaryanbooks.com. Please no queries or follow-up by fax or phone. No reading fee. Handle film, TV & foreign rights. Representation in all foreign countries.

Titles recently placed: *Birding New England*, Randi Minetor; *Birdsong for the Curious Naturalist*, Don Kroodsma; *Coves of Departure: Field Notes from the Sea of Cortez*, John S Farnsworth; *Dear Libby: Will You Answer My Questions About Friendship?*, Libby Kiszner; *Death in Acadia National Park*, Randi Minetor; *Death in Rocky Mountain National Park*, Randi Minetor; *Death on Mount Katahdin*, Randi Minetor; *Enemy Child: A Boy in the Japanese American Internment Camps of World War II*, Andrea Warren; *Historic Rocky Mountain National Park*, Randi Minetor; *Rise of the Cajun Mariners: The Race for Big Oil*, Woody Falgoux; *Rotten! Vultures, Beetles and Slime: Nature's Decomposers*, Anita Sanchez; *Smart Ass: How a Donkey Challenged Me to Accept His True Nature and Rediscover My Own*, Margie Winslow; *So You Think You Know Rock and Roll? An In-Depth Q&A Tour of the Revolutionary Dacade 1965-1975*, Peter E Meltzer; *The Complete Career Guide for Introverts*, Jane Finkle; *The Feminine Sixth: Women for the Defense*, Andrea D Lyon; *The Friendly Orange Glow: The Untold Story of the PLATO System and the Dawn of Cyberculture*, Brian Dear; *Wait Till It Gets Dark: A Kid's Guide to Exploring the Night*, Anita Sanchez, George Steele; *What's Wrong With My Marijuana Plant? A Cannabis Grower's Visual Guide to Easy Diagnosis and Organic Remedies*, David Deardorff, Kathryn Wadsworth; *Wild Wine Making: Easy & Adventurous Recipes Going Beyond Grapes*, Richard Bender

Foreign Rights: Books Crossing Borders (worldwide exc UK); Abner Stein Agency (UK & Commonwealth)

Membership(s): The Authors Guild; The Linnaean Society of New York; PEN American Center; Women's Media Group

Victoria Sanders & Associates LLC (L)
440 Buck Rd, Stone Ridge, NY 12484
Tel: 212-633-8811
E-mail: queriesvsa@gmail.com
Web Site: www.victoriasanders.com
Key Personnel
Pres: Victoria Sanders
Agent: Bernadette Baker-Baughman; Jessica Spivey
Founded: 1992
Always interested in new material & welcome all genres: literary & commercial fiction, nonfiction, memoir, women's fiction, thrillers, humor, graphic novels & motivational. No unsol mss, query first. E-mail queries only. Please include first 3 chapters (or about 25 pages) pasted into the body of the e-mail. Consult web site for further information. Handle film & TV rights & translation rights. No reading fees.

Titles recently placed: *Anonymous vs Anonymous*, Gigi Levangie; *As Good As True*, Cheryl Reid; *Black Ink*, Stephanie Stokes Oliver; *Blackbird*, Michael Fiegel; *Can't Stop Won't Stop (young adult ed)*, Jeff Chang; *Comics Will Break Your Heart*, Faith Erin Hicks; *George & Lizzie*, Nancy Pearl; *Go to Sleep, Little Creep*, Ashley Spires, David Quinn; *How to Talk to Your Cat About Gun Safety*, Zachary Auburn; *Mrs Saint and the Defectives*, Julie Lawson Timmer; *My So-Called Super Powers*, Heather Nuhfer; *Pine City*, Barbara Bourland; *Radical Hope*, Carolina De Robertis; *Rust & Stardust*, T Greenwood; *Soar*, Gail Campbell Woolley, Nick Chiles; *The Burning Edge of the World*, Carolina De Robertis; *The Freedom*

Broker, K J Howe; *The Last Mrs Parrish*, Liv Constantine; *The Lost Woman*, Sara Blaedel; *The Post*, Kevin Munoz; *The Undertaker's Daughter*, Sara Blaedel; *The Wife Between Us*, Greer Hendricks, Sarah Pekkanen; *Warrior*, Tee Hanible, Denene Millner; *When They Call You a Terrorist*, Patrisse Cullors, Asha Bandele

Schiavone Literary Agency Inc (L-D)
236 Trails End, West Palm Beach, FL 33413-2135
Tel: 561-966-9294 *Fax:* 561-966-9294
E-mail: profschia@aol.com
Web Site: www.publishersmarketplace.com/members/profschia
Key Personnel
CEO: Dr James Schiavone
Pres (Bronx, NY off): Jennifer DuVall
  E-mail: jendu77@aol.com
EVP (NY off): Kevin McAdams *E-mail:* kvn.mcadams@yahoo.com
Founded: 1996
Fiction & nonfiction, all genres: young adult, scholarly books, textbooks, business, motivational, advertising, marketing. Specialize in celebrity biography & autobiography & memoirs. No poetry or children's picture books. No unsol mss. No queries via phone, fax or post. Accept only e-mail queries consisting of one page (no attachments). No previously published work in any format. Query only one agent at the company. No fees. Commission: 15% domestic, 20% foreign. Representation in foreign markets. Send e-mail queries to individual personnel at their e-mail address noted. Also have offices in New York, NY.

Titles recently placed: *Accused*, Brittany Ducker; *Beautiful Old Dogs*, David Tabatsky; *Blending Families Successfully*, George Glass, MD; *Edwardian Cooking: 80 Recipes Inspired by Downton Abbey's Elegant Meals*, Larry Edwards; *Finding Jack: A Novel*, Gareth Crocker; *Get a Clue: Mystery Devotions for Kids*, Mark Littleton; *Hungry Love: Classy Eating, Trashy Reading*, Cindy Silvert; *The Last Meal: Defending an Accused Mass Murderer*, Dennis Shere; *The Overparenting Epidemic*, George Glass, MD, David Tabatsky; *Through the New Testament: Devotions for Kids*, Mark Littleton; *Trust Me: A Memoir*, George Kennedy; *Unlikely Liberal: Sarah Palin's Curious Record as Alaska's Governor*, Matthew Zencey

Branch Office(s)
Bronx, NY 10463-1139 (Jennifer DuVall only considers books on real estate. Kevin McAdams only considers work on contemporary music)
New York, NY (contact Kevin McAdams for musical entertainment titles, Francine Edelman for all other genres - special interest in business, marketing, advertising & self-help)

Foreign Rights: Chloe Ataroff (Central Europe, France); Asli Ermis (Turkey); Feliz Karaman (Turkey); Hamish Mackaskill (Japan); Radoslav Trenev (Bulgaria, Eastern Europe); Annisa Waharyudisti (Indonesia, Vietnam); Yang Young-Chul (Korea)

Membership(s): National Education Association (NEA)

Wendy Schmalz Agency (L)
402 Union St, Unit 831, Hudson, NY 12534
Tel: 518-672-7697
E-mail: wendy@schmalzagency.com
Web Site: www.schmalzagency.com
Key Personnel
Owner: Wendy Schmalz (AAR)
Founded: 2002
Adult & children's fiction & nonfiction. No unsol mss, e-mail queries only. See web site for submission details.

Titles recently placed: *A Lie For a Lie*, Robin Morrow MacCready; *Caroline: Little House,*

Revisited, Sarah Miller; *Snowbirds*, Crissa-Jean Chappell; *Summer of Salt and Magic*, Katrina Leno; *The White Van*, April Henry; *Threads*, Ami Polonsky; *Train I Ride*, Paul Mosier
Foreign Rights: Rights People (worldwide)

Harold Schmidt Literary Agency (L-D)
415 W 23 St, Suite 6-F, New York, NY 10011
Tel: 212-727-7473
Key Personnel
Pres: Harold D Schmidt (AAR) *E-mail:* hslanyc@aol.com
Specialize in book-length fiction & nonfiction. No unsol mss, query first by e-mail & include up to the first 5 pages of your book embedded in the e-mail; do not send as an attachment. Do not handle young adult, children's or fantasy. Telephone queries not accepted. Do not send material through the mail unless requested. Representatives in Hollywood & in all principal foreign countries.

Susan Schulman Literary Agency LLC (L-D)
454 W 44 St, New York, NY 10036
Tel: 212-713-1633
E-mail: queries@schulmanagency.com; linda@schulmanagency.com (translation & audio rts)
Key Personnel
Owner: Susan Schulman (AAR) *E-mail:* susan@schulmanagency.com
Founded: 1980
Adult book-length genre & literary fiction & nonfiction especially women's studies, biography, psychology & the social sciences. No unsol mss. Query first with SASE or by e-mail. Submit outline & 3 sample chapters. No reading fee. Co-agent in all principal foreign countries. Handles film & TV rights for other agencies & individual titles.

Foreign Rep(s): ACER Agencia Literaria (Spanish Latin America, Spanish-speaking countries); Big Apple Agency Inc (China); The English Agency (Japan) Ltd (Japan); EnterSKorea (Korea); Danny Hong Agency (Korea); Japan UNI Agency Inc (Japan); Kalem Agency (Turkey); Nurcihan Kesim Literary Agency Inc (Turkey); Duran Kim Agency (Korea); Korea Copyright Center (Korea); Agence Michelle Lapautre (France); Leipman AG (Germany); Macadamia Literary Agency (Poland); Piergiorgio Nicolazzini Literary Agency (Italy); Prava i prevodi (Eastern Europe); Sebes & Bisseling Literary Agency (Netherlands, Scandinavia); Shinwon Agency (Korea); Tuttle-Mori Agency Inc (Japan); Silke Weniger Literary Agency (Germany); Eric Yang Agency (Korea); Susanna Zevi Agenzia Letteraria (Italy)

Membership(s): The Authors Guild; The Dramatists Guild of America; Society of Children's Book Writers & Illustrators (SCBWI); Women in Film (WIF); Women's Media Group; Writers Guild of America, East (WGAE)

Laurens R Schwartz, Esquire (L-D)
5 E 22 St, Suite 15-D, New York, NY 10010-5325
Tel: 212-228-2614
Founded: 1981
Full service agency handling all media for all ages worldwide. No fees; standard commissions; WGA Signatory. No unsol mss, CD-ROMs, etc. Query first with synopsis of one project & resume. Also provide information relating to the project having been with other agents or shopped around. Enclose SASE. Require 4-week right of first refusal if request submission of entire project. Handle film, TV & licensing & merchandising rights.
Membership(s): Writers Guild of America (WGA)

S©ott Treimel NY (L)
434 Lafayette St, New York, NY 10003-6943
Tel: 212-505-8353

E-mail: general@scotttreimelny.com
Web Site: scotttreimelny.com; scotttreimelny.
  blogspot.com
Key Personnel
Owner & Pres: Scott Treimel (AAR)
Asst: Christopher R Hoyt *E-mail:* ch@
  scotttreimelny.com
Founded: 1995
Sells & administers intellectual property rights -
  foreign, dramatic, electronic, broadcast, mer-
  chandise, promotion - for children's book creators. Will only consider unsol mss upon recommendations from published authors & editors.
Titles recently placed: *¡Gracias a la Vida!*, Di-
  ane Cohn, Youme Nygyen Lu; *Cadie's Gone*,
  Dianne Warner; *Crimson*, Arthur Slade; *Kaia
  and the Bees*, Maribeth Boelts; *Persian Queen*,
  Barbara Diamond Goldin; *That's Life*, Ame
  Dyckman; *The New Kid Has Fleas*, Ame Dyckman; *The Women Who Caught the Babies*,
  Eloise Greenfield; *Tiny Barbarian*, Ame Dyckman; *Wee Beaties*, Ame Dyckman; *Willa and
  the Bear*, Philomena O'Neil; *You Don't Want a
  Dragon*, Ame Dyckman
Foreign Rep(s): Akcali Copyright (Turkey);
  Bardon Chinese Media (China); Donatalla
  d'Ormesson Agent Litteraire (France); Japan
  UNI Agency Inc (Japan); KCC Korea Copy-
  right Center Inc (KCC) (Korea); Barbara Kuper
  Literarische Agentur + Medienservice (Ger-
  many)
Membership(s): The Authors Guild; PEN Ameri-
  can Center; Society of Children's Book Writers
  & Illustrators (SCBWI)

Scovil Galen Ghosh Literary Agency Inc (L)
276 Fifth Ave, Suite 207, New York, NY 10001
Tel: 212-679-8686
E-mail: info@sgglit.com
Web Site: www.sgglit.com
Key Personnel
Pres: Russell Galen (AAR) *E-mail:* russellgalen@
  sgglit.com
Agent: Ann Behar *E-mail:* annbehar@sgglit.com
Founded: 1993
All types fiction & nonfiction, adult & juvenile.
  Handle film & TV rights. No unsol mss, query
  first. Submit outline & sample chapters. E-
  mailed queries preferred but without attach-
  ments. Does not charge fees.
Foreign Rep(s): Baror International Inc (world-
  wide exc USA)

Lynn Seligman (L)
400 Highland Ave, Upper Montclair, NJ 07043
Tel: 973-783-3631 *Fax:* 973-783-3691
E-mail: seliglit@aol.com
Founded: 1986
Adult & young adult fiction; adult nonfiction.
  Handle film & TV rights through agents in
  Hollywood. Submit letter or e-mail describ-
  ing project with short sample pasted to e-mail
  if desired. No attachments or unsol mss; query
  first with SASE if snail mail.
Titles recently placed: *Stealing Jason Wilde*, Dee
  Ernst; *Thinking Parent, Thinking Child, 2nd
  ed*, Dr. Myrna B. Shure; *Waiting for an Earl
  Like You (Masters of Seduction)*, Alexandra
  Hawkins; *You Can't Always Get the Marquis
  You Want (Masters of Seduction)*, Alexandra
  Hawkins
Foreign Rights: Books Crossing Borders (Betty
  Anne Crawford) (worldwide)
Membership(s): Women's Media Group

Seventh Avenue Literary Agency (L)
2052 124 St, South Surrey, BC V4A 9K3,
  Canada
Tel: 604-538-7252 *Fax:* 604-538-7252
E-mail: info@seventhavenuelit.com
Web Site: www.seventhavenuelit.com

Key Personnel
Pres & Dir: Robert Mackwood
  E-mail: rmackwood@seventhavenuelit.com
Founded: 1974
Nonfiction agency representing international au-
  thors from a wide range of subjects & interests.
  No unsol mss, query first by e-mail; no fees
  charged.
Titles recently placed: *Great Companies Deserve
  Great Boards: A CEO's Guide to the Board-
  room*, Beverly Behan; *Happy Healthy Gut: The
  Natural Diet Solution to Curing IBS and Other
  Chronic Digestive Disorders*, Jennifer Browne;
  *Route 66 Still Kicks: Driving America's Main
  Street*, Rick Antonson; *The Mom Shift: Women
  Share Their Thoughts of Career Success After
  Having Children*, Reva Seth; *Things That Must
  Not Be Forgotten: A Childhood in Wartime
  China (updated)*, Michael David Kwan; *Thrive
  Energy Cookbook: 150 Plant-Based Whole
  Food Recipes*, Brendan Brazier
Foreign Rights: Big Apple Agency Inc (Luc
  Kwantlen) (China, Indonesia, Taiwan); Fritz
  Agency (Christan Dittus) (Germany); Deborah
  Harris Agency (Ilana Kurshan) (Israel); Nur-
  cihan Kesim Literary Agency (Dilek Kaya)
  (Turkey); Simona Kessler Agency (Adriana
  Marinara) (Romania); Korea Copyright Agency
  (Ms MiSook Hong) (Korea); Nova Littera
  Ltd (Daria Pridatkina) (Russia); Kristin Ol-
  son Agency (Czechia); The Riff Agency (Lucia
  Riff) (Brazil, Portugal); Sebes & Bisseling Lit-
  erary Agency (Netherlands)

The Seymour Agency (L-D)
475 Miner Street Rd, Canton, NY 13617
Tel: 239-398-8209
Web Site: www.theseymouragency.com
Key Personnel
Sr Agent: Nicole Resciniti *E-mail:* nicole@
  theseymouragency.com
Agent: Marisa Cleveland *E-mail:* marisa@
  theseymouragency.com
Founded: 1992
Christian romance & women's fiction, nonfiction
  & secular romance.
Membership(s): The Authors Guild; Romance
  Writers of America (RWA); Writers Guild of
  America (WGA); Writers Guild of America,
  East (WGAE)

Charlotte Sheedy Literary Agency Inc (L)
928 Broadway, Suite 901, New York, NY 10010
Tel: 212-780-9800
Web Site: www.sheedylit.com
Key Personnel
Owner: Charlotte Sheedy *E-mail:* charlotte@
  sheedylit.com
Assoc: Evan Brown *E-mail:* evan@sheedylit.com
Agent/Rts & Perms: Joan Rosen *E-mail:* joan@
  sheedylit.com
Agent: Kevin O'Connor *E-mail:* kevin@sheedylit.
  com
Fiction & nonfiction film & TV rights. No unsol
  mss, query first (no screenplays); submit out-
  line & sample chapters; no reading fee. Agents
  in all principal countries.
Titles recently placed: *All the Wrong Questions
  (series)*, Lemony Snicket; *Hurry Up and Wait*,
  Daniel Handler, Maira Kalman; *Meanwhile,
  in San Francisco: The City in its Own Words*,
  Wendy MacNaughton; *The Blood of Emmett
  Till*, Timothy B Tyson; *The Firebrand and the
  First Lady*, Patricia Bell-Scott; *The Gutsy Girl*,
  Caroline Paul, Wendy MacNaughton (illus);
  The Odd Woman and the City, Vivian Gornick;
  The Winner's Kiss, Marie Rutkoski; *Thomas
  Jefferson: Life, Liberty and the Pursuit of Ev-
  erything*, Maira Kalman; *Tyler Makes a Cake!*,
  Tyler Florence; *Viva Frida*, Yuyi Morales
Foreign Rep(s): The English Agency (Japan);
  Agnes Krup (Australia, Germany, Italy, Por-

tugal, Switzerland); Lennart Sane (Netherlands,
  Scandinavia, Spain); Abner Stein Agency (England)

The Robert E Shepard Agency (L)
4804 Laurel Canyon Blvd, Box 592, Valley Vil-
  lage, CA 91607-3717
Web Site: www.shepardagency.com
Founded: 1994
Not currently accepting submissions.

Ken Sherman & Associates (L-D)
1275 N Hayworth, Suite 103, Los Angeles, CA
  90046
Tel: 310-273-8840
E-mail: kenshermanassociates@gmail.com
Web Site: www.kenshermanassociates.com
Key Personnel
Owner & Pres: Ken Sherman
Founded: 1989
Fiction & nonfiction books plus screenplays, tele-
  plays, film & TV rights to books & life rights.
  No unsol mss or screenplays. Accept by re-
  ferral only. Submit outline & minimum three
  sample chapters. No reading fee. International
  Advisory Board member, The Christopher Ish-
  erwood Foundation.
Titles recently placed: *Good Manners for Nice
  People Who Sometimes Say F*ck*, Amy Alkon
Membership(s): American Film Institute Third
  Decade Council; British Academy of Film &
  Television Arts/Los Angeles (BAFTA/LA);
  PEN International

Wendy Sherman Associates Inc (L)
138 W 25 St, Suite 1018, New York, NY 10001
Tel: 212-279-9027
E-mail: submissions@wsherman.com
Web Site: www.wsherman.com
Key Personnel
Founder, Owner & Pres: Wendy Sherman (AAR)
  E-mail: wendy@wsherman.com
Agent: Cherise Fisher *E-mail:* cherise@
  wsherman.com; Kelli Martin; Laura Mazer;
  Nicki Richesin *E-mail:* nicki@wsherman.com
Agency Asst: Marie Michels *E-mail:* marie@
  wsherman.com
Founded: 1999
Represents a wide range of fiction & nonfiction.
  Literary & commercial fiction, including up-
  market women's fiction; Nonfiction includes,
  memoir, narrative nonfiction, health & well-
  ness, gender issues, practical, self-help, popular
  psychology, lifestyle, home & design, fashion.
  No unsol mss, query first with SASE. For fic-
  tion, a letter & synopsis. Paste first 10 pages,
  No attachments. For nonfiction, send proposal
  & 2 sample chapters. See web site for submis-
  sion guidelines: No paper submissions. No poetry, screenplays, mysteries, romance, westerns,
  science fiction, fantasy or children's books.
Titles recently placed: *A Well Behaved Woman*,
  Therese Anne Fowler; *All That's Left of Me*,
  Janis Thomas; *Anxiety: The Missing Stage of
  Grief*, Claire Bidwell Smith; *Crystal Muse -
  Rituals for Intentional Living*, Heather Aski-
  nose, Timmi Jandro; *Elizabeth Webster and the
  Court of the King's Skull*, William Lashner;
  Emma in the Night, Wendy Walker; *Manag-
  ing the Motherload*, Rebekah Boucki; *Mantras
  in Motion*, Eroin Stutland; *Masonda Tifrere*,
  Blend; *Panorama*, Steve Kistulentz; *The Essen-
  tial Oil Hormone Solution*, Dr Mariza Snyder;
  The Kick Ass Single Mom, Emma Johnson; *The
  Recipe Box*, Viola Shipman; *The Stationery
  Shop*, Marjan Kamali; *The Summer Cottage*,
  Viola Shipman; *The Welcome Home Diner*,
  Peggy Lampman
Foreign Rights: Duran Kim Agency (Duran
  Kim) (Korea); Jenny Meyer Literary Agency
  (Jenny Meyer) (worldwide exc Asia); An-
  drew Nurnberg Associates Inc (Whitney Hsu)
  (Taiwan); Andrew Nurnberg Associates Inc

(Jackie Huang) (China); Tuttle-Mori Agency Inc (Japan)
Membership(s): Women's Media Group

Side by Side Literary Productions Inc (L)
145 E 35 St, Suite 7FE, New York, NY 10016
Tel: 212-685-6831
Web Site: sidebysidelit.com
Key Personnel
Founder & Pres: Laurie Bernstein
    E-mail: laurie@sidebysidelit.com
Founded: 2004
Handles general trade fiction & nonfiction as well as select juvenile titles. Specialize in popular health, medicine, self-help, parenting, popular culture, diet & narrative nonfiction. No unsol mss, query first. Will review hard copy & digital submissions. Handles film & TV rights.

Beverley Slopen Literary Agency (L)
131 Bloor St W, Suite 711, Toronto, ON M5S 1S3, Canada
Tel: 416-964-9598 *Fax:* 416-964-9598
Web Site: www.slopenagency.com
Key Personnel
Owner: Beverley Slopen *E-mail:* beverley@ slopenagency.ca
Founded: 1973
Serious fiction & nonfiction. No children's books, illustrated books, science fiction or fantasy. No software, no film or TV rights handled. Query letter & brief proposal sent by e-mail. Not taking on many new clients.
Titles recently placed: *A Trial in Venice*, Roberta Rich; *Albatross a Novel*, Terry Fallis; *Beyond Intelligence: Secrets for Raising Happily Productive Kids*, Dona Matthews, Joanne Foster; *Butterfly of Venus*, Susan Ferrier MacKay; *City of Fallen Angels*, Howard Engel; *Dead Reckoning*, Ken McGoogan; *Is Work Killing You?: A Doctor's Prescription for Treating Workplace Stress*, David Posen, MD; *Just Like Family*, Kate Hilton; *Life Class*, Ann Charney; *Mr Selden's Map of China: Decoding the Secrets of a Vanished Cartographer*, Tim Brook; *Music for Love or War*, Martyn Burke; *No Relation*, Terry Fallis; *Perdita*, Hilary Scharper; *The Great State*, Tim Brook; *The Home for Unwanted Girls*, Joanna Goodman; *The Memory Clinic*, Tiffany Chow
Foreign Rep(s): Julio F-Yanez Agencia Literaria SL (Spain); Paul & Peter Fritz AG (Germany); The Grayhawk Agency (Gray Tan) (China); David Grossman Literary Agency Ltd (David Grossman) (UK); The Deborah Harris Agency (Israel); International Literatuur Bureau (Netherlands); The Italian Literary Agency srl (Italy); JLM Literary Agency (Greece); Kalem (Turkey); Katai & Bolza Literary Agency (Hungary); Alexander Korzhenevski (Russia); Agence Michelle Lapautre (France); Licht & Burr Literary Agency (Scandinavia); Agencia Riff (Lucia Riff) (Brazil); Tuttle-Mori Agency Inc (Japan); Eric Yang Agency (Korea)

Michael Snell Literary Agency (L)
PO Box 1206, Truro, MA 02666-1206
Tel: 508-349-3718
Web Site: www.michaelsnellagency.com
Key Personnel
Chmn & CEO: Michael Snell
EVP: Patricia Snell *E-mail:* patricia@ michaelsnellagency.com
Founded: 1978
Adult nonfiction; all levels of business & management from popular trade to professional reference; legal, medical, health, psychology, self-help & how-to books; animals & pets; women's issues in business, family & society; popular science & business; technical & scientific; professional & general computer books; parenting & relationships; project development

& rewrite services. Welcome new authors. No unsol mss, query first. Submit outline, synopsis & up to 50 sample pages with SASE. Publication *How to Write a Book Proposal* available upon request with SASE, or consult Michael Snell's book *From Book Idea to Bestseller* (Prima Publishing). Write for information on purchasing a model book proposal. Consider new clients on an exclusive basis. No reading fee, but do arrange for developmental editors & ghostwriters who do charge a fee.
Titles recently placed: *Career Courage*, Katie C Kelley; *Don't Pay for Your MBA*, Laurie Pickard; *Excuse Me: A Guide to Business Etiquette*, Rosanne Thomas; *Finding Peace in Your Heart When Your Heart is in Pieces*, Paul Coleman; *Lead Right for Your Company Type*, William Schneider; *Springboard: Launching Your Personal Search for Success*, G Richard Shell; *Sun House*, David James Duncan; *The Long Weeping*, Jessie van Eerden; *What Keeps Leaders Up at Night: Recognizing and Resolving Your Most Troubling Management Issues*, Nicole Lipkin

Sobel Weber Associates Inc (L)
146 E 19 St, New York, NY 10003-2404
Tel: 212-420-8585
E-mail: info@sobelweber.com
Web Site: www.sobelweber.com
Key Personnel
Principal: Nat Sobel; Judith Weber
Founded: 1970
General fiction & nonfiction. No unsol mss, query first with SASE, no electronic submissions. No reading fee. Handle film, TV & foreign rights; serialization & audio rights. Representatives on the West Coast & in all major foreign countries. Consult web site for submission guidelines & client list.
Titles recently placed: *Bishop's War*, Rafael Amadeus Hines; *The Refugees*, Viet Thanh Nguyen; *Trajectory: Stories*, Richard Russo
Foreign Rights: Akcali Copyright Agency (Turkey); Agencia Literaria Carmen Balcells SA (Maribel Luque) (Spain); Tassy Barham Associates (Brazil, Portugal); Paul & Peter Fritz Agency (Germany); The Deborah Harris Agency (Israel); Katai & Bolza (Hungary); Agence Michelle Lapautre (France); Andrew Nurnberg Associates International Ltd (China, Taiwan); Kristin Olson Agency (Czechia); Prava i prevodi (Eastern Europe exc Czechia, Hungary & Slovenia, Greece, Russia); Santachiara Literary Agency (Italy); Sobel Weber Associates Inc NY (Denmark, Finland, Netherlands, Norway, Sweden); The Abner Stein Agency (UK); Tuttle-Mori Agency Inc (Indonesia, Japan, Thailand, Vietnam); Eric Yang Agency (Korea)

Spectrum Literary Agency (L)
320 Central Park W, Suite 1-D, New York, NY 10025
Tel: 212-362-4323 *Fax:* 212-362-4562
Web Site: www.spectrumliteraryagency.com
Key Personnel
Pres & Agent: Eleanor Wood
Agent: Justin Bell
Founded: 1976
Science fiction, mysteries, thrillers, horror & fantasy. No unsol mss, query first with letter, synopsis, first 10 pages & SASE. No reading fee. Agents in all principal foreign countries.
Titles recently placed: *Penric's Demon*, Lois McMaster Bujold; *Spear of Light*, Brenda Cooper; *The Genius Plague*, David Walton
Foreign Rights: Big Apple Agency Inc (Mr Luc Kwanten) (China); Book Cosmos Agency (Mihai Taru) (Korea); The Book Publishers Association of Israel (Dalia Ever-Hadani) (Israel); Julio F-Yanez Agencia Literaria SL (Montse Yanez) (Portugal, Spain); Graal Lit-

erary Agency (Lukasz Wrobel) (Poland); Japan UNI Agency Inc (Miko Yamanouchi) (Japan); Katai & Bolza Literary Agents (Peter Bolza) (Hungary); Katai & Bolza Literary Agents (Reka Bartha) (Croatia, Serbia, Slovenia); Nurcihan Kesim Literary Agency Ltd (Dilek Kayi) (Turkey); Agence Litteraire Lenclud (Anne Lenclud & Pierre Lenclud) (France); Piergiorgio Nicolazzini Literary Agency (Maura Solinas) (Italy); Nova Littera Ltd (Konstantin Palchikov & Sergei Cheredov) (Russia); Andrew Nurnberg Associates Sofia (Anna Droumeva & Mira Droumeva) (Romania); Andrew Nurnberg Associates Sofia (Mira Droumeva) (Bulgaria); Kristin Olson Literary Agency SRO (Kristin Olson & Tereza Dubova) (Czechia); Prava i prevodi (Russia); Read n Right Agency (Nike Davarinou) (Greece); Thomas Schlueck GmbH (Thomas Schlueck & Franka Zastrow) (Germany); Sebes & Bisseling Literary Agency (Lester Hekking & Jeanine Langenberg) (Netherlands)
Membership(s): Mystery Writers of America (MWA); Science Fiction & Fantasy Writers of America (SFWA)

The Spieler Agency (L)
27 W 20 St, Suite 302, New York, NY 10011
Tel: 212-757-4439 *Fax:* 212-333-2019
E-mail: spieleragency@spieleragency.com
Key Personnel
Agent: Joseph Spieler
Nonfiction & literary fiction; thrillers, children's books including middle grade, young adult & new adult. Areas of interest include: environmental issues, business; women's issues; natural history & science for religious studies, psychology; health; history; biography. No unsol mss, query first with letter (prefer e-mail), first chapter/contents or detailed proposal. No phone queries. Submit author background, description of work & sample chapter with SASE. Handle film & TV rights only for book clients. No reading fee, only commissions.
Titles recently placed: *Escape From Mr Lemoncello's Library*, Chris Grabenstein; *Pity the Billionaire: The Hard-Times Swindle and the Unlikely Comeback of the Right*, Thomas Frank; *The $14 Billion Year*, Anne Thompson; *The Financial Crisis Inquiry Report*; *The Lost Mona Lisa: The Extraordinary True Story of the Greatest Art Theft in History*, R A Scotti
Foreign Rights: The Marsh Agency (Continental Europe); Abner Stein Agency (England)

Philip G Spitzer Literary Agency Inc (L)
50 Talmage Farm Lane, East Hampton, NY 11937
Tel: 631-329-3650 *Fax:* 631-329-3651
Web Site: www.spitzeragency.com
Key Personnel
Pres: Philip Spitzer (AAR) *E-mail:* philip. spitzer@spitzeragency.com
EVP & Agent: Anne-Lise Spitzer (AAR)
    E-mail: annelise.spitzer@spitzeragency.com
Mng Agent: Lukas Ortiz (AAR) *E-mail:* lukas. ortiz@spitzeragency.com
Off Mgr: Kim Lombardini (AAR) *E-mail:* kim. lombardini@spitzeragency.com
Founded: 1969
Literary fiction, suspense/thriller, general nonfiction, sports, politics, social issues, biography, film & TV rights. No unsol mss, query first with SASE, submit outline & sample chapters. No reading fee, photocopying fee. Foreign rights agents in all major markets.
Titles recently placed: *A Private Cathedral*, James Lee Burke; *Big Man's Daughter*, Owen Fitzstephens; *Fair Warning*, Michael Connelly; *Galway Girl*, Ken Bruen; *Good Man Gone Bad*, Gar Anthony Haywood; *Green Sun*, Kent Anderson; *Last Call*, Beverly Lowry; *Rain*

Will Come, Thomas Holgate; *The Better Sister*, Alafair Burke

Foreign Rights: Big Apple Agency Inc (Luc Kwanten & Lily Chen) (China, Malaysia, Taiwan, Vietnam); Big Apple Agency Inc (Erica Zhou) (Indonesia); ELST Literary Agency (Kalina Stefanova) (Bulgaria); The Deborah Harris Agency (Efrat Lev) (Israel); International Editors' Co (Jennifer Brooke Hoge) (Latin America exc Brazil, Portugal, Spain); The Italian Literary Agency SRL (Italy); KALEM (Sedef Ilgic) (Turkey); Agence Michelle Lapautre (Catherine Lapautre) (France); Mohrbooks AG Literary Agency (Sebastian Ritcsher & Annelie Geissler) (Austria, Germany, Switzerland); Prava i prevodi (Anna Milenkovic) (Russia); Prava i prevodi (Milena Kaplarevic) (Eastern Europe exc Russia); Agencia Literaria Riff (Laura Riff & Joao Paulo Riff) (Brazil); Marianne Schoenbach Literary Agency (Netherlands); Alexander Schwarz Literary Agency (Scandinavia); Abner Stein Agency (Caspian Dennis) (UK); Tuttle-Mori Agency Inc (Misa Morikawa) (Japan); Eric Yang Agency (Sue Yang) (Korea)

Membership(s): The Authors Guild

Nancy Stauffer Associates (L)

30 Corbin Dr, Suite 1203, Darien, CT 06820

Mailing Address: PO Box 1203, Darien, CT 06820

Tel: 203-202-2500

Web Site: www.publishersmarketplace.com/members/nstauffer/

Key Personnel

Owner: Nancy Stauffer Cahoon *E-mail:* nancy@staufferliterary.com

Founded: 1989

Literary fiction, narrative nonfiction & young adult fiction. No mysteries, science fiction, fantasy, romance novels, screenplays or children's picture books. Query by e-mail only, with first 10 pages of your work. No attachments. Agents in all foreign markets.

Titles recently placed: *Our Souls at Night*, Kent Haruf; *You Don't Have to Say You Love Me: A Memoir*, Sherman Alexie

Membership(s): The Authors Guild

Michael Steinberg Literary Agent (L)

PO Box 274, Glencoe, IL 60022-0274

Tel: 847-626-1000

E-mail: michael14steinberg@comcast.net

Key Personnel

Principal: Michael Steinberg

Founded: 1980

Book-length fiction (mystery, science fiction) & nonfiction (business topics). No unsol mss, query first. Submit outline & first 3 chapters (hard copy). Will read only by personal reference from represented author or editor.

Titles recently placed: *All About Day Trading*, Jake Bernstein

Sterling Lord Literistic Inc (L)

115 Broadway, Suite 1602, New York, NY 10006

Tel: 212-780-6050 *Fax:* 212-780-6095

E-mail: info@sll.com

Web Site: www.sll.com

Key Personnel

Co-Chmn: Sterling Lord; Peter Matson

COO: Nadyne Pike

Pres: Philippa Brophy (AAR)

EVP & Mng Partner: Laurie Liss (AAR)

VP: Celeste Fine; Douglas Stewart

Agent: Elizabeth Bewley; Jessica Friedman; Robert Guinsler; Sarah Landis; Alison MacKeen; Neeti Madan; Martha Millard; Jim Rutman (AAR); Jenny Stephens

Assoc Agent: Mary Krienke

Foreign Rts Mgr & Assoc Agent: Danielle Bukowski

Foreign Rts Mgr: Szilvia Molnar

Founded: 1952

Fiction & nonfiction; film & TV rights. No unsol mss, query first; submit outline & sample chapters with SASE. No reading fee.

Foreign Rep(s): AnatoliLit Agency (Amy Spangler) (Turkey); Agence Eliane Benisti (Eliane Benisti) (France); Book/Lab Ltd (Agata Zabowska) (Poland); Paul & Peter Fritz Literary Agency (Antonia Fritz) (Austria, Germany); The Grayhawk Agency (Gray Tan) (China, Taiwan); The Grayhawk Agency (Itzel Hsu) (Indonesia, Thailand, Vietnam); The Deborah Harris Agency (Geula Geurts) (Israel); Danny Hong Agency (Danny Hong) (Korea); The Italian Literary Agency (Mariavittoria Puccetti) (Italy); JLM Literary (John Moukakos) (Greece); MB Agencia Literaria (Monica Martin) (Andorra, Catalonia, Portugal, Spain); Andrew Nurnberg Associates Baltic (Tatjana Zoldnere) (Estonia, Latvia, Lithuania, Ukraine); Andrew Nurnberg Associates Budapest (Blanka Enyi) (Croatia, Hungary); Andrew Nurnberg Associates Prague (Marta Soukopova) (Czechia, Slovakia, Slovenia); Andrew Nurnberg Associates Sofia (Mira Droumeva) (Albania, Bulgaria, North Macedonia, Romania, Serbia); Riff Agency (Laura Riff) (Brazil); Marianne Schoenbach Literary Agency (Marianne Schoenbach) (Netherlands); Tuttle-Mori Agency Inc (Ken Mori) (Japan); The Van Lear Agency (Liz Van Lear) (Russia)

Stimola Literary Studio Inc (L)

308 Livingston Ct, Edgewater, NJ 07020

Tel: 201-945-9353 *Fax:* 201-945-9353; 201-490-5920

E-mail: info@stimolaliterarystudio.com

Web Site: www.stimolaliterarystudio.com

Key Personnel

Pres: Rosemary B Stimola (AAR) *Tel:* 201-945-9565 *E-mail:* rosemary@stimolaliterarystudio.com

Dir, Opers: Nicholas Croce *Tel:* 201-248-3175 *E-mail:* nick@stimolaliterarystudio.com

Sr Agent: Erica Rand Silverman *Tel:* 917-734-3943 *E-mail:* erica@stimolaliterarystudio.com

Agent & Rts Dir: Allison Hellegers

Agent: Peter K Ryan *Tel:* 201-362-9091 *E-mail:* pete@stimolaliterarystudio.com; Adriana Stimola *Tel:* 617-784-8770 *E-mail:* adriana@stimolaliterarystudio.com

Assoc Agent: Allison Remcheck *Tel:* 216-704-5521 *E-mail:* allison@stimolaliterarystudio.com

Founded: 1997

Specialize in fiction & nonfiction, preschool through young adult in all formats, including graphic. Also representing cookbooks, farm to table, lifestyle. Queries via e-mail preferred. Respond only to those queries we wish to pursue further. No unsol attachments. See web site for submission guidelines. No fees.

Titles recently placed: *Bear Goes Sugaring*, Maxwell Eaton III; *Bear Island*, Matthew Cordell; *Bearmouth*, Liz Hyder; *Blue Barry and Pancakes*, Dan Abdo, Jason Patterson; *City Spies (series)*, James Ponti; *Dasher*, Matt Tavares; *Deposing Nathan*, Zack Smedley; *Donut Feed the Squirrels*, Mika Song; *Fell of Dark*, Caleb Roehrig; *Fly By Night*, Tara O'Connor; *Hunting November*, Adriana Mather; *I Am Love*, Susan Verde, Peter Reynolds; *Lupe Wong Won't Dance*, Donna Barba Higuera; *Mabel*, Rowboat Watkins; *Meet Me In Another Life*, Catriona Silvey; *Monsterstreet (series)*, J H Reynolds; *One of Us Is Next*, Katherine McManus; *Pitter Patterns*, Joyce Hesselberth; *The Ballad of Songbirds and Snakes*, Suzanne Collins; *The Boy Who Loved Infinity*, Amy Alznauer; *The Magic of Mindset*, Johanna Wright; *Ways to Make Sunshine*, Renee Watson

Foreign Rep(s): Intercontinental Literary Agency (translation); Schleuck Agency (Germany)

Foreign Rights: Rights People (UK)

Membership(s): American Library Association (ALA); The Authors Guild; PEN American Center; Society of Children's Book Writers & Illustrators (SCBWI)

Stonesong (L)

270 W 39 St, Suite 201, New York, NY 10018

Tel: 212-929-4600

E-mail: editors@stonesong.com

Web Site: www.stonesong.com

Key Personnel

Partner & Literary Agent: Alison Fargis

Partner & Prodn Servs: Ellen Scordato

EVP & Literary Agent: Judy Linden

Contracts Mgr & Literary Agent: Madelyn Burt

Literary Agent: Leila Campoli; Melissa Edwards; Alyssa Jennette; Emmanuelle Morgan; Maria Ribas; Adrienne Rosado

Founded: 1979

Representing nonfiction & fiction, including middle grade, young adult & adult titles. Create & develop commercial nonfiction & popular reference books on many subjects: cooking, business, how-to, self-help, memoir, beauty & fashion. Complete trade hardcover, paperback & ebook development, from concept to delivery. Consultants on backlist exploitation, acquisitions, publicity planning & editorial systems. Custom publishing for professional associations & magazines.

No unsol mss, query first. Welcome electronic queries for fiction & nonfiction. Please review agent biographies & submit query addressed to one agent to submissions@stonesong.com. Include the word "query" in the subject line. Include first chapter or first 10 pages of your work, pasted into the body of the e-mail. No attachments. Request for more material within 12 weeks if interested.

Titles recently placed: *A Common Table*, Cynthia Chen McTernan; *A Craftsman's Legacy*, Eric Gorges; *A Lady's Guide to Gossip and Murder*, Dianne Freeman; *ALFA (series)*, Milly Taiden; *All These Monsters*, Amy Tintera; *Amy Wu and the Perfect Bao*, Kat Zhang; *Baking Gold*, Jami Curl; *Batch Cocktails*, Maggie Hoffman; *Beyond Selling*, David Hoffeld; *Beyond the Point*, Claire Gibson; *Big Dreams, Daily Joys: Set goals. Get things done. Make time for what matters.*, Elise Blaha Cripe; *Bigger Bolder Baking: A Fearless Approach to Baking Anytime, Anywhere*, Gemma Stafford; *Bloom Wild*, Bari Ackerman; *Brand New Art from China*, Barbara Pollack; *Cereal City Guide: London*, Rosa Park, Rich Stapleton; *Cereal City Guide: New York*, Rosa Park, Rich Stapleton; *Cereal City Guide: Paris*, Rosa Park, Rich Stapleton; *Clean Mama's Guide to a Healthy Home: The Simple, Room-by-Room Plan for a Natural Home*, Becky Rapinchuk; *Craft the Rainbow*, Brittany Watson Jepson; *Damn Delicious Meal Prep: 115 Easy Recipes for Low-Calorie, High-Energy Living*, Chungah Rhee; *Dan, Unmasked*, Chris Negron; *Designology: How to Find Your PlaceType and Align Your Life With Design*, Sally Augustin; *Exceptional*, Dan Cable; *Find Momo Across Europe*, Andrew Knapp; *Finn and the Intergalactic Lunchbox*, Michael Buckley; *Fortuna*, Kristyn Merbeth; *From Freezer to Cooker: 75+ Whole Foods Freezer Meals for Slow Cookers and Instant Pots*, Rachel Tiemeyer, Polly Conner; *Get Off Your Acid: 7 Steps in 7 Days to Lose Weight, Fight Inflammation, and Reclaim Your Health and Energy*, Dr Daryl Gioffre; *Getting It*, Allison Moon; *Great Escapes!: True Stories of Bold Breakouts, Daring Disappearances and Death-Defying Adventures*, Michael Burgan, et al; *Half Life*, Lillian Clark; *Hello, Cookie Dough*, Kristen Tomlan; *How to Do Things:*

A Timeless Guide to a Simpler Life, William Campbell; *How to Get Ahead: A 6-Step System to Unleash Your Personal Brand and Build a World-Class Network So Opportunities Come To You*, Zak Slayback; *How to Get Sh*t Done: Why Women Need to Stop Doing Everything So They Can Achieve Anything*, Erin Falconer; *I Am Doug the Pug*, Leslie Mosier; *I Have Always Been Me*, Precious Brady-Davis; *I Just Haven't Met You Yet*, Tracy Strauss; *I Will Be Fierce*, Bea Birdsong; *Immoral Code*, Lillian Clark; *In the Company of Women*, Grace Bonney; *Into the Crooked Place*, Alexandra Christo; *It's Not You, It's Your Workplace*, Michelle King; *Lenny the Lobster Can't Stay for Dinner*, Finn Buckley, Michael Buckley; *Lightly: How to Live a Simple, Serene, and Stress-free Life*, Francine Jay; *Listen Like You Mean It: Building Better Relationships with Empathic Listening*, Ximena Vengoechea; *Lizzy Legend*, Matt Smith; *Love and Lemons Everyday*, Jeanine Donofrio; *Lucky Thirteen*, Barbara Ferrer; *Me, Myself & Ideas*, Carrie Anton, Jessica Nordskog; *Mending Matters*, Katrina Rodabaugh; *More Than Just a Pretty Face*, Syed Masood; *Nomad: Designing a Home for Escape and Adventure*, Emma Reddington; *On the Modern Farm: Portraits and Stories from the Small Farm Movement*, Aliza Eliazarov; *Once Upon a Chef, the Cookbook: 100 Tested, Perfected, and Family-Approved Recipes*, Jennifer Segal; *Own Your Weird: An Oddly Effective Way for Finding Happiness in Work, Life, and Love*, Jason Zook; *Paris in Stride: An Insider's Walking Guide*, Jessie Kanelos, Sarah Moroz; *Patterns of India*, Christine Chitnis; *Pavi Sharma's Guide to Going Home*, Bridget Farr; *Plant Tribe: How to Live Happily Ever After with Plants*, Igor Josifovic, Judith de Graaff; *Platform: The Art and Science of Personal Branding*, Cynthia Johnson; *Procrastibaking*, Erin Gardner; *Pug Pals: Yay for Vacay*, Flora Ahn; *Real Queer America: LGBT Stories from Red States*, Samantha Allen; *Ruffhouse: From the Streets of Philly to the Top of the '90s Hip Hop Charts*, Chris Schwartz; *Ruined Series*, Amy Tintera; *Sam's First Word*, Bea Birdsong; *Season: Big Flavors, Beautiful Food*, Nik Sharma; *Silence is a Sense*, Layla AlAmmar; *Start Simple*, Lukas Volger; *Sweet Laurel Savory*, Laurel Gallucci, Claire Thomas; *Terrain: Ideas and Inspirations for Decorating the Home and Garden*, Terrain; *The 28-Day Smoothie Project*, Catherine McCord; *The Art of Change: Simple Steps to Unleash Your Life*, Andy Anderson; *The Bad Muslim Discount*, Syed Masood; *The Cooks Atelier: Recipes, Techniques, and Stories from our French Cooking School*, Marjorie Taylor, Kendall Smith Franchini; *The Essential Compendium of Dad Jokes: The Best of the Worst Dad Jokes for the Painfully Punny Parent*, Thomas Nowak; *The Essential Instant Pot Keto Cookbook*, Casey Thaler; *The Many Lives of James Bond*, Mark Edlitz; *The Memory of Forgotten Things*, Kat Zhang; *The Mystery of Black Hollow Lane*, Julia Nobel; *The New Paris: The People, Places, and Ideas Fueling a Movement*, Lindsey Tramuta; *The Pact We Made*, Layla AlAmmar; *The Queens' English: The Dictionary for LGBTQIA+ Lingo*, Chloe Davis; *The Restaurant Diet: How to Eat Out Every Night and Still Lose Weight*, Fred Bollaci, Dick Smothers; *The Summer I Flew Away*, Lola St Vil; *The Ultimate Instant Pot Cookbook*, Coco Morante; *The Vegan Instant Pot Cookbook*, Coco Morante; *The Vintage Baker*, Jessie Sheehan; *This Time Around*, Barbara Ferrer; *Thorn*, Intisar Khanani; *To Kill a Kingdom*, Alexandra Christo; *Turkish Nomad: The Intellectual Journey of Talat S Halman*, Jayne L Warner; *Wild Words: Rituals, Routines, and Rhythms for Braving the Writer's Path*, Nicole Gulotta; *Woman of Color*, LaTonya Yvette; *Yes Way Rose*, Erica Blumenthal, Nikki Huganir
Foreign Rep(s): Baror International (Danny Baror); The Fielding Agency (Whitney Lee); Hodgman Literary (Sandy Hodgman)
Membership(s): American Book Producers Association (ABPA)

Straus Literary (L)
77 Van Ness Ave, Suite 101, San Francisco, CA 94102
Tel: 646-843-9950
Web Site: www.strausliterary.com
Key Personnel
Agent: Jonah Straus *E-mail:* jonah@strausliterary.com
Founded: 2003
Focus on literary fiction, historical fiction, international literature, literary mystery & thriller, cookbooks, food & travel narratives, social issues, popular science, history, international affairs, biography, memoir.
Straus Literary acts as English sub-agent for: Mertin Agency (Nicole Witt), Germany.
Operates in San Francisco & New York.
Titles recently placed: *Counternarratives*, John Keene; *Crow-Blue*, Adriana Lisboa, Alison Entrekin; *Death & Co (Cocktail Book)*, David Kaplan, Nick Fauchald; *Early: What Premature Birth Teaches about Being Human*, Sarah DiGregorio; *Ingredient: The True Elements of Cooking*, Ali Bouzari; *Molly on the Range*, Molly Yeh; *Peru: The Cookbook*, Gaston Acurio; *Poison Spring: The Secret History of the EPA*, Evaggelos Vallianatos; *Smuggler's Cove: Cocktails, Rum and the Cult of Tiki*, Martin Cate; *The Cage: The Fight for Sri Lanka and the Last Days of the Tamil Tigers*, Gordon Weiss; *The Collected Poems of Carlos Drummond de Andrade*, Carlos Drummond de Andrade, Richard Zenith; *The Cruelest Gift: Inherited Disease in the Age of DNA*, Clark Blaise; *The Descartes Highlands*, Eric Gamalinda; *The House in Smyrna*, Tatiana Salem Levy; *The La Cocina Cookbook*, Caleb Zigas and Leticia Landa; *The Lowering Days*, Gregory Brown
Foreign Rights: AK Agency (Alex Korzhenevski) (Baltic States, Russia, Ukraine); Amo Agency (Amo Noh) (Korea); Silvia Bastos Agency (Pau Centellas) (Latin America exc Brazil, Portugal, Spain); Big Apple Agency (Luc Kwanten) (China, Southeast Asia, Thailand); DS Budapest (Szabolcs Torok) (Hungary); ELST Literary Agency (Kalina Stefanova) (Bulgaria); The English Agency (Tsutomu Yawata) (Japan); Graal Literary Agency (Filip Wojiechowski) (Poland); Deborah Harris Agency (Rena Rossner) (Israel); Iris Literary (Catherine Fragou) (Greece); Kalem Agency (Sedef Ligic) (Turkey); Simona Kessler International Copyright Agency (Adriana Marina) (Romania); Agence Michelle Lapautre (Catherine Lapautre) (France, Quebec, CN, Switzerland (French-speaking)); Clementina Liuzzi Agency (Italy); Michael Meller Agency (Regina Seitz) (Austria, Germany, Switzerland (German-speaking)); Andrew Nurnberg, Prague (Petra Tobiskova) (Czechia, Slovakia); Plima Literary (Vuk Perisic) (Albania, Bosnia and Herzegovina, Croatia, Montenegro, North Macedonia, Serbia); Riff Agency (Joao Paulo Riff) (Brazil); Lennart Sane Agency (Philip Sane) (Netherlands, Scandinavia)

Robin Straus Agency Inc (L)
229 E 79 St, Suite 5A, New York, NY 10075
Tel: 212-472-3282 *Fax:* 212-472-3833
E-mail: info@robinstrausagency.com
Web Site: www.robinstrausagency.com
Key Personnel
Pres: Robin Straus (AAR) *E-mail:* robin@robinstrausagency.com

Jr Agent: Katelyn Hales
Founded: 1983
High quality fiction & nonfiction. Handle film & TV rights for represented clients' books. Foreign agents in all major foreign countries. No unsol mss, query first. No screenplays, plays, romance, westerns, horror, children's or poetry. E-mail query with outline or synopsis, short author biography & sample chapters; or send brief e-mail letter describing book project (no downloads). No reading fees.
Foreign Rights: AnatoliaLit Agency (Turkey); Deborah Harris (Israel); JLM Literary Agency (Greece); Andrew Nurnberg Associates (worldwide exc Greece, Japan, Korea, Thailand & Turkey); Tuttle-Mori Agency Inc (Japan, Thailand); Eric Yang Agency (Korea)

Strothman Agency LLC (L)
63 E Ninth St, 10X, New York, NY 10003
E-mail: info@strothmanagency.com
Web Site: www.strothmanagency.com
Key Personnel
Principal & Agent: Wendy Strothman (AAR)
Agent: Lauren E MacLeod (AAR)
Founded: 2003
Dedicated to promoting authors of significant books through the entire publishing cycle. No unsol mss, query first by e-mail only. Submit query letter, synopsis & first 10 pages to strothmanagency@gmail.com, no attachments. Submissions will be acknowledged by an autoresponder. No fees charged.
Titles recently placed: *American Madness*, Amy Ellis Nutt; *Before She Ignites (Trilogy)*, Jodi Meadows; *Eight Bears: Close and Closer Encounters Around the World*, Gloria Dickie; *Hunting for Hamilton*, Joanne Freeman; *Killers on the Trail: Love, Murder, and the Quest for Justice in America's Wild Places*, Kathryn Miles; *Tell Me How You Really Feel*, Aminah Mae Safi; *We Are Lost and Found*, Helene Dunbar
Membership(s): The Authors Guild; Copyright Clearance Center (CCC)

Carolyn Swayze Literary Agency Ltd (L)
7360 137 St, Suite 319, Surrey, BC V3W 1A3, Canada
Tel: 604-503-3895
E-mail: reception@swayzeagency.com
Web Site: www.swayzeagency.com
Key Personnel
Pres: Carolyn Swayze *E-mail:* carolyn@swayzeagency.com
Founded: 1994
Representing emerging & established authors of literary fiction, some commercial fiction, nonfiction, middle grade & young adult books. No science fiction, no self-help, no picture books. An inquiry must include an author bio, a short description of the available project & short sample. No fees charged. Authors may consult web site for current submission guidelines. Mostly Canadian authors & US Pacific Northwest.
Titles recently placed: *A Place to Call Home*, Jen Sookfong Lee; *Blackberry Cove*, Roxanne Snopek; *Bravo Beavers*, Frances Backhouse; *Buffy Sainte-Marie: The Authorized Biography*, Andrea Warner; *Chinese New Year: A Celebration for Everyone*, Jen Sookfong Lee; *Five Ways to Disappear*, R M Greenaway; *Generation Robot*, Terri Favro; *Going the Distance*, William Steele; *River of Lies*, R M Greenaway; *Tangled On Tour*, Alexandra Holden; *The Animals of Chinese New Year*, Jen Sookfong Lee; *The Chocolate Comeback*, Roxanne Snopek; *The Court of Better Fiction*, Debra Komar; *The Forbidden Purple City*, Philip Huynh; *The Kitchen: A journey through time to find the perfect design*, John Ota; *The Shadow List*, Jen Sookfong Lee; *To Make a Prairie*, Katie

Welch; *You Don't Have to Die in the End*, Anita Daher

Foreign Rep(s): L'Autre Agence (Corinne Marotte) (France)

Foreign Rights: AM Heath & Co Ltd, Authors' Agents (UK); AnatoliaLit Agency (Turkey); L'Autre Agence (France); Chinese Connection Agency (China, Taiwan); Paul Christoph Literary Agency (Brazil, Portugal); Silvia Donzelli Agency (Stefania Fietta) (Italy); ELST Literary Agency (Kalina Stefanova) (Bulgaria); International Copyright Agency (Simona Kessler) (Moldova, Romania); Duran Kim Agency (Korea); Lex Copyright (Hungary); Mohr Books (Germany); Andrew Nurnberg Associates (Baltic States); O A Literary Agency (Greece); Sebes & Bisseling Literary Agency (Denmark, Finland, Netherlands, Norway, Scandinavia, Sweden); Maria Starz-Kanska (Poland); Livia Stioia Literary Agency (Albania, Belarus, Bosnia and Herzegovina, Croatia, Georgia, North Macedonia, Russia, Serbia, Slovakia, Slovenia, Ukraine); Tuttle-Mori Agency Inc (Japan)

Tessler Literary Agency LLC (L)
27 W 20 St, Suite 1003, New York, NY 10011
Tel: 212-242-0466
Web Site: www.tessleragency.com
Key Personnel
Pres: Michelle Tessler (AAR)
Founded: 2004
Full service boutique agency dedicated to writers of high quality fiction & nonfiction. Nonfiction list includes narrative, popular science, memoir, history, psychology, business, biography, food & travel. In fiction, represents literary, women's & commercial. No unsol mss, query first via web form. No fees charged.
Titles recently placed: *Big Dog, Little Dog*, Seth Casteel; *Dear Miss Kopp (A Kopp Sisters Novel)*, Amy Stewart; *Franchise: The Golden Arches in Black America*, Marcia Chatelain; *Good Talk: A Memoir in Conversations*, Mira Jacob; *Mama's Last Hug: Animal Emotions and What They Tell Us about Ourselves*, Frans de Waal; *Nuking the Moon: And Other Intelligence Schemes and Military Plots Left on the Drawing Board*, Vincent Houghton; *Salt Houses*, Hala Alyan; *Slime: How Algae Created Us, Plague Us, and Just Might Save Us*, Ruth Kassinger; *Superpower Interrupted: The Chinese History of the World*, Michael Schuman; *The Biography of Resistance: The Epic Battle Between People and Pathogens*, Muhammad H Zaman; *The Chaos Cure: Clean Your House and Calm Your Soul in 15 Minutes*, Marla Cilley; *The Drunken Botanist*, Amy Stewart; *The House on Fripp Island*, Rebecca Kauffman; *The Jetsetters*, Amanda Eyre Ward; *The Language of Butterflies: How Thieves, Hoarders, Scientists, and Other Obsessives Unlocked the Secrets of the World's Favorite Insect*, Wendy Williams; *The Sober Lush: A Hedonist's Guide to Living a Decadent, Adventurous, Soulful Life—Alcohol Free*, Amanda Eyre Ward, Jardine Labaire; *This View of Life: Completing the Darwinian Revolution*, David Sloan Wilson; *War Doctor: Surgery on the Front Line*, David Nott; *Wayfinding: The Science and Mystery of How Humans Navigate the World*, M R O'Connor
Foreign Rights: The Deborah Harris Agency (Israel); Andrew Nurnberg & Associates (China, Europe, Latin America); Tuttle-Mori Agency Inc (Japan); Eric Yang Agency (Korea)
Membership(s): Women's Media Group

3 Seas Literary Agency (L)
PO Box 444, Sun Prairie, WI 53590
Tel: 608-834-9317
E-mail: threeseaslit@aol.com
Web Site: threeseasagency.com

Key Personnel
Literary Agent: Stacey Graham; Michelle Grajkowski (AAR); Cori Deyoe *E-mail:* cori@threeseaslit.com; Linda Scalissi
Founded: 2000
E-mail queries only. For fiction titles, query with first chapter & synopsis embedded in the e-mail. For nonfiction, query with complete proposal attached. For picture books, query with complete text. Illustrations are not necessary. Considers simultaneous submissions. Responds within one month to e-mail submissions. No snail mail queries. 3 Seas will not respond to queries that are sent to e-mail addresses other than queries@threeseaslit.com. Obtains most new clients through recommendations from others & conferences. No fees charged.
Titles recently placed: *A Navy SEAL'S Surprise Baby*, Laura Marie Altom; *A Time for Home*, Alexis Morgan; *Captive*, KM Fawcett; *Changed by His Son*, Robin Gianakopoulus; *Do or Diner: A Comfort Food Mystery*, Christine Wenger; *Every Breath She Takes*, Norah Wilson; *Forever Friday*, Timothy Lewis; *Haley's Mountain Man*, Tracy Madison; *Her Perfect Cowboy*, Trish Milburn; *His Uptown Girl*, Liz Talley; *How to Write a Book in 30 Days*, Karen Wiesner; *Jimmie Joe Johnson: Manwhore*, Lindsey Brookes; *Just Perfect*, JoMarie DeGioia; *Must Love Dukes*, Elizabeth Michaels; *One Night with the Sheikh*, Kristi Gold; *Passion and Pretense*, Susan Gee Heino; *Queen of Song and Souls*, C L Wilson; *Queen of the Sylphs*, L J McDonald; *Say It With Roses*, Devon Vaughn Archer; *Six Months Later*, Natalie D Richards; *The Art of Stealing Time*, Katie MacAlister; *The Bride Next Door*, Winnie Griggs; *The Casanova Code*, Donna MacMeans; *The Champion*, Carla Capshaw; *The Rancher's Homecoming*, Cathy McDavid; *The Sister Season*, Jennifer Brown; *The Vampire With a Dragon Tattoo*, Kerrelyn Sparks; *The Winter King*, C L Wilson; *Thousand Words*, Jennifer Brown; *Three Days on Mimosa Lane*, Anna DeStefano
Foreign Rights: Marleen Seegers (China, France, Holland, Scandinavia); Ingo Stein (Germany)
Membership(s): Romance Writers of America (RWA)

The Tomasino Agency Inc (L)
70 Chestnut St, Dobbs Ferry, NY 10522
Tel: 914-674-9659 *Fax:* 914-693-0381
E-mail: info@tomasinoagency.com
Web Site: www.tomasinoagency.com
Key Personnel
Pres: Christine K Tomasino
Founded: 1998
Commercial & literary fiction & nonfiction. Represent all subrights for book clients only. Specialize in conventional & mind/body health, women's issues, self-improvement, spirituality/esoterica, narrative nonfiction, lifestyle, adult illustrated & packaged books, sports. Translation of nonbook content into book-related formats for corporate & nonprofit organizational clients such as major web businesses & museums. No poetry, genre fiction, plays, science fiction or purely scholarly work. Foreign agents in all major markets. No unsol mss, query first.

Transatlantic Agency (L)
2 Bloor St E, Suite 3500, Toronto, ON M4W 1A8, Canada
Tel: 416-488-9214
E-mail: info@transatlanticagency.com
Web Site: www.transatlanticagency.com
Key Personnel
Pres: Samantha Haywood *E-mail:* samantha@transatlanticagency.com
Treas: Lynn Bennett *E-mail:* lynn@transatlanticagency.com

Partner & Agent: Shaun Bradley *E-mail:* shaun@transatlanticagency.com
Sr Agent: Elizabeth Bennett; Carolyn Forde; Jodell Sadler; Stephanie Sinclair
Agent: Sandra Bishop; Andrea Cascardi; Brenna English-Loeb; Fiona Kenshole *E-mail:* fiona@transatlanticagency.com; Timothy Travaglini
Speakers' Agent & Literary Agent: Rob Firing
Assoc Agent: Evan Brown; Laura Cameron; Chelene Knight; Amy Tompkins *E-mail:* amy@transatlanticagency.com
Asst Agent: Leonicka Valcius
Contracts Admin: Laura Cook
Founded: 1993
Children's, adult literary fiction & literary nonfiction. Markets Canadian & American literary properties to English language publishers in the UK, US & CN & through sub-agents to publishers around the world. Handles film & TV rights for literary properties only: no film scripts or teleplays. No unsol mss; initial letter of inquiry essential. No reading fees. See web site for individual agents' submission details.
Titles recently placed: *Boundless*, Kathleen Winter; *McKenna - American Girl*, Mary Casanova; *Punishment*, Linden MacIntyre; *Tell It to the World*, Eliott Behar; *The Circus Dogs of Prague*, Rachelle Delaney; *The Devil You Know*, Elizabeth de Mariaffi; *The Gospel Truth*, Carolyn Pignat; *The Gypsy King*, Maureen Fergus; *The Silent Wife*, A S A Harrison; *The Unlikely Hero of 13B*, Teresa Toten; *They Left Us Everything*, Plum Johnson; *Walking Home*, Eric Walters; *Will Starling*, Ian Weir
Foreign Rights: Akcali Copyright (Turkey); ANAW Literary Agency (Poland); Berla & Griffini Rights Agency (Italy); The Book Publishers Association of Israel (Israel); ELST Literary Agency (Bulgaria); The English Agency (Japan) Ltd (Japan); Agence Litteraire Lora Fountain (France, Portugal, Spain); International Editors' Co (Spanish- & Portuguese-speaking countries); Japan UNI Agency Inc (Japan); The Anna Jarota Agency (France); JLM Literary Agency (Greece); Katai & Bolza Literary Agents (Hungary); Liepman AG (Germany); Literarische Agentur+Medienservice (Germany); Mo Literary Services (Netherlands, Scandinavia); Andrew Nurnberg Associates International Ltd (China, Hong Kong, Taiwan); Kristin Olson Literary Agency sro (Czechia); Orange Agency (Korea); Agencia Literaria RIFF (Brazil); Shinwon Agency Co (Korea); THE agency (Korea); Tuttle-Mori Agency Inc (Indonesia, Japan, Malaysia, Thailand, Vietnam); Young Agency (Korea)

Treimel, S©ott, NY, see S©ott Treimel NY

TriadaUS Literary Agency (L)
PO Box 561, Sewickley, PA 15143
Tel: 412-401-3376
Web Site: www.triadaus.com
Key Personnel
Founder & Sr Agent: Dr Uwe Stender (AAR) *E-mail:* uwe@triadaus.com
Agent & Subs Rts Mgr: Brent Taylor *E-mail:* brent@triadaus.com
Assoc Agent: Laura Crockett *E-mail:* laura@triadaus.com; Lauren Spieller *E-mail:* lauren@triadaus.com
Asst Agent: Amelia Appel *E-mail:* amelia@triadaus.com
Founded: 2004
Full service literary agency including fiction & nonfiction. Also international sales, film & TV options. No unsol mss, query first.
Titles recently placed: *Always Young and Restless*, Melody Thomas Scott; *Don't Call the Wolf*, Aleksandra Ross; *Fort Builders*, Dee Romito; *Free Lunch*, Rex Ogle; *Ghost Wood Song*, Erica Waters; *Ink*, Tori Bovalino; *Loathe at First Sight*, Suzanne Park; *Malice*,

Heather Walter; *Midsummer's Mayhem*, Rajani LaRocca; *Northranger*, Rey Terciero, Bre Indigo; *Once More With Chutzpah*, Haley Neil; *Our Way Back to Always*, Nina Moreno; *Poultrygeist*, Eric Geron; *Roman and Jewel*, Dana Davis; *She's Too Pretty to Burn*, Wendy Heard; *The Chaos Curse*, Sayantani DasGupta; *The Derby Daredevils*, Kit Rosewater; *The Feminist Agenda of Jemima Kincaid*, Kate Hattemer; *The Gravity of Us*, Phil Stamper; *The Henna Wars*, Adiba Jaigirdar; *The Jasmine Throne*, Tasha Suri; *These Violent Delights*, Chloe Gong; *Turtle Under Ice*, Juleah del Rosario; *When All Cheerleaders Were Boys*, Robyn Ryle

Foreign Rights: Arika Interrights Agency (Indonesia, Thailand, Vietnam); Big Apple Agency (China); Blackbird Literary Agency (Netherlands); Book/lab Literary Agency (Poland); Corto Literary (Bulgaria, Croatia, Czechia); Donatella d'Ormesson Agent Litteraire (France); The Deborah Harris Agency (Israel); IMC Literary Agency (Mexico, Spain); Japan UNI Agency Inc (Japan); Kalem Literary Agency (Turkey); Alexander Korzhenevski Agency (Baltic States, Russia); Agencia Das Letras (Portugal); Piergiorgio Nicolazzini Literary Agency (Italy); Plima Literary (Serbia); Riff Agency (Brazil); Thomas Schlueck Agency (Germany); Eric Yang Agency (Korea)

Membership(s): Association of American Publishers (AAP)

Trident Media Group LLC (L)

41 Madison Ave, 36th fl, New York, NY 10010
Tel: 212-333-1511
E-mail: info@tridentmediagroup.com; press@tridentmediagroup.com
Web Site: www.tridentmediagroup.com
Key Personnel
Chmn: Robert Gottlieb
CEO: Daniel Strone
EVP: Ellen Levine (AAR); Scott Miller; John Silbersack
SVP: Don Fehr
SVP, Literary Agent & Motion Picture/Television Agent: Erica Spellman-Silverman
Dir, Foreign Rts: Nora Rawn; Sylvie Rosokoff; Dorothy Vincent
Foreign Rts Mgr: Martin Rouse
Audio Rts Agent: Meagan Cohen
Dom Agent: Alex Slater
Sr Foreign Rts Agent: Lucinda Karter
Foreign Rts Agent: Nicola DeRobertis-Theye; Jennifer Helinek; Adrienne Santamaria
Literary Agent: Amanda O'Connor Annis; Mark Gottlieb; Alyssa Eisner Henkin
Assoc Agent: Alice Fugate; Sulamita Garbuz; Logan Harper; Martha Wydysh
Founded: 2000
General fiction & nonfiction. No unsol mss, query first by e-mail. Submit outline & sample chapters if requested. No reading fee. Handle film & TV rights for clients only. Representation in Hollywood.
Titles recently placed: *365 Days of Wonder: Mr Browne's Book of Precepts*, R J Palacio; *A Fall From Grace*, Adam Mitzner; *Alluring Indulgence*, Nicole Edwards; *Angel Killer*, Andrew Mayne; *Avenged*, Daniel Judson; *Bad Blood*, Mark Sennen; *Blacklist*, Sylvia Day; *Bound by Night*, Larissa Ione; *Breaking Nova*, Jessica Sorensen; *Call Me*, Kristina Knight; *Chained by Night*, Larissa Ione; *Cloud City: An Anna Strong Novella*, Jeanne Stein; *Collateral Damage*, Kyra Davis; *Cut Dead*, Mark Sennen; *Dangerous Alliance*, Kyra Davis; *Deceptive Innocence*, Kyra Davis; *Family by Design*, Kristina Knight; *Future Humans: The Ongoing Evolution of Homo Sapiens*, Prof Scott Solomon; *Green Girl*, Kate Zambreno; *Hemingway's War*, Terry Mort; *In Pursuit: The Saga of the Nazi Hunters*, Andrew Nagorski; *In the Skin of a Lion*, Michael Ondaatje; *Light My Fire*, Kristina Knight; *Music Class Today!*, David Weinstone; *Mystique*, Julie Berry; *No Time to Die*, Kira Peikoff; *Pics*, Nathan Jurgenson; *President Me: The America That's in My Head*, Adam Carolla; *Rebel Democracy: Digital Warriors and Islamic World*, Haroon Ullah; *Resistance*, Ryk Brown; *Ruin*, Rachel Van Dyken; *Running in the Family*, Michael Ondaatje; *Sistering*, Hannah Roberts-McKinnon; *Slow Burn (series)*, Maya Banks; *Starfire*, Dale Brown; *Start Me Up*, Kristina Knight; *The Birth of Capitalism in Islam*, Benedikt Koehler; *The Confessors' Club*, Jack Fredrickson; *The Distance Between Lost and Found*, Kathryn Holmes; *The Ever After of Ella and Micha*, Jessica Sorensen; *The Great Surge*, Steven Radelet; *The Julian Chapter: A Wonder Story*, R J Palacio; *The Last Days*, Joel Rosenberg; *The Last Jihad*, Joel Rosenberg; *The Last Rescue*, Howard Wasdin, Debbie Wasdin; *The Monet Murders*, Terry Mort; *The Mountain*, T Jefferson Parker; *The New Abolition*, Gary Dorrien; *The Other Side of Impossible: How to Let Go of the Life You Planned and Find a Happy Ending*, Tracey Cleantis; *The Rose Hotel*, Rahimeh Andalibian; *The Scandalous Sisterhood of Prickwillow Place*, Julie Berry; *The Struggle for Liberation*, Gary Dorrien; *The Winter Place*, Alexander Yates; *The Youngs: The Brothers Who Built AC/DC*, Jesse Fink; *Thieves Road: General George Custer and the Invasion of the Black Hills*, Terry Mort; *To Silence the Screaming Dead*, Jack Fredrickson; *Touch*, Mark Sennen; *Tower of Winds*, Ilana Myer; *Toxic*, Rachel Van Dyken; *Transit Girl*, Jamie Shupak; *Treading on Thin Air*, Dr Elizabeth Austin; *True Lies*, Monica Murphy; *Unspeakable Things*, Kathleen Spivack; *Welcome to Dog Beach*, Lisa Greenwald; *Werewolf Cop*, Andrew Klavan

2M Communications Ltd (L)

19 W 21 St, Suite 501, New York, NY 10010
Tel: 212-741-1509 *Fax:* 212-691-4460
Web Site: www.2mcommunications.com
Key Personnel
Pres: Madeleine Morel (AAR) *E-mail:* morel@2mcommunications.com
Founded: 1982
Only represent previously published ghostwriters & collaborators who work with platformed authors already represented by recognized literary agents or acquired by publishing houses. Numerous New York Times bestsellers but all confidential. No unsol mss, query first. Submit CV or resume.
Membership(s): PEN American Center; Women's Media Group

United Talent Agency (L-D)

9336 Civic Center Dr, Beverly Hills, CA 90210
Tel: 310-273-6700 *Fax:* 310-247-1111
Web Site: www.unitedtalent.com
Key Personnel
CEO: Jeremy Zimmer
Co-Pres: David Kramer; Jay Sures
Head, Corp Communs: Seth Oster
Founded: 1991
Fiction, nonfiction. Handle film & TV rights. No unsol mss, query first; reading fee.
Branch Office(s)
888 Seventh Ave, 9th fl, New York, NY 10106
Tel: 212-659-2600

Janis Vallely Literary Agency (L)

11 Raup Rd, Chatham, NY 12037
Tel: 518-392-0897
E-mail: janvall@aol.com
Web Site: www.janisvallely.com
Key Personnel
Owner & Literary Agent: Janis Vallely
Founded: 2014

Represents upscale commercial nonfiction: self-help, diet, narrative nonfiction, popular psychology & health, functional medicine, new science, spirituality. No unsol mss; no phone calls, no reading fee. Submit query letter & book proposal by e-mail only. Representation on the West Coast & in foreign countries. No fiction or young adult.
Titles recently placed: *Dirty Genes*, Dr Ben Lynch; *Eat Right 4 Your Type*, Dr Peter J Dadamo; *The Chemistry of Joy*, Henry Emmons, MD; *The Microbiome Diet*, Raphael Kellman, MD; *The Whole Brain*, Raphael Kellman, MD

Wales Literary Agency Inc (L)

1508 Tenth Ave E, No 401, Seattle, WA 98102
Tel: 206-284-7114
E-mail: waleslit@waleslit.com
Web Site: www.waleslit.com
Key Personnel
Owner & Literary Agent: Elizabeth Wales (AAR)
Asst Agent & Foreign Rts: Neal Swain
Founded: 1990
Specialize in quality mainstream fiction & nonfiction. Does not handle screenplays, children's books, genre fiction or most category nonfiction. No unsol mss, query first by e-mail only (no attachments). No phone queries. Accept electronic submissions only. Simultaneous submissions accepted. Response provided within 3 weeks to queries, 3 months to mss.
Titles recently placed: *Edgar: An Autobiography*, Edgar Martinez, Larry Stone; *Every Penguin in the World*, Charles Bergman; *Frog Church*, Lyanda Lynn Haupt; *Half-Broke*, Ginger Gaffney; *The ABCs of Savage Love*, Dan Savage, Joe Newton (illus)
Foreign Rights: Big Apple Agency Inc (China, Taiwan); Nurcihan Kesim Literary & Licensing Agency (Turkey); Agence Michelle Lapautre (France); Mohrbooks AG Literary Agency (Austria, Germany, Switzerland); Andrew Nurnberg Associates (Croatia, Hungary); Reiser Agency (Italy); Sebes & Bisseling Literary Agency (Netherlands, Scandinavia); Shinwon Agency (Korea); Silk Road Agency (Thailand); Abner Stein Agency (UK); Tuttle-Mori Agency Inc (Japan)

The Wallace Literary Agency (L)

229 E 79 St, No 5A, New York, NY 10075
Tel: 212-472-3282 *Fax:* 212-472-3833
E-mail: info@wallaceliteraryagency.com
Key Personnel
Pres: Robin Straus *E-mail:* robin@wallaceliteraryagency.com
Asst: Katelyn Hales
Founded: 1988
Handle film & TV rights for agency clients only. No unsol mss. The agency is not accepting new clients.
Foreign Rights: AnatoliaLit Agency (Turkey); Deborah Harris (Israel); JLM Literary Agency (Greece); Andrew Nurnberg Associates (worldwide exc Greece, Israel, Japan, Korea & Turkey); Tuttle-Mori Agency Inc (Japan); Eric Yang Agency (Korea)

Warwick Associates (L)

18340 Sonoma Hwy, Sonoma, CA 95476
Tel: 707-939-9212 *Fax:* 707-938-3515
E-mail: warwick@vom.com
Web Site: www.warwickassociates.com
Key Personnel
Pres: Simon Warwick-Smith
Founded: 1985
A "one-stop" agency handling any or all parts of literary agenting through publicity & sales, etc. Specialize in spirituality, metaphysics, religion & psychology, celebrity memoirs, business & self-help, pop culture. Literary agent for a

number of celebrity spiritual authors. No reading fee. Accept unsol mss, but query first with 2 chapters & SASE. No fiction or poetry.

Waterside Productions Inc (L)
2055 Oxford Ave, Cardiff, CA 92007
Tel: 760-632-9190 *Fax:* 760-632-9295
E-mail: admin@waterside.com
Web Site: www.waterside.com
Key Personnel
Founder & Literary Agent: Bill Gladstone
    E-mail: bgladstone@waterside.com
VP & Agent: Carole Jelen *Tel:* 925-968-9066
    E-mail: carole@jelenpub.com
Sr Agent: Margot Maley Hutchison *Tel:* 858-483-0426 *E-mail:* mmaley@waterside.com
Foreign Rts Dir & Agent: Kimberly Brabec
    E-mail: kimberly@waterside.com
Agent: Jill Kramer *Tel:* 760-201-5737
    E-mail: WatersideAgentJK@aol.com; Johanna Maaghul *E-mail:* johanna@waterside.com; David Nelson
Founded: 1982
Specialize in nonfiction. Professional how-to: technology, business, software, test prep, etc. General: self-help, spiritual, health, human interest, etc. No phone calls. No unsol mss. Submit a full book proposal per guidelines found at, or query through, the web site form. No reading fee. Handles software, film & TV rights with co-agents. In-house international division. Affiliations with PR agencies. Waterside now has its own print on demand & ebook publishing division at end of description of services.

Watkins/Loomis Agency Inc (L)
PO Box 20925, New York, NY 10025
Tel: 212-532-0080 *Fax:* 646-383-2449
E-mail: assistant@watkinsloomis.com
Web Site: www.watkinsloomis.com
Key Personnel
Pres: Gloria Loomis
Agent: Julia Masnik
Founded: 1908
Literary fiction, memoir, political nonfiction, biography. No unsol material.
Foreign Rights: The Marsh Agency; Abner Stein Agency (UK)

Waxman Literary Agency (L)
Affiliate of Diversion Publishing Corp
443 Park Ave S, No 1004, New York, NY 10016
Tel: 212-675-5556
Web Site: www.waxmanliteraryagency.com
Key Personnel
Founder & Agent: Scott Waxman
Sr Agent: Larry Kirshbaum
Agent: Susan Canavan; Fleetwood Robbins
Founded: 1997
Fiction & nonfiction. No unsol mss, query first via e-mail. No reading fee, charge for reproductions.

Cherry Weiner Literary Agency (L)
925 Oak Bluff Ct, Dacula, GA 30019-6660
Tel: 732-446-2096 *Fax:* 732-792-0506
E-mail: cherry8486@aol.com
Key Personnel
Owner: Cherry Weiner
Founded: 1977
Science fiction, general fiction. No nonfiction. No unsol mss. Referred authors submit letter saying who referred. Submissions or recommendations only. Query letter where applicable, no downloads. No reading fee. Handle film & TV rights. Foreign representatives in England, Germany, Italy, Japan, Netherlands, Scandinavia, Russia, Spain, Eastern Europe & France.
Titles recently placed: *Alien Infiltrator*, Weston Ochse; *Silver Grass*, John D Nesbitt; *Sons of Philo Gaines*, Michael R Ritt; *The Preacher's*

Daughter, Weston Ochse; *The Skin Man*, Tim Waggoner; *Trusty Dawson (1st & 2nd in series)*, Larry D Sweazy; *Your Turn to Suffer*, Tim Waggoner

The Weingel-Fidel Agency (L)
310 E 46 St, Suite 21-E, New York, NY 10017
Tel: 212-599-2959 *Fax:* 212-286-1986
E-mail: queries@theweingel-fidelagency.com
Key Personnel
Owner: Loretta Weingel-Fidel *E-mail:* lwf@theweingel-fidelagency.com
Founded: 1989
General fiction & nonfiction. Provide services to book authors/writers. No unsol mss, query first, by referral only; no reading fee.
Foreign Rep(s): Mary Clemmey (UK); Fritz Agency (Germany); Japan UNI Agency Inc (Japan); Agence Michelle Lapautre (France); Lennart Sane (Netherlands, Scandinavia, Spain)
Foreign Rights: Jill Hughes (Albania, Bulgaria, Croatia, Estonia, Hungary, Latvia, Lithuania, Montenegro, North Macedonia, Romania, Serbia, Slovakia, Slovenia)

Westwood Creative Artists Ltd (L)
138 Sussex Mews, Toronto, ON M5S-2K1, Canada
Tel: 416-964-3302 *Fax:* 416-964-3302
E-mail: wca_office@wcaltd.com
Web Site: www.wcaltd.com
Key Personnel
Founder & CEO: Bruce Westwood
Chmn: Michael Levine
Pres & COO: Jackie Kaiser
EVP: Hilary McMahon
Intl Rts Dir: Meg Wheeler
Agent: John Pearce
Off Mgr & Literary Asst: Stephanie Thompson
Exec Asst & Intl Rts Asst: Meg Wheeler
Exec Asst: Liz Culotti
Founded: 1995
General trade fiction & nonfiction for international marketplace. Canadian authors only. No unsol mss, query first. Handle film & TV rights. No screenwriters. No reading fee. For submission guidelines, please visit us at www.wcaltd.com/submission-guidelines.
Foreign Rep(s): Akcali Copyright (Kezban Akcali & Atilla Izgi Turgut) (Turkey); Sandra Bruna Literary Agency (Sandra Bruna & Natalia Berenguer) (Brazil, Latin America, Portugal, Spain); The English Agency (Hamish Macaskill) (Japan); Graal Literary Agency (Marcin Biegal & Maria Starz-Kanska) (Poland); The Deborah Harris Agency (Efrat Lev) (Israel); International Copyright Agency (Simona Kessler) (Romania); The Italian Literary Agency SRL (Italy); Japan UNI Agency Inc (Miko Suga Yamanouchi) (Japan); Anna Jarota Agency (Sandrine Bilan & Anna Jarota) (France); JLM Literary Agency (John Moukakos) (Greece); Katai & Bolza (Peter Bolza) (Hungary); Liepman Agency (Suzanne de Roche & Ruth Weibel) (Germany); Maxima Creative Agency (Santo Manurung) (Indonesia); NiKa (Vania Kadiyska) (Bulgaria); Andrew Nurnberg & Associates (Lisa Brannstrom & Eleonoora Kirk) (Netherlands, Scandinavia); Andrew Nurnberg Associates International (Whitney Hsu) (China); Kristin Olson (Czechia); PLIMA (Vuk Perisic) (Croatia, Serbia, Slovenia); Shin Won Agency (Tae Eun Kim) (Korea); Synopsis (Natalia Sanina) (Russia); Tuttle-Mori Agency Inc (Thananchai Pandey) (Thailand); Tuttle-Mori Agency Inc (Ken Mori) (Japan)
Membership(s): Professional Association of Canadian Literary Agents (PACLA)

Rhoda Weyr Agency, see Dunham Literary Inc

Witherspoon Associates Inc, see InkWell Management

WME (L-D)
11 Madison Ave, 18th fl, New York, NY 10010
Tel: 212-586-5100
Web Site: www.wmeentertainment.com
Key Personnel
Partner: Dorian Karchmar (AAR)
Head, NY Literary Dept: Suzanne Gluck
Dept Head: Eric Simonoff
Agent: Mel Berger *E-mail:* mmb@wmeentertainment.com; Margaret Riley King *E-mail:* mrk@wmeentertainment.com
Contact: Jay Mandel
All subjects; handle software, film & TV rights. No unsol mss, query first; no reading fee.
Foreign Office(s): Center Point, 100 New Oxford St, London WC1A 1HB, United Kingdom
    Tel: (020) 7534 6800 *Fax:* (020) 7534 6900

Writers House (L)
21 W 26 St, New York, NY 10010
Tel: 212-685-2400
Web Site: www.writershouse.com
Key Personnel
Founder & Sr Agent: Albert Zuckerman
    E-mail: azuckerman@writershouse.com
Pres & Sr Agent: Amy Berkower (AAR)
    E-mail: aberkower@writershouse.com
Sr Agent: Stephen Barr *E-mail:* sbarr@writershouse.com; Johanna V Castillo *E-mail:* jcastillo@writershouse.com; Susan Cohen (AAR) *E-mail:* scohensubmissions@writershouse.com; Dan Conaway (AAR) *E-mail:* conawaysubmissions@writershouse.com; Lisa DiMona; Susan Ginsburg (AAR) *E-mail:* sginsburgsubmissions@writershouse.com; Susan Golomb (AAR) *E-mail:* sgolombsubmissions@writershouse.com; Merrilee Heifetz (AAR) *E-mail:* mheifetzsubmissions@writershouse.com; Brianne Johnson *E-mail:* bjohnsonsubmissions@writershouse.com; Dan Lazar (AAR) *E-mail:* dlazar@writershouse.com; Simon Lipskar (AAR) *E-mail:* slipskar@writershouse.com; Steven Malk *E-mail:* smalk@writershouse.com; Jodi Reamer, Esq (AAR) *E-mail:* jreamer@writershouse.com; Robin Rue (AAR) *E-mail:* rrue@writershouse.com
Sr Agent, Juv & Young Adult: Rebecca Sherman
    E-mail: rebeccasubmissions@writershouse.com
Sr Agent: Geri Thoma (AAR)
    E-mail: gerisubmissions@writershouse.com
Exec Dir, Global Licensing & Dom Partnerships: Cecelia de la Campa
Mng Dir, Global Licensing: Maja Nikolic
UK Rts Dir: Peggy Boulos Smith
Rights Mgr: Kathryn Stuart
Founded: 1973
Represents writers of fiction & nonfiction, for both adult & juvenile books as wells as illustrators. Agents work with literary & commercial fiction, women's fiction, science fiction/fantasy, narrative nonfiction, history, memoirs, biographies, psychology, science, parenting, cookbooks, how-to, self-help, business, finance, young adult & juvenile fiction/nonfiction & picture books. Interested in & work with authors at all stages of their career. Please e-mail query letter, which includes your credentials, an explanation of what makes your book unique & special, & a synopsis. Some agents within the agency have different requirements. Please contact their individual Publisher's Marketplace (PM) profile for details. Respond to all queries, generally within 6-8 weeks. Do not represent original screenplays.
Branch Office(s)
7660 Fay Ave, No 338H, La Jolla, CA 92037, Sr Agent: Steven Malk *E-mail:* smalk@writershouse.com

Foreign Rights: Akcali Copyright (Turkey); ANA (Judit Hermann) (Hungary); ANA (Petra Tobiskova) (Czechia, Slovakia); ANA Baltics (Baltic States); Anthea Agency (Katalina Sabeva) (Bulgaria); Ia Atterholm (Scandinavia); Bardon-Chinese Media Agency (China, Taiwan); Agence Eliane Benisti (France); Book Publishers Association of Israel (Israel); BookLabs Ltd (Poland); The Deborah Harris Agency (children's) (Israel); The Italian Literary Agency SRL (Italy); Japan UNI Agency Inc (Japan); JLM Literary Agency (Greece); Simona Kessler Copyright Agency (Romania); Korea Copyright Center Inc (Korea); Maxima Creative Agency (Indonesia); Mo Literary Services (children's) (Netherlands); Plima Literary Agency (Croatia, Serbia, Slovenia); RDC Agencia Literaria (Portugal, Spain); Agencia Riff (Brazil); Thomas Schlueck Literary Agency (Germany); Sebes & van Gelderen Literary Agency (Netherlands); Synopsis Agency (Natalia Sanina) (Russia); Tuttle-Mori Thailand (Thailand)

Writers' Productions (L-D)
PO Box 630, Westport, CT 06881-0630
Tel: 203-227-8199
Key Personnel
Owner & Pres: David L Meth *E-mail:* dlm67@mac.com
Founded: 1977
Literary quality fiction & nonfiction. Handle film, TV & licensing rights. Foreign reps available as & where needed. No fees. No unsol mss; not accepting new clients. No mss or samples by e-mail. No phone calls.
Membership(s): Academy of American Poets; The Dramatists Guild of America; PEN American Center

Writers' Representatives LLC (L)
116 W 14 St, 11th fl, New York, NY 10011-7305
Tel: 212-620-9009 *Fax:* 212-620-0023
E-mail: transom@writersreps.com
Web Site: www.writersreps.com
Key Personnel
Principal: Lynn Chu; Glen Hartley *E-mail:* glen@writersreps.com
Founded: 1985
Represents authors of book-length works of nonfiction & literary fiction for adults. Once WR agrees to represent an author, we give advice on how best to structure or edit a book proposal, discuss ideas for book pojects & comment on finished ms material, with the goal of placing a book with the right publisher on the best possible terms for our author. We also dis-

cuss our authors' backgrounds & interests with publishers to promote upcoming projects or to find new ones. We sell to major publishers in the US & abroad. Prefer to see ms material rather than synopses. Background about an author's professional experience, particularly that which is relevant to the book, as well as a list of previously published works. We respond within 4-6 weeks on average. We require that all authors fully advise us as to whether any project has been previously submitted to a publisher & what the response was & if the project has been submitted to another agent. Postal submissions should be accompanied by SASE. No reading fees.
Titles recently placed: *Falstaff: Give Me Life*, Harold Bloom; *The Road to Character*, David Brooks; *The Second World Wars*, Victor Davis Hanson
Foreign Rights: Agencia Literaria Carmen Balcells SA (Anna Bofill) (Portugal); Agencia Literaria Carmen Balcells SA (Maribel Luque) (Spain); Tassy Barham Associates (Tassy Barham) (Brazil); Eggers & Landwehr KG (Petra Eggers) (Germany); Japan UNI Agency Inc (Miko Yamanouchi) (Japan); Susanna Zevi Agencia Letteraria (Susanna Zevi) (Italy)

The Wylie Agency LLC (L)
250 W 57 St, Suite 2114, New York, NY 10107
Tel: 212-246-0069 *Fax:* 212-586-8953
E-mail: mail@wylieagency.com
Web Site: www.wylieagency.com
Key Personnel
Founder & Pres: Andrew Wylie
Literary Agent: Jin Auh; Sarah Chalfant; Jeffrey Posternak
Founded: 1980
Literary fiction & nonfiction; no unsol mss; query first with SASE. Handle film & TV rights. Contact for fee information.
Foreign Office(s): The Wylie Agency (UK) Ltd, 17 Bedford Sq, London WC1B 3JA, United Kingdom *Tel:* (020) 7908 5900 *Fax:* (020) 7908 5901 *E-mail:* mail@wylieagency.co.uk
Foreign Rights: The Wylie Agency (UK) Ltd (UK)

The Yao Enterprises (Literary Agents) LLC (L-D)
Division of The Yao Enterprises LLC
67 Banksville Rd, Armonk, NY 10504
Tel: 914-765-0296
E-mail: yaollc@gmail.com
Key Personnel
Pres: Mei C Yao
Founded: 1995

Specializes in original literary creations & subsequent world language translation of books on the art of living & practical spirituality. No unsol mss, query first (e-mail queries welcome). No reading fee. Handle software & film & TV rights.
Member of Souami School of Ikebana (Japan) & Aesthetic Pruning Assn (US).
Titles recently placed: *Cancer Is Not a Disease: It's a Healing Mechanism*, Andreas Moritz
Foreign Rights: SinoStar/Chinese Connection Agency (China, Hong Kong, Taiwan)

The Young Agency (L)
213 Bennett Ave, No 3H, New York, NY 10040
Tel: 212-229-2612
Key Personnel
Prop: Marian Young
Founded: 1986
Fiction & nonfiction. No unsol mss; no reading fees. Handle film & TV rights after book is sold.

Barbara J Zitwer Agency (L-D)
525 West End Ave, Unit 11-H, New York, NY 10024
Tel: 212-501-8423
E-mail: zitwer@gmail.com
Key Personnel
Pres: Barbara J Zitwer *E-mail:* zitwer@gmail.com
Founded: 1991
Winner of 2016 International Literary Agent of the Year Award. Specialize in fiction & narrative nonfiction by writers from all over the world. Represents the best writers from Korea including Booker short listed, Han Kang, Man Asian Prize winner, Kyouing sook Shin. We look for new, exciting literary voices from every country on the globe.
Titles recently placed: *Not Without Her Daughter*, Andrea Claudia Hoffmann; *Painter of the Wind*, J M Lee; *Raif Badawi: The Voice of Freedom*, Ensaf Haidar, Andrea Claudia Hoffmann; *Swallowing Mercury*, Wioletta Greg; *The Accusation*, Bandi; *The Girl Who Beat Isis*, Farida Khalaf, Claudia Andrea Hoffmann; *The Vegetarian*, Han Kang; *The White Book*, Han Kang
Foreign Rights: Gabriella Ambrosioni (Italy); Donatalla D'Ormesson (France); Anoukh Foerg Litteraire Agent (Germany); Deborah Harris Agency (Israel); KL Management (China, Japan, Korea); MO Literary Agency (Scandinavia); Andrew Nurnberg Agency (Whitney Hsu) (Taiwan); Prava i prevodi (Eastern Europe, Russia); SalmaiaLit (Portugal, Spanish-speaking countries)

Illustration Agents

Artworks Illustration
PO Box 453, New York, NY 10156
Tel: 212-239-4946
E-mail: artworksillustration@earthlink.net
Web Site: www.artworksillustration.com
Founded: 1990
Represents 30 artists.
Membership(s): Society of Illustrators

Carol Bancroft & Friends
PO Box 2030, Danbury, CT 06813
Tel: 203-730-8270 *Fax:* 203-730-8275
E-mail: cbfriends@sbcglobal.net; artists@
carolbancroft.com
Web Site: www.carolbancroft.com
Key Personnel
Owner: Joy Elton Tricarico
Founded: 1972
Represents many fine illustrators specializing in
art for children of all ages. Servicing the pub-
lishing industry including, but not limited to,
picture/mass market books & educational ma-
terials. We work with packagers, studios, toy
companies & corporations in addition to licens-
ing art to related products. Promotional packets
sent upon request.
Unsol artwork & mss are not accepted.
Membership(s): Graphic Artists Guild; Society of Children's Book Writers & Illustrators
(SCBWI); Society of Illustrators

Benoit & Associates
744 Stockton Heights Ct, Bourbonnais, IL 60914
Tel: 815-932-2582 *Fax:* 815-932-2594
Web Site: www.benoit-associates.com
Key Personnel
Pres: Michael J Benoit *E-mail:* mbenoit@benoit-
associates.com
Full service design & advertising studio. Specialize in technical & color airbrush illustration &
computer generated art (Mac & IBM) design,
art direction, in-house photography, elementary
through college textbook cover & newsletters,
brochures, letterheads & annual reports. High
volume, high quality, quick turnaround & satisfaction guaranteed.

Bernstein & Andriulli Inc
190 Bowery, 3rd fl, New York, NY 10012
Tel: 212-682-1490 *Fax:* 212-286-1890
E-mail: info@ba-reps.com
Web Site: www.ba-reps.com
Key Personnel
Illustration: Louisa St Pierre
Commercial illustration & photography.
Represents 82 artists.
Branch Office(s)
Rm 207, Block 1, 427 Ju Men Rd, Huangl'u Dis-
trict, Shanghai 200023, China, Pres: Jonathan
Tay *E-mail:* jonathan.tay@amanacliq.com
49 Borough High St, London SE1 1NB, United
Kingdom, Illustration Rep: Sam Summerskill
Tel: (0207) 645 3337 *E-mail:* sam@ba-reps.
com

Byer-Sprinzeles Agency
5800 Arlington Ave, Suite 16-C, Riverdale, NY
10471
Tel: 718-543-9399
Web Site: www.maggiebyersprinzeles.com
Key Personnel
Agent: Maggie Byer-Sprinzeles *E-mail:* maggie@
maggiebyersprinzeles.com
Founded: 1991

Represents children's book illustrators.
Represents 27 artists.
Membership(s): Society of Children's Book Writ-
ers & Illustrators (SCBWI)

The CAT Agency Inc
Formerly Christina A Tugeau Artist Agency LLC
PO Box 1390, Fairfield, CT 06825
Tel: 917-434-3141
Web Site: www.catugeau.com
Key Personnel
Owner & Agent: Christy Ewers *E-mail:* christy@
catagencyinc.com
Agent: Chad W Beckerman *E-mail:* chad@
catagencyinc.com
Founded: 1994
Strictly represents illustrators +/or au-
thors/illustrators for children's literature. Il-
lustrators: Send 4-6 jpegs of samples, live link
to web site & short letter of introduction. Au-
thor/illustrators: E-mail brief synopsis of ms &
several accompanying illustrations or samples
of artwork.
Represents 30 artists.
Membership(s): Society of Children's Book Writers & Illustrators (SCBWI)

Cornell & Co LLC
44 Jog Hill Rd, Trumbull, CT 06611
Tel: 203-454-4210
Web Site: www.cornellandco.com
Key Personnel
Owner: Merial Cornell *E-mail:* merial@
cornellandco.com
Founded: 1989
Professional illustrators, specializing in the chil-
dren's book markets; educational, trade & mass
market. Representing over 35 artists with a va-
riety of styles & techniques.
Membership(s): Graphic Artists Guild; Soci-
ety of Children's Book Writers & Illustrators
(SCBWI)

Craven Design Inc
229 E 85 St, New York, NY 10028
Mailing Address: PO Box 282, New York, NY
10028-9998
Tel: 212-288-1022 *Fax:* 212-249-9910
E-mail: cravendesign@mac.com
Web Site: www.cravendesignstudios.com
Key Personnel
Artist Rep: Meryl Jones
Founded: 1981
Artist's representative: book illustration (text &
trade), juvenile through adult; humorous, re-
alistic, decorative & technical; maps, charts,
graphs.
Represents 20 artists.

Deborah Wolfe Ltd
731 N 24 St, Philadelphia, PA 19130
Tel: 215-232-6666 *Fax:* 215-232-6585
E-mail: info@illustrationonline.com
Web Site: www.illustrationonline.com
Founded: 1978
Commercial illustrators & animators representa-
tive.
Represents 30 artists.

**Fort Ross Inc - International Representation
for Artists**
Division of Fort Ross Inc
26 Arthur Place, Yonkers, NY 10701
Tel: 914-375-6448

Key Personnel
Pres & Exec Dir: Dr Vladimir P Kartsev
E-mail: vkartsev2000@gmail.com
Founded: 1992
Foreign sales of secondary rights for illustrations,
photographs & covers made by American &
Canadian artists. Representation of Russian &
East European artists & photographers in the
US & CN.
Represents 50 artists.

Carol Guenzi Agents Inc
Subsidiary of Artagent.com
865 Delaware St, Denver, CO 80204
Tel: 303-820-2599 *Toll Free Tel:* 800-417-5120
Fax: 303-820-2598
E-mail: art@artagent.com
Web Site: www.artagent.com
Key Personnel
Pres: Carol Guenzi
Founded: 1984
A wide selection of talent in all areas of visual
communications.
Represents 25 artists.
Membership(s): AIGA, the professional associa-
tion for design; Art Directors Club of Denver
(ADCD)

Herman Agency
350 Central Park W, Apt 4I, New York, NY
10025
Tel: 212-749-4907
Web Site: www.hermanagencyinc.com
Key Personnel
Owner & Pres: Ronnie Ann Herman
E-mail: ronnie@hermanagencyinc.com
Founded: 1999
Represent illustrators, authors & au-
thor/illustrators of children's books, trade &
educational.
Represents 19 artists.
Membership(s): The Authors Guild; Society
of Children's Book Writers & Illustrators
(SCBWI)

The Ivy League of Artists Inc
18 Edgemere Rd, Livingston, NJ 07039
Tel: 973-992-4048 *Fax:* 973-992-4049
E-mail: ilartists2@gmail.com
Key Personnel
Owner & Pres: Ivy Mindlin
Illustration, spot drawings, comps, storyboards,
design, infographics, PowerPoint & mechanical
art.

Levy Creative Management LLC
425 E 58 St, Suite 37F, New York, NY 10022
Tel: 212-687-6463 *Fax:* 212-661-4839
E-mail: info@levycreative.com
Web Site: www.levycreative.com
Key Personnel
Pres & Founder: Sari Schorr *E-mail:* sari@
levycreative.com
Founded: 1996
Boutique agency representing only award-winning
international artists.

Lindgren & Smith
888C Eighth Ave, No 329, New York, NY 10019
Tel: 212-397-7330
E-mail: info@lindgrensmith.com
Web Site: lindgrensmith.com
Key Personnel
Owner: Pat Lindgren *E-mail:* pat@lindgrensmith.

com; Piper Smith *E-mail:* piper@
lindgrensmith.com
Founded: 1987
Do not accept mss; examples of illustrator's work
can be requested via e-mail. The best way to
contact us is by e-mail. Represents 25 artists.

Lott Representatives Ltd
PO Box 3607, New York, NY 10163
Tel: 212-755-5737
Web Site: www.lottreps.com
Key Personnel
Pres: Peter Lott *E-mail:* peter@lottreps.com
Represent commercial illustrators.

MB Artists
775 Sixth Ave, Suite 6, New York, NY 10001
Tel: 212-689-7830 *Fax:* 212-689-7829
Web Site: www.mbartists.com
Key Personnel
Pres & Agent: Mela Bolinao *E-mail:* mela@
mbartists.com
Founded: 1986
Represents illustrators whose work is intended for
juvenile market.
Represents 64 artists.
Membership(s): The Children's Book Council
(CBC); Graphic Artists Guild; Society of Chil-
dren's Book Writers & Illustrators (SCBWI);
Society of Illustrators

Melissa Turk & the Artist Network
9 Babbling Brook Lane, Suffern, NY 10901
Tel: 845-368-8606
E-mail: melissa@melissaturk.com
Web Site: www.melissaturk.com
Key Personnel
Contact: Dorothy Ziff
Founded: 1986
Represents professional artists supplying quality
illustration, calligraphy & cartography. Special-
ize in children's trade & educational illustration
as well as natural science illustration (wildlife,
botanical, medical, etc), publishing & interpre-
tive signage.
Represents 12 artists.
Membership(s): Graphic Artists Guild; Soci-
ety of Children's Book Writers & Illustrators
(SCBWI)

Morgan Gaynin Inc
149 Madison Ave, Suite 1140, New York, NY
10016
Tel: 212-475-0440
E-mail: info@morgangaynin.com
Web Site: www.morgangaynin.com
Key Personnel
Owner, Principal & Rep: Gail Gaynin
Rep: Kate Kelly
Founded: 1974
Illustrator's representative.
Represents 40 artists.
Membership(s): Graphic Artists Guild; Soci-
ety of Children's Book Writers & Illustrators
(SCBWI); Society of Illustrators

Wanda Nowak Creative Illustrators Agency
231 E 76 St, Suite 5-D, New York, NY 10021
Tel: 212-535-0438
E-mail: wanda@wandanow.com
Web Site: www.wandanow.com
Key Personnel
Pres: Wanda Nowak
Founded: 1995
Children's trade books, elementary & secondary
textbook illustration & book cover illustration.
Represents 16 artists.

Painted-Words Inc
310 W 97 St, Suite 24, New York, NY 10025

Tel: 212-663-2311 *Fax:* 212-663-2891
E-mail: info@painted-words.com
Web Site: painted-words.com
Key Personnel
Agent: Claire Easton; Lori Nowicki
E-mail: lori@painted-words.com
Founded: 1992 (as Lori Nowicki & Associates)
Artist & literary agent.
Represents 41 artists.
Membership(s): Society of Children's Book Writ-
ers & Illustrators (SCBWI)

Portfolio Solutions LLC
136 Jameson Hill Rd, Clinton Corners, NY 12514
Tel: 845-266-1001
Web Site: www.portfoliosolutionsllc.com
Key Personnel
Owner & Agent: Bernadette Szost *E-mail:* b.
szost@portfoliosolutionsllc.com
Founded: 1999
Agency representing illustrators of children's
books & related materials.
Represents 35 artists.
Membership(s): The Authors Guild; Society
of Children's Book Writers & Illustrators
(SCBWI)

Gerald & Cullen Rapp
41 N Main St, Suite 103, South Norwalk, CT
06854
Tel: 212-889-3337
E-mail: info@rappart.com
Web Site: www.rappart.com
Key Personnel
Rep: Nancy Moore *Tel:* 212-889-3337 ext 103
E-mail: nancy@rappart.com
Founded: 1944
Represent leading commercial illustrators on an
exclusive basis. Sell to magazine & book pub-
lishers, ad agencies, design firms & major cor-
porations.
Represents 60 artists.
Membership(s): Graphic Artists Guild; Society of
Illustrators

Kerry Reilly: Representatives
1826 Asheville Place, Charlotte, NC 28203
Tel: 704-372-6007
E-mail: kerry@reillyreps.com
Web Site: www.reillyreps.com
Animation, illustration & photography.
Represents 25 artists.

Renaissance House
Imprint of Laredo Publishing Co
465 Westview Ave, Englewood, NJ 07631
Tel: 201-408-4048
Web Site: www.renaissancehouse.net
Key Personnel
Pres: Sam Laredo *E-mail:* laredo@
renaissancehouse.net
VP & Exec Ed: Raquel Benatar *E-mail:* raquel@
renaissancehouse.net
Founded: 1991
Book developer that specializes in children's
books, educational materials & bilingual market (English/Spanish). Represents illustrators
who specialize in art for children that provide
a wide variety of styles & techniques. Services
the advertising & publishing industries, including children's books & educational materials.
Multicultural artists are available. Promotional
booklet sent upon request.
Represents 90 artists.

Rosenthal Represents
23725 Hartland St, West Hills, CA 91307
Tel: 818-430-3850
E-mail: eliselicenses@earthlink.net
Key Personnel
Pres: Elise Rosenthal

Sales & Mktg & Artists Rep: Neil Sandler
Founded: 1979
Illustrate book covers, children's & adult books.
Licensing agents.
Represents 35 artists.
Membership(s): Licensing Industry Merchandis-
ers' Association (LIMA); Society of Illustrators

Salzman International
1751 Charles Ave, Arcata, CA 95521
Tel: 415-285-8267 *Fax:* 707-822-5500
Web Site: www.salzint.com
Key Personnel
Owner: Richard Salzman *E-mail:* rs@salzint.com
Founded: 1982
Agents for visual artists for educational & trade
books specializing in art illustrators. Feature art
for magazines & periodicals. Editorial services
available.
Represents 25 artists.

Richard W Salzman Artists' Representative,
see Salzman International

The Schuna Group Inc
1503 Briarknoll Dr, Arden Hills, MN 55112
Tel: 651-631-8480
Web Site: www.schunagroup.com
Key Personnel
Pres: Jo Anne Schuna *E-mail:* joanne@
schunagroup.com
Represents 8 artists.

Storybook Arts Inc
414 Poplar Hill Rd, Dover Plains, NY 12522
Mailing Address: PO Box 672, Dover Plains, NY
12522
Tel: 845-877-3305
Web Site: www.storybookartsinc.com
Key Personnel
Owner & Pres: Janet De Carlo *E-mail:* janet@
storybookartsinc.com
Founded: 2005
Artist representative agency.
Represents 26 artists.
Membership(s): Society of Children's Book Writ-
ers & Illustrators (SCBWI)

Christina A Tugeau Artist Agency LLC, see
The CAT Agency Inc

Tugeau 2 Inc
2231 Grandview Ave, Cleveland Heights, OH
44106
Tel: 216-707-0854
Web Site: www.tugeau2.com
Key Personnel
Owner: Nicole Tugeau *E-mail:* nicole@tugeau2.
com
Founded: 2003
Agency for artist representation in the children's
publishing industry.
Represents 35 artists.
Membership(s): Society of Children's Book Writ-
ers & Illustrators (SCBWI)

WendyLynn & Co
504 Wilson Rd, Annapolis, MD 21401
Tel: 410-224-2729; 410-507-1059
Web Site: wendylynn.com
Key Personnel
Pres & Illustration Agent: Wendy Mays
E-mail: wendy@wendylynn.com
Busn Mgr & Illustration Agent: Janice Onken
E-mail: janice@wendylynn.com
Founded: 2002
Specialize in the children's publishing market.
Represent & promote our illustrators to pub-
lishing companies which produce work for
children & young adults.

Represents 25 artists.
Membership(s): Society of Children's Book Writers & Illustrators (SCBWI)

Wilkinson Studios Inc
2955 Kelly Dr, Elgin, IL 60124-4349
Tel: 312-286-3683
Web Site: www.wilkinsonstudios.com

Key Personnel
Founder & Pres: Christine Wilkinson
  E-mail: chris@wilkinsonstudios.com
Founded: 1999
Specializing in representing illustrators & managing art programs for educational, trade book & mass market publishing, children's magazines, games & related fields. Over 100 illustrators offering age appropriate artwork for PreK-college in a wide range of styles, techniques & media, both conventional & electronic. Project management of large volume blackline or color illustration programs by dedicated staff with art & design backgrounds, working directly with the publisher or interfacing with design & development house vendors.
Represents 100 artists.
Membership(s): Graphic Artists Guild; Society of Children's Book Writers & Illustrators (SCBWI)

Lecture Agents

Listed below are some of the most active lecture agents who handle tours and single engagements for writers.

American Program Bureau Inc
One Gateway Center, Suite 751, Newton, MA 02458
Tel: 617-614-1600 *Fax:* 617-965-6610
E-mail: apb@apbspeakers.com
Web Site: www.apbspeakers.com
Key Personnel
COO, Sales Dir: Andrew Walker *Tel:* 617-614-1611 *E-mail:* awalker@apbspeakers.com
Mktg Coord: Drew Sullivan *Tel:* 617-614-1638 *E-mail:* dsullivan@apbspeakers.com
Founded: 1965
Lecture representation/speakers bureau. Branches located in CA, IL & NJ.
Membership(s): International Association of Speakers Bureaus (IASB); NACA

The Barnabas Agency
Division of The B&B Media Group Inc
PO Box 3113, Corsicana, TX 75151-3113
Tel: 903-654-1319
E-mail: info@barnabasagency.com
Web Site: www.barnabasagency.com
Key Personnel
Pres & CEO: Tina Jacobson *E-mail:* tina@barnabasagency.com
VP & COO: Rick Roberson *E-mail:* rick@barnabasagency.com
VP, PR: Diane Morrow *E-mail:* diane@barnabasagency.com
Founded: 2002
Objectives: To increase recognition of the client, his/her ministry, products & service; to establish client's credibility, help achieve long-term & short-term goals & help client develop a vision. Services range from consulting to full-scale personal management of the client & implementation of the various components of the campaign.
Membership(s): Public Relations Society of America Inc (PRSA)

Burns Entertainment & Sports Marketing
820 Davis St, Suite 222, Evanston, IL 60201
Tel: 847-866-9400 *Fax:* 847-491-9778
E-mail: burnsl@burnsent.com
Web Site: burnsent.com
Key Personnel
CEO & COO: Bob Williams *E-mail:* bobwilliams@burnsent.com
Pres & Gen Coun: Marc Ippolito
Pres: Doug Shabelman
Founded: 1970
Sports & entertainment marketing, match corporations with talent celebrities for appearances, speeches & endorsements.
Branch Office(s)
333 Seventh Ave, Suite 1702, New York, NY 10001

CreativeWell Inc
PO Box 3130, Memorial Sta, Upper Montclair, NJ 07043
Tel: 973-783-7575
E-mail: info@creativewell.com
Web Site: www.creativewell.com
Key Personnel
Pres: George M Greenfield *E-mail:* george@creativewell.com
Founded: 2003
Literary, lecture & arts management.

The Fischer Ross Group Inc
75 Holly Hill Lane, Suite 100, Greenwich, CT 06830
Tel: 203-622-4950 *Fax:* 203-531-4132
E-mail: frgstaff@frg-speakers.com
Web Site: www.frg-speakers.com
Key Personnel
Pres: Grada Fischer
Exclusive lecture agents for authors (fiction, non-fiction, trade) & journalists (print & broadcast), as well as nationally known celebrities & personalities. Arrange lecture tours, individual speaking engagements, product endorsements, public openings & appearances for the university, association & corporate markets.

Greater Talent Network Inc
437 Fifth Ave, New York, NY 10016
Tel: 212-645-4200 *Toll Free Tel:* 800-326-4211 *Fax:* 212-627-1471
E-mail: info@greatertalent.com
Web Site: www.greatertalent.com
Key Personnel
CEO: Don R Epstein
Founded: 1981
Exclusive lecture & entertainment management. Represent authors, journalists & nationally & internationally known individuals. Arrange speaking engagements & tours for corporations, associations, colleges & universities, town halls, hospitals & other organizations, as well as literary, motion picture, television & radio representation.
Membership(s): International Association of Speakers Bureaus (IASB)

ICM Lecture Division
Division of International Creative Management
730 Fifth Ave, New York, NY 10019
Tel: 212-556-5600 *Fax:* 212-556-5665
Web Site: www.icmtalent.com
Exclusively represents a long list of authors, entertainers & distinguished clients & celebrities from all fields for lectures & personal appearances.
Branch Office(s)
10250 Constellation Blvd, Los Angeles, CA 90067 *Tel:* 310-550-4000
Marlborough House, 3rd fl, 10 Earlham St, London WC2H 9LN, United Kingdom *Tel:* (020) 7836 8564

International Entertainment Bureau
3612 N Washington Blvd, Indianapolis, IN 46205-3592
Tel: 317-926-7566
E-mail: ieb@prodigy.net
Key Personnel
Founder: David Leonards
Founded: 1972
Database, resource center & clearing house. Information on speakers, celebrities & entertainers available in the marketplace. Planning, consulting & booking.
Membership(s): Indiana Association of Fairs, Festivals & Events (INAFFE); Indiana Society of Association Executives (ISAE); Meeting Professionals International (MPI)

Penguin Random House Speakers Bureau, A Penguin Random House Company
1745 Broadway, Mail Drop 13-1, New York, NY 10019
Tel: 212-572-2013
E-mail: speakers@penguinrandomhouse.com
Web Site: www.prhspeakers.com
Key Personnel
SVP & Dir, Publicity: Susan Corcoran
VP & Exec Dir: Tiffany Tomlin
Sr Agent Dir: Jayme Boucher *Tel:* 212-366-2166 *E-mail:* jboucher@penguinrandomhouse.com; Kim Thornton Ingenito *Tel:* 212-572-2299 *E-mail:* kthornton@penguinrandomhouse.com; Caitlin McCaskey *Tel:* 212-782-8661 *E-mail:* cmccaskey@penguinrandomhouse.com
Agent Dir: Christine Labov; Kate Berner
Lecture Agent: Madeleine Denman; Catherine Mikula
Assoc Mgr, Sales: Mallory Conder
Founded: 2006
Full service lecture agency that represents best-selling authors, literary legends, cutting-edge thinkers & current tastemakers.
Membership(s): International Association of Speakers Bureaus (IASB)

Random House Speakers Bureau, see Penguin Random House Speakers Bureau, A Penguin Random House Company

Royce Carlton Inc
866 United Nations Plaza, Suite 587, New York, NY 10017-1880
Tel: 212-355-7700 *Toll Free Tel:* 800-LECTURE (532-8873) *Fax:* 212-888-8659
E-mail: info@roycecarlton.com
Web Site: www.roycecarlton.com
Key Personnel
Pres: Carlton Sedgeley *Tel:* 212-822-0999 *E-mail:* carlton@roycecarlton.com
EVP: Lucy Lepage *Tel:* 212-822-0979 *E-mail:* lucy@roycecarlton.com
VP: Helen Churko *Tel:* 212-822-0981 *E-mail:* helen@roycecarlton.com
Founded: 1968
Agents, managers & brokers for speakers.

Jodi Solomon Speakers Bureau
295 Huntington Ave, Suite 211, Boston, MA 02115
Tel: 617-266-3450 *Fax:* 617-266-5660
E-mail: inquiries@jodisolomonspeakers.com
Web Site: www.jodisolomonspeakers.com
Founded: 1990
Lecture & performing arts management.
Membership(s): NACA

Speakers Unlimited
7532 Courtyard Place, Cary, NC 27519
Tel: 919-466-7676 *Toll Free Tel:* 888-333-6676
E-mail: prospeak@aol.com
Web Site: www.speakersunlimited.com
Key Personnel
Owner: Mike Frank
Founded: 1971
Full service speakers bureau.
Membership(s): National Speakers Association (NSA)

The Tuesday Agency
132 1/2 E Washington St, Iowa City, IA 52240

Tel: 319-338-7080
E-mail: trinity@tuesdayagency.com
Web Site: tuesdayagency.com
Key Personnel
Pres: Trinity Ray
VP: Kevin Mills
Sr Agent: Sarah Murphy Mannheimer; Rachel
    Yoder
Founded: 2011
Exclusive speaker representation.

World Class Speakers & Entertainers
5200 Kanan Rd, Suite 210, Agoura Hills, CA
    91301
Tel: 818-991-5400
E-mail: wcse@wcspeakers.com
Web Site: www.wcspeakers.com
Key Personnel
Pres: Joseph I Kessler *E-mail:* jkessler@
    wcspeakers.com
Founded: 1970
Represents world class speakers & entertainers.
    Database of 25,000 speakers & entertainers;
    directory/guide available.

Writers' League of Texas (WLT)
611 S Congress Ave, Suite 200 A-3, Austin, TX
    78704
Tel: 512-499-8914
E-mail: wlt@writersleague.org
Web Site: www.writersleague.org
Key Personnel
Prog Dir: Michael Noll *E-mail:* michael@
    writersleague.org
Founded: 1981

Associations, Events, Courses & Awards

Book Trade & Allied Associations — Index

Book Trade & Allied Associations

Listed here are associations and organizations that are concerned with books, literacy, language and speech, media and communications as well as groups who provide services to the publishing community.

AAP, see Association of American Publishers (AAP)

AAP PreK-12 Learning Group
Division of Association of American Publishers (AAP)
455 Massachusetts Ave NW, Suite 700, Washington, DC 20001
Tel: 202-347-3375
Web Site: www.publishers.org
Founded: 2013 (merger of AAP School Division & Association of Educational Publishers (AEP))
Represents book & journal publishers in the US on matters of law & policy.
Number of Members: 350

AAR, see Association of Authors' Representatives Inc (AAR)

ABA, see American Booksellers Association

ABAC/ALAC
11 Marie St, Ottawa, ON K1N 9M5, Canada
Tel: 416-364-2376
E-mail: info@abac.org
Web Site: www.abac.org
Key Personnel
Pres: Robert Wright
Treas: Marvin Post
Founded: 1966
The association's aim is to foster an interest in rare books & mss & to maintain high standards in the antiquarian book trade.
Number of Members: 70
Publication(s): *ABAC/ALAC Membership Directory* (free by request)
Membership(s): International League of Antiquarian Booksellers

The Academy of American Poets Inc
75 Maiden Lane, Suite 901, New York, NY 10038
Tel: 212-274-0343
E-mail: academy@poets.org
Web Site: www.poets.org
Key Personnel
Pres & Exec Dir: Jennifer Benka
  E-mail: jenbenka@poets.org
Devt, Membership & Communs Sr Mgr: Molly Walsh *E-mail:* mwalsh@poets.org
Ad & Mktg Sr Mgr: Michelle Campagna
  E-mail: mcampagna@poets.org
Sr Progs Mgr: Nikay Paredes *Tel:* 212-274-0343 ext 13 *E-mail:* nparedes@poets.org
Founded: 1934
The country's largest nonprofit association devoted to poetry. Sponsors the James Laughlin Award, Walt Whitman Award, Harold Morton Landon Translation Award, Wallace Stevens Award, Lenore Marshall Poetry Prize & annual college poetry prizes; awards fellowship to American poets for distinguished poetic achievement. Publishes biannual journal. Also produces National Poetry Month.
Number of Members: 6,000
Publication(s): *American Poets* (semiannual, magazine)

Academy of Motion Picture Arts & Sciences (AMPAS)
8949 Wilshire Blvd, Beverly Hills, CA 90211
Tel: 310-247-3000 *Fax:* 310-859-9619
E-mail: ampas@oscars.org
Web Site: www.oscars.org
Key Personnel
CEO: Dawn Hudson
To advance the arts & sciences of motion pictures & to foster cooperation among the creative leadership of the motion picture industry for cultural, educational & technological progress. Confer annual awards of merit, serving as a constant incentive within the industry & focusing public attention upon the best in motion pictures.
Number of Members: 5,024
Publication(s): *Academy Players Directory, Annual Index to Motion Picture Credits, Nominations & Winners, List of Eligible Releases* (bulletin)

Academy of Television Arts & Sciences (ATAS), see Television Academy

Access Copyright, The Canadian Copyright Licensing Agency
56 Wellesley St W, Suite 401A, Toronto, ON M5S 2S3, Canada
Tel: 416-868-1620 *Toll Free Tel:* 800-893-5777
  Fax: 416-868-1621
E-mail: info@accesscopyright.ca
Web Site: www.accesscopyright.ca
Key Personnel
Pres & CEO: Roanie Levy
Founded: 1988
Number of Members: 36
Publication(s): *Online Access* (quarterly, newsletter, free, electronic)
Membership(s): Book & Periodical Council; International Federation of Reproduction Rights Organizations (IFRRO)

ACUP+, see Association of College & University Printers

Advertising Research Foundation (ARF)
432 Park Ave S, 4th fl, New York, NY 10016-8013
Tel: 212-751-5656 *Fax:* 212-689-1859
E-mail: help@thearf.org
Web Site: thearf.org
Key Personnel
Pres & CEO: Scott McDonald
COO & CFO: Thomas M Higgins
Chief Mktg Offr: Marc Rappin
Chief Res Offr: Paul Donato
EVP, Res & Innovation: Chris Bacon
EVP, Res & Innovation: Global & Ad Effectiveness: Horst Stipp, PhD
EVP, Memb Needs & Value: Michael Heitner
SVP, Events Prog Prodr: Rachael Feigenbaum
Dir, Busn Devt & Growth: Kelly Flynn
Founded: 1936
Advertising research service trade association.
Publication(s): *Journal of Advertising Research (JAR)* (quarterly, $365 standard subn; includes 4 print issues & 2-yr online archive)

AIGA, the professional association for design
222 Broadway, New York, NY 10038

Tel: 212-807-1990 *Fax:* 212-807-1799
E-mail: general@aiga.org
Web Site: www.aiga.org
Key Personnel
Exec Dir: Bennie F Johnson
Sr Dir, Admin: Amy Chapman *Tel:* 212-710-3137
Mng Ed: Sophia Ahn *Tel:* 212-710-3123
Founded: 1914
National nonprofit organization for graphic design profession. Organizes competitions, exhibitions, publications, educational activities & projects in the public interest to promote excellence in the graphic design industry.
Number of Members: 25,000
New Election: Annually in June
Meeting(s): AIGA Design Conference

ALA, see The American Library Association (ALA)

Alcuin Society
PO Box 3216, Sta Terminal, Vancouver, BC V6B 3X8, Canada
Tel: 604-732-5403
E-mail: info@alcuinsociety.com; awards@alcuinsociety.com
Web Site: alcuinsociety.com
Key Personnel
Chair, Book Design Competition: Leah Gordon
Judges book design; publishes articles on book arts, collecting, typography, private presses, book collections, book binding.
Number of Members: 275
New Election: March 2021
Publication(s): *Amphora* (3 issues/yr, journal, $50/yr membs, $75 instns)

Alliance for Audited Media (AAM)
48 W Seegers Rd, Arlington Heights, IL 60005
Tel: 224-366-6939 *Fax:* 224-366-6949
Web Site: auditedmedia.com
Key Personnel
Pres, CEO & Mng Dir: Tom Drouillard
  Tel: 224-366-6500 *E-mail:* tom.drouillard@auditedmedia.com
Cooperative association of advertisers, advertising agencies & publishers of newspapers, magazines, farm & business publications. Audit & report circulation, web site & additional digital edition analytics, including mobile application activity for publisher brands in North America.
Number of Members: 4,500
Branch Office(s)
28 W 44 St, Suite 1011, New York, NY 10036
  Tel: 212-867-8992 *Fax:* 212-867-8947
151 Bloor St W, Suite 850, Toronto, ON M5S 1S4, Canada, VP & Gen Mgr: Joan Brehl
  Tel: 416-962-5840 *Fax:* 416-962-5844
  E-mail: joan.brehl@auditedmedia.com

Alliance for Women in Media (AWM)
1250 24 St NW, Suite 300, Washington, DC 20037
Tel: 202-750-3664 *Fax:* 202-750-3664
E-mail: info@allwomeninmedia.org
Web Site: allwomeninmedia.org
Key Personnel
Exec Dir: Becky Brooks
Founded: 1951
For members of the electronic & media industries.

Number of Members: 3,000
Publication(s): *FastForward* (enewsletter)

American Academy of Arts & Sciences (AAAS)

Norton's Woods, 136 Irving St, Cambridge, MA 02138
Tel: 617-576-5000 *Fax:* 617-576-5050
E-mail: aaas@amacad.org
Web Site: www.amacad.org
Key Personnel
Pres: Jonathan Fanton
Promote interchange of ideas through seminars & publications.
Number of Members: 6,000
Publication(s): *Daedalus*

American Academy of Political & Social Science

202 S 36 St, Philadelphia, PA 19104-3806
Tel: 215-746-6500 *Fax:* 215-573-2667
Web Site: www.aapss.org
Key Personnel
Exec Dir: Tom Kecskemethy *Tel:* 215-746-7321
  E-mail: tom.kecskemethy@asc.upenn.edu
Assoc Dir & Mng Ed: Emily W Babson *Tel:* 215-898-5081 *E-mail:* emily.babson@asc.upenn.edu
Founded: 1889
Nonprofit organization.
Publication(s): *The Annals of American Academy of Political & Social Science* (6 issues/yr, $126/yr indivs, $1,016/yr instns (e-access), $1,129/yr (print & e-access))

American Antiquarian Society (AAS)

185 Salisbury St, Worcester, MA 01609-1634
Tel: 508-755-5221 *Fax:* 508-753-3311
E-mail: library@americanantiquarian.org
Web Site: www.americanantiquarian.org
Key Personnel
Pres: Ellen S Dunlap *Tel:* 508-471-2161
  E-mail: edunlap@mwa.org
Founded: 1812
Maintain research library in American history & culture through 1876.
Number of Members: 1,028

American Association for the Advancement of Science (AAAS)

1200 New York Ave NW, Washington, DC 20005
Tel: 202-326-6400
E-mail: media@aaas.org
Web Site: www.aaas.org
Key Personnel
CEO: Sudip Parikh
Chief Communs Offr & Dir, Off Public Progs: Tiffany Lohwater
Founded: 1848
Mission is to further the work of scientists, to facilitate cooperation among them, foster scientific freedom & responsibility, improve effectiveness of science in the promotion of human welfare & to increase public understanding & appreciation of the importance & promise of the methods of science in human progress. There are many membership organizations & professional societies which have similar aims or have interest in supporting these objectives. For further information, contact the AAAS Office of News & Information at the above address. US regional divisions: Arctic; Caribbean; Pacific; Southwest & Rocky Mountains.
New Election: Annually in the Fall
2021 Meeting(s): Annual Meeting (Serving Society Through Science Policy), Phoenix, AZ, Feb 11-14, 2021
2022 Meeting(s): Annual Meeting (Serving Society Through Science Policy), Philadelphia, PA, Feb 17-20, 2022
Publication(s): *Science* (weekly, journal, $10/issue, $135/yr prof rate); *Science Advances*

(journal); *Science Immunology* (journal); *Science Signaling* (journal); *Science Translational Medicine* (journal)

American Auto Racing Writers & Broadcasters

922 N Pass Ave, Burbank, CA 91505
Tel: 818-842-7005 *Fax:* 818-842-7020
Key Personnel
Pres: Ms Dusty Brandel
Media people who cover auto racing.
Number of Members: 300

American Book Producers Association (ABPA)

31 W Eighth St, 2nd fl, New York, NY 10011
Tel: 212-675-1363 *Fax:* 212-675-1364
E-mail: office@abpaonline.org
Web Site: www.abpaonline.org
Key Personnel
Pres: Richard Rothschild
VP: Nancy Hall
Treas: Valerie Tomaselli
Bd of Dirs: Leslie Carola; Karen Matsu Greenberg; Susan Knopf
Founded: 1980
An organization of independent book producing companies in the US & CN.
Number of Members: 60
Publication(s): *Booknews* (membs only)

American Booksellers Association

333 Westchester Ave, Suite S202, White Plains, NY 10604
Tel: 914-406-7500 *Toll Free Tel:* 800-637-0037
  Fax: 914-417-4013
E-mail: info@bookweb.org
Web Site: www.bookweb.org
Key Personnel
CEO: Allison Hill
COO: Joy Dallanegra-Sanger *Tel:* 800-637-0037 ext 7518 *E-mail:* joy@bookweb.org
CFO: PK Sindwani
Sr Strategy Offr: Dan Cullen *Tel:* 800-637-0037 ext 7560 *E-mail:* dan@bookweb.org
Meetings & Planning Offr: Jill Perlstein *Tel:* 800-637-0037 ext 7542 *E-mail:* jill@bookweb.org
Dir, Devt & Publr Rel: Matthew Zoni *Tel:* 800-637-0037 ext 7551 *E-mail:* matthew@bookweb.org
Dir, Public Policy & Advocacy: David Grogan *Tel:* 800-637-0037 ext 7562 *E-mail:* dave@bookweb.org
Content Dir: Sydney Jarrard *Tel:* 914-406-7563 *E-mail:* sydney@bookweb.org
Technol Dir: Greg Galloway *Tel:* 800-637-0037 ext 7568 *E-mail:* greg@bookweb.org
Sr Mgr, IndieCommerce: Geetha Nathan *Tel:* 800-637-0037 ext 7526 *E-mail:* geetha@bookweb.org
Sr Membership Mgr: Daniel O'Brien
ABC Group Mgr: Gen de Botton *Tel:* 800-637-0037 ext 7545 *E-mail:* gen@bookweb.org
Educ Mgr: Lisa Winn
Prog Mgr: Peter Reynolds *Tel:* 800-637-0037 ext 7535 *E-mail:* peter@bookweb.org
Meetings & Off Coord: Maria Rodriguez
Soc Media Coord: Akira McKinzie
Founded: 1900
Trade organization representing independent booksellers. Co-sponsor of BookExpo along with Association of American Publishers (AAP) & Association of Authors' Representatives Inc (AAR).
Number of Members: 3,500
Publication(s): *Book Buyers Handbook* (electronic); *Bookselling This Week* (electronic)
Membership(s): Book Industry Study Group (BISG)

American Christian Writers

PO Box 110390, Nashville, TN 37222-0390

Tel: 615-331-8668 *Toll Free Tel:* 800-21-WRITE (219-7483)
E-mail: acwriters@aol.com
Web Site: regaforder.wordpress.com
Key Personnel
Pres: Reg A Forder
2021 Meeting(s): Mentoring Retreat, Nashville, TN, April 9-10, 2021; Mentoring Retreat, Grand Rapids, MI, June 4-5, 2021; Mentoring Retreat, Atlanta, GA, July 9-10, 2021; Mentoring Retreat, Minneapolis, MN, Aug 6-7, 2021; Mentoring Retreat, Phoenix, AZ, Sept 10-11, 2021; Mentoring Retreat, Nashville, TN, Oct 1-2, 2021; Mentoring Retreat, Orlando, FL, Nov 12-13, 2021
Membership(s): Evangelical Christian Publishers Association (ECPA); Evangelical Press Association (EPA); Global Network of Christian Ministries

American Civil Liberties Union

125 Broad St, 18th fl, New York, NY 10004
Tel: 212-549-2500
E-mail: media@aclu.org
Web Site: www.aclu.org
Key Personnel
Pres: Susan N Herman
Chief Communs Offr: Michele Moore
Exec Dir: Anthony D Romero
Protection of constitutional rights & civil liberties through litigation, legislative lobbying & public education; 250 branch offices.
Number of Members: 500,000

American Council on Education

One Dupont Circle NW, Washington, DC 20036
Tel: 202-939-9300 *Fax:* 202-939-9302
E-mail: pubs@acenet.edu
Web Site: www.acenet.edu
Key Personnel
Pres: Ted Mitchell
Asst VP, Pub Aff: Jon Riskind *E-mail:* jriskind@acenet.edu
Founded: 1918
The nation's major coordinating body for postsecondary education. Professional books & guides in higher education (special studies & reports on higher education).
Number of Members: 1,850
2021 Meeting(s): 103rd Annual Meeting, Washington Marriott Wardman Park, Washington, DC, March 20-22, 2021

American Forest & Paper Association (AF&PA)

1101 "K" St NW, Suite 700, Washington, DC 20005
Tel: 202-463-2700
E-mail: info@afandpa.org
Web Site: www.afandpa.org
Key Personnel
Pres & CEO: Donna A Harman
VP, Admin & CFO: Samuel Kerns
VP, Gen Coun & Corp Secy: Jan A Poling
Founded: 1993
National trade association of the forest products industry.
Number of Members: 120
2021 Meeting(s): Paper2021, The Whitley Atlanta Buckhead, Atlanta, GA, March 14-16, 2021

American Institute of Graphic Arts, see AIGA, the professional association for design

American Jewish Committee (AJC)

Affiliate of Institute of Human Relations
Jacob Blaustein Bldg, 165 E 56 St, New York, NY 10022
Tel: 212-751-4000; 212-891-1456 (membership)
  Fax: 212-891-1450
Web Site: www.ajc.org

Key Personnel
Exec Dir: David A Harris *E-mail:* harrisd@ajc.
org
Dir, Pubns: Lawrence Grossman *Tel:* 212-751-
4000 ext 308 *E-mail:* grossmanl@ajc.org
Founded: 1906
Civic & religious rights of Jews in the US &
abroad; intergroup relations & human rights.
Number of Members: 43,000
Branch Office(s)
2027 Massachusetts Ave NW, Washington, DC
20036

The American Library Association (ALA)
225 N Michigan Ave, Suite 1300, Chicago, IL
60601
Tel: 312-944-6780; 312-280-4299 (memb & cust
serv) *Toll Free Tel:* 800-545-2433 *Fax:* 312-
440-9374
E-mail: ala@ala.org; customerservice@ala.org
Web Site: www.ala.org
Key Personnel
Exec Dir: Tracie D Hall
Founded: 1876
ALA is the oldest & largest library association in
the world. ALA promotes the highest quality
library & information services & public access
to information. Offers professional services &
publications to members & nonmembers.
Number of Members: 60,000
2021 Meeting(s): Midwinter Meeting, Indianapolis, IN, Jan 22-26, 2021; National Library
Week, Nationwide throughout the USA, April
4-10, 2021; Annual Conference, Chicago, IL,
June 24-29, 2021
2022 Meeting(s): National Library Week, Nationwide throughout the USA, April 3-9, 2022; Annual Conference, Washington, DC, June 23-28,
2022
2023 Meeting(s): National Library Week, Nationwide throughout the USA, April 23-29, 2023;
Annual Conference, Chicago, IL, June 22-27,
2023
2024 Meeting(s): Annual Conference, San Diego,
CA, June 27-July 2, 2024
Publication(s): *American Libraries* (6 issues/yr,
magazine, free to membs, $70/yr instns US &
CN, $80/yr instns foreign)
Branch Office(s)
1615 New Hampshire Ave NW, 1st fl, Washington, DC 20009-2520 *Tel:* 202-628-8410 *Toll
Free Tel:* 800-941-8478 *Fax:* 202-628-8419

American Literacy Council
1441 Mariposa Ave, Boulder, CO 80302
Tel: 303-440-7385
Web Site: www.americanliteracy.com
Key Personnel
Pres: Alan Mole *E-mail:* president@
americanliteracy.com
Dir & Opers Mgr: Joseph R Little *Tel:* 212-
663-4200 *E-mail:* spellingprogress@
americanliteracy.com
Founded: 1876
To convey information on new solutions, inno-
vative technologies & tools for engaging more
boldly in the battle for literacy.
Number of Members: 12

American Literary Translators Association (ALTA)
University of Arizona, Esquire Bldg, No 205,
1230 N Park Ave, Tucson, AZ 85721
Tel: 520-621-1757
Web Site: www.literarytranslators.org
Key Personnel
Exec Dir: Elisabeth Jaquette *E-mail:* elisabeth@
literarytranslators.org
Communs & Awards Mgr: Rachael Daum
Tel: 413-200-0459 *E-mail:* rachaeldaum@
literarytranslators.org

Prog Mgr: Kelsi Vananda *E-mail:* kelsi@
literarytranslators.org
Secy: Jessica Sue Vocatura *E-mail:* jessica@
literarytranslators.org
Founded: 1978
Literary translation & translators. ALTA's pro-
grams are supported in part by a grant from the
National Endowment for the Arts.
Number of Members: 800
Publication(s): *Translation Review* (3 issues/yr,
$100/yr indivs, $30/students)

American Marketing Association
130 E Randolph St, 22nd fl, Chicago, IL 60601
Tel: 312-542-9000 *Toll Free Tel:* 800-AMA-1150
(262-1150)
Web Site: www.ama.org
Key Personnel
CEO: Russ Klein *E-mail:* rklein@ama.org
COO: Jeremy Van Ek *E-mail:* jvanek@ama.org
Chief Alliances Offr: Barbara Grobicki
E-mail: bgrobicki@ama.org
Chief Content Offr: Andy Friedman
E-mail: afriedman@ama.org
Chief Experience Offr: Jennifer Severns
E-mail: jseverns@ama.org
Dir, Integrated Academic Content: Matt Weingar-
den *Tel:* 312-542-9012 *E-mail:* mweingarden@
ama.org
Founded: 1937
A nonprofit, educational institution. Offers online
marketing info. Sponsors seminars, conferences
& student marketing clubs & doctoral consor-
tium. Publish books, journals, magazines &
proceedings of conferences.
Number of Members: 30,000
Publication(s): *Journal of International Marketing*
(quarterly); *Journal of Marketing* (6 issues/yr);
Journal of Marketing Research (6 issues/yr);
Journal of Public Policy & Marketing (semiannual); *Marketing News* (monthly)

American Medical Association
AMA Plaza, 330 N Wabash, Suite 39300,
Chicago, IL 60611-5885
Tel: 312-464-5000 *Toll Free Tel:* 800-621-8335
Web Site: www.ama-assn.org
Key Personnel
CEO & EVP: James L Madara, MD
SVP & Publr, Periodic Pubns: Thomas J Easley
Promotes the science & art of medicine & bet-
terment of public health. Association of physi-
cians.
Publication(s): *JAMA: Dermatology* (monthly);
JAMA: Facial Plastic Surgery (6 issues/yr);
JAMA: Internal Medicine (monthly); *JAMA:
Neurology* (monthly); *JAMA: Ophthalmology*
(monthly); *JAMA: Otolaryngology* (monthly);
JAMA: Pediatrics (monthly); *JAMA: Psychiatry*
(monthly); *JAMA: Surgery* (monthly); *JAMA:
The Journal of the American Medical Associa-
tion* (weekly)
Branch Office(s)
119 Cherry Hill Rd, Parsippany, NJ 07054

American Medical Writers Association (AMWA)
30 W Gude Dr, Suite 525, Rockville, MD 20850-
4357
Tel: 240-238-0940 *Fax:* 301-294-9006
E-mail: amwa@amwa.org
Web Site: www.amwa.org
Key Personnel
Exec Dir: Susan Krug *Tel:* 240-238-0940 ext 109
E-mail: skrug@amwa.org
Deputy Dir: Shari Rager *Tel:* 240-238-0940 ext
107 *E-mail:* srager@amwa.org
Founded: 1940
Professional organization for writers, editors &
other communicators of medical information.
Number of Members: 5,300

2021 Meeting(s): Annual Conference, Chicago
Marriott Downtown Magnificent Mile, Chicago,
IL, Oct 27-30, 2021
Publication(s): *AMWA Journal* (quarterly, journal,
free to membs, $75/yr nonmembs); *Freelance
Directory* (online, directory, free); *Jobs Online*
(monthly, classified listing)

American Political Science Association
1527 New Hampshire Ave NW, Washington, DC
20036-1203
Tel: 202-483-2512 *Fax:* 202-483-2657
E-mail: apsa@apsanet.org; membership@apsanet.
org; press@apsanet.org
Web Site: www.apsanet.org
Key Personnel
Exec Dir: Steven Rathgeb Smith
E-mail: smithsr@apsanet.org
Founded: 1903
Provide services to facilitate research, teaching &
professional development in political science,
including publications & services to assist col-
lege faculty, graduate students & researchers.
Number of Members: 15,000
2021 Meeting(s): Annual Meeting & Exhibition,
Seattle, WA, Sept 29-Oct 3, 2021
2022 Meeting(s): Annual Meeting & Exhibition,
Montreal, QB, CN, Sept 14-18, 2022
Publication(s): *American Political Science Review*
(quarterly); *The Journal of Political Science
Education* (quarterly); *Perspectives on Politics*
(quarterly); *PS: Political Science & Politics*
(quarterly)

American Printing History Association
PO Box 4519, Grand Central Sta, New York, NY
10163
E-mail: secretary@printinghistory.org
Web Site: printinghistory.org
Key Personnel
Pres: Haven Hawley
VP, Membership: Charles Cuykendall Carter
VP, Progs: Jesse Erickson
VP, Pubns: Katherine McCanless Ruffin
Treas: David Goodrich
Secy: Virginia Bartow
Exec Secy: Lyndsi Barnes
Local chapters in New York City, Upstate New
York, New England, Inland, Chesapeake, Ohio
River Valley, Southern & Northern California.
Number of Members: 700
New Election: Annually in Jan

American Public Human Services Association
1133 19 St NW, Suite 400, Washington, DC
20036
Tel: 202-682-0100 *Fax:* 202-289-6555
E-mail: memberservice@aphsa.org
Web Site: www.aphsa.org
Key Personnel
Pres & CEO: Tracy Wareing Evans *Tel:* 202-682-
0100 ext 231 *E-mail:* tracy.wareing@aphsa.org
Communs Mgr: Jessica Garon *Tel:* 202-682-0100
ext 223 *E-mail:* jgaron@aphsa.org
Membership & Mktg Mgr: Guy DeSilva *Tel:* 202-
682-0100 ext 280 *E-mail:* gdesilva@aphsa.org
Founded: 1930
Membership organization of public human ser-
vices professionals.
Number of Members: 5,000
New Election: Annually in Dec
Publication(s): *Policy & Practice* (6 issues/yr,
magazine, $65 single copy, $75 single copy
intl, $400/yr, $475/yr intl); *This Week In Washington* (weekly when Congress is in session,
newsletter, free, electronic)

American Society for Indexing Inc (ASI)
1628 E Southern Ave, Suite 9-223, Tempe, AZ
85282
Tel: 480-245-6750
E-mail: info@asindexing.org

Web Site: www.asindexing.org
Key Personnel
Exec Dir: Gwen Henson *E-mail:* gwen@
asindexing.org
Founded: 1968
Educational programs for indexing field.
Number of Members: 450
New Election: Annually in May
Publication(s): *KeyWords* (monthly, magazine,
free to membs, $40 nonmembs)

American Society of Composers, Authors & Publishers (ASCAP)

1900 Broadway, New York City, NY 10023
Tel: 212-621-6000 *Fax:* 212-612-8453
E-mail: info@ascap.com
Web Site: www.ascap.com
Key Personnel
Chmn of the Bd & Pres: Paul Williams
E-mail: pwilliams@ascap.com
CEO: Elizabeth Matthews *E-mail:* ematthews@
ascap.com
EVP & COO: Brian Roberts
CTO: Tristan Boutros
EVP & Chief Mktg Offr: Lauren Iossa
E-mail: liossa@ascap.com
EVP, Membership: John Titta *E-mail:* jtitta@
ascap.com
Assoc Dir, Global Writer & Publr Servs: Ryan
O'Grady
Founded: 1914
License nondramatic right of public performance
of members' copyrighted musical compositions
& distribute royalties to members on basis of
performances. Members are composers, song-
writers, lyricists & music publishers.
Number of Members: 500,000
Branch Office(s)
7920 W Sunset Blvd, 3rd fl, Los Angeles, CA
90046 *Tel:* 323-883-1000 *Fax:* 323-883-1049
420 Lincoln Rd, Suite 502, Miami Beach, FL
33139 *Tel:* 305-673-3446 *Fax:* 305-673-2446
950 Joseph E Lowery Blvd NW, Suite 23, Atlanta, GA 30318 *Tel:* 404-685-8699 *Fax:* 404-
685-8701
Two Music Sq W, Nashville, TN 37203 *Tel:* 615-
742-5000 *Fax:* 615-742-5020
Ave Martinez Nadal, c/ Hill Side 623, San
Juan 00920, Puerto Rico *Tel:* 787-707-0782
Fax: 787-707-0783
4 Millbank, 2nd fl, London SW1P 3JA, United
Kingdom *Tel:* (020) 7439 0909 *Fax:* (020)
7434 0073

American Society of Journalists and Authors (ASJA)

355 Lexington Ave, 15th fl, New York, NY
10017-6603
Tel: 212-997-0947
Web Site: asja.org
Key Personnel
Exec Dir: Holly Koenig *E-mail:* director@asja.org
Founded: 1948
Service organization providing exchange of ideas
& market information. Regular meetings with
speakers from the industry, annual writers con-
ference; medical plans available. Professional
referral service, annual membership directory;
first amendment advocacy group.
Number of Members: 1,400
Publication(s): *ASJA Monthly* (11 issues/yr online,
printed quarterly, newsletter, membs only)

American Society of Magazine Editors (ASME)

PO Box 112, New York, NY 10163
Tel: 212-872-3737
E-mail: asme@asme.media
Web Site: www.asme.media
Key Personnel
Exec Dir: Sid Holt *Tel:* 212-872-3723
E-mail: sholt@asme.media

Dir of Opers: Nina Fortuna *E-mail:* nfortuna@
asme.media
Founded: 1963
Professional society for senior magazine edi-
tors. Sponsor the National Magazine Awards
in association with the Columbia Journalism
School; hold monthly luncheons for members
& conduct periodic seminars.
Number of Members: 700
New Election: Annually in April

American Society of Media Photographers Inc

PO Box 31207, Bethesda, MD 20804
Toll Free Tel: 877-771-2767 *Fax:* 231-946-6180
E-mail: asmp@vpassociations.com
Web Site: asmp.org
Key Personnel
CEO: James Edmund Datri *E-mail:* jdatri@asmp.
org
Founded: 1944
Maintain & promote high professional standards
& ethics in photography; cultivate mutual un-
derstanding among professional photographers;
protect & promote interests of photographers
whose work is for publication.
Number of Members: 5,785
Publication(s): *The ASMP Guide to New Markets
in Photography* ($24.95); *ASMP Professional
Business Practices in Photography, 7th Ed*
($23.21); *Digital Photography Best Practices
& Workflow & Handbook* ($17.92 membs)

American Society of News Editors (ASNE)

209 Reynolds Journalism Institute, Missouri
School of Journalism, Columbia, MO 65211
Tel: 573-882-2430 *Fax:* 573-884-3824
Web Site: asne.org
Key Personnel
Exec Dir: Teri Hayt *Tel:* 573-882-9854
E-mail: thayt@asne.org
Freelance Event Coord: Megan Morrison
E-mail: mschumacher@asne.org
Communs Coord: Jiyoung Won *E-mail:* jwon@
asne.org
Founded: 1922
Nonprofit professional organization focused on
leadership development & journalism-related
issues.

American Sociological Association (ASA)

1430 "K" St NW, Suite 600, Washington, DC
20005-4701
Tel: 202-383-9005 *Fax:* 202-638-0882
Web Site: www.asanet.org
Key Personnel
Exec Offr: Nancy Kidd *Tel:* 202-383-9005 ext
316 *E-mail:* executive.office@asanet.org
Pubns Dir: Karen Gray Edwards *Tel:* 202-383-
9005 ext 319 *E-mail:* publications@asanet.org
Founded: 1905
Nonprofit membership association dedicated to
advancing sociology as a scientific discipline &
profession serving the public good. Encompass
sociologists who are faculty members at colleges & universities, researchers, practitioners
& students.
Number of Members: 13,000
New Election: Annually in Aug
2021 Meeting(s): Annual Meeting, Hyatt Regency
Chicago, Chicago, IL, Aug 14-17, 2021
2022 Meeting(s): Annual Meeting, Los Angeles
Convention Center, Los Angeles, CA, Aug 13-
16, 2022
2023 Meeting(s): Annual Meeting, Philadelphia Convention Center, Marriott & Loews,
Philadelphia, PA, Aug 18-21, 2023
2024 Meeting(s): Annual Meeting, Palais des
Congres de Montreal, Montreal, QC, CN, Aug
10-13, 2024
Publication(s): *American Sociological Review*
(6 issues/yr, $45 membs, $30 student membs,
$695 instns (print/online), $625 instns (online

only); *Contemporary Sociology* (6 issues/yr,
$45 membs, $30 student membs, $553 instns
(print/online), $499 instns (online only); *Con-
texts* (quarterly, magazine, $45 membs, $30 student membs, $339 instns (print/online), $307
instns (online only); *Footnotes* (newsletter,
free online); *Journal of Health & Social Behavior* (quarterly, $45 membs (print), $30 student membs (print), $491 instns (print/online),
$443 instns (online only), online access free to
membs); *Social Psychology Quarterly* (quarterly, $45 membs (print), $30 student membs
(print), $491 instns (print/online), $443 instns
(online only), online access free to membs);
Sociological Methodology (annual, $45 membs
(print), $30 student membs (print), $491 instns (print/online), $443 instns (online only),
online access free to membs); *Sociological
Theory* (quarterly, $45 membs (print), $30
student membs (print), $491 instns (print/on-
line), $443 instns (online only), online access
free to membs); *Sociology of Education* (quarterly, $45 membs (print), $30 student membs
(print), $491 instns (print/online), $443 instns
(online only), online access free to membs);
Teaching Sociology ($45 membs (print), $30
student membs (print), $491 instns (print/on-
line), $443 instns (online only), online access
free to membs)

American Speech-Language-Hearing Association (ASHA)

2200 Research Blvd, Rockville, MD 20850-3289
Tel: 301-296-5700 *Toll Free Tel:* 800-638-
8255 (nonmembs); 800-498-2071 (membs)
Fax: 301-296-5777; 301-296-8580
E-mail: actioncenter@asha.org
Web Site: www.asha.org
Founded: 1925
Membership organization for speech-language
pathologists & audiologists. Provide consumers with information & referral on speech,
language & hearing. Publish information
brochures & packets.
Number of Members: 186,000
New Election: Annually in Sept
Publication(s): *American Journal of Audiology*
(quarterly, journal, $15/single article for 24
hours, $30 for entire site for 24 hours, $110/yr
electronic nonmembs, $270/yr electronic instns,
$160/yr online archive nonmembs & instns);
*American Journal of Speech-Language Pathol-
ogy* (quarterly, journal, $15/single article for 24
hours, $30 for entire site for 24 hours, $110/yr
electronic nonmembs, $270/yr electronic in-
stns, $197/yr online archives nonmembs &
instns); *The ASHA Leader* (monthly, newspaper, $129/yr nonmembs, $172/yr foreign nonmembs, $194/instns, $243 foreign instns); *Journal of Speech, Language & Hearing Research*
(monthly, journal, $15/single article for 24
hours, $30 for entire site for 24 hours, $230/yr
electronic nonmembs, $648/yr electronic in-
stns, $461/yr online archives nonmembs & in-
stns); *Language, Speech & Hearing Services
In Schools* (quarterly, journal, $15/single ar-
ticle for 24 hours, $30 for entire site for 24
hours, $110/yr electronic nonmembs, $270/yr
electronic instns, $197/yr online archives non-
membs & instns)
Branch Office(s)
444 N Capitol St NW, Suite 715, Washington,
DC 20001 *Tel:* 202-624-5884

American Translators Association (ATA)

225 Reinekers Lane, Suite 590, Alexandria, VA
22314
Tel: 703-683-6100 *Fax:* 703-683-6122
E-mail: ata@atanet.org
Web Site: www.atanet.org
Key Personnel
Exec Dir: Walter W Bacak, Jr *E-mail:* walter@
atanet.org

Founded: 1959

Membership consists of those professionally engaged in translating, interpreting or closely allied work, as well as those who are interested in these fields. Membership: $190/yr indivs, $350/yr corps, $235/yr instl, $80/yr students.

Number of Members: 11,000

2021 Meeting(s): Annual Conference, Minneapolis, MN, Oct 27-30, 2021

2022 Meeting(s): Annual Conference, Los Angeles, CA, Oct 12-15, 2022

2023 Meeting(s): Annual Conference, Miami, FL, Oct 25-28, 2023

2024 Meeting(s): Annual Conference, Portland, OR, Oct 30-Nov 2, 2024

Publication(s): *The ATA Chronicle* (6 issues/yr, $65, $90 CN & Mexico, $110 all other countries); *Directory of Translators and Interpreters* (online only)

Membership(s): Federation of International Translators

Antiquarian Booksellers' Association of America (ABAA)

20 W 44 St, Suite 507, New York, NY 10036

Tel: 212-944-8291 *Fax:* 212-944-8293

E-mail: hq@abaa.org

Web Site: www.abaa.org

Key Personnel

Exec Dir: Susan Benne *E-mail:* sbenne@abaa.org

Founded: 1949

Chapters: Northern California, Southern California, Midwest, Middle Atlantic, New England, Southeast, Southwest & Pacific Northwest. Membership open to antiquarian booksellers only. ABAA sponsors 3 or 4 international book fairs per year in Los Angeles & San Francisco (alternately) in Midwinter; in NY in the Spring; in Boston in late Autumn.

Number of Members: 450

Meeting(s): New York International Antiquarian Book Fair

2021 Meeting(s): California International Antiquarian Book Fair, Oakland Marriott City Center, 1001 Broadway, Oakland, CA,, Feb 12-14, 2021

Publication(s): *Newsletter* (quarterly, free, electronic)

Antiquarian Booksellers' Association of Canada/Association de la Librairie Ancienne du Canada, see ABAC/ALAC

ASHA, see American Speech-Language-Hearing Association (ASHA)

Asian American Writers' Workshop

112 W 27 St, Suite 600, New York, NY 10001

Tel: 212-494-0061

E-mail: desk@aaww.org

Web Site: aaww.org; facebook.com/AsianAmericanWritersWorkshop

Key Personnel

Exec Dir: Jafreen Uddin

Public Events & Workshops Coord: Tiffany Tran Lee

Edit Coord: Yasmin Adele Majeed

Ed-in-Chief: Jyothi Natarajan

Sr Ed: Noel T Pangilinan

Founded: 1991

Not-for-profit arts organization devoted to the creating, publishing, developing & disseminating of creative writing by Asian Americans.

ASMP, see American Society of Media Photographers Inc

Aspen Words

110 E Hallam St, Suite 116, Aspen, CO 81611

Tel: 970-925-3122 *Fax:* 970-920-5700

E-mail: aspenwords@aspeninstitute.org

Web Site: www.aspenwords.org

Key Personnel

Exec Dir: Adrienne Brodeur *Tel:* 646-461-3554 *E-mail:* adrienne.brodeur@aspeninstitute.org

Mng Dir: Jamie Kravitz *Tel:* 970-925-3122 ext 2 *E-mail:* jamie.kravitz@aspeninstitute.org

Sr Prog Assoc, Mktg & Communs: Caroline Tory *Tel:* 970-925-3122 ext 3 *E-mail:* caroline.tory@aspeninstitute.org

Founded: 1976

Program of the Aspen Institute. Encourages writers, inspires readers & connects people through the exchange of words, stories & ideas.

Meeting(s): Aspen Summer Words Writing Conference & Literary Festival, Aspen, CO, June

Associated Business Writers of America Inc

Division of National Writers Association

10940 S Parker Rd, Suite 508, Parker, CO 80134

Tel: 303-841-0246

E-mail: natlwritersassn@hotmail.com

Web Site: www.nationalwriters.com

Key Personnel

Exec Dir: Sandy Whelchel *E-mail:* authorsandy@hotmail.com

To help business writers & those seeking their services.

Number of Members: 80

Associated Press Broadcast

1100 13 St NW, Suite 500, Washington, DC 20005

Tel: 202-641-9000 *Toll Free Tel:* 800-821-4747 *Fax:* 202-370-2710

E-mail: info@ap.org

Web Site: www.ap.org

Number of Members: 5,800

Publication(s): *AP Stylebook* (annual, $20.95)

Association canadienne des reviseurs, see Editors' Association of Canada (Association canadienne des reviseurs)

Association des Editeurs de Langue Anglaise du Quebec, see The Association of English-Language Publishers of Quebec-AELAQ (Association des Editeurs de Langue Anglaise du Quebec)

Association des Libraires du Quebec (ALQ)

483, blvd St Joseph E, Montreal, QC H2J 1J8, Canada

Tel: 514-526-3349 *Fax:* 514-526-3340

E-mail: info@alq.qc.ca

Web Site: www.alq.qc.ca

Key Personnel

CEO: Katherine Fafard *E-mail:* kfafard@alq.qc.ca

Founded: 1969

Quebec association of booksellers.

Number of Members: 125

Association for Information & Image Management International (AIIM)

1100 Wayne Ave, Suite 1100, Silver Spring, MD 20910

Tel: 301-587-8202 *Toll Free Tel:* 800-477-2446 *Fax:* 301-587-2711

E-mail: aiim@aiim.org; info@aiim.org

Web Site: www.aiim.org

Key Personnel

Pres & CEO: Peggy Winston

VP, Mktg: Anthony Paille *E-mail:* apaille@aiim.org

Dir, Sales: Joe Ryan *E-mail:* jryan@aiim.org

Digital Mktg Mgr: Sean McGauley *E-mail:* smcgauley@aiim.org

Global association bringing together the users of document technologies with the providers of that technology.

Number of Members: 9,197

Branch Office(s)

AIIM Europe, Broomhall Business Centre, Lower Broomhall Farm, Broomhall Lane, WR5 2NT, United Kingdom *Tel:* (01905) 727600; (01905) 679164; (07484) 731465 (cell)

Association for Information Science & Technology (ASIS&T)

8555 16 St, Suite 850, Silver Spring, MD 20910

Tel: 301-495-0900 *Fax:* 301-495-0810

E-mail: asist@asist.org

Web Site: www.asist.org

Key Personnel

Exec Dir: Lydia Middleton *E-mail:* lmiddleton@asist.org

Dir, Fin & Admin: Humberto Doldan *E-mail:* hdoldan@asist.org

Dir, Meetings & Events: DeVonne Parks *E-mail:* dparks@asist.org

Dir, Meetings & Membership: Maureen Markey *E-mail:* mmarkey@asist.org

Mgr, Memb Servs & Communs: Stephan Addo *E-mail:* saddo@asist.org

Acctg Asst & Meeting Registrar: Carline Haynes *E-mail:* chaynes@asist.org

Founded: 1937

To foster & lead the advancement of information science & technology.

Number of Members: 4,000

2021 Meeting(s): ASIS&T Annual Meeting, Salt Lake City, UT, Oct 29-Nov 3, 2021

Publication(s): *Bulletin of the Association for Information Science & Technology* (6 issues/yr); *Journal of the Association for Information Science & Technology (JASIST)*

Association for PRINT Technologies (APTech)

1896 Preston White Dr, Reston, VA 20191

Tel: 703-264-7200 *Fax:* 703-620-0994

E-mail: aptech@aptech.org

Web Site: www.printtechnologies.org

Key Personnel

Pres: Thayer Long *E-mail:* thayer_long@aptech.org

VP, Mktg & Communs: Sarah Markfield *E-mail:* smarkfield@aptech.org

Dir, Mktg & Communs: Jane Pratt *E-mail:* jpratt@aptech.org

Founded: 1933 (as the National Printing Equipment Association)

US trade association representing more than 650 companies that manufacture & distribute equipment, software & supplies used across the workflow of printing, publishing & converting processes. Owns & produces the global PRINT® exhibition, the most comprehensive exhibition in the Americas for the printing & digital imaging industries.

Number of Members: 650

Publication(s): *NPES Pressroom Safety Manual*; *Safe Cleaning of Offset Sheetfed Presses*; *Safe Cleaning of Offset Webfed Presses*

Membership(s): American Society of Association Executives (ASAE); Council of Manufacturing Associations; International Association of Exhibitions and Events® (IAEE); National Association of Manufacturers (NAM)

Association Media & Publishing (AM&P)

Division of Connectiv

1090 Vermont Ave NW, 6th fl, Washington, DC 20005-4905

Tel: 212-784-6398

E-mail: info@associationmediaandpublishing.org; sales@associationmediaandpublishing.org

Web Site: www.siia.net/amp

Key Personnel

Exec Dir: Michael Marchesano *Tel:* 646-568-1309 *E-mail:* executivedirector@associationmediaandpublishing.org

Dir, Strategic Partnerships: Heather Cejovic *Tel:* 908-612-0134

Mktg & Communs Mgr: Allison Bostrom
Tel: 703-554-4632
Founded: 1963 (as Society of National Association Publications)
A nonprofit professional society that serves the needs of association & society publications & their staff to represent, promote & advance the common interest of periodicals of voluntary associations & societies.
Number of Members: 1,400
Publication(s): *Signature* (6 issues/yr, magazine)

Association nationale des editeurs de livres
2514, blvd Rosemont, Montreal, QC H1Y 1K4, Canada
Tel: 514-273-8130 *Toll Free Tel:* 866-900-ANEL (900-2635)
E-mail: info@anel.qc.ca
Web Site: www.anel.qc.ca
Key Personnel
Dir Gen: Richard Prieur *E-mail:* prieur@anel.qc.ca
Deputy Dir Gen: Karine Vachon
  E-mail: vachon@anel.qc.ca
Mgr, Memb Servs: Helene Letourneau
  E-mail: letourneau@anel.qc.ca
Founded: 1992
Professional association of French publishers in Canada.
Number of Members: 100

Association of American Editorial Cartoonists
PO Box 460673, Fort Lauderdale, FL 33346
Tel: 954-356-4945
Web Site: www.editorialcartoonists.com
Key Personnel
Pres: Adam Zyglis
Gen Mgr: Stephanie McMillan *E-mail:* steph@minimumsecurity.net
Founded: 1957
Professional association.
Number of Members: 260
Publication(s): *Notebook* (quarterly, free to membs, $40/yr nonmembs)

Association of American Publishers (AAP)
455 Massachusetts Ave NW, Suite 700, Washington, DC 20001-2777
Tel: 202-347-3375 *Fax:* 202-347-3690
E-mail: info@publishers.org
Web Site: publishers.org
Key Personnel
Pres & CEO: Maria Pallante
EVP & Gen Coun: Allan R Adler
Asst Gen Coun: Sofia Castillo
SVP, Communs: John McKay
VP, Admin & Bd Liaison: Syreeta N Swann
VP, Communs: Cara Duckworth; Susanna Hinds
VP, Fin & Strategic Planning: Karen McInnis
VP, Global Policy: M Lui Simpson
VP, Public Policy: Matthew Barblan
Mng Dir, Meetings & Progs: Sara Pinto
Sr Dir, Educ Policy & Progs: Kelly L Denson
Policy Specialist: Amanda Straub
Founded: 1970
Monitor & promote the US publishing industry. Members are those actively engaged in the creation, publication & production of books, journals, electronic media, testing materials & a range of educational materials. Co-sponsor of BookExpo along with American Booksellers Association (ABA) & Association of Authors' Representatives Inc (AAR).
Number of Members: 450
Meeting(s): PSP Annual Conference
Publication(s): *AAP Export Sales Report* (annual); *AAP StatShot* (monthly)
Membership(s): Book Industry Study Group (BISG)

Association of Authors' Representatives Inc (AAR)
302A W 12 St, No 122, New York, NY 10014
Tel: 212-840-5770
E-mail: administrator@aaronline.org
Web Site: www.aaronline.org
Founded: 1991
Voluntary & elective professional association of literary & play agents whose individual members subscribe to certain ethical practices. Members meet to discuss industry developments & problems of mutual interest. Co-sponsor of BookExpo along with American Booksellers Association (ABA) & Association of American Publishers (AAP).
Number of Members: 386
New Election: Annually in June

Association of Book Publishers of British Columbia
Affiliate of Association of Canadian Publishers
600-402 W Pender St, Vancouver, BC V6B 1T6, Canada
Tel: 604-684-0228
E-mail: admin@books.bc.ca
Web Site: www.books.bc.ca
Key Personnel
Exec Dir: Heidi Waechtler
Founded: 1974
Trade association representing the interests of Canadian-owned & operated book publishing companies based in BC.
Number of Members: 30
New Election: Annually in April

Association of Canadian Publishers (ACP)
174 Spadina Ave, Suite 306, Toronto, ON M5T 2C2, Canada
Tel: 416-487-6116 *Fax:* 416-487-8815
E-mail: admin@canbook.org
Web Site: publishers.ca
Key Personnel
Exec Dir: Kate Edwards *Tel:* 416-487-6116 ext 2340 *E-mail:* kate_edwards@canbook.org
Founded: 1976
Association of English language Canadian owned book publishing companies in Canada. Sponsor professional development seminars for book publishers. Publish membership directories, studies & reports.
Number of Members: 115

Association of Canadian University Presses
10 Saint Mary St, Suite 700, Toronto, ON M4Y 2W8, Canada
Tel: 416-978-2239 ext 237 *Fax:* 416-978-4738
Web Site: www.acup.ca
Key Personnel
Admin: Charley La Rose *E-mail:* clarose@utpress.utoronto.ca
Founded: 1972
Number of Members: 17
New Election: Annually in Autumn

Association of Catholic Publishers Inc
4725 Dorsey Hall Dr, Suite A, PMB 709, Ellicott City, MD 21042
Tel: 410-988-2926 *Fax:* 410-571-4946
E-mail: info@catholicpublishers.org
Web Site: www.catholicsread.org; www.catholicpublishers.org; www.midatlanticcongress.org
Key Personnel
Exec Dir: Therese Brown
Facilitate the sharing of professional information, networking, cooperation & friendship among those involved in Catholic book publishing in the US & abroad. Offers trade co-op catalog, mailing list, Catholic bestsellers, advertising insert program & professional skills workshops.
Number of Members: 100
New Election: Annually in Dec

Meeting(s): Mid-Atlantic Congress
Publication(s): *Promotional Brochure* (annually)

Association of College & University Printers
PO Box 285, Carrabelle, FL 32322
Tel: 850-570-5241
Web Site: www.acup-edu.org
Key Personnel
Admin Dir: Jennifer Bowers *E-mail:* jennifer.bowers@acup-edu.org
Number of Members: 300
Meeting(s): Annual Conference

The Association of English-Language Publishers of Quebec-AELAQ (Association des Editeurs de Langue Anglaise du Quebec)
Atwater Library, 1200 Atwater Ave, Suite 3, Westmount, QC H3Z 1X4, Canada
Tel: 514-932-5633
E-mail: admin@aelaq.org
Web Site: aelaq.org
Key Personnel
Pres: Keith Henderson
Exec Dir: Julia Kater
Advance the publication, distribution & promotion of English language books from Quebec.
Number of Members: 18
Publication(s): *Montreal Review of Books* (3 times/yr, report, free)

Association of Free Community Papers (AFCP)
135 Old Cove Rd, Suite 210, Liverpool, NY 13090
Toll Free Tel: 877-203-2327 *Fax:* 781-459-7770
E-mail: afcp@afcp.org
Web Site: www.afcp.org
Key Personnel
Exec Dir: Loren Colburn *E-mail:* loren@afcp.org
Founded: 1950
Organization of publishers serving the free-circulation community publication industry.
Number of Members: 250
Meeting(s): Annual Conference & Trade Show
Publication(s): *Freepaper Ink* (monthly, newsletter, free)

Association of Jewish Libraries (AJL) Inc
Affiliate of American Library Association (ALA)
PO Box 1118, Teaneck, NJ 07666
Tel: 201-371-3255
E-mail: info@jewishlibraries.org
Web Site: jewishlibraries.org
Key Personnel
Pres: Amalia Warshenbrot
Member libraries in two divisions: RAS (Research Libraries, Archives & Special Collections) & SCC (Schools, Synagogues & Centers). Promote librarianship, services & standards in the field of Judaica. Also affiliate of the American Theological Library Association.
Number of Members: 600
Meeting(s): AJL Annual Conference
Publication(s): *AJL Conference Proceedings* (annual); *AJL News* (quarterly); *AJL Reviews* (quarterly); *Judaica Librarianship* (semiannual, journal)

Association of Manitoba Book Publishers
100 Arthur St, Suite 404, Winnipeg, MB R3B 1H3, Canada
Tel: 204-947-3335
E-mail: ambp@mts.net
Web Site: ambp.ca
Key Personnel
Exec Dir: Michelle Peters
Projs Coord: Karen San Filippo
Founded: 1979
Publishing industry association.
Number of Members: 13

Publication(s): *Prairie Books Now* (3 issues/yr, magazine)

Membership(s): Association of Canadian Publishers (ACP)

Association of Marketing Service Providers (AMSP), see Epicomm

The Association of Medical Illustrators (AMI)
201 E Main St, Suite 1405, Lexington, KY 40507
Toll Free Tel: 866-393-4264 *Fax:* 859-514-9166
E-mail: hq@ami.org; info@ami.org
Web Site: www.ami.org
Key Personnel
Exec Dir: Melanie Bowzer *E-mail:* mbowzer@amrms.com
Founded: 1945
Promote the use of high-quality artwork in medical publications to advance medical education.
Number of Members: 850

Association of National Advertisers (ANA)
10 Grand Central, 155 E 44 St, New York, NY 10017
Tel: 212-697-5950 *Fax:* 212-302-6714
Web Site: www.ana.net
Key Personnel
CEO: Bob Liodice *Tel:* 212-455-8050
E-mail: bliodice@ana.net
Pres & COO: Christine Manna *Tel:* 212-455-8060
E-mail: cmanna@ana.net
VP: Barbara Markfield *Tel:* 212-455-8077
E-mail: bmarkfield@ana.net
Dir, PR: John Wolfe *Tel:* 212-455-8011
E-mail: jwolfe@ana.net
Founded: 1917
A member organization representing the direct marketing business to legislators, regulators & the media, also offering educational & networking experiences for members.
Meeting(s): ANA Masters of Data & Technology
Branch Office(s)
2020 "K" St NW, Suite 660, Washington, DC 20006 *Tel:* 202-861-2441 *Fax:* 202-861-2441

Association of Publishers for Special Sales (APSS)
PO Box 715, Avon, CT 06001-0715
Tel: 860-675-1344
Web Site: www.bookapss.org
Key Personnel
Exec Dir: Brian Jud *E-mail:* brianjud@bookapss.org
Busn Mgr: Kaye Krassner
A trade association for independent presses, self-publishers & pro-active authors who want to sell more books.
Publication(s): *The Sales Informer* (monthly)

Association of University Presses (AUPresses)
1412 Broadway, Suite 2135, New York, NY 10018
Tel: 212-989-1010 *Fax:* 212-989-0275
E-mail: info@aupresses.org
Web Site: www.aupresses.org
Key Personnel
Exec Dir: Peter Berkery *Tel:* 917-288-5594
E-mail: pberkery@aupresses.org
Asst Dir & Cont: Tim Muench *Tel:* 917-244-1463
E-mail: tmuench@aupresses.org
Membership & Events Dir: Susan Patton
Tel: 917-244-1915 *E-mail:* spatton@aupresses.org
Res & Communs Dir: Brenna McLaughlin
Tel: 917-244-2051 *E-mail:* bmclaughlin@aupresses.org
Busn Mgr: Kim Miller *Tel:* 917-244-1264
E-mail: kmiller@aupresses.org
Communs Prog Mgr: Kate Kolendo
External Communs Mgr: Annette Windhorn

Communs Coord: John Michael Eadicicco
Tel: 917-244-3859 *E-mail:* jeadicicco@aupresses.org
Prog Coord: Angelica DeVoe
Prog Asst: Bailey Bretz *Tel:* 917-244-2665
E-mail: bbretz@aupresses.org
Membership & affiliation consists of university presses in North America & abroad that function as the publishing arms of their respective universities, issuing some 11,000 titles & more than 600 journals annually. AUPresses helps these presses do their work more economically, creatively & effectively through its own activities in professional development; fund raising; statistical research & analysis; promoting the value of university presses; community & institutional relations & through its marketing programs.
Number of Members: 141
2021 Meeting(s): Annual Meeting, Fairmont Queen Elizabeth, 900 Rene Levesque Blvd W, Montreal, QC, CN, June 15-17, 2021
2022 Meeting(s): Annual Meeting, Marriott Marquis Washington, DC, 901 Massachusetts Ave NW, Washington, DC, June 18-20, 2022
Publication(s): *AAUP Book, Jacket & Journal Show* (catalog, $20 current yr, $15 past yrs); *Annual Directory* ($30); *The Exchange* (quarterly, newsletter, free); *University Press Books for Public & Secondary School Libraries* (annual, free)
Branch Office(s)
1775 Massachusetts Ave NW, Washington, DC 20036
Membership(s): Book Industry Study Group (BISG)

Association of Writers & Writing Programs (AWP)
University of Maryland, 5245 Greenbelt Rd, Box 246, College Park, MD 20740
Mailing Address: University of Maryland, 5700 Rivertech Ct, Suite 225, Riverdale Park, MD 20737-1250
Tel: 240-696-7700
E-mail: awp@awpwriter.org; press@awpwriter.org
Web Site: www.awpwriter.org
Key Personnel
Dir, Conferences: Cynthia Sherman
Dir, Devt: Pamela Mills
Dir, Pubns: Supriya Bhatnagar
Assoc Ed: Christopher Kondrich
Mgr, Conference Events: Colleen Cable
Founded: 1967
Magazine, publications, directory, competitions for awards (including publication), advocacy for literature & education, annual meeting, job placement.
Number of Members: 34,000
2021 Meeting(s): Annual Conference & Bookfair, Kansas City Convention Center, Kansas City, MO, March 3-6, 2021
2022 Meeting(s): Annual Conference & Bookfair, Pennsylvania Convention Center, Philadelphia, PA, March 23-26, 2022
Publication(s): *The Writer's Chronicle* (6 issues/yr, free to membs)

Association pour l'Avancement des Sciences et des Techniques de la Documentation
2065 rue Parthenais, Bureau 387, Montreal, QC H2K 3T1, Canada
Tel: 514-281-5012 *Fax:* 514-281-8219
E-mail: info@asted.org
Web Site: www.asted.org
Key Personnel
Exec Dir: Lionel Villalonga *E-mail:* lvillalonga@asted.org
Objective is the promotion of standards of excellence in the services & personnel of libraries, documentation & information centers.
Number of Members: 550

New Election: Annually during congress
Publication(s): *Documentation et Bibliotheques* (quarterly, $185/yr CN, $225/yr elsewhere)

ASTED, see Association pour l'Avancement des Sciences et des Techniques de la Documentation

Atlantic Provinces Library Association (APLA)
Dalhouse University, Kenneth C Rowe Management Bldg, 6100 University Ave, Suite 4010, Halifax, NS B3H 4R2, Canada
Mailing Address: PO Box 15000, Halifax, NS B3H 4R2, Canada
Web Site: www.apla.ca
Key Personnel
Pres: Trecia Schell *E-mail:* president@apla.ca
Secy: Amy Lorencz *Tel:* 902-420-5174
E-mail: secretary@apla.ca
Founded: 1934
Promotes the interests of libraries in the Atlantic provinces while fostering the development of librarians, library technicians & information professionals through cooperative efforts & the promotion of library interests.
2021 Meeting(s): Annual Conference, Acadia University, Wolfville, NS, CN, June 8-11, 2021
Publication(s): *APLA Bulletin* (quarterly)

Authors Alliance
2705 Webster St, No 5805, Berkeley, CA 94705
E-mail: info@authorsalliance.org
Web Site: www.authorsalliance.org
Key Personnel
Exec Dir: Brianna Schofield *E-mail:* brianna@authorsalliance.org
Communs & Opers Mgr: Erika Wilson
E-mail: erika@authorsalliance.org
Further public interest in facilitating widespread access to works of authorship by assisting & representing authors who want to disseminate knowledge & products of the imagination broadly.

The Authors Guild
31 E 32 St, 7th fl, New York, NY 10016
Tel: 212-563-5904 *Fax:* 212-564-8363
E-mail: staff@authorsguild.org
Web Site: www.authorsguild.org
Key Personnel
Gen Coun: Cheryl L Davis
Pres: Douglas Preston
VP: Monique Truong
Exec Dir: Mary Rasenberger
Founded: 1912
National membership organization for nonfiction & fiction book authors & freelance journalists. Deals with the business & professional interests of authors in such fields as book contracts, copyright, subsidiary rights, free expression, taxes & others. Offer free contract reviews, web site development & hosting.
Number of Members: 9,000
Publication(s): *The Bulletin* (quarterly, free to membs)

The Authors League Fund
31 E 32 St, 7th fl, New York, NY 10016
Tel: 212-268-1208 *Fax:* 212-564-5363
E-mail: staff@authorsleaguefund.org
Web Site: www.authorsleaguefund.org
Key Personnel
Pres: Pat Cummings
VP: Sidney Offit
Exec Dir: Isabel Howe
Secy: Peter Straub
Treas: James B Stewart
Founded: 1917
Provides emergency assistance to professional writers facing financial hardship.
Number of Members: 900

The Authors League of America Inc, see The Authors Guild

The Authors Registry Inc
31 E 32 St, 7th fl, New York, NY 10016
Tel: 212-563-6920 *Fax:* 212-564-5363
E-mail: staff@authorsregistry.org
Web Site: www.authorsregistry.org
Key Personnel
Opers Dir: Terry King *E-mail:* tking@
authorsregistry.org
A nonprofit corporation that provides a royalty collection & distribution service.
Number of Members: 40,000

The Baker Street Irregulars (BSI)
7938 Mill Stream Circle, Indianapolis, IN 46278
Tel: 317-293-2212; 317-956-6666 (cell)
Web Site: bakerstreetjournal.com
Key Personnel
Wiggins, Chmn: Michael F Whelan
Literary society with a small press operation including a quarterly journal with a Christmas annual & 3-4 published books annually.
Number of Members: 300
Publication(s): *The Baker Street Journal* (quarterly & Christmas annual, $41.95/yr, $55/yr foreign)

Before Columbus Foundation
The Raymond House, 655 13 St, Suite 302, Oakland, CA 94612
SAN: 159-2955
Tel: 916-425-7916
E-mail: beforecolumbusfoundation@gmail.com
Web Site: www.beforecolumbusfoundation.com
Key Personnel
Founder: Ishmael Reed
Founded: 1976
Provide information, research, consultation & promotional services for contemporary American multicultural writers & publishers. A nonprofit service organization that also sponsors classes, workshops, readings, public events & the annual American Book Awards.

Bibliographical Society of America
PO Box 1537, Lenox Hill Sta, New York, NY 10021-0043
Tel: 212-734-2500 *Fax:* 212-452-2710
E-mail: bsa@bibsocamer.org
Web Site: www.bibsocamer.org
Key Personnel
Pres: Barbara A Shailor
VP: Michael T Ryan
Secy: Jennifer J Love
Treas: G Scott Clemons
Exec Dir: Michele E Randall
Learned society. Sponsors short-term fellowships for bibliographic projects. Membership open to anyone interested in bibliographic projects & process.
Number of Members: 1,000
New Election: Annually in Jan
Meeting(s): Annual Meeting, New York, NY, Jan (Friday following the 4th Thursday)
Publication(s): *The Papers of the Bibliographical Society of America* (quarterly, free for membs)

Bibliographical Society of the University of Virginia
c/o Alderman Library, University of Virginia, McCormick Rd, Charlottesville, VA 22904
Mailing Address: PO Box 400152, Charlottesville, VA 22904-4152
Tel: 434-924-7013 *Fax:* 434-924-1431
E-mail: bibsoc@virginia.edu
Web Site: bsuva.org
Key Personnel
Pres: G Thomas Tanselle

Exec Secy-Treas: Anne G Ribble *E-mail:* ar3g@
virginia.edu
Founded: 1947
Scholarly society promoting the study of books as physical objects, the history of the book & of printing & publishing.
Number of Members: 400
Publication(s): *Studies in Bibliography* (annual, $55)

Binding Industries Association (BIA)
Affiliate of PRINTING United Alliance
301 Brush Creek Rd, Warrendale, PA 15086-7529
Tel: 412-741-6860 *Toll Free Tel:* 800-910-4283
Fax: 412-741-2311
Web Site: www.printing.org/bia
Key Personnel
Dir: Michael Packard *Tel:* 412-741-6860
E-mail: mpackard@printing.org
Founded: 1955
Trade finishers & loose-leaf manufacturers united to conduct seminars, hold conventions, formulate & maintain industry standards. Bestow annual product of excellence awards.
Number of Members: 100
Publication(s): *The Binding Edge* (quarterly, magazine); *Bound for Excellence* (monthly, newsletter, membs only); *Membership Directory* (in print biennially & online, book)

BISG, see Book Industry Study Group Inc (BISG)

BlackPressUSA, see National Newspaper Publishers Association (NNPA)

BMI®
7 World Trade Center, 250 Greenwich St, New York, NY 10007-0030
Tel: 212-220-3000 *Toll Free Tel:* 888-689-5264 (sales)
E-mail: newyork@bmi.com
Web Site: www.bmi.com
Key Personnel
Pres & CEO: Michael O'Neill
Founded: 1939
Secure & license the performing rights of music on behalf of its creators.
Number of Members: 600,000
Publication(s): *BMI MusicWorld Online* (monthly)
Branch Office(s)
8730 Sunset Blvd, 3rd fl W, West Hollywood, CA 90069-2211 *Tel:* 310-659-9109
E-mail: losangeles@bmi.com
Miami, FL 33139 *Tel:* 305-673-5148
E-mail: miami@bmi.com
3340 Peachtree Rd NE, Suite 570, Atlanta, GA 30326 *Tel:* 404-261-5151 *E-mail:* atlanta@bmi.com
10 Music Sq E, Nashville, TN 37203-4399
Tel: 615-401-2000 *E-mail:* nashville@bmi.com
San Jose Bldg, Suite 1008, 1250 Ave Ponce de Leon, Santurce 00907, Puerto Rico *Tel:* 787-754-6490
84 Harley House, Marylebone Rd, London NW1 5HN, United Kingdom *Tel:* (020) 7486 2036
E-mail: london@bmi.com

Book & Periodical Council (BPC)
192 Spadina Ave, Suite 107, Toronto, ON M5T 2C2, Canada
Tel: 416-975-9366 *Fax:* 416-975-1839
E-mail: info@thebpc.ca
Web Site: www.thebpc.ca
Key Personnel
Exec Dir: Anne McClelland
Founded: 1975
Umbrella organization for Canadian associations that are, or whose members are, primarily involved with the writing, editing, translating,

publishing, producing, distributing, lending, marketing, reading & selling of written words.
Number of Members: 32
Publication(s): *Dividends: The Value of Public Libraries in Canada* (free); *Freedom to Read Kit* (annual); *When the Censor Comes* (free online)

Book Industry Guild of New York
PO Box 2001, New York, NY 10113-2001
E-mail: admin@bookindustryguildofny.org
Web Site: bigny.org
Key Personnel
Pres: Jody Saunders Ray
VP: Martha Hanson
Fin Secy: Richard Bretan
Treas: Michael Kwan
Founded: 1925
For book publishing production, editorial, design & manufacturing people from the book community. Monthly dinner meetings, book show & educational seminars.
Number of Members: 800

Book Industry Study Group Inc (BISG)
1412 Broadway, Suite 2119, New York, NY 10018
Tel: 646-336-7141
E-mail: info@bisg.org
Web Site: bisg.org
Key Personnel
Exec Dir: Brian O'Leary
Opers Mgr: Jonathan Fiedler
Founded: 1975
Trade association for policy, standards & research. The member-driven organization uniquely represents all segments of our industry, from publishers & e-publishers to paper manufacturers, libraries, authors, printers, wholesalers, retailers & e-tailers, as well as organizations concerned with the book industry as a whole. For over 40 years, BISG has provided a forum for all industry professionals to come together & efficiently address issues & concerns to advance the book community.
Number of Members: 150
New Election: Annually in Sept
Meeting(s): BISG Annual Meeting of Members
Membership(s): American Library Association (ALA); Association of American Publishers (AAP); Book Industry Communication (BIC); BookNetCanada; EDItEUR; Independent Book Publishers Association (IBPA); National Information Standards Organization (NISO)

Book Manufacturers' Institute Inc (BMI)
PO Box 731388, Ormond Beach, FL 32173
Tel: 386-986-4552 *Fax:* 386-986-4553
E-mail: info@bmibook.com
Web Site: www.bmibook.org
Key Personnel
EVP: Daniel N Bach *E-mail:* dbach@bmibook.com
Founded: 1933
BMI is the leading nationally recognized trade association of the book manufacturing industry.
Number of Members: 80
Meeting(s): BMI Management Conference; BMI Annual Conference
Membership(s): Book Industry Guild of New York; National Association of Manufacturers (NAM)

Book Publicists of Southern California
714 Crescent Dr, Beverly Hills, CA 90210
Tel: 323-461-3921 *Fax:* 323-461-0917
Web Site: www.bookpublicists.org
Key Personnel
Founder: Irwin Zucker *Tel:* 310-497-4001 (cell)
E-mail: irwin@promotioninmotion.net
Pres: Bruce Braunstein
VP: Bill Frank
Membership: Valinda Rothman

Mktg: Melinda Sue Norin
Publicity: Rhonda Rees
Founded: 1976
Literary club. Bimonthly meetings at Sportsmen's Lodge, Studio City, CA, varied topics-anything pertinent to promotion of books & authors.
Number of Members: 1,200
New Election: Annually in Nov
Publication(s): *Know Thy Shelf* (6 issues/yr, newsletter, free to membs)

The Book Publishers Association of Alberta (BPAA)
Affiliate of Association of Canadian Publishers (ACP)
10523 100 Ave, Edmonton, AB T5J 0A8, Canada
Tel: 780-424-5060
E-mail: info@bookpublishers.ab.ca
Web Site: www.bookpublishers.ab.ca
Key Personnel
Exec Dir: Kieran Leblanc *E-mail:* kleblanc@bookpublishers.ab.ca
Sponsor professional development seminars, workshops & Alberta Book Publishing Awards.
Number of Members: 32
Publication(s): *Membership Directory* (free)

Bookbuilders of Boston
115 Webster Woods Lane, North Andover, MA 01845
Tel: 781-378-1361 *Fax:* 419-821-2171
E-mail: office@bbboston.org
Web Site: www.bbboston.org
Key Personnel
Pres: Iris Febres
Meetings, New England Book Show, seminars & scholarships; nonprofit organization.
New Election: Annually in April or May
Publication(s): *Directory* (annual, free to membs)

Boston Authors Club Inc
2400 Beacon St, No 208, Chestnut, MA 02467
Tel: 617-552-4031
E-mail: bostonauthorsclub@gmail.com
Web Site: bostonauthorsclub.org
Key Personnel
Pres: Mary Cronin
VP: Shirley Moskow *Tel:* 781-862-7697 *E-mail:* shirley.moskow@rtr.com
Membership Dir: Nancy Tupper Ling *E-mail:* ntupper@finelinepoets.com
Founded: 1899
Nonprofit organization promoting discussion & community among Boston area authors. Honors outstanding authors at the annual Julia Ward Howe Book Awards program.
Number of Members: 100
New Election: Annually in May

BPA Worldwide
100 Beard Sawmill Rd, 6th fl, Shelton, CT 06484
Tel: 203-447-2800 *Fax:* 203-447-2900
E-mail: info@bpaww.com
Web Site: www.bpaww.com
Key Personnel
Pres & CEO: Glenn J Hansen *E-mail:* ghansen@bpaww.com
SVP, Auditing: Richard J Murphy *E-mail:* rmurphy@bpaww.com
VP: Linda Petersell
Founded: 1931
International, independent, not-for-profit organization whose membership consists of advertiser companies, advertising agencies & publications. Audit all-paid, all-controlled or any combination of paid & controlled circulation for more than 2,600 media properties including business, technical, professional publications, consumer magazines, newspapers, web sites, e-mail, newsletters & face-to-face events-expos & shows as well as more than 2,700 advertising & agency members.

Number of Members: 4,100
Branch Office(s)
CCAB (div of BPA Worldwide Inc), 111 Queen St E, No 450, Toronto, ON M5C 1S2, Canada, VP: Tim Peel *Tel:* 416-487-2418 *Fax:* 416-487-6405 *E-mail:* mpeel@bpaww.com
CCAB (div of BPA Worldwide Inc), 6500 Rte Transcanadienne, Pointe-Claire, QC H9R 0A5, Canada, Dir: Matt Pasquale *Tel:* 514-845-0003 *Fax:* 514-845-0905 *E-mail:* mpasquale@bpaww.com
Suite 505, Bldg 4, China Central Place, 89 Jianguo Rd, Chaoyang District, Beijing 100025, China, Gen Mgr: Doreen Chan *Tel:* (010) 8591 0691 *Fax:* (010) 8591 0589 *E-mail:* dchan@bpaww.com
PO Box 502458, Dubai Media City, Dubai, United Arab Emirates, Dir: Rina Hariz *Tel:* (04) 3692468 *Fax:* (04) 3697073 *E-mail:* rhariz@bpaww.com
Central Working Shoreditch, 6-8 Bonhill St, London EC2A 4BX, United Kingdom, Dir, European Opers: Francis Stones *Tel:* (020) 3752 6844 *E-mail:* fstones@bpaww.com

Broadcast Music Inc, see BMI®

Business Forms Management Association (BFMA)
1147 Fleetwood Ave, Madison, WI 53716-1417
Toll Free Tel: 888-367-3078
E-mail: bfma@bfma.org
Web Site: www.bfma.org
Key Personnel
Pres: Olufunke Somefun
VP, Opers & CFO: Ray Killam
VP, Membership & Mktg: Shantelle Boatright
VP, Progs: Margaret Tassin
Dir, Educ: Bruce Boswell
Dir, Membership: Tammy McBride
Founded: 1958
Sponsor professional training in all aspects of information resource management; classes are conducted in major cities in the US & CN. Bestow the association's highest award, the Jo Warner Award, to professionals in the information resources industry. Recipients do not have to be BFMA members.
Number of Members: 600

Business Marketing Association (BMA)
Division of Association of National Advertisers (ANA)
708 Third Ave, New York, NY 10017
Tel: 212-697-5950 *Fax:* 212-687-7310
E-mail: info@marketing.org
Web Site: www.marketing.org
Key Personnel
Exec Dir: Michael Palmer *Tel:* 646-369-4898 *E-mail:* mpalmer@marketing.org
Sr Dir: Arthur Tharpe *Tel:* 212-455-8004 *E-mail:* atharpe@marketing.org
Fin Dir: Lana Mavreshko *Tel:* 212-340-0087 *E-mail:* lmavreshko@marketing.org
Founded: 1922 (as National Industrial Advertising Association)
Provides information & resources to business-to-business marketers & marketing communicators.
Number of Members: 2,200
Publication(s): *BMA Buzz* (monthly, newsletter)

California Independent Booksellers Alliance (CALIBA)
651 Broadway, 2nd fl, Sonoma, CA 95476
Mailing Address: PO Box 280, Sonoma, CA 95476
Tel: 415-561-7686 *Fax:* 415-561-7685
E-mail: info@caliballiance.org
Web Site: www.caliballiance.org

Key Personnel
Exec Dir: Calvin Crosby *Tel:* 415-561-7686 ext 102 *E-mail:* calvin@ncaliballiance.org
Dir, Opers: Ann Seaton *Tel:* 415-561-7686 ext 101 *E-mail:* ann@caliballiance.org
Founded: 1981
Support, nurture & promote independent retail bookselling in California.
Publication(s): *California Rep Directory* (free online); *Holiday Catalog*
Membership(s): American Booksellers Association (ABA)

Canada Council for the Arts (Conseil des arts du Canada)
150 Elgin St, 2nd fl, Ottawa, ON K2P 1L4, Canada
Mailing Address: PO Box 1047, Ottawa, ON K1P 5V8, Canada
Tel: 613-566-4414 *Toll Free Tel:* 800-263-5588 (CN only) *Fax:* 613-566-4390
E-mail: info@canadacouncil.ca; assistance@canadacouncil.ca (technical support)
Web Site: www.canadacouncil.ca; www.apply.canadacouncil.ca
Key Personnel
Admin Coord, Writing & Publg Section: Brigitte Fontille *Tel:* 613-566-4414 ext 4571 *E-mail:* brigitte.fontille@canadacouncil.ca
Federal cultural granting agency for Canadian literature. See web site for various awards, prize contests, fellowships & grants.

Canadian Authors Association (CAA)
6 West St N, Suite 203, Orillia, ON L3V 5B8, Canada
Tel: 705-325-3926
E-mail: admin@canadianauthors.org
Web Site: www.canadianauthors.org
Key Personnel
Exec Dir: Anita Purcell
Founded: 1921
Encourage & develop a climate favorable to the literary arts in Canada. Assistance to professional & emerging writers. Represent the concerns & interests of members.
Number of Members: 600
Publication(s): *Canadian Writers Guide* ($36)

Canadian Bookbinders and Book Artists Guild (CBBAG)
180 Shaw St, Unit 102, Toronto, ON M6J 2W5, Canada
Tel: 416-581-1071
E-mail: cbbag@cbbag.ca
Web Site: www.cbbag.ca
Key Personnel
Pres: Jose Villa-Arce
Founded: 1983
Presents workshops & courses on a wide variety of topics, including bookbinding, box making, paper making & decorating, letterpress printing, paper conservation & more. Also maintains a reference library & DVD catalogue.
Number of Members: 600
Publication(s): *Book Arts arts du livre Canada* (May & Nov, magazine)

Canadian Cataloguing in Publication Program
Library & Archives Canada, 395 Wellington St, Ottawa, ON K1A 0N4, Canada
Tel: 819-994-6881 *Toll Free Tel:* 866-578-7777 (CN) *Fax:* 819-934-6777
E-mail: bac.cip.lac@canada.ca
Web Site: www.bac-lac.gc.ca/eng/services/cip/pages/cip.aspx
Voluntary program of cooperation between publishers & libraries.
Publication(s): *Livres a Paraitre/Forthcoming Books* (monthly, free)

Canadian Children's Book Centre
40 Orchard View Blvd, Suite 217, Toronto, ON
M4R 1B9, Canada
Tel: 416-975-0010 *Fax:* 416-975-8970
E-mail: info@bookcentre.ca
Web Site: www.bookcentre.ca
Key Personnel
Exec Dir: Charlotte Teeple *E-mail:* charlotte@
bookcentre.ca
Lib Coord: Meghan Howe *E-mail:* meghan@
bookcentre.ca
Mktg & Web Site Coord: Camilia Kahrizi
E-mail: camilia@bookcentre.ca
Prog Coord: Shannon Howe Barnes
E-mail: shannon@bookcentre.ca
Founded: 1976
National not-for-profit organization to promote
the reading, writing & illustrating of Canadian
books for young readers. We provide programs,
publications & resources for teachers, librari-
ans, authors, illustrators, publishers, booksellers
& parents.
Number of Members: 558
Publication(s): *Best Books for Kids & Teens*
(semiannual, catalog, $5.95/issue); *Canadian
Children's Book News* (quarterly, magazine,
$4.95/issue, $24.95/single subn includes copies
of Best Books for Kids & Teens)

Canadian Circulations Audit Board, see CCAB
Inc

Canadian Institute for Studies in Publishing
Simon Fraser University at Harbour Centre, 515
W Hastings St, Suite 3576, Vancouver, BC
V6B 5K3, Canada
Tel: 778-782-5242
E-mail: pub-info@sfu.ca
Web Site: publishing.sfu.ca
Key Personnel
Prog Mgr: Jo-Anne Ray
Founded: 1987
Undergraduate, graduate & noncredit courses; re-
search on print & digital publishing.

Canadian Publishers' Council (CPC)
3080 Yonge St, Suite 6060, Toronto, ON M4N
3N1, Canada
Tel: 647-255-8880
Web Site: pubcouncil.ca
Key Personnel
Exec Dir, External Rel: David Swail
E-mail: dswail@pubcouncil.ca
Acctg Offr: Joanna Ames *Tel:* 647-255-8879
E-mail: james@pubcouncil.ca
Founded: 1910
Represents the interests of Canadian publishing
companies that publish books & other media
for elementary & secondary schools, colleges
& universities, professional & reference mar-
kets, the retail & library markets.
Number of Members: 20
New Election: Annually in Feb
Publication(s): *Publishing: A View from the Inside*
($2 plus GST); *Who Buys Books?* ($50 plus
GST)
Membership(s): International Federation of Re-
production Rights Organizations (IFRRO); International Publishers Association (IPA)

**Canadian Society of Children's Authors,
Illustrators & Performers (CANSCAIP)**
720 Bathurst St, Suite 503, Toronto, ON M5S
2R4, Canada
Tel: 416-515-1559
E-mail: office@canscaip.org
Web Site: www.canscaip.org
Key Personnel
Pres: Sharon Jennings
VP: Jennifer Maruno
Admin Dir: Helena Aalto
Founded: 1977

Dedicated to the celebration & promotion of
Canadian children's authors, illustrators & per-
formers & their work. Provide promotional &
networking opportunities.
Number of Members: 1,000
New Election: April even-numbered yrs
Meeting(s): Packaging Your Imagination, Toronto,
ON, CN, annually in Nov
Publication(s): *CANSCAIP News* (quarterly, $45/
yr nonmembs, free to membs, electronic)

CASW, see Council for the Advancement of
Science Writing (CASW)

Catholic Library Association
8550 United Plaza Blvd, Suite 1001, Baton
Rouge, LA 70809
Tel: 225-408-4417 *Fax:* 225-408-4422
E-mail: cla2@cathla.org
Web Site: cathla.org
Key Personnel
Exec Dir: Bland O'Connor
Founded: 1921
Initiate, foster & encourage activities & library
programs that promote literature & libraries of
a Catholic nature & of an ecumenical spirit.
Number of Members: 500
Publication(s): *Catholic Library World* (3 issues/
yr, $100 nonmembs US; $140/yr foreign & $25
S&H)

**Catholic Press Association of the United States
& Canada**
205 W Monroe St, Suite 470, Chicago, IL 60606
Tel: 312-380-6789 *Fax:* 312-361-0256
E-mail: journalist@catholicpress.org
Web Site: www.catholicpress.org
Key Personnel
Exec Dir: Timothy M Walter *E-mail:* twalter@
catholicpress.org
Founded: 1911
Writing, publishing, advertising; all facets of pub-
lishing.
Number of Members: 800
Meeting(s): Catholic Media Conference
Publication(s): *The Catholic Journalist* (monthly
(exc Aug), $18/yr US, $24/yr CN & else-
where); *Catholic Press Directory* (annual)

CCAB Inc
Division of BPA Worldwide
111 Queen St E, Suite 450, Toronto, ON M5C
1S2, Canada
Tel: 416-487-2418 *Fax:* 416-487-6405
Web Site: www.bpaww.com
Key Personnel
VP: Tim Peel *E-mail:* mpeel@bpaww.com
Founded: 1931
Number of Members: 550
Branch Office(s)
8-211, blvd Brien, Suite 433, Repentigny, QC
J6A 0A4, Canada

The Center for Book Arts
28 W 27 St, 3rd fl, New York, NY 10001
Tel: 212-481-0295
E-mail: info@centerforbookarts.org
Web Site: www.centerforbookarts.org
Key Personnel
Exec Dir & Curator: Alexander Campos
Founded: 1974
Nonprofit, provides workspace, education, exhi-
bitions & slide registry for book artists, hand
papermakers & letter press printers; publication
of fine art editions, lectures, outreach program.
Number of Members: 6,500
Publication(s): *Exhibition Catalogs* (quarterly, $15
membs, $20 nonmembs)

**The Center for Exhibition Industry Research
(CEIR)**
12700 Park Central Dr, Suite 308, Dallas, TX
75251
Tel: 972-687-9242 *Fax:* 972-692-6020
E-mail: info@ceir.org
Web Site: www.ceir.org
Key Personnel
CEO: Cathy Breden *Tel:* 972-687-9201
E-mail: cbreden@ceir.org
Promote the exhibition industry by promoting the
value & benefits of exhibitions in an integrated
marketing program through research, informa-
tion & communication.
Number of Members: 600

The Center for Fiction
17 E 47 St, New York, NY 10017
Tel: 212-755-6710
E-mail: info@centerforfiction.org
Web Site: centerforfiction.org
Key Personnel
Chmn of the Bd: Erroll McDonald
Mng Dir: Kristin Henley
Devt Dir: Linda Cicely Morgan
Dir, Public Programming: Melanie McNair
Head Libn & Educ Dir: Allison Escoto
PR & Mktg Mgr: Carla Cain-Walther
E-mail: carla@centerforfiction.org
Writing Progs Mgr: Thierry Kehou
E-mail: thierry@centerforfiction.org
Founded: 1820 (as the Mercantile Library)
Devoted to the vital art of fiction & to encour-
age people to read & value fiction. Circulating
library of mainly fiction titles. Monthly pro-
grams, literary lectures & readings. Writers'
studio. Inquiries invited.
Number of Members: 500

**The Center for the Book in the Library of
Congress**
The Library of Congress, 101 Independence Ave
SE, Washington, DC 20540-4920
Tel: 202-707-5221 *Fax:* 202-707-0269
E-mail: cfbook@loc.gov
Web Site: www.read.gov; www.read.gov/cfb
Key Personnel
Dir: John Van Oudenaren
Commns Offr: Guy Lamolinara
Founded: 1977 (est by law)
Uses the influence & resources of the Library of
Congress to stimulate public interest in books
& reading & to encourage the study of books.
Its program of symposia, projects, lectures,
exhibitions & publications is supported by tax-
deductible contributions from corporations &
individuals. National reading promotion net-
work includes more than 50 affiliated state
centers & more than 80 educational & civic
organizations.

Chicago Women in Publishing
PO Box 268107, Chicago, IL 60626
Tel: 773-508-0351 *Fax:* 303-942-7164
E-mail: info@cwip.org
Web Site: www.cwip.org
Key Personnel
Pres: Mejhann Workman *E-mail:* president@cwip.
org
Secy: Fiona Saltmarsh *E-mail:* secretary@cwip.
org
Founded: 1972
Jobline employment listing service, monthly
newsletter, monthly program meetings, free-
lance directory, membership directory.
Number of Members: 300
New Election: Annually in May

The Children's Book Council (CBC)
54 W 39 St, 14th fl, New York, NY 10018
Tel: 212-966-1990
E-mail: cbc.info@cbcbooks.org
Web Site: www.cbcbooks.org

Key Personnel
Exec Dir: Carl Lennertz *E-mail:* carl.lennertz@
cbcbooks.org
Assoc Exec Dir/Programming & Strategic Partnerships Dir: Shaina Birkhead *E-mail:* shaina.
birkhead@cbcbooks.org
Communs Coord: Emma Kantor *E-mail:* emma.
kantor@cbcbooks.com
Founded: 1945
Nonprofit trade association of children's book
publishers & related companies. Publish reading promotion display & informational materials. New electronic edition of Children's
Books: Awards & Prizes; provides professional
education & online member services.
Number of Members: 70
New Election: Annually in Sept
2021 Meeting(s): Children's Book Week, Nationwide across the USA, May 3-9, 2021
Publication(s): *Awards & Prizes Online* (online
database, annual, $150); *CBC Features* (semi-
annual, $60 one-time charge)

Christian Retail Association Inc (CRA)
200 West Bay Dr, Largo, FL 33770
Tel: 727-596-7625 *Toll Free Tel:* 800-868-4388
Toll Free Fax: 855-815-9277
E-mail: service@munce.com
Web Site: www.christianretailassociation.org
Key Personnel
Pres: Bob Munce
Founded: 2018
Created to help build community within the
Christian retail industry & to bring beneficial
assets to store owners & vendors. Offers ser-
vices, tradeshows, networking, training & edu-
cational materials.
Number of Members: 110
2021 Meeting(s): CPE (Christian Products
Expo™), Embassy Suites & Concord Conven-
tion, 5400 John Q Hammons Dr NW, Concord,
NC, Feb 14-16. 2021; CPE (Christian Products
Expo™), Embassy Suites & St Charles Con-
vention Center, St Charles, MO, Aug 15-17,
2021
Publication(s): *CRA Today* (quarterly, ezine, free
to membs)

CIP Program, see Canadian Cataloguing in
Publication Program

City & Regional Magazine Association
287 Richards Ave, Norwalk, CT 06850
Tel: 203-515-9294
E-mail: admin@citymag.org
Web Site: www.citymag.org
Key Personnel
Pres: Bob Fernald *E-mail:* rfernald@downeast.
com
VP: Betsy Benson *E-mail:* bbenson@
pittsburghmagazine.com
Secy: Shelly Crowley *E-mail:* scrowley@
mspmag.com
Treas: Remy Spreeuw *E-mail:* remy@5280.com
Exec Dir: Cate Sanderson *E-mail:* cate@
sandersonmgt.com
The purpose of the association is to facilitate pro-
fessional development & training opportunities
for member magazines & provide opportuni-
ties to exchange information & ideas. Also the
sponsor of CRMA Awards Competition, The
City & Regional Magazine Award Program at
the University of Missouri School of Journalism; city & regional magazine competition as
well as an annual conference.
Number of Members: 89
2021 Meeting(s): Winter Publishers Retreat,
Naples Grand Beach Resort, 475 Seagate Dr,
Naples, FL, Jan 28-30, 2021
Publication(s): *CRMA Newsletter* (free to membs,
electronic)

Colorado Authors' League
PO Box 24905, Denver, CO 80224
Web Site: coloradoauthors.org
Key Personnel
Pres: Denny Dressman
Founded: 1931
Organization of independent, professional writers
united to further members' success.
Number of Members: 250

Committee on Scholarly Editions
Subsidiary of Modern Language Association of
America (MLA)
c/o Modern Language Association of America,
85 Broad St, Suite 500, New York, NY 10004-
2434
Tel: 646-576-5044 *Fax:* 646-458-0030
E-mail: cse@mla.org
Web Site: www.mla.org
Key Personnel
Sr Acqs Ed: James C Hatch
Founded: 1979
Assists editors & publishers in preparing reliable
scholarly editions.
Number of Members: 9

Community of Literary Magazines & Presses (CLMP)
154 Christopher St, Suite 3C, New York, NY
10014-9110
Tel: 212-741-9110
E-mail: info@clmp.org
Web Site: www.clmp.org
Key Personnel
Exec Dir: Mary Gannon
Dir, Membership: Ted Dodson
Progs Dir: David Gibbs *E-mail:* dgibbs@clmp.org
Founded: 1967
A national nonprofit organization that provides
services to small independent literary magazine
& book publishers, including technical assis-
tance, various publications, marketing work-
shops, an online directory of literary maga-
zines & grant programs for literary magazines
& presses.
Number of Members: 500

Connecticut Authors & Publishers Association (CAPA)
PO Box 715, Avon, CT 06001-0715
Tel: 860-675-1344 *Toll Free Tel:* 800-562-6457
Web Site: www.aboutcapa.com
Key Personnel
Founder: Brian Jud *E-mail:* brianjud@comcast.net
Founded: 1994
Number of Members: 150
Meeting(s): Monthly Meeting, Sycamore Hills
Park Community Center, Avon, CT, 3rd Satur-
day of the month
Publication(s): *The Authority* (monthly, newsletter,
free to membs)

Conseil des arts du Canada, see Canada
Council for the Arts (Conseil des arts du
Canada)

Copywriters' Council of America™ (CCA)
Division of The Linick Group Inc
CCA Bldg, 7 Putter Lane, Middle Island, NY
11953-1920
Mailing Address: PO Box 102, Middle Island,
NY 11953-0102
Tel: 631-924-3888; 631-775-6075 *Fax:* 631-924-
8555
Key Personnel
Chmn, Consulting Group: Andrew S Linick, PhD
E-mail: cca4dmcopy@gmail.com
Pres: Gaylen Andrews
EVP: Roger Dextor
Dir, Spec Projs: Barbara Deal

Freelance digital & direct response advertising
copywriters, direct marketing consultants, PR
& communication specialists & marketing
researchers. Cover business-to-business, consumer & industrial markets. Creative services
covering all media, all products & services A-
Z, e-commerce, e-marketing, e-targeted public relations. Provide comprehensive graphic
redesign/new web site content development,
interactive services with marketing web site
makeover advice for first-time authors, self-
publishers, professionals & entrepreneurs. Specializes in online advertising/PR, links to top
search engines, consulting on a 100% satisfaction guarantee. Free site evaluation marketing
checklist (a $250 value) for LMP readers.
Number of Members: 35,000
Publication(s): *The Digest* (quarterly, for membs
only, ezine, $40)
Branch Office(s)
7 Lincoln Ave, Smithtown, NY 11787

Corporation for Public Broadcasting (CPB)
401 Ninth St NW, Washington, DC 20004-2129
Tel: 202-879-9600
Web Site: www.cpb.org
Key Personnel
Pres & CEO: Patricia de Stacy Harrison
EVP & COO: Michael Levy
Treas & CFO: William P Tayman, Jr
SVP & Gen Coun: Westwood Smithers, Jr
SVP & Corp Secy: Teresa Safon
Supports the nation's public TV & public radio
stations through federally appropriated funds.
Conducts support services to stimulate the cre-
ation of programming on TV, radio & online.

Corporation of Professional Librarians of Quebec
1453, rue Beaubien Est, Bureau 215, Montreal,
QC H2G 3C6, Canada
Tel: 514-845-3327 *Fax:* 514-845-1618
E-mail: info@cbpq.qc.ca
Web Site: www.cbpq.qc.ca
Key Personnel
Exec Dir: Regine Horinstein
Founded: 1969
Publications, continuing education for information
professionals.
Number of Members: 700
Publication(s): *Argus* (3 issues/yr, $48 CN, $50
foreign)

Council for Advancement & Support of Education (CASE)
1307 New York Ave NW, Suite 1000, Washing-
ton, DC 20005-4701
Tel: 202-328-CASE (328-2273) *Fax:* 202-387-
4973
E-mail: membersupportcenter@case.org
Web Site: www.case.org
Key Personnel
Pres: Sue Cunningham
VP, Busn & Fin: Donald Falkenstein *Tel:* 202-
478-5637 *E-mail:* falkenstein@case.org
Dir, Communs: Pam Russell *Tel:* 202-478-5680
E-mail: russell@case.org
Founded: 1974
International association of educational institu-
tions. Helps its members build stronger re-
lationships with their alumni & donors, raise
funds for campus projects, produce recruitment
materials, market their institutions to prospec-
tive students, diversity the profession & foster
public support of education.
Number of Members: 81,000
Publication(s): *Currents* (9 issues/yr (3 double is-
sues), $150/yr, $220/2 yrs, $180/yr intl, $280/2
yrs intl)
Branch Office(s)
Berlin 18 4to piso, Colonia Juarez, Delegacion
Cuauhtemoc, 06600 Mexico, DF, Mexico

Tel: (0155) 2709 15 77 *E-mail:* americalatina@
case.org
Shaw Foundation Alumni House, Unit 05-03, 11
Kent Ridge Dr, Singapore, Singapore *Tel:* 6778
3285 *Fax:* 6778 3286 *E-mail:* asia-pacific@
case.org
Paxton House, 3rd fl, 30 Artillery Lane, London
E1 7LS, United Kingdom *Tel:* (020) 7448 9940
Fax: (020) 7377 5944 *E-mail:* europe@case.org

Council for the Advancement of Science Writing (CASW)

PO Box 910, Hedgesville, WV 25427
Tel: 304-754-6786
Web Site: www.casw.org
Key Personnel
Exec Dir: Rosalind Reid *E-mail:* rosreid@gmail.
com
Admin: Diane McGurgan *E-mail:* diane@casw.
org
Founded: 1959
To advance science writing.
Meeting(s): New Horizons in Science, annually in
Oct

Crime Writers of Canada (CWC)

4C-240 Westwood Rd, Guelph, ON N1H 7W9,
Canada
E-mail: info@crimewriterscanada.com
Web Site: www.crimewriterscanada.com
Key Personnel
Exec Dir: Alison Bruce *E-mail:* ed@
crimewriterscanada.com
Asst Exec Dir & Arthur Ellis Awards Mgr: Lud-
vica Boota *E-mail:* aed@crimewriterscanada.
com
Founded: 1982
National nonprofit organization for Canadian
mystery & crime writers, associated profession-
als & others with a serious interest in Canadian
crime writing.
Publication(s): *Cool Canadian Crime* (quarterly);
Crime Beat (newsletter)

CWA/SCA Canada

Affiliate of Canadian Labour Congress
2200 Prince of Wales Dr, Suite 301, Ottawa, ON
K2E 6Z9, Canada
Tel: 613-820-9777 *Toll Free Tel:* 877-486-4292
Fax: 613-820-8188
E-mail: info@cwa-scacanada.ca
Web Site: www.cwa-scacanada.ca
Key Personnel
Pres: Martin O'Hanlon *Tel:* 613-820-8460
E-mail: mohanlon@cwa-scacanada.ca
Contracts Coord: Marj Botsford
E-mail: mbotsford@cwa-scacanada.ca
Fin Coord: Joanne Scheel *E-mail:* jscheel@cwa-
scacanada.ca
Founded: 1995 (as TNG Canada)
Media union representing members in Canada.
Affiliate of: The Newspaper Guild, Communica-
tion Workers of America (CWA) & Canadian
Labour Congress.
Number of Members: 7,000

Deadline Club

Division of Society of Professional Journalists
c/o Salmagundi Club, 47 Fifth Ave, New York,
NY 10003
Tel: 646-481-7584
Web Site: www.deadlineclub.org
Key Personnel
Pres: Claire Regan
Secy: Joanna Hernandez
Treas: Michael Rizzo
VP, Awards Contest: Daniel Roberts
VP, Awards Dinner: Colin DeVries
VP, Communs: Melissa Heule
VP, Events: Jessica Seigel
VP, Membership: Polly Whittell
VP, Spec Projs: Janell Crispyn

Founded: 1925
Monthly meetings. Members include professionals
working in print, broadcast, online & journalism education. Professional membership $30,
student membership $20. Must be SPJ member.
Number of Members: 300
Meeting(s): Annual Awards Dinner, Waldorf Astoria, New York, NY, May
Publication(s): *Deadliner Express* (newsletter);
Quill (6 issues/yr, magazine, free to membs,
$75/yr nonmembs); *SPJ Leads* (weekly,
newsletter, free to membs)

Dog Writers' Association of America Inc (DWAA)

PO Box 787, Hughesville, MD 20637
E-mail: info@dogwriters.org
Web Site: dogwriters.org
Key Personnel
Pres: Jen Reeder *E-mail:* jen@jenreeder.com
VP: Laura Coffey *E-mail:* laura.coffey@nbcuni.
com
Treas: Marsha Pugh *E-mail:* marsha_pugh01@
comcast.com
Secy: Laurren Darr *E-mail:* laurrendarr@
leftpawpress.com
Founded: 1935
Provide information about dogs (sport, breeding
& ownership) & assist writers in gaining access
to exhibitions. Annual writing competition.
Number of Members: 545
Meeting(s): Annual Meeting, Hotel Pennsylvania,
401 Seventh Ave, New York, NY, Feb
Publication(s): *Ruff Drafts* (quarterly, newsletter,
free to membs)

EdCan Network

60 St Clair Ave E, Suite 703, Toronto, ON M4T
1N5, Canada
Tel: 416-591-6300 *Toll Free Tel:* 866-803-9549
Fax: 416-591-5345 *Toll Free Fax:* 866-803-
9549
E-mail: info@edcan.ca
Web Site: www.edcan.ca
Key Personnel
COO: Gilles Latour *Tel:* 416-591-6300 ext 237
E-mail: glatour@edcan.ca
Dir, Communs: Max Cooke *Tel:* 416-591-6300
ext 225 *E-mail:* mcooke@edcan.ca
Founded: 1891
A national bilingual, charitable organization that
promotes transformation in education.
Number of Members: 304
New Election: Annually in Sept or Oct
Publication(s): *Education Canada* (4 issues/yr,
magazine, free to membs; available for pur-
chase through subn servs)

Editorial Freelancers Association (EFA)

266 W 37 St, 20th fl, New York, NY 10018
Tel: 212-920-4816 *Toll Free Tel:* 866-929-5425
E-mail: office@the-efa.org
Web Site: www.the-efa.org
Key Personnel
Co-Exec: Christina Frey; William P Keenan, Jr
Founded: 1970
A not-for-profit 501(c)(6), volunteer-based profes-
sional association of freelance editors, writers,
copy editors, proofreaders, indexers, production
specialists, researchers & translators. Provides
job listing service, courses, member directory
& related professional services. More than 20
chapters nationwide.
Number of Members: 2,300
Publication(s): *EFA Directory* (online, free); *EFA
Newsletter* (6 issues/yr, newsletter, free to
membs)

Editors' Association of Canada (Association canadienne des reviseurs)

1507-180 Dundas St W, Toronto, ON M5G 1Z8,
Canada

Tel: 416-975-1379 *Toll Free Tel:* 866-CAN-EDIT
(226-3348) *Fax:* 416-975-1637
E-mail: info@editors.ca; info@reviseurs.ca
Web Site: www.editors.ca; www.reviseurs.ca
Key Personnel
Exec Dir: John Yip-Chuck
E-mail: executivedirector@editors.ca
Sr Communs Mgr: Michelle Ou
E-mail: communications@editors.ca
Membership & Conference Coord: Caitlin Stewart
Founded: 1979
Promotes professional editing as key in producing
effective communication. Our members work
with individuals in the corporate, technical,
government, not-for-profit & publishing sectors.
Sponsor professional development seminars,
promotes & maintains high standards of editing
& publishing in Canada, establishes guidelines
to help editors secure fair pay & good working
conditions, helps both in-house & freelance editors to network & cooperates with other publishing associations in areas of common concern. The association is incorporated federally
as a not-for-profit organization & is governed
at the national level by an executive council.
Number of Members: 1,500
New Election: Annually in June
Publication(s): *Active Voice (La Voix Active)*
(semiannual, newsletter, free to membs)
Membership(s): Book & Periodical Council; Cultural Human Resources Council (CHRC)

Education Writers Association (EWA)

3516 Connecticut Ave NW, Washington, DC
20008
Tel: 202-452-9830 *Fax:* 202-452-9837
E-mail: ewa@ewa.org
Web Site: www.ewa.org
Key Personnel
COO: George Dieter *E-mail:* gdieter@ewa.org
Exec Dir: Caroline W Hendrie *E-mail:* chendrie@
ewa.org
Asst Dir: Lori Crouch *E-mail:* lcrouch@ewa.org
Founded: 1947
Professional organization of members of the me-
dia who cover education at all levels with a
mission to increase the quality & quantity of
education coverage to create a better informed
society. Conferences, seminars, newsletters,
publications, employment services, freelance
referral, workshops & national awards.
Number of Members: 3,000
Publication(s): *Standards for Education Reporters*
(free)

Educational Book & Media Association (EBMA)

11 Main St, Suite D, Warrenton, VA 20186
Mailing Address: PO Box 3363, Warrenton, VA
20188
Tel: 540-318-7770 *Fax:* 202-962-3939
E-mail: info@edupaperback.org
Web Site: www.edupaperback.org
Key Personnel
Pres: Jill Faherty
VP: Joyce Skokut
Treas: Nancy Stetzinger
Exec Dir: Brian Gorg
Meeting Mgr: Maureen Gelwicks
Founded: 1975
To develop better techniques & procedures for the
sales, marketing & distribution of paperback
books, prebound books & related media in the
school & library markets. Regular membership
consists of educational paperback & prebound
book wholesalers; associate members are pa-
perback publishers.
Number of Members: 125
2021 Meeting(s): EBMA Annual Meeting, El
Conquistador Tucson, Tucson, AZ, Jan 11-14,
2021

Epicomm

1800 Diagonal Rd, Suite 320, Alexandria, VA 22314-2862
Tel: 703-836-9200
E-mail: webmaster@epicomm.org
Web Site: epicomm.org
Key Personnel
Pres & CEO: Ken Garner *Tel:* 703-972-2730
   E-mail: kgarner@epicomm.org
EVP: Dean D'Ambrosi *Tel:* 201-523-6314
   E-mail: ddambrosi@epicomm.org
SVP & Chief Economist: Andrew D Paparozzi
   Tel: 201-523-6353 *E-mail:* apaparozzi@
   epicomm.org
Founded: 2014 (through merger of AMSP, NAPL & NAQP)
Association for leaders in print, mail, fulfillment & marketing services. Epicomm provides management tools & learning & professional development opportunities to help make informed business decisions in an ever-changing market environment.
Number of Members: 3,600
Publication(s): *Bottom Line* (6 issues/yr, magazine); *Management Bulletin* (quarterly, newsletter); *Owner Operator* (quarterly, newsletter); *REVIEW* (monthly, newsletter, electronic); *State of the Industry Update* (quarterly, newsletter)
Branch Office(s)
One Meadowlands Plaza, Suite 1511, East Rutherford, NJ 07073 *Tel:* 201-634-9600

Evangelical Christian Publishers Association (ECPA)

5801 S McClintock Dr, Suite 104, Tempe, AZ 85283
Tel: 480-966-3998 *Fax:* 480-966-1944
E-mail: info@ecpa.org
Web Site: www.ecpa.org
Key Personnel
Exec Dir: Stan Jantz
Founded: 1974
Trade association supporting Christian publishers worldwide. Provides professional seminars, compiles statistical studies & presents religious book awards.
Number of Members: 280
2021 Meeting(s): ECPA Leadership Summit, Hilton Philadelphia at Penn's Landing & the American Bible Society, both in Philadelphia, PA, May 5-6, 2021
Membership(s): Book Industry Study Group (BISG)

Evangelical Press Association (EPA)

PO Box 1787, Queen Creek, AZ 85142
Toll Free Tel: 888-311-1731
E-mail: info@evangelicalpress.com
Web Site: www.evangelicalpress.com
Key Personnel
Exec Dir: Lamar Keener
Founded: 1948
Professional association of Christian freelancers, associates, magazines, newsletters, newspapers & content-rich web sites.
Number of Members: 329
2021 Meeting(s): Annual Convention, Lancaster, PA, April 28-30, 2021
Publication(s): *Liaison* (quarterly, newsletter)

FAPA, see Florida Authors & Publishers Association Inc (FAPA)

Federation of BC Writers

PO Box 16028, 617 Belmont St, New Westminster, BC V3M 6W6, Canada
E-mail: info@bcwriters.ca
Web Site: bcwriters.ca
Key Personnel
Pres: Coco Aders-Weremczuk
Exec Dir: Craig Spence
Founded: 1976

Not-for-profit organization established to contribute to a supportive environment for writing in the province. Writers of all levels working in all genres & specialties welcome. We publish a magazine & hold readings, workshops & literary competitions.
Number of Members: 400
New Election: Annually in May
Publication(s): *WordWorks*

Florida Antiquarian Booksellers Association (FABA)

14046 Fifth St, Dade City, FL 33525
Tel: 727-234-7759
E-mail: floridabooksellers@gmail.com
Web Site: floridabooksellers.com
Key Personnel
Pres: William Chrisant
VP: Madlyn Blom
Secy: Richard Oates
Treas: Robert A Hittel
Dedicated to enhancing the business of buying & selling rare & unusual books, vintage photographs, antique maps & ephemera by promoting high standards of excellence in the industry. FABA is a membership organization & does not purchase books or provide evaluations.
2021 Meeting(s): Florida Antiquarian Book Fair, The Coliseum, 535 Fourth Ave N, St Petersburg, FL, April 23-25, 2021

Florida Authors & Publishers Association Inc (FAPA)

1702 N Woodland Blvd, Suite 116, Box 145, Deland, FL 32720
E-mail: member.services@
   floridapublishersassociation.com
Web Site: www.floridapublishersassociation.com
Key Personnel
Pres: Terri Gerrell *E-mail:* president@
   floridapublishersassociation.com
Founded: 1983
Networking seminars, newsletter, publishing, book shows, workshops, small presses, independents & self-publishers; annual President's Book Award competition. Affiliate of IBPA (Independent Book Publishers Association), AAP (Association of American Publishers) & APSS (Association of Publishers for Small Sales).
Number of Members: 144
Publication(s): *FAPA REaD* (monthly, newsletter, free to membs, media, booksellers, libraries & reviewers, electronic)

Florida Freelance Writers Association

Affiliate of Writers-Editors Network
45 Main St, North Stratford, NH 03590
Mailing Address: PO Box A, North Stratford, NH 03590
Tel: 603-922-8338 *Fax:* 603-922-8339
E-mail: ffwa@writers-editors.com; info@writers-editors.com
Web Site: www.writers-editors.com; www.ffwamembers.com
Key Personnel
Exec Dir: Dana K Cassell *E-mail:* dana@writers-editors.com
Founded: 1982
Network of freelance writers & editors, offering a job bank, Florida Markets directory, newsletter, etc.
Number of Members: 200
Publication(s): *Directory of Florida Markets for Writers* (newsletter & electronic formats, $35, free to membs); *Freelance Writer's Report* (monthly, free to membs); *Guide to WEN/FFWA Writers* (continuously updated, free to qualified publishing companies & businesses)

Florida Graphics Alliance (FGA)

Affiliate of PRINTING United Alliance
5770 Hoffner Ave, Suite 103, Orlando, FL 32822
Tel: 407-240-8009 *Toll Free Tel:* 800-331-0461
   Fax: 407-240-8333
E-mail: info@floridagraphics.org
Web Site: www.floridagraphics.org
Key Personnel
Pres: Gabriel Hernandez *E-mail:* gabe@
   floridagraphics.org
Dir, Communs: Aaron Elliott *Tel:* 407-845-0602
   E-mail: aaron@floridagraphics.org
Mgr, Memb Servs: Kasondra Weeks *Tel:* 407-845-0599 *E-mail:* kasondra@floridagraphics.org
Event Coord/Membership Mgr: Ana Cintron
   E-mail: ana@floridagraphics.org
Founded: 1939
Trade association for the graphic arts industry.
Number of Members: 380
Meeting(s): Graphics of the Americas (GOA)
Publication(s): *Graphics Update* (monthly, free to membs)

Florida Outdoor Writers Association Inc

235 Apollo Beach Blvd, Unit 271, Apollo Beach, FL 33572
Tel: 813-579-0990
E-mail: info@fowa.org
Web Site: www.fowa.org
Key Personnel
Chmn of the Bd: Tom Van Horn
Pres: Bob Bramblet
1st VP: JoNell Modys
2nd VP: Rob Modys
Secy: Kathy Barker
Treas: Bob Wattendorf
Exec Dir: Butch Newell
Founded: 1946
Not-for-profit 501(c)(3) statewide paid professional communicators organization made up of outdoor communicators who report & reflect upon Florida's diverse interests in the outdoors to educate & encourage the public in ways that protect & conserve our natural heritage.
Number of Members: 200
New Election: Annually in Sept
Publication(s): *The Market Edge* (6 issues/yr, newsletter, free to membs, electronic)

Florida Writers Association Inc

PO Box 66069, St Pete Beach, FL 33736-6069
Web Site: www.floridawriters.net
Key Personnel
Pres: Cheyenne Williams *E-mail:* ckwilliams@
   onlinebinding.com
EVP: Jade Kerrion
VP, Admin & Fin: Larry Kokko
VP, Fin: Robyn Weinbaum
Founded: 2001
Association of "writers helping writers" to improve writing skills, produce good work in all genres & successfully publish.
Number of Members: 1,500
Publication(s): *The Florida Writer* (quarterly, $4.95, free to membs)

Foil & Specialty Effects Association (FSEA)

2150 SW Westport Dr, Suite 101, Topeka, KS 66614
Tel: 785-271-5816 *Fax:* 785-271-6404
E-mail: info@fsea.com
Web Site: www.fsea.com
Key Personnel
Exec Dir: Jeff Peterson *E-mail:* jeff@fsea.com
Asst Dir: Dianna Brodine *E-mail:* dianna@
   petersonpublications.com
Sales Dir: Gayla Peterson *E-mail:* gayla@
   petersonpublications.com
Founded: 1992
Trade association for graphics finishing industry.
Number of Members: 325

La Fondation Emile Nelligan
100, rue Sherbrooke, Suite 202, Montreal, QC
H2X 1C3, Canada
Tel: 514-278-4657
E-mail: info@fondation-nelligan.org
Web Site: www.fondation-nelligan.org
Key Personnel
CEO: Manon Gagnon
Pres: Michel Dallaire
VP: Marie-Andree Beaudet
Treas/Secy: Michel Gonneville
Founded: 1979
Sponsoring organization.

**4A's (American Association of Advertising
Agencies)**
1065 Avenue of the Americas, 16th fl, New York,
NY 10018
Tel: 212-682-2500
Web Site: www.aaaa.org
Key Personnel
Pres & CEO: Marla Kaplowitz
E-mail: mkaplowitz@aaaa.org
EVP, COO & CFO: Todd Hittle *E-mail:* thittle@
aaaa.org
Chief Mktg Offr: Alison Fahey *E-mail:* afahey@
aaaa.org
EVP, Agency Rel & Membership: Mollie Rosen
E-mail: mrosen@aaaa.org
Founded: 1917
National trade association for the advertising
agency business.
Number of Members: 430
Branch Office(s)
9595 Wilshire Blvd, Suite 900, Beverly Hills,
CA 90212, EVP, Western Reg: Jerry McGee
Tel: 310-300-3422
1707 "L" St NW, Suite 600, Washington, DC
20036, EVP: Dick O'Brien *Tel:* 202-331-7345
3050 Bellingrath Blvd, Roswell, GA 30076, VP,
Agency Rel & Membership: Greg Walker
Tel: 770-639-6720 (cell)
111 Wacker Dr, No 4006, Chicago, IL 60611,
VP, Agency Rel & Membership: Laurie Stearn
Tel: 312-388-7470
11020 David Taylor Dr, Suite 305, Charlotte, NC
28262-1103 *Tel:* 704-594-6270

**GardenComm: Garden Communicators
International**
355 Lexington Ave, 15th fl, New York, NY
10017
Tel: 212-297-2198
E-mail: info@gardenwriters.org
Web Site: www.gardenwriters.org
Founded: 1948
Professional association garden communica-
tors working as staff or freelance as newspa-
per columnists, magazine columnists, pho-
tographers & radio/TV hosts. Sponsor annual
writer's contest & annual Garden Media award
program for published articles or books, as
well as an annual symposium.
Number of Members: 1,400
Meeting(s): GardenComm Annual Conference &
Expo
Publication(s): *Quill & Trowel* (6 issues/yr,
newsletter)

The Graphic Artists Guild Inc
31 W 34 St, 8th fl, New York, NY 10001
Tel: 212-791-3400 *Fax:* 212-791-0333
E-mail: admin@graphicartistsguild.org;
membership@graphicartistsguild.org
Web Site: www.graphicartistsguild.org
Key Personnel
Pres: Lara Kisielewska *E-mail:* president@
graphicartistsguild.org
Founded: 1967
Labor organization which advocates the advance-
ment of artists' rights. Members are illustrators,

graphic designers, surface & textile designers,
computer graphics artists, cartoonists & others.
Number of Members: 1,100
Publication(s): *Pricing & Ethical Guidelines, 14th
ed* ($39.99)

Graphic Arts Association
Affiliate of PRINTING United Alliance
1210 Northbrook Dr, Suite 200, Trevose, PA
19053
Tel: 215-396-2300 *Fax:* 215-396-9890
Web Site: www.graphicartsassociation.org
Key Personnel
Pres: Melissa Jones *E-mail:* mjones@gaaonline.
org
Off Mgr: Rita Donlan *E-mail:* rdonlan@
gaaonline.org
Founded: 1888
Regional trade association representing printing
& graphic arts professionals in Pennsylvania,
Central & Southern New Jersey & Delaware.
Meeting(s): Graphically Speaking Educational
Forum, annually in Oct

Gravure Association of the Americas Inc
8281 Pine Lake Rd, Denver, NC 28037
Tel: 201-523-6042 *Fax:* 201-523-6048
E-mail: gaa@gaa.org
Web Site: www.gaa.org
Key Personnel
Exec Dir: Philip Pimlott *Tel:* 812-406-5434
E-mail: ppimlott@gaa.org
Dir, Planning & Admin: Pamela W Schenk
Tel: 585-288-2297 *E-mail:* pwschenk@gaa.org
Foster the advancement of gravure printing indus-
try. Sponsor of the Golden Cylinder Awards.
Number of Members: 200

Great Lakes Graphics Association
Affiliate of PRINTING United Alliance
W232 N2950 Roundy Circle E, Pewaukee, WI
53072
Tel: 262-522-2210 *Toll Free Tel:* 855-522-2210
Fax: 262-522-2211
E-mail: admin@glga.info
Web Site: glga.info
Key Personnel
Pres: Joe Lyman
Founded: 1886
Number of Members: 410
Publication(s): *NewScan* (electronic, newsletter,
free to membs)

**Great Lakes Independent Booksellers
Association (GLIBA)**
250 Woodstock Ave, Clarendon Hills, IL 60514
Tel: 630-841-8129
Web Site: www.gliba.org
Key Personnel
Exec Dir: Larry Law *E-mail:* larry@gliba.org
Founded: 1989
Promotes independent bookselling; strengthens
partnerships among members in all aspects of
the bookselling industry; promotes the Great
Lakes region as a vital marketplace. The Great
Lakes states are Illinois, Indiana, Kentucky,
Michigan, Ohio & Wisconsin.
Meeting(s): GLIBA Spring Forum, annually in
April; Heartland Fall Forum, annually in Oct

Guild of Book Workers
521 Fifth Ave, New York, NY 10175
Tel: 212-292-4444
E-mail: communications@guildofbookworkers.org
Web Site: www.guildofbookworkers.org
Key Personnel
Pres: Bexx Caswell *Tel:* 520-682-7241
E-mail: president@guildofbookworkers.org
VP: Brien Beidler *E-mail:* vicepresident@
guildofbookworkers.org

Secy: Rebecca Smyrl *Tel:* 214-363-7946
E-mail: secretary@guildofbookworkers.org
Treas: Laura Bedford *E-mail:* treasurer@
guildofbookworkers.org
Founded: 1906
A national nonprofit educational organization
which fosters the hand book arts: binding, cal-
ligraphy, illumination, paper decorating. Spon-
sor exhibits, lectures, workshops. See web site
for membership fee information.
Number of Members: 850
Publication(s): *Journal* (annual, free to membs);
Newsletter (6 issues/yr, free to membs)

Horror Writers Association (HWA)
PO Box 56687, Sherman Oaks, CA 91413
Tel: 818-220-3965
E-mail: admin@horror.org
Web Site: horror.org
Key Personnel
Pres: Lisa Morton *E-mail:* president@horror.org
VP: John Palisano *E-mail:* vp@horror.org
Treas: Leslie Klinger *E-mail:* treasurer@horror.
org
Secy: Joe McKinney *E-mail:* secretary@horror.
org
Admin: Brad Hodson *E-mail:* admin@horror.org
Founded: 1985
To encourage public interest in & foster an ap-
preciation of good horror & dark fantasy liter-
ature. Publishes monthly newsletter, provides
online information & resources, Hardship Fund,
Grievance Committee, scholarships. Sponsors
Bram Stoker Awards® & presents an annual
Lifetime Achievement Award.
Membership fees: $69 indiv, $48 supporting,
$115 corp, $89 family.
Number of Members: 1,500
Meeting(s): StokerCon™
Publication(s): *Horror Writers Association
Newsletter* (monthly, electronic, free)

The Ibsen Society of America (ISA)
c/o Indiana University, Global & Intl Studies
Bldg 3111, 355 N Jordan Ave, Bloomington,
IN 47405-1105
Web Site: www.ibsensociety.org
Key Personnel
Pres: Olivia Noble Gunn *E-mail:* ogunn@uw.edu
VP: Dean Krouk *E-mail:* krouk@wisc.edu
Treas: Gergana May *E-mail:* ggmay@indiana.edu
Secy: Maren Anderson Johnson
E-mail: johnma29@luther.edu
Founded: 1978
Nonprofit corporation which fosters an under-
standing of Ibsen's works through lectures,
readings, performances, conferences & publi-
cations.
Number of Members: 250
Publication(s): *Ibsen News & Comment* (annual,
free to membs)

ICEA, see The Institute for Cooperation on Adult
Education (Institut de Cooperation pour
l'Education des Adultes-ICEA)

**In-Plant Printing & Mailing Association
(IPMA)**
455 S Sam Barr Dr, Suite 203, Kearney, MO
64060
Tel: 816-919-1691
E-mail: ipmainfo@ipma.org
Web Site: www.ipma.org
Key Personnel
Exec Dir: Carma Goin *E-mail:* cgoin@ipma.org
Fin Coord & Off Asst: Jennifer Chambers
E-mail: jchambers@ipma.org
Founded: 1964
Professional association dedicated to the specific
needs of all industry segments of in-house pro-
fessionals who provide graphic design, copy,
print, mail & distribution services to their or-

ganizations. Annual Educational Conference & Vendor Fair.
Number of Members: 500
Publication(s): *Inside Edge* (monthly, newsletter)

The Independent Book Publishers Association (IBPA)
1020 Manhattan Beach Blvd, Suite 204, Manhattan Beach, CA 90266
Tel: 310-546-1818
E-mail: info@ibpa-online.org
Web Site: www.ibpa-online.org
Key Personnel
CEO: Angela Bole *E-mail:* angela@ibpa-online. org
COO: Terry Nathan *E-mail:* terry@ibpa-online. org
Founded: 1983 (as Publishers Association of Southern California)
A national nonprofit publishers' co-operative which coordinates discounted participation in major book & library exhibits & trade shows throughout the country, as well as ad placement in major publications & direct mail programs. Sponsor workshops, awards & prizes.
Number of Members: 3,000
Publication(s): *IBPA Independent* (monthly, magazine, free to membs, $60/yr nonmembs); *Membership & Service Directory* (free to membs)

Independent Publishers of New England (IPNE)
10 Court St, No 206, Arlington, MA 02476-0206
Tel: 339-368-8229
E-mail: talktous@ipne.org
Web Site: www.ipne.org
Key Personnel
Pres: Eddie Vincent
Organization of professionals, authors & companies who collaborate to help each other learn & succeed in the independent book publishing field. Serves as an advocate for the regional independent publishing community. Offers educational programs, networking, marketing opportunities, advocacy & information about publishing.
Number of Members: 200

Independent Writers of Chicago (IWOC)
332 S Michigan Ave, Suite 1032, Chicago, IL 60604
Toll Free Tel: 800-804-IWOC (804-4962)
E-mail: info@iwoc.org
Web Site: www.iwoc.org
Key Personnel
Pres: Laura Stigler
Monthly meetings, workshops & seminars dealing with the business aspects of independent writing. Writers' line job referral. Speakers' bureau.
Number of Members: 85

InScribe Christian Writers' Fellowship (ICWF)
PO Box 6201, Wetaskiwin, AB T9A 2E9, Canada
Tel: 780-646-3068 *Fax:* 780-635-2190
E-mail: inscribe.mail@gmail.com
Web Site: inscribe.org
Key Personnel
Pres: Ruth L Snyder *E-mail:* president@inscribe. org
Treas: Bobbi Junior *E-mail:* payments@inscribe. org
Secy: Pat Gerbrandt *E-mail:* pageware71@gmail. com
Founded: 1980 (as Alberta Christian Writers' Fellowship)
Stimulate, encourage & support Christians who write anywhere across Canada, to advance effective Christian writing & to promote the influence of all Christians who write.
Number of Members: 180

Meeting(s): Fall Conference, Annually last weekend in Sept
Publication(s): *FellowScript* (quarterly, magazine, $50/yr PDF, $70/yr hardcover, $100/yr family hardcover, $130/2 yrs hardcover, free to membs)

Institut de Cooperation pour l'Education des Adultes, see The Institute for Cooperation on Adult Education (Institut de Cooperation pour l'Education des Adultes-ICEA)

The Institute for Cooperation on Adult Education (Institut de Cooperation pour l'Education des Adultes-ICEA)
4321, ave Papineau, Montreal, QC H2H 1T3, Canada
Tel: 514-948-2044 *Fax:* 514-948-2046
E-mail: icae@icea.qc.ca
Web Site: www.icea.qc.ca
Key Personnel
Dir Gen: Daniel Baril *Tel:* 514-948-2039
    E-mail: dbaril@icea.qc.ca
Founded: 1946
Adult education lifelong learning.
Number of Members: 107
Publication(s): *ICEA News* (newsletter, free to membs)

Inter American Press Association (IAPA)
3511 NW 91 Ave, Miami, FL 33172
Tel: 305-634-2465 *Fax:* 305-860-4264
E-mail: info@sipiapa.org
Web Site: www.sipiapa.org
Key Personnel
Exec Dir: Ricardo Trotti *E-mail:* rtrotti@sipiapa. org
Founded: 1942
To guard freedom of speech & freedom of the press; to foster & protect the general & specific interests of the daily & periodical press of the Americas; to promote & maintain the dignity, rights & responsibilities of journalism; to encourage uniform standards of professional & business conduct; to exchange ideas & information which contribute to the cultural, material & technical development of the press; to foster a wider knowledge & greater interchange in support of the basic principles of a free society & individual liberty.
Number of Members: 900
Meeting(s): General Assembly, annually in Oct
Publication(s): *Hora de Cierre* (quarterly); *IAPA Annual Report*; *IAPA News* (quarterly); *IAPA Semiannual Report*; *Notisip* (quarterly)

International Association of Business Communicators (IABC)
649 Mission St, 5th fl, San Francisco, CA 94105
Tel: 415-544-4700 *Toll Free Tel:* 800-776-4222
    (US & CN) *Fax:* 415-544-4747
E-mail: leader_centre@iabc.com;
    member_relations@iabc.com
Web Site: www.iabc.com
Key Personnel
Exec Dir: Stephanie Doute *Tel:* 415-544-4731
    E-mail: sdoute@iabc.com
Sr Mktg Mgr: Mike Holden *E-mail:* mholden@ iabc.com
Sr Membership Mgr: Jamie Recio *Tel:* 415-544-4728 *E-mail:* jrecio@iabc.com
Founded: 1970
Communication association.
Number of Members: 14,000
Meeting(s): IABC World Conference
Publication(s): *Communication World* (monthly)

International Association of Crime Writers Inc, North American Branch
243 Fifth Ave, Suite 537, New York, NY 10016
Tel: 212-243-8966 *Fax:* 815-361-1477

E-mail: info@crimewritersna.org
Web Site: www.crimewritersna.org
Key Personnel
Exec Dir: Mary A Frisque *E-mail:* mfrisque@igc. org
Pres: J Madison Davis
Secy-Treas: Jim Weikart
Secy: Steven Steinbock
Founded: 1987
Promote communication among crime writers worldwide & enhance awareness & encourage translations of the genre in the US & abroad.
Number of Members: 285
Publication(s): *Border Patrol* (quarterly, free to membs)

International Encyclopedia Society
3689 Campbell Ct, Yorktown Heights, NY 10598
Tel: 914-962-3287 *Fax:* 914-962-3287
Key Personnel
Pres & Ed: George Thomas Kurian
    E-mail: gtkurian@aol.com
Publication of books & journals; conferences; award of prizes.
Number of Members: 210

International Literacy Association (ILA)
258 Chapman Rd, Suite 203, Newark, DE 19702
Mailing Address: PO Box 8139, Newark, DE 19714-8139
Tel: 302-731-1600 *Toll Free Tel:* 800-336-7323
    (US & CN) *Fax:* 302-731-1057
E-mail: customerservice@reading.org
Web Site: www.literacyworldwide.org; www. reading.org
Key Personnel
Exec Dir: Marcie Craig Post
Founded: 1956
Conferences; publications, research, membership services; publications on reading & related topics; professional journals.
Number of Members: 60,000
2021 Meeting(s): Annual Conference, Indianapolis, IN, Oct 14-17, 2021

International Society of Latino Authors
c/o Latino Literacy Now, 3445 Catalina Dr, Carlsbad, CA 92010
Tel: 760-434-1223 *Fax:* 760-434-7476
Key Personnel
COO: Kirk Whisler *E-mail:* kirk@whisler.com
Open to published & unpublished Latino authors or any author writing about the Latino experience/issues, all publishers & related service providers who support Latino literacy, nationally or internationally.

International Society of Weekly Newspaper Editors
Missouri Southern State University, 3950 E Newman Rd, Joplin, MO 64801-1595
Tel: 417-625-9736 *Fax:* 417-659-4445
Web Site: www.iswne.org
Key Personnel
Exec Dir: Dr Chad Stebbins *E-mail:* stebbins-c@ mssu.edu
Founded: 1955
Help those in weekly press to improve standards of editorial writing & news reporting. Encourages strong independent editorial voices.
Number of Members: 300
2021 Meeting(s): ISWNE Conference, University of Nevada, Reno, NV, June 23-27, 2021
Publication(s): *Grassroots Editor* (quarterly, $25/ yr US & CN, $28 elsewhere)

International Standard Book Numbering (ISBN) US Agency, A Cambridge Information Group Co
Affiliate of R R Bowker LLC
630 Central Ave, New Providence, NJ 07974
Toll Free Tel: 877-310-7333 *Fax:* 908-219-0188
E-mail: isbn-san@bowker.com

Web Site: www.isbn.org
Coordinate implementation of the ISBN & SAN standards.
Number of Members: 400,000

The International Women's Writing Guild (IWWG)

5 Penn Plaza, 19th fl, PMB 19059, New York, NY 10001
Tel: 917-720-6959
E-mail: iwwgquestions@iwwg.org
Web Site: www.iwwg.org
Key Personnel
Exec Dir: Michelle Miller *E-mail:* michelle@iwwg.org
Founded: 1976
Network for the empowerment of women through writing. Services include updated list of close to 35 literary agents, independent small presses & other writing services. Writing conferences & events annually, subscriptionn to the newsletter *Network*, regional clusters & opportunities for publications. IWWG is a supportive network open to any woman regardless of portfolio. As such, it has established a remarkable record of achievement in the publishing world as well as in circles where lifelong learning & personal information are valued for their own sake.
Number of Members: 5,000
Publication(s): *Network* (quarterly, free)

Investigative Reporters & Editors

Missouri School of Journalism, 141 Neff Annex, Columbia, MO 65211
Tel: 573-882-2042 *Fax:* 573-882-5431
E-mail: info@ire.org
Web Site: www.ire.org
Key Personnel
Exec Dir: Doug Haddix *E-mail:* doug@ire.org
Founded: 1975
Nonprofit organization to improve the quality of investigative journalism.
Number of Members: 5,000
Publication(s): *The IRE Journal* (quarterly, free with membership, $70/yr nonmembs, $125/yr instns, $85/yr libs, $90/yr foreign nonmembs, $150/yr foreign instns)

ISBN Canada

Unit of Library & Archives Canada
Library & Archives Canada, 395 Wellington St, Ottawa, ON K1A 0N4, Canada
Tel: 819-994-6872 *Toll Free Tel:* 866-578-7777 (CN & US) *Fax:* 819-934-7535
E-mail: bac.isbn.lac@canada.ca
Web Site: www.bac-lac.gc.ca/eng/services/isbn-canada/pages/isbn-canada.aspx
Key Personnel
ISBN/ISMB Contact: Heidi Poapst; Angelique Regimbal

Jewish Book Council

520 Eighth Ave, 4th fl, New York, NY 10018
Tel: 212-201-2920 *Fax:* 212-532-4952
E-mail: jbc@jewishbooks.org
Web Site: www.jewishbookcouncil.org
Key Personnel
Exec Dir: Naomi Firestone-Teeter
Prog Dir: Evie Saphire-Bernstein *E-mail:* evie@jewishbooks.org
Founded: 1925
Sponsors programs based on its conviction that books of Jewish interest are an invaluable contribution to the welfare of the Jewish people. Works to promote the reading, writing, publishing & distribution of worthy books of Jewish content. Honors excellence in all fields of Jewish literary endeavor with awards to writers & citations to publishers. Serves as a resource providing guidance, program tools & publications; acts as a clearinghouse for information on all aspects of Jewish literature & publishing in North America.
2021 Meeting(s): Jewish Book Month, Nationwide throughout the USA, Oct 28-Nov 28, 2021
2022 Meeting(s): Jewish Book Month, Nationwide throughout the USA, Nov 18-Dec 18, 2022
2023 Meeting(s): Jewish Book Month, Nationwide throughout the USA, Nov 7-Dec 7, 2023
2024 Meeting(s): Jewish Book Month, Nationwide throughout the USA, Nov 25-Dec 25, 2024
Publication(s): *Paper Brigade* (annually, journal, $25/yr)

The League of Canadian Poets

2 Carlton St, Suite 1519, Toronto, ON M5B 1J3, Canada
Tel: 416-504-1657
E-mail: info@poets.ca
Web Site: poets.ca
Key Personnel
Exec Dir: Lesley Fletcher *E-mail:* lesley@poets.ca
Commun Coord: Laura O'Brien *E-mail:* laura@poets.com
Founded: 1966
Promote Canadian poetry & poets.
Number of Members: 700
New Election: Annually in June
Publication(s): *Poetry Markets for Canadians* (online only, $20/yr public, $100/yr schools or libs)

League of Vermont Writers Inc

PO Box 5046, Burlington, VT 05402
E-mail: lvw@leagueofvermontwriters.org
Web Site: leagueofvermontwriters.org
Founded: 1929
Four meetings per year (Jan, April, July, Sept), reader & promotional services; occasional instructional seminars & workshops, publication of anthologies of members' work, writer's service.
Number of Members: 275
New Election: Annually in Jan
Publication(s): *League Lines* (quarterly, newsletter); *Vermont Voices Jubilee, 75th Anniversary Edition*; *Vermont Voices III, An Anthology*

Library Association of Alberta (LAA)

80 Baker Crescent NW, Calgary, AB T2L 1R4, Canada
Tel: 403-284-5818 *Toll Free Tel:* 877-522-5550
E-mail: info@laa.ca
Web Site: www.laa.ca
Key Personnel
Conference Coord: Christine Sheppard
Founded: 1930
Nonprofit organization.
Number of Members: 700
2021 Meeting(s): Alberta Library Conference, Fairmont Jasper Park Lodge, Jasper, AB, CN, April 29-May 2, 2021
2022 Meeting(s): Alberta Library Conference, Fairmont Jasper Park Lodge, Jasper, AB, CN, April 28-May 1, 2022
2023 Meeting(s): Alberta Library Conference, Fairmont Jasper Park Lodge, Jasper, AB, CN, April 27-30, 2023

Library of American Broadcasting (LAB)

Unit of University of Maryland Libraries
University of Maryland, Hornbake Library, College Park, MD 20742
Tel: 301-405-9160
Web Site: www.lib.umd.edu/special/collections/massmedia/about-us
Key Personnel
Dir & Donor Rel: Laura Schnitker
E-mail: lschnitk@umd.edu

Founded: 1972
Library devoted to history of public & commercial broadcasting including collections of audio & video recordings, books, pamphlets, periodicals, personal collections, oral histories, photographs, scripts & vertical files. Referral center to other sources of broadcast history.
Number of Members: 21
New Election: Annually in Nov
Publication(s): *Airwaves* (semiannual, newsletter)

Linguistic Society of America

522 21 St NW, Suite 120, Washington, DC 20006-5012
Tel: 202-835-1714 *Fax:* 202-835-1717
E-mail: lsa@lsadc.org
Web Site: www.linguisticsociety.org
Key Personnel
Exec Dir: Alyson Reed *E-mail:* areed@lsadc.org
Dir, Membership & Meetings: David Robinson
E-mail: drobinson@lsadc.org
Founded: 1924
Advancing the scientific study of language.
Number of Members: 4,500
New Election: Annually in Sept
Publication(s): *Language* (quarterly, free to membs, $140-190/yr organizations); *LSA Meeting Handbook* (annual, free, electronic)

The Literary Press Group of Canada

425 Adelaide St W, Suite 700, Toronto, ON M5V 3C1, Canada
Tel: 416-483-1321
Web Site: www.lpg.ca
Key Personnel
Exec Dir: Christen Thomas *Tel:* 416-483-1321 ext 1 *E-mail:* christen@lpg.ca
Busn Mgr: Barb Phillips *Tel:* 416-483-1321 ext 2 *E-mail:* barb@lpg.ca
National trade association providing cooperative sales, marketing, advertising & publicity services to members.
Number of Members: 52
New Election: Annually in May

Literary Translators' Association of Canada

Concordia University, LB 601, 1455 De Maisonneuve W, Montreal, QC H3G 1M8, Canada
Tel: 514-848-2424 (ext 8702)
E-mail: info@attlc-ltac.org
Web Site: www.attlc-ltac.org
Key Personnel
Pres: Beatriz Hausner
Founded: 1975
As the only organization representing literary translators in Canada, LTAC highlights the importance of literary translation by providing access to Canada's culture, nationally & internationally & by actively participating in Canada's literary life. It does this in part by organizing public readings, lectures & panel discussions, usually in partnership with literary festivals, universities & other organizations.
Number of Members: 180
New Election: Annually in June

Livestock Publications Council

200 W Exchange Ave, Fort Worth, TX 76164
Tel: 817-336-1130
Web Site: www.livestockpublications.com
Key Personnel
Exec Dir: Diane E Johnson *E-mail:* diane@livestockpublications.com
Founded: 1974
A nonprofit organization designed to serve the livestock communications industry.
Number of Members: 195
New Election: Annually in July
Publication(s): *Actiongram* (monthly, newsletter)

Livres Canada Books

One Nicholas, Suite 504, Ottawa, ON K1N 7B7, Canada
Tel: 613-562-2324 *Fax:* 613-562-2329
E-mail: info@livrescanadabooks.com
Web Site: www.livrescanadabooks.com
Key Personnel
Exec Dir: Francois Charette *Tel:* 613-562-2324 ext 223 *E-mail:* fcharette@livrescanadabooks. com
Mgr, Digital Publg & Intl Mkts: Gabrielle Etcheverry *Tel:* 613-562-2324 ext 229 *E-mail:* getcheverry@livrescanadabooks.com
Mgr, Progs: Christy Doucet *Tel:* 613-562-2324 ext 225 *E-mail:* cdoucet@livrescanadabooks. com

As the only national trade association that connects English & French language publishers across Canada, Livres Canada Books has a mandate to foster Canadian publishers' export sales. Coordinates Canadian publishers' presence at international book fairs, promotes Canadian titles abroad through its catalogues, exhibits & web site, provides market intelligence & acts as a liaison between Canadian publishers & foreign buyers. Also assists the industry by providing funding assistance for Canadian publishers' international marketing strategies & activities.
Publication(s): *Canadian Studies Collection* (annual, free); *Rights Canada Catalogue* (annual, free)

Magazine Publishers of America, see MPA - The Association of Magazine Media

Magazines Canada (MC)

555 Richmond St W, Suite 604, Mailbox 201, Toronto, ON M5V 3B1, Canada
Tel: 416-504-0274 *Fax:* 416-504-0437
E-mail: info@magazinescanada.ca
Web Site: magazinescanada.ca
Key Personnel
Pres & CEO: Matthew Holmes *Tel:* 416-504-0274 ext 223 *E-mail:* mholmes@magazinescanada.ca
Sr Dir, Fin & Admin: Masood Abid *Tel:* 416-504-0274 ext 228 *E-mail:* mabid@ magazinescanada.ca
Dir, Govt & Indus Engagement: Melanie Rutledge *Tel:* 613-816-0823 *E-mail:* mrutledge@ magazinescanada.ca
Dir, Memb Servs & Devt: Evan Dickson *Tel:* 416-504-0274 ext 222 *E-mail:* edickson@ magazinescanada.ca
Mgr, Communs: Brianne DiAngelo *Tel:* 416-504-0274 ext 227 *E-mail:* bdiangelo@ magazinescanada.ca
Memb Servs & Events Coord: Kiley Pole *Tel:* 416-504-0274 ext 238 *E-mail:* kpole@ magazinescanada.ca
Founded: 1973
Distribution, promotion, professional development & lobbying for Canadian magazines.
Number of Members: 350
Meeting(s): MagNet

Maine Writers & Publishers Alliance

Glickman Family Library, 314 Forest Ave, Rm 318, Portland, ME 04101
Tel: 207-228-8263
E-mail: info@mainewriters.org
Web Site: mainewriters.org
Key Personnel
Exec Dir: Gibson Fay-LeBlanc *E-mail:* director@ mainewriters.org
Assoc Dir: Taryn Bowe *Tel:* 207-780-4671 *E-mail:* taryn@mainewriters.org
Prog Dir: Hannah Perry *Tel:* 207-228-8257 *E-mail:* hannah@mainewriters.org
Founded: 1975
Writing retreats, writing workshops, information services.

Number of Members: 1,600
Publication(s): *Ex Libris Maine* (monthly, newsletter, membs, supporters & parenting organizations); *The Peavey* (weekly, newsletter, membs only)

Manitoba Arts Council

525-93 Lombard Ave, Winnipeg, MB R3B 3B1, Canada
Tel: 204-945-2237 *Toll Free Tel:* 866-994-2787 *Fax:* 204-945-5925
E-mail: info@artscouncil.mb.ca
Web Site: artscouncil.mb.ca
Key Personnel
CEO: Akoulina Connell
PR Agent: Elyse Saurette *E-mail:* esaurette@ artscouncil.mb.ca
Founded: 1965
Provincial arts council that funds professional Manitoban artists & arts organizations.

The Manitoba Writers' Guild Inc

218-100 Arthur St, Winnipeg, MB R3B 1H3, Canada
Tel: 204-944-8013
E-mail: manitobawritersguild3@gmail.com
Web Site: www.mbwriter.mb.ca
Founded: 1981
Provides professional & personal support to Manitoba writers throughout their writing lives. Membership: $60/yr regular, $30/yr students & low income, $10/yr youth under 18.
Number of Members: 300

Media Alliance

2830 20 St, Suite 102, San Francisco, CA 94110
Tel: 415-746-9475
E-mail: information@media-alliance.org
Web Site: www.media-alliance.org
Key Personnel
Exec Dir: Tracy Rosenberg *Tel:* 510-684-6853 (cell) *E-mail:* tracy@media-alliance.org
Info Coord: Phavia Kujichagulia *E-mail:* jobfile@ media-alliance.org
Educational programs in editing, writing & journalism skills. Media relations & advocacy & hands-on computer skills. Job listings & resources, media watchdog activities.
Number of Members: 3,200
Publication(s): *Media How-to Guide* (book, $15 membs, $20 nonmembs)

Media Coalition Inc

19 Fulton St, Suite 407, New York, NY 10038
Tel: 212-587-4025
E-mail: info@mediacoalition.org
Web Site: mediacoalition.org
Key Personnel
Exec Dir: David Horowitz *Tel:* 212-587-4025 ext 3 *E-mail:* horowitz@mediacoalition.org
Founded: 1973
Trade association, defends first amendment rights to produce & distribute constitutionally-protected books, magazines, recordings, home video & video games.
Number of Members: 8
Publication(s): *Sense and Censorship: The Vanity of Bonfires* (free online); *Shooting the Messenger: Why Censorship Won't Stop Violence* (free online)

The Melville Society

Johns Hopkins University Press, PO Box 19966, Baltimore, MD 21211-0966
Web Site: melvillesociety.org
Key Personnel
Pres: Arimichi Makino
Treas: Steven Olsen-Smith
Exec Secy: Colin Dewey
Assoc Secy, Progs & Conferences: Meredith Farmer

Ed, Leviathan: Samuel Otter
Founded: 1945
Annual & special meetings & publications. Conferences in association with the Modern Language Association annual convention & American Literature Association annual convention.
Number of Members: 760
New Election: Annually in Spring
Publication(s): *Leviathan: A Journal of Melville Studies* (3 issues/yr, free to membs)

Michigan Library Association (MLA)

3410 Belle Chase Way, Lansing, MI 48911
Tel: 517-394-2774
E-mail: mla@milibraries.org
Web Site: www.milibraries.org
Key Personnel
Exec Dir: Deborah E Mikula *Tel:* 517-394-2774 ext 224 *E-mail:* dmikula@milibraries.org
Membership & Communs Dir: Rachel Ash *Tel:* 517-394-2774 ext 225 *E-mail:* rfash@ milibraries.org
Prog & Event Dir: Amber Sheerin *Tel:* 517-394-2774 ext 223 *E-mail:* asheerin@milibraries.org
Founded: 1891
Leads the advancement of all Michigan libraries through advocacy, education & engagement. Membership includes more than 325 libraries & 1,400 individuals throughout Michigan from public, academic, school & special libraries & organizations supportive of libraries.
2021 Meeting(s): Spring Institute for Youth Services, Mount Pleasant, MI, March 11-21, 2021; MLA Annual Conference, Port Huron, MI, Oct 13-15, 2021

Midwest Independent Booksellers Association (MIBA)

1375 St Anthony Ave, Suite 202-3, St Paul, MN 55104
Tel: 612-208-6279 *Toll Free Fax:* 844-273-4119
E-mail: info@midwestbooksellers.org
Web Site: www.midwestbooksellers.org
Key Personnel
Exec Dir: Carrie Obry *E-mail:* carrie@ midwestbooksellers.org
Dir, Opers: Robert Martin *Tel:* 612-520-1482 *E-mail:* robert@midwestbooksellers.org
Prog Specialist: Kate Scott
Founded: 1981
Association of independent bookstores in Midwest: Illinois, Iowa, Kansas, Minnesota, Missouri, Nebraska, North Dakota, South Dakota & Wisconsin. Annual trade show & meeting. Book catalog for member stores to use with consumers. Sponsors educational programs for booksellers, Spring meeting, Midwest Booksellers' Choice Awards & "Midwest Connections" regional marketing program.
Number of Members: 225
Publication(s): *Membership Directory* (online); *MIBA Trade Show Program* (annual); *Midwest Booksellers Association Winter Catalog* (annual)

Midwest Travel Journalists Inc

902 S Randall Rd, Suite C311, St Charles, IL 60174
Toll Free Tel: 888-551-8184 *Fax:* 847-622-8015
E-mail: admin@mtja.us
Web Site: www.mtja.us
Key Personnel
Pres: Gary Knowles *E-mail:* openair@aol.com
VP: Amy Lynch *E-mail:* amy@amylynch.com
Assoc VP: Jessica O'Riley *E-mail:* Jessica. ORiley@IowaEDA.com
Secy: Alan Carr *E-mail:* alan@carrstrategies.com
Treas: David Hoekman *E-mail:* david@grouptour. com
Founded: 2017

Not-for-profit organization for professional travel journalists & destination marketing representatives.
Number of Members: 100

Midwest Travel Writers Association, see Midwest Travel Journalists Inc

Miniature Book Society Inc
702 Rosecrans St, San Diego, CA 92106-3013
Tel: 619-226-4441 *Fax:* 619-226-4441
E-mail: minibook@cox.net
Web Site: www.mbs.org
Key Personnel
Pres: Stephen Byrne
Secy: Jim Brogan
Founded: 1983
Number of Members: 302
Publication(s): *Miniature Book Society Newsletter* (3 issues/yr, newsletter, $40/yr)
Membership(s): Fellowship of American Bibliophilic Societies (FABS)

Modern Language Association of America (MLA)
85 Broad St, Suite 500, New York, NY 10004-2434
SAN: 202-6422
Tel: 646-576-5000 *Fax:* 646-458-0030
E-mail: convention@mla.org
Web Site: www.mla.org
Key Personnel
Exec Dir: Paula Krebs
Founded: 1883
Convention; employment information, professional organization, scholarly publications.
Number of Members: 24,000
2021 Meeting(s): Annual Convention, Toronto, ON, CN, Jan 7-10, 2021
2022 Meeting(s): Annual Convention, Washington, DC, Jan 6-9, 2022
Publication(s): *MLA International Bibliography* (annual, inquire); *MLA Newsletter* (quarterly, free to membs); *PMLA* (5 issues/yr, $12/issue); *Profession* (annual, journal, free to membs, $7.50 nonmembs, online)

Motion Picture Association of America Inc (MPAA)
1301 "K" St NE, Suite 900E, Washington, DC 20005
Tel: 202-293-1966 *Fax:* 202-296-7410
E-mail: contactus@mpaa.org
Web Site: www.mpaa.org
Key Personnel
CEO: Charles Rivkin
Global Gen Coun: Karyn Temple
Founded: 1922
Trade association for the major motion picture producers & distributors. Administer motion picture industry's system of self-regulation & are spokespeople for production & distribution of motion pictures for theatrical, home video & TV use in the USA.
Number of Members: 60
Branch Office(s)
15301 Ventura Blvd, Bldg E, Sherman Oaks, CA 91403 *Tel:* 818-995-6600 *Fax:* 818-285-4403
3470 NW 82 Ave, Suite 680, Doral, FL 33122 *Tel:* 786-999-1359
12650 N Beach St, Suite 114, No 6, Fort Worth, TX 76244 *Tel:* 817-205-6330
55 Saint Clair Ave W, Suite 210, Toronto, ON M4V 2Y7, Canada *Tel:* 416-961-1888 *Fax:* 416-968-1016 *E-mail:* info@mpa-canada.org *Web Site:* www.mpa-canada.org
FSA 74, Driver Ave, Moore Park, NSW 2021, Australia
Avenue des Arts 46, 8th fl, 1000 Brussels, Belgium *Tel:* (02) 778 27 11 *Fax:* (02) 778 27 00

Rm 508, No 16 Bldg, Jianwai SOHO, 39 Dongsanhuan Zhonglu Rd, Beijing 100022, China
215 Atrium, A 206, Chakala, Andheri-Kurla Rd, Andheri (East), Mumbai 400 059, India
Nihon Seimei Ichibancho Bldg, 6F 23-3, Inchiben-Cho, Chiyoda-ku, Tokyo 102-0082, Japan
No 04-07 Central Mall, No 1 Magazine Rd, Singapore 059567, Singapore *Tel:* 6253 1033 *Fax:* 6255 1838 *Web Site:* www.mpa-i.org
1007, 10th fl, Monaco Bldg, 1316-5 Seocho-dong, Seocho-gu, Seoul 137-856, South Korea

MPA - The Association of Magazine Media
757 Third Ave, 11th fl, New York, NY 10012
Tel: 212-872-3700 *Fax:* 212-888-4217
Web Site: www.magazine.org
Key Personnel
Pres & CEO: Linda Thomas Brooks *Tel:* 212-872-3710
VP, Creative Servs & Events: Patty Bogie *Tel:* 212-872-3729 *E-mail:* pbogie@magazine.org
Founded: 1919
Promote the value of magazines.
Number of Members: 265
Branch Office(s)
1211 Connecticut Ave NW, Washington, DC 20036, EVP, Govt Aff: James Cregan *Tel:* 202-296-7277 *Fax:* 202-296-0343 *E-mail:* jcregan@magazine.org

Music Publishers Association (MPA)
243 Fifth Ave, Suite 236, New York, NY 10016
Tel: 212-327-4044
E-mail: admin@mpa.org
Web Site: www.mpa.org
Founded: 1895
Foster trade & commerce in the interest of those in the music publishing business & encourage understanding of & compliance with the copyright law to protect musical works against piracies & infringements.
Number of Members: 300
New Election: Annually, first week of June

Mystery Writers of America (MWA)
1140 Broadway, Suite 1507, New York, NY 10001
Tel: 212-888-8171
E-mail: mwa@mysterywriters.org
Web Site: www.mysterywriters.org
Key Personnel
Admin Dir: Margery Flax
Founded: 1945
The premier organization for mystery writers & other professionals in the mystery field. MWA watches developments in legislation & tax laws, sponsors symposia & mystery conferences, presents the Edgar Awards® & provides information for mystery writers. Membership open to published authors, editors, screenwriters & other professionals in the field.
Number of Members: 3,000
Publication(s): *Mystery Writers of American Anthology*; *The Third Degree* (10 issues/yr, free to membs)

NAB, see National Association of Broadcasters (NAB)

NASW, see National Association of Science Writers (NASW)

National Association for Printing Leadership (NAPL), see Epicomm

National Association of Black Journalists (NABJ)
1100 Knight Hall, Suite 3100, College Park, MD 20742
Tel: 301-405-0248 *Fax:* 301-314-1714
E-mail: info@nabj.org; press@nabj.org
Web Site: www.nabj.org
Key Personnel
Exec Dir: Sharon Toomer *Tel:* 301-405-7547 *E-mail:* stoomer@nabj.org
Devt Dir: Kaylan Somerville
Fin Mgr: Nathaniel Chambers *Tel:* 301-405-0532 *E-mail:* nchambers@nabj.org
Membership Mgr: Veronique Dodson *Tel:* 301-405-0554 *E-mail:* vdodson@nabj.org
Communs & Media Rel Mgr: James C Durrah, II
Prog Assoc: Jovan Riley
Founded: 1975
Organization of journalists, students & media-related professionals that provides quality programs & services to & advocates on behalf of black journalists worldwide.
Number of Members: 3,300
New Election: Biennially, odd-numbered yrs
2021 Meeting(s): NABJ Annual Convention & Career Fair, Houston, TX, Aug 18-22, 2021
Publication(s): *NABJ Journal* (quarterly, journal)

National Association of Book Entrepreneurs (NABE)
PO Box 606, Cottage Grove, OR 97424
Tel: 541-942-7455 *Fax:* 541-942-7455
E-mail: nabe@bookmarketingprofits.com
Web Site: www.bookmarketingprofits.com
Key Personnel
Exec Dir: Al Galasso
Promo Dir: Russ Von Hoelscher
Assoc Dir: Ingrid Crawford
Founded: 1980
International book marketing organization of independent publishers & mail order entrepreneurs. Activities include NABE Combined Book Exhibits at national & regional conventions serving the book, educational, gift & business trade. Publishers Preview Mail Order Program, National Press Release, Electronic Marketing plus complete publisher consultation services for printing, promoting & marketing books.
Number of Members: 1,000
Publication(s): *Book Dealers World* (quarterly, circ 10,000, $5/sample, $50/yr & $90/semiannual membership)

National Association of Broadcasters (NAB)
1771 "N" St NW, Washington, DC 20036
Tel: 202-429-5300
E-mail: nab@nab.org
Web Site: www.nab.org
Key Personnel
Pres & CEO: Gordon H Smith
EVP, Conventions & Busn Opers: Mr Chris Brown *Tel:* 202-429-5335
EVP, Mktg & Communs: Michelle Lehman *E-mail:* mlehman@nab.org
Trade association for radio & television stations. Provide products, publications (over 130) & other services related to broadcasting.
Number of Members: 9,000
2021 Meeting(s): NAB Show®, Las Vegas, NV, April 10-14, 2021

National Association of College Stores (NACS)
500 E Lorain St, Oberlin, OH 44074
Toll Free Tel: 800-622-7498 *Fax:* 440-775-4769
Web Site: www.nacs.org
Key Personnel
CEO: Ed Schlichenmayer *Tel:* 800-622-7498 ext 2250 *E-mail:* eschlichenmayer@nacs.org
Sr Dir, Meetings & Expositions: Mary Adler-Kozak *Tel:* 800-622-7498 ext 2265 *E-mail:* madler-kozak@nacs.org

Dir, Meetings: Lynn Mangol *Tel:* 800-622-7498 ext 2612 *E-mail:* lmangol@nacs.org
Exhibit Sales & Serv Rep: Linda Vargo *Tel:* 800-622-7498 ext 2302 *E-mail:* lvargo@nacs.org
Trade association for college store industry.
Number of Members: 4,000
2021 Meeting(s): CAMEX (Campus Market Expo), Atlanta Convention Center, Atlanta, GA, Feb 19-22, 2021
Publication(s): *Campus Marketplace* (weekly, newsletter, online); *The College Store* (6 issues/yr, magazine); *The Torchlight* (semiannual, newsletter)

National Association of Hispanic Publications Inc (NAHP)
529 14 St NW, Suite 923, Washington, DC 20045
Tel: 202-662-7250
E-mail: news@nahp.com
Web Site: nahp.org
Founded: 1982
Promote Hispanic media.
Number of Members: 100
Publication(s): *NAHP Newsletter* (quarterly)
Membership(s): Hispanic Association on Corporate Responsibility (HACR); National Hispanic Leadership Agenda (NHLA); United States Hispanic Chamber of Commerce (USHCC)

National Association of Printing Ink Manufacturers (NAPIM)
3600 E State St, Suite 306, Rockford, IL 61108
Tel: 815-708-7387
Web Site: www.napim.org
Key Personnel
Exec Dir: John Copeland *Tel:* 815-979-2341 *E-mail:* jcopeland@napim.org
Dir, Regulatory Aff & Technol: George Fuchs *Tel:* 864-884-8095 *E-mail:* gfuchs@napim.org
Memb Rel Mgr: Michele St Clair *E-mail:* mstclair@napim.org
Founded: 1916
Trade association representing the printing ink industry & providing information & assistance to members to better manage their business.
Number of Members: 83
2021 Meeting(s): Spring Convention, The Vinoy® Renaissance St Petersburg Resort & Golf Club, 501 Fifth Ave NE, St Petersburg, FL, April 16-19, 2021
Publication(s): *Introduction to Printing Ink* (booklet, $6 membs, $10 nonmembs); *Printing Ink Handbook, 7th ed* ($110 membs, $160 nonmembs); *Raw Materials Data Handbook, 3rd ed* ($275 membs, $475 nonmembs)

National Association of Quick Printers (NAQP), see Epicomm

National Association of Real Estate Editors (NAREE)
1003 NW Sixth Terr, Boca Raton, FL 33486-3455
Tel: 561-391-3599 *Fax:* 561-391-0099
Web Site: www.naree.org
Key Personnel
Pres: Daniel Taub
Exec Dir: Mary Doyle-Kimball *E-mail:* madkimba@aol.com
Contact: David Kimball *E-mail:* dakimball@aol.com
Founded: 1929
Nonprofit professional association of writers Journalism Contest & seminars in winter, spring & fall; memberships active for journalists & associate for communications professionals. Bruss Real Estate Book Awards annual competition.
Number of Members: 650
2020 Meeting(s): Annual Real Estate Journalism Conference, Kimpton Epic Hotel, Miami, FL, Dec 6-9, 2020

Publication(s): *NAREE Directory* (annual, directory, free to membs); *NAREE News* (quarterly, free to membs); *Spring Conference Book* (free to membs)

National Association of Science Writers (NASW)
PO Box 7905, Berkeley, CA 94707
Tel: 510-647-9500
Web Site: www.nasw.org
Key Personnel
Exec Dir: Tinsley Davis *E-mail:* director@nasw.org
Founded: 1934
Professional development organization for science writers.
Number of Members: 2,238
New Election: Biennially, even-numbered yrs
2021 Meeting(s): ScienceWriters2021, University of Colorado Boulder & CU Anschutz Medical Campus, Boulder, CO, Fall 2021
2022 Meeting(s): ScienceWriters2022, Chicago, IL, Fall 2022
2023 Meeting(s): ScienceWriters2023, Memphis, TN, Fall 2023
Publication(s): *ScienceWriters* (quarterly, magazine, free for membs)
Membership(s): World Federation of Science Journalists

National Cartoonists Society (NCS)
PO Box 592927, Orlando, FL 32859-2927
Tel: 407-994-6703 *Fax:* 407-442-0786
E-mail: info@reuben.org
Web Site: www.reuben.org
Key Personnel
Pres: Bill Morrison
Exec Dir: Latisha Moore
Founded: 1946
Fraternal organization of cartoonists.
Number of Members: 500
Publication(s): *The Cartoonist*

National Coalition Against Censorship (NCAC)
19 Fulton St, Suite 407, New York, NY 10038
Tel: 212-807-6222 *Fax:* 212-807-6245
E-mail: ncac@ncac.org
Web Site: www.ncac.org
Founded: 1974
Promote & defend free speech, inquiry & expression; monitor & publicize censorship incidents; sponsor public programs; assist in censorship controversies through advice, materials, contacts with local organizations & individuals. Membership is comprised of 50 national participating organizations. Reprints & informational materials available upon request.
Publication(s): *Censorship News* (semiannual, newsletter, online)

National Coalition for Literacy (NCL)
PO Box 2932, Washington, DC 20013-2932
E-mail: ncl@ncladvocacy.org
Web Site: www.national-coalition-literacy.org
Key Personnel
Pres: Debra Kennedy *Tel:* 202-364-1964
Founded: 1981
A member organization made up of major service, research & policy organizations in adult education, family literacy & English language acquisition. NCL's mission is to advance adult education, family literacy & English language acquisition in the US - from the most basic skills proficiency level across a continuum of services including the transition into postsecondary education & job training.
Number of Members: 30

National Communication Association
1765 "N" St NW, Washington, DC 20036
Tel: 202-464-4622 *Fax:* 202-464-4600

E-mail: inbox@natcom.org
Web Site: www.natcom.org
Key Personnel
COO: Mark Fernando *Tel:* 202-534-1105 *E-mail:* mfernando@natcom.org
Exec Dir: Paaige K Turner, PhD *Tel:* 202-534-1120 *E-mail:* pturner@natcom.org
Founded: 1914
To promote effective & ethical communication.
Number of Members: 7,500
2021 Meeting(s): Annual Convention, Washington State Convention Center, Seattle, WA, Nov 18-21, 2021
2022 Meeting(s): Annual Convention, New Orleans Marriott/Sheraton New Orleans, New Orleans, LA, Nov 17-20, 2022
2023 Meeting(s): Annual Convention, Gaylord National Resort & Convention Center, 201 Waterfront St, National Harbor, MD, Nov 16-19, 2023
Publication(s): *Communication and Critical/Cultural Studies*; *Communication Education* (quarterly); *Communication Monographs* (quarterly, journal); *Communication Teacher* (quarterly); *Critical Studies in Media Communication* (journal); *First Amendment Studies*; *Journal of Applied Communication Research*; *Journal of International & Intercultural Communication*; *The Quarterly Journal of Speech*; *Review of Communication*; *Text & Performance Quarterly* (journal)

National Council of Teachers of English (NCTE)
340 N Neil St, Suite 104, Champaign, IL 61820
Tel: 217-328-3870 *Toll Free Tel:* 877-369-6283 (cust serv) *Fax:* 217-328-9645
E-mail: customerservice@ncte.org
Web Site: www.ncte.org
Key Personnel
Exec Dir: Emily Kirkpatrick *Tel:* 217-278-3601 *E-mail:* ekirkpatrick@ncte.org
Proj Specialist, Communs: Lori Bianchini *E-mail:* lbianchini@ncte.org
Perms Coord: Kurt Austin *Tel:* 217-278-3619
Founded: 1911
Focus on the major concerns of teachers of English & the language arts; offer teaching aids, advice, direction & guidance for members. Publish educational books, journals, pamphlets, research reports & position papers for all levels of the English teaching profession. Hold annual convention for members in November; sponsor conferences & workshops.
Number of Members: 25,000
2021 Meeting(s): NCTE Annual Convention, Louisville, KY, Nov 18-21, 2021
Publication(s): *College Composition & Communication* (quarterly, journal, $75/yr, includes NCTE & CCCC membership); *College English* (6 issues/yr, journal, $75/yr, includes NCTE membership); *English Education* (quarterly, journal, $75/yr, includes NCTE & CEE membership); *English Journal* (6 issues/yr, $75/yr, includes NCTE membership); *English Leadership Quarterly* (journal, $75/yr, includes NCTE & CEL membership); *Language Arts* (6 issues/yr, journal, $75/yr, includes NCTE membership); *Research in the Teaching of English* (quarterly, journal, $75/yr, includes NCTE membership); *Talking Points* (semiannual, journal, $75/yr, includes NCTE & WLU membership); *Teaching English in the Two-Year College* (quarterly, journal, $75/yr, includes NCTE & TYCA membership); *Voices from the Middle* (quarterly, journal, $75/yr, includes NCTE membership)

National Education Association (NEA)
1201 16 St NW, Washington, DC 20036-3290
Tel: 202-833-4000 *Fax:* 202-822-7974
E-mail: media-relations-team@nea.org
Web Site: www.nea.org

Key Personnel
Pres: Lily Eskelsen Garcia
VP: Becky Pringle
Secy/Treas: Princess R Moss
Exec Dir: John C Stocks
Founded: 1857
Professional employee organization for over 3
million educators, with affiliates in every state
& in more than 14,000 communities committed
to advancing the cause of public education.
Number of Members: 3,200,000
Publication(s): *Higher Education Advocate* (6
issues/yr, newsletter); *The NEA Almanac of
Higher Education* (annual); *NEA Today* (quar-
terly, magazine); *NEA Today for Future Ed-
ucators* (annual, magazine); *NEA Today for
NEA-Retired Members* (quarterly, magazine);
Thought & Action (annual, journal)

**National Federation of Press Women Inc
(NFPW)**
PO Box 3007, Mechanicsville, VA 23116-0026
Tel: 804-746-1033 *Fax:* 804-335-1296
E-mail: info@nfpw.org
Web Site: www.nfpw.org
Founded: 1936
Organization of professional women & men pur-
suing careers across the communications spec-
trum.
Number of Members: 1,000
New Election: Biennially in Sept, odd-numbered
yrs
Meeting(s): Communications Conference
Publication(s): *Agenda* (quarterly)

**National Freedom of Information Coalition
(NFOIC)**
Affiliate of Missouri School of Journalism
Missouri School of Journalism, 31 Neff Annex,
Columbia, MO 65211
Tel: 573-882-4856
E-mail: nfoic@nfoic.org
Web Site: nfoic.org
Key Personnel
Exec Dir: Daniel Bevarly *E-mail:* dbevarly@
nfoic.org
Admin Mgr: Lara Dieringer *E-mail:* ldieringer@
nfoic.org
Founded: 1989 (as National Freedom of Informa-
tion Assembly)
Nonpartisan alliance of state & regional affiliates
promoting collaboration, education & advocacy
for open government; transparency & freedom
of information.
Number of Members: 62
Publication(s): *The FOI Advocate: The NFOIC
News Blog; FOI InSight* (newsletter)

**National Information Standards Organization
(NISO)**
3600 Clipper Mill Rd, Suite 302, Baltimore, MD
21211-1948
Tel: 301-654-2512 *Fax:* 410-685-5278
E-mail: nisohq@niso.org
Web Site: www.niso.org
Key Personnel
Exec Dir: Todd Carpenter *E-mail:* tcarpenter@
niso.org
Dir, Community Engagement: Alice Meadows
Dir, Content: Jill O'Neill *E-mail:* joneill@niso.
org
Dir, Strategic Initiatives: Jason Griffey
Assoc Dir, Progs: Nettie Lagace
E-mail: nlagace@niso.org
Off Mgr: Kimberly Graham *E-mail:* kgraham@
niso.org
Founded: 1939 (incorporated as US 501(c)(3) in
1982)
Developing, maintaining & publishing technical
standards used by libraries, information ser-
vices & publishers. Accredited by the Ameri-
can National Standards Institute.

Number of Members: 90
Publication(s): *Information Standards Quarterly
(ISQ)* (online)

National League of American Pen Women Inc
The Pen Arts Bldg & Arts Museum, 1300 17 St
NW, Washington, DC 20036-1973
Tel: 202-785-1997 *Fax:* 202-452-8868
E-mail: contact@nlapw.org
Web Site: www.nlapw.org
Key Personnel
Pres: Virginia Franklin Campbell
Founded: 1897
Scholarships, letters, art & music workshops,
awards & prizes. Must send SASE for infor-
mation.
Number of Members: 3,500
Publication(s): *The Pen Woman* (quarterly, maga-
zine, $25/yr, free to membs)

**National Music Publishers' Association
(NMPA)**
975 "F" St NW, Suite 375, Washington, DC
20004
Tel: 202-393-6672
E-mail: members@nmpa.org
Web Site: nmpa.org
Key Personnel
Pres & CEO: David M Israelite
EVP & Gen Coun: Danielle Aguirre
SVP, External Aff: Charlotte Sellmyer
VP & Sr Coun: Jonathan Cohen
VP & Sr Coun, Litigation: Erich Carey
VP, Indus Rel & Govt Aff: Amelia Binder
VP, Govt Aff & Coun: Shannon Sorenson
Dir, Communs: Katie McClenny
Dir, Events: Kartraice Hooper
Dir, Membership: Stephanie Li
Dir, Fin & HR: Karen Brown
Founded: 1917
Trade association representing all American mu-
sic publishers & their songwriting partners.
Number of Members: 3,000

National Newspaper Association
101 S Palafox, Unit 13323, Pensacola, FL 32591
Tel: 217-241-1400 *Fax:* 217-241-1301
E-mail: nna@nna.org
Web Site: nnaweb.org
Founded: 1885
Trade association with a mission to protect, pro-
mote & enhance America's community news-
papers.
Number of Members: 2,500
Meeting(s): Annual Convention & Trade Show
Publication(s): *Publishers Auxiliary* (monthly, on-
line)

**National Newspaper Publishers Association
(NNPA)**
1816 12 St NW, Washington, DC 20009
Tel: 202-588-8764 *Fax:* 202-588-8960
E-mail: info@nnpa.org
Web Site: www.nnpa.org; www.blackpressusa.com
Key Personnel
Chmn: Dorsey R Leavell
Pres & CEO: Benjamin F Chavis
Founded: 1941 (as the National Negro Publishers
Association)
Federation of more than 200 black community
newspapers from across the US.
Number of Members: 200

National Press Club (NPC)
529 14 St NW, 13th fl, Washington, DC 20045
Tel: 202-662-7500
Web Site: www.press.org
Key Personnel
Pres: Andrea Edney
VP: Alison Fitzgerald Kodjak
Secy: Ferdous Al-Faruque

Exec Dir: William McCarren
E-mail: wmccarren@press.org
Membership Secy: Patrick Host
Founded: 1908
Private professional organization for journalists.
Sponsors workshops, rap sessions with authors,
press forums, morning newsmakers, famous
speaker luncheons; awards prizes for consumer
journalism, environmental reporting; freedom
of the press; diplomatic writing, Washington
coverage & newsletters; book & art exhibits;
computerized reference library; annual Book
Fair & Authors' Night.
Number of Members: 4,000
Publication(s): *The Record* (weekly)

National Press Club of Canada Foundation Inc
17 York St, Suite 201, Ottawa, ON K1N 9J6,
Canada
E-mail: info@pressclubcanada.ca
Web Site: pressclubcanada.ca
Key Personnel
Pres: James Baxter
Dir: Sally Douglas; Chloe Gervan; Lois Siegel
Founded: 1928
Not-for-profit association for reporters, journal-
ists & media-related people; organizes small &
large events of interest to the media community
in & around Ottawa's political circles; awards
annual scholarships for journalism students.
Number of Members: 50

National Press Foundation
1211 Connecticut Ave NW, Suite 310, Washing-
ton, DC 20036
Tel: 202-663-7280
Web Site: nationalpress.org
Key Personnel
Pres & COO: Sandy Johnson *E-mail:* sjohnson@
nationalpress.org
Dir, Opers: Jenny Ash-Maher *E-mail:* jenny@
nationalpress.org
Dir, Progs: Chris Adams *E-mail:* cadams@
nationalpress.org
Digital Media Mgr: Tyler Mertins
E-mail: tmertins@nationalpress.org
Founded: 1976
Provide all expenses paid educational programs to
help journalists understand & report on com-
plex topics in Washington, DC & around the
world.

**National Press Photographers Association Inc
(NPPA)**
120 Hooper St, Athens, GA 30602
Tel: 706-542-2506
E-mail: info@nppa.org
Web Site: nppa.org
Key Personnel
Exec Dir: Akili Ramsess *E-mail:* aramsess@nppa.
org
Prof Servs Dir: Thomas Kenniff *Tel:* 919-237-
1782 *E-mail:* tkenniff@nppa.org
Founded: 1946
To promote & protect integrity & excellence in
visual journalism.
Number of Members: 5,500
Publication(s): *News Photographer Magazine*
(monthly, free with membership)

**National Society of Newspaper Columnists
(NSNC)**
205 Gun Hill St, Milton, MA 02186
Tel: 617-697-6854
E-mail: director@columnists.com
Web Site: www.columnists.com
Key Personnel
Exec Dir: Suzette Martinez Standring
Founded: 1977
Promotes professionalism & camaraderie among
columnists & other writers of the serial essay,
including bloggers. Advocates for columnists &
free-press issues. Membership dues: $50/yr.

Number of Members: 500
Publication(s): *Newsletter* (monthly, free)

National Writers Association
10940 S Parker Rd, Suite 508, Parker, CO 80134
Tel: 303-656-7235
E-mail: natlwritersassn@hotmail.com
Web Site: www.nationalwriters.com
Key Personnel
Exec Dir & Ed: Sandy Whelchel
  E-mail: authorsandy@hotmail.com
Founded: 1937
Nonprofit representative organization of new &
  established writers, serving freelance writers
  throughout the world.
Number of Members: 2,000
Publication(s): *Authorship* (quarterly, $20/yr);
  NWA Newsletter (monthly by e-mail only)

National Writers Union/UAW Local 1981
Affiliate of UAW International of the United Au-
  tomobile Aerospace & Agricultural Implement
  Workers of America
256 W 38 St, Suite 703, New York, NY 10018
Tel: 212-254-0279 *Fax:* 212-254-0673
E-mail: nwu@nwu.org
Web Site: www.nwu.org/
Key Personnel
Pres: Larry Goldbetter
Founded: 1981
Organizing for better treatment of freelance writers by publishers; grievance procedures; negotiate union contracts with publishers; health
  insurance; conferences. Direct services include
  the Technical Writers Job Hotline & the Publication Rights Clearinghouse, a groundbreaking
  license fee collection system. National health
  insurance programs around the country; national grievance officers & contract advisors;
  agents database online for members; Authors
  Network, a Bed & Breakfast program for tour-
  ing authors at over 160 sites throughout the
  country, including local reviewer's database, local press contacts & local bookstores/vendors.
Number of Members: 1,200
Publication(s): *National Membership News*
  (monthly, newsletter, free to membs)

NCTA, see Northern California Translators
  Association

New Atlantic Independent Booksellers Association (NAIBA)
2667 Hyacinth St, Westbury, NY 11590
Tel: 516-333-0681 *Fax:* 516-333-0689
E-mail: naibabooksellers@gmail.com
Web Site: www.naiba.com
Key Personnel
Exec Dir: Eileen Dengler *E-mail:* naibaeileen@
  gmail.com
To promote cooperation & mutual interest among
  booksellers & to foster & advance their trade
  & commerce.
Meeting(s): NAIBA Fall Conference, Annually in
  Oct

New England Independent Booksellers Association Inc (NEIBA)
One Beacon St, 15th fl, Boston, MA 02108
Tel: 617-547-3642 *Fax:* 617-830-8768
Web Site: www.newenglandbooks.org
Key Personnel
Exec Dir: Beth Ineson *E-mail:* beth@neba.org
Admin Coord: Nan Sorensen *E-mail:* nan@neba.
  org
Mktg Coord: Alexandra Schmelzle *E-mail:* ali@
  neba.org
Trade association. Fall trade show & conference
  annually in September or October; educational
  workshops, holiday gift catalog, book awards.

Number of Members: 300
Publication(s): *NEIBA News* (weekly, membs
  only)

New England Poetry Club
46 Wallace St, Somerville, MA 02144
E-mail: info@nepoetryclub.org
Web Site: www.nepoetryclub.org
Key Personnel
Pres: Mary Buchinger
VP: Hillary Sallick
Treas: Linda Haviland Conte
Membership Coord: Jennifer Markel; Ralph Pen-
  nel
Soc Media Ed: Blake Stewart
Programming: Wendy Drexler; Marjorie Thomsen
Founded: 1915
Society for poets, publishers, readers & trans-
  lators of poetry, who live in New England or
  have strong ties to the region. Sponsor poetry
  readings contests & workshops. Meetings take
  place at the Yenching Library (2 Divinity Ave
  Harvard Campus) on first & third Tuesdays,
  7pm, monthly from September-April. Special
  programs at Longfellow House Sundays May-
  August. $2,000 in prizes annually.
Number of Members: 250
Publication(s): *Member Newsletter* (monthly)
Branch Office(s)
18 Hall Ave, Apt 2, Somerville, MA 02144
  (Treas)

New Hampshire Writers' Project
2500 N River Rd, Manchester, NH 03106
Tel: 603-314-7980
E-mail: info@nhwritersproject.org
Web Site: www.nhwritersproject.org
Key Personnel
Chair: Masherl Chappelle
Treas: Rose Curry
Founded: 1988
Supports the development of individual writers
  & encourages an audience for literature in the
  state.
Number of Members: 780
Publication(s): *NH Writer* (6 issues/yr, newsletter)

New Jersey Business & Industry Association (NJBIA)
10 W Lafayette St, Trenton, NJ 08608-2002
Tel: 609-393-7707
Web Site: njbia.org
Key Personnel
Pres & CEO: Michele Siekerka
  E-mail: msiekerka@njbia.org
COO/CFO: Alice Gens *E-mail:* agens@njbia.org
Chief Busn Rel Offr: Wayne Staub
  E-mail: wstaub@njbia.org
Chief Communs Offr: Bob Considine
  E-mail: bconsidine@njbia.org
Chief Govt Aff Offr: Christine Buteas
  E-mail: cbuteas@njbia.org
Chief Mktg Offr & Publr: Vincent Schweikert
  E-mail: v.schweikert@njbia.org
Chief Memb Strategy Offr: Betty Boros
  E-mail: bboros@njbia.org
Founded: 1910
Statewide employer association providing infor-
  mation, services & advocacy for member com-
  panies.

New Mexico Book Association (NMBA)
1219 Luisa St, Suite 1, Santa Fe, NM 87505
Mailing Address: PO Box 1285, Santa Fe, NM
  87504
Tel: 505-660-6357
E-mail: admin@nmbook.org
Web Site: www.nmbook.org
Key Personnel
Pres: Paula Lozar *Tel:* 505-473-3479
  E-mail: lozarpaula@cs.com
Off Admin: Susan Waterman

Archivist & Sr Advisor: Richard Polese *Tel:* 505-
  983-1412 *E-mail:* richard@oceantree.com
Founded: 1994
Nonprofit association serving the interests of pub-
  lishing, writing, designing, editing, selling &
  marketing for book professionals throughout
  New Mexico. Open to all involved in books
  or publishing. Need not be a resident of New
  Mexico.
Number of Members: 180
Publication(s): *LIBRO Book News* (6 issues/yr,
  newsletter, $50/yr membs)
Membership(s): The Association of Publishers
  for Special Sales (APSS); Independent Book
  Publishers Association (IBPA); New Mexico
  Library Association; Publishers Association of
  the West (PubWest)

News Media Alliance
4401 N Fairfax Dr, Suite 300, Arlington, VA
  22203
Tel: 571-366-1000
E-mail: info@newsmediaalliance.org
Web Site: www.newsmediaalliance.org
Key Personnel
Pres & CEO: David Chavern *Tel:* 571-366-1100
  E-mail: david@newsmediaalliance.org
CFO: Robert Walden *Tel:* 571-366-1140
  E-mail: robert@newsmediaalliance.org
VP, HR & Opers: Sarah Burkman *Tel:* 571-366-
  1012 *E-mail:* sarah@newsmediaalliance.org
Dir, Communs: Lindsey Loving *Tel:* 571-366-
  1009 *E-mail:* lindsey@newsmediaalliance.org
Serves newspapers & newspaper executives by
  working to advance the cause of a free press;
  to encourage the efficiency & economy of the
  newspaper publishing business in all departments & aspects; to engage in & promote research of use to newspapers; to gather & distribute among its member newspapers accurate,
  reliable & useful information about newspapers
  & their environment & to promote the highest
  standard of journalism.
Number of Members: 2,000
Meeting(s): Key Executives Mega-Conference
Publication(s): *Presstime* (weekly, membs only)

News Media Canada
37 Front St E, Suite 200, Toronto, ON M5E 1B3,
  Canada
Tel: 416-923-3567 *Toll Free Tel:* 877-305-2262
  Fax: 416-923-7206
E-mail: info@newsmediacanada.ca
Web Site: www.nmc-mic.ca
Key Personnel
Pres & CEO: John Hinds *Tel:* 416-923-0858
  E-mail: jhinds@newsmediacanada.ca
Founded: 2016
An organization providing service to its members
  in the area of marketing, member services &
  contesting legislation that is potentially harm-
  ful to newspapers & freedom of the press in
  general. The association brings the wisdom &
  dedication of all its members to foster & nur-
  ture a free press committed to providing the
  best possible service to its readers.
Number of Members: 800

The NewsGuild - CWA
501 Third St NW, 6th fl, Washington, DC 20001-
  2797
Tel: 202-434-7177; 202-434-7162 (The Guild Re-
  porter) *Fax:* 202-434-1472
E-mail: guild@cwa-union.org
Web Site: www.newsguild.org
Key Personnel
Pres: Bernard Lunzer
Ed, The Guild Reporter: Sally Davidow
  E-mail: sdavidow@cwa-union.org
Founded: 1934
Labor union; AFL-CIO, CLC.

Number of Members: 26,000
Publication(s): *The Guild Reporter* (quarterly, free to membs, $20 subn rate nonmembs)

North American Agricultural Journalists (NAAJ)
6434 Hurta Lane, Bryan, TX 77808
Tel: 979-324-4302
Web Site: www.naaj.net
Key Personnel
Exec Secy & Treas: Kathleen Phillips
  E-mail: naajnews@yahoo.com
Founded: 1952
Self-improvement seminars; annual writing contest for members & nonmembers.
Number of Members: 120
2021 Meeting(s): Annual Meeting, Washington, DC, April 2021

North American Snowsports Journalists Association (NASJA)
49 Plaza Ave, Belchertown, MA 01007
E-mail: execsec@nasja.org
Web Site: nasja.org
Key Personnel
Pres: Iseult Devlin
VP: Bob Cox; Dan Geisen
Treas: Vicki Andersen
Founded: 1963 (founded as the US Ski Writers Association)
Professional group of writers, photographers, broadcasters, filmmakers, authors & editors who report ski & snowboard related news, info & features throughout the US & Canada.
Number of Members: 340
New Election: Annually in March

North Carolina Writers' Network
PO Box 21591, Winston-Salem, NC 27120-1591
Tel: 336-293-8844
Web Site: www.ncwriters.org
Key Personnel
Exec Dir: Ed Southern *E-mail:* ed@ncwriters.org
Founded: 1985
Nonprofit, statewide.
Number of Members: 1,500
Publication(s): *Writers' Network News* (semiannual, newspaper, free to membs)

Northern California Independent Booksellers Association (NCIBA), see California Independent Booksellers Alliance (CALIBA)

Northern California Translators Association
2261 Market St, Suite 160, San Francisco, CA 94114-1600
Tel: 510-845-8712
E-mail: administrator@ncta.org
Web Site: www.ncta.org
Key Personnel
Pres: Sonia Wichmann
Admin: Juliet Viola Kniffen
Founded: 1978
Professional translators & interpreters association. Chapter of the American Translators Association. Online referral service.
Number of Members: 500
New Election: Annually in Feb
Publication(s): *Translorial* (semiannual, print & online, journal, free to membs at www.translorial.com; free PDF access for *Translorial Reader* registrants at www.ncta.org)

Northwest Independent Editors Guild
7511 Greenwood Ave N, No 307, Seattle, WA 98103
E-mail: info@edsguild.org
Web Site: edsguild.org
Key Personnel
Pres: Pm Weizenbaum *E-mail:* president@edsguild.org

VP, Bd Devt: Valerie Paquin
VP, Memb Servs: Matthew Bennett
Secy: Karen Parkin
Treas: Michael Schuler
Founded: 1997
Professional association of more than 300 editors in the Pacific Northwest. Members work on all types of communication projects, from brochures & newsletters to books & web sites. The Editors Guild connects clients with professional editors, fosters community among its members & provides resources for their career development.
Number of Members: 300

Northwest Territories Public Library Services
Unit of Department of Education, Culture & Employment
75 Woodland Dr, Hay River, NT X0E 1G1, Canada
Tel: 867-874-6531 *Toll Free Tel:* 866-297-0232 (CN) *Fax:* 867-874-3321
Web Site: www.nwtpls.gov.nt.ca
Key Personnel
Territorial Libn: Brian Dawson
  E-mail: brian_dawson@gov.nt.ca
Provide leadership in coordinating public library services throughout the Northwest Territories.

NPTA Alliance
330 N Wabash Ave, Suite 2000, Chicago, IL 60611
Tel: 312-321-4092 *Toll Free Tel:* 800-355-NPTA (355-6782) *Fax:* 312-673-6736
Web Site: www.gonpta.com
Key Personnel
EVP: Matthew Bruno *E-mail:* mbruno@gonpta.com
Membership Servs Coord: Tia Crowley
  E-mail: tcrowley@gonpta.com
Mktg & Communs Coord: Claire Sereiko
  E-mail: csereiko@gonpta.com
Founded: 1903
Trade association serving the printing, publishing, catalog, direct mail, imaging, retail & corporate markets.
Number of Members: 2,600
New Election: Annually in Autumn
Publication(s): *Paper Merchant Weekly* (newsletter, free to membs, electronic)
Membership(s): National Association of Wholesaler-Distributors (NAW)

NWT Public Library Services, see Northwest Territories Public Library Services

Ontario Book Publishers Organization (OBPO)
One Rutton St, Suite 101, Toronto, ON M6P 0A1, Canada
Tel: 416-536-7584
E-mail: info@obpo.ca
Web Site: obpo.ca
Founded: 1990
Represent the needs, interests, concerns & issues of Ontario book publishers; facilitate information sharing & educational opportunities; facilitate group marketing projects.
Number of Members: 35

Ontario Library Association
2 Toronto St, 3rd fl, Toronto, ON M5C 2B6, Canada
Tel: 416-363-3388 *Toll Free Tel:* 866-873-9867 *Fax:* 416-941-9581
E-mail: info@accessola.com
Web Site: www.accessola.com
Key Personnel
Exec Dir: Shelagh Paterson *Tel:* 416-363-3388 ext 224 *E-mail:* spaterson@accessola.com
Founded: 1900

Memberships available: Personal membership (for one individual, based on salary earned in library work, whether full-time or part-time) $40-$120, Institutional Membership (for one or two-persons, transferable within an institution) $140-$190, Associate Membership (for businesses/corporations to provide support) $215.
Number of Members: 5,300
New Election: Annually in Dec
Publication(s): *The Teaching Librarian* (3 issues/yr, magazine, $36/yr CN)

Ordre des traducteurs, terminologues et interpretes agrees du quebec
Affiliate of Federation Internationale de Traducteurs
1108-2021 Ave Union, Montreal, QC H3A 2S9, Canada
Tel: 514-845-4411 *Toll Free Tel:* 800-265-4815 *Fax:* 514-845-9903
E-mail: info@ottiaq.org; direction@ottiaq.org; reception@ottiaq.org
Web Site: www.ottiaq.org
Key Personnel
Chief Exec Offr & Access to Info Offr: Diane Cousineau *Tel:* 514-845-4411 ext 227
Mgr, Communs & Cust Serv: Sophia Bekkoucha *Tel:* 514-845-4411 ext 225
  E-mail: sobekkoucha@ottiaq.org
Mgr, Prof Aff & Secy: Helene Gauthier *Tel:* 514-845-4411 ext 224 *E-mail:* hgauthier@ottiaq.org
Certification Coord: Benedicte Assogba *Tel:* 514-845-4411 ext 231 *E-mail:* bassogba@ottiaq.org
Prof Aff Asst: Lynda Godin *Tel:* 514-845-4411 ext 223 *E-mail:* lgodin@ottiaq.org
Admin Asst: Joanne Trudel *Tel:* 514-845-4411 ext 226 *E-mail:* jtrudel@ottiaq.org
Communs Asst: Marsida Nurka *Tel:* 514-845-4411 ext 221
Bring translators together to exchange information, send out offers of employment to members. Promote profession & protect public interest. Conferences, annual meeting, social activities, seminars, continuing education.
Number of Members: 2,073
Publication(s): *L'antenne express* (newsletter, free to membs); *Circuit* (quarterly, ezine, free)

Oregon Christian Writers (OCW)
1075 Willow Lake Rd N, Keizer, OR 97303
Tel: 503-393-3356
E-mail: contact@oregonchristianwriters.org
Web Site: oregonchristianwriters.org
Key Personnel
Pres: Marilyn Rhoades
Prog Chmn: Don White
Summer Conference Dir: Lindy Jacobs
  E-mail: summerconf@oregonchristianwriters.org
Registrar & Busn Mgr: Sue Miholer
Founded: 1963
Workshops & seminars for beginning & advanced writers; guest speakers & critiques by professional writers.
Number of Members: 375
New Election: Annually in Oct
Meeting(s): Fall Conference, annually in Oct
2021 Meeting(s): Winter One-Day Conference, Chemeketa Community College, Salem, OR, Feb 20, 2021; Spring One-Day Conference, First Baptist Church, Eugene, OR, May 15, 2021; Summer Conference, Red Lion on the River Hotel, Portland, OR, August 16–19, 2021
Publication(s): *Oregon Christian Writers Newsletter* (3 issues/yr)

Outdoor Writers Association of America (OWAA)
2814 Brooks St, Box 442, Missoula, MT 59801
Tel: 406-728-7434
E-mail: info@owaa.org
Web Site: www.owaa.org

Key Personnel
Exec Dir: Dr Brandon D Shuler
  E-mail: brandon@owaa.org
Membership & Conference Dir: Jessica (Pollett)
  Seitz *E-mail:* jseitz@owaa.org
Founded: 1927
A nonprofit, international organization represent-
  ing professional communicators dedicated to
  sharing the outdoor experience.
2021 Meeting(s): Annual Conference, Jay Peak
  Resort, 830 Jay Peak Rd, Jay, VT, July 9-12,
  2021

Overseas Press Club of America (OPC)
40 W 45 St, New York, NY 10036
Tel: 212-626-9220 *Fax:* 212-626-9210
E-mail: info@opcofamerica.org
Web Site: www.opcofamerica.org
Key Personnel
Exec Dir: Patricia Kranz *E-mail:* patricia@
  opcofamerica.org
Founded: 1939
Maintain an international association of journal-
  ists, encourage professional skill & integrity of
  reportage, contribute to the freedom & inde-
  pendence of journalism & the press worldwide.
Number of Members: 440
New Election: Annually in Aug
Publication(s): *Bulletin* (monthly, newsletter, free
  to membs); *Dateline* (annual, magazine, free to
  membs)

Pacific Northwest Booksellers Association (PNBA)
520 W 13 Ave, Eugene, OR 97401-3461
Tel: 541-683-4363 *Toll Free Tel:* 800-353-6764
  Fax: 541-683-3910
E-mail: info@pnba.org
Web Site: www.pnba.org
Key Personnel
Exec Dir: Brian Juenemann *E-mail:* brian@pnba.
  org
Founded: 1965
Annual trade lists of publishing companies' sales
  reps; educational seminars; work with local literacy groups & anticensorship organizations;
  sponsor annual booksellers awards presented
  for books of exceptional quality by Northwest
  writers or publishers; sponsor workshops &
  prizes.
Number of Members: 300
Publication(s): *Footnotes* (monthly e-mail,
  newsletter, free to membs); *nmbooklovers.org*
  (blog); *PNBA Member Handbook* (annual, free
  to membs, electronic)

Pacific Northwest Writers Association, see PNWA - a writer's resource

Pacific Printing Industries Association
Affiliate of PRINTING United Alliance
6825 SW Sandburg St, Portland, OR 97223
Mailing Address: PO Box 23575, Portland, OR
  97281-3575
Tel: 503-221-3944 *Toll Free Tel:* 877-762-7742
  Fax: 503-221-5691
E-mail: info@ppiassociation.org
Web Site: www.ppiassociation.org
Key Personnel
Exec Dir: Jules Van Sant *E-mail:* jules@
  ppiassociation.org
Membership Sales & Support: Chris Ryce
Trade association.
Number of Members: 230

Palm Springs Writers Guild
PO Box 947, Rancho Mirage, CA 92270-0947
Web Site: www.palmspringswritersguild.org
Key Personnel
Pres: John G Peters, Jr *E-mail:* president.pswg@
  gmail.com

VP, Membership: John Carrigan
  E-mail: vpmembership.pswg@gmail.com
Founded: 1977
Number of Members: 280

PEN America
Affiliate of PEN International
8444 Wilshire Blvd, 4th fl, Beverly Hills, CA
  90211
Tel: 323-424-4939 *Fax:* 323-424-4944
E-mail: info@pen.org
Web Site: pen.org/pen-america-los-angeles
Key Personnel
Pres: Jennifer Egan
Exec Dir: Michelle Franke *Tel:* 323-424-4939 ext
  1 *E-mail:* mfranke@pen.org
Founded: 1943
National association of poets, playwrights, screen-
  writers, essayists, editors, novelists, historians,
  critics, journalists & translators whose pur-
  pose is to foster a sense of community among
  writers in the Western US & to advance the
  freedom to write throughout the world.
Number of Members: 1,000
Publication(s): *ePen* (26 issues/yr, free); *Membership Directory* (annual, free for membs)

PEN America
Affiliate of PEN International
588 Broadway, Suite 303, New York, NY 10012
Tel: 212-334-1660 *Fax:* 212-334-2181
E-mail: info@pen.org
Web Site: pen.org
Key Personnel
CEO: Suzanne Nossel *Tel:* 212-334-1600 ext
  4811 *E-mail:* snossel@pen.org
Pres: Jennifer Egan
Intl Pres: John Ralston Saul
Sr Dir, Literary Progs & Dir, PEN World Voices
  Festival: Chip Rolley
Natl Outreach Prog Dir: Katie Zanecchia
Membership Coord: Daniel Guzman *Tel:* 212-
  334-1660 ext 4819 *E-mail:* daniel@pen.org
Asst Ed & Soc Media Assoc: Wei-Ling Woo
  Tel: 212-334-1660 ext 4832 *E-mail:* weiling@
  pen.org
An association of writers working to advance lit-
  erature, defend free expression & foster inter-
  national literary fellowship.
Regional offices located in AL, CA, DC, MI, NC,
  OK & TX.
Number of Members: 4,000
Publication(s): *Grants & Awards Available to
  American Writers* (online directory, $12)

PEN America Boston
Unit of PEN America
MIT, 14N-221A, 77 Massachusetts Ave, Cam-
  bridge, MA 02139
Tel: 617-324-1729
E-mail: penamericaboston@pen.org
Web Site: pen.org/pen-america-boston
Advance the cause of literature & reading in New
  England & defending free expression every-
  where.

PEN Canada
401 Richmond St W, Suite 258, Toronto, ON
  M5V 3A8, Canada
Tel: 416-703-8448
E-mail: queries@pencanada.ca
Web Site: www.pencanada.ca
Key Personnel
Exec Dir: Brendan de Caires *Tel:* 416-703-8448
  ext 3 *E-mail:* bdecaires@pencanada.ca
Off Mgr: Vera DeWaard *Tel:* 416-703-8448 ext 1
  E-mail: vsdewaard@pencanada.ca
Communs & Admin: Kasey Maguire *Tel:* 416-
  703-8448 ext 2 *E-mail:* kmaguire@pencanada.
  ca
Founded: 1926

Promotes freedom of expression through writing.
Number of Members: 500

PEN New England, see PEN America Boston

Photographic Society of America® (PSA®)
8241 S Walker Ave, Suite 104, Oklahoma City,
  OK 73139
Tel: 405-843-1437 *Toll Free Tel:* 855-PSA-INFO
  (772-4636)
E-mail: hq@psa-photo.org
Web Site: www.psa-photo.org
Key Personnel
Membership Mgr: John R Key
  E-mail: membership@psa-photo.org
Founded: 1934
Sponsor workshops & awards for members.
Number of Members: 6,500
2021 Meeting(s): PSA® International Conference
  of Photography, Rapid City, SD, Oct 6-9, 2021
2022 Meeting(s): PSA® International Conference
  of Photography, Colorado Springs, CO, Sept
  21-24, 2022
Publication(s): *PSA Journal* (monthly, free to
  membs)

Playwrights Guild of Canada
401 Richmond St W, Suite 350, Toronto, ON
  M5V 3A8, Canada
Tel: 416-703-0201
E-mail: info@playwrightsguild.ca; marketing@
  playwrightsguild.ca
Web Site: www.playwrightsguild.ca
Key Personnel
Exec Dir: Robin Sokoloski *E-mail:* robin@
  playwrightsguild.ca
Membership & Prof Contracts Mgr: Rebecca Bur-
  ton *E-mail:* membership@playwrightsguild.ca
PR Mgr: Monique Renaud
Founded: 1972
Professional association. Contracts, amateur agent
  productions, script service, readings, bookstore.
Number of Members: 850

PNWA - a writer's resource
1420 NW Gilman Blvd, Suite 8, PMB 2717, Is-
  saquah, WA 98027
Tel: 425-673-2665 *Fax:* 425-961-0768
E-mail: pnwa@pnwa.org
Web Site: www.pnwa.org
Key Personnel
Pres: Pam Binder
Founded: 1955
Nonprofit association. Develops writing talent
  through education, accessibility to publishing
  industry & participation in a vital writer com-
  munity.
Number of Members: 1,400

Poetry Society of America (PSA)
15 Gramercy Park, New York, NY 10003
Tel: 212-254-9628
Web Site: poetrysociety.org
Key Personnel
Pres: Allison Binns
Exec Dir: Matt Brogan *E-mail:* matt@
  poetrysociety.org
Deputy Dir: Brett Fletcher Lauer *E-mail:* brett@
  poetrysociety.org
Devt Dir: Madeline Weinfield *E-mail:* madeline@
  poetrysociety.org
Devt Asst: Azzure Alexander *E-mail:* azzure@
  poetrysociety.org
Progs Mgr: Emily Hunt *E-mail:* emily@
  poetrysociety.org
Founded: 1910
Contests, readings, lectures, symposia, seminars,
  weekly workshops for members.
Number of Members: 2,900

Poets & Writers Inc

90 Broad St, Suite 2100, New York, NY 10004
Tel: 212-226-3586 *Fax:* 212-226-3963
E-mail: admin@pw.org
Web Site: www.pw.org
Key Personnel
Exec Dir: Elliot Figman
Dir, Fin & Acctg: William F Hayes
Mng Dir: Melissa Ford Gradel *Tel:* 212-226-3586
ext 223
Founded: 1970
A nonprofit organization which offers information, support & exposure to writers at all stages in their careers. Founded to foster the development of poets & fiction writers & to promote communication throughout the literary community. It publishes the bimonthly *Poets & Writers Magazine,* which delivers to its readers profiles of noted authors & publishing professionals, practical how-to articles, a comprehensive listing of grants & awards for writers & special sections on subjects ranging from small presses to writers conferences. The Readings/Workshops Program supports public literary events through matching grants to community organizations.
Publication(s): *Poets & Writers Magazine* (6 issues/yr, $15.95/yr, $25.95/2 yrs, $5.95 single copy)
Branch Office(s)
PO Box 352110, Los Angeles, CA 90035, Dir: Jamie Fitzgerald *Tel:* 310-481-7195 *Fax:* 310-481-7193 *E-mail:* calif@pw.org

PRIMIR, see Print Industries Market Information and Research Organization (PRIMIR)

Print Industries Market Information and Research Organization (PRIMIR)

Unit of Association for Print Technologies (APTech)
1899 Preston White Dr, Reston, VA 20191
Tel: 703-264-7200
E-mail: aptech@aptech.org
Web Site: www.printtechnologies.org; www.npes.org/primirresearch/primir.aspx
Key Personnel
Dir, Mkt Data & Res: Jason Goodwin
E-mail: jgoodwin@aptech.org
Founded: 2005
Global source of data, analysis & trend information about print & related communications industries through research-initiated by the industry, for the industry. Any firm, corporation, division or separate business unit of a corporation, engaged in printing or converting by any & all processes, within the US or globally, or in the manufacture or distribution of equipment, software, materials or supplies to the graphic communications or converting industry, is eligible for PRIMIR membership.
Number of Members: 60
New Election: Annually in Dec

Printing & Graphics Association MidAtlantic (PGAMA)

Affiliate of PRINTING United Alliance
9685 Gerwig Lane, Suite A, Columbia, MD 21046-1520
Tel: 410-319-0900 *Toll Free Tel:* 877-319-0906
Fax: 410-319-0905
E-mail: info@pgama.com
Web Site: www.pgama.com
Key Personnel
Pres: Jay Goldscher *E-mail:* jay@pgama.com
Founded: 1894
Number of Members: 219

Printing Brokerage/Buyers Association International (PBBA)

74-5576 Pawai Place, No 599, Kailua Kona, HI 96740
Tel: 808-339-0880
E-mail: contactus@pbba.org
Web Site: pbba.org
Key Personnel
Chmn: Vincent Mallardi *E-mail:* vince@pbba.org
Founded: 1985
Trade association for printing, sales brokerage & purchasing.
Number of Members: 540
Publication(s): *Brokerage* (6 issues/yr, newsletter, free to membs); *Hot Markets for Print Demand Annual Rankings of Buyers, Print Products & Geographies* (annual, $995); *Hot Markets for Print Supply Annual Rankings of Providers, Intermediaries & Geographies* (annual, $995); *Law v. Print: Avoid Problems & Protect Opportunities Buying & Selling Prints* ($395); *Printing Brokerage in North America: The Survey* ($195); *Why Use a Printing Independent? Outsourcing is In* ($95)

Printing Industries Alliance

Affiliate of PRINTING United Alliance
636 N French Rd, Suite 1, Amherst, NY 14228
Tel: 716-691-3211 *Toll Free Tel:* 800-777-4742
Fax: 716-691-4249
E-mail: info@pialliance.org
Web Site: pialliance.org
Key Personnel
Pres: Timothy Freeman *E-mail:* tfreeman@pialliance.org
Mktg/Progs Dir: Kimberly Tuzzo
E-mail: ktuzzo@pialliance.org
Mgr, Membership Servs: Jerry Banks
E-mail: jerry@pialliance.org
Off Support Mgr: Caroline Wawrzyniec
E-mail: cwawrzyniec@pialliance.org
Trade association serving the graphic communications industry in New York State, Northern New Jersey & Northwestern Pennsylvania.
Branch Office(s)
195 Prospect Park W, Suite 1A, Brooklyn, NY 11215, EVP: Martin J Maloney *Tel:* 203-912-0804 *E-mail:* mmaloney@pialliance.org

Printing Industries of America (PIA), see PRINTING United Alliance

Printing Industry Association of the South (PIAS)

305 Plus Park Blvd, Nashville, TN 37217
Tel: 615-366-1094 *Fax:* 615-366-4192
E-mail: info@pias.org
Web Site: www.pias.org
Key Personnel
Pres: Ed Chalifoux
Provide services & support to the printing industry.
Number of Members: 400
Publication(s): *Print South* (monthly, magazine, free to membs)

PRINTING United Alliance

Formerly Printing Industries of America (PIA); Specialty Graphic Imaging Association (SGIA)
10015 Main St, Fairfax, VA 22031-3489
Tel: 703-385-1335 *Toll Free Tel:* 888-385-3588
Fax: 703-273-0456; 703-691-7492 (membership)
E-mail: assist@printing.org; info@printing.org
Web Site: www.printing.org; www.sgia.org
Key Personnel
Pres & CEO: Ford Bowers *E-mail:* fbowers@printing.org
EVP (PA Off): Michael F Makin
E-mail: mmakin@printing.org
EVP: James Martin *E-mail:* jmartin@printing.org
SVP, Educ & Training (PA Off): Joe Marin
E-mail: jmarin@printing.org
VP, HR Consulting (PA Off): Adriane Harrison
E-mail: aharrison@printing.org
VP, Mktg & Membership: Sarah Helminiak
E-mail: shelminiak@printing.org
VP, Govt & Regulatory Aff: Marci Kinter
E-mail: mkinter@printing.org
VP, Govt Aff (DC Off): Lisbeth A Lyons
E-mail: llyons@printing.org
VP, PR: Amanda Kliegl *E-mail:* akliegl@printing.org
VP, Fin & Acctg: Casey McAllister
E-mail: cmcallister@printing.org
VP, Busn Devt: Jack Noonan *E-mail:* jnoonan@printing.org
VP, Expositions: Lexy Olisko *E-mail:* lolisko@printing.org
VP, Technol & Res (PA Off): James A Workman
E-mail: jworkman@printing.org
Founded: 2020 (thru the merger of Printing Industries of America & Specialty Graphic Imaging Association)
Member organization providing research, educational & technical services to printing industry worldwide.
Number of Members: 14,000
2021 Meeting(s): Continuous Improvement Conference, Columbus, OH, April 18-21, 2021; COLOR21, Hilton La Jolla Torrey Pines, La Jolla, CA, June 5-8, 2021; PRINTING United, Orange County Convention Center, Orlando, FL, Oct 6-8, 2021
2022 Meeting(s): PRINTING United, Las Vegas Convention Center, Las Vegas, NV, Act 19-21, 2022
2023 Meeting(s): PRINTING United, Georgia World Congress Center, Atlanta, GA, Oct 18-20, 2023
2024 Meeting(s): PRINTING United, Las Vegas Convention Center, Las Vegas, NV, Oct 23-25, 2024
2025 Meeting(s): PRINTING United, Orange County Convention Center, Orlando, FL, Oct 22-24, 2025
2026 Meeting(s): PRINTING United, Las Vegas Convention Center, Las Vegas, NV, Oct 21-23, 2026
Publication(s): *Industry Ink* (monthly, enewsletter); *PRINTING United Journal* (quarterly)
Branch Office(s)
1325 "G" St NW, Suite 500, Washington, DC 20005 *Tel:* 202-627-6925 ext 504
2000 Corporate Dr, Suite 205, Wexford, PA 15090 *Tel:* 412-741-6860 *Toll Free Tel:* 800-910-4283 *Fax:* 412-741-2311

The Private Eye Writers of America (PWA)

3665 S Needles Hwy, 7G, Laughlin, NV 89029
Web Site: www.privateeyewriters.com
Key Personnel
Exec Dir: Robert J Randisi *E-mail:* rrandisi@sbcglobal.net
Founded: 1981
Organization devoted to Private Eye fiction. Membership is open to fans, writers & publishing professionals. Sponsor of the annual Shamus Awards for private eye novels & short stories.

Professional Writers Association of Canada (PWAC)

2800 14 Ave, Suite 210, Markham, ON L3R 0E4, Canada
Tel: 416-504-1645
Web Site: pwac.ca
Founded: 1976
Protects & promotes the rights of nonfiction writers in Canada. Helps freelancers have a strong network that circulates news, information & market data on the industry through a national newsletter, discussion boards & social media platforms. The organization is governed by a volunteer Board of Directors with representation from 5 regions in Canada: British Columbia, Prairies & the North, Ontario, Quebec & Atlantic. Chapters organize professional

development & social events for members, many of which are open to the public. The annual general meeting is held in conjunction with a national conference that focuses on professional development with some social engagement.

Protestant Church-Owned Publishers Association
6631 Westbury Oaks Ct, Springfield, VA 22152
Tel: 703-220-5989
Web Site: www.pcpaonline.org
Key Personnel
Dir: Gary Mulder *E-mail:* mulder@pcpaonline.org
Founded: 1951
Number of Members: 40

Public Relations Society of America Inc
120 Wall St, 21st fl, New York, NY 10005-4024
Tel: 212-460-1400 *Fax:* 212-995-0757
E-mail: memberservices@prsa.org
Web Site: www.prsa.org
Key Personnel
CEO: Joseph P Truncale
CFO: Philip T Bonaventura *Tel:* 212-460-1440
  E-mail: philip.bonaventura@prsa.org
SVP, Membership: Jay Starr *E-mail:* jay.starr@
  prsa.org
Chief Communs Offr: Laura Kane *E-mail:* laura.
  kane@prsa.org
Founded: 1947
Association of public relations professionals dedicated to development & ethical practice of public relations.
Publication(s): *The Public Relations Strategist* (quarterly, magazine, free online); *Public Relations Tactics* (monthly, newspaper, free online)

Publishers Association of the West Inc (PubWest)
17501 Hill Way, Lake Oswego, OR 97035
Tel: 503-901-9865
E-mail: pubwest1@gmail.com
Web Site: pubwest.org
Key Personnel
Pres: Colleen Dunn Bates
Founded: 1977
Members are small & medium-sized book publishers located throughout North America. Supply marketing & technical information to members; conduct annual educational seminars; promote sales in the region. Participates in BookExpo, MPBA & PNBA trade shows. Publisher of the *PubWest Industry Operations and Salary Report*.
Number of Members: 360
Publication(s): *PubWest Membership Directory* (annual, directory, free to membs, $25 for non-membs)

Publishers Information Bureau (PIB)®
Division of MPA - The Association of Magazine Media
757 Third Ave, 11th fl, New York, NY 10017
Tel: 212-872-3700 (MPA)
E-mail: infocenter@magazine.org
Web Site: www.magazine.org
Key Personnel
Pres & CEO: Linda Thomas Brooks *Tel:* 212-872-3710 *E-mail:* lthomasbrooks@magazine.
  org
SVP & CFO: Glenn Spoto *Tel:* 212-872-3722
  E-mail: gspoto@magazine.org
EVP, Communs: Susan Russ *Tel:* 212-872-3732
  E-mail: sruss@magazine.org
Dir, Info Servs: Sandy Jimenez *Tel:* 212-872-3795 *E-mail:* sjimenez@magazine.org
Measure advertising pages & rate card revenues in consumer magazines & newspaper supplements.
Number of Members: 250

Publishing Professionals Network
c/o Postal Annex, 274 Redwood Shores Pkwy, Redwood City, CA 94065-1173
Mailing Address: PO Box 129, Redwood City, CA 94064-0129
E-mail: operations@pubpronetwork.org
Web Site: pubpronetwork.org
Key Personnel
Pres: Brenda Ginty *E-mail:* brenda.ginty@
  cengage.com
Secy: Monique Muhlenkamp *E-mail:* monique@
  newworldlibrary.com
Treas: Tona Pearce Myers *E-mail:* tona@
  newworldlibrary.com
Founded: 1969
Specialize in supporting the book publishing industry. Offers educational programs, seminars & scholarships. Produces an annual book show & has monthly dinner meetings.
Number of Members: 400
New Election: Annually in Jan
Publication(s): *Bookbuilders West Newsletter* (5 issues/yr)

PubWest, see Publishers Association of the West Inc (PubWest)

Quebec Writers' Federation (QWF)
1200 Atwater Ave, Rm 3, Westmount, QC H3Z 1X4, Canada
Tel: 514-933-0878
E-mail: info@qwf.org
Web Site: www.qwf.org; www.hireawriter.ca
Key Personnel
Exec Dir: Lori Schubert *E-mail:* admin@qwf.org
Association of Quebec writers to promote English language writing in Quebec through literary awards, writing workshops, mentorship program & literary events.
Number of Members: 600

Reporters Committee for Freedom of the Press
1156 15 St NW, Suite 1250, Washington, DC 20005-1779
Tel: 202-795-9300 *Toll Free Tel:* 800-336-4243
E-mail: info@rcfp.org
Web Site: www.rcfp.org
Key Personnel
Exec Dir: Bruce Brown *Tel:* 703-807-2101
Communs Dir: Debra Gersh Hernandez *Tel:* 703-807-2104
Busn Mgr: Lois Loyd *Tel:* 571-481-9321
Founded: 1970
Legal defense & research services for journalists & media lawyers.
Publication(s): *Access to Electronic Communications* (handbook); *Access to Juror Questionnaires* (handbook); *Access to Juvenile Justice* (handbook); *Access to Police Records* (handbook); *Access to Terrorism Proceedings* (handbook); *Agents of Discovery* (report); *Alternative Dispute Resolution* (handbook); *Anonymous Juries* (report); *Federal FOIA Appeals Guide* (handbook); *Federal Open Government Guide* (handbook); *FERPA, HIPAA & DPPA* (handbook); *The First Amendment Handbook* (booklet); *Gag Orders* (handbook); *Grand Juries* (handbook); *Homefront Confidential* (report); *Judicial Speech* (handbook); *Jury Proceedings and Records* (handbook); *The Lost Stories* (handbook); *The News Media & the Law* (quarterly, magazine, $20/yr, free online a few weeks after released to subscribers); *Off Base: Military Court Dockets* (handbook); *Online Access to Plea Agreements* (handbook); *Open Courts Compendium* (handbook); *Open Government Guide, 6th ed* (handbook); *Photographers' Guide to Privacy* (handbook); *Police, Protesters and the Press* (handbook); *Private Eyes* (handbook); *Privatization v the Public's Right to Know* (handbook); *Privilege Compendium* (handbook); *A Reporter's Field Guide* (handbook); *A Reporter's Guide to American Indian Law* (handbook); *A Reporter's Guide to Medical Privacy Law* (handbook); *A Reporter's Guide to Military Justice* (handbook); *Reporter's Recording Guide* (handbook); *Secret Dockets* (handbook); *Secret Juries* (handbook); *SLAPP Stick* (handbook); *Sunshine Inc* (handbook); *Warrants & Wiretaps* (handbook); *White Paper: Military Dockets* (handbook)

Le Reseau EdCan, see EdCan Network

Romance Writers of America®
14615 Benfer Rd, Houston, TX 77069
Tel: 832-717-5200 *Fax:* 832-717-5201
E-mail: info@rwa.org
Web Site: www.rwa.org
Key Personnel
Exec Dir: Leslie Scantlebury *Tel:* 832-717-5200 ext 123 *E-mail:* leslie.scantlebury@rwa.org
Ed & Pubns Mgr: Erin Fry *Tel:* 832-717-5200 ext 122 *E-mail:* erin.fry@rwa.org
Mktg & PR Mgr: Jessie Edwards *Tel:* 832-717-5200 ext 128 *E-mail:* jessie.edwards@rwa.org
Spec Projs Mgr: Megan Sloan *Tel:* 832-717-5200 ext 120 *E-mail:* megan.sloan@rwa.org
Membership Servs Admin: Donna Mathoslah *Tel:* 832-717-5200 ext 121 *E-mail:* donna.
  mathoslah@rwa.org
Founded: 1980
Romance Writers of America is dedicated to advancing the professional interests of career-focused romance writers through networking & advocacy.
Membership: $99/yr, $25 processing fee (new & reinstating).
Number of Members: 10,000
2021 Meeting(s): Annual Conference, Gaylord Opryland Resort & Convention Center, 2800 Opryland Dr, Nashville, TN, July 14-17, 2021
2022 Meeting(s): Annual Conference, Gaylord Opryland Resort & Convention Center, 2800 Opryland Dr, Nashville, TN, July 27-30, 2022
Publication(s): *Romance Writers Report* (monthly, magazine, free to membs)

SABEW, see Society for Advancing Business Editing & Writing (SABEW)

Saskatchewan Arts Board
1355 Broad St, Regina, SK S4R 7V1, Canada
Tel: 306-787-4056 *Toll Free Tel:* 800-667-7526 (CN) *Fax:* 306-787-4199
E-mail: info@saskartsboard.ca
Web Site: www.saskartsboard.ca
Key Personnel
CEO: Michael Jones
Dir, Admin: Gail Paul Armstrong
Founded: 1948
Provide consultation, advice, grants, programs +/or services to individual artists, arts groups & organizations & members of the public. Programs support & encourage the development of artists, arts groups & organizations in the literary, performing, visual, media & multidisciplinary arts. Also develop & maintain a permanent collection of original works by Saskatchewan artists.
Branch Office(s)
201 Avenue "B" S, Saskatoon, SK S7M 1M3, Canada *Tel:* 306-964-1155 *Fax:* 306-964-1167

Science Fiction & Fantasy Writers of America Inc (SFWA)
PO Box 3238, Enfield, CT 06083-3238
Tel: 860-698-0536
E-mail: office@sfwa.org
Web Site: www.sfwa.org
Key Personnel
Pres: Cat Rambo *E-mail:* cat.rambo@sfwa.org
VP: Erin M Hartshorn *E-mail:* erin.hartshorn@
  sfwa.org

Treas & CFO: Bud Sparhawk *E-mail:* bud.
sparhawk@sfwa.org
Secy: Curtis Chen *E-mail:* curtis.chen@sfwa.org
Exec Dir: Kathryn Baker
Founded: 1965
An organization of professional writers, editors,
artists, agents & others in the science fiction &
fantasy field.
Number of Members: 1,900
New Election: Annually in May
Publication(s): *Annual Membership Directory;*
SFWA Bulletin (quarterly, $32/yr nonmembs,
$48/yr foreign nonmembs, $38 CN/Mexico)

SF Canada
516 Ninth St E, Saskatoon, SK S7N 0B1, Canada
Web Site: www.sfcanada.org
Key Personnel
Pres: Robert Dawson
VP: Judy McCrosky
Secy-Treas: Kristin Janz
Founded: 1989
Exists to foster a sense of community among
Canadian writers of speculative fiction, to im-
prove communication between Canadian writ-
ers of speculative fiction, to foster the growth
of quality writing in Canadian speculative fic-
tion, to lobby on behalf of Canadian writers of
speculative fiction & to encourage the transla-
tion of Canadian speculative fiction. Supports
positive social action.
Number of Members: 152

SHARP, see Society for the History of
Authorship, Reading & Publishing Inc
(SHARP)

SIBA, see Southern Independent Booksellers
Alliance

**Small Publishers, Artists & Writers Network
(SPAWN)**
1129 Maricopa Hwy, No 142, Ojai, CA 93023
E-mail: info@spawn.org
Web Site: spawn.org
Key Personnel
Pres: Kathleen Kaiser
Secy-Treas: Faith Strader
Founded: 1996
Provides education, information, resources & a
supportive networking environment for creative
individuals & small business owners interested
in the publishing process.
Number of Members: 200
Publication(s): *SPAWNews* (newsletter)

**Social Sciences & Humanities Research
Council of Canada (SSHRC)**
350 Albert St, Ottawa, ON K1P 6G4, Canada
Mailing Address: PO Box 1610, Ottawa, ON K1P
6G4, Canada
Tel: 613-992-0691; 613-996-6976
E-mail: research@sshrc-crsh.gc.ca
Web Site: www.sshrc.ca
Key Personnel
Pres: Ted Hewitt
EVP: Brent Herbert-Copley
VP & CFO: Patricia Sauve-McCuan
VP, Res Progs: Dominique Berube
Assoc VP, Future Challenges: Ursula Gobel
Offers 2 programs of support for scholarly pub-
lishing: Aid to scholarly publication program,
aid to research & transfer journal program.
Only Canadian citizens or permanent residents
of Canada are eligible to apply under either
program. SSHRC is a Federal Crown Corpora-
tion.
Number of Members: 22

Sociedad Interamericana de Prensa (SIP), see
Inter American Press Association (IAPA)

**Society for Advancing Business Editing &
Writing (SABEW)**
Walter Cronkite School of Journalism & Mass
Communication, Arizona State University,
555 N Central Ave, Suite 406E, Phoenix, AZ
85004-1248
Tel: 602-496-7862
E-mail: sabew@sabew.org
Web Site: sabew.org
Key Personnel
Exec Dir: Kathleen Graham *Tel:* 202-549-0158
E-mail: kgraham@sabew.org
Membership Coord: Tess McLaughlin *Tel:* 602-
496-7862 *E-mail:* tmclaughlin@sabew.org
Dir of New Initiatives & Partnerships: Renee Mc-
Givern *Tel:* 651-210-0911 *E-mail:* rmcgivern@
sabew.org
Founded: 1964
Professional development. Sponsor regional work-
shops. Specialize in business journalism.
Number of Members: 3,500
Meeting(s): Spring Conference

Society for Features Journalism (SFJ)
University of Maryland, Philip Merrill College of
Journalism, 1100 Knight Hall, College Park,
MD 20742
Tel: 301-314-2631 *Fax:* 301-314-9166
Web Site: featuresjournalism.org
Key Personnel
Exec Dir: Merrilee Cox *E-mail:* merrileesfj@
gmail.com
Founded: 1947 (as AASFE - American Associa-
tion of Sunday & Feature Editors)
Nonprofit trade association of Sunday & feature
editors.
Number of Members: 250
Publication(s): *Style Magazine* (annual)

Society for Scholarly Publishing (SSP)
1120 Rte 73, Suite 200, Mount Laurel, NJ 08054
Tel: 856-439-1385 *Fax:* 856-439-0525
E-mail: info@sspnet.org
Web Site: www.sspnet.org
Key Personnel
Exec Dir: Melanie Dolechek
E-mail: mdolechek@sspnet.org
Prog Dir: Helen Szigeti *E-mail:* hszigetissp@
gmail.com
Gen Mgr: Crystal Stone
Memb Servs Coord: Jan Kalne
Founded: 1978
Professional association for people in scholarly
publishing industry; 12-16 seminars/workshops
sponsored each year.
Number of Members: 1,000
2021 Meeting(s): Annual Meeting, Gaylord Na-
tional Resort, National Harbor, MD, May 26-
28, 2021
2022 Meeting(s): Annual Meeting, Sheraton
Chicago Hotel & Towers, Chicago, IL, June
1-3, 2022
2023 Meeting(s): Annual Meeting, Oregon Convention Center & Hyatt Regency Portland,
Portland, OR, May 31-June 2, 2023
2024 Meeting(s): Annual Meeting, Westin Waterfront, Boston, MA, May 29-31, 2024
2025 Meeting(s): Annual Meeting, Hilton Baltimore, Baltimore, MD, May 28-31, 2025
Publication(s): *Directory* (annual, membs only)

Society for Technical Communication
9401 Lee Hwy, Suite 300, Fairfax, VA 22031
Tel: 703-522-4114 *Fax:* 703-522-2075
E-mail: stc@stc.org
Web Site: www.stc.org
Key Personnel
CEO: Liz Pohland *Tel:* 571-366-1901 *E-mail:* liz.
pohland@stc.org
Founded: 1960 (as Society of Technical Writers
& Publishers)

Professional society dedicated to the advancement
of the theory & practice of technical communication in all media.
Number of Members: 5,000
Publication(s): *Intercom* (monthly, magazine,
electronic version free to membs; print version
$60/yr membs, $160/yr nonmembs, $185/yr
nonmembs CN, $215/yr nonmembs elsewhere);
Technical Communication (quarterly, journal,
free to membs, $275/yr nonmembs, electronic)

**Society for the History of Authorship, Reading
& Publishing Inc (SHARP)**
c/o Johns Hopkins University Press, Journals Pub-
lishing Div, PO Box 19966, Baltimore, MD
21211-0966
Tel: 410-516-6987 *Toll Free Tel:* 800-548-1784
Fax: 410-516-3866
E-mail: jrnlcirc@press.jhu.edu
Web Site: www.sharpweb.org
Founded: 1993
Promotes the study of book history among aca-
demics & nonacademics. Publishing & schol-
arly attention to its history.
Number of Members: 1,175
Publication(s): *Book History* (annual, journal, in-
cluded with indiv membership, $73/yr instns);
SHARP News (enewsletter); *SHARP Online
Membership & Periodicals Directory* (annual,
access to online included with membership)
Membership(s): American Council of Learned
Societies (ACLS)

Society of American Travel Writers (SATW)
17W110 22 St, One Parkview Plaza, Suite 800,
Oakbrook Terrace, IL 60181
E-mail: info@satw.org
Web Site: www.satw.org
Key Personnel
Exec Dir: Marla Schrager *E-mail:* mschrager@
satw.org
Membership Coord: Jocelyn Padilla *Tel:* 847-686-
2284 *E-mail:* jpadilla@satw.org
Founded: 1955
Promote responsible journalism, provide profes-
sional support & development for our mem-
bers, encourage the conservation & preserva-
tion of travel resources worldwide.
Number of Members: 1,100
Publication(s): *Membership Directory* (annual,
$250 print (+ $7.50 S&H) or as online PDF)

**Society of Children's Book Writers &
Illustrators (SCBWI)**
6363 Wilshire Blvd, Suite 425, Los Angeles, CA
90048
Tel: 323-782-1010
E-mail: membership@scbwi.org
Web Site: www.scbwi.org
Key Personnel
Chief Equity & Inclusion Offr: April Powers
Pres: Stephen Mooser *E-mail:* stephenmooser@
scbwi.org
Exec Dir: Lin Oliver *E-mail:* linoliver@scbwi.org
Dir, Community Mktg & Engagement: Tammy
Brown
Dir, Opers & Membership Coord: Gee Cee Addi-
son Bahador *E-mail:* gcaddison@scbwi.org
Founded: 1971
An organization of children's writers & illustra-
tors & others devoted to the interests of chil-
dren's literature; annual workshops & confer-
ences throughout the world.
Number of Members: 22,000
Meeting(s): Summer Conference, annually in
July/Aug
2021 Meeting(s): Winter Conference, New York
Hilton Midtown, New York, NY, Feb 19-21,
2021
Publication(s): *SCBWI Bulletin* (6 issues/yr, free
to membs)

Society of Illustrators (SI)
128 E 63 St, New York, NY 10065
Tel: 212-838-2560 *Fax:* 212-838-2561
E-mail: info@societyillustrators.org
Web Site: www.societyillustrators.org
Key Personnel
Exec Dir: Anelle Miller *E-mail:* anelle@
societyillustrators.org
Dir, Opers: John Capobianco *E-mail:* john@
societyillustrators.org
Founded: 1901
Formed to promote the art of illustration. The
society houses the Museum of American Illus-
tration.
Number of Members: 950
New Election: Annually in June
Publication(s): *American Illustration* (annual,
$45)

The Society of Midland Authors (SMA)
PO Box 10419, Chicago, IL 60610
E-mail: info@midlandauthors.com
Web Site: www.midlandauthors.com
Founded: 1915
Nonprofit writer's association that seeks to stimulate creative efforts & closer association
among Midwest writers; maintain collections of
writer's works & encourage interest in reading,
literature & writing in cooperation with other
educational & cultural institutions. Members
are qualified authors & co-authors of works
from recognized publishers or associates (non-
voting) who live in Illinois, Indiana, Kansas,
Michigan, Minnesota, Missouri or Nebraska.
Monthly literary & professional programs, annual awards dinner, $500 & recognition plaque,
for best books of previous year in six categories: adult fiction, adult nonfiction, poetry,
biography & memoirs (adult), children's fiction,
children's nonfiction.
Number of Members: 400
Publication(s): *Literary License* (8 issues/yr,
newsletter)

Society of Motion Picture & Television Engineers® (SMPTE®)
3 Barker Ave, 5th fl, White Plains, NY 10601
Tel: 914-761-1100 *Fax:* 914-761-3115
Web Site: www.smpte.org
Key Personnel
Exec Dir: Barbara Lange *Tel:* 914-205-2370
Dir, Events & Governance Liaison: Sally-Ann
D'Amato *Tel:* 914-205-2375
Dir, Membership: Roberta Gorman *Tel:* 914-205-
2376
Dir, Philanthropy: Mary Vinton *Tel:* 914-205-
2380
Dir, Standards & Engg: Howard Lukk *Tel:* 914-
205-2371
Mktg & Communs: Aimee Ricca *Tel:* 914-205-
2381
Founded: 1916
To advance theory & practice of engineering in
film, TV, motion imaging & allied arts & sci-
ences; establishment of standards & practices.
Annual membership dues are $145.
Number of Members: 6,800
Publication(s): *SMPTE Motion Imaging Jour-
nal* (8 issues/yr, journal, $185/yr US & CN,
$200/yr elsewhere, free to membs)

The Society of Southwestern Authors (SSA)
PO Box 30355, Tucson, AZ 85751-0355
E-mail: info@ssa-az.org
Web Site: www.ssa-az.org
Key Personnel
Pres: Rajendra Srivastava
E-mail: rajendrasrivastava@outlook.com
VP: Chris Stern *E-mail:* azwritten@gmail.com
Treas: Jay McCall *E-mail:* jmcca11415@msn.com
Recording Secy: Mary Ann Carman
E-mail: macarman@centurylink.net

Founded: 1972
Nonprofit association of writers & other publishing professionals. Sponsors a writing contest
which includes three categories: short story,
personal essay/memoirs & poetry.
Number of Members: 400
Publication(s): *The Write Word* (6 issues/yr,
newsletter, free to membs)

Software & Information Industry Association (SIIA)
1090 Vermont Ave NW, 6th fl, Washington, DC
20005-4905
Tel: 202-289-7442 *Fax:* 202-289-7097
Web Site: www.siia.net
Key Personnel
Pres: Jeff Joseph
VP, Fin & Opers: Carl Walker
VP, Membership & Mktg: Michelle Harris
Sr Dir, HR & Admin: Katrina Styles-Hunt
Principal trade association of the software & in-
formation industry.
Number of Members: 850
Publication(s): *Upgrade* (6 issues/yr, magazine,
free to membs, $79 nonmembs)

Southern California Independent Booksellers Association (SCIBA), see California Independent Booksellers Alliance (CALIBA)

Southern Independent Booksellers Alliance
51 Pleasant Ridge Dr, Asheville, NC 28805
Tel: 803-994-9530 *Fax:* 309-410-0211
E-mail: siba@sibaweb.com
Web Site: www.sibaweb.com
Key Personnel
Exec Dir: Linda-Marie Barrett
E-mail: lindamarie@sibaweb.com
Number of Members: 500
2021 Meeting(s): SIBA Discovery Show, Mar-
riott/Embassy Suites & Benton Convention
Center, Winston-Salem, NC, Sept 18-20, 2021
Publication(s): *SEBA Holiday Catalog*

Special Libraries Association (SLA)
7918 Jones Branch Dr, Suite 300, McLean, VA
22102
Tel: 703-647-4900 *Fax:* 703-506-3266
Web Site: www.sla.org
Key Personnel
Deputy CEO: Doug Newcomb *Tel:* 703-647-4923
E-mail: dnewcomb1@sla.org
CFO: Linda N Broussard *Tel:* 703-647-4938
E-mail: lbroussard@sla.org
Exec Dir: Amy Burke *E-mail:* aburke@sla.org
Dir, Membership: Paula Diaz *Tel:* 703-647-4926
E-mail: pdiaz@sla.org
Founded: 1909
Serial & nonserial publications; public relations;
professional development; employment clear-
inghouse; resume referral service; computer-
assisted, self-study programs; chapters, di-
visions, student groups & caucuses; govern-
ment relations; fund development; scholarships;
grants; honors & awards; annual conference &
exhibit; winter meeting; information resources
center.
Number of Members: 8,000
Meeting(s): Annual Conference & INFO-EXPO
Publication(s): *Information Outlook* (6 issues/yr,
ezine, $240)

Specialized Information Publishers Association (SIPA)
Division of Software & Information Industry Association (SIIA)
1090 Vermont Ave NW, 6th fl, Washington, DC
20005-4905
Tel: 202-289-7442 *Fax:* 202-289-7097
Web Site: www.siia.net/divisions/sipa-specialized-
information-publishers-association

Key Personnel
Mng Dir: Amanda McMaster *Tel:* 781-754-4469
E-mail: amcmaster@siia.net
Edit Dir: Ronn Levine *Tel:* 202-789-4491
E-mail: rlevine@siia.net
Members are subscription-based publishers rep-
resenting small & large companies. Activities
include e-mail, marketing, technical develop-
ments, copyright, business practices & editorial
development.
Number of Members: 200
Meeting(s): SIPA Annual Conference
Publication(s): *SIPAlert Daily*

Specialty Graphic Imaging Association (SGIA), see PRINTING United Alliance

Teachers & Writers Collaborative
540 Preston St, Booklyn, NY 11215
Tel: 212-691-6590 *Fax:* 212-675-0171
E-mail: info@twc.org
Web Site: www.twc.org
Key Personnel
Dir: Amy Swauger *E-mail:* aswauger@twc.org
Dir, Opers: Jade Triton *E-mail:* jtriton@twc.org
Educ Dir: Jordan Dann *E-mail:* jdann@twc.org
Founded: 1967
Information source for those interested in teach-
ing writing & literary arts; publish books &
magazines about creative writing; sponsor
workshops. Basic annual membership: $35.
Publication(s): *Teachers & Writers* (quarterly,
ezine, free)

Technical Association of the Pulp & Paper Industry (TAPPI)
15 Technology Pkwy S, Suite 115, Peachtree Cor-
ners, GA 30092
Tel: 770-446-1400 *Toll Free Tel:* 800-332-8686
(US); 800-446-9431 (CN) *Fax:* 770-446-6947
E-mail: memberconnection@tappi.org
Web Site: www.tappi.org
Key Personnel
Pres & CEO: Larry N Montague
Press Mgr: Jana Jensen *Tel:* 770-209-7242
E-mail: jjensen@tappi.org
Founded: 1915
Technical association/nonprofit professional so-
ciety of executives, operating managers, en-
gineers, scientists & technologists serving the
pulp, paper & allied industries.
Number of Members: 8,477
2021 Meeting(s): PaperCon, Cobb Galleria Cen-
tre, Atlanta, GA, April 25-28, 2021; TAPPI/
AICC SuperCorrExpo®, Orange County Con-
vention Center, Orlando, FL, Aug 8-12, 2021;
PEERS Conference, Rhode Island Convention
Center & Omni Hotel, Providence, RI, Oct 31-
Nov 3, 2021
Publication(s): *Paper360* (6 issues/yr, free to
membs, print & electronic); *TAPPI JOURNAL*
(monthly, free to membs, electronic); *Tissue360*
(semiannual, free to membs, print & electronic)

Television Academy
5220 Lankershim Blvd, North Hollywood, CA
91601-3109
Tel: 818-754-2800 *Fax:* 818-761-2827
Web Site: www.emmys.com
Key Personnel
CEO & Chmn of the Bd: Bruce Rosenblum
CFO: Heather Cochran
Pres: Maury McIntyre
SVP, Awards: John Leverence
Founded: 1977
Organization for those involved in national televi-
sion; bestows Emmy awards for excellence in
television; college television awards & college
internship program; inducts deserving individu-
als in "Television Academy Hall of Fame".
Number of Members: 20,000
Publication(s): *EMMY Magazine*

Texas Institute of Letters (TIL)
PO Box 609, Round Rock, TX 78680
E-mail: president@texasinstituteofletters.org;
secretary@texasinstituteofletters.org
Web Site: www.texasinstituteofletters.org
Key Personnel
Pres: Carmen Tafolla
VP: Sergio Troncoso
Secy: Ann Weisgarber
Treas: W K Stratton
Recording Secy: Kurt Heinzelman
Founded: 1936
Nonprofit honor society to celebrate Texas literature & to recognize distinctive literary achievement. The TIL awards over $20,000 annually to recognize outstanding literary works in several categories & supports the Dobie Paisano Fellowship for writers.
Number of Members: 250
Publication(s): *Newsletter* (2 issues/yr, membs only)

Texas Library Association (TLA)
3355 Bee Cave Rd, Suite 401, Austin, TX 78746-6763
Tel: 512-328-1518 *Fax:* 512-328-8852
E-mail: tla@txla.org
Web Site: www.txla.org
Key Personnel
Exec Dir: Shirley Robinson *Tel:* 512-328-1518 ext 151 *E-mail:* shirleyr@txla.org
Dir, Advocacy & Commun: Wendy Woodland *Tel:* 512-328-1518 ext 146 *E-mail:* wendyw@txla.org
Coord, Membership & Spec Servs: Kelly Dibbens *Tel:* 512-328-1518 ext 153 *E-mail:* kellyd@txla.org
Founded: 1902
TLA is the largest state library association in the country promoting librarianship & library service in Texas.
Number of Members: 6,000
2021 Meeting(s): Annual Conference, San Antonio, TX, April 20-23, 2021
2022 Meeting(s): Annual Conference, Fort Worth, TX, April 25-28, 2022
2023 Meeting(s): Annual Conference, Austin, TX, April 19-22, 2023
2024 Meeting(s): Annual Conference, San Antonio, TX, April 16-19, 2024
2025 Meeting(s): Annual Conference, Dallas, TX, April 1-4, 2025
Publication(s): *Texas Library Journal* (quarterly); *Texline* (irregular, enewsletter); *TLA Weekly Brief* (enewsletter); *TLACast Newsletter* (6-8 issues/yr)

The Society of Professional Journalists (SPJ)
Eugene S Pulliam National Journalism Ctr, 3909 N Meridian St, Suite 200, Indianapolis, IN 46208
Tel: 317-927-8000 *Fax:* 317-920-4789
E-mail: spj@spj.org
Web Site: www.spj.org
Key Personnel
Exec Dir: Alison Bethel McKenzie *Tel:* 317-920-4780 *E-mail:* abmckenzie@spj.org
Assoc Exec Dir: Tara Puckey *Tel:* 317-927-8000 ext 215 *E-mail:* tpuckey@spj.org
Creative Dir: Tony Peterson *Tel:* 317-927-8000 ext 214 *E-mail:* tpeterson@spj.org
Founded: 1909 (as Sigma Delta Chi fraternity)
Professional organization that includes broadcast, print & online journalists, journalism educators & students interested in journalism as a career.
Number of Members: 9,000
2021 Meeting(s): Excellence in Journalism, Minneapolis, MN, Sept 24-26, 2021
Publication(s): *Quill* (6 issues/yr, magazine, $75/yr, free to membs)

Theatre Library Association (TLA)
c/o The New York Public Library for the Performing Arts, 40 Lincoln Center Plaza, New York, NY 10023
E-mail: TheatreLibraryAssociation@gmail.com
Web Site: www.tla-online.org/awards/bookawards
Key Personnel
Pres: Nancy Friedland
VP: Angela Weaver
Exec Secy: Laurie Murphy
Treas: Colleen Reilly
Founded: 1937
Supports librarians & archivists affiliated with theatre, dance, popular entertainment, performance studies, motion picture & broadcasting collections.
Publication(s): *Performing Arts Resources* (irregularly, series)

United for Libraries
Division of The American Library Association (ALA)
859 W Lancaster Ave, Unit 2-1, Bryn Mawr, PA 19010
Tel: 312-280-2161 *Toll Free Tel:* 800-545-2433 (ext 2161) *Fax:* 484-698-7868
E-mail: united@ala.org
Web Site: www.ala.org/united
Key Personnel
Exec Dir: Beth Nawalinski *E-mail:* bnawalinski@ala.org
Mgr, Mktg & Membership: Jillian Wentworth *E-mail:* jwentworth@ala.org
Founded: 2009
Supports those who govern, promote, advocate & fundraise for libraries & brings together library trustees, advocates, friends & foundations into a partnership that creates a powerful force for libraries in the 21st century.
Number of Members: 4,000

United Nations Association of the United States of America
1750 Pennsylvania Ave NW, Suite 300, Washington, DC 20006
Tel: 202-887-9040
Web Site: www.unausa.org
Key Personnel
Exec Dir: Chris Whatley *E-mail:* cwhatley@unausa.org
Sr Dir, Membership & Progs: Rachel Pittman *E-mail:* rpittman@unfoundation.org
Communs Offr: Lauren Dickinson *E-mail:* ldickinson@unausa.org
Founded: 1946
Publications, nonprofit information & educational services about international affairs & organizations.
Number of Members: 25,000
Branch Office(s)
801 Second Ave, 9th fl, New York, NY 10017 *Tel:* 212-697-3315 *Fax:* 212-697-3316

US Board on Books For Young People (USBBY)
Division of International Board on Books for Young People (IBBY)
c/o V Ellis Vance, 5503 N El Adobe Dr, Fresno, CA 93711-2363
Tel: 559-351-6119
Web Site: www.usbby.org
Key Personnel
Exec Dir: V Ellis Vance *E-mail:* executive.director@usbby.org
Founded: 1953
To promote international understanding & goodwill through books for children & adolescents.
Number of Members: 500
Publication(s): *Bridges: A Publication of USBBY* (semiannual, newsletter)

Membership(s): American Library Association (ALA); The Children's Book Council (CBC); International Literacy Association (ILA); National Council of Teachers of English (NCTE)

USBE: United States Book Exchange
2969 W 25 St, Cleveland, OH 44113
Tel: 216-241-6960 *Fax:* 216-241-6966
E-mail: usbe@usbe.com
Web Site: www.usbe.com
Key Personnel
Mng Dir: John T Zubal; Marilyn Zubal
Redistribution of library materials to & from libraries.
Number of Members: 16,000

Visual Artists & Galleries Association Inc (VAGA)
111 Broadway, Suite 1006, New York, NY 10006
Tel: 212-736-6666 *Fax:* 212-736-6767
E-mail: info@vagarights.com
Web Site: vagarights.com
Key Personnel
Exec Dir: Robert Panzer *E-mail:* rpanzer@vagarights.com
Protects artists copyrights; provides art licensing & reproduction rights clearances & royalties collection for artists. Have archive of color transparencies & B&W images.
Number of Members: 18,000

Visual Media Alliance (VMA)
Affiliate of PRINTING United Alliance
665 Third St, Suite 500, San Francisco, CA 94107-1926
Tel: 415-495-8242 *Toll Free Tel:* 800-659-3363 *Toll Free Fax:* 800-824-1911
E-mail: info@vma.bz
Web Site: main.vma.bz
Key Personnel
Pres: Dan Nelson *Tel:* 415-489-7617 *E-mail:* dan@vma.bz
Trade association.
Number of Members: 950

Western Writers of America Inc (WWA)
271 CR 219, Encampment, WY 82325
Tel: 307-329-8942
Web Site: westernwriters.org
Key Personnel
Pres: Kirk Ellis *E-mail:* president@westernwriters.org
Exec Dir & Secy-Treas: Candy Moulton *E-mail:* wwa.moulton@gmail.com
Founded: 1953
Nonprofit confederation of professional writers of fiction & nonfiction pertaining to, or inspired by, tradition, legends, development & history of the American West.
Number of Members: 650
2021 Meeting(s): Annual Convention, Embassy Suites by Hilton Loveland Hotel Conference Center & Spa, 4705 Clydesdale Pkwy, Loveland, CO, June 16-19, 2021
Publication(s): *Roundup Magazine* (6 issues/yr, $40/yr)

Willamette Writers
5331 SW Macadam Ave, Suite 258, PMB 215, Portland, OR 97239
Tel: 901-200-5385
E-mail: wilwrite@willamettewriters.org
Web Site: willamettewriters.org
Key Personnel
VP & Secy: Gail Pasternack *E-mail:* secretary@willamettewriters.org
Monthly meeting (open to public); critique groups; writer referrals; monthly newsletter; annual writing contest & awards, annual conference.

Number of Members: 1,450
Publication(s): *The Willamette Writer* (monthly, free to membs)

Women Who Write Inc

PO Box 652, Madison, NJ 07940-0652
E-mail: info@womenwhowrite.org
Web Site: womenwhowrite.org
Key Personnel
Pres: Dana Faulkner-Punzo
VP, Membership: Diane Masucci
Ed, Writers' Notes: Maria Dewaik
Founded: 1988
Writing groups, writers' conference, workshops, readings, literary events, newsletter & literary magazine.
Number of Members: 120
Publication(s): *Goldfinch* (annual, magazine, $10); *Writers' Notes* (quarterly, newsletter)

Women's Fiction Writers Association (WFWA)

PO Box 190, Jefferson, OR 97352
E-mail: communications@womensfictionwriters.org; membership@womensfictionwriters.org
Web Site: www.womensfictionwriters.org
Key Personnel
Pres: Tasha Seegmiller *E-mail:* president@womensfictionwriters.org
VP, Communs: Kerstin March
VP, Fin & Treas: M M Finck *E-mail:* treasurer@womensfictionwriters.org
Membership Dir: Rebecca Hodge
Secy: Michele Montgomery *E-mail:* michele@mimont.com
Founded: 2013
Community of career-focused women's fiction writers providing networking, education & continuing support in their career growth.
Meeting(s): Annual Retreat, Sept
Publication(s): *Read ON!* (monthly, newsletter); *Write ON!* (quarterly, ezine)

Women's National Book Association Inc

PO Box 237, FDR Sta, New York, NY 10150-0231
Toll Free Tel: 866-610-WNBA (610-9622)
E-mail: info@wnba-books.org
Web Site: www.wnba-books.org; www.NationalReadingGroupMonth.org; www.wnba-centennial.org
Founded: 1917
Increase opportunities for women & recognition of women in the world of books. Sponsor WNBA Award since 1940, WNBA Pannell Award & WNBA Eastman Grant. Twelve chapters: Atlanta, Boston, Charlotte, Detroit, Greater Lansing, Los Angeles, Nashville, New Orleans, New York, San Francisco, Seattle & Washington, DC.
Number of Members: 1,000
New Election: Biennially in May, odd-numbered yrs
Publication(s): *The Bookwoman* (6 issues/yr + 2 spec issues, free to membs, www.wnba-books.org/bookwoman)

Writers' Alliance of Newfoundland & Labrador

Haymarket Sq, 223 Duckworth St, Suite 202, St John's, NL A1C 6N1, Canada
Tel: 709-739-5215 *Toll Free Tel:* 866-739-5215
E-mail: info@wanl.ca
Web Site: wanl.ca

Key Personnel
Exec Dir: Wendi Smallwood
Founded: 1987
Not-for-profit, member-based organization established to contribute to a supportive environment for writing & serve the needs & protect the rights of writers in the province.
Number of Members: 250
New Election: Annually in Fall

Writers' Federation of Nova Scotia

1113 Marginal Rd, Halifax, NS B3H 4P7, Canada
Tel: 902-423-8116 *Fax:* 902-422-0881
E-mail: contact@writers.ns.ca; programs@writers.ns.ca
Web Site: writers.ns.ca
Key Personnel
Communs & Devt Offr: Robin Spittal
Founded: 1976
Foster creative writing & the profession of writing in the province of Nova Scotia; provide advice & assistance to writers at all stages of their careers; encourage greater public recognition of Nova Scotian writers & their achievements; enhance the literary arts in our regional & national culture.
Number of Members: 600
New Election: Annually in June
Publication(s): *Eastword* (6 issues/yr, newsletter, electronic version free to membs, hard copy $45/yr)

Writers' Guild of Alberta

11759 Groat Rd, Edmonton, AB T5M 3K6, Canada
Tel: 780-422-8174 *Toll Free Tel:* 800-665-5354 (AB only) *Fax:* 780-422-2663 (attn WGA)
E-mail: mail@writersguild.ca
Web Site: writersguild.ca
Key Personnel
Exec Dir: Carol Holmes *E-mail:* carol.holmes@writersguild.ca
Communs & Partnerships Coord: Ellen Kartz *E-mail:* ellen.kartz@writersguild.ca
Memb Servs Coord: Giorgia Severini
Progs Coord: Natalie Cook *E-mail:* natalie.cook@writersguild.ca; Julie Robinson *E-mail:* julie.robinson@writersguild.ca
Founded: 1980
Our mission is to support, encourage & promote writers & writing, to safeguard the freedom to write & to read & to advocate for the well-being of writers.
Number of Members: 1,000
Publication(s): *WestWord* (quarterly, magazine)
Branch Office(s)
505 21 Ave SW, Calgary, AB T2S 0G9, Canada, Prog Coord: Samantha Warwick *Tel:* 403-265-2226 *E-mail:* samathawarwick@writersguild.ca

Writers Guild of America, East (WGAE)

250 Hudson St, Suite 700, New York, NY 10013
Tel: 212-767-7800 *Fax:* 212-582-1909
Web Site: www.wgaeast.org
Key Personnel
Exec Dir: Lowell Peterson *Tel:* 212-767-7828 *E-mail:* lpeterson@wgaeast.org
Asst Exec Dir: Ruth Gallo *Tel:* 212-767-7823 *E-mail:* rgallo@wgaeast.org; Marsha Seeman *Tel:* 212-767-7820 *E-mail:* mseeman@wgaeast.org
Dir, Communs: Jason Gordon *Tel:* 212-767-7809 *E-mail:* jgordon@wgaeast.org
Dir, Organizing: Justin Molito *Tel:* 212-767-7808 *E-mail:* jmolito@wgaeast.org

Dir, Progs: Dana Weissman *Tel:* 212-767-7835 *E-mail:* dweissman@wgaeast.org
Communs Coord: Molly Beer *Tel:* 212-767-7886 *E-mail:* mbeer@wgaeast.org
Events Coord: Nancy Hathorne *Tel:* 212-767-7812 *E-mail:* nhathorne@wgaeast.org
Membership Admin: Kelly O'Brien *Tel:* 212-767-7821 *E-mail:* kobrien@wgaeast.org
Labor union representing professional writers in motion pictures, TV, radio, as well as digital media content. Membership available only through the sale of literary material or employment for writing services in one of these areas.
Number of Members: 4,200
New Election: Annually in Sept
Publication(s): *On Writing* (online web series)

Writers Guild of America, West (WGAW)

7000 W Third St, Los Angeles, CA 90048
Tel: 323-951-4000 *Toll Free Tel:* 800-548-4532 *Fax:* 323-782-4800
Web Site: www.wga.org
Key Personnel
Pres: Howard Rodman
VP: David Goodman
Secy & Treas: Aaron Mendelsohn
Labor union: Collective bargaining representation for film, TV broadcast, interactive & new media writers. Awards dinner & seminars (sometimes for public).
Number of Members: 12,000
Publication(s): *Written By Magazine* (6 issues/yr, $50/yr)

Writers' League of Texas (WLT)

611 S Congress Ave, Suite 200 A-3, Austin, TX 78704
Tel: 512-499-8914
E-mail: wlt@writersleague.org
Web Site: www.writersleague.org
Key Personnel
Exec Dir: Becka Oliver *E-mail:* becka@writersleague.org
Prog Dir: Michael Noll *E-mail:* michael@writersleague.org
Memb Servs Mgr: Jordan Smith *E-mail:* jordan@writersleague.org
Founded: 1981
Workshops, seminars, classes, library resource center, technical assistance, newsletter, monthly programs, educational programs for young people. Memberships: $50 (indiv/family), $100 & up (premium), $250 & up (businesses & organizations).
Number of Members: 1,200
Publication(s): *Footnotes* (26 issues/yr, newsletter, free, electronic); *Scribe* (blog)

The Writers' Union of Canada (TWUC)

600-460 Richmond St W, Toronto, ON M5V 1Y1, Canada
Tel: 416-703-8982 *Fax:* 416-504-9090
E-mail: info@writersunion.ca
Web Site: www.writersunion.ca
Key Personnel
Exec Dir: John Degen *Tel:* 416-703-8982 ext 221
Assoc Dir: Siobhan O'Connor *Tel:* 416-703-8982 ext 222 *E-mail:* soconnor@writersunion.ca
Off Admin: Valerie Laws *Tel:* 416-703-8982 ext 224
Specialize in service for members & non-members including publications, newsletter, contract advice, competitions, ms evaluation & advocacy.
Number of Members: 2,000

Foundations

Listed below are foundations that are closely affiliated with the book trade.

Bridge to Asia
1505 Juanita Way, Berkeley, CA 94702-1103
Tel: 510-665-3998
E-mail: asianet@bridge.org
Web Site: www.bridge.org
Key Personnel
Pres: Jeffrey Smith
VP: Newton Liu
Founded: 1987
A nonprofit book donation program, which provides donated books, journals & Internet based research services to developing countries in Asia. Primary book donors include members of the American Council of Learned Societies, the Nebraska Book Company, Follett Higher Education Group & several thousand individual book donors.

The Canadian Writers' Foundation Inc (La Fondation des Ecrivains Canadiens)
PO Box 13281, Kanata Sta, Ottawa, ON K2K 1X4, Canada
Tel: 613-256-6937 *Fax:* 613-256-5457
E-mail: info@canadianwritersfoundation.org
Web Site: www.canadianwritersfoundation.org
Key Personnel
Pres: Marianne Scott *Tel:* 613-733-4223
  Fax: 613-733-8752
Exec Secy: Suzanne Williams *E-mail:* smw.
  enterprises@sympatico.ca
Founded: 1931
Benevolent trust. Provides financial assistance to distinguished senior Canadian writers in need.

La Foundation des Ecrivains Canadiens, see The Canadian Writers' Foundation Inc (La Fondation des Ecrivains Canadiens)

Graphic Arts Education & Research Foundation (GAERF)
1899 Preston White Dr, Reston, VA 20191
Tel: 703-264-7200
E-mail: gaerf@npes.org
Web Site: www.gaerf.org
Key Personnel
Pres: Thayer Long
EVP: Judith B Durham *E-mail:* jdurham@npes.
  org
Founded: 1983
A major source of financial support for projects & programs designed to provide a graphic communications work force for the future.

John Simon Guggenheim Memorial Foundation
90 Park Ave, New York, NY 10016
Tel: 212-687-4470 *Fax:* 212-697-3248
Web Site: www.gf.org
Key Personnel
Chmn: William P Kelly

Pres: Edward Hirsch
Founded: 1925
Provide fellowships to further the development of scholars & artists by assisting them to engage in research in any field of knowledge & creation in any of the arts; awarded to persons who have already demonstrated exceptional capacity for productive scholarship or exceptional creative ability in the arts.

The Zora Neale Hurston/Richard Wright Foundation
10 "G" St NE, Suite 600, Washington, DC 20002
Tel: 202-248-5051
E-mail: info@hurstonwright.org
Web Site: www.hurstonwright.org
Key Personnel
Co-Founder: Marita Golden; Clyde McElvane
Exec Dir: Kesha Lee
Founded: 1990
Dedicated to discovering, mentoring & honoring Black writers. Through workshops, master classes & readings, the organization preserves the voices of Black writers in the world literary canon, serves as a community for writers & continues a tradition of literary excellence in storytelling established by its namesakes. 501(c)(3) nonprofit.

Lannan Foundation
313 Read St, Santa Fe, NM 87501-2628
Tel: 505-986-8160
E-mail: info@lannan.org
Web Site: lannan.org
Key Personnel
Pres: Patrick Lannan
VP & Dir of Opers: Frank C Lawler
Prog Dir, Literary & Residency Progs: Martha Jessup
Founded: 1960
Family foundation dedicated to cultural freedom, diversity & creativity through projects supporting contemporary artists & writers. Grants given to nonprofit organizations in the areas of contemporary visual art, literature, indigenous communities & cultural freedom. Awards & fellowships also given.

National Book Foundation
90 Broad St, Suite 604, New York, NY 10004
Tel: 212-685-0261 *Fax:* 212-213-6570
E-mail: nationalbook@nationalbook.org
Web Site: www.nationalbook.org
Key Personnel
Deputy Dir: Jordan Smith *E-mail:* jsmith@
  nationalbook.org
Dir, Technol: Meredith Andrews
  E-mail: mandrews@nationalbook.org
Assoc Dir, Awards: Anna Dobben
  E-mail: adobben@nationalbook.org

Communs & Mktg Mgr: Bev Rivero
  E-mail: brivero@nationalbook.org
Public Progs Mgr: Natalie Green
  E-mail: ngreen@nationalbook.org
Admin & Devt Coord: Dhyana Taylor
  E-mail: dtaylor@nationalbook.org
Presenter of the National Book Awards. The Foundation's mission is to celebrate the best literature in America, expand its audience & ensure that books have a prominent place in American culture.

National Endowment for the Arts
400 Seventh St SW, Washington, DC 20506-0001
Tel: 202-682-5400
Web Site: www.arts.gov
Key Personnel
Dir, Admin Servs: Greg Gendron *Tel:* 202-682-5561 *E-mail:* gendrong@arts.gov
Dir, Lit: Amy Stolls *Tel:* 202-682-5771
  E-mail: stollsa@arts.gov
Dir, Strategic Communs & Pub Aff: Helen Aguirre Ferre *Tel:* 202-682-5759
  E-mail: ferreh@arts.gov
Asst Dir, Press: Victoria Hutter *Tel:* 202-682-5692
  E-mail: hutterv@arts.gov
Asst Dir, Pubns: Don Ball *Tel:* 202-682-5750
  E-mail: balld@arts.gov
Founded: 1965
Independent federal agency. Grants to organizations & individuals.

Western States Arts Federation
1743 Wazee St, Suite 300, Denver, CO 80202
Tel: 303-629-1166 *Toll Free Tel:* 888-562-7232
  Fax: 303-629-9717
E-mail: staff@westaf.org
Web Site: www.westaf.org
Key Personnel
Exec Dir: Anthony Radich *E-mail:* anthony.
  radich@westaf.org
Dir, Mktg & Communs: Leah Horn *E-mail:* leah.
  horn@westaf.org
Assoc Dir: Seyan Lucero *E-mail:* seyan.lucero@
  westaf.org
Fin Assoc: Michelle Baca *E-mail:* michelle.
  baca@westaf.org
Performing, visual & folk arts programs.

The H W Wilson Foundation
750 Third Ave, 13th fl, New York, NY 10017
Tel: 212-418-8473
Web Site: www.thwwf.org
Key Personnel
Exec Dir: William Stanton
Pres: Harold Regan
VP & Treas: William Hayden
VP & Secy: Michael Regan
Founded: 1952
Scholarship grants to ALA accredited library & information science programs.

Calendar of Book Trade & Promotional Events— Alphabetical Index of Sponsors

Calendar of Book Trade & Promotional Events—Alphabetical Index of Events

Calendar of Book Trade & Promotional Events

Arranged chronologically by year and month, this section lists book trade events worldwide. Preceding this section are two indexes: the Sponsor Index is an alphabetical list of event sponsors and includes the names and dates of the events they sponsor; the Event Index is an alphabetical list of events along with the dates on which they are held.

2020

NOVEMBER

Feria Internacional del Libro de Guadalajara
Av Alemania 1370, Colonia Moderna, 44190
  Guadalajara, Jalisco, Mexico
Tel: (033) 3810 0331; (033) 3268 0900
E-mail: fil@fil.com.mx
Web Site: www.fil.com.mx
Key Personnel
Pres: Raul Padilla Lopez
Gen Dir: Marisol Schulz Manaut *E-mail:* marisol.
  schulz@fil.com.mx
Content Mgmt: Laura Niembro Diaz
  E-mail: laura.niembro@fil.com.mx
Prog Coord: Carolina Tapia Luna
  E-mail: carolina.tapia@fil.com.mx
Exhibitors Coord: Armando Montes de Santiago
  E-mail: armando.desantiago@fil.com.mx
Location: Centro de Exposiciones, Expo Guadala-
  jara, Av Mariano Otero, 1499, Col Verde Valle,
  Guadalajara, Jalisco, Mexico
Nov 28-Dec 6, 2020

Jewish Book Month
Sponsored by Jewish Book Council
520 Eighth Ave, 4th fl, New York, NY 10018
Tel: 212-201-2920 *Fax:* 212-532-4952
E-mail: info@jewishbooks.org
Web Site: www.jewishbookcouncil.org; www.
  facebook.com/JewishBookCouncil; twitter.
  com/jewishbook
Key Personnel
Exec Dir: Naomi Firestone-Teeter
Dir: Carolyn Starman Hessel
Dedicated to the celebration of Jewish books
  held annually during the month leading up to
  Hanukkah.
Location: Nationwide throughout the USA
Nov 10-Dec 10, 2020

DECEMBER

Didac India
Sponsored by Worlddidac Association
Bollwerk 21, 3011 Bern, Switzerland
Tel: (031) 311 76 82 *Fax:* (031) 312 17 44
E-mail: info@worlddidac.org
Web Site: didacindia.com; www.facebook.com/
  DidacIndia; www.worlddidac.org
Key Personnel
Proj & Communs Mgr: Kateryna Schuetz
  E-mail: schuetz@worlddidac.org
International exhibition for education, training,
  technology & supply.
Location: Pragati Maidan, New Delhi, India
Dec 2-4, 2020

EastPack®
Sponsored by Informa Markets
2901 28 St, Suite 100, Santa Monica, CA 90405
Tel: 310-445-4200
E-mail: clientservices@ubm.com
Web Site: informamarkets.com

Location: Pennsylvania Convention Center,
  Philadelphia, PA, USA
Dec 1-3, 2020

Salon du Livre et de la Presse Jeunesse (SLPJ)
Sponsored by Centre de Promotion du Livre de
  Jeunesse (CPLJ)
3, rue Francois Debergue, 93100 Montreuil,
  France
Tel: 01 55 86 86 55 *Fax:* 01 48 57 04 62
E-mail: contact@slpj.fr
Web Site: www.slpjplus.fr
Key Personnel
Dir: Sylvie Vassallo
Leading publishing event dedicated to children's
  books.
Location: Seine-Saint-Denis, France
Dec 2-7, 2020

Sofia International Book Fair
Sponsored by Bulgarian Book Association (BBA)
blvd Vitosha 64, 2nd fl, ap 4, 1463 Sofia, Bulgaria
Tel: (02) 958 15 25; (02) 958 92 11
E-mail: office@abk.bg
Web Site: www.abk.bg
Key Personnel
Event Mgr: Anna Filipova *E-mail:* filipova@abk.
  bg
The first Sofia International Book fair was organized in 1968. Since then it brings together
  over 40,000 visitors yearly to meet with ex-
  hibiting companies from Bulgaria & abroad &
  offers unrivaled access to the national & international book publishing & bookseller communities.
Location: National Palace of Culture, One Bulgaria Blvd, Sofia, Bulgaria
Dec 8-13, 2020

2021

JANUARY

**American Library Association Midwinter
  Meeting**
Sponsored by The American Library Association
  (ALA)
225 N Michigan Ave, Suite 1300, Chicago, IL
  60601
Tel: 312-944-6780 *Toll Free Tel:* 800-545-2433
  (conference servs) *Fax:* 312-440-9374
E-mail: ala@ala.org
Web Site: www.ala.org
Key Personnel
Registration & Servs Mgr: Alicia Hamann
  Tel: 800-545-2433 ext 3229 *E-mail:* ahamann@
  ala.org
Conference Dir: Earla Jones *Tel:* 800-545-2433
  ext 3226 *E-mail:* ejones@ala.org
Meeting Coord: Donna Hunter *Tel:* 800-545-2433
  ext 3218 *E-mail:* dhunter@ala.org
Conference Coord: Lina Zabaneh *Tel:* 800-545-
  2433 ext 3227 *E-mail:* lzabaneh@ala.org
Meeting Mgr: Yvonne McLean *Tel:* 800-545-2433
  ext 3222 *E-mail:* ymclean@ala.org

Location: Indianapolis, IN, USA
Jan 22-26, 2021

APE 2021
Sponsored by digiprimo GmbH & Co KG
Lutherstr 122, 14089 Berlin, Germany
Mailing Address: PO Box 22 01 16, 14061
  Berlin, Germany
Tel: (0171) 3660392
E-mail: info@ape2021.eu; info@digiprimo.com
Web Site: www.ape2021.eu; www.digiprimo.com
Location: Berlin, Germany
Jan 11-13, 2021

**Football Writers Association of America
  Annual Meeting**
Sponsored by Football Writers Association of
  America (FWAA)
18652 Vista del Sol, Dallas, TX 75287
Tel: 214-870-6516
Web Site: www.sportswriters.net/fwaa; twitter.
  com/thefwaa
Key Personnel
Exec Dir: Steve Richardson *E-mail:* tiger@fwaa.
  com
Location: JW Marriott Marquis, 225 Biscayne
  Blvd Way, Miami. FL, USA
Jan 8-11, 2021

IS&T Electronic Imaging Conference
Sponsored by Society for Imaging Science &
  Technology (IS&T)
7003 Kilworth Lane, Springfield, VA 22151
Tel: 703-642-9090 *Fax:* 703-642-9094
E-mail: info@imaging.org; ei@imaging.org
Web Site: www.imaging.org
Key Personnel
Exec Dir: Suzanne E Grinnan *E-mail:* sgrinnan@
  imaging.org
Conference Prog Mgr: Marion S Zoretich
  E-mail: mzoretich@imaging.org
Exec Asst: Donna Smith *E-mail:* dsmith@
  imaging.org
Location: Parc 55, 55 Cyril Magnin St, San Fran-
  cisco, CA, USA
Jan 17-21, 2021

MLA Annual Convention
Sponsored by Modern Language Association of
  America (MLA)
85 Broad St, Suite 500, New York, NY 10004-
  2434
SAN: 202-6422
Tel: 646-576-5266 (convention); 646-576-5000
  Fax: 646-458-0030
E-mail: convention@mla.org
Web Site: www.mla.org/convention
Key Personnel
Dir of Convention & Events: Karin L Bagnall
  E-mail: kbagnall@mla.org
Location: Toronto, ON, CN
Jan 7-10, 2021

Remainder & Promotional Book Fair
Sponsored by Ciana Ltd
6 Battle Rd, Heathfield, Newton Abbot TQ12
  6RY, United Kingdom
Tel: (01626) 897 106 *Fax:* (01626) 897 107
E-mail: enquiries@ciana.co.uk

Web Site: www.ciana.co.uk
Key Personnel
Contact: Sarah Weedon; Robert Collie
Location: ILEC Conference Centre, 47 Lillie Rd, London, UK
Jan 17-18, 2021

FEBRUARY

Adelaide Festival
Sponsored by Adelaide Festival Corp
Level 9, 33 King William St, Adelaide, SA 5000, Australia
Mailing Address: PO Box 8221, Station Arcade, Adelaide, SA 5000, Australia
Tel: (08) 8216 4444 *Fax:* (08) 8216 4455
E-mail: info@adelaidefestival.com.au
Web Site: www.adelaidefestival.com.au; facebook.com/adelaidefestival
Key Personnel
Artistic Dir: Neil Armfield; Rachel Healy
Deputy Exec Dir: Rachael Azzopard
Exec Asst & Prog Coord: Marta Davis
Annual event highlighting the arts, including literature. Adelaide Writers' Week is one of the high-profile events held during the festival.
Location: Adelaide's Central Business District, Adelaide, SA, Australia
Feb 26-March 14, 2021

Amelia Island Book Festival
PO Box 15286, Fernandina Beach, FL 32035
Tel: 904-624-1665
E-mail: info@ameliaislandbookfestival.org
Web Site: www.ameliaislandbookfestival.org; facebook.com/ameliaislandbookfestival
Festival engages adults & young people in the joy of reading & writing through a series of public events featuring New York Times bestselling authors, independent publishers & authors, awards programs & workshops.
Location: Fernandina Beach, FL, USA
Feb 11-13, 2021

California International Antiquarian Book Fair
Sponsored by Antiquarian Booksellers' Association of America (ABAA)
20 W 44 St, Suite 507, New York, NY 10036
Tel: 212-944-8291 *Fax:* 212-944-8293
E-mail: info@cabookfair.com
Web Site: www.cabookfair.com; www.abaa.org
Key Personnel
Exec Dir: Susan Benne *E-mail:* sbenne@abaa.org
Annual event co-sponsored by International League of Antiquarian Booksellers.
Location: Oakland Marriott City Center, 1001 Broadway, Oakland, CA, USA
Feb 12-14, 2021

CAMEX
Sponsored by National Association of College Stores (NACS)
500 E Lorain St, Oberlin, OH 44074
Tel: 440-775-7777 *Toll Free Tel:* 800-622-7498
Fax: 440-775-4769
E-mail: info@nacs.org
Web Site: www.camex.org; www.nacs.org
Key Personnel
CEO: Ed Schlichenmayer *Tel:* 800-622-7498 ext 2250 *E-mail:* eschlichenmayer@nacs.org
Sr Dir, Meetings & Expositions: Mary Adler-Kozak *Tel:* 800-622-7498 ext 2265 *E-mail:* madler-kozak@nacs.org
Dir, Meetings: Lynn Mangol *Tel:* 800-622-7498 ext 2612 *E-mail:* lmangol@nacs.org
Conference & trade show dedicated exclusively to the more than $10 billion collegiate retailing industry.

Location: Atlanta Convention Center, Atlanta, GA, USA
Feb 19-22, 2021

Savannah Book Festival
37 W Fairmont Ave, Suite 216, Savannah, GA 31406
Tel: 912-598-4040
E-mail: info@savannahbookfestival.org
Web Site: www.savannahbookfestival.org
Key Personnel
Exec Dir: Erika Dongre *E-mail:* erika@savannahbookfestival.org
Assoc Dir: Tara Setter *E-mail:* tara@savannahbookfestival.org
Promote reading, writing & civil conversation.
Location: Lucas Theatre & various locations around Telfair, Chippewa & Wright Squares in downtown Savannah, GA, USA
Feb 11-14, 2021

SCBWI Winter Conference
Sponsored by Society of Children's Book Writers & Illustrators (SCBWI)
6363 Wilshire Blvd, Suite 425, Los Angeles, CA 90048
Tel: 323-782-1010
E-mail: scbwi@scbwi.org
Web Site: www.scbwi.org
Key Personnel
Exec Dir: Lin Oliver *E-mail:* linoliver@scbwi.org
Location: New York Hilton Midtown, New York, NY, USA
Feb 19-21, 2021

Texas Outdoor Writers Association Annual Conference
Sponsored by Texas Outdoor Writers Association (TOWA)
PO Box 151293, Austin, TX 78715-1293
Tel: 512-358-8000 *Fax:* 512-358-8010
E-mail: towa@towa.org
Web Site: towa.org; www.facebook.com/TXOWA
Key Personnel
Exec Dir: Burney Brown
Location: Hampton Inn & Suites Port Arthur, 7660 Memorial Blvd, Port Arthur, TX, USA
Feb 27-28, 2021

WestPack®
Sponsored by Informa Markets
2901 28 St, Suite 100, Santa Monica, CA 90405
Tel: 310-445-4200
E-mail: clientservices@ubm.com
Web Site: informamarkets.com
Location: Anaheim Convention Center, 800 W Katella Ave, Anaheim, CA, USA
Feb 9-11, 2021

SPRING

BookCon
Sponsored by ReedPOP
Division of Reed Exhibitions USA
201 Merritt 7, Norwalk, CT 06851
Tel: 203-840-5632 (cust serv); 203-840-4800 *Toll Free Tel:* 800-777-8774
E-mail: inquiry@thebookcon.com
Web Site: www.thebookcon.com; www.reedpop.com
Key Personnel
Event Mgr: Jenny Martin *Tel:* 203-840-5454 *E-mail:* jenny@reedexpo.com
Consumer event following BookExpo.
Location: Jacob K Javits Convention Center, 655 W 43 St, New York, NY, USA
Spring 2021

BookExpo
Sponsored by ReedPOP
Division of Reed Exhibitions USA
201 Merritt 7, Norwalk, CT 06851
Tel: 203-840-4800 *Toll Free Tel:* 800-840-5614 (cust serv)
E-mail: inquiry@bookexpoamerica.com (cust serv)
Web Site: www.bookexpoamerica.com; www.reedpop.com
Key Personnel
Event Mgr: Jenny Martin *Tel:* 203-840-5454 *E-mail:* jenny@reedexpo.com
Produced & managed by ReedPOP, BookExpo is sponsored by the American Booksellers Association (ABA), the Association of American Publishers Inc (AAP) & the Association of Authors' Representatives Inc (AAR).
Location: Jacob K Javits Convention Center, 655 W 43 St, New York, NY, USA
Spring 2021

MARCH

AWP Annual Conference & Bookfair
Sponsored by Association of Writers & Writing Programs (AWP)
University of Maryland, 5245 Greenbelt Rd, Box 246, College Park, MD 20740
Mailing Address: University of Maryland, 5700 Rivertech Ct, Suite 225, Riverdale Park, MD 20737-1250
Tel: 240-696-7742 (conference); 240-696-7700
E-mail: events@awpwriter.org; awp@awpwriter.org
Web Site: www.awpwriter.org/awp_conference/; www.awpwriter.org
Key Personnel
Dir, Conferences: Cynthia Sherman
Mgr, Conference Events: Colleen Cable
Coord, Conference Events: Aubrey Kamppila
Location: Kansas City Convention Center, Kansas City, MO, USA
March 3-6, 2021

Dahlonega Literary Festival
PO Box 1401, Dahlonega, GA 30533
Web Site: literaryfestival.org
Key Personnel
Contact: Ken Smoke *E-mail:* kensmoke369@hotmail.com
An annual celebration of books & authors held in historic downtown Dahlonega, Georgia. Events are open to everyone & most are free, unless otherwise noted, & include individual presentations, panel discussions, workshops, a festival book store, book signings & more.
Location: Dahlonega, GA, USA
March 5-6, 2021

Leipzig Book Fair (Leipziger Buchmesse)
Sponsored by Leipziger Messe GmbH
Messe-Allee 1, 04356 Leipzig, Germany
Mailing Address: Postfach 10 07 20, 04007 Leipzig, Germany
Tel: (0341) 678-6950 *Fax:* (0341) 678-8242
E-mail: info@leipziger-buchmesse.de
Web Site: www.leipziger-buchmesse.de
Key Personnel
Dir: Oliver Zille
Held annually in conjunction with The Leipzig Antiquarian Book Fair.
Location: Leipzig Exhibition Centre, Messe-Allee 1, Leipzig, Germany
March 18-21, 2021

Livre Paris (Book Paris)
Sponsored by Reed Expositions France
Subsidiary of Reed Exhibition Companies

52-54 quai de Dion-Bouton, CS 80001, 92806
Puteaux Cedex, France
Tel: 01 47 56 50 00 *Fax:* 01 47 56 21 90
E-mail: info@reedexpo.fr
Web Site: www.livreparis.com
Key Personnel
Dir, Mktg & Communs: Audrey Farache
E-mail: audrey.farache@reedexpo.fr
Annual international publishing event for publishers, booksellers, teachers & librarians. Open to the trade & the public.
Location: Paris Expo, Porte de Versailles, Paris, France
March 19-21, 2021

The London Book Fair
Sponsored by Reed Exhibitions UK
Division of RELX Group PLC
Gateway House, 28 The Quadrant, Richmond, Surrey TW9 1DN, United Kingdom
Tel: (020) 8271 2124
E-mail: lbf.helpline@reedexpo.co.uk
Web Site: www.londonbookfair.co.uk
Key Personnel
Conference Mgr: Orna O'Brien *Tel:* (020) 8910 7906 *E-mail:* orna.obrien@reedexpo.co.uk
The London Book Fair is the global marketplace for rights negotiation & the sale & distribution of content across print, audio, TV, film & digital channels. Taking place every spring in the world's premier publishing & cultural capital, it is a unique opportunity to hear from authors, enjoy the vibrant atmosphere & explore innovations shaping the publishing world of the future. The London Book Fair brings you 3 days of focused access to customers, content & emerging markets.
Location: Olympia London, Hammersmith Rd, Kensington, London, UK
March 9-11, 2021

Palm Beach Book Festival
PO Box 3069, Palm Beach, FL 33480
Tel: 561-429-4008
E-mail: info@palmbeachbookfestival.com
Web Site: www.palmbeachbookfestival.com
Key Personnel
Founder & Creative Dir: Lois Cahall
Promotes culture while nurturing the published, written word for children & adults. Sponsored by Batmasian Family Foundation.
Location: Florida Atlantic University, 777 Glades Rd, Boca Raton, FL, USA
March 19-20, 2021

Paper2021
Sponsored by American Forest & Paper Association (AF&PA)
1101 "K" St NW, Suite 700, Washington, DC 20005
Tel: 202-463-2700
E-mail: info@afandpa.org
Web Site: www.afandpa.org; papermeets.com
Key Personnel
Dir of Meetings: Susan Van Eaton
Sr Mgr, Meetings & Memb Servs: Kathy Smith
Co-hosted with the National Paper Trade Association (NPTA), this annual paper industry event offers participants access to decision makers from an impressive array of manufacturers, merchants, publishers, distributors of printing paper, packaging material & industrial material & supplies.
Location: The Whitley Atlanta Buckhead, Atlanta, GA, USA
March 14-16, 2021

Southeastern Young Adult Book Festival
2822 Ruland Place, Murfreesboro, TN 37128
E-mail: info@seyabookfest.com
Web Site: www.seyabookfest.com

Key Personnel
Pres: Liz Hicks
VP: Lindsey Kimery
Treas: Barbara Collie
Secy: Sonya Cox
Encourage & develop literacy in young adults by connecting them with authors. 2021 conference will be held virtually.
March 11-13, 2021

Southern Kentucky Book Fest
WKU Libraries, Cravens 106, 1906 College Heights Blvd, Bowling Green, KY 42101-1067
Tel: 270-745-4502
E-mail: sokybookfest@wku.edu
Web Site: www.sokybookfest.org
Key Personnel
Dir, Warren County Public Lib: Lisa Rice
E-mail: lisar@warrenpl.org
The Southern Kentucky Book Fest is one of the state's largest literary events & is presented by WKU Libraries, Warren County Public Library & Barnes & Noble Booksellers. Book Fest is a fundraiser for the promotion of literacy in our community.
Location: Knicely Conference Center, 645 Campbell Lane, Bowling Green, KY, USA
March 26-27, 2021

Southwest Florida Reading Festival
Sponsored by Lee County Library System
2345 Union St, Fort Myers, FL 33901
Tel: 239-533-4800 *Fax:* 239-485-1100
Web Site: readfest.org
Key Personnel
Festival Coord: Melissa Baker *E-mail:* mbaker@leegov.com
The festival celebrates the importance of reading & brings the finest literary talent to Southwest Florida.
Location: Fort Myers Regional Library Campus, 2450 First St, Fort Myers, FL, USA
March 6, 2021

Tennessee Williams & New Orleans Literary Festival
938 Lafayette St, Suite 514, New Orleans, LA 70113
Tel: 504-581-1144
E-mail: info@tennesseewilliams.net
Web Site: tennesseewilliams.net
Key Personnel
Exec Dir: Paul J Willis
Mng Dir: Tracy Cunningham
The festival serves the community through educational, theatrical, literary & musical programs as well as nurtures, supports & showcases regional, national & international writers, actors, musicians & other artists. The festival also honors Tennessee Williams.
Location: New Orleans, LA, USA
March 24-28, 2021

Virginia Festival of the Book
Sponsored by Virginia Foundation for the Humanities
145 Ednam Dr, Charlottesville, VA 22903
Tel: 434-924-3296
E-mail: vabook@virginia.edu
Web Site: www.vabook.org
Key Personnel
Dir: Jane Kulow *Tel:* 434-924-7548
Annual public festival for children & adults featuring authors, illustrators, publishers, publicists, agents & other book professionals in panel discussions & readings. Most events are free. Hundreds of authors invited annually.
Location: Charlottesville, VA, USA
March 17-21, 2021

Woodstock Bookfest
20 Sugar Bear Lane, Woodstock, NY 12498

Mailing Address: PO Box 333, Woodstock, NY 12498
E-mail: info@woodstockbookfest.com
Web Site: woodstockbookfest.com; www.facebook.com/pg/woodstockbookfest
Key Personnel
Exec Dir: Martha Frankel
E-mail: marthafrankel@me.com
Edit Dir: Kitty Sheehan *E-mail:* kitty5157@gmail.com
Features authors, aspiring writers, readers, students & teachers.
Location: Woodstock, NY, USA
March 18-21, 2021

APRIL

Alberta Library Conference
Sponsored by Library Association of Alberta (LAA)
80 Baker Crescent NW, Calgary, AB T2L 1R4, Canada
Tel: 403-284-5818 *Toll Free Tel:* 877-522-5550 *Fax:* 403-284-5818
E-mail: info@albertalibraryconference.com; info@laa.ca
Web Site: www.albertalibraryconference.com; www.facebook.com/AlbertaLibraryConference; www.laa.ca
Key Personnel
Conference Coord: Christine Sheppard
Co-hosted by Alberta Library Trustees Association (ALTA).
Location: Fairmont Jasper Park Lodge, Jasper, AB, CN
April 29-May 2, 2021

Bologna Children's Book Fair
Sponsored by BolognaFiere SpA
Piazza Costituzione, 6, 40128 Bologna, Italy
Tel: (051) 282 111
E-mail: bookfair@bolognafiere.it
Web Site: www.bolognachildrensbookfair.com; www.facebook.com/BolognaChildrensBookFair
Key Personnel
Event Mgr: Isabella Bonvicini *Tel:* (051) 282 290
E-mail: isabella.bonvicini@bolognafiere.it
Location: Bologna Fair Centre, Piazza Costituzione, 6, Bologna, Italy
April 12-15, 2021

EPA Annual Convention
Sponsored by Evangelical Press Association (EPA)
PO Box 1787, Queen Creek, AZ 85142
Toll Free Tel: 888-311-1731
Web Site: www.evangelicalpress.com
Key Personnel
Exec Dir: Lamar Keener
Annual convention for editors, publishers, writers & other staff (print & online publications). Workshop tracks & plenary sessions, opportunities for networking & fellowship.
Location: Lancaster, PA, USA
April 28-30, 2021

Florida Antiquarian Book Fair
Sponsored by Florida Antiquarian Booksellers Association (FABA)
14046 Fifth St, Dade City, FL 33525
Tel: 727-234-7759
E-mail: floridabookfair@gmail.com
Web Site: floridaantiquarianbookfair.com
Key Personnel
Mgr: Sarah Smith
Annual event.
Location: The Coliseum, 535 Fourth Ave N, St Petersburg, FL, USA
April 23-25, 2021

International Children's Book Day

Sponsored by International Board on Books for
Young People (IBBY)
Nonnenweg 12, Postfach, 4009 Basel, Switzerland
Tel: (061) 272 29 17 *Fax:* (061) 272 27 57
E-mail: ibby@ibby.org
Web Site: www.ibby.org
Key Personnel
Exec Dir: Liz Page *E-mail:* liz.page@ibby.org
Admin Asst: Franca Salerno *E-mail:* ibby.
secretariat@ibby.org
On Hans Christian Andersen's birthday, April
2nd, International Children's Book Day (ICBD)
is celebrated to inspire a love of reading & to
call attention to children's books. Each year a
different national section has the opportunity
to be the international sponsor. It decides upon
a theme & invites a prominent author to write
a message to the children of the world & a
well-known illustrator to design a poster. These
materials are used in different ways to promote
books & reading around the world.
April 2, 2021

Los Angeles Times Festival of Books

Sponsored by Los Angeles Times
2300 E Imperial Hwy, El Segundo, CA 90245
Tel: 213-283-2274
E-mail: eventinfo@latimes.com
Web Site: events.latimes.com/festivalofbooks;
www.facebook.com/latimesfob
Location: The University of Southern California
(USC), Los Angeles, CA, USA
April 17-18, 2021

Mississippi Book Festival

PO Box 1185, Jackson, MS 39215
Tel: 769-717-2648
E-mail: info@msbookfestival.com
Web Site: msbookfestival.com
Key Personnel
Exec Dir: Holly Lange *E-mail:* holly@
msbookfestival.com
Literary Dir: Ellen Rodgers Daniels
E-mail: ellen@msbookfestival.com
Proj Coord: Katie Molpus *E-mail:* katie@
msbookfestival.com
The festival draws thousands to its annual "liter-
ary lawn party" & book lovers' celebration.
Location: Mississippi State Capitol, 400 High St,
Jackson, MS, USA
April 21, 2021

NAAJ Annual Meeting

Sponsored by North American Agricultural Jour-
nalists (NAAJ)
6434 Hurta Lane, Bryan, TX 77808
Tel: 979-324-4302
Web Site: www.naaj.net
Key Personnel
Exec Secy & Treas: Kathleen Phillips
E-mail: naajnews@yahoo.com
Annual meeting, writing awards & scholarship
benefit dance.
Location: Washington, DC, USA
April 2021

NAPIM Spring Convention

Sponsored by National Association of Printing
Ink Manufacturers (NAPIM)
3600 E State St, Suite 306, Rockford, IL 61108
Tel: 815-708-7387
Web Site: www.napim.org
Key Personnel
Exec Dir: John Copeland *Tel:* 815-979-2341
E-mail: jcopeland@napim.org
Memb Rel Mgr: Michele St Clair
E-mail: mstclair@napim.org
Location: The Vinoy® Renaissance St Petersburg
Resort & Golf Club, 501 Fifth Ave NE, St Pe-
tersburg, FL, USA
April 16-19, 2021

National Library Week

Sponsored by The American Library Association
(ALA)
225 N Michigan Ave, Suite 1300, Chicago, IL
60601
Tel: 312-944-6780 *Toll Free Tel:* 800-545-2433
Fax: 312-440-9374
E-mail: ala@ala.org
Web Site: www.ala.org/nlw
Location: Nationwide throughout the USA
April 5-9, 2021

PaperCon

Sponsored by Technical Association of the Pulp
& Paper Industry (TAPPI)
15 Technology Pkwy S, Suite 115, Peachtree Cor-
ners, GA 30092
Tel: 770-446-1400 *Toll Free Tel:* 800-332-8686
(US); 800-446-9431 (CN) *Fax:* 770-446-6947;
770-209-7206
E-mail: memberconnection@tappi.org
Web Site: papercon.org; www.tappi.org
Key Personnel
Sr Meeting Mgr: Bridgette Brigham *Tel:* 770-209-
7244 *E-mail:* bbrigham@tappi.org
Location: Cobb Galleria Centre, Atlanta, GA,
USA
April 25-28, 2021

The Quest for Excellence® Conference

Sponsored by National Institute of Standards and
Technology (NIST)
100 Bureau Dr, Stop 1020, Gaithersburg, MD
20899-1070
Tel: 301-975-2036
E-mail: baldrige@nist.gov
Web Site: www.nist.gov/baldrige
Key Personnel
Conference Chair: Barbara Fischer
E-mail: barbara.fischer@nist.gov
Official conference of the Malcolm Baldrige Na-
tional Quality Award held in partnership with
American Society for Quality (ASQ).
Location: Gaylord National Harbor, 165 Water-
front St, National Harbor, MD, USA
April 11-14, 2021

San Antonio Book Festival

Sponsored by San Antonio Public Library Foun-
dation
1201 Avenue "B", Unit 1011, San Antonio, TX
78215
Tel: 210-750-8951
E-mail: sabf@saplf.org
Web Site: sabookfestival.org
Key Personnel
Exec Dir: Lilly Gonzalez *E-mail:* lilly.gonzalez@
saplf.org
Literary Dir: Clay Smith *E-mail:* clay.smith@
saplf.org
Mng Dir: Maritza Cirlos *E-mail:* maritza@saplf.
org
Literary Feast Coord: Marcia Logan
E-mail: marcia.logan@saplf.org
Through active partnerships with school districts
& community organizations focused on literary,
education & culture, the Festival connects with
educators, parents & students, pre-K through
college.
Location: Central Library, 600 Soledad St & the
neighboring Southwest School of Art, San Antonio, TX, USA
April 10, 2021

Texas Library Association Annual Conference

Sponsored by Texas Library Association (TLA)
3355 Bee Cave Rd, Suite 401, Austin, TX 78746-
6763
Tel: 512-328-1518 *Fax:* 512-328-8852
E-mail: tla@txla.org
Web Site: www.txla.org

Key Personnel
Mgr, Conferences & Events: Robin Morris
Tel: 512-328-1518 ext 148 *E-mail:* robinm@
txla.org
Mgr, Exhibits & Vendor Rel: Cindy Boyle
Tel: 512-328-1518 ext 144 *E-mail:* cindyb@
txla.org
Conference & Event Specialist: Michelle Cruz
Tel: 512-328-1518 ext 145 *E-mail:* michellec@
txla.org
Location: San Antonio, TX, USA
April 20-23, 2021

MAY

ASQ World Conference on Quality & Improvement

Sponsored by American Society for Quality
(ASQ)
600 N Plankinton Ave, Milwaukee, WI 53203
Mailing Address: PO Box 3005, Milwaukee, WI
53201-3005
Tel: 414-272-8575 *Toll Free Tel:* 800-248-1946
(US & CN) *Fax:* 414-272-1734
E-mail: help@asq.org
Web Site: www.asq.org
Key Personnel
Mgr, Event Mgmt: Amy Heppe *E-mail:* aheppe@
asq.org
Location: Anaheim, CA, USA
May 23-26, 2021

Bay Area Book Festival

1569 Solano Ave, No 635, Berkeley, CA 94707
E-mail: info@baybookfest.org
Web Site: www.baybookfest.org
Key Personnel
Festival Dir: Cherilyn Parsons
E-mail: womenlit@baybookfest.org
Celebrating books, reading & community.
Location: Various downtown Berkeley venues,
Berkeley, CA, USA
May 1-2, 2021

Children's Book Week

Sponsored by The Children's Book Council
(CBC)
54 W 39 St, 14th fl, New York, NY 10018
Tel: 212-966-1990
E-mail: cbc.info@cbcbooks.org
Web Site: www.cbcbooks.org; www.
everychildareader.net
Key Personnel
Exec Dir: Carl Lennertz *E-mail:* carl.lennertz@
cbcbooks.org
Assoc Exec Dir: Shaina Birkhead *E-mail:* shaina.
birkhead@cbcbooks.org
Celebration of children's books & reading admin-
istered by Every Child a Reader.
Location: Nationwide across the USA
May 3-9, 2021

EXPOLIT (Exposicion de Literatura Cristiana Book Fair)

Sponsored by Spanish Evangelical Publishers As-
sociation (SEPA)/Asociacion Evangelica es-
panola de Editores
8167 NW 84 St, Medley, FL 33166
Tel: 305-503-1191 *Toll Free Tel:* 800-767-7786
E-mail: info@expolit.com
Web Site: www.expolit.com
Key Personnel
Supv: Jessica Hernandez *E-mail:* jessica@expolit.
com
Media & Mktg Coord: Yadheera Baez-
Biancovitch *E-mail:* medios@expolit.com
Exhibit Coord: Angela Peralta
E-mail: exhibitors@expolit.com

Spanish Christian literature convention. Also sponsored by Editorial Unilit.
Location: DoubleTree by Hilton Hotel Miami Airport & Convention Center, 711 NW 72 Ave, Miami, FL, USA
May 13-16, 2021

SSP Annual Meeting
Sponsored by Society for Scholarly Publishing (SSP)
1120 Rte 73, Suite 200, Mount Laurel, NJ 08054
Tel: 856-439-1385 *Fax:* 856-439-0525
E-mail: info@sspnet.org
Web Site: www.sspnet.org
Key Personnel
Meeting Mgr: Tracy Mitchell
Location: Gaylord National Resort, National Harbor, MD, USA
May 26-28, 2021

Thessaloniki International Book Fair
Sponsored by Hellenic Foundation for Culture (HFC)
50 Stratigou Kallari, 154 52 Athens, Greece
Tel: 210-677-6540
Web Site: hfc-worldwide.org
Key Personnel
Pres: Konstantinos Tsoukalas *E-mail:* president@hfc.gr
Co-organized by International Exhibition & Congress Centre of Thessaloniki (HELEXPO), Hellenic Federation of Publishers & Booksellers (POEB) of the Municipality of Thessaloniki & carried out under the supervision & support of the Ministry for Culture & Sport.
Location: International Exhibition & Congress Centre of Thessaloniki (TIF-Helexpo), 154 Egnatia St, Thessaloniki, Greece
May 2021

JUNE

American Library Association Annual Conference
Sponsored by The American Library Association (ALA)
225 N Michigan Ave, Suite 1300, Chicago, IL 60601
Tel: 312-944-6780 *Toll Free Tel:* 800-545-2433 (conference servs) *Fax:* 312-440-9374
E-mail: ala@ala.org
Web Site: www.ala.org
Key Personnel
Registration & Servs Mgr: Alicia Hamann *Tel:* 800-545-2433 ext 3229 *E-mail:* ahamann@ala.org
Conference Dir: Earla Jones *Tel:* 800-545-2433 ext 3226 *E-mail:* ejones@ala.org
Meeting Coord: Donna Hunter *Tel:* 800-545-2433 ext 3218 *E-mail:* dhunter@ala.org
Conference Coord: Lina Zabaneh *Tel:* 800-545-2433 ext 3227 *E-mail:* lzabaneh@ala.org
Meeting Mgr: Yvonne McLean *Tel:* 800-545-2433 ext 3222 *E-mail:* ymclean@ala.org
Location: Chicago, IL, USA
June 24-29, 2021

AUPresses Annual Meeting
Sponsored by Association of University Presses (AUPresses)
1412 Broadway, Suite 2135, New York, NY 10018
Tel: 212-989-1010 *Fax:* 212-989-0275
E-mail: info@aupresses.org
Web Site: www.aupresses.org
Key Personnel
Exec Dir: Peter Berkery *Tel:* 917-288-5594 *E-mail:* pberkery@aupresses.org

Res & Communs Dir: Brenna McLaughlin *Tel:* 917-244-2051 *E-mail:* bmclaughlin@aupresses.org
Busn Mgr: Kim Miller *Tel:* 917-244-1264 *E-mail:* kmiller@aupresses.org
Location: Fairmont Queen Elizabeth, 900 Rene Levesque Blvd W, Montreal, QC, CN
June 15-17, 2021

EXPO PACK Guadalajara
Sponsored by PMMI: The Association for Packaging and Processing Technologies
12930 Westgate Dr, Suite 200, Herndon, VA 20170-6037
Tel: 571-612-3200 *Toll Free Tel:* 888-ASK-PMMI (275-7664) *Fax:* 703-243-8556
E-mail: expo@pmmi.org; info@pmmi.org
Web Site: www.expopackguadalajara.com.mx; www.pmmi.org
Key Personnel
VP, Meetings & Events: Patti Fee *Tel:* 571-612-3193
VP, Trade Shows: Laura Thompson *Tel:* 571-612-3217
Dir, Trade Show Opers: Allison Konczyk *Tel:* 571-612-3188
Dir, Trade Show Mktg: Tina Warren *Tel:* 571-612-3203
Dir, Exhibitor Servs: Merideth Newman *Tel:* 571-612-3208 *E-mail:* mnewman@pmmi.org
Sr Mgr, Events: Anna Hudson *Tel:* 571-612-3198
Trade Show Opers Mgr: Kelly Faist *Tel:* 571-612-3192
Trade Show Mktg Mgr: Lilly Kinney *Tel:* 571-287-6811
Trade Show Coord: Jeremy Adams *Tel:* 571-266-4407; Jessie Brown *Tel:* 571-266-4409
Trade Show Mktg Coord: Joyce Su *Tel:* 571-266-4405
Represents Western Mexico showcasing the latest solutions in processing & packaging. Biennial event held in odd-numbered years.
Location: June 15-17, 2021
Guadalajara, Mexico

IABC World Conference
Sponsored by International Association of Business Communicators (IABC)
649 Mission St, 5th fl, San Francisco, CA 94105
Tel: 415-544-4700 *Toll Free Tel:* 800-776-4222 (US & CN) *Fax:* 415-544-4747
E-mail: conference@iabc.com
Web Site: wc.iabc.com; www.iabc.com
Key Personnel
Dir, Content & Educ: Natasha Nicholson
Location: New York Marriott Marquis, 1535 Broadway, New York, NY, USA
June 27-30, 2021

JULY

Hong Kong Book Fair
Sponsored by Hong Kong Trade Development Council
c/o Exhibition Dept, Unit 13, Expo Galleria, Hong Kong Convention & Exhibition Centre, Wan Chai, Hong Kong
Tel: 1830 670; 1830 668 (cust serv) *Fax:* 2824 0026; 2824 0249
E-mail: exhibitions@hktdc.org
Web Site: hkbookfair.hktdc.com; hkbookfair.hktdc.com/en/index.html (English)
Location: Hong Kong Convention & Exhibition Center, One Harbour Rd, Wan Chai, Hong Kong
July 2021

IAML Annual Congress
Sponsored by International Association of Music Libraries, Archives & Documentation Centres Inc (IAML)
c/o Gothenburg University Library, Music & Drama Library, Box 210, 412 56 Gothenburg, Sweden
Tel: (031) 786 40 60
E-mail: contact@iaml.info
Web Site: www.iaml.info
Key Personnel
Secy Gen: Anders Cato *E-mail:* secretary@iaml.info
Location: Prague, Czechia
July 25-30, 2021

Outdoor Writers Association of America Annual Conference
Sponsored by Outdoor Writers Association of America (OWAA)
2814 Brooks St, Box 442, Missoula, MT 59801
Tel: 406-728-7434
E-mail: info@owaa.org
Web Site: www.owaa.org
Key Personnel
Membership & Conference Dir: Jessica (Pollett) Seitz *E-mail:* jseitz@owaa.org
The annual OWAA Conference is an opportunity for outdoor communicators & outdoor groups, businesses & agencies that are involved in the world of outdoor communication to learn & connect with others in the industry. It will give attendees a chance to network with other professionals, allow them to build crucial business outlets & help improve their skills. Attend sessions geared toward general business & newsmaker sessions, plus craft improvement in multiple genres of outdoor communication.
Location: Jay Peak Resort, 830 Jay Peak Rd, Jay, VT, USA
July 9-12, 2021

Payson Book Festival
Sponsored by Arizona Professional Writers (APW)
PO Box 1495, Payson, AZ 85547
E-mail: info@paysonbookfestival.org
Web Site: www.paysonbookfestival.org; www.facebook.com/PaysonBookFestival
Key Personnel
Dir: Connie Cockrell
Jointly presented by the Rim County Chapter of Arizona Professional Writers & Majestic Rim Retirement Living, the Payson Book Festival is held to promote literacy & showcase Arizona authors. Our mission is to enhance the love of reading by providing a friendly environment that encourages personal interaction between Arizona authors & readers of all ages. Proceeds will benefit the scholarship funds of both the Payson High School & the Gila Community College. Over 80 Arizona authors participate by signing books & visiting with readers of all ages. Some will speak about their books & the craft of writing. There will be a full schedule of speakers & several workshops throughout the day.
Location: Mazatzal Hotel & Casino, Hwy 87, Mile Marker 251, Payson, AZ, USA
July 17, 2021

Romance Writers of America Annual Conference
Sponsored by Romance Writers of America®
14615 Benfer Rd, Houston, TX 77069
Tel: 832-717-5200 *Fax:* 832-717-5201
E-mail: info@rwa.org
Web Site: www.rwa.org
Key Personnel
Spec Projs Mgr: Megan Sloan *Tel:* 832-717-5200 ext 120 *E-mail:* megan.sloan@rwa.org

Location: Gaylord Opryland Resort & Convention
Center, 2800 Opryland Dr, Nashville, TN, USA
July 14-17, 2021

AUGUST

Beijing International Book Fair (BIBF)
Sponsored by China National Publications Import
& Export (Group) Corp (CNPIEC)
Member of China Publishing Group Corp (CPG)
16 Gongti E Rd, Beijing 100020, China
Tel: (010) 6506 3080 *Fax:* (010) 6508 9188
Web Site: www.bibf.net
Key Personnel
Dir, Sales & Mktg: Mr Yuan Jiayang
E-mail: yuanjiyang@bibf.net
Acct Mgr, Americas & the UK: Ms Xu Ruoqing
E-mail: xuruoqing@bibf.net
Acct Mgr, Europe & Middle East: Mr Ni Hongri
E-mail: nihongri@bibf.net
Location: China International Exhibition Center,
Beijing, China
Aug 2021

**The Dorothy L Sayers Society Annual
Convention**
Sponsored by The Dorothy L Sayers Society
Witham Library, 18 Newland St, Witham CM8
2AQ, United Kingdom
Tel: (01376) 519625
E-mail: info@sayers.org.uk
Web Site: www.sayers.org.uk
Key Personnel
Convention Admin: Simon Medd
Membership Secy: Margaret Hunt
E-mail: membership@sayers.org.uk
Members only event.
Aug 2021

Edinburgh International Book Festival
5 Charlotte Sq, Edinburgh EH2 4DR, United
Kingdom
Tel: (0131) 718 5666
E-mail: admin@edbookfest.co.uk
Web Site: www.edbookfest.co.uk
Each year we welcome over 900 international au-
thors & over 250,000 visitors to the biggest
book festival in the world, turning Edinburgh's
Charlotte Square Gardens into a literary village
for 18 days every August.
Location: Charlotte Square Gardens, Edinburgh,
UK
Aug 2021

IFLA World Library & Information Congress
Sponsored by International Federation of Library
Associations & Institutions (IFLA) (Federation
internationale des associations de bibliothe-
caires et des bibliotheques)
Prins Willem-Alexanderhof 5, 2595 BE The
Hague, Netherlands
Mailing Address: Postbus 95312, 2509 CH The
Hague, Netherlands
Tel: (70) 314 08 84 *Fax:* (70) 383 48 27
E-mail: conferences@ifla.org; ifla@ifla.org
Web Site: www.ifla.org
Key Personnel
Secy Gen: Gerald Leitner
Held simultaneously with IFLA General Confer-
ence & Assembly.
Location: Rotterdam, Netherlands
Aug 19-26, 2021

Swanwick: The Writers' Summer School
Sponsored by Writers' Summer School
The Hayes Conference Centre, Hayes Ln, Swan-
wick, Alfreton DE55 1AU, United Kingdom
Tel: (01290) 552248

Web Site: www.swanwickwritersschool.org.uk
A weeklong residential writing school with top
name speakers & tutors, plus informative panels, talks & discussion groups. Comfortable
rooms with all meals & tuition included in the
price. Open to everyone, from absolute beginners to published authors. Beautiful setting,
licensed bar & evening entertainment. Believed
to be the longest established residential writers' school in the world, Swanwick, held annually in August, is a must attend event in every
writer's diary.
Location: The Hayes Conference Centre, Swanwick, Alfreton, Derbyshire, UK
Aug 7-13, 2021

TAPPI/AICC SuperCorrExpo® 2021
Sponsored by Technical Association of the Pulp
& Paper Industry (TAPPI)
15 Technology Pkwy S, Suite 115, Peachtree Cor-
ners, GA 30092
Tel: 770-446-1400 *Toll Free Tel:* 800-332-8686
(US); 800-446-9431 (CN) *Fax:* 770-446-6947;
770-209-7206
E-mail: memberconnection@tappi.org
Web Site: supercorrexpo.org; www.tappi.org
Key Personnel
Dir, Conventions, AICC: Cindy Huber *Tel:* 703-
836-2422 *E-mail:* chuber@aiccbox.org
Sr Meetings Mgr, AICC: Laura Mihalik *Tel:* 770-
836-2422 *E-mail:* lmihalick@aiccbox.org
Meeting Planner, TAPPI: Hayley King *Tel:* 770-
209-7224 *E-mail:* hking@tappi.org
Exhibit Mgr: Grayson Lutz *Tel:* 678-471-5838
E-mail: glutz@tappi.org
Sponsorship & Exhibit Sales: Linda Cohen
Tel: 914-944-0135 *E-mail:* lcohen@tappi.org
Location: Orange County Convention Center, Or-
lando, FL, USA
Aug 8-12, 2021

AUTUMN

Louisiana Book Festival
Sponsored by Louisiana Center for the Book
Subsidiary of State Library of Louisiana
701 N Fourth St, Baton Rouge, LA 70802
Tel: 225-219-9503 *Fax:* 225-219-9840
Web Site: louisianabookfestival.org
Key Personnel
Dir: Jim Davis *Tel:* 225-342-9714
E-mail: jdavis@slol.lib.la.us
Asst Dir: Robert Wilson *E-mail:* rwilson@slol.lib.
la.us
A free festival celebrating readers, writers &
books representing a variety of genres & re-
lated events for all ages, food, music.
Location: State Library of Louisiana, Louisiana
State Capitol, Capitol Park Welcome Center &
nearby locations, Baton Rouge, LA, USA
Fall 2021

NAIBA Fall Conference
Sponsored by New Atlantic Independent Book-
sellers Association (NAIBA)
2667 Hyacinth St, Westbury, NY 11590
Tel: 516-333-0681 *Fax:* 516-333-0689
E-mail: naibabooksellers@gmail.com
Web Site: www.naiba.com/page/fallconference
Key Personnel
Exec Dir: Eileen Dengler *E-mail:* naibaeileen@
gmail.com
Fall 2021

ScienceWriters2021
Sponsored by National Association of Science
Writers (NASW)
PO Box 7905, Berkeley, CA 94707

Tel: 510-647-9500
Web Site: www.nasw.org
Key Personnel
Exec Dir: Tinsley Davis *E-mail:* director@nasw.
org
Location: University of Colorado Boulder & CU
Anschutz Medical Campus, Boulder, CO, USA
Fall 2021

Texas Book Festival
1023 Springdale Rd, Bldg 14, Unit B, Austin, TX
78721
Tel: 512-477-4055
E-mail: bookfest@texasbookfestival.org
Web Site: www.texasbookfestival.org
Key Personnel
Exec Dir: Lois Kim *E-mail:* loiskim@
texasbookfestival.org
Deputy Dir: Claire Burrows *E-mail:* claire@
texasbookfestival.org
Literary Dir: Matthew Patin *E-mail:* matthew@
texasbookfestival.org
Devt Assoc: Maris Finn *E-mail:* maris@
texasbookfestival.org
Commus & Mktg Coord: Katey Psencik
E-mail: katey@texasbookfestival.org
The festival is a statewide program that promotes
reading & literacy highlighted by a 2 day festi-
val, held annually in the fall, featuring authors
from Texas & across the USA. Money raised
from the festival is distributed as grants to public libraries throughout the state.
Location: State Capitol Bldg, Austin, TX, USA
Fall 2021

Texas Teen Book Festival
Sponsored by Texas Book Festival
1023 Springdale Rd, Bldg 14, Unit B, Austin, TX
78721
Tel: 512-477-4055
E-mail: ttbfinfo@texasteenbookfestival.org
Web Site: texasteenbookfestival.org
Key Personnel
TTBF Dir: Claire Burrows
Celebration of the teen reading experience. Orga-
nized in collaboration with Texas Book Festi-
val, BookPeople & a dedicated group of librar-
ian volunteers.
Location: St Edward's University, Austin, TX,
USA
Fall 2021

SEPTEMBER

**Christian Resources Retailers & Suppliers
Retreat**
Sponsored by Christian Resources Together
Cedar Tree, 4 Ditchingham Close, Aylesbury,
Bucks HP19 7SA, United Kingdom
Tel: (01296) 489860
Web Site: www.christianresourcestogether.co.uk
Location: The Hayes Conference Centre, Swan-
wick, Alfreton, Derbyshire, UK
Sept 14-15, 2021

Distripress Annual Congress
Sponsored by Distripress
Postfach 8034, Zurich, Switzerland
Web Site: www.distripress.org
Key Personnel
Mng Dir: Tracy Jones *E-mail:* tracy.jones@
distripress.org
Annual event sponsored by Distripress, a non-
profit association for the promotion of interna-
tional press distribution.
Location: Estoril, Portugal
Sept 12-15, 2021

Excellence in Journalism
Sponsored by The Society of Professional Journalists (SPJ)
Eugene S Pulliam National Journalism Ctr, 3909 N Meridian St, Suite 200, Indianapolis, IN 46208
Tel: 317-927-8000 *Fax:* 317-920-4789
Web Site: excellenceinjournalism.org; www.spj. org
Key Personnel
Exec Dir: John Shertzer *Tel:* 317-920-4780
    E-mail: jshertzer@spj.org
Location: Minneapolis, MN, USA
Sept 24-26, 2021

Goeteborg Book Fair
Sponsored by Bok & Bibliotek i Norden AB
Maessans Gata 10, 412 94 Gothenburg, Sweden
Tel: (031) 708 84 00
E-mail: info@goteborg-bookfair.com; hej@ bokmassan.se
Web Site: www.bokmassan.se
Key Personnel
Prog Mgr: Oskar Ekstrom *Tel:* (031) 708 84 73
    E-mail: oe@bokmassan.se
Prog Coord: Malena Lindhoff *Tel:* (031) 708 82 06 *E-mail:* ml@bokmassan.se
Location: Gothenburg, Sweden
Sept 23-26, 2021

PACK EXPO Las Vegas
Sponsored by PMMI: The Association for Packaging and Processing Technologies
12930 Westgate Dr, Suite 200, Herndon, VA 20170-6037
Tel: 571-612-3200 *Toll Free Tel:* 888-ASK-PMMI (275-7664) *Fax:* 703-243-8556
E-mail: expo@pmmi.org; info@pmmi.org
Web Site: www.packexpolasvegas.com; www. packexpo.com; www.pmmi.org
Key Personnel
VP, Meetings & Events: Patti Fee *Tel:* 571-612-3193
VP, Trade Shows: Laura Thompson *Tel:* 571-612-3217
Dir, Trade Show Opers: Allison Konczyk *Tel:* 571-612-3188
Dir, Trade Show Mktg: Tina Warren *Tel:* 571-612-3203
Dir, Exhibitor Servs: Merideth Newman *Tel:* 571-612-3208 *E-mail:* mnewman@pmmi.org
Sr Mgr, Events: Anna Hudson *Tel:* 571-612-3198
Trade Show Opers Mgr: Kelly Faist *Tel:* 571-612-3192
Trade Show Mktg Mgr: Lilly Kinney *Tel:* 571-287-6811
Trade Show Coord: Jeremy Adams *Tel:* 571-266-4407; Jessie Brown *Tel:* 571-266-4409
Trade Show Mktg Coord: Joyce Su *Tel:* 571-266-4405
Biennial event held in odd-numbered years.
Location: Las Vegas Convention Center, 3150 Paradise Rd, Las Vegas, NV, USA
Sept 27-29, 2021

PacPrint 2021
Sponsored by Visual Connections Australia Ltd
Shop 4, 123 Midson Rd, Epping, NSW 2121, Australia
Tel: (02) 9868 1577 *Fax:* (02) 9869 0554
E-mail: exhibitions@visualconnections.org.au
Web Site: www.pacprint.com.au
Key Personnel
Event Mgr: Jenny Harris
Presented by Visual Connections Australia Ltd & the Printing Industries Association of Australia (PIAA), this event is held every 4 years.
Location: Melbourne Convention & Exhibitions Centre (MCEC), South Wharf, Victoria, Australia
Sept 28-Oct 1, 2021

SIBA Discovery Show
Sponsored by Southern Independent Booksellers Alliance
51 Pleasant Ridge Dr, Asheville, NC 28805
Tel: 803-994-9530 *Fax:* 309-410-0211
E-mail: siba@sibaweb.com
Web Site: www.sibaweb.com/trade-show; www. sibaweb.com
Key Personnel
Exec Dir: Linda-Marie Barrett
    E-mail: lindamarie@sibaweb.com
Members only event.
Location: Marriott/Embassy Suites & Benton Convention Center, Winston-Salem, NC, USA
Sept 18-20, 2021

OCTOBER

ACP/CMA National College Media Convention
Sponsored by Associated Collegiate Press (ACP)
Division of National Scholastic Press Association
2829 University Ave SE, Suite 720, Minneapolis, MN 55414
Tel: 612-200-9254
E-mail: info@studentpress.org
Web Site: www.studentpress.org; facebook. com/acpress
Key Personnel
Exec Dir, NSPA/ACP: Laura Widmer *Tel:* 612-200-9265
Co-sponsored by College Media Association.
Location: Sheraton, New Orleans, LA, USA
Oct 13-17, 2021

Alaska Book Week
Sponsored by Alaska Center for the Book
PO Box 24207, Anchorage, AK 99574
Tel: 907-786-4379
E-mail: akbookweek@gmail.com
Web Site: alaskabookweek.org
Key Personnel
Chair: Trish Jenkins
The statewide event annually celebrates the appreciation of books, from readings, to panels, lectures, discussions & youth activities.
Location: Statewide, AK, USA
Oct 2021

American Translators Association Annual Conference
Sponsored by American Translators Association (ATA)
225 Reinekers Lane, Suite 590, Alexandria, VA 22314
Tel: 703-683-6100 *Fax:* 703-683-6122
E-mail: ata@atanet.org
Web Site: www.atanet.org
Key Personnel
Exec Dir: Walter W Bacak, Jr *E-mail:* walter@ atanet.org
Location: Minneapolis, MN, USA
Oct 27-30, 2021

AMWA Annual Conference
Sponsored by American Medical Writers Association (AMWA)
30 W Gude Dr, Suite 525, Rockville, MD 20850-4357
Tel: 240-238-0940 *Fax:* 301-294-9006
E-mail: amwa@amwa.org
Web Site: www.amwa.org
Key Personnel
Sr Mgr, Educ & Events: Sook-Yi Yong *Tel:* 240-238-0940 ext 112 *E-mail:* sook-yi@amwa.org
Location: Chicago Marriott Downtown Magnificent Mile, Chicago, IL, USA
Oct 27-30, 2021

ASIS&T Annual Meeting
Sponsored by Association for Information Science & Technology (ASIS&T)
8555 16 St, Suite 850, Silver Spring, MD 20910
Tel: 301-495-0900 *Fax:* 301-495-0810
E-mail: asist@asist.org
Web Site: www.asist.org
Location: Salt Lake City, UT, USA
Oct 29-Nov 3, 2021

Frankfurter Buchmesse
(Frankfurt Book Fair)
Sponsored by Frankfurter Buchmesse GmbH
Braubachstr 16, 60311 Frankfurt am Main, Germany
Tel: (069) 21020 *Fax:* (069) 2102 277
E-mail: contact@book-fair.com
Web Site: www.book-fair.com
Key Personnel
CEO & Dir: Juergen Boos
Major international book & media fair attracting 7,500 exhibitors from over 110 countries & 285,000 visitors.
Location: Frankfurt Fairgrounds, Ludwig-Erhard-Anlage One, Frankfurt, Germany
Oct 20-24, 2021

ILA Annual Conference
Sponsored by International Literacy Association (ILA)
258 Chapman Rd, Suite 203, Newark, DE 19702
Mailing Address: PO Box 8139, Newark, DE 19714-8139
Tel: 302-731-1600 *Toll Free Tel:* 800-336-7323 (US & CN) *Fax:* 302-731-1057
E-mail: customerservice@reading.org
Web Site: www.literacyworldwide.org
Key Personnel
Exec Dir: Marcie Craig Post
Location: Indianapolis, IN, USA
Oct 14-17, 2021

Jewish Book Month
Sponsored by Jewish Book Council
520 Eighth Ave, 4th fl, New York, NY 10018
Tel: 212-201-2920 *Fax:* 212-532-4952
E-mail: info@jewishbooks.org
Web Site: www.jewishbookcouncil.org; www. facebook.com/JewishBookCouncil; twitter. com/jewishbook
Key Personnel
Exec Dir: Naomi Firestone-Teeter
Dir: Carolyn Starman Hessel
Dedicated to the celebration of Jewish books held annually during the month leading up to Hanukkah.
Location: Nationwide throughout the USA
Oct 28-Nov 28, 2021

Morristown Festival of Books
Sponsored by Kraft Event Management Inc
131 Woods End Dr, Basking Ridge, NJ 07920
Tel: 908-221-0448 *Fax:* 908-221-1466
Web Site: morristownbooks.org
Location: Morristown, NJ, USA
Oct 8-9, 2021

National Newspaper Association Annual Convention & Trade Show
Sponsored by National Newspaper Association
101 S Palafox, Unit 13323, Pensacola, FL 32591
Tel: 850-542-7087
Web Site: nna.org
Key Personnel
Exec Dir: Lynne Lance
Oct 2021

PEERS Conference
Sponsored by Technical Association of the Pulp & Paper Industry (TAPPI)
15 Technology Pkwy S, Suite 115, Peachtree Corners, GA 30092

Tel: 770-446-1400 *Toll Free Tel:* 800-332-8686
(US); 800-446-9431 (CN) *Fax:* 770-446-6947;
770-209-7206
E-mail: memberconnection@tappi.org
Web Site: tappipeers.org; www.tappi.org
Key Personnel
Div Mgr: Lisa Stephens *Tel:* 770-209-7319
E-mail: lstephens@tappi.org
Location: Rhode Island Convention Center &
Omni Hotel, Providence, RI, USA
Oct 31-Nov 3, 2021

**PSA® International Conference of
Photography**
Sponsored by Photographic Society of America®
(PSA®)
8241 S Walker Ave, Suite 104, Oklahoma City,
OK 73139
Tel: 405-843-1437 *Toll Free Tel:* 855-PSA-INFO
(772-4636)
E-mail: hq@psa-photo.org
Web Site: www.psa-photo.org
PSA Photo Festival is held during the conference.
Location: Rapid City, SD, USA
Oct 6-9, 2021

Twin Cities Book Festival
Sponsored by Rain Taxi
PO Box 3840, Minneapolis, MN 55403
Tel: 612-825-1528 *Fax:* 612-825-1528
E-mail: bookfest@raintaxi.com
Web Site: www.raintaxi.com/twin-cities-book-
festival
Key Personnel
Dir: Eric Lorberer
Gala celebration of books, featuring large book
fair, author readings & signings, activities, pan-
els, used book sale & children's events!
Location: Minnesota State Fairgrounds, 1265
Snelling Ave N, St Paul, MN, USA
Oct 2021

Utah Humanities Book Festival
Sponsored by Utah Humanities
Affiliate of Utah Center for the Book
202 W 300 N, Salt Lake City, UT 84103
Tel: 801-359-9670 *Fax:* 801-531-7869
Web Site: utahhumanities.org
Key Personnel
Exec Dir: Jodi Graham *Tel:* 801-359-9670 ext
101 *E-mail:* graham@utahhumanities.org
Prog Mgr: Willy Palomo *Tel:* 801-359-9670 ext
103 *E-mail:* palomo@utahhumanities.org
Dir, Communs: Deena Pyle *Tel:* 801-359-9670 ext
111 *E-mail:* pyle@utahhumanities.org
Free literary event featuring national, regional &
local authors held Oct 1-31 annually (National
Book Month).
Location: Statewide, UT, USA
Oct 1-31, 2021

NOVEMBER

**Karlsruher Buecherschau (Karlsruhe Book
Fair)**
Sponsored by Boersenverein des Deutschen Buch-
handels, Landesverband Baden-Wuerttemberg
eV (Association of Publishers & Booksellers in
Baden-Wuerttemberg eV)
Paulinenstr 53, 70178 Stuttgart, Germany
Tel: (0711) 61941-0 *Fax:* (0711) 61941-44
E-mail: post@buchhandelsverband.de
Web Site: www.karlsruher-buecherschau.de; www.
buchhandelsverband.de
Key Personnel
Contact: Carolin Schneider *Tel:* (0711) 61941-26
E-mail: schneider@buchhandelsverband.de

Location: Karlsruhe, Germany
Nov 2021

Kentucky Book Festival
Sponsored by Kentucky Humanities
206 E Maxwell Street, Lexington, KY 40508
Tel: 859-257-5932 *Fax:* 859-257-5933
E-mail: kyhumanities@kyhumanities.org
Web Site: www.kyhumanities.org
Key Personnel
Dir, Book Festival: Sara Volpi *Tel:* 859-257-4317
E-mail: sara.volpi@uky.edu
Nov 2021

Malta Book Festival
Sponsored by National Book Council
c/o Central Public Library, Prof J Mangion St,
Floriana FRN 1800, Malta
Tel: 27131574
Web Site: ktieb.org.mt
Key Personnel
Sr Mgr: Simona Cassano *E-mail:* simona.
cassano@ktieb.org.mt
Nov 2021

Miami Book Fair
Sponsored by Florida Center for the Literary Arts
c/o Miami Dade College, 300 NE Second Ave,
Miami, FL 33132
Tel: 305-237-3258
E-mail: wbookfair@mdc.edu
Web Site: www.miamibookfair.com
Key Personnel
Dir of Opers: Delia Lopez
Exhibit Coord: Giselle Hernandez
Miami Book Fair is the largest event of its kind
in the USA. First held in 1984, for more than
35 years, the fair has been held over 8 days
each November. In addition to readings by
more than 450 authors from all over the world
& the sale of thousands of books in many languages, the fair offers book-centered fun for
children, panel discussions & writing classes
in English & Spanish. For up to date information, call or visit the book fair web site at
www.miamibookfair.com.
Location: Miami Dade College, Wolfson Campus,
Miami, FL, USA
Nov 2021

**Salon du Livre de Montreal (Montreal Book
Fair)**
Sponsored by Salon du Livre de Montreal
1264, rue Sherbrooke E, Montreal, QC H2L 1M1,
Canada
Tel: 514-845-2365
E-mail: info@salondulivredemontreal.com
Web Site: www.salondulivredemontreal.com
Location: Place Bonaventure, 800 de la
Gauchetiere St W, Montreal, QC, CN
Nov 2021

Sharjah International Book Fair (SIBF)
Sponsored by Sharjah Book Authority
PO Box 73111, Sharjah, United Arab Emirates
Tel: (06) 5140000 *Fax:* (06) 5140111
E-mail: info@sibf.com
Web Site: www.sibf.com
Location: Expo Center Sharjah, Al Taawun St,
Sharjah, United Arab Emirates
Nov 2021

**Stuttgarter Buchwochen (Stuttgart Book
Weeks)**
Sponsored by Boersenverein des Deutschen Buch-
handels, Landesverband Baden-Wuerttemberg
eV (Association of Publishers & Booksellers in
Baden-Wuerttemberg eV)
Paulinenstr 53, 70178 Stuttgart, Germany
Tel: (0711) 61941-0 *Fax:* (0711) 61941-44
E-mail: post@buchhandelsverband.de

Web Site: www.buchwochen.de; www.
buchhandelsverband.de
Key Personnel
Contact: Andrea Baumann *Tel:* (0711) 61941-28
E-mail: baumann@buchhandelsverband.de
Location: Haus de Wirtschaft, Willi-Bleicher-Str
19, Stuttgart, Germany
Nov 2021

Worlddidac / Swissdidac Bern
Sponsored by Worlddidac Association
Bollwerk 21, 3011 Bern, Switzerland
Tel: (031) 311 76 82 *Fax:* (031) 312 17 44
E-mail: info@worlddidac.org
Web Site: www.worlddidac.org
International exhibition for education, training,
technology & supply. Held in conjunction with
Swissdidac Bern.
Location: Bernexpo, Mingerstr 6, Bern, Switzer-
land
Nov 22-24, 2021

2022

JANUARY

MLA Annual Convention
Sponsored by Modern Language Association of
America (MLA)
85 Broad St, Suite 500, New York, NY 10004-
2434
SAN: 202-6422
Tel: 646-576-5266 (convention); 646-576-5000
Fax: 646-458-0030
E-mail: convention@mla.org
Web Site: www.mla.org/convention
Key Personnel
Dir of Convention & Events: Karin L Bagnall
E-mail: kbagnall@mla.org
Location: Washington, DC, USA
Jan 6-9, 2022

MARCH

AWP Annual Conference & Bookfair
Sponsored by Association of Writers & Writing
Programs (AWP)
University of Maryland, 5245 Greenbelt Rd, Box
246, College Park, MD 20740
Mailing Address: University of Maryland, 5700
Rivertech Ct, Suite 225, Riverdale Park, MD
20737-1250
Tel: 240-696-7742 (conference); 240-696-7700
E-mail: events@awpwriter.org; awp@awpwriter.
org
Web Site: www.awpwriter.org/awp_conference/;
www.awpwriter.org
Key Personnel
Dir, Conferences: Cynthia Sherman
Mgr, Conference Events: Colleen Cable
Coord, Conference Events: Aubrey Kamppila
Location: Pennsylvania Convention Center,
Philadelphia, PA, USA
March 23-26, 2022

Leipzig Book Fair (Leipziger Buchmesse)
Sponsored by Leipziger Messe GmbH
Messe-Allee 1, 04356 Leipzig, Germany
Mailing Address: Postfach 10 07 20, 04007
Leipzig, Germany
Tel: (0341) 678-6950 *Fax:* (0341) 678-8242
E-mail: info@leipziger-buchmesse.de
Web Site: www.leipziger-buchmesse.de
Key Personnel
Dir: Oliver Zille

Held annually in conjunction with The Leipzig Antiquarian Book Fair.
Location: Leipzig Exhibition Centre, Messe-Allee 1, Leipzig, Germany
March 17-20, 2022

PACK EXPO East

Sponsored by PMMI: The Association for Packaging and Processing Technologies
12930 Westgate Dr, Suite 200, Herndon, VA 20170-6037
Tel: 571-612-3200 *Toll Free Tel:* 888-ASK-PMMI (275-7664) *Fax:* 703-243-8556
E-mail: expo@pmmi.org; info@pmmi.org
Web Site: www.packexpoeast.com; www.pmmi.org
Key Personnel
VP, Meetings & Events: Patti Fee *Tel:* 571-612-3193
VP, Trade Shows: Laura Thompson *Tel:* 571-612-3217
Dir, Trade Show Opers: Allison Konczyk *Tel:* 571-612-3188
Dir, Trade Show Mktg: Tina Warren *Tel:* 571-612-3203
Dir, Exhibitor Servs: Merideth Newman *Tel:* 571-612-3208 *E-mail:* mnewman@pmmi.org
Sr Mgr, Events: Anna Hudson *Tel:* 571-612-3198
Trade Show Opers Mgr: Kelly Faist *Tel:* 571-612-3192
Trade Show Mktg Mgr: Lilly Kinney *Tel:* 571-287-6811
Trade Show Coord: Jeremy Adams *Tel:* 571-266-4407; Jessie Brown *Tel:* 571-266-4409
Trade Show Mktg Coord: Joyce Su *Tel:* 571-266-4405
Biennial event focusing on packaging solutions for the East coast. Held in even-numbered years.
Location: Philadelphia, PA, USA
March 21-23, 2022

Virginia Festival of the Book

Sponsored by Virginia Foundation for the Humanities
145 Ednam Dr, Charlottesville, VA 22903
Tel: 434-924-3296
E-mail: vabook@virginia.edu
Web Site: www.vabook.org
Key Personnel
Dir: Jane Kulow *Tel:* 434-924-7548
Annual public festival for children & adults featuring authors, illustrators, publishers, publicists, agents & other book professionals in panel discussions & readings. Most events are free. Hundreds of authors invited annually.
Location: Charlottesville, VA, USA
March 16-20, 2022

APRIL

Alberta Library Conference

Sponsored by Library Association of Alberta (LAA)
80 Baker Crescent NW, Calgary, AB T2L 1R4, Canada
Tel: 403-284-5818 *Toll Free Tel:* 877-522-5550 *Fax:* 403-284-5818
E-mail: info@albertalibraryconference.com; info@laa.ca
Web Site: www.albertalibraryconference.com; www.facebook.com/AlbertaLibraryConference; www.laa.ca
Key Personnel
Conference Coord: Christine Sheppard
Co-hosted by Alberta Library Trustees Association (ALTA).

Location: Fairmont Jasper Park Lodge, Jasper, AB, CN
April 28-May 1, 2022

International Children's Book Day

Sponsored by International Board on Books for Young People (IBBY)
Nonnenweg 12, Postfach, 4009 Basel, Switzerland
Tel: (061) 272 29 17 *Fax:* (061) 272 27 57
E-mail: ibby@ibby.org
Web Site: www.ibby.org
Key Personnel
Exec Dir: Liz Page *E-mail:* liz.page@ibby.org
Admin Asst: Franca Salerno *E-mail:* ibby.secretariat@ibby.org
On Hans Christian Andersen's birthday, April 2nd, International Children's Book Day (ICBD) is celebrated to inspire a love of reading & to call attention to children's books. Each year a different national section has the opportunity to be the international sponsor. It decides upon a theme & invites a prominent author to write a message to the children of the world & a well-known illustrator to design a poster. These materials are used in different ways to promote books & reading around the world.
April 2, 2022

NAAJ Annual Meeting

Sponsored by North American Agricultural Journalists (NAAJ)
6434 Hurta Lane, Bryan, TX 77808
Tel: 979-324-4302
Web Site: www.naaj.net
Key Personnel
Exec Secy & Treas: Kathleen Phillips *E-mail:* naajnews@yahoo.com
Annual meeting, writing awards & scholarship benefit dance.
Location: Washington, DC, USA
April 2022

National Library Week

Sponsored by The American Library Association (ALA)
225 N Michigan Ave, Suite 1300, Chicago, IL 60601
Tel: 312-944-6780 *Toll Free Tel:* 800-545-2433 *Fax:* 312-440-9374
E-mail: ala@ala.org
Web Site: www.ala.org/nlw
Location: Nationwide throughout the USA
April 3-9, 2022

The Quest for Excellence® Conference

Sponsored by National Institute of Standards and Technology (NIST)
100 Bureau Dr, Stop 1020, Gaithersburg, MD 20899-1070
Tel: 301-975-2036
E-mail: baldrige@nist.gov
Web Site: www.nist.gov/baldrige
Key Personnel
Conference Chair: Barbara Fischer *E-mail:* barbara.fischer@nist.gov
Official conference of the Malcolm Baldrige National Quality Award held in partnership with American Society for Quality (ASQ).
Location: Gaylord National Harbor, 165 Waterfront St, National Harbor, MD, USA
April 3-6, 2022

Texas Library Association Annual Conference

Sponsored by Texas Library Association (TLA)
3355 Bee Cave Rd, Suite 401, Austin, TX 78746-6763
Tel: 512-328-1518 *Fax:* 512-328-8852
E-mail: tla@txla.org
Web Site: www.txla.org
Key Personnel
Mgr, Conferences & Events: Robin Morris

Tel: 512-328-1518 ext 148 *E-mail:* robinm@txla.org
Mgr, Exhibits & Vendor Rel: Cindy Boyle *Tel:* 512-328-1518 ext 144 *E-mail:* cindyb@txla.org
Conference & Event Specialist: Michelle Cruz *Tel:* 512-328-1518 ext 145 *E-mail:* michellec@txla.org
Location: Fort Worth, TX, USA
April 25-28, 2022

MAY

Thessaloniki International Book Fair

Sponsored by Hellenic Foundation for Culture (HFC)
50 Stratigou Kallari, 154 52 Athens, Greece
Tel: 210-677-6540
Web Site: hfc-worldwide.org
Key Personnel
Pres: Konstantinos Tsoukalas *E-mail:* president@hfc.gr
Co-organized by International Exhibition & Congress Centre of Thessaloniki (HELEXPO), Hellenic Federation of Publishers & Booksellers (POEB) of the Municipality of Thessaloniki & carried out under the supervision & support of the Ministry for Culture & Sport.
Location: International Exhibition & Congress Centre of Thessaloniki (TIF-Helexpo), 154 Egnatia St, Thessaloniki, Greece
May 2022

JUNE

American Library Association Annual Conference

Sponsored by The American Library Association (ALA)
225 N Michigan Ave, Suite 1300, Chicago, IL 60601
Tel: 312-944-6780 *Toll Free Tel:* 800-545-2433 (conference servs) *Fax:* 312-440-9374
E-mail: ala@ala.org
Web Site: www.ala.org
Key Personnel
Registration & Servs Mgr: Alicia Hamann *Tel:* 800-545-2433 ext 3229 *E-mail:* ahamann@ala.org
Conference Dir: Earla Jones *Tel:* 800-545-2433 ext 3226 *E-mail:* ejones@ala.org
Meeting Coord: Donna Hunter *Tel:* 800-545-2433 ext 3218 *E-mail:* dhunter@ala.org
Conference Coord: Lina Zabaneh *Tel:* 800-545-2433 ext 3227 *E-mail:* lzabaneh@ala.org
Meeting Mgr: Yvonne McLean *Tel:* 800-545-2433 ext 3222 *E-mail:* ymclean@ala.org
Location: Washington, DC, USA
June 23-28, 2022

AUPresses Annual Meeting

Sponsored by Association of University Presses (AUPresses)
1412 Broadway, Suite 2135, New York, NY 10018
Tel: 212-989-1010 *Fax:* 212-989-0275
E-mail: info@aupresses.org
Web Site: www.aupresses.org
Key Personnel
Exec Dir: Peter Berkery *Tel:* 917-288-5594 *E-mail:* pberkery@aupresses.org
Res & Communs Dir: Brenna McLaughlin *Tel:* 917-244-2051 *E-mail:* bmclaughlin@aupresses.org

Busn Mgr: Kim Miller *Tel:* 917-244-1264
    E-mail: kmiller@aupresses.org
Location: Marriott Marquis Washington, DC, 901
    Massachusetts Ave NW, Washington, DC, USA
June 18-20, 2022

IAML Annual Congress
Sponsored by International Association of Music
    Libraries, Archives & Documentation Centres
    Inc (IAML)
c/o Gothenburg University Library, Music &
    Drama Library, Box 210, 412 56 Gothenburg,
    Sweden
Tel: (031) 786 40 60
E-mail: contact@iaml.info
Web Site: www.iaml.info
Key Personnel
Secy Gen: Anders Cato *E-mail:* secretary@iaml.
    info
Location: Stellenbosch, South Africa
June 19-24, 2022

SSP Annual Meeting
Sponsored by Society for Scholarly Publishing
    (SSP)
1120 Rte 73, Suite 200, Mount Laurel, NJ 08054
Tel: 856-439-1385 *Fax:* 856-439-0525
E-mail: info@sspnet.org
Web Site: www.sspnet.org
Key Personnel
Meeting Mgr: Tracy Mitchell
Location: Sheraton Chicago Hotel & Towers,
    Chicago, IL, USA
June 1-3, 2022

JULY

Romance Writers of America Annual Conference
Sponsored by Romance Writers of America®
14615 Benfer Rd, Houston, TX 77069
Tel: 832-717-5200 *Fax:* 832-717-5201
E-mail: info@rwa.org
Web Site: www.rwa.org
Key Personnel
Spec Projs Mgr: Megan Sloan *Tel:* 832-717-5200
    ext 120 *E-mail:* megan.sloan@rwa.org
Location: Gaylord Opryland Resort & Convention
    Center, 2800 Opryland Dr, Nashville, TN, USA
July 27-30, 2022

AUGUST

Edinburgh International Book Festival
5 Charlotte Sq, Edinburgh EH2 4DR, United
    Kingdom
Tel: (0131) 718 5666
E-mail: admin@edbookfest.co.uk
Web Site: www.edbookfest.co.uk
Each year we welcome over 900 international au-
    thors & over 250,000 visitors to the biggest
    book festival in the world, turning Edinburgh's
    Charlotte Square Gardens into a literary village
    for 18 days every August.
Location: Charlotte Square Gardens, Edinburgh,
    UK
Aug 2022

IFLA World Library & Information Congress
Sponsored by International Federation of Library
    Associations & Institutions (IFLA) (Federation
    internationale des associations de bibliothe-
    caires et des bibliotheques)

Prins Willem-Alexanderhof 5, 2595 BE The
    Hague, Netherlands
Mailing Address: Postbus 95312, 2509 CH The
    Hague, Netherlands
Tel: (70) 314 08 84 *Fax:* (70) 383 48 27
E-mail: conferences@ifla.org; ifla@ifla.org
Web Site: www.ifla.org
Key Personnel
Secy Gen: Gerald Leitner
Held simultaneously with IFLA General Confer-
    ence & Assembly.
Location: Auckland, New Zealand
Aug 13-19, 2022

AUTUMN

Texas Teen Book Festival
Sponsored by Texas Book Festival
1023 Springdale Rd, Bldg 14, Unit B, Austin, TX
    78721
Tel: 512-477-4055
E-mail: ttbfinfo@texasteenbookfestival.org
Web Site: texasteenbookfestival.org
Key Personnel
TTBF Dir: Claire Burrows
Celebration of the teen reading experience. Orga-
    nized in collaboration with Texas Book Festi-
    val, BookPeople & a dedicated group of librar-
    ian volunteers.
Location: St Edward's University, Austin, TX,
    USA
Fall 2022

SEPTEMBER

Christian Resources Retailers & Suppliers Retreat
Sponsored by Christian Resources Together
Cedar Tree, 4 Ditchingham Close, Aylesbury,
    Bucks HP19 7SA, United Kingdom
Tel: (01296) 489860
Web Site: www.christianresourcestogether.co.uk
Location: The Hayes Conference Centre, Swan-
    wick, Alfreton, Derbyshire, UK
Sept 13-14, 2022

Goeteborg Book Fair
Sponsored by Bok & Bibliotek i Norden AB
Maessans Gata 10, 412 94 Gothenburg, Sweden
Tel: (031) 708 84 00
E-mail: info@goteborg-bookfair.com; hej@
    bokmassan.se
Web Site: www.bokmassan.se
Key Personnel
Prog Mgr: Oskar Ekstrom *Tel:* (031) 708 84 73
    E-mail: oe@bokmassan.se
Prog Coord: Malena Lindhoff *Tel:* (031) 708 82
    06 *E-mail:* ml@bokmassan.se
Location: Gothenburg, Sweden
Sept 22-25, 2022

International Board on Books for Young People Biennial Congress
Sponsored by International Board on Books for
    Young People (IBBY)
Nonnenweg 12, Postfach, 4009 Basel, Switzerland
Tel: (061) 272 29 17 *Fax:* (061) 272 27 57
E-mail: ibby@ibby.org
Web Site: www.ibby.org
Key Personnel
Exec Dir: Liz Page *E-mail:* liz.page@ibby.org
Admin Asst: Franca Salerno *E-mail:* ibby.
    secretariat@ibby.org
IBBY's biennial congresses, hosted by differ-
    ent countries, are the most important meeting

points for IBBY members & other people in-
    volved in children's books & reading devel-
    opment. They are wonderful opportunities to
    make contacts, exchange ideas & open hori-
    zons.
Location: Putrajaya, Malaysia
Sept 5-8, 2022

PSA® International Conference of Photography
Sponsored by Photographic Society of America®
    (PSA®)
8241 S Walker Ave, Suite 104, Oklahoma City,
    OK 73139
Tel: 405-843-1437 *Toll Free Tel:* 855-PSA-INFO
    (772-4636)
E-mail: hq@psa-photo.org
Web Site: www.psa-photo.org
PSA Photo Festival is held during the conference.
Location: Colorado Springs, CO, USA
Sept 21-24, 2022

OCTOBER

American Translators Association Annual Conference
Sponsored by American Translators Association
    (ATA)
225 Reinekers Lane, Suite 590, Alexandria, VA
    22314
Tel: 703-683-6100 *Fax:* 703-683-6122
E-mail: ata@atanet.org
Web Site: www.atanet.org
Key Personnel
Exec Dir: Walter W Bacak, Jr *E-mail:* walter@
    atanet.org
Location: Los Angeles, CA, USA
Oct 12-15, 2022

PACK EXPO International
Sponsored by PMMI: The Association for Pack-
    aging and Processing Technologies
12930 Westgate Dr, Suite 200, Herndon, VA
    20170-6037
Tel: 571-612-3200 *Toll Free Tel:* 888-ASK-PMMI
    (275-7664) *Fax:* 703-243-8556
E-mail: expo@pmmi.org; info@pmmi.org
Web Site: www.packexpointernational.com; www.
    packexpo.com; www.pmmi.org
Key Personnel
VP, Meetings & Events: Patti Fee *Tel:* 571-612-
    3193
VP, Trade Shows: Laura Thompson *Tel:* 571-612-
    3217
Dir, Trade Show Opers: Allison Konczyk
    Tel: 571-612-3188
Dir, Trade Show Mktg: Tina Warren *Tel:* 571-
    612-3203
Dir, Exhibitor Servs: Merideth Newman *Tel:* 571-
    612-3208 *E-mail:* mnewman@pmmi.org
Sr Mgr, Events: Anna Hudson *Tel:* 571-612-3198
Trade Show Opers Mgr: Kelly Faist *Tel:* 571-612-
    3192
Trade Show Mktg Mgr: Lilly Kinney *Tel:* 571-
    287-6811
Trade Show Coord: Jeremy Adams *Tel:* 571-266-
    4407; Jessie Brown *Tel:* 571-266-4409
Trade Show Mktg Coord: Joyce Su *Tel:* 571-266-
    4405
Biennial event held in even-numbered years.
Location: Chicago, IL, USA
Oct 23-26, 2022

Utah Humanities Book Festival
Sponsored by Utah Humanities
Affiliate of Utah Center for the Book
202 W 300 N, Salt Lake City, UT 84103
Tel: 801-359-9670 *Fax:* 801-531-7869
Web Site: utahhumanities.org

Key Personnel
Exec Dir: Jodi Graham *Tel:* 801-359-9670 ext 101 *E-mail:* graham@utahhumanities.org
Prog Mgr: Willy Palomo *Tel:* 801-359-9670 ext 103 *E-mail:* palomo@utahhumanities.org
Dir, Communs: Deena Pyle *Tel:* 801-359-9670 ext 111 *E-mail:* pyle@utahhumanities.org
Free literary event featuring national, regional & local authors held Oct 1-31 annually (National Book Month).
Location: Statewide, UT, USA
Oct 1-31, 2022

NOVEMBER

Jewish Book Month
Sponsored by Jewish Book Council
520 Eighth Ave, 4th fl, New York, NY 10018
Tel: 212-201-2920 *Fax:* 212-532-4952
E-mail: info@jewishbooks.org
Web Site: www.jewishbookcouncil.org; www.facebook.com/JewishBookCouncil; twitter.com/jewishbook
Key Personnel
Exec Dir: Naomi Firestone-Teeter
Dir: Carolyn Starman Hessel
Dedicated to the celebration of Jewish books held annually during the month leading up to Hanukkah.
Location: Nationwide throughout the USA
Nov 18-Dec 18, 2022

2023
MARCH

Leipzig Book Fair (Leipziger Buchmesse)
Sponsored by Leipziger Messe GmbH
Messe-Allee 1, 04356 Leipzig, Germany
Mailing Address: Postfach 10 07 20, 04007 Leipzig, Germany
Tel: (0341) 678-6950 *Fax:* (0341) 678-8242
E-mail: info@leipziger-buchmesse.de
Web Site: www.leipziger-buchmesse.de
Key Personnel
Dir: Oliver Zille
Held annually in conjunction with The Leipzig Antiquarian Book Fair.
Location: Leipzig Exhibition Centre, Messe-Allee 1, Leipzig, Germany
March 23-26, 2023

Virginia Festival of the Book
Sponsored by Virginia Foundation for the Humanities
145 Ednam Dr, Charlottesville, VA 22903
Tel: 434-924-3296
E-mail: vabook@virginia.edu
Web Site: www.vabook.org
Key Personnel
Dir: Jane Kulow *Tel:* 434-924-7548
Annual public festival for children & adults featuring authors, illustrators, publishers, publicists, agents & other book professionals in panel discussions & readings. Most events are free. Hundreds of authors invited annually.
Location: Charlottesville, VA, USA
March 22-26, 2023

APRIL

Alberta Library Conference
Sponsored by Library Association of Alberta (LAA)
80 Baker Crescent NW, Calgary, AB T2L 1R4, Canada
Tel: 403-284-5818 *Toll Free Tel:* 877-522-5550 *Fax:* 403-284-5818
E-mail: info@albertalibraryconference.com; info@laa.ca
Web Site: www.albertalibraryconference.com; www.facebook.com/AlbertaLibraryConference; www.laa.ca
Key Personnel
Conference Coord: Christine Sheppard
Co-hosted by Alberta Library Trustees Association (ALTA).
Location: Fairmont Jasper Park Lodge, Jasper, AB, CN
April 27-30, 2023

International Children's Book Day
Sponsored by International Board on Books for Young People (IBBY)
Nonnenweg 12, Postfach, 4009 Basel, Switzerland
Tel: (061) 272 29 17 *Fax:* (061) 272 27 57
E-mail: ibby@ibby.org
Web Site: www.ibby.org
Key Personnel
Exec Dir: Liz Page *E-mail:* liz.page@ibby.org
Admin Asst: Franca Salerno *E-mail:* ibby.secretariat@ibby.org
On Hans Christian Andersen's birthday, April 2nd, International Children's Book Day (ICBD) is celebrated to inspire a love of reading & to call attention to children's books. Each year a different national section has the opportunity to be the international sponsor. It decides upon a theme & invites a prominent author to write a message to the children of the world & a well-known illustrator to design a poster. These materials are used in different ways to promote books & reading around the world.
April 2, 2023

NAAJ Annual Meeting
Sponsored by North American Agricultural Journalists (NAAJ)
6434 Hurta Lane, Bryan, TX 77808
Tel: 979-324-4302
Web Site: www.naaj.net
Key Personnel
Exec Secy & Treas: Kathleen Phillips *E-mail:* naajnews@yahoo.com
Annual meeting, writing awards & scholarship benefit dance.
Location: Washington, DC, USA
April 2023

National Library Week
Sponsored by The American Library Association (ALA)
225 N Michigan Ave, Suite 1300, Chicago, IL 60601
Tel: 312-944-6780 *Toll Free Tel:* 800-545-2433 *Fax:* 312-440-9374
E-mail: ala@ala.org
Web Site: www.ala.org/nlw
Location: Nationwide throughout the USA
April 23-29, 2023

The Quest for Excellence® Conference
Sponsored by National Institute of Standards and Technology (NIST)
100 Bureau Dr, Stop 1020, Gaithersburg, MD 20899-1070
Tel: 301-975-2036
E-mail: baldrige@nist.gov
Web Site: www.nist.gov/baldrige

Key Personnel
Conference Chair: Barbara Fischer *E-mail:* barbara.fischer@nist.gov
Official conference of the Malcolm Baldrige National Quality Award held in partnership with American Society for Quality (ASQ).
Location: Gaylord National Harbor, 165 Waterfront St, National Harbor, MD, USA
April 2-5, 2023

Texas Library Association Annual Conference
Sponsored by Texas Library Association (TLA)
3355 Bee Cave Rd, Suite 401, Austin, TX 78746-6763
Tel: 512-328-1518 *Fax:* 512-328-8852
E-mail: tla@txla.org
Web Site: www.txla.org
Key Personnel
Mgr, Conferences & Events: Robin Morris *Tel:* 512-328-1518 ext 148 *E-mail:* robinm@txla.org
Mgr, Exhibits & Vendor Rel: Cindy Boyle *Tel:* 512-328-1518 ext 144 *E-mail:* cindyb@txla.org
Conference & Event Specialist: Michelle Cruz *Tel:* 512-328-1518 ext 145 *E-mail:* michellec@txla.org
Location: Austin, TX, USA
April 19-22, 2023

MAY

SSP Annual Meeting
Sponsored by Society for Scholarly Publishing (SSP)
1120 Rte 73, Suite 200, Mount Laurel, NJ 08054
Tel: 856-439-1385 *Fax:* 856-439-0525
E-mail: info@sspnet.org
Web Site: www.sspnet.org
Key Personnel
Meeting Mgr: Tracy Mitchell
Location: Oregon Convention Center & Hyatt Regency Portland, Portland, OR, USA
May 31-June 2, 2023

JUNE

American Library Association Annual Conference
Sponsored by The American Library Association (ALA)
225 N Michigan Ave, Suite 1300, Chicago, IL 60601
Tel: 312-944-6780 *Toll Free Tel:* 800-545-2433 (conference servs) *Fax:* 312-440-9374
E-mail: ala@ala.org
Web Site: www.ala.org
Key Personnel
Registration & Servs Mgr: Alicia Hamann *Tel:* 800-545-2433 ext 3229 *E-mail:* ahamann@ala.org
Conference Dir: Earla Jones *Tel:* 800-545-2433 ext 3226 *E-mail:* ejones@ala.org
Meeting Coord: Donna Hunter *Tel:* 800-545-2433 ext 3218 *E-mail:* dhunter@ala.org
Conference Coord: Lina Zabaneh *Tel:* 800-545-2433 ext 3227 *E-mail:* lzabaneh@ala.org
Meeting Mgr: Yvonne McLean *Tel:* 800-545-2433 ext 3222 *E-mail:* ymclean@ala.org
Location: Chicago, IL, USA
June 22-27, 2023

SEPTEMBER

Christian Resources Retailers & Suppliers Retreat
Sponsored by Christian Resources Together
Cedar Tree, 4 Ditchingham Close, Aylesbury, Bucks HP19 7SA, United Kingdom
Tel: (01296) 489860
Web Site: www.christianresourcestogether.co.uk
Location: The Hayes Conference Centre, Swanwick, Alfreton, Derbyshire, UK
Sept 12-13, 2023

Goeteborg Book Fair
Sponsored by Bok & Bibliotek i Norden AB
Maessans Gata 10, 412 94 Gothenburg, Sweden
Tel: (031) 708 84 00
E-mail: info@goteborg-bookfair.com; hej@bokmassan.se
Web Site: www.bokmassan.se
Key Personnel
Prog Mgr: Oskar Ekstrom *Tel:* (031) 708 84 73 *E-mail:* oe@bokmassan.se
Prog Coord: Malena Lindhoff *Tel:* (031) 708 82 06 *E-mail:* ml@bokmassan.se
Location: Gothenburg, Sweden
Sept 28-Oct 1, 2023

OCTOBER

American Translators Association Annual Conference
Sponsored by American Translators Association (ATA)
225 Reinekers Lane, Suite 590, Alexandria, VA 22314
Tel: 703-683-6100 *Fax:* 703-683-6122
E-mail: ata@atanet.org
Web Site: www.atanet.org
Key Personnel
Exec Dir: Walter W Bacak, Jr *E-mail:* walter@atanet.org
Location: Miami, FL, USA
Oct 25-28, 2023

Utah Humanities Book Festival
Sponsored by Utah Humanities
Affiliate of Utah Center for the Book
202 W 300 N, Salt Lake City, UT 84103
Tel: 801-359-9670 *Fax:* 801-531-7869
Web Site: utahhumanities.org
Key Personnel
Exec Dir: Jodi Graham *Tel:* 801-359-9670 ext 101 *E-mail:* graham@utahhumanities.org
Prog Mgr: Willy Palomo *Tel:* 801-359-9670 ext 103 *E-mail:* palomo@utahhumanities.org
Dir, Communs: Deena Pyle *Tel:* 801-359-9670 ext 111 *E-mail:* pyle@utahhumanities.org
Free literary event featuring national, regional & local authors held Oct 1-31 annually (National Book Month).
Location: Statewide, UT, USA
Oct 1-31, 2023

NOVEMBER

Jewish Book Month
Sponsored by Jewish Book Council
520 Eighth Ave, 4th fl, New York, NY 10018
Tel: 212-201-2920 *Fax:* 212-532-4952
E-mail: info@jewishbooks.org
Web Site: www.jewishbookcouncil.org; www.facebook.com/JewishBookCouncil; twitter.com/jewishbook
Key Personnel
Exec Dir: Naomi Firestone-Teeter
Dir: Carolyn Starman Hessel
Dedicated to the celebration of Jewish books held annually during the month leading up to Hanukkah.
Location: Nationwide throughout the USA
Nov 7-Dec 7, 2023

2024

MARCH

Virginia Festival of the Book
Sponsored by Virginia Foundation for the Humanities
145 Ednam Dr, Charlottesville, VA 22903
Tel: 434-924-3296
E-mail: vabook@virginia.edu
Web Site: www.vabook.org
Key Personnel
Dir: Jane Kulow *Tel:* 434-924-7548
Annual public festival for children & adults featuring authors, illustrators, publishers, publicists, agents & other book professionals in panel discussions & readings. Most events are free. Hundreds of authors invited annually.
Location: Charlottesville, VA, USA
March 20-24, 2024

APRIL

International Children's Book Day
Sponsored by International Board on Books for Young People (IBBY)
Nonnenweg 12, Postfach, 4009 Basel, Switzerland
Tel: (061) 272 29 17 *Fax:* (061) 272 27 57
E-mail: ibby@ibby.org
Web Site: www.ibby.org
Key Personnel
Exec Dir: Liz Page *E-mail:* liz.page@ibby.org
Admin Asst: Franca Salerno *E-mail:* ibby.secretariat@ibby.org
On Hans Christian Andersen's birthday, April 2nd, International Children's Book Day (ICBD) is celebrated to inspire a love of reading & to call attention to children's books. Each year a different national section has the opportunity to be the international sponsor. It decides upon a theme & invites a prominent author to write a message to the children of the world & a well-known illustrator to design a poster. These materials are used in different ways to promote books & reading around the world.
April 2, 2024

NAAJ Annual Meeting
Sponsored by North American Agricultural Journalists (NAAJ)
6434 Hurta Lane, Bryan, TX 77808
Tel: 979-324-4302
Web Site: www.naaj.net
Key Personnel
Exec Secy & Treas: Kathleen Phillips *E-mail:* naajnews@yahoo.com
Annual meeting, writing awards & scholarship benefit dance.
Location: Washington, DC, USA
April 2024

The Quest for Excellence® Conference
Sponsored by National Institute of Standards and Technology (NIST)

100 Bureau Dr, Stop 1020, Gaithersburg, MD 20899-1070
Tel: 301-975-2036
E-mail: baldrige@nist.gov
Web Site: www.nist.gov/baldrige
Key Personnel
Conference Chair: Barbara Fischer *E-mail:* barbara.fischer@nist.gov
Official conference of the Malcolm Baldrige National Quality Award held in partnership with American Society for Quality (ASQ).
Location: Gaylord National Harbor, 165 Waterfront St, National Harbor, MD, USA
April 7-10, 2024

Texas Library Association Annual Conference
Sponsored by Texas Library Association (TLA)
3355 Bee Cave Rd, Suite 401, Austin, TX 78746-6763
Tel: 512-328-1518 *Fax:* 512-328-8852
E-mail: tla@txla.org
Web Site: www.txla.org
Key Personnel
Mgr, Conferences & Events: Robin Morris *Tel:* 512-328-1518 ext 148 *E-mail:* robinm@txla.org
Mgr, Exhibits & Vendor Rel: Cindy Boyle *Tel:* 512-328-1518 ext 144 *E-mail:* cindyb@txla.org
Conference & Event Specialist: Michelle Cruz *Tel:* 512-328-1518 ext 145 *E-mail:* michellec@txla.org
Location: San Antonio, TX, USA
April 16-19, 2024

MAY

SSP Annual Meeting
Sponsored by Society for Scholarly Publishing (SSP)
1120 Rte 73, Suite 200, Mount Laurel, NJ 08054
Tel: 856-439-1385 *Fax:* 856-439-0525
E-mail: info@sspnet.org
Web Site: www.sspnet.org
Key Personnel
Meeting Mgr: Tracy Mitchell
Location: Westin Waterfront, Boston, MA, USA
May 29-31, 2024

JUNE

American Library Association Annual Conference
Sponsored by The American Library Association (ALA)
225 N Michigan Ave, Suite 1300, Chicago, IL 60601
Tel: 312-944-6780 *Toll Free Tel:* 800-545-2433 (conference servs) *Fax:* 312-440-9374
E-mail: ala@ala.org
Web Site: www.ala.org
Key Personnel
Registration & Servs Mgr: Alicia Hamann *Tel:* 800-545-2433 ext 3229 *E-mail:* ahamann@ala.org
Conference Dir: Earla Jones *Tel:* 800-545-2433 ext 3226 *E-mail:* ejones@ala.org
Meeting Coord: Donna Hunter *Tel:* 800-545-2433 ext 3218 *E-mail:* dhunter@ala.org
Conference Coord: Lina Zabaneh *Tel:* 800-545-2433 ext 3227 *E-mail:* lzabaneh@ala.org
Meeting Mgr: Yvonne McLean *Tel:* 800-545-2433 ext 3222 *E-mail:* ymclean@ala.org
Location: San Diego, CA, USA
June 27-July 2, 2024

OCTOBER

American Translators Association Annual Conference
Sponsored by American Translators Association (ATA)
225 Reinekers Lane, Suite 590, Alexandria, VA 22314
Tel: 703-683-6100 *Fax:* 703-683-6122
E-mail: ata@atanet.org
Web Site: www.atanet.org
Key Personnel
Exec Dir: Walter W Bacak, Jr *E-mail:* walter@atanet.org
Location: Portland, OR, USA
Oct 30-Nov 2, 2024

Utah Humanities Book Festival
Sponsored by Utah Humanities
Affiliate of Utah Center for the Book
202 W 300 N, Salt Lake City, UT 84103
Tel: 801-359-9670 *Fax:* 801-531-7869
Web Site: utahhumanities.org
Key Personnel
Exec Dir: Jodi Graham *Tel:* 801-359-9670 ext 101 *E-mail:* graham@utahhumanities.org
Prog Mgr: Willy Palomo *Tel:* 801-359-9670 ext 103 *E-mail:* palomo@utahhumanities.org
Dir, Communs: Deena Pyle *Tel:* 801-359-9670 ext 111 *E-mail:* pyle@utahhumanities.org
Free literary event featuring national, regional & local authors held Oct 1-31 annually (National Book Month).
Location: Statewide, UT, USA
Oct 1-31, 2024

NOVEMBER

Jewish Book Month
Sponsored by Jewish Book Council
520 Eighth Ave, 4th fl, New York, NY 10018
Tel: 212-201-2920 *Fax:* 212-532-4952
E-mail: info@jewishbooks.org
Web Site: www.jewishbookcouncil.org; www.facebook.com/JewishBookCouncil; twitter.com/jewishbook
Key Personnel
Exec Dir: Naomi Firestone-Teeter
Dir: Carolyn Starman Hessel
Dedicated to the celebration of Jewish books held annually during the month leading up to Hanukkah.
Location: Nationwide throughout the USA
Nov 25-Dec 25, 2024

2025

APRIL

International Children's Book Day
Sponsored by International Board on Books for Young People (IBBY)
Nonnenweg 12, Postfach, 4009 Basel, Switzerland
Tel: (061) 272 29 17 *Fax:* (061) 272 27 57
E-mail: ibby@ibby.org
Web Site: www.ibby.org
Key Personnel
Exec Dir: Liz Page *E-mail:* liz.page@ibby.org
Admin Asst: Franca Salerno *E-mail:* ibby.secretariat@ibby.org
On Hans Christian Andersen's birthday, April 2nd, International Children's Book Day (ICBD) is celebrated to inspire a love of reading & to call attention to children's books. Each year a different national section has the opportunity to be the international sponsor. It decides upon a theme & invites a prominent author to write a message to the children of the world & a well-known illustrator to design a poster. These materials are used in different ways to promote books & reading around the world.
April 2, 2025

NAAJ Annual Meeting
Sponsored by North American Agricultural Journalists (NAAJ)
6434 Hurta Lane, Bryan, TX 77808
Tel: 979-324-4302
Web Site: www.naaj.net
Key Personnel
Exec Secy & Treas: Kathleen Phillips *E-mail:* naajnews@yahoo.com
Annual meeting, writing awards & scholarship benefit dance.
Location: Washington, DC, USA
April 2025

Texas Library Association Annual Conference
Sponsored by Texas Library Association (TLA)
3355 Bee Cave Rd, Suite 401, Austin, TX 78746-6763
Tel: 512-328-1518 *Fax:* 512-328-8852
E-mail: tla@txla.org
Web Site: www.txla.org
Key Personnel
Mgr, Conferences & Events: Robin Morris *Tel:* 512-328-1518 ext 148 *E-mail:* robinm@txla.org
Mgr, Exhibits & Vendor Rel: Cindy Boyle *Tel:* 512-328-1518 ext 144 *E-mail:* cindyb@txla.org
Conference & Event Specialist: Michelle Cruz *Tel:* 512-328-1518 ext 145 *E-mail:* michellec@txla.org
Location: Dallas, TX, USA
April 1-4, 2025

MAY

SSP Annual Meeting
Sponsored by Society for Scholarly Publishing (SSP)
1120 Rte 73, Suite 200, Mount Laurel, NJ 08054
Tel: 856-439-1385 *Fax:* 856-439-0525
E-mail: info@sspnet.org
Web Site: www.sspnet.org
Key Personnel
Meeting Mgr: Tracy Mitchell
Location: Hilton Baltimore, Baltimore, MD, USA
May 28-31, 2025

JUNE

American Library Association Annual Conference
Sponsored by The American Library Association (ALA)
225 N Michigan Ave, Suite 1300, Chicago, IL 60601
Tel: 312-944-6780 *Toll Free Tel:* 800-545-2433 (conference servs) *Fax:* 312-440-9374
E-mail: ala@ala.org
Web Site: www.ala.org
Key Personnel
Registration & Servs Mgr: Alicia Hamann *Tel:* 800-545-2433 ext 3229 *E-mail:* ahamann@ala.org
Conference Dir: Earla Jones *Tel:* 800-545-2433 ext 3226 *E-mail:* ejones@ala.org
Meeting Coord: Donna Hunter *Tel:* 800-545-2433 ext 3218 *E-mail:* dhunter@ala.org
Conference Coord: Lina Zabaneh *Tel:* 800-545-2433 ext 3227 *E-mail:* lzabaneh@ala.org
Meeting Mgr: Yvonne McLean *Tel:* 800-545-2433 ext 3222 *E-mail:* ymclean@ala.org
Location: Philadelphia, PA, USA
June 26-July 1, 2025

OCTOBER

Utah Humanities Book Festival
Sponsored by Utah Humanities
Affiliate of Utah Center for the Book
202 W 300 N, Salt Lake City, UT 84103
Tel: 801-359-9670 *Fax:* 801-531-7869
Web Site: utahhumanities.org
Key Personnel
Exec Dir: Jodi Graham *Tel:* 801-359-9670 ext 101 *E-mail:* graham@utahhumanities.org
Prog Mgr: Willy Palomo *Tel:* 801-359-9670 ext 103 *E-mail:* palomo@utahhumanities.org
Dir, Communs: Deena Pyle *Tel:* 801-359-9670 ext 111 *E-mail:* pyle@utahhumanities.org
Free literary event featuring national, regional & local authors held Oct 1-31 annually (National Book Month).
Location: Statewide, UT, USA
Oct 1-31, 2025

Writers' Conferences & Workshops

The following lists workshops and seminars dealing with various aspects of the book trade. See **Courses for the Book Trade** for a list of college level programs and courses.

American Society of Journalists and Authors Annual Writers Conference
American Society of Journalists and Authors (ASJA)
355 Lexington Ave, 15th fl, New York, NY 10017-6603
Tel: 212-997-0947
Web Site: asja.org
Key Personnel
Exec Dir: Holly Koenig *E-mail:* director@asja.org
Inside information from editors, agents & publishers, find inspiration & gain income-boosting ideas. Open to all, the conference features topics for newer & more experienced pros. New panels & workshops will enrich you no matter where you are in your writing career.

AMWA Annual Conference
American Medical Writers Association (AMWA)
30 W Gude Dr, Suite 525, Rockville, MD 20850-4357
Tel: 240-238-0940 *Fax:* 301-294-9006
E-mail: amwa@amwa.org
Web Site: www.amwa.org
Key Personnel
Educ Mgr: Becky Philips
Annual conference includes workshops, open sessions & networking opportunities.
Location: Chicago Marriott Downtown Magnificent Mile, Chicago, IL
Date: Oct 27-30, 2021

Antioch Writers' Workshop
Antioch University Midwest
300 College Park Ave, Suite 200A, Dayton, OH 45469-0001
Tel: 937-567-2399
E-mail: info@antiochwritersworkshop.com
Web Site: www.antiochwritersworkshop.com
Key Personnel
Pres: T J Turner
Exec Dir: Sharon Short
A weeklong summer workshop featuring morning classes, midday presentations on writing profession, afternoon intensive seminars in a genre or type, evening faculty talks & readings. Non-refundable registration fee $125.

Appalachian Writers' Workshop
Hindman Settlement School
56 Education Lane, Hindman, KY 41822
Mailing Address: PO Box 844, Hindman, KY 41822-0844
Tel: 606-785-5475
E-mail: info@hindmansettlement.org
Web Site: www.hindmansettlement.org
Key Personnel
Exec Dir, Hindman Settlement School: Brent D Hutchinson *E-mail:* bdhutchinson@hindmansettlement.org
Poetry, nonfiction, short story, novel, dramatic writing & children's writing.

Arkansas Writers' Conference
National League of American Pen Women, Arkansas Pioneer Branch
Division of National League of American Pen Women
PO Box 24662, Little Rock, AR 72221
Tel: 501-833-2756
Web Site: www.arkansaswritersconference.org

Key Personnel
Dir: Brenda Iannacone *E-mail:* breannacone1@yahoo.com
Location: Crowne Plaza Hotel, Little Rock, AR
Date: Annually in June

Artists & Writers Summer Fellowships
The Constance Saltonstall Foundation for the Arts
435 Ellis Hollow Creek Rd, Ithaca, NY 14850
Tel: 607-539-3146
E-mail: artscolony@saltonstall.org
Web Site: www.saltonstall.org
Key Personnel
Exec Dir: Lesley Williamson
Provide month long summer fellowships for New York State artists & writers May-Sept.

The Association for Women in Communications
1717 E Republic Rd, Suite A, Springfield, MO 65804
Tel: 417-886-8606 *Fax:* 417-886-3685
E-mail: info@womcom.org
Web Site: www.womcom.org
Key Personnel
Chair: Kristin E Van Nort *E-mail:* chair@womcom.org
Exec Dir: Jean Harmison
Acct Mgr: Becky Lucas *E-mail:* members@womcom.org
Professional development workshops & exposition in various areas of the communications field. Ongoing webinars available.

Association pour l'Avancement des Sciences et des Techniques de la Documentation
2065 rue Parthenais, Bureau 387, Montreal, QC H2K 3T1, Canada
Tel: 514-281-5012 *Fax:* 514-281-8219
E-mail: info@asted.org
Web Site: www.asted.org
Key Personnel
Exec Dir: Lionel Villalonga *E-mail:* lvillalonga@asted.org

Atlantic Center for the Arts Master Artist-in-Residence Program
Atlantic Center for the Arts (ACA)
1414 Art Center Ave, New Smyrna Beach, FL 32168
Tel: 386-427-6975 *Toll Free Tel:* 800-393-6975 *Fax:* 386-427-5669
E-mail: program@atlanticcenterforthearts.org
Web Site: atlanticcenterforthearts.org
Key Personnel
Co-Exec Dir: Jim Frost *E-mail:* jfrost@atlanticcenterforthearts.org; Nancy Lowden Norman *E-mail:* nlowden@atlanticcenterforthearts.org
Dir, Fin & Acctg: Kevin Miller *E-mail:* kmiller@atlanticcenterforthearts.org
Residency Dir: Nick Conroy *E-mail:* nconroy@atlanticcenterforthearts.org
Mktg & Membership Mgr: Kathryn Peterson *E-mail:* kpeterson@atlanticcenterforthearts.org
Admin Asst: Kelly Timmons
Since 1982, Atlantic Center's residency program has provided artists from all artistic disciplines with spaces to live, work & collaborate during 3 week residencies. Each residency session includes 3 master artists of different disciplines.

The master artists each personally select a group of associates - talented, emerging artists - through an application process administered by ACA. During the residency, artists participate in informal sessions with their group, collaborate on projects & work independently on their own projects. The relaxed atmosphere & unstructured program provide considerable time for artistic regeneration & creation.

Bard Society Fiction Writing Workshop
Bard Society
3113 Crosby Lane, Jacksonville, FL 32216
Tel: 904-250-6045
E-mail: frankgrn@comcast.net
Key Personnel
Dir: Frank Green
Fiction writing workshop in existence for more than 35 years. Schedule: One workshop a week, Tuesday evening, 3 hours; more than 40 books published by members. No fee but contributions welcome. All lovers of the written word welcome. A tribute to workshop leader Frank Green was published, Wednesdays with Frank.

Beyond the Book
Copyright Clearance Center Inc (CCC)
222 Rosewood Dr, Danvers, MA 01923
Tel: 978-750-8400 (sales)
E-mail: beyondthebook@copyright.com
Web Site: www.copyright.com; beyondthebookcast.com
Key Personnel
VP, HR: Michele R Nivens
Programs also include online seminars & telephone conference calls with distinguished experts. Created with authors in mind, Beyond the Book seeks to provide information on the latest business issues facing the creative professions - from initial research to final publication & beyond. Your connection to leading editors, publishing analysts & information technology experts, as well as innovative authors.

Big Apple Conference
The International Women's Writing Guild (IWWG)
5 Penn Plaza, 19th fl, PMB 19059, New York, NY 10001
Tel: 917-720-6959
E-mail: iwwgquestions@iwwg.org
Web Site: www.iwwg.org
Key Personnel
Exec Dir: Michelle Miller *E-mail:* michelle@iwwg.org
Held twice annually.
Location: New York, NY
Date: April
Location: New York, NY
Date: Oct

Bread Loaf Writers' Conference
Middlebury College
5525 Middlebury College, 14 Old Chapel Rd, Middlebury, VT 05753
Tel: 802-443-5286 *Fax:* 802-443-2087
E-mail: blwc@middlebury.edu
Web Site: www.middlebury.edu/blwc
Key Personnel
Dir: Jennifer Grotz

Admin Dir: Noreen Cargill
Coord: Jason Lamb
Ten day conference for writers of poetry, fiction & nonfiction. Fellowship covers tuition, room & board. Work-study scholarship covers tuition, with pay to offset room & board. Tuition scholarship covers tuition.

Bucknell Seminar for Undergraduate Poets
Stadler Center for Poetry
Bucknell University, Bucknell Hall, Moore Ave, Lewisburg, PA 17837
Tel: 570-577-1853
E-mail: stadlercenter@bucknell.edu
Web Site: www.bucknell.edu/stadlercenter
Key Personnel
Prog Mgr: Andrew Ciotola
Ten applicants are accepted to participate in a 3 week residence in writing for undergraduate poets. Applications should include an academic transcript, 2 supporting recommendations (at least one from a poetry-writing instructor) & a 10-12 page portfolio. A letter of self-presentation (letter of intro stressing commitment to poetry writing, experience & any publications) should accompany the application. Applications must be submitted online or postmarked by Jan 31. See web site for details.
Location: Stadler Center for Poetry, Bucknell University, Lewisburg, PA
Date: June 2021

Cape Cod Writers' Center Conference
Cape Cod Writers Center
919 Main St, Osterville, MA 02655
Mailing Address: PO Box 408, Osterville, MA 02655
Tel: 508-420-0200
E-mail: writers@capecodwriterscenter.org
Web Site: capecodwriterscenter.org
Key Personnel
Pres: Barbara Struna
Exec Dir: Nancy Rubin Stuart
Annual conference to improve your literary skills as you learn from top professionals. Open to beginning & published authors. In addition to classes in fiction, nonfiction, mystery, poetry, children's, young adult, screenwriting, social media & promotion & other genres, the conference offers agent query & ms mentoring sessions for students. Faculty & student readings. Keynote luncheon with prominent author.
Date: Aug 2021

Chautauqua Writers' Workshop
The Writers' Center at Chautauqua
One Ames Ave, Chautauqua, NY 14722
Mailing Address: PO Box 28, Chautauqua, NY 14722-0408
Tel: 716-357-6316; 716-357-6250
  Toll Free Tel: 800-836-ARTS (836-2787)
  Fax: 716-357-9014
Web Site: ciweb.org
Key Personnel
VP: Sherra Babcock
Prog Dir, Writer's Ctr: Clara Silverstein
  E-mail: clrsilver@gmail.com
Dept Coord: Emily Carpenter
Writing workshop in poetry & prose at 137 year-old Chautauqua Institution, international center for the arts, education, religion & recreation.
Location: Chautauqua Institution, Chautauqua, NY
Date: Last week in June through the end of Aug

Chocorua Writing Workshop
World Fellowship Center
PO Box 2280, Conway, NH 03818-2280
Tel: 603-447-2280
E-mail: reservations@worldfellowship.org
Web Site: www.worldfellowship.org; www.facebook.com/World.Fellowship.Center

Key Personnel
Dir: Ellen Meeropol; Ekere Tallie
Can a letter be as powerful as a poem? Engage like good fiction? Persuade like an essay? Help the writer process like journaling? Yes! Two sessions of exploring letters & epistolary texts & writing our own.
Location: Conway (White Mountains), NH
Date: Annually in July

The Clarion Science Fiction & Fantasy Writers' Workshop
The Clarion Foundation
Arthur C Clarke Ctr for Human Imagination, UC San Diego, 9500 Gilman Dr, MC0445, La Jolla, CA 92093-0445
Tel: 858-534-2115
E-mail: clarion@ucsd.edu
Web Site: clarion.ucsd.edu; imagination.ucsd.edu
Key Personnel
Pres: Karen Joy Fowler
Prog Mgr: Patrick Coleman
Science fiction & fantasy writing workshop held for 6 weeks each summer. It is mandatory that students reside in Clarion housing.

Conference on Poetry
The Frost Place
158 Ridge Rd, Franconia, NH 03580
Mailing Address: PO Box 74, Franconia, NH 03580-0074
Tel: 603-823-5510
E-mail: frost@frostplace.org
Web Site: frostplace.org
Key Personnel
Exec Dir: Maudelle Driskell
Offers lectures, talks & craft panels by faculty in a 7-day program. See web site for details.
Date: Annually in Summer

Creative Writing Day & Workshops
Virginia Highlands Festival
PO Box 801, Abingdon, VA 24212-0801
Tel: 276-623-5266 *Fax:* 276-676-3076
E-mail: info@vahighlandsfestival.org
Web Site: vahighlandsfestival.org
Key Personnel
Chair: Steve Lindeman; Deborah Prescott
Exec Dir: Becky Caldwell
Lectures, readings & workshops in creative writing with noteworthy authors held each summer.

Djerassi Resident Artists Program
2325 Bear Gulch Rd, Woodside, CA 94062
Tel: 650-747-1250
E-mail: drap@djerassi.org
Web Site: www.djerassi.org
Key Personnel
Exec Dir: Margot Knight *Tel:* 650-747-1250 ext 14 *E-mail:* margot@djerassi.org
One month residencies for writers & other artists.

Education Writers Association Workshops
Education Writers Association (EWA)
3516 Connecticut Ave NW, Washington, DC 20008
Tel: 202-452-9830 *Fax:* 202-452-9837
E-mail: ewa@ewa.org
Web Site: www.ewa.org
Key Personnel
Exec Dir: Caroline W Hendrie *E-mail:* chendrie@ewa.org
National seminar, regional meetings.

Florida Writers Association Conference
Florida Writers Association Inc
PO Box 66069, St Pete Beach, FL 33736-6069
Web Site: www.floridawriters.net
Key Personnel
Pres: Cheyenne Williams *E-mail:* ckwilliams@onlinebinding.com

EVP: Jade Kerrion
VP, Admin & Fin: Larry Kokko
VP, Fin: Robyn Weinbaum
Assortment of workshops, networking, interviews with agents & editors, literary contest & banquet.
Date: Annually in Oct

Fun in the Sun Writer's Cruise Conference
Florida Romance Writers Inc (FRW)
Affiliate of Romance Writers of America®
PO Box 823414, Pembroke Pines, FL 33082
E-mail: frwfuninthesun@yahoo.com
Web Site: frwfuninthesunmain.blogspot.com/; www.frwriters.org
Key Personnel
Pres: Heidi Lynn Anderson
VP, Progs: Marcia King-Gamble
VP, Communs: Kimberly Gonzales
Secy: Aleka Nakis
Treas: Tina Stitzer
Highlights include 2 days of workshops on the art, craft & business of writing that will appeal to writers in all genres. Exclusive Q&A with our keynote speaker, editor/agent appointments, Floridian Idol (live readings), write-in, & more. Registration fees from $180-$220. Workshop speakers entitled to discounted registration fee. Group rates available for groups of 5 or more; special hotel rates for conference attendees also available. Use the mailing address for all conference correspondence.

Gell: A Finger Lakes Creative Retreat
Writers & Books
740 University Ave, Rochester, NY 14607-1259
Tel: 585-473-2590 *Fax:* 585-442-9333
Web Site: www.wab.org
Key Personnel
Dir, Opers & Programming: Kathy Pottetti
  Tel: 585-473-2590 ext 103 *E-mail:* kathyp@wab.org
Meeting center that hosts classes, workshops, conferences, etc for groups of up to 50 people.

The Glen Workshop
Image Journal
3307 Third Ave W, Seattle, WA 98119
Tel: 206-281-2988 *Fax:* 206-281-2979
E-mail: glenworkshop@imagejournal.org
Web Site: www.imagejournal.org
Key Personnel
Dir, Progs: Paul Anderson
A weeklong arts workshop for writers & visual artists that combines an intensive learning experience with a lively festival of the arts.

Gotham Writers' Workshop
555 Eighth Ave, Suite 1402, New York, NY 10018-4358
Tel: 212-974-8377
E-mail: contact@gothamwriters.com
Web Site: www.gothamwriters.com
Key Personnel
Pres: Alex Steele *E-mail:* alex@gothamwriters.com
Professional writers teach acclaimed creative writing classes online & in New York City throughout the year.

Harvard Summer Writing Program
Harvard University, Division of Continuing Education
51 Brattle St, Dept S760, Cambridge, MA 02138-3722
Tel: 617-495-4024 *Fax:* 617-495-9176
E-mail: summer@harvard.edu
Web Site: www.summer.harvard.edu
Key Personnel
Dir & Prog Contact: Dr Patricia Bellanca
Eight week program starting at the end of June; full semester college credit workshop courses

in creative, professional & expository writing. These include: beginning fiction, poetry, journalism & screenwriting; advanced creative nonfiction; writing grant proposals, effective business communication, legal writing & principles of editing; cross-cultural expository writing, writing about social & ethical issues & writing about literature.

Hedgebrook Master Class Retreat Series
Hedgebrook
PO Box 1231, Freeland, WA 98249
Tel: 360-321-4786 *Fax:* 360-321-2171
E-mail: hedgebrook@hedgebrook.org
Web Site: www.hedgebrook.org; www.facebook.com/hedgebrook
Key Personnel
Prog Dir: Vito Zingarelli *E-mail:* vitoz@hedgebrook.org
Prog Assoc: Julie O'Brien *E-mail:* julieo@hedgebrook.org
Craft-focused writing workshops, where participants have the unique opportunity to be in residence & study with a celebrated teacher. Weeklong Master Classes include 6-7 participants, each housed in her own cottage. Participants receive 5 days of writing workshops, instructor-led constructive group feedback sessions, one-on-one sessions with the instructor & an additional day of retreat time. Meals featuring produce harvested from our organic garden are prepared by Hedgebrook's chefs, Writers at all levels of experience, published or not, are accepted into Hedgebrook's Master Classes. Cost is $2,500-$3,500, which covers lodging, meals & workshops; all taxes included. A portion is tax-deductible.

Hedgebrook VORTEXT
Hedgebrook
PO Box 1231, Freeland, WA 98249
Tel: 360-321-4786 *Fax:* 360-321-2171
E-mail: hedgebrook@hedgebrook.org
Web Site: www.hedgebrook.org; www.facebook.com/hedgebrook
Key Personnel
Prog Dir: Vito Zingarelli *E-mail:* vitoz@hedgebrook.org
Prog Assoc: Julie O'Brien *E-mail:* julieo@hedgebrook.org
Weekend salon led by 6 established women writers. Connect & hone your craft in diverse & powerful small group workshops. Enjoy dynamic keynotes & discussions about opportunities & challenges for women who write. Engage in dynamic discussions on hot topics specific to women who write. Share meals, open mics, conversation & community in a stunningly beautiful setting. Held at the Whidbey Institute at Chinook on Whidbey Island, WA in late May, a registration fee of $950 includes all keynotes & 3 workshops of your choice, group sessions & free time to write as well as breakfast, lunch & daily reception.

Hedgebrook Writers in Residence Program
Hedgebrook
PO Box 1231, Freeland, WA 98249
Tel: 360-321-4786 *Fax:* 360-321-2171
E-mail: hedgebrook@hedgebrook.org
Web Site: www.hedgebrook.org; www.facebook.com/hedgebrook
Key Personnel
Prog Dir: Vito Zingarelli *E-mail:* vitoz@hedgebrook.org
Prog Assoc: Julie O'Brien *E-mail:* julieo@hedgebrook.org
Program supporting fully-funded residencies of approximately 40 women writers (6 or 7 at a time) at a retreat each year on Whidbey Island, WA. Hedgebrook is one of the few writer's colonies in the world exclusively dedicated to

supporting women writers & bringing their work to the world through innovative public programs. Emerging & established writers (all genres) worldwide attend. Each writer is housed in her own cottage. Residents share a home-cooked evening meal prepared by Hedgebrook's chefs. The community formed around the kitchen table is growing as Hedgebrook hosts alumnae gatherings, events & professional development workshops around the country. Applications for the upcoming residency season are available via our web site by mid-June, with a deadline in late July.

Highland Summer Writers' Conference
The Appalachian Regional Studies Center (ARSC)
Division of Radford University
PO Box 7014, Radford University, Cook Hall, Radford, VA 24142
Fax: 540-831-5951
Web Site: www.radford.edu/content/cehd/home/appalachian-studies.html
Key Personnel
Dir, ARSC: Dr Theresa Burriss *Tel:* 540-831-6857 *E-mail:* tburriss@radford.edu
Instructor & ARSC Assoc: Ruth Derrick *Tel:* 540-831-6152 *E-mail:* rbderrick@radford.edu
Annual program based on Appalachian culture & writing; directed for 2 weeks by a fiction writer/poet/dramatist. Elective seminar-workshop combination offers the opportunity to study & practice creative & expository writing & earn 3 hours graduate/undergraduate credit.
Location: Radford University, Radford, VA

Historical Novel Society North American Conference
Historical Novel Society
400 Dark Star Ct, Fairbanks, AK 99709
Tel: 217-581-7538 *Fax:* 217-581-7534
Web Site: www.historicalnovelsociety.org/event/hns-north-american-conference; historicalnovelsociety.org
Key Personnel
US Membership Secy: Georgine Olson *E-mail:* georgine@mosquitonet.com
Conference Prog Chair: Vanitha Sankaran *E-mail:* info@vanithasankaran.com
Held biennially, in odd-numbered years.
Location: San Antonio, TX
Date: June 24-26, 2021

Hurston/Wright Writers Week
The Zora Neale Hurston/Richard Wright Foundation
10 "G" St NE, Suite 600, Washington, DC 20002
Tel: 202-248-5051
E-mail: info@hurstonwright.org
Web Site: www.hurstonwright.org
Key Personnel
Co-Founder: Marita Golden; Clyde McElvane
Exec Dir: Kesha Lee
The Zora Neale Hurston/Richard Wright Foundation was founded in 1990 in Washington, DC & is dedicated to discovering, mentoring & honoring black writers. Through workshops, master classes & readings, the organization preserves the voices of black writers in the world literary canon, serves as a community for writers & continues a tradition of literary excellence in storytelling established by its namesakes. The Foundation is a 501(c)(3) nonprofit.

Idyllwild Arts Summer Workshops
Idyllwild Arts Summer Program
52500 Temecula Dr, Idyllwild, CA 92549-0038
Mailing Address: PO Box 38, Idyllwild, CA 92549-0038
Tel: 951-659-2171 *Fax:* 951-659-4552
E-mail: summer@idyllwildarts.org
Web Site: www.idyllwildarts.org/writersweek
Key Personnel
Summer Prog Registrar: Diane Dennis *Tel:* 951-659-2171 ext 2365 *E-mail:* dianed@idyllwildarts.org
Five-day writing workshops for adults in creative nonfiction, fiction, chapbooks, poetry, screenwriting & more. Two-week writing workshops for high school students in fiction, poetry & much more.

Indiana University Writers' Conference
Indiana University
464 Ballantine Hall, 1020 E Kirkwood Ave, Bloomington, IN 47405-7103
Tel: 812-855-1877 *Fax:* 812-855-9535
E-mail: writecon@indiana.edu
Web Site: www.iuwc.indiana.edu
Key Personnel
Dir: Bob Bledsoe
Weeklong, annual conference in June for writers of poetry, fiction, nonfiction & script writing. Second oldest such conference in the US. Past staff includes Raymond Carver, Allen Tate & Katherine Anne Porter.

Intimate & Inspiring Workshops for Children's Authors & Illustrators
Highlights Foundation
814 Court St, Honesdale, PA 18431
Tel: 570-253-1192 *Fax:* 570-253-0179
E-mail: jolloyd@highlightsfoundation.org
Web Site: www.highlightsfoundation.org
Key Personnel
Exec Dir: Kent L Brown, Jr *E-mail:* klbrown@highlightsfoundation.org
For children's writers & illustrators seeking to sharpen their focus. Helps to improve your craft with the help of a master, finding the time & space in which to work & marketing yourself & your books. Cost of workshops range from $495 & up which includes tuition, meals, conference supplies & housing.

Iowa Summer Writing Festival
Division of University of Iowa
250 Continuing Educ Facility, University of Iowa, Iowa City, IA 52242
Tel: 319-335-4160
E-mail: iswfestival@uiowa.edu
Web Site: iowasummerwritingfestival.org
Key Personnel
Dir: Amy Margolis *E-mail:* amy-margolis@uiowa.edu
Annual weeklong & weekend non-credit, intensive writing workshops in all genres, all levels (for adults).

IWWG Annual Summer Conference
The International Women's Writing Guild (IWWG)
5 Penn Plaza, 19th fl, PMB 19059, New York, NY 10001
Tel: 917-720-6959
E-mail: iwwgquestions@iwwg.org
Web Site: www.iwwg.org
Key Personnel
Exec Dir: Michelle Miller *E-mail:* michelle@iwwg.org
Each summer, the Guild brings together women for 7 full days of writing, crafting & connecting. Offer over 30 workshops to explore the spiritual, emotional, creative & technical side of writing.

Jentel Artist Residency Program
Jentel Foundation
130 Lower Piney Rd, Banner, WY 82832
Tel: 307-737-2311 *Fax:* 307-737-2305
E-mail: jentel@jentelarts.org
Web Site: www.jentelarts.org
Key Personnel
Exec Dir: Mary Jane Edwards

Prog Mgr: Lynn Reeves

Offers one month residencies throughout the year to visual artists in all media & writers in fiction, creative nonfiction & poetry. Located on a working cattle ranch in the foothills of the Big Horn Mountains, 20 miles from Sheridan, WY. The award includes comfortable accommodations, a separate private studio & a stipend. Residents are invited to share their work through various outreach opportunities in the community. For more info or an application, see web site. Deadline is Sept 15 & Jan 15 each year.

Juniper Summer Writing Institute
Juniper Institute
Affiliate of UMass Amherst MFA for Poets & Writers
c/o University Conference Services, 810 Campus Center, One Campus Center Way, Amherst, MA 01003
Tel: 413-545-5503
E-mail: juniperinstitute@hfa.umass.edu
Web Site: www.umass.edu/juniperinstitute
Key Personnel
Dir: Betsy Wheeler
Seven days of intensive writing workshops, craft sessions, readings & ms consultation in the beautiful Pioneer Valley. Scholarships available.

Kentucky Women Writers Conference
University of Kentucky
232 E Maxwell St, Lexington, KY 40506-0344
Tel: 859-257-2874
E-mail: kentuckywomenwriters@gmail.com
Web Site: www.kentuckywomenwriters.org
Key Personnel
Dir: Julie Kuzneski Wrinn
Founded in 1979, this is the oldest conference of its kind in the country featuring invited women writers offering workshops, reading & panel discussions.
Location: Lexington, KY
Date: Annually in Sept

Kentucky Writers Conference
Southern Kentucky Book Fest
1906 College Heights Blvd, Suite 11067, Bowling Green, KY 42101-1067
Tel: 270-745-4502
E-mail: sokybookfest@wku.edu
Web Site: www.sokybookfest.org
Key Personnel
Literary Outreach Coord: Sara Volpi *E-mail:* sara.volpi@wku.edu
Teaching craft workshops about everything from plotting techniques to employing poetic language to getting published. Free to the public. Limited seating.

Key West Literary Seminar
717 Love Lane, Key West, FL 33040
Tel: 305-293-9291 *Toll Free Tel:* 888-293-9291
E-mail: mail@kwls.org
Web Site: www.kwls.org/seminar
Key Personnel
Exec Dir: Arlo Haskell
A 4-day readers' event that explores a unique literary theme each January. The 2022 theme is "A Seminar Named Desire".
Location: Key West, FL
Date: Jan 6-9, 2022

Key West Literary Seminar's Writers' Workshop Program
Key West Literary Seminar
717 Love Lane, Key West, FL 33040
Tel: 305-293-9291 *Toll Free Tel:* 888-293-9291
E-mail: mail@kwls.org

Web Site: www.kwls.org; www.kwls.org/writers_workshops
Key Personnel
Exec Dir: Arlo Haskell
Provides writers at any stage of development with opportunities to explore the craft of writing. Multiple workshops each with their own focus & application requirements. Enrollment for each workshop is limited to 12 participants.
Location: Key West, FL
Date: Jan 11-15, 2021

LARB/USC Publishing Workshop
Los Angeles Review of Books
6671 Sunset Blvd, Suite 1521, Los Angeles, CA 90028
E-mail: publishingworkshop@lareviewofbooks.org
Web Site: thepublishingworkshop.com
Key Personnel
Publr & Ed-in-Chief: Tom Lutz *E-mail:* tom@lareviewofbooks.org
Dir: Irene Yoon
Asst Dir: Sarah LaBrie
Mng Dir, LARB: Jessica Kubinec *E-mail:* jessica@lareviewofbooks.org
Prog Mgr: Sonia Ali
Three-week summer program on USC campus. Open to graduating college seniors, those who have already graduated (alumni of any college/university), current graduate students, or people with significant relevant experience. Optional 5-week nonresidential guided Project Incubator. Tuition: Workshop: $3,000, Incubator: $3,000, Workshop & Incubator: $5,500. Optional USC housing & scholarships available.
Location: University of Southern California (USC), Los Angeles, CA
Date: Annually in July

Lost Lake Writers Retreat
Springfed Arts
PO Box 304, Royal Oak, MI 48068-0304
Tel: 248-589-3913
Web Site: www.springfed.org
Key Personnel
Dir: John D Lamb *E-mail:* johndlamb@ameritech.net
Poets & writers conference, good writers, food & accomodations.

Maine Writers Conference at Ocean Park
Affiliate of Ocean Park Association
14 Temple Ave, Ocean Park, ME 04063
Mailing Address: PO Box 7206, Ocean Park, ME 04063
Tel: 401-598-1424
E-mail: www.opa@oceanpark.org
Web Site: oceanpark.org
Key Personnel
Dir: Dr Jim Brosnan *E-mail:* jbrosnan@jwu.edu
An eclectic, economical & intensive annual conference in the Summer for writers of both poetry & prose of varying abilities & accomplishments.

McHugh's Rights/Permissions Workshop™
John B McHugh Publishing Consultant
PO Box 170665, Milwaukee, WI 53217-8056
Tel: 414-351-3056
E-mail: jack@johnbmchugh.com
Web Site: www.johnbmchugh.com
Key Personnel
Principal & Consultant: John B McHugh
Provide on-site customized workshops in all aspects of publishing management.

Mount Hermon Christian Writers Conference
Mount Hermon Christian Camps & Conference Center
c/o Mount Hermon Association Inc, 37 Conference Dr, Felton, CA 95018

Mailing Address: c/o Mount Hermon Association Inc, PO Box 413, Mount Hermon, CA 95041
Tel: 831-335-4466 *Toll Free Tel:* 888-MH-CAMPS (642-2677, registration) *Fax:* 831-335-9335
E-mail: info@mounthermon.org
Web Site: www.mounthermon.org/writers
Key Personnel
Adult Prog Specialist: Kathy Ide *E-mail:* kathy.ide@mounthermon.org
Two-day Head Start Mentoring Clinic for beginning writers; 5-day writers conference for all abilities, including beginning to professional. Held the weekend of Palm Sunday.

Mountain Writers Series
2804 SE 27 Ave, Suite 2, Portland, OR 97202
Tel: 503-232-4517 *Fax:* 503-232-4517
E-mail: programs@mountainwriters.org; support@mountainwriters.org
Web Site: www.mountainwriters.org
Key Personnel
Artistic Dir: Sandra Williams
Work with nationally recognized poets, fiction writers, nonfiction writers, screenwriters & agents.

MWG Writer Workshops & State Conference
Mississippi Writers Guild (MWG)
9 Janice Circle, Natchez, MS 39120
Tel: 601-442-0980
E-mail: mississippi.writersguild@outlook.com
Web Site: www.mississippiwritersguild.com
Key Personnel
Pres: G Mark Lafrances
Events Coord: Richelle Putnam
For information about this workshop or conference, please send an e-mail.
Date: Annually in Aug

Napa Valley Writers' Conference
Napa Valley College
1088 College Ave, St Helena, CA 94574
Tel: 707-967-2900 (ext 4) *Fax:* 707-967-2909
E-mail: info@napawritersconference.org; media@napawritersconference.org; fiction@napawritersconference.org; poetry@napawritersconference.org
Web Site: www.napawritersconference.org
Key Personnel
Exec Dir: Angela Pneuman
Mng Dir: Catherine Thorpe
Poetry Prog Dir: Nan Cohen
Fiction Dir: Ms Lakin Khan
Poetry & fiction sessions each year, offering small workshops, lectures & readings. Begins last Sunday in July & runs for one week.

National Society of Newspaper Columnists Annual Conference
National Society of Newspaper Columnists (NSNC)
205 Gun Hill St, Milton, MA 02186
Tel: 617-697-6854
E-mail: director@columnists.com
Web Site: www.columnists.com
Key Personnel
Exec Dir: Suzette Martinez Standring
Contest Chair: Cathy Turney
Conference & column writing contest; occasional newsletter; networking with staff, syndicated columnists & regular freelance columnists.
Date: Annually in June

New York State Writers Institute
State University of New York
Division of University at Albany/SUNY
University at Albany, Science Library 320, 1400 Washington Ave, Albany, NY 12222
Tel: 518-442-5620 *Fax:* 518-442-5621
E-mail: writers@albany.edu

Web Site: www.albany.edu/writers-inst
Key Personnel
Exec Dir: William Kennedy
Asst Dir: Suzanne Lance
Literary program organization featuring year-round visiting writers, classic film, special literary events & conferences, writing courses & workshops. Write or see web site for dates & locations.

North Carolina Writers' Network Annual Fall Conference
North Carolina Writers' Network
PO Box 21591, Winston-Salem, NC 27120-1591
Tel: 336-293-8844
E-mail: mail@ncwriters.org
Web Site: www.ncwriters.org
Key Personnel
Exec Dir: Ed Southern *E-mail:* ed@ncwriters.org
Workshops, readings, conferences, critiquing service & round table discussions, panels & meetings with agents, publishing workshops.

Odyssey: The Summer Fantasy Writing Workshop
PO Box 75, Mont Vernon, NH 03057
Tel: 603-673-6234 *Fax:* 603-673-6234
Web Site: www.odysseyworkshop.org
Key Personnel
Dir: Jeanne Cavelos *E-mail:* jcavelos@comcast.net
Intensive 6-week workshop for writers of fantasy, science fiction & horror. Dir Jeanne Cavelos is a former Sr Ed at Bantam Doubleday Dell Publishing & winner of the World Fantasy Award. Guest lecturers include some of the top writers in the field. College credit available.

Oregon Christian Writers One-Day Conferences
Oregon Christian Writers (OCW)
1075 Willow Lake Rd N, Keizer, OR 97303
Tel: 503-393-3356
E-mail: contact@oregonchristianwriters.org
Web Site: oregonchristianwriters.org
Key Personnel
Pres: Marilyn Rhoades
Prog Chmn: Don White
Registrar & Busn Mgr: Sue Miholer
Writers' workshops.
Location: Fall Conference
Date: Annually in Oct
Location: Winter Conference, Chemeketa Community College, Salem, OR
Date: Feb 20, 2021
Location: Spring Conference, First Baptist Church, Eugene, OR
Date: May 15, 2021

Oregon Christian Writers Summer Conference
Oregon Christian Writers (OCW)
1075 Willow Lake Rd N, Keizer, OR 97303
Tel: 503-393-3356
E-mail: contact@oregonchristianwriters.org
Web Site: oregonchristianwriters.org
Key Personnel
Summer Conference Dir: Lindy Jacobs
  E-mail: summerconf@oregonchristianwriters.org
Registrar & Busn Mgr: Sue Miholer
Seven hours of hands-on help from well-published professionals, many specialized workshops, consultations with editors & networking with successful writers.
Location: Red Lion on the River Hotel, Portland, OR
Date: Aug 16-19, 2021

Orientation to the Graphic Arts
PRINTING United Alliance
10015 Main St, Fairfax, VA 22031-3489

Tel: 703-385-1335 *Toll Free Tel:* 888-385-3588
  Fax: 703-273-0456
E-mail: info@printing.org; assist@printing.org
Web Site: www.printing.org
Key Personnel
Pres & CEO: Ford Bowers *E-mail:* fbowers@printing.org
SVP, Educ & Training (PA Off): Joe Marin
  E-mail: jmarin@printing.org
Ongoing online workshops & courses.

Outdoor Writers Association of America Annual Conference
Outdoor Writers Association of America (OWAA)
2814 Brooks St, Box 442, Missoula, MT 59801
Tel: 406-728-7434
E-mail: info@owaa.org
Web Site: www.owaa.org
Key Personnel
Exec Dir: Dr Brandon D Shuler
  E-mail: brandon@owaa.org
Membership & Conference Dir: Jessica (Pollett) Seitz *E-mail:* jseitz@owaa.org
Seminars & writing workshops; photography & outdoor news & conversation.
Location: Jay Peak Resort, 830 Jay Peak Rd, Jay, VT
Date: July 9-12, 2021

Ozark Creative Writers Inc Annual Conference
Ozark Creative Writers Inc
512 Walnut St, Mount Vernon, IN 47620
E-mail: ozarkcreativewriters@ozarkcreativewriters.com
Web Site: www.ozarkcreativewriters.com
Key Personnel
Pres: Clarissa Willis *E-mail:* clarissa@clarisawillis.com
Writers' conference for beginners & professionals. Contest information on web site.
Location: Ozarks Convention Center, Eureka Springs, AR
Date: Annually in Oct

Pennwriters Conference
Pennwriters Inc
PO Box 685, Dalton, PA 18414
E-mail: conferencecoordinator@pennwriters.org; info@pennwriters.org
Web Site: pennwriters.org
Key Personnel
Pres: Hilary Hauck *E-mail:* president@pennwriters.org
Conference Coord: Heather Desuta; Carol Silvis
Multi-genre conference with 40+ hours of workshops, panels & sessions with authors, agents & editors. Read & critique sessions. Agent/editor appointments.
Date: Annually in May

Philadelphia Writers' Conference
PO Box 7171, Elkins Park, PA 19027-0171
E-mail: info@pwcwriters.org
Web Site: pwcwriters.org
Educational conferences for writers, workshops, critiques, contests, featured speakers, agents, editors. Random free forums in Philadelphia in addition to annual 3-day event.
Location: Philadelphia, PA
Date: Annual 3-day event; 2nd full weekend of June

Poetry Flash Reading Series
Poetry Flash
1450 Fourth St, Suite 4, Berkeley, CA 94710
Tel: 510-525-5476 *Fax:* 510-525-6752
E-mail: editor@poetryflash.org
Web Site: poetryflash.org
Key Personnel
Ed, Publr & Exec Dir: Joyce Jenkins

Assoc Ed: Richard Silburg
Publication; conducts a reading & poetry series in conjunction with Moe's Books in Berkeley, CA & Diesel, A Bookstore in Oakland, CA. Host poets from all around the US.

Port Townsend Writers' Conference
Centrum Foundation
223 Battery Way, Port Townsend, WA 98368
Mailing Address: PO Box 1158, Port Townsend, WA 98368
Tel: 360-385-3102 *Toll Free Tel:* 800-733-3608 (ticket off) *Fax:* 360-385-2470
E-mail: info@centrum.org
Web Site: centrum.org
Key Personnel
Artistic Dir: Sam Ligon
Prog Mgr: Jordan Hartt *Tel:* 360-385-3102 ext 131 *E-mail:* jhartt@centrum.org
Workshops, lectures & readings.
Location: Port Townsend, WA
Date: Annually in July

The Publishing Game
Peanut Butter & Jelly Press LLC
PO Box 590239, Newton, MA 02459-0002
SAN: 299-7444
Tel: 617-630-0945 *Fax:* 617-630-0945 (call first)
E-mail: info@publishinggame.com; workshops@publishinggame.com
Web Site: www.publishinggame.com
Key Personnel
Publicist: Alyza Harris *E-mail:* alyza@publishinggame.com
All-day workshop covers how to find a literary agent, how to self-publish & how to successfully promote your book. Offered in 12 cities: New York, Boston, Philadelphia, DC, Boca Raton, Chicago, San Francisco, Los Angeles, Seattle, Phoenix, Dallas & several "floating cities" each year. $195 includes workshop course binder. See web site for latest locations, dates & details.

PNWA Writers Conference
PNWA - a writer's resource
1420 NW Gilman Blvd, Suite 8, PMB 2717, Issaquah, WA 98027
Tel: 425-673-2665
E-mail: pnwa@pnwa.org
Web Site: www.pnwa.org
Key Personnel
Pres: Pam Binder

Robert Quackenbush's Children's Book Writing & Illustration Workshops
Robert Quackenbush Studios
223 E 78 St, New York, NY 10075
Mailing Address: 460 E 79 St, New York, NY 10075
Tel: 212-744-3822
E-mail: rqstudios@aol.com
Web Site: www.rquackenbush.com
Four-day intensive workshop at author/artists' studio; focus on planning children's books from concept to completion.
Location: New York, NY
Date: Annually, 2nd week in July

Romance Writers of America Annual Conference
Romance Writers of America®
14615 Benfer Rd, Houston, TX 77069
Tel: 832-717-5200 *Fax:* 832-717-5201
E-mail: info@rwa.org
Web Site: www.rwa.org
Key Personnel
Exec Dir: Leslie Scantlebury *Tel:* 832-717-5200 ext 123 *E-mail:* leslie.scantlebury@rwa.org
Spec Projs Mgr: Megan Sloan *Tel:* 832-717-5200 ext 120 *E-mail:* megan.sloan@rwa.org
Promote recognition of the genre of romance writing as a serious book form. Conduct work-

shops, sponsor national & regional conferences & awards for members.
Location: Gaylord Opryland Resort & Convention Center, Nashville, TN
Date: July 14-17, 2021
Location: Gaylord Opryland Resort & Convention Center, 2800 Opryland Dr, Nashville, TN, USA
Date: July 27-30, 2022

San Diego Christian Writers' Guild Conference
San Diego Christian Writers' Guild
PO Box 270403, San Diego, CA 92198
Tel: 760-294-3269; 858-254-1402 *Fax:* 760-294-3269
E-mail: info@sandiegocwg.org
Web Site: www.sandiegocwg.org
Key Personnel
Pres: Jennie Gillespie; Robert Gillespie
One-day seminar & workshops; personal consultations with editors. Journalism, magazine writing, fiction. Seminar is always the 4th Saturday in September.

San Francisco Writers Conference
1029 Jones St, San Francisco, CA 94109
Tel: 415-673-0939
E-mail: sfwriterscon@aol.com
Web Site: www.sfwriters.org
Key Personnel
Co-Dir: Michael Larsen; Laurie McLean
Craft & market oriented writers' conference covering fiction, nonfiction, children's books, poetry, self-publishing, promotion with name authors.
Location: Hyatt Regency San Francisco, 5 Embarcadero Center, San Francisco, CA
Date: Feb 11-14, 2021

Sandhills Writers' Series
Augusta State University
Dept of English & Foreign Languages, 1120 15 St, Augusta, GA 30912
Tel: 706-729-2417
Key Personnel
Asst Professor: James Minick *E-mail:* jminick@augusta.edu
Fiction, nonfiction, creative nonfiction & poetry craft-directed readings; participants meet in consultations with literary agents that represent commercial & literary fiction, nonfiction & children's books. Enrollment limited. Ms deadline Feb.

SCBWI-FL Florida Regional Conference
Society of Children's Book Writers & Illustrators, Florida Region (SCBWI-FL)
125 E Merritt Island Causeway, Suite 209, Merritt Island, FL 32952
Tel: 321-338-7208
E-mail: florida@scbwi.org
Web Site: florida.scbwi.org
Key Personnel
Co-Regl Advisor: Linda Rodriguez Bernfeld
E-mail: florida-ra@scbwi.org; Dorian Cirrone
E-mail: florida-ra2@scbwi.org

SCBWI-FL Mid-Year Workshops
Society of Children's Book Writers & Illustrators, Florida Region (SCBWI-FL)
125 E Merritt Island Causeway, Suite 209, Merritt Island, FL 32952
Tel: 321-338-7208
E-mail: florida@scbwi.org
Web Site: florida.scbwi.org
Key Personnel
Co-Regl Advisor: Linda Rodriguez Bernfeld
E-mail: florida-ra@scbwi.org; Dorian Cirrone
E-mail: florida-ra2@scbwi.org
Workshops in writing & illustrating picture books, juvenile & young adult fiction & non-

fiction, children's magazines & marketing, given by published authors, illustrators, editors & agents. Also offer 5-7 writing boot camps across the state of Florida the last 2 weeks in Sept.

Science Fiction Writers Workshop
Center for the Study of Science Fiction
Division of University of Kansas
University of Kansas, Wescoe Hall, Rm 3001, Dept of English, 1445 Jayhawk Blvd, Lawrence, KS 66045
Tel: 785-864-2518 *Fax:* 785-864-1159
Web Site: www.sfcenter.ku.edu; www.sfcenter.ku.edu/sfworkshop; www.sfcenter.ku.edu/novel-workshop
Key Personnel
Founding Dir: James Gunn *E-mail:* jgunn@ku.edu
Dir: Christopher McKitterick *E-mail:* cmckit@ku.edu
Assoc Dir: Kij Johnson *E-mail:* kijjo@ku.edu
A noncredit, 2-week intensive workshop offered in association with the Campbell Conference on Science Fiction by the Center for the Study of Science Fiction.
Location: University of Kansas, Lawrence, KS
Date: Summer

See-More's Workshop Arts & Education Workshops
The Shadow Box Theatre
325 West End Ave, Suite 12-B, New York, NY 10023
Tel: 212-724-0677 *Fax:* 212-724-0767
E-mail: sbt@shadowboxtheatre.org
Web Site: www.shadowboxtheatre.org
Key Personnel
Exec/Artistic Dir: Sandra Robbins
E-mail: srobbins@shadowboxtheatre.org
Mng Arts & Educ Dir: Carol Prud'homme Davis
E-mail: cpdavis@shadowboxtheatre.org
Resident Workshops: Early learning through elementary grades, SBT's teaching artists guide students in the art of storytelling & curriculum exploration through puppetry, dramatics, dance & music. Professional Development Workshops: Hands-on staff development workshops provide classroom teachers with theatre & storytelling techniques. Author Workshops: Includes a trip or in-school SBT musical puppet show, our own storybooks with accompanying audio tapes/CDs & a meeting with playwright & author, Sandra Robbins. For more information contact us, as dates, times & locations change often.

Sewanee Writers' Conference
Stamler Ctr, 119 Gailor Hall, 735 University Ave, Sewanee, TN 37383
Tel: 931-598-1141; 931-598-1654
E-mail: swc@sewanee.edu
Web Site: www.sewaneewriters.org
Key Personnel
Dir: Wyatt Prunty *E-mail:* wprunty@sewanee.edu
Assoc Dir, Mktg & Admissions: Adam Latham
E-mail: allatham@sewanee.edu
Assoc Dir, Progs & Fin: Megan Roberts
E-mail: mgroberts@sewanee.edu
Workshops in poetry, fiction & playwriting.
Location: The University of the South, Sewanee, TN
Date: Annually the last 2 weeks in July

Society for Technical Communication's Annual Conference
Society for Technical Communication
9401 Lee Hwy, Suite 300, Fairfax, VA 22031
Tel: 703-522-4114 *Fax:* 703-522-2075
E-mail: stc@stc.org; summit@stc.org
Web Site: summit.stc.org; www.stc.org

Key Personnel
CEO: Liz Pohland *Tel:* 571-366-1901 *E-mail:* liz.pohland@stc.org
Educational conference for technical communicators.
Date: Annually in May

Southampton Writers' Conference
Stony Brook Southampton
239 Montauk Hwy, Southampton, NY 11968
Tel: 631-632-5007
E-mail: southamptonwriters@notes.cc.sunysb.edu; southamptonarts@stonybrook.edu
Web Site: www.stonybrook.edu/southampton/mfa/summer/cwl_home.html
Key Personnel
Conference Coord: Christian McLean
E-mail: christian.mclean@stonybrook.edu
Five & 12-day workshops including novel, short story, poetry, memoir & creative nonfiction, playwriting & screenwriting; also evening readings, performances & panels.

Southern California Writers' Conference (SCWC)
Division of Random Cove, ie
18160 Cottonwood Rd, Suite 260, Sunriver, OR 97707
Tel: 619-303-8185 *Fax:* 619-906-7462
E-mail: msg@writersconference.com
Web Site: www.writersconference.com
Key Personnel
Exec Dir: Michael Steven Gregory
Dir: Wes Albers *E-mail:* wes@writersconference.com
Asst Dir: Chrissie A Barnett *E-mail:* chrissie@writersconference.com
Annual writers' conference. Fiction, nonfiction & scriptwriting mss eligible for advance critique submission before the conference, followed by one-on-one consultation; awards given. Major speakers; banquet; workshops in fiction, nonfiction, legacy & indie publishing; conference emphasis on fiction & nonfiction; one agent panel, multiple read & critique, craft & troubleshooting workshops.
Location: Crowne Plaza San Diego, 2270 Hotel Circle N, San Diego, CA
Date: Feb 12-14, 2021

SouthWest Writers Conference Series
SouthWest Writers
3200 Carlisle Blvd NE, Suite 114, Albuquerque, NM 87110-1663
Tel: 505-830-6034
E-mail: swwriters@juno.com
Web Site: www.southwestwriters.com
Key Personnel
Pres: Sarah Baker
Series of one-day conferences, twice-monthly programs, workshops & writing classes.

Spring Time Writers Creative Writing & Journaling Workshop
Spring Time Writers
PO Box 512, Lyons, CO 80540-0512
Tel: 303-823-0997
E-mail: writers@springtimewriters.com
Web Site: www.springtimewriters.com
Key Personnel
Dir: Kathleen Spring
Creative writing & self discovery journaling workshops. Four days, including lodging, small classes, professional warm instruction in the Rocky Mountains in Colorado. Conferences held 2nd & 4th weekends June-Sept. See web site for details.

Squaw Valley Community of Writers Summer Workshops
Community of Writers at Squaw Valley

PO Box 1416, Nevada City, CA 95959
Tel: 530-470-8440
E-mail: info@communityofwriters.org
Web Site: www.communityofwriters.org
Key Personnel
Exec Dir: Ms Brett Hall Jones
Dir, Fiction: Lisa Alvarez; Louis B Jones
Dir, Poetry Workshop: Robert Hass
Dir, Screenwriting: Diana Fuller
Summer writing workshops; each workshop is
one week long.
Membership(s): Association of Writers & Writing
Programs.
Location: Poetry Workshop
Date: Annually in June
Location: Writers Workshops
Date: Annually in July

The Summer Experience
Sage Hill Writing Experience Inc
1831 College Ave, Suite 324, Regina, SK S4P
4V5, Canada
Tel: 306-537-7243
E-mail: sage.hill@sasktel.net
Web Site: www.sagehillwriting.ca
Key Personnel
Exec Dir: Tara Solheim
Prog Mgr: Caitlin Terfloth
Offers a special working & learning opportunity
to writers at different stages of development.
Top quality instruction, a low instructor-writer
ratio & the rural Saskatchewan setting offer
conditions ideal for the pursuit of excellence in
the arts of fiction & poetry. Application to The
Summer Experience is open to writers 19 years
of age & older, regardless of city, province or
country of residence.

Summer Words Writing Conference &
Literary Festival
Aspen Words
110 E Hallam St, Suite 116, Aspen, CO 81611
Tel: 970-925-3122 *Fax:* 970-920-5700
E-mail: aspenwords@aspeninstitute.org
Web Site: www.aspenwords.org
Key Personnel
Exec Dir: Adrienne Brodeur *Tel:* 646-461-3554
E-mail: adrienne.brodeur@aspeninstitute.org
Mng Dir: Jamie Kravitz *Tel:* 970-925-3122 ext 2
E-mail: jamie.kravitz@aspeninstitute.org
Sr Prog Assoc, Mktg & Communs: Caroline Tory
Tel: 970-925-3122 ext 3 *E-mail:* caroline.tory@
aspeninstitute.org
A 5-day writing retreat with morning workshops
in fiction, poetry, memoir & essay compli-
mented by a 5-day literary festival in the af-
ternoons & evenings, featuring 20 events for
readers & writers.
Location: Aspen, CO
Date: Annually in June

Summer Writing Seminar
Martha's Vineyard Institute of Creative Writing
7 E Pasture Rd, Aquinnah, MA 02535
Tel: 954-242-2903
Web Site: mvicw.com
Key Personnel
Dir/Prog Coord: Alexander Weinstein
E-mail: mvicwdirector@gmail.com
Annual comprehensive weeklong writing program, providing writers with the necessary time
to devote to their art, on the island of Martha's
Vineyard. Program fee is $975, which covers
participation in all workshops, evening readings, editing/ms consultation with one of the
visiting poets or authors & Friday night dinner with visiting writers. Fee does not include
travel or accommodations.

Tin House Summer Workshop
Tin House Books
2617 NW Thurman St, Portland, OR 97210

Tel: 503-473-8663
Web Site: tinhouse.com/workshop/summer-
workshop
Key Personnel
Workshop Dir: Lance Cleland
Asst Workshop Dir: India Downes-Le Guin
E-mail: india@tinhouse.com
Weeklong workshops, seminars, panels & read-
ings led by prominent contemporary writers.
Fees: $30 application; $1,600 tuition; $400
room & board; $800-$1,000 mentorships; $500
audit.
Location: Reed College, Portland, OR
Date: Annually in July

Tin House Winter Workshops
Tin House Books
2617 NW Thurman St, Portland, OR 97210
Tel: 503-473-8663
Web Site: tinhouse.com/winter-workshops
Key Personnel
Workshop Dir: Lance Cleland
Asst Workshop Dir: India Downes-Le Guin
E-mail: india@tinhouse.com
Weekend literary workshops-4 sessions. Fees: $30
application; $1,600 program, room & board;
$800-$1,000 mentorships.
Location: Sylvia Beach Hotel, Newport, OR
Date: Annually, Jan-Feb

Unicorn Writers' Conference
Unicorn Writers' Conference Inc
17 Church Hill Rd, Redding, CT 06896
Tel: 203-938-7405 *Fax:* 203-938-7405
E-mail: unicornwritersconference@gmail.com
Web Site: unicornwritersconference.com
Key Personnel
Chmn & Sessions Dir: Jan L Kardys *E-mail:* jan.
kardys@gmail.com
Mktg Dir: Barbara Ellis
Following the keynote address, delivered by a
best-selling author or celebrity. Offers 36 different sessions including fiction, nonfiction,
memoir, mystery, poetry, screenwriting, writing
for the children's market & other major genres.
How-to tutorials from publishing professionals
educating writers on all aspects of publishing
including contracts, copyrights, permissions,
special sales, subsidiary rights, media training, promotion & platform, social media, self-
publishing, book distribution & more. Features
4 agent panels & 2 editorial panels. One-to-
one ms reviews available with editors, agents
& faculty for an additional fee. Price $400,
breakfast, lunch & dinner included. Welcome
gift for all attendees. One-to-one sessions: $150
for a 30-minute session in-person private ms
consultation with the faculty member, agent,
editor of your choice. Query letter & book synopses reviews also available. Conference held
7:30am-8pm.

Visiting Writers Series
University of Alaska Fairbanks
English Dept, PO Box 755720, Fairbanks, AK
99775-5720
Tel: 907-474-7193 *Fax:* 907-474-5247
E-mail: faengl@uaf.edu
Web Site: www.alaska.edu/english
Key Personnel
Asst Professor: Daryl Farmer *E-mail:* dlfarmer@
alaska.edu
Readings from & discussion of own writings; po-
etry, fiction, nonfiction. Other sponsors include:
University of Alaska Foundation, Alaska State
Council on the Arts, The National Endowment
for the Arts, UAF College of Liberal Arts &
UA President's Special Project Fund.
Location: Fairbanks, AK
Date: Contact for schedule

VONA Voices Summer Writing Workshop
Voices of Our Nations Art Foundation (VONA)
Affiliate of University of Pennsylvania
3720 Spruce St, Suite 442, Philadelphia, PA
19104
Tel: 732-842-3932; 510-421-3913
E-mail: info@vonacommunity.org
Web Site: www.vonacommunity.org
Key Personnel
Exec Dir: Diem Jones *E-mail:* diem@
vonacommunity.org
VONA now makes its home at the University of
Pennsylvania & offers workshops in fiction,
poetry, memoir, essay writing, speculative fic-
tion, genre writing, political content in poetry-
fiction-prose, LGBTQ narrative, travel writing,
playwriting & residencies in prose & poetry.
Location: University of Pennsylvania, Philadel-
phia, PA
Date: Annually, June-July

Wesleyan Writers Conference
Wesleyan University
c/o Wesleyan University, Downey House, 294
High St, Rm 207, Middletown, CT 06459
Tel: 860-685-3604
Web Site: www.wesleyan.edu/writing/conference
Key Personnel
Dir: Anne Greene *E-mail:* agreene@wesleyan.edu
Seminars, readings, ms consultations & talks
focused on novels, short stories, film, poetry,
nonfiction, journalism, multimedia work, pub-
lishing; scholarships & fellowships. Participants
are welcome to attend seminars in all genres;
visits from editors & agents. Award-winning
writers as faculty & guest speakers.
Location: Wesleyan University, Middletown, CT
Date: Annually in June

Willamette Writers' Conference
Willamette Writers
5331 SW Macadam Ave, Suite 258, PMB 215,
Portland, OR 97239
Tel: 901-200-5385
E-mail: wilwrite@willamettewriters.org
Web Site: willamettewriters.org
Key Personnel
VP & Secy: Gail Pasternack *E-mail:* secretary@
willamettewriters.org
Annual summer 3-day conference: consultations
with over 50 national agents, editors, film
agents & producers; workshops (fiction, nonfiction, children's, screen/TV, genres, craft of
writing); editing room available. Year-round:
monthly meetings, writing contest, workshops,
newsletter.

Windbreak House Writing Retreat
Windbreak House
PO Box 169, Hermosa, SD 57744-0169
Tel: 605-255-4064
E-mail: info@windbreakhouse.com
Web Site: www.windbreakhouse.com
Key Personnel
Owner & Writer in Residence: Linda M Has-
selstrom *E-mail:* lindamhasselstrom@
windbreakhouse.com
Asst: Tamara Rogers
Retreats scheduled to suit applicants.

Winter Words Author Series
Aspen Words
110 E Hallam St, Suite 116, Aspen, CO 81611
Tel: 970-925-3122 *Fax:* 970-920-5700
E-mail: aspenwords@aspeninstitute.org
Web Site: www.aspenwords.org
Key Personnel
Exec Dir: Adrienne Brodeur *Tel:* 646-461-3554
E-mail: adrienne.brodeur@aspeninstitute.org
Mng Dir: Jamie Kravitz *Tel:* 970-925-3122 ext 2
E-mail: jamie.kravitz@aspeninstitute.org

Sr Prog Assoc, Mktg & Commun: Caroline Tory *Tel:* 970-925-3122 ext 3 *E-mail:* caroline.tory@ aspeninstitute.org
Series of readings with remarkable writers. Also includes book signings.
Location: Paepcke Auditorium, 1000 N Third St, Aspen, CO
Date: Annually, Jan-April

Wisconsin Annual Fall Conference
Society of Children's Book Writers and Illustrators, Wisconsin Chapter
PO Box 1463, Green Bay, WI 54305-1463
Tel: 323-782-1010 (corp off)
E-mail: wisconsin@scbwi.org
Web Site: www.scbwi.org; www.facebook.com/ SCBWIWisconsin
Key Personnel
Co-Regl Advisor: Andrea Skyberg; Miranda Paul
Workshop on writing & illustrating for children. Includes ms or portfolio critique. Guest faculty includes award-winning writers & illustrators.

Write on the Sound Writers' Conference
City of Edmonds Art Commission
Frances Anderson Center, 700 Main St, Edmonds, WA 98020
Tel: 425-771-0228 *Fax:* 425-771-0253
E-mail: wots@edmondswa.gov
Web Site: www.writeonthesound.com
Key Personnel
City of Edmonds Arts & Culture Mgr: Ms Frances Chapin
Annual event, presented the 1st weekend in October, with over 30 workshops by noted authors, educators & trade professionals. Features a keynote address, on-site book shop, ms critique appointments & a themed writing contest.

The Writers' Colony at Dairy Hollow
515 Spring St, Eureka Springs, AR 72632
Tel: 479-253-7444
E-mail: director@writerscolony.org
Web Site: www.writerscolony.org
Key Personnel
Dir: Linda Caldwell
See web site for upcoming events & fellowships.

Writers' League of Texas (WLT)
611 S Congress Ave, Suite 200 A-3, Austin, TX 78704
Tel: 512-499-8914
E-mail: wlt@writersleague.org
Web Site: www.writersleague.org
Key Personnel
Exec Dir: Becka Oliver *E-mail:* becka@ writersleague.org
Prog Dir: Michael Noll *E-mail:* michael@ writersleague.org
Conferences, workshops, seminars, classes, e-mail classes.
Location: Writer's League of Texas Resource Center/Library & other locations, ongoing programs throughout Texas
Date: Throughout year

Writers Mentoring Retreat
American Christian Writers
PO Box 110390, Nashville, TN 37222-0390
Tel: 615-331-8668 *Toll Free Tel:* 800-21-WRITE (219-7483)
E-mail: acwriters@aol.com

Web Site: regaforder.wordpress.com/mentoring; regaforder.wordpress.com
Key Personnel
Pres: Reg A Forder
Correspondence courses; 36 conferences annually, approximately 3 per month in major cities throughout the US. Monthly magazine by subscription.
Location: Nashville, TN
Date: April 9-10, 2021
Location: Grands Rapids, MI
Date: June 4-5, 2021
Location: Atlanta, GA
Date: July 9-10, 2021
Location: Minneapolis, MN
Date: Aug 6-7, 2021
Location: Phoenix, AZ
Date: Sept 10-11, 2021
Location: Nashville, TN
Date: Oct 1-2, 2021
Location: Orlando, FL
Date: Nov 11-13, 2021

Writers Retreat Workshop (WRW)
PO Box 170657, Austin, TX 78717
E-mail: info@writersretreatworkshop.com
Web Site: www.writersretreatworkshop.com
Key Personnel
Co-Founder: Gail Provost Stockwell
Dir: Jason Sitzes
Ed-in-Residence: Carol Doughtery
Coord: Lisa Willars-Pirc
Intensive workshop for writers of novels-in-progress, including private writing time & space, guest speakers & consultation with New York agent or editor, author instructor, as well as diagnostic sessions of participants' mss & daily assignments. Other retreats available, see web site for details.

The Writers Workshop
The Kenyon Review
Finn House, 102 W Wiggin St, Gambier, OH 43022
Tel: 740-427-5207 *Fax:* 740-427-5417
E-mail: kenyonreview@kenyon.edu
Web Site: www.kenyonreview.org
Key Personnel
Progs Dir, The Kenyon Review: Anna Duke Reach
Intensive writing workshops for adults & teens, June & July annually.

Writers Workshop in Children's Literature, see SCBWI-FL Mid-Year Workshops

The Writing Center
601 E Palisade Ave, Suite 4, Englewood Cliffs, NJ 07632
Tel: 201-567-4017 *Fax:* 201-567-7202
E-mail: writingcenter@optonline.net
Web Site: www.writingcenternj.com
Key Personnel
Dir: Barry Sheinkopf *E-mail:* bsheinkopf@ optonline.net
Writing seminars, editorial services, book design & publishing services.
Location: 601 Palisade Ave, Englewood Cliffs, NJ
Date: Year-round, 12 week writing seminars; Fall seminars begin Sept; Winter seminars begin Jan; Spring seminars begin April. Five week Summer session

Writing Workshops
UC Davis Extension
Affiliate of University of California, Davis
1333 Research Park Dr, Davis, CA 95618
Tel: 510-642-6362
E-mail: extension@ucdavis.edu
Web Site: extension.ucdavis.edu; writing.ucdavis. edu
Key Personnel
Dir, Univ Writing Prog: Carl Whithaus *Tel:* 530-752-0369 *E-mail:* cwwhithaus@ucdavis.edu
Workshops, courses & writing institutes.
Location: University of California, Davis & Sacramento, CA
Date: Year-round, call for dates

YA Fiction Workshop
Tin House Books
2617 NW Thurman St, Portland, OR 97210
Tel: 503-473-8663
Web Site: tinhouse.com/ya-workshop
Key Personnel
Workshop Dir: Lance Cleland
Asst Workshop Dir: India Downes-Le Guin *E-mail:* india@tinhouse.com
Weekend workshop for crafting young adult fiction. Fees: $30 application; $1,500 program, room, board & transportation; $800-$1,000 mentorships.
Location: Sylvia Beach Hotel, Newport, OR
Date: Annually in Oct/Nov

Yaddo Artists Residency
Yaddo
312 Union Ave, Saratoga Springs, NY 12866
Mailing Address: PO Box 395, Saratoga Springs, NY 12866-0395
Tel: 518-584-0746 *Fax:* 518-584-1312
E-mail: yaddo@yaddo.org
Web Site: www.yaddo.org
Key Personnel
Pres: Elaina Richardson *E-mail:* erichardson@ yaddo.org
Prog Dir: Candace Wait *E-mail:* chwait@yaddo. org
An artists' community established in Saratoga Springs, NY in 1900 by the financier Spencer Trask & his poet wife, Katrina, to offer creative artists the rare gift of a supportive environment with uninterrupted time to think, experiment & create. Over the years, Yaddo has welcomed more than 6,000 artists working in one or more of the following media: choreography, film, literature, musical composition, painting, performance art, photography, printmaking, sculpture & video. About 220 artists are invited each year for residencies lasting up to 2 months. Application deadlines are Jan 1 & Aug 1.

Young Writers' Workshop
Cape Cod Writers Center
919 Main St, Osterville, MA 02655
Mailing Address: PO Box 408, Osterville, MA 02655
Tel: 508-420-0200
E-mail: writers@capecodwriterscenter.org
Web Site: capecodwriterscenter.org
Key Personnel
Pres: Barbara Struna
Exec Dir: Nancy Rubin Stuart
This program offers unique learning opportunities to young writers ages 12-18.
Date: Feb 2021

Courses for the Book Trade

Various courses covering different phases of the book trade are given each year. Detailed information on any of these courses can be obtained by writing directly to the sponsoring organization. For related information see **Writers' Conferences & Workshops**.

Arizona State University Creative Writing Program
1102 S McAllister Ave, Rm 170, Tempe, AZ 85281
Mailing Address: Dept of English, Box 871401, Tempe, AZ 85287-1401
Tel: 480-965-3168 *Fax:* 480-965-3451
Web Site: www.asu.edu/clas/english/creativewriting
Key Personnel
Prog Dir, Creative Writing: Jenny Irish
  E-mail: jennifer.irish@asu.edu
Undergraduate & graduate courses in creative writing: workshops, theory & special topics.

Arkansas State University Graphic Communications Program
PO Box 1930, Dept of Media, State University, AR 72467-1930
Tel: 870-972-3114 *Fax:* 870-972-3321
Web Site: www.astate.edu
Key Personnel
Dept Chair: Dr Osa Amienyi *E-mail:* osami@astate.edu
Instructor, Graphic Commun: Pradeep C Mishra
  E-mail: pmishra@astate.edu
Courses include Desktop Publishing
Digital Pre-Press Workflow & File Creation
Graphic Communications - Estimating & Schedules
Graphic Production Systems
Internet Communications
Internship
Intro to Digital Publishing
Intro to Visual Communication
Mass Communication in Modern Society
Multi-Media Production Techniques
News Design Publication
Photography

Baylor University, Professional Writing Program
One Bear Place, Unit 97404, Waco, TX 76798-7404
Tel: 254-710-1768 *Fax:* 254-710-3894
Web Site: www.baylor.edu
Key Personnel
Dept Chair: Dr Kevin J Gardner
  E-mail: kevin_gardner@baylor.edu
Prog Contact: Dr Kara Poe Alexander
  E-mail: kara_alexander@baylor.edu
Comprehensive writing program.
Courses include Argumentative & Persuasive Writing
Creative Nonfiction
Internship in Professional Writing
Literacy Studies
New Media Writing & Rhetoric
Professional & Workplace Writing
Research in Writing & Rhetoric
Rhetoric of Race
Special Topics in Writing Workshop
Special Topics Lecture in Writing & Rhetoric
Spiritual Writing
Studies in Public & Civic Writing
Style & Editing
Technical Writing
Women's Writing & Rhetoric
Writing for Social Change

Binghamton University Creative Writing Program
Division of State University of New York at Binghamton
c/o Dept of English, PO Box 6000, Binghamton, NY 13902-6000
Tel: 607-777-2168 *Fax:* 607-777-2408
E-mail: cwpro@binghamton.edu
Web Site: english.binghamton.edu/cwpro
Key Personnel
Dir, Prog: Maria Gillan
Assoc Dir, Creative Writing: Christine Gelineau
Professor: Jaimee Wriston Colbert; Thomas Glave; Leslie Heywood; Liz Rosenberg
Asst Professor: Joe Weil; Alexi Zentner
Asst to Chmn, Eng: Colleen Burke
Undergraduate & graduate courses.
Courses include Advanced Workshops in Creative Writing
Fiction Workshop
Fundamentals of Creative Writing
Independent Study in Creative Writing
Intermediate Creative Writing
Poetry Workshop
Studies for Writers

Boston University Creative Writing Program
236 Bay State Rd, Boston, MA 02215
Tel: 617-353-2510 *Fax:* 617-353-3653
E-mail: crwr@bu.edu
Web Site: www.bu.edu/creativewriting
Key Personnel
Prog Dir: Ha Jin *E-mail:* xjin@bu.edu
Prog Coord: Catherine Con
Contact: Prof Robert Pinsky *E-mail:* rpinsky@bu.edu
Workshops. Offer one-year Master's degree MSA in creative writing.
Courses include Fiction
Poetry

Bowling Green State University Creative Writing Program
Dept of English, 409 East Hall, Bowling Green, OH 43403
Tel: 419-372-2576 *Fax:* 419-372-0333
Web Site: www.bgsu.edu/departments/creative-writing
Key Personnel
Dir & Advisor: Sharona Muir *E-mail:* smuir@bgsu.edu
Providers of comprehensive & rigorous education in professional writing, editing & marketing of poetry & fiction, since 1967.
Courses include Advanced Fiction Writing Workshop
Advanced Poetry Writing Workshop
Assistant Editing, Mid-American Review
Graduate Writers' Workshop in Poetry, Fiction
Studies in Contemporary Poetry, Fiction
Techniques of Fiction
Techniques of Poetry

The Center for Book Arts
28 W 27 St, 3rd fl, New York, NY 10001
Tel: 212-481-0295 *Toll Free Fax:* 866-708-8994
E-mail: info@centerforbookarts.org
Web Site: www.centerforbookarts.org
Key Personnel
Exec Dir: Alexander Campos *E-mail:* acampos@centerforbookarts.org

Offers classes & workshops year-round.
Courses include Bookbinding
Letterpress Printing
Papermaking

College of Liberal & Professional Studies, University of Pennsylvania
3440 Market St, Suite 100, Philadelphia, PA 19104-3335
Tel: 215-898-7326 *Fax:* 215-573-2053
E-mail: lps@sas.upenn.edu
Web Site: www.sas.upenn.edu/lps
Key Personnel
Vice Dean & Assoc Dir: Nora Lewis
  E-mail: nlewis@sas.upenn.edu
Dir, Mktg & Communs: Tomea Knight
  E-mail: knightt@sas.upenn.edu
Writing courses, beginning through advanced, taught by published authors; non-residential; fees vary; program catalog available for writing courses Sept-July.

Columbia Publishing Course at Columbia University
Affiliate of Columbia University School of Journalism
2950 Broadway, MC 3801, New York, NY 10027
Tel: 212-854-1898; 212-854-9775
E-mail: publishing-jrn@columbia.edu
Web Site: journalism.columbia.edu/columbia-publishing-course
Key Personnel
Dir: Shaye Areheart *E-mail:* shayepc@gmail.com
Provides an intensive introduction to book, magazine, & digital publishing. Students learn the entire publishing process from established publishing professionals & gain hands-on experience in all aspects of the business, from evaluation of original mss to the sales & marketing of finished products. CPC offers 2 programs: one in New York City, held over the course of 6 weeks during June & July, & one in Oxford, England, held over the course of 4 weeks in September. In New York, the first 3 weeks are devoted to book publishing, & the following 2 weeks are devoted to magazine & digital publishing. The sixth & last week is a combination of all the interests presented by the course. In Oxford, the focus is entirely on book publishing. In both places, lectures from industry leaders in every specialty, including CEOs & legendary graduates of the course, bookend a unique workshop experience, in which students form hypothetical publishing companies—complete with prospectuses, marketing pitches, financial documents, editorial content, & jacket & cover designs. Throughout, extensive career guidance, including a resume & cover-letter critique, is offered, along with job placement assistance. Application deadline is early March.
Courses include Academic Publishing
The Author's Perspective
Children's Publishing
Design
Diversity in Publishing
How to Generate Book Ideas
Independent Publishing
Innovations in Publishing
Literary Agencies & Scouts
Managing Editorial & Production
Marketing

Online Magazines
Podcasting
Profit & Loss
Publicity & Public Relations
Publishing Contracts
Sales
Subsidiary Rights

Columbia University School of the Arts Creative Writing Program
Division of Columbia University
609 Kent Hall, New York, NY 10027
Tel: 212-854-3774 *Fax:* 212-854-7704
E-mail: writingprogram@columbia.edu
Web Site: www.columbia.edu/cu/writing
Key Personnel
Chair: Timothy Donnelly
Dir, Creative Writing: Heidi Julavits
Prog Asst, Creative Writing: Dorla McIntosh
Courses include Fiction
Nonfiction
Poetry

The Lisa Ekus Group LLC
57 North St, Hatfield, MA 01038
Tel: 413-247-9325 *Fax:* 413-247-9873
E-mail: info@lisaekus.com
Web Site: lisaekus.com
Key Personnel
Principal & Pres: Lisa Ekus *E-mail:* lisaekus@
lisaekus.com
Mgr & Literary Assoc: Sally Ekus
E-mail: sally@lisaekus.com
Comprehensive 1- or 2-day media training programs designed for cookbook authors, chefs, product spokespeople, show hosts & food professionals. Participants will spend their day(s) under the lights & in front of the camera, taping & critiquing actual television demonstrations of varying lengths. Courses are typically held in the professional kitchen of our Hatfield, MA, offices but off-site training is available. Visit culinarymediatraining.com to learn more.
Courses include Cookbook Publishing 101
Honing Your Edge: Media Training for Culinary Professionals
One-On-One Media Training

Emerson College Department of Writing, Literature & Publishing
180 Tremont St, 10th fl, Boston, MA 02116-4624
Mailing Address: 120 Boylston St, Boston, MA 02116-4624
Tel: 617-824-8750
Web Site: www.emerson.edu; www.emerson.edu/
writing-literature-publishing
Key Personnel
Chair: Maria Koundoura
Graduate Prog Dir, MA in Publg & Writing: John Rodzvilla *E-mail:* john_rodzvilla@emerson.edu
Offers BA, MA, BFA & MFA degrees in publishing & writing.
Courses include Advanced Seminar Workshop in Nonfiction
Advanced Topics in Writing: Experimental Fiction
Advanced Topics in Writing: The Short Short
African-American Literature
After the Disaster: Post-War European Literature
American Novel 1
American Novel 2
American Women Writers
Applications for Print Publishing
Black Revolutionary Thought
Book Design & Production
Book Editing
Book Publishing Overview
Column Writing
Copyediting
Cultural Criticism
Elementary French 1
Elementary French 2

Elementary Spanish 1
Elementary Spanish 2
Fiction Workshop
Imagining the Caribbean
Intermediate Creative Writing: Comedy
Intermediate Creative Writing: Drama
Intermediate Creative Writing: Fiction
Intermediate Creative Writing: Nonfiction
Intermediate Creative Writing: Poetry
Intermediate Creative Writing: Sketch Troupe
Intermediate Magazine Writing
International Women Writers
Intro College Writing Applications
Introduction to Book Publishing
Introduction to Creative Writing: Fiction
Introduction to Creative Writing: Nonfiction
Introduction to Creative Writing: Poetry
Introduction to Electronic Publishing
Introduction to Literary Studies
Introduction to Magazine Writing
Latin American Literature & Cinema
Latin American Short Fiction
Literary Foundations
Literature, Culture & the Environment
Literature of the Gothic
Literatures in English
Magazine Design & Production
Magazine Publishing Overview
Magazine Writing
MFA Thesis
Native American Literature
Nonfiction Workshop
Novel Workshop
Poetry Workshop
Profile Writing
Publishing Management & Innovation
Research Writing-Int'l
Seminar in Short Fiction
Seminar in the Novel
Shakespearean Tragedy
Slavery & Freedom
Special Topics in Fiction Writing: Short Short Fiction
Sr Creative Thesis-all genres
Teaching College Composition
The Art of Fiction
The Art of Nonfiction
The Art of Poetry
The Editor/Writer Relationship
The Forms of Poetry: Theory and Practice
Topics in African American Literature: Afrofuturism
Topics in Community Publishing: Partnered Studio: Projections on a Large Scale
Topics in Fiction: The Literature of Extremes
Topics in Global Literature: Latin American Women Writers
Topics in Global Literature: Place, Displacement, Memory in Exile Literature
Topics in Global Literature: Utopian, Dystopian & Apoclyptic Fictions
Topics in Global Studies: Global Indigenous Literatures
Topics in Literature: Black English & its Influence on American Literature and Culture
Topics in Literature: Comic Prose
Topics in Literature: Decolonizing Literature & Anti-Colonial Theories
Topics in Literature: Democracy & American Literature
Topics in Literature: Literature of the Gothic II
Topics in Literature: Post Modern Fairy Tales
Topics in Literature: Reading & Writing Dangerous Poems
Topics in Literature: Resistance & Revolution
Topics in Literature: Shakespearean Journeys
Topics in Literature: Women Nobel-Laureates in Literature
Topics in Multiple Genres & Hybrid Forms: Literature of Evil
Topics in Multiple Genres & Hybrid Forms: Literature of Transcendence
Topics in Multiple Genres & Hybrid Forms: Translation Seminar

Topics in Multiple Genres & Hybrid: Native Northeast
Topics in Multiple Genres & Hybrid: The Writer, The Daemon, and the Craftsman
Topics in Poetry: Forms in Poetry
Topics in Poetry: The Poetic Sequence
Topics in Publishing: Writing for The Boston Globe Magazine
Topics in U.S. Multicultural Literature: Harlem Renaissance
Topics in Writing & Publishing: Introduction to Book Design
Topics in Writing & Publishing: Introduction to Book Design for Writers
Travel Literature
U.S. American Literatures
U.S. Latinx Literature
U.S. Multicultural Literatures
Web Development: Creating & Managing Content for the Web

Fordham University, Gabelli School of Business
140 W 62 St, Rm 440, New York, NY 10023
Web Site: www.fordham.edu
Key Personnel
Professor & Area Chair: John A Fortunato
E-mail: jfortunato@fordham.edu
Offers MBA degree with a major in Communications & Media Management. MBA Graduate courses & additional MBA course work.
Courses include Accounting
Marketing with Public Relations
The Book Publishing Industry
Broadcast & Cable Marketing & Advertising
Sales Business & Legal Aspects of Cable TV
Broadcast Management
Business & the Mass Media
Consumer Behavior
Coping with Global Corporate Crisis
Corporate Power & the Public
Direct Marketing
Economics
Executive Communications
Finance
Information & Communications Systems
International Marketing
Legal & Ethical Studies
Magazine Management
Managing Newspapers & Their Electronic Ventures
Marketing Management, Advertising & Media Planning
Mass Media in America
New Media & Mass Communications
Persuasion in Public Relations
Public Relations & Broadcasting
Public Relations as a Management Tool
Sales Management
Special Topics in Communications & Media Management: Book Publishing
The Press, the Law & the Corporation

Gaylord College of Journalism & Mass Communication, Professional Writing Program
Division of University of Oklahoma
c/o University of Oklahoma, 395 W Lindsey St, Rm 3000, Norman, OK 73019-0270
Tel: 405-325-2721
Web Site: www.ou.edu/gaylord; www.ou.edu/
gaylord/undergraduate/professional-writing
Key Personnel
Prof Writing Academic Adviser: Chandler Lindsey *Tel:* 405-325-3686
E-mail: chandlerlindsey@ou.edu
Coursework on writing for commercial publication.
Courses include Business of Professional Writing
Category Fiction
Introduction to Professional Writing
Theories of Professional Writing

Writing the Novel
Writing the Short Story

The Graphic Artists Guild Inc
31 W 34 St, 8th fl, New York, NY 10001
Tel: 212-791-3400 *Fax:* 212-791-0333
E-mail: admin@graphicartistsguild.org;
membership@graphicartistsguild.org
Web Site: www.graphicartistsguild.org
Key Personnel
Pres: Lara Kisielewska *E-mail:* president@
graphicartistsguild.org
Business workshops & seminars for professional
graphic artists.
Eastern, Midwestern, New England, Southern &
Western regional chapters.

Graphic Arts Association
Affiliate of PRINTING United Alliance
1210 Northbrook Dr, Suite 200, Trevose, PA
19053
Tel: 215-396-2300 *Fax:* 215-396-9890
E-mail: gaa@gaaonline.org
Web Site: www.graphicartsassociation.org
Key Personnel
Pres: Melissa Jones *E-mail:* mjones@gaaonline.
org
Off Mgr: Rita Donlan *E-mail:* rdonlan@
gaaonline.org
Regional trade association representing printing
& graphic arts professionals in Pennsylvania,
Central & Southern New Jersey & Delaware.
Courses include Computer Laptop Training
Estimating
Graphic Arts Fundamentals
Industrial Relations Training
Production
Sales & Management

Hamilton College, English/Creative Writing
English/Creative Writing Dept, 198 College Hill
Rd, Clinton, NY 13323
Tel: 315-859-4370 *Fax:* 315-859-4390
Web Site: www.hamilton.edu
Key Personnel
Chair: Margaret Thickstun *E-mail:* mthickst@
hamilton.edu
Professor, Eng & Creative Writing: Naomi
Guttman *E-mail:* nguttman@hamilton.edu
Professor, Eng: Doran Larson *E-mail:* dlarson@
hamilton.edu
Professor, Lit & Creative Writing: Onno Oerle-
mans *Tel:* 315-859-4378 *E-mail:* ooerlema@
hamilton.edu
Assoc Professor, Eng: Tina Hall *E-mail:* thall@
hamilton.edu
Academic program; students may concentrate on
creative writing.

Hofstra University, English Dept
203 Mason Hall, Hempstead, NY 11549
Tel: 516-463-5454 *Fax:* 516-463-6395
Web Site: www.hofstra.edu
Key Personnel
Professor, Eng: Joseph Fichtelberg, PhD
E-mail: joseph.fichtelberg@hofstra.edu
Assoc Professor: Erik A Brogger *E-mail:* erik.a.
brogger@hofstra.edu
Undergraduate courses in all phases of publishing
& creative writing, leading to a BA in English.
MA in English Literature & an MFA in cre-
ative writing.

Hollins University-Jackson Center for Creative Writing
7916 Williamson Rd, Roanoke, VA 24020
Tel: 540-362-6317
E-mail: creative.writing@hollins.edu
Web Site: www.hollins.edu; www.hollins.edu/
jacksoncenter/index.shtml

Key Personnel
Dir: Prof Thorpe Moeckel
BA degree in English with concentration in creative writing - 4 academic years; MFA in creative writing - 2-year program in residency.

Louisiana State University Creative Writing Program MFA
English Dept, 260 Allen Hall, Baton Rouge, LA
70803
Tel: 225-578-4086 *Fax:* 225-578-4129
E-mail: lsucrwriting@lsu.edu
Web Site: www.lsu.edu; www.lsu.edu/hss/english/
creative_writing
Key Personnel
Prof, Poetry: Laura Mullen *E-mail:* lmullen@lsu.
edu
Asst Dir: Randolph Thomas *E-mail:* rdthomas@
lsu.edu
A graduate program leading to a MFA degree in
creative writing.
Courses include Drama Workship, ENGL 7008
Fiction Workshop, ENGL 7006
Literary Nonfiction Workshop, ENGL 7001
Poetry Workshop, ENGL 7007
Screenwriting Workshop, ENGL 7009

Manhattanville College Master of Fine Arts in Creative Writing Program
2900 Purchase St, Purchase, NY 10577
Tel: 914-323-5239 *Fax:* 914-323-3122
Web Site: www.mville.edu/writing
Key Personnel
Asst Dir: Erika Stanley *E-mail:* stanleye@mville.
edu
Offers courses with faculty who are well-known
published writers & poets, all of whom are
dedicated to helping writers explore their craft,
sharpen their skills & take their writing to the
next level, all within a thriving literary com-
munity. In addition, students can build on the
skills gained in the editing & production course
through work on our award-winning journal
Inkwell, which gives them the editorial & pro-
duction experience to succeed in publishing.
Courses include Editing & Production Workshop
Fiction Workshop
Nonfiction Workshop
Poetry Workshop
Writing for Children & Young Adults
Writing the Contemporary Novel

McNeese State University, Writing Program
PO Box 92655, Lake Charles, LA 70609-0001
Tel: 337-475-5325; 337-475-5327
Web Site: www.mcneese.edu.com; www.mfa.
mcneese.edu
Key Personnel
Professor & Dir, MFA Prog: Amy Fleury
E-mail: afleury@mcneese.edu
Asst Professor, Fiction & Ed, McNeese Review:
John Griswold *E-mail:* wgriswold@mcneese.
edu
MFA program in creative writing - 60 hour pro-
gram.
Courses include Contemporary Novel
Contemporary Poetry
Creative Writing Workshop-Fiction
Creative Writing Workshop-Poetry
Form & Theory of Fiction I
Form & Theory of Fiction II
Form & Theory of Poetry I
Form & Theory of Poetry II

Mississippi Review/University of Southern Mississippi, Center for Writers
Affiliate of University of Southern Mississippi,
Dept of English
118 College Dr 5144, Hattiesburg, MS 39406-
0001
Tel: 601-266-1000

Web Site: www.usm.edu/humanities/center-writers.
php; sites.usm.edu/mississippi-review/index.
html
Key Personnel
Ed-in-Chief: Adam Clay
Graduate & undergraduate courses in poetry, fiction & nonfiction writing.
Department is also home to the *Mississippi Review*, a nationally recognized literary magazine.

New York City College of Technology
Division of City University of New York
300 Jay St, Brooklyn, NY 11201
Tel: 718-260-5500 *Fax:* 718-260-5198
E-mail: connect@citytech.cuny.edu
Web Site: www.citytech.cuny.edu
Key Personnel
Pres: Russell K Hotzler, PhD *Tel:* 718-260-5400
E-mail: rhotzler@citytech.cuny.edu
Dir, Graphic Arts Dept: Lloyd Carr *Tel:* 718-260-
5822 *E-mail:* lcarr@citytech.cuny.edu
2- or 4-year degree in graphic arts, certificates,
associates or baccalaureate.
Courses include Advertising
Printing & Publishing

New York University, Center for Publishing
Affiliate of School of Continuing Education
Midtown Ctr, Rm 429, 11 W 42 St, New York,
NY 10036
Tel: 212-992-3232 *Fax:* 212-992-3233
E-mail: pub.center@nyu.edu
Web Site: www.scps.nyu.edu/publishing
Key Personnel
Academic Prog Dir & Clinical Asst Professor:
Andrea L Chambers
Asst Dir: Lindsey Allen *E-mail:* lindsey.allen@
nyu.edu
Offers a certificate in publishing, consisting of
5 courses. Individual courses may be taken.
A total of 13 book, 14 magazine & 7 online
publishing courses. Also offers a certificate in
editing with 10 courses each year. The Summer
Publishing Institute is an intensive residential
program for recent college graduates, planning
to enter the publishing industry. Consists of
3-week module in book publishing & 3-week
module in magazine publishing, each including
an overview of the industry, lectures, workshops, field trips & professional simulations,
job fair & placement assistance. Application
deadline April 1 for MS in publishing. Program
consists of 42 graduate credits chosen from a
required core of courses in the functional areas
of publishing & a concentration in either book
or magazine publishing. Courses are all offered
in the evening.
Courses include Advanced Copyediting
Advanced Magazine Editing
Advanced Special Project in Publishing
Advertising in Magazines
Advertising Sales & Integrated Marketing for
Business-to-Business Publishers
The Basics of the Book Publishing Industry: To-
day & Tomorrow
Book Design Strategies
Book Editing
Book Marketing
Book Packaging
Book Production & Manufacturing
Book Publicity, Promotion
Books from Writer to Reader: An Overview of
the Publishing Process
Bookselling: From Publisher to Reader
The Business of Book Publishing: Financial Man-
agement in a Creative Environment
The Business of Business-to-Business Publishing
The Business of Online Publishing
The Business of Publishing for US Hispanic Mar-
kets
Children's Book Publishing
The Circulation Challenge: Newsstand, Retail &
Speciality Outlets

Controlled Circulation
Cookbook Copyediting
Copyediting & Proofreading Fundamentals
Cross-Media Programs: The Future of Magazine Advertising Sales
Developmental Editing
Disk & Online Editing
The Economics of Magazine Publishing
Economics of Publishing
Editing Periodicals
Effective Marketing in Publishing Via the Digital Channels
Electronic Content Development
Electronic Publishing for Print & Online Part 1: Survey
Electronic Publishing for Print & Online Part II: Portfolio
E-mail Newsletters
The Evolving Business of Custom Publishing
Fact Checking
Financial Analysis I: Introduction to Financial Statement Analysis in Publishing
Financial Copyediting
Freelance Book Indexing
Fundamentals of Copyediting
Fundamentals of Proofreading
Globalization & the Web
Grammar for Publishing Professionals
How to Develop Your Career in Publishing
How to Market Your Freelance Editorial Services
How to Self-Publish Successfully & Profitably in Today's Market–An Intensive Two-Day Seminar
The Independent Publisher: How to Start, Sustain & Build a Small Press
Information Technology Management in Publishing
International Magazine Publishing
International Publishing
Internship
Journal Copyediting & Production
The Laws of Book Publishing: A Practical Guide to Contracts, Copyright & More
Legal Proofreading
Magazine Advertising Sales & Marketing
Magazine Branding & Franchise Development
Magazine Circulation
Magazine Copyediting
Magazine Editorial Planning & Management
Magazine Financial Management
Magazine Production & Manufacturing
Magazine Promotion, Events & Public Relations
Magazine Research: New Techniques to Accelerate Recovery Growth
Magazines from Mission to Magic & More: An Overview
Managing the Publishing Enterprise
Manuscript Editing
Marketing for Publishing
Media Ethics for Publishing Professionals
Mentored Academic Study
Multi-Channel Sales Promotion for Books
Multimedia Marketing & Product Development
ONIX: How Good Product Information Improves Sales
Online Publishing: Business, Technology & Strategy
Principles & Applications of Publishing on the Internet
Principles of Profitability in Book Publishing
Print Technology for Publishing
Production Editing
Professional Book & Information Publishing
Publishing: Books, Magazines & Multimedia
Publishing in Cyberspace: Legal & Practical Problems of Internet & Electronic Publishing
Publishing Law: Issues in Intellectual Property
Publishing On-Line
The Role of the Literary Agent in Book Publishing
Scientific, Technical & Medical Journal Copyediting
Scientific, Technical & Medical Journal Copyediting & Production

Scientific, Technical, Professional Publishing on the Internet
Secrets to Success in Magazine Freelance Writing & Editing
Special Sales, Licensing & Merchandising for Books
Starting a Small Book Publishing Co
Summer Institute in Book & Magazine Publishing
Trade & General Book Publishing
Usability: Information Architecture & the User Experience in Publishing
Web Marketing & E-Commerce
Web Page Development With HTML

Ohio University, English Department, Creative Writing Program

Ohio University, English Dept, Ellis Hall, Athens, OH 45701
Tel: 740-593-2838 (English Dept) *Fax:* 740-593-2832
E-mail: english.department@ohio.edu
Web Site: www.ohio.edu/cas/english
Key Personnel
Dir: Dinty W Moore *E-mail:* moored4@ohio.edu
Offer PhD degree with creative writing emphasis.
Courses include Fiction
Form & Theory
Nonfiction
Novels
Poetry
Short Stories

Pace University, Master of Science in Publishing

Dept of Publishing, Rm 805-E, 551 Fifth Ave, New York, NY 10176
Tel: 212-346-1431 *Toll Free Tel:* 877-284-7670 *Fax:* 212-346-1165
Web Site: www.pace.edu/dyson/mspub
Key Personnel
Chmn & Dir, Publg Progs: Sherman Raskin *E-mail:* sraskin@pace.edu
Program educates its students in all pertinent aspects of the publishing business: books, magazines & digital publishing. Our graduates are equipped for the challenges facing the industry today.
Courses include Book Production & Design, PUB 606
Children's Book Publishing, PUB 634
Digital Issues in Publishing
Ebooks: Technology, Workflow & Business Model, PUB 621
Editorial Principles & Practices, PUB 634
Electronic Publishing for Publishers, PUB 636
Financial Aspects of Publishing, PUB 608
The Future of Publishing: Transmedia, PUB 613
General Interest Books, PUB 610
Information Systems in Publishing, PUB 612
Legal Aspects of Publishing, PUB 618
Magazine Production & Design, PUB 607
Marketing Principles & Practices in Publishing, PUB 628
Modern Technology in Publishing, PUB 620
Publishing Comics & Graphic Novels, PUB 610
Subsidiary Rights, Acquisitions & the Function of the Literary Agent, PUB 610

Parsons School of Design, Continuing Education

Division of New School University
2 W 13 St, Rm 506, New York, NY 10011
Tel: 212-229-8933
E-mail: ceinformation@newschool.edu; academy@newschool.edu
Web Site: www.newschool.edu/parsons
Comprehensive courses & advanced courses appropriate for book, magazine & advertising design.
Courses include Graphic & Advertising Design

Publishing Certificate Program at City College of New York

Division of Humanities NAC 5225, City College of New York, New York, NY 10031
Tel: 212-650-7925 *Fax:* 212-650-7912
E-mail: ccnypub@aol.com
Web Site: www.ccny.cuny.edu/publishing_certificate/index.html
Key Personnel
Dir: David Unger
Asst Dir: Retha Powers
Program for undergraduates. Take 4 of 20 courses offered & then qualify for a paid internship in a publishing house of your interest.
Courses include Books for Young Readers
Copyediting & Proofreading, etc
Ebooks & Digital Publishing
The Editorial Process
Introduction to Publishing I & II
Legal Issues in Publishing

Radcliffe Publishing Course, see Columbia Publishing Course at Columbia University

Rochester Institute of Technology, School of Media, Arts & Technology

69 Lomb Memorial Dr, Rochester, NY 14623-5603
Tel: 585-475-2728; 585-475-5336 *Fax:* 585-475-5336
E-mail: spmofc@rit.edu
Web Site: cias.rit.edu/printmedia
Key Personnel
Chmn, School of Printing: Gregory S D'Amico *E-mail:* gsdppr@rit.edu
Classes in books & magazine production, typography, printing design, computer use, desktop prepress production, management, sales, finishing & bindery, quality control, marketing, finance & legal problems of publishing.
Courses include Computer Use
Desktop Prepress Production
Finance & Legal Problems of Publishing
Finishing & Bindery
Management
Marketing
Printing Design
Quality Control
Sales
Typography

Rosemont College

Graduate Publg Prog, 1400 Montgomery Ave, Rosemont, PA 19010
Tel: 610-527-0200 (ext 2431)
Web Site: www.rosemont.edu
Key Personnel
Prog Dir, Graduate Publg: Marshall Warfield
Offers MA degree in publishing.
Courses include Business of Publishing
Children's & Young Adult
Design
Editorial

School of Visual Arts

209 E 23 St, New York, NY 10010-3994
Tel: 212-592-2100 *Fax:* 212-592-2116
Web Site: www.sva.edu
Key Personnel
Exec Dir, Admissions & Student Aff: Javier Vega
Non-degree programs beginning in Sept, Jan & June, including intensive 2-week workshops.
Courses include Advertising & Graphic Design
Artists' Books
BFA Programs in Advertising & Graphic Design
Book Cover Design & Illustration Book Design
Book Illustration & Children's Book Writing & Illustration
Cartooning
Computer Art & Photography
Computer Graphics
Copywriting

Editorial Design
Fine Arts
Illustration & Cartooning
Interior Design & Photography
MAT in Art Education
MFA Programs in Fine Arts Illustration
Photographic Printing Processes
Type & Design Agency Skills
Video Recording & Editing

Susquehanna University, Department of English & Creative Writing
514 University Ave, Selinsgrove, PA 17870
Tel: 570-372-0101
Key Personnel
Professor, Eng: Laurence Roth
Assoc Professor, Eng: Randy Robertson
Assoc Professor, Communs: Katherine Hastings
Assoc Professor, Creating Writing: Catherine Dent-Zobal
Assoc Professor, Creative Writing: Karla Kelsey
The English - Publishing & Editing major prepares students for careers in a digitally mediated publishing industry & for related careers in marketing, public relations, arts journalism, library & information science & media management. Courses focus on both the intellectual & practical uses of literary study, especially the technologies of writing & reading, the businesses of literature & craft.
Courses include Aesthetics & Interpretation, ENGL:290
Book Reviewing, ENGL:298
Editing, COMM:331 Intermediate focused subject course that focuses on the challenges & issues confronted in editing for journalism & teaches the process of editing a newspaper
English Grammar & the Writing Process, ENGL:269
History of the Book, ENGL:375
Internship, ENGL:540 Working with internships available in publishing or editing either on or off campus
Introduction to Modern Publishing, ENGL:190 Introduces students to the history of modern publishing, to the process, art & business of producing books
Marketing, MGMT:280
Professional Writing, ENGL:299
Public Relations, COMM:211
Publishing: Ethics, Entertainment, Art, Politics, ENGL:388 Analyzes changes & continuities in the cultural role of publishing from the beginning of mass printing to the current day
Small Press Publishing & Editing, WRIT:270 Intermediate focused subject course that focuses on the challenges & issues faced by small literary presses. Students learn to edit fiction, poetry, nonfiction & memoirs
Surveys in Forms of Writing, ENGL:265
Writing for New Media, COMM:182

Syracuse University Creative Writing Program
401 Hall of Languages, Syracuse, NY 13244-1170
Tel: 315-443-2173 *Fax:* 315-443-3660
Web Site: english.syr.edu/creative_writing; www.syr.edu
Key Personnel
Dir: Christopher Kennedy *E-mail:* ckennedy@syr.edu
Assoc Dir: Sarah C Harwell *Tel:* 315-443-9480
E-mail: scharwel@syr.edu
Courses include Eastern European Poetry/Translation
The Essay
Fiction Workshop
The Forms of Fiction
The Forms of Poetry
Open Workshop - Fiction
Open Workshop - Poetry
Poetry Workshop
Prose Writing

Writing of Fiction
Writing of Poetry
Writing the Novella

Syracuse University, SI Newhouse School of Public Communications
215 University Place, Syracuse, NY 13244-2100
Tel: 315-443-3627 *Fax:* 315-443-3946
E-mail: newhouse@syr.edu
Web Site: newhouse.syr.edu
Key Personnel
Dean: Lorraine Branham
Undergraduate degrees in advertising; broadcast & arts journalism, magazine, newspaper & online journalism; public relations; television, radio, film; visual & interactive communications; photography & graphics; Master's degrees in advertising; magazine; newspaper; media administration; visual & interactive communications; public relations; television-radio & film. PhD degrees in mass communications.
Courses include Advertising
Broadcast, Magazine & Newspaper Journalism
Film
Media Administration
Photography
Public Relations
Radio
Television

University of Alabama Program in Creative Writing
Affiliate of University of Alabama, Department of English
PO Box 870244, Tuscaloosa, AL 35487-0244
Tel: 205-348-5065 *Fax:* 205-348-1388
E-mail: english@ua.edu
Web Site: www.as.ua.edu/english
Key Personnel
Poet & Professor: Robin Behn *Tel:* 205-348-8488
E-mail: rbehn@ua.edu
Poet & Assoc Professor: Joel Brouwer *Tel:* 205-348-9524 *E-mail:* joel.brouwer@ua.edu
Fiction Writer & Professor: Michael Martone *Tel:* 205-348-5526 *E-mail:* mmartone@ua.edu
Fiction Writer & Assoc Professor: Wendy Rawlings *Tel:* 205-348-4507 *E-mail:* wendy.rawlings@ua.edu
Graduate Prog Coord: Jennifer Fuqua *Tel:* 205-348-9493 *E-mail:* jfuqua@as.ua.edu
Three-year MFA degree program & creative writing course for undergraduates, minor in creative writing. See web site for details.

University of Baltimore - Yale Gordon College of Arts & Sciences, Ampersand Institute for Words & Images
Division of Klein Family School of Communications Design
1420 N Charles St, Baltimore, MD 21201-5779
Tel: 410-837-6022 *Fax:* 410-837-6029
E-mail: scd@ubalt.edu
Web Site: www.ubalt.edu
Key Personnel
Dir: Dr Cheryl Wilson *E-mail:* cwilson2@ubalt.edu
Academic Prog Specialist: Jaye Crooks
Sponsors Fall & Spring lecture series, conducts advanced seminars, workshops, mini-courses & conferences on publishing topics including writing, design; also supports through the School of Communications Design, a MA program in Publications Design, an MFA in Integrated Design & an MFA in Creative Writing & Publishing Arts.

University of British Columbia Creative Writing Program
Buchanan Rm E-462, 1866 Main Mall, Vancouver, BC V6T 1Z1, Canada
Tel: 604-822-0699
Web Site: creativewriting.ubc.ca

Key Personnel
Chair: Alix Ohlin
Graduate Advisor: Andrew Gray *E-mail:* andrew.gray@ubc.ca
Undergraduate Advisor: Heather Miller
E-mail: crwr.undergrad@ubc.ca
Admin: Tania Chen *Tel:* 604-822-3024
E-mail: crwr.admin@ubc.ca
Undergraduate & graduate programs in creative writing as well as a non-credit novel writing course several times per year.

University of California Extension Professional Sequence in Copyediting & Courses in Publishing
1995 University Ave, Suite 110, Berkeley, CA 94720-7000
Tel: 510-642-6362 *Fax:* 510-643-0216
E-mail: letters@unex.berkeley.edu
Web Site: www.unex.berkeley.edu
Key Personnel
Prog Dir: Liz McDonough *Tel:* 510-643-1637
Certificate program in editing; evening/weekend courses & one-day seminars.
Courses include Editing
Management
Screenwriting
Writing (fiction, poetry, nonfiction)

University of Chicago, Graham School of General Studies
Division of Professional Programs
1427 E 60 St, Chicago, IL 60637
Tel: 773-702-1722 *Fax:* 773-702-6814
Web Site: www.grahamschool.uchicago.edu
Key Personnel
Prog Dir: Lisa Malvin *Tel:* 773-702-1720
E-mail: lmalvin@uchicago.edu
Noncredit courses.
Courses include Basic Creative Writing
Elements of Novel Writing
Getting the Story: Freelance Journalism Workshop
Intensive Short Story Workshop
Introduction to Freelance Journalism
Memoir Writing
Poetry Workshop: Outside the Self
Screenwriting Workshop
Writing Novels for Children & Young Adults
Writing the Novel 1
Writing the Novel 2
Writing the Personal Essay

University of Denver Publishing Institute
2000 E Asbury Ave, Denver, CO 80208
Tel: 303-871-2570 *Fax:* 303-871-2501
Web Site: www.du.edu/publishinginstitute
Key Personnel
Dir: Jill Smith *E-mail:* jill.smith@du.edu
Four-week graduate program in book publishing held July-Aug each year. Provides hands on workshops, lecture-teaching sessions on every phase of book publishing. Faculty consists of leading executives from publishing houses across the country. Emphasis on career counseling & job placement. Offers 6 quarter hours of graduate credit.
Courses include Children's Books
College Textbooks
E-Books
Economics of Publishing
Editing Workshop
Foreign Rights
Independent Presses
International Publishing
Marketing on the Internet
Marketing Workshop
Production & Design
Publicity & Promotion
Publishing & the Law
Scholarly Books
Trade & Scholarly Books
University Presses

University of Houston Creative Writing Program

229 Roy Cullen Bldg, Houston, TX 77204-5008
Tel: 713-743-2255 *Fax:* 713-743-3697
E-mail: cwp@uh.edu
Web Site: www.uh.edu/cwp
Key Personnel
Dir: Jay Kastely *E-mail:* jkastely@uh.edu
Asst Dir: Giuseppe Taurino *E-mail:* gtaurino@uh.edu
Offers MA, MFA & PhD in creative writing.

University of Illinois at Chicago, Program for Writers

Affiliate of University of Illinois, Department of English
College of Liberal Arts & Sciences, 2027 University Hall, 601 S Morgan St, Chicago, IL 60607-7120
Tel: 312-413-2200 (Eng dept) *Fax:* 312-413-1005
Web Site: www.uic.edu
Key Personnel
Dir, Prog for Writers: Cris Mazza *Tel:* 312-413-2795 *E-mail:* cmazza@uic.edu
Graduate program for writers. Students in this program take literature classes as well as writing workshops. Offers MA & PhD in writing. Undergraduates seeking a BA in English may also specialize in writing.
Courses include Experimental Writing Workshop
Fiction Workshop
Nonfiction Workshop
Novel Workshop
Poetry Workshop
Publication Workshop
Translation Practicum

University of Illinois, Department of Journalism

Unit of College of Communications, University of Illinois
Gregory Hall, Rm 120-A, 810 S Wright St, Urbana, IL 61801
Tel: 217-333-0709 *Fax:* 217-333-7931
E-mail: journ@uiuc.edu
Web Site: www.comm.uiuc.edu
Key Personnel
Dept Head: Prof Brian Johnson *Tel:* 217-333-2103 *E-mail:* bjohn@illinois.edu
Master's degree program.
Courses include Graphics
Magazine Article Writing
News Editing
Photojournalism
Reporting I & II

University of Iowa, Writers' Workshop, Graduate Creative Writing Program

102 Dey House, 507 N Clinton St, Iowa City, IA 52242-1000
Tel: 319-335-0416 *Fax:* 319-335-0420
Web Site: writersworkshop.uiowa.edu
Key Personnel
Dir: Lan Samantha Chang
Graduate: fiction & poetry workshops & seminars. Undergraduate: creative, fiction & poetry writing.

University of Montana, Environmental Writing Institute

Subsidiary of Environmental Studies Program
Environmental Studies, University of Montana, Missoula, MT 59812
Tel: 406-243-2904 *Fax:* 406-243-6090
Web Site: www.umt.edu/ewi
Key Personnel
Prog Mgr & Dir: Phil Condon *E-mail:* phil.condon@mso.umt.edu
Writing workshop for environmental & nature subjects.

University of Southern California, Master of Professional Writing Program

Mark Taper Hall, THH 355, 3501 Trousedale Pkwy, Los Angeles, CA 90089-0355
Tel: 213-740-3252 *Fax:* 213-740-5002
E-mail: mpw@college.usc.edu
Web Site: college.usc.edu/mpw
Key Personnel
Dir: Brighde Mullins
Prog Specialist: Howard Ho
Student Servs Advisor: Natalie Inouye
Multidisciplinary Creative Writing Master's program & Master's of Arts degree in Professional Writing.
Courses include Creative Nonfiction
Fiction
New Media
Poetry
Writing for Stage & Screen

University of Texas at Austin, New Writers Project

Dept of English, Calhoun Hall, Rm 226, 204 W 21 St, B-5000, Austin, TX 78712
Tel: 512-471-5132; 512-471-4991 *Fax:* 512-471-4909
Web Site: newwritersproject.org
Key Personnel
Chair: Elizabeth Cullingford
E-mail: cullingford@austin.utexas.edu
Chair, Poetry: Dean Young *E-mail:* deanyoung@mail.utexas.edu
Dir, New Writers Proj: Lisa Olstein
E-mail: lisaolstein@gmail.com
Assoc Dir, New Writers Proj: Elizabeth McCracken *E-mail:* elizmccrack@utexas.edu
Professor: Don Graham *E-mail:* dgbb@mail.utexas.edu; Kurt Heinzelman *E-mail:* kheinz@mail.utexas.edu; Rolando Hinojosa-Smith *E-mail:* rorro@mail.utexas.edu; Lisa Moore *E-mail:* llmoore@austin.utexas.edu
Susan Taylor McDaniel Regents Professor in Creative Writing: Peter La Salle *E-mail:* pnl315@yahoo.com
Assoc Professor: Edward Carey
E-mail: edcarey256@aol.com; Oscar Casares *E-mail:* ohcasares@utexas.edu; Deborah Paredez *E-mail:* paredez@austin.utexas.edu; Deb Unferth *E-mail:* debou@utexas.edu
Graduate Prog Coord I: Cassandra Shulter
E-mail: cshulter@austin.utexas.edu
Graduate Prog Coord II: Patricia Schaub
E-mail: pjschaub@austin.utexas.edu
Comprised of experienced teachers committed to advising young writers. Students work with established writers, gain editorial & teaching experience & develop the range of their work. Students graduate with an MFA in Creative Writing.

University of Texas at El Paso, Department of Creative Writing, MFA/Department of Creative Writing

901 EDUC, 500 W University Ave, El Paso, TX 79968-9991
Tel: 915-747-5713 *Fax:* 915-747-5523
E-mail: creativewriting@utep.edu
Web Site: www.utep.edu/cw
Key Personnel
Chair, Bilingual MFA: Lex Williford *Tel:* 915-747-5721 *E-mail:* lex@utep.edu
Dir, Online MFA & Assoc Professor: Daniel Chacon *Tel:* 915-747-6255 *E-mail:* danchacon@utep.edu
Graduate Dir & Assoc Professor: Jose de Pierola *Tel:* 915-747-6322 *E-mail:* jdepierola@utep.edu
Professor: Luis Arturo Ramos *Tel:* 915-747-6511 *E-mail:* laramos@utep.edu
Assoc Professor: Rosa Alcala *Tel:* 915-747-7020 *E-mail:* ralcala1@utep.edu
Asst Professor: Andrea Cote-Botero
E-mail: acbotero@utep.edu; Tim Z Hernandez *E-mail:* tzhernandez@utep.edu; Sasha Pimentel *Tel:* 915-747-6810 *E-mail:* srpimentel@utep.edu; Jeff Sirkin *Tel:* 915-747-5529 *E-mail:* jsirkin@utep.edu
Monolingual & bilingual workshops in fiction, poetry, playwriting, screenwriting, nonfiction & literary translation.

University of Wisconsin-Madison Continuing Studies

21 N Park St, 7th fl, Madison, WI 53715
Tel: 608-262-3447
Web Site: continuingstudies.wisc.edu
Key Personnel
Faculty Assoc: Christine DeSmet *Tel:* 608-262-3447 *E-mail:* christine.desmet@wisc.edu
Writing book trade & online writing courses offered, in-person retreats & conferences.
Courses include Critique Services
Weekend With Your Novel Retreat
Write-by-the-Lake Writer's Retreat
Writers' Institute Conference

Vermont College of Fine Arts MFA in Writing for Children & Young Adults Program

36 College St, Montpelier, VT 05602
Tel: 802-828-8637; 802-828-8696
Toll Free Tel: 866-934-VCFA (934-8232)
Fax: 802-828-8649
Web Site: www.vcfa.edu
Key Personnel
Prog Dir: Melissa Fisher *E-mail:* melissa.fisher@vcfa.edu
Asst Prog Dir: Susan Sarlo *E-mail:* susan.sarlo@vcfa.edu
Writing for children & young adults. Intensive 10-day residencies & nonresident 6-month writing projects.

Vermont College of Fine Arts, MFA in Writing Program

36 College St, Montpelier, VT 05602
Tel: 802-828-8840; 802-828-8839
Toll Free Tel: 866-934-VCFA (934-8232)
Fax: 802-828-8649
Web Site: www.vcfa.edu
Key Personnel
Prog Dir: Louise Crowley *E-mail:* louise.crowley@vcfa.edu
Asst Prog Dir: Jericho Parms *E-mail:* jericho.parms@vcfa.edu
Degree work in poetry, fiction, creative nonfiction.

Warren Wilson College, MFA Program for Writers

701 Warren Wilson Rd, Swannanoa, NC 28778
Mailing Address: PO Box 9000, Asheville, NC 28815-9000
Tel: 828-771-3717 *Fax:* 828-771-7005
E-mail: mfa@warren-wilson.edu
Web Site: www.warren-wilson.edu/programs/mfa-in-creative-writing
Key Personnel
Dir, MFA Prog: Debra Allberry *Tel:* 828-771-3716
Full-time 2-year program with winter & summer semesters. Ten-day residency of classes, workshops & lectures on campus. The 6-month project that follows is supervised through correspondence, with detailed ms criticism by faculty who are both accomplished writers & committed teachers.
Courses include Fiction
Poetry

Writer's Digest University

Division of Active Interest Media (AIM)
5720 Flatiron Pkwy, Boulder, CO 80301
Toll Free Tel: 800-759-0963; 800-333-5441
E-mail: writersdigestuniversity@aimmedia.com
Web Site: www.writersonlineworkshops.com
Course workshops are taught by active, published writers in the appropriate area, such as fiction

& nonfiction. Students participate online, via the Internet. Workshops range in length from 4 to 28 weeks. Correspondence; student has up to 2 years to complete; tuition installment plans available for most courses.

Courses include Advanced Blogging
Advanced Horror Workshop
Advanced Novel Writing
Advanced Poetry Writing
Agent One-on-One: First Ten Pages Boot Camp
Agent One-on-One: How to Craft Query Letters & Other Submission Materials That Get Noticed Boot Camp
The Art of Storytelling 101: Story Mapping & Pacing
The Art of Storytelling 102: Showing vs Telling
Blogging 101
Breaking into Copywriting 101
Build Your Novel Scene by Scene
Business Writing
Character Development: Creating Memorable Characters
Comedy Writing Workshop
Copyediting Certification Course
Creative Writing 101
Creativity & Expression
Description & Setting
Fantasy Writers
Fearless Writing
1st Person Point of View
Fitting Writing Into Your Life
Focus on the Short Story
Form & Composition
Freelance Writing
Freelance Writing for Stay at Home Moms (and Dads)

Fundamentals of Fiction
Fundamentals of Poetry Writing
Getting Started in Writing
Ghostwriting 101
Grammar & Mechanics
Horror Writing Intensive: Analyzing the Work of Genre Master Stephen King
How to Blog a Book
How to Catch an Agent's Interest with Your First Pages
How to Craft a Book that Will Sell
How to Find & Keep a Literary Agent Boot Camp
How to Hook an Agent: Queries & Beyond!-Recording
How to Plot & Structure Your Novel
How to Write an Article
Introduction to Copyediting
Literary Agent Boot Camp: Perfecting Submission Materials
Marketing Your Magazine Articles
Master in Fine Arts (Creative Writing) Application Preparation Course
Mastering Amazon for Authors
Outlining Your Novel
Picture eBook Mastery: The Unofficial Guide to Publishing & Selling Kindle Children's Books
Pitch an Article: Write for Today's Marketplace
Plot Perfect Boot Camp
Professional Copyediting: Tools of the Trade
Publishing Your Children's Book: How to Write & Pitch Young Adult, Middle Grade & Picture Book Manuscripts
Pulp Fiction
Query Letter in 14 Days
Read Like a Writer: Learn from the Masters

Revision & Self Editing
Sell Books on a Shoestring Budget
Short Story Fundamentals
Social Media 101
Successful Self-Publishing
Travel Writing
12 Weeks to a First Draft
Voice & Viewpoint
Wordbuilding in Science Fiction & Fantasy Writing
Write a Plot
Write Great Dialogue
Writing a Religious Book
Writing Historical Fiction
Writing Nonfiction for Children
Writing Nonfiction 101: Fundamentals
Writing Online Content
Writing the Memoir 101
Writing the Middle Grade Book
Writing the Mystery Novel
Writing the Nonfiction Book Proposal
Writing the Novel Proposal
Writing the Paranormal Novel
Writing the Personal Essay 101: Fundamentals
Writing the Picture Book
Writing the Romance Novel
Writing the Science Fiction & Fantasy Novel
Writing the Thriller Novel
Writing the Young Adult Novel
Writing Tips-Short Story Fundamentals
Writing Women's Fiction
Your Submission Tools: How to Write Excellent Queries, Opening Pages & Synopses Boot Camp

Awards, Prize Contests, Fellowships & Grants

Major awards given to books, authors and publishers by various organizations are, for the most part, not open for application. However, many prize contests may be applied for by writing to the sponsor (for prompt response, always include a self-addressed, stamped envelope). Also included in this section is information relating to fellowships and grants that are primarily available to authors and students who are pursuing publishing related studies.

For more complete information about scholarships, fellowships and grants-in-aid, see *The Annual Register of Grant Support* (Information Today, Inc., 121 Chanlon Road, Suite G-20, New Providence, NJ 07974-2195).

A Public Space Fellowships
A Public Space
323 Dean St, Brooklyn, NY 11217
Tel: 718-858-8067
E-mail: general@apublicspace.org
Web Site: apublicspace.org
Key Personnel
Founding Ed: Brigid Hughes
Mktg & Devt Dir: Lauren Cerand *Tel:* 917-533-0103 *E-mail:* lauren@apublicspace.org
Writers who have not yet published or been contracted to write a book-length work are eligible. International applicants are encouraged to apply, but only submissions in English are considered. One submission per person is allowed. Submittable opens for Fellowship submissions September 15. Submit cover letter & one previously unpublished prose piece. See web site for detailed submission guidelines.
Award: $1,000 honorarium & 6 months editorial support to prepare a piece of prose for the magazine
Closing Date: Oct 15
Presented: Successful applicants informed no later than Feb 15 for Fellowship period March 1-Sept 1

ABA Entrepreneurial Excellence Award
American Booksellers Association
333 Westchester Ave, Suite S202, White Plains, NY 10604
Toll Free Tel: 800-637-0037 *Fax:* 914-417-4013
E-mail: excellence@bookweb.org
Web Site: www.bookweb.org
Annual award given to 2 independent booksellers to recognize & celebrate their achievements. Open to all ABA member bookstores in good standing. Applicants may submit their application as an essay, in a video, or via audio recording. Applications should include the problem or concern the bookseller has recognized, the solution they created, the steps they took to implement the solution & the results of implementing their idea. Applicants should also provide data to support the success of their innovative idea.
Award: Full scholarship to Winter Institute 2021, Baltimore, MD, including up to 5 nights in the host hotel, reasonable travel costs & $1,000 stipend
Closing Date: Oct 21

J M Abraham Poetry Award
Writers' Federation of Nova Scotia
1113 Marginal Rd, Halifax, NS B3H 4P7, Canada
Tel: 902-423-8116 *Fax:* 902-422-0881
E-mail: contact@writers.ns.ca
Web Site: writers.ns.ca
Key Personnel
Communs & Devt Offr: Robin Spittal
Established: 1998
Presented annually to the best full-length book of poetry by an Atlantic Canadian writer who has lived in one or a combination of these provinces for at least 2 concurrent years immediately prior to the submission deadline date. Non-refundable $20 administrative fee per entry.

Award: $2,000
Closing Date: Nov 1
Presented: Halifax, NS, CN, Spring

Academy of American Poets Fellowship
The Academy of American Poets Inc
75 Maiden Lane, Suite 901, New York, NY 10038
Tel: 212-274-0343
E-mail: academy@poets.org
Web Site: www.poets.org
Key Personnel
Pres & Exec Dir: Jennifer Benka
    E-mail: jenbenka@poets.org
Devt, Membership & Communs Sr Mgr: Molly Walsh *E-mail:* mwalsh@poets.org
Ad & Mktg Sr Mgr: Michelle Campagna
    E-mail: mcampagna@poets.org
Sr Progs Mgr: Nikay Paredes *Tel:* 212-274-0343 ext 13 *E-mail:* nparedes@poets.org
Established: 1946
Awarded annually to recognize distinguished poetic achievement. No applications are accepted. Fellows are selected by majority vote of the Academy's Board of Chancellors.
Other Sponsor(s): T S Eliot Foundation
Award: $25,000 & residency at T S Eliot House, Gloucester, MA

Acclaim Film Script Competition
Acclaim Film
300 Central Ave, Suite 501, St Petersburg, FL 33701
Web Site: acclaimscripts.com
Key Personnel
Contest Coord: Frank Drouzas
Open to all writers 18 & over.
Award: $1,000 (1st place)
Closing Date: Ongoing

Acclaim TV Script Competition
Acclaim Film
300 Central Ave, Suite 501, St Petersburg, FL 33701
Web Site: acclaimscripts.com
Key Personnel
Contest Coord: Frank Drouzas
Open to all writers 18 & over. Must be original material of the author. Categories are Spec Scripts (for an existing show), Pilots & Movie of the Week.
Award: $500 for each category
Closing Date: Ongoing

The Accolades, see Cordon d' Or - Gold Ribbon International Culinary Academy Awards

The Acheven Book Prize for Young Adult Fiction
Fitzroy Books
Imprint of Regal House Publishing
c/o Regal House Publishing, 806 Oberlin Rd, No 12094, Raleigh, NC 27605
E-mail: info@regalhousepublishing.com
Web Site: regalhousepublishing.com/the-acheven-book-prize-for-young-adult-fiction/

Key Personnel
Founder, Publr & Ed-in-Chief: Jaynie Royal
Mng Ed: Pam Van Dyk
Sr Ed: Ruth Feiertag
Ed: Elizabeth Lowenstein
Established: 2019
Recognizing finely crafted works written for the Young Adult market. Submissions through Submittable or by post. Entry fee $25. Fax or e-mail submissions not accepted. See web site for submission guidelines. Five finalists announced Dec 10.
Award: Publication & $500 honorarium
Closing Date: Sept 30 (postmark)
Presented: Jan 10

Milton Acorn Poetry Awards
Prince Edward Island Writers' Guild
81 Prince St, Charlottetown, PE C1A 4R3, Canada
E-mail: peiliteraryawards@gmail.com
Web Site: www.peiwritersguild.com
Minimum 8 pages, maximum 10 pages per entry. Maximum 2 entries. Work must be original & unpublished. Entry fee for each submission is $25. Prince Edward Island residents only. See web site for complete entry requirements.
Award: Cash prizes for 1st, 2nd & 3rd place
Closing Date: Jan 31
Presented: Cox & Palmer Island Literary Awards Gala, Annually in Spring

Herbert Baxter Adams Prize
American Historical Association (AHA)
400 "A" St SE, Washington, DC 20003
Tel: 202-544-2422 *Fax:* 202-544-8307
E-mail: awards@historians.org
Web Site: www.historians.org
Established: 1905
For a distinguished book by an American author in the field of European history, from ancient times to 1815. Entry must be the author's first substantial book; must have been published in 2019 or 2020; must be citizen or permanent resident of the US or Canada. Submission of an entry may be made by an author or by a third party as well as by a publisher. Publishers may submit as many entries as they wish. Along with an application form, applicants must mail a copy of their book to each of the prize committee members who will be posted on our web site as the prize deadline approaches. All updated info on web site.
Award: Cash prize
Closing Date: May 15, 2021
Presented: AHA Annual Meeting, New Orleans, LA, Jan 2022

Willi Paul Adams Award
The Organization of American Historians (OAH)
112 N Bryan Ave, Bloomington, IN 47408-4141
Tel: 812-855-7311
E-mail: oah@oah.org
Web Site: www.oah.org/awards
Key Personnel
Exec Dir: Beth English *E-mail:* benglish@oah.org

Comm Coord: Kara Hamm *E-mail:* khamm@oah.org

Awarded biennially to the author of the best book on American history published in a foreign language. To be eligible, a book should be concerned with the past (recent or distant) or with issues of continuity & change. It should also be substantially concerned with events or processes that began, developed, or ended in the American colonies +/or the US. This award is not open to books whose mss were originally submitted for publication in English or by people for whom English is their first language. Each entry must have been published during the 2-year calendar period preceding that in which the award is given. Four copies of the essay & book must be mailed to the Willi Paul Adams Award Committee. See web site for full submission procedures.

Closing Date: May 2, 2022

Presented: OAH Annual Meeting, Los Angeles, CA, March 30–April 2, 2023

Jane Addams Children's Book Award

Jane Addams Peace Association

777 United Nations Plaza, 6th fl, New York, NY 10017

Tel: 212-682-8830

E-mail: info@janeaddamspeace.org

Web Site: www.janeaddamspeace.org

Key Personnel

Award Comm Chair: Heather Palmer

Bd Pres: Tura Campanella Cook

   E-mail: president@janeaddamspeace.org

Established: 1953

Awarded to children's books published in the US the previous year with themes stressing peace, social justice, world community & the equality of the sexes & all races. Those applying must submit 1 copy to the committee chair: Heather Palmer, Valley View Middle School, 6750 Valley View Rd, Edina, MN 55439.

Award: Certificate; Cash

Closing Date: Annually, Dec 31

Presented: Winners announced April 28; ceremony held 3rd Friday in Oct annually

AFCP's Awards

Association of Free Community Papers (AFCP)

135 Old Cove Rd, Suite 210, Liverpool, NY 13090

Toll Free Tel: 877-203-2327 *Fax:* 781-459-7770

E-mail: afcp@afcp.org

Web Site: www.afcp.org

Key Personnel

Exec Dir: Loren Colburn *E-mail:* loren@afcp.org

Established: 1970

Awards for excellence revolving around the theme of free community papers.

Award: Plaques

Closing Date: Jan 23

Presented: AFCP's Annual Conference

Agatha Awards

Malice Domestic Ltd

PO Box 8007, Gaithersburg, MD 20898

Tel: 301-730-1675

E-mail: mdregservices@gmail.com

Web Site: malicedomestic.org

Key Personnel

Malice Chair: Verena Rose *E-mail:* malicechair@comcast.net

Chair, Agatha Awards: Cindy Silberblatt

   E-mail: csilberblatt@att.net

Established: 1989

Awards for best traditional mysteries of the previous calendar year. Awards given for best novel, best first novel, best nonfiction work, best short story, best children's/young adult novel. Those registered for Malice by December 31 each year receive a ballot to nominate.

Closing Date: Annually, Dec 31

Presented: Malice Domestic Convention, Agatha Awards Banquet, Annually in May

Aggiornamento Award

Catholic Library Association

8550 United Plaza Blvd, Suite 1001, Baton Rouge, LA 70809

Tel: 225-408-4417 *Fax:* 225-408-4422

E-mail: cla2@cathla.org

Web Site: cathla.org

Established: 1980

To recognize contributions made by an individual or an organization for the renewal of parish & community life in the spirit of Pope John XXIII.

Award: Plaque

Closing Date: None; in-house votes

Presented: CLA Annual Convention, April

AIGA 50 Books|50 Covers

AIGA, the professional association for design

222 Broadway, New York, NY 10038

Tel: 212-807-1990 *Fax:* 212-807-1799

E-mail: competitions@aiga.org

Web Site: www.aiga.org

Key Personnel

Archives Dir: Heather Strelecki

   E-mail: heather_strelecki@aiga.org

Established: 1923

This annual competition aims to identify the 50 best-designed books & book covers. The selections from the 50 Books|50 Covers competition exemplify the best current work in book & book cover design. See web site for complete rules & eligibility.

Past selections from AIGA's book design competitions have been added to the online AIGA Design Archives as well as the physical archives at the Denver Art Museum & the Rare Book & Manuscript Library at Columbia University's Butler Library in New York City. Books selected this year will be housed at both the Robert B Haas Family Arts Library at Yale University & at the Rare Book & Manuscript Library at Columbia University's Butler Library.

Closing Date: Feb

Presented: Summer

AJL Jewish Fiction Award

Association of Jewish Libraries (AJL) Inc

PO Box 1118, Teaneck, NJ 07666

Tel: 201-371-3255

E-mail: info@jewishlibraries.org

Web Site: jewishlibraries.org/AJL_Jewish_Fiction_Award

Key Personnel

Comm Memb: Rachel Kamin

   E-mail: rachelkamin@gmail.com; Rosalind Reisner *E-mail:* roz@thereisners.net

Established: 2017

All works of fiction with significant Jewish thematic content written in English—novels, short story & flash fiction collections—by a single author published & available for purchase in the US during the award year are eligible for the award. Jewish thematic content means an extended grappling with Jewish themes throughout the book, including Judaism, Jewish history & culture, Jewish identity, etc.

Other Sponsor(s): Dan Wyman Books

Award: $1,000 cash prize & support to attend AJL conference

Presented: Association of Jewish Libraries Conference, June

AJL Judaica Bibliography Award

Association of Jewish Libraries (AJL) Inc

Affiliate of American Library Association (ALA)

PO Box 1118, Teaneck, NJ 07666

Tel: 201-371-3255

E-mail: info@jewishlibraries.org

Web Site: jewishlibraries.org

Key Personnel

Pres: Amalia Warshenbrot

Ref & Bibliography Awards Comm Chair: Sharon Benamou *E-mail:* benamou@library.ucla.edu

Established: 1984

Presented annually for best Judaica bibliography book published in previous calendar year.

Award: The seal of the Association

Closing Date: March

Presented: AJL Annual Convention, June

AJL Judaica Reference Award

Association of Jewish Libraries (AJL) Inc

Affiliate of American Library Association (ALA)

PO Box 1118, Teaneck, NJ 07666

Tel: 201-371-3255

E-mail: info@jewishlibraries.org

Web Site: jewishlibraries.org

Key Personnel

Pres: Amalia Warshenbrot

Ref & Bibliography Awards Comm Chair: Sharon Benamou *E-mail:* benamou@library.ucla.edu

Established: 1984

Annual award for outstanding Judaica reference book published during previous calendar year.

Award: The seal of the Association

Closing Date: March

Presented: AJL Annual Convention, June

AJL Scholarship

Association of Jewish Libraries (AJL) Inc

Affiliate of American Library Association (ALA)

PO Box 1118, Teaneck, NJ 07666

Tel: 201-371-3255

E-mail: scholarship@jewishlibraries.org; info@jewishlibraries.org

Web Site: jewishlibraries.org

In order to encourage students to train for & enter the field of Judaica librarianship, the Association of Jewish Libraries awards a scholarship to a student attending or planning to attend a graduate school of library & information science. Prospective candidates should have an interest in & demonstrate a potential for pursuing a career in Judaica librarianship. In addition, applicants must provide documentation showing participation in Judaica studies at an academic or less formal level +/or experience working in Judaica libraries.

Award: $1,000 per academic year

Closing Date: March 15-April 15 (varies by year)

Presented: AJL Annual Convention, June

Akron Poetry Prize

University of Akron Press

120 E Mill St, Suite 415, Akron, OH 44308

Tel: 330-972-6960 *Fax:* 330-972-8364

E-mail: uapress@uakron.edu

Web Site: www.uakron.edu/uapress/akron-poetry-prize

Key Personnel

Poetry Ed: Mary Biddinger *E-mail:* marybid@uakron.edu

Established: 1995

Open to all poets writing in English. Mss must be at least 48 pages. Entry fee: $25.

Award: $1,500 & publication

Closing Date: Annually April 15-June 15 (postmark)

Presented: Winner announced online Sept 30

Alabama Artists Fellowship Awards

Alabama State Council on the Arts

201 Monroe St, Suite 110, Montgomery, AL 36130-1800

Tel: 334-242-4076 *Fax:* 334-240-3269

Key Personnel

Exec Dir: Albert B Head

Lit Prog Mgr: Anne Kimzey *Tel:* 334-242-4076 ext 236 *E-mail:* anne.kimzey@arts.alabama.gov

Awarded based on quality of work +/or career status, achievement & potential; two-year residency required & service to the state.
Award: Cash; Two $5,000 fellowships
Closing Date: March 1
Presented: Annually, Oct 1

Alberta Book Publishing Awards
The Book Publishers Association of Alberta (BPAA)
10523 100 Ave, Edmonton, AB T5J 0A8, Canada
Tel: 780-424-5060
E-mail: info@bookpublishers.ab.ca
Web Site: www.bookpublishers.ab.ca
Key Personnel
Exec Dir: Kieran Leblanc *E-mail:* kleblanc@bookpublishers.ab.ca
Established: 1989
Awarded annually for excellence in publishing within the province of Alberta. Publishers are selected through a peer jury process in up to 14 award categories.
Award: Certificate
Closing Date: Feb
Presented: Sept

The Albertine Prize
Cultural Services of the French Embassy
972 Fifth Ave, New York, NY 10075
E-mail: press@albertine.com
Web Site: www.albertine.com/albertine-prize
Recognizes American Readers' favorite French language fiction title that has been translated into English & distributed in the US within the preceding calendar year. Voting takes place on the web site beginning March 14.
Other Sponsor(s): Van Cleef & Arpels
Award: $10,000 split between author & translator
Closing Date: April 30 for voting
Presented: June 6

Alcuin Society Awards for Excellence in Book Design in Canada
Alcuin Society
PO Box 3216, Sta Terminal, Vancouver, BC V6B 3X8, Canada
Tel: 604-732-5403
E-mail: awards@alcuinsociety.com
Web Site: alcuinsociety.com
Key Personnel
Chair, Book Design Competition: Leah Gordon
Established: 1981
Annual awards recognizing the work of Canadian book designers & publishers through the Alcuin Citations awarded for excellence in book design & production. Must fulfill the following criteria: titles published in Canada or titles co-published with a publisher in another country but representing a book by a Canadian book designer. Categories are: children, limited editions, pictorial, poetry, prose fiction, prose nonfiction, prose nonfiction illustrated, reference & comics.
Award: Certificate
Closing Date: March 1
Presented: Awards ceremonies in Toronto & Vancouver, Oct

A Owen Aldridge Prize
American Comparative Literature Association (ACLA)
University of South Carolina, Dept of Languages, Literature & Cultures, 1620 College St, Rm 817, Columbia, SC 29208
Tel: 803-777-3021
E-mail: info@acla.org
Web Site: www.acla.org/prize-awards/owen-aldridge-prize
Competition to encourage & recognize excellence in scholarship among graduate students & to reward the highest achievement by publication. Submissions must be sent to the Editor-in-

Chief of CLS in University Park, PA. See web site for specific guidelines.
Other Sponsor(s): Comparative Literature Studies (CLS)
Award: Prize paper published in *Comparative Literature Studies*, monetary prize including honorarium & help with travel expenses to attend the ACLA annual meeting
Closing Date: Annually in mid-Nov

Alex Awards
Young Adult Library Services Association (YALSA)
Division of The American Library Association (ALA)
50 E Huron St, Chicago, IL 60611
Tel: 312-280-4390 *Toll Free Tel:* 800-545-2433 *Fax:* 312-280-5276
E-mail: yalsa@ala.org
Web Site: www.ala.org/yalsa/alex-awards
Key Personnel
Chair: Mara Cota *E-mail:* maracotalib@gmail.com
Exec Dir: Anita Mechler
Prog Offr, Continuing Educ: Nicole Gibby-Munguia *Tel:* 800-545-2433 ext 5293 *E-mail:* nmunguia@ala.org
Communs Specialist: Anna Lam *Tel:* 800-545-2433 ext 5849 *E-mail:* alam@ala.org
Established: 1998
Awarded annually to 10 books written for adults that have special appeal to young adults, ages 12-18. The winning titles are selected from the previous year's publishing.
Other Sponsor(s): Margaret A Edwards Trust

Nelson Algren Literary Awards
Chicago Tribune
160 N Stetson Ave, Chicago, IL 60601
Tel: 312-222-3001
E-mail: ctc-arts@chicagotribune.com
Web Site: www.chicagotribune.com/entertainment/books/literary-awards; algren.submittable.com
Established: 1981
Given for an outstanding unpublished short fiction, double-spaced & no more than 8,000 words in length, by an American writer. No entry form or fee required. Entry online via Submittable.
Award: One winner ($3,500), 5 finalists ($750); Grand Prize winning story will be considered for publication in a print or digital edition of the *Chicago Tribune*
Closing Date: Jan 31
Presented: Chicago, IL, July

Alligator Juniper's National Writing Contest
Prescott College, Alligator Juniper
220 Grove Ave, Prescott, AZ 86301
Tel: 928-350-2012
E-mail: alligatorjuniper@prescott.edu
Web Site: alligatorjuniper.wordpress.com
Established: 1995
Annual prizes for fiction, creative nonfiction & poetry. Stories have a 30 page limit per entry or up to 5 poems. Entry fee: $18; no e-mail submissions. See web site for additional submission information.
Award: $1,000 plus publication & copy of spring issue for each of the 3 genres
Closing Date: Aug 15-Oct 15 (postmark)
Presented: Jan

ALSC Baker & Taylor Summer Reading Grant
Association for Library Service to Children (ALSC)
Division of The American Library Association (ALA)
50 E Huron St, Chicago, IL 60611-2795
Tel: 312-280-2163 *Toll Free Tel:* 800-545-2433 *Fax:* 312-440-9374; 312-280-5271

E-mail: alsc@ala.org
Web Site: www.ala.org/alsc
Key Personnel
Exec Dir: Aimee Strittmatter *E-mail:* astrittmatter@ala.org
Deputy Exec Dir: Alena Rivers *Tel:* 800-545-2433 ext 5866 *E-mail:* arivers@ala.org
Prog Offr, Communs: Laura Schulte-Cooper *Tel:* 800-545-2433 ext 2165 *E-mail:* lschulte@ala.org
Awards Coord: Katie Connelly *Tel:* 800-545-2433 ext 2163 *E-mail:* kconnelly@ala.org
Prog Coord: Ann Michaud *Tel:* 800-545-2433 ext 2166 *E-mail:* amichaud@ala.org
Membership/Mktg Specialist: Elizabeth Serrano *Tel:* 800-545-2433 ext 2164 *E-mail:* eserrano@ala.org
Encourages reading programs for children in a public library. Applicant must plan & present an outline for a theme-based summer reading program in a public library.
Award: $3,000
Closing Date: Annually, Nov 1
Presented: The ALA Midwinter Meeting, Announced in Dec press release

The Ambassador Richard C Holbrooke Distinguished Achievement Award
Dayton Literary Peace Prize Foundation
PO Box 461, Wright Brothers Branch, Dayton, OH 45409-0461
Tel: 937-298-5072
E-mail: sharon.rab@daytonliterarypeaceprize.org
Web Site: www.daytonliterarypeaceprize.org/holbrooke.htm
Key Personnel
Founder & Co-Chair: Sharon Rab *E-mail:* sharon.rab@woh.rr.com
Co-Chair: Mark Meister
Literary award for a body of work that focuses on a central message of peace. Nominated works must have significant & enduring literary value, appeal to a variety of audiences & be in English or translated into English.
Award: $10,000 & sculpture

Ambroggio Prize
The Academy of American Poets Inc
75 Maiden Lane, Suite 901, New York, NY 10038
Tel: 212-274-0343
E-mail: awards@poets.org
Web Site: www.poets.org
Key Personnel
Pres & Exec Dir: Jennifer Benka *E-mail:* jenbenka@poets.org
Devt, Membership & Communs Sr Mgr: Molly Walsh *E-mail:* mwalsh@poets.org
Ad & Mktg Sr Mgr: Michelle Campagna *E-mail:* mcampagna@poets.org
Sr Progs Mgr: Nikay Paredes *Tel:* 212-274-0343 ext 13 *E-mail:* nparedes@poets.org
Established: 2017
Annual publication prize for a book-length poetry ms originally written in Spanish & with an English translation. If poet collaborates with a translator, both must share the prize. Online submissions only through Submittable.
Award: $1,000
Closing Date: Feb 15
Presented: Applicants notified of prize results via e-mail by Sept 30

American Association of University Women Award for Juvenile Literature
AAUW, North Carolina Division
Affiliate of North Carolina Literary & Historical Association
4610 Mail Service Ctr, Raleigh, NC 27699-4610
Tel: 919-807-7290 *Fax:* 919-733-8807
Key Personnel
Awards Coord: Michael Hill *E-mail:* michael.hill@ncdcr.gov

Established: 1953

For a published work of juvenile fiction or non-fiction by a legal or actual resident of North Carolina for at least three years prior to the end of the contest period.

Other Sponsor(s): AAUW

Award: Cup

Closing Date: Annually, July 15

Presented: Raleigh, NC, Annually in Nov

American Book Awards

Before Columbus Foundation

The Raymond House, 655 13 St, Suite 302, Oakland, CA 94612

SAN: 159-2955

Tel: 916-425-7916

E-mail: beforecolumbusfoundation@gmail.com

Web Site: www.beforecolumbusfoundation.com

Key Personnel

Founder: Ishmael Reed

Established: 1978

To recognize outstanding literary achievement by contemporary American authors without restriction for race, sex, ethnic background or genre. The purpose is to acknowledge the excellence & multicultural diversity of American writing. The awards are nonprofit. There are no categories & all winners are accorded equal status. Award is given for books published within the current year. No application forms or fees. Must submit two copies of each entry.

Award: Plaque

Closing Date: Annually, Dec 31

Presented: San Francisco, CA, Annually in Oct

American Illustration/American Photography

Amilus Inc

Subsidiary of Fadner Media

225 W 36 St, Suite 602, New York, NY 10018

Tel: 917-408-9944 *Fax:* 212-532-2064

E-mail: info@ai-ap.com

Web Site: www.ai-ap.com

Key Personnel

Dir: Mark Heflin *E-mail:* mark@ai-ap.com

Established: 1985

For the finest illustrative work by students & professionals. Categories include: editorial, advertising & books, as well as unpublished work. Work will be published in the American Illustration annual & will include the artist's name, address & telephone. Also, similar competition & annual for photography called American Photography. Both books are published in November.

Closing Date: Annually, Jan 23 (photography), Feb 20 (illustration)

Presented: The Party, New York, NY, Annually in Nov

American Indian Youth Literature Award

American Indian Library Association

Affiliate of The American Library Association (ALA)

PO Box 41296, San Jose, CA 95160

E-mail: ailawebsite@gmail.com

Web Site: ailanet.org/activities/american-indian-youth-literature-award

Key Personnel

Exec Dir: Heather Devine-Hardy

E-mail: hhdevine@gmail.com

Established: 2006

Awarded biennially in even-numbered years to identify & honor the very best writing & illustrations by & about American Indians. See web site for specific criteria.

American Printing History Association Award

American Printing History Association

PO Box 4519, Grand Central Sta, New York, NY 10163

E-mail: secretary@printinghistory.org

Web Site: printinghistory.org

Key Personnel

Pres: Haven Hawley

VP, Membership: Charles Cuykendall Carter

VP, Progs: Jesse Erickson

VP, Pubns: Katherine McCanless Ruffin

Treas: David Goodrich

Secy: Virginia Bartow

Exec Secy: Lyndsi Barnes

Established: 1976

For a distinguished contribution to the study, recording, preservation or dissemination of printing history, in any specific area or in general terms.

Award: 2 framed award certificates, one for an individual & one for an institution

Presented: APHA meeting, New York, NY, Annually in Jan

The Amy Award

Poets & Writers Inc

90 Broad St, Suite 2100, New York, NY 10004

Tel: 212-226-3586 *Fax:* 212-226-3963

E-mail: admin@pw.org

Web Site: www.pw.org

Presented to women poets age 30 & under living in the New York metropolitan area or on Long Island.

Award: Honorarium & reading in New York City

The Anisfield-Wolf Book Awards

The Cleveland Foundation

1422 Euclid Ave, Suite 1300, Cleveland, OH 44115

Tel: 216-861-3810 *Fax:* 216-861-1729

E-mail: awinfo@clevefdn.org

Web Site: www.anisfield-wolf.org; www.clevelandfoundation.org

Key Personnel

CEO & Pres, Cleveland Foundation: Ronald B Richard

Jury Chmn: Henry Louis Gates, Jr

Mgr: Karen R Long

Established: 1935

Recognizes books that have made important contributions to our understanding of racism or our appreciation of the diversity of human cultures.

Award: $10,000 each (fiction, nonfiction, poetry & Lifetime Achievement)

Closing Date: Dec 31

Presented: Ohio Theatre, Playhouse Square, Cleveland, OH, Annually in Sept

R Ross Annett Award for Children's Literature

Writers' Guild of Alberta

11759 Groat Rd, Edmonton, AB T5M 3K6, Canada

Tel: 780-422-8174 *Toll Free Tel:* 800-665-5354 (AB only) *Fax:* 780-422-2663 (attn WGA)

E-mail: mail@writersguild.ca

Web Site: writersguild.ca

Key Personnel

Exec Dir: Carol Holmes *E-mail:* carol.holmes@writersguild.ca

Communs & Partnerships Coord: Ellen Kartz

E-mail: ellen.kartz@writersguild.ca

Memb Servs Coord: Giorgia Severini

Progs Coord: Natalie Cook *E-mail:* natalie.cook@writersguild.ca; Julie Robinson *E-mail:* julie.robinson@writersguild.ca

Established: 1982

Alternates yearly between picture & chapter books.

Award: $1,500

Closing Date: Annually, Dec 31

Presented: Alberta Literary Awards Gala

Branch Office(s)

505 21 Ave SW, Calgary, AB T2S 0G9, Canada, Prog Coord: Samantha Warwick *Tel:* 403-265-2226 *E-mail:* samantha.warwick@writersguild.ca

Annual & Rolling Grants for Artists

Vermont Arts Council

136 State St, Montpelier, VT 05602

Tel: 802-828-5425 *Fax:* 802-828-3363

E-mail: info@vermontartscouncil.org

Web Site: www.vermontartscouncil.org

Key Personnel

Artist & Community Progs Mgr: Sarah Mutrux

Tel: 802-828-5425 *E-mail:* smutrux@vermontartscouncil.org

Established: 1965

Individual grants are given to Vermont residents annually. Artist Development Grants open in July. Creation Grants open in February.

Award: $250-$1,000 Artist Development Grant; $3,000 Creation Grants

Closing Date: Artist Development Grant: rolling deadline; Creation Grant: 1st round March, 2nd round by invitation in April

Presented: Award notifications sent to applicants in Aug

The Applegate/Jackson/Parks Future Teacher Scholarship

National Institute for Labor Relations Research

5211 Port Royal Rd, Suite 510, Springfield, VA 22151

Tel: 703-321-9606 *Fax:* 703-321-7143

Web Site: www.nilrr.org

Key Personnel

Scholarship Admin: Cathy Jones *E-mail:* clj@nrtw.org

Based solely on scholastic ability demonstrating an understanding of compulsory unionism in education. Can submit application online.

Award: $1,000

Closing Date: Annually, Dec 31 (postmark or electronic submission)

Presented: Annually in April/May

The May Hill Arbuthnot Honor Lecture Award

Association for Library Service to Children (ALSC)

Division of The American Library Association (ALA)

50 E Huron St, Chicago, IL 60611-2795

Tel: 312-280-2163 *Toll Free Tel:* 800-545-2433 *Fax:* 312-440-9374; 312-280-5271

E-mail: alsc@ala.org

Web Site: www.ala.org/alsc

Key Personnel

Exec Dir: Aimee Strittmatter

E-mail: astrittmatter@ala.org

Deputy Exec Dir: Alena Rivers *Tel:* 800-545-2433 ext 5866 *E-mail:* arivers@ala.org

Prog Offr, Communs: Laura Schulte-Cooper

Tel: 800-545-2433 ext 2165 *E-mail:* lschulte@ala.org

Awards Coord: Katie Connelly *Tel:* 800-545-2433 ext 2163 *E-mail:* kconnelly@ala.org

Prog Coord: Ann Michaud *Tel:* 800-545-2433 ext 2166 *E-mail:* amichaud@ala.org

Membership/Mktg Specialist: Elizabeth Serrano

Tel: 800-545-2433 ext 2164 *E-mail:* eserrano@ala.org

Person appointed prepares a paper of significant contribution to the field of children's literature & delivers a lecture based on the paper in April. Libraries & other institutions apply to host the lecture. The paper is also published in the ALSC journal "Children & Libraries".

Award: $5,000

Closing Date: Dec 31

Presented: ALA Midwinter Meeting, Annually in Jan/Feb

The ARF David Ogilvy Awards

Advertising Research Foundation (ARF)

432 Park Ave S, 4th fl, New York, NY 10016-8013

Tel: 212-751-5656 *Fax:* 212-689-1859

E-mail: help@thearf.org

Web Site: thearf.org
Key Personnel
Events Prog Mgr: Sara Serpe *Tel:* 646-465-5700
  E-mail: sara@thearf.org
Established: 1994
The ARF David Ogilvy Awards honor the research & analytics insights behind successful advertising campaigns. The awards pay tribute to the late David Ogilvy, the ultimate "Mad-Man" & founder of the ad agency Ogilvy, because of his belief in the power of research behind effective advertising. Marketers seek creative that is grounded in strong consumer insights. Whether originating from data, research or a combination, The ARF David Ogilvy Awards are a surefire way to get marketers' attention.
Award: $500; crystal bowl; statue; etc. Trophy & case study published on the ARF & Warc web sites
Closing Date: Mid-May
Presented: New York, NY, Annually in Autumn during Advertising Week

Arkansas Diamond Primary Book Award
Arkansas State Library
Arkansas State Library, Suite 100, 900 W Capitol Ave, Little Rock, AR 72201-3108
Tel: 501-682-2860 *Fax:* 501-682-1693
Web Site: www.library.arkansas.gov; www.library. arkansas.gov
Key Personnel
Coord, Children's Progs: Cathy Howser
  E-mail: cathy@library.arkansas.gov
Established: 1999
To encourage reading for students in grades K-3. The Arkansas Department of Education & the Arkansas State Library support selected books that students all over Arkansas read or have read to them. The students vote for the one book they most enjoyed & the winning title recieves the award.
Other Sponsor(s): Arkansas Reading Association
Award: Medallion for 1st place, plaque for Honor Book
Closing Date: Annual vote in April
Presented: Little Rock, AR, Annually in Nov

Art In Literature: The Mary Lynn Kotz Award
Library of Virginia Foundation
800 E Broad St, Richmond, VA 23219
Tel: 804-692-3535
Web Site: www.lva.virginia.gov/public/litawards/ kotz.htm
Key Personnel
Devt Mgr: Dawn Greggs *E-mail:* dawn.greggs@ lva.virginia.gov
Exec Asst: Nancy Orr *E-mail:* nancy.orr@lva. virginia.gov
Established: 2013
Recognizes an outstanding book that is written primarily in response to a work (or works) of art while also showing the highest literary quality as a creative or scholarly work on its own merit. Works eligible for submission must be published for the first time in English in the US in the calendar year before the award is presented. New editions of previously published works are eligible for consideration if the new edition contains a substantial amount of new material. The topic of the book submitted must be the visual arts, excluding dramatic & performance arts, music, literature & interactive or computer art. Categories of acceptable work include: fiction, journalism, poetry, history, biography, art history, social history of art, catalogs of qualified museum exhibitions & young adult books.
Other Sponsor(s): Virginia Museum of Fine Arts
Closing Date: March 15, 2021
Presented: Oct 2021

Artist Grants
South Dakota Arts Council
Affiliate of Department of Tourism
711 E Wells Ave, Pierre, SD 57501-3369
Tel: 605-773-3301 *Fax:* 605-773-5977
E-mail: sdac@state.sd.us
Web Site: www.artscouncil.sd.gov/grants
Key Personnel
Dir: Patrick Baker
Awards made to residents of South Dakota, based on the quality of art work.
Award: $1,000-$5,000
Closing Date: Annually, March 1

Artist-in-Residence Program
New Brunswick Arts Board (Conseil des arts du Nouveau-Brunswick)
225 King St, Suite 201, Fredericton, NB E3B 1E1, Canada
Tel: 506-444-4444 *Toll Free Tel:* 866-460-ARTS (460-2787) *Fax:* 506-444-5543
Web Site: www.artsnb.ca
Key Personnel
Exec Dir: Joss Richer *Tel:* 506-478-4610
  E-mail: execdirgen@artsnb.ca
Prog Offr: Sarah Elizabeth Parker *Tel:* 506-440-0037 *E-mail:* sarahbeth@artsnb.ca
Opers Mgr: Tilly Jackson *Tel:* 506-478-4422
  E-mail: tjackson@artsnb.ca
Intended for New Brunswick public or private institutions & organizations that wish to host professional artists in order to enable them to pursue specific projects relating to their creative work. This program is also open to individual professionals who seek to advance their creative work through participation in residency opportunities at home or outside the province. The artists in residence are to contribute to the promotion & understanding of the arts by means of the artists' contact with the clientele of the establishments.
Closing Date: Feb 1

Artist Research & Development Grants
Arizona Commission on the Arts
417 W Roosevelt St, Phoenix, AZ 85003-1326
Tel: 602-771-6501 *Fax:* 602-256-0282
E-mail: info@azarts.gov
Web Site: www.azarts.gov
Key Personnel
Artists Servs Mgr: Gabriela Munoz
  E-mail: gmunoz@azarts.gov
Designed to support individual artists from all disciplines. The purpose of this grant is to aid in the development of artistic work, support the advancement of artistic research & recognize the contributions individual artists make to Arizona's communities.
The Bill Desmond Writing Award provides support to excelling nonfiction writers for specific project-related costs. This award offers funding support in the amount of $1,000 to one nonfiction writer applying for the Artist Research & Development Grant & can be offered independent of, or in addition to, the ARDG award. Funding for the Bill Desmond Writing Award is generously provided by the Bill & Kathy Desmond Endowment.
Award: $3,000-$5,000
Closing Date: Aug/Sept

Arts & Letters Awards
American Academy of Arts & Letters
633 W 155 St, New York, NY 10032
Tel: 212-368-5900 *Fax:* 212-491-4615
E-mail: academy@artsandletters.org
Web Site: artsandletters.org
Key Personnel
Exec Dir: Cody Upton
Given annually to artists, writers, composers & architects to encourage creative work in the arts.
Award: $10,000 each (8 awards to writers)

Arts Scholarships
New Brunswick Arts Board (Conseil des arts du Nouveau-Brunswick)
225 King St, Suite 201, Fredericton, NB E3B 1E1, Canada
Tel: 506-444-4444 *Toll Free Tel:* 866-460-ARTS (460-2787) *Fax:* 506-444-5543
Web Site: www.artsnb.ca
Key Personnel
Exec Dir: Joss Richer *Tel:* 506-478-4610
  E-mail: execdirgen@artsnb.ca
Prog Offr: Sarah Elizabeth Parker *Tel:* 506-440-0037 *E-mail:* sarahbeth@artsnb.ca
Opers Mgr: Tilly Jackson *Tel:* 506-478-4422
  E-mail: tjackson@artsnb.ca
Designed to recognize & encourage New Brunswick students who have demonstrated exceptional artistic talent & potential & who are pursuing a career in the arts. This program awards scholarships for full-time, part-time or short-term studies.
Closing Date: Feb 1

ASF Translation Awards
American-Scandinavian Foundation (ASF)
Scandinavia House, 58 Park Ave, New York, NY 10016
Tel: 212-879-9779; 212-779-3587 *Fax:* 212-686-2115
E-mail: grants@amscan.org
Web Site: www.amscan.org
Key Personnel
Fellowships & Grant Offr: Carl Fritscher
Established: 1980
For translations of contemporary poetry or fiction by Danish, Finnish, Icelandic, Norwegian or Swedish authors born after 1800. Write to ASF or visit the ASF web site for full copy of rules.
Award: $2,500 Nadia Christensen Prize & $2,000 Inger Sjoberg Prize (given to an individual whose literature translations have not previously been published). Both prizes include a publication of excerpt in an issue of *Scandinavian Review* & a commemorative bronze medallion
Closing Date: Annually, June 15
Presented: Varies

ASI/EIS Publishing Award for Excellence in Indexing
American Society for Indexing Inc (ASI)
1628 E Southern Ave, Suite 9-223, Tempe, AZ 85282
Tel: 480-245-6750
E-mail: info@asindexing.org
Web Site: www.asindexing.org
Key Personnel
Exec Dir: Gwen Henson *E-mail:* gwen@ asindexing.org
Established: 1978
Awarded to the indexer & the publisher of year's best index.
Award: $1,000 & citation (indexer), citation (publisher)
Closing Date: Annually in Feb
Presented: Annual Conference

Asian American Literary Awards
Asian American Writers' Workshop
112 W 27 St, Suite 600, New York, NY 10001
Tel: 212-494-0061
E-mail: aala@aaww.org
Web Site: aaww.org/aala
Honors Asian American writers for excellence in three categories: fiction, poetry & nonfiction. Entry fee: $100.
Closing Date: Annually in Spring
Presented: AAWW Food & Books Festival

Asian/Pacific American Award for Literature

Asian/Pacific American Librarians Association
Affiliate of The American Library Association
(ALA)
PO Box 677593, Orlando, FL 32867-7593
Web Site: www.apalaweb.org/awards/literature-awards
Key Personnel
Exec Dir: Buenaventura "Ven" Basco
Awarded annually to honor & recognize individual work about Asian/Pacific Americans & their heritage, based on literary & artistic merit. Five award categories: Adult fiction, adult nonfiction, children's literature, young adult literature, picture books. See web site for specific guidelines & nomination form.
Award: Plaque & press release to various national publications
Closing Date: Sept 30
Presented: ALA Annual Conference, Washington, DC

ASME Award for Fiction

American Society of Magazine Editors (ASME)
PO Box 112, New York, NY 10163
Tel: 212-872-3737
E-mail: asme@asme.media
Web Site: www.asme.media
Key Personnel
Exec Dir: Sid Holt *Tel:* 212-872-3723
  E-mail: sholt@asme.media
Dir of Opers: Nina Fortuna *E-mail:* nfortuna@asme.media
Established: 1966
Award honors print magazines & magazine web sites for overall excellence in fiction. An entry consists of 3 examples of short fiction written by one or more authors, published together or separately. Any consumer magazine or literary publication edited & distributed in print or online in the US is eligible for entry. Publications may submit only 1 entry. Entries may be submitted as print or digital content or as a combination of print & digital content. Content must be dated the year prior to the award, except that one story may be dated January of the award year. Entries must be submitted online at ellieawards.org. Entry fee: $40.
Other Sponsor(s): Columbia University Graduate School of Journalism
Award: Winner receives medal; finalists receive certificates of recognition
Closing Date: Nov 29
Presented: Ellie Awards, March

Aspen Words Literary Prize

Aspen Words
110 E Hallam St, Suite 116, Aspen, CO 81611
Tel: 970-925-3122 *Fax:* 970-920-5700
E-mail: literary.prize@aspeninstitute.org
Web Site: www.aspenwords.org/programs/literary-prize/; www.aspenwords.org
Key Personnel
Exec Dir: Adrienne Brodeur *Tel:* 646-461-3554
  E-mail: adrienne.brodeur@aspeninstitute.org
Mng Dir: Jamie Kravitz *Tel:* 970-925-3122 ext 2
  E-mail: jamie.kravitz@aspeninstitute.org
Sr Prog Assoc, Mktg & Communs: Caroline Tory
  Tel: 970-925-3122 ext 3 *E-mail:* caroline.tory@aspeninstitute.org
Established: 2017
Award for an influential work of fiction that focuses on vital issues - social, political, economic, environmental or otherwise - thus demonstrating the transformative power that literature has on thought & culture. Submissions accepted from publishers only. Book must be work of fiction published by a US trade publisher in the prior calendar year. Submission process opens February 1. $30 entry fee for each title submitted. See web site for online submission form & full details.
Award: $35,000

Closing Date: Aug 1
Presented: Annually in Spring

Athenaeum of Philadelphia Literary Award

Athenaeum of Philadelphia
219 S Sixth St, Philadelphia, PA 19106
Tel: 215-925-2688 *Fax:* 215-925-3755
Web Site: www.philaathenaeum.org/literary.html
Key Personnel
Libn: Jill LeMin Lee *E-mail:* jilly@philaathenaeum.org
Established: 1950
In recognition & encouragement of outstanding literary achievement in Philadelphia & the vicinity.
Award: Citation
Closing Date: Annually, Dec 1
Presented: Annually in Spring

Atlantic Public Art Funders (APAF) Creative Residency

New Brunswick Arts Board (Conseil des arts du Nouveau-Brunswick)
225 King St, Suite 201, Fredericton, NB E3B 1E1, Canada
Tel: 506-444-4444 *Toll Free Tel:* 866-460-ARTS (460-2787) *Fax:* 506-444-5543
Web Site: www.artsnb.ca
Key Personnel
Exec Dir: Joss Richer *Tel:* 506-478-4610
  E-mail: execdirgen@artsnb.ca
Prog Offr: Sarah Elizabeth Parker *Tel:* 506-440-0037 *E-mail:* sarahbeth@artsnb.ca
Opers Mgr: Tilly Jackson *Tel:* 506-478-4422
  E-mail: tjackson@artsnb.ca
Artists from New Brunswick, Nova Scotia, PEI or Newfoundland & Labrador can apply. Covers a 1- to 3-month residency for a creation-based or professional development project in the province that isn't their own. The agreement establishes an annual exchange program that provides professional artists with opportunities for creation & professional development residencies in the participating provinces. Artists participating in this program enjoy complete autonomy & define the objectives of their period of residence & elaborate the parameters & conditions governing its realization in collaboration with an arts community organization in the territory where the period of residence is to take place.
Other Sponsor(s): Arts Nova Scotia; Newfoundland & Labrador Arts Council; Prince Edward Island Council of the Arts
Award: Up to $10,000
Closing Date: Feb 1

The Audies®

Audio Publishers Association (APA)
333 Hudson St, Suite 503, New York, NY 10013
Tel: 646-688-3044
E-mail: audies@audiopub.org; info@audiopub.org
Web Site: www.audiopub.org/members/audies
Key Personnel
Exec Dir: Michele Cobb *E-mail:* mcobb@audiopub.org
Premier awards program in the US recognizing distinction in audiobooks & spoken word entertainment. Publishers & rights holders enter titles in various categories for recognition of achievement. Finalists are selected & announced in February. From that group of finalists, one winner is awarded. Qualifying audiobooks contain at least 51% spoken word content & are available for sale in the US as CDs +/or in digital format. Entry fee: $100 members, $200 nonmembers.
Award: Medallions
Presented: Audies Awards Gala

AUPresses Book, Jacket & Journal Show

Association of University Presses (AUPresses)

1412 Broadway, Suite 2135, New York, NY 10018
Tel: 212-989-1010 *Fax:* 212-989-0275
E-mail: info@aupresses.org
Web Site: www.aupresses.org
Key Personnel
Busn Mgr: Kim Miller *Tel:* 917-244-1264
  E-mail: kmiller@aupresses.org
Prog Asst: Bailey Bretz *Tel:* 917-244-2665
  E-mail: bbretz@aupresses.org
Established: 1965
Excellence in design; competition limited to member presses.
Entry fees: $40 book, $40 journal (set), $30 book jacket/cover, $30 journal cover. Exhibition fee charged for publications selected for show: $40 each book or journal, $30 each jacket or cover.
Award: Certificate, winning entries are displayed in a traveling exhibit
Closing Date: Annually in Jan
Presented: AUPresses Annual Meeting, Annually in June

Autumn House Poetry, Fiction & Nonfiction Contests

Autumn House Press
5530 Penn Ave, Pittsburgh, PA 15206
Mailing Address: PO Box 5486, Pittsburgh, PA 15206
Tel: 412-362-2665
E-mail: info@autumnhouse.org
Web Site: www.autumnhouse.org
Poetry Prize: All full-length collections of poetry 50-80 pages in length are eligible.
Fiction Contest: Submissions should be approximately 200-300 pages. All fiction sub-genres or any combination of sub-genres are eligible.
Nonfiction Contest: Submissions should be approximately 200-300 pages. All nonfiction subjects are eligible.
Enclose $30 handling fee for each prize. See web site for complete guidelines.
Award: $1,000, book publication, advance against royalties & $1,500 travel grant
Closing Date: Annually, June 30

Award of Merit

American Academy of Arts & Letters
633 W 155 St, New York, NY 10032
Tel: 212-368-5900 *Fax:* 212-491-4615
E-mail: academy@artsandletters.org
Web Site: artsandletters.org
Key Personnel
Exec Dir: Cody Upton
Established: 1942
Given annually, in rotation, to an outstanding person in America representing one of the following arts: Painting, the Short Story, Sculpture, the Novel, Poetry & Drama.
Award: $25,000 & medal

AWP Award Series

Association of Writers & Writing Programs (AWP)
University of Maryland, 5245 Greenbelt Rd, Box 246, College Park, MD 20740
Tel: 240-696-7700
E-mail: awp@awpwriter.org; press@awpwriter.org
Web Site: www.awpwriter.org
Key Personnel
Dir, Conferences: Cynthia Sherman
Dir, Devt: Pamela Mills
Dir, Pubns: Supriya Bhatnagar
Assoc Ed: Christopher Kondrich
Established: 1967
An open competition for book-length mss in 4 categories: poetry, short fiction, novel & creative (nonfiction). Online submissions only.
Award: Publication by a major university press & an honorarium of $2,500 for nonfiction & novel. Donald Hall Prize in poetry-honorarium $5,500. Grace Paley Prize for short fiction-

honorarium $5,500. One winner in each category
Closing Date: Annually, Feb 28

Axiom Business Book Awards
Independent Publisher Online
Division of Jenkins Group Inc
1129 Woodmere Ave, Suite B, Traverse City, MI
 49686
Tel: 231-933-0445 *Toll Free Tel:* 800-706-4636
 Fax: 231-933-0448
E-mail: info@axiomawards.com
Web Site: www.axiomawards.com
Key Personnel
CEO: Jerrold R Jenkins *E-mail:* jrj@
 bookpublishing.com
Pres: James Kalajian *Tel:* 800-706-4636 ext 1006
 E-mail: jjk@bookpublishing.com
Mng Ed & Awards Dir: Jim Barnes *Tel:* 800-706-
 4636 ext 1011 *E-mail:* jimb@bookpublishing.
 com
Awards Coord: Amy Shamroe
Established: 2006
US based award contest focused solely on business books. The goal of the awards is to celebrate the innovative, intelligent & creative aspects of the books that make us think, see & work differently every day. The awards offer no global boundaries, giving participants from every continent the opportunity to earn further recognition for their English language titles. All publishers are eligible, ranging from large multi-title publishing houses to small one title publishers. Publishers can be throughout North America & overseas publishers who publish English language books intended for the American market. Print-on-demand & other independent authors are welcome to enter their books themselves.
Other Sponsor(s): Books Are Marketing Tools;
 Independent Publisher; Jenkins Group
Award: Gold medal (1st place), silver medal (2nd
 place) & bronze medal (3rd place)
Closing Date: Annually in Jan
Presented: BookExpo, Annually in May

Marilyn Baillie Picture Book Award
Canadian Children's Book Centre
40 Orchard View Blvd, Suite 217, Toronto, ON
 M4R 1B9, Canada
Tel: 416-975-0010 *Fax:* 416-975-8970
E-mail: info@bookcentre.ca
Web Site: www.bookcentre.ca
Key Personnel
Exec Dir: Charlotte Teeple *E-mail:* charlotte@
 bookcentre.ca
Lib Coord: Meghan Howe *E-mail:* meghan@
 bookcentre.ca
Mktg & Web Site Coord: Camilia Kahrizi
 E-mail: camilia@bookcentre.ca
Prog Coord: Shannon Howe Barnes
 E-mail: shannon@bookcentre.ca
Established: 2006
Awarded to a Canadian author & illustrator for excellence in the illustrated picture book format for children ages 3-8.
Other Sponsor(s): Charles Baillie
Award: $20,000 cash
Closing Date: Annually in mid-Dec

Baker & Taylor/YALSA Conference Grants
Young Adult Library Services Association
 (YALSA)
Division of The American Library Association
 (ALA)
50 E Huron St, Chicago, IL 60611
Tel: 312-280-4390 *Toll Free Tel:* 800-545-2433
 Fax: 312-280-5276; 312-664-7459
E-mail: yalsa@ala.org
Web Site: www.ala.org/yalsa
Key Personnel
Exec Dir: Anita Mechler

Prog Offr, Events & Conferences: Nichole
 O'Connor *Tel:* 800-545-2433 ext 4387
 E-mail: noconnor@ala.org
Communs Specialist: Anna Lam *Tel:* 800-545-
 2433 ext 5849 *E-mail:* alam@ala.org
Established: 1983
Awarded to librarians who work directly with young adults to enable them to attend the Annual Conference for the first time. Two grants given annually, one to a school librarian & one to a public librarian.
Other Sponsor(s): Baker & Taylor
Award: $1,000 each
Closing Date: Annually, Dec 1
Presented: ALA's Midwinter Meeting

Nona Balakian Citation for Excellence in Reviewing
National Book Critics Circle
c/o 310 Lewis Ave, Brooklyn, NY 11221
E-mail: info@bookcritics.org
Web Site: bookcritics.org/awards
Key Personnel
VP, Membership & Awards: Yahdon Israel
 E-mail: yahdonisrael@bookcritics.org
Comm Chair: Katherine A Powers
 E-mail: kapow3@gmail.com
Awarded annually to recognize outstanding work by a member of NBCC. Submit via e-mail up to 5 book reviews (all published during the year of the award) of no more than 5,000 words collectively. Include a note listing the venue along with title & word count of each piece submitted. Attach PDFs or screenshots of your book reviews as they appeared online or in print.
Award: $1,000

The Balcones Fiction Prize
The Balcones Center for Creative Writing
Subsidiary of Austin Community College
1212 Rio Grande St, Austin, TX 78701
Tel: 512-828-9368
E-mail: balcones@austincc.edu
Web Site: sites.austincc.edu/crw/balcones-prizes
Key Personnel
Assoc Dir: John Herndon *E-mail:* jherndon@
 austincc.edu
Recognizes an outstanding book of fiction published during the year. Books of prose may be submitted by author or publisher. Send 3 copies. Books must bear a publication date within the calendar year prior to the year of the award. Reading fee: $30.
Award: $1,500
Closing Date: Jan 31

The Balcones Poetry Prize
The Balcones Center for Creative Writing
Subsidiary of Austin Community College
1212 Rio Grande St, Austin, TX 78701
Tel: 512-828-9368
E-mail: balcones@austincc.edu
Web Site: sites.austincc.edu/crw/category/
 balcones_poetry_prize/
Key Personnel
Assoc Dir: John Herndon *E-mail:* jherndon@
 austincc.edu
Established: 1994
Recognizes an outstanding book of poetry published during the year. Books of poetry of 42 pages or more may be submitted by author or publisher. Send 3 copies. Must bear a publication date of the previous calendar year. $25 reading fee.
Award: $1,500
Closing Date: Jan 31

Ballard Spahr Prize for Poetry
Milkweed Editions
1011 Washington Ave S, Suite 300, Minneapolis,
 MN 55415-1246

Tel: 612-332-3192 *Toll Free Tel:* 800-520-6455
 Fax: 612-215-2550
Web Site: www.milkweed.org
Key Personnel
Publg Asst: Connor Lane
Established: 2011
Annual regional prize to support outstanding poets & bring their work to a national stage. Submissions accepted in hard copy only from poets currently residing in Minnesota, Iowa, North Dakota, South Dakota, Wisconsin or Michigan. No entry fee.
Other Sponsor(s): Ballard Spahr
Award: $10,000 & publication contract
Presented: April

Bancroft Prizes
Columbia University
517 Butler Library, Mail Code 1101, 535 W 114
 St, New York, NY 10027
Tel: 212-854-4746 *Fax:* 212-854-9099
Web Site: www.columbia.edu/about/awards/
 bancroft.html
Key Personnel
Communs & Devt Assoc: Matt Hampel
Established: 1948
Two awards presented annually for distinguished books in the fields of American history (including biography) & diplomacy. Award confined to books originally published in English or those with a published English translation. Books published in year preceding that in which award is made are eligible. Submit four copies & nominating letter.
Award: $10,000 each
Closing Date: Nov 1, page-proof copy may be submitted after Nov 1, provided the work will be published after that date & before Dec 31
Presented: Columbia University, Spring

Barbey Freedom to Write Award, see
 PEN/Barbey Freedom to Write Award

Bard Fiction Prize
Bard College
Campus Rd, PO Box 5000, Annandale-on-
 Hudson, NY 12504-5000
Tel: 845-758-7087
E-mail: bfp@bard.edu
Web Site: www.bard.edu/bfp
Established: 2001
Awarded to a promising emerging writer who is an American citizen age 39 years or younger at time of application. To apply, candidates should write a cover letter explaining the project they plan to work on while at Bard & submit CV along with 3 copies of the published book they feel best represents their work. No mss accepted.
Award: $30,000 & writer-in-residence at Bard
 College for 1 semester
Closing Date: June 15
Presented: Annually in Oct

Barnes & Noble Writers for Writers Award
Poets & Writers Inc
90 Broad St, Suite 2100, New York, NY 10004
Tel: 212-226-3586 *Fax:* 212-226-3963
E-mail: admin@pw.org
Web Site: www.pw.org
Established: 1996
Celebrates authors who have given generously to other writers or to the broader literary community.

Baskerville Publishers Poetry Award
Texas Christian University
Dept of English, TCU Box 298300, Fort Worth,
 TX 76129
Tel: 817-257-5907 *Fax:* 817-257-5905
E-mail: descant@tcu.edu
Web Site: www.descant.tcu.edu

Key Personnel
Mng Ed: Dan Williams *E-mail:* d.e.williams@tcu.edu
Established: 2003
Annual award for an outstanding poem or poems by a single author in an issue. All published submissions are eligible for prize consideration. There is no application process.
Other Sponsor(s): descant (publication), Dept of English, TCU
Award: $250
Closing Date: Sept 1-April 1
Presented: Winner announced in the Summer in *descant*

The Mildred L Batchelder Award

Association for Library Service to Children (ALSC)
Division of The American Library Association (ALA)
50 E Huron St, Chicago, IL 60611-2795
Tel: 312-280-2163 *Toll Free Tel:* 800-545-2433
Fax: 312-440-9374; 312-280-5271
E-mail: alsc@ala.org
Web Site: www.ala.org/alsc
Key Personnel
Exec Dir: Aimee Strittmatter
E-mail: astrittmatter@ala.org
Deputy Exec Dir: Alena Rivers *Tel:* 800-545-2433 ext 5866 *E-mail:* arivers@ala.org
Prog Offr, Communs: Laura Schulte-Cooper *Tel:* 800-545-2433 ext 2165 *E-mail:* lschulte@ala.org
Awards Coord: Katie Connelly *Tel:* 800-545-2433 ext 2163 *E-mail:* kconnelly@ala.org
Prog Coord: Ann Michaud *Tel:* 800-545-2433 ext 2166 *E-mail:* amichaud@ala.org
Membership/Mktg Specialist: Elizabeth Serrano *Tel:* 800-545-2433 ext 2164 *E-mail:* eserrano@ala.org
Established: 1966
Awarded annually to an American publisher for an outstanding book originally published in a foreign language in a foreign country & subsequently translated to English & published in the US during the previous year.
Award: Citation
Closing Date: Dec 31
Presented: ALA Midwinter Meeting, Jan/Feb

The BC Book Prizes

West Coast Book Prize Society
207 W Hastings St, Suite 901, Vancouver, BC V6B 1H7, Canada
Fax: 604-687-2435
E-mail: info@bcbookprizes.ca
Web Site: www.bcbookprizes.ca
Key Personnel
Exec Dir: Sean Cranbury *E-mail:* sean@bcbookprizes.ca
Established: 1985
The following BC Book Prizes are awarded to a resident of BC or one who has lived in BC for 3 of the past 5 years: to the author of the best work of fiction; best book written for children 16 years & younger; best original nonfiction literary work; author of the best work of poetry. The following BC Book Prizes are also offered: originating publisher of the best book judged in terms of public appeal, initiative, design, production & content (publisher must have their head office in BC); author of the book which contributes most to the appreciation & understanding of BC (published anywhere the author may reside outside BC); author & illustrator of the best picture book written for children (author/illustrator must be a BC/Yukon resident or have lived in BC or the Yukon for 3 of the past 5 years).
Other Sponsor(s): Ampersand Inc; BC Teachers' Federation; British Columbia Booksellers Association; British Columbia Library Association; Canadian Manda Group; First Choice

Books; Friends of Sheila Egoff; Friesens; Victoria Bindery; Kate Walke; WBRA
Award: $2,000 & certificate
Closing Date: Annually, Dec 1, with exceptions made for books published in Dec
Presented: The British Columbia Book Prizes Banquet, Spring

BCHF Historial Writing Competition

British Columbia Historical Federation
PO Box 448, Fort Langley, BC V1M 2R7, Canada
E-mail: info@bchistory.ca
Web Site: www.bchistory.ca/awards/historical-writing
Key Personnel
Chair: Maurice Guibord *Tel:* 604-771-3047
E-mail: maurice@bchistory.ca
Top prize is presented annually to the author whose book makes the most significant contribution to the historical literature of British Columbia. The book must be published within the competition year. Additional prizes also given.
Award: $2,500 & The BC Lieutenant-Governor's Medal for Historical Writing (1st place), $1,500 (2nd place), $500 (3rd place), Certificates of Honourable Mention, $500 Community History Award
Closing Date: Dec 31
Presented: BCHF Annual Conference Awards Banquet, May/June

James Beard Foundation Book Awards

James Beard Foundation
Office of Awards, 6 W 18 St, 10th fl, New York, NY 10011
Tel: 212-627-1111 (ext 563)
Web Site: www.jamesbeard.org/awards
Established: 1991
Book, broadcast & journalism awards in the food & beverage industry. Begins October 15 annually.
Award: Certificate, silver colored medallion & complimentary 1-year foundation membership
Presented: Annually in Spring

George Louis Beer Prize

American Historical Association (AHA)
400 "A" St SE, Washington, DC 20003
Tel: 202-544-2422 *Fax:* 202-544-8307
E-mail: awards@historians.org
Web Site: www.historians.org
Established: 1923
Recognition of outstanding historical writing in European international history since 1895 that is submitted by a scholar who is a US citizen or permanent resident. Books published in 2020 are eligible. Only books of a high scholarly historical nature should be submitted. Along with an application form, applicants must mail a copy of their book to each of the prize committee members who will be posted on our web site as the prize deadline approaches. All updated info on web site.
Award: Cash prize
Closing Date: May 15, 2021
Presented: AHA Annual Meeting, New Orleans, LA, Jan 2022

The Pura Belpre Award

Association for Library Service to Children (ALSC)
Division of The American Library Association (ALA)
50 E Huron St, Chicago, IL 60611-2795
Tel: 312-280-2163 *Toll Free Tel:* 800-545-2433
Fax: 312-440-9374; 312-280-5271
E-mail: alsc@ala.org
Web Site: www.ala.org/alsc

Key Personnel
Exec Dir: Aimee Strittmatter
E-mail: astrittmatter@ala.org
Deputy Exec Dir: Alena Rivers *Tel:* 800-545-2433 ext 5866 *E-mail:* arivers@ala.org
Prog Offr, Communs: Laura Schulte-Cooper *Tel:* 800-545-2433 ext 2165 *E-mail:* lschulte@ala.org
Awards Coord: Katie Connelly *Tel:* 800-545-2433 ext 2163 *E-mail:* kconnelly@ala.org
Prog Coord: Ann Michaud *Tel:* 800-545-2433 ext 2166 *E-mail:* amichaud@ala.org
Membership/Mktg Specialist: Elizabeth Serrano *Tel:* 800-545-2433 ext 2164 *E-mail:* eserrano@ala.org
Established: 1996
Annual award presented to a Latino/Latina writer & illustrator whose children's work best celebrates the Latino cultural experience.
Other Sponsor(s): National Association to Promote Library & Information Services to Latinos & the Spanish Speaking (REFORMA)
Award: Medal
Closing Date: Dec 31
Presented: ALA Midwinter Meeting, Jan/Feb

Benjamin Franklin Awards™

The Independent Book Publishers Association (IBPA)
1020 Manhattan Beach Blvd, Suite 204, Manhattan Beach, CA 90266
Tel: 310-546-1818
E-mail: info@ibpa-online.org
Web Site: www.ibpa-online.org; ibpabenjaminfranklinawards.com
Key Personnel
CEO: Angela Bole *E-mail:* angela@ibpa-online.org
COO: Terry Nathan *E-mail:* terry@ibpa-online.org
Established: 1987
Excellence in independent publishing in specific genre & design (books, audio & video). Trophies are presented to the publishers during a gala awards ceremony on the last evening of the Publishing University. Entry fee: membs $95/title/category; nonmembs $225/first title (includes 1 yr membership); $95/additional titles.
Award: Gold winners: Engraved crystal trophy & award certificates with gold stickers. Silver winners: Award certificates with silver stickers
Closing Date: Sept 30 (1st call) & Dec 15 (2nd call)
Presented: May

George Bennett Fellowship

Phillips Exeter Academy
Phillips Exeter Academy, Off of the Dean of Faculty, 20 Main St, Exeter, NH 03833-2460
Tel: 603-777-3645 *Fax:* 603-777-4384
E-mail: communications@exeter.edu
Web Site: www.exeter.edu
Established: 1968
Established to provide support for 1 academic year for an individual contemplating or pursuing a career as a professional writer. Selection is based on the literary promise of the ms submitted. The committee favors applicants who have not yet published a book-length work with a major publisher. See web site for online application. Application fee: $15. Applications accepted beginning October 1.
Award: $15,570, housing & meals at the Academy for the academic year, medical/dental insurance & long-term disability
Closing Date: Nov 30
Presented: Annually in April

Naomi Berber Memorial Award

PRINTING United Alliance
10015 Main St, Fairfax, VA 22031-3489

Tel: 703-385-1335 *Toll Free Tel:* 888-385-3588
 Fax: 703-273-0456
E-mail: assist@printing.org; info@printing.org
Web Site: www.printing.org/programs/awards/
 naomi-berber-memorial-award
Key Personnel
Pres & CEO: Ford Bowers *E-mail:* fbowers@
 printing.org
Established: 1976
Honors a woman who has made a major contribution to the development of the printing
 industry. A nominee must have worked in the
 printing industry for 10 years or more. See web
 site for more information.
Award: Engraved plaque
Closing Date: June
Presented: PRINTING United Alliance Meetings
Branch Office(s)
1325 "G" St NW, Suite 500, Washington, DC
 20005
2000 Corporate Dr, Suite 205, Wexford, PA
 15090 *Tel:* 412-741-6860 *Toll Free Tel:* 800-
 910-4283 *Fax:* 412-741-2311

Jessie Bernard Award

American Sociological Association (ASA)
c/o Governance Off, 1430 "K" St NW, Suite 600,
 Washington, DC 20005
Tel: 202-383-9005 *Fax:* 202-638-0882
E-mail: governance@asanet.org
Web Site: www.asanet.org
Key Personnel
Dir, Admin & Governance: Michael Murphy
 Tel: 202-383-9005 ext 327
Prog Coord: Jordan Robison *Tel:* 202-383-9005
 ext 334
For scholarly contributions that enlarge the hori-
 zons of sociology to encompass fully the role
 of women in society. Winner announced in
 Footnotes newsletter, an ASA publication. See
 web site for future awards.
Award: Plaque
Closing Date: Jan 31
Presented: ASA Annual Meeting, Montreal, QC,
 CN, Annually in Aug

The Charles Bernheimer Prize

American Comparative Literature Association
 (ACLA)
University of South Carolina, Dept of Languages,
 Literature & Cultures, 1620 College St, Rm
 817, Columbia, SC 29208
Tel: 803-777-3021
E-mail: info@acla.org
Web Site: www.acla.org/prize-awards/charles-
 bernheimer-prize
Key Personnel
Nominations Comm Chair: Antonio Barrenechea
 E-mail: abarrene@umw.edu
An outstanding dissertation in comparative liter-
 ature defended in the year prior to July 1. See
 web site for application details.
Award: $1,000 & a certificate, complimentary
 registration, airfare & hotel accommodations
 (not including food), to facilitate the recipient
 attending the ACLA annual meeting
Closing Date: Oct 1
Presented: ACLA Annual Meeting, July

Best Translated Book Award

Three Percent
c/o Open Letter, University of Rochester, Dewey
 Hall 1-219, Box 278968, Rochester, NY 14627
Tel: 585-276-5305
E-mail: msc@rochester.edu
Web Site: besttranslatedbook.org
Key Personnel
Founder & Publr: Chad Post *E-mail:* chad.post@
 rochester.edu
Established: 2007
Recognizes the previous year's best original trans-
 lation of a work of fiction & a work of poetry

into English. Long & short lists announced
 leading up to the award. Original translations
 must have been published in the previous calendar year. Reprints & retranslation are ineligible. No entry fee. Mail one copy or send
 e-version of publication to each of the appropriate panelists (see web site for list of judges
 or contact Chad Post).
Other Sponsor(s): Amazon Literary Partnership
Award: $5,000 to both author(s) & translator(s)
Presented: May

Best Workplace in the Americas (MWA)

PRINTING United Alliance
10015 Main St, Fairfax, VA 22031-3489
Tel: 703-385-1335 *Toll Free Tel:* 888-385-3588
 Fax: 703-273-0456
E-mail: assist@printing.org; info@printing.org
Web Site: www.printing.org/programs/awards/best-
 workplace-in-the-americas
Key Personnel
Pres & CEO: Ford Bowers *E-mail:* fbowers@
 printing.org
Honors distinguished printing industry leaders by
 human resources standards.
Branch Office(s)
1325 "G" St NW, Suite 500, Washington, DC
 20005
2000 Corporate Dr, Suite 205, Wexford, PA
 15090 *Tel:* 412-741-6860 *Toll Free Tel:* 800-
 910-4283 *Fax:* 412-741-2311

Doris Betts Fiction Prize

North Carolina Writers' Network
PO Box 21591, Winston-Salem, NC 27120-1591
Tel: 336-293-8844
E-mail: mail@ncwriters.org; nclrsubmissions@
 ecu.edu
Web Site: www.ncwriters.org
Key Personnel
Exec Dir: Ed Southern *E-mail:* ed@ncwriters.org
Open to any writer who is a legal resident of
 North Carolina or a member of the NCWN.
 North Carolina Literary Review subscribers
 with North Carolina connections (lives or has
 lived in NC) are also eligible. The competition
 is for previously unpublished short stories up to
 6,000 words. Multiple entries ok, but each requires a separate entry fee. No novel excerpts.
 Submit previously unpublished stories online
 at nclr.submittable.com/submit. Entry fee: $10
 NCWN members or NCLR subscribers, $20
 nonmembs/non-subscribers. Documents must
 be Microsoft Word or .rtf files. Stories should
 be double-spaced. Author's name should not
 appear on mss.
If submitting by mail, send story ms with cover
 sheet providing name, address, e-mail address,
 word count & ms title to: NCLR, ECU Mailstop, 555 English, Greenville, NC 27858-4353
 (but mail payment per instructions on web
 site).
Award: $250 1st prize & publication in the *North
 Carolina Literary Review*. Finalists also considered for publication
Closing Date: Annually, Feb 15
Presented: May 1

Beullah Rose Poetry Prize

Smartish Pace
PO Box 22161, Baltimore, MD 21203
E-mail: smartishpace@gmail.com
Web Site: www.smartishpace.com
Key Personnel
Assoc Ed: Clare Banks *E-mail:* cbsmartishpace@
 gmail.com
Established: 2005
Prize for exceptional poetry by women. All po-
 ems submitted for the prize will be considered
 for publication in *Smartish Pace*. Online sub-
 missions at www.smartishpace.com. Postal sub-
 missions: submit 3 poems along with a $10 en-

try fee. Additional poems may be submitted for
 $1 per poem. No more than 20 poems may be
 submitted. All entries must include a bio. Include SASE with entry. Include name, address,
 e-mail & telephone number on each page of
 poetry submitted. Write or print "Beullah Rose
 Poetry Prize" on top of each poem submitted.
Award: $200 & publication of winning poem in
 Smartish Pace (1st prize). All finalists will be
 published in *Smartish Pace*
Closing Date: Annually, Nov 15
Presented: Baltimore, MD

Albert J Beveridge Award in American History

American Historical Association (AHA)
400 "A" St SE, Washington, DC 20003
Tel: 202-544-2422 *Fax:* 202-544-8307
E-mail: awards@historians.org
Web Site: www.historians.org
Established: 1939
To promote & honor outstanding historical writing. The award is given for a distinguished
 book in English on the history of the US, Latin
 America, or Canada, from 1492 to the present.
 Books that employ new methodological or conceptual tools or that constitute significant re-
 examinations of important interpretive problems will be given preference. Literary merit is
 also an important criterion. Biographies, monographs & works of synthesis & interpretation
 are eligible; translations, anthologies & collections of documents are not. Books published
 in 2021 are eligible for the award; limited to 5
 titles from any one publisher & must be submitted by sending a copy to each member of
 the committee, along with an application form.
 All updated info on web site.
Award: Cash prize
Closing Date: May 15, 2021
Presented: AHA Annual Meeting, New Orleans,
 LA, Jan 2022

Albert J Beveridge Grant for Research in the History of the Western Hemisphere

American Historical Association (AHA)
400 "A" St SE, Washington, DC 20003
Tel: 202-544-2422 *Fax:* 202-544-8307
E-mail: awards@historians.org
Web Site: www.historians.org
Established: 1939
To support research in the history of the Western hemisphere (US, CN & Latin America).
 Only members of the Association are eligible.
 The grants are intended to further research in
 progress & may be used for travel to a library
 or archive, for microfilms, photographs or photocopying - a list of purposes that is meant to
 be merely illustrative not exhaustive. Preference
 will be given to those with specific research
 needs, such as the completion of a project or
 completion of a discrete segment thereof; preference will be given to PhD candidates & junior scholars. Application forms available on
 web site. Applications must include application
 form with estimated budget, curriculum vita &
 statement of no more than 750 words. A one-
 page bibliography of the most recent relevant,
 secondary works on the topic. Mailed & faxed
 submissions are not accepted.
Award: Individual grants will not exceed $1,000
Closing Date: Annually, Feb 15

BHTG - Julie Harris Playwright Award Competition

The Beverly Hills Theatre Guild
PO Box 148, Beverly Hills, CA 90213
Tel: 310-273-3390
Web Site: www.beverlyhillstheatreguild.com
Key Personnel
Pres: Carolyn Fried
Competition Coord: Candace Coster
Established: 1978

For playwrights. Application & guidelines available upon request with SASE.
Award: $3,500, $2,500 & $1,500
Closing Date: Annually, Jan 1-April 1
Presented: Los Angeles, CA, Annually, June 30 (announcement)

BHTG - Michael J Libow Youth Theatre Award

The Beverly Hills Theatre Guild
PO Box 148, Beverly Hills, CA 90213
Tel: 310-273-3390
Web Site: www.beverlyhillstheatreguild.com
Key Personnel
Pres: Carolyn Fried
Competition Coord: Candace Coster
Established: 1999
Playwright, children's theatre grade 6th-8th, 9th-12th grade.
Award: $1,200, $600
Closing Date: Annually, Jan 15 through last day of Feb (postmark)
Presented: Los Angeles, CA, Annually, June 30

Biblio Award

Biographers International Organization (BIO)
PO Box 33020, Santa Fe, NM 87594
Web Site: biographersinternational.org
Key Personnel
Admin & Membership Coord: Lori Izykowski
E-mail: lori@biographersinternational.org
Established: 2012
Presented annually to recognize a librarian or archivist who has made an exceptional contribution to the craft of biography.
Presented: Opening reception, BIO Annual Conference, May

Ray Allen Billington Prize

The Organization of American Historians (OAH)
112 N Bryan Ave, Bloomington, IN 47408-4141
Tel: 812-855-7311
E-mail: oah@oah.org
Web Site: www.oah.org/awards
Key Personnel
Exec Dir: Beth English *E-mail:* benglish@oah.org
Comm Coord: Kara Hamm *E-mail:* khamm@oah.org
Awarded biennially in odd-numbered years to the author of the best book on the history of native +/or settler peoples in frontier, border & borderland zones of intercultural contact in any century to the present & to include works that address the legacies of those zones. Each entry must be published during the 2-year calendar period preceding that in which the award is given. One copy of each entry must be mailed directly to the committee members listed on the web site.
Closing Date: Oct 1, 2022 (postmarked)
Presented: OAH Annual Meeting, Los Angeles, CA, March 30-April 2, 2023

The Geoffrey Bilson Award for Historical Fiction for Young People

Canadian Children's Book Centre
40 Orchard View Blvd, Suite 217, Toronto, ON M4R 1B9, Canada
Tel: 416-975-0010 *Fax:* 416-975-8970
E-mail: info@bookcentre.ca
Web Site: www.bookcentre.ca
Key Personnel
Exec Dir: Charlotte Teeple *E-mail:* charlotte@bookcentre.ca
Lib Coord: Meghan Howe *E-mail:* meghan@bookcentre.ca
Mktg & Web Site Coord: Camilia Kahrizi *E-mail:* camilia@bookcentre.ca
Prog Coord: Shannon Howe Barnes *E-mail:* shannon@bookcentre.ca
Established: 1988

Awarded to a Canadian author for an outstanding work of historical fiction for young people.
Award: $5,000
Closing Date: Annually in mid-Dec

Robert Bingham Prize for Debut Fiction, see PEN/Robert Bingham Prize for Debut Fiction

Binghamton University John Gardner Fiction Book Award

The Binghamton Center for Writers-State University of New York
Dept of English, General Literature & Rhetoric, Library N, Rm 1149, Vestal Pkwy E, Binghamton, NY 13902
Mailing Address: PO Box 6000, Binghamton, NY 13902-6000
Tel: 607-777-2713
Web Site: www2.binghamton.edu/english/creative-writing
Key Personnel
Dir: Maria Mazziotti Gillan *Tel:* 973-684-5904 *E-mail:* mgillan@binghamton.edu
Established: 2002
Selected by judges as the strongest novel or collection of fiction published in the previous year. Minimum press run of 500 copies. Each book submitted must be accompanied by an application form; publishers may submit more than one book for prize consideration. Submit only two copies of a submitted title. Winners will be announced in *Poets & Writers*.
Award: $1,000
Closing Date: March 1

Binghamton University Milt Kessler Poetry Book Award

The Binghamton Center for Writers-State University of New York
Dept of English, General Literature & Rhetoric, Library N, Rm 1149, Vestal Pkwy E, Binghamton, NY 13902
Mailing Address: PO Box 6000, Binghamton, NY 13902-6000
Tel: 607-777-2713
Web Site: www2.binghamton.edu/english/creative-writing
Key Personnel
Dir: Maria Mazziotti Gillan *Tel:* 973-684-5904 *E-mail:* mgillan@binghamton.edu
Established: 2002
For a book of poems, 48 pages or more in length, selected by our judges as the strongest collection of poems by a poet over 40 published in the previous year. Must be accompanied by an application; publishers may submit more than one book for prize consideration; minimum press run of 500 copies; submit only two copies of a title. Winner announced in *Poets & Writers*.
Award: $1,000
Closing Date: March 1

BIO Award

Biographers International Organization (BIO)
PO Box 33020, Santa Fe, NM 87594
Web Site: biographersinternational.org
Key Personnel
Admin & Membership Coord: Lori Izykowski
E-mail: lori@biographersinternational.org
Annual award to an individual for contributions to advancing the art & craft of biography.
Award: Bronze plaque & cash prize

Biography Fellowships

The Leon Levy Center for Biography
365 Fifth Ave, Rm 6200, New York, NY 10016
Tel: 212-817-2025
E-mail: biography@gc.cuny.edu
Web Site: llcb.ws.gc.cuny.edu/fellowships

Key Personnel
Exec Dir: Kai Bird
Assoc Dir: Thad Ziolkowski
E-mail: tziolkowski@gc.cuny.edu
Four resident fellowships offered at the Graduate Center for the academic year beginning each September. Fellows devote their time to their projects & participate in monthly seminars & public events of the Leon Levy Center for Biography, including the annual lecture & annual conference & are encouraged to join in the dynamic intellectual community of the Graduate Center. Preference in the award of fellowships is given to those who have not yet published a biography or received fellowships for the writing of a biography. Applications are also welcome from published & accomplished writers who are undertaking their first biography. The Center does not award fellowships for memoirs, essays, plays, film or fiction. Applications require brief CV or resume (3 page maximum), narrative account of applicant's career (250 words), project description (750 words), sample of proposed biography (2,500 word maximum) & 2 letters of reference. Digital/online applications only.
Award: Awards include writing space, full access to research facilities, research assistance & stipend of $72,000
Closing Date: Jan 4

Paul Birdsall Prize

American Historical Association (AHA)
400 "A" St SE, Washington, DC 20003
Tel: 202-544-2422 *Fax:* 202-544-8307
E-mail: awards@historians.org
Web Site: www.historians.org
Established: 1985
Awarded biennially for the most important work published in English on European military or strategic history since 1870. Preference will be given to early-career academics, but established scholars & nonacademic candidates will not be excluded. Books published in English & bearing a copyright date of 2020 or 2021 are eligible for the 2022 prize. Nominators must complete an online prize submission form for each book submitted. One copy of each entry must be sent to each committee member & clearly labeled "Birdsall Prize Entry." Electronic copies may be sent only to committee members who have indicated they will accept them.
Closing Date: May 15, 2021
Presented: AHA Annual Meeting, New Orleans, LA, Jan 2022

BISG Industry Awards

Book Industry Study Group Inc (BISG)
1412 Broadway, Suite 2119, New York, NY 10018
Tel: 646-336-7141
E-mail: info@bisg.org
Web Site: www.bisg.org/bisg-industry-awards
Key Personnel
Exec Dir: Brian O'Leary
Opers Mgr: Jonathan Fiedler
Established: 2014
Categories: Distinguished Service Award, Industry Champion Award, Industry Innovator Award, BISG Industry Connector Award, BISG Standards Bearer Award, Explorer Award, BISG Community Builder Award.
Presented: BISG Annual Meeting of Members, Annually in Sept

Chip Bishop Fellowship

Biographers International Organization (BIO)
PO Box 33020, Santa Fe, NM 87594
Web Site: biographersinternational.org

Key Personnel
Admin & Membership Coord: Lori Izykowski
  E-mail: lori@biographersinternational.org
Open to both members & nonmembers to help
  biographers in financial need. To apply, send
  responses to questions provided on the web site
  to Deirdre David, VP, ddavid@temple.edu.
Award: Fee waived for annual BIO Conference &
  $500 to help defray travel & lodging expenses
Closing Date: Annually in March
Presented: Annually in April

Irma S & James H Black Award
Bank Street College of Education
610 W 112 St, New York, NY 10025
Tel: 212-875-4458
E-mail: ccl@bankstreet.edu
Web Site: www.bankstreet.edu/center-childrens-
literature
Key Personnel
Dir, Lib Servs: Kristin Freda *E-mail:* kfreda@
  bankstreet.edu
Established: 1972
For unified excellence of story line, language &
  illustration in a work for young children pub-
  lished during the previous year.
Award: Scroll & Gold Seals
Closing Date: Annually in Dec
Presented: Bank Street College of Education, An-
  nually in May

Black Warrior Review Fiction, Nonfiction & Poetry Contest
Black Warrior Review
Off of Student Media, University of Alabama,
  Tuscaloosa, AL 35486-0027
Mailing Address: PO Box 870170, Tuscaloosa,
  AL 35487-0170
Tel: 205-348-4518
Web Site: www.bwr.ua.edu
Key Personnel
Mng Ed: Gail Aronson *E-mail:* managingeditor.
  bwr@gmail.com
Ed: Bronwyn Valentine
Fiction Ed: Reem Abu-Baker
Nonfiction Ed: Kayla Rae Candrilli
Poetry Ed: Shelley Feller
Established: 2005
Awards given to best nonfiction piece, short story
  & best poem entered. Submit 1 story (up to
  7,500 words) or 3 poems. Entry fee: $20 (in-
  cludes 1-year subscription). Submit online at
  bwr.ua.edu/submit/contest.
Award: $1,000 & publication (one for each cat-
  egory - poetry, nonfiction & fiction). Finalists
  noted & considered for publication
Closing Date: Annually, Sept 1

Neltje Blanchan Memorial Award
Wyoming Arts Council
Division of Wyoming Department of Parks &
  Cultural Resources
Barrett Bldg, 2nd fl, 2301 Central Ave, Cheyenne,
  WY 82002
Tel: 307-777-7742
Web Site: wyoarts.state.wy.us
Key Personnel
Public Art & Creative Sector Indivs Supv: Rachel
  Clifton *Tel:* 307-777-5305 *E-mail:* rachel.
  clifton@state.wy.us
Established: 1988
Best writing in any genre inspired by a relation-
  ship with nature. Open to Wyoming residents
  only. Blind judges, single juror.
Award: $1,000
Closing Date: Varies, see web site
Presented: Announced in the Fall

Eleanor Taylor Bland Crime Fiction Writers of Color Award
Sisters in Crime (SinC)
PO Box 442124, Lawrence, KS 66044

Tel: 785-842-1325 *Fax:* 785-856-6314
E-mail: admin@sistersincrime.org
Web Site: www.sistersincrime.org
Key Personnel
Exec Dir: Beth Wasson
Awards Coord: Stephanie Gayle
  E-mail: stephgayle@gmail.com
Established: 2014
Grant is to support the recipient in such developmental & research activities as workshops, seminars, conferences & retreats, online
  courses & other opportunities required for completion of their debut crime fiction work. Application requirements: An unpublished work of
  crime fiction, written with an adult audience in
  mind. This may be a short story or first chap-
  ter(s) of a ms in progress, 2,500-5,000 words;
  resume or biographical statement; cover letter
  that gives a sense of the applicant as an emerging writer in the genre & briefly states how the
  grant money would be used. No prior writing
  or publishing experience is required, but the
  applicant should include any relevant studies or
  experience.
Award: $2,000 grant
Closing Date: Annually in June

Theodore C Blegen Award
The Forest History Society Inc
701 William Vickers Ave, Durham, NC 27701-
3162
Tel: 919-682-9319 *Fax:* 919-682-2349
Web Site: www.foresthistory.org
Key Personnel
Admin Asst: Andrea Anderson *E-mail:* andrea.
  anderson@foresthistory.org
Established: 1972
Recognizes the best scholarship in forest & con-
  servation history published in a journal other
  than *Environmental History*.
Award: $500 & plaque
Closing Date: Early Spring (specific date varies)

Norbert Blei/August Derleth Nonfiction Book Award
Council for Wisconsin Writers
c/o 4414 W Fillmore Dr, Milwaukee, WI 53219
E-mail: wiswriters@gmail.com
Web Site: wiswriters.org/awards
Key Personnel
Contest Chair: Daniel Kentowski
  E-mail: dkento@milwaukee.gov
Established: 1966
Annual award for the best nonfiction book pub-
  lished by a Wisconsin-based author in the con-
  test year. Entry fee: $25 nonmembs.
Award: $500 & 1-week residency at Shake Rag
  Alley Center for the Arts
Closing Date: Jan 31
Presented: CWW Annual Banquet, May

Susan P Bloom Children's Book Discovery Award
PEN America Boston
Unit of PEN America
MIT, 14N-221A, 77 Massachusetts Ave, Cam-
  bridge, MA 02139
Tel: 617-324-1729
E-mail: penamericaboston@pen.org
Web Site: www.pen-ne.org/susan-p-bloom-award
Annual awards to honor emerging writers & writ-
  ers/illustrators.

The James Boatwright III Prize for Poetry
Shenandoah: The Washington & Lee University
  Review
Washington & Lee University, Mattingly House,
  204 W Washington St, Lexington, VA 24450-
  2116
Tel: 540-458-8908
E-mail: shenandoah@wlu.edu
Web Site: shenandoahliterary.org

Key Personnel
Ed: R T Smith *E-mail:* rodsmith@wlu.edu
Asst Ed: William Wright
Annual award for the best poem published in
  Shenandoah during a volume year.
Award: $1,000

Rebekah Johnson Bobbitt National Prize for Poetry
The Poetry & Literature Center, Library of
  Congress
101 Independence Ave SE, Washington, DC
  20540-4861
Tel: 202-707-5394
Web Site: www.loc.gov/poetry
Biennial prize recognizes the most distinguished
  book of poetry written by an American & pub-
  lished during the preceding 2 years.
Other Sponsor(s): Family of Rebekah Johnson
  Bobbitt
Award: $10,000

Frederick Bock Prize
Poetry Magazine
61 W Superior St, Chicago, IL 60654
Tel: 312-787-7070 *Fax:* 312-787-6650
E-mail: editors@poetrymagazine.org
Web Site: www.poetryfoundation.org
Key Personnel
Edit Asst: Holly Amos *E-mail:* hamos@
  poetrymagazine.org
Established: 1981
For poetry published during the preceding 2 vol-
  umes of *Poetry* magazine. No application nec-
  essary.
Award: $500
Presented: Annually in Dec

George Bogin Memorial Award
Poetry Society of America (PSA)
15 Gramercy Park, New York, NY 10003
Tel: 212-254-9628
Web Site: poetrysociety.org/awards
Key Personnel
Pres: Allison Binns
Exec Dir: Matt Brogan *E-mail:* matt@
  poetrysociety.org
Deputy Dir: Brett Fletcher Lauer *E-mail:* brett@
  poetrysociety.org
Prog Dir: Laurin Macios *E-mail:* laurin@
  poetrysociety.org
Established by the family & friends of George
  Bogin, for a selection of 4 or 5 poems that re-
  flects the encounter of the ordinary & the ex-
  traordinary, uses language in an original way
  & takes a stand against oppression in any of its
  forms. See web site for more information.
Award: $500
Closing Date: Annually, Oct-Dec
Presented: Annual Awards Ceremony, New York,
  NY, Annually in Spring

Bogle International Library Travel Fund
International Relations Committee
Unit of The American Library Association (ALA)
50 E Huron St, Chicago, IL 60611-2795
Tel: 312-280-3201 *Toll Free Tel:* 800-545-2433
  (ext 3201) *Fax:* 312-280-4392
E-mail: intl@ala.org
Web Site: www.ala.org
Key Personnel
Dir, Off of Chapter & Intl Rel: Michael Dowling
Prog Offr: Delin Guerra *E-mail:* dguerra@ala.org
To enable librarians to travel abroad to study +/or
  attend first international conferences.
Award: $1,000
Closing Date: Annually, Jan 1
Presented: ALA Conference, Annually in June

Laura Day Boggs Bolling Memorial
The Poetry Society of Virginia

900 Timber Creek Place, Virginia Beach, VA 23464
E-mail: poetryinva@aol.com
Web Site: poetrysocietyofvirginia.org
Key Personnel
Pres: Robert P Arthur *E-mail:* robert.peebles.arthur@gmail.com
Exec Dir: Guy Terrell *E-mail:* guy.terrell@earthlink.net
Adult Contest Chair: Steven Blythe
E-mail: stevenblythepoetry@gmail.com
All entries must be in English, original & unpublished. Submit 2 copies, both copies must have the category name & number on top left of page. Entries will not be returned. Poem written by an adult for older school-age children (10-12 yrs); any rhymed or unrhymed form; 20 line limit. Entry fee: $4 nonmembs.
Other Sponsor(s): Children of Laura Day Boggs Bolling: Alma, Flora & Glade
Award: $50 (1st prize), $30 (2nd prize), $20 (3rd prize)
Closing Date: Jan
Presented: Annual PSV Awards Ceremony, April

Bollingen Prize in American Poetry
Beinecke Rare Book & Manuscript Library
121 Wall St, New Haven, CT 06511
Tel: 203-432-2977 *Fax:* 203-432-4047
E-mail: beinecke.library@yale.edu
Web Site: beinecke.library.yale.edu
Established: 1949
Awarded biennially in odd-numbered years to an American poet to recognize a recent book or a lifetime body of work.
Award: $165,000

Book of the Year Award
American Farm Bureau Foundation for Agriculture®
600 Maryland Ave SW, Suite 1000W, Washington, DC 20024
Toll Free Tel: 800-443-8456 *Fax:* 202-314-5121
E-mail: foundation@fb.org
Web Site: www.agfoundation.org/projects/book-of-the-year-award
Key Personnel
Prog Coord: Sydney Andrews *Tel:* 202-406-3739
E-mail: sydneya@fb.org
Annual award to honor an exceptional accurate book that helps to educate & create positive public perception about agriculture & producers. Classroom curriculum is developed to add value to the book. Any publication date is accepted. Judging begins in June for the following year's award.
Presented: Flapjack Fundraiser

Book of the Year Awards
New Atlantic Independent Booksellers Association (NAIBA)
2667 Hyacinth St, Westbury, NY 11590
Tel: 516-333-0681 *Fax:* 516-333-0689
E-mail: naibabooksellers@gmail.com
Web Site: www.naiba.com/page/BooksoftheYear
Key Personnel
Exec Dir: Eileen Dengler *E-mail:* naibaeileen@gmail.com
To recognize an author who was born or lived in the region +/or a book whose story takes place in the region. The book must have been published between June 1 & May 31 (of the award year). There are 5 categories: Fiction; Nonfiction; Picture Book; Children's Literature; Special Interest.
Closing Date: June 30
Presented: NAIBA Fall Conference, Annually in Oct

Boston Globe-Horn Book Award
The Boston Globe & The Horn Book Inc

c/o Book Reviews, The Horn Book Inc, Palace Road Bldg, 300 The Fenway, Suite P-311, Boston, MA 02115-5820
Tel: 617-278-0225 *Toll Free Tel:* 888-628-0225
Fax: 617-278-6062
E-mail: info@hbook.com
Web Site: www.hbook.com
Key Personnel
Ed-in-Chief, Horn Book Pubns: Roger Sutton
E-mail: rsutton@hbook.com
Exec Ed: Elissa Gershowitz
Mng Ed: Katrina Hedeen *Tel:* 617-628-0225 ext 222 *E-mail:* khedeen@hbook.com
Established: 1967
Honors excellence in children's & young adult literature in 3 categories: fiction & poetry, nonfiction & picture books. Published books only.
Award: $500 each
Closing Date: Annually in May
Presented: Simmons Colloquium, Annually in Fall

Boulevard Magazine Short Fiction Contest for Emerging Writers
Boulevard Magazine
6614 Clayton Rd, PMB 325, Richmond Heights, MO 63117
E-mail: editors@boulevardmagazine.org
Web Site: www.boulevardmagazine.org
Key Personnel
Founding Ed & Publr: Richard Burgin
E-mail: richardburgin@att.net
Mng Ed: Dusty Freund
Sr Ed: Glenn Blake
Ed: Jessica Rogen *E-mail:* jessicarogen@boulevardmagazine.org
Open to writers who have not yet published a book of fiction, poetry or creative nonfiction with a nationally distributed press. Simultaneous submissions are allowed but previously accepted or published work is ineligible. Send typed, double-spaced mss & SAS postcard for acknowledgment of receipt. No mss will be returned. 8,000 word maximum length; cover sheets not necessary. Entry fee is $16 per story with no limit per author. Includes 1-year subscription.
Award: $1,500 & publication in the Spring or the Fall issue of *Boulevard*
Closing Date: Annually, Dec 31

Bound to Stay Bound Books Scholarship
Association for Library Service to Children (ALSC)
Division of The American Library Association (ALA)
50 E Huron St, Chicago, IL 60611-2795
Tel: 312-280-2163 *Toll Free Tel:* 800-545-2433
Fax: 312-440-9374; 312-280-5271
E-mail: alsc@ala.org
Web Site: www.ala.org/alsc
Key Personnel
Exec Dir: Aimee Strittmatter
E-mail: astrittmatter@ala.org
Deputy Exec Dir: Alena Rivers *Tel:* 800-545-2433 ext 5866 *E-mail:* arivers@ala.org
Prog Offr, Communs: Laura Schulte-Cooper
Tel: 800-545-2433 ext 2165 *E-mail:* lschulte@ala.org
Awards Coord: Katie Connelly *Tel:* 800-545-2433 ext 2163 *E-mail:* kconnelly@ala.org
Prog Coord: Ann Michaud *Tel:* 800-545-2433 ext 2166 *E-mail:* amichaud@ala.org
Membership/Mktg Specialist: Elizabeth Serrano
Tel: 800-545-2433 ext 2164 *E-mail:* eserrano@ala.org
For study in field of library service to children toward the MLS or beyond in an ALA-accredited program.
Award: $7,500 - 4 scholarships per yr
Closing Date: Annually, March 1
Presented: ALA Annual Conference, Annually in June

Barbara Bradley Prize
New England Poetry Club
46 Wallace St, Somerville, MA 02144
E-mail: info@nepoetryclub.org
Web Site: www.nepoetryclub.org
Key Personnel
Pres: Mary Buchinger
VP: Hillary Sallick
Treas: Linda Haviland Conte
Established: 1988
Prize for a poem in lyric form, under 21 lines, written by a woman. Mark name of contest on envelope, send to address above. Send poem in duplicate with name of writer on one only. See web site for additional guidelines.
Award: $250
Closing Date: May 31
Presented: Winners announced online Aug/Sept

BrainStorm Poetry Contest for Mental Health Consumers
Northern Initiative for Social Action (NISA)
36 Elgin St, 2nd fl, Sudbury, ON P3C 5B4, Canada
Tel: 705-222-6472 (ext 303)
E-mail: openminds@nisa.on.ca
Web Site: www.openmindsquarterly.com
Key Personnel
Publr & Ed: Dinah Laprairie
Established: 2003
Contest open only to people with lived experience of mental illness internationally. It aims to eliminate the stigma associated with mental illness by showcasing the talents & creativity of individuals living with mental illness. Contest details available after December 15 online. Contest runs January to end of March each year. Call or e-mail to be added to mailing list.
Award: $250 (1st prize), $150 (2nd prize), $75 (3rd prize), plus publication in *Open Minds Quarterly*
Closing Date: Annually Jan-March

Michael Braude Award
American Academy of Arts & Letters
633 W 155 St, New York, NY 10032
Tel: 212-368-5900 *Fax:* 212-491-4615
E-mail: academy@artsandletters.org
Web Site: artsandletters.org
Key Personnel
Exec Dir: Cody Upton
Triennial award given for light verse written in English regardless of the writer's country of origin.
Award: $5,000

James Henry Breasted Prize
American Historical Association (AHA)
400 "A" St SE, Washington, DC 20003
Tel: 202-544-2422 *Fax:* 202-544-8307
E-mail: awards@historians.org
Web Site: www.historians.org
Established: 1985
Best book in English in any field of history prior to 1000 AD. Different geographic area will be eligible each year. Entries must be published in 2020. Along with an application form, applicants must mail a copy of their book to each of the prize committee members who will be posted on our web site as the prize deadline approaches. All updated info on web site.
Award: Cash prize
Closing Date: May 15, 2021
Presented: AHA Annual Meeting, New Orleans, LA, Jan 2022

The Briar Cliff Review Fiction, Poetry & Creative Nonfiction Contest
The Briar Cliff Review-Briar Cliff University
3303 Rebecca St, Sioux City, IA 51104-2100
Tel: 712-279-1651 *Fax:* 712-279-5486
Web Site: www.bcreview.org

Key Personnel
Mktg Dir: Judy Thompson
Ed: Tricia Currans-Sheehan
Poetry, creative nonfiction & fiction contest. Submit unpublished story, essay or 3 poems with $20. Entrants receive issue. No name on mss. Include cover page with title(s), name, address, e-mail, phone. Send SASE for results only. Can also use Submittable.
Award: $1,000 each category & publication in Spring
Closing Date: Annually, Nov 1

Brick Road Poetry Book Contest
Brick Road Poetry Press
513 Broadway, Columbus, GA 31901-3117
Web Site: brickroadpoetrypress.com
Key Personnel
Ed: Keith Badowski; Ron Self
Book-length poetry mss only, original collection of 50-100 pages of poetry, excluding cover page, contents, acknowledgments, etc. Entry fee: $25. Submissions accepted starting August 1.
Award: $1,000, publication contract with Brick Road Poetry Press in both print & ebook formats & 25 copies of the printed book
Closing Date: Annually, Nov 1

Brinkley-Stephenson Award
The Organization of American Historians (OAH)
112 N Bryan Ave, Bloomington, IN 47408-4141
Tel: 812-855-7311
E-mail: oah@oah.org
Web Site: www.oah.org/awards
Key Personnel
Exec Dir: Beth English *E-mail:* benglish@oah.org
Comm Coord: Kara Hamm *E-mail:* khamm@oah.org
Awarded annually for the best article that appeared in the *Journal of American History* during the preceding calendar year (March, June, September, December issues).
Closing Date: Feb 2021
Presented: OAH Annual Meeting, Chicago, IL, April 15-18, 2021

Brittingham & Pollak Prizes in Poetry
University of Wisconsin Press
Dept of English, 600 N Park St, Madison, WI 53706
Web Site: www.wisc.edu/wisconsinpress
Key Personnel
Ed: Ronald Wallace
Established: 1985
Pollak & Brittingham are two prizes from one competition. For book-length mss of poetry. Mss not accepted before July 15 or after September 15; $28 reading fee required, check made payable to: University of Wisconsin Press. Mss not returned; send required business-size SASE for contest results. For guidelines check web site. Electronic submissions encouraged.
Other Sponsor(s): University of Wisconsin Creative Writing Program
Award: $1,000 & publication in University of Wisconsin Press Poetry Series for each book
Closing Date: Sept 15

Brooklyn Public Library Literary Prize
Brooklyn Public Library
10 Grand Army Plaza, Brooklyn, NY 11238
Tel: 718-230-2100
E-mail: brooklyneagles@bklynlibrary.org
Web Site: www.bklynlibrary.org/support/bpl-literary-prize
Key Personnel
Co-Chair, Eagles Leadership Comm: Emily Ashton; Divya Sashti
Established: 2015

Annual prize to recognize outstanding works of nonfiction & fiction. Nominations are made by librarians throughout BPL's 59 branches. Two categories: Nonfiction; Fiction & Poetry.
Other Sponsor(s): Brooklyn Eagles
Award: $5,000 each
Presented: Autumn

The Heywood Broun Award
The NewsGuild - CWA
501 Third St NW, 6th fl, Washington, DC 20001-2797
Tel: 202-434-7177; 202-434-7162 (The Guild Reporter) *Fax:* 202-434-1472
Web Site: www.newsguild.org
Key Personnel
Ed: Sally Davidow *E-mail:* sdavidow@cwa-union.org
Established: 1941
Journalism.
Award: $5,000
Closing Date: Last Fri in Jan
Presented: Washington, DC, Annually in May

John Nicholas Brown Prize
Medieval Academy of America
17 Dunster St, Suite 202, Cambridge, MA 02138
Tel: 617-491-1622 *Fax:* 617-492-3303
E-mail: info@themedievalacademy.org
Web Site: www.medievalacademy.org
Key Personnel
Exec Dir: Lisa Fagin Davis *E-mail:* lfd@themedievalacademy.org
Established: 1978
For a first book or monograph published in the field of medieval studies judged by the selection committee to be of outstanding quality. Author must reside in North America.
Award: $1,000 & certificate
Closing Date: Annually, Oct 15
Presented: Annually in April

Linda Bruckheimer Series in Kentucky Literature
Sarabande Books Inc
822 E Market St, Louisville, KY 40206
Tel: 502-458-4028
E-mail: info@sarabandebooks.org
Web Site: www.sarabandebooks.org/bruckheimer
Key Personnel
Pres: Sarah Gorham *E-mail:* sgorham@sarabandebooks.org
Dir, Mktg & Publicity: Joanna Englert *E-mail:* joanna@sarabandebooks.org
Established: 2005
Submissions are open to any writer of English who is a native of Kentucky, has lived in Kentucky for at least 1 year, or whose ms is set in Kentucky, about Kentucky, or about a Kentuckian. In addition, the author must be willing & able to travel to or within Kentucky for readings & public events. Translations & previously self-published collections are not eligible. Electronic submissions preferred including ms, cover letter & $15 reading fee. See web site for detailed ms requirements. Submissions via post accepted during month of July.
Award: Publication of work by Sarabande & 2-week residency at Blackacre Conservancy
Closing Date: July 31

Georges Bugnet Award for Fiction
Writers' Guild of Alberta
11759 Groat Rd, Edmonton, AB T5M 3K6, Canada
Tel: 780-422-8174 *Toll Free Tel:* 800-665-5354 (AB only) *Fax:* 780-422-2663 (attn WGA)
E-mail: mail@writersguild.ca
Web Site: writersguild.ca
Key Personnel
Exec Dir: Carol Holmes *E-mail:* carol.holmes@writersguild.ca

Commns & Partnerships Coord: Ellen Kartz *E-mail:* ellen.kartz@writersguild.ca
Memb Servs Coord: Giorgia Severini
Progs Coord: Natalie Cook *E-mail:* natalie.cook@writersguild.ca; Julie Robinson *E-mail:* julie.robinson@writersguild.ca
Established: 1982
Alberta Literary Award, author must be resident of Alberta.
Award: $1,500
Closing Date: Annually, Dec 31
Presented: Alberta Book Awards Gala
Branch Office(s)
505 21 Ave SW, Calgary, AB T2S 0G9, Canada, Prog Coord: Samantha Warwick *Tel:* 403-265-2226 *E-mail:* samantha.warwick@writersguild.ca

John Burroughs Medal
John Burroughs Association Inc
261 Floyd Ackert Rd, New York, NY 12493
Mailing Address: PO Box 439, West Park, NY 12493
Tel: 212-769-5169 *Fax:* 212-313-7182
E-mail: info@johnburroughsassociation.org
Web Site: www.johnburroughsassociation.org
Key Personnel
Pres: Joan Burroughs *E-mail:* jjjburroughs@yahoo.com
Established: 1926
Awarded to the author of a distinguished book of nature writing that combines accurate scientific information with firsthand fieldwork & creative natural history writing.
Award: Medal
Closing Date: Annually in Oct
Presented: Annual Meeting, Yale Club, New York, NY, 1st Monday in April

John Burroughs Nature Essay Award
John Burroughs Association Inc
261 Floyd Ackert Rd, New York, NY 12493
Mailing Address: PO Box 439, West Park, NY 12493
Tel: 212-769-5169 *Fax:* 212-313-7182
E-mail: info@johnburroughsassociation.org
Web Site: www.johnburroughsassociation.org
Key Personnel
Pres: Joan Burroughs *E-mail:* jjjburroughs@yahoo.com
Awarded to an outstanding published natural history essay that is scientifically accurate, yet does more by using a personal point of view in vivid writing.
Award: Certificate of Recognition
Closing Date: Annually in Feb
Presented: Annual Meeting, Yale Club, New York, NY, 1st Monday in April

CAA Award for Canadian History
Canadian Authors Association (CAA)
6 West St N, Suite 203, Orillia, ON L3V 5B8, Canada
Tel: 705-325-3926
E-mail: admin@canadianauthors.org
Web Site: www.canadianauthors.org
Key Personnel
Exec Dir: Anita Purcell
Established: 1997
All entries must be historical nonfiction, on Canadian topics by Canadian authors. The books must be English language literature for adults (not "young adults"). Translations are not eligible. Fee of $40 per entry to offset a portion of administrative costs.
Award: $1,000
Closing Date: Annually, Dec 15
Presented: CAA's Annual Conference, Awards Gala & Banquet, Annually in June

CAA Award for Fiction
Canadian Authors Association (CAA)

6 West St N, Suite 203, Orillia, ON L3V 5B8,
Canada
Tel: 705-325-3926
E-mail: admin@canadianauthors.org
Web Site: www.canadianauthors.org
Key Personnel
Exec Dir: Anita Purcell
Entries must be full-length English language liter-
ature for adults by Canadian authors. Reprints
are not eligible. Fee at $40 per entry to offset a
portion of administrative costs.
Award: $1,000
Closing Date: Annually, Dec 15
Presented: CAA's Annual Conference, Awards
Gala & Banquet, Annually in June

CAA Emerging Writer Award
Canadian Authors Association (CAA)
6 West St N, Suite 203, Orillia, ON L3V 5B8,
Canada
Tel: 705-325-3926
E-mail: admin@canadianauthors.org
Web Site: www.canadianauthors.org
Key Personnel
Exec Dir: Anita Purcell
Awarded to the Canadian writer under 30 yrs old
deemed to show the most promise in the field
of literary creation.
Award: $500 & 1 yr membership in Canadian
Authors Association
Closing Date: Annually, March 31
Presented: CAA's Annual Conference, Awards
Gala & Banquet, Annually in June

CAA Poetry Award
Canadian Authors Association (CAA)
6 West St N, Suite 203, Orillia, ON L3V 5B8,
Canada
Tel: 705-325-3926
E-mail: admin@canadianauthors.org
Web Site: www.canadianauthors.org
Key Personnel
Exec Dir: Anita Purcell
For a volume of poetry by one poet. Entry fee
$40 per title.
Award: $1,000
Closing Date: Annually, Dec 15
Presented: CAA Annual Conference, Awards Gala
& Banquet, Annually in June

Gerald Cable Book Award
Silverfish Review Press
PO Box 3541, Eugene, OR 97403
Tel: 541-344-5060
E-mail: sfrpress@earthlink.net
Web Site: www.silverfishreviewpress.com
Key Personnel
Ed & Publr: Rodger Moody
Established: 1995
Poetry Book; for author who has not yet pub-
lished a collection; selection by May. $25 read-
ing fee.
Award: $1,000 & publication by Silverfish Re-
view Press & 25 copies of the book
Closing Date: Oct 15

The Randolph Caldecott Medal
Association for Library Service to Children
(ALSC)
Division of The American Library Association
(ALA)
50 E Huron St, Chicago, IL 60611-2795
Tel: 312-280-2163 *Toll Free Tel:* 800-545-2433
Fax: 312-440-9374; 312-280-5271
E-mail: alsc@ala.org
Web Site: www.ala.org/alsc
Key Personnel
Exec Dir: Aimee Strittmatter
E-mail: astrittmatter@ala.org
Deputy Exec Dir: Alena Rivers *Tel:* 800-545-
2433 ext 5866 *E-mail:* arivers@ala.org

Prog Offr, Communs: Laura Schulte-Cooper
Tel: 800-545-2433 ext 2165 *E-mail:* lschulte@
ala.org
Awards Coord: Katie Connelly *Tel:* 800-545-2433
ext 2163 *E-mail:* kconnelly@ala.org
Prog Coord: Ann Michaud *Tel:* 800-545-2433 ext
2166 *E-mail:* amichaud@ala.org
Membership/Mktg Specialist: Elizabeth Serrano
Tel: 800-545-2433 ext 2164 *E-mail:* eserrano@
ala.org
Established: 1937
Given annually to the artist who created the most
distinguished American picture book for chil-
dren published in the US during the previous
year. The artist must be a citizen or resident of
the US.
Award: Medal
Closing Date: Dec 31
Presented: ALA Midwinter Meeting, Jan/Feb

CALIBA Golden Poppy Awards
Formerly Northern California Book Awards
California Independent Booksellers Alliance
(CALIBA)
651 Broadway, 2nd fl, Sonoma, CA 95476
Mailing Address: PO Box 280, Sonoma, CA
95476
Tel: 415-561-7686 *Fax:* 415-561-7685
E-mail: info@caliballiance.org
Web Site: www.caliballiance.org/golden-poppy-
awards.html
Key Personnel
Exec Dir: Calvin Crosby *Tel:* 415-561-7686 ext
102 *E-mail:* calvin@ncaliballiance.org
Dir, Opers: Ann Seaton *Tel:* 415-561-7686 ext
101 *E-mail:* ann@caliballiance.org
Annual awards to recognize the most distinguished books published by California writers
& artists during the publishing year November
1-October 31.
Categories: Fiction, nonfiction, cooking & food,
mystery, poetry, young adult, middle grade,
children's picture book, mirrors & windows,
regional interest.
Closing Date: June (for books published first half
of year), Oct (nominations from 2nd half of
year)
Presented: March

California Book Awards
Commonwealth Club of California
110 The Embarcadero, San Francisco, CA 94105
Tel: 415-597-6700 *Fax:* 415-597-6729
E-mail: bookawards@commonwealthclub.org
Web Site: www.commonwealthclub.org/
bookawards
Established: 1931
Honors the exceptional literary merit of California
writers & publishers. Annual awards are presented in the categories of fiction, nonfiction,
poetry, first work of fiction, juvenile literature
(up to age 10), adult literature (ages 11-16),
Californiana, works in translation & notable
contribution to publishing. To be eligible, author must be resident in California at the time
of publication & books must be published under the year in consideration.
Award: Plaques with medallions for gold & silver
awardees
Closing Date: Dec
Presented: 1st Thursday in June

Joe Pendleton Campbell Narrative Contest
The Poetry Society of Virginia
900 Timber Creek Place, Virginia Beach, VA
23464
E-mail: poetryinva@aol.com
Web Site: poetrysocietyofvirginia.org
Key Personnel
Pres: Robert P Arthur *E-mail:* robert.peebles.
arthur@gmail.com

Exec Dir: Guy Terrell *E-mail:* guy.terrell@
earthlink.net
Adult Contest Chair: Steven Blythe
E-mail: stevenblythepoetry@gmail.com
All entries must be in English, original & un-
published. Submit 2 copies, each having the
category name & number on top left of page.
Any form; any subject; narrative poem; 64 line
limit. Entry fee: $4 nonmembs.
Other Sponsor(s): Paula Savoy
Award: $50 (1st prize), $30 (2nd prize), $20 (3rd
prize)
Closing Date: Jan
Presented: Annual PSV Awards Ceremony, April

John W Campbell Memorial Award
Center for the Study of Science Fiction
University of Kansas, Wescoe Hall, Rm 3001,
Dept of English, 1445 Jayhawk Blvd,
Lawrence, KS 66045
Tel: 785-864-2518 *Fax:* 785-864-1159
Web Site: www.sfcenter.ku.edu/campbell.htm
Key Personnel
Founding Dir: James Gunn *E-mail:* jgunn@ku.
edu
Dir: Christopher McKitterick *E-mail:* cmckit@ku.
edu
Established: 1973
Selected by jury who produces a short list &
votes on that list to select a winner. Science
fiction novels published in English anywhere in
the world in the year of eligibility. Publishers
are encouraged to submit works for considera-
tion by the jury.
Award: Trophy & expense paid trip to the confer-
ence to receive the award
Presented: Campbell Conference Awards Banquet,
University of Kansas, Lawrence, KS

Canada-Japan Literary Awards
Canada Council for the Arts (Conseil des arts du
Canada)
150 Elgin St, 2nd fl, Ottawa, ON K2P 1L4,
Canada
Mailing Address: PO Box 1047, Ottawa, ON K1P
5V8, Canada
Tel: 613-566-4414 *Toll Free Tel:* 800-263-5588
(CN only) *Fax:* 613-566-4390
Web Site: canadacouncil.ca/funding/prizes/canada-
japan-literary-awards
Key Personnel
Prog Offr: Luiza Pereira *Tel:* 613-566-4414 ext
4086 *E-mail:* luiza.pereira@canadacouncil.ca
Biennial awards to recognize literary excellence
by Canadian writers & translators who write,
or translate from Japanese into English or
French, a work on Japan, on Japanese themes
or on themes that promote mutual understanding between Japan & Canada. Nominations
must be submitted by a professional book publisher.
Award: $10,000 each (1 English language work &
1 French language work)
Closing Date: April 30, even-numbered years

Alexander Patterson Cappon Prize for Fiction
New Letters
UMKC, University House, 5101 Rockhill Rd,
Kansas City, MO 64110-2499
Tel: 816-235-1169 *Fax:* 816-235-2611
E-mail: newletters@umkc.edu
Web Site: www.newletters.org
Established: 1986
Literary contest. All entries considered for publi-
cation.
Award: $1,500 & publication
Closing Date: Annually, May 18

Dorothy Churchill Cappon Prize for the Essay
New Letters
UMKC, University House, 5101 Rockhill Rd,
Kansas City, MO 64110-2499

Tel: 816-235-1169 *Fax:* 816-235-2611
E-mail: newletters@umkc.edu
Web Site: www.newletters.org
Established: 1986
Literary contest. All entries considered for publication.
Award: $1,500 & publication
Closing Date: Annually, May 18

Career Development Program

New Brunswick Arts Board (Conseil des arts du Nouveau-Brunswick)
225 King St, Suite 201, Fredericton, NB E3B 1E1, Canada
Tel: 506-444-4444 *Toll Free Tel:* 866-460-ARTS (460-2787) *Fax:* 506-444-5543
Web Site: www.artsnb.ca
Key Personnel
Exec Dir: Joss Richer *Tel:* 506-478-4610
   E-mail: execdirgen@artsnb.ca
Prog Offr: Sarah Elizabeth Parker *Tel:* 506-440-0037 *E-mail:* sarahbeth@artsnb.ca
Opers Mgr: Tilly Jackson *Tel:* 506-478-4422
   E-mail: tjackson@artsnb.ca
Program is designed to recognize & encourage arts professionals who have demonstrated exceptional artistic talent & potential & who are pursuing a career in the arts. The program is divided in 4 components:
Arts by Innovation is for assistance to present work by invitation in established arts events.
Artist in Residence is for assistance for participation in residency opportunities of 3 months & less. The artists in residence are to contribute to the promotion & understanding of the arts by means of the artists' contact with the clientele of the establishments.
Professional Development is for assistance for professional development scholarships for studies & mentorship.
Professionalization & Promotion is designed to assist artists to produce tools related to the promotion of the artist's work & career with a view to broadening the dissemination network for their work & diversifying their sources for funding.
Closing Date: Jan 1, March 1, May 1, July 1, Sept 1, Nov 1

The Carle Honors

The Eric Carle Museum of Picture Book Art
125 W Bay Rd, Amherst, MA 01002
Tel: 413-559-6300
E-mail: info@carlemuseum.org
Web Site: www.carlemuseum.org/content/carle-honors
Key Personnel
Founder & Comm Chair: Leonard S Marcus
Dir, Devt: Rebecca Miller Goggins *Tel:* 413-559-6308 *E-mail:* rebeccag@carlemuseum.org
Museum's annual benefit gala, including 4 awards celebrating individuals whose creative vision & dedication are an inspiration to everyone who values picture books & their role in arts education & literacy. The awards recognize individuals in 4 distinct forms: Artist, for lifelong innovation in the field; Menor, editors, designers & educators who champion the art form; Angel, whose generous resources are crucial to making picture books art exhibitions, education programs & related projects a reality; Bridge, individuals who have found inspired ways to bring the art of the picture book to larger audiences through work in other fields.
Presented: Sept

Andrew Carnegie Medals for Excellence in Fiction & Nonfiction

The American Library Association (ALA)
225 N Michigan Ave, Suite 1300, Chicago, IL 60601

Tel: 312-944-6780 *Toll Free Tel:* 800-545-2433
   Fax: 312-440-9374
E-mail: ala@ala.org
Web Site: www.ala.org/awardsgrants/carnegieadult
Key Personnel
Exec Dir, RUSA: Jessica Hughes
   E-mail: jhughes@ala.org
Sr Prog Offr, RUSA: Leighann Wood
   E-mail: lwood@ala.org
Established: 2012
To recognize the best fiction & nonfiction books for adult readers published in the US in the previous year, chosen by selection committee.
Other Sponsor(s): Booklist; Carnegie Corporation of New York Grant; Reference & User Services Association (RUSA)
Award: $5,000 (winning authors, 1 in each category), $1,500 (2 finalists in each category)
Presented: ALA Midwinter Meeting, Indianapolis, IN, Jan 22-26, 2021

Carnegie-Whitney Award

ALA Publishing Committee
Unit of The American Library Association (ALA)
50 E Huron St, Chicago, IL 60611
Tel: 312-280-5416 *Toll Free Tel:* 800-545-2433
   Fax: 312-280-5275; 312-440-9379
Web Site: www.ala.org
Key Personnel
Grant Admin: Mary Jo Bolduc
   E-mail: mbolduc@ala.org
For the preparation of bibliographic aids for research with scholarly intent & general applicability. Decisions made at Publishing Committee Meeting, each January. Completed proposals should be sent to the Grant Administrator.
Award: Up to $5,000 annually
Closing Date: Annually in Nov

The Robert & Ina Caro Research/Travel Fellowship

Biographers International Organization (BIO)
PO Box 33020, Santa Fe, NM 87594
Web Site: biographersinternational.org
Key Personnel
Admin & Membership Coord: Lori Izykowski
   E-mail: lori@biographersinternational.org
BIO members with a work in progress can apply to receive funding for research trips to archives or to important settings in their subject's lives. Fellowship is restricted to support of works of biography (not of history, autobiography or memoir). E-mail name, project title, brief summary, anticipated result of receipt of travel fellowship, details of where you wish to travel & why, proposed budget & abbreviated CV. See web site to apply & submit to Deirdre David, VP, ddavid@temple.edu.
Award: One $5,000 fellowship or two $2,500 fellowships
Closing Date: Feb 1
Presented: Spring

The Carter Prize For The Essay

Shenandoah: The Washington & Lee University Review
Washington & Lee University, Mattingly House, 204 W Washington St, Lexington, VA 24450-2116
Tel: 540-458-8908
E-mail: shenandoah@wlu.edu
Web Site: shenandoahliterary.org
Key Personnel
Ed: R T Smith *E-mail:* rodsmith@wlu.edu
Asst Ed: William Wright
Annual award for the best essay published in *Shenandoah* during a volume year.
Award: $1,000

Catholic Book Awards

Catholic Press Association of the United States & Canada

205 W Monroe St, Suite 470, Chicago, IL 60606
Tel: 312-380-6789 *Fax:* 312-361-0256
E-mail: cpaawards@catholicpress.org
Web Site: www.catholicpress.org
Key Personnel
Exec Dir: Timothy M Walter *E-mail:* twalter@catholicpress.org
Busn Mgr: Barbara Mastrolia
   E-mail: bmastrolia@catholicpress.com
Awards for best Catholic books in different categories.
Award: Certificate
Closing Date: Feb
Presented: Annual Convention, June

Catholic Press Association of the US & Canada Journalism Awards, see Catholic Press Awards

Catholic Press Awards

Catholic Press Association of the United States & Canada
205 W Monroe St, Suite 470, Chicago, IL 60606
Tel: 312-380-6789 *Fax:* 312-361-0256
E-mail: cpaawards@catholicpress.org
Web Site: www.catholicpress.org
Key Personnel
Exec Dir: Timothy M Walter *E-mail:* twalter@catholicpress.org
Busn Mgr: Barbara Mastrolia
   E-mail: bmastrolia@catholicpress.com
Journalism entries from member publications.
Award: Certificate
Closing Date: Annually in Feb
Presented: Annual Convention, June

CBC Diversity Outstanding Achievement Awards

The Children's Book Council (CBC)
54 W 39 St, 14th fl, New York, NY 10018
Tel: 917-890-7416
E-mail: cbc.info@cbcbooks.org
Web Site: www.cbcbooks.org
Awarded annually to professionals or organizations in the children's publishing industry who have made a significant impact on the publishing & marketing of diverse books, diversity in hiring & mentoring & efforts that create greater awareness with the public about the importance of diverse voices.
Presented: CBC Forum, Oct

The Center for Fiction First Novel Prize

The Center for Fiction
17 E 47 St, New York, NY 10017
Tel: 212-755-6710
E-mail: info@centerforfiction.org
Web Site: www.centerforfiction.org/awards/the-first-novel-prize
Key Personnel
Writing Progs Mgr: Thierry Kehou
   E-mail: thierry@centerforfiction.org
Established: 2006
Awarded to the best debut novel published between January 1 & December 31 of the award year.
Award: $10,000 (1st prize), $1,000 (shortlist award)
Presented: The Center for Fiction's Annual Benefit & Awards Dinner, Annually in Dec

Center for Publishing Departmental Scholarships

New York University, School of Continuing & Professional Studies
Midtown Ctr, Rm 429, 11 W 42 St, New York, NY 10036
Tel: 212-992-3232 *Fax:* 212-992-3233
E-mail: pub.center@nyu.edu
Web Site: www.scps.nyu.edu
Key Personnel
Asst Dir, MS in Publg: Lindsey Allen
   E-mail: lindsey.allen@nyu.edu

Awarded to students enrolled in at least 6 credits in Master of Science in publishing program (not available to students in first semester). Need excellent academic record. Based on financial need & merit.
Award: $500 & up
Presented: Annually in Fall & Spring

Jane Chambers Playwriting Award
Women & Theatre Program, Association for Theatre in Higher Education
Georgetown University, 108 David Performing Arts Ctr, Box 571063, 37 & "O" St, NW, Washington, DC 20057-1063
Web Site: www.athe.org/?page=Jane_Chambers
Key Personnel
Contact: Jen-Scott Mobley *E-mail:* jenscottmob@gmail.com; Maya E Roth *E-mail:* mer46@georgetown.edu
Established: 1984
Award for play or performance text by a woman which reflects a feminist perspective & contains a majority of roles for women performers. Scripts may be produced or unproduced; encourage experimentation with dramatic form. See web site for FAQ & past winners. Electronic submissions preferred. One play per playwright annually. Separate contest for student playwrights.
Award: $1,000 for reading of the winning piece at the award conference & free registration to the conference; student winner, submitted separate to WTP web site, is also recognized with $250 & selected reading of scenes
Closing Date: Feb 15
Presented: Annual ATHE National Conference

The Alfred & Fay Chandler Book Award
Business History Review
c/o Harvard Business School, Connell House 301A, Boston, MA 02163
Tel: 617-495-1003 *Fax:* 617-495-2705
E-mail: bhr@hbs.edu
Web Site: www.hbs.edu/businesshistory/fellowships
Key Personnel
Ed: Walter Friedman *E-mail:* wfriedman@hbs.edu
Established: 1964
Award given every 3 years for best book published in the US on the history of business. Selection by the editorial board of the Business History Review.
Award: A scroll

G S Sharat Chandra Prize for Short Fiction
BkMk Press - University of Missouri-Kansas City
University House, 5101 Rockhill Rd, Kansas City, MO 64110-2499
Tel: 816-235-2558 *Fax:* 816-235-2611
E-mail: bkmk@umkc.edu
Web Site: www.umkc.edu/bkmk
Key Personnel
Exec Ed: Robert Stewart *Tel:* 816-235-2610
E-mail: stewartr@umkc.edu
Mng Ed: Ben Furnish *E-mail:* furnishb@umkc.edu
Established: 2001
The best book-length ms of short fiction in English by a living author. Ms must be typed on standard-sized paper in English & should be 125-300 pages double-spaced. Entries must include two title pages: one with author name, address & phone number & one with no author information. Any acknowledgments should appear on a separate piece of paper. Entries must include a table of contents. Author's name must not appear anywhere on the ms. Do not submit your ms by fax or e-mail. A SASE should be included, for notification only. Note: No mss will be returned. A reading fee of $25 in US funds (check payable to BkMk Press) must accompany each ms. Processing fee for

online submissions is an additional $5. Entrants will receive a copy of the winning book when published. Entrants may also now submit online.
Award: $1,000 plus book publication of winning ms by BkMk Press
Closing Date: Annually, Jan 15
Presented: Annually in Summer

The Chautauqua Prize
Chautauqua Institution
One Ames Ave, Chautauqua, NY 14722
Mailing Address: PO Box 28, Chautauqua, NY 14722
Toll Free Tel: 800-836-ARTS (836-2787)
Web Site: www.ciweb.org/prize
Key Personnel
Contact, Educ Dept: Sara Toth *Tel:* 716-357-6376
E-mail: stoth@ciweb.org
Established: 2012
National prize for a book of fiction or literary/narrative nonfiction that provides a richly rewarding reading experience & honors the author for a significant contribution to the literary arts. Book must be written in English & published in the calendar year prior to the year of the award. Entries must include official entry form, 8 copies of each title entered & entry fee of $75. Each nominated eligible book is evaluated by 3 Chautauquan reviewers, after which the shortlist & winner are chosen by a 3-member independent, anonymous jury.
Award: $7,500 & travel/expenses to one-week summer residency at Chautauqua
Closing Date: Dec 15

Children's & Teen Choice Book Awards
The Children's Book Council (CBC)
54 W 39 St, 14th fl, New York, NY 10018
E-mail: cbc.info@cbcbooks.org
Web Site: everychildareader.net/choice
Key Personnel
Exec Dir: Carl Lennertz *E-mail:* carl.lennertz@cbcbooks.org
Assoc Exec Dir/Programming & Strategic Partnerships Dir: Shaina Birkhead *E-mail:* shaina.birkhead@cbcbooks.org
Established: 2008
The only national book awards voted on only by kids & teens. Benefits ABFE & Every Child a Reader. Not an open application process. Publishers submission only.
Presented: The Silent Art Auction, Annually, late May/early June

Children's Literature Association Article Award
Children's Literature Association (ChLA)
1301 W 22 St, Suite 202, Oak Brook, IL 60523
Tel: 630-571-4520 *Fax:* 708-876-5598
E-mail: info@childlitassn.org
Web Site: www.childlitassn.org
Award for best literary criticism article published within a given year on the topic of children's literature. See web site for application requirements.
Award: $200 plus award certificate
Presented: ChLA Annual Conference, Annually in June

Children's Literature Association Beiter Graduate Student Research Grants
Children's Literature Association (ChLA)
1301 W 22 St, Suite 202, Oak Brook, IL 60523
Tel: 630-571-4520 *Fax:* 708-876-5598
E-mail: info@childlitassn.org
Web Site: www.childlitassn.org
Key Personnel
Grants Chair: Chris McGee
Awarded for proposals of original scholarship with the expectation that the undertaking will lead to publication or a conference presentation

& contribute to the field of children's literature criticism. Winners must either be members of the Children's Literature Association or join the association before they receive any funds. Applications & supporting materials should be written in or translated into English. Encouraging new scholars to enter the field, the scholarship is intended to enable "entry-level" scholars (graduate students, instructors or assistant professors) to bring to a publishable level dissertations, theses or papers that they have written.
Award: $500-$1,500 (based on the number & needs of the winning applicants)
Closing Date: Annually, Feb 1
Presented: ChLA Annual Conference, Annually in June

Children's Literature Association Book Award
Children's Literature Association (ChLA)
1301 W 22 St, Suite 202, Oak Brook, IL 60523
Tel: 630-571-4520 *Fax:* 708-876-5598
E-mail: info@childlitassn.org
Web Site: www.childlitassn.org
Book awards given for best book on children's literature history, scholarship & criticism published as a book in a given year. See web site for application requirements.
Award: $400 plus award certificate
Presented: ChLA Annual Conference, Annually in June

Children's Literature Legacy Award
Association for Library Service to Children (ALSC)
Division of The American Library Association (ALA)
50 E Huron St, Chicago, IL 60611-2795
Tel: 312-280-2163 *Toll Free Tel:* 800-545-2433
Fax: 312-440-9374; 312-280-5271
E-mail: alsc@ala.org
Web Site: www.ala.org/alsc
Key Personnel
Exec Dir: Aimee Strittmatter
E-mail: astrittmatter@ala.org
Deputy Exec Dir: Alena Rivers *Tel:* 800-545-2433 ext 5866 *E-mail:* arivers@ala.org
Prog Offr, Communs: Laura Schulte-Cooper *Tel:* 800-545-2433 ext 2165 *E-mail:* lschulte@ala.org
Awards Coord: Katie Connelly *Tel:* 800-545-2433 ext 2163 *E-mail:* kconnelly@ala.org
Prog Coord: Ann Michaud *Tel:* 800-545-2433 ext 2166 *E-mail:* amichaud@ala.org
Membership/Mktg Specialist: Elizabeth Serrano *Tel:* 800-545-2433 ext 2164 *E-mail:* eserrano@ala.org
Established: 1954
Annual award presented to an author or illustrator whose books have made a substantial & lasting contribution to children's literature. The books must have been published in the US.
Award: Medal
Closing Date: Dec 31
Presented: ALA Midwinter Meeting, Jan/Feb

Children's Sequoyah Book Award
Oklahoma Library Association
PO Box 6550, Edmond, OK 73083
Tel: 405-525-5100 *Fax:* 405-525-5103
Web Site: www.oklibs.org
Key Personnel
Exec Dir: Kay Boies *E-mail:* execdirector@oklibs.org
Established: 1959
School children's choice of a book published by a living US author from a selected list. Students grades 3-5 who have read/listened to at least 3 books from the Children's Masterlist are eligible to vote.
Award: Plaque/medal

Closing Date: Annually, March 1
Presented: OLA Annual Conference, Annually in April

Christian Book Award®

Evangelical Christian Publishers Association (ECPA)
5801 S McClintock Dr, Suite 104, Tempe, AZ 85283
Tel: 480-966-3998 *Fax:* 480-966-1944
E-mail: info@ecpa.org
Web Site: christianbookawards.com
Key Personnel
Exec Dir: Stan Jantz
Program recognizes the highest quality in Christian books & Bibles. There are 11 categories: Bibles; Bible Reference Works; Bible Study; Ministry Resources; Biography & Memoir; Christian Living; Faith & Culture; Devotion & Gift; Children (0-8); Young People's Literature (ages 9-16 nonfiction); New Author.
See web site for detailed submission process.
Closing Date: Sept 30
Presented: May 1

The Christopher Awards

The Christophers
5 Hanover Sq, 22nd fl, New York, NY 10004-2751
Tel: 212-759-4050 *Toll Free Tel:* 888-298-4050 (orders) *Fax:* 212-838-5073
E-mail: mail@christophers.org
Web Site: www.christophers.org
Key Personnel
Prog Mgr & Event Prodr: Tony Rossi *E-mail:* t.rossi@christophers.org
Established: 1945
For adult (nonfiction only) & juvenile fiction & nonfiction published during the current calendar year. Themes must reflect "highest values of the human spirit" criteria.
Award: Bronze medallion
Closing Date: June 1 & Nov 1; books evaluated throughout the calendar year
Presented: New York, NY, Annually in May

John Ciardi Prize for Poetry

BkMk Press - University of Missouri-Kansas City
University House, 5101 Rockhill Rd, Kansas City, MO 64110-2499
Tel: 816-235-2558 *Fax:* 816-235-2611
E-mail: bkmk@umkc.edu
Web Site: www.umkc.edu/bkmk
Key Personnel
Exec Ed: Robert Stewart *Tel:* 816-235-2610 *E-mail:* stewartr@umkc.edu
Mng Ed: Ben Furnish *E-mail:* furnishb@umkc.edu
Established: 1998
Presented for the best full-length ms of poetry in English by a living author. Ms must be typed on standard-sized paper & should be approximately 50 pages minimum, 110 pages maximum, single-spaced. Entries must include two title pages: one with author name, address & phone & one with no author information. Any acknowledgements should appear on a separate piece of paper. Entries must include a table of contents. Author's name must not appear anywhere on the ms. Do not submit your ms by fax or e-mail. A SASE should be included, for notification only. Note: No mss will be returned. A reading fee of $25 in US funds (check made payable to BkMk Press) must accompany each ms. Processing fee for online submissions is an additional $5. Entrants will receive a copy of the winning book when it is published. Entrants may also now submit online.
Award: $1,000 plus publication by BkMk Press
Closing Date: Annually, Jan 15
Presented: Annually in Summer

The City of Calgary W O Mitchell Book Prize

Writers' Guild of Alberta
11759 Groat Rd, Edmonton, AB T5M 3K6, Canada
Tel: 780-422-8174 *Toll Free Tel:* 800-665-5354 (AB only) *Fax:* 780-422-2663 (attn WGA)
E-mail: mail@writersguild.ca
Web Site: writersguild.ca
Key Personnel
Exec Dir: Carol Holmes *E-mail:* carol.holmes@writersguild.ca
Communs & Partnerships Coord: Ellen Kartz *E-mail:* ellen.kartz@writersguild.ca
Memb Servs Coord: Giorgia Severini
Progs Coord: Natalie Cook *E-mail:* natalie.cook@writersguild.ca; Julie Robinson *E-mail:* julie.robinson@writersguild.ca
Recognizes literary achievement by Calgary authors. Types may be fiction, poetry, nonfiction, children's literature & drama.
Award: $5,000
Closing Date: Annually, Dec 31
Presented: Calgary Awards, Spring
Branch Office(s)
505 21 Ave SW, Calgary, AB T2S 0G9, Canada, Prog Coord: Samantha Warwick *Tel:* 403-265-2226 *E-mail:* samantha.warwick@writersguild.ca

City of Vancouver Book Award

City of Vancouver, Cultural Services Department
Woodward's Heritage Bldg, Suite 501, 111 W Hastings St, Vancouver, BC V6B 1H4, Canada
Tel: 604-871-6634 *Fax:* 604-871-6005
E-mail: culture@vancouver.ca
Web Site: vancouver.ca/bookaward
Key Personnel
Cultural Planner: Marnie Rice *E-mail:* marnie.rice@vancouver.ca
Established: 1989
Annual award for authors of books - any genre - that contribute to the appreciation & understanding of Vancouver's history, unique character or achievements of its residents.
Award: $3,000
Closing Date: May
Presented: The Mayor's Arts Awards, Sept/Oct

Page Davidson Clayton Prize for Emerging Poets

Michigan Quarterly Review
University of Michigan, 0576 Rackham Bldg, 915 E Washington St, Ann Arbor, MI 48109-1070
Tel: 734-764-9265
E-mail: mqr@umich.edu
Web Site: sites.lsa.umich.edu/mqr/
Key Personnel
Ed: Jonathan Freedman
Poetry Ed: Keith Taylor
Awarded annually to the best poet appearing in MQR who has not yet published a book.
Award: $500

Cleveland State University Poetry Center Prizes

Cleveland State University Poetry Center
2121 Euclid Ave, Cleveland, OH 44115
Tel: 216-687-3986 *Toll Free Tel:* 888-278-6473 *Fax:* 216-687-6943
E-mail: poetrycenter@csuohio.edu
Web Site: www.csupoetrycenter.com
Key Personnel
Dir: Caryl Pagel
Asst: Jessica Schantz
Established: 1986
Poetry book mss, in 2 categories, First Book or Open Competition. Minimum 48 pages of poetry (one poem per page), SASE guidelines; readers fee required; simultaneous submissions permitted; mss not returned. Open competition is limited to poets who have published a full-length collection, 48+ pp, 500+ copies. $28 reading fee.
Award: $1,000 & publication in the Cleveland State University Poetry Center series
Closing Date: March 31 (digital entry only)
Presented: July

David H Clift Scholarship

ALA Scholarship Clearinghouse
Unit of The American Library Association (ALA)
50 E Huron St, Chicago, IL 60611
Toll Free Tel: 800-545-2433 (ext 4279) *Fax:* 312-280-3256
E-mail: scholarships@ala.org
Web Site: www.ala.org/scholarships
Key Personnel
Prog Offr: Kimberly L Redd *E-mail:* klredd@ala.org
Established: 1969
Awarded annually to worthy US or Canadian citizen or permanent resident to begin an MLS degree in an ALA-accredited program.
Award: $3,000
Closing Date: March 1; applications available beginning in Sept

Coal Hill Review Poetry Chapbook Contest

Coal Hill Review
c/o Autumn House Press, PO Box 5486, Pittsburgh, PA 15206
E-mail: reviewcoalhill@gmail.com
Web Site: www.coalhillreview.com
Key Personnel
Ed: Christine Stroud
Open to all poets writing in English. Ms may be submitted by attachment to our e-mail address. Submit a ms of 12-20 pages with a $20 entry fee.
Award: $1,000 & publication by Autumn House Press & Coal Hill Review
Closing Date: Nov 1

CODiE Awards

Software & Information Industry Association (SIIA)
1090 Vermont Ave NW, 6th fl, Washington, DC 20005-4905
Tel: 202-289-7442 *Fax:* 202-289-7097
Web Site: www.siia.net
Key Personnel
Pres: Jeff Joseph
Awards Dir: Jennifer Baranowski *Tel:* 949-448-0545 *E-mail:* jbaranowski@siia.net
Established: 1986
Honors excellence in the education & business technology industries. Nomination period begins in December.
Award: Trophy
Closing Date: Annually in Feb
Presented: Annually in July

Coe College Playwriting Festival

Coe College
1220 First Ave NE, Cedar Rapids, IA 52402
Tel: 319-399-8624 *Fax:* 319-399-8557
Web Site: www.theatre.coe.edu; www.coe.edu/academics/theatrearts/theatrearts_playwritingfestival
Key Personnel
Chair, Dept of Theatre Arts: Susan Wolverton *E-mail:* swolvert@coe.edu
Established: 1992
Biennial playwriting award for new, full-length, original, unproduced & unpublished play. No musicals, adaptations, translations or collaborations. Only 1 entry/indiv.
Award: Publicly staged reading by students, faculty +/or individuals from the community, $500 & room, board, travel for one week residency
Closing Date: Nov 1, even-numbered years
Presented: Coe College, Cedar Rapids, IA, April

Carla Cohen Free Speech Award

New Atlantic Independent Booksellers Association (NAIBA)
2667 Hyacinth St, Westbury, NY 11590
Tel: 516-333-0681 *Fax:* 516-333-0689
E-mail: naibabooksellers@gmail.com
Web Site: www.naiba.com/page/cohenfreespeechaward
Key Personnel
Exec Dir: Eileen Dengler *E-mail:* naibaeileen@gmail.com
Established: 2010
Annual award presented to a children's book that best exemplifies the ideals of the First Amendment.

Morton N Cohen Award for a Distinguished Edition of Letters

Modern Language Association of America (MLA)
85 Broad St, Suite 500, New York, NY 10004-2434
SAN: 202-6422
Tel: 646-576-5141; 646-576-5000 *Fax:* 646-458-0030
E-mail: awards@mla.org
Web Site: www.mla.org
Key Personnel
Coord, Book Prizes: Annie M Reiser
  E-mail: areiser@mla.org
Established: 1989
Award for an outstanding edition of letters published in 2019 or 2020. Editions may be in single or multiple volumes. For consideration, submit 4 copies. Editors need not be members of the MLA. Presented biennially.
Award: Cash award & certificate
Closing Date: May 1
Presented: MLA Convention, Jan 2022

The Victor Cohn Prize for Excellence in Medical Science Reporting

Council for the Advancement of Science Writing (CASW)
PO Box 910, Hedgesville, WV 25427
Tel: 304-754-6786
Web Site: www.casw.org
Established: 2000
Medical science writing for the mass media within the last 5 years. Online submissions.
Award: $3,000
Closing Date: Annually, July 31
Presented: ScienceWriters Meeting, Annually in Oct/Nov

William E Colby Award

William E Colby Military Writer's Symposium, Norwich University
158 Harmon Dr, Box 60, Northfield, VT 05663
Tel: 802-485-2965
Web Site: colby.norwich.edu/award
Key Personnel
Colby Symposium Dir: W Travis Morris
Recognizes a first work of fiction or nonfiction that has made a major contribution to the understanding of military history, intelligence operations, or international affairs. The book must have been published during the previous calendar year. $60 fee per submission.
Other Sponsor(s): Pritzker Military Foundation; Pritzker Military Museum & Library
Award: $5,000 author honorarium & invitation to an appearance at the Pritzker Military Museum & Library, Chicago, IL
Closing Date: Nov 30
Presented: Norwich University, Northfield, VT

John M Collier Award for Forest History Journalism

The Forest History Society Inc
701 William Vickers Ave, Durham, NC 27701-3162
Tel: 919-682-9319 *Fax:* 919-682-2349

Web Site: www.foresthistory.org
Key Personnel
Pres: Steven Anderson *E-mail:* steven.anderson@foresthistory.org
Admin Asst: Andrea Anderson *E-mail:* andrea.anderson@foresthistory.org
Established: 1987
Recognizes contributions to forest history that are published in newspapers, trade journals & other journalistic media. Open to any newspaper, or general circulation magazine, professional or freelance journalist in North America.
Award: $1,000 & expenses for a visit to The Forest History Society Library & Archives in Durham, NC & participation in an Institutes for Journalism in Natural Resources expedition
Closing Date: Annually, Feb 28

Carr P Collins Award

Texas Institute of Letters (TIL)
PO Box 609, Round Rock, TX 78680
Tel: 512-683-5640
E-mail: president@texasinstituteofletters.org
Web Site: www.texasinstituteofletters.org
Key Personnel
Pres: Carmen Tafolla
VP: Sergio Troncoso
Secy: Ann Weisgarber
Treas: W K Stratton
Recording Secy: Kurt Heinzelman
Annual award for the best nonfiction book by a Texan or about Texas. Guidelines on the web site.
Award: $5,000
Closing Date: Annually in Jan
Presented: TIL Awards Banquet, Annually in Spring

Colorado Book Awards

Colorado Humanities & Center for the Book
7935 E Prentice Ave, Suite 450, Greenwood Village, CO 80111
Tel: 303-894-7951 (ext 19) *Fax:* 303-864-9361
E-mail: info@coloradohumanities.org
Web Site: www.coloradohumanities.org
Key Personnel
Prog Coord: Bess Maher
Established: 1991
Cash prize to Colorado authors in fiction, nonfiction, young adult, children's, poetry, romance & additional categories vary from year to year.
Award: $250 (cash)
Closing Date: Annually in Jan
Presented: Colorado Book Awards Event, Annually in Spring

Betsy Colquitt Award for Poetry

Texas Christian University
Dept of English, TCU Box 298300, Fort Worth, TX 76129
Tel: 817-257-5907 *Fax:* 817-257-5905
E-mail: descant@tcu.edu
Web Site: www.descant.tcu.edu
Key Personnel
Mng Ed: Dan Williams *E-mail:* d.e.williams@tcu.edu
Established: 1996
Annual award for best poem or series of poems by a single author in a volume. No entry fee.
Other Sponsor(s): descant (publication), Dept of English, TCU
Award: $500
Closing Date: Mss must be time stamped or postmarked Sept 15-April 1
Presented: Winner announced in the Summer in *descant*

Miles Conrad Memorial Lecture

National Information Standards Organization (NISO)
3600 Clipper Mill Rd, Suite 302, Baltimore, MD 21211-1948

Tel: 301-654-2512 *Fax:* 410-685-5278
E-mail: nisohq@niso.org
Web Site: www.niso.org
Key Personnel
Exec Dir: Todd Carpenter *E-mail:* tcarpenter@niso.org
Dir, Community Engagement: Alice Meadows
Dir, Content: Jill O'Neill *E-mail:* joneill@niso.org
Dir, Strategic Initiatives: Jason Griffey
Assoc Dir, Progs: Nettie Lagace
  E-mail: nlagace@niso.org
Off Mgr: Kimberly Graham *E-mail:* kgraham@niso.org
Established: 1968
The award is presented to an individual who, like Conrad, has made a truly significant contribution to furthering information dissemination & its role in the advancement of science & scholarship.
Award: Plaque & honorarium

The Pat Conroy Southern Book Prize, see Southern Book Prize

Constance Rooke Creative Non-Fiction Prize

The Malahat Review
University of Victoria, Box 1700, Sta CSC, Victoria, BC V8W 2Y2, Canada
Tel: 250-721-8524 *Fax:* 250-472-5051
E-mail: malahat@uvic.ca
Web Site: malahatreview.ca
Key Personnel
Ed: John Barton
Established: 2007
Invite entries from Canadian, American & overseas authors. Must be between 2,000-3,000 words. No restrictions as to subject matter. Entry fees: $35 Canadian entries, $40 US entries & $45 (US) for entries from Mexico & outside North America. See web site for additional details.
Award: $1,000
Closing Date: Annually, Aug 1

Cordon d' Or - Gold Ribbon International Culinary Academy Awards

Cordon d' Or - Gold Ribbon Inc
7312 Sixth Ave N, St Petersburg, FL 33710
Tel: 727-347-2437
E-mail: cordondor@aol.com
Web Site: www.cordondorcuisine.com; www.florida-americasculinaryparadise.com; www.culinaryambassadorofireland.com
Key Personnel
Pres & CEO: Noreen Kinney
  E-mail: ambassadornoreen@tampabay.rr.com
Established: 2003
Literary Cookbook, Illustrated Cookbook & 'Potluck' Book (any genre) & 'Culinary Arts' Awards. Categories include cookbooks, photographers, food stylists, magazines, articles, web sites, recipes & menus. Full details available on the web site. Entry forms can be downloaded.
Award: $1,000 (overall winner), Crystal Globe Trophies (presented to winners in all categories)
Closing Date: Annually, Dec 31
Presented: St Petersburg, FL, Annually in May

Jeanne Cordova Prize for Lesbian/Queer Nonfiction

Lambda Literary
5482 Wilshire Blvd, No 1595, Los Angeles, CA 90036
Tel: 323-643-4281
E-mail: awards@lambdaliterary.org; admin@lambdaliterary.org
Web Site: www.lambdaliterary.org/jeanne-cordova-prize-lesbian-nonfiction
Key Personnel
Exec Dir: Tony Valenzuela
Awards Admin: Ella Boureau

Annual award to a writer committed to nonfiction work that captures the depth & complexity of lesbian/queer life, culture +/or history. Submission period begins in January. See web site for full guidelines & requirements.
Other Sponsor(s): Amazon Literary Partnership; The David Bohnett Foundation; California Arts Council; Los Angeles County Arts Commission; National Endowment for the Arts
Award: $2,500
Closing Date: March
Presented: Annual Lambda Literary Awards Ceremony, June

Albert B Corey Prize
Canadian Historical Association (CHA) & American Historical Association (AHA)
c/o American Historical Association, 400 "A" St SE, Washington, DC 20003-3889
Tel: 202-544-2422 *Fax:* 202-544-8307
E-mail: cha-shc@cha-shc.ca
Web Site: www.historians.org/prizes; www.cha-shc.ca
Established: 1967
Awarded biennially for the best book dealing with Canadian/American relations; awarded jointly with the American Historical Association. Books bearing an imprint of 2020 or 2021 are eligible for the 2022 prize. No application form, applicants must simply mail a copy of their book to each of the prize committee members who will be posted on our web site as the prize deadline approaches. All updated info on web site.
Award: $1,000 CAD
Closing Date: May 15, 2022
Presented: AHA Annual Meeting, Philadelphia, PA, 2023

COVR Visionary Awards
The Coalition of Visionary Resources (COVR)
PO Box 1397, Palmer Lake, CO 80133
Tel: 719-487-0424
E-mail: info@covr.org
Web Site: covr.org/awards
Key Personnel
Awards Mgmt: Sue Wilhite
Awarded annually to entries selected from among the best new products in the Mind/Body/Spirit marketplace from the previous 3 years. Creators, vendors & publishers can submit entry form online, high-resolution graphic file of the product, along with entry fee of $75 per product per category. See web site for full guidelines & categories, including 22 book categories. Entries open February 1.
Other Sponsor(s): New Leaf Distributing Co
Closing Date: April 1
Presented: INATS®, June

The Terry J Cox Poetry Award
Regal House Publishing
806 Oberlin Rd, No 12094, Raleigh, NC 27605
E-mail: info@regalhousepublishing.com
Web Site: regalhousepublishing.com/the-terry-j-cox-poetry-award/
Key Personnel
Founder, Publr & Ed-in-Chief: Jaynie Royal
Mng Ed: Pam Van Dyk
Sr Ed: Ruth Feiertag
Established: 2018
Recognizes excellence in a debut poetry collection. Submissions through Submittable or by post. Entry fee $25. Fax or e-mail submissions not accepted. See web site for submission guidelines.
Award: Publication & $500 honorarium
Closing Date: Jan 31 (postmark)
Presented: March 30

Marie Coyoteblanc Award for Indigenous Writing
Prince Edward Island Writers' Guild
81 Prince St, Charlottetown, PE C1A 4R3, Canada
E-mail: peiliteraryawards@gmail.com
Web Site: www.peiwritersguild.com
Acknowledges the contribution made to PEI literary culture by Mi'kmaq writers. Indigenous stories are an important part of our culture & ultimately this category is intended to encourage more indigenous people to start writing. The prize is open to Prince Edward Island residents who are of Mi'kmaq descent, who identify as Mi'kmaq Islanders & who are accepted as such by the communities in which they live. The Prize is designed to recognize literary merit & promote works in all categories including fiction, nonfiction, poetry, writing for children & young adults, plays & scriptwriting. Maximum 2 entries. Work must be original & unpublished. Entry fee for each submission is $25. See web site for complete entry requirements.
Award: Cash prizes for 1st, 2nd & 3rd place
Closing Date: Jan 31
Presented: Cox & Palmer Island Literary Awards Gala, Annually in Spring

CPSA Prize in Comparative Politics
Canadian Political Science Association
260 rue Dalhousie St, Suite 204, Ottawa, ON K1N 7E4, Canada
Tel: 613-562-1202 *Fax:* 613-241-0019
E-mail: cpsa-acsp@cpsa-acsp.ca
Web Site: www.cpsa-acsp.ca
Key Personnel
Admin: Michelle Hopkins
Biennial prize awarded to the best book published in English or in French in the field of comparative politics. To be eligible, a book may be single or multi-authored. Single-authored: author must be a member of the CPSA in the year the book is considered for the prize. Multi-authored: at least one of the authors must be a member of the CPSA in the year the book is considered for the prize. For the 2022 award, a book must have a copyright date of 2020 or 2021.
Award: Commemorative plaque & receive/share the set of books submitted to the CPSA office
Closing Date: Dec
Presented: Annual Conference

CPSA Prize in International Relations
Canadian Political Science Association
260 rue Dalhousie St, Suite 204, Ottawa, ON K1N 7E4, Canada
Tel: 613-562-1202 *Fax:* 613-241-0019
E-mail: cpsa-acsp@cpsa-acsp.ca
Web Site: www.cpsa-acsp.ca
Key Personnel
Admin: Michelle Hopkins
This is a biennial competition. The prize was established to recognize the contribution of Canadian political scientists to the study of international relations & to encourage the best Canadian scholarship in this field. Awarded to the best book published in English or in French in the field of international relations. Book may be single-authored or multi-authored. Single-authored: author must be a member of the CPSA in the year the book is considered for the prize. Multi-authored: at least one of the authors must be a member of the CPSA in the year the book is considered for the prize. For the 2021 award, the book must have a copyright date of 2019 or 2020.
Award: Commemorative plaque & receive/share the set of books submitted to the CPSA
Closing Date: Dec
Presented: Annual Conference, University of Alberta, Edmonton, AB, CN, June 2021

Avery O Craven Award
The Organization of American Historians (OAH)
112 N Bryan Ave, Bloomington, IN 47408-4141
Tel: 812-855-7311
E-mail: oah@oah.org
Web Site: www.oah.org/awards
Key Personnel
Exec Dir: Beth English *E-mail:* benglish@oah.org
Comm Coord: Kara Hamm *E-mail:* khamm@oah.org
Awarded annually to the author of the most original book on the coming of the Civil War, the Civil War years, or the Era of Reconstruction, with the exception of works of purely military history. Each entry must be published during the calendar year preceding that in which the award is given. One copy of each entry must be mailed directly to the committee members listed on the web site.
Closing Date: Oct 1, 2021 (postmarked)
Presented: OAH Annual Meeting, Boston, MA, March 31-April 3, 2022

The Crazyhorse Fiction Prize
Crazyhorse
College of Charleston, Dept of English, 66 George St, Charleston, SC 29424
Tel: 843-953-4470
E-mail: crazyhorse@cofc.edu
Web Site: crazyhorse.cofc.edu/prizes
Key Personnel
Mng Ed: Jonathan Heinen
Award for best short story. Enter up to 25 pages fiction with $20 entry fee, which includes one-year subscription. Submissions accepted during the month of Jan. Nationally prominent writer judges. See web site for complete instructions.
Award: $2,000 & publication in *Crazyhorse*
Closing Date: Annually, Jan 31

Creation Grant Program
New Brunswick Arts Board (Conseil des arts du Nouveau-Brunswick)
225 King St, Suite 201, Fredericton, NB E3B 1E1, Canada
Tel: 506-444-4444 *Toll Free Tel:* 866-460-ARTS (460-2787) *Fax:* 506-444-5543
Web Site: www.artsnb.ca
Key Personnel
Exec Dir: Joss Richer *Tel:* 506-478-4610
  E-mail: execdirgen@artsnb.ca
Prog Offr: Sarah Elizabeth Parker *Tel:* 506-440-0037 *E-mail:* sarahbeth@artsnb.ca
Opers Mgr: Tilly Jackson *Tel:* 506-478-4422
  E-mail: tjackson@artsnb.ca
Designed to provide assistance to professional New Brunswick artists for the research, development & execution of original projects in the arts. Creation Grants are intended to allow artists to devote some or most of their time to research & creative production.
Closing Date: April 1, Oct 1

Creative Nonfiction Awards
Prince Edward Island Writers' Guild
81 Prince St, Charlottetown, PE C1A 4R3, Canada
E-mail: peiliteraryawards@gmail.com
Web Site: www.peiwritersguild.com
This nonfiction category includes humour writing, memoir, biography, essay (including personal essay), travel writing & feature articles. It involves writing about real events, people, or ideas, conveying a message through the use of literary techniques such as characterization, plot, setting, dialogue, narrative & personal reflection. In works of creative nonfiction, the writer's voice & opinion are evident. The work should be accessible to a general reading audience (not written for a specialized or academic audience). Maximum length: 2,500 words. Maximum 2 entries. Work must be original & unpublished. Prince Edward Island residents

only. Entry fee for each submission is $25. See web site for complete entry requirements.
Award: Cash prizes for 1st, 2nd & 3rd place
Closing Date: Jan 31
Presented: Cox & Palmer Island Literary Awards Gala, Annually in Spring

Crook's Corner Book Prize
Crook's Corner Book Prize Foundation
313 Country Club Rd, Chapel Hill, NC 27514
E-mail: info@crookscornerbookprize.com
Web Site: crookscornerbookprize.com
Awarded for the best debut novel set in the American South, which includes the states Alabama, Arkansas, Florida, Georgia, Kentucky, Louisiana, Maryland, Mississippi, North Carolina, Oklahoma, South Carolina, Tennessee, Texas, Virginia, West Virginia, & the District of Columbia. Books may be self-published if they have an ISBN number. However, self-published books must be available through one of the major distributors, Baker & Taylor or Ingram, under regular reseller terms. Self-published authors can arrange for such distribution for a small fee. Books that are available only as e-books are not eligible. Submissions are welcome from authors or publishers. Entry fee: $35.
Award: $5,000 & free glass of wine at Crook's Corner restaurant every day for a year
Closing Date: May 15
Presented: Jan

Crystal Kite Awards
Society of Children's Book Writers & Illustrators (SCBWI)
6363 Wilshire Blvd, Suite 425, Los Angeles, CA 90048
Tel: 323-782-1010
E-mail: grants@scbwi.org; scbwi@scbwi.org
Web Site: www.scbwi.org/awards
Key Personnel
Award Coord: Christopher Cheng E-mail: chris@chrischeng.com
Annual peer-given award to recognize excellence in the field of children's literature in 15 US & international regions. Nominated books must be a PAL book first published within the previous calendar year. Self-published books are not eligible.
Award: Crystal, engraved kite award, opportunity to present at a regional conference, silver sticker for winning book; one winner is chosen to present at the LA Summer Conference
Closing Date: March 21
Presented: May/June

Cundill History Prize
McGill University
3463 Peel St, Montreal, QC H3A 1W7, Canada
Tel: 514-398-8346
E-mail: cundill.prize@mcgill.ca
Web Site: www.cundillprize.com
Key Personnel
Prize Admin: Adriana Goreta
Established: 2008
Awarded annually to the book that embodies historical scholarship, originality, literary quality & broad appeal. Open to books published in English between June 1 of the previous year & May 31 of the year of the award. Translations welcome. Publishers may not submit more than 4 titles. Send 7 copies of each book. Longlist announced in September, shortlist in October.
Other Sponsor(s): The Peter Cundill Foundation
Award: $75,000; $10,000 each to 2 runners-up
Closing Date: June
Presented: Cundhill History Prize Gala, Montreal, QC, CN, Nov

Cunningham Commission for Youth Theatre
The Theatre School, DePaul University

Lincoln Park Campus, 2350 N Racine Ave, Chicago, IL 60614-4100
Tel: 773-325-7999 Fax: 773-325-7920
E-mail: cunninghamcommission@depaul.edu
Web Site: theatre.depaul.edu
Key Personnel
Assoc Dean & Chair, Theatre Studies: Dean Corrin E-mail: dcorrin@depaul.edu
Dir, Mktg & PR: Anna Ables E-mail: aables@depaul.edu
Established: 1991
Playwriting commission, limited to writers whose primary residence is within 100 miles of Chicago's Loop & alumni of The Theatre School.
Award: Up to $5,000 ($2,000 paid when the commission is contracted, $1,000 paid if the script moves to a workshop, $2,000 paid as royalty if the script is produced by The Theatre School)
Closing Date: Annually in April
Presented: June

Merle Curti Intellectual History Award
The Organization of American Historians (OAH)
112 N Bryan Ave, Bloomington, IN 47408-4141
Tel: 812-855-7311
E-mail: oah@oah.org
Web Site: www.oah.org/awards
Key Personnel
Exec Dir: Beth English E-mail: benglish@oah.org
Comm Coord: Kara Hamm E-mail: khamm@oah.org
Awarded annually to the author of the best book in American intellectual history. Each entry must be published during the calendar year preceding that in which the award is given. One copy of each entry must be mailed directly to the committee members listed on the web site.
Closing Date: Oct 1, 2021 (postmarked)
Presented: OAH Annual Meeting, Boston, MA, March 31-April 3, 2022

Merle Curti Social History Award
The Organization of American Historians (OAH)
112 N Bryan Ave, Bloomington, IN 47408-4141
Tel: 812-855-7311
E-mail: oah@oah.org
Web Site: www.oah.org/awards
Key Personnel
Exec Dir: Beth English E-mail: benglish@oah.org
Comm Coord: Kara Hamm E-mail: khamm@oah.org
Awarded annually to the author of the best book in American social history. Each entry must be published during the calendar year preceding that in which the award is given. One copy of each entry must be mailed directly to the committee members listed on the web site.
Closing Date: Oct 1, 2021 (postmarked)
Presented: OAH Annual Meeting, Boston, MA, March 31-April 3, 2022

C Michael Curtis Short Story Book Prize
Hub City Press
186 W Main St, Spartanburg, SC 29306
Tel: 864-577-9349 Fax: 864-577-0188
E-mail: info@hubcity.org; submit@hubcity.org
Web Site: hubcity.org/press/c-michael-curtis-short-story-book-prize
Key Personnel
Dir: Meg Reid E-mail: meg@hubcity.org
Asst Dir: Kate McMullen E-mail: kate@hubcity.org
Open to emerging writers in 13 Southern states: Alabama, Arkansas, Florida, Georgia, Kentucky, Louisiana, Mississippi, North Carolina, South Carolina, Tennessee, Texas, Virginia & West Virginia. $25 submission fee. Online submissions only beginning August 1.
Award: $10,000 & book publication
Closing Date: Jan 1

Karen & Philip Cushman Late Bloomer Award
Society of Children's Book Writers & Illustrators (SCBWI)
6363 Wilshire Blvd, Suite 425, Los Angeles, CA 90048
Tel: 323-782-1010 Fax: 323-782-1892
E-mail: grants@scbwi.org; scbwi@scbwi.org
Web Site: www.scbwi.org
Honors authors over the age of 50 who have not been traditionally published in the children's literature field.
Award: $500 & free tuition to any SCBWI conference anywhere in the world
Closing Date: March 1-31 (submit through the Work-In-Progress application)

Dana Awards
Literary Competition, 200 Fosseway Dr, Greensboro, NC 27455
Tel: 336-644-8028
E-mail: danaawards@gmail.com
Web Site: www.danaawards.com
Key Personnel
Chair: Mary Elizabeth Parker
Established: 1996
Three awards: for unpublished group of poems, short story, novel, (or novel-in-progress). Poetry: submit 5 poems of no more than 100 lines each with a $15 entry fee. Short story: submit up to 10,000 words with a $15 entry fee. Novel: the first 40 pages & a $30 entry fee. All types of novels accepted.
Award: $4,000 total; $1,000 each for short story & poetry, $2,000 for novel
Closing Date: Annually, Oct 31
Presented: All awards, checks & notification are presented by mail or e-mail

Robert Dana-Anhinga Prize for Poetry
Anhinga Press
PO Box 3665, Tallahassee, FL 32315
Tel: 850-577-0745
E-mail: info@anhinga.org
Web Site: www.anhingapress.org
Key Personnel
Co-Dir: Kristine Snodgrass E-mail: kristine.snodgrass@gmail.com
Established: 1983
Open to all poets for a ms of original poetry in English. Reading fee: $25 (by post), $28 (Submittable).
Award: $2,000 & publication
Closing Date: Annually, Feb 15-May 15 (postmark)
Presented: Tallahassee, FL

The Danahy Fiction Prize
Tampa Review
University of Tampa Press, 401 W Kennedy Blvd, Tampa, FL 33606
Tel: 813-253-6266
E-mail: utpress@ut.edu
Web Site: tampareview.ut.edu
Key Personnel
Ed: Richard Mathews
Edit Asst: Sean Donnelly
Established: 2006
Award: $1,000 & publication in Tampa Review
Closing Date: Annually, Dec 31

Benjamin H Danks Award
American Academy of Arts & Letters
633 W 155 St, New York, NY 10032
Tel: 212-368-5900 Fax: 212-491-4615
E-mail: academy@artsandletters.org
Web Site: artsandletters.org
Key Personnel
Exec Dir: Cody Upton
Established: 2003
Annual prize, in rotation, awarded to a composer of ensemble works, a playwright & a writer.
Award: $20,000

Watson Davis & Helen Miles Davis Prize

History of Science Society
Affiliate of American Council of Learned Societies
440 Geddes Hall, Notre Dame, IN 46556
Tel: 574-631-1194
E-mail: info@hssonline.org
Web Site: www.hssonline.org
Key Personnel
Exec Dir: Robert Jay Malone
Established: 1985
For the best book on the history of science directed to a broad public published during the preceding three years.
Award: $1,000 & certificate
Closing Date: April 1
Presented: Awards Banquet, Nov

Dayton Literary Peace Prize

Dayton Literary Peace Prize Foundation
25 Harman Terr, Dayton, OH 45419
Mailing Address: PO Box 461, Wright Brothers Branch, Dayton, OH 45409-0461
Tel: 937-298-5072
Web Site: daytonliterarypeaceprize.org
Key Personnel
Founder & Co-Chair: Sharon Rab *E-mail:* sharon.rab@woh.rr.com
Established: 2006
First & only annual US literary award recognizing the power of the written word to promote peace. This project is the recognition of adult fiction & nonfiction books that have led readers to a better understanding of other cultures, peoples, religions & political points of view. $100 nomination fee.
Award: $10,000 each genre (fiction & nonfiction) plus $2,500 each 1st runner-up
Closing Date: March
Presented: Benjamin & Marian Schuster Performing Arts Center, Dayton, OH, Nov

Dayton Playhouse FutureFest

The Dayton Playhouse
PO Box 3017, Dayton, OH 45401-3017
Tel: 937-424-8477 *Fax:* 937-424-0062
E-mail: futurefest@thedaytonplayhouse.com
Web Site: wordpress.daytonplayhouse.com
Key Personnel
Exec Dir: Brian Sharp
FutureFest Prog Dir: Fran Pesch
Established: 1991
National Playwriting Competition. Entry must be an original work (no musicals or plays for children) that has not been published or produced where admission was charged prior to FutureFest. Send SASE or see web site for submission guidelines.
Award: $1,000 (1st place), $100 (5 runners up) - all 6 finalists are provided travel to & housing for the FutureFest weekend
Closing Date: Aug 1-Oct 31 (postmark)
Presented: The Dayton Playhouse, Annually in July

Delaware Division of the Arts Individual Artist Fellowships

Delaware Division of the Arts
Carvel State Off Bldg, 4th fl, 820 N French St, Wilmington, DE 19801
Tel: 302-577-8278 *Fax:* 302-577-6561
E-mail: delarts@state.de.us
Web Site: www.artsdel.org
Key Personnel
Art & Artist Servs Coord: Roxanne Stanulis
Individual Artist Fellowships will be awarded to beginning or established poets & other creative writers. Applicants must be Delaware residents.
Award: A Masters Fellowship of $10,000 & established Professional Fellowships of $6,000 each & Emerging Professional Fellowships of $3,000

Closing Date: Annually, Aug 1
Presented: Annually (Master's awarded every 3 years in literature); winners notified in Dec

Rick DeMarinis Short Story Award

CUTTHROAT, A Journal of the Arts
PO Box 2414, Durango, CO 81302
Tel: 970-903-7914
E-mail: cutthroatmag@gmail.com
Web Site: www.cutthroatmag.com
Key Personnel
Ed-in-Chief: Pamela Uschuk
Mng Ed: Andrew Allport
Fiction Ed: Beth Alvarado
Submit 1 unpublished short story (5,000 word limit), any subject, any style. Mss must be 12 point font & double-spaced. Reading fee: $20.
Award: $1,300 (1st place), $250 (2nd place), both include publication in *CUTTHROAT*
Closing Date: Annually in Oct
Presented: Annually in Dec

Denver Publishing Institute Scholarship

Book Industry Charitable Foundation
3135 S State St, Suite 203, Ann Arbor, MI 48108
Toll Free Tel: 866-733-9064 *Fax:* 734-477-2806
E-mail: info@bincfoundation.org
Web Site: www.bincfoundation.org/denver-publishing-institute/
Key Personnel
Exec Dir: Pam French *E-mail:* pam@bincfoundation.org
Dir, Devt: Kathy Bartson *E-mail:* kathy@bincfoundation.org
Progs Mgr: Kit Steinaway *E-mail:* kit@bincfoundation.org; Kate Weiss *E-mail:* kate@bincfoundation.org
Established: 2019
Scholarship opportunity for current booksellers interested in exploring a career in the publishing side of the industry. Presented in collaboration with Sourcebooks & the Denver Publishing Institute.
Award: Up to $7,000 to attend the Denver Publishing Institute, including tuition, meal plan, housing & up to $2,000 to cover travel & lost wages
Closing Date: Feb 27

Der-Hovanessian Translation Prize

New England Poetry Club
46 Wallace St, Somerville, MA 02144
E-mail: info@nepoetryclub.org
Web Site: www.nepoetryclub.org
Key Personnel
Pres: Mary Buchinger
VP: Hillary Sallick
Treas: Linda Haviland Conte
For translation from any language. Include the poem in the original language along with the translation. See web site for additional guidelines.
Award: $250
Closing Date: Annually, May 31
Presented: Announced online Aug/Sept

Annual Design Competition

The Society of Publication Designers Inc
27 Union Sq W, Suite 207, New York, NY 10003
Tel: 212-223-3332 *Fax:* 212-223-5880
E-mail: mail@spd.org
Web Site: www.spd.org
Key Personnel
Exec Dir: Keisha Dean
Established: 1975
For continuing excellence in the field of publication design. Approximately 100 categories in Design, Photography & Illustration. Winners include: Magazine of the Year, Brand of the Year, App of the Year, Website of the Year, Video of the Year, Entire Issue, Redesign, Cover, Spread/Single Page & Story.

Closing Date: Jan
Presented: Awards Gala, May

Anna Dewdney Read Together Award

The Children's Book Council (CBC)
54 W 39 St, 14th fl, New York, NY 10018
Tel: 917-890-7416
Web Site: everychildreader.net/anna
Key Personnel
Assoc Exec Dir/Programming & Strategic Partnerships Dir: Shaina Birkhead *E-mail:* shaina.birkhead@cbcbooks.org
Awarded annually to a picture book that is both a superb read aloud & also sparks compassion, empathy & connection. Librarians, teachers, booksellers, parents/caregivers & children's book bloggers are encouraged to nominate up to 5 beloved read-together picture book favorites. Nominators must be 18 years of age or older.
Other Sponsor(s): Every Child A Reader; Penguin Young Readers Group
Award: $1,000
Closing Date: Feb 14
Presented: Children's Book Week

Alice Fay Di Castagnola Award

Poetry Society of America (PSA)
15 Gramercy Park, New York, NY 10003
Tel: 212-254-9628
Web Site: poetrysociety.org/awards
Key Personnel
Pres: Allison Binns
Exec Dir: Matt Brogan *E-mail:* matt@poetrysociety.org
Deputy Dir: Brett Fletcher Lauer *E-mail:* brett@poetrysociety.org
Prog Dir: Laurin Macios *E-mail:* laurin@poetrysociety.org
Established: 1965
Offered in memory of a benefactor or friend of the society. For a ms in progress (poetry, prose or verse drama). Open to society members only. See web site for complete information.
Award: $1,000
Closing Date: Annually, Oct-Dec (postmark)
Presented: Annual Awards Ceremony, New York, NY, Annually in Spring

Diamonstein-Spielvogel Award for the Art of the Essay, see PEN/Diamonstein-Spielvogel Award for the Art of the Essay

Philip K Dick Award

Philadelphia Science Fiction Society
PO Box 3447, Hoboken, NJ 07030
Tel: 201-876-2551
Web Site: www.philipkdickaward.org
Key Personnel
Admin: Patrick Lo Brutto; John Silbersack; Gordon Van Gelder
Established: 1983
Presented annually for distinguished science fiction in paperback original form in the US.
Other Sponsor(s): Philip K Dick Trust; NorthWest Science Fiction Society
Award: $1,000
Closing Date: Dec 1
Presented: Norwescon, SeaTac, WA, Easter weekend

Dickinson, Emily Award, see The Writer Magazine/Emily Dickinson Award

Annie Dillard Award for Creative Nonfiction

The Bellingham Review
Mail Stop 9053, Western Washington University, Bellingham, WA 98225
Tel: 360-650-4863
E-mail: bhreview@wwu.edu
Web Site: www.bhreview.org

Key Personnel
Ed-in-Chief: Suzanne Paola Antonetta
Mng Ed: Mike Oliphant
Established: 1993
Maximum length for prose is 6,000 words. No previously published works, or works accepted for publication, are eligible. Work may be under consideration elsewhere, but must be withdrawn from the competition if accepted for publication. All entries will receive a complimentary 1-issue subscription. Entry fee for the first entry (one nonfiction work) $20. Each additional essay $10.
Only accept submissions through Submittable. Mailed submissions are no longer accepted. All finalists are considered for publication. The winning piece is selected by a distinguished, outside judge. Entries accepted beginning December 1.
Award: $1,000 & publication in the *Bellingham Review* (1st prize), considered for publication (2nd, 3rd & finalists)
Closing Date: Annually, March 15
Presented: Annually in June

Gordon W Dillon/Richard C Peterson Memorial Essay Prize
American Orchid Society Inc
c/o Fairchild Tropical Botanic Garden, 10901 Old Cutler Rd, Coral Gables, FL 33156
Tel: 305-740-2010
E-mail: theaos@aos.org
Web Site: www.aos.org
Key Personnel
Chief Educ & Sci Offr: Ron McHatton, PhD
 E-mail: rmchatton@aos.org
Established: 1985
Essay contest (orchid topics only; new theme announced each year).
Award: Cash award & a certificate of recognition. Winning essay published in the June issue of *Orchids* magazine the following year
Closing Date: Annually, Nov 30

Discovery/Boston Review Poetry Contest
Unterberg Poetry Center
Subsidiary of 92nd Street Y/Tisch Center for the Arts
1395 Lexington Ave, New York, NY 10128
Tel: 212-415-5760
E-mail: unterberg@92y.org
Web Site: www.92y.org/discovery
Key Personnel
Mng Dir: Ricardo Maldonado
 E-mail: rickymaldonado@92y.org
For poets who have not published a full-length poetry collection; for guidelines visit web site. $15 entry fee must accompany the submission.
Other Sponsor(s): *Boston Review*
Award: Publication in *Boston Review*, reading at The Poetry Center & $500 each to the 4 winning authors
Closing Date: Jan 12
Presented: Winner will be announced in the fall on the Boston Review web site

Distinguished Scholarly Book Award
American Sociological Association (ASA)
c/o Governance Off, 1430 "K" St NW, Suite 600, Washington, DC 20005
Tel: 202-383-9005 *Fax:* 202-638-0882
E-mail: governance@asanet.org
Web Site: www.asanet.org
Key Personnel
Dir, Admin & Governance: Michael Murphy
 Tel: 202-383-9005 ext 327
Prog Coord: Jordan Robison *Tel:* 202-383-9005 ext 334
This award is given for a single book published in the 2 calendar years preceding the award year. Any member of the ASA may nominate books for consideration for this award. Nom-

inations should include name of author, title of book, date of publication, publisher & brief statements (of no more than 300 words) as to why the book should be considered. Nominations sent from publishers who are not active members of ASA will not be accepted. Send nominations to: ASA office at above address.
Award: Plaque
Closing Date: Jan 31
Presented: ASA Annual Meeting, Montreal, QC, CN, Annually in Aug

Catherine Doctorow Innovative Fiction Prize, see The FC2 Catherine Doctorow Innovative Fiction Prize

Documentation Grant Program
New Brunswick Arts Board (Conseil des arts du Nouveau-Brunswick)
225 King St, Suite 201, Fredericton, NB E3B 1E1, Canada
Tel: 506-444-4444 *Toll Free Tel:* 866-460-ARTS (460-2787) *Fax:* 506-444-5543
Web Site: www.artsnb.ca
Key Personnel
Exec Dir: Joss Richer *Tel:* 506-478-4610
 E-mail: execdirgen@artsnb.ca
Prog Offr: Sarah Elizabeth Parker *Tel:* 506-440-0037 *E-mail:* sarahbeth@artsnb.ca
Opers Mgr: Tilly Jackson *Tel:* 506-478-4422
 E-mail: tjackson@artsnb.ca
Designed to provide assistance to New Brunswick arts professionals & professional artists for the research, development & execution of original documentation & contextualization (written, film, video, multimedia) of arts activities, arts products or art history. Documentation grants are intended to foster theoretical & critical discourse in the arts. Preference will be given to proposals concerning New Brunswick art or artists.
Closing Date: April 1, Oct 1

Blake Dodd Prize
American Academy of Arts & Letters
633 W 155 St, New York, NY 10032
Tel: 212-368-5900 *Fax:* 212-491-4615
E-mail: academy@artsandletters.org
Web Site: artsandletters.org
Key Personnel
Exec Dir: Cody Upton
Established: 2014
Triennial award for a nonfiction writer.
Award: $25,000

Dog Writers' Association of America Inc (DWAA) Annual Writing Competition
Dog Writers' Association of America Inc (DWAA)
PO Box 787, Hughesville, MD 20637
E-mail: info@dogwriters.org
Web Site: dogwriters.org
Key Personnel
Pres: Jen Reeder *E-mail:* jen@jenreeder.com
VP: Laura Coffey *E-mail:* laura.coffey@nbcuni.com
Treas: Marsha Pugh *E-mail:* marsha_pugh01@comcast.net
Secy: Laurren Darr *E-mail:* laurrendarr@leftpawpress.com
Contest Chair: Su Ewing *E-mail:* dogwriter@windstream.net
Established: 1935
To give recognition to an individual, club or group which has done an outstanding job in the dog writing field in numerous categories. Only original work published between September 1 & August 31 of the competition year.
Other Sponsor(s): ACK Reunite; American Kennel Club; American Legion Post No 348; Canine Scribbles; Ceva Animal Health; James Colasanti Jr; Dogwise Publishing; Fear Free

LLC; GNFP Digital; Babette Haggerty; International Association of Pet Fashion Professionals; Morris Animal Foundation; Pet Sitters International; Westminster Kennel Club
Award: Approximately $14,000 in cash prizes; plaques, Maxwell Medallions & certificates
Closing Date: Sept 7 (postmark or submitted online)
Presented: Annual Awards Banquet, New York, NY, Feb, Saturday before Westminster Kennel Club Dog Show

The Christopher Doheny Award
The Center for Fiction
17 E 47 St, New York, NY 10017
Tel: 212-755-6710
E-mail: doheny@centerforfiction.org; info@centerforfiction.org
Web Site: www.centerforfiction.org/awards/the-christopher-doheny-award
Key Personnel
Writing Progs Mgr: Thierry Kehou
 E-mail: thierry@centerforfiction.org
Annual award to recognize excellence in fiction or nonfiction on the topic of serious physical illness by a writer who has personally dealt with or is dealing with life-threatening illness, either his or her own or that of a close relative or friend.
Other Sponsor(s): Audible Inc
Award: $10,000, publication & promotion of book in print & audio

Donner Prize
Donner Canadian Foundation
c/o Naylor and Associates, 23 Empire Ave, Toronto, ON M4M 2L3, Canada
Tel: 416-368-8253
E-mail: donnerprize@naylorandassociates.com
Web Site: donnerbookprize.com
Key Personnel
Prize Mgr: Sherry Naylor *E-mail:* sherry@naylorandassociates.com
Annual prize to recognize & reward the best public policy thinking, writing & research by a Canadian & the role it plays in determining the well-being of Canadians & the success of Canada as a whole. All entries must be published in English or French between January 1 & December 31 of the prize year. Entries must be submitted by the publisher. Six copies of each title must be delivered to the Prize Manager by the deadline. If an electronic version is available, please e-mail a copy in addition to sending printed versions. For titles published between November 3 & December 31, the publisher may submit bound galleys or mss. See web site for full eligibility & submission guidelines.
Closing Date: Nov 30

Dorothy Canfield Fisher Book Award
Vermont Department of Libraries
109 State St, Montpelier, VT 05609-0601
Tel: 802-828-2721
Web Site: libraries.vermont.gov
Key Personnel
Chpn: Hannah Peacock *E-mail:* hpeacock@colchestervt.gov
Lib Advancement Asst: Jennifer Johnson
 E-mail: jennifer.johnson@vermont.gov
Established: 1956
For a book by a living American or Canadian author published one year previous, chosen by the children of Vermont, grades 4-8, from a master list of 30 titles.
Other Sponsor(s): Friends of Dorothy Canfield Fisher
Award: Piece of artwork from a local artist
Closing Date: Annually, Dec 1
Presented: Annually in May

Dorset Prize
Tupelo Press Inc
60 Roberts Dr, Suite 308, North Adams, MA 01247
SAN: 254-3281
Tel: 413-664-9611 *Fax:* 413-664-9711
E-mail: info@tupelopress.org
Web Site: www.tupelopress.org
Key Personnel
Publr: Jeffrey Levine *E-mail:* publisher@ tupelopress.org
Ed-in-Chief: Kristina Marie Darling
   E-mail: kdarling@tupelopress.org
Established: 2003
An open book competition for poetry. Full guidelines on the web site. Entries accepted beginning September 1.
Award: $3,000, publication & national distribution
Closing Date: Dec 31
Presented: Spring

John Dos Passos Prize for Literature
Longwood University
Dept of English & Modern Languages, 201 High St, Farmville, VA 23909
Tel: 434-395-2155 *Fax:* 434-395-2145
Web Site: www.longwood.edu/english/dos-passos-prize
Key Personnel
Chpn, Dos Passos Comm: Dr David Magill
Dept Chpn: Dr Wade Edwards
Established: 1980
To honor an imaginative prose writer. Preference given to those not previously honored. Winners are nominated & selected by a jury. Applications not accepted.
Award: $2,000 & medallion
Presented: Longwood University, Farmville, VA, Generally during fall semester

Frank Nelson Doubleday Memorial Award
Wyoming Arts Council
Division of Wyoming Department of Parks & Cultural Resources
Barrett Bldg, 2nd fl, 2301 Central Ave, Cheyenne, WY 82002
Tel: 307-777-7742
Web Site: wyoarts.state.wy.us
Key Personnel
Public Art & Creative Sector Indivs Supv: Rachel Clifton *Tel:* 307-777-5305 *E-mail:* rachel.clifton@state.wy.us
Established: 1988
Best poetry, fiction, nonfiction or drama written by a woman author. Wyoming residents only. Blind judges & single juror.
Award: $1,000
Closing Date: Varies, see web site
Presented: Announced in the Fall

Dragonfly Book Awards
Story Monsters LLC
4696 W Tyson St, Chandler, AZ 85226-2903
Tel: 480-940-8182 *Fax:* 480-940-8787
E-mail: info@StoryMonsters.com
Web Site: www.DragonflyBookAwards.com
Key Personnel
Pres: Linda F Radke *E-mail:* Linda@ StoryMonsters.com
Established: 2009
The Royal Dragonfly Book Awards honor published authors of all types of literature—fiction & nonfiction—in 66 categories. Entry fees: $60 per category (on or before August 1), $65 per category (after August 1).
The Purple Dragonfly Book Awards honor accomplished authors in the field of children's literature. 54 subject categories. Entry fees: $60 per category (on or before March 15), $65 per category (after March 15).
The awards contests are open to books published in any calendar year & in any country as long as they are available for purchase. Books entered must be printed in English. Provided they adhere to the above criteria, we accept traditionally published, partnership published & self-published books.
Printed Books: Mail two (2) copies of each book for each category in which it is entered. Along with the books, send one (1) printed copy of the e-mail confirmation per title for each category in which the book is entered. When submitting more than one book, all entries can be sent in the same envelope. Mail entries to: Cristy Bertini, Attn: Dragonfly Book Awards, 1271 Turkey St, Hardwick, MA 01082.
Ebooks: E-mail one (1) electronic copy of the book & a copy of the e-mail confirmation to cristy@storymonsters.com with "Dragonfly Book Awards" as the subject.
Award: Grand prize winner $500, certificate & 100 seals; 1st place winners receive certificate & 25 award seals & go in drawing for $100 (1 winner); 2nd place winners receive certificate & 5 award seals; honorable mentions receive certificate & 3 award seals
Closing Date: Purple Dragonfly: Annually, March 1 (early), May 1 (final); Royal Dragonfly: Annually, Aug 1 (early), Oct 1 (final)
Presented: Award is mailed

Carleton Drewry Memorial
The Poetry Society of Virginia
900 Timber Creek Place, Virginia Beach, VA 23464
E-mail: poetryinva@aol.com
Web Site: poetrysocietyofvirginia.org
Key Personnel
Pres: Robert P Arthur *E-mail:* robert.peebles.arthur@gmail.com
Exec Dir: Guy Terrell *E-mail:* guy.terrell@ earthlink.net
Adult Contest Chair: Steven Blythe
   E-mail: stevenblythepoetry@gmail.com
Lyric or sonnet. Must be in English, original & unpublished. Submit 2 copies, each having the category name & number on top left of page. Entries will not be returned. Subject: farm life or working the Earth; 48 line limit. Entry fee: $4 nonmembs.
Award: $50 (1st prize), $30 (2nd prize), $20 (3rd prize)
Closing Date: Jan
Presented: Annual PSV Awards Ceremony, April

Saint Katharine Drexel Award
Catholic Library Association
8550 United Plaza Blvd, Suite 1001, Baton Rouge, LA 70809
Tel: 225-408-4417 *Fax:* 225-408-4422
E-mail: cla2@cathla.org
Web Site: cathla.org
Established: 1966
Recognizes an outstanding contribution to the growth of high school librarianship.
Award: Plaque
Closing Date: None; in-house votes
Presented: CLA Annual Convention, April

Drury University One-Act Play Competition
Drury University
900 N Benton Ave, Springfield, MO 65802-3344
Tel: 417-873-6821
Web Site: www.drury.edu
Key Personnel
Professor, Theatre: Dr Mick Sokol
   E-mail: msokol@drury.edu
Established: 1986
Biennial award for one-act plays. Open to all playwrights. Scripts are to be original, unpublished & unproduced; staged readings or workshop productions will not disqualify a script; musicals, monologues, children's plays & adaptations will not be considered; only stage plays will be judged; preference will be given to small cast, one-set shows with running times of no less than 20 & no more than 45 minutes; no more than one script per author; all scripts are to be typewritten & firmly bound; scripts cannot be acknowledged or returned unless accompanied by a SASE.
Award: $300 plus consideration for production by Drury University (1st prize); 2 honorable mentions $150 each
Closing Date: Dec 1, even-numbered years
Presented: By mail no later than April 1, odd-numbered years

Dubuque Fine Arts Players Annual One Act Play Festival
Dubuque Fine Arts Players
Subsidiary of Dubuque County Fine Arts Society
PO Box 1160, Dubuque, IA 52004-1160
Tel: 563-588-3438
E-mail: contact@dbqoneacts.org
Web Site: www.dbqoneacts.org
Key Personnel
Pres: Art Roche
Established: 1977
Annual national one-act playwriting contest. Entry form & guidelines are available at the web site. Submit the entry form, two copies of the script, a synopsis of the play & entry fee. Plays may be submitted by US mail with a $15 entry fee. SASE should be enclosed if return of the reader evaluation forms +/or the scripts is desired. Plays may be submitted online for an entry fee of $20. The higher fee pays cost of printing & binding the play. Previously published or produced works, musicals & children's plays are not accepted.
Award: $600 (1st prize), $300 (2nd prize), $200 (3rd prize), production of first 3 winning plays unless production is beyond our capacity
Closing Date: Jan 31
Presented: Mindframe Theater, 555 John F Kennedy Rd, Dubuque, IA, Mid-Sept

John H Dunning Prize in United States History
American Historical Association (AHA)
400 "A" St SE, Washington, DC 20003
Tel: 202-544-2422 *Fax:* 202-544-8307
E-mail: awards@historians.org
Web Site: www.historians.org
Established: 1927
Biennial award in recognition of outstanding historical writing in US history. To be awarded to a young scholar for an outstanding monograph in ms or in print on any subject relating to US history. To be eligible for consideration, an entry must be of a scholarly historical nature. It must be the author's first or second book, published in 2019 or 2020. Research accuracy, originality & literary merit are important factors. Along with an application form, applicants must mail a copy of their book to each of the prize committee members who will be posted on our web site as the prize deadline approaches. All updated info on web site.
Award: Cash prize
Closing Date: May 15, 2021
Presented: AHA Annual Meeting, New Orleans, LA, Jan 2022

Eaton Literary Associates Literary Awards
Eaton Literary Agency Inc
PO Box 49795, Sarasota, FL 34230-6795
Tel: 941-366-6589 *Fax:* 941-365-4679
E-mail: eatonlit@aol.com
Web Site: www.eatonliterary.com
Key Personnel
Pres: Richard Lawrence
Established: 1984
Two awards are given, one for a book-length ms & one for a short story or article. These entries should not have been previously published.

Award: $2,500 (book-length program), $500 (short story or article program)

Closing Date: Annually, March 31 (short story or article program), Aug 31 (book-length program)

Presented: Annually in April (short story or article program), Sept (book-length program)

Edgar Allan Poe Awards®, see The Edgar Awards®

The Edgar Awards®
Mystery Writers of America (MWA)
1140 Broadway, Suite 1507, New York, NY 10001
Tel: 212-888-8171
E-mail: mwa@mysterywriters.org
Web Site: theedgars.com; www.mysterywriters.org
Key Personnel
Admin Dir: Margery Flax
Established: 1945
For the best mystery novel & best first novel by an American author. Also awards for best juvenile novel & young adult, fact-crime writing, TV episode, short story, paperback original, critical/biographical work. The work must be published for the first time in the US in the calendar year prior to the award.
Award: Ceramic bust of Poe
Closing Date: Annually, Nov 30
Presented: New York, NY, Annually in late Spring

Editorial Excellence
Biographers International Organization (BIO)
PO Box 33020, Santa Fe, NM 87594
Web Site: biographersinternational.org
Key Personnel
Admin & Membership Coord: Lori Izykowski *E-mail:* lori@biographersinternational.org
Established: 2014
Awarded annually to an outstanding editor from nominations submitted by BIO members.

Editor's Award
Poets & Writers Inc
90 Broad St, Suite 2100, New York, NY 10004
Tel: 212-226-3586 *Fax:* 212-226-3963
Web Site: www.pw.org/about-us/sponsored-prizes
Key Personnel
Mng Dir: Melissa Ford Gradel *Tel:* 212-226-3586 ext 223
Established: 2009
Annual award to recognize a book editor who has made an outstanding contribution to the publication of poetry or literary prose over a sustained period of time.
Presented: Poets & Writers annual dinner

Education Award of Excellence
PRINTING United Alliance
10015 Main St, Fairfax, VA 22031-3489
Tel: 703-385-1335 *Toll Free Tel:* 888-385-3588 *Fax:* 703-273-0456
E-mail: marketing@printing.org
Web Site: www.printing.org/programs/awards/education-award-of-excellence
Key Personnel
Pres & CEO: Ford Bowers *E-mail:* fbowers@printing.org
Established: 1984
Honors one industry representative & one graphic arts educator who have each made outstanding contributions to graphic arts education +/or training. See web site for more information.
Award: Engraved plaque
Closing Date: Oct 31
Presented: TAGA Annual Technical Conference, March

Branch Office(s)
1325 "G" St NW, Suite 500, Washington, DC 20005
2000 Corporate Dr, Suite 205, Wexford, PA 15090 *Tel:* 412-741-6860 *Toll Free Tel:* 800-910-4283 *Fax:* 412-741-2311

Educators Award
The Delta Kappa Gamma Society International
PO Box 1589, Austin, TX 78767-1589
Tel: 512-478-5748 *Toll Free Tel:* 888-762-4685 *Fax:* 512-478-3961
E-mail: societyexec@dkg.org
Web Site: www.dkg.org
Key Personnel
Membership Servs Admin: Nita Scott *Tel:* 512-478-5748 ext 113 *E-mail:* nitas@dkg.org
Annual award to the woman author(s) of a book whose work may influence the direction of thought & action necessary to meet the needs of today's complex society. The content must be of more than local interest with relationship, direct or implied, to education everywhere. The author must be a woman from Canada, Costa Rica, El Salvador, Estonia, Finland, Germany, Great Britain, Guatemala, Iceland, Mexico, Netherlands, Norway, Puerto Rico, Sweden, Japan or the US; call, e-mail or download regulations. All nominations are made by publishers or authors.
Award: $2,500
Closing Date: Feb 1 (postmark), in the year after copyright
Presented: One of five regional conferences or Society's International Convention, Summer

Margaret A Edwards Award
Young Adult Library Services Association (YALSA)
Division of The American Library Association (ALA)
50 E Huron St, Chicago, IL 60611
Tel: 312-280-4390 *Toll Free Tel:* 800-545-2433 *Fax:* 312-280-5276
E-mail: yalsa@ala.org
Web Site: www.ala.org/yalsa/edwards
Key Personnel
Exec Dir: Anita Mechler
Prog Offr, Events & Conferences: Nichole O'Connor *Tel:* 800-545-2433 ext 4387 *E-mail:* noconnor@ala.org
Communs Specialist: Anna Lam *Tel:* 800-545-2433 ext 5849 *E-mail:* alam@ala.org
Established: 1988
Given to an author for lifetime achievement in helping adolescents become aware of themselves & addressing questions about their role & importance in relationships, society & in the world.
Other Sponsor(s): School Library Journal
Award: $1,000 & citation
Closing Date: Annually in June
Presented: Announced at ALA's Midwinter Meeting. Winner honored & speaks during a luncheon at ALA's Annual Conference

Edwin Markham Prize for Poetry
Reed Magazine
San Jose State University, English Dept, One Washington Sq, San Jose, CA 95192-0090
Tel: 408-924-4441
E-mail: mail@reedmag.org
Web Site: www.reedmag.org; reedmagazine.submittable.com
All submissions must be through the online system. Writers may submit up to 5 poems per entry. Submit all poems as a single document. Reading fee: $15.
Award: $1,000 & publication in *Reed Magazine*
Closing Date: Annually, Nov 1 (submissions accepted beginning June 1)

The Maureen Egen Writers Exchange Award
Poets & Writers Inc
90 Broad St, Suite 2100, New York, NY 10004
Tel: 212-226-3586 *Fax:* 212-226-3963
E-mail: admin@pw.org
Web Site: www.pw.org
Established: 1984
Introduces emerging writers to the New York literary community & provides them with a network for professional advancement.
Award: All expenses-paid trip to New York City to meet with top literary professionals & give a public reading

Wilfrid Eggleston Award for Nonfiction
Writers' Guild of Alberta
11759 Groat Rd, Edmonton, AB T5M 3K6, Canada
Tel: 780-422-8174 *Toll Free Tel:* 800-665-5354 (AB only) *Fax:* 780-422-2663 (attn WGA)
E-mail: mail@writersguild.ca
Web Site: writersguild.ca
Key Personnel
Exec Dir: Carol Holmes *E-mail:* carol.holmes@writersguild.ca
Communs & Partnerships Coord: Ellen Kartz *E-mail:* ellen.kartz@writersguild.ca
Memb Servs Coord: Giorgia Severini
Progs Coord: Natalie Cook *E-mail:* natalie.cook@writersguild.ca; Julie Robinson *E-mail:* julie.robinson@writersguild.ca
Established: 1982
Alberta Literary Award, author must be resident of Alberta.
Award: $1,500 plus leather-bound copy of book
Closing Date: Annually, Dec 31
Presented: Alberta Book Awards Gala
Branch Office(s)
505 21 Ave SW, Calgary, AB T2S 0G9, Canada, Prog Coord: Samantha Warwick *Tel:* 403-265-2226 *E-mail:* samantha.warwick@writersguild.ca

EJK Book Award, see Ezra Jack Keats Book Award

T S Eliot Prize for Poetry
Truman State University Press
100 E Normal Ave, Kirksville, MO 63501-4221
Tel: 660-785-7336 *Toll Free Tel:* 800-916-6802 *Fax:* 660-785-4480
E-mail: tsup@truman.edu
Web Site: tsup.truman.edu
Key Personnel
Dir & Ed-in-Chief: Barbara Smith-Mandell *E-mail:* bsm@truman.edu
Established: 1997
Annual award for the best unpublished book-length collection of poetry in English. Include a non-refundable reading fee of $25 for each ms submitted.
Award: $2,000 & publication
Closing Date: Oct 31
Presented: Feb

eLit Awards
Independent Publisher Online
1129 Woodmere Ave, Suite B, Traverse City, MI 49686
Tel: 231-933-0445 *Toll Free Tel:* 800-706-4636 *Fax:* 231-933-0448
E-mail: info@elitawards.com
Web Site: www.elitawards.com
Key Personnel
CEO: Jerrold R Jenkins *E-mail:* jrj@bookpublishing.com
Pres: James Kalajian *Tel:* 800-706-4636 ext 1006 *E-mail:* jjk@bookpublishing.com
Dir: Andrew Parvel *Tel:* 800-706-4636 ext 1004 *E-mail:* aparvel@bookpublishing.com
Established: 2009

To celebrate the ever growing market of electronic publishing in the wide variety of reader formats. Publishers & authors worldwide creating electronic books written in English & created for the global marketplace are eligible for entry in 65 different categories.
Other Sponsor(s): Jenkins Group
Award: Digital seal, certificate, winners featured online
Closing Date: Annually in Jan
Presented: Online, Annually in April

Van Courtlandt Elliott Prize

Medieval Academy of America
17 Dunster St, Suite 202, Cambridge, MA 02138
Tel: 617-491-1622 *Fax:* 617-492-3303
E-mail: info@themedievalacademy.org
Web Site: www.medievalacademy.org
Key Personnel
Exec Dir: Lisa Fagin Davis *E-mail:* lfd@themedievalacademy.org
Established: 1971
For a first article published in the field of medieval studies. Author must be a resident in North America.
Award: $1,000
Closing Date: Annually, Oct 15
Presented: Annually in April

Arthur Ellis Awards

Crime Writers of Canada (CWC)
716 Thicket Way, Ottawa, ON K4A 3B5, Canada
E-mail: arthur_ellis@crimewriterscanada.com
Web Site: www.crimewriterscanada.com/awards
Key Personnel
Exec Dir: Alison Bruce *E-mail:* ed@crimewriterscanada.com
Asst Exec Dir & Arthur Ellis Awards Mgr: Ludvica Boota *E-mail:* aed@crimewriterscanada.com
Established: 1984
Annual awards to acknowledge distinction in Canadian crime writing. Open to permanent residents of Canada or Canadian citizens living abroad. Seven categories: Best crime novel, best crime first novel, best crime novella, best crime short story, best French crime book (fiction & nonfiction), best juvenile or young adult crime book (fiction & nonfiction) best nonfiction crime book. An 8th category, The Unhanged Arthur for Best Unpublished Manuscript, is open to writers who are not published novelists.
Other Sponsor(s): Dundurn; Mystery Weekly; Rakuten Kobo
Closing Date: Dec 15
Presented: Arthur Ellis Awards Banquet, Toronto, ON, CN, Last Thurs in May

Ralph Ellison Award

Oklahoma Center for the Book (OCB)
200 NE 18 St, Oklahoma City, OK 73105-3205
Tel: 405-522-3383
Web Site: libraries.ok.gov/ocb/oklahoma-book-awards
Irregular award honoring a deceased Oklahoma writer.

Emerging Critics Fellowship

National Book Critics Circle
c/o 310 Lewis Ave, Brooklyn, NY 11221
E-mail: info@bookcritics.org
Web Site: bookcritics.org
Key Personnel
VP, Membership & Awards: Yahdon Israel *E-mail:* yahdonisrael@bookcritics.org
One-year fellowship for critics who have demonstrated a genuine interest & commitment to engaging in critical conversation about books. Each writer must submit a resume, 3 writing examples, 300-500 word statement of purpose

& names/contact information for 2 references. To apply, see nbcc.submittable.com/submit.
Closing Date: Jan
Presented: Announcement early March

Emerging Playwright Award

Urban Stages
555 Eighth Ave, Suite 1800, New York, NY 10018
Tel: 212-421-1380 *Fax:* 212-421-1387
E-mail: urbanstage@aol.com
Key Personnel
Artistic Dir & Founder: Frances Hill
Literary Dir: Antoinette Mullins
Scripts not previously produced; scripts should have no more than 7 characters; well-written, imaginative situations & dialog; multicultural scripts are given special attention. Playwrights in & around NYC are given special attention. No processing fee & SASE with all submissions. Selected scripts are first given a staged reading. A select number of staged readings are given intensive workshops. A select number of workshopped plays are given full off-Broadway productions. Award given to playwrights of full productions at Urban Stages.
Award: $500
Closing Date: Year-round
Presented: New York City, NY

Emerging Voices Fellowship

PEN America
Affiliate of PEN International
8444 Wilshire Blvd, 4th fl, Beverly Hills, CA 90211
Tel: 323-424-4939 *Fax:* 323-424-4944
Web Site: pen.org/emerging-voices-fellowship
Key Personnel
Exec Dir: Michelle Franke *Tel:* 323-424-4939 ext 1 *E-mail:* mfranke@pen.org
Fellowship Mgr: Amanda Fletcher *Tel:* 323-424-4939 ext 1002 *E-mail:* afletcher@pen.org
Established: 1996
Literary mentorship that aims to provide new writers who are isolated from the literary establishment with the tools, skills & knowledge they need to launch a professional writing career. Fellowship is directed toward poets & writers of fiction & creative nonfiction with clear ideas of what they hope to accomplish through their writing. Application period begins June 1.
Award: Seven-month fellowship & $1,000 stipend
Closing Date: Aug 1

The Ralph Waldo Emerson Award

The Phi Beta Kappa Society
1606 New Hampshire Ave NW, Washington, DC 20009
Tel: 202-265-3808 *Fax:* 202-986-1601
E-mail: awards@pbk.org
Web Site: www.pbk.org/bookawards
Key Personnel
Prog & Event Specialist: Laura Hartnett *Tel:* 202-745-3287 *E-mail:* lhartnett@pbk.org
Established: 1960
For scholarly studies that contribute to interpretations of the intellectual & cultural condition of humanity. To be eligible, must have been published in US by American author. Works in history, philosophy, religion & related fields such as social sciences & anthropology are eligible. Nomination must come from publisher & be submitted online.
Award: $10,000
Closing Date: Annually in Jan
Presented: Washington, DC, Annually in Dec

Empire State Award for Excellence in Literature for Young People

New York Library Association
6021 State Farm Rd, Guilderland, NY 12084

Tel: 518-432-6952 *Toll Free Tel:* 800-252-6952 *Fax:* 518-427-1697
E-mail: info@nyla.org
Web Site: www.nyla.org
Key Personnel
Exec Dir: Jeremy Johannesen *Tel:* 518-432-6952 ext 101 *E-mail:* director@nyla.org
Communs & Mktg Mgr: Kelsey Dorado *Tel:* 518-432-6952 ext 105 *E-mail:* marketing@nyla.org
Established: 1990
One-time award presented to a living author or illustrator currently residing in New York State. The award honors excellence in children's or young adult literature & a body of work that has made a significant contribution to literature for young people.
Award: Engraved medallion
Presented: Annual Conference, Annually in Oct or Nov

Engel Findley Award, see Writers' Trust Engel Findley Award

Paul Engle Prize

Iowa City UNESCO City of Literature
123 S Linn St, Iowa City, IA 52240
E-mail: info@iowacityofliterature.org
Web Site: www.iowacityofliterature.org/paul-engle-prize
Key Personnel
Exec Dir: John Kenyon *Tel:* 319-356-5245 *E-mail:* john-kenyon@iowacityofliterature.org
Dir, Opers: Rachael Carlson *Tel:* 319-887-6100 *E-mail:* rachael-carlson@iowacityofliterature.org
Mktg Asst: Sarah Nelson *E-mail:* sarah-nelson@iowacityofliterature.org
Established: 2011
Annual prize to honor an individual who represents a pioneering spirit in the world of literature through writing, editing, publishing, or teaching & whose active participation in the larger issues of the day has contributed to the betterment of the world through the literary arts. Nominations open November 1.
Award: 10,000 & one-of-a-kind work of art
Presented: Iowa City Book Festival, Iowa City, IA, Oct

Norma Epstein Foundation Awards in Creative Writing

University of Toronto - University College
15 King's College Circle, UC 165, Toronto, ON M5S 3H7, Canada
Tel: 416-978-8083 *Fax:* 416-978-8854
E-mail: uc.programs@utoronto.ca
Web Site: www.uc.utoronto.ca/writing-centre
Key Personnel
Registrar: Shelley Cornack
Academic Liaison & Asst to Vice Principal: Khamla Sengthavy *E-mail:* khamla.sengthavy@utoronto.ca
Biennial literary competition. Five categories: poetry, drama, novel, short story & other prose.
Award: Up to a total of $2,000
Closing Date: May 1, odd-numbered years
Presented: Toronto, Nov, odd-numbered years

The Ernest Sandeen & Richard Sullivan Prizes in Fiction & Poetry

University of Notre Dame Press/ND Creative Writing Program, Dept of English
356 O'Shaughnessy Hall, Notre Dame, IN 46556
Tel: 574-631-7526 *Fax:* 574-631-4795
E-mail: creativewriting@nd.edu
Web Site: english.nd.edu/creative-writing/prizes-awards/sandeen-sullivan-prizes/
Key Personnel
Dir: Prof Joyelle McSweeney
Awarded to authors who have published at least one volume of short fiction or one volume of poetry. Include a photocopy of the copyright &

the title page of your previous volume. Vanity press publications do not fulfill this requirement. Please include a vita +/or a biographical statement which includes your publishing history. We will be glad to see a selection of reviews of the earlier collection. Submit two copies of your ms & inform us if the ms is available electronically. Include a SASE for acknowledgment of receipt of your submission. If you would like your ms returned, send a SASE. A $15 administrative fee should accompany submissions.
Both prizes are awarded biannually, Ernest Sandeen Prize in even-numbered years & Richard Sullivan Prize in odd-numbered years.
Award: $1,000 prize, $500 award & $500 advance against royalties from the Notre Dame Press
Closing Date: July 1-31, 2021 (Richard Sullivan Prize); March 1-June 1, 2022 (Ernest Sandeen Prize)
Presented: Spring following submission period

Erskine J Poetry Prize
Smartish Pace
PO Box 22161, Baltimore, MD 21203
E-mail: smartishpace@gmail.com
Web Site: www.smartishpace.com
Key Personnel
Founder & Ed: Stephen Reichert
  E-mail: sreichert@smartishpace.com
Established: 2001
All poems submitted for the prize will be considered for publication in *Smartish Pace*. Online submissions at www.smartishpace.com. Postal submissions: submit 3 poems along with a $10 entry fee. Additional poems may be submitted for $1 per poem. No more than 20 poems may be submitted. All entries must include bio. Include a SASE with entry. Include name, address, e-mail & telephone number on each page of poetry submitted. Write or print "Erskine J" on the top of each poem submitted.
Award: $200 & publication of winning poem in *Smartish Pace* (1st prize). All finalists will be published in *Smartish Pace*
Closing Date: Annually, Nov 1
Presented: Baltimore, MD

ESPN Award for Literary Sports Writing, see PEN/ESPN Award for Literary Sports Writing

ESPN Lifetime Achievement Award for Literary Sports Writing, see PEN/ESPN Lifetime Achievement Award for Literary Sports Writing

David W & Beatrice C Evans Biography & Handcart Awards
Mountain West Center for Regional Studies
Division of College of Humanities & Social Sciences-Utah State University
0735 Old Main Hill, Logan, UT 84322-0735
Tel: 435-797-0299 *Fax:* 435-797-1092
E-mail: mwc@usu.edu
Web Site: mountainwest.usu.edu
Key Personnel
Prog Dir: Evelyn I Funda
Established: 1983
For the best published biography, autobiography or memoir with a significant biographical content of an individual associated with "Mormon Country" (a geographical, not religious, concept) published in 2019 or 2020.
Award: $10,000 (The Evans Biography Award); $2,500 (The Evans Handcart Award)
Closing Date: Feb 15, 2021
Presented: Utah State University, Annually in Fall

EXCEL Awards
Association Media & Publishing (AM&P)

Division of Connectiv
1090 Vermont Ave NW, 6th fl, Washington, DC 20005-4905
Tel: 212-784-6398
E-mail: awards@associationmediaandpublishing.org; info@associationmediaandpublishing.org
Web Site: www.siia.net/amp; kellencompany.com
Key Personnel
Exec Dir: Michael Marchesano *Tel:* 646-568-1309 *E-mail:* executivedirector@associationmediaandpublishing.org
Service excellence awards program for association publishers. The EXCEL program judges over 1,200 magazines, newsletters, scholarly journals, electronic publications & web sites in the areas of editorial quality, design, general excellence, most improved & more.
Award: Gold Award (1st prize) brass statues; Silver & Bronze (2nd & 3rd prizes) framed certificates; EXTRA! Award, best of the gold, silver & bronze winners
Closing Date: Annually in Jan
Presented: Excel Awards Gala, Annual Meeting

Excellence in Graphic Literature Awards
Pop Culture Classroom
2760 W Fifth Ave, Denver, CO 80204
Tel: 303-325-1236
E-mail: egl@popcultureclassroom.org
Web Site: popcultureclassroom.org/egl
Key Personnel
Exec Dir: Sam Fuqua
Established: 2018
Awards to create a greater awareness of the value the comics medium & the graphic novel format bring to the world of reading. Submissions accepted for any book-length works published during the previous calendar year. Categories: Best in Children's Books; Best in Middle Grade Books; Best in Young Books; Best in Adult Books; Mosaic Award; Book of the Year.
Other Sponsor(s): Denver Comic-Con
Award: Trophy & medallion for book promotion

John K Fairbank Prize in East Asian History
American Historical Association (AHA)
400 "A" St SE, Washington, DC 20003
Tel: 202-544-2422 *Fax:* 202-544-8307
E-mail: awards@historians.org
Web Site: www.historians.org
Established: 1968
Outstanding book on the history of China proper, Vietnam, Chinese Central Asia, Mongolia, Manchuria, Korea or Japan substantially after 1800; books published in 2020 will be eligible; anthologies, edited works & pamphlets are ineligible for the competition. Along with an application form, applicants must mail a copy of their book to each of the prize committee members who will be posted on our web site as the prize deadline approaches. All updated info on web site.
Award: Cash prize
Closing Date: May 15, 2021
Presented: AHA Annual Meeting, New Orleans, LA, Jan 2022

Tom Fairley Award for Editorial Excellence
Editors' Association of Canada (Association canadienne des reviseurs)
1507-180 Dundas St W, Toronto, ON M5G 1Z8, Canada
Tel: 416-975-1379 *Toll Free Tel:* 866-CAN-EDIT (226-3348) *Fax:* 416-975-1637
E-mail: fairley_award@editors.ca; info@editors.ca
Web Site: www.editors.ca; www.reviseurs.ca
Key Personnel
Exec Dir: John Yip-Chuck
  E-mail: executivedirector@editors.ca

Sr Communs Mgr: Michelle Ou
  E-mail: communications@editors.ca
Membership & Conference Coord: Caitlin Stewart
Established: 1983
Recognizes the editor's often invisible contribution to written communication. $100 admission fee.
Other Sponsor(s): Breakwater Books; HarperCollins; The C D Howe Institute; New Society Publishers; Orca Book Publishers; Random House of Canada; UBC Press, Madison; University of Calgary Press
Award: $2,000 cash
Closing Date: Jan of the year after the work took place for letter of nomination & supporting material must be received by the second week in Feb
Presented: National Annual Conference, June of the year after the work took place

Far Horizons Award for Poetry
The Malahat Review
University of Victoria, Box 1700, Sta CSC, Victoria, BC V8W 2Y2, Canada
Tel: 250-721-8524 *Fax:* 250-472-5051
E-mail: malahat@uvic.ca
Web Site: www.malahatreview.ca
Key Personnel
Ed: John Barton
Established: 2006
Open to writers whose poetry has yet to be published in book form. Awarded in alternate years. See web site for details.
Award: $1,000
Closing Date: May 1, even-numbered years

Far Horizons Award for Short Fiction
The Malahat Review
University of Victoria, Box 1700, Sta CSC, Victoria, BC V8W 2Y2, Canada
Tel: 250-721-8524 *Fax:* 250-472-5051
E-mail: malahat@uvic.ca
Web Site: www.malahatreview.ca
Key Personnel
Ed: John Barton
Established: 2005
Open to writers whose fiction has yet to be published in a book of their own. Limited to 3,500 words. Awarded in alternate years. See web site for details.
Award: $1,000
Closing Date: May 1, odd-numbered years

Norma Farber First Book Award
Poetry Society of America (PSA)
15 Gramercy Park, New York, NY 10003
Tel: 212-254-9628
Web Site: poetrysociety.org/awards
Key Personnel
Pres: Allison Binns
Exec Dir: Matt Brogan *E-mail:* matt@poetrysociety.org
Deputy Dir: Brett Fletcher Lauer *E-mail:* brett@poetrysociety.org
Prog Dir: Laurin Macios *E-mail:* laurin@poetrysociety.org
For a first book of original poetry written by an American poet & published in either a hard or soft cover in a standard edition.
Award: $500
Closing Date: Annually, Oct-Dec (postmark)
Presented: Annual Awards Ceremony, New York, NY, Annually in Spring

The FC2 Catherine Doctorow Innovative Fiction Prize
Fiction Collective Two Inc (FC2)
c/o University of Alabama Press, Box 870380, Tuscaloosa, AL 35487-0380
Tel: 773-702-7000
E-mail: fc2@gmail.com
Web Site: www.fc2.org

Open to any US writer in English with at least 3 books of fiction published. Submissions may include a collection of short stories, one or more novellas, or a novel of any length. Works that have previously appeared in magazines or in anthologies may be included. Electronic submissions only. Submission fee: $25 for each ms submitted separately.
Award: $15,000 & publication by FC2
Closing Date: Annually, Nov 1
Presented: Annually in May

The FC2 Ronald Sukenick Innovative Fiction Contest
Fiction Collective Two Inc (FC2)
c/o University of Alabama Press, Box 870380, Tuscaloosa, AL 35487-0380
Tel: 773-702-7000
E-mail: fc2@gmail.com
Web Site: www.fc2.org
Open to any US writer in English who has not previously published with Fiction Collective Two. Submissions may include a collection of short stories, one or more novellas, or a novel of any length. Works that have previously appeared in magazines or in anthologies may be included. Electronic submissions only. Submission fee: $25 for each ms submitted separately.
Award: $1,500 & publication by FC2
Closing Date: Annually, Nov 1
Presented: Annually in May

Fellowship Program
Rhode Island State Council on the Arts
Affiliate of Department of Rhode Island State Government
One Capital Hill, 3rd fl, Providence, RI 02908
Tel: 401-222-3880 *Fax:* 401-222-3018
Web Site: www.arts.ri.gov
Key Personnel
Dir, Indiv Artists Progs: Cristina DiChiera
  E-mail: cristina.dichiera@arts.ri.gov
Established: 1967
Applicants must be Rhode Island residents who are over 18 & not students in an arts discipline. Fellowship recipients are selected by a regional panel of writers. Categories include fiction, poetry, playwriting/screenwriting. Guidelines & applications on web site.
Award: $5,000 recipient, $1,000 merit award
Closing Date: Annually, April 1

Fellowship, Tuition Scholarship & Work Study Programs for Writers
Bread Loaf Writers' Conference
Middlebury College, 204 College St, Middlebury, VT 05753
Tel: 802-443-5286 *Fax:* 802-443-2087
E-mail: blwc@middlebury.edu
Web Site: www.middlebury.edu/blwc
Key Personnel
Dir: Michael Collier
Admin Dir: Noreen Cargill
Asst Dir: Jennifer Grotz
Coord: Jason Lamb *E-mail:* jlamb@middlebury.edu
Work study scholarship to be used during conference in August.
Award: Fellowship provides tuition, room & board during 10-day conference; Scholarship provides tuition during conference
Closing Date: Annually, Feb 15
Presented: Ripton, VT, Annually in Aug, 10-day event

Fellowships for Creative & Performing Artists & Writers
American Antiquarian Society (AAS)
185 Salisbury St, Worcester, MA 01609-1634
Tel: 508-755-5221 *Fax:* 508-754-9069
Web Site: www.americanantiquarian.org

Key Personnel
Dir, Fellowships: Man Wolverton *Tel:* 508-471-2119 *E-mail:* mwolverton@mwa.org
Established: 1994
Award: $1,350 stipend for fellows residing on campus (rent-free) in the Society's Scholars' housing; $1,850 stipend for fellows residing off campus (no travel allowance)
Closing Date: Annually in Oct

Fellowships for Historical Research
American Antiquarian Society (AAS)
185 Salisbury St, Worcester, MA 01609-1634
Tel: 508-755-5221 *Fax:* 508-754-9069
Web Site: www.americanantiquarian.org
Key Personnel
Dir, Fellowships: Man Wolverton *Tel:* 508-471-2119 *E-mail:* mwolverton@mwa.org
Given to poets, fiction writers & creative nonfiction writers for month long residencies at the American Antiquarian Society in Worcester, MA, to research pre-20th century American history & culture. Submit 10 copies of up to 25 pages of poetry, fiction or creative nonfiction, a resume, 2 letters of recommendation & a 5 page project proposal.
Award: $1,350 stipend & on-campus housing provided; fellows residing off-campus receive $1,850
Closing Date: Annually in Oct

Fence Modern Poets Series
Fence Books
Imprint of Fence Magazine Inc
University at Albany, Science Library 320, 1400 Washington Ave, Albany, NY 12222
Tel: 518-567-7006
Web Site: www.fenceportal.org
Key Personnel
Publr & Ed: Rebecca Wolff
  E-mail: rebeccafence@gmail.com
Established: 2001
For a poet of any gender or gender identity writing in English at any stage of their publishing career. Using the online submission system, submit ms 48-80 pages & $29 entry fee.
Award: $1,000 & publication
Closing Date: Annually, April 30

Shubert Fendrich Memorial Playwriting Contest
Pioneer Drama Service Inc
PO Box 4267, Englewood, CO 80155-4267
Tel: 303-779-4035 *Toll Free Tel:* 800-333-7262
  Fax: 303-779-4315
Web Site: www.pioneerdrama.com/playwrights/contest.asp
Key Personnel
Submissions Ed: Lori Conary
Established: 1990
Presented for plays suitable for publication by Pioneer Drama Service Inc. Submission must include 100-200 word synopsis, cast list, running time, CD +/or score, set design(s), proof of production or staged reading, age of intended audience, SASE for returned materials, cover letter +/or resume. See web site for detailed guidelines.
Award: $1,000 royalty advance & publication
Closing Date: Annually, Dec 31
Presented: Annually, June 1

Edna Ferber Fiction Book Award
Council for Wisconsin Writers
c/o 210 N Main St, No 204, Cedar Grove, WI 53013
E-mail: wiswriters@gmail.com
Web Site: wiswriters.org/awards
Key Personnel
Contest Chair: Sylvia Cavanaugh
  E-mail: bgirl4shadow@gmail.com
Established: 1965

Annual award for the best fiction book published by a Wisconsin-based author in the contest year. Entry fee: $25 nonmembs.
Award: $500 & 1-week residency at Shake Rag Alley Center for the Arts
Closing Date: Jan 31
Presented: CWW Annual Banquet, May

The Field Poetry Prize
Oberlin College Press
Subsidiary of Oberlin College
50 N Professor St, Oberlin, OH 44074-1091
SAN: 212-1883
Tel: 440-775-8408 *Fax:* 440-775-8124
E-mail: oc.press@oberlin.edu
Web Site: www.oberlin.edu/ocpress; www.oberlin.edu/ocpress/prize.htm (guidelines)
Key Personnel
Mng Ed: Marco Wilkinson
Ed: David Walker; David Young
Established: 1996
Original poetry ms of 50-80 pages. Open to all poets whether or not they have previously published in book form. Reading fee: $28. Includes 1-year subscription to *Field*.
Award: $1,000 & publication in the Field Poetry Series
Closing Date: Annually, May 31
Presented: Announced in Aug (on web site)

Fine Arts Work Center in Provincetown
24 Pearl St, Provincetown, MA 02657
Tel: 508-487-9960 *Fax:* 508-487-8873
E-mail: general@fawc.org
Web Site: www.fawc.org
Key Personnel
Visual Art Fellowship Coord: James Stanley
  Tel: 508-487-9960 ext 105 *E-mail:* jstanley@fawc.org
Writing Fellowship Coord: Sophia Starmack
  Tel: 508-487-9960 ext 113 *E-mail:* sstarmack@fawc.org
Established: 1968
Offer 7-month fellowships to 10 artists & 10 writers, October 1-May 1. The Center aims to aid emerging artists & writers at a critical stage of their careers. See web site for application & information.
Award: Monthly stipends of up to $650 plus free rent for writers living at the Center; same for artists. Families welcome; no pets
Closing Date: Visual Arts: Feb 1; Writers: Dec 1

Firecracker Awards
Community of Literary Magazines & Presses (CLMP)
154 Christopher St, Suite 3C, New York, NY 10014-9110
Tel: 212-741-9110
E-mail: info@clmp.org
Web Site: www.clmp.org/firecracker
Key Personnel
Progs Dir: David Gibbs *E-mail:* dgibbs@clmp.org
Celebrate & promote great literary works from independent literary publishers & self-published authors. Categories: Fiction, Creative Nonfiction & Poetry. Awards also in 3 magazine/periodical categories: Poetry, Best Debut & General Excellence.
Other Sponsor(s): American Booksellers Association
Presented: June

5 Under 35
National Book Foundation
90 Broad St, Suite 604, New York, NY 10004
Tel: 212-685-0261 *Fax:* 212-213-6570
E-mail: nationalbook@nationalbook.org
Web Site: www.nationalbook.org
Key Personnel
Deputy Dir: Jordan Smith *E-mail:* jsmith@nationalbook.org

Dir, Technol: Meredith Andrews
  E-mail: mandrews@nationalbook.org
Assoc Dir, Awards: Anna Dobben
  E-mail: adobben@nationalbook.org
Communs & Mktg Mgr: Bev Rivero
  E-mail: brivero@nationalbook.org
Public Progs Mgr: Natalie Green
  E-mail: ngreen@nationalbook.org
Admin & Devt Coord: Dhyana Taylor
  E-mail: dtaylor@nationalbook.org
Annual prize to honor 5 young & promising fiction writers, each selected by a National Book Award winner or finalist. Honorees are selected at the discretion of the current selection committee. Author cannot be a previous 5 Under 35 honoree, must be born after November 30, 1984, must be living during the award year (December 1, 2019-November 30, 2020), must have published no more than 1 novel or short story collection & pub date must be between December 1, 2015 & November 30, 2020. Translations & books originally published outside the US are eligible but must have a US publisher & be available in English.
Other Sponsor(s): Amazon.com

Norma Fleck Award for Canadian Children's Non-Fiction
Canadian Children's Book Centre
40 Orchard View Blvd, Suite 217, Toronto, ON M4R 1B9, Canada
Tel: 416-975-0010 *Fax:* 416-975-8970
E-mail: info@bookcentre.ca
Web Site: www.bookcentre.ca
Key Personnel
Exec Dir: Charlotte Teeple *E-mail:* charlotte@bookcentre.ca
Lib Coord: Meghan Howe *E-mail:* meghan@bookcentre.ca
Mktg & Web Site Coord: Camilia Kahrizi
  E-mail: camilia@bookcentre.ca
Prog Coord: Shannon Howe Barnes
  E-mail: shannon@bookcentre.ca
Established: 1999
Awarded to a Canadian author/illustrator for an outstanding work of nonfiction for young people.
Other Sponsor(s): Fleck Family Foundation
Award: $10,000
Closing Date: Annually in mid-Dec

Fordham University, Gabelli School of Business
140 W 62 St, Rm 440, New York, NY 10023
Web Site: www.fordham.edu
Key Personnel
Professor & Area Chair: John A Fortunato
  E-mail: jfortunato@fordham.edu
Established: 1969
Offers MBA degree with a major in Communications & Media Management & Master of Science (MS) in Communications & Media Management for media & entertainment industries. Its mission is to educate business professionals who can manage effectively in a range of leadership roles & who are equipped for continuous growth in a changing global environment. A variety of assistantships, fellowships & scholarships are available to highly qualified MBA candidates.
Closing Date: Ongoing
Presented: Each trimester

Foreword's INDIES Awards
Foreword Reviews
413 E Eighth St, Traverse City, MI 49686
Tel: 231-933-3699
Web Site: www.forewordreviews.com
Key Personnel
Publr: Victoria Sutherland *E-mail:* victoria@forewordreviews.com

Any independently published book, including those from self-published authors & university presses, published in the current year & available for purchase in print or ebook formats. Revised editions of previously issued books are eligible for entry only with newly issued ISBNs. Reissued editions are not eligible for entry.
Award: $1,500 each given to best book in fiction & nonfiction
Closing Date: Annually, Jan 15 for books published in previous calendar year
Presented: ALA Annual Conference

Morris D Forkosch Prize
American Historical Association (AHA)
400 "A" St SE, Washington, DC 20003
Tel: 202-544-2422 *Fax:* 202-544-8307
E-mail: awards@historians.org
Web Site: www.historians.org
In recognition of the best in English in the field of British, British Imperial or British Commonwealth history since 1485. Submissions of books relating to the shared common law heritage of the English-speaking world are particularly encouraged. Books on British, British Imperial or British Commonwealth history published in 2020 are eligible. Along with an application form, applicants must mail a copy of their book to each of the prize committee members who will be posted on our web site as the prize deadline approaches. All updated info on web site.
Closing Date: May 15, 2021
Presented: AHA Annual Meeting, New Orleans, LA, Jan 2022

E M Forster Award
American Academy of Arts & Letters
633 W 155 St, New York, NY 10032
Tel: 212-368-5900 *Fax:* 212-491-4615
E-mail: academy@artsandletters.org
Web Site: artsandletters.org
Key Personnel
Exec Dir: Cody Upton
Given to a young English writer.
Award: $20,000 toward a stay in the US

49th Parallel Poetry Award
The Bellingham Review
Mail Stop 9053, Western Washington University, Bellingham, WA 98225
Tel: 360-650-4863
E-mail: bhreview@wwu.edu
Web Site: www.bhreview.org
Key Personnel
Ed-in-Chief: Suzanne Paola Antonetta
Mng Ed: Mike Oliphant
Established: 1983
Maximum of up to 3 poems per entry. Poems within a series of poems will each be treated as a separate entry. No previously published works, or works accepted for publication, are eligible. Work may be under consideration elsewhere, but must be withdrawn from the competition if accepted for publication. All entries will receive a complimentary 1-issue subscription. Entry fee for the first entry (up to 3 poems) $20, additional entries $10.
Only accept submissions through Submittable. Mailed submissions are no longer accepted. All finalists are considered for publication. The winning piece is selected by a distinguished, outside judge. Entries accepted beginning December 1.
Award: $1,000 & publication in the *Bellingham Review* (1st prize), considered for publication (2nd, 3rd & finalists)
Closing Date: Annually, March 15
Presented: Annually in June

Foster City International Writers Contest
Foster City Parks & Recreation Department
650 Shell Blvd, Foster City, CA 94404
Tel: 650-286-3380
E-mail: fostercity_writers@yahoo.com
Web Site: www.fostercity.org
Key Personnel
Comm Chair: Ilene Shaine
Contact: Tiffany Oren
Established: 1974
For fiction, humor, poetry & personal essay, rhymed verse, blank verse. Entries must be original, previously unpublished & in English. Fiction must be no more than 3,000 words; poetry not to exceed two double-spaced typed pages in length. Open to all writers, no age or geographic limit. Send SASE for contest flyer. Non-refundable entry fee: $20.
Award: $250 in each category (1st prize); $100 (2nd prize): nonfiction, fiction, humor, poetry

Four Quartets Prize
Poetry Society of America (PSA)
15 Gramercy Park, New York, NY 10003
Tel: 212-254-9628
Web Site: poetrysociety.org/awards
Key Personnel
Pres: Allison Binns
Exec Dir: Matt Brogan *E-mail:* matt@poetrysociety.org
Deputy Dir: Brett Fletcher Lauer *E-mail:* brett@poetrysociety.org
Devt Dir: Madeline Weinfield *E-mail:* madeline@poetrysociety.org
Progs Mgr: Emily Hunt *E-mail:* emily@poetrysociety.org
Prize for a unified & complete sequence of poems published in America in a print or online journal, chapbook, or book in the year prior to the award year. Only 1 submission per author will be considered. Submissions accepted from authors, publishers & literary agents. Self-published work, multi-author work & translations are ineligible. See web site for detailed submission requirements.
Other Sponsor(s): T S Eliot Foundation
Award: $1,000 to each of 3 finalists, additional $20,000 to winner
Closing Date: Annually in Dec
Presented: Annually in Spring

Dixon Ryan Fox Manuscript Prize
Fenimore Art Museum
5798 State Hwy 80, Cooperstown, NY 13326
Mailing Address: PO Box 800, Cooperstown, NY 13326-0800
Tel: 607-547-1416
Established: 1974
Encourage original scholarship in the history of New York State. Award granted to the best unpublished ms on the history of New York State. Electronic submissions only.
Award: $3,000
Closing Date: Annually, March 1
Presented: Fenimore Art Museum Board of Trustees Annual Meeting, Cooperstown, NY, Annually in July

Frances Henne YALSA/VOYA Research Grant
Young Adult Library Services Association (YALSA)
Division of The American Library Association (ALA)
50 E Huron St, Chicago, IL 60611
Tel: 312-280-4390 *Toll Free Tel:* 800-545-2433
  Fax: 312-280-5276
E-mail: yalsa@ala.org
Web Site: www.ala.org/yalsa/awardsandgrants/franceshenne
Key Personnel
Exec Dir: Anita Mechler

Prog Offr, Events & Conferences: Nichole
O'Connor *Tel:* 800-545-2433 ext 4387
E-mail: noconnor@ala.org
Communs Specialist: Anna Lam *Tel:* 800-545-
2433 ext 5849 *E-mail:* alam@ala.org
Established: 1986
Annually recognizes a school library media spe-
cialist with 5 years or less experience who
demonstrates leadership qualities with students,
teachers & administrators to attend an AASL
conference or ALA Annual Conference for the
first time. Applicants must be AASL personal
members.
Other Sponsor(s): Voice of Youth Advocates
(VOYA)
Award: $1,000
Closing Date: Dec 1
Presented: ALA Midwinter Meeting, Jan/Feb

Prix Francophone de l'ACSP

Canadian Political Science Association
260 rue Dalhousie St, Suite 204, Ottawa, ON
K1N 7E4, Canada
Tel: 613-562-1202 *Fax:* 613-241-0019
E-mail: cpsa-acsp@cpsa-acsp.ca
Web Site: www.cpsa-acsp.ca
Key Personnel
Admin: Michelle Hopkins
Established: 2014
Biennial prize awarded to the best book published
in French in the field of political science. To
be eligible, a book may be single-authored or
multi-authored. Single-authored: author must
be a member of the CPSA in the year the book
is considered for the award. Multi-authored:
at least one of the authors must be a member
of the CPSA in the year the book is considered for the award. For the 2022 award, a book
must have a copyright date of 2020 or 2021.
Award: Commemorative plaque & receive/share
the set of books submitted to the CPSA office
Closing Date: Dec
Presented: Annual Conference

Soeurette Diehl Fraser Translation Award

Texas Institute of Letters (TIL)
PO Box 609, Round Rock, TX 78680
Tel: 512-683-5640
E-mail: president@texasinstituteofletters.org
Web Site: www.texasinstituteofletters.org
Key Personnel
Pres: Carmen Tafolla
VP: Sergio Troncoso
Secy: Ann Weisgarber
Treas: W K Stratton
Recording Secy: Kurt Heinzelman
Established: 1990
Biennial award given for the best book of trans-
lation by a Texan. Guidelines available on the
web site.
Award: $1,000
Closing Date: Jan, odd-numbered years
Presented: TIL Awards Banquet, Spring, odd-
numbered years

George Freedley Memorial Award

Theatre Library Association (TLA)
c/o The New York Public Library for the Per-
forming Arts, 111 Amsterdam Ave, New York,
NY 10023
E-mail: TLABookAwards@gmail.com;
TheatreLibraryAssociation@gmail.com
Web Site: www.tla-online.org/awards/bookawards
Key Personnel
Co-Chair, Book Awards Comm: Diana Bertolini;
Annemarie van Roessel
Established: 1968
To the author of a book in the field of theatre,
published in the US, on the basis of schol-
arship, readability & general contribution to
knowledge. Only books related to live perfor-

mance (including vaudeville, puppetry, pan-
tomime & circus) will be considered.
Award: $500 (1st prize), $250 (Special Jury
Prize); certificate
Closing Date: Feb 28
Presented: New York City, NY, Oct

The Don Freeman Memorial Grant-In-Aid

Society of Children's Book Writers & Illustrators
(SCBWI)
6363 Wilshire Blvd, Suite 425, Los Angeles, CA
90048
Tel: 323-782-1010; 310-403-0675 (cell) *Fax:* 323-
782-1892
E-mail: grants@scbwi.org; scbwi@scbwi.org
Web Site: www.scbwi.org
Key Personnel
Pres: Stephen Mooser *E-mail:* stephenmooser@
scbwi.org
Exec Dir: Lin Oliver *E-mail:* linoliver@scbwi.org
Established: 1977
To enable picture-book artists to further their understanding, training +/or work in any aspect
of the picture-book genre. Grant may be used
for the purchase of necessary materials, enrollment in illustrators' or writers' workshops or
conferences, courses in advanced illustrating or
writing techniques & travel for research or to
expose work to publishers/art directors. Open
to Society members only.
Award: Winning works shown to editors & agents
Closing Date: Annually in March
Presented: Annually in Aug

The French-American Foundation & Florence Gould Foundation Annual Translation Prize

The French-American Foundation
28 W 44 St, Suite 1420, New York, NY 10036
Tel: 212-829-8800 *Fax:* 212-829-8810
Web Site: www.frenchamerican.org
Key Personnel
VP & CEO: Dana Arifi
Prog Offr: Katie Demallie *E-mail:* kdemallie@
frenchamerican.org
Established: 1986
Award for outstanding translations of fiction &
nonfiction from French into English which
have been published in the US. Translations
must be submitted by the US publisher. Tech-
nical, poetry, scientific, reference works & chil-
dren's literature are not accepted. Works must
have been published in the previous calendar
year.
Other Sponsor(s): Florence Gould Foundation
Award: 2 awards of $10,000 (1 each for fiction &
nonfiction)
Closing Date: Jan 15
Presented: New York, NY, Spring

Horst Frenz Prize

American Comparative Literature Association
(ACLA)
University of South Carolina, Dept of Languages,
Literature & Cultures, 1620 College St, Rm
817, Columbia, SC 29208
Tel: 803-777-3021
E-mail: info@acla.org
Web Site: www.acla.org/prize-awards/horst-frenz-
prize
Key Personnel
Nominations Comm Chair: Antonio Barrenechea
E-mail: abarrene@umw.edu
Awarded annually to the best paper presented by
a graduate student at the ACLA annual meet-
ing.
Award: $300 cash, complimentary registration to
annual meeting, travel reimbursement grant up
to $300 to attend the following year's meeting
& publication of the paper in the *Yearbook of
Comparative Literature*
Closing Date: July 31

Friends of American Writers Awards

Friends of American Writers
506 Rose Ave, Des Plaines, IL 60016
Tel: 847-827-8339
Web Site: www.fawchicago.org
Key Personnel
Pres: Roberta Gates *E-mail:* robmicgates73@
gmail.com
Adult Lit Awards: Tammie Bob
E-mail: bobtam410@gmail.com
Established: 1922
For literary fiction & nonfiction books published
in the current year. Book must be author's first,
second or third work. Author must have lived
for 5 years in the Midwest, currently living in
the Midwest, or book's setting must be Mid-
western. No poetry or mss. See web site for
full details.
Award: Two cash prizes totaling $4,000
Closing Date: Annually, Dec 20
Presented: The Fortnightly, Chicago, IL, Annually
in May

Frost Medal

Poetry Society of America (PSA)
15 Gramercy Park, New York, NY 10003
Tel: 212-254-9628
Web Site: poetrysociety.org/awards
Key Personnel
Exec Dir: Matt Brogan *E-mail:* matt@
poetrysociety.org
Deputy Dir: Brett Fletcher Lauer *E-mail:* brett@
poetrysociety.org
Devt Dir: Madeline Weinfield *E-mail:* madeline@
poetrysociety.org
Awarded annually for distinguished lifetime
achievement in American poetry. By nomina-
tion only.
Other Sponsor(s): Ironwood Foundation; Klass
Family Foundation
Award: $5,000

Fulbright Scholar Program

Council for International Exchange of Scholars
Division of The Institute of International Educa-
tion
1400 "K" St NW, Washington, DC 20005
Tel: 202-686-4000
E-mail: scholars@iie.org
Web Site: www.cies.org; www.iie.org
Key Personnel
Dir, US Scholar Progs: Jordanna Enrich *Tel:* 202-
686-6233 *E-mail:* jenrich@iie.org
Dir, Outreach: Peter Van Derwater *Tel:* 202-686-
4014 *E-mail:* pvanderwater@iie.org
Established: 1946
CIES cooperates with the US Dept of State, Bureau of Educational & Cultural Affairs, in the
administration of the Fulbright scholar program, which offers approximately 800 grants
annually to US faculty & professionals for
university teaching +/or advanced research in
more than 140 countries.
Award: Grant benefits, which vary by country,
generally include a stipend & round-trip travel
for the grantee
Closing Date: Aug 1

Gabriele Rico Challenge for Nonfiction

Reed Magazine
San Jose State University, English Dept, One
Washington Sq, San Jose, CA 95192-0090
Tel: 408-924-4441
E-mail: mail@reedmag.org
Web Site: www.reedmag.org; reedmagazine.
submittable.com
All submissions must be through the online sys-
tem. Keep submissions under 5,000 words.
Reading fee: $15.
Award: $1,333 & publication in *Reed Magazine*
Closing Date: Annually, Nov 1 (submissions ac-
cepted beginning June 1)

Ernest J Gaines Award for Literary Excellence
Baton Rouge Area Foundation
100 North St, Suite 900, Baton Rouge, LA 70802
Tel: 225-387-6126
E-mail: gainesaward@braf.org
Web Site: www.ernestjgainesaward.org
Key Personnel
Dir, Communs: Mukul Verma *Tel:* 225-362-9260
 E-mail: mverma@braf.org
Annual award to recognize outstanding work
 from promising African-American fiction writ-
 ers. Nominees must not yet be widely recog-
 nized for their work & must be an African-
 American US citizen. Works of fiction (novel
 or collection of short stories) published in the
 award year are eligible. Self-published books &
 e-mailed entries are not accepted.
Award: $15,000
Closing Date: Aug 15
Presented: Jan 30

Lewis Galantiere Translation Award
American Translators Association (ATA)
225 Reinekers Lane, Suite 590, Alexandria, VA
 22314
Tel: 703-683-6100 *Fax:* 703-683-6122
E-mail: honors_awards@atanet.org
Web Site: www.atanet.org
Key Personnel
Chair, ATA Honors & Awards Comm: Lois
 Feuerle
Established: 1984
Awarded in even years for a distinguished book-
 length literary translation from any language,
 except German into English, published in the
 US.
Award: $1,000, a certificate of recognition & up
 to $500 toward expenses to attend the ATA An-
 nual Conference
Closing Date: March 1 (even years)
Presented: ATA Annual Conference

John Kenneth Galbraith Award for Nonfiction,
 see PEN/John Kenneth Galbraith Award for
 Nonfiction

Zona Gale Award for Short Fiction
Council for Wisconsin Writers
c/o 4414 W Fillmore Dr, Milwaukee, WI 53219
E-mail: wiswriters@gmail.com
Web Site: wiswriters.org/awards
Key Personnel
Contest Chair: Daniel Kentowski
 E-mail: dkento@milwaukee.gov
Established: 1966
Annual award for the best piece of short fiction
 published by a Wisconsin-based author in the
 contest year. Entry fee: $25 nonmembs.
Award: $500 & 1-week residency at Shake Rag
 Alley Center for the Arts
Closing Date: Jan 31
Presented: CWW Annual Banquet, May

**Gannon University's High School Poetry
 Contest**
Gannon University English Dept
Gannon University, 109 University Sq, Erie, PA
 16541
Tel: 814-871-7504
Web Site: www.gannon.edu/departmental/english/
 poetry.asp
Key Personnel
Professor of Eng: Berwyn Moore
 E-mail: moore001@gannon.edu
Established: 1985
High School students in grades 9-12 are invited
 to participate; must be original poetry.
Award: $100 (1st place), $75 (2nd place), $50
 (3rd place), certificate (honorable mention)
Closing Date: Annually, Feb 1 (postmark)
Presented: Gannon University, Waldron Campus
 Center, Erie, PA, April

Francois-Xavier Garneau Medal
Canadian Historical Association
130 Albert St, Suite 1201, Ottawa, ON K1P 5G4,
 Canada
Tel: 613-233-7885 *Fax:* 613-565-5445
E-mail: cha-shc@cha-shc.ca
Web Site: www.cha-shc.ca
Key Personnel
Exec Dir: Michel Duquet *E-mail:* mduquet@cha-
 shc.ca
Established: 1980
Awarded every 5 years; commemorates the first
 Canadian Historian. Applicant should be a
 Canadian citizen or a legal immigrant. Given
 for the most outstanding scholarly book in the
 field of Canadian history within the previous
 five years.
Award: Minted medal & $2,000
Presented: 2025

Alfred C Gary Memorial
The Poetry Society of Virginia
900 Timber Creek Place, Virginia Beach, VA
 23464
E-mail: poetryinva@aol.com
Web Site: poetrysocietyofvirginia.org
Key Personnel
Pres: Robert P Arthur *E-mail:* robert.peebles.
 arthur@gmail.com
Exec Dir: Guy Terrell *E-mail:* guy.terrell@
 earthlink.net
Adult Contest Chair: Steven Blythe
 E-mail: stevenblythepoetry@gmail.com
All entries must be in English, original & un-
 published. Submit 2 copies, each having the
 category name & number on top left of page.
 Entries will not be returned. Subject: a historic
 event that occurred between 1925 & 1992;
 iambic pentameter; 48 line limit. Entry fee:
 $4 nonmembs.
Other Sponsor(s): Claudia Gary
Award: $50 (1st prize), $30 (2nd prize), $20 (3rd
 prize)
Closing Date: Jan
Presented: Annual PSV Awards Ceremony, April

John Gassner Memorial Playwriting Award
The New England Theatre Conference Inc
215 Knob Hill Dr, Hamden, CT 06518
Tel: 617-851-8535 *Fax:* 203-288-5938
E-mail: mail@netconline.org
Web Site: www.netconline.org
Established: 1967
Playwriting contest for new full-length plays.
Closing Date: Annually, April 15
Presented: NETC Annual Convention, Annually
 in Nov

The Christian Gauss Award
The Phi Beta Kappa Society
1606 New Hampshire Ave NW, Washington, DC
 20009
Tel: 202-265-3808 *Fax:* 202-986-1601
E-mail: awards@pbk.org
Web Site: www.pbk.org/bookawards
Key Personnel
Prog & Event Specialist: Laura Hartnett *Tel:* 202-
 745-3287 *E-mail:* lhartnett@pbk.org
Established: 1950
For outstanding books in the field of literary
 scholarship or criticism published in the US.
 Nominations must come from publisher & be
 submitted online.
Award: $10,000
Closing Date: Annually in Jan
Presented: Washington, DC, Annually in Dec

The Gaylactic Spectrum Awards
Gaylactic Spectrum Awards Foundation
1425 "S" St NW, Washington, DC 20009
Web Site: www.spectrumawards.org

Key Personnel
Exec Dir: Rob Gates
Established: 1998
Presented to outstanding works of science fiction,
 fantasy or horror which include significant gay,
 lesbian, bisexual or transgendered characters,
 themes, or issues. Awards are given in 3 cate-
 gories: Best Novel, Best Short Fiction & Best
 Other Work.
Award: Statuette & small cash stipend for Best
 Novel & Best Short Fiction categories
Closing Date: Open between March 15 & April
 30 for works released during the previous cal-
 endar year
Presented: Varies - World Science Fiction Convention, Gaylaxicon or other, Fall

Theodor Seuss Geisel Award
The American Library Association (ALA)
225 N Michigan Ave, Suite 1300, Chicago, IL
 60601
Toll Free Tel: 800-545-2433 *Fax:* 312-280-5271
E-mail: alscawards@ala.org
Web Site: www.ala.org/awardsgrants/theodor-
 seuss-geisel-award
Key Personnel
Awards Coord: Courtney Jones *E-mail:* cjones@
 ala.org
Established: 2004
Awarded annually to the author(s) & illustrator(s)
 of the most distinguished contribution to the
 body of American children's literature known
 as beginning reader books published in the US
 during the preceding year. Winners announced
 in January at the ALA Midwinter Meeting.
Award: Bronze medal
Closing Date: Dec 31
Presented: ALA Annual Conference, June/July

Lionel Gelber Prize
Lionel Gelber Foundation
University of Toronto, Munk School of Global
 Affairs, One Devonshire Place, Toronto, ON
 M5S 3K7, Canada
Tel: 416-946-8901 *Fax:* 416-946-8915
E-mail: events.munk@utoronto.ca
Web Site: munkschool.utoronto.ca/gelber; www.
 facebook.com/GelberPrize
Established: 1989
Given to the author of the year's most outstand-
 ing work of nonfiction in the field of interna-
 tional relations. Designed to encourage authors
 who write about international relations & to
 stimulate the audience for these books to grow.
 Open to authors of all nationalities. Six copies
 of each title must be submitted by the publisher. Books must be published between January 1 & December 31 in English or English
 translation.
Other Sponsor(s): Munk School of Global Affairs
Award: $15,000
Closing Date: Oct
Presented: Short list announced Jan; prize award
 in Spring

Leo Gershoy Award
American Historical Association (AHA)
400 "A" St SE, Washington, DC 20003
Tel: 202-544-2422 *Fax:* 202-544-8307
E-mail: awards@historians.org
Web Site: www.historians.org
Established: 1975
In recognition of outstanding historical writing
 in 17th & 18th century Western European history. Books published in 2020 will be eligible. Along with an application form, applicants must mail a copy of their book (limited
 to 3 titles from any one publisher) to each
 of the prize committee members who will be
 posted on our web site as the prize deadline
 approaches. All updated info on web site.
Award: Cash prize

Closing Date: May 15, 2021
Presented: AHA Annual Meeting, New Orleans, LA, Jan 2022

Charles M Getchell Award, see Southeastern Theatre Conference New Play Project

Arrell Gibson Lifetime Achievement Award
Oklahoma Center for the Book (OCB)
200 NE 18 St, Oklahoma City, OK 73105-3205
Tel: 405-522-3383
Web Site: libraries.ok.gov/ocb/arrell-gibson/
Annual award to honor an Oklahoman who has contributed to the state's literary heritage.
Closing Date: Jan
Presented: April

Gilder Lehrman Lincoln Prize
The Gilder Lehrman Institute of American History
300 N Washington St, Campus Box 413, Gettysburg, PA 17325
Tel: 717-337-8255
E-mail: lincolnprize@gettysburg.edu
Web Site: www.gilderlehrman.org
Established: 1990
Awarded annually for the finest scholarly work in English on Abraham Lincoln, the American Civil War soldier, or the American Civil War era. Publishers, critics & authors may submit books published in the current year. No entry fee or form. Send six copies of the nominated work.
Other Sponsor(s): Gettysburg College
Award: $50,000
Closing Date: Nov 1

Gilder Lehrman Prize for Military History
The Gilder Lehrman Institute of American History
49 W 45 St, 2nd fl, New York, NY 10036
Tel: 646-366-9666
Established: 2016
Awarded annually to recognize the best book on military history in the English-speaking world distinguished by its scholarship, its contribution to the literature & its appeal to both a general & an academic audience. Publishers may submit as many titles as they wish, but must send at least 5 copies to: Michael Ryan, VP & Dir, Patricia D Klingenstein Library, New-York Historical Society, 170 Central Park W, New York, NY 10024.
Other Sponsor(s): New-York Historical Society
Award: $50,000
Closing Date: Nov 1

Giller Prize
Scotiabank
543 Logan Ave, Toronto, ON M4K 3B6, Canada
Web Site: www.scotiabankgillerprize.ca
Key Personnel
Exec Dir: Elana Rabinovitch
Submissions & Mktg Mgr: Michelle Kadarusman
Annual literary prize for fiction.
Award: $140,000
Closing Date: Aug 15

Allen Ginsberg Poetry Award
The Poetry Center at Passaic County Community College
One College Blvd, Paterson, NJ 07505-1179
Tel: 973-684-6555 *Fax:* 973-523-6085
Web Site: www.poetrycenterpccc.com
Key Personnel
Exec Dir: Maria Mazziotti Gillan
  E-mail: mgillan@pccc.edu
Mgr: Susan Balik *E-mail:* sbalik@pccc.edu
Poem should not be more than 2 ms pages. Sheets which contain the poems should not contain the poet's name. Do not submit poems

that imitate Allen Ginsberg's work. Entry fee $18.
Award: $1,000 (1st prize), $200 (2nd prize), $100 (3rd prize)
Closing Date: Annually, Feb 1

Gival Press Novel Award
Gival Press
PO Box 3812, Arlington, VA 22203
SAN: 852-9787
Tel: 703-351-0079 *Fax:* 703-351-0079 (call first)
E-mail: givalpress@yahoo.com
Web Site: www.givalpress.com; givalpress. submittable.com
Key Personnel
Publr & Ed: Robert L Giron
Established: 2005
For best literary novel.
Award: $3,000 & publication
Closing Date: Annually, May 30
Presented: Annually, Oct 1

Gival Press Oscar Wilde Award
Gival Press
PO Box 3812, Arlington, VA 22203
SAN: 852-9787
Tel: 703-351-0079 *Fax:* 703-351-0079 (call first)
E-mail: givalpress@yahoo.com
Web Site: www.givalpress.com; givalpress. submittable.com
Key Personnel
Publr & Ed: Robert L Giron
Established: 2002
For best LBGTQ poem.
Award: $100 & online publication
Closing Date: Annually, June 27
Presented: Annually, Sept 1

Gival Press Poetry Award
Gival Press
PO Box 3812, Arlington, VA 22203
SAN: 852-9787
Tel: 703-351-0079 *Fax:* 703-351-0079 (call first)
E-mail: givalpress@yahoo.com
Web Site: www.givalpress.com; givalpress. submittable.com
Key Personnel
Publr & Ed: Robert L Giron
Established: 1999
For the best collection of poetry.
Award: $1,000 & book publication
Closing Date: Annually, Dec 15
Presented: Annually, May 1

Gival Press Short Story Award
Gival Press
PO Box 3812, Arlington, VA 22203
SAN: 852-9787
Tel: 703-351-0079 *Fax:* 703-351-0079 (call first)
E-mail: givalpress@yahoo.com
Web Site: www.givalpress.com; givalpress. submittable.com
Key Personnel
Publr & Ed: Robert L Giron
Established: 2004
For best literary short story.
Award: $1,000 & online publication
Closing Date: Annually, Aug 8
Presented: Annually, Dec 1

John Glassco Translation Prize
Literary Translators' Association of Canada
Concordia University, LB 601, 1455 De Maisonneuve W, Montreal, QC H3G 1M8, Canada
Tel: 514-848-2424 (ext 8702)
E-mail: info@attlc-ltac.org
Web Site: www.attlc-ltac.org
Key Personnel
Pres: Beatriz Hausner
Established: 1982

For a first book-length literary translation into French or English published in Canada during the previous year. Must be Canadian citizen or permanent resident.
Award: $1,000
Closing Date: Annually, July 31
Presented: Annually, Sept 30

GLCA New Writers Awards
Great Lakes Colleges Association (GLCA)
535 W William St, Suite 301, Ann Arbor, MI 48103
Tel: 734-661-2350 *Fax:* 734-661-2349
Web Site: www.glca.org
Key Personnel
Dir, Prog Devt: Gregory R Wegner
Established: 1969
For a first published work of fiction or creative nonfiction or a first book of poetry. Submissions may be made only by publishers; one entry each, poetry, fiction or creative nonfiction. Submit 4 copies of the work & an author's statement agreeing to the terms. See web site for details.
Award: Reading engagements at up to 13 colleges & universities of the GLCA; each engagement includes $500 honorarium; all travel expenses are paid
Closing Date: July 25

The Danuta Gleed Literary Award
The Writers' Union of Canada (TWUC)
600-460 Richmond St W, Toronto, ON M5V 1Y1, Canada
Tel: 416-703-8982 *Fax:* 416-504-9090
E-mail: info@writersunion.ca
Web Site: www.writersunion.ca
Key Personnel
Off Admin: Valerie Laws *Tel:* 416-703-8982 ext 224
Established: 1997
Annual award for best first collection of short fiction by a Canadian published in the calendar year prior to the closing date & available through bookstores & libraries.
Award: $10,000 (1st prize), $500 (2nd & 3rd prizes)
Closing Date: Annually, Jan 31

The Goddard Riverside Stephan Russo Book Prize
Goddard Riverside Community Center
593 Columbus Ave, New York, NY 10024
Web Site: bookprize.goddard.org
Key Personnel
Contact: Jenny Pfister *Tel:* 212-873-6600 ext 354
  E-mail: jpfister@goddard.org
Annual literary award to recognize books that focus on housing, early childhood & secondary education, older adult life, city arts, social policy & other important aspects of community life that support & promote Goddard Riverside's mission. Books must be written in English & published in the US between October 1 of the previous year & September 30 of the award year. Six copies of each title should be submitted, along with prize entry form & $50 application fee.
Closing Date: May 15
Presented: Goddard Riverside's Book Fair Gala, Fall

Gold Medal
American Academy of Arts & Letters
633 W 155 St, New York, NY 10032
Tel: 212-368-5900 *Fax:* 212-491-4615
E-mail: academy@artsandletters.org
Web Site: artsandletters.org
Key Personnel
Exec Dir: Cody Upton
Rotating categories of Belles Lettres & Criticism & Painting; Biography & Music; Fiction & Sculpture; History & Architecture, includ-

ing Landscape Architecture; Poetry & Music; Drama & Graphic Art.
Award: 2 medals annually

Golden Cylindar Awards

Gravure Association of the Americas Inc
8281 Pine Lake Rd, Denver, NC 28037
Tel: 201-523-6042 *Fax:* 201-523-6048
E-mail: gaa@gaa.org
Web Site: www.gaa.org
Key Personnel
Dir, Planning & Admin: Pamela W Schenk
    Tel: 585-288-2297 *E-mail:* pwschenk@gaa.org
Encourage highest quality gravure printing from design through production.
Award: Golden Cylinders on pedestals
Closing Date: Annually in April
Presented: Leadership Summit, Annually in Fall

Golden Kite Awards

Society of Children's Book Writers & Illustrators (SCBWI)
6363 Wilshire Blvd, Suite 425, Los Angeles, CA 90048
Tel: 323-782-1010; 310-403-0675 (cell) *Fax:* 323-782-1892
E-mail: grants@scbwi.org; scbwi@scbwi.org
Web Site: www.scbwi.org
Key Personnel
Pres: Stephen Mooser *E-mail:* stephenmooser@scbwi.org
Exec Dir: Lin Oliver *E-mail:* linoliver@scbwi.org
Established: 1973
Four awards, one each for fiction, nonfiction, picture book text & picture book illustration, awarded each year to the most outstanding children's books published during that year & written or illustrated by members of the Society of Children's Book Writers & Illustrators. An honor book plaque is awarded in each category.
Award: Free transportation & accomodations to summer conference
Closing Date: Annually in Dec
Presented: Annually in Aug

The Golden Poppy Book Awards (The Poppies), see CALIBA Golden Poppy Awards

Golden Rose Award

New England Poetry Club
46 Wallace St, Somerville, MA 02144
E-mail: info@nepoetryclub.org
Web Site: www.nepoetryclub.org
Key Personnel
Pres: Mary Buchinger
VP: Hillary Sallick
Treas: Linda Haviland Conte
Established: 1920
The oldest literary award given annually to poet who has done the most for poetry during previous year or in a lifetime. Chosen by NEPC officers.
Award: Rose sculpture
Closing Date: Annually, May 31
Presented: Announced online Aug/Sept

Laurence Goldstein Poetry Prize

Michigan Quarterly Review
University of Michigan, 0576 Rackham Bldg, 915 E Washington St, Ann Arbor, MI 48109-1070
Tel: 734-764-9265
E-mail: mqr@umich.edu
Web Site: sites.lsa.umich.edu/mqr/
Key Personnel
Ed: Jonathan Freedman
Poetry Ed: Keith Taylor
Awarded to the best poem published in MQR each year. No deadline or special application process.
Award: $500

Goodreads Choice Awards

Goodreads Inc
188 Spear St, 3rd fl, San Francisco, CA 94105
E-mail: press@goodreads.com
Web Site: www.goodreads.com/award
Key Personnel
CEO: Veronica Moss
VP, Communs: Suzanne Skyvara
15 nominees in each category. Books must be published in the US in English, including works in translation & other significant rereleases. Three rounds of voting open to all registered Goodreads members.

Governor General's Literary Awards

Canada Council for the Arts (Conseil des arts du Canada)
150 Elgin St, 2nd fl, Ottawa, ON K2P 1L4, Canada
Mailing Address: PO Box 1047, Ottawa, ON K1P 5V8, Canada
Tel: 613-566-4414 *Toll Free Tel:* 800-263-5588 (CN only) *Fax:* 613-566-4390
E-mail: info@canadacouncil.ca
Web Site: canadacouncil.ca/en/council/prizes
Key Personnel
Prog Offr: Lori Knoll *Tel:* 613-566-4414 ext 5573
    E-mail: lori.knoll@canadacouncil.ca
Established: 1936
Annual awards to the best English language & French language book in each of seven categories: fiction, poetry, drama, nonfiction, children's literature-text, children's literature-illustration & translation (from French to English & English to French).
Award: $25,000 each; non-winning finalists receive $1,000; publisher of each winning book receives $3,000 to promote the book

The Gracies®

Alliance for Women in Media (AWM)
2365 Harrodsburg Rd, Suite A325, Lexington, KY 40504
Tel: 202-750-3664 *Fax:* 202-750-3664
E-mail: info@allwomeninmedia.org
Web Site: allwomeninmedia.org
Key Personnel
Exec Dir: Becky Brooks
Awarded for programming in all mediums which contributes to positive & realistic portrayals of women, addresses interests of concern to women, enhances women's image, position & welfare.
Award: Statue
Presented: Annually in May

Graduate & Undergraduate Hopwood Contest

University of Michigan, College of Literature, Science & Arts
1176 Angell Hall, 435 S State St, Ann Arbor, MI 48109-1003
Tel: 734-764-6296 *Fax:* 734-764-3128
E-mail: abeauch@umich.edu
Web Site: lsa.umich.edu/hopwood
Graduate or undergraduate awards in nonfiction, short fiction & poetry divisions. Novel, drama & screenplay divisions are combined categories in which graduates & undergraduates compete together. A qualifying writing course is mandatory. See web site for submission guidelines & list of courses.
Closing Date: Feb 7, by 12 noon

Grand Master Award

Crime Writers of Canada (CWC)
716 Thicket Way, Ottawa, ON K4A 3B5, Canada
E-mail: info@crimewriterscanada.com
Web Site: www.crimewriterscanada.com/awards
Key Personnel
Exec Dir: Alison Bruce *E-mail:* ed@crimewriterscanada.com

Asst Exec Dir & Arthur Ellis Awards Mgr: Ludvica Boota *E-mail:* aed@crimewriterscanada.com
Established: 2014
Biennial award (alternating with the Derrick Murdoch Award) to recognize a Canadian crime writer with a substantial body of work who has garnered national & international recognition. Awarded in even-numbered years.

Carla Gray Memorial Scholarship

Book Industry Charitable Foundation
713 W Ellsworth Rd, Suite A, Ann Arbor, MI 48108
Toll Free Tel: 866-733-9064 *Fax:* 734-477-2806
E-mail: info@bincfoundation.org
Web Site: www.bincfoundation.org/carla-gray/
Key Personnel
Exec Dir: Pam French *E-mail:* pam@bincfoundation.org
Dir, Devt: Kathy Bartson *E-mail:* kathy@bincfoundation.org
Progs Mgr: Kit Steinaway *E-mail:* kit@bincfoundation.org; Kate Weiss *E-mail:* kate@bincfoundation.org
Given annually to a single bookseller with fewer than 5 years of experience, working at a store with less than $500K in revenue. The bookseller will be given a scholarship for professional development, including attendance at a key industry trade show. The bookseller will have the opportunity to connect with booksellers, publishers & authors. The bookseller will also be given a stipend to support a community outreach project of his/her own creation.

James H Gray Award for Short Nonfiction

Writers' Guild of Alberta
11759 Groat Rd, Edmonton, AB T5M 3K6, Canada
Tel: 780-422-8174 *Toll Free Tel:* 800-665-5354 (AB only) *Fax:* 780-422-2663 (attn WGA)
E-mail: mail@writersguild.ca
Web Site: writersguild.ca
Key Personnel
Exec Dir: Carol Holmes *E-mail:* carol.holmes@writersguild.ca
Communs & Partnerships Coord: Ellen Kartz *E-mail:* ellen.kartz@writersguild.ca
Memb Servs Coord: Giorgia Severini
Progs Coord: Natalie Cook *E-mail:* natalie.cook@writersguild.ca; Julie Robinson *E-mail:* julie.robinson@writersguild.ca
Established: 2009
Open to published pieces on any topic by an Alberta author; no longer than 5,000 words.
Award: $700
Closing Date: Annually, Dec 31
Presented: Alberta Book Awards Gala
Branch Office(s)
505 21 Ave SW, Calgary, AB T2S 0G9, Canada, Prog Coord: Samantha Warwick *Tel:* 403-265-2226 *E-mail:* samantha.warwick@writersguild.ca

Graywolf Press Africa Prize

Graywolf Press
250 Third Ave N, Suite 600, Minneapolis, MN 55401
Tel: 651-641-0077 *Fax:* 651-641-0036
E-mail: submissions@graywolfpress.org
Web Site: www.graywolfpress.org/resources/graywolf-press-africa-prize
Awarded for a first novel ms by an African author primarily residing in Africa. All submissions must be full-length, previously unpublished novel mss. Submissions must be in English, but translations are acceptable. Applicants with prior books are eligible, so long as none of those books is a novel. Only electronic submissions will be considered through Submittable. Please follow these formatting guidelines: a

PDF or Word file (.doc & .docx), 12-point font, double-spaced text, numbered pages.
Award: $12,000 advance & publication
Closing Date: Oct 31

Graywolf Press Nonfiction Prize
Graywolf Press
250 Third Ave N, Suite 600, Minneapolis, MN 55401
Tel: 651-641-0077 *Fax:* 651-641-0036
E-mail: wolves@graywolfpress.org (no ms queries, sample chapters or proposals)
Web Site: www.graywolfpress.org/graywolf-press-nonfiction-prize
Awarded to the most promising & innovative literary nonfiction project by a writer not yet established in the genre. Awarded every other year to a ms in progress. One submission per person will be considered. Agented submissions are also welcome. Only electronic submissions are considered (upload ms file to Submittable). See web site for submission & contest guidelines.
Award: $12,000 advance & publication by Graywolf
Presented: Biennially in even-numbered years

Green Earth Book Award
The Nature Generation
3100 Clarendon Blvd, Suite 400, Arlington, VA 22201
E-mail: info@natgen.org
Web Site: www.natgen.org/green-earth-book-awards
Key Personnel
Dir, Progs: Jenny Newton Schmidt
Established: 2005
Annual environmental stewardship award for children & young adult books. There are 5 categories: Picture Book (books for young readers in which the visual & verbal narratives tell the story); Children's Fiction (novels for young readers up to age 12); Young Adult Fiction (books for readers age 13-21); Children's Nonfiction (nonfiction books for readers from infancy to age 12); Young Adult Nonfiction (nonfiction books for readers age 12-21).
Award: $1,500 to winning authors & illustrators

The Green Rose Prize in Poetry
New Issues Poetry & Prose
c/o Western Michigan University, 1903 W Michigan Ave, Kalamazoo, MI 49008-5463
Tel: 269-387-8185
E-mail: new-issues@wmich.edu
Web Site: www.wmich.edu/newissues/sub-guide.html
Key Personnel
Mng Ed: Kimberly Kolbe
Ed-in-Chief: William Olsen
Poets writing in English who have published one or more full-length collections of poetry. A $25 reading fee must accompany each ms; do not bind ms. Include a brief bio & relevant publication information, cover page with name, address, phone number, e-mail address & title of ms; include table of contents; enclose SASE. The winning ms will be named in January & published in the Spring of the following year.
Other Sponsor(s): Western Michigan University
Award: $2,000 & book publication
Closing Date: Sept 30

Bess Gresham Memorial
The Poetry Society of Virginia
900 Timber Creek Place, Virginia Beach, VA 23464
E-mail: poetryinva@aol.com
Web Site: poetrysocietyofvirginia.org
Key Personnel
Pres: Robert P Arthur *E-mail:* robert.peebles.arthur@gmail.com

Exec Dir: Guy Terrell *E-mail:* guy.terrell@earthlink.net
Adult Contest Chair: Steven Blythe
E-mail: stevenblythepoetry@gmail.com
All entries must be in English, original & unpublished. Submit 2 copies of each poem, each having the category name & number on top left of page. Only 1 poem per category; entries will not be returned. Subject: friends & friendship; 48 line limit. Entry fee: $4 nonmembs.
Award: $50 (1st place), $30 (2nd place), $20 (3rd place)
Closing Date: Jan
Presented: Annual PSV Awards Ceremony, April

Griffin Poetry Prize
The Griffin Trust for Excellence in Poetry
363 Parkridge Crescent, Oakville, ON L6M 1A8, Canada
Tel: 905-618-0420
E-mail: info@griffinpoetryprize.com; publicity@griffinpoetryprize.com
Web Site: www.griffinpoetryprize.com
Key Personnel
Founder & Chmn: Scott Griffin
E-mail: scottgriffin@griffinpoetryprize.com
Exec Dir: Ruth Smith
Press & Publicity: Melissa Shirley *Tel:* 647-389-9510
Awarded annually for the best collection of poetry in English published during the preceding year. Two categories: International & Canadian. Entries must come from publishers only. See web site for full eligibility requirements.
Award: 2 winners receive $65,000 each; finalists are awarded $10,000 each for their participation in the Shortlist Readings
Closing Date: June 30 & Dec 31
Presented: Shortlist announced in April; Awards given in June

Guggenheim Fellowships
John Simon Guggenheim Memorial Foundation
90 Park Ave, New York, NY 10016
Tel: 212-687-4470 *Fax:* 212-697-3248
Web Site: www.gf.org/about/fellowship
Established: 1925
Grants to selected individuals for 6-12 months. Fellowships are awarded through 2 annual competitions: one open to citizens & permanent residents of the US & Canada & the other open to citizens & permanent residents of Latin America & the Caribbean. Application required. Approximately 175 Fellowships awarded each year.
Poets, playwrights, screenwriters, scholars & writers of fiction & general nonfiction should submit examples of published books; do not send journal articles or essays. Published writing not regarded as appropriate includes self-published works, publications for which the author has paid, & publications by publishers who do not engage in a process of critical review of submitted work. In addition, genre work (e.g., mysteries, romance, fantasy, etc.) is considered not competitive. We do not consider children's or young adult books. Mss will not be accepted except from playwrights. Send no more than 3 different published works (it would be helpful to have 2 copies of the most recent work). Include a list of the items submitted, giving the title, publisher, & date of each, as well as the address to which the material should be returned.
Closing Date: Sept (applications), Nov (work example submissions)
Presented: US & CN announced early April, Latin America & Caribbean announced early June

Gutekunst Prize
Goethe-Institute New York

30 Irving Place, New York, NY 10003
Tel: 212-439-8700 *Fax:* 212-439-8705
E-mail: gutekunst@goethe.de
Web Site: www.goethe.de/ins/us/enkul/ser/uef/gut.html
Key Personnel
Libn: Walter Schlect *Tel:* 212-439-8697
E-mail: walter.schlect@goethe.de
Open to college students & to all translators under the age of 35 who, at the time the prize is awarded, have not yet published, nor are under contract for, a book-length translation. Applications will be accepted only from permanent residents of the US. Team translations will not be accepted. Each applicant is required to translate a literary text of approximately 22 pages, available on request from the Goethe-Institute New York. To receive the text & the application form, please send an e-mail to gutekunst@goethe.de. The translation & application form must be mailed electronically to the Goethe-Institute New York by the deadline. Full information on the submission procedure is included on the application form.
Award: $2,500
Closing Date: Mid-March
Presented: Annually in June

Hackmatack Children's Choice Book Award
Canada Council for the Arts (Conseil des arts du Canada)
150 Elgin St, 2nd fl, Ottawa, ON K2P 1L4, Canada
Mailing Address: PO Box 1047, Ottawa, ON K1P 5V8, Canada
Tel: 902-424-3774 *Fax:* 902-424-0613
E-mail: hackmatack@hackmatack.ca
Web Site: www.hackmatack.ca
Key Personnel
Prog Coord: Kate Watson
Established: 1999
Atlantic Canadian Children's Choice Award for grades 4-6. Four categories: English fiction, English nonfiction, French fiction & French nonfiction.
Other Sponsor(s): New Brunswick Public Library Service; Nova Scotia Department of Education
Award: Plaques
Closing Date: Annually, Oct 15
Presented: Award ceremony, Annually in Spring

Hackney Literary Awards
4650 Old Looney Mill Rd, Birmingham, AL 35243
E-mail: info@hackneyliteraryawards.org
Web Site: www.hackneyliteraryawards.org
Established: 1969
Short story, poetry & novel awards. Check web site or send SASE for contest guidelines. Entry fee: novels $30, short stories $20, poetry $15. Presented in the *Birmingham Arts Journal*.
Award: $600 (1st place), $400 (2nd place), $250 (3rd place), plus a $5,000 prize sponsored by Morris Hackney for an unpublished novel
Closing Date: Annually, Sept 30 for novel entries, Nov 30 for short story & poetry entries
Presented: March 30

Hadada Award
The Paris Review Foundation
544 W 27 St, New York, NY 10001
Tel: 212-343-1333
E-mail: queries@theparisreview.org
Web Site: www.theparisreview.org/about/prizes
Key Personnel
Mng Ed: Hasan Altaf
Presented annually to a distinguished member of the writing community who has made a strong & unique contribution to literature.
Presented: Spring Revel, April

Sarah Josepha Hale Award
Trustees of the Richards Library

58 N Main, Newport, NH 03773
Tel: 603-863-3430
E-mail: rfl@newport.lib.nh.us
Web Site: www.newport.lib.nh.us
Key Personnel
Lib Dir & Award Admin: Andrea Thorpe
   E-mail: athorpe@newport.lib.nh.us
Established: 1956
A distinguished literary figure in some way associated with New England. Nominations or applications are not accepted.
Award: Bronze medal & $1,000
Presented: Newport, NH

Loretta Dunn Hall Memorial
The Poetry Society of Virginia
900 Timber Creek Place, Virginia Beach, VA 23464
E-mail: poetryinva@aol.com
Web Site: poetrysocietyofvirginia.org
Key Personnel
Pres: Robert P Arthur *E-mail:* robert.peebles.
   arthur@gmail.com
Exec Dir: Guy Terrell *E-mail:* guy.terrell@
   earthlink.net
Adult Contest Chair: Steven Blythe
   E-mail: stevenblythepoetry@gmail.com
All entries must be in English, original & unpublished. Submit 2 copies, each having the category name & number on top left of page. Subject: family; any form; 24 line limit. VA residents only. Entry fee: $4 nonmembs.
Other Sponsor(s): Phyllis Hall Haislip
Award: $50 (1st prize), $30 (2nd prize), $20 (3rd prize)
Closing Date: Jan
Presented: Annual PSV Awards Ceremony, April

Virginia Hamilton Award for Lifetime Achievement, see Coretta Scott King - Virginia Hamilton Award for Lifetime Achievement

Hammett Prize
International Association of Crime Writers Inc, North American Branch
243 Fifth Ave, Suite 537, New York, NY 10016
E-mail: info@crimewritersna.org
Web Site: www.crimewritersna.org/hammett
Key Personnel
Exec Dir: Mary A Frisque *E-mail:* mfrisque@igc.
   org
Awarded annually for literary excellence in the field of crime writing, as reflected in a book published in the English language in the US +/or Canada. Submissions may be made by publishers, agents, or authors by sending 1 copy of the nominated book to each member of the Nominations Committee.
Closing Date: Dec 15

Handy Andy Prize
The Poetry Society of Virginia
900 Timber Creek Place, Virginia Beach, VA 23464
E-mail: poetryinva@aol.com
Web Site: poetrysocietyofvirginia.org
Key Personnel
Pres: Robert P Arthur *E-mail:* robert.peebles.
   arthur@gmail.com
Exec Dir: Guy Terrell *E-mail:* guy.terrell@
   earthlink.net
Adult Contest Chair: Steven Blythe
   E-mail: stevenblythepoetry@gmail.com
For a limerick. Must be in English, original & unpublished. Submit 2 copies, each having the category name & number on top left of page. Entry fee: $4 nonmembs.
Award: $25 (1st prize), $15 (2nd prize), $10 (3rd prize)
Closing Date: Jan
Presented: Annual PSV Awards Ceremony, April

Clarence H Haring Prize
American Historical Association (AHA)
400 "A" St SE, Washington, DC 20003
Tel: 202-544-2422 *Fax:* 202-544-8307
E-mail: awards@historians.org
Web Site: www.historians.org
For work by a Latin American in Latin American history during the preceding 5 years. Offered quinquennially. There is no language limitation on works submitted. Along with an application form, applicants must mail a copy of their book to each of the prize committee members who will be posted on our web site as the prize deadline approaches. Books published 2016 through 2020 will be considered. All updated info on web site.
Award: Cash prize
Closing Date: May 15, 2021
Presented: AHA Annual Meeting, New Orleans, LA, Jan 2022

Joy Harjo Poetry Award
CUTTHROAT, A Journal of the Arts
PO Box 2414, Durango, CO 81302
Tel: 970-903-7914
E-mail: cutthroatmag@gmail.com
Web Site: www.cutthroatmag.com
Key Personnel
Ed-in-Chief: Pamela Uschuk
Mng Ed: Andrew Allport
Fiction Ed: Beth Alvarado; William Luvaas
Poetry Ed: William Pitt Root
Established: 2005
Submit online up to 3 unpublished poems (100 line limit for each). Writers may submit as often as they wish. No poems that have been previously published or have won contests are eligible; $20 reading fee.
Award: $1,300 (1st place), $250 (2nd place), both include publication in *CUTTHROAT*
Closing Date: Annually in Oct
Presented: Annually in Dec

LD & LaVerne Harrell Clark Fiction Prize
Texas State University Department of English
Flowers Hall, Rm 365, 601 University Dr, San Marcos, TX 78666
Tel: 512-245-2163 *Fax:* 512-245-8546
Web Site: www.english.txstate.edu/
   clarkfictionprize.html
Key Personnel
Chair, English Dept: Victoria L Smith, PhD
   E-mail: vs13@txstate.edu
Established: 2019
Awarded annually to recognize an exceptional recently published book-length work of fiction. Prize committee solicits nominations. No applications or unsol nominations accepted.
Award: $25,000

Aurand Harris Memorial Playwriting Award
The New England Theatre Conference Inc
215 Knob Hill Dr, Hamden, CT 06518
Tel: 617-851-8535 *Fax:* 203-288-5938
E-mail: mail@netconline.org
Web Site: www.netconline.org
Established: 1997
Competition for new plays for young audiences. Scripts must be unpublished & unproduced. For guidelines, go to web site.
Closing Date: Annually, May 1
Presented: NETC Annual Convention, Annually in Nov

Julie Harris Playwright Award Competition, see BHTG - Julie Harris Playwright Award Competition

Haskins Medal Award
Medieval Academy of America
17 Dunster St, Suite 202, Cambridge, MA 02138

Tel: 617-491-1622 *Fax:* 617-492-3303
E-mail: info@themedievalacademy.org
Web Site: www.medievalacademy.org
Key Personnel
Exec Dir: Lisa Fagin Davis *E-mail:* lfd@
   themedievalacademy.org
Established: 1940
For a book of outstanding importance in the medieval field.
Award: Gold medal
Closing Date: Annually, Oct 15
Presented: Annually in Spring

Ellis W Hawley Prize
The Organization of American Historians (OAH)
112 N Bryan Ave, Bloomington, IN 47408-4141
Tel: 812-855-7311
E-mail: oah@oah.org
Web Site: www.oah.org/awards
Key Personnel
Exec Dir: Beth English *E-mail:* benglish@oah.org
Comm Coord: Kara Hamm *E-mail:* khamm@oah.
   org
Awarded annually to the author of the best book-length historical study of the political economy, politics, or institutions of the US, in its domestic or international affairs, from the Civil War to the present. Eligible works shall include book-length historical studies, written in English, published during the calendar year preceding that in which the award is given. One copy of each entry must be mailed directly to the committee members listed on the web site.
Closing Date: Oct 1, 2021 (postmarked)
Presented: OAH Annual Meeting, Boston, MA, March 31-April 3, 2022

Friedrich Hayek Lecture & Book Prize
Manhattan Institute for Policy Research
52 Vanderbilt Ave, New York, NY 10017
Tel: 212-599-7000
Web Site: www.manhattan-institute.org
Key Personnel
Contact: Dean Ball *E-mail:* dball@manhattan-
   institute.org
Honors the book published within the past two years that best reflects political philosopher & Nobel laureate F A Hayek's vision of economic & individual liberty. The winner of the prize will deliver the annual Hayek Lecture in New York in early June.
Award: $50,000
Presented: Late Feb

Headlands Center for the Arts Residency for Writers
944 Fort Barry, Sausalito, CA 94965
Tel: 415-331-2787 *Fax:* 415-331-3857
Web Site: www.headlands.org
Key Personnel
Residency Mgr: Holly Blake *Tel:* 415-331-2787
   ext 24 *E-mail:* hblake@headlands.org
Established: 1987
A 4- to 10-week residency at Headlands is granted each year to writers of the Artist in Residency Program. Call or write the HCA for deadline & other information. See web site for application & more information.
Award: 4- to 10-week stay, with optional stipend of $500/mo
Closing Date: June 2

Heartland Booksellers Award
Great Lakes Independent Booksellers Association (GLIBA)
250 Woodstock Ave, Clarendon Hills, IL 60514
Tel: 630-841-8129
Web Site: www.gliba.org/heartland-booksellers-award.html
Key Personnel
Exec Dir: Larry Law *E-mail:* larry@gliba.org
Annual joint awards program with the Midwest Independent Booksellers Association (MIBA).

A book's relationship to the Great Lakes region may consist of either the content of the book, the author's hometown, or the author's current residence. Books must be classifiable in one of 5 awarded genres: Fiction, nonfiction, poetry, young adult/middle grade, or children's picture book. Books submitted must have an on-sale date between May 1 of the year prior & April 30 of the award year. Both GLIBA & MIBA are conducting separate submission processes with publishers.

GLIBA submissions: Submit books by authors from the following states or books with content that pertains specifically to these states: Illinois, Indiana, Kentucky, Michigan & Ohio.

MIBA submissions: Submit books by authors from the following states or books with content that pertains specifically to these states: Iowa, Kansas, Minnesota, Missouri, Nebraska, North Dakota, South Dakota & Wisconsin.

Dual submissions: If the theme of your book is broadly Midwestern & pertains to both regions, please submit to both associations.

Entry fee: $25 per title.
Other Sponsor(s): Midwest Independent Booksellers Association (MIBA)
Closing Date: June 1
Presented: Heartland Fall Forum, Oct

Heartland Literary Award
Chicago Tribune
160 N Stetson Ave, Chicago, IL 60601
Tel: 312-222-3001
E-mail: ctc-arts@chicagotribune.com
Web Site: www.chicagotribune.com/entertainment/books/literary-awards
Established: 1988
Awarded annually in 2 categories: fiction & nonfiction.
Presented: Autumn

Drue Heinz Literature Prize
University of Pittsburgh Press
7500 Thomas Blvd, Pittsburgh, PA 15260
Tel: 412-383-2456 *Fax:* 412-383-2466
E-mail: info@upress.pitt.edu
Web Site: upittpress.org/prize/drue-heinz-literature-prize/; www.upress.pitt.edu
Key Personnel
Dir: Peter W Kracht *E-mail:* pkracht@upress.pitt.edu
Established: 1980
For a collection of short fiction 150-300 pages in length. Open to all writers who have published a book-length collection of short fiction or who have had 3 short stories or novellas published in commercial magazines or literary journals of national distribution. See web site for complete rules.
Other Sponsor(s): Drue Heinz & The Drue Heinz Trust
Award: $15,000 & publication by the University of Pittsburgh Press
Closing Date: Postmarked between May 1 & June 30
Presented: Pittsburgh, PA, Dec or Jan

The Hemingway Foundation/PEN Award
PEN America Boston
Unit of PEN America
MIT, 14N-221A, 77 Massachusetts Ave, Cambridge, MA 02139
Tel: 617-324-1729
E-mail: penamericaboston@pen.org
Web Site: pen.org/pen-america-boston
Key Personnel
Award Admin: Helene Atwan
Established: 1976
Given to a novel or book of short stories by an American writer who has not previously published a book of fiction. Entry fee: $50.

Award: Winner receives $25,000, a one-week residency & $5,000 honorarium in the Distinguished Visiting Writers Series (University of Idaho's MFA Creative Writing Program). The winner also receives, along with the four finalists, an Artist Residency for one month at the Ucross Foundation in Wyoming
Closing Date: Annually in Dec
Presented: JFK Library, Boston, MA, Annually in April

Cecil Hemley Memorial Award
Poetry Society of America (PSA)
15 Gramercy Park, New York, NY 10003
Tel: 212-254-9628
Web Site: poetrysociety.org/awards
Key Personnel
Pres: Allison Binns
Exec Dir: Matt Brogan *E-mail:* matt@poetrysociety.org
Deputy Dir: Brett Fletcher Lauer *E-mail:* brett@poetrysociety.org
Prog Dir: Laurin Macios *E-mail:* laurin@poetrysociety.org
Established: 1969
For an unpublished lyric poem that addresses a philosophical or epistemological concern, not to exceed 100 lines. Open to society members only. See web site for more information.
Award: $500
Closing Date: Annually, Oct-Dec (postmark)
Presented: Annual Awards Ceremony, New York, NY, Annually in Spring

Brodie Herndon Memorial
The Poetry Society of Virginia
900 Timber Creek Place, Virginia Beach, VA 23464
E-mail: poetryinva@aol.com
Web Site: poetrysocietyofvirginia.org
Key Personnel
Pres: Robert P Arthur *E-mail:* robert.peebles.arthur@gmail.com
Exec Dir: Guy Terrell *E-mail:* guy.terrell@earthlink.net
Adult Contest Chair: Steven Blythe
E-mail: stevenblythepoetry@gmail.com
Poems in any form about heroism; 48 line limit. Must be original, unpublished & in English. Submit 2 copies, each having the category name & number on top left of page. Entry fee: $4 nonmembs.
Award: $50 (1st prize), $30 (2nd prize), $20 (3rd prize)
Closing Date: Jan
Presented: Annual PSV Awards Ceremony, April

Carl Hertzog Award for Excellence in Book Design
Friends of the University Library
Subsidiary of University of Texas at El Paso
c/o Dir of the Library, University of Texas at El Paso, El Paso, TX 79968-0582
Tel: 915-747-5683 *Fax:* 915-747-5345
Web Site: www.utep.edu/library
Key Personnel
Assoc VP: Robert L Stakes *Tel:* 915-747-6710
E-mail: rlstakes@utep.edu
Biennial award for excellence in book design. There is a maximum number of 5 entries allowed & must have been printed during the 2 years prior to year in which the award is presented. While a printer, publisher or designer may submit an entry, only the designer is eligible to receive the award.
Award: $1,000, bronze medal & certificate
Closing Date: Nov 1, odd-numbered years
Presented: University of Texas, El Paso, Feb/March, even-numbered years

Hidden River Arts Playwriting Award
Hidden River™ Arts

PO Box 63927, Philadelphia, PA 19147
Tel: 610-764-0813
E-mail: hiddenriverarts@gmail.com
Web Site: www.hiddenriverarts.org; www.hiddenriverarts.com
Key Personnel
Founding Dir: Debra Leigh Scott
Established: 2002
Annual award for an unpublished, unproduced full-length play. Entry fee: $17.
Award: $1,000 (awarded by mail)
Closing Date: June 30
Presented: Dec

The High School Award
Oklahoma Library Association
PO Box 6550, Edmond, OK 73083
Tel: 405-525-5100 *Fax:* 405-525-5103
Web Site: www.oklibs.org
Key Personnel
Exec Dir: Kay Boies *E-mail:* execdirector@oklibs.org
Established: 2010
Student choice award: students in grades 9-12 who have read/listened to at least 3 titles from the High School Master list are eligible to vote.
Award: Plaque/Medal
Closing Date: Annually, March 1
Presented: OLA Annual Conference, Annually in April

Higher Education Scholarship Program
Book Industry Charitable Foundation
3135 S State St, Suite 203, Ann Arbor, MI 48108
Toll Free Tel: 866-733-9064 *Fax:* 734-477-2806
E-mail: info@bincfoundation.org
Web Site: www.bincfoundation.org/scholarship
Key Personnel
Exec Dir: Pam French *E-mail:* pam@bincfoundation.org
Dir, Devt: Kathy Bartson *E-mail:* kathy@bincfoundation.org
Progs Mgr: Kit Steinaway *E-mail:* kit@bincfoundation.org; Kate Weiss *E-mail:* kate@bincfoundation.org
Established: 2001
Seven awards to the dependents or spouses/partners of booksellers for full-or part-time study at any accredited institution in the US. The bookseller themselves must be currently employed at a brick & mortar bookstore & have been employed there for at least 90 days for their family members to be eligible.
Award: $3,500 each

The Tony Hillerman Prize
Western Writers of America Inc (WWA)
c/o St Martin's Press, 120 Broadway, New York, NY 10271
E-mail: tonyhillermanprize@stmartins.com
Web Site: us.macmillan.com/minotaurbooks/tonyhillermanprize
Established: 2007
Awarded annually for the best first mystery set in the Southwest. Entrants must submit entry form & ms online or by mail. Limit of 1 entry per person. See web site for full guidelines.
Other Sponsor(s): St Martin's Press
Award: $10,000 & publication by St Martin's Press
Closing Date: Jan 2

Hillman Prizes for Journalism
The Sidney Hillman Foundation
330 W 42 St, Suite 900, New York, NY 10036
Tel: 646-448-6413
Web Site: www.hillmanfoundation.org
Key Personnel
Pres: Bruce Raynor
Exec Dir: Alexandra Lescaze *E-mail:* alex@hillmanfoundation.org
Established: 1950

For investigative journalism that fosters social & economic justice. See web site for categories.

Award: $5,000 & certificate designed by New York cartoonist Edward Sorel

Closing Date: Jan 31

Presented: Award ceremony & cocktail party, New York, NY, Annually in mid-May

Darlene Clark Hine Award

The Organization of American Historians (OAH)
112 N Bryan Ave, Bloomington, IN 47408-4141
Tel: 812-855-7311
E-mail: oah@oah.org
Web Site: www.oah.org/awards
Key Personnel
Exec Dir: Beth English *E-mail:* benglish@oah.org
Comm Coord: Kara Hamm *E-mail:* khamm@oah.org
Awarded annually to the author of the best book in African American women's & gender history. Each entry must be published in the calendar year preceding that in which the award is given. One copy of each entry must be mailed directly to the committee members listed on the web site.
Closing Date: Oct 1, 2021 (postmarked)
Presented: OAH Annual Meeting, Boston, MA, March 31-April 3, 2022

Eric Hoffer Award

www.HofferAward.com
Subsidiary of The Eric Hoffer Project
PO Box 11, Titusville, NJ 08560
E-mail: info@hofferaward.com
Web Site: www.hofferaward.com
Key Personnel
Chair: Christopher Klim
Coord: Dawn Shows
Established: 2002
Annual award to honor independent books of exceptional merit. Open to small, academic & independent presses for books published in the last 2 years. Books published before this 2-year window may enter either the Legacy Fiction or Legacy Nonfiction categories. In addition to the grand prize, various other prizes & separate distinctions are given for presses, including the Montaigne Medal, the da Vinci Eye & the First Horizon Award. For each category registration, submit 1 book, registration form & $55 fee. See web site for complete guidelines.
Award: $2,500 grand prize
Closing Date: Nominations Jan 21
Presented: Annually in April/May

Bess Hokin Prize

Poetry Magazine
61 W Superior St, Chicago, IL 60654
Tel: 312-787-7070 *Fax:* 312-787-6650
E-mail: editors@poetrymagazine.org
Web Site: www.poetryfoundation.org
Key Personnel
Edit Asst: Holly Amos *E-mail:* hamos@poetrymagazine.org
Established: 1948
For poetry published in the preceding 2 volumes of *Poetry* magazine. No application necessary.
Award: $1,000
Presented: Annually in Dec

Honickman First Book Prize

American Poetry Review
1906 Rittenhouse Sq, Philadelphia, PA 19103
Tel: 215-309-3722
Web Site: www.aprweb.org
Key Personnel
Ed: Elizabeth Scanlon *E-mail:* escanlon@aprweb.org
Established: 1997
Awarded to any US citizen, writing in English & who has not published a book-length collection of poems with an ISBN. Poems previously published in periodicals or limited-edition chapbooks may be included in the ms, but the ms itself must not have been published as a book-length work exceeding 25 pages. No translations or multiple author entries accepted. Entry fee $25. Now accepting online submissions.
Award: $3,000
Closing Date: Oct 31 (postmark)
Presented: Winner announced in March/April issue of the *American Poetry Review*

The Hopwood Award Theodore Roethke Prize

University of Michigan, College of Literature, Science & Arts
1176 Angell Hall, 435 S State St, Ann Arbor, MI 48109-1003
Tel: 734-764-6296 *Fax:* 734-764-3128
E-mail: abeauch@umich.edu
Web Site: lsa.umich.edu/hopwood
Awarded to the best long poem or poetic sequence written by a University of Michigan student, undergraduate or graduate.
Award: $5,000
Closing Date: 1st Wednesday in Dec, by 12 noon
Presented: April

Hopwood Underclassmen Contest

University of Michigan, College of Literature, Science & Arts
1176 Angell Hall, 435 S State St, Ann Arbor, MI 48109-1003
Tel: 734-764-6296 *Fax:* 734-764-3128
E-mail: abeauch@umich.edu
Web Site: lsa.umich.edu/hopwood
Open to any first- or second-year student regularly enrolled in qualifying writing courses. Three types of writing are eligible: nonfiction, fiction & poetry. See web site for specific guidelines.
Award: $500-$2,000 each
Closing Date: 1st Wednesday in Dec, by 12 noon
Presented: Early in Winter term

Firman Houghton Prize

New England Poetry Club
46 Wallace St, Somerville, MA 02144
E-mail: info@nepoetryclub.org
Web Site: www.nepoetryclub.org
Key Personnel
Pres: Mary Buchinger
VP: Hillary Sallick
Treas: Linda Haviland Conte
Established: 1987
Award for a lyric poem in honor of the former president of the NEPC. $15 for 3 contest entries per poem entry & $3 for additional entries, free for members & students. $20 reading fee for nonmembs.
Award: $250
Closing Date: Annually, May 31
Presented: Winners announced online Aug/Sept

Tom Howard/John H Reid Fiction & Essay Contest

Winning Writers
351 Pleasant St, PMB 222, Northampton, MA 01060-3961
Tel: 413-320-1847 *Toll Free Tel:* 866-WINWRIT (946-9748) *Fax:* 413-280-0539
Web Site: www.winningwriters.com
Key Personnel
Pres: Adam Cohen *E-mail:* adam@winningwriters.com
VP: Jendi Reiter
Established: 1990
Submit short stories, essays or other works of prose, up to 6,000 words each. Must be your own original work. $20 reading fee per entry. Writers of all nations may enter, however, the works you submit should be in English. Both published & unpublished work accepted. Applications accepted October 15-April 30.
Award: $1,500 (each 1st prize, fiction & essay), $100 (10 honorable mention awards) & publication on web site for all winners
Closing Date: Annually, April 30 (postmark)
Presented: Winner announced Oct 15 on web site

Tom Howard/Margaret Reid Poetry Contest

Winning Writers
351 Pleasant St, PMB 222, Northampton, MA 01060-3961
Tel: 413-320-1847 *Toll Free Tel:* 866-WINWRIT (946-9748) *Fax:* 413-280-0539
Web Site: www.winningwriters.com
Key Personnel
Pres: Adam Cohen *E-mail:* adam@winningwriters.com
VP: Jendi Reiter
Established: 2002
The Tom Howard Prize is awarded for a poem in any style or genre. The Margaret Reid Prize is awarded for a poem that rhymes or has a traditional style. Entry fee is $12 per poem submitted up to 250 lines. See web site for complete submission details & contest results. Both published & unpublished work accepted. Poets of all nations may enter, however, the works you submit should be in English.
Award: $1,500 each (1st prize, Tom Howard & Margaret Reid), $100 each (10 honorable mention awards) & publication on web site for all winners
Closing Date: Annually, Sept 30 (postmark)
Presented: Winner announced April 15 on web site

Julia Ward Howe Book Awards

Boston Authors Club Inc
c/o Professor Mary Cronin, 2400 Beacon St, Unit 208, Beacon Hill, MA 02467
Mailing Address: 2400 Beacon St, No 208, Chestnut, MA 02467
Tel: 617-552-4031
E-mail: bostonauthorsclub@gmail.com
Web Site: bostonauthorsclub.org
Key Personnel
Pres: Mary Cronin
VP: Shirley Moskow *Tel:* 781-862-7697 *E-mail:* shirley.moskow@rtr.com
Established: 1997
Books must be published the year prior to the award. Prizes given in both adult & young reader's categories. Authors must live or have lived, worked or attended college within 100 miles of Boston the year their books are published. Submission fee of $25 per title.
Other Sponsor(s): Boston Public Library (Rare Books Div)
Award: $1,000 each for 2 books; certificates to finalists & authors of recommended books (number varies). All receive 1-year complimentary membership in the Club
Closing Date: Annually, Jan 15
Presented: Boston Public Library, Annually in Sept

The William Dean Howells Medal

American Academy of Arts & Letters
633 W 155 St, New York, NY 10032
Tel: 212-368-5900 *Fax:* 212-491-4615
E-mail: academy@artsandletters.org
Web Site: artsandletters.org
Key Personnel
Exec Dir: Cody Upton
Established: 1925
Given once every 5 years in recognition of the most distinguished American novel published during that period.

L Ron Hubbard's Writers of the Future Contest

Author Services Inc
7051 Hollywood Blvd, Hollywood, CA 90028
Tel: 323-466-3310 *Fax:* 323-466-6474
E-mail: contests@authorservicesinc.com
Web Site: www.writersofthefuture.com
Key Personnel
Contest Dir: Joni Labaqui
Coordinating Judge: David Farland
Established: 1983
Short stories & novelettes (under 17,000 words)
of science fiction & fantasy for new & amateur
writers. No entry fee required, entrants retain
all publication rights.
Award: Annually: Trophy & $5,000 (Grand
prize); Quarterly: $1,000 (1st place), $750 (2nd
place), $500 (3rd place)
Closing Date: Quarterly: March 31, June 30, Sept
30, Dec 31

Charlotte Huck Award

National Council of Teachers of English (NCTE)
340 N Neil St, Suite 104, Champaign, IL 61820
Tel: 217-328-3870 *Toll Free Tel:* 877-369-6283
(cust serv) *Fax:* 217-328-9645; 217-328-0977
E-mail: bookawards@ncte.org
Web Site: www2.ncte.org/awards
Key Personnel
Exec Dir: Emily Kirkpatrick *Tel:* 217-278-3601
E-mail: ekirkpatrick@ncte.org
Proj Specialist, Communs: Lori Bianchini
E-mail: lbianchini@ncte.org
Established: 2014
Awarded annually to promote & recognize fiction
that has the potential to transform children's
lives by inviting compassion, imagination &
wonder. Books must have been published +/or
distributed in the US during the calendar year.
Nominations of individual books may come
from publishers, NCTE membership & from
the educational community at large. One title
is singled out for the award & up to 5 honor
books are also recognized. Eight additional recommended books can be named.
Award: Winning author +/or translator receives
plaque & are the featured speaker(s) at the luncheon; Honor book author(s) +/or illustrator(s)
receive certificate & invitation to present at session following the luncheon
Closing Date: Oct 15
Presented: Children's Book Awards Luncheon,
NCTE Annual Convention

The Hugo Awards

The World Science Fiction Society
PO Box 64128, Sunnyvale, CA 94088
Web Site: www.wsfs.org/awards; www.
thehugoawards.org
Established: 1953
Fan-voted awards for science fiction & fantasy literature. During Jan-March, members of Worldcon can nominate up to 5 people or works
from the previous year in 15 categories. Shortlist of 5 finalists announced in April. Worldcon
members cast their final ballots in July.
Award: Trophy
Presented: Hugo Ceremony, World Science Fiction Convention

Lynda Hull Memorial Poetry Prize

Crazyhorse
College of Charleston, Dept of English, 66
George St, Charleston, SC 29424
Tel: 843-953-4470
E-mail: crazyhorse@cofc.edu
Web Site: crazyhorse.cofc.edu/prizes
Key Personnel
Mng Ed: Jonathan Heinen
Awarded annually for best single poem. Enter 3
poems with $20 entry fee, which includes one-
year subscription. Submissions accepted during

the month of Jan. Nationally prominent poet
judges. See web site for complete instructions.
Award: $2,000 & publication in *Crazyhorse*
Closing Date: Jan 31

Hurston/Wright Award for College Writers

The Zora Neale Hurston/Richard Wright Founda-
tion
10 "G" St NE, Suite 600, Washington, DC 20002
Tel: 202-248-5051
E-mail: info@hurstonwright.org
Web Site: www.hurstonwright.org
Key Personnel
Co-Founder: Marita Golden; Clyde McElvane
Exec Dir: Kesha Lee
Established: 1990
Literary award presented annually to honor excel-
lence in fiction writing by African-American
students enrolled as an undergraduate or grad-
uate student in any college or university. Non-
refundable application fee of $10.
Award: $1,000 & story published in literary jour-
nal (1st prize), $500 (awarded to 2 runners-up)
Closing Date: Jan 31
Presented: April

Hurston/Wright Legacy Awards

The Zora Neale Hurston/Richard Wright Founda-
tion
10 "G" St NE, Suite 600, Washington, DC 20002
Tel: 202-248-5051
E-mail: info@hurstonwright.org
Web Site: www.hurstonwright.org
Key Personnel
Co-Founder: Marita Golden; Clyde McElvane
Exec Dir: Kesha Lee
Established: 2000
Annual national literary award for debut fiction,
fiction, nonfiction & poetry for published black
writers. Application fee: $30.
Award: $10,000 for winners in 3 categories,
$5,000 for 6 runners-up (2 in each category)
Presented: Oct

IACP Cookbook Awards

International Association of Culinary Profession-
als (IACP)
45 Rockefeller Plaza, Suite 2000, New York, NY
10111
Tel: 646-358-4957 *Toll Free Tel:* 866-358-4951
Toll Free Fax: 866-358-2524
E-mail: info@iacp.com
Web Site: www.iacp.com; www.iacp.com/award/
more/cookbook
Key Personnel
Memb Progs & Opers Mgr: Shani Phelan
Established: 1985
Open to any food or beverage book published
in the English language. Allows publishers to
enter books in the category of their choice.
Through a strict, 2-tier system of judging &
balloting, the entries are narrowed to 3 nomi-
nees in each category. See submission guide-
lines at www.iacp.com/award/more/cookbook.
Presented: Annual Conference, location varies,
Date varies every year, usually in April

The Idaho Prize for Poetry

Lost Horse Press
105 Lost Horse Lane, Sandpoint, ID 83864
Tel: 208-255-4410 *Fax:* 208-255-1560
E-mail: losthorsepress@mindspring.com
Web Site: www.losthorsepress.org
Key Personnel
Publr: Christine Holbert
Established: 2003
A national competition for a book-length poetry
ms written by an American poet. Accompany
ms with $25 reading fee (check or money or-
der only). Books distributed by the University
of Washington Press. May also submit online
using submittable.com.

Award: $1,000 & publication with 20 free author
copies
Closing Date: Annually, May 15
Presented: Annually, Aug 15

ILA Children's & Young Adults' Book Awards

International Literacy Association (ILA)
PO Box 8139, Newark, DE 19714-8139
Tel: 302-731-1600 *Toll Free Tel:* 800-336-7323
(US & CN) *Fax:* 302-731-1057
E-mail: ilaawards@reading.org
Web Site: www.literacyworldwide.org
Key Personnel
Exec Dir: Marcie Craig Post
Assoc Exec Dir: Stephen Sye *E-mail:* ssye@
reading.org
Established: 1975
Awards for newly published authors who show
unusual promise in the children's or young
adult book field. Awards will be given for
fiction & nonfiction in 3 categories: Primary
(ages preschool-8), Intermediate (ages 9-13)
& Young Adult (ages 14-17). Books from any
country & published in English for the first
time during the previous calendar year will be
considered.
Award: $800 per book
Closing Date: March 15, 2021
Presented: Annual Conference, Oct 2021

Illumination Book Awards

Independent Publisher Online
Division of Jenkins Group Inc
1129 Woodmere Ave, Suite B, Traverse City, MI
49686
Tel: 231-933-0445 *Toll Free Tel:* 800-706-4636
Fax: 231-933-0448
E-mail: awards@bookpublishing.com
Web Site: www.illuminationawards.com
Key Personnel
CEO: Jerrold R Jenkins *E-mail:* jrj@
bookpublishing.com
Pres: James Kalajian *Tel:* 800-706-4636 ext 1006
E-mail: jjk@bookpublishing.com
Mng Ed & Awards Dir: Jim Barnes *Tel:* 800-706-
4636 ext 1011 *E-mail:* jimb@bookpublishing.
com
Awards Coord: Amy Shamroe
Established: 2013
With the motto "Shining a Light on Exemplary
Christian Books," the Illumination Awards are
designed to honor the year's best new titles
written & published with a Christian worldview. The contest is for published books only,
as our judging criteria include cover design,
layout, etc. Books from all methods of publishing are welcome & authors of royalty-
published books are welcome to enter their
books themselves.
Other Sponsor(s): Jenkins Group
Award: Gold medal (1st place), silver medal (2nd
place), bronze medal (3rd place), foil seals
available, winners featured in *Independent Publisher Online*
Closing Date: Annually in Nov
Presented: Online, Annually in Jan

John Phillip Immroth Memorial Award

Intellectual Freedom Round Table (IFRT)
Unit of The American Library Association (ALA)
50 E Huron St, Chicago, IL 60611
Tel: 312-280-4226 *Toll Free Tel:* 800-545-2433
E-mail: oif@ala.org
Web Site: www.ala.org/ifrt
Key Personnel
Asst Dir: Kristen Pekoll *Tel:* 312-280-4220
Established: 1979
Annual award for notable contribution to intel-
lectual freedom & demonstrations of personal
courage in defense of freedom of expression.
Award: $500 & citation

Closing Date: Annually, Dec 1
Presented: ALA Annual Conference, Annually in
June

The Independent Publisher Book Awards
Independent Publisher Online
Division of Jenkins Group Inc
1129 Woodmere Ave, Suite B, Traverse City, MI
49686
Tel: 231-933-0445 *Toll Free Tel:* 800-706-4636
Fax: 231-933-0448
E-mail: awards@bookpublishing.com
Web Site: www.independentpublisher.com/ipland/
ipawards.php
Key Personnel
CEO: Jerrold R Jenkins *E-mail:* jrj@
bookpublishing.com
Pres: James Kalajian *Tel:* 800-706-4636 ext 1006
E-mail: jjk@bookpublishing.com
Mng Ed & Awards Dir: Jim Barnes *Tel:* 800-706-
4636 ext 1011 *E-mail:* jimb@bookpublishing.
com
Awards Coord: Amy Shamroe
Established: 1996
Recognizes the works of independent publishers
in 76 national & 22 regional categories, for
excellence in literary merit, design & produc-
tion, published during previous calendar year.
Ebooks & audiobooks are welcome.
Other Sponsor(s): Jenkins Group
Award: Gold medal (1st place), silver medal (2nd
place) & bronze medal (3rd place); foil seals
available; winners featured in *Independent Publisher Magazine Online*
Closing Date: Annually in March
Presented: BookExpo, Annually in May

**Independent Publishers of New England Book
Awards**
Independent Publishers of New England (IPNE)
10 Court St, No 206, Arlington, MA 02476-0206
Tel: 339-368-8229
E-mail: bookawards@ipne.org
Web Site: www.ipne.org/awards
Key Personnel
Pres: Eddie Vincent
Categories: Informational nonfiction, narrative
nonfiction, literary nonfiction, genre fiction, de-
sign, young adult, children's, book promotional
campaign, coffee table & art books.
Entry fee: $45 per title (1 category), $25 per ad-
ditional category, nonmembs $70 per title (1
category).
Closing Date: May 31
Presented: Annually in Nov

Indiana Review Fiction Prize
Indiana Review
Ballantine Hall 529, 1020 E Kirkwood Ave,
Bloomington, IN 47405
Tel: 812-855-3439
E-mail: inreview@indiana.edu
Web Site: indianareview.org
Key Personnel
Ed: Tessa Yang
Assoc Ed: Essence London
Submit a short story of up to 8,000 words; only
1 story per entry, maximum 12 point font. Pre-
viously published works & works forthcom-
ing elsewhere cannot be considered; $20 entry
fee (which includes a subscription to *Indiana
Review*). All prize entries are considered for
publication.
Award: $1,000 & publication in *Indiana Review*
Closing Date: Annually in Oct

IndieReader Discovery Awards
IndieReader
PO Box 43121, Montclair, NJ 07043
E-mail: amy@indiereader.com
Web Site: indiereader.com/irda
Established: 2012

Annual awards open to indie authors who have
self-published books. Entry fee: $150 per title
plus additional $50 for each additional category
entered. Submit 3 copies of your work or a
shareable efile-no matter how many categories
you've entered.
Other Sponsor(s): Amazon Kindle
Award: The top winners in the fiction & nonfiction categories will receive the following:
Kindle Paperwhite 3G. First look consideration with an eye to representation from Dystel,
Goderich & Bourret Literary Management. A
free author web site for a year via Featherlight.
The winners from each sub-category (addition
to the top winners), will also receive the following: A professional IndieReader review.
Exposure to a panel of judges who can make
a difference in your book's success. An In-
dieReader "All About the Book" feature. Stick-
ers pronouncing your book an "IndieReader
Discovery Awards" winner
Closing Date: March
Presented: BookExpo/BookCon, Annually in late
May/early June

Indies Choice Book Awards
American Booksellers Association
333 Westchester Ave, Suite S202, White Plains,
NY 10604
Tel: 914-406-7500 *Toll Free Tel:* 800-637-0037
Fax: 914-417-4013
Web Site: www.bookweb.org
Established: 1991
Book finalists will be picked by a bookseller jury,
but the pool is limited to monthly +/or quar-
terly Indie Next list selections. Categories have
been revamped & expanded, now honoring the
book of the year in the following categories:
adult fiction, adult nonfiction, adult debut,
young adults, EB White Read Aloud Picture
Book; EB White Middle Reader; Picture Book
Hall of Fame & Indie Champion.
Presented: BookExpo & ABA Convention

Individual Artist Awards
Maryland State Arts Council
Affiliate of Maryland Dept of Commerce
175 W Ostend St, Suite E, Baltimore, MD 21230
Tel: 410-767-6555 *Fax:* 410-333-1062
E-mail: msac@msac.org
Web Site: www.msac.org
Key Personnel
Exec Dir: Theresa Colvin
Solely based on excellence of previous work.
Must be a Maryland resident. Applications
available. Award categories changed annually.
Check with council for individual availability.
Award: $6,000 (1st prize), $3,000 (2nd prize) &
$1,000 (3rd prize)
Closing Date: July (see web site for exact date)
Presented: Awards Reception, Early June

Individual Artist Fellowships
Maine Arts Commission
Division of State of Maine
25 State House Sta, 193 State St, Augusta, ME
04333-0025
Tel: 207-287-2726 *Fax:* 207-287-2725
Web Site: maineart.maine.gov
Key Personnel
Sr Grants Dir: Kathy Ann Shaw *E-mail:* kathy.
shaw@maine.gov
Established: 1987
Three prizes awarded annually to visual, perform-
ing & literary artists, craft, media/film, tradi-
tional arts.
Other Sponsor(s): Maine Community Foundation
Award: $5,000
Closing Date: May
Presented: Fall

Individual Artist Fellowships
Nebraska Arts Council
Division of State of Nebraska
1004 Farnam, Plaza Level, Omaha, NE 68102
Tel: 402-595-2122 *Toll Free Tel:* 800-341-4067
Fax: 402-595-2334
Web Site: www.nebraskaartscouncil.org
Key Personnel
Artist Servs & Communs Mgr: Launa Bacon
E-mail: launa.bacon@nebraska.gov
Established: 1991
Fellowship for Nebraska residents only; operates
on a 3-year cycle rotating with visual & per-
forming arts & literature.
Award: $1,000-$5,000
Closing Date: Annually, Nov 15

Individual Artist Project Grant
Florida Dept of State, Div of Cultural Affairs
500 S Bronough St, Tallahassee, FL 32399-0250
Tel: 850-245-6470 *Fax:* 850-245-6497
E-mail: info@dos.myflorida.com
Web Site: dos.myflorida.com/cultural
Key Personnel
Dir: Sandy Shaughnessy *E-mail:* sshaughnessy@
dos.myflorida.com
Arts Consultant: Hillary Crawford
E-mail: hcrawford@dos.myflorida.com
Established: 1976
Awarded annually, this fellowship program sup-
ports the general artistic & career advancement
of individual artists & recognizes the creation
of new artworks by these artists.
Award: Up to $25,000
Closing Date: June 1

Individual Artist's Fellowships
South Carolina Arts Commission (SCAC)
Division of State of South Carolina
1026 Sumter St, Suite 200, Columbia, SC 29201-
3746
Tel: 803-734-8696 *Fax:* 803-734-8526
E-mail: info@arts.sc.gov
Web Site: www.southcarolinaarts.com
Key Personnel
Communs Dir: Milly Hough *Tel:* 803-734-8698
E-mail: mhough@arts.sc.gov
Established: 2007
Non-matching funds for South Carolina residents
only. Up to 4 fellowships each year according
to rotation cycle. Online submissions only. See
commission's web site for details.
Award: $5,000 each
Closing Date: Annually, Nov (1st weekday)

Individual Excellence Awards
Ohio Arts Council
30 E Broad St, 33rd fl, Columbus, OH 43215
Tel: 614-466-2613 *Fax:* 614-466-4494
Web Site: www.oac.state.oh.us
Key Personnel
Exec Dir: Donna Collins *E-mail:* donna.collins@
oac.ohio.gov
Prog Coord: Kathy Signorino *E-mail:* kathy.
signorino@oac.ohio.gov
Indiv Prog: Ken Emerick *E-mail:* ken.emerick@
oac.ohio.gov
Established: 1978
Available to creative artists who are residents of
Ohio. Applicants must have lived in Ohio for 1
year prior to the September 1 deadline & must
remain in the state during the grant period. Applications must be submitted online.
Odd-numbered calendar years, applications accepted in the following disciplines: choreography, criticism, fiction/nonfiction, music composition, playwriting/screenplays & poetry.
Even-numbered calendar years, applications
accepted in these disciplines: crafts, design
arts/illustration, interdisciplinary/performance
art, media arts, photography & visual arts.

Award: $5,000 (number of awards given determined by panel)
Closing Date: Sept 1

Innis-Gerin Medal
Royal Society of Canada
Walter House, 282 Somerset W, Ottawa, ON K2P 0J6, Canada
Tel: 613-991-6990 (ext 106) *Fax:* 613-991-6996
E-mail: nominations@rsc-src.ca
Web Site: www.rsc-src.ca
Key Personnel
Mgr, Fellowship & Awards: Marie-Lyne Renaud
E-mail: mlrenaud@rsc-src.ca
Established: 1966
Biennial award given in even-numbered years for a distinguished & sustained contribution to literature in social science, human geography & social psychology.
Award: Bronze medal
Closing Date: March 1
Presented: RSC Annual Meeting, Nov

Innovations in Reading Prize
National Book Foundation
90 Broad St, Suite 604, New York, NY 10004
Tel: 212-685-0261 *Fax:* 212-213-6570
E-mail: nationalbook@nationalbook.org
Web Site: www.nationalbook.org/innovations_in_reading
Key Personnel
Deputy Dir: Jordan Smith *E-mail:* jsmith@nationalbook.org
Dir, Technol: Meredith Andrews
E-mail: mandrews@nationalbook.org
Assoc Dir, Awards: Anna Dobben
E-mail: adobben@nationalbook.org
Communs & Mktg Mgr: Bev Rivero
E-mail: brivero@nationalbook.org
Public Progs Mgr: Natalie Green
E-mail: ngreen@nationalbook.org
Admin & Devt Coord: Dhyana Taylor
E-mail: dtaylor@nationalbook.org
Established: 2009
Awarded annually to an individual or organization that has developed an innovative project which creates & sustains a lifelong love of reading in the community they serve. The Foundation also recognizes 4 projects to receive the designation of honorable mention. Applications open mid-January & are submitted via online form through Submittable. See application guidelines on web site.
Other Sponsor(s): Levenger Foundation
Award: $10,000 & invitation to presnt at the Why Reading Matters Conference

Intermediate Sequoyah Book Award
Oklahoma Library Association
PO Box 6550, Edmond, OK 73083
Tel: 405-525-5100 *Fax:* 405-525-5103
Web Site: www.oklibs.org
Key Personnel
Exec Dir: Kay Boies *E-mail:* execdirector@oklibs.org
Established: 1988
Student choice award; students in grades 6-8 who have read/listened to at least 3 titles from the Intermediate Masterlist are eligible to vote.
Award: Plaque/medal
Closing Date: Annually, March 1
Presented: OLA Annual Conference, Annually in April

International Latino Book Awards
Latino Literacy Now
3445 Catalina Dr, Carlsbad, CA 92010
Tel: 760-434-1223 *Fax:* 760-434-7476
Web Site: www.award.news
Key Personnel
Awards Chair: Kirk Whisler *E-mail:* kirk@whisler.com

Established: 1998
Annual book awards celebrating books by & about Latinos.
Other Sponsor(s): California State University, Dominguez Hills; Entravision; Libros Publishing; Scholastic; VISA
Closing Date: April 11
Presented: California State University, Dominguez Hills, CA, Early Sept

International Latino Unpublished Book Awards
Latino Literacy Now
3445 Catalina Dr, Carlsbad, CA 92010
Tel: 760-434-1223 *Fax:* 760-434-7476
Web Site: www.award.news
Key Personnel
Awards Chair: Kirk Whisler *E-mail:* kirk@whisler.com
Awards for achievement in Latino literature in English & Spanish. Category groups: children, youth & young adult; nonfiction; fiction; best themed. Entries must be PDF of ms. Books written in English must be written by a Latino author or have a Latino theme. Books in Spanish, Portuguese, or a bilingual format may have been written by anyone. Entry fee: $65 per entry until November 21, $90 per entry up until final deadline.
Closing Date: April 11
Presented: MiraCosta College, San Diego County, CA, Sept

International Poetry Competition
Atlanta Review
686 Cherry St NW, Suite 333, Atlanta, GA 30332-0161
E-mail: atlantareview@gatech.edu
Web Site: www.atlantareview.com
Key Personnel
Mng Ed: J C Reilly
Ed: Karen J Head, PhD
Established: 1996
Online entry at atlantareview.submittable.com.
Award: $1,000 (grand prize), publication in *Atlanta Review* (20 publication prizes)
Closing Date: Annually, March 1

InterTech™ Technology Awards
PRINTING United Alliance
10015 Main St, Fairfax, VA 22031-3489
Tel: 703-385-1335 *Toll Free Tel:* 888-385-3588
Fax: 703-273-0456
E-mail: intertech@printing.org
Web Site: www.printing.org/programs/awards/intertechtm-technology-awards
Key Personnel
Pres & CEO: Ford Bowers *E-mail:* fbowers@printing.org
Established: 1978
Honors innovative technology excellence for the graphic communications industry. The criteria for nomination stresses that the technology be recently developed, proved in industrial application, but not yet in widespread use. See web site for more information.
Award: Lucite Star
Closing Date: June
Presented: PRINTING United Alliance Awards Gala, Annually in Fall
Branch Office(s)
1325 "G" St NW, Suite 500, Washington, DC 20005
2000 Corporate Dr, Suite 205, Wexford, PA 15090 *Tel:* 412-741-6860 *Toll Free Tel:* 800-910-4283 *Fax:* 412-741-2311

IODE Jean Throop Book Award
IODE Ontario
9-45 Frid St, Hamilton, ON L8P 4M3, Canada
Tel: 905-522-9537 *Fax:* 905-522-3637
E-mail: iodeontario@bellnet.ca

Web Site: www.iodeontario.ca
Key Personnel
Convenor: Mary K Anderson
Area VP: Margo Mackinnon
Established: 1974
Children's book (Toronto area author +/or illustrator).
Award: $1,000 & certificate
Closing Date: Annually, Feb 1
Presented: Annually in April

IODE Violet Downey Book Award
The National Chapter of Canada IODE
40 Orchard View Blvd, Suite 219, Toronto, ON M4R 1B9, Canada
Tel: 416-487-4416 *Toll Free Tel:* 866-827-7428
Fax: 416-487-4417
E-mail: iodecanada@bellnet.ca
Web Site: www.iode.ca
Key Personnel
Natl Pres: Bonnie G Rees
Established: 1984
Children's book award. Must be a Canadian author with text in English. At least 500 words & printed in Canada during previous calendar year. Suitable for children 13 years & under.
Award: $5,000
Closing Date: Annually, Dec 31
Presented: The National Annual Meeting, Annually, late May

Iowa Poetry Prize
University of Iowa Press
119 W Park Rd, 100 Kuhl House, Iowa City, IA 52242-1000
SAN: 282-4868
Tel: 319-335-2000 *Fax:* 319-335-2055
E-mail: uipress@uiowa.edu
Web Site: www.uipress.uiowa.edu
Key Personnel
Dir: James McCoy *Tel:* 319-335-2013
E-mail: james-mccoy@uiowa.edu
Assoc Dir/Design & Prodn Mgr: Karen Copp
Tel: 319-335-2014 *E-mail:* karen-copp@uiowa.edu
Mktg Dir: Allison T Means *Tel:* 319-335-3440
E-mail: allison-means@uiowa.edu
Off Mgr: Angie Dickey *Tel:* 319-335-3424
E-mail: angela-dickey@uiowa.edu
Open to new as well as established poets for a book-length collection of poems written originally in English. Previous winners, current University of Iowa students & current & former University of Iowa Press employees are not eligible. Reading fee: $20.
Award: Publication by the University of Iowa Press under a standard royalty agreement
Closing Date: Postmarked during April

Iowa Prize for Literary Nonfiction
University of Iowa Press
119 W Park Rd, 100 Kuhl House, Iowa City, IA 52242-1000
SAN: 282-4868
Tel: 319-335-2000 *Fax:* 319-335-2055
E-mail: uipress@uiowa.edu
Web Site: www.uipress.uiowa.edu
Key Personnel
Dir: James McCoy *Tel:* 319-335-2013
E-mail: james-mccoy@uiowa.edu
Assoc Dir/Design & Prodn Mgr: Karen Copp
Tel: 319-335-2014 *E-mail:* karen-copp@uiowa.edu
Mktg Dir: Allison T Means *Tel:* 319-335-3440
E-mail: allison-means@uiowa.edu
Off Mgr: Angie Dickey *Tel:* 319-335-3424
E-mail: angela-dickey@uiowa.edu
Awarded for a book-length ms of literary nonfiction originally written in English. Open to both new & established writers. Ms should be at least 40,000 words long but not exceed 90,000 words. Submit only via Submittable.
Administration fee: $10.

Award: Publication by the University of Iowa Press under its standard royalty agreement & contract terms
Closing Date: Aug 15

The Iowa Review Awards
University of Iowa-The Iowa Review
308 EPB, Iowa City, IA 52242-1408
E-mail: iowa-review@uiowa.edu
Web Site: www.iowareview.org
Key Personnel
Mng Ed: Lynne Nugent
Ed: Harilaos Stecopoulos
Established: 2003
Fiction, poetry & nonfiction categories. Submit up to 25 pages of prose (double-spaced) or 10 pages of poetry (1 poem or several, but no more than 1 poem per page). Work must be previously unpublished. There is a $20 entry fee; enclose an additional $10 for a 1-year subscription to the magazine (optional). Submissions between January 1-January 31.
Award: $1,500 & publication in December issue of *Iowa Review* (1st place), $750 & publication in December issue of *Iowa Review* (1st runners-up)
Closing Date: Annually, Jan 31

The Iowa Short Fiction Award
Writers' Workshop, The University of Iowa
102 Dey House, 507 N Clinton St, Iowa City, IA 52242-1000
Tel: 319-335-0416 *Fax:* 319-335-0420
Web Site: www.uiowapress.org/authors/iowa-short-fiction.htm
Key Personnel
Prog Assoc: Connie Brothers
Dir, Writers' Workshop: Lan Samantha Chang
Established: 1970
For a previously unpublished collection of short stories of at least 150 typewritten pages by a writer who has not previously published a volume of prose fiction. Stories previously published in periodicals are eligible for inclusion. Include SASE. Write for further information.
Other Sponsor(s): University of Iowa Press
Award: Publication by University of Iowa Press under the Press's standard contract
Closing Date: Aug 1-Sept 30

Jackie White Memorial National Children's Playwriting Contest
Columbia Entertainment Co
1400 Forum Blvd, 1C No 214, Columbia, MO 65203
E-mail: jwm@cectheatre.org
Web Site: www.cectheatre.org
Key Personnel
Pres, Community Theatre: Arron Pauley
Artistic Dir: Katie Hays
Devt Dir: Michele Curry
Established: 1988
The entry should be a full-length play or musical with speaking roles for at least 7 characters. The entry may be an unpublished original work or an adaptation; $25 entry fee, send SASE for complete rules & entry form. Each author who enters the contest may receive a letter from the contest committee discussing the strengths & weaknesses of his or her play if a SASE is enclosed.
Other Sponsor(s): City of Columbia, Office of Cultural Affairs
Award: $500, for 1st place
Closing Date: Annually, Dec 31
Presented: Annually, May 31

Joseph Henry Jackson Literary Award
The San Francisco Foundation
One Embarcadero Ctr, Suite 1400, San Francisco, CA 94111
Tel: 415-733-8500

E-mail: info@sff.org; artsinfo@sff.org
Web Site: www.sff.org
Established: 1957
Award for the author of fiction (novel or short stories), nonfictional prose, poetry. Awards are intended to encourage emerging artists not yet established in the genre who are currently residing in Alameda, Contra Costa, Marin, San Francisco or San Mateo County, for an unpublished ms-in-progress. By nomination only.
Award: $2,000
Presented: Annually in Autumn

The Jackson Poetry Prize
Poets & Writers Inc
90 Broad St, Suite 2100, New York, NY 10004
Tel: 212-226-3586 *Fax:* 212-226-3963
E-mail: admin@pw.org
Web Site: www.pw.org
Established: 2006
Honors an American poet of exceptional talent who deserves wider recognition. Eligible poets must have published at least 2 books of acknowledged literary merit.
Other Sponsor(s): Liana Foundation
Award: $60,000

The Joan Leiman Jacobson Poetry Prizes, see Discovery/Boston Review Poetry Contest

J Franklin Jameson Fellowship in American History
American Historical Association (AHA)
400 "A" St SE, Washington, DC 20003
Tel: 202-544-2422 *Fax:* 202-544-8307
E-mail: awards@historians.org
Web Site: www.historians.org
Established: 1980
To support significant scholarly research for one semester in the collections of the Library of Congress by new historians. At the time of application, applicants must hold the PhD degree or equivalent; must have received this degree within the last 5 years & must not have published or had accepted for publication a book-length historical work. The fellowship will not be awarded to permit completion of a doctoral dissertation. The applicant's project in American history must be one for which the general & special collections of the Library of Congress offer unique research support. Applicants should include a statement substantiating this relationship. Residency for at least 3 months at Library of Congress is required. Application instructions & all updated info available on web site.
Other Sponsor(s): Library of Congress
Award: Certificate & stipend of $5,000 that will be awarded for 3 months to spend in full-time residence at the Library of Congress
Closing Date: April 1

Japan-US Friendship Commission Translation Prize
Japan-US Friendship Commission
Affiliate of Donald Keene Center of Japanese Culture
Columbia University, 507 Kent Hall, MC3920, New York, NY 10027
Tel: 212-854-5036 *Fax:* 212-854-4019
Web Site: www.keenecenter.org
Key Personnel
Faculty Dir: David B Lurie
Established: 1979
The Donald Keene Center of Japanese Culture at Columbia University annually awards $6,000 in Japan-US Friendship Commission Prizes for the Translation of Japanese Literature. A prize is given for the best translation of a modern work or a classical work, or the prize is divided between equally distinguished translations.

Translations must be of book-length Japanese literary works: novels, collections of short stories, manga, literary essays, memoirs, drama, or poetry. Submissions may be unpublished mss, works in press, or books published during the 2 years prior to the prize year. Translators must be citizens or permanent residents of the US. Prior recipients of the award are eligible to submit new translations.
Award: $6,000 (either to one translator or divided between classical & modern)
Closing Date: Annually, Oct 31
Presented: Columbia University, Annually in April

Jefferson Cup Award
Youth Services Forum
Unit of Virginia Library Association (VLA)
c/o Virginia Library Association (VLA), PO Box 56312, Virginia Beach, VA 23456
Tel: 757-689-0594 *Fax:* 757-447-3478
Web Site: www.vla.org
Key Personnel
VLA Exec Dir: Lisa R Varga *E-mail:* vla.lisav@cox.net
Established: 1983
Honors a distinguished biography, historical fiction or American history book written especially for young people. Two awards given, one for books published for children & one for books published for young adults.
Award: $500 & engraved silver Jefferson Cup for each
Closing Date: Jan 31
Presented: Virginia Library Association (VLA) Annual Conference, Fall

Jerome Award
Catholic Library Association
8550 United Plaza Blvd, Suite 1001, Baton Rouge, LA 70809
Tel: 225-408-4417 *Fax:* 225-408-4422
E-mail: cla2@cathla.org
Web Site: cathla.org
Established: 1992
For outstanding work in Catholic scholarship; no unsol mss.
Award: Plaque
Closing Date: None; in-house votes
Presented: CLA Annual Convention, April

Jerome Fellowship
The Playwrights' Center
2301 Franklin Ave E, Minneapolis, MN 55406-1099
Tel: 612-332-7481 *Fax:* 612-332-6037
E-mail: info@pwcenter.org
Web Site: www.pwcenter.org
Key Personnel
Producing Artistic Dir: Jeremy Cohen *Tel:* 612-332-7481 ext 113 *E-mail:* jeremyc@pwcenter.org
Assoc Artistic Dir: Hayley Finn *Tel:* 612-332-7481 ext 119 *E-mail:* hayleyf@pwcenter.org
Artistic Progs Admin: Julia Brown *Tel:* 612-332-7481 ext 115 *E-mail:* juliab@pwcenter.org
Established: 1976
Fellowships awarded annually to emerging playwrights. Provides playwrights with funds & services to aid them in the development of their craft. One year in residence required, July 1-June 30. Contact above for application & guidelines, or download from web site.
Award: $18,000
Closing Date: See web site for details

Jewel Box Theatre Playwriting Competition
3700 N Walker, Oklahoma City, OK 73118-7031
Tel: 405-521-1786
Web Site: jewelboxtheatre.org
Key Personnel
Prodn Dir: Charles Tweed
Established: 1986

Original playwriting competition.
Award: $750
Closing Date: Jan 15
Presented: Banquet in Oklahoma City, OK, May

John Steinbeck Award for Fiction
Reed Magazine
San Jose State University, English Dept, One
  Washington Sq, San Jose, CA 95192-0090
Tel: 408-924-4441
E-mail: mail@reedmag.org
Web Site: www.reedmag.org; reedmagazine.
  submittable.com
All submissions must be through the online sys-
  tem. Keep submissions under 5,000 words.
  Reading fee: $15.
Award: $1,000 & publication in *Reed Magazine*
Closing Date: Annually, Nov 1 (submissions ac-
  cepted beginning June 1)

Anson Jones MD Awards
Texas Medical Association
401 W 15 St, Austin, TX 78701
Tel: 512-370-1300 *Fax:* 512-370-1693
Web Site: www.texmed.org
Key Personnel
Outreach Coord: Tammy Wishard
Established: 1957
Annual awards in recognition of outstanding cov-
  erage of health & medical issues to the public
  by Texas Media.
Award: $500 cash award & plaque for winners
Closing Date: Jan 10

Jesse H Jones Award
Texas Institute of Letters (TIL)
PO Box 609, Round Rock, TX 78680
Tel: 512-683-5640
E-mail: president@texasinstituteofletters.org
Web Site: www.texasinstituteofletters.org
Key Personnel
Pres: Carmen Tafolla
VP: Sergio Troncoso
Secy: Ann Weisgarber
Treas: W K Stratton
Recording Secy: Kurt Heinzelman
Annual award for the best book of fiction by a
  Texan or about Texas. Guidelines on the web
  site.
Award: $6,000
Closing Date: Annually in Jan
Presented: TIL Awards Banquet, Annually in
  Spring

Judah, Sarah, Grace & Tom Memorial
The Poetry Society of Virginia
900 Timber Creek Place, Virginia Beach, VA
  23464
E-mail: poetryinva@aol.com; info@
  poetryvirginia.org
Web Site: poetrysocietyofvirginia.org
Key Personnel
Pres: Robert P Arthur *E-mail:* robert.peebles.
  arthur@gmail.com
Exec Dir: Guy Terrell *E-mail:* guy.terrell@
  earthlink.net
Adult Contest Chair: Steven Blythe
  E-mail: stevenblythepoetry@gmail.com
All entries must be in English, original & unpublished. Submit 2 copies of each poem, both
  copies must have the category name & number
  on top left of page. Only one poem per category; entries will not be returned. Subject:
  encouraging reflection on inter-ethnic relations; any form; 48 line limit. Entry fee: $4
  nonmembs.
Award: $50 (1st place), $30 (2nd place), $20 (3rd
  place)
Closing Date: Jan
Presented: Annual PSV Awards Ceremony, April

Juniper Prize for Fiction
University of Massachusetts Press
East Experiment Station, 671 N Pleasant St,
  Amherst, MA 01003
E-mail: info@umpress.umass.edu
Web Site: www.umass.edu/umpress; www.umass.
  edu/umpress/content/juniper-literary-prize-series
Key Personnel
Dir: Mary V Dougherty *Tel:* 413-545-4990
  E-mail: mvd@umpress.umass.edu
Established: 2004
Two prizes: one novel, one story. Annual prize to
  honor & publish outstanding works of literary
  fiction. Open to all writers in English, whether
  or not they are US Citizens. Entry fee is $30
  (must be drawn on US bank). Entries accepted
  beginning August 1.
Award: $1,000 upon publication
Closing Date: Sept 30 (postmark)
Presented: Winner announced on web site in
  April

Juniper Prize for Poetry
University of Massachusetts Press
East Experiment Station, 671 N Pleasant St,
  Amherst, MA 01003
E-mail: info@umpress.umass.edu
Web Site: www.umass.edu/umpress; www.umass.
  edu/umpress/content/juniper-literary-prize-series
Key Personnel
Dir: Mary V Dougherty *Tel:* 413-545-4990
  E-mail: mvd@umpress.umass.edu
Established: 1976
Two poetry prizes awarded annually for an orig-
  inal ms of poems. One prize for first publica-
  tion, one is open to poets either with or with-
  out previously published books. Entry fee: $30.
Award: $1,000 & publication
Presented: Annually in April; publication by the
  following Spring

Juvenile Literary Awards/Young People's
  Literature Awards
Friends of American Writers
506 Rose Ave, Des Plaines, IL 60016
Tel: 847-827-8339
Web Site: www.fawchicago.org
Key Personnel
Pres: Roberta Gates *E-mail:* robmicgates73@
  gmail.com
Juv Lit Awards Chair: Martha Daniel
  E-mail: mcmdaniel@mac.com
Established: 1960
For books written for young people from toddler
  through high school age & published in the
  current year, can only be author's 1st, 2nd or
  3rd book & the author must be from the Mid-
  west +/or the book must be about the Midwest.
  See web site for full details.
Award: Two $2,000 prizes
Closing Date: Annually, Dec 20
Presented: The Fortnightly, Chicago, IL, Annually
  in May

Sue Kaufman Prize for First Fiction
American Academy of Arts & Letters
633 W 155 St, New York, NY 10032
Tel: 212-368-5900 *Fax:* 212-491-4615
E-mail: academy@artsandletters.org
Web Site: artsandletters.org
Key Personnel
Exec Dir: Cody Upton
Established: 1979
For the best published first novel or collection of
  short stories of the preceding year.
Award: $5,000

Ezra Jack Keats Book Award
Ezra Jack Keats Foundation
450 14 St, Brooklyn, NY 11215-5702
E-mail: foundation@ezra-jack-keats.org
Web Site: www.ezra-jack-keats.org

Key Personnel
Exec Dir: Dr Deborah Pope
Awarded annually to an outstanding new writer
  & new illustrator to recognize & encourage
  emerging talent in the field of children's books.
Other Sponsor(s): de Gummond Children's Litera-
  ture Collection, University of Southern Missis-
  sippi
Award: $3,000 & bronze medallion for each win-
  ner
Presented: Children's Book Festival, University of
  Southern Mississippi, Hattiesburg, MS, April

Ezra Jack Keats/Kerlan Memorial Fellowship
Ezra Jack Keats Foundation
University of Minnesota, 113 Andersen Library,
  222 21 Ave S, Minneapolis, MN 55455
Tel: 612-624-4576
E-mail: asc-clrc@umn.edu
Web Site: www.lib.umn.edu/clrc
Key Personnel
Curator Kerlan Collection: Lisa Von Drasek
Awarded to a talented writer +/or illustrator of
  children's books who wish to use the Kerlan
  Collection to further his or her artistic develop-
  ment.
Award: $1,500
Closing Date: Jan 30

Joan Kelly Memorial Prize in Women's
  History
American Historical Association (AHA)
400 "A" St SE, Washington, DC 20003
Tel: 202-544-2422 *Fax:* 202-544-8307
E-mail: awards@historians.org
Web Site: www.historians.org
Established: 1984
For the book in women's history +/or feminist
  theory that best reflects the high intellectual &
  scholarly ideals exemplified by the life & work
  of Joan Kelly. Submissions shall be books in
  any chronological period, any geographical location, or in any area of feminist theory that
  incorporates an historical perspective. Books
  should demonstrate originality of research,
  creativity of insight, graceful stylistic presentation, analytical skills & a recognition of the
  important role of sex & gender in the historical process. The inter-relationship between
  women & the historical process should be addressed. Books published in 2020 are eligible.
  Along with an application form, one copy of
  each entry must be received by each of the 5
  committee members. The Association will an-
  nounce the recipients of prizes & awards at its
  annual meeting during the 1st week in Jan. All
  updated info on web site.
Award: Cash prize
Closing Date: May 15, 2021
Presented: AHA Annual Meeting, New Orleans,
  LA, Jan 2022

Robert F Kennedy Book Awards
Robert F Kennedy Center for Justice & Human
  Rights
1300 19 St NW, Suite 750, Washington, DC
  20036
Tel: 646-553-4750 *Fax:* 202-463-6606
E-mail: info@rfkhumanrights.org
Web Site: rfkhumanrights.org
Key Personnel
Contact: Jae Regala *E-mail:* regala@
  rfkhumanrights.org
Established: 1980
For a book of fiction or nonfiction that most
  faithfully & forcefully reflects Robert
  Kennedy's interests & concerns. Publishers or
  authors should mail 6 copies of the book pub-
  lished in the previous year. Submit entry form,
  press release, review, or descriptive letter &
  $75 entry fee through online submission portal.
  See web site for further details.
Award: $2,500 & bust of Robert Kennedy

Closing Date: Feb 2
Presented: May

Coretta Scott King Book Awards

The American Library Association (ALA)
225 N Michigan Ave, Suite 1300, Chicago, IL 60601
Tel: 312-944-6780 *Toll Free Tel:* 800-545-2433
   Fax: 312-440-9374
E-mail: diversity@ala.org
Web Site: www.ala.org/awardsgrants/coretta-scott-king-book-awards
Key Personnel
Dir, OLOS: Jody Gray *E-mail:* jgray@ala.org
Asst Dir, OLOS: Gwendolyn Prellwitz
   E-mail: gprellwitz@ala.org
Asst Dir, Literacy & Continuing Educ, OLOS:
   Kristin Lahurd *E-mail:* klahurd@ala.org
Prog Offr, OLOS: John Amundsen
   E-mail: jamundsen@ala.org
Established: 1970
Awarded annually to outstanding African-American authors & illustrators of books for children & young adults that demonstrate an appreciation of African-American culture & universal human values. Administered by the Ethnic Multicultural Information Exchange Round Table (EMIERT).
Other Sponsor(s): Black Caucus of the American Library Association (BCALA); DEMCO; Encyclopaedia Britannica; World Book Inc
Award: Bronze award seal & $1,000 to both author & illustrator
Closing Date: Dec 1
Presented: Coretta Scott King Awards Breakfast, ALA Annual Conference, June

Coretta Scott King - John Steptoe Award for New Talent

The American Library Association (ALA)
225 N Michigan Ave, Suite 1300, Chicago, IL 60601
Toll Free Tel: 800-545-2433 (ext 4294) *Fax:* 312-280-3256
E-mail: diversity@ala.org
Web Site: www.ala.org/awardsgrants
Key Personnel
Outreach & Communs Prog Offr: Amber Hayes
   Tel: 312-280-2140 *E-mail:* ahayes@ala.org
Coretta Scott King Book Awards Coord: Monica Chapman *Tel:* 800-545-2433 ext 4297
   E-mail: mlchapman@ala.org
Awarded annually to affirm new talent & offer visibility to excellence in writing or illustration at the beginning of a career as a published book creator. Administered by the Ethnic & Multicultural Information Exchange Round Table (EMIERT).
Other Sponsor(s): DEMCO
Award: Plaque
Closing Date: Dec 1
Presented: Coretta Scott King Book Awards Breakfast, ALA Annual Conference

Coretta Scott King - Virginia Hamilton Award for Lifetime Achievement

The American Library Association (ALA)
225 N Michigan Ave, Suite 1300, Chicago, IL 60601
Toll Free Tel: 800-545-2433
E-mail: diversity@ala.org
Web Site: www.ala.org/emiert/virginia-hamilton-award-lifetime-achievement
Key Personnel
Prog Offr, OLOS: John Amundsen
   E-mail: jamundsen@ala.org
Established: 2010
Annual award is presented in even years to an African-American author, illustrator or author/illustrator for a body of his or her published books for children +/or young adults &

who has made a significant & lasting literary contribution.
In odd years, the award is presented to a practitioner for substantial contributions through active engagement with youth using award-winning African-American literature for children +/or young adults, via implementation of reading & reading related activities/programs.
See web site for specific selection criteria.
Award: Medal & $1,500
Presented: Coretta Scott King Awards Breakfast, ALA Annual Conference, June

Kirkus Prize

Kirkus Media LLC
65 W 36 St, Suite 700, New York, NY 10018
Web Site: www.kirkusreviews.com/prize
Awarded annually to authors of fiction, nonfiction & young readers' literature. Both traditionally published & self-published books reviewed by Kirkus that earn the Kirkus Star are eligible.
Award: $50,000 each category

The Knight-Risser Prize for Western Environmental Journalism

John S Knight Journalism Fellowships
Stanford University, 450 Serra Mall, Bldg 120, Rm 424, Stanford, CA 94305-2050
Tel: 650-723-4937 *Fax:* 650-725-6154
E-mail: knightrisserprize@lists.stanford.edu
Web Site: knightrisser.stanford.edu
Key Personnel
Dir: Dawn E Garcia *E-mail:* degarcia@stanford.edu
Admin Mgr: Erika Bartholomew *Tel:* 650-725-1192
Established: 2006
Recognizes the best environmental reporting on the North American West, from Canada through the US to Mexico. Open to print, broadcast & online journalists, staffers & free-lancers. For more information, see web site.
Other Sponsor(s): Bill Lane Center for the American West at Stanford University
Award: $5,000 cash
Closing Date: Annually in March
Presented: Annual Knight-Risser Prize Symposium, Stanford University, Stanford, CA, Summer

Knightville Poetry Contest

The New Guard
PO Box 472, Brunswick, ME 04011
E-mail: info@newguardreview.com; editors@writershotel.com
Web Site: www.newguardreview.com
Key Personnel
Founding Ed & Publr: Shanna McNair
Established: 2009
Up to 3 poems per entry. Up to 150 lines per poem. Submit all 3 poems in a single document. Online submissions only. Entry fee: $20.
Award: $1,500 & publication in *The New Guard*
Closing Date: Aug 31

Kobo Emerging Writer Prize

Rakuten Kobo Inc
135 Liberty St, Suite 101, Toronto, ON M6K 1A7, Canada
E-mail: pr@kobo.com
Web Site: www.kobo.com/emergingwriterprize
Key Personnel
Sr Mgr, PR: Sinead McElhinney *Tel:* 416-977-8737 ext 3382 *E-mail:* sinead.mcelhinney@rakuten.com
Established: 2014
Annual award with the goal of kick-starting the careers of debut Canadian authors. Three categories: Nonfiction, literary fiction & genre fiction.

Award: $10,000; each winning author receives promotional, marketing & communications support throughout the award year
Closing Date: March
Presented: June

Mary Lynn Kotz Award, see Art In Literature: The Mary Lynn Kotz Award

Katherine Singer Kovacs Prize

Modern Language Association of America (MLA)
85 Broad St, Suite 500, New York, NY 10004-2434
SAN: 202-6422
Tel: 646-576-5141; 646-576-5000 *Fax:* 646-458-0030
E-mail: awards@mla.org
Web Site: www.mla.org
Key Personnel
Coord, Book Prizes: Annie M Reiser
   E-mail: areiser@mla.org
Established: 1990
Prize for an outstanding book published in 2020 in English or Spanish in the field of Latin American & Spanish literatures & cultures. Authors need not be members of MLA. For consideration, submit 6 copies. Presented annually.
Award: Cash award & certificate
Closing Date: May 1
Presented: MLA Convention

The Kraken Book Prize for Middle-Grade Fiction

Fitzroy Books
Imprint of Regal House Publishing
c/o Regal House Publishing, 806 Oberlin Rd, No 12094, Raleigh, NC 27605
E-mail: info@regalhousepublishing.com
Web Site: regalhousepublishing.com/the-kraken-book-award/
Key Personnel
Founder, Publr & Ed-in-Chief: Jaynie Royal
Mng Ed: Pam Van Dyk
Sr Ed: Ruth Feiertag
Ed: Elizabeth Lowenstein
Established: 2019
Recognizing finely crafted works written for middle grade readers. Submissions through Submittable or by post. Entry fee $25. Fax or e-mail submissions not accepted. See web site for submission guidelines. Five finalists announced May 30.
Award: Publication & $500 honorarium
Closing Date: March 30 (postmark)
Presented: June 30

Michael Kraus Research Grant in American Colonial History

American Historical Association (AHA)
400 "A" St SE, Washington, DC 20003
Tel: 202-544-2422 *Fax:* 202-544-8307
E-mail: awards@historians.org
Web Site: www.historians.org
Grant given to a member of the association to recognize the most deserving proposal relating to works in progress on a research project in American colonial history, with particular reference to the intercultural aspects of American & European relations. The grants are intended to further research in progress & may be used for travel to a library or archive, for microfilms, photographs, or photocopying. Preference will be given to those with specific research needs, such as the completion of a project or completion of a discrete segment thereof. Only members of the association are eligible to apply. See web site for additional submission guidelines & eligibility.
Award: Individual grants will not exceed $800
Closing Date: Annually, Feb 15

The Robert Kroetsch City of Edmonton Book Prize
Writers' Guild of Alberta
11759 Groat Rd, Edmonton, AB T5M 3K6, Canada
Tel: 780-422-8174 *Toll Free Tel:* 800-665-5354 (AB only) *Fax:* 780-422-2663 (attn WGA)
E-mail: mail@writersguild.ca
Web Site: writersguild.ca
Key Personnel
Exec Dir: Carol Holmes *E-mail:* carol.holmes@writersguild.ca
Communs & Partnerships Coord: Ellen Kartz *E-mail:* ellen.kartz@writersguild.ca
Memb Servs Coord: Giorgia Severini
Progs Coord: Natalie Cook *E-mail:* natalie.cook@writersguild.ca; Julie Robinson *E-mail:* julie.robinson@writersguild.ca
Entries must deal with some aspect of the City of Edmonton: history, geography, current affairs, its arts or its people or be written by an Edmonton author.
Award: $10,000 & leather-bound copy of book
Closing Date: Annually, Dec 31
Presented: Mayor's Evening for the Arts, Annually in Spring
Branch Office(s)
505 21 Ave SW, Calgary, AB T2S 0G9, Canada, Prog Coord: Samantha Warwick *Tel:* 403-265-2226 *E-mail:* samantha.warwick@writersguild.ca

Kumu Kahua/UHM Theatre & Dance Department Playwriting Contest
Kumu Kahua/UHM Theatre & Dance Department
46 Merchant St, Honolulu, HI 96813
Tel: 808-536-4441 (box off); 808-536-4222
Fax: 808-536-4226
E-mail: kumukahuatheatre@hawaiiantel.net
Web Site: www.kumukahua.org
Key Personnel
Artistic Dir: Harry L Wong, III
Hawaii Prize: Open to residents of Hawaii & non-residents; full-length (50 pages or more); play must be set in Hawaii +/or deal with the Hawaii experience.
Pacific Rim Prize: Open to residents of Hawaii & non-residents; full-length (50 pages or more); play must be set in +/or dealing with the Pacific Islands, Pacific Rim, or the Pacific/Asian-American experience.
Resident Prize: Only open to residents of Hawaii; full-length (50 pages or more) or one-acts; play can be on any topic.
Award: $600 (Hawaii Prize), $450 (Pacific Rim Prize), $250 (Resident Prize)
Closing Date: Annually, Jan 2
Presented: May

W Kaye Lamb Scholarships
British Columbia Historical Federation
PO Box 448, Fort Langley, BC V1M 2R7, Canada
E-mail: info@bchistory.ca
Web Site: www.bchistory.ca/awards/scholarships
Key Personnel
Recognition Chair: Shannon Bettles *E-mail:* shannon@bchistory.ca
Two scholarships offered annually for essays written by students in British Columbia colleges or universities on a topic relating to British Columbia history.
Award: $750 (1st or 2nd yr student), $1,000 (3rd or 4th yr student)
Closing Date: Annually, March 1
Presented: BCHF Annual Conference Awards Banquet, Annually in May/June

Lambda Literary Awards (Lammys)
Lambda Literary
5482 Wilshire Blvd, No 1595, Los Angeles, CA 90036
Tel: 323-643-4281
E-mail: admin@lambdaliterary.org
Web Site: www.lambdaliterary.org
Key Personnel
Exec Dir: Sue Landers
Awards Admin: Ella Boureau
Established: 1989
Annual award recognizing excellence in LGBTQ literature. Entry fee required. Guidelines on the web site.
Award: Trophy
Closing Date: Dec 1
Presented: New York, NY, June

Gerald Lampert Memorial Award
The League of Canadian Poets
2 Carlton St, Suite 1519, Toronto, ON M5B 1J3, Canada
Tel: 416-504-1657
E-mail: info@poets.ca
Web Site: poets.ca
Key Personnel
Exec Dir: Lesley Fletcher *E-mail:* lesley@poets.ca
Communs Coord: Laura O'Brien *E-mail:* laura@poets.com
Annual award intended to recognize the work of a Canadian writer early in his or her career. Awarded for a first book of poetry published in the preceding year. $25 handling fee.
Award: $1,000
Closing Date: Nov 1
Presented: Annual Conference, June

Langum Prize in American Historical Fiction
The Langum Charitable Trust
2809 Berkeley Dr, Birmingham, AL 35242
Tel: 360-809-0465
E-mail: langumtrust@gmail.com
Web Site: www.langumtrust.org
Key Personnel
Dir: David J Langum, Sr *E-mail:* djlangum@samford.edu
Established: 2001
Awarded to a book published by any non-subsidy press for American historical fiction set in the colonial or national periods that is both excellent fiction & excellent history.
Award: $1,000
Closing Date: Annually, Dec 1
Presented: Annually in March

Langum Prize in American Legal History or Biography
The Langum Charitable Trust
2809 Berkeley Dr, Birmingham, AL 35242
Tel: 360-809-0465
E-mail: langumtrust@gmail.com
Web Site: www.langumtrust.org
Key Personnel
Dir: David J Langum, Sr *E-mail:* djlangum@samford.edu
Established: 2001
Awarded annually to a book in the area of American legal history or American legal biography that is accessible to the educated general public, rooted in sound scholarship & with themes that touch upon matters of general concern to the American public, past or present.
Award: $1,000
Closing Date: Dec 1
Presented: March

Lannan Literary Awards & Fellowships
Lannan Foundation
313 Read St, Santa Fe, NM 87501-2628
Tel: 505-986-8160
E-mail: info@lannan.org
Web Site: lannan.org
Key Personnel
Pres: Patrick Lannan
VP & Dir of Opers: Frank C Lawler

Prog Dir, Literary & Residency Progs: Martha Jessup
Established: 1989
The awards recognize writers who have made significant contributions to English language literature. The residency fellowships recognize writers of distinctive literary merit who demonstrate potential for continued outstanding work. Award categories are poetry, fiction, nonfiction, lifetime & notable book. Candidates selected by an anonymous nomination process. Applications & letters of inquiry not accepted.

Larew, Christian, Memorial Scholarship in Library & Information Technology, see LITA/Christian Larew Memorial Scholarship in Library & Information Technology

Latino Books Into Movies Awards
Latino Literacy Now
3445 Catalina Dr, Carlsbad, CA 92010
Tel: 760-434-1223 *Fax:* 760-434-7476
Web Site: www.award.news
Key Personnel
Awards Chair: Kirk Whisler *E-mail:* kirk@whisler.com
Accept books, movie screenplays, plays & television scripts. Send 5 copies of each book or script being nominated. In the movie & television categories, the author or co-author of the book or screenplay must be Latino, Latin American, or Spanish. Categories under Latino themes by non-Latino authors or screenwriters are open only to non-Latino writers, but must be Latino themed. Books & screenplays must be in English language. If in Spanish, must be accompanied by a PDF of English translation. Entry fee: $80 per each individual entry until November 21, $100 each after that until the final deadline.
Award: Winning books distributed to pertinent motion picture studios, television networks, producers & agents, depending on genre
Closing Date: April 11
Presented: Early Sept

Latner Writers' Trust Poetry Prize
The Writers' Trust of Canada
600-460 Richmond St W, Toronto, ON M5V 1Y1, Canada
Tel: 416-504-8222 *Toll Free Tel:* 877-906-6548 *Fax:* 416-504-9090
E-mail: info@writerstrust.com
Web Site: www.writerstrust.com/awards/latner-writers-trust-poetry-prize
Key Personnel
Exec Dir: Charlie Foran *Tel:* 416-504-8222 ext 244 *E-mail:* cforan@writerstrust.com
Prog Coord: Devon Jackson *Tel:* 416-504-8222 ext 248 *E-mail:* djackson@writerstrust.com
Established: 2014
Awarded annually to a Canadian poet in recognition of a remarkable body of work & in hope of future contributions to Canadian poetry. All eligible poets in mid-career are considered. No age restrictions apply & no submission process. Jury selection.
Other Sponsor(s): Latner Family Foundation
Award: $25,000

James Lauglin Award
The Academy of American Poets Inc
75 Maiden Lane, Suite 901, New York, NY 10038
Tel: 212-274-0343
E-mail: awards@poets.org
Web Site: www.poets.org
Key Personnel
Pres & Exec Dir: Jennifer Benka *E-mail:* jenbenka@poets.org
Devt, Membership & Communs Sr Mgr: Molly Walsh *E-mail:* mwalsh@poets.org

Ad & Mktg Sr Mgr: Michelle Campagna
  E-mail: mcampagna@poets.org
Sr Progs Mgr: Nikay Paredes *Tel:* 212-274-0343
  ext 13 *E-mail:* nparedes@poets.org
Established: 1954
Awarded to recognize & support a second book
of poetry forthcoming in the next calendar
year. Entries must be at least 48 pages & submitted in ms form (or page proofs). Publishers
must send 4 copies of each ms. Submissions
are welcome from small presses, university
presses & trade publishers that have previously
published at least 4 books of poetry. Translations & new editions of previously published
books are not eligible.
Award: $5,000, all-expenses-paid weeklong res-
idency at The Betsy Hotel, Miami Beach, FL
& approximately 1,000 copies of winning book
distributed to Academy members
Closing Date: May 15
Presented: Sept

Lawrence Foundation Prize
Michigan Quarterly Review
University of Michigan, 0576 Rackham Bldg, 915
  E Washington St, Ann Arbor, MI 48109-1070
Tel: 734-764-9265
E-mail: mqr@umich.edu
Web Site: sites.lsa.umich.edu/mqr/
Key Personnel
Ed: Jonathan Freedman
Awarded to the best work of fiction published in
MQR each year. No deadline or special appli-
cation process.
Award: $1,000

Stephen Leacock Memorial Medal for Humour
The Leacock Associates
149 Peter St N, Orillia, ON L3V 4Z4, Canada
Tel: 705-326-9286
Web Site: www.leacock.ca
Key Personnel
Chair, Award Comm: Bette Walker
  E-mail: bettewalkerca@gmail.com
Pres: Nathan Taylor
Contact: Don Reid *E-mail:* don_reid@sympatico.
  ca
Established: 1946
Humorous writing by Canadian authors. All en-
tries must have been published in the year
prior to the year the award is given. Ten copies
of each book to be submitted should be sent
along with $150 fee, authors bio & a 5x7 or
larger B&W photograph. No ebooks accepted.
Winner announced late April. Books are non-
returnable.
Other Sponsor(s): TD Bank Group
Award: $15,000 TD Bank Group cash award &
silver medal, each of 4 finalists receive $1,500
Closing Date: Dec 31
Presented: Gala Award Dinner, Geneva Park,
Orillia, ON, Annually, early June

Harper Lee Prize for Legal Fiction
The University of Alabama School of Law
101 Paul Bryant Dr, Tuscaloosa, AL 35487
Tel: 205-348-5195
Web Site: www.harperleeprize.com
Key Personnel
Contact: Monique Fields *E-mail:* mfields@law.ua.
  edu
Established: 2011
Awarded annually to a published work of fiction
that best illuminates the role of lawyers in soci-
ety & their power to effect change.
Other Sponsor(s): ABA Journal
Closing Date: March 31
Presented: Prize ceremony, Sept in conjunction
with National Book Festival, Washington, DC

Legacy Award
New Atlantic Independent Booksellers Associa-
tion (NAIBA)
2667 Hyacinth St, Westbury, NY 11590
Tel: 516-333-0681 *Fax:* 516-333-0689
E-mail: naibabooksellers@gmail.com
Web Site: www.naiba.com/page/LegacyAward
Key Personnel
Exec Dir: Eileen Dengler *E-mail:* naibaeileen@
  gmail.com
Established: 2004
To recognize those individuals whose body of
work contributed significantly to the realm of
American arts & letters. Candidates must either
reside in the region served by NAIBA, or have
created work that reflects the character of the
geographical area so represented & the spirit of
the independent bookselling community found
therin.
Presented: NAIBA Fall Conference, Annually in
Oct

Waldo G Leland Prize
American Historical Association (AHA)
400 "A" St SE, Washington, DC 20003
Tel: 202-544-2422 *Fax:* 202-544-8307
E-mail: awards@historians.org
Web Site: www.historians.org
Established: 1981
Honorific award offered every 5 years for the
most outstanding reference tool in the field of
history. Reference tool encompasses bibliographies, indexes, encyclopedias & other scholarly
apparatus. Books with a copyright between
2016 & 2020 will be eligible for the prize in
2021. No application form, applicant must send
a copy of their book to each of the prize committee members who will be posted on our web
site as the prize deadline approaches. All updated info on web site.
Closing Date: May 15, 2021
Presented: AHA Annual Meeting, New Orleans,
LA, Jan 2022

Vincent Lemieux Prize
Canadian Political Science Association
260 rue Dalhousie St, Suite 204, Ottawa, ON
  K1N 7E4, Canada
Tel: 613-562-1202 *Fax:* 613-241-0019
E-mail: cpsa-acsp@cpsa-acsp.ca
Web Site: www.cpsa-acsp.ca
Key Personnel
Admin: Michelle Hopkins
Established: 1997
This is a biennial competition awarded to the best
thesis in any sub-field of political science sub-
mitted at a Canadian University, written in En-
glish or French, judged eminently worthy of
publication in the form of a book or articles.
A thesis is eligible only after nomination by
the unit in which it was defended. For the 2021
award, a thesis must have been defended in
2019 or 2020.
Award: $1,000 & commemorative certificate
Presented: Annual Conference, University of Alberta, Edmonton, AB, CN, June 2021

Leopold-Hidy Award
The Forest History Society Inc
701 William Vickers Ave, Durham, NC 27701-
3162
Tel: 919-682-9319 *Fax:* 919-682-2349
Web Site: www.foresthistory.org
Key Personnel
Admin Asst: Andrea Anderson *E-mail:* andrea.
  anderson@foresthistory.org
Established: 1996
To honor the best article in the journal they co-
publish, "Environmental History".
Other Sponsor(s): American Society for Environ-
mental History

Richard W Leopold Prize
The Organization of American Historians (OAH)
112 N Bryan Ave, Bloomington, IN 47408-4141
Tel: 812-855-7311
E-mail: oah@oah.org
Web Site: www.oah.org/awards
Key Personnel
Exec Dir: Beth English *E-mail:* benglish@oah.org
Comm Coord: Kara Hamm *E-mail:* khamm@oah.
  org
Awarded biennially to the author or editor of the
best book on foreign policy, military affairs,
historical activities of the federal government,
documentary histories, or biography written by
a US government historian or federal contract
historian. Each entry must be published during
the 2-year period January 1, 2020-December
31, 2021. The winner must have been employed as a full-time historian or federal contract historian with the US government for a
minimum of 5 years prior to the submission.
If the author has accepted an academic position, retired, or otherwise left federal service,
the book must have been published within 2
years of their separation date. Verification of
current or past employment with the US government (in the form of a letter or e-mail sent
to the publisher from the office that employs
or has employed the author) must be included
with each entry. One copy of each entry must
be mailed directly to the committee members
listed on the web site.
Closing Date: Oct 1, 2021 (postmarked)
Presented: OAH Annual Meeting, Boston, MA,
March 31-April 3, 2022

**Fenia & Yaakov Leviant Memorial Prize in
Yiddish Studies**
Modern Language Association of America (MLA)
85 Broad St, Suite 500, New York, NY 10004-
2434
SAN: 202-6422
Tel: 646-576-5141; 646-576-5000 *Fax:* 646-458-
0030
E-mail: awards@mla.org
Web Site: www.mla.org
Key Personnel
Coord, Book Prizes: Annie M Reiser
  E-mail: areiser@mla.org
Established: 2000
Awarded alternately to an outstanding scholarly
or translation work in the field of Yiddish. The
2022 prize will be awarded to a scholarly work
in English published between 2018 & 2021.
Authors need not be members of the MLA. For
consideration, submit 4 copies.
Award: Cash award & certificate
Closing Date: May 1, 2022
Presented: MLA Convention, Jan 2023

Harry Levin Prize
American Comparative Literature Association
(ACLA)
University of South Carolina, Dept of Languages,
Literature & Cultures, 1620 College St, Rm
817, Columbia, SC 29208
Tel: 803-777-3021
E-mail: info@acla.org
Web Site: www.acla.org/prize-awards/harry-levin-
prize
Key Personnel
Nominations Comm Chair: Antonio Barrenechea
  E-mail: abarrene@umw.edu
Established: 1968
Prize recognizing an outstanding first book in the
discipline of comparative literature published
during the previous 2 calendar years as the au-
thor's 1st book-length publication. Awarded
annually. See web site for nomination process.
Award: Complimentary registration for the annual
meeting, as well as hotel & airfare accommodations (not including food)

Closing Date: Oct 1
Presented: ACLA Annual Meeting, July

Kay W Levin Award for Short Nonfiction
Council for Wisconsin Writers
c/o 210 N Main St, No 204, Cedar Grove, WI
53013
E-mail: wiswriters@gmail.com
Web Site: wiswriters.org/awards
Key Personnel
Contest Chair: Sylvia Cavanaugh
  E-mail: bgirl4shadow@gmail.com
Established: 1967
Annual award for the best piece of short nonfic-
tion published by a Wisconsin-based author in
the contest year. Entry fee: $25 nonmembs.
Award: $500 & 1-week residency at Shake Rag
Alley Center for the Arts
Closing Date: Jan 31
Presented: CWW Annual Banquet, May

Lawrence W Levine Award
The Organization of American Historians (OAH)
112 N Bryan Ave, Bloomington, IN 47408-4141
Tel: 812-855-7311
E-mail: oah@oah.org
Web Site: www.oah.org/awards
Key Personnel
Exec Dir: Beth English *E-mail:* benglish@oah.org
Comm Coord: Kara Hamm *E-mail:* khamm@oah.
org
Awarded annually to the author of the best book
in American cultural history. Each entry must
be published during the calendar year preced-
ing that in which the award is given. One copy
of each entry must be mailed directly to the
committee members listed on the web site.
Closing Date: Oct 1, 2021 (postmarked)
Presented: OAH Annual Meeting, Boston, MA,
March 31-April 3, 2022

Levinson Prize
Poetry Magazine
61 W Superior St, Chicago, IL 60654
Tel: 312-787-7070 *Fax:* 312-787-6650
E-mail: editors@poetrymagazine.org
Web Site: www.poetryfoundation.org
Key Personnel
Edit Asst: Holly Amos *E-mail:* hamos@
poetrymagazine.org
Established: 1914
For poetry published in the preceding 2 volumes
of *Poetry* magazine. No application necessary.
Award: $500
Presented: Annually in Dec

Levis Reading Prize
Virginia Commonwealth University, Dept of En-
glish
PO Box 842005, Richmond, VA 23284-2005
Tel: 804-828-1331 *Fax:* 804-828-8684
Web Site: english.vcu.edu/mfa/levis/
Established: 1997
In memory of Larry Levis, awarded annually for
best first or second book of poetry (not for
self-published or chapbooks).
Award: $5,000
Closing Date: Feb 1
Presented: VCU Cabell Library, Richmond, VA,
Sept/Oct

Lewis Memorial Lifetime Achievement Award
PRINTING United Alliance
10015 Main St, Fairfax, VA 22031-3489
Tel: 703-385-1335 *Toll Free Tel:* 888-385-3588
  Fax: 703-273-0456
E-mail: assist@printing.org; info@printing.org
Web Site: www.printing.org/programs/awards/
lewis-memorial-lifetime-achievement-award
Key Personnel
Pres & CEO: Ford Bowers *E-mail:* fbowers@
printing.org

Established: 1950
Award honors business leaders who have excelled
at shaping the business of printed communications. See web site for eligibility requirements
& nomination information.
Presented: PRINTING United Alliance Fall Meetings
Branch Office(s)
1325 "G" St NW, Suite 500, Washington, DC
20005
2000 Corporate Dr, Suite 205, Wexford, PA
15090 *Tel:* 412-741-6860 *Toll Free Tel:* 800-
910-4283 *Fax:* 412-741-2311

Liberty Legacy Foundation Award
The Organization of American Historians (OAH)
112 N Bryan Ave, Bloomington, IN 47408-4141
Tel: 812-855-7311
E-mail: oah@oah.org
Web Site: www.oah.org/awards
Key Personnel
Exec Dir: Beth English *E-mail:* benglish@oah.org
Comm Coord: Kara Hamm *E-mail:* khamm@oah.
org
Awarded annually to the author of the best book
by a historian on the civil rights struggle from
the beginnings of the nation to the present.
Each entry must be published during the cal-
endar year preceding that in which the award is
given. One copy of each entry must be mailed
directly to the committee members listed on the
web site.
Closing Date: Oct 1, 2021 (postmarked)
Presented: OAH Annual Meeting, Boston, MA,
March 31-April 3, 2022

Michael J Libow Youth Theatre Award, see
BHTG - Michael J Libow Youth Theatre
Award

Library of Congress Literacy Awards
Library of Congress
101 Independence Ave SE, Washington, DC
20540-1400
Tel: 202-707-5221 (Center for the Book)
  Fax: 202-707-0269
Web Site: www.read.gov/literacyawards
Awards to 3 organizations that have made out-
standing contributions to increasing literacy in
the US or abroad.
Award: Rubenstein Prize $150,000, American
Prize $50,000, International Prize $50,000

Library of Congress Prize for American Fiction
Library of Congress
101 Independence Ave SE, Washington, DC
20540-1400
Tel: 202-707-5221 (Center for the Book)
  Fax: 202-707-0269
Web Site: www.loc.gov
Key Personnel
Communs Offr: Guy Lamolinara
Prog Asst: Diziree Amaiz
Established: 2013
Annual award to honor an American literary
writer whose body of work is distinguished not
only for its mastery of the art but for its orig-
inality of thought & imagination. The award
seeks to commend strong, unique, enduring
voices that, throughout long, consistently ac-
complished careers, have told us something
about the American experience.
Presented: Library of Congress National Book
Festival

Library of Virginia Literary Awards
Library of Virginia Foundation
800 E Broad St, Richmond, VA 23219
Tel: 804-692-3535

Web Site: www.lva.virginia.gov/public/litawards/
index.htm
Key Personnel
Devt Mgr: Dawn Greggs *E-mail:* dawn.greggs@
lva.virginia.gov
Exec Asst: Nancy Orr *E-mail:* nancy.orr@lva.
virginia.gov
Established: 1997
Awarded annually to Virginia authors in the categories of fiction & poetry & to nonfiction authors for works about a Virginia subject. Books
must have been published & distributed during
the previous calendar year. The following types
of books are not eligible: reference works, anthologies, documentary editions, children's &
juvenile literature, photographic books, self-
help books & how-to books.
Closing Date: Feb 10, 2021
Presented: Annual gala, Oct 2021

The Lieutenant-Governor's Awards for High Achievement in the Arts
New Brunswick Arts Board (Conseil des arts du
Nouveau-Brunswick)
225 King St, Suite 201, Fredericton, NB E3B
1E1, Canada
Tel: 506-444-4444 *Toll Free Tel:* 866-460-ARTS
(460-2787) *Fax:* 506-444-5543
Web Site: www.artsnb.ca
Key Personnel
Exec Dir: Joss Richer *Tel:* 506-478-4610
  E-mail: execdirgen@artsnb.ca
Prog Offr: Sarah Elizabeth Parker *Tel:* 506-440-
0037 *E-mail:* sarahbeth@artsnb.ca
Opers Mgr: Tilly Jackson *Tel:* 506-478-4422
  E-mail: tjackson@artsnb.ca
Established: 1989
To recognize the outstanding contribution of
artists to the arts in New Brunswick.
Award: $20,000/yr
Closing Date: June 15
Presented: Fredericton, NB, CN

Ruth Lilly & Dorothy Sargent Rosenberg Poetry Fellowships
Poetry Foundation
61 W Superior St, Chicago, IL 60654
Tel: 312-787-7070 *Fax:* 312-787-6650
E-mail: info@poetryfoundation.org; media@
poetryfoundation.org
Web Site: www.poetryfoundation.org
Established: 1989
Awarded to young US poets to encourage the fur-
ther study & writing of poetry. Five fellowships
are awarded annually.
Award: $25,800 each

Ruth Lilly Poetry Prize
Poetry Foundation
61 W Superior St, Chicago, IL 60654
Tel: 312-787-7070 *Fax:* 312-787-6650
E-mail: editors@poetrymagazine.org
Web Site: poetrymagazine.org
Key Personnel
Ed: Don Share
Asst Ed: Holly Amos *E-mail:* hamos@
poetrymagazine.org
Established: 1986
Awarded to a living US poet, to recognize ex-
traordinary artistic accomplishment.
Award: $100,000
Presented: Annually in May

Abraham Lincoln Institute Book Award
Abraham Lincoln Institute Inc
105 Mount Olive Lane, Ephrata, PA 17522
E-mail: secretary@lincoln-institute.org
Web Site: www.lincoln-institute.org
Key Personnel
Chmn of the Bd: Paul Pascal
Pres: Michelle Krowl
VP: Jonathan W White

Gen Secy: Clark Evans
Established: 1998
Given for the previous year's most noteworthy book on the subject of Abraham Lincoln. Prize committee members must each receive one copy of the nominated book, accompanied by a brief letter stating its merits.
Award: $1,000
Closing Date: Nov 1
Presented: ALI Symposium, Ford's Theatre, Washington, DC, Annually in March

Joseph W Lippincott Award

The American Library Association (ALA)
225 N Michigan Ave, Suite 1300, Chicago, IL 60601
Tel: 312-280-3247 *Toll Free Tel:* 800-545-2433 (ext 3247) *Fax:* 312-944-3897
E-mail: awards@ala.org
Web Site: www.ala.org
Key Personnel
Prog Offr: Cheryl M Malden *Tel:* 312-280-3247 *Fax:* 312-944-3897 *E-mail:* cmalden@ala.org
Established: 1938
Annual award presented to a librarian for distinguished service to the profession of librarianship, such service to include outstanding participation in the activities of professional library association, notable published professional writing or other significant activity on behalf of the profession & its aims.
Other Sponsor(s): Joseph W Lippincott III
Award: $1,000 & Citation
Closing Date: Dec 1
Presented: ALA Annual Conference, June

LITA/Christian Larew Memorial Scholarship in Library & Information Technology

Library & Information Technology Association (LITA)
Division of American Library Association (ALA)
c/o American Library Association, 50 E Huron St, Chicago, IL 60611-2795
Toll Free Tel: 800-545-2433 (ext 4270)
E-mail: scholarships@ala.org
Web Site: www.ala.org/lita
Key Personnel
Prog Offr, Educ Scholarships (ALA): Kimberly Redd
Established: 1999
Awarded jointly on an annual basis. The scholarship is designed to encourage the entry of qualified persons into the library & information technology field, who plan to follow a career in that field & who demonstrate academic excellence, leadership & a vision in pursuit of library & information technology. This scholarship is for study in an ALA Accredited Master of Library Science (MLS) program.
Other Sponsor(s): Baker & Taylor
Award: $3,000
Closing Date: March 1
Presented: LITA President's program held at the American Library Association Annual Conference, June

LITA/LSSI Minority Scholarship in Library & Information Technology

Library & Information Technology Association (LITA)
Division of American Library Association (ALA)
c/o American Library Association, 50 E Huron St, Chicago, IL 60611-2795
Toll Free Tel: 800-545-2433 (ext 4270)
E-mail: scholarships@ala.org
Web Site: www.ala.org/lita
Key Personnel
Prog Offr, Educ Scholarships (ALA): Kimberly Redd
Established: 1994
Scholarship is designed to encourage the entry of qualified minorities into the library & automa-

tion field who plan to follow a career in that field & who demonstrate potential in & have a strong commitment to the use of automated systems in libraries. Applicants must be qualified members of a principal minority group (American Indian or Alaskan native, Asian or Pacific Islander, African-American or Hispanic). The recipient must be a US or Canadian citizen. The scholarship is for study in an ALA Accredited Master of Library Science (MLS) program.
Other Sponsor(s): LSSI
Award: $2,500
Closing Date: Annually, March 1
Presented: LITA President's Program held at the American Library Association Annual Conference, Annually in June

LITA/OCLC Minority Scholarship in Library & Information Technology

Library & Information Technology Association (LITA)
Division of American Library Association (ALA)
c/o American Library Association, 50 E Huron St, Chicago, IL 60611-2795
Toll Free Tel: 800-545-2433 (ext 4270)
E-mail: scholarships@ala.org
Web Site: www.ala.org/lita
Key Personnel
Prog Offr, Educ Scholarships (ALA): Kimberly Redd
Established: 1991
For qualified members of a minority group. Must be US or Canadian citizen. For applicants who plan to enter a career in the library & automation field.
Other Sponsor(s): OCLC Inc
Award: $3,000
Closing Date: Annually, March 1
Presented: LITA President's Program at the American Library Association Annual Conference, Annually in June

Literary Awards

PEN America
Affiliate of PEN International
8444 Wilshire Blvd, 4th fl, Beverly Hills, CA 90211
Tel: 323-424-4939 *Fax:* 323-424-4944
E-mail: awards@pen.org; info@pen.org
Web Site: pen.org/literary-awards
Key Personnel
Exec Dir: Michelle Franke *Tel:* 323-424-4939 ext 1 *E-mail:* mfranke@pen.org
Literary Awards: Stacy Valis *Tel:* 323-424-4939 ext 3 *E-mail:* svalis@pen.org
Established: 1982
Literary awards for: fiction, creative nonfiction, poetry, translation, children's/young adult, graphic literature, drama, research nonfiction, screenplay, teleplay, journalism (print & online). Author must live west of Mississippi River. Work must have been published/produced in the year in which submissions are accepted. Annual call for submissions opens each summer. Forms must be submitted via Submittable (penawards.submittable.com). Entry fee $30, Journalism $15.
Award: Cash awards $1,000
Closing Date: Dec 31, book categories; Jan 15, journalism; Dec 31, drama; Aug 15, screenplay; July 15, teleplay
Presented: Literary Awards Festival, Fall

Literature Fellowship

Idaho Commission on the Arts
2410 N Old Penitentiary Rd, Boise, ID 83712
Mailing Address: PO Box 83720, Boise, ID 83720-0008
Tel: 208-334-2119
E-mail: info@arts.idaho.gov
Web Site: www.arts.idaho.gov

Key Personnel
Lit Dir: Jocelyn Robertson *Tel:* 208-334-2119 ext 108 *E-mail:* jocelyn.robertson@arts.idaho.gov
Five fellowships awarded triennially for literary excellence. For Idaho residents only.
Award: $5,000
Closing Date: Jan
Presented: Triennially in July

Littleton-Griswold Prize in American Law & Society

American Historical Association (AHA)
400 "A" St SE, Washington, DC 20003
Tel: 202-544-2422 *Fax:* 202-544-8307
E-mail: awards@historians.org
Web Site: www.historians.org
Established: 1985
Best book in any subject on the history of American law & society. Only books of high scholarly & literary merit published in 2020 will be eligible for consideration. Along with an application form, applicants must mail a copy of their book to each of the prize committee members who will be posted on our web site as the prize deadline approaches. All updated info on web site.
Award: Cash prize
Closing Date: May 15, 2021
Presented: AHA Annual Meeting, New Orleans, LA, Jan 2022

Littleton-Griswold Research Grants

American Historical Association (AHA)
400 "A" St SE, Washington, DC 20003
Tel: 202-544-2422 *Fax:* 202-544-8307
E-mail: awards@historians.org
Web Site: www.historians.org
For research in American legal history & the field of law & society. Only members of the Association are eligible. Applications must include application form with estimated budget, curriculum vitae & statement of no more than 750 words & a one-page bibliography of the most recent, relevant, secondary works on the topic. Application form & all updated info on web site. Preference will be given to junior scholars, PhD candidates & those without access to institutional funds.
Award: Individual grants will not exceed $1,500
Closing Date: Feb 15

Living Now Book Awards

Independent Publisher Online
Division of Jenkins Group Inc
1129 Woodmere Ave, Suite B, Traverse City, MI 49686
Tel: 231-933-0445 *Toll Free Tel:* 800-706-4636 *Fax:* 231-933-0448
E-mail: awards@bookpublishing.com
Web Site: www.livingnowawards.com
Key Personnel
CEO: Jerrold R Jenkins *E-mail:* jrj@bookpublishing.com
Pres: James Kalajian *Tel:* 800-706-4636 ext 1006 *E-mail:* jjk@bookpublishing.com
Mng Ed & Awards Dir: Jim Barnes *Tel:* 800-706-4636 ext 1011 *E-mail:* jimb@bookpublishing.com
Awards Coord: Amy Shamroe
Established: 2008
Annual award to celebrate the innovation & creativity of newly published books that can help us improve the quality of our lives, from cooking & entertaining to fitness & travel. The awards are open to all books written in English & intended for the North American market.
Other Sponsor(s): Jenkins Group
Award: Gold medal (1st place), silver medal (2nd place), bronze medal (3rd place), foil seals available, winners featured in *Independent Publisher Online*
Closing Date: July
Presented: Winner announced online in Sept

Locus Awards

Locus Science Fiction Foundation
Division of Locus Publications
655 13 St, Suite 100, Oakland, CA 94612
Tel: 510-339-9196
E-mail: locus@locusmag.com
Web Site: www.locusmag.com
Key Personnel
Publr & Ed-in-Chief: Liza Groen Trombi
Mng Ed: Kirsten Gong-Wong
Established: 1971
Presented for the best science fiction novel, best
fantasy novel, best first novel, best young adult
novel, best novella, best novelette, best short
fiction, science fiction anthology, best nonfic-
tion, art & artist, editor, magazine, best pub-
lisher & collection of the year.
Other Sponsor(s): Arisia; Norwescon
Award: Trophy & free subn
Presented: Seattle Center, Annually in June

The Gerald Loeb Awards

Anderson School of Management at UCLA
Gold Hall, Suite B-305, 110 Westwood Plaza,
Los Angeles, CA 90095-1481
Tel: 310-825-4478 *Fax:* 310-825-4479
E-mail: loeb@anderson.ucla.edu
Web Site: www.anderson.ucla.edu/gerald-loeb-
awards
Key Personnel
Exec Dir: Jonathan Daillak
Established: 1957
Distinguished business & finance journalism in
print & broadcast media. See web site for a
complete list of categories, eligibility & rules.
$100 per entry.
Award: The winning entry in each category re-
ceives a $2,000 honorarium. Honorable men-
tions in each category receive $500. Under cer-
tain special circumstances, established by the
final judges, a writer or entry may receive a
special award
Closing Date: Annually in Feb
Presented: New York, NY, Last week in June

Loft-Mentor Series in Poetry & Creative Prose

The Loft Literary Center
Open Book, Suite 200, 1011 Washington Ave S,
Minneapolis, MN 55415
Tel: 612-215-2575 *Fax:* 612-215-2576
E-mail: loft@loft.org
Web Site: www.loft.org
Key Personnel
Prog Mgr: Kathryn Savage *Tel:* 612-215-2590
E-mail: ksavage@loft.org
Established: 1980
Annual award for poetry, nonfiction & fiction
mss. Must be Minnesota State resident. Six
different residencies scheduled throughout the
year. Winners announced on web site. Open to
poets, fiction writers & nonfiction writers.
Award: Stipend to defray costs of participating in
the program & opportunity to study with six
nationally known writer-mentors in brief resi-
dence during the course of the year
Closing Date: Mid-Spring
Presented: The Loft

The Jack London Award

Titan Press
Box 17897, Encino, CA 91416-7897
E-mail: cwcsfv@gmail.com
Key Personnel
Mng Ed: Stefanya Wilson
Three quarterly competitions: fiction, poetry &
nonfiction. Monthly nominations are made for
publication & honorable mention. Of those,
one is chosen for the annual Grand Prize. Published & unpublished mss are eligible. $65 an-
nual dues are allowed; one free submission per
quarter; nonmembers; $15 reading fee per en-
try, up to 4 entries per quarter.

Award: Invitation to attend the Biannual Writer's
Conference, plaque commemorating winner as
guest of honor (give a public reading of his
work) & publication
Closing Date: Submissions accepted throughout
the year
Presented: Biannual Writer's Conference

Judy Lopez Memorial Award For Children's Literature

Women's National Book Association/Los Angeles
Chapter
1225 Selby Ave, Los Angeles, CA 90024
Tel: 310-474-9917 *Fax:* 310-474-6436
Web Site: www.wnba-books.org/la; www.
judylopezbookaward.org
Key Personnel
Pres: Natalie Obondo
Chair, Lopez Comm: Margaret Flanders
Chair, Selection Comm: Gail Kim
Established: 1986
For best books for young readers 9-12 years of
age, submitted by publishers, written by US
citizen/US resident in year that precedes the
award.
Award: Bronze medal & cash honorarium
Closing Date: Annually, Feb 1
Presented: Los Angeles, CA, 3rd Sunday in Sept

Los Angeles Times Book Prizes

Los Angeles Times
Subsidiary of Tribune Publishing Co
2300 E Imperial Hwy, El Segundo, CA 90245
Tel: 213-237-5775 *Toll Free Tel:* 800-528-4637
(ext 75775)
Web Site: www.latimesbookprizes.com
Key Personnel
Publr & CEO: Davan Maharaj
Admin: Ann Binney *E-mail:* ann.binney@latimes.
com
Established: 1980
Annual prizes to authors in the categories of fic-
tion, first fiction, autobiographical prose, young
adult literature, graphic novels, comics, mys-
tery/thriller, biography, current interest, history,
poetry, science & technology. No submissions
accepted; nominations are done by committees
of appointed judges. There is also an award for
lifetime achievement (Robert Kirsch Award)
& Innovation in Storytelling (The Innovator's
Award).
Other Sponsor(s): The Christopher Isherwood
Foundation
Award: $500 & citation (in 10 different cate-
gories). Robert Kirsch Award & Innovator's
Award at $1,000 each, Christopher Isherwood
Prize for Autobiographical prose $2,500 & a
citation
Presented: The Los Angeles Times Book Prize
Ceremony at Bovard Auditorium, USC Cam-
pus, Annually in April

Louise Louis/Emily F Bourne Student Poetry Award

Poetry Society of America (PSA)
15 Gramercy Park, New York, NY 10003
Tel: 212-254-9628
Web Site: poetrysociety.org/awards
Key Personnel
Pres: Allison Binns
Exec Dir: Matt Brogan *E-mail:* matt@
poetrysociety.org
Deputy Dir: Brett Fletcher Lauer *E-mail:* brett@
poetrysociety.org
Prog Dir: Laurin Macios *E-mail:* laurin@
poetrysociety.org
Established: 1971
For the best unpublished poem by a student in
grades 9-12 from the US. See web site for fur-
ther guidelines.
Award: $250

Closing Date: Annually, Oct-Dec
Presented: Annual Awards Ceremony, New York,
NY, Annually in Spring

Louisville Grawemeyer Award in Religion

Louisville Presbyterian Theological Seminary &
University of Louisville
1044 Alta Vista Rd, Louisville, KY 40205-1798
Tel: 502-895-3411 *Toll Free Tel:* 800-264-1839
Fax: 502-894-2286
E-mail: grawemeyer@lpts.edu
Web Site: www.grawemeyer.org
Key Personnel
Dir: Tyler Mayfield
Established: 1990
Given for a work presented or published in the 8
years preceding the year of the award. Nomi-
nations are invited from religious organizations,
appropriate academic associations, religious
leaders & scholars, presidents of universities
or schools of religion & publishers & editors
of scholarly journals. Personal nominations ac-
cepted, self-nominations not accepted.
Award: $100,000 one-time payment
Closing Date: Nominations by Jan 15
Presented: Annually in Spring

Love Creek Annual Short Play Festival

Love Creek Productions
2144 45 Ave, Long Island City, NY 11101
Tel: 646-765-6542
E-mail: LCPSubmissions@gmail.com
Key Personnel
Mng Artistic Dir: Steven Barrett
Literary Mgr: Amanda Barrett
Established: 1988
Produce 5-7 evenings of one-act plays each year.
Submissions must include a character break-
down, preferably 2—one basic (i.e. 2 men, 1
woman) & one detailed (including breakdown
of gender, age range & other information vital
to the character).
Writers should keep in mind there are mostly
women ages 17-27 in the company.
Award: Cash (1st prize), mini-showcase produc-
tion (finalists)
Closing Date: Revolving
Presented: New York, NY, various midtown
venues, Ongoing

James Russell Lowell Prize

Modern Language Association of America (MLA)
85 Broad St, Suite 500, New York, NY 10004-
2434
SAN: 202-6422
Tel: 646-576-5141; 646-576-5000 *Fax:* 646-458-
0030
E-mail: awards@mla.org
Web Site: www.mla.org
Key Personnel
Coord, Book Prizes: Annie M Reiser
E-mail: areiser@mla.org
Established: 1969
Annual prize for an outstanding literary or lin-
guistic study, a critical edition of an important
work, or critical biography by a current MLA
member published in 2019. Authors or publish-
ers should submit 6 copies & confirmation of
the author's membership in the MLA.
Award: Cash award & certificate
Closing Date: March 1
Presented: MLA Convention, Jan 2021

Pat Lowther Memorial Award

The League of Canadian Poets
2 Carlton St, Suite 1519, Toronto, ON M5B 1J3,
Canada
Tel: 416-504-1657
E-mail: info@poets.ca
Web Site: poets.ca

Key Personnel
Exec Dir: Lesley Fletcher *E-mail:* lesley@poets.
ca
Communs Coord: Laura O'Brien *E-mail:* laura@
poets.com
Annual award for the best book of poetry written by a Canadian woman & published in the preceding year. $25 handling fee.
Award: $1,000
Closing Date: Nov 1
Presented: June

Jeremiah Ludington Award
Educational Book & Media Association (EBMA)
11 Main St, Suite D, Warrenton, VA 20186
Mailing Address: PO Box 3363, Warrenton, VA 20188
Tel: 540-318-7770 *Fax:* 202-962-3939
E-mail: info@edupaperback.org
Web Site: www.edupaperback.org
Key Personnel
Exec Dir: Brian Gorg
Meeting Mgr: Maureen Gelwicks
Established: 1979
Presented annually to an individual who has made a significant contribution to the educational book & media business.
Award: Framed certificate & EBMA presents a $2,500 check to the charity of their choice
Presented: EBMA meeting, Jan

J Anthony Lukas Book Prize
Columbia University Graduate School of Journalism
2950 Broadway, New York, NY 10027
Tel: 212-854-6468
Web Site: www.journalism.columbia.edu
Key Personnel
Prog Mgr, Prof Prizes: Caroline L Martinet
E-mail: cm3443@columbia.edu
Established: 1998
Awarded annually to a book-length work of narrative nonfiction on a topic of American political or social concern that exemplifies the literary grace, commitment to serious research & social concern that characterized the distinguished work of the award's namesake. Submissions must include 4 copies of each book. Entry fee: $75 non-refundable.
Award: $10,000
Closing Date: Dec 11

J Anthony Lukas Work-in-Progress Award
Columbia University Graduate School of Journalism
2950 Broadway, New York, NY 10027
Tel: 212-854-6468
Web Site: www.journalism.columbia.edu
Key Personnel
Prog Mgr, Prof Prizes: Caroline L Martinet
E-mail: cm3443@columbia.edu
Established: 1998
Awarded annually to aid in the completion of a significant work of nonfiction on a topic of American political or social concern. Applicants should send copy of their original book proposal, sample chapter from book, photocopy of contract with US-based publisher & explanation of how award will advance progress of the book. No entry fee.
Award: $30,000
Closing Date: Dec 11

Lush Triumphant Literary Awards
subTerrain Magazine
PO Box 3008, MPO, Vancouver, BC V6B 3X5, Canada
Tel: 604-876-8710 *Fax:* 604-879-2667
E-mail: subter@portal.ca
Web Site: www.subterrain.ca
Established: 2003

Annual literary award in 3 categories: fiction, poetry & nonfiction. Entry fee: $27.50.
Award: Awarding $3,000 in cash prizes, plus publication. The winner in each category receives a $1,000 prize plus publication in the Winter issue (plus contributor's payment). The runners-up entries are published in the Spring issue of the following year (& they receive contributor's payment)
Closing Date: May 15
Presented: Vancouver, BC, Aug 15

Mark Lynton History Prize
Columbia University Graduate School of Journalism
2950 Broadway, New York, NY 10027
Tel: 212-854-6468
Web Site: www.journalism.columbia.edu
Key Personnel
Prog Mgr, Prof Prizes: Caroline L Martinet
E-mail: cm3443@columbia.edu
Established: 1998
Awarded to a book-length work of history on any topic that best combines intellectual distinction with felicity of expression. Submissions must include 4 copies of each book. Entry fee: $75 non-refundable.
Award: $10,000
Closing Date: Dec 11

Thomas J Lyon Book Award in Western American Literary and Cultural Studies
Western Literature Association
PO Box 6815, Logan, UT 84341
Web Site: www.westernlit.org/thomas-j-lyon-book-award-in-western-american-literary-and-cultural-studies; www.westernlit.org
Key Personnel
Dir, Opers: Sabine Barcatta
E-mail: WLAoperations@gmail.com
Established: 1997
Honors outstanding single-author scholarly book on the literature & culture of the American West published in the previous year. Must submit a statement of support & 3 copies of the book.
Award: Certificate
Closing Date: June 15
Presented: Annual Conference

Lyric Poetry Award
Poetry Society of America (PSA)
15 Gramercy Park, New York, NY 10003
Tel: 212-254-9628
Web Site: poetrysociety.org/awards
Key Personnel
Pres: Allison Binns
Exec Dir: Matt Brogan *E-mail:* matt@
poetrysociety.org
Deputy Dir: Brett Fletcher Lauer *E-mail:* brett@
poetrysociety.org
Prog Dir: Laurin Macios *E-mail:* laurin@
poetrysociety.org
Established: 1972
For a lyric poem on any subject, not to exceed 50 lines. Open to society members only. See web site for further information.
Award: $500
Closing Date: Annually, Oct-Dec
Presented: Annual Awards Ceremony, New York, NY, Annually in Spring

Lyric Poetry Prizes
The Lyric Foundation
PO Box 110, Jericho, VT 05465
Tel: 802-899-3993 *Fax:* 802-899-3993
E-mail: themuse@thelyricmagazine.com
Web Site: thelyricmagazine.com
Key Personnel
Ed: Jean Mellichamp Milliken
Assoc Ed: Nancy Mellichamp Savo
Collegiate Contest Coord: Tanya Cimonetti

Established: 1921
The Collegiate contest prize is awarded to undergraduates enrolled full-time in an American or Canadian college. The annual & quarterly prizes are awarded to poems published in *The Lyric.* Winners of annual awards are announced in the winter issue each year. Send SASE or provide e-mail address for guidelines. Sample copy of *The Lyric* $5, subscription $15/yr, $28/2 yrs, $38/3 yrs, $2/yr extra foreign or Canadian.
Award: Quarterly prize: $50. Annual awards: Lyric College Poetry Contest/Scholarship: $500, Lyric Memorial, Leslie Mellichamp & Roberts Memorial Prizes: $100 each, New England & Fluvanna Prizes: $50 each. Honorable mentions get one-year subn to *The Lyric.* Checks are mailed to recipients
Closing Date: Dec 1 (postmark)
Presented: Quarterly prizes awarded in the following issue, annual prizes in the winter issue

MacArthur Fellows Program
John D & Catherine T MacArthur Foundation
Office of Grants Management, 140 S Dearborn St, Chicago, IL 60603-5285
Tel: 312-726-8000 *Fax:* 312-920-6528
E-mail: 4answers@macfound.org
Web Site: www.macfound.org/programs/fellows
Key Personnel
Mng Dir: Cecilia A Conrad
Prog Dir: Marlies A Carruth
Awards unrestricted fellowships to talented individuals who have shown extraordinary originality & dedication in their creative pursuits & a marked capacity for self-direction. Recipients may be writers, scientists, artists, social scientists, humanists, teachers, entrepreneurs or those in other fields, with or without institutional affiliations.
The Fellows Program does not accept applications or unsol nominations.
Award: $625,000 stipend paid in equal quarterly installments over 5 years

Macavity Award
Mystery Readers International
7155 Marlborough Terr, Berkeley, CA 94705
Tel: 510-845-3600
Web Site: www.mysteryreaders.org
Key Personnel
Dir: Janet Rudolph *E-mail:* janet@
mysteryreaders.org
Established: 1986
Annually awarded for works nominated by & voted on by members of Mystery Readers International in categories: Best Novel, Best First Novel, Best Short Story, Best Nonfiction/Critical; Sue Feder Award for the Historical Mystery (all published in the US the previous year).
Award: Statue
Presented: Bouchercon, the World Mystery Convention, Oct

Sir John A Macdonald Prize
Canadian Historical Association
130 Albert St, Suite 1201, Ottawa, ON K1P 5G4, Canada
Tel: 613-233-7885 *Fax:* 613-565-5445
E-mail: cha-shc@cha-shc.ca
Web Site: www.cha-shc.ca
Key Personnel
Exec Dir: Michel Duquet *E-mail:* mduquet@cha-shc.ca
Established: 1976
Awarded for the best book on Canadian history. See web site for application details.
Award: $5,000
Closing Date: Annually, Dec 1
Presented: Annual meeting, Canadian Historical Association, May

MacDowell Fellowships

MacDowell
100 High St, Peterborough, NH 03458
Tel: 603-924-3886
E-mail: info@macdowell.org; admissions@macdowell.org
Web Site: www.macdowell.org
Key Personnel
Exec Dir: Philip Himberg *E-mail:* phimberg@macdowell.org
Admissions Dir: Courtney Bethel *E-mail:* cbethel@macdowell.org
Communs Mgr: Jonathan Gourlay *Tel:* 603-924-3886 ext 114 *E-mail:* jgourlay@macdowell.org
Established: 1907
Fellowships of up to 8 weeks are available for writers, composers, film/video artists, theatre artists, visual artists, architects & interdisciplinary artists. Artists-in-residence receive room, board & exclusive use of a studio. The average length of stay is 6 weeks. Talent is the sole criterion for acceptance. Established artists as well as emerging artists are encouraged to apply. Committees of distinguished professionals donate their time to judge applications, which include work samples, references & a brief project description. There are no residency fees. Grants for travel to & from MacDowell are available based on need. Financial aid for all artists is available through special grants from various foundations. An aid application will be mailed following acceptance. The Edward MacDowell medal is awarded for a career of outstanding contributions to the arts, including musical composition, visual arts or literature, architecture, film & video & interdisciplinary arts.
Closing Date: For fellowships: Jan 15, April 15 & Sept 15, see application form & guidelines online for details
Presented: Peterborough, NH
Branch Office(s)
MacDowell NYC, 521 W 23 St, 2nd fl, New York, NY 10011 *Tel:* 212-535-9690

Machigonne Fiction Contest

The New Guard
PO Box 472, Brunswick, ME 04011
E-mail: info@newguardreview.com; editors@writershotel.com
Web Site: www.newguardreview.com
Key Personnel
Founding Ed & Publr: Shanna McNair
Established: 2009
Submit a short story or novel excerpt up to 5,000 words. Online submissions only. Entry fee: $20.
Award: $1,500 & publication in *The New Guard*
Closing Date: Aug 31

Macmillan Booksellers Professional Development Scholarship

Book Industry Charitable Foundation
3135 S State St, Suite 203, Ann Arbor, MI 48108
Toll Free Tel: 866-733-9064 *Fax:* 734-477-2806
E-mail: info@bincfoundation.org
Web Site: www.bincfoundation.org/scholarship
Key Personnel
Exec Dir: Pam French *E-mail:* pam@bincfoundation.org
Dir, Devt: Kathy Bartson *E-mail:* kathy@bincfoundation.org
Progs Mgr: Kit Steinaway *E-mail:* kit@bincfoundation.org; Kate Weiss *E-mail:* kate@bincfoundation.org
Established: 2017
Aims to strengthen the industry by encouraging a greater number of individuals from underrepresented groups to choose +/or continue careers in bookselling. This scholarship will allow up to one bookseller to attend each of the fall regional trade shows.

C B MacPherson Prize

Canadian Political Science Association
260 rue Dalhousie St, Suite 204, Ottawa, ON K1N 7E4, Canada
Tel: 613-562-1202 *Fax:* 613-241-0019
E-mail: cpsa-acsp@cpsa-acsp.ca
Web Site: www.cpsa-acsp.ca
Key Personnel
Admin: Michelle Hopkins
Established: 1992
This is a biennial competition. Awarded to the best book published in English or in French in the field of political theory. A book may be single-authored or multi-authored. Single-authored book: author must be a member of the CPSA in the year the book is considered for the prize. Multi-authored book: at least one of the authors must be a member of the CPSA in the year the book is considered for the prize. For the 2022 award, a book must have a copyright date of 2020 or 2021.
Award: Commemorative plaque & receive/share the set of books submitted to the CPSA office
Presented: Annual Conference, June 2022

Magazine Merit Awards

Society of Children's Book Writers & Illustrators (SCBWI)
6363 Wilshire Blvd, Suite 425, Los Angeles, CA 90048
Tel: 323-782-1010; 310-403-0675 (cell) *Fax:* 323-782-1892
E-mail: grants@scbwi.org; scbwi@scbwi.org
Web Site: www.scbwi.org
Key Personnel
Pres: Stephen Mooser *E-mail:* stephenmooser@scbwi.org
Exec Dir: Lin Oliver *E-mail:* linoliver@scbwi.org
Established: 1988
For outstanding original magazine work for young people published during the calendar year & having been written or illustrated by SCBWI members.
Award: 4 plaques (fiction, nonfiction, illustration, poetry), 4 honor certificates
Closing Date: Annually in Dec
Presented: Annually in April

Mailer Prize

Norman Mailer Center
1841 Broadway, Suite 322, New York, NY 10023
Tel: 646-374-3940
Web Site: nmcenter.org
Key Personnel
Pres: Lawrence Schiller *E-mail:* lschiller@nmcenter.org
Established: 2009
Given to writers whose work over the years has challenged readers' perspectives on the world around them.

Maine Literary Awards

Maine Writers & Publishers Alliance
Glickman Family Library, 314 Forest Ave, Rm 318, Portland, ME 04101
Tel: 207-228-8263
E-mail: info@mainewriters.org
Web Site: mainewriters.org/programs/maine-literary-awards
Key Personnel
Prog Dir: Hannah Perry *Tel:* 207-228-8257 *E-mail:* hannah@mainewriters.org
Annual statewide competition for published books as well as drama, short works (either published or unpublished) & student writing. Maine writers may self-nominate or be nominated by others. All nominations must have been published in the previous calendar year.
Submission fees: Book Awards & Excellence in Publishing Award $25 membs, $45 nonmembs; Short Works Awards & Drama Award $10 membs, $25 nonmembs. No fee for Youth Awards.
See web site for full submission details & all categories.
Other Sponsor(s): John N Cole Family; Just Write Books; Maine Authors Publishing; Maine Poetry Society; University of Southern Maine
Closing Date: Feb 1
Presented: Mid-June

Major Achievement Award

Council for Wisconsin Writers
c/o 3225 N 91 St, Milwaukee, WI 53222
E-mail: wiswriters@gmail.com
Web Site: wiswriters.org/awards
Key Personnel
Contest Chair: Erik Richardson *E-mail:* erichardson@wi.rr.com
Awarded biennially from the Christopher Latham Sholes Award to honor the work of a Wisconsin writer, without regard to genre or category, who deserves special recognition to his/her literary merit. No entry fee.
Award: $1,000
Closing Date: Jan 31
Presented: CWW Annual Banquet, May

J Russell Major Prize

American Historical Association (AHA)
400 "A" St SE, Washington, DC 20003
Tel: 202-544-2422 *Fax:* 202-544-8307
E-mail: awards@historians.org
Web Site: www.historians.org
Established: 2001
Awarded for the best work in English on any aspect of French history. Books published in 2020 are eligible. Along with an application form, applicants must mail a copy of their book to each of the prize committee members who will be posted on our web site as the prize deadline approaches. All updated info on web site.
Award: Cash prize
Closing Date: May 15, 2021
Presented: AHA Annual Meeting, New Orleans, LA, Jan 2022

Malahat Review Long Poem Prize

The Malahat Review
University of Victoria, Box 1700, Sta CSC, Victoria, BC V8W 2Y2, Canada
Tel: 250-721-8524 *Fax:* 250-472-5051
E-mail: malahat@uvic.ca
Web Site: www.malahatreview.ca
Key Personnel
Ed: John Barton
Established: 1988
Two awards for best long poem(s). See web site for details & entry fee. Contest runs every other year (odd-numbered years). Alternates with Novella Prize (even-numbered years).
Award: $1,000 (2 prizes)
Closing Date: Feb 1, odd-numbered years

Gene E & Adele R Malott Prize for Recording Community Activism

The Langum Charitable Trust
2809 Berkeley Dr, Birmingham, AL 35242
Tel: 360-809-0465
E-mail: langumtrust@gmail.com
Web Site: www.langumtrust.org
Key Personnel
Dir: David J Langum, Sr *E-mail:* djlangum@samford.edu
Established: 2007
Biennial prize that recognizes the best literary depiction of an individual or small group of individuals whose efforts resulted in a significant improvement of their local community. Although the work of community improvement must be significant, the basis of the prize will be the skill & power of the literary or film de-

piction. Must have been published or released within the past 2 years of a prize cycle.
Award: $1,000 for the writer. If film, divided between the director & screenwriter
Closing Date: Dec 1 for materials published or released the previous 2 calendar years

Ralph Manheim Medal for Translation, see PEN/Ralph Manheim Medal for Translation

Margaret Mann Citation
Association for Library Collections & Technical Services (ALCTS)
Division of The American Library Association (ALA)
50 E Huron St, Chicago, IL 60611
SAN: 201-0062
Tel: 312-280-5037 *Toll Free Tel:* 800-545-2433
Fax: 312-280-5033
E-mail: alcts@ala.org
Web Site: www.ala.org/alcts
Key Personnel
Exec Dir: Keri Cascio *Tel:* 312-280-5030
E-mail: kcascio@ala.org
Established: 1951
Award for outstanding professional achievement in cataloging or classification in a significant publication or by participation in a professional organization. Candidates are nominated. Citation recipient selected by jury.
Other Sponsor(s): OCLC
Award: Citation & $2,000 scholarship to the US or Canadian library school of winner's choice
Closing Date: Annually, Dec 1
Presented: ALA Annual Conference, Annually in June

Many Voices Fellowships
The Playwrights' Center
2301 Franklin Ave E, Minneapolis, MN 55406-1099
Tel: 612-332-7481 *Fax:* 612-332-6037
E-mail: info@pwcenter.org
Web Site: www.pwcenter.org
Key Personnel
Producing Artistic Dir: Jeremy Cohen *Tel:* 612-332-7481 ext 113 *E-mail:* jeremyc@pwcenter.org
Assoc Artistic Dir: Hayley Finn *Tel:* 612-332-7481 ext 119 *E-mail:* hayleyf@pwcenter.org
Artistic Progs Admin: Julia Brown *Tel:* 612-332-7481 ext 115 *E-mail:* juliab@pwcenter.org
Many Voices Fellowship Coord: Christina Ham *Tel:* 612-332-7481 ext 124 *E-mail:* christinah@pwcenter.org
For writers of color. Two distinct programs to serve writers of varying skill/experience levels both locally & nationally.
Award: Many Voices Mentorship: 1 Minnesota playwright with little or no playwriting experience, $2,000 stipend; Many Voices Fellowship: 2 emerging playwrights receive $18,000 stipend, $2,000 in play development funds & dramaturgical support. One must reside in Minnesota, the other may be a resident of any US state
Closing Date: See web site for details

Marfield Prize
Arts Club of Washington
2017 "I" St NW, Washington, DC 20006-1804
E-mail: award@artsclubofwashington.org
Web Site: artsclubofwashington.org/awards
Key Personnel
Award Admin: Sass Brown
Established: 2006
Given annually to nonfiction books about the visual, literary or performing arts written for a broad audience. Works published in the US during the previous calendar year are eligible for consideration. Publishers, agents, or authors may submit books. No entry fee. Submit 3 copies of the book with prize submission form.
Award: $10,000
Closing Date: Oct 15

Marian Library Medal
University of Dayton, Marian Library
300 College Park, Dayton, OH 45469-1390
Tel: 937-229-4214 *Fax:* 937-229-4258
Web Site: campus.udayton.edu/mary/mlmedal.html
Key Personnel
Lib Dir: Sarah Cahalan
Established: 1953
To scholars in any country for outstanding achievement in Marian research.
Award: Medal

Maritime Electric Short Story Awards
Prince Edward Island Writers' Guild
81 Prince St, Charlottetown, PE C1A 4R3, Canada
E-mail: peiliteraryawards@gmail.com
Web Site: www.peiwritersguild.com
One short story, maximum 2,500 words, constitutes an entry. Maximum 2 entries. Entry fee for each submission is $25. Work must be original & unpublished. Prince Edward Island residents only. See web site for complete entry requirements.
Award: Cash prizes for 1st, 2nd & 3rd place
Closing Date: Jan 31
Presented: Cox & Palmer Island Literary Awards Gala, Annually in Spring

Morton Marr Poetry Prize
Southwest Review
PO Box 750374, Dallas, TX 75275-0374
Fax: 214-768-1408
E-mail: swr@mail.smu.edu
Web Site: www.smu.edu/southwestreview
Key Personnel
Ed-in-Chief: Greg Brownderville
Mng Ed: Preston Hutcherson *Tel:* 214-768-1036
Open to writers who have not published a book of poetry. Contestants may submit no more than 6 previously unpublished poems in a "traditional" form (e.g. sonnet, sestina, villanelle, rhymed stanzas, blank verse, etc). There is a $5 per poem entry/handling fee.
Award: $1,000 (1st prize), $500 (2nd prize) & publication in *Southwest Review*
Closing Date: Annually, Sept 30
Presented: Annually in Dec

Helen & Howard R Marraro Prize in Italian History
American Historical Association (AHA)
400 "A" St SE, Washington, DC 20003
Tel: 202-544-2422 *Fax:* 202-544-8307
E-mail: awards@historians.org
Web Site: www.historians.org
Established: 1973
Each award will be given for the book or article deemed best by the committee which treats Italian history in any epoch, Italian cultural history, or Italian-American relations. Each book must be published in 2020. Entries must first have been published in English by a historian whose usual residence is North America. Along with an application form, applicants must mail a copy of their book together with a curriculum vitae & bibliography of the author to each of the prize committee members who will be posted on our web site as the prize deadline approaches. All updated info on web site.
Other Sponsor(s): American Catholic Historical Association; Society for Italian Historical Studies
Award: Cash prize
Closing Date: May 15, 2021
Presented: AHA Annual Meeting, New Orleans, LA, Jan 2022

Howard R Marraro Prize
Modern Language Association of America (MLA)
85 Broad St, Suite 500, New York, NY 10004-2434
SAN: 202-6422
Tel: 646-576-5141; 646-576-5000 *Fax:* 646-458-0030
E-mail: awards@mla.org
Web Site: www.mla.org
Key Personnel
Coord, Book Prizes: Annie M Reiser
E-mail: areiser@mla.org
Established: 1973
Presented for an outstanding scholarly work on any phase of Italian literature or comparative literature involving Italian by an MLA member. The prize is awarded each even-numbered year. The committee solicits submissions of works published in 2020 by current members. Submit 4 copies of the work & confirm author's membership in the MLA.
Award: Cash award & certificate
Closing Date: May 1, 2021
Presented: MLA Convention, Jan 2022

Lenore Marshall Poetry Prize
The Academy of American Poets Inc
75 Maiden Lane, Suite 901, New York, NY 10038
Tel: 212-274-0343
E-mail: awards@poets.org
Web Site: www.poets.org
Key Personnel
Pres & Exec Dir: Jennifer Benka
E-mail: jenbenka@poets.org
Devt, Membership & Communs Sr Mgr: Molly Walsh *E-mail:* mwalsh@poets.org
Ad & Mktg Sr Mgr: Michelle Campagna
E-mail: mcampagna@poets.org
Sr Progs Mgr: Nikay Paredes *Tel:* 212-274-0343 ext 13 *E-mail:* nparedes@poets.org
Established: 1975
Awarded annually to recognize the most outstanding book of poetry published in the US in the previous calendar year. Self-published books are not eligible. Translations & new editions of previously published books are not eligible. Publishers should send 4 copies of each book along with $75 entry fee & entry form for each title submitted.
Award: $25,000 & 200 copies of winning book distributed to Academy members
Closing Date: May 15
Presented: Sept

Massachusetts Book Awards
Massachusetts Center for the Book
Simons College - GSLIS, 300 The Fenway, Boston, MA 02115
Tel: 617-521-2719
E-mail: bookawards@massbook.org
Web Site: www.massbook.org
Key Personnel
Exec Dir: Sharon Shaloo *E-mail:* shaloo@massbook.org
Established: 2000
The MassBooks recognize significant achievements by Massachusetts writers in fiction, nonfiction, poetry & children's literature for the previous publishing year. Also awarded, the MA Book medal for creative publishing, programming or lifetime achievement in the Massachusetts book community. Visit web site for details.
Other Sponsor(s): Massachusetts Board of Library Commissioners; Massachusetts Cultural Council; Massachusetts Library Association; Massachusetts Library System; Simmons College Graduate School of Library & Information Science

Masters Literary Awards
Titan Press
PO Box 17897, Encino, CA 91416-7897
Tel: 818-377-4006
E-mail: titan91416@yahoo.com
Key Personnel
Mng Ed: Stefanya Wilson
Established: 1981
Annual awards (including 4 quarterly prizes) for fiction, poetry & song lyrics & nonfiction. All quality published & unpublished mss are eligible, submitted from double-spaced photocopies or tearsheets. Guidelines available with No 10 SASE.
Award: $1,000 Grand Prize, 4 quarterly prizes of Honorable Mention
Closing Date: Submissions received prior to any award date are eligible for the subsequent award
Presented: Titan Press, March 15, June 15, Aug 15, Dec 15

Amy Mathers Teen Book Award
Canadian Children's Book Centre
40 Orchard View Blvd, Suite 217, Toronto, ON M4R 1B9, Canada
Tel: 416-975-0010 *Fax:* 416-975-8970
E-mail: info@bookcentre.ca
Web Site: www.bookcentre.ca
Key Personnel
Exec Dir: Charlotte Teeple *E-mail:* charlotte@bookcentre.ca
Lib Coord: Meghan Howe *E-mail:* meghan@bookcentre.ca
Mktg & Web Site Coord: Camilia Kahrizi *E-mail:* camilia@bookcentre.ca
Prog Coord: Shannon Howe Barnes *E-mail:* shannon@bookcentre.ca
Established: 2014
Awarded to a Canadian author for excellence in teen/young adult fiction.
Other Sponsor(s): Sylvan Learning
Award: $5,000
Closing Date: Annually in mid-Dec

Mathical Book Prize
Mathematical Sciences Research Institute (MSRI)
17 Gauss Way, Berkeley, CA 94720
Tel: 510-499-5181
E-mail: mathical@msri.org
Web Site: www.mathicalbooks.org
Key Personnel
Prize Coord: Kirsten Bohl
Annual award for fiction & nonfiction books that inspire children of all ages to see math in the world around them. Winners are selected in 5 grade-level categories: PreK, K-2, 3-5, 6-8 & 9-12. Publishers may submit up to 3 titles published in the year prior to the award.
Other Sponsor(s): Children's Book Council (CBC); National Council of Teachers of English (NCTE); National Council of Teachers of Mathematics (NCTM)
Presented: National Conference on Mathematics Education, Feb

Matt Cohen Prize: In Celebration of a Writing Life
The Writers' Trust of Canada
600-460 Richmond St W, Toronto, ON M5V 1Y1, Canada
Tel: 416-504-8222 *Toll Free Tel:* 877-906-6548
Fax: 416-504-9090
E-mail: info@writerstrust.com
Web Site: www.writerstrust.com
Key Personnel
Exec Dir: Charlie Foran *Tel:* 416-504-8222 ext 244 *E-mail:* cforan@writerstrust.com
Prog Coord: Devon Jackson *Tel:* 416-504-8222 ext 248 *E-mail:* djackson@writerstrust.com
Established: 2001

Recognizes a lifetime of distinguished work by a Canadian writer, working in either poetry or prose, in either French or English.
Other Sponsor(s): David & Marla Elhberg
Award: $25,000
Presented: The Writers' Trust Awards, Toronto, ON, CN, Annually in Nov

Mature Women Scholarship Grant - Art/Letters/Music
National League of American Pen Women Inc
The Pen Arts Bldg & Arts Museum, 1300 17 St NW, Washington, DC 20036-1973
Tel: 202-785-1997 *Fax:* 202-452-8868
E-mail: contact@nlapw.org
Web Site: www.nlapw.org
Key Personnel
Pres: Virginia Franklin Campbell
Established: 1976
Awarded biennially (even-numbered years). Judges in each category (art, letters, music) change for each award every award year. Must send SASE with inquiry for requirements. Include an $8 fee payable to NLAPW with entry.
Award: $1,000 (1st place), $750 (2nd place), $500 (3rd place); $150 (Photography Award), $150 (Water Media Award), $100 (Jean Baber Memorial Art Fund)
Closing Date: Oct 1, odd-numbered years
Presented: NLAPW Convention, Biennially in April, even-numbered years; mail notification March 15

Maxim Mazumdar New Play Competition
Alleyway Theatre
One Curtain Up Alley, Buffalo, NY 14202-1911
Tel: 716-852-2600
E-mail: publicrelations@alleyway.com
Web Site: alleyway.com
Key Personnel
Founder, Alleyway Theatre: Neal Radice
Literary Mgr: Joyce Stilson *Tel:* 716-852-2600 ext 202 *E-mail:* jstilson@alleyway.com
Contest limited to one submission per author, per year, per category. Entry must be a previously unproduced full-length (not less than 90 minutes) play or musical of any style, requiring no more than 8 performers & able to be presented on a unit or simple set, musicals must include CD, sheet music not necessary. One acts must be less than 20 minutes & no more than five actors. Entries will not be returned without SASE. Entry fee: $25.
Award: Cash & premiere production of entry at Alleyway Theatre
Closing Date: Annually, July 1

Janet B McCabe Poetry Prize
Ruminate Magazine
1041 N Taft Hill Rd, Fort Collins, CO 80521
Tel: 970-449-2726
E-mail: editor@ruminatemagazine.org
Web Site: www.ruminatemagazine.com
Key Personnel
Ed-in-Chief: Brianna Van Dyke
Sr Ed: Amy Lowe
Assoc Ed: Kristin George Bagdanov; Stefani Rossi
All submissions must be previously unpublished & submitted via online submission form. Up to 2 poems per entry, no longer than 40 lines each. Entry fee $20.
Award: $1,500 & publication in the prize issue (1st place), $200 & publication (2nd place)
Closing Date: Annually, May 15
Presented: Dec 15

Mary McCarthy Prize in Short Fiction
Sarabande Books Inc
822 E Market St, Louisville, KY 40206
Tel: 502-458-4028
E-mail: info@sarabandebooks.org

Web Site: www.sarabandebooks.org/mccarthy
Key Personnel
Pres: Sarah Gorham *E-mail:* sgorham@sarabandebooks.org
Dir, Mktg & Publicity: Joanna Englert *E-mail:* joanna@sarabandebooks.org
Contest is open to any short fiction writer of English. Submissions may include a collection of short stories, one or more novellas, or a short novel. Works that have previously appeared in magazines or in anthologies may be included. Translations & previously published collections are not eligible. Online submission process. See web site for full details & ms requirements. Submission fee: $28.
Award: $2,000, publication of ms, Sarabande Writing Residency & standard royalty contract
Closing Date: Feb 15
Presented: Sept

McClelland & Stewart Journey Prize, see
Writers' Trust McClelland & Stewart Journey Prize

John H McGinnis Memorial Award
Southwest Review
PO Box 750374, Dallas, TX 75275-0374
Fax: 214-768-1408
E-mail: swr@mail.smu.edu
Web Site: www.smu.edu/southwestreview
Key Personnel
Ed-in-Chief: Greg Brownderville
Mng Ed: Preston Hutcherson *Tel:* 214-768-1036
Established: 1960
For the best essay & story appearing in the *Southwest Review* during the preceding year.
Award: $500 (2-4 awards)
Presented: Annually in Jan

Harold W McGraw Jr Prize in Education
McGraw-Hill Education
2 Penn Plaza, New York, NY 10121-2298
Tel: 646-766-2000
E-mail: info@mcgrawprize.com
Web Site: www.mcgrawprize.com
Key Personnel
Dir, Communs: Tyler Reed *E-mail:* tyler.reed@mheducation.com
Established: 1988
Honors 3 individuals whose accomplishments, programs & ideas can serve as effective models for the education of future generations. Categories: K-12, Higher Education, International Education.
Other Sponsor(s): Arizona State University
Award: $50,000 & bronze sculpture
Closing Date: Oct 31
Presented: ASU GSV Education Innovation Summit, Annually in May

William Holmes McGuffey Longevity Award
Textbook & Academic Authors Association (TAA)
PO Box 367, Fountain City, WI 54629
E-mail: info@taaonline.net
Web Site: www.taaonline.net/mcguffey-longevity-award
Key Personnel
Exec Dir: Michael Spinella *Tel:* 973-943-0501 *E-mail:* michael.spinella@taaonline.net
Dir, Publg & Opers: Kim Pawlak *Tel:* 608-687-3106 *E-mail:* kim.pawlak@taaonline.net
Dir, Instl Memberships & Meetings: Maureen Foerster *Tel:* 608-687-3106 *E-mail:* maureen.foerster@taaonline.net
Membership Coord: Bekky Murphy *Tel:* 608-567-9060 *E-mail:* bekky.murphy@taaonline.net
Recognizes textbooks & learning materials whose excellence has been demonstrated over time. To be nominated, a work must have been in print 15 years & still be selling. Works are judged for merit in 4 areas: pedagogy; con-

tent/scholarship; writing; appearance & design. Nomination fee: $350 (non-refundable). See web site for nomination form & entry guidelines.
Closing Date: Dec 15
Presented: TAA Annual Conference, Annually in June

McKnight Artist Fellowship for Writers
The Loft Literary Center
Open Book, Suite 200, 1011 Washington Ave S, Minneapolis, MN 55415
Tel: 612-215-2575 *Fax:* 612-215-2576
E-mail: loft@loft.org
Web Site: www.loft.org
Key Personnel
Prog Dir: Bao Phi *Tel:* 612-215-2585
   E-mail: bphi@loft.org
Established: 1982
Contest for Minnesota residents only.
Award: Four $25,000 awards which alternate annually between poetry & creative prose; one $25,000 award in children's literature which alternates annually between writing for children 8 & under & older children
Closing Date: Annually in late Fall
Presented: The Loft, Annually in Spring

McKnight Fellowships in Playwriting
The Playwrights' Center
2301 Franklin Ave E, Minneapolis, MN 55406-1099
Tel: 612-332-7481 *Fax:* 612-332-6037
E-mail: info@pwcenter.org
Web Site: www.pwcenter.org
Key Personnel
Producing Artistic Dir: Jeremy Cohen *Tel:* 612-332-7481 ext 113 *E-mail:* jeremyc@pwcenter.org
Assoc Artistic Dir: Hayley Finn *Tel:* 612-332-7481 ext 119 *E-mail:* hayleyf@pwcenter.org
Artistic Progs Admin: Julia Brown *Tel:* 612-332-7481 ext 115 *E-mail:* juliab@pwcenter.org
Established: 1990
Grants to recognize mid-career playwrights whose work demonstrates exceptional artistic merit & potential. Playwright's primary residence must be in the state of Minnesota. Applicant must have had a minimum of one work fully produced by a professional theater at the time of application.
Award: Grants of $25,000 each

McKnight National Residency & Commission
The Playwrights' Center
2301 Franklin Ave E, Minneapolis, MN 55406-1099
Tel: 612-332-7481 *Fax:* 612-332-6037
E-mail: info@pwcenter.org
Web Site: www.pwcenter.org
Key Personnel
Producing Artistic Dir: Jeremy Cohen *Tel:* 612-332-7481 ext 113 *E-mail:* jeremyc@pwcenter.org
Assoc Artistic Dir: Hayley Finn *Tel:* 612-332-7481 ext 119 *E-mail:* hayleyf@pwcenter.org
Artistic Progs Admin: Julia Brown *Tel:* 612-332-7481 ext 115 *E-mail:* juliab@pwcenter.org
Established: 1982
Playwrights whose work has made a significant impact on the contemporary theater. Applicant must be a US citizen or permanent resident & must have had a minimum of 2 different works fully produced by professional theaters. Call or check web site for application information & deadline guidelines. Minnesota-based playwrights are not eligible for the award. Proposals for the Residency & Commission must be agent/professional only. Send writers resume, a 2- or 3-page proposal & a full-length play script.

Award: $15,000
Closing Date: See web site for details

McLaren Memorial Comedy Play Writing Competition
Midland Community Theatre
2000 W Wadley Ave, Midland, TX 79705
Tel: 432-682-2544
E-mail: tracy@mctmidland.org
Web Site: www.mctmidland.org
Key Personnel
Prodn Mgr: Tracy Alexander *E-mail:* tracy@mctmidland.org
Established: 1990
All entries must be comedies for adults, teens, or children; musical comedies no longer accepted. Requirements: full-length play (70-90 minutes); one-act plays no longer accepted. See web site for competition guidelines & required brochure with entry form. Submissions accepted beginning December 1. Attn: McLaren Competition Chairman.
Closing Date: Annually, Jan 31
Presented: McLaren Festival, Annually in early Fall

McLemore Prize
Mississippi Historical Society
Affiliate of Mississippi Dept of Archives & History
William F Winter Archives & History Bldg, 200 North St, Jackson, MS 39201
Mailing Address: PO Box 571, Jackson, MS 39205-0571
Tel: 601-576-6850 *Fax:* 601-576-6975
E-mail: mhs@mdah.ms.gov
Web Site: www.mdah.ms.gov
Key Personnel
Pres: Susannah J Ural
VP: Page Ogden
Secy-Treas, Historical Society: Elbert Hilliard
Public Info: Timothy Davis *E-mail:* tdavis@mdah.ms.gov
Established: 1980
For distinguished scholarly book published during the previous year on a subject related to Mississippi history or biography. Prize recipient is invited to be the Friday evening banquet speaker at the Society's annual meeting.
Award: $700 cash award plus $300 honorarium & reimbursement of travel expenses as banquet speaker
Closing Date: Annually, Nov 1
Presented: Annual meeting, 1st weekend in March

Phillip H McMath Post Publication Book Award
Arkansas Writers MFA Workshop, University of Central Arkansas
Dept of Writing, University of Central Arkansas, 201 Donaghey Ave, Thompson Hall 303, Conway, AR 72035
Web Site: arkansaswriters.wordpress.com
Key Personnel
Dir: Stephanie Vanderslice *Tel:* 501-450-3340
   E-mail: stephv@uca.edu
Two awards offered, one for prose & one for poetry. Any publisher, author, agent, or any legal representative of an author may enter full-length books published in the previous calendar year. Submissions may be in any genre & may not be self-published. Entry fee: $25. See web site for detailed guidelines & submission info.
Award: $500 honorarium & travel stipend to Arkatext Literary Festival in the Spring
Closing Date: Oct 15

John McMenemy Prize
Canadian Political Science Association
260 rue Dalhousie St, Suite 204, Ottawa, ON K1N 7E4, Canada

Tel: 613-562-1202 *Fax:* 613-241-0019
E-mail: cpsa-acsp@cpsa-acsp.ca
Web Site: www.cpsa-acsp.ca
Key Personnel
Admin: Michelle Hopkins
Established: 2000
To the author or authors of the best article in English or French, published in volume 50 of the *Canadian Journal of Political Science*.
Other Sponsor(s): Societe Quebecoise de Science Politique
Award: Certificate of Award & memberships in the Canadian Political Science Association & the Societe Quebecoise de Science Politique
Presented: Annual Conference, University of Alberta, Edmonton, AB, CN, June 2021

Medal for Distinguished Contribution to American Letters
National Book Foundation
90 Broad St, Suite 604, New York, NY 10004
Tel: 212-685-0261 *Fax:* 212-213-6570
E-mail: nationalbook@nationalbook.org
Web Site: www.nationalbook.org/amerletters.html
Key Personnel
Deputy Dir: Jordan Smith *E-mail:* jsmith@nationalbook.org
Dir, Technol: Meredith Andrews
   E-mail: mandrews@nationalbook.org
Assoc Dir, Awards: Anna Dobben
   E-mail: adobben@nationalbook.org
Communs & Mktg Mgr: Bev Rivero
   E-mail: brivero@nationalbook.org
Public Progs Mgr: Natalie Green
   E-mail: ngreen@nationalbook.org
Admin & Devt Coord: Dhyana Taylor
   E-mail: dtaylor@nationalbook.org
Presented by the Board of Directors, in conjunction with the conferring of the National Book Awards to a person who has enriched our literary heritage over a life of service, or a corpus of work.
Award: $10,000
Presented: Annually in Autumn

Medal of Honor for Literature
National Arts Club
15 Gramercy Park S, New York, NY 10003
Tel: 212-475-3424
E-mail: literary@thenationalartsclub.org
Web Site: www.nationalartsclub.org
Key Personnel
Chair, Literary Comm: Cherry Provost
Established: 1967
Presented for a body of work of literary excellence; nominations within the committee only & awarded by the Board of Governors.
Award: Gold medal
Presented: Gala Black Tie Dinner, at discretion of recipient

Lucille Medwick Memorial Award
Poetry Society of America (PSA)
15 Gramercy Park, New York, NY 10003
Tel: 212-254-9628
Web Site: poetrysociety.org/awards
Key Personnel
Pres: Allison Binns
Exec Dir: Matt Brogan *E-mail:* matt@poetrysociety.org
Deputy Dir: Brett Fletcher Lauer *E-mail:* brett@poetrysociety.org
Prog Dir: Laurin Macios *E-mail:* laurin@poetrysociety.org
Established: 1974
For an original poem in any form on a humanitarian theme, not to exceed 100 lines. Translations are ineligible. Open to society members only. See web site for more information.
Award: $500
Closing Date: Annually, Oct-Dec
Presented: Annual Awards Ceremony, New York, NY, Annually in Spring

Frederic G Melcher Scholarship

Association for Library Service to Children
(ALSC)
Division of The American Library Association
(ALA)
50 E Huron St, Chicago, IL 60611-2795
Tel: 312-280-2163 *Toll Free Tel:* 800-545-2433
Fax: 312-440-9374; 312-280-5271
E-mail: alsc@ala.org
Web Site: www.ala.org/alsc
Key Personnel
Exec Dir: Aimee Strittmatter
E-mail: astrittmatter@ala.org
Deputy Exec Dir: Alena Rivers *Tel:* 800-545-2433 ext 5866 *E-mail:* arivers@ala.org
Prog Offr, Communs: Laura Schulte-Cooper
Tel: 800-545-2433 ext 2165 *E-mail:* lschulte@ala.org
Awards Coord: Katie Connelly *Tel:* 800-545-2433 ext 2163 *E-mail:* kconnelly@ala.org
Prog Coord: Ann Michaud *Tel:* 800-545-2433 ext 2166 *E-mail:* amichaud@ala.org
Membership/Mktg Specialist: Elizabeth Serrano
Tel: 800-545-2433 ext 2164 *E-mail:* eserrano@ala.org
Established: 1956
Provides financial assistance for the professional education of men & women who intend to pursue an MLS degree & who plan to work in children's librarianship. This work may be serving children up to & including the age of 14 in any type of library.
Award: $7,500 - 2 scholarships per yr
Closing Date: Annually, March 1
Presented: ALA Annual Conference, Annually in June

Louise Meriwether First Book Prize

The Feminist Press at The City University of New York
365 Fifth Ave, Suite 5406, New York, NY 10016
SAN: 213-6813
Tel: 212-817-7915
E-mail: louisemeriwetherprize@gmail.com; info@feministpress.org
Web Site: www.feministpress.org/louise-meriwether-first-book-prize
Key Personnel
Exec Dir & Publr: Jamia Wilson
Established: 2016
The prize honors author Louise Meriwether by publishing a debut work by a woman or nonbinary author of color, between 30,000 & 80,000 words. Open to fiction & nonfiction. No poetry, plays, or academic texts. Submit ms as a PDF along with cover letter as a separate PDF attachment including author statement, brief bio, ms word count, how your work fits with the Feminist Press, brief list of up to 3 writers that you consider part of your writing lineage & if you are represented by a literary agent. The work submitted may not be under contract elsewhere.
Other Sponsor(s): TAYO Literary Magazine
Award: $5,000 advance (half at the time of the initial award & half upon publication) & contract to publish their book

Addison M Metcalf Award in Literature

American Academy of Arts & Letters
633 W 155 St, New York, NY 10032
Tel: 212-368-5900 *Fax:* 212-491-4615
E-mail: academy@artsandletters.org
Web Site: artsandletters.org
Key Personnel
Exec Dir: Cody Upton
Established: 1986
Biennial award to honor young writers.
Award: $10,000

Edna Meudt Poetry Book Award

Council for Wisconsin Writers

c/o 210 N Main St, No 204, Cedar Grove, WI 53013
E-mail: wiswriters@gmail.com
Web Site: wiswriters.org/awards
Key Personnel
Contest Chair: Sylvia Cavanaugh
E-mail: bgirl4shadow@gmail.com
Established: 1965
Annual award for the best book of poems published by a Wisconsin-based author in the contest year. Entry fee: $25 nonmembs.
Award: $500 & 1-week residency at Shake Rag Alley Center for the Arts
Closing Date: Jan 31
Presented: CWW Annual Banquet, May

The David Nathan Meyerson Prize for Fiction

Southwest Review
PO Box 750374, Dallas, TX 75275-0374
Fax: 214-768-1408
E-mail: swr@mail.smu.edu
Web Site: www.smu.edu/southwestreview
Key Personnel
Ed-in-Chief: Greg Brownderville
Mng Ed: Preston Hutcherson *Tel:* 214-768-1036
Open to writers who have not published a book of fiction. Submissions must be no longer than 8,000 words. A $25 reading fee must accompany each submission.
Award: $1,000 & publication in *Southwest Review*
Closing Date: Annually, May 1
Presented: Annually in Fall

Midwest Bookseller of the Year Award

Midwest Independent Booksellers Association (MIBA)
1375 St Anthony Ave, Suite 202-3, St Paul, MN 55104
Tel: 612-208-6279 *Toll Free Fax:* 844-273-4119
E-mail: info@midwestbooksellers.org
Web Site: www.midwestbooksellers.org/bookseller-of-the-year.html
Key Personnel
Exec Dir: Carrie Obry *E-mail:* carrie@midwestbooksellers.org
Dir, Opers: Robert Martin *Tel:* 612-520-1482
E-mail: robert@midwestbooksellers.org
Prog Specialist: Kate Scott
Established: 2018
Annual award to a bookseller in MIBA's region (North Dakota, South Dakota, Wisconsin, Iowa, Minnesota, Michigan's Upper Peninsula, Illinois, Kansas, Missouri & Nebraska) in recognition of excellence in the field of bookselling. Anyone working in a bookstore is eligible for the award. Nomination form opens April 1.
Closing Date: April 30
Presented: Annual Heartland Fall Forum, Winner announced July 1

Kenneth W Mildenberger Prize

Modern Language Association of America (MLA)
85 Broad St, Suite 500, New York, NY 10004-2434
SAN: 202-6422
Tel: 646-576-5141; 646-576-5000 *Fax:* 646-458-0030
E-mail: awards@mla.org
Web Site: www.mla.org
Key Personnel
Coord, Book Prizes: Annie M Reiser
E-mail: areiser@mla.org
Established: 1980
Award for a work in the field of language, culture, literacy or literature with strong application to the teaching of languages other than English. Authors need not be members of the MLA. Awarded for a book published in 2019 or 2020. For consideration, submit 4 copies. Presented biennially.
Award: Cash award & certificate

Closing Date: May 1
Presented: MLA Convention, Jan 2022

Milkweed Fellowship

Milkweed Editions
1011 Washington Ave S, Suite 300, Minneapolis, MN 55415-1246
Tel: 612-332-3192 *Toll Free Tel:* 800-520-6455
E-mail: fellowship@milkweed.org
Web Site: milkweed.org/milkweed-fellowship
Key Personnel
Art Dir: Mary Austin Speaker
E-mail: mary_austin_speaker@milkweed.org
Paid 1- to 2-year immersion program designed to offer the tools, experience & exposure necessary to pursue a career in book publishing. Position seeks to provide entry to those historically underrepresented among workers in book publishing (indigenous, people of color, LGBTQIA+ & those with disabilities). Application must include cover letter, 1- to 2-page resume & writing sample. Materials should be submitted as one combined PDF via Submittable (milkweededitions.submittable.com/submit).
Award: $30,000 salary per year, paid time off, health & dental benefits
Closing Date: June

Milkweed National Fiction Prize

Milkweed Editions
1011 Washington Ave S, Suite 300, Minneapolis, MN 55415-1246
Tel: 612-332-3192 *Toll Free Tel:* 800-520-6455
Fax: 612-215-2550
E-mail: submissions@milkweed.org
Web Site: www.milkweed.org
Key Personnel
Publr & CEO: Daniel Slager
Mng Dir: Patrick Thomas
E-mail: patrick_thomas@milkweed.org
Engagement Coord: Abby Travis
Established: 1988
Annual award for an unpublished novel or collection of short stories +/or one or more novellas. Awarded to the best work of fiction Milkweed accepts for publication during each calendar year by a writer not previously published by Milkweed Editions. Writers must request complete guidelines before submitting ms (send SASE or visit www.milkweed.org). Open year-round.
Award: $5,000 advance against royalties
Closing Date: Annually, Jan-March, July & Sept

Milner Award

Friends of the Atlanta-Fulton Public Library
One Margaret Mitchell Sq NW, Atlanta, GA 30303
Tel: 404-730-1865
E-mail: info@themilneraward.org
Web Site: www.themilneraward.org
Established: 1983
For living American authors of children's books voted on by the children of Atlanta & Fulton County. No application process.
Other Sponsor(s): Milner Award Committee
Award: Honorarium & glass sculpture (inkwell & pen) by Hans Frabel
Closing Date: Annually, April 1
Presented: Atlanta, GA

Minnesota Book Awards

The Friends of the Saint Paul Public Library
1080 Montreal Ave, Suite 2, St Paul, MN 55116
Tel: 651-222-3242 *Fax:* 651-222-1988
E-mail: friends@thefriends.org
Web Site: thefriends.org/events/mnba
Key Personnel
Dir: Alayne Hopkins *Tel:* 651-366-6488
E-mail: alayne@thefriends.org

Books created by writers, illustrators, or book artists who are Minnesotans are eligible for the awards through nominations. Awards are given each year for books published in the previous year.

Presented: Minnesota Book Awards Gala, Annually in April

Minotaur Books/Mystery Writers of America First Crime Novel Competition

Mystery Writers of America (MWA)
1140 Broadway, Suite 1507, New York, NY 10001
Tel: 212-888-8171 *Fax:* 212-888-8107
E-mail: mb-mwafirstcrimenovelcompetition@stmartins.com
Web Site: mysterywriters.org/about-mwa/st-martins; us.macmillan.com/minotaurbooks/submit-manuscript
Open to any writer, regardless of nationality, aged 18 or older, who has never been the author of any published novel (in any genre) & is not under contract with a publisher for publication of a novel. Only one ms entry is permitted per writer. Must submit online entry form & upload electronic file of ms; do not mail or e-mail ms submission to Minotaur Books.
Other Sponsor(s): Minotaur Books
Closing Date: Dec 12
Presented: Edgar Awards Banquet

Mississippi Review Prize

University of Southern Mississippi Department of English
118 College Dr, Box 5144, Hattiesburg, MS 39406-0001
E-mail: msreview@usm.edu
Web Site: www.usm.edu/mississippi-review/contest.html
Key Personnel
Ed-in-Chief: Adam Clay
Fiction & poetry prize open to all writers in English except current or former students or employees of the University of Southern Mississippi. Entry fee $16 & $15 by post.
Award: Fiction & Poetry: $1,000 each & publication in the print issue of *Mississippi Review* next Spring
Closing Date: Annually, Jan 1
Presented: Annually in May

W O Mitchell Book Prize, see The City of Calgary W O Mitchell Book Prize

MLA Prize for a Bibliography, Archive or Digital Project

Modern Language Association of America (MLA)
85 Broad St, Suite 500, New York, NY 10004-2434
SAN: 202-6422
Tel: 646-576-5141; 646-576-5000 *Fax:* 646-458-0030
E-mail: awards@mla.org
Web Site: www.mla.org
Key Personnel
Coord, Book Prizes: Annie M Reiser
  E-mail: areiser@mla.org
Established: 1998
Awarded biennially for enumerative & descriptive bibliography, archive or digital project. A multivolume bibliography is eligible if at least one volume was published in 2018 or 2019. Criteria for determining excellence include evidence of analytical rigor, meticulous scholarship, intellectual creativity & subject range & depth. Editors need not be members of MLA. For consideration, submit 4 copies.
Award: Cash award & certificate
Closing Date: May 1, 2022
Presented: MLA Convention, Jan 2023

MLA Prize for a First Book

Modern Language Association of America (MLA)
85 Broad St, Suite 500, New York, NY 10004-2434
SAN: 202-6422
Tel: 646-576-5141; 646-576-5000 *Fax:* 646-458-0030
E-mail: awards@mla.org
Web Site: www.mla.org
Key Personnel
Coord, Book Prizes: Annie M Reiser
  E-mail: areiser@mla.org
Established: 1993
Awarded annually for an outstanding scholarly work published in year prior to competition as the first book-length publication by a current member of the MLA. For consideration, submit 6 copies.
Award: Cash award & certificate
Closing Date: March 1
Presented: MLA Convention, Jan 2021

MLA Prize for a Scholarly Edition

Modern Language Association of America (MLA)
85 Broad St, Suite 500, New York, NY 10004-2434
SAN: 202-6422
Tel: 646-576-5141; 646-576-5000 *Fax:* 646-458-0030
E-mail: awards@mla.org
Web Site: www.mla.org
Key Personnel
Coord, Book Prizes: Annie M Reiser
  E-mail: areiser@mla.org
Established: 1995
Biennial prize offered in odd-numbered years. Committee solicits submissions of editions published in 2019 or 2020. A multivolume edition is eligible if at least one volume has been published during that period. The editor need not be a member of the MLA. Edition should be based on an examination of all available relevant textual sources. The source texts & the edited text's deviation from them should be fully described. The edition should exhibit the highest standards of accuracy in the presentation of its text & apparatus, which should be presented as accessibly & elegantly as possible. For consideration, submit 4 copies with letter.
Award: Cash award & certificate
Closing Date: May 1
Presented: MLA Convention, Jan 2022

MLA Prize for Independent Scholars

Modern Language Association of America (MLA)
85 Broad St, Suite 500, New York, NY 10004-2434
SAN: 202-6422
Tel: 646-576-5141; 646-576-5000 *Fax:* 646-458-0030
E-mail: awards@mla.org
Web Site: www.mla.org
Key Personnel
Coord, Book Prizes: Annie M Reiser
  E-mail: areiser@mla.org
Established: 1983
Offered as a biennial prize with competitions in even-numbered years for a distinguished scholarly book published in 2020 or 2021 in the field of English or another modern language or literature. Author enrolled in a program leading to an academic degree & did not hold a tenured, tenure-accruing, or tenure-track position in post-secondary education at the time of publication is eligible. For consideration, submit 6 copies & a completed entry form.
Award: Cash award & certificate
Closing Date: May 1
Presented: MLA Convention, Jan 2023

MLA Prize for Studies in Native American Literatures, Cultures & Languages

Modern Language Association of America (MLA)
85 Broad St, Suite 500, New York, NY 10004-2434
SAN: 202-6422
Tel: 646-576-5141; 646-576-5000 *Fax:* 646-458-0030
E-mail: awards@mla.org
Web Site: www.mla.org
Key Personnel
Coord, Book Prizes: Annie M Reiser
  E-mail: areiser@mla.org
Established: 2012
Awarded to a current MLA member for an outstanding scholarly work in the field of Native American literatures, cultures & languages published in 2020 or 2021. Selection committee is seeking works that examine & broaden understanding of the cultural expressions of first peoples or nations in the US, CN & Mexico. For consideration, submit 4 copies & a letter identifying the work.
Closing Date: May 1
Presented: MLA Convention, Jan 2023

MLA Prize in United States Latina & Latino & Chicana & Chicano Literary & Cultural Studies

Modern Language Association of America (MLA)
85 Broad St, Suite 500, New York, NY 10004-2434
SAN: 202-6422
Tel: 646-576-5141; 646-576-5000 *Fax:* 646-458-0030
E-mail: awards@mla.org
Web Site: www.mla.org
Key Personnel
Coord, Book Prizes: Annie M Reiser
  E-mail: areiser@mla.org
Established: 2002
Biennial prize offered in odd-numbered years to a current member of the association for an outstanding scholarly study in any language of United States Latina & Latino or Chicana & Chicano literature or culture published in 2019 or 2020. Books that are primarily translations will not be considered. For consideration the author or publisher should send 4 copies.
Award: Cash award, certificate & 1 year association membership
Closing Date: May 1
Presented: MLA Convention, Jan 2022

David Montgomery Award

The Organization of American Historians (OAH)
112 N Bryan Ave, Bloomington, IN 47408-4141
Tel: 812-855-7311
E-mail: oah@oah.org
Web Site: www.oah.org/awards
Key Personnel
Exec Dir: Beth English *E-mail:* benglish@oah.org
Comm Coord: Kara Hamm *E-mail:* khamm@oah.org
Awarded annually for the best book on a topic in American labor & working-class history. Eligible works shall be written in English & deal with US history in significant ways but may include comparative or transnational studies that fall within these guidelines. Each entry must be published during the calendar year preceding that in which the award is given. One copy of each entry must be mailed directly to the committee members listed on the web site.
Closing Date: Oct 1, 2021 (postmarked)
Presented: OAH Annual Meeting, Boston, MA, March 31-April 3, 2022

Lucy Maud Montgomery PEI Literature for Children Awards

Prince Edward Island Writers' Guild
81 Prince St, Charlottetown, PE C1A 4R3, Canada
E-mail: peiliteraryawards@gmail.com
Web Site: www.peiwritersguild.com

The ms must be a story written for children. Maximum length 5,000 words. Maximum 2 entries. Entry fee for each submission is $25. Work must be original & unpublished. Illustration may be submitted with the story, but are not necessary. Prince Edward Island residents only. See web site for complete entry requirements.
Award: Cash prizes for 1st, 2nd & 3rd place
Closing Date: Jan 31
Presented: Cox & Palmer Island Literary Awards Gala, Annually in Spring

Cenie H Moon Prize
The Poetry Society of Virginia
900 Timber Creek Place, Virginia Beach, VA 23464
E-mail: poetryinva@aol.com
Web Site: poetrysocietyofvirginia.org
Key Personnel
Pres: Robert P Arthur *E-mail:* robert.peebles.arthur@gmail.com
Exec Dir: Guy Terrell *E-mail:* guy.terrell@earthlink.net
Adult Contest Chair: Steven Blythe
 E-mail: stevenblythepoetry@gmail.com
All entries must be in English, original & unpublished. Submit 2 copies of each poem, each having the category name & number on top left of page. Only one poem per category; entries will not be returned. Subject: woman or women; 48 line limit; any form. Entry fee: $4 nonmembs.
Award: $50 (1st prize), $30 (2nd prize), $20 (3rd prize)
Closing Date: Jan
Presented: Annual PSV Awards Ceremony, April

Moonbeam Children's Book Awards
Independent Publisher Online
Division of Jenkins Group Inc
1129 Woodmere Ave, Suite B, Traverse City, MI 49686
Tel: 231-933-0445 *Toll Free Tel:* 800-706-4636
 Fax: 231-933-0448
E-mail: info@moonbeamawards.com
Web Site: www.moonbeamawards.com
Key Personnel
CEO: Jerrold R Jenkins *E-mail:* jrj@bookpublishing.com
Pres: James Kalajian *Tel:* 800-706-4636 ext 1006
 E-mail: jjk@bookpublishing.com
Mng Ed & Awards Dir: Jim Barnes *Tel:* 800-706-4636 ext 1011 *E-mail:* jimb@bookpublishing.com
Awards Coord: Amy Shamroe
Established: 2007
Annual award celebrating youthful curiosity, discovery & learning through books & reading. Recognizes the best children's books published each year for the North American market. Authors, illustrators, publishers & self-publishers of children's books intended for the North American market may enter.
Other Sponsor(s): Jenkins Group Inc
Award: Gold medal (1st place), silver medal (2nd place) & bronze medal (3rd place)
Closing Date: Aug
Presented: Traverse City Children's Book Festival, Nov

Jenny McKean Moore Writer-in-Washington
George Washington University
English Dept, Rome Hall, 801 22 St NW, Suite 643, Washington, DC 20052
Tel: 202-994-6180
E-mail: engldept@gwu.edu
Web Site: english.columbian.gwu.edu
Key Personnel
Dir, Creative Writing: Lisa Page
 E-mail: lpageinc@aol.com
Established: 1976

To be considered, applications must be made by letter indicating publications, teaching experience & a selection of published work. Genre alternates from year to year. Consult AWP job list for advertisement specifying genre.
Award: One-year teaching position for approximately $60,000 plus benefits
Closing Date: Annually in Dec

The William C Morris YA Debut Award
The American Library Association (ALA)
225 N Michigan Ave, Suite 1300, Chicago, IL 60601
Tel: 312-280-4390 *Toll Free Tel:* 800-545-2433 (ext 4390) *Fax:* 312-280-5276
E-mail: yalsa@ala.org
Web Site: www.ala.org/yalsa/morris
Established: 2009
Honors a debut book published by a first-time author writing for teens & celebrating impressive new voices in young adult literature. Books must have been published November 1-October 31 of the year preceding the award. Nominations by committee.
Presented: ALA Midwinter Youth Media Awards, Annually in Winter

William Morris Society in the United States Fellowships
William Morris Society in the United States
PO Box 53263, Washington, DC 20009
E-mail: us@morrissociety.org
Web Site: www.morrissociety.org
Key Personnel
Pres: Jason Martinek
Established: 1996
For scholarly or creative projects related to William Morris (1834-96); given to US citizens or permanent residents.
Award: Up to $1,000
Closing Date: Annually, Dec 1

Willie Morris Award for Southern Fiction
654 Madison Ave, Suite 703, New York, NY 10065
E-mail: info@williemorrisaward.com
Web Site: williemorrisaward.org
Sponsored by Reba White Williams & Dave Williams.
Awarded to a classic novel of at least 50,000 words & set in the South (Alabama, Arkansas, Florida, Georgia, Louisiana, Mississippi, North Carolina, South Carolina, Tennessee, Texas, Virginia). The book must have been published in the year prior to the award year. The winning book is chosen for the quality of its prose, its originality, its sense of place & period & the authenticity & appeal of its characters. Short stories & linked short stories are not eligible. Nonfictional references & passages are acceptable only if in moderation. The selected book may contain violence & despair & feature terrible events, but the final analysis must be uplifting & suggest hope & optimism.
Award: $10,000 & expense paid trip to New York City
Closing Date: Annually in March
Presented: Annually in Oct

Willie Morris Award for Southern Poetry
654 Madison Ave, Suite 703, New York, NY 10065
E-mail: info@williemorrisaward.com
Web Site: williemorrisaward.org
Honors an original, unpublished poem that exudes the American South in spirit, history, landscape, or experience.
Award: $2,500

Harold Morton Landon Translation Award
The Academy of American Poets Inc

75 Maiden Lane, Suite 901, New York, NY 10038
Tel: 212-274-0343
E-mail: awards@poets.org
Web Site: www.poets.org
Key Personnel
Pres & Exec Dir: Jennifer Benka
 E-mail: jenbenka@poets.org
Devt, Membership & Communs Sr Mgr: Molly Walsh *E-mail:* mwalsh@poets.org
Ad & Mktg Sr Mgr: Michelle Campagna
 E-mail: mcampagna@poets.org
Sr Progs Mgr: Nikay Paredes *Tel:* 212-274-0343 ext 13 *E-mail:* nparedes@poets.org
Established: 1976
Annual award to recognize a poetry collection translated from any language into English & published in the previous calendar year. Books must be published in a standard edition (48 pages or more). Collaborations by up to 2 translators are eligible. Anthologies & self-published books will not be considered.
Award: $1,000
Closing Date: Feb 15

Kathryn A Morton Prize in Poetry
Sarabande Books Inc
822 E Market St, Louisville, KY 40206
Tel: 502-458-4028
E-mail: info@sarabandebooks.org
Web Site: www.sarabandebooks.org/morton
Key Personnel
Pres: Sarah Gorham *E-mail:* sgorham@sarabandebooks.org
Dir, Mktg & Publicity: Joanna Englert
 E-mail: joanna@sarabandebooks.org
Contest is open to any poet writing in English. Individual poems from the ms may have been published previously in magazines, chapbooks of less than 48 pages, or anthologies, but the collection as a whole must be unpublished. Translations & previously published collections are not eligible. Online submission process. See web site for full details & ms requirements. Submission fee: $28.
Award: $2,000, publication of ms, Sarabande Writing Residency & standard royalty contract
Closing Date: Feb 15
Presented: Sept

George L Mosse Prize
American Historical Association (AHA)
400 "A" St SE, Washington, DC 20003
Tel: 202-544-2422 *Fax:* 202-544-8307
E-mail: awards@historians.org
Web Site: www.historians.org
Established: 2001
For an outstanding major work of extraordinary scholarly distinction, creativity & originality in the intellectual & cultural history of Europe since the Renaissance. Only books of a high scholarly distinction should be submitted. Research accuracy, originality & literary merit are important selection factors. Books with a copyright of 2020 are eligible for the 2021 award. Along with an application form, applicants must mail a copy of their book to each of the prize committee members who will be posted on our web site as the prize deadline approaches. All updated info on web site.
Award: Cash prize
Closing Date: May 15, 2021
Presented: AHA Annual Meeting, New Orleans, LA, Jan 2022

Most Promising New Textbook Award
Textbook & Academic Authors Association (TAA)
PO Box 367, Fountain City, WI 54629
E-mail: info@taaonline.net
Web Site: www.taaonline.net/promising-new-textbook-award

Key Personnel
Exec Dir: Michael Spinella *Tel:* 973-943-0501
   E-mail: michael.spinella@taaonline.net
Dir, Publg & Opers: Kim Pawlak *Tel:* 608-687-
   3106 *E-mail:* kim.pawlak@taaonline.net
Dir, Instl Memberships & Meetings: Maureen
   Foerster *Tel:* 608-687-3106 *E-mail:* maureen.
   foerster@taaonline.net
Membership Coord: Bekky Murphy *Tel:* 608-567-
   9060 *E-mail:* bekky.murphy@taaonline.net
Recognizes excellence in 1st edition textbooks
   & learning materials. Works are judged for
   merit in 4 areas: pedagogy; content/scholarship;
   writing; appearance & design. Nomination fee:
   $350 (non-refundable). See web site for nomi-
   nation form & entry guidelines.
Closing Date: Dec 15
Presented: TAA Annual Conference, Annually in
   June

**Frank Luther Mott-Kappa Tau Alpha
   Research Award**
Kappa Tau Alpha
University of Missouri, School of Journalism, 76
   Gannett Hall, Columbia, MO 65211-1200
Tel: 573-882-7685 *Fax:* 573-884-1720
E-mail: umcjourkta@missouri.edu
Web Site: www.kappataualpha.org
Key Personnel
Exec Dir: Keith P Sanders, PhD
Established: 1944
For the best research for books in journalism &
   mass communication, exclusive of textbooks,
   published in the previous year.
Award: $1,000 & plaque (1st prize)
Closing Date: Dec (see web site)
Presented: Annually in Aug

Sheila Margaret Motton Book Prize
New England Poetry Club
46 Wallace St, Somerville, MA 02144
E-mail: info@nepoetryclub.org
Web Site: www.nepoetryclub.org
Key Personnel
Pres: Mary Buchinger
VP: Hillary Sallick
Treas: Linda Haviland Conte
Prize presented annually for a book of poems
   published in the last 2 years. Send 2 copies of
   the book. Open to NEPC members only. See
   web site for additional guidelines.
Award: $250
Closing Date: May 31
Presented: Winners announced online Aug/Sept

Erika Mumford Prize
New England Poetry Club
46 Wallace St, Somerville, MA 02144
E-mail: info@nepoetryclub.org
Web Site: www.nepoetryclub.org
Key Personnel
Pres: Mary Buchinger
VP: Hillary Sallick
Treas: Linda Haviland Conte
Established: 1988
Annual contest for a poem about foreign culture
   or travel. See web site for additional guide-
   lines.
Award: $250
Closing Date: May 31
Presented: Winners announced online Aug/Sept

Derrick Murdoch Award
Crime Writers of Canada (CWC)
716 Thicket Way, Ottawa, ON K4A 3B5, Canada
E-mail: info@crimewriterscanada.com
Web Site: www.crimewriterscanada.com/awards
Key Personnel
Exec Dir: Alison Bruce *E-mail:* ed@
   crimewriterscanada.com

Asst Exec Dir & Arthur Ellis Awards Mgr: Ludvica Boota *E-mail:* aed@crimewriterscanada.
   com
Established: 1984
Biennial special achievement award (alternating
   with the Grand Master Award) for contributions
   to the crime genre. Awarded in odd-numbered
   years.

**Walter Dean Myers Awards for Outstanding
   Children's Literature**
We Need Diverse Books™
10319 Westlake Dr, No 104, Bethesda, MD
   20817
Tel: 701-404-9632 (voicemail only)
E-mail: walteraward@diversebooks.org
Web Site: diversebooks.org/our-programs/walter-
   award
Key Personnel
Co-Dir: Kathie Weinberg
   E-mail: kathieweinberg@diversebooks.org
Judging Comm Co-Chair: Maria Salvadore
Established: 2016
Annual award to recognize diverse authors (or
   co-authors) whose works feature diverse main
   characters & address diversity in a meaning-
   ful way. Applicants must identify as diverse
   & the main character of the story must also
   identify as diverse, defined as one or more of
   the following: person of color; Native American; LGBTQIA; person with a disability;
   marginalized religious or cultural minority in
   the US. Two categories: Teen & Young Reader.
   See web site for submission guidelines. Self-
   published titles are not accepted.
Closing Date: Nov 1 (postmarked)
Presented: Awards Ceremony, Library of
   Congress, Washington, DC, Winners announced
   Jan, ceremony in March

Walter Dean Myers Grant
We Need Diverse Books™
10319 Westlake Dr, No 104, Bethesda, MD
   20817
E-mail: waltergrantwndb@gmail.com
Web Site: diversebooks.org
Key Personnel
COO & SVP, Libn Servs: Dhonielle Clayton
   E-mail: dhonielleclayton@diversebooks.org
Applicants must identify as diverse, defined as
   one or more of the following: person of color;
   Native American; LGBTQIA+; person with a
   disability; marginalized religious & cultural
   minority in the US. Applicants must be unpublished illustrators +/or authors & working
   toward a career as a children's author +/or illustrator. Submit application via e-mail, including cover letter, 2 essays & work sample. See
   web site for submission guidelines. Grant is
   limited to US residents only. Five winners will
   be selected.
Award: $2,000
Closing Date: June 21

Mythopoeic Awards
Mythopoeic Society
Friends University, 2100 W University Ave, Wi-
   chita, KS 67213
Tel: 316-295-5563
E-mail: awards@mythsoc.org
Web Site: www.mythsoc.org
Key Personnel
Awards Admin: Vicki Ronn *E-mail:* ronn@
   friends.edu
Established: 1967
Awards (2) honor scholarship in the Inklings
   (JRR Tolkien, CS Lewis, Charles Williams)
   & the general fields of myth & fantasy studies;
   each is given to the author of a book published
   in the previous 3 years. The Fantasy Awards
   (2) for adult & children's literature honor nov-
   els or single-author collections in the spirit of

the Inklings; each is given to the author of a
   book published in the previous year.
Award: Statuette
Closing Date: Members make nominations Jan-
   Feb, winners picked by late July
Presented: Mythcon 43, University of Berkeley,
   Berkeley, CA, Annually in Aug

National Award for Arts Writing, see Marfield
   Prize

National Awards for Education Reporting
Education Writers Association (EWA)
3516 Connecticut Ave NW, Washington, DC
   20008
Tel: 202-452-9830 *Fax:* 202-452-9837
E-mail: ewa@ewa.org
Web Site: www.ewa.org
Key Personnel
Exec Dir: Caroline W Hendrie *E-mail:* chendrie@
   ewa.org
Asst Dir: Lori Crouch *E-mail:* lcrouch@ewa.org
Established: 1960
Best education reporting in print & broadcast me-
   dia.
Award: Grand prize, 1st prize, 2nd prize, special
   citation, in 19 categories; plaques & certificates
Presented: EWA National Seminar

National Book Awards
National Book Foundation
90 Broad St, Suite 604, New York, NY 10004
Tel: 212-685-0261 *Fax:* 212-213-6570
E-mail: nationalbook@nationalbook.org
Web Site: www.nationalbook.org
Key Personnel
Deputy Dir: Jordan Smith *E-mail:* jsmith@
   nationalbook.org
Dir, Technol: Meredith Andrews
   E-mail: mandrews@nationalbook.org
Assoc Dir, Awards: Anna Dobben
   E-mail: adobben@nationalbook.org
Commns & Mktg Mgr: Bev Rivero
   E-mail: brivero@nationalbook.org
Public Progs Mgr: Natalie Green
   E-mail: ngreen@nationalbook.org
Admin & Devt Coord: Dhyana Taylor
   E-mail: dtaylor@nationalbook.org
Established: 1950
Awards for living American authors for books
   in the US. Five categories: fiction, nonfiction,
   poetry, young people's literature & translated
   literature.
Award: $10,000 cash & bronze sculpture for win-
   ner in each genre
Closing Date: Annually in May
Presented: New York City, NY, Annually in Nov

National Book Critics Circle Award
National Book Critics Circle
c/o 310 Lewis Ave, Brooklyn, NY 11221
E-mail: info@bookcritics.org
Web Site: bookcritics.org/awards
Key Personnel
VP, Membership & Awards: Yahdon Israel
   E-mail: yahdonisrael@bookcritics.org
Awards to honor the best literature published in
   the US in 6 categories: autobiography, biog-
   raphy, criticism, fiction, nonfiction & poetry.
   Books published in English (including transla-
   tions) in the US with publication dates in the
   calendar year of the award are considered.
Closing Date: Dec 1
Presented: NBCC Awards Ceremony, Annually in
   March

The National Business Book Award
PwC
c/o Freedman & Associates Inc, 121 Richmond St
   W, Suite 605, Toronto, ON M5H 2K1, Canada
Tel: 416-868-1500

Web Site: www.nbbaward.com
Key Personnel
Contact: Mary Ann Freedman
 E-mail: mafreedman@freedmanandassociates.
 com
Established: 1985
Excellence in business writing.
Other Sponsor(s): BMO Financial Group; Globe
 & Mail; The Walrus Magazine
Award: $30,000
Closing Date: Annually in Dec
Presented: Spring/early Summer

National Federation of State Poetry Societies Annual Poetry Contest

National Federation of State Poetry Societies
 (NFSPS)
c/o 115 N Wisteria St, Mansfield, TX 76063-1835
E-mail: contestchair@nfsps.com
Web Site: www.nfsps.com
Established: 1959
Fifty poetry contests, one for students only; rules
 & categories vary. Prizes are offered by NFSPS
 affiliated poetry societies & individual donors.
 Consult NFSPS web site for specific details for
 each contest.
Other Sponsor(s): Individual states' poetry society
 as host society
Closing Date: March 15 (must not be postmarked
 before Jan 1)
Presented: NFSPS Annual Convention

The National Humanities Medal

National Endowment for the Humanities
400 Seventh St SW, Washington, DC 20506
Tel: 202-606-8400 *Toll Free Tel:* 800-NEH-1121
 (634-1121)
E-mail: questions@neh.gov
Web Site: www.neh.gov/about/awards
Key Personnel
Dir, Communs: Carmen Ingwell
 E-mail: cingwell@neh.gov
Established: 1997
Honors individuals or groups whose work has
 deepened the nation's understanding of the hu-
 manities & broadened out citizens' engagement
 with history, literature, languages, philosophy
 & other humanities subjects. Up to 12 medals
 awarded annually.

National Jewish Book Award-Children's Literature

Jewish Book Council
520 Eighth Ave, 4th fl, New York, NY 10018
Tel: 212-201-2920 *Fax:* 212-532-4952
E-mail: jbc@jewishbooks.org
Web Site: www.jewishbookcouncil.org
Key Personnel
Exec Dir: Naomi Firestone-Teeter
Prog Dir: Evie Saphire-Bernstein *E-mail:* evie@
 jewishbooks.org
Award: Certificate & publication
Closing Date: Annually in Sept
Presented: Center for Jewish History, Annually in
 March

National Jewish Book Award-Natan Book Award

Jewish Book Council
520 Eighth Ave, 4th fl, New York, NY 10018
Tel: 212-201-2920 *Fax:* 212-532-4952
E-mail: jbc@jewishbooks.org; natanbookawards@
 jewishbooks.org
Web Site: www.jewishbookcouncil.org
Key Personnel
Exec Dir: Naomi Firestone-Teeter
Prog Dir: Evie Saphire-Bernstein *E-mail:* evie@
 jewishbooks.org
This award brings Natan's values of infusing Jew-
 ish life with creativity & meaning into the in-
 tellectual arena by supporting & promoting a
 breakthrough book intended for mainstream au-

diences that will catalyze conversations around
 the issues that Natan grapples within its grant-
 making.
Award: Two-stage award, offering at most a total of $25,000, to be divided as follows: a cash
 award to the author of $10,000 to be used dur-
 ing the writing process; & customized support
 for the marketing & publicity strategy for the
 book, up to $15,000. This is a pre-publication
 award & the prize winner will be announced
 prior to the book's publication date
Closing Date: Annually in March
Presented: Center for Jewish History, Status update on finalists by May

National Jewish Book Award-Young Adult Literature

Jewish Book Council
520 Eighth Ave, 4th fl, New York, NY 10018
Tel: 212-201-2920 *Fax:* 212-532-4952
E-mail: jbc@jewishbooks.org
Web Site: www.jewishbookcouncil.org
Key Personnel
Exec Dir: Naomi Firestone-Teeter
Prog Dir: Evie Saphire-Bernstein *E-mail:* evie@
 jewishbooks.org
Award: Certificate & publication
Closing Date: Annually in Sept
Presented: Center for Jewish History, Annually in
 March

National Jewish Book Awards

Jewish Book Council
520 Eighth Ave, 4th fl, New York, NY 10018
Tel: 212-201-2920 *Fax:* 212-532-4952
E-mail: jbc@jewishbooks.org
Web Site: www.jewishbookcouncil.org
Key Personnel
Exec Dir: Naomi Firestone-Teeter
Prog Dir: Evie Saphire-Bernstein *E-mail:* evie@
 jewishbooks.org
Established: 1950
Twenty annual awards to authors & translators
 of books of outstanding scholarship & liter-
 ary merit on Jewish themes for the general, no
 specialist reader. Writing based on archival ma-
 terial, visual arts, poetry, Jewish family via il-
 lustrated children's. Categories: Children's Lit-
 erature, Holocaust, Jewish History, (Gerrard &
 Ella Berman Award), Modern Jewish Thought
 & Experience (Dorot Foundation Award),
 Sephardic Culture (Mimi Frank Award), Jew-
 ish Education (Anonymous Donor), General
 Nonfiction, Fiction & Children's Awards, Eastern European Studies (Ronald Lauder Award),
 Children's & Young Adult's Books, American
 Jewish Studies (Celebrate 350), Women's Stud-
 ies (Barbara Dobkin Award), Jewish Book of
 the Year Award (Everett Family Foundation
 Award), Biography, Autobiography & Memoir
 (The Krauss Family Award), Book Club Award
 (The Debby & Ken Miller Award), Contem-
 porary Jewish Life & Practice (Myra H Kraft
 Memorial Award), Debut Fiction (Goldberg
 Prize), Education-Jewish Identity (In Mem-
 ory of Dorothy Kripke), Fiction (J J Green-
 berg Memorial Award), Poetry (Berru Award),
 Scholarship (Nahum Sarna Memorial Award),
 Writing Based on Archival Material (The JDC-
 Herbert Katzki Award).
Award: Certificate & publication
Closing Date: Sept
Presented: Center for Jewish History, March

National Magazine Awards

National Media Awards Foundation
2300 Yonge St, Suite 1600, Toronto, ON M4P
 1E4, Canada
Tel: 416-939-6200
E-mail: staff@magazine-awards.com
Web Site: www.magazine-awards.com; twitter.
 com/magawards

Key Personnel
Mng Dir: Barbara Gould
Established: 1977
Annual award honoring excellence in Canadian
 magazine journalism with awards in 29 cate-
 gories.
Award: $1,000 Gold Award
Closing Date: Mid-Jan
Presented: Early June

The National Medal of Arts

National Endowment for the Arts
400 Seventh St SW, Washington, DC 20506-0001
Tel: 202-682-5570
Web Site: www.arts.gov/honors/medals
Key Personnel
Chmn: Jane Chu *E-mail:* chairman@arts.gov
Dir, Strategic Communs & Pub Aff: He-
 len Aguirre Ferre *Tel:* 202-682-5759
 E-mail: ferreh@arts.gov
Established: 1984
Highest award given to artists & arts patrons by
 the US government. Awarded annually by the
 President of the US.

National One-Act Playwriting Competition

Little Theatre of Alexandria
600 Wolfe St, Alexandria, VA 22314
Tel: 703-683-5778 (ext 2) *Fax:* 703-683-1378
E-mail: asklta@thelittletheatre.com
Web Site: www.thelittletheatre.com/info
Key Personnel
Chmn, One-Act: Bonnie Jourdan *Tel:* 703-960-
 5711 *E-mail:* bonniejourdan@gmail.com
Established: 1978
Open to all playwrights. Scripts must be original,
 unpublished & unproduced stage plays. Film
 & TV scripts are ineligible. Entry fee: $20 per
 play (limit 2 plays per person). Accept plays
 July 1-October 31. Prize awarded by mail by
 March 15.
Award: $350 (1st prize), $250 (2nd prize), $150
 (3rd prize), usually stage readings of top plays
Closing Date: Annually, Oct 31

National Outdoor Book Awards

National Outdoor Book Awards Foundation Inc
921 S Eighth Ave, Stop 8128, Pocatello, ID
 83209-8128
Tel: 208-282-3912 *Fax:* 208-282-2127
Web Site: www.noba-web.org
Key Personnel
Chair: Ron Watters *E-mail:* wattron@isu.edu
Established: 1995
Award recognizing the work of outstanding writ-
 ers & publishers of outdoor books. Categories
 include history/biography, outdoor literature,
 instructional texts, outdoor adventure guides,
 nature guides, children's books, design/artistic
 merit & nature & environment. Guidelines on
 the web site.
Other Sponsor(s): Association of Outdoor Recre-
 ation & Education; National Outdoor Book
 Awards Foundation
Closing Date: Annually in Aug
Presented: International Conference on Outdoor
 Recreation & Education (depending on the
 year, held in different locations in the US &
 CN), Annually in early Nov

National Poetry Series Open Competition

National Poetry Series
57 Mountain Ave, Princeton, NJ 08540
Tel: 609-430-0999 *Fax:* 609-430-9933
Web Site: nationalpoetryseries.org
Key Personnel
Founder/Dir: Daniel Halpern
Coord: Beth Dial *E-mail:* bethdial@
 nationalpoetryseries.org
Established: 1978
For book-length typed ms of poetry, previously
 unpublished in book form; online only via Sub-

mittable with $30 entrance fee per ms. See web site for guidelines.
Award: Five books to be published by trade publishers, small presses & university publishers. $10,000 cash award for each winner
Closing Date: Feb 28
Presented: Annually in Summer

National Ten-Minute Play Contest
Actors Theatre of Louisville
316 W Main St, Louisville, KY 40202-4218
Tel: 502-584-1265
Web Site: actorstheatre.org/national-ten-minute-play-contest/
Key Personnel
Literary Mgr: Jenni Page-White *Tel:* 502-584-1265 ext 3033 *E-mail:* jpage-white@actorstheatre.org
Established: 1989
Scripts should be submitted between September 1 & November 1. Accept the first 500 plays submitted.
Award: $1,000 & possible production at Actors Theatre of Louisville
Closing Date: Annually, Nov 1
Presented: Feb

National Translation Award
American Literary Translators Association (ALTA)
University of Arizona, Esquire Bldg, No 205, 1230 N Park Ave, Tucson, AZ 85721
Tel: 520-621-1757
Web Site: www.literarytranslators.org/awards/national-translation-award
Key Personnel
Exec Dir: Elisabeth Jaquette *E-mail:* elisabeth@literarytranslators.org
Communs & Awards Mgr: Rachael Daum *Tel:* 413-200-0459 *E-mail:* rachaeldaum@literarytranslators.org
Prog Mgr: Kelsi Vananda *E-mail:* kelsi@literarytranslators.org
Secy: Jessica Sue Vocatura *E-mail:* jessica@literarytranslators.org
Established: 1991
Awarded annually in poetry & in prose to literary translators who have made an outstanding contribution to literature in English by masterfully recreating the artistic force of a book of consummate quality. Submissions are accepted from publishers only beginning January each year. Publishers are invited to submit translated works of poetry or prose published in the previous calendar year. Hybrid works & drama are welcome & may be submitted to either category as determined appropriate by the publisher. Book must be translated from any language into English; must be a book-length work of literature (poetry, fiction, drama, literary nonfiction & hybrid works are accepted; must have been published in English translation anywhere in the world in the previous calendar year. To submit, complete entry form online & pay submission fee ($30 per entry for publishers with 10 or fewer titles a year, $50 per entry for publishers with more than 10 titles a year); send hard copies of the book(s) submitted to the judges requesting them. Publishers will receive the addresses to use as part of the online entry confirmation e-mail. Please do not send hard copies of the book to ALTA directly as they will not be considered submitted for the award.
Award: $5,000
Closing Date: April 16
Presented: ALTA Conference

National Writers Association Novel Contest
National Writers Association
10940 S Parker Rd, Suite 508, Parker, CO 80134
Tel: 303-656-7235
E-mail: natlwritersassn@hotmail.com
Web Site: www.nationalwriters.com
Key Personnel
Exec Dir & Ed: Sandy Whelchel
    E-mail: authorsandy@hotmail.com
Established: 1937
Novel contest for unpublished works. Entry fee: $35.
Award: $500 (1st prize), $250 (2nd prize), $150 (3rd prize)
Closing Date: Annually, April 1

Nautilus Book Awards
Lifethread Institute LLC
PO Box 2285, Vashon, WA 98070
Tel: 206-604-2250
Web Site: www.nautilusbookawards.com
Key Personnel
Owner & Dir: Mary Belknap, PhD
    E-mail: mbelknap@nautilusbookawards.com
Established: 1997
To recognize authors & titles as *Better Books for a Better World*, books that make excellent literary contributions to any of 4 themes, spiritual growth, health & wholeness, conscious living & sustainability & positive social change.
See Book Entry procedure on the web site.
Award: Winners have option for "Author Spotlight" video interview
Closing Date: Annually in Feb
Presented: Annually in May (option for exhibit at BookExpo & American Library Association Convention in June)

Phyllis Naylor Working Writer Fellowship, see PEN/Phyllis Naylor Working Writer Fellowship

NEA Creative Writing Fellowships
National Endowment for the Arts
400 Seventh St SW, Washington, DC 20506-0001
Tel: 202-682-5400; 202-682-5496 (Voice/TTY); 202-682-5034 (lit fellowships hotline)
    Fax: 202-682-5609; 202-682-5610
E-mail: litfellowships@arts.gov
Web Site: www.arts.gov
Key Personnel
Grants Dir & Contracts Offr: Nicki Jacobs
    Tel: 202-682-5546 *E-mail:* jacobsn@arts.gov
Established: 1967
Given to published writers of prose (fiction & creative nonfiction) & poetry. Variable number of fellowships, based on available program funds. Applications accepted by genre (prose-even years & poetry-odd years). Applicants are restricted to applying in one fellowship category only in the same year. Guidelines available on web site.
Award: $25,000
Closing Date: Annually in March
Presented: Notifications to be sent by e-mail in Dec

Nelligan Prize for Short Fiction
Colorado Review
Unit of Colorado State University
Colorado State University, Dept of English, Center for Literary Publishing, 9105 Campus Delivery, Fort Collins, CO 80523-9105
Tel: 970-491-5449
E-mail: creview@colostate.edu
Web Site: nelliganprize.colostate.edu
Key Personnel
Dir & Ed: Stephanie G'Schwind
Established: 2004
Awarded annually to the author of an outstanding short story, previously unpublished. Entry fee $15 per story with no limit on number of entries. Stories must be at least 10, but under 50 pages. Online entry fee $17.
Award: $2,000 & publication in Fall/Winter issue of *Colorado Review*
Closing Date: March 14

Howard Nemerov Sonnet Award
The Formalist
21 Osborne Terr, Wayne, NJ 07470
Web Site: theformalist.evansville.edu/home.htm
Key Personnel
Dir: William Baer
Annual award given for the best unpublished sonnet (no translations).
Award: $1,000 & publication in *Measure: A Review of Formal Poetry*
Closing Date: Annually, Nov 15

The Pablo Neruda Prize for Poetry
Nimrod, The University of Tulsa
Subsidary of The Nimrod Literary Awards
Nimrod International Journal, 800 S Tucker Dr, Tulsa, OK 74104
Tel: 918-631-3080 *Fax:* 918-631-3033
E-mail: nimrod@utulsa.edu
Web Site: www.utulsa.edu/nimrod
Key Personnel
Ed-in-Chief: Eilis O'Neal
Assoc Ed: Diane Burton; Cassidy McCants
Established: 1978
No previously published works. Omit author's name on mss. Must have a US address by October to enter. Works must be in English or translated by the original author. Include a cover sheet containing major title & subtitles of the work, author's name, address & phone along with 3-10 pages of poetry: 1 long poem or several short poems. Mss will not be returned. Retain the rights to publish any contest submission. Works not accepted will be released. Winners & selected finalists will be published. Include SASE & a check for $20 (includes a 1-year subscription & processing). Online submissions: nimrodjournal.submittable.com.
Award: $2,000 (1st prize), $1,000 (2nd prize); published writers receive 2 copies of the journal; winners will be flown to Tulsa for a conference & banquet
Closing Date: Annually, April 30
Presented: University of Tulsa, Annually in Oct

Neukom Institute Literary Arts Awards
Neukom Institute for Computational Science
Dartmouth College, Sudikoff Bldg, Rm 121, 9 Maynard St, Hanover, NH 03755
Web Site: sites.dartmouth.edu/neukominstitutelitawards
Key Personnel
Dir: Prof Daniel N Rockmore *E-mail:* daniel.n.rockmore@dartmouth.edu
Global award program to honor creative works around speculative fiction. Three categories: Speculative Literary Fiction; Debut Speculative Literary Fiction; Playwriting. See web site for book & play submission requirements. Books can be submitted via regular mail or e-mail to Daniel Rockmore. Playwrights can submit at goo.gl/forms/SXxELu0wy2rDYOE03.
Award: $5,000 honorarium; winner of Playwriting Award also receives 2 readings
Closing Date: Dec 31
Presented: Early May

Neustadt International Prize for Literature
World Literature Today
Affiliate of University of Oklahoma
c/o University of Oklahoma, 630 Parrington Oval, Suite 110, Norman, OK 73019-4033
Tel: 405-325-4531
Web Site: www.worldliteraturetoday.org; www.worldlit.org
Key Personnel
Exec Dir: Robert Con Davis-Undiano
    E-mail: rcdavis@ou.edu
Asst Dir & Ed-in-Chief: Daniel Simon
    E-mail: dsimon@ou.edu
Art Dir: Merleyn Bell *E-mail:* merleyn@ou.edu

Mng Ed: Michelle Johnson *E-mail:* lmjohnson@ou.edu
Book Reviews Ed: Robert Vollmar
  E-mail: rvollmar@ou.edu
Mktg Dir, Progs & Devt: Terri Stubblefield
  E-mail: tdstubb@ou.edu
Circ & Accts Specialist: Kay Blunck
  E-mail: kblunck@ou.edu
Established: 1969
To a living writer for outstanding literary achievement; prize may honor a single major work or an entire oeuvre; writer's work must be available in a representative sample in English, Spanish or French; writer must accept the award in person in ceremonies at the University of Oklahoma; a special issue of *World Literature Today* is devoted to the laureate; Candidates must be nominated by a jury member.
Award: $50,000 & an eagle feather cast in silver
Presented: University of Oklahoma, Biennially, even-numbered years

Allan Nevins Prize
Society of American Historians (SAH)
Affiliate of American Historical Association
2950 Broadway, New York, NY 10027
Tel: 212-854-6495
E-mail: amhistsociety@columbia.edu
Web Site: sah.columbia.edu
Key Personnel
Pres: Mary Kelley
VP: Ann Fabian
Exec Secy: Andie Tucher
Established: 1961
For the best written doctoral dissertation on an American subject. The dissertation must have been defended or the PhD degree received in the calendar year preceding the award presentation & must not have already been submitted for publication.
Award: $2,000, certificate & publication by an award sponsoring publication house
Closing Date: Annually, Dec 31
Presented: New York, NY, Annually in May

New England Book Awards
New England Independent Booksellers Association Inc (NEIBA)
One Beacon St, 15th fl, Boston, MA 02108
Tel: 617-547-3642 *Fax:* 617-830-8768
Web Site: www.newenglandbooks.org/bookawards
Key Personnel
Exec Dir: Beth Ineson *E-mail:* beth@neba.org
Admin Coord: Nan Sorensen *E-mail:* nan@neba.org
Mktg Coord: Alexandra Schmelzle *E-mail:* ali@neba.org
Established: 1990
Annual awards for fiction, nonfiction, children's & publishing are chosen by booksellers. Fiction, nonfiction & children's awards are awarded to specific titles either about New England, set in New England or by an author residing in New England, published between September 1 & August 31.
Award: $250 donation to charity or literary group chosen by each author
Closing Date: July
Presented: Fall trade show & conference, Sept/Oct

New Hampshire Literary Awards
New Hampshire Writers' Project
2500 N River Rd, Manchester, NH 03106
Tel: 603-314-7980
E-mail: info@nhwritersproject.org; awards@nhwritersproject.org
Web Site: www.nhwritersproject.org
Key Personnel
Chair: Masherl Chappelle
Comm Chair: Mary Russell

Treas: Rose Curry
Off Mgr: Nicole Escobar
Established: 1992
Biennial award given in odd-numbered years. Nominees must live in New Hampshire, be a native or deal with subject matter that is deemed by judges to be inherently connected with New Hampshire.
Closing Date: Varies. Typically in Spring
Presented: Nov

New Issues Poetry Prize
New Issues Poetry & Prose
c/o Western Michigan University, 1903 W Michigan Ave, Kalamazoo, MI 49008-5463
Tel: 269-387-8185
E-mail: new-issues@wmich.edu
Web Site: www.wmich.edu/newissues
Key Personnel
Mng Ed: Kimberly Kolbe
Poets writing in English who have not previously published a full-length collection of poems. Submit ms minimum 40 pages, typed on one side, single-spaced; do not bind ms. Include brief bio & relevant publication information; cover page with name, address, phone & title of ms; include table of contents. A $20 reading fee for each ms; enclose SASE.
Other Sponsor(s): Western Michigan University
Award: $2,000 & book publication
Closing Date: Nov 30

New Letters Literary Awards
New Letters
UMKC, University House, 5101 Rockhill Rd, Kansas City, MO 64110-2499
Tel: 816-235-1169 *Fax:* 816-235-2611
E-mail: newletters@umkc.edu
Web Site: www.newletters.org
Established: 1986
Annual literary contest.
Award: $1,500 & publication for each category - fiction, poetry & essay (1st prize). All entries considered for publication
Closing Date: Annually, May 18

New Letters Prize for Poetry
New Letters
UMKC, University House, 5101 Rockhill Rd, Kansas City, MO 64110-2499
Tel: 816-235-1169 *Fax:* 816-235-2611
E-mail: newletters@umkc.edu
Web Site: www.newletters.org
Established: 1986
Annual literary contest. All entries considered for publication.
Award: $1,500 & publication
Closing Date: Annually, May 18

New Mexico-Arizona Book Awards
New Mexico Book Co-op
925 Salamanca NW, Los Ranchos, NM 87107
Tel: 505-344-9382
E-mail: info@nmbookcoop.com
Web Site: www.nmbookcoop.com/BookAwards/BookAwards.html
Open to authors & publishers anywhere. Books must have a direct connection to Arizona or New Mexico, either as subject, author, or publisher. Books with a publication date or copyright date since January 1 of the preceding year are eligible. Books that won in a category in a previous New Mexico Book Award Program are not eligible for re-submission; finalists can be re-submitted. Books can be entered in more than 1 category. Each title must include the entry form (1 form for multiple categories), payment of entry fee & 3 copies of the book being considered (add 1 copy for each additional category entered for the same book). Entry fee: $50 per entry/per category. Entries received by Feb 28 of the year of the award are eligible for

a $10 discount. See web site for information on 56 award categories.
For ebooks, entries of fiction or nonfiction are accepted in epub or mobi formats & must be e-mailed. Entry fee: $25 per entry.
Closing Date: July 1
Presented: Awards Banquet, Annually in Nov

New Millennium Awards for Fiction, Poetry & Nonfiction
New Millennium Writings
4021 Garden Dr, Knoxville, TN 37918
Tel: 865-254-4880
E-mail: hello@newmillenniumwritings.org
Web Site: newmillenniumwritings.org
Key Personnel
Publr & Ed: Alexis Williams Carr *E-mail:* alexis.williams@hotmail.com
Each fiction or nonfiction prize should total no more than 6,000 words (short-short fiction no more than 1,000 words). Each poetry entry may include up to 3 poems. $17 reading fee required for each entry. See web site for further information.
Award: $1,000 each for Poem, Fiction, Nonfiction & Short-Short Fiction plus publication
Closing Date: Annually in Jan

New Women's Voices Chapbook Competition
Finishing Line Press
PO Box 1626, Georgetown, KY 40324
Tel: 502-603-0670
E-mail: finishingbooks@aol.com; flpbookstore@aol.com
Web Site: www.finishinglinepress.com
Key Personnel
Publr: Leah Maines
Mng Ed: Kevin Murphy Maines
Sr Ed: Christen Kincaid
Established: 1998
Cash & publication of a chapbook of poems for women who have not yet published a full-length collection. Winner announced on web site & in *Poets & Writers Magazine*.
Award: $1,000 & publication
Closing Date: Annually, April 15
Presented: Finishing Line Press, Aug 30

New York City Book Awards
The New York Society Library
53 E 79 St, New York, NY 10075
Tel: 212-288-6900 *Fax:* 212-744-5832
E-mail: events@nysoclib.org
Web Site: www.nysoclib.org
Key Personnel
Head of Events: Sara Holliday *Tel:* 212-288-6900 ext 222
Established: 1996
Given annually to the authors of the best books about New York City. Must submit copy of nominated book the same year of publication. $40 per book fee. Make check out to The New York Society Library.
Award: Plaque & varied monetary amount
Closing Date: Dec
Presented: The New York Society Library, Early May

The New York Public Library Helen Bernstein Book Award for Excellence in Journalism
The New York Public Library
Stephen A Schwarzman Bldg, Fifth Ave at 42 St, South Court Bldg, 3rd fl, New York, NY 10018-2788
Tel: 212-930-0876
Web Site: www.nypl.org
Key Personnel
Helen Bernstein Libn, Periodicals: Karen Gisonny *E-mail:* kgisonny@nypl.org
Established: 1987
Requires overall journalistic excellence & a published book that stems from the author's reportage & exemplifies outstanding work. Note:

nominations are for books published during the calendar year & are solicited only from publishers & editors-in-chief of major newspapers, news magazines & book publishers nationwide.
Award: $15,000
Closing Date: Oct 1 for books published in calendar year
Presented: The New York Public Library, Annually in April/May

New York State Edith Wharton Citation of Merit for Fiction Writers
New York State Writers Institute
Subsidiary of University at Albany
University at Albany, SL 320, Albany, NY 12222
Tel: 518-442-5620 *Fax:* 518-442-5621
E-mail: writers@albany.edu
Web Site: www.albany.edu/writers-inst
Key Personnel
Founder & Exec Dir: William Kennedy
Dir: Donald W Faulkner
Asst Dir: Suzanne Lance *E-mail:* slance@uamail.albany.edu
Established: 1985
State author designation for a New York State fiction writer. Applications not accepted. Nominations by advisory panel only.
Award: $10,000
Presented: Albany, NY, Biennially, even-numbered years

New York State Walt Whitman Citation of Merit for Poets
New York State Writers Institute
Subsidiary of University at Albany
University at Albany, SL 320, Albany, NY 12222
Tel: 518-442-5620 *Fax:* 518-442-5621
E-mail: writers@albany.edu
Web Site: www.albany.edu/writers-inst
Key Personnel
Founder & Exec Dir: William Kennedy
Dir: Donald W Faulkner
Asst Dir: Suzanne Lance *E-mail:* slance@uamail.albany.edu
Established: 1985
State author designation for a New York State poet. Applications not accepted. Nominations by advisory panel only.
Award: $10,000
Presented: Albany, NY, Biennially, even-numbered years

John Newbery Medal
Association for Library Service to Children (ALSC)
Division of The American Library Association (ALA)
50 E Huron St, Chicago, IL 60611-2795
Tel: 312-280-2163 *Toll Free Tel:* 800-545-2433
Fax: 312-440-9374; 312-280-5271
E-mail: alsc@ala.org
Web Site: www.ala.org/alsc
Key Personnel
Exec Dir: Aimee Strittmatter
    E-mail: astrittmatter@ala.org
Deputy Exec Dir: Alena Rivers *Tel:* 800-545-2433 ext 5866 *E-mail:* arivers@ala.org
Prog Offr, Communs: Laura Schulte-Cooper
    Tel: 800-545-2433 ext 2165 *E-mail:* lschulte@ala.org
Awards Coord: Katie Connelly *Tel:* 800-545-2433 ext 2163 *E-mail:* kconnelly@ala.org
Prog Coord: Ann Michaud *Tel:* 800-545-2433 ext 2166 *E-mail:* amichaud@ala.org
Membership/Mktg Specialist: Elizabeth Serrano
    Tel: 800-545-2433 ext 2164 *E-mail:* eserrano@ala.org
Established: 1922
Awarded annually to the author of the most distinguished writing in a children's book published during the preceding year. Restricted to authors who are citizens or residents of the US.

Award: Medal
Closing Date: Dec 31
Presented: ALA Midwinter Meeting, Jan/Feb

Newfoundland and Labrador Book Awards
Writers' Alliance of Newfoundland and Labrador (WANL)/Literary Arts Foundation of Newfoundland and Labrador
Haymarket Sq, 223 Duckworth St, St John's, NL A1C 6N1, Canada
Tel: 709-739-5215 *Toll Free Tel:* 866-739-5215
E-mail: wanl@nf.aibn.com
Web Site: wanl.ca
Key Personnel
Exec Dir: Wendi Smallwood
Memb Servs Coord: Samantha Fitzpatrick
Established: 1997
Honor excellence in Newfoundland and Labrador writing in 4 categories: fiction & children's/young adult literature (in even years), nonfiction & poetry (in odd years).
Other Sponsor(s): The Bruneau Family (children's/young adult literature); Downhome Inc (fiction); Historic Sites Association (Heritage & History Book Award); Le Grow's Travel (poetry); Rogers Cable (nonfiction)
Award: $1,500 (1st prize), $500 each to runners-up
Closing Date: Jan
Presented: May

Newfoundland and Labrador Credit Union Fresh Fish Award for Emerging Writers
Writers' Alliance of Newfoundland and Labrador (WANL)/Literary Arts Foundation of Newfoundland and Labrador
Haymarket Sq, 223 Duckworth St, St John's, NL A1C 6N1, Canada
Tel: 709-739-5215 *Toll Free Tel:* 866-739-5215
E-mail: wanl@nf.aibn.com
Web Site: wanl.ca
Key Personnel
Exec Dir: Wendi Smallwood
Memb Servs Coord: Samantha Fitzpatrick
Established: 2006
Biennial award intended to serve as an incentive for emerging writers in Newfoundland and Labrador by providing them with financial support, recognition & professional editing services for a book-length ms in any genre. Must be registered members of WANL; writers may join WANL at the time of submission.
Award: $5,200, $1,000 toward professional editing services for the winning ms & miniature sculpture; $1,200 each to runners-up
Closing Date: Sept, odd-numbered years

Don & Gee Nicholl Fellowships in Screenwriting
Academy of Motion Picture Arts & Sciences (AMPAS)
1313 Vine St, Hollywood, CA 90028
Tel: 310-247-3010 *Fax:* 310-247-3794
E-mail: nicholl@oscars.org
Web Site: www.oscars.org/nicholl
Established: 1986
Screenwriting; for information visit web site.
Award: Up to 5 awards of $35,000 each
Closing Date: Annually, May 1
Presented: Beverly Hills, CA, Annually in Nov

Mike Nichols Writing for Performance Award, see PEN/Mike Nichols Writing for Performance Award

Mary Nickliss Prize in US Women's +/or Gender History
The Organization of American Historians (OAH)
112 N Bryan Ave, Bloomington, IN 47408-4141
Tel: 812-855-7311
E-mail: oah@oah.org

Web Site: www.oah.org/awards
Key Personnel
Exec Dir: Beth English *E-mail:* benglish@oah.org
Comm Coord: Kara Hamm *E-mail:* khamm@oah.org
Established: 2015
The prize acknowledges the generations of women whose opportunities were constrained by the historical circumstances in which they lived. It is given for "the most original" book in US women's +/or gender history (including North America & the Caribbean prior to 1776). The OAH defines "the most original" book as one that is a path breaking work or challenges +/or changes widely accepted scholarly interpretations in the field. If no book submitted for the prize meets this criterion, the award shall be given for "the best" book in US women's +/or gender history. "The best" book recognizes the ideas & originality of the significant historical scholarship being done by historians of US women's +/or gender history & makes a significant contribution to the understanding of US women's +/or gender history. Each entry must be published during the calendar year preceding that in which the award is given. One copy of each entry must be mailed directly to the committee members listed on the web site.
Closing Date: Oct 1, 2021 (postmarked)
Presented: OAH Annual Meeting, Boston, MA, March 31-April 3, 2022

Lorine Niedecker Poetry Award
Council for Wisconsin Writers
c/o 3225 N 91 St, Milwaukee, WI 53222
E-mail: wiswriters@gmail.com
Web Site: wiswriters.org/awards
Key Personnel
Contest Chair: Erik Richardson
    E-mail: erichardson@wi.rr.com
Prize awarded for a group of shorter poems (2 of which must be published in the contest year) & which represent a significant achievement commensurate with the quality of Niedecker's work. Submit up to 5 poems, none longer than 50 lines each. All types of poetry are welcome. Entry fee: $25 nonmembs. No entries accepted via e-mail.
Award: $500, $50 honorable mention
Closing Date: Jan 31
Presented: CWW Annual Banquet, May

John Frederick Nims Memorial Prize
Poetry Magazine
61 W Superior St, Chicago, IL 60654
Tel: 312-787-7070 *Fax:* 312-787-6650
E-mail: editors@poetrymagazine.org
Web Site: www.poetryfoundation.org
Key Personnel
Edit Asst: Holly Amos *E-mail:* hamos@poetrymagazine.org
Established: 1999
For poetry published in the preceding 2 volumes of *Poetry* magazine. No application necessary.
Award: $500
Presented: Annually in Dec

Nonfiction Award
Young Adult Library Services Association (YALSA)
Division of The American Library Association (ALA)
50 E Huron St, Chicago, IL 60611
Toll Free Tel: 800-545-2433 (ext 4390) *Fax:* 312-280-5276
E-mail: yalsa@ala.org
Web Site: www.ala.org/yalsa/nonfiction-award
Key Personnel
Exec Dir: Anita Mechler
Prog Offr, Events & Conferences: Nichole O'Connor *Tel:* 800-545-2433 ext 4387
    E-mail: noconnor@ala.org

Communs Specialist: Anna Lam *Tel:* 800-545-2433 ext 5849 *E-mail:* alam@ala.org
Annual award to honor the best nonfiction book published for young adults (ages 12-18) during a November 1-October 31 publishing year.
Presented: ALA Youth Media Awards

North Carolina Arts Council Writers Fellowships

North Carolina Arts Council
Division of North Carolina State Government
109 E Jones St, Raleigh, NC 27601
Mailing Address: Dept of Cultural Resources, Mail Service Ctr 4632, Raleigh, NC 27699-4632
Tel: 919-807-6500 *Fax:* 919-807-6532
E-mail: ncarts@ncdcr.gov
Web Site: www.ncarts.org
Key Personnel
Exec Dir: Wayne Martin *Tel:* 919-807-6525
E-mail: wayne.martin@ncdcr.gov
Lit & Theatre Dir: David Potorti *Tel:* 919-807-6512 *E-mail:* david.potorti@ncdcr.gov
Established: 1980
Fellowships are given every 2 years to poets & writers of fiction, literary nonfiction, literary translation playwrights & screenwriters. Writers who have lived in the state for at least 1 year as of application deadline & who intend to remain instate during the fellowship year are eligible.
Award: $10,000
Closing Date: Nov 1, even-numbered years
Presented: Summer, odd-numbered years

North Street Book Prize

Winning Writers
351 Pleasant St, PMB 222, Northampton, MA 01060-3961
Tel: 413-320-1847 *Toll Free Tel:* 866-WINWRIT (946-9748) *Fax:* 413-280-0539
Web Site: www.winningwriters.com
Key Personnel
Pres: Adam Cohen *E-mail:* adam@winningwriters.com
VP: Jendi Reiter
Submit self-published books, any year of publication, in the following categories: mainstream/literary fiction; genre fiction; creative nonfiction, memoir & poetry. Up to 150,000 words in length. Applications accepted February 15-June 30, $60 entry fee per book.
Award: $3,000 (grand prize), $1,000 (1st prize, mainstream/literary fiction, genre fiction, creative nonfiction, memoir & poetry), $250 (4 honorable mentions)
Closing Date: June 30
Presented: Winner announced Feb 15 on web site

Northern California Book Awards, see CALIBA Golden Poppy Awards

Northern California Book Awards

Northern California Book Reviewers (NCBR)
c/o Poetry Flash, 1450 Fourth St, Suite 4, Berkeley, CA 94710
Tel: 510-525-5476 *Fax:* 510-525-6752
E-mail: editor@poetryflash.org; ncbr@poetryflash.org
Web Site: poetryflash.org
Key Personnel
Chmn: Joyce Jenkins
Contact: Frances Phillips *E-mail:* frances@haassr.org
Established: 1981
Awarded annually by category (fiction, poetry, nonfiction, children's literature & translation) for best book in category by a Northern California writer. Publishers Award given occasionally for special achievement by a Northern California publisher or a literary organization.

Send 3 copies of book; no application or fee necessary.
Other Sponsor(s): Friends of the San Francisco Public Library; Mechanics' Institute Library & Chess Room; PEN West; Poetry Flash; San Francisco Public Library; Women's National Book Assn (SF Chapter)
Award: Cash & certificate
Closing Date: Dec 1
Presented: Koret Auditorium, San Francisco Main Public Library, San Francisco, CA, Spring

Notable Wisconsin Authors

Wisconsin Library Association Inc
4610 S Biltmore Lane, Suite 100, Madison, WI 53718-2153
Tel: 608-245-3640 *Fax:* 608-245-3646
Web Site: wla.wisconsinlibraries.org
Key Personnel
Exec Dir: Mr Plumer Lovelace *E-mail:* lovelace@wisconsinlibraries.org
Events & Conferences: Brigitte Rupp Vacha
E-mail: ruppvacha@wisconsinlibraries.org
Established: 1973
Annual award honoring Wisconsin authors, past & present, for their literary contributions.
Award: Printed brochure with biographical information on the notable author, including a list of authors' works
Closing Date: April 15
Presented: WLA Annual Conference, Oct-Nov

Novella Prize

The Malahat Review
University of Victoria, Box 1700, Sta CSC, Victoria, BC V8W 2Y2, Canada
Tel: 250-721-8524 *Fax:* 250-472-5051
E-mail: malahat@uvic.ca
Web Site: www.malahatreview.ca
Key Personnel
Ed: John Barton
Established: 1995
Awarded biennially (even-numbered years) alternating with Long Poem Prize (odd-numbered years). See web site for details & entry fee.
Award: $1,500
Closing Date: Feb 1, even-numbered years

NSK Neustadt Prize for Children's Literature

World Literature Today
c/o University of Oklahoma, 630 Parrington Oval, Suite 110, Norman, OK 73019-4033
Tel: 405-325-4531
Web Site: www.worldliteraturetoday.org; www.worldlit.org
Key Personnel
Exec Dir: Robert Con Davis-Undiano
E-mail: rcdavis@ou.edu
Asst Dir & Ed-in-Chief: Daniel Simon
E-mail: dsimon@ou.edu
Art Dir: Merleyn Bell *E-mail:* merleyn@ou.edu
Mktg Dir, Progs & Devt: Terri Stubblefield
E-mail: tdstubb@ou.edu
Mng Ed: Michelle Johnson *E-mail:* lmjohnson@ou.edu
Book Reviews Ed: Robert Vollmar
E-mail: rvollmar@ou.edu
Circ & Accts Specialist: Kay Blunck
E-mail: kblunck@ou.edu
Established: 2003
A biennial award intended to enhance the quality of children's literature by promoting writing that contributes to the quality of their lives. Awarded to a living writer with significant achievement, either over a lifetime or in a particular publication. The essential criterion for awarding this prize is that the writer's work is having a positive impact on the quality of children's literature.
Other Sponsor(s): Nancy Barcelo; Kathy Neustadt; Susan Neustadt Schwartz; The University of Oklahoma

Award: $25,000, medal & certificate
Closing Date: No outside nominations accepted, nominations by jury member only
Presented: The University of Oklahoma, Norman, OK, Oct, odd-numbered years

Nuestras Voces National Playwriting Competition

MetLife Foundation
138 E 27 St, New York, NY 10016
Tel: 212-225-9950 *Fax:* 212-225-9085
Web Site: www.repertorio.org
Key Personnel
Spec Projs Mgr: Allison Astor Vargas
E-mail: aav@repertorio.org
Established: 2000
Award: $3,000 & full production (winner), cash awards of $500-$3,000 (top 5), stage reading (top 10)
Closing Date: Annually in June

NYC Emerging Writers Fellowships

The Center for Fiction
17 E 47 St, New York, NY 10017
Tel: 212-755-6710
E-mail: info@centerforfiction.org
Web Site: centerforfiction.org
Key Personnel
Writing Progs Mgr: Thierry Kehou
E-mail: thierry@centerforfiction.org
Supports emerging writers living in New York City whose work shows promise of excellence.
Other Sponsor(s): Jerome Foundation
Award: $5,000 grant

NYSCA/NYFA Artist Fellowships

New York Foundation for the Arts
20 Jay St, 7th fl, Brooklyn, NY 11201
Tel: 212-366-6900 *Fax:* 212-366-1778
E-mail: info@nyfa.org
Web Site: www.nyfa.org
Key Personnel
Exec Dir: Michael Royce *E-mail:* mroyce@nyfa.org
Dir, Progs: David Perry *E-mail:* dperry@nyfa.org
Exec Asst: Lauren Hilger *E-mail:* lhilger@nyfa.org
Fellowship applications limited to New York State residents. Applications open in the fall. Grants awarded in 15 artistic disciplines over a 3-year period, 5 categories per year. See web site for categories by year.
Award: $7,000
Closing Date: Annually in Dec
Presented: New York, NY

The O. Henry Prize Stories

Anchor Books
Imprint of Knopf Doubleday Publishing Group
c/o University of Texas at Austin, One University Sta, English Dept, B5000, Austin, TX 78712
Web Site: www.randomhouse.com/anchor/ohenry
Key Personnel
Series Ed: Laura Furman
Established: 1919
Annual collection of the 20 best English language short stories published in American & Canadian magazines & written in the English language during the calendar year 2 years prior to the year presented. No submissions; selections made by the series editor from those published in the approximately 260 magazines with print editions submitted to the series.
Closing Date: May 1

Joyce Carol Oates Prize, see Simpson/Joyce Carol Oates Prize

Eli M Oboler Memorial Award

Intellectual Freedom Round Table (IFRT)
Unit of The American Library Association (ALA)

50 E Huron St, Chicago, IL 60611
Tel: 312-280-4226 *Toll Free Tel:* 800-545-2433
E-mail: oif@ala.org
Web Site: www.ala.org/ifrt
Key Personnel
Asst Dir: Kristen Pekoll *Tel:* 312-280-4220
Established: 1986
Biennial award given to an author of a published
work in English, or an English translation deal-
ing with issues, events, questions or controver-
sies in the area of intellectual freedom. Must
have been published within previous 2 calendar
years prior to the ALA annual conference at
which it is granted.
Award: $500 & certificate
Closing Date: Dec 1, odd-numbered years
Presented: ALA Annual Conference, June, even-
numbered years

The Flannery O'Connor Award for Short Fiction

University of Georgia Press
Main Library, 3rd fl, 320 S Jackson St, Athens,
GA 30602
Fax: 706-542-2558
Web Site: www.ugapress.org
Key Personnel
Series Ed: Lee K Abbott
Asst Acqs Ed: Beth Snead *Tel:* 706-542-7613
E-mail: bsnead@uga.edu
Established: 1981
Collections of original short fiction. Ms should
be 40,000-75,000 words & should be accom-
panied by a $30 submission fee; ms will not
be returned. Submissions accepted between
April 1 & May 31. Open to both published &
unpublished writers. Applicants should visit
the press web site for guidelines. No phone
calls regarding the award will be accepted.
Accepting electronic submissions at georgia-
press.submishmash.com.
Award: $1,000 & publication by the University
of Georgia Press under a standard publishing
contract
Closing Date: Annually, May 31

Frank O'Connor Prize for Fiction

Texas Christian University
Dept of English, TCU Box 298300, Fort Worth,
TX 76129
Tel: 817-257-5907 *Fax:* 817-257-5905
E-mail: descant@tcu.edu
Web Site: www.descant.tcu.edu
Key Personnel
Mng Ed: Dan Williams *E-mail:* d.e.williams@tcu.
edu
Established: 1957
Best published fiction in each volume of descant.
No entry fee. Winners announced in journal.
Other Sponsor(s): descant (publication), Dept of
English, TCU
Award: $500
Closing Date: Annually, Sept 1-April 1
Presented: Winner announced in the Summer in
descant

Scott O'Dell Award for Historical Fiction

c/o Horn Book Inc, 300 The Fenway, Suite P-
311, Palace Road Bldg, Boston, MA 02215
Tel: 617-278-0225 *Toll Free Tel:* 888-628-0225
E-mail: scottodellfanpage@gmail.com
Web Site: scottodell.com/the-scott-odell-award
Key Personnel
Chair: Deborah Stevenson
Asst to Chair: Ann Carlson
Established: 1982
Presented for a work of historical fiction pub-
lished in the previous year for children or
young adults, by a US publisher & set in the
New World. Winner is selected by O'Dell
Award Committee.

Award: $5,000
Closing Date: Annually, Dec 31

Odyssey Award for Excellence in Audiobook Production

Young Adult Library Services Association
(YALSA)
Division of The American Library Association
(ALA)
50 E Huron St, Chicago, IL 60611
Toll Free Tel: 800-545-2433 (ext 4390) *Fax:* 312-
280-5276
E-mail: yalsa@ala.org
Web Site: www.ala.org/yalsa/odyssey
Key Personnel
Exec Dir: Anita Mechler
Prog Offr, Events & Conferences: Nichole
O'Connor *Tel:* 800-545-2433 ext 4387
E-mail: noconnor@ala.org
Communs Specialist: Anna Lam *Tel:* 800-545-
2433 ext 5849 *E-mail:* alam@ala.org
Annual award given to the producer of the best
audiobook produced for children +/or young
adults, available in English in the US. Admin-
istered jointly with the Association for Library
Service to Children (ALSC).
Other Sponsor(s): Booklist

Annual Off Off Broadway Short Play Festival

Samuel French Inc
235 Park Ave S, 5th fl, New York, NY 10003
Tel: 212-206-8990 *Toll Free Tel:* 866-598-8449
Fax: 212-206-1429
E-mail: oobfestival@samuelfrench.com
Web Site: www.oobfestival.com; www.
samuelfrench.com
Key Personnel
Artistic Dir: Casey McLain *E-mail:* cmclain@
samuelfrench.com
Established: 1975
Four-week submission period beginning in
November. Selected plays are presented on the
final day of the festival.
Award: Publication of top 6 plays
Closing Date: Mid-Dec
Presented: July/Aug

Dayne Ogilvie Prize

The Writers' Trust of Canada
600-460 Richmond St W, Toronto, ON M5V
1Y1, Canada
Tel: 416-504-8222 *Toll Free Tel:* 877-906-6548
Fax: 416-504-9090
E-mail: info@writerstrust.com
Web Site: www.writerstrust.com
Key Personnel
Exec Dir: Charlie Foran *Tel:* 416-504-8222 ext
244 *E-mail:* cforan@writerstrust.com
Prog Coord: Devon Jackson *Tel:* 416-504-8222
ext 248 *E-mail:* djackson@writerstrust.com
Established: 2007
Awarded to an emerging LGBTQ writer.
Other Sponsor(s): Robin Pacific
Award: $4,000
Presented: Pride Week, Toronto, ON, CN, Annu-
ally, early Summer

Howard O'Hagan Award for Short Story

Writers' Guild of Alberta
11759 Groat Rd, Edmonton, AB T5M 3K6,
Canada
Tel: 780-422-8174 *Toll Free Tel:* 800-665-5354
(AB only) *Fax:* 780-422-2663 (attn WGA)
E-mail: mail@writersguild.ca
Web Site: writersguild.ca
Key Personnel
Exec Dir: Carol Holmes *E-mail:* carol.holmes@
writersguild.ca
Communs & Partnerships Coord: Ellen Kartz
E-mail: ellen.kartz@writersguild.ca
Memb Servs Coord: Giorgia Severini

Progs Coord: Natalie Cook *E-mail:* natalie.cook@
writersguild.ca; Julie Robinson *E-mail:* julie.
robinson@writersguild.ca
Established: 1982
Alberta literary award for published short stories
only, author must be resident of Alberta; no
longer than 5,000 words.
Award: $700
Closing Date: Annually, Dec 31
Presented: Alberta Book Awards Gala
Branch Office(s)
505 21 Ave SW, Calgary, AB T2S 0G9, Canada,
Prog Coord: Samantha Warwick *Tel:* 403-265-
2226 *E-mail:* samantha.warwick@writersguild.
ca

Ohioana Book Awards

Ohioana Library Association
274 E First Ave, Suite 300, Columbus, OH 43201
Tel: 614-466-3831 *Fax:* 614-728-6974
E-mail: ohioana@ohioana.org
Web Site: www.ohioana.org
Key Personnel
Exec Dir, Ohioana Library Association: David E
Weaver *E-mail:* dweaver@ohioana.org
Established: 1942
For the best books by Ohio authors in vari-
ous fields of writing or books about Ohio or
Ohioans. Submit 2 copies of a nominated book
on or before its publication date.
Award: $1,500 cash prize for winning book in
each category: fiction, poetry, juvenile litera-
ture, middle grade/young adult literature, non-
fiction about Ohio/Ohioan
Closing Date: Dec 31
Presented: Ohioana Awards Ceremony, Oct

Ohioana Walter Rumsey Marvin Grant

Ohioana Library Association
274 E First Ave, Suite 300, Columbus, OH 43201
Tel: 614-466-3831 *Fax:* 614-728-6974
E-mail: ohioana@ohioana.org
Web Site: www.ohioana.org
Key Personnel
Exec Dir, Ohioana Library Association: David E
Weaver *E-mail:* dweaver@ohioana.org
Established: 1982
Writing competition; awarded to young (30 yrs
of age or younger), unpublished Ohio authors
who were born or have lived in Ohio 5 years
or more.
Award: $1,000 cash prize & publication of win-
ning submission in the *Ohioana Quarterly*
Closing Date: Jan 31
Presented: Ohioana Awards Ceremony, Oct

Oklahoma Book Awards

Oklahoma Center for the Book (OCB)
200 NE 18 St, Oklahoma City, OK 73105-3205
Tel: 405-522-3383
Web Site: libraries.ok.gov/ocb/ok-book-awards/
Given annually for work written by an Oklahoman or about Oklahoma. Categories: Fiction, nonfiction, children, young adult, poetry
& design/illustration.
Presented: April

Nancy Olson Bookseller Award

Southern Independent Booksellers Alliance
51 Pleasant Ridge Dr, Asheville, NC 28805
Tel: 803-994-9530 *Fax:* 309-410-0211
E-mail: siba@sibaweb.com
Web Site: www.sibaweb.com
Key Personnel
Exec Dir: Linda-Marie Barrett
E-mail: lindamarie@sibaweb.com
Established: 2019
Annual award to recognize special booksellers.
All SIBA booksellers (not owners) are eligible.
Nominations accepted from writers, readers &
store owners. Individual booksellers may nomi-
nate themselves.

Award: 2 awards of $2,000
Closing Date: Dec

Chris O'Malley Fiction Prize

The Madison Review
University of Wisconsin, 6193 Helen C White
    Hall, English Dept, 600 N Park St, Madison,
    WI 53706
E-mail: madisonrevw@gmail.com
Web Site: www.themadisonrevw.com
Key Personnel
Chmn Dept: Russ Castronovo
Faculty Advisor & Prog Coord: Ronald Kuka
    Tel: 608-263-3374 E-mail: rfkuka@wisc.edu
Size limit 30 page maximum. Only 1 submis-
    sion is allowed per person per contest. Ms
    must be previously unpublished & should be
    double-spaced with standard 1 inch margins &
    12 point font. Entry fee $10.
Award: $1,000 & publication in Spring issue of
    The Madison Review
Closing Date: Annually, Nov 1
Presented: Announcement in March

On-the-Verge Emerging Voices Award

Society of Children's Book Writers & Illustrators
    (SCBWI)
6363 Wilshire Blvd, Suite 425, Los Angeles, CA
    90048
Tel: 323-782-1010
E-mail: grants@scbwi.org
Web Site: www.scbwi.org/awards
Key Personnel
Awards & Pubns Coord: Sarah Diamond
    E-mail: sarahdiamond@scbwi.org
Established: 2012
Grant to foster the emergence of diverse voices
    in children's books. To be eligible, a writer or
    writer/illustrator must be from an ethnic +/or
    cultural background that is traditionally under-
    represented in children's literature in Amer-
    ica. This includes but is not limited to: Amer-
    ican Indian, Asian, Black or African Amer-
    ican, Hispanic, Pacific Islander. Ms must be
    an original work written in English for young
    readers & may not be under contract. Appli-
    cant must be over 18, be unpublished (self-
    published is not considered published for this
    award) & should not yet have representation.
    Applications accepted via e-mail only to sarah-
    diamond@scbwi.org. See web site for specific
    submission guidelines.
Award: 2 writers or writer/illustrators will each
    receive a paid trip & tuition to SCBWI Sum-
    mer Conference, ms consultation, press re-
    lease, publicity, ms included on secure web site
    for selected publishing professionals to view
    & professional career development guidance
    throughout the winning year
Closing Date: Nov 15

Open Chapbook Competition

Finishing Line Press
PO Box 1626, Georgetown, KY 40324
Tel: 502-603-0670
E-mail: finishingbooks@aol.com; flpbookstore@
    aol.com
Web Site: www.finishinglinepress.com
Key Personnel
Publr: Leah Maines
Mng Ed: Kevin Murphy Maines
Sr Ed: Christen Kincaid
Established: 2002
Award for an unpublished chapbook of poems.
    Winner announced on web site & in Poets &
    Writers Magazine.
Award: $1,000 & publication
Closing Date: Oct 31
Presented: Finishing Line Press

Open Season Awards

The Malahat Review

University of Victoria, Box 1700, Sta CSC, Victo-
    ria, BC V8W 2Y2, Canada
Tel: 250-721-8524 Fax: 250-472-5051
E-mail: malahat@uvic.ca
Web Site: malahatreview.ca
Key Personnel
Ed: John Barton
Established: 2009
Awards in 3 categories: poetry, short fiction &
    creative nonfiction. See web site for additional
    details.
Award: $1,500 in each of 3 categories
Closing Date: Annually, Nov 1

Opie Prize

American Folklore Society/Children's Folklore
    Section
Indiana University, Classroom-Off Bldg, 800 E
    Third St, Bloomington, IN 47405
Tel: 812-856-2379 Fax: 812-856-2483
Web Site: www.afsnet.org
Key Personnel
Exec Dir: Timothy Lloyd E-mail: timllloyd@
    indiana.edu
Assoc Dir: Lorraine Walsh Cashman
    E-mail: lcashman@indiana.edu
Annual award for the best book-length treatment
    of children's folklore. Edited volumes, collec-
    tions of folklore & authored studies published
    in English during previous 2 years are eligible.
    Authors or publishers should submit 2 copies
    of the book.
Award: $200
Closing Date: Varies
Presented: Oct

Orbis Pictus Award

National Council of Teachers of English (NCTE)
340 N Neil St, Suite 104, Champaign, IL 61820
Tel: 217-328-3870 Toll Free Tel: 877-369-6283
    (cust serv) Fax: 217-328-9645; 217-328-0977
E-mail: bookawards@ncte.org
Web Site: www2.ncte.org/awards
Key Personnel
Exec Dir: Emily Kirkpatrick Tel: 217-278-3601
    E-mail: ekirkpatrick@ncte.org
Proj Specialist, Communs: Lori Bianchini
    E-mail: lbianchini@ncte.org
Established: 1989
Awarded annually to promote & recognize excel-
    lence in nonfiction writing for children. Books
    must have been published +/or distributed in
    the US during the calendar year. Nominations
    of individual books may come from publish-
    ers, NCTE membership & from the educational
    community at large. One title is singled out for
    the award & up to 5 honor books are also rec-
    ognized. Eight additional recommended books
    can be named.
Award: Winning author +/or translator receives
    plaque & are the featured speaker(s) at the lun-
    cheon; Honor book author(s) +/or illustrator(s)
    receive certificate & invitation to present at ses-
    sion following the luncheon
Closing Date: Oct 15
Presented: Children's Book Awards Luncheon,
    NCTE Annual Convention

Oregon Book Awards

Literary Arts
925 SW Washington St, Portland, OR 97205
Tel: 503-227-2583 Fax: 503-241-4256
E-mail: la@literary-arts.org
Web Site: www.literary-arts.org
Key Personnel
Dir, Progs for Writers: Susan Moore Tel: 503-
    227-2583 ext 107 E-mail: susan@literary-arts.
    org
Established: 1988
Available for original work published or produced
    in the following categories: poetry, novel, gen-
    eral nonfiction, creative nonfiction, children's

literature, young adult literature, drama &
    graphic literature.
Closing Date: Annually in Sept
Presented: Jan

George Orwell Award

National Council of Teachers of English (NCTE)
340 N Neil St, Suite 104, Champaign, IL 61820
Tel: 217-328-3870 Toll Free Tel: 877-369-6283
    (cust serv) Fax: 217-328-0977
E-mail: publiclangawards@ncte.org
Web Site: www.ncte.org
Key Personnel
Admin Liaison & Awards Contact: Linda Walters-
    Moore
Established: 1975
Recognizes writers for distinguished contributions
    to the critical analysis of public discourse.
Other Sponsor(s): NCTE Committee on Public
    Doublespeak
Award: Certificate
Closing Date: Annually, Sept 15
Presented: NCTE Annual Convention, Late Nov

Joyce Osterweil Award for Poetry, see
    PEN/Joyce Osterweil Award for Poetry

James H Ottaway Jr Award for the Promotion of International Literature

Words Without Borders
147 Prince St, Brooklyn, NY 11201
Tel: 347-699-2914
E-mail: info@wordswithoutborders.org
Web Site: www.wordswithoutborders.org/ottaway-
    award
Key Personnel
Book Review Ed: Miguel Conde
    E-mail: miguel@wordswithoutborders.org
Recognizes individuals who have taken extraor-
    dinary steps to advance literature in translation
    into English.
Presented: Annual Gala, New York, NY, Autumn

Ottoline Prize

Fence Books
Imprint of Fence Magazine Inc
University at Albany, Science Library 320, 1400
    Washington Ave, Albany, NY 12222
Tel: 518-567-7006
Web Site: www.fenceportal.org
Key Personnel
Publr & Ed: Rebecca Wolff
    E-mail: rebeccafence@gmail.com
Established: 2013
For a book-length work of poetry by a woman
    writing in English who has previously pub-
    lished one or more full-length books of poetry.
    Submission fee: $28.
Award: $5,000 & publication, plus complimentary
    subn to Fence

Frank L & Harriet C Owsley Award

Southern Historical Association
University of Georgia, Dept of History, Athens,
    GA 30602-1602
Tel: 706-542-8848 Fax: 706-542-2455
Web Site: www.thesha.org
Key Personnel
Admin Asst: Frances Berry E-mail: manager@
    thesha.org
Established: 1985
Awarded for most distinguished book in South-
    ern history published in even-numbered years.
    Awarded in odd-numbered years.
Award: Cash
Closing Date: March 1
Presented: Annual meeting, odd-numbered years,
    Fall

Pacific Northwest Book Awards

Pacific Northwest Booksellers Association
    (PNBA)

520 W 13 Ave, Eugene, OR 97401-3461
Tel: 541-683-4363 *Fax:* 541-683-3910
E-mail: info@pnba.org; awards@pnba.org
Web Site: www.pnba.org
Key Personnel
Exec Dir: Brian Juenemann *E-mail:* brian@pnba.
org
Established: 1965
Annual awards for authors who live in Washington, Oregon, Idaho, Alaska & Montana who have published exceptional books during the calendar year.
Award: Plaque & marketing to independent bookstores of the Pacific Northwest
Closing Date: Sept 30
Presented: Early Jan

Pacific Northwest Young Reader's Choice Award

Pacific Northwest Library Association (PNLA)
Vancouver Mall Community Library, 8700 NE Vancouver Mall Dr, Suite 285, Vancouver, WA 98662
Web Site: www.pnla.org/yrca
Key Personnel
Coord: Jocie Wilson *Tel:* 780-962-2003 ext 223
Established: 1940
Nominations taken only from children, teachers, parents & librarians of the Pacific Northwest (WA, OR, AK, ID, MT, BC & AB) for titles published 3 years previously in the US or CN. Only 4th-12th graders in the Pacific Northwest vote on a selected list of titles. The categories are junior grades 4-6, intermediate grades 7-9 & senior grades 10-12. Awarded to the author of a book most popular with children. Send SASE or see web site for information.
Award: Silver Medal
Closing Date: Annually, Feb 1
Presented: Pacific Northwest Library Association's Annual Conference, Annually in Aug

The Pacific Spirit Poetry Prize

PRISM international
University of British Columbia, Buch E462, 1866 Main Mall, Vancouver, BC V6T 1Z1, Canada
Tel: 778-822-2514 *Fax:* 778-822-3616
E-mail: prismwritingcontest@gmail.com
Web Site: www.prismmagazine.ca
Key Personnel
Exec Ed: Jennifer Lori; Claire Matthews
Poetry Ed: Dominique Bernier Cormier
Prose Ed: Christopher Evans
Established: 1986
Awarded for the best original, unpublished poem (3 poems, up to 25 pages). Works of translation are eligible. Entry fee: $35 for 3 poems plus $5 for each additional entry.
Award: $1,500 grand prize, $600 (1st runner up), $400 (2nd runner up); all entries receive 1-year subn to *PRISM international*
Closing Date: Annually in Jan

PAGE International Screenwriting Awards

Production Arts Group
7190 Sunset Blvd, Suite 610, Hollywood, CA 90046
E-mail: info@pageawards.com
Web Site: www.pageawards.com
Key Personnel
Admin Dir: Jennifer Berg
Contest Coord: Zoe Simmons
Established: 2003
Each year the judges present a total of 31 awards in 10 different categories.
Award: $25,000 (grand prize) plus gold, silver & bronze prizes in all 10 categories
Closing Date: Annually in May
Presented: Hollywood, CA, Annually in Oct

Dobie Paisano Fellowship Program

University of Texas at Austin Graduate School

110 Inner Campus Dr, Stop G0400, Austin, TX 78712-0710
Fax: 512-471-7620
Web Site: dobiepaisano.utexas.edu
Key Personnel
Dir: Dr Michael Adams *E-mail:* adameve@austin.utexas.edu
Established: 1967
Provides an opportunity for creative or nonfiction writers to live & write for an extended period in an environment that offers isolation & tranquility. At the time of application, the applicant must: be a native Texan; have lived in Texas at some time for at least 3 years; or have published significant work with a Texas subject. Criteria for making the awards include quality of work, character of the proposed project & suitability of the applicant for life at Paisano, the late J Frank Dobie's ranch near Austin, TX. Applications are available at the above web site or write for more information. Application fee: $20/1 fellowship, $30/both fellowships.
Other Sponsor(s): Texas Institute of Letters (TIL)
Award: Ralph A Johnston Memorial Fellowship: $25,000 over 4 months; Jesse H Jones Writing Fellowship: $18,000 over 6 months
Closing Date: Annually, Dec 15
Presented: Annually in May

Mildred & Albert Panowski Playwriting Award

Northern Michigan University
Forest Roberts Theatre, 1401 Presque Isle Ave, Marquette, MI 49855-5364
Tel: 906-227-2553 *Fax:* 906-227-2567
E-mail: theatre@nmu.edu
Web Site: www.nmu.edu/theatre
Key Personnel
Dir: William Digneit *Tel:* 906-227-2044
E-mail: wdigneit@nmu.edu
Established: 1977
Provides students & faculty the unique opportunity to mount & produce an original work on the university stage. The playwright will benefit from seeing the work on its feet in front of an audience & from professional adjudication by guest critics. Please check the web site for theme or genre. Play must be unproduced. Only one play per playwright may be entered. Electronic submission only.
Award: $2,000 cash, airline fare, room & board for the week of production
Closing Date: Sept 1, odd-numbered years (receipt not postmark)
Presented: Forest Roberts Theatre, Northern Michigan Univ, In upcoming season

Francis Parkman Prize

Society of American Historians (SAH)
Affiliate of American Historical Association
2950 Broadway, New York, NY 10027
Tel: 212-854-6495
E-mail: amhistsociety@columbia.edu
Web Site: sah.columbia.edu
Key Personnel
Pres: Mary Kelley
VP: Ann Fabian
Exec Secy: Andie Tucher
Established: 1957
For a nonfiction book, including biography, that is distinguished by its literary merit & makes an important contribution to the history of what is now the US. The author need not be a citizen or resident of the US & the book need not be published in the US although must be published & copyrighted in the year preceding the award.
Award: $2,000 & certificate
Closing Date: Annually, Dec 1
Presented: New York, NY, Annually in May

The Paterson Poetry Prize

The Poetry Center at Passaic County Community College
One College Blvd, Paterson, NJ 07505-1179
Tel: 973-684-6555 *Fax:* 973-523-6085
Web Site: www.poetrycenterpccc.com
Key Personnel
Exec Dir: Maria Mazziotti Gillan
E-mail: mgillan@pccc.edu
Mgr: Susan Balik *E-mail:* sbalik@pccc.edu
For a book of poems, 48 pages or more in length, selected by our judges as the strongest collection of poems published in the previous year. The poet will be asked to participate in an awards ceremony & to give a reading at the Poetry Center. Publisher may submit more than one book for prize consideration.
Award: $1,000
Closing Date: Annually, Feb 1

The Paterson Prize for Books for Young People

The Poetry Center at Passaic County Community College
One College Blvd, Paterson, NJ 07505-1179
Tel: 973-684-6555 *Fax:* 973-523-6085
Web Site: www.poetrycenterpccc.com
Key Personnel
Exec Dir: Maria Mazziotti Gillan
E-mail: mgillan@pccc.edu
Mgr: Susan Balik *E-mail:* sbalik@pccc.edu
One book in each category will be selected for the most outstanding book for young people published in the previous year.
Award: $500 in each category: PreK-Grade 3, Grades 4-6, Grades 7-12
Closing Date: Annually, Feb 1

The Alicia Patterson Foundation Fellowship Program

The Alicia Patterson Foundation
1100 Vermont Ave, Suite 900, Washington, DC 20005
Tel: 202-393-5995 *Fax:* 301-951-8512
E-mail: info@aliciapatterson.org
Web Site: www.aliciapatterson.org
Key Personnel
Exec Dir: Margaret Engel
Established: 1963
Stipend (12 or 6 months), not for academic study, for professional print journalist with 5 years experience & must write/photograph for English language medium. One additional fellowship for science & environmental topics.
Award: $40,000 over 12 months, $20,000 over 6 months. Applicants choose whether they want 6 or 12 month grants
Closing Date: Annually, Oct 1
Presented: 2nd week of Dec

Deborah Pease Prize

A Public Space
323 Dean St, Brooklyn, NY 11217
Tel: 718-858-8067
E-mail: general@apublicspace.org
Web Site: apublicspace.org
Key Personnel
Founding Ed: Brigid Hughes
Mktg & Devt Dir: Lauren Cerand *Tel:* 917-533-0103 *E-mail:* lauren@apublicspace.org
Established: 2018
Awarded to a figure who has advanced the art of literature.
Presented: Dec

William Peden Prize in Fiction

The Missouri Review
357 McReynolds Hall, Columbia, MO 65211
Tel: 573-882-4474 *Toll Free Tel:* 800-949-2505
Fax: 573-884-4671
E-mail: question@moreview.com
Web Site: www.missourireview.com

Key Personnel
Assoc Ed: Evelyn Somers *Tel:* 573-884-7839
  E-mail: rogerses@missouri.edu
Awarded annually to the best story to appear in the magazine the previous volume year. Winner is selected by an outside judge. It is not a contest that writers can enter, since the winner is selected from stories already published in the magazine.
Award: $1,000
Presented: Columbia, MO

Pegasus Award for Poetry Criticism
Poetry Foundation
61 W Superior St, Chicago, IL 60654
Tel: 312-787-7070
E-mail: info@poetryfoundation.org
Web Site: www.poetryfoundation.org/foundation/criticism-award
Key Personnel
Media & Mktg Dir: Sarah Whitcher *Tel:* 312-799-8016 *E-mail:* swhitcher@poetryfoundation.org
Prog Dir: Stephen Young
Prize to honor the best book-length works of criticism published in the US in the prior calendar year, including biographies, essay collections & critical editions that consider the subject of poetry or poets.
Award: $7,500

PEN America Los Angeles Literary Award for Journalism
PEN America
8444 Wilshire Blvd, 4th fl, Beverly Hills, CA 90211
Tel: 323-424-4939
E-mail: awards@pen.org; info@pen.org
Web Site: pen.org/pen-america-los-angeles-literary-awards-festival
Key Personnel
Exec Dir: Michelle Franke *Tel:* 323-424-4939 ext 1 *E-mail:* mfranke@pen.org
Literary Awards: Stacy Valis *Tel:* 323-424-4939 ext 3 *E-mail:* svalis@pen.org
Open to journalists living west of the Mississippi. Journalists or publishers may submit work. Printed & online articles are eligible.
Award: $1,000 & 2 tickets to Fall Gala
Closing Date: March 30
Presented: Fall

The PEN Award for Poetry in Translation
PEN America
Affiliate of PEN International
588 Broadway, Suite 303, New York, NY 10012
Tel: 212-334-1660 *Fax:* 212-334-2181
E-mail: awards@pen.org
Web Site: pen.org/pen-award-poetry-translation
Key Personnel
CEO: Suzanne Nossel *Tel:* 212-334-1600 ext 4811 *E-mail:* snossel@pen.org
Pres: Jennifer Egan
Dir, Literary Progs: Paul Morris *Tel:* 212-334-1660 ext 4824 *E-mail:* paul@pen.org
Prog Dir, Literary Awards: Nadxieli Nieto *Tel:* 646-779-4813 *E-mail:* nnieto@pen.org
Recognizes book-length translations of poetry from any language into English, published during the current calendar year & is judged by a single translator of poetry appointed by the PEN Translation Committee. All books must have been published in the US, although translators may be of any nationality (US residency or citizenship is not required). Only publishers & literary agents may submit. Submitters must complete online submission form. Entry fee: $75 (fee may be waived for small presses).
Award: $3,000
Closing Date: Annually in Aug
Presented: PEN Literary Awards Ceremony, New York, NY, Annually in Spring

PEN/Barbey Freedom to Write Award
PEN America
Affiliate of PEN International
588 Broadway, Suite 303, New York, NY 10012
Tel: 212-334-1660
E-mail: awards@pen.org
Web Site: pen.org/penbarbey-freedom-to-write-award
Key Personnel
Prog Dir, Literary Awards: Nadxieli Nieto *Tel:* 646-779-4813 *E-mail:* nnieto@pen.org
Established: 2016
Designed to honor a writer imprisoned for his or her work in an effort to end the persecution of writers & defend free expression.

PEN/Bellwether Prize for Socially Engaged Fiction
PEN America
Affiliate of PEN International
588 Broadway, Suite 303, New York, NY 10012
Tel: 212-334-1660
E-mail: awards@pen.org
Web Site: pen.org/pen-bellwether-prize
Key Personnel
Dir, Literary Progs: Paul Morris *Tel:* 212-334-1660 ext 4824 *E-mail:* paul@pen.org
Prog Dir, Literary Awards: Nadxieli Nieto *Tel:* 646-779-4813 *E-mail:* nnieto@pen.org
Awarded biennially to the author of a previously unpublished novel of high literary caliber that promotes fiction that addresses issues of social justice & the impact of culture & politics on human relationships. Entry fee: $25.
Award: $25,000 & publishing contract with Algonquin Books

PEN/Diamonstein-Spielvogel Award for the Art of the Essay
PEN America
Affiliate of PEN International
588 Broadway, Suite 303, New York, NY 10012
Tel: 212-334-1660
E-mail: awards@pen.org
Web Site: pen.org/pen-diamonstein-spielvogel-award-for-the-art-of-the-essay
Key Personnel
Dir, Literary Progs: Paul Morris *Tel:* 212-334-1660 ext 4824 *E-mail:* paul@pen.org
Prog Dir, Literary Awards: Nadxieli Nieto *Tel:* 646-779-4813 *E-mail:* nnieto@pen.org
Nonfiction award which aims to preserve the dignity & esteem that the essay form imparts to literature. Submissions accepted only from publishers or literary agents.
Award: $10,000

PEN/E O Wilson Prize for Literary Science Writing
PEN America
Affiliate of PEN International
588 Broadway, Suite 303, New York, NY 10012
Tel: 212-334-1660
E-mail: awards@pen.org
Web Site: pen.org/pen-eo-wilson-prize-literary-science-writing
Key Personnel
Dir, Literary Progs: Paul Morris *Tel:* 212-334-1660 ext 4824 *E-mail:* paul@pen.org
Prog Dir, Literary Awards: Nadxieli Nieto *Tel:* 646-779-4813 *E-mail:* nnieto@pen.org
Nonfiction award which celebrates writing that exemplifies literary excellence on the subject of physical & biological sciences.
Award: $10,000

PEN/Edward & Lily Tuck Award for Paraguayan Literature
PEN America
Affiliate of PEN International
588 Broadway, Suite 303, New York, NY 10012
Tel: 212-334-1660 *Fax:* 212-334-2181

E-mail: awards@pen.org
Web Site: pen.org/pen-edward-lily-tuck-award-paraguayan-literature
Key Personnel
Prog Dir, Literary Awards: Nadxieli Nieto *Tel:* 646-779-4813 *E-mail:* nnieto@pen.org
Established: 2010
Biennial award open to both established & emerging Paraguayan writers. Accepts submissions only to PEN Paraguay with an official letter of recommendation & internal nominations from PEN members. Publishers should send 5 copies of the candidate's book & letter of recommendation to: PEN Club del Paraguay, Pacheco 4332 Asuncion, Paraguay.
Award: $3,000 to author, $3,000 also to winning translator to bring the work to the English-speaking world
Closing Date: Oct, odd-numbered years

PEN/ESPN Award for Literary Sports Writing
PEN America
Affiliate of PEN International
588 Broadway, Suite 303, New York, NY 10012
Tel: 212-334-1660
E-mail: awards@pen.org
Web Site: pen.org/pen-espn-award
Key Personnel
Dir, Literary Progs: Paul Morris *Tel:* 212-334-1660 ext 4824 *E-mail:* paul@pen.org
Prog Dir, Literary Awards: Nadxieli Nieto *Tel:* 646-779-4813 *E-mail:* nnieto@pen.org
Award to an author of a nonfiction book about sports.
Award: $5,000

PEN/ESPN Lifetime Achievement Award for Literary Sports Writing
PEN America
Affiliate of PEN International
588 Broadway, Suite 303, New York, NY 10012
Tel: 212-334-1660
E-mail: awards@pen.org
Web Site: pen.org/pen-espn-lifetime-literary-sports-writing
Key Personnel
Dir, Literary Progs: Paul Morris *Tel:* 212-334-1660 ext 4824 *E-mail:* paul@pen.org
Prog Dir, Literary Awards: Nadxieli Nieto *Tel:* 646-779-4813 *E-mail:* nnieto@pen.org
Nonfiction award to a writer for their long-time contributions to the field of literary sports writing.
Award: $5,000

PEN/Faulkner Award for Fiction
PEN/Faulkner Foundation
201 E Capitol St SE, Washington, DC 20003
Tel: 202-898-9063 *Fax:* 202-675-0360
Web Site: www.penfaulkner.org
Key Personnel
Exec Dir: Gwydion Suilebhan *E-mail:* gwydion@penfaulkner.org
Established: 1980
Annual award for the best work of fiction published by an American citizen writer (for published work only) in a single calendar year. Send 4 copies of each book or 4 bound galleys for those being published in November & December.
Award: $15,000 (1st prize), $5,000 to each of 4 finalists
Closing Date: Oct 31
Presented: Awards Ceremony, Folger Shakespeare Library, Washington, DC, May

PEN/Fusion Emerging Writers Prize
PEN America
Affiliate of PEN International
588 Broadway, Suite 303, New York, NY 10012
Tel: 212-334-1660
E-mail: awards@pen.org
Web Site: pen.org/literary-awards

Key Personnel
Dir, Literary Progs: Paul Morris *Tel:* 212-334-1660 ext 4824 *E-mail:* paul@pen.org
Prog Dir, Literary Awards: Nadxieli Nieto *Tel:* 646-779-4813 *E-mail:* nnieto@pen.org
Annual award that recognizes a promising young writer (35 & under) of an unpublished work of nonfiction that addresses a global +/or multicultural issue. Ms submission must be an original, previously unpublished work of nonfiction written by one person, in English, 8,000-80,000 words in length. Entry fee: $35.
Award: $10,000

PEN/Jacqueline Bograd Weld Award for Biography
PEN America
Affiliate of PEN International
588 Broadway, Suite 303, New York, NY 10012
Tel: 212-334-1660
E-mail: awards@pen.org
Web Site: pen.org/pen-bograd-weld-award-biography
Key Personnel
Dir, Literary Progs: Paul Morris *Tel:* 212-334-1660 ext 4824 *E-mail:* paul@pen.org
Prog Dir, Literary Awards: Nadxieli Nieto *Tel:* 646-779-4813 *E-mail:* nnieto@pen.org
Nonfiction award for excellence in the art of biography.
Award: $5,000

PEN/Jean Stein Book Award
PEN America
Affiliate of PEN International
588 Broadway, Suite 303, New York, NY 10012
Tel: 212-334-1660
E-mail: info@pen.org; awards@pen.org
Web Site: pen.org/pen-jean-stein-book-award
Key Personnel
Dir, Literary Progs: Paul Morris *Tel:* 212-334-1660 ext 4824 *E-mail:* paul@pen.org
Prog Dir, Literary Awards: Nadxieli Nieto *Tel:* 646-779-4813 *E-mail:* nnieto@pen.org
Deputy Dir, Communs: Sarah Edkins *Tel:* 212-334-1600 ext 4830 *E-mail:* sedkins@pen.org
Established: 2017
Annual award which recognizes a book-length work of any genre for its originality, merit & impact. Judging panel will serve anonymously & will nominate candidates internally & without submissions from the public.
Award: $75,000
Presented: PEN Literary Awards Ceremony, New York, NY, Annually in Feb

PEN/John Kenneth Galbraith Award for Nonfiction
PEN America
588 Broadway, Suite 303, New York, NY 10012
Tel: 212-334-1660 *Fax:* 212-334-2181
E-mail: awards@pen.org
Web Site: pen.org/pen-galbraith-award-for-nonfiction
Key Personnel
Prog Dir, Literary Awards: Nadxieli Nieto *Tel:* 646-779-4813 *E-mail:* nnieto@pen.org
Biennial prize, in odd-numbered years, to the author of a distinguished book of general nonfiction possessing notable literary merit & critical perspective that illuminates important contemporary issues & that has been published in the US during the previous 2 calendar years. Biographies, autobiographies & memoirs are not accepted. Self-published books are not eligible. Submissions are only accepted from publishers & literary agents; authors may not submit their own work. See web site for full submission guidelines. Entry fee: $85.
Award: $10,000

PEN/Joyce Osterweil Award for Poetry
PEN America
Affiliate of PEN International
588 Broadway, Suite 303, New York, NY 10012
Tel: 212-334-1660
E-mail: awards@pen.org
Web Site: pen.org/pen-osterweil-award-for-poetry
Key Personnel
Dir, Literary Progs: Paul Morris *Tel:* 212-334-1660 ext 4824 *E-mail:* paul@pen.org
Prog Dir, Literary Awards: Nadxieli Nieto *Tel:* 646-779-4813 *E-mail:* nnieto@pen.org
Awarded in odd-numbered years (alternates with PEN/Voelcker Award for Poetry). Recognizes the high literary character of the published work to date of a new & emerging American poet of any age & the promise of further literary achievement.
Award: $5,000

PEN/Malamud Award for Excellence in Short Fiction
PEN/Faulkner Foundation
201 E Capitol St SE, Washington, DC 20003
Tel: 202-898-9063 *Fax:* 202-675-0360
E-mail: awards@penfaulkner.org; info@penfaulkner.org
Web Site: www.penfaulkner.org/pen-malamud-award
Key Personnel
Exec Dir: Gwydion Suilebhan *E-mail:* gwydion@penfaulkner.org
Honors excellence in the art of short fiction.

PEN/Mike Nichols Writing for Performance Award
PEN America
588 Broadway, Suite 303, New York, NY 10012
Tel: 212-334-1660 *Fax:* 212-334-2181
E-mail: awards@pen.org
Web Site: pen.org/pen-nichols-award
Key Personnel
Prog Dir, Literary Awards: Nadxieli Nieto *Tel:* 646-779-4813 *E-mail:* nnieto@pen.org
Established: 2019
Award aims to highlight transformative works that enlighten & inspire audiences. No outside nominations. Winner is selected by a panel of judges.
Award: $25,000
Closing Date: Aug
Presented: Feb

PEN/Nabokov Award for Achievement in International Literature
PEN America
Affiliate of PEN International
588 Broadway, Suite 303, New York, NY 10012
Tel: 212-334-1660 *Fax:* 212-334-2181
E-mail: awards@pen.org
Web Site: pen.org/pen-nabokov-award
Key Personnel
Prog Dir, Literary Awards: Nadxieli Nieto *Tel:* 646-779-4813 *E-mail:* nnieto@pen.org
Dir, Literary Progs: Paul Morris *Tel:* 212-334-1660 ext 4824 *E-mail:* paul@pen.org
Deputy Dir, Communs: Sarah Edkins *Tel:* 212-334-1600 ext 4830 *E-mail:* sedkins@pen.org
Award to honor an international writer whose work, either written in or translated into English, represents the highest level of achievement in fiction, nonfiction, poetry, +/or drama & is of enduring originality & consummate craftsmanship.
Other Sponsor(s): Vladimir Nabokov Literary Foundation
Award: $50,000
Presented: PEN Literary Awards Ceremony, New York, NY, Spring

PEN/New England Awards
Boston Globe & PEN New England

MIT, 14N-221A, 77 Massachusetts Ave, Cambridge, MA 02139
Tel: 617-324-1729
E-mail: pen-newengland@mit.edu; pen-ne@lesley.edu
Web Site: www.pen-ne.org
Key Personnel
Exec Dir: Karen Wulf *E-mail:* kwulf@mit.edu
Established: 1975
To recognize the writing of New England's best in fiction, poetry & nonfiction. Eligible books must be written by New England authors or have a New England topic or setting & must have been published by a US publisher in the previous calendar year. Submit 3 copies. Entry fee is $50 for each title.
Award: 3 $1,000 awards
Closing Date: Annually in Dec
Presented: John F Kennedy Library, Boston, MA, Annually in April

PEN Open Book Award
PEN America
Affiliate of PEN International
588 Broadway, Suite 303, New York, NY 10012
Tel: 212-334-1660
E-mail: awards@pen.org
Web Site: pen.org/pen-open-book-award
Key Personnel
Dir, Literary Progs: Paul Morris *Tel:* 212-334-1660 ext 4824 *E-mail:* paul@pen.org
Prog Dir, Literary Awards: Nadxieli Nieto *Tel:* 646-779-4813 *E-mail:* nnieto@pen.org
For a book-length work by an author of color.
Award: $5,000

PEN/Phyllis Naylor Working Writer Fellowship
PEN America
Affiliate of PEN International
588 Broadway, Suite 303, New York, NY 10012
Tel: 212-334-1660 *Fax:* 212-334-2181
E-mail: awards@pen.org
Web Site: pen.org/literary-awards/grants-fellowships
Key Personnel
CEO: Suzanne Nossel *Tel:* 212-334-1600 ext 4811 *E-mail:* snossel@pen.org
Pres: Jennifer Egan
Dir, Literary Progs: Paul Morris *Tel:* 212-334-1660 ext 4824 *E-mail:* paul@pen.org
Prog Dir, Literary Awards: Nadxieli Nieto *Tel:* 646-779-4813 *E-mail:* nnieto@pen.org
Established: 2001
Annual award presented to an author of children's or young adult fiction. Provides a writer with a measure of financial sustenance in order to make possible an extended period of time to complete a book-length work-in-progress & to assist a writer at a crucial moment in his or her career when monetary support is particularly needed.
Award: $5,000
Closing Date: Summer
Presented: PEN Literary Awards Ceremony, New York, NY, Spring

PEN/Ralph Manheim Medal for Translation
PEN America
Affiliate of PEN International
588 Broadway, Suite 303, New York, NY 10012
Tel: 212-334-1660 *Fax:* 212-334-2181
E-mail: awards@pen.org
Web Site: pen.org/literary-award/penralph-manheim-medal-for-translation
Key Personnel
CEO: Suzanne Nossel *Tel:* 212-334-1600 ext 4811 *E-mail:* snossel@pen.org
Pres: Jennifer Egan
Dir, Literary Progs: Paul Morris *Tel:* 212-334-1660 ext 4824 *E-mail:* paul@pen.org

Prog Dir, Literary Awards: Nadxieli Nieto
Tel: 646-779-4813 *E-mail:* nnieto@pen.org
Established: 1982
Awarded triennially to a translator who has
demonstrated exceptional commitment to excel-
lence throughout the body of his work. Candi-
dates nominated by the PEN Translation Com-
mittee; internal nomination only. See web site
for more information.
Award: Medal
Presented: PEN Literary Awards Ceremony, New
York, NY, Triennially in Summer

PEN/Robert Bingham Prize for Debut Fiction
PEN America
Affiliate of PEN International
588 Broadway, Suite 303, New York, NY 10012
Tel: 212-334-1660 *Fax:* 212-334-2181
E-mail: awards@pen.org
Web Site: pen.org/pen-bingham-prize
Key Personnel
CEO: Suzanne Nossel *Tel:* 212-334-1600 ext
4811 *E-mail:* snossel@pen.org
Pres: Jennifer Egan
Dir, Literary Progs: Paul Morris *Tel:* 212-334-
1660 ext 4824 *E-mail:* paul@pen.org
Prog Dir, Literary Awards: Nadxieli Nieto
Tel: 646-779-4813 *E-mail:* nnieto@pen.org
Honor an exceptionally talented fiction writer
whose debut work–a first fiction novel or col-
lection of short stories–represents distinguished
literary achievement & suggests great promise.
Nominations are welcome from any source.
Candidates must be US residents but Ameri-
can citizenship is not required. Self-published
authors are not eligible. Only publishers & lit-
erary agents may apply. Entry fee: $75 (fee
may be waived for small presses).
Award: $25,000
Closing Date: Annually in Summer
Presented: PEN Literary Awards Ceremony, New
York, NY, Annually in Spring

PEN/Saul Bellow Award for Achievement in American Fiction
PEN America
Affiliate of PEN International
588 Broadway, Suite 303, New York, NY 10012
Tel: 212-334-1660 *Fax:* 212-334-2181
E-mail: awards@pen.org
Web Site: pen.org/pen-saul-bellow-award
Key Personnel
Dir, Literary Progs: Paul Morris *Tel:* 212-334-
1660 ext 4824 *E-mail:* paul@pen.org
Prog Dir, Literary Awards: Nadxieli Nieto
Tel: 646-779-4813 *E-mail:* nnieto@pen.org
Established: 2007
Award to a living American author whose scale
of achievement in fiction, over a sustained ca-
reer, places him or her in the highest rank of
American literature. Administered by internal
nomination only.
Award: $25,000

PEN Translation Prize
PEN America
Affiliate of PEN International
588 Broadway, Suite 303, New York, NY 10012
Tel: 212-334-1660 *Fax:* 212-334-2181
E-mail: awards@pen.org
Web Site: pen.org/pen-translation-prize
Key Personnel
CEO: Suzanne Nossel *Tel:* 212-334-1600 ext
4811 *E-mail:* snossel@pen.org
Pres: Jennifer Egan
Dir, Literary Progs: Paul Morris *Tel:* 212-334-
1660 ext 4824 *E-mail:* paul@pen.org
Prog Dir, Literary Awards: Nadxieli Nieto
Tel: 646-779-4813 *E-mail:* nnieto@pen.org
Established: 1963
For the best book-length translation into English
from any language published in the US during

the previous year. Technical, scientific or reference works are not eligible. See web site for
more information. Entry fee: $75 (fee may be
waived for small presses). Only publishers &
literary agents may submit.
Award: $3,000
Closing Date: Annually in Summer
Presented: PEN Literary Awards Ceremony, New
York, NY, Annually in Spring

PEN/Voelcker Award
PEN America
Affiliate of PEN International
588 Broadway, Suite 303, New York, NY 10012
Tel: 212-334-1660
E-mail: awards@pen.org
Web Site: pen.org/pen-voelcker-award-poetry
Key Personnel
Dir, Literary Progs: Paul Morris *Tel:* 212-334-
1660 ext 4824 *E-mail:* paul@pen.org
Prog Dir, Literary Awards: Nadxieli Nieto
Tel: 646-779-4813 *E-mail:* nnieto@pen.org
Awarded to a poet whose distinguished & grow-
ing body of work to date represents a notable
& accomplished presence in American litera-
ture. Only professional members of PEN may
nominate a poet.
Award: $5,000

PEN Writers' Emergency Fund
PEN America
Affiliate of PEN International
588 Broadway, Suite 303, New York, NY 10012
Tel: 212-334-1660 *Fax:* 212-334-2181
E-mail: feprogram@pen.org
Web Site: pen.org/writers-emergency-fund
Key Personnel
CEO: Suzanne Nossel *Tel:* 212-334-1600 ext
4811 *E-mail:* snossel@pen.org
Pres: Jennifer Egan
Dir, Literary Progs: Paul Morris *Tel:* 212-334-
1660 ext 4824 *E-mail:* paul@pen.org
Writer's Fund Coord: Arielle Anema *Tel:* 212-
334-1660 ext 4813 *E-mail:* arielle@pen.org
Established: 1921
Grants for professional published writers & pro-
duced playwrights in financial emergencies due
to personal circumstances. These are not liter-
ary awards. Application form available online.
Award: Up to $2,000
Closing Date: Annually, Jan 15, March 15, June
15, Sept 15

Maxwell E Perkins Award
The Center for Fiction
17 E 47 St, New York, NY 10017
Tel: 212-755-6710
E-mail: info@centerforfiction.org
Web Site: www.centerforfiction.org/awards/perkins
Key Personnel
Writing Progs Mgr: Thierry Kehou
E-mail: thierry@centerforfiction.org
Established: 2005
To honor the work of an editor, publisher, or
agent who over the course of his or her career
has discovered, nurtured & championed writers
of fiction in the US.

Aliki Perroti & Seth Frank Most Promising Young Poet Award
The Academy of American Poets Inc
75 Maiden Lane, Suite 901, New York, NY
10038
Tel: 212-274-0343
E-mail: awards@poets.org
Web Site: www.poets.org
Key Personnel
Pres & Exec Dir: Jennifer Benka
E-mail: jenbenka@poets.org
Devt, Membership & Communs Sr Mgr: Molly
Walsh *E-mail:* mwalsh@poets.org

Ad & Mktg Sr Mgr: Michelle Campagna
E-mail: mcampagna@poets.org
Sr Progs Mgr: Nikay Paredes *Tel:* 212-274-0343
ext 13 *E-mail:* nparedes@poets.org
Established: 2013
Annual award to recognize a student poet 23
years old or younger. Only a school's college
prize coordinator may submit a student's winning poem to be considered for the prize. No
applications are accepted. The prize winner
will be featured on the Academy web site & in
American Poets magazine.
Award: $1,000 cash prize

Perugia Press Prize for a First or Second Book by a Woman
Perugia Press
PO Box 60364, Florence, MA 01062
Web Site: www.perugiapress.com; perugiapress.
org
Key Personnel
Dir: Rebecca Olander
Established: 1997
For a first or second book of poetry by a woman.
Award: $1,000 & publication
Closing Date: Annually, Nov 15
Presented: Winner announced annually by April
15

The Petrichor Prize for Finely Crafted Fiction
Regal House Publishing
806 Oberlin Rd, No 12094, Raleigh, NC 27605
E-mail: info@regalhousepublishing.com
Web Site: regalhousepublishing.com/the-petrichor-
prize-for-finely-crafted-fiction/
Key Personnel
Founder, Publr & Ed-in-Chief: Jaynie Royal
Mng Ed: Pam Van Dyk
Sr Ed: Ruth Feiertag
Established: 2019
Recognizes finely crafted works of literary fiction.
Submissions through Submittable or by post.
Entry fee $25. Fax or e-mail submissions not
accepted. See web site for submission guide-
lines. Five finalists announced on Sept 10.
Award: Publication & $500 honorarium
Closing Date: July 15 (postmark)
Presented: Oct 10

Pfizer Award
History of Science Society
Affiliate of American Council of Learned Soci-
eties
440 Geddes Hall, Notre Dame, IN 46556
Tel: 574-631-1194
E-mail: info@hssonline.org
Web Site: www.hssonline.org
Key Personnel
Exec Dir: Robert Jay Malone
Established: 1958
Award given annually for an outstanding book
in English, published during the preceding 3
years, on a topic related to the history of sci-
ence.
Award: $2,500 & a medal
Closing Date: April 1
Presented: Oct or Nov

James D Phelan Literary Award
The San Francisco Foundation
One Embarcadero Ctr, Suite 1400, San Francisco,
CA 94111
Tel: 415-733-8500
E-mail: info@sff.org; artsinfo@sff.org
Web Site: www.sff.org
Established: 1935
Award for the author of fiction (novel or short
stories), nonfictional prose, poetry, spoken
word. Awards are intended to encourage
emerging artists not yet established in the genre
who are California-born & currently residing
in Alameda, Contra Costa, Marin, San Fran-

cisco or San Mateo County, for an unpublished ms-in-progress. By nomination only.
Award: $2,000
Presented: Annually in Autumn

Phi Beta Kappa Award in Science
The Phi Beta Kappa Society
1606 New Hampshire Ave NW, Washington, DC 20009
Tel: 202-265-3808 *Fax:* 202-986-1601
E-mail: awards@pbk.org
Web Site: www.pbk.org/bookawards
Key Personnel
Prog & Event Specialist: Laura Hartnett *Tel:* 202-745-3287 *E-mail:* lhartnett@pbk.org
Established: 1959
For an outstanding interpretation of science written by a scientist & published in the US during the previous year. Works in the physical & biological sciences & mathematics are eligible for the award. Highly technical works, monographs & reports on research are not eligible. Nominations must come from publisher & be submitted online.
Award: $10,000
Closing Date: Annually in Jan
Presented: Washington, DC, Annually in Dec

Robert J Pickering Award for Playwriting Excellence
Branch County Community Theatre
89 Division, Coldwater, MI 49036
Tel: 517-279-7963 *Fax:* 517-279-8095
E-mail: j7eden@aol.com
Web Site: www.branchcct.org
Key Personnel
Pres & Comm Chmn: J Richard Colbeck
Contact: Jennifer Colbeck
Established: 1984
Playwriting, must be unproduced full-length plays +/or musicals.
Award: $200 & production (1st prize), $50 (2nd prize), $25 (3rd prize)
Closing Date: Annually, Dec 31 (entries ongoing)
Presented: Tibbits Opera House, Coldwater, MI, Annually, Feb or March

Lorne Pierce Medal
Royal Society of Canada
Walter House, 282 Somerset W, Ottawa, ON K2P 0J6, Canada
Tel: 613-991-6990 (ext 106) *Fax:* 613-991-6996
E-mail: nominations@rsc-src.ca
Web Site: www.rsc-src.ca
Key Personnel
Mgr, Fellowship & Awards: Marie-Lyne Renaud
E-mail: mlrenaud@rsc-src.ca
Established: 1926
Biennial award given in even-numbered years for an achievement of significance & conspicuous merit in imaginative or critical literature.
Award: Medal
Closing Date: March 1
Presented: RSC Annual Meeting, Nov

The Pinch Writing Awards in Fiction
The Pinch Literary Journal
University of Memphis, English Dept, 435 Patterson Hall, Memphis, TN 38152
Tel: 901-678-2651 *Fax:* 901-678-2226
E-mail: editor@pinchjournal.com
Web Site: www.pinchjournal.com
Key Personnel
Ed-in-Chief: Courtney Miller Santo
Mng Ed: Severin Allgood
Asst Mng Ed: Kendra Vanderlip
Established: 1987
Awarded annually. Submit 1 previously unpublished story not to exceed 5,000 words accompanied by a $3 reading fee. No longer accepting paper submissions. Submit through online portal beginning August 15.

Award: $200 & publication in the following Spring issue of *The Pinch* (1st prize), 2nd & 3rd place winners may also be published. All entrants receive 2 free copies of the journal in which the work appears
Closing Date: March 15
Presented: Mid-Sept

The Pinch Writing Awards in Poetry
The Pinch Literary Journal
University of Memphis, English Dept, 435 Patterson Hall, Memphis, TN 38152
Tel: 901-678-2651 *Fax:* 901-678-2226
E-mail: editor@pinchjournal.com
Web Site: www.pinchjournal.com
Key Personnel
Ed-in-Chief: Courtney Miller Santo
Mng Ed: Severin Allgood
Asst Mng Ed: Kendra Vanderlip
Established: 1987
Annual award. Submit up to a max of 5 unpublished poems accompanied by a $3 reading fee. No longer accepting paper submissions. Submit through online portal beginning August 5.
Award: $200 & publication in the subsequent issue of *The Pinch* will be awarded to the 1st place winner, 2nd & 3rd place winners may also be published. All entrants receive 2 free copies of the journal in which the work appears
Closing Date: March 15
Presented: Mid-Sept

Pinckley Prizes for Crime Fiction
Women's National Book Association of New Orleans
PO Box 13926, New Orleans, LA 70185
E-mail: pinckleyprizes@gmail.com
Web Site: www.pinckleyprizes.org
Key Personnel
Admin: Susan Larson
The prizes honor 2 women writers. The Pinckley Prize for Distinguished Body of Work honors an established woman writer who has created a significant body of work in crime fiction. The winner is nominated & selected by a jury of WNBA-NO members. The Pinckley Prize for Debut Novel honors a woman writer with a first-time published novel in adult crime fiction. The winner is selected from the submissions by a three-judge panel. Entry forms must accompany all submissions for the Debut Novel Prize.
Other Sponsor(s): Greater New Orleans Foundation
Award: $2,500 & trip to New Orleans
Closing Date: Dec 31
Presented: Oct

Pinnacle Book Achievement Awards
National Association of Book Entrepreneurs (NABE)
PO Box 606, Cottage Grove, OR 97424
Tel: 541-942-7455 *Fax:* 541-942-7455
E-mail: nabe@bookmarketingprofits.com
Web Site: www.bookmarketingprofits.com
Key Personnel
Exec Dir: Al Galasso
Annual awards to recognize the finest books published by NABE members based on book content, quality, writing style, presentation & cover design. One free entry form for one book for NABE members. Additional books or additional categories can be entered for $50 per book or category for members. All printed books written in English & published in the previous 2 years or in the year of the awards are eligible.
Award: Honor & mention in upcoming issue of *Book Dealers World*, Award Winners web page, press releases, book stickers & certificates for their web site
Closing Date: Sept 5 (1st round)

Playwright Discovery Award, see The Jean Kennedy Smith VSA Playwright Discovery Award

Playwrights Project
3675 Ruffin Rd, Suite 330, San Diego, CA 92123
Tel: 858-384-2970 *Fax:* 858-384-2974
E-mail: write@playwrightsproject.org
Web Site: www.playwrightsproject.org
Key Personnel
Exec Dir: Cecelia Kouma
Devt Mgr: Linnea Searle
Established: 1985
Annual playwriting contest for Californians under 19 years of age.
Award: Professional production (location to be announced), royalty
Closing Date: June 1
Presented: Jan-Feb following application

The Plimpton Prize
The Paris Review Foundation
544 W 27 St, New York, NY 10001
Tel: 212-343-1333
E-mail: queries@theparisreview.org
Web Site: www.theparisreview.org
Key Personnel
Mng Ed: Hasan Altaf
Sr Ed: Dierdre Foley-Mendelssohn
Awarded annually to the best work of fiction publishing in *The Paris Review* that year by an emerging or previously unpublished writer.
Award: $10,000
Presented: April

Ploughshares Emerging Writer's Contest
Ploughshares
Emerson College, 120 Boylston St, Boston, MA 02116
Tel: 617-824-3757
E-mail: pshares@pshares.org
Web Site: www.pshares.org
Key Personnel
Exec Dir & Ed-in-Chief: Ladette Randolph
Awarded annually to recognize work by an emerging writer in each of 3 genres: fiction, nonfiction & poetry. Authors are considered "emerging" if they haven't published or self-published a book. Fiction & nonfiction: Under 6,000 words; Poetry: 3-5 pages. Submit 1 entry per year via the online submission manager. Entry fee: $24 (waived if subscriber through winter issue of *Ploughshares*).
Award: $2,000 & publication to 1 winner in each genre
Closing Date: May 15
Presented: Mid-Sept

Plutarch Award
Biographers International Organization (BIO)
PO Box 33020, Santa Fe, NM 87594
Tel: 505-983-4671
Web Site: biographersinternational.org
Key Personnel
Admin & Membership Coord: Lori Izykowski
E-mail: lori@biographersinternational.org
Established: 2013
Awarded by a committee of distinguished biographers for the best biographical work of the calendar year.
Closing Date: Dec 1
Presented: BIO Conference, Annually in May

PNWA Literary Contest
PNWA - a writer's resource
1420 NW Gilman Blvd, Suite 8, PMB 2717, Issaquah, WA 98027
Tel: 425-673-2665
E-mail: pnwa@pnwa.org
Web Site: www.pnwa.org

Key Personnel
Pres: Pam Binder
Multiple categories by genre.
Closing Date: Annually in Feb
Presented: Annual Summer Conference

Edgar Allan Poe Memorial
The Poetry Society of Virginia
900 Timber Creek Place, Virginia Beach, VA 23464
E-mail: poetryinva@aol.com
Web Site: poetrysocietyofvirginia.org
Key Personnel
Pres: Robert P Arthur *E-mail:* robert.peebles.arthur@gmail.com
Exec Dir: Guy Terrell *E-mail:* guy.terrell@earthlink.net
Adult Contest Chair: Steven Blythe
   E-mail: stevenblythepoetry@gmail.com
All entries must be in English, original & unpublished. Submit 2 copies of each poem, each having the category name & number on top left of page. Only 1 poem per category; any form; any subject; 48 line limit. Entries will not be returned. Entry fee: $4 nonmembs.
Award: $100
Closing Date: Jan
Presented: Annual PSV Awards Ceremony, April

Poetry Center Book Award
Poetry Center & American Poetry Archives at San Francisco State University
1600 Holloway Ave, San Francisco, CA 94132
Tel: 415-338-2227 *Fax:* 415-338-0966
E-mail: poetry@sfsu.edu
Web Site: www.sfsu.edu/~poetry
Key Personnel
Assoc Dir: Elise Ficarra
Established: 1980
For an outstanding book of poetry published in the year of the award. Volumes by individual authors only; anthologies & translations not accepted. Poets or publishers should send 1 copy of each book & a $10 fee. Include a cover letter noting author name, book title(s), name of person issuing check & check number.
Award: $500 & an invitation to read in the Poetry Center's series
Closing Date: Jan 31
Presented: Fall

Poetry Chapbook Contest
Palettes & Quills
1935 Penfield Rd, Penfield, NY 14526
Tel: 585-383-0812
E-mail: palettesnquills@gmail.com
Web Site: www.palettesnquills.com
Key Personnel
Owner, Ed & Publr: Donna M Marbach
   E-mail: dmmarbach@gmail.com
Complete submission should include ms 14-48 pages, cover sheet, statement that all poems are your own original work, title page, acknowledgements page & complete Table of Contents. Submissions may be mailed or submitted online. $20 non-refundable entry fee per submission. Hard copy submissions are preferred, but e-mailed submissions will be accepted. Simultaneous submissions are accepted as are multiple submissions (but they must be submitted individually). See web site for complete submission guidelines.
Award: Cash ($200) plus 50 copies of the published book
Closing Date: Sept, even-numbered years
Presented: Winners announced online in Dec

Karl Pohrt Tribute Award
Book Industry Charitable Foundation
3135 S State St, Suite 203, Ann Arbor, MI 48108
Toll Free Tel: 866-733-9064 *Fax:* 734-477-2806
E-mail: info@bincfoundation.org

Web Site: www.bincfoundation.org/scholarship
Key Personnel
Exec Dir: Pam French *E-mail:* pam@bincfoundation.org
Dir, Devt: Kathy Bartson *E-mail:* kathy@bincfoundation.org
Progs Mgr: Kit Steinaway *E-mail:* kit@bincfoundation.org; Kate Weiss *E-mail:* kate@bincfoundation.org
Awarded to an independent bookseller who has overcome learning adversity or is a non-traditional student. The bookstore must have a brick & mortar presence in the US & be owned by an entity deriving a substantial portion of its revenue from the sale of physical books.
Award: $5,000

The George Polk Awards
Long Island University
The Brooklyn Campus, One University Plaza, Brooklyn, NY 11201-5372
Tel: 718-488-1009
Web Site: www.liu.edu/polk
Key Personnel
Curator: John Darnton
Coord: Ralph Engelman *E-mail:* ralph.engelman@liu.edu
Established: 1949
For outstanding discernment & reporting of a news or feature story on the Internet, in newspapers, radio or television. Entries originating from publication offices, newsrooms or individual reporters are considered. In 2015, we established the George Polk Award for Documentary Film within the George Polk Awards. Only online submissions are accepted at liu.edu/polk. See web site for entry fee information & submission guidelines.
Award: Plaque & cash award
Closing Date: End of 1st week in Jan for the previous calendar year
Presented: Luncheon in New York, NY, Annually in Spring

Porchlight Book Co Business Book Awards
Porchlight Book Co
544 S First St, Milwaukee, WI 53204
Toll Free Tel: 800-236-7323
E-mail: info@porchlightbooks.com
Web Site: porchlightbooks.com
Key Personnel
Owner, Pres & CEO: Rebecca Schwartz
   E-mail: rebecca@porchlightbooks.com
Owner: Carol Grossmeyer *E-mail:* carol@porchlightbooks.com
Mktg Dir: Blyth Meier *Tel:* 414-220-4456
   E-mail: blyth@porchlightbooks.com
Awarded annually to recognize the best books in the business genre. Any business book originally published in the prior year & available in the US is eligible. Books must be submitted by the publisher, agent, or author of the book. Categories: Leadership & strategy, management & workplace culture, marketing & sales, innovation & creativity, personal development & human behavior, current events & public affairs, narrative & biography, big ideas & new perspectives.
Closing Date: Sept
Presented: Jan (Business Book of the Year & Jack Covert Award)

Katherine Anne Porter Award
American Academy of Arts & Letters
633 W 155 St, New York, NY 10032
Tel: 212-368-5900 *Fax:* 212-491-4615
E-mail: academy@artsandletters.org
Web Site: artsandletters.org
Key Personnel
Exec Dir: Cody Upton
Established: 2001

Biennial award to honor a prose writer whose achievements & dedication to the literary profession have been demonstrated.
Award: $20,000

Katherine Anne Porter Prize for Fiction
Nimrod, The University of Tulsa
Subsidiary of The Nimrod Literary Awards
Nimrod International Journal, 800 S Tucker Dr, Tulsa, OK 74104
Tel: 918-631-3080 *Fax:* 918-631-3033
E-mail: nimrod@utulsa.edu
Web Site: www.utulsa.edu/nimrod
Key Personnel
Ed-in-Chief: Eilis O'Neal
Assoc Ed: Diane Burton; Cassidy McCants
Established: 1978
Annual prize. 7,500 words maximum. No previously published works or works accepted for publication elsewhere. Must have a US address by October to enter. Works must be in English or translated by original author. Author's name must not appear on ms. Include a cover sheet containing major title & subtitles, author's name, address, phone number & e-mail address. "Contest Entry" must be on envelope. Mss will not be returned. Nimrod retains the right to publish any submission. Works not accepted will be released; SASE for results only. $20 entry fee includes processing & 1-year subscription. Online submissions: nimrodjournal.submittable.com.
Award: $2,000 (1st prize), $1,000 (2nd prize); plus each published writer receives 2 copies of the journal; winners are flown to Tulsa for a conference & banquet
Closing Date: April 30
Presented: Tulsa, OK, Oct

Prairie Schooner Annual Strousse Award
Prairie Schooner
University of Nebraska, 123 Andrews Hall, 625 N 14 St, Lincoln, NE 68508
Mailing Address: PO Box 880334, Lincoln, NE 68588-0334
Tel: 402-472-0911 *Fax:* 402-472-9771
E-mail: prairieschooner@unl.edu
Web Site: prairieschooner.unl.edu
Key Personnel
Mng Ed: Ashley Strosnider
Ed: Kwame Dawes
Established: 1975
For best poetry published in the magazine each year.
Other Sponsor(s): Friends & famliy of Fora Strousse
Award: $500
Presented: Prairie Schooner, March

Prairie Schooner Bernice Slote Award
Prairie Schooner
University of Nebraska, 123 Andrews Hall, 625 N 14 St, Lincoln, NE 68508
Mailing Address: PO Box 880334, Lincoln, NE 68588-0334
Tel: 402-472-0911 *Fax:* 402-472-9771
E-mail: prairieschooner@unl.edu
Web Site: prairieschooner.unl.edu
Key Personnel
Mng Ed: Ashley Strosnider
Ed: Kwame Dawes
Established: 1985
Annual writing prize for best work by a beginning writer published in *Prairie Schooner* in the previous year.
Award: $500
Presented: Winners announced in Spring issue of *Prairie Schooner* magazine

Prairie Schooner Book Prize Contest in Fiction
Prairie Schooner
University of Nebraska, 123 Andrews Hall, 625 N 14 St, Lincoln, NE 68508

Mailing Address: PO Box 880334, Lincoln, NE 68588-0334
Tel: 402-472-0911 *Fax:* 402-472-9771
E-mail: psbookprize@unl.edu
Web Site: prairieschooner.unl.edu
Key Personnel
Mng Ed: Ashley Strosnider
Ed: Kwame Dawes
Welcomes mss from all living writers, including non-US citizens, writing in English. Mss previously published will not be considered. Writers may enter both fiction & poetry contests. For fiction mss, at least 150 pages in length is preferred. Entry fee: $25 per submission. Mss accepted by electronic or hard copy submission beginning January 15.
Award: $3,000 & publication through the University of Nebraska Press
Closing Date: Annually, March 15

Prairie Schooner Book Prize Contest in Poetry
Prairie Schooner
University of Nebraska, 123 Andrews Hall, 625 N 14 St, Lincoln, NE 68508
Mailing Address: PO Box 880334, Lincoln, NE 68588-0334
Tel: 402-472-0911 *Fax:* 402-472-9771
E-mail: psbookprize@unl.edu
Web Site: prairieschooner.unl.edu
Key Personnel
Mng Ed: Ashley Strosnider
Ed: Kwame Dawes
Welcomes mss from all living writers, including non-US citizens, writing in English. Mss previously published will not be considered. Writers may enter both fiction & poetry contests. For poetry mss, at least 50 pages in length is preferred. Entry fee: $25 per submission. Mss accepted by electronic or hard copy submission beginning January 15.
Award: $3,000 & publication through the University of Nebraska Press
Closing Date: March 15, annually

Prairie Schooner Edward Stanley Award
Prairie Schooner
University of Nebraska, 123 Andrews Hall, 625 N 14 St, Lincoln, NE 68508
Mailing Address: PO Box 880334, Lincoln, NE 68588-0334
Tel: 402-472-0911 *Fax:* 402-472-9771
E-mail: prairieschooner@unl.edu
Web Site: prairieschooner.unl.edu
Key Personnel
Mng Ed: Ashley Strosnider
Ed: Kwame Dawes
Established: 1992
Annual writing prize for best poem or group of poems in the volume. Only contributors to the magazine are eligible.
Other Sponsor(s): Friends & family of Marion Edward Stanley (in memorium)
Award: $1,000
Presented: Winners announced in Spring issue of *Prairie Schooner* magazine

Prairie Schooner Glenna Luschei Award
Prairie Schooner
University of Nebraska, 123 Andrews Hall, 625 N 14 St, Lincoln, NE 68508
Mailing Address: PO Box 880334, Lincoln, NE 68588-0334
Tel: 402-472-0911 *Fax:* 402-472-9771
E-mail: prairieschooner@unl.edu
Web Site: prairieschooner.unl.edu
Key Personnel
Mng Ed: Ashley Strosnider
Ed: Kwame Dawes
Established: 1989
Annual writing prizes for best work published in the magazine. Only work published in *Prairie Schooner* in the previous year is considered.

Other Sponsor(s): Glenna Luschei
Award: $1,500 (1st place), $250 (10 runners up)
Presented: Winners announced in Spring issue of *Prairie Schooner* magazine

Prairie Schooner Hugh J Luke Award
Prairie Schooner
University of Nebraska, 123 Andrews Hall, 625 N 14 St, Lincoln, NE 68508
Mailing Address: PO Box 880334, Lincoln, NE 68588-0334
Tel: 402-472-0911 *Fax:* 402-472-9771
E-mail: prairieschooner@unl.edu
Web Site: prairieschooner.unl.edu
Key Personnel
Mng Ed: Ashley Strosnider
Ed: Kwame Dawes
Established: 1989
Annual writing prize for best work published in the *Prairie Schooner* magazine in the previous year.
Other Sponsor(s): Friends & family of Hugh J Luke (in memoriam)
Award: $250
Presented: Winners announced in Spring issue of *Prairie Schooner* magazine

Prairie Schooner Jane Geske Award
Prairie Schooner
University of Nebraska, 123 Andrews Hall, 625 N 14 St, Lincoln, NE 68508
Mailing Address: PO Box 880334, Lincoln, NE 68588-0334
Tel: 402-472-0911 *Fax:* 402-472-9771
E-mail: prairieschooner@unl.edu
Web Site: prairieschooner.unl.edu
Key Personnel
Mng Ed: Ashley Strosnider
Ed: Kwame Dawes
Established: 2000
Annual award for work in any genre published in *Prairie Schooner* in the previous year.
Other Sponsor(s): Family of Jane Geske
Award: $250
Presented: Winners announced in Spring issue of *Prairie Schooner* magazine

Prairie Schooner Lawrence Foundation Award
Prairie Schooner
University of Nebraska, 123 Andrews Hall, 625 N 14 St, Lincoln, NE 68508
Mailing Address: PO Box 880334, Lincoln, NE 68588-0334
Tel: 402-472-0911 *Fax:* 402-472-9771
E-mail: prairieschooner@unl.edu
Web Site: prairieschooner.unl.edu
Key Personnel
Mng Ed: Ashley Strosnider
Ed: Kwame Dawes
Established: 1978
Annual writing prize for the best short story published in *Prairie Schooner* magazine; only work published in the previous year will be considered.
Other Sponsor(s): The Lawrence Foundation of New York City
Award: $1,000
Presented: Winners announced in Spring issue of *Prairie Schooner* magazine

Prairie Schooner Virginia Faulkner Award for Excellence in Writing
Prairie Schooner
University of Nebraska, 123 Andrews Hall, 625 N 14 St, Lincoln, NE 68508
Mailing Address: PO Box 880334, Lincoln, NE 68588-0334
Tel: 402-472-0911 *Fax:* 402-472-9771
E-mail: prairieschooner@unl.edu
Web Site: prairieschooner.unl.edu
Key Personnel
Mng Ed: Ashley Strosnider

Ed: Kwame Dawes
Established: 1987
Annual writing prize for work published in *Prairie Schooner* magazine. Only work published in the previous year is considered.
Other Sponsor(s): Friends & family of Virginia Faulkner
Award: $1,000
Presented: Winners announced in Spring issue of *Prairie Schooner* magazine

Premier Print Awards
PRINTING United Alliance
10015 Main St, Fairfax, VA 22031-3489
Tel: 703-385-1335 *Toll Free Tel:* 888-385-3588 *Fax:* 703-273-0456
E-mail: assist@printing.org; info@printing.org
Web Site: www.printing.org/ppa
Key Personnel
Pres & CEO: Ford Bowers *E-mail:* fbowers@ printing.org
Events & Spec Progs Mgr (PA Off): Mike Packard *E-mail:* mpackard@printing.org
Established: 1950
Recognizes the highest quality printed pieces in various categories from around the world. See web site for more information.
Other Sponsor(s): Domtar
Award: Certificates of Merit & the highest honor; the Benny Statue
Closing Date: Annually in May
Presented: Premier Print Awards Gala, Annually in Sept
Branch Office(s)
1325 "G" St NW, Suite 500, Washington, DC 20005
2000 Corporate Dr, Suite 205, Wexford, PA 15090 *Tel:* 412-741-6860 *Toll Free Tel:* 800-910-4283 *Fax:* 412-741-2311

Presidential Master's Prize
American Comparative Literature Association (ACLA)
University of South Carolina, Dept of Languages, Literature & Cultures, 1620 College St, Rm 817, Columbia, SC 29208
Tel: 803-777-3021
E-mail: info@acla.org
Web Site: www.acla.org/prize-awards/presidential-masters-prize
Key Personnel
Nominations Comm Chair: Antonio Barrenechea *E-mail:* abarrene@umw.edu
Annual award to the best thesis, report or substantial essay nominated by a department or program at any institution. Project must be completed by July 1 of the year prior to the award. Each institution may nominate 1 student in the field of comparative literature, identified as the best without regard to actual departmental affiliation.
Award: $500, certificate, complimentary registration for annual meeting, hotel & airfare accommodations

Presidential Undergraduate Prize
American Comparative Literature Association (ACLA)
University of South Carolina, Dept of Languages, Literature & Cultures, 1620 College St, Rm 817, Columbia, SC 29208
Tel: 803-777-3021
E-mail: info@acla.org
Web Site: www.acla.org/prize-awards/presidential-undergraduate-prize
Key Personnel
Nominations Comm Chair: Antonio Barrenechea *E-mail:* abarrene@umw.edu
Annual award to the best substantial essay nominated by a department or program. Project must be completed by July 1 of the year prior to the award. Each institution may nominate 1 student in the field of comparative literature,

identified as the best without regard to actual department affiliation.
Award: $250, certificate, complimentary registration for annual meeting, hotel & airfare accommodations

Derek Price/Rod Webster Prize Award
History of Science Society
Affiliate of American Council of Learned Societies
440 Geddes Hall, Notre Dame, IN 46556
Tel: 574-631-1194
E-mail: info@hssonline.org
Web Site: www.hssonline.org
Key Personnel
Exec Dir: Robert Jay Malone
Established: 1978
For article appearing in Isis during the preceding 3 years.
Award: $1,000
Closing Date: Annually, April 1
Presented: Annual meeting, Late Oct or early Nov

Michael L Printz Award
Young Adult Library Services Association (YALSA)
Division of The American Library Association (ALA)
50 E Huron St, Chicago, IL 60611
Tel: 312-280-4390 *Toll Free Tel:* 800-545-2433
Fax: 312-280-5276
E-mail: yalsa@ala.org
Web Site: www.ala.org/yalsa/printz
Key Personnel
Exec Dir: Anita Mechler
Prog Offr, Events & Conferences: Nichole O'Connor *Tel:* 800-545-2433 ext 4387
E-mail: noconnor@ala.org
Communs Specialist: Anna Lam *Tel:* 800-545-2433 ext 5849 *E-mail:* alam@ala.org
Established: 1999
Honors excellence in literature written for young adults. May be fiction, nonfiction, poetry or an anthology & must have been published during the preceding year & designated as young adult book or ages 12-18.
Other Sponsor(s): Booklist
Closing Date: Annually, Dec 1
Presented: YALSA Printz Reception during ALA Annual Conference

PRISM international Literary Non-Fiction Contest
PRISM international
University of British Columbia, Buch E462, 1866 Main Mall, Vancouver, BC V6T 1Z1, Canada
Tel: 778-822-2514 *Fax:* 778-822-3616
E-mail: prismwritingcontest@gmail.com
Web Site: www.prismmagazine.ca
Key Personnel
Exec Ed: Jennifer Lori; Claire Matthews
Poetry Ed: Dominique Bernier Cormier
Prose Ed: Christopher Evans
Entry fee: $35 (includes a 1-year subscription); additional entries: $5.
Other Sponsor(s): University of British Columbia Bookstore
Award: $1,500 (grand prize), $600 (1st runner up), $400 (2nd runner up)
Closing Date: Annually in Nov (check web site for exact date)

Pritzker Military Museum & Library Literature Award for Lifetime Achievement in Military Writing
Pritzker Military Museum & Library
104 S Michigan Ave, Suite 400, Chicago, IL 60603
Tel: 312-374-9390 *Fax:* 312-374-9394
E-mail: info@pritzkermilitary.org
Web Site: www.pritzkermilitary.org

Established: 2007
To recognize a living author who has made a significant contribution to the understanding of American military history, including military affairs.
Other Sponsor(s): Pritzker Military Foundation
Award: $100,000, citation & gold medallion
Closing Date: Annually in March
Presented: The Pritzker Military Museum & Library Liberty Gala, Annually in Nov

Prix Alvine-Belisle
Association pour l'Avancement des Sciences et des Techniques de la Documentation
2065 rue Parthenais, Bureau 387, Montreal, QC H2K 3T1, Canada
Tel: 514-281-5012 *Fax:* 514-281-8219
E-mail: info@asted.org
Web Site: www.asted.org
Key Personnel
Exec Dir: Lionel Villalonga *E-mail:* lvillalonga@asted.org
To the best books for young people published in French in Canada during the previous year.
Closing Date: Annually, end of June
Presented: Mount Royal Centre, Montreal, QC, CN, Annually in Nov

Prix Emile-Nelligan
La Fondation Emile Nelligan
100, rue Sherbrooke, Suite 202, Montreal, QC H2X 1C3, Canada
Tel: 514-278-4657 *Toll Free Tel:* 888-849-8540
E-mail: info@fondation-nelligan.org
Web Site: www.fondation-nelligan.org
Key Personnel
CEO: Manon Gagnon
Pres: Michel Dallaire
VP: Marie-Andree Beaudet
Treas/Secy: Michel Gonneville
Established: 1979
Collection must be published between January 1-December 31 of the preceding year.
Award: $7,500 & a bronze medal
Presented: Annually in May

Prize for the Translation of Japanese Literature, see Japan-US Friendship Commission Translation Prize

Prometheus Awards
Libertarian Futurist Society
650 Castro St, Suite 120-433, Mountain View, CA 94041
Tel: 650-968-6319
Web Site: www.lfs.org
Key Personnel
Bd Pres: Bill Stoddard
VP: Charles Morrison
Established: 1979
Recognize works of fiction that champion individual freedom. The Best Novel category is limited to novels published during the previous year or so. The Hall of Fame category (for Best Classic Fiction) is broadly inclusive: Novels, novellas, short stories, poems, plays, films, TV shows (individual episodes or entire series), series & trilogies are all eligible for nomination. Works are eligible 5 years after first publication or broadcast. Best Novel & Best Classic Fiction categories are presented annually. Special Awards are occasional & focus on outstanding pro-freedom achievements that fall outside the realm of the Best Novel category.
Award: One ounce gold coin mounted on an engraved plaque for both the Prometheus Best Novel Award & the Hall of Fame Award
Closing Date: Annually, Feb 1 (Special Awards), March 1st (Best Novel), Oct 1 (Best Classic Fiction)
Presented: World Science Fiction Convention or NASFIC, Labor Day weekend

PROSE Awards
Association of American Publishers (AAP)
455 Massachusetts Ave NW, Suite 700, Washington, DC 20001-2777
Tel: 202-347-3375 *Fax:* 202-347-3690
E-mail: proseawards@publishers.org
Web Site: www.proseawards.com; publishers.org
Key Personnel
VP, Communs: Susanna Hinds
Established: 1976
The PROSE Awards honor the very best in professional & scholarly publishing. With awards in over 60 catergories, PROSE is unique in its breath & depth. AAP, PSP & AUPresses members are eligible.
Award: Plaque & glass cubes
Closing Date: Annually, Nov 1
Presented: Annually in Feb

Public Scholar Program
National Endowment for the Humanities, Division of Research Programs
400 Seventh St SW, Washington, DC 20506
Tel: 202-606-8200
E-mail: publicscholar@neh.gov
Web Site: www.neh.gov/grants
Key Personnel
NEH Chmn: Jon Parrish Peede
Supports well-researched books in the humanities intended to reach a broad readership. Fellowship periods last from 6-12 months & must be full-time & continuous. Open to both individuals affiliated with scholarly institutions & independent scholars. All applications to this program must be submitted via Grants.gov. Applications receive peer review & NEH Chairman makes all funding decisions.
Award: $4,200 monthly stipend (maximum $50,400 for 12-month period)
Closing Date: Dec 16, 2020 for programs beginning Sept 1, 2021
Presented: Aug 2021

The Publishing Triangle Literary Awards
The Publishing Triangle
332 Bleecker St, Suite D-36, New York, NY 10014
E-mail: publishingtriangle@gmail.com
Web Site: www.publishingtriangle.org
Established: 1997
Contests for poetry, debut fiction, nonfiction & trans/gender-variant literature. Books must be published in the US or CN between January 1 & December 31. Entries are accepted only between October 1 & December 1. General instructions, specific guidelines, for each award & submission form are available on web site starting October 1. For hard copy, send your mailing address to publishingtriangle@gmail.com. Entry fee: $40.
Award: $1,000 for debut fiction, nonfiction, trans/gender-variant & poetry
Closing Date: Dec 1
Presented: Ceremony in New York City, NY, Late April/early May

PubWest Book Design Awards
Publishers Association of the West Inc (PubWest)
17501 Hill Way, Lake Oswego, OR 97035
Tel: 503-901-9865
E-mail: pubwest1@gmail.com
Web Site: pubwest.org
Key Personnel
Pres: Colleen Dunn Bates
Established: 1977
Gold, silver & bronze awards are given in 24 categories. Adult trade book (illustrated), adult trade book (non-illustrated), children's/young adult (illustrated), children's/young adult (non-illustrated), artist's book, academic book/non-trade, guide/travel book, how-to book/crafts, cookbook, art/photography

book, sports/fitness/recreation book, reference book, short stories/poetry/anthologies, gift/holiday/specialty book, historical/biographical book, graphic album-new material & previously published, jacket/cover special edition, ebook fixed layout, ebook standard, book apps, fixed layout children's ebook. Entry fee $75 (PubWest membs), $100 (nonmembs).
Award: Medallions & glass award for best of show
Closing Date: April

Pulitzer Prizes
709 Journalism Bldg, Columbia University, 2950 Broadway, New York, NY 10027
Tel: 212-854-3841 *Fax:* 212-854-3342
E-mail: pulitzer@pulitzer.org
Web Site: www.pulitzer.org
Established: 1917
Given to American authors for a distinguished book of fiction, performed play, history of the US, biography or autobiography, verse or general nonfiction, as well as journalism prizes for newspaper work in US dailies or weeklies. Books must be first published in the calendar year.
Award: Gold medal for public service journalism category; $10,000 & certificate in all other categories
Closing Date: June 15 for bks published Jan 1-June 14, Oct 15 for bks published June 15-Dec 31; literary prizes, Jan 15 (music), Feb 1 (journalism), Dec 31 (drama)
Presented: Annually in Spring

Pushcart Prize: Best of the Small Presses
Pushcart Press
PO Box 380, Wainscott, NY 11975-0380
SAN: 202-9871
Tel: 631-324-9300
Web Site: www.pushcartprize.com
Key Personnel
Pres: Bill Henderson
Established: 1976
Awarded for works previously published by a small press or literary journal.
Award: Copies of the book *The Pushcart Prize: Best of the Small Presses*
Closing Date: Annually, Dec 1
Presented: Annually in Spring

Ron Pynn Award
Textbook & Academic Authors Association (TAA)
PO Box 367, Fountain City, WI 54629
E-mail: info@taaonline.net
Web Site: www.taaonline.net/ron-pynn-award
Key Personnel
Exec Dir: Michael Spinella *Tel:* 973-943-0501 *E-mail:* michael.spinella@taaonline.net
Dir, Publg & Opers: Kim Pawlak *Tel:* 608-687-3106 *E-mail:* kim.pawlak@taaonline.net
Dir, Instl Memberships & Meetings: Maureen Foerster *Tel:* 608-687-3106 *E-mail:* maureen.foerster@taaonline.net
Membership Coord: Bekky Murphy *Tel:* 608-567-9060 *E-mail:* bekky.murphy@taaonline.net
Open to TAA members who have authored, co-authored, or co-edited at least 5 textbooks, at least 2 of which are authored or edited solely by the nominee. The nominee's textbooks must be published in more than 1 discipline or more than 1 area of discipline. Any TAA member may nominate him or herself or another TAA member. One recipient is selected by the TAA Council via ballot. Submit nominee & documentation via e-mail.
Closing Date: Jan 15
Presented: TAA Annual Conference, Annually in June

QWF Literary Awards
Quebec Writers' Federation (QWF)
1200 Atwater Ave, Rm 3, Westmount, QC H3Z 1X4, Canada
Tel: 514-933-0878
E-mail: info@qwf.org
Web Site: www.qwf.org
Key Personnel
Exec Dir: Lori Schubert *E-mail:* admin@qwf.org
Established: 1988
Literary awards for Quebec, English language authors. Request submission details.
Awards: A M Klein Prize for Poetry; Paragraphe Hugh MacLennan Prize for Fiction; Mavis Gallant Prize for Nonfiction; Concordia University First Book Prize; Cole Foundation Prize for Translation; QWF Prize for Children's & Young Adult Literature.
Award: $2,000 each
Closing Date: Annually, June 1
Presented: Annually in Nov

Miriam Rachimi Memorial
The Poetry Society of Virginia
900 Timber Creek Place, Virginia Beach, VA 23464
E-mail: poetryinva@aol.com
Web Site: poetrysocietyofvirginia.org
Key Personnel
Pres: Robert P Arthur *E-mail:* robert.peebles.arthur@gmail.com
Exec Dir: Guy Terrell *E-mail:* guy.terrell@earthlink.net
Adult Contest Chair: Steven Blythe *E-mail:* stevenblythepoetry@gmail.com
All entries must be in English, original & unpublished. Submit 2 copies, each having the category name & number on top left of page. Subject: the spiritual impact of losing (or almost losing) a loved one; any form; 48 line limit. Entry fee $4 nonmembs.
Other Sponsor(s): Ben Mahgerefteh; Michal Mahgerefteh
Award: $50 (1st prize), $30 (2nd prize), $20 (3rd prize)
Closing Date: Jan
Presented: Annual PSV Awards Ceremony, April

Radcliffe Fellowship
The Radcliffe Institute for Advanced Study
8 Garden St, Cambridge, MA 02138
Tel: 617-496-1324 (application off) *Fax:* 617-495-8136
Web Site: www.radcliffe.harvard.edu
Key Personnel
Admin, Fellowships: Alison Ney
Radcliffe Institute fellowships are designed to support scholars, scientists, artists & writers of exceptional promise & demonstrated accomplishments who wish to pursue work in academic & professional fields & in the creative arts.
Award: Stipend & office space
Closing Date: Sept 15 for Creative Arts & Humanities & Social Sciences; Oct 6 for Natural Sciences & Mathematics

Thomas Raddall Atlantic Fiction Award
Writers' Federation of Nova Scotia
1113 Marginal Rd, Halifax, NS B3H 4P7, Canada
Tel: 902-423-8116 *Fax:* 902-422-0881
E-mail: contact@writers.ns.ca
Web Site: writers.ns.ca
Key Personnel
Commns & Devt Offr: Robin Spittal
Established: 1991
Awarded for a novel or book of short fiction, published by an Atlantic Canadian writer who has lived in one or a combination of these provinces for at least 2 concurrent years immediately prior to the submission deadline date.

Non-refundable $20 administrative fee per entry.
Award: $25,000
Closing Date: Nov 1
Presented: Halifax, NS, CN, Annually in Spring

The Ragan Old North State Award Cup for Nonfiction
North Carolina Literary & Historical Association
Affiliate of Historical Book Club of North Carolina
4610 Mail Service Ctr, Raleigh, NC 27699-4610
Tel: 919-807-7290 *Fax:* 919-733-8807
Web Site: www.history.ncdcr.gov/affiliates/lit-hist/awards/awards.htm
Key Personnel
Awards Coord: Michael Hill *E-mail:* michael.hill@ncdcr.gov
Established: 2003
For published book of nonfiction, not technical or scientific, by a legal or actual resident of North Carolina for at least 3 years prior to end of contest.
Award: Cup
Closing Date: Annually, July 15
Presented: Raleigh, NC, Annually in Nov

Raiziss/de Palchi Fellowship
The Academy of American Poets Inc
75 Maiden Lane, Suite 901, New York, NY 10038
Tel: 212-274-0343
E-mail: academy@poets.org
Web Site: www.poets.org
Key Personnel
Pres & Exec Dir: Jennifer Benka *E-mail:* jenbenka@poets.org
Devt, Membership & Communs Sr Mgr: Molly Walsh *E-mail:* mwalsh@poets.org
Ad & Mktg Sr Mgr: Michelle Campagna *E-mail:* mcampagna@poets.org
Sr Progs Mgr: Nikay Paredes *Tel:* 212-274-0343 ext 13 *E-mail:* nparedes@poets.org
Established: 1995
Award to recognize outstanding translations into English of modern Italian poetry. Given to enable an American translator of 20th century Italian poetry to travel, study, or otherwise advance a significant work-in-progress. Book prize is awarded in even-numbered years & fellowship awarded in odd-numbered years.
Award: $10,000 book prize & a $25,000 fellowship
Closing Date: Sept 15-Feb 15
Presented: Sept

Sir Walter Raleigh Award for Fiction
Historical Book Club of North Carolina
Affiliate of North Carolina Literary & Historical Association
4610 Mail Service Ctr, Raleigh, NC 27699-4610
Tel: 919-807-7290 *Fax:* 919-733-8807
Key Personnel
Awards Coord: Michael Hill *E-mail:* michael.hill@ncdcr.gov
Award for the best book of fiction by an author who has been a legal or actual resident of North Carolina for at least 3 years prior to the end of the contest.

Ramirez Family Award
Texas Institute of Letters (TIL)
PO Box 609, Round Rock, TX 78680
Tel: 512-683-5640
E-mail: president@texasinstituteofletters.org
Web Site: www.texasinstituteofletters.org
Key Personnel
Pres: Carmen Tafolla
VP: Sergio Troncoso
Secy: Ann Weisgarber
Treas: W K Stratton
Recording Secy: Kurt Heinzelman

Annual award for the most useful & informative scholarly book contributing to general knowledge, by a Texan or about Texas. See web site for guidelines.
Award: $2,500
Closing Date: Annually in Jan
Presented: TIL Awards Banquet, Annually in Spring

James A Rawley Prize
The Organization of American Historians (OAH)
112 N Bryan Ave, Bloomington, IN 47408-4141
Tel: 812-855-7311
E-mail: oah@oah.org
Web Site: www.oah.org/awards
Key Personnel
Exec Dir: Beth English *E-mail:* benglish@oah.org
Comm Coord: Kara Hamm *E-mail:* khamm@oah.org
Awarded annually to the author of the best book dealing with the history of race relations in the US. Each entry must be published during the calendar year preceding that in which the award is given. One copy of each entry must be mailed directly to the committee members listed on the web site.
Closing Date: Oct 1, 2021 (postmarked)
Presented: OAH Annual Meeting, Boston, MA, March 31-April 3, 2022

RBC Bronwen Wallace Award for Emerging Writers
The Writers' Trust of Canada
600-460 Richmond St W, Toronto, ON M5V 1Y1, Canada
Tel: 416-504-8222 *Toll Free Tel:* 877-906-6548
Fax: 416-504-9090
E-mail: info@writerstrust.com
Web Site: www.writerstrust.com
Key Personnel
Exec Dir: Charlie Foran *Tel:* 416-504-8222 ext 244 *E-mail:* cforan@writerstrust.com
Prog Coord: Devon Jackson *Tel:* 416-504-8222 ext 248 *E-mail:* djackson@writerstrust.com
Established: 1994
Awarded to a young author, 35 years of age & under, who has not been previously published in book form. The award alternates each year between short fiction & poetry.
Other Sponsor(s): RBC Foundation
Award: $10,000 (winner), $2,500 (finalists)
Presented: Annually in Spring

The Rea Award for the Short Story
Dungannon Foundation
53 W Church Hill Rd, Washington, CT 06794
Web Site: reaaward.org
Key Personnel
Pres: Elizabeth R Rea
Established: 1986
Established by Michael M Rea to honor a living US or Canadian writer who has made a significant contribution to the short story form. No submissions accepted. The recipient is nominated & selected by a jury.
Award: $30,000

Reading the West Book Awards
Mountains & Plains Independent Booksellers Association
208 E Lincoln Ave, Fort Collins, CO 80524
Tel: 970-484-3939 *Toll Free Tel:* 800-752-0249
Fax: 970-484-0037
E-mail: info@mountainsplains.org
Web Site: www.mountainsplains.org/reading-the-west-book-awards
Key Personnel
Exec Dir: Heather Duncan *E-mail:* heather@mountainsplains.org
Mktg & Communs Mgr: Jeremy Ellis
Opers Mgr: Kelsey Myers

Assists publishers, authors & booksellers in promoting & building sales for exceptional books & authors in the Mountains & Plains region. These adult & children's titles exemplify the best in writing +/or illustrations whose subject matter is set in the region or invokes the spirit of the region: Arizona, Colorado, Kansas, Montana, Nebraska, Nevada, New Mexico, Oklahoma, South Dakota, Texas, Utah & Wyoming. The author's place of residence is immaterial for this award. Nominations open September 1. Books must be published in the calendar year when submissions open.
Closing Date: Dec 31
Presented: May 31

Reed Environmental Writing Award
Southern Environmental Law Center (SELC)
201 W Main St, Suite 14, Charlottesville, VA 22902
Tel: 434-977-4090 *Fax:* 434-977-1483
Web Site: www.southernenvironment.org
Key Personnel
Exec Dir: Jeff Gleason
Dir, Communs: Erin Malec
Devt Assoc: Jessica Hamilton
  E-mail: jhamilton@selcva.org
Established: 1994
Annual award to recognize & encourage the writers who most effectively tell the stories of the South. Two categories: Book (nonfiction, not self-published) & Journalism (newspaper, magazine & online articles). Entries must be at least 3,000 words, published in the preceding 12 months & relate to the natural resources or special places in at least one of SELC's states: Alabama, Georgia, North Carolina, South Carolina, Tennessee, or Virginia.
Award: $2,500 each category
Closing Date: Oct 1

Regina Medal Award
Catholic Library Association
8550 United Plaza Blvd, Suite 1001, Baton Rouge, LA 70809
Tel: 225-408-4417 *Fax:* 225-408-4422
E-mail: cla2@cathla.org
Web Site: cathla.org
Established: 1959
For continued distinguished lifetime contribution to children's literature; no unsol mss.
Award: Sterling silver medal
Closing Date: None; in-house votes
Presented: CLA Annual Convention, April

Nathan Reingold Prize
History of Science Society
Affiliate of American Council of Learned Societies
440 Geddes Hall, Notre Dame, IN 46556
Tel: 574-631-1194
E-mail: info@hssonline.org
Web Site: www.hssonline.org
Key Personnel
Exec Dir: Robert Jay Malone
Established: 1955
For an original essay, not to exceed 8,000 words, in history of science & its cultural influences. Open to graduate students only. Must send in 3 copies of essay with a detachable author/title page.
Award: $500 (& up to $500 travel reimbursement)
Closing Date: Annually, June 1
Presented: Annually in Oct or Nov

Arthur Rense Prize
American Academy of Arts & Letters
633 W 155 St, New York, NY 10032
Tel: 212-368-5900 *Fax:* 212-491-4615
E-mail: academy@artsandletters.org
Web Site: artsandletters.org

Key Personnel
Exec Dir: Cody Upton
Established: 1998
Given triennially to an exceptional poet.
Award: $20,000

Residency
Millay Colony for the Arts
454 E Hill Rd, Austerlitz, NY 12017
Mailing Address: PO Box 3, Austerlitz, NY 12017-0003
Tel: 518-392-3103; 518-392-4144
E-mail: apply@millaycolony.org
Web Site: www.millaycolony.org
Key Personnel
Exec Dir: Caroline Crumpacker
  E-mail: director@millaycolony.org
Residency Dir: Calliope Nicholas
  E-mail: residency@millaycolony.org
Residencies for writers, composers & visual artists. Information & applications available by e-mail or on web site.
Award: One-month residencies offered including room, studio & meals; no cash award
Closing Date: Oct 1 & March 1

The Restless Books Prize for New Immigrant Writing
Restless Books
232 Third St, Suite A111, Brooklyn, NY 11215
E-mail: publisher@restlessbooks.com
Web Site: www.restlessbooks.org/prize-for-new-immigrant-writing
Key Personnel
Publr: Ilan Stavans
For an outstanding debut literary work by a first-generation immigrant. Awarded for fiction & nonfiction in alternating years. Only one submission is accepted per candidate per submission period. See full submission guidelines & eligibility requirements on the web site.
Award: $10,000 & publication
Closing Date: March 31 (even-numbered years for fiction, odd-numbered years for nonfiction)

The Harold U Ribalow Prize
Hadassah Magazine
40 Wall St, 8th fl, New York, NY 10005-1387
Tel: 212-451-6286 *Fax:* 212-451-6257
E-mail: magtemp3@hadassah.org
Web Site: www.hadassah.org/magazine
Key Personnel
Exec Ed: Alan M Tigay
Established: 1983
Annual award for an outstanding English-language work of fiction on a Jewish theme by an author deserving of recognition.
Other Sponsor(s): Harold U Ribalow family
Award: $3,000
Closing Date: April of the year following publication
Presented: Autumn

Evelyn Richardson Nonfiction Award
Writers' Federation of Nova Scotia
1113 Marginal Rd, Halifax, NS B3H 4P7, Canada
Tel: 902-423-8116 *Fax:* 902-422-0881
E-mail: contact@writers.ns.ca
Web Site: writers.ns.ca
Key Personnel
Communs & Devt Offr: Robin Spittal
Established: 1978
Presented to the best nonfiction book, published by a native or resident Nova Scotian who has lived in the province for at least 2 concurrent years immediately prior to the submission deadline date. Non-refundable $20 administrative fee per entry.
Award: $2,000
Closing Date: Nov 1
Presented: Halifax, NS, CN, Annually in Spring

The Ridenhour Book Prize
The Nation Institute
116 E 16 St, 8th fl, New York, NY 10003
Tel: 212-822-0250 *Fax:* 212-253-5356
E-mail: ridenhour@nationinstitute.org
Web Site: www.ridenhour.org
Key Personnel
Exec Dir & CEO: Taya Kitman *Tel:* 212-822-0252 *E-mail:* taya@nationinstitute.org
Established: 2003
Honors an outstanding work of social significance from the prior publishing year. The prize also recognizes investigative & reportorial distinction.
Other Sponsor(s): The Fertel Foundation
Award: $10,000 stipend

The Ridenhour Courage Prize
The Nation Institute
116 E 16 St, 8th fl, New York, NY 10003
Tel: 212-822-0250 *Fax:* 212-253-5356
E-mail: ridenhour@nationinstitute.org
Web Site: www.ridenhour.org
Key Personnel
Exec Dir & CEO: Taya Kitman *Tel:* 212-822-0252 *E-mail:* taya@nationinstitute.org
Established: 2003
Presented to an individual in recognition of his or her courageous & life-long defense of the public interest & passionate commitment to social justice.
Other Sponsor(s): The Fertel Foundation
Award: $10,000 stipend

The Ridenhour Prize for Truth-Telling
The Nation Institute
116 E 16 St, 8th fl, New York, NY 10003
Tel: 212-822-0250 *Fax:* 212-253-5356
E-mail: ridenhour@nationinstitute.org
Web Site: www.ridenhour.org
Key Personnel
Exec Dir & CEO: Taya Kitman *Tel:* 212-822-0252 *E-mail:* taya@nationinstitute.org
Established: 2003
Presented to a citizen, corporate or government whistleblower, investigative journalist, or organization for bringing a specific issue of social importance to the public's attention.
Other Sponsor(s): The Fertel Foundation
Award: $10,000 stipend

Rilke Prize
University of North Texas Creative Writing Program, Department of English
Auditorium Bldg, Rm 214, 1155 Union Circle, Denton, TX 76203
E-mail: untrilkeprize@unt.edu
Web Site: english.unt.edu/creative-writing/unt-rilke-prize
Key Personnel
Dir, Creative Writing: Corey Marks, PhD *Tel:* 940-565-2126 *E-mail:* corey.marks@unt.edu
Established: 2012
Annual award to recognize a book that demonstrates exceptional artistry & vision written by a mid-career poet & published in the preceding year.
Award: $10,000
Presented: April

Gwen Pharis Ringwood Award for Drama
Writers' Guild of Alberta
11759 Groat Rd, Edmonton, AB T5M 3K6, Canada
Tel: 780-422-8174 *Toll Free Tel:* 800-665-5354 (AB only) *Fax:* 780-422-2663 (attn WGA)
E-mail: mail@writersguild.ca
Web Site: writersguild.ca
Key Personnel
Exec Dir: Carol Holmes *E-mail:* carol.holmes@writersguild.ca

Communs & Partnerships Coord: Ellen Kartz *E-mail:* ellen.kartz@writersguild.ca
Memb Servs Coord: Giorgia Severini
Progs Coord: Natalie Cook *E-mail:* natalie.cook@writersguild.ca; Julie Robinson *E-mail:* julie.robinson@writersguild.ca
Established: 1982
Alberta literary award, author must be resident of Alberta, CN.
Award: $1,500 plus leather-bound copy of book
Closing Date: Annually, Dec 31
Presented: Alberta Book Awards Gala
Branch Office(s)
505 21 Ave SW, Calgary, AB T2S 0G9, Canada, Prog Coord: Samantha Warwick *Tel:* 403-265-2226 *E-mail:* samantha.warwick@writersguild.ca

The Ripped Bodice Awards for Excellence in Romantic Fiction
The Ripped Bodice
3806 Main St, Culver City, CA 90232
Tel: 424-603-4776
E-mail: therippedbodicela@gmail.com
Web Site: www.therippedbodicela.com
Key Personnel
Co-Owner: Bea Koch; Leah Koch
Established: 2019
Celebrates the best books of the year in the best-selling romance genre. Twelve honorees will be selected each year. The book must be published in the previous year & be a romance novel.
Award: $1,000 to each honoree plus $100 donation to charity of their choice
Presented: Valentine's Day

RISING STAR Award
Women's Fiction Writers Association (WFWA)
PO Box 190, Jefferson, OR 97352
E-mail: risingstar@womenfictionwriters.org
Web Site: wfwa.memberclicks.net/rising-star-award
Key Personnel
Pres: Tasha Seegmiller *E-mail:* president@womensfictionwriters.org
VP, Communs: Kerstin March
VP, Fin & Treas: M M Finck *E-mail:* treasurer@womensfictionwriters.org
Membership Dir: Rebecca Hodge
Secy: Michele Montgomery *E-mail:* michele@mimont.com
Annual award for an unpublished writer of women's fiction. Open to all unagented writers who have never been published in the book-length women's fiction of 60,000 words or more. Award is limited to the first 75 entries. Entry fee: $30 membs, $40 nonmembs. See web site for entry submission details & complete eligibility requirements.
Award: Trophy, digital badge & certificate of display within their online presence
Closing Date: April 21
Presented: WFWA Retreat Banquet, Sept

Jack D Rittenhouse Award
Publishers Association of the West Inc (PubWest)
17501 Hill Way, Lake Oswego, OR 97035
Tel: 503-901-9865
E-mail: pubwest1@gmail.com
Web Site: pubwest.org
Key Personnel
Pres: Colleen Dunn Bates
Honors individuals who have made outstanding contributions to the book community in the West.
Presented: PubWest Annual Conference

Max Ritvo Poetry Prize
Milkweed Editions
1011 Washington Ave S, Suite 300, Minneapolis, MN 55415-1246
Tel: 612-332-3192 *Toll Free Tel:* 800-520-6455

Web Site: milkweed.org/max-ritvo-poetry-prize
Key Personnel
Publr & CEO: Daniel Slager
Mktg Dir: Joanna R Demkiewicz *Tel:* 612-215-2556 *E-mail:* joanna_demkiewicz@milkweed.org
Bookseller & Events Coord: Daley Farr *Tel:* 612-215-2540 *E-mail:* daley_farr@milkweed.org
Established: 2018
Awarded to an outstanding author of a debut collection of poems. Poets may submit one complete, book-length collection, defined as a ms of 48 or more pages. Poems may have been previously published in periodicals, chapbooks, or anthologies, but the poet must not have published, nor committed to publish, a book-length collection of poems. Mss must be of original work by a single poet; translations are not eligible. The submitting poet must reside in the US. Only online submissions via Submittable will be considered. Entry fee: $25.
Award: $10,000 & publication contract
Closing Date: June 30

Riverby Awards
John Burroughs Association Inc
261 Floyd Ackert Rd, New York, NY 12493
Mailing Address: PO Box 439, West Park, NY 12493
Tel: 212-769-5169 *Fax:* 212-313-7182
E-mail: info@johnburroughsassociation.org
Web Site: www.johnburroughsassociation.org
Key Personnel
Pres: Joan Burroughs *E-mail:* jjjburroughs@yahoo.com
To recognize writers, artists & publishers who produce outstanding nature literature for young readers that contains perceptive & artistic accounts of direct experiences in the world of nature.
Award: John Burroughs Certificate of Recognition to authors, illustrators & publishers of each selected book
Closing Date: Annually in Dec
Presented: Annual Meeting, Yale Club, New York, NY, 1st Monday in April

Roanoke-Chowan Award for Poetry
North Carolina Literary & Historical Association
Affiliate of Historical Book Club of North Carolina
4610 Mail Service Ctr, Raleigh, NC 27699-4610
Tel: 919-807-7290 *Fax:* 919-733-8807
Web Site: www.history.ncdcr.gov/affiliates/lit-hist/awards/awards.htm
Key Personnel
Awards Coord: Michael Hill *E-mail:* michael.hill@ncdcr.gov
Established: 1953
Award for the best published book of poetry by a legal or actual resident of North Carolina for at least 3 years prior to the end of the contest period.
Award: Cup
Closing Date: Annually, July 15
Presented: Raleigh, NC, Annually in Nov

Rocky Mountain Book Award
PO Box 42, Lethbridge, AB T1J 3Y3, Canada
Tel: 403-381-7164
E-mail: rockymountainbookaward@shaw.ca
Web Site: www.rmba.info
Key Personnel
Contact: Michelle Dimnik
Established: 2001
Alberta children's choice book award, grades 4-7.
Closing Date: Jan 15
Presented: Winner announced electronically on April 22

Theodore Roethke Prize, see The Hopwood Award Theodore Roethke Prize

Rogers Writers' Trust Fiction Prize

The Writers' Trust of Canada
600-460 Richmond St W, Toronto, ON M5V
1Y1, Canada
Tel: 416-504-8222 *Toll Free Tel:* 877-906-6548
Fax: 416-504-9090
E-mail: info@writerstrust.com
Web Site: www.writerstrust.com
Key Personnel
Exec Dir: Charlie Foran *Tel:* 416-504-8222 ext
244 *E-mail:* cforan@writerstrust.com
Prog Coord: Devon Jackson *Tel:* 416-504-8222
ext 248 *E-mail:* djackson@writerstrust.com
Established: 1997
Awarded to the year's best novel or collection of
short stories.
Other Sponsor(s): Rogers Communications
Award: $50,000 (winner), $5,000 (finalists)
Presented: The Writers' Trust Awards, Toronto,
ON, CN, Annually in Nov

Sami Rohr Prize for Jewish Literature

Jewish Book Council
520 Eighth Ave, 4th fl, New York, NY 10018
Tel: 212-201-2920 *Fax:* 212-532-4952
E-mail: jbc@jewishbooks.org
Web Site: www.jewishbookcouncil.org
Key Personnel
Exec Dir: Naomi Firestone-Teeter
Prog Dir: Evie Saphire-Bernstein *E-mail:* evie@
jewishbooks.org
Established: 2006
Annual award which recognizes the unique role
of contemporary writers in the transmission &
examination of Jewish values & is intended to
encourage & promote outstanding writing of
Jewish interest. Rewards an emerging writer
whose work has demonstrated a fresh vision &
evidence of future potential. Recipients must
have written a book of exceptional literary
merit that stimulates an interest in themes of
Jewish concern. Fiction & nonfiction books
will be considered in alternate years.
Award: $100,000
Presented: Center for Jewish History, March

Rosenthal Family Foundation Awards

American Academy of Arts & Letters
633 W 155 St, New York, NY 10032
Tel: 212-368-5900 *Fax:* 212-491-4615
E-mail: academy@artsandletters.org
Web Site: artsandletters.org
Key Personnel
Exec Dir: Cody Upton
Award for a work of fiction published during
the preceding year that is a considerable lit-
erary achievement. Second award is given for a
young painter of distinction.
Other Sponsor(s): The Rosenthal Foundation
Award: $10,000 each

Margaret W Rossiter History of Women in Science Prize

History of Science Society
Affiliate of American Council of Learned Soci-
eties
440 Geddes Hall, Notre Dame, IN 46556
Tel: 574-631-1194
E-mail: info@hssonline.org
Web Site: www.hssonline.org
Key Personnel
Exec Dir: Robert Jay Malone
Recognition of an outstanding book (or, in even-
numbered years, article) on the history of
women in science. Books & articles published
in the preceding 4 years are eligible.
Award: $1,000
Closing Date: April 1

Rotary Club of Charlottetown Royalty Creative Writing Awards for Young People

Prince Edward Island Writers' Guild

81 Prince St, Charlottetown, PE C1A 4R3,
Canada
E-mail: peiliteraryawards@gmail.com
Web Site: www.peiwritersguild.com
Elementary, junior & high school students may
write on the topic of their choice & submit in
1 of 4 categories: Early Elementary (grades 1-
3), Late Elementary (grades 4-6), Junior High
(grades 7-9) & Senior High (grades 10-12).
A maximum of 5 pages of poetry or 10 page
short story will constitute an entry. No entry
fee. Prince Edward Island residents only. See
web site for complete entry requirements.
Award: Cash prizes for 1st, 2nd & 3rd place
Closing Date: Jan 31
Presented: Cox & Palmer Island Literary Awards
Gala, Annually in Spring

Lois Roth Award

Modern Language Association of America (MLA)
85 Broad St, Suite 500, New York, NY 10004-
2434
SAN: 202-6422
Tel: 646-576-5141; 646-576-5000 *Fax:* 646-458-
0030
E-mail: awards@mla.org
Web Site: www.mla.org
Key Personnel
Coord, Book Prizes: Annie M Reiser
E-mail: areiser@mla.org
Established: 1999
Committee solicits submissions of outstanding
translations into English of a book-length lit-
erary work. Translations published in 2020 are
eligible. For consideration, submit 6 copies &
12-15 pages of original text in its original lan-
guage taken from the beginning, middle & end
of the work & a letter identifying the translator
& the date of publication. Translators need not
be members of the association.
Award: Cash award & certificate
Closing Date: May 1, 2021
Presented: MLA Convention, Jan 2022

Hazel Rowley Prize

Biographers International Organization (BIO)
PO Box 33020, Santa Fe, NM 87594
Web Site: biographersinternational.org
Key Personnel
Admin & Membership Coord: Lori Izykowski
E-mail: lori@biographersinternational.org
Established: 2014
Annual award for the best book proposal by a
first-time biographer. Open to citizens or per-
manent residents of the US & Canada, writing
in English, working on a biography that has
not yet been commissioned, contracted, or self-
published & who have never published a biog-
raphy, history, or work of narrative nonfiction.
Applicants should submit online entry form
& upload proposal, writing sample & resume.
Application fee: $50.
Award: $2,000 & submission to an established
literary agent for consideration
Closing Date: March 1
Presented: BIO Annual Conference, May

Lexi Rudnitsky First Book Prize in Poetry

Persea Books
90 Broad St, Suite 2100, New York, NY 10004
SAN: 212-8233
Tel: 212-260-9256
E-mail: info@perseabooks.com
Web Site: www.perseabooks.com
Key Personnel
Pres & Publr: Michael Braziller
VP & Edit Dir: Karen Braziller
Poetry Ed: Gabriel Fried
Publicity: Jonah Fried
Established: 2006
First book by an American woman poet.

Award: $1,000, publication & expenses paid res-
idency at the Civitella Ranieri Foundation in
Italy
Closing Date: Oct 31

William B Ruggles Journalism Scholarship

National Institute for Labor Relations Research
5211 Port Royal Rd, Suite 510, Springfield, VA
22151
Tel: 703-321-9606 *Fax:* 703-321-7143
Web Site: www.nilrr.org
Key Personnel
Scholarship Admin: Cathy Jones *E-mail:* clj@
nrtw.org
Established: 1974
Scholarship grant for students majoring in jour-
nalism or related majors. Based on scholastic
ability demonstrating an understanding of the
economic, political & social implications of
compulsory unionism.
Award: $2,000
Closing Date: Annually, Dec 31 (postmark or
electronic submission)
Presented: Annually in April/May

Stephan Russo Book Prize, see The Goddard
Riverside Stephan Russo Book Prize

The Cornelius Ryan Award

Overseas Press Club of America (OPC)
40 W 45 St, New York, NY 10036
Tel: 212-626-9220 *Fax:* 212-626-9210
E-mail: info@opcofamerica.org
Web Site: www.opcofamerica.org
Key Personnel
Exec Dir: Patricia Kranz
Awarded annually for best nonfiction book on
international affairs.
Award: Certificate & cash award
Closing Date: Last week of Jan
Presented: New York City, NY, Late April

Dr Tony Ryan Book Award

Castleton Lyons
2469 Ironworks Pike, Lexington, KY 40511
Tel: 859-455-9222
Web Site: www.castletonlyons.com
Key Personnel
Commercial Mgr: Stuart Fitzgibbon
E-mail: sfitzgibbon@castletonlyons.com
Off Mgr: Betsy Hager *E-mail:* bhager@
castletonlyons.com
Established: 2007
Awarded to the author of the best book, in any
category, on any aspect of Thoroughbred horse
racing. The book must have been officially
released in the previous calendar year. Re-
releases or updates of previously published
books are not eligible. Six copies of each book
must be submitted along with a signed nomination form.
Award: $10,000 & trophy, finalists receive $1,000
& trophy
Closing Date: Dec 31
Presented: Annually in April

SAH Prize for Historical Fiction

Society of American Historians (SAH)
Affiliate of American Historical Association
2950 Broadway, New York, NY 10027
Tel: 212-854-6495
E-mail: amhistsociety@columbia.edu
Web Site: sah.columbia.edu
Key Personnel
Pres: Mary Kelley
VP: Ann Fabian
Exec Secy: Andie Tucher
Established: 1993
For a book of historical fiction on an American
subject which makes a significant contribution
to historical understanding, portrays authen-

tically the people & events of the historical past & displays skills in narrative construction & prose style. Must be published & have a copyright within 2 years prior to prize year. Awarded biennially in odd-numbered years.
Award: $2,000 & certificate
Closing Date: Dec 1, 2020
Presented: New York, NY, May 2021

Saint Louis Literary Award
Saint Louis University Library Associates
Pius XII Memorial Library, 3650 Lindell Blvd, St Louis, MO 63108
Tel: 314-977-3100; 314-977-3087 *Fax:* 314-977-3108
E-mail: slula@slu.edu
Web Site: lib.slu.edu/about/associates/literary-award
Key Personnel
Pres: Lana Pepper
VP: Ted Ibur
Off Admin: Donna Neeley
Established: 1967
For body of author's work. No applications; awardee chosen by committee.
Award: Honorarium, Citation
Presented: Award Ceremony, Sheldon Concert Hall, Autumn

San Francisco Writing Contest (SFWC)
San Francisco Writers Conference
1029 Jones St, San Francisco, CA 94109
Tel: 415-673-0939
E-mail: sfwriterscon@aol.com
Web Site: www.sfwriters.org
Key Personnel
Contest Dir: Laurie McLean
All entries must be original, unpublished work not submitted to this contest in previous years & be in English. Complete an official entry form & attach to the entry. Entry fee: $40. Four categories: adult fiction, nonfiction/memoir & children's/young adult. Register online at www.sfwriters.org.
Award: $500 (grand prize), $100 (1st prize in each category)
Closing Date: Dec
Presented: Annual Conference, InterContinental Mark Hopkins Hotel, San Francisco, CA

The Carl Sandburg Literary Awards
The Chicago Public Library Foundation & Chicago Public Library
20 N Michigan Ave, Suite 520, Chicago, IL 60602
Tel: 312-201-9830 *Fax:* 312-201-9833
Web Site: www.cplfoundation.org
Key Personnel
Pres & CEO: Rhona Frazin *E-mail:* rfrazin@cplfoundation.org
Established: 2000
Honors a significant work or a body of work that has enhanced the public's awareness of the written word & reflects the library's commitment to the freedom of all people reading, discovery & creativity.
Award: $10,000
Presented: The Forum, University of Illinois at Chicago, Annually in Oct

Ada Sanderson Memorial
The Poetry Society of Virginia
900 Timber Creek Place, Virginia Beach, VA 23464
E-mail: poetryinva@aol.com
Web Site: poetrysocietyofvirginia.org
Key Personnel
Pres: Robert P Arthur *E-mail:* robert.peebles.arthur@gmail.com
Exec Dir: Guy Terrell *E-mail:* guy.terrell@earthlink.net

Adult Contest Chair: Steven Blythe
E-mail: stevenblythepoetry@gmail.com
All entries must be in English, orginal & unpublished. Submit 2 copies, each having the category name & number on top left of page. Only one poem per category; entries will not be returned. Subject: nature; any form; 48 line limit. Entry fee: $4 nonmembs.
Award: $100
Closing Date: Jan
Presented: Annual PSV Awards Ceremony, April

Mari Sandoz Award
Nebraska Library Association
PO Box 21756, Lincoln, NE 68542-1756
E-mail: nebraskalibraries@gmail.com
Web Site: www.nebraskalibraries.org
Key Personnel
Exec Dir: Nicole Zink
E-mail: nlaexecutivedirector@gmail.com
Established: 1971
Given annually to a distinguished Nebraska author.
Award: Plaque
Closing Date: May 30
Presented: NLA/NSLA Fall Convention, Late Oct

Ivan Sandrof Lifetime Achievement Award
National Book Critics Circle
c/o 310 Lewis Ave, Brooklyn, NY 11221
E-mail: info@bookcritics.org
Web Site: bookcritics.org/awards
Key Personnel
VP, Membership & Awards: Yahdon Israel
E-mail: yahdonisrael@bookcritics.org
Contact: Michael Schaub *E-mail:* mschaubtx@gmail.com
Awarded annually to a person or institution who has, over time, made significant contributions to book culture. Nominations from members only.

William Saroyan International Prize for Writing
William Saroyan Foundation
Admin, Saroyan Prize Committee, Stanford University Libraries, 557 Escondido Mall, Stanford, CA 94305-6004
Tel: 650-736-9538
Web Site: library.stanford.edu/saroyan
Key Personnel
Contact: Sonia Lee *E-mail:* sonialee@stanford.edu
Established: 2002
Biennial competition for newly published books. The 2022 prize will be for books published in 2020 or 2021. Entry form & 5 copies of publication required. Entry fee: $50.
Other Sponsor(s): The Stanford University Libraries
Award: $5,000 each in fiction & nonfiction
Closing Date: Jan 31, 2022

May Sarton Award
New England Poetry Club
46 Wallace St, Somerville, MA 02144
E-mail: info@nepoetryclub.org
Web Site: www.nepoetryclub.org
Key Personnel
Pres: Mary Buchinger
VP: Hillary Sallick
Treas: Linda Haviland Conte
Honorary awards for work that inspires other poets. Chosen by board of directors.
Award: $250 & publication of poem on NEPC web site
Closing Date: Annually, May 31
Presented: Announced online Aug/Sept

May Sarton New Hampshire Poetry Prize
Bauhan Publishing LLC

44 Main St, 2nd fl, Peterborough, NH 03458
Mailing Address: PO Box 117, Peterborough, NH 03458
Tel: 603-567-4430
Web Site: www.bauhanpublishing.com
Key Personnel
Publr: Sarah Bauhan *E-mail:* sbauhan@bauhanpublishing.com
Edit Dir: Mary Ann Faughnan
E-mail: mafaughnan@bauhanpublishing.com
Established: 2010
Awarded annually for a book-length collection of poetry. The book must be previously unublished as a whole. Collection must be written or translated into English. The poetry within can be on any topic & in any form. Entry fee: $25 per ms.
Award: $1,000, book publication, 100 complimentary copies & distribution through Casemate | IPM

Sarton Women's Book Awards™
Story Circle Network
PO Box 1616, Bertram, TX 78605-1616
E-mail: sartonprize@storycircle.org
Web Site: www.storycircle.org/SartonLiteraryAward
Awarded annually to women authors writing chiefly about women in memoir, biography & fiction published in the US & Canada selected from works submitted. Limited to submissions originally written in English & published by small/independent publishers, university presses & author-publishers (self-publishing authors). Judging is conducted in 2 rounds. Professional librarians not affiliated with SCN select the winner & finalists.
Awards are presented in 5 categories: Memoir; Nonfiction: Biography, Collective biography, Edited diaries, Scholarly studies of women's literature, Anthologies; Contemporary Fiction; Historical Fiction; Young Adult & New Adult Fiction.
Lesbian entries are welcome in all categories.
Entry fees: $90 early bird, $110 regular.
See web site for full guidelines.
Closing Date: Mid-Nov

Saturnalia Books Poetry Prize
Saturnalia Books
105 Woodside Rd, Ardmore, PA 19003
Tel: 267-278-9541
Web Site: www.saturnaliabooks.org
Key Personnel
Publr: Henry Israeli *E-mail:* hisraeli@aol.com
Established: 2003
Recognizes a poetry ms of high merit.
Award: $2,000 & publication
Closing Date: Annually, April 1

SATW Foundation Lowell Thomas Travel Journalism Competition
Society of American Travel Writers Foundation
306 Summer Hill Dr, Fredericksburg, TX 78654
Tel: 281-217-2872
E-mail: awards@satwf.com
Web Site: www.satwfoundation.org
Key Personnel
Pres: David G Molyneaux
Established: 1985
Premier awards for the best work in travel journalism. Competition is open to all North American journalists & is judged by leading schools of journalism. There are 20-plus categories, including individual & publication awards. Among them: Grand Award for Travel Journalist of the Year for a portfolio of work, Best Newspaper Travel Coverage, Best Travel Magazine, Best Travel Coverage in Other Magazines, Best Guidebook, Best Travel Book, Best Online Travel Journalism Site & categories for writing, photography, audio broadcast, video

broadcast, multimedia work & apps. For entry
details & forms, see web site. New materials
usually updated early February annually.
Award: Nearly $20,000 total in prize money:
$1,500 (top prize), $500 (1st place)
Closing Date: April 1 (subject to change)
Presented: Location varies

Aldo & Jeanne Scaglione Prize for a Translation of a Literary Work
Modern Language Association of America (MLA)
85 Broad St, Suite 500, New York, NY 10004-2434
SAN: 202-6422
Tel: 646-576-5141; 646-576-5000 *Fax:* 646-458-0030
E-mail: awards@mla.org
Web Site: www.mla.org
Key Personnel
Coord, Book Prizes: Annie M Reiser
   E-mail: areiser@mla.org
Awarded annually for an outstanding translation
into English of a book-length literary work;
books must have been published in 2020.
Translators need not be members of the MLA.
For consideration, submit 6 copies & 12-15
pages of the text in its original language taken
from the beginning, middle & end of the work.
Award: Cash award & certificate
Closing Date: May 1
Presented: MLA Convention, Jan 2022

Aldo & Jeanne Scaglione Prize for a Translation of a Scholarly Study of Literature
Modern Language Association of America (MLA)
85 Broad St, Suite 500, New York, NY 10004-2434
SAN: 202-6422
Tel: 646-576-5141; 646-576-5000 *Fax:* 646-458-0030
E-mail: awards@mla.org
Web Site: www.mla.org
Key Personnel
Coord, Book Prizes: Annie M Reiser
   E-mail: areiser@mla.org
Established: 1993
Awarded biennially for an outstanding translation
into English of a book-length work of literary
history, literary criticism, philology or literary
theory published in 2019 or 2020. For consid-
eration, submit 4 copies.
Award: Cash award & certificate
Closing Date: May 1
Presented: MLA Convention, Jan 2022

Aldo & Jeanne Scaglione Prize for Comparative Literary Studies
Modern Language Association of America (MLA)
85 Broad St, Suite 500, New York, NY 10004-2434
SAN: 202-6422
Tel: 646-576-5141; 646-576-5000 *Fax:* 646-458-0030
E-mail: awards@mla.org
Web Site: www.mla.org
Key Personnel
Coord, Book Prizes: Annie M Reiser
   E-mail: areiser@mla.org
Established: 1992
Prize awarded annually for an outstanding schol-
arly work by a current member of the MLA in
the field of comparative literary studies involv-
ing at least 2 literatures, published in 2020. For
consideration, submit 4 copies.
Award: Cash award & certificate
Closing Date: May 1
Presented: MLA Convention, Jan 2022

Aldo & Jeanne Scaglione Prize for French & Francophone Studies
Modern Language Association of America (MLA)

85 Broad St, Suite 500, New York, NY 10004-2434
SAN: 202-6422
Tel: 646-576-5141; 646-576-5000 *Fax:* 646-458-0030
E-mail: awards@mla.org
Web Site: www.mla.org
Key Personnel
Coord, Book Prizes: Annie M Reiser
   E-mail: areiser@mla.org
Established: 1992
Awarded annually for an outstanding scholarly
work by a current member of the MLA in the
field of French or Francophone linguistic or lit-
erary studies published in 2020. Books that are
primarily translations will not be considered.
For consideration, submit 4 copies.
Award: Cash award & certificate
Closing Date: May 1
Presented: MLA Convention, Jan 2022

Aldo & Jeanne Scaglione Prize for Italian Studies
Modern Language Association of America (MLA)
85 Broad St, Suite 500, New York, NY 10004-2434
SAN: 202-6422
Tel: 646-576-5141; 646-576-5000 *Fax:* 646-458-0030
E-mail: awards@mla.org
Web Site: www.mla.org
Key Personnel
Coord, Book Prizes: Annie M Reiser
   E-mail: areiser@mla.org
Established: 2000
Awarded each odd-numbered year to the author
of an outstanding scholarly book on any phase
of Italian literature or culture or comparative
literature involving Italian by a current MLA
member for books published in 2020. For con-
sideration, submit 4 copies.
Award: Cash award & certificate
Closing Date: May 1
Presented: MLA Convention, Jan 2022

Aldo & Jeanne Scaglione Prize for Studies in Germanic Languages & Literatures
Modern Language Association of America (MLA)
85 Broad St, Suite 500, New York, NY 10004-2434
SAN: 202-6422
Tel: 646-576-5141; 646-576-5000 *Fax:* 646-458-0030
E-mail: awards@mla.org
Web Site: www.mla.org
Key Personnel
Coord, Book Prizes: Annie M Reiser
   E-mail: areiser@mla.org
Established: 1992
Awarded biennially in even-numbered years to a
current MLA member for an outstanding schol-
arly work on the linguistics or literatures of the
Germanic languages including Danish, Dutch,
German, Icelandic, Norwegian, Swedish &
Yiddish & published 2020 or 2021. For con-
sideration, submit 4 copies, a letter identifying
the work & confirming the author's member-
ship.
Award: Cash award & certificate
Closing Date: May 1, 2022
Presented: MLA Convention, Jan 2023

Aldo & Jeanne Scaglione Prize for Studies in Slavic Languages & Literatures
Modern Language Association of America (MLA)
85 Broad St, Suite 500, New York, NY 10004-2434
SAN: 202-6422
Tel: 646-576-5141; 646-576-5000 *Fax:* 646-458-0030
E-mail: awards@mla.org
Web Site: www.mla.org

Key Personnel
Coord, Book Prizes: Annie M Reiser
   E-mail: areiser@mla.org
Established: 1993
Awarded biennially in odd-numbered years for an
outstanding scholarly work on the linguistics or
literatures of the Slavic languages published in
2019 or 2020. Works of literary history, literary
criticism, philology & literary theory are eligible. Books that are primarily translations will
not be considered. Authors need not be members of the MLA. For consideration, submit 4
copies.
Award: Cash award & certificate
Closing Date: May 1
Presented: MLA Convention, Jan 2022

Aldo & Jeanne Scaglione Publication Award for a Manuscript in Italian Literary Studies
Modern Language Association of America (MLA)
85 Broad St, Suite 500, New York, NY 10004-2434
SAN: 202-6422
Tel: 646-576-5141; 646-576-5000 *Fax:* 646-458-0030
E-mail: awards@mla.org
Web Site: www.mla.org
Key Personnel
Coord, Book Prizes: Annie M Reiser
   E-mail: areiser@mla.org
Established: 1998
Awarded annually to the author of an outstanding
ms dealing with any aspect of the languages
& literatures of Italy, including medieval Latin
& comparative studies or intellectual history
of the work's main point is related to the hu-
manities. Ms must be under consideration or
accepted for publication by a not-for-profit
member of the AUPresses before the award
deadline; authors must be current members of
the MLA residing in the US or CN. For consideration, submit 4 copies, plus contact & biographical information.
Award: Cash award & certificate
Closing Date: June 1
Presented: MLA Convention, Washington, DC,
Jan 6-9, 2022

William Sanders Scarborough Prize
Modern Language Association of America (MLA)
85 Broad St, Suite 500, New York, NY 10004-2434
SAN: 202-6422
Tel: 646-576-5141; 646-576-5000 *Fax:* 646-458-0030
E-mail: awards@mla.org
Web Site: www.mla.org
Key Personnel
Coord, Book Prizes: Annie M Reiser
   E-mail: areiser@mla.org
Established: 2001
Annual prize for an outstanding scholarly study
of Black American literature or culture pub-
lished the previous calendar year. Author need
not be a member of the MLA. For considera-
tion, submit 4 copies.
Award: Cash award & certificate
Closing Date: May 1
Presented: MLA Convention, Jan 2022

SCBWI Work-In-Progress Grants
Society of Children's Book Writers & Illustrators
(SCBWI)
6363 Wilshire Blvd, Suite 425, Los Angeles, CA
90048
Tel: 323-782-1010; 310-403-0675 (cell) *Fax:* 323-782-1892
E-mail: grants@scbwi.org; scbwi@scbwi.org
Web Site: www.scbwi.org
Key Personnel
Pres: Stephen Mooser *E-mail:* stephenmooser@
scbwi.org

Exec Dir: Lin Oliver *E-mail:* linoliver@scbwi.org
Established: 1978

The General Work-In-Progress Grant, the Work-In-Progress Grant for Nonfiction Research, the Work-In-Progress Grant for a Contemporary Novel for Young People & the Grant for a Work by an Author Who Has Never Been Published have been established to assist children's book writers in the completion of a specific project. Must be SCBWI member to qualify.

Award: Winning works shown to editors & agents
Closing Date: Annually in March
Presented: Annually in Aug

William D Schaeffer Environmental Award
PRINTING United Alliance
10015 Main St, Fairfax, VA 22031-3489
Tel: 703-385-1335 *Toll Free Tel:* 888-385-3588
 Fax: 703-273-0456
E-mail: assist@printing.org; marketing@printing.org
Web Site: www.printing.org/programs/awards/william-d-schaeffer-environmental-award
Key Personnel
Pres & CEO: Ford Bowers *E-mail:* fbowers@printing.org
Established: 1990

Honors significant contributions to environmental awareness by an individual in the printing industry. See web site for more information.

Award: Engraved plaque
Closing Date: Jan 31
Presented: PRINTING United Alliance Spring Administrative Meeting, April-June
Branch Office(s)
1325 "G" St NW, Suite 500, Washington, DC 20005
2000 Corporate Dr, Suite 205, Wexford, PA 15090 *Tel:* 412-741-6860 *Toll Free Tel:* 800-910-4283 *Fax:* 412-741-2311

Nicholas Schaffner Award for Music in Literature
Schaffner Press
PO Box 41567, Tucson, AZ 85717
Web Site: www.schaffnerawards.com
Key Personnel
Publr: Tim Schaffner *E-mail:* tim@schaffnerpress.com

Given to the writer of an unpublished ms who submits a literary work in the English language, either fiction, poetry or nonfiction that deals in some way with the subject of music (of any genre or period) & its influence. Entry fee: $25. See web site for submission style & format.

Award: Contract & $1,000 advance for book publication
Closing Date: Jan 28

Bernadotte E Schmitt Grants
American Historical Association (AHA)
400 "A" St SE, Washington, DC 20003
Tel: 202-544-2422 *Fax:* 202-544-8307
E-mail: awards@historians.org
Web Site: www.historians.org

Awarded to support research in the history of Europe, Africa & Asia. Only members of the Association are eligible. The grants are intended to further research in progress & may be used for travel to a library or archive, for microfilms, photographs, or photocopying. Preference will be given to those with specific research needs, such as the completion of a project or completion of a discrete segment thereof. Preference will be given to advanced doctoral students, non-tenured faculty & unaffiliated scholars. All updated info on web site. Winners notified by e-mail mid-May.

Award: Individual grants will not exceed $1,500
Closing Date: Annually, Feb 15
Presented: June

Schneider Family Book Awards
The American Library Association (ALA)
225 N Michigan Ave, Suite 1300, Chicago, IL 60601
Tel: 312-944-6780 *Toll Free Tel:* 800-545-2433
 Fax: 312-440-9374
E-mail: ala@ala.org
Web Site: www.ala.org/awardsgrants/schneider-family-book-award
Key Personnel
Prog Offr: Cheryl M Malden *Tel:* 312-280-3247
 Fax: 312-944-3897 *E-mail:* cmalden@ala.org
Established: 2003

Awards to honor an author or illustrator for a book that embodies an artistic expression of the disability experience for a child & adolescent audiences. Three awards given annually: younger children (ages 0-8), middle grades (ages 9-13) & teens (ages 14-18). Full eligibility requirements & application instructions on web site.

Award: 3 awards $5,000 each & framed plaque. When a picture book wins, $5,000 is divided equally between author & illustrator
Closing Date: Dec 1

Ruth & Sylvia Schwartz Children's Book Awards
Ruth Schwartz Foundation
c/o Ontario Arts Council, 121 Bloor St E, 7th fl, Toronto, ON M4W 3M5, Canada
Tel: 416-961-1660 *Toll Free Tel:* 800-387-0058
 (ON) *Fax:* 416-961-7796 (Ontario Arts Council); 416-969-7450 (Ontario Arts Foundation)
E-mail: info@arts.on.ca; foundation@arts.on.ca
Web Site: www.arts.on.ca; ontarioartsfoundation.on.ca/pages/ruth-sylvia-schwartz-awards
Key Personnel
Exec Dir, Ontario Arts Foundation: Alan F Walker *Tel:* 416-969-7413 *E-mail:* awalker@arts.on.ca
Dir of Admin, Ontario Arts Foundation: Ann Boyd *Tel:* 416-969-7411 *E-mail:* aboyd@arts.on.ca
Assoc Awards Offr, Ontario Arts Council: Carolyn Gloude *Tel:* 416-969-7423
 E-mail: cgloude@arts.on.ca
Established: 1976

Annual awards to recognize artistic excellence in writing & illustration in Canadian children's literature.

Other Sponsor(s): Ontario Arts Council; Ontario Arts Foundation
Award: $6,000 each for picture book & young adult/middle reader
Presented: An Ontario, CN public school, May

Science in Society Journalism Awards
National Association of Science Writers (NASW)
PO Box 7905, Berkeley, CA 94707
Tel: 510-647-9500
Web Site: www.nasw.org
Key Personnel
Exec Dir: Tinsley Davis *E-mail:* director@nasw.org
Established: 1972

Awarded annually to provide recognition for investigative reporting about the sciences & their impact on society, for material published or broadcast between the period of January 1-December 31. Publishers & broadcasters will also receive certificates of recognition.

Award: $2,500, Certificate of Recognition in each category, travel to awards presentation for 1 author or representative
Closing Date: Feb 1 (postmark)
Presented: Annual Meeting, Oct

The Robert S Sergeant Memorial
The Poetry Society of Virginia
900 Timber Creek Place, Virginia Beach, VA 23464

E-mail: poetryinva@aol.com
Web Site: poetrysocietyofvirginia.org
Key Personnel
Pres: Robert P Arthur *E-mail:* robert.peebles.arthur@gmail.com
Exec Dir: Guy Terrell *E-mail:* guy.terrell@earthlink.net
Adult Contest Chair: Steven Blythe
 E-mail: stevenblythepoetry@gmail.com

All entries must be in English, original & unpublished. Submit 2 copies, each having the category name & number on top left of page. Subject: birds; any form; 48 line limit. Entry fee: $4 nonmembs.

Award: $50
Closing Date: Jan
Presented: Annual PSV Awards Ceremony, April

SFC Literary Prize
St Francis College
180 Remsen St, Brooklyn, NY 11201
Web Site: www.sfc.edu/news/sfcliteraryprize
Key Personnel
Contact: Prof Ian Maloney *E-mail:* imaloney@sfc.edu

Biennial award to offer support & encouragement to the literary community & mid-career authors who have recently published their 3rd to 5th work of fiction. Self-published books & English translations are considered.

Award: $50,000
Presented: Brooklyn Book Festival Gala, Sept 2021

SFWA Nebula Awards
Science Fiction & Fantasy Writers of America Inc (SFWA)
PO Box 3238, Enfield, CT 06083-3238
Tel: 860-698-0536
E-mail: office@sfwa.org
Web Site: www.sfwa.org
Key Personnel
Pres: Cat Rambo *E-mail:* cat.rambo@sfwa.org
VP: Erin M Hartshorn *E-mail:* erin.hartshorn@sfwa.org
Treas & CFO: Bud Sparhawk *E-mail:* bud.sparhawk@sfwa.org
Secy: Curtis Chen *E-mail:* curtis.chen@sfwa.org
Nebula Awards Comm: Dawn Bonanno
 E-mail: nac@sfwa.org
Established: 1965

Winners are selected by the members of the SFWA in the categories of novel, novella, novelette & short story. Andre Norton award for Outstanding Young Adult Fantasy or Science Fiction first presented in 2006. Also Grand Master for lifetime achievement in science fiction & fantasy, not necessarily awarded annually. Ray Bradbury Award for outstanding dramatic presentation first presented in April 2009.

Award: Lucite trophy for Grand Master & Norton; bronze sculpture for Ray Bradbury Award

Shamus Awards
The Private Eye Writers of America (PWA)
3665 S Needles Hwy, 7G, Laughlin, NV 89029
Web Site: www.privateeyewriters.com
Key Personnel
Awards Chair: Gay Toltl Kinman
 E-mail: gaykinman@gaykinman.com

Awards for private eye novels & short stories first published in the US in the year preceding the award. Eligible works must feature as a main character a person paid for investigative work but not employed for that work by a unit of government. See web site for submission guidelines. Categories: Best Hardcover PI Novel, Best First PI Novel, Best Original Paperback PI Novel, Best PI Short Story.

Closing Date: March 31
Presented: Annually in Autumn

Shaughnessy Cohen Prize for Political Writing
The Writers' Trust of Canada
600-460 Richmond St W, Toronto, ON M5V
1Y1, Canada
Tel: 416-504-8222 *Toll Free Tel:* 877-906-6548
Fax: 416-504-9090
E-mail: info@writerstrust.com
Web Site: www.writerstrust.com
Key Personnel
Exec Dir: Charlie Foran *Tel:* 416-504-8222 ext
244 *E-mail:* cforan@writerstrust.com
Prog Coord: Devon Jackson *Tel:* 416-504-8222
ext 248 *E-mail:* djackson@writerstrust.com
Established: 2000
Awarded for a nonfiction book that captures a
political subject of relevance to the Canadian
reader & enhances understanding of the issue.
The winning work combines compelling new
insights with depth of research & is of signifi-
cant literary merit.
Other Sponsor(s): Aimia Inc
Award: $25,000 (winner), $2,500 (finalists)
Presented: Politics & the Pen, Ottawa, ON, CN,
Annually in Spring

Mina P Shaughnessy Prize
Modern Language Association of America (MLA)
85 Broad St, Suite 500, New York, NY 10004-
2434
SAN: 202-6422
Tel: 646-576-5141; 646-576-5000 *Fax:* 646-458-
0030
E-mail: awards@mla.org
Web Site: www.mla.org
Key Personnel
Coord, Book Prizes: Annie M Reiser
E-mail: areiser@mla.org
Established: 1980
Biennial prize awarded in even-numbered years
for an outstanding scholarly book in the fields
of language, culture, literacy & literature with
strong application to the teaching of English,
published in 2020 or 2021. Authors need not
be a member of the MLA. For consideration,
submit 4 copies.
Award: Cash award & certificate
Closing Date: May 1
Presented: MLA Convention, Jan 2023

Shelley Memorial Award
Poetry Society of America (PSA)
15 Gramercy Park, New York, NY 10003
Tel: 212-254-9628
Web Site: poetrysociety.org/awards
Key Personnel
Exec Dir: Matt Brogan *E-mail:* matt@
poetrysociety.org
Deputy Dir: Brett Fletcher Lauer *E-mail:* brett@
poetrysociety.org
Devt Dir: Madeline Weinfield *E-mail:* madeline@
poetrysociety.org
Awarded to a poet, selected with reference to his
or her genius & need, by a jury of 3 poets. By
nomination only.
Award: $6,000-$9,000

Christopher Latham Sholes Award
Council for Wisconsin Writers
c/o 3225 N 91 St, Milwaukee, WI 53222
E-mail: wiswriters@gmail.com
Web Site: wiswriters.org/awards
Key Personnel
Contest Chair: Erik Richardson
E-mail: erichardson@wi.rr.com
Biennial award offered in alternating years from
the Major Achievement Award to honor an in-
dividual or organization for outstanding encour-
agement of Wisconsin writers. No entry fee.
Award: $500
Closing Date: Jan 31
Presented: CWW Annual Banquet, May

**Short Prose Competition for Developing
Writers**
The Writers' Union of Canada (TWUC)
600-460 Richmond St W, Toronto, ON M5V
1Y1, Canada
Tel: 416-703-8982 *Fax:* 416-504-9090
E-mail: info@writersunion.ca
Web Site: www.writersunion.ca
Key Personnel
Competitions Coord: Nancy MacLeod *Tel:* 416-
703-8982 ext 226 *E-mail:* nmacleod@
writersunion.ca
Off Admin: Valerie Laws *Tel:* 416-703-8982 ext
224
Short prose up to 2,500 words by an unpublished
Canadian writer.
Award: $2,500
Closing Date: Annually, March 1

**Edwin "Bud" Shrake Award for Best Short
Nonfiction**
Texas Institute of Letters (TIL)
PO Box 609, Round Rock, TX 78680
Tel: 512-683-5640
E-mail: president@texasinstituteofletters.org
Web Site: www.texasinstituteofletters.org
Key Personnel
Pres: Carmen Tafolla
VP: Sergio Troncoso
Secy: Ann Weisgarber
Treas: W K Stratton
Recording Secy: Kurt Heinzelman
Annual award for best nonfiction writing appear-
ing in a magazine, journal or other periodical
or in a newspaper Sunday supplement. Only
one story per entrant. Guidelines on the web
site.
Award: $1,000
Closing Date: Annually in Jan
Presented: TIL Awards Banquet, Annually in
Spring

Joe Shuster Awards
Canadian Comic Book Creator Awards Associa-
tion (CCBCAA)
305-484 Oriole Pkwy, Toronto, ON M5P 2H8,
Canada
E-mail: info@joeshusterawards.com
Web Site: joeshusterawards.com
Key Personnel
Exec Dir/Nominating & Jury Coord: Kevin A
Boyd *E-mail:* kevin@joeshusterawards.com
Art Dir: Tyrone Biljan *E-mail:* tyrone@
joeshusterawards.com
Established: 2004
Canada's national award that honors & raises the
awareness of Canadians that create, publish
& sell comics, graphic novels & webcomics.
Core categories: Cartoonist (writer/artist), artist,
writer, colorist, cover artist, publisher. Awards
chosen by jury decision. Five additional spe-
cialty awards.
Presented: Late Summer/Early Fall

Robert F Sibert Informational Book Award
Association for Library Service to Children
(ALSC)
Division of The American Library Association
(ALA)
50 E Huron St, Chicago, IL 60611-2795
Tel: 312-280-2163 *Toll Free Tel:* 800-545-2433
Fax: 312-440-9374; 312-280-5271
E-mail: alsc@ala.org
Web Site: www.ala.org/alsc
Key Personnel
Exec Dir: Aimee Strittmatter
E-mail: astrittmatter@ala.org
Deputy Exec Dir: Alena Rivers *Tel:* 800-545-
2433 ext 5866 *E-mail:* arivers@ala.org
Prog Offr, Communs: Laura Schulte-Cooper
Tel: 800-545-2433 ext 2165 *E-mail:* lschulte@
ala.org

Awards Coord: Katie Connelly *Tel:* 800-545-2433
ext 2163 *E-mail:* kconnelly@ala.org
Prog Coord: Ann Michaud *Tel:* 800-545-2433 ext
2166 *E-mail:* amichaud@ala.org
Membership/Mktg Specialist: Elizabeth Serrano
Tel: 800-545-2433 ext 2164 *E-mail:* eserrano@
ala.org
Presented annually to the author of the most dis-
tinguished informational book published in En-
glish during the previous year for its significant
contribution to children's literature.
Award: Medal
Closing Date: Dec 31
Presented: ALA Midwinter Meeting, Jan/Feb

Silver Gavel Awards
American Bar Association
321 N Clark St, Chicago, IL 60654
Tel: 312-988-5719 *Toll Free Tel:* 800-285-2221
(orders) *Fax:* 312-988-5494
Web Site: www.ambar.org/gavelawards
Key Personnel
Staff Liaison: Howard Kaplan
E-mail: howardkaplan@americanbar.org
Div Coord & Contact: Christina Cerveny
E-mail: christina.cerveny@americanbar.org
Prog Specialist & Contact: Pamela Hollins
E-mail: pamela.hollins@americanbar.org
Established: 1958
Media & arts awards competition to recognize
communications media that have been exem-
plary in fostering public understanding of the
law & the legal system during the previous cal-
endar year.
Award: Silver Gavel, Honorable Mentions
Closing Date: Jan
Presented: July

Francis B Simkins Award
Southern Historical Association
University of Georgia, Dept of History, Athens,
GA 30602-1602
Tel: 706-542-8848 *Fax:* 706-542-2455
Web Site: www.thesha.org
Key Personnel
Admin Asst: Frances Berry *E-mail:* manager@
thesha.org
Established: 1977
Awarded for the most distinguished first book by
an author in Southern history over a 2-year pe-
riod. Awarded in odd-numbered years for book
published in 2 previous calendar years.
Award: Cash
Closing Date: March 1
Presented: Annual meeting, odd-numbered years,
Fall

The John Simmons Short Fiction Award
Writers' Workshop, The University of Iowa
102 Dey House, 507 N Clinton St, Iowa City, IA
52242-1000
Tel: 319-335-0416 *Fax:* 319-335-0420
Open to any writer who has not previously published a volume of prose fiction. Revised mss
which have been previously entered may be
resubmitted as well as writers who have published a volume of poetry are eligible. Mss
must be a collection of short stories of at least
150 typewritten pages. Photo copies are acceptable; SASE return packaging must accompany
the mss or these will not be returned. No cash,
checks, or money orders accepted.
Other Sponsor(s): University of Iowa Press
Award: Publication by University of Iowa Press
under the Press's standard contract
Closing Date: Annually, Aug 1-Sept 30
Presented: Annually in Autumn

Charlie May Simon Children's Book Award
Arkansas State Library
Arkansas State Library, Suite 100, 900 W Capitol
Ave, Little Rock, AR 72201-3108
Tel: 501-682-2860 *Fax:* 501-682-1693

Web Site: www.library.arkansas.gov
Key Personnel
Coord, Children's Progs: Cathy Howser
 E-mail: cathy@library.arkansas.gov
Established: 1970
State of Arkansas upper elementary students
 read books selected by the award committee
 throughout the year & vote on favorite choice.
 Most popular book wins award (medallion)
 & 2nd place award rewarded as Honor Book
 (plaque).
Other Sponsor(s): Arkansas Department of Educa-
 tion; Arkansas Reading Association
Award: CMS Medallion for 1st place, plaque for
 Honor Book
Closing Date: Annual vote in April
Presented: Little Rock, AR, Nov

The Simpson Family Literary Prize, see
Simpson/Joyce Carol Oates Prize

Simpson/Joyce Carol Oates Prize
Formerly The Simpson Family Literary Prize
Simpson Literary Project
Lafayette Lib & Learning Ctr Foundation, 3491
 Mount Diablo Blvd, Suite 214, Lafayette, CA
 94549
Tel: 925-283-6513
E-mail: sflpweb@gmail.com
Web Site: www.simpsonliteraryproject.org/
 programs
Key Personnel
Chair, Literary Proj: Joe Di Prisco
Established: 2017
Annual award to a writer who has earned a dis-
 tinguished reputation & the approbation of
 gratitude of readers. There is no application
 process. An anonymous jury selects the recip-
 ient. The winner will give a public reading,
 make a limited number of public appearances
 & be in brief residence at the Lafayette Library
 & the University of California, Berkeley.
Award: $50,000
Presented: Spring

Skipping Stones Honor Awards
Skipping Stones Inc
166 W 12 Ave, Eugene, OR 97401
Mailing Address: PO Box 3939, Eugene, OR
 97403
Tel: 541-342-4956
E-mail: info@skippingstones.org
Web Site: www.skippingstones.org
Key Personnel
Exec Ed: Arun N Toke *E-mail:* editor@
 skippingstones.org
Established: 1993
Honors exceptional multicultural & international
 awareness books, nature/ecology books, bilingual books, teaching resources & educational
 videos/DVDs. A panel of parents, teachers, librarians, students & editors of *Skipping Stones*
 select the honors list in the above categories.
 Entry fee: $50. Winners announced in the Sum-
 mer issue of *Skipping Stones* & on our web
 site.
Award: Honor award certificates, award seals,
 reviews, press releases, e-releases, web site hy-
 perlinks. Also displayed at NAME (National
 Association for Multicultural Education) Conference in November annually. Publicity in
 many educational journals
Closing Date: Annually, Feb 1
Presented: Annually in May

The Skipping Stones Youth Honor Awards
Skipping Stones Inc
166 W 12 Ave, Eugene, OR 97401
Mailing Address: PO Box 3939, Eugene, OR
 97403
Tel: 541-342-4956
E-mail: info@skippingstones.org

Web Site: www.skippingstones.org
Key Personnel
Exec Ed: Arun N Toke *E-mail:* editor@
 skippingstones.org
Established: 1993
Recognizes 10 creative & artistic works (writing,
 art, photo, essays, etc) by young people that
 promote multicultural & nature awareness. En-
 try fee: $5. Everyone who enters the awards
 program receives the Autumn issue with 10
 winners & a few noteworthy entries.
Award: Honor award certificate, subn to *Skipping
 Stones* & 5 nature +/or multicultural books
Closing Date: Annually, June 25
Presented: Winners announced in Autumn issue
 of *Skipping Stones*

Slipstream Annual Poetry Chapbook Contest
Slipstream Press
PO Box 2071, Dept W-1, Niagara Falls, NY
 14301
Web Site: www.slipstreampress.org
Key Personnel
Co-Ed: Dan Sicoli
Established: 1986
Prize awarded to best 40-page ms of poetry. Entry
 fee: $20.
Award: $1,000 & 50 copies of book
Closing Date: Dec 1

Donald Smiley Prize
Canadian Political Science Association
260 rue Dalhousie St, Suite 204, Ottawa, ON
 K1N 7E4, Canada
Tel: 613-562-1202 *Fax:* 613-241-0019
E-mail: cpsa-acsp@cpsa-acsp.ca
Web Site: www.cpsa-acsp.ca
Key Personnel
Admin: Michelle Hopkins
Established: 1995
Awarded annually to the best book published in
 English or in French in the field relating to the
 study of government & politics in Canada. To
 be eligible, a book may be single-authored or
 multi-authored. Single-authored: author must
 be a member of the CPSA in the year the book
 is considered for the prize. Multi-authored: at
 least one of the authors must be a member of
 the CPSA in the year the book is considered
 for the prize.
Award: Commemorative plaque & receive/share
 the set of books submitted to the CPSA office
Closing Date: Dec
Presented: Annual Conference, University of Alberta, Edmonton, AB, CN, June 2021

Helen C Smith Memorial Award
Texas Institute of Letters (TIL)
PO Box 609, Round Rock, TX 78680
Tel: 512-683-5640
E-mail: president@texasinstituteofletters.org
Web Site: www.texasinstituteofletters.org
Key Personnel
Pres: Carmen Tafolla
VP: Sergio Troncoso
Secy: Ann Weisgarber
Treas: W K Stratton
Recording Secy: Kurt Heinzelman
Annual award for the first best book of poetry by
 a poet with a Texas association. Guidelines on
 the web site.
Award: $1,200
Closing Date: Jan
Presented: TIL Awards Banquet, Spring

**The Jean Kennedy Smith VSA Playwright
Discovery Award**
VSA
Affiliate of The John F Kennedy Center for the
 Performing Arts
2700 "F" St NW, Washington, DC 20566
Tel: 202-416-8898 *Fax:* 202-416-4840

E-mail: vsainfo@kennedy-center.org
Web Site: www.kennedy-center.org/pdp
Key Personnel
Admin Asst, VSA Progs: Megan Bailey *Tel:* 202-
 416-8822 *E-mail:* mebailey@kennedy-center.
 org
Established: 1984
Open to writers with disabilities & groups that include students with disabilities (ages 14-22).
 High school students are invited to explore
 the disability experience through the art of
 script writing. Young writers with disabilities
 & collaborative groups that include students
 with disabilities are encouraged to submit 10-
 minute scripts of any genre. Selected winners
 will receive exclusive access to participate in
 the Kennedy Center American College Theater
 Festival in Washington, DC in April with the
 opportunity to perform & workshop alongside
 the nation's premier collegiate playwrights as
 well as participate in the festival's award ceremony. See web site for more information &
 details on how to enter.
Award: Attend performance of their script at JFK
 Center, scholarship funds
Closing Date: Feb 1
Presented: The John F Kennedy Center for Performing Arts, Washington, DC

The Jeffrey E Smith Editors' Prize
The Missouri Review
357 McReynolds Hall, Columbia, MO 65211
Tel: 573-882-4474 *Toll Free Tel:* 800-949-2505
 Fax: 573-884-4671
Web Site: www.missourireview.com
Key Personnel
Mng Ed: Kate McIntyre *Tel:* 573-882-7127
 E-mail: mcintyrekl@missouri.edu
Established: 1991
Awarded annually in fiction, essay & poetry.
 Entry fee entitles entrant to 1-year subscrip-
 tion. Writers should consult web site or send a
 SASE for guidelines.
Award: $5,000 each (short fiction, essay & po-
 etry) & publication in the Spring issue
Closing Date: Oct 1
Presented: Spring

Kay Snow Writing Contest
Willamette Writers
5331 SW Macadam Ave, Suite 258, PMB 215,
 Portland, OR 97239
Tel: 901-200-5385
E-mail: wilwrite@willamettewriters.org
Web Site: willamettewriters.org
Key Personnel
VP & Secy: Gail Pasternack *E-mail:* secretary@
 willamettewriters.org
Awards Dir: Blythe Ayne *E-mail:* awards@
 willamettewriters.org
Established: 1971
Annual writing competition in 6 categories: fic-
 tion, nonfiction, YA/MG, poetry, screenplay &
 college student. Entry fee: $10 members, $15
 general public, $10 college students, free for
 el-hi students. Winners listed on Willamette
 Writers web site.
Award: $100 (1st prize) & 1-day admission to the
 Willamette Writers Conference, $25 (2nd prize)
 & 1-day admission to the Willamette Writers
 Conference, $50 (3rd prize)
Presented: Annual Conference, Aug

The Society of Midland Authors Awards
The Society of Midland Authors (SMA)
PO Box 10419, Chicago, IL 60610
E-mail: info@midlandauthors.com
Web Site: www.midlandauthors.com
Key Personnel
Awards Coord: Marlene Targ Brill
Established: 1915
Juried award offers prizes in each of 6 literary
 categories: children's fiction, children's non-

fiction, adult fiction & nonfiction, biography & poetry. Awarded annually to authors in any of the Midland states: Illinois, Indiana, Iowa, Kansas, Michigan, Minnesota, Missouri, Nebraska, North Dakota, Ohio, South Dakota & Wisconsin.
Award: Monetary award $500 & plaque
Closing Date: Jan
Presented: Chicago, IL, 2nd Tuesday in May

The Society of Southwestern Authors Writing Contest

The Society of Southwestern Authors (SSA)
PO Box 30355, Tucson, AZ 85751-0355
E-mail: info@ssa-az.org
Web Site: www.ssa-az.org
Key Personnel
Pres: Rajendra Srivastava
  E-mail: rajendrasrivastava@outlook.com
VP: Chris Stern *E-mail:* azwritten@gmail.com
Treas: Jay McCall *E-mail:* jmcca11415@msn.com
Recording Secy: Mary Ann Carman
  E-mail: macarman@centurylink.net
Established: 1972
Annual awards for short fiction, 2,500 words max; personal essays & memoirs, 2,500 words max; poetry, 40 lines max.
Award: $200 (1st prize), $100 (2nd prize), $50 (3rd prize)
Closing Date: Sept 30
Presented: Awards Forum, Nov

Sophie Kerr Prize

Washington College
c/o College Relations Off, 300 Washington Ave, Chestertown, MD 21620
Tel: 410-778-2800 *Toll Free Tel:* 800-422-1782
  Fax: 410-810-7150
Web Site: www.washcoll.edu
Key Personnel
Dir, Communs: Marcia Landskroener *Tel:* 410-778-7797 *E-mail:* mlandskroener2@washcoll.edu
Established: 1968
Annual literary award to graduating senior. Only open to undergraduates of Washington College.
Award: $65,000
Closing Date: April
Presented: Washington College Commencement, Chestertown, MD, May

Southeast Review Narrative Nonfiction Contest

The Southeast Review
Florida State University, Dept of English, Tallahassee, FL 32306
E-mail: southeastreview@gmail.com
Web Site: www.southeastreview.org
Key Personnel
Ed: Alex Quinlan
Established: 1986
Best previously unpublished 6,000 word (maximum) nonfiction essay. Include a brief (100 word) bio. All entries will be considered for publication. $16 entry fee per nonfiction entry.
Other Sponsor(s): Florida State University English Department Creative Writing Program
Award: $500
Closing Date: April 1 (postmark)

Southeast Review's Gearhart Poetry Contest

The Southeast Review
Florida State University, Dept of English, Tallahassee, FL 32306
E-mail: southeastreview@gmail.com
Web Site: www.southeastreview.org
Key Personnel
Ed: Alex Quinlan
Established: 1996
Award for best poem. All entries will be considered for publication. $16 entry fee for up to 3 poems, no more than 10 pages total.

Other Sponsor(s): Florida State University English Department Creative Writing Program
Award: $500
Closing Date: April 1 (postmark)

Southeastern Theatre Conference New Play Project

Southeastern Theatre Conference (SETC)
1175 Revolution Mill Dr, Suite 14, Greensboro, NC 27405
Tel: 336-272-3645 *Fax:* 336-272-8810
E-mail: info@setc.org
Web Site: www.setc.org
Key Personnel
Chair, New Play Proj: Todd Ristau
New play contest. Submission begins March 1.
Award: $1,000, travel & expenses to annual convention
Closing Date: Annually, June 1
Presented: Southeastern Theatre Conference Convention, March of the year following the closing date

Southern Book Prize

Formerly The Pat Conroy Southern Book Prize
Southern Independent Booksellers Alliance
51 Pleasant Ridge Dr, Asheville, NC 28805
Tel: 803-994-9530 *Fax:* 309-410-0211
Web Site: www.sibaweb.com/siba-book-award
Key Personnel
Exec Dir: Linda-Marie Barrett
  E-mail: lindamarie@sibaweb.com
Nominations accepted from SIBA member booksellers. Books must be Southern in nature, or by a Southern author & published in the previous calendar year.
Closing Date: Feb 14
Presented: July 4

Southern Books Competition

Southeastern Library Association
PO Box 950, Rex, GA 30273
Tel: 678-466-4334 *Fax:* 678-466-4349
Web Site: selaonline.org
Key Personnel
Chmn: Camille McCutcheon
Admin Servs: Dr Gordon N Baker
  E-mail: gordonbaker@clayton.edu
Established: 1952
Recognition for excellence in bookmaking awarded biennially in even-numbered years for a title published during the previous 2 years. Trade publishers, university presses, specialty publishers & private presses located in Alabama, Arkansas, Florida, Georgia, Kentucky, Louisiana, Mississippi, North Carolina, South Carolina, Tennessee, Virginia, West Virginia or Puerto Rico are eligible to enter the competition. Awards are given based on design, typography & quality of production. Winners are displayed at SELA Conference & in a traveling exhibit available to institutions & organizations. It has been borrowed throughout the South, Canada, Scandinavia, Russia & South Africa.
Award: Published recognition list. Rotating & permanent display of winning books
Presented: SELA Conference, even-numbered years, Oct

Southern Playwrights Competition

Jacksonville State University, Dept of English
700 Pelham Rd N, Jacksonville, AL 36265-1602
Tel: 256-782-5412
Web Site: www.jsu.edu/english/southpla.html
Key Personnel
Coord: Joy Maloney *E-mail:* jmaloney@jsu.edu
Established: 1988
Identify & encourage the best of Southern play writing. Entries accepted beginning Sept 1.
Award: $1,000 honorarium & possible production of winning entry
Closing Date: Annually, Jan 15

Terry Southern Prize

The Paris Review Foundation
544 W 27 St, New York, NY 10001
Tel: 212-343-1333
E-mail: queries@theparisreview.org
Web Site: www.theparisreview.org
Honors "humor, wit & sprezzatura" in work from either *The Paris Review* or the *Daily*.
Award: $5,000

Sovereign Award for Outstanding Writing

The Jockey Club of Canada
Woodbine Sales Pavilion, 555 Rexdale Blvd, Toronto, ON M9W 5L2, Canada
Mailing Address: PO Box 66, Sta B, Toronto, ON M9W 5K9, Canada
Tel: 416-675-7756 *Fax:* 416-675-6378
E-mail: jockeyclub@bellnet.ca
Web Site: www.jockeyclubcanada.com; www.sovereignawards.ca
Key Personnel
Exec Dir: Melanie O'Sullivan
Established: 1975
Submissions must be of Canadian Thoroughbred Racing content. See guidelines on web site.
Award: Bronze statue of Saint Simon
Closing Date: Annually, Dec 31
Presented: Ontario, CN, Annually, date TBD upon confirmation of the first day of racing for that calendar year

The Sow's Ear Poetry Prize & The Sow's Ear Chapbook Prize

The Sow's Ear Poetry Review
Division of The Word Process Inc
1748 Cave Ridge Rd, Mount Jackson, VA 22842
Tel: 540-477-3257
E-mail: sepoetryreview@gmail.com
Web Site: sowsearpoetry.org
Key Personnel
Mng Ed: Sarah Kohrs
Ed: Kristin Zimet
Established: 1988
Single poem & chapbook.
Award: $1,000 each (poem & chapbook), plus 25 copies for chapbook winner
Closing Date: Annually, May 1 (chapbook), Nov 1 (poem)

Spark Award

Society of Children's Book Writers & Illustrators (SCBWI)
6363 Wilshire Blvd, Suite 425, Los Angeles, CA 90048
Tel: 323-782-1010 *Fax:* 323-782-1892
E-mail: grants@scbwi.org; scbwi@scbwi.org
Web Site: www.scbwi.org
Key Personnel
COO: Sara Rutenberg *E-mail:* sararutenberg@scbwi.org
Established: 2013
Annual award that recognizes excellence in a children's book published through a non-traditional publishing route.
Closing Date: Dec 15
Presented: March 31

John Spray Mystery Award

Canadian Children's Book Centre
40 Orchard View Blvd, Suite 217, Toronto, ON M4R 1B9, Canada
Tel: 416-975-0010 *Fax:* 416-975-8970
E-mail: info@bookcentre.ca
Web Site: www.bookcentre.ca
Key Personnel
Exec Dir: Charlotte Teeple *E-mail:* charlotte@bookcentre.ca
Lib Coord: Meghan Howe *E-mail:* meghan@bookcentre.ca
Mktg & Web Site Coord: Camilia Kahrizi
  E-mail: camilia@bookcentre.ca

Prog Coord: Shannon Howe Barnes
E-mail: shannon@bookcentre.ca
Established: 2011
Awarded to a Canadian author for excellence in mystery writing for children & adolescents.
Other Sponsor(s): John Spray
Award: $5,000
Closing Date: Annually in mid-Dec

Spur Awards
Western Writers of America Inc (WWA)
271 CR 219, Encampment, WY 82325
Tel: 307-329-8942
E-mail: wwa.moulton@gmail.com
Web Site: westernwriters.org/spur-awards/
Key Personnel
Pres: Kirk Ellis *E-mail:* president@ westernwriters.org
Exec Dir & Secy-Treas: Candy Moulton
E-mail: wwa.moulton@gmail.com
Established: 1953
Western fiction/nonfiction (various categories).
Award: Plaques & recognition
Closing Date: Jan 4 of year following publication
Presented: Annual Convention, June

The Edna Staebler Award for Creative Non-Fiction
Wilfrid Laurier University
Office of the Dean, Faculty of Arts, 75 University Ave W, Waterloo, ON N2L 3C5, Canada
Tel: 519-884-1970 (ext 3361)
E-mail: staebleraward@wlu.ca
Web Site: wlu.ca/staebleraward
Key Personnel
Dir, Communs & Pub Aff: Kevin Crowley *Tel:* 519-884-0710 ext 3070
E-mail: kcrowley@wlu.ca
Admin Asst to Dean of Arts: Cathy Mahler
Tel: 519-884-0710 ext 3361 *E-mail:* cmahler@ wlu.ca
Established: 1991
Annual literary award for a first or second published book of creative nonfiction with a Canadian locale +/or significance published in the previous calendar year. Open to works & distinguished by first-hand research, well-crafted interpretive writing & creative use of language or approach to the subject matter. Writer must be Canadian. Award is open to print books & ebooks.
Award: $10,000
Closing Date: See web site
Presented: Wilfrid Laurier University, Nov, announcement in Sept

Stanley Drama Award
Wagner College
One Campus Rd, Staten Island, NY 10301
Tel: 718-390-3223 *Fax:* 718-390-3323
Web Site: wagner.edu/theatre/stanley-drama
Key Personnel
Assoc Professor: Todd Alan Price *E-mail:* todd. price@wagner.edu
Established: 1957
Award given for original full-length play or musical which has not been professionally produced or received trade book publication. Writers of musicals are urged to submit music on tape or CD as well as books & lyrics. Consideration will also be given to a series of 2 or 3 thematically related one-act plays. Scripts must be accompanied by a SASE. Former winners are not eligible to compete. Applications are obtained by sending SASE or online. A reading fee of $30 must accompany submission.
Award: $2,000
Closing Date: Oct 31
Presented: Annually in April

STAR Award
Women's Fiction Writers Association (WFWA)

PO Box 190, Jefferson, OR 97352
E-mail: staraward@womenfictionwriters.org
Web Site: wfwa.memberclicks.net/star-award
Key Personnel
Pres: Tasha Seegmiller *E-mail:* president@ womensfictionwriters.org
VP, Communs: Kerstin March
VP, Fin & Treas: M M Finck *E-mail:* treasurer@ womensfictionwriters.org
Membership Dir: Rebecca Hodge
Secy: Michele Montgomery *E-mail:* michele@ mimont.com
Annual awards for published women's fiction authors. Work must be book-length (60,000 words or more), have an ISBN & have a copyright date in the calendar year prior to the award year. Two categories: General & outstanding debut. Contest is limited to the first 50 entries in each category. Entry fee: $40 membs, $50 nonmembs. See web site for entry submission details & complete eligibility requirements.
Award: Trophy, digital badge for web site & stickers for book covers
Closing Date: Jan 30
Presented: Annual WFWA Retreat, Sept

Agnes Lynch Starrett Poetry Prize
University of Pittsburgh Press
7500 Thomas Blvd, Pittsburgh, PA 15260
Tel: 412-383-2456 *Fax:* 412-383-2466
E-mail: info@upress.pitt.edu
Web Site: upittpress.org/prize/agnes-lynch-starrett-poetry-prize/; www.upress.pitt.edu
Key Personnel
Dir: Peter W Kracht *E-mail:* pkracht@upress.pitt. edu
Established: 1981
Open to any poet who has not had a full-length book previously published. Submit typed 48-100 page poetry mss on white paper with SASE & check or money order of $25 for each ms submitted. See web site for complete rules.
Award: $5,000 & publication
Closing Date: March 1-April 30 (postmark)
Presented: Pittsburgh, PA, Autumn

Stegner Fellowship
Stanford University Creative Writing Program
Stanford University, Dept of English, Stanford, CA 94305-2087
Tel: 650-723-0011 *Fax:* 650-723-3679
E-mail: stegnerfellowship@stanford.edu
Web Site: creativewriting.stanford.edu
Key Personnel
Prog Asst: Katherine Batanero
Fellowship; residence required for 2 years at Stanford beginning Autumn quarter each year.
Award: $26,000, required tuition & health insurance
Closing Date: Dec 1

Jean Stein Book Award, see PEN/Jean Stein Book Award

Stephan G Stephansson Award for Poetry
Writers' Guild of Alberta
11759 Groat Rd, Edmonton, AB T5M 3K6, Canada
Tel: 780-422-8174 *Toll Free Tel:* 800-665-5354 (AB only) *Fax:* 780-422-2663 (attn WGA)
E-mail: mail@writersguild.ca
Web Site: writersguild.ca
Key Personnel
Exec Dir: Carol Holmes *E-mail:* carol.holmes@ writersguild.ca
Communs & Partnerships Coord: Ellen Kartz
E-mail: ellen.kartz@writersguild.ca
Memb Servs Coord: Giorgia Severini
Progs Coord: Natalie Cook *E-mail:* natalie.cook@ writersguild.ca; Julie Robinson *E-mail:* julie. robinson@writersguild.ca

Established: 1982
Alberta literary award, author must be resident of Alberta.
Award: $1,500 plus leather-bound copy of book
Closing Date: Annually, Dec 31
Presented: Alberta Book Awards Gala, AB, CN
Branch Office(s)
505 21 Ave SW, Calgary, AB T2S 0G9, Canada, Prog Coord: Samantha Warwick *Tel:* 403-265-2226 *Fax:* 403-234-9532 (attn: WGA)
E-mail: samantha.warwick@writersguild.ca

John Steptoe Award for New Talent, see Coretta Scott King - John Steptoe Award for New Talent

Wallace Stevens Award
The Academy of American Poets Inc
75 Maiden Lane, Suite 901, New York, NY 10038
Tel: 212-274-0343
E-mail: awards@poets.org
Web Site: www.poets.org
Key Personnel
Pres & Exec Dir: Jennifer Benka
E-mail: jenbenka@poets.org
Devt, Membership & Communs Sr Mgr: Molly Walsh *E-mail:* mwalsh@poets.org
Ad & Mktg Sr Mgr: Michelle Campagna
E-mail: mcampagna@poets.org
Sr Progs Mgr: Nikay Paredes *Tel:* 212-274-0343 ext 13 *E-mail:* nparedes@poets.org
Established: 1994
Awarded annually to recognize outstanding & proven mastery in the art of poetry. Recipients are chosen by the Academy of American Poets Board of Chancellors. No applications are accepted.

Bram Stoker Awards®
Horror Writers Association (HWA)
PO Box 56687, Sherman Oaks, CA 91413
Tel: 818-220-3965
E-mail: admin@horror.org
Web Site: horror.org/awards/stokers.htm
Key Personnel
Co-Chmn: Ron Breznay; Rena Mason
Established: 1988
11 award categories: novel, first novel, short fiction, long fiction, young adult, fiction collection, poetry collection, anthology, screenplay, graphic novel & nonfiction.

Stone Award for Lifetime Literary Achievement
Oregon State University
College of Liberal Arts, 214 Bexell Hall, Corvallis, OR 97331
Tel: 541-737-0561
Web Site: liberalarts.oregonstate.edu/stone-award
Honors a major American author who has created a body of critically acclaimed literary work & has been a dedicated mentor to succeeding generations of young writers. Awarded biennially in even-numbered years.
Other Sponsor(s): Patrick F & Vicki Stone
Award: $20,000

Stonewall Book Awards
The American Library Association Gay, Lesbian, Bisexual & Transgender Round Table
225 N Michigan Ave, Suite 1300, Chicago, IL 60601
Toll Free Tel: 800-545-2433
E-mail: adultstonewall@gmail.com; youthstonewall@gmail.com
Web Site: www.ala.org/glbtrt/award/stonewall
Key Personnel
Staff Liaison: Kristin Lahurd
Three awards presented annually to honor books of exceptional merit relating to the GLBT experience: Barbara Gittings Literature Award; Is-

rael Fishman Nonfiction Award; Mike Morgan
& Larry Romans Children's & Young Adult
Literature Award. Award is announced in January.
Award: $1,000 & commemorative plaque
Closing Date: Dec 31
Presented: ALA Annual Conference, Annually in
June/July

Story Monsters Approved! Program
Story Monsters LLC
4696 W Tyson St, Chandler, AZ 85226-2903
Tel: 480-940-8182 *Fax:* 480-940-8787
Web Site: www.StoryMonstersApproved.com
Key Personnel
Pres: Linda F Radke *E-mail:* Linda@
StoryMonsters.com
Designation to recognize & honor accomplished
authors in the field of children's literature, as
well as children's products that inspire, inform,
teach, or entertain. Each honoree gains permission to use the seal on collateral material, web
site & on reprints of book or product cover, a
fill-in-the-blank news release to send to their
own local media contacts, book or product listing on Story Monster LLC's web site & social
media pages & a book or product listing in
Story Monsters Ink® magazine.
Program is open to printed children's books published in any calendar year or any products for
children. Books entered must be printed in English. Authors age 17 & younger must have
parent or guardian permission to enter. Nonrefundable entry fee $85 for one title in one
category, $99 for one product in one category.
Award: Certificate, 50 seals & iron-on patch

The Story Prize
41 Watchung Plaza, No 384, Montclair, NJ 07042
Tel: 973-932-0324
E-mail: info@thestoryprize.org
Web Site: www.thestoryprize.org
Key Personnel
Dir: Larry Dark *E-mail:* ldark@thestoryprize.org
Established: 2004
Annual book award honoring the author of an
outstanding collection of short fiction.
Award: $20,000, $5,000 (runners up)
Closing Date: July 15 (books published Jan-June),
Nov 15 (books published July-Dec)
Presented: The New School, 66 W 12 St, New
York, NY, March

The Story Prize Spotlight Award
The Story Prize
41 Watchung Plaza, No 384, Montclair, NJ 07042
Tel: 973-932-0324
E-mail: info@thestoryprize.org
Web Site: www.thestoryprize.org
Key Personnel
Dir: Larry Dark *E-mail:* ldark@thestoryprize.org
Annual award to a short story collection of exceptional merit.
Award: $1,000
Closing Date: July 15 (books published Jan-June),
Nov 15 (books published July-Dec)
Presented: March

Elizabeth Matchett Stover Memorial Award
Southwest Review
PO Box 750374, Dallas, TX 75275-0374
Fax: 214-768-1408
E-mail: swr@mail.smu.edu
Web Site: www.smu.edu/southwestreview
Key Personnel
Ed-in-Chief: Greg Brownderville
Mng Ed: Preston Hutcherson *Tel:* 214-768-1036
Established: 1978
Awarded annually to the author of the best poem
or group of poems published in the *Southwest
Review* during the preceding year.
Award: $300

Lucien Stryk Asian Translation Prize
American Literary Translators Association
(ALTA)
University of Arizona, Esquire Bldg, No 205,
1230 N Park Ave, Tucson, AZ 85721
Tel: 520-621-1757
Web Site: literarytranslators.org/awards/lucien-
stryk-prize
Key Personnel
Exec Dir: Elisabeth Jaquette *E-mail:* elisabeth@
literarytranslators.org
Communs & Awards Mgr: Rachael Daum
Tel: 413-200-0459 *E-mail:* rachaeldaum@
literarytranslators.org
Prog Mgr: Kelsi Vananda *E-mail:* kelsi@
literarytranslators.org
Secy: Jessica Sue Vocatura *E-mail:* jessica@
literarytranslators.org
Established: 2009
Annual award to recognize the importance of
Asian translation for international literature
& to promote the translation of Asian works
into English. Both translators & publishers are
invited to submit titles. Works must be book-
length translations into English of poetry or
source texts from, but not solely commentaries
on, Zen Buddhism; translations from Chinese,
Hindi, Japanese, Kannada, Korean, Sanskrit,
Tamil, Thai, or Vietnamese into English; published in the previous calendar year. Submissions accepted beginning in January.
Award: $5,000
Closing Date: April

Jessamy Stursberg Poetry Contest for Youth
The League of Canadian Poets
2 Carlton St, Suite 1519, Toronto, ON M5B 1J3,
Canada
Tel: 416-504-1657
E-mail: info@poets.ca
Web Site: poets.ca
Key Personnel
Exec Dir: Lesley Fletcher *E-mail:* lesley@poets.
ca
Communs Coord: Laura O'Brien *E-mail:* laura@
poets.com
Established: 1995
Seeking poems by young poets across the country. Two age categories with 3 prizes awarded
in both: Junior (grades 7-9) & Senior (grades
10-12). All winning poems will be published in
the e-zine. Submission open August 1.
Award: $400 cash (1st place), $350 cash (2nd
place), $300 cash (3rd place); all winners will
be featured on the League of Canadian Poets'
web site
Closing Date: Annually, Dec 1
Presented: Annually, last week of April

Sudden Fiction Contest
Berkeley Fiction Review
c/o ASUC Publications, Univ of California, 10-B
Eshleman Hall, Berkeley, CA 94720-4500
E-mail: bfictionreview@yahoo.com
Web Site: www.ocf.berkeley.edu/~bfr/
Key Personnel
Mng Ed: Jennifer Brown; Brighton Early
All entries must be 1,000 words or less; typed,
double-spaced, with a 12 point font; include
cover letter & e-mail only. Entry fee $6 ($4
each additional story).
Award: $200 (1st place); 1st, 2nd & 3rd place are
published in upcoming newsletter

Ronald Sukenick Innovative Fiction Contest,
see The FC2 Ronald Sukenick Innovative
Fiction Contest

Hollis Summers Poetry Prize
Ohio University Press
Alden Library, Suite 101, 30 Park Place, Athens,
OH 45701-2901

Tel: 740-593-1154
Web Site: www.ohioswallow.com/poetry_prize;
ohiouniversitypress.submittable.com/submit
(online submissions)
Key Personnel
Interim Dir & Prodn Mgr: Beth Pratt *Tel:* 740-
593-1162 *E-mail:* prattb@ohio.edu
This competition invites writers to submit unpublished collections of original poems. Individual
collections must be the work of a single author.
Translations are not accepted. Submit a ms of
60-95 pages of a poetry collection & a $30 entry fee.
Award: $1,000 & publication
Closing Date: Dec 1

Sunburst Award for Excellence in Canadian
Literature of the Fantastic
The Sunburst Award Society
2 Farm Greenway, Toronto, ON M3A 3M2,
Canada
E-mail: secretary@sunburstaward.org
Web Site: www.sunburstaward.org
Juried award which celebrates exceptional writing in 3 categories: adult, young adult & short
story. The awards are presented to the best
Canadian speculative fiction novel, book-length
collection, or short story published any time
during the previous calendar year. See web site
for eligibility criteria & submissions info.
Award: $1,000 each adult & young adult, $500
short story, plus Sunburst medallion
Closing Date: Jan 31
Presented: Annually in Fall

Sydney Taylor Book Awards
Association of Jewish Libraries (AJL) Inc
Affiliate of American Library Association (ALA)
PO Box 1118, Teaneck, NJ 07666
Tel: 201-371-3255
E-mail: chair@sydneytaylorbookaward.org; info@
jewishlibraries.org
Web Site: www.sydneytaylorbookaward.org
Key Personnel
Pres: Amalia Warshenbrot
Established: 1968
Literary content for outstanding children's books
in field of Jewish literature. Three categories
of prizes: younger readers, older readers, teen
readers.
Award: $500 prize for each category; $500 award
to illustrator of Young Readers Award book
Closing Date: Dec 1
Presented: AJL Annual Convention, June

Sydney Taylor Manuscript Award
Association of Jewish Libraries (AJL) Inc
Affiliate of American Library Association (ALA)
204 Park St, Montclair, NJ 07042
Tel: 201-371-3255
E-mail: info@jewishlibraries.org
Web Site: jewishlibraries.org
Key Personnel
Chpn: Aileen Grossberg *E-mail:* stmacajl@aol.
com
Annual award to encourage outstanding Jewish
themed fiction written by an unpublished author. Story will appeal to all children ages 8-13
& to help launch new children's writers in their
careers.
Award: $1,000
Closing Date: Sept 30
Presented: AJL Annual Convention, June

Charles S Sydnor Award
Southern Historical Association
University of Georgia, Dept of History, Athens,
GA 30602-1602
Tel: 706-542-8848 *Fax:* 706-542-2455
Web Site: www.thesha.org

Key Personnel
Admin Asst: Frances Berry *E-mail:* manager@
  thesha.org
Established: 1956
Awarded for the most distinguished book in
  Southern history published in odd-numbered
  years. Awarded in even-numbered years.
Award: Cash
Closing Date: March 1
Presented: Annual meeting, even-numbered years,
  Fall

TAA Council of Fellows
Textbook & Academic Authors Association
  (TAA)
PO Box 367, Fountain City, WI 54629
E-mail: info@taaonline.net
Web Site: www.taaonline.net/council-of-fellows
Key Personnel
Exec Dir: Michael Spinella *Tel:* 973-943-0501
  E-mail: michael.spinella@taaonline.net
Dir, Publg & Opers: Kim Pawlak *Tel:* 608-687-
  3106 *E-mail:* kim.pawlak@taaonline.net
Dir, Instl Memberships & Meetings: Maureen
  Foerster *Tel:* 608-687-3106 *E-mail:* maureen.
  foerster@taaonline.net
Membership Coord: Bekky Murphy *Tel:* 608-567-
  9060 *E-mail:* bekky.murphy@taaonline.net
Honors distinguished authors who have a long
  record of successful publishing. Any author
  whose textbook or other instructional materials
  have established his/her presence in the market place over time, who has been innovative
  in the presentation of material, is qualified for
  nomination. Members are chosen by a TAA
  Selection Committee based on a set of criteria which includes their: level of participation
  in TAA activities; teaching excellence; quality
  & quantity of textbooks (if textbook authors);
  quality & quantity of professional journal articles, monographs & edited books (if academic
  authors).
Closing Date: Jan 15

The Tampa Review Prize for Poetry
Tampa Review
University of Tampa Press, 401 W Kennedy Blvd,
  Tampa, FL 33606
Tel: 813-253-6266
E-mail: utpress@ut.edu
Web Site: tampareview.ut.edu
Key Personnel
Ed: Richard Mathews
Edit Asst: Sean Donnelly
Established: 2001
Award: $2,000 & book publication in hardcover
  & paperback
Closing Date: Dec 31

Helen Tartar First Book Subvention Award
American Comparative Literature Association
  (ACLA)
University of South Carolina, Dept of Languages,
  Literature & Cultures, 1620 College St, Rm
  817, Columbia, SC 29208
Tel: 803-777-3021
E-mail: info@acla.org
Web Site: www.acla.org/prize-awards/helen-tartar-
  first-book-subvention-award
Awarded annually on a competitive basis to first-
  time ACLA-member book authors. Applicants
  who have already secured provisional contracts
  from established academic presses will be
  given special consideration, but a provisional
  contract is not a requirement for the award.
  Subventions will be paid directly to the press.
  Applications should be submitted electronically
  to the ACLA publications committee chair. See
  web site for specific guidelines.
Award: Up to 3 awards $3,500 each

Rennie Taylor & Alton Blakeslee Fellowships in Science Writing
Council for the Advancement of Science Writing
  (CASW)
PO Box 910, Hedgesville, WV 25427
Tel: 304-754-6786
Web Site: www.casw.org
Key Personnel
Exec Dir: Rosalind Reid *E-mail:* rosreid@gmail.
  com
Established: 1975
For tuition & books for graduate study only. On-
  line submissions.
Award: $5,000
Closing Date: Annually in March
Presented: ScienceWriters Meeting, Annually in
  Oct/Nov

TD Canadian Children's Literature Award
Canadian Children's Book Centre
40 Orchard View Blvd, Suite 217, Toronto, ON
  M4R 1B9, Canada
Tel: 416-975-0010 *Fax:* 416-975-8970
E-mail: info@bookcentre.ca
Web Site: www.bookcentre.ca
Key Personnel
Exec Dir: Charlotte Teeple *E-mail:* charlotte@
  bookcentre.ca
Lib Coord: Meghan Howe *E-mail:* meghan@
  bookcentre.ca
Mktg & Web Site Coord: Camilia Kahrizi
  E-mail: camilia@bookcentre.ca
Prog Coord: Shannon Howe Barnes
  E-mail: shannon@bookcentre.ca
Established: 2004
Awarded to a Canadian author/illustrator for the
  most distinguished book of the year.
Other Sponsor(s): TD Bank Group
Award: $30,000 cash each to one English lan-
  guage & one French language book, $10,000 to
  an English language honour book (maximum of
  4), $10,000 to a French language honour book
  (maximum of 4), $2,500 to the publishers of
  the grand prize winning books for promotion &
  publicity purposes
Closing Date: Annually in mid-Dec

Tennessee Arts Commission Fellowships
Tennessee Arts Commission
401 Charlotte Ave, Nashville, TN 37243-0780
Tel: 615-741-1701 *Fax:* 615-741-8559
Web Site: www.tnartscommission.org
Key Personnel
Dir, Literary Arts & Grants Analyst: Lee Baird
  Tel: 615-532-0493 *E-mail:* lee.baird@tn.gov
Annual literary fellowships given to Tennessee
  writers of every genre. Tennessee residents
  only.
Award: $5,000
Closing Date: Jan

The Tenth Gate Prize
The Word Works
Mailing Address: PO Box 42164, Washington,
  DC 20015
Tel: 301-581-9439 *Fax:* 301-581-9443
E-mail: editor@wordworksbooks.org
Web Site: www.wordworksbooks.org
Key Personnel
Pres: Nancy White *E-mail:* nancywhitepoetry@
  gmail.com
Series Ed: Leslie McGrath
Established: 2014
Annual prize for an unpublished ms of poetry
  written in English, by a poet who has previ-
  ously published at least 2 full-length collec-
  tions. Online submissions only; please visit
  web site for guidelines. Submissions should be
  48-80 pages in length. A reading fee of $25 is
  required.
Award: $1,000 & publication
Closing Date: July 15

Texas Bluebonnet Award
Texas Library Association (TLA)
3355 Bee Cave Rd, Suite 401, Austin, TX 78746-
  6763
Tel: 512-328-1518 *Fax:* 512-328-8852
E-mail: tla@txla.org
Web Site: txla.org/tools-resources/reading-lists/
  texas-bluebonnet-award/about/; www.txla.org
Key Personnel
Coord, Membership & Spec Servs: Kelly Dibbens
  Tel: 512-328-1518 ext 153 *E-mail:* kellyd@
  txla.org
Established: 1979
Awarded to favorite title on annual list, voted on
  by 200,000 children, grades 3-6.
Other Sponsor(s): Children's Round Table; Texas
  Association of School Librarians
Award: Medallion in desk mount
Closing Date: Aug 1
Presented: April

Texas Institute of Letters Awards
Texas Institute of Letters (TIL)
PO Box 609, Round Rock, TX 78680
Tel: 512-683-5640
E-mail: president@texasinstituteofletters.org
Web Site: www.texasinstituteofletters.org
Key Personnel
Pres: Carmen Tafolla
VP: Sergio Troncoso
Secy: Ann Weisgarber
Treas: W K Stratton
Recording Secy: Kurt Heinzelman
Established: 1936
Annual award for books published by Texas res-
  idents or on Texas-related subjects. Guidelines
  on the web site.
Award: Eleven cash awards, totalling $22,000
Closing Date: Jan
Presented: TIL Awards Banquet, Spring

Textbook Excellence Award
Textbook & Academic Authors Association
  (TAA)
PO Box 367, Fountain City, WI 54629
E-mail: info@taaonline.net
Web Site: www.taaonline.net/textbook-excellence-
  award
Key Personnel
Exec Dir: Michael Spinella *Tel:* 973-943-0501
  E-mail: michael.spinella@taaonline.net
Dir, Publg & Opers: Kim Pawlak *Tel:* 608-687-
  3106 *E-mail:* kim.pawlak@taaonline.net
Dir, Instl Memberships & Meetings: Maureen
  Foerster *Tel:* 608-687-3106 *E-mail:* maureen.
  foerster@taaonline.net
Membership Coord: Bekky Murphy *Tel:* 608-567-
  9060 *E-mail:* bekky.murphy@taaonline.net
Recognizes excellence in current textbooks &
  learning materials. Works are judged for merit
  in 4 areas: pedagogy; content/scholarship; writ-
  ing; appearance & design. Nomination fee:
  $350 (non-refundable). See web site for nomi-
  nation form & entry guidelines.
Closing Date: Dec 15
Presented: TAA Annual Conference, Annually in
  June

David Thelen Award
The Organization of American Historians (OAH)
112 N Bryan Ave, Bloomington, IN 47408-4141
Tel: 812-855-7311
E-mail: oah@oah.org
Web Site: www.oah.org/awards
Key Personnel
Exec Dir: Beth English *E-mail:* benglish@oah.org
Comm Coord: Kara Hamm *E-mail:* khamm@oah.
  org
Awarded biennially to the author of the best ar-
  ticle on American history written in a foreign
  language. To be eligible, an article may have
  already been published (during January 1, 2019
  through December 31, 2020) or may be an

original work that broadens the presentation of American history. The winning article will illustrate how the understanding of American history can be approached differently when it is conceived in the scholarly or public debates of a country other than the US. Submissions should be interesting, compelling & highlight a way of thinking or writing about the US that offers a perspective most American readers rarely encounter. The award is open to roundtables, keynote addresses, conference papers, or other types of scholarship. The ms should be framed & communicated to people outside the US & written in a language other than English. See web site for complete submission process.
Award: Winning article will be published in the *Journal of American History*
Closing Date: May 1, 2021 (hardcopy postmarked)
Presented: OAH Annual Meeting, Boston, MA, March 31-April 3, 2022

Third Coast Poetry & Fiction Contest
Third Coast Magazine
Western Michigan University English Dept, 1903 W Michigan Ave, Kalamazoo, MI 49008-5331
E-mail: editors@thirdcoastmagazine.com
Web Site: www.thirdcoastmagazine.com/contests
Two awards given annually for a poem & a short story. Submit up to 3 poems or a short story of up to 9,000 words with a $16 entry fee, which includes a subscription to *Third Coast*.
Award: $1,000 & publication in *Third Coast*
Closing Date: Jan 15

3-Day Novel Contest
The Geist Foundation
201-111 W Hastings St, Vancouver, BC V6B 1H4, Canada
Tel: 604-681-9161
E-mail: info@3daynovel.com
Web Site: www.3daynovel.com
Established: 1977
Annual international novel writing competition. Entry fee: $50 ($35 early bird) for US & CN entries; may be postmarked up until 1 day before contest.
Award: Publication (1st prize), $500 (2nd prize), $100 (3rd prize)
Closing Date: Friday before Labor Day (postmark)
Presented: Labor Day weekend

Thriller Awards Competition
International Thriller Writers (ITW)
PO Box 311, Eureka, CA 95502
Web Site: thrillerwriters.org
Key Personnel
Exec Dir: Liz Berry
VP, Awards: Anthony Franze *E-mail:* anthony@anthonyfranzebooks.com
To be eligible, all novels must first be published by an ITW recognized publisher or from an ITW active member during the eligibility period. Works must have been published between September 1 & August 31 of the year preceding the award. Works may be submitted to only one category: Hardcover Novel, First Novel, Short Story, Paperback Original Novel, Young Adult Novel, Ebook Original Novel.
Closing Date: Nov 1
Presented: ITW Gala Banquet, New York, NY, Annually in July

Thurber Prize for American Humor
Thurber House
77 Jefferson Ave, Columbus, OH 43215
Tel: 614-464-1032 *Fax:* 614-280-3645
E-mail: thurberhouse@thurberhouse.org
Web Site: www.thurberhouse.org
Key Personnel
Exec Dir: Laurie Lathan

Deputy Dir: Anne Touvell *Tel:* 614-464-1032 ext 10
Annual award for the most outstanding book of humor writing published in the US. The award is presented by Thurber House, a nonprofit literary center in Columbus, OH & the former home of American humorist, author & New Yorker cartoonist James Thurber.
Award: $5,000, commemorative plaque & a nationwide media campaign
Closing Date: April 1
Presented: Caroline's Comedy Club on Broadway, New York, NY, Fall

James Tiptree Jr Literary Award
James Tiptree Jr Literary Award Council
173 Anderson St, San Francisco, CA 94110
Tel: 415-641-4103
E-mail: info@tiptree.org
Web Site: tiptree.org
Key Personnel
Founder: Karen Joy Fowler; Pat Murphy
Established: 1991
Annual literary prize for science fiction or fantasy that expands or explores our understanding of gender. Nominations are accepted throughout the year on the web site.
Presented: WisCon, Madison, WI, Memorial Day weekend

Arthur Tofte/Betty Ren Wright Children's Literature Award
Council for Wisconsin Writers
c/o 3225 N 91 St, Milwaukee, WI 53222
E-mail: wiswriters@gmail.com
Web Site: wiswriters.org/awards
Key Personnel
Contest Chair: Erik Richardson
   E-mail: erichardson@wi.rr.com
Established: 1966
Annual award for the best children's book published by a Wisconsin-based writer in the contest year. Entry fee: $25 nonmembs.
Award: $500 & 1-week residency at Shake Rag Alley Center for the Arts
Closing Date: Jan 31
Presented: CWW Annual Banquet, May

Toronto Book Awards
Toronto Cultural Partnerships
Division of City of Toronto
c/o Toronto Arts & Culture, City Hall, 9E, 100 Queen St W, Toronto, ON M5H 2N2, Canada
Web Site: www.toronto.ca/book_awards
Key Personnel
Cultural Devt Offr: Christopher Jones *Tel:* 416-392-6832 *E-mail:* cjones2@toronto.ca
Established: 1974
To honor authors of books of literary or artistic merit that are evocative of Toronto published between January 1 & May 31 the preceding year.
Other Sponsor(s): Toronto Public Library (in partnership)
Award: $15,000 annually, $1,000 to each short listed book, usually 4 books, remainder to winner
Closing Date: Last weekday in April
Presented: Toronto, ON, CN, Shortlist announced in Aug & winner in Oct

Towson University Prize for Literature
Towson University
English Dept, 8000 York Rd, Towson, MD 21252
Tel: 410-704-2000 *Fax:* 410-704-3999
Web Site: www.towson.edu/english
Key Personnel
Chair: Dr H George Hahn
Established: 1979
Annual award for a single book or book-length ms of fiction, poetry, drama or imaginative nonfiction by a Maryland writer. Applicant

must have resided in Maryland at least 3 years prior to applying & must be a Maryland resident when the prize is awarded.
Award: $1,000
Closing Date: June 15
Presented: Spring

Translation Projects
National Endowment for the Arts
400 Seventh St SW, Washington, DC 20506-0001
Tel: 202-682-5400; 202-682-5496 (Voice/TTY); 202-682-5034 (lit fellowships hotline)
Fax: 202-682-5609; 202-682-5610
E-mail: litfellowships@arts.gov
Web Site: www.arts.gov
Key Personnel
Grants Dir & Contracts Offr: Nicki Jacobs
   Tel: 202-682-5546 *E-mail:* jacobsn@arts.gov
Fellowships for published translators: for translations of published literary material into English. Applications accepted by genre. Guidelines available on web site.
Award: $12,500 or $25,000, depending on the artistic excellence & merit of the project
Closing Date: Annually in Dec
Presented: Notification by mail, Annually in Aug

Treehouse Climate Action Poem Prize
The Academy of American Poets Inc
75 Maiden Lane, Suite 901, New York, NY 10038
Tel: 212-274-0343
E-mail: academy@poets.org
Web Site: www.poets.org
Key Personnel
Pres & Exec Dir: Jennifer Benka
   E-mail: jenbenka@poets.org
Devt, Membership & Communs Sr Mgr: Molly Walsh *E-mail:* mwalsh@poets.org
Ad & Mktg Sr Mgr: Michelle Campagna
   E-mail: mcampagna@poets.org
Sr Progs Mgr: Nikay Paredes *Tel:* 212-274-0343 ext 13 *E-mail:* nparedes@poets.org
Established: 2019
To honor exceptional poems that help make real for readers the gravity of the vulnerable state of our environment at present. Poets may submit only 1 poem for consideration. Poems must be original works by the poet submitting & be previously unpublished. Poems may be submitted in Spanish but must be accompanied by an English translation. Submissions accepted online only through Submittable. See web site for full guidelines.
Other Sponsor(s): Treehouse Investments
Award: $1,000 (1st prize), $750 (2nd prize), $500 (3rd prize); poems will be published in the *Poem-a-Day* series
Closing Date: Nov 1

Trillium Book Award/Prix Trillium
Ontario Media Development Corp (OMDC)
Division of Ministry of Culture, Ontario Government
South Tower, Suite 501, 175 Bloor St E, Toronto, ON M4W 3R8, Canada
Tel: 416-314-6858 (ext 698) *Fax:* 416-314-6876
Web Site: www.omdc.on.ca
Key Personnel
Consultant, Indus Initiatives: Janet Hawkins
   Tel: 416-642-6698 *E-mail:* jhawkins@omdc.on.ca
Established: 1987
Open to books in any genre; fiction, nonfiction, drama & children's books. There are no restrictions regarding the previous works of the author.
Award: $20,000 to winning authors in English & French; $2,500 to publishers of winning book in English & French
Closing Date: Jan
Presented: Award ceremony, Late Spring

Harry S Truman Book Award
Truman Library Institute
5151 Troost Ave, Suite 300, Kansas City, MO 64110
Tel: 816-400-1212 *Toll Free Tel:* 844-358-5400
Web Site: trumanlibraryinstitute.org
Key Personnel
Book Award Admin: Lisa Sullivan *E-mail:* lisa.sullivan@trumanlibraryinstitute.org
Established: 1963
Biennial award for recognition of the best book published within a 2-year period dealing primarily & substantially with some aspect of the history of the US between April 12, 1945 & January 20, 1953, or with the life or career of Harry S Truman. The award is given in even-numbered years. Five copies of each book entered must be submitted to the Book Award Administrator.
Award: $2,500
Closing Date: Before Jan 20, 2022
Presented: No later than May 8 (Truman's birthday), 2022

Trustus Playwrights' Festival
Trustus Theatre
520 Lady St, Columbia, SC 29201
Tel: 803-254-9732
Web Site: www.trustus.org
Key Personnel
Artistic Dir: Chad Henderson *E-mail:* chad@trustus.org
Established: 1988
Experimental, hard-hitting, off-the-wall comedies or dramas suitable for open-minded audiences. No topic taboo, no musicals or plays for young audiences. Two copies of synopsis, resume & completed application. Send SASE for application & guidelines. Applications available on our web site.
Award: Selected play receives public staged reading & $250, followed by a 1-year development period, full production, additional $500, plus travel/accommodations for festival opening
Closing Date: Dec 1-Feb 1
Presented: Trustus, Aug, full production

Edward & Lily Tuck Award for Paraguayan Literature, see PEN/Edward & Lily Tuck Award for Paraguayan Literature

Kate Tufts Discovery Award
Claremont Graduate University
Harper East, Unit B-7, 160 E Tenth St, Claremont, CA 91711-6165
Tel: 909-621-8974
E-mail: tufts@cgu.edu
Web Site: www.cgu.edu/tufts
Key Personnel
Poetry Awards Coord: Genevieve Kaplan
Established: 1993
Most worthy 1st book of poetry published between July 1 & June 30. Award presented annually for a 1st book by a poet of genuine promise.
Award: $10,000 cash
Closing Date: July 1
Presented: Claremont Graduate University, Claremont, CA, April

Kingsley Tufts Poetry Award
Claremont Graduate University
Harper East, Unit B-7, 160 E Tenth St, Claremont, CA 91711-6165
Tel: 909-621-8974
E-mail: tufts@cgu.edu
Web Site: www.cgu.edu/tufts
Key Personnel
Poetry Awards Coord: Genevieve Kaplan
Established: 1992
Most worthy book of poetry published between July 1 & June 30. Mss, CDs & chapbooks

not accepted. This annual award honors a poet who is past the very beginning, but has not yet reached the acknowledged pinnacle of his or her career.
Award: $100,000 cash
Closing Date: July 1
Presented: Claremont Graduate University, Claremont, CA, April

Tupelo Press Berkshire Prize for a First or Second Book of Poetry
Tupelo Press Inc
60 Roberts Dr, Suite 308, North Adams, MA 01247
SAN: 254-3281
Tel: 413-664-9611 *Fax:* 413-664-9711
E-mail: info@tupelopress.org
Web Site: www.tupelopress.org
Key Personnel
Publr: Jeffrey Levine *E-mail:* publisher@tupelopress.org
Ed-in-Chief: Kristina Marie Darling
   E-mail: kdarling@tupelopress.org
Established: 2000
An annual competition for 1st or 2nd books of poetry. Full guidelines on the web site. Entries accepted beginning January 1.
Award: $3,000 & publication & distribution
Closing Date: April 30
Presented: Summer

Tupelo Press Snowbound Series Chapbook Award
Tupelo Press Inc
60 Roberts Dr, Suite 308, North Adams, MA 01247
SAN: 254-3281
Tel: 413-664-9611 *Fax:* 413-664-9711
E-mail: info@tupelopress.org
Web Site: www.tupelopress.org
Key Personnel
Publr: Jeffrey Levine *E-mail:* publisher@tupelopress.org
Ed-in-Chief: Kristina Marie Darling
   E-mail: kdarling@tupelopress.org
Established: 2004
An annual open poetry chapbook competition. Full guidelines on the web site. Entries accepted beginning December 1.
Award: $1,000 & publication
Closing Date: Feb 28
Presented: Spring

Frederick Jackson Turner Award
The Organization of American Historians (OAH)
112 N Bryan Ave, Bloomington, IN 47408-4141
Tel: 812-855-7311
E-mail: oah@oah.org
Web Site: www.oah.org/awards
Key Personnel
Exec Dir: Beth English *E-mail:* benglish@oah.org
Comm Coord: Kara Hamm *E-mail:* khamm@oah.org
Awarded annually to the author of a first scholarly book dealing with some aspect of American history. Eligible books must be published during the calendar year preceding that in which the award is given. The author may not have previously published a book-length work of history. Submissions will be made by publishers, who may submit such books as they deem eligible. Co-authored works are eligible, as long as neither author has previously published a book of history. Authors who have previously co-authored a book of history are not eligible. One copy of each entry must be mailed directly to the committee members listed on the web site & must include a complete list of the author's publications or a statement from the publisher verifying this is the author's first book. No submission will be considered without this proof of eligibility.

Closing Date: Oct 1, 2021 (postmarked)
Presented: OAH Annual Meeting, Boston, MA, March 31-April 3, 2022

The Tusculum Review Poetry Chapbook Prize
The Tusculum Review
60 Shiloh Rd, Greeneville, TN 37745
Mailing Address: PO Box 5113, Greeneville, TN 37743
E-mail: review@tusculum.edu
Web Site: web.tusculum.edu/tusculumreview/contest
Each chapbook ms entered should consist of 20-30 pages of poems in a standard 12-point font. No more than one poem may appear on a page. Entry fee: $20 per chapbook ms. A ms need not be thematically coherent or connected through narrative. Co-authored mss are permitted. Include title page, table of contents & acknowledgements page (if any of the poems have been previously published). Please send a cover letter with your contest entry. See web site for details.
Award: $1,000 & publication in *The Tusculum Review*
Closing Date: April 1

The 25 Most "Censored" Stories Annual
Project Censored - Media Freedom Foundation
PO Box 750940, Petaluma, CA 94975
Tel: 707-241-4596
Web Site: www.projectcensored.org
Key Personnel
Pres, Media Freedom Foundation & Dir, Project Censored: Mickey Huff *E-mail:* mickey@projectcensored.org
Established: 1976
Investigative journalism.
Award: Certificate
Presented: Oct 1

Cy Twombly Award for Poetry
Foundation for Contemporary Arts
820 Greenwich St, New York, NY 10014
Tel: 212-807-7077
E-mail: info@contemporary-arts.org
Web Site: www.foundationforcontemporaryarts.org/grants/cy-twombly-award-for-poetry
Key Personnel
Exec Dir: Stacy Tenenbaum Stark
Assoc Dir: Sarah Rulfs
Prog Mgr: Alexander Thompson
Established: 2018
Annual grant to support a poet. Administered by a confidential nomination & selection process. Applications & unsol nominations are not accepted.
Other Sponsor(s): Cy Twombly Foundation
Award: $40,000
Presented: Jan

Ucross Foundation Residency Program
Ucross Foundation
30 Big Red Lane, Clearmont, WY 82835
Tel: 307-737-2291 *Fax:* 307-737-2322
E-mail: info@ucross.org
Web Site: www.ucrossfoundation.org
Key Personnel
Pres, Ucross Foundation: Sharon Dynak
   E-mail: sdynak@ucross.org
Residency Mgr: Ruth Salvatore
   E-mail: rsalvatore@ucross.org
Established: 1983
Artist & writer residency program. Approximately 100 individuals per year for 2-6 week lengths of time. Application fee: $40.
Award: Room, studio & board
Closing Date: Annually, March 1 (Fall session) & Oct 1 (Spring session)

Friedrich Ulfers Prize
New York University, Deutsches Haus
42 Washington Mews, New York, NY 10003

E-mail: info@festivalneueliteratur.org
Web Site: festivalneueliteratur.org/prize
Awarded annually to a leading publisher, writer, critic, translator, or scholar who has championed the advancement of German-language literature in the US.
Award: $5,000 grant
Presented: Festival Neue Literatur, March

Unhanged Arthur Ellis Award
Crime Writers of Canada (CWC)
716 Thicket Way, Ottawa, ON K4A 3B5, Canada
E-mail: arthur_ellis@crimewriterscanada.com
Web Site: www.crimewriterscanada.com/awards
Key Personnel
Exec Dir: Alison Bruce *E-mail:* ed@crimewriterscanada.com
Asst Exec Dir & Arthur Ellis Awards Mgr: Ludvica Boota *E-mail:* aed@crimewriterscanada.com
Established: 2007
Annual award for the best unpublished first crime novel. Open to Canadian citizens & permanent residents who have never had a novel of any kind published commercially. Contestants must have a completed novel ms (50,000-110,000 words) at the time of entry.
Other Sponsor(s): Dundurn Press
Closing Date: Oct 15
Presented: Arthur Ellis Awards Banquet, Toronto, ON, Last Thurs in May

John Updike Award
American Academy of Arts & Letters
633 W 155 St, New York, NY 10032
Tel: 212-368-5900 *Fax:* 212-491-4615
E-mail: academy@artsandletters.org
Web Site: artsandletters.org
Key Personnel
Exec Dir: Cody Upton
Biennial award to recognize a writer in mid-career who has demonstrated consistent excellence.
Award: $20,000

Utah Original Writing Competition
Utah Division of Arts & Museums
Subsidiary of Utah State Department of Heritage & Arts
617 E South Temple, Salt Lake City, UT 84102
Tel: 801-236-7555 *Fax:* 801-236-7556
Web Site: arts.utah.gov
Key Personnel
Literary Arts Specialist: Alyssa Hickman Grove *Tel:* 801-236-7548 *E-mail:* agrove@utah.gov
Established: 1958
Applicants must be Utah residents age 18 or older. Guidelines & forms posted on web site in April.
Award: $7,350 in prizes in 7 categories
Closing Date: Last Friday in June
Presented: Salt Lake City, UT, Annually in Oct/Nov

William Van Dyke Short Story Prize
Ruminate Magazine
1041 N Taft Hill Rd, Fort Collins, CO 80521
Tel: 970-449-2726
E-mail: editor@ruminatemagazine.org
Web Site: www.ruminatemagazine.com
Key Personnel
Ed-in-Chief: Brianna Van Dyke
Sr Ed: Amy Lowe
Assoc Ed: Kristin George Bagdanov; Stefani Rossi
Established: 2009
All submissions must be previously unpublished & submitted via online submission form. One short story per contest entry, 5,500 words or less. No limit on number of entries per person. Entry fee: $20.

Award: $1,500 & publication in Spring issue (1st place), $200 & publication (2nd place)
Closing Date: Annually, Feb 15
Presented: Aug 15

The William Van Wert Memorial Fiction Award
Hidden River™ Arts
PO Box 63927, Philadelphia, PA 19147
Tel: 610-764-0813
E-mail: hiddenriverarts@gmail.com
Web Site: www.hiddenriverarts.org; www.hiddenriverarts.com
Key Personnel
Founding Dir: Debra Leigh Scott
Established: 2002
Annual award for a work of unpublished short story or novel excerpt of 25 pages or less. Entry fee: $17.
Award: $1,000 (awarded by mail)
Closing Date: June 30
Presented: Dec

VanderMey Nonfiction Prize
Ruminate Magazine
1041 N Taft Hill Rd, Fort Collins, CO 80521
Tel: 970-449-2726
E-mail: editor@ruminatemagazine.org
Web Site: www.ruminatemagazine.com
Key Personnel
Ed-in-Chief: Brianna Van Dyke
Sr Ed: Amy Lowe
Assoc Ed: Kristin George Bagdanov; Stefani Rossi
Established: 2011
One nonfiction piece per entry, 5,500 words or less & must be previously unpublished. No limit on number of entries per person. Entry fee $20.
Award: $1,500 & publication in prize issue (1st place), $200 & publication (2nd place)
Closing Date: Annually, Nov 15
Presented: May 15

Daniel Varoujan Award
New England Poetry Club
46 Wallace St, Somerville, MA 02144
E-mail: info@nepoetryclub.org
Web Site: www.nepoetryclub.org
Key Personnel
Pres: Mary Buchinger
VP: Hillary Sallick
Treas: Linda Haviland Conte
Established: 1979
Award for an unpublished poem in English (not a translation) worthy of the Armenian poet, Daniel Varoujan, executed by the Turks in 1915 at the onset of the genocide of the Armenian population; $15 for up to 3 entries & $3 for each additional poem for nonmembs. Send poem in duplicate, name of writer on one only. Previous winners may not enter again. See web site for additional guidelines.
Award: $500 & publication of poem on NEPC web site
Closing Date: Annually, May 31
Presented: Winners announced online Aug/Sept

Vermont Studio Center Writer's Program Fellowships
Vermont Studio Center
80 Pearl St, Johnson, VT 05656
Mailing Address: PO Box 613, Johnson, VT 05656
Tel: 802-635-2727 *Fax:* 802-635-2730
E-mail: writing@vermontstudiocenter.org; info@vermontstudiocenter.org
Web Site: www.vermontstudiocenter.org
Key Personnel
Writing Prog Dir: Jody Gladding *E-mail:* jody@vermontstudiocenter.org

Prog Dir: Kathy Black *E-mail:* kblack@vermontstudiocenter.org
Accepts 16 writers per month year-round. Fellowship awards are given as funds are available through VSC Fellowships.
Award: Four-week residency
Closing Date: Feb 15, June 15, Oct 1; apply 6 months prior to residency date

Jill Vickers Prize
Canadian Political Science Association
260 rue Dalhousie St, Suite 204, Ottawa, ON K1N 7E4, Canada
Tel: 613-562-1202 *Fax:* 613-241-0019
E-mail: cpsa-acsp@cpsa-acsp.ca
Web Site: www.cpsa-acsp.ca
Key Personnel
Admin: Michelle Hopkins
Awarded to the author or authors of the best paper presented on the topic of gender & politics.
Award: Commemorative certificate
Closing Date: June 15
Presented: Annual Conference, June 2022

Vicky Metcalf Award for Literature for Young People
The Writers' Trust of Canada
600-460 Richmond St W, Toronto, ON M5V 1Y1, Canada
Tel: 416-504-8222 *Toll Free Tel:* 877-906-6548 *Fax:* 416-504-9090
E-mail: info@writerstrust.com
Web Site: www.writerstrust.com
Key Personnel
Exec Dir: Charlie Foran *Tel:* 416-504-8222 ext 244 *E-mail:* cforan@writerstrust.com
Prog Coord: Devon Jackson *Tel:* 416-504-8222 ext 248 *E-mail:* djackson@writerstrust.com
Awarded to a Canadian writer of young people's literature for a body of work.
Other Sponsor(s): George Cedric Metcalf Charitable Foundation
Award: $20,000
Presented: The Writers' Trust Awards, Toronto, ON, CN, Annually in Nov

The Vivian
Romance Writers of America®
14615 Benfer Rd, Houston, TX 77069
Tel: 832-717-5200 *Fax:* 832-717-5201
E-mail: contests@rwa.org
Web Site: www.rwa.org
Key Personnel
Pres: Alyssa Day
Exec Dir: Leslie Scantlebury *Tel:* 832-717-5200 ext 123 *E-mail:* leslie.scantlebury@rwa.org
Mktg & PR Mgr: Jessie Edwards *Tel:* 832-717-5200 ext 128 *E-mail:* jessie.edwards@rwa.org
Awarded in recognition of excellence in romance writing & showcases author talent & creativity.

Voelcker Award, see PEN/Voelcker Award

Harold D Vursell Memorial Award
American Academy of Arts & Letters
633 W 155 St, New York, NY 10032
Tel: 212-368-5900 *Fax:* 212-491-4615
E-mail: academy@artsandletters.org
Web Site: artsandletters.org
Key Personnel
Exec Dir: Cody Upton
Given annually to single out recent prose that merits recognition for the quality of its style.
Award: $20,000

Christopher Lightfoot Walker Award
American Academy of Arts & Letters
633 W 155 St, New York, NY 10032
Tel: 212-368-5900
E-mail: academy@artsandletters.org
Web Site: artsandletters.org

Key Personnel
Lit Coord: Ashley Fedor *E-mail:* afedor@
artsandletters.org
Established: 2018
Awarded biennially in even-numbered years to
recognize a writer of distinction who has made
a significant contribution to American literature.
Award: $100,000

Richard Wall Memorial Award
Theatre Library Association (TLA)
c/o The New York Public Library for the Per-
forming Arts, 111 Amsterdam Ave, New York,
NY 10023
E-mail: TheatreLibraryAssociation@gmail.com;
TLABookAwards@gmail.com
Web Site: www.tla-online.org/awards/bookawards
Key Personnel
Co-Chair, Book Awards Comm: Diana Bertolini;
Annemarie van Roessel
Established: 1973
Honors books published in US in the field of
recorded performance including motion picture,
TV & radio. Ineligible books are: directories,
collections from previously published sources
& reprints.
Award: $500 (1st prize), $250 (Special Jury
prize); certificate
Closing Date: Feb 28
Presented: New York, NY, Oct

Edward Lewis Wallant Award
Dr & Mrs Irving Waltman
Maurice Greenberg Center for Judaic Studies, 200
Bloomfield Ave, Harry Jack Gray E 300, West
Hartford, CT 06117
Tel: 860-768-4964 *Fax:* 860-768-5044
E-mail: mgcjs@hartford.edu
Web Site: www.hartford.edu/a_and_s/greenberg/
wallant
Key Personnel
Sponsor of Award: Fran Waltman; Irving Walt-
man
Coord, Award Comm: Avinoam Patt, PhD
Established: 1963
Awarded annually to a Jewish writer, preferably
unrecognized, whose published creative work
of fiction is deemed to have significance for the
American Jew.
Award: $500 & scroll
Closing Date: Nov 1

George Washington Book Prize
Washington College, CV Starr Center for the
Study of the American Experience
101 S Water St, Chestertown, MD 21620
Tel: 410-810-7165 *Fax:* 410-810-7175
Web Site: starrcenter.washcoll.edu/centers/starr/
george-washington-book-prize.php
Key Personnel
Book Prize Coord: Jean Wortman
E-mail: jwortman2@washcoll.edu
Established: 2005
Created to recognize outstanding published works
that contribute to a greater understanding of
America's Founding era. Books must be pub-
lished in the year prior to the year prize is
awarded. Announcement of finalists on George
Washington's Birthday, February 22. An-
nouncement of winner at Mount Vernon, VA
in May.
Other Sponsor(s): George Washington's Mount
Vernon; Gilder Lehrman Institute of American
History
Award: $50,000
Closing Date: Dec 1
Presented: Mount Vernon Estate & Gardens, 3200
Mount Vernon Memorial Hwy, Mount Vernon,
VA, Spring

Washington State Book Awards
Washington Center for the Book
c/o The Seattle Public Library, 1000 Fourth Ave,
Seattle, WA 98104-1109
Tel: 206-386-4636
E-mail: wsba@spl.org
Web Site: www.spl.org
Annual awards for outstanding books for books
published by Washington authors the previ-
ous year. A book award is given based on the
strength of the publication's literary merit, last-
ing importance & overall quality to an author
who was born in Washington state or is a cur-
rent resident & has maintained residence here
for at least 3 years. Winners & finalists are
named in 8 categories:
Books for Adults: Fiction; Poetry; Biography &
Memoir; General Nonfiction
Books for Youth: Picture Books; Books for Early
Readers (ages 6-8); Books for Middle Grade
Readers (ages 8-12); Books for Young Adults
(ages 13-18).
Other Sponsor(s): The Seattle Public Library
Foundation
Closing Date: Feb 1
Presented: Oct

The Robert Watson Literary Prizes in Fiction & Poetry
The Greensboro Review
MFA Writing Program, The Greensboro Review,
UNC-Greensboro, 3302 MHRA Bldg, Greens-
boro, NC 27402-6170
Tel: 336-334-5459 *Fax:* 336-256-1470
Web Site: www.greensbororeview.org
Key Personnel
Ed: Jim Clark *E-mail:* jlclark@uncg.edu
Assoc Ed: Terry Kennedy *E-mail:* tlkenned@
uncg.edu
Established: 1984
Short story & poetry.
Other Sponsor(s): MFA Writing Program at UNC
Greensboro
Award: $1,000 (each category)
Closing Date: Annually, Sept 15

Jacqueline Bograd Weld Award for Biography,
see PEN/Jacqueline Bograd Weld Award for
Biography

Rene Wellek Prize
American Comparative Literature Association
(ACLA)
University of South Carolina, Dept of Languages,
Literature & Cultures, 1620 College St, Rm
817, Columbia, SC 29208
Tel: 803-777-3021
E-mail: info@acla.org
Web Site: www.acla.org/prize-awards/rené-wellek-
prize
Key Personnel
Nominations Comm Chair: Antonio Barrenechea
E-mail: abarrene@umw.edu
Established: 1968
To recognize the best book published in the field
of comparative literature published in the 2 cal-
endar years prior to presentation. See web site
for nomination process.
Award: Complimentary registration for the annual
meeting as well as hotel & airfare accommoda-
tions (not including food)
Closing Date: Oct 1
Presented: ACLA Annual Meeting, July

Wergle Flomp Humor Poetry Contest
Winning Writers
351 Pleasant St, PMB 222, Northampton, MA
01060-3961
Tel: 413-320-1847 *Toll Free Tel:* 866-WINWRIT
(946-9748) *Fax:* 413-280-0539
Web Site: www.winningwriters.com

Key Personnel
Pres: Adam Cohen *E-mail:* adam@
winningwriters.com
VP: Jendi Reiter
Established: 2001
Seeks best humor poems. Both published & un-
published works are welcome. Submit poems
in English or inspired gibberish. No entry fee.
Contestants may enter one poem per year up to
250 lines. Poets from all nations welcome.
Award: $1,000 (1st prize), $250 (2nd prize), $100
(10 honorable mentions), plus publication on
web site for all winners
Closing Date: Annually, April 1
Presented: Winners announced Aug 15 on web
site

Wesley-Logan Prize
American Historical Association (AHA)
400 "A" St SE, Washington, DC 20003
Tel: 202-544-2422 *Fax:* 202-544-8307
E-mail: awards@historians.org
Web Site: www.historians.org
Established: 1992
For an outstanding book in African diaspora history. The prize is offered on some aspect of
the history of the dispersion, settlement & ad-
justment +/or return of peoples originally from
Africa. Eligible for consideration are books
in any chronological period & any geological
location. Only books of high scholarly & literary merit will be considered. Along with an
application form, applicants must mail a copy
of their book to each of the prize committee
members who will be posted on our web site
as the prize deadline approaches. All updated
info on web site. Books published in 2020 will
be considered.
Other Sponsor(s): Association for the Study of
Afro-American Life & History
Award: Cash
Closing Date: May 15, 2021
Presented: AHA Annual Meeting, New Orleans,
LA, Jan 2022

Western Heritage Awards (Wrangler Award)
National Cowboy & Western Heritage Museum®
1700 NE 63 St, Oklahoma City, OK 73111
Tel: 405-478-2250 *Fax:* 405-478-4714
E-mail: info@nationalcowboymuseum.org
Web Site: nationalcowboymuseum.org
Key Personnel
McCasland Chair of Cowboy Culture & Exhibit
Curator: Don Reeves *E-mail:* donreeves@
nationalcowboymuseum.org
Established: 1961
Awarded annually honoring works in TV, film, lit-
erary & music which preserve the spirit of the
American West.
Award: Bronze sculpture of a cowboy on horse-
back
Closing Date: Dec 31 (TV, film & literary)
Presented: Banquet & Awards Ceremonies, Na-
tional Cowboy & Western Heritage Museum,
April (must be in attendance to receive bronze
sculpture)

Hilary Weston Writers' Trust Prize for Nonfiction
The Writers' Trust of Canada
600-460 Richmond St W, Toronto, ON M5V
1Y1, Canada
Tel: 416-504-8222 *Toll Free Tel:* 877-906-6548
Fax: 416-504-9090
E-mail: info@writerstrust.com
Web Site: www.writerstrust.com
Key Personnel
Exec Dir: Charlie Foran *Tel:* 416-504-8222 ext
244 *E-mail:* cforan@writerstrust.com
Prog Coord: Devon Jackson *Tel:* 416-504-8222
ext 248 *E-mail:* djackson@writerstrust.com
Established: 1997

Awarded for literary exellence in nonfiction, which includes personal or journalistic essays, history, biography, memoirs, commentary & criticism, both social & political.
Award: $60,000 (1st prize), $5,000 (finalists)
Presented: Annually in Nov

Charles A Weyerhauser Book Award
The Forest History Society Inc
701 William Vickers Ave, Durham, NC 27701-3162
Tel: 919-682-9319 *Fax:* 919-682-2349
Web Site: www.foresthistory.org
Key Personnel
Admin Asst: Andrea Anderson *E-mail:* andrea.anderson@foresthistory.org
Established: 1977
Rewards superior scholarship in forest & conservation history. Annual award goes to an author who has exhibited fresh insight into a topic & whose narrative analysis is clear, inventive & thought-provoking. Books are selected by award giver to avoid receipt of too many ineligible books.

E B White Award
American Academy of Arts & Letters
633 W 155 St, New York, NY 10032
Tel: 212-368-5900 *Fax:* 212-491-4615
E-mail: academy@artsandletters.org
Web Site: artsandletters.org
Key Personnel
Exec Dir: Cody Upton
Established: 2013
Given to a writer for achievement in children's literature.
Award: $10,000

White, Jackie, Memorial National Children's Playwriting Contest, see Jackie White Memorial National Children's Playwriting Contest

William Allen White Children's Book Awards
Emporia State University, William Allen White Library
One Kellogg Circle, Emporia, KS 66801-5092
Mailing Address: Emporia State University, Campus Box 4051, Emporia, KS 66801-5092
Tel: 620-341-5208 *Toll Free Tel:* 877-613-7323
Fax: 620-341-6208
E-mail: wawbookaward@emporia.edu
Web Site: waw.emporia.edu/libsv/wawbookaward
Key Personnel
Exec Dir: Michelle Hammond
  E-mail: mhammon2@emporia.edu
Established: 1952
Two children's books are selected by the children of Kansas, grades 3-5 & 6-8, from 2 master lists of books chosen by a selection committee. When a student has read 2 books from either of the master lists, he or she is eligible to vote at their school (homeschooled vote at their local public library) for the annual White Award winners. Votes are recorded by each school, district or public library & submitted to the William Allen White Children Book Awards Program.
Other Sponsor(s): Trusler Foundation
Award: Two bronze medals, one for each grade level & a $2,500 check for each winner
Closing Date: Votes must be received by April 15
Presented: Emporia State University, Albert Taylor Hall, Winners announced late April & awards presented in Autumn

Whiting Awards
Mrs Giles Whiting Foundation
16 Court St, Suite 2308, Brooklyn, NY 11241
Tel: 718-701-5962
E-mail: info@whiting.org

Web Site: www.whiting.org
Key Personnel
Exec Dir: Daniel Reid
Foundation Bd Pres: Peter Pennoyer
Dir, Literary Progs: Courtney Hodell
Prog Asst: Adina Applebaum
Res & Web Asst: Katy Einerson
Established: 1985
For creative writing in fiction, nonfiction, poetry & plays. Applications not accepted by the foundation; confidential nominators propose candidates for selection committee consideration.
Award: Ten awards of $50,000 each
Presented: Annually in March

Whiting Creative Nonfiction Grant
Mrs Giles Whiting Foundation
16 Court St, Suite 2308, Brooklyn, NY 11241
Tel: 718-701-5962
E-mail: nonfiction@whiting.org; info@whiting.org
Web Site: www.whiting.org
Key Personnel
Exec Dir: Daniel Reid
Foundation Bd Pres: Peter Pennoyer
Dir, Literary Progs: Courtney Hodell
Prog Asst: Adina Applebaum
Res & Web Asst: Katy Einerson
Established: 2016
Program offers allocations to as many as 6 works in progress to enable authors to complete their books. To be eligible, writers must be under contract with a publisher & at least 2 years into their contract. Submissions welcome for nonfiction works of history, cultural or political reportage, biography, memoir, the sciences, philosophy, criticism, food or travel writing & personal essays, among other categories, for a general, not academic, readership. To apply, writers should submit their original proposal that led to the contract, as many as 3 sample chapters, a budget & schedule for completion, a letter of support from their publisher & 2 other letters of support (not to come from their agent). Writers can submit applications online at www.whiting.org/nonfiction/application.
Award: $40,000
Closing Date: May 1
Presented: Annually in Dec

Whiting Literary Magazine Prizes
Mrs Giles Whiting Foundation
16 Court St, Suite 2308, Brooklyn, NY 11241
Tel: 718-701-5962
E-mail: info@whiting.org
Web Site: www.whiting.org/writers/whiting-literary-magazine-prizes
Key Personnel
Exec Dir: Daniel Reid
Dir, Literary Progs: Courtney Hodell
Annual awards in print & digital categories to smaller & mid-sized journals with budgets of up to $500,000. Each prize includes an outright gift in the first year followed by substantial matching grants in the next 2 years & capacity building opportunities. Applicants must be not-for-profit in the US & have published at least annually for at least the last 3 years.
Closing Date: Dec

Walt Whitman Award
The Academy of American Poets Inc
75 Maiden Lane, Suite 901, New York, NY 10038
Tel: 212-274-0343
E-mail: academy@poets.org
Web Site: www.poets.org
Key Personnel
Pres & Exec Dir: Jennifer Benka
  E-mail: jenbenka@poets.org

Devt, Membership & Communs Sr Mgr: Molly Walsh *E-mail:* mwalsh@poets.org
Ad & Mktg Sr Mgr: Michelle Campagna
  E-mail: mcampagna@poets.org
Sr Progs Mgr: Nikay Paredes *Tel:* 212-274-0343 ext 13 *E-mail:* nparedes@poets.org
Established: 1975
Annual award for a book-length ms of poetry by a living American poet who has not published a book of poetry. Visit academy web site for entry form & guidelines.
Award: First book publication $5,000, publication by Graywolf Press, an all-expenses-paid 6-week residency at the Civitella Ranieri Center in Italy & distribution of the winning book to thousands of Academy of American Poet members
Closing Date: Sept 15-Nov 15
Presented: April

Jon Whyte Memorial Essay Prize
Writers' Guild of Alberta
11759 Groat Rd, Edmonton, AB T5M 3K6, Canada
Tel: 780-422-8174 *Toll Free Tel:* 800-665-5354 (AB only) *Fax:* 780-422-2663 (attn WGA)
E-mail: mail@writersguild.ca
Web Site: writersguild.ca
Key Personnel
Exec Dir: Carol Holmes *E-mail:* carol.holmes@writersguild.ca
Communs & Partnerships Coord: Ellen Kartz *E-mail:* ellen.kartz@writersguild.ca
Memb Servs Coord: Giorgia Severini
Progs Coord: Natalie Cook *E-mail:* natalie.cook@writersguild.ca; Julie Robinson *E-mail:* julie.robinson@writersguild.ca
Established: 1992
Awarded to an outstanding unpublished essay by an Alberta author; no longer than 3,000 words.
Award: $700
Closing Date: Annually, Dec 31
Presented: Alberta Book Awards Gala
Branch Office(s)
505 21 Ave SW, Calgary, AB T2S 0G9, Canada, Prog Coord: Samantha Warwick *Tel:* 403-265-2226 *E-mail:* samantha.warwick@writersguild.ca

Wichita State University Playwriting Contest
School of Performing Arts
Division of Wichita State University
1845 Fairmount St, Box 153, Wichita, KS 67260-0153
Tel: 316-978-3360 *Fax:* 316-978-3202
Web Site: www.wichita.edu
Key Personnel
Admin Specialist: Renea Goforth *Tel:* 316-978-6634
For college students only (graduate or undergraduate).
Award: Production of play, transportation & housing for playwright to attend performance
Closing Date: Annually, Jan 15
Presented: Welsbacher Theatre, Wichita State University, Wichita, KS, Annually in Spring

Thornton Wilder Prize for Translation
American Academy of Arts & Letters
633 W 155 St, New York, NY 10032
Tel: 212-368-5900 *Fax:* 212-491-4615
E-mail: academy@artsandletters.org
Web Site: artsandletters.org
Key Personnel
Exec Dir: Cody Upton
Established: 2009
Recognizes a practitioner, scholar, or patron who has made a significant contribution to the art of literary translation.
Award: $20,000

William Flanagan Memorial Creative Persons Center

Edward F Albee Foundation
14 Harrison St, New York, NY 10013
Tel: 212-226-2020 *Fax:* 212-226-5551
E-mail: info@albeefoundation.org
Web Site: www.albeefoundation.org
Key Personnel
Exec Dir: Jakob Holder
Annual residency program for writers & visual artists. The only requirements are talent & need.
Award: Room (writers); Room & Studio (visual artists)
Closing Date: Jan 1-March 1 for Summer season
Presented: The Barn, Montauk, Long Island, NY, Mid-May through mid-Oct, every writer or artist can choose 4 or 6 weeks, depending on availability

Oscar Williams/Gene Derwood Award

NY Community Trust
909 Third Ave, New York, NY 10022
Tel: 212-686-0010 *Fax:* 212-532-8528
E-mail: info@nycommunitytrust.org
Web Site: www.nycommunitytrust.org
Key Personnel
Pres: Lorie Slutsky *Tel:* 212-686-2565
VP, Communs: David Marcus *Tel:* 212-889-3963
VP, Grants: Pat Jenny *Tel:* 212-686-0010 ext 201
Dir, Grants Budgeting: Liza Lagunoff *Tel:* 212-686-7196 *E-mail:* ll@nyct-cfi.org
Asst to Pres: Barbara Wybraniec *Tel:* 212-686-0010 ext 229
Established: 1971
Annual award intended to help needy or worthy poets & artists who have had long & distinguished careers. Nominations or applications are not accepted in any form.
Award: Cash varies in amount

William Carlos Williams Award

Poetry Society of America (PSA)
15 Gramercy Park, New York, NY 10003
Tel: 212-254-9628
Web Site: poetrysociety.org/awards
Key Personnel
Pres: Allison Binns
Exec Dir: Matt Brogan *E-mail:* matt@poetrysociety.org
Deputy Dir: Brett Fletcher Lauer *E-mail:* brett@poetrysociety.org
Prog Dir: Laurin Macios *E-mail:* laurin@poetrysociety.org
For a book of poetry published by a small press or a nonprofit or university press. Submissions, accompanied by an entry form, from publishers only. See web site for complete guidelines.
Award: Purchase prize between $500 & $1,000
Closing Date: Annually, Oct-Dec
Presented: Announced on web site early April

E O Wilson Literary Science Writing Award,
see PEN/E O Wilson Prize for Literary Science Writing

Gary Wilson Award for Short Fiction

Texas Christian University
Dept of English, TCU Box 298300, Fort Worth, TX 76129
Tel: 817-257-5907 *Fax:* 817-257-5905
E-mail: descant@tcu.edu
Web Site: www.descant.tcu.edu
Key Personnel
Mng Ed: Dan Williams *E-mail:* d.e.williams@tcu.edu
Established: 2005
For an outstanding story in an issue. No application process, no entry fee; all published submissions are eligible for prize consideration. Submit work with a SASE.

Other Sponsor(s): descant (publication), Dept of English, TCU
Award: $250 cash
Closing Date: Annually, Sept 1-April 1
Presented: Winner announced in the Summer in *descant*

The H W Wilson Library Staff Development Grant

ALA Awards Program
Affiliate of The American Library Association (ALA)
50 E Huron St, Chicago, IL 60611
Tel: 312-280-3247 *Toll Free Tel:* 800-545-2433 (ext 3247) *Fax:* 312-944-3897; 312-440-9379
E-mail: awards@ala.org
Web Site: www.ala.org
Key Personnel
Prog Off: Cheryl Malden *E-mail:* cmalden@ala.org
To a library organization for a program to further its staff development goals & objectives.
Award: $3,500 & 24k gold-framed citation
Closing Date: Annually, Dec 1
Presented: ALA Annual Conference

Herbert Warren Wind Book Award

USGA Museum & Archives
77 Liberty Corner Rd, Far Hills, NJ 07931-0708
Tel: 908-234-2300
Web Site: www.usga.org
Key Personnel
Libn: Nancy Stulack *Tel:* 908-781-1107
E-mail: nstulack@usga.org
Established: 1987
Recognizes & honors outstanding contributions to golf literature. Named in honor of the famed golf writer, the annual award acknowledges & encourages outstanding research, writing & publishing about golf. The award attempts to broaden the public's interest & knowledge in the game of golf. Presented by the USGA Museum & Archives, the Book Award is the top literary prize awarded by the USGA.
Award: Silver inkwell with feather
Closing Date: Oct 31
Presented: USGA Annual Meeting, Feb

Windham-Campbell Prizes

Yale University, Windham-Campbell Prizes Endowment
Beinecke Rare Book & Manuscript Library, 121 Wall St, New Haven, CT 06511
Fax: 203-432-9033
Web Site: windhamcampbell.org
Key Personnel
Prog Dir: Michael Kelleher
Global English language awards that call attention to literary achievement & provide writers with the opportunity to focus on their work independent of financial concerns. Nomination only. Eight prizes available each year. Categories: fiction, nonfiction, drama & poetry.
Award: $165,000 unrestricted grant
Presented: Annually in Spring

Justin Winsor Prize for Library History Essay

The Library History Round Table of the American Library Association
225 N Michigan Ave, Suite 1300, Chicago, IL 60601
Tel: 312-280-4283 *Toll Free Tel:* 800-545-2433 (ext 4283) *Fax:* 312-280-4392
E-mail: ors@ala.org
Web Site: www.ala.org; ala.org/lhrt
Key Personnel
Prog Offr & LHRT Liaison: Kelsey Henke *E-mail:* khenke@ala.org
To author of an outstanding essay embodying original historical research on a significant subject of library history.

Award: $500 & invitation to have paper considered for publication in *Libraries & the Cultural Record*
Closing Date: Jan

The Wisconsin Writers Awards

Council for Wisconsin Writers
c/o 210 N Main St, No 204, Cedar Grove, WI 53013
E-mail: wiswriters@gmail.com
Web Site: wiswriters.org/awards
Key Personnel
Pres & Awards Co-Chair: Geoff Gilpin *E-mail:* geoff@geoffgilpin.com
Secy & Awards Co-Chair: Sylvia Cavanaugh *E-mail:* bgirl4shadow@gmail.com
Devt Dir & Awards Co-Chair: Erik Richardson *E-mail:* erichardson@wi.rr.com
PR Dir: Jerrianne Hayslett *E-mail:* jfarhsi@aol.com
Eight annual awards for deserving writers throughout the state & 2 biennial awards to individuals or organizations who have made significant contributions to literature in the state. Submissions accepted November 1-January 31 for work published in the year prior to the close of the contest. Entry fee: $25 nonmembs (exc Essay Award for Young Writers). Two biennial awards are offered in alternating years - Major Achievement Award & Christopher Latham Sholes Award.
Award: $500 each, $250 Essay Award for Young Writers, $1,000 for Major Achievement Award, $50 honorable mentions
Closing Date: Jan 31
Presented: CWW Annual Banquet, May

WLA Literary Award

Wisconsin Library Association Inc
4610 S Biltmore Lane, Suite 100, Madison, WI 53718-2153
Tel: 608-245-3640 *Fax:* 608-245-3646
Web Site: wla.wisconsinlibraries.org
Key Personnel
Exec Dir: Mr Plumer Lovelace *E-mail:* lovelace@wisconsinlibraries.org
Events & Conferences: Brigitte Rupp Vacha *E-mail:* ruppvacha@wisconsinlibraries.org
Established: 1974
To honor a work by a Wisconsin author for a book published in the preceding year that contributes to the world of literature & ideas.
Award: Monetary award
Closing Date: April 15
Presented: WLA Annual Conference, Oct-Nov

WNBA Pannell Award for Excellence in Children's Bookselling

Women's National Book Association Inc
PO Box 237, FDR Sta, New York, NY 10150-0231
Toll Free Tel: 866-610-WNBA (610-9622)
E-mail: WNBAPannell@gmail.com
Web Site: www.wnba-books.org; www.NationalReadingGroupMonth.org; www.wnba-books.org/awards
Key Personnel
Co-Chair: Sally M Kim; Susan Knopf *E-mail:* susan@scoutbooksandmedia.com
Established: 1981
Recognizes retail bookstores that excel at creatively bringing books & children together & inspiring children's interest in books & reading. Nominations come from customers, sales & marketing people & other book industry professionals & stores themselves. One general book store with a children's section & one children's specialty store are selected each year by a jury of 5 book industry professionals based on creativity, responsiveness to community needs, passion & understanding of children's books & young readers.

Other Sponsor(s): Estate of Lucille Micheels Pannell; Penguin Young Readers Group
Award: $2,000 (2 at $1,000 each) plus 1 piece of original art for each recipient
Closing Date: Feb
Presented: BookExpo, Late May/early June

WNBA Writing Contest
Women's National Book Association Inc
PO Box 237, FDR Sta, New York, NY 10150-0231
Toll Free Tel: 866-610-WNBA (610-9622)
E-mail: info@wnba-books.org
Web Site: www.wnba-books.org/contest
Key Personnel
Chair: Joan Gelfand E-mail: joan@joangelfand.com
Entries accepted in 4 categories: Fiction, Nonfiction, Poetry & Young Adult Fiction. Open to all adults 18 years or older writing in English. International submissions are welcome if they are able to accept the winning prize in US dollars. Multiple entries accepted but each requires a fee & separate entry. Entry fee: $15 memb, $20 nonmemb.
Award: $250 cash prize for winner in each category & publication in "The Bookwoman"
Closing Date: March 1
Presented: May 15

WNDB Internship Grants
We Need Diverse Books™
10319 Westlake Dr, No 104, Bethesda, MD 20817
Tel: 701-404-9632 (voicemail only)
E-mail: internships@diversebooks.org
Web Site: diversebooks.org/our-programs/internship-grants
Key Personnel
Head, Internship Grants Comm: Jennifer Mann E-mail: jennifermann@diversebooks.org
Communs Mgr: Alaina Leary E-mail: alainaleary@diversebooks.org
Supplemental grants to students from diverse backgrounds to help further their goals of pursuing a career in children's publishing. Applicant must identify as coming from a diverse background, be a high school graduate/GED, or currently enrolled college/university student, or college graduate, have received a paid internship offer from a participating publisher or from a qualifying literary agent. The position must be at least half time (17+ hours per week), minimum wage. For publishers, the internship must be in the children's division. For literary agencies, the internship must have a focus on children's publishing (spending at least 50% of the time on children's books).
Award: $2,500 each & 2-month public transportation stipend
Closing Date: May 31

Thomas Wolfe Fiction Prize
North Carolina Writers' Network
PO Box 21591, Winston-Salem, NC 27120-1591
E-mail: mail@ncwriters.org
Web Site: www.ncwriters.org
Key Personnel
Exec Dir: Ed Southern E-mail: ed@ncwriters.org
Competition is open to all writers regardless of geographical location or prior publication. Submit 2 copies of an unpublished fiction ms not to exceed 3,000 words. Entry fee: $15 membs, $25 nonmembs. Submissions accepted December 1-January 30. Send submissions to Thomas Wolfe Fiction Prize, Great Smokies Writing Program, UNCA, One University Heights, Asheville, NC 28804.
Award: $1,000 & possible publication in The Thomas Wolfe Review
Closing Date: Annually, Jan 30

Helen & Kurt Wolff Translator's Prize
Goethe-Institute New York
30 Irving Place, New York, NY 10003
Tel: 212-439-8700 Fax: 212-439-8705
E-mail: info-newyork@goethe.de
Web Site: www.goethe.de/ins/us/enkul/ser/uef/hkw.html
Key Personnel
Libn: Walter Schlect Tel: 212-439-8697 E-mail: walter.schlect@goethe.de
Established: 1996
Awarded annually to honor an outstanding literary translation from German into English published in the US the previous year. American publishers are invited to submit 6 copies.
Award: $10,000
Closing Date: Jan 31
Presented: June (winning translation announced mid-April)

Tobias Wolff Award for Fiction
The Bellingham Review
Mail Stop 9053, Western Washington University, Bellingham, WA 98225
Tel: 360-650-4863
E-mail: bhreview@wwu.edu
Web Site: www.bhreview.org
Key Personnel
Ed-in-Chief: Suzanne Paola Antonetta
Mng Ed: Mike Oliphant
Established: 1993
Maximum length for prose is 6,000 words. Novel excerpts up to 6,000 words are accepted. No previously published works, or works accepted for publication, are eligible. Work may be under consideration elsewhere, but must be withdrawn from the competition if accepted for publication. All entries will receive a complimentary 1-issue subscription. Entry fee for the first entry (1 short story, or novel excerpt up to 6,000 words) $20. Each additional entry $10. Only accept submissions through Submittable. Mailed submissions are no longer accepted. All finalists are considered for publication. The winning piece is selected by a distinguished, outside judge. Entries accepted beginning December 1.
Award: $1,000 & publication in The Bellingham Review (1st prize); considered for publication (2nd, 3rd & finalists)
Closing Date: Annually, March 15
Presented: Annually in June

Women's National Book Association Award
Women's National Book Association Inc
PO Box 237, FDR Sta, New York, NY 10150-0231
Toll Free Tel: 866-610-WNBA (610-9622)
Web Site: www.wnba-books.org; www.NationalReadingGroupMonth.org
Key Personnel
Natl Treas: Nicole Pilo E-mail: npilo@cplanning.com
NYC Pres: Hannah Bennett E-mail: h.bennett42@gmail.com
Secy: Celine Keating
Established: 1940
Presented to a living American woman who derives part or all of her income from books & allied arts & who has done meritorious work in the world of books beyond the duties or responsibilities of her profession or occupation. Offered biennially in even-numbered years.
Award: Citation
Presented: Varies

The J Howard & Barbara M J Wood Prize
Poetry Magazine
61 W Superior St, Chicago, IL 60654
Tel: 312-787-7070 Fax: 312-787-6650
E-mail: editors@poetrymagazine.org
Web Site: www.poetryfoundation.org
Key Personnel
Edit Asst: Holly Amos E-mail: hamos@poetrymagazine.org
Established: 1994
For poetry published in the preceding 2 volumes of Poetry magazine. No application necessary.
Award: $5,000
Presented: Annually in Dec

Carter G Woodson Book Awards
National Council for the Social Studies
8555 16 St, Suite 500, Silver Spring, MD 20910
Tel: 301-588-1800 Toll Free Tel: 800-296-7840 Fax: 301-588-2049
E-mail: excellence@ncss.org; publications@ncss.org
Web Site: www.socialstudies.org
Key Personnel
Exec Dir: Lawrence Paska E-mail: lpaska@ncss.org
Dir, External Rel & Council Communs: Ana Post Tel: 301-588-1800 ext 114 E-mail: apost@ncss.org
Dir, Meetings & Exhibits: David Bailor Tel: 301-588-1800 ext 109 E-mail: dbailor@ncss.org
Dir, Pubns: Michael Simpson Tel: 301-588-1800 ext 105 E-mail: msimpson@ncss.org
Prog Mgr: Victoria Nayiga Tel: 301-850-7455 E-mail: victoria@ncss.org
Established: 1974
Annual award to recognize the most distinguished nonfiction books for young readers which depict ethnicity in the US. Eligible books deal with the experiences of one or more racial/ethnic minority groups in the US. Publisher must provide copy of each title for submission requirements.
Award: One elementary (K-6) & one middle level (5-8), one secondary (7-12) annual award, 3 runner-up books designated Woodson Honor Books, seals are now available to publishers $.25 each for less than 1,000 & less for larger quantities
Closing Date: Sept 30
Presented: Awards Reception, NCSS Annual Conference

Word Works Washington Prize
The Word Works
Adirondack Community College, Dearlove Hall, 640 Bay Rd, Queensbury, NY 12804
Mailing Address: PO Box 42164, Washington, DC 20015
Tel: 301-581-9439 Fax: 301-581-9443
E-mail: editor@wordworksbooks.org
Web Site: www.wordworksbooks.org
Key Personnel
Chpn, Bd of Dirs: Karren L Alenier
Pres: Nancy White E-mail: nancywhitepoetry@gmail.com
Established: 1981
Annual prize for an unpublished ms of poetry. Submission may be made by any living American or Canadian writer. Include 2 title pages, one with & one without name, address, telephone number & e-mail. No entry form is required. Online submissions available. Submissions should be 48-80 pages in English; please attach $25 entry fee, acknowledgment page & brief bio. Business sized SASE mandatory with entry. Visit web site for guidelines.
Award: $1,500 & publication
Closing Date: March 15

World Fantasy Awards
World Fantasy Awards Association
PO Box 43, Mukilteo, WA 98275-0043
Web Site: www.worldfantasy.org
Key Personnel
Pres: Peter Dennis Pautz E-mail: sfexecsec@gmail.com

To acknowledge excellence in fantasy writing & art.
Award: Trophy
Closing Date: June 1
Presented: World Fantasy Convention, Halloween weekend

World's Best Short-Short Story Contest
The Southeast Review
Florida State University, Dept of English, Tallahassee, FL 32306
E-mail: southeastreview@gmail.com
Web Site: www.southeastreview.org
Key Personnel
Ed: Alex Quinlan
Established: 1986
Best 500 word (maximum) previously unpublished short-short story. All entries will be considered for publication. $16 entry fee for up to 3 stories.
Other Sponsor(s): Florida State University English Department Creative Writing Program
Award: $500
Closing Date: April 1 (postmark)

Write Now
Childsplay
900 S Mitchell Dr, Tempe, AZ 85281
Tel: 480-921-5700 *Fax:* 480-921-5777
E-mail: info@writenow.co
Web Site: www.writenow.co
Key Personnel
Founder: Dorothy Webb
Artistic Dir: Jenny Millinger *Tel:* 480-921-5770 *E-mail:* jmillinger@childsplayaz.org
Established: 1988
Biennial workshop to encourage writers to create strikingly original theatre for young audiences.
Award: $1,000, development workshop & rehearsed reading (up to 4 winners); all scripts receive dramaturgical feedback
Closing Date: May 31
Presented: Feb 2021

Writer in Residence
Idaho Commission on the Arts
2410 N Old Penitentiary Rd, Boise, ID 83712
Mailing Address: PO Box 83720, Boise, ID 83720-0008
Tel: 208-334-2119
E-mail: info@arts.idaho.gov
Web Site: www.arts.idaho.gov
Key Personnel
Lit Dir: Jocelyn Robertson *Tel:* 208-334-2119 ext 108 *E-mail:* jocelyn.robertson@arts.idaho.gov
Triennial award for artistic excellence. Open only to residents of Idaho; must have resided in Idaho at least 1 year. Recipient serves a 3-year term, tours the state & gives at least 4 annual readings (8 of 12 in rural communities).
Award: $15,000 ($5,000 annually) plus allowable travel expenses
Closing Date: Jan 31, 2022
Presented: July 2022

The Writer Magazine/Emily Dickinson Award
Poetry Society of America (PSA)
15 Gramercy Park, New York, NY 10003
Tel: 212-254-9628
Web Site: poetrysociety.org/awards
Key Personnel
Pres: Allison Binns
Exec Dir: Matt Brogan *E-mail:* matt@poetrysociety.org
Deputy Dir: Brett Fletcher Lauer *E-mail:* brett@poetrysociety.org
Prog Dir: Laurin Macios *E-mail:* laurin@poetrysociety.org
Established: 1971
For a poem inspired by Dickinson (though not necessarily in her style), not to exceed 30 lines.

Open to society members only. See web site for more information.
Award: $250
Closing Date: Annually, Oct-Dec
Presented: Annual Awards Ceremony, New York, NY, Annually in Spring

Writer's Digest Annual Writing Competition
Active Interest Media (AIM)
5720 Flatiron Pkwy, Boulder, CO 80301
Web Site: www.writersdigest.com/writing-competitions
Original, unpublished mss in 10 categories: inspirational/spiritual; memoirs/personal essay; print or online article; genre short story (mystery, romance, etc); mainstream/literary short story; rhyming poetry; non-rhyming poetry; script (stage play/television/movie script/short film); children's/young adult fiction.
Poetry entry fees: Early $20 first entry, $15 each additional entry; Regular $25 first entry, $20 each additional entry.
Ms entry fees: Early $30 first entry, $25 each additional entry; Regular $35 first entry, $30 each additional entry.
Award: Paid trip to Writer's Digest Conference with (grand prize) $5,000 cash & more, interview in *Writer's Digest*, one-year subscription to magazine. See web site for additional prizes for 1st-10th place & honorable mentions
Presented: May (early), June (regular)

Writers-Editors Network International Writing Competition
Florida Freelance Writers Association
Affiliate of Writers-Editors Network
45 Main St, North Stratford, NH 03590
Mailing Address: PO Box A, North Stratford, NH 03590
Tel: 603-922-8338 *Fax:* 603-922-8339
E-mail: contest@writers-editors.com
Web Site: www.writers-editors.com; www.ffwamembers.com
Key Personnel
Exec Dir: Dana K Cassell *E-mail:* dana@writers-editors.com
Established: 1984
Fiction, nonfiction, juvenile & poetry.
Award: Cash & certificate, critiques for most promising
Closing Date: Annually, March 15
Presented: Annually, May 31

Writers Guild of America Awards
Writers Guild of America, West (WGAW)
7000 W Third St, Los Angeles, CA 90048
Tel: 323-951-4000; 323-782-4569 *Fax:* 323-782-4800
Web Site: www.wga.org
Key Personnel
Pres: Howard Rodman
VP: David Goodman
Secy & Treas: Aaron Mendelsohn
Awards: Jennifer Burt
Established: 1948
Annual awards. Any eligible film exhibited for 1 week during calendar year; original screenplay; adapted screenplay. TV & radio awards. Only members can enter.
Award: Statuette
Presented: Annual Writer's Guild Award Show, Feb

Writers' League of Texas Book Awards
Writers' League of Texas (WLT)
611 S Congress Ave, Suite 200 A-3, Austin, TX 78704
Tel: 512-499-8914
E-mail: wlt@writersleague.org
Web Site: www.writersleague.org

Key Personnel
Prog Dir: Michael Noll *E-mail:* michael@writersleague.org
Established: 1991
Members of the Writers' League of Texas annually recognize outstanding books (fiction, nonfiction, poetry & literary prose, children's long & children's short) published in the year prior to presentation. Membership is not required. See web site for complete submission details.
Award: $1,000 each award, commemorative award & appearance at the Texas Book Festival
Closing Date: Late Feb
Presented: Autumn

Writers' Trust Engel Findley Award
The Writers' Trust of Canada
600-460 Richmond St W, Toronto, ON M5V 1Y1, Canada
Tel: 416-504-8222 *Toll Free Tel:* 877-906-6548 *Fax:* 416-504-9090
E-mail: info@writerstrust.com
Web Site: www.writerstrust.com
Key Personnel
Exec Dir: Charlie Foran *Tel:* 416-504-8222 ext 244 *E-mail:* cforan@writerstrust.com
Prog Coord: Devon Jackson *Tel:* 416-504-8222 ext 248 *E-mail:* djackson@writerstrust.com
Established: 1986
Presented to a Canadian writer in mid-career. Writers are judged on their body of work—no less than 3 works of literary merit which are predominantly fiction rather than a single book. All Canadian writers are considered.
Award: $25,000
Presented: The Writers' Trust Awards, Toronto, ON, CN, Annually in Nov

Writers' Trust McClelland & Stewart Journey Prize
The Writers' Trust of Canada
600-460 Richmond St W, Toronto, ON M5V 1Y1, Canada
Tel: 416-504-8222 *Toll Free Tel:* 877-906-6548 *Fax:* 416-504-9090
E-mail: info@writerstrust.com
Web Site: www.writerstrust.com
Key Personnel
Exec Dir: Charlie Foran *Tel:* 416-504-8222 ext 244 *E-mail:* cforan@writerstrust.com
Prog Coord: Devon Jackson *Tel:* 416-504-8222 ext 248 *E-mail:* djackson@writerstrust.com
Established: 1988
Awarded to a new & developing writer of distinction for a short story published in a Canadian literary publication.
Other Sponsor(s): James A Michener (donation of his Canadian royalty earnings from his novel *Journey*)
Award: $10,000 (winner), $2,500 (finalists)
Presented: The Writers' Trust Awards, Toronto, ON, CN, Annually in Nov

WritersWeekly.com's 24-Hour Short Story Contest
WritersWeekly
5726 Cortez Rd, Suite 349, Bradenton, FL 34210
Fax: 305-768-0261
Web Site: www.writersweekly.com
Key Personnel
Publr: Angela Hoy *E-mail:* angela@writersweekly.com
Held quarterly & limited to 500 entrants. You must be entered in the contest before the topic is posted in order to submit your story. Late stories are disqualified. Entry fee $5.
Award: $300 (1st prize), $250 (2nd place), $200 (3rd place); all winners will receive publication of their story on WritersWeekly.com & 1 Freelance Income Kit. There will be 30 honorable mentions
Closing Date: 24 hours after contest start

Wyoming Arts Council Creative Writing Fellowships

Wyoming Arts Council
Division of Wyoming Department of Parks & Cultural Resources
Barrett Bldg, 2nd fl, 2301 Central Ave, Cheyenne, WY 82002
Tel: 307-777-7742
Web Site: wyoarts.state.wy.us
Key Personnel
Public Art & Creative Sector Indivs Supv: Rachel Clifton *Tel:* 307-777-5305 *E-mail:* rachel.clifton@state.wy.us
Established: 1986
Awarded annually for the most exciting new creative writing by Wyoming residents. The 3 categories are: poetry, fiction & nonfiction. Blind judges & one juror.
Award: $3,000 each
Closing Date: Varies, see web site
Presented: Announced in the Fall

Yale Series of Younger Poets

Yale University Press
302 Temple St, New Haven, CT 06511
Mailing Address: PO Box 209040, New Haven, CT 06520-9040
Tel: 203-432-0960 *Fax:* 203-432-0948
E-mail: ysyp@yale.edu
Web Site: youngerpoets.yupnet.org
Established: 1919
Awarded annually for poetry mss, 48-64 pages, by early-career American poets who have not previously had a volume of verse published. Submission fee: $25. Mss accepted October 1-November 15. See web site for further details.
Award: Publication & royalties
Closing Date: Nov 15

YALSA/VOYA Research Grant, see Frances Henne YALSA/VOYA Research Grant

Anne & Philip Yandle Best Article Award

British Columbia Historical Federation
PO Box 448, Fort Langley, BC V1M 2R7, Canada
E-mail: info@bchistory.ca
Web Site: www.bchistory.ca/awards
Key Personnel
Recognition Chair: Shannon Bettles
  E-mail: shannon@bchistory.ca
Awarded annually to the author of an article published in *British Columbia History* that best enhances knowledge of the history of British Columbia & provides enjoyable reading. Judging is based upon subject development, writing skill, freshness of material & its appeal to a general readership interested in all aspects of the history of the province.
Award: $250 cash prize & certificate
Closing Date: Dec 31
Presented: BCHF Annual Conference Awards Banquet

YES New Play Festival

Northern Kentucky University
205 FA Theatre Dept, Nunn Dr, Highland Heights, KY 41099-1007
Tel: 859-572-6362 *Fax:* 859-572-6057
Key Personnel
Proj Dir: Corrie Danieley *E-mail:* daneileyc1@nku.edu; Michael King *E-mail:* mking@nku.edu
Established: 1983
New play contest (biennial).
Award: $500 honoraria, travel & housing for 2-3 different playwrights to attend fully produced premiers of their plays
Closing Date: Plays accepted May 1-Sept 30 in even-numbered year prior to year of presentation
Presented: April 2021

Young Lions Fiction Award

New York Public Library
445 Fifth Ave, 4th fl, New York, NY 10016
Tel: 212-930-0887 *Fax:* 212-930-0983
E-mail: younglions@nypl.org
Web Site: www.nypl.org
Key Personnel
Assoc Mgr, Young Lions Fiction Award: Kayla Ponturo *E-mail:* kaylaponturo@nypl.org
Established: 2001
Given annually to an American writer age 35 or younger for either a novel or collection of short stories.
Award: $10,000
Closing Date: Aug
Presented: The New York Public Library, June

Phyllis Smart-Young Poetry Prize

The Madison Review
University of Wisconsin, 6193 Helen C White Hall, English Dept, 600 N Park St, Madison, WI 53706
E-mail: madisonrevw@gmail.com
Web Site: www.themadisonrevw.com
Key Personnel
Chmn Dept: Russ Castronovo
Faculty Advisor & Prog Coord: Ronald Kuka *Tel:* 608-263-3374 *E-mail:* rfkuka@wisc.edu
Ed: Kiyoko Reidy
Mss must be previously unpublished & should be double-spaced with standard 1-inch margins. There is a maximum of 15 pages for combined 3 poems. Only 1 submission (3 poems) is allowed per person per contest. Entry fee $10.
Award: $1,000 & publication in Spring issue of *The Madison Review*
Closing Date: Annually, Nov 1
Presented: Announcement in March

Young Writers Award

Council for Wisconsin Writers
c/o 3225 N 91 St, Milwaukee, WI 53222
E-mail: wiswriters@gmail.com
Web Site: wiswriters.org/awards
Key Personnel
Contest Chair: Erik Richardson
  E-mail: erichardson@wi.rr.com
Annual award to recognize Wisconsin high school students who excel at creative writing. An entry is a single written work in any literary genre on any topic. Genres include poetry, drama, short fiction, essay, humor & memoir.
Award: $250, $50 honorable mention
Closing Date: Jan 31
Presented: CWW Annual Banquet, May

YoungArts

National YoungArts Foundation
2100 Biscayne Blvd, Miami, FL 33137
Tel: 305-377-1140 *Toll Free Tel:* 800-970-ARTS (970-2787)
E-mail: info@youngarts.org; apply@youngarts.org
Web Site: www.youngarts.org
Key Personnel
Media: Dejha Carrington *E-mail:* dcarrington@youngarts.org
Established: 1981
Annual cash award & scholarship opportunities for 15-18 year old artists with demonstrated talent in dance, jazz, cinematic arts, classical music, photography, theater, visual arts, voice & writing. Registration fee: $35. Applicants must be US citizens or have permanent resident status.
Other Sponsor(s): Carnival Foundation
Award: Up to $10,000 in individual awards with potential for Presidential Scholar in the Arts Award
Closing Date: Oct 14
Presented: Alumni Performance & Awards Ceremony, New World Center, Miami, FL, Jan

Morton Dauwen Zabel Award

American Academy of Arts & Letters
633 W 155 St, New York, NY 10032
Tel: 212-368-5900 *Fax:* 212-491-4615
E-mail: academy@artsandletters.org
Web Site: artsandletters.org
Key Personnel
Exec Dir: Cody Upton
Biennial award presented in even-numbered years in rotation to a poet, writer of fiction, or critic, of progressive, original & experimental tendencies.
Award: $10,000

Barbara & David Zalaznick Book Prize in American History

New-York Historical Society
170 Central Park W, New York, NY 10024
Tel: 212-873-3400 *Fax:* 212-595-5707
E-mail: info@nyhistory.org
Web Site: www.nyhistory.org/news/book-prize
Key Personnel
VP & Dir, Patricia D Klingenstein Library: Michael Ryan *Tel:* 212-485-9219
Awarded for a nonfiction book on American history or biography that is distinguished by its scholarship, its literary style & its appeal to a general, as well as an academic, audience. Publishers may submit as many titles as they wish, but must send 7 copies of each submission.
Award: Engraved medal, $50,000 cash prize to author & title of American Historian Laureate
Presented: Chairman's Council Weekend with History, Annually in April

The Jacob Zilber Prize for Short Fiction

PRISM international
University of British Columbia, Buch E462, 1866 Main Mall, Vancouver, BC V6T 1Z1, Canada
Tel: 778-822-2514 *Fax:* 778-822-3616
E-mail: prismwritingcontest@gmail.com
Web Site: www.prismmagazine.ca
Key Personnel
Exec Ed: Jennifer Lori; Claire Matthews
Poetry Ed: Dominique Bernier Cormier
Prose Ed: Christopher Evans
Established: 1986
Short fiction. Entry fee: $35 (CN), $40 (US), $45 (intl).
Award: $1,500 (grand prize), $600 (1st runner up), $400 (2nd runner up)
Closing Date: Annually in Jan (check web site for exact date)

Charlotte Zolotow Award

Cooperative Children's Book Center (CCBC)
225 N Mills St, Rm 401, Madison, WI 53706
Tel: 608-263-3720
E-mail: ccbcinfo@education.wisc.edu
Web Site: ccbs.education.wisc.edu/books/zolotow.asp
Key Personnel
Comm Chair: Megan Schliesman *Tel:* 608-262-9503 *E-mail:* schliesman@education.wisc.edu
Established: 1998
Awarded annually to the author of the best picture book text published in the US in the preceding year. Book may be fiction, nonfiction or folklore, as long as it is presented in picture book form & aimed at children from birth to age 7. Must be printed book originally written in English. Books published only as ebooks/digital books are not eligible.
Award: Bronze medallion
Closing Date: Dec
Presented: Spring

Anna Zornio Memorial Children's Theatre Playwriting Award
University of New Hampshire Department of Theatre & Dance
D22 Paul Creative Arts Center, 30 Academic Way, Durham, NH 03824
Tel: 603-862-2919 *Fax:* 603-862-0298

Web Site: cola.unh.edu/theatre-dance/resource/zornio
Key Personnel
Admin Mgr: Michael Wood *Tel:* 603-862-3038
  E-mail: mike.wood@unh.edu
Chair, Dept of Theatre & Dance: David Kaye
Established: 1980

Award for well written play or musical appropriate for young audiences, PreK-12.
Award: Cash award, up to $500 & play underwritten & produced by the UNH Theatre Department
Closing Date: March 1, 2021
Presented: University of New Hampshire, Durham, NH, Winner announced Nov 2021

Books & Magazines for the Trade

Reference Books for the Trade

A Dictionary of Modern English Usage
Published by Oxford University Press USA
198 Madison Ave, New York, NY 10016
SAN: 202-5892
Toll Free Tel: 800-451-7556 (orders) *Fax:* 212-726-6453
E-mail: orders.us@oup.com
Web Site: global.oup.com
Key Personnel
Author: H W Fowler
Editor: David Crystal
2010 (Dec): 832 pp, $17.95
First published 2009
ISBN(s): 978-0-19-958589-2

A Guide to Academic Writing
Published by Praeger
Imprint of ABC-CLIO
130 Cremona Dr, Suite C, Santa Barbara, CA 93117
Mailing Address: PO Box 1911, Santa Barbara, CA 93116-1911
Tel: 805-968-1911 *Toll Free Tel:* 800-368-6868
Fax: 805-685-9685 *Toll Free Fax:* 866-270-3856
E-mail: custserv@abc-clio.com
Web Site: www.abc-clio.com
Key Personnel
Dir, Edit-Print: Anthony Chiffolo
Author: Jeffery A Cantor
A comprehensive guide to academic writing & publishing.
200 pp, $26.95 paper, $64 hardcover
ISBN(s): 978-0-275-94660-9 (paper); 978-0-313-29017-6 (hardcover)

All-in-One Media Contacts Directory
Published by Gebbie Press Inc
PO Box 1000, New Paltz, NY 12561-0017
Tel: 845-255-7560 *Toll Free Fax:* 888-345-2790
E-mail: gebbie@gebbiepress.com
Web Site: www.gebbieinc.com
Key Personnel
Pres: Mark Gebbie
Published in 3 sections. The Daily & Weekly Newspaper Directory section lists contact information for all US daily & weekly newspapers, including Black & Spanish language papers. The Radio & Television Directory section includes radio & TV stations including Black & Spanish language stations & the Trade & Consumer Directory section includes a comprehensive listing of magazines available in various formats.
Annual (print version).
49th ed, 2020: 462 pp, $165 paper, $395 online application or text files

Almanac of Famous People
Published by Gale

Division of Cengage Learning
27500 Drake Rd, Farmington Hills, MI 48331-3535
SAN: 213-4373
Tel: 248-699-4253 *Toll Free Tel:* 800-877-4253
Fax: 248-699-8070 *Toll Free Fax:* 800-414-5043 (orders)
E-mail: gale.galeord@cengage.com
Web Site: www.gale.com
A guide to sources of biographical information on more than 30,000 famous individuals & groups. Entries provide: Subject's best-known name, complete name, nickname, name of group, dates & places of birth & death (when appropriate), nationality & occupation. Most entries include citations to sources that provide additional biographical information. Four indexes: geographic, occupation, chronological index by date & chronological index by year.
10th ed, 2011, $394 hardcover
First published 2001
ISBN(s): 978-1-4144-4548-9

American Book Prices Current
Published by Bancroft Parkman Inc
PO Box 1236, Washington, CT 06793-0236
Tel: 860-868-7408
E-mail: abpc@snet.net
Web Site: www.bookpricescurrent.com
Key Personnel
Publr: Daniel J Leab
Exec Ed: Katharine Kyes Leab
Research price guide detailing prices realized at auction in the US & abroad in the world of books, mss, autographs, maps, broadsides & charts. Now online only, continually updated.
Online price: lib or dealer $595, others $800, update $198.90
First published 1895

American Book Publishing Record® Annual
Published by Grey House Publishing Inc™
4919 Rte 22, Amenia, NY 12501
Mailing Address: PO Box 56, Amenia, NY 12501-0056
Tel: 518-789-8700 *Toll Free Tel:* 800-562-2139
Fax: 518-789-0556
E-mail: books@greyhouse.com
Web Site: greyhouse.com
Provides access to over 50,000 cataloging records for the entire previous year, for books published or distributed in the US.
Annual.
2020: 3,800 pp, $1,025/2 vol set
ISBN(s): 978-1-64265-537-7 (2 vol set)

American Book Trade Directory
Published by Information Today, Inc

121 Chanlon Rd, Suite G-20, New Providence, NJ 07974-2195
Toll Free Tel: 800-824-2470 *Fax:* 727-286-7281
E-mail: custserv@infotoday.com
Key Personnel
Mgr, Tampa Edit Opers: Debra James *Tel:* 800-824-2470 ext 2220 *E-mail:* djames@infotoday.com
Comprehensive directory of over 11,900 booksellers & wholesalers in the US & Canada, arranged by state/province & city; includes information on sidelines, appraisers, auctioneers & dealers in foreign language books.
Annual.
66th ed, 2020-2021: 1,040 pp, $399.50
ISBN(s): 978-1-57387-561-5

American Library Directory
Published by Information Today, Inc
121 Chanlon Rd, Suite G-20, New Providence, NJ 07974-2195
Toll Free Tel: 800-300-9868 (cust serv); 800-409-4929 (press 4)
E-mail: custserv@infotoday.com
Web Site: www.americanlibrarydirectory.com
Key Personnel
Consulting Ed: Stephen L Torpie *Tel:* 908-219-0278 *E-mail:* storpie@infotoday.com
Comprehensive directory of over 30,000 libraries (public, academic & special) throughout the US & Canada. Also includes listings of library schools, networks & systems, consortia & state library agencies. Automation information, as well as URLs for libraries & e-mails for library personnel included. Entries arranged geographically. Personnel Index section arranged alphabetically.
Annual.
73rd ed, 2020-2021: 3,888 pp, $399.50/2 vol set cloth
ISBN(s): 978-1-57387-562-2 (2 vol set)

American Reference Books Annual
Published by Libraries Unlimited
Imprint of ABC-CLIO
147 Castilian Dr, Santa Barbara, CA 93117
Mailing Address: PO Box 1911, Santa Barbara, CA 93116-1911
Tel: 805-968-1911 *Toll Free Tel:* 800-368-6868
Fax: 805-685-9685 *Toll Free Fax:* 866-270-3856
E-mail: customerservice@abc-clio.com
Web Site: www.abc-clio.com
Key Personnel
Assoc Ed: Juneal M Chenoweth
The premier sources of information for the library & information community for more than 3 decades. Includes descriptive & evaluative entries for recent reference publications. Reviews by subject experts of materials from more than

300 publishers & in nearly 500 subject areas. ARBA assists in answering everyday reference questions & in building a reference collection. Also available online.
Annual.
Vol 50, 2019: 552 pp, $155
ISBN(s): 978-1-4408-6913-6 (hardcover); 978-1-4408-6914-3 (ebook)

The Art & Science of Book Publishing
Published by Ohio University Press
Alden Library, Suite 101, 30 Park Place, Athens, OH 45701-2901
Tel: 740-593-1154
Web Site: www.ohioswallow.com
Key Personnel
Interim Dir & Prodn Mgr: Beth Pratt *Tel:* 740-593-1162 *E-mail:* prattb@ohio.edu
Edit Coord: Tyler Balli *E-mail:* tylerballi@ohio.edu
Author: Herbert S Bailey, Jr
Introduction to basics of book publishing.
1993 ed: 234 pp, $18.95 paper
First published 1970
ISBN(s): 978-0-8214-0970-1

The Association of American University Presses Directory
Published by Association of University Presses (AUPresses)
1412 Broadway, Suite 2135, New York, NY 10018
Tel: 212-989-1010 *Toll Free Tel:* 800-621-2736 (orders) *Fax:* 773-702-7212 (orders); 212-989-0275
E-mail: info@aupresses.org
Web Site: www.aupresses.org
A detailed introduction to the structure & staff of the AUPresses & to the publishing programs & personnel of member presses.
Annual.
2020: 260 pp, $30 print, $30 full-access digital, $7 30-day access digital
ISBN(s): 978-0-945103-42-4 (digital); 978-0-945103-44-8 (print)

Author in Progress
Published by Writer's Digest Books
Imprint of Penguin Random House LLC
1745 Broadway, New York, NY 10019
Web Site: www.writersdigest.com; www.writersdigestshop.com; www.fwmedia.com
No-nonsense guide for excelling at every step of the novel writing process, from setting goals, researching & drafting to giving a receiving critiques, polishing prose & seeking publication.
352 pp, $19.99 paper & ebook (retail)
ISBN(s): 978-1-4403-4671-2 (paper); 978-1-4403-4672-9 (ebook)

Authors, Copyright, and Publishing in the Digital Era
Published by IGI Global
701 E Chocolate Ave, Hershey, PA 17033
Tel: 717-533-8845 (ext 100) *Toll Free Tel:* 866-342-6657 *Fax:* 717-533-8661; 717-533-7115
E-mail: cust@igi-global.com
Web Site: www.igi-global.com
2014: 262 pp, $195
ISBN(s): 978-1-4666-5214-9; 978-1-4666-5215-6 (ebook)

AV Market Place (AVMP)
Published by Information Today, Inc
121 Chanlon Rd, Suite G-20, New Providence, NJ 07974-2195
Tel: 908-795-3755 *Toll Free Tel:* 800-409-4929 (press 3); 800-300-9868 (cust serv)
E-mail: custserv@infotoday.com

Key Personnel
Mng Ed: Karen Hallard *Tel:* 908-219-0277 *E-mail:* khallard@infotoday.com
A comprehensive directory of the AV market, listing the activities of almost 4,300 manufacturers, distributors & production service companies & over 1,250 products & services. Heavily indexed. Also contains information on related associations, state & local film & television commissions, awards & festivals, periodicals, reference books & AV-oriented conferences & exhibits. Covers all 50 states plus Canada.
Annual.
48th ed, 2020: 1,306 pp, $389.50 paper
ISBN(s): 978-1-57387-560-8

Awards & Prizes Online
Published by The Children's Book Council (CBC)
54 W 39 St, 14th fl, New York, NY 10018
Tel: 212-966-1990
E-mail: cbc.info@cbcbooks.org
Web Site: www.cbcbooks.org
Key Personnel
Exec Dir: Carl Lennertz *E-mail:* carl.lennertz@cbcbooks.org
Lists over 300 major US, British Commonwealth & international children's & young adult book awards; for teachers, librarians & universities with English, library or education schools teaching children's literature or creative writing. Includes indices, appendix & a list of information resources.
$150 online

Banned in the USA: A Reference Guide to Book Censorship in Schools & Public Libraries Revised & Expanded Edition
Published by Greenwood Press
Imprint of ABC-CLIO
130 Cremona Dr, Suite C, Santa Barbara, CA 93117
Mailing Address: PO Box 1911, Santa Barbara, CA 93116-1911
Tel: 805-968-1911 *Toll Free Tel:* 800-368-6868 *Fax:* 805-685-9685 *Toll Free Fax:* 866-270-3856
E-mail: customerservice@abc-clio.com
Web Site: www.abc-clio.com
Key Personnel
Dir, Edit-Print: Anthony Chiffolo
Author: Herbert N Foerstel
Foerstel's book is the perfect book to hand to students writing papers on censorship or anyone doing research on the subject.
2002: 328 pp, $72 hardcover
ISBN(s): 978-0-313-31166-6

Be the Media
Published by Natural E Creative Group LLC
1110 Jericho Tpke, 2nd fl, New Hyde Park, NY 11040
Tel: 516-488-1143 *Fax:* 516-488-4111
E-mail: info@bethemedia.com
Web Site: www.bethemedia.com
1st ed: 536 pp, $34.95 US
First published 2008
ISBN(s): 978-0-9760814-5-6

Biography and Genealogy Master Index (BGMI)
Published by Gale
Division of Cengage Learning
27500 Drake Rd, Farmington Hills, MI 48331-3535
SAN: 213-4373
Tel: 248-699-4253 *Toll Free Tel:* 800-877-4253 *Fax:* 248-699-8075 *Toll Free Fax:* 800-414-5043 (orders)
E-mail: gale.galeord@cengage.com
Web Site: www.gale.com

Provides more than 17 million citations compiled from more than 2,000 publications, covering over 5 million people. Available online, updated twice annually.

Book Blitz, Getting Your Book in the News
Published by Best Sellers
7456 Evergreen Dr, Goleta, CA 93117
Tel: 805-968-8567 *Fax:* 805-968-8567
Key Personnel
Author: Barbara Gaughen *E-mail:* bgaughenmu@aol.com; Ernest Weckbaugh
A hands-on publicity guide for authors; 60 steps for instant book success.
1996: 268 pp, $12.95
ISBN(s): 978-1-881474-02-9

Book Review Digest
Published by Grey House Publishing Inc™
4919 Rte 22, Amenia, NY 12501
Mailing Address: PO Box 56, Amenia, NY 12501-0056
Tel: 518-789-8700 *Toll Free Tel:* 800-562-2139 *Fax:* 518-789-0556
E-mail: books@greyhouse.com
Web Site: greyhouse.com
Concise critical evaluations, including citations & excerpts from book reviews, from more than 100 selected American, British & Canadian periodicals.
Annual.
2019 (2018 annual cumulation): 2,200 pp, $695
ISBN(s): 978-1-64265-372-4

Book Review Index
Published by Gale
Division of Cengage Learning
27500 Drake Rd, Farmington Hills, MI 48331-3535
SAN: 213-4373
Tel: 248-699-4253 *Toll Free Tel:* 800-877-4253 *Fax:* 248-699-8075 *Toll Free Fax:* 800-414-5043 (orders)
E-mail: gale.galeord@cengage.com
Web Site: www.gale.com
Provides quick access to reviews of books, periodicals, books on tape & electronic media representing a wide range of popular, academic & professional interests. More than 400 publications are indexed, including journals & national general interest publications & newspapers. Available as 3 issue subscription or as an annual cumulation.
2018 ed, $685 paper
ISBN(s): 978-1-41032-817-5

Bookbinding Materials & Techniques 1700-1920
Published by Canadian Bookbinders and Book Artists Guild (CBBAG)
180 Shaw St, Unit 102, Toronto, ON M6J 2W5, Canada
Tel: 416-581-1071
E-mail: cbbag@cbbag.ca
Web Site: www.cbbag.ca
Key Personnel
Author: Margaret Lock
160 pp, $20
First published 2003
ISBN(s): 978-0-9695091-9-6

Bookman's Price Index: A Guide to the Values of Rare & Other Out-of-Print Books
Published by Gale
Division of Cengage Learning
27500 Drake Rd, Farmington Hills, MI 48331-3535
SAN: 213-4373
Tel: 248-699-4253 *Toll Free Tel:* 800-877-4253 *Fax:* 248-699-8075 *Toll Free Fax:* 800-414-5043 (orders)

E-mail: gale.galeord@cengage.com
Web Site: www.gale.com
Gathers the most recent listings in the antiquarian book world in order to create a catalog of recent trends & pricing in the field of collectible books. Volumes do not supersede previous volumes. Each volume covers catalogs from the previous 4-6 months. Each entry includes title, author, edition, year published, physical description (size, binding, illustrations), condition of the book & price.
Vol 103, 2016: 1,184 pp, $814 hardcover
First published 1964
ISBN(s): 978-1-4103-1794-0

Books in Print®
Published by Grey House Publishing Inc™
4919 Rte 22, Amenia, NY 12501
Mailing Address: PO Box 56, Amenia, NY 12501-0056
Tel: 518-789-8700 *Toll Free Tel:* 800-562-2139
Fax: 518-789-0556
E-mail: books@greyhouse.com
Web Site: greyhouse.com
Serves the library & book trade communities as the definitive bibliographic resource. Features more than 1.7 million titles from more than 123,000 US publishers, to offer unparalleled coverage of the full range of books currently published or distributed in the US.
Annual.
2020-2021: 18,000 pp, $1,930/7 vol set
ISBN(s): 978-1-64265-496-7 (7 vol set)

Books in Print® Supplement
Published by Grey House Publishing Inc™
4919 Rte 22, Amenia, NY 12501
Mailing Address: PO Box 56, Amenia, NY 12501-0056
Tel: 518-789-8700 *Toll Free Tel:* 800-562-2139
Fax: 518-789-0556
E-mail: books@greyhouse.com
Web Site: greyhouse.com
This essential mid-year companion to *Books In Print®* provides the latest book publishing updates for the past 6 months. This resource is crucial in ensuring that libraries & bookstores have access to the most accurate information throughout the year.
Annual.
56th ed, 2019-2020: 8,400 pp, $1,110/3 vol set
ISBN(s): 978-1-64265-504-9 (3 vol set)

Books Out Loud™: Bowker's Guide to Audiobooks
Published by Grey House Publishing Inc™
4919 Rte 22, Amenia, NY 12501
Mailing Address: PO Box 56, Amenia, NY 12501-0056
Tel: 518-789-8700 *Toll Free Tel:* 800-562-2139
Fax: 518-789-0556
E-mail: books@greyhouse.com
Web Site: greyhouse.com
Must-have collection development & reference tool for your library or bookstore. Offers bibliographic information on over 300,000 audiobooks from over 10,000 producers & 2,100 distributors & wholesalers.
Annual.
2020: 5,800 pp, $705/2 vol set
ISBN(s): 978-1-6426-515-5 (2 vol set)

Business & Legal Forms for Authors & Self-Publishers
Published by Allworth Press
Imprint of Skyhorse Publishing Inc
307 W 36 St, 11th fl, New York, NY 10018
Tel: 212-643-6816 *Fax:* 212-643-6819
Web Site: www.allworth.com
Key Personnel
Founder & Publr: Tad Crawford
 E-mail: crawford@allworth.com

Busn Mgr: Marrissa Jones *E-mail:* mjones@skyhorsepublishing.com
Contains 32 ready-to-use forms, negotiation checklist & extra tear-out forms; digital forms available online.
4th ed, 2015: 176 pp, $24.99
ISBN(s): 978-1-62153-464-2

Cabell's Directory of Publishing Opportunities in Accounting
Published by Cabell Publishing Co
PO Box 5428, Beaumont, TX 77726-5428
Tel: 409-898-0575 *Fax:* 409-866-9554
E-mail: orders@cabells.com
Web Site: www.cabells.com
Key Personnel
Founder & Pres: David Cabell *E-mail:* dave@cabells.com
VP, Busn Devt: Lacey E Earle *E-mail:* lacey@cabells.com
VP, Global Mktg: Sheree Crosby
 E-mail: sheree@cabells.com
Online directory of information on over 517 journals in accounting.
First published 1978
ISBN(s): 978-0-911753-49-3

Cabell's Directory of Publishing Opportunities in All Directories
Published by Cabell Publishing Co
PO Box 5428, Beaumont, TX 77726-5428
Tel: 409-898-0575 *Fax:* 409-866-9554
E-mail: orders@cabells.com
Web Site: www.cabells.com
Key Personnel
Founder & Pres: David Cabell *E-mail:* dave@cabells.com
VP, Busn Devt: Lacey E Earle *E-mail:* lacey@cabells.com
VP, Global Mktg: Sheree Crosby
 E-mail: sheree@cabells.com

Cabell's Directory of Publishing Opportunities in Astronomy
Published by Cabell Publishing Co
PO Box 5428, Beaumont, TX 77726-5428
Tel: 409-898-0575 *Fax:* 409-866-9554
E-mail: orders@cabells.com
Web Site: www.cabells.com
Key Personnel
Founder & Pres: David Cabell *E-mail:* dave@cabells.com
VP, Busn Devt: Lacey E Earle *E-mail:* lacey@cabells.com
VP, Global Mktg: Sheree Crosby
 E-mail: sheree@cabells.com

Cabell's Directory of Publishing Opportunities in Biological Sciences
Published by Cabell Publishing Co
PO Box 5428, Beaumont, TX 77726-5428
Tel: 409-898-0575 *Fax:* 409-866-9554
E-mail: orders@cabells.com
Web Site: www.cabells.com
Key Personnel
Founder & Pres: David Cabell *E-mail:* dave@cabells.com
VP, Busn Devt: Lacey E Earle *E-mail:* lacey@cabells.com
VP, Global Mktg: Sheree Crosby
 E-mail: sheree@cabells.com
First published 2016
ISBN(s): 978-0-911753-76-9

Cabell's Directory of Publishing Opportunities in Business - College/Library Set
Published by Cabell Publishing Co
PO Box 5428, Beaumont, TX 77726-5428
Tel: 409-898-0575 *Fax:* 409-866-9554
E-mail: orders@cabells.com
Web Site: www.cabells.com

Key Personnel
Founder & Pres: David Cabell *E-mail:* dave@cabells.com
VP, Busn Devt: Lacey E Earle *E-mail:* lacey@cabells.com
VP, Global Mktg: Sheree Crosby
 E-mail: sheree@cabells.com
Online directory of information on over 4,617 academic journals in business.
First published 1978
ISBN(s): 978-0-911753-65-3

Cabell's Directory of Publishing Opportunities in Chemistry
Published by Cabell Publishing Co
PO Box 5428, Beaumont, TX 77726-5428
Tel: 409-898-0575 *Fax:* 409-866-9554
E-mail: orders@cabells.com
Web Site: www.cabells.com
Key Personnel
Founder & Pres: David Cabell *E-mail:* dave@cabells.com
VP, Busn Devt: Lacey E Earle *E-mail:* lacey@cabells.com
VP, Global Mktg: Sheree Crosby
 E-mail: sheree@cabells.com

Cabell's Directory of Publishing Opportunities in Computer Science-Business Information Systems
Published by Cabell Publishing Co
PO Box 5428, Beaumont, TX 77726-5428
Tel: 409-898-0575 *Fax:* 409-866-9554
E-mail: orders@cabells.com
Web Site: www.cabells.com
Key Personnel
Founder & Pres: David Cabell *E-mail:* dave@cabells.com
VP, Busn Devt: Lacey E Earle *E-mail:* lacey@cabells.com
VP, Global Mktg: Sheree Crosby
 E-mail: sheree@cabells.com
Information on over 1,618 journals in computer science & business information systems.
First published 2010
ISBN(s): 978-0-911753-70-7

Cabell's Directory of Publishing Opportunities in Economics & Finance
Published by Cabell Publishing Co
PO Box 5428, Beaumont, TX 77726-5428
Tel: 409-898-0575 *Fax:* 409-866-9554
E-mail: orders@cabells.com
Web Site: www.cabells.com
Key Personnel
Founder & Pres: David Cabell *E-mail:* dave@cabells.com
VP, Busn Devt: Lacey E Earle *E-mail:* lacey@cabells.com
VP, Global Mktg: Sheree Crosby
 E-mail: sheree@cabells.com
Online directory of information on over 1,362 journals in economics & finance.
First published 1978
ISBN(s): 978-0-911753-50-9

Cabell's Directory of Publishing Opportunities in Education, Curriculum & Methods
Published by Cabell Publishing Co
PO Box 5428, Beaumont, TX 77726-5428
Tel: 409-898-0575 *Fax:* 409-866-9554
E-mail: orders@cabells.com
Web Site: www.cabells.com
Key Personnel
Founder & Pres: David Cabell *E-mail:* dave@cabells.com
VP, Busn Devt: Lacey E Earle *E-mail:* lacey@cabells.com
VP, Global Mktg: Sheree Crosby
 E-mail: sheree@cabells.com
Online indexes of over 906 journals on 28 different topic areas related to educational curriculum & methods.

First published 1981
ISBN(s): 978-0-911753-66-0

Cabell's Directory of Publishing Opportunities in Education Set
Published by Cabell Publishing Co
PO Box 5428, Beaumont, TX 77726-5428
Tel: 409-898-0575 *Fax:* 409-866-9554
E-mail: orders@cabells.com
Web Site: www.cabells.com
Key Personnel
Founder & Pres: David Cabell *E-mail:* dave@cabells.com
VP, Busn Devt: Lacey E Earle *E-mail:* lacey@cabells.com
VP, Global Mktg: Sheree Crosby
E-mail: sheree@cabells.com
Information on over 2,119 journals in education. Electronic version only.
First published 2009
ISBN(s): 978-0-911753-69-1

Cabell's Directory of Publishing Opportunities in Educational Psychology & Administration
Published by Cabell Publishing Co
PO Box 5428, Beaumont, TX 77726-5428
Tel: 409-898-0575 *Fax:* 409-866-9554
E-mail: orders@cabells.com
Web Site: www.cabells.com
Key Personnel
Founder & Pres: David Cabell *E-mail:* dave@cabells.com
VP, Busn Devt: Lacey E Earle *E-mail:* lacey@cabells.com
VP, Global Mktg: Sheree Crosby
E-mail: sheree@cabells.com
Online indexes of over 718 journals on 28 different topic areas related to educational psychology & administration.
First published 1981
ISBN(s): 978-0-911753-67-7

Cabell's Directory of Publishing Opportunities in Educational Technology & Library Science
Published by Cabell Publishing Co
PO Box 5428, Beaumont, TX 77726-5428
Tel: 409-898-0575 *Fax:* 409-866-9554
E-mail: orders@cabells.com
Web Site: www.cabells.com
Key Personnel
Founder & Pres: David Cabell *E-mail:* dave@cabells.com
VP, Busn Devt: Lacey E Earle *E-mail:* lacey@cabells.com
VP, Global Mktg: Sheree Crosby
E-mail: sheree@cabells.com
Online directory of information on over 495 journals in educational technology & library science.
First published 2007
ISBN(s): 978-0-911753-68-4

Cabell's Directory of Publishing Opportunities in Geology
Published by Cabell Publishing Co
PO Box 5428, Beaumont, TX 77726-5428
Tel: 409-898-0575 *Fax:* 409-866-9554
E-mail: orders@cabells.com
Web Site: www.cabells.com
Key Personnel
Founder & Pres: David Cabell *E-mail:* dave@cabells.com
VP, Busn Devt: Lacey E Earle *E-mail:* lacey@cabells.com
VP, Global Mktg: Sheree Crosby
E-mail: sheree@cabells.com
First published 2016
ISBN(s): 978-0-911753-78-3

Cabell's Directory of Publishing Opportunities in Health Administration
Published by Cabell Publishing Co
PO Box 5428, Beaumont, TX 77726-5428
Tel: 409-898-0575 *Fax:* 409-866-9554
E-mail: orders@cabells.com
Web Site: www.cabells.com
Key Personnel
Founder & Pres: David Cabell *E-mail:* dave@cabells.com
VP, Busn Devt: Lacey E Earle *E-mail:* lacey@cabells.com
VP, Global Mktg: Sheree Crosby
E-mail: sheree@cabells.com
Information on 788 journals listed in health administration.
First published 2010
ISBN(s): 978-0-911753-71-4

Cabell's Directory of Publishing Opportunities in Management
Published by Cabell Publishing Co
PO Box 5428, Beaumont, TX 77726-5428
Tel: 409-898-0575 *Fax:* 409-866-9554
E-mail: orders@cabells.com
Web Site: www.cabells.com
Key Personnel
Founder & Pres: David Cabell *E-mail:* dave@cabells.com
VP, Busn Devt: Lacey E Earle *E-mail:* lacey@cabells.com
VP, Global Mktg: Sheree Crosby
E-mail: sheree@cabells.com
Online directory of information on over 2,080 journals in management.
First published 1978
ISBN(s): 978-0-911753-51-6

Cabell's Directory of Publishing Opportunities in Marketing
Published by Cabell Publishing Co
PO Box 5428, Beaumont, TX 77726-5428
Tel: 409-898-0575 *Fax:* 409-866-9554
E-mail: orders@cabells.com
Web Site: www.cabells.com
Key Personnel
Founder & Pres: David Cabell *E-mail:* dave@cabells.com
VP, Busn Devt: Lacey E Earle *E-mail:* lacey@cabells.com
VP, Global Mktg: Sheree Crosby
E-mail: sheree@cabells.com
Online directory of information on over 658 journals in marketing.
First published 1978
ISBN(s): 978-0-911753-64-6

Cabell's Directory of Publishing Opportunities in Mathematics
Published by Cabell Publishing Co
PO Box 5428, Beaumont, TX 77726-5428
Tel: 409-898-0575 *Fax:* 409-866-9554
E-mail: orders@cabells.com
Web Site: www.cabells.com
Key Personnel
Founder & Pres: David Cabell *E-mail:* dave@cabells.com
VP, Busn Devt: Lacey E Earle *E-mail:* lacey@cabells.com
VP, Global Mktg: Sheree Crosby
E-mail: sheree@cabells.com

Cabell's Directory of Publishing Opportunities in Nursing
Published by Cabell Publishing Co
PO Box 5428, Beaumont, TX 77726-5428
Tel: 409-898-0575 *Fax:* 409-866-9554
E-mail: orders@cabells.com
Web Site: www.cabells.com
Key Personnel
Founder & Pres: David Cabell *E-mail:* dave@cabells.com

VP, Busn Devt: Lacey E Earle *E-mail:* lacey@cabells.com
VP, Global Mktg: Sheree Crosby
E-mail: sheree@cabells.com
Information on over 571 academic journals in nursing. Electronic version only.
First published 2010
ISBN(s): 978-0-911753-72-1

Cabell's Directory of Publishing Opportunities in Oceanography
Published by Cabell Publishing Co
PO Box 5428, Beaumont, TX 77726-5428
Tel: 409-898-0575 *Fax:* 409-866-9554
E-mail: orders@cabells.com
Web Site: www.cabells.com
Key Personnel
Founder & Pres: David Cabell *E-mail:* dave@cabells.com
VP, Busn Devt: Lacey E Earle *E-mail:* lacey@cabells.com
VP, Global Mktg: Sheree Crosby
E-mail: sheree@cabells.com
First published 2016
ISBN(s): 978-0-911753-79-0

Cabell's Directory of Publishing Opportunities in Physics
Published by Cabell Publishing Co
PO Box 5428, Beaumont, TX 77726-5428
Tel: 409-898-0575 *Fax:* 409-866-9554
E-mail: orders@cabells.com
Web Site: www.cabells.com
Key Personnel
Founder & Pres: David Cabell *E-mail:* dave@cabells.com
VP, Busn Devt: Lacey E Earle *E-mail:* lacey@cabells.com
VP, Global Mktg: Sheree Crosby
E-mail: sheree@cabells.com
First published 2016
ISBN(s): 978-0-911753-80-6

Cabell's Directory of Publishing Opportunities in Psychology & Psychiatry
Published by Cabell Publishing Co
PO Box 5428, Beaumont, TX 77726-5428
Tel: 409-898-0575 *Fax:* 409-866-9554
E-mail: orders@cabells.com
Web Site: www.cabells.com
Key Personnel
Founder & Pres: David Cabell *E-mail:* dave@cabells.com
VP, Busn Devt: Lacey E Earle *E-mail:* lacey@cabells.com
VP, Global Mktg: Sheree Crosby
E-mail: sheree@cabells.com
Online directory of information on 1,841 journals listed in psychology & psychiatry.
First published 2002
ISBN(s): 978-0-911753-73-8

Careers in Communications & Media
Published by Grey House Publishing Inc™
4919 Rte 22, Amenia, NY 12501
Mailing Address: PO Box 56, Amenia, NY 12501-0056
Tel: 518-789-8700 *Toll Free Tel:* 800-562-2139
Fax: 518-789-0556
E-mail: csr@salempress.com
Web Site: salempress.com
Key Personnel
Ed: Michael Shally-Jensen, PhD
Provides a current overview & future outlook of specific occupations in communications & media industries. Companies in this field are involved in television & radio broadcasting, motion picture/video production, publishing, advertising & telecommunications.
Jan 2014: 375 pp, $125 (includes online access with print purchase)
ISBN(s): 978-1-61925-230-1; 978-1-61925-231-8 (ebook)

Catholic Press Association Directory
Published by Catholic Press Association of the
United States & Canada
205 W Monroe St, Suite 470, Chicago, IL 60606
Tel: 312-380-6789 *Fax:* 312-361-0256
Web Site: www.catholicpress.org
Key Personnel
Exec Dir: Timothy M Walter *E-mail:* twalter@
catholicpress.org
Busn Mgr: Barbara Mastrolia
E-mail: bmastrolia@catholicpress.com
Proj Coord: Elise Freed-Brown
Proj Asst: Carol Arnold
Complete listings of more than 600 Catholic
newspapers, magazines, newsletters & foreign
language publications in the US & Canada.
Also includes Catholic book & general publish-
ers; Diocesan directories & media services.
Annual.
2020, Free to membs, $80 for nonmembs

CCOD, see Consultants & Consulting
Organizations Directory (CCOD)

The Chicago Guide to Fact-Checking
Published by University of Chicago Press
1427 E 60 St, Chicago, IL 60637-2954
SAN: 202-5280
E-mail: custserv@press.uchicago.edu;
marketing@press.uchicago.edu
Web Site: www.press.uchicago.edu
Key Personnel
Sr Ed, Ref & Writing Guides: Mary Laur
Tel: 773-702-7326 *E-mail:* mlaur@uchicago.
edu
This book is an accessible, one-stop guide to
the why, what & how of contemporary fact-
checking. Brooke Borel covers best practices
for fact-checking in a variety of media—from
magazine articles, both print & online, to books
& documentaries—& from the perspective of
both in-house & freelance checkers. She also
offers advice on navigating relationships with
writers, editors & sources; considers the realities of fact-checking on a budget & checking one's own work; & reflects on the place of
fact-checking in today's media landscape.
1st ed: 192 pp, $55 cloth, $17 paper, $15 ebook
First published 2016
ISBN(s): 978-0-226-29076-8 (cloth); 978-0-226-
29093-5 (paper); 978-0-226-29109-3 (ebook)

The Chicago Manual of Style
Published by University of Chicago Press
1427 E 60 St, Chicago, IL 60637-2954
SAN: 202-5280
Tel: 773-702-7700; 773-702-7000 (cust serv,
print); 773-753-3347 *Toll Free Tel:* 800-621-
2736 (orders); 877-705-1878 (US & CN)
Fax: 773-702-9756
E-mail: custserv@press.uchicago.edu;
marketing@press.uchicago.edu;
cmoshelpdesk@press.uchicago.edu
Web Site: www.press.uchicago.edu; www.
chicagomanualofstyle.org
Key Personnel
Sr Ed, Ref & Writing Guides: Mary Laur
Tel: 773-702-7326 *E-mail:* mlaur@uchicago.
edu
Style manual for authors, editors & copywriters.
Also available as an online subscription.
Revised every 7-10 yrs.
17th ed, 2017: 1,184 pp, $70
ISBN(s): 978-0-226-28705-8

Children's Books in Print®
Published by Grey House Publishing Inc™
4919 Rte 22, Amenia, NY 12501
Mailing Address: PO Box 56, Amenia, NY
12501-0056
Tel: 518-789-8700 *Toll Free Tel:* 800-562-2139
Fax: 518-789-0556

E-mail: books@greyhouse.com
Web Site: greyhouse.com
Vital resource for locating children's & young
adult titles in the US, offering immediate access to over 275,000 children's books from
over 20,000 US publishers.
Annual.
51st ed, 2020: 3,500 pp, $880/3 vol set
ISBN(s): 978-1-64265-150-8 (3 vol set)

Children's Core Collection
Published by Grey House Publishing Inc™
4919 Rte 22, Amenia, NY 12501
Mailing Address: PO Box 56, Amenia, NY
12501-0056
Tel: 518-789-8700 *Toll Free Tel:* 800-562-2139
Fax: 518-789-0556
E-mail: books@greyhouse.com
Web Site: greyhouse.com
Guide to approximately 16,000 books, covering
fiction & nonfiction works, story collections,
picture books, easy readers, graphic novels
& biographies recommended for readers from
preschool through grade 6.
24th ed, Oct 2019: 3,000 pp, $240
ISBN(s): 978-1-64265-023-5

Children's Literature Review
Published by Gale
Division of Cengage Learning
27500 Drake Rd, Farmington Hills, MI 48331-
3535
SAN: 213-4373
Tel: 248-699-4253 *Toll Free Tel:* 800-877-4253
Fax: 248-699-8070 *Toll Free Fax:* 800-414-
5043 (orders)
E-mail: gale.galeord@cengage.com
Web Site: www.gale.com
Online resource providing critical information
from English language sources in the field of
children's & young adult literature. The series
currently covers more than 750 authors.

Children's Writer's Word Book
Published by Writer's Digest Books
Imprint of Penguin Random House LLC
1745 Broadway, New York, NY 10019
Web Site: www.writersdigest.com; www.
writersdigestshop.com
Handy reference book to be used along with your
dictionary or thesaurus. Gives guidelines for
sentence length, word usage & theme at each
reading level.
2nd ed: 352 pp, $19.99 paper (retail)
First published 1999
ISBN(s): 978-1-58297-413-2

**Complete Broadcasting Industry Guide:
Television, Radio, Cable & Streaming**
Formerly Complete Television, Radio & Cable
Industry Guide
Published by Grey House Publishing Inc™
4919 Rte 22, Amenia, NY 12501
Mailing Address: PO Box 56, Amenia, NY
12501-0056
Tel: 518-789-8700 *Toll Free Tel:* 800-562-2139
Fax: 518-789-0556
E-mail: books@greyhouse.com
Web Site: greyhouse.com
Station data & industry contacts in the U.S. &
Canadian television, radio & cable marketplace.
Annual.
2020: 1,641 pp, $350 (includes online access)
ISBN(s): 978-1-64265-104-1

The Complete Guide to Book Marketing
Published by Allworth Press
Imprint of Skyhorse Publishing Inc
307 W 36 St, 11th fl, New York, NY 10018
Tel: 212-643-6816 *Fax:* 212-643-6819
Web Site: www.allworth.com

Key Personnel
Founder & Publr: Tad Crawford
E-mail: crawford@allworth.com
Busn Mgr: Marrissa Jones *E-mail:* mjones@
skyhorsepublishing.com
Author: David Cole
Comprehensive resource book covering all aspects
of book marketing.
2004 (revised): 256 pp, $19.95
ISBN(s): 978-1-58115-322-4

The Complete Guide to Book Publicity
Published by Allworth Press
Imprint of Skyhorse Publishing Inc
307 W 36 St, 11th fl, New York, NY 10018
Tel: 212-643-6816 *Fax:* 212-643-6819
Web Site: www.allworth.com
Key Personnel
Founder & Publr: Tad Crawford
E-mail: crawford@allworth.com
Busn Mgr: Marrissa Jones *E-mail:* mjones@
skyhorsepublishing.com
Author: Jodee Blanco
A comprehensive resource book covering all as-
pects of book publicity.
2nd ed, 2004: 304 pp, $19.95
ISBN(s): 978-1-58115-349-1

The Complete Guide to Self-Publishing
Published by Writer's Digest Books
Imprint of Penguin Random House LLC
1745 Broadway, New York, NY 10019
Web Site: www.writersdigest.com; www.
writersdigestshop.com
Everything you need to write, publish, promote &
sell your book.
5th ed: 576 pp, $24.99 paper & ebook (retail)
First published 1991
ISBN(s): 978-1-58297-718-8 (paper); 978-1-
59963-184-4 (ebook)

The Complete Guide to Successful Publishing
Published by Cardoza Publishing
1916 E Charleston Blvd, Las Vegas, NV 89104
Tel: 702-870-7200 *Fax:* 702-822-6500
E-mail: info@cardozabooks.com
Web Site: www.cardozabooks.com
Key Personnel
Publr & Author: Avery Cardoza
This step-by-step guide shows beginning & established publishers how to successfully produce
professional-looking books that not only look
good, but sell in the open market; readers learn
how to find & develop ideas; set up the business from the ground up; design & layout a
book; find authors, work contracts & negotiate deals; get distribution; expand a publishing
company into a large enterprise & more.
3rd ed, April 2003: 416 pp, $12.97
First published 1995
ISBN(s): 978-1-58042-097-6

The Complete Handbook of Novel Writing
Published by Writer's Digest Books
Imprint of Penguin Random House LLC
1745 Broadway, New York, NY 10019
Web Site: www.writersdigest.com; www.
writersdigestshop.com
Everything you need to know about creating &
selling your work.
3rd ed: 528 pp, $19.99 paper & ebook (retail)
First published 2002
ISBN(s): 978-1-4403-4839-6 (paper); 978-1-4403-
4842-6 (ebook)

**Complete Television, Radio & Cable Industry
Guide**, see Complete Broadcasting Industry
Guide: Television, Radio, Cable & Streaming

Complete Video Directory™
Published by Grey House Publishing Inc™
4919 Rte 22, Amenia, NY 12501

Mailing Address: PO Box 56, Amenia, NY
12501-0056
Tel: 518-789-8700 *Toll Free Tel:* 800-562-2139
Fax: 518-789-0556
E-mail: books@greyhouse.com
Web Site: greyhouse.com
Extensive listing of over 72,000 entertainment &
performance titles along with educational &
special interest videos & educational programs.
Annual.
2020: 7,900 pp, $1,055/4 vol set
ISBN(s): 978-1-64265-518-6 (4 vol set)

Concise Dictionary of British Literary Biography

Published by Gale
Division of Cengage Learning
27500 Drake Rd, Farmington Hills, MI 48331-
3535
SAN: 213-4373
Tel: 248-699-4253 *Toll Free Tel:* 800-877-4253
Fax: 248-699-8070 *Toll Free Fax:* 800-414-
5043 (orders)
E-mail: gale.galeord@cengage.com
Web Site: www.gale.com
Key Personnel
Ed: Matthew J Bruccoli; Richard Layman
Illustrated set provides thorough coverage of ma-
jor British literary figures of all eras. Each vol-
ume covers 20-30 writers from all genres who
were active during a single historical period.
Vol 1: *Writers of the Middle Ages and Renais-
sance Before 1660*
Vol 2: *Writers of the Restoration and 18th Cen-
tury 1660-1789*
Vol 3: *Writers of the Romantic Period, 1789-1832*
Vol 4: *Victorian Writers, 1832-1890*
Vol 5: *Late Victorian and Edwardian Writers,
1890-1914*
Vol 6: *Modern Writers, 1914-1945*
Vol 7: *Writers After World War II, 1945-1960*
Vol 8: *Contemporary Writers, 1960-Present.*
1st ed, 1992: 24,000 pp, $1,380/8-vol set hard-
cover
ISBN(s): 978-0-8103-7980-0

Concise Major 21st-Century Writers

Published by Gale
Division of Cengage Learning
27500 Drake Rd, Farmington Hills, MI 48331-
3535
SAN: 213-4373
Tel: 248-699-4253 *Toll Free Tel:* 800-877-4253
Fax: 248-699-8070 *Toll Free Fax:* 800-414-
5043 (orders)
E-mail: gale.galeord@cengage.com
Web Site: www.gale.com
Detailed biographical & bibliographical information on approximately 700 authors who are
most often studied in college & high school.
Sketches typically include personal information, addresses, career history, writings, works
in progress, biographical/critical sources & authors' comments +/or informative essays about
their lives & work.
3rd ed, 2006: 3,890 pp, $803/5-vol set hardcover,
$883.30 ebook
ISBN(s): 978-0-7876-7539-4 (hardcover/5-vol
set); 978-1-4144-1048-7 (ebook)

Consultants & Consulting Organizations Directory (CCOD)

Published by Gale
Division of Cengage Learning
27500 Drake Rd, Farmington Hills, MI 48331-
3535
SAN: 213-4373
Tel: 248-699-4253 *Toll Free Tel:* 800-877-4253
Fax: 248-699-8069 *Toll Free Fax:* 800-414-
5043 (orders)
E-mail: gale.galeord@cengage.com;
businessproducts@cengage.com

Web Site: www.gale.com
Key Personnel
Ed: Julie A Gough *E-mail:* julie.gough@cengage.
com
Important details, including services offered, full
contact information, date founded & principal
business executives. More than 26,000 firms
& individuals listed are arranged in subject
sections under 14 general fields of consulting
activity ranging from agriculture to marketing. More than 400 specialties are represented,
including finance, computers, fund raising &
others. Also available as an ebook.
45th ed, 2020: 2,911 pp, $1,950 paper, see web
site for ebook price
ISBN(s): 978-1-4103-8537-6 (paper); 978-1-4103-
8545-1 (ebook)

Contemporary Authors

Published by Gale
Division of Cengage Learning
27500 Drake Rd, Farmington Hills, MI 48331-
3535
SAN: 213-4373
Tel: 248-699-4253 *Toll Free Tel:* 800-877-4253
Fax: 248-699-8070 *Toll Free Fax:* 800-414-
5043 (orders)
E-mail: gale.galeord@cengage.com
Web Site: www.gale.com
Find biographical information on more than
160,000 modern novelists, poets, playwrights,
nonfiction writers, journalists & scriptwriters.
Also available as an ebook.
Vol 413, 2018: 465 pp, $418 hardcover, see web
site for ebook price
ISBN(s): 978-1-4103-8026-5 (hardcover); 978-1-
4103-8030-2 (ebook)

Contemporary Literary Criticism

Published by Gale
Division of Cengage Learning
27500 Drake Rd, Farmington Hills, MI 48331-
3535
SAN: 213-4373
Tel: 248-699-4253 *Toll Free Tel:* 800-877-4253
Fax: 248-699-8070 *Toll Free Fax:* 800-414-
5043 (orders)
E-mail: gale.galeord@cengage.com
Web Site: www.gale.com
Key Personnel
Ed: Jeffrey Hunter
Covers authors who are currently active or who
died after Dec 31, 1959. Each print volume
profiles approximately 6-8 novelists, poets,
playwrights & other creative & nonfiction writers by providing full-text or excerpted criticism
taken from books, magazines, literary reviews,
newspapers & scholarly journals. Most critical
essays are full text. Each of the approximately
200 essays per volume is prefaced by a full citation & annotation & most entries in the print
series include an author portrait. Each volume
includes cumulative author name, topic & nationality indexes, as well as a volume-specific
title index. A cumulative title index to the entire series is available separately. Also available
online.
$438 hardcover

Copy Editing

Published by Cambridge University Press
One Liberty Plaza, 20th fl, New York, NY 10006
SAN: 200-206X
Tel: 212-337-5000
E-mail: newyork@cambridge.org
Web Site: www.cambridge.org/us
Key Personnel
Author: Judith Butcher
Copy Editing covers all aspects of the editorial
process involved in converting an author's ms
to the printed page. It covers the basics from
how to mark a ms for the designer & typeset-

ter, through the ground rules of house style &
consistency, to how to read & correct proofs.
4th ed, 2006: 558 pp, $120
ISBN(s): 978-521-84713-1

Critical Approaches to Literature

Published by Grey House Publishing Inc™
4919 Rte 22, Amenia, NY 12501
Mailing Address: PO Box 56, Amenia, NY
12501-0056
Tel: 518-789-8700 *Toll Free Tel:* 800-562-2139
Fax: 518-789-0556
E-mail: csr@salempress.com
Web Site: salempress.com
Key Personnel
Ed: Robert C Evans
Each volume provides literature students with the
tools necessary to study each approach to lit-
erary criticism using a unique combination of
critical contexts & analysis of several works.
Also includes in-depth critical readings of pop-
ular works.
Individual volumes:
Feminist, published Jan 2018, 359 pp
Moral, published April 2017, 300 pp
Multicultural, published July 2017, 336 pp
Psychological, published March 2017, 350 pp.
$125/vol (includes online access)
ISBN(s): 978-1-68217-272-8 (Psychological);
978-1-68217-273-5 (Psychological ebook); 978-
1-68217-274-2 (Moral); 978-1-68217-275-9
(Moral ebook); 978-1-68217-575-0 (Multi-
cultural); 978-1-68217-576-7 (Multicultural
ebook); 978-1-68217-577-4 (Feminist); 978-1-
68217-578-1 (Feminist ebook)

Critical Insights: Authors

Published by Grey House Publishing Inc™
4919 Rte 22, Amenia, NY 12501
Mailing Address: PO Box 56, Amenia, NY
12501-0056
Tel: 518-789-8700 *Toll Free Tel:* 800-562-2139
Fax: 518-789-0556
E-mail: csr@salempress.com
Web Site: salempress.com
Key Personnel
Ed, James McBride: Mildred R Mickle
Ed, Edith Wharton: Myrto Drizou
Ed, Richard Wright: Kimberly Drake
Each volume includes: General bibliography,
chronology of author's life, complete list of
author's works, publication dates of works, de-
tailed bio of the editor & general subject index.
Volumes published May-Dec 2018:
Martin Luther King Jr, 310 pp
James McBride, 292 pp
Edith Wharton, 288 pp.
Volumes published Jan-Oct 2019:
Walt Whitman, 400 pp
Oscar Wilde, 400 pp
Richard Wright, 260 pp.
$105/vol (includes online access with print pur-
chase)
ISBN(s): 978-1-64265-275-8 (Walt Whitman);
978-1-64265-309-0 (Oscar Wilde); 978-1-
68217-573-6 (Edith Wharton); 978-1-68217-
574-3 (Edith Wharton ebook); 978-1-68217-
694-8 (James McBride); 978-1-68217-695-5
(James McBride ebook); 978-1-68217-917-8
(Richard Wright); 978-1-68217-960-4 (Richard
Wright ebook)

Critical Insights: Themes

Published by Grey House Publishing Inc™
4919 Rte 22, Amenia, NY 12501
Mailing Address: PO Box 56, Amenia, NY
12501-0056
Tel: 518-789-8700 *Toll Free Tel:* 800-562-2139
Fax: 518-789-0556
E-mail: csr@salempress.com
Web Site: salempress.com

Key Personnel
Ed, Historical Fiction: Virginia Brackett
Ed, Inequality: Kimberly Drake
Ed, Survival: Robert C Evans
Ed, The Immigrant Experience: Maryse Jaya-
  suriya
Each volume explores a popular literary theme.
Volumes published Jan-Sept 2018:
Historical Fiction, 288 pp
The Immigrant Experience, 288 pp
Inequality, 276 pp
Survival, 286 pp.
Volumes published Nov 2019:
Greed, 400 pp.
$105/vol (includes online access with print pur-
  chase)
ISBN(s): 978-1-64265-277-2 (Greed); 978-1-
  68217-690-0 (Inequality); 978-1-68217-691-7
  (Inequality ebook); 978-1-68217-692-4 (The
  Immigrant Experience); 978-1-68217-693-1
  (The Immigrant Experience ebook); 978-1-
  68217-710-5 (Historical Fiction); 978-1-68217-
  711-2 (Historical Fiction ebook); 978-1-68217-
  920-8 (Survival); 978-1-68217-963-5 (Survival
  ebook)

Critical Insights: Works
Published by Grey House Publishing Inc™
4919 Rte 22, Amenia, NY 12501
Mailing Address: PO Box 56, Amenia, NY
  12501-0056
Tel: 518-789-8700 *Toll Free Tel:* 800-562-2139
  Fax: 518-789-0556
E-mail: csr@salempress.com
Web Site: salempress.com
Key Personnel
Ed, Animal Farm: Thomas Horan
Ed, The Crucible, Hamlet, Invisible Man & Par-
  adise Lost: Robert C Evans
Ed, The Outsiders: M Katherine Grimes
Ed, The Scarlett Letter: Brian Yothers
Each essay is 5,000 words in length & offers
  comprehensive, in-depth coverage of a single
  work. Each volume contains essays that break
  down the work from several different perspec-
  tives & includes a brief biography of the au-
  thor.
Volumes published Feb-Nov 2018:
Animal Farm by George Orwell, 300 pp
The Crucible by Arthur Miller, 300 pp
Invisible Man by Ralph Ellison, 300 pp
The Outsiders by S E Hinton, 288 pp
The Scarlet Letter by Nathaniel Hawthorne, 276
  pp.
Volumes published Jan-Nov 2019:
Hamlet by William Shakespeare, 328 pp
The Odyssey by Homer, 400 pp
Paradise Lost by John Milton, 344 pp
The Pearl by John Steinbeck, 400 pp
$105/vol (includes online access with print pur-
  chase)
ISBN(s): 978-1-64265-024-2 (Paradise Lost);
  978-1-64265-025-9 (Paradise Lost ebook); 978-
  1-64265-026-6 (Hamlet); 978-1-64265-027-
  3 (Hamlet ebook); 978-1-64265-271-0 (The
  Odyssey); 978-1-64265-311-3 (The Pearl); 978-
  1-68217-684-9 (The Crucible); 978-1-68217-
  685-6 (The Crucible ebook); 978-1-68217-686-
  3 (The Outsiders); 978-1-68217-687-0 (The
  Outsiders ebook); 978-1-68217-688-7 (The
  Scarlet Letter); 978-1-68217-689-4 (The Scarlet Letter ebook); 978-1-68217-918-5 (Animal
  Farm); 978-1-68217-919-2 (Invisible Man);
  978-1-68217-961-1 (Animal Farm ebook); 978-
  1-68217-962-8 (Invisible Man ebook)

Critical Survey of American Literature
Published by Grey House Publishing Inc™
4919 Rte 22, Amenia, NY 12501
Mailing Address: PO Box 56, Amenia, NY
  12501-0056
Tel: 518-789-8700 *Toll Free Tel:* 800-562-2139
  Fax: 518-789-0556

E-mail: csr@salempress.com
Web Site: salempress.com
Key Personnel
Ed: Steven G Kellman, PhD
Detailed profiles of over 400 major American au-
  thors of fiction, drama & poetry, each with sec-
  tions on biography, general analysis & analysis
  of the author's most important works. Origi-
  nally published as *Magill's Survey of American
  Literature*.
Dec 2016: 3,422 pp, $499/6 vol set (includes on-
  line access)
First published 2006
ISBN(s): 978-1-68217-128-8 (6 vol set); 978-1-
  68217-147-9 (ebook set)

Critical Survey of Drama
Published by Grey House Publishing Inc™
4919 Rte 22, Amenia, NY 12501
Mailing Address: PO Box 56, Amenia, NY
  12501-0056
Tel: 518-789-8700 *Toll Free Tel:* 800-562-2139
  Fax: 518-789-0556
E-mail: csr@salempress.com
Web Site: salempress.com
Contains 638 essays that discuss both individual
  dramatists & overview topics. Also contains a
  listing of major dramatic awards, time line of
  drama history, glossary & bibliography.
3rd ed, 2017: 4,438 pp, $599/8 vol set (includes
  online access)
ISBN(s): 978-1-68217-622-1 (8 vol set); 978-1-
  68217-639-9 (ebook set)

Critical Survey of Graphic Novels: Heroes &
  Superheroes
Published by Grey House Publishing Inc™
4919 Rte 22, Amenia, NY 12501
Mailing Address: PO Box 56, Amenia, NY
  12501-0056
Tel: 518-789-8700 *Toll Free Tel:* 800-562-2139
  Fax: 518-789-0556
E-mail: csr@salempress.com
Web Site: salempress.com
Key Personnel
Ed: Bart H Beaty; Stephen Weiner
Provides in-depth insight into over 150 of the
  most popular & studied graphic novels. Ar-
  ranged alphabetically.
2nd ed, Oct 2018: 948 pp, $295/2 vol set (in-
  cludes online access with print purchase)
ISBN(s): 978-1-68217-908-6 (2 vol set); 978-1-
  68217-956-7 (ebook set)

Critical Survey of Graphic Novels: History,
  Theme & Technique
Published by Grey House Publishing Inc™
4919 Rte 22, Amenia, NY 12501
Mailing Address: PO Box 56, Amenia, NY
  12501-0056
Tel: 518-789-8700 *Toll Free Tel:* 800-562-2139
  Fax: 518-789-0556
E-mail: csr@salempress.com
Web Site: salempress.com
Key Personnel
Ed: Bart H Beaty; Stephen Weiner
Contains over 80 essays covering themes & con-
  cepts in graphic novels, including genres, time
  periods, foreign language traditions, social rel-
  evance & craftsmanship such as lettering &
  inking.
2nd ed, 2019: 524 pp, $195 (includes online ac-
  cess with print purchase)
ISBN(s): 978-1-68217-911-6; 978-1-68217-959-8
  (ebook)

Critical Survey of Graphic Novels:
  Independents & Underground Classics
Published by Grey House Publishing Inc™
4919 Rte 22, Amenia, NY 12501
Mailing Address: PO Box 56, Amenia, NY
  12501-0056

Tel: 518-789-8700 *Toll Free Tel:* 800-562-2139
  Fax: 518-789-0556
E-mail: csr@salempress.com
Web Site: salempress.com
Key Personnel
Ed: Bart H Beaty; Stephen Weiner
215 essays covering graphic novels & core
  comics series, focusing on the independents
  & underground genre.
2019: 1,110 pp, $395 (includes online access with
  print purchase)
ISBN(s): 978-1-68217-913-0 (3 vol set); 978-1-
  68217-958-1 (ebook set)

Critical Survey of Graphic Novels: Manga
Published by Grey House Publishing Inc™
4919 Rte 22, Amenia, NY 12501
Mailing Address: PO Box 56, Amenia, NY
  12501-0056
Tel: 518-789-8700 *Toll Free Tel:* 800-562-2139
  Fax: 518-789-0556
E-mail: csr@salempress.com
Web Site: salempress.com
Key Personnel
Ed: Bart H Beaty; Stephen Weiner
Provides in-depth insight into more than 70 of the
  most popular & studied manga graphic novels,
  ranging from metaseries to stand-alone books.
Oct 2018: 412 pp, $195 (includes online access
  with print purchase)
ISBN(s): 978-1-68217-912-3; 978-1-68217-957-4
  (ebook)

Critical Survey of Long Fiction
Published by Grey House Publishing Inc™
4919 Rte 22, Amenia, NY 12501
Mailing Address: PO Box 56, Amenia, NY
  12501-0056
Tel: 518-789-8700 *Toll Free Tel:* 800-562-2139
  Fax: 518-789-0556
E-mail: csr@salempress.com
Web Site: salempress.com
Key Personnel
Ed: Carl Rollyson, PhD
Profiles of major writers of long fiction throughout history & the world, including critical analyses of their significant novels & novellas. Single hardcover & paperback volumes with the
  most popular content also available, each pro-
  filing authors & works in a particular genre or
  geography.
Original 10 volume set profiles 678 writers & is
  available for $995, contact publisher for details
  (ISBN: 978-1-58765-535-7 hardcover, ISBN:
  978-1-58765-546-3 ebook).
6,056 pp, $39.95 or $105/vol (depending on individual volume title); hardcover titles include
  online access
First published 1983
ISBN(s): 978-1-4298-3675-3 (Detective & Mystery Novelists); 978-1-4298-3676-0 (Fantasy
  Novelists); 978-1-4298-3677-7 (Novelists with
  Gay & Lesbian Themes); 978-1-4298-3680-7
  (Picaresque Novelists); 978-1-4298-3681-4 (Political Novelists); 978-1-4298-3682-1 (Psychological Novelists); 978-1-4298-3685-2 (Satirical
  Novelists); 978-1-4298-3686-9 (Religious Novelists); 978-1-4298-3691-3 (German Novelists);
  978-1-4298-3693-7 (Italian Novelists); 978-1-
  4298-3694-4 (Novelists of the Jewish Culture);
  978-1-4298-3698-2 (Spanish Novelists); 978-
  1-58765-926-3 (Detective & Mystery Novelists ebook); 978-1-58765-927-0 (Fantasy Novelists ebook); 978-1-58765-928-7 (Novelists
  with Gay & Lesbian Themes ebook); 978-1-
  58765-929-4 (Gothic Novelists ebook); 978-1-
  58765-930-0 (Naturalist Novelists ebook); 978-
  1-58765-931-7 (Picaresque Novelists ebook);
  978-1-58765-932-4 (Political Novelists ebook);
  978-1-58765-933-1 (Psychological Novelists
  ebook); 978-1-58765-934-8 (Science Fiction
  Novelists ebook); 978-1-58765-935-5 (Novelists with Feminist Themes ebook); 978-1-

58765-936-2 (Satirical Novelists ebook); 978-1-58765-937-9 (Religious Novelists ebook); 978-1-58765-938-6 (African American Culture ebook); 978-1-58765-939-3 (Asian Novelists ebook); 978-1-58765-940-9 (English Novelists ebook); 978-1-58765-941-6 (French Novelists ebook); 978-1-58765-942-3 (German Novelists ebook); 978-1-58765-943-0 (Irish Novelists ebook); 978-1-58765-944-7 (Italian Novelists ebook); 978-1-58765-945-4 (Novelists of the Jewish Culture ebook); 978-1-58765-946-1 (Latin American Novelists ebook); 978-1-58765-947-8 (Native American Novelists ebook); 978-1-58765-948-5 (Russian Novelists ebook); 978-1-58765-949-2 (Spanish Novelists ebook); 978-1-61925-717-7 (African American Culture); 978-1-61925-718-4 (Asian Novelists); 978-1-61925-719-1 (English Novelists); 978-1-61925-720-7 (French Novelists); 978-1-61925-721-4 (Gothic Novelists); 978-1-61925-722-1 (Irish Novelists); 978-1-61925-723-8 (Latin American Novelists); 978-1-61925-724-5 (Native American Novelists); 978-1-61925-725-2 (Naturalist Novelists); 978-1-61925-726-9 (Novelists with Feminist Themes); 978-1-61925-727-6 (Russian Novelists); 978-1-61925-728-3 (Science Fiction Novelists)

Critical Survey of Mystery & Detective Fiction
Published by Grey House Publishing Inc™
4919 Rte 22, Amenia, NY 12501
Mailing Address: PO Box 56, Amenia, NY 12501-0056
Tel: 518-789-8700 *Toll Free Tel:* 800-562-2139
Fax: 518-789-0556
E-mail: csr@salempress.com
Web Site: salempress.com
Key Personnel
Ed: Carl Rollyson, PhD
Provides detailed analyses of the lives & writings of major contributors to mystery & detective fiction.
Jan 2021: 2,400 pp, $399/4 vol set or ebook set
ISBN(s): 978-1-64265-707-4 (4 vol set); 978-1-64265-708-1 (ebook set)

Critical Survey of Mythology & Folklore: Gods & Goddesses
Published by Grey House Publishing Inc™
4919 Rte 22, Amenia, NY 12501
Mailing Address: PO Box 56, Amenia, NY 12501-0056
Tel: 518-789-8700 *Toll Free Tel:* 800-562-2139
Fax: 518-789-0556
E-mail: csr@salempress.com
Web Site: salempress.com
Key Personnel
Ed: Michael Shally-Jensen, PhD
Examines the major & minor deities from a broad range of regions & cultures throughout the world. Collection includes 524 essays organized into 10 world regions.
2019: 1,048 pp, $295/2 vol set (includes online access with print purchase)
ISBN(s): 978-1-64265-115-7; 978-1-64265-116-4 (ebook set)

Critical Survey of Mythology & Folklore: Heroes & Heroines
Published by Grey House Publishing Inc™
4919 Rte 22, Amenia, NY 12501
Mailing Address: PO Box 56, Amenia, NY 12501-0056
Tel: 518-789-8700 *Toll Free Tel:* 800-562-2139
Fax: 518-789-0556
E-mail: csr@salempress.com
Web Site: salempress.com
Covers a diverse range of countries & cultures, as well as important retellings in the modern tradition. Articles cover: *Birth & Prophecy, The Host of Heroines, The Culture Hero, Trial &*

Quest, Myth & Monstrosity, Survey of Myth & Folklore.
Sept 2013: 516 pp, $175 (includes online access)
ISBN(s): 978-1-61925-181-6; 978-1-61925-186-1 (ebook)

Critical Survey of Mythology & Folklore: Love, Sexuality & Desire
Published by Grey House Publishing Inc™
4919 Rte 22, Amenia, NY 12501
Mailing Address: PO Box 56, Amenia, NY 12501-0056
Tel: 518-789-8700 *Toll Free Tel:* 800-562-2139
Fax: 518-789-0556
E-mail: csr@salempress.com
Web Site: salempress.com
Each title examines familiar & unfamiliar myths, from a diverse range of countries & cultures, as well as important retellings in the modern tradition. Topics covered include: *Gods & Mortals in Love, The Myth of the Second Half, Modern Tales & Myths, Forbidden Love, Love Unrequited, The Lover's Quest.*
Jan 2013: 984 pp, $295/2 vol set (includes online access with print purchase)
ISBN(s): 978-1-4298-3765-1 (2 vol set); 978-1-4298-3768-2 (ebook set)

Critical Survey of Mythology & Folklore: World Mythology
Published by Grey House Publishing Inc™
4919 Rte 22, Amenia, NY 12501
Mailing Address: PO Box 56, Amenia, NY 12501-0056
Tel: 518-789-8700 *Toll Free Tel:* 800-562-2139
Fax: 518-789-0556
E-mail: csr@salempress.com
Web Site: salempress.com
Presents articles on myths, folktales, legends & other traditional literature. Covers a diverse range of authors, countries & cultures that span the globe. Articles begin with a summary that offers readers the major actions & characters in the tale followed by an analysis of the important cultural & social interpretations of the author & myth.
Dec 2013: 326 pp, $175 (includes online access with print purchase)
ISBN(s): 978-1-61925-182-3; 978-1-61925-187-8 (ebook)

Critical Survey of Poetry
Published by Grey House Publishing Inc™
4919 Rte 22, Amenia, NY 12501
Mailing Address: PO Box 56, Amenia, NY 12501-0056
Tel: 518-789-8700 *Toll Free Tel:* 800-562-2139
Fax: 518-789-0556
E-mail: csr@salempress.com
Web Site: salempress.com
An in-depth resource covering over 900 poets throughout history & the world. Organized into 6 subsets by geography & essay type.
American Poets, 4 vol set, 2,414 pp, $495
British, Irish & Commonwealth Poets, 3 vol set, 1,470 pp, $395
Contemporary Poets, 2 vol set, published Sept 2019, 900 pp, $295
European Poets, 3 vol set, 1,262 pp, $395
World Poets, 1 vol, 442 pp, $150
Topical Essays, 2 vol set, 924 pp, $295
Cumulative Indexes, 1 vol, 266 pp, free with purchase of more than one subset.
4th ed, Jan 2011: 6,778 pp, $1,295/14 vol set (includes online access with print purchase)
First published 2002
ISBN(s): 978-1-58765-582-1 (14 vol set); 978-1-58765-583-8 (American Poets set); 978-1-58765-588-3 (British, Irish & Commonwealth Poets set); 978-1-58765-592-0 (American Poets ebook set); 978-1-58765-593-7 (14 vol ebook set); 978-1-58765-755-9 (British, Irish & Com-

monwealth Poets ebook set); 978-1-58765-756-6 (European Poets set); 978-1-58765-760-3 (European Poets ebook set); 978-1-58765-761-0 (World Poets); 978-1-58765-762-7 (World Poets ebook); 978-1-58765-763-4 (Topical Essays set); 978-1-58765-766-5 (Topical Essays ebook set); 978-1-58765-767-2 (Cumulative Indexes); 978-1-64265-279-6 (Contemporary Poets set)

Critical Survey of Science Fiction & Fantasy Literature
Published by Grey House Publishing Inc™
4919 Rte 22, Amenia, NY 12501
Mailing Address: PO Box 56, Amenia, NY 12501-0056
Tel: 518-789-8700 *Toll Free Tel:* 800-562-2139
Fax: 518-789-0556
E-mail: csr@salempress.com
Web Site: salempress.com
Key Personnel
Ed: Paul Di Filippo
Provides descriptions of hundreds of important works of science fiction & fantasy, summarizing plots & analyzing the works in terms of their contributions to literature.
3rd ed, March 2017: 1,572 pp, $295/3 vol set (includes online access with print purchase)
ISBN(s): 978-1-68217-278-0 (3 vol set); 978-1-68217-279-7 (ebook set)

Critical Survey of Shakespeare's Plays
Published by Grey House Publishing Inc™
4919 Rte 22, Amenia, NY 12501
Mailing Address: PO Box 56, Amenia, NY 12501-0056
Tel: 518-789-8700 *Toll Free Tel:* 800-562-2139
Fax: 518-789-0556
E-mail: csr@salempress.com
Web Site: salempress.com
Key Personnel
Ed: Joseph Rosenblum
Examines all 39 of Shakespeare's most influential plays, as well as his life, style, technique & influences.
Oct 2015: 381 pp, $125 (includes online access with print purchase)
ISBN(s): 978-1-61925-864-8; 978-1-61925-865-5 (ebook)

Critical Survey of Shakespeare's Sonnets
Published by Grey House Publishing Inc™
4919 Rte 22, Amenia, NY 12501
Mailing Address: PO Box 56, Amenia, NY 12501-0056
Tel: 518-789-8700 *Toll Free Tel:* 800-562-2139
Fax: 518-789-0556
E-mail: csr@salempress.com
Web Site: salempress.com
Collection of 25 essays on the most popular sonnets written by William Shakespeare, each providing an in-depth analysis of its historical significance, literary technique & discusses its meaning to a contemporary audience.
July 2014: 355 pp, $125 (includes online access with print purchase)
ISBN(s): 978-1-61925-499-2; 978-1-61925-500-5 (ebook)

Critical Survey of Short Fiction
Published by Grey House Publishing Inc™
4919 Rte 22, Amenia, NY 12501
Mailing Address: PO Box 56, Amenia, NY 12501-0056
Tel: 518-789-8700 *Toll Free Tel:* 800-562-2139
Fax: 518-789-0556
E-mail: csr@salempress.com
Web Site: salempress.com
Key Personnel
Ed: Charles E May
625 essays providing in-depth overviews of short story writers throughout history & the world.

Organized into 5 subsets by geography & essay type.

American Writers, 4 vol set, 1,600 pp, $495
British, Irish & Commonwealth Writers, 2 vol set, 800 pp, $295
European Writers, 1 vol, 400 pp, $175
World Writers, 1 vol, 400 pp, $175
Topical Essays, 1 vol, 400 pp, $175
Cumulative Indexes, 1 vol, 400 pp, free with purchase of more than one subset.
4th ed, Jan 2012: 4,000 pp, $1,095/10 vol set (includes online access with print purchase)
ISBN(s): 978-1-58765-789-4 (10 vol set); 978-1-58765-790-0 (American Writers set); 978-1-58765-795-5 (British, Irish & Commonwealth Writers set); 978-1-58765-798-6 (European Writers); 978-1-58765-799-3 (World Writers); 978-1-58765-800-6 (Topical Essays); 978-1-58765-803-7 (Cumulative Indexes); 978-1-58765-804-4 (10 vol ebook set); 978-1-58765-805-1 (American Writers ebook set); 978-1-58765-806-8 (British, Irish & Commonwealth Writers ebook set); 978-1-58765-807-5 (European Writers ebook); 978-1-58765-808-2 (World Writers ebook); 978-1-58765-809-9 (Topical Essays ebook)

Critical Survey of World Literature
Published by Grey House Publishing Inc™
4919 Rte 22, Amenia, NY 12501
Mailing Address: PO Box 56, Amenia, NY 12501-0056
Tel: 518-789-8700 *Toll Free Tel:* 800-562-2139
Fax: 518-789-0556
E-mail: csr@salempress.com
Web Site: salempress.com
Key Personnel
Ed: Robert C Evans
Profiles major authors of fiction, drama, poetry & essays, each with sections on biography, general analysis & analysis of the author's most important works.
2018: 3,366 pp, $499/6 vol set (includes online access with print purchase)
ISBN(s): 978-1-68217-615-3 (6 vol set); 978-1-68217-638-2 (ebook set)

Critical Survey of Young Adult Literature
Published by Grey House Publishing Inc™
4919 Rte 22, Amenia, NY 12501
Mailing Address: PO Box 56, Amenia, NY 12501-0056
Tel: 518-789-8700 *Toll Free Tel:* 800-562-2139
Fax: 518-789-0556
E-mail: csr@salempress.com
Web Site: salempress.com
Key Personnel
Ed: Amy Pattee
Author biographies, genre overviews, plot summaries, theme overviews & film analysis for the young adult genre.
April 2016: 694 pp, $185 (includes online access with print purchase)
ISBN(s): 978-1-61925-971-3; 978-1-61925-972-0 (ebook)

Current Biography Cumulated Index 1940-2017
Published by Grey House Publishing Inc™
4919 Rte 22, Amenia, NY 12501
Mailing Address: PO Box 56, Amenia, NY 12501-0056
Tel: 518-789-8700 *Toll Free Tel:* 800-562-2139
Fax: 518-789-0556
E-mail: books@greyhouse.com
Web Site: greyhouse.com
Name & profession indexes to late issues in which biographies appear in *Current Biography Yearbook*.
2017: 1,100 pp, $199
ISBN(s): 978-1-68217-206-3

Current Biography Yearbook
Published by Grey House Publishing Inc™
4919 Rte 22, Amenia, NY 12501
Mailing Address: PO Box 56, Amenia, NY 12501-0056
Tel: 518-789-8700 *Toll Free Tel:* 800-562-2139
Fax: 518-789-0556
E-mail: books@greyhouse.com
Web Site: greyhouse.com
Compilation of 200 up-to-date, contemporary profiles of accomplished & rising stars of politics, industry, entertainment & the arts from the US & around the world.
Annual.
2020: 750 pp, $199
ISBN(s): 978-1-68217-709-9

Cyclopedia of Literary Characters
Published by Grey House Publishing Inc™
4919 Rte 22, Amenia, NY 12501
Mailing Address: PO Box 56, Amenia, NY 12501-0056
Tel: 518-789-8700 *Toll Free Tel:* 800-562-2139
Fax: 518-789-0556
E-mail: csr@salempress.com
Web Site: salempress.com
Key Personnel
Ed: Frank N Magill
Provides critical descriptions of more than 29,000 major characters that appear in 3,500 important works of literature. New to this edition are 245 characters published in popular works of fiction from 2000 to 2013.
4th ed, Feb 2015: 3,344 pp, $495/5 vol set (includes online access with print purchase)
ISBN(s): 978-1-61925-497-8 (5 vol set); 978-1-61925-498-5 (ebook set)

Cyclopedia of Literary Places
Published by Grey House Publishing Inc™
4919 Rte 22, Amenia, NY 12501
Mailing Address: PO Box 56, Amenia, NY 12501-0056
Tel: 518-789-8700 *Toll Free Tel:* 800-562-2139
Fax: 518-789-0556
E-mail: csr@salempress.com
Web Site: salempress.com
Key Personnel
Ed: Denise Lenchner
In-depth discussion of the use of place in over 1,400 popular literary works. Each article provides the full title of the work, author's name & vital dates, type of work, type of plot, time of plot & date of original publication.
2nd ed, April 2016: 1,304 pp, $395/3 vol set (includes online access with print purchase)
ISBN(s): 978-1-61925-884-6 (3 vol set); 978-1-61925-885-3 (ebook set)

Developmental Editing: A Handbook for Freelancers, Authors, and Publishers
Published by University of Chicago Press
1427 E 60 St, Chicago, IL 60637-2954
SAN: 202-5280
E-mail: custserv@press.uchicago.edu; marketing@press.uchicago.edu
Web Site: www.press.uchicago.edu
Key Personnel
Sr Ed, Ref & Writing Guides: Mary Laur
  Tel: 773-702-7326 *E-mail:* mlaur@uchicago.edu
Transforming a mss into a book that edifies, inspires & sells is the job of the developmental editor. Author Scott Norton starts with the core tasks of shaping the proposal, finding the hook & building the narrative or argument & then turns to the hard work of executing the plan & establishing a style. The book also includes detailed case studies featuring a variety of nonfiction books & authors ranging from first-timer to veteran, journalist to scholar.
1st ed: 252 pp, $50 cloth, $28 paper or ebook

First published 2009
ISBN(s): 978-0-226-59514-6 (cloth); 978-0-226-59515-3 (paper); 978-0-226-59516-0 (ebook)

Dictionary of Literary Biography
Published by Gale
Division of Cengage Learning
27500 Drake Rd, Farmington Hills, MI 48331-3535
SAN: 213-4373
Tel: 248-699-4253 *Toll Free Tel:* 800-877-4253
  Fax: 248-699-8070 *Toll Free Fax:* 800-414-5043 (orders)
E-mail: gale.galeord@cengage.com
Web Site: www.gale.com
Multivolume series; each volume focuses on a specific literary movement or period. Series aims to encompass all who have contributed to literary history from the Elizabethan Era to 20th century English, American, Canadian, French & German literature, drama & history. Major biographical & critical essays are presented for the most important figures of each era. Each essay includes a career chronology, list of publications & a bibliography of works by & about the subject. Also available online.
$420 hardcover

Direct Marketing Market Place® (DMMP)
Published by NRP Direct
430 Mountain Ave, Suite 403, New Providence, NJ 07974
Tel: 908-517-0780 *Toll Free Tel:* 844-592-4197
  Fax: 908-608-3012 (cust serv)
E-mail: info@nrpdirect.com
Web Site: www.dirmktgplace.com; www.nrpdirect.com
A comprehensive source of direct marketing, listing over 17,071 key personnel & over 8,672 leading direct marketing companies, suppliers & creative sources.
Annual.
$389

A Directory of American Poets & Writers
Published by Poets & Writers Inc
90 Broad St, Suite 2100, New York, NY 10004
Tel: 212-226-3586 *Fax:* 212-226-3963
E-mail: directory@pw.org
Web Site: www.pw.org/directory
Key Personnel
Exec Dir: Elliot Figman
Mng Dir: Melissa Ford Gradel *Tel:* 212-226-3586 ext 223
Names, addresses, telephone numbers & e-mail addresses of over 10,000 contemporary American writers & poets. Available online only.
Free

The Directory of Business Information Resources
Published by Grey House Publishing Inc™
4919 Rte 22, Amenia, NY 12501
Mailing Address: PO Box 56, Amenia, NY 12501-0056
Tel: 518-789-8700 *Toll Free Tel:* 800-562-2139
  Fax: 518-789-0556
E-mail: books@greyhouse.com
Web Site: greyhouse.com
Source for contacts in 104 business areas. The 24,855 detailed, informative entries include contact names, phone & fax numbers, web sites & e-mail addresses along with descriptions, membership information, ordering details & more.
Annual.
27th ed, 2020: 2,018 pp, $195 (includes online access)
First published 1992
ISBN(s): 978-1-64265-437-0

The Directory of Mail Order Catalogs
Published by Grey House Publishing Inc™

4919 Rte 22, Amenia, NY 12501
Mailing Address: PO Box 56, Amenia, NY
12501-0056
Tel: 518-789-8700 *Toll Free Tel:* 800-562-2139
Fax: 518-789-0556
E-mail: books@greyhouse.com
Web Site: greyhouse.com
Complete listing of direct-to-consumer &
business-to-business mail order catalogs, in-
cluding detailed contact information.
Annual.
34th ed, 2020: 1,000 pp, $250 (includes online
access)
First published 1981
ISBN(s): 978-1-64265-106-5

Directory of Poetry Publishers
Published by Dustbooks
PO Box 100, Paradise, CA 95967-0100
SAN: 204-1871
Tel: 530-877-6110 *Fax:* 530-877-0222
E-mail: inquiries@dustbooks.com; info@
dustbooks.com
Web Site: www.dustbooks.com
Key Personnel
Ed: Neil McIntyre
Information on more than 1,900 book & maga-
zine publishers of poetry worldwide, including
university presses & e-zines.
Annual (CD-ROM), continuously (online).
33rd ed, 2017-2018, $21 CD-ROM, $65 CD-
ROM (3 directories), $49.95 online (4 direc-
tories)
ISBN(s): 978-1-935742-47-0 (CD-ROM)

Directory of Small Press/Magazine Editors &
   Publishers
Published by Dustbooks
PO Box 100, Paradise, CA 95967-0100
SAN: 204-1871
Tel: 530-877-6110 *Fax:* 530-877-0222
E-mail: inquiries@dustbooks.com; info@
dustbooks.com
Web Site: www.dustbooks.com
Key Personnel
Ed: Neil McIntyre
Names & numbers guide to the small press &
magazine industry.
Annual (CD-ROM), continuously (online).
48th ed, 2017-2018, $21 CD-ROM, $65 CD-
ROM (3 directories), $49.95 online (4 direc-
tories)
ISBN(s): 978-1-935742-45-6 (CD-ROM)

Directory of Special Libraries and Information
   Centers (DSL)
Published by Gale
Division of Cengage Learning
27500 Drake Rd, Farmington Hills, MI 48331-
3535
SAN: 213-4373
Tel: 248-699-4253 *Toll Free Tel:* 800-877-4253
Fax: 248-699-8075 *Toll Free Fax:* 800-414-
5043 (orders)
E-mail: gale.galeord@cengage.com
Web Site: www.gale.com
Key Personnel
Content Proj Ed: Matthew Miskelly
   E-mail: matthew.miskelly@cengage.com
Vol 1, in 3 parts, provides detailed contact &
descriptive info on subject-specific resource
collections maintained by various government
agencies, businesses, publishers, educational &
nonprofit organizations & associations around
the world. Vol 2 contains geographical & personnel indexes. Available as ebook only.
44th ed: 2,937 pp, $2,374 ebook
ISBN(s): 978-1-4144-8789-2

Do-It-Yourself Book Publicity Kit
Published by Open Horizons Publishing Co
PO Box 2887, Taos, NM 87571

Tel: 575-751-3398
E-mail: books@bookmarketingbestsellers.com
Web Site: bookmarketingbestsellers.com
Key Personnel
Publr & Ed: John Kremer *E-mail:* johnkremer@
bookmarket.com
How to write a news release, put together a me-
dia kit, get reviews, schedule interviews & get
on-going national publicity.
2017: 256 pp, $30

Drama Criticism
Published by Gale
Division of Cengage Learning
27500 Drake Rd, Farmington Hills, MI 48331-
3535
SAN: 213-4373
Tel: 248-699-4253 *Toll Free Tel:* 800-877-4253
Fax: 248-699-8070 *Toll Free Fax:* 800-414-
5043 (orders)
E-mail: gale.galeord@cengage.com
Web Site: www.gale.com
Each volume covers 4-8 significant dramatists or
plays. For each play or playwright featured, a
full range of critical opinion is presented, along
with a biographical sketch, a chronological list
of the writer's major works & more. Most critical essays are full text.
Vol 59, 2018: 455 pp, $299 hardcover
ISBN(s): 978-1-4103-7845-3

E-Publishing and Digital Libraries: Legal and
   Organizational Issues
Published by IGI Global
701 E Chocolate Ave, Hershey, PA 17033
Tel: 717-533-8845 (ext 100) *Toll Free Tel:* 866-
342-6657 *Fax:* 717-533-8661; 717-533-7115
E-mail: cust@igi-global.com
Web Site: www.igi-global.com
2011: 552 pp, $180
ISBN(s): 978-1-60960-031-0; 978-1-60960-033-4
(ebook)

EFA Online Directory
Published by Editorial Freelancers Association
   (EFA)
266 W 37 St, 20th fl, New York, NY 10018
Tel: 212-920-4816 *Toll Free Tel:* 866-929-5425
E-mail: office@the-efa.org
Web Site: www.the-efa.org
Key Personnel
Co-Exec: Christina Frey; William P Keenan, Jr
National, nonprofit professional organization comprising editors, writers, indexers, proofreaders,
researchers, translators & other self-employed
workers in the publishing industry. Online directory searchable by skills, subject matter,
expertise & location. Members may post descriptions of services, resumes & contact information. Clients can directly hire the freelance
help they need.
2,300 pp, free (online)
ISBN(s): 978-1-880407-13-4

El-Hi Textbooks & Serials in Print®
Published by Grey House Publishing Inc™
4919 Rte 22, Amenia, NY 12501
Mailing Address: PO Box 56, Amenia, NY
12501-0056
Tel: 518-789-8700 *Toll Free Tel:* 800-562-2139
Fax: 518-789-0556
E-mail: books@greyhouse.com
Web Site: greyhouse.com
Includes the in-print titles of publishers of text-
books & related materials. Coverage includes
over 195,000 elementary, junior high & high
school textbooks from over 17,000 US publish-
ers.
Annual.
148th ed, 2020: 4,000 pp, $785/2 vol set
ISBN(s): 978-1-64265-523-0 (2 vol set)

The Elements of Style
Published by Pearson Arts & Sciences
Division of Pearson Education Ltd
330 Hudson St, 9th fl, New York, NY 10013-
1048
Tel: 917-981-2200
Web Site: www.pearsonhighered.com
Key Personnel
Author: William Strunk; E B White
50th Anniversary, 2008: 105 pp, $19.95
ISBN(s): 978-0-205-63264-0 (cloth)

The Emotional Craft of Fiction
Published by Writer's Digest Books
Imprint of Penguin Random House LLC
1745 Broadway, New York, NY 10019
Web Site: www.writersdigest.com; www.
writersdigestshop.com
Veteran literary agent & expert fiction instructor
Donald Maass shows you how to use story to
provoke a visceral & emotional experience in
readers.
224 pp, $16.99 paper & ebook (retail)
ISBN(s): 978-1-4403-4837-2 (paper); 978-1-4403-
4840-2 (ebook)

Encyclopedia of African-American Writing
Published by Grey House Publishing Inc™
4919 Rte 22, Amenia, NY 12501
Mailing Address: PO Box 56, Amenia, NY
12501-0056
Tel: 518-789-8700 *Toll Free Tel:* 800-562-2139
Fax: 518-789-0556
E-mail: books@greyhouse.com;
customerservice@greyhouse.com
Web Site: greyhouse.com
Highlights the role & influence of African-
American authors from the 18th century to the
present. Over 800 author biographies, with illustrations, cover the important events in each
writer's life, education, major works, awards,
family & important associates.
3rd ed, 2018: 1,134 pp, $165 hardcover (includes
online access), $206 ebook
ISBN(s): 978-1-68217-718-1; 978-1-68217-719-8
(ebook)

Encyclopedia of Associations: National
   Organizations
Published by Gale
Division of Cengage Learning
27500 Drake Rd, Farmington Hills, MI 48331-
3535
SAN: 213-4373
Tel: 248-699-4253 *Toll Free Tel:* 800-877-4253
Fax: 248-699-8075 *Toll Free Fax:* 800-414-
5043 (orders)
E-mail: gale.galeord@cengage.com
Web Site: www.gale.com
Key Personnel
Ed: Kristy Swartout *E-mail:* kristy.swartout@
cengage.com
A guide to more than 24,000 nonprofit American
membership organizations of national & inter-
national scope. Detailed entries furnish association name & complete contact information.
This information is not duplicated anywhere in
Encyclopedia of Associations. Name & key-
word indexes accompany each volume. Two
companion volumes: Vol 2: *Geographic & Executive Indexes* & Vol 3: *Supplement.*
58th ed, 2019: 3,314 pp, $1,384 print, see web
site for ebook price
ISBN(s): 978-1-4103-8215-3 (print); 978-1-4103-
8221-4 (ebook)

Fiction Core Collection
Published by Grey House Publishing Inc™
4919 Rte 22, Amenia, NY 12501
Mailing Address: PO Box 56, Amenia, NY
12501-0056

Tel: 518-789-8700 *Toll Free Tel:* 800-562-2139
Fax: 518-789-0556
E-mail: books@greyhouse.com
Web Site: greyhouse.com
Recommends works of classic & contemporary fiction. Includes over 8,500 titles plus review sources & other professional aids for librarians.
20th ed, 2020: 1,300 pp, $295
ISBN(s): 978-1-64265-316-8

Fierce on the Page
Published by Writer's Digest Books
Imprint of Penguin Random House LLC
1745 Broadway, New York, NY 10019
Web Site: www.writersdigest.com; www. writersdigestshop.com
Craft your best writing & your best life with this collection of contemplative & inspiring essays.
240 pp, $16.99 paper & ebook (retail)
ISBN(s): 978-1-59963-993-2 (paper); 978-1-59963-994-9 (ebook)

45 Master Characters
Published by Writer's Digest Books
Imprint of Penguin Random House LLC
1745 Broadway, New York, NY 10019
Web Site: www.writersdigest.com; www. writersdigestshop.com
Gives all the information you need to develop believable characters that resonate with every reader.
288 pp, $17.99 paper & ebook (retail)
First published 2001
ISBN(s): 978-1-59963-534-7 (paper); 978-1-59963-535-4 (ebook)

Gale Directory of Databases (GDD)
Published by Gale
Division of Cengage Learning
27500 Drake Rd, Farmington Hills, MI 48331-3535
SAN: 213-4373
Tel: 248-699-4253 *Toll Free Tel:* 800-877-4253
Fax: 248-699-8070 *Toll Free Fax:* 800-414-5043 (orders)
E-mail: gale.galeord@cengage.com
Web Site: www.gale.com
Current information about more than 14,000 databases & more than 3,000 producers, online services & vendors/distributors available worldwide in a variety of formats. Also available as an ebook.
40th ed, 2017: 2,556 pp, $1,051 paper, $1,101.10 ebook
ISBN(s): 978-1-4103-2675-1 (paper); 978-1-4103-2682-9 (ebook)

Gale Directory of Publications and Broadcast Media (GDPBM)
Published by Gale
Division of Cengage Learning
27500 Drake Rd, Farmington Hills, MI 48331-3535
SAN: 213-4373
Tel: 248-699-4253 *Toll Free Tel:* 800-877-4253
Fax: 248-699-8075 *Toll Free Fax:* 800-414-5043 (orders)
E-mail: gale.galeord@cengage.com
Web Site: www.gale.com
Each edition contains approximately 53,000 listings for radio & television stations, cable companies & print/online companies as well as more than 13,500 international entries. Includes phone & fax number, e-mail addresses & web site URLs, listing of key personnel & more. Also available as an ebook.
152nd ed, 2016: 5,851 pp, $1,569 hardcover, $1,725.90 ebook
First published 1869
ISBN(s): 978-1-4144-8781-6 (ebook); 978-1-4144-8802-8 (hardcover)

General Issues in Literacy/Illiteracy in the World: A Bibliography
Published by Greenwood Press
Imprint of ABC-CLIO
130 Cremona Dr, Suite C, Santa Barbara, CA 93117
Mailing Address: PO Box 1911, Santa Barbara, CA 93116-1911
Tel: 805-968-1911 *Toll Free Tel:* 800-368-6868
Fax: 805-685-9685 *Toll Free Fax:* 866-270-3856
E-mail: customerservice@abc-clio.com
Web Site: www.abc-clio.com
Key Personnel
Dir, Edit-Print: Anthony Chiffolo
Author: William Eller; John Hladczuk; Sharon Hladczuk
Literacy-illiteracy; bibliography.
1st ed, 1990: 435 pp, $106.95 hardbound
ISBN(s): 978-0-313-27327-8

Getting It Published: A Guide for Scholars & Anyone Else Serious About Serious Books
Published by University of Chicago Press
1427 E 60 St, Chicago, IL 60637-2954
SAN: 202-5280
E-mail: custserv@press.uchicago.edu; marketing@press.uchicago.edu
Web Site: www.press.uchicago.edu
Key Personnel
Edit Dir, Humanities & Sci: Alan G Thomas
  Tel: 773-702-7644 *E-mail:* athomas2@ uchicago.edu
A professor, author & 30-year veteran of the book industry, William Germano, knows what editors want & what writers need to know to get their work published. This 3rd edition of *Getting It Published* offers clear, practicable guidance on developing a compelling book proposal, finding the right publisher, evaluating a contract, negotiating the production process & emerging as a published author.
Revised every 5-7 yrs.
3rd ed: 304 pp, $60 cloth, $20 paper, $18 ebook
First published 2001
ISBN(s): 978-0-226-28137-7 (cloth); 978-0-226-28140-7 (paper); 978-0-226-28154-4 (ebook)

Gordon's Radio List
Published by North Ridge Books
PO Box 2832, Rancho Mirage, CA 92270
Tel: 949-533-5106 (cell) *Toll Free Fax:* 800-763-9881
E-mail: nrbooks@aol.com
Web Site: www.radiopublicity.net
Key Personnel
Ed: William A Gordon
Book-length database of over 900 radio shows that interview authors, updated on a day-to-day basis. Available in both Excel & Word versions.
$369 includes free e-mailed updates for 3 months with the option to purchase additional updates

Grammatically Correct
Published by Writer's Digest Books
Imprint of Penguin Random House LLC
1745 Broadway, New York, NY 10019
Web Site: www.writersdigest.com; www. writersdigestshop.com
Easy to use, quick reference & most of all, comprehensive.
2nd ed: 352 pp, $19.99 paper & ebook (retail)
First published 1997
ISBN(s): 978-1-58297-616-7 (paper); 978-1-59963-160-8 (ebook)

Grants & Awards
Published by PEN America
Affiliate of PEN International
588 Broadway, Suite 303, New York, NY 10012
Tel: 212-334-1660 *Fax:* 212-334-2181

E-mail: info@pen.org
Web Site: pen.org
Key Personnel
CEO: Suzanne Nossel *Tel:* 212-334-1600 ext 4811 *E-mail:* snossel@pen.org
Pres: Jennifer Egan
Website Ed: Antonio Aiello *Tel:* 212-334-1660 ext 114 *E-mail:* antonio@pen.org
Database with nearly 1,500 domestic & foreign grants, literary awards, fellowships & residencies.
Online annual subn: free for membs; $12 non-membs, $200 instns

Graphic Novels Core Collection
Published by Grey House Publishing Inc™
4919 Rte 22, Amenia, NY 12501
Mailing Address: PO Box 56, Amenia, NY 12501-0056
Tel: 518-789-8700 *Toll Free Tel:* 800-562-2139
Fax: 518-789-0556
E-mail: books@greyhouse.com
Web Site: greyhouse.com
Essential resource for library & media specialists looking to energize, enhance & enrich their collection with 3,500 important & highly recommended fiction & nonfiction graphic novel titles.
3rd ed, Dec 2020: 1,400 pp, $295
ISBN(s): 978-1-64265-647-3

Guide to Literary Agents
Published by Writer's Digest Books
Imprint of Penguin Random House LLC
1745 Broadway, New York, NY 10019
Web Site: www.writersdigest.com; www. writersdigestshop.com
Annual.
29th ed, 2020: 336 pp, $29.99 paper (retail)
ISBN(s): 978-1-4403-5494-6 (paper)

Guide to Writers Conferences & Writing Workshops
Published by ShawGuides
PO Box 61569, Staten Island, NY 10306-7569
Tel: 718-874-3311
E-mail: support@shawguides.com
Web Site: shawguides.com
Online directory of writing conferences, writers workshops, creative career writing programs & literary retreats. 1,466 programs available at writing.shawguides.com.

How to Get Your Book Published Free in Minutes & Marketed Worldwide in Days
Published by Communication Unlimited
185 Shevelin Rd, Novato, CA 94947
Tel: 415-884-2941 *Toll Free Tel:* 800-563-1454
Fax: 415-883-5707
E-mail: gordon@gordonburgett.com
Web Site: www.gordonburgett.com
Key Personnel
Pres: Gordon Burgett *E-mail:* glburgett@aol.com
How-to information, step-by-step process & detailed examples of "ancillary" publishing.
1st ed, 2010: 208 pp, $15 paper, $10 digital download
ISBN(s): 978-0-9826635-0-9 (digital download); 978-0-9826635-1-6 (print)

How to Write a Book Proposal
Published by Writer's Digest Books
Imprint of Penguin Random House LLC
1745 Broadway, New York, NY 10019
Web Site: www.writersdigest.com; www. writersdigestshop.com
Details how the industry works, where it's headed & how you can be part of it.
4th ed: 336 pp, $19.99 paper & ebook (retail)
First published 2003
ISBN(s): 978-1-58297-702-7 (paper); 978-1-59963-307-7 (ebook)

Hudson's Washington News Media Contacts Guide
Published by Grey House Publishing Inc™
4919 Rte 22, Amenia, NY 12501
Mailing Address: PO Box 56, Amenia, NY 12501-0056
Tel: 518-789-8700 *Toll Free Tel:* 800-562-2139
Fax: 518-789-0556
E-mail: books@greyhouse.com
Web Site: greyhouse.com
Comprehensive listing of over 3,000 news organizations & their holdings & more than 4,000 key media contacts in the Washington, DC metropolitan area.
Annual.
2019: 270 pp, $289, online database available (see web site for quote)
ISBN(s): 978-1-64265-070-9

Index to Legal Periodicals & Books
Published by Grey House Publishing Inc™
4919 Rte 22, Amenia, NY 12501
Mailing Address: PO Box 56, Amenia, NY 12501-0056
Tel: 518-789-8700 *Toll Free Tel:* 800-562-2139
Fax: 518-789-0556
E-mail: books@greyhouse.com
Web Site: greyhouse.com
A cumulative author-subject index to legal publications with a table of cases & statutes & listing of book reviews.
2020 (2019 annual cumulation): 3,000 pp, $695
ISBN(s): 978-1-64265-615-2

Indexing from A to Z
Published by Grey House Publishing Inc™
4919 Rte 22, Amenia, NY 12501
Mailing Address: PO Box 56, Amenia, NY 12501-0056
Tel: 518-789-8700 *Toll Free Tel:* 800-562-2139
Fax: 518-789-0556
E-mail: books@greyhouse.com
Web Site: greyhouse.com
Includes the latest national & international standards & recommended practices pertaining to indexes & indexing.
Available for purchase at www.hwwilsoninprint.com/index_AZ.php.
2nd ed, 1996: 569 pp, $80
First published 1991
ISBN(s): 978-0-8242-0882-0

International Directory of Little Magazines & Small Presses
Published by Dustbooks
PO Box 100, Paradise, CA 95967-0100
SAN: 204-1871
Tel: 530-877-6110 *Fax:* 530-877-0222
E-mail: inquiries@dustbooks.com; info@dustbooks.com
Web Site: www.dustbooks.com
Key Personnel
Ed: Neil McIntyre
For libraries & writers; 3,800 small book & magazine publishers with full data.
Annual (CD-ROM), continuously (online).
53rd ed, 2017-2018, $30 CD-ROM, $65 CD-ROM (3 directories), $49.95 online (4 directories)
ISBN(s): 978-1-935742-44-9 (CD-ROM)

International Literary Market Place (ILMP)
Published by Information Today, Inc
121 Chanlon Rd, Suite G-20, New Providence, NJ 07974-2195
Tel: 908-795-3755 *Toll Free Tel:* 800-409-4929 (press 3); 800-300-9868 (cust serv)
E-mail: custserv@infotoday.com
Web Site: www.literarymarketplace.com
Key Personnel
Mng Ed: Karen Hallard *Tel:* 908-219-0277
E-mail: khallard@infotoday.com

A comprehensive directory of data on the book trade industry in over 175 countries outside the US & Canada, with more than 9,000 publishers & over 3,200 book organizations including, among others, agents, booksellers & library associations. Includes information basic to conducting business in each country. The US & Canada are covered by *Literary Market Place*. Web version, which includes *Literary Market Place*, also available.
Annual.
54th ed, 2021: 1,850 pp, $369.50 paper, $459.50 online subn
ISBN(s): 978-1-57387-565-3

Introduction to Literary Context
Published by Grey House Publishing Inc™
4919 Rte 22, Amenia, NY 12501
Mailing Address: PO Box 56, Amenia, NY 12501-0056
Tel: 518-789-8700 *Toll Free Tel:* 800-562-2139
Fax: 518-789-0556
E-mail: csr@salempress.com
Web Site: salempress.com
Each volume explores literary content. Each essay examines works through the following categories: content synopsis, religious context, historical context, societal context, biographical context, scientific & technological context. Includes discussion questions, essay ideas, works cited, bibliography & general index.
Volumes published Nov 2013:
American Post-Modernist Novels, 340 pp
American Short Fiction, 290 pp.
Volumes published April-Dec 2014:
American Poetry of the 20th Century, 265 pp
English Literature, 274 pp
Plays, 262 pp
World Literature, 369 pp.
$165/vol (includes online access with print purchase)
ISBN(s): 978-1-61925-210-3 (American Post-Modernist Novels); 978-1-61925-211-0 (American Post-Modernist Novels ebook); 978-1-61925-212-7 (American Short Fiction); 978-1-61925-213-4 (American Short Fiction ebook); 978-1-61925-483-1 (World Literature); 978-1-61925-484-8 (World Literature ebook); 978-1-61925-485-5 (English Literature); 978-1-61925-486-2 (English Literature ebook); 978-1-61925-713-9 (American Poetry of the 20th Century); 978-1-61925-714-6 (American Poetry of the 20th Century ebook); 978-1-61925-715-3 (Plays); 978-1-61925-716-0 (Plays ebook)

Jeff Herman's Guide to Book Publishers, Editors and Literary Agents: Who They Are, What They Want, How to Win Them Over
Published by New World Library
Division of Whatever Publishing Inc
14 Pamaron Way, Novato, CA 94949
SAN: 211-8777
Tel: 415-884-2100 *Toll Free Tel:* 800-972-6657; 800-227-3900 (ext 52, retail orders)
Fax: 415-884-2199
Web Site: www.newworldlibrary.com
Key Personnel
Author: Jeff Herman
Writing/reference book. Directory of publishers (US, University, CN) & US literary agents. Includes interviews with editors & agents as well as additional information on submitting material to the publishing industry.
28th ed, 2018: 672 pp, $29.95 paper
First published 1990
ISBN(s): 978-1-6086-8584-4

The Joy of Publishing!
Published by Open Horizons Publishing Co
PO Box 2887, Taos, NM 87571
Tel: 575-751-3398

E-mail: books@bookmarketingbestsellers.com
Web Site: bookmarketingbestsellers.com
Key Personnel
Publr & Ed: John Kremer *E-mail:* johnkremer@bookmarket.com
Fascinating facts, anecdotes, curiosities & historic origins about books & authors, editors & publishers, bookmaking & bookselling.
2000: 256 pp, $29.99 (hardcover), $19.95 (Internet special)
First published 1996
ISBN(s): 978-0-912411-47-7

Keys to Great Writing
Published by Writer's Digest Books
Imprint of Penguin Random House LLC
1745 Broadway, New York, NY 10019
Web Site: www.writersdigest.com; www.writersdigestshop.com
From grammar to revision strategies.
1st ed: 240 pp, $14.99 (retail)
ISBN(s): 978-1-58297-492-7

Law Books & Serials in Print™
Published by Grey House Publishing Inc™
4919 Rte 22, Amenia, NY 12501
Mailing Address: PO Box 56, Amenia, NY 12501-0056
Tel: 518-789-8700 *Toll Free Tel:* 800-562-2139
Fax: 518-789-0556
E-mail: books@greyhouse.com
Web Site: greyhouse.com
Provides immediate access to current legal books, serials & multimedia publications distributed or published in the US. Offers data on 45,000 titles & 28,000 serials.
Annual.
45th ed, 2020: 3,900 pp, $2,050/3 vol set
ISBN(s): 978-1-64265-530-8 (3 vol set)

The Library & Book Trade Almanac
Published by Information Today, Inc
121 Chanlon Rd, Suite G-20, New Providence, NJ 07974-2195
Tel: 908-219-0279 *Toll Free Tel:* 800-300-9868 (cust serv)
E-mail: custserv@infotoday.com
Key Personnel
Ed: John B Bryans
Almanac of US library & book trade statistics, standards, programs & major events of the year, as well as international statistics & developments. Includes lists of library & literary awards & prizes, notable books, library schools, scholarship sources; directory of book trade & library associations at state, regional, national & international levels; employment sources; calendar of events.
Annual.
65th ed, 2020: 648 pp, $299.50 hardbound
ISBN(s): 978-1-57387-563-9

Literary Market Place (LMP)
Published by Information Today, Inc
121 Chanlon Rd, Suite G-20, New Providence, NJ 07974-2195
Tel: 908-795-3755 *Toll Free Tel:* 800-409-4929 (press 3); 800-300-9868 (cust serv)
E-mail: custserv@infotoday.com
Web Site: www.literarymarketplace.com
Key Personnel
Mng Ed: Karen Hallard *Tel:* 908-219-0277
E-mail: khallard@infotoday.com
Directory of over 23,000 companies & individuals in US & Canadian publishing. Areas covered include book publishers; associations; book trade events; courses, conferences & contests; agents & agencies; services & suppliers; direct-mail promotion; review, selection & reference; radio & television; wholesale, export & import & book manufacturing. A 2 volume set, each containing 2 alphabetical names & numbers indexes, one for key companies listed & one for

individuals. The rest of the world is covered by *International Literary Market Place*. Web version, which also includes *International Literary Market Place*, also available.
Annual.
81st ed, 2021: 1,556 pp, $459.50/2 vol set paper, $459.50 online subn
ISBN(s): 978-1-57387-567-7 (2 vol set)

Magazines for Libraries
Published by ProQuest LLC
Subsidiary of Cambridge Information Group Inc
630 Central Ave, New Providence, NJ 07974
E-mail: info@proquest.com
Web Site: www.proquest.com
Key Personnel
Gen Ed: Cheryl LaGuardia
Creator: Bill Katz
A critically annotated guide to magazine selection for public, college, school & special libraries, with approximately 5,000 periodicals critically evaluated by more than 160 subject specialists & classified under more than 160 subject headings. Includes journals (print & electronic) & newspapers.
Annual.
28th ed, 2020, $1,551 cloth
First published 1969
ISBN(s): 978-1-60030-677-8

Magill's Choice: American Ethnic Writers
Published by Grey House Publishing Inc™
4919 Rte 22, Amenia, NY 12501
Mailing Address: PO Box 56, Amenia, NY 12501-0056
Tel: 518-789-8700 *Toll Free Tel:* 800-562-2139
Fax: 518-789-0556
E-mail: csr@salempress.com
Web Site: salempress.com
Coverage of 225 ethnic writers, including summary descriptions of the writer's significance, associated ethnicities, birth/death dates, biography & thorough analysis of the writer's works.
Aug 2008: 1,000 pp, $217/3 vol set (includes online access with print purchase)
ISBN(s): 978-1-58765-462-6; 978-1-58765-466-4 (ebook)

Magill's Choice: Holocaust Literature
Published by Grey House Publishing Inc™
4919 Rte 22, Amenia, NY 12501
Mailing Address: PO Box 56, Amenia, NY 12501-0056
Tel: 518-789-8700 *Toll Free Tel:* 800-562-2139
Fax: 518-789-0556
E-mail: csr@salempress.com
Web Site: salempress.com
Key Personnel
Ed: John K Roth; Edward J Sexton
More than 100 in-depth reviews of the classics of Holocaust literature, including histories, biographies, memoirs, diaries, testimonials, philosophy, social criticism, novels, short fiction, poetry & plays.
March 2008: 960 pp, $130/2 vol set (includes online access with print purchase)
ISBN(s): 978-1-58765-375-9 (2 vol set); 978-1-58765-443-5 (ebook set)

Magill's Choice: Notable African American Writers
Published by Grey House Publishing Inc™
4919 Rte 22, Amenia, NY 12501
Mailing Address: PO Box 56, Amenia, NY 12501-0056
Tel: 518-789-8700 *Toll Free Tel:* 800-562-2139
Fax: 518-789-0556
E-mail: csr@salempress.com
Web Site: salempress.com
Biographical essays on 80 important African American writers in all genres.

2006: 2,400 pp, $217/3 vol set (includes online access with print purchase)
ISBN(s): 978-1-58765-272-1 (3 vol set); 978-1-58765-362-9 (ebook set)

Magill's Choice: Notable American Novelists
Published by Grey House Publishing Inc™
4919 Rte 22, Amenia, NY 12501
Mailing Address: PO Box 56, Amenia, NY 12501-0056
Tel: 518-789-8700 *Toll Free Tel:* 800-562-2139
Fax: 518-789-0556
E-mail: csr@salempress.com
Web Site: salempress.com
Presents biographical sketches & analytical overviews of 145 of the best known American & Canadian writers of long fiction from the 19th & 20th centuries that are studied in the core curricula of high school & undergraduate literature studies.
Aug 2007 (revised): 1,536 pp, $217/3 vol set (includes online access with print purchase)
ISBN(s): 978-1-58765-393-3 (3 vol set); 978-1-58765-410-7 (ebook set)

Magill's Choice: Notable Playwrights
Published by Grey House Publishing Inc™
4919 Rte 22, Amenia, NY 12501
Mailing Address: PO Box 56, Amenia, NY 12501-0056
Tel: 518-789-8700 *Toll Free Tel:* 800-562-2139
Fax: 518-789-0556
E-mail: csr@salempress.com
Web Site: salempress.com
Biographical sketches & critical studies of 106 of the most important & best-known dramatists, from the development of drama in ancient Greece & Rome to European, American, Asian & African writers of the present century.
Aug 2004: 1,131 pp, $217/3 vol set (includes online access with print purchase)
ISBN(s): 978-1-58765-195-3 (3 vol set); 978-1-58765-316-2 (ebook set)

Magill's Choice: Short Story Writers
Published by Grey House Publishing Inc™
4919 Rte 22, Amenia, NY 12501
Mailing Address: PO Box 56, Amenia, NY 12501-0056
Tel: 518-789-8700 *Toll Free Tel:* 800-562-2139
Fax: 518-789-0556
E-mail: csr@salempress.com
Web Site: salempress.com
Key Personnel
Ed: Charles May
Covers 146 of the most frequently taught, read & researched short fiction writers studied in American schools & colleges.
Oct 2007 (revised): 1,164 pp, $217/3 vol set (includes online access with print purchase)
ISBN(s): 978-1-58765-389-6 (3 vol set); 978-1-58765-411-4 (ebook set)

Magill's Literary Annual
Published by Grey House Publishing Inc™
4919 Rte 22, Amenia, NY 12501
Mailing Address: PO Box 56, Amenia, NY 12501-0056
Tel: 518-789-8700 *Toll Free Tel:* 800-562-2139
Fax: 518-789-0556
E-mail: csr@salempress.com
Web Site: salempress.com
Key Personnel
Ed: Jennifer Sawtelle
Offers over 150 major examples of serious literature published during the previous calendar year, covering the best of the best in fiction & nonfiction.
Annual.
2021: 700 pp, $210/2 vol set (includes online access)

First published 1954
ISBN(s): 978-1-64265-729-6 (2 vol set); 978-1-64265-732-6 (ebook set)

Managing the Publishing Process: An Annotated Bibliography
Published by Greenwood Press
Imprint of ABC-CLIO
130 Cremona Dr, Suite C, Santa Barbara, CA 93117
Mailing Address: PO Box 1911, Santa Barbara, CA 93116-1911
Tel: 805-968-1911 *Toll Free Tel:* 800-368-6868
Fax: 805-685-9685 *Toll Free Fax:* 866-270-3856
E-mail: customerservice@abc-clio.com
Web Site: www.abc-clio.com
Key Personnel
Dir, Edit-Print: Anthony Chiffolo
Author: Bruce Speck
Cites & annotates more than 1,200 books & articles on how to manage the publishing process.
1995: 360 pp, $75 hardcover
ISBN(s): 978-0-313-27956-0

Manufacturing Standards & Specifications for (El-Hi) Textbooks (MSST)
Published by State Instructional Materials Review Administrators (SIMRA)
PO Box 731388, Ormond Beach, FL 32173
Tel: 386-986-4552 *Fax:* 386-986-4553
E-mail: info@bmibook.com
Web Site: www.bmibook.org
Key Personnel
EVP & ACTS Coord: Daniel N Bach
The official Advisory Commission on Textbook Specifications (ACTS) publication detailing the approved guidelines for the manufacture of elementary & high school textbooks.
Sept 2012: 92 pp, $35 per copy looseleaf bound, adhesive bound or CD

Masterplots
Published by Grey House Publishing Inc™
4919 Rte 22, Amenia, NY 12501
Mailing Address: PO Box 56, Amenia, NY 12501-0056
Tel: 518-789-8700 *Toll Free Tel:* 800-562-2139
Fax: 518-789-0556
E-mail: csr@salempress.com
Web Site: salempress.com
Key Personnel
Ed: Laurence W Mazzeno
Fundamental reference data, plot synopses & critical evaluations of the most important works in all genres throughout history & around the world.
4th ed, Nov 2010: 7,316 pp, $1,200/12 vol set (includes online access)
First published 1976
ISBN(s): 978-1-58765-568-5 (12 vol set)

Masterplots 2010-2018 Supplement
Published by Grey House Publishing Inc™
4919 Rte 22, Amenia, NY 12501
Mailing Address: PO Box 56, Amenia, NY 12501-0056
Tel: 518-789-8700 *Toll Free Tel:* 800-562-2139
Fax: 518-789-0556
E-mail: csr@salempress.com
Web Site: salempress.com
Critically evaluates 187 major examples of serious fiction, published in English from 2010-2018, from writers in the US & around the world.
2018: 616 pp, $225/2 vol set (includes online access with print purchase)
ISBN(s): 978-1-64265-032-7; 978-1-64265-033-4 (ebook)

Medical & Health Care Books & Serials in Print™
Published by Grey House Publishing Inc™
4919 Rte 22, Amenia, NY 12501
Mailing Address: PO Box 56, Amenia, NY 12501-0056
Tel: 518-789-8700 *Toll Free Tel:* 800-562-2139
Fax: 518-789-0556
E-mail: books@greyhouse.com
Web Site: greyhouse.com
Bibliographic information on thousands of highly specialized health science & allied health titles published or distributed in the US. Provides immediate access to over 120,000 ISBNs comprising over 110,000 entries from over 15,000 publishers.
Annual.
45th ed, 2020: 6,300 pp, $990/3 vol set
ISBN(s): 978-1-64265-534-6 (3 vol set)

Middle & Junior High Core Collection
Published by Grey House Publishing Inc™
4919 Rte 22, Amenia, NY 12501
Mailing Address: PO Box 56, Amenia, NY 12501-0056
Tel: 518-789-8700 *Toll Free Tel:* 800-562-2139
Fax: 518-789-0556
E-mail: books@greyhouse.com
Web Site: greyhouse.com
Guide to over 11,000 fiction & nonfiction books recommended for children & young adolescents, grades 5-9.
14th ed, Jan 2019: 2,500 pp, $295
ISBN(s): 978-1-64265-259-8

MLRC 50-State Survey: Employment Libel & Privacy Law
Published by Media Law Resource Center Inc
North Tower, 20th fl, 520 Eighth Ave, New York, NY 10018
Tel: 212-337-0200 *Fax:* 212-337-9893
E-mail: medialaw@medialaw.org
Web Site: www.medialaw.org
Key Personnel
Exec Dir: George Freeman
Easy-to-use compendiums of the law in all US jurisdictions, state & federal, used by journalists, lawyers, judges & law schools nationwide. Each state's chapter, prepared by experts in that jurisdiction, is presented in a uniform outline format. Also available as an ebook.
Annual.
2018-2019, $215
ISBN(s): 978-1-63283-8599 (paper); 978-1-63283-8605 (ebook)

MLRC 50-State Survey: Media Libel Law
Published by Media Law Resource Center Inc
North Tower, 20th fl, 520 Eighth Ave, New York, NY 10018
Tel: 212-337-0200 *Fax:* 212-337-9893
E-mail: medialaw@medialaw.org
Web Site: www.medialaw.org
Key Personnel
Exec Dir: George Freeman
Easy-to-use compendiums of the law in all US jurisdictions, state & federal, used by journalists, lawyers, judges & law schools nationwide. Each state's chapter, prepared by experts in that jurisdiction, is presented in a uniform outline format. Also available as an ebook.
Annual.
2018-2019, $215
ISBN(s): 978-1-63283-8551 (paper); 978-1-63283-8568 (ebook)

MLRC 50-State Survey: Media Privacy & Related Law
Published by Media Law Resource Center Inc
North Tower, 20th fl, 520 Eighth Ave, New York, NY 10018
Tel: 212-337-0200 *Fax:* 212-337-9893

E-mail: medialaw@medialaw.org
Web Site: www.medialaw.org
Key Personnel
Exec Dir: George Freeman
Easy-to-use compendiums of the law in all US jurisdictions, state & federal, used by journalists, lawyers, judges & law schools nationwide. Each state's chapter, prepared by experts in that jurisdiction, is presented in a uniform outline format. Also available as an ebook.
Annual.
2018-2019, $215
ISBN(s): 978-1-63283-8575 (paper); 978-1-63283-8582 (ebook)

National Trade and Professional Associations of the United States
Published by Columbia Books & Information Services (CBIS)
4340 East-West Hwy, Suite 300, Bethesda, MD 20814
Tel: 202-464-1662 *Toll Free Tel:* 888-265-0600 (cust serv) *Fax:* 301-664-9600
E-mail: info@columbiabooks.com
Web Site: www.columbiabooks.com
Key Personnel
Sr Mktg Mgr: Jamie Herring *Tel:* 240-235-0271
    E-mail: jherring@columbiabooks.com
Covers over 8,000 trade associations, professional societies & labor unions with national memberships with such data as chief executive, size of membership & staff, budget, telephone, facsimile number, e-mail address, publications, meeting data & historical background. Includes indexes by subject, geography, budget, acronym, chief executive officer & annual meeting location. Also available online at www.associationexecs.com.
Annual.
2019: 1,920 pp, $349
First published 1965
ISBN(s): 978-1-938939-83-9 (paper)

The New York Times Manual of Style & Usage
Published by Three Rivers Press
Division of Penguin Random House LLC
1745 Broadway, New York, NY 10019
Tel: 212-782-9000 *Toll Free Tel:* 800-733-3000 (cust serv)
Web Site: www.penguinrandomhouse.com
Key Personnel
Author: William G Connolly; Allan M Siegal
5th ed, 2015, $18 paper, $12.99 ebook
ISBN(s): 978-1-10190-322-3 (ebook); 978-1-10190-544-9 (paper)

Niche Publishing: Publish Profitably Every Time
Published by Communication Unlimited
185 Shevelin Rd, Novato, CA 94947
Tel: 415-884-2941 *Toll Free Tel:* 800-563-1454
    Fax: 415-883-5707
E-mail: gordon@gordonburgett.com
Web Site: www.gordonburgett.com
Key Personnel
Pres & Ed: Gordon Burgett *E-mail:* glburgett@aol.com
How-to information, step-by-step process & detailed example of niche publishing.
2008: 208 pp, $15 paper, $10 digital download
ISBN(s): 978-0-979629-525

Nineteenth-Century Literature Criticism
Published by Gale
Division of Cengage Learning
27500 Drake Rd, Farmington Hills, MI 48331-3535
SAN: 213-4373
Tel: 248-699-4253 *Toll Free Tel:* 800-877-4253
    Fax: 248-699-8070 *Toll Free Fax:* 800-414-5043 (orders)
E-mail: gale.galeord@cengage.com

Web Site: www.gale.com
Profiles 4-8 literary figures by providing full-text or excerpted criticism taken from books, magazines, literary reviews, newspapers & scholarly journals.
$397 hardcover

Novels Into Film: Adaptations & Interpretations
Published by Grey House Publishing Inc™
4919 Rte 22, Amenia, NY 12501
Mailing Address: PO Box 56, Amenia, NY 12501-0056
Tel: 518-789-8700 *Toll Free Tel:* 800-562-2139
    Fax: 518-789-0556
E-mail: csr@salempress.com
Web Site: salempress.com
100 concise essays on significant novels & movie adaptations, ranging from classics to contemporary favorites. Providing authoritative information & scholarly analysis with a focus on narrative elements & adaptation strategies, the essays also introduce fundamental concepts in literary & film criticism & address the qualities that are specific to the two media of literature & film.
Oct 2018: 416 pp, $185 (includes online access with print purchase)
ISBN(s): 978-1-68217-907-9; 978-1-68217-955-0 (ebook)

O'Dwyer's Directory of Public Relations Firms
Published by J R O'Dwyer Co Inc
271 Madison Ave, Rm 600, New York, NY 10016
Tel: 212-679-2471 *Toll Free Tel:* 866-395-7710
    Fax: 212-683-2750
Web Site: www.odwyerpr.com
Key Personnel
Ed-in-Chief & Publr: Jack O'Dwyer
    E-mail: jack@odwyerpr.com
Assoc Publr & Ed: Jane Landers *E-mail:* jane@odwyerpr.com; John O'Dwyer *E-mail:* john@odwyerpr.com
Dir, Mktg: Christine O'Dwyer *E-mail:* christine@odwyerpr.com
Sr Ed: Fraser P Seitel *E-mail:* yusake@aol.com
Directory Ed-in-Chief: Melissa Werbell
    E-mail: melissa@odwyerpr.com
A listing of more than 1,200 PR firms in the US & abroad. Also available on web site as PDF download.
48th ed, 2018: 330 pp, $95
First published 1970
ISBN(s): 978-0-9976910-2-3

100 Things Every Writer Needs to Know
Published by TarcherPerigee
Imprint of Penguin Group USA, A Penguin Random House Company
375 Hudson St, New York, NY 10014
Tel: 212-366-2000 *Fax:* 212-366-2365
Web Site: www.penguin.com
Key Personnel
VP & Ed-in-Chief: Marian Lizzi
Author: Scott Edelstein
256 pp, $14.95
First published 1996
ISBN(s): 978-0-399-52508-7

1001 Ways to Market Your Books
Published by Open Horizons Publishing Co
PO Box 2887, Taos, NM 87571
Tel: 575-751-3398
E-mail: books@bookmarketingbestsellers.com
Web Site: bookmarketingbestsellers.com
Key Personnel
Publr & Ed: John Kremer *E-mail:* johnkremer@bookmarket.com
Outlines more than 1,000 different ways to market books. Uses many real-life examples describing how other publishers market their

books. Includes planning & design, advertising & distribution, subsidiary rights & spinoffs.
7th ed, 2016: 704 pp, $27.95 paper

1,001 Tips for Writers: Words of Wisdom About Writing, Getting Published, and Living the Literary Life
Published by North Ridge Books
PO Box 2832, Rancho Mirage, CA 92270
Tel: 949-533-5106 (cell) *Toll Free Fax:* 800-763-9881
E-mail: nrbooks@aol.com
Web Site: www.1001tipsforwriters.com
Key Personnel
Ed: William A Gordon
1,001 Tips for Writers is a quotation book offering "Words of Wisdom About Writing, Getting Published, and Living the Literary Life." The book quotes literary greats; working writers, publishers, editors on subjects such as "How to Get Traditionally Published", "Self-Publishing", "Book Publicity" & writing history, humor, novels, & journalism.
1st ed, 2014, $16.95 paper, $8.95 ebook
ISBN(s): 978-0-937813-09-6 (ebook); 978-0-937813-10-2 (paper)

The Pocket Muse 2
Published by Writer's Digest Books
Imprint of Penguin Random House LLC
1745 Broadway, New York, NY 10019
Web Site: www.writersdigest.com; www.writersdigestshop.com
Unique ideas for overcoming writer's block, creativity boosters, revision tips & more. Available as ebook only.
2nd ed, $12.99 ebook (retail)

Poetry Criticism
Published by Gale
Division of Cengage Learning
27500 Drake Rd, Farmington Hills, MI 48331-3535
SAN: 213-4373
Tel: 248-699-4253 *Toll Free Tel:* 800-877-4253
Fax: 248-699-8070 *Toll Free Fax:* 800-414-5043 (orders)
E-mail: gale.galeord@cengage.com
Web Site: www.gale.com
Each volume of this reference provides substantial critical essays & biographical information on 4-8 major poets from all eras. Entries provide an introductory biographical sketch, an author portrait, a primary bibliography, annotated full-text & excerpted criticism of the poets' works & sources for additional reading. When available, comments from the poets themselves are included. Also available online.
$297 hardcover

Poet's Market
Published by Writer's Digest Books
Imprint of Penguin Random House LLC
1745 Broadway, New York, NY 10019
Web Site: www.writersdigest.com; www.writersdigestshop.com
Where & how to get poetry published; 1,800 US & international publisher listings, also includes contests & awards, writing colonies, organizations, conferences, workshops & publications useful to poets. Also available in Kindle format.
Annual.
33rd, 2020: 480 pp, $29.99 paper (retail)
ISBN(s): 978-1-4403-5495-2 (paper)

Professional Writing: Processes, Strategies & Tips for Publishing in Education Journals
Published by Krieger Publishing Co
1725 Krieger Dr, Malabar, FL 32950
SAN: 202-6562

Tel: 321-724-9542 *Fax:* 321-951-3671
E-mail: info@krieger-publishing.com
Web Site: www.krieger-publishing.com
Key Personnel
Author: Roger Hiemstra
Provides insights, tips, strategies & recommendations for publishing in educational periodicals.
1994: 152 pp, $27.50 cloth
First published 1993
ISBN(s): 978-0-89464-660-7

Public Library Core Collection: Nonfiction
Published by Grey House Publishing Inc™
4919 Rte 22, Amenia, NY 12501
Mailing Address: PO Box 56, Amenia, NY 12501-0056
Tel: 518-789-8700 *Toll Free Tel:* 800-562-2139
Fax: 518-789-0556
E-mail: books@greyhouse.com
Web Site: greyhouse.com
Recommends reference & nonfiction books for the general adult audience. Guide to over 12,000 books, plus review sources & other professional aids for librarians & media specialists.
17th ed, 2019: 3,106 pp, $420
ISBN(s): 978-1-68217-661-0

Publish, Don't Perish: The Scholar's Guide to Academic Writing & Publishing
Published by Praeger
Imprint of ABC-CLIO
130 Cremona Dr, Suite C, Santa Barbara, CA 93117
Mailing Address: PO Box 1911, Santa Barbara, CA 93116-1911
Tel: 805-968-1911 *Toll Free Tel:* 800-368-6868
Fax: 805-685-9685 *Toll Free Fax:* 866-270-3856
E-mail: custserv@abc-clio.com
Web Site: www.abc-clio.com
Key Personnel
Dir, Edit-Print: Anthony Chiffolo
Author: Joseph M Moxley
Expressing a strongly positive view of the value of academic publishing that reaches far beyond what is implied by the book title, Moxley offers informed suggestions to faculty members for conceiving, developing & publishing scholarly documents as books or journal articles.
224 pp, $27.95 paper, $40 hardcover
First published 1992
ISBN(s): 978-0-275-94453-7 (paper); 978-0-313-27735-1 (hardcover)

Publishers Directory (PD)
Published by Gale
Division of Cengage Learning
27500 Drake Rd, Farmington Hills, MI 48331-3535
SAN: 213-4373
Tel: 248-699-4253 *Toll Free Tel:* 800-877-4253
Fax: 248-699-8070 *Toll Free Fax:* 800-414-5043 (orders)
E-mail: gale.galeord@cengage.com; businessproducts@cengage.com
Web Site: www.gale.com
Contains over 20,000 US & Canadian publishers & distributors. Entries contain full organization contact information, including corporate e-mails & web sites when provided. In addition, most entries feature a wealth of descriptive (when available), including principal officers with personal e-mails; year founded; annual sales; number of titles per year, including an estimate for current year; total title count; discount policy; percentage of sales. Also available as an ebook.
45th ed, 2020: 2,081 pp, $1,061/3 vol set paper, see web site for ebook price
ISBN(s): 978-1-4103-8628-1 (hardcover); 978-1-4103-8632-8 (ebook)

Publishers, Distributors & Wholesalers of the United States™
Published by Grey House Publishing Inc™
4919 Rte 22, Amenia, NY 12501
Mailing Address: PO Box 56, Amenia, NY 12501-0056
Tel: 518-789-8700 *Toll Free Tel:* 800-562-2139
Fax: 518-789-0556
E-mail: books@greyhouse.com
Web Site: greyhouse.com
Offers detailed data on active US publishers, distributors, wholesalers, video producers, manufacturers, audio producers, museums with publishing programs & other related businesses. Immediate access to over 500,000 publishers & over 15,000 distributors & wholesalers.
Annual.
42nd ed, 2021: 5,400 pp, $985/2 vol set hardcover
ISBN(s): 978-1-64265-540-7 (2 vol set)

Publishers' International ISBN Directory
Published by De Gruyter Saur
Imprint of Walter de Gruyter GmbH
Genthiner Str 13, 10785 Berlin, Germany
Tel: (030) 260 05-0 *Fax:* (030) 260 05-251
E-mail: service@degruyter.com
Web Site: www.degruyter.com
Seven volume set containing the names of more than 1,000,000 active publishing houses & more than 1,100,000 ISBN prefixes from 221 countries & territories.
41st ed, 2015: 9,217 pp, $2,366 hardcover, $3,346 print & ebook
ISBN(s): 978-3-11-033619-1 (hardcover/7-vol set); 978-3-11-033735-8 (eBookPLUS); 978-3-11-033736-5 (print & ebook)

Publishing for the PreK-12 Market
Published by Simba Information
Division of Market Research.com
11200 Rockville Pike, Suite 504, Rockville, MD 20852
SAN: 210-2021
Tel: 240-747-3091 *Toll Free Tel:* 888-297-4622 (cust serv) *Fax:* 240-747-3004
E-mail: customerservice@simbainformation.com
Web Site: www.simbainformation.com
Key Personnel
Sr Analyst/Mng Ed: Kathy Mickey
Sr Analyst/Ed: Karen Meaney
Up-to-date descriptions & statistics on enrollments, demographic trends, in several categories; publishers' sales, forecasts, expenditures & profiles of the leading publishers in the K-12 market place.
Annual.
2018-2019: 162 pp, $3,250 online download

Publishing in the Information Age: A New Management Framework for the Digital Era
Published by Praeger
Imprint of ABC-CLIO
130 Cremona Dr, Suite C, Santa Barbara, CA 93117
Mailing Address: PO Box 1911, Santa Barbara, CA 93116-1911
Tel: 805-968-1911 *Toll Free Tel:* 800-368-6868
Fax: 805-685-9685 *Toll Free Fax:* 866-270-3856
E-mail: custserv@abc-clio.com
Web Site: www.abc-clio.com
Key Personnel
Dir, Edit-Print: Anthony Chiffolo
Author: Douglas M Eisenhart
A comprehensive single-volume study of the transformations underway in the publishing industry attributable to the penetration of digital information technologies & how publishers can benefit from them.
$39.95 paper, $84 hardcover

First published 1999
ISBN(s): 978-0-275-95696-7 (paper); 978-0-89930-847-0 (hardcover)

Recommended Reading: 600 Classics Reviewed
Published by Grey House Publishing Inc™
4919 Rte 22, Amenia, NY 12501
Mailing Address: PO Box 56, Amenia, NY 12501-0056
Tel: 518-789-8700 *Toll Free Tel:* 800-562-2139
Fax: 518-789-0556
E-mail: csr@salempress.com
Web Site: salempress.com
Covers 600 noteworthy works of literature (fiction, nonfiction, poetry or drama) & introduces brief, ready-reference data for the user's convenience: title, author, date of first publication, type of work & brief extract of book's content or impact.
2nd ed, Oct 2015: 406 pp, $125 (includes online access with print purchase)
First published 1995
ISBN(s): 978-1-61925-867-9; 978-1-61925-868-6 (ebook)

Research Centers Directory (RCD)
Published by Gale
Division of Cengage Learning
27500 Drake Rd, Farmington Hills, MI 48331-3535
SAN: 213-4373
Tel: 248-699-4253 *Toll Free Tel:* 800-877-4253
Fax: 248-699-8075 *Toll Free Fax:* 800-414-5043 (orders)
E-mail: gale.galeord@cengage.com
Web Site: www.gale.com
Directory describes university affiliated & other nonprofit research institutes in North America. Indexes: subject, geographic, personal name & master. Also available as an ebook.
46th ed, 2016: 3,157 pp, $1,296/5 vol set paper, $1,425.60 ebook
ISBN(s): 978-1-5730-2885-1 (5 vol set paper); 978-1-5730-2891-2 (ebook)

Sears List of Subject Headings
Published by Grey House Publishing Inc™
4919 Rte 22, Amenia, NY 12501
Mailing Address: PO Box 56, Amenia, NY 12501-0056
Tel: 518-789-8700 *Toll Free Tel:* 800-562-2139
Fax: 518-789-0556
E-mail: books@greyhouse.com
Web Site: greyhouse.com
Standard thesaurus of subject terminology for small & medium-sized libraries. Also includes *Principles of the Sears List*, outlining theoretical foundations of the *Sears List* & the general principles of subject cataloging.
22nd ed, July 2018: 1,100 pp, $195 (includes online access)
First published 1923
ISBN(s): 978-1-68217-234-6

The Secrets of Story
Published by Writer's Digest Books
Imprint of Penguin Random House LLC
1745 Broadway, New York, NY 10019
Web Site: www.writersdigest.com; www.writersdigestshop.com
Provides comprehensive, audience-focused strategies for becoming a master storyteller.
368 pp, $19.99 paper & ebook (retail)
ISBN(s): 978-1-4403-4823-5 (paper); 978-1-4403-4826-6 (ebook)

Senior High Core Collection
Published by Grey House Publishing Inc™
4919 Rte 22, Amenia, NY 12501
Mailing Address: PO Box 56, Amenia, NY 12501-0056

Tel: 518-789-8700 *Toll Free Tel:* 800-562-2139
Fax: 518-789-0556
E-mail: books@greyhouse.com
Web Site: greyhouse.com
Guide to over 8,500 fiction & nonfiction books recommended for adolescents & young adults, grades 9-12.
22nd ed, Oct 2020: 2,000 pp, $295
ISBN(s): 978-1-64265-648-0

Shakespearean Criticism
Published by Gale
Division of Cengage Learning
27500 Drake Rd, Farmington Hills, MI 48331-3535
SAN: 213-4373
Tel: 248-699-4253 *Toll Free Tel:* 800-877-4253
Fax: 248-699-8070 *Toll Free Fax:* 800-414-5043 (orders)
E-mail: gale.galeord@cengage.com
Web Site: www.gale.com
Thematically arranged essays from 1960 to the present of commentary on Shakespeare's plays & poems. Illustrated series provides support to students & teachers at high school & college levels. Beginning with Vol 60, presents topical entries comprised of essays that analyze various topics or themes of Shakespeare's works. Each volume has a cumulative character index, a topic index & a topic index arranged by play title. Also available online.
Vol 175, 2017: 416 pp, $397 hardcover
ISBN(s): 978-1-4103-2946-2

Short Story Criticism: Excerpts from Criticism of the Works of Short Fiction Writers
Published by Gale
Division of Cengage Learning
27500 Drake Rd, Farmington Hills, MI 48331-3535
SAN: 213-4373
Tel: 248-699-4253 *Toll Free Tel:* 800-877-4253
Fax: 248-699-8070 *Toll Free Fax:* 800-414-5043 (orders)
E-mail: gale.galeord@cengage.com
Web Site: www.gale.com
Series presenting critical views on the most widely studied writers of short fiction. Each volume includes overview of 3-6 short story writers, works, or topics & historical survey of the critical response. Most critical essays are full text. Also available online.
$297 hardcover

Short Story Index
Published by Grey House Publishing Inc™
4919 Rte 22, Amenia, NY 12501
Mailing Address: PO Box 56, Amenia, NY 12501-0056
Tel: 518-789-8700 *Toll Free Tel:* 800-562-2139
Fax: 518-789-0556
E-mail: books@greyhouse.com
Web Site: greyhouse.com
Indexing coverage of short stories written in or translated into English & published in collections, covering all styles & genres, from classics to experimental fiction.
Annual.
2020 ed (2019 annual cumulation): 300 pp, $295
ISBN(s): 978-1-64265-363-2

The Small Press Record of Books in Print
Published by Dustbooks
PO Box 100, Paradise, CA 95967-0100
SAN: 204-1871
Tel: 530-877-6110 *Fax:* 530-877-0222
E-mail: inquiries@dustbooks.com; info@dustbooks.com
Web Site: www.dustbooks.com
Key Personnel
Ed: Neil McIntyre

More than 44,000 titles from more than 5,100 small, independent, educational & self-publishers worldwide.
43rd ed, $37.95 CD-ROM, $49.50 online (4 directories)
ISBN(s): 978-1-935742-46-3 (CD-ROM)

Software and Intellectual Property Protection: Copyright and Patent Issues for Computer and Legal Professionals
Published by Praeger
Imprint of ABC-CLIO
130 Cremona Dr, Suite C, Santa Barbara, CA 93117
Mailing Address: PO Box 1911, Santa Barbara, CA 93116-1911
Tel: 805-968-1911 *Toll Free Tel:* 800-368-6868
Fax: 805-685-9685 *Toll Free Fax:* 866-270-3856
E-mail: custserv@abc-clio.com
Web Site: www.abc-clio.com
Key Personnel
Dir, Edit-Print: Anthony Chiffolo
Author: Bernard A Galler
A succinct, readable survey of the critical issues & cases in copyright & patent law applied to computer software, intended for computer professionals, academics & lawyers.
224 pp, $84 hardcover
ISBN(s): 978-0-89930-974-3

Something About the Author
Published by Gale
Division of Cengage Learning
27500 Drake Rd, Farmington Hills, MI 48331-3535
SAN: 213-4373
Tel: 248-699-4253 *Toll Free Tel:* 800-877-4253
Fax: 248-699-8070 *Toll Free Fax:* 800-414-5043 (orders)
E-mail: gale.galeord@cengage.com
Web Site: www.gale.com
Provides illustrated biographical articles on approximately 75 children's authors & artists. The series covers more than 15,000 individuals, ranging from established award-winners to authors & illustrators who are just beginning their careers. Entries cover: personal life, career, writings, adaptation, additional sources, photographs & illustrations. Also available as an ebook.
Vol 362, 2021: 450 pp, $285
ISBN(s): 978-1-4103-8907-7

The Standard Periodical Directory
Published by Oxbridge® Communications Inc
301 W 29 St, No 301, New York, NY 10001
Key Personnel
CEO: Louis Hagood *Tel:* 212-741-0231
Over 63,000 US & Canadian periodicals arranged by subject matter into 262 classifications & indexed by title. Listings include publishing company, address, telephone number; names of editor, publisher, ad director; annotations; frequency, circulation, advertising & subscription rates; year established; trim size, print method, page count.
42nd ed, 2019: 2,112 pp, $1,995 hardcover, $995 digital, $1,995 single user CD-ROM, $2,995 print & CD-ROM
First published 1964
ISBN(s): 978-1-891783-69-2 (hardcover)

Subject Guide to Books in Print®
Published by Grey House Publishing Inc™
4919 Rte 22, Amenia, NY 12501
Mailing Address: PO Box 56, Amenia, NY 12501-0056
Tel: 518-789-8700 *Toll Free Tel:* 800-562-2139
Fax: 518-789-0556
E-mail: books@greyhouse.com
Web Site: greyhouse.com

Master subject reference to titles, authors, publishers & distributors in the US, providing access to 2.5 million titles arranged by 75,000 Library of Congress subject headings.
Annual.
2020-2021: 15,400 pp, $1,415/6 vol set
ISBN(s): 978-1-64265-508-7 (6 vol set)

Subject Guide to Children's Books in Print®
Published by Grey House Publishing Inc™
4919 Rte 22, Amenia, NY 12501
Mailing Address: PO Box 56, Amenia, NY 12501-0056
Tel: 518-789-8700 *Toll Free Tel:* 800-562-2139 *Fax:* 518-789-0556
E-mail: books@greyhouse.com
Web Site: greyhouse.com
A natural complement to *Children's Books in Print®* & valuable tool when expanding children's literature collections & new curriculum areas. Coverage includes over 500,000 titles organized by 10,000 Library of Congress subject headings.
Annual.
51st ed, 2020: 2,900 pp, $670
ISBN(s): 978-1-64265-153-9

The Subversive Copy Editor: Advice from Chicago (Or, How to Negotiate Good Relationships with Your Writers, Your Colleagues, and Yourself)
Published by University of Chicago Press
1427 E 60 St, Chicago, IL 60637-2954
SAN: 202-5280
E-mail: custserv@press.uchicago.edu; marketing@press.uchicago.edu
Web Site: www.press.uchicago.edu
Key Personnel
Sr Ed, Ref & Writing Guides: Mary Laur
Tel: 773-702-7326 *E-mail:* mlaur@uchicago.edu
Longtime mss editor & *Chicago Manual of Style* guru Carol Fisher Saller brings a refreshingly levelheaded approach to the classic battle between writers & editors. The 2nd edition reflects today's publishing practices while retaining the self-deprecating tone & sharp humor that helped make the 1st edition so popular. Saller's sage advice will prove useful & entertaining to anyone charged with the sometimes perilous task of improving the writing of others.
Revised every 5-7 yrs.
2nd ed: 200 pp, $45 cloth, $15 paper or ebook
First published 2009
ISBN(s): 978-0-226-23990-3 (cloth); 978-0-226-24007-7 (paper); 978-0-226-24010-7 (ebook)

Survey of Compensation & Personnel Practices in the Publishing Industry
Published by Association of American Publishers (AAP)
455 Massachusetts Ave NW, Suite 700, Washington, DC 20001-2777
Tel: 202-347-3375 *Fax:* 202-347-3690
E-mail: info@publishers.org
Web Site: publishers.org
Key Personnel
Pres & CEO: Maria Pallante
EVP & Gen Coun: Allan R Adler
Asst Gen Coun: Sofia Castillo
SVP, Communs: John McKay
VP, Admin & Bd Liaison: Syreeta N Swann
VP, Communs: Cara Duckworth; Susanna Hinds
VP, Fin & Strategic Planning: Karen McInnis
VP, Global Policy: M Lui Simpson
Mng Dir, Meetings & Progs: Sara Pinto
Policy Specialist: Amanda Straub
Survey report contains salary & personnel practices information for more than 120 benchmark jobs in the publishing industry.

Annual.
220 pp, Varies based on participation, company site & AAP membership status

Training Guide to Frontline Bookselling
Published by Paz & Associates
1417 Sadler Rd, PMB 274, Fernandina Beach, FL 32034
Tel: 904-277-2664 *Fax:* 904-261-6742
E-mail: mkaufman@pazbookbiz.com
Web Site: www.pazbookbiz.com
Key Personnel
Partner: Donna Paz Kaufman *E-mail:* dpaz@pazbookbiz.com
12 chapters on all aspects of bookstore operations, includes trainers outline.
4th ed, Jan 2014: 125 pp, $189 plus shipping

Travel Writer's Guide
Published by Communication Unlimited
185 Shevelin Rd, Novato, CA 94947
Tel: 415-884-2941 *Toll Free Tel:* 800-563-1454 *Fax:* 415-883-5707
E-mail: gordon@gordonburgett.com
Web Site: www.gordonburgett.com
Key Personnel
Pres: Gordon Burgett *E-mail:* glburgett@aol.com
Writing/reference.
3rd ed (revised), updated 2005: 376 pp, $15 paper, $10 digital download
ISBN(s): 978-0-9708621-1-3

Troubleshooting Your Novel
Published by Writer's Digest Books
Imprint of Penguin Random House LLC
1745 Broadway, New York, NY 10019
Web Site: www.writersdigest.com; www.writersdigestshop.com
Helpful techniques & checklists, timesaving tricks of the trade & hundreds of questions for ms analysis & revision.
368 pp, $19.99 paper & ebook (retail)
ISBN(s): 978-1-59963-980-2 (paper); 978-1-59963-982-6 (ebook)

TRUMATCH Colorfinder
Published by TRUMATCH Inc
122 Mill Pond Lane, Water Mill, NY 11976
Mailing Address: PO Box 501, Water Mill, NY 11976-0501
Tel: 631-204-9100 *Toll Free Tel:* 800-TRU-9100 (878-9100, US & CN)
E-mail: info@trumatch.com
Web Site: www.trumatch.com
Key Personnel
Pres: Steven J Abramson
VP: Jane E Nichols *E-mail:* janen@trumatch.com
Digital guides for 4-color printing.
$85 paper for coated ed or uncoated ed

Twentieth-Century Literary Criticism
Published by Gale
Division of Cengage Learning
27500 Drake Rd, Farmington Hills, MI 48331-3535
SAN: 213-4373
Tel: 248-699-4253 *Toll Free Tel:* 800-877-4253 *Fax:* 248-699-8070 *Toll Free Fax:* 800-414-5043 (orders)
E-mail: gale.galeord@cengage.com
Web Site: www.gale.com
Key Personnel
Ed: Linda Pavlovski
Presents overviews of authors & furnishes full texts from representative criticism on the great novelists, poets, playwrights & literary theorists of the period 1900-1999. Each volume presents overviews of 4-8 authors. Every fourth volume covers literary topics including major literary movements, trends & other topics related to 20th century literature.
$397 hardcover

20 Master Plots
Published by Writer's Digest Books
Imprint of Penguin Random House LLC
1745 Broadway, New York, NY 10019
Web Site: www.writersdigest.com; www.writersdigestshop.com
How to take timeless storytelling structures & make them immediate, now, for fiction that's universal in how it speaks to the reader's heart.
1st ed: 288 pp, $16.99 paper, $14.99 ebook (retail)
First published 2003
ISBN(s): 978-1-59963-537-8 (paper); 978-1-59963-538-5 (ebook)

Ulrich's Periodicals Directory
Published by ProQuest LLC
Subsidiary of Cambridge Information Group Inc
630 Central Ave, New Providence, NJ 07974
Tel: 908-795-3659 (edit) *Toll Free Tel:* 800-346-6049 (Ulrich's hotline, US only)
E-mail: ulrichs@proquest.com; core_service@proquest.com (orders)
Web Site: www.ulrichsweb.com; www.proquest.com
Online only.
First published 1932

Walden's Paper Catalog
Published by Walden-Mott Corp
225 N Franklin Tpke, Ramsey, NJ 07446-1600
Tel: 201-818-8630 *Fax:* 201-818-8720
Web Site: www.waldenmott.com
Key Personnel
Ed: Alfred F Walden *Tel:* 201-818-8630 ext 11
National directory for information on commercial printing & writing papers. Brand names are listed alphabetically & by classification of paper. Paper distributors are listed geographically to help printers source from a local supplier.
2 issues/yr.
$85/yr
First published 1914

Walden's Paper Handbook
Published by Walden-Mott Corp
225 N Franklin Tpke, Ramsey, NJ 07446-1600
Tel: 201-818-8630 *Fax:* 201-818-8720
Web Site: www.waldenmott.com
Key Personnel
Ed: Alfred F Walden *Tel:* 201-818-8630 ext 11
Pulp & paper industry pocket guide.
3rd ed: 277 pp, $25

What Editors Do: The Art, Craft, and Business of Book Editing
Published by University of Chicago Press
1427 E 60 St, Chicago, IL 60637-2954
SAN: 202-5280
E-mail: custserv@press.uchicago.edu; marketing@press.uchicago.edu
Web Site: www.press.uchicago.edu
Key Personnel
Sr Ed, Ref & Writing Guides: Mary Laur
Tel: 773-702-7326 *E-mail:* mlaur@uchicago.edu
In this volume, Peter Ginna gathers essays from 27 leading editors in book publishing about their work. Representing both large houses & small & encompassing trade, textbook, academic & children's publishing, the contributors shed light on such issues as how editors acquire books, what constitutes a strong author-editor relationship & the editor's vital role at each stage of the publishing process. The book serves as a resource both for those entering the profession (or already in it) & for those outside publishing who seek an understanding of it.
1st ed: 320 pp, $75 cloth, $25 paper, $18 ebook
First published 2017
ISBN(s): 978-0-226-29983-9 (cloth); 978-0-226-29997-6 (paper); 978-0-226-30003-0 (ebook)

Word Painting
Published by Writer's Digest Books
Imprint of Penguin Random House LLC
1745 Broadway, New York, NY 10019
Web Site: www.writersdigest.com; www.
  writersdigestshop.com
Combines direct instruction with intriguing word
  exercises to teach you how to "paint" evocative
  descriptions that capture the images of your
  mind's eye & improve your writing.
Revised ed: 272 pp, $18.99 paper & ebook (re-
  tail)
First published 2000
ISBN(s): 978-1-59963-868-3 (paper); 978-1-
  59963-870-6 (ebook)

World Authors 2000-2005
Published by Grey House Publishing Inc™
4919 Rte 22, Amenia, NY 12501
Mailing Address: PO Box 56, Amenia, NY
  12501-0056
Tel: 518-789-8700 *Toll Free Tel:* 800-562-2139
  Fax: 518-789-0556
E-mail: books@greyhouse.com
Web Site: greyhouse.com
Covers some 300 novelists, poets, dramatists, essayists, scientists, biographers & other authors
  whose books, published 2000 through 2005,
  represent the dawn of a new millenium of great
  literature.
Available
  for purchase at www.hwwilsoninprint.com/
  world_authors05.php.
2007: 800 pp, $170
ISBN(s): 978-0-8242-1077-9

Write Naked
Published by Writer's Digest Books
Imprint of Penguin Random House LLC
1745 Broadway, New York, NY 10019
Web Site: www.writersdigest.com; www.
  writersdigestshop.com
Lessons & craft advice every writer needs in order to carve out a rewarding career in the romance genre.
240 pp, $16.99 paper & ebook (retail)
ISBN(s): 978-1-4403-4734-4 (paper); 978-1-4403-
  4740-5 (ebook)

Writer's Guide to Character Traits
Published by Writer's Digest Books
Imprint of Penguin Random House LLC
1745 Broadway, New York, NY 10019
Web Site: www.writersdigest.com; www.
  writersdigestshop.com
Profiles the mental, emotional & physical quali-
  ties of dozens of different personality types.
384 pp, $17.99 paper (retail)
First published 1999
ISBN(s): 978-1-58297-390-6

**The Writer's Guide to Crafting Stories for
  Children**
Published by Writer's Digest Books
Imprint of Penguin Random House LLC
1745 Broadway, New York, NY 10019
Web Site: www.writersdigest.com; www.
  writersdigestshop.com
Insightful advice for mastering storytelling ba-
  sics with dozens of examples that illustrate a
  variety of plot-building techniques.
1st ed: 192 pp, $16.99 paper (retail)
First published 2001
ISBN(s): 978-1-58297-052-3

**The Writer's Idea Book 10th Anniversary
  Edition**
Published by Writer's Digest Books
Imprint of Penguin Random House LLC
1745 Broadway, New York, NY 10019
Web Site: www.writersdigest.com; www.
  writersdigestshop.com
Helps you to jump-start your creativity & develop
  original ideas.
352 pp, $19.99 paper & ebook (retail)
First published 2002
ISBN(s): 978-1-59963-386-2 (paper); 978-1-
  59963-387-9 (ebook)

Writer's Market
Published by Writer's Digest Books
Imprint of Penguin Random House LLC
1745 Broadway, New York, NY 10019
Web Site: www.writersmarket.com; www.
  writersdigest.com; www.writersdigestshop.com
Lists more than 4,000 places where freelance
  writers can sell articles, books, novels, stories,
  fillers & scripts. Also available in Kindle format.
Annual.
99th ed, 2020: 896 pp, $29.99 paper (retail)
ISBN(s): 978-1-4403-0122-3 (paper)

**The Writer's Market Guide to Getting
  Published**
Published by Writer's Digest Books
Imprint of Penguin Random House LLC
1745 Broadway, New York, NY 10019
Web Site: www.writersdigest.com; www.
  writersdigestshop.com
Sound information on professional writing issues,
  focusing on everything from contracts to cre-
  ativity. Available as an ebook only.
$19.99 ebook (retail)
First published 2004
ISBN(s): 978-1-59963-151-6

Writing Creative Nonfiction
Published by Writer's Digest Books
Imprint of Penguin Random House LLC
1745 Broadway, New York, NY 10019
Web Site: www.writersdigest.com; www.
  writersdigestshop.com
More than thirty essays examining every key element of the craft, from researching ideas &
  structuring the story, to reportage & personal
  reflection.
400 pp, $18.99 paper (retail)
First published 2001
ISBN(s): 978-1-884910-50-0

**Writing Down the Bones: Freeing the Writer
  Within**
Published by Shambhala Publications Inc
4720 Walnut St, No 106, Boulder, CO 80301
Tel: 303-222-9598; 978-829-2599 (intl callers)
  Toll Free Tel: 888-424-2329 (cust serv); 866-
  424-0030 (off) *Fax:* 617-236-1563
E-mail: editorialdept@shambhala.com
Web Site: www.shambhala.com
Key Personnel
Owner & EVP: Sara Bercholz
Pres: Nikko Odiseos
Mng Ed: Liz Shaw
Author: Natalie Goldberg
Brings together Zen meditation & writing.
224 pp, $14 paper, $18.95 hardcover
First published 2005
ISBN(s): 978-1-59030-261-3 (paper); 978-1-
  59030-794-6 (hardcover); 987-0-8348-2113-2
  (ebook)

Writing Life Stories
Published by Writer's Digest Books
Imprint of Penguin Random House LLC
1745 Broadway, New York, NY 10019
Web Site: www.writersdigest.com; www.
  writersdigestshop.com
How to capture your own experiences & turn
  them into personal essays & book-length memoirs.
304 pp, $16.99 paper & ebook (retail)
First published 1998
ISBN(s): 978-1-58297-527-6 (paper); 978-1-
  58297-707-2 (ebook)

Writing the Breakout Novel
Published by Writer's Digest Books
Imprint of Penguin Random House LLC
1745 Broadway, New York, NY 10019
Web Site: www.writersdigest.com; www.
  writersdigestshop.com
How to take your prose to the next level & write
  a breakout novel.
1st ed: 256 pp, $17.99 paper (retail)
First published 2001
ISBN(s): 978-1-58297-182-7

The Yearbook of Experts®
Published by Broadcast Interview Source Inc
2500 Wisconsin Ave NW, Suite 949, Washington,
  DC 20007-4132
Tel: 202-333-5000 *Fax:* 202-342-5411
E-mail: expertclick@gmail.com
Web Site: www.expertclick.com
Key Personnel
Publr & Ed: Mitchell P Davis *Tel:* 203-333-4904
  E-mail: mitchell@yearbookofexperts.com
Listings of contacts at publishers, trade associ-
  ations & public interest groups that welcome
  media contacts; for both print & broadcast
  journalist use. Also available online.
Annual.
36th ed, 2020: 317 pp, $39.95 print ed
First published 1984
ISBN(s): 978-0-934333-12-2

**The Yearbook of Experts, Authorities &
  Spokespersons®**, see The Yearbook of
  Experts®

You Can Write Children's Books Workbook
Published by Writer's Digest Books
Imprint of Penguin Random House LLC
1745 Broadway, New York, NY 10019
Web Site: www.writersdigest.com; www.
  writersdigestshop.com
Provides hands-on instruction for finishing a ms,
  preparing it for publication & getting it published. Available as ebook only.
2nd ed, $14.99 ebook (retail)
First published 2004

Young Adult Fiction Core Collection
Published by Grey House Publishing Inc™
4919 Rte 22, Amenia, NY 12501
Mailing Address: PO Box 56, Amenia, NY
  12501-0056
Tel: 518-789-8700 *Toll Free Tel:* 800-562-2139
  Fax: 518-789-0556
E-mail: books@greyhouse.com
Web Site: greyhouse.com
Essential resource for library & media specialists
  looking to enhance & enrich their collection
  with more than 2,500 important & highly rec-
  ommended titles for young adult readers.
3rd ed, 2019: 500 pp, $255
ISBN(s): 978-1-64265-022-8

Magazines for the Trade

The magazines listed have been selected because they are published specifically for the book trade industry (apart from book review and index journals, which are listed in **Book Review & Index Journals & Services** in volume 2) or because they are widely used in the industry for reference. Also included in this section are literary journals.

For a comprehensive international directory of periodicals, see *Ulrich's Periodicals Directory* (online only, compiled by ProQuest LLC, 630 Central Avenue, New Providence, NJ 07974), which lists magazines by subject and includes notations indicating those that carry book reviews.

Ad Age
Published by Crain Communications Inc
685 Third Ave, New York, NY 10017-4024
Tel: 212-210-0100 *Toll Free Tel:* 877-320-1721
E-mail: adageeditor@adage.com; info@adage.com; customerservice@adage.com
Web Site: adage.com
Key Personnel
Pres & Publr: Josh Golden *E-mail:* jgolden@adage.com
Assoc Publr, Gen Mgr, Mktg & Brand: Heidi Waldusky *E-mail:* hwaldusky@adage.com
Exec Ed: Judann Pollack *E-mail:* jpollack@adage.com
Ed: Brian Braiker *E-mail:* bbraiker@adage.com
Covers advertising in business, media, trade newspapers & magazines. Print & digital.
First published 1930
Frequency: 24 issues/yr
Circulation: 58,000
$109/yr (All Access), $279/yr (Insider), $1,199/yr (Editor's Circle)
ISSN: 0001-8899 (print); 1557-7414 (online)
Trim Size: 10 x 13
Ad Rates: 4-color full page (1-5x) $35,190; B&W full page (1-5x) $27,060

Adweek
Published by Adweek LLC
261 Madison Ave, 8th fl, New York, NY 10016
Tel: 212-493-4262
Web Site: www.adweek.com
Subscription Address: PO Box 15, Congers, NY 10920 *Toll Free Tel:* 877-674-8161 (US); 845-267-3007 (outside US) *E-mail:* subscriptions@adweek.com
Key Personnel
Ed & SVP, Programming: Lisa Granatstein *E-mail:* lisa.granatstein@adweek.com
Edit Dir: James Cooper *E-mail:* james.cooper@adweek.com
First published 1979
Frequency: 33 issues/yr
$99/yr digital, $149/yr digital & print
ISSN: 1549-9553
Trim Size: 9 x 10 3/4
Ad Rates: Full page $29,400 (1x); 1/2 page $17,600 (1x)

American Poetry Review
1906 Rittenhouse Sq, Philadelphia, PA 19103
Tel: 215-309-3722
Web Site: www.aprweb.org
Key Personnel
Busn Mgr: Michael Duffy
Ed: Elizabeth Scanlon *E-mail:* escanlon@aprweb.org
Poetry, general essays, fiction, translations, columns & interviews.
First published 1972
Book Use: Excerpts & serial rights, reviews
Frequency: 6 issues/yr
Avg pages per issue: 44
Circulation: 8,000
$5/issue, $28/yr
ISSN: 0360-3709
Ad Rates: B&W full page $950; see web site for additional rates

The American Spectator
Published by The American Spectator Foundation
122 S Royal St, Suite 1, Alexandria, VA 22314
Tel: 703-807-2011
E-mail: editor@spectator.org
Web Site: spectator.org
Key Personnel
Publr: Melissa Mackenzie
Edit Dir: Wladyslaw Pleszczynski
Ed-in-Chief: R Emmett Tyrrell, Jr
Occasional book reviews & articles featuring books. Online only.
First published 1924

ANQ: A Quarterly Journal of Short Articles, Notes & Reviews
Published by Taylor & Francis Inc
530 Walnut St, Suite 850, Philadelphia, PA 19106
Tel: 215-625-8900 (ext 4) *Toll Free Tel:* 800-354-1420 *Fax:* 215-207-0050; 215-207-0046 (cust serv)
E-mail: support@tandfonline.com
Web Site: www.tandfonline.com; www.routledge.com
Key Personnel
Global Publg Dir, Journals: Leon Heward-Mills
Mng Ed: Geraldine Richards
Short, incisive research-based articles about the literature of the English-speaking world & the language of literature. Contributors unravel obscure allusions, explain sources & analogues & supply variant ms readings. Also included are Old English word studies, textual emendations & rare correspondence from neglected archives. The journal is an essential source for professors & students, as well as archivists, bibliographers, biographers, editors, lexicographers & textual scholars. Also available online.
First published 1987
Book Use: Reviews
Frequency: Quarterly
Avg pages per issue: 72
Circulation: 500
Indivs: $108/yr (print only or print & online); Instns: $276/yr (online only), $325/yr (print & online)
ISSN: 0895-769X (print); 1940-3364 (online)
Trim Size: 7 x 10
Ad Rates: Full page $550; 1/2 page $350
Ad Closing Date(s): Winter, Dec 1; Spring, March 21; Summer, June 18; Fall, Sept 19

Artists Magazine
Published by Golden Peak Media
9912 Carver Rd, Blue Ash, OH 45242
E-mail: info@artistsnetwork.com
Web Site: www.artistsnetwork.com
Subscription Address: PO Box 421751, Palm Coast, FL 32142-1751 *Tel:* 386-246-3370 *Toll Free Tel:* 800-333-0440 (US only)
Key Personnel
Sr Art Dir: Brian Roeth
Mng Ed: Brian Riley
Sr Ed: Holly Davis
Ed: Maureen Bloomfield
Assoc Ed: McKenzie Graham; Michael Woodson
Art instruction & advice for the working artist.
First published 1984

Book Use: Occasional book reviews (art-related titles only)
Frequency: 10 issues/yr
Avg pages per issue: 100
Circulation: 60,000
$17.99/yr digital, $21.99/yr US print only, $23.99/yr US print & digital, $31.99/yr CN print only, $33.99/yr CN print & digital, $36.99/yr intl print only, $39.99/yr intl print & digital
ISSN: 0741-3351
Trim Size: 7 3/4 x 10 1/2

AudioFile®
Published by AudioFile® Publications Inc
37 Silver St, Portland, ME 04101
Tel: 207-774-7563 *Toll Free Tel:* 800-506-1212 *Fax:* 207-775-3744
E-mail: info@audiofilemagazine.com; editorial@audiofilemagazine.com
Web Site: www.audiofilemagazine.com
Key Personnel
Founder & Ed: Robin F Whitten *E-mail:* robin@audiofilemagazine.com
Publr: Michele L Cobb *E-mail:* michele@audiofilemagazine.com
Art Dir: Jennifer Steele
Mng Ed: Jennifer M Dowell *E-mail:* jennifer@audiofilemagazine.com
Review Ed: Elizabeth K Dodge
Edit Asst: Alisha Langerman; Joanne Simonean
Audiobook reviews & recommendations. Focus on the listening experience & the unique aspects of the audio performance. Reviews published weekly on web site. Also narrator & author profiles. Award exceptional performances with AudioFile's Earphone Awards.
First published 1992
Frequency: 6 issues/yr
Avg pages per issue: 72
Circulation: 20,000
$19.95/yr, $26.95/2 yrs, $60/yr (prof subn with annual "Audiobook Reference Guide"); $10/issue
ISSN: 1063-0244
Avg reviews per issue: 400
Trim Size: 8 3/8 x 10 7/8
Ad Rates: Full page $3,250

Authorship
Published by National Writers Association
10940 S Parker Rd, Suite 508, Parker, CO 80134
Tel: 303-656-7235
E-mail: natlwritersassn@hotmail.com
Web Site: www.nationalwriters.com
Key Personnel
Exec Dir & Ed: Sandy Whelchel *E-mail:* authorsandy@hotmail.com
Only take submissions dealing with writing. Also available online.
Book Use: Review books for writers (in-house staff)
Frequency: Quarterly
Avg pages per issue: 28
Circulation: 8,000
$20/yr
ISSN: 1092-9347

Book Dealers World

Published by National Association of Book Entrepreneurs (NABE)
PO Box 606, Cottage Grove, OR 97424
Tel: 541-942-7455 *Fax:* 541-942-7455
E-mail: bookdealersworld@bookmarketingprofits.com
Web Site: www.bookmarketingprofits.com
Key Personnel
Exec Dir: Al Galasso
Assoc Dir: Ingrid Crawford
Features the latest marketing ideas, publisher profiles, advertising tips, prime contacts & promotional strategies.
First published 1980
Book Use: From NABE members
Frequency: 3 issues/yr (Jan, May & Sept)
Avg pages per issue: 32
Circulation: 5,000
$50/yr US, $55/yr CN, $70/yr foreign; free to membs
ISSN: 1098-8521
Ad Rates: Full page $500; 1/2 page $250; 1/4 page $150

BookPage

Published by ProMotion Inc
2143 Belcourt Ave, Nashville, TN 37212
Tel: 615-292-8926 *Fax:* 615-292-8249
Web Site: bookpage.com
Key Personnel
Founder & Pres: Michael A Zibart
Publr & Ed-in-Chief: Trisha Ping *E-mail:* trisha@bookpage.com
Assoc Publr: Elizabeth Grace Herbert *Tel:* 615-292-8926 ext 34 *E-mail:* elizabeth@bookpage.com
Book reviews, author interviews; focus on general interest new releases. Columns on romance, mystery, audio & paperback, plus individual reviews on books in all categories. Focus is completely on new releases; no backlist reviewed. Hardcover & paperback titles reviewed.
First published 1988
Book Use: Reviews
Frequency: Monthly
Avg pages per issue: 32
Circulation: 400,000
Trim Size: 9 x 10.9
Ad Rates: Full page color $9,650; 1/2 page $5,600

Bookselling This Week

Published by American Booksellers Association
333 Westchester Ave, Suite S202, White Plains, NY 10604
Tel: 914-406-7500 *Toll Free Tel:* 800-637-0037
Fax: 914-417-4013
E-mail: info@bookweb.org
Web Site: www.bookweb.org
Key Personnel
Content Dir: Sydney Jarrard *Tel:* 914-406-7563
E-mail: sydney@bookweb.org
Book industry & ABA membership news. Available online only.
Frequency: Weekly
Circulation: 12,000

Canadian Children's Book News

Published by Canadian Children's Book Centre
40 Orchard View Blvd, Suite 217, Toronto, ON M4R 1B9, Canada
Tel: 416-975-0010 *Fax:* 416-975-8970
E-mail: info@bookcentre.ca
Web Site: www.bookcentre.ca
Key Personnel
Ed: Sandra O'Brien *E-mail:* sandra@bookcentre.ca
News, book reviews (only reviews books by Canadian authors & illustrators), author & illustrator profiles & information about the world of children's books in Canada. Visit web site

for media kit. CCBN is available with membership to the Canadian Children's Book Centre; also available in bulk subns & on newsstands across Canada.
First published 1977
Frequency: Quarterly
Avg pages per issue: 40
Circulation: 4,000
$4.95/issue; $24.95/single-copy subn (add $25 shipping for intl orders); contact CCBC for bulk rates
ISSN: 1705-7809
Trim Size: 8 1/8 x 10 7/8

Catholic Library World

Published by Catholic Library Association
8550 United Plaza Blvd, Suite 1001, Baton Rouge, LA 70809
Tel: 225-408-4417 *Fax:* 225-408-4422
E-mail: cla2@cathla.org
Web Site: cathla.org
Key Personnel
Gen Ed: Sigrid Kelsey *E-mail:* sigridkelsey@gmail.com
Articles, book & media reviews for library information professionals.
First published 1929
Book Use: Regularly publish reviews of books & other media
Frequency: 3 issues/yr
Avg pages per issue: 90
$15/issue, $55/yr membs, $100/yr nonmembs US, $125/yr nonmembs outside US
ISSN: 0008-820X
Trim Size: 6 7/8 x 9 1/2
Ad Rates: Full page $425; 2/3 page $360; 1/2 page $295; 1/3 page $230; 1/6 page $185; preferred space also available, color additional
Ad Closing Date(s): Feb 1 (March issue), Aug 1 (Sept issue), Nov 1 (Dec issue)

The Bulletin of the Center for Children's Books

Published by Johns Hopkins University Press
2715 N Charles St, Baltimore, MD 21218-4363
SAN: 202-7348
Tel: 410-516-6900; 410-516-6987 (journal orders outside US & CN); 217-244-0324 (bulletin info) *Toll Free Tel:* 800-548-1784 (journal orders) *Fax:* 410-516-6968
E-mail: bccb@illinois.edu; jlorder@jhupress.jhu.edu
Web Site: bccb.ischool.illinois.edu; www.press.jhu.edu/journals/bulletin-center-childrens-books
Key Personnel
Ed: Deborah Stevenson
Asst Ed: Kate Quealy-Gainer
For teachers, librarians, parents & booksellers
First published 1947
Book Use: Reviews of children's & young adult books for teachers, librarians, parents & booksellers
Frequency: 11 issues/yr
Avg pages per issue: 40
Circulation: 6,500
Indivs: $55/yr, $99/2 yrs (print), $64.82/yr, $117/2 yrs (electronic); Instns: $120/yr, $240/2 yrs (print)
ISSN: 0008-9036

Christian Retailing

Published by Charisma Media
600 Rinehart Rd, Lake Mary, FL 32746
Tel: 407-333-0600 *Fax:* 407-333-7133
E-mail: retailing@charismamedia.com
Web Site: www.christianretailing.com; www.charismamedia.com
Key Personnel
Ed: Christine D Johnson *E-mail:* chris.johnson@charismamedia.com
This trade publication for the Christian products industry includes industry news, best-

seller lists, industry expert Q&As & columns & Christian retail features. Advertising targets Christian retail store owners & buyers.
First published 1955
Book Use: News & reviews of new releases
Frequency: 3 issues/yr
Avg pages per issue: 50
Circulation: 4,300
$40/yr, $65/yr CN, $80/yr foreign, free to qualified readers
ISSN: 0892-0281

The Chronicle of Higher Education

1255 23 St NW, Suite 700, Washington, DC 20037
Tel: 202-466-1000 *Fax:* 202-452-1033
E-mail: editor@chronicle.com
Web Site: www.chronicle.com
Key Personnel
Pres & Ed-in-Chief: Michael G Riley
E-mail: michael.riley@chronicle.com
Mng Ed: Brock Read
Deputy Mng Ed: Jennifer Ruark *E-mail:* jennifer.ruark@chronicle.com
Weekly newspaper covering higher education, including scholarly & publishing news.
First published 1966
Book Use: Articles on books of interest to an academic audience & on academic aspects of the publishing industry. Lists new books on higher education & new scholarly books; short- & medium-length excerpts from books on academic & literary issues
Frequency: Weekly (except for 2 issues in Dec & 1 in Aug)
Avg pages per issue: 100
Circulation: 350,000
$6.99/issue; digital & print: $99.95/yr, $169.95/2 yrs
ISSN: 0009-5982

College & Research Libraries (C&RL)

Published by Association of College & Research Libraries (ACRL)
Division of The American Library Association (ALA)
50 E Huron St, Chicago, IL 60611
Tel: 312-280-2516 *Toll Free Tel:* 800-545-2433 (ext 2516) *Fax:* 312-280-2520
E-mail: acrl@ala.org
Web Site: www.ala.org/acrl
Key Personnel
Sr Prodn Ed: Dawn Mueller
Ed: Wendi Arant Kaspar
Online only scholarly research journal. Theory & research relevant to academic & research librarians. See web site for submission guidelines.
First published 1939
Book Use: Reviews
Frequency: 6 issues/yr
Free

Columbia Journalism Review

Published by Columbia Graduate School of Journalism
Affiliate of Columbia University
801 Pulitzer Hall, 2950 Broadway, New York, NY 10027
Tel: 212-854-1881; 212-854-2718 (busn)
Toll Free Tel: 888-425-7782 (US subns)
Fax: 212-854-8367
E-mail: editors@cjr.org
Web Site: www.cjr.org
Key Personnel
Ed-in-Chief & Publr: Kyle Pope
Mng Ed: Betsy Morais
Sr Digital Ed: Justin Ray
Assoc Ed: Brendan Fitzgerald
Sr Writer & Sr Delacorte Fellow: Alexandria Neason
CJR's mission is to be the intellectual leader in the rapidly changing world of journalism. It is

the most respected voice on press criticism &
it shapes the ideas that make media leaders &
journalists smarter about their work. Through
its fast-turn analysis & deep reporting, CJR
is an essential venue not just for journalists,
but also for the thousands of professionals in
communications, technology, academia & other
fields reliant on solid media industry knowledge.
First published 1961
Frequency: Semiannual
Circulation: 30,000
Free online; print: $50/yr US, $75/yr CN & intl
ISSN: 0010-194X
Ad Rates: E-mail for rates

Connections
Published by Printing Industries of New England
5 Crystal Pond Rd, Southborough, MA 01772-
1758
Tel: 508-804-4171 *Toll Free Tel:* 800-365-7463
Web Site: www.pine.org
Key Personnel
Pres & Publr: Christine Hadopian
Members only trade magazine for printing &
graphic communication companies in New
England.
First published 1938
Frequency: 6 issues/yr
Avg pages per issue: 48
Circulation: 1,200
Free to membs
ISSN: 0162-8771
Trim Size: 8 1/2 x 11
Ad Closing Date(s): 10th of the month preceding
publication

Consequence Magazine
PO Box 323, Cohasset, MA 02025-0323
E-mail: consequence.mag@gmail.com
Web Site: www.consequencemagazine.org
Key Personnel
Ed: Catherine Parnell
Art Feature Ed: Anne Kovach
Layout Ed: Jane Widiger
Reviews Ed: John R Coats
Independent nonprofit literary magazine focus-
ing on the culture & consequences of war.
Publishes short fiction, poetry, nonfiction, in-
terviews, visual art & reviews. Also available
online.
Frequency: Annual
$10/yr, $19/2 yrs, $28/3 yrs; Intl: $20/yr, $39/2
yrs, $58/3 yrs

**Editors' Association of Canada - Online
Directory of Editors**
Published by Editors' Association of Canada (As-
sociation canadienne des reviseurs)
1507-180 Dundas St W, Toronto, ON M5G 1Z8,
Canada
Tel: 416-975-1379 *Toll Free Tel:* 866-CAN-EDIT
(226-3348) *Fax:* 416-975-1637
E-mail: info@editors.ca
Web Site: www.editors.ca
Key Personnel
Exec Dir: John Yip-Chuck
E-mail: executivedirector@editors.ca
Sr Communs Mgr: Michelle Ou
E-mail: communications@editors.ca
Membership & Conference Coord: Caitlin Stewart
Online directory of descriptive listings of current
association members indexed by specialty.
$80/yr CN

Educational Marketer
Published by Simba Information
Division of Market Research.com
11200 Rockville Pike, Suite 504, Rockville, MD
20852
SAN: 210-2021

Tel: 240-747-3091 *Toll Free Tel:* 888-297-4622
(cust serv) *Fax:* 240-747-3004
E-mail: customerservice@simbainformation.com
Web Site: www.simbainformation.com; www.
educationalmarketer.net
Key Personnel
Sr Analyst/Mng Ed: Kathy Mickey
Sr Analyst/Ed: Karen Meaney
Newsletter; reports on educational publishing field
(el-hi & college): enrollments, demographics,
funding, mergers & acquisitions, new product
developments & personnel changes. For pub-
lishers, suppliers & dealers in the educational
market.
First published 1968
Frequency: 24 issues/yr
Avg pages per issue: 8
$695/yr
ISSN: 1013-1806

Electronic Education Report
Published by Simba Information
Division of Market Research.com
11200 Rockville Pike, Suite 504, Rockville, MD
20852
SAN: 210-2021
Tel: 240-747-3091 *Toll Free Tel:* 888-297-4622
(cust serv) *Fax:* 240-747-3004
E-mail: customerservice@simbainformation.com
Web Site: www.simbainformation.com
Key Personnel
Sr Analyst/Mng Ed: Kathy Mickey
Sr Analyst/Ed: Karen Meaney
Published twice each month to provide industry
top executives & decision-makers with criti-
cal news & informed perspective on the K-12
electronic instructional materials market. Each
issue contains insight into the current oppor-
tunities & challenges facing instructional soft-
ware providers, as well as relevant analysis of
emergent technology.
First published 1994
Frequency: 24 issues/yr
$650/yr PDF download
ISSN: 1077-9949
Trim Size: 8 1/2 x 11

Event
Published by Douglas College
700 Royal Ave, New Westminster, BC V3M 5Z5,
Canada
Mailing Address: PO Box 2503, New Westmin-
ster, BC V3L 5B2, Canada
Tel: 604-527-5293 *Fax:* 604-527-5095
E-mail: event@douglascollege.ca
Web Site: www.eventmagazine.ca
Key Personnel
Mng Ed: Ian Cockfield
Ed: Shashi Bhat
Fiction Ed: Christine Dewar
Poetry Ed: Joanne Arnott
Reviews Ed: Susan Wasserman
Literary journal. Occasionally publish unsol re-
views but should query first. Publish mostly
Canadian writers, but are open to anyone writ-
ing in English. Do not read mss in Jan, July,
Aug & Dec. Buy fiction, poetry, creative non-
fiction.
First published 1971
Frequency: 3 issues/yr
Avg pages per issue: 128
Circulation: 950
$11.95/issue, $29.95/yr
ISSN: 0315-3770
Trim Size: 6 x 9
Ad Rates: Full page $200; 1/2 page $100
Ad Closing Date(s): March 15 (Summer), July 15
(Fall/Winter), Nov 15 (Spring)

Facilities & Destinations
Published by Facilities Media Group
55 E 59 St, 20th fl, New York, NY 10022

Tel: 212-532-4150 *Fax:* 212-213-6382
Web Site: facilitiesonline.com
Key Personnel
Assoc Publr: Michael Caffin *E-mail:* mcaffin@
facilitiesonline.com
Edit Dir: George Seli *E-mail:* gseli@
facilitiesonline.com
Trade magazine chronicling the facility, event &
convention marketplace.
First published 1991
Frequency: Quarterly
Avg pages per issue: 48
Circulation: 29,000
Free to qualified readers

Facilities & Event Management
Published by Facilities Media Group
55 E 59 St, 20th fl, New York, NY 10022
Tel: 212-532-4150 *Fax:* 212-213-6382
Web Site: facilitiesonline.com
Key Personnel
Assoc Publr: Michael Caffin *E-mail:* mcaffin@
facilitiesonline.com
Edit Dir: George Seli *E-mail:* gseli@
facilitiesonline.com
Trade magazine chronicling the facility, event &
convention marketplace.
First published 1991
Frequency: Semiannual
Free to qualified readers

**Folio: The Magazine for Magazine
Management**
Published by Access Intelligence
761 Main Ave, 2nd fl, Norwalk, CT 06851
Tel: 203-854-6730; 203-899-8433
Web Site: www.foliomag.com
Key Personnel
Publr: Robbie Caploe *Tel:* 917-974-0640
E-mail: rcaploe@accessintel.com
Assoc Publr: Danielle Sikes *E-mail:* dsikes@
accessintel.com
Content Dir: Caysey Welton *Tel:* 203-899-8431
E-mail: cwelton@accessintel.com
Sr Ed: Greg Dool *Tel:* 212-621-4979
E-mail: gdool@accessintel.com
Asst Ed: Kayleigh Barber *Tel:* 203-899-8455
E-mail: kbarber@accessintel.com
News & articles for the magazine publishing ex-
ecutive.
First published 1972
Book Use: Excerpts & condensations
Frequency: Monthly
Avg pages per issue: 60
Circulation: 8,500
ISSN: 0046-4333

Forecast
Published by Baker & Taylor LLC
2550 W Tyvola Rd, Suite 300, Charlotte, NC
28217
Mailing Address: PO Box 6885, Bridgewater, NJ
08807-0855
Tel: 704-998-3100 *Toll Free Tel:* 800-775-
1800 (info servs); 800-775-1700 (cust serv)
Toll Free Fax: 866-557-3396 (cust serv)
E-mail: btinfo@baker-taylor.com
Web Site: www.baker-taylor.com
Key Personnel
Dir, Mdsg, Ad Sales & Edit: Lynn Bond
Ed: Charles Pizar
Mktg Specialist: Donna Heffner
Promotes new & forthcoming adult hardcover,
paperback & spoken word audio titles. Digital
only.
Avg pages per issue: 87
Free

Foreword Reviews
Division of Foreword Magazine Inc
413 E Eighth St, Traverse City, MI 49686
Tel: 231-933-3699

E-mail: sales@forewordreviews.com
Web Site: www.forewordreviews.com
Key Personnel
Publr: Victoria Sutherland *E-mail:* victoria@
forewordreviews.com
Assoc Publr: Bill Harper *E-mail:* bill@
forewordreviews.com
Ed-in-Chief: Matt Sutherland *E-mail:* matt@
forewordreviews.com
Mng Ed: Michelle Anne Schingler
E-mail: mschingler@forewordreviews.com
Ad Sales: Stacy Price *E-mail:* stacy@
forewordreviews.com
Review journal of books from independent
presses, university presses & self-publishers.
Distributed to librarians & booksellers for col-
lection development.
First published 1998
Frequency: Quarterly
Avg pages per issue: 64
Circulation: 15,000
$19.95/yr US, $39.95/yr CN, $59.95/yr foreign
(print), $9.99/yr (online)
ISSN: 1099-2642
Trim Size: 8 1/2 x 11
Ad Rates: B&W full page $2,257; 1/2 page
$1,349
Ad Closing Date(s): 3 weeks prior to issue date

**Gateway Journalism Review/St Louis
Journalism Review**
Published by Southern Illinois University Carbon-
dale, School of Journalism, College of Mass
Communication & Media Arts
Communications Bldg, 1100 Lincoln Dr, Mail
Code 6601, Carbondale, IL 62901
Tel: 618-453-3262; 618-536-3361 (subns)
E-mail: gatewayjr@siu.edu (subns)
Web Site: gatewayjr.org
Key Personnel
Publr: William Freivogel *E-mail:* wfreivogel@
gmail.com
Ed: Jackie Spinner *Tel:* 202-441-0228
E-mail: jspinner@colum.edu
Critically analyzes the mass media in the Mid-
west. The publication's goal is to regularly re-
view journalism new media, photojournalism,
advertising, public relations & entertainment
media to help ensure the public has the most
credible, fair media possible.
First published 1970
Book Use: Book review & excerpts
Frequency: Quarterly
Avg pages per issue: 36
Circulation: 1,250
$20/yr, $35/2 yrs, $45/3 yrs
ISSN: 0036-2972
Trim Size: 8 1/2 x 11
Ad Closing Date(s): 20th of each month

Geist
Published by The Geist Foundation
201-111 W Hastings St, Vancouver, BC V6B
1H4, Canada
Tel: 604-681-9161 *Toll Free Tel:* 888-GEIST-EH
(434-7834) *Fax:* 604-677-6319
E-mail: geist@geist.com
Web Site: www.geist.com
Key Personnel
Publr: Michal Kozlowski
Assoc Publr: AnnMarie MacKinnon
Canadian ideas & culture with a strong literary
focus. The 'Geist' tone is intelligent, plain-
talking, inclusive & offbeat. Submissions must
have a Canadian angle content or author. Mail-
in submissions only (except for contests).
First published 1990
Frequency: Quarterly
Avg pages per issue: 72
Circulation: 7,000
$24.95/yr CN, $40/yr US, $45/yr intl, $39.95/2
yrs CN, $54.95/3 yrs CN

ISSN: 1181-6554
Ad Rates: Full page $970; 2/3 page $735; 1/2
page $685; 1/3 page $425; 1/6 page $270; ad
rates decrease with frequent advertisement

Graphic Monthly
Published by North Island Publishing Ltd
1606 Sedlescomb Dr, Suite 8, Mississauga, ON
L4X 1M6, Canada
Tel: 905-625-7070 *Toll Free Tel:* 800-331-7408
(US only) *Fax:* 905-625-4856
E-mail: editor@graphicmonthly.ca; circulation@
graphicmonthly.ca
Web Site: www.graphicmonthly.ca
Key Personnel
Publr: Alexander (Sandy) Donald *E-mail:* s.
donald@northisland.ca
Online printing industry reference tool for owners
& managers delivering expert how-to advice,
product & service information & insightful
analysis.
First published 1980
Frequency: 6 issues/yr

Growing Minds
Published by Baker & Taylor LLC
2550 W Tyvola Rd, Suite 300, Charlotte, NC
28217
Mailing Address: PO Box 6885, Bridgewater, NJ
08807-0855
Tel: 704-998-3100 *Toll Free Tel:* 800-775-
1800 (info servs); 800-775-1700 (cust serv)
Toll Free Fax: 866-557-3396 (cust serv)
E-mail: btinfo@baker-taylor.com
Web Site: www.baker-taylor.com
Key Personnel
Dir, Mdsg, Ad Sales & Edit: Lynn Bond
Ed: Pamela Day
Mktg Specialist: Donna Heffner
Comprehensive guide to children's & teen selec-
tions featuring titles of interest to all levels,
from toddlers to young adults. Digital only.
Frequency: 10 issues/yr (combined June/July &
Nov/Dec issues)
Free

Guild of Book Workers Newsletter
Published by Guild of Book Workers
521 Fifth Ave, New York, NY 10175
Tel: 212-292-4444
E-mail: newsletter@guildofbookworkers.org;
communications@guildofbookworkers.org
Web Site: www.guildofbookworkers.org
Key Personnel
Pres: Bexx Caswell *Tel:* 520-682-7241
E-mail: president@guildofbookworkers.org
VP: Brien Beidler *E-mail:* vicepresident@
guildofbookworkers.org
Secy: Rebecca Smyrl *Tel:* 214-363-7946
E-mail: secretary@guildofbookworkers.org
Treas: Laura Bedford *E-mail:* treasurer@
guildofbookworkers.org
Newsletter Ed: Lang Ingalls
Articles, calendar of activities related to the book
arts.
Frequency: 6 issues/yr
Avg pages per issue: 24
Circulation: 900
Free with membership
Trim Size: 8 1/2 x 11
Ad Rates: Full page $265; 1/2 page $140; 1/4
page $75; 1/8 page $40
Ad Closing Date(s): First Fri of the prior month

The Horn Book Guide
Published by Horn Book Inc
300 The Fenway, Suite P-311, Palace Road Bldg,
Boston, MA 02115
Tel: 617-278-0225 *Toll Free Tel:* 888-628-0225
Fax: 617-278-6062
E-mail: info@hbook.com
Web Site: www.hbook.com

Subscription Address: 7585 Industrial Pkwy, Plain
City, OH 43064 *Toll Free Tel:* 877-523-6072
Fax: 760-317-2335
Key Personnel
Group Publr: Rebecca T Miller *Tel:* 646-380-
0738 *E-mail:* rmiller@mediasourceinc.com
Creative Dir: Lolly Robinson *Tel:* 617-628-0225
ext 226 *E-mail:* lrobinson@hbook.com
Ed-in-Chief: Roger Sutton
Mng Ed: Katrina Hedeen *E-mail:* khedeen@
hbook.com
Assoc Ed: Cynthia K Ritter *E-mail:* critter@
hbook.com
Brief critical reviews of virtually every hardcover
trade children's & young adult books published
in the US & recommended by The Horn Book.
Publishers should submit 2 copies of appropriate new titles preferably 3 months in advance
of publication date. Publisher must be included
in *Literary Market Place* to be considered. Digital only.
First published 1990
Frequency: Semiannual
Circulation: 2,600
$48/yr

The Horn Book Magazine
Published by Horn Book Inc
300 The Fenway, Suite P-311, Palace Road Bldg,
Boston, MA 02115
Tel: 617-278-0225 *Toll Free Tel:* 888-628-0225
Fax: 617-278-6062
E-mail: info@hbook.com
Web Site: www.hbook.com
Subscription Address: 7585 Industrial Pkwy, Plain
City, OH 43064 *Toll Free Tel:* 877-523-6072
Fax: 760-317-2335
Key Personnel
Group Publr: Rebecca T Miller *Tel:* 646-380-
0738 *E-mail:* rmiller@mediasourceinc.com
Creative Dir: Lolly Robinson *Tel:* 617-628-0225
ext 226 *E-mail:* lrobinson@hbook.com
Ed-in-Chief: Roger Sutton
Book Review Ed: Martha V Parravano
E-mail: mvp@hbook.com
Exec Ed: Elissa Gershowitz
E-mail: egershowitz@hbook.com
Asst Ed: Shoshana Flax *E-mail:* sflax@hbook.
com
Children's literature journal featuring reviews,
articles, essays, columns, interviews with chil-
dren's book authors & illustrators, current an-
nouncements.
First published 1924
Book Use: Reviews & occasional excerpts
Frequency: 6 issues/yr
Avg pages per issue: 128
Circulation: 8,500
$72/yr
ISSN: 0018-5078
Trim Size: 6 x 9
Ad Rates: Color covers 2, 3 & 4 $2,577/each; full
page interior $2,150
Ad Closing Date(s): 2 months before publication
date

Independent Publisher
Published by Jenkins Group Inc
1129 Woodmere Ave, Suite B, Traverse City, MI
49686
Tel: 231-933-0445 *Toll Free Tel:* 800-706-4636
Fax: 231-933-0448
Web Site: www.independentpublisher.com
Key Personnel
CEO: Jerrold R Jenkins *Tel:* 231-933-0445 ext
1008 *E-mail:* jrj@bookpublishing.com
Pres & COO: James Kalajian *Tel:* 231-933-0445
ext 1006 *E-mail:* jjk@bookpublishing.com
Mng Ed, Independent Publisher Online: Jim
Barnes *E-mail:* jimb@bookpublishing.com
Article topics relevant to the business of inde-
pendent book publishing & retailing, including

marketing, book awards, promotion & distribution. Available online since 2000.
First published 1983
Book Use: Featured reviews & individual reviews from independently published works of the current year
Frequency: Monthly
Avg pages per issue: 80
Circulation: 10,000
Free online; sent monthly via e-mail
ISSN: 1098-5735
Avg reviews per issue: 40

Information Today

Published by Information Today, Inc
143 Old Marlton Pike, Medford, NJ 08055-8750
Tel: 609-654-6266 *Toll Free Tel:* 800-300-9868 (cust serv) *Fax:* 609-654-4309
E-mail: custserv@infotoday.com
Web Site: www.infotoday.com/IT/default.asp; bookstore.infotoday.com/naintom9ispe.html (digital subn); bookstore.infotoday.com/intom9ispery.html (print + digital subn)
Key Personnel
Publr/Pres & CEO: Thomas H Hogan
Ed: Brandi Scardilli *E-mail:* bscardilli@infotoday.com
The newsmagazine for users & producers of digital information services. Subscription options include print, PDF, or print + PDF.
First published 1983
Frequency: 9 issues/yr
Avg pages per issue: 40
Circulation: 8,000
Print: $99.95/yr, $188/2 yrs, $288/3 yrs US; $128/yr CN & Mexico; $143/yr other; Digital/PDF: $99.95/yr, $188/2 yrs, $288/3 yrs; Print & Digital/PDF: $124.95/yr, $234/2 yrs, $360/3 yrs US; $160/yr CN & Mexico; $179/yr other
ISSN: 8755-6286
Trim Size: 8 1/2 x 11
Ad Rates: See web site for complete details

Journal of International Marketing

Published by American Marketing Association
130 E Randolph St, 22nd fl, Chicago, IL 60601
Tel: 312-542-9000 *Toll Free Tel:* 800-AMA-1150 (262-1150)
E-mail: jim@ama.org; customersupport@ama.org; amasubs@subscriptionoffice.com
Web Site: www.ama.org
Key Personnel
VP, Pubns: David W Stewart
Ed-in-Chief: Constantine S Katsikeas
International peer-reviewed journal dedicated to advancing international marketing practice, research & theory. Contributions addressing any aspects of international marketing are welcome. The journal presents scholarly & managerially relevant articles on international marketing. Aimed at both international marketing/business scholars & practitioners at senior- & mid-level international marketing positions, the journal's prime objective is to bridge the gap between theory & practice in international marketing.
Frequency: Quarterly
Avg pages per issue: 144
Circulation: 1,300
Indivs: $50/issue, $140/yr online only, $152/yr print only, $155/yr print & online; Instns: $81/issue, $294/yr print or online only, $353/yr print & online
ISSN: 1069-031X (print); 1547-7215 (online)

Journal of Marketing

Published by American Marketing Association
130 E Randolph St, 22nd fl, Chicago, IL 60601
Tel: 312-542-9000 *Toll Free Tel:* 800-AMA-1150 (262-1150)
E-mail: jom@ama.org; amasubs@subscriptionoffice.com

Web Site: www.ama.org/journal-of-marketing
Key Personnel
VP, Pubns: David W Stewart
Ed-in-Chief: Christine Moorman
Develops & disseminates knowledge about real-world marketing questions useful to scholars, educators, managers, policy makers, consumers & other societal stakeholders around the world. It is the premier outlet for substantive research in marketing.
First published 1936
Book Use: Some reviews & excerpts
Frequency: 6 issues/yr
Avg pages per issue: 144
Circulation: 8,200
Indivs: $41/issue, $171/yr online only, $186/yr print only, $190/yr print & online; Instns: $82/issue, $449/yr print or online only, $540/yr print & online
ISSN: 0022-2429 (print); 1547-7185 (online)

Journal of Marketing Research

Published by American Marketing Association
130 E Randolph St, 22nd fl, Chicago, IL 60601
Tel: 312-542-9000 *Toll Free Tel:* 800-AMA-1150 (262-1150)
E-mail: jmr@ama.org; customersupport@ama.org; amasubs@subscriptionoffice.com
Web Site: www.ama.org
Key Personnel
VP, Pubns: David W Stewart
Ed: Rajdeep Grewal
Articles representing the entire spectrum of topics in marketing. It welcomes diverse theoretical perspectives & a wide variety of data & methodological approaches. Seeks papers that make methodological, substantive +/or theoretical contributions. Empirical studies in papers that seek to make a theoretical +/or substantive contribution may involve experimental +/or observational designs & rely on primary data (including qualitative date) +/or secondary data (including meta-analytic data sets).
First published 1963
Book Use: Some reviews
Frequency: 6 issues/yr
Avg pages per issue: 128
Circulation: 4,400
Indivs: $41/issue, $171/yr online only, $186/yr print only, $190/yr print & online; Instns: $82/issue, $449/yr print or online only, $540/yr print & online
ISSN: 0022-2437 (print); 1547-7193 (online)

Journal of Scholarly Publishing

Published by University of Toronto Press Journals Division
Division of University of Toronto Press Inc
5201 Dufferin St, Toronto, ON M3H 5T8, Canada
Tel: 416-667-7810 *Toll Free Tel:* 800-221-9985 (CN) *Fax:* 416-667-7832
E-mail: jsp@utpress.utoronto.ca; journals@utpress.utoronto.ca
Web Site: utpjournals.press/loi/jsp
Key Personnel
Dir, Journals: Antonia Pop *Tel:* 416-667-7838 *E-mail:* apop@utpress.utoronto.ca
Ed-in-Chief: Robert Brown; Alex Holzman
Sales & Ad Rep, Journals: Lauren Gowing *Tel:* 416-667-7806 *E-mail:* lgowing@utpress.utoronto.ca
Articles on the writing, publication & use of serious nonfiction addressed to scholars, authors, publishers, reviewers, editors & librarians. Also available online.
First published 1969
Book Use: Reviews of books relating to publishing
Frequency: Quarterly
Avg pages per issue: 64
Circulation: 800
Indivs: $48/yr (student, print & online), $40/yr (online only), $60/yr (print only), $77/yr

(print & online); Instns: $140/yr (online only), $180/yr (print only), $199/yr (print & online)
ISSN: 1198-9742 (print); 1710-1166 (online)
Trim Size: 6 x 9

Journalism & Mass Communication Quarterly

Published by SAGE Publishing
2455 Teller Rd, Thousand Oaks, CA 91320
Toll Free Tel: 800-818-7243 *Toll Free Fax:* 800-583-2665
E-mail: jmcq.electronic@gmail.com; journals@sagepub.com
Web Site: www.sagepub.com
Key Personnel
Book Review Ed: Daniel C Hallin
Ed: Louisa Ha
Research in journalism & mass communication. Also available online.
First published 1924
Frequency: Quarterly
Avg pages per issue: 300
Circulation: 5,000
Indivs: $185 (print only); Instns: $370 (electronic only), $403 (print only), $411 (print & electronic)
ISSN: 1077-6990 (print); 2161-430X (online)

The Kenyon Review

Subsidiary of Kenyon College
Finn House, 102 W Wiggin St, Gambier, OH 43022
Tel: 740-427-5208 *Fax:* 740-427-5417
E-mail: kenyonreview@kenyon.edu
Web Site: www.kenyonreview.org
Key Personnel
Mng Ed: Abigail Wadsworth Serfass *Tel:* 740-427-5389 *E-mail:* serfassam@kenyon.edu
Ed: David Lynn
Assoc Ed: Kristen Reach
Fiction, poetry, essays, book reviews, drama.
First published 1939
Book Use: Reviews of 12 books
Frequency: 6 issues/yr
Avg pages per issue: 120
Circulation: 7,500
$35/yr, $60/2 yrs, $85/3 yrs
ISSN: 0163-075X
Trim Size: 6 1/8 x 10
Ad Rates: Full page $375
Ad Closing Date(s): Nov 10, Jan 10, March 10, May 10, July 10, Sept 10

Knowledge Quest

Published by American Association of School Librarians
Division of The American Library Association (ALA)
50 E Huron St, Chicago, IL 60611
Tel: 312-944-6780 *Toll Free Tel:* 800-545-2433 *Fax:* 312-280-5276
E-mail: aasl@ala.org
Web Site: knowledgequest.aasl.org
Key Personnel
Ed: Meg Featheringham *Tel:* 312-280-1396
Devoted to offering substantive information to assist in building-level school librarians, supervisors, library educators & other decision makers concerned with the development of school library programs & services. Articles address the integration of theory & practice in school librarianship & new developments in education, learning theory & relevant disciplines.
First published 1997
Frequency: 5 issues/yr
Avg pages per issue: 80
Circulation: 7,000
$12/issue, $50/yr nonmembs US, $60/yr nonmembs foreign
ISSN: 1094-9046
Trim Size: 8 x 10 1/2
Ad Rates: 4-color full page (1x) $1,480; B&W full page (1x) $830

LARB Quarterly Journal

Published by Los Angeles Review of Books
6671 Sunset Blvd, Suite 1521, Los Angeles, CA 90028
Tel: 323-952-3950
E-mail: info@lareviewofbooks.org; editorial@lareviewofbooks.org
Web Site: lareviewofbooks.org
Key Personnel
Publr & Ed-in-Chief: Tom Lutz *E-mail:* tom@lareviewofbooks.org
Mng Dir: Jessica Kubinec *E-mail:* jessica@lareviewofbooks.org
Exec Ed: Boris Dralyuk *E-mail:* boris@lareviewofbooks.org
Mng Ed: Medaya Ocher *E-mail:* medaya@lareviewofbooks.org
Literary journal featuring original art, essays, poetry & fiction.
First published 2013
Frequency: Quarterly
Avg pages per issue: 144
Circulation: 1,250
$10/mo or $100/yr (LARB membership)
Trim Size: 7.5 x 9.2
Ad Rates: Contact Bill Harper, bill@lareviewofbooks.org for ad rates & closing dates

Latin American Literary Review

Published by Ubiquity Press
Cornell University, Dept Comparative Literature, Goldwin Smith Hall, Ithaca, NY 14853
Web Site: www.lalrp.net; lalronline.wordpress.com
Key Personnel
Ed: Debra A Castillo *E-mail:* dac9@cornell.edu
Book Review Ed: Luis Carcamo Huechante
   E-mail: carcamohuechante@austin.utexas.edu
Ed, Creative Writing Section: Lina Meruane
   E-mail: lina.meruane@nyu.edu
Peer-reviewed scholarly journal devoted to the literature of Latin America (including the US) & Brazil. Published in English, Spanish & Portuguese. Bringing to its readers the most recent writing of some of the leading scholars & critics in the fields of Hispanic & Portuguese literature, the *Latin American Literary Review* is of interest to all libraries & institutions of higher learning, especially to all departments of English, Modern Languages, Latin American Studies & Comparative Literature. Back content can be found on JSTOR or PROQUEST.
See www.lalrp.net/about/submissions for complete submission guidelines.
First published 1972
Frequency: Semiannual
Avg pages per issue: 150
Circulation: 1,500
Print copies of back issues: $32 indiv domestic, $55 instl domestic, $42 indiv foreign, $58 instl foreign; for airmail add $12
ISSN: 0047-4134
Trim Size: 9 x 6

Library Journal

Published by Media Source Inc
123 William St, Suite 802, New York, NY 10038
Tel: 646-380-0700 *Toll Free Tel:* 800-588-1030
   Fax: 646-380-0756
E-mail: ljinfo@mediasourceinc.com
Web Site: www.libraryjournal.com
Key Personnel
Pres & CEO: Steve Zales *Tel:* 614-873-7940
   E-mail: szales@mediasourceinc.com
Group Publr: Rebecca T Miller *Tel:* 646-380-0738 *E-mail:* rmiller@mediasourceinc.com
Ed-in-Chief: Meredith Schwartz *Tel:* 646-380-0745 *E-mail:* mschwartz@mediasourceinc.com
Mng Ed: Bette-Lee Fox *Tel:* 646-380-0717
   E-mail: blfox@mediasourceinc.com
Reviews over 8,000 books, audiobooks, DVDs, databases & web sites annually & provides coverage of technology, management, policy &

other professional concerns through our print journal, weekly newsletters, online reporting & digital & live events. Over 75,000 library directors, administrators & staff in public, academic & special libraries read *Library Journal*.
First published 1876
Book Use: Reviews, news, technology, best practices
Frequency: Semimonthly (exc monthly during Jan, July, Aug & Dec)
Avg pages per issue: 104
Circulation: 12,000
$157.99/yr US, $199.99/yr CN & Mexico, $219.99/yr foreign
ISSN: 0363-0277

The Library Quarterly

Published by University of Chicago Press, Journals Division
University of Maryland, College of Information Studies, 4105 Hornbake Bldg, South Wing, College Park, MD 20742
Fax: 301-314-9145
E-mail: lq@press.uchicago.edu
Web Site: www.journals.uchicago.edu
Subscription Address: 1427 E 60 St, Chicago, IL 60637 *Tel:* 773-753-3347 (subns) *Toll Free Tel:* 877-705-1878 (subns)
Key Personnel
Mng Ed: Karen Kettnich *E-mail:* kkettnic@umd.edu
Ed: Ursula Gorham; Paul Jaeger; Natalie Greene Taylor
Reviews Ed: Lindsay Inge Carpenter; Rachel Gammons
Library & information science & related subjects. Also available online.
First published 1931
Book Use: Reviews
Frequency: Quarterly
Avg pages per issue: 128
Circulation: 432 (print)
Indivs: $17/issue, $48/yr (electronic only), $49/yr (print only), $54/yr (electronic & print); Students: $17/issue, $27/yr (electronic only); Instns: $84/issue, $280/yr (print only), see web site for pricing by instn type
ISSN: 0024-2519 (print); 1549-652X (online)
Trim Size: 6 x 9
Ad Rates: Full page $760

Locus: The Magazine of the Science Fiction & Fantasy Field

Published by Locus Science Fiction Foundation
655 13 St, Suite 100, Oakland, CA 94612
Tel: 510-339-9196
E-mail: locus@locusmag.com
Web Site: www.locusmag.com
Key Personnel
Publr & Ed-in-Chief: Liza Groen Trombi
Mng Ed: Kirsten Gong-Wong
Includes publishing news, book reviews, literary awards, author interviews & annual analysis of the science fiction, fantasy, horror & young-adult field, monthly bestseller list & a complete monthly listing of new publications. Primarily a trade magazine for publishing professionals, writers, booksellers & libraries.
First published 1968
Book Use: Reviews
Frequency: Monthly
Avg pages per issue: 72
Circulation: 6,000
$8.99/issue + S&H, $75/yr (print & digital)
ISSN: 0047-4959
Trim Size: 8 3/8 x 10 7/8
Ad Rates: Color full page $1,500; 2/3 page $1,050; 1/2 page $800; 1/3 page $525; 1/4 page $400; 1/6 page $275
Ad Closing Date(s): 20th of the month, 6 weeks before issue date

Medical Reference Services Quarterly

Published by Routledge
Member of Taylor & Francis Group, an Informa Business
530 Walnut St, Suite 850, Philadelphia, PA 19106
Tel: 215-625-8900 *Toll Free Tel:* 800-354-1420
Web Site: www.tandfonline.com
Key Personnel
Ed: Jonquil D Feldman
Working tool journal for medical & health sciences librarians. Regularly publishes brief practice-oriented articles relating to medical reference services, with an emphasis on user education, database searching & electronic information.
First published 1982
Book Use: Reviews
Frequency: Quarterly
Avg pages per issue: 116
Indivs: $170/yr online only, $194/yr print & online; Instns: $618/yr online only, $727/yr print & online
ISSN: 0276-3869 (print); 1540-9597 (online)

Mergers & Acquisitions

Published by SourceMedia LLC
One State Street Plaza, 27th fl, New York, NY 10004
Tel: 212-803-8200; 212-803-6079 (subns); 212-803-8500 (cust serv)
E-mail: help@sourcemedia.com
Web Site: www.themiddlemarket.com
Key Personnel
Publr: Harry Nikpour *E-mail:* harry.nikpour@sourcemedia.com
Ed-in-Chief: Mary Kathleen Flynn *Tel:* 212-803-3871 *E-mail:* marykathleen.flynn@sourcemedia.com
Asst Mng Ed: Demitri Diakantonis *Tel:* 212-803-8704 *E-mail:* demitri.diakantonis@sourcemedia.com
Professional journal; covers the latest trends & influences impacting the buying & selling of businesses. Articles cover how to make money, save money & avoid disaster in the constantly changing merger & acquisition environment.
First published 1965
Frequency: Monthly
Avg pages per issue: 56
Circulation: 20,000
$449/yr (print & digital), free 2-wk trial available
ISSN: 0026-0010

MLQ (Modern Language Quarterly): A Journal of Literary History

Published by Duke University Press
c/o University of Washington, English Dept, Box 354330, Seattle, WA 98195-4430
Tel: 206-543-6827 *Fax:* 206-685-2673
E-mail: mlq@u.washington.edu
Web Site: www.dukeupress.edu/modern-language-quarterly
Subscription Address: Duke University Press, 905 W Main St, Suite 18-B, Durham, NC 27701 *Tel:* 919-688-5134 *Toll Free Tel:* 888-651-0122 US *Toll Free Fax:* 888-651-0124 US *E-mail:* subscriptions@dukeupress.edu
Key Personnel
Journals Dir: Rob Dilworth
   E-mail: journalsdirector@dukeupress.edu
Dir, Mktg & Sales: Cason Lynley
Ed: Marshall Brown
Assoc Ed: Jeffrey Knight; Juliet Shields
Asst Ed: Matthew Poland
Scholarly articles on literary history.
First published 1940
Book Use: Reviews
Frequency: Quarterly
Avg pages per issue: 130
Circulation: 1,350
Indivs: $20/yr online only, $35/yr print & online; Students: $18/yr print & online; Instns: $334/yr

online only, $416/yr print only, $436/yr print &
online; add $14 postage CN, $18 postage intl
ISSN: 0026-7929 (print); 1527-1943 (online)
Ad Rates: B&W full page $300; 1/2 page $225

Network

Published by The International Women's Writing
Guild (IWWG)
5 Penn Plaza, 19th fl, PMB 19059, New York,
NY 10001
Tel: 917-720-6959
E-mail: iwwgquestions@iwwg.org
Web Site: www.iwwg.org
Key Personnel
Exec Dir: Michelle Miller *E-mail:* michelle@
iwwg.org
Member news, regional clusters, correspondence
corner, letters to the editor, environmental, spe-
cial offerings, profile of guild members. Several
hundred opportunities for publication & sub-
mission in every issue.
First published 1978
Frequency: Quarterly
Avg pages per issue: 32
Circulation: 3,000
Free to membs

New Millennium Writings

4021 Garden Dr, Knoxville, TN 37918
Tel: 865-254-4880
E-mail: hello@newmillenniumwritings.org
Web Site: newmillenniumwritings.org
Key Personnel
Publr & Ed: Alexis Williams Carr *E-mail:* alexis.
williams@hotmail.com
Contains fiction, poetry & creative nonfiction by
both emerging & well known writers. Regu-
larly features profiles, interviews & essay on
famous writers. Also includes writing tips &
commentary by the editor.
First published 1996

News & Tech, see Newspapers & Technology

Newspapers & Technology

Published by Conley Magazines LLC
PO Box 478, Beaver Dam, WI 53916
Tel: 303-575-9595
E-mail: editor@newsandtech.com
Web Site: www.newsandtech.com
Key Personnel
Publr & Editor-in-Chief: Mary Van Meter
E-mail: vanmeternt@aol.com
Trade publication for newspaper publishers &
department managers involved in applying &
integrating technology. Written by industry ex-
perts who provide regular coverage of the fol-
lowing departments: prepress, press, postpress
& new media.
First published 1988
Frequency: 6 issues/yr
Avg pages per issue: 48
Circulation: 15,000
Free to qualified personnel
ISSN: 1052-5572

North Carolina Literary Review (NCLR)

Published by East Carolina University/North Car-
olina Literary & Historical Association/Univer-
sity of North Carolina Press
East Carolina University, English Dept, ECU
Mailstop 555 English, Greenville, NC 27858-
4353
Tel: 252-328-1537 *Fax:* 252-328-4889
E-mail: ncluser@ecu.edu
Web Site: www.nclr.ecu.edu
Key Personnel
Ed: Margaret Bauer *E-mail:* bauerm@ecu.edu
Articles, essays, interviews, fiction/poetry by &
about North Carolina writers & literature, cul-
ture & history.

First published 1992
Book Use: Excerpts from forthcoming books
when relevant & appropriate; essay reviews
only - 2 or more books treated thematically
Frequency: Annual
Avg pages per issue: 200
Circulation: 750
$15/issue, $25/2 yr subn, $25/yr instn, $50/issue
foreign, $50/yr subn foreign
ISSN: 1063-0724
Avg reviews per issue: 8-12
Ad Rates: Full page $250; 1/2 page $150; 1/4
page $100
Ad Closing Date(s): Feb 1

Poetics Today

Published by Duke University Press
Ohio State University, Dept of English, 164 W
Annie & John Glenn Ave, Columbus, OH
43210
Tel: 614-292-6065 *Fax:* 614-292-7816
E-mail: poeticstoday@osu.edu
Web Site: www.dukeupress.edu/poetics-today
Subscription Address: Duke University Press,
905 W Main St, Suite 18-B, Durham, NC
27701 *Tel:* 919-688-5134 *Toll Free Tel:* 888-
651-0122 US *Toll Free Fax:* 888-651-0124 US
E-mail: subscriptions@dukepress.edu
Key Personnel
Journals Dir: Rob Dilworth
E-mail: journalsdirector@dukeupress.edu
Dir, Mktg & Sales: Cason Lynley
Ed: Brian McHale
Book Review Ed: Eyal Segal
International journal for theory & analysis of lit-
erature & communication.
Book Use: Book reviews
Frequency: Quarterly
Avg pages per issue: 200
Circulation: 800
Indivs: $25/yr online only, $40/yr print & online;
Students: $20/yr print & online; Instns: $422/yr
online only, $524/yr print only, $556/yr print &
online; add $14 postage CN, $18 postage intl
ISSN: 0333-5372 (print); 1527-5507 (online)
Ad Rates: B&W full page $300; 1/2 page $225

Poetry

Published by Poetry Foundation
61 W Superior St, Chicago, IL 60654
Tel: 312-787-7070 *Fax:* 312-787-6650
E-mail: editors@poetrymagazine.org
Web Site: www.poetryfoundation.org/
poetrymagazine
Subscription Address: PO Box 421141, Palm
Coast, FL 32142-1141
Key Personnel
Ed: Don Share
Asst Ed: Holly Amos *E-mail:* hamos@
poetrymagazine.org
Poetry, essays & book reviews. Complete submis-
sion guidelines can be found on the web site.
First published 1912
Frequency: Monthly
Avg pages per issue: 100
Circulation: 25,000
US: $3.75/issue, $35/yr indivs, $38/yr instns; For-
eign: $47/yr indivs, $50/yr instns
ISSN: 0032-2032
Trim Size: 5 1/2 x 9
Ad Rates: Full page $800; 1/2 page $500; 1/4
page $375
Ad Closing Date(s): 15th of the 3rd month before
issue date

Poets & Writers Magazine

Published by Poets & Writers Inc
90 Broad St, Suite 2100, New York, NY 10004
Tel: 212-226-3586 *Fax:* 212-226-3963
E-mail: editor@pw.org
Web Site: www.pw.org

Key Personnel
Ed-in-Chief: Kevin Larimer
Prodn Ed: Ariel Davis
News for & about the contemporary literary com-
munity in the US. Pertinent articles, grants &
awards, publishing opportunities, essays, inter-
views with writers.
First published 1973
Book Use: First serial, excerpts, author interviews
Frequency: 6 issues/yr
Avg pages per issue: 132
Circulation: 60,000
$5.95/issue, $12.95/yr, $19.95/2 yrs
ISSN: 0891-6136

PRISM international

Published by University of British Columbia
Creative Writing Program UBC, 1866 Main Mall,
Buch E-462, Vancouver, BC V6T 1Z1, Canada
Tel: 604-822-2514 *Fax:* 604-822-3616
E-mail: circulation@prismmagazine.ca;
promotions@prismmagazine.ca; reviews@
prismmagazine.ca
Web Site: prismmagazine.ca
Key Personnel
Exec Ed, Circ: Molly Cross-Blanchard
Exec Ed, Promos: Olga Holin
Exec Ed, Reviews: Cara Nelissen
Contemporary writing & translation from Canada
& around the world.
First published 1959
Frequency: Quarterly
Avg pages per issue: 90
Circulation: 1,200
$35/yr CN, $40/yr US, $45/yr intl, $55/2 yrs CN,
$63/2 yrs US, $69/2 yrs intl
Trim Size: 6 x 9
Ad Rates: Full page $220; 1/2 page $160; inside
cover front or back $295

Professional Photographer - The Magazine

Published by PPA Publications & Events Inc
229 Peachtree St NE, Suite 2300, Atlanta, GA
30303
Tel: 404-522-8600 *Toll Free Tel:* 800-786-6277
E-mail: csc@ppa.com
Web Site: www.ppa.com; ppmag.com
Key Personnel
Dir, Sales & Strategic Alliances: Wayne Jones
Tel: 404-522-8600 ext 248 *E-mail:* wjones@
ppa.com
Illustrated feature articles about photographers,
business & photographic techniques & trends;
for practicing professional photographers (portrait, wedding, commercial, illustration, freelance, industrial, biomedical & scientific).
First published 1907
Frequency: Monthly
Avg pages per issue: 80
$19.95/yr US (print or digital), $29.95/yr US
(print & digital), $19.95/yr CN (digital only),
$35.95/yr CN (print only), $45.95/yr CN (print
& digital)

ProtoView

Published by Ringgold Inc
7515 NE Ambassador Place, Suite A, Portland,
OR 97220
Tel: 503-281-9230
E-mail: info@protoview.com
Web Site: www.protoview.com
Key Personnel
Ed: Eithne O'Leyne *E-mail:* eithne.oleyne@
ringgold.com
Subscription database incorporating reference &
research & *SciTech Book News*. Abstracts, bib-
liographic & expanded metadata on scholarly
works in all media. ProtoView content licensed
to Discovery channels, including vendors &
related products owned by Baker & Taylor,
ProQuest, Gale/Cengage & others.
ISSN: 2372-3424

Publishers Weekly
Published by PWxyz LLC
71 W 23 St, Suite 1608, New York, NY 10010
Tel: 212-377-5500 *Fax:* 212-377-2733
Web Site: www.publishersweekly.com
Key Personnel
Pres: George Slowik, Jr *E-mail:* george@
 publishersweekly.com
Publr: Cevin Bryerman *Tel:* 212-377-5703
 E-mail: cbryerman@publishersweekly.com
VP, Busn Devt: Carl Pritzkat *E-mail:* cpritzkat@
 publishersweekly.com
VP, Opers: Patrick Turner *E-mail:* patrick@
 publishersweekly.com
Adult Book Dir: Louisa Ermelino
 E-mail: lermelino@publishersweekly.com
Art Dir: Clive Chiu *E-mail:* cchiu@
 publishersweekly.com
Edit Dir: Jim Milliot *Tel:* 212-377-5705
 E-mail: jmilliot@publishersweekly.com
News Dir: Rachel Deahl *E-mail:* rdeahl@
 publishersweekly.com
Exec Ed: Jonathan Segura *E-mail:* jsegura@
 publishersweekly.com
Mng Ed: Dan Berchenko *E-mail:* dberchenko@
 publishersweekly.com
Sr Writer: Andrew R Albanese
 E-mail: aalbanese@publishersweekly.com
Sr Ed: Mark Rotella *E-mail:* mrotella@
 publishersweekly.com
Sr News Ed: Calvin Reid *E-mail:* creid@
 publishersweekly.com
Children's Book Ed: Diane Roback
 E-mail: roback@publishersweekly.com
Digital Ed & Assoc News Ed: John Maher
 E-mail: jmaher@publishersweekly.com
Fiction Reviews Ed: David Varno
Assoc Ed, Children's Books: Emma Kantor
 E-mail: ekantor@publishersweekly.com
Assoc Reviews Ed: Phoebe Cramer
Asst Ed, Children's Books: Matia Burnett
 E-mail: mburnett@publishersweekly.com
Features Ed: Carolyn Juris *E-mail:* cjuris@
 publishersweekly.com
Religion News Ed: Emma Koonse
 E-mail: ekoonse@publishersweekly.com
Religion Reviews Ed: Seth Satterlee
 E-mail: ssatterlee@publishersweekly.com
Sr Religion Ed: Lynn Garrett *E-mail:* lgarrett@
 publishersweekly.com
Sr Reviews Ed: Peter Cannon; Rose Fox
Reviews Ed: Alex Crowley; Annie Coreno; Ev-
 erett Jones
BookLife Ed: Adam Boretz *E-mail:* aboretz@
 publishersweekly.com
Bookselling & Intl News Ed: Ed Nawotka
 E-mail: enawotka@publishersweekly.com
Copy Ed: Hannah Kushnick *E-mail:* hkushnick@
 publishersweekly.com
Mktg/Licensing Mgr: Christi Cassidy
 E-mail: ccassidy@publishersweekly.com
News for the book trade.
First published 1872
Book Use: Reviews, excerpts, news, features &
 statistics
Frequency: Weekly (51 issues/yr)
Avg pages per issue: 112
Circulation: 68,000 print; 1,000,000 online
Print, digital & online: $289.99/yr US, $339.99/yr
 CN; Digital & online: $229.99/yr US & CN
ISSN: 0000-0019 (print); 2150-4000 (digital)
Trim Size: 7 7/8 x 10 1/2

Publishing Perspectives
30 Irving Place, 4th fl, New York, NY 10003
Tel: 212-794-2851
Web Site: publishingperspectives.com
Key Personnel
Publr: Hannah Johnson *E-mail:* hannah@
 publishingperspectives.com
Online trade magazine for the international pub-
 lishing industry.
First published 2009

Frequency: Daily (Mon-Fri)
Free

Quill & Quire
Published by St Joseph Communications
111 Queen St E, Suite 320, Toronto, ON M5C
 1S2, Canada
Tel: 416-364-3333 *Fax:* 416-595-5415
Web Site: www.quillandquire.com
Key Personnel
Publr: Alison Jones *Tel:* 416-364-3333 ext 3119
 E-mail: ajones@quillandquire.com
Ed: Sue Carter
Articles & features on book selling, publishing &
 Canadian libraries for writers, booksellers, pub-
 lishers & librarians. Includes section, *Books for
 Young People*, with news & reviews of chil-
 dren's books & authors; review section for
 books for adults.
First published 1935
Book Use: Reviews
Frequency: 10 issues/yr
Avg pages per issue: 42
Circulation: 2,500
$89.50/yr CN, $150/2 yrs CN, $125/yr outside
 CN
ISSN: 0033-6491

Quill & Scroll
Published by Quill and Scroll Society
University of Iowa, School of Journalism, W111
 Adler Journalism Bldg, Iowa City, IA 52242
Tel: 319-335-3457
E-mail: quill-scroll@uiowa.edu
Web Site: quillandscroll.org
Key Personnel
Exec Dir: Jeffrey Browne
Off Mgr: Judy M Hauge
Scholastic journalism publishing, editing, writing,
 design, legal, ethics, broadcast & multimedia
 production. Digital only.
First published 1926
Frequency: Semiannual during school yr
Avg pages per issue: 24
ISSN: 0033-6505

Quill Magazine
Published by The Society of Professional Journal-
 ists (SPJ)
Eugene S Pulliam National Journalism Ctr, 3909
 N Meridian St, Suite 200, Indianapolis, IN
 46208
Tel: 317-927-8000 *Fax:* 317-920-4789
E-mail: spj@spj.org
Web Site: www.spj.org/quill.asp; www.spj.org
Key Personnel
Ed: Lou Harry
Examines the issues, changes & trends that influ-
 ence the journalism profession.
First published 1912
Book Use: Book reviews, excerpts from books
 with journalism themes
Frequency: Quarterly
Avg pages per issue: 32
Circulation: 7,000
$75/yr, free for membs
ISSN: 0033-6475
Trim Size: 8 1/2 x 10 3/4
Ad Rates: Full page color: $2,000 (1x), $1,900
 (2x), $1,800 (4x); 1/2 page: $1,000 (1x), $900
 (2x), $800 (4x); 1/4 page: $600 (1x), $500
 (2x), $400 (4x); back inside cover: $2,500 (1x),
 $2,400 (2x), $2,300 (4x); front inside cover:
 $2,500 (1x), $2,400 (2x), $2,300 (4x)
Ad Closing Date(s): Jan 18, April 19, June 21,
 Oct 18

Radio-TV Interview Report (RTIR)
Published by Bradley Communications Corp
390 Reed Rd, Broomall, PA 19008
Tel: 484-477-4220
E-mail: info@rtir.com

Web Site: www.rtir.com; rtironline.com
Key Personnel
Publr: Steve Harrison
Lists authors, experts, celebrities, entrepreneurs &
 others available for live & in-studio interviews.
 Electronic only.
Frequency: 2 issues/wk
Circulation: 4,000
Free to qualified personnel

Reference & User Services Quarterly (RUSQ)
Published by Reference & User Services Associa-
 tion
Division of The American Library Association
 (ALA)
50 E Huron St, Chicago, IL 60611
SAN: 201-0062
Tel: 312-280-4395 *Toll Free Tel:* 800-545-2433
 Fax: 312-280-5273
E-mail: rusa@ala.org
Web Site: www.ala.org/rusa
Key Personnel
Contact: Leighann Wood
First published 1960
Frequency: Quarterly
Circulation: 3,825
$25/issue, $65/yr CN & Mexico, $75/yr all other
 foreign
ISSN: 2163-5242
Avg reviews per issue: 35-40

Rosebud Magazine
Published by Rosebud Inc
PO Box 459, Cambridge, WI 53523
Tel: 608-423-9780
Web Site: www.rsbd.net
Key Personnel
Publr & Mng Ed: Roderick Clark
 E-mail: jrodclark@rsbd.net
Short story, poetry & nonfiction.
First published 1993
Book Use: Excerpts
Frequency: 2 issues/yr
Avg pages per issue: 136
Circulation: 6,000
$7.95/issue, $24/2 yrs, $40/4 yrs
ISSN: 1072-1681
Ad Rates: Full page $750; 1/2 page $400; 1/4
 page $250

Sales & Marketing Management Magazine
Published by Mach1 Business Media LLC
27020 Noble Rd, Excelsior, MN 55331
Mailing Address: PO Box 247, Excelsior, MN
 55331-0247
Tel: 952-401-1283 *Fax:* 952-401-7899
Web Site: www.salesandmarketing.com
Key Personnel
Pres & Publr: Mike Murrell *Tel:* 952-401-1283
 E-mail: mike@salesandmarketing.com
Audience Mktg Dir: Vicki Blomquist
 E-mail: vicki@salesandmarketing.com
Ed-in-Chief: Paul Nolan *Tel:* 763-350-3411
 E-mail: paul@salesandmarketing.com
Print & online magazine providing information on
 major marketing, sales & management trends.
First published 1918
Book Use: Reviews
Frequency: Updated 2-3 times a week
Avg pages per issue: 36
Circulation: 25,000 print
Free online. Print free to qualified recipients. Oth-
 erwise $48 US; $67 CN; $146 other countries
ISSN: 0163-7517
Trim Size: 8 x 10 3/4
Ad Rates: 2-page spread: $13,995 (1x), $13,695
 (3x), $13,265 (6x); full page: $9,395 (1x),
 $8,695 (3x), $8,265 (6x); 1/2 page $6,075 (1x),
 $5,765 (3x), $5,460 (6x)
Ad Closing Date(s): See media kit online

School Library Connection
Published by Libraries Unlimited

147 Castilian Dr, Santa Barbara, CA 93117
Mailing Address: PO Box 1911, Santa Barbara,
CA 93116-1911
Toll Free Tel: 800-368-6868 *Toll Free Fax:* 866-
270-3856
E-mail: customerservice@abc-clio.com
Web Site: schoollibraryconnection.com
Key Personnel
Mng Ed: David Paige
K-12 school librarians & educators. See web site
for information regarding ad rates & ad closing
dates as well as submission & reviewer infor-
mation.
First published 1982
Book Use: Reviews; articles written by school
librarians
Frequency: 6 print issues/school yr plus 4 online
issues
Avg pages per issue: 84
$89/yr
ISSN: 1542-4715

School Library Journal
Published by Media Source Inc
123 William St, Suite 802, New York, NY 10038
Tel: 646-380-0752 *Toll Free Tel:* 800-595-1066
Fax: 646-380-0756
E-mail: slj@mediasourceinc.com; sljsubs@
pcspublink.com
Web Site: www.slj.com; www.facebook.com/
schoollibraryjournal; twitter.com/sljournal
Subscription Address: PO Box 461119, Escon-
dido, CA 92046
Key Personnel
Group Publr: Rebecca T Miller *Tel:* 646-380-
0738 *E-mail:* rmiller@mediasourceinc.com
Reviews Dir: Kiera Parrott *E-mail:* kparrott@
mediasourceinc.com
Ed-in-Chief: Kathy Ishizuka *E-mail:* kishizuka@
mediasourceinc.com
Mng Ed, SLJ Reviews: Luann Toth *Tel:* 646-380-
0749 *E-mail:* ltoth@mediasourceinc.com
Sr Ed, Young Adult: Katy Hershberger
E-mail: khershberger@mediasourceinc.com
Articles about library service to children & young
adults; reviews of new books & multimedia
products for children & young adults by school
& public librarians.
First published 1954
Book Use: Reviews
Frequency: Monthly
Avg pages per issue: 115
Circulation: 38,000
$15/issue newsstand; Indivs: $136.99/yr (print or
digital), $159.99/yr (print & digital); Instns:
$136.99/yr (print only), $249.99/yr (digital
only), $349.99/yr (print & digital)
ISSN: 0362-8930

Science & Technology Libraries
Published by Routledge
Member of Taylor & Francis Group, an Informa
Business
530 Walnut St, Suite 850, Philadelphia, PA 19106
Tel: 215-625-8900 *Toll Free Tel:* 800-354-1420
Web Site: www.tandfonline.com
Key Personnel
Ed-in-Chief: Tony Stankus *E-mail:* tstankus@
uark.edu
Topics relevant to management, operations, col-
lections, services & staffing of specialized li-
braries in science & technology fields.
First published 1980
Book Use: Reviews
Frequency: Quarterly
Avg pages per issue: 105
Circulation: 343
Indivs: $176/yr online only, $200/yr print & on-
line or print only; Instns: $710/yr online only,
$835/yr print & online
ISSN: 0194-262X (print); 1541-1109 (online)

The Serials Librarian
Published by Routledge
Member of Taylor & Francis Group, an Informa
Business
530 Walnut St, Suite 850, Philadelphia, PA 19106
Tel: 215-625-8900 *Toll Free Tel:* 800-354-1420
Web Site: www.tandfonline.com
Key Personnel
Ed-in-Chief: Sharon Dyas-Correia
Assoc Ed: Courtney McAllister
Serials librarianship in academic, public, medical,
law & other special libraries.
First published 1976
Book Use: Reviews
Frequency: Quarterly
Avg pages per issue: 154
Circulation: 712
Indivs: $332/yr online only, $379/yr print & on-
line; Instns: $1,202/yr online only, $1,414/yr
print & online
ISSN: 0361-526X (print); 1541-1095 (online)

Story Monsters Ink®
Published by Story Monsters Press
Imprint of Story Monsters LLC
4696 W Tyson St, Chandler, AZ 85226-2903
Tel: 480-940-8182 *Fax:* 480-940-8787
Web Site: www.StoryMonsters.com
Key Personnel
Pres: Linda F Radke *E-mail:* Linda@
StoryMonsters.com
Ed-in-Chief: Cristy Bertini *Tel:* 413-477-1105
E-mail: cristy@storymonsters.com
E-mail article submissions to
cristy@storymonsters.com.
First published 2014
Frequency: Monthly
Avg pages per issue: 64
Circulation: 130,000
$7.95/issue, $39/yr
ISSN: 2374-4413
Trim Size: 8.375 x 10.875
Ad Rates: $95-$1,600
Ad Closing Date(s): 1st of each month

subTerrain Magazine
Published by subTerrain Literary Collective Soci-
ety
PO Box 3008, MPO, Vancouver, BC V6B 3X5,
Canada
Tel: 604-876-8710
E-mail: subter@portal.ca
Web Site: www.subterrain.ca
Key Personnel
Ed-in-Chief: Brian Kaufman
Literary magazine with the motto "Strong Words
for a Polite Nation".
First published 1988
Frequency: 3 issues/yr
Avg pages per issue: 80
Circulation: 4,000
$7/issue US, $8 issue/CN; $18/yr, $32/2 yrs (US
& CN)
ISSN: 0840-7533
Trim Size: 6 1/2 x 9
Ad Rates: Back cover-color $900; inside front/
back cover $800; inside full page color $847;
1/2 page color $575. Prices in Canadian dol-
lars. For other sizes & B&W rates, see web
site
Ad Closing Date(s): Feb 13, June 15, Oct 15

The Wordsworth Circle
Published by University of Chicago Press
1427 E 60 St, Chicago, IL 60637-2954
SAN: 202-5280
Tel: 773-753-3347 *Toll Free Tel:* 877-705-
1878 (US & CN) *Fax:* 773-753-0811
Toll Free Fax: 877-705-1879 (US & CN)
E-mail: subscriptions@press.uchicago.edu;
journalsupport@press.uchicago.edu
Web Site: www.journals.uchicago.edu/twc

Key Personnel
Ed: Marilyn Gaull *E-mail:* mgaull@bu.edu
Peer-reviewed essays on all areas of British Ro-
manticism.
First published 1970
Frequency: Quarterly
Avg pages per issue: 125
Circulation: 4,600
Indiv: $45/yr; Instl: $120-$210 tiered electronic
only, $193-$339 tiered print & electronic
ISSN: 0043-8006 (print); 2640-7310 (online)
Trim Size: 6 x 9
Ad Rates: Full page $724; 1/2 page $546
Ad Closing Date(s): Feb 1 (Spring), May 1 (Sum-
mer), Aug 1 (Autumn), Nov 1 (Winter)

World Literature Today
Published by University of Oklahoma
630 Parrington Oval, Suite 110, Norman, OK
73019-4033
Tel: 405-325-4531
E-mail: wlt@ou.edu
Web Site: www.worldliteraturetoday.org
Key Personnel
Exec Dir: Robert Con Davis-Undiano
Asst Dir & Ed-in-Chief: Daniel Simon
E-mail: dsimon@ou.edu
Art Dir: Jennifer Blair
Mktg Dir, Progs & Devt: Terry D Stubblefield
E-mail: tdstubb@ou.edu
Mng Ed: Michelle Johnson *E-mail:* lmjohnson@
ou.edu
Book Reviews Ed: Robert Vollmar
Circ & Accts Specialist: Kay Blunck
E-mail: kblunck@ou.edu
Critical essays & reviews covering all the major
& most of the smaller languages & literatures
of the world. Also available online.
First published 1927
Frequency: 6 issues/yr
Avg pages per issue: 96
Circulation: 300,000
$8.95/issue, $35/yr indivs, $60/yr foreign indivs,
$135/yr instns, $205/yr foreign instns
ISSN: 0196-3570 (print); 1945-8134 (online)
Ad Rates: Full page $500; 1/2 page $350; inside
cover (front or back) $700; back cover $1,000

The Writer
Published by Madavor Media LLC
25 Braintree Hill Office Park, Suite 404, Brain-
tree, MA 02184
Tel: 903-636-1120 (cust serv) *Toll Free Tel:* 877-
252-8139 (cust serv) *Fax:* 617-536-0102
E-mail: customerservice@the-writer.us
Web Site: www.writermag.com
Key Personnel
Sr Ed: Nicki Porter *E-mail:* nporter@madavor.
com
Instructional articles on fiction, nonfiction & free-
lance writing, plus markets for ms sales. See
guidelines on web site. Accept unsol mss.
First published 1887
Book Use: Regular book review section
Frequency: Monthly
Avg pages per issue: 60
Circulation: 30,000
$8/issue, $28.95/yr US, $38.95/yr CN, $43.95/yr
elsewhere
ISSN: 0043-9517 (print); 2163-0046 (online)
Trim Size: 8 x 10 1/2
Ad Rates: 4-color full page $2,794; 1/2 page
$1,649; 1/4 page $894

Writer's Digest Magazine
Published by Active Interest Media (AIM)
5720 Flatiron Pkwy, Boulder, CO 80301
E-mail: wdsubmissions@aimmedia.com
Web Site: www.writersdigest.com
Key Personnel
Mng Content Dir: Amy Jones
Ed-in-Chief: Ericka McIntyre
Assoc Mng Ed: Cassie Lipp

Sr Ed: Jeanne Veillette Bowerman; Robert Lee
  Brewer
Focus is on the craft & business of writing.
First published 1920
Book Use: Excerpts, profiles of authors, tips &
  techniques
Frequency: 8 issues/yr
Circulation: 60,000 paid
$19.96/yr, $29.96/2 yrs
ISSN: 0043-9525
Trim Size: 7 3/4 x 10 1/2

The Yale Review
Published by Yale University
314 Prospect St, New Haven, CT 06511
Mailing Address: PO Box 208343, New Haven,
  CT 06520-8243
Tel: 203-432-0499 *Fax:* 203-432-0510
Web Site: yalereview.yale.edu
Subscription Address: John Wiley & Sons Inc,
  Wiley Subscription Services, 111 River St,
  Hoboken, NJ 07030-5774 *Toll Free Tel:* 800-
  835-6770 *E-mail:* cs-journals@wiley.com

Key Personnel
Ed: Meghan O'Rourke
Literary work, essays & reviews.
First published 1911
Frequency: Quarterly
Indivs: $43/yr print & online North & South
  America, 46 GBP/yr UK & rest of world; In-
  stns: $244/yr print & online North & South
  America, 189 GBP/yr UK & rest of world
Ad Rates: Full page $425; 1/2 page $300; inside
  back cover $475; series discount 10% (3x or
  more)

Company Index

Included in this index are the names, addresses, telecommunication numbers and electronic addresses of the organizations included in this volume of *LMP*. Entries also include the page number(s) on which the listings appear.

Sections not represented in this index are **Imprints, Subsidiaries & Distributors; Calendar of Book Trade & Promotional Events; Reference Books for the Trade** and **Magazines for the Trade.**

A+ English LLC/Book-Editing.com/Book Editing Associates, PO Box 1369, Mansfield, TX 76063 *Tel:* 469-789-3030 *E-mail:* editingnetwork@gmail. com *Web Site:* www.editing-writing.com; www.book-editing.com; www.helpwithstatistics.com; www. apawriting.com; childrensbookeditors.com; www. christianeditorsnetwork.com; dissertationwriting.com; statisticstutors.com, pg 457

A Public Space Fellowships, 323 Dean St, Brooklyn, NY 11217 *Tel:* 718-858-8067 *E-mail:* general@ apublicspace.org *Web Site:* apublicspace.org, pg 589

A-R Editions Inc, 1600 Aspen Commons, Suite 100, Middleton, WI 53562 *Tel:* 608-836-9000 *Toll Free Tel:* 800-736-0070 (North America book orders only) *Fax:* 608-831-8200 *E-mail:* info@areditions.com; orders@areditions.com *Web Site:* www.areditions.com, pg 1

A 2 Z Press LLC, 3670 Woodbridge Rd, Deland, FL 32720 *Tel:* 440-241-3126 *E-mail:* sizemore3630@ aol.com *Web Site:* www.a2zpress.com; www. bestlittleonlinebookstore.com, pg 1

A Westport Wordsmith, 101 Winfield St, Norwalk, CT 06855 *Tel:* 203-939-9484 *E-mail:* pj104daily@aol. com, pg 457

AAA Books Unlimited, 3060 Blackthorn Rd, Riverwoods, IL 60015 *Tel:* 847-444-1220 *Fax:* 847-607-8335 *Web Site:* www.aaabooksunlimited.com, pg 473

AAAI Press, 2275 E Bayshore Rd, Suite 160, Palo Alto, CA 94303 *Tel:* 650-328-3123 *Fax:* 650-321-4457 *E-mail:* publications20@aaai.org *Web Site:* www.aaai. org/Press/press.php, pg 1

AACC International, 3340 Pilot Knob Rd, St Paul, MN 55121 *Tel:* 651-454-7250 *Fax:* 651-454-0766 *E-mail:* aacc@scisoc.org *Web Site:* www.aaccnet.org, pg 1

AAH Graphics Inc, 9293 Fort Valley Rd, Fort Valley, VA 22652 *Tel:* 540-933-6210 *Fax:* 540-933-6523 *E-mail:* aah@aahgraphics.com *Web Site:* www. aahgraphics.com, pg 457

The Aaland Agency, PO Box 849, Inyokern, CA 93527-0849 *Tel:* 760-384-3910 *E-mail:* anniejo41@gmail. com *Web Site:* www.the-aaland-agency.com, pg 473

AAP PreK-12 Learning Group, 455 Massachusetts Ave NW, Suite 700, Washington, DC 20001 *Tel:* 202-347-3375 *Web Site:* www.publishers.org, pg 521

AAPG (American Association of Petroleum Geologists), 1444 S Boulder Ave, Tulsa, OK 74119 *Tel:* 918-584-2555 *Toll Free Tel:* 800-364-AAPG (364-2274) *Fax:* 918-580-2665 *E-mail:* info@aapg.org *Web Site:* www.aapg.org, pg 1

Aaron-Spear, PO Box 42, Brooksville, ME 04617 *Tel:* 207-326-8764, pg 457

ABA Entrepreneurial Excellence Award, 333 Westchester Ave, Suite S202, White Plains, NY 10604 *Toll Free Tel:* 800-637-0037 *Fax:* 914-417-4013 *E-mail:* excellence@bookweb.org *Web Site:* www. bookweb.org, pg 589

ABAC/ALAC, 11 Marie St, Ottawa, ON K1N 9M5, Canada *Tel:* 416-364-2376 *E-mail:* info@abac.org *Web Site:* www.abac.org, pg 521

Abaris Books, 70 New Canaan Ave, Norwalk, CT 06850 *Tel:* 203-838-8402 *Fax:* 203-857-0730 *E-mail:* abaris@abarisbooks.com *Web Site:* abarisbooks.com, pg 1

Abbeville Press, 655 Third Ave, New York, NY 10017 *Tel:* 212-366-5585 *Toll Free Tel:* 800-ART-BOOK (278-2665); 800-343-4499 (orders) *Fax:* 646-375-2359 *Toll Free Fax:* 800-351-5073 (orders) *E-mail:* abbeville@abbeville.com; sales@abbeville. com; marketing@abbeville.com; rights@abbeville.com *Web Site:* www.abbeville.com, pg 2

Abbeville Publishing Group, 655 Third Ave, New York, NY 10017 *Tel:* 646-375-2136 *Fax:* 646-375-2359 *E-mail:* abbeville@abbeville.com; marketing@ abbeville.com; sales@abbeville.com; rights@abbeville. com *Web Site:* www.abbeville.com, pg 2

ABC-CLIO, 130 Cremona Dr, Santa Barbara, CA 93117 *Tel:* 805-968-1911 *Toll Free Tel:* 800-368-6868 *Fax:* 805-685-9685 *Toll Free Fax:* 866-270-3856 *E-mail:* customerservice@abc-clio.com *Web Site:* www.abc-clio.com, pg 2

ABDO Publishing Co Inc, 8000 W 78 St, Suite 310, Edina, MN 55439 *Tel:* 952-698-2403 *Toll Free Tel:* 800-800-1312 *Fax:* 952-831-1632 *Toll Free Fax:* 800-862-3480 *E-mail:* customerservice@ abdopublishing.com; info@abdopublishing.com *Web Site:* abdopublishing.com, pg 2

Dominick Abel Literary Agency Inc, 146 W 82 St, Suite 1-A, New York, NY 10024 *Tel:* 212-877-0710 *Fax:* 212-595-3133 *E-mail:* agency@dalainc.com *Web Site:* www.dalainc.com, pg 473

Abingdon Press, 2222 Rosa L Parks Blvd, Nashville, TN 37228 *Tel:* 615-749-6000 (academic books) *Toll Free Tel:* 800-251-3320 (orders) *Fax:* 615-749-6056 (academic books) *Toll Free Fax:* 800-836-7802 (orders) *E-mail:* orders@abingdonpress.com; permissions@abingdonpress.com *Web Site:* www. abingdonpress.com, pg 2

About Books Inc, 1001 Taurus Dr, Colorado Springs, CO 80906 *Tel:* 719-440-8932 *Fax:* 719-213-2602 *Web Site:* www.about-books.com, pg 457

J M Abraham Poetry Award, 1113 Marginal Rd, Halifax, NS B3H 4P7, Canada *Tel:* 902-423-8116 *Fax:* 902-422-0881 *E-mail:* contact@writers.ns.ca *Web Site:* writers.ns.ca, pg 589

Abrams Artists Agency, 275 Seventh Ave, 26th fl, New York, NY 10001 *Tel:* 646-486-4600 *Fax:* 646-486-0100 *E-mail:* literary@abramsartny.com *Web Site:* www.abramsartists.com, pg 473

Harry N Abrams Inc, 195 Broadway, 9th fl, New York, NY 10007 *Tel:* 212-206-7715 *Toll Free Tel:* 800-345-1359 *Fax:* 212-519-1210 *E-mail:* abrams@ abramsbooks.com *Web Site:* www.abramsbooks.com, pg 2

Abrams Learning Trends, 16310 Bratton Lane, Suite 250, Austin, TX 78728-2403 *Toll Free Tel:* 800-227-9120 *Toll Free Fax:* 800-737-3322 *E-mail:* customerservice@abramslearningtrends.com (orders, cust serv); contactus@abramslearningtrends. com *Web Site:* www.abramslearningtrends.com (orders, cust serv), pg 3

Acacia House Publishing Services Ltd, 51 Chestnut Ave, Brantford, ON N3T 4C3, Canada *Tel:* 519-752-0978 *Fax:* 519-752-0978, pg 473

Academic Press, 50 Hampshire St, 5th fl, Cambridge, MA 02139 *Tel:* 781-663-5200 *Fax:* 937-247-0808 *Web Site:* www.elsevier.com/books-and-journals/ academic-press, pg 3

Academica Press, 1727 Massachusetts Ave NW, Suite 507, Washington, DC 20036 *Tel:* 978-829-2577 *E-mail:* editorial@academicapress.com *Web Site:* www.academicapress.com, pg 3

Academy Chicago, 814 N Franklin St, Chicago, IL 60610 *Tel:* 312-337-0747 *Toll Free Tel:* 800-888-4741 (orders) *Fax:* 312-337-5110 *E-mail:* frontdesk@ chicagoreviewpress.com *Web Site:* www. chicagoreviewpress.com, pg 3

Academy of American Poets Fellowship, 75 Maiden Lane, Suite 901, New York, NY 10038 *Tel:* 212-274-0343 *E-mail:* academy@poets.org *Web Site:* www. poets.org, pg 589

The Academy of American Poets Inc, 75 Maiden Lane, Suite 901, New York, NY 10038 *Tel:* 212-274-0343 *E-mail:* academy@poets.org *Web Site:* www.poets.org, pg 521

Academy of Motion Picture Arts & Sciences (AMPAS), 8949 Wilshire Blvd, Beverly Hills, CA 90211 *Tel:* 310-247-3000 *Fax:* 310-859-9619 *E-mail:* ampas@oscars.org *Web Site:* www.oscars.org, pg 521

Academy of Nutrition & Dietetics, 120 S Riverside Plaza, Suite 2190, Chicago, IL 60606-6995 *Tel:* 312-899-0040 (ext 5000) *Toll Free Tel:* 800-877-1600 *E-mail:* sales@eatright.org *Web Site:* www.eatright.org, pg 3

ACC Art Books, 6 W 18 St, Suite 4B, New York, NY 10011 *Tel:* 212-645-1111 *Toll Free Tel:* 800-252-5231 *Fax:* 212-989-3205 *E-mail:* ussales@ accpublishinggroup.com *Web Site:* www.accartbooks. com/us/, pg 4

Access Copyright, The Canadian Copyright Licensing Agency, 56 Wellesley St W, Suite 401A, Toronto, ON M5S 2S3, Canada *Tel:* 416-868-1620 *Toll Free Tel:* 800-893-5777 *Fax:* 416-868-1621 *E-mail:* info@ accesscopyright.ca *Web Site:* www.accesscopyright.ca, pg 521

Acclaim Film Script Competition, 300 Central Ave, Suite 501, St Petersburg, FL 33701 *Web Site:* acclaimscripts. com, pg 589

Acclaim TV Script Competition, 300 Central Ave, Suite 501, St Petersburg, FL 33701 *Web Site:* acclaimscripts. com, pg 589

Accuity, 1007 Church St, 6th fl, Evanston, IL 60201 *Tel:* 847-676-9600 *Toll Free Tel:* 800-321-3373 *Fax:* 847-933-8101 *E-mail:* customerservice@accuity. com *Web Site:* www.accuity.com, pg 4

Accurate Writing & More, 16 Barstow Lane, Hadley, MA 01035 *Tel:* 413-586-2388 *Web Site:* www. accuratewriting.com; www.frugalmarketing.com; www. goingbeyondsustainability.com; www.transformpreneur. com; www.greenandprofitable.com; www.twitter. com/shelhorowitz, pg 457

The Acheven Book Prize for Young Adult Fiction, c/o Regal House Publishing, 806 Oberlin Rd, No 12094, Raleigh, NC 27605 *E-mail:* info@regalhousepublishing.com *Web Site:* regalhousepublishing.com/the-acheven-book-prize-for-young-adult-fiction/, pg 589

Milton Acorn Poetry Awards, 81 Prince St, Charlottetown, PE C1A 4R3, Canada *E-mail:* peiliteraryawards@gmail.com *Web Site:* www. peiwritersguild.com, pg 589

Acres USA, 501 Eighth Ave, Greenley, CO 80631 *Tel:* 512-892-4400 *Toll Free Tel:* 800-355-5313 *E-mail:* orders@acresusa.com; editor@acresusa.com; info@acresusa.com *Web Site:* www.acresusa.com, pg 4

Acroterion Books, 5305 Harvard Rd, Lawrence, KS 66049-4781 *Tel:* 785-917-0773 *E-mail:* info@acroterionbooks.com *Web Site:* www.acroterionbooks.com, pg 447

ACTA Press, 200-4040 Bowness Rd NW, Calgary, AB T3B 3R7, Canada *Tel:* 403-288-1195 *Fax:* 403-247-6851 *E-mail:* journals@actapress.com; publish@actapress.com; sales@actapress.com *Web Site:* www.actapress.com, pg 415

ACTA Publications, 4848 N Clark St, Chicago, IL 60640 *Toll Free Tel:* 800-397-2282 *E-mail:* actapublications@actapublications.com *Web Site:* www.actapublications.com, pg 4

ACU Press, 1648 Campus Ct, Abilene, TX 79601 *Tel:* 325-674-2720 *Toll Free Tel:* 877-816-4455 *Web Site:* www.acupressbooks.com; www.leafwoodpublishers.com, pg 4

Adams & Ambrose Publishing, PO Box 259684, Madison, WI 53725-9684 *Tel:* 608-977-1825 *E-mail:* info@adamsambrose.com, pg 4

Herbert Baxter Adams Prize, 400 "A" St SE, Washington, DC 20003 *Tel:* 202-544-2422 *Fax:* 202-544-8307 *E-mail:* awards@historians.org *Web Site:* www.historians.org, pg 589

Adams Media, 57 Littlefield St, Avon, MA 02322 *Tel:* 508-427-7100 *Web Site:* www.simonandschuster.com, pg 4

Adams-Pomeroy Press, 103 N Jackson St, Albany, WI 53502 *Tel:* 608-862-3645 *Toll Free Tel:* 877-862-3645 *Fax:* 608-862-3647 *E-mail:* adamspomeroy@tds.net, pg 447

Willi Paul Adams Award, 112 N Bryan Ave, Bloomington, IN 47408-4141 *Tel:* 812-855-7311 *E-mail:* oah@oah.org *Web Site:* www.oah.org/awards, pg 589

Jane Addams Children's Book Award, 777 United Nations Plaza, 6th fl, New York, NY 10017 *Tel:* 212-682-8830 *E-mail:* info@janeaddamspeace.org *Web Site:* www.janeaddamspeace.org, pg 590

Addicus Books Inc, PO Box 45327, Omaha, NE 68145 *Tel:* 402-330-7493 *Fax:* 402-330-1707 *E-mail:* info@addicusbooks.com; addicusbks@aol.com *Web Site:* www.addicusbooks.com, pg 4

J Adel Art & Design, 586 Ramapo Rd, Teaneck, NJ 07666 *Tel:* 201-836-2606 *E-mail:* jadelnj@aol.com, pg 457

Adirondack Mountain Club (ADK), 814 Goggins Rd, Lake George, NY 12845-4117 *Tel:* 518-668-4447 *Toll Free Tel:* 800-395-8080 *Fax:* 518-668-3746 *E-mail:* info@adk.org *Web Site:* www.adk.org, pg 5

Advance Publishing Inc, 6950 Fulton St, Houston, TX 77022 *Tel:* 713-695-0600 *Toll Free Tel:* 800-917-9630 *Fax:* 713-695-8585 *E-mail:* info@advancepublishing.com *Web Site:* www.advancepublishing.com, pg 5

Adventure House, 914 Laredo Rd, Silver Spring, MD 20901 *Tel:* 301-754-1589 *Web Site:* www.adventurehouse.com, pg 5

AdventureKEEN, 2204 First Ave S, Suite 102, Birmingham, AL 35233 *Tel:* 763-689-9800 *Toll Free Tel:* 800-678-7006 *Fax:* 763-689-9039 *Toll Free Fax:* 877-374-9016 *E-mail:* info@adventurewithkeen.com *Web Site:* adventurewithkeen.com, pg 5

Adventures Unlimited Press (AUP), One Adventure Place, Kempton, IL 60946 *Tel:* 815-253-6390 *Fax:* 815-253-6300 *E-mail:* adventuresunlimitedpress.com *Web Site:* www.adventuresunlimitedpress.com, pg 5

Advertising Research Foundation (ARF), 432 Park Ave S, 4th fl, New York, NY 10016-8013 *Tel:* 212-751-5656 *Fax:* 212-689-1859 *E-mail:* help@thearf.org *Web Site:* thearf.org, pg 521

The AEI Press, 1789 Massachusetts Ave NW, Washington, DC 20036 *Tel:* 202-862-5800 *Fax:* 202-862-7177 *Web Site:* www.aei.org, pg 5

AEIOU Inc, 894 Piermont Ave, Piermont, NY 10968 *Tel:* 845-359-1911, pg 457

Aevitas Creative Management, 19 W 21 St, Suite 501, New York, NY 10010 *Tel:* 212-765-6900 *Web Site:* aevitascreative.com, pg 474

AFB Press, 1401 S Clark St, Suite 730, Arlington, VA 22202 *Tel:* 304-710-3043 *Toll Free Tel:* 800-232-3044 (orders) *Fax:* 917-210-3979 (orders) *E-mail:* afbpress@afb.net *Web Site:* www.afb.org, pg 5

AFCP's Awards, 135 Old Cove Rd, Suite 210, Liverpool, NY 13090 *Toll Free Tel:* 877-203-2327 *Fax:* 781-459-7770 *E-mail:* afcp@afcp.org *Web Site:* www.afcp.org, pg 590

Africa World Press Inc, 541 W Ingham Ave, Suite B, Trenton, NJ 08638 *Tel:* 609-695-3200 *Fax:* 609-695-6466 *E-mail:* customerservice@africaworldpressbooks.com *Web Site:* www.africaworldpressbooks.com, pg 5

African American Images, PO Box 1799, Chicago Heights, IL 60412 *Tel:* 708-672-4909 (cust serv) *Fax:* 708-672-0466 *E-mail:* customersvc@africanamericanimages.com *Web Site:* www.africanamericanimages.com, pg 5

Agatha Awards, PO Box 8007, Gaithersburg, MD 20898 *Tel:* 301-730-1675 *E-mail:* mdregservices@gmail.com *Web Site:* malicedomestic.org, pg 590

Agency Chicago, 7000 Phoenix Ave NE, Suite 202, Albuquerque, NM 87110 *E-mail:* agency.chicago@usa.com, pg 474

Aggiornamento Award, 8550 United Plaza Blvd, Suite 1001, Baton Rouge, LA 70809 *Tel:* 225-408-4417 *Fax:* 225-408-4422 *E-mail:* cla2@cathla.org *Web Site:* cathla.org, pg 590

The Ahearn Agency Inc, 2021 Pine St, New Orleans, LA 70118 *Tel:* 504-861-8395 *Fax:* 504-866-6434 *Web Site:* www.ahearnagency.com, pg 474

Ahsahta Press, Boise State University, Mail Stop 1580, 1910 University Dr, Boise, ID 83725-1580 *Tel:* 208-519-6726 *E-mail:* ahsahta@boisestate.edu *Web Site:* ahsahtapress.org, pg 5

AICPA Professional Publications, 220 Leigh Farm Rd, Durham, NC 27707 *Tel:* 919-402-4500 *Toll Free Tel:* 888-777-7077 (memb serv ctr) *Fax:* 919-402-4505 *Toll Free Fax:* 800-362-5066 (memb serv ctr) *E-mail:* acquisitions@aicpa.org; service@aicpa.org *Web Site:* www.aicpa.org, pg 6

AIGA 50 Books|50 Covers, 222 Broadway, New York, NY 10038 *Tel:* 212-807-1990 *Fax:* 212-807-1799 *E-mail:* competitions@aiga.org *Web Site:* www.aiga.org, pg 590

AIGA, the professional association for design, 222 Broadway, New York, NY 10038 *Tel:* 212-807-1990 *Fax:* 212-807-1799 *E-mail:* general@aiga.org *Web Site:* www.aiga.org, pg 521

AJL Jewish Fiction Award, PO Box 1118, Teaneck, NJ 07666 *Tel:* 201-371-3255 *E-mail:* info@jewishlibraries.org *Web Site:* jewishlibraries.org/AJL_Jewish_Fiction_Award, pg 590

AJL Judaica Bibliography Award, PO Box 1118, Teaneck, NJ 07666 *Tel:* 201-371-3255 *E-mail:* info@jewishlibraries.org *Web Site:* jewishlibraries.org, pg 590

AJL Judaica Reference Award, PO Box 1118, Teaneck, NJ 07666 *Tel:* 201-371-3255 *E-mail:* info@jewishlibraries.org *Web Site:* jewishlibraries.org, pg 590

AJL Scholarship, PO Box 1118, Teaneck, NJ 07666 *Tel:* 201-371-3255 *E-mail:* scholarship@jewishlibraries.org *Web Site:* jewishlibraries.org, pg 590

AK Press Distribution, 370 Ryan Ave, Unit 100, Chico, CA 95973 *Tel:* 510-208-1700 *Fax:* 510-208-1701 *E-mail:* info@akpress.org *Web Site:* www.akpress.org, pg 6

Akashic Books, 232 Third St, Suite A-115, Brooklyn, NY 11215 *Tel:* 718-643-9193 *Fax:* 718-643-9195 *E-mail:* info@akashicbooks.com *Web Site:* www.akashicbooks.com, pg 6

Akron Poetry Prize, 120 E Mill St, Suite 415, Akron, OH 44308 *Tel:* 330-972-6960 *Fax:* 330-972-8364 *E-mail:* uapress@uakron.edu *Web Site:* www.uakron.edu/uapress/akron-poetry-prize, pg 590

ALA Neal-Schuman, 50 E Huron St, Chicago, IL 60611 *Toll Free Tel:* 800-545-2433 *Fax:* 312-280-5860 *E-mail:* editionsmarketing@ala.org *Web Site:* www.alastore.ala.org, pg 6

Alabama Artists Fellowship Awards, 201 Monroe St, Suite 110, Montgomery, AL 36130-1800 *Tel:* 334-242-4076 *Fax:* 334-240-3269, pg 590

Alaska Native Language Center, PO Box 757680, Fairbanks, AK 99775-7680 *Fax:* 907-474-6586 *E-mail:* uaf-anlc@alaska.edu (orders) *Web Site:* www.uaf.edu/anlc, pg 6

Alazar Press, 201 Orchard Lane, Carrboro, NC 27510 *Tel:* 919-274-0653 *E-mail:* alazar.press@gmail.com *Web Site:* www.alazar-press.com, pg 447

Albert Whitman & Co, 250 S Northwest Hwy, Suite 320, Park Ridge, IL 60068 *Tel:* 847-232-2800 *Toll Free Tel:* 800-255-7675 *Fax:* 847-581-0039 *E-mail:* mail@albertwhitman.com *Web Site:* www.albertwhitman.com, pg 6

Alberta Book Publishing Awards, 10523 100 Ave, Edmonton, AB T5J 0A8, Canada *Tel:* 780-424-5060 *E-mail:* info@bookpublishers.ab.ca *Web Site:* www.bookpublishers.ab.ca, pg 591

The Albertine Prize, 972 Fifth Ave, New York, NY 10075 *E-mail:* press@albertine.com *Web Site:* www.albertine.com/albertine-prize, pg 591

Rodelinde Albrecht, PO Box 444, Lenox Dale, MA 01242-0444 *Tel:* 413-243-4350 *E-mail:* rodelinde@gmail.com, pg 457

Alcuin Society, PO Box 3216, Sta Terminal, Vancouver, BC V6B 3X8, Canada *Tel:* 604-732-5403 *E-mail:* info@alcuinsociety.com; awards@alcuinsociety.com *Web Site:* alcuinsociety.com, pg 521

Alcuin Society Awards for Excellence in Book Design in Canada, PO Box 3216, Sta Terminal, Vancouver, BC V6B 3X8, Canada *Tel:* 604-732-5403 *E-mail:* awards@alcuinsociety.com *Web Site:* alcuinsociety.com, pg 591

A Owen Aldridge Prize, University of South Carolina, Dept of Languages, Literature & Cultures, 1620 College St, Rm 817, Columbia, SC 29208 *Tel:* 803-777-3021 *E-mail:* info@acla.org *Web Site:* www.acla.org/prize-awards/owen-aldridge-prize, pg 591

Alex Awards, 50 E Huron St, Chicago, IL 60611 *Tel:* 312-280-4390 *Toll Free Tel:* 800-545-2433 *Fax:* 312-280-5276 *E-mail:* yalsa@ala.org *Web Site:* www.ala.org/yalsa/alex-awards, pg 591

The Alexander Graham Bell Association for the Deaf & Hard of Hearing, 3417 Volta Place NW, Washington, DC 20007 *Tel:* 202-337-5220 *Toll Free Tel:* 866-337-5220 (orders) *Fax:* 202-337-8314 *E-mail:* info@agbell.org; publications@agbell.org *Web Site:* www.agbell.org, pg 6

Alexander Street, a ProQuest Company, 99 Canal Center Plaza, Suite 200, Alexandria, VA 22314 *Tel:* 703-212-8520 *Toll Free Tel:* 800-889-5937 *E-mail:* sales@alexanderstreet.com; marketing@alexanderstreet.com; info@alexanderstreet.com *Web Site:* alexanderstreet.com, pg 6

Alfred Music, PO Box 10003, Van Nuys, CA 91410 *Tel:* 818-891-5999 (dealer sales, intl) *Toll Free Tel:* 800-292-6122 (dealer sales, US & CN); 800-628-1528 (cust serv) *Fax:* 818-893-5560 (dealer sales); 818-830-6252 (cust serv) *Toll Free Fax:* 800-632-1928 (dealer sales) *E-mail:* customerservice@alfred.com; sales@alfred.com *Web Site:* www.alfred.com, pg 7

Algonquin Books, 400 Silver Cedar Ct, Suite 300, Chapel Hill, NC 27514-1585 *Tel:* 919-967-0108 *Fax:* 919-933-0272 *E-mail:* inquiry@algonquin.com *Web Site:* www.workman.com/algonquin, pg 7

Algora Publishing, 1732 First Ave, No 20330, New York, NY 10128 *Tel:* 212-678-0232 *Fax:* 212-666-3682 *E-mail:* editors@algora.com *Web Site:* www.algora.com, pg 7

Nelson Algren Literary Awards, 160 N Stetson Ave, Chicago, IL 60601 *Tel:* 312-222-3001 *E-mail:* ctc-arts@chicagotribune.com *Web Site:* www.chicagotribune.com/entertainment/books/literary-awards; algren.submittable.com, pg 591

Alice James Books, 114 Prescott St, Farmington, ME 04938 *Tel:* 207-778-7071 *Fax:* 207-778-7766 *E-mail:* info@alicejamesbooks.org *Web Site:* alicejamesbooks.org, pg 7

All About Kids Publishing, PO Box 159, Gilroy, CA 95021 *Tel:* 408-337-1152 *E-mail:* info@allaboutkidspub.com *Web Site:* www.allaboutkidspub.com, pg 7

All Things That Matter Press, 79 Jones Rd, Somerville, ME 04348 *E-mail:* allthingsthatmatterpress@gmail.com *Web Site:* www.allthingsthatmatterpress.com, pg 8

Alliance for Audited Media (AAM), 48 W Seegers Rd, Arlington Heights, IL 60005 *Tel:* 224-366-6939 *Fax:* 224-366-6949 *Web Site:* auditedmedia.com, pg 521

Alliance for Women in Media (AWM), 1250 24 St NW, Suite 300, Washington, DC 20037 *Tel:* 202-750-3664 *Fax:* 202-750-3664 *E-mail:* info@allwomeninmedia.org *Web Site:* allwomeninmedia.org, pg 521

Alligator Juniper's National Writing Contest, 220 Grove Ave, Prescott, AZ 86301 *Tel:* 928-350-2012 *E-mail:* alligatorjuniper@prescott.edu *Web Site:* alligatorjuniper.wordpress.com, pg 591

Allium Press of Chicago, 1530 Elgin Ave, Forest Park, IL 60130 *Tel:* 708-689-9323 *E-mail:* info@alliumpress.com *Web Site:* www.alliumpress.com, pg 8

Alloy Entertainment LLC, 30 Hudson Yards, 22nd fl, New York, NY 10001 *E-mail:* collaborative@alloyentertainment.com, pg 8

Allworth Press, 307 W 36 St, 11th fl, New York, NY 10018 *Tel:* 212-643-6816 *Fax:* 212-643-6819 *Web Site:* www.allworth.com, pg 8

AllWrite Advertising & Publishing, 3300 Buckeye Rd, Suite 264, Atlanta, GA 30341 *Tel:* 770-284-8983 *Fax:* 770-284-8986 *E-mail:* questions@allwritepublishing.com; support@allwritepublishing.com (orders & returns) *Web Site:* allwritepublishing.com, pg 8

AllWrite Advertising & Publishing, 3300 Buckeye Rd, Suite 264, Atlanta, GA 30341 *Tel:* 770-284-8983 *Fax:* 770-284-8986 *E-mail:* questions@allwritepublishing.com *Web Site:* allwritepublishing.com, pg 457

Jeanette Almada, 452 W Aldine, Unit 215, Chicago, IL 60657 *Tel:* 773-404-9350 *E-mail:* jmalmada@sbcglobal.net, pg 457

Alpha Books, 6081 E 82 St, 4th fl, Indianapolis, IN 46250 *Tel:* 212-366-2000 *E-mail:* ecommerce@us.penguingroup.com *Web Site:* www.dk.com, pg 8

ALSC Baker & Taylor Summer Reading Grant, 50 E Huron St, Chicago, IL 60611-2795 *Tel:* 312-280-2163 *Toll Free Tel:* 800-545-2433 *Fax:* 312-440-9374; 312-280-5271 *E-mail:* alsc@ala.org *Web Site:* www.ala.org/alsc, pg 591

Amadeus Press, 200 Park Ave S, Suite 1109, New York, NY 10003 *Tel:* 212-529-3888 *Fax:* 212-529-4223 *Web Site:* www.rowman.com, pg 8

Amakella Publishing, PO Box 9445, Arlington, VA 22219 *Tel:* 202-239-8660 *E-mail:* info@amakella.com *Web Site:* www.amakella.com, pg 8

Frank Amato Publications Inc, 4040 SE Wister St, Milwaukie, OR 97222 *Tel:* 503-653-8108 *Toll Free Tel:* 800-541-9498 *Fax:* 503-653-2766 *E-mail:* customerservice@amatobooks.com; info@amatobooks.com *Web Site:* www.amatobooks.com, pg 8

Ambassador International, 411 University Ridge, Suite B14, Greenville, SC 29601 *Tel:* 864-751-4844 *E-mail:* info@emeraldhouse.com; publisher@emeraldhouse.com (ms submissions); sales@emeraldhouse.com (orders/order inquiries); media@emeraldhouse.com *Web Site:* ambassador-international.com; www.facebook.com/AmbassadorIntl; twitter.com/ambassadorintl, pg 8

The Ambassador Richard C Holbrooke Distinguished Achievement Award, PO Box 461, Wright Brothers Branch, Dayton, OH 45409-0461 *Tel:* 937-298-5072 *E-mail:* sharon.rab@daytonliterarypeaceprize.org *Web Site:* www.daytonliterarypeaceprize.org/holbrooke.htm, pg 591

Amber Lotus Publishing, PO Box 11329, Portland, OR 97211 *Tel:* 503-284-6400 *Toll Free Tel:* 800-326-2375 (orders only) *Fax:* 503-284-6417 *E-mail:* info@amberlotus.com *Web Site:* www.amberlotus.com, pg 8

Ambroggio Prize, 75 Maiden Lane, Suite 901, New York, NY 10038 *Tel:* 212-274-0343 *E-mail:* awards@poets.org *Web Site:* www.poets.org, pg 591

America West Publishers, 5872 Government Way, Unit 1-10, Dalton Gardens, ID 83814 *Tel:* 208-762-0633 *Toll Free Tel:* 800-729-4131 *Web Site:* www.nohoax.com, pg 9

American Academy of Arts & Sciences (AAAS), Norton's Woods, 136 Irving St, Cambridge, MA 02138 *Tel:* 617-576-5000 *Fax:* 617-576-5050 *E-mail:* aaas@amacad.org *Web Site:* www.amacad.org, pg 522

American Academy of Environmental Engineers & Scientists®, 147 Old Solomons Island Rd, Suite 303, Annapolis, MD 21401 *Tel:* 410-266-3311 *Fax:* 410-266-7653 *E-mail:* info@aaees.org *Web Site:* www.aaees.org, pg 9

American Academy of Pediatrics, 345 Park Blvd, Itasca, IL 60143 *Toll Free Tel:* 888-227-1770 *Fax:* 847-228-1281 *Web Site:* www.aap.org; shop.aap.org; publishing.aap.org, pg 9

American Academy of Political & Social Science, 202 S 36 St, Philadelphia, PA 19104-3806 *Tel:* 215-746-6500 *Fax:* 215-573-2667 *Web Site:* www.aapss.org, pg 522

The American Alpine Club Press, 710 Tenth St, Suite 100, Golden, CO 80401 *Tel:* 303-384-0110 *Fax:* 303-384-0111 *E-mail:* info@americanalpineclub.org *Web Site:* americanalpineclub.org, pg 9

American Anthropological Association (AAA), 2300 Clarendon Blvd, Suite 1301, Arlington, VA 22201 *Tel:* 703-528-1902 *Fax:* 703-528-3546 *E-mail:* pubs@americananthro.org *Web Site:* www.americananthro.org, pg 9

American Antiquarian Society (AAS), 185 Salisbury St, Worcester, MA 01609-1634 *Tel:* 508-755-5221 *Fax:* 508-753-3311 *E-mail:* library@americanantiquarian.org *Web Site:* www.americanantiquarian.org, pg 522

American Association for the Advancement of Science (AAAS), 1200 New York Ave NW, Washington, DC 20005 *Tel:* 202-326-6400 *E-mail:* media@aaas.org *Web Site:* www.aaas.org, pg 522

American Association for Vocational Instructional Materials, 220 Smithonia Rd, Winterville, GA 30683 *Tel:* 706-742-5355 *Fax:* 706-742-7005 *E-mail:* sales@aavim.com, pg 9

American Association of Blood Banks, North Tower, 4550 Montgomery Ave, Suite 700, Bethesda, MD 20814 *Tel:* 301-907-6977 *Toll Free Tel:* 866-222-2498 (sales) *Fax:* 301-907-6895 *E-mail:* aabb@aabb.org; sales@aabb.org (ordering); publications1@aabb.org (catalog) *Web Site:* www.aabb.org, pg 9

American Association of Collegiate Registrars & Admissions Officers (AACRAO), One Dupont Circle NW, Suite 520, Washington, DC 20036 *Tel:* 202-293-9161 *Fax:* 202-872-8857 *Web Site:* www.aacrao.org, pg 9

American Association of University Women Award for Juvenile Literature, 4610 Mail Service Ctr, Raleigh, NC 27699-4610 *Tel:* 919-807-7290 *Fax:* 919-733-8807, pg 591

American Auto Racing Writers & Broadcasters, 922 N Pass Ave, Burbank, CA 91505 *Tel:* 818-842-7005 *Fax:* 818-842-7020, pg 522

American Bar Association, 321 N Clark St, Chicago, IL 60654 *Tel:* 312-988-5000 *Toll Free Tel:* 800-285-2221 (orders) *Fax:* 312-988-6281 *E-mail:* orders@abanet.org *Web Site:* www.americanbar.org, pg 9

American Bible Society, 101 N Independence Mall E, 8th fl, Philadelphia, PA 19106-2112 *Tel:* 215-309-0900 *Toll Free Tel:* 800-322-4253 (cust serv); 888-596-6296 *E-mail:* info@americanbible.org *Web Site:* www.americanbible.org, pg 9

American Book Awards, The Raymond House, 655 13 St, Suite 302, Oakland, CA 94612 *Tel:* 916-425-7916 *E-mail:* beforecolumbusfoundation@gmail.com *Web Site:* www.beforecolumbusfoundation.com, pg 592

American Book Producers Association (ABPA), 31 W Eighth St, 2nd fl, New York, NY 10011 *Tel:* 212-675-1363 *Fax:* 212-675-1364 *E-mail:* office@abpaonline.org *Web Site:* www.abpaonline.org, pg 522

American Booksellers Association, 333 Westchester Ave, Suite S202, White Plains, NY 10604 *Tel:* 914-406-7500 *Toll Free Tel:* 800-637-0037 *Fax:* 914-417-4013 *E-mail:* info@bookweb.org *Web Site:* www.bookweb.org, pg 522

American Carriage House Publishing, 400 Idaho Maryland Rd, Grass Valley, CA 95945 *Tel:* 530-432-8860 *Toll Free Tel:* 866-986-2665 *E-mail:* editor@carriagehousepublishing.com *Web Site:* www.americancarriagehousepublishing.com, pg 10

American Catholic Press (ACP), 16565 S State St, South Holland, IL 60473 *Tel:* 708-331-5485 *Fax:* 708-331-5484 *E-mail:* acp@acpress.org *Web Site:* www.acpress.org, pg 10

The American Ceramic Society, 550 Polaris Pkwy, Suite 510, Westerville, OH 43082 *Tel:* 240-646-7054 *Toll Free Tel:* 866-721-3322 *Fax:* 240-396-5637 *E-mail:* customerservice@ceramics.org *Web Site:* ceramics.org, pg 10

The American Chemical Society, 1155 16 St NW, Washington, DC 20036 *Tel:* 202-872-4600 *Toll Free Tel:* 800-227-5558 (US) *Fax:* 202-872-6067 *E-mail:* help@acs.org *Web Site:* www.acs.org, pg 10

American Christian Writers, PO Box 110390, Nashville, TN 37222-0390 *Tel:* 615-331-8668 *Toll Free Tel:* 800-21-WRITE (219-7483) *E-mail:* acwriters@aol.com *Web Site:* regaforder.wordpress.com, pg 522

American Civil Liberties Union, 125 Broad St, 18th fl, New York, NY 10004 *Tel:* 212-549-2500 *E-mail:* media@aclu.org *Web Site:* www.aclu.org, pg 522

American College, 270 S Bryn Mawr Ave, Bryn Mawr, PA 19010 *Tel:* 610-526-1000 *Toll Free Tel:* 888-263-7265 *Fax:* 610-526-1310 *Web Site:* www.theamericancollege.edu, pg 10

American College of Surgeons, 633 N Saint Clair St, Chicago, IL 60611-3211 *Tel:* 312-202-5000 *Fax:* 312-202-5001 *E-mail:* postmaster@facs.org *Web Site:* www.facs.org, pg 10

American Correctional Association, 206 N Washington St, Suite 200, Alexandria, VA 22314 *Tel:* 703-224-0000 *Toll Free Tel:* 800-222-5646 *Fax:* 703-224-0179 *E-mail:* publications@aca.org *Web Site:* www.aca.org, pg 10

American Council on Education, One Dupont Circle NW, Washington, DC 20036 *Tel:* 202-939-9300; 202-939-9452 (publg dept); 301-632-6757 (orders) *E-mail:* pubs@acenet.edu *Web Site:* www.acenet.edu, pg 10

American Council on Education, One Dupont Circle NW, Washington, DC 20036 *Tel:* 202-939-9300 *Fax:* 202-939-9302 *E-mail:* pubs@acenet.edu *Web Site:* www.acenet.edu, pg 522

American Counseling Association, 6101 Stevenson Ave, Suite 600, Alexandria, VA 22304 *Tel:* 703-823-9800 *Toll Free Tel:* 800-298-2276 *Fax:* 703-823-0252

Toll Free Fax: 800-473-2329 *E-mail:* membership@counseling.org (book orders) *Web Site:* www.counseling.org, pg 10

American Diabetes Association, 2451 Crystal Dr, Suite 900, Arlington, VA 22202 *Toll Free Tel:* 800-342-2383 *E-mail:* booksinfo@diabetes.org *Web Site:* www.diabetes.org, pg 10

American Federation of Arts, 305 E 47 St, 10th fl, New York, NY 10017 *Tel:* 212-988-7700 *Toll Free Tel:* 800-232-0270 *Fax:* 212-861-2487 *E-mail:* pubinfo@amfedarts.org *Web Site:* www.amfedarts.org, pg 10

American Federation of Astrologers Inc, 6535 S Rural Rd, Tempe, AZ 85283-3746 *Tel:* 480-838-1751 *Toll Free Tel:* 888-301-7630 *Fax:* 480-838-8293 *Web Site:* www.astrologers.com, pg 11

American Fisheries Society, 425 Barlow Place, Suite 110, Bethesda, MD 20814-2144 *Tel:* 301-897-8616; 703-661-1570 (book orders) *Fax:* 301-897-8096; 703-996-1010 (book orders) *E-mail:* main@fisheries.org *Web Site:* www.fisheries.org, pg 11

American Forest & Paper Association (AF&PA), 1101 "K" St NW, Suite 700, Washington, DC 20005 *Tel:* 202-463-2700 *E-mail:* info@afandpa.org *Web Site:* www.afandpa.org, pg 522

American Geophysical Union (AGU), 2000 Florida Ave NW, Washington, DC 20009 *Tel:* 202-462-6900 *Toll Free Tel:* 800-966-2481 (North America) *Fax:* 202-328-0566 *E-mail:* service@agu.org (cust serv); earthspacescience@agu.org *Web Site:* www.agu.org, pg 11

American Geosciences Institute (AGI), 4220 King St, Alexandria, VA 22302-1502 *Tel:* 703-379-2480 (ext 246) *Fax:* 703-379-7563 *E-mail:* agi@americangeosciences.org *Web Site:* www.americangeosciences.org, pg 11

American Girl Publishing, 8400 Fairway Place, Middleton, WI 53562 *Tel:* 608-836-4848; 608-831-5210 (outside US & CN) *Toll Free Tel:* 800-233-0264; 800-360-1861; 800-845-0005 (US & CN) *Fax:* 608-836-1999 *Web Site:* www.americangirl.com, pg 11

American Historical Association (AHA), 400 "A" St SE, Washington, DC 20003 *Tel:* 202-544-2422 *Fax:* 202-544-8307 *E-mail:* aha@historians.org; awards@historians.org *Web Site:* www.historians.org, pg 11

American Illustration/American Photography, 225 W 36 St, Suite 602, New York, NY 10018 *Tel:* 917-408-9944 *Fax:* 212-532-2064 *E-mail:* info@ai-ap.com *Web Site:* www.ai-ap.com, pg 592

American Indian Youth Literature Award, PO Box 41296, San Jose, CA 95160 *E-mail:* ailawebsite@gmail.com *Web Site:* ailanet.org/activities/american-indian-youth-literature-award, pg 592

American Industrial Hygiene Association - AIHA, 3141 Fairview Park Dr, Suite 777, Falls Church, VA 22042 *Tel:* 703-849-8888 *Fax:* 703-207-3561 *E-mail:* infonet@aiha.org *Web Site:* www.aiha.org, pg 11

American Institute for Economic Research (AIER), 250 Division St, Great Barrington, MA 01230 *Tel:* 413-528-1216 *Toll Free Tel:* 888-528-1216 (orders) *E-mail:* info@aier.org *Web Site:* www.aier.org, pg 11

American Institute of Aeronautics & Astronautics (AIAA), 12700 Sunrise Valley Dr, Suite 200, Reston, VA 20191-5807 *Tel:* 703-264-7500 *Toll Free Tel:* 800-639-AIAA (639-2422) *Fax:* 703-264-7551 *E-mail:* custserv@aiaa.org *Web Site:* www.aiaa.org, pg 11

American Institute of Chemical Engineers (AIChE), 120 Wall St, 23rd fl, New York, NY 10005-4020 *Tel:* 203-702-7660 *Toll Free Tel:* 800-242-4363 *Fax:* 203-775-5177 *E-mail:* customerservice@aiche.org *Web Site:* www.aiche.org, pg 12

American Institute of Physics, One Physics Ellipse, College Park, MD 20740-3843 *Tel:* 516-576-2200; 301-209-3100 (orders) *E-mail:* help@aip.org *Web Site:* www.aip.org, pg 12

American Jewish Committee (AJC), Jacob Blaustein Bldg, 165 E 56 St, New York, NY 10022 *Tel:* 212-751-4000; 212-891-1456 (membership) *Fax:* 212-891-1450 *Web Site:* www.ajc.org, pg 522

American Law Institute, 4025 Chestnut St, Philadelphia, PA 19104-3099 *Tel:* 215-243-1600 *Toll Free Tel:* 800-253-6397 *Fax:* 215-243-1636 *E-mail:* ali@ali.org; custserv@ali.org *Web Site:* www.ali.org, pg 12

American Law Institute Continuing Legal Education (ALI CLE), 4025 Chestnut St, Philadelphia, PA 19104 *Tel:* 215-243-1600 *Toll Free Tel:* 800-CLE-NEWS (253-6397) *Fax:* 215-243-1664; 215-243-1608 *Web Site:* www.ali-cle.org, pg 12

The American Library Association (ALA), 225 N Michigan Ave, Suite 1300, Chicago, IL 60601 *Tel:* 312-944-6780 *Toll Free Tel:* 800-545-2433 *Fax:* 312-280-5275 *E-mail:* editionsmarketing@ala.org *Web Site:* www.alastore.ala.org, pg 12

The American Library Association (ALA), 225 N Michigan Ave, Suite 1300, Chicago, IL 60601 *Tel:* 312-944-6780; 312-280-4299 (memb & cust serv) *Toll Free Tel:* 800-545-2433 *Fax:* 312-440-9374 *E-mail:* ala@ala.org; customerservice@ala.org *Web Site:* www.ala.org, pg 523

American Literacy Council, 1441 Mariposa Ave, Boulder, CO 80302 *Tel:* 303-440-7385 *Web Site:* www.americanliteracy.com, pg 523

American Literary Translators Association (ALTA), University of Arizona, Esquire Bldg, No 205, 1230 N Park Ave, Tucson, AZ 85721 *Tel:* 520-621-1757 *Web Site:* www.literarytranslators.org, pg 523

American Map Corp, 36-36 33 St, 4th fl, Long Island City, NY 11106 *Tel:* 718-784-0055 *Toll Free Tel:* 888-774-7979 *Fax:* 718-784-0640 (admin); 718-784-1216 (sales & orders) *E-mail:* info@kappamapgroup.com *Web Site:* www.kappamapgroup.com, pg 12

American Marketing Association, 130 E Randolph St, 22nd fl, Chicago, IL 60601 *Tel:* 312-542-9000 *Toll Free Tel:* 800-AMA-1150 (262-1150) *Web Site:* www.ama.org, pg 523

American Mathematical Society, 201 Charles St, Providence, RI 02904-2213 *Tel:* 401-455-4000 *Toll Free Tel:* 800-321-4267 *Fax:* 401-331-3842; 401-455-4046 (cust serv) *E-mail:* ams@ams.org; cust-serv@ams.org *Web Site:* www.ams.org, pg 12

American Medical Association, AMA Plaza, 330 N Wabash, Suite 39300, Chicago, IL 60611-5885 *Tel:* 312-464-5000 *Toll Free Tel:* 800-621-8335 *Web Site:* www.ama-assn.org, pg 12, 523

American Medical Writers Association (AMWA), 30 W Gude Dr, Suite 525, Rockville, MD 20850-4357 *Tel:* 240-238-0940 *Fax:* 301-294-9006 *E-mail:* amwa@amwa.org *Web Site:* www.amwa.org, pg 523

American Numismatic Society, 75 Varick St, 11th fl, New York, NY 10013 *Tel:* 212-571-4470 *Fax:* 212-571-4479 *E-mail:* ans@numismatics.org *Web Site:* www.numismatics.org, pg 13

American Philosophical Society, 104 S Fifth St, Philadelphia, PA 19106 *Tel:* 215-440-3425 *Fax:* 215-440-3450 *E-mail:* orders@dianepublishing.net *Web Site:* www.amphilsoc.org, pg 13

American Political Science Association, 1527 New Hampshire Ave NW, Washington, DC 20036-1203 *Tel:* 202-483-2512 *Fax:* 202-483-2657 *E-mail:* apsa@apsanet.org; membership@apsanet.org; press@apsanet.org *Web Site:* www.apsanet.org, pg 523

American Press, 60 State St, Suite 700, Boston, MA 02109 *Tel:* 617-247-0022 *E-mail:* americanpress@flash.net *Web Site:* www.americanpresspublishers.com, pg 13

American Printing History Association, PO Box 4519, Grand Central Sta, New York, NY 10163 *E-mail:* secretary@printinghistory.org *Web Site:* printinghistory.org, pg 523

American Printing History Association Award, PO Box 4519, Grand Central Sta, New York, NY 10163 *E-mail:* secretary@printinghistory.org *Web Site:* printinghistory.org, pg 592

American Printing House for the Blind Inc, 1839 Frankfort Ave, Louisville, KY 40206 *Tel:* 502-895-2405 *Toll Free Tel:* 800-223-1839 (cust serv) *Fax:* 502-899-2274 *E-mail:* info@aph.org *Web Site:* www.aph.org; shop.aph.org, pg 13

American Program Bureau Inc, One Gateway Center, Suite 751, Newton, MA 02458 *Tel:* 617-614-1600 *Fax:* 617-965-6610 *E-mail:* apb@apbspeakers.com *Web Site:* www.apbspeakers.com, pg 515

American Psychiatric Association Publishing, 800 Maine Ave SW, Suite 900, Washington, DC 20024 *Tel:* 202-459-9722 *Toll Free Tel:* 800-368-5777 *Fax:* 202-403-3094 *E-mail:* appi@psych.org *Web Site:* www.appi.org; www.psychiatryonline.org, pg 13

American Psychological Association, 750 First St NE, Washington, DC 20002-4242 *Tel:* 202-336-5510 *Toll Free Tel:* 800-374-2721 *Fax:* 202-336-5502 *E-mail:* order@apa.org *Web Site:* www.apa.org/books, pg 13

American Public Human Services Association, 1133 19 St NW, Suite 400, Washington, DC 20036 *Tel:* 202-682-0100 *Fax:* 202-289-6555 *E-mail:* memberservice@aphsa.org *Web Site:* www.aphsa.org, pg 523

American Public Works Association (APWA), 1200 Main St, Suite 1400, Kansas City, MO 64105-2100 *Tel:* 816-472-6100 *Toll Free Tel:* 800-848-APWA (848-2792) *Fax:* 816-472-1610 *Web Site:* www.apwa.net, pg 13

American Quilter's Society, 5801 Kentucky Dam Rd, Paducah, KY 42003-9323 *Tel:* 270-898-7903 *Toll Free Tel:* 800-626-5420 (orders) *Fax:* 270-898-1173 *E-mail:* orders@americanquilter.com *Web Site:* www.americanquilter.com, pg 14

American Society for Indexing Inc (ASI), 1628 E Southern Ave, Suite 9-223, Tempe, AZ 85282 *Tel:* 480-245-6750 *E-mail:* info@asindexing.org *Web Site:* www.asindexing.org, pg 523

American Society for Nondestructive Testing, 1711 Arlingate Lane, Columbus, OH 43228-0518 *Tel:* 614-274-6003 *Toll Free Tel:* 800-222-2768 *Fax:* 614-274-6899 *Web Site:* www.asnt.org, pg 14

American Society for Quality (ASQ), 600 N Plankinton Ave, Milwaukee, WI 53203 *Tel:* 414-272-8575 *Toll Free Tel:* 800-248-1946 (US & CN); 800-514-1564 (Mexico) *Fax:* 414-272-1734 *E-mail:* help@asq.org *Web Site:* www.asq.org, pg 14

American Society of Agricultural & Biological Engineers (ASABE), 2950 Niles Rd, St Joseph, MI 49085-9659 *Tel:* 269-429-0300 *Toll Free Tel:* 800-371-2723 *Fax:* 269-429-3852 *E-mail:* hq@asabe.org *Web Site:* www.asabe.org, pg 14

American Society of Agronomy, 5585 Guilford Rd, Madison, WI 53711-5801 *Tel:* 608-273-8080 *Fax:* 608-273-2021 *E-mail:* headquarters@sciencesocieties.org *Web Site:* www.agronomy.org, pg 14

American Society of Civil Engineers (ASCE), 1801 Alexander Bell Dr, Reston, VA 20191-4400 *Tel:* 703-295-6300 *Toll Free Tel:* 800-548-ASCE (548-2723) *Toll Free Fax:* 866-913-6085 *E-mail:* ascelibrary@asce.org; pubsful@asce.org *Web Site:* www.asce.org, pg 14

American Society of Composers, Authors & Publishers (ASCAP), 1900 Broadway, New York City, NY 10023 *Tel:* 212-621-6000 *Fax:* 212-612-8453 *E-mail:* info@ascap.com *Web Site:* www.ascap.com, pg 524

American Society of Health-System Pharmacists (ASHP), 4500 East-West Hwy, Suite 900, Bethesda, MD 20814 *Tel:* 301-657-3000; 301-664-8700 *Toll Free Tel:* 866-279-0681 (orders) *Fax:* 301-657-1251 (orders) *E-mail:* custserv@ashp.org *Web Site:* www.ashp.org, pg 14

American Society of Journalists and Authors (ASJA), 355 Lexington Ave, 15th fl, New York, NY 10017-6603 *Tel:* 212-997-0947 *Web Site:* asja.org, pg 524

American Society of Journalists and Authors Annual Writers Conference, 355 Lexington Ave, 15th fl, New York, NY 10017-6603 *Tel:* 212-997-0947 *Web Site:* asja.org, pg 573

American Society of Magazine Editors (ASME), PO Box 112, New York, NY 10163 *Tel:* 212-872-3737 *E-mail:* asme@asme.media *Web Site:* www.asme. media, pg 524

American Society of Mechanical Engineers (ASME), 2 Park Ave, New York, NY 10016-5990 *Tel:* 212-591-7000 *Toll Free Tel:* 800-843-2763 (cust serv-US, CN & Mexico) *Fax:* 973-882-1717 (orders & inquiries) *E-mail:* customercare@asme.org *Web Site:* www.asme. org, pg 14

American Society of Media Photographers Inc, PO Box 31207, Bethesda, MD 20804 *Toll Free Tel:* 877-771-2767 *Fax:* 231-946-6180 *E-mail:* asmp@ vpassociations.com *Web Site:* asmp.org, pg 524

American Society of News Editors (ASNE), 209 Reynolds Journalism Institute, Missouri School of Journalism, Columbia, MO 65211 *Tel:* 573-882-2430 *Fax:* 573-884-3824 *Web Site:* asne.org, pg 524

American Society of Plant Taxonomists, University of Wyoming, Dept of Botany 3165, 1000 E University Ave, Laramie, WY 82071 *Tel:* 307-766-2556 *Fax:* 307-766-2851 *E-mail:* aspt@uwyo.edu *Web Site:* www.aspt.net, pg 14

American Sociological Association (ASA), 1430 "K" St NW, Suite 600, Washington, DC 20005-4701 *Tel:* 202-383-9005 *Fax:* 202-638-0882 *Web Site:* www.asanet. org, pg 524

American Speech-Language-Hearing Association (ASHA), 2200 Research Blvd, Rockville, MD 20850-3289 *Tel:* 301-296-5700 *Toll Free Tel:* 800-638-8255 (nonmembs); 800-498-2071 (membs) *Fax:* 301-296-5777; 301-296-8580 *E-mail:* actioncenter@asha.org *Web Site:* www.asha.org, pg 524

American Technical Publishers Inc, 10100 Orland Pkwy, Suite 200, Orland Park, IL 60467-5756 *Toll Free Tel:* 800-323-3471 *Fax:* 708-957-1101 *E-mail:* service@atplearning.com; order@atplearning. com *Web Site:* www.atplearning.com, pg 15

American Translators Association (ATA), 225 Reinekers Lane, Suite 590, Alexandria, VA 22314 *Tel:* 703-683-6100 *Fax:* 703-683-6122 *E-mail:* ata@atanet.org *Web Site:* www.atanet.org, pg 524

American Water Works Association (AWWA), 6666 W Quincy Ave, Denver, CO 80235-3098 *Tel:* 303-794-7711 *Toll Free Tel:* 800-926-7337 *E-mail:* service@ awwa.org (cust serv) *Web Site:* www.awwa.org, pg 15

Amherst Media Inc, PO Box 538, Buffalo, NY 14213 *Tel:* 716-874-4450 *E-mail:* marketing@amherstmedia. com *Web Site:* www.amherstmedia.com, pg 15

Amicus, PO Box 1329, Mankato, MN 56002 *Tel:* 507-388-9357 *Fax:* 507-388-9357 *E-mail:* info@ amicuspublishing.us; orders@amicuspublishing.us *Web Site:* www.amicuspublishing.us, pg 15

AMMO Books LLC, 5022 N Eagle Rock Blvd, Los Angeles, CA 90041 *Tel:* 323-223-AMMO (223-2666) *Fax:* 323-978-4200 *E-mail:* weborders@ammobooks. com; orders@ammobooks.com *Web Site:* ammobooks. com, pg 15

Ampersand Group, 1136 Maritime Way, Suite 717, Kanata, ON K2K 0M1, Canada *Tel:* 613-435-5066, pg 457

Ampersand Inc/Professional Publishing Services, 515 Madison St, New Orleans, LA 70116 *Tel:* 312-280-8905 *Fax:* 312-944-1582 *E-mail:* info@ ampersandworks.com *Web Site:* www. ampersandworks.com, pg 15

Betsy Amster Literary Enterprises, 607 Foothill Blvd, No 1061, La Canada Flintridge, CA 91012 *Tel:* 626-529-5667 *E-mail:* rights@amsterlit.com (rts inquiries); b.amster.assistant@gmail.com (adult book queries); b. amster.kidsbooks@gmail.com (children & young adult book queries) *Web Site:* www.amsterlit.com, pg 474

AMWA Annual Conference, 30 W Gude Dr, Suite 525, Rockville, MD 20850-4357 *Tel:* 240-238-0940 *Fax:* 301-294-9006 *E-mail:* amwa@amwa.org *Web Site:* www.amwa.org, pg 573

The Amy Award, 90 Broad St, Suite 2100, New York, NY 10004 *Tel:* 212-226-3586 *Fax:* 212-226-3963 *E-mail:* admin@pw.org *Web Site:* www.pw.org, pg 592

Anaphora Literary Press, 1108 W Third St, Quanah, TX 79252 *Tel:* 470-289-6395 *Web Site:* anaphoraliterary. com, pg 15

Anchor Books, c/o Penguin Random House Inc, 1745 Broadway, New York, NY 10019 *Tel:* 212-572-2420 *E-mail:* vintageanchorpublicity@randomhouse.com *Web Site:* knopfdoubleday.com/imprint/anchor, pg 15

Ancient Faith Publishing, 2427 Bond St, University Park, IL 60484 *Tel:* 219-728-2216 *Toll Free Tel:* 800-967-7377 *Toll Free Fax:* 866-599-5208 *E-mail:* info@ancientfaith.com; orders@ancientfaith. com *Web Site:* www.ancientfaith.com/publishing, pg 16

Barbara S Anderson, 706 W Davis Ave, Ann Arbor, MI 48103-4855 *Tel:* 734-995-0125 *E-mail:* bsa@ watercolorbarbara.com, pg 457

Denice A Anderson, 210 E Church St, Clinton, MI 49236 *Tel:* 517-456-4990 *Fax:* 517-456-4990 *E-mail:* deniceanderson@frontier.com, pg 457

Jim Anderson, 77 S Second St, Brooklyn, NY 11249 *Tel:* 718-388-1083 *E-mail:* jim.and@att.net, pg 457

Anderson Literary Management LLC, 244 Fifth Ave, 11th fl, New York, NY 10001 *Tel:* 212-645-6045 *Fax:* 212-741-1936 *E-mail:* info@andersonliterary.com *Web Site:* www.andersonliterary.com, pg 474

Sara Anderson Children's Books, PO Box 47182, Seattle, WA 98146 *Tel:* 206-285-1520 *Web Site:* www. saranderson.com, pg 16

Andrews McMeel Publishing LLC, 1130 Walnut St, Kansas City, MO 64106-2109 *Toll Free Tel:* 800-851-8923; 800-943-9839 (cust serv) *Toll Free Fax:* 800-943-9831 (orders) *E-mail:* sales@amuniversal.com *Web Site:* www.andrewsmcmeel.com; publishing. andrewsmcmeel.com, pg 16

Andrews University Press, Sutherland House, 8360 W Campus Circle Dr, Berrien Springs, MI 49104-1700 *Tel:* 269-471-6134 *Toll Free Tel:* 800-467-6369 (Visa, MC & American Express orders only) *Fax:* 269-471-6224 *E-mail:* aupo@andrews.edu; aup@andrews.edu; aupress@andrews.edu *Web Site:* www.universitypress. andrews.edu, pg 16

Andy Ross Literary Agency, 767 Santa Ray Ave, Oakland, CA 94610 *Tel:* 510-238-8965 *E-mail:* andyrossagency@hotmail.com *Web Site:* www. andyrossagency.com, pg 474

Angel City Press, 2118 Wilshire Blvd, Suite 880, Santa Monica, CA 90403 *Tel:* 310-395-9982 *Toll Free Tel:* 800-949-8039 *Fax:* 310-395-3353 *E-mail:* info@ angelcitypress.com *Web Site:* www.angelcitypress.com, pg 16

Angel Editing Services, PO Box 752, Mountain Ranch, CA 95246 *Tel:* 209-728-8364 *E-mail:* info@ stephaniemarohn.com *Web Site:* www. stephaniemarohn.com, pg 457

Angels Editorial Services, 1630 Main St, No 41, Coventry, CT 06238 *Tel:* 860-742-5279 *E-mail:* angelsus@aol.com, pg 458

Angelus Press, 2915 Forest Ave, Kansas City, MO 64109 *Tel:* 816-753-3150 *Toll Free Tel:* 800-966-7337 *Fax:* 816-753-3557 *E-mail:* support@angeluspress.org *Web Site:* www.angeluspress.org, pg 16

Anhinga Press, PO Box 3665, Tallahassee, FL 32315 *Tel:* 850-577-0745 *E-mail:* info@anhinga.org *Web Site:* www.anhingapress.org; www.facebook. com/anhingapress, pg 16

Animal Media Group LLC, 100 First Ave, Suite 1100, Pittsburgh, PA 15222-1519 *Tel:* 412-566-5656 *Fax:* 412-566-5656 *E-mail:* info@animalmediagroup. com *Web Site:* www.animalmediagroup.com, pg 16

The Anisfield-Wolf Book Awards, 1422 Euclid Ave, Suite 1300, Cleveland, OH 44115 *Tel:* 216-861-3810 *Fax:* 216-861-1729 *E-mail:* awinfo@clevefdn. org *Web Site:* www.anisfield-wolf.org; www. clevelandfoundation.org, pg 592

R Ross Annett Award for Children's Literature, 11759 Groat Rd, Edmonton, AB T5M 3K6, Canada *Tel:* 780-422-8174 *Toll Free Tel:* 800-665-5354 (AB only) *Fax:* 780-422-2663 (attn WGA) *E-mail:* mail@ writersguild.ca *Web Site:* writersguild.ca, pg 592

Annick Press Ltd, 15 Patricia Ave, Toronto, ON M2M 1H9, Canada *Tel:* 416-221-4802 *Fax:* 416-221-8400 *E-mail:* annickpress@annickpress.com *Web Site:* www. annickpress.com, pg 415

Annual & Rolling Grants for Artists, 136 State St, Montpelier, VT 05602 *Tel:* 802-828-5425 *Fax:* 802-828-3363 *E-mail:* info@vermontartscouncil.org *Web Site:* www.vermontartscouncil.org, pg 592

Annual Reviews, 4139 El Camino Way, Palo Alto, CA 94306 *Tel:* 650-493-4400 *Toll Free Tel:* 800-523-8635 *Fax:* 650-424-0910; 650-855-9815 *E-mail:* service@ annualreviews.org *Web Site:* www.annualreviews.org, pg 17

ANR Publications University of California, 2801 Second St, Davis, CA 95618 *Tel:* 530-400-0725 (cust serv) *Toll Free Tel:* 800-994-8849 *E-mail:* anrcatalog@ ucanr.edu *Web Site:* anrcatalog.ucanr.edu, pg 17

Antioch Writers' Workshop, 300 College Park Ave, Suite 200A, Dayton, OH 45469-0001 *Tel:* 937-567-2399 *E-mail:* info@antiochwritersworkshop.com *Web Site:* www.antiochwritersworkshop.com, pg 573

Antiquarian Booksellers' Association of America (ABAA), 20 W 44 St, Suite 507, New York, NY 10036 *Tel:* 212-944-8291 *Fax:* 212-944-8293 *E-mail:* hq@abaa.org *Web Site:* www.abaa.org, pg 525

Antrim House, 21 Goodrich Rd, Simsbury, CT 06070-1804 *Tel:* 860-217-0023 *E-mail:* eds@ antrimhousebooks.com *Web Site:* www. antrimhousebooks.com, pg 17

Anvil Press Publishers, 278 E First Ave, Vancouver, BC V5T 1A6, Canada *Tel:* 604-876-8710 *Fax:* 604-879-2667 *E-mail:* info@anvilpress.com *Web Site:* www. anvilpress.com, pg 415

AOCS Press, 2710 S Boulder Dr, Urbana, IL 61802-6996 *Tel:* 217-693-4838 *Fax:* 217-351-8091 *E-mail:* general@aocs.org *Web Site:* www.aocs.org, pg 17

AOTA Press, 6116 Executive Blvd, Suite 200, North Bethesda, MD 20852-4929 *Tel:* 301-652-6611 *Toll Free Tel:* 877-404-AOTA (404-2682, orders) *Fax:* 770-238-0414 (orders) *E-mail:* aotapress@aota.org; customerservice@aota.org *Web Site:* www.aota. org/Publications-News/AOTAPress.aspx; www.aota. org; store.aota.org, pg 17

APA Talent & Literary Agency, 405 S Beverly Dr, Beverly Hills, CA 90212 *Tel:* 310-888-4200 *Web Site:* www.apa-agency.com, pg 474

APC Publishing, PO Box 461166, Aurora, CO 80046-1166 *Tel:* 303-660-2158 *Toll Free Tel:* 800-660-5107 (sales & orders) *E-mail:* mail@4wdbooks.com; orders@4wdbooks.com *Web Site:* www.4wdbooks. com, pg 17

Aperture Books, 547 W 27 St, 4th fl, New York, NY 10001 *Tel:* 212-505-5555 *Toll Free Fax:* 888-623-6908 *E-mail:* customerservice@aperture.org *Web Site:* aperture.org, pg 17

The Apocryphile Press, 1700 Shattuck Ave, Suite 81, Berkeley, CA 94709 *Tel:* 510-290-4349 *E-mail:* apocryphile@me.com *Web Site:* www. apocryphilepress.com, pg 17

Apogee Press, 2308 Sixth St, Berkeley, CA 94710 *E-mail:* editors.apogee@gmail.com *Web Site:* www. apogeepress.com, pg 17

Apollo Managed Care Inc, 1100 Town & Country Rd, Suite 1250, Orange, CA 92868 *Toll Free Tel:* 888-276-5563 *E-mail:* info@apollomanagedcare.com *Web Site:* www.apollomanagedcare.com, pg 18

APPA: The Association of Higher Education Facilities Officers, 1643 Prince St, Alexandria, VA 22314-2818 *Tel:* 703-684-1446 *Fax:* 703-549-2772 *Web Site:* www.appa.org, pg 18

Appalachian Mountain Club Books, 5 Joy St, Boston, MA 02114 *Tel:* 617-523-0655 *Toll Free Tel:* 800-262-4455 (orders) *Fax:* 617-523-0722 *E-mail:* amcbooks@outdoors.org *Web Site:* www.outdoors.org, pg 18

Appalachian Trail Conservancy (ATC), 799 Washington St, Harpers Ferry, WV 25425 *Tel:* 304-535-6331 *Toll Free Tel:* 888-287-8673 (orders only) *Fax:* 304-535-2667 *E-mail:* publisher@appalachiantrail.org *Web Site:* www.appalachiantrail.org; www.atctrailstore.org, pg 18

Appalachian Writers' Workshop, 56 Education Lane, Hindman, KY 41822 *Tel:* 606-785-5475 *E-mail:* info@hindmansettlement.org *Web Site:* www.hindmansettlement.org, pg 573

Applause Theatre & Cinema Books, PO Box 1520, Wayne, NJ 07470-1520 *Tel:* 973-987-5363 *E-mail:* info@applausepub.com *Web Site:* www.applausepub.com, pg 18

The Applegate/Jackson/Parks Future Teacher Scholarship, 5211 Port Royal Rd, Suite 510, Springfield, VA 22151 *Tel:* 703-321-9606 *Fax:* 703-321-7143 *Web Site:* www.nilrr.org, pg 592

Applewood Books Inc, One River Rd, Carlisle, MA 01741 *Tel:* 781-271-0055 *Toll Free Tel:* 800-277-5312 (orders) *Fax:* 781-271-0056 *E-mail:* bookorder@awb.com; customercare@awb.com *Web Site:* www.awb.com, pg 18

Appraisal Institute, 200 W Madison, Suite 1500, Chicago, IL 60606 *Tel:* 312-335-4100 *Toll Free Tel:* 888-756-4624 *Fax:* 312-335-4400 *E-mail:* aiservice@appraisalinstitute.org *Web Site:* www.appraisalinstitute.org, pg 18

Apress Media LLC, 233 Spring St, 6th fl, New York, NY 10013 *Tel:* 212-460-1500 *E-mail:* editorial@apress.com; customerservice@springernature.com *Web Site:* www.apress.com, pg 18

APS PRESS, 3340 Pilot Knob Rd, St Paul, MN 55121 *Tel:* 651-454-7250 *Toll Free Tel:* 800-328-7560 *Fax:* 651-454-0766 *E-mail:* aps@scisoc.org *Web Site:* www.shopapspress.org, pg 18

Aptara Inc, 2901 Telestar Ct, Suite 522, Falls Church, VA 22042 *Tel:* 703-352-0001 *E-mail:* moreinfo@aptaracorp.com *Web Site:* www.aptaracorp.com, pg 458

Aquila Communications Inc, 281 rue Alice-Carriere St, Beaconsville, QC H9W 6E6, Canada *Toll Free Tel:* 800-667-7071 *Fax:* 514-505-4579 *Toll Free Fax:* 866-338-1948 *Web Site:* www.aquilacommunications.com, pg 415

Arbordale Publishing, 612 Johnnie Dodds Blvd, Suite A2, Mount Pleasant, SC 29464 *Tel:* 843-971-6722 *Toll Free Tel:* 877-243-3457 *Fax:* 843-216-3804 *E-mail:* info@arbordalepublishing.com *Web Site:* www.arbordalepublishing.com, pg 19

The May Hill Arbuthnot Honor Lecture Award, 50 E Huron St, Chicago, IL 60611-2795 *Tel:* 312-280-2163 *Toll Free Tel:* 800-545-2433 *Fax:* 312-440-9374; 312-280-5271 *E-mail:* alsc@ala.org *Web Site:* www.ala.org/alsc, pg 592

Arbutus Press, 2364 Pinehurst Trail, Traverse City, MI 49696 *Tel:* 231-946-7240 *E-mail:* info@arbutuspress.com *Web Site:* www.arbutuspress.com, pg 19

Arcade Publishing Inc, 307 W 36 St, 11th fl, New York, NY 10018 *Tel:* 212-643-6816 *Fax:* 212-643-6819 *E-mail:* info@skyhorsepublishing.com (subs & foreign rts) *Web Site:* www.arcadepub.com, pg 19

Arcadia, 159 Lake Place S, Danbury, CT 06810-7261 *Tel:* 203-797-0993 *E-mail:* arcadialit@gmail.com, pg 475

Arcadia Publishing Inc, 420 Wando Park Blvd, Mount Pleasant, SC 29464 *Tel:* 843-853-2070 *Toll Free Tel:* 888-313-2665 (orders only) *Fax:* 843-853-0044 *E-mail:* sales@arcadiapublishing.com *Web Site:* www.arcadiapublishing.com, pg 19

Archon Editorial LLC, 815 King St, Suite 204, Alexandria, VA 22314 *Tel:* 703-838-1650 *E-mail:* stoddardbc@gmail.com *Web Site:* www.archoneditorial.com, pg 458

ARE Press, 215 67 St, Virginia Beach, VA 23451 *Tel:* 757-428-3588 *Toll Free Tel:* 800-333-4499 *Web Site:* www.edgarcayce.org, pg 19

The ARF David Ogilvy Awards, 432 Park Ave S, 4th fl, New York, NY 10016-8013 *Tel:* 212-751-5656 *Fax:* 212-689-1859 *E-mail:* help@thearf.org *Web Site:* thearf.org, pg 592

Ariadne Press, 270 Goins Ct, Riverside, CA 92507 *Tel:* 951-684-9202 *Fax:* 951-779-0449 *E-mail:* ariadnepress@aol.com *Web Site:* www.ariadnebooks.com, pg 19

Ariel Press, 2317 Quail Cove Dr, Jasper, GA 30143 *Tel:* 770-894-4226 *E-mail:* lig201@lightariel.com *Web Site:* www.lightariel.com, pg 19

The Arion Press, The Presidio, 1802 Hays St, San Francisco, CA 94129 *Tel:* 415-668-2542 *Fax:* 415-668-2550 *E-mail:* arionpress@arionpress.com *Web Site:* www.arionpress.com, pg 20

Arizona State University Creative Writing Program, 1102 S McAllister Ave, Rm 170, Tempe, AZ 85281 *Tel:* 480-965-3168 *Fax:* 480-965-3451 *Web Site:* www.asu.edu/clas/english/creativewriting, pg 581

Arkansas Diamond Primary Book Award, Arkansas State Library, Suite 100, 900 W Capitol Ave, Little Rock, AR 72201-3108 *Tel:* 501-682-2860 *Fax:* 501-682-1693 *Web Site:* www.library.arkansas.gov; www.library.arkansas.gov, pg 593

Arkansas State University Graphic Communications Program, PO Box 1930, Dept of Media, State University, AR 72467-1930 *Tel:* 870-972-3114 *Fax:* 870-972-3321 *Web Site:* www.astate.edu, pg 581

Arkansas Writers' Conference, PO Box 24662, Little Rock, AR 72221 *Tel:* 501-833-2756 *Web Site:* www.arkansaswritersconference.org, pg 573

Arkham House Publishers Inc, PO Box 546, Sauk City, WI 53583 *Tel:* 608-643-4500 *Fax:* 608-643-5043 *E-mail:* sales@arkhamhouse.com *Web Site:* www.arkhamhouse.com, pg 20

Aro Book Publishing Co, 130 S 800 W, Salt Lake City, UT 84104-1120 *Tel:* 801-637-9115 *Fax:* 801-419-0125 *E-mail:* arobook@yahoo.com *Web Site:* www.arobookpublishing.com, pg 20

Jason Aronson Inc, 4501 Forbes Blvd, Suite 200, Lanham, MD 20706 *Tel:* 301-459-3366 *Toll Free Tel:* 800-462-6420 ext 3024 (cust serv) *Fax:* 301-429-5748 *Toll Free Fax:* 800-338-4550 (cust serv) *E-mail:* orders@rowman.com; customercare@rowman.com *Web Site:* www.rowman.com, pg 20

Arsenal Pulp Press, 211 E Georgia St, No 202, Vancouver, BC V6A 1Z6, Canada *Tel:* 604-687-4233 *Toll Free Tel:* 888-600-PULP (600-7857) *Fax:* 604-687-4283 *E-mail:* info@arsenalpulp.com *Web Site:* www.arsenalpulp.com, pg 415

Art Image Publications, PO Box 160, Derby Line, VT 05830 *Toll Free Tel:* 800-361-2598 *Toll Free Fax:* 800-559-2598 *E-mail:* info@artimagepublications.com; customer.service@artimagepublications.com *Web Site:* www.artimagepublications.com, pg 20

Art In Literature: The Mary Lynn Kotz Award, 800 E Broad St, Richmond, VA 23219 *Tel:* 804-692-3535 *Web Site:* www.lva.virginia.gov/public/litawards/kotz.htm, pg 593

The Art Institute of Chicago, 111 S Michigan Ave, Chicago, IL 60603-6404 *Tel:* 312-443-3600; 312-443-3540 (pubns) *Fax:* 312-443-1334 (pubns) *Web Site:* www.artic.edu; www.artinstituteshop.org, pg 20

Art of Living, PrimaMedia Inc, 1050 Second St Pike, Unit 1373, Southampton, PA 18966 *Tel:* 215-660-5045 *E-mail:* primamedia4@yahoo.com, pg 20

ArtAge Publications, PO Box 19955, Portland, OR 97280 *Tel:* 503-246-3000 *Toll Free Tel:* 800-858-4998 *Web Site:* www.seniortheatre.com, pg 20

Arte Publico Press, University of Houston, Bldg 19, Rm 100, 4902 Gulf Fwy, Houston, TX 77204-2004 *Tel:* 713-743-2998 (sales) *Toll Free Tel:* 800-633-2783 *Fax:* 713-743-2847 (sales) *E-mail:* appinfo@uh.edu; bkorders@uh.edu *Web Site:* artepublicopress.com, pg 20

Artech House®, 685 Canton St, Norwood, MA 02062 *Tel:* 781-769-9750 *Toll Free Tel:* 800-225-9977 *Fax:* 781-769-6334 *E-mail:* artech@artechhouse.com *Web Site:* www.artechhouse.com, pg 21

Artisan, 225 Varick St, New York, NY 10014-4381 *Tel:* 212-254-5900 *Toll Free Tel:* 800-722-7202 *Fax:* 212-677-6692 *E-mail:* artisaninfo@artisanbooks.com *Web Site:* www.artisanbooks.com; www.workman.com/artisanbooks, pg 21

Artisan Bookworks, 921 S Third Ave, No 8, Sequim, WA 98382 *Tel:* 425-954-5277 *E-mail:* books@artisanbookworks.com *Web Site:* www.artisanbookworks.com, pg 21

Artist Grants, 711 E Wells Ave, Pierre, SD 57501-3369 *Tel:* 605-773-3301 *Fax:* 605-773-5977 *E-mail:* sdac@state.sd.us *Web Site:* www.artscouncil.sd.gov/grants, pg 593

Artist-in-Residence Program, 225 King St, Suite 201, Fredericton, NB E3B 1E1, Canada *Tel:* 506-444-4444 *Toll Free Tel:* 866-460-ARTS (460-2787) *Fax:* 506-444-5543 *Web Site:* www.artsnb.ca, pg 593

Artist Research & Development Grants, 417 W Roosevelt St, Phoenix, AZ 85003-1326 *Tel:* 602-771-6501 *Fax:* 602-256-0282 *E-mail:* info@azarts.gov *Web Site:* www.azarts.gov, pg 593

Artists & Writers Summer Fellowships, 435 Ellis Hollow Creek Rd, Ithaca, NY 14850 *Tel:* 607-539-3146 *E-mail:* artscolony@saltonstall.org *Web Site:* www.saltonstall.org, pg 573

Arts & Letters Awards, 633 W 155 St, New York, NY 10032 *Tel:* 212-368-5900 *Fax:* 212-491-4615 *E-mail:* academy@artsandletters.org *Web Site:* artsandletters.org, pg 593

Arts Scholarships, 225 King St, Suite 201, Fredericton, NB E3B 1E1, Canada *Tel:* 506-444-4444 *Toll Free Tel:* 866-460-ARTS (460-2787) *Fax:* 506-444-5543 *Web Site:* www.artsnb.ca, pg 593

Artworks Illustration, PO Box 453, New York, NY 10156 *Tel:* 212-239-4946 *E-mail:* artworksillustration@earthlink.net *Web Site:* www.artworksillustration.com, pg 511

ArtWrite Productions, 1555 Gardena Ave NE, Minneapolis, MN 55432-5848 *Tel:* 612-803-0436 *E-mail:* artwriteprod@gmail.com *Web Site:* artwriteproductions.com; adaptedclassics.com, pg 21

ASCD, 1703 N Beauregard St, Alexandria, VA 22311-1714 *Tel:* 703-578-9600 *Toll Free Tel:* 800-933-2723 *Fax:* 703-575-5400 *E-mail:* member@ascd.org *Web Site:* www.ascd.org, pg 21

Ascend Books LLC, 7221 W 79 St, Suite 206, Overland Park, KS 66204 *Tel:* 913-948-5500 *Web Site:* www.ascendbooks.com, pg 21

Ascension Press, PO Box 1990, West Chester, PA 19380 *Tel:* 610-696-7795; 484-875-4550 (admin) *Toll Free Tel:* 800-376-0520 (sales & cust serv) *Web Site:* ascensionpress.com, pg 21

ASCP Press, 33 W Monroe St, Suite 1600, Chicago, IL 60603 *Tel:* 312-541-4999 *Toll Free Tel:* 800-267-2727 *Fax:* 312-541-4998 *Web Site:* www.ascp.org, pg 22

ASCSA Publications, 6-8 Charlton St, Princeton, NJ 08540-5232 *Tel:* 609-683-0800 *Fax:* 609-924-0578 *Web Site:* www.ascsa.edu.gr/publications, pg 22

ASET - The Neurodiagnostic Society, 402 E Bannister Rd, Suite A, Kansas City, MO 64131-3019 *Tel:* 816-931-1120 *Fax:* 816-931-1145 *E-mail:* info@aset.org *Web Site:* www.aset.org, pg 22

717

Ballinger Publishing, 314 N Spring St, Suite A, Pensacola, FL 32501 *Tel:* 850-433-1166 *Fax:* 850-435-9174 *E-mail:* info@ballingerpublishing.com *Web Site:* www.ballingerpublishing.com, pg 27

Carol Bancroft & Friends, PO Box 2030, Danbury, CT 06813 *Tel:* 203-730-8270 *Fax:* 203-730-8275 *E-mail:* cbfriends@sbcglobal.net; artists@carolbancroft.com *Web Site:* www.carolbancroft.com, pg 511

Bancroft Press, 3209 Bancroft Rd, Baltimore, MD 21215 *Tel:* 410-358-0658 *Web Site:* www.bancroftpress.com, pg 27

Bancroft Prizes, 517 Butler Library, Mail Code 1101, 535 W 114 St, New York, NY 10027 *Tel:* 212-854-4746 *Fax:* 212-854-9099 *Web Site:* www.columbia.edu/about/awards/bancroft.html, pg 595

Bandanna Books, 1212 Punta Gorda St, No 13, Santa Barbara, CA 93103 *E-mail:* bandanna@cox.net *Web Site:* www.bandannabooks.com; www.mudbornpress.us; www.betabooks.us; www.shakespeareplaybook.com; www.bookdoc.us; catandbirdiebooks.com, pg 27

B&H Publishing Group, One LifeWay Plaza, Nashville, TN 37234 *Toll Free Tel:* 800-251-3225 (retailers); 800-448-8032 (consumers); 800-458-2772 (churches) *Fax:* 615-251-3914 (consumers); 615-251-5933 (churches) *Toll Free Fax:* 800-296-4036 (retailers) *E-mail:* customerservice@lifeway.com; bhcustomerservice@lifeway.com; bhtradesales@lifeway.com *Web Site:* www.bhpublishinggroup.com, pg 27

Banner of Truth, 63 E Louther St, Carlisle, PA 17013 *Tel:* 717-249-5747 *Toll Free Tel:* 800-263-8085 (orders) *Fax:* 717-249-0604 *E-mail:* banneroftruth.org *Web Site:* www.banneroftruth.org, pg 27

A Richard Barber/Peter Berinstein & Associates, 60 E Eighth St, Suite 21-N, New York, NY 10003 *Tel:* 212-737-7266 *Fax:* 860-927-3942 *E-mail:* barberrich@aol.com, pg 475

Barbour Publishing Inc, 1810 Barbour Dr, Uhrichsville, OH 44683 *Tel:* 740-922-6045 *Fax:* 740-922-5948 *E-mail:* info@barbourbooks.com *Web Site:* www.barbourbooks.com, pg 27

Barcelona Publishers LLC, 10231 N Plano Rd, Dallas, TX 75238 *Tel:* 214-553-9785 *E-mail:* warehouse@barcelonapublishers.com *Web Site:* www.barcelonapublishers.com, pg 28

Bard Fiction Prize, Campus Rd, PO Box 5000, Annandale-on-Hudson, NY 12504-5000 *Tel:* 845-758-7087 *E-mail:* bfp@bard.edu *Web Site:* www.bard.edu/bfp, pg 595

Bard Society Fiction Writing Workshop, 3113 Crosby Lane, Jacksonville, FL 32216 *Tel:* 904-250-6045 *E-mail:* frankgrn@comcast.net, pg 573

Barefoot Books, 2067 Massachusetts Ave, 5th fl, Cambridge, MA 02140 *Tel:* 617-576-0660 *Toll Free Tel:* 866-215-1756 (cust serv); 866-417-2369 (orders) *Fax:* 617-576-0049 *E-mail:* help@barefootbooks.com *Web Site:* www.barefootbooks.com, pg 28

The Barnabas Agency, PO Box 3113, Corsicana, TX 75151-3113 *Tel:* 903-654-1319 *E-mail:* info@barnabasagency.com *Web Site:* www.barnabasagency.com, pg 515

Barnes & Noble Writers for Writers Award, 90 Broad St, Suite 2100, New York, NY 10004 *Tel:* 212-226-3586 *Fax:* 212-226-3963 *E-mail:* admin@pw.org *Web Site:* www.pw.org, pg 595

Kathleen Barnes, 238 W Fourth St, Suite 3-C, New York, NY 10014 *Tel:* 212-924-8084 *E-mail:* kbarnes@compasscommunications.org, pg 459

Barnhardt & Ashe Publishing Inc, 444 Brickell Ave, Suite 51, PMB 432, Miami, FL 33131 *Toll Free Tel:* 800-283-6360 (orders) *E-mail:* barnhardtashe@aol.com, pg 28

Baror International Inc, PO Box 868, Armonk, NY 10504-0868 *Tel:* 914-273-9199 *Fax:* 914-273-5058 *Web Site:* www.barorint.com, pg 475

Barranca Press, 17 Rockridge Rd, Mount Vernon, NY 10552 *Tel:* 347-820-2363 *E-mail:* editor@barrancapress.com *Web Site:* www.barrancapress.com, pg 28

Loretta Barrett Books Inc, 101 Fifth Ave, 11th fl, New York, NY 10003 *Tel:* 212-242-3420 *E-mail:* lbbagencymail@gmail.com *Web Site:* www.lorettabarrettbooks.com, pg 475

Barricade Books Inc, 2037 LeMoine Ave, Fort Lee, NJ 07024 *Tel:* 201-944-7600 *E-mail:* info@barricadebooks.com *Web Site:* www.barricadebooks.com, pg 28

Barringer Publishing, 770 Glendale Ave, Naples, FL 34110 *Tel:* 239-293-1289 *E-mail:* schlesadv@gmail.com *Web Site:* www.barringerpublishing.com, pg 28

Barrytown/Station Hill Press, 120 Station Hill Rd, Barrytown, NY 12507 *Tel:* 845-758-5293 *E-mail:* publishers@stationhill.org *Web Site:* www.stationhill.org, pg 28

Diana Barth, 535 W 51 St, Suite 3-A, New York, NY 10019 *Tel:* 212-307-5465 *E-mail:* diabarth@juno.com, pg 459

Anita Bartholomew, 16650 SE Sunridge Lane, Portland, OR 97267 *Tel:* 774-264-8205 *E-mail:* anita@anitabartholomew.com *Web Site:* www.anitabartholomew.com, pg 459

Bartleby Press, 8926 Baltimore St, No 858, Savage, MD 20763 *Tel:* 301-589-5831 *Toll Free Tel:* 800-953-9929 *E-mail:* inquiries@bartlebythepublisher.com *Web Site:* www.bartlebythepublisher.com, pg 28

Basic Health Publications, 4507 Charlotte Ave, Suite 100, Nashville, TN 37209 *Tel:* 615-255-2665 *E-mail:* marketing@turnerpublishing.com, pg 28

Baskerville Publishers Poetry Award, Dept of English, TCU Box 298300, Fort Worth, TX 76129 *Tel:* 817-257-5907 *Fax:* 817-257-5905 *E-mail:* descant@tcu.edu *Web Site:* www.descant.tcu.edu, pg 595

The Mildred L Batchelder Award, 50 E Huron St, Chicago, IL 60611-2795 *Tel:* 312-280-2163 *Toll Free Tel:* 800-545-2433 *Fax:* 312-440-9374; 312-280-5271 *E-mail:* alsc@ala.org *Web Site:* www.ala.org/alsc, pg 596

Mark E Battersby, PO Box 527, Ardmore, PA 19003-0527 *Tel:* 610-924-9157 *Fax:* 610-924-9159 *E-mail:* mebatt12@earthlink.net *Web Site:* www.thetaxscribe.com, pg 459

Bay Tree Publishing LLC, 225 E Richmond Ave, Point Richmond, CA 94801 *Tel:* 510-619-6338 *Web Site:* www.baytreepublish.com, pg 28

Bayeux Arts Inc, 2403, 510-Sixth Ave SE, Calgary, AB T2G 1L7, Canada *E-mail:* mail@bayeux.com *Web Site:* bayeux.com, pg 416

Baylor University Press, Baylor University, One Bear Place, Waco, TX 76798-7363 *Tel:* 254-710-3164 *Web Site:* www.baylorpress.com, pg 29

Baylor University, Professional Writing Program, One Bear Place, Unit 97404, Waco, TX 76798-7404 *Tel:* 254-710-1768 *Fax:* 254-710-3894 *Web Site:* www.baylor.edu, pg 581

The BC Book Prizes, 207 W Hastings St, Suite 901, Vancouver, BC V6B 1H7, Canada *Fax:* 604-687-2435 *E-mail:* info@bcbookprizes.ca *Web Site:* www.bcbookprizes.ca, pg 596

BCHF Historial Writing Competition, PO Box 448, Fort Langley, BC V1M 2R7, Canada *E-mail:* info@bchistory.ca *Web Site:* www.bchistory.ca/awards/historical-writing, pg 596

Beach Lloyd Publishers LLC, 231 Sunnyside Rd, West Grove, PA 19390 *Tel:* 215-407-4570 (cell) *E-mail:* beachlloyd@erols.com *Web Site:* beachlloyd.com, pg 29

Beacon Hill Press of Kansas City, PO Box 419527, Kansas City, MO 64141 *Tel:* 816-931-1900 *Toll Free Tel:* 800-877-0700 (cust serv) *Fax:* 816-531-0923 *Toll Free Fax:* 800-849-9827 *E-mail:* orders@

thefoundrypublishing.com; customercare@thefoundrypublishing.com *Web Site:* www.thefoundrypublishing.com, pg 29

Beacon Press, 24 Farnsworth St, Boston, MA 02210-1409 *Tel:* 617-742-2110 *Fax:* 617-723-3097; 617-742-2290 *Web Site:* www.beacon.org, pg 29

Bear & Bobcat Books, 5212 Venice Blvd, Los Angeles, CA 90019 *Toll Free Tel:* 866-918-6173 *Fax:* 858-369-5201 *E-mail:* info@hameraypublishing.com (cust serv); sales@hameraypublishing.com (sales) *Web Site:* www.bearandbobcat.com, pg 29

Bear & Co Inc, One Park St, Rochester, VT 05767 *Tel:* 802-767-3174 *Toll Free Tel:* 800-932-3277 *Fax:* 802-767-3726 *E-mail:* customerservice@InnerTraditions.com *Web Site:* InnerTraditions.com, pg 29

James Beard Foundation Book Awards, Office of Awards, 6 W 18 St, 10th fl, New York, NY 10011 *Tel:* 212-627-1111 (ext 563) *Web Site:* www.jamesbeard.org/awards, pg 596

BearManor Media, PO Box 71426, Albany, GA 31708 *Tel:* 580-252-3547 *E-mail:* orders@benohmart.com; books@benohmart.com *Web Site:* www.bearmanormedia.com, pg 30

Bearport Publishing Co Inc, 45 W 21 St, Suite 3B, New York, NY 10010 *Tel:* 212-337-8577 *Toll Free Tel:* 877-337-8577 *Fax:* 212-337-8557 *Toll Free Fax:* 866-337-8557 *E-mail:* service@bearportpublishing; info@bearportpublishing.com *Web Site:* www.bearportpublishing.com, pg 30

Beaver Wood Associates, 655 Alstead Center Rd, Alstead, NH 03602 *Tel:* 603-835-7900 *Web Site:* www.beaverwood.com, pg 459

Beaver's Pond Press Inc, 939 Seventh St W, St Paul, MN 55102 *Tel:* 952-829-8818 *E-mail:* info@beaverspondpress.com *Web Site:* www.beaverspondpress.com, pg 30

Bedford/St Martin's, One New York Plaza, 46th fl, New York, NY 10004 *Tel:* 212-576-9400; 212-375-7000 *E-mail:* press.inquiries@macmillan.com *Web Site:* www.macmillanlearning.com/college/us, pg 30

Beehive Books, 4700 Kingsessing Ave, Suite C, Philadelphia, PA 19143 *E-mail:* beehivebook@gmail.com *Web Site:* www.beehivebooks.net, pg 30

Beekman Books Inc, 300 Old All Angels Hill Rd, Wappingers Falls, NY 12590 *Tel:* 845-297-2690 *E-mail:* beekmanbooks@yahoo.com *Web Site:* www.beekmanbooks.com, pg 30

George Louis Beer Prize, 400 "A" St SE, Washington, DC 20003 *Tel:* 202-544-2422 *Fax:* 202-544-8307 *E-mail:* awards@historians.org *Web Site:* www.historians.org, pg 596

Before Columbus Foundation, The Raymond House, 655 13 St, Suite 302, Oakland, CA 94612 *Tel:* 916-425-7916 *E-mail:* beforecolumbusfoundation@gmail.com *Web Site:* www.beforecolumbusfoundation.com, pg 528

Begell House Inc Publishers, 50 North St, Danbury, CT 06810 *Tel:* 203-456-6161 *Fax:* 203-456-6167 *E-mail:* orders@begellhouse.com *Web Site:* www.begellhouse.com, pg 30

Behrman House Inc, 11 Edison Place, Springfield, NJ 07081 *Tel:* 973-379-7200 *Toll Free Tel:* 800-221-2755 *Fax:* 973-379-7280 *E-mail:* customersupport@behrmanhouse.com *Web Site:* store.behrmanhouse.com, pg 30

Frederic C Beil Publisher Inc, 609 Whitaker St, Savannah, GA 31401 *Tel:* 912-233-2446 *E-mail:* fcb@beil.com *Web Site:* www.beil.com, pg 31

Beliveau Editeur, 567 rue Bienville, Boucherville, QC J4B 2Z5, Canada *Tel:* 450-679-1933 *Web Site:* www.beliveauediteur.com, pg 416

Bell Springs Publishing, PO Box 1240, Willits, CA 95490-1240 *Tel:* 707-272-3472 *E-mail:* publisher@bellsprings.com *Web Site:* bellsprings.com; aboutpinball.com, pg 31

Bella Books, PO Box 10543, Tallahassee, FL 32302 *Tel:* 850-576-2370 *Toll Free Tel:* 800-729-4992 *Fax:* 850-576-3498 *E-mail:* info@bellabooks.com; orders@bellabooks.com; ebooks@bellabooks.com *Web Site:* www.bellabooks.com, pg 31

BelleBooks, PO Box 300921, Memphis, TN 38130 *Tel:* 901-344-9024 *Fax:* 901-344-9068 *E-mail:* bellebooks@bellebooks.com *Web Site:* www.bellebooks.com, pg 31

Bellerophon Books, PO Box 21307, Santa Barbara, CA 93121-1307 *Tel:* 805-965-7034 *Toll Free Tel:* 800-253-9943 *Fax:* 805-965-8286 *e-mail:* sales.bellerophon@gmail.com *Web Site:* www.bellerophonbooks.com, pg 31

Bellevue Literary Press, 90 Broad St, Suite 2100, New York, NY 10004 *Tel:* 917-732-3603 *Web Site:* blpress.org, pg 31

The Pura Belpre Award, 50 E Huron St, Chicago, IL 60611-2795 *Tel:* 312-280-2163 *Toll Free Tel:* 800-545-2433 *Fax:* 312-440-9374; 312-280-5271 *E-mail:* alsc@ala.org *Web Site:* www.ala.org/alsc, pg 596

Ben Yehuda Press, 122 Ayers Ct, No 1B, Teaneck, NJ 07666 *E-mail:* orders@benyehudapress.com; yudel@benyehudapress.com *Web Site:* www.benyehudapress.com, pg 31

BenBella Books Inc, 10300 N Central Expwy, Suite 400, Dallas, TX 75231 *Tel:* 214-750-3600 *E-mail:* feedback@benbellabooks.com *Web Site:* www.benbellabooks.com; www.smartpopbooks.com, pg 31

R James Bender Publishing, PO Box 23456, San Jose, CA 95153-3456 *Tel:* 408-225-5777 *Fax:* 408-225-4739 *Web Site:* www.bender-publishing.com, pg 31

Benjamin Franklin Awards™, 1020 Manhattan Beach Blvd, Suite 204, Manhattan Beach, CA 90266 *Tel:* 310-546-1818 *E-mail:* info@ibpa-online.org *Web Site:* www.ibpa-online.org; ibpabenjaminfranklinawards.com, pg 596

John Benjamins Publishing Co, 10 Meadowbrook Rd, Brunswick, ME 04011 *Toll Free Tel:* 800-562-5666 (orders) *Web Site:* www.benjamins.com, pg 31

George Bennett Fellowship, Phillips Exeter Academy, Off of the Dean of Faculty, 20 Main St, Exeter, NH 03833-2460 *Tel:* 603-777-3645 *Fax:* 603-777-4384 *E-mail:* communications@exeter.edu *Web Site:* www.exeter.edu, pg 596

Benoit & Associates, 744 Stockton Heights Ct, Bourbonnais, IL 60914 *Tel:* 815-932-2582 *Fax:* 815-932-2594 *Web Site:* www.benoit-associates.com, pg 511

Bentley Publishers, 1734 Massachusetts Ave, Cambridge, MA 02138-1804 *Tel:* 617-547-4170 *Toll Free Tel:* 800-423-4595 *Fax:* 617-876-9235 *E-mail:* sales@bentleypublishers.com *Web Site:* www.bentleypublishers.com, pg 32

BePuzzled, 2030 Harrison St, San Francisco, CA 94110 *Tel:* 415-503-1600 *Toll Free Tel:* 800-347-4818 *Fax:* 415-503-0085 *E-mail:* info@ugames.com *Web Site:* www.ugames.com, pg 32

Naomi Berber Memorial Award, 10015 Main St, Fairfax, VA 22031-3489 *Tel:* 703-385-1335 *Toll Free Tel:* 888-385-3588 *Fax:* 703-273-0456 *E-mail:* assist@printing.org; info@printing.org *Web Site:* www.printing.org/programs/awards/naomi-berber-memorial-award, pg 596

Berghahn Books, 20 Jay St, Suite 512, Brooklyn, NY 11201 *Tel:* 212-233-6004 *Fax:* 212-233-6007 *E-mail:* info@berghahnbooks.com; salesus@berghahnbooks.com; editorial@journals.berghahnbooks.com *Web Site:* www.berghahnbooks.com, pg 32

Barbara Bergstrom MA LLC, 13 Stockton Way, Howell, NJ 07731 *Tel:* 732-363-8372, pg 459

Berkley Publishing Group, 1745 Broadway, 19th fl, New York, NY 10019 *Tel:* 212-366-2000 *Web Site:* www.penguin.com, pg 32

Berkshire Publishing Group LLC, PO Box 177, Great Barrington, MA 01230 *E-mail:* info@berkshirepublishing.com *Web Site:* www.berkshirepublishing.com, pg 32

Bernan, 4501 Forbes Blvd, Suite 200, Lanham, MD 20706 *Tel:* 717-794-3800 (cust serv & orders) *Toll Free Tel:* 800-462-6420 (cust serv & orders) *Fax:* 717-794-3803 *Toll Free Fax:* 800-338-4550 *E-mail:* customercare@bernan.com *Web Site:* rowman.com/page/bernan, pg 32

Jessie Bernard Award, c/o Governance Off, 1430 "K" St NW, Suite 600, Washington, DC 20005 *Tel:* 202-383-9005 *Fax:* 202-638-0882 *E-mail:* governance@asanet.org *Web Site:* www.asanet.org, pg 597

The Charles Bernheimer Prize, University of South Carolina, Dept of Languages, Literature & Cultures, 1620 College St, Rm 817, Columbia, SC 29208 *Tel:* 803-777-3021 *E-mail:* info@acla.org *Web Site:* www.acla.org/prize-awards/charles-bernheimer-prize, pg 597

Bernstein & Andriulli Inc, 190 Bowery, 3rd fl, New York, NY 10012 *Tel:* 212-682-1490 *Fax:* 212-286-1890 *E-mail:* info@ba-reps.com *Web Site:* www.ba-reps.com, pg 511

Meredith Bernstein Literary Agency Inc, 2095 Broadway, Suite 505, New York, NY 10023 *Tel:* 212-799-1007 *Fax:* 212-799-1145 *E-mail:* MGoodBern@aol.com *Web Site:* www.meredithbernsteinliteraryagency.com, pg 475

Berrett-Koehler Publishers Inc, 1333 Broadway, Suite 1000, Oakland, CA 94612 *Tel:* 510-817-2277 *Fax:* 510-817-2278 *E-mail:* bkpub@bkpub.com *Web Site:* www.bkconnection.com, pg 32

Bess Press, 3565 Harding Ave, Honolulu, HI 96816 *Tel:* 808-734-7159 *Fax:* 808-732-3627 *E-mail:* customerservice@besspress.com *Web Site:* www.besspress.com, pg 32

A M Best Co, One Ambest Rd, Oldwick, NJ 08858 *Tel:* 908-439-2200 (ext 5311, sales); 908-439-2200 *E-mail:* customer_service@ambest.com; sales@ambest.com *Web Site:* www.ambest.com, pg 33

Best Translated Book Award, c/o Open Letter, University of Rochester, Dewey Hall 1-219, Box 278968, Rochester, NY 14627 *Tel:* 585-276-5305 *E-mail:* msc@rochester.edu *Web Site:* besttranslatedbook.org, pg 597

Best Workplace in the Americas (MWA), 10015 Main St, Fairfax, VA 22031-3489 *Tel:* 703-385-1335 *Toll Free Tel:* 888-385-3588 *Fax:* 703-273-0456 *E-mail:* assist@printing.org; info@printing.org *Web Site:* www.printing.org/programs/awards/best-workplace-in-the-americas, pg 597

Bethany House Publishers, 11400 Hampshire Ave S, Bloomington, MN 55438 *Tel:* 952-829-2500 *Toll Free Tel:* 800-877-2665 (orders) *Fax:* 952-829-2568 *Toll Free Fax:* 800-398-3111 (orders) *Web Site:* www.bethanyhouse.com; www.bakerpublishinggroup.com, pg 33

The Bethel Agency, PO Box 21043, Park West Sta, New York, NY 10025 *Tel:* 212-864-4510 *E-mail:* bethelagcy@aol.com, pg 475

Bethlehem Books, 10194 Garfield St S, Bathgate, ND 58216 *Toll Free Tel:* 800-757-6831 *Fax:* 701-265-3716 *E-mail:* contact@bethlehembooks.com *Web Site:* bethlehembooks.com, pg 33

Betterway Books, 1745 Broadway, New York, NY 10019 *Tel:* 212-782-9000 *Web Site:* www.penguinrandomhouse.com, pg 33

Doris Betts Fiction Prize, PO Box 21591, Winston-Salem, NC 27120-1591 *Tel:* 336-293-8844 *E-mail:* mail@ncwriters.org; nclrsubmissions@ecu.edu *Web Site:* www.ncwriters.org, pg 597

Between the Lines, 401 Richmond St W, No 277, Toronto, ON M5V 3A8, Canada *Tel:* 416-535-9914 *Toll Free Tel:* 800-718-7201 *Fax:* 416-535-1484 *E-mail:* info@btlbooks.com *Web Site:* btlbooks.com, pg 416

Beullah Rose Poetry Prize, PO Box 22161, Baltimore, MD 21203 *E-mail:* smartishpace@gmail.com *Web Site:* www.smartishpace.com, pg 597

Albert J Beveridge Award in American History, 400 "A" St SE, Washington, DC 20003 *Tel:* 202-544-2422 *Fax:* 202-544-8307 *E-mail:* awards@historians.org *Web Site:* www.historians.org, pg 597

Albert J Beveridge Grant for Research in the History of the Western Hemisphere, 400 "A" St SE, Washington, DC 20003 *Tel:* 202-544-2422 *Fax:* 202-544-8307 *E-mail:* awards@historians.org *Web Site:* www.historians.org, pg 597

Beyond the Book, 222 Rosewood Dr, Danvers, MA 01923 *Tel:* 978-750-8400 (sales) *E-mail:* beyondthebook@copyright.com *Web Site:* www.copyright.com; beyondthebookcast.com, pg 573

Bhaktivedanta Book Trust (BBT), 9701 Venice Blvd, Suite 3, Los Angeles, CA 90034 *Tel:* 310-837-5283 *Toll Free Tel:* 800-927-4152 *Fax:* 310-837-1056 *E-mail:* store@krishna.com *Web Site:* www.krishna.com, pg 33

BHTG - Julie Harris Playwright Award Competition, PO Box 148, Beverly Hills, CA 90213 *Tel:* 310-273-3390 *Web Site:* www.beverlyhillstheatreguild.com, pg 597

BHTG - Michael J Libow Youth Theatre Award, PO Box 148, Beverly Hills, CA 90213 *Tel:* 310-273-3390 *Web Site:* www.beverlyhillstheatreguild.com, pg 598

Biblio Award, PO Box 33020, Santa Fe, NM 87594 *Web Site:* biographersinternational.org, pg 598

BiblioGenesis, 152 Coddington Rd, Ithaca, NY 14850 *Tel:* 607-277-9660 *Web Site:* www.bibliogenesis.com, pg 459

Bibliographical Society of America, PO Box 1537, Lenox Hill Sta, New York, NY 10021-0043 *Tel:* 212-734-2500 *Fax:* 212-452-2710 *E-mail:* bsa@bibsocamer.org *Web Site:* www.bibsocamer.org, pg 528

Bibliographical Society of the University of Virginia, c/o Alderman Library, University of Virginia, McCormick Rd, Charlottesville, VA 22904 *Tel:* 434-924-7013 *Fax:* 434-924-1431 *E-mail:* bibsoc@virginia.edu *Web Site:* bsuva.org, pg 528

Bick Publishing House, 75 Mungertown Rd, Madison, CT 06443 *Tel:* 203-245-0341 *Fax:* 203-208-5253 *E-mail:* bickpubhse@aol.com *Web Site:* www.bickpubhouse.com, pg 33

Big Apple Conference, 5 Penn Plaza, 19th fl, PMB 19059, New York, NY 10001 *Tel:* 917-720-6959 *E-mail:* iwwgquestions@iwwg.org *Web Site:* www.iwwg.org, pg 573

Big Guy Books, 6866 Embarcadero Lane, Carlsbad, CA 92011 *Tel:* 760-652-5360 *Toll Free Tel:* 800-536-3030 (booksellers' cust serv) *Fax:* 760-652-5361 *E-mail:* info@bigguybooks.com *Web Site:* www.bigguybooks.com, pg 33

Vicky Bijur Literary Agency, 27 W 20 St, Suite 1003, New York, NY 10011 *Tel:* 212-580-4108 *E-mail:* queries@vickybijuragency.com *Web Site:* www.vickybijuragency.com, pg 475

Ray Allen Billington Prize, 112 N Bryan Ave, Bloomington, IN 47408-4141 *Tel:* 812-855-7311 *E-mail:* oah@oah.org *Web Site:* www.oah.org/awards, pg 598

The Geoffrey Bilson Award for Historical Fiction for Young People, 40 Orchard View Blvd, Suite 217, Toronto, ON M4R 1B9, Canada *Tel:* 416-975-0010 *Fax:* 416-975-8970 *E-mail:* info@bookcentre.ca *Web Site:* www.bookcentre.ca, pg 598

Binding Industries Association (BIA), 301 Brush Creek Rd, Warrendale, PA 15086-7529 *Tel:* 412-741-6860 *Toll Free Tel:* 800-910-4283 *Fax:* 412-741-2311 *Web Site:* www.printing.org/bia, pg 528

Binghamton University Creative Writing Program, c/o Dept of English, PO Box 6000, Binghamton, NY 13902-6000 *Tel:* 607-777-2168 *Fax:* 607-777-2408 *E-mail:* cwpro@binghamton.edu *Web Site:* english.binghamton.edu/cwpro, pg 581

George Bogin Memorial Award, 15 Gramercy Park, New York, NY 10003 *Tel:* 212-254-9628 *Web Site:* poetrysociety.org/awards, pg 599

Bogle International Library Travel Fund, 50 E Huron St, Chicago, IL 60611-2795 *Tel:* 312-280-3201 *Toll Free Tel:* 800-545-2433 (ext 3201) *Fax:* 312-280-4392 *E-mail:* intl@ala.org *Web Site:* www.ala.org, pg 599

Editions du Bois-de-Coulonge, 1140 Ave de Montigny, Sillery, QC G1S 3T7, Canada *Tel:* 418-683-6332 *Web Site:* www.ebc.qc.ca, pg 416

Bolchazy-Carducci Publishers Inc, 1570 Baskin Rd, Mundelein, IL 60060 *Tel:* 847-526-4344 *Fax:* 847-526-2867 *E-mail:* info@bolchazy.com; orders@bolchazy.com *Web Site:* www.bolchazy.com, pg 37

Bold Strokes Books Inc, 648 S Cambridge Rd, Bldg A, Johnsonville, NY 12094 *Tel:* 518-677-5127 *E-mail:* service@boldstrokesbooks.com *Web Site:* www.boldstrokesbooks.com, pg 37

Laura Day Boggs Bolling Memorial, 900 Timber Creek Place, Virginia Beach, VA 23464 *E-mail:* poetryinva@aol.com *Web Site:* poetrysocietyofvirginia.org, pg 599

Bollingen Prize in American Poetry, 121 Wall St, New Haven, CT 06511 *Tel:* 203-432-2977 *Fax:* 203-432-4047 *E-mail:* beinecke.library@yale.edu *Web Site:* beinecke.library.yale.edu, pg 600

Alison Bond Literary Agency, 171 W 79 St, No 143, New York, NY 10024, pg 476

Bond Literary Agency, 201 Milwaukee St, Suite 200, Denver, CO 80206 *Tel:* 303-781-9305 *E-mail:* queries@bondliteraryagency.com *Web Site:* bondliteraryagency.com, pg 476

Book & Periodical Council (BPC), 192 Spadina Ave, Suite 107, Toronto, ON M5T 2C2, Canada *Tel:* 416-975-9366 *Fax:* 416-975-1839 *E-mail:* info@thebpc.ca *Web Site:* www.thebpc.ca, pg 528

Book Industry Guild of New York, PO Box 2001, New York, NY 10113-2001 *E-mail:* admin@bookindustryguildofny.org *Web Site:* bigny.org, pg 528

Book Industry Study Group Inc (BISG), 1412 Broadway, Suite 2119, New York, NY 10018 *Tel:* 646-336-7141 *E-mail:* info@bisg.org *Web Site:* bisg.org, pg 528

Book Manufacturers' Institute Inc (BMI), PO Box 731388, Ormond Beach, FL 32173 *Tel:* 386-986-4552 *Fax:* 386-986-4553 *E-mail:* info@bmibook.com *Web Site:* www.bmibook.org, pg 528

Book Marketing Works LLC, 50 Lovely St (Rte 177), Avon, CT 06001 *Tel:* 860-675-1344 *Web Site:* www.bookmarketingworks.com, pg 37

Book of the Year Award, 600 Maryland Ave SW, Suite 1000W, Washington, DC 20024 *Toll Free Tel:* 800-443-8456 *Fax:* 202-314-5121 *E-mail:* foundation@fb.org *Web Site:* www.agfoundation.org/projects/book-of-the-year-award, pg 600

Book of the Year Awards, 2667 Hyacinth St, Westbury, NY 11590 *Tel:* 516-333-0681 *Fax:* 516-333-0689 *E-mail:* naibabooksellers@gmail.com *Web Site:* www.naiba.com/page/BooksoftheYear, pg 600

Book Peddlers, 18925 Lake Ave, Deephaven, MN 55391 *Tel:* 952-544-1154 *Web Site:* www.bookpeddlers.com, pg 38

Book Publicists of Southern California, 714 Crescent Dr, Beverly Hills, CA 90210 *Tel:* 323-461-3921 *Fax:* 323-461-0917 *Web Site:* www.bookpublicists.com, pg 528

The Book Publishers Association of Alberta (BPAA), 10523 100 Ave, Edmonton, AB T5J 0A8, Canada *Tel:* 780-424-5060 *E-mail:* info@bookpublishers.ab.ca *Web Site:* www.bookpublishers.ab.ca, pg 529

Book Sales, 142 W 36 St, 4th fl, New York, NY 10018 *Tel:* 212-779-4972; 212-779-4971 *Fax:* 212-779-6058 *Web Site:* www.quartoknows.com, pg 38

The Book Tree, 3316 Adams Ave, Suite A, San Diego, CA 92116 *Tel:* 619-280-1263 *Toll Free Tel:* 800-700-8733 (orders) *Fax:* 619-280-1285 *E-mail:* orders@thebooktree.com; info@thebooktree.com *Web Site:* thebooktree.com, pg 38

Bookbuilders of Boston, 115 Webster Woods Lane, North Andover, MA 01845 *Tel:* 781-378-1361 *Fax:* 419-821-2171 *E-mail:* office@bbboston.org *Web Site:* www.bbboston.org, pg 529

BookCrafters LLC, Box C, Convent Station, NJ 07961 *Web Site:* bookcraftersllc.com, pg 459

BookEnds Literary Agency, 136 Long Hill Rd, Gillette, NJ 07933 *Web Site:* www.bookendsliterary.com, pg 476

Bookhaven Press LLC, 302 Scenic Ct, Moon Township, PA 15108 *Tel:* 412-494-6926 *E-mail:* info@bookhavenpress.com; orders@bookhavenpress.com *Web Site:* bookhavenpress.com, pg 38

BookLogix, 1264 Old Alpharetta Rd, Alpharetta, GA 30005 *Tel:* 470-239-8547 *Toll Free Fax:* 888-564-7890 *E-mail:* publishing@booklogix.com *Web Site:* www.booklogix.com, pg 38

The Bookmill, 501 Palisades Dr, No 315, Pacific Palisades, CA 90272-2848 *Tel:* 310-459-0190 *E-mail:* thebookmill1@verizon.net *Web Site:* www.thebookmill.us, pg 459

Books & Such, 52 Mission Circle, Suite 122, PMB 170, Santa Rosa, CA 95409-5370 *Tel:* 707-538-4184 *Web Site:* booksandsuch.com, pg 476

Books In Motion, 9922 E Montgomery, Suite 31, Spokane Valley, WA 99206 *Tel:* 509-922-1646 *Toll Free Tel:* 800-752-3199 *Fax:* 509-922-1445 *E-mail:* info@booksinmotion.com *Web Site:* www.booksinmotion.com, pg 38

Books on Tape™, 1745 Broadway, New York, NY 10019 *Toll Free Tel:* 800-733-3000 (cust serv) *Toll Free Fax:* 800-940-7046 *Web Site:* www.booksontape.com, pg 38

BookStop Literary Agency LLC, 67 Meadow View Rd, Orinda, CA 94563 *E-mail:* info@bookstopliterary.com *Web Site:* www.bookstopliterary.com, pg 477

Boom! Studios, 5670 Wilshire Blvd, Suite 400, Los Angeles, CA 90036 *Web Site:* www.boom-studios.com, pg 38

Georges Borchardt Inc, 136 E 57 St, New York, NY 10022 *Tel:* 212-753-5785 *E-mail:* georges@gbagency.com *Web Site:* www.gbagency.com, pg 477

Borealis Press Ltd, 8 Mohawk Crescent, Nepean, ON K2H 7G6, Canada *Tel:* 613-829-0150 *Toll Free Tel:* 877-696-2585 *Fax:* 613-829-7783 *E-mail:* drt@borealispress.com *Web Site:* www.borealispress.com, pg 417

Boson Books™, 1262 Sunnyoaks Circle, Altadena, CA 91001 *Tel:* 626-507-8033 *Fax:* 626-818-1842 *Web Site:* bitingduckpress.com, pg 38

Boston Authors Club Inc, 2400 Beacon St, No 208, Chestnut, MA 02467 *Tel:* 617-552-4031 *E-mail:* bostonauthorsclub@gmail.com *Web Site:* bostonauthorsclub.org, pg 529

Boston Globe-Horn Book Award, c/o Book Reviews, The Horn Book Inc, Palace Road Bldg, 300 The Fenway, Suite P-311, Boston, MA 02115-5820 *Tel:* 617-278-0225 *Toll Free Tel:* 888-628-0225 *Fax:* 617-278-6062 *E-mail:* info@hbook.com *Web Site:* www.hbook.com, pg 600

Boston Informatics, 35 Byard Lane, Westborough, MA 01581 *Tel:* 508-366-8176 *Web Site:* bostoninformatics.com, pg 459

The Boston Mills Press, 50 Staples Ave, Unit 1, Richmond Hill, ON L4B 0A7, Canada *Tel:* 416-499-8412 *Toll Free Tel:* 800-387-6192 *Fax:* 416-499-8313 *Toll Free Fax:* 800-450-0391 *E-mail:* service@fireflybooks.com *Web Site:* www.fireflybooks.com, pg 417

Boston Road Communications, 227 Boston Rd, Groton, MA 01450-1959 *Tel:* 978-448-8133, pg 459

Boston University Creative Writing Program, 236 Bay State Rd, Boston, MA 02215 *Tel:* 617-353-2510 *Fax:* 617-353-3653 *E-mail:* crwr@bu.edu *Web Site:* www.bu.edu/creativewriting, pg 581

Bottom Dog Press, 813 Seneca Ave, Huron, OH 44839 *Tel:* 419-602-1556 *Fax:* 419-616-3966 *Web Site:* smithdocs.net, pg 39

Boulevard Magazine Short Fiction Contest for Emerging Writers, 6614 Clayton Rd, PMB 325, Richmond Heights, MO 63117 *E-mail:* editors@boulevardmagazine.org *Web Site:* www.boulevardmagazine.org, pg 600

Bound to Stay Bound Books Scholarship, 50 E Huron St, Chicago, IL 60611-2795 *Tel:* 312-280-2163 *Toll Free Tel:* 800-545-2433 *Fax:* 312-440-9374; 312-280-5271 *E-mail:* alsc@ala.org *Web Site:* www.ala.org/alsc, pg 600

R R Bowker LLC, 789 E Eisenhower Pkwy, Ann Arbor, MI 48106 *Tel:* 908-286-1090 *Toll Free Tel:* 888-269-5372 (edit & cust serv, press 2 for returns) *Fax:* 908-219-0098; (020) 7832 1710 (UK for intl) *Toll Free Fax:* 877-337-7015 (US & CN) *E-mail:* orders@proquest.com (domestic orders); isbn-san@bowker.com *Web Site:* www.bowker.com, pg 39

Bowling Green State University Creative Writing Program, Dept of English, 409 East Hall, Bowling Green, OH 43403 *Tel:* 419-372-2576 *Fax:* 419-372-0333 *Web Site:* www.bgsu.edu/departments/creative-writing, pg 581

Boydell & Brewer Inc, 668 Mount Hope Ave, Rochester, NY 14620-2731 *Tel:* 585-275-0419 *Fax:* 585-271-8778 *E-mail:* boydell@boydellusa.net *Web Site:* www.boydellandbrewer.com, pg 39

Boyds Mills & Kane, 250 Park Ave, 7th fl, New York, NY 10177 *E-mail:* info@bmkbooks.com *Web Site:* www.boydsmillsandkane.com, pg 39

Boys Town Press, 13603 Flanagan Blvd, 2nd fl, Boys Town, NE 68010 *Tel:* 531-355-1320 *Toll Free Tel:* 800-282-6657 *Fax:* 531-355-1310 *E-mail:* btpress@boystown.org *Web Site:* www.boystownpress.org, pg 39

BPA Worldwide, 100 Beard Sawmill Rd, 6th fl, Shelton, CT 06484 *Tel:* 203-447-2800 *Fax:* 203-447-2900 *E-mail:* info@bpaww.com *Web Site:* www.bpaww.com, pg 529

BPC, 415 Farm Rd, Summertown, TN 38483 *Tel:* 931-964-3571 *Toll Free Tel:* 888-260-8458 *Fax:* 931-964-3518 *E-mail:* info@bookpubco.com *Web Site:* www.bookpubco.com, pg 39

BPS Books, 47 Anderson Ave, Toronto, ON M5P 1H6, Canada *Tel:* 416-609-2004 *Web Site:* www.bpsbooks.com, pg 417

Bradford Literary Agency, 5694 Mission Center Rd, Suite 347, San Diego, CA 92108 *Tel:* 619-521-1201 *E-mail:* queries@bradfordlit.com *Web Site:* www.bradfordlit.com, pg 477

Barbara Bradley Prize, 46 Wallace St, Somerville, MA 02144 *E-mail:* info@nepoetryclub.org *Web Site:* www.nepoetryclub.org, pg 600

Brady Literary Management, PO Box 64, Hartland Four Corners, VT 05049 *Tel:* 802-436-2455, pg 459

BrainStorm Poetry Contest for Mental Health Consumers, 36 Elgin St, 2nd fl, Sudbury, ON P3C 5B4, Canada *Tel:* 705-222-6472 (ext 303) *E-mail:* openminds@nisa.on.ca *Web Site:* www.openmindsquarterly.com, pg 600

Brandt & Hochman Literary Agents Inc, 1501 Broadway, Suite 2310, New York, NY 10036 *Tel:* 212-840-5760 *Fax:* 212-840-5776 *Web Site:* brandthochman.com, pg 477

The Joan Brandt Agency, 788 Wesley Dr NW, Atlanta, GA 30305 *Tel:* 404-351-8877 *Fax:* 404-351-0068, pg 477

Brandylane Publishers Inc, 5 S First St, Richmond, VA 23219 *Tel:* 804-644-3090 *Fax:* 804-644-3092 *Web Site:* brandylanepublishers.com, pg 39

Michael Braude Award, 633 W 155 St, New York, NY 10032 *Tel:* 212-368-5900 *Fax:* 212-491-4615 *E-mail:* academy@artsandletters.org *Web Site:* artsandletters.org, pg 600

Brault & Bouthillier, 700 ave Beaumont, Montreal, QC H3N 1V5, Canada *Tel:* 514-273-9186 *Toll Free Tel:* 800-361-0378 *Fax:* 514-273-8627 *Toll Free Fax:* 800-361-0378 *E-mail:* ventes@bb.ca *Web Site:* bb.ca, pg 417

Barbara Braun Associates Inc, 7 E 14 St, Suite 19F, New York, NY 10003 *Tel:* 917-414-3022 *Web Site:* www. barbarabraunagency.com, pg 478

George Braziller Inc, 277 Broadway, Suite 708, New York, NY 10007 *Tel:* 212-260-9256 *Fax:* 212-267-3165 *E-mail:* submissions@georgebraziller.com *Web Site:* www.georgebraziller.com, pg 40

Bread Loaf Writers' Conference, 5525 Middlebury College, 14 Old Chapel Rd, Middlebury, VT 05753 *Tel:* 802-443-5286 *Fax:* 802-443-2087 *E-mail:* blwc@ middlebury.edu *Web Site:* www.middlebury.edu/blwc, pg 573

Breakaway Books, PO Box 24, Halcottsville, NY 12438-0024 *Tel:* 607-326-4805 *E-mail:* breakawaybooks@ gmail.com *Web Site:* www.breakawaybooks.com, pg 40

Breakthrough Publications Inc, 3 Iroquois St, Barn, Emmaus, PA 18049 *Toll Free Tel:* 800-824-5001 (ext 12) *Fax:* 610-928-4064 *E-mail:* dot@booksonhorses. com; ruth@booksonhorses.com *Web Site:* www. booksonhorses.com, pg 40

Breakwater Books Ltd, One Stamp's Lane, St John's, NL A1C 6E6, Canada *Tel:* 709-722-6680 *Toll Free Tel:* 800-563-3333 (orders) *Fax:* 709-753-0708 *E-mail:* info@breakwaterbooks.com; orders@breakwaterbooks.com *Web Site:* www. breakwaterbooks.com, pg 417

Nicholas Brealey Publishing, 53 State St, 9th fl, Boston, MA 02109 *Tel:* 617-523-3801 *E-mail:* info@ nicholasbrealey.com; sales-us@nicholasbrealey.com *Web Site:* www.nicholasbrealey.com, pg 40

James Henry Breasted Prize, 400 "A" St SE, Washington, DC 20003 *Tel:* 202-544-2422 *Fax:* 202-544-8307 *E-mail:* awards@historians.org *Web Site:* www. historians.org, pg 600

Brentwood Christian Press, PO Box 4773, Columbus, GA 31914-4773 *Toll Free Tel:* 800-334-8861 *E-mail:* brentwood@aol.com *Web Site:* www. brentwoodbooks.com, pg 40

Brethren Press, 1451 Dundee Ave, Elgin, IL 60120 *Tel:* 847-742-5100 *Toll Free Tel:* 800-323-8039 *Toll Free Fax:* 800-667-8188 *E-mail:* brethrenpress@ brethren.org *Web Site:* www.brethrenpress.com, pg 40

Brewers Publications, 1327 Spruce St, Boulder, CO 80302 *Tel:* 303-447-0816 *Toll Free Tel:* 888-822-6273 (CN & US) *Fax:* 303-447-2825 *E-mail:* info@brewersassociation.org *Web Site:* www. brewersassociation.org, pg 40

The Briar Cliff Review Fiction, Poetry & Creative Nonfiction Contest, 3303 Rebecca St, Sioux City, IA 51104-2100 *Tel:* 712-279-1651 *Fax:* 712-279-5486 *Web Site:* www.bcreview.org, pg 600

Brick Books, 22 Spencer Ave, Toronto, ON M6K 2J6, Canada *Tel:* 416-455-8385 *E-mail:* brenda@ brickbooks.ca *Web Site:* www.brickbooks.ca, pg 417

Brick Mantel Books, 4719 Holly Hills Ave, St Louis, MO 63116 *Tel:* 314-827-6567 *E-mail:* info@ brickmantelbooks.com *Web Site:* brickmantelbooks. com, pg 40

Brick Road Poetry Book Contest, 513 Broadway, Columbus, GA 31901-3117 *Web Site:* brickroadpoetrypress.com, pg 601

Brick Tower Press, Manhanset House, PO Box 342, Shelter Island Heights, NY 11965-0342 *Tel:* 212-427-7139 *Toll Free Tel:* 800-68-BRICK (682-7425) *E-mail:* bricktower@aol.com *Web Site:* bricktowerpress.com, pg 40

BrickHouse Books Inc, 306 Suffolk Rd, Baltimore, MD 21218 *Fax:* 410-235-7690 *Web Site:* brickhousebooks. wordpress.com, pg 40

Bridge-Logos, 1426W Newberry Rd, No 409, Newberry, FL 32669-2765 *Toll Free Tel:* 800-320-4108 *Web Site:* www.bridgelogos.com, pg 41

Bridge Publications Inc, 5600 E Olympic Blvd, Commerce, CA 90022 *Tel:* 323-888-6200 *Toll Free Tel:* 800-722-1733 *Fax:* 323-888-6202 *E-mail:* info@ bridgepub.com *Web Site:* www.bridgepub.com, pg 41

Bridge to Asia, 1505 Juanita Way, Berkeley, CA 94702-1103 *Tel:* 510-665-3998 *E-mail:* asianet@bridge.org *Web Site:* www.bridge.org, pg 551

Brigantine Media, 211 North Ave, St Johnsbury, VT 05819 *Tel:* 802-751-8802 *Fax:* 802-751-8804 *Web Site:* brigantinemedia.com, pg 41

M Courtney Briggs Esq, Authors Representative, Chase Tower, 28th fl, 100 N Broadway Ave, Oklahoma City, OK 73102, pg 478

Bright Connections Media, A World Book Encyclopedia Company, 180 N LaSalle St, Suite 900, Chicago, IL 60601 *Tel:* 312-729-5800 *Web Site:* www. brightconnectionsmedia.com, pg 41

Brill Inc, 2 Liberty Sq, 11th fl, Boston, MA 02109 *Tel:* 617-263-2323 *Toll Free Tel:* 800-962-4406; 800-337-9255 (orders - USA & CN) *Fax:* 617-263-2324 *E-mail:* sales-us@brill.com *Web Site:* www.brill.com, pg 41

Brilliance Audio, 1704 Eaton Dr, Grand Haven, MI 49417 *Tel:* 616-846-5256 *Toll Free Tel:* 800-648-2312 (orders only) *Fax:* 616-846-0630 *E-mail:* customerservice@brillianceaudio.com *Web Site:* www.brillianceaudio.com, pg 41

Brindle & Glass Publishing Ltd, 1075 Pendergast St, Suite 103, Victoria, BC V8V 0A1, Canada *Tel:* 250-360-0829 *Fax:* 250-386-0829 *E-mail:* info@ touchwoodeditions.com *Web Site:* www. touchwoodeditions.com, pg 417

Brinkley-Stephenson Award, 112 N Bryan Ave, Bloomington, IN 47408-4141 *Tel:* 812-855-7311 *E-mail:* oah@oah.org *Web Site:* www.oah.org/awards, pg 601

Bristol Park Books, 252 W 38 St, Suite 206, New York, NY 10018 *Tel:* 212-842-0700 *Fax:* 212-842-1771 *E-mail:* info@bristolparkbooks.com *Web Site:* bristolparkbooks.com, pg 41

Brittingham & Pollak Prizes in Poetry, Dept of English, 600 N Park St, Madison, WI 53706 *Web Site:* www. wisc.edu/wisconsinpress, pg 601

Broadview Press, 280 Perry St, Unit 5, Peterborough, ON K9J 2J4, Canada *Tel:* 705-743-8990 *Fax:* 705-743-8353 *E-mail:* customerservice@broadviewpress. com *Web Site:* www.broadviewpress.com, pg 417

Brockman Inc, 260 Fifth Ave, 10th fl, New York, NY 10001 *Tel:* 212-935-8900 *Fax:* 212-935-5535 *E-mail:* rights@brockman.com *Web Site:* www. brockman.com, pg 478

Broden Books LLC, 3824 Sunset Dr, Spring Park, MN 55384 *Tel:* 952-471-1066 *E-mail:* media@ brodenbooks.com *Web Site:* www.brodenbooks.com, pg 41

Paul H Brookes Publishing Co Inc, PO Box 10624, Baltimore, MD 21285-0624 *Tel:* 410-337-9580 (outside US & CN) *Toll Free Tel:* 800-638-3775 (US & CN) *Fax:* 410-337-8539 *E-mail:* custserv@ brookespublishing.com *Web Site:* www. brookespublishing.com, pg 42

The Brookings Institution Press, 1775 Massachusetts Ave NW, Washington, DC 20036-2188 *Tel:* 202-797-6000 *E-mail:* permissions@brookings.edu *Web Site:* www. brookings.edu, pg 42

Brookline Books, 8 Trumbull Rd, Suite B-001, Northampton, MA 01060 *Tel:* 603-669-7032 (orders) *Toll Free Tel:* 800-666-2665 (orders) *Fax:* 413-584-6184 *E-mail:* brbooks@yahoo.com, pg 42

Brooklyn Public Library Literary Prize, 10 Grand Army Plaza, Brooklyn, NY 11238 *Tel:* 718-230-2100 *E-mail:* brooklyneagles@bklynlibrary.com *Web Site:* www.bklynlibrary.org/support/bpl-literary-prize, pg 601

Brooklyn Publishers LLC, PO Box 248, Cedar Rapids, IA 52406 *Tel:* 319-368-8012 *Toll Free Tel:* 888-473-8521 *Fax:* 319-368-8011 *E-mail:* customerservice@ brookpub.com *Web Site:* www.brookpub.com, pg 42

Broquet Inc, 97-B, Montee des Bouleaux, St-Constant, QC J5A 1A9, Canada *Tel:* 450-638-3338 *Fax:* 450-638-4338 *E-mail:* info@broquet.qc.ca *Web Site:* www. broquet.qc.ca, pg 417

The Heywood Broun Award, 501 Third St NW, 6th fl, Washington, DC 20001-2797 *Tel:* 202-434-7177; 202-434-7162 (The Guild Reporter) *Fax:* 202-434-1472 *Web Site:* www.newsguild.org, pg 601

Brown Books Publishing Group, 16250 Knoll Trail, Suite 205, Dallas, TX 75248 *Tel:* 972-381-0009 *Fax:* 972-248-4336 *E-mail:* publishing@brownbooks. com *Web Site:* www.brownbooks.com, pg 42

Curtis Brown Ltd, 228 E 45 St, 3rd fl, New York, NY 10017 *Tel:* 212-473-5400 *Web Site:* www.curtisbrown. com, pg 478

John Nicholas Brown Prize, 17 Dunster St, Suite 202, Cambridge, MA 02138 *Tel:* 617-491-1622 *Fax:* 617-492-3303 *E-mail:* info@themedievalacademy.org *Web Site:* www.medievalacademy.org, pg 601

Karen Brown Guides LLC, PO Box 70, San Mateo, CA 94401-0070 *Fax:* 650-342-9153 *Web Site:* www. karenbrown.com, pg 42

Marie Brown Associates, 412 W 154 St, New York, NY 10032 *Tel:* 212-939-9725 *E-mail:* submissions. mbrownlit@gmail.com, pg 478

Browne & Miller Literary Associates, 52 Village Place, Hinsdale, IL 60521 *Tel:* 312-922-3063 *E-mail:* mail@ browneandmiller.com *Web Site:* www.browneandmiller. com, pg 478

Linda Bruckheimer Series in Kentucky Literature, 822 E Market St, Louisville, KY 40206 *Tel:* 502-458-4028 *E-mail:* info@sarabandebooks.org *Web Site:* www. sarabandebooks.org/bruckheimer, pg 601

Brush Education Inc, 6531-111 St, Edmonton, AB T6H 4R5, Canada *Tel:* 780-989-0910 *Toll Free Tel:* 855-283-0900 *Fax:* 780-989-0930 *Toll Free Fax:* 855-283-6947 *E-mail:* contact@brusheducation.ca *Web Site:* www.brusheducation.ca, pg 418

J B Bryans Literary, 7 Meetinghouse Ct, Indian Mills, NJ 08088 *Tel:* 609-922-0369 *E-mail:* info@brylit.com *Web Site:* brylit.com, pg 478

Don Buchwald & Associates Inc, 10 E 44 St, New York, NY 10017 *Tel:* 212-867-1200 *Fax:* 212-867-2434 *E-mail:* info@buchwald.com *Web Site:* www. buchwald.com, pg 478

Bucknell Seminar for Undergraduate Poets, Bucknell University, Bucknell Hall, Moore Ave, Lewisburg, PA 17837 *Tel:* 570-577-1853 *E-mail:* stadlercenter@ bucknell.edu *Web Site:* www.bucknell.edu/ stadlercenter, pg 574

Bucknell University Press, One Dent Dr, Lewisburg, PA 17837 *Tel:* 570-577-3674 *E-mail:* universitypress@ bucknell.edu *Web Site:* www.bucknell.edu/ universitypress, pg 42

Judith Buckner Literary Agency, 12721 Hart St, North Hollywood, CA 91605 *Tel:* 818-982-8202 *Fax:* 818-764-6844, pg 478

Georges Bugnet Award for Fiction, 11759 Groat Rd, Edmonton, AB T5M 3K6, Canada *Tel:* 780-422-8174 *Toll Free Tel:* 800-665-5354 (AB only) *Fax:* 780-422-2663 (attn WGA) *E-mail:* mail@writersguild.ca *Web Site:* writersguild.ca, pg 601

BuilderBooks, 1201 15 St NW, Washington, DC 20005 *Tel:* 202-822-0200 *Toll Free Tel:* 800-223-2665 *Fax:* 202-266-8096 (edit) *E-mail:* info@nahb.com *Web Site:* builderbooks.com, pg 42

The Bukowski Agency Ltd, 14 Prince Arthur Ave, Suite 202, Toronto, ON M5R 1A9, Canada *Tel:* 416-928-6728 *Fax:* 416-963-9978 *E-mail:* info@ bukowskiagency.com *Web Site:* www.bukowskiagency. com, pg 478

Bull Publishing Co, PO Box 1377, Boulder, CO 80306 *Tel:* 303-545-6350 *Toll Free Tel:* 800-676-2855 *Fax:* 303-545-6354 *E-mail:* bullpublishing@msn.com *Web Site:* www.bullpub.com, pg 42

The Bureau for At-Risk Youth, 40 Aero Rd, Unit 2, Bohemia, NY 11716 *Toll Free Tel:* 800-99YOUTH (999-6884) *Toll Free Fax:* 800-262-1886 *Web Site:* www.at-risk.com, pg 43

Bureau of Economic Geology, c/o The University of Texas at Austin, 10100 Burnet Rd, Bldg 130, Austin, TX 78758 *Tel:* 512-471-1534 *Fax:* 512-471-0140 *E-mail:* pubsales@beg.utexas.edu *Web Site:* www.beg.utexas.edu, pg 43

Burford Books, 101 E State St, No 301, Ithaca, NY 14850 *Tel:* 607-319-4373 *Fax:* 607-319-4373 *Toll Free Fax:* 866-212-7750 *E-mail:* info@burfordbooks.com *Web Site:* www.burfordbooks.com, pg 43

Hilary R Burke, 59 Sparks St, Ottawa, ON K1P 6C3, Canada *Tel:* 613-237-4658 *E-mail:* hburke99@yahoo.com, pg 460

Burns Archive Press, 140 E 38 St, New York, NY 10016 *Tel:* 212-889-1938 *E-mail:* info@burnsarchive.com *Web Site:* www.burnsarchive.com, pg 43

Burns Entertainment & Sports Marketing, 820 Davis St, Suite 222, Evanston, IL 60201 *Tel:* 847-866-9400 *Fax:* 847-491-9778 *E-mail:* burnsl@burnsent.com *Web Site:* burnsent.com, pg 515

John Burroughs Medal, 261 Floyd Ackert Rd, New York, NY 12493 *Tel:* 212-769-5169 *Fax:* 212-313-7182 *E-mail:* info@johnburroughsassociation.org *Web Site:* www.johnburroughsassociation.org, pg 601

John Burroughs Nature Essay Award, 261 Floyd Ackert Rd, New York, NY 12493 *Tel:* 212-769-5169 *Fax:* 212-313-7182 *E-mail:* info@johnburroughsassociation.org *Web Site:* www.johnburroughsassociation.org, pg 601

Business Expert Press, 222 E 46 St, Suite 203, New York, NY 10017-2906 *Tel:* 919-612-6706 *E-mail:* sales@businessexpertpress.com *Web Site:* www.businessexpertpress.com, pg 43

Business Forms Management Association (BFMA), 1147 Fleetwood Ave, Madison, WI 53716-1417 *Toll Free Tel:* 888-367-3078 *E-mail:* bfma@bfma.org *Web Site:* www.bfma.org, pg 529

Business Marketing Association (BMA), 708 Third Ave, New York, NY 10017 *Tel:* 212-697-5950 *Fax:* 212-687-7310 *E-mail:* info@marketing.org *Web Site:* www.marketing.org, pg 529

Business Research Services Inc, PO Box 42674, Washington, DC 20015 *Tel:* 301-229-5561 *Toll Free Fax:* 877-516-0818 *E-mail:* brspubs@sba8a.com *Web Site:* www.sba8a.com; www.setasidealert.com, pg 43

BWL Publishing Inc, 100 Chinook Winds Place SW, Unit 4105, Airdrie, AB T4B-4B4, Canada *Tel:* 403-710-4869 *E-mail:* bwlgeneral@telus.net *Web Site:* bookswelove.net; www.facebook.com/groups/153824114796417, pg 418

Byer-Sprinzeles Agency, 5800 Arlington Ave, Suite 16-C, Riverdale, NY 10471 *Tel:* 718-543-9399 *Web Site:* www.maggiebyersprinzeles.com, pg 511

Sheree Bykofsky Associates Inc, PO Box 706, Brigantine, NJ 08203 *E-mail:* submitbee@aol.com *Web Site:* www.shereebee.com, pg 479

Bywater Books Inc, PO Box 3671, Ann Arbor, MI 48106-3671 *Tel:* 734-662-8815 *Web Site:* bywaterbooks.com, pg 43

BZ/Rights & Permissions Inc, 145 W 86 St, New York, NY 10024 *Tel:* 212-924-3000 *Fax:* 212-924-2525 *E-mail:* info@bzrights.com *Web Site:* www.bzrights.com, pg 460

CAA Award for Canadian History, 6 West St N, Suite 203, Orillia, ON L3V 5B8, Canada *Tel:* 705-325-3926 *E-mail:* admin@canadianauthors.org *Web Site:* www.canadianauthors.org, pg 601

CAA Award for Fiction, 6 West St N, Suite 203, Orillia, ON L3V 5B8, Canada *Tel:* 705-325-3926 *E-mail:* admin@canadianauthors.org *Web Site:* www.canadianauthors.org, pg 601

CAA Emerging Writer Award, 6 West St N, Suite 203, Orillia, ON L3V 5B8, Canada *Tel:* 705-325-3926 *E-mail:* admin@canadianauthors.org *Web Site:* www.canadianauthors.org, pg 602

CAA Poetry Award, 6 West St N, Suite 203, Orillia, ON L3V 5B8, Canada *Tel:* 705-325-3926 *E-mail:* admin@canadianauthors.org *Web Site:* www.canadianauthors.org, pg 602

Gerald Cable Book Award, PO Box 3541, Eugene, OR 97403 *Tel:* 541-344-5060 *E-mail:* sfrpress@earthlink.net *Web Site:* www.silverfishreviewpress.com, pg 602

Caissa Editions, PO Box 151, Yorklyn, DE 19736-0151 *Tel:* 302-239-4608 *Web Site:* www.chessbookstore.com, pg 43

The Randolph Caldecott Medal, 50 E Huron St, Chicago, IL 60611-2795 *Tel:* 312-280-2163 *Toll Free Tel:* 800-545-2433 *Fax:* 312-440-9374; 312-280-5271 *E-mail:* alsc@ala.org *Web Site:* www.ala.org/alsc, pg 602

CALIBA Golden Poppy Awards, 651 Broadway, 2nd fl, Sonoma, CA 95476 *Tel:* 415-561-7686 *Fax:* 415-561-7685 *E-mail:* info@caliballiance.org *Web Site:* www.caliballiance.org/golden-poppy-awards.html, pg 602

California Book Awards, 110 The Embarcadero, San Francisco, CA 94105 *Tel:* 415-597-6700 *Fax:* 415-597-6729 *E-mail:* bookawards@commonwealthclub.org *Web Site:* www.commonwealthclub.org/bookawards, pg 602

California Independent Booksellers Alliance (CALIBA), 651 Broadway, 2nd fl, Sonoma, CA 95476 *Tel:* 415-561-7686 *Fax:* 415-561-7685 *E-mail:* info@caliballiance.org *Web Site:* www.caliballiance.org, pg 529

Callawind Publications Inc, 3551 St Charles Blvd, Suite 179, Kirkland, QC H9H 3C4, Canada *Tel:* 514-685-9109 *E-mail:* info@callawind.com *Web Site:* www.callawind.com, pg 418

Cambridge University Press, One Liberty Plaza, 20th fl, New York, NY 10006 *Tel:* 212-924-3900; 212-337-5000 *Fax:* 212-691-3239; 845-353-4141 *E-mail:* newyork@cambridge.org; customer_service@cambridge.org *Web Site:* www.cambridge.org/us, pg 43

Kimberley Cameron & Associates LLC, 1550 Tiburon Blvd, Suite 704, Tiburon, CA 94920 *Tel:* 415-789-9191 *Fax:* 415-789-9177 *Web Site:* www.kimberleycameron.com, pg 479

Camino Books Inc, PO Box 59026, Philadelphia, PA 19102-9026 *Tel:* 215-413-1917 *Fax:* 215-413-3255 *E-mail:* camino@caminobooks.com *Web Site:* www.caminobooks.com, pg 44

Joe Pendleton Campbell Narrative Contest, 900 Timber Creek Place, Virginia Beach, VA 23464 *E-mail:* poetryinva@aol.com *Web Site:* poetrysocietyofvirginia.org, pg 602

John W Campbell Memorial Award, University of Kansas, Wescoe Hall, Rm 3001, Dept of English, 1445 Jayhawk Blvd, Lawrence, KS 66045 *Tel:* 785-864-2518 *Fax:* 785-864-1159 *Web Site:* www.sfcenter.ku.edu/campbell.htm, pg 602

Campfield & Campfield Publishing LLC, 6521 Cutler St, Philadelphia, PA 19126 *Toll Free Tel:* 888-518-2440 *Fax:* 215-224-6696 *E-mail:* info@campfieldspublishing.com *Web Site:* www.campfieldspublishing.com, pg 44

Canada Council for the Arts (Conseil des arts du Canada), 150 Elgin St, 2nd fl, Ottawa, ON K2P 1L4, Canada *Tel:* 613-566-4414 *Toll Free Tel:* 800-263-5588 (CN only) *Fax:* 613-566-4390 *E-mail:* info@canadacouncil.ca; assistance@canadacouncil.ca (technical support) *Web Site:* www.canadacouncil.ca; www.apply.canadacouncil.ca, pg 529

Canada-Japan Literary Awards, 150 Elgin St, 2nd fl, Ottawa, ON K2P 1L4, Canada *Tel:* 613-566-4414 *Toll Free Tel:* 800-263-5588 (CN only) *Fax:* 613-566-4390 *Web Site:* canadacouncil.ca/funding/prizes/canada-japan-literary-awards, pg 602

Canada Law Book®, One Corporate Plaza, 2075 Kennedy Rd, Toronto, ON M1T 3V4, Canada *Tel:* 416-609-3800 (cust rel & orders) *Toll Free Tel:* 800-387-5351 (cust rel, CN & US only); 800-347-5164 (cust rel & orders, CN & US) *Fax:* 416-298-5082 (cust rel & orders, Toronto) *Toll Free Fax:* 877-750-9041 (cust rel & orders, CN only) *E-mail:* customersupport.legaltaxcanada@tr.com *Web Site:* www.carswell.com, pg 418

Canadian Authors Association (CAA), 6 West St N, Suite 203, Orillia, ON L3V 5B8, Canada *Tel:* 705-325-3926 *E-mail:* admin@canadianauthors.org *Web Site:* www.canadianauthors.org, pg 529

Canadian Bible Society, 10 Carnforth Rd, Toronto, ON M4A 2S4, Canada *Tel:* 416-757-4171 *Toll Free Tel:* 800-465-2425 *Fax:* 416-757-3376 *E-mail:* custserv@biblesociety.ca *Web Site:* www.biblescanada.com; www.biblesociety.ca, pg 418

Canadian Bookbinders and Book Artists Guild (CBBAG), 180 Shaw St, Unit 102, Toronto, ON M6J 2W5, Canada *Tel:* 416-581-1071 *E-mail:* cbbag@cbbag.ca *Web Site:* www.cbbag.ca, pg 529

Canadian Cataloguing in Publication Program, Library & Archives Canada, 395 Wellington St, Ottawa, ON K1A 0N4, Canada *Tel:* 819-994-6881 *Toll Free Tel:* 866-578-7777 (CN) or 819-934-6777 *E-mail:* bac.cip.lac@canada.ca *Web Site:* www.bac-lac.gc.ca/eng/services/cip/pages/cip.aspx, pg 529

Canadian Children's Book Centre, 40 Orchard View Blvd, Suite 217, Toronto, ON M4R 1B9, Canada *Tel:* 416-975-0010 *Fax:* 416-975-8970 *E-mail:* info@bookcentre.ca *Web Site:* www.bookcentre.ca, pg 530

Canadian Circumpolar Institute (CCI) Press, 1-16 Rutherford Library South, 11204 89 Ave NW, Edmonton, AB T6G-2J4, Canada *Tel:* 780-492-3662 *Fax:* 780-492-0719 *Web Site:* www.uap.ualberta.ca, pg 418

Canadian Council on Social Development (Conseil canadien de developpement social), 190 O'Connor St, Suite 100, Ottawa, ON K2P 2R3, Canada *Tel:* 613-236-8977 *Fax:* 613-236-2750 *E-mail:* info@ccsd.ca *Web Site:* www.ccsd.ca, pg 418

Canadian Energy Research Institute, 3512 33 St NW, Suite 150, Calgary, AB T2L 2A6, Canada *Tel:* 403-282-1231 *Fax:* 403-290-2251 *E-mail:* info@ceri.ca *Web Site:* www.ceri.ca, pg 418

Canadian Institute for Studies in Publishing, Simon Fraser University at Harbour Centre, 515 W Hastings St, Suite 3576, Vancouver, BC V6B 5K3, Canada *Tel:* 778-782-5242 *E-mail:* pub-info@sfu.ca *Web Site:* publishing.sfu.ca, pg 530

Canadian Institute of Resources Law (L'Institut canadien du droit des ressources), Faculty of Law, University of Calgary, 2500 University Dr NW, MFH 3353, Calgary, AB T2N 1N4, Canada *Tel:* 403-220-3200 *Fax:* 403-282-6182 *E-mail:* cirl@ucalgary.ca *Web Site:* www.cirl.ca, pg 419

Canadian Institute of Ukrainian Studies Press, University of Toronto, 256 McCaul St, Rm 308, Toronto, ON M5T 1W5, Canada *Tel:* 416-946-7326 *Fax:* 416-978-2672 *E-mail:* cius@ualberta.ca *Web Site:* www.ciuspress.com, pg 419

Canadian Museum of History (Musee canadien de l'histoire), 100 Laurier St, Gatineau, QC K1A 0M8, Canada *Tel:* 819-776-7000 *Toll Free Tel:* 800-555-5621 (North American orders only) *Fax:* 819-776-7187 *Web Site:* www.historymuseum.ca, pg 419

Canadian Publishers' Council (CPC), 3080 Yonge St, Suite 6060, Toronto, ON M4N 3N1, Canada *Tel:* 647-255-8880 *Web Site:* pubcouncil.ca, pg 530

Canadian Scholars' Press Inc, 425 Adelaide St W, Suite 200, Toronto, ON M5V 3C1, Canada *Tel:* 416-929-2774 *Toll Free Tel:* 800-463-1998 *Fax:* 416-929-1926 *E-mail:* info@cspi.org; info@canadianscholars.ca; editorial@canadianscholars.ca; orders@canadianscholars.ca *Web Site:* www.canadianscholars.ca; www.womenspress.ca, pg 419

Canadian Society of Children's Authors, Illustrators & Performers (CANSCAIP), 720 Bathurst St, Suite 503, Toronto, ON M5S 2R4, Canada *Tel:* 416-515-1559 *E-mail:* office@canscaip.org *Web Site:* www.canscaip. org, pg 530

The Canadian Writers' Foundation Inc (La Fondation des Ecrivains Canadiens), PO Box 13281, Kanata Sta, Ottawa, ON K2K 1X4, Canada *Tel:* 613-256-6937 *Fax:* 613-256-5457 *E-mail:* info@ canadianwritersfoundation.org *Web Site:* www. canadianwritersfoundation.org, pg 551

Candied Plums, 7548 Ravenna Ave NE, Seattle, WA 98115 *E-mail:* candiedplums@gmail.com *Web Site:* www.candiedplums.com, pg 44

Candlewick Press, 99 Dover St, Somerville, MA 02144-2825 *Tel:* 617-661-3330 *Fax:* 617-661-0565 *E-mail:* bigbear@candlewick.com; salesinfo@ candlewick.com *Web Site:* www.candlewick.com, pg 44

C&T Publishing Inc, 1651 Challenge Dr, Concord, CA 94520-5206 *Tel:* 925-677-0377 *Toll Free Tel:* 800-284-1114 *Fax:* 925-677-0373 *E-mail:* support@ctpub.com *Web Site:* www.ctpub.com, pg 44

Cape Cod Writers' Center Conference, 919 Main St, Osterville, MA 02655 *Tel:* 508-420-0200 *E-mail:* writers@capecodwriterscenter.org *Web Site:* capecodwriterscenter.org, pg 574

Capitol Enquiry Inc, 1034 Emerald Bay Rd, No 435, South Lake Tahoe, CA 96150 *Tel:* 916-442-1434 *Toll Free Tel:* 800-922-7486 *Fax:* 916-244-2704 *E-mail:* info@capenq.com *Web Site:* govbuddy.com, pg 44

Alexander Patterson Cappon Prize for Fiction, UMKC, University House, 5101 Rockhill Rd, Kansas City, MO 64110-2499 *Tel:* 816-235-1169 *Fax:* 816-235-2611 *E-mail:* newletters@umkc.edu *Web Site:* www. newletters.org, pg 602

Dorothy Churchill Cappon Prize for the Essay, UMKC, University House, 5101 Rockhill Rd, Kansas City, MO 64110-2499 *Tel:* 816-235-1169 *Fax:* 816-235-2611 *E-mail:* newletters@umkc.edu *Web Site:* www. newletters.org, pg 602

Capstone Publishers™, 1710 Roe Crest Dr, North Mankato, MN 56003 *Toll Free Tel:* 800-747-4992 (cust serv) *Toll Free Tel:* 888-262-0705 *E-mail:* customer.service@capstonepub.com *Web Site:* www.capstonepub.com, pg 44

Captain Fiddle Music & Publications, 94 Wiswall Rd, Lee, NH 03861 *Tel:* 603-659-2658 *E-mail:* cfiddle@ tiac.net *Web Site:* captainfiddle.com, pg 44

Captus Press Inc, 1600 Steeles Ave W, Units 14 & 15, Concord, ON L4K 4M2, Canada *Tel:* 416-736-5537 *Fax:* 416-736-5793 *E-mail:* info@captus.com *Web Site:* www.captus.com, pg 419

Cardiotext Publishing, 3405 W 44 St, Minneapolis, MN 55410 *Tel:* 612-925-2053 *Toll Free Tel:* 888-999-9174 *Fax:* 612-922-7556 *E-mail:* info@cardiotext.com *Web Site:* www.cardiotextpublishing.com, pg 44

Cardoza Publishing, 1916 E Charleston Blvd, Las Vegas, NV 89104 *Tel:* 702-870-7200 *Toll Free Tel:* 800-577-WINS (577-9467) *E-mail:* info@cardozabooks.com *Web Site:* www.cardozabooks.com, pg 45

Career Development Program, 225 King St, Suite 201, Fredericton, NB E3B 1E1, Canada *Tel:* 506-444-4444 *Toll Free Tel:* 866-460-ARTS (460-2787) *Fax:* 506-444-5543 *Web Site:* www.artsnb.ca, pg 603

The Carle Honors, 125 W Bay Rd, Amherst, MA 01002 *Tel:* 413-559-6300 *E-mail:* info@carlemuseum.org *Web Site:* www.carlemuseum.org/content/carle-honors, pg 603

Carlisle Press - Walnut Creek, 2673 Township Rd 421, Sugarcreek, OH 44681 *Tel:* 330-852-1900 *Toll Free Tel:* 800-852-4482 *Fax:* 330-852-3285, pg 45

Andrew Carnegie Medals for Excellence in Fiction & Nonfiction, 225 N Michigan Ave, Suite 1300, Chicago, IL 60601 *Tel:* 312-944-6780 *Toll Free*

Tel: 800-545-2433 *Fax:* 312-440-9374 *E-mail:* ala@ ala.org *Web Site:* www.ala.org/awardsgrants/ carnegieadult, pg 603

Carnegie Mellon University Press, 5032 Forbes Ave, Pittsburgh, PA 15289-1021 *Tel:* 412-268-2861 *Fax:* 412-268-8706 *E-mail:* carnegiemellonuniversitypress@gmail.com *Web Site:* www.cmu.edu/universitypress, pg 45

Carnegie-Whitney Award, 50 E Huron St, Chicago, IL 60611 *Tel:* 312-280-5416 *Toll Free Tel:* 800-545-2433 *Fax:* 312-280-5275; 312-440-9379 *Web Site:* www.ala. org, pg 603

The Robert & Ina Caro Research/Travel Fellowship, PO Box 33020, Santa Fe, NM 87594 *Web Site:* biographersinternational.org, pg 603

Carolina Academic Press, 700 Kent St, Durham, NC 27701 *Tel:* 919-489-7486 *Toll Free Tel:* 800-489-7486 *Fax:* 919-493-5668 *E-mail:* cap@cap-press.com *Web Site:* www.cap-press.com; www.caplaw.com, pg 45

Carolrhoda Books Inc, 241 First Ave N, Minneapolis, MN 55401 *Tel:* 612-332-3344 *Toll Free Tel:* 800-328-4929 *Fax:* 612-332-7615 *Toll Free Fax:* 800-332-1132 *E-mail:* info@lernerbooks.com; custserve@ lernerbooks.com *Web Site:* www.lernerbooks.com; www.facebook.com/lernerbooks, pg 45

Carolrhoda Lab™, 241 First Ave N, Minneapolis, MN 55401 *Tel:* 612-332-3344 *Toll Free Tel:* 800-328-4929 *Fax:* 612-332-7615 *Toll Free Fax:* 800-332-1132 *E-mail:* info@lernerbooks.com; custserve@ lernerbooks.com *Web Site:* www.lernerbooks.com; www.facebook.com/lernerbooks, pg 45

Carpe Indexum, 1960 Deer Run Rd, LaFayette, NY 13084 *Tel:* 315-677-3030 *E-mail:* info@carpeindexum. com *Web Site:* www.carpeindexum.com, pg 460

Carroll Publishing, 4701 Sangamore Rd, Suite S-155, Bethesda, MD 20816 *Tel:* 301-263-9800 *Fax:* 301-263-9805 *E-mail:* info@carrollpub.com; customersvc@carrollpub.com *Web Site:* www. carrollpublishing.com, pg 45

R E Carsch, MS-Consultant, 1453 Rhode Island St, San Francisco, CA 94107-3248 *Tel:* 415-533-8356 *E-mail:* recarsch@mzinfo.com, pg 460

Carson Dellosa Publishing LLC, PO Box 35665, Greensboro, NC 27425-5665 *Tel:* 336-632-0084 *Toll Free Tel:* 800-321-0943 *Fax:* 336-632-0087 *Toll Free Fax:* 800-535-2669 *E-mail:* custsvc@carsondellosa. com *Web Site:* www.carsondellosa.com, pg 45

Carswell, One Corporate Plaza, 2075 Kennedy Rd, Toronto, ON M1T 3V4, Canada *Tel:* 416-609-5811 (sales); 416-609-3800 *Toll Free Tel:* 800-387-5164 (CN & US) *Fax:* 416-298-5094 (sales); 416-298-5082 *Toll Free Fax:* 877-750-9041 (CN only) *E-mail:* customersupport.legaltaxcanada@tr.com *Web Site:* store.thomsonreuters.ca, pg 419

Carol Cartaino, 2000 Flat Run Rd, Seaman, OH 45679 *Tel:* 937-764-1303 *Fax:* 937-764-1303 *E-mail:* cartaino@aol.com, pg 460

CarTech Inc, 838 Lake St S, Forest Lake, MN 55025 *Tel:* 651-277-1200 *Toll Free Tel:* 800-551-4754 *Fax:* 651-277-1203 *E-mail:* info@cartechbooks.com *Web Site:* www.cartechbooks.com, pg 45

The Carter Prize For The Essay, Washington & Lee University, Mattingly House, 204 W Washington St, Lexington, VA 24450-2116 *Tel:* 540-458-8908 *E-mail:* shenandoah@wlu.edu *Web Site:* shenandoahliterary.org, pg 603

Claudia Caruana, PO Box 654, Murray Hill Sta, New York, NY 10016 *Tel:* 516-488-5815 *E-mail:* ccaruana29@hotmail.com, pg 460

Maria Carvainis Agency Inc, Rockefeller Center, 1270 Avenue of the Americas, Suite 2320, New York, NY 10020 *Tel:* 212-245-6365 *Fax:* 212-245-7196 *E-mail:* mca@mariacarvainisagency.com *Web Site:* mariacarvainisagency.com, pg 479

Casa Bautista de Publicaciones, 7000 Alabama St, El Paso, TX 79904 *Tel:* 915-566-9656 *Toll Free Tel:* 800-755-5958 (cust serv & orders) *Fax:* 915-565-9008 (orders) *E-mail:* orders@editorialmh.org *Web Site:* www.editorialmh.org, pg 46

Casemate | publishers, 1950 Lawrence Rd, Havertown, PA 19083 *Tel:* 610-853-9131 *Fax:* 610-853-9146 *E-mail:* casemate@casematepublishers.com *Web Site:* www.casematepublishers.com, pg 46

Castle Connolly Medical Ltd, 42 W 24 St, 2nd fl, New York, NY 10010 *Tel:* 212-367-8400 *Fax:* 212-367-0964 *Web Site:* www.castleconnolly.com, pg 46

The CAT Agency Inc, PO Box 1390, Fairfield, CT 06825 *Tel:* 917-434-3141 *Web Site:* www.catugeau. com, pg 511

Catalyst Communication Arts, 94 Chuparrosa Dr, San Luis Obispo, CA 93401 *Tel:* 805-235-2351 *Fax:* 805-543-7140 *Web Site:* www.sonsieconroy.com, pg 460

Catalyst Creative Services, 619 Marion Plaza, Palo Alto, CA 94301-4251 *Tel:* 650-325-1500 *E-mail:* afriendlyghostwriter@gmail.com *Web Site:* www.catalystcreative.us, pg 460

Catholic Book Awards, 205 W Monroe St, Suite 470, Chicago, IL 60606 *Tel:* 312-380-6789 *Fax:* 312-361-0256 *E-mail:* cpaawards@catholicpress.org *Web Site:* www.catholicpress.org, pg 603

Catholic Book Publishing Corp, 77 West End Rd, Totowa, NJ 07512 *Tel:* 973-890-2400 *Toll Free Tel:* 877-228-2665 *Fax:* 973-890-2410 *E-mail:* info@ catholicbookpublishing.com *Web Site:* www. catholicbookpublishing.com, pg 46

The Catholic Health Association of the United States, 4455 Woodson Rd, St Louis, MO 63134-3797 *Tel:* 314-427-2500 *Fax:* 314-427-0029 *E-mail:* servicecenter@chausa.org *Web Site:* www. chausa.org, pg 46

Catholic Library Association, 8550 United Plaza Blvd, Suite 1001, Baton Rouge, LA 70809 *Tel:* 225-408-4417 *Fax:* 225-408-4422 *E-mail:* cla2@cathla.org *Web Site:* cathla.org, pg 530

Catholic Press Association of the United States & Canada, 205 W Monroe St, Suite 470, Chicago, IL 60606 *Tel:* 312-380-6789 *Fax:* 312-361-0256 *E-mail:* journalist@catholicpress.org *Web Site:* www. catholicpress.org, pg 530

Catholic Press Awards, 205 W Monroe St, Suite 470, Chicago, IL 60606 *Tel:* 312-380-6789 *Fax:* 312-361-0256 *E-mail:* cpaawards@catholicpress.org *Web Site:* www.catholicpress.org, pg 603

The Catholic University of America Press, 240 Leahy Hall, 620 Michigan Ave NE, Washington, DC 20064 *Tel:* 202-319-5052 *Toll Free Tel:* 800-537-5487 (orders only) *Fax:* 202-319-4985 *E-mail:* cua-press@cua.edu *Web Site:* cuapress.org, pg 46

Cato Institute, 1000 Massachusetts Ave NW, Washington, DC 20001-5403 *Tel:* 202-842-0200 *Toll Free Tel:* 800-767-1241 *Fax:* 202-842-3490 *E-mail:* catostore@cato. org *Web Site:* www.cato.org, pg 46

Jeanne Cavelos Editorial Services, PO Box 75, Mont Vernon, NH 03057 *Tel:* 603-673-6234 *Web Site:* jeannecavelos.com, pg 460

Caxton Press, 312 Main St, Caldwell, ID 83605-3299 *Tel:* 208-459-7421 *Toll Free Tel:* 800-657-6465 *Fax:* 208-459-7450 *E-mail:* publish@caxtonpress.com *Web Site:* www.caxtonpress.com, pg 46

CBC Diversity Outstanding Achievement Awards, 54 W 39 St, 14th fl, New York, NY 10018 *Tel:* 917-890-7416 *E-mail:* cbc.info@cbcbooks.org *Web Site:* www. cbcbooks.org, pg 603

CCAB Inc, 111 Queen St E, Suite 450, Toronto, ON M5C 1S2, Canada *Tel:* 416-487-2418 *Fax:* 416-487-6405 *Web Site:* www.bpaww.com, pg 530

CCH, a Wolters Kluwer business, 2700 Lake Cook Rd, Riverwoods, IL 60015 *Tel:* 847-267-7000 *Web Site:* www.cch.com, pg 47

CeciBooks Editorial & Publishing Consultation, 7057 26 Ave NW, Seattle, WA 98117 *E-mail:* ceci@cecibooks. com *Web Site:* www.cecibooks.com, pg 460

725

Cedar Fort Inc, 2373 W 700 S, Springville, UT 84663 *Tel:* 801-489-4084 *Toll Free Tel:* 800-SKY-BOOK (759-2665) *Web Site:* cedarfort.com, pg 47

Cedar Grove Publishing, 3205 Elmhurst St, Rowlett, TX 75088 *Tel:* 415-364-8292 *E-mail:* queries@ cedargrovebooks.com *Web Site:* www. cedargrovebooks.com, pg 47

Cedar Tree Books, PO Box 4256, Wilmington, DE 19807 *Tel:* 302-998-4171 *Fax:* 302-998-4185 *E-mail:* books@ctpress.com *Web Site:* www. cedartreebooks.com, pg 47

CEF Press, 17482 State Hwy M, Warrenton, MO 63383-0348 *Tel:* 636-456-4321 *Toll Free Tel:* 800-748-7710 (cust serv); 800-300-4033 (USA ministries) *Fax:* 636-456-2078 (cust serv) *E-mail:* custserv@cefonline.com *Web Site:* cefonline.com, pg 47

Celebra, 375 Hudson St, New York, NY 10014 *Tel:* 212-366-2000 *E-mail:* ecommerce@us.penguingroup.com *Web Site:* www.penguin.com, pg 47

Cengage Learning, 20 Channel Center St, Boston, MA 02210 *Tel:* 617-289-7700 *Toll Free Tel:* 800-354-9706 *Fax:* 617-289-7844 *E-mail:* esales@cengage.com *Web Site:* www.cengage.com, pg 47

The Center for Book Arts, 28 W 27 St, 3rd fl, New York, NY 10001 *Tel:* 212-481-0295 *E-mail:* info@centerforbookarts.org *Web Site:* www. centerforbookarts.org, pg 530

The Center for Book Arts, 28 W 27 St, 3rd fl, New York, NY 10001 *Tel:* 212-481-0295 *Toll Free Fax:* 866-708-8994 *E-mail:* info@centerforbookarts. org *Web Site:* www.centerforbookarts.org, pg 581

Center for Creative Leadership LLC, One Leadership Place, Greensboro, NC 27410-9427 *Tel:* 336-545-2810; 336-288-7210 *Fax:* 336-282-3284 *E-mail:* info@ccl.org *Web Site:* www.ccl.org/ publications, pg 47

Center for East Asian Studies (CEAS), Western Washington University, 516 High St, Bellingham, WA 98225 *Tel:* 360-650-3339 *Fax:* 360-650-6110 *E-mail:* eas@wwu.edu *Web Site:* www.wwu.edu/eas, pg 48

The Center for Exhibition Industry Research (CEIR), 12700 Park Central Dr, Suite 308, Dallas, TX 75251 *Tel:* 972-687-9242 *Fax:* 972-692-6020 *E-mail:* info@ ceir.org *Web Site:* www.ceir.org, pg 530

The Center for Fiction, 17 E 47 St, New York, NY 10017 *Tel:* 212-755-6710 *E-mail:* info@ centerforfiction.org *Web Site:* centerforfiction.org, pg 530

The Center for Fiction First Novel Prize, 17 E 47 St, New York, NY 10017 *Tel:* 212-755-6710 *E-mail:* info@centerforfiction.org *Web Site:* www. centerforfiction.org/awards/the-first-novel-prize, pg 603

Center for Futures Education Inc, 345 Erie St, Grove City, PA 16127 *Tel:* 724-458-5860 *Fax:* 724-458-5962 *E-mail:* info@thectr.com *Web Site:* www.thectr.com, pg 48

The Center for Learning, 10200 Jefferson Blvd, Culver City, CA 90232 *Tel:* 310-839-2436 *Toll Free Tel:* 800-421-4246 *Fax:* 310-839-2249 *Toll Free Fax:* 800-944-5432 *E-mail:* access@socialstudies.com *Web Site:* www.centerforlearning.org, pg 48

Center for Publishing Departmental Scholarships, Midtown Ctr, Rm 429, 11 W 42 St, New York, NY 10036 *Tel:* 212-992-3232 *Fax:* 212-992-3233 *E-mail:* pub.center@nyu.edu *Web Site:* www.scps.nyu. edu, pg 603

The Center for the Book in the Library of Congress, The Library of Congress, 101 Independence Ave SE, Washington, DC 20540-4920 *Tel:* 202-707-5221 *Fax:* 202-707-0269 *E-mail:* cfbook@loc.gov *Web Site:* www.read.gov; www.read.gov/cfb, pg 530

Center for the Collaborative Classroom, 1001 Marina Village Pkwy, Suite 110, Alameda, CA 94501-1042 *Tel:* 510-533-0213 *Toll Free Tel:* 800-666-7270 *Fax:* 510-464-3670 *E-mail:* info@ collaborativeclassroom.org; clientsupport@ collaborativeclassroom.org *Web Site:* www. collaborativeclassroom.org, pg 48

Centering Corp, 7230 Maple St, Omaha, NE 68134 *Tel:* 402-553-1200 *Toll Free Tel:* 866-218-0101 *Fax:* 402-553-0507 *E-mail:* orders@centering.org *Web Site:* www.centering.org, pg 48

Centerstream Publishing LLC, PO Box 17878, Anaheim Hills, CA 92817-7878 *Tel:* 714-779-9390 *E-mail:* centerstrm@aol.com *Web Site:* www. centerstream-usa.com, pg 48

Central Conference of American Rabbis/CCAR Press, 355 Lexington Ave, New York, NY 10017 *Tel:* 212-972-3636 *Fax:* 212-692-0819 *E-mail:* info@ccarpress. org *Web Site:* www.ccarpress.org, pg 48

Central Recovery Press (CRP), 3321 N Buffalo Dr, Suite 275, Las Vegas, NV 89129 *Tel:* 702-868-5830 *Fax:* 702-868-5831 *E-mail:* sales@centralrecovery.com *Web Site:* centralrecoverypress.com, pg 48

Centre for Reformation & Renaissance Studies (CRRS), 71 Queen's Park Crescent E, Toronto, ON M5S 1K7, Canada *Tel:* 416-585-4465 *Fax:* 416-585-4430 (attn: CRRS) *E-mail:* crrs.publications@utoronto.ca *Web Site:* crrs.ca, pg 419

Centre Franco-Ontarien de Ressources en Alphabetisation (Centre FORA), PO Box 56, Hanmer, ON P3P 1S9, Canada *Tel:* 705-524-3672 *Toll Free Tel:* 888-814-4422 (orders, CN only) *Fax:* 705-524-8535 *E-mail:* info@centrefora.on.ca *Web Site:* www. centrefora.on.ca, pg 419

Cenveo Publisher Services, 555 Virginia Dr, Fort Washington, PA 19034 *Tel:* 267-470-1590 *Fax:* 215-591-9093 *E-mail:* info.psg@cenveo.com *Web Site:* www.cenveopublisherservices.com, pg 460

Chain Store Guide (CSG), 3710 Corporex Park Dr, Suite 310, Tampa, FL 33619 *Toll Free Tel:* 800-927-9292 (orders) *Fax:* 813-627-6888 *E-mail:* webmaster@csgis. com *Web Site:* www.csgis.com, pg 48

Chalice Press, 483 E Lockwood Ave, Suite 100, St Louis, MO 63119 *Tel:* 314-231-8500 *Toll Free Tel:* 800-366-3383 *Fax:* 314-231-8524; 770-280-4039 (orders) *E-mail:* customerservice@chalicepress.com *Web Site:* www.chalicepress.com, pg 48

Jane Chambers Playwriting Award, Georgetown University, 108 David Performing Arts Ctr, Box 571063, 37 & "O" St, NW, Washington, DC 20057-1063 *Web Site:* www.athe.org/?page=Jane_Chambers, pg 604

The Alfred & Fay Chandler Book Award, c/o Harvard Business School, Connell House 301A, Boston, MA 02163 *Tel:* 617-495-1003 *Fax:* 617-495-2705 *E-mail:* bhr@hbs.edu *Web Site:* www.hbs.edu/ businesshistory/fellowships, pg 604

G S Sharat Chandra Prize for Short Fiction, University House, 5101 Rockhill Rd, Kansas City, MO 64110-2499 *Tel:* 816-235-2558 *Fax:* 816-235-2611 *E-mail:* bkmk@umkc.edu *Web Site:* www.umkc. edu/bkmk, pg 604

Channel Photographics, 980 Lincoln Ave, Suite 200-B, San Rafael, CA 94901 *Tel:* 415-456-2934 *Fax:* 415-456-4124 *Web Site:* www.channelphotographics.com, pg 49

Chaosium Inc, 3450 Wooddale Ct, Ann Arbor, MI 48104 *Tel:* 734-972-9551 *E-mail:* customerservice@ chaosium.com *Web Site:* www.chaosium.com, pg 49

Charisma Media, 600 Rinehart Rd, Lake Mary, FL 32746 *Tel:* 407-333-0600 (all imprints) *Toll Free Tel:* 800-283-8494 (Charisma Media, Siloam Press, Creation House); 800-665-1468 *Fax:* 407-333-7100 (all imprints) *E-mail:* charisma@charismamedia.com *Web Site:* www.charismamedia.com, pg 49

Charles Press Publishers, 230 N 21 St, Suite 312, Philadelphia, PA 19103 *Tel:* 215-470-5977 *E-mail:* mail@charlespresspub.com *Web Site:* charlespresspub.com, pg 49

Charles River Media, 20 Channel Center St, Boston, MA 02210 *Tel:* 617-289-7700 *Fax:* 617-289-7844 *Web Site:* www.cengage.com; www.delmarlearning. com/charlesriver, pg 49

Charles Scribner's Sons®, 27500 Drake Rd, Farmington Hills, MI 48331-3535 *Toll Free Tel:* 800-877-4253 *Toll Free Tel:* 800-414-5043 *E-mail:* gale.galeord@ cengage.com *Web Site:* www.gale.com/scribners, pg 49

Charlesbridge Publishing Inc, 85 Main St, Watertown, MA 02472 *Tel:* 617-926-0329 *Toll Free Tel:* 800-225-3214 *Fax:* 617-926-5720 *Toll Free Fax:* 800-926-5775 *E-mail:* books@charlesbridge.com *Web Site:* www. charlesbridge.com, pg 49

The Charlton Press Corp, 991 Victoria St N, Kitchener, ON N2B 3C7, Canada *Tel:* 416-962-2665 *Toll Free Tel:* 866-663-8827 *Fax:* 519-579-0532 *E-mail:* chpress@charltonpress.com *Web Site:* www. charltonpress.com, pg 419

Chartered Professional Accountants of Canada (CPA Canada), 277 Wellington St W, Toronto, ON M5V 3H2, Canada *Tel:* 416-977-3222 *Toll Free Tel:* 800-268-3793 *Fax:* 416-977-8585 *E-mail:* member. services@cpacanada.ca *Web Site:* www.cpacanada.ca; www.facebook.com/CPACanada/, pg 419

The Chautauqua Prize, One Ames Ave, Chautauqua, NY 14722 *Toll Free Tel:* 800-836-ARTS (836-2787) *Web Site:* www.ciweb.org/prize, pg 604

Chautauqua Writers' Workshop, One Ames Ave, Chautauqua, NY 14722 *Tel:* 716-357-6316; 716-357-6250 *Toll Free Tel:* 800-836-ARTS (836-2787) *Fax:* 716-357-9014 *Web Site:* ciweb.org, pg 574

Margaret Cheasebro, 5709 Holmes Dr, Farmington, NM 87402 *Tel:* 505-325-1557 *E-mail:* mwriter4571@ yahoo.com *Web Site:* www.margaretcheasebro.com, pg 460

Chelsea Green Publishing Co, 85 N Main St, Suite 120, White River Junction, VT 05001 *Tel:* 802-295-6300 *Toll Free Tel:* 800-639-4099 (cust serv & orders) *Fax:* 802-295-6444 *E-mail:* customerservice@ chelseagreen.com; editorial@chelseagreen.com; publicity@chelseagreen.com; rights@chelseagreen.com *Web Site:* www.chelseagreen.com, pg 49

Chelsea House, 132 W 31 St, 17th fl, New York, NY 10001 *Toll Free Tel:* 800-322-8755 *Toll Free Fax:* 800-678-3633 *E-mail:* custserv@ factsonfile.com; info@infobase.com *Web Site:* www. infobasepublishing.com; www.infobase.com, pg 50

ChemTec Publishing, 38 Earswick Dr, Toronto, ON M1E 1C6, Canada *Tel:* 416-265-2603 *Fax:* 416-265-1399 *E-mail:* orderdesk@chemtec.org *Web Site:* www. chemtec.org, pg 420

Cheneliere Education Inc, 5800, rue St Denis, bureau 900, Montreal, QC H2S 3L5, Canada *Tel:* 514-273-1066 *Toll Free Tel:* 800-565-5531 *Fax:* 514-276-0324 *Toll Free Fax:* 800-814-0324 *E-mail:* info@cheneliere. ca *Web Site:* www.cheneliere.ca, pg 420

Cheng & Tsui Co Inc, 25 West St, 2nd fl, Boston, MA 02111-1213 *Tel:* 617-988-2400 *Toll Free Tel:* 800-554-1963 *Fax:* 617-426-3669; 617-556-8964 *E-mail:* service@cheng-tsui.com; orders@cheng-tsui. com *Web Site:* www.cheng-tsui.com, pg 50

Ruth Chernia, 198 Victor Ave, Toronto, ON M4K 1B2, Canada *Tel:* 416-466-0164 *E-mail:* rchernia@editors. ca; rchernia@sympatico.ca *Web Site:* www.editors. ca/profile/444/ruth-chernia, pg 460

Cherry Hill Publishing LLC, 24344 Del Amo Rd, Ramona, CA 92065 *Tel:* 858-829-5550 *Toll Free Tel:* 800-407-1072 *Fax:* 760-203-1200 *E-mail:* operations@cherryhillpublishing.com; sales@cherryhillpublishing.com *Web Site:* www. cherryhillpublishing.com, pg 50

Linda Chester Literary Agency, 630 Fifth Ave, Suite 2000, New York, NY 10111 *Tel:* 212-218-3350 *E-mail:* submissions@lindachester.com *Web Site:* www.lindachester.com, pg 479

Chicago Review Press, 814 N Franklin St, Chicago, IL 60610 *Tel:* 312-337-0747 *Toll Free Tel:* 800-888-4741 *Fax:* 312-337-5110 *E-mail:* frontdesk@ chicagoreviewpress.com *Web Site:* www. chicagoreviewpress.com, pg 50

CN Times Books, 100 Jericho Quadrangle, Suite 337, Jericho, NY 11791 *Tel:* 516-719-0886 *E-mail:* yanliu@cntimesbooks.com *Web Site:* www.cntimesbooks.com, pg 54

Coach House Books, 80 bpNichol Lane, Toronto, ON M5S 3J4, Canada *Tel:* 416-979-2217 *Toll Free Tel:* 800-367-6360 (outside Toronto) *Fax:* 416-977-1158 *E-mail:* mail@chbooks.com *Web Site:* www.chbooks.com, pg 420

Coaches Choice, 5 Harris Ct, Bldg N, Suite 4, Monterey, CA 93940 *Toll Free Tel:* 888-229-5745 *Fax:* 831-372-6075 *E-mail:* info@coacheschoice.com *Web Site:* www.coacheschoice.com, pg 54

Coachlight Press LLC, 1704 Craig's Store Rd, Afton, VA 22920-2017 *Tel:* 434-823-1692 *E-mail:* sales@coachlightpress.com *Web Site:* www.coachlightpress.com, pg 54

Coal Hill Review Poetry Chapbook Contest, c/o Autumn House Press, PO Box 5486, Pittsburgh, PA 15206 *E-mail:* reviewcoalhill@gmail.com *Web Site:* www.coalhillreview.com, pg 605

Coastside Editorial, PO Box 181, Moss Beach, CA 94038 *E-mail:* bevjoe@pacific.net, pg 461

Codhill Press, One Arden Lane, New Paltz, NY 12561 *E-mail:* codhillpress@aol.com *Web Site:* www.codhill.com, pg 54

CODiE Awards, 1090 Vermont Ave NW, 6th fl, Washington, DC 20005-4905 *Tel:* 202-289-7442 *Fax:* 202-289-7097 *Web Site:* www.siia.net, pg 605

Coe College Playwriting Festival, 1220 First Ave NE, Cedar Rapids, IA 52402 *Tel:* 319-399-8624 *Fax:* 319-399-8557 *Web Site:* www.theatre.coe.edu; www.coe.edu/academics/theatrearts/theatrearts_playwritingfestival, pg 605

Coffee House Press, 79 13 Ave NE, Suite 110, Minneapolis, MN 55413 *Tel:* 612-338-0125 *Fax:* 612-338-4004 *E-mail:* info@coffeehousepress.org *Web Site:* coffeehousepress.org, pg 54

Cognizant Communication Corp, 18 Peekskill Hollow Rd, Putnam Valley, NY 10579-0037 *Tel:* 845-603-6440; 845-603-6441 (warehouse & orders) *Fax:* 845-603-6442 *E-mail:* inquiries@cognizantcommunication.com; sales@cognizantcommunication.com *Web Site:* www.cognizantcommunication.com, pg 54

Carla Cohen Free Speech Award, 2667 Hyacinth St, Westbury, NY 11590 *Tel:* 516-333-0681 *Fax:* 516-333-0689 *E-mail:* naibabooksellers@gmail.com *Web Site:* www.naiba.com/page/cohenfreespeechaward, pg 606

Morton N Cohen Award for a Distinguished Edition of Letters, 85 Broad St, Suite 500, New York, NY 10004-2434 *Tel:* 646-576-5141; 646-576-5000 *Fax:* 646-458-0030 *E-mail:* awards@mla.org *Web Site:* www.mla.org, pg 606

Robert L Cohen, 182-12 Horace Harding Expwy, Suite 2M, Fresh Meadows, NY 11365 *Tel:* 718-762-1195 *Toll Free Tel:* 866-EDITING (334-8464) *Fax:* 917-781-0703 *E-mail:* wordsmith@sterlingmp.com *Web Site:* www.rlcwordsandmusic.com; www.linkedin.com/in/robertcohen17, pg 461

Cohesion®, 511 W Bay St, Suite 480, Tampa, FL 33606 *Tel:* 813-999-3111 *Toll Free Tel:* 866-727-6800 *Web Site:* www.cohesion.com, pg 461

The Victor Cohn Prize for Excellence in Medical Science Reporting, PO Box 910, Hedgesville, WV 25427 *Tel:* 304-754-6786 *Web Site:* www.casw.org, pg 606

William E Colby Award, 158 Harmon Dr, Box 60, Northfield, VT 05663 *Tel:* 802-485-2965 *Web Site:* colby.norwich.edu/award, pg 606

Cold Spring Harbor Laboratory Press, One Bungtown Rd, Cold Spring Harbor, NY 11724 *Tel:* 516-422-4100 *Toll Free Tel:* 800-843-4388 *Fax:* 516-422-4097; 516-422-4092 (submissions) *E-mail:* cshpress@cshl.edu *Web Site:* www.cshlpress.com, pg 54

Collector Grade Publications Inc, PO Box 1046, Cobourg, ON K9A 4W5, Canada *Tel:* 905-342-3434 *Fax:* 905-342-3688 *E-mail:* info@collectorgrade.com *Web Site:* www.collectorgrade.com, pg 420

The College Board, 250 Vesey St, New York, NY 10281 *Tel:* 212-713-8000 *Toll Free Tel:* 866-630-9305 *Web Site:* www.collegeboard.com, pg 55

College of Liberal & Professional Studies, University of Pennsylvania, 3440 Market St, Suite 100, Philadelphia, PA 19104-3335 *Tel:* 215-898-7326 *Fax:* 215-573-2053 *E-mail:* lps@sas.upenn.edu *Web Site:* www.sas.upenn.edu/lps, pg 581

College Publishing, 12309 Lynwood Dr, Glen Allen, VA 23059 *Tel:* 804-364-8410 *Fax:* 804-364-8408 *E-mail:* collegepub@mindspring.com *Web Site:* www.collegepublishing.us, pg 55

Collier Associates, 309 Kelsey Park Circle, Palm Beach Gardens, FL 33410 *Tel:* 561-514-6548 *E-mail:* dmccabooks@gmail.com, pg 479

John M Collier Award for Forest History Journalism, 701 William Vickers Ave, Durham, NC 27701-3162 *Tel:* 919-682-9319 *Fax:* 919-682-2349 *Web Site:* www.foresthistory.org, pg 606

Frances Collin Literary Agency, PO Box 33, Wayne, PA 19087 *E-mail:* queries@francescollin.com *Web Site:* www.francescollin.com, pg 480

Carr P Collins Award, PO Box 609, Round Rock, TX 78680 *Tel:* 512-683-5640 *E-mail:* president@texasinstituteofletters.org *Web Site:* www.texasinstituteofletters.org, pg 606

The Colonial Williamsburg Foundation, PO Box 1776, Williamsburg, VA 23187-1776 *Tel:* 757-229-1000 *Toll Free Tel:* 800-HISTORY (447-8679) *E-mail:* geninfo@cwf.org *Web Site:* www.colonialwilliamsburg.org, pg 55

Colorado Authors' League, PO Box 24905, Denver, CO 80224 *Web Site:* coloradoauthors.org, pg 531

Colorado Book Awards, 7935 E Prentice Ave, Suite 450, Greenwood Village, CO 80111 *Tel:* 303-894-7951 (ext 19) *Fax:* 303-864-9361 *E-mail:* info@coloradohumanities.org *Web Site:* www.coloradohumanities.org, pg 606

Betsy Colquitt Award for Poetry, Dept of English, TCU Box 298300, Fort Worth, TX 76129 *Tel:* 817-257-5907 *Fax:* 817-257-5905 *E-mail:* descant@tcu.edu *Web Site:* www.descant.tcu.edu, pg 606

Columbia Books & Information Services (CBIS), 4340 East-West Hwy, Suite 300, Bethesda, MD 20814 *Tel:* 202-464-1662 *Fax:* 301-664-9600 *E-mail:* info@columbiabooks.com *Web Site:* www.columbiabooks.com; www.lobbyists.info; www.associationexecs.com, pg 55

Columbia Publishing Course at Columbia University, 2950 Broadway, MC 3801, New York, NY 10027 *Tel:* 212-854-1898; 212-854-9775 *E-mail:* publishing-jrn@columbia.edu *Web Site:* journalism.columbia.edu/columbia-publishing-course, pg 581

Columbia University Press, 61 W 62 St, New York, NY 10023 *Tel:* 212-459-0600 *Toll Free Tel:* 800-944-8648 *Fax:* 212-459-3678 *Web Site:* cup.columbia.edu, pg 55

Columbia University School of the Arts Creative Writing Program, 609 Kent Hall, New York, NY 10027 *Tel:* 212-854-3774 *Fax:* 212-854-7704 *E-mail:* writingprogram@columbia.edu *Web Site:* www.columbia.edu/cu/writing, pg 582

Comex Systems Inc, 9380 Nastrand Circle, Port Charlotte, FL 33981 *Tel:* 908-881-6301 *E-mail:* mail@comexsystems.com *Web Site:* www.comexsystems.com, pg 55

Committee on Scholarly Editions, c/o Modern Language Association of America, 85 Broad St, Suite 500, New York, NY 10004-2434 *Tel:* 646-576-5044 *Fax:* 646-458-0030 *E-mail:* cse@mla.org *Web Site:* www.mla.org, pg 531

Commonwealth Editions, One River Rd, Carlisle, MA 01741 *Tel:* 781-271-0055 *Toll Free Tel:* 800-277-5312 *Fax:* 781-271-0056 *E-mail:* customercare@awb.com *Web Site:* www.awb.com, pg 55

Community of Literary Magazines & Presses (CLMP), 154 Christopher St, Suite 3C, New York, NY 10014-9110 *Tel:* 212-741-9110 *E-mail:* info@clmp.org *Web Site:* www.clmp.org, pg 531

Company's Coming Publishing Ltd, 87 E Pender St, Vancouver, BC V6A 1S9, Canada *Tel:* 780-450-6223 (orders & inquiries) *Toll Free Tel:* 800-661-9017 (CN); 800-518-3541 (US) *Fax:* 780-450-1857 *E-mail:* info@companyscoming.com *Web Site:* www.companyscoming.com, pg 420

Concordia Publishing House, 3558 S Jefferson Ave, St Louis, MO 63118-3968 *Tel:* 314-268-1000; 314-268-1268 (bookshop) *Toll Free Tel:* 800-325-3040 (cust serv) *Toll Free Fax:* 800-490-9889 (cust serv) *E-mail:* order@cph.org *Web Site:* www.cph.org, pg 56

The Conference Board Inc, 845 Third Ave, New York, NY 10022-6600 *Tel:* 212-759-0900; 212-339-0345 (cust serv) *E-mail:* customer.service@conferenceboard.org; membership@conferenceboard.org *Web Site:* www.conference-board.org; www.linkedin.com/company/the-conference-board, pg 56

Conference on Poetry, 158 Ridge Rd, Franconia, NH 03580 *Tel:* 603-823-5510 *E-mail:* frost@frostplace.org *Web Site:* frostplace.org, pg 574

Don Congdon Associates Inc, 110 William St, Suite 2202, New York, NY 10038-3914 *Tel:* 212-645-1229 *Fax:* 212-727-2688 *E-mail:* dca@doncongdon.com *Web Site:* www.doncongdon.com, pg 480

Connecticut Authors & Publishers Association (CAPA), PO Box 715, Avon, CT 06001-0715 *Tel:* 860-675-1344 *Toll Free Tel:* 800-562-6457 *Web Site:* www.aboutcapa.com, pg 531

The Connecticut Law Tribune, 201 Ann Uccello St, 4th fl, Hartford, CT 06103 *Tel:* 860-527-7900 *Toll Free Tel:* 877-256-2472 *Web Site:* www.law.com/ctlawtribune/, pg 56

Miles Conrad Memorial Lecture, 3600 Clipper Mill Rd, Suite 302, Baltimore, MD 21211-1948 *Tel:* 301-654-2512 *Fax:* 410-685-5278 *E-mail:* nisohq@niso.org *Web Site:* www.niso.org, pg 606

Constance Rooke Creative Non-Fiction Prize, University of Victoria, Box 1700, Sta CSC, Victoria, BC V8W 2Y2, Canada *Tel:* 250-721-8524 *Fax:* 250-472-5051 *E-mail:* malahat@uvic.ca *Web Site:* malahatreview.ca, pg 606

Consumer Press, 13326 SW 28 St, Suite 102, Fort Lauderdale, FL 33330-1102 *Tel:* 954-370-9153 *Fax:* 954-472-1008 *E-mail:* info@consumerpress.com *Web Site:* www.consumerpress.com, pg 56

Contemporary Publishing Co of Raleigh Inc, 5849 Lease Lane, Raleigh, NC 27617 *Tel:* 919-851-8221 *Fax:* 919-851-6666 *E-mail:* questions@contemporarypublishing.com *Web Site:* www.contemporarypublishing.com, pg 56

Continental AfrikaPublishers, 182 Stribling Circle, Spartanburg, SC 29301 *E-mail:* afrikalion@aol.com; profafrikadzatadeku@yahoo.com; profafrikadzatadeku@facebook.com *Web Site:* www.afrikacentricity.com, pg 56

The Continuing Legal Education Society of British Columbia (CLEBC), 500-1155 W Pender St, Vancouver, BC V6E 2P4, Canada *Tel:* 604-669-3544; 604-893-2121 (cust serv) *Toll Free Tel:* 800-663-0437 (CN) *Fax:* 604-669-9260 *E-mail:* custserv@cle.bc.ca *Web Site:* www.cle.bc.ca, pg 420

David C Cook, 4050 Lee Vance Dr, Colorado Springs, CO 80918 *Tel:* 719-536-0100 *Toll Free Tel:* 800-708-5550; 800-323-7543 (orders & cust serv) *Toll Free Fax:* 800-430-0726 (cust serv) *Web Site:* www.davidccook.org, pg 56

The Doe Coover Agency, PO Box 668, Winchester, MA 01890 *Tel:* 781-721-6000 *Fax:* 781-721-6727 *E-mail:* info@doecooveragency.com *Web Site:* www.doecooveragency.com, pg 480

Copper Canyon Press, Fort Worden State Park, Bldg 313, Port Townsend, WA 98368 *Tel:* 360-385-4925 *Toll Free Tel:* 877-501-1393 (orders) *Fax:* 360-385-4985 *E-mail:* poetry@coppercanyonpress.org *Web Site:* www.coppercanyonpress.org, pg 56

Copywriters' Council of America™ (CCA), CCA Bldg, 7 Putter Lane, Middle Island, NY 11953-1920 *Tel:* 631-924-3888; 631-775-6075 *Fax:* 631-924-8555, pg 461, 531

Cordon d' Or - Gold Ribbon International Culinary Academy Awards, 7312 Sixth Ave N, St Petersburg, FL 33710 *Tel:* 727-347-2437 *E-mail:* cordondor@ aol.com *Web Site:* www.cordondorcuisine.com; www.florida-americasculinaryparadise.com; www. culinaryambassadorofireland.com, pg 606

Jeanne Cordova Prize for Lesbian/Queer Nonfiction, 5482 Wilshire Blvd, No 1595, Los Angeles, CA 90036 *Tel:* 323-643-4281 *E-mail:* awards@ lambdaliterary.org; admin@lambdaliterary.org *Web Site:* www.lambdaliterary.org/jeanne-cordova-prize-lesbian-nonfiction, pg 606

Albert B Corey Prize, c/o American Historical Association, 400 "A" St SE, Washington, DC 20003-3889 *Tel:* 202-544-2422 *Fax:* 202-544-8307 *E-mail:* cha-shc@cha-shc.ca *Web Site:* www.historians. org/prizes; www.cha-shc.ca, pg 607

Cormorant Books Inc, 260 Spadina Ave, Suite 502, Toronto, ON M4Y 1P9, Canada *Tel:* 416-925-8887 *E-mail:* info@cormorantbooks.com *Web Site:* www. cormorantbooks.com, pg 420

Cornell & Co LLC, 44 Jog Hill Rd, Trumbull, CT 06611 *Tel:* 203-454-4210 *Web Site:* www.cornellandco.com, pg 511

Cornell Maritime Press, 4880 Lower Valley Rd, Atglen, PA 19310 *Tel:* 610-593-1777 *Fax:* 610-593-2002 *E-mail:* info@schifferbooks.com *Web Site:* www. schifferbooks.com, pg 57

Cornell University Press, Sage House, 512 E State St, Ithaca, NY 14850 *Tel:* 607-253-2338 *Fax:* 607-253-2374 *E-mail:* cupressinfo@cornell.edu; cupress-sales@ cornell.edu *Web Site:* www.cornellpress.cornell.edu, pg 57

Cornerstone Book Publishers, PO Box 24652, New Orleans, LA 70184 *E-mail:* info@ cornerstonepublishers.com; 1cornerstonebooks@gmail. com *Web Site:* www.cornerstonepublishers.com, pg 57

Corporation for Public Broadcasting (CPB), 401 Ninth St NW, Washington, DC 20004-2129 *Tel:* 202-879-9600 *Web Site:* www.cpb.org, pg 531

Corporation of Professional Librarians of Quebec, 1453, rue Beaubien Est, Bureau 215, Montreal, QC H2G 3C6, Canada *Tel:* 514-845-3327 *Fax:* 514-845-1618 *E-mail:* info@cbpq.qc.ca *Web Site:* www.cbpq.qc.ca, pg 531

Corwin, 2455 Teller Rd, Thousand Oaks, CA 91320 *Tel:* 805-499-9734 *Toll Free Tel:* 800-233-9936 *Fax:* 805-499-5323 *Toll Free Fax:* 800-417-2466 *E-mail:* info@corwin.com; order@corwin.com *Web Site:* www.corwin.com, pg 57

Cosimo Inc, Old Chelsea Sta, PO Box 416, New York, NY 10011-0416 *Tel:* 212-989-3616 *Fax:* 212-989-3662 *E-mail:* info@cosimobooks.com *Web Site:* www. cosimobooks.com, pg 57

Cotsen Institute of Archaeology Press, 308 Charles E Young Dr N, Fowler A163, Box 951510, Los Angeles, CA 90095 *Tel:* 310-206-9384 *Fax:* 310-206-4723 *E-mail:* cioapress@ioa.ucla.edu *Web Site:* www.ioa. ucla.edu, pg 57

Council for Advancement & Support of Education (CASE), 1307 New York Ave NW, Suite 1000, Washington, DC 20005-4701 *Tel:* 202-328-CASE (328-2273) *Fax:* 202-387-4973 *E-mail:* membersupportcenter@case.org *Web Site:* www.case.org, pg 531

Council for Exceptional Children (CEC), 2900 Crystal Dr, Suite 100, Arlington, VA 22202 *Toll Free Tel:* 888-232-7733; 866-915-5000 (TTY) *E-mail:* service@cec.sped.org *Web Site:* www.cec. sped.org, pg 57

Council for Research in Values & Philosophy, The Catholic University of America, Gibbons Hall, Rm B-12, 620 Michigan Ave NE, Washington, DC 20064 *Tel:* 202-319-6089 *Fax:* 202-319-6089 *E-mail:* cua-rvp@cua.edu *Web Site:* www.crvp.org, pg 58

Council for the Advancement of Science Writing (CASW), PO Box 910, Hedgesville, WV 25427 *Tel:* 304-754-6786 *Web Site:* www.casw.org, pg 532

Council of State Governments, 1776 Avenue of the States, Lexington, KY 40511 *Tel:* 859-244-8000 *Toll Free Tel:* 800-800-1910 *Fax:* 859-244-8001 *E-mail:* sales@csg.org *Web Site:* www.csg.org; csgstore.org, pg 58

Council on Foreign Relations Press, The Harold Pratt House, 58 E 68 St, New York, NY 10065 *Tel:* 212-434-9400 *Fax:* 212-434-9800 *E-mail:* publications@ cfr.org *Web Site:* www.cfr.org, pg 58

Counterpath Press, 7935 E 14 Ave, Denver, CO 80220 *E-mail:* counterpath@counterpathpress.org *Web Site:* www.counterpathpress.org, pg 58

Counterpoint Press LLC, 2560 Ninth St, Suite 318, Berkeley, CA 94710 *Tel:* 510-704-0230 *Fax:* 510-704-0268 *E-mail:* info@counterpointpress.com *Web Site:* counterpointpress.com; softskull.com, pg 58

Country Music Foundation Press, 222 Fifth Ave S, Nashville, TN 37203 *Tel:* 615-416-2001 *Fax:* 615-255-2245 *E-mail:* info@countrymusichalloffame.org *Web Site:* www.countrymusichalloffame.org, pg 58

The Countryman Press, c/o W W Norton & Company Inc, 500 Fifth Ave, New York, NY 10110 *Tel:* 212-354-5500 *Fax:* 212-869-0856 *E-mail:* countrymanpress@wwnorton.com *Web Site:* wwnorton.com/the-countryman-press, pg 58

Course Crafters Inc, 243 Greenleaf Rd, Anson, ME 04911 *Tel:* 207-696-4050 *E-mail:* info@coursecrafters. com *Web Site:* www.coursecrafters.com, pg 461

La Courte Echelle, 4388, rue Saint-Denis, Suite 315, Montreal, QC H2J 2L1, Canada *Tel:* 514-312-6950 *E-mail:* info@courteechelle.com *Web Site:* courteechelle.groupecourteechelle.com, pg 420

Covenant Communications Inc, 1226 S 630 E, Suite 4, American Fork, UT 84003 *Tel:* 801-756-1041 *E-mail:* info@covenant-lds.com *Web Site:* www. covenant-lds.com, pg 59

COVR Visionary Awards, PO Box 1397, Palmer Lake, CO 80133 *Tel:* 719-487-0424 *E-mail:* info@covr.org *Web Site:* covr.org/awards, pg 607

The Terry J Cox Poetry Award, 806 Oberlin Rd, No 12094, Raleigh, NC 27605 *E-mail:* info@regalhousepublishing.com *Web Site:* regalhousepublishing.com/the-terry-j-cox-poetry-award/, pg 607

Coyote Press, PO Box 3377, Salinas, CA 93912-3377 *Tel:* 831-422-4912 *Fax:* 831-422-4913 *E-mail:* orders@coyotepress.com *Web Site:* www. coyotepress.com, pg 59

Marie Coyoteblanc Award for Indigenous Writing, 81 Prince St, Charlottetown, PE C1A 4R4, Canada *E-mail:* peiliteraryawards@gmail.com *Web Site:* www. peiwritersguild.com, pg 607

CPSA Prize in Comparative Politics, 260 rue Dalhousie St, Suite 204, Ottawa, ON K1N 7E4, Canada *Tel:* 613-562-1202 *Fax:* 613-241-0019 *E-mail:* cpsa-acsp@cpsa-acsp.ca *Web Site:* www.cpsa-acsp.ca, pg 607

CPSA Prize in International Relations, 260 rue Dalhousie St, Suite 204, Ottawa, ON K1N 7E4, Canada *Tel:* 613-562-1202 *Fax:* 613-241-0019 *E-mail:* cpsa-acsp@cpsa-acsp.ca *Web Site:* www.cpsa-acsp.ca, pg 607

CQ Press, 2600 Virginia Ave NW, Suite 600, Washington, DC 20037 *Tel:* 202-729-1900; 202-729-1800 *Toll Free Tel:* 866-4CQ-PRESS (427-7737) *E-mail:* customerservice@cqpress.com *Web Site:* www.cqpress.com; library.cqpress.com, pg 59

Crabtree Publishing Co, 347 Fifth Ave, Suite 1402-145, New York, NY 10016 *Tel:* 212-496-5040 *Toll Free Tel:* 800-387-7650 *Toll Free Fax:* 800-355-7166 *E-mail:* custserv@crabtreebooks.com *Web Site:* www. crabtreebooks.com, pg 59

Crabtree Publishing Co Ltd, 616 Welland Ave, St Catharines, ON L2M 5V6, Canada *Tel:* 905-682-5221 *Toll Free Tel:* 800-387-7650 *Fax:* 905-682-7166 *Toll Free Fax:* 800-355-7166 *E-mail:* custserv@ crabtreebooks.com; sales@crabtreebooks.com; orders@crabtreebooks.com *Web Site:* www. crabtreebooks.com, pg 420

Craftsman Book Co, 6058 Corte Del Cedro, Carlsbad, CA 92011 *Tel:* 760-438-7828 *Toll Free Tel:* 800-829-8123 *Fax:* 760-438-0398 *Web Site:* www.craftsman-book.com, pg 59

Avery O Craven Award, 112 N Bryan Ave, Bloomington, IN 47408-4141 *Tel:* 812-855-7311 *E-mail:* oah@oah. org *Web Site:* www.oah.org/awards, pg 607

Craven Design Inc, 229 E 85 St, New York, NY 10028 *Tel:* 212-288-1022 *Fax:* 212-249-9910 *E-mail:* cravendesign@mac.com *Web Site:* www. cravendesignstudios.com, pg 511

The Crazyhorse Fiction Prize, College of Charleston, Dept of English, 66 George St, Charleston, SC 29424 *Tel:* 843-953-4470 *E-mail:* crazyhorse@cofc.edu *Web Site:* crazyhorse.cofc.edu/prizes, pg 607

CRC Press, 6000 Broken Sound Pkwy NW, Suite 300, Boca Raton, FL 33487 *Toll Free Tel:* 800-272-7737 (orders) *Toll Free Fax:* 800-374-3401 (orders) *E-mail:* orders@taylorandfrancis.com *Web Site:* www. crcpress.com, pg 59

Creation Grant Program, 225 King St, Suite 201, Fredericton, NB E3B 1E1, Canada *Tel:* 506-444-4444 *Toll Free Tel:* 866-460-ARTS (460-2787) *Fax:* 506-444-5543 *Web Site:* www.artsnb.ca, pg 607

Creative Editions, PO Box 227, Mankato, MN 56002 *Tel:* 507-388-6273 *Toll Free Tel:* 800-445-6209 *Fax:* 507-388-2746 *E-mail:* info@thecreativecompany. us; orders@thecreativecompany.us *Web Site:* www. thecreativecompany.us, pg 59

Creative Freelancers Inc, PO Box 366, Tallevast, FL 34270 *Toll Free Tel:* 800-398-9544 *Web Site:* www. freelancers1.com, pg 461

Creative Homeowner, 1970 Broad St, East Petersburg, PA 17520 *Tel:* 717-560-4703 *Toll Free Tel:* 844-307-3677 *Toll Free Fax:* 888-369-2885 *E-mail:* customerservice@foxchapelpublishing.com; sales@foxchapelpublishing.com *Web Site:* www. foxchapelB2B.com, pg 59

Creative Nonfiction Awards, 81 Prince St, Charlottetown, PE C1A 4R3, Canada *E-mail:* peiliteraryawards@ gmail.com *Web Site:* www.peiwritersguild.com, pg 607

Creative Writing Day & Workshops, PO Box 801, Abingdon, VA 24212-0801 *Tel:* 276-623-5266 *Fax:* 276-676-3076 *E-mail:* info@vahighlandsfestival. org *Web Site:* vahighlandsfestival.org, pg 574

CreativeWell Inc, PO Box 3130, Memorial Sta, Upper Montclair, NJ 07043 *Tel:* 973-783-7575 *E-mail:* info@ creativewell.com *Web Site:* www.creativewell.com, pg 480, 515

Crichton & Associates Inc, 6940 Carroll Ave, Takoma Park, MD 20912 *Tel:* 301-495-9663 *E-mail:* cricht1@ aol.com *Web Site:* www.crichton-associates.com, pg 480

Cricket Cottage Publishing LLC, 1500 Beville Rd, Suite 606-346, Daytona Beach, FL 32114 *Tel:* 323-207-6213 *E-mail:* thecricketpublishing@gmail.com *Web Site:* thecricketpublishing.com; www.facebook. com/CricketCottagePublishing, pg 59

Crime Writers of Canada (CWC), 4C-240 Westwood Rd, Guelph, ON N1H 7W9, Canada *E-mail:* info@ crimewriterscanada.com *Web Site:* www. crimewriterscanada.com, pg 532

Crook's Corner Book Prize, 313 Country Club Rd, Chapel Hill, NC 27514 *E-mail:* info@crookscornerbookprize. com *Web Site:* crookscornerbookprize.com, pg 608

Cross-Cultural Communications, 239 Wynsum Ave, Merrick, NY 11566-4725 *Tel:* 516-868-5635 *Fax:* 516-379-1901 *E-mail:* cccbarkan@optonline. net; cccpoetry@aol.com *Web Site:* www.facebook. com/CrossCulturalCommunications.NY/, pg 60

Crossquarter Publishing Group, PO Box 23749, Santa Fe, NM 87502 *Tel:* 505-690-3923 *Fax:* 214-975-9715 *E-mail:* sales@crossquarter.com; info@crossquarter.com *Web Site:* www.crossquarter.com, pg 60

The Crossroad Publishing Co, 831 Chestnut Ridge Rd, Chestnut Ridge, NY 10977 *Tel:* 845-517-0180 *Toll Free Tel:* 800-888-4741 (orders) *E-mail:* info@crossroadpublishing.com *Web Site:* www.CrossroadPublishing.com, pg 60

Crossway, 1300 Crescent St, Wheaton, IL 60187 *Tel:* 630-682-4300 *Toll Free Tel:* 800-635-7993 (orders); 800-543-1659 (cust serv) *Fax:* 630-682-4785 *E-mail:* info@crossway.org *Web Site:* www.crossway.org, pg 60

Crown House Publishing Co LLC, 81 Brook Hills Circle, White Plains, NY 10605 *Tel:* 914-946-3517 *Toll Free Tel:* 877-925-1213 (cust serv) *Fax:* 914-946-1160 *E-mail:* info@chpus.com *Web Site:* www.crownhousepublishing.com, pg 60

Crown Publishing Group, 1745 Broadway, New York, NY 10019 *Tel:* 212-782-9000 *Toll Free Tel:* 888-264-1745 *Fax:* 212-940-7408 *E-mail:* crownosm@penguinrandomhouse.com *Web Site:* crownpublishing.com, pg 60

Crystal Clarity Publishers, 14618 Tyler Foote Rd, Nevada City, CA 95959 *Tel:* 530-478-7600 *Toll Free Tel:* 800-424-1055 *Fax:* 530-478-7562 *E-mail:* clarity@crystalclarity.com *Web Site:* www.crystalclarity.com, pg 61

Crystal Kite Awards, 6363 Wilshire Blvd, Suite 425, Los Angeles, CA 90048 *Tel:* 323-782-1010 *E-mail:* grants@scbwi.org; scbwi@scbwi.org *Web Site:* www.scbwi.org/awards, pg 608

CS International Literary Agency, 43 W 39 St, New York, NY 10018 *Tel:* 212-921-1610; 212-391-9208 *E-mail:* query@csliterary.com; csliterary08@gmail.com *Web Site:* www.csliterary.com, pg 461

The CSIS Press, 1616 Rhode Island Ave NW, Washington, DC 20036 *Tel:* 202-887-0200 *Fax:* 202-775-3199 *E-mail:* books@csis.org *Web Site:* www.csis.org, pg 61

CSLI Publications, Stanford University, Cordura Hall, 220 Panama St, Stanford, CA 94305-4115 *Tel:* 650-723-1839 *Fax:* 650-725-2166 *E-mail:* pubs@csli.stanford.edu *Web Site:* cslipublications.stanford.edu, pg 61

CSWE Press, 1701 Duke St, Suite 200, Alexandria, VA 22314-3457 *Tel:* 703-683-8080 *Fax:* 703-683-8493 *E-mail:* publications@cswe.org; info@cswe.org *Web Site:* www.cswe.org, pg 61

Cultural Studies & Analysis, 1123 Montrose St, Philadelphia, PA 19147-3721 *Tel:* 215-592-8544 *E-mail:* info@culturalanalysis.com *Web Site:* www.culturalanalysis.com, pg 461

Cundill History Prize, 3463 Peel St, Montreal, QC H3A 1W7, Canada *Tel:* 514-398-8346 *E-mail:* cundill.prize@mcgill.ca *Web Site:* www.cundillprize.com, pg 608

Cunningham Commission for Youth Theatre, Lincoln Park Campus, 2350 N Racine Ave, Chicago, IL 60614-4100 *Tel:* 773-325-7999 *Fax:* 773-325-7920 *E-mail:* cunninghamcommission@depaul.edu *Web Site:* theatre.depaul.edu, pg 608

Cup of Tea Books, PO Box 21133, Columbus, OH 43221 *E-mail:* sales@pagespringpublishing.com; weditor@pagespringpublishing.com; submissions@pagespringpublishing.com *Web Site:* www.cupofteabooks.com, pg 61

Merle Curti Intellectual History Award, 112 N Bryan Ave, Bloomington, IN 47408-4141 *Tel:* 812-855-7311 *E-mail:* oah@oah.org *Web Site:* www.oah.org/awards, pg 608

Merle Curti Social History Award, 112 N Bryan Ave, Bloomington, IN 47408-4141 *Tel:* 812-855-7311 *E-mail:* oah@oah.org *Web Site:* www.oah.org/awards, pg 608

C Michael Curtis Short Story Book Prize, 186 W Main St, Spartanburg, SC 29306 *Tel:* 864-577-9349 *Fax:* 864-577-0188 *E-mail:* info@hubcity.org; submit@hubcity.org *Web Site:* hubcity.org/press/c-michael-curtis-short-story-book-prize, pg 608

Richard Curtis Associates Inc, 200 E 72 St, Suite 28J, New York, NY 10021 *Tel:* 212-772-7363 *E-mail:* info@curtisagency.com *Web Site:* www.curtisagency.com, pg 480

Karen & Philip Cushman Late Bloomer Award, 6363 Wilshire Blvd, Suite 425, Los Angeles, CA 90048 *Tel:* 323-782-1010 *Fax:* 323-782-1892 *E-mail:* grants@scbwi.org; scbwi@scbwi.org *Web Site:* www.scbwi.org, pg 608

CWA/SCA Canada, 2200 Prince of Wales Dr, Suite 301, Ottawa, ON K2E 6Z9, Canada *Tel:* 613-820-9777 *Toll Free Tel:* 877-486-4292 *Fax:* 613-820-8188 *E-mail:* info@cwa-scacanada.ca *Web Site:* www.cwa-scacanada.ca, pg 532

Cycle Publishing LLC, 1282 Seventh Ave, San Francisco, CA 94122-2526 *Tel:* 415-665-8214 *Fax:* 415-753-8572 *Web Site:* www.cyclepublishing.com, pg 61

Cypress House, 155 Cypress St, Fort Bragg, CA 95437 *Tel:* 707-964-9520 *Toll Free Tel:* 800-773-7782 *Fax:* 707-964-7531 *Web Site:* www.cypresshouse.com, pg 61, 461

Dalkey Archive Press, University of Houston-Victoria, 3402 N Ben Wilson, Victoria, TX 77901 *E-mail:* contact@dalkeyarchive.com *Web Site:* www.dalkeyarchive.com, pg 61

Dana Awards, Literary Competition, 200 Fosseway Dr, Greensboro, NC 27455 *Tel:* 336-644-8028 *E-mail:* danaawards@gmail.com *Web Site:* www.danaawards.com, pg 608

Robert Dana-Anhinga Prize for Poetry, PO Box 3665, Tallahassee, FL 32315 *Tel:* 850-577-0745 *E-mail:* info@anhinga.org *Web Site:* www.anhingapress.org, pg 608

The Danahy Fiction Prize, University of Tampa Press, 401 W Kennedy Blvd, Tampa, FL 33606 *Tel:* 813-253-6266 *E-mail:* utpress@ut.edu *Web Site:* tampareview.ut.edu, pg 608

Dancing Dakini Press, 77 Morning Sun Dr, Sedona, AZ 86336 *Tel:* 505-466-1887 *E-mail:* editor@dancingdakinipress.com *Web Site:* www.dancingdakinipress.com, pg 61

Dancing Lemur Press LLC, PO Box 383, Pikeville, NC 27863-0383 *E-mail:* inquiries@dancinglemurpressllc.com *Web Site:* www.dancinglemurpressllc.com, pg 61

John Daniel & Co, PO Box 2790, McKinleyville, CA 95519-2790 *Tel:* 707-839-3495 *Toll Free Tel:* 800-662-8351 *E-mail:* dandd@danielpublishing.com *Web Site:* www.danielpublishing.com, pg 62

John M Daniel Literary Services, PO Box 2790, McKinleyville, CA 95519 *Tel:* 707-839-3495 *E-mail:* jmd@danielpublishing.com *Web Site:* www.danielpublishing.com/litserv.htm, pg 462

Benjamin H Danks Award, 633 W 155 St, New York, NY 10032 *Tel:* 212-368-5900 *Fax:* 212-491-4615 *E-mail:* academy@artsandletters.org *Web Site:* artsandletters.org, pg 608

Darhansoff & Verrill, 133 W 72 St, Rm 304, New York, NY 10023 *Tel:* 917-305-1300 *E-mail:* permissions@dvagency.com *Web Site:* www.dvagency.com, pg 480

Dark Horse Comics, 10956 SE Main St, Milwaukie, OR 97222 *Tel:* 503-652-8815 *Fax:* 503-654-9440 *E-mail:* dhcomics@darkhorse.com *Web Site:* www.darkhorse.com, pg 62

Darla Bruno Writing Coach, Developmental Editor, 42 Trenton Ave, Frenchtown, NJ 08825 *E-mail:* editor@darlabruno.com *Web Site:* www.darlabruno.com, pg 462

The Dartnell Corporation, 2222 Sedwick Dr, Durham, NC 27713 *Toll Free Tel:* 800-223-8720; 800-472-0148 (cust serv) *Toll Free Fax:* 800-508-2592 *E-mail:* customerservice@dartnellcorp.com *Web Site:* www.dartnellcorp.com, pg 62

Data Trace Publishing Co (DTP), 110 West Rd, Suite 227, Towson, MD 21204-2316 *Tel:* 410-494-4994 *Toll Free Tel:* 800-342-0454 *Fax:* 410-494-0515 *E-mail:* info@datatrace.com; customerservice@datatrace.com; salesandmarketing@datatrace.com; editorial@datatrace.com *Web Site:* www.datatrace.com, pg 62

Database Directories, 588 Dufferin Ave, London, ON N6B 2A4, Canada *Tel:* 519-433-1666 *Fax:* 519-430-1131 *E-mail:* mail@databasedirectory.com *Web Site:* www.databasedirectory.com, pg 421

May Davenport Publishers, 26313 Purissima Rd, Los Altos Hills, CA 94022 *Tel:* 650-947-6499 *E-mail:* mdbooks@earthlink.net *Web Site:* www.maydavenportpublishers.org, pg 62

The Davies Group Publishers, PO Box 440140, Aurora, CO 80044-0140 *Tel:* 303-750-8374 *E-mail:* daviesgroup@msn.com (orders) *Web Site:* www.thedaviesgrouppublishers.com, pg 62

Davies Publishing Inc, 32 S Raymond Ave, Suites 4 & 5, Pasadena, CA 91105-1961 *Tel:* 626-792-3046 *Toll Free Tel:* 877-792-0005 *Fax:* 626-792-5308 *E-mail:* info@daviespublishing.com *Web Site:* daviespublishing.com, pg 62

F A Davis Co, 1915 Arch St, Philadelphia, PA 19103 *Tel:* 215-568-2270; 215-440-3001 *Toll Free Tel:* 800-523-4049 *Fax:* 215-568-5065; 215-440-3016 *E-mail:* info@fadavis.com; orders@fadavis.com *Web Site:* www.fadavis.com, pg 62

Watson Davis & Helen Miles Davis Prize, 440 Geddes Hall, Notre Dame, IN 46556 *Tel:* 574-631-1194 *E-mail:* info@hssonline.org *Web Site:* www.hssonline.org, pg 609

DAW Books Inc, 375 Hudson St, New York, NY 10014 *Tel:* 212-366-2096 *Fax:* 212-366-2090 *E-mail:* daw@penguinrandomhouse.com *Web Site:* www.dawbooks.com; www.penguin.com; www.penguinrandomhouse.com, pg 63

The Dawn Horse Press, 12040 N Seigler Rd, Middletown, CA 95461 *Tel:* 707-928-6590 *Toll Free Tel:* 877-770-0772 *Fax:* 707-928-5068 *E-mail:* dhp@adidam.org *Web Site:* www.dawnhorsepress.com, pg 63

Dawn Publications Inc, 12402 Bitney Springs Rd, Nevada City, CA 95959 *Tel:* 530-274-7775 *Toll Free Tel:* 800-545-7475 *Fax:* 530-274-7778 *E-mail:* nature@dawnpub.com; orders@dawnpub.com *Web Site:* www.dawnpub.com, pg 63

DawnSignPress, 6130 Nancy Ridge Dr, San Diego, CA 92121-3223 *Tel:* 858-625-0600 *Toll Free Tel:* 800-549-5350 *Fax:* 858-625-2336 *E-mail:* contactus@dawnsign.com *Web Site:* www.dawnsign.com, pg 63

Liza Dawson Associates, 121 W 27 St, Suite 1201, New York, NY 10001 *Tel:* 212-465-9071 *Web Site:* www.lizadawsonassociates.com, pg 480

Dayton Literary Peace Prize, 25 Harman Terr, Dayton, OH 45419 *Tel:* 937-298-5072 *Web Site:* daytonliterarypeaceprize.org, pg 609

Dayton Playhouse FutureFest, PO Box 3017, Dayton, OH 45401-3017 *Tel:* 937-424-8477 *Fax:* 937-424-0062 *E-mail:* futurefest@thedaytonplayhouse.com *Web Site:* wordpress.daytonplayhouse.com, pg 609

dbS Productions, PO Box 94, Charlottesville, VA 22902 *Tel:* 434-293-5502 *Toll Free Tel:* 800-745-1581 *E-mail:* info@dbs-sar.com *Web Site:* www.dbs-sar.com, pg 63

DC Canada Education Publishing (DCCED), 180 Metcalfe St, Suite 204, Ottawa, ON K2P 1P5, Canada *Tel:* 613-565-8885 *Toll Free Tel:* 888-565-0262 *Fax:* 613-565-8881 *E-mail:* info@dc-canada.ca *Web Site:* www.dc-canada.ca, pg 421

DC Comics Inc, 4000 Warner Blvd, Burbank, CA 91522 *Web Site:* www.dccomics.com; www.dcentertainment.com; www.madmag.com, pg 63

Walter De Gruyter Inc, 121 High St, 3rd fl, Boston, MA 02110 *Tel:* 857-284-7073 *Fax:* 857-284-7358 *E-mail:* service@degruyter.com *Web Site:* www.degruyter.com, pg 63

J de S Associates Inc, 9 Shagbark Rd, South Norwalk, CT 06854 *Tel:* 203-838-7571 *Fax:* 203-866-2713 *Web Site:* www.jdesassociates.com, pg 481

Deadline Club, c/o Salmagundi Club, 47 Fifth Ave, New York, NY 10003 *Tel:* 646-481-7584 *Web Site:* www. deadlineclub.org, pg 532

Deborah Wolfe Ltd, 731 N 24 St, Philadelphia, PA 19130 *Tel:* 215-232-6666 *Fax:* 215-232-6585 *E-mail:* info@illustrationonline.com *Web Site:* www. illustrationonline.com, pg 511

The Jennifer DeChiara Literary Agency, 245 Park Ave, 39th fl, New York, NY 10167 *Tel:* 212-372-8989 *Web Site:* www.jdlit.com, pg 481

Deep River Books LLC, PO Box 310, Sisters, OR 97759 *Tel:* 541-549-1139 *E-mail:* info@deepriverbooks.com *Web Site:* deepriverbooks.com, pg 63

DeFiore and Company Literary Management Inc, 47 E 19 St, 3rd fl, New York, NY 10003 *Tel:* 212-925-7744 *Fax:* 212-925-9803 *E-mail:* info@defliterary. com; submissions@defliterary.com *Web Site:* www. defliterary.com, pg 481

Delaware Division of the Arts Individual Artist Fellowships, Carvel State Off Bldg, 4th fl, 820 N French St, Wilmington, DE 19801 *Tel:* 302-577-8278 *Fax:* 302-577-6561 *E-mail:* delarts@state.de.us *Web Site:* www.artsdel.org, pg 609

Joelle Delbourgo Associates Inc, 101 Park St, Montclair, NJ 07042 *Tel:* 973-773-0836 (call only during standard business hours) *Web Site:* www.delbourgo. com, pg 481

Delphinium Books, 16350 Ventura Blvd, Suite D, Encino, CA 91436 *Tel:* 917-301-7496 (e-mail first) *Web Site:* www.delphiniumbooks.com, pg 64

Rick DeMarinis Short Story Award, PO Box 2414, Durango, CO 81302 *Tel:* 970-903-7914 *E-mail:* cutthroatmag@gmail.com *Web Site:* www. cutthroatmag.com, pg 609

Demos Medical Publishing, 11 W 42 St, 15th fl, New York, NY 10036 *Tel:* 212-683-0072 *E-mail:* cs@ springerpub.com *Web Site:* www.springerpub.com/ medicine; www.springerpub.com/consumer-health, pg 64

Denver Publishing Institute Scholarship, 3135 S State St, Suite 203, Ann Arbor, MI 48108 *Toll Free Tel:* 866-733-9064 *Fax:* 734-477-2806 *E-mail:* info@ bincfoundation.org *Web Site:* www.bincfoundation. org/denver-publishing-institute/, pg 609

Der-Hovanessian Translation Prize, 46 Wallace St, Somerville, MA 02144 *E-mail:* info@nepoetryclub.org *Web Site:* www.nepoetryclub.org, pg 609

Deseret Book Co, 57 W South Temple, Salt Lake City, UT 84101-1511 *Tel:* 801-517-3309; 801-534-1515 (corp) *Toll Free Tel:* 800-453-4532 (orders); 888-846-7302 (orders) *Fax:* 801-517-3126 *E-mail:* service@ deseretbook.com *Web Site:* www.deseretbook.com, pg 64

Annual Design Competition, 27 Union Sq W, Suite 207, New York, NY 10003 *Tel:* 212-223-3332 *Fax:* 212-223-5880 *E-mail:* mail@spd.org *Web Site:* www.spd. org, pg 609

DEStech Publications Inc, 439 N Duke St, Lancaster, PA 17602-4967 *Tel:* 717-290-1660 *Toll Free Tel:* 877-500-4DES (500-4337) *Fax:* 717-509-6100 *E-mail:* info@ destechpub.com *Web Site:* www.destechpub.com, pg 64

Destiny Image Inc, 167 Walnut Bottom Rd, Shippensburg, PA 17257-0310 *Tel:* 717-532-3040 *Toll Free Tel:* 800-722-6774 (orders only) *Fax:* 717-532-9291 *Web Site:* www.destinyimage.com, pg 64

DeVorss & Co, 553 Constitution Ave, Camarillo, CA 93012-8510 *Tel:* 805-322-9010 *Toll Free Tel:* 800-843-5743 *Fax:* 805-322-9011 *E-mail:* service@devorss.com *Web Site:* www.devorss.com, pg 64

Anna Dewdney Read Together Award, 54 W 39 St, 14th fl, New York, NY 10018 *Tel:* 917-890-7416 *Web Site:* everychildareader.net/anna, pg 609

Dewey Publications Inc, 1840 Wilson Blvd, Suite 203, Arlington, VA 22201 *Tel:* 703-524-1355 *Fax:* 703-524-1463 *E-mail:* deweypublications@gmail.com *Web Site:* www.deweypub.com, pg 64

Dharma Publishing, 35788 Hauser Bridge Rd, Cazadero, CA 95421 *Tel:* 707-847-3717 *Fax:* 707-847-3380 *E-mail:* contact@dharmapublishing.com *Web Site:* www.dharmapublishing.com, pg 64

Alice Fay Di Castagnola Award, 15 Gramercy Park, New York, NY 10003 *Tel:* 212-254-9628 *Web Site:* poetrysociety.org/awards, pg 609

Christina Di Martino Literary Services, 87 Hamilton Place, No 7G, New York, NY 10031 *Tel:* 212-996-9086; 561-283-1549 *E-mail:* writealotmail@gmail. com, pg 462

diacriTech Inc, 4 S Market St, 4th fl, Boston, MA 02109 *Tel:* 617-600-3366 *Fax:* 617-848-2938 *Web Site:* www. diacritech.com, pg 462

Dial Books for Young Readers, 345 Hudson St, New York, NY 10014 *Tel:* 212-366-2000 *Toll Free Tel:* 800-733-3000 (orders) *Fax:* 212-414-3396 *Web Site:* www.penguin.com/publishers/ dialbooksforyoungreaders/, pg 64

Philip K Dick Award, PO Box 3447, Hoboken, NJ 07030 *Tel:* 201-876-2551 *Web Site:* www. philipkdickaward.org, pg 609

D4EO Literary Agency, 7 Indian Valley Rd, Weston, CT 06883 *Tel:* 203-544-7180 *Fax:* 203-544-7160 *Web Site:* www.d4eoliteraryagency.com; www. publishersmarketplace.com/members/d4eo/; twitter. com/d4eo, pg 481

Sandra Dijkstra Literary Agency, 1155 Camino del Mar, PMB 515, Del Mar, CA 92014-2605 *Web Site:* dijkstraagency.com, pg 482

Annie Dillard Award for Creative Nonfiction, Mail Stop 9053, Western Washington University, Bellingham, WA 98225 *Tel:* 360-650-4863 *E-mail:* bhreview@ wwu.edu *Web Site:* www.bhreview.org, pg 609

Gordon W Dillon/Richard C Peterson Memorial Essay Prize, c/o Fairchild Tropical Botanic Garden, 10901 Old Cutler Rd, Coral Gables, FL 33156 *Tel:* 305-740-2010 *E-mail:* theaos@aos.org *Web Site:* www.aos.org, pg 610

DiscoverNet Publishing, 2474 Walnut St, Suite 105, Cary, NC 27518 *Tel:* 919-301-0109 *Fax:* 919-557-2261 *E-mail:* info@discovernet.com *Web Site:* www. discovernet.com, pg 64

Discovery/Boston Review Poetry Contest, 1395 Lexington Ave, New York, NY 10128 *Tel:* 212-415-5760 *E-mail:* unterberg@92y.org *Web Site:* www.92y. org/discovery, pg 610

Discovery House Publishers, 3000 Kraft Ave SE, Grand Rapids, MI 49512 *Tel:* 616-942-2803 *Toll Free Tel:* 800-653-8333 (cust serv) *E-mail:* support@dhp. org; customerservice@dhp.org *Web Site:* www.dhp.org, pg 65

Disney-Hyperion Books, 1101 Flower St, Glendale, CA 91201 *Web Site:* books.disney.com, pg 65

Disney Press, 1101 Flower St, Glendale, CA 91201 *Web Site:* books.disney.com, pg 65

Disney Publishing Worldwide, 1101 Flower St, Glendale, CA 91201 *Web Site:* books.disney.com, pg 65

Dissertation.com, 200 Spectrum Center Dr, 3rd fl, Irvine, CA 92618 *Tel:* 561-750-4344 *Toll Free Tel:* 800-636-8329 *Fax:* 561-750-6797 *Web Site:* www.dissertation. com, pg 65

Distinguished Scholarly Book Award, c/o Governance Off, 1430 "K" St NW, Suite 600, Washington, DC 20005 *Tel:* 202-383-9005 *Fax:* 202-638-0882 *E-mail:* governance@asanet.org *Web Site:* www.asanet. org, pg 610

Diversion Books, 443 Park Ave S, Suite 1008, New York, NY 10016 *Tel:* 212-961-6390 *E-mail:* info@ diversionbooks.com *Web Site:* www.diversionbooks. com, pg 65

Djerassi Resident Artists Program, 2325 Bear Gulch Rd, Woodside, CA 94062 *Tel:* 650-747-1250 *E-mail:* drap@djerassi.org *Web Site:* www.djerassi.org, pg 574

DK Publishing, 1450 Broadway, Suite 801, New York, NY 10018 *Tel:* 646-674-4000 *Toll Free Tel:* 800-733-3000 *Fax:* 646-674-4020 *E-mail:* marketing@dk.com; publicity@dk.com; csorders@penguinrandomhouse. com; ecustomerservice@randomhouse.com *Web Site:* www.dk.com; www.penguin.com, pg 65

DK Research Inc, 9 Wicks Dr, Commack, NY 11725-3921 *Tel:* 631-543-5537 *Fax:* 631-543-5549 *E-mail:* dkresearch@optimum.net *Web Site:* www. dkresearchinc.com, pg 462

Documentation Grant Program, 225 King St, Suite 201, Fredericton, NB E3B 1E1, Canada *Tel:* 506-444-4444 *Toll Free Tel:* 866-460-ARTS (460-2787) *Fax:* 506-444-5543 *Web Site:* www.artsnb.ca, pg 610

Blake Dodd Prize, 633 W 155 St, New York, NY 10032 *Tel:* 212-368-5900 *Fax:* 212-491-4615 *E-mail:* academy@artsandletters.org *Web Site:* artsandletters.org, pg 610

Dog Writers' Association of America Inc (DWAA), PO Box 787, Hughesville, MD 20637 *E-mail:* info@ dogwriters.org *Web Site:* dogwriters.org, pg 532

Dog Writers' Association of America Inc (DWAA) Annual Writing Competition, PO Box 787, Hughesville, MD 20637 *E-mail:* info@dogwriters.org *Web Site:* dogwriters.org, pg 610

Dogwise Publishing, 403 S Mission St, Wenatchee, WA 98801 *Tel:* 509-663-9115 *Toll Free Tel:* 800-776-2665 *E-mail:* mail@dogwise.com *Web Site:* www.dogwise. com, pg 66

The Christopher Doheny Award, 17 E 47 St, New York, NY 10017 *Tel:* 212-755-6710 *E-mail:* doheny@ centerforfiction.org; info@centerforfiction.org *Web Site:* www.centerforfiction.org/awards/the-christopher-doheny-award, pg 610

Tom Doherty Associates, LLC, 120 Broadway, New York, NY 10271 *Tel:* 646-307-5511 *Toll Free Tel:* 800-455-0340 *Web Site:* us.macmillan.com/ torforge, pg 66

Janis A Donnaud & Associates Inc, 77 Bleecker St, No C1-25, New York, NY 10012 *Tel:* 212-431-2663 *Fax:* 212-431-2667 *E-mail:* jdonnaud@aol.com, pg 482

Donner Prize, c/o Naylor and Associates, 23 Empire Ave, Toronto, ON M4M 2L3, Canada *Tel:* 416-368-8253 *E-mail:* donnerprize@naylorandassociates.com *Web Site:* donnerbookprize.com, pg 610

The Donning Company Publishers, 731 S Brunswick St, Brookfield, MO 64628 *Toll Free Tel:* 800-369-2646 (ext 3377) *Web Site:* www.donning.com, pg 66

Jim Donovan Literary, 5635 SMU Blvd, Suite 201, Dallas, TX 75206 *Tel:* 214-696-9411 *E-mail:* jdlqueries@sbcglobal.net, pg 482

Doodle and Peck Publishing, 413 Cedarburg Ct, Yukon, OK 73099 *Tel:* 405-354-7422 *E-mail:* contact@ doodleandpeck.com *Web Site:* www.doodleandpeck. com, pg 66

Dordt Press, 700 Seventh St NE, Sioux Center, IA 51250-1671 *Tel:* 712-722-6420 *Toll Free Tel:* 800-343-6738 *Fax:* 712-722-6035 *E-mail:* dordtpress@ dordt.edu; bookstore@dordt.edu *Web Site:* www.dordt. edu/about-dordt/publications/dordt-press-catalog, pg 66

Dorothy Canfield Fisher Book Award, 109 State St, Montpelier, VT 05609-0601 *Tel:* 802-828-2721 *Web Site:* libraries.vermont.gov, pg 610

Dorrance Publishing Co Inc, 585 Alpha Dr, Suite 103, Pittsburgh, PA 15238 *Toll Free Tel:* 800-695-9599; 800-788-7654 (gen cust orders) *Fax:* 412-387-1319 *E-mail:* dorrinfo@dorrancepublishing.com; dorrordr@ dorrancepublishing.com (book orders) *Web Site:* www. dorrancepublishing.com, pg 66

Dorset Prize, 60 Roberts Dr, Suite 308, North Adams, MA 01247 *Tel:* 413-664-9611 *Fax:* 413-664-9711 *E-mail:* info@tupelopress.org *Web Site:* www. tupelopress.org, pg 611

John Dos Passos Prize for Literature, Dept of English & Modern Languages, 201 High St, Farmville, VA 23909 *Tel:* 434-395-2155 *Fax:* 434-395-2145 *Web Site:* www.longwood.edu/english/dos-passos-prize, pg 611

Double Dragon Publishing Inc, 1-5762 Hwy 7 E, Markham, ON L3P 7Y4, Canada *E-mail:* sales@double-dragon-ebooks.com *Web Site:* www.double-dragon-ebooks.com, pg 421

Double Play, 303 Hillcrest Rd, Belton, MO 64012-1852 *Tel:* 816-651-7118, pg 462

Doubleday, c/o Penguin Random House Inc, 1745 Broadway, New York, NY 10019 *Tel:* 212-751-2600 *Fax:* 212-572-2662 (foreign rts) *E-mail:* ddaypub@randomhouse.com *Web Site:* knopfdoubleday.com, pg 66

Doubleday Canada, 320 Front St W, Suite 1400, Toronto, ON M5V 3B6, Canada *Tel:* 416-364-4449 *Fax:* 416-598-7764 *Web Site:* www.penguinrandomhouse.ca, pg 421

Frank Nelson Doubleday Memorial Award, Barrett Bldg, 2nd fl, 2301 Central Ave, Cheyenne, WY 82002 *Tel:* 307-777-7742 *Web Site:* wyoarts.state.wy.us, pg 611

Douglas & McIntyre (2013) Ltd, 4437 Rondeview Rd, Madeira Park, BC V0N 2H1, Canada *Toll Free Tel:* 800-667-2988 *E-mail:* info@douglas-mcintyre.com *Web Site:* www.douglas-mcintyre.com, pg 421

Dover Publications Inc, 31 E Second St, Mineola, NY 11501-3852 *Tel:* 516-294-7000 *Toll Free Tel:* 800-223-3130 (orders) *Fax:* 516-742-6953 *E-mail:* rights@doverpublications.com; service@doverpublications.com; doversales@doverpublications.com *Web Site:* store.doverdirect.com; www.doverpublications.com, pg 67

Down East Books, 4501 Forbes Blvd, Suite 200, Lanham, MD 20706 *Tel:* 301-459-3366 *Fax:* 301-429-5748 *E-mail:* orders@rowman.com; customercare@rowman.com *Web Site:* rowman.com/page/downeastbooks, pg 67

Down The Shore Publishing Corp, 106 Stafford Forge Rd, West Creek, NJ 08092 *Tel:* 609-812-5076 *Fax:* 609-812-5098 *E-mail:* dtsbooks@comcast.net; info@down-the-shore.com *Web Site:* www.down-the-shore.com, pg 67

Dragon Door Publications, 2999 Yorkton Blvd, Suite 2, Little Canada, MN 55117 *Tel:* 651-487-2180 *E-mail:* support@dragondoor.com *Web Site:* www.dragondoor.com, pg 67

Dragonfly Book Awards, 4696 W Tyson St, Chandler, AZ 85226-2903 *Tel:* 480-940-8182 *Fax:* 480-940-8787 *E-mail:* info@StoryMonsters.com *Web Site:* www.DragonflyBookAwards.com, pg 611

Dramatic Publishing Co, 311 Washington St, Woodstock, IL 60098-3308 *Tel:* 815-338-7170 *Toll Free Tel:* 800-448-7469 *Fax:* 815-338-8981 *Toll Free Fax:* 800-334-5302 *E-mail:* plays@dramaticpublishing.com; customerservice@dpcplays.com *Web Site:* www.dramaticpublishing.com, pg 67

Dramatists Play Service Inc, 440 Park Ave S, New York, NY 10016 *Tel:* 212-683-8960 *Fax:* 212-213-1539 *E-mail:* postmaster@dramatists.com; orders@dramatists.com; publications@dramatists.com *Web Site:* www.dramatists.com, pg 67

Dreaming Robot Press, 1214 San Francisco Ave, Las Vegas, NM 87701 *Tel:* 505-264-3830 *E-mail:* books@dreamingrobotpress.com *Web Site:* dreamingrobotpress.com, pg 67

Dreamscape Media LLC, 1417 Timberwolf Dr, Holland, OH 43528 *Tel:* 419-867-6965 *Toll Free Tel:* 877-983-7326 *E-mail:* info@dreamscapeab.com *Web Site:* www.dreamscapepublishing.com, pg 67

Drennan Communications, 6 Robin Lane, East Kingston, NH 03827 *Tel:* 603-642-8002 *Fax:* 603-642-8002, pg 462

Drennan Literary Agency, 6 Robin Lane, East Kingston, NH 03827 *Tel:* 603-642-8002 *Fax:* 603-642-8002, pg 482

Carleton Drewry Memorial, 900 Timber Creek Place, Virginia Beach, VA 23464 *E-mail:* poetryinva@aol.com *Web Site:* poetrysocietyofvirginia.org, pg 611

Saint Katharine Drexel Award, 8550 United Plaza Blvd, Suite 1001, Baton Rouge, LA 70809 *Tel:* 225-408-4417 *Fax:* 225-408-4422 *E-mail:* cla2@cathla.org *Web Site:* cathla.org, pg 611

Drummond Books, 2111 Cleveland St, Evanston, IL 60202 *Tel:* 847-302-2534 *E-mail:* drummondbooks@gmail.com, pg 462

Drury University One-Act Play Competition, 900 N Benton Ave, Springfield, MO 65802-3344 *Tel:* 417-873-6821 *Web Site:* www.drury.edu, pg 611

Dubuque Fine Arts Players Annual One Act Play Festival, PO Box 1160, Dubuque, IA 52004-1160 *Tel:* 563-588-3438 *E-mail:* contact@dbqoneacts.org *Web Site:* www.dbqoneacts.org, pg 611

Dufour Editions Inc, PO Box 7, Chester Springs, PA 19425 *Tel:* 610-458-5005 *E-mail:* info@dufoureditions.com *Web Site:* www.dufoureditions.com, pg 67

Duke University Press, 905 W Main St, Suite 18B, Durham, NC 27701 *Tel:* 919-688-5134 *Toll Free Tel:* 888-651-0122 (US) *Fax:* 919-688-2615 *Toll Free Fax:* 888-651-0124 *E-mail:* orders@dukeupress.edu *Web Site:* www.dukeupress.edu, pg 67

Dumbarton Oaks, 1703 32 St NW, Washington, DC 20007 *Tel:* 202-339-6400 *Fax:* 202-339-6401; 202-298-8407 *E-mail:* doaksbooks@doaks.org; press@doaks.org *Web Site:* www.doaks.org, pg 68

Dun & Bradstreet, 103 JFK Pkwy, Short Hills, NJ 07078 *Tel:* 973-921-5500 *Toll Free Tel:* 844-869-8244; 800-234-3867 (cust serv) *Web Site:* www.dnb.com, pg 68

Dundurn Press Ltd, 3 Church St, Suite 500, Toronto, ON M5E 1M2, Canada *Tel:* 416-214-5544 *E-mail:* info@dundurn.com; publicity@dundurn.com; sales@dundurn.com *Web Site:* www.dundurn.com, pg 421

Dunham Literary Inc, 110 William St, Suite 2202, New York, NY 10038 *Tel:* 212-929-0994 *Web Site:* dunhamlit.com, pg 482

John H Dunning Prize in United States History, 400 "A" St SE, Washington, DC 20003 *Tel:* 202-544-2422 *Fax:* 202-544-8307 *E-mail:* awards@historians.org *Web Site:* www.historians.org, pg 611

Dunow, Carlson & Lerner Literary Agency Inc, 27 W 20 St, Suite 1107, New York, NY 10011 *Tel:* 212-645-7606 *E-mail:* mail@dclagency.com *Web Site:* www.dclagency.com, pg 482

Dupree, Miller & Associates Inc, 4311 Oak Lawn Ave, Suite 650, Dallas, TX 75219 *Tel:* 214-559-2665 *Fax:* 214-559-7243 *E-mail:* editorial@dupreemiller.com *Web Site:* www.dupreemiller.com, pg 482

Dustbooks, PO Box 100, Paradise, CA 95967-0100 *Tel:* 530-877-6110 *Fax:* 530-877-0222 *E-mail:* inquiries@dustbooks.com; info@dustbooks.com *Web Site:* www.dustbooks.com, pg 68

Dutton, 1745 Broadway, New York, NY 10019 *Tel:* 212-366-2000 *Fax:* 212-366-2262 *E-mail:* duttonpublicity@us.penguingroup.com *Web Site:* www.penguin.com, pg 68

Dutton Children's Books, 345 Hudson St, New York, NY 10014 *Tel:* 212-366-2000 *Web Site:* www.penguin.com/publishers/duttonchildrensbooks/, pg 68

DWJ BOOKS LLC, 14 Hill Side Lane, East Hampton, NY 11937 *Tel:* 631-267-8270 *E-mail:* info@dwjbooks.com *Web Site:* www.dwjbooks.com, pg 462

Dystel, Goderich & Bourret LLC, One Union Sq W, Suite 904, New York, NY 10003 *Tel:* 212-627-9100 *Fax:* 212-627-9313 *Web Site:* www.dystel.com, pg 482

Eakin Press, PO Box 331779, Fort Worth, TX 76163 *Tel:* 817-344-7036 *Toll Free Tel:* 888-982-8270 *Fax:* 817-344-7036 *Web Site:* www.eakinpress.com, pg 68

Earth Edit, PO Box 114, Maiden Rock, WI 54750 *Tel:* 715-448-3009, pg 462

East Asian Legal Studies Program (EALSP), 500 W Baltimore St, Rm 254, Baltimore, MD 21201-1786 *Tel:* 410-706-3870 *Fax:* 410-706-0407 *E-mail:* eastasia@law.umaryland.edu *Web Site:* www.law.umaryland.edu/programs/international/eastasia, pg 68

East Mountain Editing Services, PO Box 1895, Tijeras, NM 87059-1895 *Tel:* 505-281-8422 *Web Site:* www.spanishindexing.com, pg 462

East West Discovery Press, PO Box 3585, Manhattan Beach, CA 90266 *Tel:* 310-545-3730 *Fax:* 310-545-3731 *E-mail:* info@eastwestdiscovery.com *Web Site:* www.eastwestdiscovery.com, pg 68

Eastland Press, 2421 29 Ave W, Seattle, WA 98199 *Tel:* 206-931-6957 (cust serv) *Fax:* 206-283-7084 (orders) *E-mail:* info@eastlandpress.com; orders@eastlandpress.com *Web Site:* www.eastlandpress.com, pg 69

Easy Money Press, 82-5800 Napo'opo'o Rd, Captain Cook, HI 96704 *Tel:* 808-313-2808 *E-mail:* easymoneypress@yahoo.com, pg 69

Eaton Literary Associates Literary Awards, PO Box 49795, Sarasota, FL 34230-6795 *Tel:* 941-366-6589 *Fax:* 941-365-4679 *E-mail:* eatonlit@aol.com *Web Site:* www.eatonliterary.com, pg 611

Eclectic Book Press, 72 Glenmaura National Blvd, Suite 104B, Moosic, PA 18507 *Tel:* 862-251-2296; 570-878-7960 *E-mail:* info@endlessmountainspublishing.com *Web Site:* endlessmountainspublishing.com, pg 69

Ecrits des Forges, 992-A rue Royale, Trois-Rivieres, QC G9A 4H9, Canada *Tel:* 819-840-8492 *E-mail:* ecritsdesforges@gmail.com *Web Site:* www.ecritsdesforges.com, pg 421

ECS Publishing Group, 1727 Larkin Williams Rd, Fenton, MO 63026 *Tel:* 636-305-0100 *Toll Free Tel:* 800-647-2117 *Web Site:* ecspublishing.com; www.facebook.com/ecspublishing, pg 69

ECW Press, 665 Gerrard St E, Toronto, ON M4M 1Y2, Canada *Tel:* 416-694-3348 *E-mail:* info@ecwpress.com *Web Site:* www.ecwpress.com, pg 421

EDC Publishing, 5402 S 122 E Ave, Tulsa, OK 74146 *Tel:* 918-622-4522 *Toll Free Tel:* 800-475-4522 *Fax:* 918-665-7919 *Toll Free Fax:* 800-743-5660 *E-mail:* edc@edcpub.com *Web Site:* www.edcpub.com, pg 69

EdCan Network, 60 St Clair Ave E, Suite 703, Toronto, ON M4T 1N5, Canada *Tel:* 416-591-6300 *Toll Free Tel:* 866-803-9549 *Fax:* 416-591-5345 *Toll Free Fax:* 866-803-9549 *E-mail:* info@edcan.ca *Web Site:* www.edcan.ca, pg 532

Anne Edelstein Literary Agency LLC, 404 Riverside Dr, New York, NY 10025 *Tel:* 212-414-4923 *E-mail:* info@aeliterary.com; rights@aeliterary.com *Web Site:* www.aeliterary.com, pg 483

The Edgar Awards®, 1140 Broadway, Suite 1507, New York, NY 10001 *Tel:* 212-888-8171 *E-mail:* mwa@mysterywriters.org *Web Site:* theedgars.com; www.mysterywriters.org, pg 612

EDGE Science Fiction & Fantasy Publishing Inc, PO Box 1714, Calgary, AB T2P 2L7, Canada *Tel:* 403-254-0160 *Fax:* 403-254-0456 *E-mail:* admin@hadespublications.com *Web Site:* www.edgewebsite.com, pg 422

Edgewise Press Inc, 24 Fifth Ave, Suite 224, New York, NY 10011 *Tel:* 212-982-4818 *Fax:* 212-982-1364 *E-mail:* epinc@mindspring.com *Web Site:* www.edgewisepress.org, pg 69

ediciones Lerner, 241 First Ave N, Minneapolis, MN 55401 *Tel:* 612-332-3344 *Toll Free Tel:* 800-328-4929 *Fax:* 612-332-7615 *Toll Free Fax:* 800-332-1132 *E-mail:* info@lernerbooks.com; custserve@lernerbooks.com *Web Site:* www.lernerbooks.com; www.facebook.com/lernerbooks, pg 69

Edit Etc, 26 Country Lane, Brunswick, ME 04011 *Tel:* 914-715-5849 *E-mail:* atkedit@cs.com *Web Site:* www.anntkeene.com, pg 462

Wm B Eerdmans Publishing Co, 4035 Park East Ct SE, Grand Rapids, MI 49546 *Tel:* 616-459-4591 *Toll Free Tel:* 800-253-7521 *Fax:* 616-459-6540 *E-mail:* customerservice@eerdmans.com; sales@ eerdmans.com *Web Site:* www.eerdmans.com, pg 70

The Maureen Egen Writers Exchange Award, 90 Broad St, Suite 2100, New York, NY 10004 *Tel:* 212-226-3586 *Fax:* 212-226-3963 *E-mail:* admin@pw.org *Web Site:* www.pw.org, pg 612

Wilfrid Eggleston Award for Nonfiction, 11759 Groat Rd, Edmonton, AB T5M 3K6, Canada *Tel:* 780-422-8174 *Toll Free Tel:* 800-665-5354 (AB only) *Fax:* 780-422-2663 (attn WGA) *E-mail:* mail@ writersguild.ca *Web Site:* writersguild.ca, pg 612

Diane Eickhoff, 3808 Genessee St, Kansas City, MO 64111 *Tel:* 816-561-6693 *E-mail:* diane.eickhoff@ gmail.com, pg 463

Eifrig Publishing LLC, PO Box 66, Lemont, PA 16851 *Toll Free Tel:* 888-340-6543 *E-mail:* info@ eifrigpublishing.com *Web Site:* www.eifrigpublishing. com, pg 70

Eisenbrauns, 820 N University Dr, USB 1, Suite C, University Park, PA 16802 *Tel:* 814-865-1327 *Toll Free Tel:* 800-326-9180 *Fax:* 814-863-1408 *Toll Free Fax:* 877-778-2665 *E-mail:* orders@eisenbrauns.org *Web Site:* www.eisenbrauns.org, pg 70

The Lisa Ekus Group LLC, 57 North St, Hatfield, MA 01038 *Tel:* 413-247-9325 *Fax:* 413-247-9873 *E-mail:* info@lisaekus.com *Web Site:* lisaekus.com, pg 483, 582

Elderberry Press Inc, 1393 Old Homestead Dr, Oakland, OR 97462-9690 *Tel:* 541-459-6043 *Web Site:* www. elderberrypress.com, pg 70

The Electrochemical Society (ECS), 65 S Main St, Bldg D, Pennington, NJ 08534-2839 *Tel:* 609-737-1902 *Fax:* 609-737-0629 *E-mail:* publications@ electrochem.org; customerservice@electrochem.org *Web Site:* www.electrochem.org, pg 70

Edward Elgar Publishing Inc, The William Pratt House, 9 Dewey Ct, Northampton, MA 01060-3815 *Tel:* 413-584-5551 *Toll Free Tel:* 800-390-3149 (orders) *Fax:* 413-584-9933 *E-mail:* elgarinfo@e-elgar. com; elgarsales@e-elgar.com; elgarsubmissions@e-elgar.com (edit) *Web Site:* www.e-elgar.com; www. elgaronline.com (ebooks & journals), pg 70

T S Eliot Prize for Poetry, 100 E Normal Ave, Kirksville, MO 63501-4221 *Tel:* 660-785-7336 *Toll Free Tel:* 800-916-6802 *Fax:* 660-785-4480 *E-mail:* tsup@truman.edu *Web Site:* tsup.truman.edu, pg 612

eLit Awards, 1129 Woodmere Ave, Suite B, Traverse City, MI 49686 *Tel:* 231-933-0445 *Toll Free Tel:* 800-706-4636 *Fax:* 231-933-0448 *E-mail:* info@elitawards. com *Web Site:* www.elitawards.com, pg 612

Elite Books, PO Box 442, Fulton, CA 95439 *Tel:* 707-525-9292 *Toll Free Fax:* 800-330-9798 *E-mail:* support@eftuniverse.com *Web Site:* www. elitebooksonline.com, pg 71

Ethan Ellenberg Literary Agency, 155 Suffolk St, Suite 2R, New York, NY 10002 *Tel:* 212-431-4554 *E-mail:* agent@ethanellenberg.com *Web Site:* www. ethanellenberg.com, pg 483

Van Courtlandt Elliott Prize, 17 Dunster St, Suite 202, Cambridge, MA 02138 *Tel:* 617-491-1622 *Fax:* 617-492-3303 *E-mail:* info@themedievalacademy.org *Web Site:* www.medievalacademy.org, pg 613

Arthur Ellis Awards, 716 Thicket Way, Ottawa, ON K4A 3B5, Canada *E-mail:* arthur_ellis@crimewriterscanada. com *Web Site:* www.crimewriterscanada.com/awards, pg 613

Nicholas Ellison Agency, 3 Tara Dr, Brookfield, CT 06804-2324 *Web Site:* www.thenicholasellisonagency. com, pg 483

Ralph Ellison Award, 200 NE 18 St, Oklahoma City, OK 73105-3205 *Tel:* 405-522-3383 *Web Site:* libraries.ok. gov/ocb/oklahoma-book-awards, pg 613

Irene Elmer, 2806 Cherry St, Berkeley, CA 94705-2310 *Tel:* 510-883-1265 *E-mail:* ielmer@lmi.net, pg 463

Elsevier Engineering Information (Ei), 230 Park Ave, 8th fl, New York, NY 10169-0123 *Tel:* 212-989-5800 *Fax:* 212-633-3990 *E-mail:* eicustomersupport@ elsevier.com *Web Site:* www.elsevier.com/solutions/ engineering-village, pg 71

Elsevier, Health Sciences Division, 1600 John F Kennedy Blvd, Suite 1800, Philadelphia, PA 19103-2899 *Tel:* 215-239-3900 *Toll Free Tel:* 800-523-1649 *Fax:* 215-239-3990 *Web Site:* www.us.elsevierhealth. com, pg 71

Elsevier Inc, 230 Park Ave, Suite 800, New York, NY 10169 *Tel:* 212-989-5800 *Fax:* 212-633-3990 *Web Site:* www.elsevier.com, pg 71

Elva Resa Publishing, 8362 Tamarack Village, Suite 119-106, St Paul, MN 55125 *Tel:* 651-357-8770 *Fax:* 501-641-0777 *E-mail:* staff@elvaresa.com *Web Site:* www. elvaresa.com; www.militaryfamilybooks.com, pg 71

Catherine C Elverston ELS, 3242 NW 5 St, Gainesville, FL 32609 *Tel:* 352-222-0625 (cell) *E-mail:* celverston@gmail.com, pg 463

R Elwell Indexing, 193 Main St, Cold Spring, NY 10516 *Tel:* 845-667-1036 *E-mail:* r.elwell.indexing@gmail. com, pg 463

EMC Publishing LLC, 875 Montreal Way, St Paul, MN 55102 *Tel:* 651-290-2800 (corp) *Toll Free Tel:* 888-851-7094 *Fax:* info@carnegielearning.com *Web Site:* www.emcp.com, pg 71

Emerald Books, PO Box 55787, Seattle, WA 98155 *Tel:* 425-771-1153 *Toll Free Tel:* 800-922-2143 *Fax:* 425-775-2383 *E-mail:* books@ywampublishing. com *Web Site:* www.ywampublishing.com, pg 71

Emerging Critics Fellowship, c/o 310 Lewis Ave, Brooklyn, NY 11221 *E-mail:* info@bookcritics.org *Web Site:* bookcritics.org, pg 613

Emerging Playwright Award, 555 Eighth Ave, Suite 1800, New York, NY 10018 *Tel:* 212-421-1380 *Fax:* 212-421-1387 *E-mail:* urbanstage@aol.com, pg 613

Emerging Voices Fellowship, 8444 Wilshire Blvd, 4th fl, Beverly Hills, CA 90211 *Tel:* 323-424-4939 *Fax:* 323-424-4944 *Web Site:* pen.org/emerging-voices-fellowship, pg 613

Emerson College Department of Writing, Literature & Publishing, 180 Tremont St, 10th fl, Boston, MA 02116-4624 *Tel:* 617-824-8750 *Web Site:* www. emerson.edu; www.emerson.edu/writing-literature-publishing, pg 582

The Ralph Waldo Emerson Award, 1606 New Hampshire Ave NW, Washington, DC 20009 *Tel:* 202-265-3808 *Fax:* 202-986-1601 *E-mail:* awards@pbk.org *Web Site:* www.pbk.org/bookawards, pg 613

Emmaus Road Publishing Inc, 1468 Parkview Circle, Steubenville, OH 43952 *Tel:* 740-283-2880 (outside US) *Toll Free Tel:* 800-398-5470 (orders) *Fax:* 740-283-4011 (orders) *E-mail:* questions@emmausroad.org *Web Site:* www.emmausroad.org, pg 71

Emond Montgomery Publications Ltd, 60 Shaftesbury Ave, Toronto, ON M4T 1A3, Canada *Tel:* 416-975-3925 *Toll Free Tel:* 888-837-0815 *Fax:* 416-975-3924 *E-mail:* orders@emp.ca *Web Site:* www.emp.ca, pg 425

Empire Publishing Service, PO Box 1344, Studio City, CA 91614-0344 *Tel:* 818-784-8918 *Fax:* 818-990-2477 *E-mail:* empirepubsvc@att.net, pg 71

Empire State Award for Excellence in Literature for Young People, 6021 State Farm Rd, Guilderland, NY 12084 *Tel:* 518-432-6952 *Toll Free Tel:* 800-252-6952 *Fax:* 518-427-1697 *E-mail:* info@nyla.org *Web Site:* www.nyla.org, pg 613

Enchanted Lion Books, 67 West St, Studio 317A, Brooklyn, NY 11222 *Tel:* 646-785-9272 *E-mail:* enchantedlion.community@gmail.com *Web Site:* www.enchantedlion.com, pg 72

Encounter Books, 900 Broadway, Suite 601, New York, NY 10003 *Tel:* 212-871-6310 *Toll Free Tel:* 800-343-4499 *Fax:* 212-871-6311 *E-mail:* publicity@ encounterbooks.com *Web Site:* www.encounterbooks. com, pg 72

Encyclopaedia Britannica Inc, 325 N La Salle St, Suite 200, Chicago, IL 60654 *Tel:* 312-347-7000 (all other countries) *Toll Free Tel:* 800-323-1229 (US & CN) *Fax:* 312-294-2104 *E-mail:* contact@eb.com *Web Site:* www.britannica.com, pg 72

Endless Mountains Publishing Co, 72 Glenmaura National Blvd, Suite 104B, Moosic, PA 18507 *Tel:* 862-251-2296; 570-878-7960 *E-mail:* info@ endlessmountainspublishing.com *Web Site:* www. endlessmountainspublishing.com, pg 72

Energy Psychology Press, 1490 Mark West Springs Rd, Santa Rosa, CA 95404 *Tel:* 707-525-9292 *Toll Free Fax:* 800-330-9798 *E-mail:* energypsychologypress@ gmail.com; support@eftuniverse.com *Web Site:* www. energypsychologypress.com; www.elitebooksonline. com, pg 72

Paul Engle Prize, 123 S Linn St, Iowa City, IA 52240 *E-mail:* info@iowacityofliterature.org *Web Site:* www. iowacityofliterature.org/paul-engle-prize, pg 613

Enough Said, 3959 NW 29 Lane, Gainesville, FL 32606 *Tel:* 352-262-2971 *E-mail:* enoughsaid@cox.net, pg 463

Enslow Publishing LLC, 101 W 23 St, Suite 240, New York, NY 10011 *Toll Free Tel:* 800-398-2504 *Fax:* 908-771-0925 *Toll Free Fax:* 877-980-4454 *E-mail:* customerservice@enslow.com *Web Site:* www. enslow.com, pg 72

Entangled Publishing LLC, 2614 S Timberline Rd, Suite 105, Fort Collins, CO 80525 *Toll Free Tel:* 877-677-9451 *E-mail:* publisher@entangledpublishing.com *Web Site:* www.entangledpublishing.com, pg 72

Entomological Society of America, 3 Park Place, Suite 307, Annapolis, MD 21401-3722 *Tel:* 301-731-4535 *Fax:* 301-731-4538 *E-mail:* esa@entsoc.org *Web Site:* www.entsoc.org, pg 72

Environmental Law Institute, 1730 "M" St NW, Suite 700, Washington, DC 20036 *Tel:* 202-939-3800 *Toll Free Tel:* 800-433-5120 *Fax:* 202-939-3868 *E-mail:* law@eli.org *Web Site:* www.eli.org, pg 73

Epicenter Press Inc, 6524 NE 181 St, Suite 2, Kenmore, WA 98028 *Tel:* 425-485-6822 (edit, mktg, busn off) *Fax:* 425-481-8253 *E-mail:* info@epicenterpress.com *Web Site:* www.epicenterpress.com, pg 73

Epicomm, 1800 Diagonal Rd, Suite 320, Alexandria, VA 22314-2862 *Tel:* 703-836-9200 *E-mail:* webmaster@ epicomm.org *Web Site:* epicomm.org, pg 533

EPS/School Specialty Literacy & Intervention, 625 Mount Auburn St, 3rd fl, Cambridge, MA 02138-3039 *Toll Free Tel:* 800-225-5750 *Toll Free Fax:* 888-440-2665 *E-mail:* customerservice@schoolspecialty. com *Web Site:* eps.schoolspecialty.com, pg 73

Norma Epstein Foundation Awards in Creative Writing, 15 King's College Circle, UC 165, Toronto, ON M5S 3H7, Canada *Tel:* 416-978-8083 *Fax:* 416-978-8854 *E-mail:* uc.programs@utoronto.ca *Web Site:* www.uc. utoronto.ca/writing-centre, pg 613

The Ernest Sandeen & Richard Sullivan Prizes in Fiction & Poetry, 356 O'Shaughnessy Hall, Notre Dame, IN 46556 *Tel:* 574-631-7526 *Fax:* 574-631-4795 *E-mail:* creativewriting@nd.edu *Web Site:* english. nd.edu/creative-writing/prizes-awards/sandeen-sullivan-prizes/, pg 613

Erskine J Poetry Prize, PO Box 22161, Baltimore, MD 21203 *E-mail:* smartishpace@gmail.com *Web Site:* www.smartishpace.com, pg 614

Felicia Eth Literary Representation, 555 Bryant St, Suite 350, Palo Alto, CA 94301 *Tel:* 415-970-9717 *E-mail:* feliciaeth.literary@gmail.com *Web Site:* www. ethliterary.com, pg 483

Etruscan Press, Wilkes University, 84 W South St, Wilkes-Barre, PA 18766 *Tel:* 570-408-4546 *Fax:* 570-408-3333 *E-mail:* books@etruscanpress.org *Web Site:* www.etruscanpress.org, pg 73

Europa Editions, 214 W 29 St, Suite 1003, New York, NY 10001 *Tel:* 212-868-6844 *Fax:* 212-868-6845 *E-mail:* info@europaeditions.com *Web Site:* www.europaeditions.com, pg 73

Evan-Moor Educational Publishers, 18 Lower Ragsdale Dr, Monterey, CA 93940-5746 *Tel:* 831-649-5901 *Toll Free Tel:* 800-777-4362 (orders) *Fax:* 831-649-6256 *Toll Free Fax:* 800-777-4332 (orders) *E-mail:* sales@evan-moor.com; marketing@evan-moor.com *Web Site:* www.evan-moor.com, pg 73

Evangelical Christian Publishers Association (ECPA), 5801 S McClintock Dr, Suite 104, Tempe, AZ 85283 *Tel:* 480-966-3998 *Fax:* 480-966-1944 *E-mail:* info@ecpa.org *Web Site:* www.ecpa.org, pg 533

Evangelical Press Association (EPA), PO Box 1787, Queen Creek, AZ 85142 *Toll Free Tel:* 888-311-1731 *E-mail:* info@evangelicalpress.com *Web Site:* www.evangelicalpress.com, pg 533

David W & Beatrice C Evans Biography & Handcart Awards, 0735 Old Main Hill, Logan, UT 84322-0735 *Tel:* 435-797-0299 *Fax:* 435-797-1092 *E-mail:* mwc@usu.edu *Web Site:* mountainwest.usu.edu, pg 614

M Evans & Company, c/o Rowman & Littlefield Publishing Group, 4501 Forbes Blvd, Suite 200, Lanham, MD 20706 *Tel:* 301-459-3366 *Fax:* 301-429-5748 *Web Site:* rowman.com, pg 73

Mary Evans Inc, 242 E Fifth St, New York, NY 10003-8501 *Tel:* 212-979-0880 *Fax:* 212-979-5344 *E-mail:* info@maryevansinc.com *Web Site:* www.maryevansinc.com, pg 484

Evergreen Pacific Publishing Ltd, 4204 Russell Rd, Suite M, Mukilteo, WA 98275-5424 *Tel:* 425-493-1451 *Fax:* 425-493-1453 *E-mail:* sales@evergreenpacific.com *Web Site:* www.evergreenpacific.com, pg 74

Everyman's Library, c/o Penguin Random House Inc, 1745 Broadway, New York, NY 10019 *Tel:* 212-751-2600 *Fax:* 212-572-2662 (foreign rts) *Web Site:* knopfdoubleday.com, pg 74

Everything Goes Media LLC, PO Box 1524, Milwaukee, WI 53201 *Tel:* 312-226-8400 *E-mail:* info@everythinggoesmedia.com *Web Site:* www.everythinggoesmedia.com, pg 74

Excalibur Publications, PO Box 89667, Tucson, AZ 85752-9667 *Tel:* 520-575-9057 *E-mail:* excaliburpublications@centurylink.net, pg 74

EXCEL Awards, 1090 Vermont Ave NW, 6th fl, Washington, DC 20005-4905 *Tel:* 212-784-6398 *E-mail:* awards@associationmediaandpublishing.org; info@associationmediaandpublishing.org *Web Site:* www.siia.net/amp; kellencompany.com, pg 614

Excellence in Graphic Literature Awards, 2760 W Fifth Ave, Denver, CO 80204 *Tel:* 303-325-1236 *E-mail:* egl@popcultureclassroom.org *Web Site:* popcultureclassroom.org/egl, pg 614

Excelsior Editions, 10 N Pearl St, 4th fl, Albany, NY 12207 *Tel:* 518-944-2800 *Toll Free Tel:* 866-430-7869 *Fax:* 518-320-1592 *E-mail:* info@sunypress.edu *Web Site:* www.sunypress.edu, pg 74

The Experiment, 220 E 23 St, Suite 600, New York, NY 10010-4658 *Tel:* 212-889-1659 *E-mail:* info@theexperimentpublishing.com *Web Site:* www.theexperimentpublishing.com, pg 74

Eye in the Ear Children's Audio, 5 Crescent St, Portland, ME 04102 *Toll Free Tel:* 855-99-STORY (997-8679) *Fax:* 207-699-1380 (attn: Laurence Kelly) *E-mail:* info@eyeintheear.com *Web Site:* www.eyeintheear.com, pg 74

Facts On File, 132 W 31 St, 17th fl, New York, NY 10001 *Tel:* 212-967-8800 *Toll Free Tel:* 800-322-8755 *Toll Free Fax:* 800-678-3633 *E-mail:* custserv@factsonfile.com *Web Site:* infobasepublishing.com, pg 74

Fair Winds Press, 100 Cummings Ctr, Suite 265-D, Beverly, MA 01915 *Tel:* 978-282-9590 *Fax:* 978-282-7765 *E-mail:* sales@quarto.com *Web Site:* www.quartoknows.com, pg 75

John K Fairbank Prize in East Asian History, 400 "A" St SE, Washington, DC 20003 *Tel:* 202-544-2422 *Fax:* 202-544-8307 *E-mail:* awards@historians.org *Web Site:* www.historians.org, pg 614

Fairchild Books, 1385 Broadway, 5th fl, New York, NY 10018 *Tel:* 212-419-5300 *Toll Free Tel:* 800-932-4724; 888-330-8477 (orders) *Web Site:* bloomsbury.com/us/academic/fairchildbooks, pg 75

Fairleigh Dickinson University Press, 842 Cambie St, Vancouver, BC V6B 2P6, Canada *Tel:* 604-648-4476 *Fax:* 604-648-4489 *E-mail:* fdupress@fdu.edu *Web Site:* www.fdupress.org, pg 425

Tom Fairley Award for Editorial Excellence, 1507-180 Dundas St W, Toronto, ON M5G 1Z8, Canada *Tel:* 416-975-1379 *Toll Free Tel:* 866-CAN-EDIT (226-3348) *Fax:* 416-975-1637 *E-mail:* fairley_award@editors.ca; info@editors.ca *Web Site:* www.editors.ca; www.reviseurs.ca, pg 614

The Fairmont Press Inc, 700 Indian Trail, Lilburn, GA 30047 *Tel:* 770-925-9388 *Fax:* 770-381-9865 *Web Site:* www.fairmontpress.com, pg 75

Fairwinds Press, PO Box 668, Lions Bay, BC V0N 2E0, Canada *Tel:* 604-913-0649 *E-mail:* orders@fairwinds-press.com *Web Site:* www.fairwinds-press.com, pg 425

Faith & Fellowship Publishing, 1020 W Alcott Ave, Fergus Falls, MN 56537 *Tel:* 218-736-7357 *Toll Free Tel:* 800-332-9232 *E-mail:* ffpublishing@clba.org *Web Site:* www.clba.org, pg 75

Faith Library Publications, PO Box 50126, Tulsa, OK 74150-0126 *Tel:* 918-258-1588 (ext 2218) *Toll Free Tel:* 888-258-0999 (orders) *Fax:* 918-872-7710 (orders) *E-mail:* flp@rhema.org *Web Site:* www.rhema.org/store, pg 75

Faithlife Corp, 1313 Commercial St, Bellingham, WA 98225 *Tel:* 360-527-1700 *Toll Free Tel:* 800-875-6467 *Fax:* 360-527-1707 *E-mail:* sales@faithlife.com; customerservice@faithlife.com *Web Site:* faithlife.com, pg 75

FaithWalk Publishing, 5450 N Dixie Hwy, Lima, OH 45807 *Tel:* 419-227-1818 *Toll Free Tel:* 800-537-1030 (orders, non-bookstore mkts) *Fax:* 419-224-9184 *E-mail:* orders@csspub.com *Web Site:* www.faithwalkpub.com, pg 75

Familius, 1254 Commerce Way, Sanger, CA 93657 *Tel:* 559-876-2170 *Fax:* 559-876-2180 *E-mail:* orders@familius.com *Web Site:* www.familius.com, pg 75

Far Horizons Award for Poetry, University of Victoria, Box 1700, Sta CSC, Victoria, BC V8W 2Y2, Canada *Tel:* 250-721-8524 *Fax:* 250-472-5051 *E-mail:* malahat@uvic.ca *Web Site:* www.malahatreview.ca, pg 614

Far Horizons Award for Short Fiction, University of Victoria, Box 1700, Sta CSC, Victoria, BC V8W 2Y2, Canada *Tel:* 250-721-8524 *Fax:* 250-472-5051 *E-mail:* malahat@uvic.ca *Web Site:* www.malahatreview.ca, pg 614

Norma Farber First Book Award, 15 Gramercy Park, New York, NY 10003 *Tel:* 212-254-9628 *Web Site:* poetrysociety.org/awards, pg 614

Farcountry Press, 2750 Broadwater Ave, Helena, MT 59602-9202 *Tel:* 406-422-1263 *Toll Free Tel:* 800-821-3874 (sales off) *Fax:* 406-443-5480 *E-mail:* books@farcountrypress.com; sales@farcountrypress.com *Web Site:* www.farcountrypress.com, pg 75

Farrar, Straus & Giroux Books for Young Readers, 120 Broadway, New York, NY 10271 *Tel:* 212-741-6900 *Toll Free Tel:* 888-330-8477 (orders) *Fax:* 212-633-9385 *Web Site:* us.macmillan.com/mackids; www.mackidsbooks.com, pg 75

Farrar, Straus & Giroux, LLC, 175 Varick St, 9th fl, New York, NY 10014 *Tel:* 212-741-6900 *E-mail:* fsg.publicity@fsgbooks.com *Web Site:* us.macmillan.com/fsg.aspx, pg 76

Farrar Writing & Editing, 4638 Manchester Rd, Mound, MN 55364 *Tel:* 952-451-5982 *Fax:* 952-472-6874 (call first) *Web Site:* www.writeandedit.net, pg 463

Father & Son Publishing Inc, 4909 N Monroe St, Tallahassee, FL 32303-7015 *Tel:* 850-562-2712 *Toll Free Tel:* 800-741-2712 (orders only) *Fax:* 850-562-0916 *Web Site:* www.fatherson.com, pg 76

The FC2 Catherine Doctorow Innovative Fiction Prize, c/o University of Alabama Press, Box 870380, Tuscaloosa, AL 35487-0380 *Tel:* 773-702-7000 *E-mail:* fc2@gmail.com *Web Site:* www.fc2.org, pg 614

The FC2 Ronald Sukenick Innovative Fiction Contest, c/o University of Alabama Press, Box 870380, Tuscaloosa, AL 35487-0380 *Tel:* 773-702-7000 *E-mail:* fc2@gmail.com *Web Site:* www.fc2.org, pg 615

FC&A Publishing, 103 Clover Green, Peachtree City, GA 30269 *Tel:* 770-487-6307 *Toll Free Tel:* 800-226-8024 *E-mail:* customer_service@fca.com *Web Site:* www.fca.com, pg 76

Federal Bar Association, 1220 N Filmore St, Suite 444, Arlington, VA 22201 *Tel:* 571-481-9100 *Fax:* 571-481-9090 *E-mail:* fba@fedbar.org *Web Site:* www.fedbar.org, pg 76

Federal Street Press, 25-13 Old Kings Hwy N, No 277, Darien, CT 06820 *Tel:* 203-852-1280 *Toll Free Tel:* 877-886-2830 *Fax:* 203-852-1389 *E-mail:* info@federalstreetpress.com; sales@federalstreetpress.com; customerservice@federalstreetpress.com; orders@federalstreetpress.com *Web Site:* federalstreetpress.com, pg 76

Federation of BC Writers, PO Box 16028, 617 Belmont St, New Westminster, BC V3M 6W6, Canada *E-mail:* info@bcwriters.ca *Web Site:* bcwriters.ca, pg 533

Feigenbaum Publishing Consultants Inc, 61 Bounty Lane, Jericho, NY 11753 *Tel:* 516-647-8314 (cell), pg 484

Betsy Feist Resources, 140 E 81 St, Unit 7-E, New York, NY 10028-1875 *Tel:* 212-861-2014 *E-mail:* bfresources@rcn.com, pg 463

Feldheim Publishers, 208 Airport Executive Park, Nanuet, NY 10954 *Tel:* 845-356-2282 *Toll Free Tel:* 800-237-7149 (orders) *Fax:* 845-425-1908 *E-mail:* sales@feldheim.com *Web Site:* www.feldheim.com, pg 76

Fellowship Program, One Capital Hill, 3rd fl, Providence, RI 02908 *Tel:* 401-222-3880 *Fax:* 401-222-3018 *Web Site:* www.arts.ri.gov, pg 615

Fellowship, Tuition Scholarship & Work Study Programs for Writers, Middlebury College, 204 College St, Middlebury, VT 05753 *Tel:* 802-443-5286 *Fax:* 802-443-2087 *E-mail:* blwc@middlebury.edu *Web Site:* www.middlebury.edu/blwc, pg 615

Fellowships for Creative & Performing Artists & Writers, 185 Salisbury St, Worcester, MA 01609-1634 *Tel:* 508-755-5221 *Fax:* 508-754-9069 *Web Site:* www.americanantiquarian.org, pg 615

Fellowships for Historical Research, 185 Salisbury St, Worcester, MA 01609-1634 *Tel:* 508-755-5221 *Fax:* 508-754-9069 *Web Site:* www.americanantiquarian.org, pg 615

Jerry Felsen, 3960 NW 196 St, Miami Gardens, FL 33055-1869 *Tel:* 305-625-5012 *E-mail:* jfelsen0@att.net, pg 463

The Feminist Press at The City University of New York, 365 Fifth Ave, Suite 5406, New York, NY 10016 *Tel:* 212-817-7915 *Fax:* 212-817-1593 *E-mail:* info@feministpress.org *Web Site:* www.feministpress.org, pg 76

Fence Books, University at Albany, Science Library 320, 1400 Washington Ave, Albany, NY 12222 *Tel:* 518-567-7006 *Web Site:* www.fenceportal.org, pg 77

Fence Modern Poets Series, University at Albany, Science Library 320, 1400 Washington Ave, Albany, NY 12222 *Tel:* 518-567-7006 *Web Site:* www.fenceportal.org, pg 615

Shubert Fendrich Memorial Playwriting Contest, PO Box 4267, Englewood, CO 80155-4267 Tel: 303-779-4035 Toll Free Tel: 800-333-7262 Fax: 303-779-4315 Web Site: www.pioneerdrama.com/playwrights/contest.asp, pg 615

Feral House, 1240 W Sims Way, Suite 124, Port Townsend, WA 98368 Tel: 323-666-3311 E-mail: info@feralhouse.com Web Site: feralhouse.com, pg 77

Edna Ferber Fiction Book Award, c/o 210 N Main St, No 204, Cedar Grove, WI 53013 E-mail: wiswriters@gmail.com Web Site: wiswriters.org/awards, pg 615

Ferguson Publishing, 132 W 31 St, 17th fl, New York, NY 10001 Tel: 212-967-8800 Toll Free Tel: 800-322-8755 Toll Free Fax: 800-678-3633 E-mail: custserv@factsonfile.com Web Site: infobasepublishing.com, pg 77

Fernwood Publishing, 32 Oceanvista Lane, Black Point, NS B0J 1B0, Canada Tel: 902-857-1388 Fax: 902-857-1328 E-mail: info@fernpub.ca; roseway@fernpub.ca Web Site: fernwoodpublishing.ca, pg 426

Fiction Collective Two Inc (FC2), c/o University of Alabama Press, Box 870380, Tuscaloosa, AL 35487-0380 Tel: 773-702-7000 Web Site: www.fc2.org, pg 77

The Field Poetry Prize, 50 N Professor St, Oberlin, OH 44074-1091 Tel: 440-775-8408 Fax: 440-775-8124 E-mail: oc.press@oberlin.edu Web Site: www.oberlin.edu/ocpress; www.oberlin.edu/ocpress/prize.htm (guidelines), pg 615

Fifth Estate Publishing, 2795 County Hwy 57, Blounstville, AL 35031 Tel: 256-631-5107 Toll Free Tel: 855-299-2160 E-mail: josephlumpkin@hotmail.com Web Site: fifthestatepub.com, pg 77

Fifth House Publishers, 195 Allstate Pkwy, Markham, ON L3R 4T8, Canada Tel: 905-477-9700 Toll Free Tel: 800-387-9776 E-mail: godwit@fitzhenry.ca; bookinfo@fitzhenry.ca (cust serv) Web Site: www.fifthhousepublishers.ca, pg 426

Filsinger & Company Ltd, 288 W 12 St, Suite 2R, New York, NY 10014 Tel: 212-243-7421 (by appt) E-mail: filsingercompany@gmail.com Web Site: www.filsingerco.com, pg 447

Filter Press LLC, PO Box 95, Palmer Lake, CO 80133 Tel: 719-481-2420 Toll Free Tel: 888-570-2663 Fax: 719-481-2420 E-mail: info@filterpressbooks.com; orders@filterpressbooks.com Web Site: filterpressbooks.com, pg 77

Financial Executives Research Foundation Inc (FERF), West Tower, 7th fl, 1250 Headquarters Plaza, Morristown, NJ 07960-6837 Tel: 973-765-1000 Fax: 973-765-1018 Web Site: www.financialexecutives.org, pg 77

Financial Times Press, 800 E 96 St, Indianapolis, IN 46240 E-mail: customer-service@informit.com; community@informit.com Web Site: www.informit.com/ftpress, pg 77

Finding My Way Books, 3512 SW Huntoon St, Topeka, KS 66604-1748 Tel: 785-273-6239 E-mail: findingmywaybooks@gmail.com Web Site: www.findingmywaybooks.net, pg 78

Fine Arts Work Center in Provincetown, 24 Pearl St, Provincetown, MA 02657 Tel: 508-487-9960 Fax: 508-487-8873 E-mail: general@fawc.org Web Site: www.fawc.org, pg 615

Fine Creative Media, Inc, 589 Eighth Ave, 6th fl, New York, NY 10018 Tel: 212-595-3500 Fax: 212-202-4195 E-mail: info@mjfbooks.com Web Site: www.mjfbooks.com, pg 77

Fine Wordworking, PO Box 3041, Monterey, CA 93942-3041 Tel: 831-375-6278 E-mail: info@finewordworking.com Web Site: marilynch.com, pg 463

FineEdge.com LLC, 902 Eighth St, Anacortes, WA 98221 Tel: 360-299-8500 Fax: 360-299-0535 E-mail: orders@fineedge.com Web Site: www.fineedge.com; waggonerguide.com, pg 78

FinePrint Literary Management, 207 W 106 St, Suite 1D, New York, NY 10025 Tel: 212-279-6214 E-mail: assist@fineprint.com Web Site: www.fineprintlit.com, pg 484

Fire Engineering Books & Videos, 1421 S Sheridan Rd, Tulsa, OK 74112 Tel: 918-831-9421 Toll Free Tel: 800-752-9764 Fax: 918-831-9555 E-mail: sales@pennwell.com Web Site: www.pennwellbooks.com, pg 78

Firecracker Awards, 154 Christopher St, Suite 3C, New York, NY 10014-9110 Tel: 212-741-9110 E-mail: info@clmp.org Web Site: www.clmp.org/firecracker, pg 615

Firefall Editions, 4905 Tunlaw St, Alexandria, VA 22312 Tel: 510-549-2461 E-mail: literary@att.net Web Site: www.firefallmedia.com, pg 78

Firefly Books Ltd, 50 Staples Ave, Unit 1, Richmond Hill, ON L4B 0A7, Canada Tel: 416-499-8412 Toll Free Tel: 800-387-6192 (CN); 800-387-5085 (US) Fax: 416-499-8313 Toll Free Fax: 800-450-0391 (CN); 800-565-6034 (US) E-mail: service@fireflybooks.com Web Site: www.fireflybooks.com, pg 426

First Avenue Editions, 241 First Ave N, Minneapolis, MN 55401 Tel: 612-332-3344 Toll Free Tel: 800-328-4929 Fax: 612-332-7615 Toll Free Fax: 800-332-1132 E-mail: info@lernerbooks.com; custserve@lernerbooks.com Web Site: www.lernerbooks.com; www.facebook.com/lernerbooks, pg 78

The Fischer-Harbage Agency Inc, 540 President St, 3rd fl, Brooklyn, NY 11215 Tel: 212-695-7105 E-mail: info@fischerharbage.com Web Site: www.fischerharbage.com, pg 484

The Fischer Ross Group Inc, 75 Holly Hill Lane, Suite 100, Greenwich, CT 06830 Tel: 203-622-4950 Fax: 203-531-4132 E-mail: frgstaff@frg-speakers.com Web Site: www.frg-speakers.com, pg 515

Fitzhenry & Whiteside Limited, 195 Allstate Pkwy, Markham, ON L3R 4T8, Canada Tel: 905-477-9700 Toll Free Tel: 800-387-9776 Fax: 905-477-2834 Toll Free Fax: 800-260-9777 E-mail: bookinfo@fitzhenry.ca; godwit@fitzhenry.ca Web Site: www.fitzhenry.ca, pg 426

Fitzroy Books, c/o Regal House Publishing, 806 Oberlin Rd, No 12094, Raleigh, NC 27605 E-mail: info@regalhousepublishing.com Web Site: fitzroybooks.com, pg 78

5 Under 35, 90 Broad St, Suite 604, New York, NY 10004 Tel: 212-685-0261 Fax: 212-213-6570 E-mail: nationalbook@nationalbook.org Web Site: www.nationalbook.org, pg 615

FJH Music Co Inc, 2525 Davie Rd, Suite 360, Fort Lauderdale, FL 33317-7424 Tel: 954-382-6061 Toll Free Tel: 800-262-8744 Fax: 954-382-3073 E-mail: custserv@fjhmusic.com; sales@fjhmusic.com Web Site: www.fjhmusic.com, pg 78

Flammarion Quebec, 375 Ave Laurier W, Montreal, QC H2V 2K3, Canada Tel: 514-277-8807 Fax: 514-278-2085 E-mail: info@flammarion.qc.ca Web Site: www.flammarion.qc.ca, pg 426

Flanker Press Ltd, 1243 Kenmount Rd, Unit 1, Paradise, NL A1L 0V8, Canada Tel: 709-739-4477 Toll Free Tel: 866-739-4420 Fax: 709-739-4420 E-mail: info@flankerpress.com; sales@flankerpress.com Web Site: www.flankerpress.com, pg 427

Flannery Literary, 1140 Wickfield Ct, Naperville, IL 60563 Web Site: flanneryliterary.com, pg 484

Flashlight Press, 527 Empire Blvd, Brooklyn, NY 11225 Tel: 718-288-8300 Fax: 718-972-6307 Web Site: www.flashlightpress.com, pg 79

Norma Fleck Award for Canadian Children's Non-Fiction, 40 Orchard View Blvd, Suite 217, Toronto, ON M4R 1B9, Canada Tel: 416-975-0010 Fax: 416-975-8970 E-mail: info@bookcentre.ca Web Site: www.bookcentre.ca, pg 616

FleetSeek, 6190 Powers Ferry Rd, Suite 320, Atlanta, GA 30339 Tel: 540-899-9872 Toll Free Tel: 888-ONLY-TTS (665-9887) Fax: 540-899-1948 E-mail: fleetseek@fleetseek.com Web Site: www.fleetseek.com, pg 79

Peter Fleming Agency, PO Box 458, Pacific Palisades, CA 90272 Tel: 310-454-1373 E-mail: peterfleming408@gmail.com, pg 484

Florida Antiquarian Booksellers Association (FABA), 14046 Fifth St, Dade City, FL 33525 Tel: 727-234-7759 E-mail: floridabooksellers@gmail.com Web Site: floridabooksellers.com, pg 533

Florida Authors & Publishers Association Inc (FAPA), 1702 N Woodland Blvd, Suite 116, Box 145, Deland, FL 32720 E-mail: member.services@floridapublishersassociation.com Web Site: www.floridapublishersassociation.com, pg 533

Florida Freelance Writers Association, 45 Main St, North Stratford, NH 03590 Tel: 603-922-8338 Fax: 603-922-8339 E-mail: ffwa@writers-editors.com; info@writers-editors.com Web Site: www.writers-editors.com; www.ffwamembers.com, pg 533

Florida Graphics Alliance (FGA), 5770 Hoffner Ave, Suite 103, Orlando, FL 32822 Tel: 407-240-8009 Toll Free Tel: 800-331-0461 Fax: 407-240-8333 E-mail: info@floridagraphics.org Web Site: www.floridagraphics.org, pg 533

Florida Outdoor Writers Association Inc, 235 Apollo Beach Blvd, Unit 271, Apollo Beach, FL 33572 Tel: 813-579-0990 E-mail: info@fowa.org Web Site: www.fowa.org, pg 533

Florida Writers Association Conference, PO Box 66069, St Pete Beach, FL 33736-6069 Web Site: www.floridawriters.net, pg 574

Florida Writers Association Inc, PO Box 66069, St Pete Beach, FL 33736-6069 Web Site: www.floridawriters.net, pg 533

Flowerpot Press, 2160 S Service Rd W, Oakville, ON L6L 5N1, Canada Tel: 416-479-0695 Toll Free Tel: 866-927-5001 E-mail: info@flowerpotpress.com; order@flowerpotpress.com Web Site: www.flowerpotpress.com, pg 427

Focus, PO Box 390007, Cambridge, MA 02139-0001 Tel: 317-635-9250 Fax: 317-635-9292 E-mail: customer@hackettpublishing.com; editorial@hackettpublishing.com Web Site: focusbookstore.com; www.hackettpublishing.com, pg 79

Focus on the Family, 8605 Explorer Dr, Colorado Springs, CO 80920-1051 Tel: 719-531-5181 Toll Free Tel: 800-A-FAMILY (232-6459) Fax: 719-531-3424 Web Site: www.focusonthefamily.com; www.facebook.com/focusonthefamily, pg 79

Focus Strategic Communications Inc, 2474 Waterford St, Oakville, ON L6L 5E6, Canada Tel: 905-825-8757 E-mail: info@focussc.com Web Site: www.focussc.com, pg 463

Fodor's Travel, 909 N Sepulveda Blvd, El Segundo, CA 90245 E-mail: marketing@fodors.com Web Site: www.fodors.com, pg 79

Sheldon Fogelman Agency Inc, 420 E 72 St, New York, NY 10021 Tel: 212-532-7250 Fax: 212-685-8939 E-mail: info@sheldonfogelmanagency.com Web Site: sheldonfogelmanagency.com, pg 484

Foil & Specialty Effects Association (FSEA), 2150 SW Westport Dr, Suite 101, Topeka, KS 66614 Tel: 785-271-5816 Fax: 785-271-6404 E-mail: info@fsea.com Web Site: www.fsea.com, pg 533

Folio Literary Management, The Film Center Bldg, 630 Ninth Ave, Suite 1101, New York, NY 10036 Tel: 212-400-1494 Fax: 212-967-0977 Web Site: www.foliolit.com, pg 484

Folklore Publishing, 11717-9B Ave NW, Unit 2, Edmonton, AB T6J 7B7, Canada Tel: 780-435-2376 Web Site: www.folklorepublishing.com, pg 427

La Fondation Emile Nelligan, 100, rue Sherbrooke, Suite 202, Montreal, QC H2X 1C3, Canada Tel: 514-278-4657 E-mail: info@fondation-nelligan.org Web Site: www.fondation-nelligan.org, pg 534

Fons Vitae, 49 Mockingbird Valley Dr, Louisville, KY 40207-1366 *Tel:* 502-897-3641 *Fax:* 502-893-7373 *E-mail:* fonsvitaeky@aol.com *Web Site:* www.fonsvitae.com, pg 79

Fordham University, Gabelli School of Business, 140 W 62 St, Rm 440, New York, NY 10023 *Web Site:* www.fordham.edu, pg 582, 616

Fordham University Press, Joseph A Martino Hall, 45 Columbus Ave, New York, NY 10023 *Fax:* 347-842-3083 *Web Site:* www.fordhampress.com, pg 79

Foreword's INDIES Awards, 413 E Eighth St, Traverse City, MI 49686 *Tel:* 231-933-3699 *Web Site:* www.forewordreviews.com, pg 616

Morris D Forkosch Prize, 400 "A" St SE, Washington, DC 20003 *Tel:* 202-544-2422 *Fax:* 202-544-8307 *E-mail:* awards@historians.org *Web Site:* www.historians.org, pg 616

E M Forster Award, 633 W 155 St, New York, NY 10032 *Tel:* 212-368-5900 *Fax:* 212-491-4615 *E-mail:* academy@artsandletters.org *Web Site:* artsandletters.org, pg 616

Fort Ross Inc - International Representation for Artists, 26 Arthur Place, Yonkers, NY 10701 *Tel:* 914-375-6448, pg 485, 511

49th Parallel Poetry Award, Mail Stop 9053, Western Washington University, Bellingham, WA 98225 *Tel:* 360-650-4863 *E-mail:* bhreview@wwu.edu *Web Site:* www.bhreview.org, pg 616

Forum Publishing Co, 383 E Main St, Centerport, NY 11721 *Tel:* 631-754-5000 *Toll Free Tel:* 800-635-7654 *Fax:* 631-754-0630 *E-mail:* forumpublishing@aol.com *Web Site:* www.forum123.com, pg 80

Forward Movement, 412 Sycamore St, Cincinnati, OH 45202-4110 *Tel:* 513-721-6659 *Toll Free Tel:* 800-543-1813 *Fax:* 513-721-0729 (orders) *E-mail:* orders@forwardmovement.org (orders & cust serv) *Web Site:* www.forwardmovement.org, pg 80

Foster City International Writers Contest, 650 Shell Blvd, Foster City, CA 94404 *Tel:* 650-286-3380 *E-mail:* fostercity_writers@yahoo.com *Web Site:* www.fostercity.org, pg 616

Foster Travel Publishing, 1623 Martin Luther King Jr Way, Berkeley, CA 94709 *Tel:* 510-549-2202 *Web Site:* www.fostertravel.com, pg 463

Walter Foster Publishing Inc, 6 Orchard Rd, Suite 100, Lake Forest, CA 92630 *Tel:* 949-380-7510 *Toll Free Tel:* 800-426-0099; 800-759-0190 (orders) *Fax:* 949-380-7575 *E-mail:* walterfoster@quarto.com *Web Site:* www.quartoknows.com/walter-foster, pg 80

Foundation Center, 32 Old Slip, 24th fl, New York, NY 10005-3500 *Tel:* 212-620-4230 *Toll Free Tel:* 800-424-9836 *Fax:* 212-807-3677 *E-mail:* customerservice@foundationcenter.org *Web Site:* foundationcenter.org, pg 80

Foundation Press, c/o West Academic, 444 Cedar St, Suite 700, St Paul, MN 55101 *Toll Free Tel:* 877-888-1330 *E-mail:* customerservice@westacademic.com *Web Site:* www.westacademic.com, pg 80

Foundation Publications, 900 S Euclid St, La Habra, CA 90631 *Tel:* 714-879-2286 *E-mail:* info@foundationpublications.com *Web Site:* www.foundationpublications.com, pg 80

Four Quartets Prize, 15 Gramercy Park, New York, NY 10003 *Tel:* 212-254-9628 *Web Site:* poetrysociety.org/awards, pg 616

4A's (American Association of Advertising Agencies), 1065 Avenue of the Americas, 16th fl, New York, NY 10018 *Tel:* 212-682-2500 *Web Site:* www.aaaa.org, pg 534

Fowler Museum at UCLA, PO Box 951549, Los Angeles, CA 90095-1549 *Tel:* 310-825-4361 *Fax:* 310-206-7007 *E-mail:* fowlerws@arts.ucla.edu *Web Site:* www.fowler.ucla.edu, pg 80

Fox Chapel Publishing Co Inc, 1970 Broad St, East Petersburg, PA 17520 *Tel:* 717-560-4703 *Toll Free Tel:* 800-457-9112 *Fax:* 717-560-4702 *E-mail:* customerservice@foxchapelpublishing.com *Web Site:* www.foxchapelpublishing.com, pg 80

Dixon Ryan Fox Manuscript Prize, 5798 State Hwy 80, Cooperstown, NY 13326 *Tel:* 607-547-1416, pg 616

Frances Henne YALSA/VOYA Research Grant, 50 E Huron St, Chicago, IL 60611 *Tel:* 312-280-4390 *Toll Free Tel:* 800-545-2433 *Fax:* 312-280-5276 *E-mail:* yalsa@ala.org *Web Site:* www.ala.org/yalsa/awardsandgrants/franceshenne, pg 616

Franciscan Media, 28 W Liberty St, Cincinnati, OH 45202 *Tel:* 513-241-5615 *Toll Free Tel:* 800-488-0488 *E-mail:* admin@franciscanmedia.org *Web Site:* www.franciscanmedia.org, pg 80

Prix Francophone de l'ACSP, 260 rue Dalhousie St, Suite 204, Ottawa, ON K1N 7E4, Canada *Tel:* 613-562-1202 *Fax:* 613-241-0019 *E-mail:* cpsa-acsp@cpsa-acsp.ca *Web Site:* www.cpsa-acsp.ca, pg 617

Sandi Frank, 8 Fieldcrest Ct, Cortlandt Manor, NY 10567 *Tel:* 914-739-7088 *E-mail:* sfrankmail@aol.com, pg 463

Franklin, Beedle & Associates Inc, 2154 NE Broadway, Suite 100, Portland, OR 97232 *Tel:* 503-284-6348 *Toll Free Tel:* 800-322-2665 *Fax:* 503-625-4434 *Web Site:* www.fbeedle.com, pg 81

Lynn C Franklin Associates Ltd, 1350 Broadway, Suite 2015, New York, NY 10018 *Tel:* 212-868-6311 *Fax:* 212-868-6312 *E-mail:* agency@franklinandsiegal.com, pg 485

Soeurette Diehl Fraser Translation Award, PO Box 609, Round Rock, TX 78680 *Tel:* 512-683-5640 *E-mail:* president@texasinstituteofletters.org *Web Site:* www.texasinstituteofletters.org, pg 617

Frederick Fell Publishers Inc, 7519 LaPaz Blvd, Suite C303, Boca Raton, FL 33433 *Tel:* 954-925-5242 *E-mail:* fellpub@aol.com (admin only) *Web Site:* www.fellpub.com, pg 81

Jeanne Fredericks Literary Agency Inc, 221 Benedict Hill Rd, New Canaan, CT 06840 *Tel:* 203-972-3011 *Fax:* 203-972-3011 *E-mail:* jeanne.fredericks@gmail.com (no unsol attachments) *Web Site:* www.jeannefredericks.com, pg 485

Free Spirit Publishing Inc, 6325 Sandburg Rd, Suite 100, Minneapolis, MN 55427 *Tel:* 612-338-2068 *Toll Free Tel:* 800-735-7323 *Fax:* 612-337-5050 *Toll Free Fax:* 866-419-5199 *E-mail:* help4kids@freespirit.com *Web Site:* www.freespirit.com, pg 81

George Freedley Memorial Award, c/o The New York Public Library for the Performing Arts, 111 Amsterdam Ave, New York, NY 10023 *E-mail:* TLABookAwards@gmail.com; TheatreLibraryAssociation@gmail.com *Web Site:* www.tla-online.org/awards/bookawards, pg 617

Robert A Freedman Dramatic Agency Inc, 1501 Broadway, Suite 2310, New York, NY 10036 *Tel:* 212-840-5760 *Fax:* 212-840-5776, pg 485

The Don Freeman Memorial Grant-In-Aid, 6363 Wilshire Blvd, Suite 425, Los Angeles, CA 90048 *Tel:* 323-782-1010; 310-403-0675 (cell) *Fax:* 323-782-1892 *E-mail:* grants@scbwi.org; scbwi@scbwi.org *Web Site:* www.scbwi.org, pg 617

W H Freeman, 41 Madison Ave, New York, NY 10010 *Tel:* 212-576-9400 *Fax:* 212-689-2383 *Web Site:* www.macmillanlearning.com, pg 81

The French-American Foundation & Florence Gould Foundation Annual Translation Prize, 28 W 44 St, Suite 1420, New York, NY 10036 *Tel:* 212-829-8800 *Fax:* 212-829-8810 *Web Site:* www.frenchamerican.org, pg 617

Samuel French Inc, 235 Park Ave S, 5th fl, New York, NY 10003 *Tel:* 212-206-8990 *Toll Free Tel:* 866-598-8449 *Fax:* 212-206-1429 *E-mail:* info@samuelfrench.com *Web Site:* www.samuelfrench.com, pg 81

Horst Frenz Prize, University of South Carolina, Dept of Languages, Literature & Cultures, 1620 College St, Rm 817, Columbia, SC 29208 *Tel:* 803-777-3021 *E-mail:* info@acla.org *Web Site:* www.acla.org/prize-awards/horst-frenz-prize, pg 617

Fresh Air Books, 1908 Grand Ave, Nashville, TN 37212 *Tel:* 615-340-7200 *Toll Free Tel:* 800-972-0433 (orders) *Web Site:* books.upperroom.org, pg 81

Sarah Jane Freymann Literary Agency LLC, 59 W 71 St, Suite 9-B, New York, NY 10023 *Tel:* 212-362-9277 *E-mail:* submissions@sarahjanefreymann.com *Web Site:* www.sarahjanefreymann.com, pg 485

Fredrica S Friedman & Co Inc, 857 Fifth Ave, New York, NY 10065 *Tel:* 212-639-9455 *E-mail:* info@fredricafriedman.com *Web Site:* www.fredricafriedman.com, pg 485

Friends of American Writers Awards, 506 Rose Ave, Des Plaines, IL 60016 *Tel:* 847-827-8339 *Web Site:* www.fawchicago.org, pg 617

Friends United Press, 101 Quaker Hill Dr, Richmond, IN 47374 *Tel:* 765-962-7573 *Fax:* 765-966-1293 *E-mail:* friendspress@fum.org; orders@fum.org *Web Site:* www.friendsunitedmeeting.org; bookstore.friendsunitedmeeting.org, pg 81

Fromer, 1606 Noyes Dr, Silver Spring, MD 20910-2224 *Tel:* 301-585-8827, pg 463

Frost Medal, 15 Gramercy Park, New York, NY 10003 *Tel:* 212-254-9628 *Web Site:* poetrysociety.org/awards, pg 617

Candice Fuhrman Literary Agency, 10 Cypress Hollow Dr, Tiburon, CA 94920 *Tel:* 415-383-1014 *E-mail:* fuhrmancandice@gmail.com, pg 485

Fulbright Scholar Program, 1400 "K" St NW, Washington, DC 20005 *Tel:* 202-686-4000 *E-mail:* scholars@iie.org *Web Site:* www.cies.org; www.iie.org, pg 617

Fulcrum Publishing Inc, 4690 Table Mountain Dr, Suite 100, Golden, CO 80403 *Tel:* 303-277-1623 *Toll Free Tel:* 800-992-2908 *Fax:* 303-279-7111 *Toll Free Fax:* 800-726-7112 *E-mail:* info@fulcrumbooks.com; orders@fulcrumbooks.com *Web Site:* www.fulcrumbooks.com, pg 82

Fun in the Sun Writer's Cruise Conference, PO Box 823414, Pembroke Pines, FL 33082 *E-mail:* frwfuninthesun@yahoo.com *Web Site:* frwfuninthesunmain.blogspot.com/; www.frwriters.org, pg 574

FurnitureCore, 1389 Peachtree St NE, Suite 310, Atlanta, GA 30309 *Tel:* 404-961-3734 *Toll Free Tel:* 800-826-8868 *Fax:* 404-961-3749 *E-mail:* info@furniturecore.com *Web Site:* www.furniturecore.com, pg 82

Future Horizons Inc, 721 W Abram St, Arlington, TX 76013 *Tel:* 817-277-0727 *Toll Free Tel:* 800-489-0727 *Fax:* 817-277-2270 *E-mail:* info@fhautism.com *Web Site:* www.fhautism.com, pg 82

Gabriele Rico Challenge for Nonfiction, San Jose State University, English Dept, One Washington Sq, San Jose, CA 95192-0090 *Tel:* 408-924-4441 *E-mail:* mail@reedmag.org *Web Site:* www.reedmag.org; reedmagazine.submittable.com, pg 617

Gaetan Morin Editeur, 5800, rue St-Denis, bureau 900, Montreal, QC H2S 3L5, Canada *Tel:* 514-273-1066 *Toll Free Tel:* 800-565-5531 *Fax:* 514-276-0324 *Toll Free Fax:* 800-814-0324 *E-mail:* info@cheneliere.ca *Web Site:* www.cheneliere.ca, pg 427

Gagosian Gallery, 980 Madison Ave, New York, NY 10075 *Tel:* 212-744-2313 *Fax:* 212-772-7962 *E-mail:* newyork@gagosian.com *Web Site:* www.gagosian.com, pg 82

Ernest J Gaines Award for Literary Excellence, 100 North St, Suite 900, Baton Rouge, LA 70802 *Tel:* 225-387-6126 *E-mail:* gainesaward@braf.org *Web Site:* www.ernestjgainesaward.org, pg 618

Lewis Galantiere Translation Award, 225 Reinekers Lane, Suite 590, Alexandria, VA 22314 *Tel:* 703-683-6100 *Fax:* 703-683-6122 *E-mail:* honors_awards@atanet.org *Web Site:* www.atanet.org, pg 618

Galaxy Press, 7051 Hollywood Blvd, Hollywood, CA 90028 *Tel:* 323-466-3310 *Toll Free Tel:* 877-8GALAXY (842-5299) *E-mail:* info@galaxypress.com; customers@galaxypress.com *Web Site:* www.galaxypress.com, pg 82

Galde Press Inc, PO Box 774, Hendersonville, NC 28793 *Tel:* 828-702-3032 *Web Site:* www.galdepress.com, pg 82

Gale, 27500 Drake Rd, Farmington Hills, MI 48331-3535 *Tel:* 248-699-4253 *Toll Free Tel:* 800-877-4253 *Toll Free Fax:* 800-414-5043 (orders) *E-mail:* gale.customercare@cengage.com *Web Site:* www.gale.com, pg 82

Zona Gale Award for Short Fiction, c/o 4414 W Fillmore Dr, Milwaukee, WI 53219 *E-mail:* wiswriters@gmail.com *Web Site:* wiswriters.org/awards, pg 618

Galen Press Ltd, PO Box 64400-WB, Tucson, AZ 85728-4400 *Tel:* 520-577-8363 *Fax:* 520-529-6459 *E-mail:* sales@galenpress.com *Web Site:* www.galenpress.com, pg 82

Gallaudet University Press, 800 Florida Ave NE, Washington, DC 20002-3695 *Tel:* 202-651-5488 *Fax:* 202-651-5489 *E-mail:* gupress@gallaudet.edu *Web Site:* gupress.gallaudet.edu, pg 82

Gallery Books, 1230 Avenue of the Americas, New York, NY 10020 *Toll Free Tel:* 800-456-6798 *Fax:* 212-698-7284 *E-mail:* consumer.customerservice@simonandschuster.com *Web Site:* www.simonandschuster.com, pg 82

Diane Gallo, 49 Hilton St, Gilbertsville, NY 13776 *Tel:* 607-783-2386 *Fax:* 607-783-2386 *E-mail:* dgallo@stny.rr.com *Web Site:* www.dianegallo.com, pg 464

Gallopade International Inc, 611 Hwy 74 S, Suite 2000, Peachtree City, GA 30269 *Tel:* 770-631-4222 *Toll Free Tel:* 800-536-2GET (536-2438) *Fax:* 770-631-4810 *Toll Free Tel:* 800-871-2979 *E-mail:* customerservice@gallopade.com *Web Site:* www.gallopade.com, pg 83

Gannon University's High School Poetry Contest, Gannon University, 109 University Sq, Erie, PA 16541 *Tel:* 814-871-7504 *Web Site:* www.gannon.edu/departmental/english/poetry.asp, pg 618

The Garamond Agency Inc, 12 Horton St, Newburyport, MA 01950 *E-mail:* query@garamondagency.com *Web Site:* www.garamondagency.com, pg 485

GardenComm: Garden Communicators International, 355 Lexington Ave, 15th fl, New York, NY 10017 *Tel:* 212-297-2198 *E-mail:* info@gardenwriters.org *Web Site:* www.gardenwriters.org, pg 534

Gareth Stevens Publishing, 111 E 14 St, Suite 349, New York, NY 10003 *Toll Free Tel:* 800-542-2595 *Toll Free Fax:* 877-542-2596 (cust serv) *E-mail:* customerservice@gspub.com *Web Site:* garethstevens.com, pg 83

Francois-Xavier Garneau Medal, 130 Albert St, Suite 1201, Ottawa, ON K1P 5G4, Canada *Tel:* 613-233-7885 *Fax:* 613-565-5445 *E-mail:* cha-shc@cha-shc.ca *Web Site:* www.cha-shc.ca, pg 618

Max Gartenberg Literary Agency, 912 N Pennsylvania Ave, Yardley, PA 19067 *Tel:* 215-295-9230 *Web Site:* www.maxgartenberg.com, pg 485

Alfred C Gary Memorial, 900 Timber Creek Place, Virginia Beach, VA 23464 *E-mail:* poetryinva@aol.com *Web Site:* poetrysocietyofvirginia.org, pg 618

The Gary-Paul Agency, 1549 Main St, Stratford, CT 06615 *Tel:* 203-345-6167 *Web Site:* www.thegarypaulagency.com; www.nutmegpictures.com, pg 464

John Gassner Memorial Playwriting Award, 215 Knob Hill Dr, Hamden, CT 06518 *Tel:* 617-851-8535 *Fax:* 203-288-5938 *E-mail:* mail@netconline.org *Web Site:* www.netconline.org, pg 618

Gatekeeper Press, 2167 Stringtown Rd, Suite 109, Columbus, OH 43123 *Toll Free Tel:* 866-535-0913 *Fax:* 216-803-0350 *E-mail:* info@gatekeeperpress.com *Web Site:* www.gatekeeperpress.com, pg 83

Gateways Books & Tapes, PO Box 370, Nevada City, CA 95959 *Tel:* 530-271-2239 *Toll Free Tel:* 800-869-0658 *E-mail:* info@gatewaysbooksandtapes.com *Web Site:* www.gatewaysbooksandtapes.com; www.retrosf.com (Retro Science Fiction imprint), pg 83

The Christian Gauss Award, 1606 New Hampshire Ave NW, Washington, DC 20009 *Tel:* 202-265-3808 *Fax:* 202-986-1601 *E-mail:* awards@pbk.org *Web Site:* www.pbk.org/bookawards, pg 618

Gauthier Publications Inc, PO Box 806241, St Clair Shores, MI 48080 *Tel:* 313-458-7141 *Fax:* 586-279-1515 *E-mail:* info@gauthierpublications.com *Web Site:* www.gauthierpublications.com, pg 83

The Gaylactic Spectrum Awards, 1425 "S" St NW, Washington, DC 20009 *Web Site:* www.spectrumawards.org, pg 618

Gaylord College of Journalism & Mass Communication, Professional Writing Program, c/o University of Oklahoma, 395 W Lindsey St, Rm 3000, Norman, OK 73019-0270 *Tel:* 405-325-2721 *Web Site:* www.ou.edu/gaylord; www.ou.edu/gaylord/undergraduate/professional-writing, pg 582

Fred Gebhart, PO Box 111, Gold Hill, OR 97525 *Tel:* 541-855-8975 *E-mail:* fgebhart@pobox.com *Web Site:* www.fredgebhart.com, pg 464

Gefen Books, c/o Storch, 255 Central Ave, B-206, Lawrence, NY 11559 *Tel:* 516-593-1234 *Toll Free Tel:* 800-477-5257 *Fax:* 516-295-2739 *E-mail:* gefenny@gefenpublishing.com; info@gefenpublishing.com *Web Site:* www.gefenpublishing.com, pg 84

Theodor Seuss Geisel Award, 225 N Michigan Ave, Suite 1300, Chicago, IL 60601 *Toll Free Tel:* 800-545-2433 *Fax:* 312-280-5271 *E-mail:* alscawards@ala.org *Web Site:* www.ala.org/awardsgrants/theodor-seuss-geisel-award, pg 618

Lionel Gelber Prize, University of Toronto, Munk School of Global Affairs, One Devonshire Place, Toronto, ON M5S 3K7, Canada *Tel:* 416-946-8901 *Fax:* 416-946-8915 *E-mail:* events.munk@utoronto.ca *Web Site:* munkschool.utoronto.ca/gelber; www.facebook.com/GelberPrize, pg 618

Gelfman Schneider/ICM Partners, 850 Seventh Ave, Suite 903, New York, NY 10019 *Tel:* 212-245-1993 *Fax:* 212-245-8678 *E-mail:* mail@gelfmanschneider.com *Web Site:* gelfmanschneider.com, pg 486

Gell: A Finger Lakes Creative Retreat, 740 University Ave, Rochester, NY 14607-1259 *Tel:* 585-473-2590 *Fax:* 585-442-9333 *Web Site:* www.wab.org, pg 574

Gelles-Cole Literary Enterprises, 2163 Lima Loop, PMB 01-408, Laredo, TX 78045-9452 *Tel:* 845-810-0029 *Web Site:* www.literaryenterprises.com, pg 464

Gem Guides Book Co, 1155 W Ninth St, Upland, CA 91786 *Tel:* 626-855-1611 *Toll Free Tel:* 800-824-5118 (orders) *Fax:* 626-855-1610 *E-mail:* info@gemguidesbooks.com; sales@gemguidesbooks.com (orders) *Web Site:* www.gemguidesbooks.com, pg 84

GemStone Press, 4507 Charlotte Ave, Suite 100, Nashville, TN 37209 *Tel:* 615-255-BOOK (255-2665) *Fax:* 615-255-5081 *E-mail:* marketing@turnerpublishing.com *Web Site:* gemstonepress.com; www.turnerpublishing.com, pg 84

Genealogical Publishing Co, 3600 Clipper Mill Rd, Suite 229, Baltimore, MD 21211 *Tel:* 410-837-8271 *Toll Free Tel:* 800-296-6687 *Fax:* 410-752-8492 *Toll Free Fax:* 800-599-9561 *E-mail:* info@genealogical.com; web@genealogical.com *Web Site:* www.genealogical.com, pg 84

Genesis Press Inc, PO Box 101, Columbus, MS 39701 *Toll Free Tel:* 888-463-4461 (orders only), pg 84

Geological Society of America (GSA), 3300 Penrose Place, Boulder, CO 80301-1806 *Tel:* 303-357-1000 *Fax:* 303-357-1070 *E-mail:* pubs@geosociety.org (prodn); editing@geosociety.org (edit) *Web Site:* www.geosociety.org, pg 84

GeoLytics Inc, 3322 Rte 22, Suite 806, Branchburg, NJ 08876 *Tel:* 908-707-1505 *Toll Free Tel:* 800-577-6717 *Fax:* 908-707-1595 *E-mail:* support@geolytics.com; questions@geolytics.com *Web Site:* www.geolytics.com, pg 85

Georgetown University Press, 3520 Prospect St NW, Suite 140, Washington, DC 20007 *Tel:* 202-687-5889 (busn) *Fax:* 202-687-6340 (edit) *E-mail:* gupress@georgetown.edu *Web Site:* press.georgetown.edu, pg 85

The Gersh Agency (TGA), 41 Madison Ave, 33rd fl, New York, NY 10010 *Tel:* 212-997-1818 *Web Site:* gershbooks.com, pg 486

Leo Gershoy Award, 400 "A" St SE, Washington, DC 20003 *Tel:* 202-544-2422 *Fax:* 202-544-8307 *E-mail:* awards@historians.org *Web Site:* www.historians.org, pg 618

Nancy C Gerth PhD, 1431 Harlan's Trail, Sagle, ID 83860 *Tel:* 208-304-9066 *E-mail:* docnangee@nancygerth.com *Web Site:* www.nancygerth.com, pg 464

Gestalt Journal Press, PO Box 278, Gouldsboro, ME 04607-0278 *Tel:* 207-404-9954 *Fax:* 207-510-4889 *E-mail:* press@gestalt.org *Web Site:* gestalt.org, pg 85

Getty Publications, 1200 Getty Center Dr, Suite 500, Los Angeles, CA 90049-1682 *Tel:* 310-440-7365 *Toll Free Tel:* 800-223-3431 (orders) *Fax:* 310-440-7758 *E-mail:* pubsinfo@getty.edu *Web Site:* www.getty.edu/publications, pg 85

GGP Publishing Inc, 105 Calvert St, Suite 201, Harrison, NY 10528-3138 *Tel:* 914-834-8896 *Fax:* 914-834-7566 *Web Site:* www.GGPPublishing.com, pg 464, 486

GIA Publications Inc, 7404 S Mason Ave, Chicago, IL 60638 *Tel:* 708-496-3800 *Toll Free Tel:* 800-GIA-1358 (442-1358) *Fax:* 708-496-3828 *E-mail:* custserv@giamusic.com *Web Site:* www.giamusic.com, pg 85

Gibbs Smith Publisher, 1877 E Gentile St, Layton, UT 84041 *Tel:* 801-544-9800 *Toll Free Tel:* 800-748-5439; 800-835-4993 (orders) *Fax:* 801-544-5582 *Toll Free Fax:* 800-213-3023 (orders only) *E-mail:* info@gibbs-smith.com; tradeorders@gibbs-smith.com *Web Site:* www.gibbs-smith.com, pg 85

Arrell Gibson Lifetime Achievement Award, 200 NE 18 St, Oklahoma City, OK 73105-3205 *Tel:* 405-522-3383 *Web Site:* libraries.ok.gov/ocb/arrell-gibson/, pg 619

Gifted Education Press, 10201 Yuma Ct, Manassas, VA 20109 *Tel:* 703-369-5017 *Web Site:* www.giftededpress.com, pg 85

Gifted Unlimited LLC, 12340 US Hwy 42, No 453, Goshen, KY 40026 *Tel:* 502-715-6306 *E-mail:* info@giftedunlimitedllc.com; orders@giftedunlimitedllc.com *Web Site:* www.giftedunlimitedllc.com, pg 86

Sheri Gilbert, 123 Van Voorhis Ave, Rochester, NY 14617 *Tel:* 585-342-0331 *E-mail:* shergilb@aol.com *Web Site:* www.permissionseditor.com, pg 464

Gilder Lehrman Lincoln Prize, 300 N Washington St, Campus Box 413, Gettysburg, PA 17325 *Tel:* 717-337-8255 *E-mail:* lincolnprize@gettysburg.edu *Web Site:* www.gilderlehrman.org, pg 619

Gilder Lehrman Prize for Military History, 49 W 45 St, 2nd fl, New York, NY 10036 *Tel:* 646-366-9666, pg 619

Giller Prize, 543 Logan Ave, Toronto, ON M4K 3B6, Canada *Web Site:* www.scotiabankgillerprize.ca, pg 619

Gingko Press Inc, 1321 Fifth St, Berkeley, CA 94710 *Tel:* 510-898-1195 *Fax:* 510-898-1196 *E-mail:* books@gingkopress.com *Web Site:* www.gingkopress.com, pg 86

Allen Ginsberg Poetry Award, One College Blvd, Paterson, NJ 07505-1179 *Tel:* 973-684-6555 *Fax:* 973-523-6085 *Web Site:* www.poetrycenterpccc.com, pg 619

Gival Press, 5200 N First St, Arlington, VA 22203 *Tel:* 703-351-0079 *Fax:* 703-351-0079 (call first) *E-mail:* givalpress@yahoo.com *Web Site:* www.givalpress.com, pg 86

Gival Press Novel Award, PO Box 3812, Arlington, VA 22203 *Tel:* 703-351-0079 *Fax:* 703-351-0079 (call first) *E-mail:* givalpress@yahoo.com *Web Site:* www.givalpress.com; givalpress.submittable.com, pg 619

Gival Press Oscar Wilde Award, PO Box 3812, Arlington, VA 22203 *Tel:* 703-351-0079 *Fax:* 703-351-0079 (call first) *E-mail:* givalpress@yahoo.com *Web Site:* www.givalpress.com; givalpress.submittable. com, pg 619

Gival Press Poetry Award, PO Box 3812, Arlington, VA 22203 *Tel:* 703-351-0079 *Fax:* 703-351-0079 (call first) *E-mail:* givalpress@yahoo.com *Web Site:* www. givalpress.com; givalpress.submittable.com, pg 619

Gival Press Short Story Award, PO Box 3812, Arlington, VA 22203 *Tel:* 703-351-0079 *Fax:* 703-351-0079 (call first) *E-mail:* givalpress@yahoo.com *Web Site:* www. givalpress.com; givalpress.submittable.com, pg 619

John Glassco Translation Prize, Concordia University, LB 601, 1455 De Maisonneuve W, Montreal, QC H3G 1M8, Canada *Tel:* 514-848-2424 (ext 8702) *E-mail:* info@attlc-ltac.org *Web Site:* www.attlc-ltac. org, pg 619

GLCA New Writers Awards, 535 W William St, Suite 301, Ann Arbor, MI 48103 *Tel:* 734-661-2350 *Fax:* 734-661-2349 *Web Site:* www.glca.org, pg 619

Susan Gleason, 325 Riverside Dr, Suite 41, New York, NY 10025 *Tel:* 212-662-3876 *E-mail:* sgleasonliteraryagent@gmail.com, pg 486

The Danuta Gleed Literary Award, 600-460 Richmond St W, Toronto, ON M5V 1Y1, Canada *Tel:* 416-703-8982 *Fax:* 416-504-9090 *E-mail:* info@writersunion.ca *Web Site:* www.writersunion.ca, pg 619

The Glen Workshop, 3307 Third Ave W, Seattle, WA 98119 *Tel:* 206-281-2988 *Fax:* 206-281-2979 *E-mail:* glenworkshop@imagejournal.org *Web Site:* www.imagejournal.org, pg 574

Peter Glenn Publications, 306 NE Second St, 2nd fl, Delray Beach, FL 33483 *Web Site:* pgdirect.com, pg 86

Glitterati Editions, 311 W 43 St, 12th fl, New York, NY 10036 *Tel:* 646-584-6382 *Fax:* 646-607-4433 *E-mail:* media@glitteratieditions.com *Web Site:* glitteratieditions.com, pg 86

Global Authors Publications (GAP), 38 Bluegrass, Middleberg, FL 32068 *Tel:* 904-425-1608 *E-mail:* gapbook@yahoo.com *Web Site:* www. globalauthorspublications.com, pg 86

Global Lion Intellectual Property Management Inc, PO Box 669238, Pompano Beach, FL 33066 *Tel:* 754-222-6948 *Fax:* 754-222-6948 *E-mail:* queriesgloballionmgt@gmail.com *Web Site:* www.globallionmanagement.com, pg 486

Global Publishing, Sales & Distribution, 135 Third St, Suite 150, San Rafael, CA 94901 *Tel:* 415-456-2934 *Fax:* 415-456-4124 *E-mail:* info@globalpsd.com *Web Site:* www.globalpsd.com, pg 86

Global Training Center Inc, 550 S Mesa Hills Dr, Suite E4, El Paso, TX 79912 *Tel:* 915-534-7900 *Toll Free Tel:* 800-860-5030 *Fax:* 915-534-7903 *E-mail:* contact@globaltrainingcenter.com *Web Site:* www.globaltrainingcenter.com, pg 86

The Globe Pequot Press, 246 Goose Lane, Guilford, CT 06437 *Tel:* 203-458-4500 *Toll Free Tel:* 800-243-0495 (orders only); 888-249-7586 (cust serv) *Fax:* 203-458-4601 *Toll Free Fax:* 800-820-2329 (orders & cust serv) *E-mail:* editorial@globepequot.com; info@rowman.com; orders@rowman.com *Web Site:* rowman.com, pg 86

Globo Libros Literary Management, 450 E 63 St, New York, NY 10065 *Web Site:* www.globo-libros.com; www.publishersmarketplace.com/members/dstockwell, pg 486

The Goddard Riverside Stephan Russo Book Prize, 593 Columbus Ave, New York, NY 10024 *Web Site:* bookprize.goddard.org, pg 619

David R Godine Inc, 15 Court Sq, Suite 320, Boston, MA 02108-2536 *Tel:* 617-451-9600 *Fax:* 617-350-0250 *E-mail:* info@godine.com *Web Site:* www. godine.com, pg 87

Gold Medal, 633 W 155 St, New York, NY 10032 *Tel:* 212-368-5900 *Fax:* 212-491-4615 *E-mail:* academy@artsandletters.org *Web Site:* artsandletters.org, pg 619

Golden Cylindar Awards, 8281 Pine Lake Rd, Denver, NC 28037 *Tel:* 201-523-6042 *Fax:* 201-523-6048 *E-mail:* gaa@gaa.org *Web Site:* www.gaa.org, pg 620

Golden Kite Awards, 6363 Wilshire Blvd, Suite 425, Los Angeles, CA 90048 *Tel:* 323-782-1010; 310-403-0675 (cell) *Fax:* 323-782-1892 *E-mail:* grants@scbwi.org; scbwi@scbwi.org *Web Site:* www.scbwi.org, pg 620

Golden Meteorite Press, 11919 82 St NW, Suite 103, Edmonton, AB T5B 2W4, Canada *Tel:* 780-378-0063 *Fax:* 780-378-0063, pg 427

Golden Rose Award, 46 Wallace St, Somerville, MA 02144 *E-mail:* info@nepoetryclub.org *Web Site:* www. nepoetryclub.org, pg 620

Golden West Cookbooks, 5738 N Central Ave, Phoenix, AZ 85012-1316 *Tel:* 602-234-1574 *Toll Free Tel:* 800-521-9221 *Fax:* 602-234-3062 *E-mail:* info@americantravelerpress.com *Web Site:* www. americantravelerpress.com, pg 87

Goldfarb & Associates, 721 Gibbon St, Alexandria, VA 22314 *Tel:* 202-466-3030 *Fax:* 703-836-5644 *E-mail:* rlglawlit@gmail.com *Web Site:* www. ronaldgoldfarb.com, pg 486

Frances Goldin Literary Agency, Inc, 214 W 29 St, Suite 410, New York, NY 10001 *Tel:* 212-777-0047 *Fax:* 212-228-1660 *E-mail:* agency@goldinlit.com *Web Site:* www.goldinlit.com, pg 486

Donald Goldstein, 1500 E 17 St, Brooklyn, NY 11230 *Tel:* 718-375-9346 *E-mail:* dgoldsbkyn@aol.com, pg 464

Laurence Goldstein Poetry Prize, University of Michigan, 0576 Rackham Bldg, 915 E Washington St, Ann Arbor, MI 48109-1070 *Tel:* 734-764-9265 *E-mail:* mqr@umich.edu *Web Site:* sites.lsa.umich. edu/mqr/, pg 620

Goodheart-Willcox Publisher, 18604 W Creek Dr, Tinley Park, IL 60477-6243 *Tel:* 708-687-5000 *Toll Free Tel:* 800-323-0440 *Toll Free Fax:* 888-409-3900 *E-mail:* custserv@g-w.com; orders@g-w.com *Web Site:* www.g-w.com, pg 87

Irene Goodman Literary Agency, 27 W 24 St, Suite 700B, New York, NY 10010 *Tel:* 212-604-0330 *E-mail:* queries@irenegoodman.com *Web Site:* www. irenegoodman.com, pg 486

Robert M Goodman, 140 West End Ave, Unit 11-J, New York, NY 10023 *Tel:* 917-439-1097 *E-mail:* bobbybgood@gmail.com, pg 464

Goodreads Choice Awards, 188 Spear St, 3rd fl, San Francisco, CA 94105 *E-mail:* press@goodreads.com *Web Site:* www.goodreads.com/award, pg 620

Goose Lane Editions, 500 Beaverbrook Ct, Suite 330, Fredericton, NB E3B 5X4, Canada *Tel:* 506-450-4251 *Toll Free Tel:* 888-926-8377 *Fax:* 506-459-4991 *E-mail:* info@gooselane.com; customerservice@gooselane.com *Web Site:* www.gooselane.com, pg 427

Goose River Press, 3400 Friendship Rd, Waldoboro, ME 04572-6337 *Tel:* 207-832-6665 *E-mail:* gooseriverpress@gmail.com *Web Site:* gooseriverpress.com, pg 87

Goosebottom Books, PO Box 150764, San Rafael, CA 94915-0764 *Tel:* 415-717-6300 *E-mail:* info@goosebottombooks.com *Web Site:* goosebottombooks. com, pg 87

P M Gordon Associates Inc, 2115 Wallace St, Philadelphia, PA 19130 *Tel:* 215-769-2525 *Web Site:* www.pmgordonassociates.com, pg 464

Gorgias Press LLC, PO Box 6939, Piscataway, NJ 08854-6939 *Tel:* 732-885-8900 *Fax:* 732-885-8908 *E-mail:* helpdesk@gorgiaspress.com *Web Site:* www. gorgiaspress.com, pg 87

Gospel Publishing House, 1445 Boonville Ave, Springfield, MO 65802 *Tel:* 417-862-2781; 417-831-8000 (outside US) *Toll Free Tel:* 800-641-

4310 *Fax:* 417-862-5881 *Toll Free Fax:* 800-328-0294 *E-mail:* custsrvorders@ag.org *Web Site:* www. gospelpublishing.com, pg 87

Gotham Writers' Workshop, 555 Eighth Ave, Suite 1402, New York, NY 10018-4358 *Tel:* 212-974-8377 *E-mail:* contact@gothamwriters.com *Web Site:* www. gothamwriters.com, pg 574

Sherry Gottlieb, 300 W Ninth St, No 126, Oxnard, CA 93030-7098 *Tel:* 805-382-3425 *E-mail:* writer@wordservices.com *Web Site:* www.wordservices.com, pg 464

Governor General's Literary Awards, 150 Elgin St, 2nd fl, Ottawa, ON K2P 1L4, Canada *Tel:* 613-566-4414 *Toll Free Tel:* 800-263-5588 (CN only) *Fax:* 613-566-4390 *E-mail:* info@canadacouncil.ca *Web Site:* canadacouncil.ca/en/council/prizes, pg 620

The Gracies®, 2365 Harrodsburg Rd, Suite A325, Lexington, KY 40504 *Tel:* 202-750-3664 *Fax:* 202-750-3664 *E-mail:* info@allwomeninmedia.org *Web Site:* allwomeninmedia.org, pg 620

Doug Grad Literary Agency Inc, 68 Jay St, Suite W11, Brooklyn, NY 11201-1189 *Tel:* 718-788-6067 *E-mail:* query@dgliterary.com *Web Site:* www. dgliterary.com, pg 486

Graduate & Undergraduate Hopwood Contest, 1176 Angell Hall, 435 S State St, Ann Arbor, MI 48109-1003 *Tel:* 734-764-6296 *Fax:* 734-763-3128 *E-mail:* abeauch@umich.edu *Web Site:* lsa.umich. edu/hopwood, pg 620

The Graduate Group/Booksellers, 86 Norwood Rd, West Hartford, CT 06117-2236 *Tel:* 860-233-2330 *E-mail:* graduategroup@hotmail.com *Web Site:* www. graduategroup.com, pg 87

Graham Agency, 115 W 45 St, Suite 505, New York, NY 10036 *Tel:* 212-489-7730, pg 487

Grand & Archer Publishing, 463 Coyote, Cathedral City, CA 92234 *Tel:* 323-493-2785 *E-mail:* grandandarcher@gmail.com, pg 87

Grand Central Publishing, 1290 Avenue of the Americas, New York, NY 10104 *Tel:* 212-364-1100 *Web Site:* www.hachettebookgroup.com, pg 88

Grand Master Award, 716 Thicket Way, Ottawa, ON K4A 3B5, Canada *E-mail:* info@crimewriterscanada. com *Web Site:* www.crimewriterscanada.com/awards, pg 620

Donald M Grant Publisher Inc, PO Box 187, Hampton Falls, NH 03844-0187 *Tel:* 603-778-7191 *Fax:* 603-778-7191 *E-mail:* office@grantbooks.com *Web Site:* secure.grantbooks.com, pg 88

The Graphic Artists Guild Inc, 31 W 34 St, 8th fl, New York, NY 10001 *Tel:* 212-791-3400 *Fax:* 212-791-0333 *E-mail:* admin@graphicartistsguild.org; membership@graphicartistsguild.org *Web Site:* www. graphicartistsguild.org, pg 534, 583

Graphic Arts Association, 1210 Northbrook Dr, Suite 200, Trevose, PA 19053 *Tel:* 215-396-2300 *Fax:* 215-396-9890 *Web Site:* www.graphicartsassociation.org, pg 534

Graphic Arts Association, 1210 Northbrook Dr, Suite 200, Trevose, PA 19053 *Tel:* 215-396-2300 *Fax:* 215-396-9890 *E-mail:* gaa@gaaonline.org *Web Site:* www. graphicartsassociation.org, pg 583

Graphic Arts Education & Research Foundation (GAERF), 1899 Preston White Dr, Reston, VA 20191 *Tel:* 703-264-7200 *E-mail:* gaerf@npes.org *Web Site:* www.gaerf.org, pg 551

Graphic Universe™, 241 First Ave N, Minneapolis, MN 55401 *Tel:* 612-332-3344 *Toll Free Tel:* 800-328-4929 *Fax:* 612-332-7615 *Toll Free Fax:* 800-332-1132 *E-mail:* info@lernerbooks.com; custserve@lernerbooks.com *Web Site:* www.lernerbooks.com; www.facebook.com/lernerbooks, pg 88

Graphic World Publishing Services, 11687 Adie Rd, St Louis, MO 63043 *Tel:* 314-567-9854 *Fax:* 314-567-7178 *E-mail:* quote@gwinc.com *Web Site:* www. gwinc.com, pg 464

Health Communications Inc, 3201 SW 15 St, Deerfield Beach, FL 33442 *Tel:* 954-360-0909 *Toll Free Tel:* 800-851-9100; 800-441-5569 (cust serv & orders) *Fax:* 954-360-0034 *Toll Free Fax:* 800-424-7652 (cust serv & orders) *E-mail:* customerservice2@hcibooks. com *Web Site:* www.hcibooks.com, pg 96

Health Forum Inc, 155 N Wacker Dr, Suite 400, Chicago, IL 60606 *Tel:* 312-893-6800 *Toll Free Tel:* 800-242-2626 *Fax:* 312-422-4500 *E-mail:* hfcustsvc@healthforum.com *Web Site:* www. ahaonlinestore.com; www.healthforum.com, pg 97

Health Professions Press, 409 Washington Ave, Suite 500, Towson, MD 21204 *Tel:* 410-337-9585 *Toll Free Tel:* 888-337-8808 *Fax:* 410-337-8539 *Web Site:* www. healthpropress.com, pg 97

Heartland Booksellers Award, 250 Woodstock Ave, Clarendon Hills, IL 60514 *Tel:* 630-841-8129 *Web Site:* www.gliba.org/heartland-booksellers-award. html, pg 622

Heartland Literary Award, 160 N Stetson Ave, Chicago, IL 60601 *Tel:* 312-222-3001 *E-mail:* ctc-arts@ chicagotribune.com *Web Site:* www.chicagotribune. com/entertainment/books/literary-awards, pg 623

HeartMath LLC, 14700 W Park Ave, Boulder Creek, CA 95006 *Tel:* 831-338-8500 *Toll Free Tel:* 800-711-6221 *Fax:* 831-338-8504 *E-mail:* info@heartmath.org; inquiry@heartmath.org *Web Site:* www.heartmath.org, pg 97

Hearts 'n Tummies Cookbook Co, 3544 Blakslee St, Wever, IA 52658 *Tel:* 319-372-7480 *Toll Free Tel:* 800-571-2665 *Fax:* 319-372-7485 *E-mail:* quixotepress@gmail.com; heartsntummies@ gmail.com *Web Site:* www.heartsntummies.com, pg 97

Anne Hebenstreit, 20 Tip Top Way, Berkeley Heights, NJ 07922 *Tel:* 908-665-0536, pg 464

Hebrew Union College Press, 3101 Clifton Ave, Cincinnati, OH 45220 *Tel:* 513-221-1875 *Fax:* 513-221-0321 *Web Site:* press.huc.edu, pg 97

Hedgebrook Master Class Retreat Series, PO Box 1231, Freeland, WA 98249 *Tel:* 360-321-4786 *Fax:* 360-321-2171 *E-mail:* hedgebrook@hedgebrook.org *Web Site:* www.hedgebrook.org; www.facebook. com/hedgebrook, pg 575

Hedgebrook VORTEXT, PO Box 1231, Freeland, WA 98249 *Tel:* 360-321-4786 *Fax:* 360-321-2171 *E-mail:* hedgebrook@hedgebrook.org *Web Site:* www. hedgebrook.org; www.facebook.com/hedgebrook, pg 575

Hedgebrook Writers in Residence Program, PO Box 1231, Freeland, WA 98249 *Tel:* 360-321-4786 *Fax:* 360-321-2171 *E-mail:* hedgebrook@hedgebrook. org *Web Site:* www.hedgebrook.org; www.facebook. com/hedgebrook, pg 575

Heimburger House Publishing Co, 7236 W Madison St, Forest Park, IL 60130 *Tel:* 708-366-1973 *Fax:* 708-366-1973 *E-mail:* info@heimburgerhouse.com *Web Site:* www.heimburgerhouse.com, pg 97

William S Hein & Co Inc, 2350 N Forest Rd, Getzville, NY 14068 *Tel:* 716-882-2600 *Toll Free Tel:* 800-828-7571 *Fax:* 716-883-8100 *E-mail:* mail@wshein.com; marketing@wshein.com *Web Site:* www.wshein.com, pg 97

Heinemann, 361 Hanover St, Portsmouth, NH 03801-3912 *Tel:* 603-431-7894 *Toll Free Tel:* 800-225-5800 (US) *Fax:* 603-431-2214 *Toll Free Fax:* 877-231-6980 (US) *E-mail:* custserv@heinemann.com *Web Site:* www.heinemann.com, pg 97

Drue Heinz Literature Prize, 7500 Thomas Blvd, Pittsburgh, PA 15260 *Tel:* 412-383-2456 *Fax:* 412-383-2466 *E-mail:* info@upress.pitt.edu *Web Site:* upittpress.org/prize/drue-heinz-literature-prize/; www.upress.pitt.edu, pg 623

Hellgate Press, PO Box 3531, Ashland, OR 97520 *Tel:* 541-973-5154 *Toll Free Tel:* 800-795-4059 *E-mail:* sales@hellgatepress.com *Web Site:* www. hellgatepress.com, pg 98

Helm Editorial Services, 300 Canopy Walk Lane, Unit 325, Palm Coast, FL 33237 *Tel:* 954-525-5626 *E-mail:* lynnehelm12@aol.com, pg 464

The Hemingway Foundation/PEN Award, MIT, 14N-221A, 77 Massachusetts Ave, Cambridge, MA 02139 *Tel:* 617-324-1729 *E-mail:* penamericaboston@pen.org *Web Site:* pen.org/pen-america-boston, pg 623

Cecil Hemley Memorial Award, 15 Gramercy Park, New York, NY 10003 *Tel:* 212-254-9628 *Web Site:* poetrysociety.org/awards, pg 623

Hendrickson Publishers Inc, PO Box 3473, Peabody, MA 01961-3473 *Tel:* 978-532-6546 *Toll Free Tel:* 800-358-3111 *Fax:* 978-573-8111 *E-mail:* customerservice@ hendricksonrose.com; info@hendricksonrose.com *Web Site:* www.hendricksonrose.com, pg 98

Her Own Words LLC, PO Box 5264, Madison, WI 53705-0264 *Tel:* 608-271-7083 *Fax:* 608-271-0209 *Web Site:* www.herownwords.com; www. nontraditionalcareers.com, pg 98

Herald Press, PO Box 866, Harrisonburg, VA 22803 *Toll Free Tel:* 800-245-7894 (orders) *Fax:* 540-242-4476 *Toll Free Fax:* 877-271-0760 *E-mail:* info@ mennomedia.org; customerservice@mennomedia.org *Web Site:* www.heraldpress.com; store.mennomedia. org, pg 98

Herald Publishing House, 1001 W Walnut St, Independence, MO 64050-3562 *Tel:* 816-521-3015 *Toll Free Tel:* 800-767-8181 *Fax:* 816-521-3066 *E-mail:* sales@heraldhouse.org *Web Site:* www. heraldhouse.org, pg 98

Heritage Books Inc, 5810 Ruatan St, Berwyn Heights, MD 20740 *Toll Free Tel:* 800-876-6103 *Toll Free Fax:* 800-876-6103; 800-297-9954 *E-mail:* orders@ heritagebooks.com; submissions@heritagebooks.com *Web Site:* www.heritagebooks.com, pg 98

The Heritage Foundation, 214 Massachusetts Ave NE, Washington, DC 20002-4999 *Tel:* 202-546-4400 *Toll Free Tel:* 800-544-4843 *Fax:* 202-546-8328 *E-mail:* info@heritage.org *Web Site:* www.heritage.org, pg 98

Heritage House Publishing Co Ltd, 1075 Pendergast St, No 103, Victoria, BC V8V 0A1, Canada *Tel:* 250-360-0829 *Fax:* 250-386-0829 *E-mail:* heritage@ heritagehouse.ca *Web Site:* www.heritagehouse.ca, pg 429

Herman Agency, 350 Central Park W, Apt 4I, New York, NY 10025 *Tel:* 212-749-4907 *Web Site:* www. hermanagencyinc.com, pg 511

The Jeff Herman Agency LLC, 29 Park St, Stockbridge, MA 01262 *Tel:* 413-298-0077 *E-mail:* submissions@ jeffherman.com *Web Site:* www.jeffherman.com, pg 488

Brodie Herndon Memorial, 900 Timber Creek Place, Virginia Beach, VA 23464 *E-mail:* poetryinva@aol. com *Web Site:* poetrysocietyofvirginia.org, pg 623

Herr's Indexing Service, 76-340 Kealoha St, Kailua Kona, HI 96740 *Tel:* 808-365-4348 *E-mail:* linda@ herrsindexing.com *Web Site:* www.herrsindexing.com, pg 465

Carl Hertzog Award for Excellence in Book Design, c/o Dir of the Library, University of Texas at El Paso, El Paso, TX 79968-0582 *Tel:* 915-747-5683 *Fax:* 915-747-5345 *Web Site:* www.utep.edu/library, pg 623

Heuer Publishing LLC, PO Box 248, Cedar Rapids, IA 52406 *Tel:* 319-368-8008 *Toll Free Tel:* 800-950-7529 *Fax:* 319-368-8011 *E-mail:* orders@heuerpub.com; customerservice@heuerpub.com *Web Site:* www. hitplays.com, pg 98

Les Heures bleues, 4455 Coolbrook Ave, No 2, Montreal, QC H4A 3G1, Canada *Tel:* 438-399-2077 *Fax:* 450-671-7718 *E-mail:* editions.lesheuresbleues@ gmail.com *Web Site:* www.heuresbleues.com, pg 429

Hewitt Homeschooling Resources, 8117 N Division, Suite D, Spokane, WA 99208 *Toll Free Tel:* 800-348-1750 *Fax:* 360-835-8697 *E-mail:* sales@hewitthomeschooling.com *Web Site:* hewitthomeschooling.com, pg 98

Heyday, 1808 San Pablo Ave, Suite A, Berkeley, CA 94702 *Tel:* 510-549-3564 *E-mail:* heyday@ heydaybooks.com *Web Site:* heydaybooks.com, pg 98

Hi Willow Research & Publishing, 123 E Second Ave, Suite 1106, Salt Lake City, UT 84103 *Tel:* 801-755-1122 *E-mail:* lmcsourcesales@gmail.com *Web Site:* www.lmcsource.com; www.davidvl.org, pg 99

Hidden River Arts Playwriting Award, PO Box 63927, Philadelphia, PA 19147 *Tel:* 610-764-0813 *E-mail:* hiddenriverarts@gmail.com *Web Site:* www. hiddenriverarts.org; www.hiddenriverarts.com, pg 623

Higginson Book Co, 10 Colonial Rd, Suite 5-6, Salem, MA 01970 *Tel:* 978-745-7170 *Fax:* 978-745-8025 *E-mail:* higginsonbookcompany@gmail.com *Web Site:* www.higginsonbooks.com, pg 99

High Plains Press, PO Box 123, Glendo, WY 82213 *Tel:* 307-735-4370 *Toll Free Tel:* 800-552-7819 *Fax:* 307-735-4590 *E-mail:* editor@highplainspress. com *Web Site:* highplainspress.com, pg 99

The High School Award, PO Box 6550, Edmond, OK 73083 *Tel:* 405-525-5100 *Fax:* 405-525-5103 *Web Site:* www.oklibs.org, pg 623

High Tide Press, 301 Veterans Pkwy, New Lenox, IL 60451 *E-mail:* orders@cherryhillhightide.com *Web Site:* www.cherryhillhightide.com, pg 99

Higher Education Scholarship Program, 3135 S State St, Suite 203, Ann Arbor, MI 48108 *Toll Free Tel:* 866-733-9064 *Fax:* 734-477-2806 *E-mail:* info@ bincfoundation.org *Web Site:* www.bincfoundation. org/scholarship, pg 623

Highland Summer Writers' Conference, PO Box 7014, Radford University, Cook Hall, Radford, VA 24142 *Fax:* 540-831-5951 *Web Site:* www.radford.edu/ content/cehd/home/appalachian-studies.html, pg 575

Highlights for Children Inc, 815 Church St, Honesdale, PA 18431 *Tel:* 570-253-1164 *Toll Free Tel:* 800-490-5111 *Fax:* 570-253-0179 *E-mail:* salesandmarketing@ highlightspress.com *Web Site:* www.highlightspress. com; www.highlights.com; www.facebook.com/ HighlightsforChildren, pg 99

Hill & Wang, 175 Varick St, New York, NY 10014 *Tel:* 212-741-6900 *Fax:* 212-633-9385 *E-mail:* fsg. publicity@fsgbooks.com; fsg.editorial@fsgbooks. com; sales@fsgbooks.com *Web Site:* us.macmillan. com/hillandwang.aspx, pg 99

Hill Nadell Literary Agency, 6442 Santa Monica Blvd, Suite 201, Los Angeles, CA 90038 *Tel:* 310-860-9605 *Fax:* 323-380-5206 *E-mail:* queries@hillnadell.com; rights@hillnadell.com (rts & perms) *Web Site:* www. hillnadell.com, pg 488

The Tony Hillerman Prize, c/o St Martin's Press, 120 Broadway, New York, NY 10271 *E-mail:* tonyhillermanprize@stmartins.com *Web Site:* us.macmillan.com/minotaurbooks/ tonyhillermanprize, pg 623

Hillman Prizes for Journalism, 330 W 42 St, Suite 900, New York, NY 10036 *Tel:* 646-448-6413 *Web Site:* www.hillmanfoundation.org, pg 623

Hillsdale College Press, 33 E College St, Hillsdale, MI 49242 *Tel:* 517-437-7341 *Toll Free Tel:* 800-437-2268 *Fax:* 517-607-2658 *E-mail:* pr@hillsdale.edu *Web Site:* www.hillsdale.edu, pg 99

Hillsdale Educational Publishers Inc, 39 North St, Hillsdale, MI 49242 *Tel:* 517-437-3179 *Fax:* 517-437-0531 *E-mail:* davestory@aol.com *Web Site:* www. hillsdalepublishers.com; michbooks.com, pg 99

Hilton Publishing Co, 1630 45 St, Suite B101, Munster, IN 46321 *Tel:* 219-922-4868 *Fax:* 219-924-6811 *E-mail:* info@hiltonpub.com *Web Site:* www.hiltonpub. com, pg 99

Himalayan Institute Press, 952 Bethany Tpke, Honesdale, PA 18431 *Tel:* 570-253-5551 *Toll Free Tel:* 800-822-4547 *E-mail:* trade@himalayaninstitute.org *Web Site:* www.himalayaninstitute.org, pg 100

Darlene Clark Hine Award, 112 N Bryan Ave, Bloomington, IN 47408-4141 *Tel:* 812-855-7311 *E-mail:* oah@oah.org *Web Site:* www.oah.org/awards, pg 624

Hippocrene Books Inc, 171 Madison Ave, Suite 1605, New York, NY 10016 *Tel:* 212-685-4373 *E-mail:* info@hippocrenebooks.com; orderdept@ hippocrenebooks.com (orders) *Web Site:* www. hippocrenebooks.com, pg 100

L Anne Hirschel DDS, 5990 Highgate Ave, East Lansing, MI 48823 *Tel:* 517-333-1748 *E-mail:* alicerichard@comcast.net, pg 465

The Historic New Orleans Collection, 533 Royal St, New Orleans, LA 70130 *Tel:* 504-523-4662 *Fax:* 504-598-7108 *E-mail:* wrc@hnoc.org *Web Site:* www.hnoc. org, pg 100

Historical Novel Society North American Conference, 400 Dark Star Ct, Fairbanks, AK 99709 *Tel:* 217-581-7538 *Fax:* 217-581-7534 *Web Site:* www. historicalnovelsociety.org/event/hns-north-american-conference; historicalnovelsociety.org, pg 575

History Publishing Co LLC, PO Box 700, Palisades, NY 10964 *Tel:* 845-359-1765 *Fax:* 845-818-3730 (sales) *E-mail:* info@historypublishingco.com *Web Site:* www.historypublishingco.com, pg 100

Histria Books, 7181 N Hualapai Way, Suite 130-86, Las Vegas, NV 89166 *Tel:* 561-299-0802 *E-mail:* info@ histriabooks.com; orders@histriabooks.com; rights@ histriabooks.com *Web Site:* histriabooks.com, pg 100

W D Hoard & Sons Co, 28 W Milwaukee Ave, Fort Atkinson, WI 53538 *Tel:* 920-563-5551 *Fax:* 920-563-7298 *E-mail:* hdbooks@hoards.com; editors@hoards. com *Web Site:* www.hoards.com, pg 100

Hobblebush Books, 17-A Old Milford Rd, Brookline, NH 03033 *Tel:* 603-672-4317 *Fax:* 603-672-4317 *E-mail:* info@hobblebush.com *Web Site:* www. hobblebush.com, pg 100

Eric Hoffer Award, PO Box 11, Titusville, NJ 08560 *E-mail:* info@hofferaward.com *Web Site:* www. hofferaward.com, pg 624

Hofstra University, English Dept, 203 Mason Hall, Hempstead, NY 11549 *Tel:* 516-463-5454 *Fax:* 516-463-6395 *Web Site:* www.hofstra.edu, pg 583

The Barbara Hogenson Agency Inc, 165 West End Ave, Suite 19-C, New York, NY 10023 *Tel:* 212-874-8084 *Fax:* 212-595-6748 *E-mail:* bhogenson@aol.com, pg 488

Hogrefe Publishing Corp, 361 Newbury St, 5th fl, Boston, MA 02115 *Tel:* 857-880-2002 *E-mail:* customerservice@hogrefe.com *Web Site:* us. hogrefe.com, pg 101

Hohm Press, PO Box 4410, Chino Valley, AZ 86323 *Tel:* 928-636-3331 *Toll Free Tel:* 800-381-2700 *Fax:* 928-636-7519 *E-mail:* publisher@hohmpress.com *Web Site:* www.hohmpress.com, pg 101

Bess Hokin Prize, 61 W Superior St, Chicago, IL 60654 *Tel:* 312-787-7070 *Fax:* 312-787-6650 *E-mail:* editors@poetrymagazine.org *Web Site:* www. poetryfoundation.org, pg 624

Holiday House Publishing Inc, 50 Broad St, New York, NY 10004 *Tel:* 212-688-0085 *Fax:* 212-421-6134 *E-mail:* info@holidayhouse.com *Web Site:* www. holidayhouse.com, pg 101

Hollins University-Jackson Center for Creative Writing, 7916 Williamson Rd, Roanoke, VA 24020 *Tel:* 540-362-6317 *E-mail:* creative.writing@hollins.edu *Web Site:* www.hollins.edu; www.hollins.edu/ jacksoncenter/index.shtml, pg 583

Hollym International Corp, 2647 Gateway Rd, No 105-223, Carlsbad, CA 92009 *Tel:* 760-814-9880 *Fax:* 908-353-0255 *E-mail:* contact@hollym.com *Web Site:* www.hollym.com, pg 101

Hollywood Film Archive, 8391 Beverly Blvd, No 321, Los Angeles, CA 90048 *Web Site:* hfarchive.com, pg 101

Burnham Holmes, 182 Lakeview Hill Rd, Poultney, VT 05764-9179 *Tel:* 802-287-9707 *Fax:* 802-287-9707 (computer fax/modem) *E-mail:* burnham.holmes@ castleton.edu, pg 465

Henry Holmes Literary Agent/Book Publicist/Marketing Consultant, Mitchell Heights, Apt 205, 2100 S Main St, Fall River, MA 02724 *Tel:* 508-672-2258; 508-415-4062 (cell), pg 465, 489

Holmes Publishing Group LLC, PO Box 2370, Sequim, WA 98382 *Tel:* 360-681-2900 *E-mail:* holmespub@ fastmail.fm *Web Site:* www.jdholmes.com, pg 101

Henry Holt and Company, LLC, 120 Broadway, 23rd fl, New York, NY 10271 *Tel:* 646-307-5151 *Toll Free Tel:* 888-330-8477 (orders) *Fax:* 646-307-5285 *Web Site:* www.henryholt.com, pg 101

Holy Cow! Press, PO Box 3170, Mount Royal Sta, Duluth, MN 55803 *Tel:* 218-724-1653 *E-mail:* holycow@holycowpress.org *Web Site:* www. holycowpress.org, pg 102

Holy Cross Orthodox Press, 50 Goddard Ave, Brookline, MA 02445 *Tel:* 617-731-3500; 617-850-1321 *E-mail:* press@hchc.edu *Web Site:* www.hchc.edu, pg 102

Homa & Sekey Books, 140 E Ridgewood Ave, Paramus, NJ 07652 *Tel:* 201-261-8810 *Toll Free Tel:* 800-870-HOMA (870-4662 orders) *Fax:* 201-261-8890 *E-mail:* info@homabooks.com *Web Site:* www. homabooks.com, pg 102

Homestead Publishing, Box 193, Moose, WY 83012-0193 *Tel:* 307-733-6248 *Fax:* 307-733-6248 *E-mail:* orders@homesteadpublishing.net *Web Site:* www.homesteadpublishing.net, pg 102

Honickman First Book Prize, 1906 Rittenhouse Sq, Philadelphia, PA 19103 *Tel:* 215-309-3722 *Web Site:* www.aprweb.org, pg 624

Hoover Institution Press, Stanford University, 434 Galvez Mall, Stanford, CA 94305-6003 *Tel:* 650-723-3373 *Toll Free Tel:* 800-935-2882 *Fax:* 650-723-8626 *E-mail:* hooverpress@stanford.edu *Web Site:* www. hooverpress.org; www.hoover.org, pg 102

Hoover's Inc, 7700 W Parmer Lane, Bldg A, Austin, TX 78729 *Tel:* 512-374-4500 *Toll Free Tel:* 855-858-5974 *Web Site:* www.hoovers.com, pg 102

Hope Publishing Co, 380 S Main Place, Carol Stream, IL 60188 *Tel:* 630-665-3200 *Toll Free Tel:* 800-323-1049 *E-mail:* hope@hopepublishing.com *Web Site:* www.hopepublishing.com, pg 102

The Hopwood Award Theodore Roethke Prize, 1176 Angell Hall, 435 S State St, Ann Arbor, MI 48109-1003 *Tel:* 734-764-6296 *Fax:* 734-764-3128 *E-mail:* abeauch@umich.edu *Web Site:* lsa.umich. edu/hopwood, pg 624

Hopwood Underclassmen Contest, 1176 Angell Hall, 435 S State St, Ann Arbor, MI 48109-1003 *Tel:* 734-764-6296 *Fax:* 734-764-3128 *E-mail:* abeauch@umich.edu *Web Site:* lsa.umich.edu/hopwood, pg 624

Horizon Publishers & Distributors Inc, 191 N 650 E, Bountiful, UT 84010-3628 *Tel:* 801-292-7102 *E-mail:* ldshorizonpublishers1@gmail.com *Web Site:* www.ldshorizonpublishers.com, pg 102

Hornfischer Literary Management LP, PO Box 50544, Austin, TX 78763 *Tel:* 512-472-0011 *E-mail:* queries@hornfischerlit.com *Web Site:* www. hornfischerlit.com, pg 489

Horror Writers Association (HWA), PO Box 56687, Sherman Oaks, CA 91413 *Tel:* 818-220-3965 *E-mail:* admin@horror.org *Web Site:* horror.org, pg 534

Hospital & Healthcare Compensation Service, 3 Post Rd, Suite 3, Oakland, NJ 07436 *Tel:* 201-405-0075 *Fax:* 201-405-2110 *E-mail:* allinfo@hhcsinc.com *Web Site:* www.hhcsinc.com, pg 103

Host Publications, 3408 West Ave, Austin, TX 78705 *Tel:* 512-236-1290 *Fax:* 512-236-1208 *Web Site:* www. hostpublications.com, pg 103

Firman Houghton Prize, 46 Wallace St, Somerville, MA 02144 *E-mail:* info@nepoetryclub.org *Web Site:* www. nepoetryclub.org, pg 624

Houghton Mifflin Harcourt, 125 High St, Boston, MA 02110 *Tel:* 617-351-5000 *Toll Free Tel:* 855-969-4642; 800-225-5425 (K-12 educ materials); 800-323-9540

(assessment materials); 877-219-1537 (SkillsTutor); 888-242-6747 (Innovation in Educ Group); 800-225-3362 (Trade & Ref Div) *Toll Free Fax:* 800-269-5232 *E-mail:* myhmhco@hmhco.com *Web Site:* www. hmhco.com, pg 103

Houghton Mifflin Harcourt Assessments, One Pierce Place, Itasca, IL 60143 *Tel:* 630-467-7000 *Toll Free Tel:* 800-323-9540 *Fax:* 630-467-7192 (cust serv) *E-mail:* assessmentorders@hmhco.com *Web Site:* www.hmhco.com/classroom-solutions/ assessment, pg 103

Houghton Mifflin Harcourt K-12 Publishers, 125 High St, Boston, MA 02110 *Tel:* 617-351-5020 *E-mail:* corporate.communications@hmhco.com *Web Site:* www.hmhco.com/classroom (solutions); www.hmhco.com, pg 103

Houghton Mifflin Harcourt Trade & Reference Division, 125 High St, Boston, MA 02110 *Tel:* 617-351-5000 *Web Site:* www.hmhco.com, pg 103

House of Anansi Press Inc, 128 Sterling Rd, Lower Level, Toronto, ON M6R 2B7, Canada *Tel:* 416-363-4343 *Fax:* 416-363-1017 *E-mail:* customerservice@ houseofanansi.com *Web Site:* www.houseofanansi.com, pg 429

House of Collectibles, 1745 Broadway, New York, NY 10019 *Tel:* 212-782-9000 *Web Site:* www. penguinrandomhouse.com, pg 104

House to House Publications, 11 Toll Gate Rd, Lititz, PA 17543 *Tel:* 717-627-1996 *Toll Free Tel:* 800-848-5892 *Fax:* 717-627-4004 *E-mail:* h2hp@dcfi.org *Web Site:* www.h2hp.com, pg 104

Housing Assistance Council, 1025 Vermont Ave NW, Suite 606, Washington, DC 20005 *Tel:* 202-842-8600 *Fax:* 202-347-3441 *E-mail:* hac@ruralhome.org *Web Site:* www.ruralhome.org, pg 104

Tom Howard/John H Reid Fiction & Essay Contest, 351 Pleasant St, PMB 222, Northampton, MA 01060-3961 *Tel:* 413-320-1847 *Toll Free Tel:* 866-WINWRIT (946-9748) *Fax:* 413-280-0539 *Web Site:* www. winningwriters.com, pg 624

Tom Howard/Margaret Reid Poetry Contest, 351 Pleasant St, PMB 222, Northampton, MA 01060-3961 *Tel:* 413-320-1847 *Toll Free Tel:* 866-WINWRIT (946-9748) *Fax:* 413-280-0539 *Web Site:* www. winningwriters.com, pg 624

C D Howe Institute, 67 Yonge St, Suite 300, Toronto, ON M5E 1J8, Canada *Tel:* 416-865-1904 *Fax:* 416-865-1866 *E-mail:* cdhowe@cdhowe.org *Web Site:* www.cdhowe.org, pg 430

Julia Ward Howe Book Awards, c/o Professor Mary Cronin, 2400 Beacon St, Unit 208, Beacon Hill, MA 02467 *Tel:* 617-552-4031 *E-mail:* bostonauthorsclub@ gmail.com *Web Site:* bostonauthorsclub.org, pg 624

The William Dean Howells Medal, 633 W 155 St, New York, NY 10032 *Tel:* 212-368-5900 *Fax:* 212-491-4615 *E-mail:* academy@artsandletters.org *Web Site:* artsandletters.org, pg 624

HRD Press, 22 Amherst Rd, Amherst, MA 01002-9709 *Tel:* 413-253-3488 *Toll Free Tel:* 800-822-2801 *Fax:* 413-253-3490 *E-mail:* info@hrdpress. com; customerservice@hrdpress.com *Web Site:* www. hrdpress.com, pg 104

L Ron Hubbard's Writers of the Future Contest, 7051 Hollywood Blvd, Hollywood, CA 90028 *Tel:* 323-466-3310 *Fax:* 323-466-6474 *E-mail:* contests@ authorservicesinc.com *Web Site:* www. writersofthefuture.com, pg 625

Charlotte Huck Award, 340 N Neil St, Suite 104, Champaign, IL 61820 *Tel:* 217-328-3870 *Toll Free Tel:* 877-369-6283 (cust serv) *Fax:* 217-328-9645; 217-328-0977 *E-mail:* bookawards@ncte.org *Web Site:* www2.ncte.org/awards, pg 625

Hudson Institute, 1201 Pennsylvania Ave NW, Suite 400, Washington, DC 20004 *Tel:* 202-974-2400 *Fax:* 202-974-2410 *E-mail:* info@hudson.org *Web Site:* www. hudson.org, pg 104

The Hugo Awards, PO Box 64128, Sunnyvale, CA 94088 *Tel:* www.wsfs.org/awards; www. thehugoawards.org, pg 625

Lynda Hull Memorial Poetry Prize, College of Charleston, Dept of English, 66 George St, Charleston, SC 29424 *Tel:* 843-953-4470 *E-mail:* crazyhorse@cofc.edu *Web Site:* crazyhorse.cofc.edu/prizes, pg 625

Human Kinetics Inc, 1607 N Market St, Champaign, IL 61820 *Tel:* 217-351-5076 *Toll Free Tel:* 800-747-4457 *Fax:* 217-351-1549 (orders/cust serv) *E-mail:* info@hkusa.com *Web Site:* www.humankinetics.com, pg 104

Human Rights Watch, 350 Fifth Ave, 34th fl, New York, NY 10118-3299 *Tel:* 212-290-4700 *Fax:* 212-736-1300 *E-mail:* hrwpress@hrw.org *Web Site:* www.hrw.org, pg 105

Humanix Books LLC, 8 W 40 St, 20th fl, New York, NY 10804 *Toll Free Tel:* 855-371-7810 *E-mail:* info@humanixbooks.com *Web Site:* www.humanixbooks.com, pg 105

Huntington Press Publishing, 3665 Procyon St, Las Vegas, NV 89103-1907 *Tel:* 702-252-0655 *Toll Free Tel:* 800-244-2224 *Fax:* 702-252-0675 *E-mail:* editor@huntingtonpress.com *Web Site:* www.huntingtonpress.com, pg 105

Hurston/Wright Award for College Writers, 10 "G" St NE, Suite 600, Washington, DC 20002 *Tel:* 202-248-5051 *E-mail:* info@hurstonwright.org *Web Site:* www.hurstonwright.org, pg 625

Hurston/Wright Legacy Awards, 10 "G" St NE, Suite 600, Washington, DC 20002 *Tel:* 202-248-5051 *E-mail:* info@hurstonwright.org *Web Site:* www.hurstonwright.org, pg 625

Hurston/Wright Writers Week, 10 "G" St NE, Suite 600, Washington, DC 20002 *Tel:* 202-248-5051 *E-mail:* info@hurstonwright.org *Web Site:* www.hurstonwright.org, pg 575

The Zora Neale Hurston/Richard Wright Foundation, 10 "G" St NE, Suite 600, Washington, DC 20002 *Tel:* 202-248-5051 *E-mail:* info@hurstonwright.org *Web Site:* www.hurstonwright.org, pg 551

Hutton Publishing, 140D Heritage Village, Southbury, CT 06488 *Tel:* 203-405-6227 *E-mail:* huttonbooks@hotmail.com, pg 105

IACP Cookbook Awards, 45 Rockefeller Plaza, Suite 2000, New York, NY 10111 *Tel:* 646-358-4957 *Toll Free Tel:* 866-358-4951 *Toll Free Fax:* 866-358-2524 *E-mail:* info@iacp.com *Web Site:* www.iacp.com/award/more/cookbook, pg 625

Ibex Publishers, PO Box 30087, Bethesda, MD 20824 *Tel:* 301-718-8188 *Toll Free Tel:* 888-718-8188 *Fax:* 301-907-8707 *E-mail:* info@ibexpub.com *Web Site:* ibexpub.com, pg 105

IBFD North America Inc (International Bureau of Fiscal Documentation), 8300 Boone Blvd, Suite 380, Vienna, VA 22182 *Tel:* 703-442-7757 *E-mail:* info@ibfd.org *Web Site:* www.ibfd.org, pg 105

The Ibsen Society of America (ISA), c/o Indiana University, Global & Intl Studies Bldg 3111, 355 N Jordan Ave, Bloomington, IN 47405-1105 *Web Site:* www.ibsensociety.org, pg 534

ICM Lecture Division, 730 Fifth Ave, New York, NY 10019 *Tel:* 212-556-5600 *Fax:* 212-556-5665 *Web Site:* www.icmtalent.com, pg 515

ICM Partners, 65 E 55 St, New York, NY 10022 *Tel:* 212-556-5600 *Web Site:* www.icmtalent.com, pg 489

The Idaho Prize for Poetry, 105 Lost Horse Lane, Sandpoint, ID 83864 *Tel:* 208-255-4410 *Fax:* 208-255-1560 *E-mail:* losthorsepress@mindspring.com *Web Site:* www.losthorsepress.org, pg 625

Idyll Arbor Inc, 39129 264 Ave SE, Enumclaw, WA 98022 *Tel:* 360-825-7797 *Fax:* 360-825-5670 *E-mail:* sales@idyllarbor.com *Web Site:* www.idyllarbor.com, pg 105

Idyllwild Arts Summer Workshops, 52500 Temecula Dr, Idyllwild, CA 92549-0038 *Tel:* 951-659-2171 *Fax:* 951-659-4552 *E-mail:* summer@idyllwildarts.org *Web Site:* www.idyllwildarts.org/writersweek, pg 575

IEEE Computer Society, 2001 "L" St NW, Suite 700, Washington, DC 20036-4928 *Tel:* 202-371-0101 *Toll Free Tel:* 800-678-4333 (memb info) *Fax:* 202-728-9614 *E-mail:* help@computer.org *Web Site:* www.computer.org, pg 105

IEEE Press, 445 Hoes Lane, Piscataway, NJ 08854 *Tel:* 732-981-0060 *Fax:* 732-867-9946 *E-mail:* pressbooks@ieee.org (proposals & info) *Web Site:* www.ieee.org/press, pg 106

IET USA Inc, 379 Thornall St, Edison, NJ 08837 *Tel:* 732-321-5575 *Fax:* 732-321-5702 *E-mail:* ietusa@theiet.org *Web Site:* www.theiet.org, pg 106

Ignatius Press, 1348 Tenth Ave, San Francisco, CA 94122-2304 *Toll Free Tel:* 800-651-1531 (orders); 888-615-3186 (cust serv) *Fax:* 415-387-0896 *E-mail:* info@ignatius.com *Web Site:* www.ignatius.com, pg 106

IHS Press, 222 W 21 St, Suite F-122, Norfolk, VA 23517 *Toll Free Tel:* 877-447-7737 *Toll Free Fax:* 877-447-7737 *E-mail:* info@ihspress.com; tradesales@ihspress.com (wholesale sales); order@ihspress.com *Web Site:* www.ihspress.com, pg 106

ILA Children's & Young Adults' Book Awards, PO Box 8139, Newark, DE 19714-8139 *Tel:* 302-731-1600 *Toll Free Tel:* 800-336-7323 (US & CN) *Fax:* 302-731-1057 *E-mail:* ilaawards@reading.org *Web Site:* www.literacyworldwide.org, pg 625

Illinois State Museum Society, 502 S Spring St, Springfield, IL 62706-5000 *Tel:* 217-782-7386 *Fax:* 217-782-1254 *E-mail:* subscriptions@museum.state.il.us *Web Site:* www.illinoisstatemuseum.org, pg 106

Illuminating Engineering Society of North America (IES), 120 Wall St, 17th fl, New York, NY 10005-4001 *Tel:* 212-248-5000 *Fax:* 212-248-5017; 212-248-5018 *E-mail:* ies@ies.org *Web Site:* www.ies.org, pg 106

Illumination Book Awards, 1129 Woodmere Ave, Suite B, Traverse City, MI 49686 *Tel:* 231-933-0445 *Toll Free Tel:* 800-706-4636 *Fax:* 231-933-0448 *E-mail:* awards@bookpublishing.com *Web Site:* www.illuminationawards.com, pg 625

Imagination Publishing Group, PO Box 1304, Dunedin, FL 34697 *Toll Free Tel:* 888-701-6481 *Fax:* 727-361-0584 *E-mail:* info@imaginationpublishinggroup.com *Web Site:* www.imaginationpublishinggroup.com, pg 106

Imago Press, 3710 E Edison St, Tucson, AZ 85716 *Tel:* 520-444-2265 *Web Site:* www.oasisjournal.org, pg 106

ImaJinn Books, PO Box 300921, Memphis, TN 38130 *Tel:* 901-344-9024 *Fax:* 901-344-9068 *E-mail:* bellebooks@bellebooks.com *Web Site:* www.imajinnbooks.com, pg 106

Immedium, 535 Rockdale Dr, San Francisco, CA 94127 *Tel:* 415-452-8546 *Fax:* 360-937-6272 *E-mail:* orders@immedium.com; sales@immedium.com *Web Site:* www.immedium.com, pg 107

John Phillip Immroth Memorial Award, 50 E Huron St, Chicago, IL 60611 *Tel:* 312-280-4226 *Toll Free Tel:* 800-545-2433 *E-mail:* oif@ala.org *Web Site:* www.ala.org/ifrt, pg 625

Impact Publications/Development Concepts Inc, 7820 Sudley Rd, Suite 100, Manassas, VA 20109 *Tel:* 703-361-7300 *Toll Free Tel:* 800-361-1055 (cust serv) *Fax:* 703-335-9486 *E-mail:* query@impactpublications.com *Web Site:* www.impactpublications.com; www.veteransworld.com, pg 107

In-Plant Printing & Mailing Association (IPMA), 455 S Sam Barr Dr, Suite 203, Kearney, MO 64060 *Tel:* 816-919-1691 *E-mail:* ipmainfo@ipma.org *Web Site:* www.ipma.org, pg 534

In the Garden Publishing, 7525 Paragon Rd, No 752252, Dayton, OH 45459 *Tel:* 937-317-0859 *E-mail:* editor@inthegardenpublishing.com *Web Site:* www.inthegardenpublishing.com, pg 107

Incentive Publications by World Book, 180 N LaSalle St, Suite 900, Chicago, IL 60101 *Toll Free Tel:* 800-967-5325; 800-975-3250; 888-482-9764 (trade dept) *Toll Free Fax:* 888-922-3766 *E-mail:* tradeorders@worldbook.com *Web Site:* www.incentivepublications.com, pg 107

Inclusion Press International, 47 Indian Trail, Toronto, ON M6R 1Z8, Canada *Tel:* 416-658-5363 *Fax:* 416-658-5067 *E-mail:* inclusionpress@inclusion.com *Web Site:* www.inclusion.com, pg 430

The Independent Book Publishers Association (IBPA), 1020 Manhattan Beach Blvd, Suite 204, Manhattan Beach, CA 90266 *Tel:* 310-546-1818 *E-mail:* info@ibpa-online.org *Web Site:* www.ibpa-online.org, pg 535

Independent Information Publications, 3357 21 St, San Francisco, CA 94110 *Tel:* 415-643-8600 *E-mail:* sharisteiner@gmail.com *Web Site:* www.movedoc.com, pg 107

Independent Institute, 100 Swan Way, Suite 200, Oakland, CA 94621-1428 *Tel:* 510-632-1366 *Toll Free Tel:* 800-927-8733 *Fax:* 510-568-6040 *E-mail:* orders@independent.org *Web Site:* www.independent.org, pg 107

The Independent Publisher Book Awards, 1129 Woodmere Ave, Suite B, Traverse City, MI 49686 *Tel:* 231-933-0445 *Toll Free Tel:* 800-706-4636 *Fax:* 231-933-0448 *E-mail:* awards@bookpublishing.com *Web Site:* www.independentpublisher.com/ipland/ipawards.php, pg 626

Independent Publishers of New England (IPNE), 10 Court St, No 206, Arlington, MA 02476-0206 *Tel:* 339-368-8229 *E-mail:* talktous@ipne.org *Web Site:* www.ipne.org, pg 535

Independent Publishers of New England Book Awards, 10 Court St, No 206, Arlington, MA 02476-0206 *Tel:* 339-368-8229 *E-mail:* bookawards@ipne.org *Web Site:* www.ipne.org/awards, pg 626

Independent Writers of Chicago (IWOC), 332 S Michigan Ave, Suite 1032, Chicago, IL 60604 *Toll Free Tel:* 800-804-IWOC (804-4962) *E-mail:* info@iwoc.org *Web Site:* www.iwoc.org, pg 535

IndexEmpire Indexing Services, 16740 Orville Wright Dr, Riverside, CA 92518 *Tel:* 951-697-2819 *E-mail:* indexempire@gmail.com, pg 465

Indexing by the Book, PO Box 12513, Tucson, AZ 85732-2513 *Tel:* 520-750-8439 *E-mail:* indextran@cox.net *Web Site:* www.indexingbythebook.com, pg 465

Indiana Historical Society Press, 450 W Ohio St, Indianapolis, IN 46202-3269 *Tel:* 317-232-1882; 317-234-0026 (orders); 317-234-2716 (edit) *Toll Free Tel:* 800-447-1830 (orders) *Fax:* 317-234-0562 (orders); 317-233-0857 (edit) *E-mail:* ihspress@indianahistory.org; orders@indianahistory.org (orders) *Web Site:* www.indianahistory.org; shop.indianahistory.org (orders), pg 107

Indiana Review Fiction Prize, Ballantine Hall 529, 1020 E Kirkwood Ave, Bloomington, IN 47405 *Tel:* 812-855-3439 *E-mail:* inreview@indiana.edu *Web Site:* indianareview.org, pg 626

Indiana University African Studies Program, Indiana University, 355 N Jordan, Rm GA 3072, Bloomington, IN 47405 *Tel:* 812-855-8284 *Fax:* 812-855-6734 *E-mail:* afrist@indiana.edu *Web Site:* www.indiana.edu/~afrist; www.go.iu.edu/afrist, pg 107

Indiana University Press, Herman B Wells Library 350, 1320 E Tenth St, Bloomington, IN 47405-3907 *Tel:* 812-855-8817 *Toll Free Tel:* 800-842-6796 (orders only) *Fax:* 812-855-7931; 812-855-8507 *E-mail:* iupress@indiana.edu; iuporder@indiana.edu (orders) *Web Site:* www.iupress.indiana.edu, pg 107

Indiana University Writers' Conference, 464 Ballantine Hall, 1020 E Kirkwood Ave, Bloomington, IN 47405-7103 *Tel:* 812-855-1877 *Fax:* 812-855-9535 *E-mail:* writecon@indiana.edu *Web Site:* www.iuwc.indiana.edu, pg 575

IndieReader Discovery Awards, PO Box 43121, Montclair, NJ 07043 *E-mail:* amy@indiereader.com *Web Site:* indiereader.com/irda, pg 626

Indies Choice Book Awards, 333 Westchester Ave, Suite S202, White Plains, NY 10604 *Tel:* 914-406-7500 *Toll Free Tel:* 800-637-0037 *Fax:* 914-417-4013 *Web Site:* www.bookweb.org, pg 626

Individual Artist Awards, 175 W Ostend St, Suite E, Baltimore, MD 21230 *Tel:* 410-767-6555 *Fax:* 410-333-1062 *E-mail:* msac@msac.org *Web Site:* www.msac.org, pg 626

Individual Artist Fellowships, 1004 Farnam, Plaza Level, Omaha, NE 68102 *Tel:* 402-595-2122 *Toll Free Tel:* 800-341-4067 *Fax:* 402-595-2334 *Web Site:* www.nebraskaartscouncil.org, pg 626

Individual Artist Fellowships, 25 State House Sta, 193 State St, Augusta, ME 04333-0025 *Tel:* 207-287-2726 *Fax:* 207-287-2725 *Web Site:* mainearts.maine.gov, pg 626

Individual Artist Project Grant, 500 S Bronough St, Tallahassee, FL 32399-0250 *Tel:* 850-245-6470 *Fax:* 850-245-6497 *E-mail:* info@dos.myflorida.com *Web Site:* dos.myflorida.com/cultural, pg 626

Individual Artist's Fellowships, 1026 Sumter St, Suite 200, Columbia, SC 29201-3746 *Tel:* 803-734-8696 *Fax:* 803-734-8526 *E-mail:* info@arts.sc.gov *Web Site:* www.southcarolinaarts.com, pg 626

Individual Excellence Awards, 30 E Broad St, 33rd fl, Columbus, OH 43215 *Tel:* 614-466-2613 *Fax:* 614-466-4494 *Web Site:* www.oac.state.oh.us, pg 626

Industrial Press Inc, 32 Haviland St, Suite 3, Norwalk, CT 06854 *Tel:* 203-956-5593 ext 0 (cust serv) *Toll Free Tel:* 888-528-7852 ext 0 (cust serv) *Fax:* 203-354-9391 (cust serv) *E-mail:* info@industrialpress.com (cust serv) *Web Site:* books.industrialpress.com; ebooks.industrialpress.com, pg 108

Information Age Publishing Inc, PO Box 79049, Charlotte, NC 28271-7047 *Tel:* 704-752-9125 *Fax:* 704-752-9113 *E-mail:* infoage@infoagepub.com *Web Site:* www.infoagepub.com, pg 108

Information Gatekeepers Inc (IGI), PO Box 606, Winchester, MA 01890 *Tel:* 617-782-5033 *Fax:* 617-507-8338 *E-mail:* info@igigroup.com *Web Site:* www.igigroup.com, pg 108

Information Today, Inc, 143 Old Marlton Pike, Medford, NJ 08055-8750 *Tel:* 609-654-6266 *Toll Free Tel:* 800-300-9868 (cust serv) *Fax:* 609-654-4309 *E-mail:* custserv@infotoday.com *Web Site:* www.infotoday.com, pg 108

Infosources Publishing, 140 Norma Rd, Teaneck, NJ 07666 *Tel:* 201-836-7072 *Web Site:* www.infosourcespub.com, pg 108

Inkwater Press, 6750 SW Franklin St, Suite A, Portland, OR 97223 *Tel:* 503-968-6777 *Fax:* 503-968-6779 *E-mail:* orders@inkwaterbooks.com *Web Site:* www.inkwater.com, pg 109

InkWell Management, 521 Fifth Ave, 26th fl, New York, NY 10175 *Tel:* 212-922-3500 *Fax:* 212-922-0535 *E-mail:* info@inkwellmanagement.com *Web Site:* inkwellmanagement.com, pg 489

Inner Traditions International Ltd, One Park St, Rochester, VT 05767 *Tel:* 802-767-3174 *Toll Free Tel:* 800-246-8648 *Fax:* 802-767-3726 *E-mail:* customerservice@InnerTraditions.com *Web Site:* www.InnerTraditions.com, pg 109

Innis-Gerin Medal, Walter House, 282 Somerset W, Ottawa, ON K2P 0J6, Canada *Tel:* 613-991-6990 (ext 106) *Fax:* 613-991-6996 *E-mail:* nominations@rsc-src.ca *Web Site:* www.rsc-src.ca, pg 627

The Innovation Press, 1001 Fourth Ave, Suite 3200, Seattle, WA 98154 *Tel:* 360-870-9988 *E-mail:* info@theinnovationpress.com *Web Site:* theinnovationpress.com, pg 109

Innovations in Reading Prize, 90 Broad St, Suite 604, New York, NY 10004 *Tel:* 212-685-0261 *Fax:* 212-213-6570 *E-mail:* nationalbook@nationalbook.org *Web Site:* www.nationalbook.org/innovations_in_reading, pg 627

InScribe Christian Writers' Fellowship (ICWF), PO Box 6201, Wetaskiwin, AB T9A 2E9, Canada *Tel:* 780-646-3068 *Fax:* 780-635-2190 *E-mail:* inscribe.mail@gmail.com *Web Site:* inscribe.org, pg 535

Insight Editions, 800 "A" St, San Rafael, CA 94901 *Tel:* 415-526-1370 *Toll Free Tel:* 800-809-3792 *Toll Free Fax:* 866-509-0515 *E-mail:* info@insighteditions.com; marketing@insighteditions.com *Web Site:* insighteditions.com, pg 109

Insomniac Press, 520 Princess Ave, London, ON N6B 2B8, Canada *Tel:* 519-266-3556 *Web Site:* www.insomniacpress.com, pg 430

The Institute for Cooperation on Adult Education (Institut de Cooperation pour l'Education des Adultes-ICEA), 4321, ave Papineau, Montreal, QC H2H 1T3, Canada *Tel:* 514-948-2044 *Fax:* 514-948-2046 *E-mail:* icae@icea.qc.ca *Web Site:* www.icea.qc.ca, pg 535

Institute for Research on Public Policy (IRPP), 1470 Peel St, No 200, Montreal, QC H3A 1T1, Canada *Tel:* 514-985-2461 *Fax:* 514-985-2559 *E-mail:* irpp@irpp.org *Web Site:* irpp.org, pg 430

Institute of Continuing Legal Education, 1020 Greene St, Ann Arbor, MI 48109-1444 *Tel:* 734-764-0533 *Toll Free Tel:* 877-229-4350 *Fax:* 734-763-2412 *Toll Free Fax:* 877-229-4351 *E-mail:* icle@umich.edu *Web Site:* www.icle.org, pg 109

Institute of Environmental Sciences & Technology - IEST, 1827 Walden Office Sq, Suite 400, Schaumburg, IL 60173 *Tel:* 847-981-0100 *Fax:* 847-981-4130 *E-mail:* information@iest.org *Web Site:* www.iest.org, pg 109

Institute of Governmental Studies, 109 Moses Hall, No 2370, Berkeley, CA 94720-2370 *Tel:* 510-642-1428 *E-mail:* igspress@berkeley.edu *Web Site:* www.igs.berkeley.edu, pg 109

Institute of Intergovernmental Relations, Queen's University, Robert Sutherland Hall, Rm 412, Kingston, ON K7L 3N6, Canada *Tel:* 613-533-2080 *Fax:* 613-533-6868 *E-mail:* iigr@queensu.ca *Web Site:* www.queensu.ca/iigr, pg 430

Institute of Jesuit Sources (IJS), Boston College, Institute for Advanced Jesuit Studies, 140 Commonwealth Ave, Chestnut, MA 02467 *Tel:* 617-552-2568 *Fax:* 617-552-2575 *E-mail:* jesuitsources@bc.edu *Web Site:* jesuitsources.bc.edu, pg 110

Institute of Mathematical Geography, 1964 Boulder Dr, Ann Arbor, MI 48104 *Tel:* 734-975-0246 *E-mail:* image@imagenet.org *Web Site:* www.imagenet.org, pg 110

Institute of Police Technology & Management, 12000 Alumni Dr, Jacksonville, FL 32224-2678 *Tel:* 904-620-4786 *Fax:* 904-620-2453 *E-mail:* info@iptm.org *Web Site:* www.iptm.org, pg 110

Institute of Psychological Research, Inc., 76 Ave, Mozart W, Montreal, QC H2S 1C4, Canada *Tel:* 514-382-3000 *Toll Free Tel:* 800-363-7800 *Fax:* 514-382-3007 *Toll Free Fax:* 888-382-3007 *E-mail:* info@irpcanada.com *Web Site:* www.irpcanada.com, pg 430

Institute of Public Administration of Canada, 1075 Bay St, Suite 401, Toronto, ON M5S 2B1, Canada *Tel:* 416-924-8787 *Fax:* 416-924-4992 *E-mail:* ntl@ipac.ca *Web Site:* www.ipac.ca, pg 430

The Institutes™, 720 Providence Rd, Suite 100, Malvern, PA 19355-3433 *Tel:* 610-644-2100 *Toll Free Tel:* 800-644-2101 *Fax:* 610-640-9576 *E-mail:* customerservice@theinstitutes.org *Web Site:* www.theinstitutes.org, pg 110

Integra Software Services Inc, 1110 Jorie Blvd, Suite 200, Oak Brook, IL 60523 *Tel:* 630-586-2579 *Fax:* 630-586-2599 *E-mail:* marketing@integra.co.in *Web Site:* www.integra.co.in, pg 465

Inter-American Development Bank, 1300 New York Ave NW, Washington, DC 20577 *Tel:* 202-623-1000 *Fax:* 202-623-3096 *E-mail:* pic@iadb.org *Web Site:* publications.iadb.org, pg 110

Inter American Press Association (IAPA), 3511 NW 91 Ave, Miami, FL 33172 *Tel:* 305-634-2465 *Fax:* 305-860-4264 *E-mail:* info@sipiapa.org *Web Site:* www.sipiapa.org, pg 535

Inter-University Consortium for Political & Social Research (ICPSR), 330 Packard St, Ann Arbor, MI 48104 *Tel:* 734-647-5000 *Fax:* 734-647-8200 *E-mail:* help@icpsr.umich.edu *Web Site:* www.icpsr.umich.edu, pg 110

Intercultural Development Research Association (IDRA), 5815 Callaghan Rd, Suite 101, San Antonio, TX 78228 *Tel:* 210-444-1710 *Fax:* 210-444-1714 *E-mail:* contact@idra.org *Web Site:* www.idra.org, pg 110

Intercultural Press Inc, 53 State St, Boston, MA 02109 *Tel:* 617-523-3801 *E-mail:* info@nicholasbrealey.com *Web Site:* nbuspublishing.com, pg 110

InterLicense Ltd, 110 Country Club Dr, Suite A, Mill Valley, CA 94941 *Tel:* 415-381-9780 *Fax:* 415-381-6485 *E-mail:* foreignrights@interlicense.net *Web Site:* interlicense.net, pg 489

Interlink Publishing Group Inc, 46 Crosby St, Northampton, MA 01060 *Tel:* 413-582-7054 *Toll Free Tel:* 800-238-LINK (238-5465) *Fax:* 413-582-7057 *E-mail:* info@interlinkbooks.com *Web Site:* www.interlinkbooks.com, pg 110

Intermediate Sequoyah Book Award, PO Box 6550, Edmond, OK 73083 *Tel:* 405-525-5100 *Fax:* 405-525-5103 *Web Site:* www.oklibs.org, pg 627

International Association of Business Communicators (IABC), 649 Mission St, 5th fl, San Francisco, CA 94105 *Tel:* 415-544-4700 *Toll Free Tel:* 800-776-4222 (US & CN) *Fax:* 415-544-4747 *E-mail:* leader_centre@iabc.com; member_relations@iabc.com *Web Site:* www.iabc.com, pg 535

International Association of Crime Writers Inc, North American Branch, 243 Fifth Ave, Suite 537, New York, NY 10016 *Tel:* 212-243-8966 *Fax:* 815-361-1477 *E-mail:* info@crimewritersna.org *Web Site:* www.crimewritersna.org, pg 535

International Book Centre Inc, 2391 Auburn Rd, Shelby Township, MI 48317 *Tel:* 586-254-7230 *Fax:* 586-254-7230 *E-mail:* ibc@ibcbooks.com *Web Site:* www.ibcbooks.com, pg 110

International City/County Management Association (ICMA), 777 N Capitol St NE, Suite 500, Washington, DC 20002-4201 *Tel:* 202-289-4262 *Toll Free Tel:* 800-745-8780 *Fax:* 202-962-3500 *E-mail:* customerservices@icma.org *Web Site:* icma.org, pg 110

International Code Council Inc, 3060 Saturn St, Suite 100, Brea, CA 92821 *Tel:* 562-699-0541 *Toll Free Tel:* 888-422-7233 *Fax:* 562-908-5524 *Toll Free Fax:* 866-891-1695 *E-mail:* order@icc-es.org *Web Site:* www.iccsafe.org, pg 111

International Council of Shopping Centers (ICSC), 1221 Avenue of the Americas, 41st fl, New York, NY 10020-1099 *Web Site:* www.icsc.org, pg 111

International Encyclopedia Society, 3689 Campbell Ct, Yorktown Heights, NY 10598 *Tel:* 914-962-3287 *Fax:* 914-962-3287, pg 535

International Entertainment Bureau, 3612 N Washington Blvd, Indianapolis, IN 46205-3592 *Tel:* 317-926-7566 *E-mail:* ieb@prodigy.net, pg 515

International Food Policy Research Institute, 1201 Eye St NW, Washington, DC 20005-3915 *Tel:* 202-862-5600 *Fax:* 202-862-5606 *E-mail:* ifpri@cgiar.org *Web Site:* www.ifpri.org, pg 111

International Foundation of Employee Benefit Plans, 18700 W Bluemound Rd, Brookfield, WI 53045 *Tel:* 262-786-6700 *Toll Free Tel:* 888-334-3327 *Fax:* 262-786-8780 *E-mail:* editor@ifebp.org *Web Site:* www.ifebp.org, pg 111

The International Institute of Islamic Thought, 500 Grove St, Suite 200, Herndon, VA 20170 *Tel:* 703-471-1133 *Fax:* 703-471-3922 *E-mail:* iiit@iiit.org *Web Site:* www.iiit.org, pg 111

International Latino Book Awards, 3445 Catalina Dr, Carlsbad, CA 92010 *Tel:* 760-434-1223 *Fax:* 760-434-7476 *Web Site:* www.award.news, pg 627

International Latino Unpublished Book Awards, 3445 Catalina Dr, Carlsbad, CA 92010 *Tel:* 760-434-1223 *Fax:* 760-434-7476 *Web Site:* www.award.news, pg 627

International Linguistics Corp, 12220 Blue Ridge Blvd, Suite G, Kansas City, MO 64030 *Tel:* 816-765-8855 *Toll Free Tel:* 800-237-1830 (orders) *E-mail:* learnables@sbcglobal.net *Web Site:* www.learnables.com, pg 111

International Literacy Association (ILA), 258 Chapman Rd, Suite 203, Newark, DE 19702 *Tel:* 302-731-1600 *Toll Free Tel:* 800-336-7323 (US & CN) *Fax:* 302-731-1057 *E-mail:* customerservice@reading.org *Web Site:* www.literacyworldwide.org; www.reading.org, pg 111, 535

International Monetary Fund (IMF), Editorial & Publications Division, 700 19 St NW, HQ1-5-355, Washington, DC 20431 *Tel:* 202-623-7430 *Fax:* 202-623-7201 *E-mail:* publications@imf.org *Web Site:* bookstore.imf.org; elibrary.imf.org (online collection), pg 111

International Poetry Competition, 686 Cherry St NW, Suite 333, Atlanta, GA 30332-0161 *E-mail:* atlantareview@gatech.edu *Web Site:* www.atlantareview.com, pg 627

International Press of Boston Inc, 387 Somerville Ave, Somerville, MA 02143 *Tel:* 617-623-3016 *Fax:* 617-623-3101 *E-mail:* ipb-orders@intlpress.com *Web Site:* www.intlpress.com, pg 111

International Publishers Co Inc, 235 W 23 St, New York, NY 10011 *Tel:* 212-366-9816 *Fax:* 212-366-9820 *E-mail:* service@intpubnyc.com *Web Site:* www.intpubnyc.com, pg 111

International Risk Management Institute Inc, 12222 Merit Dr, Suite 1600, Dallas, TX 75251-2266 *Tel:* 972-960-7693 *Fax:* 972-371-5120 *E-mail:* info27@irmi.com *Web Site:* www.irmi.com, pg 111

International Self-Counsel Press Ltd, 1481 Charlotte Rd, North Vancouver, BC V7J 1H1, Canada *Tel:* 604-986-3366 *Toll Free Tel:* 800-663-3007 *E-mail:* orders@self-counsel.com; sales@self-counsel.com *Web Site:* www.self-counsel.com, pg 430

International Society for Technology in Education, 1530 Wilson Blvd, Suite 730, Arlington, VA 22209 *Tel:* 503-342-2848 (intl) *Toll Free Tel:* 800-336-5191 (US & CN) *E-mail:* iste@iste.org *Web Site:* www.iste.org; www.isteconference.org, pg 112

International Society of Automation (ISA), 67 T W Alexander Dr, Research Triangle Park, NC 27709-0185 *Tel:* 919-549-8411 *Fax:* 919-549-8288 *E-mail:* info@isa.org *Web Site:* www.isa.org, pg 112

International Society of Latino Authors, c/o Latino Literacy Now, 3445 Catalina Dr, Carlsbad, CA 92010 *Tel:* 760-434-1223 *Fax:* 760-434-7476, pg 535

International Society of Weekly Newspaper Editors, Missouri Southern State University, 3950 E Newman Rd, Joplin, MO 64801-1595 *Tel:* 417-625-9736 *Fax:* 417-659-4445 *Web Site:* www.iswne.org, pg 535

International Standard Book Numbering (ISBN) US Agency, A Cambridge Information Group Co, 630 Central Ave, New Providence, NJ 07974 *Toll Free Tel:* 877-310-7333 *Fax:* 908-219-0188 *E-mail:* isbn-san@bowker.com *Web Site:* www.isbn.org, pg 535

International Titles, 931 E 56 St, Austin, TX 78751-1724 *Tel:* 512-909-2447 *Web Site:* www.internationaltitles.com, pg 489

International Transactions Inc, 28 Alope Way, Gila, NM 88038 *Tel:* 845-373-9696 *Fax:* 480-393-5162 *E-mail:* info@internationaltransactions.us *Web Site:* www.intltrans.com, pg 489

International Wealth Success Inc, PO Box 186, Merrick, NY 11566-0186 *Tel:* 516-766-5850 *Toll Free Tel:* 800-323-0548 *Fax:* 516-766-5919 *E-mail:* admin@iwsmoney.com *Web Site:* www.iwsmoney.com, pg 112

The International Women's Writing Guild (IWWG), 5 Penn Plaza, 19th fl, PMB 19059, New York, NY 10001 *Tel:* 917-720-6959 *E-mail:* iwwgquestions@iwwg.org *Web Site:* www.iwwg.org, pg 536

InterTech™ Technology Awards, 10015 Main St, Fairfax, VA 22031-3489 *Tel:* 703-385-1335 *Toll Free Tel:* 888-385-3588 *Fax:* 703-273-0456 *E-mail:* intertech@printing.org *Web Site:* www.printing.org/programs/awards/intertechtm-technology-awards, pg 627

InterVarsity Press, 430 Plaza Dr, Westmont, IL 60559-1234 *Tel:* 630-734-4000 *Toll Free Tel:* 800-843-9487 *Fax:* 630-734-4200 *E-mail:* email@ivpress.com *Web Site:* www.ivpress.com, pg 112

Interweave Press LLC, 4868 Innovation Dr, Fort Collins, CO 80525 *Web Site:* www.interweave.com, pg 112

Intimate & Inspiring Workshops for Children's Authors & Illustrators, 814 Court St, Honesdale, PA 18431 *Tel:* 570-253-1192 *Fax:* 570-253-0179 *E-mail:* jolloyd@highlightsfoundation.org *Web Site:* www.highlightsfoundation.org, pg 575

Investigative Reporters & Editors, Missouri School of Journalism, 141 Neff Annex, Columbia, MO 65211 *Tel:* 573-882-2042 *Fax:* 573-882-5431 *E-mail:* info@ire.org *Web Site:* www.ire.org, pg 536

IODE Jean Throop Book Award, 9-45 Frid St, Hamilton, ON L8P 4M3, Canada *Tel:* 905-522-9537 *Fax:* 905-522-3637 *E-mail:* iodeontario@bellnet.ca *Web Site:* www.iodeontario.ca, pg 627

IODE Violet Downey Book Award, 40 Orchard View Blvd, Suite 219, Toronto, ON M4R 1B9, Canada *Tel:* 416-487-4416 *Toll Free Tel:* 866-827-7428 *Fax:* 416-487-4417 *E-mail:* iodecanada@bellnet.ca *Web Site:* www.iode.ca, pg 627

Iowa Poetry Prize, 119 W Park Rd, 100 Kuhl House, Iowa City, IA 52242-1000 *Tel:* 319-335-2000 *Fax:* 319-335-2055 *E-mail:* uipress@uiowa.edu *Web Site:* www.uipress.uiowa.edu, pg 627

Iowa Prize for Literary Nonfiction, 119 W Park Rd, 100 Kuhl House, Iowa City, IA 52242-1000 *Tel:* 319-335-2000 *Fax:* 319-335-2055 *E-mail:* uipress@uiowa.edu *Web Site:* www.uipress.uiowa.edu, pg 627

The Iowa Review Awards, 308 EPB, Iowa City, IA 52242-1408 *E-mail:* iowa-review@uiowa.edu *Web Site:* www.iowareview.org, pg 628

The Iowa Short Fiction Award, 102 Dey House, 507 N Clinton St, Iowa City, IA 52242-1000 *Tel:* 319-335-0416 *Fax:* 319-335-0420 *Web Site:* www.uiowapress.org/authors/iowa-short-fiction.htm, pg 628

Iowa Summer Writing Festival, 250 Continuing Educ Facility, University of Iowa, Iowa City, IA 52242 *Tel:* 319-335-4160 *E-mail:* iswfestival@uiowa.edu *Web Site:* iowasummerwritingfestival.org, pg 575

Iris Press, 969 Oak Ridge Tpke, No 328, Oak Ridge, TN 37830 *Web Site:* www.irisbooks.com, pg 112

Iron Gate Publishing, PO Box 999, Niwot, CO 80544 *Tel:* 303-530-2551 *Fax:* 303-530-5273 *E-mail:* editor@irongate.com *Web Site:* www.irongate.com, pg 112

Irwin Law Inc, 14 Duncan St, Suite 206, Toronto, ON M5H 3G8, Canada *Tel:* 416-862-7690 *Toll Free Tel:* 888-314-9014 *Fax:* 416-862-9236 *E-mail:* info@irwinlaw.com; contact@irwinlaw.com *Web Site:* www.irwinlaw.com, pg 431

ISBN Canada, Library & Archives Canada, 395 Wellington St, Ottawa, ON K1A 0N4, Canada *Tel:* 819-994-6872 *Toll Free Tel:* 866-578-7777 (CN & US) *Fax:* 819-934-7535 *E-mail:* bac.isbn.lac@canada.ca *Web Site:* www.bac-lac.gc.ca/eng/services/isbn-canada/pages/isbn-canada.aspx, pg 536

ISI Books, 3901 Centerville Rd, Wilmington, DE 19807-1938 *Tel:* 302-652-4600 *Toll Free Tel:* 800-526-7022 *Fax:* 302-652-1760 *E-mail:* info@isi.org; isibooks@isi.org *Web Site:* www.isibooks.org, pg 112

Island Press, 2000 "M" St NW, Suite 650, Washington, DC 20036 *Tel:* 202-232-7933 *Toll Free Tel:* 800-828-1302 *Fax:* 202-234-1328 *E-mail:* info@islandpress.org *Web Site:* www.islandpress.org, pg 112

Islandport Press, 247 Portland St, Bldg C, Yarmouth, ME 04096 *Tel:* 207-846-3344 *Fax:* 207-619-9975 *E-mail:* info@islandportpress.com *Web Site:* www.islandportpress.com, pg 112

Italica Press, 99 Wall St, Suite 650, New York, NY 10005 *Tel:* 917-371-0563 *E-mail:* inquiries@italicapress.com *Web Site:* www.italicapress.com, pg 113

Italics Publishing, 100 Northcliffe Dr, No 223, Gulf Breeze, FL 32561 *E-mail:* submissions@italicspublishing.com (submissions) *Web Site:* italicspublishing.com, pg 113

ITMB Publishing Ltd, 12300 Bridgeport Rd, Richmond, BC V6V 1J5, Canada *Tel:* 604-273-1400 *Fax:* 604-273-1488 *E-mail:* itmb@itmb.com *Web Site:* www.itmb.com, pg 431

iUniverse, 1663 Liberty Dr, Bloomington, IN 47403 *Toll Free Tel:* 800-AUTHORS (288-4677) *Web Site:* www.iuniverse.com, pg 113

Richard Ivey School of Business, Ivey Business School at Western University, 1255 Western Rd, London, ON N6G 0N1, Canada *Tel:* 519-661-3206; 519-661-3208 *Toll Free Tel:* 800-649-6355 *Fax:* 519-661-3485; 519-661-3882 *E-mail:* cases@ivey.uwo.ca *Web Site:* www.iveycases.com; www.ivey.uwo.ca, pg 431

The Ivy League of Artists Inc, 18 Edgemere Rd, Livingston, NJ 07039 *Tel:* 973-992-4048 *Fax:* 973-992-4049 *E-mail:* ilartists2@gmail.com, pg 511

IWWG Annual Summer Conference, 5 Penn Plaza, 19th fl, PMB 19059, New York, NY 10001 *Tel:* 917-720-6959 *E-mail:* iwwgquestions@iwwg.org *Web Site:* www.iwwg.org, pg 575

JABberwocky Literary Agency Inc, 49 W 45 St, 12th fl, New York, NY 10036 *Tel:* 917-388-3010 *Fax:* 917-388-2998 *Web Site:* www.awfulagent.com, pg 489

Jackie White Memorial National Children's Playwriting Contest, 1400 Forum Blvd, 1C No 214, Columbia, MO 65203 *E-mail:* jwm@cectheatre.org *Web Site:* www.cectheatre.org, pg 628

Joseph Henry Jackson Literary Award, One Embarcadero Ctr, Suite 1400, San Francisco, CA 94111 *Tel:* 415-733-8500 *E-mail:* info@sff.org; artsinfo@sff.org *Web Site:* www.sff.org, pg 628

Melanie Jackson Agency LLC, 41 W 72 St, Suite 3F, New York, NY 10023 *Tel:* 212-873-3373, pg 490

The Jackson Poetry Prize, 90 Broad St, Suite 2100, New York, NY 10004 *Tel:* 212-226-3586 *Fax:* 212-226-3963 *E-mail:* admin@pw.org *Web Site:* www.pw.org, pg 628

Jain Publishing Co, PO Box 3523, Fremont, CA 94539 *Tel:* 510-659-8272 *Fax:* 510-659-0501 *E-mail:* mail@jainpub.com *Web Site:* www.jainpub.com, pg 113

J Franklin Jameson Fellowship in American History, 400 "A" St SE, Washington, DC 20003 *Tel:* 202-544-2422 *Fax:* 202-544-8307 *E-mail:* awards@historians.org *Web Site:* www.historians.org, pg 628

Jan Williams Indexing Services, 300 Dartmouth College Hwy, Lyme, NH 03768-3207 *Tel:* 603-795-4924 *Web Site:* www.janwilliamsindexing.com, pg 465

Janklow & Nesbit Associates, 285 Madison Ave, 21st fl, New York, NY 10017 *Tel:* 212-421-1700 *Fax:* 212-355-1403 *E-mail:* info@janklow.com *Web Site:* janklowandnesbit.com, pg 490

Janus Literary Agency, PO Box 837, Methuen, MA 01844 *Tel:* 978-273-4227 *E-mail:* janusliteraryagency@gmail.com *Web Site:* janusliteraryagency.com, pg 490

Japan-US Friendship Commission Translation Prize, Columbia University, 507 Kent Hall, MC3920, New York, NY 10027 *Tel:* 212-854-5036 *Fax:* 212-854-4019 *Web Site:* www.keenecenter.org, pg 628

Jefferson Cup Award, c/o Virginia Library Association (VLA), PO Box 56312, Virginia Beach, VA 23456 *Tel:* 757-689-0594 *Fax:* 757-447-3478 *Web Site:* www.vla.org, pg 628

Jellinek & Murray Literary Agency, 47-231 Kamakoi Rd, Kaneohe, HI 96744 *Tel:* 808-239-8451, pg 490

Jenkins Group Inc, 1129 Woodmere Ave, Suite B, Traverse City, MI 49686 *Tel:* 231-933-0445 *Toll Free Tel:* 800-706-4636 *Fax:* 231-933-0448 *E-mail:* info@ bookpublishing.com *Web Site:* www.bookpublishing. com, pg 465

Carolyn Jenks Agency, 30 Cambridge Park Dr, Suite 3140, Cambridge, MA 02140 *Tel:* 617-233-9130 *E-mail:* queries@carolynjenksagency.com (submissions) *Web Site:* www.carolynjenksagency.com, pg 490

Jentel Artist Residency Program, 130 Lower Piney Rd, Banner, WY 82832 *Tel:* 307-737-2311 *Fax:* 307-737-2305 *E-mail:* jentel@jentelarts.org *Web Site:* www. jentelarts.org, pg 575

Jerome Award, 8550 United Plaza Blvd, Suite 1001, Baton Rouge, LA 70809 *Tel:* 225-408-4417 *Fax:* 225-408-4422 *E-mail:* cla2@cathla.org *Web Site:* cathla. org, pg 628

Jerome Fellowship, 2301 Franklin Ave E, Minneapolis, MN 55406-1099 *Tel:* 612-332-7481 *Fax:* 612-332-6037 *E-mail:* info@pwcenter.org *Web Site:* www. pwcenter.org, pg 628

JET Literary Associates Inc, 941 Calle Mejia, Suite 507, Santa Fe, NM 87501 *Tel:* 505-780-0721 *Web Site:* www.jetliterary.wordpress.com, pg 490

Jewel Box Theatre Playwriting Competition, 3700 N Walker, Oklahoma City, OK 73118-7031 *Tel:* 405-521-1786 *Web Site:* jewelboxtheatre.org, pg 628

Jewish Book Council, 520 Eighth Ave, 4th fl, New York, NY 10018 *Tel:* 212-201-2920 *Fax:* 212-532-4952 *E-mail:* jbc@jewishbooks.org *Web Site:* www. jewishbookcouncil.org, pg 536

Jewish Lights, 4507 Charlotte Ave, Suite 100, Nashville, TN 37209 *Tel:* 615-255-BOOK (255-2665) *Fax:* 615-255-5081 *E-mail:* marketing@turnerpublishing.com *Web Site:* jewishlights.com; www.turnerpublishing. com, pg 113

Jewish Publication Society, 2100 Arch St, Philadelphia, PA 19103 *Tel:* 215-832-0600 *Toll Free Tel:* 800-234-3151 *Fax:* 215-568-2017 *Web Site:* www.jps.org, pg 113

JFE Editorial, 190 Ocean Dr, Gun Barrel City, TX 75156 *Tel:* 817-560-7018 *E-mail:* jford@jfe-editorial.com; juneford1@gmail.com, pg 465

Jhpiego, 1615 Thames St, Baltimore, MD 21231-3492 *Tel:* 410-537-1800 *Fax:* 410-537-1473 *E-mail:* info@ jhpiego.net *Web Site:* www.jhpiego.org, pg 113

JIST Publishing, 875 Montreal Way, St Paul, MN 55102 *Toll Free Tel:* 800-328-1452 *Toll Free Fax:* 800-328-4564 *E-mail:* educate@emcp.com *Web Site:* jist.emcp. com, pg 113

JL Communications, 10205 Green Holly Terr, Silver Spring, MD 20902 *Tel:* 301-593-0640, pg 465

JMW Group Inc, 347 Rte 6, No 867, Mahopac, NY 10541 *Tel:* 914-841-7105 *Fax:* 914-248-8861 *E-mail:* jmwgroup@jmwgroup.net *Web Site:* jmwgroup.net, pg 490

Jody Rein Books Inc, 7741 S Ash Ct, Centennial, CO 80122 *Tel:* 303-694-9386 *Web Site:* www. jodyreinbooks.com, pg 490

John Deere Publishing, 5440 Corporate Park Dr, Davenport, IA 52807 *Toll Free Tel:* 800-522-7448 (orders) *Fax:* 563-355-3690 *E-mail:* deere_bookstore_support@midlandcorp.com *Web Site:* techpubs.deere.com, pg 113

John Steinbeck Award for Fiction, San Jose State University, English Dept, One Washington Sq, San Jose, CA 95192-0090 *Tel:* 408-924-4441 *E-mail:* mail@reedmag.org *Web Site:* www.reedmag. org; reedmagazine.submittable.com, pg 629

Johns Hopkins University Press, 2715 N Charles St, Baltimore, MD 21218-4363 *Tel:* 410-516-6900; 410-516-6987 (journal orders outside US & CN) *Toll Free Tel:* 800-537-5487 (book orders & cust serv); 800-548-1784 (journal orders) *Fax:* 410-516-6968; 410-516-3866 (journal orders); 410-516-

6998 (orders) *E-mail:* hfscustserv@press.jhu.edu (cust serv); jrnlcirc@press.jhu.edu (journal orders) *Web Site:* www.press.jhu.edu; muse.jhu.edu, pg 113

Lyndon B Johnson School of Public Affairs, University of Texas at Austin, 2315 Red River St, Austin, TX 78712-1536 *Tel:* 512-471-3200 *Fax:* 512-471-4697 *E-mail:* lbjdeansoffice@austin.utexas.edu *Web Site:* www.utexas.edu/lbj, pg 114

Jones & Bartlett Learning LLC, 5 Wall St, Burlington, MA 01803 *Tel:* 978-443-5000 *Toll Free Tel:* 800-832-0034 *Fax:* 978-443-8000 *E-mail:* info@jblearning.com *Web Site:* www.jblearning.com, pg 114

Anson Jones MD Awards, 401 W 15 St, Austin, TX 78701 *Tel:* 512-370-1300 *Fax:* 512-370-1693 *Web Site:* www.texmed.org, pg 629

Jones Hutton Literary Associates, 140D Heritage Village, Southbury, CT 06488 *Tel:* 203-558-4478 *E-mail:* huttonbooks@hotmail.com, pg 490

Jesse H Jones Award, PO Box 609, Round Rock, TX 78680 *Tel:* 512-683-5640 *E-mail:* president@ texasinstituteofletters.org *Web Site:* www. texasinstituteofletters.org, pg 629

Joshua Tree Publishing, 3 Golf Ctr, Suite 201, Hoffman Estates, IL 60169 *Tel:* 312-893-7525 *E-mail:* info@ joshuatreepublishing.com *Web Site:* www. joshuatreepublishing.com; www.centaurbooks.com (imprint); www.chiralhouse.com (imprint), pg 114

Judah, Sarah, Grace & Tom Memorial, 900 Timber Creek Place, Virginia Beach, VA 23464 *E-mail:* poetryinva@aol.com; info@poetryvirginia.org *Web Site:* poetrysocietyofvirginia.org, pg 629

Judaica Press Inc, 123 Ditmas Ave, Brooklyn, NY 11218 *Tel:* 718-972-6200 *Toll Free Tel:* 800-972-6201 *Fax:* 718-972-6204 *E-mail:* info@judaicapress.com; orders@judaicapress.com; submissions@judaicapress. com *Web Site:* www.judaicapress.com, pg 114

Judson Press, 1075 First Ave, King of Prussia, PA 19406 *Toll Free Tel:* 800-458-3766 *Fax:* 610-768-2107 *Web Site:* www.judsonpress.com, pg 114

Jump!, 5357 Penn Ave, Minneapolis, MN 55419 *Toll Free Tel:* 888-799-1860 *Toll Free Fax:* 800-675-6679 *E-mail:* customercare@jumplibrary.com *Web Site:* www.jumplibrary.com, pg 115

Jump at the Sun, 125 West End Ave, 3rd fl, New York, NY 10023 *Web Site:* books.disney.com, pg 115

Juniper Prize for Fiction, East Experiment Station, 671 N Pleasant St, Amherst, MA 01003 *E-mail:* info@ umpress.umass.edu *Web Site:* www.umass.edu/ umpress; www.umass.edu/umpress/content/juniper-literary-prize-series, pg 629

Juniper Prize for Poetry, East Experiment Station, 671 N Pleasant St, Amherst, MA 01003 *E-mail:* info@ umpress.umass.edu *Web Site:* www.umass.edu/ umpress; www.umass.edu/umpress/content/juniper-literary-prize-series, pg 629

Juniper Summer Writing Institute, c/o University Conference Services, 810 Campus Center, One Campus Center Way, Amherst, MA 01003 *Tel:* 413-545-5503 *E-mail:* juniperinstitute@hfa.umass.edu *Web Site:* www.umass.edu/juniperinstitute, pg 576

Just Creative Writing & Indexing Services (JCR), 301 Wood Duck Dr, Greensboro, MD 21639 *Tel:* 443-262-2136 *E-mail:* judy@justcreativewriting.com *Web Site:* www.justcreativewriting.com, pg 465

Just World Books LLC, PO Box 5484, Charlottesville, VA 22905 *Toll Free Tel:* 888-506-3769 *E-mail:* sales@ justworldbooks.com *Web Site:* justworldbooks.com, pg 115

Juvenile Literary Awards/Young People's Literature Awards, 506 Rose Ave, Des Plaines, IL 60016 *Tel:* 847-827-8339 *Web Site:* www.fawchicago.org, pg 629

Kabbalah Publishing, 1062 S Robertson Blvd, Los Angeles, CA 90035 *Tel:* 310-657-5404 *E-mail:* kcla@kabbalah.com; losangeles@kabbalah. com *Web Site:* www.kabbalah.com, pg 115

Kaeden Corp, PO Box 16190, Rocky River, OH 44116-0190 *Tel:* 440-617-1400 *Toll Free Tel:* 800-890-7323 *Fax:* 440-617-1403 *E-mail:* info@kaeden.com *Web Site:* www.kaeden.com, pg 115

Kalaniot Books, 72 Glenmaura National Blvd, Suite 104B, Moosic, PA 18507 *Tel:* 862-251-2296; 570-878-7960 *E-mail:* info@endlessmountainspublishing. com *Web Site:* www.endlessmountainspublishing.com, pg 115

Kalmbach Publishing Co, 21027 Crossroads Circle, Waukesha, WI 53186 *Tel:* 262-796-8776 *Toll Free Tel:* 800-533-6644 (cust serv & orders); 800-558-1544 *Fax:* 262-798-6592 *E-mail:* customerservice@ kalmbach.com *Web Site:* www.kalmbach.com, pg 115

Kamehameha Publishing, 1887 Makukone St, Pauahi Admin Bldg, Suite 211, Honolulu, HI 96817 *E-mail:* publishing@ksbe.edu *Web Site:* kamehamehapublishing.org, pg 115

Kane Miller Books, 4901 Morena Blvd, Suite 213, San Diego, CA 92117 *E-mail:* submissions@kanemiller. com; info@kanemiller.com *Web Site:* www.kanemiller. com, pg 115

Kapp Books LLC, 3602 Rocky Meadow Ct, Fairfax, VA 22033 *Tel:* 703-261-9171 *Fax:* 703-621-7162 *E-mail:* info@kappbooks.com *Web Site:* www. kappbooks.com, pg 115

Kar-Ben Publishing, 241 First Ave N, Minneapolis, MN 55401 *Tel:* 612-332-3344 *Toll Free Tel:* 800-4-KARBEN (452-7236) *Fax:* 612-332-7615 *Toll Free Fax:* 800-332-1132 *Web Site:* www.karben.com, pg 115

The Karpfinger Agency, 357 W 20 St, New York, NY 10011-3379 *Tel:* 212-691-2690 *Fax:* 212-691-7129 *E-mail:* info@karpfinger.com (no queries or submissions) *Web Site:* karpfinger.com, pg 490

Sue Kaufman Prize for First Fiction, 633 W 155 St, New York, NY 10032 *Tel:* 212-368-5900 *Fax:* 212-491-4615 *E-mail:* academy@artsandletters.org *Web Site:* artsandletters.org, pg 629

Kazi Publications Inc, 3023 W Belmont Ave, Chicago, IL 60618 *Tel:* 773-267-7001 *Fax:* 773-267-7002 *E-mail:* info@kazi.org *Web Site:* www.kazi.org, pg 116

Ezra Jack Keats Book Award, 450 14 St, Brooklyn, NY 11215-5702 *E-mail:* foundation@ezra-jack-keats.org *Web Site:* www.ezra-jack-keats.org, pg 629

Ezra Jack Keats/Kerlan Memorial Fellowship, University of Minnesota, 113 Andersen Library, 222 21 Ave S, Minneapolis, MN 55455 *Tel:* 612-624-4576 *E-mail:* asc-clrc@umn.edu *Web Site:* www.lib.umn. edu/clrc, pg 629

Keim Publishing, 66 Main St, Suite 807, Yonkers, NY 10701 *Tel:* 917-655-7190, pg 465

J J Keller & Associates, Inc, 3003 Breezewood Lane, Neenah, WI 54957 *Tel:* 920-722-2848 *Toll Free Tel:* 877-564-2333 *Toll Free Fax:* 800-727-7516 *E-mail:* contactus@jjkeller.com; customerservice@ jjkeller.com *Web Site:* www.jjkeller.com, pg 116

Keller Media Inc, 578 Washington Blvd, No 745, Marina del Rey, CA 90292 *Toll Free Tel:* 800-278-8706 *E-mail:* query@kellermedia.com *Web Site:* kellermedia.com/query, pg 490

Joan Kelly Memorial Prize in Women's History, 400 "A" St SE, Washington, DC 20003 *Tel:* 202-544-2422 *Fax:* 202-544-8307 *E-mail:* awards@historians.org *Web Site:* www.historians.org, pg 629

Kelsey Street Press, 2824 Kelsey St, Berkeley, CA 94705 *E-mail:* info@kelseyst.com *Web Site:* www.kelseyst. com, pg 116

Kendall Hunt Publishing Co, 4050 Westmark Dr, Dubuque, IA 52002-2624 *Tel:* 563-589-1000 *Toll Free Tel:* 800-228-0810 (orders) *Fax:* 563-589-1046 *Toll Free Fax:* 800-772-9165 *E-mail:* orders@kendallhunt. com *Web Site:* www.kendallhunt.com, pg 116

Kennedy Information Inc, 24 Railroad St, Keene, NH 03431 *Tel:* 603-357-8103 *Toll Free Tel:* 800-531-0140, pg 116

Robert F Kennedy Book Awards, 1300 19 St NW, Suite 750, Washington, DC 20036 *Tel:* 646-553-4750 *Fax:* 202-463-6606 *E-mail:* info@rfkhumanrights.org *Web Site:* rfkhumanrights.org, pg 629

Kensington Publishing Corp, 119 W 40 St, New York, NY 10018 *Tel:* 212-407-1500 *Toll Free Tel:* 800-221-2647 *Fax:* 212-935-0699 *Web Site:* www.kensingtonbooks.com, pg 116

Kent State University Press, 1118 University Library Bldg, 1125 Risman Dr, Kent, OH 44242 *Tel:* 330-672-7913 *Fax:* 330-672-3104 *E-mail:* ksupress@kent.edu *Web Site:* www.kentstateuniversitypress.com, pg 116

Kentucky Women Writers Conference, 232 E Maxwell St, Lexington, KY 40506-0344 *Tel:* 859-257-2874 *E-mail:* kentuckywomenwriters@gmail.com *Web Site:* www.kentuckywomenwriters.org, pg 576

Kentucky Writers Conference, 1906 College Heights Blvd, Suite 11067, Bowling Green, KY 42101-1067 *Tel:* 270-745-4502 *E-mail:* sokybookfest@wku.edu *Web Site:* www.sokybookfest.org, pg 576

Natasha Kern Literary Agency Inc, PO Box 1069, White Salmon, WA 98672 *Tel:* 509-493-3803 *Web Site:* www.natashakernliterary.com, pg 491

Kessinger Publishing LLC, PO Box 1404, Whitefish, MT 59937 *Web Site:* www.kessinger.net, pg 117

Jascha Kessler, 218 16 St, Santa Monica, CA 90402-2216 *Tel:* 310-393-7968 *Fax:* 310-393-7968 (by request only) *E-mail:* urim.urim@gmail.com *Web Site:* www.jfkessler.com; www.xlibris.com, pg 466

Louise B Ketz Agency, 414 E 78 St, Suite 1-B, New York, NY 10075 *Tel:* 212-249-0668 *E-mail:* ketzagency@aol.com, pg 491

Key West Literary Seminar, 717 Love Lane, Key West, FL 33040 *Tel:* 305-293-9291 *Toll Free Tel:* 888-293-9291 *E-mail:* mail@kwls.org *Web Site:* www.kwls.org/seminar, pg 576

Key West Literary Seminar's Writers' Workshop Program, 717 Love Lane, Key West, FL 33040 *Tel:* 305-293-9291 *Toll Free Tel:* 888-293-9291 *E-mail:* mail@kwls.org *Web Site:* www.kwls.org; www.kwls.org/writers_workshops, pg 576

Virginia Kidd Agency Inc, 538 E Harford St, PO Box 278, Milford, PA 18337 *Tel:* 570-296-6205 *Web Site:* vk-agency.com, pg 491

Kids Can Press Ltd, 25 Dockside Dr, Toronto, ON M5A 0B5, Canada *Tel:* 416-479-7000 *Toll Free Tel:* 800-265-0884 *Fax:* 416-960-5437 *E-mail:* info@kidscan.com; customerservice@kidscan.com *Web Site:* www.kidscanpress.com; www.kidscanpress.ca, pg 431

Kidsbooks LLC, 3535 W Peterson Ave, Chicago, IL 60659 *Tel:* 773-509-0707 *Fax:* 773-509-0404 *E-mail:* customerservice@kidsbooks.com *Web Site:* www.kidsbooks.com, pg 117

Kindred Productions, 1310 Taylor Ave, Winnipeg, MB R3M 3Z6, Canada *Tel:* 204-669-6575 *Toll Free Tel:* 800-545-7322 *Fax:* 204-654-1865 *E-mail:* kindred@mbchurches.ca *Web Site:* www.kindredproductions.com, pg 431

Kinesiology Books Publisher, 212 Robert St (side basement door), Toronto, ON M5S 2K7, Canada *Tel:* 416-323-9438 *Fax:* 416-966-9022 *E-mail:* sbp@sportbookspub.com; kbp@kinesiology101.com *Web Site:* www.sportbookspub.com, pg 431

Coretta Scott King Book Awards, 225 N Michigan Ave, Suite 1300, Chicago, IL 60601 *Tel:* 312-944-6780 *Toll Free Tel:* 800-545-2433 *Fax:* 312-440-9374 *E-mail:* diversity@ala.org *Web Site:* www.ala.org/awardsgrants/coretta-scott-king-book-awards, pg 630

Coretta Scott King - John Steptoe Award for New Talent, 225 N Michigan Ave, Suite 1300, Chicago, IL 60601 *Toll Free Tel:* 800-545-2433 (ext 4294) *Fax:* 312-280-3256 *E-mail:* diversity@ala.org *Web Site:* www.ala.org/awardsgrants, pg 630

Coretta Scott King - Virginia Hamilton Award for Lifetime Achievement, 225 N Michigan Ave, Suite 1300, Chicago, IL 60601 *Toll Free Tel:* 800-545-2433

E-mail: diversity@ala.org *Web Site:* www.ala.org/emiert/virginia-hamilton-award-lifetime-achievement, pg 630

Jessica Kingsley Publishers Inc, 400 Market St, Suite 400, Philadelphia, PA 19106 *Tel:* 215-922-1161 *Toll Free Tel:* 866-416-1078 (cust serv) *Fax:* 215-922-1474 *E-mail:* hello.usa@jkp.com *Web Site:* www.jkp.com, pg 117

Kinship Books, 305 Cedar Heights Rd, Rhinebeck, NY 12572 *Tel:* 845-876-4592 (orders) *E-mail:* kinship@hvc.rr.com *Web Site:* www.kinshipny.com, pg 117

Kirchoff/Wohlberg Inc, 897 Boston Post Rd, Madison, CT 06443 *Tel:* 203-245-7308 *Fax:* 203-245-3218 *E-mail:* info@kirchoffwohlberg.com *Web Site:* www.kirchoffwohlberg.com, pg 491

Kirkbride Bible Co Inc, 1102 Deloss St, Indianapolis, IN 46203 *Tel:* 317-633-1900 *Toll Free Tel:* 800-428-4385 *Fax:* 317-633-1444 *E-mail:* sales@kirkbride.com; info@kirkbride.com *Web Site:* www.kirkbride.com, pg 117

Kirkus Prize, 65 W 36 St, Suite 700, New York, NY 10018 *Web Site:* www.kirkusreviews.com/prize, pg 630

Kiva Publishing Inc, 10 Bella Loma, Santa Fe, NM 87506 *Tel:* 909-896-0518 *E-mail:* kivapub@aol.com *Web Site:* www.kivapub.com, pg 117

Harvey Klinger Inc, 300 W 55 St, Suite 11V, New York, NY 10019 *Tel:* 212-581-7068 *Fax:* 212-315-3823 *E-mail:* queries@harveyklinger.com *Web Site:* www.harveyklinger.com, pg 491

Klutz, 524 Broadway, 5th fl, New York, NY 10012 *Tel:* 212-343-6360 *Toll Free Tel:* 800-737-4123 (cust serv) *E-mail:* sales@klutz.com (all sales inquires); marketing@klutz.com (all mktg inquiries); publicity@klutz.com (all publicity inquires) *Web Site:* www.klutz.com; store.scholastic.com, pg 117

Kneerim & Williams Agency, 90 Canal St, Boston, MA 02114 *Tel:* 617-303-1650 *Web Site:* www.kwlit.com, pg 491

The Knight Agency Inc, 232 W Washington St, Madison, GA 30650 *E-mail:* admin@knightagency.net *Web Site:* www.knightagency.net, pg 491

The Knight-Risser Prize for Western Environmental Journalism, Stanford University, 450 Serra Mall, Bldg 120, Rm 424, Stanford, CA 94305-2050 *Tel:* 650-723-4937 *Fax:* 650-725-6154 *E-mail:* knightrisserprize@lists.stanford.edu *Web Site:* knightrisser.stanford.edu, pg 630

Knightville Poetry Contest, PO Box 472, Brunswick, ME 04011 *E-mail:* info@newguardreview.com; editors@writershotel.com *Web Site:* www.newguardreview.com, pg 630

Alfred A Knopf, c/o Penguin Random House Inc, 1745 Broadway, New York, NY 10019 *Tel:* 212-751-2600 *Fax:* 212-572-2662 (foreign rts) *Web Site:* knopfdoubleday.com, pg 117

Knopf Canada, 320 Front St W, Suite 1400, Toronto, ON M5V 3B6, Canada *Tel:* 416-364-4449 *Toll Free Tel:* 888-523-9292 *Fax:* 416-598-7764 *Web Site:* www.penguinrandomhouse.ca, pg 431

Kobo Emerging Writer Prize, 135 Liberty St, Suite 101, Toronto, ON M6K 1A7, Canada *E-mail:* pr@kobo.com *Web Site:* www.kobo.com/emergingwriterprize, pg 630

Kodansha USA Inc, 451 Park Ave S, 7th fl, New York, NY 10016 *Tel:* 917-322-6200 *Fax:* 212-935-6929 *E-mail:* info@kodansha-usa.com *Web Site:* www.kodanshausa.com, pg 118

Bill Koehnlein, 236 E Fifth St, New York, NY 10003-8545 *Tel:* 212-674-9145 *E-mail:* koehnlein.bill@gmail.com, pg 466

Barry R Koffler, Featherside, 14 Ginger Rd, High Falls, NY 12440 *Tel:* 845-687-9851 *E-mail:* barkof@feathersite.com, pg 466

Kogan Page, c/o Martin P Hill Consulting, 122 W 27 St, 10th fl, New York, NY 10001 *Tel:* 929-362-7262 *E-mail:* info@koganpage.com *Web Site:* www.koganpage.com, pg 118

Paul Kohner Agency, 9300 Wilshire Blvd, Suite 555, Beverly Hills, CA 90212 *Tel:* 310-550-1060 *Fax:* 310-276-1083, pg 492

Koho Pono LLC, 15024 SE Pinegrove Loop, Clackamas, OR 97015 *Tel:* 503-723-7392 *E-mail:* info@kohopono.com; orders@ingrambook.com *Web Site:* kohopono.com, pg 118

KOK Edit, 15 Hare Lane, East Setauket, NY 11733-3606 *Tel:* 631-997-8191 *Fax:* 631-474-9849 *E-mail:* editor@kokedit.com *Web Site:* www.kokedit.com; twitter.com/kokedit; www.facebook.com/K.OmooreKlopf; www.linkedin.com/in/kokedit; www.editor-mom.blogspot.com, pg 466

Konecky & Konecky LLC, 72 Ayers Point Rd, Old Saybrook, CT 06475 *Tel:* 860-388-0878 *E-mail:* sean.konecky@gmail.com *Web Site:* www.koneckyandkonecky.com, pg 118

Linda Konner Literary Agency, 10 W 15 St, Suite 1918, New York, NY 10011 *Tel:* 212-691-3419 *Fax:* 212-691-0935 *Web Site:* www.lindakonnerliteraryagency.com, pg 492

Barbara S Kouts Literary Agency LLC, PO Box 560, Bellport, NY 11713 *Tel:* 631-286-1278 *Fax:* 631-286-1538 *E-mail:* bkouts@aol.com, pg 492

Katherine Singer Kovacs Prize, 85 Broad St, Suite 500, New York, NY 10004-2434 *Tel:* 646-576-5141; 646-576-5000 *Fax:* 646-458-0030 *E-mail:* awards@mla.org *Web Site:* www.mla.org, pg 630

The Kraken Book Prize for Middle-Grade Fiction, c/o Regal House Publishing, 806 Oberlin Rd, No 12094, Raleigh, NC 27605 *E-mail:* info@regalhousepublishing.com *Web Site:* regalhousepublishing.com/the-kraken-book-award/, pg 630

Eileen Kramer, 336 Great Rd, Stow, MA 01775 *Tel:* 978-897-4121 *E-mail:* kramer@tiac.net, pg 466

HJ Kramer Inc, PO Box 1082, Tiburon, CA 94920 *Tel:* 415-884-2100 (ext 10) *Toll Free Tel:* 800-972-6657 *Fax:* 415-435-5364 *E-mail:* hjkramer@jps.net *Web Site:* www.hjkramer.com; www.newworldlibrary.com, pg 118

Michael Kraus Research Grant in American Colonial History, 400 "A" St SE, Washington, DC 20003 *Tel:* 202-544-2422 *Fax:* 202-544-8307 *E-mail:* awards@historians.org *Web Site:* www.historians.org, pg 630

Krause Publications Inc, 1745 Broadway, New York, NY 10019 *Tel:* 212-782-9000 *Web Site:* www.penguinrandomhouse.com, pg 118

Kregel Publications, 2450 Oak Industrial Dr NE, Grand Rapids, MI 49505 *Tel:* 616-451-4775 *Toll Free Tel:* 800-733-2607 *Fax:* 616-451-9330 *E-mail:* kregelbooks@kregel.com *Web Site:* www.kregel.com, pg 118

Stuart Krichevsky Literary Agency Inc, 6 E 39 St, Suite 500, New York, NY 10016 *Tel:* 212-725-5288 *Fax:* 212-725-5275 *E-mail:* query@skagency.com *Web Site:* skagency.com, pg 492

Krieger Publishing Co, 1725 Krieger Lane, Malabar, FL 32950 *Tel:* 321-724-9542 *Fax:* 321-951-3671 *E-mail:* info@krieger-publishing.com *Web Site:* www.krieger-publishing.com, pg 119

The Robert Kroetsch City of Edmonton Book Prize, 11759 Groat Rd, Edmonton, AB T5M 3K6, Canada *Tel:* 780-422-8174 *Toll Free Tel:* 800-665-5354 (AB only) *Fax:* 780-422-2663 (attn WGA) *E-mail:* mail@writersguild.ca *Web Site:* writersguild.ca, pg 631

Lynn C Kronzek, Richard A Flom & Robert Flom, 145 S Glenoaks Blvd, Suite 240, Burbank, CA 91502 *Tel:* 818-768-7688, pg 466

KTAV Publishing House Inc, 527 Empire Blvd, Brooklyn, NY 11225 *Tel:* 201-963-9524; 718-972-5449 *Fax:* 718-972-6307 *E-mail:* orders@ktav.com *Web Site:* www.ktav.com, pg 119

Kumarian Press, 1800 30 St, Suite 314, Boulder, CO 80301 Tel: 303-444-6684 Fax: 303-444-0824 E-mail: questions@rienner.com Web Site: www.rienner.com, pg 119

Polly Kummel LLC, 624 Boardman Rd, Aiken, SC 29803 Tel: 803-641-6831 E-mail: editor@amazinphrasin.com; pollyk1@msn.com Web Site: www.amazinphrasin.com, pg 466

Kumon Publishing North America, 300 Frank Burr Blvd, Suite 6, Teaneck, NJ 07666 Tel: 201-836-2105 Fax: 201-836-1559 E-mail: books@kumon.com Web Site: www.kumonbooks.com, pg 119

Kumu Kahua/UHM Theatre & Dance Department Playwriting Contest, 46 Merchant St, Honolulu, HI 96813 Tel: 808-536-4441 (box off); 808-536-4222 Fax: 808-536-4226 E-mail: kumukahuatheatre@hawaiiantel.net Web Site: www.kumukahua.org, pg 631

The LA Literary Agency, 1264 N Hayworth Ave, Los Angeles, CA 90046 Tel: 323-654-5288 E-mail: laliteraryagency@mac.com Web Site: www.laliteraryagency.com, pg 492

Lachina Creative Inc, 3791 S Green Rd, Cleveland, OH 44122 Tel: 216-292-7959 E-mail: info@lachina.com Web Site: www.lachina.com, pg 466

Lynne Lackenbach Editorial Services, 31 Pillsbury Rd, East Hampstead, NH 03826 Tel: 603-329-8133 E-mail: lynnelack@gmail.com, pg 466

Ladderbird Literary Agency, 45 Midland St, Worcester, MA 01602 Tel: 508-459-9590 Web Site: www.ladderbird.com, pg 492

Lake Superior Publishing LLC, 109 W Superior St, Suite 200, Duluth, MN 55802 Tel: 218-722-5002 Toll Free Tel: 888-BIG-LAKE (244-5253) Fax: 218-722-4096 E-mail: edit@lakesuperior.com Web Site: www.lakesuperior.com, pg 119

LAMA Books, 2381 Sleepy Hollow Ave, Hayward, CA 94545-3429 Tel: 510-785-1091 Toll Free Tel: 888-452-6244 Fax: 510-785-1099 Web Site: www.lamabooks.com, pg 119

W Kaye Lamb Scholarships, PO Box 448, Fort Langley, BC V1M 2R7, Canada E-mail: info@bchistory.ca Web Site: www.bchistory.ca/awards/scholarships, pg 631

Lambda Literary Awards (Lammys), 5482 Wilshire Blvd, No 1595, Los Angeles, CA 90036 Tel: 323-643-4281 E-mail: admin@lambdaliterary.org Web Site: www.lambdaliterary.org, pg 631

Peter Lampack Agency Inc, 350 Fifth Ave, Suite 5300, New York, NY 10118 Tel: 212-687-9106 Fax: 212-687-9109 Web Site: www.peterlampackagency.com, pg 492

Gerald Lampert Memorial Award, 2 Carlton St, Suite 1519, Toronto, ON M5B 1J3, Canada Tel: 416-504-1657 E-mail: info@poets.ca Web Site: poets.ca, pg 631

Lanahan Publishers Inc, 324 Hawthorne Rd, Baltimore, MD 21210-2303 Tel: 410-366-2434 Toll Free Tel: 866-345-1949 Fax: 410-366-8798 E-mail: lanahan@aol.com Web Site: www.lanahanpublishers.com, pg 119

Land on Demand, 20 Long Crescent Dr, Bristol, VA 24201 Tel: 423-366-0513 E-mail: landondemand@gmail.com Web Site: boblandedits.blogspot.com, pg 466

Landauer Publishing, 1970 Broad St, East Petersburg, PA 17520 Tel: 717-560-4703 Toll Free Tel: 800-457-9112 Fax: 717-560-4702 E-mail: customerservice@foxchapelpublishing.com Web Site: landauerpub.com, pg 119

Peter Lang Publishing Inc, 80 Broadway, 5th fl, New York, NY 10004 Tel: 703-661-1584 Toll Free Tel: 800-770-5264 (cust serv) Fax: 703-996-1010 E-mail: newyork.editorial@peterlang.com; customerservice@plang.com Web Site: www.peterlang.com, pg 119

Langmarc Publishing, 7500 Shadowridge Run, No 28, Austin, TX 78749 Tel: 512-394-0989 Toll Free Tel: 800-864-1648 (orders) E-mail: langmarc@booksails.com Web Site: www.langmarc.com, pg 120

Langum Prize in American Historical Fiction, 2809 Berkeley Dr, Birmingham, AL 35242 Tel: 360-809-0465 E-mail: langumtrust@gmail.com Web Site: www.langumtrust.org, pg 631

Langum Prize in American Legal History or Biography, 2809 Berkeley Dr, Birmingham, AL 35242 Tel: 360-809-0465 E-mail: langumtrust@gmail.com Web Site: www.langumtrust.org, pg 631

Lannan Foundation, 313 Read St, Santa Fe, NM 87501-2628 Tel: 505-986-8160 E-mail: info@lannan.org Web Site: lannan.org, pg 551

Lannan Literary Awards & Fellowships, 313 Read St, Santa Fe, NM 87501-2628 Tel: 505-986-8160 E-mail: info@lannan.org Web Site: lannan.org, pg 631

Lantern Books, 128 Second Place, Garden Suite, Brooklyn, NY 11231 Tel: 212-414-2275 E-mail: editorial@lanternbooks.com; info@lanternmedia.net Web Site: lanternbooks.presswarehouse.com/home/home.aspx, pg 120

LARB Books, 6671 Sunset Blvd, Suite 1521, Los Angeles, CA 90028 Tel: 323-952-3950 E-mail: larbbooks@lareviewofbooks.org Web Site: larbbooks.org, pg 120

LARB/USC Publishing Workshop, 6671 Sunset Blvd, Suite 1521, Los Angeles, CA 90028 E-mail: publishingworkshop@lareviewofbooks.org Web Site: thepublishingworkshop.com, pg 576

Laredo Publishing Co, 465 Westview Ave, Englewood, NJ 07631 Tel: 201-408-4048 E-mail: info@laredopublishing.com Web Site: www.laredopublishing.com, pg 120

Lark Crafts, 1166 Avenue of the Americas, 17th fl, New York, NY 10036 Tel: 212-532-7160 E-mail: editorial@sterlingpub.com; customerservice@sterlingpublishing.com Web Site: larkcrafts.com; www.facebook.com/LarkCrafts; www.sterlingpublishing.com, pg 120

Larson Publications, 4936 State Rte 414, Burdett, NY 14818 Tel: 607-546-9342 Toll Free Tel: 800-828-2197 Fax: 607-546-9344 E-mail: custserv@larsonpublications.com Web Site: www.larsonpublications.com, pg 120

Lasaria Creative Publishing, 4094 Majestic Lane, Suite 352, Fairfax, VA 22033 E-mail: info@lasariacreative.com Web Site: www.lasariacreative.com, pg 120

Latino Books Into Movies Awards, 3445 Catalina Dr, Carlsbad, CA 92010 Tel: 760-434-1223 Fax: 760-434-7476 Web Site: www.award.news, pg 631

Latner Writers' Trust Poetry Prize, 600-460 Richmond St W, Toronto, ON M5V 1Y1, Canada Tel: 416-504-8222 Toll Free Tel: 877-906-6548 Fax: 416-504-9090 E-mail: info@writerstrust.com Web Site: www.writerstrust.com/awards/latner-writers-trust-poetry-prize, pg 631

Laughing Elephant Books, 3645 Interlake N, Seattle, WA 98103 Tel: 206-447-9229 Toll Free Tel: 800-354-0400 Fax: 206-447-9189 E-mail: support@laughingelephant.com Web Site: www.laughingelephant.com, pg 120

James Lauglin Award, 75 Maiden Lane, Suite 901, New York, NY 10038 Tel: 212-274-0343 E-mail: awards@poets.org Web Site: www.poets.org, pg 631

Laurier Books Ltd, PO Box 8493, Ottawa, ON K1G 3H9, Canada Tel: 613-738-2163 Toll Free Tel: 855-736-9160 E-mail: laurierbooks@yahoo.com, pg 432

Law School Admission Council, 662 Penn St, Newtown, PA 18940 Tel: 215-968-1101 E-mail: lsacaccounts@lsac.org Web Site: www.lsac.org, pg 120

The Lawbook Exchange Ltd, 33 Terminal Ave, Clark, NJ 07066-1321 Tel: 732-382-1800 Toll Free Tel: 800-422-6686 Fax: 732-382-1887 E-mail: law@lawbookexchange.com Web Site: www.lawbookexchange.com, pg 121

Lawrence Foundation Prize, University of Michigan, 0576 Rackham Bldg, 915 E Washington St, Ann Arbor, MI 48109-1070 Tel: 734-764-9265 E-mail: mqr@umich.edu Web Site: sites.lsa.umich.edu/mqr/, pg 632

Merloyd Lawrence Inc, 102 Chestnut St, Boston, MA 02108 Tel: 617-523-5895 Fax: 617-263-2749, pg 121

Lawyers & Judges Publishing Co Inc, 917 N Swan Rd, Suite 300, Tucson, AZ 85711 Tel: 520-323-1500 Fax: 520-323-0055 E-mail: sales@lawyersandjudges.com Web Site: www.lawyersandjudges.com, pg 121

Stephen Leacock Memorial Medal for Humour, 149 Peter St N, Orillia, ON L3V 4Z4, Canada Tel: 705-326-9286 Web Site: www.leacock.ca, pg 632

Leadership Connect, 1407 Broadway, Suite 318, New York, NY 10018 Tel: 212-627-4140 Toll Free Tel: 800-627-0311 Fax: 212-645-0931 E-mail: info@leadershipconnect.io Web Site: www.leadershipconnect.io, pg 121

Leadership Ministries Worldwide, 1928 Central Ave, Chattanooga, TN 37408 Tel: 423-855-2181 Toll Free Tel: 800-987-8790 E-mail: info@lmw.org Web Site: lmw.org; store.lmw.org, pg 121

Leaf Storm Press, PO Box 4670, Santa Fe, NM 87502-4670 Tel: 505-216-6155 E-mail: leafstormpress@gmail.com Web Site: leafstormpress.com, pg 121

The League of Canadian Poets, 2 Carlton St, Suite 1519, Toronto, ON M5B 1J3, Canada Tel: 416-504-1657 E-mail: info@poets.ca Web Site: poets.ca, pg 536

League of Vermont Writers Inc, PO Box 5046, Burlington, VT 05402 E-mail: lvw@leagueofvermontwriters.org Web Site: leagueofvermontwriters.org, pg 536

THE Learning Connection®, 4100 Silverstar Rd, Suite D, Orlando, FL 32808 Toll Free Tel: 800-218-8489 Fax: 407-292-2123 E-mail: tlc@tlconnection.com Web Site: www.tlconnection.com, pg 121

Learning Links Inc, 26 Haypress Rd, Cranbury, NJ 08512 Tel: 516-437-9071 Toll Free Tel: 800-724-2616 Fax: 516-437-5392 Toll Free Fax: 888-960-2508 E-mail: info@learninglinks.com Web Site: www.learninglinks.com, pg 121

The Learning Source Ltd, 644 Tenth St, Brooklyn, NY 11215 E-mail: info@learningsourceltd.com Web Site: www.learningsourceltd.com, pg 466

LearningExpress, 224 W 29 St, 3rd fl, New York, NY 10001 Toll Free Tel: 800-295-9556 (ext 2) Web Site: learningexpresshub.com, pg 121

The Ned Leavitt Agency, 752 Creeklocks Rd, Rosendale, NY 12472 Tel: 845-658-3333 Web Site: www.nedleavittagency.com, pg 492

Lectorum Publications Inc, 205 Chubb Ave, Lyndhurst, NJ 07071 Toll Free Tel: 800-345-5946 Fax: 201-559-2201 Toll Free Fax: 877-532-8676 E-mail: lectorum@lectorum.com Web Site: www.lectorum.com, pg 121

Lederer Books, 6120 Day Long Lane, Clarksville, MD 21029 Tel: 410-531-6644 Toll Free Tel: 800-410-7367 (orders) Fax: 410-531-9440 Toll Free Fax: 800-327-0048 E-mail: customerservice@messianicjewish.net Web Site: www.messianicjewish.net, pg 122

Lee & Low Books Inc, 95 Madison Ave, Suite 1205, New York, NY 10016 Tel: 212-779-4400 Toll Free Tel: 888-320-3190 (ext 28, orders only) Fax: 212-683-1894 (orders only); 212-532-6035 E-mail: general@leeandlow.com Web Site: www.leeandlow.com, pg 122

Harper Lee Prize for Legal Fiction, 101 Paul Bryant Dr, Tuscaloosa, AL 35487 Tel: 205-348-5195 Web Site: www.harperleeprize.com, pg 632

Legacy Award, 2667 Hyacinth St, Westbury, NY 11590 Tel: 516-333-0681 Fax: 516-333-0689 E-mail: naibabooksellers@gmail.com Web Site: www.naiba.com/page/LegacyAward, pg 632

Legacy Bound, 5 N Central Ave, Ely, MN 55731 Tel: Toll Free Tel: 800-909-9698 E-mail: orders@legacybound.net Web Site: www.legacybound.net, pg 122

COMPANY INDEX

Lehigh University Press, B-040 Christmas-Saucon Hall, 14 E Packer Ave, Bethlehem, PA 18015 *Tel:* 610-758-3933 *Fax:* 610-758-6331 *E-mail:* inlup@lehigh.edu *Web Site:* lupress.cas2.lehigh.edu, pg 122

Leisure Arts Inc, 104 Champs Blvd, Suite 100, Maumelle, AR 72113 *Tel:* 501-868-8800 *Toll Free Tel:* 800-643-8030 *Toll Free Fax:* 877-710-5603 (catalog) *E-mail:* customer_service@leisurearts.com *Web Site:* www.leisurearts.com, pg 122

Waldo G Leland Prize, 400 "A" St SE, Washington, DC 20003 *Tel:* 202-544-2422 *Fax:* 202-544-8307 *E-mail:* awards@historians.org *Web Site:* www.historians.org, pg 632

Vincent Lemieux Prize, 260 rue Dalhousie St, Suite 204, Ottawa, ON K1N 7E4, Canada *Tel:* 613-562-1202 *Fax:* 613-241-0019 *E-mail:* cpsa-acsp@cpsa-acsp.ca *Web Site:* www.cpsa-acsp.ca, pg 632

Debra Lemonds, PO Box 5516, Pasadena, CA 91117-0516 *Tel:* 626-844-9363 *E-mail:* dlemonds@zoho.com, pg 466

The Lentz Leadership Institute LLC, 540 Arlington Lane, Grayslake, IL 60030 *Tel:* 702-719-9214 *E-mail:* orders@lentzleadership.com; www.lentzleadership.com; www.refractivethinker.com; www.pensieropress.com; www.narratorepress.com, pg 122

Leopold-Hidy Award, 701 William Vickers Ave, Durham, NC 27701-3162 *Tel:* 919-682-9319 *Fax:* 919-682-2349 *Web Site:* www.foresthistory.org, pg 632

Richard W Leopold Prize, 112 N Bryan Ave, Bloomington, IN 47408-4141 *Tel:* 812-855-7311 *E-mail:* oah@oah.org *Web Site:* www.oah.org/awards, pg 632

Lerner Publications, 241 First Ave N, Minneapolis, MN 55401 *Tel:* 612-332-3344 *Toll Free Tel:* 800-328-4929 *Fax:* 612-332-7615 *Toll Free Fax:* 800-332-1132 *E-mail:* info@lernerbooks.com; custserve@lernerbooks.com *Web Site:* www.lernerbooks.com; www.facebook.com/lernerbooks, pg 122

Lerner Publishing Group Inc, 241 First Ave N, Minneapolis, MN 55401 *Tel:* 612-332-3344 *Toll Free Tel:* 800-328-4929 *Fax:* 612-332-7615 *Toll Free Fax:* 800-332-1132 *E-mail:* info@lernerbooks.com; custserve@lernerbooks.com *Web Site:* www.lernerbooks.com; www.facebook.com/lernerbooks, pg 122

LernerClassroom, 241 First Ave N, Minneapolis, MN 55401 *Tel:* 612-332-3344 *Toll Free Tel:* 800-328-4929 *Fax:* 612-332-7615 *Toll Free Fax:* 800-332-1132 *E-mail:* info@lernerbooks.com; custserve@lernerbooks.com *Web Site:* www.lernerbooks.com; www.facebook.com/lernerbooks, pg 123

Letterbox/Papyrus of London Publishers USA, 10501 Broom Hill Dr, Suite 1-F, Las Vegas, NV 89134-7339 *Tel:* 702-256-3838 *E-mail:* lb27383@cox.net, pg 123

Fenia & Yaakov Leviant Memorial Prize in Yiddish Studies, 85 Broad St, Suite 500, New York, NY 10004-2434 *Tel:* 646-576-5141; 646-576-5000 *Fax:* 646-458-0030 *E-mail:* awards@mla.org *Web Site:* www.mla.org, pg 632

Harry Levin Prize, University of South Carolina, Dept of Languages, Literature & Cultures, 1620 College St, Rm 817, Columbia, SC 29208 *Tel:* 803-777-3021 *E-mail:* info@acla.org *Web Site:* www.acla.org/prize-awards/harry-levin-prize, pg 632

Kay W Levin Award for Short Nonfiction, c/o 210 N Main St, No 204, Cedar Grove, WI 53013 *E-mail:* wiswriters@gmail.com *Web Site:* wiswriters.org/awards, pg 633

Levine|Greenberg|Rostan Literary Agency, 307 Seventh Ave, Suite 2407, New York, NY 10001 *Tel:* 212-337-0934 *Fax:* 212-337-0948 *Web Site:* lgrliterary.com, pg 493

Lawrence W Levine Award, 112 N Bryan Ave, Bloomington, IN 47408-4141 *Tel:* 812-855-7311 *E-mail:* oah@oah.org *Web Site:* www.oah.org/awards, pg 633

Levinson Prize, 61 W Superior St, Chicago, IL 60654 *Tel:* 312-787-7070 *Fax:* 312-787-6650 *E-mail:* editors@poetrymagazine.org *Web Site:* www.poetryfoundation.org, pg 633

Levis Reading Prize, PO Box 842005, Richmond, VA 23284-2005 *Tel:* 804-828-1331 *Fax:* 804-828-8684 *Web Site:* english.vcu.edu/mfa/levis/, pg 633

Levy Creative Management LLC, 425 E 58 St, Suite 37F, New York, NY 10022 *Tel:* 212-687-6463 *Fax:* 212-661-4839 *E-mail:* info@levycreative.com *Web Site:* www.levycreative.com, pg 511

Lewis Memorial Lifetime Achievement Award, 10015 Main St, Fairfax, VA 22031-3489 *Tel:* 703-385-1335 *Toll Free Tel:* 888-385-3588 *Fax:* 703-273-0456 *E-mail:* assist@printing.org; info@printing.org *Web Site:* www.printing.org/programs/awards/lewis-memorial-lifetime-achievement-award, pg 633

Lexington Books, 4501 Forbes Blvd, Suite 200, Lanham, MD 20706 *Tel:* 301-459-3366 *Web Site:* rowman.com/page/lexington, pg 123

LexisNexis®, 230 Park Ave, Suite 7, New York, NY 10169 *Tel:* 212-309-8100 *Toll Free Fax:* 800-437-8674 *Web Site:* www.lexisnexis.com, pg 123

LexisNexis® Canada Inc, 111 Gordon Baker Rd, Suite 900, Toronto, ON M2H 3R1, Canada *Tel:* 905-479-2665 *Toll Free Tel:* 800-668-6481; 800-387-0899 (cust care); 800-255-5174 (sales) *E-mail:* service@lexisnexis.ca (cust serv); sales@lexisnexis.ca *Web Site:* www.lexisnexis.ca, pg 432

LexisNexis® Matthew Bender®, 701 E Water St, Charlottesville, VA 22902 *Tel:* 434-972-7600 *Web Site:* www.lexisnexis.com, pg 123

Liberty Fund Inc, 11301 N Meridian St, Carmel, IN 46032-4564 *Tel:* 317-842-0880 *Toll Free Tel:* 800-955-8335; 800-866-3520 *Fax:* 317-579-6060 (cust serv); 708-534-7803 *E-mail:* books@libertyfund.org; info@libertyfund.org *Web Site:* www.libertyfund.org, pg 123

Liberty Legacy Foundation Award, 112 N Bryan Ave, Bloomington, IN 47408-4141 *Tel:* 812-855-7311 *E-mail:* oah@oah.org *Web Site:* www.oah.org/awards, pg 633

Libraries Unlimited, 147 Castilian Dr, Santa Barbara, CA 93117 *Tel:* 805-968-1911 *Toll Free Tel:* 800-368-6868 *Toll Free Fax:* 888-873-7017 *E-mail:* customerservice@abc-clio.com *Web Site:* www.abc-clio.com, pg 123

Library Association of Alberta (LAA), 80 Baker Crescent NW, Calgary, AB T2L 1R4, Canada *Tel:* 403-284-5818 *Toll Free Tel:* 877-522-5550 *E-mail:* info@laa.ca *Web Site:* www.laa.ca, pg 536

The Library of America, 14 E 60 St, New York, NY 10022-1006 *Tel:* 212-308-3360 *Fax:* 212-750-8352 *E-mail:* info@loa.org *Web Site:* www.loa.org, pg 124

Library of American Broadcasting (LAB), University of Maryland, Hornbake Library, College Park, MD 20742 *Tel:* 301-405-9160 *Web Site:* www.lib.umd.edu/special/collections/massmedia/about-us, pg 536

Library of Congress Literacy Awards, 101 Independence Ave SE, Washington, DC 20540-1400 *Tel:* 202-707-5221 (Center for the Book) *Fax:* 202-707-0269 *Web Site:* www.read.gov/literacyawards, pg 633

Library of Congress Prize for American Fiction, 101 Independence Ave SE, Washington, DC 20540-1400 *Tel:* 202-707-5221 (Center for the Book) *Fax:* 202-707-0269 *Web Site:* www.loc.gov, pg 633

Library of Virginia Literary Awards, 800 E Broad St, Richmond, VA 23219 *Tel:* 804-692-3535 *Web Site:* www.lva.virginia.gov/public/litawards/index.htm, pg 633

Lidec Inc, 800, blvd Industriel, bureau 202, Saint-Jean-sur-Richlieu, QC J3B 8G4, Canada *Tel:* 514-843-5991 *Toll Free Tel:* 800-350-5991 (CN only) *Fax:* 514-843-5252 *E-mail:* lidec@lidec.qc.ca *Web Site:* www.lidec.qc.ca, pg 432

Robert Lieberman Agency, 475 Nelson Rd, Ithaca, NY 14850 *Tel:* 607-273-8801 *Web Site:* www.kewgardensmovie.com/CUPeople/users/rhl10, pg 493

Mary Ann Liebert Inc, 140 Huguenot St, 3rd fl, New Rochelle, NY 10801-5215 *Tel:* 914-740-2100 *Toll Free Fax:* 914-740-2101 *E-mail:* info@liebertpub.com *Web Site:* www.liebertonline.com, pg 124

The Lieutenant-Governor's Awards for High Achievement in the Arts, 225 King St, Suite 201, Fredericton, NB E3B 1E1, Canada *Tel:* 506-444-4444 *Toll Free Tel:* 866-460-ARTS (460-2787) *Fax:* 506-444-5543 *Web Site:* www.artsnb.ca, pg 633

Life Cycle Books, PO Box 799, Fort Collins, CO 80522 *Toll Free Tel:* 800-214-5849 *E-mail:* orders@lifecyclebooks.com *Web Site:* www.lifecyclebooks.com, pg 124

Life Cycle Books Ltd, 11 Progress Ave, Unit 6, Toronto, ON M1P 4S7, Canada *Toll Free Tel:* 866-880-5860 *Toll Free Fax:* 866-260-8172 *E-mail:* orders@lifecyclebooks.ca; billing@lifecyclebooks.ca; support@lifecyclebooks.ca *Web Site:* www.lifecyclebooks.com, pg 432

Light-Beams Publishing, 36 Blandings Way, Biddeford, ME 04005 *Tel:* 603-659-1300 *E-mail:* info@light-beams.com *Web Site:* www.light-beams.com, pg 124

Light Publications, Hope Artiste Village, 1005 Main St, Suite 1212, Pawtucket, RI 02806 *Tel:* 401-484-0228 *E-mail:* info@lightpublications.com *Web Site:* lightpublications.com, pg 124

Light Technology Publishing LLC, 4030 E Huntington Dr, Flagstaff, AZ 86004 *Tel:* 928-526-1345 *Toll Free Tel:* 800-450-0985 *Fax:* 928-714-1132 *E-mail:* publishing@lighttechnology.net *Web Site:* www.lighttechnology.com, pg 124

Lighthouse Publishing of the Carolinas, 2333 Barton Oaks Dr, Raleigh, NC 27614-7940 *E-mail:* lighthousepublishingcarolinas@gmail.com *Web Site:* lpcbooks.com, pg 124

Liguori Publications, One Liguori Dr, Liguori, MO 63057-1000 *Tel:* 636-464-2500 *Toll Free Tel:* 800-325-9521 *Toll Free Fax:* 800-325-9526 (sales) *E-mail:* liguori@liguori.org (sales & cust serv) *Web Site:* www.liguori.org, pg 124

Ruth Lilly & Dorothy Sargent Rosenberg Poetry Fellowships, 61 W Superior St, Chicago, IL 60654 *Tel:* 312-787-7070 *Fax:* 312-787-6650 *E-mail:* info@poetryfoundation.org; media@poetryfoundation.org *Web Site:* www.poetryfoundation.org, pg 633

Ruth Lilly Poetry Prize, 61 W Superior St, Chicago, IL 60654 *Tel:* 312-787-7070 *Fax:* 312-787-6650 *E-mail:* editors@poetrymagazine.org *Web Site:* poetrymagazine.org, pg 633

Limelight Editions, PO Box 1520, Wayne, NJ 07470-1520 *Tel:* 973-987-5363 *Web Site:* limelighteditions.com, pg 124

Abraham Lincoln Institute Book Award, 105 Mount Olive Lane, Ephrata, PA 17522 *E-mail:* secretary@lincoln-institute.org *Web Site:* www.lincoln-institute.org, pg 633

Linden Publishing Co Inc, 2006 S Mary St, Fresno, CA 93721 *Tel:* 559-233-6633 *Toll Free Tel:* 800-345-4447 (orders) *Fax:* 559-233-6933 *Web Site:* lindenpub.com, pg 125

Lindgren & Smith, 888C Eighth Ave, No 329, New York, NY 10019 *Tel:* 212-397-7330 *E-mail:* info@lindgrensmith.com *Web Site:* lindgrensmith.com, pg 511

LinguaText LLC, 103 Walker Way, Newark, DE 19711 *Tel:* 302-453-8695 *E-mail:* text@linguatextbooks.com *Web Site:* www.linguatextbooks.com, pg 125

Linguistic Society of America, 522 21 St NW, Suite 120, Washington, DC 20006-5012 *Tel:* 202-835-1714 *Fax:* 202-835-1717 *E-mail:* lsa@lsadc.org *Web Site:* www.linguisticsociety.org, pg 536

Andrew S Linick PhD, The Copyologist®, Linick Bldg, 7 Putter Lane, Middle Island, NY 11953 *Tel:* 631-924-3888; 631-775-6075 *Fax:* 631-924-8555 *E-mail:* linickgroup@gmail.com *Web Site:* topmarketingadvisor.com, pg 466

Love Creek Annual Short Play Festival, 2144 45 Ave, Long Island City, NY 11101 *Tel:* 646-765-6542 *E-mail:* LCPSubmissions@gmail.com, pg 635

Love Inspired Books, 233 Broadway, Suite 1001, New York, NY 10279 *Tel:* 212-553-4200 *Toll Free Tel:* 888-432-4879 *Fax:* 212-227-8969 *E-mail:* customerservice@harlequin.ca *Web Site:* www. harlequin.com, pg 128

Loving Healing Press Inc, 5145 Pontiac Trail, Ann Arbor, MI 48105 *Tel:* 734-417-4266 *Toll Free Tel:* 888-761-6268 (US & CN) *Fax:* 734-663-6861 *E-mail:* info@lovinghealing.com; info@lhpress. com *Web Site:* www.lovinghealing.com; www. modernhistorypress.com (imprint), pg 128

James Russell Lowell Prize, 85 Broad St, Suite 500, New York, NY 10004-2434 *Tel:* 646-576-5141; 646-576-5000 *Fax:* 646-458-0030 *E-mail:* awards@mla.org *Web Site:* www.mla.org, pg 635

Lowenstein Associates Inc, 115 E 23 St, 4th fl, New York, NY 10010 *Tel:* 212-206-1630 *E-mail:* assistant@bookhaven.com (queries, no attachments) *Web Site:* www.lowensteinassociates.com, pg 493

Pat Lowther Memorial Award, 2 Carlton St, Suite 1519, Toronto, ON M5B 1J3, Canada *Tel:* 416-504-1657 *E-mail:* info@poets.ca *Web Site:* poets.ca, pg 635

Loyola Press, 3441 N Ashland Ave, Chicago, IL 60657 *Tel:* 773-281-1818 *Toll Free Tel:* 800-621-1008 *Fax:* 773-281-0555 (cust serv); 773-281-4129 (edit) *E-mail:* customerservice@loyolapress.com *Web Site:* www.loyolapress.com, pg 128

LPD Press/Rio Grande Books, 925 Salamanca NW, Los Ranchos de Albuquerque, NM 87107-5647 *Tel:* 505-344-9382 *E-mail:* lpdpress@q.com *Web Site:* nmsantos.com, pg 129

LRP Publications, 360 Hiatt Dr, Palm Beach Gardens, FL 33418 *Tel:* 561-622-6520 *Toll Free Tel:* 800-341-7874 *Fax:* 561-622-2423 *E-mail:* custserve@lrp.com *Web Site:* www.lrp.com; www.shoplrp.com, pg 129

LRS, 19146 Van Ness Ave, Torrance, CA 90501 *Tel:* 310-354-2610 *Toll Free Tel:* 800-255-5002 *Fax:* 310-354-2601 *E-mail:* largeprintsb@aol.com *Web Site:* lrs-largeprint.com, pg 129

Lucent Press, 29 E 21 St, New York, NY 10010 *Toll Free Tel:* 800-237-9932 *Toll Free Fax:* 888-436-4643 *Web Site:* rosenpublishing.com, pg 129

Lucky Marble Books, 2671 Bristol Rd, Columbus, OH 43221 *Tel:* 614-264-5588 *E-mail:* sales@ pagespringpublishing.com *Web Site:* www. luckymarblebooks.com, pg 129

Jeremiah Ludington Award, 11 Main St, Suite D, Warrenton, VA 20186 *Tel:* 540-318-7770 *Fax:* 202-962-3939 *E-mail:* info@edupaperback.org *Web Site:* www.edupaperback.org, pg 636

J Anthony Lukas Book Prize, 2950 Broadway, New York, NY 10027 *Tel:* 212-854-6468 *Web Site:* www. journalism.columbia.edu, pg 636

J Anthony Lukas Work-in-Progress Award, 2950 Broadway, New York, NY 10027 *Tel:* 212-854-6468 *Web Site:* www.journalism.columbia.edu, pg 636

Lumina Datamatics Inc, 4 Collins Ave, Plymouth, MA 02360 *Tel:* 508-746-0300 *Fax:* 508-746-3233 *Web Site:* luminadatamatics.com, pg 466

Luna Bisonte Prods, 137 Leland Ave, Columbus, OH 43214 *Tel:* 614-846-4126 *Web Site:* www. johnmbennett.net; www.lulu.com/spotlight/ lunabisonteprods, pg 129

Lush Triumphant Literary Awards, PO Box 3008, MPO, Vancouver, BC V6B 3X5, Canada *Tel:* 604-876-8710 *Fax:* 604-879-2667 *E-mail:* subter@portal.ca *Web Site:* www.subterrain.ca, pg 636

Lutheran Braille Workers Inc, 13471 California St, Yucaipa, CA 92399 *Tel:* 909-795-8977 *Toll Free Tel:* 800-925-6092 *Fax:* 909-795-8970 *E-mail:* lbw@ lbwinc.org *Web Site:* www.lbwinc.org, pg 129

Mark Lynton History Prize, 2950 Broadway, New York, NY 10027 *Tel:* 212-854-6468 *Web Site:* www. journalism.columbia.edu, pg 636

Lynx House Press, 420 W 24 St, Spokane, WA 99203 *Tel:* 509-624-4894 *E-mail:* lynxhousepress@gmail.com *Web Site:* www.lynxhousepress.com, pg 129

Elizabeth Lyon, 1980 Cleveland St, Eugene, OR 97405 *Tel:* 541-357-4181 *E-mail:* elyon123@comcast.net *Web Site:* www.elizabethlyon.com, pg 467

Thomas J Lyon Book Award in Western American Literary and Cultural Studies, PO Box 6815, Logan, UT 84341 *Web Site:* www.westernlit.org/thomas-j-lyon-book-award-in-western-american-literary-and-cultural-studies; www.westernlit.org, pg 636

The Lyons Press, 246 Goose Lane, Guilford, CT 06437 *Tel:* 203-458-4500 *Fax:* 201-458-4601 *E-mail:* info@ rowman.com *Web Site:* rowman.com/page/lyonspress, pg 129

Lyric Poetry Award, 15 Gramercy Park, New York, NY 10003 *Tel:* 212-254-9628 *Web Site:* poetrysociety. org/awards, pg 636

Lyric Poetry Prizes, PO Box 110, Jericho, VT 05465 *Tel:* 802-899-3993 *Fax:* 802-899-3993 *E-mail:* themuse@thelyricmagazine.com *Web Site:* thelyricmagazine.com, pg 636

Donald Maass Literary Agency, 1000 Dean St, Suite 252, Brooklyn, NY 11238 *Tel:* 212-727-8383 *E-mail:* info@maassagency.com *Web Site:* www. maassagency.com, pg 493

MacArthur Fellows Program, Office of Grants Management, 140 S Dearborn St, Chicago, IL 60603-5285 *Tel:* 312-726-8000 *Fax:* 312-920-6528 *E-mail:* 4answers@macfound.org *Web Site:* www. macfound.org/programs/fellows, pg 636

Macavity Award, 7155 Marlborough Terr, Berkeley, CA 94705 *Tel:* 510-845-3600 *Web Site:* www. mysteryreaders.org, pg 636

Gina Maccoby Literary Agency, PO Box 60, Chappaqua, NY 10514-0060 *Tel:* 914-238-5630 *E-mail:* query@ maccobylit.com *Web Site:* www.publishersmarketplace. com/members/GinaMaccoby, pg 494

Sir John A Macdonald Prize, 130 Albert St, Suite 1201, Ottawa, ON K1P 5G4, Canada *Tel:* 613-233-7885 *Fax:* 613-565-5445 *E-mail:* cha-shc@cha-shc.ca *Web Site:* www.cha-shc.ca, pg 636

MacDowell Fellowships, 100 High St, Peterborough, NH 03458 *Tel:* 603-924-3886 *E-mail:* info@macdowell. org; admissions@macdowell.org *Web Site:* www. macdowell.org, pg 637

Machigonne Fiction Contest, PO Box 472, Brunswick, ME 04011 *E-mail:* info@newguardreview. com; editors@writershotel.com *Web Site:* www. newguardreview.com, pg 637

Macmillan, 120 Broadway, 22nd fl, New York, NY 10271 *Tel:* 646-307-5151 *E-mail:* press.inquiries@ macmillan.com *Web Site:* www.macmillan.com, pg 129

Macmillan Audio, 120 Broadway, 22nd fl, New York, NY 10271 *Tel:* 646-307-5151 *Toll Free Tel:* 888-330-8477 (cust serv) *Web Site:* www.macmillanaudio.com, pg 130

Macmillan Booksellers Professional Development Scholarship, 3135 S State St, Suite 203, Ann Arbor, MI 48108 *Toll Free Tel:* 866-733-9064 *Fax:* 734-477-2806 *E-mail:* info@bincfoundation.org *Web Site:* www.bincfoundation.org/scholarship, pg 637

Macmillan Learning, 41 Madison Ave, New York, NY 10010 *Tel:* 212-576-9400 *Fax:* 212-689-2383 *Web Site:* www.macmillanlearning.com, pg 130

Macmillan Reference USA™, 27500 Drake Rd, Farmington Hills, MI 48331-3535 *Tel:* 248-699-4253 *Toll Free Tel:* 800-877-4253 *Toll Free Fax:* 877-363-4253 *E-mail:* gale.customercare@cengage.com *Web Site:* www.gale.cengage.com/macmillan, pg 130

C B MacPherson Prize, 260 rue Dalhousie St, Suite 204, Ottawa, ON K1N 7E4, Canada *Tel:* 613-562-1202 *Fax:* 613-241-0019 *E-mail:* cpsa-acsp@cpsa-acsp.ca *Web Site:* www.cpsa-acsp.ca, pg 637

Madonna House Publications, 2888 Dafoe Rd, Combermere, ON K0J 1L0, Canada *Tel:* 613-756-3728 *Toll Free Tel:* 888-703-7110 *Fax:* 613-756-0103 *Toll Free Fax:* 877-717-2888 *E-mail:* publications@ madonnahouse.org *Web Site:* www.madonnahouse. org/publications, pg 432

Magazine Merit Awards, 6363 Wilshire Blvd, Suite 425, Los Angeles, CA 90048 *Tel:* 323-782-1010; 310-403-0675 (cell) *Fax:* 323-782-1892 *E-mail:* grants@scbwi. org; scbwi@scbwi.org *Web Site:* www.scbwi.org, pg 637

Magazines Canada (MC), 555 Richmond St W, Suite 604, Mailbox 201, Toronto, ON M5V 3B1, Canada *Tel:* 416-504-0274 *Fax:* 416-504-0437 *E-mail:* info@ magazinescanada.ca *Web Site:* magazinescanada.ca, pg 537

Mage Publishers Inc, 4601 N Park Ave, No 1616, Chevy Chase, MD 20815 *Web Site:* www.mage.com, pg 130

The Magni Co, 7106 Wellington Point Rd, McKinney, TX 75070 *Tel:* 972-540-2050 *Fax:* 972-540-1057 *E-mail:* sales@magnico.com; info@magnico.com *Web Site:* www.magnico.com, pg 130

Maharishi University of Management Press, 1000 N Fourth St, Dept 1155, Fairfield, IA 52557-1155 *Tel:* 641-472-1101 *Toll Free Tel:* 800-831-6523 *Fax:* 641-472-1122 *E-mail:* mumpress@mum.edu *Web Site:* www.mumpress.com, pg 130

Mailer Prize, 1841 Broadway, Suite 322, New York, NY 10023 *Tel:* 646-374-3940 *Web Site:* nmcenter.org, pg 637

Maine Literary Awards, Glickman Family Library, 314 Forest Ave, Rm 318, Portland, ME 04101 *Tel:* 207-228-8263 *E-mail:* info@mainewriters.org *Web Site:* mainewriters.org/programs/maine-literary-awards, pg 637

Maine Writers & Publishers Alliance, Glickman Family Library, 314 Forest Ave, Rm 318, Portland, ME 04101 *Tel:* 207-228-8263 *E-mail:* info@mainewriters.org *Web Site:* mainewriters.org, pg 537

Maine Writers Conference at Ocean Park, 14 Temple Ave, Ocean Park, ME 04063 *Tel:* 401-598-1424 *E-mail:* www.opa@oceanpark.org *Web Site:* oceanpark.org, pg 576

Major Achievement Award, c/o 3225 N 91 St, Milwaukee, WI 53222 *E-mail:* wiswriters@gmail.com *Web Site:* wiswriters.org/awards, pg 637

J Russell Major Prize, 400 "A" St SE, Washington, DC 20003 *Tel:* 202-544-2422 *Fax:* 202-544-8307 *E-mail:* awards@historians.org *Web Site:* www. historians.org, pg 637

Malahat Review Long Poem Prize, University of Victoria, Box 1700, Sta CSC, Victoria, BC V8W 2Y2, Canada *Tel:* 250-721-8524 *Fax:* 250-472-5051 *E-mail:* malahat@uvic.ca *Web Site:* www. malahatreview.ca, pg 637

Gene E & Adele R Malott Prize for Recording Community Activism, 2809 Berkeley Dr, Birmingham, AL 35242 *Tel:* 360-809-0465 *E-mail:* langumtrust@ gmail.com *Web Site:* www.langumtrust.org, pg 637

Management Advisory Services & Publications (MASP), PO Box 81151, Wellesley Hills, MA 02481-0001 *Tel:* 781-235-2895 *Fax:* 781-235-5446 *E-mail:* info@ masp.com *Web Site:* www.masp.com, pg 130

Management Sciences for Health, 200 Rivers Edge Dr, Medford, MA 02155 *Tel:* 617-250-9500 *Fax:* 617-250-9090 *E-mail:* bookstore@msh.org *Web Site:* www.msh. org, pg 130

Mandala Earth, 800 "A" St, San Rafael, CA 94901 *Tel:* 415-526-1370 *Toll Free Fax:* 866-509-0515 *E-mail:* info@mandalapublishing.com *Web Site:* www. mandalaeartheditions.com, pg 131

Mandel Vilar Press, 19 Oxford Ct, Simsbury, CT 06070 *Tel:* 806-790-4731 *E-mail:* info@mvpress.org *Web Site:* mvpress.org, pg 131

Manhattanville College Master of Fine Arts in Creative Writing Program, 2900 Purchase St, Purchase, NY 10577 *Tel:* 914-323-5239 *Fax:* 914-323-3122 *Web Site:* www.mville.edu/writing, pg 583

Manic D Press Inc, 250 Banks St, San Francisco, CA 94110-0804 *Tel:* 415-648-8288 *E-mail:* info@manicdpress.com *Web Site:* www.manicdpress.com, pg 131

Manitoba Arts Council, 525-93 Lombard Ave, Winnipeg, MB R3B 3B1, Canada *Tel:* 204-945-2237 *Toll Free Tel:* 866-994-2787 *Fax:* 204-945-5925 *E-mail:* info@artscouncil.mb.ca *Web Site:* artscouncil.mb.ca, pg 537

The Manitoba Writers' Guild Inc, 218-100 Arthur St, Winnipeg, MB R3B 1H3, Canada *Tel:* 204-944-8013 *E-mail:* manitobawritersguild3@gmail.com *Web Site:* www.mbwriter.mb.ca, pg 537

Carol Mann Agency, 55 Fifth Ave, 18th fl, New York, NY 10003 *Tel:* 212-206-5635 *Fax:* 212-675-4809 *E-mail:* submissions@carolmannagency.com *Web Site:* www.carolmannagency.com, pg 494

Margaret Mann Citation, 50 E Huron St, Chicago, IL 60611 *Tel:* 312-280-5037 *Toll Free Tel:* 800-545-2433 *Fax:* 312-280-5033 *E-mail:* alcts@ala.org *Web Site:* www.ala.org/alcts, pg 638

Phyllis Manner, 17 Springdale Rd, New Rochelle, NY 10804 *Tel:* 914-834-4707 *Fax:* 914-834-4707 *E-mail:* pmanner@aol.com; manneredit@gmail.com, pg 467

Manning Publications Co, 20 Baldwin Rd, PO Box 761, Shelter Island, NY 11964 *Tel:* 203-626-1510 *E-mail:* sales@manning.com; support@manning.com (cust serv) *Web Site:* www.manning.com, pg 131

Freya Manston Associates Inc, 145 W 58 St, New York, NY 10019 *Tel:* 212-247-3075, pg 494

ManuscriptCritique.com, PO Box 362, Clay, AL 35048 *Web Site:* www.manuscriptcritique.com, pg 467

Many Voices Fellowships, 2301 Franklin Ave E, Minneapolis, MN 55406-1099 *Tel:* 612-332-7481 *Fax:* 612-332-6037 *E-mail:* info@pwcenter.org *Web Site:* www.pwcenter.org, pg 638

MapEasy Inc, PO Box 80, Wainscott, NY 11975-0080 *Tel:* 631-537-6213 *Fax:* 631-537-4541 *E-mail:* info@mapeasy.com *Web Site:* www.mapeasy.com, pg 131

MAR*CO Products Inc, PO Box 686, Hatfield, PA 19440 *Tel:* 215-956-0313 *Toll Free Tel:* 800-448-2197 *Fax:* 215-956-9041 *E-mail:* help@marcoproducts.com; sales@marcoproducts.com *Web Site:* www.marcoproducts.com, pg 131

Marathon Press, 1500 Square Turn Blvd, Norfolk, NE 68701 *Tel:* 402-371-5040 *Toll Free Tel:* 800-228-0629 *Fax:* 402-371-9382 *E-mail:* info@marathonpress.net *Web Site:* www.marathonpress.com, pg 132

March Tenth Inc, 24 Hillside Terr, Montvale, NJ 07645 *Tel:* 201-387-6551 *Fax:* 201-387-6552 *Web Site:* www.march10th.com, pg 494

Denise Marcil Literary Agency LLC, 483 Westover Rd, Stamford, CT 06902 *Tel:* 203-327-9970 *Fax:* 203-327-9970 *Web Site:* www.marcilofarrellagency.com, pg 494

Danny Marcus Word Worker, 62 Washington St, Suite 2, Marblehead, MA 01945-3553 *Tel:* 781-631-3886; 781-290-9174 (cell) *Fax:* 781-631-3886 *E-mail:* emildanelle@yahoo.com, pg 467

Maren Green Publishing Inc, 5630 Memorial Ave N, Suite 3, Oak Park Heights, MN 55082 *Tel:* 651-439-4500 *Toll Free Tel:* 800-287-1512 *Fax:* 651-439-4532 *E-mail:* info@marengreen.com *Web Site:* www.marengreen.com, pg 132

Marfield Prize, 2017 "I" St NW, Washington, DC 20006-1804 *E-mail:* award@artsclubofwashington.org *Web Site:* artsclubofwashington.org/awards, pg 638

Marian Library Medal, 300 College Park, Dayton, OH 45469-1390 *Tel:* 937-229-4214 *Fax:* 937-229-4258 *Web Site:* campus.udayton.edu/mary/mlmedal.html, pg 638

Marick Press, PO Box 36253, Grosse Pointe Farms, MI 48236 *Tel:* 313-407-9236 *E-mail:* orders@marickpress.com *Web Site:* www.marickpress.com, pg 132

Marine Education Textbooks, 124 N Van Ave, Houma, LA 70363-5895 *Tel:* 985-879-3866 *Fax:* 985-879-3911 *E-mail:* email@marineeducationtextbooks.com *Web Site:* www.marineeducationtextbooks.com, pg 132

Marine Techniques Publishing, 311 W River Rd, Augusta, ME 04330-3991 *Tel:* 207-622-7984 *E-mail:* promariner@roadrunner.com *Web Site:* marinetechpublishing.com; www.groups.yahoo.com/group/marinetechniquespublishing, pg 132

Maritime Electric Short Story Awards, 81 Prince St, Charlottetown, PE C1A 4R3, Canada *E-mail:* peiliteraryawards@gmail.com *Web Site:* www.peiwritersguild.com, pg 638

Markowski International Publishers, One Oakglade Circle, Hummelstown, PA 17036-9525 *Tel:* 717-566-0468 *E-mail:* info@possibilitypress.com *Web Site:* www.possibilitypress.com; www.aeronauticalpublishers.com, pg 132

Mildred Marmur Associates Ltd, 2005 Palmer Ave, PMB 127, Larchmont, NY 10538 *Tel:* 914-834-1170 *Fax:* 914-833-1175 *E-mail:* marmur@westnet.com, pg 494

Marquette University Press, 1415 W Wisconsin Ave, Milwaukee, WI 53233 *Tel:* 414-288-1564 *Fax:* 414-288-7813 *Web Site:* www.marquette.edu/mupress, pg 132

Marquis Who's Who, 100 Connell Dr, Suite 2300, Berkeley Heights, NJ 07922 *Tel:* 908-673-0100 *Toll Free Tel:* 844-394-6946 *Fax:* 908-356-0184 *E-mail:* info@marquisww.com; customerservice@marquisww.com (cust serv, sales) *Web Site:* www.marquiswhoswho.com, pg 132

Morton Marr Poetry Prize, PO Box 750374, Dallas, TX 75275-0374 *Fax:* 214-768-1408 *E-mail:* swr@mail.smu.edu *Web Site:* www.smu.edu/southwestreview, pg 638

Helen & Howard R Marraro Prize in Italian History, 400 "A" St SE, Washington, DC 20003 *Tel:* 202-544-2422 *Fax:* 202-544-8307 *E-mail:* awards@historians.org *Web Site:* www.historians.org, pg 638

Howard R Marraro Prize, 85 Broad St, Suite 500, New York, NY 10004-2434 *Tel:* 646-576-5141; 646-576-5000 *Fax:* 646-458-0030 *E-mail:* awards@mla.org *Web Site:* www.mla.org, pg 638

Marriage Transformation LLC, PO Box 249, Harrison, TN 37341 *Tel:* 423-599-0153 *Web Site:* www.marriagetransformation.com; www.transformationlearningcenter.com, pg 132

Marsal Lyon Literary Agency LLC, 665 San Rodolfo Dr, Suite 124, PMB 121, Solana Beach, CA 92075 *Tel:* 760-814-8507 *Web Site:* www.marsallyonliteraryagency.com, pg 494

Marshall Cavendish Education, 99 White Plains Rd, Tarrytown, NY 10591-9001 *Tel:* 914-332-8888 *Toll Free Tel:* 800-821-9881 *Fax:* 914-332-1082 *E-mail:* mce@marshallcavendish.com; customerservice@marshallcavendish.com *Web Site:* www.mceducation.us, pg 133

The Evan Marshall Agency, One Pacio Ct, Roseland, NJ 07068-1121 *Tel:* 973-287-6216 *Web Site:* www.evanmarshallagency.com, pg 495

Lenore Marshall Poetry Prize, 75 Maiden Lane, Suite 901, New York, NY 10038 *Tel:* 212-274-0343 *E-mail:* awards@poets.org *Web Site:* www.poets.org, pg 638

The Martell Agency, 1350 Avenue of the Americas, Suite 1205, New York, NY 10019 *Tel:* 212-317-2672 *Web Site:* www.themartellagency.com, pg 495

Martin Literary Management, 15601 32 Ave SE, Mill Creek, WA 98012 *Tel:* 206-466-1773 (no phone queries) *Fax:* 206-466-1774 *Web Site:* www.martinliterarymanagement.com, pg 495

Martin-McLean Literary Associates LLC, 5023 W 120 Ave, Suite 228, Broomfield, CO 80020 *Tel:* 303-465-2056 *Fax:* 303-465-2056 *E-mail:* martinmcleanlit@aol.com *Web Site:* www.martinmcleanlit.com, pg 495

Martindale LLC, 121 Chanlon Rd, Suite 110, New Providence, NJ 07974 *Tel:* 908-464-6800; 908-771-7777 (intl) *Toll Free Tel:* 800-526-4902 *Fax:* 908-771-8704 *E-mail:* info@martindale.com *Web Site:* www.martindale.com, pg 133

Martingale®, 19021 120 Ave NE, Suite 102, Bothell, WA 98011 *Tel:* 425-483-3313 *Toll Free Tel:* 800-426-3126 *Fax:* 425-486-7596 *E-mail:* info@martingale-pub.com *Web Site:* www.martingale-pub.com, pg 133

Maryland Historical Society, 201 W Monument St, Baltimore, MD 21201 *Tel:* 410-685-3750 *Fax:* 410-385-2105 *Web Site:* www.mdhs.org, pg 133

Maryland History Press, PO Box 206, Fruitland, MD 21826-0206 *Tel:* 443-397-0912 *E-mail:* ehpatterson@earthlink.net *Web Site:* www.marylandhistorypress.com, pg 133

Mason Crest Publishers, 450 Parkway Dr, Suite D, Broomall, PA 19008 *Tel:* 610-543-6200 *Toll Free Tel:* 866-MCP-BOOK (627-2665) *Fax:* 610-543-3878 *Web Site:* www.masoncrest.com, pg 133

Massachusetts Book Awards, Simons College - GSLIS, 300 The Fenway, Boston, MA 02115 *Tel:* 617-521-2719 *E-mail:* bookawards@massbook.org *Web Site:* www.massbook.org, pg 638

The Massachusetts Historical Society, 1154 Boylston St, Boston, MA 02215-3695 *Tel:* 617-536-1608 *Fax:* 617-859-0074 *E-mail:* publications@masshist.org *Web Site:* www.masshist.org, pg 133

Massachusetts Institute of Technology Libraries, 77 Massachusetts Ave, Bldg 14, Rm 0551, Cambridge, MA 02139-4307 *E-mail:* docs@mit.edu *Web Site:* libraries.mit.edu/docs, pg 133

Master Books®, 3142 Hwy 103 N, Green Forest, AR 72638 *Tel:* 870-438-5288 *Toll Free Tel:* 800-999-3777 *E-mail:* sales@masterbooks.com; nlp@nlpg.com; submissions@newleafpress.net *Web Site:* www.masterbooks.com; www.nlpg.com/imprint/master-books, pg 134

Master Point Press, 214 Merton St, Suite 205, Toronto, ON M4S 1A6, Canada *Tel:* 647-956-4933 *E-mail:* info@masterpointpress.com *Web Site:* www.masterpointpress.com; www.ebooksbridge.com (ebook sales), pg 432

Masters Literary Awards, PO Box 17897, Encino, CA 91416-7897 *Tel:* 818-377-4006 *E-mail:* titan91416@yahoo.com, pg 639

Mastery Education, PO Box 513, Saddle Brook, NJ 07663-0513 *Tel:* 201-712-0090 *Toll Free Tel:* 800-822-1080 *Fax:* 201-712-0045 *E-mail:* cs@masteryeducation.com *Web Site:* masteryeducation.com; www.measuringuplive2.com, pg 134

Materials Research Society, 506 Keystone Dr, Warrendale, PA 15086-7537 *Tel:* 724-779-3003 *Fax:* 724-779-8313 *E-mail:* info@mrs.org *Web Site:* www.mrs.org, pg 134

Math Solutions®, One Harbor Dr, Suite 101, Sausalito, CA 94965 *Toll Free Tel:* 877-234-7323 *Toll Free Fax:* 800-724-4716 *E-mail:* info@mathsolutions.com; orders@mathsolutions.com *Web Site:* www.mathsolutions.com; store.mathsolutions.com, pg 134

Math Teachers Press Inc, 4850 Park Glen Rd, Minneapolis, MN 55416 *Tel:* 952-545-6535 *Toll Free Tel:* 800-852-2435 *Fax:* 952-546-7502 *E-mail:* info@movingwithmath.com *Web Site:* www.movingwithmath.com, pg 134

The Mathematical Association of America, 1529 18 St NW, Washington, DC 20036-1358 *Tel:* 202-387-5200 *Toll Free Tel:* 800-741-9415 *Fax:* 202-265-2384 *E-mail:* maahq@maa.org; advertising@maa.org (pubns) *Web Site:* www.maa.org, pg 134

Amy Mathers Teen Book Award, 40 Orchard View Blvd, Suite 217, Toronto, ON M4R 1B9, Canada *Tel:* 416-975-0010 *Fax:* 416-975-8970 *E-mail:* info@bookcentre.ca *Web Site:* www.bookcentre.ca, pg 639

Mathical Book Prize, 17 Gauss Way, Berkeley, CA 94720 *Tel:* 510-499-5181 *E-mail:* mathical@msri.org *Web Site:* www.mathicalbooks.org, pg 639

Joy Matkowski, 212 Ridge Hill Rd, Mechanicsburg, PA 17050 *Tel:* 717-620-8490 *E-mail:* jmatkowski1@comcast.net, pg 467

Matt Cohen Prize: In Celebration of a Writing Life, 600-460 Richmond St W, Toronto, ON M5V 1Y1, Canada *Tel:* 416-504-8222 *Toll Free Tel:* 877-906-6548 *Fax:* 416-504-9090 *E-mail:* info@writerstrust.com *Web Site:* www.writerstrust.com, pg 639

Mature Women Scholarship Grant - Art/Letters/Music, The Pen Arts Bldg & Arts Museum, 1300 17 St NW, Washington, DC 20036-1973 *Tel:* 202-785-1997 *Fax:* 202-452-8868 *E-mail:* contact@nlapw.org *Web Site:* www.nlapw.org, pg 639

Maven House Press, 4 Snead Ct, Palmyra, VA 22963 *Tel:* 610-883-7988 *E-mail:* info@mavenhousepress.com *Web Site:* mavenhousepress.com, pg 134

Mawenzi House Publishers Ltd, 39 Woburn Ave (B), Toronto, ON M5W 1K5, Canada *Tel:* 416-483-7191 *E-mail:* info@mawenzihouse.com *Web Site:* www.mawenzihouse.com, pg 432

Peter Mayeux, 8148 Regent Dr, Lincoln, NE 68507-3366 *Tel:* 402-466-8547 *E-mail:* pm41923@windstream.net, pg 467

Mazda Publishers Inc, PO Box 2603, Costa Mesa, CA 92628 *Tel:* 714-751-5252 *Fax:* 714-751-4805 *E-mail:* mazdapub@aol.com *Web Site:* www.mazdapublishers.com, pg 134

Maxim Mazumdar New Play Competition, One Curtain Up Alley, Buffalo, NY 14202-1911 *Tel:* 716-852-2600 *E-mail:* publicrelations@alleyway.com *Web Site:* alleyway.com, pg 639

MB Artists, 775 Sixth Ave, Suite 6, New York, NY 10001 *Tel:* 212-689-7830 *Fax:* 212-689-7829 *Web Site:* www.mbartists.com, pg 512

McBooks Press, 246 Goose Lane, Guildord, CT 06357 *Tel:* 203-458-4500 *E-mail:* info@rowman.com *Web Site:* www.mcbooks.com, pg 134

Margret McBride Literary Agency, PO Box 9128, La Jolla, CA 92038 *Tel:* 858-454-1550 *E-mail:* staff@mcbridelit.com *Web Site:* www.mcbrideliterary.com, pg 496

Janet B McCabe Poetry Prize, 1041 N Taft Hill Rd, Fort Collins, CO 80521 *Tel:* 970-449-2726 *E-mail:* editor@ruminatemagazine.org *Web Site:* www.ruminatemagazine.com, pg 639

E J McCarthy Agency, 405 Maple St, Suite H, Mill Valley, CA 94941 *Tel:* 415-383-6639 *E-mail:* ejmagency@gmail.com *Web Site:* www.publishersmarketplace.com/members/ejmccarthy, pg 496

Mary McCarthy Prize in Short Fiction, 822 E Market St, Louisville, KY 40206 *Tel:* 502-458-4028 *E-mail:* info@sarabandebooks.org *Web Site:* www.sarabandebooks.org/mccarthy, pg 639

Gerard McCauley Agency Inc, PO Box 844, Katonah, NY 10536-0844 *Tel:* 914-232-5700, pg 496

Anita D McClellan Associates, 464 Common St, Suite 142, Belmont, MA 02478-2704 *Tel:* 617-575-9203 *E-mail:* adm@anitamcclellan.com *Web Site:* www.anitamcclellan.com, pg 467, 496

McClelland & Stewart Ltd, 320 Front St W, Suite 1400, Toronto, ON M5V 3B6, Canada *Tel:* 416-364-4449 *Fax:* 416-598-7764 *E-mail:* customerservicescanada@penguinrandomhouse.com; publicity@ca.penguingroup.com *Web Site:* penguinrandomhouse.ca/imprints/mcclelland-stewart, pg 432

The McDonald & Woodward Publishing Co, 695 Tall Oaks Dr, Newark, OH 43055 *Tel:* 740-641-2691 *Toll Free Tel:* 800-233-8787 *Fax:* 740-641-2692 *E-mail:* mwpubco@mwpubco.com *Web Site:* www.mwpubco.com, pg 134

McFarland, 960 NC Hwy 88 W, Jefferson, NC 28640 *Tel:* 336-246-4460 *Toll Free Tel:* 800-253-2187 (orders) *Fax:* 336-246-5018; 336-246-4403 (orders) *E-mail:* info@mcfarlandpub.com *Web Site:* mcfarlandbooks.com, pg 135

McGill-Queen's University Press, 1010 Sherbrooke W, Suite 1720, Montreal, QC H3A 2R7, Canada *Tel:* 514-398-3750 *Fax:* 514-398-4333 *E-mail:* mqup@mqup.ca *Web Site:* www.mqup.ca, pg 433

John H McGinnis Memorial Award, PO Box 750374, Dallas, TX 75275-0374 *Fax:* 214-768-1408 *E-mail:* swr@mail.smu.edu *Web Site:* www.smu.edu/southwestreview, pg 639

Harold W McGraw Jr Prize in Education, 2 Penn Plaza, New York, NY 10121-2298 *Tel:* 646-766-2000 *E-mail:* info@mcgrawprize.com *Web Site:* www.mcgrawprize.com, pg 639

McGraw-Hill Career Education, 1333 Burr Ridge Pkwy, Burr Ridge, IL 60527 *Tel:* 630-789-4000 *Toll Free Tel:* 800-338-3987 (cust serv) *Fax:* 630-789-5523; 614-755-5645 (cust serv) *Web Site:* www.mhhe.com, pg 135

McGraw-Hill Contemporary Learning Series, 501 Bell St, Dubuque, IA 52001 *Toll Free Tel:* 800-243-6532 *Web Site:* www.mhcls.com, pg 135

McGraw-Hill Create, 2 Penn Plaza, New York, NY 10121 *Toll Free Tel:* 800-962-9342 *E-mail:* mhhe.create@mheducation.com *Web Site:* create.mheducation.com; shop.mheducation.com, pg 135

McGraw-Hill Education, 2 Penn Plaza, New York, NY 10121-2298 *Tel:* 212-904-2000 *E-mail:* international_cs@mheducation.com; seg_customerservice@mheducation.com (PreK-12); hep_customerservice@mheducation.com (higher education) *Web Site:* www.mheducation.com, pg 135

McGraw-Hill Higher Education, 1333 Burr Ridge Pkwy, Burr Ridge, IL 60527 *Tel:* 630-789-4000 *Toll Free Tel:* 800-338-3987 (cust serv) *Fax:* 614-755-5645 (cust serv) *Web Site:* www.mhhe.com, pg 135

McGraw-Hill Humanities, Social Sciences, Languages, 2 Penn Plaza, 21st fl, New York, NY 10121 *Tel:* 212-904-2000 *Toll Free Tel:* 800-338-3987 (cust serv) *Fax:* 614-755-5645 (cust serv) *Web Site:* www.mhhe.com, pg 136

McGraw-Hill/Irwin, 1333 Burr Ridge Pkwy, Burr Ridge, IL 60527 *Tel:* 630-789-4000 *Toll Free Tel:* 800-338-3987 (cust serv) *Fax:* 630-789-6942; 614-755-5645 (cust serv) *Web Site:* www.mhhe.com, pg 136

McGraw-Hill Professional Publishing Group, 2 Penn Plaza, New York, NY 10121 *Tel:* 646-766-2000 *Web Site:* www.mhprofessional.com; www.mheducation.com, pg 136

McGraw-Hill Ryerson, 300 Water St, Whitby, ON L1N 9B6, Canada *Tel:* 905-430-5000 *Toll Free Tel:* 800-565-5758 (cust serv) *Fax:* 905-430-5020 *Toll Free Fax:* 800-463-5885 *Web Site:* www.mheducation.ca, pg 433

McGraw-Hill School Education Group, 8787 Orion Place, Columbus, OH 43240 *Tel:* 614-430-4000 *Toll Free Tel:* 800-848-1567 *Web Site:* www.mheducation.com, pg 136

McGraw-Hill Science, Engineering, Mathematics, 501 Bell St, Dubuque, IA 52001 *Tel:* 563-584-6000 *Toll Free Tel:* 800-338-3987 (cust serv) *Fax:* 614-755-5645 (cust serv) *Web Site:* www.mhhe.com, pg 136

William Holmes McGuffey Longevity Award, PO Box 367, Fountain City, WI 54629 *E-mail:* info@taaonline.net *Web Site:* www.taaonline.net/mcguffey-longevity-award, pg 639

McHugh's Rights/Permissions Workshop™, PO Box 170665, Milwaukee, WI 53217-8056 *Tel:* 414-351-3056 *E-mail:* jack@johnbmchugh.com *Web Site:* www.johnbmchugh.com, pg 576

McIntosh and Otis Inc, 207 E 37 St, Suite BG, New York, NY 10016 *Tel:* 212-687-7400 *Fax:* 212-687-6894 *E-mail:* info@mcintoshandotis.com *Web Site:* www.mcintoshandotis.com, pg 496

McKnight Artist Fellowship for Writers, Open Book, Suite 200, 1011 Washington Ave S, Minneapolis, MN 55415 *Tel:* 612-215-2575 *Fax:* 612-215-2576 *E-mail:* loft@loft.org *Web Site:* www.loft.org, pg 640

McKnight Fellowships in Playwriting, 2301 Franklin Ave E, Minneapolis, MN 55406-1099 *Tel:* 612-332-7481 *Fax:* 612-332-6037 *E-mail:* info@pwcenter.org *Web Site:* www.pwcenter.org, pg 640

McKnight National Residency & Commission, 2301 Franklin Ave E, Minneapolis, MN 55406-1099 *Tel:* 612-332-7481 *Fax:* 612-332-6037 *E-mail:* info@pwcenter.org *Web Site:* www.pwcenter.org, pg 640

Pamela Dittmer McKuen, 87 Tanglewood Dr, Glen Ellyn, IL 60137 *Tel:* 630-545-0867 *E-mail:* pmckuen@gmail.com *Web Site:* www.pamelamckuen.com; www.allthewriteplaces.com, pg 467

McLaren Memorial Comedy Play Writing Competition, 2000 W Wadley Ave, Midland, TX 79705 *Tel:* 432-682-2544 *E-mail:* tracy@mctmidland.org *Web Site:* www.mctmidland.org, pg 640

McLemore Prize, William F Winter Archives & History Bldg, 200 North St, Jackson, MS 39201 *Tel:* 601-576-6850 *Fax:* 601-576-6975 *E-mail:* mhs@mdah.ms.gov *Web Site:* www.mdah.ms.gov, pg 640

Phillip H McMath Post Publication Book Award, Dept of Writing, University of Central Arkansas, 201 Donaghey Ave, Thompson Hall 303, Conway, AR 72035 *Web Site:* arkansaswriters.wordpress.com, pg 640

John McMenemy Prize, 260 rue Dalhousie St, Suite 204, Ottawa, ON K1N 7E4, Canada *Tel:* 613-562-1202 *Fax:* 613-241-0019 *E-mail:* cpsa@cpsa-acsp.ca *Web Site:* www.cpsa-acsp.ca, pg 640

Sally Hill McMillan LLC, 429 E Kingston Ave, Charlotte, NC 28203 *Tel:* 704-334-0897 *E-mail:* mcmagency@aol.com, pg 496

Pat McNees, 10643 Weymouth St, Suite 204, Bethesda, MD 20814 *Tel:* 301-897-8557 *E-mail:* patmcnees@gmail.com *Web Site:* www.patmcnees.com; www.writersandeditors.com, pg 467

McNeese State University, Writing Program, PO Box 92655, Lake Charles, LA 70609-0001 *Tel:* 337-475-5325; 337-475-5327 *Web Site:* www.mcneese.edu.com; www.mfa.mcneese.edu, pg 583

McPherson & Co, 148 Smith Ave, Kingston, NY 12401 *Tel:* 845-331-5807 *E-mail:* bmcphersonco@gmail.com *Web Site:* www.mcphersonco.com, pg 136

McSweeney's Publishing, 849 Valencia St, San Francisco, CA 94110 *Tel:* 415-642-5609 (cust serv) *E-mail:* custserv@mcsweeneys.net *Web Site:* www.mcsweeneys.net, pg 136

MC2 Solutions LLC, 5101 Violet Lane, Madison, WI 53714 *Tel:* 608-240-4959, pg 467

MDR, A D&B Co, 6 Armstrong Rd, Suite 301, Shelton, CT 06484 *Tel:* 203-926-4800 *Toll Free Tel:* 800-333-8802 *Fax:* 203-225-4603 *Toll Free Fax:* 866-532-7097 *E-mail:* mdrinfo@dnb.com *Web Site:* mdreducation.com, pg 136

me+mi publishing inc, 2600 Beverly Dr, Unit 113, Aurora, IL 60502 *Tel:* 630-588-9801 *Toll Free Tel:* 888-251-1444 *Web Site:* www.memima.com, pg 137

R S Means from The Gordian Group, 1099 Hingham St, Suite 201, Rockland, MA 02370 *Toll Free Tel:* 800-448-8182 (cust serv); 800-334-3509 (sales) *Toll Free Fax:* 800-632-6732 *Web Site:* www.rsmeans.com, pg 137

Medal for Distinguished Contribution to American Letters, 90 Broad St, Suite 604, New York, NY 10004 *Tel:* 212-685-0261 *Fax:* 212-213-6570 *E-mail:* nationalbook@nationalbook.org *Web Site:* www.nationalbook.org/amerletters.html, pg 640

Medal of Honor for Literature, 15 Gramercy Park S, New York, NY 10003 *Tel:* 212-475-3424 *E-mail:* literary@thenationalartsclub.org *Web Site:* www.nationalartsclub.org, pg 640

Medals of America Press, 114 Southchase Blvd, Fountain Inn, SC 29644 *Toll Free Tel:* 800-605-4001 *Toll Free Fax:* 800-407-8640 *Web Site:* moapress.com, pg 137

MedBooks Inc, PO Box 12805, Dallas, TX 75225 *Tel:* 972-643-1809; 972-643-1802 *Fax:* 972-643-1859 *E-mail:* medbooks@medbooks.com; customerservice@ medbooks.com; sales@medbooks.com *Web Site:* www. medbooks.com, pg 137

Media Alliance, 2830 20 St, Suite 102, San Francisco, CA 94110 *Tel:* 415-746-9475 *E-mail:* information@ media-alliance.org *Web Site:* www.media-alliance.org, pg 537

Media Coalition Inc, 19 Fulton St, Suite 407, New York, NY 10038 *Tel:* 212-587-4025 *E-mail:* info@ mediacoalition.org *Web Site:* mediacoalition.org, pg 537

Medical Group Management Association (MGMA), 104 Inverness Terr E, Englewood, CO 80112-5306 *Tel:* 303-799-1111; 303-799-1111 (ext 1888, book orders) *Toll Free Tel:* 877-275-6462 *E-mail:* support@ mgma.com; infocenter@mgma.com *Web Site:* www. mgma.com, pg 137

Medical Physics Publishing Corp (MPP), 4555 Helgesen Dr, Madison, WI 53718 *Tel:* 608-262-4021; 608-224-4508 *Toll Free Tel:* 800-442-5778 (cust serv) *Fax:* 608-224-5016 *E-mail:* mpp@medicalphysics.org *Web Site:* www.medicalphysics.org, pg 137

Medieval Institute Publications, WMU East Campus, 100-E Walwood Hall, Kalamazoo, MI 49008 *Tel:* 269-387-8754 *Fax:* 269-387-8750 *Web Site:* www.wmich. edu/medievalpublications, pg 137

MedMaster Inc, 3337 Hollywood Oaks Dr, Fort Lauderdale, FL 33312 *Tel:* 954-962-8414 *Toll Free Tel:* 800-335-3480 *Fax:* 954-962-4508 *E-mail:* mmbks@aol.com *Web Site:* www.medmaster. net, pg 137

Lucille Medwick Memorial Award, 15 Gramercy Park, New York, NY 10003 *Tel:* 212-254-9628 *Web Site:* poetrysociety.org/awards, pg 640

Mel Bay Publications Inc, 1734 Gilsinn Lane, Fenton, MO 63026 *Tel:* 636-257-3970 *Toll Free Tel:* 800-863-5229 *Fax:* 636-257-5062 *Toll Free Fax:* 800-660-9818 *E-mail:* email@melbay.com *Web Site:* www.melbay. com, pg 137

Frederic G Melcher Scholarship, 50 E Huron St, Chicago, IL 60611-2795 *Tel:* 312-280-2163 *Toll Free Tel:* 800-545-2433 *Fax:* 312-440-9374; 312-280-5271 *E-mail:* alsc@ala.org *Web Site:* www.ala.org/alsc, pg 641

Melissa Turk & the Artist Network, 9 Babbling Brook Lane, Suffern, NY 10901 *Tel:* 845-368-8606 *E-mail:* melissa@melissaturk.com *Web Site:* www. melissaturk.com, pg 512

The Edwin Mellen Press, 240 Portage Rd, Lewiston, NY 14092 *Tel:* 716-754-2266; 716-754-2788 (order fulfillment) *Fax:* 716-754-4056 *E-mail:* editor@ mellenpress.com *Web Site:* www.mellenpress.com, pg 137

Tom Mellers Publishing Services (TMPS), 60 Second Ave, Suite 8, New York, NY 10003 *Tel:* 212-254-4958 *E-mail:* tmps71@yahoo.com, pg 467

The Melville Society, Johns Hopkins University Press, PO Box 19966, Baltimore, MD 21211-0966 *Web Site:* melvillesociety.org, pg 537

Menasha Ridge Press, 2204 First Ave S, Suite 102, Birmingham, AL 35233 *Toll Free Tel:* 888-604-4537 *Fax:* 205-326-1012 *E-mail:* info@adventurewithkeen. com *Web Site:* www.menasharidge.com; www. adventurewithkeen.com, pg 138

Fred C Mench Professor of Classics Emeritus, 207 Saint Martins Lane, Smyrna, TN 37167 *Tel:* 615-459-0765 *E-mail:* fmench@earthlink.net, pg 468

Mendel Media Group LLC, 115 W 30 St, Suite 209, New York, NY 10001 *Tel:* 646-239-9896 *Web Site:* www.mendelmedia.com, pg 496

MennoMedia, 100 S Mason St, Suite B, Harrisonburg, VA 22801 *Toll Free Tel:* 800-245-7894 (orders & cust serv US) *Toll Free Fax:* 877-271-0760 *E-mail:* info@ mennomedia.org *Web Site:* www.mennomedia.org, pg 138

Mercer University Press, 368 Orange St, Macon, GA 31201 *Tel:* 478-301-2880 *Toll Free Tel:* 866-895-1472 *Fax:* 478-301-2585 *E-mail:* mupressorders@mercer. edu *Web Site:* www.mupress.org, pg 138

Scott Meredith Literary Agency LP, 125 Park Ave, 25th fl, New York, NY 10017 *Tel:* 646-218-9240 *Fax:* 212-977-5997 *E-mail:* info@scottmeredith.com *Web Site:* www.scottmeredith.com, pg 496

Louise Meriwether First Book Prize, 365 Fifth Ave, Suite 5406, New York, NY 10016 *Tel:* 212-817-7915 *E-mail:* louisemeriwetherprize@gmail.com; info@feministpress.org *Web Site:* www.feministpress. org/louise-meriwether-first-book-prize, pg 641

Meriwether Publishing, c/o Pioneer Drama Service, 9707-A E Easter Lane, Englewood, CO 80112 *Tel:* 303-779-4035 *Toll Free Tel:* 800-333-7262 *Fax:* 303-779-4315 *E-mail:* books@pioneerdrama.com *Web Site:* www.pioneerdrama.com, pg 138

Merriam Press, 489 South St, Hoosick Falls, NY 12090 *Tel:* 518-949-0882 *E-mail:* merriampress@gmail.com *Web Site:* www.merriam-press.com, pg 138

Merriam-Webster Inc, 47 Federal St, Springfield, MA 01102 *Tel:* 413-734-3134 *Toll Free Tel:* 800-828-1880 (orders & cust serv) *Fax:* 413-731-5979 (sales) *E-mail:* support@merriam-webster.com *Web Site:* www.merriam-webster.com, pg 138

Mesorah Publications Ltd, 4401 Second Ave, Brooklyn, NY 11232 *Tel:* 718-921-9000 *Toll Free Tel:* 800-637-6724 *Fax:* 718-680-1875 *E-mail:* info@artscroll.com; orders@artscroll.com *Web Site:* www.artscroll.com, pg 138

Messianic Jewish Publishers, 6120 Day Long Lane, Clarksville, MD 21029 *Tel:* 410-531-6644; 616-970-2449 *Toll Free Tel:* 800-410-7367 (orders) *Fax:* 410-531-9440; 717-761-7273 (orders) *Toll Free Fax:* 800-327-0048 (orders) *E-mail:* editor@messianicjewish. net; customerservice@messianicjewish.net *Web Site:* messianicjewish.net/publish, pg 138

Metamorphosis Literary Agency, 12837 S Seminole Dr, Olathe, KS 66062 *Tel:* 646-397-1640 *E-mail:* info@ metamorphosisliteraryagency.com *Web Site:* www. metamorphosisliteraryagency.com, pg 497

Addison M Metcalf Award in Literature, 633 W 155 St, New York, NY 10032 *Tel:* 212-368-5900 *Fax:* 212-491-4615 *E-mail:* academy@artsandletters.org *Web Site:* artsandletters.org, pg 641

Metropolitan Classics, 26 Arthur Place, Yonkers, NY 10701 *Tel:* 914-375-6448 *Web Site:* www.fortrossinc. com, pg 138

Metropolitan Editorial & Writing Service, 4455 Douglas Ave, Riverdale, NY 10471 *Tel:* 718-549-5518, pg 468

The Metropolitan Museum of Art, 1000 Fifth Ave, New York, NY 10028 *Tel:* 212-535-7710 *E-mail:* editorial@metmuseum.org *Web Site:* www. metmuseum.org, pg 139

Edna Meudt Poetry Book Award, c/o 210 N Main St, No 204, Cedar Grove, WI 53013 *E-mail:* wiswriters@ gmail.com *Web Site:* wiswriters.org/awards, pg 641

The David Nathan Meyerson Prize for Fiction, PO Box 750374, Dallas, TX 75275-0374 *Fax:* 214-768-1408 *E-mail:* swr@mail.smu.edu *Web Site:* www.smu. edu/southwestreview, pg 641

MFA Publications, 465 Huntington Ave, Boston, MA 02115 *Tel:* 617-369-4233 *E-mail:* publications@mfa. org *Web Site:* www.mfa.org/publications, pg 139

Michelin Maps & Guides, One Parkway S, Greenville, SC 29615-5022 *E-mail:* michelin.guides@michelin. com *Web Site:* guide.michelin.com; michelinmedia. com, pg 139

Michigan Library Association (MLA), 3410 Belle Chase Way, Lansing, MI 48911 *Tel:* 517-394-2774 *E-mail:* mla@milibraries.org *Web Site:* www. milibraries.org, pg 537

Michigan Municipal League, 1675 Green Rd, Ann Arbor, MI 48105 *Tel:* 734-662-3246 *Toll Free Tel:* 800-653-2483 *E-mail:* contact@mml.org *Web Site:* www.mml.org, pg 139

Michigan State University Press (MSU Press), Manly Miles Bldg, Suite 25, 1405 S Harrison Rd, East Lansing, MI 48823-5245 *Tel:* 517-355-9543 *Fax:* 517-432-2611 *Web Site:* msupress.org, pg 139

Susan T Middleton, 366A Norton Hill Rd, Ashfield, MA 01330-9601 *Tel:* 413-628-4039 *E-mail:* smiddle@ crocker.com, pg 468

Midnight Marquee Press Inc, 9721 Britinay Lane, Baltimore, MD 21234 *Tel:* 410-665-1198 *E-mail:* mmarquee@aol.com *Web Site:* www.midmar. com, pg 139

Midwest Bookseller of the Year Award, 1375 St Anthony Ave, Suite 202-3, St Paul, MN 55104 *Tel:* 612-208-6279 *Toll Free Fax:* 844-273-4119 *E-mail:* info@midwestbooksellers.org *Web Site:* www. midwestbooksellers.org/bookseller-of-the-year.html, pg 641

Midwest Independent Booksellers Association (MIBA), 1375 St Anthony Ave, Suite 202-3, St Paul, MN 55104 *Tel:* 612-208-6279 *Toll Free Tel:* 844-273-4119 *E-mail:* info@midwestbooksellers.org *Web Site:* www. midwestbooksellers.org, pg 537

Midwest Travel Journalists Inc, 902 S Randall Rd, Suite C311, St Charles, IL 60174 *Toll Free Tel:* 888-551-8184 *Fax:* 847-622-8015 *E-mail:* admin@mtja.us *Web Site:* www.mtja.us, pg 537

Mighty Media Press, 1201 Currie Ave, Minneapolis, MN 55403 *Tel:* 612-455-0252; 612-399-1969 *Fax:* 612-338-4817 *E-mail:* info@mightymedia.com *Web Site:* www.mightymediapress.com, pg 139

Mike Murach & Associates Inc, 4340 N Knoll Ave, Fresno, CA 93722 *Tel:* 559-440-9071 *Toll Free Tel:* 800-221-5528 *Fax:* 559-440-0963 *E-mail:* murachbooks@murach.com *Web Site:* www. murach.com, pg 139

Milady, Executive Woods, 5 Maxwell Dr, Clifton Park, NY 12065-2919 *Tel:* 518-348-2300 *Toll Free Tel:* 800-998-7498 *Fax:* 518-373-6309 *E-mail:* info@milady. com *Web Site:* milady.cengage.com, pg 139

Kenneth W Mildenberger Prize, 85 Broad St, Suite 500, New York, NY 10004-2434 *Tel:* 646-576-5141; 646-576-5000 *Fax:* 646-458-0030 *E-mail:* awards@mla.org *Web Site:* www.mla.org, pg 641

Military Info Publishing, PO Box 41211, Plymouth, MN 55442 *Tel:* 763-533-8627 *E-mail:* publisher@military-info.com *Web Site:* www.military-info.com, pg 140

Military Living Publications, 333 Maple Ave E, Suite 3130, Vienna, VA 22180-4717 *Tel:* 703-237-0203 *Fax:* 703-552-8855 *E-mail:* customerservice@ militaryliving.com; sales@militaryliving.com; editor@ militaryliving.com *Web Site:* www.militaryliving.com, pg 140

Milkweed Editions, 1011 Washington Ave S, Suite 300, Minneapolis, MN 55415-1246 *Tel:* 612-332-3192 *Toll Free Tel:* 800-520-6455 *Fax:* 612-215-2550 *Web Site:* milkweed.org, pg 140

Milkweed Fellowship, 1011 Washington Ave S, Suite 300, Minneapolis, MN 55415-1246 *Tel:* 612-332-3192 *Toll Free Tel:* 800-520-6455 *E-mail:* fellowship@ milkweed.org *Web Site:* milkweed.org/milkweed-fellowship, pg 641

Milkweed National Fiction Prize, 1011 Washington Ave S, Suite 300, Minneapolis, MN 55415-1246 *Tel:* 612-332-3192 *Toll Free Tel:* 800-520-6455 *Fax:* 612-215-2550 *E-mail:* submissions@milkweed. org *Web Site:* www.milkweed.org, pg 641

Millbrook Press, 241 First Ave N, Minneapolis, MN 55401 *Tel:* 612-332-3344 *Toll Free Tel:* 800-328-4929 *Fax:* 612-332-7615 *Toll Free Fax:* 800-332-1132 *E-mail:* info@lernerbooks.com; custserve@ lernerbooks.com *Web Site:* www.lernerbooks.com; www.facebook.com/millbrookpress, pg 140

The Miller Agency Inc, 630 Ninth Ave, Suite 1102, New York, NY 10036 *Tel:* 212-206-0913 *Fax:* 212-206-1473, pg 497

Richard K Miller Associates, 2413 Main St, Suite 331, Miramar, FL 33025 *Toll Free Tel:* 888-928-RKMA (928-7562) *Toll Free Fax:* 877-928-7562 *Web Site:* rkma.com, pg 140

Stephen M Miller Inc, 15727 S Madison Dr, Olathe, KS 66062 *Tel:* 913-768-7997 *Web Site:* www.stephenmillerbooks.com, pg 468

Milliken Publishing Co, 501 E Third St, Dayton, OH 45402 *Tel:* 937-228-6118 *Toll Free Tel:* 800-444-1144 *Fax:* 937-223-2042 *E-mail:* order@lorenz.com *Web Site:* www.lorenzeducationalpress.com, pg 140

Kathleen Mills Editorial Services, 327 E King St, Chardon, OH 44024 *Tel:* 440-285-4347 *E-mail:* mills_edit@yahoo.com, pg 468

Milner Award, One Margaret Mitchell Sq NW, Atlanta, GA 30303 *Tel:* 404-730-1865 *E-mail:* info@themilneraward.org *Web Site:* www.themilneraward.org, pg 641

The Minerals, Metals & Materials Society (TMS), 5700 Corporate Dr, Suite 750, Pittsburgh, PA 15237 *Tel:* 724-776-9000 *Toll Free Tel:* 800-759-4867 *Fax:* 724-776-3770 *E-mail:* publications@tms.org (orders) *Web Site:* www.tms.org/bookstore (orders); www.tms.org, pg 140

Miniature Book Society Inc, 702 Rosecrans St, San Diego, CA 92106-3013 *Tel:* 619-226-4441 *Fax:* 619-226-4441 *E-mail:* minibook@cox.net *Web Site:* www.mbs.org, pg 538

Minnesota Book Awards, 1080 Montreal Ave, Suite 2, St Paul, MN 55116 *Tel:* 651-222-3242 *Fax:* 651-222-1988 *E-mail:* friends@thefriends.org *Web Site:* thefriends.org/events/mnba, pg 641

Minnesota Historical Society Press, 345 Kellogg Blvd W, St Paul, MN 55102-1906 *Tel:* 651-259-3205 *Fax:* 651-297-1345 *E-mail:* info-mnhspress@mnhs.org *Web Site:* www.mnhs.org/mnhspress, pg 140

Minotaur Books/Mystery Writers of America First Crime Novel Competition, 1140 Broadway, Suite 1507, New York, NY 10001 *Tel:* 212-888-8171 *Fax:* 212-888-8107 *E-mail:* mb-mwafirstcrimenovelcompetition@stmartins.com *Web Site:* mysterywriters.org/about-mwa/st-martins; us.macmillan.com/minotaurbooks/submit-manuscript, pg 642

Mississippi Review Prize, 118 College Dr, Box 5144, Hattiesburg, MS 39406-0001 *E-mail:* msreview@usm.edu *Web Site:* www.usm.edu/mississippi-review/contest.html, pg 642

Mississippi Review/University of Southern Mississippi, Center for Writers, 118 College Dr 5144, Hattiesburg, MS 39406-0001 *Tel:* 601-266-1000 *Web Site:* www.usm.edu/humanities/center-writers.php; sites.usm.edu/mississippi-review/index.html, pg 583

MIT List Visual Arts Center, MIT E 15-109, 20 Ames St, Cambridge, MA 02139 *Tel:* 617-253-4400; 617-253-4680 *E-mail:* listinfo@mit.edu *Web Site:* listart.mit.edu, pg 141

The MIT Press, One Rogers St, Cambridge, MA 02142 *Tel:* 617-253-5255 *Toll Free Tel:* 800-405-1619 (orders) *Fax:* 617-258-6779; 617-577-1545 (orders) *Web Site:* mitpress.mit.edu, pg 141

Mitchell Lane Publishers Inc, 2001 SW 31 Ave, Hallandale, FL 33009 *Tel:* 954-985-9400 *Toll Free Tel:* 800-223-3251 *Fax:* 954-987-2200 *E-mail:* customerservice@mitchelllane.com *Web Site:* www.mitchelllane.com, pg 141

MLA Prize for a Bibliography, Archive or Digital Project, 85 Broad St, Suite 500, New York, NY 10004-2434 *Tel:* 646-576-5141; 646-576-5000 *Fax:* 646-458-0030 *E-mail:* awards@mla.org *Web Site:* www.mla.org, pg 642

MLA Prize for a First Book, 85 Broad St, Suite 500, New York, NY 10004-2434 *Tel:* 646-576-5141; 646-576-5000 *Fax:* 646-458-0030 *E-mail:* awards@mla.org *Web Site:* www.mla.org, pg 642

MLA Prize for a Scholarly Edition, 85 Broad St, Suite 500, New York, NY 10004-2434 *Tel:* 646-576-5141; 646-576-5000 *Fax:* 646-458-0030 *E-mail:* awards@mla.org *Web Site:* www.mla.org, pg 642

MLA Prize for Independent Scholars, 85 Broad St, Suite 500, New York, NY 10004-2434 *Tel:* 646-576-5141; 646-576-5000 *Fax:* 646-458-0030 *E-mail:* awards@mla.org *Web Site:* www.mla.org, pg 642

MLA Prize for Studies in Native American Literatures, Cultures & Languages, 85 Broad St, Suite 500, New York, NY 10004-2434 *Tel:* 646-576-5141; 646-576-5000 *Fax:* 646-458-0030 *E-mail:* awards@mla.org *Web Site:* www.mla.org, pg 642

MLA Prize in United States Latina & Latino & Chicana & Chicano Literary & Cultural Studies, 85 Broad St, Suite 500, New York, NY 10004-2434 *Tel:* 646-576-5141; 646-576-5000 *Fax:* 646-458-0030 *E-mail:* awards@mla.org *Web Site:* www.mla.org, pg 642

Sondra Mochson, 18 Overlook Dr, Port Washington, NY 11050 *Tel:* 516-883-0961, pg 468

Modern Language Association of America (MLA), 85 Broad St, Suite 500, New York, NY 10004-2434 *Tel:* 646-576-5000 *Fax:* 646-458-0030 *Web Site:* www.mla.org, pg 141

Modern Language Association of America (MLA), 85 Broad St, Suite 500, New York, NY 10004-2434 *Tel:* 646-576-5000 *Fax:* 646-458-0030 *E-mail:* convention@mla.org *Web Site:* www.mla.org, pg 538

Modern Memoirs, 34 Main St, No 6, Amherst, MA 01002-2367 *Tel:* 413-253-2353 *Web Site:* www.modernmemoirs.com; www.whitepoppypress.com, pg 141

Modern Publishing, 6198 Butler Pike, Suite 200, Blue Bell, PA 19422 *Tel:* 215-643-6385 *Fax:* 215-628-3571 *Web Site:* kappabooks.com, pg 141

Modus Vivendi Publishing Inc, 55, rue Jean-Talon Ouest, Montreal, QC H2R-2W8, Canada *Tel:* 514-272-0433 *Fax:* 514-272-7234 *E-mail:* info@groupemodus.com *Web Site:* www.groupemodus.com, pg 433

The Monacelli Press, 65 Bleecker St, 8th fl, New York, NY 10012 *Tel:* 212-229-9925 *E-mail:* contact@monacellipress.com *Web Site:* www.monacellipress.com, pg 141

Mondial, 203 W 107 St, Suite 6-C, New York, NY 10025 *Tel:* 646-807-8031 *Fax:* 208-361-2863 *E-mail:* contact@mondialbooks.com *Web Site:* www.mondialbooks.com, pg 142

Mondo Publishing, 980 Avenue of the Americas, New York, NY 10018 *Tel:* 212-268-3560 *Toll Free Tel:* 888-88-MONDO (886-6636) *Toll Free Fax:* 888-532-4492 *E-mail:* info@mondopub.com *Web Site:* www.mondopub.com, pg 142

The Mongolia Society Inc, Indiana University, 703 Eigenmann Hall, 1900 E Tenth St, Bloomington, IN 47406-7512 *Tel:* 812-855-4078 *Fax:* 812-855-4078 *E-mail:* monsoc@indiana.edu *Web Site:* mongoliasociety.org, pg 142

Monkfish Book Publishing Co, 22 E Market St, Suite 304, Rhinebeck, NY 12572 *Tel:* 845-876-4861 *E-mail:* monkfish@monkfishpublishing.com *Web Site:* www.monkfishpublishing.com, pg 142

Montemayor Press, 663 Hyland Hill Rd, Washington, VT 05675 *Tel:* 802-552-0750 *E-mail:* mail@montemayorpress.com *Web Site:* www.montemayorpress.com, pg 142

David Montgomery Award, 112 N Bryan Ave, Bloomington, IN 47408-4141 *Tel:* 812-855-7311 *E-mail:* oah@oah.org *Web Site:* www.oah.org/awards, pg 642

Lucy Maud Montgomery PEI Literature for Children Awards, 81 Prince St, Charlottetown, PE C1A 4R3, Canada *E-mail:* peiliteraryawards@gmail.com *Web Site:* www.peiwritersguild.com, pg 642

Monthly Review Press, 134 W 29 St, Suite 706, New York, NY 10001 *Tel:* 212-691-2555 *E-mail:* mreview@igc.org *Web Site:* monthlyreview.org, pg 142

Montreal-Contacts/The Rights Agency, 1350 Sherbrooke St E, Suite 1, Montreal, QC H2L 1M4, Canada *Tel:* 514-400-7075 *Fax:* 514-400-1045 *Web Site:* www.montreal-contacts.com/?lang=en, pg 497

Moody Publishers, 820 N La Salle Blvd, Chicago, IL 60610 *Tel:* 312-329-2101 *Toll Free Tel:* 800-678-8812 *Fax:* 312-329-2144 *Toll Free Fax:* 800-678-3329 *E-mail:* mpcustomerservice@moody.edu; mporders@moody.edu; publicity@moody.edu *Web Site:* www.moodypublishers.com, pg 142

Cenie H Moon Prize, 900 Timber Creek Place, Virginia Beach, VA 23464 *E-mail:* poetryinva@aol.com *Web Site:* poetrysocietyofvirginia.org, pg 643

Moonbeam Children's Book Awards, 1129 Woodmere Ave, Suite B, Traverse City, MI 49686 *Tel:* 231-933-0445 *Toll Free Tel:* 800-706-4636 *Fax:* 231-933-0448 *E-mail:* info@moonbeamawards.com *Web Site:* www.moonbeamawards.com, pg 643

Moonshine Cove Publishing LLC, 150 Willow Point, Abbeville, SC 29620 *E-mail:* publisher@moonshinecovepublishing.com *Web Site:* moonshinecovepublishing.com, pg 142

Moonstone Press LLC, 4816 Carrington Circle, Sarasota, FL 34243 *Tel:* 301-765-1081 *Fax:* 301-765-0510 *E-mail:* mazeprod@erols.com *Web Site:* www.moonstonepress.net, pg 447

Jenny McKean Moore Writer-in-Washington, English Dept, Rome Hall, 801 22 St NW, Suite 643, Washington, DC 20052 *Tel:* 202-994-6180 *E-mail:* engldept@gwu.edu *Web Site:* english.columbian.gwu.edu, pg 643

Moose Hide Books, 684 Walls Rd, Prince Township, ON P6A 6K4, Canada *Tel:* 705-779-3331 *Fax:* 705-779-3331 *E-mail:* mooseenterprises@on.aibn.com *Web Site:* www.moosehidebooks.com, pg 433

Morehouse Publishing, 19 E 34 St, New York, NY 10016 *Tel:* 212-592-1800 *Toll Free Tel:* 800-242-1918 (retail orders only) *E-mail:* churchpublishingorders@pbd.com *Web Site:* www.churchpublishing.org, pg 142

Morgan Gaynin Inc, 149 Madison Ave, Suite 1140, New York, NY 10016 *Tel:* 212-475-0440 *E-mail:* info@morgangaynin.com *Web Site:* www.morgangaynin.com, pg 512

Morgan James Publishing, 5 Penn Plaza, 23rd fl, New York, NY 10001 *Tel:* 212-655-5470 *Fax:* 516-908-4496 *E-mail:* support@morganjamespublishing.com *Web Site:* www.morganjamespublishing.com, pg 143

Morgan Kaufmann, 50 & 60 Hampshire St, 5th fl, Cambridge, MA 02139 *Web Site:* www.elsevier.com/books-and-journals/morgan-kaufmann, pg 143

Howard Morhaim Literary Agency Inc, 30 Pierrepont St, Brooklyn, NY 11201-3371 *Tel:* 718-222-8400 *E-mail:* info@morhaimliterary.com *Web Site:* www.morhaimliterary.com, pg 497

Moriah Books, PO Box 1094, Casper, WY 82602 *Web Site:* moriahbook.com, pg 143

Morning Sun Books Inc, 1200 County Rd 523, Flemington, NJ 08822 *Tel:* 908-806-6216 *Fax:* 908-237-2407 *E-mail:* sales@morningsunbooks.com *Web Site:* morningsunbooks.com, pg 143

The William C Morris YA Debut Award, 225 N Michigan Ave, Suite 1300, Chicago, IL 60601 *Tel:* 312-280-4390 *Toll Free Tel:* 800-545-2433 (ext 4390) *Fax:* 312-280-5276 *E-mail:* yalsa@ala.org *Web Site:* www.ala.org/yalsa/morris, pg 643

William Morris Society in the United States Fellowships, PO Box 53263, Washington, DC 20009 *E-mail:* us@morrissociety.org *Web Site:* www.morrissociety.org, pg 643

Willie Morris Award for Southern Fiction, 654 Madison Ave, Suite 703, New York, NY 10065 *E-mail:* info@williemorrisaward.com *Web Site:* williemorrisaward.org, pg 643

Willie Morris Award for Southern Poetry, 654 Madison Ave, Suite 703, New York, NY 10065 *E-mail:* info@williemorrisaward.com *Web Site:* williemorrisaward.org, pg 643

Henry Morrison Inc, PO Box 235, Bedford Hills, NY 10507-0235 *Tel:* 914-666-3500 *E-mail:* hmorrison1@aol.com, pg 497

Harold Morton Landon Translation Award, 75 Maiden Lane, Suite 901, New York, NY 10038 *Tel:* 212-274-0343 *E-mail:* awards@poets.org *Web Site:* www.poets.org, pg 643

Kathryn A Morton Prize in Poetry, 822 E Market St, Louisville, KY 40206 *Tel:* 502-458-4028 *E-mail:* info@sarabandebooks.org *Web Site:* www.sarabandebooks.org/morton, pg 643

Morton Publishing Co, 925 W Kenyon Ave, Unit 12, Englewood, CO 80110 *Tel:* 303-761-4805 *Fax:* 303-762-9923 *E-mail:* contact@morton-pub.com; returns@morton-pub.com *Web Site:* www.morton-pub.com, pg 143

Mosaic Press, 1252 Speers Rd, Units 1 & 2, Oakville, ON L6L 5N9, Canada *Tel:* 905-825-2130 *Fax:* 905-825-2130 *E-mail:* info@mosaic-press.com *Web Site:* www.mosaic-press.com, pg 433

George L Mosse Prize, 400 "A" St SE, Washington, DC 20003 *Tel:* 202-544-2422 *Fax:* 202-544-8307 *E-mail:* awards@historians.org *Web Site:* www.historians.org, pg 643

Most Promising New Textbook Award, PO Box 367, Fountain City, WI 54629 *E-mail:* info@taaonline.net *Web Site:* www.taaonline.net/promising-new-textbook-award, pg 643

Motion Picture Association of America Inc (MPAA), 1301 "K" St NE, Suite 900E, Washington, DC 20005 *Tel:* 202-293-1966 *Fax:* 202-296-7410 *E-mail:* contactus@mpaa.org *Web Site:* www.mpaa.org, pg 538

Frank Luther Mott-Kappa Tau Alpha Research Award, University of Missouri, School of Journalism, 76 Gannett Hall, Columbia, MO 65211-1200 *Tel:* 573-882-7685 *Fax:* 573-884-1720 *E-mail:* umcjourkta@missouri.edu *Web Site:* www.kappataualpha.org, pg 644

Sheila Margaret Motton Book Prize, 46 Wallace St, Somerville, MA 02144 *E-mail:* info@nepoetryclub.org *Web Site:* www.nepoetryclub.org, pg 644

Mount Hermon Christian Writers Conference, c/o Mount Hermon Association Inc, 37 Conference Dr, Felton, CA 95018 *Tel:* 831-335-4466 *Toll Free Tel:* 888-MH-CAMPS (642-2677, registration) *Fax:* 831-335-9335 *E-mail:* info@mounthermon.org *Web Site:* www.mounthermon.org/writers, pg 576

Mountain n' Air Books, 2947-A Honolulu Ave, La Crescenta, CA 91214 *Tel:* 818-248-9345 *Toll Free Tel:* 800-446-9696 *Toll Free Fax:* 800-303-5578 *E-mail:* contact@mountain-n-air.com *Web Site:* www.mountain-n-air.com, pg 143

Mountain Press Publishing Co, 1301 S Third W, Missoula, MT 59801 *Tel:* 406-728-1900 *Toll Free Tel:* 800-234-5308 *Fax:* 406-728-1635 *E-mail:* info@mtnpress.com *Web Site:* www.mountain-press.com, pg 143

Mountain Writers Series, 2804 SE 27 Ave, Suite 2, Portland, OR 97202 *Tel:* 503-232-4517 *Fax:* 503-232-4517 *E-mail:* programs@mountainwriters.org; support@mountainwriters.org *Web Site:* www.mountainwriters.org, pg 576

The Mountaineers Books, 1001 SW Klickitat Way, Suite 201, Seattle, WA 98134 *Tel:* 206-223-6303 *Fax:* 206-223-6306 *E-mail:* mbooks@mountaineersbooks.org; customerservice@mountaineersbooks.org *Web Site:* www.mountaineersbooks.org, pg 143

De Gruyter Mouton, 125 Pearl St, Boston, MA 02110 *Tel:* 857-284-7073 *Fax:* 857-284-7358 *E-mail:* service@degruyter.com *Web Site:* www.degruyter.com, pg 143

Movable Type Management, 244 Madison Ave, Suite 334, New York, NY 10016 *Web Site:* www.movabletm.com, pg 497

Moznaim Publishing Corp, 4304 12 Ave, Brooklyn, NY 11219 *Tel:* 718-438-7680 *Fax:* 718-438-1305 *E-mail:* sales@moznaim.com *Web Site:* www.moznaim.com, pg 144

MPA - The Association of Magazine Media, 757 Third Ave, 11th fl, New York, NY 10012 *Tel:* 212-872-3700 *Fax:* 212-888-4217 *Web Site:* www.magazine.org, pg 538

MRTS, PO Box 874402, Tempe, AZ 85287-4402 *Tel:* 480-727-6503 *Toll Free Tel:* 800-621-2736 (orders) *Fax:* 480-965-1681 *Toll Free Fax:* 800-621-8476 (orders) *E-mail:* mrts@asu.edu *Web Site:* acmrspress.com, pg 144

Mary Mueller, 516 Bartram Rd, Moorestown, NJ 08057 *Tel:* 856-778-4769 *E-mail:* mamam49@aol.com, pg 468

Multicultural Publications Inc, 1939 Manchester Rd, Akron, OH 44314 *Tel:* 330-865-9578 *Fax:* 330-865-9578 *E-mail:* multiculturalpub@prodigy.net *Web Site:* www.multiculturalpub.net, pg 144

Multnomah, 10807 New Allegiance Dr, Suite 500, Colorado Springs, CO 80921 *Tel:* 719-590-4999 *Toll Free Tel:* 800-603-7051 (orders) *Fax:* 719-590-8977 *Toll Free Fax:* 800-294-5686 (orders) *E-mail:* info@waterbrookmultnomah.com *Web Site:* waterbrookmultnomah.com, pg 144

Erika Mumford Prize, 46 Wallace St, Somerville, MA 02144 *E-mail:* info@nepoetryclub.org *Web Site:* www.nepoetryclub.org, pg 644

Municipal Analysis Services Inc, PO Box 13453, Austin, TX 78711-3453 *Tel:* 512-704-7194 *E-mail:* munilysis@gmail.com *Web Site:* sites.google.com/site/gregmichels/home, pg 144

Derrick Murdoch Award, 716 Thicket Way, Ottawa, ON K4A 3B5, Canada *E-mail:* info@crimewriterscanada.com *Web Site:* www.crimewriterscanada.com/awards, pg 644

The Museum of Modern Art (MoMA), Publications Dept, 11 W 53 St, New York, NY 10019 *Tel:* 212-708-9443 *E-mail:* moma_publications@moma.org *Web Site:* www.moma.org, pg 144

Museum of New Mexico Press, 725 Camino Lejo, Suite C, Santa Fe, NM 87505 *Tel:* 505-476-1155; 505-272-7777 (orders) *Toll Free Tel:* 800-249-7737 (orders) *Fax:* 505-476-1156 *Toll Free Fax:* 800-622-8667 (orders) *Web Site:* www.mnmpress.org, pg 144

Music Publishers Association (MPA), 243 Fifth Ave, Suite 236, New York, NY 10016 *Tel:* 212-327-4044 *E-mail:* admin@mpa.org *Web Site:* www.mpa.org, pg 538

Mutual Publishing LLC, 1215 Center St, Suite 210, Honolulu, HI 96816 *Tel:* 808-732-1709 *Fax:* 808-734-4094 *E-mail:* info@mutualpublishing.com *Web Site:* www.mutualpublishing.com, pg 144

MWG Writer Workshops & State Conference, 9 Janice Circle, Natchez, MS 39120 *Tel:* 601-442-0980 *E-mail:* mississippi.writersguild@outlook.com *Web Site:* www.mississippiwritersguild.com, pg 576

Walter Dean Myers Awards for Outstanding Children's Literature, 10319 Westlake Dr, No 104, Bethesda, MD 20817 *Tel:* 701-404-9632 (voicemail only) *E-mail:* walteraward@diversebooks.org *Web Site:* diversebooks.org/our-programs/walter-award, pg 644

Walter Dean Myers Grant, 10319 Westlake Dr, No 104, Bethesda, MD 20817 *E-mail:* waltergrantwndb@gmail.com *Web Site:* diversebooks.org, pg 644

Mystery Writers of America (MWA), 1140 Broadway, Suite 1507, New York, NY 10001 *Tel:* 212-888-8171 *E-mail:* mwa@mysterywriters.org *Web Site:* www.mysterywriters.org, pg 538

Mythopoeic Awards, Friends University, 2100 W University Ave, Wichita, KS 67213 *Tel:* 316-295-5563 *E-mail:* awards@mythsoc.org *Web Site:* www.mythsoc.org, pg 644

NACE International, 15835 Park Ten Place, Houston, TX 77084 *Tel:* 281-228-6200; 281-228-6223 *Toll Free Tel:* 800-797-NACE (797-6223) *Fax:* 281-228-6300 *E-mail:* firstservice@nace.org *Web Site:* www.nace.org, pg 144

Jean V Naggar Literary Agency Inc (JVNLA), 216 E 75 St, Suite 1-E, New York, NY 10021 *Tel:* 212-794-1082 *E-mail:* jvnla@jvnla.com *Web Site:* www.jvnla.com, pg 497

Napa Valley Writers' Conference, 1088 College Ave, St Helena, CA 94574 *Tel:* 707-967-2900 (ext 4) *Fax:* 707-967-2909 *E-mail:* info@napawritersconference.org; media@napawritersconference.org; fiction@napawritersconference.org; poetry@napawritersconference.org *Web Site:* www.napawritersconference.org, pg 576

Narada Press, 3165-133 Weber St N, Waterloo, ON N2J 3G9, Canada *Tel:* 519-886-1969, pg 433

NASW Press, 750 First St NE, Suite 800, Washington, DC 20002 *Tel:* 202-408-8600 *Fax:* 203-336-8312 *E-mail:* press@naswdc.org *Web Site:* www.naswpress.org, pg 145

Nataraj Books, 7967 Twist Lane, Springfield, VA 22153 *Tel:* 703-455-4996 *Fax:* 703-455-4001 *E-mail:* nataraj@erols.com; orders@natarajbooks.com; natarajbooks@gmail.com *Web Site:* www.natarajbooks.com, pg 145

National Academies Press (NAP), Lockbox 285, 500 Fifth St NW, Washington, DC 20001 *Toll Free Tel:* 800-624-6242 *Fax:* 202-334-2451 (cust serv); 202-334-2793 (mktg dept) *E-mail:* customer_service@nap.edu *Web Site:* www.nap.edu, pg 145

National Association of Black Journalists (NABJ), 1100 Knight Hall, Suite 3100, College Park, MD 20742 *Tel:* 301-405-0248 *Fax:* 301-314-1714 *E-mail:* info@nabj.org; press@nabj.org *Web Site:* www.nabj.org, pg 538

National Association of Book Entrepreneurs (NABE), PO Box 606, Cottage Grove, OR 97424 *Tel:* 541-942-7455 *Fax:* 541-942-7455 *E-mail:* nabe@bookmarketingprofits.com *Web Site:* www.bookmarketingprofits.com, pg 538

National Association of Broadcasters (NAB), 1771 "N" St NW, Washington, DC 20036 *Tel:* 202-429-5300 *E-mail:* nab@nab.org *Web Site:* www.nab.org, pg 145, 538

National Association of College Stores (NACS), 500 E Lorain St, Oberlin, OH 44074 *Toll Free Tel:* 800-622-7498 *Fax:* 440-775-4769 *Web Site:* www.nacs.org, pg 538

National Association of Hispanic Publications Inc (NAHP), 529 14 St NW, Suite 923, Washington, DC 20045 *Tel:* 202-662-7250 *E-mail:* news@nahp.com *Web Site:* nahp.org, pg 539

National Association of Insurance Commissioners, 1100 Walnut St, Suite 1500, Kansas City, MO 64106-2197 *Tel:* 816-842-3600 *Fax:* 816-783-8175 *E-mail:* prodserv@naic.org *Web Site:* www.naic.org, pg 145

National Association of Printing Ink Manufacturers (NAPIM), 3600 E State St, Suite 306, Rockford, IL 61108 *Tel:* 815-708-7387 *Web Site:* www.napim.org, pg 539

National Association of Real Estate Editors (NAREE), 1003 NW Sixth Terr, Boca Raton, FL 33486-3455 *Tel:* 561-391-3599 *Fax:* 561-391-0099 *Web Site:* www.naree.org, pg 539

National Association of Science Writers (NASW), PO Box 7905, Berkeley, CA 94707 *Tel:* 510-647-9500 *Web Site:* www.nasw.org, pg 539

National Association of Secondary School Principals (NASSP), 1904 Association Dr, Reston, VA 20191-1537 *Tel:* 703-860-0200 *Toll Free Tel:* 800-253-7746; 866-647-7253 (sales) *E-mail:* membership@nassp.org *Web Site:* www.nassp.org, pg 145

National Awards for Education Reporting, 3516 Connecticut Ave NW, Washington, DC 20008 *Tel:* 202-452-9830 *Fax:* 202-452-9837 *E-mail:* ewa@ewa.org *Web Site:* www.ewa.org, pg 644

National Book Awards, 90 Broad St, Suite 604, New York, NY 10004 *Tel:* 212-685-0261 *Fax:* 212-213-6570 *E-mail:* nationalbook@nationalbook.org *Web Site:* www.nationalbook.org, pg 644

National Book Co, PO Box 8795, Portland, OR 97280-8795 *Tel:* 503-228-6345 *Fax:* 810-885-5811 *E-mail:* info@eralearning.com *Web Site:* www.eralearning.com, pg 145

National Book Critics Circle Award, c/o 310 Lewis Ave, Brooklyn, NY 11221 *E-mail:* info@bookcritics.org *Web Site:* bookcritics.org/awards, pg 644

National Book Foundation, 90 Broad St, Suite 604, New York, NY 10004 *Tel:* 212-685-0261 *Fax:* 212-213-6570 *E-mail:* nationalbook@nationalbook.org *Web Site:* www.nationalbook.org, pg 551

National Braille Press, 88 Saint Stephen St, Boston, MA 02115-4312 *Tel:* 617-266-6160 *Toll Free Tel:* 800-548-7323 (cust serv); 888-965-8965 *Fax:* 617-437-0456 *E-mail:* contact@nbp.org *Web Site:* www.nbp.org, pg 145

The National Business Book Award, c/o Freedman & Associates Inc, 121 Richmond St W, Suite 605, Toronto, ON M5H 2K1, Canada *Tel:* 416-868-1500 *Web Site:* www.nbbaward.com, pg 644

National Cartoonists Society (NCS), PO Box 592927, Orlando, FL 32859-2927 *Tel:* 407-994-6703 *Fax:* 407-442-0786 *E-mail:* info@reuben.org *Web Site:* www.reuben.org, pg 539

National Catholic Educational Association, 1005 N Glebe Rd, Suite 525, Arlington, VA 22201 *Tel:* 571-257-0010 *Toll Free Tel:* 800-711-6232 *Fax:* 703-243-0025 *E-mail:* nceaadmin@ncea.org *Web Site:* www.ncea.org, pg 145

National Center for Children in Poverty, 722 W 168 St, New York, NY 10032 *Tel:* 646-284-9600; 212-304-6073 *E-mail:* info@nccp.org *Web Site:* www.nccp.org, pg 146

National Center For Employee Ownership (NCEO), 1629 Telegraph Ave, Suite 200, Oakland, CA 94612 *Tel:* 510-208-1300 *Fax:* 510-272-9510 *E-mail:* customerservice@nceo.org *Web Site:* www.nceo.org, pg 146

National Coalition Against Censorship (NCAC), 19 Fulton St, Suite 407, New York, NY 10038 *Tel:* 212-807-6222 *Fax:* 212-807-6245 *E-mail:* ncac@ncac.org *Web Site:* www.ncac.org, pg 539

National Coalition for Literacy (NCL), PO Box 2932, Washington, DC 20013-2932 *E-mail:* ncl@ncladvocacy.org *Web Site:* www.national-coalition-literacy.org, pg 539

National Communication Association, 1765 "N" St NW, Washington, DC 20036 *Tel:* 202-464-4622 *Fax:* 202-464-4600 *E-mail:* inbox@natcom.org *Web Site:* www.natcom.org, pg 539

National Conference of State Legislatures (NCSL), 7700 E First Place, Denver, CO 80230 *Tel:* 303-364-7700 *Fax:* 303-364-7800 *E-mail:* books@ncsl.org *Web Site:* www.ncsl.org, pg 146

National Council of Teachers of English (NCTE), 340 N Neil St, Suite 104, Champaign, IL 61820 *Tel:* 217-328-3870 *Toll Free Tel:* 877-369-6283 (cust serv) *Fax:* 217-328-9645 *E-mail:* customerservice@ncte.org *Web Site:* www.ncte.org, pg 146, 539

National Council of Teachers of Mathematics (NCTM), 1906 Association Dr, Reston, VA 20191-1502 *Tel:* 703-620-9840 *Toll Free Tel:* 800-235-7566 *Fax:* 703-476-2970 *E-mail:* nctm@nctm.org *Web Site:* www.nctm.org, pg 146

National Education Association (NEA), 1201 16 St NW, Washington, DC 20036-3290 *Tel:* 202-833-4000 *Fax:* 202-822-7974 *Web Site:* www.nea.org, pg 146

National Education Association (NEA), 1201 16 St NW, Washington, DC 20036-3290 *Tel:* 202-833-4000 *Fax:* 202-822-7974 *E-mail:* media-relations-team@nea.org *Web Site:* www.nea.org, pg 539

National Endowment for the Arts, 400 Seventh St SW, Washington, DC 20506-0001 *Tel:* 202-682-5400 *Web Site:* www.arts.gov, pg 551

National Federation of Press Women Inc (NFPW), PO Box 3007, Mechanicsville, VA 23116-0026 *Tel:* 804-746-1033 *Fax:* 804-335-1296 *E-mail:* info@nfpw.org *Web Site:* www.nfpw.org, pg 540

National Federation of State Poetry Societies Annual Poetry Contest, c/o 115 N Wisteria St, Mansfield, TX 76063-1835 *E-mail:* contestchair@nfsps.com *Web Site:* www.nfsps.com, pg 645

National Freedom of Information Coalition (NFOIC), Missouri School of Journalism, 31 Neff Annex, Columbia, MO 65211 *Tel:* 573-882-4856 *E-mail:* nfoic@nfoic.org *Web Site:* nfoic.org, pg 540

National Gallery of Art, Sixth & Constitution Ave NW, Washington, DC 20565 *Tel:* 202-842-6200 *Fax:* 202-408-8530 *E-mail:* publishingoffice@nga.gov *Web Site:* www.nga.gov, pg 146

National Gallery of Canada Boutique, 380 Sussex Dr, Ottawa, ON K1N 9N4, Canada *Tel:* 613-990-0962 (mail order sales) *E-mail:* ngcbook@gallery.ca *Web Site:* www.gallery.ca, pg 433

National Geographic Books, 1145 17 St NW, Washington, DC 20036-4688 *Tel:* 202-857-7000 *Toll Free Tel:* 877-866-6486 *E-mail:* ngbooks@cdsfulfillment.com *Web Site:* www.nationalgeographic.com/books/; ngbooks.buysub.com, pg 146

National Geographic Learning, 20 Channel Center St, Boston, MA 02210 *Tel:* 617-289-7796 *E-mail:* schoolcustomerservice@cengage.com *Web Site:* www.ngl.cengage.com/school, pg 146

National Golf Foundation, 501 N Hwy A1A, Jupiter, FL 33477-4577 *Tel:* 561-744-6006 *Toll Free Tel:* 888-275-4643 *Fax:* 561-744-6107 *E-mail:* general@ngf.org *Web Site:* www.ngf.org, pg 147

The National Humanities Medal, 400 Seventh St SW, Washington, DC 20506 *Tel:* 202-606-8400 *Toll Free Tel:* 800-NEH-1121 (634-1121) *E-mail:* questions@neh.gov *Web Site:* www.neh.gov/about/awards, pg 645

National Information Standards Organization (NISO), 3600 Clipper Mill Rd, Suite 302, Baltimore, MD 21211-1948 *Tel:* 301-654-2512 *Fax:* 410-685-5278 *E-mail:* nisohq@niso.org *Web Site:* www.niso.org, pg 147, 540

National Institute for Trial Advocacy (NITA), 1685 38 St, Suite 200, Boulder, CO 80301-2735 *Tel:* 720-890-4860 *Toll Free Tel:* 877-648-2632; 800-225-6482 (orders & returns) *Fax:* 720-890-7069 *E-mail:* customerservice@nita.org; sales@nita.org *Web Site:* www.nita.org, pg 147

National Jewish Book Award-Children's Literature, 520 Eighth Ave, 4th fl, New York, NY 10018 *Tel:* 212-201-2920 *Fax:* 212-532-4952 *E-mail:* jbc@jewishbooks.org *Web Site:* www.jewishbookcouncil.org, pg 645

National Jewish Book Award-Natan Book Award, 520 Eighth Ave, 4th fl, New York, NY 10018 *Tel:* 212-201-2920 *Fax:* 212-532-4952 *E-mail:* jbc@jewishbooks.org; natanbookawards@jewishbooks.org *Web Site:* www.jewishbookcouncil.org, pg 645

National Jewish Book Award-Young Adult Literature, 520 Eighth Ave, 4th fl, New York, NY 10018 *Tel:* 212-201-2920 *Fax:* 212-532-4952 *E-mail:* jbc@jewishbooks.org *Web Site:* www.jewishbookcouncil.org, pg 645

National Jewish Book Awards, 520 Eighth Ave, 4th fl, New York, NY 10018 *Tel:* 212-201-2920 *Fax:* 212-532-4952 *E-mail:* jbc@jewishbooks.org *Web Site:* www.jewishbookcouncil.org, pg 645

National League of American Pen Women Inc, The Pen Arts Bldg & Arts Museum, 1300 17 St NW, Washington, DC 20036-1973 *Tel:* 202-785-1997 *Fax:* 202-452-8868 *E-mail:* contact@nlapw.org *Web Site:* www.nlapw.org, pg 540

National Learning Corp, 212 Michael Dr, Syosset, NY 11791 *Tel:* 516-921-8888 *Toll Free Tel:* 800-632-8888 *Fax:* 516-921-8743 *E-mail:* info@passbooks.com *Web Site:* www.passbooks.com, pg 147

National Magazine Awards, 2300 Yonge St, Suite 1600, Toronto, ON M4P 1E4, Canada *Tel:* 416-939-6200 *E-mail:* staff@magazine-awards.com *Web Site:* www.magazine-awards.com; twitter.com/magawards, pg 645

The National Medal of Arts, 400 Seventh St SW, Washington, DC 20506-0001 *Tel:* 202-682-5570 *Web Site:* www.arts.gov/honors/medals, pg 645

National Music Publishers' Association (NMPA), 975 "F" St NW, Suite 375, Washington, DC 20004 *Tel:* 202-393-6672 *E-mail:* members@nmpa.org *Web Site:* nmpa.org, pg 540

National Newspaper Association, 101 S Palafox, Unit 13323, Pensacola, FL 32591 *Tel:* 217-241-1400 *Fax:* 217-241-1301 *E-mail:* nna@nna.org *Web Site:* nnaweb.org, pg 540

National Newspaper Publishers Association (NNPA), 1816 12 St NW, Washington, DC 20009 *Tel:* 202-588-8764 *Fax:* 202-588-8960 *E-mail:* info@nnpa.org *Web Site:* www.nnpa.org; www.blackpressusa.com, pg 540

National Notary Association (NNA), 9350 De Soto Ave, Chatsworth, CA 91311-4926 *Tel:* 818-739-4000 *Toll Free Tel:* 800-876-6827 *Toll Free Fax:* 800-833-1211 *E-mail:* services@nationalnotary.org *Web Site:* www.nationalnotary.org, pg 147

National One-Act Playwriting Competition, 600 Wolfe St, Alexandria, VA 22314 *Tel:* 703-683-5778 (ext 2) *Fax:* 703-683-1378 *E-mail:* asklta@thelittletheatre.com *Web Site:* www.thelittletheatre.com/info, pg 645

National Outdoor Book Awards, 921 S Eighth Ave, Stop 8128, Pocatello, ID 83209-8128 *Tel:* 208-282-3912 *Fax:* 208-282-2127 *Web Site:* www.noba-web.org, pg 645

National Poetry Series Open Competition, 57 Mountain Ave, Princeton, NJ 08540 *Tel:* 609-430-0999 *Fax:* 609-430-9933 *Web Site:* nationalpoetryseries.org, pg 645

National Press Club (NPC), 529 14 St NW, 13th fl, Washington, DC 20045 *Tel:* 202-662-7500 *Web Site:* www.press.org, pg 540

National Press Club of Canada Foundation Inc, 17 York St, Suite 201, Ottawa, ON K1N 9J6, Canada *E-mail:* info@pressclubcanada.ca *Web Site:* pressclubcanada.ca, pg 540

National Press Foundation, 1211 Connecticut Ave NW, Suite 310, Washington, DC 20036 *Tel:* 202-663-7280 *Web Site:* nationalpress.org, pg 540

National Press Photographers Association Inc (NPPA), 120 Hooper St, Athens, GA 30602 *Tel:* 706-542-2506 *E-mail:* info@nppa.org *Web Site:* nppa.org, pg 540

National Resource Center for Youth Services, Schusterman Ctr, Bldg 4W, 4502 E 41 St, Tulsa, OK 74135-2512 *Tel:* 918-660-3700 *Toll Free Tel:* 800-274-2687 *Fax:* 918-660-3737 *Web Site:* www.nrcys.ou.edu, pg 147

National Science Teachers Association (NSTA), 1840 Wilson Blvd, Arlington, VA 22201-3000 *Tel:* 703-312-9205 *Toll Free Tel:* 800-277-5300 (orders) *Toll Free Fax:* 888-433-0526 (orders) *E-mail:* publisher@nsta.org (gen info); orders@nsta.org *Web Site:* www.nsta.org/publications/press/; www.nsta.org/store, pg 147

National Society of Newspaper Columnists (NSNC), 205 Gun Hill St, Milton, MA 02186 *Tel:* 617-697-6854 *E-mail:* director@columnists.com *Web Site:* www.columnists.com, pg 540

National Society of Newspaper Columnists Annual Conference, 205 Gun Hill St, Milton, MA 02186 *Tel:* 617-697-6854 *E-mail:* director@columnists.com *Web Site:* www.columnists.com, pg 576

National Ten-Minute Play Contest, 316 W Main St, Louisville, KY 40202-4218 *Tel:* 502-584-1265 *Web Site:* actorstheatre.org/national-ten-minute-play-contest/, pg 646

National Translation Award, University of Arizona, Esquire Bldg, No 205, 1230 N Park Ave, Tucson, AZ 85721 *Tel:* 520-621-1757 *Web Site:* www.literarytranslators.org/awards/national-translation-award, pg 646

The National Underwriter Co, 4157 Olympic Blvd, Suite 225, Erlanger, KY 41018 *Tel:* 859-692-2100 *Toll Free Tel:* 800-543-0874 *Toll Free Fax:* 800-874-1916 *E-mail:* customerservice@nuco.com *Web Site:* www.nationalunderwriter.com, pg 147

National Wildlife Federation, 11100 Wildlife Center Dr, Reston, VA 20190-5362 *Toll Free Tel:* 800-477-5034 *Web Site:* www.zoobooks.com, pg 147

National Writers Association, 10940 S Parker Rd, Suite 508, Parker, CO 80134 *Tel:* 303-656-7235 *E-mail:* natlwritersassn@hotmail.com *Web Site:* www.nationalwriters.com, pg 541

National Writers Association Novel Contest, 10940 S Parker Rd, Suite 508, Parker, CO 80134 *Tel:* 303-656-7235 *E-mail:* natlwritersassn@hotmail.com *Web Site:* www.nationalwriters.com, pg 646

National Writers Union/UAW Local 1981, 256 W 38 St, Suite 703, New York, NY 10018 *Tel:* 212-254-0279 *Fax:* 212-254-0673 *E-mail:* nwu@nwu.org *Web Site:* www.nwu.org/, pg 541

Nautilus Book Awards, PO Box 2285, Vashon, WA 98070 *Tel:* 206-604-2250 *Web Site:* www.nautilusbookawards.com, pg 646

Naval Institute Press, 291 Wood Rd, Annapolis, MD 21402-5034 *Tel:* 410-268-6110 *Toll Free Tel:* 800-233-8764 *Fax:* 410-295-1084; 410-571-1703 (cust serv) *E-mail:* webmaster@navalinstitute.org; customer@navalinstitute.org (cust serv) *Web Site:* www.nip.org; www.usni.org, pg 147

NavPress Publishing Group, 3820 N 30 St, Colorado Springs, CO 80904 *Tel:* 719-598-1212 *Toll Free Tel:* 800-323-9400; 855-277-9400 (cust serv) *Toll Free Fax:* 800-684-0247 *Web Site:* www.navpress.com, pg 148

NBM Publishing Inc, 160 Broadway, E Wing, Suite 700, New York, NY 10038 *Tel:* 646-559-4681 *Toll Free Tel:* 800-886-1223 *Fax:* 212-643-1545 *E-mail:* admin@nbmpub.com *Web Site:* www.nbmpub.com, pg 148

NEA Creative Writing Fellowships, 400 Seventh St SW, Washington, DC 20506-0001 *Tel:* 202-682-5400; 202-682-5496 (Voice/TTY); 202-682-5034 (lit fellowships hotline) *Fax:* 202-682-5609; 202-682-5610 *E-mail:* litfellowships@arts.gov *Web Site:* www.arts.gov, pg 646

Neibauer Press, 20 Industrial Dr, Warminster, PA 18974 *Tel:* 215-322-6200 *Toll Free Tel:* 800-322-6203 (orders) *Fax:* 215-322-2495 *E-mail:* info@neibauer.com *Web Site:* www.neibauer.com; www.churchsupplier.com (orders), pg 148

Nina Neimark Editorial Services, 543 Third St, Brooklyn, NY 11215 *Tel:* 718-499-6804 *E-mail:* pneimark@hotmail.com, pg 468

Nelligan Prize for Short Fiction, Colorado State University, Dept of English, Center for Literary Publishing, 9105 Campus Delivery, Fort Collins, CO 80523-9105 *Tel:* 970-491-5449 *E-mail:* creview@colostate.edu *Web Site:* nelliganprize.colostate.edu, pg 646

Nelson Education Ltd, 1120 Birchmount Rd, Scarborough, ON M1K 5G4, Canada *Tel:* 416-752-9100 *Toll Free Tel:* 800-268-2222 (cust serv) *Fax:* 416-752-8101 *Toll Free Fax:* 800-430-4445 *E-mail:* peopleandengagement@nelson.com *Web Site:* www.nelson.com, pg 433

Nelson Literary Agency LLC, 1732 Wazee St, Suite 207, Denver, CO 80202-1284 *Tel:* 303-292-2805 *E-mail:* info@nelsonagency.com *Web Site:* www.nelsonagency.com, pg 497

Howard Nemerov Sonnet Award, 21 Osborne Terr, Wayne, NJ 07470 *Web Site:* theformalist.evansville.edu/home.htm, pg 646

The Pablo Neruda Prize for Poetry, Nimrod International Journal, 800 S Tucker Dr, Tulsa, OK 74104 *Tel:* 918-631-3080 *Fax:* 918-631-3033 *E-mail:* nimrod@utulsa.edu *Web Site:* www.utulsa.edu/nimrod, pg 646

Neukom Institute Literary Arts Awards, Dartmouth College, Sudikoff Bldg, Rm 121, 9 Maynard St, Hanover, NH 03755 *Web Site:* sites.dartmouth.edu/neukominstituteliawards, pg 646

Neustadt International Prize for Literature, c/o University of Oklahoma, 630 Parrington Oval, Suite 110, Norman, OK 73019-4033 *Tel:* 405-325-4531 *Web Site:* www.worldliteraturetoday.org; www.worldlit.org, pg 646

Allan Nevins Prize, 2950 Broadway, New York, NY 10027 *Tel:* 212-854-6495 *E-mail:* amhistsociety@columbia.edu *Web Site:* sah.columbia.edu, pg 647

New Atlantic Independent Booksellers Association (NAIBA), 2667 Hyacinth St, Westbury, NY 11590 *Tel:* 516-333-0681 *Fax:* 516-333-0689 *E-mail:* naibabooksellers@gmail.com *Web Site:* www.naiba.com, pg 541

New Author Publishing, 4 E Fulford Place, Brockville, ON K6V 2Z8, Canada *Tel:* 613-865-7471 *Web Site:* www.newauthorpublishing.com, pg 434

New City Press, 202 Comforter Blvd, Hyde Park, NY 12538 *Tel:* 845-229-0335 *Toll Free Tel:* 800-462-5980 (orders only) *Fax:* 845-229-0351 *E-mail:* info@newcitypress.com; orders@newcitypress.com *Web Site:* www.newcitypress.com, pg 148

New Concepts Publishing, 5265 Humphreys Rd, Lake Park, GA 31636 *E-mail:* newconcepts@newconceptspublishing.com *Web Site:* www.newconceptspublishing.com, pg 148

New Directions Publishing Corp, 80 Eighth Ave, 19th fl, New York, NY 10011 *Tel:* 212-255-0230 *E-mail:* editorial@ndbooks.com; publicity@ndbooks.com *Web Site:* ndbooks.com, pg 148

New England Book Awards, One Beacon St, 15th fl, Boston, MA 02108 *Tel:* 617-547-3642 *Fax:* 617-830-8768 *Web Site:* www.newenglandbooks.org/bookawards, pg 647

New England Independent Booksellers Association Inc (NEIBA), One Beacon St, 15th fl, Boston, MA 02108 *Tel:* 617-547-3642 *Fax:* 617-830-8768 *Web Site:* www.newenglandbooks.org, pg 541

New England Poetry Club, 46 Wallace St, Somerville, MA 02144 *E-mail:* info@nepoetryclub.org *Web Site:* www.nepoetryclub.org, pg 541

New Forums Press Inc, 1018 S Lewis St, Stillwater, OK 74074 *Tel:* 405-372-6158 *Toll Free Tel:* 800-606-3766 *Fax:* 405-377-2237 *E-mail:* submissions@newforums.com *Web Site:* www.newforums.com, pg 148

New Hampshire Literary Awards, 2500 N River Rd, Manchester, NH 03106 *Tel:* 603-314-7980 *E-mail:* info@nhwritersproject.org; awards@nhwritersproject.org *Web Site:* www.nhwritersproject.org, pg 647

New Hampshire Writers' Project, 2500 N River Rd, Manchester, NH 03106 *Tel:* 603-314-7980 *E-mail:* info@nhwritersproject.org *Web Site:* www.nhwritersproject.org, pg 541

New Harbinger Publications Inc, 5674 Shattuck Ave, Oakland, CA 94609 *Tel:* 510-652-0215 *Toll Free Tel:* 800-748-6273 (orders only) *Fax:* 510-652-5472 *Toll Free Fax:* 800-652-1613 *E-mail:* nhhelp@newharbinger.com; customerservice@newharbinger.com *Web Site:* www.newharbinger.com, pg 148

New Horizon Press, PO Box 669, Far Hills, NJ 07931-0669 *Tel:* 908-604-6311 *E-mail:* nhp@newhorizonpressbooks.com *Web Site:* www.newhorizonpressbooks.com, pg 148

New Issues Poetry & Prose, c/o Western Michigan University, 1903 W Michigan Ave, Kalamazoo, MI 49008-5463 *Tel:* 269-387-8185 *E-mail:* new-issues@wmich.edu *Web Site:* www.wmich.edu/newissues, pg 149

New Issues Poetry Prize, c/o Western Michigan University, 1903 W Michigan Ave, Kalamazoo, MI 49008-5463 *Tel:* 269-387-8185 *E-mail:* new-issues@wmich.edu *Web Site:* www.wmich.edu/newissues, pg 647

New Jersey Business & Industry Association (NJBIA), 10 W Lafayette St, Trenton, NJ 08608-2002 *Tel:* 609-393-7707 *Web Site:* njbia.org, pg 541

New Leaf Press, 3142 Hwy 103 N, Green Forest, AR 72638-2233 *Tel:* 870-438-5288 *Toll Free Tel:* 800-999-3777 *Fax:* 870-438-5120 *E-mail:* nlp@newleafpress.net; submissions@newleafpress.net *Web Site:* www.nlpg.com, pg 149

New Letters Literary Awards, UMKC, University House, 5101 Rockhill Rd, Kansas City, MO 64110-2499 *Tel:* 816-235-1169 *Fax:* 816-235-2611 *E-mail:* newletters@umkc.edu *Web Site:* www.newletters.org, pg 647

New Letters Prize for Poetry, UMKC, University House, 5101 Rockhill Rd, Kansas City, MO 64110-2499 *Tel:* 816-235-1169 *Fax:* 816-235-2611 *E-mail:* newletters@umkc.edu *Web Site:* www.newletters.org, pg 647

New Mexico-Arizona Book Awards, 925 Salamanca NW, Los Ranchos, NM 87107 *Tel:* 505-344-9382 *E-mail:* info@nmbookcoop.com *Web Site:* www.nmbookcoop.com/BookAwards/BookAwards.html, pg 647

New Mexico Book Association (NMBA), 1219 Luisa St, Suite 1, Santa Fe, NM 87505 *Tel:* 505-660-6357 *E-mail:* admin@nmbook.org *Web Site:* www.nmbook.org, pg 541

New Millennium Awards for Fiction, Poetry & Nonfiction, 4021 Garden Dr, Knoxville, TN 37918 *Tel:* 865-254-4880 *E-mail:* hello@newmillenniumwritings.org *Web Site:* newmillenniumwritings.org, pg 647

The New Press, 120 Wall St, 31st fl, New York, NY 10005 *Tel:* 212-629-8802 *Toll Free Tel:* 800-343-4489 (orders) *Fax:* 212-629-8617 *Toll Free Fax:* 800-351-5073 (orders) *E-mail:* newpress@thenewpress.com *Web Site:* www.thenewpress.com, pg 149

New Readers Press, 104 Marcellus, Syracuse, NY 13204 *Tel:* 315-422-9121 *Toll Free Tel:* 800-448-8878 *Toll Free Fax:* 866-894-2100 *E-mail:* nrp@proliteracy.org *Web Site:* www.newreaderspress.com, pg 149

New Rivers Press, c/o Minnesota State University Moorhead, 1104 Seventh Ave S, Moorhead, MN 56563 *Tel:* 218-477-5870 *Fax:* 218-477-2236 *E-mail:* nrp@mnstate.edu *Web Site:* www.newriverspress.com; www.mnstate.edu/newriverspress, pg 149

New Star Books Ltd, 107-3477 Commercial St, Vancouver, BC V5N 4E8, Canada *Tel:* 604-738-9429 *E-mail:* info@newstarbooks.com *Web Site:* www.newstarbooks.com, pg 434

New Win Publishing, 9682 Telstar Ave, Suite 110, El Monte, CA 91731 *Tel:* 626-448-3448 *Fax:* 626-602-3817 *E-mail:* info@academiclearningcompany.com *Web Site:* newwinpublishing.com; wbusinessbooks.com, pg 149

New Women's Voices Chapbook Competition, PO Box 1626, Georgetown, KY 40324 *Tel:* 502-603-0670 *E-mail:* finishingbooks@aol.com; flpbookstore@aol.com *Web Site:* www.finishinglinepress.com, pg 647

New World Library, 14 Pamaron Way, Novato, CA 94949 *Tel:* 415-884-2100 *Toll Free Tel:* 800-227-3900 (ext 52, retail orders); 800-972-6657 *Fax:* 415-884-2199 *E-mail:* escort@newworldlibrary.com *Web Site:* www.newworldlibrary.com, pg 149

New World Publishing (Canada), PO Box 36075, Halifax, NS B3J 3S9, Canada *Tel:* 902-576-2055 (inquiries) *Toll Free Tel:* 877-211-3334 (orders) *Fax:* 902-576-2095 *Web Site:* www.newworldpublishing.com, pg 434

New York Academy of Sciences (NYAS), 7 World Trade Center, 40th fl, 250 Greenwich St, New York, NY 10007-2157 *Tel:* 212-298-8600 *Toll Free Tel:* 800-843-6927 *Fax:* 212-298-3650 *E-mail:* nyas@nyas.org; annals@nyas.org; customerservice@nyas.org *Web Site:* www.nyas.org, pg 150

The New York Botanical Garden Press, 2900 Southern Blvd, Bronx, NY 10458-5126 *Tel:* 718-817-8721 *Fax:* 718-817-8842 *E-mail:* nybgpress@nybg.org *Web Site:* www.nybgpress.org, pg 150

759

Norwood House Press, PO Box 1306, Fairport, NY 14450 *Tel:* 773-467-0837 *Toll Free Tel:* 866-565-2900 *Fax:* 773-467-9686 *Toll Free Fax:* 866-565-2901 *E-mail:* customerservice@norwoodhousepress.com *Web Site:* www.norwoodhousepress.com, pg 153

Notable Wisconsin Authors, 4610 S Biltmore Lane, Suite 100, Madison, WI 53718-2153 *Tel:* 608-245-3640 *Fax:* 608-245-3646 *Web Site:* wla.wisconsinlibraries.org, pg 649

Nova Press, PO Box 692023, West Hollywood, CA 90069 *Tel:* 310-601-8551 *E-mail:* novapress@aol.com *Web Site:* www.novapress.net, pg 153

Nova Science Publishers Inc, 400 Oser Ave, Suite 1600, Hauppauge, NY 11788-3619 *Tel:* 631-231-7269 *Fax:* 631-231-8175 *E-mail:* nova.main@novapublishers.com *Web Site:* www.novapublishers.com, pg 153

Novalis Publishing, 10 Lower Spadina Ave, Suite 400, Toronto, ON M5V 2Z2, Canada *Tel:* 416-363-3303 *Toll Free Tel:* 877-702-7773 *Fax:* 416-363-9409 *Toll Free Fax:* 877-702-7775 *E-mail:* books@novalis.ca *Web Site:* www.novalis.ca, pg 434

Novella Prize, University of Victoria, Box 1700, Sta CSC, Victoria, BC V8W 2Y2, Canada *Tel:* 250-721-8524 *Fax:* 250-472-5051 *E-mail:* malahat@uvic.ca *Web Site:* www.malahatreview.ca, pg 649

Wanda Nowak Creative Illustrators Agency, 231 E 76 St, Suite 5-D, New York, NY 10021 *Tel:* 212-535-0438 *E-mail:* wanda@wandanow.com *Web Site:* www.wandanow.com, pg 512

NPTA Alliance, 330 N Wabash Ave, Suite 2000, Chicago, IL 60611 *Tel:* 312-321-4092 *Toll Free Tel:* 800-355-NPTA (355-6782) *Fax:* 312-673-6736 *Web Site:* www.gonpta.com, pg 542

NRP Direct, 430 Mountain Ave, Suite 403, New Providence, NJ 07974 *Tel:* 908-517-0780 *Toll Free Tel:* 844-592-4197 *Fax:* 908-608-3012 (cust serv) *E-mail:* info@nrpdirect.com *Web Site:* www.nrpdirect.com, pg 153

NSK Neustadt Prize for Children's Literature, c/o University of Oklahoma, 630 Parrington Oval, Suite 110, Norman, OK 73019-4033 *Tel:* 405-325-4531 *Web Site:* www.worldliteraturetoday.org; www.worldlit.org, pg 649

Nuestras Voces National Playwriting Competition, 138 E 27 St, New York, NY 10016 *Tel:* 212-225-9950 *Fax:* 212-225-9085 *Web Site:* www.repertorio.org, pg 649

Nursesbooks.org, The Publishing Program of ANA, 8515 Georgia Ave, Suite 400, Silver Spring, MD 20910-3492 *Tel:* 301-628-5000 *Toll Free Tel:* 800-274-4262; 800-637-0323 (orders) *Fax:* 301-628-5342 *E-mail:* anp@ana.org *Web Site:* www.Nursesbooks.org; www.NursingWorld.org, pg 153

NYC Emerging Writers Fellowships, 17 E 47 St, New York, NY 10017 *Tel:* 212-755-6710 *E-mail:* info@centerforfiction.org *Web Site:* centerforfiction.org, pg 649

NYSCA/NYFA Artist Fellowships, 20 Jay St, 7th fl, Brooklyn, NY 11201 *Tel:* 212-366-6900 *Fax:* 212-366-1778 *E-mail:* info@nyfa.org *Web Site:* www.nyfa.org, pg 649

Nystrom Education, 10200 Jefferson Blvd, Culver City, CA 90232 *Tel:* 310-839-2436 *Toll Free Tel:* 800-421-4246 *Fax:* 310-839-2249 *Toll Free Fax:* 800-944-5432 *E-mail:* access@nystromeducation.com; customerservice@nystromeducation.com *Web Site:* www.nystromeducation.com, pg 153

The O. Henry Prize Stories, c/o University of Texas at Austin, One University Sta, English Dept, B5000, Austin, TX 78712 *Web Site:* www.randomhouse.com/anchor/ohenry, pg 649

OAG Worldwide, 801 Warrenville Rd, Suite 555, Lisle, IL 60532 *Tel:* 630-515-5300 *Toll Free Tel:* 800-342-5624 (cust serv) *E-mail:* contactus@oag.com *Web Site:* www.oag.com, pg 153

Oak Knoll Press, 310 Delaware St, New Castle, DE 19720 *Tel:* 302-328-7232 *Toll Free Tel:* 800-996-2556 *Fax:* 302-328-7274 *E-mail:* oakknoll@oakknoll.com; publishing@oakknoll.com *Web Site:* www.oakknoll.com, pg 153

The Oaklea Press, 41 Old Mill Rd, Richmond, VA 23226-3111 *Tel:* 804-218-2394 *Web Site:* oakleapress.com, pg 154

Oberlin College Press, 50 N Professor St, Oberlin, OH 44074-1091 *Tel:* 440-775-8408 *Fax:* 440-775-8124 *E-mail:* oc.press@oberlin.edu *Web Site:* www.oberlin.edu/ocpress, pg 154

Oberon Press, 145 Spruce St, Suite 205, Ottawa, ON K1R 6P1, Canada *Tel:* 613-238-3275 *Fax:* 613-238-3275 *E-mail:* oberon@sympatico.ca *Web Site:* www.oberonpress.ca, pg 435

Objective Entertainment, 609 Greenwich St, 6th fl, New York, NY 10014 *Tel:* 212-431-5454 *Fax:* 917-464-6394 *Web Site:* www.objectiveent.com, pg 498

Eli M Oboler Memorial Award, 50 E Huron St, Chicago, IL 60611 *Tel:* 312-280-4226 *Toll Free Tel:* 800-545-2433 *E-mail:* oif@ala.org *Web Site:* www.ala.org/ifrt, pg 649

Ocean Tree Books, 1325 Cerro Gordo Rd, Santa Fe, NM 87501 *Tel:* 505-983-1412 *Fax:* 505-983-0899 *E-mail:* richard@oceantree.com *Web Site:* www.oceantree.com, pg 154

Oceanview Publishing Inc, 1620 Main St, Suite 11, Sarasota, FL 34236 *Tel:* 941-387-8500 *Web Site:* oceanviewpub.com, pg 154

The Flannery O'Connor Award for Short Fiction, Main Library, 3rd fl, 320 S Jackson St, Athens, GA 30602 *Fax:* 706-542-2558 *Web Site:* www.ugapress.org, pg 650

Frank O'Connor Prize for Fiction, Dept of English, TCU Box 298300, Fort Worth, TX 76129 *Tel:* 817-257-5907 *Fax:* 817-257-5905 *E-mail:* descant@tcu.edu *Web Site:* www.descant.tcu.edu, pg 650

OCP, 5536 NE Hassalo St, Portland, OR 97213 *Tel:* 503-281-1191 *Toll Free Tel:* 800-548-8749 *Fax:* 503-282-3486 *Toll Free Fax:* 800-843-8181 *E-mail:* liturgy@ocp.org *Web Site:* www.ocp.org, pg 154

Octane Press, 815A Brazos St, No 658, Austin, TX 78701 *Tel:* 512-334-9441; 512-761-4555 (sales) *Fax:* 512-430-5343 *E-mail:* info@octanepress.com; sales@octanepress.com *Web Site:* octanepress.com/content/submissions, pg 154

Scott O'Dell Award for Historical Fiction, c/o Horn Book Inc, 300 The Fenway, Suite P-311, Palace Road Bldg, Boston, MA 02215 *Tel:* 617-278-0225 *Toll Free Tel:* 888-628-0225 *E-mail:* scottodellfanpage@gmail.com *Web Site:* scottodell.com/the-scott-odell-award, pg 650

Odyssey Award for Excellence in Audiobook Production, 50 E Huron St, Chicago, IL 60611 *Toll Free Tel:* 800-545-2433 (ext 4390) *Fax:* 312-280-5276 *E-mail:* yalsa@ala.org *Web Site:* www.ala.org/yalsa/odyssey, pg 650

Odyssey Books, 2421 Redwood Ct, Longmont, CO 80503-8155 *Tel:* 720-494-1473 *Fax:* 720-494-1471 *E-mail:* books@odysseybooks.net, pg 154

Odyssey: The Summer Fantasy Writing Workshop, PO Box 75, Mont Vernon, NH 03057 *Tel:* 603-673-6234 *Fax:* 603-673-6234 *Web Site:* www.odysseyworkshop.org, pg 577

OECD Washington Center, 1776 "I" St NW, Suite 450, Washington, DC 20006 *Tel:* 202-785-6323 *Toll Free Tel:* 800-456-6323 (dist ctr/pubns orders) *Fax:* 202-785-0350 *E-mail:* washington.contact@oecd.org; oecdilibrary@oecd.org (sales) *Web Site:* www.oecd-ilibrary.org, pg 154

Annual Off Off Broadway Short Play Festival, 235 Park Ave S, 5th fl, New York, NY 10003 *Tel:* 212-206-8990 *Toll Free Tel:* 866-598-8449 *Fax:* 212-206-1429 *E-mail:* oobfestival@samuelfrench.com *Web Site:* www.oobfestival.com; www.samuelfrench.com, pg 650

Dayne Ogilvie Prize, 600-460 Richmond St W, Toronto, ON M5V 1Y1, Canada *Tel:* 416-504-8222 *Toll Free Tel:* 877-906-6548 *Fax:* 416-504-9090 *E-mail:* info@writerstrust.com *Web Site:* www.writerstrust.com, pg 650

Howard O'Hagan Award for Short Story, 11759 Groat Rd, Edmonton, AB T5M 3K6, Canada *Tel:* 780-422-8174 *Toll Free Tel:* 800-665-5354 (AB only) *Fax:* 780-422-2663 (attn WGA) *E-mail:* mail@writersguild.ca *Web Site:* writersguild.ca, pg 650

Ohio Genealogical Society, 611 State Rte 97 W, Bellville, OH 44813-8813 *Tel:* 419-886-1903 *Fax:* 419-886-0092 *E-mail:* ogs@ogs.org *Web Site:* www.ogs.org, pg 154

Ohio State University Foreign Language Publications, 198 Hagerty Hall, 1775 College Rd, Columbus, OH 43210-1309 *Tel:* 614-292-3838 *Toll Free Tel:* 800-678-6999 *E-mail:* flpubs@osu.edu *Web Site:* flpubs.osu.edu, pg 155

The Ohio State University Press, 180 Pressey Hall, 1070 Carmack Rd, Columbus, OH 43210-1002 *Tel:* 614-292-6930 *Fax:* 614-292-2065 *Toll Free Fax:* 800-621-8476 *E-mail:* info@osupress.org *Web Site:* ohiostatepress.org, pg 155

Ohio University, English Department, Creative Writing Program, Ohio University, English Dept, Ellis Hall, Athens, OH 45701 *Tel:* 740-593-2838 (English Dept) *Fax:* 740-593-2832 *E-mail:* english.department@ohio.edu *Web Site:* www.ohio.edu/cas/english, pg 584

Ohio University Press, Alden Library, Suite 101, 30 Park Place, Athens, OH 45701-2901 *Tel:* 740-593-1154 *Web Site:* www.ohioswallow.com, pg 155

Ohioana Book Awards, 274 E First Ave, Suite 300, Columbus, OH 43201 *Tel:* 614-466-3831 *Fax:* 614-728-6974 *E-mail:* ohioana@ohioana.org *Web Site:* www.ohioana.org, pg 650

Ohioana Walter Rumsey Marvin Grant, 274 E First Ave, Suite 300, Columbus, OH 43201 *Tel:* 614-466-3831 *Fax:* 614-728-6974 *E-mail:* ohioana@ohioana.org *Web Site:* www.ohioana.org, pg 650

Oklahoma Book Awards, 200 NE 18 St, Oklahoma City, OK 73105-3205 *Tel:* 405-522-3383 *Web Site:* libraries.ok.gov/ocb/ok-book-awards/, pg 650

Olde & Oppenheim Publishers, 3219 N Margate Place, Chandler, AZ 85224 *E-mail:* olde_oppenheim@hotmail.com, pg 155

Veronica Oliva, 304 Lily St, San Francisco, CA 94102-5608 *Tel:* 415-337-7707 *E-mail:* veronicaoliva@sbcglobal.net, pg 468

Nancy Olson Bookseller Award, 51 Pleasant Ridge Dr, Asheville, NC 28805 *Tel:* 803-994-9530 *Fax:* 309-410-0211 *E-mail:* siba@sibaweb.com *Web Site:* www.sibaweb.com, pg 650

Chris O'Malley Fiction Prize, University of Wisconsin, 6193 Helen C White Hall, English Dept, 600 N Park St, Madison, WI 53706 *E-mail:* madisonrevw@gmail.com *Web Site:* www.themadisonrevw.com, pg 651

Omnibus Press, 180 Madison Ave, 24th fl, New York, NY 10016 *Tel:* 212-254-2100 *Toll Free Tel:* 800-431-7187 *Fax:* 212-254-2013 *Toll Free Fax:* 800-345-6842 *E-mail:* info@omnibuspress.com *Web Site:* www.omnibuspress.com; www.musicsales.com, pg 155

Omnidawn Publishing, 2200 Adeline St, Suite 150, Oakland, CA 94607 *Tel:* 510-237-5472 *Toll Free Tel:* 800-792-4957 *Fax:* 510-232-8525 *E-mail:* manager@omnidawn.com *Web Site:* www.omnidawn.com, pg 155

Omnigraphics Inc, 615 Griswold, Suite 520, Detroit, MI 48226 *Tel:* 610-461-3548 *Toll Free Tel:* 800-234-1340 (cust serv) *Fax:* 610-532-9001 *Toll Free Fax:* 800-875-1340 (cust serv) *E-mail:* contact@omnigraphics.com; customerservice@omnigraphics.com *Web Site:* omnigraphics.com, pg 155

Omniscient Publishing, 14728 Shirley St, Omaha, NE 68144 *Tel:* 402-334-1676 *Fax:* 402-334-4437 *Web Site:* www.thevaticanfiles.com, pg 447

Omohundro Institute of Early American History & Culture, Swem Library, Ground fl, 400 Landrum Dr, Williamsburg, VA 23185 *Tel:* 757-221-1110 *Fax:* 757-221-1047 *E-mail:* ieahc1@wm.edu *Web Site:* oieahc.wm.edu, pg 155

On-the-Verge Emerging Voices Award, 6363 Wilshire Blvd, Suite 425, Los Angeles, CA 90048 *Tel:* 323-782-1010 *E-mail:* grants@scbwi.org *Web Site:* www.scbwi.org/awards, pg 651

One Act Play Depot, 618 Memorial Dr, PO Box 335, Spiritwood, SK S0J 2M0, Canada *E-mail:* plays@oneactplays.net; orders@oneactplays.net *Web Site:* oneactplays.net, pg 435

One On One Book Publishing/Film-Video Publications, 7944 Capistrano Ave, West Hills, CA 91304 *Tel:* 818-340-6620; 818-340-0175 *Fax:* 818-340-6620 *E-mail:* onebookpro@aol.com, pg 155

Ontario Book Publishers Organization (OBPO), One Rutton St, Suite 101, Toronto, ON M6P 0A1, Canada *Tel:* 416-536-7584 *E-mail:* info@obpo.ca *Web Site:* obpo.ca, pg 542

Ontario Library Association, 2 Toronto St, 3rd fl, Toronto, ON M5C 2B6, Canada *Tel:* 416-363-3388 *Toll Free Tel:* 866-873-9867 *Fax:* 416-941-9581 *E-mail:* info@accessola.com *Web Site:* www.accessola.com, pg 542

Oolichan Books, PO Box 2278, Fernie, BC V0B 1M0, Canada *Tel:* 250-423-6113 *E-mail:* info@oolichan.com *Web Site:* www.oolichan.com, pg 435

Ooligan Press, Portland State University, PO Box 751, Portland, OR 97207 *Tel:* 503-725-9748 *Fax:* 503-725-3561 *E-mail:* ooligan@ooliganpress.pdx.edu *Web Site:* ooligan.pdx.edu, pg 155

Open Books Press, 4735 S State Rd 446, Bloomington, IN 47401 *Tel:* 314-827-6567; 812-837-9226 *E-mail:* info@openbookspress.com *Web Site:* openbookspress.com, pg 156

Open Chapbook Competition, PO Box 1626, Georgetown, KY 40324 *Tel:* 502-603-0670 *E-mail:* finishingbooks@aol.com; flpbookstore@aol.com *Web Site:* www.finishinglinepress.com, pg 651

Open Court Publishing Co, 70 E Lake St, Suite 800, Chicago, IL 60601 *Tel:* 312-701-1720 *Toll Free Tel:* 800-815-2280 *Fax:* 312-701-1728 *E-mail:* opencourt@cricketmedia.com *Web Site:* www.opencourtbooks.com, pg 156

Open Horizons Publishing Co, PO Box 2887, Taos, NM 87571 *Tel:* 575-751-3398 *E-mail:* books@bookmarketingbestsellers.com *Web Site:* bookmarketingbestsellers.com, pg 156

Open Season Awards, University of Victoria, Box 1700, Sta CSC, Victoria, BC V8W 2Y2, Canada *Tel:* 250-721-8524 *Fax:* 250-472-5051 *E-mail:* malahat@uvic.ca *Web Site:* malahatreview.ca, pg 651

Opie Prize, Indiana University, Classroom-Off Bldg, 800 E Third St, Bloomington, IN 47405 *Tel:* 812-856-2379 *Fax:* 812-856-2483 *Web Site:* www.afsnet.org, pg 651

The Optical Society (OSA), 2010 Massachusetts Ave NW, Washington, DC 20036-1023 *Tel:* 202-223-8130 *Toll Free Tel:* 800-766-4672 *E-mail:* custserv@osa.org *Web Site:* www.osa.org, pg 156

Optometric Extension Program Foundation (OEP), 2300 York Rd, Suite 113, Timonium, MD 21093 *Tel:* 410-561-3791 *E-mail:* admin@oepf.org *Web Site:* www.oepf.org, pg 156

OptumInsight™, 11000 Optum Circle, Eden Prairie, MN 55344 *Tel:* 952-833-7100 *Toll Free Tel:* 888-445-8745 *Web Site:* www.optum.com, pg 156

Orange Frazer Press Inc, 37 1/2 W Main St, Wilmington, OH 45177 *Tel:* 937-382-3196 *Fax:* 937-383-3159 *E-mail:* ofrazer@erinet.com *Web Site:* www.orangefrazer.com, pg 156

Orbis Books, PO Box 302, Maryknoll, NY 10545-0302 *Tel:* 914-941-7636 *Toll Free Tel:* 800-258-5838 (orders, Mon-Fri 8AM-4PM EST) *Fax:* 914-941-7005 *E-mail:* orbisbooks@maryknoll.org *Web Site:* orbisbooks.com, pg 156

Orbis Pictus Award, 340 N Neil St, Suite 104, Champaign, IL 61820 *Tel:* 217-328-3870 *Toll Free Tel:* 877-369-6283 (cust serv) *Fax:* 217-328-9645; 217-328-0977 *E-mail:* bookawards@ncte.org *Web Site:* www2.ncte.org/awards, pg 651

Orbit, 1290 Avenue of the Americas, New York, NY 10104 *Tel:* 212-364-1100 *Toll Free Tel:* 800-759-0190 *Web Site:* www.orbitbooks.net, pg 156

Orca Book Publishers, 1016 Balmoral Rd, Victoria, BC V8T 1A8, Canada *Toll Free Tel:* 800-210-5277 *Toll Free Fax:* 877-408-1551 *E-mail:* orca@orcabook.com *Web Site:* www.orcabook.com, pg 435

Ordre des traducteurs, terminologues et interpretes agrees du quebec, 1108-2021 Ave Union, Montreal, QC H3A 2S9, Canada *Tel:* 514-845-4411 *Toll Free Tel:* 800-265-4815 *Fax:* 514-845-9903 *E-mail:* info@ottiaq.org; direction@ottiaq.org; reception@ottiaq.org *Web Site:* www.ottiaq.org, pg 542

Oregon Book Awards, 925 SW Washington St, Portland, OR 97205 *Tel:* 503-227-2583 *Fax:* 503-241-4256 *E-mail:* la@literary-arts.org *Web Site:* www.literary-arts.org, pg 651

Oregon Christian Writers (OCW), 1075 Willow Lake Rd N, Keizer, OR 97303 *Tel:* 503-393-3356 *E-mail:* contact@oregonchristianwriters.org *Web Site:* oregonchristianwriters.org, pg 542

Oregon Christian Writers One-Day Conferences, 1075 Willow Lake Rd N, Keizer, OR 97303 *Tel:* 503-393-3356 *E-mail:* contact@oregonchristianwriters.org *Web Site:* oregonchristianwriters.org, pg 577

Oregon Christian Writers Summer Conference, 1075 Willow Lake Rd N, Keizer, OR 97303 *Tel:* 503-393-3356 *E-mail:* contact@oregonchristianwriters.org *Web Site:* oregonchristianwriters.org, pg 577

Oregon State University Press, 121 The Valley Library, Corvallis, OR 97331-4501 *Tel:* 541-737-3166, pg 157

O'Reilly Media Inc, 1005 Gravenstein Hwy N, Sebastopol, CA 95472 *Tel:* 707-827-7000; 707-827-7019 (cust support) *Toll Free Tel:* 800-998-9938; 800-889-8969 *Fax:* 707-829-0104; 707-824-8268 *E-mail:* orders@oreilly.com; support@oreilly.com *Web Site:* www.oreilly.com, pg 157

Oriental Institute Publications, 1155 E 58 St, Chicago, IL 60637 *Tel:* 773-702-5967 *Fax:* 773-702-9853 *E-mail:* oi-publications@uchicago.edu *Web Site:* oi.uchicago.edu, pg 157

Orientation to the Graphic Arts, 10015 Main St, Fairfax, VA 22031-3489 *Tel:* 703-385-1335 *Toll Free Tel:* 888-385-3588 *Fax:* 703-273-0456 *E-mail:* info@printing.org; assist@printing.org *Web Site:* www.printing.org, pg 577

The Original Falcon Press, 1753 E Broadway Rd, No 101-277, Tempe, AZ 85282 *Tel:* 602-708-1409 *E-mail:* info@originalfalcon.com *Web Site:* www.originalfalcon.com, pg 157

ORO editions, 31 Commercial Blvd, Suite F, Novato, CA 94949 *Tel:* 415-883-3300 *Fax:* 415-883-3309 *E-mail:* info@oroeditions.com *Web Site:* www.oroeditions.com, pg 157

George Orwell Award, 340 N Neil St, Suite 104, Champaign, IL 61820 *Tel:* 217-328-3870 *Toll Free Tel:* 877-369-6283 (cust serv) *Fax:* 217-328-0977 *E-mail:* publiclangawards@ncte.org *Web Site:* www.ncte.org, pg 651

Fifi Oscard Agency Inc, 1440 Broadway, 23rd fl, New York, NY 10018 *Tel:* 212-764-1100 *E-mail:* agency@fifioscard.com *Web Site:* fifioscard.com, pg 498

Other Press, 267 Fifth Ave, 6th fl, New York, NY 10016 *Tel:* 212-414-0054 *Toll Free Tel:* 877-843-6843 *Fax:* 212-414-0939 *E-mail:* editor@otherpress.com; marketing@otherpress.com; publicity@otherpress.com *Web Site:* www.otherpress.com, pg 158

James H Ottaway Jr Award for the Promotion of International Literature, 147 Prince St, Brooklyn, NY 11201 *Tel:* 347-699-2914 *E-mail:* info@wordswithoutborders.org *Web Site:* www.wordswithoutborders.org/ottaway-award, pg 651

Ottoline Prize, University at Albany, Science Library 320, 1400 Washington Ave, Albany, NY 12222 *Tel:* 518-567-7006 *Web Site:* www.fenceportal.org, pg 651

Our Sunday Visitor Publishing, 200 Noll Plaza, Huntington, IN 46750 *Tel:* 260-356-8400 *Toll Free Tel:* 800-348-2440 (orders) *Fax:* 260-356-8472 *Toll Free Fax:* 800-498-6709 *E-mail:* osvbooks@osv.com (book orders) *Web Site:* www.osv.com, pg 157

Outdoor Writers Association of America (OWAA), 2814 Brooks St, Box 442, Missoula, MT 59801 *Tel:* 406-728-7434 *E-mail:* info@owaa.org *Web Site:* www.owaa.org, pg 542

Outdoor Writers Association of America Annual Conference, 2814 Brooks St, Box 442, Missoula, MT 59801 *Tel:* 406-728-7434 *E-mail:* info@owaa.org *Web Site:* www.owaa.org, pg 577

The Overlook Press, 195 Broadway, 9th fl, New York, NY 10007 *Tel:* 212-673-2210; 845-679-6838 (orders & dist) *E-mail:* abrams@abramsbooks.com; sales@abramsbooks.com (orders) *Web Site:* www.abramsbooks.com/imprints/overlookpress/; www.abramsbooks.com/overlooksales/, pg 158

Overseas Press Club of America (OPC), 40 W 45 St, New York, NY 10036 *Tel:* 212-626-9220 *Fax:* 212-626-9210 *E-mail:* info@opcofamerica.org *Web Site:* www.opcofamerica.org, pg 543

Richard C Owen Publishers Inc, PO Box 585, Katonah, NY 10536-0585 *Tel:* 914-232-3903 *Toll Free Tel:* 800-336-5588 *Fax:* 914-232-3977 *Web Site:* www.rcowen.com, pg 158

Owl About Books Publisher Inc, 1632 Royalwood Circle, Joshua, TX 76058 *Tel:* 682-553-9078 *Fax:* 817-558-8983 *E-mail:* owlaboutbooks@gmail.com *Web Site:* www.owlaboutbooks.com, pg 158

Owlkids Books Inc, 10 Lower Spadina Ave, Suite 400, Toronto, ON M5V 2Z2, Canada *Tel:* 416-340-2700 *Fax:* 416-340-9769 *E-mail:* owlkids@owlkids.com *Web Site:* www.owlkidsbooks.com, pg 435

Frank L & Harriet C Owsley Award, University of Georgia, Dept of History, Athens, GA 30602-1602 *Tel:* 706-542-8848 *Fax:* 706-542-2455 *Web Site:* www.thesha.org, pg 651

Oxford University Press USA, 198 Madison Ave, New York, NY 10016 *Toll Free Tel:* 800-451-7556 (orders); 800-445-9714 (cust serv) *Fax:* 919-677-1303 *E-mail:* custserv.us@oup.com *Web Site:* global.oup.com, pg 158

Oyster River Press, 36 Oyster River Rd, Durham, NH 03824-3029 *Tel:* 603-868-5006 *E-mail:* oysterriverpress@comcast.net *Web Site:* www.oysterriverbooks.com; www.facebook.com/OysterRiverPress, pg 468

Ozark Creative Writers Inc Annual Conference, 512 Walnut St, Mount Vernon, IN 47620 *E-mail:* ozarkcreativewriters@ozarkcreativewriters.com *Web Site:* www.ozarkcreativewriters.com, pg 577

Ozark Mountain Publishing Inc, PO Box 754, Huntsville, AR 72740-0754 *Tel:* 479-738-2348 *Toll Free Tel:* 800-935-0045 *Fax:* 479-738-2448 *E-mail:* info@ozarkmt.com *Web Site:* www.ozarkmt.com, pg 158

P & R Publishing Co, 1102 Marble Hill Rd, Phillipsburg, NJ 08865 *Tel:* 908-454-0505 *Toll Free Tel:* 800-631-0094 *Fax:* 908-859-2390 *E-mail:* sales@prpbooks.com; info@prpbooks.com *Web Site:* www.prpbooks.com, pg 158

Pace University, Master of Science in Publishing, Dept of Publishing, Rm 805-E, 551 Fifth Ave, New York, NY 10176 *Tel:* 212-346-1431 *Toll Free Tel:* 877-284-7670 *Fax:* 212-346-1165 *Web Site:* www.pace.edu/dyson/mspub, pg 584

Pace University Press, MS in Publishing, 8th fl, 551 Fifth Ave, New York, NY 10176 *Tel:* 212-346-1417 *Fax:* 212-346-1165 *Web Site:* www.pace.edu/press, pg 158

Pacific Educational Press, c/o UBC Press, 2029 West Mall, Vancouver, BC V6T 1Z2, Canada *Tel:* 604-822-5959; 604-827-2232 (cust serv) *Toll Free Tel:* 855-827-2232 *E-mail:* pep.admin@ubc.ca; pep.sales@ubc.ca *Web Site:* pacificedpress.ca, pg 435

Pacific Northwest Book Awards, 520 W 13 Ave, Eugene, OR 97401-3461 *Tel:* 541-683-4363 *Fax:* 541-683-3910 *E-mail:* info@pnba.org; awards@pnba.org *Web Site:* www.pnba.org, pg 651

Pacific Northwest Booksellers Association (PNBA), 520 W 13 Ave, Eugene, OR 97401-3461 *Tel:* 541-683-4363 *Toll Free Tel:* 800-353-6764 *Fax:* 541-683-3910 *E-mail:* info@pnba.org *Web Site:* www.pnba.org, pg 543

Pacific Northwest Young Reader's Choice Award, Vancouver Mall Community Library, 8700 NE Vancouver Mall Dr, Suite 285, Vancouver, WA 98662 *Web Site:* www.pnla.org/yrca, pg 652

Pacific Press® Publishing Association, 1350 N Kings Rd, Nampa, ID 83687-3193 *Tel:* 208-465-2500 *Toll Free Tel:* 800-447-7377 *Fax:* 208-465-2531 *Web Site:* www.pacificpress.com, pg 158

Pacific Printing Industries Association, 6825 SW Sandburg St, Portland, OR 97223 *Tel:* 503-221-3944 *Toll Free Tel:* 877-762-7742 *Fax:* 503-221-5691 *E-mail:* info@ppiassociation.org *Web Site:* www.ppiassociation.org, pg 543

Pacific Publishing Services, PO Box 1150, Capitola, CA 95010-1150 *Tel:* 831-476-8284 *Fax:* 831-476-8294 *E-mail:* pacpubs@attglobal.net, pg 468

The Pacific Spirit Poetry Prize, University of British Columbia, Buch E462, 1866 Main Mall, Vancouver, BC V6T 1Z1, Canada *Tel:* 778-822-2514 *Fax:* 778-822-3616 *E-mail:* prismwritingcontest@gmail.com *Web Site:* www.prismmagazine.ca, pg 652

Pact Press, c/o Regal House Publishing, 806 Oberlin Rd, No 12094, Raleigh, NC 27605 *E-mail:* info@regalhousepublishing.com *Web Site:* pactpress.com, pg 159

PAGE International Screenwriting Awards, 7190 Sunset Blvd, Suite 610, Hollywood, CA 90046 *E-mail:* info@pageawards.com *Web Site:* www.pageawards.com, pg 652

Paintbox Press, 275 Madison Ave, Suite 600, New York, NY 10016 *Tel:* 212-878-6610 *E-mail:* info@paintboxpress.com *Web Site:* www.paintboxpress.com, pg 159

Painted Hills Publishing, 16500 Dakota Ridge Rd, Longmont, CO 80503 *Tel:* 303-823-6642 *E-mail:* cw@livingimagescjw.com *Web Site:* www.wildhoofbeats.com; www.livingimagescjw.com, pg 447

Painted-Words Inc, 310 W 97 St, Suite 24, New York, NY 10025 *Tel:* 212-663-2311 *Fax:* 212-663-2891 *E-mail:* info@painted-words.com *Web Site:* painted-words.com, pg 512

Dobie Paisano Fellowship Program, 110 Inner Campus Dr, Stop G0400, Austin, TX 78712-0710 *Tel:* 512-471-7620 *Web Site:* dobiepaisano.utexas.edu; pg 652

Palgrave Macmillan, One New York Plaza, Suite 4500, New York, NY 10004-1562 *Tel:* 212-726-9200 *E-mail:* sales-ny@springernature.com *Web Site:* www.palgrave.com; www.springernature.com, pg 159

Palimpsest Press, 1171 Eastlawn Ave, Windsor, ON N8S 3J1, Canada *Tel:* 519-259-2112 *E-mail:* publicity@palimpsestpress.ca *Web Site:* www.palimpsestpress.ca, pg 435

Palladium Books Inc, 39074 Webb Ct, Westland, MI 48185 *Tel:* 734-721-2903 (orders) *Web Site:* www.palladiumbooks.com, pg 159

Palm Island Press, 3607 Maine Ave, Sebring, FL 33870 *Tel:* 305-296-3102 *E-mail:* pipress2@gmail.com, pg 159

Palm Springs Writers Guild, PO Box 947, Rancho Mirage, CA 92270-0947 *Web Site:* www.palmspringswritersguild.org, pg 543

Palmetto Bug Books, 1345 NE 105 St, No 2, Miami Shores, FL 33138 *Tel:* 305-531-9813 *E-mail:* palmettobugbooks@gmail.com, pg 159

Pangaea Publications, 402 Church St, Wisconsin Dells, WI 53965 *Tel:* 651-226-2032 *Fax:* 651-226-2032 *E-mail:* info@pangaea.org *Web Site:* pangaea.org, pg 159

Karen L Pangallo, 27 Buffum St, Salem, MA 01970 *Tel:* 978-744-8796 *E-mail:* pangallo@noblenet.org; kpangallo@gmail.com, pg 468

Mildred & Albert Panowski Playwriting Award, Forest Roberts Theatre, 1401 Presque Isle Ave, Marquette, MI 49855-5364 *Tel:* 906-227-2553 *Fax:* 906-227-2567 *E-mail:* theatre@nmu.edu *Web Site:* www.nmu.edu/theatre, pg 652

Pantheon Books, c/o Penguin Random House Inc, 1745 Broadway, New York, NY 10019 *Tel:* 212-751-2600 *Fax:* 212-572-2662 (foreign rts) *Web Site:* knopfdoubleday.com, pg 159

Pants On Fire Press, 2062 Harbor Cove Way, Winter Garden, FL 34787 *Tel:* 863-546-0760 *E-mail:* submission@pantsonfirepress.com *Web Site:* www.pantsonfirepress.com, pg 159

Papercutz, 160 Broadway, E Wing, Suite 700, New York, NY 10038 *Tel:* 646-559-4681 *Toll Free Tel:* 800-886-1223 *Fax:* 212-643-1545 *E-mail:* papercutz@papercutz.com *Web Site:* www.papercutz.com, pg 160

Parachute Publishing LLC, 157 Columbus Ave, Suite 518, New York, NY 10023 *Tel:* 212-691-1422, pg 160

Paraclete Press Inc, 36 Southern Eagle Cartway, Brewster, MA 02631 *Tel:* 508-255-4685 *Toll Free Tel:* 800-451-5006 *Fax:* 508-255-5705 *E-mail:* mail@paracletepress.com; customerservice@paracletepress.com *Web Site:* www.paracletepress.com, pg 160

Paradigm Publications, 202 Bendix Dr, Taos, NM 87571 *Tel:* 575-758-7758 *Toll Free Tel:* 800-873-3946 (US); 888-873-3947 (CN) *Fax:* 575-758-7768 *E-mail:* info@paradigm-pubs.com *Web Site:* www.paradigm-pubs.com; www.redwingbooks.com, pg 160

Paradise Cay Publications Inc, 120 Monda Way, Blue Lake, CA 95525 *Tel:* 707-822-9063 *Toll Free Tel:* 800-736-4509 *Fax:* 707-822-9163 *E-mail:* info@paracay.com; orders@paracay.com *Web Site:* www.paracay.com, pg 160

Paragon House, 3600 Labore Rd, Suite 1, St Paul, MN 55110-4144 *Tel:* 651-644-3087 *Toll Free Tel:* 800-447-3709 *Fax:* 651-644-0997 *E-mail:* paragon@paragonhouse.com *Web Site:* www.paragonhouse.com, pg 160

Parallax Press, 2236B Sixth St, Berkeley, CA 94710 *Tel:* 510-540-6411 *Toll Free Tel:* 800-863-5290 (orders) *Fax:* 510-981-1157 *Web Site:* www.parallax.org, pg 160

Paramount Market Publishing Inc, 274 N Goodman St, Suite D214, Rochester, NY 14607 *Tel:* 607-275-8100 *E-mail:* editors@paramountbooks.com *Web Site:* www.paramountbooks.com, pg 160

Parenting Press, 13751 Lake City Way NE, Suite 110, Seattle, WA 98125 *Tel:* 206-364-2900 *Toll Free Tel:* 800-99-BOOKS (992-6657) *Fax:* 206-364-0702 *E-mail:* office@parentingpress.com; marketing@parentingpress.com *Web Site:* www.parentingpress.com, pg 161

Park Place Publications, 591 Lighthouse Ave, Suite 10, Pacific Grove, CA 93950 *Tel:* 831-649-6640 *E-mail:* publishingbiz@sbcglobal.net *Web Site:* www.parkplacepublications.com, pg 161

Francis Parkman Prize, 2950 Broadway, New York, NY 10027 *Tel:* 212-854-6495 *E-mail:* amhistsociety@columbia.edu *Web Site:* sah.columbia.edu, pg 652

Parmenides Publishing, 3753 Howard Hughes Pkwy, Suite 200, Las Vegas, NV 89169 *Tel:* 702-892-3934 *Fax:* 702-892-3939 *E-mail:* info@parmenides.com *Web Site:* www.parmenides.com, pg 161

Parsons School of Design, Continuing Education, 2 W 13 St, Rm 506, New York, NY 10011 *Tel:* 212-229-8933 *E-mail:* ceinformation@newschool.edu; academy@newschool.edu *Web Site:* www.newschool.edu/parsons, pg 584

The Paterson Poetry Prize, One College Blvd, Paterson, NJ 07505-1179 *Tel:* 973-684-6555 *Fax:* 973-523-6085 *Web Site:* www.poetrycenterpccc.com, pg 652

The Paterson Prize for Books for Young People, One College Blvd, Paterson, NJ 07505-1179 *Tel:* 973-684-6555 *Fax:* 973-523-6085 *Web Site:* www.poetrycenterpccc.com, pg 652

Path Press Inc, 708 Washington St, Evanston, IL 60202 *Tel:* 847-492-0177 *E-mail:* pathpressinc@aol.com, pg 161

Pathfinder Publishing Inc, 120 S Houghton Rd, Suite 138, Tucson, AZ 85748 *Tel:* 520-647-0158 *Web Site:* www.pathfinderpublishing.com, pg 161

Kathi J Paton Literary Agency, Box 2044, Radio City Sta, New York, NY 10101-2044 *Tel:* 212-265-6586 *E-mail:* kjplitbiz@optonline.net *Web Site:* www.patonliterary.com, pg 498

Diane Patrick, 140 Carver Loop, No 21A, Bronx, NY 10475-2954 *E-mail:* dpatrickediting@aol.com *Web Site:* www.dianepatrick.net, pg 468

The Alicia Patterson Foundation Fellowship Program, 1100 Vermont Ave, Suite 900, Washington, DC 20005 *Tel:* 202-393-5995 *Fax:* 301-951-8512 *E-mail:* info@aliciapatterson.org *Web Site:* www.aliciapatterson.org, pg 652

Paul Dry Books, 1700 Sansom St, Suite 700, Philadelphia, PA 19103 *Tel:* 215-231-9939 *E-mail:* editor@pauldrybooks.com *Web Site:* www.pauldrybooks.com, pg 161

Pauline Books & Media, 50 Saint Paul's Ave, Boston, MA 02130 *Tel:* 617-522-8911 *Toll Free Tel:* 800-876-4463 (orders); 800-836-9723 (cust serv) *Fax:* 617-541-9805 *E-mail:* editorial@paulinemedia.com (ms submissions); orderentry@pauline.org (cust serv) *Web Site:* www.pauline.org/pbmpublishing, pg 161

Paulines Editions, 5610 rue Beaubien est, Montreal, QC H1T 1X5, Canada *Tel:* 514-253-5610 *Fax:* 514-253-1907 *E-mail:* fsp-paulines@videotron.ca *Web Site:* www.editions.paulines.qc.ca, pg 435

Paulist Press, 997 Macarthur Blvd, Mahwah, NJ 07430-9990 *Tel:* 201-825-7300 *Toll Free Tel:* 800-218-1903 *Fax:* 201-825-6921 *Toll Free Fax:* 800-836-3161 *E-mail:* info@paulistpress.com; publicity@paulistpress.com *Web Site:* www.paulistpress.com, pg 161

Peabody Museum Press, 11 Divinity Ave, Cambridge, MA 02138 *Tel:* 617-495-4255; 617-495-3938 (edit) *E-mail:* peapub@fas.harvard.edu *Web Site:* www.peabody.harvard.edu/publications, pg 162

Peachpit Press, 1301 Sansome St, San Francisco, CA 94111 *Toll Free Tel:* 800-283-9444 *E-mail:* info@peachpit.com; ask@peachpit.com *Web Site:* www.peachpit.com, pg 162

Peachtree Publishing Co Inc, 1700 Chattahoochee Ave, Atlanta, GA 30318-2112 *Tel:* 404-876-8761 *Toll Free Tel:* 800-241-0113 *Fax:* 404-875-2578 *Toll Free Fax:* 800-875-8909 *E-mail:* hello@peachtree-online.com; orders@peachtree-online.com; sales@peachtree-online.com *Web Site:* www.peachtree-online.com, pg 162

PearlCo Literary Agency, LLC, 6596 Heronswood Cove, Memphis, TN 38119 *Tel:* 901-754-5276 *Web Site:* www.pearlcoliteraryagency.com, pg 498

Pearson Allyn & Bacon, 501 Boylston St, Boston, MA 02116 *Tel:* 617-848-6000 *Toll Free Tel:* 800-428-4466 *Fax:* 617-848-6016 *Web Site:* home.pearsonhighered.com, pg 162

Pearson Arts & Sciences, 221 River St, Hoboken, NJ 07030 *Tel:* 917-981-2200 *Web Site:* www.pearsonhighered.com, pg 162

Pearson Benjamin Cummings, 1301 Sansome St, San Francisco, CA 94111-1122 *Tel:* 415-402-2500 *Toll Free Tel:* 800-922-0579 (orders) *Toll Free Fax:* 800-445-6991 (orders) *Web Site:* home.pearsonhighered.com, pg 162

Pearson Business Publishing, 221 River St, Hoboken, NJ 07030-4772 *Tel:* 201-236-7000 *Web Site:* www.pearsonhighered.com, pg 162

Pearson Education Canada, 26 Prince Andrew Place, North York, ON M3C 2H4, Canada *Toll Free Tel:* 800-567-3800 *Fax:* 416-447-7755 *Toll Free Fax:* 800-263-7733 *E-mail:* cdn.ordr@pearsoned.com *Web Site:* www.pearson.com/ca; www.mypearsonstore.ca, pg 436

Pearson Education Ltd, 225 River St, Hoboken, NJ 07030-4772 *Tel:* 201-236-7000 *Fax:* 201-236-6549 *Web Site:* www.pearsoned.com, pg 162

Pearson ELT, 221 River St, Hoboken, NJ 07030 *Toll Free Tel:* 877-202-4572 *Toll Free Fax:* 800-445-6991 *E-mail:* english@pearson.com *Web Site:* www.pearsonelt.com, pg 162

Pearson ERPI, 1611 Cremazie Blvd E, 10th fl, Montreal, QC H2M 2P2, Canada *Tel:* 514-334-2690 *Toll Free Tel:* 800-263-3678 *Fax:* 514-334-4720 *Toll Free Fax:* 800-643-4720 *E-mail:* bienvenue@pearsonerpi.com *Web Site:* pearsonerpi.com; pearsonplc.ca, pg 436

Pearson Higher Education, 225 River St, Hoboken, NJ 07030-4772 *Tel:* 201-236-7000 *Web Site:* www.pearson.com/us/higher-education.html, pg 162

Pearson Learning Solutions, 501 Boyleston St, Suite 900, Boston, MA 02116 *Tel:* 617-671-3300 *Toll Free Tel:* 800-428-4466 (orders); 800-635-1579 *E-mail:* pcp@pearson.com *Web Site:* www.pearsoned.com, pg 162

Deborah Pease Prize, 323 Dean St, Brooklyn, NY 11217 *Tel:* 718-858-8067 *E-mail:* general@apublicspace.org *Web Site:* apublicspace.org, pg 652

William Peden Prize in Fiction, 357 McReynolds Hall, Columbia, MO 65211 *Tel:* 573-882-4474 *Toll Free Tel:* 800-949-2505 *Fax:* 573-884-4671 *E-mail:* question@moreview.com *Web Site:* www.missourireview.com, pg 652

T H Peek Publisher, PO Box 7406, Ann Arbor, MI 48107 *Tel:* 734-222-8205 *Fax:* 734-661-0136 *E-mail:* info@thpeekpublisher.com *Web Site:* www.thpeekpublisher.com, pg 162

Pegasus Award for Poetry Criticism, 61 W Superior St, Chicago, IL 60654 *Tel:* 312-787-7070 *E-mail:* poetryfoundation.org *Web Site:* www.poetryfoundation.org/foundation/criticism-award, pg 653

Pelican Publishing Co, 400 Poydras St, Suite 900, New Orleans, LA 70130 *Tel:* 504-368-1175 *Toll Free Tel:* 800-843-1724 *Fax:* 504-368-1195 *E-mail:* sales@pelicanpub.com (sales); office@pelicanpub.com (permission); promo@pelicanpub.com (publicity) *Web Site:* www.pelicanpub.com, pg 162

Pembroke Publishers Ltd, 538 Hood Rd, Markham, ON L3R 3K9, Canada *Tel:* 905-477-0650 *Toll Free Tel:* 800-997-9807 *Fax:* 905-477-3691 *Toll Free Fax:* 800-339-5568 *Web Site:* www.pembrokepublishers.com, pg 436

PEN America, 588 Broadway, Suite 303, New York, NY 10012 *Tel:* 212-334-1660 *Fax:* 212-334-2181 *E-mail:* info@pen.org *Web Site:* pen.org, pg 543

PEN America, 8444 Wilshire Blvd, 4th fl, Beverly Hills, CA 90211 *Tel:* 323-424-4939 *Fax:* 323-424-4944 *E-mail:* info@pen.org *Web Site:* pen.org/pen-america-los-angeles, pg 543

PEN America Boston, MIT, 14N-221A, 77 Massachusetts Ave, Cambridge, MA 02139 *Tel:* 617-324-1729 *E-mail:* penamericaboston@pen.org *Web Site:* pen.org/pen-america-boston, pg 543

PEN America Los Angeles Literary Award for Journalism, 8444 Wilshire Blvd, 4th fl, Beverly Hills, CA 90211 *Tel:* 323-424-4939 *E-mail:* awards@pen.org; info@pen.org *Web Site:* pen.org/pen-america-los-angeles-literary-awards-festival, pg 653

Pen & Publish LLC, 4719 Holly Hills Ave, St Louis, MO 63116 *Tel:* 314-827-6567 *E-mail:* info@penandpublish.com *Web Site:* www.penandpublish.com, pg 163

The PEN Award for Poetry in Translation, 588 Broadway, Suite 303, New York, NY 10012 *Tel:* 212-334-1660 *Fax:* 212-334-2181 *E-mail:* awards@pen.org *Web Site:* pen.org/pen-award-poetry-translation, pg 653

PEN/Barbey Freedom to Write Award, 588 Broadway, Suite 303, New York, NY 10012 *Tel:* 212-334-1660 *E-mail:* awards@pen.org *Web Site:* pen.org/penbarbey-freedom-to-write-award, pg 653

PEN/Bellwether Prize for Socially Engaged Fiction, 588 Broadway, Suite 303, New York, NY 10012 *Tel:* 212-334-1660 *E-mail:* awards@pen.org *Web Site:* pen.org/pen-bellwether-prize, pg 653

PEN Canada, 401 Richmond St W, Suite 258, Toronto, ON M5V 3A8, Canada *Tel:* 416-703-8448 *E-mail:* queries@pencanada.ca *Web Site:* www.pencanada.ca, pg 543

PEN/Diamonstein-Spielvogel Award for the Art of the Essay, 588 Broadway, Suite 303, New York, NY 10012 *Tel:* 212-334-1660 *E-mail:* awards@pen.org *Web Site:* pen.org/pen-diamonstein-spielvogel-award-for-the-art-of-the-essay, pg 653

PEN/E O Wilson Prize for Literary Science Writing, 588 Broadway, Suite 303, New York, NY 10012 *Tel:* 212-334-1660 *E-mail:* awards@pen.org *Web Site:* pen.org/pen-eo-wilson-prize-literary-science-writing, pg 653

PEN/Edward & Lily Tuck Award for Paraguayan Literature, 588 Broadway, Suite 303, New York, NY 10012 *Tel:* 212-334-1660 *Fax:* 212-334-2181 *E-mail:* awards@pen.org *Web Site:* pen.org/pen-edward-lily-tuck-award-paraguayan-literature, pg 653

PEN/ESPN Award for Literary Sports Writing, 588 Broadway, Suite 303, New York, NY 10012 *Tel:* 212-334-1660 *E-mail:* awards@pen.org *Web Site:* pen.org/pen-espn-award, pg 653

PEN/ESPN Lifetime Achievement Award for Literary Sports Writing, 588 Broadway, Suite 303, New York, NY 10012 *Tel:* 212-334-1660 *E-mail:* awards@pen.org *Web Site:* pen.org/pen-espn-lifetime-literary-sports-writing, pg 653

PEN/Faulkner Award for Fiction, 201 E Capitol St SE, Washington, DC 20003 *Tel:* 202-898-9063 *Fax:* 202-675-0360 *Web Site:* www.penfaulkner.org, pg 653

PEN/Fusion Emerging Writers Prize, 588 Broadway, Suite 303, New York, NY 10012 *Tel:* 212-334-1660 *E-mail:* awards@pen.org *Web Site:* pen.org/literary-awards, pg 653

PEN/Jacqueline Bograd Weld Award for Biography, 588 Broadway, Suite 303, New York, NY 10012 *Tel:* 212-334-1660 *E-mail:* awards@pen.org *Web Site:* pen.org/pen-bograd-weld-award-biography, pg 654

PEN/Jean Stein Book Award, 588 Broadway, Suite 303, New York, NY 10012 *Tel:* 212-334-1660 *E-mail:* info@pen.org; awards@pen.org *Web Site:* pen.org/pen-jean-stein-book-award, pg 654

PEN/John Kenneth Galbraith Award for Nonfiction, 588 Broadway, Suite 303, New York, NY 10012 *Tel:* 212-334-1660 *Fax:* 212-334-2181 *E-mail:* awards@pen.org *Web Site:* pen.org/pen-galbraith-award-for-nonfiction, pg 654

PEN/Joyce Osterweil Award for Poetry, 588 Broadway, Suite 303, New York, NY 10012 *Tel:* 212-334-1660 *E-mail:* awards@pen.org *Web Site:* pen.org/pen-osterweil-award-for-poetry, pg 654

Pen-L Publishing, 12 W Dickson St, No 4455, Fayetteville, AR 72702 *Web Site:* www.pen-l.com, pg 163

PEN/Malamud Award for Excellence in Short Fiction, 201 E Capitol St SE, Washington, DC 20003 *Tel:* 202-898-9063 *Fax:* 202-675-0360 *E-mail:* awards@penfaulkner.org; info@penfaulkner.org *Web Site:* www.penfaulkner.org/pen-malamud-award, pg 654

PEN/Mike Nichols Writing for Performance Award, 588 Broadway, Suite 303, New York, NY 10012 *Tel:* 212-334-1660 *Fax:* 212-334-2181 *E-mail:* awards@pen.org *Web Site:* pen.org/pen-nichols-award, pg 654

PEN/Nabokov Award for Achievement in International Literature, 588 Broadway, Suite 303, New York, NY 10012 *Tel:* 212-334-1660 *Fax:* 212-334-2181 *E-mail:* awards@pen.org *Web Site:* pen.org/pen-nabokov-award, pg 654

PEN/New England Awards, MIT, 14N-221A, 77 Massachusetts Ave, Cambridge, MA 02139 *Tel:* 617-324-1729 *E-mail:* pen-newengland@mit.edu; pen-ne@lesley.edu *Web Site:* www.pen-ne.org, pg 654

PEN Open Book Award, 588 Broadway, Suite 303, New York, NY 10012 *Tel:* 212-334-1660 *E-mail:* awards@pen.org *Web Site:* pen.org/pen-open-book-award, pg 654

PEN/Phyllis Naylor Working Writer Fellowship, 588 Broadway, Suite 303, New York, NY 10012 *Tel:* 212-334-1660 *Fax:* 212-334-2181 *E-mail:* awards@pen.org *Web Site:* pen.org/literary-awards/grants-fellowships, pg 654

PEN/Ralph Manheim Medal for Translation, 588 Broadway, Suite 303, New York, NY 10012 *Tel:* 212-334-1660 *Fax:* 212-334-2181 *E-mail:* awards@pen.org *Web Site:* pen.org/literary-award/penralph-manheim-medal-for-translation, pg 654

PEN/Robert Bingham Prize for Debut Fiction, 588 Broadway, Suite 303, New York, NY 10012 *Tel:* 212-334-1660 *Fax:* 212-334-2181 *E-mail:* awards@pen.org *Web Site:* pen.org/pen-bingham-prize, pg 655

PEN/Saul Bellow Award for Achievement in American Fiction, 588 Broadway, Suite 303, New York, NY 10012 *Tel:* 212-334-1660 *Fax:* 212-334-2181 *E-mail:* awards@pen.org *Web Site:* pen.org/pen-saul-bellow-award, pg 655

PEN Translation Prize, 588 Broadway, Suite 303, New York, NY 10012 *Tel:* 212-334-1660 *Fax:* 212-334-2181 *E-mail:* awards@pen.org *Web Site:* pen.org/pen-translation-prize, pg 655

PEN/Voelcker Award, 588 Broadway, Suite 303, New York, NY 10012 *Tel:* 212-334-1660 *E-mail:* awards@pen.org *Web Site:* pen.org/pen-voelcker-award-poetry, pg 655

PEN Writers' Emergency Fund, 588 Broadway, Suite 303, New York, NY 10012 *Tel:* 212-334-1660 *Fax:* 212-334-2181 *E-mail:* feprogram@pen.org *Web Site:* pen.org/writers-emergency-fund, pg 655

Pendragon Press, 52 White Hill Rd, Hillsdale, NY 12529-5839 *Tel:* 518-325-6100 *Toll Free Tel:* 877-656-6381 (orders) *E-mail:* editor@pendragonpress.com; orders@pendragonpress.com *Web Site:* www.pendragonpress.com, pg 163

Penfield Books, 215 Brown St, Iowa City, IA 52245 *Tel:* 319-337-9998 *Toll Free Tel:* 800-728-9998 *Fax:* 319-351-6846 *E-mail:* penfield@penfieldbooks.com; orders@penfieldbooks.com *Web Site:* www.penfieldbooks.com, pg 163

Penguin Books, 375 Hudson St, New York, NY 10014 *Tel:* 212-366-2000 *E-mail:* penguinpublicity@us.penguingroup.com *Web Site:* www.penguinclassics.com; www.penguin.com, pg 163

Penguin Group (Canada), 320 Front St W, Suite 1400, Toronto, ON M5V 3B6, Canada *Tel:* 416-364-4449 *Fax:* 416-598-7764 *E-mail:* customerservicescanada@penguinrandomhouse.com; publicity@ca.penguingroup.com *Web Site:* penguinrandomhouse.ca/imprints/penguin-canada, pg 436

Penguin Group USA, A Penguin Random House Company, 375 Hudson St, New York, NY 10014 *Tel:* 212-366-2000 *Toll Free Tel:* 800-847-5515 (inside sales); 800-631-8571 (cust serv) *Fax:* 212-366-2666; 607-775-4829 (inside sales) *E-mail:* online@us.penguingroup.com *Web Site:* www.penguin.com, pg 163

The Penguin Press, 375 Hudson St, New York, NY 10014 *Web Site:* thepenguinpress.com, pg 164

Penguin Random House Audio Publishing, 1745 Broadway, New York, NY 10019 *E-mail:* audio@penguinrandomhouse.com *Web Site:* www.penguinrandomhouseaudio.com, pg 164

Penguin Random House Canada, 320 Front St W, Suite 1400, Toronto, ON M5V 3B6, Canada *Tel:* 416-364-4449 *Toll Free Tel:* 888-523-9292 (cust serv) *Fax:* 416-598-7764 *Web Site:* www. penguinrandomhouse.ca, pg 436

Penguin Random House Large Print, 1745 Broadway, New York, NY 10019 *Tel:* 212-782-9000 *Web Site:* www.penguinrandomhouse.com, pg 164

Penguin Random House LLC, 1745 Broadway, New York, NY 10019 *Tel:* 212-782-9000 *Toll Free Tel:* 800-726-0600 *Web Site:* www. penguinrandomhouse.com, pg 164

Penguin Random House Speakers Bureau, A Penguin Random House Company, 1745 Broadway, Mail Drop 13-1, New York, NY 10019 *Tel:* 212-572-2013 *E-mail:* speakers@penguinrandomhouse.com *Web Site:* www.prhspeakers.com, pg 515

Penguin Workshop, 1745 Broadway, New York, NY 10019 *Tel:* 212-366-2000 *Web Site:* www.penguin. com/publishers/penguinworkshop/, pg 165

Penguin Young Readers Group, 345 Hudson St, New York, NY 10014 *Tel:* 212-366-2000; 212-414-3553 *Fax:* 212-414-3340 *Web Site:* www.penguin.com/ children, pg 165

Penn State University Press, University Support Bldg 1, Suite C, 820 N University Dr, University Park, PA 16802-1003 *Tel:* 814-865-1327 *Toll Free Tel:* 800-326-9180 *Fax:* 814-863-1408 *Toll Free Fax:* 877-778-2665 *E-mail:* orders@psupress.org; orders@eisenbrauns.org *Web Site:* www.psupress.org; www.eisenbrauns.org, pg 166

Pennsylvania Historical & Museum Commission, State Museum Bldg, 300 North St, Harrisburg, PA 17120-0053 *Tel:* 717-787-3362; 717-787-5526 (orders) *E-mail:* ra-shoppaheritage@pa.gov *Web Site:* www. phmc.pa.gov; www.shoppaheritage.com, pg 166

Pennsylvania State Data Center, Penn State Harrisburg, 777 W Harrisburg Pike, Middletown, PA 17057-4898 *Tel:* 717-948-6336 *Fax:* 717-948-6754 *E-mail:* pasdc@ psu.edu *Web Site:* pasdc.hbg.psu.edu, pg 166

PennWell Books, 1421 S Sheridan Rd, Tulsa, OK 74112 *Tel:* 918-831-9421 *Toll Free Tel:* 800-752-9764 *Fax:* 918-831-9555 *E-mail:* sales@pennwell.com *Web Site:* www.pennwellbooks.com, pg 166

Pennwriters Conference, PO Box 685, Dalton, PA 18414 *E-mail:* conferencecoordinator@pennwriters.org; info@pennwriters.org *Web Site:* pennwriters.org, pg 577

Penny-Farthing Productions, One Sugar Creek Center Blvd, Suite 820, Sugar Land, TX 77478 *Tel:* 713-780-0300 *Toll Free Tel:* 800-926-2669 *Fax:* 713-780-4004 *E-mail:* corp@pfproductions.com *Web Site:* www. pfproductions.com, pg 166

Pentecostal Publishing House, 36 Research Park Ct, Weldon Spring, MO 63304 *Tel:* 314-837-7300 *Toll Free Tel:* 866-819-7667 *Fax:* 314-837-6574 (orders) *Web Site:* www.pentecostalpublishing.com; wordaflamepress.com, pg 166

PeopleSpeak, 25401 Alicia Pkwy, Suite L-512, Laguna Hills, CA 92653 *Tel:* 949-581-6190 *Fax:* 949-581-4958 *E-mail:* pplspeak@att.net *Web Site:* www. detailsplease.com/peoplespeak, pg 468

Rebecca Pepper, 434 NE Floral Place, Portland, OR 97232 *Tel:* 503-236-5802 *E-mail:* rpepper@rpepper. net, pg 468

Peradam Press, PO Box 6, North San Juan, CA 95960-0006 *Tel:* 530-277-9324 *Fax:* 530-559-0754 *E-mail:* peradam@earthlink.net, pg 167

Dan Peragine Literary Agency, 227 Beechwood Ave, Bogota, NJ 07603 *Tel:* 201-390-0468 *Fax:* 201-390-0468 *E-mail:* dpliterary@aol.com, pg 498

Perfection Learning, 1000 N Second Ave, Logan, IA 51546 *Tel:* 712-644-2831 *Toll Free Tel:* 800-831-4190 *Toll Free Fax:* 800-543-2745 *E-mail:* orders@ perfectionlearning.com *Web Site:* perfectionlearning. com, pg 167

Maxwell E Perkins Award, 17 E 47 St, New York, NY 10017 *Tel:* 212-755-6710 *E-mail:* info@ centerforfiction.org *Web Site:* www.centerforfiction. org/awards/perkins, pg 655

The Permanent Press, 4170 Noyac Rd, Sag Harbor, NY 11963 *Tel:* 631-725-1101 *Web Site:* www. thepermanentpress.com, pg 167

The Permissions Group Inc, 401 S Milwaukee Ave, Suite 180, Wheeling, IL 60090 *Tel:* 847-635-6550 *Toll Free Tel:* 800-374-7985 *Fax:* 847-635-6968 *E-mail:* info@permissionsgroup.com *Web Site:* www. permissionsgroup.com, pg 468

Aliki Perroti & Seth Frank Most Promising Young Poet Award, 75 Maiden Lane, Suite 901, New York, NY 10038 *Tel:* 212-274-0343 *E-mail:* awards@poets.org *Web Site:* www.poets.org, pg 655

Persea Books, 90 Broad St, Suite 2100, New York, NY 10004 *Tel:* 212-260-9256 *E-mail:* info@perseabooks. com; poetry@perseabooks.com; publicity@ perseabooks.com *Web Site:* www.perseabooks.com, pg 167

Perseus Books, 1290 Avenue of the Americas, New York, NY 10104 *Tel:* 212-340-8100 *Toll Free Tel:* 800-343-4499 (cust serv) *Fax:* 212-340-8105 *Web Site:* www.perseusbooks.com, pg 167

Perugia Press Prize for a First or Second Book by a Woman, PO Box 60364, Florence, MA 01062 *Web Site:* www.perugiapress.com; perugiapress.org, pg 655

Peter Pauper Press, Inc, 202 Mamaroneck Ave, Suite 400, White Plains, NY 10601-5376 *Tel:* 914-681-0144 *Fax:* 914-681-0389 *E-mail:* customerservice@ peterpauper.com; orders@peterpauper.com; marketing@peterpauper.com *Web Site:* www. peterpauper.com, pg 168

Elsa Peterson Ltd, 41 East Ave, Norwalk, CT 06851-3919 *Tel:* 203-846-8331 *E-mail:* epltd@earthlink.net, pg 469

Peterson Institute for International Economics (PIIE), 1750 Massachusetts Ave NW, Washington, DC 20036-1903 *Tel:* 202-328-9000 *Fax:* 202-328-5432 *E-mail:* media@piie.com *Web Site:* piie.com, pg 168

Peterson's, 8740 Lucent Blvd, Suite 400, Highlands Ranch, CO 80129 *Tel:* 609-896-1800 *Toll Free Tel:* 800-338-3282 *E-mail:* pubmarketing@petersons. com *Web Site:* www.petersons.com, pg 168

The Petrichor Prize for Finely Crafted Fiction, 806 Oberlin Rd, No 12094, Raleigh, NC 27605 *E-mail:* info@regalhousepublishing.com *Web Site:* regalhousepublishing.com/the-petrichor-prize-for-finely-crafted-fiction/, pg 655

Petroleum Extension Service (PETEX), JJ Pickle Research Campus, 10100 Burnet Rd, Bldg 2, Austin, TX 78758-4445 *Tel:* 512-471-5940 *Toll Free Tel:* 800-687-4132 *Fax:* 512-471-9410 *Toll Free Fax:* 800-687-7839 *E-mail:* info@petex.utexas.edu *Web Site:* cee. utexas.edu/ce/petex, pg 168

Evelyn Walters Pettit, 114 S Park Ave, Suite E, Winter Park, FL 32789-7012 *Tel:* 407-620-0131 (cell); 407-644-1711 *Fax:* 407-644-1711 *E-mail:* bookseller@ brandywinebooks.com, pg 469

Pfizer Award, 440 Geddes Hall, Notre Dame, IN 46556 *Tel:* 574-631-1194 *E-mail:* info@hssonline.org *Web Site:* www.hssonline.org, pg 655

Pflaum Publishing Group, 3055 Kettering Blvd, Suite 100, Dayton, OH 45439 *Toll Free Tel:* 800-523-4625; 800-543-4383 (ext 1136, cust serv) *Toll Free Fax:* 800-370-4450 *E-mail:* service@pflaum.com *Web Site:* www.pflaum.com, pg 168

Phaidon, 65 Bleecker St, 8th fl, New York, NY 10012 *Tel:* 212-652-5400 *Toll Free Tel:* 800-759-0190 (cust serv) *Fax:* 212-652-5410 *Toll Free Fax:* 800-286-9471 (cust serv) *E-mail:* enquiries@phaidon.com *Web Site:* www.phaidon.com, pg 168

James D Phelan Literary Award, One Embarcadero Ctr, Suite 1400, San Francisco, CA 94111 *Tel:* 415-733-8500 *E-mail:* info@sff.org; artsinfo@sff.org *Web Site:* www.sff.org, pg 655

Phi Beta Kappa Award in Science, 1606 New Hampshire Ave NW, Washington, DC 20009 *Tel:* 202-265-3808 *Fax:* 202-986-1601 *E-mail:* awards@pbk.org *Web Site:* www.pbk.org/bookawards, pg 656

Phi Delta Kappa International®, 1820 N Fort Myer Dr, Suite 320, Arlington, VA 22209 *Tel:* 812-339-1156 *Toll Free Tel:* 800-766-1156 *Fax:* 812-339-0018 *E-mail:* memberservices@pdkintl.org *Web Site:* www. pdkintl.org, pg 169

Philadelphia Museum of Art, PO Box 7646, Philadelphia, PA 19101-7646 *Tel:* 215-763-8100 *Fax:* 215-236-4465 *Web Site:* www.philamuseum.org, pg 169

Philadelphia Writers' Conference, PO Box 7171, Elkins Park, PA 19027-0171 *E-mail:* info@pwcwriters.org *Web Site:* pwcwriters.org, pg 577

Meredith Phillips, 4127 Old Adobe Rd, Palo Alto, CA 94306 *Tel:* 650-857-9555 *E-mail:* mphillips0743@ comcast.net, pg 469

Philomel, 345 Hudson St, New York, NY 10014 *Tel:* 212-366-2000 *Web Site:* www.penguin.com/ publishers/philomel, pg 169

Philosophical Library Inc, 275 Central Park W, Suite 12D, New York, NY 10024 *Tel:* 212-873-6070 *Fax:* 212-873-6070 *E-mail:* editors@philosophicallibrary.com *Web Site:* philosophicallibrary.com, pg 169

Philosophy Documentation Center, PO Box 7147, Charlottesville, VA 22906-7147 *Tel:* 434-220-3300 *Toll Free Tel:* 800-444-2419 *Fax:* 434-220-3301 *E-mail:* order@pdcnet.org *Web Site:* www.pdcnet.org, pg 169

PhotoEdit Inc, 3505 Cadillac Ave, Suite P-101, Costa Mesa, CA 92626 *Toll Free Tel:* 888-450-0946 *Fax:* 714-434-5937 *Toll Free Fax:* 800-804-3707 *Web Site:* www.photoeditinc.com, pg 469

Photographic Society of America® (PSA®), 8241 S Walker Ave, Suite 104, Oklahoma City, OK 73139 *Tel:* 405-843-1437 *Toll Free Tel:* 855-PSA-INFO (772-4636) *E-mail:* hq@psa-photo.org *Web Site:* www.psa-photo.org, pg 543

Piano Press, 1425 Ocean Ave, Suite 5, Del Mar, CA 92014 *Tel:* 619-884-1401 *Fax:* 858-755-1104 *E-mail:* pianopress@pianopress.com *Web Site:* www. pianopress.com, pg 169

Picador, 120 Broadway, New York, NY 10271 *Tel:* 646-307-5151 *Fax:* 212-253-9627 *E-mail:* publicity@ picadorusa.com *Web Site:* us.macmillan.com/picador, pg 169

Alison Picard Literary Agent, PO Box 2000, Cotuit, MA 02635 *Tel:* 508-477-7192 *Fax:* 508-477-7192 (call first) *E-mail:* ajpicard@aol.com, pg 498

The Picasso Project, 1109 Geary Blvd, San Francisco, CA 94109 *Tel:* 415-292-6500 *Fax:* 415-292-6594 *E-mail:* editeur@earthlink.net (edit); picasso@art-books.com (orders) *Web Site:* www.art-books.com, pg 169

Piccadilly Books Ltd, PO Box 25203, Colorado Springs, CO 80936-5203 *Tel:* 719-550-9887 *E-mail:* orders@ piccadillybooks.com *Web Site:* www.piccadillybooks. com, pg 169

Robert J Pickering Award for Playwriting Excellence, 89 Division, Coldwater, MI 49036 *Tel:* 517-279-7963 *Fax:* 517-279-8095 *E-mail:* j7eden@aol.com *Web Site:* www.branchcct.org, pg 656

Pictures & Words Editorial Services, 3100 "B" Ave, Anacortes, WA 98221 *Tel:* 360-293-8476 *E-mail:* editor@picturesandwords.com *Web Site:* www. picturesandwords.com/words, pg 469

Pieces of Learning Inc, 1112 N Carbon St, Suite A, Marion, IL 62959-8976 *Tel:* 618-964-9426 *Toll Free Tel:* 800-729-5137 *Toll Free Fax:* 800-844-0455 *E-mail:* info@piecesoflearning.com *Web Site:* piecesoflearning.com, pg 169

Lorne Pierce Medal, Walter House, 282 Somerset W, Ottawa, ON K2P 0J6, Canada *Tel:* 613-991-6990 (ext 106) *Fax:* 613-991-6996 *E-mail:* nominations@rsc-src.ca *Web Site:* www.rsc-src.ca, pg 656

The Pilgrim Press/United Church Press, 700 Prospect Ave, Cleveland, OH 44115-1100 *Tel:* 216-736-2100 *Toll Free Tel:* 800-537-3394 (orders) *E-mail:* permissions@thepilgrimpress.com; store@ucc.org (orders) *Web Site:* www.thepilgrimpress.com, pg 170

The Pinch Writing Awards in Fiction, University of Memphis, English Dept, 435 Patterson Hall, Memphis, TN 38152 *Tel:* 901-678-2651 *Fax:* 901-678-2226 *E-mail:* editor@pinchjournal.com *Web Site:* www.pinchjournal.com, pg 656

The Pinch Writing Awards in Poetry, University of Memphis, English Dept, 435 Patterson Hall, Memphis, TN 38152 *Tel:* 901-678-2651 *Fax:* 901-678-2226 *E-mail:* editor@pinchjournal.com *Web Site:* www.pinchjournal.com, pg 656

Pinckley Prizes for Crime Fiction, PO Box 13926, New Orleans, LA 70185 *E-mail:* pinckleyprizes@gmail.com *Web Site:* www.pinckleyprizes.org, pg 656

Caroline Pincus Book Midwife, 101 Wool St, San Francisco, CA 94110 *Tel:* 415-516-6206 *E-mail:* cpincus1958@gmail.com *Web Site:* www.carolinepincus.com, pg 469

Pinder Lane & Garon-Brooke Associates Ltd, 159 W 53 St, New York, NY 10019 *Tel:* 212-489-0880 *Fax:* 212-489-7104 *E-mail:* pinderlanegaronbrooke@gmail.com *Web Site:* www.pinderlaneandgaronbrooke.com, pg 498

Pineapple Press, 203 Royal Poinciana Way, Suite E, Palm Beach, FL 33480 *Web Site:* www.pineapplepress.com, pg 170

Pinnacle Book Achievement Awards, PO Box 606, Cottage Grove, OR 97424 *Tel:* 541-942-7455 *Fax:* 541-942-7455 *E-mail:* nabe@bookmarketingprofits.com *Web Site:* www.bookmarketingprofits.com, pg 656

Pippin Press, 229 E 85 St, New York, NY 10028 *Tel:* 212-288-4920 *Fax:* 908-237-2407, pg 170

Pippin Properties Inc, 110 W 40 St, Suite 1704, New York, NY 10018 *Tel:* 212-338-9310 *E-mail:* info@pippinproperties.com *Web Site:* www.pippinproperties.com; www.facebook.com/pippinproperties, pg 498

Planert Creek Press, E4843 395 Ave, Menomonie, WI 54751 *Tel:* 715-235-4110 *E-mail:* publisher@planertcreekpress.com *Web Site:* www.planertcreekpress.com, pg 170

Planners Press, 205 N Michigan Ave, Suite 1200, Chicago, IL 60601 *Tel:* 312-431-9100 *Fax:* 312-786-6700 *E-mail:* customerservice@planning.org *Web Site:* www.planning.org, pg 170

Platinum Press LLC, 281 Hicks St, Brooklyn, NY 11201 *Tel:* 718-875-4092 *Fax:* 718-875-5065, pg 170

Platypus Media LLC, 725 Eighth St SE, Washington, DC 20003 *Tel:* 202-546-1674 *Toll Free Tel:* 877-PLATYPS (752-8977) *Fax:* 202-546-2356 *E-mail:* info@platypusmedia.com *Web Site:* www.platypusmedia.com, pg 170

Playwrights Guild of Canada, 401 Richmond St W, Suite 350, Toronto, ON M5V 3A8, Canada *Tel:* 416-703-0201 *E-mail:* info@playwrightsguild.ca; marketing@playwrightsguild.ca *Web Site:* www.playwrightsguild.ca, pg 543

Playwrights Project, 3675 Ruffin Rd, Suite 330, San Diego, CA 92123 *Tel:* 858-384-2970 *Fax:* 858-384-2974 *E-mail:* write@playwrightsproject.org *Web Site:* www.playwrightsproject.org, pg 656

Pleasure Boat Studio: A Literary Press, 3710 SW Barton St, Seattle, WA 98126 *Tel:* 206-962-0460 *E-mail:* pleasboatpublishing@gmail.com *Web Site:* www.pleasureboatstudio.com, pg 170

Plexus Publishing, Inc, 143 Old Marlton Pike, Medford, NJ 08055 *Tel:* 609-654-6500 *Fax:* 609-654-4309 *E-mail:* info@plexuspublishing.com *Web Site:* www.plexuspublishing.com, pg 170

The Plimpton Prize, 544 W 27 St, New York, NY 10001 *Tel:* 212-343-1333 *E-mail:* queries@theparisreview.org *Web Site:* www.theparisreview.org, pg 656

Plough Publishing House, 151 Bowne Dr, Walden, NY 12586-2832 *Tel:* 845-572-3455 *Toll Free Tel:* 800-521-8011 *E-mail:* info@plough.com; editor@plough.com *Web Site:* www.plough.com, pg 170

Ploughshares, Emerson College, 120 Boylston St, Boston, MA 02116 *Tel:* 617-824-3757 *E-mail:* pshares@pshares.org *Web Site:* www.pshares.org, pg 171

Ploughshares Emerging Writer's Contest, Emerson College, 120 Boylston St, Boston, MA 02116 *Tel:* 617-824-3757 *E-mail:* pshares@pshares.org *Web Site:* www.pshares.org, pg 656

Plowshare Media, 405 Vincente Way, La Jolla, CA 92037 *Tel:* 858-454-5446 *E-mail:* sales@plowsharemedia.com *Web Site:* plowsharemedia.com, pg 171

Plum Tree Books, 2151 Market St, Camp Hill, PA 17011 *Tel:* 717-730-0711 *E-mail:* info@classicalsubjects.com *Web Site:* www.plumtreebooks.com, pg 171

Plume, 375 Hudson St, New York, NY 10014 *Tel:* 212-366-2000 *Fax:* 212-243-6002 *Web Site:* www.penguin.com/publishers/plume, pg 171

Plunkett Research Ltd, PO Drawer 541737, Houston, TX 77254-1737 *Tel:* 713-932-0000 *Fax:* 713-932-7080 *E-mail:* customersupport@plunkettresearch.com *Web Site:* www.plunkettresearch.com, pg 171

Plutarch Award, PO Box 33020, Santa Fe, NM 87594 *Tel:* 505-983-4671 *Web Site:* biographersinternational.org, pg 656

PNWA Literary Contest, 1420 NW Gilman Blvd, Suite 8, PMB 2717, Issaquah, WA 98027 *Tel:* 425-673-2665 *E-mail:* pnwa@pnwa.org *Web Site:* www.pnwa.org, pg 656

PNWA - a writer's resource, 1420 NW Gilman Blvd, Suite 8, PMB 2717, Issaquah, WA 98027 *Tel:* 425-673-2665 *Fax:* 425-961-0768 *E-mail:* pnwa@pnwa.org *Web Site:* www.pnwa.org, pg 543

J P Pochron Writer for Hire, 830 Lake Orchid Circle, No 203, Vero Beach, FL 32962 *Tel:* 772-569-2967 *E-mail:* hotwriter15@hotmail.com, pg 469

Pocket Press Inc, PO Box 25124, Portland, OR 97298-0124 *Toll Free Tel:* 888-237-2110 *Toll Free Fax:* 877-643-3732 *E-mail:* sales@pocketpressinc.com *Web Site:* www.pocketpressinc.com, pg 171

Pocol Press, 320 Sutton St, Punxsutawney, PA 15767 *Tel:* 703-870-9611 *E-mail:* info@pocolpress.com *Web Site:* www.pocolpress.com, pg 171

Edgar Allan Poe Memorial, 900 Timber Creek Place, Virginia Beach, VA 23464 *E-mail:* poetryinva@aol.com *Web Site:* poetrysocietyofvirginia.org, pg 657

Poetry Center Book Award, 1600 Holloway Ave, San Francisco, CA 94132 *Tel:* 415-338-2227 *Fax:* 415-338-0966 *E-mail:* poetry@sfsu.edu *Web Site:* www.sfsu.edu/~poetry, pg 657

Poetry Chapbook Contest, 1935 Penfield Rd, Penfield, NY 14526 *Tel:* 585-383-0812 *E-mail:* palettesnquills@gmail.com *Web Site:* www.palettesnquills.com, pg 657

Poetry Flash Reading Series, 1450 Fourth St, Suite 4, Berkeley, CA 94710 *Tel:* 510-525-5476 *Fax:* 510-525-6752 *E-mail:* editor@poetryflash.org *Web Site:* poetryflash.org, pg 577

Poetry Society of America (PSA), 15 Gramercy Park, New York, NY 10003 *Tel:* 212-254-9628 *Web Site:* poetrysociety.org, pg 543

Poets & Writers Inc, 90 Broad St, Suite 2100, New York, NY 10004 *Tel:* 212-226-3586 *Fax:* 212-226-3963 *E-mail:* admin@pw.org *Web Site:* www.pw.org, pg 544

Karl Pohrt Tribute Award, 3135 S State St, Suite 203, Ann Arbor, MI 48108 *Toll Free Tel:* 866-733-9064 *Fax:* 734-477-2806 *E-mail:* info@bincfoundation.org *Web Site:* www.bincfoundation.org/scholarship, pg 657

Pointed Leaf Press, 136 Baxter St, New York, NY 10013 *Tel:* 212-941-1800 *Fax:* 212-941-1822 *E-mail:* info@pointedleafpress.com *Web Site:* www.pointedleafpress.com, pg 171

Poisoned Pen Press, 4014 N Goldwater Blvd, Suite 201, Scottsdale, AZ 85251 *Tel:* 480-945-3375 *Toll Free Tel:* 800-421-3976 *Fax:* 480-949-1707 *E-mail:* info@poisonedpenpress.com *Web Site:* www.poisonedpenpress.com, pg 171

Polar Bear & Company, 8 Brook St, Solon, ME 04979 *Tel:* 207-319-4727 *Web Site:* polarbearandco.com, pg 171

Polebridge Press, PO Box 346, Farmington, MN 55024 *Tel:* 651-200-2372 *E-mail:* orders@westarinstitute.org *Web Site:* www.westarinstitute.org, pg 172

Wendy Polhemus-Annibell, PO Box 464, Peconic, NY 11958 *Tel:* 631-833-6942 *E-mail:* wannibell@gmail.com, pg 469

Police Executive Research Forum, 1120 Connecticut Ave NW, Suite 930, Washington, DC 20036 *Tel:* 202-466-7820 *Web Site:* www.policeforum.org, pg 172

Polis Books, 1201 Hudson St, No 211S, Hoboken, NJ 07030 *E-mail:* info@polisbooks.com; submissions@polisbooks.com *Web Site:* www.polisbooks.com; facebook.com/PolisBooks; twitter.com/PolisBooks, pg 172

The George Polk Awards, The Brooklyn Campus, One University Plaza, Brooklyn, NY 11201-5372 *Tel:* 718-488-1009 *Web Site:* www.liu.edu/polk, pg 657

Pom Inc, 18-15 215 St, Bayside, NY 11360 *Tel:* 516-487-3441, pg 498

Pomegranate Communications Inc, 19018 NE Portal Way, Portland, OR 97230 *Tel:* 503-328-6500 *Toll Free Tel:* 800-227-1428 *Fax:* 503-328-9330 *Toll Free Fax:* 800-848-4376 *E-mail:* contactus@pomegranate.com *Web Site:* www.pomegranate.com, pg 172

Pontifical Institute of Mediaeval Studies, Department of Publications, 59 Queen's Park Crescent E, Toronto, ON M5S 2C4, Canada *Tel:* 416-926-7142 *Fax:* 416-926-7258 *Web Site:* www.pims.ca, pg 437

Porchlight Book Co Business Book Awards, 544 S First St, Milwaukee, WI 53204 *Toll Free Tel:* 800-236-7323 *E-mail:* info@porchlightbooks.com *Web Site:* porchlightbooks.com, pg 657

Porcupine's Quill Inc, 68 Main St, Erin, ON N0B 1T0, Canada *Tel:* 519-833-9158 *E-mail:* pql@sentex.net *Web Site:* porcupinesquill.ca; www.facebook.com/theporcupinesquill, pg 437

Port Townsend Writers' Conference, 223 Battery Way, Port Townsend, WA 98368 *Tel:* 360-385-3102 *Toll Free Tel:* 800-733-3608 (ticket off) *Fax:* 360-385-2470 *E-mail:* info@centrum.org *Web Site:* centrum.org, pg 577

Portage & Main Press, 318 McDermot, Suite 100, Winnipeg, MB R3A 0A2, Canada *Tel:* 204-987-3500 *Toll Free Tel:* 800-667-9673 *Fax:* 204-947-0080 *Toll Free Fax:* 866-734-8477 *E-mail:* customerservice@portageandmainpress.com *Web Site:* www.portageandmainpress.com, pg 437

Katherine Anne Porter Award, 633 W 155 St, New York, NY 10032 *Tel:* 212-368-5900 *Fax:* 212-491-4615 *E-mail:* academy@artsandletters.org *Web Site:* artsandletters.org, pg 657

Katherine Anne Porter Prize for Fiction, Nimrod International Journal, 800 S Tucker Dr, Tulsa, OK 74104 *Tel:* 918-631-3080 *Fax:* 918-631-3033 *E-mail:* nimrod@utulsa.edu *Web Site:* www.utulsa.edu/nimrod, pg 657

Portfolio, 375 Hudson St, New York, NY 10014 *Web Site:* www.penguin.com/meet/publishers/portfolio, pg 172

Portfolio Solutions LLC, 136 Jameson Hill Rd, Clinton Corners, NY 12514 *Tel:* 845-266-1001 *Web Site:* www.portfoliosolutionsllc.com, pg 512

PRO-ED Inc, 8700 Shoal Creek Blvd, Austin, TX 78757-6897 *Tel:* 512-451-3246 *Toll Free Tel:* 800-897-3202 *Fax:* 512-451-8542 *Toll Free Fax:* 800-397-7633 *E-mail:* info@proedinc.com *Web Site:* www.proedinc.com, pg 175

Pro Lingua Associates Inc, 74 Cotton Mill Hill, Suite A-315, Brattleboro, VT 05301 *Tel:* 802-257-7779 *Toll Free Tel:* 800-366-4775 *Fax:* 802-257-5117 *E-mail:* info@prolinguaassociates.com *Web Site:* www.prolinguaassociates.com, pg 175

Productive Publications, 380 Brooke Ave, Lower Level, North York, ON M5M 2L6, Canada *Tel:* 416-483-0634 *Toll Free Tel:* 877-879-2669 (orders) *Fax:* 416-322-7434 *E-mail:* productivepublications@rogers.com *Web Site:* www.productivepublications.ca, pg 438

Productivity Press, 711 Third Ave, 8th fl, New York, NY 10017 *Tel:* 212-216-7800 *Toll Free Tel:* 800-634-7064 (orders); 800-797-3803 *E-mail:* orders@taylorandfrancis.com *Web Site:* www.crcpress.com, pg 175

Professional Communications Inc, 1223 W Main, Suite 1427, Durant, OK 74702-1427 *Tel:* 580-745-9838 *Toll Free Tel:* 800-337-9838 *Fax:* 580-745-9837 *E-mail:* info@pcibooks.com *Web Site:* www.pcibooks.com, pg 175

The Professional Education Group LLC (PEG), 700 Twelve Oaks Center Dr, Suite 104, Wayzata, MN 55391 *Tel:* 952-933-9990 *Toll Free Tel:* 800-229-2531 *E-mail:* orders@proedgroup.com *Web Site:* www.proedgroup.com, pg 176

Professional Resource Press, 3251 New England St, Sarasota, FL 34231 *Tel:* 941-343-9601 *Toll Free Tel:* 800-443-3364 (orders & cust serv) *Fax:* 941-343-9201 *Toll Free Fax:* 866-804-4843 (orders only) *E-mail:* cs@prpress.com *Web Site:* www.prpress.com, pg 176

The Professional Writer, 175 W 12 St, Suite 6D, New York, NY 10011 *Tel:* 212-414-0188; 917-658-1946 (cell) *E-mail:* paul@theprofessionalwriter.com, pg 469

Professional Writers Association of Canada (PWAC), 2800 14 Ave, Suite 210, Markham, ON L3R 0E4, Canada *Tel:* 416-504-1645 *Web Site:* pwac.ca, pg 544

Progressive Press, 3716 37 St, San Diego, CA 92105-2409 *Tel:* 619-892-7781 *Fax:* 619-892-7781 *E-mail:* info@progressivepress.com *Web Site:* www.progressivepress.com, pg 176

Prometheus Awards, 650 Castro St, Suite 120-433, Mountain View, CA 94041 *Tel:* 650-968-6319 *Web Site:* www.lfs.org, pg 659

Prometheus Books, 59 John Glenn Dr, Amherst, NY 14228-2119 *Tel:* 716-691-0133 *Fax:* 716-691-0137 *E-mail:* marketing@prometheusbooks.com; editorial@prometheusbooks.com; rights@prometheusbooks.com *Web Site:* www.prometheusbooks.com, pg 176

Pronk Media Inc, PO Box 340, Beaverton, ON L0K 1A0, Canada *Tel:* 416-441-3760 *E-mail:* info@pronk.com *Web Site:* www.pronk.com, pg 469

Proofed to Perfection Editing Services, 6519 Sherrill Baggett Rd, Godwin, NC 28344 *Tel:* 910-980-0832 *E-mail:* inquiries@proofedtoperfection.com *Web Site:* www.proofedtoperfection.com, pg 469

ProQuest LLC, 789 E Eisenhower Pkwy, Ann Arbor, MI 48108 *Tel:* 734-761-4700 *Toll Free Tel:* 800-521-0600; 877-779-6768 (sales) *E-mail:* sales@proquest.com *Web Site:* www.proquest.com, pg 176

PROSE Awards, 455 Massachusetts Ave NW, Suite 700, Washington, DC 20001-2777 *Tel:* 202-347-3375 *Fax:* 202-347-3690 *E-mail:* proseawards@publishers.org *Web Site:* www.proseawards.com; publishers.org, pg 659

Prospect Agency, 285 Fifth Ave, PMB 445, Brooklyn, NY 11215 *Tel:* 718-788-3217 *Fax:* 718-360-9582 *Web Site:* www.prospectagency.com, pg 499

Prospect Park Books, 2359 Lincoln Ave, Altadena, CA 91001 *Tel:* 626-793-9796 *E-mail:* info@prospectparkbooks.com *Web Site:* www.prospectparkbooks.com, pg 177

ProStar Publications Inc, 226 W Florence Ave, Inglewood, CA 90301 *Toll Free Tel:* 800-481-6277 *E-mail:* editor@prostarpublications.com *Web Site:* www.prostarpublications.com, pg 177

Protestant Church-Owned Publishers Association, 6631 Westbury Oaks Ct, Springfield, VA 22152 *Tel:* 703-220-5989 *Web Site:* www.pcpaonline.org, pg 545

The PRS Group Inc, 5800 Heritage Landing Dr, Suite E, East Syracuse, NY 13057-9358 *Tel:* 315-431-0511 *Fax:* 315-431-0200 *E-mail:* custserv@prsgroup.com *Web Site:* www.prsgroup.com, pg 177

Prufrock Press, PO Box 8813, Waco, TX 76714-8813 *Tel:* 254-756-3337 *Toll Free Tel:* 800-998-2208 *Fax:* 254-756-3339 *Toll Free Fax:* 800-240-0333 *E-mail:* info@prufrock.com *Web Site:* www.prufrock.com, pg 177

PSMJ Resources Inc, 10 Midland Ave, Newton, MA 02458 *Tel:* 617-965-0055 *Toll Free Tel:* 800-537-PSMJ (537-7765) *Fax:* 617-965-5152 *Web Site:* www.psmj.com, pg 177

Psychological Assessment Resources Inc (PAR), 16204 N Florida Ave, Lutz, FL 33549 *Tel:* 813-449-4065 *Toll Free Tel:* 800-331-8378 *Fax:* 813-961-2196 *Toll Free Fax:* 800-727-9329 *Web Site:* www.parinc.com, pg 177

Public Citizen, 1600 20 St NW, Washington, DC 20009 *Tel:* 202-588-1000 *Web Site:* www.citizen.org, pg 177

Public Relations Society of America Inc, 120 Wall St, 21st fl, New York, NY 10005-4024 *Tel:* 212-460-1400 *Fax:* 212-995-0757 *E-mail:* memberservices@prsa.org *Web Site:* www.prsa.org, pg 545

Public Scholar Program, 400 Seventh St SW, Washington, DC 20506 *Tel:* 202-606-8200 *E-mail:* publicscholar@neh.gov *Web Site:* www.neh.gov/grants, pg 659

Publication Consultants, 8370 Eleusis Dr, Anchorage, AK 99502 *Tel:* 907-349-2424 *Fax:* 907-349-2426 *E-mail:* books@publicationconsultants.com *Web Site:* www.publicationconsultants.com, pg 177

Les Publications du Quebec, 1000, rte de l'Eqalise, Bureau 500, Quebec, QC G1V 3V9, Canada *Tel:* 418-643-5150 *Toll Free Tel:* 800-463-2100 (Quebec province only) *Fax:* 418-643-6177 *Toll Free Fax:* 800-561-3479 *E-mail:* publicationsduquebec@cspq.gouv.qc.ca *Web Site:* www.publicationsduquebec.gouv.qc.ca, pg 438

Publications International Ltd (PIL), 8140 N Lehigh Ave, Morton Grove, IL 60053 *Tel:* 847-676-3470 *Fax:* 847-676-3671 *E-mail:* customer_service@pubint.com *Web Site:* pilbooks.com, pg 177

Publishers Association of the West Inc (PubWest), 17501 Hill Way, Lake Oswego, OR 97035 *Tel:* 503-901-9865 *E-mail:* pubwest1@gmail.com *Web Site:* pubwest.org, pg 545

Publishers Information Bureau (PIB)®, 757 Third Ave, 11th fl, New York, NY 10017 *Tel:* 212-872-3700 (MPA) *E-mail:* infocenter@magazine.org *Web Site:* www.magazine.org, pg 545

Publishing Certificate Program at City College of New York, Division of Humanities NAC 5225, City College of New York, New York, NY 10031 *Tel:* 212-650-7925 *Fax:* 212-650-7912 *E-mail:* ccnypub@aol.com *Web Site:* www.ccny.cuny.edu/publishing_certificate/index.html, pg 584

The Publishing Game, PO Box 590239, Newton, MA 02459-0002 *Tel:* 617-630-0945 *Fax:* 617-630-0945 (call first) *E-mail:* info@publishinggame.com; workshops@publishinggame.com *Web Site:* www.publishinggame.com, pg 577

Publishing Professionals Network, c/o Postal Annex, 274 Redwood Shores Pkwy, Redwood City, CA 94065-1173 *E-mail:* operations@pubpronetwork.org *Web Site:* pubpronetwork.org, pg 545

Publishing Resources Inc, 425 Carr 693, PMB 160, Dorado, PR 00646 *Tel:* 787-647-9342 *E-mail:* pri@chevako.net *Web Site:* www.publishingresources.net, pg 469

Publishing Synthesis Ltd, 39 Crosby St, New York, NY 10013 *Tel:* 212-219-0135 *E-mail:* mainmail@pubsyn.com *Web Site:* www.pubsyn.com, pg 469

The Publishing Triangle Literary Awards, 332 Bleecker St, Suite D-36, New York, NY 10014 *E-mail:* publishingtriangle@gmail.com *Web Site:* www.publishingtriangle.org, pg 659

PubWest Book Design Awards, 17501 Hill Way, Lake Oswego, OR 97035 *Tel:* 503-901-9865 *E-mail:* pubwest1@gmail.com *Web Site:* pubwest.org, pg 659

Puddingstone Literary, Authors' Agents, 11 Mabro Dr, Denville, NJ 07834-9607 *Tel:* 973-366-3622, pg 499

Puffin Books, 345 Hudson St, New York, NY 10014 *Tel:* 212-366-2000 *Web Site:* www.penguin.com/publishers/puffin, pg 177

Pulitzer Prizes, 709 Journalism Bldg, Columbia University, 2950 Broadway, New York, NY 10027 *Tel:* 212-854-3841 *Fax:* 212-854-3342 *E-mail:* pulitzer@pulitzer.org *Web Site:* www.pulitzer.org, pg 660

Purdue University Press, Stewart Ctr 190, 504 W State St, West Lafayette, IN 47907-2058 *Tel:* 765-494-2038 *Fax:* 765-496-2442 *E-mail:* pupress@purdue.edu *Web Site:* www.thepress.purdue.edu, pg 178

Purple House Press, 8100 US Hwy 62 E, Cynthiana, KY 41031 *Tel:* 859-235-9970 *Web Site:* www.purplehousepress.com, pg 178

Purple Mountain Press Ltd, 1064 Main St, Fleischmanns, NY 12430 *Tel:* 845-254-4062 *Toll Free Tel:* 800-325-2665 (orders) *Fax:* 845-254-4476 *E-mail:* purple@catskill.net *Web Site:* www.catskill.net/purple, pg 178

Pushcart Press, PO Box 380, Wainscott, NY 11975-0380 *Tel:* 631-324-9300 *Web Site:* www.pushcartprize.com/pushcartpress, pg 178

Pushcart Prize: Best of the Small Presses, PO Box 380, Wainscott, NY 11975-0380 *Tel:* 631-324-9300 *Web Site:* www.pushcartprize.com, pg 660

GP Putnam's Sons (Children's), 345 Hudson St, New York, NY 10014 *Tel:* 212-366-2000 *Fax:* 212-414-3393 *Web Site:* www.penguin.com/publishers/gpputnamssonsbooksforyoungread, pg 178

GP Putnam's Sons (Hardcover), 375 Hudson St, New York, NY 10014 *Tel:* 212-366-2000 *Fax:* 212-366-2643 *E-mail:* online@penguinputnam.com *Web Site:* www.penguin.com/publishers/gpputnamssons, pg 178

PNWA Writers Conference, 1420 NW Gilman Blvd, Suite 8, PMB 2717, Issaquah, WA 98027 *Tel:* 425-673-2665 *E-mail:* pnwa@pnwa.org *Web Site:* www.pnwa.org, pg 577

Pyncheon House, 6 University Dr, Suite 105, Amherst, MA 01002, pg 178

Ron Pynn Award, PO Box 367, Fountain City, WI 54629 *E-mail:* info@taaonline.net *Web Site:* www.taaonline.net/ron-pynn-award, pg 660

QA International (QAI), 329 De la Commune W, 3rd fl, Montreal, QC H2Y 2E1, Canada *Tel:* 514-499-3000 *Fax:* 514-499-3010 *Web Site:* www.qa-international.com, pg 438

Robert Quackenbush's Children's Book Writing & Illustration Workshops, 223 E 78 St, New York, NY 10075 *Tel:* 212-744-3822 *E-mail:* rqstudios@aol.com *Web Site:* www.rquackenbush.com, pg 577

Quail Ridge Press (QRP), 2451 Atrium Way, Nashville, TN 37214 *Toll Free Tel:* 800-358-0560 *Fax:* 615-391-2815 *Web Site:* www.swphbooks.com/quail-ridge-press.html, pg 178

Quality Medical Publishing Inc, 11802 Borman Dr, St Louis, MO 63146 *Tel:* 314-878-7808 *E-mail:* customerservice@qmp.com *Web Site:* www.qmp.com, pg 178

Quarto Publishing Group USA Inc, 100 Cummings Ctr, Suite 265D, Beverly, MA 01915 *Tel:* 978-282-9590 *Toll Free Tel:* 800-328-0590 (sales) *Fax:* 978-283-2742 *E-mail:* sales@quartous.com *Web Site:* www.quartoknows.com, pg 178

Regent Press Publishers & Printers, 2747 Regent St, Berkeley, CA 94705 *Tel:* 510-845-1196 *E-mail:* regentpress@mindspring.com *Web Site:* www. regentpress.net, pg 184

Regina Medal Award, 8550 United Plaza Blvd, Suite 1001, Baton Rouge, LA 70809 *Tel:* 225-408-4417 *Fax:* 225-408-4422 *E-mail:* cla2@cathla.org *Web Site:* cathla.org, pg 661

Regnery Publishing, 300 New Jersey Ave NW, Washington, DC 20001 *Tel:* 202-216-0600 *Toll Free Tel:* 888-219-4747 *Fax:* 202-393-1795 *Web Site:* www. regnery.com, pg 184

Regular Baptist Press, 3715 N Ventura Dr, Arlington Heights, IL 60004 *Tel:* 847-843-1600 *Toll Free Tel:* 800-727-4440 (cust serv) *Fax:* 847-843-3757 *E-mail:* orders@rbpstore.org *Web Site:* regularbaptistpress.org, pg 184

Kerry Reilly: Representatives, 1826 Asheville Place, Charlotte, NC 28203 *Tel:* 704-372-6007 *E-mail:* kerry@reillyreps.com *Web Site:* www. reillyreps.com, pg 512

Nathan Reingold Prize, 440 Geddes Hall, Notre Dame, IN 46556 *Tel:* 574-631-1194 *E-mail:* info@hssonline. org *Web Site:* www.hssonline.org, pg 661

Remember Point Inc, PO Box 1448, Pacific Palisades, CA 90272 *Tel:* 310-896-8716 *E-mail:* info@ rememberpoint.com *Web Site:* www.rememberpoint. com; www.longfellowfindsahome.com, pg 184

Renaissance House, 465 Westview Ave, Englewood, NJ 07631 *Tel:* 201-408-4048 *Web Site:* www. renaissancehouse.net, pg 184, 512

Renaissance Literary & Talent, PO Box 17379, Beverly Hills, CA 90209 *Tel:* 323-848-8305 *E-mail:* query@ renaissancemgmt.net *Web Site:* renaissancemgmt.net, pg 499

The Amy Rennert Agency Inc, 1550 Tiburon Blvd, Suite 302, Tiburon, CA 94920 *Tel:* 415-789-8955 *E-mail:* queries@amyrennert.com (no unsol queries) *Web Site:* amyrennert.com, pg 499

Arthur Rense Prize, 633 W 155 St, New York, NY 10032 *Tel:* 212-368-5900 *Fax:* 212-491-4615 *E-mail:* academy@artsandletters.org *Web Site:* artsandletters.org, pg 661

Reporters Committee for Freedom of the Press, 1156 15 St NW, Suite 1250, Washington, DC 20005-1779 *Tel:* 202-795-9300 *Toll Free Tel:* 800-336-4243 *E-mail:* info@rcfp.org *Web Site:* rcfp.org, pg 545

Research & Education Association (REA), 258 Prospect Plains Rd, Cranbury, NJ 08512 *Tel:* 732-819-8880 *Fax:* 732-819-8808 (orders) *E-mail:* info@rea.com *Web Site:* www.rea.com, pg 184

Research Press, 2612 N Mattis Ave, Champaign, IL 61822 *Tel:* 217-352-3273 *Toll Free Tel:* 800-519-2707 *Fax:* 217-352-1221 *E-mail:* rp@researchpress. com; orders@researchpress.com *Web Site:* www. researchpress.com, pg 184

Research Research, 240 E 27 St, Suite 20-K, New York, NY 10016-9238 *Tel:* 212-779-9540 *Fax:* 212-779-9540 *E-mail:* ehtac@msn.com, pg 469

Residency, 454 E Hill Rd, Austerlitz, NY 12017 *Tel:* 518-392-3103; 518-392-4144 *E-mail:* apply@ millaycolony.org *Web Site:* www.millaycolony.org, pg 661

Resilient Publishing, 406 S Third St, Boise, ID 83702 *Tel:* 208-258-9544 *E-mail:* submissions@ resilientpublishing.com *Web Site:* www. resilientpublishing.com; www.facebook.com/ ResilientPub, pg 184

The Restless Books Prize for New Immigrant Writing, 232 Third St, Suite A111, Brooklyn, NY 11215 *E-mail:* publisher@restlessbooks.com *Web Site:* www. restlessbooks.org/prize-for-new-immigrant-writing, pg 661

Revell, PO Box 6287, Grand Rapids, MI 49516-6287 *Tel:* 616-676-9185 *Toll Free Tel:* 800-877-2665; 800-679-1957 *Fax:* 616-676-9573 *Web Site:* www. bakerpublishinggroup.com, pg 185

The Harold U Ribalow Prize, 40 Wall St, 8th fl, New York, NY 10005-1387 *Tel:* 212-451-6286 *Fax:* 212-451-6257 *E-mail:* magtemp3@hadassah.org *Web Site:* www.hadassah.org/magazine, pg 661

Evelyn Richardson Nonfiction Award, 1113 Marginal Rd, Halifax, NS B3H 4P7, Canada *Tel:* 902-423-8116 *Fax:* 902-422-0881 *E-mail:* contact@writers.ns.ca *Web Site:* writers.ns.ca, pg 661

The Ridenhour Book Prize, 116 E 16 St, 8th fl, New York, NY 10003 *Tel:* 212-822-0250 *Fax:* 212-253-5356 *E-mail:* ridenhour@nationinstitute.org *Web Site:* www.ridenhour.org, pg 662

The Ridenhour Courage Prize, 116 E 16 St, 8th fl, New York, NY 10003 *Tel:* 212-822-0250 *Fax:* 212-253-5356 *E-mail:* ridenhour@nationinstitute.org *Web Site:* www.ridenhour.org, pg 662

The Ridenhour Prize for Truth-Telling, 116 E 16 St, 8th fl, New York, NY 10003 *Tel:* 212-822-0250 *Fax:* 212-253-5356 *E-mail:* ridenhour@nationinstitute.org *Web Site:* www.ridenhour.org, pg 662

Lynne Rienner Publishers Inc, 1800 30 St, Suite 314, Boulder, CO 80301 *Tel:* 303-444-6684 *Fax:* 303-444-0824 *E-mail:* questions@rienner.com; cservice@ rienner.com *Web Site:* www.rienner.com, pg 185

Rilke Prize, Auditorium Bldg, Rm 214, 1155 Union Circle, Denton, TX 76203 *E-mail:* untrilkeprize@ unt.edu *Web Site:* english.unt.edu/creative-writing/unt-rilke-prize, pg 662

Gwen Pharis Ringwood Award for Drama, 11759 Groat Rd, Edmonton, AB T5M 3K6, Canada *Tel:* 780-422-8174 *Toll Free Tel:* 800-665-5354 (AB only) *Fax:* 780-422-2663 (attn WGA) *E-mail:* mail@ writersguild.ca *Web Site:* writersguild.ca, pg 662

Rio Nuevo Publishers, 451 N Bonita Ave, Tucson, AZ 85745 *Tel:* 520-623-9558 *Toll Free Tel:* 800-969-9558 *Fax:* 520-624-5888 *Toll Free Fax:* 800-715-5888 *E-mail:* info@rionuevo.com (cust serv) *Web Site:* www.rionuevo.com, pg 185

The Ripped Bodice Awards for Excellence in Romantic Fiction, 3806 Main St, Culver City, CA 90232 *Tel:* 424-603-4776 *E-mail:* therippedbodicela@gmail. com *Web Site:* www.therippedbodicela.com, pg 662

RISING STAR Award, PO Box 190, Jefferson, OR 97352 *E-mail:* risingstar@womenfictionwriters.org *Web Site:* wfwa.memberclicks.net/rising-star-award, pg 662

Rising Sun Publishing, PO Box 70906, Marietta, GA 30007-0906 *Tel:* 770-518-0369 *Toll Free Tel:* 800-524-2813 *Fax:* 770-587-0862 *E-mail:* info@rspublishing. com *Web Site:* www.rspublishing.com, pg 185

Ann Rittenberg Literary Agency Inc, 15 Maiden Lane, Suite 206, New York, NY 10038 *Tel:* 212-684-6936 *Fax:* 212-684-6929 *E-mail:* info@rittlit.com *Web Site:* www.rittlit.com, pg 499

Jack D Rittenhouse Award, 17501 Hill Way, Lake Oswego, OR 97035 *Tel:* 503-901-9865 *E-mail:* pubwest1@gmail.com *Web Site:* pubwest.org, pg 662

Max Ritvo Poetry Prize, 1011 Washington Ave S, Suite 300, Minneapolis, MN 55415-1246 *Tel:* 612-332-3192 *Toll Free Tel:* 800-520-6455 *Web Site:* milkweed. org/max-ritvo-poetry-prize, pg 662

Judith Riven Literary Agent LLC, 250 W 16 St, Suite 4F, New York, NY 10011 *Tel:* 212-255-1009 *Fax:* 212-255-8547 *E-mail:* rivenlitqueries@gmail.com *Web Site:* rivenlit.com, pg 469, 499

River City Publishing LLC, 1719 Mulberry St, Montgomery, AL 36106 *Tel:* 334-265-6753, pg 185

Riverby Awards, 261 Floyd Ackert Rd, New York, NY 12493 *Tel:* 212-769-5169 *Fax:* 212-313-7182 *E-mail:* info@johnburroughsassociation.org *Web Site:* www.johnburroughsassociation.org, pg 662

Riverdale Avenue Books (RAB), 5676 Riverdale Ave, Bronx, NY 10471 *Tel:* 212-279-6418 *E-mail:* customerservice@riverdaleavebooks.com *Web Site:* www.riverdaleavebooks.com, pg 185

Riverhead Books, 375 Hudson St, New York, NY 10014 *Tel:* 212-366-2000 *Web Site:* www.penguin. com/publishers/riverhead, pg 185

Riverside Literary Agency, 41 Simon Keets Rd, Leyden, MA 01337 *Tel:* 413-772-0067 *Fax:* 413-772-0969 *E-mail:* rivlit@sover.net *Web Site:* www. riversideliteraryagency.com, pg 500

Rizzoli International Publications Inc, 300 Park Ave S, 4th fl, New York, NY 10010-5399 *Tel:* 212-387-3400 *Toll Free Tel:* 800-522-6657 (orders only) *Fax:* 212-387-3535 *E-mail:* publicity@rizzoliusa.com *Web Site:* www.rizzoliusa.com, pg 185

RMA, 85 Lincoln St, 1st fl, Meriden, CT 06451 *Tel:* 718-434-1893 *Fax:* 203-440-1013 *Web Site:* www. ricia.com, pg 500

The RoadRunner Press, 124 NW 32 St, Oklahoma City, OK 73118 *Tel:* 405-524-6205 *Fax:* 405-524-6312 *E-mail:* info@theroadrunnerpress.com; orders@theroadrunnerpress.com *Web Site:* www. theroadrunnerpress.com, pg 186

Roam Agency, 45 Main St, Suite 727, Brooklyn, NY 11201-1076 *E-mail:* roam@roamagency.com *Web Site:* www.roamagency.com, pg 500

Roanoke-Chowan Award for Poetry, 4610 Mail Service Ctr, Raleigh, NC 27699-4610 *Tel:* 919-807-7290 *Fax:* 919-733-8807 *Web Site:* www.history.ncdcr. gov/affiliates/lit-hist/awards/awards.htm, pg 662

Roaring Brook Press, 120 Broadway, New York, NY 10271 *Tel:* 646-307-5151 *Web Site:* us.macmillan. com/publishers/roaring-brook-press, pg 186

Roaring Forties Press, 1053 Santa Fe Ave, Berkeley, CA 94706 *Tel:* 510-527-5461 *E-mail:* info@ roaringfortiespress.com *Web Site:* www. roaringfortiespress.com, pg 186

B J Robbins Literary Agency, 5130 Bellaire Ave, North Hollywood, CA 91607 *E-mail:* robbinsliterary@gmail. com, pg 500

The Roberts Group, 12803 Eastview Curve, Apple Valley, MN 55124 *Tel:* 952-322-4005 *E-mail:* info@ editorialservice.com *Web Site:* www.editorialservice. com, pg 470

Rochester Institute of Technology, School of Media, Arts & Technology, 69 Lomb Memorial Dr, Rochester, NY 14623-5603 *Tel:* 585-475-2728; 585-475-5336 *Fax:* 585-475-5336 *E-mail:* spmofc@rit.edu *Web Site:* cias.rit.edu/printmedia, pg 584

The Rockefeller University Press, 950 Third Ave, 2nd fl, New York, NY 10022 *Tel:* 212-327-7938 *E-mail:* rupress@rockefeller.edu *Web Site:* www. rupress.org, pg 186

RockHill Publishing LLC, PO Box 62241, Virginia Beach, VA 23466-2241 *Tel:* 757-692-2021 *E-mail:* jlh@rockhillpublishing.com *Web Site:* rockhillpublishing.com, pg 186

Rocky Mountain Book Award, PO Box 42, Lethbridge, AB T1J 3Y3, Canada *Tel:* 403-381-7164 *E-mail:* rockymountainbookaward@shaw.ca *Web Site:* www.rmba.info, pg 662

Rocky Mountain Books Ltd (RMB), 103-1075 Pendergast St, Victoria, BC V8V 0A1, Canada *Tel:* 250-360-0829 *Fax:* 250-386-0829 *Web Site:* www. rmbooks.com, pg 438

Rocky Mountain Mineral Law Foundation, 9191 Sheridan Blvd, Suite 203, Westminster, CO 80031 *Tel:* 303-321-8100 *Fax:* 303-321-7657 *E-mail:* info@ rmmlf.org *Web Site:* www.rmmlf.org, pg 186

Rod & Staff Publishers Inc, 14193 Hwy 172, Crockett, KY 41413 *Tel:* 606-522-4348 *Fax:* 606-522-4896, pg 186

Roger Williams Agency, 17 Paddock Dr, Lawrence Twp, NJ 08648 *Tel:* 860-973-2439 *E-mail:* roger@ rogerwilliamsagency.com *Web Site:* www. rogerwilliamsagency.com, pg 500

Rogers Writers' Trust Fiction Prize, 600-460 Richmond St W, Toronto, ON M5V 1Y1, Canada *Tel:* 416-504-8222 *Toll Free Tel:* 877-906-6548 *Fax:* 416-504-9090 *E-mail:* info@writerstrust.com *Web Site:* www.writerstrust.com, pg 663

Linda Roghaar Literary Agency LLC, 133 High Point Dr, Amherst, MA 01002 *Tel:* 413-256-1921 *E-mail:* contact@lindaroghaar.com *Web Site:* www.lindaroghaar.com, pg 500

Sami Rohr Prize for Jewish Literature, 520 Eighth Ave, 4th fl, New York, NY 10018 *Tel:* 212-201-2920 *Fax:* 212-532-4952 *E-mail:* jbc@jewishbooks.org *Web Site:* www.jewishbookcouncil.org, pg 663

The Roistacher Literary Agency, 545 W 111 St, Suite 7J, New York, NY 10025-1965 *Tel:* 212-222-1405, pg 500

Roman Catholic Books, PO Box 2286, Fort Collins, CO 80522-2286 *Tel:* 970-490-2735 *Fax:* 904-493-8781 *Web Site:* www.booksforcatholics.com, pg 186

Romance Writers of America®, 14615 Benfer Rd, Houston, TX 77069 *Tel:* 832-717-5200 *Fax:* 832-717-5201 *E-mail:* info@rwa.org *Web Site:* www.rwa.org, pg 545

Romance Writers of America Annual Conference, 14615 Benfer Rd, Houston, TX 77069 *Tel:* 832-717-5200 *Fax:* 832-717-5201 *E-mail:* info@rwa.org *Web Site:* www.rwa.org, pg 577

Roncorp Music, PO Box 1210, Coatesville, PA 19320 *Tel:* 610-679-5400 *E-mail:* info@nemusicpub.com *Web Site:* www.nemusicpub.com, pg 186

Ronin Publishing Inc, PO Box 3436, Oakland, CA 94609 *Tel:* 510-420-3669 *Fax:* 510-420-3672 *E-mail:* ronin@roninpub.com *Web Site:* www.roninpub.com, pg 186

Ronsdale Press Ltd, 3350 W 21 Ave, Vancouver, BC V6S 1G7, Canada *Tel:* 604-738-4688 *Fax:* 604-731-4548 *E-mail:* ronsdale@shaw.ca *Web Site:* ronsdalepress.com, pg 438

Peter Rooney, 332 Bleecker St, PMB X-6, New York, NY 10014-2980 *Tel:* 917-376-1792 *Fax:* 212-226-8047 *E-mail:* magneticreports@gmail.com *Web Site:* www.magneticreports.xyz, pg 470

Rootstock Publishing, 27 Main St, Suite 6, Montpelier, VT 05602 *Tel:* 802-839-0371 *E-mail:* info@rootstockpublishing.com *Web Site:* www.rootstockpublishing.com, pg 187

Robert Rose Inc, 120 Eglinton Ave E, Suite 800, Toronto, ON M4P 1E2, Canada *Tel:* 416-322-6552 *Fax:* 416-322-6936 *Web Site:* www.robertrose.ca, pg 438

Rosemont College, Graduate Publg Prog, 1400 Montgomery Ave, Rosemont, PA 19010 *Tel:* 610-527-0200 (ext 2431) *Web Site:* www.rosemont.edu, pg 584

The Rosen Publishing Group Inc, 29 E 21 St, New York, NY 10010 *Toll Free Tel:* 800-237-9932 *Toll Free Fax:* 888-436-4643 *E-mail:* info@rosenpub.com *Web Site:* www.rosenpublishing.com, pg 187

The Rosenberg Group, 23 Lincoln Ave, Marblehead, MA 01945 *Tel:* 781-990-1341 *Fax:* 781-990-1344 *E-mail:* rosenberglitsubmit@icloud.com *Web Site:* www.rosenberggroup.com, pg 500

Rita Rosenkranz Literary Agency, 440 West End Ave, Suite 15D, New York, NY 10024-5358 *Tel:* 212-873-6333 *Fax:* 212-873-5225 *Web Site:* www.ritarosenkranzliteraryagency.com, pg 500

Rosenthal Family Foundation Awards, 633 W 155 St, New York, NY 10032 *Tel:* 212-368-5900 *Fax:* 212-491-4615 *E-mail:* academy@artsandletters.org *Web Site:* artsandletters.org, pg 663

Rosenthal Represents, 23725 Hartland St, West Hills, CA 91307 *Tel:* 818-430-3850 *E-mail:* eliselicenses@earthlink.net, pg 512

RosettaBooks, 125 Park Ave, 25th fl, New York, NY 10017 *Tel:* 646-274-1970 *Fax:* 212-977-5997 (e-fax) *E-mail:* rights@rosettabooks.com; production@rosettabooks.com *Web Site:* www.rosettabooks.com, pg 187

Ross Books, PO Box 4340, Berkeley, CA 94704-0340 *Tel:* 510-841-2474 *Fax:* 510-295-2531 *E-mail:* sales@rossbooks.com *Web Site:* www.rossbooks.com, pg 187

Margaret W Rossiter History of Women in Science Prize, 440 Geddes Hall, Notre Dame, IN 46556 *Tel:* 574-631-1194 *E-mail:* info@hssonline.org *Web Site:* www.hssonline.org, pg 663

Rotary Club of Charlottetown Royalty Creative Writing Awards for Young People, 81 Prince St, Charlottetown, PE C1A 4R3, Canada *E-mail:* peiliteraryawards@gmail.com *Web Site:* www.peiwritersguild.com, pg 663

Lois Roth Award, 85 Broad St, Suite 500, New York, NY 10004-2434 *Tel:* 646-576-5141; 646-576-5000 *Fax:* 646-458-0030 *E-mail:* awards@mla.org *Web Site:* www.mla.org, pg 663

Rothstein Associates Inc, 4 Arapaho Rd, Brookfield, CT 06804-3104 *Tel:* 203-740-7400 *Toll Free Tel:* 888-768-4783 *Fax:* 203-740-7401 *E-mail:* info@rothstein.com *Web Site:* www.rothstein.com; www.rothsteinpublishing.com, pg 187

Jane Rotrosen Agency LLC, 85 Broad St, 28th fl, New York, NY 10004 *Tel:* 212-593-4330 *Fax:* 212-935-6985 *Web Site:* janerotrosen.com, pg 500

The Rough Notes Co Inc, 11690 Technology Dr, Carmel, IN 46032-5600 *Tel:* 317-582-1600 *Toll Free Tel:* 800-428-4384 (cust serv) *Fax:* 317-816-1000 *Toll Free Fax:* 800-321-1909 *E-mail:* rnc@roughnotes.com *Web Site:* www.roughnotes.com, pg 187

Round Table Companies, 1027 Kenton Rd, Deerfield, IL 60015 *Tel:* 949-375-1006 *Fax:* 815-346-2398 *Web Site:* www.roundtablecompanies.com, pg 187

Routledge, 711 Third Ave, New York, NY 10017 *Tel:* 212-216-7800 *Toll Free Tel:* 800-634-7064 (order enquiries, cust serv) *Fax:* 212-564-7854 *Web Site:* www.routledge.com, pg 187

Rowe Publishing LLC, 655 Old Lifsey Springs Rd, Molena, GA 30258 *Tel:* 785-302-0451 *E-mail:* info@rowepub.com *Web Site:* www.rowepub.com, pg 188

Hazel Rowley Prize, PO Box 33020, Santa Fe, NM 87594 *Web Site:* biographersinternational.org, pg 663

Rowman & Littlefield, 4501 Forbes Blvd, Suite 200, Lanham, MD 20706 *Tel:* 301-459-3366 *Toll Free Tel:* 800-462-6420 (ext 3024, cust serv) *Fax:* 301-429-5748 *Web Site:* rowman.com, pg 188

Dick Rowson, 4701 Connecticut Ave NW, Suite 503, Washington, DC 20008 *Tel:* 202-244-8104 *E-mail:* rcrowson2@aol.com, pg 470

Royal Fireworks Press, PO Box 399, Unionville, NY 10988 *Tel:* 845-726-4444 *Fax:* 845-726-3824 *E-mail:* mail@rfwp.com *Web Site:* www.rfwp.com, pg 188

Royal Ontario Museum Press, 100 Queen's Park, Toronto, ON M5S 2C6, Canada *Tel:* 416-586-8000 *Fax:* 416-586-5642 *E-mail:* info@rom.on.ca *Web Site:* www.rom.on.ca, pg 439

Royce Carlton Inc, 866 United Nations Plaza, Suite 587, New York, NY 10017-1880 *Tel:* 212-355-7700 *Toll Free Tel:* 800-LECTURE (532-8873) *Fax:* 212-888-8659 *E-mail:* info@roycecarlton.com *Web Site:* www.roycecarlton.com, pg 515

Lexi Rudnitsky First Book Prize in Poetry, 90 Broad St, Suite 2100, New York, NY 10004 *Tel:* 212-260-9256 *E-mail:* info@perseabooks.com *Web Site:* www.perseabooks.com, pg 663

William B Ruggles Journalism Scholarship, 5211 Port Royal Rd, Suite 510, Springfield, VA 22151 *Tel:* 703-321-9606 *Fax:* 703-321-7143 *Web Site:* www.nilrr.org, pg 663

Russell Sage Foundation, 112 E 64 St, New York, NY 10065 *Tel:* 212-750-6000 *Toll Free Tel:* 800-524-6401 *Fax:* 212-371-4761 *E-mail:* info@rsage.org *Web Site:* www.russellsage.org, pg 188

Russian Information Services Inc, PO Box 567, Montpelier, VT 05601 *Tel:* 802-223-4955 *Toll Free Tel:* 800-639-4301 *E-mail:* orders@russianlife.com *Web Site:* www.russianlife.com, pg 188

Rutgers University Press, 106 Somerset St, 3rd fl, New Brunswick, NJ 08901 *Tel:* 848-445-7762; 848-445-7761 (sales) *Fax:* 732-745-4935 *E-mail:* sales@rutgersuniversitypress.org *Web Site:* www.rutgersuniversitypress.org, pg 188

The Cornelius Ryan Award, 40 W 45 St, New York, NY 10036 *Tel:* 212-626-9220 *Fax:* 212-626-9210 *E-mail:* info@opcofamerica.org *Web Site:* www.opcofamerica.org, pg 663

Dr Tony Ryan Book Award, 2469 Ironworks Pike, Lexington, KY 40511 *Tel:* 859-455-9222 *Web Site:* www.castletonlyons.com, pg 663

Regina Ryan Books, 251 Central Park W, Suite 7-D, New York, NY 10024 *Tel:* 212-787-5589 *E-mail:* queries@reginaryanbooks.com *Web Site:* www.reginaryanbooks.com, pg 500

Sachem Publishing Associates Inc, 402 W Lyon Farm Dr, Greenwich, CT 06831 *Tel:* 203-813-3077 *E-mail:* sachempub@optonline.net, pg 470

Saddleback Educational Publishing, 151 Kalmus Dr, Suite J-1, Costa Mesa, CA 92626 *Tel:* 714-640-5200 *Toll Free Tel:* 888-SDLBACK (735-2225); 800-637-8715 *Fax:* 714-640-5297 *Toll Free Fax:* 888-734-4010 *E-mail:* contact@sdlback.com *Web Site:* www.sdlback.com, pg 189

William H Sadlier Inc, 9 Pine St, New York, NY 10005 *Tel:* 212-227-2120 *Toll Free Tel:* 800-221-5175 (cust serv) *Fax:* 212-312-6080 *E-mail:* customerservice@sadlier.com *Web Site:* www.sadlier.com, pg 189

SAE (Society of Automotive Engineers International), 400 Commonwealth Dr, Warrendale, PA 15096-0001 *Tel:* 724-776-4841; 724-776-4970 (outside US & CN) *Toll Free Tel:* 877-606-7323 (cust serv) *Fax:* 724-776-0790 (cust serv) *E-mail:* publications@sae.org; customerservice@sae.org *Web Site:* www.sae.org, pg 189

Safari Press, 15621 Chemical Lane, Bldg B, Huntington Beach, CA 92649 *Tel:* 714-894-9080 *Toll Free Tel:* 800-451-4788 *Fax:* 714-894-4949 *E-mail:* info@safaripress.com *Web Site:* www.safaripress.com, pg 189

Safer Society Foundation Inc, 33 Park St, Brandon, VT 05733 *Tel:* 802-247-3132 *Fax:* 802-247-4233 *E-mail:* info@safersociety.org *Web Site:* www.safersociety.org, pg 189

Sagamore Publishing LLC, 3611 N Staley Rd, Suite B, Champaign, IL 61822 *Tel:* 217-359-5940 *Toll Free Tel:* 800-327-5557 (orders) *Fax:* 217-359-5975 *E-mail:* web@sagamorepub.com *Web Site:* www.sagamorepub.com, pg 189

SAGE Publishing, 2455 Teller Rd, Thousand Oaks, CA 91320 *Toll Free Tel:* 800-818-7243 *Toll Free Fax:* 800-583-2665 *E-mail:* info@sagepub.com; orders@sagepub.com *Web Site:* www.sagepublishing.com, pg 189

SAH Prize for Historical Fiction, 2950 Broadway, New York, NY 10027 *Tel:* 212-854-6495 *E-mail:* amhistsociety@columbia.edu *Web Site:* sah.columbia.edu, pg 663

St Andrews University Press, 1700 Dogwood Mile, Laurinburg, NC 28352-5598 *Tel:* 910-277-5555 *Toll Free Tel:* 800-763-0198 *Fax:* 910-277-5020 *Web Site:* www.sa.edu/st-andrews-university-press, pg 190

St Augustine's Press Inc, PO Box 2285, South Bend, IN 46680-2285 *Tel:* 574-291-3500 *Fax:* 574-291-3700 *E-mail:* bruce@staugustine.net *Web Site:* www.staugustine.net, pg 190

Saint Herman Press, 4430 Mushroom Lane, Platina, CA 96076 *Tel:* 530-352-4430 *Fax:* 530-352-4432 *E-mail:* stherman@stherman.com *Web Site:* www.sainthermanmonastery.com, pg 190

St James Press®, 27500 Drake Rd, Farmington Hills, MI 48331-3535 *Tel:* 248-699-4253 *Toll Free Tel:* 800-877-4253 (orders) *Toll Free Fax:* 877-363-4253 *E-mail:* gale.customerservice@cengage.com *Web Site:* www.gale.com, pg 190

Guy Saint-Jean Editeur Inc, 4490, rue Garand, Laval, QC H7L 5Z6, Canada *Tel:* 450-663-1777 *E-mail:* info@saint-jeanediteur.com *Web Site:* saint-jeanediteur.com, pg 439

Saint Johann Press, 315 Schraalenburgh Rd, Haworth, NJ 07641 *Tel:* 201-387-1529 *Fax:* 201-501-0698 *Web Site:* www.stjohannpress.com, pg 190

St Joseph's University Press, 5600 City Ave, Philadelphia, PA 19131-1395 *Tel:* 610-660-3402 *Fax:* 610-660-3412 *E-mail:* sjupress@sju.edu *Web Site:* www.sjupress.com, pg 190

Saint Louis Literary Award, Pius XII Memorial Library, 3650 Lindell Blvd, St Louis, MO 63108 *Tel:* 314-977-3100; 314-977-3087 *Fax:* 314-977-3108 *E-mail:* slula@slu.edu *Web Site:* lib.slu.edu/about/associates/literary-award, pg 664

St Martin's Press, LLC, 120 Broadway, New York, NY 10271 *Tel:* 646-307-5151 *Web Site:* us.macmillan.com/smp, pg 190

Saint Mary's Press, 702 Terrace Heights, Winona, MN 55987-1320 *Tel:* 507-457-7900 *Toll Free Tel:* 800-533-8095 *Toll Free Fax:* 800-344-9225 *E-mail:* smpress@smp.org *Web Site:* www.smp.org, pg 191

Saint Nectarios Press, 10300 Ashworth Ave N, Seattle, WA 98133-9410 *Tel:* 206-522-4471 *Toll Free Tel:* 800-643-4233 *E-mail:* orders@stnectariospress.com *Web Site:* www.stnectariospress.com, pg 191

St Pauls, 2187 Victory Blvd, Staten Island, NY 10314-6603 *Tel:* 718-761-0047 (edit & prodn); 718-698-2759 (mktg & billing) *Toll Free Tel:* 800-343-2522 *Fax:* 718-761-0057 *E-mail:* sales@stpauls.us; marketing@stpauls.us *Web Site:* www.stpauls.us, pg 191

Salem Press, 2 University Plaza, Suite 310, Hackensack, NJ 07601 *Tel:* 201-968-0500 *Toll Free Tel:* 800-221-1592 *Fax:* 201-968-0511 *E-mail:* csr@salempress.com *Web Site:* salempress.com, pg 191

Salina Bookshelf Inc, 1120 W University Ave, Suite 102, Flagstaff, AZ 86001 *Toll Free Tel:* 877-527-0070 *Fax:* 928-526-0386 *Web Site:* www.salinabookshelf.com, pg 191

Salmon Bay Indexing, PO Box 2362, Vashon, WA 98070 *Tel:* 206-612-3993 *Web Site:* salmonbayindexing.com, pg 470

Barbara S Salz LLC Photo Research, 127 Prospect Place, South Orange, NJ 07079 *Tel:* 646-734-5949 *E-mail:* bsalz.photo@gmail.com, pg 470

Salzman International, 1751 Charles Ave, Arcata, CA 95521 *Tel:* 415-285-8267 *Fax:* 707-822-5500 *Web Site:* www.salzint.com, pg 512

SAMS Technical Publishing LLC, 9850 E 30 St, Indianapolis, IN 46229 *Toll Free Tel:* 800-428-7267 *E-mail:* customercare@samswebsite.com *Web Site:* www.samswebsite.com, pg 191

Paul Samuelson, 117 Oak Dr, San Rafael, CA 94901 *Tel:* 415-517-0700 (cell) *E-mail:* paul@storywrangler.com *Web Site:* www.storywrangler.com, pg 470

San Diego Christian Writers' Guild Conference, PO Box 270403, San Diego, CA 92198 *Tel:* 760-294-3269; 858-254-1402 *Fax:* 760-294-3269 *E-mail:* info@sandiegocwg.org *Web Site:* www.sandiegocwg.org, pg 578

San Diego State University Press, Arts & Letters 283/MC 6020, 5500 Campanile Dr, San Diego, CA 92182-6020 *Tel:* 619-594-6220 (orders); 619-594-1524 (returns) *Fax:* 619-594-4998 (returns) *E-mail:* memo@sdsu.edu *Web Site:* sdsupress.sdsu.edu, pg 191

San Francisco Writers Conference, 1029 Jones St, San Francisco, CA 94109 *Tel:* 415-673-0939 *E-mail:* sfwriterscon@aol.com *Web Site:* www.sfwriters.org, pg 578

San Francisco Writing Contest (SFWC), 1029 Jones St, San Francisco, CA 94109 *Tel:* 415-673-0939 *E-mail:* sfwriterscon@aol.com *Web Site:* www.sfwriters.org, pg 664

The Carl Sandburg Literary Awards, 20 N Michigan Ave, Suite 520, Chicago, IL 60602 *Tel:* 312-201-9830 *Fax:* 312-201-9833 *Web Site:* www.cplfoundation.org, pg 664

Victoria Sanders & Associates LLC, 440 Buck Rd, Stone Ridge, NY 12484 *Tel:* 212-633-8811 *E-mail:* queriesvsa@gmail.com *Web Site:* www.victoriasanders.com, pg 501

Ada Sanderson Memorial, 900 Timber Creek Place, Virginia Beach, VA 23464 *E-mail:* poetryinva@aol.com *Web Site:* poetrysocietyofvirginia.org, pg 664

Sandhills Writers' Series, Dept of English & Foreign Languages, 1120 15 St, Augusta, GA 30912 *Tel:* 706-729-2417, pg 578

Mari Sandoz Award, PO Box 21756, Lincoln, NE 68542-1756 *E-mail:* nebraskalibraries@gmail.com *Web Site:* www.nebraskalibraries.org, pg 664

Ivan Sandrof Lifetime Achievement Award, c/o 310 Lewis Ave, Brooklyn, NY 11221 *E-mail:* info@bookcritics.org *Web Site:* bookcritics.org/awards, pg 664

Santa Monica Press LLC, 16236 San Dieguito Rd, Suite 1-28, Rancho Santa Fe, CA 92067 *Tel:* 858-793-1890 *Toll Free Tel:* 800-784-9553 *E-mail:* books@santamonicapress.com *Web Site:* www.santamonicapress.com, pg 191

Santillana USA Publishing Co, 2023 NW 84 Ave, Doral, FL 33122 *Tel:* 305-591-9522 *Toll Free Tel:* 800-245-8584 *E-mail:* customerservice@santillanausa.com *Web Site:* www.santillanausa.com, pg 192

Sara Jordan Publishing, RPO Lakeport Box 28105, St Catharines, ON L2N 7P8, Canada *Tel:* 905-938-5050 *Toll Free Tel:* 800-567-7733 *Fax:* 905-938-9970 *Toll Free Fax:* 800-229-3855 *Web Site:* www.sara-jordan.com, pg 439

Sarabande Books Inc, 822 E Market St, Louisville, KY 40206 *Tel:* 502-458-4028 *Fax:* 502-458-4065 *E-mail:* info@sarabandebooks.org *Web Site:* www.sarabandebooks.org, pg 192

William Saroyan International Prize for Writing, Admin, Saroyan Prize Committee, Stanford University Libraries, 557 Escondido Mall, Stanford, CA 94305-6004 *Tel:* 650-736-9538 *Web Site:* library.stanford.edu/saroyan, pg 664

May Sarton Award, 46 Wallace St, Somerville, MA 02144 *E-mail:* info@nepoetryclub.org *Web Site:* www.nepoetryclub.org, pg 664

May Sarton New Hampshire Poetry Prize, 44 Main St, 2nd fl, Peterborough, NH 03458 *Tel:* 603-567-4430 *Web Site:* www.bauhanpublishing.com, pg 664

Sarton Women's Book Awards™, PO Box 1616, Bertram, TX 78605-1616 *E-mail:* sartonprize@storycircle.org *Web Site:* www.storycircle.org/SartonLiteraryAward, pg 664

SAS Press, 100 SAS Campus Dr, Cary, NC 27513-2414 *Tel:* 919-677-8000 *Toll Free Tel:* 800-727-0025 *Fax:* 919-677-4444 *E-mail:* saspress@sas.com *Web Site:* support.sas.com/en/books.html, pg 192

Saskatchewan Arts Board, 1355 Broad St, Regina, SK S4R 7V1, Canada *Tel:* 306-787-4056 *Toll Free Tel:* 800-667-7526 (CN) *Fax:* 306-787-4199 *E-mail:* info@saskartsboard.ca *Web Site:* www.saskartsboard.ca, pg 545

Sasquatch Books, 1904 S Third Ave, Suite 710, Seattle, WA 98101 *Tel:* 206-467-4300 *Toll Free Tel:* 800-775-0817 *Fax:* 206-467-4301 *E-mail:* custserv@sasquatchbooks.com *Web Site:* sasquatchbooks.com, pg 192

Saturnalia Books Poetry Prize, 105 Woodside Rd, Ardmore, PA 19003 *Tel:* 267-278-9541 *Web Site:* www.saturnaliabooks.org, pg 664

SATW Foundation Lowell Thomas Travel Journalism Competition, 306 Summer Hill Dr, Fredericksburg, TX 78654 *Tel:* 281-217-2872 *E-mail:* awards@satwf.com *Web Site:* www.satwfoundation.org, pg 664

Satya House Publications, 22 Turkey St, Hardwick, MA 01037 *Tel:* 413-477-8743 *E-mail:* info@satyahouse.com; orders@satyahouse.com *Web Site:* www.satyahouse.com, pg 192

Savant Books & Publications LLC, 2630 Kapiolani Blvd, Suite 1601, Honolulu, HI 96826 *Tel:* 808-941-3927 (9AM-noon HST) *E-mail:* savantbooks@gmail.com; savantdistribution@gmail.com *Web Site:* www.savantbooksandpublications.com; www.savantdistribution.com, pg 192

Savvas Learning Co LLC, 15 E Midland Ave, Suite 502, Paramus, NJ 07652 *Toll Free Tel:* 800-848-9500 *Web Site:* www.savvas.com, pg 193

SBL Press, The Luce Ctr, Suite 350, 825 Houston Mill Rd, Atlanta, GA 30329 *Tel:* 404-727-3100 *Fax:* 404-727-3101 (corp) *E-mail:* sbl@sbl-site.org *Web Site:* www.sbl-site.org, pg 193

Aldo & Jeanne Scaglione Prize for a Translation of a Literary Work, 85 Broad St, Suite 500, New York, NY 10004-2434 *Tel:* 646-576-5141; 646-576-5000 *Fax:* 646-458-0030 *E-mail:* awards@mla.org *Web Site:* www.mla.org, pg 665

Aldo & Jeanne Scaglione Prize for a Translation of a Scholarly Study of Literature, 85 Broad St, Suite 500, New York, NY 10004-2434 *Tel:* 646-576-5141; 646-576-5000 *Fax:* 646-458-0030 *E-mail:* awards@mla.org *Web Site:* www.mla.org, pg 665

Aldo & Jeanne Scaglione Prize for Comparative Literary Studies, 85 Broad St, Suite 500, New York, NY 10004-2434 *Tel:* 646-576-5141; 646-576-5000 *Fax:* 646-458-0030 *E-mail:* awards@mla.org *Web Site:* www.mla.org, pg 665

Aldo & Jeanne Scaglione Prize for French & Francophone Studies, 85 Broad St, Suite 500, New York, NY 10004-2434 *Tel:* 646-576-5141; 646-576-5000 *Fax:* 646-458-0030 *E-mail:* awards@mla.org *Web Site:* www.mla.org, pg 665

Aldo & Jeanne Scaglione Prize for Italian Studies, 85 Broad St, Suite 500, New York, NY 10004-2434 *Tel:* 646-576-5141; 646-576-5000 *Fax:* 646-458-0030 *E-mail:* awards@mla.org *Web Site:* www.mla.org, pg 665

Aldo & Jeanne Scaglione Prize for Studies in Germanic Languages & Literatures, 85 Broad St, Suite 500, New York, NY 10004-2434 *Tel:* 646-576-5141; 646-576-5000 *Fax:* 646-458-0030 *E-mail:* awards@mla.org *Web Site:* www.mla.org, pg 665

Aldo & Jeanne Scaglione Prize for Studies in Slavic Languages & Literatures, 85 Broad St, Suite 500, New York, NY 10004-2434 *Tel:* 646-576-5141; 646-576-5000 *Fax:* 646-458-0030 *E-mail:* awards@mla.org *Web Site:* www.mla.org, pg 665

Aldo & Jeanne Scaglione Publication Award for a Manuscript in Italian Literary Studies, 85 Broad St, Suite 500, New York, NY 10004-2434 *Tel:* 646-576-5141; 646-576-5000 *Fax:* 646-458-0030 *E-mail:* awards@mla.org *Web Site:* www.mla.org, pg 665

William Sanders Scarborough Prize, 85 Broad St, Suite 500, New York, NY 10004-2434 *Tel:* 646-576-5141; 646-576-5000 *Fax:* 646-458-0030 *E-mail:* awards@mla.org *Web Site:* www.mla.org, pg 665

Scarsdale Publishing Ltd, 333 Mamaroneck Ave, White Plains, NY 10607 *E-mail:* scarsdale@scarsdalepublishing.com *Web Site:* scarsdalepublishing.com, pg 193

SCBWI-FL Florida Regional Conference, 125 E Merritt Island Causeway, Suite 209, Merritt Island, FL 32952 *Tel:* 321-338-7208 *E-mail:* florida@scbwi.org *Web Site:* florida.scbwi.org, pg 578

SCBWI-FL Mid-Year Workshops, 125 E Merritt Island Causeway, Suite 209, Merritt Island, FL 32952 *Tel:* 321-338-7208 *E-mail:* florida@scbwi.org *Web Site:* florida.scbwi.org, pg 578

SCBWI Work-In-Progress Grants, 6363 Wilshire Blvd, Suite 425, Los Angeles, CA 90048 *Tel:* 323-782-1010; 310-403-0675 (cell) *Fax:* 323-782-1892 *E-mail:* grants@scbwi.org; scbwi@scbwi.org *Web Site:* www.scbwi.org, pg 665

Skinner House Books, c/o Unitarian Universalist Assn, 24 Farnsworth St, Boston, MA 02210-1409 *Tel:* 617-742-2100 *Fax:* 617-948-6466 *E-mail:* skinnerhouse@uua.org *Web Site:* www.skinnerhouse.org, pg 200

Skipping Stones Honor Awards, 166 W 12 Ave, Eugene, OR 97401 *Tel:* 541-342-4956 *E-mail:* info@skippingstones.org *Web Site:* www.skippingstones.org, pg 668

The Skipping Stones Youth Honor Awards, 166 W 12 Ave, Eugene, OR 97401 *Tel:* 541-342-4956 *E-mail:* info@skippingstones.org *Web Site:* www.skippingstones.org, pg 668

Sky Pony Press, 307 W 36 St, 11th fl, New York, NY 10018 *Tel:* 212-643-6816 *Fax:* 212-643-6819 *E-mail:* skypony@skyhorsepublishing.com; info@skyhorsepublishing.com; submissions@skyhorsepublishing.com *Web Site:* www.skyponypress.com, pg 200

SkyLight Paths, 4507 Charlotte Ave, Suite 100, Nashville, TN 37209 *Tel:* 615-255-BOOK (255-2665) *Fax:* 615-255-5081 *E-mail:* marketing@turnerpublishing.com *Web Site:* www.skylightpaths.com; www.turnerpublishing.com, pg 200

SLACK® Incorporated, A Wyanoke Group Company, 6900 Grove Rd, Thorofare, NJ 08086-9447 *Tel:* 856-848-1000 *Toll Free Tel:* 800-257-8290 *Fax:* 856-848-6091 *E-mail:* sales@slackinc.com; editor@slackinc.com; customerservice@slackinc.com *Web Site:* www.healio.com/books, pg 201

Sleeping Bear Press™, 2395 S Huron Pkwy, Suite 200, Ann Arbor, MI 48104 *Toll Free Tel:* 800-487-2323 *Fax:* 734-794-0004 *E-mail:* customerservice@sleepingbearpress.com *Web Site:* www.sleepingbearpress.com, pg 201

Slipstream Annual Poetry Chapbook Contest, PO Box 2071, Dept W-1, Niagara Falls, NY 14301 *Web Site:* www.slipstreampress.org, pg 668

Beverley Slopen Literary Agency, 131 Bloor St W, Suite 711, Toronto, ON M5S 1S3, Canada *Tel:* 416-964-9598 *Fax:* 416-964-9598 *Web Site:* www.slopenagency.com, pg 503

Small Beer Press, 150 Pleasant St, No 306, Easthampton, MA 01027 *Tel:* 413-203-1636 *Fax:* 413-203-1636 *E-mail:* info@smallbeerpress.com *Web Site:* smallbeerpress.com, pg 201

Small Business Advisors Inc, 2005 Park St, Atlantic Beach, NY 11509 *Tel:* 516-374-1387 *Fax:* 516-374-1175 *E-mail:* info@smallbusinessadvice.com *Web Site:* www.smallbusinessadvice.com, pg 201

Small Publishers, Artists & Writers Network (SPAWN), 1129 Maricopa Hwy, No 142, Ojai, CA 93023 *E-mail:* info@spawn.org *Web Site:* spawn.org, pg 546

SME (Society of Manufacturing Engineers), 1000 Town Ctr, Suite 1910, Southfield, MI 48075 *Tel:* 313-425-3000 *Toll Free Tel:* 800-733-4763 (cust serv) *Fax:* 313-425-3400 *E-mail:* publications@sme.org *Web Site:* www.sme.org, pg 201

Donald Smiley Prize, 260 rue Dalhousie St, Suite 204, Ottawa, ON K1N 7E4, Canada *Tel:* 613-562-1202 *Fax:* 613-241-0019 *E-mail:* cpsa-acsp@cpsa-acsp.ca *Web Site:* www.cpsa-acsp.ca, pg 668

Smith & Kraus Publishers Inc, 177 Lyme Rd, Hanover, NH 03755 *Tel:* 618-783-0519 *Toll Free Tel:* 877-668-8680 *Fax:* 618-783-0520 *E-mail:* editor@smithandkraus.com; info@smithandkraus.com; customerservice@smithandkraus.com *Web Site:* www.smithandkraus.com, pg 201

Helen C Smith Memorial Award, PO Box 609, Round Rock, TX 78680 *Tel:* 512-683-5640 *E-mail:* president@texasinstituteofletters.org *Web Site:* www.texasinstituteofletters.org, pg 668

The Jean Kennedy Smith VSA Playwright Discovery Award, 2700 "F" St NW, Washington, DC 20566 *Tel:* 202-416-8898 *Fax:* 202-416-4840 *E-mail:* vsainfo@kennedy-center.org *Web Site:* www.kennedy-center.org/pdp, pg 668

The Jeffrey E Smith Editors' Prize, 357 McReynolds Hall, Columbia, MO 65211 *Tel:* 573-882-4474 *Toll Free Tel:* 800-949-2505 *Fax:* 573-884-4671 *Web Site:* www.missourireview.com, pg 668

M Lee Smith Publishers, 100 Winners Circle, Suite 300, Brentwood, TN 37027 *Tel:* 615-373-7517 *Toll Free Tel:* 800-274-6774; 800-727-5257 *E-mail:* custserv@mleesmith.com; service@blr.com *Web Site:* www.mleesmith.com; www.blr.com, pg 201

Roger W Smith, 59-67 58 Rd, Maspeth, NY 11378-3211 *Tel:* 718-416-1334 *E-mail:* brandeis106@gmail.com, pg 471

Steve Smith Autosports, PO Box 11631, Santa Ana, CA 92711-1631 *Tel:* 714-639-7681 *Fax:* 714-639-9741 *Web Site:* www.stevesmithautosports.com, pg 202

Smithsonian Institution Scholarly Press, Aerospace Bldg, 704-A, MRC 957, Washington, DC 20013 *Tel:* 202-633-3017 *Fax:* 202-633-6877 *E-mail:* schol_press@si.edu *Web Site:* scholarlypress.si.edu, pg 202

Smyth & Helwys Publishing Inc, 6316 Peake Rd, Macon, GA 31210-3960 *Tel:* 478-757-0564 *Toll Free Tel:* 800-747-3016 (orders only) *Fax:* 478-757-1305 *E-mail:* information@helwys.com *Web Site:* www.helwys.com, pg 202

Michael Snell Literary Agency, PO Box 1206, Truro, MA 02666-1206 *Tel:* 508-349-3718 *Web Site:* www.michaelsnellagency.com, pg 503

Kay Snow Writing Contest, 5331 SW Macadam Ave, Suite 258, PMB 215, Portland, OR 97239 *Tel:* 901-200-5385 *E-mail:* wilwrite@willamettewriters.org *Web Site:* willamettewriters.org, pg 668

Snow Lion, 4720 Walnut St, Boulder, CO 80301 *E-mail:* customercare@shambhala.com *Web Site:* www.shambhala.com/snowlion, pg 202

Sobel Weber Associates Inc, 146 E 19 St, New York, NY 10003-2404 *Tel:* 212-420-8585 *E-mail:* info@sobelweber.com *Web Site:* www.sobelweber.com, pg 503

Social Sciences & Humanities Research Council of Canada (SSHRC), 350 Albert St, Ottawa, ON K1P 6G4, Canada *Tel:* 613-992-0691; 613-996-6976 *E-mail:* research@sshrc-crsh.gc.ca *Web Site:* www.sshrc.ca, pg 546

Society for Advancing Business Editing & Writing (SABEW), Walter Cronkite School of Journalism & Mass Communication, Arizona State University, 555 N Central Ave, Suite 406E, Phoenix, AZ 85004-1248 *Tel:* 602-496-7862 *E-mail:* sabew@sabew.org *Web Site:* sabew.org, pg 546

Society for Features Journalism (SFJ), University of Maryland, Philip Merrill College of Journalism, 1100 Knight Hall, College Park, MD 20742 *Tel:* 301-314-2631 *Fax:* 301-314-9166 *Web Site:* featuresjournalism.org, pg 546

Society for Human Resource Management (SHRM), 1800 Duke St, Alexandria, VA 22314 *Tel:* 703-548-3440 *Toll Free Tel:* 800-283-7476 (orders) *E-mail:* books@shrm.org *Web Site:* www.shrm.org, pg 202

Society for Industrial & Applied Mathematics, 3600 Market St, 6th fl, Philadelphia, PA 19104-2688 *Tel:* 215-382-9800 *Toll Free Tel:* 800-447-7426 *Fax:* 215-386-7999 *E-mail:* siambooks@siam.org *Web Site:* www.siam.org, pg 202

Society for Mining, Metallurgy & Exploration, 12999 E Adam Aircraft Circle, Englewood, CO 80112 *Tel:* 303-948-4200 *Toll Free Tel:* 800-763-3132 *Fax:* 303-973-3845 *E-mail:* cs@smenet.org; books@smenet.org *Web Site:* www.smenet.org, pg 202

Society for Scholarly Publishing (SSP), 1120 Rte 73, Suite 200, Mount Laurel, NJ 08054 *Tel:* 856-439-1385 *Fax:* 856-439-0525 *E-mail:* info@sspnet.org *Web Site:* www.sspnet.org, pg 546

Society for Technical Communication, 9401 Lee Hwy, Suite 300, Fairfax, VA 22031 *Tel:* 703-522-4114 *Fax:* 703-522-2075 *E-mail:* stc@stc.org *Web Site:* www.stc.org, pg 546

Society for Technical Communication's Annual Conference, 9401 Lee Hwy, Suite 300, Fairfax, VA 22031 *Tel:* 703-522-4114 *Fax:* 703-522-2075 *E-mail:* stc@stc.org; summit@stc.org *Web Site:* summit.stc.org; www.stc.org, pg 578

Society for the History of Authorship, Reading & Publishing Inc (SHARP), c/o Johns Hopkins University Press, Journals Publishing Div, PO Box 19966, Baltimore, MD 21211-0966 *Tel:* 410-516-6987 *Toll Free Tel:* 800-548-1784 *Fax:* 410-516-3866 *E-mail:* jrnlcirc@press.jhu.edu *Web Site:* www.sharpweb.org, pg 546

Society of American Archivists, 17 N State St, Suite 1425, Chicago, IL 60602-4061 *Tel:* 312-606-0722 *Toll Free Tel:* 866-722-7858 *Fax:* 312-606-0728 *Web Site:* www.archivists.org, pg 202

Society of American Travel Writers (SATW), 17W110 22 St, One Parkview Plaza, Suite 800, Oakbrook Terrace, IL 60181 *E-mail:* info@satw.org *Web Site:* www.satw.org, pg 546

Society of Children's Book Writers & Illustrators (SCBWI), 6363 Wilshire Blvd, Suite 425, Los Angeles, CA 90048 *Tel:* 323-782-1010 *E-mail:* membership@scbwi.org *Web Site:* www.scbwi.org, pg 546

Society of Environmental Toxicology & Chemistry (SETAC), 229 S Baylen St, 2nd fl, Pensacola, FL 32502 *Tel:* 850-469-1500 *Toll Free Fax:* 888-296-4136 *E-mail:* setac@setac.org *Web Site:* www.setac.org, pg 202

Society of Exploration Geophysicists, 8801 S Yale Ave, Suite 500, Tulsa, OK 74137 *Tel:* 918-497-5500 *Fax:* 918-497-5557 *E-mail:* web@seg.org *Web Site:* www.seg.org, pg 202

Society of Illustrators (SI), 128 E 63 St, New York, NY 10065 *Tel:* 212-838-2560 *Fax:* 212-838-2561 *E-mail:* info@societyillustrators.org *Web Site:* www.societyillustrators.org, pg 547

The Society of Midland Authors (SMA), PO Box 10419, Chicago, IL 60610 *E-mail:* info@midlandauthors.com *Web Site:* www.midlandauthors.com, pg 547

The Society of Midland Authors Awards, PO Box 10419, Chicago, IL 60610 *E-mail:* info@midlandauthors.com *Web Site:* www.midlandauthors.com, pg 668

Society of Motion Picture & Television Engineers® (SMPTE®), 3 Barker Ave, 5th fl, White Plains, NY 10601 *Tel:* 914-761-1100 *Fax:* 914-761-3115 *Web Site:* www.smpte.org, pg 547

The Society of Naval Architects & Marine Engineers (SNAME), 99 Canal Center Plaza, Suite 310, Alexandria, VA 22314 *Tel:* 703-997-6701 *Toll Free Tel:* 800-798-2188 *Fax:* 703-997-6702 *Web Site:* www.sname.org, pg 203

The Society of Southwestern Authors (SSA), PO Box 30355, Tucson, AZ 85751-0355 *E-mail:* info@ssa-az.org *Web Site:* www.ssa-az.org, pg 547

The Society of Southwestern Authors Writing Contest, PO Box 30355, Tucson, AZ 85751-0355 *E-mail:* info@ssa-az.org *Web Site:* www.ssa-az.org, pg 669

Software & Information Industry Association (SIIA), 1090 Vermont Ave NW, 6th fl, Washington, DC 20005-4905 *Tel:* 202-289-7442 *Fax:* 202-289-7097 *Web Site:* www.siia.net, pg 547

Soho Press Inc, 853 Broadway, New York, NY 10003 *Tel:* 212-260-1900 *E-mail:* soho@sohopress.com; publicity@sohopress.com *Web Site:* sohopress.com, pg 203

Soil Science Society of America (SSSA), 5585 Guilford Rd, Madison, WI 53711-5801 *Tel:* 608-273-8080 *Fax:* 608-273-2021 *Web Site:* www.soils.org, pg 203

Solano Press Books, PO Box 773, Point Arena, CA 95468 *Tel:* 707-884-4508 *Toll Free Tel:* 800-931-9373 *Fax:* 707-884-4109 *E-mail:* spbooks@solano.com *Web Site:* www.solano.com, pg 203

Jodi Solomon Speakers Bureau, 295 Huntington Ave, Suite 211, Boston, MA 02115 *Tel:* 617-266-3450 *Fax:* 617-266-5660 *E-mail:* inquiries@jodisolomonspeakers.com *Web Site:* jodisolomonspeakers.com, pg 515

Solution Tree, 555 N Morton St, Bloomington, IN 47404 *Tel:* 812-336-7700 *Toll Free Tel:* 800-733-6786 *Fax:* 812-336-7790 *E-mail:* pubs@solutiontree.com; orders@solutiontree.com *Web Site:* www.solutiontree. com, pg 203

Somerset Hall Press, 416 Commonwealth Ave, Suite 612, Boston, MA 02215 *Tel:* 617-236-5126 *E-mail:* info@somersethallpress.com *Web Site:* www. somersethallpress.com, pg 203

Soncino Press Ltd, 123 Ditmas Ave, Brooklyn, NY 11218 *Tel:* 718-972-6200 *Toll Free Tel:* 800-972-6201 *Fax:* 718-972-6204 *E-mail:* info@soncino.com *Web Site:* www.soncino.com, pg 203

Sophia Institute Press®, 18 Celina Ave, Unit 1, Nashua, NH 03063 *Tel:* 603-641-9344 *Toll Free Tel:* 800-888-9344 *Fax:* 603-641-8108 *Toll Free Fax:* 888-288-2259 *E-mail:* orders@sophiainstitute.com *Web Site:* www. sophiainstitute.com, pg 203

Sophie Kerr Prize, c/o College Relations Off, 300 Washington Ave, Chestertown, MD 21620 *Tel:* 410-778-2800 *Toll Free Tel:* 800-422-1782 *Fax:* 410-810-7150 *Web Site:* www.washcoll.edu, pg 669

Soul Mate Publishing, 3210 Sherwood Dr, Walworth, NY 14568 *Web Site:* www.soulmatepublishing.com, pg 203

Gordon Soules Book Publishers Ltd, 2372 Haywood Ave, West Vancouver, BC V7V 1X7, Canada *Tel:* 604-922-6588 *Fax:* 604-922-6574 *E-mail:* books@ gordonsoules.com *Web Site:* www.gordonsoules.com, pg 441

Sound Feelings Publishing, 18375 Ventura Blvd, No 8000, Tarzana, CA 91356 *Tel:* 818-757-0600 *E-mail:* information@soundfeelings.com *Web Site:* www.soundfeelings.com, pg 203

Sounds True Inc, 413 S Arthur Ave, Louisville, CO 80027 *Tel:* 303-665-3151 *Toll Free Tel:* 800-333-9185 (US); 888-303-9185 (US & CN) *E-mail:* customerservice@soundstrue.com; stpublicity@soundstrue.com *Web Site:* www. soundstrue.com, pg 204

Sourcebooks LLC, 1935 Brookdale Rd, Suite 139, Naperville, IL 60563 *Tel:* 630-961-3900 *Toll Free Tel:* 800-432-7444 *Fax:* 630-961-2168 *E-mail:* info@ sourcebooks.com; customersupport@sourcebooks.com *Web Site:* www.sourcebooks.com, pg 204

Sourced Media Books, 15 Via Picato, San Clemente, CA 92673 *Tel:* 949-813-0182 *E-mail:* editor@sourcedmediabooks.com *Web Site:* sourcedmediabooks.com, pg 204

South Carolina Bar, Continuing Legal Education Div, 950 Taylor St, Columbia, SC 29201 *Tel:* 803-799-6653 *Toll Free Tel:* 800-768-7787 *E-mail:* scbar-info@scbar. org *Web Site:* www.scbar.org, pg 204

South Dakota Historical Society Press, 900 Governors Dr, Pierre, SD 57501 *Tel:* 605-773-6009 *Fax:* 605-773-6041 *E-mail:* info@sdshspress.com; orders@ sdshspress.com *Web Site:* sdshspress.com, pg 205

South Platte Press, PO Box 163, David City, NE 68632-0163 *Tel:* 402-367-3554 *E-mail:* railroads@ windstream.net *Web Site:* www.southplattepress.net, pg 205

Southampton Writers' Conference, 239 Montauk Hwy, Southampton, NY 11968 *Tel:* 631-632-5007 *E-mail:* southamptonwriters@notes.cc.sunysb.edu; southamptonarts@stonybrook.edu *Web Site:* www. stonybrook.edu/southampton/mfa/summer/cwl_home. html, pg 578

Southeast Review Narrative Nonfiction Contest, Florida State University, Dept of English, Tallahassee, FL 32306 *E-mail:* southeastreview@gmail.com *Web Site:* www.southeastreview.org, pg 669

Southeast Review's Gearhart Poetry Contest, Florida State University, Dept of English, Tallahassee, FL 32306 *E-mail:* southeastreview@gmail.com *Web Site:* www.southeastreview.org, pg 669

Southeastern Theatre Conference New Play Project, 1175 Revolution Mill Dr, Suite 14, Greensboro, NC 27405 *Tel:* 336-272-3645 *Fax:* 336-272-8810 *E-mail:* info@ setc.org *Web Site:* www.setc.org, pg 669

Southern Book Prize, 51 Pleasant Ridge Dr, Asheville, NC 28805 *Tel:* 803-994-9530 *Fax:* 309-410-0211 *Web Site:* www.sibaweb.com/siba-book-award, pg 669

Southern Books Competition, PO Box 950, Rex, GA 30273 *Tel:* 678-466-4334 *Fax:* 678-466-4349 *Web Site:* selaonline.org, pg 669

Southern California Writers' Conference (SCWC), 18160 Cottonwood Rd, Suite 260, Sunriver, OR 97707 *Tel:* 619-303-8185 *Fax:* 619-906-7462 *E-mail:* msg@writersconference.com *Web Site:* www. writersconference.com, pg 578

Southern Historical Press Inc, 375 W Broad St, Greenville, SC 29601 *Tel:* 864-233-2346 *Toll Free Tel:* 800-233-0152 *E-mail:* southernhistoricalpress@ gmail.com *Web Site:* www.southernhistoricalpress.com, pg 205

Southern Illinois University Press, 1915 University Press Dr, SIUC Mail Code 6806, Carbondale, IL 62901-4323 *Tel:* 618-453-2281 *Fax:* 618-453-1221 *Web Site:* www.siupress.com, pg 205

Southern Independent Booksellers Alliance, 51 Pleasant Ridge Dr, Asheville, NC 28805 *Tel:* 803-994-9530 *Fax:* 309-410-0211 *E-mail:* siba@sibaweb.com *Web Site:* www.sibaweb.com, pg 547

Southern Playwrights Competition, 700 Pelham Rd N, Jacksonville, AL 36265-1602 *Tel:* 256-782-5412 *Web Site:* www.jsu.edu/english/southpla.html, pg 669

Terry Southern Prize, 544 W 27 St, New York, NY 10001 *Tel:* 212-343-1333 *E-mail:* queries@ theparisreview.org *Web Site:* www.theparisreview.org, pg 669

SouthWest Writers Conference Series, 3200 Carlisle Blvd NE, Suite 114, Albuquerque, NM 87110-1663 *Tel:* 505-830-6034 *E-mail:* swwriters@juno.com *Web Site:* www.southwestwriters.com, pg 578

Sovereign Award for Outstanding Writing, Woodbine Sales Pavilion, 555 Rexdale Blvd, Toronto, ON M9W 5L2, Canada *Tel:* 416-675-7756 *Fax:* 416-675-6378 *E-mail:* jockeyclub@bellnet.ca *Web Site:* www. jockeyclubcanada.com; www.sovereignawards.ca, pg 669

The Sow's Ear Poetry Prize & The Sow's Ear Chapbook Prize, 1748 Cave Ridge Rd, Mount Jackson, VA 22842 *Tel:* 540-477-3257 *E-mail:* sepoetryreview@ gmail.com *Web Site:* sowsearpoetry.org, pg 669

Soyinfo Center, 1021 Dolores Dr, Lafayette, CA 94549-0234 *Tel:* 925-283-2991 *Web Site:* www.soyinfocenter. com, pg 205

Spark Award, 6363 Wilshire Blvd, Suite 425, Los Angeles, CA 90048 *Tel:* 323-782-1010 *Fax:* 323-782-1892 *E-mail:* grants@scbwi.org; scbwi@scbwi.org *Web Site:* www.scbwi.org, pg 669

Speakers Unlimited, 7532 Courtyard Place, Cary, NC 27519 *Tel:* 919-466-7676 *Toll Free Tel:* 888-333-6676 *E-mail:* prospeak@aol.com *Web Site:* www. speakersunlimited.com, pg 515

Special Libraries Association (SLA), 7918 Jones Branch Dr, Suite 300, McLean, VA 22102 *Tel:* 703-647-4900 *Fax:* 703-506-3266 *Web Site:* www.sla.org, pg 547

Specialized Information Publishers Association (SIPA), 1090 Vermont Ave NW, 6th fl, Washington, DC 20005-4095 *Tel:* 202-289-7442 *Fax:* 202-289-7097 *Web Site:* www.siia.net/divisions/sipa-specialized-information-publishers-association, pg 547

Spectrum Literary Agency, 320 Central Park W, Suite 1-D, New York, NY 10025 *Tel:* 212-362-4323 *Fax:* 212-362-4562 *Web Site:* www.spectrumliteraryagency.com, pg 503

SPIE, 1000 20 St, Bellingham, WA 98225-6705 *Tel:* 360-676-3290 *Toll Free Tel:* 888-504-8171 (orders) *Fax:* 360-647-1445 *E-mail:* help@spie.org; customerservice@spie.org (orders) *Web Site:* www. spie.org, pg 205

The Spieler Agency, 27 W 20 St, Suite 302, New York, NY 10011 *Tel:* 212-757-4439 *Fax:* 212-333-2019 *E-mail:* spieleragency@spieleragency.com, pg 503

Spinsters Ink, PO Box 10543, Tallahassee, FL 32302 *Tel:* 850-576-2370 *Toll Free Tel:* 800-729-4992 *E-mail:* info@bellabooks.com *Web Site:* www. bellabooks.com/Publisher-spinsters-ink-cat.html, pg 205

Philip G Spitzer Literary Agency Inc, 50 Talmage Farm Lane, East Hampton, NY 11937 *Tel:* 631-329-3650 *Fax:* 631-329-3651 *Web Site:* www.spitzeragency.com, pg 503

Spizzirri Publishing Inc, PO Box 9397, Rapid City, SD 57709-9397 *Tel:* 605-348-2749 *Toll Free Tel:* 800-325-9819 *Fax:* 605-348-6251 *Toll Free Fax:* 800-322-9819 *E-mail:* spizzpub@aol.com *Web Site:* www.spizzirri. com, pg 205

John Spray Mystery Award, 40 Orchard View Blvd, Suite 217, Toronto, ON M4R 1B9, Canada *Tel:* 416-975-0010 *Fax:* 416-975-8970 *E-mail:* info@ bookcentre.ca *Web Site:* www.bookcentre.ca, pg 669

Spring Time Writers Creative Writing & Journaling Workshop, PO Box 512, Lyons, CO 80540-0512 *Tel:* 303-823-0997 *E-mail:* writers@springtimewriters. com *Web Site:* www.springtimewriters.com, pg 578

Springer, 233 Spring St, New York, NY 10013-1578 *Tel:* 212-460-1500 *Toll Free Tel:* 800-SPRINGER (777-4643) *Fax:* 212-460-1700 *E-mail:* customerservice@springer.com *Web Site:* www.springer.com, pg 205

Springer Publishing Co, 11 W 42 St, 15th fl, New York, NY 10036-8002 *Tel:* 212-431-4370 *Toll Free Tel:* 877-687-7476 *E-mail:* marketing@springerpub.com; cs@ springerpub.com (orders); textbook@springerpub. com; specialsales@springerpub.com *Web Site:* www. springerpub.com, pg 205

Spur Awards, 271 CR 219, Encampment, WY 82325 *Tel:* 307-329-8942 *E-mail:* wwa.moulton@gmail.com *Web Site:* westernwriters.org/spur-awards/, pg 670

Square One Publishers Inc, 115 Herricks Rd, Garden City Park, NY 11040 *Tel:* 516-535-2010 *Toll Free Tel:* 877-900-BOOK (900-2665) *Fax:* 516-535-2014 *E-mail:* sq1publish@aol.com *Web Site:* www. squareonepublishers.com, pg 206

Squaw Valley Community of Writers Summer Workshops, PO Box 1416, Nevada City, CA 95959 *Tel:* 530-470-8440 *E-mail:* info@communityofwriters. org *Web Site:* www.communityofwriters.org, pg 578

SSPC: The Society for Protective Coatings, 800 Trumbull Dr, Pittsburgh, PA 15205-4365 *Tel:* 412-281-2331 *Toll Free Tel:* 877-281-7772 (US only) *Fax:* 412-444-3591 *E-mail:* info@sspc.org *Web Site:* www.sspc. org, pg 206

Stackler Editorial Agency, 200 Woodland Ave, Summit, NJ 07901 *Tel:* 510-912-9187 *E-mail:* ed.stackler@ gmail.com *Web Site:* www.fictioneditor.com, pg 471

Stackpole Books, 31 E Main St, New Kingstown, PA 17072 *Tel:* 717-590-8974 *Web Site:* www. stackpolebooks.com, pg 206

The Edna Staebler Award for Creative Non-Fiction, Office of the Dean, Faculty of Arts, 75 University Ave W, Waterloo, ON N2L 3C5, Canada *Tel:* 519-884-1970 (ext 3361) *E-mail:* staebleraward@wlu.ca *Web Site:* wlu.ca/staebleraward, pg 670

Standard Publishing, 4050 Lee Vance Dr, Colorado Springs, CO 80918 *Toll Free Tel:* 800-323-7543 *Toll Free Fax:* 800-430-0726 *Web Site:* www.standardpub. com, pg 206

Standard Publishing Corp, 10 High St, Boston, MA 02110 *Tel:* 617-457-0600 *Toll Free Tel:* 800-682-5759 *Fax:* 617-457-0608 *Web Site:* www.spcpub.com, pg 206

Stanford University Press, 425 Broadway St, Redwood City, CA 94063-3126 *Tel:* 650-723-9434 *Fax:* 650-725-3457 *E-mail:* info@www.sup.org; publicity@ www.sup.org; sales@www.sup.org *Web Site:* www. sup.org, pg 206

Teacher's Discovery, 2741 Paldan Dr, Auburn Hills, MI 48326 *Toll Free Tel:* 800-832-2437 *Toll Free Fax:* 800-287-4509 *E-mail:* help@teachersdiscovery. com *Web Site:* www.teachersdiscovery.com, pg 214

Teaching & Learning Co, 501 E Third St, Dayton, OH 45402 *Tel:* 937-228-6118 *Toll Free Tel:* 800-444-1144 *Fax:* 937-223-2042 *E-mail:* info@lorenz.com *Web Site:* www.lorenzeducationalpress.com, pg 214

Teaching Strategies LLC, 4500 East-West Hwy, Suite 300, Bethesda, MD 20814 *Tel:* 301-634-0818 *Toll Free Tel:* 800-637-3652 *Fax:* 301-657-0250; 301-634-0833 *E-mail:* info@teachingstrategies.com *Web Site:* www. teachingstrategies.com, pg 214

Technical Association of the Pulp & Paper Industry (TAPPI), 15 Technology Pkwy S, Suite 115, Peachtree Corners, GA 30092 *Tel:* 770-446-1400 *Toll Free Tel:* 800-332-8686 (US); 800-446-9431 (CN) *Fax:* 770-446-6947 *E-mail:* memberconnection@tappi. org *Web Site:* www.tappi.org, pg 547

Television Academy, 5220 Lankershim Blvd, North Hollywood, CA 91601-3109 *Tel:* 818-754-2800 *Fax:* 818-761-2827 *Web Site:* www.emmys.com, pg 547

Temple University Press, 1852 N Tenth St, Philadelphia, PA 19122-6099 *Tel:* 215-926-2140 *Toll Free Tel:* 800-621-2736 *Fax:* 215-926-2141 *E-mail:* tempress@ temple.edu *Web Site:* tupress.temple.edu, pg 214

Templegate Publishers, 302 E Adams St, Springfield, IL 62701 *Tel:* 217-522-3353 (edit & sales) *Toll Free Tel:* 800-367-4844 (orders only) *E-mail:* wisdom@ templegate.com; orders@templegate.com (sales) *Web Site:* www.templegate.com, pg 214

Templeton Press, 300 Conshohocken State Rd, Suite 550, West Conshohocken, PA 19428 *Tel:* 484-531-8380 *Fax:* 484-531-8382 *E-mail:* tpinfo@templetonpress.org *Web Site:* www.templetonpress.org, pg 214

Temporal Mechanical Press, 6760 Hwy 7, Estes Park, CO 80517-6404 *Tel:* 970-586-4706 *E-mail:* info@ enosmills.com *Web Site:* www.enosmills.com, pg 215

Ten Speed Press, 6001 Shellmound St, Suite 600, Emeryville, CA 94608 *Tel:* 510-285-3000 *Toll Free Tel:* 800-841-BOOK (841-2665) *Web Site:* crownpublishing.com/imprint/ten-speed-press, pg 215

Tennessee Arts Commission Fellowships, 401 Charlotte Ave, Nashville, TN 37243-0780 *Tel:* 615-741-1701 *Fax:* 615-741-8559 *Web Site:* www.tnartscommission. org, pg 672

The Tenth Gate Prize, *Tel:* 301-581-9439 *Fax:* 301-581-9443 *E-mail:* editor@wordworksbooks.org *Web Site:* www.wordworksbooks.org, pg 672

Teora USA LLC, 9443 Rosehill Dr, Bethesda, MD 20817 *Tel:* 301-986-6990 *E-mail:* teorausa@gmail.com *Web Site:* www.teora.com, pg 215

Terra Nova Books, 33 Alondra Rd, Santa Fe, NM 87508 *Tel:* 505-670-9319 *Fax:* 509-461-9333 *E-mail:* publisher@terranovabooks.com; marketing@ terranovabooks.com *Web Site:* www.terranovabooks. com, pg 215

TESOL International Association, 1925 Ballenger Ave, Alexandria, VA 22314-6820 *Tel:* 703-836-0774 *Fax:* 703-836-7864; 703-836-6447 *E-mail:* publications@tesol.org; info@tesol.org; members@tesol.org *Web Site:* www.tesol.org, pg 215

Tessler Literary Agency LLC, 27 W 20 St, Suite 1003, New York, NY 10011 *Tel:* 212-242-0466 *Web Site:* www.tessleragency.com, pg 506

Teton NewMedia Inc, 90 E Simpson, Suite 110, Jackson, WY 83001 *Tel:* 307-732-0028 *Toll Free Tel:* 877-306-9793 *Fax:* 307-734-0841 *E-mail:* sales@tetonnm.com *Web Site:* www.tetonnm.com, pg 215

Texas A&M University Press, John H Lindsey Bldg, Lewis St, 4354 TAMU, College Station, TX 77843-4354 *Tel:* 979-845-1436 *Toll Free Tel:* 800-826-8911 (orders) *Fax:* 979-847-8752 *Toll Free Fax:* 888-617-2421 (orders) *E-mail:* bookorders@tamu.edu *Web Site:* www.tamupress.com, pg 215

Texas Bluebonnet Award, 3355 Bee Cave Rd, Suite 401, Austin, TX 78746-6763 *Tel:* 512-328-1518 *Fax:* 512-328-8852 *E-mail:* tla@txla.org *Web Site:* txla.org/tools-resources/reading-lists/texas-bluebonnet-award/about/; www.txla.org, pg 672

Texas Institute of Letters (TIL), PO Box 609, Round Rock, TX 78680 *E-mail:* president@ texasinstituteofletters.org; secretary@ texasinstituteofletters.org *Web Site:* www. texasinstituteofletters.org, pg 548

Texas Institute of Letters Awards, PO Box 609, Round Rock, TX 78680 *Tel:* 512-683-5640 *E-mail:* president@texasinstituteofletters.org *Web Site:* www.texasinstituteofletters.org, pg 672

Texas Library Association (TLA), 3355 Bee Cave Rd, Suite 401, Austin, TX 78746-6763 *Tel:* 512-328-1518 *Fax:* 512-328-8852 *E-mail:* tla@txla.org *Web Site:* www.txla.org, pg 548

Texas State Historical Association, 3001 Lake Austin Blvd, Suite 3.116, Austin, TX 78703 *Tel:* 512-471-2600 *Fax:* 512-473-8691 *Web Site:* www.tshaonline. org, pg 216

Texas Tech University Press, 1120 Main St, 2nd fl, Lubbock, TX 79401 *Tel:* 806-742-2982 *Toll Free Tel:* 800-832-4042 *E-mail:* ttup@ttu.edu *Web Site:* www.ttupress.org, pg 216

University of Texas Press, 3001 Lake Austin Blvd, 2.200, Austin, TX 78703 *Tel:* 512-471-7233 *Fax:* 512-232-7178 *E-mail:* utpress@uts.cc.utexas.edu; info@ utpress.utexas.edu *Web Site:* utpress.utexas.edu, pg 216

Texas Western Press, c/o University of Texas at El Paso, 500 W University Ave, El Paso, TX 79968-0633 *Tel:* 915-747-5688 *Toll Free Tel:* 800-488-3798 (orders only) *Fax:* 915-747-5345 *E-mail:* twpress@utep.edu *Web Site:* twp.utep.edu, pg 216

Textbook Excellence Award, PO Box 367, Fountain City, WI 54629 *E-mail:* info@taaonline.net *Web Site:* www. taaonline.net/textbook-excellence-award, pg 672

TFH Publications Inc, PO Box 427, Neptune, NJ 07754 *Toll Free Tel:* 855-273-7527 (cust serv) *Fax:* 732-988-5466 (cust serv); 732-776-8763 (sales) *E-mail:* info@ tfh.com (cust serv); sales@tfh.com *Web Site:* www. tfhpublications.com; www.tfh.com; www.facebook. com/TfhPetBooks, pg 216

Thames & Hudson, 500 Fifth Ave, New York, NY 10110 *Tel:* 212-354-3763 *Toll Free Tel:* 800-233-4830 *Fax:* 212-398-1252 *E-mail:* bookinfo@thames. wwnorton.com *Web Site:* www.thamesandhudsonusa. com, pg 216

The Society of Professional Journalists (SPJ), Eugene S Pulliam National Journalism Ctr, 3909 N Meridian St, Suite 200, Indianapolis, IN 46208 *Tel:* 317-927-8000 *Fax:* 317-920-4789 *E-mail:* spj@spj.org *Web Site:* www.spj.org, pg 548

Theatre Communications Group, 520 Eighth Ave, 24th fl, New York, NY 10018-4156 *Tel:* 212-609-5900 *Fax:* 212-609-5901 *E-mail:* info@tcg.org *Web Site:* www.tcg.org, pg 216

Theatre Library Association (TLA), c/o The New York Public Library for the Performing Arts, 40 Lincoln Center Plaza, New York, NY 10023 *E-mail:* TheatreLibraryAssociation@gmail.com *Web Site:* www.tla-online.org/awards/bookawards, pg 548

David Thelen Award, 112 N Bryan Ave, Bloomington, IN 47408-4141 *Tel:* 812-855-7311 *E-mail:* oah@oah. org *Web Site:* www.oah.org/awards, pg 672

Theosophical University Press, PO Box C, Pasadena, CA 91109-7107 *Tel:* 626-798-3378 *E-mail:* tupress@ theosociety.org *Web Site:* www.theosociety.org, pg 217

Theytus Books Ltd, 154 Enowkin Trail, RR 2, Site 50, Comp 8, Penticton, BC V2A 6J7, Canada *Tel:* 250-493-7181 *Fax:* 250-493-5302 *E-mail:* order@theytus. com; marketing@theytus.com *Web Site:* www.theytus. com, pg 441

Thieme Medical Publishers Inc, 333 Seventh Ave, 18th fl, New York, NY 10001 *Tel:* 212-760-0888 *Toll Free Tel:* 800-782-3488 *Fax:* 212-947-1112 *E-mail:* customerservice@thieme.com *Web Site:* www. thieme.com, pg 217

Third Coast Poetry & Fiction Contest, Western Michigan University English Dept, 1903 W Michigan Ave, Kalamazoo, MI 49008-5331 *E-mail:* editors@ thirdcoastmagazine.com *Web Site:* www. thirdcoastmagazine.com/contests, pg 673

Third World Press, 7822 S Dobson Ave, Chicago, IL 60619 *Tel:* 773-651-0700 *Fax:* 773-651-7286 *E-mail:* twpbooks@thirdworldpressfoundation.org *Web Site:* thirdworldpressfoundation.org, pg 217

Thistledown Press, 410 Second Ave, Saskatoon, SK S7K 2C3, Canada *Tel:* 306-244-1722 *Fax:* 306-244-1762 *E-mail:* tdpress@thistledownpress.com; editorial@ thistledownpress.com; marketing@thistledownpress. com *Web Site:* www.thistledownpress.com, pg 441

Thodestool Fiction Editing, 40 McDougall Rd, Waterloo, ON N2L 2W5, Canada *Web Site:* www.thodestool.ca, pg 471

Charles C Thomas Publisher Ltd, 2600 S First St, Springfield, IL 62704 *Tel:* 217-789-8980 *Toll Free Tel:* 800-258-8980 *Fax:* 217-789-9130 *E-mail:* books@ccthomas.com *Web Site:* www. ccthomas.com, pg 217

Thomas Nelson, 501 Nelson Place, Nashville, TN 37214 *Tel:* 615-889-9000 *Toll Free Tel:* 800-251-4000 *Fax:* 615-902-1548 *Web Site:* www.thomasnelson.com, pg 217

Thompson Educational Publishing Inc, 20 Ripley Ave, Toronto, ON M6S 3N9, Canada *Tel:* 416-766-2763 (admin & orders) *Toll Free Tel:* 877-366-2763 *Fax:* 416-766-0398 (admin & orders) *E-mail:* info@ thompsonbooks.com *Web Site:* www.thompsonbooks. com, pg 441

Thomson West, 610 Opperman Dr, Eagan, MN 55123 *Tel:* 651-687-7000 *Toll Free Tel:* 844-209-1086 (sales); 800-328-4880 (cust serv) *Web Site:* legalsolutions. thomsonreuters.com, pg 217

Thorndike Press®, 10 Water St, Suite 310, Waterville, ME 04901 *Toll Free Tel:* 800-223-1244 (ext 4, cust serv/orders) *Toll Free Fax:* 800-558-4676 (orders) *E-mail:* gale.printorders@cengage.com; international@cengage.com (cust orders outside US & CN) *Web Site:* www.gale.com/thorndike, pg 217

Susan Thornton, 6090 Liberty Ave, Vermilion, OH 44089 *Tel:* 440-967-1757 *E-mail:* allenthornton@ earthlink.net, pg 471

3-Day Novel Contest, 201-111 W Hastings St, Vancouver, BC V6B 1H4, Canada *Tel:* 604-681-9161 *Fax:* info@3daynovel.com *Web Site:* www. 3daynovel.com, pg 673

3 Seas Literary Agency, PO Box 444, Sun Prairie, WI 53590 *Tel:* 608-834-9317 *E-mail:* threeseaslit@aol. com *Web Site:* threeseasagency.com, pg 506

Three Wishes Publishing Company, 26500 W Agoura Rd, Suite 102-754, Calabasas, CA 91302 *Tel:* 818-878-0902 *Fax:* 818-878-1805 *E-mail:* Alva710@ aol.com *Web Site:* www.threewishespublishing.com, pg 448

Thriller Awards Competition, PO Box 311, Eureka, CA 95502 *Web Site:* thrillerwriters.org, pg 673

ThunderStone Books, 6575 Horse Dr, Las Vegas, NV 89131 *E-mail:* info@thunderstonebooks.com *Web Site:* www.thunderstonebooks.com, pg 217

Thurber Prize for American Humor, 77 Jefferson Ave, Columbus, OH 43215 *Tel:* 614-464-1032 *Fax:* 614-280-3645 *E-mail:* thurberhouse@thurberhouse.org *Web Site:* www.thurberhouse.org, pg 673

Tide-mark Press, 207 Oakwood Ave, West Hartford, CT 06119 *Tel:* 860-310-3370 *Toll Free Tel:* 800-338-2508 *Fax:* 860-310-3654 *E-mail:* customerservice@tide-mark.com, pg 218

Tiger Tales, 5 River Rd, Suite 128, Wilton, CT 06897-4069 *Tel:* 920-387-2333 *Fax:* 920-387-9994 *Web Site:* www.tigertalesbooks.com, pg 218

Tilbury House Publishers, 12 Starr St, Thomaston, ME 04861 *Tel:* 207-582-1899 *Toll Free Tel:* 800-582-1899 (orders) *Fax:* 207-582-8227 *E-mail:* tilbury@tilburyhouse.com *Web Site:* www.tilburyhouse.com, pg 218

Tiller Press, 1230 Avenue of the Americas, New York, NY 10020, pg 218

Timber Press Inc, 133 SW Second Ave, Suite 450, Portland, OR 97204 *Tel:* 503-227-2878 *Toll Free Tel:* 800-327-5680 *Fax:* 503-227-3070 *E-mail:* info@timberpress.com *Web Site:* www.timberpress.com, pg 218

Tin House Summer Workshop, 2617 NW Thurman St, Portland, OR 97210 *Tel:* 503-473-8663 *Web Site:* tinhouse.com/workshop/summer-workshop, pg 579

Tin House Winter Workshops, 2617 NW Thurman St, Portland, OR 97210 *Tel:* 503-473-8663 *Web Site:* tinhouse.com/winter-workshops, pg 579

James Tiptree Jr Literary Award, 173 Anderson St, San Francisco, CA 94110 *Tel:* 415-641-4103 *E-mail:* info@tiptree.org *Web Site:* tiptree.org, pg 673

TJ Publishers Inc, PO Box 702701, Dallas, TX 75370 *Toll Free Tel:* 800-999-1168 *Fax:* 972-416-0944 *E-mail:* TJPubinc@aol.com, pg 448

The Toby Press LLC, PO Box 8531, New Milford, CT 06776-8531 *Tel:* 203-830-8508 *Fax:* 203-830-8512 *E-mail:* toby@tobypress.com; sales@korenpub.com *Web Site:* www.tobypress.com; www.korenpub.com, pg 218

Todd Publications, 15494 Fiorenza Circle, Delray Beach, FL 33446 *Tel:* 561-910-0440 *Fax:* 561-910-0440 *E-mail:* toddpub@yahoo.com, pg 218

Arthur Tofte/Betty Ren Wright Children's Literature Award, c/o 3225 N 91 St, Milwaukee, WI 53222 *E-mail:* wiswriters@gmail.com *Web Site:* wiswriters.org/awards, pg 673

The Tomasino Agency Inc, 70 Chestnut St, Dobbs Ferry, NY 10522 *Tel:* 914-674-9659 *Fax:* 914-693-0381 *E-mail:* info@tomasinoagency.com *Web Site:* www.tomasinoagency.com, pg 506

Tommy Nelson®, 501 Nelson Place, Nashville, TN 37214 *Tel:* 615-889-9000; 615-902-1485 (cust serv) *Toll Free Tel:* 800-251-4000 *Web Site:* www.tommynelson.com, pg 218

Top of the Mountain Publishing, 4837 62 St N, St Petersburg, FL 33709 *Tel:* 727-391-3958, pg 219

Top Publications Ltd, 2745 Dallas Pkwy, Suite 420, Plano, TX 75093 *Tel:* 972-628-6414 *Fax:* 972-233-0713 *E-mail:* bill@toppub.com *Web Site:* toppub.com, pg 219

Torah Umesorah Publications, 620 Foster Ave, Brooklyn, NY 11230 *Tel:* 718-259-1223 *Fax:* 718-259-1795 *E-mail:* publications@torah-umesorah.org, pg 219

Toronto Book Awards, c/o Toronto Arts & Culture, City Hall, 9E, 100 Queen St W, Toronto, ON M5H 2N2, Canada *Web Site:* www.toronto.ca/book_awards, pg 673

Tortuga Press, 2777 Yulupa Ave, PMB 181, Santa Rosa, CA 95405 *Tel:* 707-544-4720 *Fax:* 707-595-5331 *E-mail:* info@tortugapress.com *Web Site:* www.tortugapress.com, pg 219

TotalRecall Publications Inc, 1103 Middlecreek, Friendswood, TX 77546 *Tel:* 281-992-3131 *E-mail:* sales@totalrecallpress.com *Web Site:* www.totalrecallpress.com, pg 219

TouchWood Editions, 103-1075 Pendergast St, Victoria, BC V8V 0A1, Canada *Tel:* 250-360-0829 *Fax:* 250-386-0829 *E-mail:* info@touchwoodeditions.com *Web Site:* www.touchwoodeditions.com, pg 441

Tower Publishing Co, 650 Cape Rd, Standish, ME 04084 *Tel:* 207-642-5400 *Toll Free Tel:* 800-969-8693 *E-mail:* info@towerpub.com *Web Site:* www.towerpub.com, pg 219

Townson Publishing Co Ltd, PO Box 1404, Sta A, Vancouver, BC V6C 2P7, Canada *Tel:* 604-886-0594 *E-mail:* admin@gpub.com; rights@gpub.ca *Web Site:* generalpublishing.com, pg 441

Towson University Prize for Literature, English Dept, 8000 York Rd, Towson, MD 21252 *Tel:* 410-704-2000 *Fax:* 410-704-3999 *Web Site:* www.towson.edu/english, pg 673

Tracks Publishing, 458 Dorothy Ave, Ventura, CA 93003 *Tel:* 805-754-0248 *E-mail:* tracks@cox.net *Web Site:* www.startupsports.com, pg 219

Tradewind Books, 202-1807 Maritime Mews, Vancouver, BC V6H 3W7, Canada *Tel:* 604-662-4405 *E-mail:* tradewindbooks@yahoo.com; tradewindbooks@gmail.com *Web Site:* www.tradewindbooks.com, pg 442

Trafalgar Square Books, 388 Howe Hill Rd, North Pomfret, VT 05053 *Tel:* 802-457-1911 *Toll Free Tel:* 800-423-4525 *Fax:* 802-457-1913 *E-mail:* contact@trafalgarbooks.com *Web Site:* www.trafalgarbooks.com; www.horseandriderbooks.com, pg 219

Trafford, 1663 Liberty Dr, Bloomington, IN 47403 *Toll Free Tel:* 888-232-4444 *E-mail:* customersupport@trafford.com; sales@trafford.com *Web Site:* www.trafford.com, pg 219

Tralco-Lingo Fun, PO Box 79008, RPO Garth, Hamilton, ON L9C 7N6, Canada *Tel:* 905-575-5717 *Toll Free Tel:* 888-487-2526 *Fax:* sales@tralco.com *Web Site:* www.tralco.com, pg 442

Trans-Atlantic Publications Inc, 33 Ashley Dr, Schwenksville, PA 19473 *Tel:* 215-925-2762 *Fax:* 215-925-1912 *Web Site:* www.transatlanticpub.com; www.businesstitles.com, pg 219

Transatlantic Agency, 2 Bloor St E, Suite 3500, Toronto, ON M4W 1A8, Canada *Tel:* 416-488-9214 *E-mail:* info@transatlanticagency.com *Web Site:* www.transatlanticagency.com, pg 506

Transcontinental Music Publications (TMP), 1375 Remington Rd, Suite M, Schaumburg, IL 60173-4844 *Tel:* 847-781-7800 *Fax:* 847-781-7801 *E-mail:* tmp@accantors.org *Web Site:* www.transcontinentalmusic.com, pg 220

Translation Projects, 400 Seventh St SW, Washington, DC 20506-0001 *Tel:* 202-682-5400; 202-682-5496 (Voice/TTY); 202-682-5034 (lit fellowships hotline) *Fax:* 202-682-5609; 202-682-5610 *E-mail:* litfellowships@arts.gov *Web Site:* www.arts.gov, pg 673

Transportation Research Board (TRB), 500 Fifth St NW, Washington, DC 20001 *Tel:* 202-334-3213 (orders); 202-334-3072 (subns) *Fax:* 202-334-2519 *E-mail:* trbsales@nas.edu *Web Site:* trb.org, pg 220

Travel Keys, PO Box 160691, Sacramento, CA 95816-0691 *Tel:* 916-452-5200 *Fax:* 916-452-5200, pg 220

Travelers' Tales, 2320 Bowdoin St, Palo Alto, CA 94306 *Tel:* 650-462-2110 *E-mail:* ttales@travelerstales.com *Web Site:* travelerstales.com, pg 220

Treasure Bay Inc, PO Box 119, Novato, CA 94948 *Tel:* 415-884-2888 *Fax:* 415-884-2840 *E-mail:* customerservice@treasurebaybooks.com *Web Site:* www.treasurebaybooks.com, pg 220

Treehaus Communications Inc, PO Box 249, Loveland, OH 45140-0249 *Tel:* 513-683-5716 *Toll Free Tel:* 800-638-4287 (orders) *Fax:* 513-683-2882 (orders) *E-mail:* treehaus@treehaus1.com *Web Site:* www.treehaus1.com, pg 220

Treehouse Climate Action Poem Prize, 75 Maiden Lane, Suite 901, New York, NY 10038 *Tel:* 212-274-0343 *E-mail:* academy@poets.org *Web Site:* www.poets.org, pg 673

Triad Publishing Co, PO Box 13355, Gainesville, FL 32604 *Fax:* 304-727-9345 *Toll Free Fax:* 800-854-4947 *E-mail:* orders@triadpublishing.com *Web Site:* www.triadpublishing.com, pg 220

TriadaUS Literary Agency, PO Box 561, Sewickley, PA 15143 *Tel:* 412-401-3376 *Web Site:* www.triadaus.com, pg 506

Trident Media Group LLC, 41 Madison Ave, 36th fl, New York, NY 10010 *Tel:* 212-333-1511 *E-mail:* info@tridentmediagroup.com; press@tridentmediagroup.com *Web Site:* www.tridentmediagroup.com, pg 507

Trillium Book Award/Prix Trillium, South Tower, Suite 501, 175 Bloor St E, Toronto, ON M4W 3R8, Canada *Tel:* 416-314-6858 (ext 698) *Fax:* 416-314-6876 *Web Site:* www.omdc.on.ca, pg 673

The Trinity Foundation, PO Box 68, Unicoi, TN 37692-0068 *Tel:* 423-743-0199 *Fax:* 423-743-2005 *Web Site:* www.trinityfoundation.org, pg 220

Trinity University Press, One Trinity Place, San Antonio, TX 78212-7200 *Tel:* 210-999-8884 *Fax:* 210-999-8838 *E-mail:* books@trinity.edu *Web Site:* www.tupress.org, pg 220

TripBuilder Media Inc, 180 Post Rd E, Suite 200, Westport, CT 06880 *Tel:* 203-227-1255 *Toll Free Tel:* 800-525-9745 *Fax:* 203-227-1257 *E-mail:* info@tripbuildermedia.com *Web Site:* www.tripbuildermedia.com, pg 220

TriQuarterly Books, 629 Noyes St, Evanston, IL 60208 *Tel:* 847-491-7420 *Toll Free Tel:* 800-621-2736 (orders only) *Fax:* 847-491-8150 *E-mail:* nupress@northwestern.edu *Web Site:* www.nupress.northwestern.edu, pg 220

TRISTAN Publishing, 2355 Louisiana Ave N, Minneapolis, MN 55427 *Tel:* 763-545-1383 *Toll Free Tel:* 866-545-1383 *Fax:* 763-545-1387 *E-mail:* info@tristanpublishing.com *Web Site:* www.tristanpublishing.com, pg 221

Triumph Books, 814 N Franklin St, Chicago, IL 60610 *Tel:* 312-337-0747 *Toll Free Tel:* 800-888-4741 (cust serv) *Fax:* 312-280-5470; 312-337-5985 *Web Site:* www.triumphbooks.com, pg 221

Triumph Learning LLC, 80 Northwest Blvd, Nashua, NH 03063 *Toll Free Tel:* 800-225-5700 (cust serv) *E-mail:* customerservice.eps@schoolspecialty.com *Web Site:* eps.schoolspecialty.com/coach, pg 221

Harry S Truman Book Award, 5151 Troost Ave, Suite 300, Kansas City, MO 64110 *Tel:* 816-400-1212 *Toll Free Tel:* 844-358-5400 *Web Site:* trumanlibraryinstitute.org, pg 674

Truman State University Press, 100 E Normal Ave, Kirksville, MO 63501-4221 *Tel:* 660-785-7336 *Toll Free Tel:* 800-916-6802 *Fax:* 660-785-4480 *E-mail:* tsup@truman.edu *Web Site:* tsup.truman.edu, pg 221

Trusted Media Brands Inc, 750 Third Ave, 3rd fl, New York, NY 10017 *Tel:* 646-293-6299 *Toll Free Tel:* 877-732-4438 (cust serv) *Fax:* 646-293-6251 *E-mail:* customercare@trustedmediabrands.com; press@trustedmediabrands.com *Web Site:* www.trustedmediabrands.com; www.rd.com, pg 221

Trustus Playwrights' Festival, 520 Lady St, Columbia, SC 29201 *Tel:* 803-254-9732 *Web Site:* www.trustus.org, pg 674

TSG Publishing Foundation Inc, 28641 N 63 Place, Cave Creek, AZ 85331 *Tel:* 480-502-1909 *Fax:* 480-502-0713 *E-mail:* info@tsgfoundation.org *Web Site:* www.tsgfoundation.org, pg 221

Tudor Publishers Inc, 3109 Shady Lawn Dr, Greensboro, NC 27408 *Tel:* 336-288-5395 *E-mail:* tudorpublishers@triad.rr.com, pg 221

The Tuesday Agency, 132 1/2 E Washington St, Iowa City, IA 52240 *Tel:* 319-338-7080 *E-mail:* trinity@tuesdayagency.com *Web Site:* tuesdayagency.com, pg 515

Kate Tufts Discovery Award, Harper East, Unit B-7, 160 E Tenth St, Claremont, CA 91711-6165 *Tel:* 909-621-8974 *E-mail:* tufts@cgu.edu *Web Site:* www.cgu.edu/tufts, pg 674

Kingsley Tufts Poetry Award, Harper East, Unit B-7, 160 E Tenth St, Claremont, CA 91711-6165 *Tel:* 909-621-8974 *E-mail:* tufts@cgu.edu *Web Site:* www.cgu.edu/tufts, pg 674

Tugeau 2 Inc, 2231 Grandview Ave, Cleveland Heights, OH 44106 *Tel:* 216-707-0854 *Web Site:* www.tugeau2. com, pg 512

Tughra Books, 335 Clifton Ave, Clifton, NJ 07011 *Tel:* 646-415-9331 *Fax:* 646-827-6228 *E-mail:* info@ tughrabooks.com *Web Site:* www.tughrabooks.com, pg 221

Tumblehome Learning Inc, 201 Newbury St, Suite 201, Boston, MA 02116 *E-mail:* info@ tumblehomelearning.com *Web Site:* www. tumblehomelearning.com, pg 221

Tundra Books, 320 Front St W, Suite 1400, Toronto, ON M5V 3B6, Canada *Tel:* 416-364-4449 *Toll Free Tel:* 888-523-9292 (orders); 800-588-1074 *Fax:* 416-598-7764 *Toll Free Fax:* 888-562- 9924 (orders) *E-mail:* tundra@mcclelland.com *Web Site:* tundrabooks.wordpress.com, pg 442

Tupelo Press Berkshire Prize for a First or Second Book of Poetry, 60 Roberts Dr, Suite 308, North Adams, MA 01247 *Tel:* 413-664-9611 *Fax:* 413-664- 9711 *E-mail:* info@tupelopress.org *Web Site:* www. tupelopress.org, pg 674

Tupelo Press Inc, 60 Roberts Dr, Suite 308, North Adams, MA 01247 *Tel:* 413-664-9611 *Fax:* 413-664- 9711 *E-mail:* info@tupelopress.org *Web Site:* www. tupelopress.org, pg 222

Tupelo Press Snowbound Series Chapbook Award, 60 Roberts Dr, Suite 308, North Adams, MA 01247 *Tel:* 413-664-9611 *Fax:* 413-664-9711 *E-mail:* info@ tupelopress.org *Web Site:* www.tupelopress.org, pg 674

Frederick Jackson Turner Award, 112 N Bryan Ave, Bloomington, IN 47408-4141 *Tel:* 812-855-7311 *E-mail:* oah@oah.org *Web Site:* www.oah.org/awards, pg 674

Turner Publishing Co, 4507 Charlotte Ave, Suite 100, Nashville, TN 37209 *Tel:* 615-255-BOOK (255- 2665) *Fax:* 615-255-5081 *E-mail:* marketing@ turnerpublishing.com; submissions@turnerpublishing. com; editorial@turnerpublishing.com *Web Site:* www. turnerpublishing.com; www.facebook.com/turner. publishing, pg 222

Turnstone Press, Artspace Bldg, 206-100 Arthur St, Winnipeg, MB R3B 1H3, Canada *Tel:* 204-947- 1555 *Toll Free Tel:* 888-363-7718 *Fax:* 204-942-1556 *E-mail:* info@turnstonepress.com *Web Site:* www. turnstonepress.com, pg 442

Turtle Point Press, 208 Java St, 5th fl, Brooklyn, NY 11222-5748 *Tel:* 212-741-1393 *E-mail:* info@ turtlepointpress.com *Web Site:* www.turtlepointpress. com, pg 222

The Tusculum Review Poetry Chapbook Prize, 60 Shiloh Rd, Greeneville, TN 37745 *E-mail:* review@tusculum. edu *Web Site:* web.tusculum.edu/tusculumreview/ contest, pg 674

Tuttle Publishing, Airport Business Park, 364 Innovation Dr, North Clarendon, VT 05759-9436 *Tel:* 802- 773-8930 *Toll Free Tel:* 800-526-2778 *Fax:* 802- 773-6993 *Toll Free Fax:* 800-FAX-TUTL (329- 8885) *E-mail:* info@tuttlepublishing.com; orders@ tuttlepublishing.com *Web Site:* www.tuttlepublishing. com, pg 222

Tuxedo Press, 546 E Springville Rd, Carlisle, PA 17015 *Tel:* 717-258-9733 *Fax:* 717-243-0074 *E-mail:* info@ tuxedo-press.com *Web Site:* tuxedo-press.com, pg 222

Twenty-First Century Books, 241 First Ave N, Minneapolis, MN 55401 *Tel:* 612-332-3344 *Toll Free Tel:* 800-328-4929 *Fax:* 612-332-7615 *Toll Free Fax:* 800-332-1132 *E-mail:* info@lernerbooks. com; custserve@lernerbooks.com *Web Site:* www. lernerbooks.com; www.facebook.com/lernerbooks, pg 222

The 25 Most "Censored" Stories Annual, PO Box 750940, Petaluma, CA 94975 *Tel:* 707-241-4596 *Web Site:* www.projectcensored.org, pg 674

Twenty-Third Publications, One Montauk Ave, Suite 200, New London, CT 06320 *Tel:* 860-437-3012 *Toll Free Tel:* 800-321-0411 (orders) *Toll Free Fax:* 800-

572-0788 *E-mail:* resources@twentythirdpublications. com *Web Site:* www.twentythirdpublications.com, pg 222

Twilight Times Books, PO Box 3340, Kingsport, TN 37664-0340 *Tel:* 423-323-0183 *Fax:* 423-323-0183 *E-mail:* publisher@twilighttimes.com *Web Site:* www. twilighttimesbooks.com, pg 223

Twin Oaks Indexing, 138 Twin Oaks Rd, Suite W, Louisa, VA 23093 *Tel:* 540-894-5126 *Web Site:* www. twinoakscommunity.org, pg 471

Two Thousand Three Associates, 135 Chilean Ave, Palm Beach, FL 33480 *Tel:* 386-690-2503 *E-mail:* ttta1@att. net *Web Site:* www.twothousandthree.com, pg 223

2M Communications Ltd, 19 W 21 St, Suite 501, New York, NY 10010 *Tel:* 212-741-1509 *Fax:* 212-691- 4460 *Web Site:* www.2mcommunications.com, pg 507

Cy Twombly Award for Poetry, 820 Greenwich St, New York, NY 10014 *Tel:* 212-807-7077 *E-mail:* info@contemporary-arts.org *Web Site:* www. foundationforcontemporaryarts.org/grants/cy-twombly- award-for-poetry, pg 674

Tyndale House Publishers Inc, 351 Executive Dr, Carol Stream, IL 60188 *Tel:* 630-668-8300 *Toll Free Tel:* 800-323-9400; 855-277-9400 *Toll Free Fax:* 866- 622-9474 *Web Site:* www.tyndale.com, pg 223

UCLA Latin American Center Publications, UCLA Latin American Institute, 10343 Bunche Hall, Los Angeles, CA 90095 *Tel:* 310-825-4571 *Fax:* 310- 206-6859 *E-mail:* latinamctr@international.ucla.edu *Web Site:* www.international.ucla.edu/lai, pg 223

Ucross Foundation Residency Program, 30 Big Red Lane, Clearmont, WY 82835 *Tel:* 307-737- 2291 *Fax:* 307-737-2322 *E-mail:* info@ucross.org *Web Site:* www.ucrossfoundation.org, pg 674

Ugly Duckling Presse, The Old American Can Factory, 232 Third St, Suite E303, Brooklyn, NY 11215 *Tel:* 347-948-5170 *E-mail:* office@uglyducklingpresse. org; orders@uglyducklingpresse.org; publicity@ uglyducklingpresse.org; rights@uglyducklingpresse.org *Web Site:* uglyducklingpresse.org, pg 223

Friedrich Ulfers Prize, 42 Washington Mews, New York, NY 10003 *E-mail:* info@festivalneueliteratur.org *Web Site:* festivalneueliteratur.org/prize, pg 674

Ulysses Press, 195 Montague St, 14th fl, Brooklyn, NY 11201 *Tel:* 510-601-8301 *Toll Free Tel:* 800-377-2542 *Fax:* 510-601-8307 *E-mail:* ulysses@ulyssespress.com *Web Site:* www.ulyssespress.com, pg 223

Ulysses Travel Guides, 4176, rue Saint-Denis, Montreal, QC H2W 2M5, Canada *Tel:* 514-843-9882 (ext 2232); 514-843-9447 (bookstore) *Toll Free Tel:* 800-748- 9171 *Fax:* 514-843-9448 *E-mail:* info@ulysses.ca; st- denis@ulysses.ca *Web Site:* www.ulyssesguides.com, pg 442

Unarius Academy of Science Publications, 145 S Magnolia Ave, El Cajon, CA 92020-4522 *Tel:* 619- 444-7062 *Toll Free Tel:* 800-475-7062 *Fax:* 619- 444-9637 *E-mail:* uriel@unarius.org *Web Site:* www. unarius.org, pg 223

Unhanged Arthur Ellis Award, 716 Thicket Way, Ottawa, ON K4A 3B5, Canada *E-mail:* arthur_ellis@ crimewriterscanada.com *Web Site:* www. crimewriterscanada.com/awards, pg 675

Unicorn Writers' Conference, 17 Church Hill Rd, Redding, CT 06896 *Tel:* 203-938-7405 *Fax:* 203-938- 7405 *E-mail:* unicornwritersconference@gmail.com *Web Site:* unicornwritersconference.com, pg 579

Editorial Unilit, 8167 NW 84 St, Medley, FL 33166 *Tel:* 305-592-6136 *Toll Free Tel:* 800-767-7726 *Fax:* 305-592-0087 *E-mail:* info@editorialunilit.com; customerservice@editorialunilit.com *Web Site:* www. editorialunilit.com, pg 224

United for Libraries, 859 W Lancaster Ave, Unit 2-1, Bryn Mawr, PA 19010 *Tel:* 312-280-2161 *Toll Free Tel:* 800-545-2433 (ext 2161) *Fax:* 484-698-7868 *E-mail:* united@ala.org *Web Site:* www.ala.org/united, pg 548

United Nations Association of the United States of America, 1750 Pennsylvania Ave NW, Suite 300, Washington, DC 20006 *Tel:* 202-887-9040 *Web Site:* www.unausa.org, pg 548

United Nations Publications, 300 E 42 St, 9th fl, New York, NY 10017 *Tel:* 703-661-1571 *Fax:* 703-996- 1010 *E-mail:* publications@un.org *Web Site:* shop.un. org, pg 224

United States Holocaust Memorial Museum, 100 Raoul Wallenberg Place SW, Washington, DC 20024-2126 *Tel:* 202-488-0400; 202-314-7837; 202-488-6144 (orders) *Toll Free Tel:* 800-259- 9998 (orders) *Fax:* 202-479-9726; 202-488-0438 (orders) *E-mail:* cahs_publications@ushmm.org *Web Site:* www.ushmm.org, pg 224

United States Institute of Peace Press, 2301 Constitution Ave NW, Washington, DC 20037 *Tel:* 703-661-1590 (cust serv) *Toll Free Tel:* 800-868-8064 (cust serv) *E-mail:* usipmail@presswarehouse.com (orders) *Web Site:* bookstore.usip.org, pg 224

United States Pharmacopeia, 12601 Twinbrook Pkwy, Rockville, MD 20852-1790 *Tel:* 301-881-0666 *Toll Free Tel:* 800-227-8772 *Fax:* 301-816-8237 (mktg) *E-mail:* marketing@usp.org *Web Site:* www.usp.org, pg 224

United States Tennis Association, 70 W Red Oak Lane, White Plains, NY 10604 *Tel:* 914-696-7000 *Fax:* 914- 696-7027 *Web Site:* www.usta.com, pg 224

United Talent Agency, 9336 Civic Center Dr, Beverly Hills, CA 90210 *Tel:* 310-273-6700 *Fax:* 310-247- 1111 *Web Site:* www.unitedtalent.com, pg 507

Univelt Inc, 740 Metcalf St, No 13, Escondido, CA 92025 *Tel:* 760-746-4005 *Fax:* 760-746-3139 *E-mail:* sales@univelt.com *Web Site:* www.univelt. com; www.astronautical.org, pg 224

Universal-Publishers Inc, 200 Spectrum Center Dr, 3rd fl, Irvine, CA 92618-5004 *Tel:* 561-750-4344 *Toll Free Tel:* 800-636-8329 (US only) *Fax:* 561-750-6797 *Web Site:* www.universal-publishers.com, pg 225

Universe Publishing, 300 Park Ave S, 4th fl, New York, NY 10010 *Tel:* 212-387-3400 *Fax:* 212-387-3535 *Web Site:* www.rizzoliusa.com, pg 225

University Council for Educational Administration (UCEA), Michigan State University, College of Education, 620 Farm Lane, 432 Erickson Hall, East Lansing, MI 48824 *Tel:* 434-243-1041 *E-mail:* ucea@ msu.edu *Web Site:* www.ucea.org, pg 225

University of Alabama Press, 200 Hackberry Lane, 2nd fl, Tuscaloosa, AL 35487 *Tel:* 205-348-5180 *Fax:* 205- 348-9201 *Web Site:* www.uapress.ua.edu, pg 225

University of Alabama Program in Creative Writing, PO Box 870244, Tuscaloosa, AL 35487-0244 *Tel:* 205- 348-5065 *Fax:* 205-348-1388 *E-mail:* english@ua.edu *Web Site:* www.as.ua.edu/english, pg 585

University of Alaska Press, Elmer E Rasmuson Library, 1732 Tanana Loop, Suite 402, Fairbanks, AK 99775 *Tel:* 907-474-5831 *Toll Free Tel:* 888-252-6657 (US only) *Fax:* 907-474-5502 *Web Site:* www.alaska. edu/uapress, pg 225

University of Alberta Press, Ring House 2, Edmonton, AB T6G 2E1, Canada *Tel:* 780-492-3662 *Fax:* 780- 492-0719 *Web Site:* www.uap.ualberta.ca, pg 442

The University of Arizona Press, 1510 E University Blvd, Tucson, AZ 85721 *Tel:* 520-621-1441 *Toll Free Tel:* 800-426-3797 (orders) *Fax:* 520-621-8899 *Toll Free Fax:* 800-426-3797 *E-mail:* uap@uapress.arizona. edu *Web Site:* www.uapress.arizona.edu, pg 225

The University of Arkansas Press, McIlroy House, 105 N McIlroy Ave, Fayetteville, AR 72701 *Tel:* 479- 575-7544 *E-mail:* info@uapress.com *Web Site:* www. uapress.com, pg 225

University of Baltimore - Yale Gordon College of Arts & Sciences, Ampersand Institute for Words & Images, 1420 N Charles St, Baltimore, MD 21201-5779 *Tel:* 410-837-6022 *Fax:* 410-837-6029 *E-mail:* scd@ ubalt.edu *Web Site:* www.ubalt.edu, pg 585

University of British Columbia Creative Writing Program, Buchanan Rm E-462, 1866 Main Mall, Vancouver, BC V6T 1Z1, Canada *Tel:* 604-822-0699 *Web Site:* creativewriting.ubc.ca, pg 585

University of British Columbia Press, 2029 West Mall, Vancouver, BC V6T 1Z2, Canada *Tel:* 604-822-5959 *Toll Free Tel:* 877-377-9378 *Fax:* 604-822-6083 *Toll Free Fax:* 800-668-0821 *E-mail:* frontdesk@ubcpress. ca *Web Site:* www.ubcpress.ca, pg 443

University of Calgary Press, 2500 University Dr NW, Calgary, AB T2N 1N4, Canada *Tel:* 403-220-7578 *Fax:* 403-282-0085 *E-mail:* ucpress@ucalgary.ca *Web Site:* press.ucalgary.ca, pg 443

University of California Extension Professional Sequence in Copyediting & Courses in Publishing, 1995 University Ave, Suite 110, Berkeley, CA 94720-7000 *Tel:* 510-642-6362 *Fax:* 510-643-0216 *E-mail:* letters@unex.berkeley.edu *Web Site:* www. unex.berkeley.edu, pg 585

University of California Institute on Global Conflict & Cooperation, 9500 Gilman Dr, MC 0518, La Jolla, CA 92093-0518 *Tel:* 858-534-6106 *Fax:* 858-534-7655 *E-mail:* igcc-communications@ucsd.edu *Web Site:* igcc.ucsd.edu, pg 226

University of California Press, 155 Grand Ave, Suite 400, Oakland, CA 94612-3758 *Tel:* 510-883-8232 *Fax:* 510-836-8910 *E-mail:* generalmailbox@ucpress. edu *Web Site:* www.ucpress.edu, pg 226

University of Chicago, Graham School of General Studies, 1427 E 60 St, Chicago, IL 60637 *Tel:* 773-702-1722 *Fax:* 773-702-6814 *Web Site:* www. grahamschool.uchicago.edu, pg 585

University of Chicago Press, 1427 E 60 St, Chicago, IL 60637-2954 *Tel:* 773-702-7700; 773-702-7600 *Toll Free Tel:* 800-621-2736 (orders) *Fax:* 773-702-9756; 773-660-2235 (orders); 773-702-2708 *E-mail:* custserv@press.uchicago.edu; marketing@ press.uchicago.edu *Web Site:* www.press.uchicago.edu, pg 226

University of Delaware Press, 200A Morris Library, 181 S College Ave, Newark, DE 19717-5267 *Tel:* 302-831-1149 *Fax:* 302-831-6549 *E-mail:* ud-press@udel.edu *Web Site:* library.udel.edu/udpress, pg 227

University of Denver Publishing Institute, 2000 E Asbury Ave, Denver, CO 80208 *Tel:* 303-871-2570 *Fax:* 303-871-2501 *Web Site:* www.du.edu/publishinginstitute, pg 585

University of Georgia Press, Main Library, 3rd fl, 320 S Jackson St, Athens, GA 30602 *Fax:* 706-542-2558; 706-542-6770 *Web Site:* www.ugapress.org, pg 227

University of Hawaii Press, 2840 Kolowalu St, Honolulu, HI 96822-1888 *Tel:* 808-956-8255 *Toll Free Tel:* 888-UHPRESS (847-7377) *Fax:* 808-988-6052 *Toll Free Fax:* 800-650-7811 *E-mail:* uhpbooks@hawaii.edu *Web Site:* www.uhpress.hawaii.edu, pg 227

University of Houston Creative Writing Program, 229 Roy Cullen Bldg, Houston, TX 77204-5008 *Tel:* 713-743-2255 *Fax:* 713-743-3697 *E-mail:* cwp@uh.edu *Web Site:* www.uh.edu/cwp, pg 586

University of Illinois at Chicago, Program for Writers, College of Liberal Arts & Sciences, 2027 University Hall, 601 S Morgan St, Chicago, IL 60607-7120 *Tel:* 312-413-2200 (Eng dept) *Fax:* 312-413-1005 *Web Site:* www.uic.edu, pg 586

University of Illinois, Department of Journalism, Gregory Hall, Rm 120-A, 810 S Wright St, Urbana, IL 61801 *Tel:* 217-333-0709 *Fax:* 217-333-7931 *E-mail:* journ@ uiuc.edu *Web Site:* www.comm.uiuc.edu, pg 586

University of Illinois Press, 1325 S Oak St, MC-566, Champaign, IL 61820-6903 *Tel:* 217-333-0950 *Fax:* 217-244-8082 *E-mail:* uipress@uillinois.edu; journals@uillinois.edu *Web Site:* www.press.uillinois. edu, pg 227

University of Iowa Press, 119 W Park Rd, 100 Kuhl House, Iowa City, IA 52242-1000 *Tel:* 319-335-2000 *Toll Free Tel:* 800-621-2736 (orders only) *Fax:* 319-335-2055 *Toll Free Fax:* 800-621-8476 (orders only) *E-mail:* uipress@uiowa.edu *Web Site:* www.uipress. uiowa.edu, pg 227

University of Iowa, Writers' Workshop, Graduate Creative Writing Program, 102 Dey House, 507 N Clinton St, Iowa City, IA 52242-1000 *Tel:* 319-335-0416 *Fax:* 319-335-0420 *Web Site:* writersworkshop. uiowa.edu, pg 586

University of Louisiana at Lafayette Press, PO Box 43558, Lafayette, LA 70504-3558 *Tel:* 337-482-6027 *E-mail:* press.submissions@louisiana.edu *Web Site:* ulpress.org, pg 228

University of Manitoba Press, University of Manitoba, 301 St Johns College, 92 Dysart Rd, Winnipeg, MB R3T 2M5, Canada *Tel:* 204-474-9495 *Fax:* 204-474-7566 *E-mail:* uofmpress@umanitoba.ca *Web Site:* uofmpress.ca, pg 443

University of Massachusetts Press, East Experiment Station, 671 N Pleasant St, Amherst, MA 01003 *Tel:* 413-545-2217 *Fax:* 413-545-1226 *E-mail:* info@ umpress.umass.edu *Web Site:* www.umass.edu/ umpress, pg 228

University of Michigan Press, 839 Greene St, Ann Arbor, MI 48104-3209 *Tel:* 734-764-4388 *Fax:* 734-615-1540 *E-mail:* um.press@umich.edu *Web Site:* www.press.umich.edu, pg 228

University of Minnesota Press, 111 Third Ave S, Suite 290, Minneapolis, MN 55401-2520 *Tel:* 612-301-1990 *Fax:* 612-301-1980 *E-mail:* ump@umn.edu *Web Site:* www.upress.umn.edu, pg 228

University of Missouri Press, 113 Heinkel Bldg, 201 S Seventh St, Columbia, MO 65211 *Tel:* 573-882-7641; 573-882-3000 (publicity & sales enquiries) *Toll Free Tel:* 800-621-2736 (orders) *Fax:* 573-884-4498 *Toll Free Fax:* 800-621-8476 (orders) *E-mail:* upress@ missouri.edu; umpmarketing@missouri.edu (publicity & sales enquiries) *Web Site:* upress.missouri.edu, pg 228

University of Montana, Environmental Writing Institute, Environmental Studies, University of Montana, Missoula, MT 59812 *Tel:* 406-243-2904 *Fax:* 406-243-6090 *Web Site:* www.umt.edu/ewi, pg 586

University of Nebraska Press, 1111 Lincoln Mall, Lincoln, NE 68588-0630 *Tel:* 402-472-3581; 919-966-7449 (cust serv & foreign orders) *Toll Free Tel:* 800-848-6224 (cust serv & US orders) *Fax:* 402-472-6214; 919-962-2704 (cust serv & foreign orders) *Toll Free Fax:* 800-526-2617 (cust serv & US orders) *E-mail:* pressmail@unl.edu *Web Site:* www. nebraskapress.unl.edu, pg 229

University of Nevada Press, c/o University of Nevada, Continuing Educ Bldg, MS 0166, Reno, NV 89557-0166 *Tel:* 775-784-6573 *Fax:* 775-784-6200 *Web Site:* www.unpress.nevada.edu, pg 229

University of New Mexico Press, One University of New Mexico, Albuquerque, NM 87131-0001 *Tel:* 505-272-7777 *Fax:* 505-277-3343 *E-mail:* custserv@unm.edu (order dept) *Web Site:* unmpress.com, pg 229

University of New Orleans Press, 2000 Lakeshore Dr, New Orleans, LA 70148 *Tel:* 504-280-7457 *E-mail:* unopress@uno.edu *Web Site:* www.uno. edu/unopress, pg 229

The University of North Carolina Press, 116 S Boundary St, Chapel Hill, NC 27514-3808 *Tel:* 919-966-3561 *E-mail:* uncpress@unc.edu *Web Site:* www.uncpress. org, pg 229

University of North Texas Press, Willis Library, Rm 251P, 1506 Highland St, Denton, TX 76201 *Tel:* 940-565-2142 *Fax:* 940-369-8760 *Web Site:* untpress.unt. edu, pg 229

University of Notre Dame Press, 310 Flanner Hall, Notre Dame, IN 46556 *Tel:* 574-631-6346 *Fax:* 574-631-8148 *E-mail:* undpress@nd.edu *Web Site:* www. undpress.nd.edu, pg 230

University of Oklahoma Press, 2800 Venture Dr, Norman, OK 73069-8216 *Tel:* 405-325-2000 *Web Site:* www.oupress.com, pg 230

University of Ottawa Press (Presses de l'Université d'Ottawa), 542 King Edward Ave, Ottawa, ON K1N 6N5, Canada *Tel:* 613-562-5246 *Fax:* 613-562-5247 *E-mail:* puo-uop@uottawa.ca; acquisitions@uottawa.ca *Web Site:* press.uottawa.ca, pg 443

University of Pennsylvania Museum of Archaeology & Anthropology, 3260 South St, Philadelphia, PA 19104-6324 *Tel:* 215-898-4119; 215-898-4000 *E-mail:* publications@pennmuseum.org *Web Site:* www.penn.museum, pg 230

University of Pennsylvania Press, 3905 Spruce St, Philadelphia, PA 19104 *Tel:* 215-898-6261 *Fax:* 215-898-0404 *E-mail:* custserv@pobox.upenn.edu *Web Site:* www.pennpress.org, pg 230

University of Pittsburgh Press, 7500 Thomas Blvd, Pittsburgh, PA 15260 *Tel:* 412-383-2456 *Fax:* 412-383-2466 *E-mail:* info@upress.pitt.edu *Web Site:* www.upress.pitt.edu, pg 230

University of Puerto Rico Press, Edificio La Editorial (level 2), Carr No 1, KM 12.0, Jardin Botanico Norte, San Juan, PR 00927 *Tel:* 787-250-0435; 787-250-0550 *Toll Free Tel:* 877-338-7788 *Fax:* 787-753-9116 *E-mail:* info@laeditorialupr.com *Web Site:* www. laeditorialupr.com, pg 231

University of Regina Press, 2 Research Dr, Suite 246, Regina, SK S4S 7H9, Canada *Tel:* 306-585-4758 *Fax:* 306-585-4699 *E-mail:* uofrpress@uregina.ca *Web Site:* uofrpress.ca, pg 444

University of Rochester Press, 668 Mount Hope Ave, Rochester, NY 14620-2731 *Tel:* 585-275-0419 *Fax:* 585-271-8778 *E-mail:* boydell@boydellusa.net *Web Site:* www.urpress.com, pg 231

University of South Carolina Press, 1600 Hampton St, Suite 544, Columbia, SC 29208 *Tel:* 803-777-5245 *Toll Free Tel:* 800-768-2500 (orders) *Fax:* 803-777-0160 *Toll Free Fax:* 800-868-0740 (orders) *Web Site:* www.sc.edu/uscpress, pg 231

University of Southern California, Master of Professional Writing Program, Mark Taper Hall, THH 355, 3501 Trousedale Pkwy, Los Angeles, CA 90089-0355 *Tel:* 213-740-3252 *Fax:* 213-740-5002 *E-mail:* mpw@ college.usc.edu *Web Site:* college.usc.edu/mpw, pg 586

University of Tennessee Press, 110 Conference Center Bldg, 600 Henley St, Knoxville, TN 37996-4108 *Tel:* 865-974-3321 *Toll Free Tel:* 800-621-2736 (orders) *Fax:* 865-974-3724 *Toll Free Fax:* 800-621-8476 (orders) *E-mail:* custserv@utpress.org *Web Site:* www.utpress.org, pg 231

University of Texas at Arlington College of Architecture, Planning & Public Affairs, 601 S Nedderman Dr, Suite 203, Arlington, TX 76019 *E-mail:* cappa@uta. edu *Web Site:* www.uta.edu/cappa, pg 231

University of Texas at Austin, New Writers Project, Dept of English, Calhoun Hall, Rm 226, 204 W 21 St, B-5000, Austin, TX 78712 *Tel:* 512-471-5132; 512-471-4991 *Fax:* 512-471-4909 *Web Site:* newwritersproject. org, pg 586

University of Texas at El Paso, Department of Creative Writing, MFA/Department of Creative Writing, 901 EDUC, 500 W University Ave, El Paso, TX 79968-9991 *Tel:* 915-747-5713 *Fax:* 915-747-5523 *E-mail:* creativewriting@utep.edu *Web Site:* www.utep. edu/cw, pg 586

University of Toronto Press, 10 St Mary St, Suite 700, Toronto, ON M4Y 2W8, Canada *Tel:* 416-978-2239 *Fax:* 416-978-4738 *E-mail:* info@utpress. utoronto.ca *Web Site:* www.utpress.utoronto.ca; www. utppublishing.com, pg 444

The University of Utah Press, J Willard Marriott Library, Suite 5400, 295 S 1500 E, Salt Lake City, UT 84112-0860 *Tel:* 801-585-9786 *Fax:* 801-581-3365 *E-mail:* hannah.new@utah.edu *Web Site:* www. uofupress.com, pg 231

The University of Virginia Press, PO Box 400318, Charlottesville, VA 22904-4318 *Tel:* 434-924-3468 (cust serv); 434-924-3469 (cust serv) *Toll Free Tel:* 800-831-3406 (orders) *Fax:* 434-982-2655 *Toll Free Fax:* 877-288-6400 *E-mail:* vapress@virginia.edu *Web Site:* www.upress.virginia.edu, pg 231

University of Washington Press, 4333 Brooklyn Ave NE, Seattle, WA 98105-9570 *Tel:* 206-543-4050 *Toll Free Tel:* 800-537-5487 (orders) *Fax:* 206-543-3932; 410-516-6998 (orders) *E-mail:* uwapress@uw.edu *Web Site:* uwapress.uw.edu, pg 232

University of Wisconsin-Madison Continuing Studies, 21 N Park St, 7th fl, Madison, WI 53715 *Tel:* 608-262-3447 *Web Site:* continuingstudies.wisc.edu, pg 586

University of Wisconsin Press, 728 State St, Suite 443, Madison, WI 53706-1418 *Tel:* 608-263-1110; 608-263-0668 (journal orders) *Toll Free Tel:* 800-621-2736 (book orders) *Fax:* 608-263-1173 *Toll Free Fax:* 800-621-2736 (book orders) *E-mail:* uwiscpress@uwpress.wisc.edu *Web Site:* uwpress.wisc.edu, pg 232

University Press of America Inc, 4501 Forbes Blvd, Suite 200, Lanham, MD 20706 *Tel:* 301-459-3366 *Toll Free Tel:* 800-462-6420 *Fax:* 301-429-5748 *Toll Free Fax:* 800-338-4550 *Web Site:* www.univpress.com, pg 232

University Press of Colorado, 245 Century Circle, Suite 202, Louisville, CO 80027 *Tel:* 720-406-8849 *Toll Free Tel:* 800-621-2736 (orders) *Fax:* 720-406-3443 *Web Site:* www.upcolorado.com, pg 232

University Press of Florida, 2046 NE Waldo Rd, Suite 2100, Gainesville, FL 32609 *Tel:* 352-392-1351 *Toll Free Tel:* 800-226-3822 (orders only) *Fax:* 352-392-0590 *Toll Free Fax:* 800-680-1955 (orders only) *E-mail:* press@upress.ufl.edu; orders@upress.ufl.edu *Web Site:* www.upf.com, pg 232

University Press of Kansas, 2502 Westbrooke Circle, Lawrence, KS 66045-4444 *Tel:* 785-864-4154; 785-864-4155 (orders) *Fax:* 785-864-4586 *E-mail:* upress@ku.edu; upkorders@ku.edu (orders) *Web Site:* www.kansaspress.ku.edu, pg 233

The University Press of Kentucky, 663 S Limestone St, Lexington, KY 40508-4008 *Tel:* 859-257-8400 *Fax:* 859-257-8481 *Web Site:* www.kentuckypress.com, pg 233

University Press of Mississippi, 3825 Ridgewood Rd, Jackson, MS 39211-6492 *Tel:* 601-432-6205 *Toll Free Tel:* 800-737-7788 (orders & cust serv) *Fax:* 601-432-6217 *E-mail:* press@mississippi.edu *Web Site:* www.upress.state.ms.us, pg 233

University Publishing House, PO Box 1664, Mannford, OK 74044 *Tel:* 918-865-4726 *E-mail:* upub5@outlook.com *Web Site:* www.universitypublishinghouse.net, pg 233

University Science Books, 20 Edgeshill Rd, Mill Valley, CA 94941 *Tel:* 703-661-1572 (cust serv, orders) *Fax:* 703-661-1572 (cust serv, orders) *E-mail:* usbmail@presswarehouse.com (cust serv, orders) *Web Site:* www.uscibooks.com, pg 233

UnKnownTruths.com Publishing Co, 8815 Conroy Windermere Rd, Suite 190, Orlando, FL 32835 *Tel:* 407-929-9207 *E-mail:* info@unknowntruths.com *Web Site:* unknowntruths.com, pg 234

Unlimited Publishing LLC, PO Box 99, Nashville, IN 47448, pg 234

John Updike Award, 633 W 155 St, New York, NY 10032 *Tel:* 212-368-5900 *Fax:* 212-491-4615 *E-mail:* academy@artsandletters.org *Web Site:* artsandletters.org, pg 675

W E Upjohn Institute for Employment Research, 300 S Westnedge Ave, Kalamazoo, MI 49007-4686 *Tel:* 269-343-5541; 269-343-4330 (orders) *Toll Free Tel:* 888-227-8569 *Fax:* 269-343-7310 *E-mail:* publications@upjohn.org; communications@upjohn.org *Web Site:* www.upjohn.org, pg 234

Upper Access Inc, 87 Upper Access Rd, Hinesburg, VT 05461 *Tel:* 802-482-2988 *E-mail:* upperaccessbooks@gmail.com *Web Site:* www.upperaccess.com, pg 234

Upper Room Books, 1908 Grand Ave, Nashville, TN 37212 *Tel:* 615-340-7200 *Toll Free Tel:* 800-972-0433 *Web Site:* books.upperroom.org, pg 234

Upstart Books™, PO Box 7488, Madison, WI 53707 *Tel:* 608-241-1201 *Toll Free Tel:* 800-356-1200 (orders); 800-962-4463 (cust serv) *Toll Free Fax:* 800-245-1329 (orders) *E-mail:* custserv@demco.com; order@demco.com *Web Site:* www.demco.com/upstart, pg 234

Urim Publications, 527 Empire Blvd, Brooklyn, NY 11225-3121 *Tel:* 718-972-5449 *Fax:* 718-972-6307 *E-mail:* urimpublisher@gmail.com *Web Site:* www.urimpublications.com, pg 234

US Board on Books For Young People (USBBY), c/o V Ellis Vance, 5503 N El Adobe Dr, Fresno, CA 93711-2363 *Tel:* 559-351-6119 *Web Site:* www.usbby.org, pg 548

US Conference of Catholic Bishops, USCCB Publishing, 3211 Fourth St NE, Washington, DC 20017 *Toll Free Tel:* 800-235-8722 *Fax:* 301-779-8596 (orders) *E-mail:* css@usccb.org *Web Site:* store.usccb.org, pg 234

US Games Systems Inc, 179 Ludlow St, Stamford, CT 06902 *Tel:* 203-353-8400 *Toll Free Tel:* 800-54-GAMES (544-2637) *Fax:* 203-353-8431 *E-mail:* info@usgamesinc.com *Web Site:* www.usgamesinc.com, pg 234

US Government Publishing Office (GPO), Superintendent of Documents, 732 N Capitol St NW, Washington, DC 20401 *Tel:* 202-512-1800 *Toll Free Tel:* 866-512-1800 (orders) *Fax:* 202-512-1998 *E-mail:* contactcenter@gpo.gov *Web Site:* www.gpo.gov; bookstore.gpo.gov (sales), pg 235

USBE: United States Book Exchange, 2969 W 25 St, Cleveland, OH 44113 *Tel:* 216-241-6960 *Fax:* 216-241-6966 *E-mail:* usbe@usbe.com *Web Site:* www.usbe.com, pg 548

Utah Geological Survey, 1594 W North Temple, Suite 3110, Salt Lake City, UT 84116-3154 *Tel:* 801-537-3300 *Toll Free Tel:* 888-UTAH-MAP (882-4627, bookstore) *Fax:* 801-537-3400 *E-mail:* geostore@utah.gov *Web Site:* geology.utah.gov, pg 235

Utah Original Writing Competition, 617 E South Temple, Salt Lake City, UT 84102 *Tel:* 801-236-7555 *Fax:* 801-236-7556 *Web Site:* arts.utah.gov, pg 675

Utah State University Press, 3078 Old Main Hill, Logan, UT 84322-3078 *Tel:* 435-797-1362 *Web Site:* www.usupress.com, pg 235

Janis Vallely Literary Agency, 11 Raup Rd, Chatham, NY 12037 *Tel:* 518-392-0897 *E-mail:* janvall@aol.com *Web Site:* www.janisvallely.com, pg 507

William Van Dyke Short Story Prize, 1041 N Taft Hill Rd, Fort Collins, CO 80521 *Tel:* 970-449-2726 *E-mail:* editor@ruminatemagazine.org *Web Site:* www.ruminatemagazine.com, pg 675

The William Van Wert Memorial Fiction Award, PO Box 63927, Philadelphia, PA 19147 *Tel:* 610-764-0813 *E-mail:* hiddenriverarts@gmail.com *Web Site:* www.hiddenriverarts.org; www.hiddenriverarts.com, pg 675

VanDam Inc, The VanDam Bldg, 121 W 27 St, New York, NY 10001 *Tel:* 212-929-0416 *Toll Free Tel:* 800-UNFOLDS (863-6537) *Fax:* 212-929-0426 *E-mail:* info@vandam.com *Web Site:* www.vandam.com, pg 235

Vandamere Press, 3580 Morris St N, St Petersburg, FL 33713 *Tel:* 727-556-0950 *Toll Free Tel:* 800-551-7776 *Fax:* 727-556-2560 *E-mail:* orders@vandamere.com *Web Site:* www.vandamere.com, pg 235

Vanderbilt University Press, 2301 Vanderbilt Place, PMB 401813, Nashville, TN 37240-1813 *Tel:* 615-322-3585 *Toll Free Tel:* 800-848-6224 (orders only) *Fax:* 615-343-0308 *E-mail:* vupress@vanderbilt.edu *Web Site:* www.vanderbiltuniversitypress.com, pg 235

VanderMey Nonfiction Prize, 1041 N Taft Hill Rd, Fort Collins, CO 80521 *Tel:* 970-449-2726 *E-mail:* editor@ruminatemagazine.org *Web Site:* www.ruminatemagazine.com, pg 675

Daniel Varoujan Award, 46 Wallace St, Somerville, MA 02144 *E-mail:* info@nepoetryclub.org *Web Site:* www.nepoetryclub.org, pg 675

Vault.com Inc, 132 W 31 St, 16th fl, New York, NY 10001 *Tel:* 212-366-4212 *Toll Free Tel:* 800-535-2074 *Fax:* 212-366-6117 (cust serv) *E-mail:* editors@vault.com; customerservice@vault.com *Web Site:* www.vault.com, pg 235

Vedanta Press, 1946 Vedanta Place, Hollywood, CA 90068 *Tel:* 323-960-1728; 323-960-1736 (catalog) *Fax:* 323-465-9568 *E-mail:* vpress@vedanta.com *Web Site:* www.vedanta.com, pg 235

Vehicule Press, PO Box 42094, CP Roy, Montreal, QC H2W-2T3, Canada *Tel:* 514-844-6073 *E-mail:* vp@vehiculepress.com; admin@vehiculepress.com *Web Site:* www.vehiculepress.com, pg 445

Velazquez Press, 9682 Telstar Ave, Suite 110, El Monte, CA 91731 *Tel:* 626-448-3448 *Fax:* 626-602-3817 *E-mail:* info@academiclearningcompany.com *Web Site:* www.velazquezpress.com, pg 235

The Vendome Press, 244 Fifth Ave, Suite 2043, New York, NY 10001 *Tel:* 212-737-1857 *E-mail:* info@vendomepress.com *Web Site:* www.vendomepress.com, pg 235

Vermont College of Fine Arts MFA in Writing for Children & Young Adults Program, 36 College St, Montpelier, VT 05602 *Tel:* 802-828-8637; 802-828-8696 *Toll Free Tel:* 866-934-VCFA (934-8232) *Fax:* 802-828-8649 *Web Site:* www.vcfa.edu, pg 586

Vermont College of Fine Arts, MFA in Writing Program, 36 College St, Montpelier, VT 05602 *Tel:* 802-828-8840; 802-828-8839 *Toll Free Tel:* 866-934-VCFA (934-8232) *Fax:* 802-828-8649 *Web Site:* www.vcfa.edu, pg 586

Vermont Studio Center Writer's Program Fellowships, 80 Pearl St, Johnson, VT 05656 *Tel:* 802-635-2727 *Fax:* 802-635-2730 *E-mail:* writing@vermontstudiocenter.org; info@vermontstudiocenter.org *Web Site:* www.vermontstudiocenter.org, pg 675

Vernon Press, 1000 N West St, Suite 1200, Wilmington, DE 19801 *Tel:* 302-250-4440 *E-mail:* info@vernonpress.com *Web Site:* www.vernonpress.com, pg 235

Verso, 20 Jay St, Suite 1010, Brooklyn, NY 11201 *Tel:* 718-246-8160 *Fax:* 718-246-8165 *E-mail:* verso@versobooks.com *Web Site:* www.versobooks.com, pg 235

Vesuvian Books, 2817 West End Ave, No 126-283, Nashville, TN 37203 *E-mail:* info@vesuvianmedia.com *Web Site:* www.vesuvianbooks.com, pg 236

Jill Vickers Prize, 260 rue Dalhousie St, Suite 204, Ottawa, ON K1N 7E4, Canada *Tel:* 613-562-1202 *Fax:* 613-241-0019 *E-mail:* cpsa-acsp@cpsa-acsp.ca *Web Site:* www.cpsa-acsp.ca, pg 675

Vicky Metcalf Award for Literature for Young People, 600-460 Richmond St W, Toronto, ON M5V 1Y1, Canada *Tel:* 416-504-8222 *Toll Free Tel:* 877-906-6548 *Fax:* 416-504-9090 *E-mail:* info@writerstrust.com *Web Site:* www.writerstrust.com, pg 675

Viking, 375 Hudson St, New York, NY 10014 *Tel:* 212-366-2000 *Fax:* 212-243-6002 *Web Site:* www.penguin.com/publishers/vikingbooks, pg 236

Viking Children's Books, 345 Hudson St, New York, NY 10014 *Fax:* 212-414-3393 *E-mail:* youngreaderspublicity@us.penguingroup.com *Web Site:* www.penguin.com/publishers/vikingchildrensbooks, pg 236

Viking Studio, 375 Hudson St, New York, NY 10014 *Tel:* 212-366-2000 *Fax:* 212-366-2636 *E-mail:* averystudiopublicity@us.penguingroup.com *Web Site:* www.penguin.com, pg 236

Carl Vinson Institute of Government, University of Georgia, 201 N Milledge Ave, Athens, GA 30602 *Tel:* 706-542-2736 *Fax:* 706-542-9301 *Web Site:* www.cviog.uga.edu, pg 236

Vintage Books, c/o Penguin Random House Inc, 1745 Broadway, New York, NY 10019 *Tel:* 212-572-2420 *E-mail:* vintageanchorpublicity@randomhouse.com *Web Site:* knopfdoubleday.com/imprint/vintage, pg 236

Visible Ink Press®, 43311 Joy Rd, Suite 414, Canton, MI 48187-2075 *Tel:* 734-667-3211 *Fax:* 734-667-4311 *E-mail:* info@visibleinkpress.com *Web Site:* www.visibleinkpress.com, pg 236

Visiting Writers Series, English Dept, PO Box 755720, Fairbanks, AK 99775-5720 *Tel:* 907-474-7193 *Fax:* 907-474-5247 *E-mail:* faengl@uaf.edu *Web Site:* www.alaska.edu/english, pg 579

Visual Artists & Galleries Association Inc (VAGA), 111 Broadway, Suite 1006, New York, NY 10006 *Tel:* 212-736-6666 *Fax:* 212-736-6767 *E-mail:* info@vagarights.com *Web Site:* vagarights.com, pg 548

Visual Media Alliance (VMA), 665 Third St, Suite 500, San Francisco, CA 94107-1926 *Tel:* 415-495-8242 *Toll Free Tel:* 800-659-3363 *Toll Free Fax:* 800-824-1911 *E-mail:* info@vma.bz *Web Site:* main.vma.bz, pg 548

Visual Profile Books Inc, 389 Fifth Ave, Suite 1105, New York, NY 10016 *Tel:* 516-445-0116 *Web Site:* www.visualprofilebooks.com, pg 237

The Vivian, 14615 Benfer Rd, Houston, TX 77069 *Tel:* 832-717-5200 *Fax:* 832-717-5201 *E-mail:* contests@rwa.org *Web Site:* www.rwa.org, pg 675

VLB editeur, 4545, rue Frontenac, 3rd fl, Montreal, QC H2H 2R7, Canada *Tel:* 514-849-5259 *Web Site:* www.edvlb.com, pg 445

Ludwig von Mises Institute, 518 W Magnolia Ave, Auburn, AL 36832 *Tel:* 334-321-2100 *Fax:* 334-321-2119 *E-mail:* info@mises.org *Web Site:* www.mises.org, pg 237

VONA Voices Summer Writing Workshop, 3720 Spruce St, Suite 442, Philadelphia, PA 19104 *Tel:* 732-842-3932; 510-421-3913 *E-mail:* info@vonacommunity.org *Web Site:* www.vonacommunity.org, pg 579

Voyager Sopris Learning Inc, 17855 Dallas Pkwy, Suite 400, Dallas, TX 75287 *Tel:* 303-651-2829 *Toll Free Tel:* 800-547-6747 *Fax:* 303-776-5934 *Toll Free Fax:* 888-819-7767 *E-mail:* customerservice@voyagersopris.com *Web Site:* www.voyagersopris.com, pg 237

Harold D Vursell Memorial Award, 633 W 155 St, New York, NY 10032 *Tel:* 212-368-5900 *Fax:* 212-491-4615 *E-mail:* academy@artsandletters.org *Web Site:* artsandletters.org, pg 675

Wake Forest University Press, 2518 Reynolda Rd, Winston-Salem, NC 27106 *Tel:* 336-758-5448 *Fax:* 336-842-3853 *E-mail:* wfupress@wfu.edu *Web Site:* wfupress.wfu.edu, pg 237

Walch Education, 40 Walch Dr, Portland, ME 04103-1286 *Tel:* 207-772-2846 *Toll Free Tel:* 800-558-2846 *Fax:* 207-772-3105 *Toll Free Fax:* 888-991-5755 *E-mail:* customerservice@walch.com *Web Site:* www.walch.com, pg 237

Waldorf Publishing, 2140 Hall Johnson Rd, No 102-345, Grapevine, TX 76051 *Tel:* 972-674-3131 *E-mail:* info@waldorfpublishing.com *Web Site:* www.waldorfpublishing.com, pg 237

Wales Literary Agency Inc, 1508 Tenth Ave E, No 401, Seattle, WA 98102 *Tel:* 206-284-7114 *E-mail:* waleslit@waleslit.com *Web Site:* www.waleslit.com, pg 507

Christopher Lightfoot Walker Award, 633 W 155 St, New York, NY 10032 *Tel:* 212-368-5900 *E-mail:* academy@artsandletters.org *Web Site:* artsandletters.org, pg 675

Richard Wall Memorial Award, c/o The New York Public Library for the Performing Arts, 111 Amsterdam Ave, New York, NY 10023 *E-mail:* TheatreLibraryAssociation@gmail.com; TLABookAwards@gmail.com *Web Site:* www.tla-online.org/awards/bookawards, pg 676

The Wallace Literary Agency, 229 E 79 St, No 5A, New York, NY 10075 *Tel:* 212-472-3282 *Fax:* 212-472-3833 *E-mail:* info@wallaceliteraryagency.com, pg 507

Edward Lewis Wallant Award, Maurice Greenberg Center for Judaic Studies, 200 Bloomfield Ave, Harry Jack Gray E 300, West Hartford, CT 06117 *Tel:* 860-768-4964 *Fax:* 860-768-5044 *E-mail:* mgcjs@hartford.edu *Web Site:* www.hartford.edu/a_and_s/greenberg/wallant, pg 676

Wambtac Communications, 1512 E Santa Clara Ave, Santa Ana, CA 92705 *Tel:* 714-954-0580 *Toll Free Tel:* 800-641-3936 *E-mail:* wambtac@wambtac.com *Web Site:* www.wambtac.com; claudiasuzanne.com (prof servs), pg 471

Warner Press, 2902 Enterprise Dr, Anderson, IN 46013 *Tel:* 765-644-7721 *Toll Free Tel:* 800-741-7721 (orders) *Fax:* 765-640-8005 *E-mail:* wporders@warnerpress.org *Web Site:* www.warnerpress.org, pg 237

Warren Wilson College, MFA Program for Writers, 701 Warren Wilson Rd, Swannanoa, NC 28778 *Tel:* 828-771-3717 *Fax:* 828-771-7005 *E-mail:* mfa@warren-wilson.edu *Web Site:* www.warren-wilson.edu/programs/mfa-in-creative-writing, pg 586

Warwick Associates, 18340 Sonoma Hwy, Sonoma, CA 95476 *Tel:* 707-939-9212 *Fax:* 707-938-3515 *E-mail:* warwick@vom.com *Web Site:* www.warwickassociates.com, pg 507

George Washington Book Prize, 101 S Water St, Chestertown, MD 21620 *Tel:* 410-810-7165 *Fax:* 410-810-7175 *Web Site:* starrcenter.washcoll.edu/centers/starr/george-washington-book-prize.php, pg 676

Washington State Book Awards, c/o The Seattle Public Library, 1000 Fourth Ave, Seattle, WA 98104-1109 *Tel:* 206-386-4636 *E-mail:* wsba@spl.org *Web Site:* www.spl.org, pg 676

Washington State University Press, Cooper Publications Bldg, 2300 Grimes Way, Pullman, WA 99164-5910 *Tel:* 509-335-7880 *Toll Free Tel:* 800-354-7360 (orders) *E-mail:* wsupress@wsu.edu *Web Site:* wsupress.wsu.edu, pg 237

Water Environment Federation, 601 Wythe St, Alexandria, VA 22314-1994 *Tel:* 703-684-2400 *Toll Free Tel:* 800-666-0206 (cust serv) *Fax:* 703-684-2492 *E-mail:* inquiry@wef.org *Web Site:* www.wef.org, pg 237

Water Resources Publications LLC, PO Box 630026, Highlands Ranch, CO 80163-0026 *Tel:* 720-873-0171 *Toll Free Tel:* 800-736-2405 *Fax:* 720-873-0173 *Toll Free Fax:* 800-616-1971 *E-mail:* info@wrpllc.com *Web Site:* www.wrpllc.com, pg 237

WaterBrook, 10807 New Allegiance Dr, Suite 500, Colorado Springs, CO 80921 *Tel:* 719-590-4999 *Toll Free Tel:* 800-603-7051 (orders) *Fax:* 719-590-8977 *Toll Free Fax:* 800-294-5686 (orders) *E-mail:* info@waterbrookmultnomah.com *Web Site:* waterbrookmultnomah.com, pg 237

Watermark Publishing, 1000 Bishop St, Suite 806, Honolulu, HI 96813 *Tel:* 808-587-7766 *Toll Free Tel:* 866-900-BOOK (900-2665) *Fax:* 808-521-3461 *E-mail:* info@bookshawaii.net *Web Site:* www.bookshawaii.net, pg 238

Waterside Productions Inc, 2055 Oxford Ave, Cardiff, CA 92007 *Tel:* 760-632-9190 *Fax:* 760-632-9295 *E-mail:* admin@waterside.com *Web Site:* www.waterside.com, pg 508

Watkins/Loomis Agency Inc, PO Box 20925, New York, NY 10025 *Tel:* 212-532-0080 *Fax:* 646-383-2449 *E-mail:* assistant@watkinsloomis.com *Web Site:* www.watkinsloomis.com, pg 508

Watson-Guptill Publications, c/o Ten Speed Press, 6001 Shellmount St, Suite 600, Emeryville, CA 94608 *Web Site:* crownpublishing.com/imprint/watson-guptill, pg 238

Watson Publishing International LLC, 349 Old Plymouth Rd, Sagamore Beach, MA 02562 *E-mail:* orders@shpusa.com *Web Site:* www.shpusa.com; www.watsonpublishing.com, pg 238

The Robert Watson Literary Prizes in Fiction & Poetry, MFA Writing Program, The Greensboro Review, UNC-Greensboro, 3302 MHRA Bldg, Greensboro, NC 27402-6170 *Tel:* 336-334-5459 *Fax:* 336-256-1470 *Web Site:* www.greensbororeview.org, pg 676

Waveland Press Inc, 4180 IL Rte 83, Suite 101, Long Grove, IL 60047-9580 *Tel:* 847-634-0081 *Fax:* 847-634-9501 *E-mail:* info@waveland.com *Web Site:* www.waveland.com, pg 238

Waxman Literary Agency, 443 Park Ave S, No 1004, New York, NY 10016 *Tel:* 212-675-5556 *Web Site:* www.waxmanliteraryagency.com, pg 508

Wayne State University Press, Leonard N Simons Bldg, 4809 Woodward Ave, Detroit, MI 48201-1309 *Tel:* 313-577-6120 *Toll Free Tel:* 800-978-7323 *Fax:* 313-577-6131 *E-mail:* bookorders@wayne.edu *Web Site:* www.wsupress.wayne.edu, pg 238

Wayside Publishing, 2 Stonewood Dr, Freeport, ME 04032 *Toll Free Tel:* 888-302-2519 *E-mail:* info@waysidepublishing.com; support@waysidepublishing.com *Web Site:* waysidepublishing.com, pg 238

Weigl Educational Publishers Ltd, 6325 Tenth St SE, Calgary, AB T2H 2Z9, Canada *Tel:* 403-233-7747 *Toll Free Tel:* 800-668-0766 *Fax:* 403-233-7769 *Toll Free Fax:* 866-449-3445 *E-mail:* orders@weigl.com *Web Site:* www.weigl.ca; av2books.com, pg 445

Cherry Weiner Literary Agency, 925 Oak Bluff Ct, Dacula, GA 30019-6660 *Tel:* 732-446-2096 *Fax:* 732-792-0506 *E-mail:* cherry8486@aol.com, pg 508

The Weingel-Fidel Agency, 310 E 46 St, Suite 21-E, New York, NY 10017 *Tel:* 212-599-2959 *Fax:* 212-286-1986 *E-mail:* queries@theweingel-fidelagency.com, pg 508

Welcome Enterprises Inc, 300 Park Ave S, New York, NY 10010 *Tel:* 212-387-3400 *Web Site:* www.rizzoliusa.com, pg 238

Welcome Rain Publishers LLC, 217 Thompson St, Suite 473, New York, NY 10012 *Tel:* 212-686-1909 *Web Site:* welcomerain.com, pg 238

Welcome to My Worlds, 1630 W Gail Dr, Chandler, AZ 85224-4045 *Tel:* 480-773-8958 *Web Site:* kbshawauthor.com, pg 238

Well-Trained Mind Press, 18021 The Glebe Lane, Charles City, VA 23030 *Tel:* 804-829-5043 *Toll Free Tel:* 877-322-3445 (orders) *Fax:* 804-829-5704 *E-mail:* support@welltrainedmind.com *Web Site:* welltrainedmind.com, pg 238

Rene Wellek Prize, University of South Carolina, Dept of Languages, Literature & Cultures, 1620 College St, Rm 817, Columbia, SC 29208 *Tel:* 803-777-3021 *E-mail:* info@acla.org *Web Site:* www.acla.org/prize-awards/rené-wellek-prize, pg 676

Wellington Press, 9601-30 Miccosukee Rd, Tallahassee, FL 32309 *E-mail:* peacegames@aol.com *Web Site:* www.peacegames.com, pg 238

WendyLynn & Co, 504 Wilson Rd, Annapolis, MD 21401 *Tel:* 410-224-2729; 410-507-1059 *Web Site:* wendylynn.com, pg 512

Wergle Flomp Humor Poetry Contest, 351 Pleasant St, PMB 222, Northampton, MA 01060-3961 *Tel:* 413-320-1847 *Toll Free Tel:* 866-WINWRIT (946-9748) *Fax:* 413-280-0539 *Web Site:* www.winningwriters.com, pg 676

Eliot Werner Publications Inc, 31 Willow Lane, Clinton Corners, NY 12514 *Tel:* 845-266-4241 *Fax:* 845-266-3317 *E-mail:* eliotwerner217@gmail.com *Web Site:* www.eliotwerner.com, pg 238

Toby Wertheim, 240 E 76 St, New York, NY 10021 *Tel:* 212-472-8587 *E-mail:* tobywertheim@yahoo.com, pg 471

Wesley-Logan Prize, 400 "A" St SE, Washington, DC 20003 *Tel:* 202-544-2422 *Fax:* 202-544-8307 *E-mail:* awards@historians.org *Web Site:* www.historians.org, pg 676

Wesleyan Publishing House, 13300 Olio Rd, Fishers, IN 46037 *Tel:* 317-774-3853 *Toll Free Tel:* 800-493-7539 *Fax:* 317-774-3865 *Toll Free Fax:* 800-788-3535 *E-mail:* wph@wesleyan.org *Web Site:* www.wesleyan.org/books, pg 239

Wesleyan University Press, 215 Long Lane, Middletown, CT 06459-0433 *Tel:* 860-685-7712 *Fax:* 860-685-7712 *Web Site:* www.wesleyan.edu/wespress, pg 239

Wesleyan Writers Conference, c/o Wesleyan University, Downey House, 294 High St, Rm 207, Middletown, CT 06459 *Tel:* 860-685-3604 *Web Site:* www.wesleyan.edu/writing/conference, pg 579

West Academic, 444 Cedar St, Suite 700, St Paul, MN 55101 *Toll Free Tel:* 877-888-1330 *E-mail:* customerservice@westacademic.com; support@westacademic.com; media@westacademic.com *Web Site:* www.westacademic.com, pg 239

Wilshire Book Co, 22647 Ventura Blvd, No 314, Woodland Hills, CA 91364-1416 *Tel:* 818-700-1522 *E-mail:* sales@mpowers.com *Web Site:* www.mpowers.com, pg 242

Gary Wilson Award for Short Fiction, Dept of English, TCU Box 298300, Fort Worth, TX 76129 *Tel:* 817-257-5907 *Fax:* 817-257-5905 *E-mail:* descant@tcu.edu *Web Site:* www.descant.tcu.edu, pg 678

The H W Wilson Foundation, 750 Third Ave, 13th fl, New York, NY 10017 *Tel:* 212-418-8473 *Web Site:* www.thwwf.org, pg 551

The H W Wilson Library Staff Development Grant, 50 E Huron St, Chicago, IL 60611 *Tel:* 312-280-3247 *Toll Free Tel:* 800-545-2433 (ext 3247) *Fax:* 312-944-3897; 312-440-9379 *E-mail:* awards@ala.org *Web Site:* www.ala.org, pg 678

Wimmer Cookbooks, 4650 Shelby Air Dr, Memphis, TN 38118 *Toll Free Tel:* 800-548-2537 *Fax:* 901-363-1771 *E-mail:* info@wimmerco.com *Web Site:* www.wimmerco.com, pg 242

Herbert Warren Wind Book Award, 77 Liberty Corner Rd, Far Hills, NJ 07931-0708 *Tel:* 908-234-2300 *Web Site:* www.usga.org, pg 678

Windbreak House Writing Retreat, PO Box 169, Hermosa, SD 57744-0169 *Tel:* 605-255-4064 *E-mail:* info@windbreakhouse.com *Web Site:* www.windbreakhouse.com, pg 579

Windham-Campbell Prizes, Beinecke Rare Book & Manuscript Library, 121 Wall St, New Haven, CT 06511 *Fax:* 203-432-9033 *Web Site:* windhamcampbell.org, pg 678

Windhaven®, 466 Rte 10, Orford, NH 03777 *Tel:* 603-512-9251 (cell) *Web Site:* www.windhavenpress.com, pg 471

Windsor Books, 260 W Main St, Suite 5, Bayshore, NY 11706 *Tel:* 631-665-6688 *Toll Free Tel:* 800-321-5934 *E-mail:* windsor.books@att.net *Web Site:* www.windsorpublishing.com, pg 242

Wings Press, PO Box 591176, San Antonio, TX 78259 *E-mail:* wingspresspublishing@gmail.com *Web Site:* www.wingspress.com, pg 242

Justin Winsor Prize for Library History Essay, 225 N Michigan Ave, Suite 1300, Chicago, IL 60601 *Tel:* 312-280-4283 *Toll Free Tel:* 800-545-2433 (ext 4283) *Fax:* 312-280-4392 *E-mail:* ors@ala.org *Web Site:* www.ala.org; ala.org/lhrt, pg 678

Winter Words Author Series, 110 E Hallam St, Suite 116, Aspen, CO 81611 *Tel:* 970-925-3122 *Fax:* 970-920-5700 *E-mail:* aspenwords@aspeninstitute.org *Web Site:* www.aspenwords.org, pg 579

Winters Publishing, 705 E Washington St, Greensburg, IN 47240 *Tel:* 812-663-4948 *Toll Free Tel:* 800-457-3230 *Fax:* 812-663-4948 *E-mail:* winterspublishing@gmail.com *Web Site:* www.winterspublishing.com, pg 242

Winterthur Museum, Garden & Library, 5105 Kennett Pike, Winterthur, DE 19735 *Tel:* 302-888-4663 *Toll Free Tel:* 800-448-3883 *Fax:* 302-888-4950 *Web Site:* www.winterthur.org, pg 242

Winterwolf Press, 1810 E Sahara Ave, Suite 737, Las Vegas, NV 89014 *Toll Free Tel:* 855-ICE-WOLF (423-9653) *E-mail:* info@winterwolfpress.com; questions@winterwolfpress.com; admin@winterwolfpress.com (orders) *Web Site:* winterwolfpress.com, pg 243

Wisconsin Annual Fall Conference, PO Box 1463, Green Bay, WI 54305-1463 *Tel:* 323-782-1010 (corp off) *E-mail:* wisconsin@scbwi.org *Web Site:* www.scbwi.org; www.facebook.com/SCBWIWisconsin, pg 580

Wisconsin Department of Public Instruction, 125 S Webster St, Madison, WI 53703 *Tel:* 608-266-2188 *Toll Free Tel:* 800-441-4563 (US only); 800-243-8782 (US only) *E-mail:* pubsales@dpi.wi.gov *Web Site:* pubsales.dpi.wi.gov, pg 243

The Wisconsin Writers Awards, c/o 210 N Main St, No 204, Cedar Grove, WI 53013 *E-mail:* wiswriters@gmail.com *Web Site:* wiswriters.org/awards, pg 678

Wisdom Publications Inc, 199 Elm St, Somerville, MA 02144 *Tel:* 617-776-7416 *Toll Free Tel:* 800-272-4050 (orders) *Fax:* 617-776-7841 *E-mail:* info@wisdompubs.org; submission@wisdompubs.org *Web Site:* www.wisdompubs.org, pg 243

Wizards of the Coast LLC, 1600 Lind Ave SW, Suite 400, Renton, WA 98057-3305 *Tel:* 425-226-6500 *E-mail:* press@wizards.com *Web Site:* company.wizards.com; www.wizards.com, pg 243

WLA Literary Award, 4610 S Biltmore Lane, Suite 100, Madison, WI 53718-2153 *Tel:* 608-245-3640 *Fax:* 608-245-3646 *Web Site:* wla.wisconsinlibraries.org, pg 678

WME, 11 Madison Ave, 18th fl, New York, NY 10010 *Tel:* 212-586-5100 *Web Site:* www.wmeentertainment.com, pg 508

WNBA Pannell Award for Excellence in Children's Bookselling, PO Box 237, FDR Sta, New York, NY 10150-0231 *Toll Free Tel:* 866-610-WNBA (610-9622) *E-mail:* WNBAPannell@gmail.com *Web Site:* www.wnba-books.org; www.NationalReadingGroupMonth.org; www.wnba-books.org/awards, pg 678

WNBA Writing Contest, PO Box 237, FDR Sta, New York, NY 10150-0231 *Toll Free Tel:* 866-610-WNBA (610-9622) *E-mail:* info@wnba-books.org *Web Site:* www.wnba-books.org/contest, pg 679

WNDB Internship Grants, 10319 Westlake Dr, No 104, Bethesda, MD 20817 *Tel:* 701-404-9632 (voicemail only) *E-mail:* internships@diversebooks.org *Web Site:* diversebooks.org/our-programs/internship-grants, pg 679

Alan Wofsy Fine Arts, 1109 Geary Blvd, San Francisco, CA 94109 *Tel:* 415-292-6500 *Toll Free Tel:* 800-660-6403 *Fax:* 415-292-6594 (off & cust serv); 510-251-1840 (acctg) *E-mail:* order@art-books.com (orders); editeur@earthlink.net (edit); beauxarts@earthlink.net (cust serv) *Web Site:* www.art-books.com, pg 243

Thomas Wolfe Fiction Prize, PO Box 21591, Winston-Salem, NC 27120-1591 *E-mail:* mail@ncwriters.org *Web Site:* www.ncwriters.org, pg 679

Helen & Kurt Wolff Translator's Prize, 30 Irving Place, New York, NY 10003 *Tel:* 212-439-8700 *Fax:* 212-439-8705 *E-mail:* info-newyork@goethe.de *Web Site:* www.goethe.de/ins/us/enkul/ser/uef/hkw.html, pg 679

Tobias Wolff Award for Fiction, Mail Stop 9053, Western Washington University, Bellingham, WA 98225 *Tel:* 360-650-4863 *E-mail:* bhreview@wwu.edu *Web Site:* www.bhreview.org, pg 679

Wolfman Books, 410 13 St, Oakland, CA 94612 *Tel:* 510-679-4650 *E-mail:* hello@wolfmanhomerepair.com *Web Site:* wolfmanhomerepair.com, pg 243

Wolters Kluwer Law & Business, 76 Ninth Ave, 7th fl, New York, NY 10011-5201 *Tel:* 212-771-0600; 301-698-7100 (cust serv outside US) *Toll Free Tel:* 800-234-1660 (cust serv) *E-mail:* customer.service@wolterskluwer.com; lrusmedia@wolterskluwer.com *Web Site:* lrus.wolterskluwer.com, pg 243

Wolters Kluwer US Corp, 2700 Lake Cook Rd, Riverwoods, IL 60015 *Tel:* 847-267-7000 *Fax:* 847-580-5192 *E-mail:* info@wolterskluwer.com *Web Site:* www.wolterskluwer.com, pg 243

Women Who Write Inc, PO Box 652, Madison, NJ 07940-0652 *E-mail:* info@womenwhowrite.org *Web Site:* www.womenwhowrite.org, pg 549

Women's Fiction Writers Association (WFWA), PO Box 190, Jefferson, OR 97352 *E-mail:* communications@womensfictionwriters.org; membership@womensfictionwriters.org *Web Site:* www.womensfictionwriters.org, pg 549

Women's National Book Association Award, PO Box 237, FDR Sta, New York, NY 10150-0231 *Toll Free Tel:* 866-610-WNBA (610-9622) *Web Site:* www.wnba-books.org; www.NationalReadingGroupMonth.org, pg 679

Women's National Book Association Inc, PO Box 237, FDR Sta, New York, NY 10150-0231 *Toll Free Tel:* 866-610-WNBA (610-9622) *E-mail:* info@wnba-books.org *Web Site:* www.wnba-books.org; www.NationalReadingGroupMonth.org; www.wnba-centennial.org, pg 549

The J Howard & Barbara M J Wood Prize, 61 W Superior St, Chicago, IL 60654 *Tel:* 312-787-7070 *Fax:* 312-787-6650 *E-mail:* editors@poetrymagazine.org *Web Site:* www.poetryfoundation.org, pg 679

Wood Lake Publishing Inc, 485 Beaver Lake Rd, Kelowna, BC V4V 1S5, Canada *Tel:* 250-766-2778 *Toll Free Tel:* 800-663-2775 (orders & cust serv) *Fax:* 250-766-2736 *Toll Free Fax:* 888-841-9991 (orders & cust serv) *E-mail:* info@woodlake.com; customerservice@woodlake.com *Web Site:* www.woodlakebooks.com, pg 445

Woodbine House, 6510 Bells Mill Rd, Bethesda, MD 20817 *Tel:* 301-897-3570 *Toll Free Tel:* 800-843-7323 *Fax:* 301-897-5838 *E-mail:* info@woodbinehouse.com *Web Site:* www.woodbinehouse.com, pg 243

Woodrow Wilson Center Press, One Woodrow Wilson Plaza, 1300 Pennsylvania Ave NW, Washington, DC 20004-3027 *Tel:* 202-691-4122 *Web Site:* wilsoncenter.org/woodrow-wilson-center-press, pg 244

Carter G Woodson Book Awards, 8555 16 St, Suite 500, Silver Spring, MD 20910 *Tel:* 301-588-1800 *Toll Free Tel:* 800-296-7840 *Fax:* 301-588-2049 *E-mail:* excellence@ncss.org; publications@ncss.org *Web Site:* www.socialstudies.org, pg 679

WoodstockArts, PO Box 1342, Woodstock, NY 12498 *Tel:* 845-679-8111; 845-679-8555 *Fax:* 419-793-3452 *E-mail:* info@woodstockarts.com *Web Site:* woodstockarts.com, pg 244

Word Works Washington Prize, Adirondack Community College, Dearlove Hall, 640 Bay Rd, Queensbury, NY 12804 *Tel:* 301-581-9439 *Fax:* 301-581-9443 *E-mail:* editor@wordworksbooks.org *Web Site:* www.wordworksbooks.org, pg 679

WordCo Indexing Services Inc, 49 Church St, Norwich, CT 06360 *Tel:* 860-886-2532 *Toll Free Tel:* 877-WORDCO-3 (967-3263) *Fax:* 860-886-1155 *E-mail:* office@wordco.com *Web Site:* www.wordco.com, pg 471

Words into Print, 208 Java St, 5th fl, Brooklyn, NY 11222 *E-mail:* query@wordsintoprint.org *Web Site:* wordsintoprint.org, pg 471

Workers Compensation Research Institute, 955 Massachusetts Ave, Cambridge, MA 02139 *Tel:* 617-661-9274 *Fax:* 617-661-9284 *E-mail:* wcri@wcrinet.org *Web Site:* www.wcrinet.org, pg 244

Working With Words, 5320 SW Mayfair Ct, Beaverton, OR 97005 *Tel:* 503-644-4317 *E-mail:* editor@zzz.com, pg 472

Workman Publishing Co Inc, 225 Varick St, 9th fl, New York, NY 10014-4381 *Tel:* 212-254-5900 *Toll Free Tel:* 800-722-7202 *Fax:* 212-254-8098 *E-mail:* info@workman.com; orders@workman.com *Web Site:* www.workman.com, pg 244

World Almanac®, 307 W 36 St, 11 fl, New York, NY 10018 *Tel:* 212-643-6816 *Toll Free Tel:* 800-322-8755 *Fax:* 212-643-6819 *E-mail:* info@skyhorsepublishing.com *Web Site:* www.skyhorsepublishing.com, pg 244

World Bank Publications, Office of the Publisher, 1818 "H" St NW, U-11-1104, Washington, DC 20433 *Tel:* 202-458-4497; 202-473-1000 *Toll Free Tel:* 800-645-7247 (cust serv) *Fax:* 202-522-2631 *E-mail:* books@worldbank.org; pubrights@worldbank.org (foreign rts) *Web Site:* www.worldbank.org/en/research, pg 244

World Book Inc, 180 N LaSalle, Suite 900, Chicago, IL 60601 *Tel:* 312-729-5800 *Toll Free Tel:* 800-967-5325 (consumer sales, US); 800-463-8845 (consumer sales, CN); 800-975-3250 (school & lib sales, US); 800-837-5365 (school & lib sales, CN); 866-586-5200 (web sales) *Fax:* 312-729-5600; 312-729-5606 *Toll Free Fax:* 800-433-9330 (school & lib sales, US); 888-690-4002 (school & lib sales, CN) *E-mail:* customercare@worldbook.com *Web Site:* www.worldbook.com, pg 245

World Citizens, PO Box 131, Mill Valley, CA 94942-0131 *Tel:* 415-380-8020; 415-233-2822 (direct) *Toll Free Tel:* 800-247-6553 (orders only), pg 245

World Class Speakers & Entertainers, 5200 Kanan Rd, Suite 210, Agoura Hills, CA 91301 *Tel:* 818-991-5400 *E-mail:* wcse@wcspeakers.com *Web Site:* www.wcspeakers.com, pg 516

World Fantasy Awards, PO Box 43, Mukilteo, WA 98275-0043 *Web Site:* www.worldfantasy.org, pg 679

World Resources Institute, 10 "G" St NE, Suite 800, Washington, DC 20002 *Tel:* 202-729-7600 *Fax:* 202-729-7610 *Web Site:* www.wri.org, pg 245

World Scientific Publishing Co Inc, 27 Warren St, Suite 401-402, Hackensack, NJ 07601 *Tel:* 201-487-9655 *Fax:* 201-487-9656 *E-mail:* wspc_us@wspc.com; sales@wspc.com; mkt@wspc.com; editor@wspc.com *Web Site:* www.worldscientific.com, pg 245

World Trade Press LLC, 616 E Eighth St, Suite 7, Traverse City, MI 49686 *Tel:* 707-778-1124 *Toll Free Tel:* 800-833-8586 *Fax:* 231-642-5300 *Web Site:* www.worldtradepress.com, pg 245

World's Best Short-Short Story Contest, Florida State University, Dept of English, Tallahassee, FL 32306 *E-mail:* southeastreview@gmail.com *Web Site:* www.southeastreview.org, pg 680

WorldTariff, 220 Montgomery St, Suite 448, San Francisco, CA 94104-3410 *Tel:* 415-391-7501 *Toll Free Tel:* 866-268-7602 *Web Site:* ftn.fedex.com/wtonline, pg 245

Worldwide Library, 225 Duncan Mill Rd, Don Mills, ON M3B 3K9, Canada *Tel:* 416-445-5860 *Toll Free Tel:* 888-432-4879 *E-mail:* customerservice@harlequin.com *Web Site:* www.harlequin.com, pg 446

Worth Publishers, One New York Plaza, 46th fl, New York, NY 10004 *Tel:* 212-576-9400; 212-375-7000 *E-mail:* press.inquiries@macmillan.com *Web Site:* www.macmillanlearning.com/college/us, pg 245

Worthy & James Publishing, PO Box 362015, Milpitas, CA 95036 *Tel:* 408-945-3963 *E-mail:* worthy1234@sbcglobal.net; mail@worthyjames.com *Web Site:* www.worthyjames.com, pg 448

Wright Information Indexing Services, PO Box 658, Sandia Park, NM 87047 *Tel:* 505-281-2600 *Web Site:* www.wrightinformation.com, pg 472

Write for Success Editing Services, PO Box 292153, Los Angeles, CA 90029-8653 *Tel:* 323-356-8833 *E-mail:* writeforsuccessediting@gmail.com *Web Site:* www.write-for-success.com, pg 472

Write Now, 900 S Mitchell Dr, Tempe, AZ 85281 *Tel:* 480-921-5700 *Fax:* 480-921-5777 *E-mail:* info@writenow.co *Web Site:* www.writenow.co, pg 680

Write on the Sound Writers' Conference, Frances Anderson Center, 700 Main St, Edmonds, WA 98020 *Tel:* 425-771-0228 *Fax:* 425-771-0253 *E-mail:* wots@edmondswa.gov *Web Site:* www.writeonthesound.com, pg 580

Write Stuff Enterprises LLC, 1001 S Andrews Ave, Suite 200, Fort Lauderdale, FL 33316 *Tel:* 954-462-6657 *Fax:* 954-462-6023 *E-mail:* info@writestuffbooks.com *Web Site:* www.writestuffbooks.com, pg 245

The Write Way, 3048 Horizon Lane, Suite 1102, Naples, FL 34109 *Tel:* 239-273-9145 *E-mail:* darekane@gmail.com, pg 472

WriteLife Publishing, 960 Oaktree Blvd, Christianburg, VA 24073 *E-mail:* writelife@boutiqueofqualitybooks.com *Web Site:* www.writelife.com; www.facebook.com/writelife, pg 245

Writer in Residence, 2410 N Old Penitentiary Rd, Boise, ID 83712 *Tel:* 208-334-2119 *E-mail:* info@arts.idaho.gov *Web Site:* www.arts.idaho.gov, pg 680

The Writer Magazine/Emily Dickinson Award, 15 Gramercy Park, New York, NY 10003 *Tel:* 212-254-9628 *Web Site:* poetrysociety.org/awards, pg 680

Writer's Digest Annual Writing Competition, 5720 Flatiron Pkwy, Boulder, CO 80301 *Web Site:* www.writersdigest.com/writing-competitions, pg 680

Writer's Alliance of Newfoundland & Labrador, Haymarket Sq, 223 Duckworth St, Suite 202, St John's, NL A1C 6N1, Canada *Tel:* 709-739-5215 *Toll Free Tel:* 866-739-5215 *E-mail:* info@wanl.ca *Web Site:* wanl.ca, pg 549

Writer's AudioShop, 1316 Overland Stage Rd, Dripping Springs, TX 78620 *Tel:* 512-476-1616 *E-mail:* wrtaudshop@aol.com *Web Site:* www.writersaudio.com, pg 246

The Writers' Colony at Dairy Hollow, 515 Spring St, Eureka Springs, AR 72632 *Tel:* 479-253-7444 *E-mail:* director@writerscolony.org *Web Site:* www.writerscolony.org, pg 580

Writer's Digest Books, 1745 Broadway, New York, NY 10019, pg 246

Writer's Digest University, 5720 Flatiron Pkwy, Boulder, CO 80301 *Toll Free Tel:* 800-759-0963; 800-333-5441 *E-mail:* writersdigestuniversity@aimmedia.com *Web Site:* www.writersonlineworkshops.com, pg 586

Writers-Editors Network International Writing Competition, 45 Main St, North Stratford, NH 03590 *Tel:* 603-922-8338 *Fax:* 603-922-8339 *E-mail:* contest@writers-editors.com *Web Site:* www.writers-editors.com; www.ffwamembers.com, pg 680

Writers' Federation of Nova Scotia, 1113 Marginal Rd, Halifax, NS B3H 4P7, Canada *Tel:* 902-423-8116 *Fax:* 902-422-0881 *E-mail:* contact@writers.ns.ca; programs@writers.ns.ca *Web Site:* writers.ns.ca, pg 549

Writers' Guild of Alberta, 11759 Groat Rd, Edmonton, AB T5M 3K6, Canada *Tel:* 780-422-8174 *Toll Free Tel:* 800-665-5354 (AB only) *Fax:* 780-422-2663 (attn WGA) *E-mail:* mail@writersguild.ca *Web Site:* writersguild.ca, pg 549

Writers Guild of America Awards, 7000 W Third St, Los Angeles, CA 90048 *Tel:* 323-951-4000; 323-782-4569 *Fax:* 323-782-4800 *Web Site:* www.wga.org, pg 680

Writers Guild of America, East (WGAE), 250 Hudson St, Suite 700, New York, NY 10013 *Tel:* 212-767-7800 *Fax:* 212-582-1909 *Web Site:* www.wgaeast.org, pg 549

Writers Guild of America, West (WGAW), 7000 W Third St, Los Angeles, CA 90048 *Tel:* 323-951-4000 *Toll Free Tel:* 800-548-4532 *Fax:* 323-782-4800 *Web Site:* www.wga.org, pg 549

Writers House, 21 W 26 St, New York, NY 10010 *Tel:* 212-685-2400 *Web Site:* www.writershouse.com, pg 508

Writers' League of Texas (WLT), 611 S Congress Ave, Suite 200 A-3, Austin, TX 78704 *Tel:* 512-499-8914 *E-mail:* wlt@writersleague.org *Web Site:* www.writersleague.org, pg 516, 549, 580

Writers' League of Texas Book Awards, 611 S Congress Ave, Suite 200 A-3, Austin, TX 78704 *Tel:* 512-499-8914 *E-mail:* wlt@writersleague.org *Web Site:* www.writersleague.org, pg 680

The Writer's Lifeline Inc, 400 S Burnside Ave, Suite 11B, Los Angeles, CA 90036 *Tel:* 323-932-1685 *Web Site:* www.thewriterslifeline.com, pg 472

Writers Mentoring Retreat, PO Box 110390, Nashville, TN 37222-0390 *Tel:* 615-331-8668 *Toll Free Tel:* 800-21-WRITE (219-7483) *E-mail:* acwriters@aol.com *Web Site:* regaforder.wordpress.com/mentoring; regaforder.wordpress.com, pg 580

Writers' Productions, PO Box 630, Westport, CT 06881-0630 *Tel:* 203-227-8199, pg 509

Writer's Relief, Inc, 18766 John J Williams Hwy, Unit 4, Box 335, Rehoboth Beach, DE 19971 *Toll Free Tel:* 866-405-3003 *Fax:* 201-641-1253 *E-mail:* info@writersrelief.com *Web Site:* www.WritersRelief.com, pg 472

Writers' Representatives LLC, 116 W 14 St, 11th fl, New York, NY 10011-7305 *Tel:* 212-620-9009 *Fax:* 212-620-0023 *E-mail:* transom@writersreps.com *Web Site:* www.writersreps.com, pg 509

Writers Retreat Workshop (WRW), PO Box 170657, Austin, TX 78717 *E-mail:* info@writersretreatworkshop.com *Web Site:* www.writersretreatworkshop.com, pg 580

Writers' Trust Engel Findley Award, 600-460 Richmond St W, Toronto, ON M5V 1Y1, Canada *Tel:* 416-504-8222 *Toll Free Tel:* 877-906-6548 *Fax:* 416-504-9090 *E-mail:* info@writerstrust.com *Web Site:* www.writerstrust.com, pg 680

Writers' Trust McClelland & Stewart Journey Prize, 600-460 Richmond St W, Toronto, ON M5V 1Y1, Canada *Tel:* 416-504-8222 *Toll Free Tel:* 877-906-6548 *Fax:* 416-504-9090 *E-mail:* info@writerstrust.com *Web Site:* www.writerstrust.com, pg 680

The Writers' Union of Canada (TWUC), 600-460 Richmond St W, Toronto, ON M5V 1Y1, Canada *Tel:* 416-703-8982 *Fax:* 416-504-9090 *E-mail:* info@writersunion.ca *Web Site:* www.writersunion.ca, pg 549

The Writers Workshop, Finn House, 102 W Wiggin St, Gambier, OH 43022 *Tel:* 740-427-5207 *Fax:* 740-427-5417 *E-mail:* kenyonreview@kenyon.edu *Web Site:* www.kenyonreview.org, pg 580

WritersWeekly.com's 24-Hour Short Story Contest, 5726 Cortez Rd, Suite 349, Bradenton, FL 34210 *Fax:* 305-768-0261 *Web Site:* www.writersweekly.com, pg 680

The Writing Center, 601 E Palisade Ave, Suite 4, Englewood Cliffs, NJ 07632 *Tel:* 201-567-4017 *Fax:* 201-567-7202 *E-mail:* writingcenter@optonline.net *Web Site:* www.writingcenternj.com, pg 580

Writing Workshops, 1333 Research Park Dr, Davis, CA 95618 *Tel:* 510-642-6362 *E-mail:* extension@ucdavis.edu *Web Site:* extension.ucdavis.edu; writing.ucdavis.edu, pg 580

The Wylie Agency LLC, 250 W 57 St, Suite 2114, New York, NY 10107 *Tel:* 212-246-0069 *Fax:* 212-586-8953 *E-mail:* mail@wylieagency.com *Web Site:* www.wylieagency.com, pg 509

Wyman Indexing, 1311 Delaware Ave SW, No S332, Washington, DC 20024 *Tel:* 443-336-5497 *Web Site:* www.wymanindexing.com, pg 472

Wyndham Hall Press, 10372 W Munro Lake Dr, Levering, MI 49755 *Tel:* 419-648-9124 *E-mail:* orders@wyndhamhallpress.com *Web Site:* www.wyndhamhallpress.com, pg 246

Wyoming Arts Council Creative Writing Fellowships, Barrett Bldg, 2nd fl, 2301 Central Ave, Cheyenne, WY 82002 *Tel:* 307-777-7742 *Web Site:* wyoarts.state.wy.us, pg 681

Xist Publishing, PO Box 61593, Irvine, CA 92602 *Tel:* 949-478-2568 *E-mail:* info@xistpublishing.com *Web Site:* www.xistpublishing.com, pg 246

Xlibris Corp, 1663 Liberty Dr, Suite 200, Bloomington, IN 47403 *Toll Free Tel:* 844-714-8691; 888-795-4274 *Fax:* 610-915-0294 *E-mail:* info@xlibris.com; media@xlibris.com *Web Site:* www.xlibris.com; www.authorsolutions.com/our-imprints/xlibris, pg 246

XML Press, 24310 Moulton Pkwy, Suite O-175, Laguna Hills, CA 92637 *Tel:* 970-231-3624 *E-mail:* publisher@xmlpress.net *Web Site:* xmlpress.net, pg 246

YA Fiction Workshop, 2617 NW Thurman St, Portland, OR 97210 *Tel:* 503-473-8663 *Web Site:* tinhouse.com/ya-workshop, pg 580

Yaddo Artists Residency, 312 Union Ave, Saratoga Springs, NY 12866 *Tel:* 518-584-0746 *Fax:* 518-584-1312 *E-mail:* yaddo@yaddo.org *Web Site:* www.yaddo.org, pg 580

Yale Center for British Art, 1080 Chapel St, New Haven, CT 06510-2302 *Tel:* 203-432-8929 *Fax:* 203-432-1626 *E-mail:* ycba.publications@yale.edu *Web Site:* britishart.yale.edu, pg 246

Yale Series of Younger Poets, 302 Temple St, New Haven, CT 06511 *Tel:* 203-432-0960 *Fax:* 203-432-0948 *E-mail:* ysyp@yale.edu *Web Site:* youngerpoets.yupnet.org, pg 681

Yale University Press, 302 Temple St, New Haven, CT 06511-8909 *Tel:* 203-432-0960; 203-432-0966 (sales); 401-531-2800 (cust serv) *Toll Free Tel:* 800-405-1619 (cust serv) *Fax:* 203-432-0948; 203-432-8485 (sales); 401-531-2801 (cust serv) *Toll Free Fax:* 800-406-9145 (cust serv) *E-mail:* sales.press@yale.edu (sales); customer.care@triliteral.org (cust serv) *Web Site:* www.yalebooks.com; yalepress.yale.edu/yupbooks, pg 246

Anne & Philip Yandle Best Article Award, PO Box 448, Fort Langley, BC V1M 2R7, Canada *E-mail:* info@bchistory.ca *Web Site:* www.bchistory.ca/awards, pg 681

The Yao Enterprises (Literary Agents) LLC, 67 Banksville Rd, Armonk, NY 10504 *Tel:* 914-765-0296 *E-mail:* yaollc@gmail.com, pg 509

Yard Dog Press, 710 W Redbud Lane, Alma, AR 72921-7247 *Tel:* 479-632-4693 *Fax:* 479-632-4693 *Web Site:* www.yarddogpress.com, pg 247

YBK Publishers Inc, 39 Crosby St, New York, NY 10013 *Tel:* 212-219-0135 *E-mail:* readmybook@ybkpublishers.com; info@ybkpublishers.com *Web Site:* www.ybkpublishers.com, pg 247

YES New Play Festival, 205 FA Theatre Dept, Nunn Dr, Highland Heights, KY 41099-1007 *Tel:* 859-572-6362 *Fax:* 859-572-6057, pg 681

Yeshiva University Press, 500 W 185 St, New York, NY 10033 *Tel:* 212-960-5400 *Web Site:* www.yu.edu/books, pg 247

YMAA Publication Center Inc, PO Box 480, Wolfeboro, NH 03894 *Tel:* 603-569-7988 *Toll Free Tel:* 800-669-8892 *Fax:* 603-569-1889 *E-mail:* info@ymaa.com *Web Site:* www.ymaa.com, pg 247

Yotzeret Publishing, PO Box 18662, St Paul, MN 55118-0662 *Tel:* 651-470-3853 *Fax:* 651-224-7447 *E-mail:* info@yotzeretpublishing.com; orders@yotzeretpublishing.com *Web Site:* yotzeretpublishing.com, pg 247

The Young Agency, 213 Bennett Ave, No 3H, New York, NY 10040 *Tel:* 212-229-2612, pg 509

Young Lions Fiction Award, 445 Fifth Ave, 4th fl, New York, NY 10016 *Tel:* 212-930-0887 *Fax:* 212-930-0983 *E-mail:* younglions@nypl.org *Web Site:* www.nypl.org, pg 681

Phyllis Smart-Young Poetry Prize, University of Wisconsin, 6193 Helen C White Hall, English Dept, 600 N Park St, Madison, WI 53706 *E-mail:* madisonrevw@gmail.com *Web Site:* www.themadisonrevw.com, pg 681

Young Writers Award, c/o 3225 N 91 St, Milwaukee, WI 53222 *E-mail:* wiswriters@gmail.com *Web Site:* wiswriters.org/awards, pg 681

Young Writers' Workshop, 919 Main St, Osterville, MA 02655 *Tel:* 508-420-0200 *E-mail:* writers@capecodwriterscenter.org *Web Site:* capecodwriterscenter.org, pg 580

YoungArts, 2100 Biscayne Blvd, Miami, FL 33137 *Tel:* 305-377-1140 *Toll Free Tel:* 800-970-ARTS (970-2787) *E-mail:* info@youngarts.org; apply@youngarts.org *Web Site:* www.youngarts.org, pg 681

YWAM Publishing, PO Box 55787, Seattle, WA 98155-0787 *Tel:* 425-771-1153 *Toll Free Tel:* 800-922-2143 *Fax:* 425-775-2383 *E-mail:* books@ywampublishing.com *Web Site:* www.ywampublishing.com, pg 247

Morton Dauwen Zabel Award, 633 W 155 St, New York, NY 10032 *Tel:* 212-368-5900 *Fax:* 212-491-4615 *E-mail:* academy@artsandletters.org *Web Site:* artsandletters.org, pg 681

Zagat Inc, 424 Broadway, 5th fl, New York, NY 10013 *Toll Free Tel:* 800-540-9609 *E-mail:* feedback@zagat.com; press@zagat.com *Web Site:* www.zagat.com, pg 247

Barbara & David Zalaznick Book Prize in American History, 170 Central Park W, New York, NY 10024 *Tel:* 212-873-3400 *Fax:* 212-595-5707 *E-mail:* info@nyhistory.org *Web Site:* www.nyhistory.org/news/book-prize, pg 681

Zaner-Bloser Inc, 1400 Goodale Blvd, Suite 200, Grandview Heights, OH 43212 *Toll Free Tel:* 800-421-3018 (cust serv) *Toll Free Fax:* 800-992-6087 (orders) *E-mail:* customerexperience@zaner-bloser.com *Web Site:* www.zaner-bloser.com, pg 247

Zebra Communications, 230 Deerchase Dr, Woodstock, GA 30188-4438 *Tel:* 770-924-0528 *E-mail:* bobbie@zebraeditor.com *Web Site:* www.zebraeditor.com, pg 472

Zeig, Tucker & Theisen Inc, 2632 E Thomas Rd, Suite 201, Phoenix, AZ 85016 *Tel:* 480-389-4342 *Web Site:* www.zeigtucker.com, pg 248

Zest Books, 241 First Ave N, Minneapolis, MN 55401 *Tel:* 612-332-3344 *Toll Free Tel:* 800-328-4929 *Toll Free Fax:* 800-332-1132 *E-mail:* info@lernerbooks.com; publicity@lernerbooks.com; custserve@lernerbooks.com (orders) *Web Site:* lernerbooks.com, pg 248

The Jacob Zilber Prize for Short Fiction, University of British Columbia, Buch E462, 1866 Main Mall, Vancouver, BC V6T 1Z1, Canada *Tel:* 778-822-2514 *Fax:* 778-822-3616 *E-mail:* prismwritingcontest@gmail.com *Web Site:* www.prismmagazine.ca, pg 681

Barbara J Zitwer Agency, 525 West End Ave, Unit 11-H, New York, NY 10024 *Tel:* 212-501-8423 *E-mail:* zitwer@gmail.com, pg 509

Robert Zolnerzak, 101 Clark St, Unit 20-K, Brooklyn, NY 11201 *Tel:* 718-522-0591 *E-mail:* rzolnerzak@gmail.com, pg 472

Charlotte Zolotow Award, 225 N Mills St, Rm 401, Madison, WI 53706 *Tel:* 608-263-3720 *E-mail:* ccbcinfo@education.wisc.edu *Web Site:* ccbs.education.wisc.edu/books/zolotow.asp, pg 681

Zondervan, 3900 Sparks Dr, Grand Rapids, MI 49546 *Tel:* 616-698-6900 *Toll Free Tel:* 800-226-1122; 800-727-1309 (retail orders) *Fax:* 616-698-3350 *Toll Free Fax:* 800-698-3256 (retail orders) *Web Site:* www.zondervan.com, pg 248

Zone Books, 633 Vanderbilt St, Brooklyn, NY 11218 *Tel:* 718-686-0048 *Fax:* 718-686-9045 *E-mail:* info@zonebooks.org *Web Site:* www.zonebooks.org, pg 248

Anna Zornio Memorial Children's Theatre Playwriting Award, D22 Paul Creative Arts Center, 30 Academic Way, Durham, NH 03824 *Tel:* 603-862-2919 *Fax:* 603-862-0298 *Web Site:* cola.unh.edu/theatre-dance/resource/zornio, pg 682

Zumaya Publications LLC, 3209 S Interstate 35, Suite 1086, Austin, TX 78741 *Tel:* 512-333-4055 *Fax:* 512-276-6745 *E-mail:* publisher@zumayapublications.com; acquisitions@zumayapublications.com *Web Site:* www.zumayapublications.com, pg 248

Personnel Index

Included in this index are the personnel included in the entries in this volume of *LMP*, along with the page number(s) on which they appear. Not included in this index are those individuals associated with listings in the **Calendar of Book Trade & Promotional Events; Reference Books for the Trade** and **Magazines for the Trade** sections. Also, personnel associated with secondary addresses within listings (such as branch offices, sales offices, editorial offices, etc.) are not included.

Aalto, Helena, Canadian Society of Children's Authors, Illustrators & Performers (CANSCAIP), 720 Bathurst St, Suite 503, Toronto, ON M5S 2R4, Canada *Tel:* 416-515-1559 *E-mail:* office@canscaip.org *Web Site:* www.canscaip.org, pg 530

Aardema, John, Sourcebooks LLC, 1935 Brookdale Rd, Suite 139, Naperville, IL 60563 *Tel:* 630-961-3900 *Toll Free Tel:* 800-432-7444 *Fax:* 630-961-2168 *E-mail:* info@sourcebooks.com; customersupport@sourcebooks.com *Web Site:* www.sourcebooks.com, pg 204

Aaron, David H, Hebrew Union College Press, 3101 Clifton Ave, Cincinnati, OH 45220 *Tel:* 513-221-1875 *Fax:* 513-221-0321 *Web Site:* press.huc.edu, pg 97

Aaronson, Deborah, Phaidon, 65 Bleecker St, 8th fl, New York, NY 10012 *Tel:* 212-652-5400 *Toll Free Tel:* 800-759-0190 (cust serv) *Fax:* 212-652-5410 *Toll Free Fax:* 800-286-9471 (cust serv) *E-mail:* enquiries@phaidon.com *Web Site:* www.phaidon.com, pg 168

Aaronson, Whitney, Random House Children's Books, 1745 Broadway, 10th fl, New York, NY 10019 *Tel:* 212-782-9000 *Web Site:* www.randomhousekids.com, pg 181

Abbate, Gabriella, Houghton Mifflin Harcourt Trade & Reference Division, 125 High St, Boston, MA 02110 *Tel:* 617-351-5000 *Web Site:* www.hmhco.com, pg 104

Abbate, Megan, Roaring Brook Press, 120 Broadway, New York, NY 10271 *Tel:* 646-307-5151 *Web Site:* us.macmillan.com/publishers/roaring-brook-press, pg 186

Abbey, Caroline, Random House Children's Books, 1745 Broadway, 10th fl, New York, NY 10019 *Tel:* 212-782-9000 *Web Site:* www.randomhousekids.com, pg 180

Abbott, George, AFB Press, 1401 S Clark St, Suite 730, Arlington, VA 22202 *Tel:* 304-710-3043 *Toll Free Tel:* 800-232-3044 (orders) *Fax:* 917-210-3979 (orders) *E-mail:* afbpress@afb.net *Web Site:* www.afb.org, pg 5

Abbott, Joseph P Jr, Houghton Mifflin Harcourt, 125 High St, Boston, MA 02110 *Tel:* 617-351-5000 *Toll Free Tel:* 855-969-4642; 800-225-5425 (K-12 educ materials); 800-323-9540 (assessment materials); 877-219-1537 (SkillsTutor); 888-242-6747 (Innovation in Educ Group); 800-225-3362 (Trade & Ref Div) *Toll Free Fax:* 800-269-5232 *E-mail:* myhmhco@hmhco.com *Web Site:* www.hmhco.com, pg 103

Abbott, Lee K, The Flannery O'Connor Award for Short Fiction, Main Library, 3rd fl, 320 S Jackson St, Athens, GA 30602 *Fax:* 706-542-2558 *Web Site:* www.ugapress.org, pg 650

Abdelmoumen, Melikah, Les Editions de l'Hexagone, 4545, rue Frontenac, 3rd fl, Montreal, QC H2H 2R7, Canada *Tel:* 514-849-5259 *Web Site:* www.edhexagone.com, pg 422

Abdelmoumen, Melikah, VLB editeur, 4545, rue Frontenac, 3rd fl, Montreal, QC H2H 2R7, Canada *Tel:* 514-849-5259 *Web Site:* www.edvlb.com, pg 445

Abdo, Jim, ABDO Publishing Co Inc, 8000 W 78 St, Suite 310, Edina, MN 55439 *Tel:* 952-698-2403 *Toll Free Tel:* 800-800-1312 *Fax:* 952-831-1632 *Toll Free Fax:* 800-862-3480 *E-mail:* customerservice@abdopublishing.com; info@abdopublishing.com *Web Site:* abdopublishing.com, pg 2

Abdo, Paul, ABDO Publishing Co Inc, 8000 W 78 St, Suite 310, Edina, MN 55439 *Tel:* 952-698-2403 *Toll Free Tel:* 800-800-1312 *Fax:* 952-831-1632 *Toll

Free Fax:* 800-862-3480 *E-mail:* customerservice@abdopublishing.com; info@abdopublishing.com *Web Site:* abdopublishing.com, pg 2

Abe, Carol, University of Hawaii Press, 2840 Kolowalu St, Honolulu, HI 96822-1888 *Tel:* 808-956-8255 *Toll Free Tel:* 888-UHPRESS (847-7377) *Fax:* 808-988-6052 *Toll Free Fax:* 800-650-7811 *E-mail:* uhpbooks@hawaii.edu *Web Site:* www.uhpress.hawaii.edu, pg 227

Abel, Dominick, Dominick Abel Literary Agency Inc, 146 W 82 St, Suite 1-A, New York, NY 10024 *Tel:* 212-877-0710 *Fax:* 212-595-3133 *E-mail:* agency@dalainc.com *Web Site:* www.dalainc.com, pg 473

Abell, Whitley, The Jennifer DeChiara Literary Agency, 245 Park Ave, 39th fl, New York, NY 10167 *Tel:* 212-372-8989 *Web Site:* www.jdlit.com, pg 481

Abellera, Lisa, Kimberley Cameron & Associates LLC, 1550 Tiburon Blvd, Suite 704, Tiburon, CA 94920 *Tel:* 415-789-9191 *Fax:* 415-789-9177 *Web Site:* www.kimberleycameron.com, pg 479

Abfier, Mel, StarGroup International Inc, 1194 Old Dixie Hwy, Suite 201, West Palm Beach, FL 33413 *Tel:* 561-547-0667 *Fax:* 561-843-8530 *E-mail:* info@stargroupinternational.com *Web Site:* www.stargroupinternational.com, pg 207

Abid, Masood, Magazines Canada (MC), 555 Richmond St W, Suite 604, Mailbox 201, Toronto, ON M5V 3B1, Canada *Tel:* 416-504-0274 *Fax:* 416-504-0437 *E-mail:* info@magazinescanada.ca *Web Site:* magazinescanada.ca, pg 537

Abkemeier, Laurie, DeFiore and Company Literary Management Inc, 47 E 19 St, 3rd fl, New York, NY 10003 *Tel:* 212-925-7744 *Fax:* 212-925-9803 *E-mail:* info@defliterary.com; submissions@defliterary.com *Web Site:* www.defliterary.com, pg 481

Ableman, Brian, The Learning Source Ltd, 644 Tenth St, Brooklyn, NY 11215 *E-mail:* info@learningsourceltd.com *Web Site:* www.learningsourceltd.com, pg 466

Ables, Anna, Cunningham Commission for Youth Theatre, Lincoln Park Campus, 2350 N Racine Ave, Chicago, IL 60614-4100 *Tel:* 773-325-7999 *Fax:* 773-325-7920 *E-mail:* cunninghamcommission@depaul.edu *Web Site:* theatre.depaul.edu, pg 608

Abraham, Tree, Bloomsbury Publishing Inc, 1385 Broadway, 5th fl, New York, NY 10018 *Tel:* 212-419-5300 *E-mail:* marketingusa@bloomsbury.com; adultpublicityusa@bloomsbury.com; askacademic@bloomsbury.com *Web Site:* www.bloomsbury.com, pg 36

Abrahamsen, Eric, Candied Plums, 7548 Ravenna Ave NE, Seattle, WA 98115 *E-mail:* candiedplums@gmail.com *Web Site:* www.candiedplums.com, pg 44

Abrami, Jenny, Sasquatch Books, 1904 S Third Ave, Suite 710, Seattle, WA 98101 *Tel:* 206-467-4300 *Toll Free Tel:* 800-775-0817 *Fax:* 206-467-4301 *E-mail:* custserv@sasquatchbooks.com *Web Site:* sasquatchbooks.com, pg 192

Abramo, Lauren E, Dystel, Goderich & Bourret LLC, One Union Sq W, Suite 904, New York, NY 10003 *Tel:* 212-627-9100 *Fax:* 212-627-9313 *Web Site:* www.dystel.com, pg 482

Abrams, Joanne, Square One Publishers Inc, 115 Herricks Rd, Garden City Park, NY 11040 *Tel:* 516-535-2010 *Toll Free Tel:* 877-900-BOOK (900-2665) *Fax:* 516-535-2014 *E-mail:* sq1publish@aol.com *Web Site:* www.squareonepublishers.com, pg 206

Abrams, Liesa, Simon & Schuster Children's Publishing, 1230 Avenue of the Americas, New York, NY 10020 *Tel:* 212-698-7000 *Web Site:* www.simonandschuster.com/kids; www.simonandschuster.com/teen; simonandschuster.net; simonandschuster.biz, pg 199

Abrams, Robert, Columbia University Press, 61 W 62 St, New York, NY 10023 *Tel:* 212-459-0600 *Toll Free Tel:* 800-944-8648 *Fax:* 212-459-3678 *Web Site:* cup.columbia.edu, pg 55

Abrams, Robert E, Abbeville Press, 655 Third Ave, New York, NY 10017 *Tel:* 212-366-5585 *Toll Free Tel:* 800-ART-BOOK (278-2665); 800-343-4499 (orders) *Fax:* 646-375-2359 *Toll Free Fax:* 800-351-5073 (orders) *E-mail:* abbeville@abbeville.com; sales@abbeville.com; marketing@abbeville.com; rights@abbeville.com *Web Site:* www.abbeville.com, pg 2

Abrams, Robert E, Abbeville Publishing Group, 655 Third Ave, New York, NY 10017 *Tel:* 646-375-2136 *Fax:* 646-375-2359 *E-mail:* abbeville@abbeville.com; marketing@abbeville.com; sales@abbeville.com; rights@abbeville.com *Web Site:* www.abbeville.com, pg 2

Abu-Baker, Reem, Black Warrior Review Fiction, Nonfiction & Poetry Contest, Off of Student Media, University of Alabama, Tuscaloosa, AL 35486-0027 *Tel:* 205-348-4518 *Web Site:* www.bwr.ua.edu, pg 599

Accardi, Ben, Andrews McMeel Publishing LLC, 1130 Walnut St, Kansas City, MO 64106-2109 *Toll Free Tel:* 800-851-8923; 800-943-9839 (cust serv) *Toll Free Fax:* 800-943-9831 (orders) *E-mail:* sales@amuniversal.com *Web Site:* www.andrewsmcmeel.com; publishing.andrewsmcmeel.com, pg 16

Acevedo, Amanda, Houghton Mifflin Harcourt Trade & Reference Division, 125 High St, Boston, MA 02110 *Tel:* 617-351-5000 *Web Site:* www.hmhco.com, pg 104

Aceves Garcia, Alexis, Counterpoint Press LLC, 2560 Ninth St, Suite 318, Berkeley, CA 94710 *Tel:* 510-704-0230 *Fax:* 510-704-0268 *E-mail:* info@counterpointpress.com *Web Site:* counterpointpress.com; softskull.com, pg 58

Ackell, Melinda, Random House Children's Books, 1745 Broadway, 10th fl, New York, NY 10019 *Tel:* 212-782-9000 *Web Site:* www.randomhousekids.com, pg 180

Ackerman, Jon, Highlights for Children Inc, 815 Church St, Honesdale, PA 18431 *Tel:* 570-253-1164 *Toll Free Tel:* 800-490-5111 *Fax:* 570-253-0179 *E-mail:* salesandmarketing@highlightspress.com *Web Site:* www.highlightspress.com; www.highlights.com; www.facebook.com/HighlightsforChildren, pg 99

Ackerman, Larissa, Kensington Publishing Corp, 119 W 40 St, New York, NY 10018 *Tel:* 212-407-1500 *Toll Free Tel:* 800-221-2647 *Fax:* 212-935-0699 *Web Site:* www.kensingtonbooks.com, pg 116

Acland, Marigold, Cambridge University Press, One Liberty Plaza, 20th fl, New York, NY 10006 *Tel:* 212-924-3900; 212-337-5000 *Fax:* 212-691-3239; 845-353-4141 *E-mail:* newyork@cambridge.org; customer_service@cambridge.org *Web Site:* www.cambridge.org/us, pg 43

Acquarola, Amy, Swedenborg Foundation, 320 N Church St, West Chester, PA 19380 *Tel:* 610-430-3222 *Toll Free Tel:* 800-355-3222 (cust serv) *Fax:* 610-430-7982 *E-mail:* info@swedenborg.com *Web Site:* swedenborg.com, pg 211

Adamo, John, Random House Children's Books, 1745 Broadway, 10th fl, New York, NY 10019 *Tel:* 212-782-9000 *Web Site:* www.randomhousekids.com, pg 180

Adams, Benjamin, Perseus Books, 1290 Avenue of the Americas, New York, NY 10104 *Tel:* 212-340-8100 *Toll Free Tel:* 800-343-4499 (cust serv) *Fax:* 212-340-8105 *Web Site:* www.perseusbooks.com, pg 167

Adams, Carrie Olivia, University of Chicago Press, 1427 E 60 St, Chicago, IL 60637-2954 *Tel:* 773-702-7700; 773-702-7600 *Toll Free Tel:* 800-621-2736 (orders) *Fax:* 773-702-9756; 773-660-2235 (orders); 773-702-2708 *E-mail:* custserv@press.uchicago.edu; marketing@press.uchicago.edu *Web Site:* www.press.uchicago.edu, pg 226

Adams, Chris, National Press Foundation, 1211 Connecticut Ave NW, Suite 310, Washington, DC 20036 *Tel:* 202-663-7280 *Web Site:* nationalpress.org, pg 540

Adams, Chuck, Algonquin Books, 400 Silver Cedar Ct, Suite 300, Chapel Hill, NC 27514-1585 *Tel:* 919-967-0108 *Fax:* 919-933-0272 *E-mail:* inquiry@algonquin.com *Web Site:* www.workman.com/algonquin, pg 7

Adams, Devinn, Arcadia Publishing Inc, 420 Wando Park Blvd, Mount Pleasant, SC 29464 *Tel:* 843-853-2070 *Toll Free Tel:* 888-313-2665 (orders only) *Fax:* 843-853-0044 *E-mail:* sales@arcadiapublishing.com *Web Site:* www.arcadiapublishing.com, pg 19

Adams, Jen, Sounds True Inc, 413 S Arthur Ave, Louisville, CO 80027 *Tel:* 303-665-3151 *Toll Free Tel:* 800-333-9185 (US); 888-303-9185 (US & CN) *E-mail:* customerservice@soundstrue.com; stpublicity@soundstrue.com *Web Site:* www.soundstrue.com, pg 204

Adams, Katie Henderson, W W Norton & Company Inc, 500 Fifth Ave, New York, NY 10110-0017 *Tel:* 212-354-5500 *Toll Free Tel:* 800-233-4830 (orders & cust serv) *Fax:* 212-869-0856 *Toll Free Fax:* 800-458-6515 *E-mail:* orders@wwnorton.com *Web Site:* wwnorton.com, pg 152

Adams, Kelli, Counterpoint Press LLC, 2560 Ninth St, Suite 318, Berkeley, CA 94710 *Tel:* 510-704-0230 *Fax:* 510-704-0268 *E-mail:* info@counterpointpress.com *Web Site:* counterpointpress.com; softskull.com, pg 58

Adams, Lauren, Random House Children's Books, 1745 Broadway, 10th fl, New York, NY 10019 *Tel:* 212-782-9000 *Web Site:* www.randomhousekids.com, pg 181

Adams, Lisa, The Garamond Agency Inc, 12 Horton St, Newburyport, MA 01950 *E-mail:* query@garamondagency.com *Web Site:* www.garamondagency.com, pg 485

Adams, Martha, Leisure Arts Inc, 104 Champs Blvd, Suite 100, Maumelle, AR 72113 *Tel:* 501-868-8800 *Toll Free Tel:* 800-643-8030 *Toll Free Fax:* 877-710-5603 (catalog) *E-mail:* customer_service@leisurearts.com *Web Site:* www.leisurearts.com, pg 122

Adams, Matthew, Between the Lines, 401 Richmond St W, No 277, Toronto, ON M5V 3A8, Canada *Tel:* 416-535-9914 *Toll Free Tel:* 800-718-7201 *Fax:* 416-535-1484 *E-mail:* info@btlbooks.com *Web Site:* btlbooks.com, pg 416

Adams, Dr Michael, Dobie Paisano Fellowship Program, 110 Inner Campus Dr, Stop G0400, Austin, TX 78712-0710 *Fax:* 512-471-7620 *Web Site:* dobiepaisano.utexas.edu, pg 652

Adams, Stephanie, Stanford University Press, 425 Broadway St, Redwood City, CA 94063-3126 *Tel:* 650-723-9434 *Fax:* 650-725-3457 *E-mail:* info@www.sup.org; publicity@www.sup.org; sales@www.sup.org *Web Site:* www.sup.org, pg 206

Adams, Terry, Little, Brown and Company, 1290 Avenue of the Americas, New York, NY 10104 *Tel:* 212-364-1100 *Fax:* 212-364-0952 *E-mail:* firstname.lastname@hbgusa.com *Web Site:* www.littlebrown.com; www.hachettebookgroup.com, pg 125

Adams, Wesley, Farrar, Straus & Giroux Books for Young Readers, 120 Broadway, New York, NY 10271 *Tel:* 212-741-6900 *Toll Free Tel:* 888-330-8477 (orders) *Fax:* 212-633-9385 *Web Site:* us.macmillan.com/mackids, pg 76

Adams, William, University of South Carolina Press, 1600 Hampton St, Suite 544, Columbia, SC 29208 *Tel:* 803-777-5245 *Toll Free Tel:* 800-768-2500 (orders) *Fax:* 803-777-0160 *Toll Free Fax:* 800-868-0740 (orders) *Web Site:* www.sc.edu/uscpress, pg 231

Addo, Michelle, Kensington Publishing Corp, 119 W 40 St, New York, NY 10018 *Tel:* 212-407-1500 *Toll Free Tel:* 800-221-2647 *Fax:* 212-935-0699 *Web Site:* www.kensingtonbooks.com, pg 116

Addo, Stephan, Association for Information Science & Technology (ASIS&T), 8555 16 St, Suite 850, Silver Spring, MD 20910 *Tel:* 301-495-0900 *Fax:* 301-495-0810 *E-mail:* asist@asist.org *Web Site:* www.asist.org, pg 525

Adel, Judith, J Adel Art & Design, 586 Ramapo Rd, Teaneck, NJ 07666 *Tel:* 201-836-2606 *E-mail:* jadelnj@aol.com, pg 457

Aders-Weremczuk, Coco, Federation of BC Writers, PO Box 16028, 617 Belmont St, New Westminster, BC V3M 6W6, Canada *E-mail:* info@bcwriters.ca *Web Site:* bcwriters.ca, pg 533

Adjemian, Robert, Vedanta Press, 1946 Vedanta Place, Hollywood, CA 90068 *Tel:* 323-960-1728; 323-960-1736 (catalog) *Fax:* 323-465-9568 *E-mail:* vpress@vedanta.com *Web Site:* www.vedanta.com, pg 235

Adkins, David, Council of State Governments, 1776 Avenue of the States, Lexington, KY 40511 *Tel:* 859-244-8000 *Toll Free Tel:* 800-800-1910 *Fax:* 859-244-8001 *E-mail:* sales@csg.org *Web Site:* www.csg.org; csgstore.org, pg 58

Adler, Allan R, Association of American Publishers (AAP), 455 Massachusetts Ave NW, Suite 700, Washington, DC 20001-2777 *Tel:* 202-347-3375 *Fax:* 202-347-3690 *E-mail:* info@publishers.org *Web Site:* publishers.org, pg 526

Adler, Allison, Andrews McMeel Publishing LLC, 1130 Walnut St, Kansas City, MO 64106-2109 *Toll Free Tel:* 800-851-8923; 800-943-9839 (cust serv) *Toll Free Fax:* 800-943-9831 (orders) *E-mail:* sales@amuniversal.com *Web Site:* www.andrewsmcmeel.com; publishing.andrewsmcmeel.com, pg 16

Adler, Alyssa, Penguin Group USA, A Penguin Random House Company, 375 Hudson St, New York, NY 10014 *Tel:* 212-366-2000 *Toll Free Tel:* 800-847-5515 (inside sales); 800-631-8571 (cust serv) *Fax:* 212-366-2666; 607-775-4829 (inside sales) *E-mail:* online@us.penguingroup.com *Web Site:* www.penguin.com, pg 163

Adler, Alyssa, Portfolio, 375 Hudson St, New York, NY 10014 *Web Site:* www.penguin.com/meet/publishers/portfolio, pg 172

Adler, Ellen, The New Press, 120 Wall St, 31st fl, New York, NY 10005 *Tel:* 212-629-8802 *Toll Free Tel:* 800-343-4489 (orders) *Fax:* 212-629-8617 *Toll Free Fax:* 800-351-5073 (orders) *E-mail:* newpress@thenewpress.com *Web Site:* www.thenewpress.com, pg 149

Adler, Eve, Sterling Publishing Co Inc, 1166 Avenue of the Americas, 17th fl, New York, NY 10036-2715 *Tel:* 212-532-7160 *Toll Free Tel:* 800-367-9692 *Fax:* 212-213-2495 *Toll Free Fax:* 800-542-7567 *E-mail:* custservice@sterlingpublishing.com; customerservice@sterlingpublishing.com; editorial@sterlingpublishing.com; tradesales@sterlingpublishing.com *Web Site:* www.sterlingpublishing.com, pg 208

Adler, Laina, HarperCollins General Books Group, 195 Broadway, New York, NY 10007 *Tel:* 212-207-7000 *Web Site:* www.harpercollins.com, pg 93

Adler-Kozak, Mary, National Association of College Stores (NACS), 500 E Lorain St, Oberlin, OH 44074 *Toll Free Tel:* 800-622-7498 *Fax:* 440-775-4769 *Web Site:* www.nacs.org, pg 538

Agnew, Tim, Concordia Publishing House, 3558 S Jefferson Ave, St Louis, MO 63118-3968 *Tel:* 314-268-1000; 314-268-1268 (bookshop) *Toll Free Tel:* 800-325-3040 (cust serv) *Toll Free Fax:* 800-490-9889 (cust serv) *E-mail:* order@cph.org *Web Site:* www.cph.org, pg 56

Agree, Peter A, University of Pennsylvania Press, 3905 Spruce St, Philadelphia, PA 19104 *Tel:* 215-898-6261 *Fax:* 215-898-0404 *E-mail:* custserv@pobox.upenn.edu *Web Site:* www.pennpress.org, pg 230

Agro, Janine, Soho Press Inc, 853 Broadway, New York, NY 10003 *Tel:* 212-260-1900 *E-mail:* soho@sohopress.com; publicity@sohopress.com *Web Site:* sohopress.com, pg 203

Aguilo, Maria Jesus, Berrett-Koehler Publishers Inc, 1333 Broadway, Suite 1000, Oakland, CA 94612 *Tel:* 510-817-2277 *Fax:* 510-817-2278 *E-mail:* bkpub@bkpub.com *Web Site:* www.bkconnection.com, pg 32

Aguirre, Danielle, National Music Publishers' Association (NMPA), 975 "F" St NW, Suite 375, Washington, DC 20004 *Tel:* 202-393-6672 *E-mail:* members@nmpa.org *Web Site:* nmpa.org, pg 540

Agyemang, Elizabeth, Houghton Mifflin Harcourt Trade & Reference Division, 125 High St, Boston, MA 02110 *Tel:* 617-351-5000 *Web Site:* www.hmhco.com, pg 104

Ahadi, Julia, Penny-Farthing Productions, One Sugar Creek Center Blvd, Suite 820, Sugar Land, TX 77478 *Tel:* 713-780-0300 *Toll Free Tel:* 800-926-2669 *Fax:* 713-780-4004 *E-mail:* corp@pfproductions.com *Web Site:* www.pfproductions.com, pg 166

Ahearn, Pamela G, The Ahearn Agency Inc, 2021 Pine St, New Orleans, LA 70118 *Tel:* 504-861-8395 *Fax:* 504-866-6434 *Web Site:* www.ahearnagency.com, pg 474

Ahern, G Thomas, Capstone Publishers™, 1710 Roe Crest Dr, North Mankato, MN 56003 *Toll Free Tel:* 800-747-4992 (cust serv) *Toll Free Fax:* 888-262-0705 *E-mail:* customer.service@capstonepub.com *Web Site:* www.capstonepub.com, pg 44

Aherne, Tavy, Indiana University African Studies Program, Indiana University, 355 N Jordan, Rm GA 3072, Bloomington, IN 47405 *Tel:* 812-855-8284 *Fax:* 812-855-6734 *E-mail:* afrist@indiana.edu *Web Site:* www.indiana.edu/~afrist; www.go.iu.edu/afrist, pg 107

Ahlquist, Susan, Second Chance Press, 4170 Noyac Rd, Sag Harbor, NY 11963 *Tel:* 631-725-1101 *E-mail:* info@thepermanentpress.com *Web Site:* www.thepermanentpress.com, pg 196

Ahmad, Ibrahim, Akashic Books, 232 Third St, Suite A-115, Brooklyn, NY 11215 *Tel:* 718-643-9193 *Fax:* 718-643-9195 *E-mail:* info@akashicbooks.com *Web Site:* www.akashicbooks.com, pg 6

Ahn, Sophia, AIGA, the professional association for design, 222 Broadway, New York, NY 10038 *Tel:* 212-807-1990 *Fax:* 212-807-1799 *E-mail:* general@aiga.org *Web Site:* www.aiga.org, pg 521

Ahuja, Parveen, Kapp Books LLC, 3602 Rocky Meadow Ct, Fairfax, VA 22033 *Tel:* 703-261-9171 *Fax:* 703-621-7162 *E-mail:* info@kappbooks.com *Web Site:* www.kappbooks.com, pg 115

Aielli, Michelle, Perseus Books, 1290 Avenue of the Americas, New York, NY 10104 *Tel:* 212-340-8100 *Toll Free Tel:* 800-343-4499 (cust serv) *Fax:* 212-340-8105 *Web Site:* www.perseusbooks.com, pg 167

Ainsley, Martin, Goose Lane Editions, 500 Beaverbrook Ct, Suite 330, Fredericton, NB E3B 5X4, Canada *Tel:* 506-450-4251 *Toll Free Tel:* 888-926-8377 *Fax:* 506-459-4991 *E-mail:* info@gooselane.com; customerservice@gooselane.com *Web Site:* www.gooselane.com, pg 427

Aippersbach, Kim, Tradewind Books, 202-1807 Maritime Mews, Vancouver, BC V6H 3W7, Canada *Tel:* 604-662-4405 *E-mail:* tradewindbooks@yahoo.com; tradewindbooks@gmail.com *Web Site:* www.tradewindbooks.com, pg 442

Aitken, Daniel T, Wisdom Publications Inc, 199 Elm St, Somerville, MA 02144 *Tel:* 617-776-7416 *Toll Free Tel:* 800-272-4050 (orders) *Fax:* 617-776-7841 *E-mail:* info@wisdompubs.org; submission@wisdompubs.org *Web Site:* www.wisdompubs.org, pg 243

Aiwuyor, Jessica, Association of Research Libraries (ARL), 21 Dupont Circle NW, Suite 800, Washington, DC 20036 *Tel:* 202-296-2296 *Fax:* 202-872-0884 *E-mail:* webmgr@arl.org *Web Site:* www.arl.org, pg 23

Akers, Terrie, Other Press, 267 Fifth Ave, 6th fl, New York, NY 10016 *Tel:* 212-414-0054 *Toll Free Tel:* 877-843-6843 *Fax:* 212-414-0939 *E-mail:* editor@otherpress.com; marketing@otherpress.com; publicity@otherpress.com *Web Site:* www.otherpress.com, pg 157

Akinaka, James, Penguin Young Readers Group, 345 Hudson St, New York, NY 10014 *Tel:* 212-366-2000; 212-414-3553 *Fax:* 212-414-3340 *Web Site:* www.penguin.com/children, pg 165

Akoury-Ross, Lisa, SDP Publishing Solutions LLC, 36 Captain's Way, East Bridgewater, MA 02333 *Tel:* 617-775-0656 *Web Site:* www.sdppublishingsolutions.com, pg 470

Al-Faruque, Ferdous, National Press Club (NPC), 529 14 St NW, 13th fl, Washington, DC 20045 *Tel:* 202-662-7500 *Web Site:* www.press.org, pg 540

Al-Hillal, Semareh, Groundwood Books, 128 Sterling Rd, Lower Level, Toronto, ON M6R 2B7, Canada *Tel:* 416-363-4343 *Fax:* 416-363-1017 *E-mail:* genmail@groundwoodbooks.com *Web Site:* www.houseofanansi.com, pg 428

Alain, Louise, Les Editions Alire, 120 cote du Passage, Levis, QC G6V 5S9, Canada *Tel:* 418-835-4441 *Fax:* 418-838-4443 *E-mail:* info@alire.com *Web Site:* www.alire.com, pg 422

Alain, Marc, Modus Vivendi Publishing Inc, 55, rue Jean-Talon Ouest, Montreal, QC H2R-2W8, Canada *Tel:* 514-272-0433 *Fax:* 514-272-7234 *E-mail:* info@groupemodus.com *Web Site:* www.groupemodus.com, pg 433

Albanese, Frank, HarperCollins Publishers, 195 Broadway, New York, NY 10007 *Tel:* 212-207-7000 *Fax:* 212-207-7145 *Web Site:* www.harpercollins.com, pg 94

Albers, Wes, Southern California Writers' Conference (SCWC), 18160 Cottonwood Rd, Suite 260, Sunriver, OR 97707 *Tel:* 619-303-8185 *Fax:* 619-906-7462 *E-mail:* msg@writersconference.com *Web Site:* www.writersconference.com, pg 578

Albert, M Jean-Pierre, Les Editions Fides, 7333 place des Roseraies, bureau 100, Anjou, QC H1M 2X6, Canada *Tel:* 514-745-4290 *Fax:* 514-745-4299 *E-mail:* editions@groupefides.com *Web Site:* www.editionsfides.com, pg 423

Albiniak, Mike, Teton NewMedia Inc, 90 E Simpson, Suite 110, Jackson, WY 83001 *Tel:* 307-732-0028 *Toll Free Tel:* 877-306-9793 *Fax:* 307-734-0841 *E-mail:* sales@tetonnm.com *Web Site:* www.tetonnm.com, pg 215

Albrecht, Ms Geri, Heuer Publishing LLC, PO Box 248, Cedar Rapids, IA 52406 *Tel:* 319-368-8008 *Toll Free Tel:* 800-950-7529 *Fax:* 319-368-8011 *E-mail:* orders@heuerpub.com; customerservice@heuerpub.com *Web Site:* www.hitplays.com, pg 98

Alcala, Rosa, University of Texas at El Paso, Department of Creative Writing, MFA/Department of Creative Writing, 901 EDUC, 500 W University Ave, El Paso, TX 79968-9991 *Tel:* 915-747-5713 *Fax:* 915-747-5523 *E-mail:* creativewriting@utep.edu *Web Site:* www.utep.edu/cw, pg 586

Alcid, Dominick, Federal Bar Association, 1220 N Filmore St, Suite 444, Arlington, VA 22201 *Tel:* 571-481-9100 *Fax:* 571-481-9090 *E-mail:* fba@fedbar.org *Web Site:* www.fedbar.org, pg 76

Alcid, Edmond, Moose Hide Books, 684 Walls Rd, Prince Township, ON P6A 6K4, Canada *Tel:* 705-779-3331 *Fax:* 705-779-3331 *E-mail:* mooseenterprises@on.aibn.com *Web Site:* www.moosehidebooks.com, pg 433

Aldana, Patricia, Greystone Books Ltd, 343 Railway St, Suite 201, Vancouver, BC V6A 1A4, Canada *Tel:* 604-875-1550 *Fax:* 604-875-1556 *E-mail:* info@greystonebooks.com *Web Site:* www.greystonebooks.com, pg 427

Alden, Laura, Judson Press, 1075 First Ave, King of Prussia, PA 19406 *Toll Free Tel:* 800-458-3766 *Fax:* 610-768-2107 *Web Site:* www.judsonpress.com, pg 115

Aldis, Sherri, United Nations Publications, 300 E 42 St, 9th fl, New York, NY 10017 *Tel:* 703-661-1571 *Fax:* 703-996-1010 *E-mail:* publications@un.org *Web Site:* shop.un.org, pg 224

Alenier, Karren L, Word Works Washington Prize, Adirondack Community College, Dearlove Hall, 640 Bay Rd, Queensbury, NY 12804 *Tel:* 301-581-9439 *Fax:* 301-581-9443 *E-mail:* editor@wordworksbooks.org *Web Site:* www.wordworksbooks.org, pg 679

Alesse, Craig, Amherst Media Inc, PO Box 538, Buffalo, NY 14213 *Tel:* 716-874-4450 *E-mail:* marketing@amherstmedia.com *Web Site:* www.amherstmedia.com, pg 15

Alessi, Darren, Perseus Books, 1290 Avenue of the Americas, New York, NY 10104 *Tel:* 212-340-8100 *Toll Free Tel:* 800-343-4499 (cust serv) *Fax:* 212-340-8105 *Web Site:* www.perseusbooks.com, pg 168

Alewel, Rex, Marathon Press, 1500 Square Turn Blvd, Norfolk, NE 68701 *Tel:* 402-371-5040 *Toll Free Tel:* 800-228-0629 *Fax:* 402-371-9382 *E-mail:* info@marathonpress.net *Web Site:* www.marathonpress.com, pg 132

Alexander, Azzure, Poetry Society of America (PSA), 15 Gramercy Park, New York, NY 10003 *Tel:* 212-254-9628 *Web Site:* poetrysociety.org, pg 543

Alexander, J Trent, Inter-University Consortium for Political & Social Research (ICPSR), 330 Packard St, Ann Arbor, MI 48104 *Tel:* 734-647-5000 *Fax:* 734-647-8200 *E-mail:* help@icpsr.umich.edu *Web Site:* www.icpsr.umich.edu, pg 110

Alexander, Jeff, Words into Print, 208 Java St, 5th fl, Brooklyn, NY 11222 *E-mail:* query@wordsintoprint.org *Web Site:* wordsintoprint.org, pg 471

Alexander, Dr Kara Poe, Baylor University, Professional Writing Program, One Bear Place, Unit 97404, Waco, TX 76798-7404 *Tel:* 254-710-1768 *Fax:* 254-710-3894 *Web Site:* www.baylor.edu, pg 581

Alexander, Lee Ann, Pentecostal Publishing House, 36 Research Park Ct, Weldon Spring, MO 63304 *Tel:* 314-837-7300 *Toll Free Tel:* 866-819-7667 *Fax:* 314-837-6574 (orders) *Web Site:* www.pentecostalpublishing.com; wordaflamepress.com, pg 167

Alexander, Pamela, Oberlin College Press, 50 N Professor St, Oberlin, OH 44074-1091 *Tel:* 440-775-8408 *Fax:* 440-775-8124 *E-mail:* oc.press@oberlin.edu *Web Site:* www.oberlin.edu/ocpress, pg 154

Alexander, Patrick, Penn State University Press, University Support Bldg 1, Suite C, 820 N University Dr, University Park, PA 16802-1003 *Tel:* 814-865-1327 *Toll Free Tel:* 800-326-9180 *Fax:* 814-863-1408 *Toll Free Fax:* 877-778-2665 *E-mail:* orders@psupress.org; orders@eisenbrauns.org *Web Site:* www.psupress.org; www.eisenbrauns.org, pg 166

Alexander, Richard, Bristol Park Books, 252 W 38 St, Suite 206, New York, NY 10018 *Tel:* 212-842-0700 *Fax:* 212-842-1771 *E-mail:* info@bristolparkbooks.com *Web Site:* bristolparkbooks.com, pg 41

Alexander, Ms Sandy, University Press of Mississippi, 3825 Ridgewood Rd, Jackson, MS 39211-6492 *Tel:* 601-432-6205 *Toll Free Tel:* 800-737-7788 (orders & cust serv) *Fax:* 601-432-6217 *E-mail:* press@mississippi.edu *Web Site:* www.upress.state.ms.us, pg 233

Alexander, Shara, Houghton Mifflin Harcourt Trade & Reference Division, 125 High St, Boston, MA 02110 *Tel:* 617-351-5000 *Web Site:* www.hmhco.com, pg 104

Alexander, Susanne, Goose Lane Editions, 500 Beaverbrook Ct, Suite 330, Fredericton, NB E3B 5X4, Canada *Tel:* 506-450-4251 *Toll Free Tel:* 888-926-8377 *Fax:* 506-459-4991 *E-mail:* info@gooselane.com; customerservice@gooselane.com *Web Site:* www.gooselane.com, pg 427

Alexander, Susanne M, Marriage Transformation LLC, PO Box 249, Harrison, TN 37341 *Tel:* 423-599-0153 *Web Site:* www.marriagetransformation.com; www.transformationlearningcenter.com, pg 132

Alexander, Tracy, McLaren Memorial Comedy Play Writing Competition, 2000 W Wadley Ave, Midland, TX 79705 *Tel:* 432-682-2544 *E-mail:* tracy@mctmidland.org *Web Site:* www.mctmidland.org, pg 640

Algar, Liza, Chronicle Books, 680 Second St, San Francisco, CA 94107 *Tel:* 415-537-4200 *Toll Free Tel:* 800-759-0190 (cust serv) *Fax:* 415-537-4460 *Toll Free Tel:* 800-858-7787 (orders); 800-286-9471 (cust serv) *E-mail:* frontdesk@chroniclebooks.com *Web Site:* www.chroniclebooks.com, pg 51

Alguire, Julie, Crabtree Publishing Co, 347 Fifth Ave, Suite 1402-145, New York, NY 10016 *Tel:* 212-496-5040 *Toll Free Tel:* 800-387-7650 *Toll Free Fax:* 800-355-7166 *E-mail:* custserv@crabtreebooks.com *Web Site:* www.crabtreebooks.com, pg 59

Alguire, Julie, Crabtree Publishing Co Ltd, 616 Welland Ave, St Catharines, ON L2M 5V6, Canada *Tel:* 905-682-5221 *Toll Free Tel:* 800-387-7650 *Fax:* 905-682-7166 *Toll Free Fax:* 800-355-7166 *E-mail:* custserv@crabtreebooks.com; sales@crabtreebooks.com; orders@crabtreebooks.com *Web Site:* www.crabtreebooks.com, pg 421

Ali, Kazim, Oberlin College Press, 50 N Professor St, Oberlin, OH 44074-1091 *Tel:* 440-775-8408 *Fax:* 440-775-8124 *E-mail:* oc.press@oberlin.edu *Web Site:* www.oberlin.edu/ocpress, pg 154

Ali, Liaquat, Kazi Publications Inc, 3023 W Belmont Ave, Chicago, IL 60618 *Tel:* 773-267-7001 *Fax:* 773-267-7002 *E-mail:* info@kazi.org *Web Site:* www.kazi.org, pg 116

Ali, Sonia, LARB/USC Publishing Workshop, 6671 Sunset Blvd, Suite 1521, Los Angeles, CA 90028 *E-mail:* publishingworkshop@lareviewofbooks.org *Web Site:* thepublishingworkshop.com, pg 576

Aliotti, Tracee, International Society for Technology in Education, 1530 Wilson Blvd, Suite 730, Arlington, VA 22209 *Tel:* 503-342-2848 (intl) *Toll Free Tel:* 800-336-5191 (US & CN) *E-mail:* iste@iste.org *Web Site:* www.iste.org; www.isteconference.org, pg 112

All, Emma, American Psychological Association, 750 First St NE, Washington, DC 20002-4242 *Tel:* 202-336-5510 *Toll Free Tel:* 800-374-2721 *Fax:* 202-336-5502 *E-mail:* order@apa.org *Web Site:* www.apa.org/books, pg 13

Allan, Richard, The Aaland Agency, PO Box 849, Inyokern, CA 93527-0849 *Tel:* 760-384-3910 *E-mail:* anniejo41@gmail.com *Web Site:* www.the-aaland-agency.com, pg 473

Allannic, Rica, David Black Agency, 335 Adams St, 27th fl, Suite 2707, Brooklyn, NY 11201 *Tel:* 718-852-5500 *Fax:* 718-852-5539 *Web Site:* www.davidblackagency.com, pg 476

Allberry, Debra, Warren Wilson College, MFA Program for Writers, 701 Warren Wilson Rd, Swannanoa, NC 28778 *Tel:* 828-771-3717 *Fax:* 828-771-7005 *E-mail:* mfa@warren-wilson.edu *Web Site:* www.warren-wilson.edu/programs/mfa-in-creative-writing, pg 586

Allen, Charlie, Princeton University Press, 41 William St, Princeton, NJ 08540-5237 *Tel:* 609-258-4900 *Fax:* 609-258-6305 *Web Site:* press.princeton.edu, pg 175

Allen, Heather, Harlequin Enterprises Ltd, Bay Adelaide Centre, East Tower, 22 Adelaide St W, 41st fl, Toronto, ON M5H 4E3, Canada *Tel:* 416-445-5860 *Toll Free Tel:* 888-432-4879; 800-370-5838 (ebook inquiries) *E-mail:* customerservice@harlequin.com *Web Site:* www.harlequin.com, pg 429

Allen, John R, The Brookings Institution Press, 1775 Massachusetts Ave NW, Washington, DC 20036-2188 *Tel:* 202-797-6000 *E-mail:* permissions@brookings.edu *Web Site:* www.brookings.edu, pg 42

Allen, Lindsey, Center for Publishing Departmental Scholarships, Midtown Ctr, Rm 429, 11 W 42 St, New York, NY 10036 *Tel:* 212-992-3232 *Fax:* 212-992-3233 *E-mail:* pub.center@nyu.edu *Web Site:* www.scps.nyu.edu, pg 603

Allen, Lindsey, New York University, Center for Publishing, Midtown Ctr, Rm 429, 11 W 42 St, New York, NY 10036 *Tel:* 212-992-3232 *Fax:* 212-992-3233 *E-mail:* pub.center@nyu.edu *Web Site:* www.scps.nyu.edu/publishing, pg 583

Allen, Marc, New World Library, 14 Pamaron Way, Novato, CA 94949 *Tel:* 415-884-2100 *Toll Free Tel:* 800-227-3900 (ext 52, retail orders); 800-972-6657 *Fax:* 415-884-2199 *E-mail:* escort@newworldlibrary.com *Web Site:* www.newworldlibrary.com, pg 149

Allen, Pete, JMW Group Inc, 347 Rte 6, No 867, Mahopac, NY 10541 *Tel:* 914-841-7105 *Fax:* 914-248-8861 *E-mail:* jmwgroup@jmwgroup.net *Web Site:* jmwgroup.net, pg 490

Allen, Rebecca, TCU Press, 3000 Sandage Ave, Fort Worth, TX 76109 *Tel:* 817-257-7822 *Toll Free Tel:* 800-826-8911 (orders) *Fax:* 817-257-5075 *Web Site:* www.prs.tcu.edu, pg 213

Allen, Robert, Macmillan Audio, 120 Broadway, 22nd fl, New York, NY 10271 *Tel:* 646-307-5151 *Toll Free Fax:* 888-330-8477 (cust serv) *Web Site:* www.macmillanaudio.com, pg 130

Allen, Ron, International Risk Management Institute Inc, 12222 Merit Dr, Suite 1600, Dallas, TX 75251-2266 *Tel:* 972-960-7693 *Fax:* 972-371-5120 *E-mail:* info27@irmi.com *Web Site:* www.irmi.com, pg 111

Allen, Samantha, Chronicle Books, 680 Second St, San Francisco, CA 94107 *Tel:* 415-537-4200 *Toll Free Tel:* 800-759-0190 (cust serv) *Fax:* 415-537-4460 *Toll Free Fax:* 800-858-7787 (orders); 800-286-9471 (cust serv) *E-mail:* frontdesk@chroniclebooks.com *Web Site:* www.chroniclebooks.com, pg 52

Allen, Simon, McGraw-Hill Education, 2 Penn Plaza, New York, NY 10121-2298 *Tel:* 212-904-2000 *E-mail:* international_cs@mheducation.com; seg_customerservice@mheducation.com (PreK-12); hep_customerservice@mheducation.com (higher education) *Web Site:* www.mheducation.com, pg 135

Allen, Thomas M, Sterling Publishing Co Inc, 1166 Avenue of the Americas, 17th fl, New York, NY 10036-2715 *Tel:* 212-532-7160 *Toll Free Tel:* 800-367-9692 *Fax:* 212-213-2495 *Toll Free Fax:* 800-542-7567 *E-mail:* custservice@sterlingpublishing.com; customerservice@sterlingpublishing.com; editorial@sterlingpublishing.com; tradesales@sterlingpublishing.com *Web Site:* www.sterlingpublishing.com, pg 208

Allen, Tom, Sophia Institute Press®, 18 Celina Ave, Unit 1, Nashua, NH 03063 *Tel:* 603-641-9344 *Toll Free Tel:* 800-888-9344 *Fax:* 603-641-8108 *Toll Free Fax:* 888-288-2259 *E-mail:* orders@sophiainstitute.com *Web Site:* www.sophiainstitute.com, pg 203

Allender, David, David R Godine Inc, 15 Court Sq, Suite 320, Boston, MA 02108-2536 *Tel:* 617-451-9600 *Fax:* 617-350-0250 *E-mail:* info@godine.com *Web Site:* www.godine.com, pg 87

Aller, Gary, Gallaudet University Press, 800 Florida Ave NE, Washington, DC 20002-3695 *Tel:* 202-651-5488 *Fax:* 202-651-5489 *E-mail:* gupress@gallaudet.edu *Web Site:* gupress.gallaudet.edu, pg 82

Allessi, Ana Maria, Workman Publishing Co Inc, 225 Varick St, 9th fl, New York, NY 10014-4381 *Tel:* 212-254-5900 *Toll Free Tel:* 800-722-7202 *Fax:* 212-254-8098 *E-mail:* info@workman.com; orders@workman.com *Web Site:* www.workman.com, pg 244

Allgood, Severin, The Pinch Writing Awards in Fiction, University of Memphis, English Dept, 435 Patterson Hall, Memphis, TN 38152 *Tel:* 901-678-2651 *Fax:* 901-678-2226 *E-mail:* editor@pinchjournal.com *Web Site:* www.pinchjournal.com, pg 656

Allgood, Severin, The Pinch Writing Awards in Poetry, University of Memphis, English Dept, 435 Patterson Hall, Memphis, TN 38152 *Tel:* 901-678-2651 *Fax:* 901-678-2226 *E-mail:* editor@pinchjournal.com *Web Site:* www.pinchjournal.com, pg 656

Allin, Mark, John Wiley & Sons Inc, 111 River St, Hoboken, NJ 07030-5774 *Tel:* 201-748-6000 *Toll Free Tel:* 800-225-5945 (cust serv) *Fax:* 201-748-6088 *E-mail:* info@wiley.com *Web Site:* www.wiley.com, pg 241

Allman, Karen, Rowman & Littlefield, 4501 Forbes Blvd, Suite 200, Lanham, MD 20706 *Tel:* 301-459-3366 *Toll Free Tel:* 800-462-6420 (ext 3024, cust serv) *Fax:* 301-429-5748 *Web Site:* rowman.com, pg 188

Allport, Andrew, Rick DeMarinis Short Story Award, PO Box 2414, Durango, CO 81302 *Tel:* 970-903-7914 *E-mail:* cutthroatmag@gmail.com *Web Site:* www.cutthroatmag.com, pg 609

Allport, Andrew, Joy Harjo Poetry Award, PO Box 2414, Durango, CO 81302 *Tel:* 970-903-7914 *E-mail:* cutthroatmag@gmail.com *Web Site:* www.cutthroatmag.com, pg 622

Allyn, Pam, Scholastic Education, 557 Broadway, New York, NY 10012 *Tel:* 212-343-6100 *Fax:* 212-343-6189 *Web Site:* www.scholastic.com, pg 194

Almahdi, Nadia, Houghton Mifflin Harcourt Trade & Reference Division, 125 High St, Boston, MA 02110 *Tel:* 617-351-5000 *Web Site:* www.hmhco.com, pg 104

Almeida, Alia, Houghton Mifflin Harcourt Trade & Reference Division, 125 High St, Boston, MA 02110 *Tel:* 617-351-5000 *Web Site:* www.hmhco.com, pg 104

Alonso-Mendoza, Emilio, The Alexander Graham Bell Association for the Deaf & Hard of Hearing, 3417 Volta Place NW, Washington, DC 20007 *Tel:* 202-337-5220 *Toll Free Tel:* 866-337-5220 (orders) *Fax:* 202-337-8314 *E-mail:* info@agbell.org; publications@agbell.org *Web Site:* www.agbell.org, pg 6

Alperen, Jennifer, The Betsy Nolan Literary Agency, 112 E 17 St, Suite 1W, New York, NY 10003 *Tel:* 212-967-8200 *Fax:* 212-967-7292 *E-mail:* dblehr@cs.com, pg 498

Alpert, Sarah, Algonquin Books, 400 Silver Cedar Ct, Suite 300, Chapel Hill, NC 27514-1585 *Tel:* 919-967-0108 *Fax:* 919-933-0272 *E-mail:* inquiry@algonquin.com *Web Site:* www.workman.com/algonquin, pg 7

Alps, Marisa, Harbour Publishing Co Ltd, 4437 Rondeview Rd, Madeira Park, BC V0N 2H0, Canada *Tel:* 604-883-2730 *Toll Free Tel:* 800-667-2988 *Fax:* 604-883-9451 *E-mail:* info@harbourpublishing.com *Web Site:* www.harbourpublishing.com, pg 429

Altaf, Hasan, Hadada Award, 544 W 27 St, New York, NY 10001 *Tel:* 212-343-1333 *E-mail:* queries@theparisreview.org *Web Site:* www.theparisreview.org/about/prizes, pg 621

Altaf, Hasan, The Plimpton Prize, 544 W 27 St, New York, NY 10001 *Tel:* 212-343-1333 *E-mail:* queries@theparisreview.org *Web Site:* www.theparisreview.org, pg 656

Altman, David G, Center for Creative Leadership LLC, One Leadership Place, Greensboro, NC 27410-9427 *Tel:* 336-545-2810; 336-288-7210 *Fax:* 336-282-3284 *E-mail:* info@ccl.org *Web Site:* www.ccl.org/publications, pg 47

Altman, Mary, Sourcebooks LLC, 1935 Brookdale Rd, Suite 139, Naperville, IL 60563 *Tel:* 630-961-3900 *Toll Free Tel:* 800-432-7444 *Fax:* 630-961-2168 *E-mail:* info@sourcebooks.com; customersupport@sourcebooks.com *Web Site:* www.sourcebooks.com, pg 204

Altshuler, Miriam, DeFiore and Company Literary Management Inc, 47 E 19 St, 3rd fl, New York, NY 10003 *Tel:* 212-925-7744 *Fax:* 212-925-9803 *E-mail:* info@defliterary.com; submissions@defliterary.com *Web Site:* www.defliterary.com, pg 481

Alvarado, Beth, Rick DeMarinis Short Story Award, PO Box 2414, Durango, CO 81302 *Tel:* 970-903-7914 *E-mail:* cutthroatmag@gmail.com *Web Site:* www.cutthroatmag.com, pg 609

Alvarado, Beth, Joy Harjo Poetry Award, PO Box 2414, Durango, CO 81302 *Tel:* 970-903-7914 *E-mail:* cutthroatmag@gmail.com *Web Site:* www.cutthroatmag.com, pg 622

Alvarado, Veronica, Tiller Press, 1230 Avenue of the Americas, New York, NY 10020, pg 218

Alvarez, Awilda, Hippocrene Books Inc, 171 Madison Ave, Suite 1605, New York, NY 10016 *Tel:* 212-685-4373 *E-mail:* info@hippocrenebooks.com; orderdept@hippocrenebooks.com (orders) *Web Site:* www.hippocrenebooks.com, pg 100

Alvarez, Iria, Penguin Random House LLC, 1745 Broadway, New York, NY 10019 *Tel:* 212-782-9000 *Toll Free Tel:* 800-726-0600 *Web Site:* www.penguinrandomhouse.com, pg 164

Alvarez, Jessica, BookEnds Literary Agency, 136 Long Hill Rd, Gillette, NJ 07933 *Web Site:* www.bookendsliterary.com, pg 476

Alvarez, Lisa, Squaw Valley Community of Writers Summer Workshops, PO Box 1416, Nevada City, CA 95959 *Tel:* 530-470-8440 *E-mail:* info@communityofwriters.org *Web Site:* www.communityofwriters.org, pg 579

Alward, Kathy, Piano Press, 1425 Ocean Ave, Suite 5, Del Mar, CA 92014 *Tel:* 619-884-1401 *Fax:* 858-755-1104 *E-mail:* pianopress@pianopress.com *Web Site:* www.pianopress.com, pg 169

Amaiz, Diziree, Library of Congress Prize for American Fiction, 101 Independence Ave SE, Washington, DC 20540-1400 *Tel:* 202-707-5221 (Center for the Book) *Fax:* 202-707-0269 *Web Site:* www.loc.gov, pg 633

Amato, Frank W, Frank Amato Publications Inc, 4040 SE Wister St, Milwaukie, OR 97222 *Tel:* 503-653-8108 *Toll Free Tel:* 800-541-9498 *Fax:* 503-653-2766 *E-mail:* customerservice@amatobooks.com; info@amatobooks.com *Web Site:* www.amatobooks.com, pg 8

Amato, Nick S, Frank Amato Publications Inc, 4040 SE Wister St, Milwaukie, OR 97222 *Tel:* 503-653-8108 *Toll Free Tel:* 800-541-9498 *Fax:* 503-653-2766 *E-mail:* customerservice@amatobooks.com; info@amatobooks.com *Web Site:* www.amatobooks.com, pg 8

Amato, Tony F, Frank Amato Publications Inc, 4040 SE Wister St, Milwaukie, OR 97222 *Tel:* 503-653-8108 *Toll Free Tel:* 800-541-9498 *Fax:* 503-653-2766 *E-mail:* customerservice@amatobooks.com; info@amatobooks.com *Web Site:* www.amatobooks.com, pg 8

Ambrose, Ann, Princeton University Press, 41 William St, Princeton, NJ 08540-5237 *Tel:* 609-258-4900 *Fax:* 609-258-6305 *Web Site:* press.princeton.edu, pg 174

Ambrosio, Dan, Perseus Books, 1290 Avenue of the Americas, New York, NY 10104 *Tel:* 212-340-8100 *Toll Free Tel:* 800-343-4499 (cust serv) *Fax:* 212-340-8105 *Web Site:* www.perseusbooks.com, pg 167

Amendolara, Paula, Simon & Schuster Sales Division, 1230 Avenue of the Americas, New York, NY 10020 *Tel:* 212-698-7000, pg 200

Amer, Morgan, Chronicle Books, 680 Second St, San Francisco, CA 94107 *Tel:* 415-537-4200 *Toll Free Tel:* 800-759-0190 (cust serv) *Fax:* 415-537-4460 *Toll Free Fax:* 800-858-7787 (orders); 800-286-9471 (cust serv) *E-mail:* frontdesk@chroniclebooks.com *Web Site:* www.chroniclebooks.com, pg 52

Ames, Joanna, Canadian Publishers' Council (CPC), 3080 Yonge St, Suite 6060, Toronto, ON M4N 3N1, Canada *Tel:* 647-255-8880 *Web Site:* pubcouncil.ca, pg 530

Ames, Steve, World Citizens, PO Box 131, Mill Valley, CA 94942-0131 *Tel:* 415-380-8020; 415-233-2822 (direct) *Toll Free Tel:* 800-247-6553 (orders only), pg 245

Amienyi, Dr Osa, Arkansas State University Graphic Communications Program, PO Box 1930, Dept of Media, State University, AR 72467-1930 *Tel:* 870-972-3114 *Fax:* 870-972-3321 *Web Site:* www.astate.edu, pg 581

Anderson, Monty, Westminster John Knox Press (WJK), 100 Witherspoon St, Louisville, KY 40202-1396 *Tel:* 502-569-5052 *Toll Free Tel:* 800-523-1631 (US & CN) *Fax:* 502-569-8308 *Toll Free Fax:* 800-541-5113 (US & CN) *E-mail:* customer_service@wjkbooks.com; orders@wjkbooks.com *Web Site:* www.wjkbooks.com, pg 239

Anderson, Paul, The Glen Workshop, 3307 Third Ave W, Seattle, WA 98119 *Tel:* 206-281-2988 *Fax:* 206-281-2979 *E-mail:* glenworkshop@imagejournal.org *Web Site:* www.imagejournal.org, pg 574

Anderson, Robert, Bloomberg Law Book Division, 1801 S Bell St, Arlington, VA 22202 *Tel:* 732-476-6397 *Toll Free Tel:* 800-960-1220 *Fax:* 732-346-1624 *E-mail:* books@bloomberglaw.com *Web Site:* www. bna.com/bloomberglaw/, pg 35

Anderson, Roshe, TarcherPerigee, 375 Hudson St, New York, NY 10014 *Tel:* 212-366-2000 *Fax:* 212-366-2643 *E-mail:* customerservice@penguinrandomhouse. com (cust serv); TarcherPerigeePublicity@ penguinrandomhouse.com (media queries) *Web Site:* www.tarcherbooks.com; www.facebook. com/TarcherPerigee/; www.penguin.com/publishers/ tarcherperigee, pg 213

Anderson, Samara, Robert A Freedman Dramatic Agency Inc, 1501 Broadway, Suite 2310, New York, NY 10036 *Tel:* 212-840-5760 *Fax:* 212-840-5776, pg 485

Anderson, Sara, Sara Anderson Children's Books, PO Box 47182, Seattle, WA 98146 *Tel:* 206-285-1520 *Web Site:* www.saranderson.com, pg 16

Anderson, Steven, John M Collier Award for Forest History Journalism, 701 William Vickers Ave, Durham, NC 27701-3162 *Tel:* 919-682-9319 *Fax:* 919-682-2349 *Web Site:* www.foresthistory.org, pg 606

Andonian, Mr Aramais, Blue Crane Books Inc, 36 Hazel St, Watertown, MA 02472 *Tel:* 617-926-8989, pg 36

Andrabi, Waseem, Cenveo Publisher Services, 555 Virginia Dr, Fort Washington, PA 19034 *Tel:* 267-470-1590 *Fax:* 215-591-9093 *E-mail:* info.psg@cenveo. com *Web Site:* www.cenveopublisherservices.com, pg 460

Andrade, Jamie, Perseus Books, 1290 Avenue of the Americas, New York, NY 10104 *Tel:* 212-340-8100 *Toll Free Tel:* 800-343-4499 (cust serv) *Fax:* 212-340-8105 *Web Site:* www.perseusbooks.com, pg 167

Andre, Laura, Ohio University Press, Alden Library, Suite 101, 30 Park Place, Athens, OH 45701-2901 *Tel:* 740-593-1154 *Web Site:* www.ohioswallow.com, pg 155

Andreadis, Tina, HarperCollins General Books Group, 195 Broadway, New York, NY 10007 *Tel:* 212-207-7000 *Web Site:* www.harpercollins.com, pg 93

Andree, Courtney J, University of Massachusetts Press, East Experiment Station, 671 N Pleasant St, Amherst, MA 01003 *Tel:* 413-545-2217 *Fax:* 413-545-1226 *E-mail:* info@umpress.umass.edu *Web Site:* www. umass.edu/umpress, pg 228

Andreou, George, Harvard University Press, 79 Garden St, Cambridge, MA 02138-1499 *Tel:* 617-495-2600; 401-531-2800 (intl orders) *Toll Free Tel:* 800-405-1619 (orders) *Fax:* 617-495-5898 (gen); 617-496-4677 (edit & rts); 401-531-2801 (intl orders) *Toll Free Fax:* 800-406-9145 (orders) *E-mail:* contact_hup@ harvard.edu *Web Site:* www.hup.harvard.edu, pg 95

Andrews, Emily, Cornell University Press, Sage House, 512 E State St, Ithaca, NY 14850 *Tel:* 607-253-2338 *Fax:* 607-253-2374 *E-mail:* cupressinfo@cornell.edu; cupress-sales@cornell.edu *Web Site:* www.cornellpress. cornell.edu, pg 57

Andrews, Gaylen, Copywriters' Council of America™ (CCA), CCA Bldg, 7 Putter Lane, Middle Island, NY 11953-1920 *Tel:* 631-924-3888; 631-775-6075 *Fax:* 631-924-8555, pg 531

Andrews, Hugh, Andrews McMeel Publishing LLC, 1130 Walnut St, Kansas City, MO 64106-2109 *Toll Free Tel:* 800-851-8923; 800-943-9839 (cust serv)

Toll Free Fax: 800-943-9831 (orders) *E-mail:* sales@ amuniversal.com *Web Site:* www.andrewsmcmeel.com; publishing.andrewsmcmeel.com, pg 16

Andrews, James, Andrews McMeel Publishing LLC, 1130 Walnut St, Kansas City, MO 64106-2109 *Toll Free Tel:* 800-851-8923; 800-943-9839 (cust serv) *Toll Free Fax:* 800-943-9831 (orders) *E-mail:* sales@ amuniversal.com *Web Site:* www.andrewsmcmeel.com; publishing.andrewsmcmeel.com, pg 16

Andrews, Meredith, 5 Under 35, 90 Broad St, Suite 604, New York, NY 10004 *Tel:* 212-685-0261 *Fax:* 212-213-6570 *E-mail:* nationalbook@nationalbook.org *Web Site:* www.nationalbook.org, pg 616

Andrews, Meredith, Innovations in Reading Prize, 90 Broad St, Suite 604, New York, NY 10004 *Tel:* 212-685-0261 *Fax:* 212-213-6570 *E-mail:* nationalbook@ nationalbook.org *Web Site:* www.nationalbook.org/ innovations_in_reading, pg 627

Andrews, Meredith, Medal for Distinguished Contribution to American Letters, 90 Broad St, Suite 604, New York, NY 10004 *Tel:* 212-685-0261 *Fax:* 212-213-6570 *E-mail:* nationalbook@ nationalbook.org *Web Site:* www.nationalbook.org/ amerletters.html, pg 640

Andrews, Meredith, National Book Awards, 90 Broad St, Suite 604, New York, NY 10004 *Tel:* 212-685-0261 *Fax:* 212-213-6570 *E-mail:* nationalbook@ nationalbook.org *Web Site:* www.nationalbook.org, pg 644

Andrews, Meredith, National Book Foundation, 90 Broad St, Suite 604, New York, NY 10004 *Tel:* 212-685-0261 *Fax:* 212-213-6570 *E-mail:* nationalbook@ nationalbook.org *Web Site:* www.nationalbook.org, pg 551

Andrews, Sydney, Book of the Year Award, 600 Maryland Ave SW, Suite 1000W, Washington, DC 20024 *Toll Free Tel:* 800-443-8456 *Fax:* 202-314-5121 *E-mail:* foundation@fb.org *Web Site:* www. agfoundation.org/projects/book-of-the-year-award, pg 600

Andrews, Vaughn, Workman Publishing Co Inc, 225 Varick St, 9th fl, New York, NY 10014-4381 *Tel:* 212-254-5900 *Toll Free Tel:* 800-722-7202 *Fax:* 212-254-8098 *E-mail:* info@workman.com; orders@workman. com *Web Site:* www.workman.com, pg 244

Andrus, Raven, HarperCollins General Books Group, 195 Broadway, New York, NY 10007 *Tel:* 212-207-7000 *Web Site:* www.harpercollins.com, pg 94

Anema, Arielle, PEN Writers' Emergency Fund, 588 Broadway, Suite 303, New York, NY 10012 *Tel:* 212-334-1660 *Fax:* 212-334-2181 *E-mail:* feprogram@pen. org *Web Site:* pen.org/writers-emergency-fund, pg 655

Angel, Mitzi, Farrar, Straus & Giroux, LLC, 175 Varick St, 9th fl, New York, NY 10014 *Tel:* 212-741-6900 *E-mail:* fsg.publicity@fsgbooks.com *Web Site:* us. macmillan.com/fsg.aspx, pg 76

Angel, Mitzi, Macmillan, 120 Broadway, 22nd fl, New York, NY 10271 *Tel:* 646-307-5151 *E-mail:* press. inquiries@macmillan.com *Web Site:* www.macmillan. com, pg 129

Angelilli, Brenda, Harry N Abrams Inc, 195 Broadway, 9th fl, New York, NY 10007 *Tel:* 212-206-7715 *Toll Free Tel:* 800-345-1359 *Fax:* 212-519-1210 *E-mail:* abrams@abramsbooks.com *Web Site:* www. abramsbooks.com, pg 3

Angelilli, Chris, Random House Children's Books, 1745 Broadway, 10th fl, New York, NY 10019 *Tel:* 212-782-9000 *Web Site:* www.randomhousekids.com, pg 180

Angress, Miriam, Duke University Press, 905 W Main St, Suite 18B, Durham, NC 27701 *Tel:* 919-688-5134 *Toll Free Tel:* 888-651-0122 (US) *Fax:* 919-688-2615 *Toll Free Fax:* 888-651-0124 *E-mail:* orders@ dukeupress.edu *Web Site:* www.dukeupress.edu, pg 68

Angulo, Albert, Perseus Books, 1290 Avenue of the Americas, New York, NY 10104 *Tel:* 212-340-8100 *Toll Free Tel:* 800-343-4499 (cust serv) *Fax:* 212-340-8105 *Web Site:* www.perseusbooks.com, pg 168

Annis, Amanda O'Connor, Trident Media Group LLC, 41 Madison Ave, 36th fl, New York, NY 10010 *Tel:* 212-333-1511 *E-mail:* info@tridentmediagroup. com; press@tridentmediagroup.com *Web Site:* www. tridentmediagroup.com, pg 507

Anthony, Graham, August House Inc, 3500 Piedmont Rd NE, Suite 310, Atlanta, GA 30305 *Tel:* 404-442-4420 *Toll Free Tel:* 800-284-8784 *Fax:* 404-442-4435 *E-mail:* ahinfo@augusthouse.com *Web Site:* www. augusthouse.com, pg 25

Anthony, Joya, Chronicle Books, 680 Second St, San Francisco, CA 94107 *Tel:* 415-537-4200 *Toll Free Tel:* 800-759-0190 (cust serv) *Fax:* 415-537-4460 *Toll Free Fax:* 800-858-7787 (orders); 800-286-9471 (cust serv) *E-mail:* frontdesk@chroniclebooks.com *Web Site:* www.chroniclebooks.com, pg 52

Antoine, Marie-Claire, Lynne Rienner Publishers Inc, 1800 30 St, Suite 314, Boulder, CO 80301 *Tel:* 303-444-6684 *Fax:* 303-444-0824 *E-mail:* questions@ rienner.com; cservice@rienner.com *Web Site:* www. rienner.com, pg 185

Antonetta, Suzanne Paola, Annie Dillard Award for Creative Nonfiction, Mail Stop 9053, Western Washington University, Bellingham, WA 98225 *Tel:* 360-650-4863 *E-mail:* bhreview@wwu.edu *Web Site:* www.bhreview.org, pg 610

Antonetta, Suzanne Paola, 49th Parallel Poetry Award, Mail Stop 9053, Western Washington University, Bellingham, WA 98225 *Tel:* 360-650-4863 *E-mail:* bhreview@wwu.edu *Web Site:* www.bhreview. org, pg 616

Antonetta, Suzanne Paola, Tobias Wolff Award for Fiction, Mail Stop 9053, Western Washington University, Bellingham, WA 98225 *Tel:* 360-650-4863 *E-mail:* bhreview@wwu.edu *Web Site:* www.bhreview. org, pg 679

Antonson, Lori, The Axelrod Agency, 55 Main St, Chatham, NY 12037 *Tel:* 518-392-2100, pg 475

Antony, Peter, The Metropolitan Museum of Art, 1000 Fifth Ave, New York, NY 10028 *Tel:* 212-535-7710 *E-mail:* editorial@metmuseum.org *Web Site:* www. metmuseum.org, pg 139

Antony, Wayne, Fernwood Publishing, 32 Oceanvista Lane, Black Point, NS B0J 1B0, Canada *Tel:* 902-857-1388 *Fax:* 902-857-1328 *E-mail:* info@fernpub.ca; roseway@fernpub.ca *Web Site:* fernwoodpublishing.ca, pg 426

Anzuoni, Nicole, Pauline Books & Media, 50 Saint Paul's Ave, Boston, MA 02130 *Tel:* 617-522-8911 *Toll Free Tel:* 800-876-4463 (orders); 800-836-9723 (cust serv) *Fax:* 617-541-9805 *E-mail:* editorial@ paulinemedia.com (ms submissions); orderentry@ pauline.org (cust serv) *Web Site:* www.pauline.org/ pbmpublishing, pg 161

Apelian, Bill, BJU Press, 1430 Wade Hampton Blvd, Greenville, SC 29609-5046 *Tel:* 864-770-1317; 864-546-4600 *Toll Free Tel:* 800-845-5731 *E-mail:* bjupinfo@bju.edu *Web Site:* www.bjupress. com, pg 34

Appel, Amelia, TriadaUS Literary Agency, PO Box 561, Sewickley, PA 15143 *Tel:* 412-401-3376 *Web Site:* www.triadaus.com, pg 506

Appel, Celeste, Unarius Academy of Science Publications, 145 S Magnolia Ave, El Cajon, CA 92020-4522 *Tel:* 619-444-7062 *Toll Free Tel:* 800-475-7062 *Fax:* 619-444-9637 *E-mail:* uriel@unarius.org *Web Site:* www.unarius.org, pg 224

Appel, Fred, Princeton University Press, 41 William St, Princeton, NJ 08540-5237 *Tel:* 609-258-4900 *Fax:* 609-258-6305 *Web Site:* press.princeton.edu, pg 174

Appelbaum, David, Codhill Press, One Arden Lane, New Paltz, NY 12561 *E-mail:* codhillpress@aol.com *Web Site:* www.codhill.com, pg 54

Apperson, Laura, St Martin's Press, LLC, 120 Broadway, New York, NY 10271 *Tel:* 646-307-5151 *Web Site:* us. macmillan.com/smp, pg 190

Axelrod, Glen, TFH Publications Inc, PO Box 427, Neptune, NJ 07754 *Toll Free Tel:* 855-273-7527 (cust serv) *Fax:* 732-988-5466 (cust serv); 732-776-8763 (sales) *E-mail:* info@tfh.com (cust serv); sales@tfh.com *Web Site:* www.tfhpublications.com; www.tfh.com; www.facebook.com/TfhPetBooks, pg 216

Axelrod, Steven, The Axelrod Agency, 55 Main St, Chatham, NY 12037 *Tel:* 518-392-2100, pg 475

Axelson-Berry, Kitty, Modern Memoirs, 34 Main St, No 6, Amherst, MA 01002-2367 *Tel:* 413-253-2353 *Web Site:* www.modernmemoirs.com; www.whitepoppypress.com, pg 141

Axford, Elizabeth C, Piano Press, 1425 Ocean Ave, Suite 5, Del Mar, CA 92014 *Tel:* 619-884-1401 *Fax:* 858-755-1104 *E-mail:* pianopress@pianopress.com *Web Site:* www.pianopress.com, pg 169

Aycock, David, Baylor University Press, Baylor University, One Bear Place, Waco, TX 76798-7363 *Tel:* 254-710-3164 *Web Site:* www.baylorpress.com, pg 29

Ayer, Paula, Greystone Books Ltd, 343 Railway St, Suite 201, Vancouver, BC V6A 1A4, Canada *Tel:* 604-875-1550 *Fax:* 604-875-1556 *E-mail:* info@greystonebooks.com *Web Site:* www.greystonebooks.com, pg 427

Ayers, James, University of New Mexico Press, One University of New Mexico, Albuquerque, NM 87131-0001 *Tel:* 505-272-7777 *Fax:* 505-277-3343 *E-mail:* custserv@unm.edu (order dept) *Web Site:* unmpress.com, pg 229

Ayne, Blythe, Kay Snow Writing Contest, 5331 SW Macadam Ave, Suite 258, PMB 215, Portland, OR 97239 *Tel:* 901-200-5385 *E-mail:* wilwrite@willamettewriters.org *Web Site:* willamettewriters.org, pg 668

Ayubi, Emily, American Psychological Association, 750 First St NE, Washington, DC 20002-4242 *Tel:* 202-336-5510 *Toll Free Tel:* 800-374-2721 *Fax:* 202-336-5502 *E-mail:* order@apa.org *Web Site:* www.apa.org/books, pg 13

Ayuso, Daniela, Doubleday, c/o Penguin Random House Inc, 1745 Broadway, New York, NY 10019 *Tel:* 212-751-2600 *Fax:* 212-572-2662 (foreign rts) *E-mail:* ddaypub@randomhouse.com *Web Site:* knopfdoubleday.com, pg 66

Aziz, Duriva, Scholastic International, 557 Broadway, New York, NY 10012 *Tel:* 212-343-6100; 646-330-5288 (intl cust serv) *Toll Free Tel:* 800-SCHOLASTIC (724-6527) *Fax:* 646-837-7878 *E-mail:* international@scholastic.com, pg 194

Aziz, Ms Nurjehan, Mawenzi House Publishers Ltd, 39 Woburn Ave (B), Toronto, ON M5W 1K5, Canada *Tel:* 416-483-7191 *E-mail:* info@mawenzihouse.com *Web Site:* www.mawenzihouse.com, pg 432

Baake, Mike, Self-Realization Fellowship Publishers, 3208 Humboldt St, Los Angeles, CA 90031 *Tel:* 323-276-6002 *Toll Free Tel:* 888-773-8680 *Fax:* 323-927-1624 *E-mail:* sales@yogananda-srf.org *Web Site:* www.yogananda-srf.org; bookstore.yogananda-srf.org/ (orders), pg 196

Baar, Emily, Oceanview Publishing Inc, 1620 Main St, Suite 11, Sarasota, FL 34236 *Tel:* 941-387-8500 *Web Site:* oceanviewpub.com, pg 154

Babcock, Michael, David R Godine Inc, 15 Court Sq, Suite 320, Boston, MA 02108-2536 *Tel:* 617-451-9600 *Fax:* 617-350-0250 *E-mail:* info@godine.com *Web Site:* www.godine.com, pg 87

Babcock, Sherra, Chautauqua Writers' Workshop, One Ames Ave, Chautauqua, NY 14722 *Tel:* 716-357-6316; 716-357-6250 *Toll Free Tel:* 800-836-ARTS (836-2787) *Fax:* 716-357-9014 *Web Site:* ciweb.org, pg 574

Babler, Linda, Atwood Publishing, PO Box 3185, Madison, WI 53704 *Tel:* 608-242-7101 *Toll Free Tel:* 888-242-7101 *Fax:* 608-242-7102 *E-mail:* customerservice@atwoodpublishing.com *Web Site:* www.atwoodpublishing.com, pg 24

Babson, Emily W, American Academy of Political & Social Science, 202 S 36 St, Philadelphia, PA 19104-3806 *Tel:* 215-746-6500 *Fax:* 215-573-2667 *Web Site:* www.aapss.org, pg 522

Baca, Michelle, Western States Arts Federation, 1743 Wazee St, Suite 300, Denver, CO 80202 *Tel:* 303-629-1166 *Toll Free Tel:* 888-562-7232 *Fax:* 303-629-9717 *E-mail:* staff@westaf.org *Web Site:* www.westaf.org, pg 551

Bacak, Walter W Jr, American Translators Association (ATA), 225 Reinekers Lane, Suite 590, Alexandria, VA 22314 *Tel:* 703-683-6100 *Fax:* 703-683-6122 *E-mail:* ata@atanet.org *Web Site:* www.atanet.org, pg 524

Bace, Marjan, Manning Publications Co, 20 Baldwin Rd, PO Box 761, Shelter Island, NY 11964 *Tel:* 203-626-1510 *E-mail:* sales@manning.com; support@manning.com (cust serv) *Web Site:* www.manning.com, pg 131

Bach, Daniel N, Book Manufacturers' Institute Inc (BMI), PO Box 731388, Ormond Beach, FL 32173 *Tel:* 386-986-4552 *Fax:* 386-986-4553 *E-mail:* info@bmibook.com *Web Site:* www.bmibook.org, pg 528

Bach, Lisa, Chronicle Books, 680 Second St, San Francisco, CA 94107 *Tel:* 415-537-4200 *Toll Free Tel:* 800-759-0190 (cust serv) *Fax:* 415-537-4460 *Toll Free Fax:* 800-858-7787 (orders); 800-286-9471 (cust serv) *E-mail:* frontdesk@chroniclebooks.com *Web Site:* www.chroniclebooks.com, pg 51

Bacha, Diane M, Kalmbach Publishing Co, 21027 Crossroads Circle, Waukesha, WI 53186 *Tel:* 262-796-8776 *Toll Free Tel:* 800-533-6644 (cust serv & orders); 800-558-1544 *Fax:* 262-798-6592 *E-mail:* customerservice@kalmbach.com *Web Site:* www.kalmbach.com, pg 115

Bacigalupi, John, The Taunton Press Inc, 63 S Main St, Newtown, CT 06470 *Tel:* 203-426-8171 *Toll Free Tel:* 800-477-8727 (cust serv); 800-888-8286 (orders) *Fax:* 203-426-3434 *E-mail:* booksales@taunton.com *Web Site:* www.taunton.com, pg 213

Backman, Elizabeth H, Elizabeth H Backman, 86 Johnnycake Hollow Rd, Pine Plains, NY 12567 *Tel:* 518-398-9344 *Fax:* 518-398-6368 *E-mail:* bethcountry@fairpoint.net, pg 475

Backman, John, Backman Writing & Communications, 32 Hillview Ave, Rensselaer, NY 12144 *Tel:* 518-449-4985 *Web Site:* www.backwrite.com, pg 458

Bacon, Chris, Advertising Research Foundation (ARF), 432 Park Ave S, 4th fl, New York, NY 10016-8013 *Tel:* 212-751-5656 *Fax:* 212-689-1859 *E-mail:* help@thearf.org *Web Site:* thearf.org, pg 521

Bacon, Launa, Individual Artist Fellowships, 1004 Farnam, Plaza Level, Omaha, NE 68102 *Tel:* 402-595-2122 *Toll Free Tel:* 800-341-4067 *Fax:* 402-595-2334 *Web Site:* www.nebraskaartscouncil.org, pg 626

Badalian, Alvart, Blue Crane Books Inc, 36 Hazel St, Watertown, MA 02472 *Tel:* 617-926-8989, pg 36

Bader, Rachel, Random House Children's Books, 1745 Broadway, 10th fl, New York, NY 10019 *Tel:* 212-782-9000 *Web Site:* www.randomhousekids.com, pg 180

Badowski, Keith, Brick Road Poetry Book Contest, 513 Broadway, Columbus, GA 31901-3117 *Web Site:* brickroadpoetrypress.com, pg 601

Baechler, Ryan, Academy of Nutrition & Dietetics, 120 S Riverside Plaza, Suite 2190, Chicago, IL 60606-6995 *Tel:* 312-899-0040 (ext 5000) *Toll Free Tel:* 800-877-1600 *E-mail:* sales@eatright.org *Web Site:* www.eatright.org, pg 3

Baer, D Richard, Hollywood Film Archive, 8391 Beverly Blvd, No 321, Los Angeles, CA 90048 *Web Site:* hfarchive.com, pg 101

Baer, William, Howard Nemerov Sonnet Award, 21 Osborne Terr, Wayne, NJ 07470 *Web Site:* theformalist.evansville.edu/home.htm, pg 646

Baffa, Grace, Mason Crest Publishers, 450 Parkway Dr, Suite D, Broomall, PA 19008 *Tel:* 610-543-6200 *Toll Free Tel:* 866-MCP-BOOK (627-2665) *Fax:* 610-543-3878 *Web Site:* www.masoncrest.com, pg 133

Bagatella, Andrew, Whitecap Books, 314 W Cordova St, Suite 209, Vancouver, BC V6B 1E8, Canada *Tel:* 604-681-6181 *Toll Free Tel:* 800-387-9776 *Toll Free Fax:* 800-260-9777 *Web Site:* www.whitecap.ca, pg 445

Bagdanov, Kristin George, Janet B McCabe Poetry Prize, 1041 N Taft Hill Rd, Fort Collins, CO 80521 *Tel:* 970-449-2726 *E-mail:* editor@ruminatemagazine.org *Web Site:* www.ruminatemagazine.com, pg 639

Bagdanov, Kristin George, William Van Dyke Short Story Prize, 1041 N Taft Hill Rd, Fort Collins, CO 80521 *Tel:* 970-449-2726 *E-mail:* editor@ruminatemagazine.org *Web Site:* www.ruminatemagazine.com, pg 675

Bagdanov, Kristin George, VanderMey Nonfiction Prize, 1041 N Taft Hill Rd, Fort Collins, CO 80521 *Tel:* 970-449-2726 *E-mail:* editor@ruminatemagazine.org *Web Site:* www.ruminatemagazine.com, pg 675

Bagshaw, Sean, The Optical Society (OSA), 2010 Massachusetts Ave NW, Washington, DC 20036-1023 *Tel:* 202-223-8130 *Toll Free Tel:* 800-766-4672 *E-mail:* custserv@osa.org *Web Site:* www.osa.org, pg 156

Bahador, Gee Cee Addison, Society of Children's Book Writers & Illustrators (SCBWI), 6363 Wilshire Blvd, Suite 425, Los Angeles, CA 90048 *Tel:* 323-782-1010 *E-mail:* membership@scbwi.org *Web Site:* www.scbwi.org, pg 546

Bahr, Ed, Pacific Press® Publishing Association, 1350 N Kings Rd, Nampa, ID 83687-3193 *Tel:* 208-465-2500 *Toll Free Tel:* 800-447-7377 *Fax:* 208-465-2531 *Web Site:* www.pacificpress.com, pg 158

Bailey, Anne G, Westernlore Press, PO Box 35305, Tucson, AZ 85740-5305 *Tel:* 520-297-5491, pg 239

Bailey, Diane, HarperCollins Publishers, 195 Broadway, New York, NY 10007 *Tel:* 212-207-7000 *Fax:* 212-207-7145 *Web Site:* www.harpercollins.com, pg 94

Bailey, Jocelyn, Thomas Nelson, 501 Nelson Place, Nashville, TN 37214 *Tel:* 615-889-9000 *Toll Free Tel:* 800-251-4000 *Fax:* 615-902-1548 *Web Site:* www.thomasnelson.com, pg 217

Bailey, Jocelyn, Zondervan, 3900 Sparks Dr, Grand Rapids, MI 49546 *Tel:* 616-698-6900 *Toll Free Tel:* 800-226-1122; 800-727-1309 (retail orders) *Fax:* 616-698-3350 *Toll Free Fax:* 800-698-3256 (retail orders) *Web Site:* www.zondervan.com, pg 248

Bailey, Lynn R, Westernlore Press, PO Box 35305, Tucson, AZ 85740-5305 *Tel:* 520-297-5491, pg 239

Bailey, Megan, The Jean Kennedy Smith VSA Playwright Discovery Award, 2700 "F" St NW, Washington, DC 20566 *Tel:* 202-416-8898 *Fax:* 202-416-4840 *E-mail:* vsainfo@kennedy-center.org *Web Site:* www.kennedy-center.org/pdp, pg 668

Bailor, David, Carter G Woodson Book Awards, 8555 16 St, Suite 500, Silver Spring, MD 20910 *Tel:* 301-588-1800 *Toll Free Tel:* 800-296-7840 *Fax:* 301-588-2049 *E-mail:* excellence@ncss.org; publications@ncss.org *Web Site:* www.socialstudies.org, pg 679

Baines, Jennika, Indiana University Press, Herman B Wells Library 350, 1320 E Tenth St, Bloomington, IN 47405-3907 *Tel:* 812-855-8817 *Toll Free Tel:* 800-842-6796 (orders only) *Fax:* 812-855-7931; 812-855-8507 *E-mail:* iupress@indiana.edu; iuporder@indiana.edu (orders) *Web Site:* www.iupress.indiana.edu, pg 108

Baines, Rebecca, National Geographic Books, 1145 17 St NW, Washington, DC 20036-4688 *Tel:* 202-857-7000 *Toll Free Tel:* 877-866-6486 *E-mail:* ngbooks@cdsfulfillment.com *Web Site:* www.nationalgeographic.com/books/; ngbooks.buysub.com, pg 146

Baird, Andrea, Chicago Review Press, 814 N Franklin St, Chicago, IL 60610 *Tel:* 312-337-0747 *Toll Free Tel:* 800-888-4741 *Fax:* 312-337-5110 *E-mail:* frontdesk@chicagoreviewpress.com *Web Site:* www.chicagoreviewpress.com, pg 50

Barnes, Jacqline, Naval Institute Press, 291 Wood Rd, Annapolis, MD 21402-5034 *Tel:* 410-268-6110 *Toll Free Tel:* 800-233-8764 *Fax:* 410-295-1084; 410-571-1703 (cust serv) *E-mail:* webmaster@navalinstitute.org; customer@navalinstitute.org (cust serv) *Web Site:* www.nip.org; www.usni.org, pg 147

Barnes, Janet, Bentley Publishers, 1734 Massachusetts Ave, Cambridge, MA 02138-1804 *Tel:* 617-547-4170 *Toll Free Tel:* 800-423-4595 *Fax:* 617-876-9235 *E-mail:* sales@bentleypublishers.com *Web Site:* www.bentleypublishers.com, pg 32

Barnes, Jim, Axiom Business Book Awards, 1129 Woodmere Ave, Suite B, Traverse City, MI 49686 *Tel:* 231-933-0445 *Toll Free Tel:* 800-706-4636 *Fax:* 231-933-0448 *E-mail:* info@axiomawards.com *Web Site:* www.axiomawards.com, pg 595

Barnes, Jim, Illumination Book Awards, 1129 Woodmere Ave, Suite B, Traverse City, MI 49686 *Tel:* 231-933-0445 *Toll Free Tel:* 800-706-4636 *Fax:* 231-933-0448 *E-mail:* awards@bookpublishing.com *Web Site:* www.illuminationawards.com, pg 625

Barnes, Jim, The Independent Publisher Book Awards, 1129 Woodmere Ave, Suite B, Traverse City, MI 49686 *Tel:* 231-933-0445 *Toll Free Tel:* 800-706-4636 *Fax:* 231-933-0448 *E-mail:* awards@bookpublishing.com *Web Site:* www.independentpublisher.com/ipland/ipawards.php, pg 626

Barnes, Jim, Jenkins Group Inc, 1129 Woodmere Ave, Suite B, Traverse City, MI 49686 *Tel:* 231-933-0445 *Toll Free Tel:* 800-706-4636 *Fax:* 231-933-0448 *E-mail:* info@bookpublishing.com *Web Site:* www.bookpublishing.com, pg 465

Barnes, Jim, Living Now Book Awards, 1129 Woodmere Ave, Suite B, Traverse City, MI 49686 *Tel:* 231-933-0445 *Toll Free Tel:* 800-706-4636 *Fax:* 231-933-0448 *E-mail:* awards@bookpublishing.com *Web Site:* www.livingnowawards.com, pg 634

Barnes, Jim, Moonbeam Children's Book Awards, 1129 Woodmere Ave, Suite B, Traverse City, MI 49686 *Tel:* 231-933-0445 *Toll Free Tel:* 800-706-4636 *Fax:* 231-933-0448 *E-mail:* info@moonbeamawards.com *Web Site:* www.moonbeamawards.com, pg 643

Barnes, Jonathan, The Astronomical Society of the Pacific, 390 Ashton Ave, San Francisco, CA 94112 *Tel:* 415-337-1100 *Fax:* 415-337-5205 *Web Site:* www.astrosociety.org, pg 24

Barnes, Lyndsi, American Printing History Association, PO Box 4519, Grand Central Sta, New York, NY 10163 *E-mail:* secretary@printinghistory.org *Web Site:* printinghistory.org, pg 523

Barnes, Lyndsi, American Printing History Association Award, PO Box 4519, Grand Central Sta, New York, NY 10163 *E-mail:* secretary@printinghistory.org *Web Site:* printinghistory.org, pg 592

Barnes, Marcy, Beacon Press, 24 Farnsworth St, Boston, MA 02210-1409 *Tel:* 617-742-2110 *Fax:* 617-723-3097; 617-742-2290 *Web Site:* www.beacon.org, pg 29

Barnes, Meredith, Harlequin Enterprises Ltd, 195 Broadway, 24th fl, New York, NY 10007 *Tel:* 212-207-7000 *Toll Free Tel:* 888-432-4879 *E-mail:* customerservice@harlequin.com *Web Site:* www.harlequin.com, pg 93

Barnes, Shannon Howe, Marilyn Baillie Picture Book Award, 40 Orchard View Blvd, Suite 217, Toronto, ON M4R 1B9, Canada *Tel:* 416-975-0010 *Fax:* 416-975-8970 *E-mail:* info@bookcentre.ca *Web Site:* www.bookcentre.ca, pg 595

Barnes, Shannon Howe, The Geoffrey Bilson Award for Historical Fiction for Young People, 40 Orchard View Blvd, Suite 217, Toronto, ON M4R 1B9, Canada *Tel:* 416-975-0010 *Fax:* 416-975-8970 *E-mail:* info@bookcentre.ca *Web Site:* www.bookcentre.ca, pg 598

Barnes, Shannon Howe, Canadian Children's Book Centre, 40 Orchard View Blvd, Suite 217, Toronto, ON M4R 1B9, Canada *Tel:* 416-975-0010 *Fax:* 416-975-8970 *E-mail:* info@bookcentre.ca *Web Site:* www.bookcentre.ca, pg 530

Barnes, Shannon Howe, Norma Fleck Award for Canadian Children's Non-Fiction, 40 Orchard View Blvd, Suite 217, Toronto, ON M4R 1B9, Canada *Tel:* 416-975-0010 *Fax:* 416-975-8970 *E-mail:* info@bookcentre.ca *Web Site:* www.bookcentre.ca, pg 616

Barnes, Shannon Howe, Amy Mathers Teen Book Award, 40 Orchard View Blvd, Suite 217, Toronto, ON M4R 1B9, Canada *Tel:* 416-975-0010 *Fax:* 416-975-8970 *E-mail:* info@bookcentre.ca *Web Site:* www.bookcentre.ca, pg 639

Barnes, Shannon Howe, John Spray Mystery Award, 40 Orchard View Blvd, Suite 217, Toronto, ON M4R 1B9, Canada *Tel:* 416-975-0010 *Fax:* 416-975-8970 *E-mail:* info@bookcentre.ca *Web Site:* www.bookcentre.ca, pg 670

Barnes, Shannon Howe, TD Canadian Children's Literature Award, 40 Orchard View Blvd, Suite 217, Toronto, ON M4R 1B9, Canada *Tel:* 416-975-0010 *Fax:* 416-975-8970 *E-mail:* info@bookcentre.ca *Web Site:* www.bookcentre.ca, pg 672

Barnet, Anna Kyoko, American Federation of Arts, 305 E 47 St, 10th fl, New York, NY 10017 *Tel:* 212-988-7700 *Toll Free Tel:* 800-232-0270; 212-861-2487 *E-mail:* pubinfo@amfedarts.org *Web Site:* www.amfedarts.org, pg 10

Barnett, Bob, University of Texas Press, 3001 Lake Austin Blvd, 2.200, Austin, TX 78703 *Tel:* 512-471-7233 *Fax:* 512-232-7178 *E-mail:* utpress@uts.cc.utexas.edu; info@utpress.utexas.edu *Web Site:* utpress.utexas.edu, pg 216

Barnett, Chrissie A, Southern California Writers' Conference (SCWC), 18160 Cottonwood Rd, Suite 260, Sunriver, OR 97707 *Tel:* 619-303-8185 *Fax:* 619-906-7462 *E-mail:* msg@writersconference.com *Web Site:* www.writersconference.com, pg 578

Barnett, Robin, Zondervan, 3900 Sparks Dr, Grand Rapids, MI 49546 *Tel:* 616-698-6900 *Toll Free Tel:* 800-226-1122; 800-727-1309 (retail orders) *Fax:* 616-698-3350 *Toll Free Fax:* 800-698-3256 (retail orders) *Web Site:* www.zondervan.com, pg 248

Barney, Jenny, Publications International Ltd (PIL), 8140 N Lehigh Ave, Morton Grove, IL 60053 *Tel:* 847-676-3470 *Fax:* 847-676-3671 *E-mail:* customer_service@pubint.com *Web Site:* pilbooks.com, pg 177

Barney, Stacey, GP Putnam's Sons (Children's), 345 Hudson St, New York, NY 10014 *Tel:* 212-366-2000 *Fax:* 212-414-3393 *Web Site:* www.penguin.com/publishers/gpputnamssonsbooksforyoungread, pg 178

Baron, Carole, Alfred A Knopf, c/o Penguin Random House Inc, 1745 Broadway, New York, NY 10019 *Tel:* 212-751-2600 *Fax:* 212-572-2662 (foreign rts) *Web Site:* knopfdoubleday.com, pg 118

Baror, Danny, Baror International Inc, PO Box 868, Armonk, NY 10504-0868 *Tel:* 914-273-9199 *Fax:* 914-273-5058 *Web Site:* www.barorint.com, pg 475

Baror-Shapiro, Heather, Baror International Inc, PO Box 868, Armonk, NY 10504-0868 *Tel:* 914-273-9199 *Fax:* 914-273-5058 *Web Site:* www.barorint.com, pg 475

Barot, Len, Bold Strokes Books Inc, 648 S Cambridge Rd, Bldg A, Johnsonville, NY 12094 *Tel:* 518-677-5127 *E-mail:* service@boldstrokesbooks.com *Web Site:* www.boldstrokesbooks.com, pg 37

Barr, Stephen, Writers House, 21 W 26 St, New York, NY 10010 *Tel:* 212-685-2400 *Web Site:* www.writershouse.com, pg 508

Barrales-Saylor, Kelly, Sourcebooks LLC, 1935 Brookdale Rd, Suite 139, Naperville, IL 60563 *Tel:* 630-961-3900 *Toll Free Tel:* 800-432-7444 *Fax:* 630-961-2168 *E-mail:* info@sourcebooks.com; customersupport@sourcebooks.com *Web Site:* www.sourcebooks.com, pg 204

Barras, Lise, Pearson ERPI, 1611 Cremazie Blvd E, 10th fl, Montreal, QC H2M 2P2, Canada *Tel:* 514-334-2690 *Toll Free Tel:* 800-263-3678 *Fax:* 514-334-4720

Toll Free Fax: 800-643-4720 *E-mail:* bienvenue@pearsonerpi.com *Web Site:* pearsonerpi.com; pearsonplc.ca, pg 436

Barreiros, Arleen, Winterwolf Press, 1810 E Sahara Ave, Suite 737, Las Vegas, NV 89014 *Toll Free Tel:* 855-ICE-WOLF (423-9653) *E-mail:* info@winterwolfpress.com; questions@winterwolfpress.com; admin@winterwolfpress.com (orders) *Web Site:* winterwolfpress.com, pg 243

Barrenechea, Antonio, The Charles Bernheimer Prize, University of South Carolina, Dept of Languages, Literature & Cultures, 1620 College St, Rm 817, Columbia, SC 29208 *Tel:* 803-777-3021 *E-mail:* info@acla.org *Web Site:* www.acla.org/prize-awards/charles-bernheimer-prize, pg 597

Barrenechea, Antonio, Horst Frenz Prize, University of South Carolina, Dept of Languages, Literature & Cultures, 1620 College St, Rm 817, Columbia, SC 29208 *Tel:* 803-777-3021 *E-mail:* info@acla.org *Web Site:* www.acla.org/prize-awards/horst-frenz-prize, pg 617

Barrenechea, Antonio, Harry Levin Prize, University of South Carolina, Dept of Languages, Literature & Cultures, 1620 College St, Rm 817, Columbia, SC 29208 *Tel:* 803-777-3021 *E-mail:* info@acla.org *Web Site:* www.acla.org/prize-awards/harry-levin-prize, pg 632

Barrenechea, Antonio, Presidential Master's Prize, University of South Carolina, Dept of Languages, Literature & Cultures, 1620 College St, Rm 817, Columbia, SC 29208 *Tel:* 803-777-3021 *E-mail:* info@acla.org *Web Site:* www.acla.org/prize-awards/presidential-masters-prize, pg 658

Barrenechea, Antonio, Presidential Undergraduate Prize, University of South Carolina, Dept of Languages, Literature & Cultures, 1620 College St, Rm 817, Columbia, SC 29208 *Tel:* 803-777-3021 *E-mail:* info@acla.org *Web Site:* www.acla.org/prize-awards/presidential-undergraduate-prize, pg 658

Barrenechea, Antonio, Rene Wellek Prize, University of South Carolina, Dept of Languages, Literature & Cultures, 1620 College St, Rm 817, Columbia, SC 29208 *Tel:* 803-777-3021 *E-mail:* info@acla.org *Web Site:* www.acla.org/prize-awards/rené-wellek-prize, pg 676

Barrett, Amanda, Love Creek Annual Short Play Festival, 2144 45 Ave, Long Island City, NY 11101 *Tel:* 646-765-6542 *E-mail:* LCPSubmissions@gmail.com, pg 635

Barrett, Dave, little bee books, 251 Park Ave S, 12th fl, New York, NY 10010 *Toll Free Tel:* 844-321-0237 *E-mail:* info@littlebeebooks.com *Web Site:* littlebeebooks.com, pg 125

Barrett, Lauren, Ohio State University Foreign Language Publications, 198 Hagerty Hall, 1775 College Rd, Columbus, OH 43210-1309 *Tel:* 614-292-3838 *Toll Free Tel:* 800-678-6999 *E-mail:* flpubs@osu.edu *Web Site:* flpubs.osu.edu, pg 155

Barrett, Linda-Marie, Nancy Olson Bookseller Award, 51 Pleasant Ridge Dr, Asheville, NC 28805 *Tel:* 803-994-9530 *Fax:* 309-410-0211 *E-mail:* siba@sibaweb.com *Web Site:* www.sibaweb.com, pg 650

Barrett, Linda-Marie, Southern Book Prize, 51 Pleasant Ridge Dr, Asheville, NC 28805 *Tel:* 803-994-9530 *Fax:* 309-410-0211 *Web Site:* www.sibaweb.com/siba-book-award, pg 669

Barrett, Linda-Marie, Southern Independent Booksellers Alliance, 51 Pleasant Ridge Dr, Asheville, NC 28805 *Tel:* 803-994-9530 *Fax:* 309-410-0211 *E-mail:* siba@sibaweb.com *Web Site:* www.sibaweb.com, pg 547

Barrett, Sheila, Harvard University Press, 79 Garden St, Cambridge, MA 02138-1499 *Tel:* 617-495-2600; 401-531-2800 (intl orders) *Toll Free Tel:* 800-405-1619 (orders) *Fax:* 617-495-5898 (gen); 617-496-4677 (edit & rts); 401-531-2801 (intl orders) *Toll Free Fax:* 800-406-9145 (orders) *E-mail:* contact_hup@harvard.edu *Web Site:* www.hup.harvard.edu, pg 102

Barrett, Steven, Love Creek Annual Short Play Festival, 2144 45 Ave, Long Island City, NY 11101 *Tel:* 646-765-6542 *E-mail:* LCPSubmissions@gmail.com, pg 635

Barricklow, Pamela, HarperCollins General Books Group, 195 Broadway, New York, NY 10007 *Tel:* 212-207-7000 *Web Site:* www.harpercollins.com, pg 93

Barrow, Bebe, Chronicle Books, 680 Second St, San Francisco, CA 94107 *Tel:* 415-537-4200 *Toll Free Tel:* 800-759-0190 (cust serv) *Fax:* 415-537-4460 *Toll Free Fax:* 800-858-7787 (orders); 800-286-9471 (cust serv) *E-mail:* frontdesk@chroniclebooks.com *Web Site:* www.chroniclebooks.com, pg 52

Barrs, Michael, Perseus Books, 1290 Avenue of the Americas, New York, NY 10104 *Tel:* 212-340-8100 *Toll Free Tel:* 800-343-4499 (cust serv) *Fax:* 212-340-8105 *Web Site:* www.perseusbooks.com, pg 167

Barry, Beth, Demos Medical Publishing, 11 W 42 St, 15th fl, New York, NY 10036 *Tel:* 212-683-0072 *E-mail:* cs@springerpub.com *Web Site:* www.springerpub.com/medicine; www.springerpub.com/consumer-health, pg 64

Barry, Beth Kaufman, Springer Publishing Co, 11 W 42 St, 15th fl, New York, NY 10036-8002 *Tel:* 212-431-4370 *Toll Free Tel:* 877-687-7476 *E-mail:* marketing@springerpub.com; cs@springerpub.com (orders); textbook@springerpub.com; specialsales@springerpub.com *Web Site:* www.springerpub.com, pg 206

Barry, Bridget, University of Nebraska Press, 1111 Lincoln Mall, Lincoln, NE 68588-0630 *Tel:* 402-472-3581; 919-966-7449 (cust serv & foreign orders) *Toll Free Tel:* 800-848-6224 (cust serv & US orders) *Fax:* 402-472-6214; 919-962-2704 (cust serv & foreign orders) *Toll Free Fax:* 800-526-2617 (cust serv & US orders) *E-mail:* pressmail@unl.edu *Web Site:* www.nebraskapress.unl.edu, pg 229

Barry, Graham, Chronicle Books, 680 Second St, San Francisco, CA 94107 *Tel:* 415-537-4200 *Toll Free Tel:* 800-759-0190 (cust serv) *Fax:* 415-537-4460 *Toll Free Fax:* 800-858-7787 (orders); 800-286-9471 (cust serv) *E-mail:* frontdesk@chroniclebooks.com *Web Site:* www.chroniclebooks.com, pg 51

Bartels, Lynn, Lucky Marble Books, 2671 Bristol Rd, Columbus, OH 43221 *Tel:* 614-264-5588 *E-mail:* sales@pagespringpublishing.com *Web Site:* www.luckymarblebooks.com, pg 129

Barth, Jennifer, HarperCollins General Books Group, 195 Broadway, New York, NY 10007 *Tel:* 212-207-7000 *Web Site:* www.harpercollins.com, pg 93

Bartholomew, Erika, The Knight-Risser Prize for Western Environmental Journalism, Stanford University, 450 Serra Mall, Bldg 120, Rm 424, Stanford, CA 94305-2050 *Tel:* 650-723-4937 *Fax:* 650-725-6154 *E-mail:* knightrisserprize@lists.stanford.edu *Web Site:* knightrisser.stanford.edu, pg 630

Bartholomew, Marie, Kids Can Press Ltd, 25 Dockside Dr, Toronto, ON M5A 0B5, Canada *Tel:* 416-479-7000 *Toll Free Tel:* 800-265-0884 *Fax:* 416-960-5437 *E-mail:* info@kidscan.com; customerservice@kidscan.com *Web Site:* www.kidscanpress.com; www.kidscanpress.ca, pg 431

Bartleson, Katelynn, Jessica Kingsley Publishers Inc, 400 Market St, Suite 400, Philadelphia, PA 19106 *Tel:* 215-922-1161 *Toll Free Tel:* 866-416-1078 (cust serv) *Fax:* 215-922-1474 *E-mail:* hello.usa@jkp.com *Web Site:* www.jkp.com, pg 117

Bartlett, Danielle, HarperCollins General Books Group, 195 Broadway, New York, NY 10007 *Tel:* 212-207-7000 *Web Site:* www.harpercollins.com, pg 93

Bartok, Josh, Wisdom Publications Inc, 199 Elm St, Somerville, MA 02144 *Tel:* 617-776-7416 *Toll Free Tel:* 800-272-4050 (orders) *Fax:* 617-776-7841 *E-mail:* info@wisdompubs.org; submission@wisdompubs.org *Web Site:* www.wisdompubs.org, pg 243

Barton, Beth, Simon & Schuster Children's Publishing, 1230 Avenue of the Americas, New York, NY 10020 *Tel:* 212-698-7000 *Web Site:* www.simonandschuster.com/kids; www.simonandschuster.com/teen; simonandschuster.net; simonandschuster.biz, pg 199

Barton, John, Constance Rooke Creative Non-Fiction Prize, University of Victoria, Box 1700, Sta CSC, Victoria, BC V8W 2Y2, Canada *Tel:* 250-721-8524 *Fax:* 250-472-5051 *E-mail:* malahat@uvic.ca *Web Site:* malahatreview.ca, pg 606

Barton, John, Far Horizons Award for Poetry, University of Victoria, Box 1700, Sta CSC, Victoria, BC V8W 2Y2, Canada *Tel:* 250-721-8524 *Fax:* 250-472-5051 *E-mail:* malahat@uvic.ca *Web Site:* www.malahatreview.ca, pg 614

Barton, John, Far Horizons Award for Short Fiction, University of Victoria, Box 1700, Sta CSC, Victoria, BC V8W 2Y2, Canada *Tel:* 250-721-8524 *Fax:* 250-472-5051 *E-mail:* malahat@uvic.ca *Web Site:* www.malahatreview.ca, pg 614

Barton, John, Malahat Review Long Poem Prize, University of Victoria, Box 1700, Sta CSC, Victoria, BC V8W 2Y2, Canada *Tel:* 250-721-8524 *Fax:* 250-472-5051 *E-mail:* malahat@uvic.ca *Web Site:* www.malahatreview.ca, pg 637

Barton, John, Novella Prize, University of Victoria, Box 1700, Sta CSC, Victoria, BC V8W 2Y2, Canada *Tel:* 250-721-8524 *Fax:* 250-472-5051 *E-mail:* malahat@uvic.ca *Web Site:* www.malahatreview.ca, pg 649

Barton, John, Open Season Awards, University of Victoria, Box 1700, Sta CSC, Victoria, BC V8W 2Y2, Canada *Tel:* 250-721-8524 *Fax:* 250-472-5051 *E-mail:* malahat@uvic.ca *Web Site:* malahatreview.ca, pg 651

Bartow, Virginia, American Printing History Association, PO Box 4519, Grand Central Sta, New York, NY 10163 *E-mail:* secretary@printinghistory.org *Web Site:* printinghistory.org, pg 523

Bartow, Virginia, American Printing History Association Award, PO Box 4519, Grand Central Sta, New York, NY 10163 *E-mail:* secretary@printinghistory.org *Web Site:* printinghistory.org, pg 592

Bartram, Brent, Andrews McMeel Publishing LLC, 1130 Walnut St, Kansas City, MO 64106-2109 *Toll Free Tel:* 800-851-8923; 800-943-9839 (cust serv) *Toll Free Fax:* 800-943-9831 (orders) *E-mail:* sales@amuniversal.com *Web Site:* www.andrewsmcmeel.com; publishing.andrewsmcmeel.com, pg 16

Bartson, Kathy, Denver Publishing Institute Scholarship, 3135 S State St, Suite 203, Ann Arbor, MI 48108 *Toll Free Tel:* 866-733-9064 *Fax:* 734-477-2806 *E-mail:* info@bincfoundation.org *Web Site:* www.bincfoundation.org/denver-publishing-institute/, pg 609

Bartson, Kathy, Carla Gray Memorial Scholarship, 713 W Ellsworth Rd, Suite A, Ann Arbor, MI 48108 *Toll Free Tel:* 866-733-9064 *Fax:* 734-477-2806 *E-mail:* info@bincfoundation.org *Web Site:* www.bincfoundation.org/carla-gray/, pg 620

Bartson, Kathy, Higher Education Scholarship Program, 3135 S State St, Suite 203, Ann Arbor, MI 48108 *Toll Free Tel:* 866-733-9064 *Fax:* 734-477-2806 *E-mail:* info@bincfoundation.org *Web Site:* bincfoundation.org/scholarship, pg 623

Bartson, Kathy, Macmillan Booksellers Professional Development Scholarship, 3135 S State St, Suite 203, Ann Arbor, MI 48108 *Toll Free Tel:* 866-733-9064 *Fax:* 734-477-2806 *E-mail:* info@bincfoundation.org *Web Site:* www.bincfoundation.org/scholarship, pg 637

Bartson, Kathy, Karl Pohrt Tribute Award, 3135 S State St, Suite 203, Ann Arbor, MI 48108 *Toll Free Tel:* 866-733-9064 *Fax:* 734-477-2806 *E-mail:* info@bincfoundation.org *Web Site:* www.bincfoundation.org/scholarship, pg 657

Bartz, Olivia, Houghton Mifflin Harcourt Trade & Reference Division, 125 High St, Boston, MA 02110 *Tel:* 617-351-5000 *Web Site:* www.hmhco.com, pg 104

Barz, Otto, YBK Publishers Inc, 39 Crosby St, New York, NY 10013 *Tel:* 212-219-0135 *E-mail:* readmybook@ybkpublishers.com; info@ybkpublishers.com *Web Site:* www.ybkpublishers.com, pg 247

Barz, Otto H, Publishing Synthesis Ltd, 39 Crosby St, New York, NY 10013 *Tel:* 212-219-0135 *E-mail:* mainmail@pubsyn.com *Web Site:* www.pubsyn.com, pg 469

Basch, Richard, Don Buchwald & Associates Inc, 10 E 44 St, New York, NY 10017 *Tel:* 212-867-1200 *Fax:* 212-867-2434 *E-mail:* info@buchwald.com *Web Site:* www.buchwald.com, pg 478

Basco, Buenaventura "Ven", Asian/Pacific American Award for Literature, PO Box 677593, Orlando, FL 32867-7593 *Web Site:* www.apalaweb.org/awards/literature-awards, pg 594

Bascom, Jordan, Milkweed Editions, 1011 Washington Ave S, Suite 300, Minneapolis, MN 55415-1246 *Tel:* 612-332-3192 *Toll Free Tel:* 800-520-6455 *Fax:* 612-215-2550 *Web Site:* milkweed.org, pg 140

Bashirrad, Avideh, Random House Publishing Group, 1745 Broadway, New York, NY 10019 *Toll Free Tel:* 800-200-3552 *Web Site:* www.randomhousebooks.com, pg 181

Baskin, John, Orange Frazer Press Inc, 37 1/2 W Main St, Wilmington, OH 45177 *Tel:* 937-382-3196 *Fax:* 937-383-3159 *E-mail:* ofrazer@erinet.com *Web Site:* www.orangefrazer.com, pg 156

Bass, Chonise, Simon & Schuster, 1230 Avenue of the Americas, New York, NY 10020 *Tel:* 212-698-7000 *Toll Free Tel:* 800-223-2348 (cust serv); 800-223-2336 (orders) *Toll Free Fax:* 800-943-9831 (orders) *Web Site:* www.simonandschuster.com, pg 198

Bass, Judy, Industrial Press Inc, 32 Haviland St, Suite 3, Norwalk, CT 06854 *Tel:* 203-956-5593 ext 0 (cust serv) *Toll Free Tel:* 888-528-7852 ext 0 (cust serv) *Fax:* 203-354-9391 (cust serv) *E-mail:* info@industrialpress.com (cust serv) *Web Site:* books.industrialpress.com; ebooks.industrialpress.com, pg 108

Bass, Patrik, HarperCollins General Books Group, 195 Broadway, New York, NY 10007 *Tel:* 212-207-7000 *Web Site:* www.harpercollins.com, pg 93

Basseches, John, Royal Ontario Museum Press, 100 Queen's Park, Toronto, ON M5S 2C6, Canada *Tel:* 416-586-8000 *Fax:* 416-586-5642 *E-mail:* info@rom.on.ca *Web Site:* www.rom.on.ca, pg 439

Bassel, Katie, St Martin's Press, LLC, 120 Broadway, New York, NY 10271 *Tel:* 646-307-5151 *Web Site:* us.macmillan.com/smp, pg 191

Bast, Tom, Triumph Books, 814 N Franklin St, Chicago, IL 60610 *Tel:* 312-337-0747 *Toll Free Tel:* 800-888-4741 (cust serv) *Fax:* 312-280-5470; 312-337-5985 *Web Site:* www.triumphbooks.com, pg 221

Bastian, Donald G, BPS Books, 47 Anderson Ave, Toronto, ON M5P 1H6, Canada *Tel:* 416-609-2004 *Web Site:* www.bpsbooks.com, pg 417

Basu, Anwesha, HarperCollins General Books Group, 195 Broadway, New York, NY 10007 *Tel:* 212-207-7000 *Web Site:* www.harpercollins.com, pg 93

Basu, Nita, Hachette Audio, 1290 Avenue of the Americas, New York, NY 10104 *Tel:* 212-364-1100 *Web Site:* www.hachetteaudio.com, pg 90

Batana, Rosario, Vernon Press, 1000 N West St, Suite 1200, Wilmington, DE 19801 *Tel:* 302-250-4440 *E-mail:* info@vernonpress.com *Web Site:* www.vernonpress.com, pg 235

Batanero, Katherine, Stegner Fellowship, Stanford University, Dept of English, Stanford, CA 94305-2087 *Tel:* 650-723-0011 *Fax:* 650-723-3679 *E-mail:* stegnerfellowship@stanford.edu *Web Site:* creativewriting.stanford.edu, pg 670

Batcheller, Susan, Candlewick Press, 99 Dover St, Somerville, MA 02144-2825 *Tel:* 617-661-3330 *Fax:* 617-661-0565 *E-mail:* bigbear@candlewick.com; salesinfo@candlewick.com *Web Site:* www.candlewick.com, pg 44

Batchelor, Justina, Grove Atlantic Inc, 154 W 14 St, 12th fl, New York, NY 10011 *Tel:* 212-614-7850 *Toll Free Tel:* 800-521-0178 *Fax:* 212-614-7886 *E-mail:* info@groveatlantic.com; sales@groveatlantic.com; publicity@groveatlantic.com; rights@groveatlantic.com *Web Site:* www.groveatlantic.com, pg 89

Bateman, Lewis, Cambridge University Press, One Liberty Plaza, 20th fl, New York, NY 10006 *Tel:* 212-924-3900; 212-337-5000 *Fax:* 212-691-3239; 845-353-4141 *E-mail:* newyork@cambridge.org; customer_service@cambridge.org *Web Site:* www.cambridge.org/us, pg 43

Bates, Anika, Random House Children's Books, 1745 Broadway, 10th fl, New York, NY 10019 *Tel:* 212-782-9000 *Web Site:* www.randomhousekids.com, pg 181

Bates, Colleen Dunn, Prospect Park Books, 2359 Lincoln Ave, Altadena, CA 91001 *Tel:* 626-793-9796 *E-mail:* info@prospectparkbooks.com *Web Site:* www.prospectparkbooks.com, pg 177

Bates, Colleen Dunn, Publishers Association of the West Inc (PubWest), 17501 Hill Way, Lake Oswego, OR 97035 *Tel:* 503-901-9865 *E-mail:* pubwest1@gmail.com *Web Site:* pubwest.org, pg 545

Bates, Colleen Dunn, PubWest Book Design Awards, 17501 Hill Way, Lake Oswego, OR 97035 *Tel:* 503-901-9865 *E-mail:* pubwest1@gmail.com *Web Site:* pubwest.org, pg 659

Bates, Colleen Dunn, Jack D Rittenhouse Award, 17501 Hill Way, Lake Oswego, OR 97035 *Tel:* 503-901-9865 *E-mail:* pubwest1@gmail.com *Web Site:* pubwest.org, pg 662

Bates, Vicki, University of South Carolina Press, 1600 Hampton St, Suite 544, Columbia, SC 29208 *Tel:* 803-777-5245 *Toll Free Tel:* 800-768-2500 (orders) *Fax:* 803-777-0160 *Toll Free Fax:* 800-868-0740 (orders) *Web Site:* www.sc.edu/uscpress, pg 231

Bathgate, Linda, Washington State University Press, Cooper Publications Bldg, 2300 Grimes Way, Pullman, WA 99164-5910 *Tel:* 509-335-7880 *Toll Free Tel:* 800-354-7360 (orders) *E-mail:* wsupress@wsu.edu *Web Site:* wsupress.wsu.edu, pg 237

Batiz-Benet, Mercedes, Bayeux Arts Inc, 2403, 510-Sixth Ave SE, Calgary, AB T2G 1L7, Canada *E-mail:* mail@bayeux.com *Web Site:* bayeux.com, pg 416

Batmanglij, Mohammad, Mage Publishers Inc, 4601 N Park Ave, No 1616, Chevy Chase, MD 20815 *Web Site:* www.mage.com, pg 130

Batmanglij, Najmieh, Mage Publishers Inc, 4601 N Park Ave, No 1616, Chevy Chase, MD 20815 *Web Site:* www.mage.com, pg 130

Batt, Adria, Shambhala Publications Inc, 4720 Walnut St, Boulder, CO 80301 *Tel:* 303-222-9598 *Toll Free Tel:* 866-424-0030 (off); 888-424-2329 (cust serv) *E-mail:* customercare@shambhala.com *Web Site:* www.shambhala.com, pg 197

Battaglia, Dana, Paul H Brookes Publishing Co Inc, PO Box 10624, Baltimore, MD 21285-0624 *Tel:* 410-337-9580 (outside US & CN) *Toll Free Tel:* 800-638-3775 (US & CN) *Fax:* 410-337-8539 *E-mail:* custserv@brookespublishing.com *Web Site:* www.brookespublishing.com, pg 42

Battista, Dino, The University of North Carolina Press, 116 S Boundary St, Chapel Hill, NC 27514-3808 *Tel:* 919-966-3561 *E-mail:* uncpress@unc.edu *Web Site:* www.uncpress.org, pg 229

Battista, Garth, Breakaway Books, PO Box 24, Halcottsville, NY 12438-0024 *Tel:* 607-326-4805 *E-mail:* breakawaybooks@gmail.com *Web Site:* www.breakawaybooks.com, pg 40

Batura, Paul, Focus on the Family, 8605 Explorer Dr, Colorado Springs, CO 80920-1051 *Tel:* 719-531-5181 *Toll Free Tel:* 800-A-FAMILY (232-6459) *Fax:* 719-531-3424 *Web Site:* www.focusonthefamily.com; www.facebook.com/focusonthefamily, pg 79

Bauchner, Howard C MD, American Medical Association, AMA Plaza, 330 N Wabash, Suite 39300, Chicago, IL 60611-5885 *Tel:* 312-464-5000 *Toll Free Tel:* 800-621-8335 *Web Site:* www.ama-assn.org, pg 12

Bauer, Nate, University of Alaska Press, Elmer E Rasmuson Library, 1732 Tanana Loop, Suite 402, Fairbanks, AK 99775 *Tel:* 907-474-5831 *Toll Free Tel:* 888-252-6657 (US only) *Fax:* 907-474-5502 *Web Site:* www.alaska.edu/uapress, pg 225

Bauer, Susan Wise, Well-Trained Mind Press, 18021 The Glebe Lane, Charles City, VA 23030 *Tel:* 804-829-5043 *Toll Free Tel:* 877-322-3445 (orders) *Fax:* 804-829-5704 *E-mail:* support@welltrainedmind.com *Web Site:* welltrainedmind.com, pg 238

Bauerle, Chris, Sourcebooks LLC, 1935 Brookdale Rd, Suite 139, Naperville, IL 60563 *Tel:* 630-961-3900 *Toll Free Tel:* 800-432-7444 *Fax:* 630-961-2168 *E-mail:* info@sourcebooks.com; customersupport@sourcebooks.com *Web Site:* www.sourcebooks.com, pg 204

Baugher, Matt, Thomas Nelson, 501 Nelson Place, Nashville, TN 37214 *Tel:* 615-889-9000 *Toll Free Tel:* 800-251-4000 *Fax:* 615-902-1548 *Web Site:* www.thomasnelson.com, pg 217

Baughman, Jeff, Fox Chapel Publishing Co Inc, 1970 Broad St, East Petersburg, PA 17520 *Tel:* 717-560-4703 *Toll Free Tel:* 800-457-9112 *Fax:* 717-560-4702 *E-mail:* customerservice@foxchapelpublishing.com *Web Site:* www.foxchapelpublishing.com, pg 80

Bauhan, Sarah, May Sarton New Hampshire Poetry Prize, 44 Main St, 2nd fl, Peterborough, NH 03458 *Tel:* 603-567-4430 *Web Site:* www.bauhanpublishing.com, pg 664

Baule, Deirdre, Hachette Nashville, 6100 Tower Circle, Room 210, Franklin, TN 37067 *Tel:* 615-221-0996 *Fax:* 615-221-0962 *Web Site:* www.hachettebookgroup.com, pg 91

Bauman, Erica, Aevitas Creative Management, 19 W 21 St, Suite 501, New York, NY 10010 *Tel:* 212-765-6900 *Web Site:* aevitascreative.com, pg 474

Baumann, David, University of Pittsburgh Press, 7500 Thomas Blvd, Pittsburgh, PA 15260 *Tel:* 412-383-2456 *Fax:* 412-383-2466 *E-mail:* info@upress.pitt.edu *Web Site:* www.upress.pitt.edu, pg 230

Baumer, Jan, Folio Literary Management, The Film Center Bldg, 630 Ninth Ave, Suite 1101, New York, NY 10036 *Tel:* 212-400-1494 *Fax:* 212-967-0977 *Web Site:* www.foliolit.com, pg 484

Baumstein, Hali, Bloomsbury Publishing Inc, 1385 Broadway, 5th fl, New York, NY 10018 *Tel:* 212-419-5300 *E-mail:* marketingusa@bloomsbury.com; adultpublicityusa@bloomsbury.com; askacademic@bloomsbury.com *Web Site:* www.bloomsbury.com, pg 36

Bautista, Fr Tony, St Pauls, 2187 Victory Blvd, Staten Island, NY 10314-6603 *Tel:* 718-761-0047 (edit & prodn); 718-698-2759 (mktg & billing) *Toll Free Tel:* 800-343-2522 *Fax:* 718-761-0057 *E-mail:* sales@stpauls.us; marketing@stpauls.us *Web Site:* www.stpauls.us, pg 191

Baxter, Carol, The Mathematical Association of America, 1529 18 St NW, Washington, DC 20036-1358 *Tel:* 202-387-5200 *Toll Free Tel:* 800-741-9415 *Fax:* 202-265-2384 *E-mail:* maahq@maa.org; advertising@maa.org (pubns) *Web Site:* www.maa.org, pg 134

Baxter, James, National Press Club of Canada Foundation Inc, 17 York St, Suite 201, Ottawa, ON K1N 9J6, Canada *E-mail:* info@pressclubcanada.ca *Web Site:* pressclubcanada.ca, pg 540

Bay, Bill, Mel Bay Publications Inc, 1734 Gilsinn Lane, Fenton, MO 63026 *Tel:* 636-257-3970 *Toll Free Tel:* 800-863-5229 *Fax:* 636-257-5062 *Toll Free Fax:* 800-660-9818 *E-mail:* email@melbay.com *Web Site:* www.melbay.com, pg 137

Bay, Linda, Penguin Group USA, A Penguin Random House Company, 375 Hudson St, New York, NY 10014 *Tel:* 212-366-2000 *Toll Free Tel:* 800-847-5515 (inside sales); 800-631-8571 (cust serv) *Fax:* 212-366-2666; 607-775-4829 (inside sales) *E-mail:* online@us.penguingroup.com *Web Site:* www.penguin.com, pg 163

Bay, Stephanie, Random House Children's Books, 1745 Broadway, 10th fl, New York, NY 10019 *Tel:* 212-782-9000 *Web Site:* www.randomhousekids.com, pg 181

Bayer, Lisa, University of Georgia Press, Main Library, 3rd fl, 320 S Jackson St, Athens, GA 30602 *Fax:* 706-542-2558; 706-542-6770 *Web Site:* www.ugapress.org, pg 227

Bayers, William, Houghton Mifflin Harcourt, 125 High St, Boston, MA 02110 *Tel:* 617-351-5000 *Toll Free Tel:* 855-969-4642; 800-225-5425 (K-12 educ materials); 800-323-9540 (assessment materials); 877-219-1537 (SkillsTutor); 888-242-6747 (Innovation in Educ Group); 800-225-3362 (Trade & Ref Div) *Toll Free Fax:* 800-269-5232 *E-mail:* myhmhco@hmhco.com *Web Site:* www.hmhco.com, pg 103

Bays, Susan, Arbutus Press, 2364 Pinehurst Trail, Traverse City, MI 49696 *Tel:* 231-946-7240 *E-mail:* info@arbutuspress.com *Web Site:* www.arbutuspress.com, pg 19

Bazzy, William M, Artech House®, 685 Canton St, Norwood, MA 02062 *Tel:* 781-769-9750 *Toll Free Tel:* 800-225-9977 *Fax:* 781-769-6334 *E-mail:* artech@artechhouse.com *Web Site:* www.artechhouse.com, pg 21

Beachy, Michael, Wm B Eerdmans Publishing Co, 4035 Park East Ct SE, Grand Rapids, MI 49546 *Tel:* 616-459-4591 *Toll Free Tel:* 800-253-7521 *Fax:* 616-459-6540 *E-mail:* customerservice@eerdmans.com; sales@eerdmans.com *Web Site:* www.eerdmans.com, pg 70

Beard, Elliott, The Brookings Institution Press, 1775 Massachusetts Ave NW, Washington, DC 20036-2188 *Tel:* 202-797-6000 *E-mail:* permissions@brookings.edu *Web Site:* www.brookings.edu, pg 42

Beard, Morgan, Swedenborg Foundation, 320 N Church St, West Chester, PA 19380 *Tel:* 610-430-3222 *Toll Free Tel:* 800-355-3222 (cust serv) *Fax:* 610-430-7982 *E-mail:* info@swedenborg.com *Web Site:* swedenborg.com, pg 211

Beard, Stephanie, Turner Publishing Co, 4507 Charlotte Ave, Suite 100, Nashville, TN 37209 *Tel:* 615-255-BOOK (255-2665) *Fax:* 615-255-5081 *E-mail:* marketing@turnerpublishing.com; submissions@turnerpublishing.com; editorial@turnerpublishing.com *Web Site:* www.turnerpublishing.com; www.facebook.com/turner.publishing, pg 222

Beardow, Jim, International Monetary Fund (IMF), Editorial & Publications Division, 700 19 St NW, HQ1-5-355, Washington, DC 20431 *Tel:* 202-623-7430 *Fax:* 202-623-7201 *E-mail:* publications@imf.org *Web Site:* bookstore.imf.org; elibrary.imf.org (online collection), pg 111

Beasley, J Malcolm, Professional Communications Inc, 1223 W Main, Suite 1427, Durant, OK 74702-1427 *Tel:* 580-745-9838 *Toll Free Tel:* 800-337-9838 *Fax:* 580-745-9837 *E-mail:* info@pcibooks.com *Web Site:* www.pcibooks.com, pg 176

Beaudet, Marie-Andree, La Fondation Emile Nelligan, 100, rue Sherbrooke, Suite 202, Montreal, QC H2X 1C3, Canada *E-mail:* info@fondation-nelligan.org *Web Site:* www.fondation-nelligan.org, pg 534

Beaudet, Marie-Andree, Prix Emile-Nelligan, 100, rue Sherbrooke, Suite 202, Montreal, QC H2X 1C3, Canada *Tel:* 514-278-4657 *Toll Free Tel:* 888-849-8540 *E-mail:* info@fondation-nelligan.org *Web Site:* www.fondation-nelligan.org, pg 659

Beaudoin, Andre, Les Editions Ganesha Inc, CP 484, succursale d'Youville, Montreal, QC H2P 2W1, Canada *Tel:* 450-641-2395 *E-mail:* courriel@editions-ganesha.qc.ca *Web Site:* www.editions-ganesha.qc.ca, pg 424

Beaumier, Fr Casey, Institute of Jesuit Sources (IJS), Boston College, Institute for Advanced Jesuit Studies, 140 Commonwealth Ave, Chestnut, MA 02467 *Tel:* 617-552-2568 *Fax:* 617-552-2575 *E-mail:* jesuitsources@bc.edu *Web Site:* jesuitsources.bc.edu, pg 110

Becerra, Nannette, Gem Guides Book Co, 1155 W Ninth St, Upland, CA 91786 *Tel:* 626-855-1611 *Toll Free Tel:* 800-824-5118 (orders) *Fax:* 626-855-1610 *E-mail:* info@gemguidesbooks.com; sales@gemguidesbooks.com (orders) *Web Site:* www.gemguidesbooks.com, pg 84

Becher, Bill, AuthorHouse, 1663 Liberty Dr, Bloomington, IN 47403 *Tel:* 812-339-6000 (outside US) *Toll Free Tel:* 888-519-5121 *E-mail:* authorsupport@authorhouse.com *Web Site:* www.authorhouse.com, pg 25

Becher, Bill, iUniverse, 1663 Liberty Dr, Bloomington, IN 47403 *Toll Free Tel:* 800-AUTHORS (288-4677) *Web Site:* www.iuniverse.com, pg 113

Becher, Bill, Trafford, 1663 Liberty Dr, Bloomington, IN 47403 *Toll Free Tel:* 888-232-4444 *E-mail:* customersupport@trafford.com; sales@trafford.com *Web Site:* www.trafford.com, pg 219

Becher, Bill, Xlibris Corp, 1663 Liberty Dr, Suite 200, Bloomington, IN 47403 *Toll Free Tel:* 844-714-8691; 888-795-4274 *Fax:* 610-915-0294 *E-mail:* info@xlibris.com; media@xlibris.com *Web Site:* www.xlibris.com; www.authorsolutions.com/our-imprints/xlibris, pg 246

Bechthold, Mike, Wilfrid Laurier University Press, 75 University Ave W, Waterloo, ON N2L 3C5, Canada *Tel:* 519-884-0710 *Toll Free Tel:* 866-836-5551 (CN & US) *Fax:* 519-725-1399 *E-mail:* press@wlu.ca *Web Site:* www.wlupress.wlu.ca, pg 445

Beck, Eric, Seedling Publications Inc, 520 E Bainbridge St, Elizabethtown, PA 17022 *Toll Free Tel:* 800-233-0759 *Toll Free Tel:* 888-834-1303 *E-mail:* edcsr@continentalpress.com *Web Site:* www.continentalpress.com, pg 196

Beck, Rachel, Liza Dawson Associates, 121 W 27 St, Suite 1201, New York, NY 10001 *Tel:* 212-465-9071 *Web Site:* www.lizadawsonassociates.com, pg 481

Becker, Matt, University of Massachusetts Press, East Experiment Station, 671 N Pleasant St, Amherst, MA 01003 *Tel:* 413-545-2217 *Fax:* 413-545-1226 *E-mail:* info@umpress.umass.edu *Web Site:* www.umass.edu/umpress, pg 228

Becker, Ulrich, Mondial, 203 W 107 St, Suite 6-C, New York, NY 10025 *Tel:* 646-807-8031 *Fax:* 208-361-2863 *E-mail:* contact@mondialbooks.com *Web Site:* www.mondialbooks.com, pg 142

Beckerman, Chad W, The CAT Agency Inc, PO Box 1390, Fairfield, CT 06825 *Tel:* 917-434-3141 *Web Site:* www.catugeau.com, pg 511

Beckett, Autumn, Oceanview Publishing Inc, 1620 Main St, Suite 11, Sarasota, FL 34236 *Tel:* 941-387-8500 *Web Site:* oceanviewpub.com, pg 154

Beckman, Andrew, Timber Press Inc, 133 SW Second Ave, Suite 450, Portland, OR 97204 *Tel:* 503-227-2878 *Toll Free Tel:* 800-327-5680 *Fax:* 503-227-3070 *E-mail:* info@timberpress.com *Web Site:* www.timberpress.com, pg 218

Bedard, Rachel, Les Editions du Remue-Menage, La Maison Parent-Roback, 110 rue Sainte-Therese, bureau 303, Montreal, QC H2Y 1E6, Canada *Tel:* 514-876-0097 *Fax:* 514-876-7951 *E-mail:* info@editions-rm.ca *Web Site:* www.editions-rm.ca, pg 423

Bedford, Laura, Guild of Book Workers, 521 Fifth Ave, New York, NY 10175 *Tel:* 212-292-4444 *E-mail:* communications@guildofbookworkers.org *Web Site:* www.guildofbookworkers.org, pg 534

Bedford, Stephen, Simon & Schuster, 1230 Avenue of the Americas, New York, NY 10020 *Tel:* 212-698-7000 *Toll Free Tel:* 800-223-2348 (cust serv); 800-223-2336 (orders) *Toll Free Fax:* 800-943-9831 (orders) *Web Site:* www.simonandschuster.com, pg 198

Bedi, Satbir, Scholastic Inc, 557 Broadway, New York, NY 10012 *Tel:* 212-343-6100 *Toll Free Tel:* 800-SCHOLASTIC (724-6527) *Web Site:* www.scholastic.com, pg 194

Bedick, Cara, Chronicle Books, 680 Second St, San Francisco, CA 94107 *Tel:* 415-537-4200 *Toll Free Tel:* 800-759-0190 (cust serv) *Fax:* 415-537-4460 *Toll Free Fax:* 800-858-7787 (orders); 800-286-9471 (cust serv) *E-mail:* frontdesk@chroniclebooks.com *Web Site:* www.chroniclebooks.com, pg 52

Bedingfield, Sarah, Levine|Greenberg|Rostan Literary Agency, 307 Seventh Ave, Suite 2407, New York, NY 10001 *Tel:* 212-337-0934 *Fax:* 212-337-0948 *Web Site:* lgrliterary.com, pg 493

Beditz, Dr Joseph, National Golf Foundation, 501 N Hwy A1A, Jupiter, FL 33477-4577 *Tel:* 561-744-6006 *Toll Free Tel:* 888-275-4643 *Fax:* 561-744-6107 *E-mail:* general@ngf.org *Web Site:* www.ngf.org, pg 147

Bednarik, Joseph, Copper Canyon Press, Fort Worden State Park, Bldg 313, Port Townsend, WA 98368 *Tel:* 360-385-4925 *Toll Free Tel:* 877-501-1393 (orders) *Fax:* 360-385-4985 *E-mail:* poetry@coppercanyonpress.org *Web Site:* www.coppercanyonpress.org, pg 56

Bedrick, Claudia, Enchanted Lion Books, 67 West St, Studio 317A, Brooklyn, NY 11222 *Tel:* 646-785-9272 *E-mail:* enchantedlion.community@gmail.com *Web Site:* www.enchantedlion.com, pg 72

Beeke, Joel R, Reformation Heritage Books, 2965 Leonard St NE, Grand Rapids, MI 49525 *Tel:* 616-977-0889 *Fax:* 616-285-3246 *E-mail:* orders@heritagebooks.org *Web Site:* www.heritagebooks.org, pg 184

Beeny, Martyn, Cornell University Press, Sage House, 512 E State St, Ithaca, NY 14850 *Tel:* 607-253-2338 *Fax:* 607-253-2374 *E-mail:* cupressinfo@cornell.edu; cupress-sales@cornell.edu *Web Site:* www.cornellpress.cornell.edu, pg 57

Beer, Molly, Writers Guild of America, East (WGAE), 250 Hudson St, Suite 700, New York, NY 10013 *Tel:* 212-767-7800 *Fax:* 212-582-1909 *Web Site:* www.wgaeast.org, pg 549

Beers, Ron, Tyndale House Publishers Inc, 351 Executive Dr, Carol Stream, IL 60188 *Tel:* 630-668-8300 *Toll Free Tel:* 800-323-9400; 855-277-9400 *Toll Free Fax:* 866-622-9474 *Web Site:* www.tyndale.com, pg 223

Begay, Corey, Salina Bookshelf Inc, 1120 W University Ave, Suite 102, Flagstaff, AZ 86001 *Toll Free Tel:* 877-527-0070 *Fax:* 928-526-0386 *Web Site:* www.salinabookshelf.com, pg 191

Beguiristain, Luisa, Roaring Brook Press, 120 Broadway, New York, NY 10271 *Tel:* 646-307-5151 *Web Site:* us.macmillan.com/publishers/roaring-brook-press, pg 186

Behal, Hayley, Arcadia Publishing Inc, 420 Wando Park Blvd, Mount Pleasant, SC 29464 *Tel:* 843-853-2070 *Toll Free Tel:* 888-313-2665 (orders only) *Fax:* 843-853-0044 *E-mail:* sales@arcadiapublishing.com *Web Site:* www.arcadiapublishing.com, pg 19

Behar, Ann, Scovil Galen Ghosh Literary Agency Inc, 276 Fifth Ave, Suite 207, New York, NY 10001 *Tel:* 212-679-8686 *E-mail:* info@sgglit.com *Web Site:* www.sgglit.com, pg 502

Behar, Tracy, Little, Brown and Company, 1290 Avenue of the Americas, New York, NY 10104 *Tel:* 212-364-1100 *Fax:* 212-364-0952 *E-mail:* firstname.lastname@hbgusa.com *Web Site:* www.littlebrown.com; www.hachettebookgroup.com, pg 125

Behm, Melissa, Health Professions Press, 409 Washington Ave, Suite 500, Towson, MD 21204 *Tel:* 410-337-9585 *Toll Free Tel:* 888-337-8808 *Fax:* 410-337-8539 *Web Site:* www.healthpropress.com, pg 97

Behm, Melissa A, Paul H Brookes Publishing Co Inc, PO Box 10624, Baltimore, MD 21285-0624 *Tel:* 410-337-9580 (outside US & CN) *Toll Free Tel:* 800-638-3775 (US & CN) *Fax:* 410-337-8539 *E-mail:* custserv@brookespublishing.com *Web Site:* www.brookespublishing.com, pg 42

Behn, Robin, University of Alabama Program in Creative Writing, PO Box 870244, Tuscaloosa, AL 35487-0244 *Tel:* 205-348-5065 *Fax:* 205-348-1388 *E-mail:* english@ua.edu *Web Site:* www.as.ua.edu/english, pg 585

Behning, Janet, Princeton Architectural Press, 202 Warren St, Hudson, NY 12534 *Tel:* 518-671-6100 *Toll Free Tel:* 800-722-6657 (dist); 800-759-0190 (sales) *E-mail:* sales@papress.com *Web Site:* www.papress.com, pg 174

Behrend-Wilcox, Talia, Harry N Abrams Inc, 195 Broadway, 9th fl, New York, NY 10007 *Tel:* 212-206-7715 *Toll Free Tel:* 800-345-1359 *Fax:* 212-519-1210 *E-mail:* abrams@abramsbooks.com *Web Site:* www.abramsbooks.com, pg 3

Behrman, David, Behrman House Inc, 11 Edison Place, Springfield, NJ 07081 *Tel:* 973-379-7200 *Toll Free Tel:* 800-221-2755 *Fax:* 973-379-7280 *E-mail:* customersupport@bchrmanhouse.com *Web Site:* store.behrmanhouse.com, pg 30

Beidler, Brien, Guild of Book Workers, 521 Fifth Ave, New York, NY 10175 *Tel:* 212-292-4444 *E-mail:* communications@guildofbookworkers.org *Web Site:* www.guildofbookworkers.org, pg 534

Beier, Elizabeth, St Martin's Press, LLC, 120 Broadway, New York, NY 10271 *Tel:* 646-307-5151 *Web Site:* us.macmillan.com/smp, pg 190

Beil, Frederic C, Frederic C Beil Publisher Inc, 609 Whitaker St, Savannah, GA 31401 *Tel:* 912-233-2446 *E-mail:* fcb@beil.com *Web Site:* www.beil.com, pg 31

Beilenson, Esther, Peter Pauper Press, Inc, 202 Mamaroneck Ave, Suite 400, White Plains, NY 10601-5376 *Tel:* 914-681-0144 *Fax:* 914-681-0389 *E-mail:* customerservice@peterpauper.com; orders@peterpauper.com; marketing@peterpauper.com *Web Site:* www.peterpauper.com, pg 168

Beilenson, Laurence, Peter Pauper Press, Inc, 202 Mamaroneck Ave, Suite 400, White Plains, NY 10601-5376 *Tel:* 914-681-0144 *Fax:* 914-681-0389 *E-mail:* customerservice@peterpauper.com; orders@peterpauper.com; marketing@peterpauper.com *Web Site:* www.peterpauper.com, pg 168

Beit-Arie, Oren, ProQuest LLC, 789 E Eisenhower Pkwy, Ann Arbor, MI 48108 *Tel:* 734-761-4700 *Toll Free Tel:* 800-521-0600; 877-779-6768 (sales) *E-mail:* sales@proquest.com *Web Site:* www.proquest.com, pg 176

Beitzel, Tim, Kendall Hunt Publishing Co, 4050 Westmark Dr, Dubuque, IA 52002-2624 *Tel:* 563-589-1000 *Toll Free Tel:* 800-228-0810 (orders) *Fax:* 563-589-1046 *Toll Free Fax:* 800-772-9165 *E-mail:* orders@kendallhunt.com *Web Site:* www.kendallhunt.com, pg 116

Bekkoucha, Sophia, Ordre des traducteurs, terminologues et interpretes agrees du quebec, 1108-2021 Ave Union, Montreal, QC H3A 2S9, Canada *Tel:* 514-845-4411 *Toll Free Tel:* 800-265-4815 *Fax:* 514-845-9903 *E-mail:* info@ottiaq.org; direction@ottiaq.org; reception@ottiaq.org *Web Site:* www.ottiaq.org, pg 542

Belan, Allison, Duke University Press, 905 W Main St, Suite 18B, Durham, NC 27701 *Tel:* 919-688-5134 *Toll Free Tel:* 888-651-0122 (US) *Fax:* 919-688-2615 *Toll Free Fax:* 888-651-0124 *E-mail:* orders@dukeupress.edu *Web Site:* www.dukeupress.edu, pg 68

Belanger, Paul, Les Editions du Noroit, 4609, rue D'Iberville, espace 202, Montreal, QC H2H 2L9, Canada *Tel:* 514-727-0005 *E-mail:* lenoroit@lenoroit.com *Web Site:* www.lenoroit.com, pg 423

Belden, Kathryn, Scribner, 1230 Avenue of the Americas, New York, NY 10020, pg 195

Belderis, Ina, Theosophical University Press, PO Box C, Pasadena, CA 91109-7107 *Tel:* 626-798-3378 *E-mail:* tupress@theosociety.org *Web Site:* www.theosociety.org, pg 217

Belfiglio, Brian, Scribner, 1230 Avenue of the Americas, New York, NY 10020, pg 195

Beliveau, Mathieu, Beliveau Editeur, 567 rue Bienville, Boucherville, QC J4B 2Z5, Canada *Tel:* 450-679-1933 *Web Site:* www.beliveauediteur.com, pg 416

Belknap, Mary PhD, Nautilus Book Awards, PO Box 2285, Vashon, WA 98070 *Tel:* 206-604-2250 *Web Site:* www.nautilusbookawards.com, pg 646

Bell, Aimee, Gallery Books, 1230 Avenue of the Americas, New York, NY 10020 *Toll Free Tel:* 800-456-6798 *Fax:* 212-698-2615 *E-mail:* consumer.customerservice@simonandschuster.com *Web Site:* www.simonandschuster.com, pg 83

Bell, Aurora, University of South Carolina Press, 1600 Hampton St, Suite 544, Columbia, SC 29208 Tel: 803-777-5245 Toll Free Tel: 800-768-2500 (orders) Fax: 803-777-0160 Toll Free Fax: 800-868-0740 (orders) Web Site: www.sc.edu/uscpress, pg 231

Bell, Duncan, Columbia Books & Information Services (CBIS), 4340 East-West Hwy, Suite 300, Bethesda, MD 20814 Tel: 202-464-1662 Fax: 301-664-9600 E-mail: info@columbiabooks.com Web Site: www.columbiabooks.com; www.lobbyists.info; www.associationexecs.com, pg 55

Bell, E, Haynes North America Inc, 859 Lawrence Dr, Newbury Park, CA 91320-1514 Tel: 805-498-6703 Toll Free Tel: 800-4-HAYNES (442-9637) Fax: 805-498-2867 E-mail: cstn@haynes.com Web Site: www.haynes.com, pg 96

Bell, Emily, Farrar, Straus & Giroux, LLC, 175 Varick St, 9th fl, New York, NY 10014 Tel: 212-741-6900 E-mail: fsg.publicity@fsgbooks.com Web Site: us.macmillan.com/fsg.aspx, pg 76

Bell, Justin, Spectrum Literary Agency, 320 Central Park W, Suite 1-D, New York, NY 10025 Tel: 212-362-4323 Fax: 212-362-4562 Web Site: www.spectrumliteraryagency.com, pg 503

Bell, Merleyn, Neustadt International Prize for Literature, c/o University of Oklahoma, 630 Parrington Oval, Suite 110, Norman, OK 73019-4033 Tel: 405-325-4531 Web Site: www.worldliteraturetoday.org; www.worldlit.org, pg 646

Bell, Merleyn, NSK Neustadt Prize for Children's Literature, c/o University of Oklahoma, 630 Parrington Oval, Suite 110, Norman, OK 73019-4033 Tel: 405-325-4531 Web Site: www.worldliteraturetoday.org; www.worldlit.org, pg 649

Bellanca, Dr Patricia, Harvard Summer Writing Program, 51 Brattle St, Dept S760, Cambridge, MA 02138-3722 Tel: 617-495-4024 Fax: 617-495-9176 E-mail: summer@harvard.edu Web Site: www.summer.harvard.edu, pg 574

Belleris, Christine, Health Communications Inc, 3201 SW 15 St, Deerfield Beach, FL 33442 Tel: 954-360-0909 Toll Free Tel: 800-851-9100; 800-441-5569 (cust serv & orders) Fax: 954-360-0034 Toll Free Fax: 800-424-7652 (cust serv & orders) E-mail: customerservice2@hcibooks.com Web Site: www.hcibooks.com, pg 96

Belozerskaya, Marina, Fowler Museum at UCLA, PO Box 951549, Los Angeles, CA 90095-1549 Tel: 310-825-4361 Fax: 310-206-7007 E-mail: fowlerws@arts.ucla.edu Web Site: www.fowler.ucla.edu, pg 80

Ben, Crystal, Orbit, 1290 Avenue of the Americas, New York, NY 10104 Tel: 212-364-1100 Toll Free Tel: 800-759-0190 Web Site: www.orbitbooks.net, pg 156

Benamou, Sharon, AJL Judaica Bibliography Award, PO Box 1118, Teaneck, NJ 07666 Tel: 201-371-3255 E-mail: info@jewishlibraries.org Web Site: jewishlibraries.org, pg 590

Benamou, Sharon, AJL Judaica Reference Award, PO Box 1118, Teaneck, NJ 07666 Tel: 201-371-3255 E-mail: info@jewishlibraries.org Web Site: jewishlibraries.org, pg 590

Benamy, Talia, Philomel, 345 Hudson St, New York, NY 10014 Tel: 212-366-2000 Web Site: www.penguin.com/publishers/philomel, pg 169

Benard, Mary, Skinner House Books, c/o Unitarian Universalist Assn, 24 Farnsworth St, Boston, MA 02110-1409 Tel: 617-742-2100 Fax: 617-948-6466 E-mail: skinnerhouse@uua.org Web Site: www.skinnerhouse.org, pg 200

Benatar, Raquel, Laredo Publishing Co, 465 Westview Ave, Englewood, NJ 07631 Tel: 201-408-4048 E-mail: info@laredopublishing.com Web Site: www.laredopublishing.com, pg 120

Benatar, Raquel, Renaissance House, 465 Westview Ave, Englewood, NJ 07631 Tel: 201-408-4048 Web Site: www.renaissancehouse.net, pg 184, 512

Bender, Robert, Simon & Schuster, 1230 Avenue of the Americas, New York, NY 10020 Tel: 212-698-7000 Toll Free Tel: 800-223-2348 (cust serv); 800-223-2336 (orders) Toll Free Fax: 800-943-9831 (orders) Web Site: www.simonandschuster.com, pg 198

Bender, Robyn, Penguin Young Readers Group, 345 Hudson St, New York, NY 10014 Tel: 212-366-2000; 212-414-3553 Fax: 212-414-3340 Web Site: www.penguin.com/children, pg 165

Bender, Roger J, R James Bender Publishing, PO Box 23456, San Jose, CA 95153-3456 Tel: 408-225-5777 Fax: 408-225-4739 Web Site: www.bender-publishing.com, pg 31

Benedetto, Lynn, Cornell University Press, Sage House, 512 E State St, Ithaca, NY 14850 Tel: 607-253-2338 Fax: 607-253-2374 E-mail: cupressinfo@cornell.edu; cupress-sales@cornell.edu Web Site: www.cornellpress.cornell.edu, pg 57

Benedict, Holly, Quincannon Publishing Group, PO Box 8100, Glen Ridge, NJ 07028-8100 Tel: 973-380-9942 E-mail: editors@quincannongroup.com (query first via e-mail) Web Site: www.quincannongroup.com, pg 179

Benevento, Nicole, Holiday House Publishing Inc, 50 Broad St, New York, NY 10004 Tel: 212-688-0085 Fax: 212-421-6134 E-mail: info@holidayhouse.com Web Site: www.holidayhouse.com, pg 101

Benjey, Thomas R, Tuxedo Press, 546 E Springville Rd, Carlisle, PA 17015 Tel: 717-258-9733 Fax: 717-243-0074 E-mail: info@tuxedo-press.com Web Site: tuxedo-press.com, pg 222

Benka, Jennifer, Academy of American Poets Fellowship, 75 Maiden Lane, Suite 901, New York, NY 10038 Tel: 212-274-0343 E-mail: academy@poets.org Web Site: www.poets.org, pg 589

Benka, Jennifer, The Academy of American Poets Inc, 75 Maiden Lane, Suite 901, New York, NY 10038 Tel: 212-274-0343 E-mail: academy@poets.org Web Site: www.poets.org, pg 521

Benka, Jennifer, Ambroggio Prize, 75 Maiden Lane, Suite 901, New York, NY 10038 Tel: 212-274-0343 E-mail: awards@poets.org Web Site: www.poets.org, pg 591

Benka, Jennifer, James Lauglin Award, 75 Maiden Lane, Suite 901, New York, NY 10038 Tel: 212-274-0343 E-mail: awards@poets.org Web Site: www.poets.org, pg 631

Benka, Jennifer, Lenore Marshall Poetry Prize, 75 Maiden Lane, Suite 901, New York, NY 10038 Tel: 212-274-0343 E-mail: awards@poets.org Web Site: www.poets.org, pg 638

Benka, Jennifer, Harold Morton Landon Translation Award, 75 Maiden Lane, Suite 901, New York, NY 10038 Tel: 212-274-0343 E-mail: awards@poets.org Web Site: www.poets.org, pg 643

Benka, Jennifer, Aliki Perroti & Seth Frank Most Promising Young Poet Award, 75 Maiden Lane, Suite 901, New York, NY 10038 Tel: 212-274-0343 E-mail: awards@poets.org Web Site: www.poets.org, pg 655

Benka, Jennifer, Raiziss/de Palchi Fellowship, 75 Maiden Lane, Suite 901, New York, NY 10038 Tel: 212-274-0343 E-mail: academy@poets.org Web Site: www.poets.org, pg 660

Benka, Jennifer, Wallace Stevens Award, 75 Maiden Lane, Suite 901, New York, NY 10038 Tel: 212-274-0343 E-mail: awards@poets.org Web Site: www.poets.org, pg 670

Benka, Jennifer, Treehouse Climate Action Poem Prize, 75 Maiden Lane, Suite 901, New York, NY 10038 Tel: 212-274-0343 E-mail: academy@poets.org Web Site: www.poets.org, pg 673

Benka, Jennifer, Walt Whitman Award, 75 Maiden Lane, Suite 901, New York, NY 10038 Tel: 212-274-0343 E-mail: academy@poets.org Web Site: www.poets.org, pg 677

Benko, Kamilla, Bloomsbury Publishing Inc, 1385 Broadway, 5th fl, New York, NY 10018 Tel: 212-419-5300 E-mail: marketingusa@bloomsbury.com; adultpublicityusa@bloomsbury.com; askacademic@bloomsbury.com Web Site: www.bloomsbury.com, pg 36

Benne, Susan, Antiquarian Booksellers' Association of America (ABAA), 20 W 44 St, Suite 507, New York, NY 10036 Tel: 212-944-8291 Fax: 212-944-8293 E-mail: hq@abaa.org Web Site: www.abaa.org, pg 525

Benner, Deborah J, Goose River Press, 3400 Friendship Rd, Waldoboro, ME 04572-6337 Tel: 207-832-6665 E-mail: gooseriverpress@gmail.com Web Site: gooseriverpress.com, pg 87

Bennett, Barbara, Kensington Publishing Corp, 119 W 40 St, New York, NY 10018 Tel: 212-407-1500 Toll Free Tel: 800-221-2647 Fax: 212-935-0699 Web Site: www.kensingtonbooks.com, pg 116

Bennett, Elizabeth, Transatlantic Agency, 2 Bloor St E, Suite 3500, Toronto, ON M4W 1A8, Canada Tel: 416-488-9214 E-mail: info@transatlanticagency.com Web Site: www.transatlanticagency.com, pg 506

Bennett, Hannah, Cleis Press, 101 Hudson St, 37th fl, Suite 3705, Jersey City, NJ 07302 Tel: 646-257-4343 E-mail: cleis@cleispress.com Web Site: www.cleispress.com; www.vivaeditions.com, pg 53

Bennett, Hannah, Women's National Book Association Award, PO Box 237, FDR Sta, New York, NY 10150-0231 Toll Free Tel: 866-610-WNBA (610-9622) Web Site: www.wnba-books.org; www.NationalReadingGroupMonth.org, pg 679

Bennett, Jed, Penguin Young Readers Group, 345 Hudson St, New York, NY 10014 Tel: 212-366-2000; 212-414-3553 Fax: 212-414-3340 Web Site: www.penguin.com/children, pg 165

Bennett, John M, Luna Bisonte Prods, 137 Leland Ave, Columbus, OH 43214 Tel: 614-846-4126 Web Site: www.johnmbennett.net; www.lulu.com/spotlight/lunabisonteprods, pg 129

Bennett, Katherine, Perseus Books, 1290 Avenue of the Americas, New York, NY 10104 Tel: 212-340-8100 Toll Free Tel: 800-343-4499 (cust serv) Fax: 212-340-8105 Web Site: www.perseusbooks.com, pg 168

Bennett, Katie, HarperCollins Publishers, 195 Broadway, New York, NY 10007 Tel: 212-207-7000 Fax: 212-207-7145 Web Site: www.harpercollins.com, pg 94

Bennett, Lynn, Transatlantic Agency, 2 Bloor St E, Suite 3500, Toronto, ON M4W 1A8, Canada Tel: 416-488-9214 E-mail: info@transatlanticagency.com Web Site: www.transatlanticagency.com, pg 506

Bennett, Matthew, Northwest Independent Editors Guild, 7511 Greenwood Ave N, No 307, Seattle, WA 98103 E-mail: info@edsguild.org Web Site: edsguild.org, pg 542

Bennett, Meagan, Phaidon, 65 Bleecker St, 8th fl, New York, NY 10012 Tel: 212-652-5400 Toll Free Tel: 800-759-0190 (cust serv) Fax: 212-652-5410 Toll Free Fax: 800-286-9471 (cust serv) E-mail: enquiries@phaidon.com Web Site: www.phaidon.com, pg 168

Bennett, Millicent, Houghton Mifflin Harcourt Trade & Reference Division, 125 High St, Boston, MA 02110 Tel: 617-351-5000 Web Site: www.hmhco.com, pg 104

Bennie, Dale, University of Oklahoma Press, 2800 Venture Dr, Norman, OK 73069-8216 Tel: 405-325-2000 Web Site: www.oupress.com, pg 230

Benoit, Michael J, Benoit & Associates, 744 Stockton Heights Ct, Bourbonnais, IL 60914 Tel: 815-932-2582 Fax: 815-932-2594 Web Site: www.benoit-associates.com, pg 511

Bensaid, Barbara, US Games Systems Inc, 179 Ludlow St, Stamford, CT 06902 Tel: 203-353-8400 Toll Free Tel: 800-54-GAMES (544-2637) Fax: 203-353-8431 E-mail: info@usgamesinc.com Web Site: usgamesinc.com, pg 234

Benshoff, Emma, Random House Children's Books, 1745 Broadway, 10th fl, New York, NY 10019 Tel: 212-782-9000 Web Site: www.randomhousekids.com, pg 180

Benshoff, Kirk, Roaring Brook Press, 120 Broadway, New York, NY 10271 Tel: 646-307-5151 Web Site: us.macmillan.com/publishers/roaring-brook-press, pg 186

Bensky, Dan, Eastland Press, 2421 29 Ave W, Seattle, WA 98199 Tel: 206-931-6957 (cust serv) Fax: 206-283-7084 (orders) E-mail: info@eastlandpress.com; orders@eastlandpress.com Web Site: www.eastlandpress.com, pg 69

Benson, Betsy, City & Regional Magazine Association, 287 Richards Ave, Norwalk, CT 06850 Tel: 203-515-9294 E-mail: admin@citymag.org Web Site: www.citymag.org, pg 531

Benson, Ms Frances, Cornell University Press, Sage House, 512 E State St, Ithaca, NY 14850 Tel: 607-253-2338 Fax: 607-253-2374 E-mail: cupressinfo@cornell.edu; cupress-sales@cornell.edu Web Site: www.cornellpress.cornell.edu, pg 57

Benson, Ingrid, Integra Software Services Inc, 1110 Jorie Blvd, Suite 200, Oak Brook, IL 60523 Tel: 630-586-2579 Fax: 630-586-2599 E-mail: marketing@integra.co.in Web Site: www.integra.co.in, pg 465

Bentley, Michael, Bentley Publishers, 1734 Massachusetts Ave, Cambridge, MA 02138-1804 Tel: 617-547-4170 Toll Free Tel: 800-423-4595 Fax: 617-876-9235 E-mail: sales@bentleypublishers.com Web Site: www.bentleypublishers.com, pg 32

Benton, Lori, Scholastic Trade Division, 557 Broadway, New York, NY 10012 Tel: 212-343-6100; 212-343-4685 (export sales) Fax: 212-343-4714 (export sales) Web Site: www.scholastic.com, pg 194

Benvenuto, Kerri, Random House Children's Books, 1745 Broadway, 10th fl, New York, NY 10019 Tel: 212-782-9000 Web Site: www.randomhousekids.com, pg 180

Bercholz, Ivan, Shambhala Publications Inc, 4720 Walnut St, Boulder, CO 80301 Tel: 303-222-9598 Toll Free Tel: 866-424-0030 (off); 888-424-2329 (cust serv) E-mail: customercare@shambhala.com Web Site: www.shambhala.com, pg 197

Bercholz, Samuel, Shambhala Publications Inc, 4720 Walnut St, Boulder, CO 80301 Tel: 303-222-9598 Toll Free Tel: 866-424-0030 (off); 888-424-2329 (cust serv) E-mail: customercare@shambhala.com Web Site: www.shambhala.com, pg 197

Bercholz, Sara, Shambhala Publications Inc, 4720 Walnut St, Boulder, CO 80301 Tel: 303-222-9598 Toll Free Tel: 866-424-0030 (off); 888-424-2329 (cust serv) E-mail: customercare@shambhala.com Web Site: www.shambhala.com, pg 197

Beresford, Lea, Bloomsbury Publishing Inc, 1385 Broadway, 5th fl, New York, NY 10018 Tel: 212-419-5300 E-mail: marketingusa@bloomsbury.com; adultpublicityusa@bloomsbury.com; askacademic@bloomsbury.com Web Site: www.bloomsbury.com, pg 36

Berg, Jennifer, PAGE International Screenwriting Awards, 7190 Sunset Blvd, Suite 610, Hollywood, CA 90046 E-mail: info@pageawards.com Web Site: www.pageawards.com, pg 652

Berge, Pablo Agrest, STOCKCERO Inc, 3785 NW 82 Ave, Suite 302, Doral, FL 33166 Tel: 305-722-7628 Fax: 305-722-7628 E-mail: academicservices@stockcero.com; sales@stockcero.com Web Site: www.stockcero.com, pg 209

Bergen, Glenn, University of Manitoba Press, University of Manitoba, 301 St Johns College, 92 Dysart Rd, Winnipeg, MB R3T 2M5, Canada Tel: 204-474-9495 Fax: 204-474-7566 E-mail: uofmpress@umanitoba.ca Web Site: uofmpress.ca, pg 443

Bergen, Julia, Tom Doherty Associates, LLC, 120 Broadway, New York, NY 10271 Tel: 646-307-5511 Toll Free Tel: 800-455-0340 Web Site: us.macmillan.com/torforge, pg 66

Berger, Andrew, Quality Medical Publishing Inc, 11802 Borman Dr, St Louis, MO 63146 Tel: 314-878-7808 E-mail: customerservice@qmp.com Web Site: www.qmp.com, pg 178

Berger, Annie, Sourcebooks LLC, 1935 Brookdale Rd, Suite 139, Naperville, IL 60563 Tel: 630-961-3900 Toll Free Tel: 800-432-7444 Fax: 630-961-2168 E-mail: info@sourcebooks.com; customersupport@sourcebooks.com Web Site: www.sourcebooks.com, pg 204

Berger, Courtney, Duke University Press, 905 W Main St, Suite 18B, Durham, NC 27701 Tel: 919-688-5134 Toll Free Tel: 888-651-0122 (US) Fax: 919-688-2615 Toll Free Fax: 888-651-0124 E-mail: orders@dukeupress.edu Web Site: www.dukeupress.edu, pg 68

Berger, Ellie, Scholastic Inc, 557 Broadway, New York, NY 10012 Tel: 212-343-6100 Toll Free Tel: 800-SCHOLASTIC (724-6527) Web Site: www.scholastic.com, pg 194

Berger, Ellie, Scholastic Trade Division, 557 Broadway, New York, NY 10012 Tel: 212-343-6100; 212-343-4685 (export sales) Fax: 212-343-4714 (export sales) Web Site: www.scholastic.com, pg 194

Berger, Erin M, Scholastic Trade Division, 557 Broadway, New York, NY 10012 Tel: 212-343-6100; 212-343-4685 (export sales) Fax: 212-343-4714 (export sales) Web Site: www.scholastic.com, pg 194

Berger, Dr John, Cambridge University Press, One Liberty Plaza, 20th fl, New York, NY 10006 Tel: 212-924-3900; 212-337-5000 Fax: 212-691-3239; 845-353-4141 E-mail: newyork@cambridge.org; customer_service@cambridge.org Web Site: www.cambridge.org/us, pg 43

Berger, Karen, Dark Horse Comics, 10956 SE Main St, Milwaukie, OR 97222 Tel: 503-652-8815 Fax: 503-654-9440 E-mail: dhcomics@darkhorse.com Web Site: www.darkhorse.com, pg 62

Berger, Mel, WME, 11 Madison Ave, 18th fl, New York, NY 10010 Tel: 212-586-5100 Web Site: www.wmeentertainment.com, pg 508

Berger, Whitney, Sasquatch Books, 1904 S Third Ave, Suite 710, Seattle, WA 98101 Tel: 206-467-4300 Toll Free Tel: 800-775-0817 Fax: 206-467-4301 E-mail: custserv@sasquatchbooks.com Web Site: sasquatchbooks.com, pg 192

Bergera, Gary James, Signature Books Publishing LLC, 564 W 400 N, Salt Lake City, UT 84116-3411 Toll Free Tel: 800-356-5687 E-mail: people@signaturebooks.com Web Site: www.signaturebooks.com; www.signaturebookslibrary.org, pg 198

Bergeron, Amanda, Berkley Publishing Group, 1745 Broadway, 19th fl, New York, NY 10019 Tel: 212-366-2000 Web Site: www.penguin.com, pg 32

Bergeron, Catherine, Johns Hopkins University Press, 2715 N Charles St, Baltimore, MD 21218-4363 Tel: 410-516-6900; 410-516-6987 (journal orders outside US & CN) Toll Free Tel: 800-537-5487 (book orders & cust serv); 800-548-1784 (journal orders) Fax: 410-516-6968; 410-516-3866 (journal orders); 410-516-6998 (orders) E-mail: hfscustserv@press.jhu.edu (cust serv); jrnlcirc@press.jhu.edu (journal orders) Web Site: www.press.jhu.edu; muse.jhu.edu, pg 114

Bergeron, Laura, Watson Publishing International LLC, 349 Old Plymouth Rd, Sagamore Beach, MA 02562 E-mail: orders@shpusa.com Web Site: www.shpusa.com; www.watsonpublishing.com, pg 238

Bergh, Lily, Canadian Scholars' Press Inc, 425 Adelaide St W, Suite 200, Toronto, ON M5V 3C1, Canada Tel: 416-929-2774 Toll Free Tel: 800-463-1998 Fax: 416-929-1926 E-mail: info@cspi.org; info@canadianscholars.ca; editorial@canadianscholars.ca; orders@canadianscholars.ca Web Site: www.canadianscholars.ca; www.womenspress.ca, pg 419

Berghahn, Dr Marion, Berghahn Books, 20 Jay St, Suite 512, Brooklyn, NY 11201 Tel: 212-233-6004 Fax: 212-233-6007 E-mail: info@berghahnbooks.com; salesus@berghahnbooks.com; editorial@journals.berghahnbooks.com Web Site: www.berghahnbooks.com, pg 32

Berghahn, Vivian, Berghahn Books, 20 Jay St, Suite 512, Brooklyn, NY 11201 Tel: 212-233-6004 Fax: 212-233-6007 E-mail: info@berghahnbooks.com;

salesus@berghahnbooks.com; editorial@journals.berghahnbooks.com Web Site: www.berghahnbooks.com, pg 32

Bergkamp, Will, Augsburg Fortress Publishers, Publishing House of the Evangelical Lutheran Church in America, 510 Marquette Ave S, Minneapolis, MN 55402 Tel: 612-330-3300 Toll Free Tel: 800-426-0115 (ext 639, subns); 800-328-4648 (orders) Fax: 612-330-3455 E-mail: info@augsburgfortress.org; copyright@augsburgfortress.org (reprint permission requests); customercare@augsburgfortress.org Web Site: www.augsburgfortress.org; www.1517.media, pg 25

Bergonzi, Megan, Seedling Publications Inc, 520 E Bainbridge St, Elizabethtown, PA 17022 Toll Free Tel: 800-233-0759 Toll Free Fax: 888-834-1303 E-mail: edcsr@continentalpress.com Web Site: www.continentalpress.com, pg 196

Bergstrom, Jennifer, Gallery Books, 1230 Avenue of the Americas, New York, NY 10020 Toll Free Tel: 800-456-6798 Fax: 212-698-7284 E-mail: consumer.customerservice@simonandschuster.com Web Site: www.simonandschuster.com, pg 83

Bergstrom, Jennifer, Simon & Schuster, Inc, 1230 Avenue of the Americas, New York, NY 10020 Tel: 212-698-7000 Toll Free Tel: 800-223-2336 (orders) Fax: 212-698-7007 Toll Free Fax: 800-943-9831 (orders) E-mail: firstname.lastname@simonandschuster.com; purchaseorders@simonandschuster.com (orders) Web Site: www.simonandschuster.com, pg 199

Berinstein, Peter, A Richard Barber/Peter Berinstein & Associates, 60 E Eighth St, Suite 21-N, New York, NY 10003 Tel: 212-737-7266 Fax: 860-927-3942 E-mail: barberrich@aol.com, pg 475

Berk, Adina Popescu, Yale University Press, 302 Temple St, New Haven, CT 06511-8909 Tel: 203-432-0960; 203-432-0966 (sales); 401-531-2800 (cust serv) Toll Free Tel: 800-405-1619 (cust serv) Fax: 203-432-0948; 203-432-8485 (sales); 401-531-2801 (cust serv) Toll Free Fax: 800-406-9145 (cust serv) E-mail: sales.press@yale.edu (sales); customer.care@triliteral.org (cust serv) Web Site: www.yalebooks.com; yalepress.yale.edu/yupbooks, pg 246

Berkery, Peter, Association of University Presses (AUPresses), 1412 Broadway, Suite 2135, New York, NY 10018 Tel: 212-989-1010 Fax: 212-989-0275 E-mail: info@aupresses.org Web Site: www.aupresses.org, pg 527

Berkey, Jane Rotrosen, Jane Rotrosen Agency LLC, 85 Broad St, 28th fl, New York, NY 10004 Tel: 212-593-4330 Fax: 212-935-6985 Web Site: janerotrosen.com, pg 500

Berkin, Adam, Scholastic Education, 557 Broadway, New York, NY 10012 Tel: 212-343-6100 Fax: 212-343-6189 Web Site: www.scholastic.com, pg 194

Berkman, Hilary, Candlewick Press, 99 Dover St, Somerville, MA 02144-2825 Tel: 617-661-3330 Fax: 617-661-0565 E-mail: bigbear@candlewick.com; salesinfo@candlewick.com Web Site: www.candlewick.com, pg 44

Berkower, Amy, Writers House, 21 W 26 St, New York, NY 10010 Tel: 212-685-2400 Web Site: www.writershouse.com, pg 508

Berman, Ari, Yeshiva University Press, 500 W 185 St, New York, NY 10033 Tel: 212-960-5400 Web Site: www.yu.edu/books, pg 247

Berman, Sam, The Rough Notes Co Inc, 11690 Technology Dr, Carmel, IN 46032-5600 Tel: 317-582-1600 Toll Free Tel: 800-428-4384 (cust serv) Fax: 317-816-1000 Toll Free Fax: 800-321-1909 E-mail: rnc@roughnotes.com Web Site: www.roughnotes.com, pg 187

Berman, Todd, Penguin Random House LLC, 1745 Broadway, New York, NY 10019 Tel: 212-782-9000 Toll Free Tel: 800-726-0600 Web Site: www.penguinrandomhouse.com, pg 164

Bermudez, Melanie, Random House Children's Books, 1745 Broadway, 10th fl, New York, NY 10019 Tel: 212-782-9000 Web Site: www.randomhousekids.com, pg 181

Bernard, Alec, Puddingstone Literary, Authors' Agents, 11 Mabro Dr, Denville, NJ 07834-9607 *Tel:* 973-366-3622, pg 499

Bernard, Megan, Tom Doherty Associates, LLC, 120 Broadway, New York, NY 10271 *Tel:* 646-307-5511 *Toll Free Tel:* 800-455-0340 *Web Site:* us.macmillan.com/torforge, pg 66

Berndt, Kirstin, Simon & Schuster, 1230 Avenue of the Americas, New York, NY 10020 *Tel:* 212-698-7000 *Toll Free Tel:* 800-223-2348 (cust serv); 800-223-2336 (orders) *Toll Free Fax:* 800-943-9831 (orders) *Web Site:* www.simonandschuster.com, pg 198

Berner, Kate, Penguin Random House Speakers Bureau, A Penguin Random House Company, 1745 Broadway, Mail Drop 13-1, New York, NY 10019 *Tel:* 212-572-2013 *E-mail:* speakers@penguinrandomhouse.com *Web Site:* www.prhspeakers.com, pg 515

Bernfeld, Linda Rodriguez, SCBWI-FL Florida Regional Conference, 125 E Merritt Island Causeway, Suite 209, Merritt Island, FL 32952 *Tel:* 321-338-7208 *E-mail:* florida@scbwi.org *Web Site:* florida.scbwi.org, pg 578

Bernfeld, Linda Rodriguez, SCBWI-FL Mid-Year Workshops, 125 E Merritt Island Causeway, Suite 209, Merritt Island, FL 32952 *Tel:* 321-338-7208 *E-mail:* florida@scbwi.org *Web Site:* florida.scbwi.org, pg 578

Bernier, Jean, Les Editions du Boreal, 4447, rue St-Denis, Montreal, QC H2J 2L2, Canada *Tel:* 514-287-7401 *Fax:* 514-287-7664 *E-mail:* boreal@editionsboreal.qc.ca *Web Site:* www.editionsboreal.qc.ca, pg 423

Bernstein, Barbara, Hampton Press Inc, 307 Seventh Ave, Suite 506, New York, NY 10001 *Tel:* 646-638-3800 *Toll Free Tel:* 800-894-8955 *Fax:* 646-638-3802 *E-mail:* hamptonpr1@aol.com *Web Site:* www.hamptonpress.com, pg 92

Bernstein, Jonathan, Barricade Books Inc, 2037 LeMoine Ave, Fort Lee, NJ 07024 *Tel:* 201-944-7600 *E-mail:* info@barricadebooks.com *Web Site:* www.barricadebooks.com, pg 28

Bernstein, Laurie, Side by Side Literary Productions Inc, 145 E 35 St, Suite 7FE, New York, NY 10016 *Tel:* 212-685-6831 *Web Site:* sidebysidelit.com, pg 503

Bernstein, Meredith, Meredith Bernstein Literary Agency Inc, 2095 Broadway, Suite 505, New York, NY 10023 *Tel:* 212-799-1007 *Fax:* 212-799-1145 *E-mail:* MGoodBern@aol.com *Web Site:* www.meredithbernsteinliteraryagency.com, pg 475

Berry, Erin, BoardSource, 750 Ninth St NW, Suite 650, Washington, DC 20001-4793 *Tel:* 202-349-2580 *Toll Free Tel:* 877-892-6273 *E-mail:* members@boardsource.org *Web Site:* www.boardsource.org, pg 37

Berry, Frances, Frank L & Harriet C Owsley Award, University of Georgia, Dept of History, Athens, GA 30602-1602 *Tel:* 706-542-8848 *Fax:* 706-542-2455 *Web Site:* www.thesha.org, pg 651

Berry, Frances, Francis B Simkins Award, University of Georgia, Dept of History, Athens, GA 30602-1602 *Tel:* 706-542-8848 *Fax:* 706-542-2455 *Web Site:* www.thesha.org, pg 667

Berry, Frances, Charles S Sydnor Award, University of Georgia, Dept of History, Athens, GA 30602-1602 *Tel:* 706-542-8848 *Fax:* 706-542-2455 *Web Site:* www.thesha.org, pg 672

Berry, Liz, Thriller Awards Competition, PO Box 311, Eureka, CA 95502 *Web Site:* thrillerwriters.org, pg 673

Bershtel, Sara, Henry Holt and Company, LLC, 120 Broadway, 23rd fl, New York, NY 10271 *Tel:* 646-307-5151 *Toll Free Tel:* 888-330-8477 (orders) *Fax:* 646-307-5285 *Web Site:* www.henryholt.com, pg 101

Bertoli, Monique, Les Editions du Vermillon, 305, rue St-Patrick, Ottawa, ON K1N 5K4, Canada *Tel:* 613-241-4032 *Fax:* 613-241-3109 *E-mail:* leseditionsduvermillon@rogers.com *Web Site:* www.leseditionsduvermillon.ca, pg 423

Bertolini, Diana, George Freedley Memorial Award, c/o The New York Public Library for the Performing Arts, 111 Amsterdam Ave, New York, NY 10023 *E-mail:* TLABookAwards@gmail.com; TheatreLibraryAssociation@gmail.com *Web Site:* www.tla-online.org/awards/bookawards, pg 617

Bertolini, Diana, Richard Wall Memorial Award, c/o The New York Public Library for the Performing Arts, 111 Amsterdam Ave, New York, NY 10023 *E-mail:* TheatreLibraryAssociation@gmail.com; TLABookAwards@gmail.com *Web Site:* www.tla-online.org/awards/bookawards, pg 676

Bertrand, Alfred, Georgetown University Press, 3520 Prospect St NW, Suite 140, Washington, DC 20007 *Tel:* 202-687-5889 (busn) *Fax:* 202-687-6340 (edit) *E-mail:* gupress@georgetown.edu *Web Site:* press.georgetown.edu, pg 85

Bertrand, Daniel, Les Editions JCL, 688, rue St-Joseph, Marieville, QC J3M 1H1, Canada *Tel:* 450-460-4438 *E-mail:* info@jcl.qc.ca *Web Site:* www.jcl.qc.ca, pg 424

Berube, Dominique, Social Sciences & Humanities Research Council of Canada (SSHRC), 350 Albert St, Ottawa, ON K1P 6G4, Canada *Tel:* 613-992-0691; 613-996-6976 *E-mail:* research@sshrc-crsh.gc.ca *Web Site:* www.sshrc.ca, pg 546

Berube, Patty, Wood Lake Publishing Inc, 485 Beaver Lake Rd, Kelowna, BC V4V 1S5, Canada *Tel:* 250-766-2778 *Toll Free Tel:* 800-663-2775 (orders & cust serv) *Fax:* 250-766-2736 *Toll Free Fax:* 888-841-9991 (orders & cust serv) *E-mail:* info@woodlake.com; customerservice@woodlake.com *Web Site:* www.woodlakebooks.com, pg 445

Besel, Jen, Black Rabbit Books, 2140 Howard Dr W, North Mankato, MN 56003 *Tel:* 507-388-1609 *Fax:* 507-388-2746 *E-mail:* info@blackrabbitbooks.com; orders@blackrabbitbooks.com *Web Site:* www.blackrabbitbooks.com, pg 34

Bess, Benjamin E, Bess Press, 3565 Harding Ave, Honolulu, HI 96816 *Tel:* 808-734-7159 *Fax:* 808-732-3627 *E-mail:* customerservice@besspress.com *Web Site:* www.besspress.com, pg 32

Besser, Jennifer, Farrar, Straus & Giroux Books for Young Readers, 120 Broadway, New York, NY 10271 *Tel:* 212-741-6900 *Toll Free Tel:* 888-330-8477 (orders) *Fax:* 212-633-9385 *Web Site:* us.macmillan.com/mackids; www.mackidsbooks.com, pg 75

Besser, Jennifer, Roaring Brook Press, 120 Broadway, New York, NY 10271 *Tel:* 646-307-5151 *Web Site:* us.macmillan.com/publishers/roaring-brook-press, pg 186

Bestler, Emily, Atria Books, 1230 Avenue of the Americas, New York, NY 10020 *Tel:* 212-698-7000 *Fax:* 212-698-7007 *Web Site:* www.simonandschuster.com, pg 24

Betancourt, John, Wildside Press LLC, 7945 MacArthur Blvd, Suite 215, Cabin John, MD 20818 *Tel:* 301-762-1305 *Fax:* 301-762-1306 *E-mail:* wildside@wildsidepress.com; wildsidepress@yahoo.com *Web Site:* wildsidepress.com, pg 241

Betancourt, Lorraine, Oxford University Press USA, 198 Madison Ave, New York, NY 10016 *Toll Free Tel:* 800-451-7556 (orders); 800-445-9714 (cust serv) *Fax:* 919-677-1303 *E-mail:* custserv.us@oup.com *Web Site:* global.oup.com, pg 158

Bethel, Courtney, MacDowell Fellowships, 100 High St, Peterborough, NH 03458 *Tel:* 603-924-3886 *E-mail:* info@macdowell.org; admissions@macdowell.org *Web Site:* www.macdowell.org, pg 637

Betters, Michelle, Beacon Press, 24 Farnsworth St, Boston, MA 02210-1409 *Tel:* 617-742-2110 *Fax:* 617-723-3097; 617-742-2290 *Web Site:* www.beacon.org, pg 29

Bettles, Shannon, W Kaye Lamb Scholarships, PO Box 448, Fort Langley, BC V1M 2R7, Canada *E-mail:* info@bchistory.ca *Web Site:* www.bchistory.ca/awards/scholarships, pg 631

Bettles, Shannon, Anne & Philip Yandle Best Article Award, PO Box 448, Fort Langley, BC V1M 2R7, Canada *E-mail:* info@bchistory.ca *Web Site:* www.bchistory.ca/awards, pg 681

Beullac, Paul, B & B Publishing, 4823 Sherbrooke St W, Off 275, Westmount, QC H3Z 1G7, Canada *Tel:* 514-932-9466 *Fax:* 514-932-5929 *E-mail:* editions@ebbp.ca, pg 416

Bevarly, Daniel, National Freedom of Information Coalition (NFOIC), Missouri School of Journalism, 31 Neff Annex, Columbia, MO 65211 *Tel:* 573-882-4856 *E-mail:* nfoic@nfoic.org *Web Site:* nfoic.org, pg 540

Bevington, Stan, Coach House Books, 80 bpNichol Lane, Toronto, ON M5S 3J4, Canada *Tel:* 416-979-2217 *Toll Free Tel:* 800-367-6360 (outside Toronto) *Fax:* 416-977-1158 *E-mail:* mail@chbooks.com *Web Site:* www.chbooks.com, pg 420

Bewley, Elizabeth, Sterling Lord Literistic Inc, 115 Broadway, Suite 1602, New York, NY 10006 *Tel:* 212-780-6050 *Fax:* 212-780-6095 *E-mail:* info@sll.com *Web Site:* www.sll.com, pg 504

Bhatnagar, Supriya, Association of Writers & Writing Programs (AWP), University of Maryland, 5245 Greenbelt Rd, Box 246, College Park, MD 20740 *Tel:* 240-696-7700 *E-mail:* awp@awpwriter.org; press@awpwriter.org *Web Site:* www.awpwriter.org, pg 527

Bhatnagar, Supriya, AWP Award Series, University of Maryland, 5245 Greenbelt Rd, Box 246, College Park, MD 20740 *Tel:* 240-696-7700 *E-mail:* awp@awpwriter.org; press@awpwriter.org *Web Site:* www.awpwriter.org, pg 594

Bi, Faye, Bloomsbury Publishing Inc, 1385 Broadway, 5th fl, New York, NY 10018 *Tel:* 212-419-5300 *E-mail:* marketingusa@bloomsbury.com; adultpublicityusa@bloomsbury.com; askacademic@bloomsbury.com *Web Site:* www.bloomsbury.com, pg 36

Bialer, Matt, Sanford J Greenburger Associates Inc, 55 Fifth Ave, New York, NY 10003 *Tel:* 212-206-5600 *Fax:* 212-463-8718 *Web Site:* greenburger.com; www.sjga.com, pg 487

Bialosky, Jill, W W Norton & Company Inc, 500 Fifth Ave, New York, NY 10110-0017 *Tel:* 212-354-5500 *Toll Free Tel:* 800-233-4830 (orders & cust serv) *Fax:* 212-869-0856 *Toll Free Fax:* 800-458-6515 *E-mail:* orders@wwnorton.com, pg 152

Bianchini, Bob, Random House Children's Books, 1745 Broadway, 10th fl, New York, NY 10019 *Tel:* 212-782-9000 *Web Site:* www.randomhousekids.com, pg 181

Bianchini, Lori, Charlotte Huck Award, 340 N Neil St, Suite 104, Champaign, IL 61820 *Tel:* 217-328-3870 *Toll Free Tel:* 877-369-6283 (cust serv) *Fax:* 217-328-9645; 217-328-0977 *E-mail:* bookawards@ncte.org *Web Site:* www2.ncte.org/awards, pg 625

Bianchini, Lori, National Council of Teachers of English (NCTE), 340 N Neil St, Suite 104, Champaign, IL 61820 *Tel:* 217-328-3870 *Toll Free Tel:* 877-369-6283 (cust serv) *Fax:* 217-328-9645 *E-mail:* customerservice@ncte.org *Web Site:* www.ncte.org, pg 539

Bianchini, Lori, Orbis Pictus Award, 340 N Neil St, Suite 104, Champaign, IL 61820 *Tel:* 217-328-3870 *Toll Free Tel:* 877-369-6283 (cust serv) *Fax:* 217-328-9645; 217-328-0977 *E-mail:* bookawards@ncte.org *Web Site:* www2.ncte.org/awards, pg 651

Bianco, Kristen, GP Putnam's Sons (Hardcover), 375 Hudson St, New York, NY 10014 *Tel:* 212-366-2000 *Fax:* 212-366-2643 *E-mail:* online@penguinputnam.com *Web Site:* www.penguin.com/publishers/gpputnamssons, pg 178

Bicknell, Liz, Candlewick Press, 99 Dover St, Somerville, MA 02144-2825 *Tel:* 617-661-3330 *Fax:* 617-661-0565 *E-mail:* bigbear@candlewick.com; salesinfo@candlewick.com *Web Site:* www.candlewick.com, pg 44

Biddinger, Mary, Akron Poetry Prize, 120 E Mill St, Suite 415, Akron, OH 44308 Tel: 330-972-6960 Fax: 330-972-8364 E-mail: uapress@uakron.edu Web Site: www.uakron.edu/uapress/akron-poetry-prize, pg 590

Biedenharn, Isabella, Random House Publishing Group, 1745 Broadway, New York, NY 10019 Toll Free Tel: 800-200-3552 Web Site: www.randomhousebooks. com, pg 181

Bieker, Lauren, FinePrint Literary Management, 207 W 106 St, Suite 1D, New York, NY 10025 Tel: 212-279-6214 E-mail: assist@fineprint.com Web Site: www. fineprintlit.com, pg 484

Bieker, Mike, The University of Arkansas Press, McIlroy House, 105 N McIlroy Ave, Fayetteville, AR 72701 Tel: 479-575-7544 E-mail: info@uapress.com Web Site: www.uapress.com, pg 225

Bielstein, Susan, University of Chicago Press, 1427 E 60 St, Chicago, IL 60637-2954 Tel: 773-702-7700; 773-702-7600 Toll Free Tel: 800-621-2736 (orders) Fax: 773-702-9756; 773-660-2235 (orders); 773-702-2708 E-mail: custserv@press.uchicago.edu; marketing@press.uchicago.edu Web Site: www.press. uchicago.edu, pg 226

Biesel, David, Saint Johann Press, 315 Schraalenburgh Rd, Haworth, NJ 07641 Tel: 201-387-1529 Fax: 201-501-0698 Web Site: www.stjohannpress.com, pg 190

Biesel, Diane, Saint Johann Press, 315 Schraalenburgh Rd, Haworth, NJ 07641 Tel: 201-387-1529 Fax: 201-501-0698 Web Site: www.stjohannpress.com, pg 190

Bigler, Amy, Zondervan, 3900 Sparks Dr, Grand Rapids, MI 49546 Tel: 616-698-6900 Toll Free Tel: 800-226-1122; 800-727-1309 (retail orders) Fax: 616-698-3350 Toll Free Fax: 800-698-3256 (retail orders) Web Site: www.zondervan.com, pg 248

Bijur, Vicky, Vicky Bijur Literary Agency, 27 W 20 St, Suite 1003, New York, NY 10011 Tel: 212-580-4108 E-mail: queries@vickybijuragency.com Web Site: www.vickybijuragency.com, pg 475

Biljan, Tyrone, Joe Shuster Awards, 305-484 Oriole Pkwy, Toronto, ON M5P 2H8, Canada E-mail: info@ joeshusterawards.com Web Site: joeshusterawards.com, pg 667

Billingsley, Sarah, Chronicle Books, 680 Second St, San Francisco, CA 94107 Tel: 415-537-4200 Toll Free Tel: 800-759-0190 (cust serv) Fax: 415-537-4460 Toll Free Fax: 800-858-7787 (orders); 800-286-9471 (cust serv) E-mail: frontdesk@chroniclebooks.com Web Site: www.chroniclebooks.com, pg 51

Bily, Beth, Lake Superior Publishing LLC, 109 W Superior St, Suite 200, Duluth, MN 55802 Tel: 218-722-5002 Toll Free Tel: 888-BIG-LAKE (244-5253) Fax: 218-722-4096 E-mail: edit@lakesuperior.com Web Site: www.lakesuperior.com, pg 119

Binder, Amelia, National Music Publishers' Association (NMPA), 975 "F" St NW, Suite 375, Washington, DC 20004 Tel: 202-393-6672 E-mail: members@nmpa.org Web Site: nmpa.org, pg 540

Binder, Pam, PNWA Literary Contest, 1420 NW Gilman Blvd, Suite 8, PMB 2717, Issaquah, WA 98027 Tel: 425-673-2665 E-mail: pnwa@pnwa.org Web Site: www.pnwa.org, pg 657

Binder, Pam, PNWA - a writer's resource, 1420 NW Gilman Blvd, Suite 8, PMB 2717, Issaquah, WA 98027 Tel: 425-673-2665 Fax: 425-961-0768 E-mail: pnwa@pnwa.org Web Site: www.pnwa.org, pg 543

Binder, Pam, PNWA Writers Conference, 1420 NW Gilman Blvd, Suite 8, PMB 2717, Issaquah, WA 98027 Tel: 425-673-2665 E-mail: pnwa@pnwa.org Web Site: www.pnwa.org, pg 577

Binford, Susan, Lyndon B Johnson School of Public Affairs, University of Texas at Austin, 2315 Red River St, Austin, TX 78712-1536 Tel: 512-471-3200 Fax: 512-471-4697 E-mail: lbjdeansoffice@austin. utexas.edu Web Site: www.utexas.edu/lbj, pg 114

Bingham, Chelsea, David R Godine Inc, 15 Court Sq, Suite 320, Boston, MA 02108-2536 Tel: 617-451-9600 Fax: 617-350-0250 E-mail: info@godine.com Web Site: www.godine.com, pg 87

Bingham, Tony, Association for Talent Development (ATD) Press, 1640 King St, Box 1443, Alexandria, VA 22313-1443 Tel: 703-683-8100 Toll Free Tel: 800-628-2783 Fax: 703-299-8723; 703-683-1523 (cust care) E-mail: customercare@td.org Web Site: www. astd.org; www.td.org, pg 23

Binney, Ann, Los Angeles Times Book Prizes, 2300 E Imperial Hwy, El Segundo, CA 90245 Tel: 213-237-5775 Toll Free Tel: 800-528-4637 (ext 75775) Web Site: www.latimesbookprizes.com, pg 635

Binns, Allison, George Bogin Memorial Award, 15 Gramercy Park, New York, NY 10003 Tel: 212-254-9628 Web Site: poetrysociety.org/awards, pg 599

Binns, Allison, Alice Fay Di Castagnola Award, 15 Gramercy Park, New York, NY 10003 Tel: 212-254-9628 Web Site: poetrysociety.org/awards, pg 609

Binns, Allison, Norma Farber First Book Award, 15 Gramercy Park, New York, NY 10003 Tel: 212-254-9628 Web Site: poetrysociety.org/awards, pg 614

Binns, Allison, Four Quartets Prize, 15 Gramercy Park, New York, NY 10003 Tel: 212-254-9628 Web Site: poetrysociety.org/awards, pg 616

Binns, Allison, Cecil Hemley Memorial Award, 15 Gramercy Park, New York, NY 10003 Tel: 212-254-9628 Web Site: poetrysociety.org/awards, pg 623

Binns, Allison, Louise Louis/Emily F Bourne Student Poetry Award, 15 Gramercy Park, New York, NY 10003 Tel: 212-254-9628 Web Site: poetrysociety. org/awards, pg 635

Binns, Allison, Lyric Poetry Award, 15 Gramercy Park, New York, NY 10003 Tel: 212-254-9628 Web Site: poetrysociety.org/awards, pg 636

Binns, Allison, Lucille Medwick Memorial Award, 15 Gramercy Park, New York, NY 10003 Tel: 212-254-9628 Web Site: poetrysociety.org/awards, pg 640

Binns, Allison, Poetry Society of America (PSA), 15 Gramercy Park, New York, NY 10003 Tel: 212-254-9628 Web Site: poetrysociety.org, pg 543

Binns, Allison, William Carlos Williams Award, 15 Gramercy Park, New York, NY 10003 Tel: 212-254-9628 Web Site: poetrysociety.org/awards, pg 678

Binns, Allison, The Writer Magazine/Emily Dickinson Award, 15 Gramercy Park, New York, NY 10003 Tel: 212-254-9628 Web Site: poetrysociety.org/awards, pg 680

Binns, Beth, Woodbine House, 6510 Bells Mill Rd, Bethesda, MD 20817 Tel: 301-897-3570 Toll Free Tel: 800-843-7323 Fax: 301-897-5838 E-mail: info@ woodbinehouse.com Web Site: www.woodbinehouse. com, pg 244

Binyominson, Yerachmiel, Hachai Publishing, 527 Empire Blvd, Brooklyn, NY 11225 Tel: 718-633-0100 Fax: 718-633-0103 E-mail: info@hachai.com Web Site: www.hachai.com, pg 90

Biondello, Sarah J, Teachers College Press, 1234 Amsterdam Ave, New York, NY 10027 Tel: 212-678-3929 Fax: 212-678-4149 E-mail: tcpress@tc.edu Web Site: www.tcpress.com, pg 214

Bird, Kai, Biography Fellowships, 365 Fifth Ave, Rm 6200, New York, NY 10016 Tel: 212-817-2025 E-mail: biography@gc.cuny.edu Web Site: llcb.ws. gc.cuny.edu/fellowships, pg 598

Birdsell, Mary, Finding My Way Books, 3512 SW Huntoon St, Topeka, KS 66604-1748 Tel: 785-273-6239 E-mail: findingmywaybooks@gmail.com Web Site: www.findingmywaybooks.net, pg 78

Birkhead, Shaina, Children's & Teen Choice Book Awards, 54 W 39 St, 14th fl, New York, NY 10018 E-mail: cbc.info@cbcbooks.org Web Site: everychildareader.net/choice, pg 604

Birkhead, Shaina, The Children's Book Council (CBC), 54 W 39 St, 14th fl, New York, NY 10018 Tel: 212-966-1990 E-mail: cbc.info@cbcbooks.org Web Site: www.cbcbooks.org, pg 531

Birkhead, Shaina, Anna Dewdney Read Together Award, 54 W 39 St, 14th fl, New York, NY 10018 Tel: 917-890-7416 Web Site: everychildareader.net/anna, pg 609

Birkholz, Linda, Peradam Press, PO Box 6, North San Juan, CA 95960-0006 Tel: 530-277-9324 Fax: 530-559-0754 E-mail: peradam@earthlink.net, pg 167

Birmingham, Sara, HarperCollins General Books Group, 195 Broadway, New York, NY 10007 Tel: 212-207-7000 Web Site: www.harpercollins.com, pg 93

Birnbaum, Agnes, Bleecker Street Associates Inc, 215 Thompson St, Suite 519, New York, NY 10012 Tel: 212-677-4492 Fax: 212-388-0001, pg 476

Bisch, Florence, Groupe Sogides Inc, 955 rue Amherst, Montreal, QC H2L 3K4, Canada Tel: 514-523-1182 Fax: 514-597-0370 Web Site: sogides.com, pg 428

Bischel, Dr Margaret, Apollo Managed Care Inc, 1100 Town & Country Rd, Suite 1250, Orange, CA 92868 Toll Free Tel: 888-276-5563 E-mail: info@apollomanagedcare.com Web Site: www. apollomanagedcare.com, pg 18

Bishop, Amy Elizabeth, Dystel, Goderich & Bourret LLC, One Union Sq W, Suite 904, New York, NY 10003 Tel: 212-627-9100 Fax: 212-627-9313 Web Site: www.dystel.com, pg 482

Bishop, Sandra, Transatlantic Agency, 2 Bloor St E, Suite 3500, Toronto, ON M4W 1A8, Canada Tel: 416-488-9214 E-mail: info@transatlanticagency.com Web Site: www.transatlanticagency.com, pg 506

Bisk, Alison L, Bisk Education, 9417 Princess Palm Ave, Suite 400, Tampa, FL 33619 Tel: 813-621-6200 Toll Free Tel: 800-280-9718 (cust serv) E-mail: customerservice@bisk.com Web Site: www. bisk.com, pg 33

Bisk, Michael, Bisk Education, 9417 Princess Palm Ave, Suite 400, Tampa, FL 33619 Tel: 813-621-6200 Toll Free Tel: 800-280-9718 (cust serv) E-mail: customerservice@bisk.com Web Site: www. bisk.com, pg 33

Bissonnette, Melanie, Les Editions Alire, 120 cote du Passage, Levis, QC G6V 5S9, Canada Tel: 418-835-4441 Fax: 418-838-4443 E-mail: info@alire.com Web Site: www.alire.com, pg 422

Biter, Amy, Hachette Nashville, 6100 Tower Circle, Room 210, Franklin, TN 37067 Tel: 615-221-0996 Fax: 615-221-0962 Web Site: www.hachettebookgroup. com, pg 91

Bixler, Gina, University of Notre Dame Press, 310 Flanner Hall, Notre Dame, IN 46556 Tel: 574-631-6346 Fax: 574-631-8148 E-mail: undpress@nd.edu Web Site: www.undpress.nd.edu, pg 230

Bjerke, Paisius, Saint Herman Press, 4430 Mushroom Lane, Platina, CA 96076 Tel: 530-352-4430 Fax: 530-352-4432 E-mail: sherman@stherman.com Web Site: www.sainthermanmonastery.com, pg 190

Blachere, Natalie, McGill-Queen's University Press, 1010 Sherbrooke W, Suite 1720, Montreal, QC H3A 2R7, Canada Tel: 514-398-3750 Fax: 514-398-4333 E-mail: mqup@mqup.ca Web Site: www.mqup.ca, pg 433

Black, Dr Adam, Macmillan Learning, 41 Madison Ave, New York, NY 10010 Tel: 212-576-9400 Fax: 212-689-2383 Web Site: www.macmillanlearning.com, pg 130

Black, Amy, Doubleday Canada, 320 Front St W, Suite 1400, Toronto, ON M5V 3B6, Canada Tel: 416-364-4449 Fax: 416-598-7764 Web Site: www. penguinrandomhouse.ca, pg 421

Black, David, David Black Agency, 335 Adams St, 27th fl, Suite 2707, Brooklyn, NY 11201 Tel: 718-852-5500 Fax: 718-852-5539 Web Site: www.davidblackagency. com, pg 475

Black, Hannah, Random House Children's Books, 1745 Broadway, 10th fl, New York, NY 10019 Tel: 212-782-9000 Web Site: www.randomhousekids.com, pg 181

Blumenstock, Sarah, Berkley Publishing Group, 1745 Broadway, 19th fl, New York, NY 10019 *Tel:* 212-366-2000 *Web Site:* www.penguin.com, pg 32

Blumenthal, Scott, Scobre Press Corp, 2255 Calle Clara, La Jolla, CA 92037 *Fax:* 858-551-1232 *E-mail:* info@scobre.com *Web Site:* www.scobre.com; scobre. bookbuddyaudio.com, pg 195

Blunck, Kay, Neustadt International Prize for Literature, c/o University of Oklahoma, 630 Parrington Oval, Suite 110, Norman, OK 73019-4033 *Tel:* 405-325-4531 *Web Site:* www.worldliteraturetoday.org; www. worldlit.org, pg 647

Blunck, Kay, NSK Neustadt Prize for Children's Literature, c/o University of Oklahoma, 630 Parrington Oval, Suite 110, Norman, OK 73019-4033 *Tel:* 405-325-4531 *Web Site:* www.worldliteraturetoday.org; www.worldlit.org, pg 649

Blythe, Heather, Society for Industrial & Applied Mathematics, 3600 Market St, 6th fl, Philadelphia, PA 19104-2688 *Tel:* 215-382-9800 *Toll Free Tel:* 800-447-7426 *Fax:* 215-386-7999 *E-mail:* siambooks@siam.org *Web Site:* www.siam.org, pg 202

Blythe, Steven, Laura Day Boggs Bolling Memorial, 900 Timber Creek Place, Virginia Beach, VA 23464 *E-mail:* poetryinva@aol.com *Web Site:* poetrysocietyofvirginia.org, pg 600

Blythe, Steven, Joe Pendleton Campbell Narrative Contest, 900 Timber Creek Place, Virginia Beach, VA 23464 *E-mail:* poetryinva@aol.com *Web Site:* poetrysocietyofvirginia.org, pg 602

Blythe, Steven, Carleton Drewry Memorial, 900 Timber Creek Place, Virginia Beach, VA 23464 *E-mail:* poetryinva@aol.com *Web Site:* poetrysocietyofvirginia.org, pg 611

Blythe, Steven, Alfred C Gary Memorial, 900 Timber Creek Place, Virginia Beach, VA 23464 *E-mail:* poetryinva@aol.com *Web Site:* poetrysocietyofvirginia.org, pg 618

Blythe, Steven, Bess Gresham Memorial, 900 Timber Creek Place, Virginia Beach, VA 23464 *E-mail:* poetryinva@aol.com *Web Site:* poetrysocietyofvirginia.org, pg 621

Blythe, Steven, Loretta Dunn Hall Memorial, 900 Timber Creek Place, Virginia Beach, VA 23464 *E-mail:* poetryinva@aol.com *Web Site:* poetrysocietyofvirginia.org, pg 622

Blythe, Steven, Handy Andy Prize, 900 Timber Creek Place, Virginia Beach, VA 23464 *E-mail:* poetryinva@aol.com *Web Site:* poetrysocietyofvirginia.org, pg 622

Blythe, Steven, Brodie Herndon Memorial, 900 Timber Creek Place, Virginia Beach, VA 23464 *E-mail:* poetryinva@aol.com *Web Site:* poetrysocietyofvirginia.org, pg 623

Blythe, Steven, Judah, Sarah, Grace & Tom Memorial, 900 Timber Creek Place, Virginia Beach, VA 23464 *E-mail:* poetryinva@aol.com; info@poetryvirginia.org *Web Site:* poetrysocietyofvirginia.org, pg 629

Blythe, Steven, Cenie H Moon Prize, 900 Timber Creek Place, Virginia Beach, VA 23464 *E-mail:* poetryinva@aol.com *Web Site:* poetrysocietyofvirginia.org, pg 643

Blythe, Steven, Edgar Allan Poe Memorial, 900 Timber Creek Place, Virginia Beach, VA 23464 *E-mail:* poetryinva@aol.com *Web Site:* poetrysocietyofvirginia.org, pg 657

Blythe, Steven, Miriam Rachimi Memorial, 900 Timber Creek Place, Virginia Beach, VA 23464 *E-mail:* poetryinva@aol.com *Web Site:* poetrysocietyofvirginia.org, pg 660

Blythe, Steven, Ada Sanderson Memorial, 900 Timber Creek Place, Virginia Beach, VA 23464 *E-mail:* poetryinva@aol.com *Web Site:* poetrysocietyofvirginia.org, pg 664

Blythe, Steven, The Robert S Sergeant Memorial, 900 Timber Creek Place, Virginia Beach, VA 23464 *E-mail:* poetryinva@aol.com *Web Site:* poetrysocietyofvirginia.org, pg 666

Blyzwick, Cara, SSPC: The Society for Protective Coatings, 800 Trumbull Dr, Pittsburgh, PA 15205-4365 *Tel:* 412-281-2331 *Toll Free Tel:* 877-281-7772 (US only) *Fax:* 412-444-3591 *E-mail:* info@sspc.org *Web Site:* www.sspc.org, pg 206

Boardman, Ted, Indiana University Press, Herman B Wells Library 350, 1320 E Tenth St, Bloomington, IN 47405-3907 *Tel:* 812-855-8817 *Toll Free Tel:* 800-842-6796 (orders only) *Fax:* 812-855-7931; 812-855-8507 *E-mail:* iupress@indiana.edu; iuporder@indiana.edu (orders) *Web Site:* www.iupress.indiana.edu, pg 108

Boates, Reid, Reid Boates Literary Agency, 69 Cooks Crossroad, Pittstown, NJ 08867-0328 *Tel:* 908-797-8087 *E-mail:* reid.boates@gmail.com, pg 476

Boatright, Shantelle, Business Forms Management Association (BFMA), 1147 Fleetwood Ave, Madison, WI 53716-1417 *Toll Free Tel:* 888-367-3078 *E-mail:* bfma@bfma.org *Web Site:* www.bfma.org, pg 529

Bob, Tammie, Friends of American Writers Awards, 506 Rose Ave, Des Plaines, IL 60016 *Tel:* 847-827-8339 *Web Site:* www.fawchicago.org, pg 617

Bobak, Cathy, Random House Children's Books, 1745 Broadway, 10th fl, New York, NY 10019 *Tel:* 212-782-9000 *Web Site:* www.randomhousekids.com, pg 181

Bobbitt, Michael D, Twilight Times Books, PO Box 3340, Kingsport, TN 37664-0340 *Tel:* 423-323-0183 *Fax:* 423-323-0183 *E-mail:* publisher@twilighttimes. com *Web Site:* www.twilighttimesbooks.com, pg 223

Boccardi, Paul, Little, Brown and Company, 1290 Avenue of the Americas, New York, NY 10104 *Tel:* 212-364-1100 *Fax:* 212-364-0952 *E-mail:* firstname.lastname@hbgusa. com *Web Site:* www.littlebrown.com; www. hachettebookgroup.com, pg 125

Bode, Jaime, Macmillan, 120 Broadway, 22nd fl, New York, NY 10271 *Tel:* 646-307-5151 *E-mail:* press. inquiries@macmillan.com *Web Site:* www.macmillan. com, pg 130

Bodnar, Georgia, Viking, 375 Hudson St, New York, NY 10014 *Tel:* 212-366-2000 *Fax:* 212-243-6002 *Web Site:* www.penguin.com/publishers/vikingbooks, pg 236

Boehm, Ronald, ABC-CLIO, 130 Cremona Dr, Santa Barbara, CA 93117 *Tel:* 805-968-1911 *Toll Free Tel:* 800-368-6868 *Fax:* 805-685-9685 *Toll Free Fax:* 866-270-3856 *E-mail:* customerservice@abc-clio.com *Web Site:* www.abc-clio.com, pg 2

Boehmer, Gabriella, HeartMath LLC, 14700 W Park Ave, Boulder Creek, CA 95006 *Tel:* 831-338-8500 *Toll Free Tel:* 800-711-6221 *Fax:* 831-338-8504 *E-mail:* info@heartmath.org; inquiry@heartmath.org *Web Site:* www.heartmath.org, pg 97

Boehmer, Susan Wallace, Harvard University Press, 79 Garden St, Cambridge, MA 02138-1499 *Tel:* 617-495-2600; 401-531-2800 (intl orders) *Toll Free Tel:* 800-405-1619 (orders) *Fax:* 617-495-5898 (gen); 617-496-4677 (edit & rts); 401-531-2801 (intl orders) *Toll Free Fax:* 800-406-9145 (orders) *E-mail:* contact_hup@harvard.edu *Web Site:* www.hup.harvard.edu, pg 95

Boer, Faye, Folklore Publishing, 11717-9B Ave NW, Unit 2, Edmonton, AB T6J 7B7, Canada *Tel:* 780-435-2376 *Web Site:* www.folklorepublishing.com, pg 427

Boer, Peter J, Blue Bike Books, 4811-51 Ave, Stony Plain, AB T7Z 1C4, Canada *Tel:* 780-435-2376 *Web Site:* www.bluebikebooks.com, pg 416

Boersma, Karen, Owlkids Books Inc, 10 Lower Spadina Ave, Suite 400, Toronto, ON M5V 2Z2, Canada *Tel:* 416-340-2700 *Fax:* 416-340-9769 *E-mail:* owlkids@owlkids.com *Web Site:* www. owlkidsbooks.com, pg 435

Boesch, William, US Government Publishing Office (GPO), Superintendent of Documents, 732 N Capitol St NW, Washington, DC 20401 *Tel:* 202-512-1800 *Toll Free Tel:* 866-512-1800 (orders) *Fax:* 202-512-1998 *E-mail:* contactcenter@gpo.gov *Web Site:* www.gpo. gov; bookstore.gpo.gov (sales), pg 235

Bogaards, Paul, Alfred A Knopf, c/o Penguin Random House Inc, 1745 Broadway, New York, NY 10019 *Tel:* 212-751-2600 *Fax:* 212-572-2662 (foreign rts) *Web Site:* knopfdoubleday.com, pg 118

Bogaards, Paul, Pantheon Books, c/o Penguin Random House Inc, 1745 Broadway, New York, NY 10019 *Tel:* 212-751-2600 *Fax:* 212-572-2662 (foreign rts) *Web Site:* knopfdoubleday.com, pg 159

Bogie, Patty, MPA - The Association of Magazine Media, 757 Third Ave, 11th fl, New York, NY 10012 *Tel:* 212-872-3700 *Fax:* 212-888-4217 *Web Site:* www. magazine.org, pg 538

Bohl, Kirsten, Mathical Book Prize, 17 Gauss Way, Berkeley, CA 94720 *Tel:* 510-499-5181 *E-mail:* mathical@msri.org *Web Site:* www. mathicalbooks.org, pg 639

Boies, Kay, Children's Sequoyah Book Award, PO Box 6550, Edmond, OK 73083 *Tel:* 405-525-5100 *Fax:* 405-525-5103 *Web Site:* www.oklibs.org, pg 604

Boies, Kay, The High School Award, PO Box 6550, Edmond, OK 73083 *Tel:* 405-525-5100 *Fax:* 405-525-5103 *Web Site:* www.oklibs.org, pg 623

Boies, Kay, Intermediate Sequoyah Book Award, PO Box 6550, Edmond, OK 73083 *Tel:* 405-525-5100 *Fax:* 405-525-5103 *Web Site:* www.oklibs.org, pg 627

Boileau, Kendra, Penn State University Press, University Support Bldg 1, Suite C, 820 N University Dr, University Park, PA 16802-1003 *Tel:* 814-865-1327 *Toll Free Tel:* 800-326-9180 *Fax:* 814-863-1408 *Toll Free Fax:* 877-778-2665 *E-mail:* orders@psupress.org; orders@eisenbrauns.org *Web Site:* www.psupress.org; www.eisenbrauns.org, pg 166

Boitnott, Sally, Pelican Publishing Co, 400 Poydras St, Suite 900, New Orleans, LA 70130 *Tel:* 504-368-1175 *Toll Free Tel:* 800-843-1724 *Fax:* 504-368-1195 *E-mail:* sales@pelicanpub.com (sales); office@pelicanpub.com (permission); promo@pelicanpub.com (publicity) *Web Site:* www.pelicanpub.com, pg 162

Bol, Robert, Revell, PO Box 6287, Grand Rapids, MI 49516-6287 *Tel:* 616-676-9185 *Toll Free Tel:* 800-877-2665; 800-679-1957 *Fax:* 616-676-9573 *Web Site:* www.bakerpublishinggroup.com, pg 185

Bolan, Michael, LinguaText LLC, 103 Walker Way, Newark, DE 19711 *Tel:* 302-453-8695 *E-mail:* text@linguatextbooks.com *Web Site:* www.linguatextbooks. com, pg 125

Boland, John, Trusted Media Brands Inc, 750 Third Ave, 3rd fl, New York, NY 10017 *Tel:* 646-293-6299 *Toll Free Tel:* 877-732-4438 (cust serv) *Fax:* 646-293-6251 *E-mail:* customercare@trustedmediabrands. com; press@trustedmediabrands.com *Web Site:* www. trustedmediabrands.com; www.rd.com, pg 221

Boland, Katie, Counterpoint Press LLC, 2560 Ninth St, Suite 318, Berkeley, CA 94710 *Tel:* 510-704-0230 *Fax:* 510-704-0268 *E-mail:* info@counterpointpress. com *Web Site:* counterpointpress.com; softskull.com, pg 58

Boldrick, Penelope, Ignatius Press, 1348 Tenth Ave, San Francisco, CA 94122-2304 *Toll Free Tel:* 800-651-1531 (orders); 888-615-3186 (cust serv) *Fax:* 415-387-0896 *E-mail:* info@ignatius.com *Web Site:* www. ignatius.com, pg 106

Bolduc, Mary Jo, The American Library Association (ALA), 225 N Michigan Ave, Suite 1300, Chicago, IL 60601 *Tel:* 312-944-6780 *Toll Free Tel:* 800-545-2433 *Fax:* 312-280-5275 *E-mail:* editionsmarketing@ala.org *Web Site:* www.alastore.ala.org, pg 12

Bolduc, Mary Jo, Carnegie-Whitney Award, 50 E Huron St, Chicago, IL 60611 *Tel:* 312-280-5416 *Toll Free Tel:* 800-545-2433 *Fax:* 312-280-5275; 312-440-9379 *Web Site:* www.ala.org, pg 603

Bole, Angela, Benjamin Franklin Awards™, 1020 Manhattan Beach Blvd, Suite 204, Manhattan Beach, CA 90266 *Tel:* 310-546-1818 *E-mail:* info@ibpa-online.org *Web Site:* www.ibpa-online.org; ibpabenjaminfranklinawards.com, pg 596

Bowes, Matt, NeWest Press, 8540 109 St, No 201, Edmonton, AB T6G 1E6, Canada *Tel:* 780-432-9427 *Fax:* 780-433-3179 *E-mail:* info@newestpress.com; orders@newestpress.com *Web Site:* www.newestpress.com, pg 434

Bowker, Scott, Houghton Mifflin Harcourt, 125 High St, Boston, MA 02110 *Tel:* 617-351-5000 *Toll Free Tel:* 855-969-4642; 800-225-5425 (K-12 educ materials); 800-323-9540 (assessment materials); 877-219-1537 (SkillsTutor); 888-242-6747 (Innovation in Educ Group); 800-225-3362 (Trade & Ref Div) *Toll Free Fax:* 800-269-5232 *E-mail:* myhmhco@hmhco.com *Web Site:* www.hmhco.com, pg 103

Bowlin, Sarah, Aevitas Creative Management, 19 W 21 St, Suite 501, New York, NY 10010 *Tel:* 212-765-6900 *Web Site:* aevitascreative.com, pg 474

Bowman, Hannah, Liza Dawson Associates, 121 W 27 St, Suite 1201, New York, NY 10001 *Tel:* 212-465-9071 *Web Site:* www.lizadawsonassociates.com, pg 481

Bowman, Ryland, Carolina Academic Press, 700 Kent St, Durham, NC 27701 *Tel:* 919-489-7486 *Toll Free Tel:* 800-489-7486 *Fax:* 919-493-5668 *E-mail:* cap@cap-press.com *Web Site:* www.cap-press.com; www.caplaw.com, pg 45

Bowyer, Clifford B, Silver Leaf Books LLC, 13 Temi Rd, Holliston, MA 01746 *E-mail:* sales@silverleafbooks.com; editor@silverleafbooks.com; customerservice@silverleafbooks.com *Web Site:* www.silverleafbooks.com, pg 198

Bowzer, Melanie, The Association of Medical Illustrators (AMI), 201 E Main St, Suite 1405, Lexington, KY 40507 *Toll Free Tel:* 866-393-4264 *Fax:* 859-514-9166 *E-mail:* hq@ami.org; info@ami.org *Web Site:* www.ami.org, pg 527

Boyd, Ann, Ruth & Sylvia Schwartz Children's Book Awards, c/o Ontario Arts Council, 121 Bloor St E, 7th fl, Toronto, ON M4W 3M5, Canada *Tel:* 416-961-1660 *Toll Free Tel:* 800-387-0058 (ON) *Fax:* 416-961-7796 (Ontario Arts Council); 416-969-7450 (Ontario Arts Foundation) *E-mail:* info@arts.on.ca; foundation@arts.on.ca *Web Site:* www.arts.on.ca; ontarioartsfoundation.on.ca/pages/ruth-sylvia-schwartz-awards, pg 666

Boyd, Cat, Simon & Schuster, 1230 Avenue of the Americas, New York, NY 10020 *Tel:* 212-698-7000 *Toll Free Tel:* 800-223-2348 (cust serv); 800-223-2336 (orders) *Toll Free Fax:* 800-943-9831 (orders) *Web Site:* www.simonandschuster.com, pg 198

Boyd, Jon, InterVarsity Press, 430 Plaza Dr, Westmont, IL 60559-1234 *Tel:* 630-734-4000 *Toll Free Tel:* 800-843-9487 *Fax:* 630-734-4200 *E-mail:* email@ivpress.com *Web Site:* www.ivpress.com, pg 112

Boyd, Kevin A, Joe Shuster Awards, 305-484 Oriole Pkwy, Toronto, ON M5P 2H8, Canada *E-mail:* info@joeshusterawards.com *Web Site:* joeshusterawards.com, pg 667

Boyd, Matt, The Penguin Press, 375 Hudson St, New York, NY 10014 *Web Site:* thepenguinpress.com, pg 164

Boyd, Taryn, Brindle & Glass Publishing Ltd, 1075 Pendergast St, Suite 103, Victoria, BC V8V 0A1, Canada *Tel:* 250-360-0829 *Fax:* 250-386-0829 *E-mail:* info@touchwoodeditions.com *Web Site:* www.touchwoodeditions.com, pg 417

Boyd, Taryn, TouchWood Editions, 103-1075 Pendergast St, Victoria, BC V8V 0A1, Canada *Tel:* 250-360-0829 *Fax:* 250-386-0829 *E-mail:* info@touchwoodeditions.com *Web Site:* www.touchwoodeditions.com, pg 441

Boyd, Vicki, Heinemann, 361 Hanover St, Portsmouth, NH 03801-3912 *Tel:* 603-431-7894 *Toll Free Tel:* 800-225-5800 (US) *Fax:* 603-431-2214 *Toll Free Fax:* 877-231-6980 (US) *E-mail:* custserv@heinemann.com *Web Site:* www.heinemann.com, pg 97

Boyd, Vicki, Houghton Mifflin Harcourt, 125 High St, Boston, MA 02110 *Tel:* 617-351-5000 *Toll Free Tel:* 855-969-4642; 800-225-5425 (K-12 educ materials); 800-323-9540 (assessment materials); 877-219-1537 (SkillsTutor); 888-242-6747 (Innovation in

Educ Group); 800-225-3362 (Trade & Ref Div) *Toll Free Fax:* 800-269-5232 *E-mail:* myhmhco@hmhco.com *Web Site:* www.hmhco.com, pg 103

Boyer, Heather, Island Press, 2000 "M" St NW, Suite 650, Washington, DC 20036 *Tel:* 202-232-7933 *Toll Free Tel:* 800-828-1302 *Fax:* 202-234-1328 *E-mail:* info@islandpress.org *Web Site:* www.islandpress.org, pg 112

Boyer, Jennifer, American Association of Blood Banks, North Tower, 4550 Montgomery Ave, Suite 700, Bethesda, MD 20814 *Tel:* 301-907-6977 *Toll Free Tel:* 866-222-2498 (sales) *Fax:* 301-907-6895 *E-mail:* aabb@aabb.org; sales@aabb.org (ordering); publications1@aabb.org (catalog) *Web Site:* www.aabb.org, pg 9

Boyle, Aileen, Plume, 375 Hudson St, New York, NY 10014 *Tel:* 212-366-2000 *Fax:* 212-243-6002 *Web Site:* www.penguin.com/publishers/plume, pg 171

Boyle, Colleen, The Penguin Press, 375 Hudson St, New York, NY 10014 *Web Site:* thepenguinpress.com, pg 164

Boyle, Corinne, Peradam Press, PO Box 6, North San Juan, CA 95960-0006 *Tel:* 530-277-9324 *Fax:* 530-559-0754 *E-mail:* peradam@earthlink.net, pg 167

Boynton, Suki, The Feminist Press at The City University of New York, 365 Fifth Ave, Suite 5406, New York, NY 10016 *Tel:* 212-817-7915 *Fax:* 212-817-1593 *E-mail:* info@feministpress.org *Web Site:* www.feministpress.org, pg 77

Boynton-Trigg, Anne, Scholastic International, 557 Broadway, New York, NY 10012 *Tel:* 212-343-6100; 646-330-5288 (intl cust serv) *Toll Free Tel:* 800-SCHOLASTIC (724-6527) *Fax:* 646-837-7878 *E-mail:* international@scholastic.com, pg 194

Bozzi, Debra, Yale University Press, 302 Temple St, New Haven, CT 06511-8909 *Tel:* 203-432-0960; 203-432-0966 (sales); 401-531-2800 (cust serv) *Toll Free Tel:* 800-405-1619 (cust serv) *Fax:* 203-432-0948; 203-432-8485 (sales); 401-531-2801 (cust serv) *Toll Free Fax:* 800-406-9145 (cust serv) *E-mail:* sales.press@yale.edu (sales); customer.care@triliteral.org (cust serv) *Web Site:* www.yalebooks.com; yalepress.yale.edu/yupbooks, pg 246

Braaten, Douglas PhD, New York Academy of Sciences (NYAS), 7 World Trade Center, 40th fl, 250 Greenwich St, New York, NY 10007-2157 *Tel:* 212-298-8600 *Toll Free Tel:* 800-843-6927 *Fax:* 212-298-3650 *E-mail:* nyas@nyas.org; annals@nyas.org; customerservice@nyas.org *Web Site:* www.nyas.org, pg 150

Braaten, Hannah, Gallery Books, 1230 Avenue of the Americas, New York, NY 10020 *Toll Free Tel:* 800-456-6798 *Fax:* 212-698-7284 *E-mail:* consumer.customerservice@simonandschuster.com *Web Site:* www.simonandschuster.com, pg 83

Brabec, Kimberly, Waterside Productions Inc, 2055 Oxford Ave, Cardiff, CA 92007 *Tel:* 760-632-9190 *Fax:* 760-632-9295 *E-mail:* admin@waterside.com *Web Site:* www.waterside.com, pg 508

Brach, Courtney, Rutgers University Press, 106 Somerset St, 3rd fl, New Brunswick, NJ 08901 *Tel:* 848-445-7762; 848-445-7761 (sales) *Fax:* 732-745-4935 *E-mail:* sales@rutgersuniversitypress.org *Web Site:* www.rutgersuniversitypress.org, pg 188

Brachfeld, Janea, Storey Publishing LLC, 210 MASS MoCA Way, North Adams, MA 01247 *Tel:* 413-346-2100 *Toll Free Tel:* 800-441-5700 (orders); 800-827-7444 (cust serv) *Fax:* 413-346-2199 *Toll Free Fax:* 800-865-3429 (cust serv) *E-mail:* sales@storey.com; feedback@storey.com *Web Site:* www.storey.com, pg 209

Bracken, Don, History Publishing Co LLC, PO Box 700, Palisades, NY 10964 *Tel:* 845-359-1765 *Fax:* 845-818-3730 (sales) *E-mail:* info@historypublishingco.com *Web Site:* www.historypublishingco.com, pg 100

Brackob, Dana, Histria Books, 7181 N Hualapai Way, Suite 130-86, Las Vegas, NV 89166 *Tel:* 561-299-0802 *E-mail:* info@histriabooks.com; orders@histriabooks.com; rights@histriabooks.com *Web Site:* histriabooks.com, pg 100

Brackob, Kurt, Histria Books, 7181 N Hualapai Way, Suite 130-86, Las Vegas, NV 89166 *Tel:* 561-299-0802 *E-mail:* info@histriabooks.com; orders@histriabooks.com; rights@histriabooks.com *Web Site:* histriabooks.com, pg 100

Bradford, Laura, Bradford Literary Agency, 5694 Mission Center Rd, Suite 347, San Diego, CA 92108 *Tel:* 619-521-1201 *E-mail:* queries@bradfordlit.com *Web Site:* www.bradfordlit.com, pg 477

Bradie, Ian R, Cambridge University Press, One Liberty Plaza, 20th fl, New York, NY 10006 *Tel:* 212-924-3900; 212-337-5000 *Fax:* 212-691-3239; 845-353-4141 *E-mail:* newyork@cambridge.org; customer_service@cambridge.org *Web Site:* www.cambridge.org/us, pg 43

Bradley, Cheryl, NASW Press, 750 First St NE, Suite 800, Washington, DC 20002 *Tel:* 202-408-8600 *Fax:* 203-336-8312 *E-mail:* press@naswdc.org *Web Site:* www.naswpress.org, pg 145

Bradley, Fern Marshall, Chelsea Green Publishing Co, 85 N Main St, Suite 120, White River Junction, VT 05001 *Tel:* 802-295-6300 *Toll Free Tel:* 800-639-4099 (cust serv & orders) *Fax:* 802-295-6444 *E-mail:* customerservice@chelseagreen.com; editorial@chelseagreen.com; publicity@chelseagreen.com; rights@chelseagreen.com *Web Site:* www.chelseagreen.com, pg 49

Bradley, Joanna, Fresh Air Books, 1908 Grand Ave, Nashville, TN 37212 *Tel:* 615-340-7200 *Toll Free Tel:* 800-972-0433 (orders) *Web Site:* books.upperroom.org, pg 81

Bradley, Joanna, Upper Room Books, 1908 Grand Ave, Nashville, TN 37212 *Tel:* 615-340-7200 *Toll Free Tel:* 800-972-0433 *Web Site:* books.upperroom.org, pg 234

Bradley, Kevin J, Taylor & Francis Inc, 530 Walnut St, Suite 850, Philadelphia, PA 19106 *Tel:* 215-625-8900 *Toll Free Tel:* 800-354-1420 *Fax:* 215-207-0050; 215-207-0046 (cust serv) *E-mail:* support@tandfonline.com *Web Site:* www.taylorandfrancis.com, pg 213

Bradley, Shaun, Transatlantic Agency, 2 Bloor St E, Suite 3500, Toronto, ON M4W 1A8, Canada *Tel:* 416-488-9214 *E-mail:* info@transatlanticagency.com *Web Site:* www.transatlanticagency.com, pg 506

Bradshaw, Jenny, McClelland & Stewart Ltd, 320 Front St W, Suite 1400, Toronto, ON M5V 3B6, Canada *Tel:* 416-364-4449 *Fax:* 416-598-7764 *E-mail:* customerservicescanada@penguinrandomhouse.com; publicity@ca.penguingroup.com *Web Site:* penguinrandomhouse.ca/imprints/mcclelland-stewart, pg 433

Brady, Hillary, DK Publishing, 1450 Broadway, Suite 801, New York, NY 10018 *Tel:* 646-674-4000 *Toll Free Tel:* 800-733-3000 *Fax:* 646-674-4020 *E-mail:* marketing@dk.com; publicity@dk.com; csorders@penguinrandomhouse.com; ecustomerservice@randomhouse.com *Web Site:* www.dk.com; www.penguin.com, pg 65

Brady, Laura, House of Anansi Press Inc, 128 Sterling Rd, Lower Level, Toronto, ON M6R 2B7, Canada *Tel:* 416-363-4343 *Fax:* 416-363-1017 *E-mail:* customerservice@houseofanansi.com *Web Site:* www.houseofanansi.com, pg 429

Brady, Dr Philip, Etruscan Press, Wilkes University, 84 W South St, Wilkes-Barre, PA 18766 *Tel:* 570-408-4546 *Fax:* 570-408-3333 *E-mail:* books@etruscanpress.org *Web Site:* www.etruscanpress.org, pg 73

Brady, Robert L, BLR®—Business & Legal Resources, 100 Winners Circle, Suite 300, Brentwood, TN 37027 *Tel:* 860-510-0100 *Toll Free Tel:* 800-727-5257 *E-mail:* service@blr.com *Web Site:* www.blr.com, pg 36

Brady, Sally R, Brady Literary Management, PO Box 64, Hartland Four Corners, VT 05049 *Tel:* 802-436-2455, pg 459

Brailsford, Karen, Aevitas Creative Management, 19 W 21 St, Suite 501, New York, NY 10010 *Tel:* 212-765-6900 *Web Site:* aevitascreative.com, pg 474

Bramblet, Bob, Florida Outdoor Writers Association Inc, 235 Apollo Beach Blvd, Unit 271, Apollo Beach, FL 33572 *Tel:* 813-579-0990 *E-mail:* info@fowa.org *Web Site:* www.fowa.org, pg 533

Branch, Justin, Greenleaf Book Group LLC, 3 Park Place, 4005 Banister Lane, Suite B, Austin, TX 78704 *Tel:* 512-891-6100 *Fax:* 512-891-6150 *E-mail:* contact@greenleafbookgroup.com *Web Site:* www.greenleafbookgroup.com, pg 89

Brand, Amy, The MIT Press, One Rogers St, Cambridge, MA 02142 *Tel:* 617-253-5255 *Toll Free Tel:* 800-405-1619 (orders) *Fax:* 617-258-6779; 617-577-1545 (orders) *Web Site:* mitpress.mit.edu, pg 141

Brand, Dionne, McClelland & Stewart Ltd, 320 Front St W, Suite 1400, Toronto, ON M5V 3B6, Canada *Tel:* 416-364-4449 *Fax:* 416-598-7764 *E-mail:* customerservicescanada@penguinrandomhouse.com; publicity@ca.penguingroup.com *Web Site:* penguinrandomhouse.ca/imprints/mcclelland-stewart, pg 433

Brand, Megan, University of British Columbia Press, 2029 West Mall, Vancouver, BC V6T 1Z2, Canada *Tel:* 604-822-5959 *Toll Free Tel:* 877-377-9378 *Fax:* 604-822-6083 *Toll Free Fax:* 800-668-0821 *E-mail:* frontdesk@ubcpress.ca *Web Site:* www.ubcpress.ca, pg 443

Brandel, Ms Dusty, American Auto Racing Writers & Broadcasters, 922 N Pass Ave, Burbank, CA 91505 *Tel:* 818-842-7005 *Fax:* 818-842-7020, pg 522

Brandenburgh, Greg, Red Wheel/Weiser, 65 Parker St, Suite 7, Newburyport, MA 01950 *Tel:* 978-465-0504 *Toll Free Tel:* 800-423-7087 (orders) *Fax:* 978-465-0243 *E-mail:* info@rwwbooks.com *Web Site:* www.redwheelweiser.com, pg 183

Brander, Jacob, Mesorah Publications Ltd, 4401 Second Ave, Brooklyn, NY 11232 *Tel:* 718-921-9000 *Toll Free Tel:* 800-637-6724 *Fax:* 718-680-1875 *E-mail:* info@artscroll.com; orders@artscroll.com *Web Site:* www.artscroll.com, pg 138

Brandreth, Dale, Caissa Editions, PO Box 151, Yorklyn, DE 19736-0151 *Tel:* 302-239-4608 *Web Site:* www.chessbookstore.com, pg 43

Brandt, Eric, The University of Virginia Press, PO Box 400318, Charlottesville, VA 22904-4318 *Tel:* 434-924-3468 (cust serv); 434-924-3469 (cust serv) *Toll Free Tel:* 800-831-3406 (orders) *Fax:* 434-982-2655 *Toll Free Fax:* 877-288-6400 *E-mail:* vapress@virginia.edu *Web Site:* www.upress.virginia.edu, pg 231

Brandt, Joan, The Joan Brandt Agency, 788 Wesley Dr NW, Atlanta, GA 30305 *Tel:* 404-351-8877 *Fax:* 404-351-0068, pg 477

Brandt, Rosemary, The University of Arizona Press, 1510 E University Blvd, Tucson, AZ 85721 *Tel:* 520-621-1441 *Toll Free Tel:* 800-426-3797 (orders) *Fax:* 520-621-8899 *Toll Free Fax:* 800-426-3797 *E-mail:* uap@uapress.arizona.edu *Web Site:* www.uapress.arizona.edu, pg 225

Brandt, Suzanne, Feldheim Publishers, 208 Airport Executive Park, Nanuet, NY 10954 *Tel:* 845-356-2282 *Toll Free Tel:* 800-237-7149 (orders) *Fax:* 845-425-1908 *E-mail:* sales@feldheim.com *Web Site:* www.feldheim.com, pg 76

Brandt, William, Arcadia Publishing Inc, 420 Wando Park Blvd, Mount Pleasant, SC 29464 *Tel:* 843-853-2070 *Toll Free Tel:* 888-313-2665 (orders only) *Fax:* 843-853-0044 *E-mail:* sales@arcadiapublishing.com *Web Site:* www.arcadiapublishing.com, pg 19

Branham, Lorraine, Syracuse University, SI Newhouse School of Public Communications, 215 University Place, Syracuse, NY 13244-2100 *Tel:* 315-443-3627 *Fax:* 315-443-3946 *E-mail:* newhouse@syr.edu *Web Site:* newhouse.syr.edu, pg 585

Brants, Keith, Martingale®, 19021 120 Ave NE, Suite 102, Bothell, WA 98011 *Tel:* 425-483-3313 *Toll Free Tel:* 800-426-3126 *Fax:* 425-486-7596 *E-mail:* info@martingale-pub.com *Web Site:* www.martingale-pub.com, pg 133

Braswell, Bess, Harlequin Enterprises Ltd, 195 Broadway, 24th fl, New York, NY 10007 *Tel:* 212-207-7000 *Toll Free Tel:* 888-432-4879 *E-mail:* customerservice@harlequin.com *Web Site:* www.harlequin.com, pg 93

Bratcher, Joe W III, Host Publications, 3408 West Ave, Austin, TX 78705 *Tel:* 512-236-1290 *Fax:* 512-236-1208 *Web Site:* www.hostpublications.com, pg 103

Brault, Yves, Brault & Bouthillier, 700 ave Beaumont, Montreal, QC H3N 1V5, Canada *Tel:* 514-273-9186 *Toll Free Tel:* 800-361-0378 *Fax:* 514-273-8627 *Toll Free Fax:* 800-361-0378 *E-mail:* ventes@bb.ca *Web Site:* bb.ca, pg 417

Braun, Barbara, Barbara Braun Associates Inc, 7 E 14 St, Suite 19F, New York, NY 10003 *Tel:* 917-414-3022 *Web Site:* www.barbarabraunagency.com, pg 478

Braunstein, Bruce, Book Publicists of Southern California, 714 Crescent Dr, Beverly Hills, CA 90210 *Tel:* 323-461-3921 *Fax:* 323-461-0917 *Web Site:* www.bookpublicists.org, pg 528

Bray, Donna, HarperCollins Children's Books, 195 Broadway, New York, NY 10007 *Tel:* 212-207-7000 *Web Site:* www.harpercollins.com/childrens, pg 93

Brayda, Stephen, HarperCollins General Books Group, 195 Broadway, New York, NY 10007 *Tel:* 212-207-7000 *Web Site:* www.harpercollins.com, pg 93

Braziller, Karen, Persea Books, 90 Broad St, Suite 2100, New York, NY 10004 *Tel:* 212-260-9256 *E-mail:* info@perseabooks.com; poetry@perseabooks.com; publicity@perseabooks.com *Web Site:* www.perseabooks.com, pg 167

Braziller, Karen, Lexi Rudnitsky First Book Prize in Poetry, 90 Broad St, Suite 2100, New York, NY 10004 *Tel:* 212-260-9256 *E-mail:* info@perseabooks.com *Web Site:* www.perseabooks.com, pg 663

Braziller, Michael, George Braziller Inc, 277 Broadway, Suite 708, New York, NY 10007 *Tel:* 212-260-9256 *Fax:* 212-267-3165 *E-mail:* submissions@georgebraziller.com *Web Site:* www.georgebraziller.com, pg 40

Braziller, Michael, Persea Books, 90 Broad St, Suite 2100, New York, NY 10004 *Tel:* 212-260-9256 *E-mail:* info@perseabooks.com; poetry@perseabooks.com; publicity@perseabooks.com *Web Site:* www.perseabooks.com, pg 167

Braziller, Michael, Lexi Rudnitsky First Book Prize in Poetry, 90 Broad St, Suite 2100, New York, NY 10004 *Tel:* 212-260-9256 *E-mail:* info@perseabooks.com *Web Site:* www.perseabooks.com, pg 663

Brazis, Tamar, Viking Children's Books, 345 Hudson St, New York, NY 10014 *Tel:* 212-414-3393 *E-mail:* youngreaderspublicity@us.penguingroup.com *Web Site:* www.penguin.com/publishers/vikingchildrensbooks, pg 236

Brebner, Nicole, Harlequin Enterprises Ltd, Bay Adelaide Centre, East Tower, 22 Adelaide St W, 41st fl, Toronto, ON M5H 4E3, Canada *Tel:* 416-445-5860 *Toll Free Tel:* 888-432-4879; 800-370-5838 (ebook inquiries) *E-mail:* customerservice@harlequin.com *Web Site:* www.harlequin.com, pg 429

Brecker, Lora, Ascension Press, PO Box 1990, West Chester, PA 19380 *Tel:* 610-696-7795; 484-875-4550 (admin) *Toll Free Tel:* 800-376-0520 (sales & cust serv) *Web Site:* ascensionpress.com, pg 22

Breden, Cathy, The Center for Exhibition Industry Research (CEIR), 12700 Park Central Dr, Suite 308, Dallas, TX 75251 *Tel:* 972-687-9242 *Fax:* 972-692-6020 *E-mail:* info@ceir.org *Web Site:* www.ceir.org, pg 530

Breeden, Elizabeth, Simon & Schuster, 1230 Avenue of the Americas, New York, NY 10020 *Tel:* 212-698-7000 *Toll Free Tel:* 800-223-2348 (cust serv); 800-223-2336 (orders) *Toll Free Fax:* 800-943-9831 (orders) *Web Site:* www.simonandschuster.com, pg 198

Breeden, Kristi, Hachette Nashville, 6100 Tower Circle, Room 210, Franklin, TN 37067 *Tel:* 615-221-0996 *Fax:* 615-221-0962 *Web Site:* www.hachettebookgroup.com, pg 91

Breeden, Vickie, AuthorHouse, 1663 Liberty Dr, Bloomington, IN 47403 *Tel:* 812-339-6000 (outside US) *Toll Free Tel:* 888-519-5121 *E-mail:* authorsupport@authorhouse.com *Web Site:* www.authorhouse.com, pg 25

Breen, Jessica, Perseus Books, 1290 Avenue of the Americas, New York, NY 10104 *Tel:* 212-340-8100 *Toll Free Tel:* 800-343-4499 (cust serv) *Fax:* 212-340-8105 *Web Site:* www.perseusbooks.com, pg 167

Breichner, William M, Johns Hopkins University Press, 2715 N Charles St, Baltimore, MD 21218-4363 *Tel:* 410-516-6900; 410-516-6987 (journal orders outside US & CN) *Toll Free Tel:* 800-537-5487 (book orders & cust serv); 800-548-1784 (journal orders) *Fax:* 410-516-6968; 410-516-3866 (journal orders); 410-516-6998 (orders) *E-mail:* hfscustserv@press.jhu.edu (cust serv); jrnlcirc@press.jhu.edu (journal orders) *Web Site:* www.press.jhu.edu; muse.jhu.edu, pg 114

Breier, Davida, Johns Hopkins University Press, 2715 N Charles St, Baltimore, MD 21218-4363 *Tel:* 410-516-6900; 410-516-6987 (journal orders outside US & CN) *Toll Free Tel:* 800-537-5487 (book orders & cust serv); 800-548-1784 (journal orders) *Fax:* 410-516-6968; 410-516-3866 (journal orders); 410-516-6998 (orders) *E-mail:* hfscustserv@press.jhu.edu (cust serv); jrnlcirc@press.jhu.edu (journal orders) *Web Site:* www.press.jhu.edu; muse.jhu.edu, pg 114

Brendan, Stephen, Light Publications, Hope Artiste Village, 1005 Main St, Suite 1212, Pawtucket, RI 02806 *Tel:* 401-484-0228 *E-mail:* info@lightpublications.com *Web Site:* lightpublications.com, pg 124

Brengelman, Laura, Industrial Press Inc, 32 Haviland St, Suite 3, Norwalk, CT 06854 *Tel:* 203-956-5593 ext 0 (cust serv) *Toll Free Tel:* 888-528-7852 ext 0 (cust serv) *Fax:* 203-354-9391 (cust serv) *E-mail:* info@industrialpress.com (cust serv) *Web Site:* books.industrialpress.com; ebooks.industrialpress.com, pg 108

Brennan, Linda, Phaidon, 65 Bleecker St, 8th fl, New York, NY 10012 *Tel:* 212-652-5400 *Toll Free Tel:* 800-759-0190 (cust serv) *Fax:* 212-652-5410 *Toll Free Fax:* 800-286-9471 (cust serv) *E-mail:* enquiries@phaidon.com *Web Site:* www.phaidon.com, pg 168

Brennan, Nancy, Candlewick Press, 99 Dover St, Somerville, MA 02144-2825 *Tel:* 617-661-3330 *Fax:* 617-661-0565 *E-mail:* bigbear@candlewick.com; salesinfo@candlewick.com *Web Site:* www.candlewick.com, pg 44

Brennan, Stephen J PhD, Omniscient Publishing, 14728 Shirley St, Omaha, NE 68144 *Tel:* 402-334-1676 *Fax:* 402-334-4437 *Web Site:* www.thevaticanfiles.com, pg 447

Brent, Barbara, Two Thousand Three Associates, 135 Chilean Ave, Palm Beach, FL 33480 *Tel:* 386-690-2503 *E-mail:* ttta1@att.net *Web Site:* www.twothousandthree.com, pg 223

Breschini, Gary PhD, Coyote Press, PO Box 3377, Salinas, CA 93912-3377 *Tel:* 831-422-4912 *Fax:* 831-422-4913 *E-mail:* orders@coyotepress.com *Web Site:* www.coyotepress.com, pg 59

Breslin, Ramsay, Kelsey Street Press, 2824 Kelsey St, Berkeley, CA 94705 *E-mail:* info@kelseyst.com *Web Site:* www.kelseyst.com, pg 116

Bressler, Rachel, Harlequin Enterprises Ltd, 195 Broadway, 24th fl, New York, NY 10007 *Tel:* 212-207-7000 *Toll Free Tel:* 888-432-4879 *E-mail:* customerservice@harlequin.com *Web Site:* www.harlequin.com, pg 93

Bretan, Richard, Book Industry Guild of New York, PO Box 2001, New York, NY 10113-2001 *E-mail:* admin@bookindustryguildofny.org *Web Site:* bigny.org, pg 528

Bretz, Bailey, Association of University Presses (AUPresses), 1412 Broadway, Suite 2135, New York, NY 10018 *Tel:* 212-989-1010 *Fax:* 212-989-0275 *E-mail:* info@aupresses.org *Web Site:* www.aupresses.org, pg 527

Bretz, Bailey, AUPresses Book, Jacket & Journal Show, 1412 Broadway, Suite 2135, New York, NY 10018 *Tel:* 212-989-1010 *Fax:* 212-989-0275 *E-mail:* info@ aupresses.org *Web Site:* www.aupresses.org, pg 594

Breunig, Kevin, Appalachian Mountain Club Books, 5 Joy St, Boston, MA 02114 *Tel:* 617-523-0655 *Toll Free:* 800-262-4455 (orders) *Fax:* 617-523-0722 *E-mail:* amcbooks@outdoors.org *Web Site:* www. outdoors.org, pg 18

Brewer, Amy, Metamorphosis Literary Agency, 12837 S Seminole Dr, Olathe, KS 66062 *Tel:* 646-397-1640 *E-mail:* info@metamorphosisliteraryagency.com *Web Site:* www.metamorphosisliteraryagency.com, pg 497

Brewer, Andrew, Princeton University Press, 41 William St, Princeton, NJ 08540-5237 *Tel:* 609-258-4900 *Fax:* 609-258-6305 *Web Site:* press.princeton.edu, pg 174

Brezack, Hannah, Perseus Books, 1290 Avenue of the Americas, New York, NY 10104 *Tel:* 212-340-8100 *Toll Free Tel:* 800-343-4499 (cust serv) *Fax:* 212-340-8105 *Web Site:* www.perseusbooks.com, pg 167

Breznay, Ron, Bram Stoker Awards®, PO Box 56687, Sherman Oaks, CA 91413 *Tel:* 818-220-3965 *E-mail:* admin@horror.org *Web Site:* horror.org/ awards/stokers.htm, pg 670

Brianik, Christina, Teachers College Press, 1234 Amsterdam Ave, New York, NY 10027 *Tel:* 212-678-3929 *Fax:* 212-678-4149 *E-mail:* tcpress@tc.edu *Web Site:* www.tcpress.com, pg 214

Bricsoe, Kisha, National Catholic Educational Association, 1005 N Glebe Rd, Suite 525, Arlington, VA 22201 *Tel:* 571-257-0010 *Toll Free Tel:* 800-711-6232 *Fax:* 703-243-0025 *E-mail:* nceaadmin@ncea.org *Web Site:* www.ncea.org, pg 145

Bridges, Lois, Scholastic Education, 557 Broadway, New York, NY 10012 *Tel:* 212-343-6100 *Fax:* 212-343-6189 *Web Site:* www.scholastic.com, pg 194

Briel, Barbara, Sourcebooks LLC, 1935 Brookdale Rd, Suite 139, Naperville, IL 60563 *Tel:* 630-961-3900 *Toll Free Tel:* 800-432-7444 *Fax:* 630-961-2168 *E-mail:* info@sourcebooks.com; customersupport@ sourcebooks.com *Web Site:* www.sourcebooks.com, pg 204

Briggs, Christopher, Independent Institute, 100 Swan Way, Suite 200, Oakland, CA 94621-1428 *Tel:* 510-632-1366 *Toll Free Tel:* 800-927-8733 *Fax:* 510-568-6040 *E-mail:* orders@independent.org *Web Site:* www. independent.org, pg 107

Briggs, M Courtney, M Courtney Briggs Esq, Authors Representative, Chase Tower, 28th fl, 100 N Broadway Ave, Oklahoma City, OK 73102, pg 478

Bright, Harry, Maharishi University of Management Press, 1000 N Fourth St, Dept 1155, Fairfield, IA 52557-1155 *Tel:* 641-472-1101 *Toll Free Tel:* 800-831-6523 *Fax:* 641-472-1122 *E-mail:* mumpress@mum. edu *Web Site:* www.mumpress.com, pg 130

Brigido, Adrianne, Springer Publishing Co, 11 W 42 St, 15th fl, New York, NY 10036-8002 *Tel:* 212-431-4370 *Toll Free Tel:* 877-687-7476 *E-mail:* marketing@ springerpub.com; cs@springerpub.com (orders); textbook@springerpub.com; specialsales@springerpub. com *Web Site:* www.springerpub.com, pg 206

Brill, Calista, Roaring Brook Press, 120 Broadway, New York, NY 10271 *Tel:* 646-307-5151 *Web Site:* us. macmillan.com/publishers/roaring-brook-press, pg 186

Brill, L Chip, Peter Glenn Publications, 306 NE Second St, 2nd fl, Delray Beach, FL 33483 *Web Site:* pgdirect. com, pg 86

Brill, Marlene Targ, The Society of Midland Authors Awards, PO Box 10419, Chicago, IL 60610 *E-mail:* info@midlandauthors.com *Web Site:* www. midlandauthors.com, pg 668

Brill, Paula, Between the Lines, 401 Richmond St W, No 277, Toronto, ON M5V 3A8, Canada *Tel:* 416-535-9914 *Toll Free Tel:* 800-718-7201 *Fax:* 416-535-1484 *E-mail:* info@btlbooks.com *Web Site:* btlbooks.com, pg 416

Brinati, Teresa, Society of American Archivists, 17 N State St, Suite 1425, Chicago, IL 60602-4061 *Tel:* 312-606-0722 *Toll Free Tel:* 866-722-7858 *Fax:* 312-606-0728 *Web Site:* www.archivists.org, pg 202

Brinker, Spencer, Bearport Publishing Co Inc, 45 W 21 St, Suite 3B, New York, NY 10010 *Tel:* 212-337-8577 *Toll Free Tel:* 877-337-8577 *Fax:* 212-337-8557 *Toll Free Tel:* 866-337-8557 *E-mail:* service@ bearportpublishing.com; info@bearportpublishing.com *Web Site:* www.bearportpublishing.com, pg 30

Briskin, Dennis Alan, Catalyst Creative Services, 619 Marion Plaza, Palo Alto, CA 94301-4251 *Tel:* 650-325-1500 *E-mail:* afriendlyghostwriter@gmail.com *Web Site:* www.catalystcreative.us, pg 460

Britt, Nadine, Penguin Young Readers Group, 345 Hudson St, New York, NY 10014 *Tel:* 212-366-2000; 212-414-3553 *Fax:* 212-414-3340 *Web Site:* www. penguin.com/children, pg 165

Britton, Gregory M, Johns Hopkins University Press, 2715 N Charles St, Baltimore, MD 21218-4363 *Tel:* 410-516-6900; 410-516-6987 (journal orders outside US & CN) *Toll Free Tel:* 800-537-5487 (book orders & cust serv); 800-548-1784 (journal orders) *Fax:* 410-516-6968; 410-516-3866 (journal orders); 410-516-6998 (orders) *E-mail:* hfscustserv@press.jhu. edu (cust serv); jrnlcirc@press.jhu.edu (journal orders) *Web Site:* www.press.jhu.edu; muse.jhu.edu, pg 114

Britton, Laurel, The Metropolitan Museum of Art, 1000 Fifth Ave, New York, NY 10028 *Tel:* 212-535-7710 *E-mail:* editorial@metmuseum.org *Web Site:* www. metmuseum.org, pg 139

Broaddus, Katie, Hachette Nashville, 6100 Tower Circle, Room 210, Franklin, TN 37067 *Tel:* 615-221-0996 *Fax:* 615-221-0962 *Web Site:* www.hachettebookgroup. com, pg 91

Brochu, Karen, House of Anansi Press Inc, 128 Sterling Rd, Lower Level, Toronto, ON M6R 2B7, Canada *Tel:* 416-363-4343 *Fax:* 416-363-1017 *E-mail:* customerservice@houseofanansi.com *Web Site:* www.houseofanansi.com, pg 429

Brochu, Ron, Lake Superior Publishing LLC, 109 W Superior St, Suite 200, Duluth, MN 55802 *Tel:* 218-722-5002 *Toll Free Tel:* 888-BIG-LAKE (244-5253) *Fax:* 218-722-4096 *E-mail:* edit@lakesuperior.com *Web Site:* www.lakesuperior.com, pg 119

Brochu, Yvon, Editions FouLire, 4339, rue des Becassines, Quebec, QC G1G 1V5, Canada *Tel:* 418-628-4029 *Toll Free Tel:* 877-628-4029 (CN & US) *Fax:* 418-628-4801 *E-mail:* info@foulire.com; edition@foulire.com *Web Site:* www.foulire.com, pg 423

Brock, Emily, Dutton, 1745 Broadway, New York, NY 10019 *Tel:* 212-366-2000 *Fax:* 212-366-2262 *E-mail:* duttonpublicity@us.penguingroup.com *Web Site:* www.penguin.com, pg 68

Brock, John, Texas Tech University Press, 1120 Main St, 2nd fl, Lubbock, TX 79401 *Tel:* 806-742-2982 *Toll Free Tel:* 800-832-4042 *E-mail:* ttup@ttu.edu *Web Site:* www.ttupress.org, pg 216

Brockenbrough, Gina, SLACK® Incorporated, A Wyanoke Group Company, 6900 Grove Rd, Thorofare, NJ 08086-9447 *Tel:* 856-848-1000 *Toll Free Tel:* 800-257-8290 *Fax:* 856-848-6091 *E-mail:* sales@slackinc. com; editor@slackinc.com; customerservice@slackinc. com *Web Site:* www.healio.com/books, pg 201

Brockman, John, Brockman Inc, 260 Fifth Ave, 10th fl, New York, NY 10001 *Tel:* 212-935-8900 *Fax:* 212-935-5535 *E-mail:* rights@brockman.com *Web Site:* www.brockman.com, pg 478

Brockman, Max, Brockman Inc, 260 Fifth Ave, 10th fl, New York, NY 10001 *Tel:* 212-935-8900 *Fax:* 212-935-5535 *E-mail:* rights@brockman.com *Web Site:* www.brockman.com, pg 478

Brodeur, Adrienne, Aspen Words, 110 E Hallam St, Suite 116, Aspen, CO 81611 *Tel:* 970-925-3122 *Fax:* 970-920-5700 *E-mail:* aspenwords@ aspeninstitute.org *Web Site:* www.aspenwords.org, pg 525

Brodeur, Adrienne, Aspen Words Literary Prize, 110 E Hallam St, Suite 116, Aspen, CO 81611 *Tel:* 970-925-3122 *Fax:* 970-920-5700 *E-mail:* literary.prize@ aspeninstitute.org *Web Site:* www.aspenwords.org/ programs/literary-prize/; www.aspenwords.org, pg 594

Brodeur, Adrienne, Summer Words Writing Conference & Literary Festival, 110 E Hallam St, Suite 116, Aspen, CO 81611 *Tel:* 970-925-3122 *Fax:* 970-920-5700 *E-mail:* aspenwords@aspeninstitute.org *Web Site:* www.aspenwords.org, pg 579

Brodeur, Adrienne, Winter Words Author Series, 110 E Hallam St, Suite 116, Aspen, CO 81611 *Tel:* 970-925-3122 *Fax:* 970-920-5700 *E-mail:* aspenwords@ aspeninstitute.org *Web Site:* www.aspenwords.org, pg 579

Brodeur, Kristin, Houghton Mifflin Harcourt Trade & Reference Division, 125 High St, Boston, MA 02110 *Tel:* 617-351-5000 *Web Site:* www.hmhco.com, pg 104

Brodine, Dianna, Foil & Specialty Effects Association (FSEA), 2150 SW Westport Dr, Suite 101, Topeka, KS 66614 *Tel:* 785-271-5816 *Fax:* 785-271-6404 *E-mail:* info@fsea.com *Web Site:* www.fsea.com, pg 533

Brodsly, Eve, Chronicle Books, 680 Second St, San Francisco, CA 94107 *Tel:* 415-537-4200 *Toll Free Tel:* 800-759-0190 (cust serv) *Fax:* 415-537-4460 *Toll Free Tel:* 800-858-7787 (orders); 800-286-9471 (cust serv) *E-mail:* frontdesk@chroniclebooks.com *Web Site:* www.chroniclebooks.com, pg 52

Brody, Deb, Houghton Mifflin Harcourt Trade & Reference Division, 125 High St, Boston, MA 02110 *Tel:* 617-351-5000 *Web Site:* www.hmhco.com, pg 104

Brody, Samantha, Maria Carvainis Agency Inc, Rockefeller Center, 1270 Avenue of the Americas, Suite 2320, New York, NY 10020 *Tel:* 212-245-6365 *Fax:* 212-245-7196 *E-mail:* mca@mariacarvainisagency.com *Web Site:* www.mariacarvainisagency.com, pg 479

Brogan, Jim, Miniature Book Society Inc, 702 Rosecrans St, San Diego, CA 92106-3013 *Tel:* 619-226-4441 *Fax:* 619-226-4441 *E-mail:* minibook@cox.net *Web Site:* www.mbs.org, pg 538

Brogan, Matt, George Bogin Memorial Award, 15 Gramercy Park, New York, NY 10003 *Tel:* 212-254-9628 *Web Site:* poetrysociety.org/awards, pg 599

Brogan, Matt, Alice Fay Di Castagnola Award, 15 Gramercy Park, New York, NY 10003 *Tel:* 212-254-9628 *Web Site:* poetrysociety.org/awards, pg 609

Brogan, Matt, Norma Farber First Book Award, 15 Gramercy Park, New York, NY 10003 *Tel:* 212-254-9628 *Web Site:* poetrysociety.org/awards, pg 614

Brogan, Matt, Four Quartets Prize, 15 Gramercy Park, New York, NY 10003 *Tel:* 212-254-9628 *Web Site:* poetrysociety.org/awards, pg 616

Brogan, Matt, Frost Medal, 15 Gramercy Park, New York, NY 10003 *Tel:* 212-254-9628 *Web Site:* poetrysociety.org/awards, pg 617

Brogan, Matt, Cecil Hemley Memorial Award, 15 Gramercy Park, New York, NY 10003 *Tel:* 212-254-9628 *Web Site:* poetrysociety.org/awards, pg 623

Brogan, Matt, Louise Louis/Emily F Bourne Student Poetry Award, 15 Gramercy Park, New York, NY 10003 *Tel:* 212-254-9628 *Web Site:* poetrysociety. org/awards, pg 635

Brogan, Matt, Lyric Poetry Award, 15 Gramercy Park, New York, NY 10003 *Tel:* 212-254-9628 *Web Site:* poetrysociety.org/awards, pg 636

Brogan, Matt, Lucille Medwick Memorial Award, 15 Gramercy Park, New York, NY 10003 *Tel:* 212-254-9628 *Web Site:* poetrysociety.org/awards, pg 640

Brogan, Matt, Poetry Society of America (PSA), 15 Gramercy Park, New York, NY 10003 *Tel:* 212-254-9628 *Web Site:* poetrysociety.org, pg 543

Brown, Jonathan, David C Cook, 4050 Lee Vance Dr, Colorado Springs, CO 80918 *Tel:* 719-536-0100 *Toll Free Tel:* 800-708-5550; 800-323-7543 (orders & cust serv) *Toll Free Fax:* 800-430-0726 (cust serv) *Web Site:* www.davidccook.org, pg 56

Brown, Julia, Jerome Fellowship, 2301 Franklin Ave E, Minneapolis, MN 55406-1099 *Tel:* 612-332-7481 *Fax:* 612-332-6037 *E-mail:* info@pwcenter.org *Web Site:* www.pwcenter.org, pg 628

Brown, Julia, Many Voices Fellowships, 2301 Franklin Ave E, Minneapolis, MN 55406-1099 *Tel:* 612-332-7481 *Fax:* 612-332-6037 *E-mail:* info@pwcenter.org *Web Site:* www.pwcenter.org, pg 638

Brown, Julia, McKnight Fellowships in Playwriting, 2301 Franklin Ave E, Minneapolis, MN 55406-1099 *Tel:* 612-332-7481 *Fax:* 612-332-6037 *E-mail:* info@pwcenter.org *Web Site:* www.pwcenter.org, pg 640

Brown, Julia, McKnight National Residency & Commission, 2301 Franklin Ave E, Minneapolis, MN 55406-1099 *Tel:* 612-332-7481 *Fax:* 612-332-6037 *E-mail:* info@pwcenter.org *Web Site:* www.pwcenter.org, pg 640

Brown, Karen, National Music Publishers' Association (NMPA), 975 "F" St NW, Suite 375, Washington, DC 20004 *Tel:* 202-393-6672 *E-mail:* members@nmpa.org *Web Site:* nmpa.org, pg 540

Brown, Kate, Quirk Books, 215 Church St, Philadelphia, PA 19106 *Tel:* 215-627-3581 *Fax:* 215-627-5220 *E-mail:* general@quirkbooks.com *Web Site:* www.quirkbooks.com, pg 179

Brown, Kate, Yale University Press, 302 Temple St, New Haven, CT 06511-8909 *Tel:* 203-432-0960; 203-432-0966 (sales); 401-531-2800 (cust serv) *Toll Free Tel:* 800-405-1619 (cust serv) *Fax:* 203-432-0948; 203-432-8485 (sales); 401-531-2801 (cust serv) *Toll Free Fax:* 800-406-9145 (cust serv) *E-mail:* sales. press@yale.edu (sales); customer.care@triliteral.org (cust serv) *Web Site:* www.yalebooks.com; yalepress.yale.edu/yupbooks, pg 246

Brown, Kent, Dramatic Publishing Co, 311 Washington St, Woodstock, IL 60098-3308 *Tel:* 815-338-7170 *Toll Free Tel:* 800-448-7469 *Fax:* 815-338-8981 *Toll Free Fax:* 800-334-5302 *E-mail:* plays@dramaticpublishing.com; customerservice@dpcplays.com *Web Site:* www.dramaticpublishing.com, pg 67

Brown, Kent L Jr, Intimate & Inspiring Workshops for Children's Authors & Illustrators, 814 Court St, Honesdale, PA 18431 *Tel:* 570-253-1192 *Fax:* 570-253-0179 *E-mail:* jolloyd@highlightsfoundation.org *Web Site:* www.highlightsfoundation.org, pg 575

Brown, Laini, Hachette Nashville, 6100 Tower Circle, Room 210, Franklin, TN 37067 *Tel:* 615-221-0996 *Fax:* 615-221-0962 *Web Site:* www.hachettebookgroup.com, pg 91

Brown, Laura, Harlequin Enterprises Ltd, 195 Broadway, 24th fl, New York, NY 10007 *Tel:* 212-207-7000 *Toll Free Tel:* 888-432-4879 *E-mail:* customerservice@harlequin.com *Web Site:* www.harlequin.com, pg 93

Brown, Linda, American Society of Plant Taxonomists, University of Wyoming, Dept of Botany 3165, 1000 E University Ave, Laramie, WY 82071 *Tel:* 307-766-2556 *Fax:* 307-766-2851 *E-mail:* aspt@uwyo.edu *Web Site:* www.aspt.net, pg 14

Brown, Lucia, The Feminist Press at The City University of New York, 365 Fifth Ave, Suite 5406, New York, NY 10016 *Tel:* 212-817-7915 *Fax:* 212-817-1593 *E-mail:* feministpress.org *Web Site:* www.feministpress.org, pg 76

Brown, Marian, Henry Holt and Company, LLC, 120 Broadway, 23rd fl, New York, NY 10271 *Tel:* 646-307-5151 *Toll Free Tel:* 888-330-8477 (orders) *Fax:* 646-307-5285 *Web Site:* www.henryholt.com, pg 102

Brown, Marian, Plume, 375 Hudson St, New York, NY 10014 *Tel:* 212-366-2000 *Fax:* 212-243-6002 *Web Site:* www.penguin.com/publishers/plume, pg 171

Brown, Marie D, Marie Brown Associates, 412 W 154 St, New York, NY 10032 *Tel:* 212-939-9725 *E-mail:* submissions.mbrownlit@gmail.com, pg 478

Brown, Mark, Beacon Hill Press of Kansas City, PO Box 419527, Kansas City, MO 64141 *Tel:* 816-931-1900 *Toll Free Tel:* 800-877-0700 (cust serv) *Fax:* 816-531-0923 *Toll Free Fax:* 800-849-9827 *E-mail:* orders@thefoundrypublishing.com; customercare@thefoundrypublishing.com *Web Site:* www.thefoundrypublishing.com, pg 29

Brown, Marlena, Picador, 120 Broadway, New York, NY 10271 *Tel:* 646-307-5151 *Fax:* 212-253-9627 *E-mail:* publicity@picadorusa.com *Web Site:* us.macmillan.com/picador, pg 169

Brown, Marlena, Tiller Press, 1230 Avenue of the Americas, New York, NY 10020, pg 218

Brown, Marty, Oregon State University Press, 121 The Valley Library, Corvallis, OR 97331-4501 *Tel:* 541-737-3166, pg 157

Brown, Merle, Harry N Abrams Inc, 195 Broadway, 9th fl, New York, NY 10007 *Tel:* 212-206-7715 *Toll Free Tel:* 800-345-1359 *Fax:* 212-519-1210 *E-mail:* abrams@abramsbooks.com *Web Site:* www.abramsbooks.com, pg 3

Brown, Milli, Brown Books Publishing Group, 16250 Knoll Trail, Suite 205, Dallas, TX 75248 *Tel:* 972-381-0009 *Fax:* 972-248-4336 *E-mail:* publishing@brownbooks.com *Web Site:* www.brownbooks.com, pg 42

Brown, Pamela, Little, Brown and Company, 1290 Avenue of the Americas, New York, NY 10104 *Tel:* 212-364-1100 *Fax:* 212-364-0952 *E-mail:* firstname.lastname@hbgusa.com *Web Site:* www.littlebrown.com; www.hachettebookgroup.com, pg 125

Brown, Richard, University of South Carolina Press, 1600 Hampton St, Suite 544, Columbia, SC 29208 *Tel:* 803-777-5245 *Toll Free Tel:* 800-768-2500 (orders) *Fax:* 803-777-0160 *Toll Free Fax:* 800-868-0740 (orders) *Web Site:* www.sc.edu/uscpress, pg 231

Brown, Rose, Clerical Plus, 97 Blueberry Lane, Shelton, CT 06484 *Tel:* 203-225-0879 *Fax:* 203-225-0879 *E-mail:* clericalplus@aol.com *Web Site:* www.clericalplus.net, pg 461

Brown, Sammy, Houghton Mifflin Harcourt Trade & Reference Division, 125 High St, Boston, MA 02110 *Tel:* 617-351-5000 *Web Site:* www.hmhco.com, pg 104

Brown, Sass, Marfield Prize, 2017 "I" St NW, Washington, DC 20006-1804 *E-mail:* award@artsclubofwashington.org *Web Site:* artsclubofwashington.org/awards, pg 638

Brown, Sherri L, Atlantic Publishing Group Inc, 1405 SW Sixth Ave, Ocala, FL 34471 *Tel:* 352-622-1825 *Fax:* 352-622-1875 *E-mail:* sales@atlantic-pub.com *Web Site:* www.atlantic-pub.com, pg 24

Brown, Stephanie, Vandamere Press, 3580 Morris St N, St Petersburg, FL 33713 *Tel:* 727-556-0950 *Toll Free Tel:* 800-551-7776 *Fax:* 727-556-2560 *E-mail:* orders@vandamere.com *Web Site:* www.vandamere.com, pg 235

Brown, Stephen, Random House Children's Books, 1745 Broadway, 10th fl, New York, NY 10019 *Tel:* 212-782-9000 *Web Site:* www.randomhousekids.com, pg 181

Brown, Steven, Nelson Education Ltd, 1120 Birchmount Rd, Scarborough, ON M1K 5G4, Canada *Tel:* 416-752-9100 *Toll Free Tel:* 800-268-2222 (cust serv) *Fax:* 416-752-8101 *Toll Free Fax:* 800-430-4445 *E-mail:* peopleandengagement@nelson.com *Web Site:* www.nelson.com, pg 434

Brown, Susan, Macmillan Learning, 41 Madison Ave, New York, NY 10010 *Tel:* 212-576-9400 *Fax:* 212-689-2383 *Web Site:* www.macmillanlearning.com, pg 130

Brown, Tammy, Society of Children's Book Writers & Illustrators (SCBWI), 6363 Wilshire Blvd, Suite 425, Los Angeles, CA 90048 *Tel:* 323-782-1010 *E-mail:* membership@scbwi.org *Web Site:* www.scbwi.org, pg 546

Brown, Therese, Association of Catholic Publishers Inc, 4725 Dorsey Hall Dr, Suite A, PMB 709, Ellicott City, MD 21042 *Tel:* 410-988-2926 *Fax:* 410-571-4946

E-mail: info@catholicpublishers.org *Web Site:* www.catholicsread.org; www.catholicpublishers.org; www.midatlanticcongress.org, pg 526

Brownderville, Greg, Morton Marr Poetry Prize, PO Box 750374, Dallas, TX 75275-0374 *Fax:* 214-768-1408 *E-mail:* swr@mail.smu.edu *Web Site:* www.smu.edu/southwestreview, pg 638

Brownderville, Greg, John H McGinnis Memorial Award, PO Box 750374, Dallas, TX 75275-0374 *Fax:* 214-768-1408 *E-mail:* swr@mail.smu.edu *Web Site:* www.smu.edu/southwestreview, pg 639

Brownderville, Greg, The David Nathan Meyerson Prize for Fiction, PO Box 750374, Dallas, TX 75275-0374 *Fax:* 214-768-1408 *E-mail:* swr@mail.smu.edu *Web Site:* www.smu.edu/southwestreview, pg 641

Brownderville, Greg, Elizabeth Matchett Stover Memorial Award, PO Box 750374, Dallas, TX 75275-0374 *Fax:* 214-768-1408 *E-mail:* swr@mail.smu.edu *Web Site:* www.smu.edu/southwestreview, pg 671

Browne, Anne, Scholastic Canada Ltd, 604 King St W, Toronto, ON M5V 1E1, Canada *Tel:* 905-887-7323 *Toll Free Tel:* 800-268-3860 (CN) *Toll Free Fax:* 866-387-4944 *E-mail:* custserve@scholastic.ca *Web Site:* www.scholastic.ca, pg 439

Browne, Renni, The Editorial Department LLC, 8476 E Speedway Blvd, Suite 202, Tucson, AZ 85710 *Tel:* 520-546-9992 *E-mail:* admin@editorialdepartment.com *Web Site:* www.editorialdepartment.com, pg 463

Browne, Ross, The Editorial Department LLC, 8476 E Speedway Blvd, Suite 202, Tucson, AZ 85710 *Tel:* 520-546-9992 *E-mail:* admin@editorialdepartment.com *Web Site:* www.editorialdepartment.com, pg 463

Brownfield, Renee, National Association of Insurance Commissioners, 1100 Walnut St, Suite 1500, Kansas City, MO 64106-2197 *Tel:* 816-842-3600 *Fax:* 816-783-8175 *E-mail:* prodserv@naic.org *Web Site:* www.naic.org, pg 145

Browning, Guy, Macmillan, 120 Broadway, 22nd fl, New York, NY 10271 *Tel:* 646-307-5151 *E-mail:* press.inquiries@macmillan.com *Web Site:* www.macmillan.com, pg 129

Brownoff, Alan, University of Alberta Press, Ring House 2, Edmonton, AB T6G 2E1, Canada *Tel:* 780-492-3662 *Fax:* 780-492-0719 *Web Site:* www.uap.ualberta.ca, pg 442

Bruce, Alison, Crime Writers of Canada (CWC), 4C-240 Westwood Rd, Guelph, ON N1H 7W9, Canada *E-mail:* info@crimewriterscanada.com *Web Site:* www.crimewriterscanada.com, pg 532

Bruce, Alison, Arthur Ellis Awards, 716 Thicket Way, Ottawa, ON K4A 3B5, Canada *E-mail:* arthur_ellis@crimewriterscanada.com *Web Site:* www.crimewriterscanada.com/awards, pg 613

Bruce, Alison, Grand Master Award, 716 Thicket Way, Ottawa, ON K4A 3B5, Canada *E-mail:* info@crimewriterscanada.com *Web Site:* www.crimewriterscanada.com/awards, pg 620

Bruce, Alison, Derrick Murdoch Award, 716 Thicket Way, Ottawa, ON K4A 3B5, Canada *E-mail:* info@crimewriterscanada.com *Web Site:* www.crimewriterscanada.com/awards, pg 644

Bruce, Alison, Unhanged Arthur Ellis Award, 716 Thicket Way, Ottawa, ON K4A 3B5, Canada *E-mail:* arthur_ellis@crimewriterscanada.com *Web Site:* www.crimewriterscanada.com/awards, pg 675

Bruce, Sandra, Milady, Executive Woods, 5 Maxwell Dr, Clifton Park, NY 12065-2919 *Tel:* 518-348-2300 *Toll Free Tel:* 800-998-7498 *Fax:* 518-373-6309 *E-mail:* info@milady.com *Web Site:* milady.cengage.com, pg 139

Bruce, Taylor, Arcadia Publishing Inc, 420 Wando Park Blvd, Mount Pleasant, SC 29464 Tel: 843-853-2070 Toll Free Tel: 888-313-2665 (orders only) Fax: 843-853-0044 E-mail: sales@arcadiapublishing.com Web Site: www.arcadiapublishing.com, pg 19

Bruce-Eddings, Carla, Algonquin Books, 400 Silver Cedar Ct, Suite 300, Chapel Hill, NC 27514-1585 Tel: 919-967-0108 Fax: 919-933-0272 E-mail: inquiry@algonquin.com Web Site: www.workman.com/algonquin, pg 7

Bruce-Eddings, Carla, Counterpoint Press LLC, 2560 Ninth St, Suite 318, Berkeley, CA 94710 Tel: 510-704-0230 Fax: 510-704-0268 E-mail: info@counterpointpress.com Web Site: counterpointpress.com; softskull.com, pg 58

Brugger, Deborah, Saint Johann Press, 315 Schraalenburgh Rd, Haworth, NJ 07641 Tel: 201-387-1529 Fax: 201-501-0698 Web Site: www.stjohannpress.com, pg 190

Brumley, Mark, Ignatius Press, 1348 Tenth Ave, San Francisco, CA 94122-2304 Toll Free Tel: 800-651-1531 (orders); 888-615-3186 (cust serv) Fax: 415-387-0896 E-mail: info@ignatius.com Web Site: www.ignatius.com, pg 106

Brumwell, Barbara, LexisNexis® Canada Inc, 111 Gordon Baker Rd, Suite 900, Toronto, ON M2H 3R1, Canada Tel: 905-479-2665 Toll Free Tel: 800-668-6481; 800-387-0899 (cust care); 800-255-5174 (sales) E-mail: service@lexisnexis.ca (cust serv); sales@lexisnexis.ca Web Site: www.lexisnexis.ca, pg 432

Brunette, Paul, Concordia Publishing House, 3558 S Jefferson Ave, St Louis, MO 63118-3968 Tel: 314-268-1000; 314-268-1268 (bookshop) Toll Free Tel: 800-325-3040 (cust serv) Toll Free Fax: 800-490-9889 (cust serv) E-mail: order@cph.org Web Site: www.cph.org, pg 56

Brunn, Jennifer, Harry N Abrams Inc, 195 Broadway, 9th fl, New York, NY 10007 Tel: 212-206-7715 Toll Free Tel: 800-345-1359 Fax: 212-519-1210 E-mail: abrams@abramsbooks.com Web Site: www.abramsbooks.com, pg 3

Brunn, Peter, Center for the Collaborative Classroom, 1001 Marina Village Pkwy, Suite 110, Alameda, CA 94501-1042 Tel: 510-533-0213 Toll Free Tel: 800-666-7270 Fax: 510-464-3670 E-mail: info@collaborativeclassroom.org; clientsupport@collaborativeclassroom.org Web Site: www.collaborativeclassroom.org, pg 48

Bruno, Matthew, NPTA Alliance, 330 N Wabash Ave, Suite 2000, Chicago, IL 60611 Tel: 312-321-4092 Toll Free Tel: 800-355-NPTA (355-6782) Fax: 312-673-6736 Web Site: www.gonpta.com, pg 542

Brunsek, Judy, Owlkids Books Inc, 10 Lower Spadina Ave, Suite 400, Toronto, ON M5V 2Z2, Canada Tel: 416-340-2700 Fax: 416-340-9769 E-mail: owlkids@owlkids.com Web Site: www.owlkidsbooks.com, pg 435

Bruschi, Alexandra, TarcherPerigee, 375 Hudson St, New York, NY 10014 Tel: 212-366-2000 Fax: 212-366-2643 E-mail: customerservice@penguinrandomhouse.com (cust serv); TarcherPerigeePublicity@penguinrandomhouse.com (media queries) Web Site: www.tarcherbooks.com; www.facebook.com/TarcherPerigee; www.penguin.com/publishers/tarcherperigee, pg 213

Bruscia, Kenneth E, Barcelona Publishers LLC, 10231 N Plano Rd, Dallas, TX 75238 Tel: 214-553-9785 E-mail: warehouse@barcelonapublishers.com Web Site: www.barcelonapublishers.com, pg 28

Brussel, Gail, The Penguin Press, 375 Hudson St, New York, NY 10014 Web Site: thepenguinpress.com, pg 164

Bryan, Heather, Nimbus Publishing Ltd, 3731 Mackintosh St, Halifax, NS B3K 5A5, Canada Tel: 902-455-4286 Toll Free Tel: 800-NIMBUS9 (646-2879) Fax: 902-455-5440 Toll Free Fax: 888-253-3133 E-mail: customerservice@nimbus.ca Web Site: www.nimbus.ca, pg 434

Bryan, Nancy, University of Texas Press, 3001 Lake Austin Blvd, 2.200, Austin, TX 78703 Tel: 512-471-7233 Fax: 512-232-7178 E-mail: utpress@uts.cc.utexas.edu; info@utpress.utexas.edu Web Site: utpress.utexas.edu, pg 216

Bryans, John B, J B Bryans Literary, 7 Meetinghouse Ct, Indian Mills, NJ 08088 Tel: 609-922-0369 E-mail: info@brylit.com Web Site: brylit.com, pg 478

Bryant, Elizabeth, Graywolf Press, 250 Third Ave N, Suite 600, Minneapolis, MN 55401 Tel: 651-641-0077 Fax: 651-641-0036 E-mail: wolves@graywolfpress.org (no ms queries, sample chapters or proposals) Web Site: www.graywolfpress.org, pg 88

Bryant, L J, Wildflower Press, c/o Oakbrook Press, 3301 S Valley Dr, Rapid City, SD 57703 Tel: 605-381-6385 E-mail: info@wildflowerpress.org Web Site: www.wildflowerpress.org, pg 241

Bryant, Virginia Veiga, Georgetown University Press, 3520 Prospect St NW, Suite 140, Washington, DC 20007 Tel: 202-687-5889 (busn) Fax: 202-687-6340 (edit) E-mail: gupress@georgetown.edu Web Site: press.georgetown.edu, pg 85

Bryerose, Cathy C, Regal Crest Enterprises, 2028 E Ben White Blvd, No 240-1113, Austin, TX 78741 Tel: 409-527-1188 Toll Free Fax: 866-294-9628 E-mail: info@regalcrestbooks.biz Web Site: www.regalcrest.biz, pg 184

Bucaria, Catherine, Penguin Random House Audio Publishing, 1745 Broadway, New York, NY 10019 E-mail: audio@penguinrandomhouse.com Web Site: www.penguinrandomhouseaudio.com, pg 164

Bucca, Lauren, Princeton University Press, 41 William St, Princeton, NJ 08540-5237 Tel: 609-258-4900 Fax: 609-258-6305 Web Site: press.princeton.edu, pg 175

Bucci, Chris, Aevitas Creative Management, 19 W 21st, Suite 501, New York, NY 10010 Tel: 212-765-6900 Web Site: aevitascreative.com, pg 474

Buccieri, Laura, Copper Canyon Press, Fort Worden State Park, Bldg 313, Port Townsend, WA 98368 Tel: 360-385-4925 Toll Free Tel: 877-501-1393 (orders) Fax: 360-385-4985 E-mail: poetry@coppercanyonpress.org Web Site: www.coppercanyonpress.org, pg 57

Buchanan, Holly, University Press of America Inc, 4501 Forbes Blvd, Suite 200, Lanham, MD 20706 Tel: 301-459-3366 Toll Free Tel: 800-462-6420 Fax: 301-429-5748 Toll Free Fax: 800-338-4550 Web Site: www.univpress.com, pg 232

Buchanan, Matt, Tanglewood Publishing, 1060 N Capitol Ave, Suite E-395, Indianapolis, IN 46204 Tel: 812-877-9488 Toll Free Tel: 800-788-3123 (orders) E-mail: info@tanglewoodbooks.com; orders@tanglewoodbooks.com Web Site: www.tanglewoodbooks.com, pg 212

Buchanan, Melissa, University of Georgia Press, Main Library, 3rd fl, 320 S Jackson St, Athens, GA 30602 Fax: 706-542-2558; 706-542-6770 Web Site: www.ugapress.org, pg 227

Buchinger, Mary, Barbara Bradley Prize, 46 Wallace St, Somerville, MA 02144 E-mail: info@nepoetryclub.org Web Site: www.nepoetryclub.org, pg 600

Buchinger, Mary, Der-Hovanessian Translation Prize, 46 Wallace St, Somerville, MA 02144 E-mail: info@nepoetryclub.org Web Site: www.nepoetryclub.org, pg 609

Buchinger, Mary, Golden Rose Award, 46 Wallace St, Somerville, MA 02144 E-mail: info@nepoetryclub.org Web Site: www.nepoetryclub.org, pg 620

Buchinger, Mary, Firman Houghton Prize, 46 Wallace St, Somerville, MA 02144 E-mail: info@nepoetryclub.org Web Site: www.nepoetryclub.org, pg 624

Buchinger, Mary, Sheila Margaret Motton Book Prize, 46 Wallace St, Somerville, MA 02144 E-mail: info@nepoetryclub.org Web Site: www.nepoetryclub.org, pg 644

Buchinger, Mary, Erika Mumford Prize, 46 Wallace St, Somerville, MA 02144 E-mail: info@nepoetryclub.org Web Site: www.nepoetryclub.org, pg 644

Buchinger, Mary, New England Poetry Club, 46 Wallace St, Somerville, MA 02144 E-mail: info@nepoetryclub.org Web Site: www.nepoetryclub.org, pg 541

Buchinger, Mary, May Sarton Award, 46 Wallace St, Somerville, MA 02144 E-mail: info@nepoetryclub.org Web Site: www.nepoetryclub.org, pg 664

Buchinger, Mary, Daniel Varoujan Award, 46 Wallace St, Somerville, MA 02144 E-mail: info@nepoetryclub.org Web Site: www.nepoetryclub.org, pg 675

Buchwald, Don, Don Buchwald & Associates Inc, 10 E 44 St, New York, NY 10017 Tel: 212-867-1200 Fax: 212-867-2434 E-mail: info@buchwald.com Web Site: www.buchwald.com, pg 478

Buckles, Kristen, The University of Arizona Press, 1510 E University Blvd, Tucson, AZ 85721 Tel: 520-621-1441 Toll Free Tel: 800-426-3797 (orders) Fax: 520-621-8899 Toll Free Fax: 800-426-3797 E-mail: uap@uapress.arizona.edu Web Site: www.uapress.arizona.edu, pg 225

Buckley, Carol, Piano Press, 1425 Ocean Ave, Suite 5, Del Mar, CA 92014 Tel: 619-884-1401 Fax: 858-755-1104 E-mail: pianopress@pianopress.com Web Site: www.pianopress.com, pg 169

Buckley, Cicely, Oyster River Press, 36 Oyster River Rd, Durham, NH 03824-3029 Tel: 603-868-5006 E-mail: oysterriverpress@comcast.net Web Site: www.oysterriverbooks.com; www.facebook.com/OysterRiverPress, pg 468

Buckley, Kerri, Harlequin Enterprises Ltd, 195 Broadway, 24th fl, New York, NY 10007 Tel: 212-207-7000 Toll Free Tel: 888-432-4879 E-mail: customerservice@harlequin.com Web Site: www.harlequin.com, pg 93

Buckley, Paul, Viking, 375 Hudson St, New York, NY 10014 Tel: 212-366-2000 Fax: 212-243-6002 Web Site: www.penguin.com/publishers/vikingbooks, pg 236

Buckner, Judith, Judith Buckner Literary Agency, 12721 Hart St, North Hollywood, CA 91605 Tel: 818-982-8202 Fax: 818-764-6844, pg 478

Buckner, Richard E, Beacon Hill Press of Kansas City, PO Box 419527, Kansas City, MO 64141 Tel: 816-931-1900 Toll Free Tel: 800-877-0700 (cust serv) Fax: 816-531-0923 Toll Free Fax: 800-849-9827 E-mail: orders@thefoundrypublishing.com; customercare@thefoundrypublishing.com Web Site: www.thefoundrypublishing.com, pg 29

Budak, Melissa, Liturgy Training Publications, 3949 S Racine Ave, Chicago, IL 60609-2523 Tel: 773-579-4900 Toll Free Tel: 800-933-1800 (US & CN only orders) Fax: 773-579-4929 E-mail: orders@ltp.org Web Site: www.ltp.org, pg 126

Budde, Mark, Carolrhoda Books Inc, 241 First Ave N, Minneapolis, MN 55401 Tel: 612-332-3344 Toll Free Tel: 800-328-4929 Fax: 612-332-7615 Toll Free Fax: 800-332-1132 E-mail: info@lernerbooks.com; custserve@lernerbooks.com Web Site: www.lernerbooks.com; www.facebook.com/lernerbooks, pg 45

Budde, Mark, Carolrhoda Lab™, 241 First Ave N, Minneapolis, MN 55401 Tel: 612-332-3344 Toll Free Tel: 800-328-4929 Fax: 612-332-7615 Toll Free Fax: 800-332-1132 E-mail: info@lernerbooks.com; custserve@lernerbooks.com Web Site: www.lernerbooks.com; www.facebook.com/lernerbooks, pg 45

Budde, Mark, ediciones Lerner, 241 First Ave N, Minneapolis, MN 55401 Tel: 612-332-3344 Toll Free Tel: 800-328-4929 Fax: 612-332-7615 Toll Free Fax: 800-332-1132 E-mail: info@lernerbooks.com; custserve@lernerbooks.com Web Site: www.lernerbooks.com; www.facebook.com/lernerbooks, pg 69

Budde, Mark, First Avenue Editions, 241 First Ave N, Minneapolis, MN 55401 Tel: 612-332-3344 Toll Free Tel: 800-328-4929 Fax: 612-332-7615 Toll Free Fax: 800-332-1132 E-mail: info@lernerbooks.

Butler, Butch, StarGroup International Inc, 1194 Old Dixie Hwy, Suite 201, West Palm Beach, FL 33413 *Tel:* 561-547-0667 *Fax:* 561-843-8530 *E-mail:* info@stargroupinternational.com *Web Site:* stargroupinternational.com, pg 207

Butler, Leigh, Penguin Group USA, A Penguin Random House Company, 375 Hudson St, New York, NY 10014 *Tel:* 212-366-2000 *Toll Free Tel:* 800-847-5515 (inside sales); 800-631-8571 (cust serv) *Fax:* 212-366-2666; 607-775-4829 (inside sales) *E-mail:* online@us.penguingroup.com *Web Site:* www.penguin.com, pg 163

Butler, Shannon, Islandport Press, 247 Portland St, Bldg C, Yarmouth, ME 04096 *Tel:* 207-846-3344 *Fax:* 207-619-9975 *E-mail:* info@islandport.com *Web Site:* www.islandportpress.com, pg 112

Butterfield, Natalie, Chronicle Books, 680 Second St, San Francisco, CA 94107 *Tel:* 415-537-4200 *Toll Free Tel:* 800-759-0190 (cust serv) *Fax:* 415-537-4460 *Toll Free Tel:* 800-858-7787 (orders); 800-286-9471 (cust serv) *E-mail:* frontdesk@chroniclebooks.com *Web Site:* www.chroniclebooks.com, pg 52

Byer-Sprinzeles, Maggie, Byer-Sprinzeles Agency, 5800 Arlington Ave, Suite 16-C, Riverdale, NY 10471 *Tel:* 718-543-9399 *Web Site:* www.maggiebyersprinzeles.com, pg 511

Bykofsky, Sheree, Sheree Bykofsky Associates Inc, PO Box 706, Brigantine, NJ 08203 *E-mail:* submitbee@aol.com *Web Site:* www.shereebee.com, pg 479

Bylander, John, Teachers College Press, 1234 Amsterdam Ave, New York, NY 10027 *Tel:* 212-678-3929 *Fax:* 212-678-4149 *E-mail:* tcpress@tc.edu *Web Site:* www.tcpress.com, pg 214

Bynum, Robert C, Travel Keys, PO Box 160691, Sacramento, CA 95816-0691 *Tel:* 916-452-5200 *Fax:* 916-452-5200, pg 220

Byrd, Elizabeth, Princeton University Press, 41 William St, Princeton, NJ 08540-5237 *Tel:* 609-258-4900 *Fax:* 609-258-6305 *Web Site:* press.princeton.edu, pg 174

Byrd, John, Cinco Puntos Press, 701 Texas Ave, El Paso, TX 79901 *Tel:* 915-838-1625 *Toll Free Tel:* 800-566-9072 *Fax:* 915-838-1635 *E-mail:* info@cincopuntos.com *Web Site:* www.cincopuntos.com, pg 52

Byrd, Lee, Cinco Puntos Press, 701 Texas Ave, El Paso, TX 79901 *Tel:* 915-838-1625 *Toll Free Tel:* 800-566-9072 *Fax:* 915-838-1635 *E-mail:* info@cincopuntos.com *Web Site:* www.cincopuntos.com, pg 52

Byrne, Stephen, Miniature Book Society Inc, 702 Rosecrans St, San Diego, CA 92106-3013 *Tel:* 619-226-4441 *Fax:* 619-226-4441 *E-mail:* minibook@cox.net *Web Site:* www.mbs.org, pg 538

Byrne-Jimenez, Monica, University Council for Educational Administration (UCEA), Michigan State University, College of Education, 620 Farm Lane, 432 Erickson Hall, East Lansing, MI 48824 *Tel:* 434-243-1041 *E-mail:* ucea@msu.edu *Web Site:* www.ucea.org, pg 225

Byrns, Bob, Paulist Press, 997 Macarthur Blvd, Mahwah, NJ 07430-9990 *Tel:* 201-825-7300 *Toll Free Tel:* 800-218-1903 *Fax:* 201-825-6921 *Toll Free Fax:* 800-836-3161 *E-mail:* info@paulistpress.com; publicity@paulistpress.com *Web Site:* www.paulistpress.com, pg 161

Caban, Isa, Tom Doherty Associates, LLC, 120 Broadway, New York, NY 10271 *Tel:* 646-307-5511 *Toll Free Tel:* 800-455-0340 *Web Site:* us.macmillan.com/torforge, pg 66

Cabaza, Becky, Words into Print, 208 Java St, 5th fl, Brooklyn, NY 11222 *E-mail:* query@wordsintoprint.org *Web Site:* wordsintoprint.com, pg 471

Cabezas, Sue, Applewood Books Inc, One River Rd, Carlisle, MA 01741 *Tel:* 781-271-0055 *Toll Free Tel:* 800-277-5312 (orders) *Fax:* 781-271-0056 *E-mail:* bookorder@awb.com; customercare@awb.com *Web Site:* www.awb.com, pg 18

Cabin, John, Vandamere Press, 3580 Morris St N, St Petersburg, FL 33713 *Tel:* 727-556-0950 *Toll Free Tel:* 800-551-7776 *Fax:* 727-556-2560 *E-mail:* orders@vandamere.com *Web Site:* www.vandamere.com, pg 235

Cable, Colleen, Association of Writers & Writing Programs (AWP), University of Maryland, 5245 Greenbelt Rd, Box 246, College Park, MD 20740 *Tel:* 240-696-7700 *E-mail:* awp@awpwriter.org; press@awpwriter.org *Web Site:* www.awpwriter.org, pg 527

Cabrera, Javier, Santillana USA Publishing Co, 2023 NW 84 Ave, Doral, FL 33122 *Tel:* 305-591-9522 *Toll Free Tel:* 800-245-8584 *E-mail:* customerservice@santillanausa.com *Web Site:* www.santillanausa.com, pg 192

Cabrera, Luis, Lonely Planet, 124 Linden St, Oakland, CA 94607 *Tel:* 510-250-6400 *Toll Free Tel:* 800-275-8555 (orders) *E-mail:* info@lonelyplanet.com *Web Site:* www.lonelyplanet.com, pg 127

Caffery, Dr Joshua, University of Louisiana at Lafayette Press, PO Box 43558, Lafayette, LA 70504-3558 *Tel:* 337-482-6027 *E-mail:* press.submissions@louisiana.edu *Web Site:* ulpress.org, pg 228

Caggiula, Samuel M, Casemate | publishers, 1950 Lawrence Rd, Havertown, PA 19083 *Tel:* 610-853-9131 *Fax:* 610-853-9146 *E-mail:* casemate@casematepublishers.com *Web Site:* www.casematepublishers.com, pg 46

Cahalan, Sarah, Marian Library Medal, 300 College Park, Dayton, OH 45469-1390 *Tel:* 937-229-4214 *Fax:* 937-229-4258 *Web Site:* campus.udayton.edu/mary/mlmedal.html, pg 638

Cahill, Alexandra, DEStech Publications Inc, 439 N Duke St, Lancaster, PA 17602-4967 *Tel:* 717-290-1660 *Toll Free Tel:* 877-500-4DES (500-4337) *Fax:* 717-509-6100 *E-mail:* info@destechpub.com *Web Site:* www.destechpub.com, pg 64

Cahill, Brendan, Penguin Random House LLC, 1745 Broadway, New York, NY 10019 *Tel:* 212-782-9000 *Toll Free Tel:* 800-726-0600 *Web Site:* www.penguinrandomhouse.com, pg 164

Cahill, Kerry, American Psychological Association, 750 First St NE, Washington, DC 20002-4242 *Tel:* 202-336-5510 *Toll Free Tel:* 800-374-2721 *Fax:* 202-336-5502 *E-mail:* order@apa.org *Web Site:* www.apa.org/books, pg 13

Cahoon, Nancy Stauffer, Nancy Stauffer Associates, 30 Corbin Dr, Suite 1203, Darien, CT 06820 *Tel:* 203-202-2500 *Web Site:* www.publishersmarketplace.com/members/nstauffer/, pg 504

Caiati, Michael, Random House Children's Books, 1745 Broadway, 10th fl, New York, NY 10019 *Tel:* 212-782-9000 *Web Site:* www.randomhousekids.com, pg 181

Cain-Walther, Carla, The Center for Fiction, 17 E 47 St, New York, NY 10017 *Tel:* 212-755-6710 *E-mail:* info@centerforfiction.org *Web Site:* centerforfiction.org, pg 530

Calamia, Joseph, University of Chicago Press, 1427 E 60 St, Chicago, IL 60637-2954 *Tel:* 773-702-7700; 773-702-7600 *Toll Free Tel:* 800-621-2736 (orders) *Fax:* 773-702-9756; 773-660-2235 (orders); 773-702-2708 *E-mail:* custserv@press.uchicago.edu; marketing@press.uchicago.edu *Web Site:* www.press.uchicago.edu, pg 226

Calderara, Theo, Oxford University Press USA, 198 Madison Ave, New York, NY 10016 *Tel:* 800-451-7556 (orders); 800-445-9714 (cust serv) *Fax:* 919-677-1303 *E-mail:* custserv.us@oup.com *Web Site:* global.oup.com, pg 158

Caldwell, Amy, Beacon Press, 24 Farnsworth St, Boston, MA 02210-1409 *Tel:* 617-742-2110 *Fax:* 617-723-3097; 617-742-2290 *Web Site:* www.beacon.org, pg 29

Caldwell, Becky, Creative Writing Day & Workshops, PO Box 801, Abingdon, VA 24212-0801 *Tel:* 276-623-5266 *Fax:* 276-676-3076 *E-mail:* info@vahighlandsfestival.org *Web Site:* vahighlandsfestival.org, pg 574

Caldwell, Claire, Annick Press Ltd, 15 Patricia Ave, Toronto, ON M2M 1H9, Canada *Tel:* 416-221-4802 *Fax:* 416-221-8400 *E-mail:* annickpress@annickpress.com *Web Site:* www.annickpress.com, pg 415

Caldwell, Linda, The Writers' Colony at Dairy Hollow, 515 Spring St, Eureka Springs, AR 72632 *Tel:* 479-253-7444 *E-mail:* director@writerscolony.org *Web Site:* www.writerscolony.org, pg 580

Caldwell, Patrice, Howard Morhaim Literary Agency Inc, 30 Pierrepont St, Brooklyn, NY 11201-3371 *Tel:* 718-222-8400 *E-mail:* info@morhaimliterary.com *Web Site:* www.morhaimliterary.com, pg 497

Calella, Christine, Simon & Schuster, 1230 Avenue of the Americas, New York, NY 10020 *Tel:* 212-698-7000 *Toll Free Tel:* 800-223-2348 (cust serv); 800-223-2336 (orders) *Toll Free Fax:* 800-943-9831 (orders) *Web Site:* www.simonandschuster.com, pg 198

Calistro, Paddy, Angel City Press, 2118 Wilshire Blvd, Suite 880, Santa Monica, CA 90403 *Tel:* 310-395-9982 *Toll Free Tel:* 800-949-8039 *Fax:* 310-395-3353 *E-mail:* info@angelcitypress.com *Web Site:* www.angelcitypress.com, pg 16

Callahan, Alison, Gallery Books, 1230 Avenue of the Americas, New York, NY 10020 *Toll Free Tel:* 800-456-6798 *Fax:* 212-698-7284 *E-mail:* consumer.customerservice@simonandschuster.com *Web Site:* www.simonandschuster.com, pg 83

Callahan, Annie, CRC Press, 6000 Broken Sound Pkwy NW, Suite 300, Boca Raton, FL 33487 *Toll Free Tel:* 800-272-7737 (orders) *Toll Free Fax:* 800-374-3401 (orders) *E-mail:* orders@taylorandfrancis.com *Web Site:* www.crcpress.com, pg 59

Callahan, Laurie, New Directions Publishing Corp, 80 Eighth Ave, 19th fl, New York, NY 10011 *Tel:* 212-255-0230 *E-mail:* editorial@ndbooks.com; publicity@ndbooks.com *Web Site:* ndbooks.com, pg 148

Callahan, Pat, University of South Carolina Press, 1600 Hampton St, Suite 544, Columbia, SC 29208 *Tel:* 803-777-5245 *Toll Free Tel:* 800-768-2500 (orders) *Fax:* 803-777-0160 *Toll Free Fax:* 800-868-0740 (orders) *Web Site:* www.sc.edu/uscpress, pg 231

Callahan, Sabrina, Little, Brown and Company, 1290 Avenue of the Americas, New York, NY 10104 *Tel:* 212-364-1100 *Fax:* 212-364-0952 *E-mail:* firstname.lastname@hbgusa.com *Web Site:* www.littlebrown.com; www.hachettebookgroup.com, pg 125

Callanan, Annie, Taylor & Francis Inc, 530 Walnut St, Suite 850, Philadelphia, PA 19106 *Tel:* 215-625-8900 *Toll Free Tel:* 800-354-1420 *Fax:* 215-207-0050; 215-207-0046 (cust serv) *E-mail:* support@tandfonline.com *Web Site:* www.taylorandfrancis.com, pg 213

Callaway, Jaimee, Perseus Books, 1290 Avenue of the Americas, New York, NY 10104 *Tel:* 212-340-8100 *Toll Free Tel:* 800-343-4499 (cust serv) *Fax:* 212-340-8105 *Web Site:* www.perseusbooks.com, pg 167

Callaway, MaryKatherine, Louisiana State University Press, 338 Johnston Hall, Baton Rouge, LA 70803 *Tel:* 225-578-6294 *E-mail:* lsupress@lsu.edu *Web Site:* lsupress.org, pg 128

Callery, Maryann, Plowshare Media, 405 Vincente Way, La Jolla, CA 92037 *Tel:* 858-454-5446 *E-mail:* sales@plowsharemedia.com *Web Site:* plowsharemedia.com, pg 171

Callow, Phil, OAG Worldwide, 801 Warrenville Rd, Suite 555, Lisle, IL 60532 *Tel:* 630-515-5300 *Toll Free Tel:* 800-342-5624 (cust serv) *E-mail:* contactus@oag.com *Web Site:* www.oag.com, pg 153

Calusine, Lyndsay, Houghton Mifflin Harcourt Trade & Reference Division, 125 High St, Boston, MA 02110 *Tel:* 617-351-5000 *Web Site:* www.hmhco.com, pg 104

Calvert, Cordelia, W W Norton & Company Inc, 500 Fifth Ave, New York, NY 10110-0017 *Tel:* 212-354-5500 *Toll Free Tel:* 800-233-4830 (orders & cust serv) *Fax:* 212-869-0856 *Toll Free Fax:* 800-458-6515 *E-mail:* orders@wwnorton.com *Web Site:* wwnorton.com, pg 152

Carroll-Davis, Julie, ProQuest LLC, 789 E Eisenhower Pkwy, Ann Arbor, MI 48108 *Tel:* 734-761-4700 *Toll Free Tel:* 800-521-0600; 877-779-6768 (sales) *E-mail:* sales@proquest.com *Web Site:* www.proquest.com, pg 176

Carruth, Marlies A, MacArthur Fellows Program, Office of Grants Management, 140 S Dearborn St, Chicago, IL 60603-5285 *Tel:* 312-726-8000 *Fax:* 312-920-6528 *E-mail:* 4answers@macfound.org *Web Site:* www.macfound.org/programs/fellows, pg 636

Carruthers, Madeline, Chronicle Books, 680 Second St, San Francisco, CA 94107 *Tel:* 415-537-4200 *Toll Free Tel:* 800-759-0190 (cust serv) *Fax:* 415-537-4460 *Toll Free Fax:* 800-858-7787 (orders); 800-286-9471 (cust serv) *E-mail:* frontdesk@chroniclebooks.com *Web Site:* www.chroniclebooks.com, pg 52

Carson, Dina C, Iron Gate Publishing, PO Box 999, Niwot, CO 80544 *Tel:* 303-530-2551 *Fax:* 303-530-5273 *E-mail:* editor@irongate.com *Web Site:* www.irongate.com, pg 112

Carson, Ken, Cengage Learning, 20 Channel Center St, Boston, MA 02210 *Tel:* 617-289-7700 *Toll Free Tel:* 800-354-9706 *Fax:* 617-289-7844 *E-mail:* esales@cengage.com *Web Site:* www.cengage.com, pg 47

Carstens, Sarah, Rizzoli International Publications Inc, 300 Park Ave S, 4th fl, New York, NY 10010-5399 *Tel:* 212-387-3400 *Toll Free Tel:* 800-522-6657 (orders only) *Fax:* 212-387-3535 *E-mail:* publicity@rizzoliusa.com *Web Site:* www.rizzoliusa.com, pg 185

Carswell, Christine, Chronicle Books, 680 Second St, San Francisco, CA 94107 *Tel:* 415-537-4200 *Toll Free Tel:* 800-759-0190 (cust serv) *Fax:* 415-537-4460 *Toll Free Fax:* 800-858-7787 (orders); 800-286-9471 (cust serv) *E-mail:* frontdesk@chroniclebooks.com *Web Site:* www.chroniclebooks.com, pg 51

Carter, Dr Allyson, The University of Arizona Press, 1510 E University Blvd, Tucson, AZ 85721 *Tel:* 520-621-1441 *Toll Free Tel:* 800-426-3797 (orders) *Fax:* 520-621-8899 *Toll Free Fax:* 800-426-3797 *E-mail:* uap@uapress.arizona.edu *Web Site:* www.uapress.arizona.edu, pg 225

Carter, Brenda, American Psychological Association, 750 First St NE, Washington, DC 20002-4242 *Tel:* 202-336-5510 *Toll Free Tel:* 800-374-2721 *Fax:* 202-336-5502 *E-mail:* order@apa.org *Web Site:* www.apa.org/books, pg 13

Carter, Brittany, Columbia Books & Information Services (CBIS), 4340 East-West Hwy, Suite 300, Bethesda, MD 20814 *Tel:* 202-464-1662 *Fax:* 301-664-9600 *E-mail:* info@columbiabooks.com *Web Site:* www.columbiabooks.com; www.lobbyists.info; www.associationexecs.com, pg 55

Carter, Charles Cuykendall, American Printing History Association, PO Box 4519, Grand Central Sta, New York, NY 10163 *E-mail:* secretary@printinghistory.org *Web Site:* printinghistory.org, pg 523

Carter, Charles Cuykendall, American Printing History Association Award, PO Box 4519, Grand Central Sta, New York, NY 10163 *E-mail:* secretary@printinghistory.org *Web Site:* printinghistory.org, pg 592

Carter Eaton, Eryn, Hampton Roads Publishing, 65 Parker St, Suite 7, Newburyport, MA 01950-4600 *Tel:* 978-465-0504 *Toll Free Tel:* 800-423-7087 (orders) *Fax:* 978-465-0243 *Toll Free Fax:* 877-337-3309 *E-mail:* orders@rwwbooks.com *Web Site:* redwheelweiser.com, pg 92

Carter, Jill, Crossway, 1300 Crescent St, Wheaton, IL 60187 *Tel:* 630-682-4300 *Toll Free Tel:* 800-635-7993 (orders); 800-543-1659 (cust serv) *Fax:* 630-682-4785 *E-mail:* info@crossway.org *Web Site:* www.crossway.org, pg 60

Caruso, Emma, Random House Publishing Group, 1745 Broadway, New York, NY 10019 *Toll Free Tel:* 800-200-3552 *Web Site:* www.randomhousebooks.com, pg 181

Carvainis, Maria, Maria Carvainis Agency Inc, Rockefeller Center, 1270 Avenue of the Americas, Suite 2320, New York, NY 10020 *Tel:* 212-245-6365 *Fax:* 212-245-7196 *E-mail:* mca@mariacarvainisagency.com *Web Site:* mariacarvainisagency.com, pg 479

Carvalho, Julia, Chronicle Books, 680 Second St, San Francisco, CA 94107 *Tel:* 415-537-4200 *Toll Free Tel:* 800-759-0190 (cust serv) *Fax:* 415-537-4460 *Toll Free Fax:* 800-858-7787 (orders); 800-286-9471 (cust serv) *E-mail:* frontdesk@chroniclebooks.com *Web Site:* www.chroniclebooks.com, pg 51

Carver, Peter, Red Deer Press Inc, 195 Allstate Pkwy, Markham, ON L3R 4T8, Canada *Tel:* 905-477-9700 *Toll Free Tel:* 800-387-9776 (orders) *E-mail:* rdp@reddeerpress.com; bookinfo@fitzhenry.ca *Web Site:* www.reddeerpress.com, pg 438

Casares, Oscar, University of Texas at Austin, New Writers Project, Dept of English, Calhoun Hall, Rm 226, 204 W 21 St, B-5000, Austin, TX 78712 *Tel:* 512-471-5132; 512-471-4991 *Fax:* 512-471-4909 *Web Site:* newwritersproject.org, pg 586

Cascardi, Andrea, Transatlantic Agency, 2 Bloor St E, Suite 3500, Toronto, ON M4W 1A8, Canada *Tel:* 416-488-9214 *E-mail:* info@transatlanticagency.com *Web Site:* www.transatlanticagency.com, pg 506

Cascio, Keri, Margaret Mann Citation, 50 E Huron St, Chicago, IL 60611 *Tel:* 312-280-5037 *Toll Free Tel:* 800-545-2433 *Fax:* 312-280-5033 *E-mail:* alcts@ala.org *Web Site:* www.ala.org/alcts, pg 638

Casey, Adrianne, Channel Photographics, 980 Lincoln Ave, Suite 200-B, San Rafael, CA 94901 *Tel:* 415-456-2934 *Fax:* 415-456-4124 *Web Site:* www.channelphotographics.com, pg 49

Casey, Adrianne, Global Publishing, Sales & Distribution, 135 Third St, Suite 150, San Rafael, CA 94901 *Tel:* 415-456-2934 *Fax:* 415-456-4124 *E-mail:* info@globalpsd.com *Web Site:* www.globalpsd.com, pg 86

Casey, Alec, Trusted Media Brands Inc, 750 Third Ave, 3rd fl, New York, NY 10017 *Tel:* 646-293-6296 *Toll Free Tel:* 877-732-4438 (cust serv) *Fax:* 646-293-6251 *E-mail:* customercare@trustedmediabrands.com; press@trustedmediabrands.com *Web Site:* www.trustedmediabrands.com; www.rd.com, pg 221

Casey, Barbara, Strategic Media Books LLC, 782 Wofford St, Rock Hill, SC 29730 *Tel:* 803-366-5440 *E-mail:* contact@strategicmediabooks.com *Web Site:* strategicmediabooks.com, pg 210

Casey, Maribeth, Storey Publishing LLC, 210 MASS MoCA Way, North Adams, MA 01247 *Tel:* 413-346-2100 *Toll Free Tel:* 800-441-5700 (orders); 800-827-7444 (cust serv) *Fax:* 413-346-2199 *Toll Free Fax:* 800-865-3429 (cust serv) *E-mail:* sales@storey.com; feedback@storey.com *Web Site:* www.storey.com, pg 209

Casey, Megan, University of Missouri Press, 113 Heinkel Bldg, 201 S Seventh St, Columbia, MO 65211 *Tel:* 573-882-7641; 573-882-3000 (publicity & sales enquiries) *Toll Free Tel:* 800-621-2736 (orders) *Fax:* 573-884-4498 *Toll Free Fax:* 800-621-8476 (orders) *E-mail:* upress@missouri.edu; umpmarketing@missouri.edu (publicity & sales enquiries) *Web Site:* upress.missouri.edu, pg 228

Cash, Amy Opperman, Larson Publications, 4936 State Rte 414, Burdett, NY 14818 *Tel:* 607-546-9342 *Toll Free Tel:* 800-828-2197 *Fax:* 607-546-9344 *E-mail:* custserv@larsonpublications.com *Web Site:* www.larsonpublications.com, pg 120

Cash, Mary, Holiday House Publishing Inc, 50 Broad St, New York, NY 10004 *Tel:* 212-688-0085 *Fax:* 212-421-6134 *E-mail:* info@holidayhouse.com *Web Site:* www.holidayhouse.com, pg 101

Cashion, David, Harry N Abrams Inc, 195 Broadway, 9th fl, New York, NY 10007 *Tel:* 212-206-7715 *Toll Free Tel:* 800-345-1359 *Fax:* 212-519-1210 *E-mail:* abrams@abramsbooks.com *Web Site:* www.abramsbooks.com, pg 3

Cashman, Ann, The LA Literary Agency, 1264 N Hayworth Ave, Los Angeles, CA 90046 *Tel:* 323-654-5288 *E-mail:* laliteraryagency@mac.com *Web Site:* www.laliteraryagency.com, pg 492

Cashman, Lorraine Walsh, Opie Prize, Indiana University, Classroom-Off Bldg, 800 E Third St, Bloomington, IN 47405 *Tel:* 812-856-2379 *Fax:* 812-856-2483 *Web Site:* www.afsnet.org, pg 651

Cashman, Michelle, St Martin's Press, LLC, 120 Broadway, New York, NY 10271 *Tel:* 646-307-5151 *Web Site:* us.macmillan.com/smp, pg 190

Casolaro, Frank, Hachette Book Group, 1290 Avenue of the Americas, New York, NY 10104 *Tel:* 212-364-1100 *Toll Free Tel:* 800-759-0190 (cust serv) *Fax:* 212-364-0933 (intl orders) *Toll Free Fax:* 800-286-9471 (cust serv) *Web Site:* www.hachettebookgroup.com, pg 91

Cason, Mary, Philadelphia Museum of Art, PO Box 7646, Philadelphia, PA 19101-7646 *Tel:* 215-763-8100 *Fax:* 215-236-4465 *Web Site:* www.philamuseum.org, pg 169

Cassaday, Kate, HarperCollins Canada Ltd, 2 Bloor St E, 20th fl, Toronto, ON M4W 1A8, Canada *Tel:* 416-975-9334 *Fax:* 416-975-5223 *E-mail:* hcorder@harpercollins.com *Web Site:* www.harpercollins.ca, pg 429

Cassell, Dana K, Florida Freelance Writers Association, 45 Main St, North Stratford, NH 03590 *Tel:* 603-922-8338 *Fax:* 603-922-8339 *E-mail:* ffwa@writers-editors.com; info@writers-editors.com *Web Site:* www.writers-editors.com; www.ffwamembers.com, pg 533

Cassell, Dana K, Writers-Editors Network International Writing Competition, 45 Main St, North Stratford, NH 03590 *Tel:* 603-922-8338 *Fax:* 603-922-8339 *E-mail:* contest@writers-editors.com *Web Site:* www.writers-editors.com; www.ffwamembers.com, pg 680

Cassidy, Kyran, HarperCollins Publishers, 195 Broadway, New York, NY 10007 *Tel:* 212-207-7000 *Fax:* 212-207-7145 *Web Site:* www.harpercollins.com, pg 94

Cassity, Liza, Berkley Publishing Group, 1745 Broadway, 19th fl, New York, NY 10019 *Tel:* 212-366-2000 *Web Site:* www.penguin.com, pg 32

Cassity, Liza, Dutton, 1745 Broadway, New York, NY 10019 *Tel:* 212-366-2000 *Fax:* 212-366-2262 *E-mail:* duttonpublicity@us.penguingroup.com *Web Site:* www.penguin.com, pg 68

Cassity, Liza, Plume, 375 Hudson St, New York, NY 10014 *Tel:* 212-366-2000 *Fax:* 212-243-6002 *Web Site:* www.penguin.com/publishers/plume, pg 171

Cassity, Liza, GP Putnam's Sons (Children's), 345 Hudson St, New York, NY 10014 *Tel:* 212-366-2000 *Fax:* 212-414-3393 *Web Site:* www.penguin.com/publishers/gpputnamssonsbooksforyoungread, pg 178

Cassity, Liza, GP Putnam's Sons (Hardcover), 375 Hudson St, New York, NY 10014 *Tel:* 212-366-2000 *Fax:* 212-366-2643 *E-mail:* online@penguinputnam.com *Web Site:* www.penguin.com/publishers/gpputnamssons, pg 178

Cassola, Lexy, Dutton, 1745 Broadway, New York, NY 10019 *Tel:* 212-366-2000 *Fax:* 212-366-2262 *E-mail:* duttonpublicity@us.penguingroup.com *Web Site:* www.penguin.com, pg 68

Castaldo, John, G Schirmer Inc/Associated Music Publishers Inc, 180 Madison Ave, 24th fl, New York, NY 10016 *Tel:* 212-254-2100 *Fax:* 212-254-2013 *E-mail:* schirmer@schirmer.com *Web Site:* www.musicsalesclassical.com, pg 193

Castellani, Mary Kate, Bloomsbury Publishing Inc, 1385 Broadway, 5th fl, New York, NY 10018 *Tel:* 212-419-5300 *E-mail:* marketingusa@bloomsbury.com; adultpublicityusa@bloomsbury.com; askacademic@bloomsbury.com *Web Site:* www.bloomsbury.com, pg 35

Castillo, Johanna V, Writers House, 21 W 26 St, New York, NY 10010 *Tel:* 212-685-2400 *Web Site:* www.writershouse.com, pg 508

Castillo, Sofia, Association of American Publishers (AAP), 455 Massachusetts Ave NW, Suite 700, Washington, DC 20001-2777 *Tel:* 202-347-3375 *Fax:* 202-347-3690 *E-mail:* info@publishers.org *Web Site:* publishers.org, pg 526

Chalfant, Sarah, The Wylie Agency LLC, 250 W 57 St, Suite 2114, New York, NY 10107 *Tel:* 212-246-0069 *Fax:* 212-586-8953 *E-mail:* mail@wylieagency.com *Web Site:* www.wylieagency.com, pg 509

Chalifoux, Ed, Printing Industry Association of the South (PIAS), 305 Plus Park Blvd, Nashville, TN 37217 *Tel:* 615-366-1094 *Fax:* 615-366-4192 *E-mail:* info@pias.org *Web Site:* www.pias.org, pg 544

Chalker, Bob, NACE International, 15835 Park Ten Place, Houston, TX 77084 *Tel:* 281-228-6200; 281-228-6223 *Toll Free Tel:* 800-797-NACE (797-6223) *Fax:* 281-228-6300 *E-mail:* firstservice@nace.org *Web Site:* www.nace.org, pg 144

Challender, Gary, Books In Motion, 9922 E Montgomery, Suite 31, Spokane Valley, WA 99206 *Tel:* 509-922-1646 *Toll Free Tel:* 800-752-3199 *Fax:* 509-922-1445 *E-mail:* info@booksinmotion.com *Web Site:* www.booksinmotion.com, pg 38

Challice, John, Oxford University Press USA, 198 Madison Ave, New York, NY 10016 *Toll Free Tel:* 800-451-7556 (orders); 800-445-9714 (cust serv) *Fax:* 919-677-1303 *E-mail:* custserv.us@oup.com *Web Site:* global.oup.com, pg 158

Chamberlain, Laura, Anchor Books, c/o Penguin Random House Inc, 1745 Broadway, New York, NY 10019 *Tel:* 212-572-2420 *E-mail:* vintageanchorpublicity@randomhouse.com *Web Site:* knopfdoubleday.com/imprint/anchor, pg 15

Chamberlain, Laura, Vintage Books, c/o Penguin Random House Inc, 1745 Broadway, New York, NY 10019 *Tel:* 212-572-2420 *E-mail:* vintageanchorpublicity@randomhouse.com *Web Site:* knopfdoubleday.com/imprint/vintage, pg 236

Chambers, Andrea L, New York University, Center for Publishing, Midtown Ctr, Rm 429, 11 W 42 St, New York, NY 10036 *Tel:* 212-992-3232 *Fax:* 212-992-3233 *E-mail:* pub.center@nyu.edu *Web Site:* www.scps.nyu.edu/publishing, pg 583

Chambers, Jennifer, In-Plant Printing & Mailing Association (IPMA), 455 S Sam Barr Dr, Suite 203, Kearney, MO 64060 *Tel:* 816-919-1691 *E-mail:* ipmainfo@ipma.org *Web Site:* www.ipma.org, pg 534

Chambers, Lewis R, The Bethel Agency, PO Box 21043, Park West Sta, New York, NY 10025 *Tel:* 212-864-4510 *E-mail:* bethelagcy@aol.com, pg 475

Chambers, Nathaniel, National Association of Black Journalists (NABJ), 1100 Knight Hall, Suite 3100, College Park, MD 20742 *Tel:* 301-405-0248 *Fax:* 301-314-1714 *E-mail:* info@nabj.org; press@nabj.org *Web Site:* www.nabj.org, pg 538

Chambers, Samantha, Chronicle Books, 680 Second St, San Francisco, CA 94107 *Tel:* 415-537-4200 *Toll Free Tel:* 800-759-0190 (cust serv) *Fax:* 415-537-4460 *Toll Free Fax:* 800-858-7787 (orders); 800-286-9471 (cust serv) *E-mail:* frontdesk@chroniclebooks.com *Web Site:* www.chroniclebooks.com, pg 52

Chamblee, Ruth, National Geographic Books, 1145 17 St NW, Washington, DC 20036-4688 *Tel:* 202-857-7000 *Toll Free Tel:* 877-866-6486 *E-mail:* ngbooks@cdsfulfillment.com *Web Site:* www.nationalgeographic.com/books/; ngbooks.buysub.com, pg 146

Chambliss, Jamie, Folio Literary Management, The Film Center Bldg, 630 Ninth Ave, Suite 1101, New York, NY 10036 *Tel:* 212-400-1494 *Fax:* 212-967-0977 *Web Site:* www.foliolit.com, pg 484

Chamenko, Tiffany, Information Today, Inc, 143 Old Marlton Pike, Medford, NJ 08055-8750 *Tel:* 609-654-6266 *Toll Free Tel:* 800-300-9868 (cust serv) *Fax:* 609-654-4309 *E-mail:* custserv@infotoday.com *Web Site:* www.infotoday.com, pg 108

Chance, Rachel, The American Library Association (ALA), 225 N Michigan Ave, Suite 1300, Chicago, IL 60601 *Tel:* 312-944-6780 *Toll Free Tel:* 800-545-2433 *Fax:* 312-280-5275 *E-mail:* editionsmarketing@ala.org *Web Site:* www.alastore.ala.org, pg 141

Chanda, Justin, Simon & Schuster Children's Publishing, 1230 Avenue of the Americas, New York, NY 10020 *Tel:* 212-698-7000 *Web Site:* www.simonandschuster.com/kids; www.simonandschuster.com/teen; simonandschuster.net; simonandschuster.biz, pg 199

Chandlee, Chad M, Kendall Hunt Publishing Co, 4050 Westmark Dr, Dubuque, IA 52002-2624 *Tel:* 563-589-1000 *Toll Free Tel:* 800-228-0810 (orders) *Fax:* 563-589-1046 *Toll Free Fax:* 800-772-9165 *E-mail:* orders@kendallhunt.com *Web Site:* www.kendallhunt.com, pg 116

Chandler, Pamela Siege, Foundation Press, c/o West Academic, 444 Cedar St, Suite 700, St Paul, MN 55101 *Toll Free Tel:* 877-888-1330 *E-mail:* customerservice@westacademic.com *Web Site:* www.westacademic.com, pg 80

Chaney, Margo, University of Illinois Press, 1325 S Oak St, MC-566, Champaign, IL 61820-6903 *Tel:* 217-333-0950 *Fax:* 217-244-8082 *E-mail:* uipress@uillinois.edu; journals@uillinois.edu *Web Site:* www.press.uillinois.edu, pg 227

Chang, Lan Samantha, The Iowa Short Fiction Award, 102 Dey House, 507 N Clinton St, Iowa City, IA 52242-1000 *Tel:* 319-335-0416 *Fax:* 319-335-0420 *Web Site:* www.uiowapress.org/authors/iowa-short-fiction.htm, pg 628

Chang, Lan Samantha, University of Iowa, Writers' Workshop, Graduate Creative Writing Program, 102 Dey House, 507 N Clinton St, Iowa City, IA 52242-1000 *Tel:* 319-335-0416 *Fax:* 319-335-0420 *Web Site:* writersworkshop.uiowa.edu, pg 586

Chang, Melanie, Harry N Abrams Inc, 195 Broadway, 9th fl, New York, NY 10007 *Tel:* 212-206-7715 *Toll Free Tel:* 800-345-1359 *Fax:* 212-519-1210 *E-mail:* abrams@abramsbooks.com *Web Site:* www.abramsbooks.com, pg 3

Chang, Melanie, Stewart, Tabori & Chang, 195 Broadway, 9th fl, New York, NY 10007 *Tel:* 212-206-7715 *Fax:* 212-519-1210 *E-mail:* abrams@abramsbooks.com *Web Site:* www.abramsbooks.com/imprints/stc, pg 208

Chang, Ms Minju, BookStop Literary Agency LLC, 67 Meadow View Rd, Orinda, CA 94563 *E-mail:* info@bookstopliterary.com *Web Site:* www.bookstopliterary.com, pg 477

Chang, Susan, Tom Doherty Associates, LLC, 120 Broadway, New York, NY 10271 *Tel:* 646-307-5511 *Toll Free Tel:* 800-455-0340 *Web Site:* us.macmillan.com/torforge, pg 66

Chang, Wah-Ming, Counterpoint Press LLC, 2560 Ninth St, Suite 318, Berkeley, CA 94710 *Tel:* 510-704-0230 *Fax:* 510-704-0268 *E-mail:* info@counterpointpress.com *Web Site:* counterpointpress; softskull.com, pg 58

Chanter, Dr Carol, Scholastic Education, 557 Broadway, New York, NY 10012 *Tel:* 212-343-6100 *Fax:* 212-343-6189 *Web Site:* www.scholastic.com, pg 194

Chao, Victoria, Chronicle Books, 680 Second St, San Francisco, CA 94107 *Tel:* 415-537-4200 *Toll Free Tel:* 800-759-0190 (cust serv) *Fax:* 415-537-4460 *Toll Free Fax:* 800-858-7787 (orders); 800-286-9471 (cust serv) *E-mail:* frontdesk@chroniclebooks.com *Web Site:* www.chroniclebooks.com, pg 52

Chapin, Amy, Avery Color Studios, 511 "D" Ave, Gwinn, MI 49841 *Tel:* 906-346-3908 *Toll Free Tel:* 800-722-9925 *Fax:* 906-346-3015 *E-mail:* averycolor@averycolorstudios.com *Web Site:* www.averycolorstudios.com, pg 26

Chapin, Ms Frances, Write on the Sound Writers' Conference, Frances Anderson Center, 700 Main St, Edmonds, WA 98020 *Tel:* 425-771-0228 *Fax:* 425-771-0253 *E-mail:* wots@edmondswa.gov *Web Site:* www.writeonthesound.com, pg 580

Chapin, Wells, Avery Color Studios, 511 "D" Ave, Gwinn, MI 49841 *Tel:* 906-346-3908 *Toll Free Tel:* 800-722-9925 *Fax:* 906-346-3015 *E-mail:* averycolor@averycolorstudios.com *Web Site:* www.averycolorstudios.com, pg 26

Chaplin, Candice, Penguin Random House LLC, 1745 Broadway, New York, NY 10019 *Tel:* 212-782-9000 *Toll Free Tel:* 800-726-0600 *Web Site:* www.penguinrandomhouse.com, pg 164

Chapman, Amy, AIGA, the professional association for design, 222 Broadway, New York, NY 10038 *Tel:* 212-807-1990 *Fax:* 212-807-1799 *E-mail:* general@aiga.org *Web Site:* www.aiga.org, pg 521

Chapman, Ian, Simon & Schuster, Inc, 1230 Avenue of the Americas, New York, NY 10020 *Tel:* 212-698-7000 *Toll Free Tel:* 800-223-2336 (orders) *Fax:* 212-698-7007 *Toll Free Fax:* 800-943-9831 (orders) *E-mail:* firstname.lastname@simonandschuster.com; purchaseorders@simonandschuster.com (orders) *Web Site:* www.simonandschuster.com, pg 199

Chapman, Monica, Coretta Scott King - John Steptoe Award for New Talent, 225 N Michigan Ave, Suite 1300, Chicago, IL 60601 *Toll Free Tel:* 800-545-2433 (ext 4294) *Fax:* 312-280-3256 *E-mail:* diversity@ala.org *Web Site:* www.ala.org/awardsgrants, pg 630

Chapman, Robyn, Roaring Brook Press, 120 Broadway, New York, NY 10271 *Tel:* 646-307-5151 *Web Site:* us.macmillan.com/publishers/roaring-brook-press, pg 186

Chapnick, Laura, Groundwood Books, 128 Sterling Rd, Lower Level, Toronto, ON M6R 2B7, Canada *Tel:* 416-363-4343 *Fax:* 416-363-1017 *E-mail:* genmail@groundwoodbooks.com *Web Site:* www.houseofanansi.com, pg 428

Chappell, Chris, Berghahn Books, 20 Jay St, Suite 512, Brooklyn, NY 11201 *Tel:* 212-233-6004 *Fax:* 212-233-6007 *E-mail:* info@berghahnbooks.com; salesus@berghahnbooks.com; editorial@journals.berghahnbooks.com *Web Site:* www.berghahnbooks.com, pg 32

Chappell, John, Lumina Datamatics Inc, 4 Collins Ave, Plymouth, MA 02360 *Tel:* 508-746-0300 *Fax:* 508-746-3233 *Web Site:* luminadatamatics.com, pg 467

Chappelle, Masherl, New Hampshire Literary Awards, 2500 N River Rd, Manchester, NH 03106 *Tel:* 603-314-7980 *E-mail:* info@nhwritersproject.org; awards@nhwritersproject.org *Web Site:* www.nhwritersproject.org, pg 647

Chappelle, Masherl, New Hampshire Writers' Project, 2500 N River Rd, Manchester, NH 03106 *Tel:* 603-314-7980 *E-mail:* info@nhwritersproject.org *Web Site:* www.nhwritersproject.org, pg 541

Charbonneau, Annie-Pier, University of Ottawa Press (Presses de l'Université d'Ottawa), 542 King Edward Ave, Ottawa, ON K1N 6N5, Canada *Tel:* 613-562-5246 *Fax:* 613-562-5247 *E-mail:* puo-uop@uottawa.ca; acquisitions@uottawa.ca *Web Site:* press.uottawa.ca, pg 444

Charbonneau, Catherine, La Courte Echelle, 4388, rue Saint-Denis, Suite 315, Montreal, QC H2J 2L1, Canada *Tel:* 514-312-6950 *E-mail:* info@courteechelle.com *Web Site:* courteechelle.groupecourteechelle.com, pg 420

Charette, Francois, Livres Canada Books, One Nicholas, Suite 504, Ottawa, ON K1N 7B7, Canada *Tel:* 613-562-2324 *Fax:* 613-562-2329 *E-mail:* info@livrescanadabooks.com *Web Site:* www.livrescanadabooks.com, pg 537

Charles, Kristi, National Resource Center for Youth Services, Schusterman Ctr, Bldg 4W, 4502 E 41 St, Tulsa, OK 74135-2512 *Tel:* 918-660-3700 *Toll Free Tel:* 800-274-2687 *Fax:* 918-660-3737 *Web Site:* www.nrcys.ou.edu, pg 147

Charlip, Christine, ASM Press, 1752 "N" St NW, Washington, DC 20036-2904 *Tel:* 202-737-3600 *Fax:* 202-942-9342 *E-mail:* books@asmusa.org *Web Site:* www.asmscience.org, pg 22

Chasan, Gail, Harlequin Enterprises Ltd, 195 Broadway, 24th fl, New York, NY 10007 *Tel:* 212-207-7000 *Toll Free Tel:* 888-432-4879 *E-mail:* customerservice@harlequin.com *Web Site:* www.harlequin.com, pg 93

Chase, Cameron, Pippin Properties Inc, 110 W 40 St, Suite 1704, New York, NY 10018 *Tel:* 212-338-9310 *E-mail:* info@pippinproperties.com *Web Site:* www.pippinproperties.com; www.facebook.com/pippinproperties, pg 498

Chatterjee, Jaya Aninda, Yale University Press, 302 Temple St, New Haven, CT 06511-8909 *Tel:* 203-432-0960; 203-432-0966 (sales); 401-531-2800 (cust serv) *Toll Free Tel:* 800-405-1619 (cust serv) *Fax:* 203-432-0948; 203-432-8485 (sales); 401-531-2801 (cust serv) *Toll Free Fax:* 800-406-9145 (cust serv) *E-mail:* sales. press@yale.edu (sales); customer.care@triliteral.org (cust serv) *Web Site:* www.yalebooks.com; yalepress. yale.edu/yupbooks, pg 246

Chauhan, Bhavna, Doubleday Canada, 320 Front St W, Suite 1400, Toronto, ON M5V 3B6, Canada *Tel:* 416-364-4449 *Fax:* 416-598-7764 *Web Site:* www. penguinrandomhouse.ca, pg 421

Chauncey, Caroline, Harvard Education Publishing Group, 8 Story St, 1st fl, Cambridge, MA 02138 *Tel:* 617-495-3432 *Fax:* 617-496-3584 *Web Site:* www. hepg.org, pg 94

Chavern, David, News Media Alliance, 4401 N Fairfax Dr, Suite 300, Arlington, VA 22203 *Tel:* 571-366-1000 *E-mail:* info@newsmediaalliance.org *Web Site:* www. newsmediaalliance.org, pg 541

Chavis, Benjamin F, National Newspaper Publishers Association (NNPA), 1816 12 St NW, Washington, DC 20009 *Tel:* 202-588-8764 *Fax:* 202-588-8960 *E-mail:* info@nnpa.org *Web Site:* www.nnpa.org; www.blackpressusa.com, pg 540

Checole, Kassahun, Africa World Press Inc, 541 W Ingham Ave, Suite B, Trenton, NJ 08638 *Tel:* 609-695-3200 *Fax:* 609-695-6466 *E-mail:* customerservice@africaworldpressbooks.com *Web Site:* www.africaworldpressbooks.com, pg 5

Checole, Senait Kassahun, The Red Sea Press Inc, 541 W Ingham Ave, Suite B, Trenton, NJ 08638 *Tel:* 609-695-3200 *Fax:* 609-695-6466 *E-mail:* customerservice@africaworldpressbooks.com *Web Site:* www.africaworldpressbooks.com, pg 183

Cheiffetz, Julia, Atria Books, 1230 Avenue of the Americas, New York, NY 10020 *Tel:* 212-698-7000 *Fax:* 212-698-7007 *Web Site:* www.simonandschuster. com, pg 24

Chen, Curtis, Science Fiction & Fantasy Writers of America Inc (SFWA), PO Box 3238, Enfield, CT 06083-3238 *Tel:* 860-698-0536 *E-mail:* office@sfwa. org *Web Site:* www.sfwa.org, pg 546

Chen, Curtis, SFWA Nebula Awards, PO Box 3238, Enfield, CT 06083-3238 *Tel:* 860-698-0536 *E-mail:* office@sfwa.org *Web Site:* www.sfwa.org, pg 666

Chen, May, HarperCollins General Books Group, 195 Broadway, New York, NY 10007 *Tel:* 212-207-7000 *Web Site:* www.harpercollins.com, pg 93

Chen, Tania, University of British Columbia Creative Writing Program, Buchanan Rm E-462, 1866 Main Mall, Vancouver, BC V6T 1Z1, Canada *Tel:* 604-822-0699 *Web Site:* creativewriting.ubc.ca, pg 585

Chenault, Earlita, Parallax Press, 2236B Sixth St, Berkeley, CA 94710 *Tel:* 510-540-6411 *Toll Free Tel:* 800-863-5290 (orders) *Fax:* 510-981-1157 *Web Site:* www.parallax.org, pg 160

Cheney, Margaret, Ohio Genealogical Society, 611 State Rte 97 W, Bellville, OH 44813-8813 *Tel:* 419-886-1903 *Fax:* 419-886-0092 *E-mail:* ogs@ogs.org *Web Site:* www.ogs.org, pg 154

Cheng, Christopher, Crystal Kite Awards, 6363 Wilshire Blvd, Suite 425, Los Angeles, CA 90048 *Tel:* 323-782-1010 *E-mail:* grants@scbwi.org; scbwi@scbwi.org *Web Site:* www.scbwi.org/awards, pg 608

Cheng, Jill, Cheng & Tsui Co Inc, 25 West St, 2nd fl, Boston, MA 02111-1213 *Tel:* 617-988-2400 *Toll Free Tel:* 800-554-1963 *Fax:* 617-426-3669; 617-556-8964 *E-mail:* service@cheng-tsui.com; orders@cheng-tsui. com *Web Site:* www.cheng-tsui.com, pg 50

Cheng, Vivian, Marshall Cavendish Education, 99 White Plains Rd, Tarrytown, NY 10591-9001 *Tel:* 914-332-8888 *Toll Free Tel:* 800-821-9881 *Fax:* 914-332-1082 *E-mail:* mce@marshallcavendish. com; customerservice@marshallcavendish.com *Web Site:* www.mceducation.us, pg 133

Chenoweth, Allie, Second Story Press, 20 Maud St, Suite 401, Toronto, ON M5V 2M5, Canada *Tel:* 416-537-7850 *Fax:* 416-537-0588 *E-mail:* info@ secondstorypress.ca *Web Site:* secondstorypress.ca, pg 439

Chepesiuk, Ron, Strategic Media Books LLC, 782 Wofford St, Rock Hill, SC 29730 *Tel:* 803-366-5440 *E-mail:* contact@strategicmediabooks.com *Web Site:* strategicmediabooks.com, pg 210

Cheregotis, Stacy, BePuzzled, 2030 Harrison St, San Francisco, CA 94110 *Tel:* 415-503-1600 *Toll Free Tel:* 800-347-4818 *Fax:* 415-503-0085 *E-mail:* info@ ugames.com *Web Site:* www.ugames.com, pg 32

Chernoff, Mitch, Society for Industrial & Applied Mathematics, 3600 Market St, 6th fl, Philadelphia, PA 19104-2688 *Tel:* 215-382-9800 *Toll Free Tel:* 800-447-7426 *Fax:* 215-386-7999 *E-mail:* siambooks@siam.org *Web Site:* www.siam.org, pg 202

Cherrington, Janelle, Scholastic Education, 557 Broadway, New York, NY 10012 *Tel:* 212-343-6100 *Fax:* 212-343-6189 *Web Site:* www.scholastic.com, pg 194

Cherry, Amy, W W Norton & Company Inc, 500 Fifth Ave, New York, NY 10110-0017 *Tel:* 212-354-5500 *Toll Free Tel:* 800-233-4830 (orders & cust serv) *Fax:* 212-869-0856 *Toll Free Fax:* 800-458-6515 *E-mail:* orders@wwnorton.com *Web Site:* wwnorton. com, pg 152

Cherullo, Helen, The Mountaineers Books, 1001 SW Klickitat Way, Suite 201, Seattle, WA 98134 *Tel:* 206-223-6303 *Fax:* 206-223-6306 *E-mail:* mbooks@mountaineersbooks. org; customerservice@mountaineersbooks. org *Web Site:* www.mountaineersbooks.org, pg 143

Chesman, Andrea, Little Chicago Editorial Services, 154 Natural Tpke, Ripton, VT 05766 *Tel:* 802-388-9782 *Web Site:* andreachesman.com, pg 466

Chester, Linda, Linda Chester Literary Agency, 630 Fifth Ave, Suite 2000, New York, NY 10111 *Tel:* 212-218-3350 *E-mail:* submissions@lindachester.com *Web Site:* www.lindachester.com, pg 479

Cheuse, Sonya, HarperCollins General Books Group, 195 Broadway, New York, NY 10007 *Tel:* 212-207-7000 *Web Site:* www.harpercollins.com, pg 93

Chevako, Anne W, Publishing Resources Inc, 425 Carr 693, PMB 160, Dorado, PR 00646 *Tel:* 787-647-9342 *E-mail:* pri@chevako.net *Web Site:* www. publishingresources.net, pg 469

Chevako, Jay A, Publishing Resources Inc, 425 Carr 693, PMB 160, Dorado, PR 00646 *Tel:* 787-647-9342 *E-mail:* pri@chevako.net *Web Site:* www. publishingresources.net, pg 469

Chevako, Ronald J, Publishing Resources Inc, 425 Carr 693, PMB 160, Dorado, PR 00646 *Tel:* 787-647-9342 *E-mail:* pri@chevako.net *Web Site:* www. publishingresources.net, pg 469

Chew, Mieke, New Directions Publishing Corp, 80 Eighth Ave, 19th fl, New York, NY 10011 *Tel:* 212-255-0230 *E-mail:* editorial@ndbooks.com; publicity@ ndbooks.com *Web Site:* ndbooks.com, pg 148

Chia, Douglas, The Conference Board Inc, 845 Third Ave, New York, NY 10022-6600 *Tel:* 212-759-0900; 212-339-0345 (cust serv) *E-mail:* customer.service@ conferenceboard.org; membership@conferenceboard. org *Web Site:* www.conference-board.org; linkedin.com/company/the-conference-board, pg 56

Chidiac, Dana, Dial Books for Young Readers, 345 Hudson St, New York, NY 10014 *Tel:* 212-366-2000 *Toll Free Tel:* 800-733-3000 (orders) *Fax:* 212-414-3396 *Web Site:* www.penguin.com/publishers/ dialbooksforyoungreaders/, pg 64

Chidley, Sam, The Karpfinger Agency, 357 W 20 St, New York, NY 10011-3379 *Tel:* 212-691-2690 *Fax:* 212-691-7129 *E-mail:* info@karpfinger.com (no queries or submissions) *Web Site:* karpfinger.com, pg 490

Chidlow-Irvin, Georgina, Hachette Nashville, 6100 Tower Circle, Room 210, Franklin, TN 37067 *Tel:* 615-221-0996 *Fax:* 615-221-0962 *Web Site:* www. hachettebookgroup.com, pg 91

Childress, David H, Adventures Unlimited Press (AUP), One Adventure Place, Kempton, IL 60946 *Tel:* 815-253-6390 *Fax:* 815-253-6300 *E-mail:* info@ adventuresunlimitedpress.com *Web Site:* www. adventuresunlimitedpress.com, pg 5

Childs, Faith Hampton, Faith Childs Literary Agency Inc, 915 Broadway, Suite 1009, New York, NY 10010 *Tel:* 212-995-9600 *Web Site:* faithchildsliteraryagency. com, pg 479

Childs, Jennifer, Penguin Random House LLC, 1745 Broadway, New York, NY 10019 *Tel:* 212-782-9000 *Toll Free Tel:* 800-726-0600 *Web Site:* www. penguinrandomhouse.com, pg 164

Chiles, Nick, Aevitas Creative Management, 19 W 21 St, Suite 501, New York, NY 10010 *Tel:* 212-765-6900 *Web Site:* aevitascreative.com, pg 474

Chillot, Rick, Quirk Books, 215 Church St, Philadelphia, PA 19106 *Tel:* 215-627-3581 *Fax:* 215-627-5220 *E-mail:* general@quirkbooks.com *Web Site:* www. quirkbooks.com, pg 179

Chin, Brenda, BelleBooks, PO Box 300921, Memphis, TN 38130 *Tel:* 901-344-9024 *Fax:* 901-344-9068 *E-mail:* bellebooks@bellebooks.com *Web Site:* www. bellebooks.com, pg 31

Chin, Kristine, American Institute of Chemical Engineers (AIChE), 120 Wall St, 23rd fl, New York, NY 10005-4020 *Tel:* 203-702-7660 *Toll Free Tel:* 800-242-4363 *Fax:* 203-775-5177 *E-mail:* customerservice@aiche. org *Web Site:* www.aiche.org, pg 12

Chin, Oliver, Immedium, 535 Rockdale Dr, San Francisco, CA 94127 *Tel:* 415-452-8546 *Fax:* 360-937-6272 *E-mail:* orders@immedium.com; sales@ immedium.com *Web Site:* www.immedium.com, pg 107

Ching, Angela, Simon & Schuster, 1230 Avenue of the Americas, New York, NY 10020 *Tel:* 212-698-7000 *Toll Free Tel:* 800-223-2348 (cust serv); 800-223-2336 (orders) *Toll Free Fax:* 800-943-9831 (orders) *Web Site:* www.simonandschuster.com, pg 198

Chinski, Eric, Farrar, Straus & Giroux, LLC, 175 Varick St, 9th fl, New York, NY 10014 *Tel:* 212-741-6900 *E-mail:* fsg.publicity@fsgbooks.com *Web Site:* us. macmillan.com/fsg.aspx, pg 76

Chipponeri, Kelli, Chronicle Books, 680 Second St, San Francisco, CA 94107 *Tel:* 415-537-4200 *Toll Free Tel:* 800-759-0190 (cust serv) *Fax:* 415-537-4460 *Toll Free Fax:* 800-858-7787 (orders); 800-286-9471 (cust serv) *E-mail:* frontdesk@chroniclebooks.com *Web Site:* www.chroniclebooks.com, pg 51

Chlebowski, Rachel, Random House Children's Books, 1745 Broadway, 10th fl, New York, NY 10019 *Tel:* 212-782-9000 *Web Site:* www.randomhousekids. com, pg 180

Chmiel, Barbara R, The Blackburn Press, PO Box 287, Caldwell, NJ 07006-0287 *Tel:* 973-228-7077 *Fax:* 973-228-7276 *Web Site:* www.blackburnpress. com, pg 34

Cho, Barbara, little bee books, 251 Park Ave S, 12th fl, New York, NY 10010 *Toll Free Tel:* 844-321-0237 *E-mail:* info@littlebeebooks.com *Web Site:* littlebeebooks.com, pg 125

Chodosh, Ellen, New York University Press, 838 Broadway, 3rd fl, New York, NY 10003-4812 *Tel:* 212-998-2575 (edit) *Toll Free Tel:* 800-996-6987 (orders) *Fax:* 212-995-4798 (orders) *E-mail:* nyupressinfo@nyu.edu; orders@nyupress.org *Web Site:* www.nyupress.org, pg 150

Choi, Jennifer, Harlequin Enterprises Ltd, 195 Broadway, 24th fl, New York, NY 10007 *Tel:* 212-207-7000 *Toll Free Tel:* 888-432-4879 *E-mail:* customerservice@ harlequin.com *Web Site:* www.harlequin.com, pg 93

Choix, Paul, Regnery Publishing, 300 New Jersey Ave NW, Washington, DC 20001 *Tel:* 202-216-0600 *Toll Free Tel:* 888-219-4747 *Fax:* 202-393-1795 *Web Site:* www.regnery.com, pg 184

Chong, Anita, McClelland & Stewart Ltd, 320 Front St W, Suite 1400, Toronto, ON M5V 3B6, Canada *Tel:* 416-364-4449 *Fax:* 416-598-7764 *E-mail:* customerservicescanada@ penguinrandomhouse.com; publicity@ca.penguingroup. com *Web Site:* penguinrandomhouse.ca/imprints/ mcclelland-stewart, pg 433

Chong, Michele, Michael Wiese Productions, 12400 Ventura Blvd, No 1111, Studio City, CA 91604 *Tel:* 818-379-8799 *Toll Free Tel:* 800-833-5738 (orders) *Fax:* 818-986-3408 *E-mail:* mwpsales@ earthlink.net; fulfillment@portcity.com *Web Site:* www.mwp.com, pg 241

Chopin, Stefan, Leadership Connect, 1407 Broadway, Suite 318, New York, NY 10018 *Tel:* 212-627-4140 *Toll Free Tel:* 800-627-0311 *Fax:* 212-645-0931 *E-mail:* info@leadershipconnect.io *Web Site:* www. leadershipconnect.io, pg 121

Choron, Harry, March Tenth Inc, 24 Hillside Terr, Montvale, NJ 07645 *Tel:* 201-387-6551 *Fax:* 201-387-6552 *Web Site:* www.march10th.com, pg 494

Choron, Sandra, March Tenth Inc, 24 Hillside Terr, Montvale, NJ 07645 *Tel:* 201-387-6551 *Fax:* 201-387-6552 *Web Site:* www.march10th.com, pg 494

Chorpenning, Rev Joseph F, St Joseph's University Press, 5600 City Ave, Philadelphia, PA 19131-1395 *Tel:* 610-660-3402 *Fax:* 610-660-3412 *E-mail:* sjupress@sju.edu *Web Site:* www.sjupress. com, pg 190

Chou, Arthur, New Win Publishing, 9682 Telstar Ave, Suite 110, El Monte, CA 91731 *Tel:* 626-448-3448 *Fax:* 626-602-3817 *E-mail:* info@academiclearningcompany.com *Web Site:* newwinpublishing.com; wbusinessbooks. com, pg 149

Chou, Arthur, Velazquez Press, 9682 Telstar Ave, Suite 110, El Monte, CA 91731 *Tel:* 626-448-3448 *Fax:* 626-602-3817 *E-mail:* info@ academiclearningcompany.com *Web Site:* www. velazquezpress.com, pg 235

Chou, Shelly, Agency Chicago, 7000 Phoenix Ave NE, Suite 202, Albuquerque, NM 87110 *E-mail:* agency. chicago@usa.com, pg 474

Choy, May, Orbit, 1290 Avenue of the Americas, New York, NY 10104 *Tel:* 212-364-1100 *Toll Free Tel:* 800-759-0190 *Web Site:* www.orbitbooks.net, pg 156

Choyce, Lesley, Pottersfield Press, 248 Leslie Rd, East Lawrencetown, NS B2Z 1T4, Canada *Toll Free Tel:* 800-646-2879 (orders only) *E-mail:* pottersfieldcreative@gmail.com *Web Site:* www.pottersfieldpress.com, pg 437

Chrisant, William, Florida Antiquarian Booksellers Association (FABA), 14046 Fifth St, Dade City, FL 33525 *Tel:* 727-234-7759 *E-mail:* floridabooksellers@ gmail.com *Web Site:* floridabooksellers.com, pg 533

Chrisman Jacques, Kelly, University Press of Kansas, 2502 Westbrooke Circle, Lawrence, KS 66045-4444 *Tel:* 785-864-4154; 785-864-4155 (orders) *Fax:* 785-864-4586 *E-mail:* upress@ku.edu; upkorders@ku.edu (orders) *Web Site:* www.kansaspress.ku.edu, pg 233

Chrisman, Ronald, University of North Texas Press, Willis Library, Rm 251P, 1506 Highland St, Denton, TX 76201 *Tel:* 940-565-2142 *Fax:* 940-369-8760 *Web Site:* untpress.unt.edu, pg 229

Christensen, Daniel, Random House Publishing Group, 1745 Broadway, New York, NY 10019 *Toll Free Tel:* 800-200-3552 *Web Site:* www.randomhousebooks. com, pg 181

Christensen, Karen, Berkshire Publishing Group LLC, PO Box 177, Great Barrington, MA 01230 *E-mail:* info@berkshirepublishing.com *Web Site:* www.berkshirepublishing.com, pg 32

Christian, Abigail, Society of American Archivists, 17 N State St, Suite 1425, Chicago, IL 60602-4061 *Tel:* 312-606-0722 *Toll Free Tel:* 866-722-7858 *Fax:* 312-606-0728 *Web Site:* www.archivists.org, pg 202

Christian, Alayne Kay, Blue Whale Press, 237 Rainbow Dr, No 13702, Livingston, TX 77399-2037 *Toll Free Tel:* 800-848-1631 *E-mail:* info@bluewhalepress. com; sales@bluewhalepress.com *Web Site:* www. bluewhalepress.com, pg 37

Christmas, Bobbie, Zebra Communications, 230 Deerchase Dr, Woodstock, GA 30188-4438 *Tel:* 770-924-0528 *E-mail:* bobbie@zebraeditor.com *Web Site:* www.zebraeditor.com, pg 472

Christon, Alexa, Pearson Education Ltd, 225 River St, Hoboken, NJ 07030-4772 *Tel:* 201-236-7000 *Fax:* 201-236-6549 *Web Site:* www.pearsoned.com, pg 162

Christopher, Rob, ALA Neal-Schuman, 50 E Huron St, Chicago, IL 60611 *Toll Free Tel:* 800-545-2433 *Fax:* 312-280-5860 *E-mail:* editionsmarketing@ala.org *Web Site:* www.alastore.ala.org, pg 6

Christopher, Rob, The American Library Association (ALA), 225 N Michigan Ave, Suite 1300, Chicago, IL 60601 *Tel:* 312-944-6780 *Toll Free Tel:* 800-545-2433 *Fax:* 312-280-5275 *E-mail:* editionsmarketing@ala.org *Web Site:* www.alastore.ala.org, pg 12

Chu, Elaine, Immedium, 535 Rockdale Dr, San Francisco, CA 94127 *Tel:* 415-452-8546 *Fax:* 360-937-6272 *E-mail:* orders@immedium.com; sales@ immedium.com *Web Site:* www.immedium.com, pg 107

Chu, Jane, The National Medal of Arts, 400 Seventh St SW, Washington, DC 20506-0001 *Tel:* 202-682-5570 *Web Site:* www.arts.gov/honors/medals, pg 645

Chu, Lily, Captus Press Inc, 1600 Steeles Ave W, Units 14 & 15, Concord, ON L4K 4M2, Canada *Tel:* 416-736-5537 *Fax:* 416-736-5793 *E-mail:* info@captus. com *Web Site:* www.captus.com, pg 419

Chu, Lynn, Writers' Representatives LLC, 116 W 14 St, 11th fl, New York, NY 10011-7305 *Tel:* 212-620-9009 *Fax:* 212-620-0023 *E-mail:* transom@writersreps.com *Web Site:* www.writersreps.com, pg 509

Chuirazzi, Sara, Penguin Books, 375 Hudson St, New York, NY 10014 *Tel:* 212-366-2000 *E-mail:* penguinpublicity@us.penguingroup.com *Web Site:* www.penguinclassics.com; www.penguin. com, pg 163

Chuirazzi, Sara, Viking, 375 Hudson St, New York, NY 10014 *Tel:* 212-366-2000 *Fax:* 212-243-6002 *Web Site:* www.penguin.com/publishers/vikingbooks, pg 236

Chun, Jessica, Little, Brown and Company, 1290 Avenue of the Americas, New York, NY 10104 *Tel:* 212-364-1100 *Fax:* 212-364-0952 *E-mail:* firstname.lastname@ hbgusa.com *Web Site:* www.littlebrown.com; www. hachettebookgroup.com, pg 125

Chun, Stephanie, University of Hawaii Press, 2840 Kolowalu St, Honolulu, HI 96822-1888 *Tel:* 808-956-8255 *Toll Free Tel:* 888-UHPRESS (847-7377) *Fax:* 808-988-6052 *Toll Free Fax:* 800-650-7811 *E-mail:* uhpbooks@hawaii.edu *Web Site:* www. uhpress.hawaii.edu, pg 227

Chung, Nicole, Counterpoint Press LLC, 2560 Ninth St, Suite 318, Berkeley, CA 94710 *Tel:* 510-704-0230 *Fax:* 510-704-0268 *E-mail:* info@counterpointpress. com *Web Site:* counterpointpress.com; softskull.com, pg 58

Church, Dawson, Energy Psychology Press, 1490 Mark West Springs Rd, Santa Rosa, CA 95404 *Tel:* 707-525-9292 *Toll Free Fax:* 800-330-9798 *E-mail:* energypsychologypress@gmail. com; support@eftuniverse.com *Web Site:* www. energypsychologypress.com; www.elitebooksonline. com, pg 72

Church, Doug, Pacific Press® Publishing Association, 1350 N Kings Rd, Nampa, ID 83687-3193 *Tel:* 208-465-2500 *Toll Free Tel:* 800-447-7377 *Fax:* 208-465-2531 *Web Site:* www.pacificpress.com, pg 159

Church, Natalie, Dutton, 1745 Broadway, New York, NY 10019 *Tel:* 212-366-2000 *Fax:* 212-366-2262 *E-mail:* duttonpublicity@us.penguingroup.com *Web Site:* www.penguin.com, pg 68

Church, Natalie, Penguin Group USA, A Penguin Random House Company, 375 Hudson St, New York, NY 10014 *Tel:* 212-366-2000 *Toll Free Tel:* 800-847-5515 (inside sales); 800-631-8571 (cust serv) *Fax:* 212-366-2666; 607-775-4829 (inside sales) *E-mail:* online@us.penguingroup.com *Web Site:* www. penguin.com, pg 163

Church, Natalie, Plume, 375 Hudson St, New York, NY 10014 *Tel:* 212-366-2000 *Fax:* 212-243-6002 *Web Site:* www.penguin.com/publishers/plume, pg 171

Churko, Helen, Royce Carlton Inc, 866 United Nations Plaza, Suite 587, New York, NY 10017-1880 *Tel:* 212-355-7700 *Toll Free Tel:* 800-LECTURE (532-8873) *Fax:* 212-888-8659 *E-mail:* info@roycecarlton.com *Web Site:* www.roycecarlton.com, pg 515

Chutjian, Lisa, The Alexander Graham Bell Association for the Deaf & Hard of Hearing, 3417 Volta Place NW, Washington, DC 20007 *Tel:* 202-337-5220 *Toll Free Tel:* 866-337-5220 (orders) *Fax:* 202-337-8314 *E-mail:* info@agbell.org; publications@agbell.org *Web Site:* www.agbell.org, pg 6

Cianfrone, Amy, Perseus Books, 1290 Avenue of the Americas, New York, NY 10104 *Tel:* 212-340-8100 *Toll Free Tel:* 800-343-4499 (cust serv) *Fax:* 212-340-8105 *Web Site:* www.perseusbooks.com, pg 167

Ciani, Nicholas, Atria Books, 1230 Avenue of the Americas, New York, NY 10020 *Tel:* 212-698-7000 *Fax:* 212-698-7007 *Web Site:* www.simonandschuster. com, pg 24

Cicciarelli, Joellyn, Loyola Press, 3441 N Ashland Ave, Chicago, IL 60657 *Tel:* 773-281-1818 *Toll Free Tel:* 800-621-1008 *Fax:* 773-281-0555 (cust serv); 773-281-4129 (edit) *E-mail:* customerservice@ loyolapress.com *Web Site:* www.loyolapress.com, pg 128

Cicel, Terezia, Viking, 375 Hudson St, New York, NY 10014 *Tel:* 212-366-2000 *Fax:* 212-243-6002 *Web Site:* www.penguin.com/publishers/vikingbooks, pg 236

Ciecierski, Andrea, Stylus Publishing LLC, 22883 Quicksilver Dr, Sterling, VA 20166-2019 *Tel:* 703-661-1504 (edit & sales) *Toll Free Tel:* 800-232-0223 (orders & cust serv) *Fax:* 703-661-1547 *E-mail:* stylusmail@styluspub.com (orders & cust serv); stylusinfo@styluspub.com *Web Site:* styluspub. presswarehouse.com, pg 210

Cigich, Bradley, Alexander Street, a ProQuest Company, 99 Canal Center Plaza, Suite 200, Alexandria, VA 22314 *Tel:* 703-212-8520 *Toll Free Tel:* 800-889-5937 *E-mail:* sales@alexanderstreet.com; marketing@ alexanderstreet.com; info@alexanderstreet.com *Web Site:* alexanderstreet.com, pg 7

Ciletti, Barbara, Odyssey Books, 2421 Redwood Ct, Longmont, CO 80503-8155 *Tel:* 720-494-1473 *Fax:* 720-494-1471 *E-mail:* books@odysseybooks.net, pg 154

Cilurso, Ed, Taylor & Francis Inc, 530 Walnut St, Suite 850, Philadelphia, PA 19106 *Tel:* 215-625-8900 *Toll Free Tel:* 800-354-1420 *Fax:* 215-207-0050; 215-207-0046 (cust serv) *E-mail:* support@tandfonline.com *Web Site:* www.taylorandfrancis.com, pg 213

Cimina, Dominique, Random House Children's Books, 1745 Broadway, 10th fl, New York, NY 10019 *Tel:* 212-782-9000 *Web Site:* www.randomhousekids. com, pg 180

Ciminera, Siobhan, Simon & Schuster Children's Publishing, 1230 Avenue of the Americas, New York, NY 10020 *Tel:* 212-698-7000 *Web Site:* www. simonandschuster.com/kids; www.simonandschuster. com/teen; simonandschuster.net; simonandschuster.biz, pg 199

Cimino, Antoinette, Springer, 233 Spring St, New York, NY 10013-1578 *Tel:* 212-460-1500 *Toll Free Tel:* 800-SPRINGER (777-4643) *Fax:* 212-460-1700 *E-mail:* customerservice@springer.com *Web Site:* www.springer.com, pg 205

Cimonetti, Tanya, Lyric Poetry Prizes, PO Box 110, Jericho, VT 05465 *Tel:* 802-899-3993 *Fax:* 802-899-3993 *E-mail:* themuse@thelyricmagazine.com *Web Site:* thelyricmagazine.com, pg 636

Coffey, Laura, Dog Writers' Association of America Inc (DWAA) Annual Writing Competition, PO Box 787, Hughesville, MD 20637 *E-mail:* info@dogwriters.org *Web Site:* dogwriters.org, pg 610

Coffey, Roland, Yale University Press, 302 Temple St, New Haven, CT 06511-8909 *Tel:* 203-432-0960; 203-432-0966 (sales); 401-531-2800 (cust serv) *Toll Free Tel:* 800-405-1619 (cust serv) *Fax:* 203-432-0948; 203-432-8485 (sales); 401-531-2801 (cust serv) *Toll Free Fax:* 800-406-9145 (cust serv) *E-mail:* sales. press@yale.edu (sales); customer.care@triliteral.org (cust serv) *Web Site:* www.yalebooks.com; yalepress. yale.edu/yupbooks, pg 246

Cogbill, Monet, Theatre Communications Group, 520 Eighth Ave, 24th fl, New York, NY 10018-4156 *Tel:* 212-609-5900 *Fax:* 212-609-5901 *E-mail:* info@ tcg.org *Web Site:* www.tcg.org, pg 216

Coggins, Cara, Houghton Mifflin Harcourt, 125 High St, Boston, MA 02110 *Tel:* 617-351-5000 *Toll Free Tel:* 855-969-4642; 800-225-5425 (K-12 educ materials); 800-323-9540 (assessment materials); 877-219-1537 (SkillsTutor); 888-242-6747 (Innovation in Educ Group); 800-225-3362 (Trade & Ref Div) *Toll Free Fax:* 800-269-5232 *E-mail:* myhmhco@hmhco. com *Web Site:* www.hmhco.com, pg 103

Coggins, Joel, University of Pittsburgh Press, 7500 Thomas Blvd, Pittsburgh, PA 15260 *Tel:* 412-383-2456 *Fax:* 412-383-2466 *E-mail:* info@upress.pitt.edu *Web Site:* www.upress.pitt.edu, pg 230

Cohan, Darcy, Insight Editions, 800 "A" St, San Rafael, CA 94901 *Tel:* 415-526-1370 *Toll Free Tel:* 800-809-3792 *Toll Free Fax:* 866-509-0515 *E-mail:* info@ insighteditions.com; marketing@insighteditions.com *Web Site:* insighteditions.com, pg 109

Cohen, Adam, Tom Howard/John H Reid Fiction & Essay Contest, 351 Pleasant St, PMB 222, Northampton, MA 01060-3961 *Tel:* 413-320-1847 *Toll Free Tel:* 866-WINWRIT (946-9748) *Fax:* 413-280-0539 *Web Site:* www.winningwriters.com, pg 624

Cohen, Adam, Tom Howard/Margaret Reid Poetry Contest, 351 Pleasant St, PMB 222, Northampton, MA 01060-3961 *Tel:* 413-320-1847 *Toll Free Tel:* 866-WINWRIT (946-9748) *Fax:* 413-280-0539 *Web Site:* www.winningwriters.com, pg 624

Cohen, Adam, North Street Book Prize, 351 Pleasant St, PMB 222, Northampton, MA 01060-3961 *Tel:* 413-320-1847 *Toll Free Tel:* 866-WINWRIT (946-9748) *Fax:* 413-280-0539 *Web Site:* www.winningwriters. com, pg 649

Cohen, Adam, Wergle Flomp Humor Poetry Contest, 351 Pleasant St, PMB 222, Northampton, MA 01060-3961 *Tel:* 413-320-1847 *Toll Free Tel:* 866-WINWRIT (946-9748) *Fax:* 413-280-0539 *Web Site:* www. winningwriters.com, pg 676

Cohen, Bill, Harrington Park Press, 9 E Eighth St, Box 331, New York, NY 10003 *Tel:* 347-882-3545 (edit & publicity) *Fax:* 646-602-1349 (edit & publicity) *Web Site:* harringtonparkpress.com, pg 94

Cohen, Brett, Quirk Books, 215 Church St, Philadelphia, PA 19106 *Tel:* 215-627-3581 *Fax:* 215-627-5220 *E-mail:* general@quirkbooks.com *Web Site:* www. quirkbooks.com, pg 179

Cohen, Christine M, Virginia Kidd Agency Inc, 538 E Harford St, PO Box 278, Milford, PA 18337 *Tel:* 570-296-6205 *Web Site:* vk-agency.com, pg 491

Cohen, Craig, powerHouse Books, 32 Adams St, Brooklyn, NY 11201 *Tel:* 212-604-9074 *E-mail:* info@powerhousebooks.com *Web Site:* www. powerhousebooks.com, pg 172

Cohen, Herbert J, Platinum Press LLC, 281 Hicks St, Brooklyn, NY 11201 *Tel:* 718-875-4092 *Fax:* 718-875-5065, pg 170

Cohen, Jeremy, Jerome Fellowship, 2301 Franklin Ave E, Minneapolis, MN 55406-1099 *Tel:* 612-332-7481 *Fax:* 612-332-6037 *E-mail:* info@pwcenter.org *Web Site:* www.pwcenter.org, pg 628

Cohen, Jeremy, Many Voices Fellowships, 2301 Franklin Ave E, Minneapolis, MN 55406-1099 *Tel:* 612-332-7481 *Fax:* 612-332-6037 *E-mail:* info@pwcenter.org *Web Site:* www.pwcenter.org, pg 638

Cohen, Jeremy, McKnight Fellowships in Playwriting, 2301 Franklin Ave E, Minneapolis, MN 55406-1099 *Tel:* 612-332-7481 *Fax:* 612-332-6037 *E-mail:* info@ pwcenter.org *Web Site:* www.pwcenter.org, pg 640

Cohen, Jeremy, McKnight National Residency & Commission, 2301 Franklin Ave E, Minneapolis, MN 55406-1099 *Tel:* 612-332-7481 *Fax:* 612-332-6037 *E-mail:* info@pwcenter.org *Web Site:* www.pwcenter. org, pg 640

Cohen, Jodie, Algonquin Books, 400 Silver Cedar Ct, Suite 300, Chapel Hill, NC 27514-1585 *Tel:* 919-967-0108 *Fax:* 919-933-0272 *E-mail:* inquiry@algonquin. com *Web Site:* www.workman.com/algonquin, pg 7

Cohen, Jonathan, Kensington Publishing Corp, 119 W 40 St, New York, NY 10018 *Tel:* 212-407-1500 *Toll Free Tel:* 800-221-2647 *Fax:* 212-935-0699 *Web Site:* www. kensingtonbooks.com, pg 116

Cohen, Jonathan, National Music Publishers' Association (NMPA), 975 "F" St NW, Suite 375, Washington, DC 20004 *Tel:* 202-393-6672 *E-mail:* members@nmpa.org *Web Site:* nmpa.org, pg 540

Cohen, Katia Segre, GeoLytics Inc, 3322 Rte 22, Suite 806, Branchburg, NJ 08876 *Tel:* 908-707-1505 *Toll Free Tel:* 800-577-6717 *Fax:* 908-707-1595 *E-mail:* support@geolytics.com; questions@geolytics. com *Web Site:* www.geolytics.com, pg 85

Cohen, Kelly, The Optical Society (OSA), 2010 Massachusetts Ave NW, Washington, DC 20036-1023 *Tel:* 202-223-8130 *Toll Free Tel:* 800-766-4672 *E-mail:* custserv@osa.org *Web Site:* www.osa.org, pg 156

Cohen, Leslie, Chronicle Books, 680 Second St, San Francisco, CA 94107 *Tel:* 415-537-4200 *Toll Free Tel:* 800-759-0190 (cust serv) *Fax:* 415-537-4460 *Toll Free Fax:* 800-858-7787 (orders); 800-286-9471 (cust serv) *E-mail:* frontdesk@chroniclebooks.com *Web Site:* www.chroniclebooks.com, pg 51

Cohen, Lord, Alan Wofsy Fine Arts, 1109 Geary Blvd, San Francisco, CA 94109 *Tel:* 415-292-6500 *Toll Free Tel:* 800-660-6403 *Fax:* 415-292-6594 (off & cust serv); 510-251-1840 (acctg) *E-mail:* order@art-books. com (orders); editeur@earthlink.net (edit); beauxarts@ earthlink.net (cust serv) *Web Site:* www.art-books.com, pg 243

Cohen, Louis, Mason Crest Publishers, 450 Parkway Dr, Suite D, Broomall, PA 19008 *Tel:* 610-543-6200 *Toll Free Tel:* 866-MCP-BOOK (627-2665) *Fax:* 610-543-3878 *Web Site:* www.masoncrest.com, pg 133

Cohen, Meagan, Trident Media Group LLC, 41 Madison Ave, 36th fl, New York, NY 10010 *Tel:* 212-333-1511 *E-mail:* info@tridentmediagroup.com; press@tridentmediagroup.com *Web Site:* www. tridentmediagroup.com, pg 507

Cohen, Michael R, Puddingstone Literary, Authors' Agents, 11 Mabro Dr, Denville, NJ 07834-9607 *Tel:* 973-366-3622, pg 499

Cohen, Nan, Napa Valley Writers' Conference, 1088 College Ave, St Helena, CA 94574 *Tel:* 707-967-2900 (ext 4) *Fax:* 707-967-2909 *E-mail:* info@napawritersconference. org; media@napawritersconference.org; fiction@napawritersconference.org; poetry@ napawritersconference.org *Web Site:* www. napawritersconference.org, pg 576

Cohen, Paul, Monkfish Book Publishing Co, 22 E Market St, Suite 304, Rhinebeck, NY 12572 *Tel:* 845-876-4861 *E-mail:* monkfish@monkfishpublishing.com *Web Site:* www.monkfishpublishing.com, pg 142

Cohen, Peter, McGraw-Hill Higher Education, 1333 Burr Ridge Pkwy, Burr Ridge, IL 60527 *Tel:* 630-789-4000 *Toll Free Tel:* 800-338-3987 (cust serv) *Fax:* 614-755-5645 (cust serv) *Web Site:* www.mhhe.com, pg 135

Cohen, Samantha, Simon & Schuster, Inc, 1230 Avenue of the Americas, New York, NY 10020 *Tel:* 212-698-7000 *Toll Free Tel:* 800-223-2336 (orders) *Fax:* 212-698-7007 *Toll Free Fax:* 800-943-9831 (orders) *E-mail:* firstname.lastname@simonandschuster.com; purchaseorders@simonandschuster.com (orders) *Web Site:* www.simonandschuster.com, pg 199

Cohen, Sandra, Little, Brown Books for Young Readers, 1290 Avenue of the Americas, New York, NY 10104 *Tel:* 212-364-1100 *Toll Free Tel:* 800-759-0190 (cust serv) *Web Site:* www.hachettebookgroup.com, pg 126

Cohen, Steve, St Martin's Press, LLC, 120 Broadway, New York, NY 10271 *Tel:* 646-307-5151 *Web Site:* us. macmillan.com/smp, pg 190

Cohen, Susan, Writers House, 21 W 26 St, New York, NY 10010 *Tel:* 212-685-2400 *Web Site:* www. writershouse.com, pg 508

Cohen, Susan Lee, Riverside Literary Agency, 41 Simon Keets Rd, Leyden, MA 01337 *Tel:* 413-772-0067 *Fax:* 413-772-0969 *E-mail:* rivlit@sover.net *Web Site:* www.riversideliteraryagency.com, pg 500

Cohen, Susan Perlman, PearlCo Literary Agency, LLC, 6596 Heronswood Cove, Memphis, TN 38119 *Tel:* 901-754-5276 *Web Site:* www. pearlcoliteraryagency.com, pg 498

Cohn, Anthony G, AAAI Press, 2275 E Bayshore Rd, Suite 160, Palo Alto, CA 94303 *Tel:* 650-328-3123 *Fax:* 650-321-4457 *E-mail:* publications20@aaai.org *Web Site:* www.aaai.org/Press/press.php, pg 1

Colangelo, Brook, Houghton Mifflin Harcourt, 125 High St, Boston, MA 02110 *Tel:* 617-351-5000 *Toll Free Tel:* 855-969-4642; 800-225-5425 (K-12 educ materials); 800-323-9540 (assessment materials); 877-219-1537 (SkillsTutor); 888-242-6747 (Innovation in Educ Group); 800-225-3362 (Trade & Ref Div) *Toll Free Fax:* 800-269-5232 *E-mail:* myhmhco@hmhco. com *Web Site:* www.hmhco.com, pg 103

Colbeck, J Richard, Robert J Pickering Award for Playwriting Excellence, 89 Division, Coldwater, MI 49036 *Tel:* 517-279-7963 *Fax:* 517-279-8095 *E-mail:* j7eden@aol.com *Web Site:* www.branchcct. org, pg 656

Colbeck, Jennifer, Robert J Pickering Award for Playwriting Excellence, 89 Division, Coldwater, MI 49036 *Tel:* 517-279-7963 *Fax:* 517-279-8095 *E-mail:* j7eden@aol.com *Web Site:* www.branchcct. org, pg 656

Colbert, Jaimee Wriston, Binghamton University Creative Writing Program, c/o Dept of English, PO Box 6000, Binghamton, NY 13902-6000 *Tel:* 607-777-2168 *Fax:* 607-777-2408 *E-mail:* cwpro@binghamton. edu *Web Site:* english.binghamton.edu/cwpro, pg 581

Colburn, Loren, AFCP's Awards, 135 Old Cove Rd, Suite 210, Liverpool, NY 13090 *Toll Free Tel:* 877-203-2327 *Fax:* 781-459-7770 *E-mail:* afcp@afcp.org *Web Site:* www.afcp.org, pg 590

Colburn, Loren, Association of Free Community Papers (AFCP), 135 Old Cove Rd, Suite 210, Liverpool, NY 13090 *Toll Free Tel:* 877-203-2327 *Fax:* 781-459-7770 *E-mail:* afcp@afcp.org *Web Site:* www.afcp.org, pg 526

Colby, John T Jr, Brick Tower Press, Manhanset House, PO Box 342, Shelter Island Heights, NY 11965-0342 *Tel:* 212-427-7139 *Toll Free Tel:* 800-68-BRICK (682-7425) *E-mail:* bricktower@aol.com *Web Site:* bricktowerpress.com, pg 40

Colding, Robert, Information Today, Inc, 143 Old Marlton Pike, Medford, NJ 08055-8750 *Tel:* 609-654-6266 *Toll Free Tel:* 800-300-9868 (cust serv) *Fax:* 609-654-4309 *E-mail:* custserv@infotoday.com *Web Site:* www.infotoday.com, pg 108

Colding, Robert, Plexus Publishing, Inc, 143 Old Marlton Pike, Medford, NJ 08055 *Tel:* 609-654-6500 *Fax:* 609-654-4309 *E-mail:* info@plexuspublishing. com *Web Site:* www.plexuspublishing.com, pg 170

Cole, Becky, Plume, 375 Hudson St, New York, NY 10014 *Tel:* 212-366-2000 *Fax:* 212-243-6002 *Web Site:* www.penguin.com/publishers/plume, pg 171

Cole, David, Bay Tree Publishing LLC, 225 E Richmond Ave, Point Richmond, CA 94801 *Tel:* 510-619-6338 *Web Site:* www.baytreepublish.com, pg 28

Cole, Maureen, HarperCollins General Books Group, 195 Broadway, New York, NY 10007 *Tel:* 212-207-7000 *Web Site:* www.harpercollins.com, pg 93

Coleburn, Carolyn, Viking, 375 Hudson St, New York, NY 10014 *Tel:* 212-366-2000 *Fax:* 212-243-6002 *Web Site:* www.penguin.com/publishers/vikingbooks, pg 236

Coleman, David, The College Board, 250 Vesey St, New York, NY 10281 *Tel:* 212-713-8000 *Toll Free Tel:* 866-630-9305 *Web Site:* www.collegeboard.com, pg 55

Coleman, Jason, The University of Virginia Press, PO Box 400318, Charlottesville, VA 22904-4318 *Tel:* 434-924-3468 (cust serv); 434-924-3469 (cust serv) *Toll Free Tel:* 800-831-3406 (orders) *Fax:* 434-982-2655 *Toll Free Fax:* 877-288-6400 *E-mail:* vapress@virginia.edu *Web Site:* www.upress.virginia.edu, pg 231

Coleman, Patrick, The Clarion Science Fiction & Fantasy Writers' Workshop, Arthur C Clarke Ctr for Human Imagination, UC San Diego, 9500 Gilman Dr, MC0445, La Jolla, CA 92093-0445 *Tel:* 858-534-2115 *E-mail:* clarion@ucsd.edu *Web Site:* clarion.ucsd.edu; imagination.ucsd.edu, pg 574

Coleman, Robin W, Johns Hopkins University Press, 2715 N Charles St, Baltimore, MD 21218-4363 *Tel:* 410-516-6900; 410-516-6987 (journal orders outside US & CN) *Toll Free Tel:* 800-537-5487 (book orders & cust serv); 800-548-1784 (journal orders) *Fax:* 410-516-6968; 410-516-3866 (journal orders); 410-516-6998 (orders) *E-mail:* hfscustserv@press.jhu.edu (cust serv); jrnlcirc@press.jhu.edu (journal orders) *Web Site:* www.press.jhu.edu; muse.jhu.edu, pg 114

Colgan, Tom, Berkley Publishing Group, 1745 Broadway, 19th fl, New York, NY 10019 *Tel:* 212-366-2000 *Web Site:* www.penguin.com, pg 32

Collette, Ann, Rees Literary Agency, 14 Beacon St, Suite 710, Boston, MA 02108 *Tel:* 617-227-9014 *Fax:* 617-227-8762 *Web Site:* www.reesagency.com, pg 499

Collicelli, Gilles, Editions Mediaspaul, 3965, blvd Henri-Bourassa E, Montreal, QC H1H 1L1, Canada *Tel:* 514-322-7341 *Fax:* 514-322-4281 *E-mail:* editeur@mediaspaul.ca *Web Site:* mediaspaul.ca, pg 424

Collier, Abby, University of Pittsburgh Press, 7500 Thomas Blvd, Pittsburgh, PA 15260 *Tel:* 412-383-2456 *Fax:* 412-383-2466 *E-mail:* info@upress.pitt.edu *Web Site:* www.upress.pitt.edu, pg 230

Collier, Diana G, Clarity Press Inc, 2625 Piedmont Rd NE, Suite 56, Atlanta, GA 30324 *Tel:* 404-647-6501 *E-mail:* claritypress@usa.net (foreign rts & perms) *Web Site:* www.claritypress.com, pg 53

Collier, Dianna, Collier Associates, 309 Kelsey Park Circle, Palm Beach Gardens, FL 33410 *Tel:* 561-514-6548 *E-mail:* dmccabooks@gmail.com, pg 479

Collier, MacKenzie Fraser-Bub, University of South Carolina Press, 1600 Hampton St, Suite 544, Columbia, SC 29208 *Tel:* 803-777-5245 *Toll Free Tel:* 800-768-2500 (orders) *Fax:* 803-777-0160 *Toll Free Fax:* 800-868-0740 (orders) *Web Site:* www.sc.edu/uscpress, pg 231

Collier, Michael, Fellowship, Tuition Scholarship & Work Study Programs for Writers, Middlebury College, 204 College St, Middlebury, VT 05753 *Tel:* 802-443-5286 *Fax:* 802-443-2087 *E-mail:* blwc@middlebury.edu *Web Site:* www.middlebury.edu/blwc, pg 615

Collier, Theresa, Artisan, 225 Varick St, New York, NY 10014-4381 *Tel:* 212-254-5900 *Toll Free Tel:* 800-722-7202 *Fax:* 212-677-6692 *E-mail:* artisaninfo@artisanbooks.com *Web Site:* www.artisanbooks.com; www.workman.com/artisanbooks, pg 21

Collignon, Kimberly, Data Trace Publishing Co (DTP), 110 West Rd, Suite 227, Towson, MD 21204-2316 *Tel:* 410-494-4994 *Toll Free Tel:* 800-342-0454 *Fax:* 410-494-0515 *E-mail:* info@datatrace.com; customerservice@datatrace.com; salesandmarketing@datatrace.com; editorial@datatrace.com *Web Site:* www.datatrace.com, pg 62

Collin, Frances, Frances Collin Literary Agency, PO Box 33, Wayne, PA 19087 *E-mail:* queries@francescollin.com *Web Site:* www.francescollin.com, pg 480

Collin, Rachel, Mitchell Lane Publishers Inc, 2001 SW 31 Ave, Hallandale, FL 33009 *Tel:* 954-985-9400 *Toll Free Tel:* 800-223-3251 *Fax:* 954-987-2200 *E-mail:* customerservice@mitchelllane.com *Web Site:* www.mitchelllane.com, pg 141

Collins, Anne, Knopf Canada, 320 Front St W, Suite 1400, Toronto, ON M5V 3B6, Canada *Tel:* 416-364-4449 *Toll Free Tel:* 888-523-9292 *Fax:* 416-598-7764 *Web Site:* www.penguinrandomhouse.ca, pg 431

Collins, Beth, Beacon Press, 24 Farnsworth St, Boston, MA 02210-1409 *Tel:* 617-742-2110 *Fax:* 617-723-3097; 617-742-2290 *Web Site:* www.beacon.org, pg 29

Collins, Camille, HarperCollins General Books Group, 195 Broadway, New York, NY 10007 *Tel:* 212-207-7000 *Web Site:* www.harpercollins.com, pg 94

Collins, Christy, White Cloud Press, 300 E Hersey St, Suite 11, Ashland, OR 97520 *Tel:* 541-488-6415 *Fax:* 541-482-7708 *E-mail:* info@whitecloudpress.com *Web Site:* www.whitecloudpress.com, pg 240

Collins, Donna, Individual Excellence Awards, 30 E Broad St, 33rd fl, Columbus, OH 43215 *Tel:* 614-466-2613 *Fax:* 614-466-4494 *Web Site:* www.oac.state.oh.us, pg 626

Collins, Martha, Oberlin College Press, 50 N Professor St, Oberlin, OH 44074-1091 *Tel:* 440-775-8408 *Fax:* 440-775-8124 *E-mail:* oc.press@oberlin.edu *Web Site:* www.oberlin.edu/ocpress, pg 154

Collins, Nate, Samuel French Inc, 235 Park Ave S, 5th fl, New York, NY 10003 *Tel:* 212-206-8990 *Toll Free Tel:* 866-598-8449 *Fax:* 212-206-1429 *E-mail:* info@samuelfrench.com *Web Site:* www.samuelfrench.com, pg 81

Collins, Nick, The Permanent Press, 4170 Noyac Rd, Sag Harbor, NY 11963 *Tel:* 631-725-1101 *Web Site:* www.thepermanentpress.com, pg 167

Collins, Nick, Second Chance Press, 4170 Noyac Rd, Sag Harbor, NY 11963 *Tel:* 631-725-1101 *E-mail:* info@thepermanentpress.com *Web Site:* www.thepermanentpress.com, pg 196

Collins, Teresa Wells, The University Press of Kentucky, 663 S Limestone St, Lexington, KY 40508-4008 *Tel:* 859-257-8400 *Fax:* 859-257-8481 *Web Site:* www.kentuckypress.com, pg 233

Colom, Wilbur O, Genesis Press Inc, PO Box 101, Columbus, MS 39701 *Toll Free Tel:* 888-463-4461 (orders only), pg 84

Columbus, Nadya, Nova Science Publishers Inc, 400 Oser Ave, Suite 1600, Hauppauge, NY 11788-3619 *Tel:* 631-231-7269 *Fax:* 631-231-8175 *E-mail:* nova.main@novapublishers.com *Web Site:* www.novapublishers.com, pg 153

Colvin, Andrea, Little, Brown Books for Young Readers, 1290 Avenue of the Americas, New York, NY 10104 *Tel:* 212-364-1100 *Toll Free Tel:* 800-759-0190 (cust serv) *Web Site:* www.hachettebookgroup.com, pg 126

Colvin, Rod, Addicus Books Inc, PO Box 45327, Omaha, NE 68145 *Tel:* 402-330-7493 *Fax:* 402-330-1707 *E-mail:* info@addicusbooks.com; addicusbks@aol.com *Web Site:* www.addicusbooks.com, pg 4

Colvin, Theresa, Individual Artist Awards, 175 W Ostend St, Suite E, Baltimore, MD 21230 *Tel:* 410-767-6555 *Fax:* 410-333-1062 *E-mail:* msac@msac.org *Web Site:* www.msac.org, pg 626

Combs, Michele, Carpe Indexum, 1960 Deer Run Rd, LaFayette, NY 13084 *Tel:* 315-677-3030 *E-mail:* info@carpeindexum.com *Web Site:* www.carpeindexum.com, pg 460

Comeau, Jennifer, University of Illinois Press, 1325 S Oak St, MC-566, Champaign, IL 61820-6903 *Tel:* 217-333-0950 *Fax:* 217-244-8082 *E-mail:* uipress@uillinois.edu; journals@uillinois.edu *Web Site:* www.press.uillinois.edu, pg 227

Comeau, Kimberly, Scarsdale Publishing Ltd, 333 Mamaroneck Ave, White Plains, NY 10607 *E-mail:* scarsdale@scarsdalepublishing.com *Web Site:* scarsdalepublishing.com, pg 193

Comer, Heather, Mercer University Press, 368 Orange St, Macon, GA 31201 *Tel:* 478-301-2880 *Toll Free Tel:* 866-895-1472 *Fax:* 478-301-2585 *E-mail:* mupressorders@mercer.edu *Web Site:* www.mupress.org, pg 138

Comerford, Rachel, Macmillan Learning, 41 Madison Ave, New York, NY 10010 *Tel:* 212-576-9400 *Fax:* 212-689-2383 *Web Site:* www.macmillanlearning.com, pg 130

Comfort, Anna, Harbour Publishing Co Ltd, 4437 Rondeview Rd, Madeira Park, BC V0N 2H0, Canada *Tel:* 604-883-2730 *Toll Free Tel:* 800-667-2988 *Fax:* 604-883-9451 *E-mail:* info@harbourpublishing.com *Web Site:* www.harbourpublishing.com, pg 429

Comrie, Tim, YMAA Publication Center Inc, PO Box 480, Wolfeboro, NH 03894 *Tel:* 603-569-7988 *Toll Free Tel:* 800-669-8892 *Fax:* 603-569-1889 *E-mail:* info@ymaa.com *Web Site:* www.ymaa.com, pg 247

Comtois, Celine, La Courte Echelle, 4388, rue Saint-Denis, Suite 315, Montreal, QC H2J 2L1, Canada *Tel:* 514-312-6950 *E-mail:* info@courteechelle.com *Web Site:* courteechelle.groupecourteechelle.com, pg 420

Con, Catherine, Boston University Creative Writing Program, 236 Bay State Rd, Boston, MA 02215 *Tel:* 617-353-2510 *Fax:* 617-353-3653 *E-mail:* crwr@bu.edu *Web Site:* www.bu.edu/creativewriting, pg 581

Conary, Lori, Shubert Fendrich Memorial Playwriting Contest, PO Box 4267, Englewood, CO 80155-4267 *Tel:* 303-779-4035 *Toll Free Tel:* 800-333-7262 *Fax:* 303-779-4315 *Web Site:* www.pioneerdrama.com/playwrights/contest.asp, pg 615

Conary, Lori, Meriwether Publishing, c/o Pioneer Drama Service, 9707-A E Easter Lane, Englewood, CO 80112 *Tel:* 303-779-4035 *Toll Free Tel:* 800-333-7262 *Fax:* 303-779-4315 *E-mail:* books@pioneerdrama.com *Web Site:* www.pioneerdrama.com, pg 138

Conaway, Dan, Writers House, 21 W 26 St, New York, NY 10010 *Tel:* 212-685-2400 *Web Site:* www.writershouse.com, pg 508

Concannon, Sean, No Starch Press, 245 Eighth St, San Francisco, CA 94103 *Tel:* 415-863-9900 *Toll Free Tel:* 800-420-7240 *Fax:* 415-863-9950 *E-mail:* info@nostarch.com; sales@nostarch.com *Web Site:* www.nostarch.com, pg 150

Concepcion, Cristina, Don Congdon Associates Inc, 110 William St, Suite 2202, New York, NY 10038-3914 *Tel:* 212-645-1229 *Fax:* 212-727-2688 *E-mail:* dca@doncongdon.com *Web Site:* www.doncongdon.com, pg 480

Conde, Miguel, James H Ottaway Jr Award for the Promotion of International Literature, 147 Prince St, Brooklyn, NY 11201 *Tel:* 347-699-2914 *E-mail:* info@wordswithoutborders.org *Web Site:* www.wordswithoutborders.org/ottaway-award, pg 651

Conde, Sidney, St Martin's Press, LLC, 120 Broadway, New York, NY 10271 *Tel:* 646-307-5151 *Web Site:* us.macmillan.com/smp, pg 190

Conder, Mallory, Penguin Random House Speakers Bureau, A Penguin Random House Company, 1745 Broadway, Mail Drop 13-1, New York, NY 10019 *Tel:* 212-572-2013 *E-mail:* speakers@penguinrandomhouse.com *Web Site:* www.prhspeakers.com, pg 515

Condit, Carl Daniel, Sunstone Press, PO Box 2321, Santa Fe, NM 87504-2321 *Tel:* 505-988-4418 *Toll Free Tel:* 800-243-5644 *Fax:* 505-988-1025 (orders only) *Web Site:* www.sunstonepress.com, pg 211

Condon, Alicia, Kensington Publishing Corp, 119 W 40 St, New York, NY 10018 *Tel:* 212-407-1500 *Toll Free Tel:* 800-221-2647 *Fax:* 212-935-0699 *Web Site:* www.kensingtonbooks.com, pg 116

Corbett, Sara, Workman Publishing Co Inc, 225 Varick St, 9th fl, New York, NY 10014-4381 *Tel:* 212-254-5900 *Toll Free Tel:* 800-722-7202 *Fax:* 212-254-8098 *E-mail:* info@workman.com; orders@workman.com *Web Site:* www.workman.com, pg 244

Corbia, Thomas, Marshall Cavendish Education, 99 White Plains Rd, Tarrytown, NY 10591-9001 *Tel:* 914-332-8888 *Toll Free Tel:* 800-821-9881 *Fax:* 914-332-1082 *E-mail:* mce@marshallcavendish. com; customerservice@marshallcavendish.com *Web Site:* www.mceducation.us, pg 133

Corbin, Kim, New World Library, 14 Pamaron Way, Novato, CA 94949 *Tel:* 415-884-2100 *Toll Free Tel:* 800-227-3900 (ext 52, retail orders); 800-972-6657 *Fax:* 415-884-2199 *E-mail:* escort@ newworldlibrary.com *Web Site:* www.newworldlibrary. com, pg 149

Corcoran, Jennifer, HarperCollins Children's Books, 195 Broadway, New York, NY 10007 *Tel:* 212-207-7000 *Web Site:* www.harpercollins.com/childrens, pg 93

Corcoran, Susan, Penguin Random House Speakers Bureau, A Penguin Random House Company, 1745 Broadway, Mail Drop 13-1, New York, NY 10019 *Tel:* 212-572-2013 *E-mail:* speakers@ penguinrandomhouse.com *Web Site:* www.prhspeakers. com, pg 515

Corcoran, Susan, Random House Publishing Group, 1745 Broadway, New York, NY 10019 *Toll Free Tel:* 800-200-3552 *Web Site:* www.randomhousebooks. com, pg 181

Corcoran-Lytle, Katherine, Adams Media, 57 Littlefield St, Avon, MA 02322 *Tel:* 508-427-7100 *Web Site:* www.simonandschuster.com, pg 4

Cordero, Yojaira, Jessica Kingsley Publishers Inc, 400 Market St, Suite 400, Philadelphia, PA 19106 *Tel:* 215-922-1161 *Toll Free Tel:* 866-416-1078 (cust serv) *Fax:* 215-922-1474 *E-mail:* hello.usa@jkp.com *Web Site:* www.jkp.com, pg 117

Cordova, Alyssa, Regnery Publishing, 300 New Jersey Ave NW, Washington, DC 20001 *Tel:* 202-216-0600 *Toll Free Tel:* 888-219-4747 *Fax:* 202-393-1795 *Web Site:* www.regnery.com, pg 184

Corenswet, John, Paul Dry Books, 1700 Sansom St, Suite 700, Philadelphia, PA 19103 *Tel:* 215-231-9939 *E-mail:* editor@pauldrybooks.com *Web Site:* www. pauldrybooks.com, pg 161

Corey, David, Jessica Kingsley Publishers Inc, 400 Market St, Suite 400, Philadelphia, PA 19106 *Tel:* 215-922-1161 *Toll Free Tel:* 866-416-1078 (cust serv) *Fax:* 215-922-1474 *E-mail:* hello.usa@jkp.com *Web Site:* www.jkp.com, pg 117

Corey, Robin, Random House Children's Books, 1745 Broadway, 10th fl, New York, NY 10019 *Tel:* 212-782-9000 *Web Site:* www.randomhousekids.com, pg 181

Cormier, Dominique Bernier, The Pacific Spirit Poetry Prize, University of British Columbia, Buch E462, 1866 Main Mall, Vancouver, BC V6T 1Z1, Canada *Tel:* 778-822-2514 *Fax:* 778-822-3616 *E-mail:* prismwritingcontest@gmail.com *Web Site:* www.prismmagazine.ca, pg 652

Cormier, Dominique Bernier, PRISM international Literary Non-Fiction Contest, University of British Columbia, Buch E462, 1866 Main Mall, Vancouver, BC V6T 1Z1, Canada *Tel:* 778-822-2514 *Fax:* 778-822-3616 *E-mail:* prismwritingcontest@gmail.com *Web Site:* www.prismmagazine.ca, pg 659

Cormier, Dominique Bernier, The Jacob Zilber Prize for Short Fiction, University of British Columbia, Buch E462, 1866 Main Mall, Vancouver, BC V6T 1Z1, Canada *Tel:* 778-822-2514 *Fax:* 778-822-3616 *E-mail:* prismwritingcontest@gmail.com *Web Site:* www.prismmagazine.ca, pg 681

Cormier, Ellen, Dial Books for Young Readers, 345 Hudson St, New York, NY 10014 *Tel:* 212-366-2000 *Toll Free Tel:* 800-733-3000 (orders) *Fax:* 212-414-3396 *Web Site:* www.penguin.com/publishers/ dialbooksforyoungreaders/, pg 64

Cormier, Helene, Les Presses de l'Universite Laval, 2180, Chemin Sainte-Foy, 1st fl, Quebec, QC G1V 0A6, Canada *Tel:* 418-656-2803 *Fax:* 418-656-3305 *E-mail:* presses@pul.ulaval.ca *Web Site:* www.pulaval. com, pg 437

Cormier, Stephane, Editions Prise de parole, 109 Elm St, Suite 205, Sudbury, ON P3C 1T4, Canada *Tel:* 705-675-6491 *Fax:* 705-673-1817 *E-mail:* info@ prisedeparole.ca *Web Site:* www.prisedeparole.ca, pg 438

Corn, Alison, Insight Editions, 800 "A" St, San Rafael, CA 94901 *Tel:* 415-526-1370 *Toll Free Tel:* 800-809-3792 *Toll Free Fax:* 866-509-0515 *E-mail:* info@ insighteditions.com; marketing@insighteditions.com *Web Site:* insighteditions.com, pg 109

Cornack, Shelley, Norma Epstein Foundation Awards in Creative Writing, 15 King's College Circle, UC 165, Toronto, ON M5S 3H7, Canada *Tel:* 416-978-8083 *Fax:* 416-978-8854 *E-mail:* uc.programs@utoronto.ca *Web Site:* www.uc.utoronto.ca/writing-centre, pg 613

Cornell, Merial, Cornell & Co LLC, 44 Jog Hill Rd, Trumbull, CT 06611 *Tel:* 203-454-4210 *Web Site:* www.cornellandco.com, pg 511

Corrado, Susan, Naval Institute Press, 291 Wood Rd, Annapolis, MD 21402-5034 *Tel:* 410-268-6110 *Toll Free Tel:* 800-233-8764 *Fax:* 410-295-1084; 410-571-1703 (cust serv) *E-mail:* webmaster@ navalinstitute.org; customer@navalinstitute.org (cust serv) *Web Site:* www.nip.org; www.usni.org, pg 147

Corral, Rodrigo, Farrar, Straus & Giroux, LLC, 175 Varick St, 9th fl, New York, NY 10014 *Tel:* 212-741-6900 *E-mail:* fsg.publicity@fsgbooks.com *Web Site:* us.macmillan.com/fsg.aspx, pg 76

Correa, Alex, Lectorum Publications Inc, 205 Chubb Ave, Lyndhurst, NJ 07071 *Toll Free Tel:* 800-345-5946 *Fax:* 201-559-2201 *Toll Free Fax:* 877-532-8676 *E-mail:* lectorum@lectorum.com *Web Site:* www. lectorum.com, pg 121

Correa, Maria, Random House Children's Books, 1745 Broadway, 10th fl, New York, NY 10019 *Tel:* 212-782-9000 *Web Site:* www.randomhousekids.com, pg 180

Correa, Nick, Cambridge University Press, One Liberty Plaza, 20th fl, New York, NY 10006 *Tel:* 212-924-3900; 212-337-5000 *Fax:* 212-691-3239; 845-353-4141 *E-mail:* newyork@cambridge.org; customer_service@cambridge.org *Web Site:* www. cambridge.org/us, pg 43

Corrin, Dean, Cunningham Commission for Youth Theatre, Lincoln Park Campus, 2350 N Racine Ave, Chicago, IL 60614-4100 *Tel:* 773-325-7999 *Fax:* 773-325-7920 *E-mail:* cunninghamcommission@depaul.edu *Web Site:* theatre.depaul.edu, pg 608

Corson, Karyl, FaithWalk Publishing, 5450 N Dixie Hwy, Lima, OH 45807 *Tel:* 419-227-1818 *Toll Free Tel:* 800-537-1030 (orders, non-bookstore mkts) *Fax:* 419-224-9184 *E-mail:* orders@csspub.com *Web Site:* www.faithwalkpub.com, pg 75

Cosgrove, Jay, Yale University Press, 302 Temple St, New Haven, CT 06511-8909 *Tel:* 203-432-0960; 203-432-0966 (sales); 401-531-2800 (cust serv) *Toll Free Tel:* 800-405-1619 (cust serv) *Fax:* 203-432-0948; 203-432-8485 (sales); 401-531-2801 (cust serv) *Toll Free Fax:* 800-406-9145 (cust serv) *E-mail:* sales. press@yale.edu (sales); customer.care@triliteral.org (cust serv) *Web Site:* www.yalebooks.com; yalepress. yale.edu/yupbooks, pg 246

Cosseboom, Joel, University of Hawaii Press, 2840 Kolowalu St, Honolulu, HI 96822-1888 *Tel:* 808-956-8255 *Toll Free Tel:* 888-UHPRESS (847-7377) *Fax:* 808-988-6052 *Toll Free Fax:* 800-650-7811 *E-mail:* uhpbooks@hawaii.edu *Web Site:* www. uhpress.hawaii.edu, pg 227

Costantini MFA, Lana, Center for the Collaborative Classroom, 1001 Marina Village Pkwy, Suite 110, Alameda, CA 94501-1042 *Tel:* 510-533-0213 *Toll Free Tel:* 800-666-7270 *Fax:* 510-464-3670 *E-mail:* info@collaborativeclassroom. org; clientsupport@collaborativeclassroom.org *Web Site:* www.collaborativeclassroom.org, pg 48

Costanzo, Gerald, Carnegie Mellon University Press, 5032 Forbes Ave, Pittsburgh, PA 15289-1021 *Tel:* 412-268-2861 *Fax:* 412-268-8706 *E-mail:* carnegiemellonuniversitypress@gmail.com *Web Site:* www.cmu.edu/universitypress, pg 45

Costello, John, The MIT Press, One Rogers St, Cambridge, MA 02142 *Tel:* 617-253-5255 *Toll Free Tel:* 800-405-1619 (orders) *Fax:* 617-258-6779; 617-577-1545 (orders) *Web Site:* mitpress.mit.edu, pg 141

Coster, Candace, BHTG - Julie Harris Playwright Award Competition, PO Box 148, Beverly Hills, CA 90213 *Tel:* 310-273-3390 *Web Site:* www. beverlyhillstheatreguild.com, pg 597

Coster, Candace, BHTG - Michael J Libow Youth Theatre Award, PO Box 148, Beverly Hills, CA 90213 *Tel:* 310-273-3390 *Web Site:* www. beverlyhillstheatreguild.com, pg 598

Cota, Mara, Alex Awards, 50 E Huron St, Chicago, IL 60611 *Tel:* 312-280-4390 *Toll Free Tel:* 800-545-2433 *Fax:* 312-280-5276 *E-mail:* yalsa@ala.org *Web Site:* www.ala.org/yalsa/alex-awards, pg 591

Cote, Marc, Cormorant Books Inc, 260 Spadina Ave, Suite 502, Toronto, ON M4Y 1P9, Canada *Tel:* 416-925-8887 *E-mail:* info@cormorantbooks.com *Web Site:* www.cormorantbooks.com, pg 420

Cote-Botero, Andrea, University of Texas at El Paso, Department of Creative Writing, MFA/Department of Creative Writing, 901 EDUC, 500 W University Ave, El Paso, TX 79968-9991 *Tel:* 915-747-5713 *Fax:* 915-747-5523 *E-mail:* creativewriting@utep.edu *Web Site:* www.utep.edu/cw, pg 586

Cott, Sharon, The Metropolitan Museum of Art, 1000 Fifth Ave, New York, NY 10028 *Tel:* 212-535-7710 *E-mail:* editorial@metmuseum.org *Web Site:* www. metmuseum.org, pg 139

Cotter, Glenda, The University of Utah Press, J Willard Marriott Library, Suite 5400, 295 S 1500 E, Salt Lake City, UT 84112-0860 *Tel:* 801-585-9786 *Fax:* 801-581-3365 *E-mail:* hannah.new@utah.edu *Web Site:* www.uofupress.com, pg 231

Cottle, Anna, Cine/Lit Representation, PO Box 802918, Santa Clarita, CA 91380-2918 *Tel:* 661-513-0268 *E-mail:* cinelit@att.net, pg 479

Cottrell, Sophie, Hachette Book Group, 1290 Avenue of the Americas, New York, NY 10104 *Tel:* 212-364-1100 *Toll Free Tel:* 800-759-0190 (cust serv) *Fax:* 212-364-0933 (intl orders) *Toll Free Fax:* 800-286-9471 (cust serv) *Web Site:* www. hachettebookgroup.com, pg 90

Couch, Mora, Holiday House Publishing Inc, 50 Broad St, New York, NY 10004 *Tel:* 212-688-0085 *Fax:* 212-421-6134 *E-mail:* info@holidayhouse.com *Web Site:* www.holidayhouse.com, pg 101

Couch, Peg, Leisure Arts Inc, 104 Champs Blvd, Suite 100, Maumelle, AR 72113 *Tel:* 501-868-8800 *Toll Free Tel:* 800-643-8030 *Toll Free Fax:* 877-710-5603 (catalog) *E-mail:* customer_service@leisurearts.com *Web Site:* www.leisurearts.com, pg 122

Coughlan, Robert, Capstone Publishers™, 1710 Roe Crest Dr, North Mankato, MN 56003 *Toll Free Tel:* 800-747-4992 (cust serv) *Toll Free Fax:* 888-262-0705 *E-mail:* customer.service@capstonepub.com *Web Site:* www.capstonepub.com, pg 44

Counts, Nicole, Random House Publishing Group, 1745 Broadway, New York, NY 10019 *Toll Free Tel:* 800-200-3552 *Web Site:* www.randomhousebooks.com, pg 181

Coupe, Carla, Wildside Press LLC, 7945 MacArthur Blvd, Suite 215, Cabin John, MD 20818 *Tel:* 301-762-1305 *Fax:* 301-762-1306 *E-mail:* wildside@ wildsidepress.com; wildsidepress@yahoo.com *Web Site:* wildsidepress.com, pg 241

Courage, Rachel Ekstrom, Folio Literary Management, The Film Center Bldg, 630 Ninth Ave, Suite 1101, New York, NY 10036 *Tel:* 212-400-1494 *Fax:* 212-967-0977 *Web Site:* www.foliolit.com, pg 484

Cousineau, Diane, Ordre des traducteurs, terminologues et interpretes agrees du quebec, 1108-2021 Ave Union, Montreal, QC H3A 2S9, Canada *Tel:* 514-845-4411 *Toll Free Tel:* 800-265-4815 *Fax:* 514-845-9903 *E-mail:* info@ottiaq.org; direction@ottiaq.org; reception@ottiaq.org *Web Site:* www.ottiaq.org, pg 542

Cousineau, Helene, Pearson ERPI, 1611 Cremazie Blvd E, 10th fl, Montreal, QC H2M 2P2, Canada *Tel:* 514-334-2690 *Toll Free Tel:* 800-263-3678 *Fax:* 514-334-4720 *Toll Free Fax:* 800-643-4720 *E-mail:* bienvenue@pearsonerpi.com *Web Site:* pearsonerpi.com; pearsonplc.ca, pg 436

Coveney, Chris, The Massachusetts Historical Society, 1154 Boylston St, Boston, MA 02215-3695 *Tel:* 617-536-1608 *Fax:* 617-859-0074 *E-mail:* publications@masshist.org *Web Site:* www.masshist.org, pg 133

Covrett, Katya, Zondervan, 3900 Sparks Dr, Grand Rapids, MI 49546 *Tel:* 616-698-6900 *Toll Free Tel:* 800-226-1122; 800-727-1309 (retail orders) *Fax:* 616-698-3350 *Toll Free Fax:* 800-698-3256 (retail orders) *Web Site:* www.zondervan.com, pg 248

Cowan, Michael, American Society of Mechanical Engineers (ASME), 2 Park Ave, New York, NY 10016-5990 *Tel:* 212-591-7000 *Toll Free Tel:* 800-843-2763 (cust serv-US, CN & Mexico) *Fax:* 973-882-1717 (orders & inquiries) *E-mail:* customercare@asme.org *Web Site:* www.asme.org, pg 14

Cowles, Lauren, Cambridge University Press, One Liberty Plaza, 20th fl, New York, NY 10006 *Tel:* 212-924-3900; 212-337-5000 *Fax:* 212-691-3239; 845-353-4141 *E-mail:* newyork@cambridge.org; customer_service@cambridge.org *Web Site:* www.cambridge.org/us, pg 43

Cox, Bob, North American Snowsports Journalists Association (NASJA), 49 Plaza Ave, Belchertown, MA 01007 *E-mail:* execsec@nasja.org *Web Site:* nasja.org, pg 542

Cox, Clare, The Lyons Press, 246 Goose Lane, Guilford, CT 06437 *Tel:* 203-458-4500 *Fax:* 201-458-4601 *E-mail:* info@rowman.com *Web Site:* rowman.com/page/lyonspress, pg 129

Cox, Clare, Rowman & Littlefield, 4501 Forbes Blvd, Suite 200, Lanham, MD 20706 *Tel:* 301-459-3366 *Toll Free Tel:* 800-462-6420 (ext 3024, cust serv) *Fax:* 301-429-5748 *Web Site:* rowman.com, pg 188

Cox, Clare, University Press of America Inc, 4501 Forbes Blvd, Suite 200, Lanham, MD 20706 *Tel:* 301-459-3366 *Toll Free Tel:* 800-462-6420 *Fax:* 301-429-5748 *Toll Free Fax:* 800-338-4550 *Web Site:* www.univpress.com, pg 232

Cox, Merrilee, Society for Features Journalism (SFJ), University of Maryland, Philip Merrill College of Journalism, 1100 Knight Hall, College Park, MD 20742 *Tel:* 301-314-2631 *Fax:* 301-314-9166 *Web Site:* featuresjournalism.org, pg 546

Cox, Ron, Kamehameha Publishing, 1887 Makukone St, Pauahi Admin Bldg, Suite 211, Honolulu, HI 96817 *E-mail:* publishing@ksbe.edu *Web Site:* kamehamehapublishing.org, pg 115

Cox, Scott, Publications International Ltd (PIL), 8140 N Lehigh Ave, Morton Grove, IL 60053 *Tel:* 847-676-3470 *Fax:* 847-676-3671 *E-mail:* customer_service@pubint.com *Web Site:* pilbooks.com, pg 177

Cox, Tom, Penguin Random House LLC, 1745 Broadway, New York, NY 10019 *Tel:* 212-782-9000 *Toll Free Tel:* 800-726-0600 *Web Site:* www.penguinrandomhouse.com, pg 164

Cox, Tom, Whitaker House, 1030 Hunt Valley Circle, New Kensington, PA 15068 *Tel:* 724-334-7000 *Toll Free Tel:* 800-444-4484 (sales) *Fax:* 724-334-1200 *E-mail:* publisher@whitakerhouse.com; sales@whitakerhouse.com *Web Site:* www.whitakerhouse.com, pg 240

Coxon, Khadija, McGill-Queen's University Press, 1010 Sherbrooke W, Suite 1720, Montreal, QC H3A 2R7, Canada *Tel:* 514-398-3750 *Fax:* 514-398-4333 *E-mail:* mqup@mqup.ca *Web Site:* www.mqup.ca, pg 433

Coyle, Lily, Beaver's Pond Press Inc, 939 Seventh St W, St Paul, MN 55102 *Tel:* 952-829-8818 *E-mail:* info@beaverspondpress.com *Web Site:* www.beaverspondpress.com, pg 30

Coyne, Brendan, Penn State University Press, University Support Bldg 1, Suite C, 820 N University Dr, University Park, PA 16802-1003 *Tel:* 814-865-1327 *Toll Free Tel:* 800-326-9180 *Fax:* 814-863-1408 *Toll Free Fax:* 877-778-2665 *E-mail:* orders@psupress.org; orders@eisenbrauns.org *Web Site:* www.psupress.org; www.eisenbrauns.org, pg 166

Coyne, Christopher, Marshall Cavendish Education, 99 White Plains Rd, Tarrytown, NY 10591-9001 *Tel:* 914-332-8888 *Toll Free Tel:* 800-821-9881 *Fax:* 914-332-1082 *E-mail:* mce@marshallcavendish.com; customerservice@marshallcavendish.com *Web Site:* www.mceducation.us, pg 133

Coyne, Frank, George T Bisel Co Inc, 710 S Washington Sq, Philadelphia, PA 19106-3519 *Tel:* 215-922-5760 *Toll Free Tel:* 800-247-3526 *Fax:* 215-922-2235 *E-mail:* gbisel@bisel.com *Web Site:* www.bisel.com, pg 33

Craanen, Beth, The Electrochemical Society (ECS), 65 S Main St, Bldg D, Pennington, NJ 08534-2839 *Tel:* 609-737-1902 *Fax:* 609-737-0629 *E-mail:* publications@electrochem.org; customerservice@electrochem.org *Web Site:* www.electrochem.org, pg 70

Crabtree, Andrea, Crabtree Publishing Co, 347 Fifth Ave, Suite 1402-145, New York, NY 10016 *Tel:* 212-496-5040 *Toll Free Tel:* 800-387-7650 *Toll Free Fax:* 800-355-7166 *E-mail:* custserv@crabtreebooks.com *Web Site:* www.crabtreebooks.com, pg 59

Crabtree, Andrea, Crabtree Publishing Co Ltd, 616 Welland Ave, St Catharines, ON L2M 5V6, Canada *Tel:* 905-682-5221 *Toll Free Tel:* 800-387-7650 *Fax:* 905-682-7166 *Toll Free Fax:* 800-355-7166 *E-mail:* custserv@crabtreebooks.com; sales@crabtreebooks.com; orders@crabtreebooks.com *Web Site:* www.crabtreebooks.com, pg 421

Crabtree, Peter A, Crabtree Publishing Co, 347 Fifth Ave, Suite 1402-145, New York, NY 10016 *Tel:* 212-496-5040 *Toll Free Tel:* 800-387-7650 *Toll Free Fax:* 800-355-7166 *E-mail:* custserv@crabtreebooks.com *Web Site:* www.crabtreebooks.com, pg 59

Crabtree, Peter A, Crabtree Publishing Co Ltd, 616 Welland Ave, St Catharines, ON L2M 5V6, Canada *Tel:* 905-682-5221 *Toll Free Tel:* 800-387-7650 *Fax:* 905-682-7166 *Toll Free Fax:* 800-355-7166 *E-mail:* custserv@crabtreebooks.com; sales@crabtreebooks.com; orders@crabtreebooks.com *Web Site:* www.crabtreebooks.com, pg 421

Crabtree, Tamara, Abingdon Press, 2222 Rosa L Parks Blvd, Nashville, TN 37228 *Tel:* 615-749-6000 (academic books) *Toll Free Tel:* 800-251-3320 (orders) *Fax:* 615-749-6056 (academic books) *Toll Free Fax:* 800-836-7802 (orders) *E-mail:* orders@abingdonpress.com; permissions@abingdonpress.com *Web Site:* www.abingdonpress.com, pg 2

Crago, Jonathan, McGill-Queen's University Press, 1010 Sherbrooke W, Suite 1720, Montreal, QC H3A 2R7, Canada *Tel:* 514-398-3750 *Fax:* 514-398-4333 *E-mail:* mqup@mqup.ca *Web Site:* www.mqup.ca, pg 433

Crahan, Eric, Princeton University Press, 41 William St, Princeton, NJ 08540-5237 *Tel:* 609-258-4900 *Fax:* 609-258-6305 *Web Site:* press.princeton.edu, pg 174

Craig, Bryce H, P & R Publishing Co, 1102 Marble Hill Rd, Phillipsburg, NJ 08865 *Tel:* 908-454-0505 *Toll Free Tel:* 800-631-0094 *Fax:* 908-859-2390 *E-mail:* sales@prpbooks.com; info@prpbooks.com *Web Site:* www.prpbooks.com, pg 158

Craig, Noah, Leadership Ministries Worldwide, 1928 Central Ave, Chattanooga, TN 37408 *Tel:* 423-855-2181 *Toll Free Tel:* 800-987-8790 *E-mail:* info@lmw.org *Web Site:* lmw.org; store.lmw.org, pg 121

Cram, Liz, Chartered Professional Accountants of Canada (CPA Canada), 277 Wellington St W, Toronto, ON M5V 3H2, Canada *Tel:* 416-977-

3222 *Toll Free Tel:* 800-268-3793 *Fax:* 416-977-8585 *E-mail:* member.services@cpacanada.ca *Web Site:* www.cpacanada.ca; www.facebook.com/CPACanada/, pg 419

Cranbury, Sean, The BC Book Prizes, 207 W Hastings St, Suite 901, Vancouver, BC V6B 1H7, Canada *Fax:* 604-687-2435 *E-mail:* info@bcbookprizes.ca *Web Site:* www.bcbookprizes.ca, pg 596

Crandell, Leslie, Berrett-Koehler Publishers Inc, 1333 Broadway, Suite 1000, Oakland, CA 94612 *Tel:* 510-817-2277 *Fax:* 510-817-2278 *E-mail:* bkpub@bkpub.com *Web Site:* www.bkconnection.com, pg 32

Cranford, Garry, Flanker Press Ltd, 1243 Kenmount Rd, Unit 1, Paradise, NL A1L 0V8, Canada *Tel:* 709-739-4477 *Toll Free Tel:* 866-739-4420 *Fax:* 709-739-4420 *E-mail:* info@flankerpress.com; sales@flankerpress.com *Web Site:* www.flankerpress.com, pg 427

Cranford, Jerry, Flanker Press Ltd, 1243 Kenmount Rd, Unit 1, Paradise, NL A1L 0V8, Canada *Tel:* 709-739-4477 *Toll Free Tel:* 866-739-4420 *Fax:* 709-739-4420 *E-mail:* info@flankerpress.com; sales@flankerpress.com *Web Site:* www.flankerpress.com, pg 427

Crassons, Kate, Lehigh University Press, B-040 Christmas-Saucon Hall, 14 E Packer Ave, Bethlehem, PA 18015 *Tel:* 610-758-3933 *Fax:* 610-758-6331 *E-mail:* inlup@lehigh.edu *Web Site:* lupress.cas2.lehigh.edu, pg 122

Craven, Ashleigh, Gryphon House Inc, 6848 Leon's Way, Lewisville, NC 27023 *Toll Free Tel:* 800-638-0928 *Toll Free Fax:* 877-638-7576 *E-mail:* info@ghbooks.com *Web Site:* www.gryphonhouse.com, pg 90

Craven, Robert H Jr, F A Davis Co, 1915 Arch St, Philadelphia, PA 19103 *Tel:* 215-568-2270; 215-440-3001 *Toll Free Tel:* 800-523-4049 *Fax:* 215-568-5065; 215-440-3016 *E-mail:* info@fadavis.com; orders@fadavis.com *Web Site:* www.fadavis.com, pg 62

Craven, Robert H Sr, F A Davis Co, 1915 Arch St, Philadelphia, PA 19103 *Tel:* 215-568-2270; 215-440-3001 *Toll Free Tel:* 800-523-4049 *Fax:* 215-568-5065; 215-440-3016 *E-mail:* info@fadavis.com; orders@fadavis.com *Web Site:* www.fadavis.com, pg 62

Craven, Victoria, The Monacelli Press, 65 Bleecker St, 8th fl, New York, NY 10012 *Tel:* 212-229-9925 *E-mail:* contact@monacellipress.com *Web Site:* www.monacellipress.com, pg 141

Crawford, Ann H, Geological Society of America (GSA), 3300 Penrose Place, Boulder, CO 80301-1806 *Tel:* 303-357-1000 *Fax:* 303-357-1070 *E-mail:* pubs@geosociety.org (prodn); editing@geosociety.org (edit) *Web Site:* www.geosociety.org, pg 84

Crawford, Edward, Hachette Nashville, 6100 Tower Circle, Room 210, Franklin, TN 37067 *Tel:* 615-221-0996 *Fax:* 615-221-0962 *Web Site:* www.hachettebookgroup.com, pg 91

Crawford, Hillary, Individual Artist Project Grant, 500 S Bronough St, Tallahassee, FL 32399-0250 *Tel:* 850-245-6470 *Fax:* 850-245-6497 *E-mail:* info@dos.myflorida.com *Web Site:* dos.myflorida.com/cultural, pg 626

Crawford, Ingrid, National Association of Book Entrepreneurs (NABE), PO Box 606, Cottage Grove, OR 97424 *Tel:* 541-942-7455 *Fax:* 541-942-7455 *E-mail:* nabe@bookmarketingprofits.com *Web Site:* www.bookmarketingprofits.com, pg 538

Crawford, Kelly, Paintbox Press, 275 Madison Ave, Suite 600, New York, NY 10016 *Tel:* 212-878-6610 *E-mail:* info@paintboxpress.com *Web Site:* paintboxpress.com, pg 159

Crawford, Kristen, Arcadia Publishing Inc, 420 Wando Park Blvd, Mount Pleasant, SC 29464 *Tel:* 843-853-2070 *Toll Free Tel:* 888-313-2665 (orders only) *Fax:* 843-853-0044 *E-mail:* sales@arcadiapublishing.com *Web Site:* www.arcadiapublishing.com, pg 19

Crawford, Mark, MC2 Solutions LLC, 5101 Violet Lane, Madison, WI 53714 *Tel:* 608-240-4959, pg 467

Crawford, Rachel, Naval Institute Press, 291 Wood Rd, Annapolis, MD 21402-5034 *Tel:* 410-268-6110 *Toll Free Tel:* 800-233-8764 *Fax:* 410-295-1084;

410-571-1703 (cust serv) E-mail: webmaster@ navalinstitute.org; customer@navalinstitute.org (cust serv) Web Site: www.nip.org; www.usni.org, pg 147

Crawford, Tad, Allworth Press, 307 W 36 St, 11th fl, New York, NY 10018 Tel: 212-643-6816 Fax: 212-643-6819 Web Site: www.allworth.com, pg 8

Crawford, William R Sr, Military Living Publications, 333 Maple Ave E, Suite 3130, Vienna, VA 22180-4717 Tel: 703-237-0203 Fax: 703-552-8855 E-mail: customerservice@militaryliving.com; sales@ militaryliving.com; editor@militaryliving.com Web Site: www.militaryliving.com, pg 140

Crean, Patrick, HarperCollins Canada Ltd, 2 Bloor St E, 20th fl, Toronto, ON M4W 1A8, Canada Tel: 416-975-9334 Fax: 416-975-5223 E-mail: hcorder@ harpercollins.com Web Site: www.harpercollins.ca, pg 429

Creekmore, Sylvan, St Martin's Press, LLC, 120 Broadway, New York, NY 10271 Tel: 646-307-5151 Web Site: us.macmillan.com/smp, pg 190

Crespo, Paola, Orbit, 1290 Avenue of the Americas, New York, NY 10104 Tel: 212-364-1100 Toll Free Tel: 800-759-0190 Web Site: www.orbitbooks.net, pg 156

Crevier, Yvonne, University of Massachusetts Press, East Experiment Station, 671 N Pleasant St, Amherst, MA 01003 Tel: 413-545-2217 Fax: 413-545-1226 E-mail: info@umpress.umass.edu Web Site: www. umass.edu/umpress, pg 228

Crewe, Jennifer, Columbia University Press, 61 W 62 St, New York, NY 10023 Tel: 212-459-0600 Toll Free Tel: 800-944-8648 Fax: 212-459-3678 Web Site: cup. columbia.edu, pg 55

Crews, Shaquona, Quirk Books, 215 Church St, Philadelphia, PA 19106 Tel: 215-627-3581 Fax: 215-627-5220 E-mail: general@quirkbooks.com Web Site: www.quirkbooks.com, pg 179

Crichton, Sarah, Henry Holt and Company, LLC, 120 Broadway, 23rd fl, New York, NY 10271 Tel: 646-307-5151 Toll Free Tel: 888-330-8477 (orders) Fax: 646-307-5285 Web Site: www.henryholt.com, pg 101

Crichton, Sha-Shana, Crichton & Associates Inc, 6940 Carroll Ave, Takoma Park, MD 20912 Tel: 301-495-9663 E-mail: cricht1@aol.com Web Site: www. crichton-associates.com, pg 480

Crider, Andrew K, Christian Light Publications Inc, 1051 Mount Clinton Pike, Harrisonburg, VA 22802 Tel: 540-434-1003 Toll Free Tel: 800-776-0478 Fax: 540-433-8896 E-mail: info@clp.org; orders@ clp.org Web Site: www.clp.org, pg 51

Crilly, Donna, Paulist Press, 997 Macarthur Blvd, Mahwah, NJ 07430-9990 Tel: 201-825-7300 Toll Free Tel: 800-218-1903 Fax: 201-825-6921 Toll Free Fax: 800-836-3161 E-mail: info@paulistpress. com; publicity@paulistpress.com Web Site: www. paulistpress.com, pg 161

Crippen, Cynthia, AEIOU Inc, 894 Piermont Ave, Piermont, NY 10968 Tel: 845-359-1911, pg 457

Crisp, Laura, Anchor Books, c/o Penguin Random House Inc, 1745 Broadway, New York, NY 10019 Tel: 212-572-2420 E-mail: vintageanchorpublicity@ randomhouse.com Web Site: knopfdoubleday.com/ imprint/anchor, pg 15

Crisp, Laura, Vintage Books, c/o Penguin Random House Inc, 1745 Broadway, New York, NY 10019 Tel: 212-572-2420 E-mail: vintageanchorpublicity@ randomhouse.com Web Site: knopfdoubleday.com/ imprint/vintage, pg 236

Crispyn, Janell, Deadline Club, c/o Salmagundi Club, 47 Fifth Ave, New York, NY 10003 Tel: 646-481-7584 Web Site: www.deadlineclub.org, pg 532

Criss, Shannon, Diversion Books, 443 Park Ave S, Suite 1008, New York, NY 10016 Tel: 212-961-6390 E-mail: info@diversionbooks.com Web Site: www. diversionbooks.com, pg 65

Crist, Connie, Warner Press, 2902 Enterprise Dr, Anderson, IN 46013 Tel: 765-644-7721 Toll Free Tel: 800-741-7721 (orders) Fax: 765-640-8005 E-mail: wporders@warnerpress.org Web Site: www. warnerpress.org, pg 237

Cristofaro, Joe, Groupe Educalivres Inc, 1699, blvd le Corbusier, bureau 350, Laval, QC H7S 1Z3, Canada Tel: 514-334-8466 Toll Free Tel: 800-567-3671 (info serv) Fax: 514-334-8387 Toll Free Fax: 800-267-4387 E-mail: infoservice@granduc.com Web Site: www. educalivres.com, pg 428

Croce, Mr Carmen R, St Joseph's University Press, 5600 City Ave, Philadelphia, PA 19131-1395 Tel: 610-660-3402 Fax: 610-660-3412 E-mail: sjupress@sju.edu Web Site: www.sjupress.com, pg 190

Croce, Nicholas, Stimola Literary Studio Inc, 308 Livingston Ct, Edgewater, NJ 07020 Tel: 201-945-9353 Fax: 201-945-9353; 201-490-5920 E-mail: info@stimolaliterarystudio.com Web Site: www.stimolaliterarystudio.com, pg 504

Crocker, Amanda, Between the Lines, 401 Richmond St W, No 277, Toronto, ON M5V 3A8, Canada Tel: 416-535-9914 Toll Free Tel: 800-718-7201 Fax: 416-535-1484 E-mail: info@btlbooks.com Web Site: btlbooks. com, pg 416

Crocker, Harry W III, Regnery Publishing, 300 New Jersey Ave NW, Washington, DC 20001 Tel: 202-216-0600 Toll Free Tel: 888-219-4747 Fax: 202-393-1795 Web Site: www.regnery.com, pg 184

Crockett, Laura, TriadaUS Literary Agency, PO Box 561, Sewickley, PA 15143 Tel: 412-401-3376 Web Site: www.triadaus.com, pg 506

Croll, Jennifer, Greystone Books Ltd, 343 Railway St, Suite 201, Vancouver, BC V6A 1A4, Canada Tel: 604-875-1550 Fax: 604-875-1556 E-mail: info@ greystonebooks.com Web Site: www.greystonebooks. com, pg 427

Cromie, Eric, McSweeney's Publishing, 849 Valencia St, San Francisco, CA 94110 Tel: 415-642-5609 (cust serv) E-mail: custserv@mcsweeneys.net Web Site: www.mcsweeneys.net, pg 136

Cronin, Denise, Random House Publishing Group, 1745 Broadway, New York, NY 10019 Toll Free Tel: 800-200-3552 Web Site: www.randomhousebooks.com, pg 181

Cronin, Mary, Boston Authors Club Inc, 2400 Beacon St, No 208, Chestnut, MA 02467 Tel: 617-552-4031 E-mail: bostonauthorsclub@gmail.com Web Site: bostonauthorsclub.org, pg 529

Cronin, Mary, Julia Ward Howe Book Awards, c/o Professor Mary Cronin, 2400 Beacon St, Unit 208, Beacon Hill, MA 02467 Tel: 617-552-4031 E-mail: bostonauthorsclub@gmail.com Web Site: bostonauthorsclub.org, pg 624

Cronin, Sam, Nelson Literary Agency LLC, 1732 Wazee St, Suite 207, Denver, CO 80202-1284 Tel: 303-292-2805 E-mail: info@nelsonagency.com Web Site: www. nelsonagency.com, pg 497

Cronshaw, Francine, East Mountain Editing Services, PO Box 1895, Tijeras, NM 87059-1895 Tel: 505-281-8422 Web Site: www.spanishindexing.com, pg 462

Crooks, Cathie, University of Alberta Press, Ring House 2, Edmonton, AB T6G 2E1, Canada Tel: 780-492-3662 Fax: 780-492-0719 Web Site: www.uap.ualberta. ca, pg 442

Crooks, Jaye, University of Baltimore - Yale Gordon College of Arts & Sciences, Ampersand Institute for Words & Images, 1420 N Charles St, Baltimore, MD 21201-5779 Tel: 410-837-6022 Fax: 410-837-6029 E-mail: scd@ubalt.edu Web Site: www.ubalt.edu, pg 585

Crooms, Sandy, University of Pittsburgh Press, 7500 Thomas Blvd, Pittsburgh, PA 15260 Tel: 412-383-2456 Fax: 412-383-2466 E-mail: info@upress.pitt.edu Web Site: www.upress.pitt.edu, pg 230

Crosby, Calvin, CALIBA Golden Poppy Awards, 651 Broadway, 2nd fl, Sonoma, CA 95476 Tel: 415-561-7686 Fax: 415-561-7685 E-mail: info@caliballiance. org Web Site: www.caliballiance.org/golden-poppy-awards.html, pg 602

Crosby, Calvin, California Independent Booksellers Alliance (CALIBA), 651 Broadway, 2nd fl, Sonoma, CA 95476 Tel: 415-561-7686 Fax: 415-561-7685 E-mail: info@caliballiance.org Web Site: www. caliballiance.org, pg 529

Crosby, Jeff, InterVarsity Press, 430 Plaza Dr, Westmont, IL 60559-1234 Tel: 630-734-4000 Toll Free Tel: 800-843-9487 Fax: 630-734-4200 E-mail: email@ivpress. com Web Site: www.ivpress.com, pg 112

Crosby, Michael, Leadership Connect, 1407 Broadway, Suite 318, New York, NY 10018 Tel: 212-627-4140 Toll Free Tel: 800-627-0311 Fax: 212-645-0931 E-mail: info@leadershipconnect.io Web Site: www. leadershipconnect.io, pg 121

Cross, Claudia, Folio Literary Management, The Film Center Bldg, 630 Ninth Ave, Suite 1101, New York, NY 10036 Tel: 212-400-1494 Fax: 212-967-0977 Web Site: www.foliolit.com, pg 484

Cross, Jamie, Math Solutions®, One Harbor Dr, Suite 101, Sausalito, CA 94965 Tel: 877-234-7323 Toll Free Tel: 800-724-4716 E-mail: info@ mathsolutions.com; orders@mathsolutions. com Web Site: www.mathsolutions.com; store. mathsolutions.com, pg 134

Cross, John C Esq, Standard Publishing Corp, 10 High St, Boston, MA 02110 Tel: 617-457-0600 Toll Free Tel: 800-682-5759 Fax: 617-457-0608 Web Site: www. spcpub.com, pg 206

Crotty, Kevin, ICM Partners, 65 E 55 St, New York, NY 10022 Tel: 212-556-5600 Web Site: www.icmtalent. com, pg 489

Crouch, Lori, Education Writers Association (EWA), 3516 Connecticut Ave NW, Washington, DC 20008 Tel: 202-452-9830 Fax: 202-452-9837 E-mail: ewa@ ewa.org Web Site: www.ewa.org, pg 532

Crouch, Lori, National Awards for Education Reporting, 3516 Connecticut Ave NW, Washington, DC 20008 Tel: 202-452-9830 Fax: 202-452-9837 E-mail: ewa@ ewa.org Web Site: www.ewa.org, pg 644

Crouchet, Mike, Cardiotext Publishing, 3405 W 44 St, Minneapolis, MN 55410 Tel: 612-925-2053 Toll Free Tel: 888-999-9174 Fax: 612-922-7556 E-mail: info@ cardiotext.com Web Site: www.cardiotextpublishing. com, pg 44

Crowe, Sara, Pippin Properties Inc, 110 W 40 St, Suite 1704, New York, NY 10018 Tel: 212-338-9310 E-mail: info@pippinproperties.com Web Site: www.pippinproperties.com; www.facebook. com/pippinproperties, pg 498

Crowley, Kevin, The Edna Staebler Award for Creative Non-Fiction, Office of the Dean, Faculty of Arts, 75 University Ave W, Waterloo, ON N2L 3C5, Canada Tel: 519-884-1970 (ext 3361) E-mail: staebleraward@ wlu.ca Web Site: wlu.ca/staebleraward, pg 670

Crowley, Louise, Vermont College of Fine Arts, MFA in Writing Program, 36 College St, Montpelier, VT 05602 Tel: 802-828-8840; 802-828-8839 Toll Free Tel: 866-934-VCFA (934-8232) Fax: 802-828-8649 Web Site: www.vcfa.edu, pg 586

Crowley, Michael, Berrett-Koehler Publishers Inc, 1333 Broadway, Suite 1000, Oakland, CA 94612 Tel: 510-817-2277 Fax: 510-817-2278 E-mail: bkpub@bkpub. com Web Site: www.bkconnection.com, pg 32

Crowley, Shelly, City & Regional Magazine Association, 287 Richards Ave, Norwalk, CT 06850 Tel: 203-515-9294 E-mail: admin@citymag.org Web Site: www. citymag.org, pg 531

Crowley, Tia, NPTA Alliance, 330 N Wabash Ave, Suite 2000, Chicago, IL 60611 Tel: 312-321-4092 Toll Free Tel: 800-355-NPTA (355-6782) Fax: 312-673-6736 Web Site: www.gonpta.com, pg 542

Crowther, Duane S, Horizon Publishers & Distributors Inc, 191 N 650 E, Bountiful, UT 84010-3628 Tel: 801-292-7102 E-mail: ldshorizonpublishers1@ gmail.com Web Site: www.ldshorizonpublishers.com, pg 102

Daillak, Jonathan, The Gerald Loeb Awards, Gold Hall, Suite B-305, 110 Westwood Plaza, Los Angeles, CA 90095-1481 *Tel:* 310-825-4478 *Fax:* 310-825-4479 *E-mail:* loeb@anderson.ucla.edu *Web Site:* www. anderson.ucla.edu/gerald-loeb-awards, pg 635

Daily, Peggy, A Westport Wordsmith, 101 Winfield St, Norwalk, CT 06855 *Tel:* 203-939-9484 *E-mail:* pj104daily@aol.com, pg 457

Dallaire, Michel, La Fondation Emile Nelligan, 100, rue Sherbrooke, Suite 202, Montreal, QC H2X 1C3, Canada *Tel:* 514-278-4657 *E-mail:* info@fondation-nelligan.org *Web Site:* www.fondation-nelligan.org, pg 534

Dallaire, Michel, Prix Emile-Nelligan, 100, rue Sherbrooke, Suite 202, Montreal, QC H2X 1C3, Canada *Tel:* 514-278-4657 *Toll Free Tel:* 888-849-8540 *E-mail:* info@fondation-nelligan.org *Web Site:* www.fondation-nelligan.org, pg 659

Dallam, Josie, little bee books, 251 Park Ave S, 12th fl, New York, NY 10010 *Toll Free Tel:* 844-321-0237 *E-mail:* info@littlebeebooks.com *Web Site:* littlebeebooks.com, pg 125

Dallanegra-Sanger, Joy, American Booksellers Association, 333 Westchester Ave, Suite S202, White Plains, NY 10604 *Tel:* 914-406-7500 *Toll Free Tel:* 800-637-0037 *Fax:* 914-417-4013 *E-mail:* info@bookweb.org *Web Site:* www.bookweb.org, pg 522

Dalpe, Marianne, La Courte Echelle, 4388, rue Saint-Denis, Suite 315, Montreal, QC H2J 2L1, Canada *Tel:* 514-312-6950 *E-mail:* info@courteechelle.com *Web Site:* courteechelle.groupecourteechelle.com, pg 420

Dalton, Emily, Northwestern University Press, 629 Noyes St, Evanston, IL 60208-4210 *Tel:* 847-491-2046 *Toll Free Tel:* 800-621-2736 (orders only) *Fax:* 847-491-8150 *E-mail:* nupress@northwestern.edu *Web Site:* www.nupress.northwestern.edu, pg 152

Dalton, Heather, Living Language, c/o Penguin Random House, 1745 Broadway, New York, NY 10019 *Tel:* 212-782-9000 *Toll Free Tel:* 800-733-3000 (orders) *E-mail:* support@livinglanguage.com *Web Site:* www.livinglanguage.com, pg 126

Dalton, Heather, Penguin Random House Audio Publishing, 1745 Broadway, New York, NY 10019 *E-mail:* audio@penguinrandomhouse.com *Web Site:* www.penguinrandomhouseaudio.com, pg 164

Daluga, Emily, Harry N Abrams Inc, 195 Broadway, 9th fl, New York, NY 10007 *Tel:* 212-206-7715 *Toll Free Tel:* 800-345-1359 *Fax:* 212-519-1210 *E-mail:* abrams@abramsbooks.com *Web Site:* www.abramsbooks.com, pg 3

Daly, Emma, Human Rights Watch, 350 Fifth Ave, 34th fl, New York, NY 10118-3299 *Tel:* 212-290-4700 *Fax:* 212-736-1300 *E-mail:* hrwpress@hrw.org *Web Site:* www.hrw.org, pg 105

Daly, John, WriteLife Publishing, 960 Oaktree Blvd, Christianburg, VA 24073 *E-mail:* writelife@boutiqueofqualitybooks.com *Web Site:* www.writelife.com; www.facebook.com/writelife, pg 246

Daly, Laura, Adams Media, 57 Littlefield St, Avon, MA 02322 *Tel:* 508-427-7100 *Web Site:* www.simonandschuster.com, pg 4

Daly, Patrick, Banner of Truth, 63 E Louther St, Carlisle, PA 17013 *Tel:* 717-249-5747 *Toll Free Tel:* 800-263-8085 (orders) *Fax:* 717-249-0604 *E-mail:* info@banneroftruth.org *Web Site:* www.banneroftruth.org, pg 27

Daly, Peter H, Naval Institute Press, 291 Wood Rd, Annapolis, MD 21402-5034 *Tel:* 410-268-6110 *Toll Free Tel:* 800-233-8764 *Fax:* 410-295-1084; 410-571-1703 (cust serv) *E-mail:* webmaster@navalinstitute.org; customer@navalinstitute.org (cust serv) *Web Site:* www.nip.org; www.usni.org, pg 147

Daly, Trish, Portfolio, 375 Hudson St, New York, NY 10014 *Web Site:* www.penguin.com/meet/publishers/portfolio, pg 172

Damascene, Abbott, Saint Herman Press, 4430 Mushroom Lane, Platina, CA 96076 *Tel:* 530-352-4430 *Fax:* 530-352-4432 *E-mail:* stherman@stherman.com *Web Site:* www.sainthermanmonastery.com, pg 190

Damkoehler, Katrina, Random House Children's Books, 1745 Broadway, 10th fl, New York, NY 10019 *Tel:* 212-782-9000 *Web Site:* www.randomhousekids.com, pg 180

Damle, Vaishali, IEEE Press, 445 Hoes Lane, Piscataway, NJ 08854 *Tel:* 732-981-0060 *Fax:* 732-867-9946 *E-mail:* pressbooks@ieee.org (proposals & info) *Web Site:* www.ieee.org/press, pg 106

Damp, Dennis V, Bookhaven Press LLC, 302 Scenic Ct, Moon Township, PA 15108 *Tel:* 412-494-6926 *E-mail:* info@bookhavenpress.com; orders@bookhavenpress.com *Web Site:* bookhavenpress.com, pg 38

Danaczko, Melissa, Stuart Krichevsky Literary Agency Inc, 6 E 39 St, Suite 500, New York, NY 10016 *Tel:* 212-725-5288 *Fax:* 212-725-5275 *E-mail:* query@skagency.com *Web Site:* skagency.com, pg 492

Dancy, David, American Public Works Association (APWA), 1200 Main St, Suite 1400, Kansas City, MO 64105-2100 *Tel:* 816-472-6100 *Toll Free Tel:* 800-848-APWA (848-2792) *Fax:* 816-472-1610 *Web Site:* www.apwa.net, pg 13

Danek, Annette, Penguin Random House LLC, 1745 Broadway, New York, NY 10019 *Tel:* 212-782-9000 *Toll Free Tel:* 800-726-0600 *Web Site:* www.penguinrandomhouse.com, pg 164

Danforth, Randi, Cotsen Institute of Archaeology Press, 308 Charles E Young Dr N, Fowler A163, Box 951510, Los Angeles, CA 90095 *Tel:* 310-206-9384 *Fax:* 310-206-4723 *E-mail:* cioapress@ioa.ucla.edu *Web Site:* www.ioa.ucla.edu, pg 57

Danforth, Scott, University of Tennessee Press, 110 Conference Center Bldg, 600 Henley St, Knoxville, TN 37996-4108 *Tel:* 865-974-3321 *Toll Free Tel:* 800-621-2736 (orders) *Fax:* 865-974-3724 *Toll Free Fax:* 800-621-8476 (orders) *E-mail:* custserv@utpress.org *Web Site:* www.utpress.org, pg 231

Dang, Mei, DC Canada Education Publishing (DCCED), 180 Metcalfe St, Suite 204, Ottawa, ON K2P 1P5, Canada *Tel:* 613-565-8885 *Toll Free Tel:* 888-565-0262 *Fax:* 613-565-8881 *E-mail:* info@dc-canada.ca *Web Site:* www.dc-canada.ca, pg 421

Daniel, John, John Daniel & Co, PO Box 2790, McKinleyville, CA 95519-2790 *Tel:* 707-839-3495 *Toll Free Tel:* 800-662-8351 *E-mail:* dandd@danielpublishing.com *Web Site:* www.danielpublishing.com, pg 62

Daniel, John M, John M Daniel Literary Services, PO Box 2790, McKinleyville, CA 95519 *Tel:* 707-839-3495 *E-mail:* jmd@danielpublishing.com *Web Site:* www.danielpublishing.com/litserv.htm, pg 462

Daniel, Martha, Juvenile Literary Awards/Young People's Literature Awards, 506 Rose Ave, Des Plaines, IL 60016 *Tel:* 847-827-8339 *Web Site:* www.fawchicago.org, pg 629

Daniel, Susan, John Daniel & Co, PO Box 2790, McKinleyville, CA 95519-2790 *Tel:* 707-839-3495 *Toll Free Tel:* 800-662-8351 *E-mail:* dandd@danielpublishing.com *Web Site:* www.danielpublishing.com, pg 62

Daniel, Tina, Human Kinetics Inc, 1607 N Market St, Champaign, IL 61820 *Tel:* 217-351-5076 *Toll Free Tel:* 800-747-4457 *Fax:* 217-351-1549 (orders/cust serv) *E-mail:* info@hkusa.com *Web Site:* www.humankinetics.com, pg 105

Danieley, Corrie, YES New Play Festival, 205 FA Theatre Dept, Nunn Dr, Highland Heights, KY 41099-1007 *Tel:* 859-572-6362 *Fax:* 859-572-6057, pg 681

Daniels, Diana, Mason Crest Publishers, 450 Parkway Dr, Suite D, Broomall, PA 19008 *Tel:* 610-543-6200 *Toll Free Tel:* 866-MCP-BOOK (627-2665) *Fax:* 610-543-3878 *Web Site:* www.masoncrest.com, pg 133

Dann, Jordan, Teachers & Writers Collaborative, 540 Preston St, Booklyn, NY 11215 *Tel:* 212-691-6590 *Fax:* 212-675-0171 *E-mail:* info@twc.org *Web Site:* www.twc.org, pg 547

Dannis, Joe, DawnSignPress, 6130 Nancy Ridge Dr, San Diego, CA 92121-3223 *Tel:* 858-625-0600 *Toll Free Tel:* 800-549-5350 *Fax:* 858-625-2336 *E-mail:* contactus@dawnsign.com *Web Site:* www.dawnsign.com, pg 63

Dano, Yvette, Penguin Group USA, A Penguin Random House Company, 375 Hudson St, New York, NY 10014 *Tel:* 212-366-2000 *Toll Free Tel:* 800-847-5515 (inside sales); 800-631-8571 (cust serv) *Fax:* 212-366-2666; 607-775-4829 (inside sales) *E-mail:* online@us.penguingroup.com *Web Site:* www.penguin.com, pg 163

Danzinger, Sheldon, Russell Sage Foundation, 112 E 64 St, New York, NY 10065 *Tel:* 212-750-6000 *Toll Free Tel:* 800-524-6401 *Fax:* 212-371-4761 *E-mail:* info@rsage.org *Web Site:* www.russellsage.org, pg 188

Darby, George, University of New Orleans Press, 2000 Lakeshore Dr, New Orleans, LA 70148 *Tel:* 504-280-7457 *E-mail:* unopress@uno.edu *Web Site:* www.uno.edu/unopress, pg 229

Dardick, Simon, Vehicule Press, PO Box 42094, CP Roy, Montreal, QC H2W-2T3, Canada *Tel:* 514-844-6073 *E-mail:* vp@vehiculepress.com; admin@vehiculepress.com *Web Site:* www.vehiculepress.com, pg 445

Darga, Jon Michael, Aevitas Creative Management, 19 W 21 St, Suite 501, New York, NY 10010 *Tel:* 212-765-6900 *Web Site:* aevitascreative.com, pg 474

Darhansoff, Liz, Darhansoff & Verrill, 133 W 72 St, Rm 304, New York, NY 10023 *Tel:* 917-305-1300 *E-mail:* permissions@dvagency.com *Web Site:* www.dvagency.com, pg 480

Dark, Larry, The Story Prize, 41 Watchung Plaza, No 384, Montclair, NJ 07042 *Tel:* 973-932-0324 *E-mail:* info@thestoryprize.org *Web Site:* www.thestoryprize.org, pg 671

Dark, Larry, The Story Prize Spotlight Award, 41 Watchung Plaza, No 384, Montclair, NJ 07042 *Tel:* 973-932-0324 *E-mail:* info@thestoryprize.org *Web Site:* www.thestoryprize.org, pg 671

Darling, Benjamin, Laughing Elephant Books, 3645 Interlake N, Seattle, WA 98103 *Tel:* 206-447-9229 *Toll Free Tel:* 800-354-0400 *Fax:* 206-447-9189 *E-mail:* support@laughingelephant.com *Web Site:* www.laughingelephant.com, pg 120

Darling, Karen Merikangas, University of Chicago Press, 1427 E 60 St, Chicago, IL 60637-2954 *Tel:* 773-702-7700; 773-702-7600 *Toll Free Tel:* 800-621-2736 (orders) *Fax:* 773-702-9756; 773-660-2235 (orders); 773-702-2708 *E-mail:* custserv@press.uchicago.edu; marketing@press.uchicago.edu *Web Site:* www.press.uchicago.edu, pg 226

Darling, Kristina Marie, Dorset Prize, 60 Roberts Dr, Suite 308, North Adams, MA 01247 *Tel:* 413-664-9611 *Fax:* 413-664-9711 *E-mail:* info@tupelopress.org *Web Site:* www.tupelopress.org, pg 611

Darling, Kristina Marie, Tupelo Press Berkshire Prize for a First or Second Book of Poetry, 60 Roberts Dr, Suite 308, North Adams, MA 01247 *Tel:* 413-664-9611 *Fax:* 413-664-9711 *E-mail:* info@tupelopress.org *Web Site:* www.tupelopress.org, pg 674

Darling, Kristina Marie, Tupelo Press Inc, 60 Roberts Dr, Suite 308, North Adams, MA 01247 *Tel:* 413-664-9611 *Fax:* 413-664-9711 *E-mail:* info@tupelopress.org *Web Site:* www.tupelopress.org, pg 222

Darling, Kristina Marie, Tupelo Press Snowbound Series Chapbook Award, 60 Roberts Dr, Suite 308, North Adams, MA 01247 *Tel:* 413-664-9611 *Fax:* 413-664-9711 *E-mail:* info@tupelopress.org *Web Site:* www.tupelopress.org, pg 674

Darlington, Gary, Springer Publishing Co, 11 W 42 St, 15th fl, New York, NY 10036-8002 *Tel:* 212-431-4370 *Toll Free Tel:* 877-687-7476 *E-mail:* marketing@springerpub.com; cs@springerpub.com (orders); textbook@springerpub.com; specialsales@springerpub.com *Web Site:* www.springerpub.com, pg 206

Darnall, Kerry, Washington State University Press, Cooper Publications Bldg, 2300 Grimes Way, Pullman, WA 99164-5910 *Tel:* 509-335-7880 *Toll Free Tel:* 800-354-7360 (orders) *E-mail:* wsupress@wsu.edu *Web Site:* wsupress.wsu.edu, pg 237

Darnton, John, The George Polk Awards, The Brooklyn Campus, One University Plaza, Brooklyn, NY 11201-5372 *Tel:* 718-488-1009 *Web Site:* www.liu.edu/polk, pg 657

Darr, Carolyn, GP Putnam's Sons (Hardcover), 375 Hudson St, New York, NY 10014 *Tel:* 212-366-2000 *Fax:* 212-366-2643 *E-mail:* online@penguinputnam. com *Web Site:* www.penguin.com/publishers/ gpputnamssons, pg 178

Darr, Laurren, Dog Writers' Association of America Inc (DWAA), PO Box 787, Hughesville, MD 20637 *E-mail:* info@dogwriters.org *Web Site:* dogwriters.org, pg 532

Darr, Laurren, Dog Writers' Association of America Inc (DWAA) Annual Writing Competition, PO Box 787, Hughesville, MD 20637 *E-mail:* info@dogwriters.org *Web Site:* dogwriters.org, pg 610

Daswani, Deepak, Simon & Schuster, Inc, 1230 Avenue of the Americas, New York, NY 10020 *Tel:* 212-698-7000 *Toll Free Tel:* 800-223-2336 (orders) *Fax:* 212-698-7007 *Toll Free Fax:* 800-943-9831 (orders) *E-mail:* firstname.lastname@simonandschuster.com; purchaseorders@simonandschuster.com (orders) *Web Site:* www.simonandschuster.com, pg 199

Datri, James Edmund, American Society of Media Photographers Inc, PO Box 31207, Bethesda, MD 20804 *Toll Free Tel:* 877-771-2767 *Fax:* 231-946-6180 *E-mail:* asmp@vpassociations.com *Web Site:* asmp. org, pg 524

Dattorre, Michael, Ash Tree Publishing, PO Box 64, Woodstock, NY 12498 *Tel:* 845-246-8081 *Fax:* 845-246-8081 *Web Site:* www.ashtreepublishing.com, pg 22

Datz, Arielle, Dunow, Carlson & Lerner Literary Agency Inc, 27 W 20 St, Suite 1107, New York, NY 10011 *Tel:* 212-645-7606 *E-mail:* mail@dclagency.com *Web Site:* www.dclagency.com, pg 482

Daugherty, Peter, Princeton University Press, 41 William St, Princeton, NJ 08540-5237 *Tel:* 609-258-4900 *Fax:* 609-258-6305 *Web Site:* press.princeton.edu, pg 175

Daulton, Sue, Penguin Random House Audio Publishing, 1745 Broadway, New York, NY 10019 *E-mail:* audio@penguinrandomhouse.com *Web Site:* www.penguinrandomhouseaudio.com, pg 164

Daum, Rachael, American Literary Translators Association (ALTA), University of Arizona, Esquire Bldg, No 205, 1230 N Park Ave, Tucson, AZ 85721 *Tel:* 520-621-1757 *Web Site:* www.literarytranslators. org, pg 523

Daum, Rachael, National Translation Award, University of Arizona, Esquire Bldg, No 205, 1230 N Park Ave, Tucson, AZ 85721 *Tel:* 520-621-1757 *Web Site:* www. literarytranslators.org/awards/national-translation-award, pg 646

Daum, Rachael, Lucien Stryk Asian Translation Prize, University of Arizona, Esquire Bldg, No 205, 1230 N Park Ave, Tucson, AZ 85721 *Tel:* 520-621-1757 *Web Site:* literarytranslators.org/awards/lucien-stryk-prize, pg 671

Davenport, Elaine, Writer's AudioShop, 1316 Overland Stage Rd, Dripping Springs, TX 78620 *Tel:* 512-476-1616 *E-mail:* wrtaudshop@aol.com *Web Site:* www. writersaudio.com, pg 246

Davenport, May, May Davenport Publishers, 26313 Purissima Rd, Los Altos Hills, CA 94022 *Tel:* 650-947-6499 *E-mail:* mdbooks@earthlink.net *Web Site:* www.maydavenportpublishers.org, pg 62

David, Jack, ECW Press, 665 Gerrard St E, Toronto, ON M4M 1Y2, Canada *Tel:* 416-694-3348 *E-mail:* info@ ecwpress.com *Web Site:* www.ecwpress.com, pg 421

David, Kim, McGraw-Hill Higher Education, 1333 Burr Ridge Pkwy, Burr Ridge, IL 60527 *Tel:* 630-789-4000 *Toll Free Tel:* 800-338-3987 (cust serv) *Fax:* 614-755-5645 (cust serv) *Web Site:* www.mhhe.com, pg 135

David, Kim, McGraw-Hill Humanities, Social Sciences, Languages, 2 Penn Plaza, 21st fl, New York, NY 10121 *Tel:* 212-904-2000 *Toll Free Tel:* 800-338-3987 (cust serv) *Fax:* 614-755-5645 (cust serv) *Web Site:* www.mhhe.com, pg 136

David, Kim, McGraw-Hill/Irwin, 1333 Burr Ridge Pkwy, Burr Ridge, IL 60527 *Tel:* 630-789-4000 *Toll Free Tel:* 800-338-3987 (cust serv) *Fax:* 630-789-6942; 614-755-5645 (cust serv) *Web Site:* www.mhhe.com, pg 136

David, Kim, McGraw-Hill Science, Engineering, Mathematics, 501 Bell St, Dubuque, IA 52001 *Tel:* 563-584-6000 *Toll Free Tel:* 800-338-3987 (cust serv) *Fax:* 614-755-5645 (cust serv) *Web Site:* www. mhhe.com, pg 136

Davidow, Sally, The Heywood Broun Award, 501 Third St NW, 6th fl, Washington, DC 20001-2797 *Tel:* 202-434-7177; 202-434-7162 (The Guild Reporter) *Fax:* 202-434-1472 *Web Site:* www.newsguild.org, pg 601

Davidow, Sally, The NewsGuild - CWA, 501 Third St NW, 6th fl, Washington, DC 20001-2797 *Tel:* 202-434-7177; 202-434-7162 (The Guild Reporter) *Fax:* 202-434-1472 *E-mail:* guild@cwa-union.org *Web Site:* www.newsguild.org, pg 541

Davidson, Andrew J, University of Missouri Press, 113 Heinkel Bldg, 201 S Seventh St, Columbia, MO 65211 *Tel:* 573-882-7641; 573-882-3000 (publicity & sales enquiries) *Toll Free Tel:* 800-621-2736 (orders) *Fax:* 573-884-4498 *Toll Free Fax:* 800-621-8476 (orders) *E-mail:* upress@missouri.edu; umpmarketing@missouri.edu (publicity & sales enquiries) *Web Site:* upress.missouri.edu, pg 228

Davidson, Gary, Hachette Nashville, 6100 Tower Circle, Room 210, Franklin, TN 37067 *Tel:* 615-221-0996 *Fax:* 615-221-0962 *Web Site:* www.hachettebookgroup. com, pg 91

Davidson, Scott, McGraw-Hill Career Education, 1333 Burr Ridge Pkwy, Burr Ridge, IL 60527 *Tel:* 630-789-4000 *Toll Free Tel:* 800-338-3987 (cust serv) *Fax:* 630-789-5523; 614-755-5645 (cust serv) *Web Site:* www.mhhe.com, pg 135

Davies, Mr Glyn, Rothstein Associates Inc, 4 Arapaho Rd, Brookfield, CT 06804-3104 *Tel:* 203-740-7400 *Toll Free Tel:* 888-768-4783 *Fax:* 203-740-7401 *E-mail:* info@rothstein.com *Web Site:* www.rothstein. com; www.rothsteinpublishing.com, pg 187

Davies, Jeremy, Farrar, Straus & Giroux, LLC, 175 Varick St, 9th fl, New York, NY 10014 *Tel:* 212-741-6900 *E-mail:* fsg.publicity@fsgbooks.com *Web Site:* us.macmillan.com/fsg.aspx, pg 76

Davies, Jon, University of Georgia Press, Main Library, 3rd fl, 320 S Jackson St, Athens, GA 30602 *Fax:* 706-542-2558; 706-542-6770 *Web Site:* www.ugapress.org, pg 227

Davies, Michael, Davies Publishing Inc, 32 S Raymond Ave, Suites 4 & 5, Pasadena, CA 91105-1961 *Tel:* 626-792-3046 *Toll Free Tel:* 877-792-0005 *Fax:* 626-792-5308 *E-mail:* info@daviespublishing. com *Web Site:* daviespublishing.com, pg 62

Daving, Kyle, William S Hein & Co Inc, 2350 N Forest Rd, Getzville, NY 14068 *Tel:* 716-882-2600 *Toll Free Tel:* 800-828-7571 *Fax:* 716-883-8100 *E-mail:* mail@ wshein.com; marketing@wshein.com *Web Site:* www. wshein.com, pg 97

Davis, Carol Prud'homme, See-More's Workshop Arts & Education Workshops, 325 West End Ave, Suite 12-B, New York, NY 10023 *Tel:* 212-724-0677 *Fax:* 212-724-0767 *E-mail:* sbt@shadowboxtheatre.org *Web Site:* www.shadowboxtheatre.org, pg 578

Davis, Cheryl L, The Authors Guild, 31 E 32 St, 7th fl, New York, NY 10016 *Tel:* 212-563-5904 *Fax:* 212-564-8363 *E-mail:* staff@authorsguild.org *Web Site:* www.authorsguild.org, pg 527

Davis, Christine, Institute of Environmental Sciences & Technology - IEST, 1827 Walden Office Sq, Suite 400, Schaumburg, IL 60173 *Tel:* 847-981-0100 *Fax:* 847-981-4130 *E-mail:* information@iest.org *Web Site:* www.iest.org, pg 109

Davis, Dawn, Simon & Schuster, 1230 Avenue of the Americas, New York, NY 10020 *Tel:* 212-698-7000 *Toll Free Tel:* 800-223-2348 (cust serv); 800-223-2336 (orders) *Toll Free Fax:* 800-943-9831 (orders) *Web Site:* www.simonandschuster.com, pg 198

Davis, Deanna, University of Missouri Press, 113 Heinkel Bldg, 201 S Seventh St, Columbia, MO 65211 *Tel:* 573-882-7641; 573-882-3000 (publicity & sales enquiries) *Toll Free Tel:* 800-621-2736 (orders) *Fax:* 573-884-4498 *Toll Free Tel:* 800-621-8476 (orders) *E-mail:* upress@missouri.edu; umpmarketing@missouri.edu (publicity & sales enquiries) *Web Site:* upress.missouri.edu, pg 228

Davis, Dina, Harlequin Enterprises Ltd, 195 Broadway, 24th fl, New York, NY 10007 *Tel:* 212-207-7000 *Toll Free Tel:* 888-432-4879 *E-mail:* customerservice@ harlequin.com *Web Site:* www.harlequin.com, pg 93

Davis, Gary, The Learning Source Ltd, 644 Tenth St, Brooklyn, NY 11215 *E-mail:* info@learningsourceltd. com *Web Site:* www.learningsourceltd.com, pg 466

Davis, J Madison, International Association of Crime Writers Inc, North American Branch, 243 Fifth Ave, Suite 537, New York, NY 10016 *Tel:* 212-243-8966 *Fax:* 815-361-1477 *E-mail:* info@crimewritersna.org *Web Site:* www.crimewritersna.org, pg 535

Davis, James B, Practice Management Information Corp (PMIC), 4727 Wilshire Blvd, Suite 302, Los Angeles, CA 90010 *Tel:* 323-954-0224 *Fax:* 323-954-0253 *E-mail:* customer.service@pmiconline.com *Web Site:* pmiconline.stores.yahoo.net, pg 173

Davis, Janet, Health Administration Press, One N Franklin St, Suite 1700, Chicago, IL 60606-3491 *Tel:* 312-424-2800 *Fax:* 312-424-0014 *E-mail:* hapbooks@ache.org *Web Site:* www.ache. org/hap (orders), pg 96

Davis, John, Central Recovery Press (CRP), 3321 N Buffalo Dr, Suite 275, Las Vegas, NV 89129 *Tel:* 702-868-5830 *Fax:* 702-868-5831 *E-mail:* sales@ centralrecovery.com *Web Site:* centralrecoverypress. com, pg 48

Davis, Julie, Indiana University Press, Herman B Wells Library 350, 1320 E Tenth St, Bloomington, IN 47405-3907 *Tel:* 812-855-8817 *Toll Free Tel:* 800-842-6796 (orders only) *Fax:* 812-855-7931; 812-855-8507 *E-mail:* iupress@indiana.edu; iuporder@indiana.edu (orders) *Web Site:* www.iupress.indiana.edu, pg 108

Davis, Lanie, Alloy Entertainment LLC, 30 Hudson Yards, 22nd fl, New York, NY 10001 *E-mail:* collaborative@alloyentertainment.com, pg 8

Davis, Lisa, University of Tennessee Press, 110 Conference Center Bldg, 600 Henley St, Knoxville, TN 37996-4108 *Tel:* 865-974-3321 *Toll Free Tel:* 800-621-2736 (orders) *Fax:* 865-974-3724 *Toll Free Fax:* 800-621-8476 (orders) *E-mail:* custserv@utpress. org *Web Site:* www.utpress.org, pg 231

Davis, Lisa Fagin, John Nicholas Brown Prize, 17 Dunster St, Suite 202, Cambridge, MA 02138 *Tel:* 617-491-1622 *Fax:* 617-492-3303 *E-mail:* info@ themedievalacademy.org *Web Site:* www. medievalacademy.org, pg 601

Davis, Lisa Fagin, Van Courtlandt Elliott Prize, 17 Dunster St, Suite 202, Cambridge, MA 02138 *Tel:* 617-491-1622 *Fax:* 617-492-3303 *E-mail:* info@ themedievalacademy.org *Web Site:* www. medievalacademy.org, pg 613

Davis, Lisa Fagin, Haskins Medal Award, 17 Dunster St, Suite 202, Cambridge, MA 02138 *Tel:* 617-491-1622 *Fax:* 617-492-3303 *E-mail:* info@ themedievalacademy.org *Web Site:* www. medievalacademy.org, pg 622

Davis, Lizzie, Coffee House Press, 79 13 Ave NE, Suite 110, Minneapolis, MN 55413 *Tel:* 612-338-0125 *Fax:* 612-338-4004 *E-mail:* info@coffeehousepress.org *Web Site:* coffeehousepress.org, pg 54

Davis, Matthew, Society for Human Resource Management (SHRM), 1800 Duke St, Alexandria, VA 22314 *Tel:* 703-548-3440 *Toll Free Tel:* 800-283-7476 (orders) *E-mail:* books@shrm.org *Web Site:* www.shrm.org, pg 202

Davis, Melodie, MennoMedia, 100 S Mason St, Suite B, Harrisonburg, VA 22801 *Toll Free Tel:* 800-245-7894 (orders & cust serv US) *Toll Free Fax:* 877-271-0760 *E-mail:* info@mennomedia.org *Web Site:* www.mennomedia.org, pg 138

Davis, Michele, J J Keller & Associates, Inc, 3003 Breezewood Lane, Neenah, WI 54957 *Tel:* 920-722-2848 *Toll Free Tel:* 877-564-2333 *Toll Free Fax:* 800-727-7516 *E-mail:* contactus@jjkeller.com; customerservice@jjkeller.com *Web Site:* www.jjkeller.com, pg 116

Davis, Naomi, BookEnds Literary Agency, 136 Long Hill Rd, Gillette, NJ 07933 *Web Site:* www.bookendsliterary.com, pg 476

Davis, Patti, The PRS Group Inc, 5800 Heritage Landing Dr, Suite E, East Syracuse, NY 13057-9358 *Tel:* 315-431-0511 *Fax:* 315-431-0200 *E-mail:* custserv@prsgroup.com *Web Site:* www.prsgroup.com, pg 177

Davis, Reiko, DeFiore and Company Literary Management Inc, 47 E 19 St, 3rd fl, New York, NY 10003 *Tel:* 212-925-7744 *Fax:* 212-925-9803 *E-mail:* info@defliterary.com; submissions@defliterary.com *Web Site:* www.defliterary.com, pg 481

Davis, Robert, Tom Doherty Associates, LLC, 120 Broadway, New York, NY 10271 *Tel:* 646-307-5511 *Toll Free Tel:* 800-455-0340 *Web Site:* us.macmillan.com/torforge, pg 66

Davis, Susan M, Sagamore Publishing LLC, 3611 N Staley Rd, Suite B, Champaign, IL 61822 *Tel:* 217-359-5940 *Toll Free Tel:* 800-327-5557 (orders) *Fax:* 217-359-5975 *E-mail:* web@sagamorepub.com *Web Site:* www.sagamorepub.com, pg 189

Davis, Timothy, McLemore Prize, William F Winter Archives & History Bldg, 200 North St, Jackson, MS 39201 *Tel:* 601-576-6850 *Fax:* 601-576-6975 *E-mail:* mhs@mdah.ms.gov *Web Site:* www.mdah.ms.gov, pg 640

Davis, Timothy S Esq, Close Up Publishing, 1330 Braddock Place, Suite 400, Alexandria, VA 22314 *Tel:* 703-706-3300 *Toll Free Tel:* 800-CLOSE-UP (256-7387) *E-mail:* info@closeup.org *Web Site:* www.closeup.org, pg 54

Davis, Tinsley, National Association of Science Writers (NASW), PO Box 7905, Berkeley, CA 94707 *Tel:* 510-647-9500 *Web Site:* www.nasw.org, pg 539

Davis, Tinsley, Science in Society Journalism Awards, PO Box 7905, Berkeley, CA 94707 *Tel:* 510-647-9500 *Web Site:* www.nasw.org, pg 666

Davis, Wendy, The Learning Source Ltd, 644 Tenth St, Brooklyn, NY 11215 *E-mail:* info@learningsourceltd.com *Web Site:* www.learningsourceltd.com, pg 466

Davis-Undiano, Robert Con, Neustadt International Prize for Literature, c/o University of Oklahoma, 630 Parrington Oval, Suite 110, Norman, OK 73019-4033 *Tel:* 405-325-4531 *Web Site:* www.worldliteraturetoday.org; www.worldlit.org, pg 646

Davis-Undiano, Robert Con, NSK Neustadt Prize for Children's Literature, c/o University of Oklahoma, 630 Parrington Oval, Suite 110, Norman, OK 73019-4033 *Tel:* 405-325-4531 *Web Site:* www.worldliteraturetoday.org; www.worldlit.org, pg 649

Davulis, Laura, Johns Hopkins University Press, 2715 N Charles St, Baltimore, MD 21218-4363 *Tel:* 410-516-6900; 410-516-6987 (journal orders outside US & CN) *Toll Free Tel:* 800-537-5487 (book orders & cust serv); 800-548-1784 (journal orders) *Fax:* 410-516-6968; 410-516-3866 (journal orders); 410-516-6998 (orders) *E-mail:* hfscustserv@press.jhu.edu (cust serv); jrnlcirc@press.jhu.edu (journal orders) *Web Site:* www.press.jhu.edu; muse.jhu.edu, pg 114

Davy, Martin, Houghton Mifflin Harcourt, 125 High St, Boston, MA 02110 *Tel:* 617-351-5000 *Toll Free Tel:* 855-969-4642; 800-225-5425 (K-12 educ

materials); 800-323-9540 (assessment materials); 877-219-1537 (SkillsTutor); 888-242-6747 (Innovation in Educ Group); 800-225-3362 (Trade & Ref Div) *Toll Free Fax:* 800-269-5232 *E-mail:* myhmhco@hmhco.com *Web Site:* www.hmhco.com, pg 103

Dawes, John, Piano Press, 1425 Ocean Ave, Suite 5, Del Mar, CA 92014 *Tel:* 619-884-1401 *Fax:* 858-755-1104 *E-mail:* pianopress@pianopress.com *Web Site:* www.pianopress.com, pg 169

Dawes, Kwame, Prairie Schooner Annual Strousse Award, University of Nebraska, 123 Andrews Hall, 625 N 14 St, Lincoln, NE 68508 *Tel:* 402-472-0911 *Fax:* 402-472-9771 *E-mail:* prairieschooner@unl.edu *Web Site:* prairieschooner.unl.edu, pg 657

Dawes, Kwame, Prairie Schooner Bernice Slote Award, University of Nebraska, 123 Andrews Hall, 625 N 14 St, Lincoln, NE 68508 *Tel:* 402-472-0911 *Fax:* 402-472-9771 *E-mail:* prairieschooner@unl.edu *Web Site:* prairieschooner.unl.edu, pg 657

Dawes, Kwame, Prairie Schooner Book Prize Contest in Fiction, University of Nebraska, 123 Andrews Hall, 625 N 14 St, Lincoln, NE 68508 *Tel:* 402-472-0911 *Fax:* 402-472-9771 *E-mail:* psbookprize@unl.edu *Web Site:* prairieschooner.unl.edu, pg 658

Dawes, Kwame, Prairie Schooner Book Prize Contest in Poetry, University of Nebraska, 123 Andrews Hall, 625 N 14 St, Lincoln, NE 68508 *Tel:* 402-472-0911 *Fax:* 402-472-9771 *E-mail:* psbookprize@unl.edu *Web Site:* prairieschooner.unl.edu, pg 658

Dawes, Kwame, Prairie Schooner Edward Stanley Award, University of Nebraska, 123 Andrews Hall, 625 N 14 St, Lincoln, NE 68508 *Tel:* 402-472-0911 *Fax:* 402-472-9771 *E-mail:* prairieschooner@unl.edu *Web Site:* prairieschooner.unl.edu, pg 658

Dawes, Kwame, Prairie Schooner Glenna Luschei Award, University of Nebraska, 123 Andrews Hall, 625 N 14 St, Lincoln, NE 68508 *Tel:* 402-472-0911 *Fax:* 402-472-9771 *E-mail:* prairieschooner@unl.edu *Web Site:* prairieschooner.unl.edu, pg 658

Dawes, Kwame, Prairie Schooner Hugh J Luke Award, University of Nebraska, 123 Andrews Hall, 625 N 14 St, Lincoln, NE 68508 *Tel:* 402-472-0911 *Fax:* 402-472-9771 *E-mail:* prairieschooner@unl.edu *Web Site:* prairieschooner.unl.edu, pg 658

Dawes, Kwame, Prairie Schooner Jane Geske Award, University of Nebraska, 123 Andrews Hall, 625 N 14 St, Lincoln, NE 68508 *Tel:* 402-472-0911 *Fax:* 402-472-9771 *E-mail:* prairieschooner@unl.edu *Web Site:* prairieschooner.unl.edu, pg 658

Dawes, Kwame, Prairie Schooner Lawrence Foundation Award, University of Nebraska, 123 Andrews Hall, 625 N 14 St, Lincoln, NE 68508 *Tel:* 402-472-0911 *Fax:* 402-472-9771 *E-mail:* prairieschooner@unl.edu *Web Site:* prairieschooner.unl.edu, pg 658

Dawes, Kwame, Prairie Schooner Virginia Faulkner Award for Excellence in Writing, University of Nebraska, 123 Andrews Hall, 625 N 14 St, Lincoln, NE 68508 *Tel:* 402-472-0911 *Fax:* 402-472-9771 *E-mail:* prairieschooner@unl.edu *Web Site:* prairieschooner.unl.edu, pg 658

Dawson, Bart, Hachette Nashville, 6100 Tower Circle, Room 210, Franklin, TN 37067 *Tel:* 615-221-0996 *Fax:* 615-221-0962 *Web Site:* www.hachettebookgroup.com, pg 91

Dawson, Brian, Northwest Territories Public Library Services, 75 Woodland Dr, Hay River, NT X0E 1G1, Canada *Tel:* 867-874-6531 *Toll Free Tel:* 866-297-0232 (CN) *Fax:* 867-874-3321 *Web Site:* www.nwtpls.gov.nt.ca, pg 542

Dawson, Havis, Liza Dawson Associates, 121 W 27 St, Suite 1201, New York, NY 10001 *Tel:* 212-465-9071 *Web Site:* www.lizadawsonassociates.com, pg 481

Dawson, Kathy, Penguin Young Readers Group, 345 Hudson St, New York, NY 10014 *Tel:* 212-366-2000; 212-414-3553 *Fax:* 212-414-3340 *Web Site:* www.penguin.com/children, pg 165

Dawson, Liza, Liza Dawson Associates, 121 W 27 St, Suite 1201, New York, NY 10001 *Tel:* 212-465-9071 *Web Site:* www.lizadawsonassociates.com, pg 481

Dawson, Mariel, Farrar, Straus & Giroux Books for Young Readers, 120 Broadway, New York, NY 10271 *Tel:* 212-741-6900 *Toll Free Tel:* 888-330-8477 (orders) *Fax:* 212-633-9385 *Web Site:* us.macmillan.com/mackids; www.mackidsbooks.com, pg 76

Dawson, Mariel, Roaring Brook Press, 120 Broadway, New York, NY 10271 *Tel:* 646-307-5151 *Web Site:* us.macmillan.com/publishers/roaring-brook-press, pg 186

Dawson, Robert, SF Canada, 516 Ninth St E, Saskatoon, SK S7N 0B1, Canada *Web Site:* www.sfcanada.org, pg 546

Day, Alyson, HarperCollins Children's Books, 195 Broadway, New York, NY 10007 *Tel:* 212-207-7000 *Web Site:* www.harpercollins.com/childrens, pg 93

Day, Alyssa, The Vivian, 14615 Benfer Rd, Houston, TX 77069 *Tel:* 832-717-5200 *Fax:* 832-717-5201 *E-mail:* contests@rwa.org *Web Site:* www.rwa.org, pg 675

Day, Emily, Macmillan, 120 Broadway, 22nd fl, New York, NY 10271 *Tel:* 646-307-5151 *E-mail:* press.inquiries@macmillan.com *Web Site:* www.macmillan.com, pg 130

Day, Lawson, Amber Lotus Publishing, PO Box 11329, Portland, OR 97211 *Tel:* 503-284-6400 *Toll Free Tel:* 800-326-2375 (orders only) *Fax:* 503-284-6417 *E-mail:* info@amberlotus.com *Web Site:* www.amberlotus.com, pg 9

Day, Susie, Monthly Review Press, 134 W 29 St, Suite 706, New York, NY 10001 *Tel:* 212-691-2555 *E-mail:* mreview@igc.org *Web Site:* monthlyreview.org, pg 142

de Alteriis, Antoinette, Arcadia Publishing Inc, 420 Wando Park Blvd, Mount Pleasant, SC 29464 *Tel:* 843-853-2070 *Toll Free Tel:* 888-313-2665 (orders only) *Fax:* 843-853-0044 *E-mail:* sales@arcadiapublishing.com *Web Site:* www.arcadiapublishing.com, pg 19

de Alteriis, Antoinette, Pelican Publishing Co, 400 Poydras St, Suite 900, New Orleans, LA 70130 *Tel:* 504-368-1175 *Toll Free Tel:* 800-843-1724 *Fax:* 504-368-1195 *E-mail:* sales@pelicanpub.com (sales); office@pelicanpub.com (permission); promo@pelicanpub.com (publicity) *Web Site:* www.pelicanpub.com, pg 162

De Boer, Rebecca, University of Notre Dame Press, 310 Flanner Hall, Notre Dame, IN 46556 *Tel:* 574-631-6346 *Fax:* 574-631-8148 *E-mail:* undpress@nd.edu *Web Site:* www.undpress.nd.edu, pg 230

de Botton, Gen, American Booksellers Association, 333 Westchester Ave, Suite S202, White Plains, NY 10604 *Tel:* 914-406-7500 *Toll Free Tel:* 800-637-0037 *Fax:* 914-417-4013 *E-mail:* info@bookweb.org *Web Site:* www.bookweb.org, pg 522

de Caires, Brendan, PEN Canada, 401 Richmond St W, Suite 258, Toronto, ON M5V 3A8, Canada *Tel:* 416-703-8448 *E-mail:* queries@pencanada.ca *Web Site:* www.pencanada.ca, pg 543

De Carlo, Janet, Storybook Arts Inc, 414 Poplar Hill Rd, Dover Plains, NY 12522 *Tel:* 845-877-3305 *Web Site:* www.storybookartsinc.com, pg 512

De Guire, Eileen, The American Ceramic Society, 550 Polaris Pkwy, Suite 510, Westerville, OH 43082 *Tel:* 240-646-7054 *Toll Free Tel:* 866-721-3322 *Fax:* 240-396-5637 *E-mail:* customerservice@ceramics.org *Web Site:* ceramics.org, pg 10

de Guzman, Beth, Grand Central Publishing, 1290 Avenue of the Americas, New York, NY 10104 *Tel:* 212-364-1100 *Web Site:* www.hachettebookgroup.com, pg 88

de Guzman, Trisha, Farrar, Straus & Giroux Books for Young Readers, 120 Broadway, New York, NY 10271 *Tel:* 212-741-6900 *Toll Free Tel:* 888-330-8477 (orders) *Fax:* 212-633-9385 *Web Site:* us.macmillan.com/mackids; www.mackidsbooks.com, pg 76

De Jackmo, Nicole, Quirk Books, 215 Church St, Philadelphia, PA 19106 *Tel:* 215-627-3581 *Fax:* 215-627-5220 *E-mail:* general@quirkbooks.com *Web Site:* www.quirkbooks.com, pg 179 de la Campa, Cecelia, Writers House, 21 W 26 St, New York, NY 10010 Tel: 212-685-2400 Web Site: www. writershouse.com, pg 508

de las Heras, Nicole, Random House Children's Books, 1745 Broadway, 10th fl, New York, NY 10019 Tel: 212-782-9000 Web Site: www.randomhousekids. com, pg 180

de Menil, Joy, Harvard University Press, 79 Garden St, Cambridge, MA 02138-1499 Tel: 617-495-2600; 401-531-2800 (intl orders) Toll Free Tel: 800-405-1619 (orders) Fax: 617-495-5898 (gen); 617-496-4677 (edit & rts); 401-531-2801 (intl orders) Toll Free Fax: 800-406-9145 (orders) E-mail: contact_hup@harvard.edu Web Site: www.hup.harvard.edu, pg 95

De Mers, Martin, Algora Publishing, 1732 First Ave, No 20330, New York, NY 10128 Tel: 212-678-0232 Fax: 212-666-3682 E-mail: editors@algora.com Web Site: www.algora.com, pg 7

De Pasture, Madris, New Concepts Publishing, 5265 Humphreys Rd, Lake Park, GA 31636 E-mail: newconcepts@newconceptspublishing.com Web Site: www.newconceptspublishing.com, pg 148

de Pierola, Jose, University of Texas at El Paso, Department of Creative Writing, MFA/Department of Creative Writing, 901 EDUC, 500 W University Ave, El Paso, TX 79968-9991 Tel: 915-747-5713 Fax: 915-747-5523 E-mail: creativewriting@utep.edu Web Site: www.utep.edu/cw, pg 586

De Souza, Kathleen, Mary Ann Liebert Inc, 140 Huguenot St, 3rd fl, New Rochelle, NY 10801-5215 Tel: 914-740-2100 Toll Free Tel: 800-654-3237 Fax: 914-740-2101 E-mail: info@liebertpub.com Web Site: www.liebertonline.com, pg 124

De Spelder, Lynne Ann, Pacific Publishing Services, PO Box 1150, Capitola, CA 95010-1150 Tel: 831-476-8284 Fax: 831-476-8294 E-mail: pacpubs@attglobal. net, pg 468

De Spirito, Sal, Encyclopaedia Britannica Inc, 325 N La Salle St, Suite 200, Chicago, IL 60654 Tel: 312-347-7000 (all other countries) Toll Free Tel: 800-323-1229 (US & CN) Fax: 312-294-2104 E-mail: contact@eb. com Web Site: www.britannica.com, pg 72

de Spoelberch, Jacques, J de S Associates Inc, 9 Shagbark Rd, South Norwalk, CT 06854 Tel: 203-838-7571 Fax: 203-866-2713 Web Site: www. jdesassociates.com, pg 481

De Vivo, Frank, Practising Law Institute, 1177 Avenue of the Americas, New York, NY 10036 Tel: 212-824-5700 Toll Free Tel: 800-260-4PLI (260-4754, cust serv) Toll Free Fax: 800-321-0093 (local) E-mail: info@pli.edu (cust serv) Web Site: www.pli. edu, pg 173

Deal, Barbara, Copywriters' Council of America™ (CCA), CCA Bldg, 7 Putter Lane, Middle Island, NY 11953-1920 Tel: 631-924-3888; 631-775-6075 Fax: 631-924-8555, pg 461, 531

Dean, Bridget PhD, Bolchazy-Carducci Publishers Inc, 1570 Baskin Rd, Mundelein, IL 60060 Tel: 847-526-4344 Fax: 847-526-2867 E-mail: info@bolchazy.com; orders@bolchazy.com Web Site: www.bolchazy.com, pg 37

Dean, Jeff, Harvard University Press, 79 Garden St, Cambridge, MA 02138-1499 Tel: 617-495-2600; 401-531-2800 (intl orders) Toll Free Tel: 800-405-1619 (orders) Fax: 617-495-5898 (gen); 617-496-4677 (edit & rts); 401-531-2801 (intl orders) Toll Free Fax: 800-406-9145 (orders) E-mail: contact_hup@harvard.edu Web Site: www.hup.harvard.edu, pg 95

Dean, Keisha, Annual Design Competition, 27 Union Sq W, Suite 207, New York, NY 10003 Tel: 212-223-3332 Fax: 212-223-5880 E-mail: mail@spd.org Web Site: www.spd.org, pg 609

Dean, Mary Catherine, Abingdon Press, 2222 Rosa L Parks Blvd, Nashville, TN 37228 Tel: 615-749-6000 (academic books) Toll Free Tel: 800-251-3320 (orders) Fax: 615-749-6056 (academic books) Toll Free Fax: 800-836-7802 (orders) E-mail: orders@ abingdonpress.com; permissions@abingdonpress.com Web Site: www.abingdonpress.com, pg 2

Dean, Sheri E, Business Expert Press, 222 E 46 St, Suite 203, New York, NY 10017-2906 Tel: 919-612-6706 E-mail: sales@businessexpertpress.com Web Site: www.businessexpertpress.com, pg 43

Deane, Chuck, Sourcebooks LLC, 1935 Brookdale Rd, Suite 139, Naperville, IL 60563 Tel: 630-961-3900 Toll Free Tel: 800-432-7444 Fax: 630-961-2168 E-mail: info@sourcebooks.com; customersupport@ sourcebooks.com Web Site: www.sourcebooks.com, pg 204

Deans, Meghan, HarperCollins General Books Group, 195 Broadway, New York, NY 10007 Tel: 212-207-7000 Web Site: www.harpercollins.com, pg 93

Dearborn, Rhonda, Springer Publishing Co, 11 W 42 St, 15th fl, New York, NY 10036-8002 Tel: 212-431-4370 Toll Free Tel: 877-687-7476 E-mail: marketing@ springerpub.com; cs@springerpub.com (orders); textbook@springerpub.com; specialsales@springerpub. com Web Site: www.springerpub.com, pg 206

DeBois, Jena, Random House Children's Books, 1745 Broadway, 10th fl, New York, NY 10019 Tel: 212-782-9000 Web Site: www.randomhousekids.com, pg 181

DeCaires, Angela, BookLogix, 1264 Old Alpharetta Rd, Alpharetta, GA 30005 Tel: 470-239-8547 Toll Free Fax: 888-564-7890 E-mail: publishing@booklogix. com Web Site: www.booklogix.com, pg 38

DeChiara, Jennifer, The Jennifer DeChiara Literary Agency, 245 Park Ave, 39th fl, New York, NY 10167 Tel: 212-372-8989 Web Site: www.jdlit.com, pg 481

Decker, Kate Delano-Condax, Resilient Publishing, 406 S Third St, Boise, ID 83702 Tel: 208-258-9544 E-mail: submissions@resilientpublishing. com Web Site: www.resilientpublishing.com; www. facebook.com/ResilientPub, pg 184

Decker, Stacia, Dunow, Carlson & Lerner Literary Agency Inc, 27 W 20 St, Suite 1107, New York, NY 10011 Tel: 212-645-7606 E-mail: mail@dclagency. com Web Site: www.dclagency.com, pg 482

Decter, Jackuelen, The Vendome Press, 244 Fifth Ave, Suite 2043, New York, NY 10001 Tel: 212-737-1857 E-mail: info@vendomepress.com Web Site: www. vendomepress.com, pg 235

Deen, John, Rizzoli International Publications Inc, 300 Park Ave S, 4th fl, New York, NY 10010-5399 Tel: 212-387-3400 Toll Free Tel: 800-522-6657 (orders only) Fax: 212-387-3535 E-mail: publicity@rizzoliusa. com Web Site: www.rizzoliusa.com, pg 185

DeFiore, Brian, DeFiore and Company Literary Management Inc, 47 E 19 St, 3rd fl, New York, NY 10003 Tel: 212-925-7744 Fax: 212-925-9803 E-mail: info@defliterary.com; submissions@ defliterary.com Web Site: www.defliterary.com, pg 481

Degen, John, The Writers' Union of Canada (TWUC), 600-460 Richmond St W, Toronto, ON M5V 1Y1, Canada Tel: 416-703-8982 Fax: 416-504-9090 E-mail: info@writersunion.ca Web Site: www. writersunion.ca, pg 549

DeGenaro, Angelo T, McGraw-Hill Education, 2 Penn Plaza, New York, NY 10121-2298 Tel: 212-904-2000 E-mail: international_cs@mheducation.com; seg_customerservice@mheducation.com (PreK-12); hep_customerservice@mheducation.com (higher education) Web Site: www.mheducation.com, pg 135

DeGennaro, Denise, Random House Children's Books, 1745 Broadway, 10th fl, New York, NY 10019 Tel: 212-782-9000 Web Site: www.randomhousekids. com, pg 180

DeGiglio, Peter, Entangled Publishing LLC, 2614 S Timberline Rd, Suite 105, Fort Collins, CO 80525 Toll Free Tel: 877-677-9451 E-mail: publisher@ entangledpublishing.com Web Site: www. entangledpublishing.com, pg 72

Dehmler, Mari Lynch, Fine Wordworking, PO Box 3041, Monterey, CA 93942-3041 Tel: 831-375-6278 E-mail: info@finewordworking.com Web Site: marilynch.com, pg 463

Deisinger, Robert D, American Technical Publishers Inc, 10100 Orland Pkwy, Suite 200, Orland Park, IL 60467-5756 Toll Free Tel: 800-323-3471 Fax: 708-957-1101 E-mail: service@atplearning.com; order@ atplearning.com Web Site: www.atplearning.com, pg 15

Deist, Jeff, Ludwig von Mises Institute, 518 W Magnolia Ave, Auburn, AL 36832 Tel: 334-321-2100 Fax: 334-321-2119 E-mail: info@mises.org Web Site: www. mises.org, pg 237

Deitch, Lisa, F A Davis Co, 1915 Arch St, Philadelphia, PA 19103 Tel: 215-568-2270; 215-440-3001 Toll Free Tel: 800-523-4049 Fax: 215-568-5065; 215-440-3016 E-mail: info@fadavis.com; orders@fadavis.com Web Site: www.fadavis.com, pg 62

Deitcher, Jessica, Anchor Books, c/o Penguin Random House Inc, 1745 Broadway, New York, NY 10019 Tel: 212-572-2420 E-mail: vintageanchorpublicity@ randomhouse.com Web Site: knopfdoubleday.com/ imprint/anchor, pg 15

Deitcher, Jessica, Vintage Books, c/o Penguin Random House Inc, 1745 Broadway, New York, NY 10019 Tel: 212-572-2420 E-mail: vintageanchorpublicity@ randomhouse.com Web Site: knopfdoubleday.com/ imprint/vintage, pg 236

Deku, Prof Afrikadzata PhD, Continental AfrikaPublishers, 182 Stribling Circle, Spartanburg, SC 29301 E-mail: afrikalion@ aol.com; profafrikadzatadeku@yahoo.com; profafrikadzatadeku@facebook.com Web Site: www. afrikacentricity.com, pg 56

Del Mar, Zoe, Houghton Mifflin Harcourt Trade & Reference Division, 125 High St, Boston, MA 02110 Tel: 617-351-5000 Web Site: www.hmhco.com, pg 104

Del Priore, Lucy, Roaring Brook Press, 120 Broadway, New York, NY 10271 Tel: 646-307-5151 Web Site: us. macmillan.com/publishers/roaring-brook-press, pg 186

Del Valle, Daniel, Farrar, Straus & Giroux, LLC, 175 Varick St, 9th fl, New York, NY 10014 Tel: 212-741-6900 E-mail: fsg.publicity@fsgbooks.com Web Site: us.macmillan.com/fsg.aspx, pg 76

Delaney, Ian, Chronicle Books, 680 Second St, San Francisco, CA 94107 Tel: 415-537-4200 Toll Free Tel: 800-759-0190 (cust serv) Fax: 415-537-4460 Toll Free Fax: 800-858-7787 (orders); 800-286-9471 (cust serv) E-mail: frontdesk@chroniclebooks.com Web Site: www.chroniclebooks.com, pg 52

Delaney, Jacqueline, Princeton University Press, 41 William St, Princeton, NJ 08540-5237 Tel: 609-258-4900 Fax: 609-258-6305 Web Site: press.princeton. edu, pg 175

Delaney, Kelly, Random House Children's Books, 1745 Broadway, 10th fl, New York, NY 10019 Tel: 212-782-9000 Web Site: www.randomhousekids.com, pg 180

DeLappe, Kathryn, Firefall Editions, 4905 Tunlaw St, Alexandria, VA 22312 Tel: 510-549-2461 E-mail: literary@att.net Web Site: www.firefallmedia. com, pg 78

Delbourgo, Joelle, Joelle Delbourgo Associates Inc, 101 Park St, Montclair, NJ 07042 Tel: 973-773-0836 (call only during standard business hours) Web Site: www. delbourgo.com, pg 481

Delman, Scott, Association for Computing Machinery, 2 Penn Plaza, Suite 701, New York, NY 10121-0701 Tel: 212-869-7440 Toll Free Tel: 800-342-6626 Fax: 212-944-1318 (memb servs) E-mail: acmhelp@ acm.org Web Site: www.acm.org, pg 23

Delman, Stephanie, Sanford J Greenburger Associates Inc, 55 Fifth Ave, New York, NY 10003 Tel: 212-206-5600 Fax: 212-463-8718 Web Site: greenburger.com; www.sjga.com, pg 487

Delorme, Alain, Les Editions Goelette Inc, 1350 Marie-Victorin, St-Bruno-de-Montarville, Quebec, QC J3V 6B9, Canada Tel: 450-653-1337 Toll Free Tel: 800-463-4961 Fax: 450-653-9924 E-mail: info@ boutiquegoelette.com Web Site: www.boutiquegoelette. com, pg 424

DeLozier, Sara, Penguin Books, 375 Hudson St, New York, NY 10014 *Tel:* 212-366-2000 *E-mail:* penguinpublicity@us.penguingroup.com *Web Site:* www.penguinclassics.com; www.penguin. com, pg 163

DeLozier, Sara, Penguin Group USA, A Penguin Random House Company, 375 Hudson St, New York, NY 10014 *Tel:* 212-366-2000 *Toll Free Tel:* 800-847-5515 (inside sales); 800-631-8571 (cust serv) *Fax:* 212-366-2666; 607-775-4829 (inside sales) *E-mail:* online@us.penguingroup.com *Web Site:* www. penguin.com, pg 163

DeLozier, Sara, Viking, 375 Hudson St, New York, NY 10014 *Tel:* 212-366-2000 *Fax:* 212-243-6002 *Web Site:* www.penguin.com/publishers/vikingbooks, pg 236

DeLuca, David, Bess Press, 3565 Harding Ave, Honolulu, HI 96816 *Tel:* 808-734-7159 *Fax:* 808-732-3627 *E-mail:* customerservice@besspress.com *Web Site:* www.besspress.com, pg 32

Deluca, Michael J, Small Beer Press, 150 Pleasant St, No 306, Easthampton, MA 01027 *Tel:* 413-203-1636 *Fax:* 413-203-1636 *E-mail:* info@smallbeerpress.com *Web Site:* smallbeerpress.com, pg 201

DeLucci, Theresa, Tom Doherty Associates, LLC, 120 Broadway, New York, NY 10271 *Tel:* 646-307-5511 *Toll Free Tel:* 800-455-0340 *Web Site:* us.macmillan. com/torforge, pg 66

DeLuise, Janelle, Little, Brown Books for Young Readers, 1290 Avenue of the Americas, New York, NY 10104 *Tel:* 212-364-1100 *Toll Free Tel:* 800-759-0190 (cust serv) *Web Site:* www.hachettebookgroup. com, pg 126

Dema, Leslie, Broadview Press, 280 Perry St, Unit 5, Peterborough, ON K9J 2J4, Canada *Tel:* 705-743-8990 *Fax:* 705-743-8353 *E-mail:* customerservice@ broadviewpress.com *Web Site:* www.broadviewpress. com, pg 417

DeMaiolo, James, Tachyon Publications LLC, 1459 18 St, No 139, San Francisco, CA 94107 *Tel:* 415-285-5615 *E-mail:* tachyon@tachyonpublications.com *Web Site:* www.tachyonpublications.com, pg 212

Demallie, Katie, The French-American Foundation & Florence Gould Foundation Annual Translation Prize, 28 W 44 St, Suite 1420, New York, NY 10036 *Tel:* 212-829-8800 *Fax:* 212-829-8810 *Web Site:* www. frenchamerican.org, pg 617

DeMarco, Karah, Water Environment Federation, 601 Wythe St, Alexandria, VA 22314-1994 *Tel:* 703-684-2400 *Toll Free Tel:* 800-666-0206 (cust serv) *Fax:* 703-684-2492 *E-mail:* inquiry@wef.org *Web Site:* www.wef.org, pg 237

Demary, Mensah, Counterpoint Press LLC, 2560 Ninth St, Suite 318, Berkeley, CA 94710 *Tel:* 510-704-0230 *Fax:* 510-704-0268 *E-mail:* info@counterpointpress. com *Web Site:* counterpointpress.com; softskull.com, pg 58

DeMier, Chrissy, Morton Publishing Co, 925 W Kenyon Ave, Unit 12, Englewood, CO 80110 *Tel:* 303-761-4805 *Fax:* 303-762-9923 *E-mail:* contact@morton-pub.com; returns@morton-pub.com *Web Site:* morton-pub.com, pg 143

Demkiewicz, Joanna R, Milkweed Editions, 1011 Washington Ave S, Suite 300, Minneapolis, MN 55415-1246 *Tel:* 612-332-3192 *Toll Free Tel:* 800-520-6455 *Fax:* 612-215-2550 *Web Site:* milkweed.org, pg 140

Demkiewicz, Joanna R, Max Ritvo Poetry Prize, 1011 Washington Ave S, Suite 300, Minneapolis, MN 55415-1246 *Tel:* 612-332-3192 *Toll Free Tel:* 800-520-6455 *Web Site:* milkweed.org/max-ritvo-poetry-prize, pg 662

DeMonico, Michael, Sophia Institute Press®, 18 Celina Ave, Unit 1, Nashua, NH 03063 *Tel:* 603-641-9344 *Toll Free Tel:* 800-888-9344 *Fax:* 603-641-8108 *Toll Free Fax:* 888-288-2259 *E-mail:* orders@ sophiainstitute.com *Web Site:* www.sophiainstitute. com, pg 203

Dempsey, Luke, HarperCollins General Books Group, 195 Broadway, New York, NY 10007 *Tel:* 212-207-7000 *Web Site:* www.harpercollins.com, pg 93

Dempsey, Nora, Quincannon Publishing Group, PO Box 8100, Glen Ridge, NJ 07028-8100 *Tel:* 973-380-9942 *E-mail:* editors@quincannongroup.com (query first via e-mail) *Web Site:* www.quincannongroup.com, pg 179

DeMuzio, Stephanie, Jessica Kingsley Publishers Inc, 400 Market St, Suite 400, Philadelphia, PA 19106 *Tel:* 215-922-1161 *Toll Free Tel:* 866-416-1078 (cust serv) *Fax:* 215-922-1474 *E-mail:* hello.usa@jkp.com *Web Site:* www.jkp.com, pg 117

DeNardo, Melanie, Random House Publishing Group, 1745 Broadway, New York, NY 10019 *Toll Free Tel:* 800-200-3552 *Web Site:* www.randomhousebooks. com, pg 181

Denato, Sr Maria Grace, Pauline Books & Media, 50 Saint Paul's Ave, Boston, MA 02130 *Tel:* 617-522-8911 *Toll Free Tel:* 800-876-4463 (orders); 800-836-9723 (cust serv) *Fax:* 617-541-9805 *E-mail:* editorial@paulinemedia.com (ms submissions); orderentry@pauline.org (cust serv) *Web Site:* www.pauline.org/pbmpublishing, pg 161

Denehy, Debby, Petroleum Extension Service (PETEX), JJ Pickle Research Campus, 10100 Burnet Rd, Bldg 2, Austin, TX 78758-4445 *Tel:* 512-471-5940 *Toll Free Tel:* 800-687-4132 *Fax:* 512-471-9410 *Toll Free Fax:* 800-687-7839 *E-mail:* info@petex.utexas.edu *Web Site:* cee.utexas.edu/ce/petex, pg 168

Denekamp, Hope, Kneerim & Williams Agency, 90 Canal St, Boston, MA 02114 *Tel:* 617-303-1650 *Web Site:* www.kwlit.com, pg 491

Dengler, Eileen, Book of the Year Awards, 2667 Hyacinth St, Westbury, NY 11590 *Tel:* 516-333-0681 *Fax:* 516-333-0689 *E-mail:* naibabooksellers@gmail. com *Web Site:* www.naiba.com/page/BooksoftheYear, pg 600

Dengler, Eileen, Carla Cohen Free Speech Award, 2667 Hyacinth St, Westbury, NY 11590 *Tel:* 516-333-0681 *Fax:* 516-333-0689 *E-mail:* naibabooksellers@ gmail.com *Web Site:* www.naiba.com/page/ cohenfreespeechaward, pg 606

Dengler, Eileen, Legacy Award, 2667 Hyacinth St, Westbury, NY 11590 *Tel:* 516-333-0681 *Fax:* 516-333-0689 *E-mail:* naibabooksellers@gmail.com *Web Site:* www.naiba.com/page/LegacyAward, pg 632

Dengler, Eileen, New Atlantic Independent Booksellers Association (NAIBA), 2667 Hyacinth St, Westbury, NY 11590 *Tel:* 516-333-0681 *Fax:* 516-333-0689 *E-mail:* naibabooksellers@gmail.com *Web Site:* www. naiba.com, pg 541

Denis, Casey, The Penguin Press, 375 Hudson St, New York, NY 10014 *Web Site:* thepenguinpress.com, pg 164

Denman, Madeleine, Penguin Random House Speakers Bureau, A Penguin Random House Company, 1745 Broadway, Mail Drop 13-1, New York, NY 10019 *Tel:* 212-572-2013 *E-mail:* speakers@ penguinrandomhouse.com *Web Site:* www.prhspeakers. com, pg 515

Dennis, Diane, Idyllwild Arts Summer Workshops, 52500 Temecula Dr, Idyllwild, CA 92549-0038 *Tel:* 951-659-2171 *Fax:* 951-659-4552 *E-mail:* summer@idyllwildarts.org *Web Site:* www. idyllwildarts.org/writersweek, pg 575

Dennis, Josh, Crossway, 1300 Crescent St, Wheaton, IL 60187 *Tel:* 630-682-4300 *Toll Free Tel:* 800-635-7993 (orders); 800-543-1659 (cust serv) *Fax:* 630-682-4785 *E-mail:* info@crossway.org *Web Site:* www.crossway. org, pg 60

Dennison, Brittany, New Directions Publishing Corp, 80 Eighth Ave, 19th fl, New York, NY 10011 *Tel:* 212-255-0230 *E-mail:* editorial@ndbooks.com; publicity@ ndbooks.com *Web Site:* ndbooks.com, pg 148

Dennys, Louise, Knopf Canada, 320 Front St W, Suite 1400, Toronto, ON M5V 3B6, Canada *Tel:* 416-364-4449 *Toll Free Tel:* 888-523-9292 *Fax:* 416-598-7764 *Web Site:* www.penguinrandomhouse.ca, pg 431

Dennys, Louise, Penguin Random House Canada, 320 Front St W, Suite 1400, Toronto, ON M5V 3B6, Canada *Tel:* 416-364-4449 *Toll Free Tel:* 888-523-9292 (cust serv) *Fax:* 416-598-7764 *Web Site:* www. penguinrandomhouse.ca, pg 436

Denson, Kelly L, Association of American Publishers (AAP), 455 Massachusetts Ave NW, Suite 700, Washington, DC 20001-2777 *Tel:* 202-347-3375 *Fax:* 202-347-3690 *E-mail:* info@publishers.org *Web Site:* publishers.org, pg 526

Dent-Zobal, Catherine, Susquehanna University, Department of English & Creative Writing, 514 University Ave, Selinsgrove, PA 17870 *Tel:* 570-372-0101, pg 585

Deol, Amar, Atria Books, 1230 Avenue of the Americas, New York, NY 10020 *Tel:* 212-698-7000 *Fax:* 212-698-7007 *Web Site:* www.simonandschuster.com, pg 24

Depken, Kristen, Random House Children's Books, 1745 Broadway, 10th fl, New York, NY 10019 *Tel:* 212-782-9000 *Web Site:* www.randomhousekids.com, pg 180

Deraco, Anthony A, DEStech Publications Inc, 439 N Duke St, Lancaster, PA 17602-4967 *Tel:* 717-290-1660 *Toll Free Tel:* 877-500-4DES (500-4337) *Fax:* 717-509-6100 *E-mail:* info@destechpub.com *Web Site:* www.destechpub.com, pg 64

Derleth, Damon, Arkham House Publishers Inc, PO Box 546, Sauk City, WI 53583 *Tel:* 608-643-4500 *Fax:* 608-643-5043 *E-mail:* sales@arkhamhouse.com *Web Site:* www.arkhamhouse.com, pg 20

DeRobertis-Theye, Nicola, Trident Media Group LLC, 41 Madison Ave, 36th fl, New York, NY 10010 *Tel:* 212-333-1511 *E-mail:* info@tridentmediagroup. com; press@tridentmediagroup.com *Web Site:* www. tridentmediagroup.com, pg 507

Derrick, Ruth, Highland Summer Writers' Conference, PO Box 7014, Radford University, Cook Hall, Radford, VA 24142 *Fax:* 540-831-5951 *Web Site:* www.radford.edu/content/cehd/home/ appalachian-studies.html, pg 575

Derviskadic, Dado, Folio Literary Management, The Film Center Bldg, 630 Ninth Ave, Suite 1101, New York, NY 10036 *Tel:* 212-400-1494 *Fax:* 212-967-0977 *Web Site:* www.foliolit.com, pg 484

Des Jardines, David E, University of Georgia Press, Main Library, 3rd fl, 320 S Jackson St, Athens, GA 30602 *Fax:* 706-542-2558; 706-542-6770 *Web Site:* www.ugapress.org, pg 227

Desai, Amit, DC Comics Inc, 4000 Warner Blvd, Burbank, CA 91522 *Web Site:* www.dccomics.com; www.dcentertainment.com; www.madmag.com, pg 63

Desautels, Jon, Bear & Co Inc, One Park St, Rochester, VT 05767 *Tel:* 802-767-3174 *Toll Free Tel:* 800-932-3277 *Fax:* 802-767-3726 *E-mail:* customerservice@ InnerTraditions.com *Web Site:* InnerTraditions.com, pg 29

Desautels, Jon, Inner Traditions International Ltd, One Park St, Rochester, VT 05767 *Tel:* 802-767-3174 *Toll Free Tel:* 800-246-8648 *Fax:* 802-767-3726 *E-mail:* customerservice@InnerTraditions.com *Web Site:* www.InnerTraditions.com, pg 109

Deschenes, Sophie, Les Editions de l'Hexagone, 4545, rue Frontenac, 3rd fl, Montreal, QC H2H 2R7, Canada *Tel:* 514-849-5259 *Web Site:* www.edhexagone.com, pg 422

Deschenes, Sophie, VLB editeur, 4545, rue Frontenac, 3rd fl, Montreal, QC H2H 2R7, Canada *Tel:* 514-849-5259 *Web Site:* www.edvlb.com, pg 445

DeSilva, Guy, American Public Human Services Association, 1133 19 St NW, Suite 400, Washington, DC 20036 *Tel:* 202-682-0100 *Fax:* 202-289-6555 *E-mail:* memberservice@aphsa.org *Web Site:* www. aphsa.org, pg 523

Desir, Christa, Sourcebooks LLC, 1935 Brookdale Rd, Suite 139, Naperville, IL 60563 *Tel:* 630-961-3900 *Toll Free Tel:* 800-432-7444 *Fax:* 630-961-2168

E-mail: info@sourcebooks.com; customersupport@ sourcebooks.com **Web Site:** www.sourcebooks.com, pg 204

Desjardins, Daniel, Ulysses Travel Guides, 4176, rue Saint-Denis, Montreal, QC H2W 2M5, Canada **Tel:** 514-843-9882 (ext 2232); 514-843-9447 (bookstore) **Toll Free Tel:** 800-748-9171 **Fax:** 514-843-9448 **E-mail:** info@ulysses.ca; st-denis@ulysses.ca **Web Site:** www.ulyssesguides.com, pg 442

Desjardins, Francoise, Art Image Publications, PO Box 160, Derby Line, VT 05830 **Toll Free Tel:** 800-361-2598 **Toll Free Fax:** 800-559-2598 **E-mail:** info@artimagepublications.com; customer. service@artimagepublications.com **Web Site:** www. artimagepublications.com, pg 20

DeSmet, Christine, University of Wisconsin-Madison Continuing Studies, 21 N Park St, 7th fl, Madison, WI 53715 **Tel:** 608-262-3447 **Web Site:** continuingstudies. wisc.edu, pg 586

Desmond, Sean, Grand Central Publishing, 1290 Avenue of the Americas, New York, NY 10104 **Tel:** 212-364-1100 **Web Site:** www.hachettebookgroup.com, pg 88

DeSmyter, DJ, St Martin's Press, LLC, 120 Broadway, New York, NY 10271 **Tel:** 646-307-5151 **Web Site:** us. macmillan.com/smp, pg 190

Despain, Ashley, Chronicle Books, 680 Second St, San Francisco, CA 94107 **Tel:** 415-537-4200 **Toll Free Tel:** 800-759-0190 (cust serv) **Fax:** 415-537-4460 **Toll Free Fax:** 800-858-7787 (orders); 800-286-9471 (cust serv) **E-mail:** frontdesk@chroniclebooks.com **Web Site:** www.chroniclebooks.com, pg 52

Despins, Paul, Savvas Learning Co LLC, 15 E Midland Ave, Suite 502, Paramus, NJ 07652 **Toll Free Tel:** 800-848-9500 **Web Site:** www.savvas.com, pg 193

Desser, Robin, Random House Publishing Group, 1745 Broadway, New York, NY 10019 **Toll Free Tel:** 800-200-3552 **Web Site:** www.randomhousebooks.com, pg 181

Desuta, Heather, Pennwriters Conference, PO Box 685, Dalton, PA 18414 **E-mail:** conferencecoordinator@ pennwriters.org; info@pennwriters.org **Web Site:** pennwriters.org, pg 577

Dettman, Tracey, Fifth House Publishers, 195 Allstate Pkwy, Markham, ON L3R 4T8, Canada **Tel:** 905-477-9700 **Toll Free Tel:** 800-387-9776 **E-mail:** godwit@ fitzhenry.ca; bookinfo@fitzhenry.ca (cust serv) **Web Site:** www.fifthhousepublishers.ca, pg 426

Detweiler, Katelyn, Jill Grinberg Literary Management LLC, 392 Vanderbilt Ave, Brooklyn, NY 11238 **Tel:** 212-620-5883 **E-mail:** info@jillgrinbergliterary. com **Web Site:** www.jillgrinbergliterary.com, pg 487

Devens, Robert, University of Texas Press, 3001 Lake Austin Blvd, 2.200, Austin, TX 78703 **Tel:** 512-471-7233 **Fax:** 512-232-7178 **E-mail:** utpress@uts.cc. utexas.edu; info@utpress.utexas.edu **Web Site:** utpress. utexas.edu, pg 216

Devine, Tracy, Random House Publishing Group, 1745 Broadway, New York, NY 10019 **Toll Free Tel:** 800-200-3552 **Web Site:** www.randomhousebooks.com, pg 181

Devine-Hardy, Heather, American Indian Youth Literature Award, PO Box 41296, San Jose, CA 95160 **E-mail:** ailawebsite@gmail.com **Web Site:** ailanet. org/activities/american-indian-youth-literature-award, pg 592

Devineni, Ram, Rattapallax Press, 532 La Guadia Place, Suite 353, New York, NY 10012 **Web Site:** www. rattapallax.com, pg 182

DeVinney, Karen, University of North Texas Press, Willis Library, Rm 251P, 1506 Highland St, Denton, TX 76201 **Tel:** 940-565-2142 **Fax:** 940-369-8760 **Web Site:** untpress.unt.edu, pg 229

Devlin, Anne G, Max Gartenberg Literary Agency, 912 N Pennsylvania Ave, Yardley, PA 19067 **Tel:** 215-295-9230 **Web Site:** www.maxgartenberg.com, pg 485

Devlin, Iseult, North American Snowsports Journalists Association (NASJA), 49 Plaza Ave, Belchertown, MA 01007 **E-mail:** execsec@nasja.org **Web Site:** nasja.org, pg 542

Devlin, Jeanne, The RoadRunner Press, 124 NW 32 St, Oklahoma City, OK 73118 **Tel:** 405-524-6205 **Fax:** 405-524-6312 **E-mail:** info@theroadrunnerpress. com; orders@theroadrunnerpress.com **Web Site:** www. theroadrunnerpress.com, pg 186

DeVoe, Angelica, Association of University Presses (AUPresses), 1412 Broadway, Suite 2135, New York, NY 10018 **Tel:** 212-989-1010 **Fax:** 212-989-0275 **E-mail:** info@aupresses.org **Web Site:** www.aupresses. org, pg 527

Devoll, Julie, Harvard Business Review Press, 20 Guest St, Suite 700, Brighton, MA 02135 **Tel:** 617-783-7400 **Fax:** 617-783-7489 **E-mail:** custserv@hbsp.harvard.edu **Web Site:** www.harvardbusiness.org, pg 94

deVries, Anna, Picador, 120 Broadway, New York, NY 10271 **Tel:** 646-307-5151 **Fax:** 212-253-9627 **E-mail:** publicity@picadorusa.com **Web Site:** us. macmillan.com/picador, pg 169

DeVries, Colin, Deadline Club, c/o Salmagundi Club, 47 Fifth Ave, New York, NY 10003 **Tel:** 646-481-7584 **Web Site:** www.deadlineclub.org, pg 532

DeVries, Tom, Wm B Eerdmans Publishing Co, 4035 Park East Ct SE, Grand Rapids, MI 49546 **Tel:** 616-459-4591 **Toll Free Tel:** 800-253-7521 **Fax:** 616-459-6540 **E-mail:** customerservice@eerdmans.com; sales@ eerdmans.com **Web Site:** www.eerdmans.com, pg 70

Dew, Dr Jay, Texas A&M University Press, John H Lindsey Bldg, Lewis St, 4354 TAMU, College Station, TX 77843-4354 **Tel:** 979-845-1436 **Toll Free Tel:** 800-826-8911 (orders) **Fax:** 979-847-8752 **Toll Free Fax:** 888-617-2421 (orders) **E-mail:** bookorders@ tamu.edu **Web Site:** www.tamupress.com, pg 215

DeWaard, Vera, PEN Canada, 401 Richmond St W, Suite 258, Toronto, ON M5V 3A8, Canada **Tel:** 416-703-8448 **E-mail:** queries@pencanada.ca **Web Site:** www. pencanada.ca, pg 543

Dewaik, Maria, Women Who Write Inc, PO Box 652, Madison, NJ 07940-0652 **E-mail:** info@ womenwhowrite.org **Web Site:** womenwhowrite.org, pg 549

DeWall, Jan, Search Institute Press®, The Banks Bldg, Suite 125, 615 First Ave NE, Minneapolis, MN 55413 **Tel:** 612-376-8955; 612-692-5520 **Toll Free Tel:** 800-888-7828 **Fax:** 612-692-5553 **E-mail:** si@search-institute.org **Web Site:** www.search-institute.org, pg 196

DeWerd, Andrea, Houghton Mifflin Harcourt Trade & Reference Division, 125 High St, Boston, MA 02110 **Tel:** 617-351-5000 **Web Site:** www.hmhco.com, pg 104

Dewey, Arthur J, Polebridge Press, PO Box 346, Farmington, MN 55024 **Tel:** 651-200-2372 **E-mail:** orders@westarinstitute.org **Web Site:** www. westarinstitute.org, pg 172

Dewey, Colin, The Melville Society, Johns Hopkins University Press, PO Box 19966, Baltimore, MD 21211-0966 **Web Site:** melvillesociety.org, pg 537

Dewey, Nicole, Little, Brown and Company, 1290 Avenue of the Americas, New York, NY 10104 **Tel:** 212-364-1100 **Fax:** 212-364-0952 **E-mail:** firstname.lastname@hbgusa. com **Web Site:** www.littlebrown.com; www. hachettebookgroup.com, pg 126

DeWitt, David, little bee books, 251 Park Ave S, 12th fl, New York, NY 10010 **Toll Free Tel:** 844-321-0237 **E-mail:** info@littlebeebooks.com **Web Site:** littlebeebooks.com, pg 125

Dextor, Roger, Copywriters' Council of America™ (CCA), CCA Bldg, 7 Putter Lane, Middle Island, NY 11953-0102 **Tel:** 631-924-3888; 631-775-6075 **Fax:** 631-924-8555, pg 461, 531

Dextor, Roger, Andrew S Linick PhD, The Copyologist®, Linick Bldg, 7 Putter Lane, Middle Island, NY 11953 **Tel:** 631-924-3888; 631-775-6075 **Fax:** 631-924-8555 **E-mail:** linickgroup@gmail.com **Web Site:** topmarketingadvisor.com, pg 466

Dextre, Natalia, Random House Children's Books, 1745 Broadway, 10th fl, New York, NY 10019 **Tel:** 212-782-9000 **Web Site:** www.randomhousekids.com, pg 181

Deyoe, Cori, 3 Seas Literary Agency, PO Box 444, Sun Prairie, WI 53590 **Tel:** 608-834-9317 **E-mail:** threeseaslit@aol.com **Web Site:** threeseasagency.com, pg 506

DeYoung, Christina, Harvard Education Publishing Group, 8 Story St, 1st fl, Cambridge, MA 02138 **Tel:** 617-495-3432 **Fax:** 617-496-3584 **Web Site:** www. hepg.org, pg 94

Dhar, Uday K, Mondial, 203 W 107 St, Suite 6-C, New York, NY 10025 **Tel:** 646-807-8031 **Fax:** 208-361-2863 **E-mail:** contact@mondialbooks.com **Web Site:** www.mondialbooks.com, pg 142

Di Blasi, Sara, Tom Doherty Associates, LLC, 120 Broadway, New York, NY 10271 **Tel:** 646-307-5511 **Toll Free Tel:** 800-455-0340 **Web Site:** us.macmillan. com/torforge, pg 66

Di Gioia, Tony, George T Bisel Co Inc, 710 S Washington Sq, Philadelphia, PA 19106-3519 **Tel:** 215-922-5760 **Toll Free Tel:** 800-247-3526 **Fax:** 215-922-2235 **E-mail:** gbisel@bisel.com **Web Site:** www.bisel.com, pg 33

Di Martino, Christina, Christina Di Martino Literary Services, 87 Hamilton Place, No 7G, New York, NY 10031 **Tel:** 212-996-9086; 561-283-1549 **E-mail:** writealotmail@gmail.com, pg 462

Di Prisco, Joe, Simpson/Joyce Carol Oates Prize, Lafayette Lib & Learning Ctr Foundation, 3491 Mount Diablo Blvd, Suite 214, Lafayette, CA 94549 **Tel:** 925-283-6513 **E-mail:** sflpweb@gmail.com **Web Site:** www.simpsonliteraryproject.org/programs, pg 668

Dial, Beth, National Poetry Series Open Competition, 57 Mountain Ave, Princeton, NJ 08540 **Tel:** 609-430-0999 **Fax:** 609-430-9933 **Web Site:** nationalpoetryseries.org, pg 645

Diamond, Sarah, On-the-Verge Emerging Voices Award, 6363 Wilshire Blvd, Suite 425, Los Angeles, CA 90048 **Tel:** 323-782-1010 **E-mail:** grants@scbwi.org **Web Site:** www.scbwi.org/awards, pg 651

DiAngelo, Brianne, Magazines Canada (MC), 555 Richmond St W, Suite 604, Mailbox 201, Toronto, ON M5V 3B1, Canada **Tel:** 416-504-0274 **Fax:** 416-504-0437 **E-mail:** info@magazinescanada.ca **Web Site:** magazinescanada.ca, pg 537

Dias-Mandoly, Melissa, University of Pittsburgh Press, 7500 Thomas Blvd, Pittsburgh, PA 15260 **Tel:** 412-383-2456 **Fax:** 412-383-2466 **E-mail:** info@upress. pitt.edu **Web Site:** www.upress.pitt.edu, pg 230

Diaz, Paula, Special Libraries Association (SLA), 7918 Jones Branch Dr, Suite 300, McLean, VA 22102 **Tel:** 703-647-4900 **Fax:** 703-506-3266 **Web Site:** www. sla.org, pg 547

Diaz, Stefanie, Sanford J Greenburger Associates Inc, 55 Fifth Ave, New York, NY 10003 **Tel:** 212-206-5600 **Fax:** 212-463-8718 **Web Site:** greenburger.com; www.sjga.com, pg 487

Dibbens, Kelly, Texas Bluebonnet Award, 3355 Bee Cave Rd, Suite 401, Austin, TX 78746-6763 **Tel:** 512-328-1518 **Fax:** 512-328-8852 **E-mail:** tla@txla.org **Web Site:** txla.org/tools-resources/reading-lists/texas-bluebonnet-award/about/; www.txla.org, pg 672

Dibbens, Kelly, Texas Library Association (TLA), 3355 Bee Cave Rd, Suite 401, Austin, TX 78746-6763 **Tel:** 512-328-1518 **Fax:** 512-328-8852 **E-mail:** tla@ txla.org **Web Site:** www.txla.org, pg 548

DiBiase, Diane, Poisoned Pen Press, 4014 N Goldwater Blvd, Suite 201, Scottsdale, AZ 85251 **Tel:** 480-945-3375 **Toll Free Tel:** 800-421-3976 **Fax:** 480-949-1707 **E-mail:** info@poisonedpenpress.com **Web Site:** www. poisonedpenpress.com, pg 171

DiChiera, Cristina, Fellowship Program, One Capital Hill, 3rd fl, Providence, RI 02908 **Tel:** 401-222-3880 **Fax:** 401-222-3018 **Web Site:** www.arts.ri.gov, pg 615

Dick, Janet L, Museum of New Mexico Press, 725 Camino Lejo, Suite C, Santa Fe, NM 87505 *Tel:* 505-476-1155; 505-272-7777 (orders) *Toll Free Tel:* 800-249-7737 (orders) *Fax:* 505-476-1156 *Toll Free Fax:* 800-622-8667 (orders) *Web Site:* www.mnmpress.org, pg 144

Dickemper, Cheryl, Houghton Mifflin Harcourt Trade & Reference Division, 125 High St, Boston, MA 02110 *Tel:* 617-351-5000 *Web Site:* www.hmhco.com, pg 104

Dickerman, Colin, Farrar, Straus & Giroux, LLC, 175 Varick St, 9th fl, New York, NY 10014 *Tel:* 212-741-6900 *E-mail:* fsg.publicity@fsgbooks.com *Web Site:* us.macmillan.com/fsg.aspx, pg 76

Dickey, Angie, Iowa Poetry Prize, 119 W Park Rd, 100 Kuhl House, Iowa City, IA 52242-1000 *Tel:* 319-335-2000 *Fax:* 319-335-2055 *E-mail:* uipress@uiowa.edu *Web Site:* www.uipress.uiowa.edu, pg 627

Dickey, Angie, Iowa Prize for Literary Nonfiction, 119 W Park Rd, 100 Kuhl House, Iowa City, IA 52242-1000 *Tel:* 319-335-2000 *Fax:* 319-335-2055 *E-mail:* uipress@uiowa.edu *Web Site:* www.uipress.uiowa.edu, pg 627

Dickey, Angie, University of Iowa Press, 119 W Park Rd, 100 Kuhl House, Iowa City, IA 52242-1000 *Tel:* 319-335-2000 *Toll Free Tel:* 800-621-2736 (orders only) *Fax:* 319-335-2055 *Toll Free Fax:* 800-621-8476 (orders only) *E-mail:* uipress@uiowa.edu *Web Site:* www.uipress.uiowa.edu, pg 228

Dickey, Sonia, University of New Mexico Press, One University of New Mexico, Albuquerque, NM 87131-0001 *Tel:* 505-272-7777 *Fax:* 505-277-3343 *E-mail:* custserv@unm.edu (order dept) *Web Site:* unmpress.com, pg 229

Dickinson, Jan, Wheatherstone Press, 11595 SW Butner Rd, No 22, Portland, OR 97225 *Tel:* 503-244-8929 *E-mail:* relocntr@nwlink.com *Web Site:* www.wheatherstonepress.com, pg 240

Dickinson, Lauren, United Nations Association of the United States of America, 1750 Pennsylvania Ave NW, Suite 300, Washington, DC 20006 *Tel:* 202-887-9040 *Web Site:* www.unausa.org, pg 548

Dickson, Barbara, AOTA Press, 6116 Executive Blvd, Suite 200, North Bethesda, MD 20852-4929 *Tel:* 301-652-6611 *Toll Free Tel:* 877-404-AOTA (404-2682, orders) *Fax:* 770-238-0414 (orders) *E-mail:* aotapress@aota.org; customerservice@aota.org *Web Site:* www.aota.org/Publications-News/AOTAPress.aspx; www.aota.org; store.aota.org, pg 17

Dickson, Evan, Magazines Canada (MC), 555 Richmond St W, Suite 604, Mailbox 201, Toronto, ON M5V 3B1, Canada *Tel:* 416-504-0274 *Fax:* 416-504-0437 *E-mail:* info@magazinescanada.ca *Web Site:* magazinescanada.ca, pg 537

Didier, Rebecca, Trafalgar Square Books, 388 Howe Hill Rd, North Pomfret, VT 05053 *Tel:* 802-457-1911 *Toll Free Tel:* 800-423-4525 *Fax:* 802-457-1913 *E-mail:* contact@trafalgarbooks.com *Web Site:* www.trafalgarbooks.com; www.horseandriderbooks.com, pg 219

Didio, Dan, DC Comics Inc, 4000 Warner Blvd, Burbank, CA 91522 *Web Site:* www.dccomics.com; www.dcentertainment.com; www.madmag.com, pg 63

Diebel, Rachel, St Martin's Press, LLC, 120 Broadway, New York, NY 10271 *Tel:* 646-307-5151 *Web Site:* us.macmillan.com/smp, pg 190

Diehl, Debra, University Press of Kansas, 2502 Westbrooke Circle, Lawrence, KS 66045-4444 *Tel:* 785-864-4154; 785-864-4155 (orders) *Fax:* 785-864-4586 *E-mail:* upress@ku.edu; upkorders@ku.edu (orders) *Web Site:* www.kansaspress.ku.edu, pg 233

Dienstfrey, Patricia, Kelsey Street Press, 2824 Kelsey St, Berkeley, CA 94705 *E-mail:* info@kelseyst.com *Web Site:* www.kelseyst.com, pg 116

Dieringer, Lara, National Freedom of Information Coalition (NFOIC), Missouri School of Journalism, 31 Neff Annex, Columbia, MO 65211 *Tel:* 573-882-4856 *E-mail:* nfoic@nfoic.org *Web Site:* nfoic.org, pg 540

Dieter, George, Education Writers Association (EWA), 3516 Connecticut Ave NW, Washington, DC 20008 *Tel:* 202-452-9830 *Fax:* 202-452-9837 *E-mail:* ewa@ewa.org *Web Site:* www.ewa.org, pg 532

Dieterich, Danielle, Penguin Group USA, A Penguin Random House Company, 375 Hudson St, New York, NY 10014 *Tel:* 212-366-2000 *Toll Free Tel:* 800-847-5515 (inside sales); 800-631-8571 (cust serv) *Fax:* 212-366-2666; 607-775-4829 (inside sales) *E-mail:* online@us.penguingroup.com *Web Site:* www.penguin.com, pg 163

Dieterich, Danielle, GP Putnam's Sons (Hardcover), 375 Hudson St, New York, NY 10014 *Tel:* 212-366-2000 *Fax:* 212-366-2643 *E-mail:* online@penguinputnam.com *Web Site:* www.penguin.com/publishers/gpputnamssons, pg 178

Diethelm, Lauren, Random House Children's Books, 1745 Broadway, 10th fl, New York, NY 10019 *Tel:* 212-782-9000 *Web Site:* www.randomhousekids.com, pg 181

Diforio, Robert (Bob) G, D4EO Literary Agency, 7 Indian Valley Rd, Weston, CT 06883 *Tel:* 203-544-7180 *Fax:* 203-544-7160 *Web Site:* www.d4eoliteraryagency.com; www.publishersmarketplace.com/members/d4eo/; twitter.com/d4eo, pg 482

Digneit, William, Mildred & Albert Panowski Playwriting Award, Forest Roberts Theatre, 1401 Presque Isle Ave, Marquette, MI 49855-5364 *Tel:* 906-227-2553 *Fax:* 906-227-2567 *E-mail:* theatre@nmu.edu *Web Site:* www.nmu.edu/theatre, pg 652

Dijkstra, Sandra, Sandra Dijkstra Literary Agency, 1155 Camino del Mar, PMB 515, Del Mar, CA 92014-2605 *Web Site:* dijkstraagency.com, pg 482

Dilanyan, Rema, Peter Lampack Agency Inc, 350 Fifth Ave, Suite 5300, New York, NY 10118 *Tel:* 212-687-9106 *Fax:* 212-687-9109 *Web Site:* www.peterlampackagency.com, pg 492

Dilger, Lynn, Sourcebooks LLC, 1935 Brookdale Rd, Suite 139, Naperville, IL 60563 *Tel:* 630-961-3900 *Toll Free Tel:* 800-432-7444 *Fax:* 630-961-2168 *E-mail:* info@sourcebooks.com; customersupport@sourcebooks.com *Web Site:* www.sourcebooks.com, pg 204

Dillman, Susanne Edes, Standard Publishing Corp, 10 High St, Boston, MA 02110 *Tel:* 617-457-0600 *Toll Free Tel:* 800-682-5759 *Fax:* 617-457-0608 *Web Site:* www.spcpub.com, pg 206

Dillon, Sanyu, Penguin Random House LLC, 1745 Broadway, New York, NY 10019 *Tel:* 212-782-9000 *Toll Free Tel:* 800-726-0600 *Web Site:* www.penguinrandomhouse.com, pg 164

Dillon-Fried, Rachel, Sanford J Greenburger Associates Inc, 55 Fifth Ave, New York, NY 10003 *Tel:* 212-206-5600 *Fax:* 212-463-8718 *Web Site:* greenburger.com; www.sjga.com, pg 487

Dilworth, Rob, Duke University Press, 905 W Main St, Suite 18B, Durham, NC 27701 *Tel:* 919-688-5134 *Toll Free Tel:* 888-651-0122 (US) *Fax:* 919-688-2615 *Toll Free Fax:* 888-651-0124 *E-mail:* orders@dukepress.edu *Web Site:* www.dukeupress.edu, pg 68

DiMasi, Theresa, Simon & Schuster, Inc, 1230 Avenue of the Americas, New York, NY 10020 *Tel:* 212-698-7000 *Toll Free Tel:* 800-223-2336 (orders) *Fax:* 212-698-7007 *Toll Free Fax:* 800-943-9831 (orders) *E-mail:* firstname.lastname@simonandschuster.com; purchaseorders@simonandschuster.com (orders) *Web Site:* www.simonandschuster.com, pg 199

DiMasi, Theresa, Tiller Press, 1230 Avenue of the Americas, New York, NY 10020, pg 218

Dimbleby, Robert, Hogrefe Publishing Corp, 361 Newbury St, 5th fl, Boston, MA 02115 *Tel:* 857-880-2002 *E-mail:* customerservice@hogrefe.com *Web Site:* us.hogrefe.com, pg 101

Dimeff, Alex, University of New Orleans Press, 2000 Lakeshore Dr, New Orleans, LA 70148 *Tel:* 504-280-7457 *E-mail:* unopress@uno.edu *Web Site:* www.uno.edu/unopress, pg 229

Dimnik, Michelle, Rocky Mountain Book Award, PO Box 42, Lethbridge, AB T1J 3Y3, Canada *Tel:* 403-381-7164 *E-mail:* rockymountainbookaward@shaw.ca *Web Site:* www.rmba.info, pg 662

Dimock, Kate, Springer Publishing Co, 11 W 42 St, 15th fl, New York, NY 10036-8002 *Tel:* 212-431-4370 *Toll Free Tel:* 877-687-7476 *E-mail:* marketing@springerpub.com; cs@springerpub.com (orders); textbook@springerpub.com; specialsales@springerpub.com *Web Site:* www.springerpub.com, pg 206

DiMona, Lisa, Writers House, 21 W 26 St, New York, NY 10010 *Tel:* 212-685-2400 *Web Site:* www.writershouse.com, pg 508

Dinardo, Jeff, Red Chair Press, PO Box 333, South Egremont, MA 01258-0333 *Tel:* 413-528-2398 (edit off) *Toll Free Tel:* 800-328-4929 (orders & cust serv) *E-mail:* info@redchairpress.com *Web Site:* www.redchairpress.com, pg 182

Dinas, Jackie, Kensington Publishing Corp, 119 W 40 St, New York, NY 10018 *Tel:* 212-407-1500 *Toll Free Tel:* 800-221-2647 *Fax:* 212-935-0699 *Web Site:* www.kensingtonbooks.com, pg 116

Ding, Kristine, University of Illinois Press, 1325 S Oak St, MC-566, Champaign, IL 61820-6903 *Tel:* 217-333-0950 *Fax:* 217-244-8082 *E-mail:* uipress@uillinois.edu; journals@uillinois.edu *Web Site:* www.press.uillinois.edu, pg 227

Dinger, Angela, William H Sadlier Inc, 9 Pine St, New York, NY 10005 *Tel:* 212-227-2120 *Toll Free Tel:* 800-221-5175 (cust serv) *Fax:* 212-312-6080 *E-mail:* customerservice@sadlier.com *Web Site:* www.sadlier.com, pg 189

Dinger, Frank S, William H Sadlier Inc, 9 Pine St, New York, NY 10005 *Tel:* 212-227-2120 *Toll Free Tel:* 800-221-5175 (cust serv) *Fax:* 212-312-6080 *E-mail:* customerservice@sadlier.com *Web Site:* www.sadlier.com, pg 189

Dinkins, Joyce, Discovery House Publishers, 3000 Kraft Ave SE, Grand Rapids, MI 49512 *Tel:* 616-942-2803 *Toll Free Tel:* 800-653-8333 (cust serv) *E-mail:* support@dhp.org; customerservice@dhp.org *Web Site:* www.dhp.org, pg 65

Dinovis, Marisa, Random House Children's Books, 1745 Broadway, 10th fl, New York, NY 10019 *Tel:* 212-782-9000 *Web Site:* www.randomhousekids.com, pg 181

Dinstman, Lee, APA Talent & Literary Agency, 405 S Beverly Dr, Beverly Hills, CA 90212 *Tel:* 310-888-4200 *Web Site:* www.apa-agency.com, pg 474

Dion, Denis, Les Presses de l'Universite Laval, 2180, Chemin Sainte-Foy, 1st fl, Quebec, QC G1V 0A6, Canada *Tel:* 418-656-2803 *Fax:* 418-656-3305 *E-mail:* presses@pul.ulaval.ca *Web Site:* www.pulaval.com, pg 437

Dionne, Richard, Red Deer Press Inc, 195 Allstate Pkwy, Markham, ON L3R 4T8, Canada *Tel:* 905-477-9700 *Toll Free Tel:* 800-387-9776 (orders) *E-mail:* rdp@reddeerpress.com; bookinfo@fitzhenry.ca *Web Site:* www.reddeerpress.com, pg 438

DiSabatino, Nicholas, Beacon Press, 24 Farnsworth St, Boston, MA 02210-1409 *Tel:* 617-742-2110 *Fax:* 617-723-3097; 617-742-2290 *Web Site:* www.beacon.org, pg 29

DiSanto, Drohan, Vanderbilt University Press, 2301 Vanderbilt Place, PMB 401813, Nashville, TN 37240-1813 *Tel:* 615-322-3585 *Toll Free Tel:* 800-848-6224 (orders only) *Fax:* 615-343-0308 *E-mail:* vupress@vanderbilt.edu *Web Site:* www.vanderbiltuniversitypress.com, pg 235

DiSarro, Lisa, Houghton Mifflin Harcourt Trade & Reference Division, 125 High St, Boston, MA 02110 *Tel:* 617-351-5000 *Web Site:* www.hmhco.com, pg 104

Disbrow, Ethan, Amber Lotus Publishing, PO Box 11329, Portland, OR 97211 *Tel:* 503-284-6400 *Toll Free Tel:* 800-326-2375 (orders only) *Fax:* 503-284-6417 *E-mail:* info@amberlotus.com *Web Site:* www.amberlotus.com, pg 9

Dissen, Matthew, Melanie Jackson Agency LLC, 41 W 72 St, Suite 3F, New York, NY 10023 *Tel:* 212-873-3373, pg 490

Dissinger, Deanne, American Law Institute, 4025 Chestnut St, Philadelphia, PA 19104-3099 *Tel:* 215-243-1600 *Toll Free Tel:* 800-253-6397 *Fax:* 215-243-1636 *E-mail:* ali@ali.org; custserv@ali.org *Web Site:* www.ali.org, pg 12

Distelberg, Brian, Perseus Books, 1290 Avenue of the Americas, New York, NY 10104 *Tel:* 212-340-8100 *Toll Free Tel:* 800-343-4499 (cust serv) *Fax:* 212-340-8105 *Web Site:* www.perseusbooks.com, pg 167

Ditchik, Seth, Yale University Press, 302 Temple St, New Haven, CT 06511-8909 *Tel:* 203-432-0960; 203-432-0966 (sales); 401-531-2800 (cust serv) *Toll Free Tel:* 800-405-1619 (cust serv) *Fax:* 203-432-0948; 203-432-8485 (sales); 401-531-2801 (cust serv) *Toll Free Fax:* 800-406-9145 (cust serv) *E-mail:* sales.press@yale.edu (sales); customer.care@triliteral.org (cust serv) *Web Site:* www.yalebooks.com; yalepress.yale.edu/yupbooks, pg 246

Diver, Lucienne, The Knight Agency Inc, 232 W Washington St, Madison, GA 30650 *E-mail:* admin@knightagency.net *Web Site:* www.knightagency.net, pg 491

DiVietro, Philip, American Society of Mechanical Engineers (ASME), 2 Park Ave, New York, NY 10016-5990 *Tel:* 212-591-7000 *Toll Free Tel:* 800-843-2763 (cust serv-US, CN & Mexico) *Fax:* 973-882-1717 (orders & inquiries) *E-mail:* customercare@asme.org *Web Site:* www.asme.org, pg 14

Dixon, Debra, BelleBooks, PO Box 300921, Memphis, TN 38130 *Tel:* 901-344-9024 *Fax:* 901-344-9068 *E-mail:* bellebooks@bellebooks.com *Web Site:* www.bellebooks.com, pg 31

Djangi, Taraneh, Penguin Random House Audio Publishing, 1745 Broadway, New York, NY 10019 *E-mail:* audio@penguinrandomhouse.com *Web Site:* www.penguinrandomhouseaudio.com, pg 164

Dlouhy, Caitlyn, Simon & Schuster Children's Publishing, 1230 Avenue of the Americas, New York, NY 10020 *Tel:* 212-698-7000 *Web Site:* www.simonandschuster.com/kids; www.simonandschuster.com/teen; simonandschuster.net; simonandschuster.biz, pg 199

Do, Quynh, W W Norton & Company Inc, 500 Fifth Ave, New York, NY 10110-0017 *Tel:* 212-354-5500 *Toll Free Tel:* 800-233-4830 (orders & cust serv) *Fax:* 212-869-0856 *Toll Free Fax:* 800-458-6515 *E-mail:* orders@wwnorton.com *Web Site:* wwnorton.com, pg 152

Dobben, Anna, 5 Under 35, 90 Broad St, Suite 604, New York, NY 10004 *Tel:* 212-685-0261 *Fax:* 212-213-6570 *E-mail:* nationalbook@nationalbook.org *Web Site:* www.nationalbook.org, pg 616

Dobben, Anna, Innovations in Reading Prize, 90 Broad St, Suite 604, New York, NY 10004 *Tel:* 212-685-0261 *Fax:* 212-213-6570 *E-mail:* nationalbook@nationalbook.org *Web Site:* www.nationalbook.org/innovations_in_reading, pg 627

Dobben, Anna, Medal for Distinguished Contribution to American Letters, 90 Broad St, Suite 604, New York, NY 10004 *Tel:* 212-685-0261 *Fax:* 212-213-6570 *E-mail:* nationalbook@nationalbook.org *Web Site:* www.nationalbook.org/amerletters.html, pg 640

Dobben, Anna, National Book Awards, 90 Broad St, Suite 604, New York, NY 10004 *Tel:* 212-685-0261 *Fax:* 212-213-6570 *E-mail:* nationalbook@nationalbook.org *Web Site:* www.nationalbook.org, pg 644

Dobben, Anna, National Book Foundation, 90 Broad St, Suite 604, New York, NY 10004 *Tel:* 212-685-0261 *Fax:* 212-213-6570 *E-mail:* nationalbook@nationalbook.org *Web Site:* www.nationalbook.org, pg 551

Dobinick, Susan, Bloomsbury Publishing Inc, 1385 Broadway, 5th fl, New York, NY 10018 *Tel:* 212-419-5300 *E-mail:* marketingusa@bloomsbury.com; adultpublicityusa@bloomsbury.com; askacademic@bloomsbury.com *Web Site:* www.bloomsbury.com, pg 36

Dobles, Gustavo, Wolters Kluwer Law & Business, 76 Ninth Ave, 7th fl, New York, NY 10011-5201 *Tel:* 212-771-0600; 301-698-7100 (cust serv outside US) *Toll Free Tel:* 800-234-1660 (cust serv) *E-mail:* customer.service@wolterskluwer.com; lrusmedia@wolterskluwer.com *Web Site:* lrus.wolterskluwer.com, pg 243

Dobson, Allison, Penguin Group USA, A Penguin Random House Company, 375 Hudson St, New York, NY 10014 *Tel:* 212-366-2000 *Toll Free Tel:* 800-847-5515 (inside sales); 800-631-8571 (cust serv) *Fax:* 212-366-2666; 607-775-4829 (inside sales) *E-mail:* online@us.penguingroup.com *Web Site:* www.penguin.com, pg 163

Dobson, David, Presbyterian Publishing Corp (PPC), 100 Witherspoon St, Louisville, KY 40202 *Tel:* 502-569-5000 *Toll Free Tel:* 800-523-1631 (US only) *Fax:* 502-569-5113 *E-mail:* customerservice@presbypub.com *Web Site:* www.wjkbooks.com, pg 173

Dobson, David, Westminster John Knox Press (WJK), 100 Witherspoon St, Louisville, KY 40202-1396 *Tel:* 502-569-5052 *Toll Free Tel:* 800-523-1631 (US & CN) *Fax:* 502-569-8308 *Toll Free Fax:* 800-541-5113 (US & CN) *E-mail:* customer_service@wjkbooks.com; orders@wjkbooks.com *Web Site:* www.wjkbooks.com, pg 239

Dobson, Megan, Zondervan, 3900 Sparks Dr, Grand Rapids, MI 49546 *Tel:* 616-698-6900 *Toll Free Tel:* 800-226-1122; 800-727-1309 (retail orders) *Fax:* 616-698-3350 *Toll Free Fax:* 800-698-3256 (retail orders) *Web Site:* www.zondervan.com, pg 248

Dodd, Michael A, Liturgy Training Publications, 3949 S Racine Ave, Chicago, IL 60609-2523 *Tel:* 773-579-4900 *Toll Free Tel:* 800-933-1800 (US & CN only orders) *Fax:* 773-579-4929 *E-mail:* orders@ltp.org *Web Site:* www.ltp.org, pg 126

Dodds, Andy, Grand Central Publishing, 1290 Avenue of the Americas, New York, NY 10104 *Tel:* 212-364-1100 *Web Site:* www.hachettebookgroup.com, pg 88

Dodes, Jeff, St Martin's Press, LLC, 120 Broadway, New York, NY 10271 *Tel:* 646-307-5151 *Web Site:* us.macmillan.com/smp, pg 190

Dodillet, Katie, Tyndale House Publishers Inc, 351 Executive Dr, Carol Stream, IL 60188 *Tel:* 630-668-8300 *Toll Free Tel:* 800-323-9400; 855-277-9400 *Toll Free Fax:* 866-622-9474 *Web Site:* www.tyndale.com, pg 223

Dodson, Ted, Community of Literary Magazines & Presses (CLMP), 154 Christopher St, Suite 3C, New York, NY 10014-9110 *Tel:* 212-741-9110 *E-mail:* info@clmp.org *Web Site:* www.clmp.org, pg 531

Dodson, Veronique, National Association of Black Journalists (NABJ), 1100 Knight Hall, Suite 3100, College Park, MD 20742 *Tel:* 301-405-0248 *Fax:* 301-314-1714 *E-mail:* info@nabj.org; press@nabj.org *Web Site:* www.nabj.org, pg 538

Doerr, Jennifer, Yale University Press, 302 Temple St, New Haven, CT 06511-8909 *Tel:* 203-432-0960; 203-432-0966 (sales); 401-531-2800 (cust serv) *Toll Free Tel:* 800-405-1619 (cust serv) *Fax:* 203-432-0948; 203-432-8485 (sales); 401-531-2801 (cust serv) *Toll Free Fax:* 800-406-9145 (cust serv) *E-mail:* sales.press@yale.edu (sales); customer.care@triliteral.org (cust serv) *Web Site:* www.yalebooks.com; yalepress.yale.edu/yupbooks, pg 246

Doerr, Susan, University of Minnesota Press, 111 Third Ave S, Suite 290, Minneapolis, MN 55401-2520 *Tel:* 612-301-1990 *Fax:* 612-301-1980 *E-mail:* ump@umn.edu *Web Site:* www.upress.umn.edu, pg 228

Doerrer, David, Abrams Artists Agency, 275 Seventh Ave, 26th fl, New York, NY 10001 *Tel:* 646-486-4600 *Fax:* 646-486-0100 *E-mail:* literary@abramsartny.com *Web Site:* www.abramsartists.com, pg 473

Doherty, Patricia, Macmillan, 120 Broadway, 22nd fl, New York, NY 10271 *Tel:* 646-307-5151 *E-mail:* press.inquiries@macmillan.com *Web Site:* www.macmillan.com, pg 130

Doherty, Thomas, Tom Doherty Associates, LLC, 120 Broadway, New York, NY 10271 *Tel:* 646-307-5511 *Toll Free Tel:* 800-455-0340 *Web Site:* us.macmillan.com/torforge, pg 66

Doherty, Thomas, Macmillan, 120 Broadway, 22nd fl, New York, NY 10271 *Tel:* 646-307-5151 *E-mail:* press.inquiries@macmillan.com *Web Site:* www.macmillan.com, pg 129

Doig, Stephanie, Harlequin Enterprises Ltd, Bay Adelaide Centre, East Tower, 22 Adelaide St W, 41st fl, Toronto, ON M5H 4E3, Canada *Tel:* 416-445-5860 *Toll Free Tel:* 888-432-4879; 800-370-5838 (ebook inquiries) *E-mail:* customerservice@harlequin.com *Web Site:* www.harlequin.com, pg 429

Dolan, Eamon, Simon & Schuster, 1230 Avenue of the Americas, New York, NY 10020 *Tel:* 212-698-7000 *Toll Free Tel:* 800-223-2348 (cust serv); 800-223-2336 (orders) *Toll Free Fax:* 800-943-9831 (orders) *Web Site:* www.simonandschuster.com, pg 198

Dolce, Holly, Harry N Abrams Inc, 195 Broadway, 9th fl, New York, NY 10007 *Tel:* 212-206-7715 *Toll Free Tel:* 800-345-1359 *Fax:* 212-519-1210 *E-mail:* abrams@abramsbooks.com *Web Site:* www.abramsbooks.com, pg 3

Doldan, Humberto, Association for Information Science & Technology (ASIS&T), 8555 16 St, Suite 850, Silver Spring, MD 20910 *Tel:* 301-495-0900 *Fax:* 301-495-0810 *E-mail:* asist@asist.org *Web Site:* www.asist.org, pg 525

Dolechek, Melanie, Society for Scholarly Publishing (SSP), 1120 Rte 73, Suite 200, Mount Laurel, NJ 08054 *Tel:* 856-439-1385 *Fax:* 856-439-0525 *E-mail:* info@sspnet.org *Web Site:* www.sspnet.org, pg 546

Dolence, Travis, New Rivers Press, c/o Minnesota State University Moorhead, 1104 Seventh Ave S, Moorhead, MN 56563 *Tel:* 218-477-5870 *Fax:* 218-477-2236 *E-mail:* nrp@mnstate.edu *Web Site:* www.newriverspress.com; www.mnstate.edu/newriverspress, pg 149

Doliveux, Maelle, Beehive Books, 4700 Kingsessing Ave, Suite C, Philadelphia, PA 19143 *E-mail:* beehivebook@gmail.com *Web Site:* www.beehivebooks.net, pg 30

Doll, Holly, Fitzhenry & Whiteside Limited, 195 Allstate Pkwy, Markham, ON L3R 4T8, Canada *Tel:* 905-477-9700 *Toll Free Tel:* 800-387-9776 *Fax:* 905-477-2834 *Toll Free Tel:* 800-260-9777 *E-mail:* bookinfo@fitzhenry.ca; godwit@fitzhenry.ca *Web Site:* www.fitzhenry.ca, pg 426

Dollar, Douglas, New Forums Press Inc, 1018 S Lewis St, Stillwater, OK 74074 *Tel:* 405-372-6158 *Toll Free Tel:* 800-606-3766 *Fax:* 405-377-2237 *E-mail:* submissions@newforums.com *Web Site:* www.newforums.com, pg 148

Dols, Amy, The Child's World Inc, 1980 Lookout Dr, North Mankato, MN 56003-1705 *Tel:* 507-385-1044 *Toll Free Tel:* 800-599-READ (599-7323) *Toll Free Fax:* 888-320-2329 *E-mail:* sales@childsworld.com *Web Site:* childsworld.com, pg 51

Dominguez, Ginny, Farrar, Straus & Giroux Books for Young Readers, 120 Broadway, New York, NY 10271 *Tel:* 212-741-6900 *Toll Free Tel:* 888-330-8477 (orders) *Fax:* 212-633-9385 *Web Site:* us.macmillan.com/mackids; www.mackidsbooks.com, pg 76

Dominguez, Ginny, Henry Holt and Company, LLC, 120 Broadway, 23rd fl, New York, NY 10271 *Tel:* 646-307-5151 *Toll Free Tel:* 888-330-8477 (orders) *Fax:* 646-307-5285 *Web Site:* www.henryholt.com, pg 102

Dominguez, Ginny, Roaring Brook Press, 120 Broadway, New York, NY 10271 *Tel:* 646-307-5151 *Web Site:* us.macmillan.com/publishers/roaring-brook-press, pg 186

Dominguez, Maria, Scholastic Trade Division, 557 Broadway, New York, NY 10012 *Tel:* 212-343-6100; 212-343-4685 (export sales) *Fax:* 212-343-4714 (export sales) *Web Site:* www.scholastic.com, pg 194

Dominguez, Sonia, DeVorss & Co, 553 Constitution Ave, Camarillo, CA 93012-8510 *Tel:* 805-322-9010 *Toll Free Tel:* 800-843-5743 *Fax:* 805-322-9011 *E-mail:* service@devorss.com *Web Site:* www.devorss. com, pg 64

Dominici, Philip, Dover Publications Inc, 31 E Second St, Mineola, NY 11501-3852 *Tel:* 516-294-7000 *Toll Free Tel:* 800-223-3130 (orders) *Fax:* 516-742-6953 *E-mail:* rights@doverpublications.com; service@doverpublications.com; doversales@ doverpublications.com *Web Site:* store.doverdirect.com; www.doverpublications.com, pg 67

Donaher, Br Edward, St Pauls, 2187 Victory Blvd, Staten Island, NY 10314-6603 *Tel:* 718-761-0047 (edit & prodn); 718-698-2759 (mktg & billing) *Toll Free Tel:* 800-343-2522 *Fax:* 718-761-0057 *E-mail:* sales@ stpauls.us; marketing@stpauls.us *Web Site:* www. stpauls.us, pg 191

Donahue, Bevin, North Atlantic Books, 2526 Martin Luther King Jr Way, Berkeley, CA 94704 *Tel:* 510-549-4270 *Fax:* 510-549-4276 *Web Site:* www. northatlanticbooks.com, pg 151

Donahue, Jed, ISI Books, 3901 Centerville Rd, Wilmington, DE 19807-1938 *Tel:* 302-652-4600 *Toll Free Tel:* 800-526-7022 *Fax:* 302-652-1760 *E-mail:* info@isi.org; isibooks@isi.org *Web Site:* www.isibooks.org, pg 112

Donatich, John, Yale University Press, 302 Temple St, New Haven, CT 06511-8909 *Tel:* 203-432-0960; 203-432-0966 (sales); 401-531-2800 (cust serv) *Toll Free Tel:* 800-405-1619 (cust serv) *Fax:* 203-432-0948; 203-432-8485 (sales); 401-531-2801 (cust serv) *Toll Free Fax:* 800-406-9145 (cust serv) *E-mail:* sales. press@yale.edu (sales); customer.care@triliteral.org (cust serv) *Web Site:* www.yalebooks.com; yalepress. yale.edu/yupbooks, pg 246

Donato, Paul, Advertising Research Foundation (ARF), 432 Park Ave S, 4th fl, New York, NY 10016-8013 *Tel:* 212-751-5656 *Fax:* 212-689-1859 *E-mail:* help@ thearf.org *Web Site:* thearf.org, pg 521

Donavan, Lisa, Michigan Municipal League, 1675 Green Rd, Ann Arbor, MI 48105 *Tel:* 734-662-3246 *Toll Free Tel:* 800-653-2483 *E-mail:* contact@mml.org *Web Site:* www.mml.org, pg 139

Donlan, Rita, Graphic Arts Association, 1210 Northbrook Dr, Suite 200, Trevose, PA 19053 *Tel:* 215-396-2300 *Fax:* 215-396-9890 *Web Site:* www. graphicartsassociation.org, pg 534

Donlan, Rita, Graphic Arts Association, 1210 Northbrook Dr, Suite 200, Trevose, PA 19053 *Tel:* 215-396-2300 *Fax:* 215-396-9890 *E-mail:* gaa@ gaaonline.org *Web Site:* www.graphicartsassociation. org, pg 583

Donnaud, Janis A, Janis A Donnaud & Associates Inc, 77 Bleecker St, No C1-25, New York, NY 10012 *Tel:* 212-431-2663 *Fax:* 212-431-2667 *E-mail:* jdonnaud@aol.com, pg 482

Donnelly, Patrick, AOCS Press, 2710 S Boulder Dr, Urbana, IL 61802-6996 *Tel:* 217-693-4838 *Fax:* 217-351-8091 *E-mail:* general@aocs.org *Web Site:* www. aocs.org, pg 17

Donnelly, Sean, The Danahy Fiction Prize, University of Tampa Press, 401 W Kennedy Blvd, Tampa, FL 33606 *Tel:* 813-253-6266 *E-mail:* utpress@ut.edu *Web Site:* tampareview.ut.edu, pg 608

Donnelly, Sean, The Tampa Review Prize for Poetry, University of Tampa Press, 401 W Kennedy Blvd, Tampa, FL 33606 *Tel:* 813-253-6266 *E-mail:* utpress@ ut.edu *Web Site:* tampareview.ut.edu, pg 672

Donnelly, Shannon, Diversion Books, 443 Park Ave S, Suite 1008, New York, NY 10016 *Tel:* 212-961-6390 *E-mail:* info@diversionbooks.com *Web Site:* www. diversionbooks.com, pg 65

Donnelly, Susan, Harvard University Press, 79 Garden St, Cambridge, MA 02138-1499 *Tel:* 617-495-2600; 401-531-2800 (intl orders) *Toll Free Tel:* 800-405-1619 (orders) *Fax:* 617-495-5898 (gen); 617-496-4677 (edit & rts); 401-531-2801 (intl orders) *Toll Free Fax:* 800-406-9145 (orders) *E-mail:* contact_hup@ harvard.edu *Web Site:* www.hup.harvard.edu, pg 95

Donnelly, Timothy, Columbia University School of the Arts Creative Writing Program, 609 Kent Hall, New York, NY 10027 *Tel:* 212-854-3774 *Fax:* 212-854-7704 *E-mail:* writingprogram@columbia.edu *Web Site:* www.columbia.edu/cu/writing, pg 582

Donovan, Amy, United States Holocaust Memorial Museum, 100 Raoul Wallenberg Place SW, Washington, DC 20024-2126 *Tel:* 202-488-0400; 202-314-7837; 202-488-6144 (orders) *Toll Free Tel:* 800-259-9998 (orders) *Fax:* 202-479-9726; 202-488-0438 (orders) *E-mail:* cahs_publications@ushmm.org *Web Site:* www.ushmm.org, pg 224

Donovan, Jennifer, Penguin Random House Audio Publishing, 1745 Broadway, New York, NY 10019 *E-mail:* audio@penguinrandomhouse.com *Web Site:* www.penguinrandomhouseaudio.com, pg 164

Donovan, Jim, Jim Donovan Literary, 5635 SMU Blvd, Suite 201, Dallas, TX 75206 *Tel:* 214-696-9411 *E-mail:* jdlqueries@sbcglobal.net, pg 482

Donovan, Lauren, Scholastic Trade Division, 557 Broadway, New York, NY 10012 *Tel:* 212-343-6100; 212-343-4685 (export sales) *Fax:* 212-343-4714 (export sales) *Web Site:* www.scholastic.com, pg 194

Donovan, Mary Lee, Candlewick Press, 99 Dover St, Somerville, MA 02144-2825 *Tel:* 617-661-3330 *Fax:* 617-661-0565 *E-mail:* bigbear@candlewick. com; salesinfo@candlewick.com *Web Site:* www. candlewick.com, pg 44

Doob, Gabriella, HarperCollins General Books Group, 195 Broadway, New York, NY 10007 *Tel:* 212-207-7000 *Web Site:* www.harpercollins.com, pg 93

Dooley, Theresa, HarperCollins General Books Group, 195 Broadway, New York, NY 10007 *Tel:* 212-207-7000 *Web Site:* www.harpercollins.com, pg 94

Dooley, Tim, OCP, 5536 NE Hassalo St, Portland, OR 97213 *Tel:* 503-281-1191 *Toll Free Tel:* 800-548-8749 *Fax:* 503-282-3486 *Toll Free Fax:* 800-843-8181 *E-mail:* liturgy@ocp.org *Web Site:* www.ocp.org, pg 154

Dooley-Dorocke, Erica, Solution Tree, 555 N Morton St, Bloomington, IN 47404 *Tel:* 812-336-7700 *Toll Free Tel:* 800-733-6786 *Fax:* 812-336-7790 *E-mail:* pubs@solutiontree.com; orders@solutiontree. com *Web Site:* www.solutiontree.com, pg 203

Doornbos, Cris, David C Cook, 4050 Lee Vance Dr, Colorado Springs, CO 80918 *Tel:* 719-536-0100 *Toll Free Tel:* 800-708-5550; 800-323-7543 (orders & cust serv) *Toll Free Fax:* 800-430-0726 (cust serv) *Web Site:* www.davidccook.org, pg 56

Dorado, Kelsey, Empire State Award for Excellence in Literature for Young People, 6021 State Farm Rd, Guilderland, NY 12084 *Tel:* 518-432-6952 *Toll Free Tel:* 800-252-6952 *Fax:* 518-427-1697 *E-mail:* info@ nyla.org *Web Site:* www.nyla.org, pg 613

Dorff, Patricia, Council on Foreign Relations Press, The Harold Pratt House, 58 E 68 St, New York, NY 10065 *Tel:* 212-434-9400 *Fax:* 212-434-9800 *E-mail:* publications@cfr.org *Web Site:* www.cfr.org, pg 58

Dorfman, Debra, Scholastic Trade Division, 557 Broadway, New York, NY 10012 *Tel:* 212-343-6100; 212-343-4685 (export sales) *Fax:* 212-343-4714 (export sales) *Web Site:* www.scholastic.com, pg 194

Dorfman, Larry, Capstone Publishers™, 1710 Roe Crest Dr, North Mankato, MN 56003 *Toll Free Tel:* 800-747-4992 (cust serv) *Toll Free Fax:* 888-262-0705 *E-mail:* customer.service@capstonepub.com *Web Site:* www.capstonepub.com, pg 44

Dorman, Dr Jessica, The Historic New Orleans Collection, 533 Royal St, New Orleans, LA 70130 *Tel:* 504-523-4662 *Fax:* 504-598-7108 *E-mail:* wrc@ hnoc.org *Web Site:* www.hnoc.org, pg 100

Dorman, Pamela, Viking, 375 Hudson St, New York, NY 10014 *Tel:* 212-366-2000 *Fax:* 212-243-6002 *Web Site:* www.penguin.com/publishers/vikingbooks, pg 236

Dosik, Anita, APPA: The Association of Higher Education Facilities Officers, 1643 Prince St, Alexandria, VA 22314-2818 *Tel:* 703-684-1446 *Fax:* 703-549-2772 *Web Site:* www.appa.org, pg 18

Dossov, Tatiana, Peter Lampack Agency Inc, 350 Fifth Ave, Suite 5300, New York, NY 10118 *Tel:* 212-687-9106 *Fax:* 212-687-9109 *Web Site:* www. peterlampackagency.com, pg 492

Doten, Mark, Soho Press Inc, 853 Broadway, New York, NY 10003 *Tel:* 212-260-1900 *E-mail:* soho@ sohopress.com; publicity@sohopress.com *Web Site:* www. sohopress.com, pg 203

Dotson, Anne Dean, The University Press of Kentucky, 663 S Limestone St, Lexington, KY 40508-4008 *Tel:* 859-257-8400 *Fax:* 859-257-8481 *Web Site:* www. kentuckypress.com, pg 233

Dotto, Gabriel, Michigan State University Press (MSU Press), Manly Miles Bldg, Suite 25, 1405 S Harrison Rd, East Lansing, MI 48823-5245 *Tel:* 517-355-9543 *Fax:* 517-432-2611 *Web Site:* msupress.org, pg 139

Doucet, Christy, Livres Canada Books, One Nicholas, Suite 504, Ottawa, ON K1N 7B7, Canada *Tel:* 613-562-2324 *Fax:* 613-562-2329 *E-mail:* info@livrescanadabooks.com *Web Site:* www. livrescanadabooks.com, pg 537

Dougherty, Adria, Sterling Publishing Co Inc, 1166 Avenue of the Americas, 17th fl, New York, NY 10036-2715 *Tel:* 212-532-7160 *Toll Free Tel:* 800-367-9692 *Fax:* 212-213-2495 *Toll Free Fax:* 800-542-7567 *E-mail:* custservice@sterlingpublishing.com; customerservice@sterlingpublishing.com; editorial@ sterlingpublishing.com; tradesales@sterlingpublishing. com *Web Site:* www.sterlingpublishing.com, pg 208

Dougherty, Mary V, Juniper Prize for Fiction, East Experiment Station, 671 N Pleasant St, Amherst, MA 01003 *E-mail:* info@umpress.umass.edu *Web Site:* www.umass.edu/umpress; www.umass. edu/umpress/content/juniper-literary-prize-series, pg 629

Dougherty, Mary V, Juniper Prize for Poetry, East Experiment Station, 671 N Pleasant St, Amherst, MA 01003 *E-mail:* info@umpress.umass.edu *Web Site:* www.umass.edu/umpress; www.umass. edu/umpress/content/juniper-literary-prize-series, pg 629

Dougherty, Mary V, University of Massachusetts Press, East Experiment Station, 671 N Pleasant St, Amherst, MA 01003 *Tel:* 413-545-2217 *Fax:* 413-545-1226 *E-mail:* info@umpress.umass.edu *Web Site:* www. umass.edu/umpress, pg 228

Doughtery, Carol, Writers Retreat Workshop (WRW), PO Box 170657, Austin, TX 78717 *E-mail:* info@ writersretreatworkshop.com *Web Site:* www. writersretreatworkshop.com, pg 580

Doughty, Sarah, Adams Media, 57 Littlefield St, Avon, MA 02322 *Tel:* 508-427-7100 *Web Site:* www. simonandschuster.com, pg 4

Doughty, Todd, Doubleday, c/o Penguin Random House Inc, 1745 Broadway, New York, NY 10019 *Tel:* 212-751-2600 *Fax:* 212-572-2662 (foreign rts) *E-mail:* ddaypub@randomhouse.com *Web Site:* knopfdoubleday.com, pg 66

Douglas, Alecia, McIntosh and Otis Inc, 207 E 37 St, Suite BG, New York, NY 10016 *Tel:* 212-687-7400 *Fax:* 212-687-6894 *E-mail:* info@mcintoshandotis.com *Web Site:* www.mcintoshandotis.com, pg 496

Douglas, Deron, Double Dragon Publishing Inc, 1-5762 Hwy 7 E, Markham, ON L3P 7Y4, Canada *E-mail:* sales@double-dragon-ebooks.com *Web Site:* www.double-dragon-ebooks.com, pg 421

Douglas, Sally, National Press Club of Canada Foundation Inc, 17 York St, Suite 201, Ottawa, ON K1N 9J6, Canada *E-mail:* info@pressclubcanada.ca *Web Site:* pressclubcanada.ca, pg 540

Douglas, Sarah L, Abrams Artists Agency, 275 Seventh Ave, 26th fl, New York, NY 10001 *Tel:* 646-486-4600 *Fax:* 646-486-0100 *E-mail:* literary@abramsartny.com *Web Site:* www.abramsartists.com, pg 473

Duckson, Scott, West Academic, 444 Cedar St, Suite 700, St Paul, MN 55101 *Toll Free Tel:* 877-888-1330 *E-mail:* customerservice@westacademic.com; support@westacademic.com; media@westacademic.com *Web Site:* www.westacademic.com, pg 239

Duckworth, Cara, Association of American Publishers (AAP), 455 Massachusetts Ave NW, Suite 700, Washington, DC 20001-2777 *Tel:* 202-347-3375 *Fax:* 202-347-3690 *E-mail:* info@publishers.org *Web Site:* publishers.org, pg 526

Dudding, Michael, Houghton Mifflin Harcourt, 125 High St, Boston, MA 02110 *Tel:* 617-351-5000 *Toll Free Tel:* 855-969-4642; 800-225-5425 (K-12 educ materials); 800-323-9540 (assessment materials); 877-219-1537 (SkillsTutor); 888-242-6747 (Innovation in Educ Group); 800-225-3362 (Trade & Ref Div) *Toll Free Fax:* 800-269-5232 *E-mail:* myhmhco@hmhco.com *Web Site:* www.hmhco.com, pg 103

Dudley, Tim, Master Books®, 3142 Hwy 103 N, Green Forest, AR 72638 *Tel:* 870-438-5288 *Toll Free Tel:* 800-999-3777 *E-mail:* sales@masterbooks.com; nlp@nlpg.com; submissions@newleafpress.net *Web Site:* www.masterbooks.com; www.nlpg.com/imprint/master-books, pg 134

Dudley, Tim, New Leaf Press, 3142 Hwy 103 N, Green Forest, AR 72638-2233 *Tel:* 870-438-5288 *Toll Free Tel:* 800-999-3777 *Fax:* 870-438-5120 *E-mail:* nlp@newleafpress.net; submissions@newleafpress.net *Web Site:* www.nlpg.com, pg 149

Dudzik, Andy, Leaf Storm Press, PO Box 4670, Santa Fe, NM 87502-4670 *Tel:* 505-216-6155 *E-mail:* leafstormpress@gmail.com *Web Site:* leafstormpress.com, pg 121

Dufault, Christopher, Doubleday, c/o Penguin Random House Inc, 1745 Broadway, New York, NY 10019 *Tel:* 212-751-2600 *Fax:* 212-572-2662 (foreign rts) *E-mail:* ddaypub@randomhouse.com *Web Site:* knopfdoubleday.com, pg 66

Dufault, Christopher, Alfred A Knopf, c/o Penguin Random House Inc, 1745 Broadway, New York, NY 10019 *Tel:* 212-751-2600 *Fax:* 212-572-2662 (foreign rts) *Web Site:* knopfdoubleday.com, pg 117

Dufault, Christopher, Penguin Random House LLC, 1745 Broadway, New York, NY 10019 *Tel:* 212-782-9000 *Toll Free Tel:* 800-726-0600 *Web Site:* www.penguinrandomhouse.com, pg 164

Dufresne, Collette, Editions Michel Quintin, 2259 Papineau Ave, Suite 104, Montreal, QC H2K 4J5, Canada *Tel:* 514-379-3774 *E-mail:* info@editionsmichelquintin.ca *Web Site:* www.editionsmichelquintin.ca, pg 424

Dufresne, Jean-Sebastien, Montreal-Contacts/The Rights Agency, 1350 Sherbrooke St E, Suite 1, Montreal, QC H2L 1M4, Canada *Tel:* 514-400-7075 *Fax:* 514-400-1045 *Web Site:* www.montreal-contacts.com/?lang=en, pg 497

Duft, Todd, RAND Corp, 1776 Main St, Santa Monica, CA 90407-2138 *Tel:* 310-393-0411 *Fax:* 310-393-4818 *Web Site:* www.rand.org, pg 180

Duggins, Linda, Grand Central Publishing, 1290 Avenue of the Americas, New York, NY 10104 *Tel:* 212-364-1100 *Web Site:* www.hachettebookgroup.com, pg 88

Duhaime, Jeanne, Les Editions Vents d'Ouest, 109, rue Wright, bureau 202, Gatineau, QC J8X 2G7, Canada *Tel:* 819-770-6377 *E-mail:* info@ventsdouest.ca *Web Site:* www.ventsdouest.ca, pg 425

Duhe, Mary, University of Louisiana at Lafayette Press, PO Box 43558, Lafayette, LA 70504-3558 *Tel:* 337-482-6027 *E-mail:* press.submissions@louisiana.edu *Web Site:* ulpress.org, pg 228

Dujack, Stephen, Environmental Law Institute, 1730 "M" St NW, Suite 700, Washington, DC 20036 *Tel:* 202-939-3800 *Toll Free Tel:* 800-433-5120 *Fax:* 202-939-3868 *E-mail:* law@eli.org *Web Site:* www.eli.org, pg 73

Dujan, Patricio, Math Solutions®, One Harbor Dr, Suite 101, Sausalito, CA 94965 *Toll Free Tel:* 877-234-7323 *Toll Free Fax:* 800-724-4716 *E-mail:* info@mathsolutions.com; orders@mathsolutions.com *Web Site:* www.mathsolutions.com; store.mathsolutions.com, pg 134

Duke, Celeste, BLR®—Business & Legal Resources, 100 Winners Circle, Suite 300, Brentwood, TN 37027 *Tel:* 860-510-0100 *Toll Free Tel:* 800-727-5257 *E-mail:* service@blr.com *Web Site:* www.blr.com, pg 36

Duke, Mary, Chronicle Books, 680 Second St, San Francisco, CA 94107 *Tel:* 415-537-4200 *Toll Free Tel:* 800-759-0190 (cust serv) *Fax:* 415-537-4460 *Toll Free Fax:* 800-858-7787 (orders); 800-286-9471 (cust serv) *E-mail:* frontdesk@chroniclebooks.com *Web Site:* www.chroniclebooks.com, pg 51

Dukeshire, Deborah, Standard Publishing Corp, 10 High St, Boston, MA 02110 *Tel:* 617-457-0600 *Toll Free Tel:* 800-682-5759 *Fax:* 617-457-0608 *Web Site:* www.spcpub.com, pg 206

Dulaney, Kristin, Farrar, Straus & Giroux Books for Young Readers, 120 Broadway, New York, NY 10271 *Tel:* 212-741-6900 *Toll Free Tel:* 888-330-8477 (orders) *Fax:* 212-633-9385 *Web Site:* us.macmillan.com/mackids; www.mackidsbooks.com, pg 76

Dulaney, Kristin, Roaring Brook Press, 120 Broadway, New York, NY 10271 *Tel:* 646-307-5151 *Web Site:* us.macmillan.com/publishers/roaring-brook-press, pg 186

Duncan, Andrew, Grand Central Publishing, 1290 Avenue of the Americas, New York, NY 10104 *Tel:* 212-364-1100 *Web Site:* www.hachettebookgroup.com, pg 88

Duncan, Heather, Reading the West Book Awards, 208 E Lincoln Ave, Fort Collins, CO 80524 *Tel:* 970-484-3939 *Toll Free Tel:* 800-752-0249 *Fax:* 970-484-0037 *E-mail:* info@mountainsplains.org *Web Site:* www.mountainsplains.org/reading-the-west-book-awards, pg 661

Duncan, Michael, Cambridge University Press, One Liberty Plaza, 20th fl, New York, NY 10006 *Tel:* 212-924-3900; 212-337-5000 *Fax:* 212-691-3239; 845-353-4141 *E-mail:* newyork@cambridge.org; customer_service@cambridge.org *Web Site:* www.cambridge.org/us, pg 43

Duncan, Virginia, HarperCollins Children's Books, 195 Broadway, New York, NY 10007 *Tel:* 212-207-7000 *Web Site:* www.harpercollins.com/childrens, pg 93

Dunham, Gary, Indiana University Press, Herman B Wells Library 350, 1320 E Tenth St, Bloomington, IN 47405-3907 *Tel:* 812-855-8817 *Toll Free Tel:* 800-842-6796 (orders only) *Fax:* 812-855-7931; 812-855-8507 (orders) *E-mail:* iupress@indiana.edu; iuporder@indiana.edu *Web Site:* www.iupress.indiana.edu, pg 108

Dunham, Jennie, Dunham Literary Inc, 110 William St, Suite 2202, New York, NY 10038 *Tel:* 212-929-0994 *Web Site:* dunhamlit.com, pg 482

Dunkin, Amy, Houghton Mifflin Harcourt, 125 High St, Boston, MA 02110 *Tel:* 617-351-5000 *Toll Free Tel:* 855-969-4642; 800-225-5425 (K-12 educ materials); 800-323-9540 (assessment materials); 877-219-1537 (SkillsTutor); 888-242-6747 (Innovation in Educ Group); 800-225-3362 (Trade & Ref Div) *Toll Free Fax:* 800-269-5232 *E-mail:* myhmhco@hmhco.com *Web Site:* www.hmhco.com, pg 103

Dunlap, Chris, The Arion Press, The Presidio, 1802 Hays St, San Francisco, CA 94129 *Tel:* 415-668-2542 *Fax:* 415-668-2550 *E-mail:* arionpress@arionpress.com *Web Site:* www.arionpress.com, pg 20

Dunlap, Ellen S, American Antiquarian Society (AAS), 185 Salisbury St, Worcester, MA 01609-1634 *Tel:* 508-755-5221 *Fax:* 508-753-3311 *E-mail:* library@americanantiquarian.org *Web Site:* www.americanantiquarian.org, pg 522

Dunn, Aimee Parent, Palimpsest Press, 1171 Eastlawn Ave, Windsor, ON N8S 3J1, Canada *Tel:* 519-259-2112 *E-mail:* publicity@palimpsestpress.ca *Web Site:* www.palimpsestpress.ca, pg 435

Dunn, Shaun, Palimpsest Press, 1171 Eastlawn Ave, Windsor, ON N8S 3J1, Canada *Tel:* 519-259-2112 *E-mail:* publicity@palimpsestpress.ca *Web Site:* www.palimpsestpress.ca, pg 435

Dunn, Stephen P, W W Norton & Company Inc, 500 Fifth Ave, New York, NY 10110-0017 *Tel:* 212-354-5500 *Toll Free Tel:* 800-233-4830 (orders & cust serv) *Fax:* 212-869-0856 *Toll Free Fax:* 800-458-6515 *E-mail:* orders@wwnorton.com *Web Site:* wwnorton.com, pg 152

Dunnihoo, Jeff, Pragma Media, PO Box 413, Bertam, TX 78605 *Tel:* 512-436-0606 *E-mail:* soicandfriends@pragma.media *Web Site:* soicnsot.pragma.media, pg 447

Dunnington, Jack, The Experiment, 220 E 23 St, Suite 600, New York, NY 10010-4658 *Tel:* 212-889-1659 *E-mail:* info@theexperimentpublishing.com *Web Site:* www.theexperimentpublishing.com, pg 74

Dunow, Henry, Dunow, Carlson & Lerner Literary Agency Inc, 27 W 20 St, Suite 1107, New York, NY 10011 *Tel:* 212-645-7606 *E-mail:* mail@dclagency.com *Web Site:* www.dclagency.com, pg 482

Dunton, David, Harvey Klinger Inc, 300 W 55 St, Suite 11V, New York, NY 10019 *Tel:* 212-581-7068 *Fax:* 212-315-3823 *E-mail:* queries@harveyklinger.com *Web Site:* www.harveyklinger.com, pg 491

DuPont, Charles, Alan Wofsy Fine Arts, 1109 Geary Blvd, San Francisco, CA 94109 *Tel:* 415-292-6500 *Toll Free Tel:* 800-660-6403 *Fax:* 415-292-6594 (off & cust serv); 510-251-1840 (acctg) *E-mail:* order@art-books.com (orders); editeur@earthlink.net (edit); beauxarts@earthlink.net (cust serv) *Web Site:* www.art-books.com, pg 243

Duquet, Michel, Francois-Xavier Garneau Medal, 130 Albert St, Suite 1201, Ottawa, ON K1P 5G4, Canada *Tel:* 613-233-7885 *Fax:* 613-565-5445 *E-mail:* cha-shc@cha-shc.ca *Web Site:* www.cha-shc.ca, pg 618

Duquet, Michel, Sir John A Macdonald Prize, 130 Albert St, Suite 1201, Ottawa, ON K1P 5G4, Canada *Tel:* 613-233-7885 *Fax:* 613-565-5445 *E-mail:* cha-shc@cha-shc.ca *Web Site:* www.cha-shc.ca, pg 636

Duquette, Brett, little bee books, 251 Park Ave S, 12th fl, New York, NY 10010 *Toll Free Tel:* 844-321-0237 *E-mail:* info@littlebeebooks.com *Web Site:* littlebeebooks.com, pg 125

Duran, Bernardo, NACE International, 15835 Park Ten Place, Houston, TX 77084 *Tel:* 281-228-6200; 281-228-6223 *Toll Free Tel:* 800-797-NACE (797-6223) *Fax:* 281-228-6300 *E-mail:* firstservice@nace.org *Web Site:* www.nace.org, pg 144

Durante, Dawn, University of Texas Press, 3001 Lake Austin Blvd, 2.200, Austin, TX 78703 *Tel:* 512-471-7233 *Fax:* 512-232-7178 *E-mail:* utpress@uts.cc.utexas.edu; info@utpress.utexas.edu *Web Site:* utpress.utexas.edu, pg 216

Durbin, Dean, Trusted Media Brands Inc, 750 Third Ave, 3rd fl, New York, NY 10017 *Tel:* 646-293-6299 *Toll Free Tel:* 877-732-4438 (cust serv) *Fax:* 646-293-6251 *E-mail:* customercare@trustedmediabrands.com; press@trustedmediabrands.com *Web Site:* www.trustedmediabrands.com; www.rd.com, pg 221

Durbin, Jon, W W Norton & Company Inc, 500 Fifth Ave, New York, NY 10110-0017 *Tel:* 212-354-5500 *Toll Free Tel:* 800-233-4830 (orders & cust serv) *Fax:* 212-869-0856 *Toll Free Fax:* 800-458-6515 *E-mail:* orders@wwnorton.com *Web Site:* wwnorton.com, pg 152

Durham, Daphne, Farrar, Straus & Giroux, LLC, 175 Varick St, 9th fl, New York, NY 10014 *Tel:* 212-741-6900 *E-mail:* fsg.publicity@fsgbooks.com *Web Site:* us.macmillan.com/fsg.aspx, pg 76

Durham, Judith B, Graphic Arts Education & Research Foundation (GAERF), 1899 Preston White Dr, Reston, VA 20191 *Tel:* 703-264-7200 *E-mail:* gaerf@npes.org *Web Site:* www.gaerf.org, pg 551

Durham, Rusty, StarGroup International Inc, 1194 Old Dixie Hwy, Suite 201, West Palm Beach, FL 33413 *Tel:* 561-547-0667 *Fax:* 561-843-8530 *E-mail:* info@stargroupinternational.com *Web Site:* stargroupinternational.com, pg 207

Durkin, Cletus, Penguin Random House LLC, 1745 Broadway, New York, NY 10019 Tel: 212-782-9000 Toll Free Tel: 800-726-0600 Web Site: www.penguinrandomhouse.com, pg 164

Durrah, James C II, National Association of Black Journalists (NABJ), 1100 Knight Hall, Suite 3100, College Park, MD 20742 Tel: 301-405-0248 Fax: 301-314-1714 E-mail: info@nabj.org; press@nabj.org Web Site: www.nabj.org, pg 538

Durrant, Jennifer, Sourced Media Books, 15 Via Picato, San Clemente, CA 92673 Tel: 949-813-0182 E-mail: editor@sourcedmediabooks.com Web Site: sourcedmediabooks.com, pg 204

Duval, Emily, Random House Children's Books, 1745 Broadway, 10th fl, New York, NY 10019 Tel: 212-782-9000 Web Site: www.randomhousekids.com, pg 181

Duval, Nathalie, Alexander Street, a ProQuest Company, 99 Canal Center Plaza, Suite 200, Alexandria, VA 22314 Tel: 703-212-8520 Toll Free Tel: 800-889-5937 E-mail: sales@alexanderstreet.com; marketing@alexanderstreet.com; info@alexanderstreet.com Web Site: alexanderstreet.com, pg 7

DuVall, Jennifer, Schiavone Literary Agency Inc, 236 Trails End, West Palm Beach, FL 33413-2135 Tel: 561-966-9294 Fax: 561-966-9294 E-mail: profschia@aol.com Web Site: www.publishersmarketplace.com/members/profschia, pg 501

Dworkin, Brooke, Disney Press, 1101 Flower St, Glendale, CA 91201 Web Site: books.disney.com, pg 65

Dwyer, Corinne A, North Star Press of Saint Cloud Inc, 19485 Estes Rd, Clearwater, MN 55320 Tel: 320-558-9062 E-mail: info@northstarpress.com Web Site: www.northstarpress.com, pg 152

Dwyer, Peter, Cistercian Publications, Saint John's Abbey, PO Box 7500, Collegeville, MN 56321 Tel: 320-363-2213 Toll Free Tel: 800-436-8431 Fax: 320-363-3299 Toll Free Fax: 800-445-5899 E-mail: sales@litpress.org Web Site: www.cistercianpublications.org, pg 52

Dwyer, Peter, Liturgical Press, PO Box 7500, St John's Abbey, Collegeville, MN 56321-7500 Tel: 320-363-2213 Toll Free Tel: 800-858-5450 Fax: 320-363-3299 Toll Free Fax: 800-445-5899 E-mail: sales@litpress.org Web Site: www.litpress.org, pg 126

Dye, Ann, HarperCollins Children's Books, 195 Broadway, New York, NY 10007 Tel: 212-207-7000 Web Site: www.harpercollins.com/childrens, pg 93

Dye, Ann, Houghton Mifflin Harcourt Trade & Reference Division, 125 High St, Boston, MA 02110 Tel: 617-351-5000 Web Site: www.hmhco.com, pg 104

Dye, Skip, Books on Tape™, 1745 Broadway, New York, NY 10019 Toll Free Tel: 800-733-3000 (cust serv) Toll Free Fax: 800-940-7046 Web Site: www.booksontape.com, pg 38

Dye, Skip, Penguin Random House LLC, 1745 Broadway, New York, NY 10019 Tel: 212-782-9000 Toll Free Tel: 800-726-0600 Web Site: www.penguinrandomhouse.com, pg 164

Dyer, Phoebe, Bloomsbury Publishing Inc, 1385 Broadway, 5th fl, New York, NY 10018 Tel: 212-419-5300 E-mail: marketingusa@bloomsbury.com; adultpublicityusa@bloomsbury.com; askacademic@bloomsbury.com Web Site: www.bloomsbury.com, pg 36

Dyke, George, Earth Edit, PO Box 114, Maiden Rock, WI 54750 Tel: 715-448-3009, pg 462

Dykstra, LeeAnna, Broadview Press, 280 Perry St, Unit 5, Peterborough, ON K9J 2J4, Canada Tel: 705-743-8990 Fax: 705-743-8353 E-mail: customerservice@broadviewpress.com Web Site: www.broadviewpress.com, pg 417

Dynak, Sharon, Ucross Foundation Residency Program, 30 Big Red Lane, Clearmont, WY 82835 Tel: 307-737-2291 Fax: 307-737-2322 E-mail: info@ucross.org Web Site: www.ucrossfoundation.org, pg 674

Dyson, Elizabeth Branch, University of Chicago Press, 1427 E 60 St, Chicago, IL 60637-2954 Tel: 773-702-7700; 773-702-7600 Toll Free Tel: 800-621-2736 (orders) Fax: 773-702-9756; 773-660-2235 (orders); 773-702-2708 E-mail: custserv@press.uchicago.edu; marketing@press.uchicago.edu Web Site: www.press.uchicago.edu, pg 226

Dyssegaard, Elisabeth, St Martin's Press, LLC, 120 Broadway, New York, NY 10271 Tel: 646-307-5151 Web Site: us.macmillan.com/smp, pg 190

Dyssou, Nanda, LARB Books, 6671 Sunset Blvd, Suite 1521, Los Angeles, CA 90028 Tel: 323-952-3950 E-mail: larbbooks@lareviewofbooks.org Web Site: larbbooks.org, pg 120

Dystel, Jane, Dystel, Goderich & Bourret LLC, One Union Sq W, Suite 904, New York, NY 10003 Tel: 212-627-9100 Fax: 212-627-9313 Web Site: www.dystel.com, pg 482

Dziena, David, Pflaum Publishing Group, 3055 Kettering Blvd, Suite 100, Dayton, OH 45439 Toll Free Tel: 800-523-4625; 800-543-4383 (ext 1136, cust serv) Toll Free Fax: 800-370-4450 E-mail: service@pflaum.com Web Site: www.pflaum.com, pg 168

Dzienkonski, Karen, Penguin Random House Audio Publishing, 1745 Broadway, New York, NY 10019 E-mail: audio@penguinrandomhouse.com Web Site: www.penguinrandomhouseaudio.com, pg 164

Eadicicco, John Michael, Association of University Presses (AUPresses), 1412 Broadway, Suite 2135, New York, NY 10018 Tel: 212-989-1010 Fax: 212-989-0275 E-mail: info@aupresses.org Web Site: www.aupresses.org, pg 527

Eagle, Sara, Alfred A Knopf, c/o Penguin Random House Inc, 1745 Broadway, New York, NY 10019 Tel: 212-751-2600 Fax: 212-572-2662 (foreign rts) Web Site: knopfdoubleday.com, pg 118

Eagle, Sara, Pantheon Books, c/o Penguin Random House Inc, 1745 Broadway, New York, NY 10019 Tel: 212-751-2600 Fax: 212-572-2662 (foreign rts) Web Site: knopfdoubleday.com, pg 159

Eagle, Sara, Schocken Books, c/o Penguin Random House Inc, 1745 Broadway, New York, NY 10019 Tel: 212-751-2600 Fax: 212-572-2662 (foreign rts) Web Site: knopfdoubleday.com, pg 193

Eaker, Noah, HarperCollins General Books Group, 195 Broadway, New York, NY 10007 Tel: 212-207-7000 Web Site: www.harpercollins.com, pg 93

Earle, Kathryn, Bloomsbury Academic, 1385 Broadway, 5th fl, New York, NY 10018 Tel: 212-419-5300 Web Site: www.bloomsbury.com/us/academic, pg 35

Earle, Kathryn, Bloomsbury Publishing Inc, 1385 Broadway, 5th fl, New York, NY 10018 Tel: 212-419-5300 E-mail: marketingusa@bloomsbury.com; adultpublicityusa@bloomsbury.com; askacademic@bloomsbury.com Web Site: www.bloomsbury.com, pg 36

Earley, Diane, Charlesbridge Publishing Inc, 85 Main St, Watertown, MA 02472 Tel: 617-926-0329 Toll Free Tel: 800-225-3214 Fax: 617-926-5720 Toll Free Fax: 800-926-5775 E-mail: books@charlesbridge.com Web Site: www.charlesbridge.com, pg 49

Early, Brighton, Sudden Fiction Contest, c/o ASUC Publications, Univ of California, 10-B Eshleman Hall, Berkeley, CA 94720-4500 E-mail: bfictionreview@yahoo.com Web Site: www.ocf.berkeley.edu/~bfr/, pg 671

Easley, Thomas J, American Medical Association, AMA Plaza, 330 N Wabash, Suite 39300, Chicago, IL 60611-5885 Tel: 312-464-5000 Toll Free Tel: 800-621-8335 Web Site: www.ama-assn.org, pg 12, 523

Easton, Claire, Painted-Words Inc, 310 W 97 St, Suite 24, New York, NY 10025 Tel: 212-663-2311 Fax: 212-663-2891 E-mail: info@painted-words.com Web Site: painted-words.com, pg 512

Easton, Emily, Random House Children's Books, 1745 Broadway, 10th fl, New York, NY 10019 Tel: 212-782-9000 Web Site: www.randomhousekids.com, pg 180

Eastright, Josh, Bloomberg Law Book Division, 1801 S Bell St, Arlington, VA 22202 Tel: 732-476-6397 Toll Free Tel: 800-960-1220 Fax: 732-346-1624 E-mail: books@bloomberglaw.com Web Site: www.bna.com/bloomberglaw/, pg 35

Eastwood, Hilary, Mazda Publishers Inc, PO Box 2603, Costa Mesa, CA 92628 Tel: 714-751-5252 Fax: 714-751-4805 E-mail: mazdapub@aol.com Web Site: www.mazdapublishers.com, pg 134

Eaton, Brenda, Interlink Publishing Group Inc, 46 Crosby St, Northampton, MA 01060 Tel: 413-582-7054 Toll Free Tel: 800-238-LINK (238-5465) Fax: 413-582-7057 E-mail: info@interlinkbooks.com Web Site: www.interlinkbooks.com, pg 110

Eaton, Dena, Bitingduck Press LLC, 1262 Sunnyoaks Circle, Altadena, CA 91001 Tel: 626-507-8033 E-mail: notifications@bitingduckpress.com Web Site: bitingduckpress.com, pg 34

Eaton, Eryn, Red Wheel/Weiser, 65 Parker St, Suite 7, Newburyport, MA 01950 Tel: 978-465-0504 Toll Free Tel: 800-423-7087 (orders) Fax: 978-465-0243 E-mail: info@rwwbooks.com Web Site: www.redwheelweiser.com, pg 183

Eaton, Jonathan, Tilbury House Publishers, 12 Starr St, Thomaston, ME 04861 Tel: 207-582-1899 Toll Free Tel: 800-582-1899 (orders) Fax: 207-582-8227 E-mail: tilbury@tilburyhouse.com Web Site: www.tilburyhouse.com, pg 218

Eaton, Sandi, Chelsea Green Publishing Co, 85 N Main St, Suite 120, White River Junction, VT 05001 Tel: 802-295-6300 Toll Free Tel: 800-639-4099 (cust serv & orders) Fax: 802-295-6444 E-mail: customerservice@chelseagreen.com; editorial@chelseagreen.com; publicity@chelseagreen.com; rights@chelseagreen.com Web Site: www.chelseagreen.com, pg 49

Eberle, Katie, Parallax Press, 2236B Sixth St, Berkeley, CA 94710 Tel: 510-540-6411 Toll Free Tel: 800-863-5290 (orders) Fax: 510-981-1157 Web Site: www.parallax.org, pg 160

Eck, Caitlin, Chicago Review Press, 814 N Franklin St, Chicago, IL 60610 Tel: 312-337-0747 Toll Free Tel: 800-888-4741 Fax: 312-337-5110 E-mail: frontdesk@chicagoreviewpress.com Web Site: www.chicagoreviewpress.com, pg 50

Ecklebarger, David, Editorial Unilit, 8167 NW 84 St, Medley, FL 33166 Tel: 305-592-6136 Toll Free Tel: 800-767-7726 Fax: 305-592-0087 E-mail: info@editorialunilit.com; customerservice@editorialunilit.com Web Site: www.editorialunilit.com, pg 224

Eckstut, Arielle, Levine|Greenberg|Rostan Literary Agency, 307 Seventh Ave, Suite 2407, New York, NY 10001 Tel: 212-337-0934 Fax: 212-337-0948 Web Site: lgrliterary.com, pg 493

Eddy, Claire, Tom Doherty Associates, LLC, 120 Broadway, New York, NY 10271 Tel: 646-307-5511 Toll Free Tel: 800-455-0340 Web Site: us.macmillan.com/torforge, pg 66

Eddy, Holly, Islandport Press, 247 Portland St, Bldg C, Yarmouth, ME 04096 Tel: 207-846-3344 Fax: 207-619-9975 E-mail: info@islandportpress.com Web Site: www.islandportpress.com, pg 112

Eddy, Jim, Psychological Assessment Resources Inc (PAR), 16204 N Florida Ave, Lutz, FL 33549 Tel: 813-449-4065 Toll Free Tel: 800-331-8378 Fax: 813-961-2196 Toll Free Fax: 800-727-9329 Web Site: www.parinc.com, pg 177

Edelman, Maggie, Chronicle Books, 680 Second St, San Francisco, CA 94107 Tel: 415-537-4200 Toll Free Tel: 800-759-0190 (cust serv) Fax: 415-537-4460 Toll Free Fax: 800-858-7787 (orders); 800-286-9471 (cust serv) E-mail: frontdesk@chroniclebooks.com Web Site: www.chroniclebooks.com, pg 52

Edelson, Libby, HarperCollins General Books Group, 195 Broadway, New York, NY 10007 Tel: 212-207-7000 Web Site: www.harpercollins.com, pg 93

Ekus, Lisa, The Lisa Ekus Group LLC, 57 North St, Hatfield, MA 01038 *Tel:* 413-247-9325 *Fax:* 413-247-9873 *E-mail:* info@lisaekus.com, pg 483, 582 *Web Site:* lisaekus.com, pg 483, 582

Ekus, Sally, The Lisa Ekus Group LLC, 57 North St, Hatfield, MA 01038 *Tel:* 413-247-9325 *Fax:* 413-247-9873 *E-mail:* info@lisaekus.com *Web Site:* lisaekus.com, pg 483, 582

Elancheran, Maran, Newgen North America Inc, 2714 Bee Cave Rd, Suite 201, Austin, TX 78746 *Tel:* 512-478-5341 *Fax:* 512-476-4756 *E-mail:* sales@newgen.co *Web Site:* www.newgen.co, pg 468

Elbe, Susan, John Wiley & Sons Inc Global Education, 111 River St, Hoboken, NJ 07030-5774 *Tel:* 201-748-6000 *Toll Free Tel:* 800-225-5945 (cust serv) *Fax:* 201-748-6008 *E-mail:* info@wiley.com *Web Site:* www.wiley.com, pg 242

Elblonk, Matthew, DeFiore and Company Literary Management Inc, 47 E 19 St, 3rd fl, New York, NY 10003 *Tel:* 212-925-7744 *Fax:* 212-925-9803 *E-mail:* info@defiliterary.com; submissions@defiliterary.com *Web Site:* www.defiliterary.com, pg 481

Eldred, Jake, Penguin Random House LLC, 1745 Broadway, New York, NY 10019 *Tel:* 212-782-9000 *Toll Free Tel:* 800-726-0600 *Web Site:* www.penguinrandomhouse.com, pg 164

Eldredge, Samantha, SDP Publishing Solutions LLC, 36 Captain's Way, East Bridgewater, MA 02333 *Tel:* 617-775-0656 *Web Site:* www.sdppublishingsolutions.com, pg 470

Elias, Lindsey, Penguin Random House LLC, 1745 Broadway, New York, NY 10019 *Tel:* 212-782-9000 *Toll Free Tel:* 800-726-0600 *Web Site:* www.penguinrandomhouse.com, pg 164

Elinsky, Rachel, HarperCollins Publishers, 195 Broadway, New York, NY 10007 *Tel:* 212-207-7000 *Fax:* 212-207-7145 *Web Site:* www.harpercollins.com, pg 94

Elizalde, Steve, Greenleaf Book Group LLC, 3 Park Place, 4005 Banister Lane, Suite B, Austin, TX 78704 *Tel:* 512-891-6100 *Fax:* 512-891-6150 *E-mail:* contact@greenleafbookgroup.com *Web Site:* www.greenleafbookgroup.com, pg 89

Ellen, Joan, World Citizens, PO Box 131, Mill Valley, CA 94942-0131 *Tel:* 415-380-8020; 415-233-2822 (direct) *Toll Free Tel:* 800-247-6553 (orders only), pg 245

Ellenberg, Ethan, Ethan Ellenberg Literary Agency, 155 Suffolk St, Suite 2R, New York, NY 10002 *Tel:* 212-431-4554 *E-mail:* agent@ethanellenberg.com *Web Site:* www.ethanellenberg.com, pg 483

Ellenson, David, Hebrew Union College Press, 3101 Clifton Ave, Cincinnati, OH 45220 *Tel:* 513-221-1875 *Fax:* 513-221-0321 *Web Site:* press.huc.edu, pg 97

Eller, Beth, Bloomsbury Publishing Inc, 1385 Broadway, 5th fl, New York, NY 10018 *Tel:* 212-419-5300 *E-mail:* marketingusa@bloomsbury.com; adultpublicityusa@bloomsbury.com; askacademic@bloomsbury.com *Web Site:* www.bloomsbury.com, pg 35

Ellerbeck, Brian, Teachers College Press, 1234 Amsterdam Ave, New York, NY 10027 *Tel:* 212-678-3929 *Fax:* 212-678-4149 *E-mail:* tcpress@tc.edu *Web Site:* www.tcpress.com, pg 214

Elliott, Aaron, Florida Graphics Alliance (FGA), 5770 Hoffner Ave, Suite 103, Orlando, FL 32822 *Tel:* 407-240-8009 *Toll Free Tel:* 800-331-0461 *Fax:* 407-240-8333 *E-mail:* info@floridagraphics.org *Web Site:* www.floridagraphics.org, pg 533

Elliott, Bill, iUniverse, 1663 Liberty Dr, Bloomington, IN 47403 *Toll Free Tel:* 800-AUTHORS (288-4677) *Web Site:* www.iuniverse.com, pg 113

Elliott, Bill, Trafford, 1663 Liberty Dr, Bloomington, IN 47403 *Toll Free Tel:* 888-232-4444 *E-mail:* customersupport@trafford.com; sales@trafford.com *Web Site:* www.trafford.com, pg 219

Elliott, Bill, Xlibris Corp, 1663 Liberty Dr, Suite 200, Bloomington, IN 47403 *Toll Free Tel:* 844-714-8691; 888-795-4274 *Fax:* 610-915-0294 *E-mail:* info@xlibris.com; media@xlibris.com *Web Site:* www.xlibris.com; www.authorsolutions.com/our-imprints/xlibris, pg 246

Elliott, Jennifer, International Linguistics Corp, 12220 Blue Ridge Blvd, Suite G, Kansas City, MO 64030 *Tel:* 816-765-8855 *Toll Free Tel:* 800-237-1830 (orders) *E-mail:* learnables@sbcglobal.net *Web Site:* www.learnables.com, pg 111

Elliott, Miranda, Dufour Editions Inc, PO Box 7, Chester Springs, PA 19425 *Tel:* 610-458-5005 *E-mail:* info@dufoureditions.com *Web Site:* www.dufoureditions.com, pg 67

Elliott, Stephanie, Wesleyan University Press, 215 Long Lane, Middletown, CT 06459-0433 *Tel:* 860-685-7712 *Fax:* 860-685-7712 *Web Site:* www.wesleyan.edu/wespress, pg 239

Elliott, Stephen P, Sachem Publishing Associates Inc, 402 W Lyon Farm Dr, Greenwich, CT 06831 *Tel:* 203-813-3077 *E-mail:* sachempub@optonline.net, pg 470

Elliott, William, AuthorHouse, 1663 Liberty Dr, Bloomington, IN 47403 *Tel:* 812-339-6000 (outside US) *Toll Free Tel:* 888-519-5121 *E-mail:* authorsupport@authorhouse.com *Web Site:* www.authorhouse.com, pg 25

Ellis, Barbara, Unicorn Writers' Conference, 17 Church Hill Rd, Redding, CT 06896 *Tel:* 203-938-7405 *Fax:* 203-938-7405 *E-mail:* unicornwritersconference@gmail.com *Web Site:* unicornwritersconference.com, pg 579

Ellis, Clare, Stone Pier Press, PO Box 170572, San Francisco, CA 94117 *Tel:* 415-484-2821 *E-mail:* hello@stonepierpress.org *Web Site:* www.stonepierpress.org, pg 209

Ellis, Elaina, Copper Canyon Press, Fort Worden State Park, Bldg 313, Port Townsend, WA 98368 *Tel:* 360-385-4925 *Toll Free Tel:* 877-501-1393 (orders) *Fax:* 360-385-4985 *E-mail:* poetry@coppercanyonpress.org *Web Site:* www.coppercanyonpress.org, pg 56

Ellis, Jane, University Science Books, 20 Edgeshill Rd, Mill Valley, CA 94941 *Tel:* 703-661-1572 (cust serv, orders) *Fax:* 703-661-1572 (cust serv, orders) *E-mail:* usbmail@presswarehouse.com (cust serv, orders) *Web Site:* www.uscibooks.com, pg 233

Ellis, Jeremy, Reading the West Book Awards, 208 E Lincoln Ave, Fort Collins, CO 80524 *Tel:* 970-484-3939 *Toll Free Tel:* 800-752-0249 *Fax:* 970-484-0037 *E-mail:* info@mountainsplains.org *Web Site:* www.mountainsplains.org/reading-the-west-book-awards, pg 661

Ellis, Kirk, Spur Awards, 271 CR 219, Encampment, WY 82325 *Tel:* 307-329-8942 *E-mail:* wwa.moulton@gmail.com *Web Site:* westernwriters.org/spur-awards/, pg 670

Ellis, Kirk, Western Writers of America Inc (WWA), 271 CR 219, Encampment, WY 82325 *Tel:* 307-329-8942 *Web Site:* westernwriters.org, pg 548

Ellis, Mercury, Chronicle Books, 680 Second St, San Francisco, CA 94107 *Tel:* 415-537-4200 *Toll Free Tel:* 800-759-0190 (cust serv) *Fax:* 415-537-4460 *Toll Free Fax:* 800-858-7787 (orders); 800-286-9471 (cust serv) *E-mail:* frontdesk@chroniclebooks.com *Web Site:* www.chroniclebooks.com, pg 51

Ellis, Molly, Farrar, Straus & Giroux Books for Young Readers, 120 Broadway, New York, NY 10271 *Tel:* 212-741-6900 *Toll Free Tel:* 888-330-8477 (orders) *Fax:* 212-633-9385 *Web Site:* us.macmillan.com/mackids; www.mackidsbooks.com, pg 76

Ellis, Molly, Roaring Brook Press, 120 Broadway, New York, NY 10271 *Tel:* 646-307-5151 *Web Site:* us.macmillan.com/publishers/roaring-brook-press, pg 186

Ellison, Nicholas, Nicholas Ellison Agency, 3 Tara Dr, Brookfield, CT 06804-2324 *Web Site:* www.thenicholasellisonagency.com, pg 483

Ellsberg, Robert, Orbis Books, PO Box 302, Maryknoll, NY 10545-0302 *Tel:* 914-941-7636 *Toll Free Tel:* 800-258-5838 (orders, Mon-Fri 8AM-4PM EST) *Fax:* 914-941-7005 *E-mail:* orbisbooks@maryknoll.org *Web Site:* orbisbooks.com, pg 156

Ellsworth, Thomas N, Vesuvian Books, 2817 West End Ave, No 126-283, Nashville, TN 37203 *E-mail:* info@vesuvianmedia.com *Web Site:* www.vesuvianbooks.com, pg 236

Ellul, Nicole, Simon & Schuster Children's Publishing, 1230 Avenue of the Americas, New York, NY 10020 *Tel:* 212-698-7000 *Web Site:* www.simonandschuster.com/kids; www.simonandschuster.com/teen; simonandschuster.net; simonandschuster.biz, pg 199

Elmer, Derek, Random House Children's Books, 1745 Broadway, 10th fl, New York, NY 10019 *Tel:* 212-782-9000 *Web Site:* www.randomhousekids.com, pg 180

Elnan, Hannah, Sasquatch Books, 1904 S Third Ave, Suite 710, Seattle, WA 98101 *Tel:* 206-467-4300 *Toll Free Tel:* 800-775-0817 *Fax:* 206-467-4301 *E-mail:* custserv@sasquatchbooks.com *Web Site:* sasquatchbooks.com, pg 192

Elwell, James, Tyndale House Publishers Inc, 351 Executive Dr, Carol Stream, IL 60188 *Tel:* 630-668-8300 *Toll Free Tel:* 800-323-9400; 855-277-9400 *Toll Free Fax:* 866-622-9474 *Web Site:* www.tyndale.com, pg 223

Emerick, Ken, Individual Excellence Awards, 30 E Broad St, 33rd fl, Columbus, OH 43215 *Tel:* 614-466-2613 *Fax:* 614-466-4494 *Web Site:* www.oac.state.oh.us, pg 626

Emmett, Jennifer, National Geographic Books, 1145 17 St NW, Washington, DC 20036-4688 *Tel:* 202-857-7000 *Toll Free Tel:* 877-866-6486 *E-mail:* ngbooks@cdsfulfillment.com *Web Site:* www.nationalgeographic.com/books/; ngbooks.buysub.com, pg 146

Emmrich, Terry, University of Wisconsin Press, 728 State St, Suite 443, Madison, WI 53706-1418 *Tel:* 608-263-1110; 608-263-0668 (journal orders) *Toll Free Tel:* 800-621-2736 (book orders) *Fax:* 608-263-1173 *Toll Free Fax:* 800-621-2736 (book orders) *E-mail:* uwiscpress@uwpress.wisc.edu *Web Site:* uwpress.wisc.edu, pg 232

Emond, D Paul, Emond Montgomery Publications Ltd, 60 Shaftesbury Ave, Toronto, ON M4T 1A3, Canada *Tel:* 416-975-3925 *Toll Free Tel:* 888-837-0815 *Fax:* 416-975-3924 *E-mail:* orders@emp.ca *Web Site:* www.emp.ca, pg 425

Enderle, Kristine, American Psychological Association, 750 First St NE, Washington, DC 20002-4242 *Tel:* 202-336-5510 *Toll Free Tel:* 800-374-2721 *Fax:* 202-336-5502 *E-mail:* order@apa.org *Web Site:* www.apa.org/books, pg 13

Enderlin, Jennifer, St Martin's Press, LLC, 120 Broadway, New York, NY 10271 *Tel:* 646-307-5151 *Web Site:* us.macmillan.com/smp, pg 190

Endler, Abby, Alfred A Knopf, c/o Penguin Random House Inc, 1745 Broadway, New York, NY 10019 *Tel:* 212-751-2600 *Fax:* 212-572-2662 (foreign rts) *Web Site:* knopfdoubleday.com, pg 118

Eng, Dave, Frank Amato Publications Inc, 4040 SE Wister St, Milwaukie, OR 97222 *Tel:* 503-653-8108 *Toll Free Tel:* 800-541-9498 *Fax:* 503-653-2766 *E-mail:* customerservice@amatobooks.com; info@amatobooks.com *Web Site:* www.amatobooks.com, pg 8

Eng, Kenneth, Macmillan, 120 Broadway, 22nd fl, New York, NY 10271 *Tel:* 646-307-5151 *E-mail:* press.inquiries@macmillan.com *Web Site:* www.macmillan.com, pg 129

Engel, Jackie, Little, Brown Books for Young Readers, 1290 Avenue of the Americas, New York, NY 10104 *Tel:* 212-364-1100 *Toll Free Tel:* 800-759-0190 (cust serv) *Web Site:* www.hachettebookgroup.com, pg 126

Engel, Margaret, The Alicia Patterson Foundation Fellowship Program, 1100 Vermont Ave, Suite 900, Washington, DC 20005 *Tel:* 202-393-5995 *Fax:* 301-951-8512 *E-mail:* info@aliciapatterson.org *Web Site:* www.aliciapatterson.org, pg 652

Engelman, Ralph, The George Polk Awards, The Brooklyn Campus, One University Plaza, Brooklyn, NY 11201-5372 *Tel:* 718-488-1009 *Web Site:* www. liu.edu/polk, pg 657

Engelmann, Sarah, Doubleday, c/o Penguin Random House Inc, 1745 Broadway, New York, NY 10019 *Tel:* 212-751-2600 *Fax:* 212-572-2662 (foreign rts) *E-mail:* ddaypub@randomhouse.com *Web Site:* knopfdoubleday.com, pg 66

Engelsma, Jonathan, Reformation Heritage Books, 2965 Leonard St NE, Grand Rapids, MI 49525 *Tel:* 616-977-0889 *Fax:* 616-285-3246 *E-mail:* orders@ heritagebooks.org *Web Site:* www.heritagebooks.org, pg 184

Engler, Hannah, Doubleday, c/o Penguin Random House Inc, 1745 Broadway, New York, NY 10019 *Tel:* 212-751-2600 *Fax:* 212-572-2662 (foreign rts) *E-mail:* ddaypub@randomhouse.com *Web Site:* knopfdoubleday.com, pg 66

Englert, Bradley, Orbit, 1290 Avenue of the Americas, New York, NY 10104 *Tel:* 212-364-1100 *Toll Free Tel:* 800-759-0190 *Web Site:* www.orbitbooks.net, pg 156

Englert, Joanna, Linda Bruckheimer Series in Kentucky Literature, 822 E Market St, Louisville, KY 40206 *Tel:* 502-458-4028 *E-mail:* info@sarabandebooks.org *Web Site:* www.sarabandebooks.org/bruckheimer, pg 601

Englert, Joanna, Mary McCarthy Prize in Short Fiction, 822 E Market St, Louisville, KY 40206 *Tel:* 502-458-4028 *E-mail:* info@sarabandebooks.org *Web Site:* www.sarabandebooks.org/mccarthy, pg 639

Englert, Joanna, Kathryn A Morton Prize in Poetry, 822 E Market St, Louisville, KY 40206 *Tel:* 502-458-4028 *E-mail:* info@sarabandebooks.org *Web Site:* www. sarabandebooks.org/morton, pg 643

Englert, Joanna, Sarabande Books Inc, 822 E Market St, Louisville, KY 40206 *Tel:* 502-458-4028 *Fax:* 502-458-4065 *E-mail:* info@sarabandebooks.org *Web Site:* www.sarabandebooks.org, pg 192

Engles, Eric W PhD, EditCraft Editorial Services, 422 Pine St, Grass Valley, CA 95945 *Tel:* 530-273-3934 *Web Site:* www.editcraft.com, pg 463

English, Beth, Willi Paul Adams Award, 112 N Bryan Ave, Bloomington, IN 47408-4141 *Tel:* 812-855-7311 *E-mail:* oah@oah.org *Web Site:* www.oah.org/awards, pg 589

English, Beth, Ray Allen Billington Prize, 112 N Bryan Ave, Bloomington, IN 47408-4141 *Tel:* 812-855-7311 *E-mail:* oah@oah.org *Web Site:* www.oah.org/awards, pg 598

English, Beth, Brinkley-Stephenson Award, 112 N Bryan Ave, Bloomington, IN 47408-4141 *Tel:* 812-855-7311 *E-mail:* oah@oah.org *Web Site:* www.oah.org/awards, pg 601

English, Beth, Avery O Craven Award, 112 N Bryan Ave, Bloomington, IN 47408-4141 *Tel:* 812-855-7311 *E-mail:* oah@oah.org *Web Site:* www.oah.org/awards, pg 607

English, Beth, Merle Curti Intellectual History Award, 112 N Bryan Ave, Bloomington, IN 47408-4141 *Tel:* 812-855-7311 *E-mail:* oah@oah.org *Web Site:* www.oah.org/awards, pg 608

English, Beth, Merle Curti Social History Award, 112 N Bryan Ave, Bloomington, IN 47408-4141 *Tel:* 812-855-7311 *E-mail:* oah@oah.org *Web Site:* www.oah. org/awards, pg 608

English, Beth, Ellis W Hawley Prize, 112 N Bryan Ave, Bloomington, IN 47408-4141 *Tel:* 812-855-7311 *E-mail:* oah@oah.org *Web Site:* www.oah.org/awards, pg 622

English, Beth, Darlene Clark Hine Award, 112 N Bryan Ave, Bloomington, IN 47408-4141 *Tel:* 812-855-7311 *E-mail:* oah@oah.org *Web Site:* www.oah.org/awards, pg 624

English, Beth, Richard W Leopold Prize, 112 N Bryan Ave, Bloomington, IN 47408-4141 *Tel:* 812-855-7311 *E-mail:* oah@oah.org *Web Site:* www.oah.org/awards, pg 632

English, Beth, Lawrence W Levine Award, 112 N Bryan Ave, Bloomington, IN 47408-4141 *Tel:* 812-855-7311 *E-mail:* oah@oah.org *Web Site:* www.oah.org/awards, pg 633

English, Beth, Liberty Legacy Foundation Award, 112 N Bryan Ave, Bloomington, IN 47408-4141 *Tel:* 812-855-7311 *E-mail:* oah@oah.org *Web Site:* www.oah. org/awards, pg 633

English, Beth, David Montgomery Award, 112 N Bryan Ave, Bloomington, IN 47408-4141 *Tel:* 812-855-7311 *E-mail:* oah@oah.org *Web Site:* www.oah.org/awards, pg 642

English, Beth, Mary Nickliss Prize in US Women's +/or Gender History, 112 N Bryan Ave, Bloomington, IN 47408-4141 *Tel:* 812-855-7311 *E-mail:* oah@oah.org *Web Site:* www.oah.org/awards, pg 648

English, Beth, James A Rawley Prize, 112 N Bryan Ave, Bloomington, IN 47408-4141 *Tel:* 812-855-7311 *E-mail:* oah@oah.org *Web Site:* www.oah.org/awards, pg 661

English, Beth, David Thelen Award, 112 N Bryan Ave, Bloomington, IN 47408-4141 *Tel:* 812-855-7311 *E-mail:* oah@oah.org *Web Site:* www.oah.org/awards, pg 672

English, Beth, Frederick Jackson Turner Award, 112 N Bryan Ave, Bloomington, IN 47408-4141 *Tel:* 812-855-7311 *E-mail:* oah@oah.org *Web Site:* www.oah. org/awards, pg 674

English-Loeb, Brenna, Transatlantic Agency, 2 Bloor St E, Suite 3500, Toronto, ON M4W 1A8, Canada *Tel:* 416-488-9214 *E-mail:* info@transatlanticagency. com *Web Site:* www.transatlanticagency.com, pg 506

Engstrand, Vida, Kensington Publishing Corp, 119 W 40 St, New York, NY 10018 *Tel:* 212-407-1500 *Toll Free Tel:* 800-221-2647 *Fax:* 212-935-0699 *Web Site:* www. kensingtonbooks.com, pg 116

Engstrom, Krister, Random House Children's Books, 1745 Broadway, 10th fl, New York, NY 10019 *Tel:* 212-782-9000 *Web Site:* www.randomhousekids. com, pg 180

Enrich, Jordanna, Fulbright Scholar Program, 1400 "K" St NW, Washington, DC 20005 *Tel:* 202-686-4000 *E-mail:* scholars@iie.org *Web Site:* www.cies.org; www.iie.org, pg 617

Enright, Katrina, Sky Pony Press, 307 W 36 St, 11th fl, New York, NY 10018 *Tel:* 212-643-6816 *Fax:* 212-643-6819 *E-mail:* skypony@skyhorsepublishing. com; info@skyhorsepublishing.com; submissions@ skyhorsepublishing.com *Web Site:* www.skyponypress. com, pg 200

Ensor, Kendra, Rand McNally, 9855 Woods Dr, Skokie, IL 60077 *Tel:* 847-329-8100 *Toll Free Tel:* 877-446-4863 *Toll Free Fax:* 877-469-1298 *E-mail:* mediarelations@randmcnally.com; tndsupport@randmcnally.com *Web Site:* www. randmcnally.com, pg 180

Entrekin, Morgan, Grove Atlantic Inc, 154 W 14 St, 12th fl, New York, NY 10011 *Tel:* 212-614-7850 *Toll Free Tel:* 800-521-0178 *Fax:* 212-614-7886 *E-mail:* info@ groveatlantic.com; sales@groveatlantic.com; publicity@groveatlantic.com; rights@groveatlantic.com *Web Site:* www.groveatlantic.com, pg 89

Entricken, Kevin, Wolters Kluwer US Corp, 2700 Lake Cook Rd, Riverwoods, IL 60015 *Tel:* 847-267-7000 *Fax:* 847-580-5192 *E-mail:* info@wolterskluwer.com *Web Site:* www.wolterskluwer.com, pg 243

Eoyle, Claire, McSweeney's Publishing, 849 Valencia St, San Francisco, CA 94110 *Tel:* 415-642-5609 (cust serv) *E-mail:* custserv@mcsweeneys.net *Web Site:* www.mcsweeneys.net, pg 136

Epler, Barbara, New Directions Publishing Corp, 80 Eighth Ave, 19th fl, New York, NY 10011 *Tel:* 212-255-0230 *E-mail:* editorial@ndbooks.com; publicity@ ndbooks.com *Web Site:* ndbooks.com, pg 148

Epstein, Don R, Greater Talent Network Inc, 437 Fifth Ave, New York, NY 10016 *Tel:* 212-645-4200 *Toll Free Tel:* 800-326-4211 *Fax:* 212-627-1471 *E-mail:* info@greatertalent.com *Web Site:* www. greatertalent.com, pg 515

Epstein, Richard, Atlantic Law Book Co, 22 Grassmere Ave, West Hartford, CT 06110-1215 *Tel:* 860-231-9300 *Toll Free Tel:* 800-259-5534 *E-mail:* atlanticlawbooks@aol.com *Web Site:* www. atlanticlawbooks.com, pg 24

Erickson, Anna, Creative Editions, PO Box 227, Mankato, MN 56002 *Tel:* 507-388-6273 *Toll Free Tel:* 800-445-6209 *Fax:* 507-388-2746 *E-mail:* info@ thecreativecompany.us; orders@thecreativecompany.us *Web Site:* www.thecreativecompany.us, pg 59

Erickson, Jesse, American Printing History Association, PO Box 4519, Grand Central Sta, New York, NY 10163 *E-mail:* secretary@printinghistory.org *Web Site:* printinghistory.org, pg 523

Erickson, Jesse, American Printing History Association Award, PO Box 4519, Grand Central Sta, New York, NY 10163 *E-mail:* secretary@printinghistory.org *Web Site:* printinghistory.org, pg 592

Erickson, Leslie, University of British Columbia Press, 2029 West Mall, Vancouver, BC V6T 1Z2, Canada *Tel:* 604-822-5959 *Toll Free Tel:* 877-377-9378 *Fax:* 604-822-6083 *Toll Free Fax:* 800-668-0821 *E-mail:* frontdesk@ubcpress.ca *Web Site:* www. ubcpress.ca, pg 443

Erickson, Lisa, HarperCollins General Books Group, 195 Broadway, New York, NY 10007 *Tel:* 212-207-7000 *Web Site:* www.harpercollins.com, pg 93

Erickson, Stephen, St Martin's Press, LLC, 120 Broadway, New York, NY 10271 *Tel:* 646-307-5151 *Web Site:* us.macmillan.com/smp, pg 191

Erickson, Tim, RAND Corp, 1776 Main St, Santa Monica, CA 90407-2138 *Tel:* 310-393-0411 *Fax:* 310-393-4818 *Web Site:* www.rand.org, pg 180

Ernest, James, Wm B Eerdmans Publishing Co, 4035 Park East Ct SE, Grand Rapids, MI 49546 *Tel:* 616-459-4591 *Toll Free Tel:* 800-253-7521 *Fax:* 616-459-6540 *E-mail:* customerservice@eerdmans.com; sales@ eerdmans.com *Web Site:* www.eerdmans.com, pg 70

Ernst, Christopher D, Artech House®, 685 Canton St, Norwood, MA 02062 *Tel:* 781-769-9750 *Toll Free Tel:* 800-225-9977 *Fax:* 781-769-6334 *E-mail:* artech@artechhouse.com *Web Site:* www. artechhouse.com, pg 21

Errico, Kristin, Harlequin Enterprises Ltd, 195 Broadway, 24th fl, New York, NY 10007 *Tel:* 212-207-7000 *Toll Free Tel:* 888-432-4879 *E-mail:* customerservice@harlequin.com *Web Site:* www.harlequin.com, pg 93

Errico, Vincent, Trusted Media Brands Inc, 750 Third Ave, 3rd fl, New York, NY 10017 *Tel:* 646-293-6299 *Toll Free Tel:* 877-732-4438 (cust serv) *Fax:* 646-293-6251 *E-mail:* customercare@trustedmediabrands. com; press@trustedmediabrands.com *Web Site:* www. trustedmediabrands.com; www.rd.com, pg 221

Ertl, Julie, Anchor Books, c/o Penguin Random House Inc, 1745 Broadway, New York, NY 10019 *Tel:* 212-572-2420 *E-mail:* vintageanchorpublicity@ randomhouse.com *Web Site:* knopfdoubleday.com/ imprint/anchor, pg 15

Ertl, Julie, Vintage Books, c/o Penguin Random House Inc, 1745 Broadway, New York, NY 10019 *Tel:* 212-572-2420 *E-mail:* vintageanchorpublicity@ randomhouse.com *Web Site:* knopfdoubleday.com/ imprint/vintage, pg 236

Esco, Melinda, TCU Press, 3000 Sandage Ave, Fort Worth, TX 76109 *Tel:* 817-257-7822 *Toll Free Tel:* 800-826-8911 (orders) *Fax:* 817-257-5075 *Web Site:* www.prs.tcu.edu, pg 213

Escobar, Nicole, New Hampshire Literary Awards, 2500 N River Rd, Manchester, NH 03106 *Tel:* 603-314-7980 *E-mail:* info@nhwritersproject.org; awards@ nhwritersproject.org *Web Site:* www.nhwritersproject. org, pg 647

Escoto, Allison, The Center for Fiction, 17 E 47 St, New York, NY 10017 *Tel:* 212-755-6710 *E-mail:* info@centerforfiction.org *Web Site:* centerforfiction.org, pg 530

Esersky, Gareth, Carol Mann Agency, 55 Fifth Ave, 18th fl, New York, NY 10003 *Tel:* 212-206-5635 *Fax:* 212-675-4809 *E-mail:* submissions@carolmannagency.com *Web Site:* www.carolmannagency.com, pg 494

Essary, Loris, International Titles, 931 E 56 St, Austin, TX 78751-1724 *Tel:* 512-909-2447 *Web Site:* www.internationaltitles.com, pg 489

Ester, Alicia, Beaver's Pond Press Inc, 939 Seventh St W, St Paul, MN 55102 *Tel:* 952-829-8818 *E-mail:* info@beaverspondpress.com *Web Site:* www.beaverspondpress.com, pg 30

Etcheson, Amy, Southern Illinois University Press, 1915 University Press Dr, SIUC Mail Code 6806, Carbondale, IL 62901-4323 *Tel:* 618-453-2281 *Fax:* 618-453-1221 *Web Site:* www.siupress.com, pg 205

Etcheverry, Gabrielle, Livres Canada Books, One Nicholas, Suite 504, Ottawa, ON K1N 7B7, Canada *Tel:* 613-562-2324 *Fax:* 613-562-2329 *E-mail:* info@livrescanadabooks.com *Web Site:* www.livrescanadabooks.com, pg 537

Eth, Felicia, Felicia Eth Literary Representation, 555 Bryant St, Suite 350, Palo Alto, CA 94301 *Tel:* 415-970-9717 *E-mail:* feliciaeth.literary@gmail.com *Web Site:* www.ethliterary.com, pg 483

Etra, Judith, Whittier Publications Inc, 3115 Long Beach Rd, Oceanside, NY 11572 *Tel:* 516-432-8120 *Toll Free Tel:* 800-897-TEXT (897-8398) *Fax:* 516-889-0341 *E-mail:* info@whitbooks.com *Web Site:* www.whitbooks.com, pg 240

Etsch, Janet, The Conference Board Inc, 845 Third Ave, New York, NY 10022-6600 *Tel:* 212-759-0900; 212-339-0345 (cust serv) *E-mail:* customer.service@conferenceboard.org; membership@conferenceboard.org *Web Site:* www.conference-board.org; www.linkedin.com/company/the-conference-board, pg 56

Etsell, Christopher, The Guilford Press, 370 Seventh Ave, Suite 1200, New York, NY 10001-1020 *Tel:* 212-431-9800 *Toll Free Tel:* 800-365-7006 *Fax:* 212-966-6708 *E-mail:* info@guilford.com *Web Site:* www.guilford.com, pg 90

Ettinger, Kathryn, Perseus Books, 1290 Avenue of the Americas, New York, NY 10104 *Tel:* 212-340-8100 *Toll Free Tel:* 800-343-4499 (cust serv) *Fax:* 212-340-8105 *Web Site:* www.perseusbooks.com, pg 167

Etzkorn, Laura, Tom Doherty Associates, LLC, 120 Broadway, New York, NY 10271 *Tel:* 646-307-5511 *Toll Free Tel:* 800-455-0340 *Web Site:* us.macmillan.com/torforge, pg 66

Eubanks, Debra, American Psychiatric Association Publishing, 800 Maine Ave SW, Suite 900, Washington, DC 20024 *Tel:* 202-459-9722 *Toll Free Tel:* 800-368-5777 *Fax:* 202-403-3094 *E-mail:* appi@psych.org *Web Site:* www.appi.org; www.psychiatryonline.org, pg 13

Eulau, Dennis, Simon & Schuster, Inc, 1230 Avenue of the Americas, New York, NY 10020 *Tel:* 212-698-7000 *Toll Free Tel:* 800-223-2336 (orders) *Fax:* 212-698-7007 *Toll Free Fax:* 800-943-9831 (orders) *E-mail:* firstname.lastname@simonandschuster.com; purchaseorders@simonandschuster.com (orders) *Web Site:* www.simonandschuster.com, pg 199

Evans, Ashten, Ulysses Press, 195 Montague St, 14th fl, Brooklyn, NY 11201 *Tel:* 510-601-8301 *Toll Free Tel:* 800-377-2542 *Fax:* 510-601-8307 *E-mail:* ulysses@ulyssespress.com *Web Site:* www.ulyssespress.com, pg 223

Evans, Christopher, The Pacific Spirit Poetry Prize, University of British Columbia, Buch E462, 1866 Main Mall, Vancouver, BC V6T 1Z1, Canada *Tel:* 778-822-2514 *Fax:* 778-822-3616 *E-mail:* prismwritingcontest@gmail.com *Web Site:* www.prismmagazine.ca, pg 652

Evans, Christopher, PRISM international Literary Non-Fiction Contest, University of British Columbia, Buch E462, 1866 Main Mall, Vancouver, BC V6T

1Z1, Canada *Tel:* 778-822-2514 *Fax:* 778-822-3616 *E-mail:* prismwritingcontest@gmail.com *Web Site:* www.prismmagazine.ca, pg 659

Evans, Christopher, The Jacob Zilber Prize for Short Fiction, University of British Columbia, Buch E462, 1866 Main Mall, Vancouver, BC V6T 1Z1, Canada *Tel:* 778-822-2514 *Fax:* 778-822-3616 *E-mail:* prismwritingcontest@gmail.com *Web Site:* www.prismmagazine.ca, pg 681

Evans, Claire Lewis, University of Alabama Press, 200 Hackberry Lane, 2nd fl, Tuscaloosa, AL 35487 *Tel:* 205-348-5180 *Fax:* 205-348-9201 *Web Site:* www.uapress.ua.edu, pg 225

Evans, Clark, Abraham Lincoln Institute Book Award, 105 Mount Olive Lane, Ephrata, PA 17522 *E-mail:* secretary@lincoln-institute.org *Web Site:* www.lincoln-institute.org, pg 634

Evans, Jennifer, Springer, 233 Spring St, New York, NY 10013-1578 *Tel:* 212-460-1500 *Toll Free Tel:* 800-SPRINGER (777-4643) *Fax:* 212-460-1700 *E-mail:* customerservice@springer.com *Web Site:* www.springer.com, pg 205

Evans, Mary, Mary Evans Inc, 242 E Fifth St, New York, NY 10003-8501 *Tel:* 212-979-0880 *Fax:* 212-979-5344 *E-mail:* info@maryevansinc.com *Web Site:* www.maryevansinc.com, pg 484

Evans, Megan, Harry N Abrams Inc, 195 Broadway, 9th fl, New York, NY 10007 *Tel:* 212-206-7715 *Toll Free Tel:* 800-345-1359 *Fax:* 212-519-1210 *E-mail:* abrams@abramsbooks.com *Web Site:* www.abramsbooks.com, pg 3

Evans, Mike, Houghton Mifflin Harcourt, 125 High St, Boston, MA 02110 *Tel:* 617-351-5000 *Toll Free Tel:* 855-969-4642; 800-225-5425 (K-12 educ materials); 800-323-9540 (assessment materials); 877-219-1537 (SkillsTutor); 888-242-6747 (Innovation in Educ Group); 800-225-3362 (Trade & Ref Div) *Toll Free Fax:* 800-269-5232 *E-mail:* myhmhco@hmhco.com *Web Site:* www.hmhco.com, pg 103

Evans, Nivia, Orbit, 1290 Avenue of the Americas, New York, NY 10104 *Tel:* 212-364-1100 *Toll Free Tel:* 800-759-0190 *Web Site:* www.orbitbooks.net, pg 156

Evans, Suzy, Sandra Dijkstra Literary Agency, 1155 Camino del Mar, PMB 515, Del Mar, CA 92014-2605 *Web Site:* dijkstraagency.com, pg 482

Evans, Tracy Wareing, American Public Human Services Association, 1133 19 St NW, Suite 400, Washington, DC 20036 *Tel:* 202-682-0100 *Fax:* 202-289-6555 *E-mail:* memberservice@aphsa.org *Web Site:* www.aphsa.org, pg 523

Evans, William, Evan-Moor Educational Publishers, 18 Lower Ragsdale Dr, Monterey, CA 93940-5746 *Tel:* 831-649-5901 *Toll Free Tel:* 800-777-4362 (orders) *Fax:* 831-649-6256 *Toll Free Fax:* 800-777-4332 (orders) *E-mail:* sales@evan-moor.com; marketing@evan-moor.com *Web Site:* www.evan-moor.com, pg 73

Eveleigh, Douglas, Encyclopaedia Britannica Inc, 325 N La Salle St, Suite 200, Chicago, IL 60654 *Tel:* 312-347-7000 (all other countries) *Toll Free Tel:* 800-323-1229 (US & CN) *Fax:* 312-294-2104 *E-mail:* contact@eb.com *Web Site:* www.britannica.com, pg 72

Everhart, Deborah L, Andrews University Press, Sutherland House, 8360 W Campus Circle Dr, Berrien Springs, MI 49104-1700 *Tel:* 269-471-6134 *Toll Free Tel:* 800-467-6369 (Visa, MC & American Express orders only) *Fax:* 269-471-6224 *E-mail:* aupo@andrews.edu; aup@andrews.edu; aupress@andrews.edu *Web Site:* www.universitypress.andrews.edu, pg 16

Everhart, Sean, David C Cook, 4050 Lee Vance Dr, Colorado Springs, CO 80918 *Tel:* 719-536-0100 *Toll Free Tel:* 800-708-5550; 800-323-7543 (orders & cust serv) *Toll Free Fax:* 800-430-0726 (cust serv) *Web Site:* www.davidccook.org, pg 56

Ewen, Laura, Bloomsbury Academic, 1385 Broadway, 5th fl, New York, NY 10018 *Tel:* 212-419-5300 *Web Site:* www.bloomsbury.com/us/academic, pg 35

Ewers, Christy, The CAT Agency Inc, PO Box 1390, Fairfield, CT 06825 *Tel:* 917-434-3141 *Web Site:* www.catugeau.com, pg 511

Ewing, Su, Dog Writers' Association of America Inc (DWAA) Annual Writing Competition, PO Box 787, Hughesville, MD 20637 *E-mail:* info@dogwriters.org *Web Site:* dogwriters.org, pg 610

Eyring, Teresa, Theatre Communications Group, 520 Eighth Ave, 24th fl, New York, NY 10018-4156 *Tel:* 212-609-5900 *Fax:* 212-609-5901 *E-mail:* info@tcg.org *Web Site:* www.tcg.org, pg 216

Faber, Kathy, HarperCollins General Books Group, 195 Broadway, New York, NY 10007 *Tel:* 212-207-7000 *Web Site:* www.harpercollins.com, pg 93

Fabian, Ann, Allan Nevins Prize, 2950 Broadway, New York, NY 10027 *Tel:* 212-854-6495 *E-mail:* amhistsociety@columbia.edu *Web Site:* sah.columbia.edu, pg 647

Fabian, Ann, Francis Parkman Prize, 2950 Broadway, New York, NY 10027 *Tel:* 212-854-6495 *E-mail:* amhistsociety@columbia.edu *Web Site:* sah.columbia.edu, pg 652

Fabian, Ann, SAH Prize for Historical Fiction, 2950 Broadway, New York, NY 10027 *Tel:* 212-854-6495 *E-mail:* amhistsociety@columbia.edu *Web Site:* sah.columbia.edu, pg 663

Fabian, Elizabeth, Random House Publishing Group, 1745 Broadway, New York, NY 10019 *Toll Free Tel:* 800-200-3552 *Web Site:* www.randomhousebooks.com, pg 181

Fabricant, David, Abbeville Press, 655 Third Ave, New York, NY 10017 *Tel:* 212-366-5585 *Toll Free Tel:* 800-ART-BOOK (278-2665); 800-343-4499 (orders) *Fax:* 646-375-2359 *Toll Free Fax:* 800-351-5073 (orders) *E-mail:* abbeville@abbeville.com; sales@abbeville.com; marketing@abbeville.com; rights@abbeville.com *Web Site:* www.abbeville.com, pg 2

Fabricant, David, Abbeville Publishing Group, 655 Third Ave, New York, NY 10017 *Tel:* 646-375-2136 *Fax:* 646-375-2359 *E-mail:* abbeville@abbeville.com; marketing@abbeville.com; sales@abbeville.com; rights@abbeville.com *Web Site:* www.abbeville.com, pg 2

Fabricant, Shannon Connors, Perseus Books, 1290 Avenue of the Americas, New York, NY 10104 *Tel:* 212-340-8100 *Toll Free Tel:* 800-343-4499 (cust serv) *Fax:* 212-340-8105 *Web Site:* www.perseusbooks.com, pg 167

Faccenda, Jenna, Casemate | publishers, 1950 Lawrence Rd, Havertown, PA 19083 *Tel:* 610-853-9131 *Fax:* 610-853-9146 *E-mail:* casemate@casematepublishers.com *Web Site:* www.casematepublishers.com, pg 46

Faderin, Kemi, Dystel, Goderich & Bourret LLC, One Union Sq W, Suite 904, New York, NY 10003 *Tel:* 212-627-9100 *Fax:* 212-627-9313 *Web Site:* www.dystel.com, pg 482

Fafard, Katherine, Association des Libraires du Quebec (ALQ), 483, blvd St Joseph E, Montreal, QC H2J 1J8, Canada *Tel:* 514-526-3349 *Fax:* 514-526-3340 *E-mail:* info@alq.qc.ca *Web Site:* www.alq.qc.ca, pg 525

Fagan, John, University of Pittsburgh Press, 7500 Thomas Blvd, Pittsburgh, PA 15260 *Tel:* 412-383-2456 *Fax:* 412-383-2466 *E-mail:* info@upress.pitt.edu *Web Site:* www.upress.pitt.edu, pg 230

Fagan, Raymond, William H Sadlier Inc, 9 Pine St, New York, NY 10005 *Tel:* 212-227-2120 *Toll Free Tel:* 800-221-5175 (cust serv) *Fax:* 212-312-6080 *E-mail:* customerservice@sadlier.com *Web Site:* www.sadlier.com, pg 189

Faherty, Jill, Educational Book & Media Association (EBMA), 11 Main St, Suite D, Warrenton, VA 20186 *Tel:* 540-318-7770 *Fax:* 202-962-3939 *E-mail:* info@edupaperback.org *Web Site:* www.edupaperback.org, pg 532

Fahey, Alison, 4A's (American Association of Advertising Agencies), 1065 Avenue of the Americas, 16th fl, New York, NY 10018 *Tel:* 212-682-2500 *Web Site:* www.aaaa.org, pg 534

Fahlgren, Erik, W W Norton & Company Inc, 500 Fifth Ave, New York, NY 10110-0017 *Tel:* 212-354-5500 *Toll Free Tel:* 800-233-4830 (orders & cust serv) *Fax:* 212-869-0856 *Toll Free Fax:* 800-458-6515 *E-mail:* orders@wwnorton.com *Web Site:* wwnorton. com, pg 152

Faktorovich, Dr Anna, Anaphora Literary Press, 1108 W Third St, Quanah, TX 79252 *Tel:* 470-289-6395 *Web Site:* anaphoraliterary.com, pg 15

Falb, Mark C, Kendall Hunt Publishing Co, 4050 Westmark Dr, Dubuque, IA 52002-2624 *Tel:* 563-589-1000 *Toll Free Tel:* 800-228-0810 (orders) *Fax:* 563-589-1046 *Toll Free Fax:* 800-772-9165 *E-mail:* orders@kendallhunt.com *Web Site:* www. kendallhunt.com, pg 116

Faley, Erin, Academy of Nutrition & Dietetics, 120 S Riverside Plaza, Suite 2190, Chicago, IL 60606-6995 *Tel:* 312-899-0040 (ext 5000) *Toll Free Tel:* 800-877-1600 *E-mail:* sales@eatright.org *Web Site:* www. eatright.org, pg 3

Falkenstein, Donald, Council for Advancement & Support of Education (CASE), 1307 New York Ave NW, Suite 1000, Washington, DC 20005-4701 *Tel:* 202-328-CASE (328-2273) *Fax:* 202-387-4973 *E-mail:* membersupportcenter@case.org *Web Site:* www.case.org, pg 531

Fallon, Claire, Coffee House Press, 79 13 Ave NE, Suite 110, Minneapolis, MN 55413 *Tel:* 612-338-0125 *Fax:* 612-338-4004 *E-mail:* info@coffeehousepress.org *Web Site:* coffeehousepress.org, pg 54

Falter, Sarah, Perseus Books, 1290 Avenue of the Americas, New York, NY 10104 *Tel:* 212-340-8100 *Toll Free Tel:* 800-343-4499 (cust serv) *Fax:* 212-340-8105 *Web Site:* www.perseusbooks.com, pg 168

Fan, Shenggen, International Food Policy Research Institute, 1201 Eye St NW, Washington, DC 20005-3915 *Tel:* 202-862-5600 *Fax:* 202-862-5606 *E-mail:* ifpri@cgiar.org *Web Site:* www.ifpri.org, pg 111

Fanton, Jonathan, American Academy of Arts & Sciences (AAAS), Norton's Woods, 136 Irving St, Cambridge, MA 02138 *Tel:* 617-576-5000 *Fax:* 617-576-5050 *E-mail:* aaas@amacad.org *Web Site:* www. amacad.org, pg 522

Fargis, Alison, Stonesong, 270 W 39 St, Suite 201, New York, NY 10018 *Tel:* 212-929-4600 *E-mail:* editors@ stonesong.com *Web Site:* www.stonesong.com, pg 504

Fariel, Quinn, Perseus Books, 1290 Avenue of the Americas, New York, NY 10104 *Tel:* 212-340-8100 *Toll Free Tel:* 800-343-4499 (cust serv) *Fax:* 212-340-8105 *Web Site:* www.perseusbooks.com, pg 167

Faris, Curran, Fernwood Publishing, 32 Oceanvista Lane, Black Point, NS B0J 1B0, Canada *Tel:* 902-857-1388 *Fax:* 902-857-1328 *E-mail:* info@fernpub.ca; roseway@fernpub.ca *Web Site:* fernwoodpublishing.ca, pg 426

Farkas, Sam, Jill Grinberg Literary Management LLC, 392 Vanderbilt Ave, Brooklyn, NY 11238 *Tel:* 212-620-5883 *E-mail:* info@jillgrinbergliterary.com *Web Site:* www.jillgrinbergliterary.com, pg 487

Farland, David, L Ron Hubbard's Writers of the Future Contest, 7051 Hollywood Blvd, Hollywood, CA 90028 *Tel:* 323-466-3310 *Fax:* 323-466-6474 *E-mail:* contests@authorservicesinc.com *Web Site:* www.writersofthefuture.com, pg 625

Farmer, Brad, Gibbs Smith Publisher, 1877 E Gentile St, Layton, UT 84041 *Tel:* 801-544-9800 *Toll Free Tel:* 800-748-5439; 800-835-4993 (orders) *Fax:* 801-544-5582 *Toll Free Fax:* 800-213-3023 (orders only) *E-mail:* info@gibbs-smith.com; tradeorders@gibbs-smith.com *Web Site:* www.gibbs-smith.com, pg 85

Farmer, Brent Jr, Charlesbridge Publishing Inc, 85 Main St, Watertown, MA 02472 *Tel:* 617-926-0329 *Toll Free Tel:* 800-225-3214 *Fax:* 617-926-5720 *Toll Free Fax:* 800-926-5775 *E-mail:* books@charlesbridge.com *Web Site:* www.charlesbridge.com, pg 49

Farmer, Brent, Charlesbridge Publishing Inc, 85 Main St, Watertown, MA 02472 *Tel:* 617-926-0329 *Toll Free Tel:* 800-225-3214 *Fax:* 617-926-5720 *Toll Free Fax:* 800-926-5775 *E-mail:* books@charlesbridge.com *Web Site:* www.charlesbridge.com, pg 49

Farmer, Chris, University of Texas Press, 3001 Lake Austin Blvd, 2.200, Austin, TX 78703 *Tel:* 512-471-7233 *Fax:* 512-232-7178 *E-mail:* utpress@uts.cc. utexas.edu; info@utpress.utexas.edu *Web Site:* utpress. utexas.edu, pg 216

Farmer, Daryl, Visiting Writers Series, English Dept, PO Box 755720, Fairbanks, AK 99775-5720 *Tel:* 907-474-7193 *Fax:* 907-474-5247 *E-mail:* faengl@uaf.edu *Web Site:* www.alaska.edu/english, pg 579

Farmer, Gary, American Association for Vocational Instructional Materials, 220 Smithonia Rd, Winterville, GA 30683 *Tel:* 706-742-5355 *Fax:* 706-742-7005 *E-mail:* sales@aavim.com, pg 9

Farmer, Meredith, The Melville Society, Johns Hopkins University Press, PO Box 19966, Baltimore, MD 21211-0966 *Web Site:* melvillesociety.org, pg 537

Farmer, Susan, DEStech Publications Inc, 439 N Duke St, Lancaster, PA 17602-4967 *Tel:* 717-290-1660 *Toll Free Tel:* 877-500-4DES (500-4337) *Fax:* 717-509-6100 *E-mail:* info@destechpub.com *Web Site:* www. destechpub.com, pg 64

Farnol, Jane, Astor Indexers, 22 S Commons, Kent, CT 06757 *Tel:* 860-592-0225; 570-534-8951 (cell), pg 458

Farnsworth, David, Casemate | publishers, 1950 Lawrence Rd, Havertown, PA 19083 *Tel:* 610-853-9131 *Fax:* 610-853-9146 *E-mail:* casemate@ casematepublishers.com *Web Site:* www. casematepublishers.com, pg 46

Farnsworth, Sarah, Casemate | publishers, 1950 Lawrence Rd, Havertown, PA 19083 *Tel:* 610-853-9131 *Fax:* 610-853-9146 *E-mail:* casemate@ casematepublishers.com *Web Site:* www. casematepublishers.com, pg 46

Farr, Daley, Coffee House Press, 79 13 Ave NE, Suite 110, Minneapolis, MN 55413 *Tel:* 612-338-0125 *Fax:* 612-338-4004 *E-mail:* info@coffeehousepress.org *Web Site:* coffeehousepress.org, pg 54

Farr, Daley, Max Ritvo Poetry Prize, 1011 Washington Ave S, Suite 300, Minneapolis, MN 55415-1246 *Tel:* 612-332-3192 *Toll Free Tel:* 800-520-6455 *Web Site:* milkweed.org/max-ritvo-poetry-prize, pg 662

Farrace, Bob, National Association of Secondary School Principals (NASSP), 1904 Association Dr, Reston, VA 20191-1537 *Tel:* 703-860-0200 *Toll Free Tel:* 800-253-7746; 866-647-7253 (sales) *E-mail:* membership@ nassp.org *Web Site:* www.nassp.org, pg 145

Farranto, Amy, Cornell University Press, Sage House, 512 E State St, Ithaca, NY 14850 *Tel:* 607-253-2338 *Fax:* 607-253-2374 *E-mail:* cupressinfo@cornell.edu; cupress-sales@cornell.edu *Web Site:* www.cornellpress. cornell.edu, pg 57

Farranto, Amy, Northern Illinois University Press, 2280 Bethany Rd, DeKalb, IL 60115 *Tel:* 815-753-1075 *Fax:* 815-753-1631 *Web Site:* cornellpress.cornell. edu/imprints/northern-illinois-university-press, pg 152

Farrar, Amy E, Farrar Writing & Editing, 4638 Manchester Rd, Mound, MN 55364 *Tel:* 952-451-5982 *Fax:* 952-472-6874 (call first) *Web Site:* www. writeandedit.net, pg 463

Farrell, Dan, Crossway, 1300 Crescent St, Wheaton, IL 60187 *Tel:* 630-682-4300 *Toll Free Tel:* 800-635-7993 (orders); 800-543-1659 (cust serv) *Fax:* 630-682-4785 *E-mail:* info@crossway.org *Web Site:* www.crossway. org, pg 60

Farrin, Cassandra, Polebridge Press, PO Box 346, Farmington, MN 55024 *Tel:* 651-200-2372 *E-mail:* orders@westarinstitute.org *Web Site:* www. westarinstitute.org, pg 172

Farris, Sienna, Simon & Schuster, Inc, 1230 Avenue of the Americas, New York, NY 10020 *Tel:* 212-698-7000 *Toll Free Tel:* 800-223-2336 (orders) *Fax:* 212-698-7007 *Toll Free Fax:* 800-943-9831 (orders)

E-mail: firstname.lastname@simonandschuster.com; purchaseorders@simonandschuster.com (orders) *Web Site:* www.simonandschuster.com, pg 199

Fassett, David, InterVarsity Press, 430 Plaza Dr, Westmont, IL 60559-1234 *Tel:* 630-734-4000 *Toll Free Tel:* 800-843-9487 *Fax:* 630-734-4200 *E-mail:* email@ ivpress.com *Web Site:* www.ivpress.com, pg 112

Fassler, Kristin, Atria Books, 1230 Avenue of the Americas, New York, NY 10020 *Tel:* 212-698-7000 *Fax:* 212-698-7007 *Web Site:* www.simonandschuster. com, pg 24

Fastiggi, Ray, The Rockefeller University Press, 950 Third Ave, 2nd fl, New York, NY 10022 *Tel:* 212-327-7938 *E-mail:* rupress@rockefeller.edu *Web Site:* www. rupress.org, pg 186

Faughnan, Mary Ann, May Sarton New Hampshire Poetry Prize, 44 Main St, 2nd fl, Peterborough, NH 03458 *Tel:* 603-567-4430 *Web Site:* www. bauhanpublishing.com, pg 664

Faulkner, Donald W, New York State Edith Wharton Citation of Merit for Fiction Writers, University at Albany, SL 320, Albany, NY 12222 *Tel:* 518-442-5620 *Fax:* 518-442-5621 *E-mail:* writers@albany.edu *Web Site:* www.albany.edu/writers-inst, pg 648

Faulkner, Donald W, New York State Walt Whitman Citation of Merit for Poets, University at Albany, SL 320, Albany, NY 12222 *Tel:* 518-442-5620 *Fax:* 518-442-5621 *E-mail:* writers@albany.edu *Web Site:* www. albany.edu/writers-inst, pg 648

Faulkner-Punzo, Dana, Women Who Write Inc, PO Box 652, Madison, NJ 07940-0652 *E-mail:* info@ womenwhowrite.org *Web Site:* womenwhowrite.org, pg 549

Faulner, Melissa, Dutton Children's Books, 345 Hudson St, New York, NY 10014 *Tel:* 212-366-2000 *Web Site:* www.penguin.com/publishers/ duttonchildrensbooks/, pg 68

Fausset, Katherine, Curtis Brown Ltd, 228 E 45 St, 3rd fl, New York, NY 10017 *Tel:* 212-473-5400 *Web Site:* www.curtisbrown.com, pg 478

Faust, Harmony, Gale, 27500 Drake Rd, Farmington Hills, MI 48331-3535 *Tel:* 248-699-4253 *Toll Free Tel:* 800-877-4253 *Toll Free Fax:* 800-414-5043 (orders) *E-mail:* gale.customercare@cengage.com *Web Site:* www.gale.com, pg 82

Faust, Harmony, Macmillan Reference USA™, 27500 Drake Rd, Farmington Hills, MI 48331-3535 *Tel:* 248-699-4253 *Toll Free Tel:* 800-877-4253 *Toll Free Fax:* 877-363-4253 *E-mail:* gale.customercare@ cengage.com *Web Site:* www.gale.cengage.com/ macmillan, pg 130

Faust, Jessica H, BookEnds Literary Agency, 136 Long Hill Rd, Gillette, NJ 07933 *Web Site:* www. bookendsliterary.com, pg 476

Favreau, Marc, The New Press, 120 Wall St, 31st fl, New York, NY 10005 *Tel:* 212-629-8802 *Toll Free Tel:* 800-343-4489 (orders) *Fax:* 212-629-8617 *Toll Free Fax:* 800-351-5073 (orders) *E-mail:* newpress@ thenewpress.com *Web Site:* www.thenewpress.com, pg 149

Fay-LeBlanc, Gibson, Maine Writers & Publishers Alliance, Glickman Family Library, 314 Forest Ave, Rm 318, Portland, ME 04101 *Tel:* 207-228-8263 *E-mail:* info@mainewriters.org *Web Site:* mainewriters.org, pg 537

Fazzalaro, Kristina, Penguin Books, 375 Hudson St, New York, NY 10014 *Tel:* 212-366-2000 *E-mail:* penguinpublicity@us.penguingroup.com *Web Site:* www.penguinclassics.com; www.penguin. com, pg 163

Fazzalaro, Kristina, Penguin Group USA, A Penguin Random House Company, 375 Hudson St, New York, NY 10014 *Tel:* 212-366-2000 *Toll Free Tel:* 800-847-5515 (inside sales); 800-631-8571 (cust serv) *Fax:* 212-366-2666; 607-775-4829 (inside sales) *E-mail:* online@us.penguingroup.com *Web Site:* www. penguin.com, pg 163

Forney, Emily, BookEnds Literary Agency, 136 Long Hill Rd, Gillette, NJ 07933 *Web Site:* www. bookendsliterary.com, pg 476

Forrer, David, InkWell Management, 521 Fifth Ave, 26th fl, New York, NY 10175 *Tel:* 212-922-3500 *Fax:* 212-922-0535 *E-mail:* info@inkwellmanagement.com *Web Site:* inkwellmanagement.com, pg 489

Forrie, Allan, Thistledown Press, 410 Second Ave, Saskatoon, SK S7K 2C3, Canada *Tel:* 306-244-1722 *Fax:* 306-244-1762 *E-mail:* tdpress@thistledownpress. com; editorial@thistledownpress.com; marketing@ thistledownpress.com *Web Site:* www.thistledownpress. com, pg 441

Forrie, Jackie, Thistledown Press, 410 Second Ave, Saskatoon, SK S7K 2C3, Canada *Tel:* 306-244-1722 *Fax:* 306-244-1762 *E-mail:* tdpress@thistledownpress. com; editorial@thistledownpress.com; marketing@ thistledownpress.com *Web Site:* www.thistledownpress. com, pg 441

Forrister, Brad, M Lee Smith Publishers, 100 Winners Circle, Suite 300, Brentwood, TN 37027 *Tel:* 615-373-7517 *Toll Free Tel:* 800-274-6774; 800-727-5257 *E-mail:* custserv@mleesmith.com; service@blr.com *Web Site:* www.mleesmith.com; www.blr.com, pg 202

Forsa, Bethlam, Savvas Learning Co LLC, 15 E Midland Ave, Suite 502, Paramus, NJ 07652 *Toll Free Tel:* 800-848-9500 *Web Site:* www.savvas.com, pg 193

Forte, Fran, The New Press, 120 Wall St, 31st fl, New York, NY 10005 *Tel:* 212-629-8802 *Toll Free Tel:* 800-343-4489 (orders) *Fax:* 212-629-8617 *Toll Free Fax:* 800-351-5073 (orders) *E-mail:* newpress@ thenewpress.com *Web Site:* www.thenewpress.com, pg 149

Fortier, Gary, Cengage Learning, 20 Channel Center St, Boston, MA 02210 *Tel:* 617-289-7700 *Toll Free Tel:* 800-354-9706 *Fax:* 617-289-7844 *E-mail:* esales@cengage.com *Web Site:* www.cengage. com, pg 47

Fortin, Jacques, QA International (QAI), 329 De la Commune W, 3rd fl, Montreal, QC H2Y 2E1, Canada *Tel:* 514-499-3000 *Fax:* 514-499-3010 *Web Site:* www. qa-international.com, pg 438

Fortin, Ms Josee, Broquet Inc, 97-B, Montee des Bouleaux, St-Constant, QC J5A 1A9, Canada *Tel:* 450-638-3338 *Fax:* 450-638-4338 *E-mail:* info@ broquet.qc.ca *Web Site:* www.broquet.qc.ca, pg 417

Fortner, Shannon T, Johns Hopkins University Press, 2715 N Charles St, Baltimore, MD 21218-4363 *Tel:* 410-516-6900; 410-516-6987 (journal orders outside US & CN) *Toll Free Tel:* 800-537-5487 (book orders & cust serv); 800-548-1784 (journal orders) *Fax:* 410-516-6968; 410-516-3866 (journal orders); 410-516-6998 (orders) *E-mail:* hfscustserv@press.jhu. edu (cust serv); jrnlcirc@press.jhu.edu (journal orders) *Web Site:* www.press.jhu.edu; muse.jhu.edu, pg 114

Fortuna, Nina, American Society of Magazine Editors (ASME), PO Box 112, New York, NY 10163 *Tel:* 212-872-3737 *E-mail:* asme@asme.media *Web Site:* www.asme.media, pg 524

Fortuna, Nina, ASME Award for Fiction, PO Box 112, New York, NY 10163 *Tel:* 212-872-3737 *E-mail:* asme@asme.media *Web Site:* www.asme. media, pg 594

Fortunato, John A, Fordham University, Gabelli School of Business, 140 W 62 St, Rm 440, New York, NY 10023 *Web Site:* www.fordham.edu, pg 582, 616

Fortune, John, Math Solutions®, One Harbor Dr, Suite 101, Sausalito, CA 94965 *Toll Free Tel:* 877-234-7323 *Toll Free Fax:* 800-724-4716 *E-mail:* info@ mathsolutions.com; orders@mathsolutions.com *Web Site:* www.mathsolutions.com; store. mathsolutions.com, pg 134

Fosado, Gisela, Duke University Press, 905 W Main St, Suite 18B, Durham, NC 27701 *Tel:* 919-688-5134 *Toll Free Tel:* 888-651-0122 (US) *Fax:* 919-688-2615 *Toll Free Fax:* 888-651-0124 *E-mail:* orders@dukeupress. edu *Web Site:* www.dukeupress.edu, pg 68

Foster, Corrin, Greenleaf Book Group LLC, 3 Park Place, 4005 Banister Lane, Suite B, Austin, TX 78704 *Tel:* 512-891-6100 *Fax:* 512-891-6150 *E-mail:* contact@greenleafbookgroup.com *Web Site:* www.greenleafbookgroup.com, pg 89

Foster, Cynthia, University Press of Mississippi, 3825 Ridgewood Rd, Jackson, MS 39211-6492 *Tel:* 601-432-6205 *Toll Free Tel:* 800-737-7788 (orders & cust serv) *Fax:* 601-432-6217 *E-mail:* press@mississippi. edu *Web Site:* www.upress.state.ms.us, pg 233

Foster, Dianne, Amber Lotus Publishing, PO Box 11329, Portland, OR 97211 *Tel:* 503-284-6400 *Toll Free Tel:* 800-326-2375 (orders only) *Fax:* 503-284-6417 *E-mail:* info@amberlotus.com *Web Site:* www. amberlotus.com, pg 9

Foster, Frank, Medals of America Press, 114 Southchase Blvd, Fountain Inn, SC 29644 *Toll Free Tel:* 800-605-4001 *Toll Free Fax:* 800-407-8640 *Web Site:* moapress.com, pg 137

Foster, Lee, Foster Travel Publishing, 1623 Martin Luther King Jr Way, Berkeley, CA 94709 *Tel:* 510-549-2202 *Web Site:* www.fostertravel.com, pg 463

Foster, Roz, Frances Goldin Literary Agency, Inc, 214 W 29 St, Suite 410, New York, NY 10001 *Tel:* 212-777-0047 *Fax:* 212-228-1660 *E-mail:* agency@goldinlit. com *Web Site:* www.goldinlit.com, pg 486

Foster, Susan, Bitingduck Press LLC, 1262 Sunnyoaks Circle, Altadena, CA 91001 *Tel:* 626-507-8033 *E-mail:* notifications@bitingduckpress.com *Web Site:* bitingduckpress.com, pg 34

Fotinos, Joel, St Martin's Press, LLC, 120 Broadway, New York, NY 10271 *Tel:* 646-307-5151 *Web Site:* us. macmillan.com/smp, pg 190

Foulon, Alexandrine, Editions Hurtubise, 1815, ave De Lorimier, Montreal, QC H2K 3W6, Canada *Tel:* 514-523-1523 *Toll Free Tel:* 800-361-1664 *Fax:* 514-523-9969 *Web Site:* www.editionshurtubise.com, pg 424

Foulon, Arnaud, Editions Hurtubise, 1815, ave De Lorimier, Montreal, QC H2K 3W6, Canada *Tel:* 514-523-1523 *Toll Free Tel:* 800-361-1664 *Fax:* 514-523-9969 *Web Site:* www.editionshurtubise.com, pg 424

Foulon, Herve, Editions Hurtubise, 1815, ave De Lorimier, Montreal, QC H2K 3W6, Canada *Tel:* 514-523-1523 *Toll Free Tel:* 800-361-1664 *Fax:* 514-523-9969 *Web Site:* www.editionshurtubise.com, pg 424

Fournier, Holly, Fire Engineering Books & Videos, 1421 S Sheridan Rd, Tulsa, OK 74112 *Tel:* 918-831-9421 *Toll Free Tel:* 800-752-9764 *Fax:* 918-831-9555 *E-mail:* sales@pennwell.com *Web Site:* www. pennwellbooks.com, pg 78

Fournier, Holly, PennWell Books, 1421 S Sheridan Rd, Tulsa, OK 74112 *Tel:* 918-831-9421 *Toll Free Tel:* 800-752-9764 *Fax:* 918-831-9555 *E-mail:* sales@ pennwell.com *Web Site:* www.pennwellbooks.com, pg 166

Fournier, Sarah, Heinemann, 361 Hanover St, Portsmouth, NH 03801-3912 *Tel:* 603-431-7894 *Toll Free Tel:* 800-225-5800 (US) *Fax:* 603-431-2214 *Toll Free Fax:* 877-231-6980 (US) *E-mail:* custserv@ heinemann.com *Web Site:* www.heinemann.com, pg 98

Fowler, Karen Joy, The Clarion Science Fiction & Fantasy Writers' Workshop, Arthur C Clarke Ctr for Human Imagination, UC San Diego, 9500 Gilman Dr, MC0445, La Jolla, CA 92093-0445 *Tel:* 858-534-2115 *E-mail:* clarion@ucsd.edu *Web Site:* clarion.ucsd.edu; imagination.ucsd.edu, pg 574

Fowler, Karen Joy, James Tiptree Jr Literary Award, 173 Anderson St, San Francisco, CA 94110 *Tel:* 415-641-4103 *E-mail:* info@tiptree.org *Web Site:* tiptree.org, pg 673

Fox, Anna, ChemTec Publishing, 38 Earswick Dr, Toronto, ON M1E 1C6, Canada *Tel:* 416-265-2603 *Fax:* 416-265-1399 *E-mail:* orderdesk@chemtec.org *Web Site:* www.chemtec.org, pg 420

Fox, Graham, Institute for Research on Public Policy (IRPP), 1470 Peel St, No 200, Montreal, QC H3A 1T1, Canada *Tel:* 514-985-2461 *Fax:* 514-985-2559 *E-mail:* irpp@irpp.org *Web Site:* irpp.org, pg 430

Fox, Jim, Silman-James Press Inc, 141 N Clark Dr, Unit 1, West Hollywood, CA 90048 *Tel:* 310-205-0665 *Fax:* 323-214-7943 *E-mail:* info@silmanjamespress. com *Web Site:* www.silmanjamespress.com, pg 198

Fox, Keith, Phaidon, 65 Bleecker St, 8th fl, New York, NY 10012 *Tel:* 212-652-5400 *Toll Free Tel:* 800-759-0190 (cust serv) *Fax:* 212-652-5410 *Toll Free Fax:* 800-286-9471 (cust serv) *E-mail:* enquiries@ phaidon.com *Web Site:* www.phaidon.com, pg 168

Fox, Laurie, Linda Chester Literary Agency, 630 Fifth Ave, Suite 2000, New York, NY 10111 *Tel:* 212-218-3350 *E-mail:* submissions@lindachester.com *Web Site:* www.lindachester.com, pg 479

Fox, Leisette, Wildflower Press, c/o Oakbrook Press, 3301 S Valley Dr, Rapid City, SD 57703 *Tel:* 605-381-6385 *E-mail:* info@wildflowerpress.org *Web Site:* www.wildflowerpress.org, pg 241

Fox, Nancy, Gem Guides Book Co, 1155 W Ninth St, Upland, CA 91786 *Tel:* 626-855-1611 *Toll Free Tel:* 800-541-7760 (orders) *Fax:* 626-855-1610 *E-mail:* info@gemguidesbooks.com; sales@ gemguidesbooks.com (orders) *Web Site:* www. gemguidesbooks.com, pg 84

Fox, R K, American Press, 60 State St, Suite 700, Boston, MA 02109 *Tel:* 617-247-0022 *E-mail:* americanpress@flash.net *Web Site:* www. americanpresspublishers.com, pg 13

Fox, Steven A, Central Conference of American Rabbis/CCAR Press, 355 Lexington Ave, New York, NY 10017 *Tel:* 212-972-3636 *Fax:* 212-692-0819 *E-mail:* info@ccarpress.org *Web Site:* www.ccarpress. org, pg 48

Foxman, Ariel, Aevitas Creative Management, 19 W 21 St, Suite 501, New York, NY 10010 *Tel:* 212-765-6900 *Web Site:* aevitascreative.com, pg 474

Foxman, Janet, The University of Arkansas Press, McIlroy House, 105 N McIlroy Ave, Fayetteville, AR 72701 *Tel:* 479-575-7544 *E-mail:* info@uapress.com *Web Site:* www.uapress.com, pg 226

Foy, Fritz, Tom Doherty Associates, LLC, 120 Broadway, New York, NY 10271 *Tel:* 646-307-5511 *Toll Free Tel:* 800-455-0340 *Web Site:* us.macmillan. com/torforge, pg 66

Fradkoff, Lindsay, Perseus Books, 1290 Avenue of the Americas, New York, NY 10104 *Tel:* 212-340-8100 *Toll Free Tel:* 800-343-4499 (cust serv) *Fax:* 212-340-8105 *Web Site:* www.perseusbooks.com, pg 167

Franceschelli, Christopher, Handprint Books Inc, 413 Sixth Ave, Brooklyn, NY 11215-3310 *Tel:* 718-768-3696 *Toll Free Tel:* 800-722-6657 (orders) *Fax:* 718-369-0844 *Toll Free Fax:* 800-858-7787 (orders) *E-mail:* info@handprintbooks.com *Web Site:* www. handprintbooks.com, pg 92

Franceschelli, Joe, HarperCollins Publishers, 195 Broadway, New York, NY 10007 *Tel:* 212-207-7000 *Fax:* 212-207-7145 *Web Site:* www.harpercollins.com, pg 94

Franceschi, Susan, American Water Works Association (AWWA), 6666 W Quincy Ave, Denver, CO 80235-3098 *Tel:* 303-794-7711 *Toll Free Tel:* 800-926-7337 *E-mail:* service@awwa.org (cust serv) *Web Site:* www. awwa.org, pg 15

Francet, Cris, Pants On Fire Press, 2062 Harbor Cove Way, Winter Garden, FL 34787 *Tel:* 863-546-0760 *E-mail:* submission@pantsonfirepress.com *Web Site:* www.pantsonfirepress.com, pg 159

Francis, Barbara, Pippin Press, 229 E 85 St, New York, NY 10028 *Tel:* 212-288-4920 *Fax:* 908-237-2407, pg 170

Francis, Fred, Perseus Books, 1290 Avenue of the Americas, New York, NY 10104 *Tel:* 212-340-8100 *Toll Free Tel:* 800-343-4499 (cust serv) *Fax:* 212-340-8105 *Web Site:* www.perseusbooks.com, pg 167

Francis, Jason, Signature Books Publishing LLC, 564 W 400 N, Salt Lake City, UT 84116-3411 *Toll Free Tel:* 800-356-5687 *E-mail:* people@signaturebooks. com *Web Site:* www.signaturebooks.com; www. signaturebookslibrary.org, pg 198

French, Pam, Karl Pohrt Tribute Award, 3135 S State St, Suite 203, Ann Arbor, MI 48108 *Toll Free Tel:* 866-733-9064 *Fax:* 734-477-2806 *E-mail:* info@ bincfoundation.org *Web Site:* www.bincfoundation. org/scholarship, pg 657

Frerich, Stephanie, Simon & Schuster, 1230 Avenue of the Americas, New York, NY 10020 *Tel:* 212-698-7000 *Toll Free Tel:* 800-223-2348 (cust serv); 800-223-2336 (orders) *Toll Free Fax:* 800-943-9831 (orders) *Web Site:* www.simonandschuster.com, pg 198

Frescas Macias, Stephanie, Cinco Puntos Press, 701 Texas Ave, El Paso, TX 79901 *Tel:* 915-838-1625 *Toll Free Tel:* 800-566-9072 *Fax:* 915-838-1635 *E-mail:* info@cincopuntos.com *Web Site:* www. cincopuntos.com, pg 52

Frese, Alan, Pippin Press, 229 E 85 St, New York, NY 10028 *Tel:* 212-288-4920 *Fax:* 908-237-2407, pg 170

Freund, Dusty, Boulevard Magazine Short Fiction Contest for Emerging Writers, 6614 Clayton Rd, PMB 325, Richmond Heights, MO 63117 *E-mail:* editors@boulevardmagazine.org *Web Site:* www.boulevardmagazine.org, pg 600

Frey, Christina, Editorial Freelancers Association (EFA), 266 W 37 St, 20th fl, New York, NY 10018 *Tel:* 212-920-4816 *Toll Free Tel:* 866-929-5425 *E-mail:* office@ the-efa.org *Web Site:* www.the-efa.org, pg 532

Freyer, Emily, Teachers College Press, 1234 Amsterdam Ave, New York, NY 10027 *Tel:* 212-678-3929 *Fax:* 212-678-4149 *E-mail:* tcpress@tc.edu *Web Site:* www.tcpress.com, pg 214

Freymann, Sarah Jane, Sarah Jane Freymann Literary Agency LLC, 59 W 71 St, Suite 9-B, New York, NY 10023 *Tel:* 212-362-9277 *E-mail:* submissions@sarahjanefreymann.com *Web Site:* www.sarahjanefreymann.com, pg 485

Frick, Amalia, GP Putnam's Sons (Children's), 345 Hudson St, New York, NY 10014 *Tel:* 212-366-2000 *Fax:* 212-414-3393 *Web Site:* www.penguin. com/publishers/gpputnamssonsbooksforyoungread, pg 178

Frick, Whitney, Random House Publishing Group, 1745 Broadway, New York, NY 10019 *Toll Free Tel:* 800-200-3552 *Web Site:* www.randomhousebooks.com, pg 181

Fried, Brett, Silver Leaf Books LLC, 13 Temi Rd, Holliston, MA 01746 *E-mail:* sales@silverleafbooks. com; editor@silverleafbooks.com; customerservice@ silverleafbooks.com *Web Site:* www.silverleafbooks. com, pg 198

Fried, Carolyn, BHTG - Julie Harris Playwright Award Competition, PO Box 148, Beverly Hills, CA 90213 *Tel:* 310-273-3390 *Web Site:* www. beverlyhillstheatreguild.com, pg 597

Fried, Carolyn, BHTG - Michael J Libow Youth Theatre Award, PO Box 148, Beverly Hills, CA 90213 *Tel:* 310-273-3390 *Web Site:* www. beverlyhillstheatreguild.com, pg 598

Fried, Gabriel, Persea Books, 90 Broad St, Suite 2100, New York, NY 10004 *Tel:* 212-260-9256 *E-mail:* info@perseabooks.com; poetry@perseabooks. com; publicity@perseabooks.com *Web Site:* www. perseabooks.com, pg 167

Fried, Gabriel, Lexi Rudnitsky First Book Prize in Poetry, 90 Broad St, Suite 2100, New York, NY 10004 *Tel:* 212-260-9256 *E-mail:* info@perseabooks. com *Web Site:* www.perseabooks.com, pg 663

Fried, Ian, Close Up Publishing, 1330 Braddock Place, Suite 400, Alexandria, VA 22314 *Tel:* 703-706-3300 *Toll Free Tel:* 800-CLOSE-UP (256-7387) *E-mail:* info@closeup.org *Web Site:* www.closeup.org, pg 54

Fried, Jonah, Persea Books, 90 Broad St, Suite 2100, New York, NY 10004 *Tel:* 212-260-9256 *E-mail:* info@perseabooks.com; poetry@perseabooks. com; publicity@perseabooks.com *Web Site:* www. perseabooks.com, pg 167

Fried, Jonah, Lexi Rudnitsky First Book Prize in Poetry, 90 Broad St, Suite 2100, New York, NY 10004 *Tel:* 212-260-9256 *E-mail:* info@perseabooks.com *Web Site:* www.perseabooks.com, pg 663

Fried, Marilyn, Silver Leaf Books LLC, 13 Temi Rd, Holliston, MA 01746 *E-mail:* sales@silverleafbooks. com; editor@silverleafbooks.com; customerservice@ silverleafbooks.com *Web Site:* www.silverleafbooks. com, pg 198

Fried, Melanie, Harlequin Enterprises Ltd, Bay Adelaide Centre, East Tower, 22 Adelaide St W, 41st fl, Toronto, ON M5H 4E3, Canada *Tel:* 416-445-5860 *Toll Free Tel:* 888-432-4879; 800-370-5838 (ebook inquiries) *E-mail:* customerservice@harlequin.com *Web Site:* www.harlequin.com, pg 429

Friedland, Nancy, Theatre Library Association (TLA), c/o The New York Public Library for the Performing Arts, 40 Lincoln Center Plaza, New York, NY 10023 *E-mail:* TheatreLibraryAssociation@gmail.com *Web Site:* www.tla-online.org/awards/bookawards, pg 548

Friedman, Andy, American Marketing Association, 130 E Randolph St, 22nd fl, Chicago, IL 60601 *Tel:* 312-542-9000 *Toll Free Tel:* 800-AMA-1150 (262-1150) *Web Site:* www.ama.org, pg 523

Friedman, Caitlin, Scholastic Trade Division, 557 Broadway, New York, NY 10012 *Tel:* 212-343-6100; 212-343-4685 (export sales) *Fax:* 212-343-4714 (export sales) *Web Site:* www.scholastic.com, pg 194

Friedman, Dina, Accurate Writing & More, 16 Barstow Lane, Hadley, MA 01035 *Tel:* 413-586-2388 *Web Site:* www.accuratewriting.com; www. frugalmarketing.com; www.goingbeyondsustainability. com; www.transformpreneur.com; www. greenandprofitable.com; www.twitter.com/ shelhorowitz, pg 457

Friedman, Fredrica S, Fredrica S Friedman & Co Inc, 857 Fifth Ave, New York, NY 10065 *Tel:* 212-639-9455 *E-mail:* info@fredricafriedman.com *Web Site:* www.fredricafriedman.com, pg 485

Friedman, Jessica, Sterling Lord Literistic Inc, 115 Broadway, Suite 1602, New York, NY 10006 *Tel:* 212-780-6050 *Fax:* 212-780-6095 *E-mail:* info@sll.com *Web Site:* www.sll.com, pg 504

Friedman, Tully M, The AEI Press, 1789 Massachusetts Ave NW, Washington, DC 20036 *Tel:* 202-862-5800 *Fax:* 202-862-7177 *Web Site:* www.aei.org, pg 5

Friedman, Walter, The Alfred & Fay Chandler Book Award, c/o Harvard Business School, Connell House 301A, Boston, MA 02163 *Tel:* 617-495-1003 *Fax:* 617-495-2705 *E-mail:* bhr@hbs.edu *Web Site:* www.hbs.edu/businesshistory/fellowships, pg 604

Friedman, Yali, Logos Press, 3909 Witmer Rd, Suite 416, Niagara Falls, NY 14305 *Fax:* 815-346-3514 *E-mail:* info@logos-press.com *Web Site:* www.logos-press.com, pg 127

Friel, Emily, Integra Software Services Inc, 1110 Jorie Blvd, Suite 200, Oak Brook, IL 60523 *Tel:* 630-586-2579 *Fax:* 630-586-2599 *E-mail:* marketing@integra. co.in *Web Site:* www.integra.co.in, pg 465

Friesen, Desirae, Tom Doherty Associates, LLC, 120 Broadway, New York, NY 10271 *Tel:* 646-307-5511 *Toll Free Tel:* 800-455-0340 *Web Site:* us.macmillan. com/torforge, pg 66

Friesen, Ron, The Continuing Legal Education Society of British Columbia (CLEBC), 500-1155 W Pender St, Vancouver, BC V6E 2P4, Canada *Tel:* 604-669-3544; 604-893-2121 (cust serv) *Toll Free Tel:* 800-663-0437 (CN) *Fax:* 604-669-9260 *E-mail:* custserv@cle.bc.ca *Web Site:* www.cle.bc.ca, pg 420

Frisch, Janice, Indiana University Press, Herman B Wells Library 350, 1320 E Tenth St, Bloomington, IN 47405-3907 *Tel:* 812-855-8817 *Toll Free Tel:* 800-842-6796 (orders only) *Fax:* 812-855-7931; 812-855-8507 *E-mail:* iupress@indiana.edu; iuporder@indiana.edu (orders) *Web Site:* www.iupress.indiana.edu, pg 108

Frisch, Shelley, Markus Wiener Publishers Inc, 231 Nassau St, Princeton, NJ 08542 *Tel:* 609-921-1141 *Fax:* 609-921-1140 *E-mail:* publisher@markuswiener. com *Web Site:* www.markuswiener.com, pg 241

Frisque, Mary A, Hammett Prize, 243 Fifth Ave, Suite 537, New York, NY 10016 *E-mail:* info@ crimewritersna.org *Web Site:* www.crimewritersna. org/hammett, pg 622

Frisque, Mary A, International Association of Crime Writers Inc, North American Branch, 243 Fifth Ave, Suite 537, New York, NY 10016 *Tel:* 212-243-8966 *Fax:* 815-361-1477 *E-mail:* info@crimewritersna.org *Web Site:* www.crimewritersna.org, pg 535

Fritscher, Carl, ASF Translation Awards, Scandinavia House, 58 Park Ave, New York, NY 10016 *Tel:* 212-879-9779; 212-779-3587 *Fax:* 212-686-2115 *E-mail:* grants@amscan.org *Web Site:* www.amscan. org, pg 593

Froman, Craig, Master Books®, 3142 Hwy 103 N, Green Forest, AR 72638 *Tel:* 870-438-5288 *Toll Free Tel:* 800-999-3777 *E-mail:* sales@masterbooks. com; nlp@nlpg.com; submissions@newleafpress. net *Web Site:* www.masterbooks.com; www.nlpg. com/imprint/master-books, pg 134

Froman, Craig, New Leaf Press, 3142 Hwy 103 N, Green Forest, AR 72638-2233 *Tel:* 870-438-5288 *Toll Free Tel:* 800-999-3777 *Fax:* 870-438-5120 *E-mail:* nlp@newleafpress.net; submissions@ newleafpress.net *Web Site:* www.nlpg.com, pg 149

Fromer, Margot J, Fromer, 1606 Noyes Dr, Silver Spring, MD 20910-2224 *Tel:* 301-585-8827, pg 463

Frontera, Samantha, Triumph Books, 814 N Franklin St, Chicago, IL 60610 *Tel:* 312-337-0747 *Toll Free Tel:* 800-888-4741 (cust serv) *Fax:* 312-280-5470; 312-337-5985 *Web Site:* www.triumphbooks.com, pg 221

Frost, Jim, Atlantic Center for the Arts Master Artist-in-Residence Program, 1414 Art Center Ave, New Smyrna Beach, FL 32168 *Tel:* 386-427-6975 *Toll Free Tel:* 800-393-6975 *Fax:* 386-427-5669 *E-mail:* program@atlanticcenterforthearts.org *Web Site:* atlanticcenterforthearts.org, pg 573

Fry, Erin, Romance Writers of America®, 14615 Benfer Rd, Houston, TX 77069 *Tel:* 832-717-5200 *Fax:* 832-717-5201 *E-mail:* info@rwa.org, pg 545

Fry, Sonali, Random House Children's Books, 1745 Broadway, 10th fl, New York, NY 10019 *Tel:* 212-782-9000 *Web Site:* www.randomhousekids.com, pg 180

Fryer, Janice, Adams Media, 57 Littlefield St, Avon, MA 02322 *Tel:* 508-427-7100 *Web Site:* www. simonandschuster.com, pg 4

Fryman, Alona, Bloomsbury Publishing Inc, 1385 Broadway, 5th fl, New York, NY 10018 *Tel:* 212-419-5300 *E-mail:* marketingusa@bloomsbury.com; adultpublicityusa@bloomsbury.com; askacademic@ bloomsbury.com *Web Site:* www.bloomsbury.com, pg 36

Fuchs, George, National Association of Printing Ink Manufacturers (NAPIM), 3600 E State St, Suite 306, Rockford, IL 61108 *Tel:* 815-708-7387 *Web Site:* www.napim.org, pg 539

Fuchs, Robert E, Wildflower Press, c/o Oakbrook Press, 3301 S Valley Dr, Rapid City, SD 57703 *Tel:* 605-381-6385 *E-mail:* info@wildflowerpress.org *Web Site:* www.wildflowerpress.org, pg 241

Fuersich, Larry, Visual Profile Books Inc, 389 Fifth Ave, Suite 1105, New York, NY 10016 *Tel:* 516-445-0116 *Web Site:* www.visualprofilebooks.com, pg 237

Fugate, Alice, Trident Media Group LLC, 41 Madison Ave, 36th fl, New York, NY 10010 *Tel:* 212-333-1511 *E-mail:* info@tridentmediagroup.com; press@tridentmediagroup.com *Web Site:* www. tridentmediagroup.com, pg 507

Fugliese, Susan, Newbury Street Press, 99-101 Newbury St, Boston, MA 02116 *Tel:* 617-226-1206 *Toll Free Tel:* 888-296-3447 (NEHGS membership) *Fax:* 617-536-7307 *E-mail:* sales@nehgs.org *Web Site:* www. americanancestors.org, pg 150

Fuhrman, Candice, Candice Fuhrman Literary Agency, 10 Cypress Hollow Dr, Tiburon, CA 94920 *Tel:* 415-383-1014 *E-mail:* fuhrmancandice@gmail.com, pg 485

Fujimoto, Grace, Perseus Books, 1290 Avenue of the Americas, New York, NY 10104 *Tel:* 212-340-8100 *Toll Free Tel:* 800-343-4499 (cust serv) *Fax:* 212-340-8105 *Web Site:* www.perseusbooks.com, pg 167

Fuller, Barbara, Editcetera, 2034 Blake St, Suite 5, Berkeley, CA 94704 *Tel:* 510-849-1110 *E-mail:* info@editcetera.com *Web Site:* www.editcetera.com, pg 462

Fuller, Diana, Squaw Valley Community of Writers Summer Workshops, PO Box 1416, Nevada City, CA 95959 *Tel:* 530-470-8440 *E-mail:* info@communityofwriters.org *Web Site:* www.communityofwriters.org, pg 579

Fulton, Scott, Environmental Law Institute, 1730 "M" St NW, Suite 700, Washington, DC 20036 *Tel:* 202-939-3800 *Toll Free Tel:* 800-433-5120 *Fax:* 202-939-3868 *E-mail:* law@eli.org *Web Site:* www.eli.org, pg 73

Fund, Ken, Quarto Publishing Group USA Inc, 100 Cummings Ctr, Suite 265D, Beverly, MA 01915 *Tel:* 978-282-9590 *Toll Free Tel:* 800-328-0590 (sales) *Fax:* 978-283-2742 *E-mail:* sales@quartous.com *Web Site:* www.quartoknows.com, pg 178

Funda, Evelyn I, David W & Beatrice C Evans Biography & Handcart Awards, 0735 Old Main Hill, Logan, UT 84322-0735 *Tel:* 435-797-0299 *Fax:* 435-797-1092 *E-mail:* mwc@usu.edu *Web Site:* mountainwest.usu.edu, pg 614

Funk, Cameon, MAR*CO Products Inc, PO Box 686, Hatfield, PA 19440 *Tel:* 215-956-0313 *Toll Free Tel:* 800-448-2197 *Fax:* 215-956-9041 *E-mail:* help@marcoproducts.com; sales@marcoproducts.com *Web Site:* www.marcoproducts.com, pg 131

Funk, Warren, MAR*CO Products Inc, PO Box 686, Hatfield, PA 19440 *Tel:* 215-956-0313 *Toll Free Tel:* 800-448-2197 *Fax:* 215-956-9041 *E-mail:* help@marcoproducts.com; sales@marcoproducts.com *Web Site:* www.marcoproducts.com, pg 131

Fuqua, Jennifer, University of Alabama Program in Creative Writing, PO Box 870244, Tuscaloosa, AL 35487-0244 *Tel:* 205-348-5065 *Fax:* 205-348-1388 *E-mail:* english@ua.edu *Web Site:* www.as.ua.edu/english, pg 585

Fuqua, Sam, Excellence in Graphic Literature Awards, 2760 W Fifth Ave, Denver, CO 80204 *Tel:* 303-325-1236 *E-mail:* egl@popcultureclassroom.org *Web Site:* popcultureclassroom.org/egl, pg 614

Furman, Laura, The O. Henry Prize Stories, c/o University of Texas at Austin, One University Sta, English Dept, B5000, Austin, TX 78712 *Web Site:* www.randomhouse.com/anchor/ohenry, pg 649

Furnish, Ben, BkMk Press - University of Missouri-Kansas City, University House, 5101 Rockhill Rd, Kansas City, MO 64110-2499 *Tel:* 816-235-2558 *Fax:* 816-235-2611 *E-mail:* bkmk@umkc.edu *Web Site:* www.umkc.edu/bkmk, pg 34

Furnish, Ben, G S Sharat Chandra Prize for Short Fiction, University House, 5101 Rockhill Rd, Kansas City, MO 64110-2499 *Tel:* 816-235-2558 *Fax:* 816-235-2611 *E-mail:* bkmk@umkc.edu *Web Site:* www.umkc.edu/bkmk, pg 604

Furnish, Ben, John Ciardi Prize for Poetry, University House, 5101 Rockhill Rd, Kansas City, MO 64110-2499 *Tel:* 816-235-2558 *Fax:* 816-235-2611 *E-mail:* bkmk@umkc.edu *Web Site:* www.umkc.edu/bkmk, pg 605

Furr, Madison, Farrar, Straus & Giroux Books for Young Readers, 120 Broadway, New York, NY 10271 *Tel:* 212-741-6900 *Toll Free Tel:* 888-330-8477 (orders) *Fax:* 212-633-9385 *Web Site:* us.macmillan.com/mackids; www.mackidsbooks.com, pg 76

Furr, Madison, Roaring Brook Press, 120 Broadway, New York, NY 10271 *Tel:* 646-307-5151 *Web Site:* us.macmillan.com/publishers/roaring-brook-press, pg 186

Furr, Patti, FaithWalk Publishing, 5450 N Dixie Hwy, Lima, OH 45807 *Tel:* 419-227-1818 *Toll Free Tel:* 800-537-1030 (orders, non-bookstore mkts) *Fax:* 419-224-9184 *E-mail:* orders@csspub.com *Web Site:* www.faithwalkpub.com, pg 75

Furtak, Shannon, William S Hein & Co Inc, 2350 N Forest Rd, Getzville, NY 14068 *Tel:* 716-882-2600 *Toll Free Tel:* 800-828-7571 *Fax:* 716-883-8100 *E-mail:* mail@wshein.com; marketing@wshein.com *Web Site:* www.wshein.com, pg 97

Furuta, Evelyn, Chronicle Books, 680 Second St, San Francisco, CA 94107 *Tel:* 415-537-4200 *Toll Free Tel:* 800-759-0190 (cust serv) *Fax:* 415-537-4460 *Toll Free Fax:* 800-858-7787 (orders); 800-286-9471 (cust serv) *E-mail:* frontdesk@chroniclebooks.com *Web Site:* www.chroniclebooks.com, pg 52

Fusting, Donald W, Lanahan Publishers Inc, 324 Hawthorne Rd, Baltimore, MD 21210-2303 *Tel:* 410-366-2434 *Toll Free Tel:* 866-345-1949 *Fax:* 410-366-8798 *E-mail:* lanahan@aol.com *Web Site:* www.lanahanpublishers.com, pg 119

G'Schwind, Stephanie, Nelligan Prize for Short Fiction, Colorado State University, Dept of English, Center for Literary Publishing, 9105 Campus Delivery, Fort Collins, CO 80523-9105 *Tel:* 970-491-5449 *E-mail:* creview@colostate.edu *Web Site:* nelliganprize.colostate.edu, pg 646

Gabel, Claudia, HarperCollins Children's Books, 195 Broadway, New York, NY 10007 *Tel:* 212-207-7000 *Web Site:* www.harpercollins.com/childrens, pg 93

Gadd, Laurence, North River Press Publishing Corp, 27 Rosseter St, Great Barrington, MA 01230 *Tel:* 413-528-0034 *Toll Free Tel:* 800-486-2665 *Fax:* 413-528-3163 *Toll Free Fax:* 800-BOOK-FAX (266-5329) *E-mail:* info@northriverpress.com *Web Site:* www.northriverpress.com, pg 152

Gadney, Alan, One On One Book Publishing/Film-Video Publications, 7944 Capistrano Ave, West Hills, CA 91304 *Tel:* 818-340-6620; 818-340-0175 *Fax:* 818-340-6620 *E-mail:* onebookpro@aol.com, pg 155

Gadney, Nancy, One On One Book Publishing/Film-Video Publications, 7944 Capistrano Ave, West Hills, CA 91304 *Tel:* 818-340-6620; 818-340-0175 *Fax:* 818-340-6620 *E-mail:* onebookpro@aol.com, pg 155

Gadoury, Bill, Macmillan Learning, 41 Madison Ave, New York, NY 10010 *Tel:* 212-576-9400 *Fax:* 212-689-2383 *Web Site:* www.macmillanlearning.com, pg 130

Gadow, Katharina, Workman Publishing Co Inc, 225 Varick St, 9th fl, New York, NY 10014-4381 *Tel:* 212-254-5900 *Toll Free Tel:* 800-722-7202 *Fax:* 212-254-8098 *E-mail:* info@workman.com; orders@workman.com *Web Site:* www.workman.com, pg 244

Gaffney, Theresa, Penguin Books, 375 Hudson St, New York, NY 10014 *Tel:* 212-366-2000 *E-mail:* penguinpublicity@us.penguingroup.com *Web Site:* www.penguinclassics.com; www.penguin.com, pg 163

Gaffney, Theresa, Viking, 375 Hudson St, New York, NY 10014 *Tel:* 212-366-2000 *Fax:* 212-243-6002 *Web Site:* www.penguin.com/publishers/vikingbooks, pg 236

Gafron, Stephanie, Sourcebooks LLC, 1935 Brookdale Rd, Suite 139, Naperville, IL 60563 *Tel:* 630-961-3900 *Toll Free Tel:* 800-432-7444 *Fax:* 630-961-2168 *E-mail:* info@sourcebooks.com; customersupport@sourcebooks.com *Web Site:* www.sourcebooks.com, pg 204

Gage, Michael, Kirkbride Bible Co Inc, 1102 Deloss St, Indianapolis, IN 46203 *Tel:* 317-633-1900 *Toll Free Tel:* 800-428-4385 *Fax:* 317-633-1444 *E-mail:* sales@kirkbride.com; info@kirkbride.com *Web Site:* www.kirkbride.com, pg 117

Gagliano, Gina, Random House Children's Books, 1745 Broadway, 10th fl, New York, NY 10019 *Tel:* 212-782-9000 *Web Site:* www.randomhousekids.com, pg 180

Gagnon, Andre, Editions Hurtubise, 1815, ave De Lorimier, Montreal, QC H2K 3W6, Canada *Tel:* 514-523-1523 *Toll Free Tel:* 800-361-1664 *Fax:* 514-523-9969 *Web Site:* www.editionshurtubise.com, pg 424

Gagnon, Manon, La Fondation Emile Nelligan, 100, rue Sherbrooke, Suite 202, Montreal, QC H2X 1C3, Canada *Tel:* 514-278-4657 *E-mail:* info@fondation-nelligan.org *Web Site:* www.fondation-nelligan.org, pg 534

Gagnon, Manon, Prix Emile-Nelligan, 100, rue Sherbrooke, Suite 202, Montreal, QC H2X 1C3, Canada *Tel:* 514-278-4657 *Toll Free Tel:* 888-849-8540 *E-mail:* info@fondation-nelligan.org *Web Site:* www.fondation-nelligan.org, pg 659

Gagnon, Matt, Boom! Studios, 5670 Wilshire Blvd, Suite 400, Los Angeles, CA 90036 *Web Site:* www.boom-studios.com, pg 38

Galardo, Elsa, Les Editions JCL, 688, rue St-Joseph, Marieville, QC J3M 1H1, Canada *Tel:* 450-460-4438 *E-mail:* info@jcl.qc.ca *Web Site:* www.jcl.qc.ca, pg 424

Galassi, Jonathan, Farrar, Straus & Giroux, LLC, 175 Varick St, 9th fl, New York, NY 10014 *Tel:* 212-741-6900 *E-mail:* fsg.publicity@fsgbooks.com *Web Site:* us.macmillan.com/fsg.aspx, pg 76

Galasso, Al, National Association of Book Entrepreneurs (NABE), PO Box 606, Cottage Grove, OR 97424 *Tel:* 541-942-7455 *Fax:* 541-942-7455 *E-mail:* nabe@bookmarketingprofits.com *Web Site:* www.bookmarketingprofits.com, pg 538

Galasso, Al, Pinnacle Book Achievement Awards, PO Box 606, Cottage Grove, OR 97424 *Tel:* 541-942-7455 *Fax:* 541-942-7455 *E-mail:* nabe@bookmarketingprofits.com *Web Site:* www.bookmarketingprofits.com, pg 656

Galat, Danielle, New World Library, 14 Pamaron Way, Novato, CA 94949 *Tel:* 415-884-2100 *Toll Free Tel:* 800-227-3900 (ext 52, retail orders); 800-972-6657 *Fax:* 415-884-2199 *E-mail:* escort@newworldlibrary.com *Web Site:* www.newworldlibrary.com, pg 149

Galbraith, Judy, Free Spirit Publishing Inc, 6325 Sandburg Rd, Suite 100, Minneapolis, MN 55427 *Tel:* 612-338-2068 *Toll Free Tel:* 800-735-7323 *Fax:* 612-337-5050 *Toll Free Fax:* 866-419-5199 *E-mail:* help4kids@freespirit.com *Web Site:* www.freespirit.com, pg 81

Galde, Phyllis, Galde Press Inc, PO Box 774, Hendersonville, NC 28793 *Tel:* 828-702-3032 *Web Site:* www.galdepress.com, pg 82

Gale, Kate, Red Hen Press, PO Box 40820, Pasadena, CA 91114 *Tel:* 626-356-4760 *Fax:* 626-356-9974 *Web Site:* www.redhen.org, pg 183

Gale, Meighan, Zone Books, 633 Vanderbilt St, Brooklyn, NY 11218 *Tel:* 718-686-0048 *Fax:* 718-686-9045 *E-mail:* info@zonebooks.org *Web Site:* www.zonebooks.org, pg 248

Galen, Russell, Scovil Galen Ghosh Literary Agency Inc, 276 Fifth Ave, Suite 207, New York, NY 10001 *Tel:* 212-679-8686 *E-mail:* info@sgglit.com *Web Site:* www.sgglit.com, pg 502

Gall, John, Alfred A Knopf, c/o Penguin Random House Inc, 1745 Broadway, New York, NY 10019 *Tel:* 212-751-2600 *Fax:* 212-572-2662 (foreign rts) *Web Site:* knopfdoubleday.com, pg 117

Gallagher, Amy, North River Press Publishing Corp, 27 Rosseter St, Great Barrington, MA 01230 *Tel:* 413-528-0034 *Toll Free Tel:* 800-486-2665 *Fax:* 413-528-3163 *Toll Free Fax:* 800-BOOK-FAX (266-5329) *E-mail:* info@northriverpress.com *Web Site:* www.northriverpress.com, pg 152

Gallagher, Caitlin, Yale University Press, 302 Temple St, New Haven, CT 06511-8909 *Tel:* 203-432-0960; 203-432-0966 (sales); 401-531-2800 (cust serv) *Toll Free Tel:* 800-405-1619 (cust serv) *Fax:* 203-432-0948; 203-432-8485 (sales); 401-531-2801 (cust serv) *Toll Free Fax:* 800-406-9145 (cust serv) *E-mail:* sales.press@yale.edu (sales); customer.care@triliteral.org (cust serv) *Web Site:* www.yalebooks.com; yalepress.yale.edu/yupbooks, pg 246

Gallagher, Charles, Arcadia Publishing Inc, 420 Wando Park Blvd, Mount Pleasant, SC 29464 *Tel:* 843-853-2070 *Toll Free Tel:* 888-313-2665 (orders only) *Fax:* 843-853-0044 *E-mail:* sales@arcadiapublishing.com *Web Site:* www.arcadiapublishing.com, pg 19

Gallagher, Conor, TAN Books, PO Box 269, Gastonia, NC 28053 *Tel:* 704-731-0651 *Toll Free Tel:* 800-437-5876 *Fax:* 815-226-7770 *E-mail:* customerservice@tanbooks.com *Web Site:* www.tanbooks.com, pg 212

Gallagher, Julia, Holiday House Publishing Inc, 50 Broad St, New York, NY 10004 *Tel:* 212-688-0085 *Fax:* 212-421-6134 *E-mail:* info@holidayhouse.com *Web Site:* www.holidayhouse.com, pg 101

Gallagher, Laird, Farrar, Straus & Giroux, LLC, 175 Varick St, 9th fl, New York, NY 10014 *Tel:* 212-741-6900 *E-mail:* fsg.publicity@fsgbooks.com *Web Site:* us.macmillan.com/fsg.aspx, pg 76

Gallagher, Lisa, DeFiore and Company Literary Management Inc, 47 E 19 St, 3rd fl, New York, NY 10003 *Tel:* 212-925-7744 *Fax:* 212-925-9803 *E-mail:* info@defliterary.com; submissions@defliterary.com *Web Site:* www.defliterary.com, pg 481

Gallagher, Mike, Penguin Group USA, A Penguin Random House Company, 375 Hudson St, New York, NY 10014 *Tel:* 212-366-2000 *Toll Free Tel:* 800-847-5515 (inside sales); 800-631-8571 (cust serv) *Fax:* 212-366-2666; 607-775-4829 (inside sales) *E-mail:* online@us.penguingroup.com *Web Site:* www.penguin.com, pg 163

Gallagher, Richard, Annual Reviews, 4139 El Camino Way, Palo Alto, CA 94306 *Tel:* 650-493-4400 *Toll Free Tel:* 800-523-8635 *Fax:* 650-424-0910; 650-855-9815 *E-mail:* service@annualreviews.org *Web Site:* www.annualreviews.org, pg 17

Gallagher, Robert, TAN Books, PO Box 269, Gastonia, NC 28053 *Tel:* 704-731-0651 *Toll Free Tel:* 800-437-5876 *Fax:* 815-226-7770 *E-mail:* customerservice@tanbooks.com *Web Site:* www.tanbooks.com, pg 212

Gallancy, Shawna C, American Federation of Arts, 305 E 47 St, 10th fl, New York, NY 10017 *Tel:* 212-988-7700 *Toll Free Tel:* 800-232-0270 *Fax:* 212-861-2487 *E-mail:* pubinfo@amfedarts.org *Web Site:* www.amfedarts.org, pg 10

Gallant, Barry, Doubleday Canada, 320 Front St W, Suite 1400, Toronto, ON M5V 3B6, Canada *Tel:* 416-364-4449 *Fax:* 416-598-7764 *Web Site:* www.penguinrandomhouse.ca, pg 421

Gallant, Barry, Knopf Canada, 320 Front St W, Suite 1400, Toronto, ON M5V 3B6, Canada *Tel:* 416-364-4449 *Toll Free Tel:* 888-523-9292 *Fax:* 416-598-7764 *Web Site:* www.penguinrandomhouse.ca, pg 431

Gallant, Barry, Penguin Group (Canada), 320 Front St W, Suite 1400, Toronto, ON M5V 3B6, Canada *Tel:* 416-364-4449 *Fax:* 416-598-7764 *E-mail:* customerservicescanada@penguinrandomhouse.com; publicity@ca.penguingroup.com *Web Site:* penguinrandomhouse.ca/imprints/penguin-canada, pg 436

Gallant, Barry, Penguin Random House Canada, 320 Front St W, Suite 1400, Toronto, ON M5V 3B6, Canada *Tel:* 416-364-4449 *Toll Free Tel:* 888-523-9292 (cust serv) *Fax:* 416-598-7764 *Web Site:* www.penguinrandomhouse.ca, pg 436

Gallant, Barry, Seal Books, 320 Front St W, Suite 1400, Toronto, ON M5V 3B6, Canada *Tel:* 416-364-4449 *Toll Free Tel:* 888-523-9292 (order desk) *Fax:* 416-598-7764 *Web Site:* www.penguinrandomhouse.ca, pg 439

Gallegos, Anna, Museum of New Mexico Press, 725 Camino Lejo, Suite C, Santa Fe, NM 87505 *Tel:* 505-476-1155; 505-272-7777 (orders) *Toll Free Tel:* 800-249-7737 (orders) *Fax:* 505-476-1156 *Toll Free Fax:* 800-622-8667 (orders) *Web Site:* www.mnmpress.org, pg 144

Gallo, Irene, Tom Doherty Associates, LLC, 120 Broadway, New York, NY 10271 *Tel:* 646-307-5511 *Toll Free Tel:* 800-455-0340 *Web Site:* us.macmillan.com/torforge, pg 66

Gallo, Ruth, Writers Guild of America, East (WGAE), 250 Hudson St, Suite 700, New York, NY 10013 *Tel:* 212-767-7800 *Fax:* 212-582-1909 *Web Site:* www.wgaeast.org, pg 549

Gallo, Vincent, William H Sadlier Inc, 9 Pine St, New York, NY 10005 *Tel:* 212-227-2120 *Toll Free Tel:* 800-221-5175 (cust serv) *Fax:* 212-312-6080 *E-mail:* customerservice@sadlier.com *Web Site:* www.sadlier.com, pg 189

Galloway, Erin, Berkley Publishing Group, 1745 Broadway, 19th fl, New York, NY 10019 *Tel:* 212-366-2000 *Web Site:* www.penguin.com, pg 32

Galloway, Greg, American Booksellers Association, 333 Westchester Ave, Suite S202, White Plains, NY 10604 *Tel:* 914-406-7500 *Toll Free Tel:* 800-637-0037 *Fax:* 914-417-4013 *E-mail:* info@bookweb.org *Web Site:* www.bookweb.org, pg 522

Galston, David, Polebridge Press, PO Box 346, Farmington, MN 55024 *Tel:* 651-200-2372 *E-mail:* orders@westarinstitute.org *Web Site:* www.westarinstitute.org, pg 172

Galusha, Dale, Pacific Press® Publishing Association, 1350 N Kings Rd, Nampa, ID 83687-3193 *Tel:* 208-465-2500 *Toll Free Tel:* 800-447-7377 *Fax:* 208-465-2531 *Web Site:* www.pacificpress.com, pg 159

Galvin, Lori, Aevitas Creative Management, 19 W 21 St, Suite 501, New York, NY 10010 *Tel:* 212-765-6900 *Web Site:* aevitascreative.com, pg 474

Galvin, Tom, Triumph Books, 814 N Franklin St, Chicago, IL 60610 *Tel:* 312-337-0747 *Toll Free Tel:* 800-888-4741 (cust serv) *Fax:* 312-280-5470; 312-337-5985 *Web Site:* www.triumphbooks.com, pg 221

Galyan, Sheyna, Yotzeret Publishing, PO Box 18662, St Paul, MN 55118-0662 *Tel:* 651-470-3853 *Fax:* 651-224-7447 *E-mail:* info@yotzeretpublishing.com; orders@yotzeretpublishing.com *Web Site:* yotzeretpublishing.com, pg 247

Gamelli, Katie, Abrams Artists Agency, 275 Seventh Ave, 26th fl, New York, NY 10001 *Tel:* 646-486-4600 *Fax:* 646-486-0100 *E-mail:* literary@abramsartny.com *Web Site:* www.abramsartists.com, pg 473

Gammel, David, Entomological Society of America, 3 Park Place, Suite 307, Annapolis, MD 21401-3722 *Tel:* 301-731-4535 *Fax:* 301-731-4538 *E-mail:* esa@entsoc.org *Web Site:* www.entsoc.org, pg 73

Gammons, Keith, Smyth & Helwys Publishing Inc, 6316 Peake Rd, Macon, GA 31210-3960 *Tel:* 478-757-0564 *Toll Free Tel:* 800-747-3016 (orders only) *Fax:* 478-757-1305 *E-mail:* information@helwys.com *Web Site:* www.helwys.com, pg 202

Gandolfo, Italia, Vesuvian Books, 2817 West End Ave, No 126-283, Nashville, TN 37203 *E-mail:* info@vesuvianmedia.com *Web Site:* www.vesuvianbooks.com, pg 236

Gannon, Mary, Community of Literary Magazines & Presses (CLMP), 154 Christopher St, Suite 3C, New York, NY 10014-9110 *Tel:* 212-741-9110 *E-mail:* info@clmp.org *Web Site:* www.clmp.org, pg 531

Gannon, Melissa, Berghahn Books, 20 Jay St, Suite 512, Brooklyn, NY 11201 *Tel:* 212-233-6004 *Fax:* 212-233-6007 *E-mail:* info@berghahnbooks.com; salesus@berghahnbooks.com; editorial@journals.berghahnbooks.com *Web Site:* www.berghahnbooks.com, pg 32

Gantz, Gabrielle, St Martin's Press, LLC, 120 Broadway, New York, NY 10271 *Tel:* 646-307-5151 *Web Site:* us.macmillan.com/smp, pg 190

Gao, Carrie, Chronicle Books, 680 Second St, San Francisco, CA 94107 *Tel:* 415-537-4200 *Toll Free Tel:* 800-759-0190 (cust serv) *Fax:* 415-537-4460 *Toll Free Fax:* 800-858-7787 (orders); 800-286-9471 (cust serv) *E-mail:* frontdesk@chroniclebooks.com *Web Site:* www.chroniclebooks.com, pg 52

Garbuz, Sulamita, Trident Media Group LLC, 41 Madison Ave, 36th fl, New York, NY 10010 *Tel:* 212-333-1511 *E-mail:* info@tridentmediagroup.com; press@tridentmediagroup.com *Web Site:* www.tridentmediagroup.com, pg 507

Garceau, Peter, Perseus Books, 1290 Avenue of the Americas, New York, NY 10104 *Tel:* 212-340-8100 *Toll Free Tel:* 800-343-4499 (cust serv) *Fax:* 212-340-8105 *Web Site:* www.perseusbooks.com, pg 168

Garces, Christina, Chronicle Books, 680 Second St, San Francisco, CA 94107 *Tel:* 415-537-4200 *Toll Free Tel:* 800-759-0190 (cust serv) *Fax:* 415-537-4460 *Toll Free Tel:* 800-858-7787 (orders); 800-286-9471 (cust serv) *E-mail:* frontdesk@chroniclebooks.com *Web Site:* www.chroniclebooks.com, pg 52

Garcia, Dawn E, The Knight-Risser Prize for Western Environmental Journalism, Stanford University, 450 Serra Mall, Bldg 120, Rm 424, Stanford, CA 94305-2050 *Tel:* 650-723-4937 *Fax:* 650-725-6154 *E-mail:* knightrisserprize@lists.stanford.edu *Web Site:* knightrisser.stanford.edu, pg 630

Garcia, Lily Eskelsen, National Education Association (NEA), 1201 16 St NW, Washington, DC 20036-3290 *Tel:* 202-833-4000 *Fax:* 202-822-7974 *Web Site:* www.nea.org, pg 146

Garcia, Lily Eskelsen, National Education Association (NEA), 1201 16 St NW, Washington, DC 20036-3290 *Tel:* 202-833-4000 *Fax:* 202-822-7974 *E-mail:* media-relations-team@nea.org *Web Site:* www.nea.org, pg 540

Garcia-Brown, Pilar, Houghton Mifflin Harcourt Trade & Reference Division, 125 High St, Boston, MA 02110 *Tel:* 617-351-5000 *Web Site:* www.hmhco.com, pg 104

Gardiner, Eileen, Italica Press, 99 Wall St, Suite 650, New York, NY 10005 *Tel:* 917-371-0563 *E-mail:* inquiries@italicapress.com *Web Site:* www.italicapress.com, pg 113

Gardner, Annie, Random House Children's Books, 1745 Broadway, 10th fl, New York, NY 10019 *Tel:* 212-782-9000 *Web Site:* www.randomhousekids.com, pg 181

Gardner, Jason, New World Library, 14 Pamaron Way, Novato, CA 94949 *Tel:* 415-884-2100 *Toll Free Tel:* 800-227-3900 (ext 52, retail orders); 800-972-6657 *Fax:* 415-884-2199 *E-mail:* escort@newworldlibrary.com *Web Site:* www.newworldlibrary.com, pg 149

Gardner, Joseph, Child's Play®, 250 Minot Ave, Auburn, ME 04210 *Tel:* 207-784-7252 *Toll Free Tel:* 800-639-6404 *Fax:* 207-784-7358 *Toll Free Fax:* 800-854-6989 *E-mail:* chpmaine@aol.com *Web Site:* www.childs-play.com, pg 51

Gardner, Dr Kevin J, Baylor University, Professional Writing Program, One Bear Place, Unit 97404, Waco, TX 76798-7404 *Tel:* 254-710-1768 *Fax:* 254-710-3894 *Web Site:* www.baylor.edu, pg 581

Gardner, Rachelle, Books & Such, 52 Mission Circle, Suite 122, PMB 170, Santa Rosa, CA 95409-5370 *Tel:* 707-538-4184 *Web Site:* booksandsuch.com, pg 477

Garfield, Valerie, Simon & Schuster Children's Publishing, 1230 Avenue of the Americas, New York, NY 10020 *Tel:* 212-698-7000 *Web Site:* www.simonandschuster.com/kids; www.simonandschuster.com/teen; simonandschuster.net; simonandschuster.biz, pg 199

Garner, Ken, Epicomm, 1800 Diagonal Rd, Suite 320, Alexandria, VA 22314-2862 *Tel:* 703-836-9200 *E-mail:* webmaster@epicomm.org *Web Site:* epicomm.org, pg 533

Garner, Marion, Penguin Random House Canada, 320 Front St W, Suite 1400, Toronto, ON M5V 3B6, Canada *Tel:* 416-364-4449 *Toll Free Tel:* 888-523-9292 (cust serv) *Fax:* 416-598-7764 *Web Site:* www.penguinrandomhouse.ca, pg 436

Garnett, Callie, Bloomsbury Publishing Inc, 1385 Broadway, 5th fl, New York, NY 10018 *Tel:* 212-419-5300 *E-mail:* marketingusa@bloomsbury.com; adultpublicityusa@bloomsbury.com; askacademic@bloomsbury.com *Web Site:* www.bloomsbury.com, pg 36

Gaynin, Gail, Morgan Gaynin Inc, 149 Madison Ave, Suite 1140, New York, NY 10016 *Tel:* 212-475-0440 *E-mail:* info@morgangaynin.com *Web Site:* www.morgangaynin.com, pg 512

Gazlay, Laura, The Library of America, 14 E 60 St, New York, NY 10022-1006 *Tel:* 212-308-3360 *Fax:* 212-750-8352 *E-mail:* info@loa.org *Web Site:* www.loa.org, pg 124

Gazzolo, Paul, Gale, 27500 Drake Rd, Farmington Hills, MI 48331-3535 *Tel:* 248-699-4253 *Toll Free Tel:* 800-877-4253 *Toll Free Fax:* 800-414-5043 (orders) *E-mail:* gale.customercare@cengage.com *Web Site:* www.gale.com, pg 82

Gazzolo, Paul, Macmillan Reference USA™, 27500 Drake Rd, Farmington Hills, MI 48331-3535 *Tel:* 248-699-4253 *Toll Free Tel:* 800-877-4253 *Toll Free Fax:* 877-363-4253 *E-mail:* gale.customercare@cengage.com *Web Site:* www.gale.cengage.com/macmillan, pg 130

Geary, William III, Bisk Education, 9417 Princess Palm Ave, Suite 400, Tampa, FL 33619 *Tel:* 813-621-6200 *Toll Free Tel:* 800-280-9718 (cust serv) *E-mail:* customerservice@bisk.com *Web Site:* www.bisk.com, pg 33

Gebhardt, Phyllis, Trusted Media Brands Inc, 750 Third Ave, 3rd fl, New York, NY 10017 *Tel:* 646-293-6299 *Toll Free Tel:* 877-732-4438 (cust serv) *Fax:* 646-293-6251 *E-mail:* customercare@trustedmediabrands.com; press@trustedmediabrands.com *Web Site:* www.trustedmediabrands.com; www.rd.com, pg 221

Geck, Steve, Sourcebooks LLC, 1935 Brookdale Rd, Suite 139, Naperville, IL 60563 *Tel:* 630-961-3900 *Toll Free Tel:* 800-432-7444 *Fax:* 630-961-2168 *E-mail:* info@sourcebooks.com; customersupport@sourcebooks.com *Web Site:* www.sourcebooks.com, pg 204

Gee, Jim, Leadership Connect, 1407 Broadway, Suite 318, New York, NY 10018 *Tel:* 212-627-4140 *Toll Free Tel:* 800-627-0311 *Fax:* 212-645-0931 *E-mail:* info@leadershipconnect.io *Web Site:* www.leadershipconnect.io, pg 121

Geer, David, Samuel French Inc, 235 Park Ave S, 5th fl, New York, NY 10003 *Tel:* 212-206-8990 *Toll Free Tel:* 866-598-8449 *Fax:* 212-206-1429 *E-mail:* info@samuelfrench.com *Web Site:* www.samuelfrench.com, pg 81

Geeter, Camille, Chronicle Books, 680 Second St, San Francisco, CA 94107 *Tel:* 415-537-4200 *Toll Free Tel:* 800-759-0190 (cust serv) *Fax:* 415-537-4460 *Toll Free Fax:* 800-858-7787 (orders); 800-286-9471 (cust serv) *E-mail:* frontdesk@chroniclebooks.com *Web Site:* www.chroniclebooks.com, pg 52

Geffen, Brian, Henry Holt and Company, LLC, 120 Broadway, 23rd fl, New York, NY 10271 *Tel:* 646-307-5151 *Toll Free Tel:* 888-330-8477 (orders) *Fax:* 646-307-5285 *Web Site:* www.henryholt.com, pg 102

Gehy, Farah, Peachtree Publishing Co Inc, 1700 Chattahoochee Ave, Atlanta, GA 30318-2112 *Tel:* 404-876-8761 *Toll Free Tel:* 800-241-0113 *Fax:* 404-875-2578 *Toll Free Fax:* 800-875-8909 *E-mail:* hello@peachtree-online.com; orders@peachtree-online.com; sales@peachtree-online.com *Web Site:* www.peachtree-online.com, pg 162

Geiger, Ellen, Frances Goldin Literary Agency, Inc, 214 W 29 St, Suite 410, New York, NY 10001 *Tel:* 212-777-0047 *Fax:* 212-228-1660 *E-mail:* agency@goldinlit.com *Web Site:* www.goldinlit.com, pg 486

Geiger, Rachel, Chronicle Books, 680 Second St, San Francisco, CA 94107 *Tel:* 415-537-4200 *Toll Free Tel:* 800-759-0190 (cust serv) *Fax:* 415-537-4460 *Toll Free Fax:* 800-858-7787 (orders); 800-286-9471 (cust serv) *E-mail:* frontdesk@chroniclebooks.com *Web Site:* www.chroniclebooks.com, pg 51

Geisen, Dan, North American Snowsports Journalists Association (NASJA), 49 Plaza Ave, Belchertown, MA 01007 *E-mail:* execsec@nasja.org *Web Site:* nasja.org, pg 542

Geisler, Anna, Guernica Editions Inc, 1569 Heritage Way, Oakville, ON L6M 2Z7, Canada *Tel:* 905-599-5304 *E-mail:* info@guernicaeditions.com *Web Site:* www.guernicaeditions.com; www.facebook.com/guernicaed, pg 428

Geissler, Cynara, Arsenal Pulp Press, 211 E Georgia St, No 202, Vancouver, BC V6A 1Z6, Canada *Tel:* 604-687-4233 *Toll Free Tel:* 888-600-PULP (600-7857) *Fax:* 604-687-4283 *E-mail:* info@arsenalpulp.com *Web Site:* www.arsenalpulp.com, pg 415

Geist, Jennifer, Brick Mantel Books, 4719 Holly Hills Ave, St Louis, MO 63116 *Tel:* 314-827-6567 *E-mail:* info@brickmantel.com *Web Site:* brickmantelbooks.com, pg 40

Geist, Jennifer, Open Books Press, 4735 S State Rd 446, Bloomington, IN 47401 *Tel:* 314-827-6567; 812-837-9226 *E-mail:* info@openbookspress.com *Web Site:* openbookspress.com, pg 156

Geist, Jennifer, Pen & Publish LLC, 4719 Holly Hills Ave, St Louis, MO 63116 *Tel:* 314-827-6567 *E-mail:* info@penandpublish.com *Web Site:* www.penandpublish.com, pg 163

Geist, Ken, Scholastic Trade Division, 557 Broadway, New York, NY 10012 *Tel:* 212-343-6100; 212-343-4685 (export sales) *Fax:* 212-343-4714 (export sales) *Web Site:* www.scholastic.com, pg 194

Gelb, Joe, Small Business Advisors Inc, 2005 Park St, Atlantic Beach, NY 11509 *Tel:* 516-374-1387 *Fax:* 516-374-1175 *E-mail:* info@smallbusinessadvice.com *Web Site:* www.smallbusinessadvice.com, pg 201

Gelbman, Leslie, St Martin's Press, LLC, 120 Broadway, New York, NY 10271 *Tel:* 646-307-5151 *Web Site:* us.macmillan.com/smp, pg 190

Gelfand, Joan, WNBA Writing Contest, PO Box 237, FDR Sta, New York, NY 10150-0231 *Toll Free Tel:* 866-610-WNBA (610-9622) *E-mail:* info@wnba-books.org *Web Site:* www.wnba-books.org/contest, pg 679

Gelfand, Dr Sergei, American Mathematical Society, 201 Charles St, Providence, RI 02904-2213 *Tel:* 401-455-4000 *Toll Free Tel:* 800-321-4267 *Fax:* 401-331-3842; 401-455-4046 (cust serv) *E-mail:* ams@ams.org; cust-serv@ams.org *Web Site:* www.ams.org, pg 12

Gelfman, Jane, Gelfman Schneider/ICM Partners, 850 Seventh Ave, Suite 903, New York, NY 10019 *Tel:* 212-245-1993 *Fax:* 212-245-8678 *E-mail:* mail@gelfmanschneider.com *Web Site:* gelfmanschneider.com, pg 486

Gelineau, Christine, Binghamton University Creative Writing Program, c/o Dept of English, PO Box 6000, Binghamton, NY 13902-6000 *Tel:* 607-777-2168 *Fax:* 607-777-2408 *E-mail:* cwpro@binghamton.edu *Web Site:* english.binghamton.edu/cwpro, pg 581

Geller, Nick, Yale University Press, 302 Temple St, New Haven, CT 06511-8909 *Tel:* 203-432-0960; 203-432-0966 (sales); 401-531-2800 (cust serv) *Toll Free Tel:* 800-405-1619 (cust serv) *Fax:* 203-432-0948; 203-432-8485 (sales); 401-531-2801 (cust serv) *Toll Free Fax:* 800-406-9145 (cust serv) *E-mail:* sales.press@yale.edu (sales); customer.care@triliteral.org (cust serv) *Web Site:* www.yalebooks.com; yalepress.yale.edu/yupbooks, pg 246

Geller, Sandra R, Practising Law Institute, 1177 Avenue of the Americas, New York, NY 10036 *Tel:* 212-824-5700 *Toll Free Tel:* 800-260-4PLI (260-4754, cust serv) *Toll Free Fax:* 800-321-0093 (local) *E-mail:* info@pli.edu (cust serv) *Web Site:* www.pli.edu, pg 173

Gelles-Cole, Sandi, Gelles-Cole Literary Enterprises, 2163 Lima Loop, PMB 01-408, Laredo, TX 78045-9452 *Tel:* 845-810-0029 *Web Site:* www.literaryenterprises.com, pg 464

Gellman, Rachel, American Society of Health-System Pharmacists (ASHP), 4500 East-West Hwy, Suite 900, Bethesda, MD 20814 *Tel:* 301-657-3000; 301-664-8700 *Toll Free Tel:* 866-279-0681 (orders) *Fax:* 301-657-1251 (orders) *E-mail:* custserv@ashp.org *Web Site:* www.ashp.org, pg 14

Gelwicks, Maureen, Educational Book & Media Association (EBMA), 11 Main St, Suite D, Warrenton, VA 20186 *Tel:* 540-318-7770 *Fax:* 202-962-3939 *E-mail:* info@edupaperback.org *Web Site:* www.edupaperback.org, pg 532

Gelwicks, Maureen, Jeremiah Ludington Award, 11 Main St, Suite D, Warrenton, VA 20186 *Tel:* 540-318-7770 *Fax:* 202-962-3939 *E-mail:* info@edupaperback.org *Web Site:* www.edupaperback.org, pg 636

Gendler, Anne, Northwestern University Press, 629 Noyes St, Evanston, IL 60208-4210 *Tel:* 847-491-2046 *Toll Free Tel:* 800-621-2736 (orders only) *Fax:* 847-491-8150 *E-mail:* nupress@northwestern.edu *Web Site:* www.nupress.northwestern.edu, pg 152

Gendron, Greg, National Endowment for the Arts, 400 Seventh St SW, Washington, DC 20506-0001 *Tel:* 202-682-5400 *Web Site:* www.arts.gov, pg 551

Genet, Pascal, Les Editions XYZ inc, 1815, ave De Lorimier, Montreal, QC H2K 3W6, Canada *Tel:* 514-525-2170 *Fax:* 514-525-7537 *E-mail:* info@editionsxyz.com *Web Site:* www.editionsxyz.com, pg 425

Genna, Victoria, Farrar, Straus & Giroux, LLC, 175 Varick St, 9th fl, New York, NY 10014 *Tel:* 212-741-6900 *E-mail:* fsg.publicity@fsgbooks.com *Web Site:* us.macmillan.com/fsg.aspx, pg 76

Genna, Victoria, Hill & Wang, 175 Varick St, New York, NY 10014 *Tel:* 212-741-6900 *Fax:* 212-633-9385 *E-mail:* fsg.publicity@fsgbooks.com; fsg.editorial@fsgbooks.com; sales@fsgbooks.com *Web Site:* us.macmillan.com/hillandwang.aspx, pg 99

Gens, Alice, New Jersey Business & Industry Association (NJBIA), 10 W Lafayette St, Trenton, NJ 08608-2002 *Tel:* 609-393-7707 *Web Site:* njbia.org, pg 541

Gensch, Chris, The Alexander Graham Bell Association for the Deaf & Hard of Hearing, 3417 Volta Place NW, Washington, DC 20007 *Tel:* 202-337-5220 *Toll Free Tel:* 866-337-5220 (orders) *Fax:* 202-337-8314 *E-mail:* info@agbell.org; publications@agbell.org *Web Site:* www.agbell.org, pg 6

Gentile, Michael, Penguin Group USA, A Penguin Random House Company, 375 Hudson St, New York, NY 10014 *Tel:* 212-366-2000 *Toll Free Tel:* 800-847-5515 (inside sales); 800-631-8571 (cust serv) *Fax:* 212-366-2666; 607-775-4829 (inside sales) *E-mail:* online@us.penguingroup.com *Web Site:* www.penguin.com, pg 163

Gentile, Michael, Penguin Random House LLC, 1745 Broadway, New York, NY 10019 *Tel:* 212-782-9000 *Toll Free Tel:* 800-726-0600 *Web Site:* www.penguinrandomhouse.com, pg 164

Gentile, Michael, Penguin Young Readers Group, 345 Hudson St, New York, NY 10014 *Tel:* 212-366-2000; 212-414-3553 *Fax:* 212-414-3340 *Web Site:* www.penguin.com/children, pg 165

Gentillo, Eileen, Simon & Schuster Sales Division, 1230 Avenue of the Americas, New York, NY 10020 *Tel:* 212-698-7000, pg 200

George, Bob, FurnitureCore, 1389 Peachtree St NE, Suite 310, Atlanta, GA 30309 *Tel:* 404-961-3734 *Toll Free Tel:* 800-826-8868 *Fax:* 404-961-3749 *E-mail:* info@furniturecore.com *Web Site:* www.furniturecore.com, pg 82

George, Denise, Thomas Nelson, 501 Nelson Place, Nashville, TN 37214 *Tel:* 615-889-9000 *Toll Free Tel:* 800-251-4000 *Fax:* 615-902-1548 *Web Site:* www.thomasnelson.com, pg 217

George, Kallie, Greystone Books Ltd, 343 Railway St, Suite 201, Vancouver, BC V6A 1A4, Canada *Tel:* 604-875-1550 *Fax:* 604-875-1556 *E-mail:* info@greystonebooks.com *Web Site:* www.greystonebooks.com, pg 427

George, Kayleigh, HarperCollins General Books Group, 195 Broadway, New York, NY 10007 *Tel:* 212-207-7000 *Web Site:* www.harpercollins.com, pg 93

George, Leigh, Macmillan, 120 Broadway, 22nd fl, New York, NY 10271 *Tel:* 646-307-5151 *E-mail:* press.inquiries@macmillan.com *Web Site:* www.macmillan.com, pg 130

George, Peter, Houghton Mifflin Harcourt, 125 High St, Boston, MA 02110 *Tel:* 617-351-5000 *Toll Free Tel:* 855-969-4642; 800-225-5425 (K-12 educ materials); 800-323-9540 (assessment materials); 877-219-1537 (SkillsTutor); 888-242-6747 (Innovation in Educ Group); 800-225-3362 (Trade & Ref Div) *Toll Free Fax:* 800-269-5232 *E-mail:* myhmhco@hmhco. com *Web Site:* www.hmhco.com, pg 103

Geraghty, Joe, Close Up Publishing, 1330 Braddock Place, Suite 400, Alexandria, VA 22314 *Tel:* 703-706-3300 *Toll Free Tel:* 800-CLOSE-UP (256-7387) *E-mail:* info@closeup.org *Web Site:* www.closeup.org, pg 54

Geraghty, Kate, Macmillan Learning, 41 Madison Ave, New York, NY 10010 *Tel:* 212-576-9400 *Fax:* 212-689-2383 *Web Site:* www.macmillanlearning.com, pg 130

Geraghty, Patrick, Whitecap Books, 314 W Cordova St, Suite 209, Vancouver, BC V6B 1E8, Canada *Tel:* 604-681-6181 *Toll Free Tel:* 800-387-9776 *Toll Free Fax:* 800-260-9777 *Web Site:* www.whitecap.ca, pg 445

Gerak, Margaret, Workman Publishing Co Inc, 225 Varick St, 9th fl, New York, NY 10014-4381 *Tel:* 212-254-5900 *Toll Free Tel:* 800-722-7202 *Fax:* 212-254-8098 *E-mail:* info@workman.com; orders@workman. com *Web Site:* www.workman.com, pg 244

Gerardi, Jan, Random House Children's Books, 1745 Broadway, 10th fl, New York, NY 10019 *Tel:* 212-782-9000 *Web Site:* www.randomhousekids.com, pg 180

Gerbasi, Catherine, Portage & Main Press, 318 McDermot, Suite 100, Winnipeg, MB R3A 0A2, Canada *Tel:* 204-987-3500 *Toll Free Tel:* 800-667-9673 *Fax:* 204-947-0080 *Toll Free Fax:* 866-734-8477 *E-mail:* customerservice@portageandmainpress.com *Web Site:* www.portageandmainpress.com, pg 437

Gerber, Marty, Terra Nova Books, 33 Alondra Rd, Santa Fe, NM 87508 *Tel:* 505-670-9319 *Fax:* 509-461-9333 *E-mail:* publisher@terranovabooks.com; marketing@ terranovabooks.com *Web Site:* www.terranovabooks. com, pg 215

Gerber, Scott, Terra Nova Books, 33 Alondra Rd, Santa Fe, NM 87508 *Tel:* 505-670-9319 *Fax:* 509-461-9333 *E-mail:* publisher@terranovabooks.com; marketing@ terranovabooks.com *Web Site:* www.terranovabooks. com, pg 215

Gerbrandt, Pat, InScribe Christian Writers' Fellowship (ICWF), PO Box 6201, Wetaskiwin, AB T9A 2E9, Canada *Tel:* 780-646-3068 *Fax:* 780-635-2190 *E-mail:* inscribe.mail@gmail.com *Web Site:* inscribe. org, pg 535

German, Amanda, Workman Publishing Co Inc, 225 Varick St, 9th fl, New York, NY 10014-4381 *Tel:* 212-254-5900 *Toll Free Tel:* 800-722-7202 *Fax:* 212-254-8098 *E-mail:* info@workman.com; orders@workman. com *Web Site:* www.workman.com, pg 244

German, Donna, Arbordale Publishing, 612 Johnnie Dodds Blvd, Suite A2, Mount Pleasant, SC 29464 *Tel:* 843-971-6722 *Toll Free Tel:* 877-243-3457 *Fax:* 843-216-3804 *E-mail:* info@arbordalepublishing. com *Web Site:* www.arbordalepublishing.com, pg 19

German, Lee, Arbordale Publishing, 612 Johnnie Dodds Blvd, Suite A2, Mount Pleasant, SC 29464 *Tel:* 843-971-6722 *Toll Free Tel:* 877-243-3457 *Fax:* 843-216-3804 *E-mail:* info@arbordalepublishing.com *Web Site:* www.arbordalepublishing.com, pg 19

Gernenz, Heather, University of Illinois Press, 1325 S Oak St, MC-566, Champaign, IL 61820-6903 *Tel:* 217-333-0950 *Fax:* 217-244-8082 *E-mail:* uipress@uillinois.edu; journals@uillinois.edu *Web Site:* www.press.uillinois.edu, pg 227

Gerrell, Terri, Florida Authors & Publishers Association Inc (FAPA), 1702 N Woodland Blvd, Suite 116, Box 145, Deland, FL 32720 *E-mail:* member.services@ floridapublishersassociation.com *Web Site:* www. floridapublishersassociation.com, pg 533

Gershenowitz, Deborah, The University of North Carolina Press, 116 S Boundary St, Chapel Hill, NC 27514-3808 *Tel:* 919-966-3561 *E-mail:* uncpress@unc. edu *Web Site:* www.uncpress.org, pg 229

Gershowitz, Elissa, Boston Globe-Horn Book Award, c/o Book Reviews, The Horn Book Inc, Palace Road Bldg, 300 The Fenway, Suite P-311, Boston, MA 02115-5820 *Tel:* 617-278-0225 *Toll Free Tel:* 888-628-0225 *Fax:* 617-278-6062 *E-mail:* info@hbook.com *Web Site:* www.hbook.com, pg 600

Gerstle, Dan, W W Norton & Company Inc, 500 Fifth Ave, New York, NY 10110-0017 *Tel:* 212-354-5500 *Toll Free Tel:* 800-233-4830 (orders & cust serv) *Fax:* 212-869-0856 *Toll Free Fax:* 800-458-6515 *E-mail:* orders@wwnorton.com *Web Site:* wwnorton. com, pg 152

Gerth, Rob, The Electrochemical Society (ECS), 65 S Main St, Bldg D, Pennington, NJ 08534-2839 *Tel:* 609-737-1902 *Fax:* 609-737-0629 *E-mail:* publications@electrochem.org; customerservice@electrochem.org *Web Site:* www. electrochem.org, pg 70

Gervan, Chloe, National Press Club of Canada Foundation Inc, 17 York St, Suite 201, Ottawa, ON K1N 9J6, Canada *E-mail:* info@pressclubcanada.ca *Web Site:* pressclubcanada.ca, pg 540

Gervasio, Janet, HarperCollins Publishers, 195 Broadway, New York, NY 10007 *Tel:* 212-207-7000 *Fax:* 212-207-7145 *Web Site:* www.harpercollins.com, pg 94

Gharib, Linda, Wolters Kluwer Law & Business, 76 Ninth Ave, 7th fl, New York, NY 10011-5201 *Tel:* 212-771-0600; 301-698-7100 (cust serv outside US) *Toll Free Tel:* 800-234-1660 (cust serv) *E-mail:* customer.service@wolterskluwer. com; lrusmedia@wolterskluwer.com *Web Site:* lrus. wolterskluwer.com, pg 243

Gharib, Linda, Wolters Kluwer US Corp, 2700 Lake Cook Rd, Riverwoods, IL 60015 *Tel:* 847-267-7000 *Fax:* 847-580-5192 *E-mail:* info@wolterskluwer. com *Web Site:* www.wolterskluwer.com, pg 243

Ghione, Yvette, Kids Can Press Ltd, 25 Dockside Dr, Toronto, ON M5A 0B5, Canada *Tel:* 416-479-7000 *Toll Free Tel:* 800-265-0884 *Fax:* 416-960-5437 *E-mail:* info@kidscan.com; customerservice@ kidscan.com *Web Site:* www.kidscanpress.com; www. kidscanpress.ca, pg 431

Ghoura, Judy, Fitzhenry & Whiteside Limited, 195 Allstate Pkwy, Markham, ON L3R 4T8, Canada *Tel:* 905-477-9700 *Toll Free Tel:* 800-387-9776 *Fax:* 905-477-2834 *Toll Free Fax:* 800-260-9777 *E-mail:* bookinfo@fitzhenry.ca; godwit@fitzhenry.ca *Web Site:* www.fitzhenry.ca, pg 426

Ghoura, Judy, Red Deer Press Inc, 195 Allstate Pkwy, Markham, ON L3R 4T8, Canada *Tel:* 905-477-9700 *Toll Free Tel:* 800-387-9776 (orders) *E-mail:* rdp@reddeerpress.com; bookinfo@fitzhenry.ca *Web Site:* www.reddeerpress.com, pg 438

Giagnocavo, Alan, Fox Chapel Publishing Co Inc, 1970 Broad St, East Petersburg, PA 17520 *Tel:* 717-560-4703 *Toll Free Tel:* 800-457-9112 *Fax:* 717-560-4702 *E-mail:* customerservice@foxchapelpublishing.com *Web Site:* www.foxchapelpublishing.com, pg 80

Giangreco, Karen, The Experiment, 220 E 23 St, Suite 600, New York, NY 10010-4658 *Tel:* 212-889-1659 *E-mail:* info@theexperimentpublishing.com *Web Site:* www.theexperimentpublishing.com, pg 74

Giarratano, Matt, Penguin Books, 375 Hudson St, New York, NY 10014 *Tel:* 212-366-2000 *E-mail:* penguinpublicity@us.penguingroup.com *Web Site:* www.penguinclassics.com; www.penguin. com, pg 163

Giarratano, Matt, Plume, 375 Hudson St, New York, NY 10014 *Tel:* 212-366-2000 *Fax:* 212-243-6002 *Web Site:* www.penguin.com/publishers/plume, pg 171

Giarratano, Michael, Perseus Books, 1290 Avenue of the Americas, New York, NY 10104 *Tel:* 212-340-8100 *Toll Free Tel:* 800-343-4499 (cust serv) *Fax:* 212-340-8105 *Web Site:* www.perseusbooks.com, pg 168

Gibbons, Meg, Sourcebooks LLC, 1935 Brookdale Rd, Suite 139, Naperville, IL 60563 *Tel:* 630-961-3900 *Toll Free Tel:* 800-432-7444 *Fax:* 630-961-2168

E-mail: info@sourcebooks.com; customersupport@ sourcebooks.com *Web Site:* www.sourcebooks.com, pg 204

Gibbons, Melissa, William H Sadlier Inc, 9 Pine St, New York, NY 10005 *Tel:* 212-227-2120 *Toll Free Tel:* 800-221-5175 (cust serv) *Fax:* 212-312-6080 *E-mail:* customerservice@sadlier.com *Web Site:* www. sadlier.com, pg 189

Gibbs, David, Community of Literary Magazines & Presses (CLMP), 154 Christopher St, Suite 3C, New York, NY 10014-9110 *Tel:* 212-741-9110 *E-mail:* info@clmp.org *Web Site:* www.clmp.org, pg 531

Gibbs, David, Firecracker Awards, 154 Christopher St, Suite 3C, New York, NY 10014-9110 *Tel:* 212-741-9110 *E-mail:* info@clmp.org *Web Site:* www.clmp. org/firecracker, pg 615

Gibbs, Naomi, Houghton Mifflin Harcourt Trade & Reference Division, 125 High St, Boston, MA 02110 *Tel:* 617-351-5000 *Web Site:* www.hmhco.com, pg 104

Gibby-Munguia, Nicole, Alex Awards, 50 E Huron St, Chicago, IL 60611 *Tel:* 312-280-4390 *Toll Free Tel:* 800-545-2433 *Fax:* 312-280-5276 *E-mail:* yalsa@ ala.org *Web Site:* www.ala.org/yalsa/alex-awards, pg 591

Gibeley, Andrew, Harry N Abrams Inc, 195 Broadway, 9th fl, New York, NY 10007 *Tel:* 212-206-7715 *Toll Free Tel:* 800-345-1359 *Fax:* 212-519-1210 *E-mail:* abrams@abramsbooks.com *Web Site:* www. abramsbooks.com, pg 3

Gibson, Angela, Modern Language Association of America (MLA), 85 Broad St, Suite 500, New York, NY 10004-2434 *Tel:* 646-576-5000 *Fax:* 646-458-0030 *Web Site:* www.mla.org, pg 141

Gibson, Bethany, Goose Lane Editions, 500 Beaverbrook Ct, Suite 330, Fredericton, NB E3B 5X4, Canada *Tel:* 506-450-4251 *Toll Free Tel:* 888-926-8377 *Fax:* 506-459-4991 *E-mail:* info@gooselane.com; customerservice@gooselane.com *Web Site:* www. gooselane.com, pg 427

Gibson, George, Grove Atlantic Inc, 154 W 14 St, 12th fl, New York, NY 10011 *Tel:* 212-614-7850 *Toll Free Tel:* 800-521-0178 *Fax:* 212-614-7886 *E-mail:* info@ groveatlantic.com; sales@groveatlantic.com; publicity@groveatlantic.com; rights@groveatlantic.com *Web Site:* www.groveatlantic.com, pg 89

Gibson, Jack, International Risk Management Institute Inc, 12222 Merit Dr, Suite 1600, Dallas, TX 75251-2266 *Tel:* 972-960-7693 *Fax:* 972-371-5120 *E-mail:* info27@irmi.com *Web Site:* www.irmi.com, pg 111

Gibson, Maggie, Random House Children's Books, 1745 Broadway, 10th fl, New York, NY 10019 *Tel:* 212-782-9000 *Web Site:* www.randomhousekids.com, pg 181

Giddens, Mary, SteinerBooks Inc, 610 Main St, Suite 1, Great Barrington, MA 01230 *Tel:* 413-528-8233 *E-mail:* service@steinerbooks.org; friends@ steinerbooks.org *Web Site:* steiner.presswarehouse.com, pg 208

Gier, Lora, Trusted Media Brands Inc, 750 Third Ave, 3rd fl, New York, NY 10017 *Tel:* 646-293-6299 *Toll Free Tel:* 877-732-4438 (cust serv) *Fax:* 646-293-6251 *E-mail:* customercare@trustedmediabrands. com; press@trustedmediabrands.com *Web Site:* www. trustedmediabrands.com; www.rd.com, pg 221

Gifford, James, Fairleigh Dickinson University Press, 842 Cambie St, Vancouver, BC V6B 2P6, Canada *Tel:* 604-648-4476 *Fax:* 604-648-4489 *E-mail:* fdupress@fdu.edu *Web Site:* www.fdupress. org, pg 425

Gifford, James M PhD, The Jesse Stuart Foundation (JSF), 4440 13 St, Ashland, KY 41102 *Tel:* 606-326-1667 *Fax:* 606-325-2519 *E-mail:* jsf@jsfbooks.com *Web Site:* www.jsfbooks.com, pg 210

Giffuni, Cathe, Research Research, 240 E 27 St, Suite 20-K, New York, NY 10016-9238 *Tel:* 212-779-9540 *Fax:* 212-779-9540 *E-mail:* ehtac@msn.com, pg 469

Gift, Patricia, Hay House Inc, 2776 Loker Ave W, Carlsbad, CA 92010 Tel: 760-431-7695 (ext 2, intl) Toll Free Tel: 800-654-5126 (ext 2, US) Toll Free Fax: 800-650-5115 E-mail: info@hayhouse.com; editorial@hayhouse.com Web Site: www.hayhouse.com, pg 96

Gignilliat-Day, Leslie, Amber Lotus Publishing, PO Box 11329, Portland, OR 97211 Tel: 503-284-6400 Toll Free Tel: 800-326-2375 (orders only) Fax: 503-284-6417 E-mail: info@amberlotus.com Web Site: www.amberlotus.com, pg 9

Gil, Samantha, Workman Publishing Co Inc, 225 Varick St, 9th fl, New York, NY 10014-4381 Tel: 212-254-5900 Toll Free Tel: 800-722-7202 Fax: 212-254-8098 E-mail: info@workman.com; orders@workman.com Web Site: www.workman.com, pg 244

Gilbert, Alexis, Grand Central Publishing, 1290 Avenue of the Americas, New York, NY 10104 Tel: 212-364-1100 Web Site: www.hachettebookgroup.com, pg 88

Gilbert, Cristina, Macmillan, 120 Broadway, 22nd fl, New York, NY 10271 Tel: 646-307-5151 E-mail: press.inquiries@macmillan.com Web Site: www.macmillan.com, pg 129

Gilbert, Deborah, Soul Mate Publishing, 3210 Sherwood Dr, Walworth, NY 14568 Web Site: www.soulmatepublishing.com, pg 203

Gilbert, Frances, Random House Children's Books, 1745 Broadway, 10th fl, New York, NY 10019 Tel: 212-782-9000 Web Site: www.randomhousekids.com, pg 180

Gilbert, Jennifer G, Galen Press Ltd, PO Box 64400-WB, Tucson, AZ 85728-4400 Tel: 520-577-8363 Fax: 520-529-6459 E-mail: sales@galenpress.com Web Site: www.galenpress.com, pg 82

Gilbert, Jon, Seven Stories Press, 140 Watts St, New York, NY 10013 Tel: 212-226-8760 Toll Free Tel: 800-733-3000 (orders) Fax: 212-226-1411 E-mail: sevenstories@sevenstories.com Web Site: www.sevenstories.com, pg 197

Gilbert, Sheila E, DAW Books Inc, 375 Hudson St, New York, NY 10014 Tel: 212-366-2096 Fax: 212-366-2090 E-mail: daw@penguinrandomhouse.com Web Site: www.dawbooks.com; www.penguin.com; www.penguinrandomhouse.com, pg 63

Gilbert, Tara, The Jennifer DeChiara Literary Agency, 245 Park Ave, 39th fl, New York, NY 10167 Tel: 212-372-8989 Web Site: www.jdlit.com, pg 481

Gilbride, Tara, Penguin Group USA, A Penguin Random House Company, 375 Hudson St, New York, NY 10014 Tel: 212-366-2000 Toll Free Tel: 800-847-5515 (inside sales); 800-631-8571 (cust serv) Fax: 212-366-2666; 607-775-4829 (inside sales) E-mail: online@us.penguingroup.com Web Site: www.penguin.com, pg 163

Gilbride, Tara, Portfolio, 375 Hudson St, New York, NY 10014 Web Site: www.penguin.com/meet/publishers/portfolio, pg 172

Gildea, Kelly, Penguin Random House Audio Publishing, 1745 Broadway, New York, NY 10019 E-mail: audio@penguinrandomhouse.com Web Site: www.penguinrandomhouseaudio.com, pg 164

Gildea, Matthew, Arcadia Publishing Inc, 420 Wando Park Blvd, Mount Pleasant, SC 29464 Tel: 843-853-2070 Toll Free Tel: 888-313-2665 (orders only) Fax: 843-853-0044 E-mail: sales@arcadiapublishing.com Web Site: www.arcadiapublishing.com, pg 19

Gilewicz, John, Adirondack Mountain Club (ADK), 814 Goggins Rd, Lake George, NY 12845-4117 Tel: 518-668-4447 Toll Free Tel: 800-395-8080 Fax: 518-668-3746 E-mail: info@adk.org Web Site: www.adk.org, pg 5

Gill, Craig, University Press of Mississippi, 3825 Ridgewood Rd, Jackson, MS 39211-6492 Tel: 601-432-6205 Toll Free Tel: 800-737-7788 (orders & cust serv) Fax: 601-432-6217 E-mail: press@mississippi.edu Web Site: www.upress.state.ms.us, pg 233

Gillan, Maria, Binghamton University Creative Writing Program, c/o Dept of English, PO Box 6000, Binghamton, NY 13902-6000 Tel: 607-777-2168 Fax: 607-777-2408 E-mail: cwpro@binghamton.edu Web Site: english.binghamton.edu/cwpro, pg 581

Gillan, Maria Mazziotti, Binghamton University John Gardner Fiction Book Award, Dept of English, General Literature & Rhetoric, Library N, Rm 1149, Vestal Pkwy E, Binghamton, NY 13902 Tel: 607-777-2713 Web Site: www2.binghamton.edu/english/creative-writing, pg 598

Gillan, Maria Mazziotti, Binghamton University Milt Kessler Poetry Book Award, Dept of English, General Literature & Rhetoric, Library N, Rm 1149, Vestal Pkwy E, Binghamton, NY 13902 Tel: 607-777-2713 Web Site: www2.binghamton.edu/english/creative-writing, pg 598

Gillan, Maria Mazziotti, Allen Ginsberg Poetry Award, One College Blvd, Paterson, NJ 07505-1179 Tel: 973-684-6555 Fax: 973-523-6085 Web Site: www.poetrycenterpccc.com, pg 619

Gillan, Maria Mazziotti, The Paterson Poetry Prize, One College Blvd, Paterson, NJ 07505-1179 Tel: 973-684-6555 Fax: 973-523-6085 Web Site: www.poetrycenterpccc.com, pg 652

Gillan, Maria Mazziotti, The Paterson Prize for Books for Young People, One College Blvd, Paterson, NJ 07505-1179 Tel: 973-684-6555 Fax: 973-523-6085 Web Site: www.poetrycenterpccc.com, pg 652

Gillerman, Sharon, Hebrew Union College Press, 3101 Clifton Ave, Cincinnati, OH 45220 Tel: 513-221-1875 Fax: 513-221-0321 Web Site: press.huc.edu, pg 97

Gilles, Misti, Sagamore Publishing LLC, 3611 N Staley Rd, Suite B, Champaign, IL 61822 Tel: 217-359-5940 Toll Free Tel: 800-327-5557 (orders) Fax: 217-359-5975 E-mail: web@sagamorepub.com Web Site: www.sagamorepub.com, pg 189

Gillespie, Christine, Alfred A Knopf, c/o Penguin Random House Inc, 1745 Broadway, New York, NY 10019 Tel: 212-751-2600 Fax: 212-572-2662 (foreign rts) Web Site: knopfdoubleday.com, pg 117

Gillespie, Christine, Pantheon Books, c/o Penguin Random House Inc, 1745 Broadway, New York, NY 10019 Tel: 212-751-2600 Fax: 212-572-2662 (foreign rts) Web Site: knopfdoubleday.com, pg 159

Gillespie, Jennie, San Diego Christian Writers' Guild Conference, PO Box 270403, San Diego, CA 92198 Tel: 760-294-3269; 858-254-1402 Fax: 760-294-3269 E-mail: info@sandiegocwg.org Web Site: www.sandiegocwg.org, pg 578

Gillespie, Robert, San Diego Christian Writers' Guild Conference, PO Box 270403, San Diego, CA 92198 Tel: 760-294-3269; 858-254-1402 Fax: 760-294-3269 E-mail: info@sandiegocwg.org Web Site: www.sandiegocwg.org, pg 578

Gilliam, Ashley, Scribner, 1230 Avenue of the Americas, New York, NY 10020, pg 195

Gilligan, Rev Michael PhD, American Catholic Press (ACP), 16565 S State St, South Holland, IL 60473 Tel: 708-331-5485 Fax: 708-331-5484 E-mail: acp@acpress.org Web Site: www.acpress.org, pg 10

Gillingham, Sara, Greystone Books Ltd, 343 Railway St, Suite 201, Vancouver, BC V6A 1A4, Canada Tel: 604-875-1550 Fax: 604-875-1556 E-mail: info@greystonebooks.com Web Site: www.greystonebooks.com, pg 427

Gilliss, Sonya, Fitzhenry & Whiteside Limited, 195 Allstate Pkwy, Markham, ON L3R 4T8, Canada Tel: 905-477-9700 Toll Free Tel: 800-387-9776 Fax: 905-477-2834 Toll Free Fax: 800-260-9777 E-mail: bookinfo@fitzhenry.ca; godwit@fitzhenry.ca Web Site: www.fitzhenry.ca, pg 426

Gilliss, Sonya, Red Deer Press Inc, 195 Allstate Pkwy, Markham, ON L3R 4T8, Canada Tel: 905-477-9700 Toll Free Tel: 800-387-9776 (orders) E-mail: rdp@reddeerpress.com; bookinfo@fitzhenry.ca Web Site: www.reddeerpress.com, pg 438

Gilly, Holly, Human Kinetics Inc, 1607 N Market St, Champaign, IL 61820 Tel: 217-351-5076 Toll Free Tel: 800-747-4457 Fax: 217-351-1549 (orders/cust serv) E-mail: info@hkusa.com Web Site: www.humankinetics.com, pg 105

Gilman, Dana S, J J Keller & Associates, Inc, 3003 Breezewood Lane, Neenah, WI 54957 Tel: 920-722-2848 Toll Free Tel: 877-564-2333 Toll Free Fax: 800-727-7516 E-mail: contactus@jjkeller.com; customerservice@jjkeller.com Web Site: www.jjkeller.com, pg 116

Gilmer, Rachel, Sourcebooks LLC, 1935 Brookdale Rd, Suite 139, Naperville, IL 60563 Tel: 630-961-3900 Toll Free Tel: 800-432-7444 Fax: 630-961-2168 E-mail: info@sourcebooks.com; customersupport@sourcebooks.com Web Site: www.sourcebooks.com, pg 204

Gilmore, David, Random House Children's Books, 1745 Broadway, 10th fl, New York, NY 10019 Tel: 212-782-9000 Web Site: www.randomhousekids.com, pg 181

Gilo, Jessica A, The Monacelli Press, 65 Bleecker St, 8th fl, New York, NY 10012 Tel: 212-229-9925 E-mail: contact@monacellipress.com Web Site: www.monacellipress.com, pg 141

Gilpin, Geoff, The Wisconsin Writers Awards, c/o 210 N Main St, No 204, Cedar Grove, WI 53013 E-mail: wiswriters@gmail.com Web Site: wiswriters.org/awards, pg 678

Gilsinger, Jayne, PennWell Books, 1421 S Sheridan Rd, Tulsa, OK 74112 Tel: 918-831-9421 Toll Free Tel: 800-752-9764 Fax: 918-831-9555 E-mail: sales@pennwell.com Web Site: www.pennwellbooks.com, pg 166

Gilson, Kristin, Simon & Schuster Children's Publishing, 1230 Avenue of the Americas, New York, NY 10020 Tel: 212-698-7000 Web Site: www.simonandschuster.com/kids; www.simonandschuster.com/teen; simonandschuster.net; simonandschuster.biz, pg 199

Gingerich, Amy, Herald Press, PO Box 866, Harrisonburg, VA 22803 Toll Free Tel: 800-245-7894 (orders) Fax: 540-242-4476 Toll Free Fax: 877-271-0760 E-mail: info@mennomedia.org; customerservice@mennomedia.org Web Site: www.heraldpress.com; store.mennomedia.org, pg 98

Gingerich, Amy, MennoMedia, 100 S Mason St, Suite B, Harrisonburg, VA 22801 Toll Free Tel: 800-245-7894 (orders & cust serv US) Toll Free Fax: 877-271-0760 E-mail: info@mennomedia.org Web Site: www.mennomedia.org, pg 138

Gingras, Dominique, Les Presses de l'Universite Laval, 2180, Chemin Sainte-Foy, 1st fl, Quebec, QC G1V 0A6, Canada Tel: 418-656-2803 Fax: 418-656-3305 E-mail: presses@pul.ulaval.ca Web Site: www.pulaval.com, pg 437

Ginsberg, Jordan, McClelland & Stewart Ltd, 320 Front St W, Suite 1400, Toronto, ON M5V 3B6, Canada Tel: 416-364-4449 Fax: 416-598-7764 E-mail: customerservicescanada@penguinrandomhouse.com; publicity@ca.penguingroup.com Web Site: penguinrandomhouse.ca/imprints/mcclelland-stewart, pg 433

Ginsberg, Peter L, Curtis Brown Ltd, 228 E 45 St, 3rd fl, New York, NY 10017 Tel: 212-473-5400 Web Site: www.curtisbrown.com, pg 478

Ginsburg, Susan, Writers House, 21 W 26 St, New York, NY 10010 Tel: 212-685-2400 Web Site: www.writershouse.com, pg 508

Ginty, Brenda, Publishing Professionals Network, c/o Postal Annex, 274 Redwood Shores Pkwy, Redwood City, CA 94065-1173 E-mail: operations@pubpronetwork.org Web Site: pubpronetwork.org, pg 545

Giovinazzo, Elena, Pippin Properties Inc, 110 W 40 St, Suite 1704, New York, NY 10018 Tel: 212-338-9310 E-mail: info@pippinproperties.com Web Site: www.pippinproperties.com; www.facebook.com/pippinproperties, pg 498

Gipson, Kyle, Johns Hopkins University Press, 2715 N Charles St, Baltimore, MD 21218-4363 Tel: 410-516-6900; 410-516-6987 (journal orders outside US

& CN) *Toll Free Tel:* 800-537-5487 (book orders & cust serv); 800-548-1784 (journal orders) *Fax:* 410-516-6968; 410-516-3866 (journal orders); 410-516-6998 (orders) *E-mail:* hfscustserv@press.jhu.edu (cust serv); jrnlcirc@press.jhu.edu (journal orders) *Web Site:* www.press.jhu.edu; muse.jhu.edu, pg 114

Gipson, Scott, Caxton Press, 312 Main St, Caldwell, ID 83605-3299 *Tel:* 208-459-7421 *Toll Free Tel:* 800-657-6465 *Fax:* 208-459-7450 *E-mail:* publish@caxtonpress.com *Web Site:* www.caxtonpress.com, pg 47

Giron, Robert L, Gival Press, 5200 N First St, Arlington, VA 22203 *Tel:* 703-351-0079 *Fax:* 703-351-0079 (call first) *E-mail:* givalpress@yahoo.com *Web Site:* www.givalpress.com, pg 86

Giron, Robert L, Gival Press Novel Award, PO Box 3812, Arlington, VA 22203 *Tel:* 703-351-0079 *Fax:* 703-351-0079 (call first) *E-mail:* givalpress@yahoo.com *Web Site:* www.givalpress.com; givalpress.submittable.com, pg 619

Giron, Robert L, Gival Press Oscar Wilde Award, PO Box 3812, Arlington, VA 22203 *Tel:* 703-351-0079 *Fax:* 703-351-0079 (call first) *E-mail:* givalpress@yahoo.com *Web Site:* www.givalpress.com; givalpress.submittable.com, pg 619

Giron, Robert L, Gival Press Poetry Award, PO Box 3812, Arlington, VA 22203 *Tel:* 703-351-0079 *Fax:* 703-351-0079 (call first) *E-mail:* givalpress@yahoo.com *Web Site:* www.givalpress.com; givalpress.submittable.com, pg 619

Giron, Robert L, Gival Press Short Story Award, PO Box 3812, Arlington, VA 22203 *Tel:* 703-351-0079 *Fax:* 703-351-0079 (call first) *E-mail:* givalpress@yahoo.com *Web Site:* www.givalpress.com; givalpress.submittable.com, pg 619

Giroux, Greg, Bartleby Press, 8926 Baltimore St, No 858, Savage, MD 20763 *Tel:* 301-589-5831 *Toll Free Tel:* 800-953-9929 *E-mail:* inquiries@bartlebythepublisher.com *Web Site:* www.bartlebythepublisher.com, pg 28

Giroux, Steve, Teacher's Discovery, 2741 Paldan Dr, Auburn Hills, MI 48326 *Toll Free Tel:* 800-832-2437 *Toll Free Fax:* 800-287-4509 *E-mail:* help@teachersdiscovery.com *Web Site:* www.teachersdiscovery.com, pg 214

Girsch, Laurie Y, Professional Resource Press, 3251 New England St, Sarasota, FL 34231 *Tel:* 941-343-9601 *Toll Free Tel:* 800-443-3364 (orders & cust serv) *Fax:* 941-343-9201 *Toll Free Fax:* 866-804-4843 (orders only) *E-mail:* cs@prpress.com *Web Site:* www.prpress.com, pg 176

Gisonny, Karen, The New York Public Library Helen Bernstein Book Award for Excellence in Journalism, Stephen A Schwarzman Bldg, Fifth Ave at 42 St, South Court Bldg, 3rd fl, New York, NY 10018-2788 *Tel:* 212-930-0876 *Web Site:* www.nypl.org, pg 647

Gissinger-Rivera, Beth, Adams Media, 57 Littlefield St, Avon, MA 02322 *Tel:* 508-427-7100 *Web Site:* www.simonandschuster.com, pg 4

Giuffrida, Amy, The Jennifer DeChiara Literary Agency, 245 Park Ave, 39th fl, New York, NY 10167 *Tel:* 212-372-8989 *Web Site:* www.jdlit.com, pg 481

Gladding, Jody, Vermont Studio Center Writer's Program Fellowships, 80 Pearl St, Johnson, VT 05656 *Tel:* 802-635-2727 *Fax:* 802-635-2730 *E-mail:* writing@vermontstudiocenter.org; info@vermontstudiocenter.org *Web Site:* www.vermontstudiocenter.org, pg 675

Gladstone, Bill, Waterside Productions Inc, 2055 Oxford Ave, Cardiff, CA 92007 *Tel:* 760-632-9190 *Fax:* 760-632-9295 *E-mail:* admin@waterside.com *Web Site:* www.waterside.com, pg 508

Glaser, Rebecca, Amicus, PO Box 1329, Mankato, MN 56002 *Tel:* 507-388-9357 *Fax:* 507-388-9357 *E-mail:* info@amicuspublishing.us; orders@amicuspublishing.us *Web Site:* www.amicuspublishing.us, pg 15

Glasner, Lynne, Associated Editors, 27 W 96 St, New York, NY 10025 *Tel:* 212-662-9703 *Fax:* 212-662-9703, pg 458

Glass, Erica, Penguin Group USA, A Penguin Random House Company, 375 Hudson St, New York, NY 10014 *Tel:* 212-366-2000 *Toll Free Tel:* 800-847-5515 (inside sales); 800-631-8571 (cust serv) *Fax:* 212-366-2666; 607-775-4829 (inside sales) *E-mail:* online@us.penguingroup.com *Web Site:* www.penguin.com, pg 163

Glass, Joy L, Edgewise Press Inc, 24 Fifth Ave, Suite 224, New York, NY 10011 *Tel:* 212-982-4818 *Fax:* 212-982-1364 *E-mail:* epinc@mindspring.com *Web Site:* www.edgewisepress.org, pg 69

Glasser, Carla, The Betsy Nolan Literary Agency, 112 E 17 St, Suite 1W, New York, NY 10003 *Tel:* 212-967-8200 *Fax:* 212-967-7292 *E-mail:* dblehr@cs.com, pg 498

Glavash, Keith, Massachusetts Institute of Technology Libraries, 77 Massachusetts Ave, Bldg 14, Rm 0551, Cambridge, MA 02139-4307 *E-mail:* docs@mit.edu *Web Site:* libraries.mit.edu/docs, pg 134

Glave, Thomas, Binghamton University Creative Writing Program, c/o Dept of English, PO Box 6000, Binghamton, NY 13902-6000 *Tel:* 607-777-2168 *Fax:* 607-777-2408 *E-mail:* cwpro@binghamton.edu *Web Site:* english.binghamton.edu/cwpro, pg 581

Glaz, Linda, Hartline Literary Agency LLC, 123 Queenston Dr, Pittsburgh, PA 15235 *Tel:* 412-829-2483 *Toll Free Fax:* 888-279-6007 *Web Site:* www.hartlineliterary.com, pg 488

Glazer, Lori, Houghton Mifflin Harcourt Trade & Reference Division, 125 High St, Boston, MA 02110 *Tel:* 617-351-5000 *Web Site:* www.hmhco.com, pg 104

Glazner, Steve, APPA: The Association of Higher Education Facilities Officers, 1643 Prince St, Alexandria, VA 22314-2818 *Tel:* 703-684-1446 *Fax:* 703-549-2772 *Web Site:* www.appa.org, pg 18

Gleason, Ben, Wisdom Publications Inc, 199 Elm St, Somerville, MA 02144 *Tel:* 617-776-7416 *Toll Free Tel:* 800-272-4050 (orders) *Fax:* 617-776-7841 *E-mail:* info@wisdompubs.org; submission@wisdompubs.org *Web Site:* www.wisdompubs.org, pg 243

Gleason, Bill, Society for Mining, Metallurgy & Exploration, 12999 E Adam Aircraft Circle, Englewood, CO 80112 *Tel:* 303-948-4200 *Toll Free Tel:* 800-763-3132 *Fax:* 303-973-3845 *E-mail:* cs@smenet.org; books@smenet.org *Web Site:* www.smenet.org, pg 202

Gleason, Bob, Tom Doherty Associates, LLC, 120 Broadway, New York, NY 10271 *Tel:* 646-307-5511 *Toll Free Tel:* 800-455-0340 *Web Site:* us.macmillan.com/torforge, pg 66

Gleason, Jeff, Reed Environmental Writing Award, 201 W Main St, Suite 14, Charlottesville, VA 22902 *Tel:* 434-977-4090 *Fax:* 434-977-1483 *Web Site:* www.southernenvironment.org, pg 661

Gleason, Laura, Louisiana State University Press, 338 Johnston Hall, Baton Rouge, LA 70803 *Tel:* 225-578-6294 *E-mail:* lsupress@lsu.edu *Web Site:* lsupress.org, pg 128

Gleick, Betsy, Algonquin Books, 400 Silver Cedar Ct, Suite 300, Chapel Hill, NC 27514-1585 *Tel:* 919-967-0108 *Fax:* 919-933-0272 *E-mail:* inquiry@algonquin.com *Web Site:* www.workman.com/algonquin, pg 7

Glemot, Suzanne, University of Iowa Press, 119 W Park Rd, 100 Kuhl House, Iowa City, IA 52242-1000 *Tel:* 319-335-2000 *Toll Free Tel:* 800-621-2736 (orders only) *Fax:* 319-335-2055 *Toll Free Fax:* 800-621-8476 (orders only) *E-mail:* uipress@uiowa.edu *Web Site:* www.uipress.uiowa.edu, pg 228

Glenn, Mary, Humanix Books LLC, 8 W 40 St, 20th fl, New York, NY 10804 *Toll Free Tel:* 855-371-7810 *E-mail:* info@humanixbooks.com *Web Site:* www.humanixbooks.com, pg 105

Glennon, Robin, Abingdon Press, 2222 Rosa L Parks Blvd, Nashville, TN 37228 *Tel:* 615-749-6000 (academic books) *Toll Free Tel:* 800-251-3320 (orders) *Fax:* 615-749-6056 (academic books) *Toll Free Fax:* 800-836-7802 (orders) *E-mail:* orders@abingdonpress.com; permissions@abingdonpress.com *Web Site:* www.abingdonpress.com, pg 2

Glesne, Mark, Thomas Nelson, 501 Nelson Place, Nashville, TN 37214 *Tel:* 615-889-9000 *Toll Free Tel:* 800-251-4000 *Fax:* 615-902-1548 *Web Site:* www.thomasnelson.com, pg 217

Glick, Jon, Chronicle Books, 680 Second St, San Francisco, CA 94107 *Tel:* 415-537-4200 *Toll Free Tel:* 800-759-0190 (cust serv) *Fax:* 415-537-4460 *Toll Free Fax:* 800-858-7787 (orders); 800-286-9471 (cust serv) *E-mail:* frontdesk@chroniclebooks.com *Web Site:* www.chroniclebooks.com, pg 52

Glick, Stacey Kendall, Dystel, Goderich & Bourret LLC, One Union Sq W, Suite 904, New York, NY 10003 *Tel:* 212-627-9100 *Fax:* 212-627-9313 *Web Site:* www.dystel.com, pg 482

Glidden, Hanna, Random House Children's Books, 1745 Broadway, 10th fl, New York, NY 10019 *Tel:* 212-782-9000 *Web Site:* www.randomhousekids.com, pg 180

Glider, Kate, Random House Children's Books, 1745 Broadway, 10th fl, New York, NY 10019 *Tel:* 212-782-9000 *Web Site:* www.randomhousekids.com, pg 181

Glosband, Oliver, Shambhala Publications Inc, 4720 Walnut St, Boulder, CO 80301 *Tel:* 303-222-9598 *Toll Free Tel:* 866-424-0030 (off); 888-424-2329 (cust serv) *E-mail:* customercare@shambhala.com *Web Site:* www.shambhala.com, pg 197

Gloude, Carolyn, Ruth & Sylvia Schwartz Children's Book Awards, c/o Ontario Arts Council, 121 Bloor St E, 7th fl, Toronto, ON M4W 3M5, Canada *Tel:* 416-961-1660 *Toll Free Tel:* 800-387-0058 (ON) *Fax:* 416-961-7796 (Ontario Arts Council); 416-969-7450 (Ontario Arts Foundation) *E-mail:* info@arts.on.ca; foundation@arts.on.ca *Web Site:* www.arts.on.ca; ontarioartsfoundation.on.ca/pages/ruth-sylvia-schwartz-awards, pg 666

Glover, Elizabeth, University of Pennsylvania Press, 3905 Spruce St, Philadelphia, PA 19104 *Tel:* 215-898-6261 *Fax:* 215-898-0404 *E-mail:* custserv@pobox.upenn.edu *Web Site:* www.pennpress.org, pg 230

Glover, Josh, Penguin Random House Canada, 320 Front St W, Suite 1400, Toronto, ON M5V 3B6, Canada *Tel:* 416-364-4449 *Toll Free Tel:* 888-523-9292 (cust serv) *Fax:* 416-598-7764 *Web Site:* www.penguinrandomhouse.ca, pg 436

Glover, Sally, Lynne Rienner Publishers Inc, 1800 30 St, Suite 314, Boulder, CO 80301 *Tel:* 303-444-6684 *Fax:* 303-444-0824 *E-mail:* questions@rienner.com; cservice@rienner.com *Web Site:* www.rienner.com, pg 185

Gluck, Suzanne, WME, 11 Madison Ave, 18th fl, New York, NY 10010 *Tel:* 212-586-5100 *Web Site:* www.wmeentertainment.com, pg 508

Glusman, John, W W Norton & Company Inc, 500 Fifth Ave, New York, NY 10110-0017 *Tel:* 212-354-5500 *Toll Free Tel:* 800-233-4830 (orders & cust serv) *Fax:* 212-869-0856 *Toll Free Fax:* 800-458-6515 *E-mail:* orders@wwnorton.com *Web Site:* wwnorton.com, pg 152

Glynn, John, Harlequin Enterprises Ltd, 195 Broadway, 24th fl, New York, NY 10007 *Tel:* 212-207-7000 *Toll Free Tel:* 888-432-4879 *E-mail:* customerservice@harlequin.com *Web Site:* www.harlequin.com, pg 93

Go, Sarah Lin, Chronicle Books, 680 Second St, San Francisco, CA 94107 *Tel:* 415-537-4200 *Toll Free Tel:* 800-759-0190 (cust serv) *Fax:* 415-537-4460 *Toll Free Fax:* 800-858-7787 (orders); 800-286-9471 (cust serv) *E-mail:* frontdesk@chroniclebooks.com *Web Site:* www.chroniclebooks.com, pg 52

Gobel, Ursula, Social Sciences & Humanities Research Council of Canada (SSHRC), 350 Albert St, Ottawa, ON K1P 6G4, Canada *Tel:* 613-992-0691; 613-996-6976 *E-mail:* research@sshrc-crsh.gc.ca *Web Site:* www.sshrc.ca, pg 546

Goderich, Miriam, Dystel, Goderich & Bourret LLC, One Union Sq W, Suite 904, New York, NY 10003 *Tel:* 212-627-9100 *Fax:* 212-627-9313 *Web Site:* www. dystel.com, pg 482

Godin, Lynda, Ordre des traducteurs, terminologues et interpretes agrees du quebec, 1108-2021 Ave Union, Montreal, QC H3A 2S9, Canada *Tel:* 514-845-4411 *Toll Free Tel:* 800-265-4815 *Fax:* 514-845-9903 *E-mail:* info@ottiaq.org; direction@ottiaq.org; reception@ottiaq.org *Web Site:* www.ottiaq.org, pg 542

Godine, David R, David R Godine Inc, 15 Court Sq, Suite 320, Boston, MA 02108-2536 *Tel:* 617-451-9600 *Fax:* 617-350-0250 *E-mail:* info@godine.com *Web Site:* www.godine.com, pg 87

Godoff, Ann, Penguin Group USA, A Penguin Random House Company, 375 Hudson St, New York, NY 10014 *Tel:* 212-366-2000 *Toll Free Tel:* 800-847-5515 (inside sales); 800-631-8571 (cust serv) *Fax:* 212-366-2666; 607-775-4829 (inside sales) *E-mail:* online@ us.penguingroup.com *Web Site:* www.penguin.com, pg 163

Godoff, Ann, The Penguin Press, 375 Hudson St, New York, NY 10014 *Web Site:* thepenguinpress.com, pg 164

Godwin, Laura, Henry Holt and Company, LLC, 120 Broadway, 23rd fl, New York, NY 10271 *Tel:* 646-307-5151 *Toll Free Tel:* 888-330-8477 (orders) *Fax:* 646-307-5285 *Web Site:* www.henryholt.com, pg 101

Goedkoop, Annie, The Electrochemical Society (ECS), 65 S Main St, Bldg D, Pennington, NJ 08534-2839 *Tel:* 609-737-1902 *Fax:* 609-737-0629 *E-mail:* publications@electrochem.org; customerservice@electrochem.org *Web Site:* www. electrochem.org, pg 70

Goel, Atul, Cenveo Publisher Services, 555 Virginia Dr, Fort Washington, PA 19034 *Tel:* 267-470-1590 *Fax:* 215-591-9093 *E-mail:* info.psg@cenveo.com *Web Site:* www.cenveopublisherservices.com, pg 460

Goel, Sonali, Macmillan, 120 Broadway, 22nd fl, New York, NY 10271 *Tel:* 646-307-5151 *E-mail:* press. inquiries@macmillan.com *Web Site:* www.macmillan. com, pg 130

Goeser, Nicholas J PhD, Soil Science Society of America (SSSA), 5585 Guilford Rd, Madison, WI 53711-5801 *Tel:* 608-273-8080 *Fax:* 608-273-2021 *Web Site:* www.soils.org, pg 203

Goeser, Nichols J PhD, American Society of Agronomy, 5585 Guilford Rd, Madison, WI 53711-5801 *Tel:* 608-273-8080 *Fax:* 608-273-2021 *E-mail:* headquarters@ sciencesocieties.org *Web Site:* www.agronomy.org, pg 14

Goettler, Peter, Cato Institute, 1000 Massachusetts Ave NW, Washington, DC 20001-5403 *Tel:* 202-842-0200 *Toll Free Tel:* 800-767-1241 *Fax:* 202-842-3490 *E-mail:* catostore@cato.org *Web Site:* www.cato.org, pg 46

Goetz, Adria, Martin Literary Management, 15601 32 Ave SE, Mill Creek, WA 98012 *Tel:* 206-466-1773 (no phone queries) *Fax:* 206-466-1774 *Web Site:* www. martinliterarymanagement.com, pg 495

Goetz, Barbara, Small Business Advisors Inc, 2005 Park St, Atlantic Beach, NY 11509 *Tel:* 516-374-1387 *Fax:* 516-374-1175 *E-mail:* info@smallbusinessadvice. com *Web Site:* www.smallbusinessadvice.com, pg 201

Goff, Anthony, Hachette Audio, 1290 Avenue of the Americas, New York, NY 10104 *Tel:* 212-364-1100 *Web Site:* www.hachetteaudio.com, pg 90

Goff, Anthony, Hachette Book Group, 1290 Avenue of the Americas, New York, NY 10104 *Tel:* 212-364-1100 *Toll Free Tel:* 800-759-0190 (cust serv) *Fax:* 212-364-0933 (intl orders) *Toll Free Fax:* 800-286-9471 (cust serv) *Web Site:* www. hachettebookgroup.com, pg 91

Goff, Gordon, ORO editions, 31 Commercial Blvd, Suite F, Novato, CA 94949 *Tel:* 415-883-3300 *Fax:* 415-883-3309 *E-mail:* info@oroeditions.com *Web Site:* www.oroeditions.com, pg 157

Goff, Jacqui, Insight Editions, 800 "A" St, San Rafael, CA 94901 *Tel:* 415-526-1370 *Toll Free Tel:* 800-809-3792 *Toll Free Fax:* 866-509-0515 *E-mail:* info@ insighteditions.com; marketing@insighteditions.com *Web Site:* insighteditions.com, pg 109

Goff, Jacqui, Mandala Earth, 800 "A" St, San Rafael, CA 94901 *Tel:* 415-526-1370 *Toll Free Fax:* 866-509-0515 *E-mail:* info@mandalapublishing.com *Web Site:* www. mandalaeartheditions.com, pg 131

Goff, Michaela, Casemate | publishers, 1950 Lawrence Rd, Havertown, PA 19083 *Tel:* 610-853-9131 *Fax:* 610-853-9146 *E-mail:* casemate@ casematepublishers.com *Web Site:* www. casematepublishers.com, pg 46

Goff, Raoul, Insight Editions, 800 "A" St, San Rafael, CA 94901 *Tel:* 415-526-1370 *Toll Free Tel:* 800-809-3792 *Toll Free Fax:* 866-509-0515 *E-mail:* info@ insighteditions.com; marketing@insighteditions.com *Web Site:* insighteditions.com, pg 109

Goff, Raoul, Mandala Earth, 800 "A" St, San Rafael, CA 94901 *Tel:* 415-526-1370 *Toll Free Fax:* 866-509-0515 *E-mail:* info@mandalapublishing.com *Web Site:* www. mandalaeartheditions.com, pg 131

Goff, Steven, Channel Photographics, 980 Lincoln Ave, Suite 200-B, San Rafael, CA 94901 *Tel:* 415-456-2934 *Fax:* 415-456-4124 *Web Site:* www. channelphotographics.com, pg 49

Goff, Steven, Global Publishing, Sales & Distribution, 135 Third St, Suite 150, San Rafael, CA 94901 *Tel:* 415-456-2934 *Fax:* 415-456-4124 *E-mail:* info@ globalpsd.com *Web Site:* www.globalpsd.com, pg 86

Goforth, Renea, Wichita State University Playwriting Contest, 1845 Fairmount St, Box 153, Wichita, KS 67260-0153 *Tel:* 316-978-3360 *Fax:* 316-978-3202 *Web Site:* www.wichita.edu, pg 677

Goggins, Rebecca Miller, The Carle Honors, 125 W Bay Rd, Amherst, MA 01002 *Tel:* 413-559-6300 *E-mail:* info@carlemuseum.org *Web Site:* www. carlemuseum.org/content/carle-honors, pg 603

Goh, Jaymee, Tachyon Publications LLC, 1459 18 St, No 139, San Francisco, CA 94107 *Tel:* 415-285-5615 *E-mail:* tachyon@tachyonpublications.com *Web Site:* www.tachyonpublications.com, pg 212

Goin, Carma, In-Plant Printing & Mailing Association (IPMA), 455 S Sam Barr Dr, Suite 203, Kearney, MO 64060 *Tel:* 816-919-1691 *E-mail:* ipmainfo@ipma.org *Web Site:* www.ipma.org, pg 534

Goin, Kenn, Bearport Publishing Co Inc, 45 W 21 St, Suite 3B, New York, NY 10010 *Tel:* 212-337-8577 *Toll Free Tel:* 877-337-8577 *Fax:* 212-337-8557 *Toll Free Fax:* 866-337-8557 *E-mail:* service@ bearportpublishing.com; info@bearportpublishing.com *Web Site:* www.bearportpublishing.com, pg 30

Gold, Heather, Yale University Press, 302 Temple St, New Haven, CT 06511-8909 *Tel:* 203-432-0960; 203-432-0966 (sales); 401-531-2800 (cust serv) *Toll Free Tel:* 800-405-1619 (cust serv) *Fax:* 203-432-0948; 203-432-8485 (sales); 401-531-2801 (cust serv) *Toll Free Fax:* 800-406-9145 (cust serv) *E-mail:* sales. press@yale.edu (sales); customer.care@triliteral.org (cust serv) *Web Site:* www.yalebooks.com; yalepress. yale.edu/yupbooks, pg 246

Gold, Jerry, Black Heron Press, PO Box 614, Anacortes, WA 98221 *Tel:* 360-899-9335 *Web Site:* blackheronpress.com, pg 34

Gold, Leslie J, PRB Productions, 963 Peralta Ave, Albany, CA 94706-2144 *Tel:* 510-526-0722 *E-mail:* prbprdns@aol.com *Web Site:* www.prbmusic. com, pg 173

Goldbaum, Milton J, Alan Wofsy Fine Arts, 1109 Geary Blvd, San Francisco, CA 94109 *Tel:* 415-292-6500 *Toll Free Tel:* 800-660-6403 *Fax:* 415-292-6594 (off & cust serv); 510-251-1840 (acctg) *E-mail:* order@ art-books.com (orders); editeur@earthlink.net (edit); beauxarts@earthlink.net (cust serv) *Web Site:* www. art-books.com, pg 243

Goldberg, Anne, Phaidon, 65 Bleecker St, 8th fl, New York, NY 10012 *Tel:* 212-652-5400 *Toll Free Tel:* 800-759-0190 (cust serv) *Fax:* 212-652-5410 *Toll Free Fax:* 800-286-9471 (cust serv) *E-mail:* enquiries@phaidon.com *Web Site:* www. phaidon.com, pg 168

Goldberg, David, The MIT Press, One Rogers St, Cambridge, MA 02142 *Tel:* 617-253-5255 *Toll Free Tel:* 800-405-1619 (orders) *Fax:* 617-258-6779; 617-577-1545 (orders) *Web Site:* mitpress.mit.edu, pg 141

Goldberg, Michael, MedMaster Inc, 3337 Hollywood Oaks Dr, Fort Lauderdale, FL 33312 *Tel:* 954-962-8414 *Toll Free Tel:* 800-335-3480 *Fax:* 954-962-4508 *E-mail:* mmbks@aol.com *Web Site:* www.medmaster. net, pg 137

Goldberg, Sarah, Scribner, 1230 Avenue of the Americas, New York, NY 10020, pg 195

Goldberg, Stephen, MedMaster Inc, 3337 Hollywood Oaks Dr, Fort Lauderdale, FL 33312 *Tel:* 954-962-8414 *Toll Free Tel:* 800-335-3480 *Fax:* 954-962-4508 *E-mail:* mmbks@aol.com *Web Site:* www.medmaster. net, pg 137

Goldbetter, Larry, National Writers Union/UAW Local 1981, 256 W 38 St, Suite 703, New York, NY 10018 *Tel:* 212-254-0279 *Fax:* 212-254-0673 *E-mail:* nwu@ nwu.org *Web Site:* www.nwu.org/, pg 541

Golden, Lori, Health Communications Inc, 3201 SW 15 St, Deerfield Beach, FL 33442 *Tel:* 954-360-0909 *Toll Free Tel:* 800-851-9100; 800-441-5569 (cust serv & orders) *Fax:* 954-360-0034 *Toll Free Fax:* 800-424-7652 (cust serv & orders) *E-mail:* customerservice2@ hcibooks.com *Web Site:* www.hcibooks.com, pg 96

Golden, Marita, Hurston/Wright Award for College Writers, 10 "G" St NE, Suite 600, Washington, DC 20002 *Tel:* 202-248-5051 *E-mail:* info@hurstonwright. org *Web Site:* www.hurstonwright.org, pg 625

Golden, Marita, Hurston/Wright Legacy Awards, 10 "G" St NE, Suite 600, Washington, DC 20002 *Tel:* 202-248-5051 *E-mail:* info@hurstonwright.org *Web Site:* www.hurstonwright.org, pg 625

Golden, Marita, Hurston/Wright Writers Week, 10 "G" St NE, Suite 600, Washington, DC 20002 *Tel:* 202-248-5051 *E-mail:* info@hurstonwright.org *Web Site:* www.hurstonwright.org, pg 575

Golden, Marita, The Zora Neale Hurston/Richard Wright Foundation, 10 "G" St NE, Suite 600, Washington, DC 20002 *Tel:* 202-248-5051 *E-mail:* info@ hurstonwright.org *Web Site:* www.hurstonwright.org, pg 551

Golden, Tim, Sourcebooks LLC, 1935 Brookdale Rd, Suite 139, Naperville, IL 60563 *Tel:* 630-961-3900 *Toll Free Tel:* 800-432-7444 *Fax:* 630-961-2168 *E-mail:* info@sourcebooks.com; customersupport@ sourcebooks.com *Web Site:* www.sourcebooks.com, pg 204

Goldfarb, Ronald L, Goldfarb & Associates, 721 Gibbon St, Alexandria, VA 22314 *Tel:* 202-466-3030 *Fax:* 703-836-5644 *E-mail:* rlglawlit@gmail.com *Web Site:* www.ronaldgoldfarb.com, pg 486

Goldinger, Sharon, PeopleSpeak, 25401 Alicia Pkwy, Suite L-512, Laguna Hills, CA 92653 *Tel:* 949-581-6190 *Fax:* 949-581-4958 *E-mail:* pplspeak@att.net *Web Site:* www.detailsplease.com/peoplespeak, pg 468

Goldklang, Janice, Other Press, 267 Fifth Ave, 6th fl, New York, NY 10016 *Tel:* 212-414-0054 *Toll Free Tel:* 877-843-6843 *Fax:* 212-414-0939 *E-mail:* editor@otherpress.com; marketing@ otherpress.com; publicity@otherpress.com *Web Site:* www.otherpress.com, pg 157

Goldman, Erika, Bellevue Literary Press, 90 Broad St, Suite 2100, New York, NY 10004 *Tel:* 917-732-3603 *Web Site:* blpress.org, pg 31

Goldman, Gloria, Judaica Press Inc, 123 Ditmas Ave, Brooklyn, NY 11218 *Tel:* 718-972-6200 *Toll Free Tel:* 800-972-6201 *Fax:* 718-972-6204 *E-mail:* info@judaicapress.com; orders@judaicapress. com; submissions@judaicapress.com *Web Site:* www. judaicapress.com, pg 114

Goodwin, Hannah, The Feminist Press at The City University of New York, 365 Fifth Ave, Suite 5406, New York, NY 10016 *Tel:* 212-817-7915 *Fax:* 212-817-1593 *E-mail:* info@feministpress.org *Web Site:* www.feministpress.org, pg 77

Goodwin, Jason, Print Industries Market Information and Research Organization (PRIMIR), 1899 Preston White Dr, Reston, VA 20191 *Tel:* 703-264-7200 *E-mail:* aptech@aptech.org *Web Site:* www.printtechnologies.org; www.npes.org/primirresearch/primir.aspx, pg 544

Goodwin, John, Galaxy Press, 7051 Hollywood Blvd, Hollywood, CA 90028 *Tel:* 323-466-3310 *Toll Free Tel:* 877-8GALAXY (842-5299) *E-mail:* info@galaxypress.com; customers@galaxypress.com *Web Site:* www.galaxypress.com, pg 82

Goody, Margo, Macmillan Audio, 120 Broadway, 22nd fl, New York, NY 10271 *Tel:* 646-307-5151 *Toll Free Tel:* 888-330-8477 (cust serv) *Web Site:* www.macmillanaudio.com, pg 130

Goossen, Chad, PrairieView Press, 625 Seventh St, Gretna, MB R0G 0V0, Canada *Tel:* 204-327-6543 *Toll Free Tel:* 800-477-7377 *Toll Free Fax:* 866-480-0253 *Web Site:* prairieviewpress.com, pg 437

Goossen, Chester, PrairieView Press, 625 Seventh St, Gretna, MB R0G 0V0, Canada *Tel:* 204-327-6543 *Toll Free Tel:* 800-477-7377 *Toll Free Fax:* 866-480-0253 *Web Site:* prairieviewpress.com, pg 437

Gorder, Alisha, Counterpoint Press LLC, 2560 Ninth St, Suite 318, Berkeley, CA 94710 *Tel:* 510-704-0230 *Fax:* 510-704-0268 *E-mail:* info@counterpointpress.com *Web Site:* counterpointpress.com; softskull.com, pg 58

Gordon, Annette, Clarity Press Inc, 2625 Piedmont Rd NE, Suite 56, Atlanta, GA 30324 *Tel:* 404-647-6501 *E-mail:* claritypress@usa.net (foreign rts & perms) *Web Site:* www.claritypress.com, pg 53

Gordon, Ariel, University of Manitoba Press, University of Manitoba, 301 St Johns College, 92 Dysart Rd, Winnipeg, MB R3T 2M5, Canada *Tel:* 204-474-9495 *Fax:* 204-474-7566 *E-mail:* uofmpress@umanitoba.ca *Web Site:* uofmpress.ca, pg 443

Gordon, Clayton, Illuminating Engineering Society of North America (IES), 120 Wall St, 17th fl, New York, NY 10005-4001 *Tel:* 212-248-5000 *Fax:* 212-248-5017; 212-248-5018 *E-mail:* ies@ies.org *Web Site:* www.ies.org, pg 106

Gordon, Douglas C, P M Gordon Associates Inc, 2115 Wallace St, Philadelphia, PA 19130 *Tel:* 215-769-2525 *Web Site:* www.pmgordonassociates.com, pg 464

Gordon, Emma, Houghton Mifflin Harcourt Trade & Reference Division, 125 High St, Boston, MA 02110 *Tel:* 617-351-5000 *Web Site:* www.hmhco.com, pg 104

Gordon, Jason, Writers Guild of America, East (WGAE), 250 Hudson St, Suite 700, New York, NY 10013 *Tel:* 212-767-7800 *Fax:* 212-582-1909 *Web Site:* www.wgaeast.org, pg 549

Gordon, Kathryn, HarperCollins General Books Group, 195 Broadway, New York, NY 10007 *Tel:* 212-207-7000 *Web Site:* www.harpercollins.com, pg 93

Gordon, Leah, Alcuin Society, PO Box 3216, Sta Terminal, Vancouver, BC V6B 3X8, Canada *Tel:* 604-732-5403 *E-mail:* info@alcuinsociety.com; awards@alcuinsociety.com *Web Site:* alcuinsociety.com, pg 521

Gordon, Leah, Alcuin Society Awards for Excellence in Book Design in Canada, PO Box 3216, Sta Terminal, Vancouver, BC V6B 3X8, Canada *Tel:* 604-732-5403 *E-mail:* awards@alcuinsociety.com *Web Site:* alcuinsociety.com, pg 591

Gordon, Leah, Perseus Books, 1290 Avenue of the Americas, New York, NY 10104 *Tel:* 212-340-8100 *Toll Free Tel:* 800-343-4499 (cust serv) *Fax:* 212-340-8105 *Web Site:* www.perseusbooks.com, pg 167

Gordon, Lindsay, Avery, 1745 Broadway, New York, NY 10019 *Tel:* 212-366-2000 *Fax:* 212-366-2636 *E-mail:* averypublicity@penguinrandomhouse.com *Web Site:* www.penguin.com/publishers/avery; www.penguinrandomhouse.com, pg 26

Gordon, Lindsay, TarcherPerigee, 375 Hudson St, New York, NY 10014 *Tel:* 212-366-2000 *Fax:* 212-366-2643 *E-mail:* customerservice@penguinrandomhouse.com (cust serv); TarcherPerigeePublicity@penguinrandomhouse.com (media queries) *Web Site:* www.tarcherbooks.com; www.facebook.com/TarcherPerigee/; www.penguin.com/publishers/tarcherperigee, pg 213

Gordon, Marilyn, Baker Books, 6030 E Fulton Rd, Ada, MI 49301 *Tel:* 616-676-9185 *Toll Free Tel:* 800-877-2665 (orders) *Fax:* 616-676-9573 *Toll Free Fax:* 800-398-3111 (orders) *E-mail:* media@bakerpublishinggroup.com; orders@bakerpublishinggroup.com; sales@bakerpublishinggroup.com *Web Site:* www.bakerpublishinggroup.com, pg 27

Gordon, Marilyn, Revell, PO Box 6287, Grand Rapids, MI 49516-6287 *Tel:* 616-676-9185 *Toll Free Tel:* 800-877-2665; 800-679-1957 *Fax:* 616-676-9573 *Web Site:* www.bakerpublishinggroup.com, pg 185

Gordon, Peggy M, P M Gordon Associates Inc, 2115 Wallace St, Philadelphia, PA 19130 *Tel:* 215-769-2525 *Web Site:* www.pmgordonassociates.com, pg 464

Gordon, Peter, Cambridge University Press, One Liberty Plaza, 20th fl, New York, NY 10006 *Tel:* 212-924-3900; 212-337-5000 *Fax:* 212-691-3239; 845-353-4141 *E-mail:* newyork@cambridge.org; customer_service@cambridge.org *Web Site:* www.cambridge.org/us, pg 43

Gore, Clelia, Martin Literary Management, 15601 32 Ave SE, Mill Creek, WA 98012 *Tel:* 206-466-1773 (no phone queries) *Fax:* 206-466-1774 *Web Site:* www.martinliterarymanagement.com, pg 495

Goreta, Adriana, Cundill History Prize, 3463 Peel St, Montreal, QC H3A 1W7, Canada *Tel:* 514-398-8346 *E-mail:* cundill.prize@mcgill.ca *Web Site:* www.cundillprize.com, pg 608

Gorg, Brian, Educational Book & Media Association (EBMA), 11 Main St, Suite D, Warrenton, VA 20186 *Tel:* 540-318-7770 *Fax:* 202-962-3939 *E-mail:* info@edupaperback.org *Web Site:* www.edupaperback.org, pg 532

Gorg, Brian, Jeremiah Ludington Award, 11 Main St, Suite D, Warrenton, VA 20186 *Tel:* 540-318-7770 *Fax:* 202-962-3939 *E-mail:* info@edupaperback.org *Web Site:* www.edupaperback.org, pg 636

Gorham, Sarah, Linda Bruckheimer Series in Kentucky Literature, 822 E Market St, Louisville, KY 40206 *Tel:* 502-458-4028 *E-mail:* info@sarabandebooks.org *Web Site:* www.sarabandebooks.org/bruckheimer, pg 601

Gorham, Sarah, Mary McCarthy Prize in Short Fiction, 822 E Market St, Louisville, KY 40206 *Tel:* 502-458-4028 *E-mail:* info@sarabandebooks.org *Web Site:* www.sarabandebooks.org/mccarthy, pg 639

Gorham, Sarah, Kathryn A Morton Prize in Poetry, 822 E Market St, Louisville, KY 40206 *Tel:* 502-458-4028 *E-mail:* info@sarabandebooks.org *Web Site:* www.sarabandebooks.org/morton, pg 643

Gorham, Sarah, Sarabande Books Inc, 822 E Market St, Louisville, KY 40206 *Tel:* 502-458-4028 *Fax:* 502-458-4065 *E-mail:* info@sarabandebooks.org *Web Site:* www.sarabandebooks.org, pg 192

Gorman, Don, Rocky Mountain Books Ltd (RMB), 103-1075 Pendergast St, Victoria, BC V8V 0A1, Canada *Tel:* 250-360-0829 *Fax:* 250-386-0829 *Web Site:* www.rmbooks.com, pg 438

Gorman, Roberta, Society of Motion Picture & Television Engineers® (SMPTE®), 3 Barker Ave, 5th fl, White Plains, NY 10601 *Tel:* 914-761-1100 *Fax:* 914-761-3115 *Web Site:* www.smpte.org, pg 547

Gosling, Anthony, Crossway, 1300 Crescent St, Wheaton, IL 60187 *Tel:* 630-682-4300 *Toll Free Tel:* 800-635-7993 (orders); 800-543-1659 (cust serv) *Fax:* 630-682-4785 *E-mail:* info@crossway.org *Web Site:* www.crossway.org, pg 60

Gosling, Nicole, Crossway, 1300 Crescent St, Wheaton, IL 60187 *Tel:* 630-682-4300 *Toll Free Tel:* 800-635-7993 (orders); 800-543-1659 (cust serv) *Fax:* 630-682-4785 *E-mail:* info@crossway.org *Web Site:* www.crossway.org, pg 60

Gosse, Jonathan F, American Technical Publishers Inc, 10100 Orland Pkwy, Suite 200, Orland Park, IL 60467-5756 *Toll Free Tel:* 800-323-3471 *Fax:* 708-957-1101 *E-mail:* service@atplearning.com; order@atplearning.com *Web Site:* www.atplearning.com, pg 15

Gottier, Aaron, P & R Publishing Co, 1102 Marble Hill Rd, Phillipsburg, NJ 08865 *Tel:* 908-454-0505 *Toll Free Tel:* 800-631-0094 *Fax:* 908-859-2390 *E-mail:* sales@prpbooks.com; info@prpbooks.com *Web Site:* www.prpbooks.com, pg 158

Gottlieb, Mark, Trident Media Group LLC, 41 Madison Ave, 36th fl, New York, NY 10010 *Tel:* 212-333-1511 *E-mail:* info@tridentmediagroup.com; press@tridentmediagroup.com *Web Site:* www.tridentmediagroup.com, pg 507

Gottlieb, Richard, Grey House Publishing Inc™, 4919 Rte 22, Amenia, NY 12501 *Tel:* 518-789-8700 *Toll Free Tel:* 800-562-2139 *Fax:* 518-789-0556 *E-mail:* books@greyhouse.com; customerservice@greyhouse.com *Web Site:* greyhouse.com, pg 89

Gottlieb, Robert, Trident Media Group LLC, 41 Madison Ave, 36th fl, New York, NY 10010 *Tel:* 212-333-1511 *E-mail:* info@tridentmediagroup.com; press@tridentmediagroup.com *Web Site:* www.tridentmediagroup.com, pg 507

Gougeon, Guy, Flammarion Quebec, 375 Ave Laurier W, Montreal, QC H2V 2K3, Canada *Tel:* 514-277-8807 *Fax:* 514-278-2085 *E-mail:* info@flammarion.qc.ca *Web Site:* www.flammarion.qc.ca, pg 426

Gould, Barbara, National Magazine Awards, 2300 Yonge St, Suite 1600, Toronto, ON M4P 1E4, Canada *Tel:* 416-939-6200 *E-mail:* staff@magazine-awards.com *Web Site:* www.magazine-awards.com; twitter.com/magawards, pg 645

Gould, Morgan, Houghton Mifflin Harcourt, 125 High St, Boston, MA 02110 *Tel:* 617-351-5000 *Toll Free Tel:* 855-969-4642; 800-225-5425 (K-12 educ materials); 800-323-9540 (assessment materials); 877-219-1537 (SkillsTutor); 888-242-6747 (Innovation in Educ Group); 800-225-3362 (Trade & Ref Div) *Toll Free Fax:* 800-269-5232 *E-mail:* myhmhco@hmhco.com *Web Site:* www.hmhco.com, pg 103

Gould, Robert, Big Guy Books, 6866 Embarcadero Lane, Carlsbad, CA 92011 *Tel:* 760-652-5360 *Toll Free Tel:* 800-536-3030 (booksellers' cust serv) *Fax:* 760-652-5361 *E-mail:* info@bigguybooks.com *Web Site:* www.bigguybooks.com, pg 33

Gourlay, Jonathan, MacDowell Fellowships, 100 High St, Peterborough, NH 03458 *Tel:* 603-924-3886 *E-mail:* info@macdowell.org; admissions@macdowell.org *Web Site:* www.macdowell.org, pg 637

Gouws, Johann, Alfred Music, PO Box 10003, Van Nuys, CA 91410 *Tel:* 818-891-5999 (dealer sales, intl) *Toll Free Tel:* 800-292-6122 (dealer sales, US & CN); 800-628-1528 (cust serv) *Fax:* 818-893-5560 (dealer sales); 818-830-6252 (cust serv) *Toll Free Fax:* 800-632-1928 (dealer sales) *E-mail:* customerservice@alfred.com; sales@alfred.com *Web Site:* www.alfred.com, pg 7

Gouzoules, Leon, Firefly Books Ltd, 50 Staples Ave, Unit 1, Richmond Hill, ON L4B 0A7, Canada *Tel:* 416-499-8412 *Toll Free Tel:* 800-387-6192 (CN); 800-387-5085 (US) *Fax:* 416-499-8313 *Toll Free Fax:* 800-450-0391 (CN); 800-565-6034 (US) *E-mail:* service@fireflybooks.com *Web Site:* www.fireflybooks.com, pg 426

Governa, Mark, Perseus Books, 1290 Avenue of the Americas, New York, NY 10104 *Tel:* 212-340-8100 *Toll Free Tel:* 800-343-4499 (cust serv) *Fax:* 212-340-8105 *Web Site:* www.perseusbooks.com, pg 168

Grace, Bill, Little, Brown Books for Young Readers, 1290 Avenue of the Americas, New York, NY 10104 *Tel:* 212-364-1100 *Toll Free Tel:* 800-759-0190 (cust serv) *Web Site:* www.hachettebookgroup.com, pg 126

Grad, Doug, Doug Grad Literary Agency Inc, 68 Jay St, Suite W11, Brooklyn, NY 11201-1189 *Tel:* 718-788-6067 *E-mail:* query@dgliterary.com *Web Site:* www.dgliterary.com, pg 486

Gradel, Melissa Ford, Editor's Award, 90 Broad St, Suite 2100, New York, NY 10004 *Tel:* 212-226-3586 *Fax:* 212-226-3963 *Web Site:* www.pw.org/about-us/sponsored-prizes, pg 612

Gradel, Melissa Ford, Poets & Writers Inc, 90 Broad St, Suite 2100, New York, NY 10004 *Tel:* 212-226-3586 *Fax:* 212-226-3963 *E-mail:* admin@pw.org *Web Site:* www.pw.org, pg 544

Grady, Lynn, Princeton Architectural Press, 202 Warren St, Hudson, NY 12534 *Tel:* 518-671-6100 *Toll Free Tel:* 800-722-6657 (dist); 800-759-0190 (sales) *E-mail:* sales@papress.com *Web Site:* www.papress.com, pg 174

Graff, Emily, Simon & Schuster, 1230 Avenue of the Americas, New York, NY 10020 *Tel:* 212-698-7000 *Toll Free Tel:* 800-223-2348 (cust serv); 800-223-2336 (orders) *Toll Free Fax:* 800-943-9831 (orders) *Web Site:* www.simonandschuster.com, pg 198

Graham, Alexander T, Council for Exceptional Children (CEC), 2900 Crystal Dr, Suite 100, Arlington, VA 22202 *Toll Free Tel:* 888-232-7733; 866-915-5000 (TTY) *E-mail:* service@cec.sped.org *Web Site:* www.cec.sped.org, pg 57

Graham, Bonny, National Council of Teachers of English (NCTE), 340 N Neil St, Suite 104, Champaign, IL 61820 *Tel:* 217-328-3870 *Toll Free Tel:* 877-369-6283 (cust serv) *Fax:* 217-328-9645 *E-mail:* customerservice@ncte.org *Web Site:* www.ncte.org, pg 146

Graham, Don, University of Texas at Austin, New Writers Project, Dept of English, Calhoun Hall, Rm 226, 204 W 21 St, B-5000, Austin, TX 78712 *Tel:* 512-471-5132; 512-471-4991 *Fax:* 512-471-4909 *Web Site:* newwritersproject.org, pg 586

Graham, Earl, Graham Agency, 115 W 45 St, Suite 505, New York, NY 10036 *Tel:* 212-489-7730, pg 487

Graham, Jon, Bear & Co Inc, One Park St, Rochester, VT 05767 *Tel:* 802-767-3174 *Toll Free Tel:* 800-932-3277 *Fax:* 802-767-3726 *E-mail:* customerservice@InnerTraditions.com *Web Site:* InnerTraditions.com, pg 29

Graham, Jon, Inner Traditions International Ltd, One Park St, Rochester, VT 05767 *Tel:* 802-767-3174 *Toll Free Tel:* 800-246-8648 *Fax:* 802-767-3726 *E-mail:* customerservice@InnerTraditions.com *Web Site:* www.InnerTraditions.com, pg 109

Graham, Joseph, The American Chemical Society, 1155 16 St NW, Washington, DC 20036 *Tel:* 202-872-4600 *Toll Free Tel:* 800-227-5558 (US) *Fax:* 202-872-6067 *E-mail:* help@acs.org *Web Site:* www.acs.org, pg 10

Graham, Kathleen, Society for Advancing Business Editing & Writing (SABEW), Walter Cronkite School of Journalism & Mass Communication, Arizona State University, 555 N Central Ave, Suite 406E, Phoenix, AZ 85004-1248 *Tel:* 602-496-7862 *E-mail:* sabew@sabew.org *Web Site:* sabew.org, pg 546

Graham, Kimberly, Miles Conrad Memorial Lecture, 3600 Clipper Mill Rd, Suite 302, Baltimore, MD 21211-1948 *Tel:* 301-654-2512 *Fax:* 410-685-5278 *E-mail:* nisohq@niso.org *Web Site:* www.niso.org, pg 606

Graham, Kimberly, National Information Standards Organization (NISO), 3600 Clipper Mill Rd, Suite 302, Baltimore, MD 21211-1948 *Tel:* 301-654-2512 *Fax:* 410-685-5278 *E-mail:* nisohq@niso.org *Web Site:* www.niso.org, pg 147, 540

Graham, Nan, Scribner, 1230 Avenue of the Americas, New York, NY 10020, pg 195

Graham, Nan, Simon & Schuster, Inc, 1230 Avenue of the Americas, New York, NY 10020 *Tel:* 212-698-7000 *Toll Free Tel:* 800-223-2336 (orders) *Fax:* 212-698-7007 *Toll Free Fax:* 800-943-9831 (orders) *E-mail:* firstname.lastname@simonandschuster.com; purchaseorders@simonandschuster.com (orders) *Web Site:* www.simonandschuster.com, pg 199

Graham, Rachel, National Geographic Books, 1145 17 St NW, Washington, DC 20036-4688 *Tel:* 202-857-7000 *Toll Free Tel:* 877-866-6486 *E-mail:* ngbooks@cdsfulfillment.com *Web Site:* www.nationalgeographic.com/books/; ngbooks.buysub.com, pg 146

Graham, Stacey, 3 Seas Literary Agency, PO Box 444, Sun Prairie, WI 53590 *Tel:* 608-834-9317 *E-mail:* threeseaslit@aol.com *Web Site:* threeseasagency.com, pg 506

Grahek, Greg, AACC International, 3340 Pilot Knob Rd, St Paul, MN 55121 *Tel:* 651-454-7250 *Fax:* 651-454-0766 *E-mail:* aacc@scisoc.org *Web Site:* www.aaccnet.org, pg 1

Grahek, Greg, APS PRESS, 3340 Pilot Knob Rd, St Paul, MN 55121 *Tel:* 651-454-7250 *Toll Free Tel:* 800-328-7560 *Fax:* 651-454-0766 *E-mail:* aps@scisoc.org *Web Site:* www.shopapspress.org, pg 18

Grainger, Jeremy, Rutgers University Press, 106 Somerset St, 3rd fl, New Brunswick, NJ 08901 *Tel:* 848-445-7762; 848-445-7761 (sales) *Fax:* 732-745-4935 *E-mail:* sales@rutgersuniversitypress.org *Web Site:* www.rutgersuniversitypress.org, pg 188

Grajkowski, Michelle, 3 Seas Literary Agency, PO Box 444, Sun Prairie, WI 53590 *Tel:* 608-834-9317 *E-mail:* threeseaslit@aol.com *Web Site:* threeseasagency.com, pg 506

Grames, Juliet, Soho Press Inc, 853 Broadway, New York, NY 10003 *Tel:* 212-260-1900 *E-mail:* soho@sohopress.com; publicity@sohopress.com *Web Site:* sohopress.com, pg 203

Granada, Lina, Brandt & Hochman Literary Agents Inc, 1501 Broadway, Suite 2310, New York, NY 10036 *Tel:* 212-840-5760 *Fax:* 212-840-5776 *Web Site:* brandthochman.com, pg 477

Grandstaff, Emily, The University of Virginia Press, PO Box 400318, Charlottesville, VA 22904-4318 *Tel:* 434-924-3468 (cust serv); 434-924-3469 (cust serv) *Toll Free Tel:* 800-831-3406 (orders) *Fax:* 434-982-2655 *Toll Free Fax:* 877-288-6400 *E-mail:* vapress@virginia.edu *Web Site:* www.upress.virginia.edu, pg 231

Granger, David, Aevitas Creative Management, 19 W 21 St, Suite 501, New York, NY 10010 *Tel:* 212-765-6900 *Web Site:* aevitascreative.com, pg 474

Grant, Donna, University of Regina Press, 2 Research Dr, Suite 246, Regina, SK S4S 7H9, Canada *Tel:* 306-585-4758 *Fax:* 306-585-4699 *E-mail:* uofrpress@uregina.ca *Web Site:* uofrpress.ca, pg 444

Grant, Gavin J, Small Beer Press, 150 Pleasant St, No 306, Easthampton, MA 01027 *Tel:* 413-203-1636 *Fax:* 413-203-1636 *E-mail:* info@smallbeerpress.com *Web Site:* smallbeerpress.com, pg 201

Grant, Janet Kobobel, Books & Such, 52 Mission Circle, Suite 122, PMB 170, Santa Rosa, CA 95409-5370 *Tel:* 707-538-4184 *Web Site:* booksandsuch.com, pg 476

Grantham, Charles E, Contemporary Publishing Co of Raleigh Inc, 5849 Lease Lane, Raleigh, NC 27617 *Tel:* 919-851-8221 *Fax:* 919-851-6666 *E-mail:* questions@contemporarypublishing.com *Web Site:* www.contemporarypublishing.com, pg 56

Grassi, Laurie, Simon & Schuster Canada, 166 King St E, Suite 300, Toronto, ON M5A 1J3, Canada *Tel:* 647-427-8882 *Toll Free Tel:* 800-387-0446; 800-268-3216 (orders) *Fax:* 647-430-9446 *Toll Free Fax:* 888-849-8151 (orders) *E-mail:* info@simonandschuster.ca *Web Site:* www.simonandschuster.ca, pg 440

Grathwohl, Casper, Oxford University Press USA, 198 Madison Ave, New York, NY 10016 *Toll Free Tel:* 800-451-7556 (orders); 800-445-9714 (cust serv) *Fax:* 919-677-1303 *E-mail:* custserv.us@oup.com *Web Site:* global.oup.com, pg 158

Gratz, Mike, Olde & Oppenheim Publishers, 3219 N Margate Place, Chandler, AZ 85224 *E-mail:* olde_oppenheim@hotmail.com, pg 155

Grauman, Judith, The Guilford Press, 370 Seventh Ave, Suite 1200, New York, NY 10001-1020 *Tel:* 212-431-9800 *Toll Free Tel:* 800-365-7006 *Fax:* 212-966-6708 *E-mail:* info@guilford.com *Web Site:* www.guilford.com, pg 90

Gray, Alyssa, Hebrew Union College Press, 3101 Clifton Ave, Cincinnati, OH 45220 *Tel:* 513-221-1875 *Fax:* 513-221-0321 *Web Site:* press.huc.edu, pg 97

Gray, Andrew, University of British Columbia Creative Writing Program, Buchanan Rm E-462, 1866 Main Mall, Vancouver, BC V6T 1Z1, Canada *Tel:* 604-822-0699 *Web Site:* creativewriting.ubc.ca, pg 585

Gray, Catherine Moreton, BLR®—Business & Legal Resources, 100 Winners Circle, Suite 300, Brentwood, TN 37027 *Tel:* 860-510-0100 *Toll Free Tel:* 800-727-5257 *E-mail:* service@blr.com *Web Site:* www.blr.com, pg 36

Gray, David, Gray & Company Publishers, 1588 E 40 St, Suite 1B, Cleveland, OH 44103 *Tel:* 216-431-2665 *Toll Free Tel:* 800-915-3609 *E-mail:* sales@grayco.com; editorial@grayco.com; support@grayco.com; publicity@grayco.com *Web Site:* www.grayco.com, pg 88

Gray, Jody, Coretta Scott King Book Awards, 225 N Michigan Ave, Suite 1300, Chicago, IL 60601 *Tel:* 312-944-6780 *Toll Free Tel:* 800-545-2433 *Fax:* 312-440-9374 *E-mail:* diversity@ala.org *Web Site:* www.ala.org/awardsgrants/coretta-scott-king-book-awards, pg 630

Gray, Kim, Simon & Schuster Sales Division, 1230 Avenue of the Americas, New York, NY 10020 *Tel:* 212-698-7000, pg 200

Gray, Phil, Self-Realization Fellowship Publishers, 3208 Humboldt St, Los Angeles, CA 90031 *Tel:* 323-276-6002 *Toll Free Tel:* 888-773-8680 *Fax:* 323-927-1624 *E-mail:* sales@yogananda-srf.org *Web Site:* www.yogananda-srf.org; bookstore.yogananda-srf.org/ (orders), pg 196

Gray, Thomas, Upper Access Inc, 87 Upper Access Rd, Hinesburg, VT 05461 *Tel:* 802-482-2988 *E-mail:* upperaccessbooks@gmail.com *Web Site:* www.upperaccess.com, pg 234

Grazian, Natalie, Martin Literary Management, 15601 32 Ave SE, Mill Creek, WA 98012 *Tel:* 206-466-1773 (no phone queries) *Fax:* 206-466-1774 *Web Site:* www.martinliterarymanagement.com, pg 495

Graziani, Mike, SLACK® Incorporated, A Wyanoke Group Company, 6900 Grove Rd, Thorofare, NJ 08086-9447 *Tel:* 856-848-1000 *Toll Free Tel:* 800-257-8290 *Fax:* 856-848-6091 *E-mail:* sales@slackinc.com; editor@slackinc.com; customerservice@slackinc.com *Web Site:* www.healio.com/books, pg 201

Greco, Al, Carson Dellosa Publishing LLC, PO Box 35665, Greensboro, NC 27425-5665 *Tel:* 336-632-0084 *Toll Free Tel:* 800-321-0943 *Fax:* 336-632-0087 *Toll Free Fax:* 800-535-2669 *E-mail:* custsvc@carsondellosa.com *Web Site:* www.carsondellosa.com, pg 45

Greco, Gabrielle, Workman Publishing Co Inc, 225 Varick St, 9th fl, New York, NY 10014-4381 *Tel:* 212-254-5900 *Toll Free Tel:* 800-722-7202 *Fax:* 212-254-8098 *E-mail:* info@workman.com; orders@workman.com *Web Site:* www.workman.com, pg 244

Greco, John, American Bible Society, 101 N Independence Mall E, 8th fl, Philadelphia, PA 19106-2112 *Tel:* 215-309-0900 *Toll Free Tel:* 800-322-4253 (cust serv); 888-596-6296 *E-mail:* info@americanbible.org *Web Site:* www.americanbible.org, pg 9

Greco, Kristin, Psychological Assessment Resources Inc (PAR), 16204 N Florida Ave, Lutz, FL 33549 *Tel:* 813-449-4065 *Toll Free Tel:* 800-331-8378 *Fax:* 813-961-2196 *Toll Free Fax:* 800-727-9329 *Web Site:* www.parinc.com, pg 177

Greco, Marilyn, Schoolhouse Network, PO Box 1518, Northampton, MA 01061 *Tel:* 480-427-4836 *E-mail:* schoolhousenetwork@gmail.com, pg 470

Greco, Tim, Macmillan, 120 Broadway, 22nd fl, New York, NY 10271 *Tel:* 646-307-5151 *E-mail:* press.inquiries@macmillan.com *Web Site:* www.macmillan.com, pg 129

Grotz, Jennifer, Bread Loaf Writers' Conference, 5525 Middlebury College, 14 Old Chapel Rd, Middlebury, VT 05753 *Tel:* 802-443-5286 *Fax:* 802-443-2087 *E-mail:* blwc@middlebury.edu *Web Site:* www. middlebury.edu/blwc, pg 573

Grotz, Jennifer, Fellowship, Tuition Scholarship & Work Study Programs for Writers, Middlebury College, 204 College St, Middlebury, VT 05753 *Tel:* 802-443-5286 *Fax:* 802-443-2087 *E-mail:* blwc@middlebury.edu *Web Site:* www.middlebury.edu/blwc, pg 615

Grove, Alyssa Hickman, Utah Original Writing Competition, 617 E South Temple, Salt Lake City, UT 84102 *Tel:* 801-236-7555 *Fax:* 801-236-7556 *Web Site:* arts.utah.gov, pg 675

Grove, Tara, The New Press, 120 Wall St, 31st fl, New York, NY 10005 *Tel:* 212-629-8802 *Toll Free Tel:* 800-343-4489 (orders) *Fax:* 212-629-8617 *Toll Free Fax:* 800-351-5073 (orders) *E-mail:* newpress@thenewpress.com *Web Site:* www.thenewpress.com, pg 149

Grow, KJ, Shambhala Publications Inc, 4720 Walnut St, Boulder, CO 80301 *Tel:* 303-222-9598 *Toll Free Tel:* 866-424-0030 (off); 888-424-2329 (cust serv) *E-mail:* customercare@shambhala.com *Web Site:* www.shambhala.com, pg 197

Grubb, Nora, Doubleday, c/o Penguin Random House Inc, 1745 Broadway, New York, NY 10019 *Tel:* 212-751-2600 *Fax:* 212-572-2662 (foreign rts) *E-mail:* ddaypub@randomhouse.com *Web Site:* knopfdoubleday.com, pg 66

Grubb, Randell C, Theosophical University Press, PO Box C, Pasadena, CA 91109-7107 *Tel:* 626-798-3378 *E-mail:* tupress@theosociety.org *Web Site:* www. theosociety.org, pg 217

Gruber, Pam, Irene Goodman Literary Agency, 27 W 24 St, Suite 700B, New York, NY 10010 *Tel:* 212-604-0330 *E-mail:* queries@irenegoodman.com *Web Site:* www.irenegoodman.com, pg 486

Gruninger, Susanna, Kensington Publishing Corp, 119 W 40 St, New York, NY 10018 *Tel:* 212-407-1500 *Toll Free Tel:* 800-221-2647 *Fax:* 212-935-0699 *Web Site:* www.kensingtonbooks.com, pg 116

Grutjen, Wibke, Hachette Book Group, 1290 Avenue of the Americas, New York, NY 10104 *Tel:* 212-364-1100 *Toll Free Tel:* 800-759-0190 (cust serv) *Fax:* 212-364-0933 (intl orders) *Toll Free Fax:* 800-286-9471 (cust serv) *Web Site:* hachettebookgroup.com, pg 90

Gu, Wendi, Sanford J Greenburger Associates Inc, 55 Fifth Ave, New York, NY 10003 *Tel:* 212-206-5600 *Fax:* 212-463-8718 *Web Site:* greenburger.com; www. sjga.com, pg 487

Guacci, Julie, Little, Brown and Company, 1290 Avenue of the Americas, New York, NY 10104 *Tel:* 212-364-1100 *Fax:* 212-364-0952 *E-mail:* firstname.lastname@hbgusa.com *Web Site:* www.littlebrown.com; www. hachettebookgroup.com, pg 126

Guarin, Imelda, Marshall Cavendish Education, 99 White Plains Rd, Tarrytown, NY 10591-9001 *Tel:* 914-332-8888 *Toll Free Tel:* 800-821-9881 *Fax:* 914-332-1082 *E-mail:* mce@marshallcavendish.com; customerservice@marshallcavendish.com *Web Site:* www.mceducation.us, pg 133

Guay, Marie-Noelle, Editions Yvon Blais, 75-4700 rue Queen, Montreal, QC H3C 2N6, Canada *Tel:* 514-842-3937 *Toll Free Tel:* 800-363-3047 *Fax:* 450-263-9256 *E-mail:* editionsyvonblais.commandes@thomsonreuters.com (cust serv) *Web Site:* www. editionsyvonblais.com, pg 425

Guenzel, Andrea L, The Electrochemical Society (ECS), 65 S Main St, Bldg D, Pennington, NJ 08534-2839 *Tel:* 609-737-1902 *Fax:* 609-737-0629 *E-mail:* publications@electrochem.org; customerservice@electrochem.org *Web Site:* www. electrochem.org, pg 70

Guenzi, Carol, Carol Guenzi Agents Inc, 865 Delaware St, Denver, CO 80204 *Tel:* 303-820-2599 *Toll Free Tel:* 800-417-5120 *Fax:* 303-820-2598 *E-mail:* art@artagent.com *Web Site:* www.artagent.com, pg 511

Guerin, Tom, Little, Brown Books for Young Readers, 1290 Avenue of the Americas, New York, NY 10104 *Tel:* 212-364-1100 *Toll Free Tel:* 800-759-0190 (cust serv) *Web Site:* www.hachettebookgroup.com, pg 126

Guerra, Delin, Bogle International Library Travel Fund, 50 E Huron St, Chicago, IL 60611-2795 *Tel:* 312-280-3201 *Toll Free Tel:* 800-545-2433 (ext 3201) *Fax:* 312-280-4392 *E-mail:* intl@ala.org *Web Site:* www.ala.org, pg 599

Guerra, Margie, The Experiment, 220 E 23 St, Suite 600, New York, NY 10010-4658 *Tel:* 212-889-1659 *E-mail:* info@theexperimentpublishing.com *Web Site:* www.theexperimentpublishing.com, pg 74

Guerth, Jan-Erik, BlueBridge, PO Box 601, Katonah, NY 10536 *Tel:* 914-301-5901 *Web Site:* www. bluebridgebooks.com, pg 37

Guess, Elizabeth, Little, Brown and Company, 1290 Avenue of the Americas, New York, NY 10104 *Tel:* 212-364-1100 *Fax:* 212-364-0952 *E-mail:* firstname.lastname@hbgusa.com *Web Site:* www.littlebrown.com; www. hachettebookgroup.com, pg 126

Guest, Tracey, St Martin's Press, LLC, 120 Broadway, New York, NY 10271 *Tel:* 646-307-5151 *Web Site:* us.macmillan.com/smp, pg 190

Guevara, Linda L, All About Kids Publishing, PO Box 159, Gilroy, CA 95021 *Tel:* 408-337-1152 *E-mail:* info@allaboutkidspub.com *Web Site:* www. allaboutkidspub.com, pg 7

Guevin, John R, Biographical Publishing Co, 95 Sycamore Dr, Prospect, CT 06712-1011 *Tel:* 203-758-3661 *Fax:* 253-793-2618 *E-mail:* biopub@aol.com *Web Site:* www.biopub.us, pg 33

Guibord, Maurice, BCHF Historial Writing Competition, PO Box 448, Fort Langley, BC V1M 2R7, Canada *E-mail:* info@bchistory.ca *Web Site:* www.bchistory.ca/awards/historical-writing, pg 596

Guido, Umberto III, Peter Glenn Publications, 306 NE Second St, 2nd fl, Delray Beach, FL 33483 *Web Site:* pgdirect.com, pg 86

Guidone, Kimberly, The Jennifer DeChiara Literary Agency, 245 Park Ave, 39th fl, New York, NY 10167 *Tel:* 212-372-8989 *Web Site:* www.jdlit.com, pg 481

Guignard, Gayla, The Alexander Graham Bell Association for the Deaf & Hard of Hearing, 3417 Volta Place NW, Washington, DC 20007 *Tel:* 202-337-5220 *Toll Free Tel:* 866-337-5220 (orders) *Fax:* 202-337-8314 *E-mail:* info@agbell.org; publications@agbell.org *Web Site:* www.agbell.org, pg 6

Guilfoyle, Virginia, Federal Street Press, 25-13 Old Kings Hwy N, No 277, Darien, CT 06820 *Tel:* 203-852-1280 *Toll Free Tel:* 877-886-2830 *Fax:* 203-852-1389 *E-mail:* info@federalstreetpress.com; sales@federalstreetpress.com; customerservice@federalstreetpress.com; orders@federalstreetpress.com *Web Site:* federalstreetpress.com, pg 76

Guili, Lisa, Educational Insights, 152 W Walnut St, Suite 201, Gardena, CA 90248 *Toll Free Tel:* 800-995-4436 *Toll Free Fax:* 888-892-8731 *E-mail:* cs@educationalinsights.com *Web Site:* www. educationalinsights.com, pg 70

Guinsler, Robert, Sterling Lord Literistic Inc, 115 Broadway, Suite 1602, New York, NY 10006 *Tel:* 212-780-6050 *Fax:* 212-780-6095 *E-mail:* info@sll.com *Web Site:* www.sll.com, pg 504

Guinta, Kimberly, Rutgers University Press, 106 Somerset St, 3rd fl, New Brunswick, NJ 08901 *Tel:* 848-445-7762; 848-445-7761 (sales) *Fax:* 732-745-4935 *E-mail:* sales@rutgersuniversitypress.org *Web Site:* www.rutgersuniversitypress.org, pg 188

Guiod, Suzanne, Bucknell University Press, One Dent Dr, Lewisburg, PA 17837 *Tel:* 570-577-3674 *E-mail:* universitypress@bucknell.edu *Web Site:* www. bucknell.edu/universitypress, pg 42

Guiterman, Carina, Simon & Schuster, 1230 Avenue of the Americas, New York, NY 10020 *Tel:* 212-698-7000 *Toll Free Tel:* 800-223-2348 (cust serv); 800-223-2336 (orders) *Toll Free Fax:* 800-943-9831 (orders) *Web Site:* www.simonandschuster.com, pg 198

Gulick, Lisa, Sunbelt Publications Inc, 1250 Fayette St, El Cajon, CA 92020-1511 *Tel:* 619-258-4911 *Toll Free Tel:* 800-626-6579 (cust serv) *Fax:* 619-258-4916 *E-mail:* service@sunbeltpub.com; info@sunbeltpub.com *Web Site:* sunbeltpublications.com, pg 210

Gulla, Joseph, Alazar Press, 201 Orchard Lane, Carrboro, NC 27510 *Tel:* 919-274-0653 *E-mail:* alazar.press@gmail.com *Web Site:* www.alazar-press.com, pg 447

Gulla, Rosemarie, Alazar Press, 201 Orchard Lane, Carrboro, NC 27510 *Tel:* 919-274-0653 *E-mail:* alazar.press@gmail.com *Web Site:* www.alazar-press.com, pg 447

Gundry, Stanley N, Zondervan, 3900 Sparks Dr, Grand Rapids, MI 49546 *Tel:* 616-698-6900 *Toll Free Tel:* 800-226-1122; 800-727-1309 (retail orders) *Fax:* 616-698-3350 *Toll Free Fax:* 800-698-3256 (retail orders) *Web Site:* www.zondervan.com, pg 248

Gunn, David, Regular Baptist Press, 3715 N Ventura Dr, Arlington Heights, IL 60004 *Tel:* 847-843-1600 *Toll Free Tel:* 800-727-4440 (cust serv) *Fax:* 847-843-3757 *E-mail:* orders@rbpstore.org *Web Site:* regularbaptistpress.org, pg 184

Gunn, James, John W Campbell Memorial Award, University of Kansas, Wescoe Hall, Rm 3001, Dept of English, 1445 Jayhawk Blvd, Lawrence, KS 66045 *Tel:* 785-864-2518 *Fax:* 785-864-1159 *Web Site:* www. sfcenter.ku.edu/campbell.htm, pg 602

Gunn, James, Science Fiction Writers Workshop, University of Kansas, Wescoe Hall, Rm 3001, Dept of English, 1445 Jayhawk Blvd, Lawrence, KS 66045 *Tel:* 785-864-2518 *Fax:* 785-864-1159 *Web Site:* www. sfcenter.ku.edu; www.sfcenter.ku.edu/sfworkshop; www.sfcenter.ku.edu/novel-workshop, pg 578

Gunn, Olivia Noble, The Ibsen Society of America (ISA), c/o Indiana University, Global & Intl Studies Bldg 3111, 355 N Jordan Ave, Bloomington, IN 47405-1105 *Web Site:* www.ibsensociety.org, pg 534

Gunnison, John P, Adventure House, 914 Laredo Rd, Silver Spring, MD 20901 *Tel:* 301-754-1589 *Web Site:* www.adventurehouse.com, pg 5

Gunnison, Toni, University of Wisconsin Press, 728 State St, Suite 443, Madison, WI 53706-1418 *Tel:* 608-263-1110; 608-263-0668 (journal orders) *Toll Free Tel:* 800-621-2736 (book orders) *Fax:* 608-263-1173 *Toll Free Fax:* 800-621-2736 (book orders) *E-mail:* uwiscpress@uwpress.wisc.edu *Web Site:* uwpress.wisc.edu, pg 232

Guo, Janalyn, The University of Utah Press, J Willard Marriott Library, Suite 5400, 295 S 1500 E, Salt Lake City, UT 84112-0860 *Tel:* 801-585-9786 *Fax:* 801-581-3365 *E-mail:* hannah.new@utah.edu *Web Site:* www.uofupress.com, pg 231

Gupta, Ashis, Bayeux Arts Inc, 2403, 510-Sixth Ave SE, Calgary, AB T2G 1L7, Canada *E-mail:* mail@bayeux.com *Web Site:* bayeux.com, pg 416

Gupta, Swapna, Bayeux Arts Inc, 2403, 510-Sixth Ave SE, Calgary, AB T2G 1L7, Canada *E-mail:* mail@bayeux.com *Web Site:* bayeux.com, pg 416

Gurewich, Judith, Other Press, 267 Fifth Ave, 6th fl, New York, NY 10016 *Tel:* 212-414-0054 *Toll Free Tel:* 877-843-6843 *Fax:* 212-414-0939 *E-mail:* editor@otherpress.com; marketing@otherpress.com; publicity@otherpress.com *Web Site:* www.otherpress.com, pg 157

Gurney, James, Blue Mountain Arts Inc, 2905 Wilderness Place, Suite 100, Boulder, CO 80301 *Tel:* 303-449-0536 *Toll Free Tel:* 800-525-0642 *Fax:* 303-417-6472 *Toll Free Fax:* 800-545-8573 *E-mail:* info@sps.com *Web Site:* www.sps.com, pg 36

Gurreri, Wayne, Harry N Abrams Inc, 195 Broadway, 9th fl, New York, NY 10007 *Tel:* 212-206-7715 *Toll Free Tel:* 800-345-1359 *Fax:* 212-519-1210 *E-mail:* abrams@abramsbooks.com *Web Site:* www. abramsbooks.com, pg 3

Gusinde-Duffy, Mick, University of Georgia Press, Main Library, 3rd fl, 320 S Jackson St, Athens, GA 30602 *Fax:* 706-542-2558; 706-542-6770 *Web Site:* www. ugapress.org, pg 227

Gustafson, Lauraine, Classical Academic Press, 515 S 32 St, Camp Hill, PA 17011 *Tel:* 717-730-0711 *Toll Free Tel:* 866-730-0711 *Fax:* 717-730-0721 *Toll Free Fax:* 866-730-0721 *E-mail:* info@ classicalsubjects.com; orders@classicalsubjects.com *Web Site:* classicalacademicpress.com, pg 53

Gutierrez, Morgan, Chronicle Books, 680 Second St, San Francisco, CA 94107 *Tel:* 415-537-4200 *Toll Free Tel:* 800-759-0190 (cust serv) *Fax:* 415-537-4460 *Toll Free Tel:* 800-858-7787 (orders); 800-286-9471 (cust serv) *E-mail:* frontdesk@chroniclebooks.com *Web Site:* www.chroniclebooks.com, pg 52

Gutierrez, Romi, University Press of Florida, 2046 NE Waldo Rd, Suite 2100, Gainesville, FL 32609 *Tel:* 352-392-1351 *Toll Free Tel:* 800-226-3822 (orders only) *Fax:* 352-392-0590 *Toll Free Fax:* 800-680-1955 (orders only) *E-mail:* press@upress.ufl.edu; orders@ upress.ufl.edu *Web Site:* www.upf.com, pg 232

Gutin, Julie, NASW Press, 750 First St NE, Suite 800, Washington, DC 20002 *Tel:* 202-408-8600 *Fax:* 203-336-8312 *E-mail:* press@naswdc.org *Web Site:* www. naswpress.org, pg 145

Gutmajer, Shoshana, Artisan, 225 Varick St, New York, NY 10014-4381 *Tel:* 212-254-5900 *Toll Free Tel:* 800-722-7202 *Fax:* 212-677-6692 *E-mail:* artisaninfo@ artisanbooks.com *Web Site:* www.artisanbooks.com; www.workman.com/artisanbooks, pg 21

Gutman, Cassie, Sourcebooks LLC, 1935 Brookdale Rd, Suite 139, Naperville, IL 60563 *Tel:* 630-961-3900 *Toll Free Tel:* 800-432-7444 *Fax:* 630-961-2168 *E-mail:* info@sourcebooks.com; customersupport@ sourcebooks.com *Web Site:* www.sourcebooks.com, pg 204

Guttman, Joseph, University of Pennsylvania Press, 3905 Spruce St, Philadelphia, PA 19104 *Tel:* 215-898-6261 *Fax:* 215-898-0404 *E-mail:* custserv@pobox.upenn. edu *Web Site:* www.pennpress.org, pg 230

Guttman, Naomi, Hamilton College, English/Creative Writing, English/Creative Writing Dept, 198 College Hill Rd, Clinton, NY 13323 *Tel:* 315-859-4370 *Fax:* 315-859-4390 *Web Site:* www.hamilton.edu, pg 583

Guy, Connor, Perseus Books, 1290 Avenue of the Americas, New York, NY 10104 *Tel:* 212-340-8100 *Toll Free Tel:* 800-343-4499 (cust serv) *Fax:* 212-340-8105 *Web Site:* www.perseusbooks.com, pg 167

Guzman, Daniel, PEN America, 588 Broadway, Suite 303, New York, NY 10012 *Tel:* 212-334-1660 *Fax:* 212-334-2181 *E-mail:* info@pen.org *Web Site:* pen.org, pg 543

Guzman, Martha, Maria Carvainis Agency Inc, Rockefeller Center, 1270 Avenue of the Americas, Suite 2320, New York, NY 10020 *Tel:* 212-245-6365 *Fax:* 212-245-7196 *E-mail:* mca@mariacarvainisagency.com *Web Site:* mariacarvainisagency.com, pg 479

Guzman, Robert, Penguin Random House Audio Publishing, 1745 Broadway, New York, NY 10019 *E-mail:* audio@penguinrandomhouse.com *Web Site:* www.penguinrandomhouseaudio.com, pg 164

Guzzardo, Lindsay, The Editorial Department LLC, 8476 E Speedway Blvd, Suite 202, Tucson, AZ 85710 *Tel:* 520-546-9992 *E-mail:* admin@ editorialdepartment.com *Web Site:* www. editorialdepartment.com, pg 463

Gwiazda, Ron, Abrams Artists Agency, 275 Seventh Ave, 26th fl, New York, NY 10001 *Tel:* 646-486-4600 *Fax:* 646-486-0100 *E-mail:* literary@abramsartny.com *Web Site:* www.abramsartists.com, pg 473

Gyllenhaal, Rebecca, Quirk Books, 215 Church St, Philadelphia, PA 19106 *Tel:* 215-627-3581 *Fax:* 215-627-5220 *E-mail:* general@quirkbooks.com *Web Site:* www.quirkbooks.com, pg 179

Ha, Paul C, MIT List Visual Arts Center, MIT E 15-109, 20 Ames St, Cambridge, MA 02139 *Tel:* 617-253-4400; 617-253-4680 *E-mail:* listinfo@mit.edu *Web Site:* listart.mit.edu, pg 141

Haas, Linda, StarGroup International Inc, 1194 Old Dixie Hwy, Suite 201, West Palm Beach, FL 33413 *Tel:* 561-547-0667 *Fax:* 561-843-8530 *E-mail:* info@stargroupinternational.com *Web Site:* stargroupinternational.com, pg 207

Haas, Maggie, Chronicle Books, 680 Second St, San Francisco, CA 94107 *Tel:* 415-537-4200 *Toll Free Tel:* 800-759-0190 (cust serv) *Fax:* 415-537-4460 *Toll Free Tel:* 800-858-7787 (orders); 800-286-9471 (cust serv) *E-mail:* frontdesk@chroniclebooks.com *Web Site:* www.chroniclebooks.com, pg 52

Haase, H W, Quintessence Publishing Co Inc, 411 N Raddant Rd, Batavia, IL 60510 *Tel:* 630-736-3600 *Toll Free Tel:* 800-621-0387 *Fax:* 630-736-3633 *E-mail:* contact@quintbook.com; service@quintbook. com *Web Site:* www.quintpub.com, pg 179

Haav, Julia, Princeton University Press, 41 William St, Princeton, NJ 08540-5237 *Tel:* 609-258-4900 *Fax:* 609-258-6305 *Web Site:* press.princeton.edu, pg 174

Habegger, Larry, Travelers' Tales, 2320 Bowdoin St, Palo Alto, CA 94306 *Tel:* 650-462-2110 *E-mail:* ttales@travelerstales.com *Web Site:* travelerstales.com, pg 220

Hackenberg, Rev Rachel, The Pilgrim Press/United Church Press, 700 Prospect Ave, Cleveland, OH 44115-1100 *Tel:* 216-736-2100 *Toll Free Tel:* 800-537-3394 (orders) *E-mail:* permissions@thepilgrimpress. com; store@ucc.org (orders) *Web Site:* www. thepilgrimpress.com, pg 170

Hackett, Ann, University of New Orleans Press, 2000 Lakeshore Dr, New Orleans, LA 70148 *Tel:* 504-280-7457 *E-mail:* unopress@uno.edu *Web Site:* www.uno. edu/unopress, pg 232

Hackett, Danielle, Arkham House Publishers Inc, PO Box 546, Sauk City, WI 53583 *Tel:* 608-643-4500 *Fax:* 608-643-5043 *E-mail:* sales@arkhamhouse.com *Web Site:* www.arkhamhouse.com, pg 20

Hackinson, Frank J, FJH Music Co Inc, 2525 Davie Rd, Suite 360, Fort Lauderdale, FL 33317-7424 *Tel:* 954-382-6061 *Toll Free Tel:* 800-262-8744 *Fax:* 954-382-3073 *E-mail:* custserv@fjhmusic.com; sales@fjhmusic. com *Web Site:* www.fjhmusic.com, pg 79

Hackinson, Kevin, FJH Music Co Inc, 2525 Davie Rd, Suite 360, Fort Lauderdale, FL 33317-7424 *Tel:* 954-382-6061 *Toll Free Tel:* 800-262-8744 *Fax:* 954-382-3073 *E-mail:* custserv@fjhmusic.com; sales@fjhmusic. com *Web Site:* www.fjhmusic.com, pg 79

Hackinson, Kyle, FJH Music Co Inc, 2525 Davie Rd, Suite 360, Fort Lauderdale, FL 33317-7424 *Tel:* 954-382-6061 *Toll Free Tel:* 800-262-8744 *Fax:* 954-382-3073 *E-mail:* custserv@fjhmusic.com; sales@fjhmusic. com *Web Site:* www.fjhmusic.com, pg 79

Haddix, Doug, Investigative Reporters & Editors, Missouri School of Journalism, 141 Neff Annex, Columbia, MO 65211 *Tel:* 573-882-2042 *Fax:* 573-882-5431 *E-mail:* info@ire.org *Web Site:* www.ire.org, pg 536

Hades, Brian, EDGE Science Fiction & Fantasy Publishing Inc, PO Box 1714, Calgary, AB T2P 2L7, Canada *Tel:* 403-254-0160 *Fax:* 403-254-0456 *E-mail:* admin@hadespublications.com *Web Site:* www.edgewebsite.com, pg 422

Hadley, Candida, Fernwood Publishing, 32 Oceanvista Lane, Black Point, NS B0J 1B0, Canada *Tel:* 902-857-1388 *Fax:* 902-857-1328 *E-mail:* info@fernpub.ca; roseway@fernpub.ca *Web Site:* fernwoodpublishing.ca, pg 426

Hagaman, Jane, Red Wheel/Weiser, 65 Parker St, Suite 7, Newburyport, MA 01950 *Tel:* 978-465-0504 *Toll Free Tel:* 800-423-7087 (orders) *Fax:* 978-465-0243 *E-mail:* info@rwwbooks.com *Web Site:* www. redwheelweiser.com, pg 183

Hagan, Lisa, Lisa Hagan Literary, 110 Martin Dr, Bracey, VA 23919 *Tel:* 434-636-4138 *E-mail:* LisaHaganLiterary@yahoo.com *Web Site:* www.publishersmarketplace.com/members/ LisaHagan, pg 487

Hagan, Peter, Dramatists Play Service Inc, 440 Park Ave S, New York, NY 10016 *Tel:* 212-683-8960 *Fax:* 212-213-1539 *E-mail:* postmaster@dramatists. com; orders@dramatists.com; publications@dramatists. com *Web Site:* www.dramatists.com, pg 67

Hagenberg, Mark, Perfection Learning, 1000 N Second Ave, Logan, IA 51546 *Tel:* 712-644-2831 *Toll Free Tel:* 800-831-4190 *Toll Free Fax:* 800-543-2745 *E-mail:* orders@perfectionlearning.com *Web Site:* perfectionlearning.com, pg 167

Hager, Betsy, Dr Tony Ryan Book Award, 2469 Ironworks Pike, Lexington, KY 40511 *Tel:* 859-455-9222 *Web Site:* www.castletonlyons.com, pg 663

Haggar, Darren, The Penguin Press, 375 Hudson St, New York, NY 10014 *Web Site:* thepenguinpress.com, pg 164

Haggen, Michael, Scholastic Education, 557 Broadway, New York, NY 10012 *Tel:* 212-343-6100 *Fax:* 212-343-6189 *Web Site:* www.scholastic.com, pg 194

Hagman, Lorri, University of Washington Press, 4333 Brooklyn Ave NE, Seattle, WA 98105-9570 *Tel:* 206-543-4050 *Toll Free Tel:* 800-537-5487 (orders) *Fax:* 206-543-3932; 410-516-6998 (orders) *E-mail:* uwapress@uw.edu *Web Site:* uwapress.uw.edu, pg 232

Hahn, Dr H George, Towson University Prize for Literature, English Dept, 8000 York Rd, Towson, MD 21252 *Tel:* 410-704-2000 *Fax:* 410-704-3999 *Web Site:* www.towson.edu/english, pg 673

Haines, Cameron, Arcadia Publishing Inc, 420 Wando Park Blvd, Mount Pleasant, SC 29464 *Tel:* 843-853-2070 *Toll Free Tel:* 888-313-2665 (orders only) *Fax:* 843-853-0044 *E-mail:* sales@arcadiapublishing. com *Web Site:* www.arcadiapublishing.com, pg 19

Haire, Timothy, Yale University Press, 302 Temple St, New Haven, CT 06511-8909 *Tel:* 203-432-0960; 203-432-0966 (sales); 401-531-2800 (cust serv) *Toll Free Tel:* 800-405-1619 (cust serv) *Fax:* 203-432-0948; 203-432-8485 (sales); 401-531-2801 (cust serv) *Toll Free Fax:* 800-406-9145 (cust serv) *E-mail:* sales. press@yale.edu (sales); customer.care@triliteral.org (cust serv) *Web Site:* www.yalebooks.com; yalepress. yale.edu/yupbooks, pg 246

Hajnoczky, Helen, University of Calgary Press, 2500 University Dr NW, Calgary, AB T2N 1N4, Canada *Tel:* 403-220-7578 *Fax:* 403-282-0085 *E-mail:* ucpress@ucalgary.ca *Web Site:* press.ucalgary. ca, pg 443

Hake, Jesse, Classical Academic Press, 515 S 32 St, Camp Hill, PA 17011 *Tel:* 717-730-0711 *Toll Free Tel:* 866-730-0711 *Fax:* 717-730-0721 *Toll Free Fax:* 866-730-0721 *E-mail:* info@ classicalsubjects.com; orders@classicalsubjects.com *Web Site:* classicalacademicpress.com, pg 53

Haldoupis, Nicole, Thistledown Press, 410 Second Ave, Saskatoon, SK S7K 2C3, Canada *Tel:* 306-244-1722 *Fax:* 306-244-1762 *E-mail:* tdpress@thistledownpress. com; editorial@thistledownpress.com; marketing@ thistledownpress.com *Web Site:* www.thistledownpress. com, pg 441

Hale, Charles, The MIT Press, One Rogers St, Cambridge, MA 02142 *Tel:* 617-253-5255 *Toll Free Tel:* 800-405-1619 (orders) *Fax:* 617-258-6779; 617-577-1545 (orders) *Web Site:* mitpress.mit.edu, pg 141

Hales, Katelyn, Robin Straus Agency Inc, 229 E 79 St, Suite 5A, New York, NY 10075 *Tel:* 212-472-3282 *Fax:* 212-472-3833 *E-mail:* info@robinstrausagency. com *Web Site:* www.robinstrausagency.com, pg 505

Hales, Katelyn, The Wallace Literary Agency, 229 E 79 St, No 5A, New York, NY 10075 *Tel:* 212-472-3282 *Fax:* 212-472-3833 *E-mail:* info@ wallaceliteraryagency.com, pg 507

Haley, Elma, Arbordale Publishing, 612 Johnnie Dodds Blvd, Suite A2, Mount Pleasant, SC 29464 *Tel:* 843-971-6722 *Toll Free Tel:* 877-243-3457 *Fax:* 843-216-3804 *E-mail:* info@arbordalepublishing.com *Web Site:* www.arbordalepublishing.com, pg 19

Haley, Jolene, Marsal Lyon Literary Agency LLC, 665 San Rodolfo Dr, Suite 124, PMB 121, Solana Beach, CA 92075 Tel: 760-814-8507 Web Site: www. marsallyonliteraryagency.com, pg 494

Hall, Andrea, Albert Whitman & Co, 250 S Northwest Hwy, Suite 320, Park Ridge, IL 60068 Tel: 847-232-2800 Toll Free Tel: 800-255-7675 Fax: 847-581-0039 E-mail: mail@albertwhitman.com Web Site: www. albertwhitman.com, pg 6

Hall, Anna, Perseus Books, 1290 Avenue of the Americas, New York, NY 10104 Tel: 212-340-8100 Toll Free Tel: 800-343-4499 (cust serv) Fax: 212-340-8105 Web Site: www.perseusbooks.com, pg 168

Hall, Eric, The Rough Notes Co Inc, 11690 Technology Dr, Carmel, IN 46032-5600 Tel: 317-582-1600 Toll Free Tel: 800-428-4384 (cust serv) Fax: 317-816-1000 Toll Free Fax: 800-321-1909 E-mail: rnc@roughnotes. com Web Site: www.roughnotes.com, pg 187

Hall, Heather, Sourcebooks LLC, 1935 Brookdale Rd, Suite 139, Naperville, IL 60563 Tel: 630-961-3900 Toll Free Tel: 800-432-7444 Fax: 630-961-2168 E-mail: info@sourcebooks.com; customersupport@ sourcebooks.com Web Site: www.sourcebooks.com, pg 204

Hall, Kit, Financial Executives Research Foundation Inc (FERF), West Tower, 7th fl, 1250 Headquarters Plaza, Morristown, NJ 07960-6837 Tel: 973-765-1000 Fax: 973-765-1018 Web Site: www.financialexecutives. org, pg 77

Hall, Laurie, US Government Publishing Office (GPO), Superintendent of Documents, 732 N Capitol St NW, Washington, DC 20401 Tel: 202-512-1800 Toll Free Tel: 866-512-1800 (orders) Fax: 202-512-1998 E-mail: contactcenter@gpo.gov Web Site: www.gpo. gov; bookstore.gpo.gov (sales), pg 235

Hall, Lindsey, Tom Doherty Associates, LLC, 120 Broadway, New York, NY 10271 Tel: 646-307-5511 Toll Free Tel: 800-455-0340 Web Site: us.macmillan. com/torforge, pg 66

Hall, Marie, Fordham University Press, Joseph A Martino Hall, 45 Columbus Ave, New York, NY 10023 Fax: 347-842-3083 Web Site: www. fordhampress.com, pg 79

Hall, Megan, Athabasca University Press, Edmonton Learning Ctr, Peace Hills Trust Tower, 1200, 10011-109 St, Edmonton, AB T5J 3S8, Canada Tel: 780-497-3412 Fax: 780-421-3298 E-mail: aupress@athabascau. ca Web Site: www.aupress.ca, pg 415

Hall, Nancy, American Book Producers Association (ABPA), 31 W Eighth St, 2nd fl, New York, NY 10011 Tel: 212-675-1363 Fax: 212-675-1364 E-mail: office@abpaonline.org Web Site: www. abpaonline.org, pg 522

Hall, Mr Sidney Jr, Hobblebush Books, 17-A Old Milford Rd, Brookline, NH 03033 Tel: 603-672-4317 Fax: 603-672-4317 E-mail: info@hobblebush.com Web Site: www.hobblebush.com, pg 100

Hall, Tanya, Greenleaf Book Group LLC, 3 Park Place, 4005 Banister Lane, Suite B, Austin, TX 78704 Tel: 512-891-6100 Fax: 512-891-6150 E-mail: contact@greenleafbookgroup.com Web Site: www.greenleafbookgroup.com, pg 89

Hall, Tina, Hamilton College, English/Creative Writing, English/Creative Writing Dept, 198 College Hill Rd, Clinton, NY 13323 Tel: 315-859-4370 Fax: 315-859-4390 Web Site: www.hamilton.edu, pg 583

Hall, Tracie D, The American Library Association (ALA), 225 N Michigan Ave, Suite 1300, Chicago, IL 60601 Tel: 312-944-6780 Toll Free Tel: 800-545-2433 Fax: 312-280-5275 E-mail: editionsmarketing@ala.org Web Site: www.alastore.ala.org, pg 12

Hall, Tracie D, The American Library Association (ALA), 225 N Michigan Ave, Suite 1300, Chicago, IL 60601 Tel: 312-944-6780; 312-280-4299 (memb & cust serv) Toll Free Tel: 800-545-2433 Fax: 312-440-9374 E-mail: ala@ala.org; customerservice@ala.org Web Site: www.ala.org, pg 523

Hallak, Natalie, Harlequin Enterprises Ltd, 195 Broadway, 24th fl, New York, NY 10007 Tel: 212-207-7000 Toll Free Tel: 888-432-4879 E-mail: customerservice@harlequin.com Web Site: www.harlequin.com, pg 93

Haller, Jennifer, Penguin Young Readers Group, 345 Hudson St, New York, NY 10014 Tel: 212-366-2000; 212-414-3553 Fax: 212-414-3340 Web Site: www. penguin.com/children, pg 165

Hallett, Marta, Glitterati Editions, 311 W 43 St, 12th fl, New York, NY 10036 Tel: 646-584-6382 Fax: 646-607-4433 E-mail: media@glitteratieditions.com Web Site: glitteratieditions.com, pg 86

Halley, Brian, University of Massachusetts Press, East Experiment Station, 671 N Pleasant St, Amherst, MA 01003 Tel: 413-545-2217 Fax: 413-545-1226 E-mail: info@umpress.umass.edu Web Site: www. umass.edu/umpress, pg 228

Halliday, Dorothea, Yale University Press, 302 Temple St, New Haven, CT 06511-8909 Tel: 203-432-0960; 203-432-0966 (sales); 401-531-2800 (cust serv) Toll Free Tel: 800-405-1619 (cust serv) Fax: 203-432-0948; 203-432-8485 (sales); 401-531-2801 (cust serv) Toll Free Fax: 800-406-9145 (cust serv) E-mail: sales. press@yale.edu (sales); customer.care@triliteral.org (cust serv) Web Site: www.yalebooks.com; yalepress. yale.edu/yupbooks, pg 246

Hallinger, Linda Herr, Herr's Indexing Service, 76-340 Kealoha St, Kailua Kona, HI 96740 Tel: 808-365-4348 E-mail: linda@herrsindexing.com Web Site: www. herrsindexing.com, pg 465

Halpern, Daniel, HarperCollins General Books Group, 195 Broadway, New York, NY 10007 Tel: 212-207-7000 Web Site: www.harpercollins.com, pg 93

Halpern, Daniel, National Poetry Series Open Competition, 57 Mountain Ave, Princeton, NJ 08540 Tel: 609-430-0999 Fax: 609-430-9933 Web Site: nationalpoetryseries.org, pg 645

Halpern, Hugh Nathanial, US Government Publishing Office (GPO), Superintendent of Documents, 732 N Capitol St NW, Washington, DC 20401 Tel: 202-512-1800 Toll Free Tel: 866-512-1800 (orders) Fax: 202-512-1998 E-mail: contactcenter@gpo.gov Web Site: www.gpo.gov; bookstore.gpo.gov (sales), pg 235

Halpern, Ilsa PhD, LearningExpress, 224 W 29 St, 3rd fl, New York, NY 10001 Toll Free Tel: 800-295-9556 (ext 2) Web Site: learningexpresshub.com, pg 121

Halsey, Jennifer, International Society of Automation (ISA), 67 T W Alexander Dr, Research Triangle Park, NC 27709-0185 Tel: 919-549-8411 Fax: 919-549-8288 E-mail: info@isa.org Web Site: www.isa.org, pg 112

Halverson, Pete, University Press of Mississippi, 3825 Ridgewood Rd, Jackson, MS 39211-6492 Tel: 601-432-6205 Toll Free Tel: 800-737-7788 (orders & cust serv) Fax: 601-432-6217 E-mail: press@mississippi. edu Web Site: www.upress.state.ms.us, pg 233

Ham, Christina, Many Voices Fellowships, 2301 Franklin Ave E, Minneapolis, MN 55406-1099 Tel: 612-332-7481 Fax: 612-332-6037 E-mail: info@pwcenter.org Web Site: www.pwcenter.org, pg 638

Hamblen, Carol, Johns Hopkins University Press, 2715 N Charles St, Baltimore, MD 21218-4363 Tel: 410-516-6900; 410-516-6987 (journal orders outside US & CN) Toll Free Tel: 800-537-5487 (book orders & cust serv); 800-548-1784 (journal orders) Fax: 410-516-6968; 410-516-3866 (journal orders); 410-516-6998 (orders) E-mail: hfscustserv@press.jhu.edu (cust serv); jrnlcirc@press.jhu.edu (journal orders) Web Site: www.press.jhu.edu; muse.jhu.edu, pg 114

Hambrick, Elizabeth, Chronicle Books, 680 Second St, San Francisco, CA 94107 Tel: 415-537-4200 Toll Free Tel: 800-759-0190 (cust serv) Fax: 415-537-4460 Toll Free Fax: 800-858-7787 (orders); 800-286-9471 (cust serv) E-mail: frontdesk@chroniclebooks.com Web Site: www.chroniclebooks.com, pg 52

Hamel, Gillian, Omnidawn Publishing, 2200 Adeline St, Suite 150, Oakland, CA 94607 Tel: 510-237-5472 Toll Free Fax: 800-792-4957 Fax: 510-232-8525 E-mail: manager@omnidawn.com Web Site: omnidawn.com, pg 155

Hames, Charles, New York University Press, 838 Broadway, 3rd fl, New York, NY 10003-4812 Tel: 212-998-2575 (edit) Toll Free Tel: 800-996-6987 (orders) Fax: 212-995-4798 (orders) E-mail: nyupressinfo@nyu.edu; orders@nyupress.org Web Site: www.nyupress.org, pg 150

Hamilton, Bonni, Hampton Roads Publishing, 65 Parker St, Suite 7, Newburyport, MA 01950-4600 Tel: 978-465-0504 Toll Free Tel: 800-423-7087 (orders) Fax: 978-465-0243 Toll Free Fax: 877-337-3309 E-mail: info@rwwbooks.com Web Site: redwheelweiser.com, pg 92

Hamilton, Bonni, Red Wheel/Weiser, 65 Parker St, Suite 7, Newburyport, MA 01950 Tel: 978-465-0504 Toll Free Tel: 800-423-7087 (orders) Fax: 978-465-0243 E-mail: info@rwwbooks.com Web Site: www. redwheelweiser.com, pg 183

Hamilton, Bridget, National Geographic Books, 1145 17 St NW, Washington, DC 20036-4688 Tel: 202-857-7000 Toll Free Tel: 877-866-6486 E-mail: ngbooks@ cdsfulfillment.com Web Site: www.nationalgeographic. com/books/; ngbooks.buysub.com, pg 146

Hamilton, Carol, AAAI Press, 2275 E Bayshore Rd, Suite 160, Palo Alto, CA 94303 Tel: 650-328-3123 Fax: 650-321-4457 E-mail: publications20@aaai.org Web Site: www.aaai.org/Press/press.php, pg 1

Hamilton, Cindy, HarperCollins Children's Books, 195 Broadway, New York, NY 10007 Tel: 212-207-7000 Web Site: www.harpercollins.com/childrens, pg 93

Hamilton, David M, AAAI Press, 2275 E Bayshore Rd, Suite 160, Palo Alto, CA 94303 Tel: 650-328-3123 Fax: 650-321-4457 E-mail: publications20@aaai.org Web Site: www.aaai.org/Press/press.php, pg 1

Hamilton, Emily, University of Minnesota Press, 111 Third Ave S, Suite 290, Minneapolis, MN 55401-2520 Tel: 612-301-1990 Fax: 612-301-1980 E-mail: ump@ umn.edu Web Site: www.upress.umn.edu, pg 228

Hamilton, Jessica, Reed Environmental Writing Award, 201 W Main St, Suite 14, Charlottesville, VA 22902 Tel: 434-977-4090 Fax: 434-977-1483 Web Site: www. southernenvironment.org, pg 661

Hamilton, Julie, Insight Editions, 800 "A" St, San Rafael, CA 94901 Tel: 415-526-1370 Toll Free Tel: 800-809-3792 Toll Free Fax: 866-509-0515 E-mail: info@ insighteditions.com; marketing@insighteditions.com Web Site: insighteditions.com, pg 109

Hamilton, Julie, Mandala Earth, 800 "A" St, San Rafael, CA 94901 Tel: 415-526-1370 Toll Free Fax: 866-509-0515 E-mail: info@mandalapublishing.com Web Site: www.mandalaeartheditions.com, pg 131

Hamilton, Liz, Northwestern University Press, 629 Noyes St, Evanston, IL 60208-4210 Tel: 847-491-2046 Toll Free Tel: 800-621-2736 (orders only) Fax: 847-491-8150 E-mail: nupress@northwestern.edu Web Site: www.nupress.northwestern.edu, pg 152

Hamilton, Michaela, Kensington Publishing Corp, 119 W 40 St, New York, NY 10018 Tel: 212-407-1500 Toll Free Tel: 800-221-2647 Fax: 212-935-0699 Web Site: www.kensingtonbooks.com, pg 116

Hamilton, Patricia, Park Place Publications, 591 Lighthouse Ave, Suite 10, Pacific Grove, CA 93950 Tel: 831-649-6640 E-mail: publishingbiz@sbcglobal. net Web Site: www.parkplacepublications.com, pg 161

Hamilton, Richard, XML Press, 24310 Moulton Pkwy, Suite O-175, Laguna Hills, CA 92637 Tel: 970-231-3624 E-mail: publisher@xmlpress.net Web Site: xmlpress.net, pg 246

Hamlin, Faith, Sanford J Greenburger Associates Inc, 55 Fifth Ave, New York, NY 10003 Tel: 212-206-5600 Fax: 212-463-8718 Web Site: greenburger.com; www.sjga.com, pg 487

Hamlin, Kairi, Tanglewood Publishing, 1060 N Capitol Ave, Suite E-395, Indianapolis, IN 46204 Tel: 812-877-9488 Toll Free Tel: 800-788-3123 (orders) E-mail: info@tanglewoodbooks.com; orders@tanglewoodbooks.com Web Site: www. tanglewoodbooks.com, pg 212

Hamm, Kara, Willi Paul Adams Award, 112 N Bryan Ave, Bloomington, IN 47408-4141 *Tel:* 812-855-7311 *E-mail:* oah@oah.org *Web Site:* www.oah.org/awards, pg 590

Hamm, Kara, Ray Allen Billington Prize, 112 N Bryan Ave, Bloomington, IN 47408-4141 *Tel:* 812-855-7311 *E-mail:* oah@oah.org *Web Site:* www.oah.org/awards, pg 598

Hamm, Kara, Brinkley-Stephenson Award, 112 N Bryan Ave, Bloomington, IN 47408-4141 *Tel:* 812-855-7311 *E-mail:* oah@oah.org *Web Site:* www.oah.org/awards, pg 601

Hamm, Kara, Avery O Craven Award, 112 N Bryan Ave, Bloomington, IN 47408-4141 *Tel:* 812-855-7311 *E-mail:* oah@oah.org *Web Site:* www.oah.org/awards, pg 607

Hamm, Kara, Merle Curti Intellectual History Award, 112 N Bryan Ave, Bloomington, IN 47408-4141 *Tel:* 812-855-7311 *E-mail:* oah@oah.org *Web Site:* www.oah.org/awards, pg 608

Hamm, Kara, Merle Curti Social History Award, 112 N Bryan Ave, Bloomington, IN 47408-4141 *Tel:* 812-855-7311 *E-mail:* oah@oah.org *Web Site:* www.oah.org/awards, pg 608

Hamm, Kara, Ellis W Hawley Prize, 112 N Bryan Ave, Bloomington, IN 47408-4141 *Tel:* 812-855-7311 *E-mail:* oah@oah.org *Web Site:* www.oah.org/awards, pg 622

Hamm, Kara, Darlene Clark Hine Award, 112 N Bryan Ave, Bloomington, IN 47408-4141 *Tel:* 812-855-7311 *E-mail:* oah@oah.org *Web Site:* www.oah.org/awards, pg 624

Hamm, Kara, Richard W Leopold Prize, 112 N Bryan Ave, Bloomington, IN 47408-4141 *Tel:* 812-855-7311 *E-mail:* oah@oah.org *Web Site:* www.oah.org/awards, pg 632

Hamm, Kara, Lawrence W Levine Award, 112 N Bryan Ave, Bloomington, IN 47408-4141 *Tel:* 812-855-7311 *E-mail:* oah@oah.org *Web Site:* www.oah.org/awards, pg 633

Hamm, Kara, Liberty Legacy Foundation Award, 112 N Bryan Ave, Bloomington, IN 47408-4141 *Tel:* 812-855-7311 *E-mail:* oah@oah.org *Web Site:* www.oah.org/awards, pg 633

Hamm, Kara, David Montgomery Award, 112 N Bryan Ave, Bloomington, IN 47408-4141 *Tel:* 812-855-7311 *E-mail:* oah@oah.org *Web Site:* www.oah.org/awards, pg 642

Hamm, Kara, Mary Nickliss Prize in US Women's +/or Gender History, 112 N Bryan Ave, Bloomington, IN 47408-4141 *Tel:* 812-855-7311 *E-mail:* oah@oah.org *Web Site:* www.oah.org/awards, pg 648

Hamm, Kara, James A Rawley Prize, 112 N Bryan Ave, Bloomington, IN 47408-4141 *Tel:* 812-855-7311 *E-mail:* oah@oah.org *Web Site:* www.oah.org/awards, pg 661

Hamm, Kara, David Thelen Award, 112 N Bryan Ave, Bloomington, IN 47408-4141 *Tel:* 812-855-7311 *E-mail:* oah@oah.org *Web Site:* www.oah.org/awards, pg 672

Hamm, Kara, Frederick Jackson Turner Award, 112 N Bryan Ave, Bloomington, IN 47408-4141 *Tel:* 812-855-7311 *E-mail:* oah@oah.org *Web Site:* www.oah.org/awards, pg 674

Hammack, Brice, Rutgers University Press, 106 Somerset St, 3rd fl, New Brunswick, NJ 08901 *Tel:* 848-445-7762; 848-445-7761 (sales) *Fax:* 732-745-4935 *E-mail:* sales@rutgersuniversitypress.org *Web Site:* www.rutgersuniversitypress.org, pg 188

Hammer, Daniel, The Historic New Orleans Collection, 533 Royal St, New Orleans, LA 70130 *Tel:* 504-523-4662 *Fax:* 504-598-7108 *E-mail:* wrc@hnoc.org *Web Site:* www.hnoc.org, pg 100

Hammer, Jennifer, New York University Press, 838 Broadway, 3rd fl, New York, NY 10003-4812 *Tel:* 212-998-2575 (edit) *Toll Free Tel:* 800-996-6987 (orders) *Fax:* 212-995-4798 (orders) *E-mail:* nyupressinfo@nyu.edu; orders@nyupress.org *Web Site:* www.nyupress.org, pg 150

Hammond, Michelle, William Allen White Children's Book Awards, One Kellogg Circle, Emporia, KS 66801-5092 *Tel:* 620-341-5208 *Toll Free Tel:* 877-613-7323 *Fax:* 620-341-6208 *E-mail:* wawbookaward@emporia.edu *Web Site:* waw.emporia.edu/libsv/wawbookaward, pg 677

Hamon, Donna L, Triad Publishing Co, PO Box 13355, Gainesville, FL 32604 *Fax:* 304-727-9345 *Toll Free Fax:* 800-854-4947 *E-mail:* orders@triadpublishing.com *Web Site:* www.triadpublishing.com, pg 220

Hampel, Matt, Bancroft Prizes, 517 Butler Library, Mail Code 1101, 535 W 114 St, New York, NY 10027 *Tel:* 212-854-4746 *Fax:* 212-854-9099 *Web Site:* www.columbia.edu/about/awards/bancroft.html, pg 595

Hamre, John J, The CSIS Press, 1616 Rhode Island Ave NW, Washington, DC 20036 *Tel:* 202-887-0200 *Fax:* 202-775-3199 *E-mail:* books@csis.org *Web Site:* www.csis.org, pg 61

Hamrick, Dave, University of Texas Press, 3001 Lake Austin Blvd, 2.200, Austin, TX 78703 *Tel:* 512-471-7233 *Fax:* 512-232-7178 *E-mail:* utpress@uts.cc.utexas.edu; info@utpress.utexas.edu *Web Site:* utpress.utexas.edu, pg 216

Hamstra, Paul, Evergreen Pacific Publishing Ltd, 4204 Russell Rd, Suite M, Mukilteo, WA 98275-5424 *Tel:* 425-493-1451 *Fax:* 425-493-1453 *E-mail:* sales@evergreenpacific.com *Web Site:* www.evergreenpacific.com, pg 74

Hamza, Dr Mohamed H, ACTA Press, 200-4040 Bowness Rd NW, Calgary, AB T3B 3R7, Canada *Tel:* 403-288-1195 *Fax:* 403-247-6851 *E-mail:* journals@actapress.com; publish@actapress.com; sales@actapress.com *Web Site:* www.actapress.com, pg 415

Hanas, Jim, HarperCollins General Books Group, 195 Broadway, New York, NY 10007 *Tel:* 212-207-7000 *Web Site:* www.harpercollins.com, pg 93

Hanas, Jim, HarperCollins Publishers, 195 Broadway, New York, NY 10007 *Tel:* 212-207-7000 *Fax:* 212-207-7145 *Web Site:* www.harpercollins.com, pg 94

Hancock, David, Hancock House Publishers Ltd, 19313 Zero Ave, Surrey, BC V3S 9R9, Canada *Tel:* 604-538-1114 *Toll Free Tel:* 800-938-1114 *Fax:* 604-538-2262 *Toll Free Fax:* 800-983-2262 *E-mail:* sales@hancockhouse.com; info@hancockhouse.com *Web Site:* www.hancockhouse.com, pg 428

Hancock, David L, Morgan James Publishing, 5 Penn Plaza, 23rd fl, New York, NY 10001 *Tel:* 212-655-5470 *Fax:* 516-908-4496 *E-mail:* support@morganjamespublishing.com *Web Site:* www.morganjamespublishing.com, pg 143

Handberg, Ryan, THE Learning Connection®, 4100 Silverstar Rd, Suite D, Orlando, FL 32808 *Toll Free Tel:* 800-218-8489 *Fax:* 407-292-2123 *E-mail:* tlc@tlconnection.com *Web Site:* www.tlconnection.com, pg 121

Handelman, Jessica, Houghton Mifflin Harcourt Trade & Reference Division, 125 High St, Boston, MA 02110 *Tel:* 617-351-5000 *Web Site:* www.hmhco.com, pg 104

Hanes, Peter, Flanker Press Ltd, 1243 Kenmount Rd, Unit 1, Paradise, NL A1L 0V8, Canada *Tel:* 709-739-4477 *Toll Free Tel:* 866-739-4420 *Fax:* 709-739-4420 *E-mail:* info@flankerpress.com; sales@flankerpress.com *Web Site:* www.flankerpress.com, pg 427

Hanesalo, Bruce A, Military Info Publishing, PO Box 41211, Plymouth, MN 55442 *Tel:* 763-533-8627 *E-mail:* publisher@military-info.com *Web Site:* www.military-info.com, pg 140

Haney, Scott, Chronicle Books, 680 Second St, San Francisco, CA 94107 *Tel:* 415-537-4200 *Toll Free Tel:* 800-759-0190 (cust serv) *Fax:* 415-537-4460 *Toll Free Fax:* 800-858-7787 (orders); 800-286-9471 (cust serv) *E-mail:* frontdesk@chroniclebooks.com *Web Site:* www.chroniclebooks.com, pg 51

Hanger, Nancy C, Windhaven®, 466 Rte 10, Orford, NH 03777 *Tel:* 603-512-9251 (cell) *Web Site:* www.windhavenpress.com, pg 471

Hanjian, Cassie, DeFiore and Company Literary Management Inc, 47 E 19 St, 3rd fl, New York, NY 10003 *Tel:* 212-925-7744 *Fax:* 212-925-9803 *E-mail:* info@defliterary.com; submissions@defliterary.com *Web Site:* www.defliterary.com, pg 481

Hankshaw, Hank, Two Thousand Three Associates, 135 Chilean Ave, Palm Beach, FL 33480 *Tel:* 386-690-2503 *E-mail:* ttta1@att.net *Web Site:* www.twothousandthree.com, pg 223

Hanley, Jordan, Tom Doherty Associates, LLC, 120 Broadway, New York, NY 10271 *Tel:* 646-307-5511 *Toll Free Tel:* 800-455-0340 *Web Site:* us.macmillan.com/torforge, pg 66

Hanna, Bill, Acacia House Publishing Services Ltd, 51 Chestnut Ave, Brantford, ON N3T 4C3, Canada *Tel:* 519-752-0978 *Fax:* 519-752-0978, pg 473

Hannan, Jack, McGill-Queen's University Press, 1010 Sherbrooke W, Suite 1720, Montreal, QC H3A 2R7, Canada *Tel:* 514-398-3750 *Fax:* 514-398-4333 *E-mail:* mqup@mqup.ca *Web Site:* www.mqup.ca, pg 433

Hansard, Patrick, American Psychiatric Association Publishing, 800 Maine Ave SW, Suite 900, Washington, DC 20024 *Tel:* 202-459-9722 *Toll Free Tel:* 800-368-5777 *Fax:* 202-403-3094 *E-mail:* appi@psych.org *Web Site:* www.appi.org; www.psychiatryonline.org, pg 13

Hansen, Glenn J, BPA Worldwide, 100 Beard Sawmill Rd, 6th fl, Shelton, CT 06484 *Tel:* 203-447-2800 *Fax:* 203-447-2900 *E-mail:* info@bpaww.com *Web Site:* www.bpaww.com, pg 529

Hansen, Heather, Princeton University Press, 41 William St, Princeton, NJ 08540-5237 *Tel:* 609-258-4900 *Fax:* 609-258-6305 *Web Site:* press.princeton.edu, pg 174

Hansen, Jill, ABDO Publishing Co Inc, 8000 W 78 St, Suite 310, Edina, MN 55439 *Tel:* 952-698-2403 *Toll Free Tel:* 800-800-1312 *Fax:* 952-831-1632 *Toll Free Fax:* 800-862-3480 *E-mail:* customerservice@abdopublishing.com; info@abdopublishing.com *Web Site:* abdopublishing.com, pg 2

Hansen, Kathleen M, Modern Language Association of America (MLA), 85 Broad St, Suite 500, New York, NY 10004-2434 *Tel:* 646-576-5000 *Fax:* 646-458-0030 *Web Site:* www.mla.org, pg 141

Hansen, Michael, Cengage Learning, 20 Channel Center St, Boston, MA 02210 *Tel:* 617-289-7700 *Toll Free Tel:* 800-354-9706 *Fax:* 617-289-7844 *E-mail:* esales@cengage.com *Web Site:* www.cengage.com, pg 47

Hansen, Mike, Hal Leonard Corp, 7777 W Bluemound Rd, Milwaukee, WI 53213 *Tel:* 414-774-3630 *Fax:* 414-774-3259 *E-mail:* halinfo@halleonard.com *Web Site:* www.halleonard.com, pg 91

Hansen, Stephanie, Metamorphosis Literary Agency, 12837 S Seminole Dr, Olathe, KS 66062 *Tel:* 646-397-1640 *E-mail:* info@metamorphosisliteraryagency.com *Web Site:* www.metamorphosisliteraryagency.com, pg 497

Hansen, Vaughne L, Virginia Kidd Agency Inc, 538 E Harford St, PO Box 278, Milford, PA 18337 *Tel:* 570-296-6205 *Web Site:* vk-agency.com, pg 491

Hanson, Andy, Illinois State Museum Society, 502 S Spring St, Springfield, IL 62706-5000 *Tel:* 217-782-7386 *Fax:* 217-782-1254 *E-mail:* subscriptions@museum.state.il.us *Web Site:* www.illinoisstatemuseum.org, pg 106

Hanson, Brooks, American Geophysical Union (AGU), 2000 Florida Ave NW, Washington, DC 20009 *Tel:* 202-462-6900 *Toll Free Tel:* 800-966-2481 (North America) *Fax:* 202-328-0566 *E-mail:* service@agu.org (cust serv); earthspacescience@agu.org *Web Site:* www.agu.org, pg 11

Hanson, Eliza, Gallery Books, 1230 Avenue of the Americas, New York, NY 10020 *Toll Free Tel:* 800-456-6798 *Fax:* 212-698-7284 *E-mail:* consumer.customerservice@simonandschuster.com *Web Site:* www.simonandschuster.com, pg 83

Hanson, John, Indiana University African Studies Program, Indiana University, 355 N Jordan, Rm GA 3072, Bloomington, IN 47405 *Tel:* 812-855-8284 *Fax:* 812-855-6734 *E-mail:* afrist@indiana.edu *Web Site:* www.indiana.edu/~afrist; www.go.iu.edu/afrist, pg 107

Hanson, Kevin, Simon & Schuster Canada, 166 King St E, Suite 300, Toronto, ON M5A 1J3, Canada *Tel:* 647-427-8882 *Toll Free Tel:* 800-387-0446; 800-268-3216 (orders) *Fax:* 647-430-9446 *Toll Free Fax:* 888-849-8151 (orders) *E-mail:* info@simonandschuster.ca *Web Site:* www.simonandschuster.ca, pg 440

Hanson, Kevin, Simon & Schuster, Inc, 1230 Avenue of the Americas, New York, NY 10020 *Tel:* 212-698-7000 *Toll Free Tel:* 800-223-2336 (orders) *Fax:* 212-698-7007 *Toll Free Fax:* 800-943-9831 (orders) *E-mail:* firstname.lastname@simonandschuster.com; purchaseorders@simonandschuster.com (orders) *Web Site:* www.simonandschuster.com, pg 199

Hanson, Martha, Book Industry Guild of New York, PO Box 2001, New York, NY 10113-2001 *E-mail:* admin@bookindustryguildofny.org *Web Site:* bigny.org, pg 528

Hanson, Todd, Medical Physics Publishing Corp (MPP), 4555 Helgesen Dr, Madison, WI 53718 *Tel:* 608-262-4021; 608-224-4508 *Toll Free Tel:* 800-442-5778 (cust serv) *Fax:* 608-224-5016 *E-mail:* mpp@medicalphysics.org *Web Site:* www.medicalphysics.org, pg 137

Haproff, David, Russell Sage Foundation, 112 E 64 St, New York, NY 10065 *Tel:* 212-750-6000 *Toll Free Tel:* 800-524-6401 *Fax:* 212-371-4761 *E-mail:* info@rsage.org *Web Site:* www.russellsage.org, pg 188

Harding, Elizabeth, Curtis Brown Ltd, 228 E 45 St, 3rd fl, New York, NY 10017 *Tel:* 212-473-5400 *Web Site:* www.curtisbrown.com, pg 478

Hardy, Lynn, Resilient Publishing, 406 S Third St, Boise, ID 83702 *Tel:* 208-258-9544 *E-mail:* submissions@resilientpublishing.com *Web Site:* www.resilientpublishing.com; www.facebook.com/ResilientPub, pg 184

Hare, Robbie Anna, Goldfarb & Associates, 721 Gibbon St, Alexandria, VA 22314 *Tel:* 202-466-3030 *Fax:* 703-836-5644 *E-mail:* rlglawlit@gmail.com *Web Site:* www.ronaldgoldfarb.com, pg 486

Haring, Sara Beth, St Martin's Press, LLC, 120 Broadway, New York, NY 10271 *Tel:* 646-307-5151 *Web Site:* us.macmillan.com/smp, pg 190

Harley, Megan, Algonquin Books, 400 Silver Cedar Ct, Suite 300, Chapel Hill, NC 27514-1585 *Tel:* 919-967-0108 *Fax:* 919-933-0272 *E-mail:* inquiry@algonquin.com *Web Site:* www.workman.com/algonquin, pg 7

Harman, Donna A, American Forest & Paper Association (AF&PA), 1101 "K" St NW, Suite 700, Washington, DC 20005 *Tel:* 202-463-2700 *E-mail:* info@afandpa.org *Web Site:* www.afandpa.org, pg 522

Harmison, Jean, The Association for Women in Communications, 1717 E Republic Rd, Suite A, Springfield, MO 65804 *Tel:* 417-886-8606 *Fax:* 417-886-3685 *E-mail:* info@womcom.org *Web Site:* www.womcom.org, pg 573

Harmsworth, Esmond, Aevitas Creative Management, 19 W 21 St, Suite 501, New York, NY 10010 *Tel:* 212-765-6900 *Web Site:* aevitascreative.com, pg 474

Harp, Gabe, The MIT Press, One Rogers St, Cambridge, MA 02142 *Tel:* 617-253-5255 *Toll Free Tel:* 800-405-1619 (orders) *Fax:* 617-258-6779; 617-577-1545 (orders) *Web Site:* mitpress.mit.edu, pg 141

Harper, Logan, Trident Media Group LLC, 41 Madison Ave, 36th fl, New York, NY 10010 *Tel:* 212-333-1511 *E-mail:* info@tridentmediagroup.com; press@tridentmediagroup.com *Web Site:* www.tridentmediagroup.com, pg 507

Harper, Matt, HarperCollins General Books Group, 195 Broadway, New York, NY 10007 *Tel:* 212-207-7000 *Web Site:* www.harpercollins.com, pg 93

Harper, Michael, The Little Entrepreneur, c/o Harper Arrington Media, 18701 Grand River, Suite 105, Detroit, MI 48223 *Toll Free Tel:* 888-435-9234 *Fax:* 248-281-0373 *E-mail:* info@startingaclothingline.com *Web Site:* www.thelittlee.com, pg 126

Harpster, Kristin, Wayne State University Press, Leonard N Simons Bldg, 4809 Woodward Ave, Detroit, MI 48201-1309 *Tel:* 313-577-6120 *Toll Free Tel:* 800-978-7323 *Fax:* 313-577-6131 *E-mail:* bookorders@wayne.edu *Web Site:* www.wsupress.wayne.edu, pg 238

Harrell, Casey, Thomas Nelson, 501 Nelson Place, Nashville, TN 37214 *Tel:* 615-889-9000 *Toll Free Tel:* 800-251-4000 *Fax:* 615-902-1548 *Web Site:* www.thomasnelson.com, pg 217

Harrell, Rachel, Chronicle Books, 680 Second St, San Francisco, CA 94107 *Tel:* 415-537-4200 *Toll Free Tel:* 800-759-0190 (cust serv) *Fax:* 415-537-4460 *Toll Free Fax:* 800-858-7787 (orders); 800-286-9471 (cust serv) *E-mail:* frontdesk@chroniclebooks.com *Web Site:* www.chroniclebooks.com, pg 52

Harri, Kaitlin, HarperCollins General Books Group, 195 Broadway, New York, NY 10007 *Tel:* 212-207-7000 *Web Site:* www.harpercollins.com, pg 93

Harrington, Dorota, Owl About Books Publisher Inc, 1632 Royalwood Circle, Joshua, TX 76058 *Tel:* 682-553-9078 *Fax:* 817-558-8983 *E-mail:* owlaboutbooks@gmail.com *Web Site:* www.owlaboutbooks.com, pg 158

Harrington, Joyce, Adams & Ambrose Publishing, PO Box 259684, Madison, WI 53725-9684 *Tel:* 608-977-1825 *E-mail:* info@adamsambrose.com, pg 4

Harrington, Mark, Harry N Abrams Inc, 195 Broadway, 9th fl, New York, NY 10007 *Tel:* 212-206-7715 *Toll Free Tel:* 800-345-1359 *Fax:* 212-519-1210 *E-mail:* abrams@abramsbooks.com *Web Site:* www.abramsbooks.com, pg 3

Harrington, Meghan, St Martin's Press, LLC, 120 Broadway, New York, NY 10271 *Tel:* 646-307-5151 *Web Site:* us.macmillan.com/smp, pg 191

Harrington, Dr Robert M, American Mathematical Society, 201 Charles St, Providence, RI 02904-2213 *Tel:* 401-455-4000 *Toll Free Tel:* 800-321-4267 *Fax:* 401-331-3842; 401-455-4046 (cust serv) *E-mail:* ams@ams.org; cust-serv@ams.org *Web Site:* www.ams.org, pg 12

Harrington, Roby, W W Norton & Company Inc, 500 Fifth Ave, New York, NY 10110-0017 *Tel:* 212-354-5500 *Toll Free Tel:* 800-233-4830 (orders & cust serv) *Fax:* 212-869-0856 *Toll Free Fax:* 800-458-6515 *E-mail:* orders@wwnorton.com *Web Site:* wwnorton.com, pg 152

Harrington, Timothy, Little, Brown and Company, 1290 Avenue of the Americas, New York, NY 10104 *Tel:* 212-364-1100 *Fax:* 212-364-0952 *E-mail:* firstname.lastname@hbgusa.com *Web Site:* www.littlebrown.com; www.hachettebookgroup.com, pg 126

Harriot, Michael, Folio Literary Management, The Film Center Bldg, 630 Ninth Ave, Suite 1101, New York, NY 10036 *Tel:* 212-400-1494 *Fax:* 212-967-0977 *Web Site:* www.foliolit.com, pg 484

Harris, Alec, GIA Publications Inc, 7404 S Mason Ave, Chicago, IL 60638 *Tel:* 708-496-3800 *Toll Free Tel:* 800-GIA-1358 (442-1358) *Fax:* 708-496-3828 *E-mail:* custserv@giamusic.com *Web Site:* www.giamusic.com, pg 85

Harris, Alyza, The Publishing Game, PO Box 590239, Newton, MA 02459-0002 *Tel:* 617-630-0945 *Fax:* 617-630-0945 (call first) *E-mail:* info@publishinggame.com; workshops@publishinggame.com *Web Site:* www.publishinggame.com, pg 577

Harris, David A, American Jewish Committee (AJC), Jacob Blaustein Bldg, 165 E 56 St, New York, NY 10022 *Tel:* 212-751-4000; 212-891-1456 (membership) *Fax:* 212-891-1450 *Web Site:* www.ajc.org, pg 523

Harris, Debra, All Things That Matter Press, 79 Jones Rd, Somerville, ME 04348 *E-mail:* allthingsthatmatterpress@gmail.com *Web Site:* www.allthingsthatmatterpress.com, pg 8

Harris, Erin, Folio Literary Management, The Film Center Bldg, 630 Ninth Ave, Suite 1101, New York, NY 10036 *Tel:* 212-400-1494 *Fax:* 212-967-0977 *Web Site:* www.foliolit.com, pg 484

Harris, Jake, United States Institute of Peace Press, 2301 Constitution Ave NW, Washington, DC 20037 *Tel:* 703-661-1590 (cust serv) *Toll Free Tel:* 800-868-8064 (cust serv) *E-mail:* usipmail@presswarehouse.com (orders) *Web Site:* bookstore.usip.org, pg 224

Harris, Joy, The Joy Harris Literary Agency Inc, 1501 Broadway, Suite 2310, New York, NY 10036 *Tel:* 212-924-6269 *Fax:* 212-840-5776 *E-mail:* contact@joyharrisliterary.com *Web Site:* www.joyharrisliterary.com, pg 488

Harris, Kathy, Paul H Brookes Publishing Co Inc, PO Box 10624, Baltimore, MD 21285-0624 *Tel:* 410-337-9580 (outside US & CN) *Toll Free Tel:* 800-638-3775 (US & CN) *Fax:* 410-337-8539 *E-mail:* custserv@brookespublishing.com *Web Site:* www.brookespublishing.com, pg 42

Harris, Melissa, Aperture Books, 547 W 27 St, 4th fl, New York, NY 10001 *Tel:* 212-505-5555 *Toll Free Fax:* 888-623-6908 *E-mail:* customerservice@aperture.org *Web Site:* aperture.org, pg 17

Harris, Michelle, Software & Information Industry Association (SIIA), 1090 Vermont Ave NW, 6th fl, Washington, DC 20005-4905 *Tel:* 202-289-7442 *Fax:* 202-289-7097 *Web Site:* www.siia.net, pg 547

Harris, Peter, Penguin Group USA, A Penguin Random House Company, 375 Hudson St, New York, NY 10014 *Tel:* 212-366-2000 *Toll Free Tel:* 800-847-5515 (inside sales); 800-631-8571 (cust serv) *Fax:* 212-366-2666; 607-775-4829 (inside sales) *E-mail:* online@us.penguingroup.com *Web Site:* www.penguin.com, pg 163

Harris, Ross, Stuart Krichevsky Literary Agency Inc, 6 E 39 St, Suite 500, New York, NY 10016 *Tel:* 212-725-5288 *Fax:* 212-725-5275 *E-mail:* query@skagency.com *Web Site:* skagency.com, pg 492

Harris, Sloan, ICM Partners, 65 E 55 St, New York, NY 10022 *Tel:* 212-556-5600 *Web Site:* www.icmtalent.com, pg 489

Harris, Steve, Concordia Publishing House, 3558 S Jefferson Ave, St Louis, MO 63118-3968 *Tel:* 314-268-1000; 314-268-1268 (bookshop) *Toll Free Tel:* 800-325-3040 (cust serv) *Toll Free Fax:* 800-490-9889 (cust serv) *E-mail:* order@cph.org *Web Site:* www.cph.org, pg 56

Harrison, Adriane, PRINTING United Alliance, 10015 Main St, Fairfax, VA 22031-3489 *Tel:* 703-385-1335 *Toll Free Tel:* 888-385-3588 *Fax:* 703-273-0456; 703-691-7492 (membership) *E-mail:* assist@printing.org; info@printing.org *Web Site:* www.printing.org; www.sgia.org, pg 544

Harrison, Colin, Scribner, 1230 Avenue of the Americas, New York, NY 10020, pg 195

Harrison, DeSales, Oberlin College Press, 50 N Professor St, Oberlin, OH 44074-1091 *Tel:* 440-775-8408 *Fax:* 440-775-8124 *E-mail:* oc.press@oberlin.edu *Web Site:* www.oberlin.edu/ocpress, pg 154

Harrison, Heather, Parallax Press, 2236B Sixth St, Berkeley, CA 94710 *Tel:* 510-540-6411 *Toll Free Tel:* 800-863-5290 (orders) *Fax:* 510-981-1157 *Web Site:* www.parallax.org, pg 160

Harrison, Joyce, University Press of Kansas, 2502 Westbrooke Circle, Lawrence, KS 66045-4444 *Tel:* 785-864-4154; 785-864-4155 (orders) *Fax:* 785-864-4586 *E-mail:* upress@ku.edu; upkorders@ku.edu (orders) *Web Site:* www.kansaspress.ku.edu, pg 233

Harrison, Kate, Dial Books for Young Readers, 345 Hudson St, New York, NY 10014 *Tel:* 212-366-2000 *Toll Free Tel:* 800-733-3000 (orders) *Fax:* 212-414-3396 *Web Site:* www.penguin.com/publishers/dialbooksforyoungreaders/, pg 64

Harrison, Katherine, Random House Children's Books, 1745 Broadway, 10th fl, New York, NY 10019 *Tel:* 212-782-9000 *Web Site:* www.randomhousekids.com, pg 180

Harrison, Kristen, The Brookings Institution Press, 1775 Massachusetts Ave NW, Washington, DC 20036-2188 *Tel:* 202-797-6000 *E-mail:* permissions@brookings. edu *Web Site:* www.brookings.edu, pg 42

Harrison, Patricia de Stacy, Corporation for Public Broadcasting (CPB), 401 Ninth St NW, Washington, DC 20004-2129 *Tel:* 202-879-9600 *Web Site:* www. cpb.org, pg 531

Harriss, Clarinda, BrickHouse Books Inc, 306 Suffolk Rd, Baltimore, MD 21218 *Fax:* 410-235-7690 *Web Site:* brickhousebooks.wordpress.com, pg 41

Hart, Becca, Beaver's Pond Press Inc, 939 Seventh St W, St Paul, MN 55102 *Tel:* 952-829-8818 *E-mail:* info@beaverspondpress.com *Web Site:* www. beaverspondpress.com, pg 30

Hart, Cate, Harvey Klinger Inc, 300 W 55 St, Suite 11V, New York, NY 10019 *Tel:* 212-581-7068 *Fax:* 212-315-3823 *E-mail:* queries@harveyklinger. com *Web Site:* www.harveyklinger.com, pg 491

Hart, Jim, Hartline Literary Agency LLC, 123 Queenston Dr, Pittsburgh, PA 15235 *Tel:* 412-829-2483 *Toll Free Fax:* 888-279-6007 *Web Site:* www.hartlineliterary. com, pg 488

Hart, Joyce, Hartline Literary Agency LLC, 123 Queenston Dr, Pittsburgh, PA 15235 *Tel:* 412-829-2483 *Toll Free Fax:* 888-279-6007 *Web Site:* www. hartlineliterary.com, pg 488

Hart, Laura, Bellevue Literary Press, 90 Broad St, Suite 2100, New York, NY 10004 *Tel:* 917-732-3603 *Web Site:* blpress.org, pg 31

Hart, Tara, Penguin Random House Audio Publishing, 1745 Broadway, New York, NY 10019 *E-mail:* audio@penguinrandomhouse.com *Web Site:* www.penguinrandomhouseaudio.com, pg 164

Hartke, Elizabeth, BuilderBooks, 1201 15 St NW, Washington, DC 20005 *Tel:* 202-822-0200 *Toll Free Tel:* 800-223-2665 *Fax:* 202-266-8096 (edit) *E-mail:* info@nahb.com *Web Site:* builderbooks.com, pg 42

Hartley, Emily, Random House Publishing Group, 1745 Broadway, New York, NY 10019 *Toll Free Tel:* 800-200-3552 *Web Site:* www.randomhousebooks.com, pg 181

Hartley, Glen, Writers' Representatives LLC, 116 W 14 St, 11th fl, New York, NY 10011-7305 *Tel:* 212-620-9009 *Fax:* 212-620-0023 *E-mail:* transom@ writersreps.com *Web Site:* www.writersreps.com, pg 509

Hartley, John, Peter Pauper Press, Inc, 202 Mamaroneck Ave, Suite 400, White Plains, NY 10601-5376 *Tel:* 914-681-0144 *Fax:* 914-681-0389 *E-mail:* customerservice@peterpauper.com; orders@ peterpauper.com; marketing@peterpauper.com *Web Site:* www.peterpauper.com, pg 168

Hartman, Charles, National Council of Teachers of English (NCTE), 340 N Neil St, Suite 104, Champaign, IL 61820 *Tel:* 217-328-3870 *Toll Free Tel:* 877-369-6283 (cust serv) *Fax:* 217-328-9645 *E-mail:* customerservice@ncte.org *Web Site:* www. ncte.org, pg 146

Hartman, Erinn, Alfred A Knopf, c/o Penguin Random House Inc, 1745 Broadway, New York, NY 10019 *Tel:* 212-751-2600 *Fax:* 212-572-2662 (foreign rts) *Web Site:* knopfdoubleday.com, pg 118

Hartman, Mark, Hartman Publishing Inc, 1313 Iron Ave SW, Albuquerque, NM 87102 *Tel:* 505-291-1274 *Toll Free Tel:* 800-999-9534 *Toll Free Fax:* 800-474-6106 *E-mail:* info@hartmanonline.com *Web Site:* www. hartmanonline.com, pg 94

Hartman, William, Quintessence Publishing Co Inc, 411 N Raddant Rd, Batavia, IL 60510 *Tel:* 630-736-3600 *Toll Free Tel:* 800-621-0387 *Fax:* 630-736-3633 *E-mail:* contact@quintbook.com; service@quintbook. com *Web Site:* www.quintpub.com, pg 179

Hartnett, Laura, The Ralph Waldo Emerson Award, 1606 New Hampshire Ave NW, Washington, DC 20009 *Tel:* 202-265-3808 *Fax:* 202-986-1601 *E-mail:* awards@pbk.org *Web Site:* www.pbk.org/ bookawards, pg 613

Hartnett, Laura, The Christian Gauss Award, 1606 New Hampshire Ave NW, Washington, DC 20009 *Tel:* 202-265-3808 *Fax:* 202-986-1601 *E-mail:* awards@pbk.org *Web Site:* www.pbk.org/bookawards, pg 618

Hartnett, Laura, Phi Beta Kappa Award in Science, 1606 New Hampshire Ave NW, Washington, DC 20009 *Tel:* 202-265-3808 *Fax:* 202-986-1601 *E-mail:* awards@pbk.org *Web Site:* www.pbk.org/ bookawards, pg 656

Hartogh, Frances, Rocky Mountain Mineral Law Foundation, 9191 Sheridan Blvd, Suite 203, Westminster, CO 80031 *Tel:* 303-321-8100 *Fax:* 303-321-7657 *E-mail:* info@rmmlf.org *Web Site:* www. rmmlf.org, pg 186

Hartshorn, Erin M, Science Fiction & Fantasy Writers of America Inc (SFWA), PO Box 3238, Enfield, CT 06083-3238 *Tel:* 860-698-0536 *E-mail:* office@sfwa. org *Web Site:* www.sfwa.org, pg 545

Hartshorn, Erin M, SFWA Nebula Awards, PO Box 3238, Enfield, CT 06083-3238 *Tel:* 860-698-0536 *E-mail:* office@sfwa.org *Web Site:* www.sfwa.org, pg 666

Hartson, Kate, Hachette Nashville, 6100 Tower Circle, Room 210, Franklin, TN 37067 *Tel:* 615-221-0996 *Fax:* 615-221-0962 *Web Site:* www.hachettebookgroup. com, pg 91

Hartt, Jordan, Port Townsend Writers' Conference, 223 Battery Way, Port Townsend, WA 98368 *Tel:* 360-385-3102 *Toll Free Tel:* 800-733-3608 (ticket off) *Fax:* 360-385-2470 *E-mail:* info@centrum.org *Web Site:* centrum.org, pg 577

Harty, Pamela, The Knight Agency Inc, 232 W Washington St, Madison, GA 30650 *E-mail:* admin@ knightagency.net *Web Site:* www.knightagency.net, pg 491

Harvey, Dr Alan, Stanford University Press, 425 Broadway St, Redwood City, CA 94063-3126 *Tel:* 650-723-9434 *Fax:* 650-725-3457 *E-mail:* info@ www.sup.org; publicity@www.sup.org; sales@www. sup.org *Web Site:* www.sup.org, pg 206

Harwell, Andrew, HarperCollins Children's Books, 195 Broadway, New York, NY 10007 *Tel:* 212-207-7000 *Web Site:* www.harpercollins.com/childrens, pg 93

Harwell, Sarah C, Syracuse University Creative Writing Program, 401 Hall of Languages, Syracuse, NY 13244-1170 *Tel:* 315-443-2173 *Fax:* 315-443-3660 *Web Site:* english.syr.edu/creative_writing; www.syr. edu, pg 585

Hashimoto, Meika, Random House Children's Books, 1745 Broadway, 10th fl, New York, NY 10019 *Tel:* 212-782-9000 *Web Site:* www.randomhousekids. com, pg 180

Haskell, Arlo, Key West Literary Seminar, 717 Love Lane, Key West, FL 33040 *Tel:* 305-293-9291 *Toll Free Tel:* 888-293-9291 *E-mail:* mail@kwls.org *Web Site:* www.kwls.org/seminar, pg 576

Haskell, Arlo, Key West Literary Seminar's Writers' Workshop Program, 717 Love Lane, Key West, FL 33040 *Tel:* 305-293-9291 *Toll Free Tel:* 888-293-9291 *E-mail:* mail@kwls.org *Web Site:* www.kwls.org; www.kwls.org/writers_workshops, pg 576

Hass, Julia, Chronicle Books, 680 Second St, San Francisco, CA 94107 *Tel:* 415-537-4200 *Toll Free Tel:* 800-759-0190 (cust serv) *Fax:* 415-537-4460 *Toll Free Fax:* 800-858-7787 (orders); 800-286-9471 (cust serv) *E-mail:* frontdesk@chroniclebooks.com *Web Site:* www.chroniclebooks.com, pg 52

Hass, Robert, Squaw Valley Community of Writers Summer Workshops, PO Box 1416, Nevada City, CA 95959 *Tel:* 530-470-8440 *E-mail:* info@ communityofwriters.org *Web Site:* www. communityofwriters.org, pg 579

Hassan, Shannon, Marsal Lyon Literary Agency LLC, 665 San Rodolfo Dr, Suite 124, PMB 121, Solana Beach, CA 92075 *Tel:* 760-814-8507 *Web Site:* www. marsallyonliteraryagency.com, pg 494

Hasselstrom, Linda M, Windbreak House Writing Retreat, PO Box 169, Hermosa, SD 57744-0169 *Tel:* 605-255-4064 *E-mail:* info@windbreakhouse.com *Web Site:* www.windbreakhouse.com, pg 579

Hasso, M (May) H, Boston Informatics, 35 Byard Lane, Westborough, MA 01581 *Tel:* 508-366-8176 *Web Site:* www.bostoninformatics.com, pg 459

Hastings, Katherine, Susquehanna University, Department of English & Creative Writing, 514 University Ave, Selinsgrove, PA 17870 *Tel:* 570-372-0101, pg 585

Hastings, Robert, Pacific Press® Publishing Association, 1350 N Kings Rd, Nampa, ID 83687-3193 *Tel:* 208-465-2500 *Toll Free Tel:* 800-447-7377 *Fax:* 208-465-2531 *Web Site:* www.pacificpress.com, pg 159

Hastings, Vinsula, Modern Memoirs, 34 Main St, No 6, Amherst, MA 01002-2367 *Tel:* 413-253-2353 *Web Site:* www.modernmemoirs.com; www. whitepoppypress.com, pg 141

Hatch, James C, Committee on Scholarly Editions, c/o Modern Language Association of America, 85 Broad St, Suite 500, New York, NY 10004-2434 *Tel:* 646-576-5044 *Fax:* 646-458-0030 *E-mail:* cse@mla.org *Web Site:* www.mla.org, pg 531

Hatch, John, Signature Books Publishing LLC, 564 W 400 N, Salt Lake City, UT 84116-3411 *Toll Free Tel:* 800-356-5687 *E-mail:* people@signaturebooks. com *Web Site:* www.signaturebooks.com; www. signaturebookslibrary.org, pg 198

Hatch, Ronald, Ronsdale Press Ltd, 3350 W 21 Ave, Vancouver, BC V6S 1G7, Canada *Tel:* 604-738-4688 *Fax:* 604-731-4548 *E-mail:* ronsdale@shaw.ca *Web Site:* ronsdalepress.com, pg 438

Hatch, Veronica, Ronsdale Press Ltd, 3350 W 21 Ave, Vancouver, BC V6S 1G7, Canada *Tel:* 604-738-4688 *Fax:* 604-731-4548 *E-mail:* ronsdale@shaw.ca *Web Site:* ronsdalepress.com, pg 438

Hathorne, Nancy, Writers Guild of America, East (WGAE), 250 Hudson St, Suite 700, New York, NY 10013 *Tel:* 212-767-7800 *Fax:* 212-582-1909 *Web Site:* www.wgaeast.org, pg 549

Hatton, Kelly, BOA Editions Ltd, 250 N Goodman St, Suite 306, Rochester, NY 14607 *Tel:* 585-546-3410 *Fax:* 585-546-3913 *E-mail:* contact@boaeditions.org *Web Site:* www.boaeditions.org, pg 37

Hauber, Janine, Sheldon Fogelman Agency Inc, 420 E 72 St, New York, NY 10021 *Tel:* 212-532-7250 *Fax:* 212-685-8939 *E-mail:* info@sheldonfogelmanagency.com *Web Site:* sheldonfogelmanagency.com, pg 484

Haubner, Julianna, Avid Reader Press, 1230 Avenue of the Americas, New York, NY 10020 *Web Site:* avidreaderpress.com, pg 26

Hauck, Hilary, Pennwriters Conference, PO Box 685, Dalton, PA 18414 *E-mail:* conferencecoordinator@ pennwriters.org; info@pennwriters.org *Web Site:* pennwriters.org, pg 577

Haugh, Clare, Perseus Books, 1290 Avenue of the Americas, New York, NY 10104 *Tel:* 212-340-8100 *Toll Free Tel:* 800-343-4499 (cust serv) *Fax:* 212-340-8105 *Web Site:* www.perseusbooks.com, pg 167

Haugh, Mark, PennWell Books, 1421 S Sheridan Rd, Tulsa, OK 74112 *Tel:* 918-831-9421 *Toll Free Tel:* 800-752-9764 *Fax:* 918-831-9555 *E-mail:* sales@ pennwell.com *Web Site:* www.pennwellbooks.com, pg 166

Haughian, Karen, Signature Editions, PO Box 206, RPO Corydon, Winnipeg, MB R3M 3S7, Canada *Tel:* 204-779-7803 *E-mail:* submissions@signature-editions. com; orders@signature-editions.com *Web Site:* www. signature-editions.com, pg 440

Haun, Sue, Teton NewMedia Inc, 90 E Simpson, Suite 110, Jackson, WY 83001 *Tel:* 307-732-0028 *Toll Free Tel:* 877-306-9793 *Fax:* 307-734-0841 *E-mail:* sales@ tetonnm.com *Web Site:* www.tetonnm.com, pg 215

Hauser, Robert M, American Philosophical Society, 104 S Fifth St, Philadelphia, PA 19106 *Tel:* 215-440-3425 *Fax:* 215-440-3450 *E-mail:* orders@dianepublishing. net *Web Site:* www.amphilsoc.org, pg 13

Hausner, Beatriz, John Glassco Translation Prize, Concordia University, LB 601, 1455 De Maisonneuve W, Montreal, QC H3G 1M8, Canada *Tel:* 514-848-2424 (ext 8702) *E-mail:* info@attlc-ltac.org *Web Site:* www.attlc-ltac.org, pg 619

Hausner, Beatriz, Literary Translators' Association of Canada, Concordia University, LB 601, 1455 De Maisonneuve W, Montreal, QC H3G 1M8, Canada *Tel:* 514-848-2424 (ext 8702) *E-mail:* info@attlc-ltac. org *Web Site:* www.attlc-ltac.org, pg 536

Haut, Judith, Random House Children's Books, 1745 Broadway, 10th fl, New York, NY 10019 *Tel:* 212-782-9000 *Web Site:* www.randomhousekids.com, pg 180

Hawkes, Gwen, St Martin's Press, LLC, 120 Broadway, New York, NY 10271 *Tel:* 646-307-5151 *Web Site:* us. macmillan.com/smp, pg 190

Hawkins, Anne, John Hawkins and Associates Inc, 80 Maiden Lane, Suite 1503, New York, NY 10038 *Tel:* 212-807-7040 *E-mail:* jha@jhalit.com *Web Site:* jhalit.com, pg 488

Hawkins, Bob Jr, Harvest House Publishers Inc, PO Box 41210, Eugene, OR 97404-0322 *Tel:* 541-343-0123 *Toll Free Tel:* 888-501-6991 *Fax:* 541-342-6410 *E-mail:* admin@harvesthousepublishers. com; permissions@harvesthousepublishers.com *Web Site:* harvesthousepublishers.com, pg 95

Hawkins, Drew, Canadian Scholars' Press Inc, 425 Adelaide St W, Suite 200, Toronto, ON M5V 3C1, Canada *Tel:* 416-929-2774 *Toll Free Tel:* 800-463-1998 *Fax:* 416-929-1926 *E-mail:* info@cspi.org; info@canadianscholars.ca; editorial@canadianscholars. ca; orders@canadianscholars.ca *Web Site:* www. canadianscholars.ca; www.womenspress.ca, pg 419

Hawkins, Jaclyn, Sounds True Inc, 413 S Arthur Ave, Louisville, CO 80027 *Tel:* 303-665-3151 *Toll Free Tel:* 800-333-9185 (US); 888-303-9185 (US & CN) *E-mail:* customerservice@soundstrue. com; stpublicity@soundstrue.com *Web Site:* www. soundstrue.com, pg 204

Hawkins, Janet, Trillium Book Award/Prix Trillium, South Tower, Suite 501, 175 Bloor St E, Toronto, ON M4W 3R8, Canada *Tel:* 416-314-6858 (ext 698) *Fax:* 416-314-6876 *Web Site:* www.omdc.on.ca, pg 673

Hawley, Haven, American Printing History Association, PO Box 4519, Grand Central Sta, New York, NY 10163 *E-mail:* secretary@printinghistory.org *Web Site:* printinghistory.org, pg 523

Hawley, Haven, American Printing History Association Award, PO Box 4519, Grand Central Sta, New York, NY 10163 *E-mail:* secretary@printinghistory.org *Web Site:* printinghistory.org, pg 592

Hawley, Marcy, Orange Frazer Press Inc, 37 1/2 W Main St, Wilmington, OH 45177 *Tel:* 937-382-3196 *Fax:* 937-383-3159 *E-mail:* ofrazer@erinet.com *Web Site:* www.orangefrazer.com, pg 156

Hawley, Sarah, Orange Frazer Press Inc, 37 1/2 W Main St, Wilmington, OH 45177 *Tel:* 937-382-3196 *Fax:* 937-383-3159 *E-mail:* ofrazer@erinet.com *Web Site:* www.orangefrazer.com, pg 156

Hay, Louise, Hay House Inc, 2776 Loker Ave W, Carlsbad, CA 92010 *Tel:* 760-431-7695 (ext 2, intl) *Toll Free Tel:* 800-654-5126 (ext 2, US) *Toll Free Fax:* 800-650-5115 *E-mail:* info@hayhouse.com; editorial@hayhouse.com *Web Site:* www.hayhouse. com, pg 96

Hayden, Jeffrey, International Monetary Fund (IMF), Editorial & Publications Division, 700 19 St NW, HQ1-5-355, Washington, DC 20431 *Tel:* 202-623-7430 *Fax:* 202-623-7201 *E-mail:* publications@imf.org *Web Site:* bookstore.imf.org; elibrary.imf.org (online collection), pg 111

Hayden, Patrick Nielsen, Tom Doherty Associates, LLC, 120 Broadway, New York, NY 10271 *Tel:* 646-307-5511 *Toll Free Tel:* 800-455-0340 *Web Site:* us. macmillan.com/torforge, pg 66

Hayden, Thomas K, National Notary Association (NNA), 9350 De Soto Ave, Chatsworth, CA 91311-4926 *Tel:* 818-739-4000 *Toll Free Tel:* 800-876-6827 *Toll Free Fax:* 800-833-1211 *E-mail:* services@ nationalnotary.org *Web Site:* www.nationalnotary.org, pg 147

Hayden, William, The H W Wilson Foundation, 750 Third Ave, 13th fl, New York, NY 10017 *Tel:* 212-418-8473 *Web Site:* www.thwwf.org, pg 551

Haydon, Roger, Cornell University Press, Sage House, 512 E State St, Ithaca, NY 14850 *Tel:* 607-253-2338 *Fax:* 607-253-2374 *E-mail:* cupressinfo@cornell.edu; cupress-sales@cornell.edu *Web Site:* www.cornellpress. cornell.edu, pg 57

Hayes, Amber, Coretta Scott King - John Steptoe Award for New Talent, 225 N Michigan Ave, Suite 1300, Chicago, IL 60601 *Toll Free Tel:* 800-545-2433 (ext 4294) *Fax:* 312-280-3256 *E-mail:* diversity@ala.org *Web Site:* www.ala.org/awardsgrants, pg 630

Hayes, Caroline A, W W Norton & Company Inc, 500 Fifth Ave, New York, NY 10110-0017 *Tel:* 212-354-5500 *Toll Free Tel:* 800-233-4830 (orders & cust serv) *Fax:* 212-869-0856 *Toll Free Fax:* 800-458-6515 *E-mail:* orders@wwnorton.com *Web Site:* wwnorton. com, pg 152

Hayes, Kevin, Omnigraphics Inc, 615 Griswold, Suite 520, Detroit, MI 48226 *Tel:* 610-461-3548 *Toll Free Tel:* 800-234-1340 (cust serv) *Fax:* 610-532-9001 *Toll Free Fax:* 800-875-1340 (cust serv) *E-mail:* contact@ omnigraphics.com; customerservice@omnigraphics. com *Web Site:* omnigraphics.com, pg 155

Hayes, Regina, Viking Children's Books, 345 Hudson St, New York, NY 10014 *Fax:* 212-414-3393 *E-mail:* youngreaderspublicity@us.penguingroup. com *Web Site:* www.penguin.com/publishers/ vikingchildrensbooks, pg 236

Hayes, Ryan, Chronicle Books, 680 Second St, San Francisco, CA 94107 *Tel:* 415-537-4200 *Toll Free Tel:* 800-759-0190 (cust serv) *Fax:* 415-537-4460 *Toll Free Fax:* 800-858-7787 (orders); 800-286-9471 (cust serv) *E-mail:* frontdesk@chroniclebooks.com *Web Site:* www.chroniclebooks.com, pg 52

Hayes, William F, Poets & Writers Inc, 90 Broad St, Suite 2100, New York, NY 10004 *Tel:* 212-226-3586 *Fax:* 212-226-3963 *E-mail:* admin@pw.org *Web Site:* www.pw.org, pg 544

Haynes, Carline, Association for Information Science & Technology (ASIS&T), 8555 16 St, Suite 850, Silver Spring, MD 20910 *Tel:* 301-495-0900 *Fax:* 301-495-0810 *E-mail:* asist@asist.org *Web Site:* www.asist.org, pg 525

Hays, John, Bear & Co Inc, One Park St, Rochester, VT 05767 *Tel:* 802-767-3174 *Toll Free Tel:* 800-932-3277 *Fax:* 802-767-3726 *E-mail:* customerservice@ InnerTraditions.com *Web Site:* InnerTraditions.com, pg 29

Hays, John, Inner Traditions International Ltd, One Park St, Rochester, VT 05767 *Tel:* 802-767-3174 *Toll Free Tel:* 800-246-8648 *Fax:* 802-767-3726 *E-mail:* customerservice@InnerTraditions.com *Web Site:* www.InnerTraditions.com, pg 109

Hays, Katie, Jackie White Memorial National Children's Playwriting Contest, 1400 Forum Blvd, 1C No 214, Columbia, MO 65203 *E-mail:* jwm@cectheatre.org *Web Site:* www.cectheatre.org, pg 628

Hays, Michael, McGraw-Hill Higher Education, 1333 Burr Ridge Pkwy, Burr Ridge, IL 60527 *Tel:* 630-789-4000 *Toll Free Tel:* 800-338-3987 (cust serv) *Fax:* 614-755-5645 (cust serv) *Web Site:* www.mhhe. com, pg 135

Hayskar, Bonnie, Pangaea Publications, 402 Church St, Wisconsin Dells, WI 53965 *Tel:* 651-226-2032 *Fax:* 651-226-2032 *E-mail:* info@pangaea.org *Web Site:* pangaea.org, pg 159

Hayslett, Jerrianne, The Wisconsin Writers Awards, c/o 210 N Main St, No 204, Cedar Grove, WI 53013 *E-mail:* wiswriters@gmail.com *Web Site:* wiswriters. org/awards, pg 678

Hayt, Teri, American Society of News Editors (ASNE), 209 Reynolds Journalism Institute, Missouri School of Journalism, Columbia, MO 65211 *Tel:* 573-882-2430 *Fax:* 573-884-3824 *Web Site:* asne.org, pg 524

Haywood, Samantha, Transatlantic Agency, 2 Bloor St E, Suite 3500, Toronto, ON M4W 1A8, Canada *Tel:* 416-488-9214 *E-mail:* info@transatlanticagency. com *Web Site:* www.transatlanticagency.com, pg 506

Hazboun, Alma, Judson Press, 1075 First Ave, King of Prussia, PA 19406 *Toll Free Tel:* 800-458-3766 *Fax:* 610-768-2107 *Web Site:* www.judsonpress.com, pg 115

Heacock, Kait, University of Washington Press, 4333 Brooklyn Ave NE, Seattle, WA 98105-9570 *Tel:* 206-543-4050 *Toll Free Tel:* 800-537-5487 (orders) *Fax:* 206-543-3932; 410-516-6998 (orders) *E-mail:* uwpress@uw.edu *Web Site:* uwapress.uw.edu, pg 232

Head, Albert B, Alabama Artists Fellowship Awards, 201 Monroe St, Suite 110, Montgomery, AL 36130-1800 *Tel:* 334-242-4076 *Fax:* 334-240-3269, pg 590

Head, Karen J PhD, International Poetry Competition, 686 Cherry St NW, Suite 333, Atlanta, GA 30332-0161 *E-mail:* atlantareview@gatech.edu *Web Site:* www.atlantareview.com, pg 627

Headley, Jennifer, BJU Press, 1430 Wade Hampton Blvd, Greenville, SC 29609-5046 *Tel:* 864-770-1317; 864-546-4600 *Toll Free Tel:* 800-845-5731 *E-mail:* bjupinfo@bju.edu *Web Site:* www.bjupress. com, pg 34

Healey, Helen, Penguin Group USA, A Penguin Random House Company, 375 Hudson St, New York, NY 10014 *Tel:* 212-366-2000 *Toll Free Tel:* 800-847-5515 (inside sales); 800-631-8571 (cust serv) *Fax:* 212-366-2666; 607-775-4829 (inside sales) *E-mail:* online@ us.penguingroup.com *Web Site:* www.penguin.com, pg 163

Healey, Helen, Portfolio, 375 Hudson St, New York, NY 10014 *Web Site:* www.penguin.com/meet/publishers/ portfolio, pg 172

Healy, Chuck, Liguori Publications, One Liguori Dr, Liguori, MO 63057-1000 *Tel:* 636-464-2500 *Toll Free Tel:* 800-325-9521 *Toll Free Fax:* 800-325-9526 (sales) *E-mail:* liguori@liguori.org (sales & cust serv) *Web Site:* www.liguori.org, pg 124

Healy, Nick, Capstone Publishers™, 1710 Roe Crest Dr, North Mankato, MN 56003 *Toll Free Tel:* 800-747-4992 (cust serv) *Toll Free Fax:* 888-262-0705 *E-mail:* customer.service@capstonepub.com *Web Site:* www.capstonepub.com, pg 44

Heard, Janet, Davies Publishing Inc, 32 S Raymond Ave, Suites 4 & 5, Pasadena, CA 91105-1961 *Tel:* 626-792-3046 *Toll Free Tel:* 877-792-0005 *Fax:* 626-792-5308 *E-mail:* info@daviespublishing.com *Web Site:* daviespublishing.com, pg 62

Heater, Maria, Nelson Literary Agency LLC, 1732 Wazee St, Suite 207, Denver, CO 80202-1284 *Tel:* 303-292-2805 *E-mail:* info@nelsonagency.com *Web Site:* www.nelsonagency.com, pg 497

Heath, Mary, University Press of Mississippi, 3825 Ridgewood Rd, Jackson, MS 39211-6492 *Tel:* 601-432-6205 *Toll Free Tel:* 800-737-7788 (orders & cust serv) *Fax:* 601-432-6217 *E-mail:* press@mississippi. edu *Web Site:* www.upress.state.ms.us, pg 233

Heaton, Ashleigh, Random House Publishing Group, 1745 Broadway, New York, NY 10019 *Toll Free Tel:* 800-200-3552 *Web Site:* www.randomhousebooks. com, pg 181

Hebel, Brad, Columbia University Press, 61 W 62 St, New York, NY 10023 *Tel:* 212-459-0600 *Toll Free Tel:* 800-944-8648 *Fax:* 212-459-3678 *Web Site:* cup. columbia.edu, pg 55

Hebert, Jean-Francois, Editions du CHU Sainte-Justine, 3175, chemin de la Cote-Sainte-Catherine, Montreal, QC H3T 1C5, Canada *Tel:* 514-345-4671 *Fax:* 514-345-4631 *E-mail:* edition.hsj@ssss.gouv.qc.ca *Web Site:* www.editions-chu-sainte-justine.org, pg 423

Heckenthorn, Steve, Medals of America Press, 114 Southchase Blvd, Fountain Inn, SC 29644 *Toll Free Tel:* 800-605-4001 *Toll Free Fax:* 800-407-8640 *Web Site:* moapress.com, pg 137

Hecker, J L, Stipes Publishing LLC, 204 W University Ave, Champaign, IL 61820 *Tel:* 217-356-8391 *Fax:* 217-356-5753 *E-mail:* stipes01@sbcglobal.net *Web Site:* www.stipes.com, pg 208

Hecker, Mel, United States Holocaust Memorial Museum, 100 Raoul Wallenberg Place SW, Washington, DC 20024-2126 *Tel:* 202-488-0400; 202-314-7837; 202-488-6144 (orders) *Toll Free Tel:* 800-259-9998 (orders) *Fax:* 202-479-9726; 202-488-0438 (orders) *E-mail:* cahs_publications@ushmm.org *Web Site:* www.ushmm.org, pg 224

Hedden, Andrew, Scholastic Inc, 557 Broadway, New York, NY 10012 *Tel:* 212-343-6100 *Toll Free Tel:* 800-SCHOLASTIC (724-6527) *Web Site:* www.scholastic.com, pg 194

Heddle, Jennifer, Disney Publishing Worldwide, 1101 Flower St, Glendale, CA 91201 *Web Site:* books.disney.com, pg 65

Hedeen, Katrina, Boston Globe-Horn Book Award, c/o Book Reviews, The Horn Book Inc, Palace Road Bldg, 300 The Fenway, Suite P-311, Boston, MA 02115-5820 *Tel:* 617-278-0225 *Toll Free Tel:* 888-628-0225 *Fax:* 617-278-6062 *E-mail:* info@hbook.com *Web Site:* www.hbook.com, pg 600

Hedman, Susan Alvare, Hartman Publishing Inc, 1313 Iron Ave SW, Albuquerque, NM 87102 *Tel:* 505-291-1274 *Toll Free Tel:* 800-999-9534 *Toll Free Fax:* 800-474-6106 *E-mail:* info@hartmanonline.com *Web Site:* www.hartmanonline.com, pg 94

Hedrick, Chris, Scholastic Education, 557 Broadway, New York, NY 10012 *Tel:* 212-343-6100 *Fax:* 212-343-6189 *Web Site:* www.scholastic.com, pg 194

Heffron, Tom, Octane Press, 815A Brazos St, No 658, Austin, TX 78701 *Tel:* 512-334-9441; 512-761-4555 (sales) *Fax:* 512-430-5343 *E-mail:* info@octanepress.com; sales@octanepress.com *Web Site:* octanepress.com/content/submissions, pg 154

Heflin, Mark, American Illustration/American Photography, 225 W 36 St, Suite 602, New York, NY 10018 *Tel:* 917-408-9944 *Fax:* 212-532-2064 *E-mail:* info@ai-ap.com *Web Site:* www.ai-ap.com, pg 592

Heifetz, Merrilee, Writers House, 21 W 26 St, New York, NY 10010 *Tel:* 212-685-2400 *Web Site:* www.writershouse.com, pg 508

Heilman, Erika, Harvard Business Review Press, 20 Guest St, Suite 700, Brighton, MA 02135 *Tel:* 617-783-7400 *Fax:* 617-783-7489 *E-mail:* custserv@hbsp.harvard.edu *Web Site:* www.harvardbusiness.org, pg 94

Heimbouch, Hollis, HarperCollins General Books Group, 195 Broadway, New York, NY 10007 *Tel:* 212-207-7000 *Web Site:* www.harpercollins.com, pg 93

Heimburger, Donald J, Heimburger House Publishing Co, 7236 W Madison St, Forest Park, IL 60130 *Tel:* 708-366-1973 *Fax:* 708-366-1973 *E-mail:* info@heimburgerhouse.com *Web Site:* www.heimburgerhouse.com, pg 97

Heimert, Lara, Perseus Books, 1290 Avenue of the Americas, New York, NY 10104 *Tel:* 212-340-8100 *Toll Free Tel:* 800-343-4499 (cust serv) *Fax:* 212-340-8105 *Web Site:* www.perseusbooks.com, pg 167

Hein, Kristi, Pictures & Words Editorial Services, 3100 "B" Ave, Anacortes, WA 98221 *Tel:* 360-293-8476 *E-mail:* editor@picturesandwords.com *Web Site:* www.picturesandwords.com/words, pg 469

Hein, W Shannon, William S Hein & Co Inc, 2350 N Forest Rd, Getzville, NY 14068 *Tel:* 716-882-2600 *Toll Free Tel:* 800-828-7571 *Fax:* 716-883-8100 *E-mail:* mail@wshein.com; marketing@wshein.com *Web Site:* www.wshein.com, pg 97

Hein, William S Jr, William S Hein & Co Inc, 2350 N Forest Rd, Getzville, NY 14068 *Tel:* 716-882-2600 *Toll Free Tel:* 800-828-7571 *Fax:* 716-883-8100 *E-mail:* mail@wshein.com; marketing@wshein.com *Web Site:* www.wshein.com, pg 97

Heinen, Jonathan, The Crazyhorse Fiction Prize, College of Charleston, Dept of English, 66 George St, Charleston, SC 29424 *Tel:* 843-953-4470 *E-mail:* crazyhorse@cofc.edu *Web Site:* crazyhorse.cofc.edu/prizes, pg 607

Heinen, Jonathan, Lynda Hull Memorial Poetry Prize, College of Charleston, Dept of English, 66 George St, Charleston, SC 29424 *Tel:* 843-953-4470 *E-mail:* crazyhorse@cofc.edu *Web Site:* crazyhorse.cofc.edu/prizes, pg 625

Heinzelman, Kurt, Carr P Collins Award, PO Box 609, Round Rock, TX 78680 *Tel:* 512-683-5640 *E-mail:* president@texasinstituteofletters.org *Web Site:* www.texasinstituteofletters.org, pg 606

Heinzelman, Kurt, Soeurette Diehl Fraser Translation Award, PO Box 609, Round Rock, TX 78680 *Tel:* 512-683-5640 *E-mail:* president@texasinstituteofletters.org *Web Site:* www.texasinstituteofletters.org, pg 617

Heinzelman, Kurt, Jesse H Jones Award, PO Box 609, Round Rock, TX 78680 *Tel:* 512-683-5640 *E-mail:* president@texasinstituteofletters.org *Web Site:* www.texasinstituteofletters.org, pg 629

Heinzelman, Kurt, Ramirez Family Award, PO Box 609, Round Rock, TX 78680 *Tel:* 512-683-5640 *E-mail:* president@texasinstituteofletters.org *Web Site:* www.texasinstituteofletters.org, pg 660

Heinzelman, Kurt, Edwin "Bud" Shrake Award for Best Short Nonfiction, PO Box 609, Round Rock, TX 78680 *Tel:* 512-683-5640 *E-mail:* president@texasinstituteofletters.org *Web Site:* www.texasinstituteofletters.org, pg 667

Heinzelman, Kurt, Helen C Smith Memorial Award, PO Box 609, Round Rock, TX 78680 *Tel:* 512-683-5640 *E-mail:* president@texasinstituteofletters.org *Web Site:* www.texasinstituteofletters.org, pg 668

Heinzelman, Kurt, Texas Institute of Letters (TIL), PO Box 609, Round Rock, TX 78680 *E-mail:* president@texasinstituteofletters.org; secretary@texasinstituteofletters.org *Web Site:* www.texasinstituteofletters.org, pg 548

Heinzelman, Kurt, Texas Institute of Letters Awards, PO Box 609, Round Rock, TX 78680 *Tel:* 512-683-5640 *E-mail:* president@texasinstituteofletters.org *Web Site:* www.texasinstituteofletters.org, pg 672

Heinzelman, Kurt, University of Texas at Austin, New Writers Project, Dept of English, Calhoun Hall, Rm 226, 204 W 21 St, B-5000, Austin, TX 78712 *Tel:* 512-471-5132; 512-471-4991 *Fax:* 512-471-4909 *Web Site:* newwritersproject.org, pg 586

Heiser, Christopher, University of Chicago Press, 1427 E 60 St, Chicago, IL 60637-2954 *Tel:* 773-702-7700; 773-702-7600 *Toll Free Tel:* 800-621-2736 (orders) *Fax:* 773-702-9756; 773-660-2235 (orders); 773-702-2708 *E-mail:* custserv@press.uchicago.edu; marketing@press.uchicago.edu *Web Site:* www.press.uchicago.edu, pg 226

Heitner, Michael, Advertising Research Foundation (ARF), 432 Park Ave S, 4th fl, New York, NY 10016-8013 *Tel:* 212-751-5656 *Fax:* 212-689-1859 *E-mail:* help@thearf.org *Web Site:* thearf.org, pg 521

Held, Ivan, Dutton, 1745 Broadway, New York, NY 10019 *Tel:* 212-366-2000 *Fax:* 212-366-2262 *E-mail:* duttonpublicity@us.penguingroup.com *Web Site:* www.penguin.com, pg 68

Held, Ivan, Penguin Group USA, A Penguin Random House Company, 375 Hudson St, New York, NY 10014 *Tel:* 212-366-2000 *Toll Free Tel:* 800-847-5515 (inside sales); 800-631-8571 (cust serv) *Fax:* 212-366-2666; 607-775-4829 (inside sales) *E-mail:* online@us.penguingroup.com *Web Site:* www.penguin.com, pg 163

Held, Ivan, GP Putnam's Sons (Hardcover), 375 Hudson St, New York, NY 10014 *Tel:* 212-366-2000 *Fax:* 212-366-2643 *E-mail:* online@penguinputnam.com *Web Site:* www.penguin.com/publishers/gpputnamssons, pg 178

Helfand, Debra, Farrar, Straus & Giroux, LLC, 175 Varick St, 9th fl, New York, NY 10014 *Tel:* 212-741-6900 *E-mail:* fsg.publicity@fsgbooks.com *Web Site:* us.macmillan.com/fsg.aspx, pg 76

Helferty, Molly, Kids Can Press Ltd, 25 Dockside Dr, Toronto, ON M5A 0B5, Canada *Tel:* 416-479-7000 *Toll Free Tel:* 800-265-0884 *Fax:* 416-960-5437 *E-mail:* info@kidscan.com; customerservice@kidscan.com *Web Site:* www.kidscanpress.com; www.kidscanpress.ca, pg 431

Helgesen, Jeff, Research Press, 2612 N Mattis Ave, Champaign, IL 61822 *Tel:* 217-352-3273 *Toll Free Tel:* 800-519-2707 *Fax:* 217-352-1221 *E-mail:* rp@researchpress.com; orders@researchpress.com *Web Site:* www.researchpress.com, pg 184

Helinek, Jennifer, Trident Media Group LLC, 41 Madison Ave, 36th fl, New York, NY 10010 *Tel:* 212-333-1511 *E-mail:* info@tridentmediagroup.com; press@tridentmediagroup.com *Web Site:* www.tridentmediagroup.com, pg 507

Helleberg, Tom, The Mountaineers Books, 1001 SW Klickitat Way, Suite 201, Seattle, WA 98134 *Tel:* 206-223-6303 *Fax:* 206-223-6306 *E-mail:* mbooks@mountaineersbooks.org; customerservice@mountaineersbooks.org *Web Site:* www.mountaineersbooks.org, pg 143

Hellegers, Allison, Stimola Literary Studio Inc, 308 Livingston Ct, Edgewater, NJ 07020 *Tel:* 201-945-9353 *Fax:* 201-945-9353; 201-490-5920 *E-mail:* info@stimolaliterarystudio.com *Web Site:* www.stimolaliterarystudio.com, pg 504

Heller, Allyson, Simon & Schuster Children's Publishing, 1230 Avenue of the Americas, New York, NY 10020 *Tel:* 212-698-7000 *Web Site:* www.simonandschuster.com/kids; www.simonandschuster.com/teen; simonandschuster.net; simonandschuster.biz, pg 199

Heller, Brian, Macmillan, 120 Broadway, 22nd fl, New York, NY 10271 *Tel:* 646-307-5151 *E-mail:* press.inquiries@macmillan.com *Web Site:* www.macmillan.com, pg 129

Heller, Chelsey, Aevitas Creative Management, 19 W 21 St, Suite 501, New York, NY 10010 *Tel:* 212-765-6900 *Web Site:* aevitascreative.com, pg 474

Heller, Moshe, KTAV Publishing House Inc, 527 Empire Blvd, Brooklyn, NY 11225 *Tel:* 201-963-9524; 718-972-5449 *Fax:* 718-972-6307 *E-mail:* orders@ktav.com *Web Site:* www.ktav.com, pg 119

Helm, Kevin, ASET - The Neurodiagnostic Society, 402 E Bannister Rd, Suite A, Kansas City, MO 64131-3019 *Tel:* 816-931-1120 *Fax:* 816-931-1145 *E-mail:* info@aset.org *Web Site:* www.aset.org, pg 22

Helminiak, Sarah, PRINTING United Alliance, 10015 Main St, Fairfax, VA 22031-3489 *Tel:* 703-385-1335 *Toll Free Tel:* 888-385-3588 *Fax:* 703-273-0456; 703-691-7492 (membership) *E-mail:* assist@printing.org; info@printing.org *Web Site:* www.printing.org; www.sgia.org, pg 544

Helms, Derek, University Press of Kansas, 2502 Westbrooke Circle, Lawrence, KS 66045-4444 *Tel:* 785-864-4154; 785-864-4155 (orders) *Fax:* 785-864-4586 *E-mail:* upress@ku.edu; upkorders@ku.edu (orders) *Web Site:* www.kansaspress.ku.edu, pg 233

Helstien, Dylan, St Martin's Press, LLC, 120 Broadway, New York, NY 10271 *Tel:* 646-307-5151 *Web Site:* us.macmillan.com/smp, pg 191

Heltzel, Anne, Harry N Abrams Inc, 195 Broadway, 9th fl, New York, NY 10007 *Tel:* 212-206-7715 *Toll Free Tel:* 800-345-1359 *Fax:* 212-519-1210 *E-mail:* abrams@abramsbooks.com *Web Site:* www.abramsbooks.com, pg 3

Hemperly, Becky S, Candlewick Press, 99 Dover St, Somerville, MA 02144-2825 *Tel:* 617-661-3330 *Fax:* 617-661-0565 *E-mail:* bigbear@candlewick.com; salesinfo@candlewick.com *Web Site:* www.candlewick.com, pg 44

Hempstead, Andrew, Summerthought Publishing, PO Box 2309, Banff, AB T1L 1C1, Canada *Tel:* 403-762-0535 *Fax:* 403-762-3095 *Toll Free Fax:* 800-762-3095 (orders) *E-mail:* info@summerthought.com; sales@ summerthought.com *Web Site:* summerthought.com, pg 441

Henderson, Bill, Pushcart Press, PO Box 380, Wainscott, NY 11975-0380 *Tel:* 631-324-9300 *Web Site:* www. pushcartprize.com/pushcartpress, pg 178

Henderson, Bill, Pushcart Prize: Best of the Small Presses, PO Box 380, Wainscott, NY 11975-0380 *Tel:* 631-324-9300 *Web Site:* www.pushcartprize.com, pg 660

Henderson, Chad, Trustus Playwrights' Festival, 520 Lady St, Columbia, SC 29201 *Tel:* 803-254-9732 *Web Site:* www.trustus.org, pg 674

Henderson, Diane, Homestead Publishing, Box 193, Moose, WY 83012-0193 *Tel:* 307-733-6248 *Fax:* 307-733-6248 *E-mail:* orders@homesteadpublishing.net *Web Site:* www.homesteadpublishing.net, pg 102

Henderson, Keith, The Association of English-Language Publishers of Quebec-AELAQ (Association des Editeurs de Langue Anglaise du Quebec), Atwater Library, 1200 Atwater Ave, Suite 3, Westmount, QC H3Z 1X4, Canada *Tel:* 514-932-5633 *E-mail:* admin@ aelaq.org *Web Site:* aelaq.org, pg 526

Henderson, Nicholas, Farrar, Straus & Giroux Books for Young Readers, 120 Broadway, New York, NY 10271 *Tel:* 212-741-6900 *Toll Free Tel:* 888-330-8477 (orders) *Fax:* 212-633-9385 *Web Site:* us.macmillan. com/mackids; www.mackidsbooks.com, pg 76

Henderson-Brown, Zakia, The New Press, 120 Wall St, 31st fl, New York, NY 10005 *Tel:* 212-629-8802 *Toll Free Tel:* 800-343-4489 (orders) *Fax:* 212-629-8617 *Toll Free Fax:* 800-351-5073 (orders) *E-mail:* newpress@thenewpress.com *Web Site:* www. thenewpress.com, pg 149

Hendricks, Kent, Zondervan, 3900 Sparks Dr, Grand Rapids, MI 49546 *Tel:* 616-698-6900 *Toll Free Tel:* 800-226-1122; 800-727-1309 (retail orders) *Fax:* 616-698-3350 *Toll Free Fax:* 800-698-3256 (retail orders) *Web Site:* www.zondervan.com, pg 248

Hendricksen, Sara, University of Nevada Press, c/o University of Nevada, Continuing Educ Bldg, MS 0166, Reno, NV 89557-0166 *Tel:* 775-784-6573 *Fax:* 775-784-6200 *Web Site:* www.unpress.nevada. edu, pg 229

Hendrie, Caroline W, Education Writers Association (EWA), 3516 Connecticut Ave NW, Washington, DC 20008 *Tel:* 202-452-9830 *Fax:* 202-452-9837 *E-mail:* ewa@ewa.org *Web Site:* www.ewa.org, pg 532

Hendrie, Caroline W, Education Writers Association Workshops, 3516 Connecticut Ave NW, Washington, DC 20008 *Tel:* 202-452-9830 *Fax:* 202-452-9837 *E-mail:* ewa@ewa.org *Web Site:* www.ewa.org, pg 574

Hendrie, Caroline W, National Awards for Education Reporting, 3516 Connecticut Ave NW, Washington, DC 20008 *Tel:* 202-452-9830 *Fax:* 202-452-9837 *E-mail:* ewa@ewa.org *Web Site:* www.ewa.org, pg 644

Hendrix, Dr Erika, Peter Lang Publishing Inc, 80 Broadway, 5th fl, New York, NY 10004 *Tel:* 703-661-1584 *Toll Free Tel:* 800-770-5264 (cust serv) *Fax:* 703-996-1010 *E-mail:* newyork.editorial@ peterlang.com; customerservice@plang.com *Web Site:* www.peterlang.com, pg 119

Henebry, Martha, American Association of Collegiate Registrars & Admissions Officers (AACRAO), One Dupont Circle NW, Suite 520, Washington, DC 20036 *Tel:* 202-293-9161 *Fax:* 202-872-8857 *Web Site:* www. aacrao.org, pg 9

Henke, Kelsey, Justin Winsor Prize for Library History Essay, 225 N Michigan Ave, Suite 1300, Chicago, IL 60601 *Tel:* 312-280-4283 *Toll Free Tel:* 800-545-2433 (ext 4283) *Fax:* 312-280-4392 *E-mail:* ors@ala.org *Web Site:* www.ala.org; ala.org/lhrt, pg 678

Henkin, Alyssa Eisner, Trident Media Group LLC, 41 Madison Ave, 36th fl, New York, NY 10010 *Tel:* 212-333-1511 *E-mail:* info@tridentmediagroup. com; press@tridentmediagroup.com *Web Site:* www. tridentmediagroup.com, pg 507

Henley, Kristin, The Center for Fiction, 17 E 47 St, New York, NY 10017 *Tel:* 212-755-6710 *E-mail:* info@ centerforfiction.org *Web Site:* centerforfiction.org, pg 530

Henn, J Garrett, McGraw-Hill Professional Publishing Group, 2 Penn Plaza, New York, NY 10121 *Tel:* 646-766-2000 *Web Site:* www.mhprofessional.com; www. mheducation.com, pg 136

Henney, Eric, Perseus Books, 1290 Avenue of the Americas, New York, NY 10104 *Tel:* 212-340-8100 *Toll Free Tel:* 800-343-4499 (cust serv) *Fax:* 212-340-8105 *Web Site:* www.perseusbooks.com, pg 167

Hennigan, Shane, Arcadia Publishing Inc, 420 Wando Park Blvd, Mount Pleasant, SC 29464 *Tel:* 843-853-2070 *Toll Free Tel:* 888-313-2665 (orders only) *Fax:* 843-853-0044 *E-mail:* sales@arcadiapublishing. com *Web Site:* www.arcadiapublishing.com, pg 19

Henning-Stout, Sara, Princeton University Press, 41 William St, Princeton, NJ 08540-5237 *Tel:* 609-258-4900 *Fax:* 609-258-6305 *Web Site:* press.princeton. edu, pg 175

Henoch, Larissa, Health Communications Inc, 3201 SW 15 St, Deerfield Beach, FL 33442 *Tel:* 954-360-0909 *Toll Free Tel:* 800-851-9100; 800-441-5569 (cust serv & orders) *Fax:* 954-360-0034 *Toll Free Fax:* 800-424-7652 (cust serv & orders) *E-mail:* customerservice2@ hcibooks.com *Web Site:* www.hcibooks.com, pg 96

Henriques, Sasha, Random House Children's Books, 1745 Broadway, 10th fl, New York, NY 10019 *Tel:* 212-782-9000 *Web Site:* www.randomhousekids. com, pg 180

Henry, Christie, Princeton University Press, 41 William St, Princeton, NJ 08540-5237 *Tel:* 609-258-4900 *Fax:* 609-258-6305 *Web Site:* press.princeton.edu, pg 174

Henry, Claire, Fairchild Books, 1385 Broadway, 5th fl, New York, NY 10018 *Tel:* 212-419-5300 *Toll Free Tel:* 800-932-4724; 888-330-8477 (orders) *Web Site:* bloomsbury.com/us/academic/fairchildbooks, pg 75

Henry, Gray, Fons Vitae, 49 Mockingbird Valley Dr, Louisville, KY 40207-1366 *Tel:* 502-897-3641 *Fax:* 502-893-7373 *E-mail:* fonsvitaeky@aol.com *Web Site:* www.fonsvitae.com, pg 79

Henry, Jack, World Citizens, PO Box 131, Mill Valley, CA 94942-0131 *Tel:* 415-380-8020; 415-233-2822 (direct) *Toll Free Tel:* 800-247-6553 (orders only), pg 245

Henry, Lynn, Knopf Canada, 320 Front St W, Suite 1400, Toronto, ON M5V 3B6, Canada *Tel:* 416-364-4449 *Toll Free Tel:* 888-523-9292 *Fax:* 416-598-7764 *Web Site:* www.penguinrandomhouse.ca, pg 431

Hensley, Alan, McGraw-Hill Career Education, 1333 Burr Ridge Pkwy, Burr Ridge, IL 60527 *Tel:* 630-789-4000 *Toll Free Tel:* 800-338-3987 (cust serv) *Fax:* 630-789-5523; 614-755-5645 (cust serv) *Web Site:* www.mhhe.com, pg 135

Hensley, Kate, Princeton University Press, 41 William St, Princeton, NJ 08540-5237 *Tel:* 609-258-4900 *Fax:* 609-258-6305 *Web Site:* press.princeton.edu, pg 175

Hensley, Todd, C&T Publishing Inc, 1651 Challenge Dr, Concord, CA 94520-5206 *Tel:* 925-677-0377 *Toll Free Tel:* 800-284-1114 *Fax:* 925-677-0373 *E-mail:* support@ctpub.com *Web Site:* www.ctpub. com, pg 44

Hensley, Tony, C&T Publishing Inc, 1651 Challenge Dr, Concord, CA 94520-5206 *Tel:* 925-677-0377 *Toll Free Tel:* 800-284-1114 *Fax:* 925-677-0373 *E-mail:* support@ctpub.com *Web Site:* www.ctpub. com, pg 44

Henson, Gwen, American Society for Indexing Inc (ASI), 1628 E Southern Ave, Suite 9-223, Tempe, AZ 85282 *Tel:* 480-245-6750 *E-mail:* info@asindexing.org *Web Site:* www.asindexing.org, pg 524

Henson, Gwen, ASI/EIS Publishing Award for Excellence in Indexing, 1628 E Southern Ave, Suite 9-223, Tempe, AZ 85282 *Tel:* 480-245-6750 *E-mail:* info@asindexing.org *Web Site:* www. asindexing.org, pg 593

Henson, Kristi, University of Alabama Press, 200 Hackberry Lane, 2nd fl, Tuscaloosa, AL 35487 *Tel:* 205-348-5180 *Fax:* 205-348-9201 *Web Site:* www. uapress.ua.edu, pg 225

Hentz, Brad, Sourcebooks LLC, 1935 Brookdale Rd, Suite 139, Naperville, IL 60563 *Tel:* 630-961-3900 *Toll Free Tel:* 800-432-7444 *Fax:* 630-961-2168 *E-mail:* info@sourcebooks.com; customersupport@ sourcebooks.com *Web Site:* www.sourcebooks.com, pg 204

Herbert, Karen Brown, Karen Brown Guides LLC, PO Box 70, San Mateo, CA 94401-0070 *Fax:* 650-342-9153 *Web Site:* www.karenbrown.com, pg 42

Herbert-Copley, Brent, Social Sciences & Humanities Research Council of Canada (SSHRC), 350 Albert St, Ottawa, ON K1P 6G4, Canada *Tel:* 613-992-0691; 613-996-6976 *E-mail:* research@sshrc-crsh.gc.ca *Web Site:* www.sshrc.ca, pg 546

Herchenroeder, Jen, Bancroft Press, 3209 Bancroft Rd, Baltimore, MD 21215 *Tel:* 410-358-0658 *Web Site:* www.bancroftpress.com, pg 27

Herder, Dr Gwendolin, The Crossroad Publishing Co, 831 Chestnut Ridge Rd, Chestnut Ridge, NY 10977 *Tel:* 845-517-0180 *Toll Free Tel:* 800-888-4741 (orders) *E-mail:* info@crossroadpublishing.com *Web Site:* www.CrossroadPublishing.com, pg 60

Hergenroeder, Jennifer, The Experiment, 220 E 23 St, Suite 600, New York, NY 10010-4658 *Tel:* 212-889-1659 *E-mail:* info@theexperimentpublishing.com *Web Site:* www.theexperimentpublishing.com, pg 74

Herits, Noreen, Random House Children's Books, 1745 Broadway, 10th fl, New York, NY 10019 *Tel:* 212-782-9000 *Web Site:* www.randomhousekids.com, pg 180

Herman, Cheryl, Books on Tape™, 1745 Broadway, New York, NY 10019 *Toll Free Tel:* 800-733-3000 (cust serv) *Toll Free Fax:* 800-940-7046 *Web Site:* www.booksontape.com, pg 38

Herman, Gilles, Les Editions du Septentrion, 835 Turnbull Ave, Quebec City, QC G1R 2X4, Canada *Tel:* 418-688-3556 *Fax:* 418-527-4978 *E-mail:* info@ septentrion.qc.ca *Web Site:* www.septentrion.qc.ca, pg 423

Herman, Heather, Morton Publishing Co, 925 W Kenyon Ave, Unit 12, Englewood, CO 80110 *Tel:* 303-761-4805 *Fax:* 303-762-9923 *E-mail:* contact@morton-pub.com; returns@morton-pub.com *Web Site:* www. morton-pub.com, pg 143

Herman, Jeffrey H, The Jeff Herman Agency LLC, 29 Park St, Stockbridge, MA 01262 *Tel:* 413-298-0077 *E-mail:* submissions@jeffherman.com *Web Site:* www. jeffherman.com, pg 488

Herman, Kate, Chronicle Books, 680 Second St, San Francisco, CA 94107 *Tel:* 415-537-4200 *Toll Free Tel:* 800-759-0190 (cust serv) *Fax:* 415-537-4460 *Toll Free Fax:* 800-858-7787 (orders); 800-286-9471 (cust serv) *E-mail:* frontdesk@chroniclebooks.com *Web Site:* www.chroniclebooks.com, pg 51

Herman, Rhonda, McFarland, 960 NC Hwy 88 W, Jefferson, NC 28640 *Tel:* 336-246-4460 *Toll Free Tel:* 800-253-2187 (orders) *Fax:* 336-246-5018; 336-246-4403 (orders) *E-mail:* info@mcfarlandpub.com *Web Site:* mcfarlandbooks.com, pg 135

Herman, Ronnie Ann, Herman Agency, 350 Central Park W, Apt 4I, New York, NY 10025 *Tel:* 212-749-4907 *Web Site:* www.hermanagencyinc.com, pg 511

Herman, Susan N, American Civil Liberties Union, 125 Broad St, 18th fl, New York, NY 10004 *Tel:* 212-549-2500 *E-mail:* media@aclu.org *Web Site:* www.aclu. org, pg 522

Hermann, Sara, Parmenides Publishing, 3753 Howard Hughes Pkwy, Suite 200, Las Vegas, NV 89169 *Tel:* 702-892-3934 *Fax:* 702-892-3939 *E-mail:* info@ parmenides.com *Web Site:* www.parmenides.com, pg 161

Hermann, Suzanne, American Institute for Economic Research (AIER), 250 Division St, Great Barrington, MA 01230 *Tel:* 413-528-1216 *Toll Free Tel:* 888-528-1216 (orders) *E-mail:* info@aier.org *Web Site:* www.aier.org, pg 11

Hermelin, Christopher, The Fischer-Harbage Agency Inc, 540 President St, 3rd fl, Brooklyn, NY 11215 *Tel:* 212-695-7105 *E-mail:* info@fischerharbage.com *Web Site:* www.fischerharbage.com, pg 484

Hermes, Sr Kathryn James, Pauline Books & Media, 50 Saint Paul's Ave, Boston, MA 02130 *Tel:* 617-522-8911 *Toll Free Tel:* 800-876-4463 (orders); 800-836-9723 (cust serv) *Fax:* 617-541-9805 *E-mail:* editorial@paulinemedia.com (ms submissions); orderentry@pauline.org (cust serv) *Web Site:* www.pauline.org/pbmpublishing, pg 161

Hernandez, Carlos, Editorial Unilit, 8167 NW 84 St, Medley, FL 33166 *Tel:* 305-592-6136 *Toll Free Tel:* 800-767-7726 *Fax:* 305-592-0087 *E-mail:* info@editorialunilit.com; customerservice@editorialunilit.com *Web Site:* www.editorialunilit.com, pg 224

Hernandez, Debra Gersh, Reporters Committee for Freedom of the Press, 1156 15 St NW, Suite 1250, Washington, DC 20005-1779 *Tel:* 202-795-9300 *Toll Free Tel:* 800-336-4243 *E-mail:* info@rcfp.org *Web Site:* www.rcfp.org, pg 545

Hernandez, Gabriel, Florida Graphics Alliance (FGA), 5770 Hoffner Ave, Suite 103, Orlando, FL 32822 *Tel:* 407-240-8009 *Toll Free Tel:* 800-331-0461 *Fax:* 407-240-8333 *E-mail:* info@floridagraphics.org *Web Site:* www.floridagraphics.org, pg 533

Hernandez, Joanna, Deadline Club, c/o Salmagundi Club, 47 Fifth Ave, New York, NY 10003 *Tel:* 646-481-7584 *Web Site:* www.deadlineclub.org, pg 532

Hernandez, Laura, Random House Children's Books, 1745 Broadway, 10th fl, New York, NY 10019 *Tel:* 212-782-9000 *Web Site:* www.randomhousekids.com, pg 181

Hernandez, Tim Z, University of Texas at El Paso, Department of Creative Writing, MFA/Department of Creative Writing, 901 EDUC, 500 W University Ave, El Paso, TX 79968-9991 *Tel:* 915-747-5713 *Fax:* 915-747-5523 *E-mail:* creativewriting@utep.edu *Web Site:* www.utep.edu/cw, pg 586

Herndon, John, The Balcones Fiction Prize, 1212 Rio Grande St, Austin, TX 78701 *Tel:* 512-828-9368 *E-mail:* balcones@austincc.edu *Web Site:* sites.austincc.edu/crw/balcones-prizes, pg 595

Herndon, John, The Balcones Poetry Prize, 1212 Rio Grande St, Austin, TX 78701 *Tel:* 512-828-9368 *E-mail:* balcones@austincc.edu *Web Site:* sites.austincc.edu/crw/category/balcones_poetry_prize/, pg 595

Herrera, Aida, BenBella Books Inc, 10300 N Central Expwy, Suite 400, Dallas, TX 75231 *Tel:* 214-750-3600 *E-mail:* feedback@benbellabooks.com *Web Site:* www.benbellabooks.com; www.smartpopbooks.com, pg 31

Herrera, Jennifer, David Black Agency, 335 Adams St, 27th fl, Suite 2707, Brooklyn, NY 11201 *Tel:* 718-852-5500 *Fax:* 718-852-5539 *Web Site:* www.davidblackagency.com, pg 476

Herrera Mulligan, Michelle, Atria Books, 1230 Avenue of the Americas, New York, NY 10020 *Tel:* 212-698-7000 *Fax:* 212-698-7007 *Web Site:* www.simonandschuster.com, pg 24

Herrick, Becky, Sky Pony Press, 307 W 36 St, 11th fl, New York, NY 10018 *Tel:* 212-643-6816 *Fax:* 212-643-6819 *E-mail:* skypony@skyhorsepublishing.com; info@skyhorsepublishing.com; submissions@skyhorsepublishing.com *Web Site:* www.skyponypress.com, pg 200

Herring, Jamie, Columbia Books & Information Services (CBIS), 4340 East-West Hwy, Suite 300, Bethesda, MD 20814 *Tel:* 202-464-1662 *Fax:* 301-664-9600 *E-mail:* info@columbiabooks.com *Web Site:* www.columbiabooks.com; www.lobbyists.info; www.associationexecs.com, pg 55

Herrington, Jennifer, Harvey Klinger Inc, 300 W 55 St, Suite 11V, New York, NY 10019 *Tel:* 212-581-7068 *Fax:* 212-315-3823 *E-mail:* queries@harveyklinger.com *Web Site:* www.harveyklinger.com, pg 491

Herrmann, Laurie, Beaver's Pond Press Inc, 939 Seventh St W, St Paul, MN 55102 *Tel:* 952-829-8818 *E-mail:* info@beaverspondpress.com *Web Site:* www.beaverspondpress.com, pg 30

Hershey, Elena, Doubleday, c/o Penguin Random House Inc, 1745 Broadway, New York, NY 10019 *Tel:* 212-751-2600 *Fax:* 212-572-2662 (foreign rts) *E-mail:* ddaypub@randomhouse.com *Web Site:* knopfdoubleday.com, pg 66

Hershey, Jennifer, Random House Publishing Group, 1745 Broadway, New York, NY 10019 *Toll Free Tel:* 800-200-3552 *Web Site:* www.randomhousebooks.com, pg 181

Hershon, Robert, Hanging Loose Press, 231 Wyckoff St, Brooklyn, NY 11217 *Tel:* 347-529-4738 *Fax:* 347-227-8215 *E-mail:* print225@aol.com *Web Site:* www.hangingloosepress.com, pg 92

Herz, Suzanne, Anchor Books, c/o Penguin Random House Inc, 1745 Broadway, New York, NY 10019 *Tel:* 212-572-2420 *E-mail:* vintageanchorpublicity@randomhouse.com *Web Site:* knopfdoubleday.com/imprint/anchor, pg 15

Herz, Suzanne, Doubleday, c/o Penguin Random House Inc, 1745 Broadway, New York, NY 10019 *Tel:* 212-751-2600 *Fax:* 212-572-2662 (foreign rts) *E-mail:* ddaypub@randomhouse.com *Web Site:* knopfdoubleday.com, pg 66

Herz, Suzanne, Vintage Books, c/o Penguin Random House Inc, 1745 Broadway, New York, NY 10019 *Tel:* 212-572-2420 *E-mail:* vintageanchorpublicity@randomhouse.com *Web Site:* knopfdoubleday.com/imprint/vintage, pg 236

Heschke, Christa, McIntosh and Otis Inc, 207 E 37 St, Suite BG, New York, NY 10016 *Tel:* 212-687-7400 *Fax:* 212-687-6894 *E-mail:* info@mcintoshandotis.com *Web Site:* www.mcintoshandotis.com, pg 496

Hess, Stephanie, Orbit, 1290 Avenue of the Americas, New York, NY 10104 *Tel:* 212-364-1100 *Toll Free Tel:* 800-759-0190 *Web Site:* www.orbitbooks.net, pg 156

Hesse, Lauren, Little, Brown and Company, 1290 Avenue of the Americas, New York, NY 10104 *Tel:* 212-364-1100 *Fax:* 212-364-0952 *E-mail:* firstname.lastname@hbgusa.com *Web Site:* www.littlebrown.com; www.hachettebookgroup.com, pg 125

Hetrick, J Thomas, Pocol Press, 320 Sutton St, Punxsutawney, PA 15767 *Tel:* 703-870-9611 *E-mail:* info@pocolpress.com *Web Site:* www.pocolpress.com, pg 171

Heule, Melissa, Deadline Club, c/o Salmagundi Club, 47 Fifth Ave, New York, NY 10003 *Tel:* 646-481-7584 *Web Site:* www.deadlineclub.org, pg 532

Heustess, Todd, Peter Glenn Publications, 306 NE Second St, 2nd fl, Delray Beach, FL 33483 *Web Site:* pgdirect.com, pg 86

Heward-Mills, Leon, Taylor & Francis Inc, 530 Walnut St, Suite 850, Philadelphia, PA 19106 *Tel:* 215-625-8900 *Toll Free Tel:* 800-354-1420 *Fax:* 215-207-0050; 215-207-0046 (cust serv) *E-mail:* support@tandfonline.com *Web Site:* www.taylorandfrancis.com, pg 213

Hewitt, Kristen, Chronicle Books, 680 Second St, San Francisco, CA 94107 *Tel:* 415-537-4200 *Toll Free Tel:* 800-759-0190 (cust serv) *Fax:* 415-537-4460 *Toll Free Fax:* 800-858-7787 (orders); 800-286-9471 (cust serv) *E-mail:* frontdesk@chroniclebooks.com *Web Site:* www.chroniclebooks.com, pg 51

Hewitt, Ted, Social Sciences & Humanities Research Council of Canada (SSHRC), 350 Albert St, Ottawa, ON K1P 6G4, Canada *Tel:* 613-992-0691; 613-996-6976 *E-mail:* research@sshrc-crsh.gc.ca *Web Site:* www.sshrc.ca, pg 546

Hewlett, Ashley, GP Putnam's Sons (Hardcover), 375 Hudson St, New York, NY 10014 *Tel:* 212-366-2000 *Fax:* 212-366-2643 *E-mail:* online@penguinputnam.com *Web Site:* www.penguin.com/publishers/gpputnamssons, pg 178

Hewlett, Moneta, Quirk Books, 215 Church St, Philadelphia, PA 19106 *Tel:* 215-627-3581 *Fax:* 215-627-5220 *E-mail:* general@quirkbooks.com *Web Site:* www.quirkbooks.com, pg 179

Heydt, David, HarperCollins General Books Group, 195 Broadway, New York, NY 10007 *Tel:* 212-207-7000 *Web Site:* www.harpercollins.com, pg 93

Heydweiller, Tracy, Random House Children's Books, 1745 Broadway, 10th fl, New York, NY 10019 *Tel:* 212-782-9000 *Web Site:* www.randomhousekids.com, pg 180

Heymann, Thomas A, National Notary Association (NNA), 9350 De Soto Ave, Chatsworth, CA 91311-4926 *Tel:* 818-739-4000 *Toll Free Tel:* 800-876-6827 *Toll Free Fax:* 800-833-1211 *E-mail:* services@nationalnotary.org *Web Site:* www.nationalnotary.org, pg 147

Heyward, William, The Penguin Press, 375 Hudson St, New York, NY 10014 *Web Site:* thepenguinpress.com, pg 164

Heywood, Leslie, Binghamton University Creative Writing Program, c/o Dept of English, PO Box 6000, Binghamton, NY 13902-6000 *Tel:* 607-777-2168 *Fax:* 607-777-2408 *E-mail:* cwpro@binghamton.edu *Web Site:* english.binghamton.edu/cwpro, pg 581

Hicks, David, International Wealth Success Inc, PO Box 186, Merrick, NY 11566-0186 *Tel:* 516-766-5850 *Toll Free Tel:* 800-323-0548 *Fax:* 516-766-5919 *E-mail:* admin@iwsmoney.com *Web Site:* www.iwsmoney.com, pg 112

Hicks, Patricia, Peradam Press, PO Box 6, North San Juan, CA 95960-0006 *Tel:* 530-277-9324 *Fax:* 530-559-0754 *E-mail:* peradam@earthlink.net, pg 167

Higbee, Alexa, Bloomsbury Publishing Inc, 1385 Broadway, 5th fl, New York, NY 10018 *Tel:* 212-419-5300 *E-mail:* marketingusa@bloomsbury.com; adultpublicityusa@bloomsbury.com; askacademic@bloomsbury.com *Web Site:* www.bloomsbury.com, pg 36

Higgins, Thomas M, Advertising Research Foundation (ARF), 432 Park Ave S, 4th fl, New York, NY 10016-8013 *Tel:* 212-751-5656 *Fax:* 212-689-1859 *E-mail:* help@thearf.org *Web Site:* thearf.org, pg 521

High, Holly, DEStech Publications Inc, 439 N Duke St, Lancaster, PA 17602-4967 *Tel:* 717-290-1660 *Toll Free Tel:* 877-500-4DES (500-4337) *Fax:* 717-509-6100 *E-mail:* info@destechpub.com *Web Site:* www.destechpub.com, pg 64

High, Sara, Workman Publishing Co Inc, 225 Varick St, 9th fl, New York, NY 10014-4381 *Tel:* 212-254-5900 *Toll Free Tel:* 800-722-7202 *Fax:* 212-254-8098 *E-mail:* info@workman.com; orders@workman.com *Web Site:* www.workman.com, pg 244

Hildebrand, Douglas, University of Alberta Press, Ring House 2, Edmonton, AB T6G 2E1, Canada *Tel:* 780-492-3662 *Fax:* 780-492-0719 *Web Site:* www.uap.ualberta.ca, pg 442

Hildreth, Mary Anne, Tower Publishing Co, 650 Cape Rd, Standish, ME 04084 *Tel:* 207-642-5400 *Toll Free Tel:* 800-969-8693 *E-mail:* info@towerpub.com *Web Site:* www.towerpub.com, pg 219

Hiles, Rachel, Chronicle Books, 680 Second St, San Francisco, CA 94107 *Tel:* 415-537-4200 *Toll Free Tel:* 800-759-0190 (cust serv) *Fax:* 415-537-4460 *Toll Free Fax:* 800-858-7787 (orders); 800-286-9471 (cust serv) *E-mail:* frontdesk@chroniclebooks.com *Web Site:* www.chroniclebooks.com, pg 52

Hilferty, Dan, Mason Crest Publishers, 450 Parkway Dr, Suite D, Broomall, PA 19008 *Tel:* 610-543-6200 *Toll Free Tel:* 866-MCP-BOOK (627-2665) *Fax:* 610-543-3878 *Web Site:* www.masoncrest.com, pg 133

Hilger, Lauren, NYSCA/NYFA Artist Fellowships, 20 Jay St, 7th fl, Brooklyn, NY 11201 *Tel:* 212-366-6900 *Fax:* 212-366-1778 *E-mail:* info@nyfa.org *Web Site:* www.nyfa.org, pg 649

Hite, Robyn, Wimmer Cookbooks, 4650 Shelby Air Dr, Memphis, TN 38118 *Toll Free Tel:* 800-548-2537 *Fax:* 901-363-1771 *E-mail:* info@wimmerco.com *Web Site:* www.wimmerco.com, pg 242

Hittel, Robert A, Florida Antiquarian Booksellers Association (FABA), 14046 Fifth St, Dade City, FL 33525 *Tel:* 727-234-7759 *E-mail:* floridabooksellers@gmail.com *Web Site:* floridabooksellers.com, pg 533

Hittle, Todd, 4A's (American Association of Advertising Agencies), 1065 Avenue of the Americas, 16th fl, New York, NY 10018 *Tel:* 212-682-2500 *Web Site:* www.aaaa.org, pg 534

Hivnor, Maggie, University of Chicago Press, 1427 E 60 St, Chicago, IL 60637-2954 *Tel:* 773-702-7700; 773-702-7600 *Toll Free Tel:* 800-621-2736 (orders) *Fax:* 773-702-9756; 773-660-2235 (orders); 773-702-2708 *E-mail:* custserv@press.uchicago.edu; marketing@press.uchicago.edu *Web Site:* www.press.uchicago.edu, pg 226

Hlavac, Julia, Sleeping Bear Press™, 2395 S Huron Pkwy, Suite 200, Ann Arbor, MI 48104 *Toll Free Tel:* 800-487-2323 *Fax:* 734-794-0004 *E-mail:* customerservice@sleepingbearpress.com *Web Site:* www.sleepingbearpress.com, pg 201

Ho, Howard, University of Southern California, Master of Professional Writing Program, Mark Taper Hall, THH 355, 3501 Trousedale Pkwy, Los Angeles, CA 90089-0355 *Tel:* 213-740-3252 *Fax:* 213-740-5002 *E-mail:* mpw@college.usc.edu *Web Site:* college.usc.edu/mpw, pg 586

Hoagland, Nancy, Duke University Press, 905 W Main St, Suite 18B, Durham, NC 27701 *Tel:* 919-688-5134 *Toll Free Tel:* 888-651-0122 (US) *Fax:* 919-688-2615 *Toll Free Fax:* 888-651-0124 *E-mail:* orders@dukeupress.edu *Web Site:* www.dukeupress.edu, pg 68

Hoak, Michael, Yale University Press, 302 Temple St, New Haven, CT 06511-8909 *Tel:* 203-432-0960; 203-432-0966 (sales); 401-531-2800 (cust serv) *Toll Free Tel:* 800-405-1619 (cust serv) *Fax:* 203-432-0948; 203-432-8485 (sales); 401-531-2801 (cust serv) *Toll Free Fax:* 800-406-9145 (cust serv) *E-mail:* sales.press@yale.edu (sales); customer.care@triliteral.org (cust serv) *Web Site:* www.yalebooks.com; yalepress.yale.edu/yupbooks, pg 246

Hoard, Trish, The Library of America, 14 E 60 St, New York, NY 10022-1006 *Tel:* 212-308-3360 *Fax:* 212-750-8352 *E-mail:* info@loa.org *Web Site:* www.loa.org, pg 124

Hoare, Steve, Black Dome Press Corp, 649 Delaware Ave, Delmar, NY 12054 *Tel:* 518-439-6512 *E-mail:* blackdomep@aol.com *Web Site:* www.blackdomepress.com, pg 34

Hobeika, Joelle, Alloy Entertainment LLC, 30 Hudson Yards, 22nd fl, New York, NY 10001 *E-mail:* collaborative@alloyentertainment.com, pg 8

Hocherman, Riva, Henry Holt and Company, LLC, 120 Broadway, 23rd fl, New York, NY 10271 *Tel:* 646-307-5151 *Toll Free Tel:* 888-330-8477 (orders) *Fax:* 646-307-5285 *Web Site:* www.henryholt.com, pg 102

Hochman, Gail, Brandt & Hochman Literary Agents Inc, 1501 Broadway, Suite 2310, New York, NY 10036 *Tel:* 212-840-5760 *Fax:* 212-840-5776 *Web Site:* brandthochman.com, pg 477

Hochman, Paul, St Martin's Press, LLC, 120 Broadway, New York, NY 10271 *Tel:* 646-307-5151 *Web Site:* us.macmillan.com/smp, pg 190

Hodapp, Angie, Nelson Literary Agency LLC, 1732 Wazee St, Suite 207, Denver, CO 80202-1284 *Tel:* 303-292-2805 *E-mail:* info@nelsonagency.com *Web Site:* www.nelsonagency.com, pg 497

Hodell, Courtney, Whiting Awards, 16 Court St, Suite 2308, Brooklyn, NY 11241 *Tel:* 718-701-5962 *E-mail:* info@whiting.org *Web Site:* www.whiting.org, pg 677

Hodell, Courtney, Whiting Creative Nonfiction Grant, 16 Court St, Suite 2308, Brooklyn, NY 11241 *Tel:* 718-701-5962 *E-mail:* nonfiction@whiting.org; info@whiting.org *Web Site:* www.whiting.org, pg 677

Hodell, Courtney, Whiting Literary Magazine Prizes, 16 Court St, Suite 2308, Brooklyn, NY 11241 *Tel:* 718-701-5962 *E-mail:* info@whiting.org *Web Site:* www.whiting.org/writers/whiting-literary-magazine-prizes, pg 677

Hodge, Joelle, Classical Academic Press, 515 S 32 St, Camp Hill, PA 17011 *Tel:* 717-730-0711 *Toll Free Tel:* 866-730-0711 *Fax:* 717-730-0721 *Toll Free Fax:* 866-730-0721 *E-mail:* info@classicalsubjects.com; orders@classicalsubjects.com *Web Site:* classicalacademicpress.com, pg 53

Hodge, Rebecca, RISING STAR Award, PO Box 190, Jefferson, OR 97352 *E-mail:* risingstar@womenfictionwriters.org *Web Site:* wfwa.memberclicks.net/rising-star-award, pg 662

Hodge, Rebecca, STAR Award, PO Box 190, Jefferson, OR 97352 *E-mail:* staraward@womenfictionwriters.org *Web Site:* wfwa.memberclicks.net/star-award, pg 670

Hodge, Rebecca, Women's Fiction Writers Association (WFWA), PO Box 190, Jefferson, OR 97352 *E-mail:* communications@womensfictionwriters.org; membership@womensfictionwriters.org *Web Site:* www.womensfictionwriters.org, pg 549

Hodson, Brad, Horror Writers Association (HWA), PO Box 56687, Sherman Oaks, CA 91413 *Tel:* 818-220-3965 *E-mail:* admin@horror.org *Web Site:* horror.org, pg 534

Hodson, Nancy, Cold Spring Harbor Laboratory Press, One Bungtown Rd, Cold Spring Harbor, NY 11724 *Tel:* 516-422-4100 *Toll Free Tel:* 800-843-4388 *Fax:* 516-422-4097; 516-422-4092 (submissions) *E-mail:* cshpress@cshl.edu *Web Site:* www.cshlpress.com, pg 54

Hodus, Brett, Scobre Press Corp, 2255 Calle Clara, La Jolla, CA 92037 *Fax:* 858-551-1232 *E-mail:* info@scobre.com *Web Site:* www.scobre.com; scobre.bookbuddyaudio.com, pg 195

Hoekman, David, Midwest Travel Journalists Inc, 902 S Randall Rd, Suite C311, St Charles, IL 60174 *Toll Free Tel:* 888-551-8184 *Fax:* 847-622-8015 *E-mail:* admin@mtja.us *Web Site:* www.mtja.us, pg 537

Hoeler, Tom, Penguin Random House LLC, 1745 Broadway, New York, NY 10019 *Tel:* 212-782-9000 *Toll Free Tel:* 800-726-0600 *Web Site:* www.penguinrandomhouse.com, pg 164

Hoesly, Sherry, The Permissions Group Inc, 401 S Milwaukee Ave, Suite 180, Wheeling, IL 60090 *Tel:* 847-635-6550 *Toll Free Tel:* 800-374-7985 *Fax:* 847-635-6968 *E-mail:* info@permissionsgroup.com *Web Site:* www.permissionsgroup.com, pg 468

Hofeldt, Sara E, Tapestry Press Ltd, 19 Nashoba Rd, Littleton, MA 01460 *Tel:* 978-486-0200 *Toll Free Tel:* 800-535-2007 *E-mail:* publish@tapestrypress.com *Web Site:* www.tapestrypress.com, pg 213

Hoff, Alexandra, University of New Mexico Press, One University of New Mexico, Albuquerque, NM 87131-0001 *Tel:* 505-272-7777 *Fax:* 505-277-3343 *E-mail:* custserv@unm.edu (order dept) *Web Site:* unmpress.com, pg 229

Hoffman, Jonathan, School Zone Publishing Co, 1819 Industrial Dr, Grand Haven, MI 49417 *Tel:* 616-846-5030 *Toll Free Tel:* 800-253-0564 *Fax:* 616-846-6181 *Web Site:* www.schoolzone.com, pg 195

Hoffman, Lauren, Simon & Schuster Children's Publishing, 1230 Avenue of the Americas, New York, NY 10020 *Tel:* 212-698-7000 *Web Site:* www.simonandschuster.com/kids; www.simonandschuster.com/teen; simonandschuster.net; simonandschuster.biz, pg 199

Hoffman, Mitch, The Aaron M Priest Literary Agency Inc, 200 W 41 St, 21st fl, New York, NY 10036 *Tel:* 212-818-0344 *Fax:* 212-573-9417 *E-mail:* info@aaronpriest.com *Web Site:* www.aaronpriest.com, pg 499

Hoffman, Philip, Penguin Random House LLC, 1745 Broadway, New York, NY 10019 *Tel:* 212-782-9000 *Toll Free Tel:* 800-726-0600 *Web Site:* www.penguinrandomhouse.com, pg 164

Hoffman, Randy, Captus Press Inc, 1600 Steeles Ave W, Units 14 & 15, Concord, ON L4K 4M2, Canada *Tel:* 416-736-5537 *Fax:* 416-736-5793 *E-mail:* info@captus.com *Web Site:* www.captus.com, pg 419

Hoffman, Scott, Folio Literary Management, The Film Center Bldg, 630 Ninth Ave, Suite 1101, New York, NY 10036 *Tel:* 212-400-1494 *Fax:* 212-967-0977 *Web Site:* www.foliolit.com, pg 484

Hoffman, Stefanie, Little, Brown Books for Young Readers, 1290 Avenue of the Americas, New York, NY 10104 *Tel:* 212-364-1100 *Toll Free Tel:* 800-759-0190 (cust serv) *Web Site:* www.hachettebookgroup.com, pg 126

Hoffman, Stuart A, Star Publishing Co Inc, PO Box 5165, Belmont, CA 94002-5165 *Tel:* 650-591-3505 *E-mail:* starpublishing@gmail.com *Web Site:* www.starpublishing.com, pg 207

Hoffnagle, Jerry, Rizzoli International Publications Inc, 300 Park Ave S, 4th fl, New York, NY 10010-5399 *Tel:* 212-387-3400 *Toll Free Tel:* 800-522-6657 (orders only) *Fax:* 212-387-3535 *E-mail:* publicity@rizzoliusa.com *Web Site:* www.rizzoliusa.com, pg 185

Hofmann, Ashley, AOTA Press, 6116 Executive Blvd, Suite 200, North Bethesda, MD 20852-4929 *Tel:* 301-652-6611 *Toll Free Tel:* 877-404-AOTA (404-2682, orders) *Fax:* 770-238-0414 (orders) *E-mail:* aotapress@aota.org; customerservice@aota.org *Web Site:* www.aota.org/Publications-News/AOTAPress.aspx; www.aota.org; store.aota.org, pg 17

Hofmann, Deborah, David Black Agency, 335 Adams St, 27th fl, Suite 2707, Brooklyn, NY 11201 *Tel:* 718-852-5500 *Fax:* 718-852-5539 *Web Site:* www.davidblackagency.com, pg 476

Hogan, John P, Council for Research in Values & Philosophy, The Catholic University of America, Gibbons Hall, Rm B-12, 620 Michigan Ave NE, Washington, DC 20064 *Tel:* 202-319-6089 *Fax:* 202-319-6089 *E-mail:* cua-rvp@cua.edu *Web Site:* www.crvp.org, pg 58

Hogan, Mary S, Plexus Publishing, Inc, 143 Old Marlton Pike, Medford, NJ 08055 *Tel:* 609-654-6500 *Fax:* 609-654-4309 *E-mail:* info@plexuspublishing.com *Web Site:* www.plexuspublishing.com, pg 170

Hogan, Megan, Simon & Schuster, 1230 Avenue of the Americas, New York, NY 10020 *Tel:* 212-698-7000 *Toll Free Tel:* 800-223-2348 (cust serv); 800-223-2336 (orders) *Toll Free Fax:* 800-943-9831 (orders) *Web Site:* www.simonandschuster.com, pg 198

Hogan, Michelle, Our Sunday Visitor Publishing, 200 Noll Plaza, Huntington, IN 46750 *Tel:* 260-356-8400 *Toll Free Tel:* 800-348-2440 (orders) *Fax:* 260-356-8472 *Toll Free Fax:* 800-498-6709 *E-mail:* osvbooks@osv.com (book orders) *Web Site:* www.osv.com, pg 157

Hogan, Patrick, The American Library Association (ALA), 225 N Michigan Ave, Suite 1300, Chicago, IL 60601 *Tel:* 312-944-6780 *Toll Free Tel:* 800-545-2433 *Fax:* 312-280-5275 *E-mail:* editionsmarketing@ala.org *Web Site:* www.alastore.ala.org, pg 12

Hogan, Thomas Jr, Information Today, Inc, 143 Old Marlton Pike, Medford, NJ 08055-8750 *Tel:* 609-654-6266 *Toll Free Tel:* 800-300-9868 (cust serv) *Fax:* 609-654-4309 *E-mail:* custserv@infotoday.com *Web Site:* www.infotoday.com, pg 108

Hogan, Thomas Jr, Plexus Publishing, Inc, 143 Old Marlton Pike, Medford, NJ 08055 *Tel:* 609-654-6500 *Fax:* 609-654-4309 *E-mail:* info@plexuspublishing.com *Web Site:* www.plexuspublishing.com, pg 170

Hogan, Thomas H, Information Today, Inc, 143 Old Marlton Pike, Medford, NJ 08055-8750 *Tel:* 609-654-6266 *Toll Free Tel:* 800-300-9868 (cust serv) *Fax:* 609-654-4309 *E-mail:* custserv@infotoday.com *Web Site:* www.infotoday.com, pg 108

Hogan, Thomas H, Plexus Publishing, Inc, 143 Old Marlton Pike, Medford, NJ 08055 *Tel:* 609-654-6500 *Fax:* 609-654-4309 *E-mail:* info@plexuspublishing.com *Web Site:* www.plexuspublishing.com, pg 170

Hoge, Steve, W W Norton & Company Inc, 500 Fifth Ave, New York, NY 10110-0017 *Tel:* 212-354-5500 *Toll Free Tel:* 800-233-4830 (orders & cust serv) *Fax:* 212-869-0856 *Toll Free Fax:* 800-458-6515 *E-mail:* orders@wwnorton.com *Web Site:* wwnorton. com, pg 152

Hogeland, Kim, Oregon State University Press, 121 The Valley Library, Corvallis, OR 97331-4501 *Tel:* 541-737-3166, pg 157

Hogenson, Barbara, The Barbara Hogenson Agency Inc, 165 West End Ave, Suite 19-C, New York, NY 10023 *Tel:* 212-874-8084 *Fax:* 212-595-6748 *E-mail:* bhogenson@aol.com, pg 489

Hoggutt, Brenda Jo, University of Texas Press, 3001 Lake Austin Blvd, 2.200, Austin, TX 78703 *Tel:* 512-471-7233 *Fax:* 512-232-7178 *E-mail:* utpress@uts.cc. utexas.edu; info@utpress.utexas.edu *Web Site:* utpress. utexas.edu, pg 216

Hogrebe, Christina, Jane Rotrosen Agency LLC, 85 Broad St, 28th fl, New York, NY 10004 *Tel:* 212-593-4330 *Fax:* 212-935-6985 *Web Site:* janerotrosen.com, pg 500

Hokanson, Sarah, Random House Children's Books, 1745 Broadway, 10th fl, New York, NY 10019 *Tel:* 212-782-9000 *Web Site:* www.randomhousekids. com, pg 180

Hoke, Dylan, Hachette Book Group, 1290 Avenue of the Americas, New York, NY 10104 *Tel:* 212-364-1100 *Toll Free Tel:* 800-759-0190 (cust serv) *Fax:* 212-364-0933 (intl orders) *Toll Free Fax:* 800-286-9471 (cust serv) *Web Site:* www.hachettebookgroup.com, pg 91

Holahan, Jessica, Yale University Press, 302 Temple St, New Haven, CT 06511-8909 *Tel:* 203-432-0960; 203-432-0966 (sales); 401-531-2800 (cust serv) *Toll Free Tel:* 800-405-1619 (cust serv) *Fax:* 203-432-0948; 203-432-8485 (sales); 401-531-2801 (cust serv) *Toll Free Fax:* 800-406-9145 (cust serv) *E-mail:* sales. press@yale.edu (sales); customer.care@triliteral.org (cust serv) *Web Site:* www.yalebooks.com; yalepress. yale.edu/yupbooks, pg 246

Holbert, Christine, The Idaho Prize for Poetry, 105 Lost Horse Lane, Sandpoint, ID 83864 *Tel:* 208-255-4410 *Fax:* 208-255-1560 *E-mail:* losthorsepress@ mindspring.com *Web Site:* www.losthorsepress.org, pg 625

Holbert, Christine, Lost Horse Press, 105 Lost Horse Lane, Sandpoint, ID 83864 *Tel:* 208-255-4410 *E-mail:* losthorsepress@mindspring.com *Web Site:* www.losthorsepress.org, pg 128

Holden, Mike, International Association of Business Communicators (IABC), 649 Mission St, 5th fl, San Francisco, CA 94105 *Tel:* 415-544-4700 *Toll Free Tel:* 800-776-4222 (US & CN) *Fax:* 415-544-4747 *E-mail:* leader_centre@iabc.com; member_relations@ iabc.com *Web Site:* www.iabc.com, pg 535

Holder, Jakob, William Flanagan Memorial Creative Persons Center, 14 Harrison St, New York, NY 10013 *Tel:* 212-226-2020 *Fax:* 212-226-5551 *E-mail:* info@ albeefoundation.org *Web Site:* www.albeefoundation. org, pg 678

Holdridge, Jefferson, Wake Forest University Press, 2518 Reynolda Rd, Winston-Salem, NC 27106 *Tel:* 336-758-5448 *Fax:* 336-842-3853 *E-mail:* wfupress@wfu. edu *Web Site:* wfupress.wfu.edu, pg 237

Holland, Mark, Rocky Mountain Mineral Law Foundation, 9191 Sheridan Blvd, Suite 203, Westminster, CO 80031 *Tel:* 303-321-8100 *Fax:* 303-321-7657 *E-mail:* info@rmmlf.org *Web Site:* www. rmmlf.org, pg 186

Hollander, Eli M, Feldheim Publishers, 208 Airport Executive Park, Nanuet, NY 10954 *Tel:* 845-356-2282 *Toll Free Tel:* 800-237-7149 (orders) *Fax:* 845-425-1908 *E-mail:* sales@feldheim.com *Web Site:* www. feldheim.com, pg 76

Hollein, Max, The Metropolitan Museum of Art, 1000 Fifth Ave, New York, NY 10028 *Tel:* 212-535-7710 *E-mail:* editorial@metmuseum.org *Web Site:* www. metmuseum.org, pg 139

Holliday, Sara, New York City Book Awards, 53 E 79 St, New York, NY 10075 *Tel:* 212-288-6900 *Fax:* 212-744-5832 *E-mail:* events@nysoclib.org *Web Site:* www.nysoclib.org, pg 647

Hollingsworth, Jonathan, Macmillan, 120 Broadway, 22nd fl, New York, NY 10271 *Tel:* 646-307-5151 *E-mail:* press.inquiries@macmillan.com *Web Site:* www.macmillan.com, pg 130

Hollins, Pamela, Silver Gavel Awards, 321 N Clark St, Chicago, IL 60654 *Tel:* 312-988-5719 *Toll Free Tel:* 800-285-2221 (orders) *Fax:* 312-988-5494 *Web Site:* www.ambar.org/gavelawards, pg 667

Hollins-Alexander, Sonja EdD, Corwin, 2455 Teller Rd, Thousand Oaks, CA 91320 *Tel:* 805-499-9734 *Toll Free Tel:* 800-233-9936 *Fax:* 805-499-5323 *Toll Free Fax:* 800-417-2466 *E-mail:* info@corwin.com; order@ corwin.com *Web Site:* www.corwin.com, pg 57

Holloway, J David, American Technical Publishers Inc, 10100 Orland Pkwy, Suite 200, Orland Park, IL 60467-5756 *Toll Free Tel:* 800-323-3471 *Fax:* 708-957-1101 *E-mail:* service@atplearning.com; order@ atplearning.com *Web Site:* www.atplearning.com, pg 15

Holman, Tim, Hachette Book Group, 1290 Avenue of the Americas, New York, NY 10104 *Tel:* 212-364-1100 *Toll Free Tel:* 800-759-0190 (cust serv) *Fax:* 212-364-0933 (intl orders) *Toll Free Fax:* 800-286-9471 (cust serv) *Web Site:* www. hachettebookgroup.com, pg 90

Holman, Tim, Orbit, 1290 Avenue of the Americas, New York, NY 10104 *Tel:* 212-364-1100 *Toll Free Tel:* 800-759-0190 *Web Site:* www.orbitbooks.net, pg 156

Holmes, Carol, R Ross Annett Award for Children's Literature, 11759 Groat Rd, Edmonton, AB T5M 3K6, Canada *Tel:* 780-422-8174 *Toll Free Tel:* 800-665-5354 (AB only) *Fax:* 780-422-2663 (attn WGA) *E-mail:* mail@writersguild.ca *Web Site:* writersguild. ca, pg 592

Holmes, Carol, Georges Bugnet Award for Fiction, 11759 Groat Rd, Edmonton, AB T5M 3K6, Canada *Tel:* 780-422-8174 *Toll Free Tel:* 800-665-5354 (AB only) *Fax:* 780-422-2663 (attn WGA) *E-mail:* mail@ writersguild.ca *Web Site:* writersguild.ca, pg 601

Holmes, Carol, The City of Calgary W O Mitchell Book Prize, 11759 Groat Rd, Edmonton, AB T5M 3K6, Canada *Tel:* 780-422-8174 *Toll Free Tel:* 800-665-5354 (AB only) *Fax:* 780-422-2663 (attn WGA) *E-mail:* mail@writersguild.ca *Web Site:* writersguild. ca, pg 605

Holmes, Carol, Wilfrid Eggleston Award for Nonfiction, 11759 Groat Rd, Edmonton, AB T5M 3K6, Canada *Tel:* 780-422-8174 *Toll Free Tel:* 800-665-5354 (AB only) *Fax:* 780-422-2663 (attn WGA) *E-mail:* mail@ writersguild.ca *Web Site:* writersguild.ca, pg 612

Holmes, Carol, James H Gray Award for Short Nonfiction, 11759 Groat Rd, Edmonton, AB T5M 3K6, Canada *Tel:* 780-422-8174 *Toll Free Tel:* 800-665-5354 (AB only) *Fax:* 780-422-2663 (attn WGA) *E-mail:* mail@writersguild.ca *Web Site:* writersguild. ca, pg 620

Holmes, Carol, The Robert Kroetsch City of Edmonton Book Prize, 11759 Groat Rd, Edmonton, AB T5M 3K6, Canada *Tel:* 780-422-8174 *Toll Free Tel:* 800-665-5354 (AB only) *Fax:* 780-422-2663 (attn WGA) *E-mail:* mail@writersguild.ca *Web Site:* writersguild. ca, pg 631

Holmes, Carol, Howard O'Hagan Award for Short Story, 11759 Groat Rd, Edmonton, AB T5M 3K6, Canada *Tel:* 780-422-8174 *Toll Free Tel:* 800-665-5354 (AB only) *Fax:* 780-422-2663 (attn WGA) *E-mail:* mail@ writersguild.ca *Web Site:* writersguild.ca, pg 650

Holmes, Carol, Gwen Pharis Ringwood Award for Drama, 11759 Groat Rd, Edmonton, AB T5M 3K6, Canada *Tel:* 780-422-8174 *Toll Free Tel:* 800-665-5354 (AB only) *Fax:* 780-422-2663 (attn WGA) *E-mail:* mail@writersguild.ca *Web Site:* writersguild. ca, pg 662

Holmes, Carol, Stephan G Stephansson Award for Poetry, 11759 Groat Rd, Edmonton, AB T5M 3K6, Canada *Tel:* 780-422-8174 *Toll Free Tel:* 800-665-5354 (AB only) *Fax:* 780-422-2663 (attn WGA) *E-mail:* mail@writersguild.ca *Web Site:* writersguild. ca, pg 670

Holmes, Carol, Jon Whyte Memorial Essay Prize, 11759 Groat Rd, Edmonton, AB T5M 3K6, Canada *Tel:* 780-422-8174 *Toll Free Tel:* 800-665-5354 (AB only) *Fax:* 780-422-2663 (attn WGA) *E-mail:* mail@ writersguild.ca *Web Site:* writersguild.ca, pg 677

Holmes, Carol, Writers' Guild of Alberta, 11759 Groat Rd, Edmonton, AB T5M 3K6, Canada *Tel:* 780-422-8174 *Toll Free Tel:* 800-665-5354 (AB only) *Fax:* 780-422-2663 (attn WGA) *E-mail:* mail@ writersguild.ca *Web Site:* writersguild.ca, pg 549

Holmes, Henry, Henry Holmes Literary Agent/Book Publicist/Marketing Consultant, Mitchell Heights, Apt 205, 2100 S Main St, Fall River, MA 02724 *Tel:* 508-672-2258; 508-415-4062 (cell), pg 465, 489

Holmes, J D, Holmes Publishing Group LLC, PO Box 2370, Sequim, WA 98382 *Tel:* 360-681-2900 *E-mail:* holmespub@fastmail.fm *Web Site:* www. jdholmes.com, pg 101

Holmes, Jack, Johns Hopkins University Press, 2715 N Charles St, Baltimore, MD 21218-4363 *Tel:* 410-516-6900; 410-516-6987 (journal orders outside US & CN) *Toll Free Tel:* 800-537-5487 (book orders & cust serv); 800-548-1784 (journal orders) *Fax:* 410-516-6968; 410-516-3866 (journal orders); 410-516-6998 (orders) *E-mail:* hfscustserv@press.jhu.edu (cust serv); jrnlcirc@press.jhu.edu (journal orders) *Web Site:* www.press.jhu.edu; muse.jhu.edu, pg 114

Holmes, James, ProQuest LLC, 789 E Eisenhower Pkwy, Ann Arbor, MI 48108 *Tel:* 734-761-4700 *Toll Free Tel:* 800-521-0600; 877-779-6768 (sales) *E-mail:* sales@proquest.com *Web Site:* www.proquest. com, pg 176

Holmes, Prof Janet, Ahsahta Press, Boise State University, Mail Stop 1580, 1910 University Dr, Boise, ID 83725-1580 *Tel:* 208-519-6726 *E-mail:* ahsahta@boisestate.edu *Web Site:* ahsahtapress.org, pg 6

Holmes, Matthew, Magazines Canada (MC), 555 Richmond St W, Suite 604, Mailbox 201, Toronto, ON M5V 3B1, Canada *Tel:* 416-504-0274 *Fax:* 416-504-0437 *E-mail:* info@magazinescanada.ca *Web Site:* magazinescanada.ca, pg 537

Holstein, Stephanie, Princeton Architectural Press, 202 Warren St, Hudson, NY 12534 *Tel:* 518-671-6100 *Toll Free Tel:* 800-722-6657 (dist); 800-759-0190 (sales) *E-mail:* sales@papress.com *Web Site:* www.papress. com, pg 174

Holt, Matt, BenBella Books Inc, 10300 N Central Expwy, Suite 400, Dallas, TX 75231 *Tel:* 214-750-3600 *E-mail:* feedback@benbellabooks. com *Web Site:* www.benbellabooks.com; www. smartpopbooks.com, pg 31

Holt, Sid, American Society of Magazine Editors (ASME), PO Box 112, New York, NY 10163 *Tel:* 212-872-3737 *E-mail:* asme@asme.media *Web Site:* www.asme.media, pg 524

Holt, Sid, ASME Award for Fiction, PO Box 112, New York, NY 10163 *Tel:* 212-872-3737 *E-mail:* asme@ asme.media *Web Site:* www.asme.media, pg 594

Holtzer, Mastan, Rand McNally, 9855 Woods Dr, Skokie, IL 60077 *Tel:* 847-329-8100 *Toll Free Tel:* 877-446-4863 *Toll Free Fax:* 877-469-1298 *E-mail:* mediarelations@randmcnally.com; tndsupport@randmcnally.com *Web Site:* www. randmcnally.com, pg 180

Holung, Lindsay, House of Anansi Press Inc, 128 Sterling Rd, Lower Level, Toronto, ON M6R 2B7, Canada *Tel:* 416-363-4343 *Fax:* 416-363-1017 *E-mail:* customerservice@houseofanansi.com *Web Site:* www.houseofanansi.com, pg 429

Holway, Pamela, Athabasca University Press, Edmonton Learning Ctr, Peace Hills Trust Tower, 1200, 10011-109 St, Edmonton, AB T5J 3S8, Canada *Tel:* 780-497-3412 *Fax:* 780-421-3298 *E-mail:* aupress@athabascau. ca *Web Site:* www.aupress.ca, pg 416

Horst, Ines ter, University of Texas Press, 3001 Lake Austin Blvd, 2.200, Austin, TX 78703 *Tel:* 512-471-7233 *Fax:* 512-232-7178 *E-mail:* utpress@uts.cc. utexas.edu; info@utpress.utexas.edu *Web Site:* utpress. utexas.edu, pg 216

Horton, Chelsea, American Anthropological Association (AAA), 2300 Clarendon Blvd, Suite 1301, Arlington, VA 22201 *Tel:* 703-528-1902 *Fax:* 703-528-3546 *E-mail:* pubs@americananthro.org *Web Site:* www. americananthro.org, pg 9

Horton, David, Bethany House Publishers, 11400 Hampshire Ave S, Bloomington, MN 55438 *Tel:* 952-829-2500 *Toll Free Tel:* 800-877-2665 (orders) *Fax:* 952-829-2568 *Toll Free Fax:* 800-398-3111 (orders) *Web Site:* www.bethanyhouse.com; www. bakerpublishinggroup.com, pg 33

Horton, Kelsey, Random House Children's Books, 1745 Broadway, 10th fl, New York, NY 10019 *Tel:* 212-782-9000 *Web Site:* www.randomhousekids.com, pg 180

Horvath, Dave, University Press of America Inc, 4501 Forbes Blvd, Suite 200, Lanham, MD 20706 *Tel:* 301-459-3366 *Toll Free Tel:* 800-462-6420 *Fax:* 301-429-5748 *Toll Free Fax:* 800-338-4550 *Web Site:* www. univpress.com, pg 232

Hosea, Beata, The Art Institute of Chicago, 111 S Michigan Ave, Chicago, IL 60603-6404 *Tel:* 312-443-3600; 312-443-3540 (pubns) *Fax:* 312-443-1334 (pubns) *Web Site:* www.artic.edu; www. artinstituteshop.org, pg 20

Hoshijo, Amara, Soho Press Inc, 853 Broadway, New York, NY 10003 *Tel:* 212-260-1900 *E-mail:* soho@ sohopress.com; publicity@sohopress.com *Web Site:* sohopress.com, pg 203

Hosier, Erin, Dunow, Carlson & Lerner Literary Agency Inc, 27 W 20 St, Suite 1107, New York, NY 10011 *Tel:* 212-645-7606 *E-mail:* mail@dclagency.com *Web Site:* www.dclagency.com, pg 482

Hoskin, Christine, Schoolhouse Indexing, 10-B Parade Ground Rd, Etna, NH 03750 *Tel:* 603-643-1617 *Web Site:* schoolhouseindexing.com, pg 470

Host, Patrick, National Press Club (NPC), 529 14 St NW, 13th fl, Washington, DC 20045 *Tel:* 202-662-7500 *Web Site:* www.press.org, pg 540

Hottensen, Judy, Grove Atlantic Inc, 154 W 14 St, 12th fl, New York, NY 10011 *Tel:* 212-614-7850 *Toll Free Tel:* 800-521-0178 *Fax:* 212-614-7886 *E-mail:* info@ groveatlantic.com; sales@groveatlantic.com; publicity@groveatlantic.com; rights@groveatlantic.com *Web Site:* www.groveatlantic.com, pg 89

Hotzler, Russell K PhD, New York City College of Technology, 300 Jay St, Brooklyn, NY 11201 *Tel:* 718-260-5500 *Fax:* 718-260-5198 *E-mail:* connect@citytech.cuny.edu *Web Site:* www. citytech.cuny.edu, pg 583

Houck, Anna, Carnegie Mellon University Press, 5032 Forbes Ave, Pittsburgh, PA 15289-1021 *Tel:* 412-268-2861 *Fax:* 412-268-8706 *E-mail:* carnegiemellonuniversitypress@gmail.com *Web Site:* www.cmu.edu/universitypress, pg 45

Houder, Daniel, Kennedy Information Inc, 24 Railroad St, Keene, NH 03431 *Tel:* 603-357-8103 *Toll Free Tel:* 800-531-0140, pg 116

Hough, Milly, Individual Artist's Fellowships, 1026 Sumter St, Suite 200, Columbia, SC 29201-3746 *Tel:* 803-734-8696 *Fax:* 803-734-8526 *E-mail:* info@ arts.sc.gov *Web Site:* www.southcarolinaarts.com, pg 626

Houghton, Harmon, Clear Light Publishers, 823 Don Diego Ave, Santa Fe, NM 87505 *Tel:* 505-989-9590 *Toll Free Tel:* 800-253-2747 (orders) *E-mail:* info@ clearlightbooks.com *Web Site:* www.clearlightbooks. com, pg 53

Houghton, Quincy, The Metropolitan Museum of Art, 1000 Fifth Ave, New York, NY 10028 *Tel:* 212-535-7710 *E-mail:* editorial@metmuseum.org *Web Site:* www.metmuseum.org, pg 139

Houghton, Stephen, Parallax Press, 2236B Sixth St, Berkeley, CA 94710 *Tel:* 510-540-6411 *Toll Free Tel:* 800-863-5290 (orders) *Fax:* 510-981-1157 *Web Site:* www.parallax.org, pg 160

Hourigan, Katherine, Doubleday, c/o Penguin Random House Inc, 1745 Broadway, New York, NY 10019 *Tel:* 212-751-2600 *Fax:* 212-572-2662 (foreign rts) *E-mail:* ddaypub@randomhouse.com *Web Site:* knopfdoubleday.com, pg 66

Hourigan, Katherine, Alfred A Knopf, c/o Penguin Random House Inc, 1745 Broadway, New York, NY 10019 *Tel:* 212-751-2600 *Fax:* 212-572-2662 (foreign rts) *Web Site:* knopfdoubleday.com, pg 118

House, Jack, Townson Publishing Co Ltd, PO Box 1404, Sta A, Vancouver, BC V6C 2P7, Canada *Tel:* 604-886-0594 *E-mail:* admin@gpub.com; rights@gpub.ca *Web Site:* generalpublishing.com, pg 441

Houser, David, Psychological Assessment Resources Inc (PAR), 16204 N Florida Ave, Lutz, FL 33549 *Tel:* 813-449-4065 *Toll Free Tel:* 800-331-8378 *Fax:* 813-961-2196 *Toll Free Fax:* 800-727-9329 *Web Site:* www.parinc.com, pg 177

Housley, Jim, Bloom's Literary Criticism, 132 W 31 St, 17th fl, New York, NY 10001 *Toll Free Tel:* 800-322-8755 *Toll Free Fax:* 800-678-3633 *E-mail:* custserv@ factsonfile.com *Web Site:* www.infobasepublishing. com, pg 35

Housley, Jim, Chelsea House, 132 W 31 St, 17th fl, New York, NY 10001 *Toll Free Tel:* 800-322-8755 *Toll Free Fax:* 800-678-3633 *E-mail:* custserv@ factsonfile.com; info@infobase.com *Web Site:* www. infobasepublishing.com; www.infobase.com, pg 50

Housley, Jim, Facts On File, 132 W 31 St, 17th fl, New York, NY 10001 *Tel:* 212-967-8800 *Toll Free Tel:* 800-322-8755 *Toll Free Fax:* 800-678-3633 *E-mail:* custserv@factsonfile.com *Web Site:* infobasepublishing.com, pg 74

Housley, Jim, Ferguson Publishing, 132 W 31 St, 17th fl, New York, NY 10001 *Tel:* 212-967-8800 *Toll Free Tel:* 800-322-8755 *Toll Free Fax:* 800-678-3633 *E-mail:* custserv@factsonfile.com *Web Site:* infobasepublishing.com, pg 77

Houtz, Julie, ASCD, 1703 N Beauregard St, Alexandria, VA 22311-1714 *Tel:* 703-578-9600 *Toll Free Tel:* 800-933-2723 *Fax:* 703-575-5400 *E-mail:* member@ascd. org *Web Site:* www.ascd.org, pg 21

Howard, Assuanta, Asta Publications LLC, 275 W Clarkstown Rd, New City, NY 10956 *Tel:* 678-814-1320 *Toll Free Tel:* 800-482-4190 *Fax:* 678-814-1370 *E-mail:* info@astapublications.com *Web Site:* www. astapublications.com, pg 23

Howard, Brent, Dutton, 1745 Broadway, New York, NY 10019 *Tel:* 212-366-2000 *Fax:* 212-366-2262 *E-mail:* duttonpublicity@us.penguingroup.com *Web Site:* www.penguin.com, pg 68

Howard, Elise, Algonquin Books, 400 Silver Cedar Ct, Suite 300, Chapel Hill, NC 27514-1585 *Tel:* 919-967-0108 *Fax:* 919-933-0272 *E-mail:* inquiry@algonquin. com *Web Site:* www.workman.com/algonquin, pg 7

Howard, Gerry, Doubleday, c/o Penguin Random House Inc, 1745 Broadway, New York, NY 10019 *Tel:* 212-751-2600 *Fax:* 212-572-2662 (foreign rts) *E-mail:* ddaypub@randomhouse.com *Web Site:* knopfdoubleday.com, pg 66

Howard, Glenda, Harlequin Enterprises Ltd, 195 Broadway, 24th fl, New York, NY 10007 *Tel:* 212-207-7000 *Toll Free Tel:* 888-432-4879 *E-mail:* customerservice@harlequin.com *Web Site:* www.harlequin.com, pg 93

Howard, J Kirk, Simon & Pierre Publishing Co Ltd, 3 Church St, Suite 500, Toronto, ON M5E 1M2, Canada *Tel:* 416-214-5544 *E-mail:* info@dundurn.com *Web Site:* www.dundurn.com, pg 440

Howard, Jackson, Farrar, Straus & Giroux, LLC, 175 Varick St, 9th fl, New York, NY 10014 *Tel:* 212-741-6900 *E-mail:* fsg.publicity@fsgbooks.com *Web Site:* us.macmillan.com/fsg.aspx, pg 76

Howard, Jeff, Rand-Smith Publishing, 204 College Ave, Ashland, VA 23005 *Tel:* 804-874-6012 *E-mail:* randsmithllc@gmail.com *Web Site:* www.rand-smith.com, pg 180

Howard, Kait, Perseus Books, 1290 Avenue of the Americas, New York, NY 10104 *Tel:* 212-340-8100 *Toll Free Tel:* 800-343-4499 (cust serv) *Fax:* 212-340-8105 *Web Site:* www.perseusbooks.com, pg 168

Howard, Kirk, Dundurn Press Ltd, 3 Church St, Suite 500, Toronto, ON M5E 1M2, Canada *Tel:* 416-214-5544 *E-mail:* info@dundurn.com; publicity@dundurn. com; sales@dundurn.com *Web Site:* www.dundurn. com, pg 421

Howard, MacKenzie, Thomas Nelson, 501 Nelson Place, Nashville, TN 37214 *Tel:* 615-889-9000 *Toll Free Tel:* 800-251-4000 *Fax:* 615-902-1548 *Web Site:* www. thomasnelson.com, pg 217

Howard, MacKenzie, Tommy Nelson®, 501 Nelson Place, Nashville, TN 37214 *Tel:* 615-889-9000; 615-902-1485 (cust serv) *Toll Free Tel:* 800-251-4000 *Web Site:* www.tommynelson.com, pg 219

Howard, Marilyn, Creative Freelancers Inc, PO Box 366, Tallevast, FL 34270 *Toll Free Tel:* 800-398-9544 *Web Site:* www.freelancers1.com, pg 461

Howard, Meredith, Columbia University Press, 61 W 62 St, New York, NY 10023 *Tel:* 212-459-0600 *Toll Free Tel:* 800-944-8648 *Fax:* 212-459-3678 *Web Site:* cup. columbia.edu, pg 55

Howe, Isabel, The Authors League Fund, 31 E 32 St, 7th fl, New York, NY 10016 *Tel:* 212-268-1208 *Fax:* 212-564-5363 *E-mail:* staff@authorsleaguefund. org *Web Site:* www.authorsleaguefund.org, pg 527

Howe, Meghan, Marilyn Baillie Picture Book Award, 40 Orchard View Blvd, Suite 217, Toronto, ON M4R 1B9, Canada *Tel:* 416-975-0010 *Fax:* 416-975-8970 *E-mail:* info@bookcentre.ca *Web Site:* www. bookcentre.ca, pg 595

Howe, Meghan, The Geoffrey Bilson Award for Historical Fiction for Young People, 40 Orchard View Blvd, Suite 217, Toronto, ON M4R 1B9, Canada *Tel:* 416-975-0010 *Fax:* 416-975-8970 *E-mail:* info@ bookcentre.ca *Web Site:* www.bookcentre.ca, pg 598

Howe, Meghan, Canadian Children's Book Centre, 40 Orchard View Blvd, Suite 217, Toronto, ON M4R 1B9, Canada *Tel:* 416-975-0010 *Fax:* 416-975-8970 *E-mail:* info@bookcentre.ca *Web Site:* www. bookcentre.ca, pg 530

Howe, Meghan, Norma Fleck Award for Canadian Children's Non-Fiction, 40 Orchard View Blvd, Suite 217, Toronto, ON M4R 1B9, Canada *Tel:* 416-975-0010 *Fax:* 416-975-8970 *E-mail:* info@bookcentre.ca *Web Site:* www.bookcentre.ca, pg 616

Howe, Meghan, Amy Mathers Teen Book Award, 40 Orchard View Blvd, Suite 217, Toronto, ON M4R 1B9, Canada *Tel:* 416-975-0010 *Fax:* 416-975-8970 *E-mail:* info@bookcentre.ca *Web Site:* www. bookcentre.ca, pg 639

Howe, Meghan, John Spray Mystery Award, 40 Orchard View Blvd, Suite 217, Toronto, ON M4R 1B9, Canada *Tel:* 416-975-0010 *Fax:* 416-975-8970 *E-mail:* info@ bookcentre.ca *Web Site:* www.bookcentre.ca, pg 669

Howe, Meghan, TD Canadian Children's Literature Award, 40 Orchard View Blvd, Suite 217, Toronto, ON M4R 1B9, Canada *Tel:* 416-975-0010 *Fax:* 416-975-8970 *E-mail:* info@bookcentre.ca *Web Site:* www. bookcentre.ca, pg 672

Howe, Sally, Scribner, 1230 Avenue of the Americas, New York, NY 10020, pg 195

Howell, Christopher, Lynx House Press, 420 W 24 St, Spokane, WA 99203 *Tel:* 509-624-4894 *E-mail:* lynxhousepress@gmail.com *Web Site:* www. lynxhousepress.org, pg 129

Howell, Heather, Turner Publishing Co, 4507 Charlotte Ave, Suite 100, Nashville, TN 37209 *Tel:* 615-255-BOOK (255-2665) *Fax:* 615-255-5081 *E-mail:* marketing@turnerpublishing.com; submissions@turnerpublishing.com; editorial@ turnerpublishing.com *Web Site:* www.turnerpublishing. com; www.facebook.com/turner.publishing, pg 222

Hyde, Mallory, Sourcebooks LLC, 1935 Brookdale Rd, Suite 139, Naperville, IL 60563 Tel: 630-961-3900 Toll Free Tel: 800-432-7444 Fax: 630-961-2168 E-mail: info@sourcebooks.com; customersupport@sourcebooks.com Web Site: www.sourcebooks.com, pg 204

Hyman, Alan, The Picasso Project, 1109 Geary Blvd, San Francisco, CA 94109 Tel: 415-292-6500 Fax: 415-292-6594 E-mail: editeur@earthlink.net (edit); picasso@art-books.com (orders) Web Site: www.art-books.com, pg 169

Hyman, Ben, Bloomsbury Publishing Inc, 1385 Broadway, 5th fl, New York, NY 10018 Tel: 212-419-5300 E-mail: marketingusa@bloomsbury.com; adultpublicityusa@bloomsbury.com; askacademic@bloomsbury.com Web Site: www.bloomsbury.com, pg 36

Hymer, Bennett, Mutual Publishing LLC, 1215 Center St, Suite 210, Honolulu, HI 96816 Tel: 808-732-1709 Fax: 808-734-4094 E-mail: info@mutualpublishing.com Web Site: www.mutualpublishing.com, pg 144

Hynes, Alicia, Alice James Books, 114 Prescott St, Farmington, ME 04938 Tel: 207-778-7071 Fax: 207-778-7766 E-mail: info@alicejamesbooks.org Web Site: alicejamesbooks.org, pg 7

Iacobelli, Luciano, Quattro Books Inc, 12 Concord Ave, 2nd fl, Toronto, ON M6H 2P1, Canada Tel: 647-748-7484 E-mail: info@quattrobooks.ca Web Site: www.quattrobooks.ca, pg 438

Iannacone, Brenda, Arkansas Writers' Conference, PO Box 24662, Little Rock, AR 72221 Tel: 501-833-2756 Web Site: www.arkansaswritersconference.org, pg 573

Iannotta, Ben, American Institute of Aeronautics & Astronautics (AIAA), 12700 Sunrise Valley Dr, Suite 200, Reston, VA 20191-5807 Tel: 703-264-7500 Toll Free Tel: 800-639-AIAA (639-2422) Fax: 703-264-7551 E-mail: custserv@aiaa.org Web Site: www.aiaa.org, pg 11

Iaquinta, Gina, W W Norton & Company Inc, 500 Fifth Ave, New York, NY 10110-0017 Tel: 212-354-5500 Toll Free Tel: 800-233-4830 (orders & cust serv) Fax: 212-869-0856 Toll Free Fax: 800-458-6515 E-mail: orders@wwnorton.com Web Site: wwnorton.com, pg 152

Iaria, Carmela, Penguin Young Readers Group, 345 Hudson St, New York, NY 10014 Tel: 212-366-2000; 212-414-3553 Fax: 212-414-3340 Web Site: www.penguin.com/children, pg 165

Iarrera, Linda, McGill-Queen's University Press, 1010 Sherbrooke W, Suite 1720, Montreal, QC H3A 2R7, Canada Tel: 514-398-3750 Fax: 514-398-4333 E-mail: mqup@mqup.ca Web Site: www.mqup.ca, pg 433

Ibarra, Allan, Groundwood Books, 128 Sterling Rd, Lower Level, Toronto, ON M6R 2B7, Canada Tel: 416-363-4343 Fax: 416-363-1017 E-mail: genmail@groundwoodbooks.com Web Site: www.houseofanansi.com, pg 428

Ibur, Ted, Saint Louis Literary Award, Pius XII Memorial Library, 3650 Lindell Blvd, St Louis, MO 63108 Tel: 314-977-3100; 314-977-3087 Fax: 314-977-3108 E-mail: slula@slu.edu Web Site: lib.slu.edu/about/associates/literary-award, pg 664

Ichniowski, Liz, Penguin Group USA, A Penguin Random House Company, 375 Hudson St, New York, NY 10014 Tel: 212-366-2000 Toll Free Tel: 800-847-5515 (inside sales); 800-631-8571 (cust serv) Fax: 212-366-2666; 607-775-4829 (inside sales) E-mail: online@us.penguingroup.com Web Site: www.penguin.com, pg 163

Ide, Kathy, Mount Hermon Christian Writers Conference, c/o Mount Hermon Association Inc, 37 Conference Dr, Felton, CA 95018 Tel: 831-335-4466 Toll Free Tel: 888-MH-CAMPS (642-2677, registration) Fax: 831-335-9335 E-mail: info@mounthermon.org Web Site: www.mounthermon.org/writers, pg 576

Idil, Ahmet, Tughra Books, 335 Clifton Ave, Clifton, NJ 07011 Tel: 646-415-9331 Fax: 646-827-6228 E-mail: info@tughrabooks.com Web Site: www.tughrabooks.com, pg 221

Igarashi, Yuka, Counterpoint Press LLC, 2560 Ninth St, Suite 318, Berkeley, CA 94710 Tel: 510-704-0230 Fax: 510-704-0268 E-mail: info@counterpointpress.com Web Site: counterpointpress.com; softskull.com, pg 58

Ignatius, Adi, Harvard Business Review Press, 20 Guest St, Suite 700, Brighton, MA 02135 Tel: 617-783-7400 Fax: 617-783-7489 E-mail: custserv@hbsp.harvard.edu Web Site: www.harvardbusiness.org, pg 94

Igoe, Robert B Jr, North Country Books Inc, 220 Lafayette St, Utica, NY 13502-4312 Tel: 315-735-4877 Toll Free Tel: 800-342-7409 (orders) Fax: 315-738-4342 E-mail: ncbooks@verizon.net Web Site: www.northcountrybooks.com, pg 151

Iguchi, Yasuyo, The MIT Press, One Rogers St, Cambridge, MA 02142 Tel: 617-253-5255 Toll Free Tel: 800-405-1619 (orders) Fax: 617-258-6779; 617-577-1545 (orders) Web Site: mitpress.mit.edu, pg 141

Ikeda, Masako, University of Hawaii Press, 2840 Kolowalu St, Honolulu, HI 96822-1888 Tel: 808-956-8255 Toll Free Tel: 888-UHPRESS (847-7377) Fax: 808-988-6052 Toll Free Fax: 800-650-7811 E-mail: uhpbooks@hawaii.edu Web Site: www.uhpress.hawaii.edu, pg 227

Ilgunas, Charlie, little bee books, 251 Park Ave S, 12th fl, New York, NY 10010 Toll Free Tel: 844-321-0237 E-mail: info@littlebeebooks.com Web Site: littlebeebooks.com, pg 125

Impey, Alison, Random House Children's Books, 1745 Broadway, 10th fl, New York, NY 10019 Tel: 212-782-9000 Web Site: www.randomhousekids.com, pg 180

Imranyi, Erika, Harlequin Enterprises Ltd, 195 Broadway, 24th fl, New York, NY 10007 Tel: 212-207-7000 Toll Free Tel: 888-432-4879 E-mail: customerservice@harlequin.com Web Site: www.harlequin.com, pg 93

Imranyi, Erika, Harlequin Enterprises Ltd, Bay Adelaide Centre, East Tower, 22 Adelaide St W, 41st fl, Toronto, ON M5H 4E3, Canada Tel: 416-445-5860 Toll Free Tel: 888-432-4879; 800-370-5838 (ebook inquiries) E-mail: customerservice@harlequin.com Web Site: www.harlequin.com, pg 429

Indrigo, Miranda, Harlequin Enterprises Ltd, Bay Adelaide Centre, East Tower, 22 Adelaide St W, 41st fl, Toronto, ON M5H 4E3, Canada Tel: 416-445-5860 Toll Free Tel: 888-432-4879; 800-370-5838 (ebook inquiries) E-mail: customerservice@harlequin.com Web Site: www.harlequin.com, pg 429

Ineson, Beth, New England Book Awards, One Beacon St, 15th fl, Boston, MA 02108 Tel: 617-547-3642 Fax: 617-830-8768 Web Site: www.newenglandbooks.org/bookawards, pg 647

Ineson, Beth, New England Independent Booksellers Association Inc (NEIBA), One Beacon St, 15th fl, Boston, MA 02108 Tel: 617-547-3642 Fax: 617-830-8768 Web Site: www.newenglandbooks.org, pg 541

Ingalls, Johanna, Akashic Books, 232 Third St, Suite A-115, Brooklyn, NY 11215 Tel: 718-643-9193 Fax: 718-643-9195 E-mail: info@akashicbooks.com Web Site: www.akashicbooks.com, pg 6

Ingenito, Kim Thornton, Penguin Random House Speakers Bureau, A Penguin Random House Company, 1745 Broadway, Mail Drop 13-1, New York, NY 10019 Tel: 212-572-2013 E-mail: speakers@penguinrandomhouse.com Web Site: www.prhspeakers.com, pg 515

Ingersoll, Tessa, Chronicle Books, 680 Second St, San Francisco, CA 94107 Tel: 415-537-4200 Toll Free Tel: 800-759-0190 (cust serv) Fax: 415-537-4460 Toll Free Tel: 800-858-7787 (orders); 800-286-9471 (cust serv) E-mail: frontdesk@chroniclebooks.com Web Site: www.chroniclebooks.com, pg 51

Ingerson, Audrey, Random House Children's Books, 1745 Broadway, 10th fl, New York, NY 10019 Tel: 212-782-9000 Web Site: www.randomhousekids.com, pg 180

Ingle, Stephen, WordCo Indexing Services Inc, 49 Church St, Norwich, CT 06360 Tel: 860-886-2532 Toll Free Tel: 877-WORDCO-3 (967-3263) Fax: 860-886-1155 E-mail: office@wordco.com Web Site: www.wordco.com, pg 471

Inglis, John, Cold Spring Harbor Laboratory Press, One Bungtown Rd, Cold Spring Harbor, NY 11724 Tel: 516-422-4100 Toll Free Tel: 800-843-4388 Fax: 516-422-4097; 516-422-4092 (submissions) E-mail: cshpress@cshl.edu Web Site: www.cshlpress.com, pg 54

Inglis, Sharon, Newbury Street Press, 99-101 Newbury St, Boston, MA 02116 Tel: 617-226-1206 Toll Free Tel: 888-296-3447 (NEHGS membership) Fax: 617-536-7307 E-mail: sales@nehgs.org Web Site: www.americanancestors.org, pg 150

Ingwell, Carmen, The National Humanities Medal, 400 Seventh St SW, Washington, DC 20506 Tel: 202-606-8400 Toll Free Tel: 800-NEH-1121 (634-1121) E-mail: questions@neh.gov Web Site: www.neh.gov/about/awards, pg 645

Inkster, Tim, Porcupine's Quill Inc, 68 Main St, Erin, ON N0B 1T0, Canada Tel: 519-833-9158 E-mail: pql@sentex.net Web Site: porcupinesquill.ca; www.facebook.com/theporcupinesquill, pg 437

Inouye, Natalie, University of Southern California, Master of Professional Writing Program, Mark Taper Hall, THH 355, 3501 Trousedale Pkwy, Los Angeles, CA 90089-0355 Tel: 213-740-3252 Fax: 213-740-5002 E-mail: mpw@college.usc.edu Web Site: college.usc.edu/mpw, pg 586

Inteli, Nancy, HarperCollins Children's Books, 195 Broadway, New York, NY 10007 Tel: 212-207-7000 Web Site: www.harpercollins.com/childrens, pg 93

Inzetta, Jenn, Random House Children's Books, 1745 Broadway, 10th fl, New York, NY 10019 Tel: 212-782-9000 Web Site: www.randomhousekids.com, pg 181

Iossa, Lauren, American Society of Composers, Authors & Publishers (ASCAP), 1900 Broadway, New York City, NY 10023 Tel: 212-621-6000 Fax: 212-612-8453 E-mail: info@ascap.com Web Site: www.ascap.com, pg 524

Ippolito, Marc, Burns Entertainment & Sports Marketing, 820 Davis St, Suite 222, Evanston, IL 60201 Tel: 847-866-9400 Fax: 847-491-9778 E-mail: burnsl@burnsent.com Web Site: burnsent.com, pg 515

Ireland, Elizabeth, Counterpoint Press LLC, 2560 Ninth St, Suite 318, Berkeley, CA 94710 Tel: 510-704-0230 Fax: 510-704-0268 E-mail: info@counterpointpress.com Web Site: counterpointpress.com; softskull.com, pg 58

Ireland, Pamela, BelleBooks, PO Box 300921, Memphis, TN 38130 Tel: 901-344-9024 Fax: 901-344-9068 E-mail: bellebooks@bellebooks.com Web Site: www.bellebooks.com, pg 31

Irish, Jenny, Arizona State University Creative Writing Program, 1102 S McAllister Ave, Rm 170, Tempe, AZ 85281 Tel: 480-965-3168 Fax: 480-965-3451 Web Site: www.asu.edu/clas/english/creativewriting, pg 581

Irvin, Margo, Stanford University Press, 425 Broadway St, Redwood City, CA 94063-3126 Tel: 650-723-9434 Fax: 650-725-3457 E-mail: info@www.sup.org; publicity@www.sup.org; sales@www.sup.org Web Site: www.sup.org, pg 206

Irvine, Marie Aline, Reference Publications Inc, 218 Saint Clair River Dr, Algonac, MI 48001 Tel: 810-794-5722 E-mail: referencepub@sbcglobal.net, pg 183

Irwin, Mark, Insight Editions, 800 "A" St, San Rafael, CA 94901 Tel: 415-526-1370 Toll Free Tel: 800-809-3792 Toll Free Fax: 866-509-0515 E-mail: info@insighteditions.com; marketing@insighteditions.com Web Site: insighteditions.com, pg 109

Irwin-Diehl, Rebecca, Judson Press, 1075 First Ave, King of Prussia, PA 19406 Toll Free Tel: 800-458-3766 Fax: 610-768-2107 Web Site: www.judsonpress.com, pg 115

Isaac, Joanne, American Numismatic Society, 75 Varick St, 11th fl, New York, NY 10013 *Tel:* 212-571-4470 *Fax:* 212-571-4479 *E-mail:* ans@numismatics.org *Web Site:* www.numismatics.org, pg 13

Isaacs, Beth, Vesuvian Books, 2817 West End Ave, No 126-283, Nashville, TN 37203 *E-mail:* info@vesuvianmedia.com *Web Site:* www.vesuvianbooks.com, pg 236

Isaacs, Suzanne Talbot, Ampersand Inc/Professional Publishing Services, 515 Madison St, New Orleans, LA 70116 *Tel:* 312-280-8905 *Fax:* 312-944-1582 *E-mail:* info@ampersandworks.com *Web Site:* www.ampersandworks.com, pg 15

Isaacson, Walter, Arcadia Publishing Inc, 420 Wando Park Blvd, Mount Pleasant, SC 29464 *Tel:* 843-853-2070 *Toll Free Tel:* 888-313-2665 (orders only) *Fax:* 843-853-0044 *E-mail:* sales@arcadiapublishing.com *Web Site:* www.arcadiapublishing.com, pg 19

Isayeff, Emily, Random House Publishing Group, 1745 Broadway, New York, NY 10019 *Toll Free Tel:* 800-200-3552 *Web Site:* www.randomhousebooks.com, pg 181

Isdahl, Danika, Sarabande Books Inc, 822 E Market St, Louisville, KY 40206 *Tel:* 502-458-4028 *Fax:* 502-458-4065 *E-mail:* info@sarabandebooks.org *Web Site:* www.sarabandebooks.org, pg 192

Iserson, Mary Lou, Galen Press Ltd, PO Box 64400-WB, Tucson, AZ 85728-4400 *Tel:* 520-577-8363 *Fax:* 520-529-6459 *E-mail:* sales@galenpress.com *Web Site:* www.galenpress.com, pg 82

Ishay-Cohen, Michelle, Artisan, 225 Varick St, New York, NY 10014-4381 *Tel:* 212-254-5900 *Toll Free Tel:* 800-722-7202 *Fax:* 212-677-6692 *E-mail:* artisaninfo@artisanbooks.com *Web Site:* www.artisanbooks.com; www.workman.com/artisanbooks, pg 21

Israel, Yahdon, Nona Balakian Citation for Excellence in Reviewing, c/o 310 Lewis Ave, Brooklyn, NY 11221 *E-mail:* info@bookcritics.org *Web Site:* bookcritics.org/awards, pg 595

Israel, Yahdon, Emerging Critics Fellowship, c/o 310 Lewis Ave, Brooklyn, NY 11221 *E-mail:* info@bookcritics.org *Web Site:* bookcritics.org, pg 613

Israel, Yahdon, National Book Critics Circle Award, c/o 310 Lewis Ave, Brooklyn, NY 11221 *E-mail:* info@bookcritics.org *Web Site:* bookcritics.org/awards, pg 644

Israel, Yahdon, Ivan Sandrof Lifetime Achievement Award, c/o 310 Lewis Ave, Brooklyn, NY 11221 *E-mail:* info@bookcritics.org *Web Site:* bookcritics.org/awards, pg 664

Israeli, Henry, Saturnalia Books Poetry Prize, 105 Woodside Rd, Ardmore, PA 19003 *Tel:* 267-278-9541 *Web Site:* www.saturnaliabooks.org, pg 664

Israelite, David M, National Music Publishers' Association (NMPA), 975 "F" St NW, Suite 375, Washington, DC 20004 *Tel:* 202-393-6672 *E-mail:* members@nmpa.org *Web Site:* nmpa.org, pg 540

Itkin, Bridget Monroe, Artisan, 225 Varick St, New York, NY 10014-4381 *Tel:* 212-254-5900 *Toll Free Tel:* 800-722-7202 *Fax:* 212-677-6692 *E-mail:* artisaninfo@artisanbooks.com *Web Site:* www.artisanbooks.com; www.workman.com/artisanbooks, pg 21

Itterly, Allison, WriteLife Publishing, 960 Oaktree Blvd, Christianburg, VA 24073 *E-mail:* writelife@boutiqueofqualitybooks.com *Web Site:* www.writelife.com; www.facebook.com/writelife, pg 246

Iverson, Anne, Mountain Press Publishing Co, 1301 S Third W, Missoula, MT 59801 *Tel:* 406-728-1900 *Toll Free Tel:* 800-234-5308 *Fax:* 406-728-1635 *E-mail:* info@mtnpress.com *Web Site:* www.mountainpress.com, pg 143

Iverson, Haven, Sounds True Inc, 413 S Arthur Ave, Louisville, CO 80027 *Tel:* 303-665-3151 *Toll Free Tel:* 800-333-9185 (US); 888-303-9185

(US & CN) *E-mail:* customerservice@soundstrue.com; stpublicity@soundstrue.com *Web Site:* www.soundstrue.com, pg 204

Iwasutiak, Adria, Simon & Schuster Canada, 166 King St E, Suite 300, Toronto, ON M5A 1J3, Canada *Tel:* 647-427-8882 *Toll Free Tel:* 800-387-0446; 800-268-3216 (orders) *Fax:* 647-430-9446 *Toll Free Fax:* 888-849-8151 (orders) *E-mail:* info@simonandschuster.ca *Web Site:* www.simonandschuster.ca, pg 440

Izykowski, Lori, Biblio Award, PO Box 33020, Santa Fe, NM 87594 *Web Site:* biographersinternational.org, pg 598

Izykowski, Lori, BIO Award, PO Box 33020, Santa Fe, NM 87594 *Web Site:* biographersinternational.org, pg 598

Izykowski, Lori, Chip Bishop Fellowship, PO Box 33020, Santa Fe, NM 87594 *Web Site:* biographersinternational.org, pg 599

Izykowski, Lori, The Robert & Ina Caro Research/Travel Fellowship, PO Box 33020, Santa Fe, NM 87594 *Web Site:* biographersinternational.org, pg 603

Izykowski, Lori, Editorial Excellence, PO Box 33020, Santa Fe, NM 87594 *Web Site:* biographersinternational.org, pg 612

Izykowski, Lori, Plutarch Award, PO Box 33020, Santa Fe, NM 87594 *Tel:* 505-983-4671 *Web Site:* biographersinternational.org, pg 656

Izykowski, Lori, Hazel Rowley Prize, PO Box 33020, Santa Fe, NM 87594 *Web Site:* biographersinternational.org, pg 663

Izzo, Ben, Abrams Artists Agency, 275 Seventh Ave, 26th fl, New York, NY 10001 *Tel:* 646-486-4600 *Fax:* 646-486-0100 *E-mail:* literary@abramsartny.com *Web Site:* www.abramsartists.com, pg 473

Jabbari, Dr A Kamron, Mazda Publishers Inc, PO Box 2603, Costa Mesa, CA 92628 *Tel:* 714-751-5252 *Fax:* 714-751-4805 *E-mail:* mazdapub@aol.com *Web Site:* www.mazdapublishers.com, pg 134

Jabbour, Anthony, Dun & Bradstreet, 103 JFK Pkwy, Short Hills, NJ 07078 *Tel:* 973-921-5500 *Toll Free Tel:* 844-869-8244; 800-234-3867 (cust serv) *Web Site:* www.dnb.com, pg 68

Jablonski, Lauren, St Martin's Press, LLC, 120 Broadway, New York, NY 10271 *Tel:* 646-307-5151 *Web Site:* us.macmillan.com/smp, pg 190

Jackson, Bobby L, Multicultural Publications Inc, 1939 Manchester Rd, Akron, OH 44314 *Tel:* 330-865-9578 *Fax:* 330-865-9578 *E-mail:* multiculturalpub@prodigy.net *Web Site:* www.multiculturalpub.net, pg 144

Jackson, Christopher, Random House Publishing Group, 1745 Broadway, New York, NY 10019 *Toll Free Tel:* 800-200-3552 *Web Site:* www.randomhousebooks.com, pg 181

Jackson, Devon, Latner Writers' Trust Poetry Prize, 600-460 Richmond St W, Toronto, ON M5V 1Y1, Canada *Tel:* 416-504-8222 *Toll Free Tel:* 877-906-6548 *Fax:* 416-504-9090 *E-mail:* info@writerstrust.com *Web Site:* www.writerstrust.com/awards/latner-writers-trust-poetry-prize, pg 631

Jackson, Devon, Matt Cohen Prize: In Celebration of a Writing Life, 600-460 Richmond St W, Toronto, ON M5V 1Y1, Canada *Tel:* 416-504-8222 *Toll Free Tel:* 877-906-6548 *Fax:* 416-504-9090 *E-mail:* info@writerstrust.com *Web Site:* www.writerstrust.com, pg 639

Jackson, Devon, Dayne Ogilvie Prize, 600-460 Richmond St W, Toronto, ON M5V 1Y1, Canada *Tel:* 416-504-8222 *Toll Free Tel:* 877-906-6548 *Fax:* 416-504-9090 *E-mail:* info@writerstrust.com *Web Site:* www.writerstrust.com, pg 650

Jackson, Devon, RBC Bronwen Wallace Award for Emerging Writers, 600-460 Richmond St W, Toronto, ON M5V 1Y1, Canada *Tel:* 416-504-8222 *Toll Free Tel:* 877-906-6548 *Fax:* 416-504-9090 *E-mail:* info@writerstrust.com *Web Site:* www.writerstrust.com, pg 661

Jackson, Devon, Rogers Writers' Trust Fiction Prize, 600-460 Richmond St W, Toronto, ON M5V 1Y1, Canada *Tel:* 416-504-8222 *Toll Free Tel:* 877-906-6548 *Fax:* 416-504-9090 *E-mail:* info@writerstrust.com *Web Site:* www.writerstrust.com, pg 663

Jackson, Devon, Shaughnessy Cohen Prize for Political Writing, 600-460 Richmond St W, Toronto, ON M5V 1Y1, Canada *Tel:* 416-504-8222 *Toll Free Tel:* 877-906-6548 *Fax:* 416-504-9090 *E-mail:* info@writerstrust.com *Web Site:* www.writerstrust.com, pg 667

Jackson, Devon, Vicky Metcalf Award for Literature for Young People, 600-460 Richmond St W, Toronto, ON M5V 1Y1, Canada *Tel:* 416-504-8222 *Toll Free Tel:* 877-906-6548 *Fax:* 416-504-9090 *E-mail:* info@writerstrust.com *Web Site:* www.writerstrust.com, pg 675

Jackson, Devon, Hilary Weston Writers' Trust Prize for Nonfiction, 600-460 Richmond St W, Toronto, ON M5V 1Y1, Canada *Tel:* 416-504-8222 *Toll Free Tel:* 877-906-6548 *Fax:* 416-504-9090 *E-mail:* info@writerstrust.com *Web Site:* www.writerstrust.com, pg 676

Jackson, Devon, Writers' Trust Engel Findley Award, 600-460 Richmond St W, Toronto, ON M5V 1Y1, Canada *Tel:* 416-504-8222 *Toll Free Tel:* 877-906-6548 *Fax:* 416-504-9090 *E-mail:* info@writerstrust.com *Web Site:* www.writerstrust.com, pg 680

Jackson, Devon, Writers' Trust McClelland & Stewart Journey Prize, 600-460 Richmond St W, Toronto, ON M5V 1Y1, Canada *Tel:* 416-504-8222 *Toll Free Tel:* 877-906-6548 *Fax:* 416-504-9090 *E-mail:* info@writerstrust.com *Web Site:* www.writerstrust.com, pg 680

Jackson, Eleanor, Dunow, Carlson & Lerner Literary Agency Inc, 27 W 20 St, Suite 1107, New York, NY 10011 *Tel:* 212-645-7606 *E-mail:* mail@dclagency.com *Web Site:* www.dclagency.com, pg 482

Jackson, Jennifer, Doubleday, c/o Penguin Random House Inc, 1745 Broadway, New York, NY 10019 *Tel:* 212-751-2600 *Fax:* 212-572-2662 (foreign rts) *E-mail:* ddaypub@randomhouse.com *Web Site:* knopfdoubleday.com, pg 66

Jackson, Jennifer, Alfred A Knopf, c/o Penguin Random House Inc, 1745 Broadway, New York, NY 10019 *Tel:* 212-751-2600 *Fax:* 212-572-2662 (foreign rts) *Web Site:* knopfdoubleday.com, pg 118

Jackson, Jennifer, Donald Maass Literary Agency, 1000 Dean St, Suite 252, Brooklyn, NY 11238 *Tel:* 212-727-8383 *E-mail:* info@maassagency.com *Web Site:* www.maassagency.com, pg 493

Jackson, Joe, Princeton University Press, 41 William St, Princeton, NJ 08540-5237 *Tel:* 609-258-4900 *Fax:* 609-258-6305 *Web Site:* press.princeton.edu, pg 174

Jackson, Karen, Thomas Nelson, 501 Nelson Place, Nashville, TN 37214 *Tel:* 615-889-9000 *Toll Free Tel:* 800-251-4000 *Fax:* 615-902-1548 *Web Site:* www.thomasnelson.com, pg 217

Jackson, Lauren, Gallery Books, 1230 Avenue of the Americas, New York, NY 10020 *Toll Free Tel:* 800-456-6798 *Fax:* 212-698-7284 *E-mail:* consumer.customerservice@simonandschuster.com *Web Site:* www.simonandschuster.com, pg 83

Jackson, Melanie, Melanie Jackson Agency LLC, 41 W 72 St, Suite 3F, New York, NY 10023 *Tel:* 212-873-3373, pg 490

Jackson, Regina, Warner Press, 2902 Enterprise Dr, Anderson, IN 46013 *Tel:* 765-644-7721 *Toll Free Tel:* 800-741-7721 (orders) *Fax:* 765-640-8005 *E-mail:* wporders@warnerpress.org *Web Site:* www.warnerpress.org, pg 237

Jackson, Tilly, Artist-in-Residence Program, 225 King St, Suite 201, Fredericton, NB E3B 1E1, Canada *Tel:* 506-444-4444 *Toll Free Tel:* 866-460-ARTS (460-2787) *Fax:* 506-444-5543 *Web Site:* www.artsnb.ca, pg 593

Jackson, Tilly, Arts Scholarships, 225 King St, Suite 201, Fredericton, NB E3B 1E1, Canada *Tel:* 506-444-4444 *Toll Free Tel:* 866-460-ARTS (460-2787) *Fax:* 506-444-5543 *Web Site:* www.artsnb.ca, pg 593

Jackson, Tilly, Atlantic Public Art Funders (APAF) Creative Residency, 225 King St, Suite 201, Fredericton, NB E3B 1E1, Canada *Tel:* 506-444-4444 *Toll Free Tel:* 866-460-ARTS (460-2787) *Fax:* 506-444-5543 *Web Site:* www.artsnb.ca, pg 594

Jackson, Tilly, Career Development Program, 225 King St, Suite 201, Fredericton, NB E3B 1E1, Canada *Tel:* 506-444-4444 *Toll Free Tel:* 866-460-ARTS (460-2787) *Fax:* 506-444-5543 *Web Site:* www.artsnb.ca, pg 603

Jackson, Tilly, Creation Grant Program, 225 King St, Suite 201, Fredericton, NB E3B 1E1, Canada *Tel:* 506-444-4444 *Toll Free Tel:* 866-460-ARTS (460-2787) *Fax:* 506-444-5543 *Web Site:* www.artsnb.ca, pg 607

Jackson, Tilly, Documentation Grant Program, 225 King St, Suite 201, Fredericton, NB E3B 1E1, Canada *Tel:* 506-444-4444 *Toll Free Tel:* 866-460-ARTS (460-2787) *Fax:* 506-444-5543 *Web Site:* www.artsnb.ca, pg 610

Jackson, Tilly, The Lieutenant-Governor's Awards for High Achievement in the Arts, 225 King St, Suite 201, Fredericton, NB E3B 1E1, Canada *Tel:* 506-444-4444 *Toll Free Tel:* 866-460-ARTS (460-2787) *Fax:* 506-444-5543 *Web Site:* www.artsnb.ca, pg 633

Jackson, William, Workman Publishing Co Inc, 225 Varick St, 9th fl, New York, NY 10014-4381 *Tel:* 212-254-5900 *Toll Free Tel:* 800-722-7202 *Fax:* 212-254-8098 *E-mail:* info@workman.com; orders@workman.com *Web Site:* www.workman.com, pg 244

Jacob, Chris, HeartMath LLC, 14700 W Park Ave, Boulder Creek, CA 95006 *Tel:* 831-338-8500 *Toll Free Tel:* 800-711-6221 *Fax:* 831-338-8504 *E-mail:* info@heartmath.org; inquiry@heartmath.org *Web Site:* www.heartmath.org, pg 97

Jacob, Mary Ann, Texas A&M University Press, John H Lindsey Bldg, Lewis St, 4354 TAMU, College Station, TX 77843-4354 *Tel:* 979-845-1436 *Toll Free Tel:* 800-826-8911 (orders) *Fax:* 979-847-8752 *Toll Free Fax:* 888-617-2421 (orders) *E-mail:* bookorders@tamu.edu *Web Site:* www.tamupress.com, pg 215

Jacobs, Andrea, The Globe Pequot Press, 246 Goose Lane, Guilford, CT 06437 *Tel:* 203-458-4500 *Toll Free Tel:* 800-243-0495 (orders only); 888-249-7586 (cust serv) *Fax:* 203-458-4601 *Toll Free Fax:* 800-820-2329 (orders & cust serv) *E-mail:* editorial@globepequot.com; info@rowman.com; orders@rowman.com *Web Site:* rowman.com, pg 86

Jacobs, Ben, Bloom's Literary Criticism, 132 W 31 St, 17th fl, New York, NY 10001 *Toll Free Tel:* 800-322-8755 *Toll Free Fax:* 800-678-3633 *E-mail:* custserv@factsonfile.com *Web Site:* www.infobasepublishing.com, pg 35

Jacobs, Ben, Chelsea House, 132 W 31 St, 17th fl, New York, NY 10001 *Toll Free Tel:* 800-322-8755 *Toll Free Fax:* 800-678-3633 *E-mail:* custserv@factsonfile.com; info@infobase.com *Web Site:* www.infobasepublishing.com; www.infobase.com, pg 50

Jacobs, Ben, Facts On File, 132 W 31 St, 17th fl, New York, NY 10001 *Tel:* 212-967-8800 *Toll Free Tel:* 800-322-8755 *Toll Free Fax:* 800-678-3633 *E-mail:* custserv@factsonfile.com *Web Site:* infobasepublishing.com, pg 75

Jacobs, Ben, Ferguson Publishing, 132 W 31 St, 17th fl, New York, NY 10001 *Tel:* 212-967-8800 *Toll Free Tel:* 800-322-8755 *Toll Free Fax:* 800-678-3633 *E-mail:* custserv@factsonfile.com *Web Site:* infobasepublishing.com, pg 77

Jacobs, Donald, Georgetown University Press, 3520 Prospect St NW, Suite 140, Washington, DC 20007 *Tel:* 202-687-5889 (busn) *Tel:* 202-687-6340 (edit) *E-mail:* gupress@georgetown.edu *Web Site:* press.georgetown.edu, pg 85

Jacobs, Farrin, Little, Brown Books for Young Readers, 1290 Avenue of the Americas, New York, NY 10104 *Tel:* 212-364-1100 *Toll Free Tel:* 800-759-0190 (cust serv) *Web Site:* www.hachettebookgroup.com, pg 126

Jacobs, Katherine, Roaring Brook Press, 120 Broadway, New York, NY 10271 *Tel:* 646-307-5151 *Web Site:* us.macmillan.com/publishers/roaring-brook-press, pg 186

Jacobs, Laurence, Craftsman Book Co, 6058 Corte Del Cedro, Carlsbad, CA 92011 *Tel:* 760-438-7828 *Toll Free Tel:* 800-829-8123 *Fax:* 760-438-0398 *Web Site:* www.craftsman-book.com, pg 59

Jacobs, Lindy, Oregon Christian Writers (OCW), 1075 Willow Lake Rd N, Keizer, OR 97303 *Tel:* 503-393-3356 *E-mail:* contact@oregonchristianwriters.org *Web Site:* oregonchristianwriters.org, pg 542

Jacobs, Lindy, Oregon Christian Writers Summer Conference, 1075 Willow Lake Rd N, Keizer, OR 97303 *Tel:* 503-393-3356 *E-mail:* contact@oregonchristianwriters.org *Web Site:* oregonchristianwriters.org, pg 577

Jacobs, Michael, Harry N Abrams Inc, 195 Broadway, 9th fl, New York, NY 10007 *Tel:* 212-206-7715 *Toll Free Tel:* 800-345-1359 *Fax:* 212-519-1210 *E-mail:* abrams@abramsbooks.com *Web Site:* www.abramsbooks.com, pg 3

Jacobs, Michael, Stewart, Tabori & Chang, 195 Broadway, 9th fl, New York, NY 10007 *Tel:* 212-206-7715 *Fax:* 212-519-1210 *E-mail:* abrams@abramsbooks.com *Web Site:* www.abramsbooks.com/imprints/stc, pg 208

Jacobs, Nicki, NEA Creative Writing Fellowships, 400 Seventh St SW, Washington, DC 20506-0001 *Tel:* 202-682-5400; 202-682-5496 (Voice/TTY); 202-682-5034 (lit fellowships hotline) *Fax:* 202-682-5609; 202-682-5610 *E-mail:* litfellowships@arts.gov *Web Site:* www.arts.gov, pg 646

Jacobs, Nicki, Translation Projects, 400 Seventh St SW, Washington, DC 20506-0001 *Tel:* 202-682-5400; 202-682-5496 (Voice/TTY); 202-682-5034 (lit fellowships hotline) *Fax:* 202-682-5609; 202-682-5610 *E-mail:* litfellowships@arts.gov *Web Site:* www.arts.gov, pg 673

Jacobs, Robert H, Univelt Inc, 740 Metcalf St, No 13, Escondido, CA 92025 *Tel:* 760-746-4005 *Fax:* 760-746-3139 *E-mail:* sales@univelt.com *Web Site:* www.univelt.com; www.astronautical.org, pg 225

Jacobson, Hillary, ICM Partners, 65 E 55 St, New York, NY 10022 *Tel:* 212-556-5600 *Web Site:* www.icmtalent.com, pg 489

Jacobson, Kip, Blue Apple Books, 515 Valley St, Suite 170, Maplewood, NJ 07040 *Tel:* 973-763-8191 *E-mail:* info@blueapplebooks.com *Web Site:* blueapplebooks.com, pg 36

Jacobson, Tina, The Barnabas Agency, PO Box 3113, Corsicana, TX 75151-3113 *Tel:* 903-654-1319 *E-mail:* info@barnabasagency.com *Web Site:* www.barnabasagency.com, pg 515

Jacobson, Wendy, Martingale®, 19021 120 Ave NE, Suite 102, Bothell, WA 98011 *Tel:* 425-483-3313 *Toll Free Tel:* 800-426-3126 *Fax:* 425-486-7596 *E-mail:* info@martingale-pub.com *Web Site:* www.martingale-pub.com, pg 133

Jacoby, Judy, Doubleday, c/o Penguin Random House Inc, 1745 Broadway, New York, NY 10019 *Tel:* 212-751-2600 *Fax:* 212-572-2662 (foreign rts) *E-mail:* ddaypub@randomhouse.com *Web Site:* knopfdoubleday.com, pg 66

Jacques, Julia, Adams Media, 57 Littlefield St, Avon, MA 02322 *Tel:* 508-427-7100 *Web Site:* www.simonandschuster.com, pg 4

Jade, Miranda, Imagination Publishing Group, PO Box 1304, Dunedin, FL 34697 *Toll Free Tel:* 888-701-6481 *Fax:* 727-361-0584 *E-mail:* info@imaginationpublishinggroup.com *Web Site:* www.imaginationpublishinggroup.com, pg 106

Jaeger, Christine, Tom Doherty Associates, LLC, 120 Broadway, New York, NY 10271 *Tel:* 646-307-5511 *Toll Free Tel:* 800-455-0340 *Web Site:* us.macmillan.com/torforge, pg 66

Jaeger, Christine, Macmillan, 120 Broadway, 22nd fl, New York, NY 10271 *Tel:* 646-307-5151 *E-mail:* press.inquiries@macmillan.com *Web Site:* www.macmillan.com, pg 130

Jaffe, Gary, Linda Chester Literary Agency, 630 Fifth Ave, Suite 2000, New York, NY 10111 *Tel:* 212-218-3350 *E-mail:* submissions@lindachester.com *Web Site:* www.lindachester.com, pg 479

Jaffe, Sarah, Penguin Random House Audio Publishing, 1745 Broadway, New York, NY 10019 *E-mail:* audio@penguinrandomhouse.com *Web Site:* www.penguinrandomhouseaudio.com, pg 164

Jaffee, Pamela, HarperCollins General Books Group, 195 Broadway, New York, NY 10007 *Tel:* 212-207-7000 *Web Site:* www.harpercollins.com, pg 93

Jaffery, Zareen, Penguin Young Readers Group, 345 Hudson St, New York, NY 10014 *Tel:* 212-366-2000; 212-414-3553 *Fax:* 212-414-3340 *Web Site:* www.penguin.com/children, pg 165

Jahns, Randy, Crossway, 1300 Crescent St, Wheaton, IL 60187 *Tel:* 630-682-4300 *Toll Free Tel:* 800-635-7993 (orders); 800-543-1659 (cust serv) *Fax:* 630-682-4785 *E-mail:* info@crossway.org *Web Site:* www.crossway.org, pg 60

Jain, Amanda, BookEnds Literary Agency, 136 Long Hill Rd, Gillette, NJ 07933 *Web Site:* www.bookendsliterary.com, pg 476

Jain, Mukesh, Jain Publishing Co, PO Box 3523, Fremont, CA 94539 *Tel:* 510-659-8272 *Fax:* 510-659-0501 *E-mail:* mail@jainpub.com *Web Site:* www.jainpub.com, pg 113

Jaksha, Joseph, Hazelden Publishing, 15251 Pleasant Valley Rd, Center City, MN 55012-0011 *Tel:* 651-213-4200 *Toll Free Tel:* 800-257-7810; 866-328-9000 *Fax:* 651-213-4793 *E-mail:* productionformation@hazeldenbettyford.org *Web Site:* www.hazelden.org, pg 96

Jalbert, Sarah, Editions MultiMondes, 1815, Avenue de Lorimier, Montreal, QC H2K 3W6, Canada *Tel:* 514-523-1523 *Toll Free Tel:* 800-361-1664 *Fax:* 514-523-9969 *Web Site:* www.multim.com, pg 425

James, Angela, Harlequin Enterprises Ltd, Bay Adelaide Centre, East Tower, 22 Adelaide St W, 41st fl, Toronto, ON M5H 4E3, Canada *Tel:* 416-445-5860 *Toll Free Tel:* 888-432-4879; 800-370-5838 (ebook inquiries) *E-mail:* customerservice@harlequin.com *Web Site:* www.harlequin.com, pg 429

James, Casey Blue, Penguin Group USA, A Penguin Random House Company, 375 Hudson St, New York, NY 10014 *Tel:* 212-366-2000 *Toll Free Tel:* 800-847-5515 (inside sales); 800-631-8571 (cust serv) *Fax:* 212-366-2666; 607-775-4829 (inside sales) *E-mail:* online@us.penguingroup.com *Web Site:* www.penguin.com, pg 163

James, Diane, Worthy & James Publishing, PO Box 362015, Milpitas, CA 95036 *Tel:* 408-945-3963 *E-mail:* worthy1234@sbcglobal.net; mail@worthyjames.com *Web Site:* www.worthyjames.com, pg 448

James, Kay Coles, The Heritage Foundation, 214 Massachusetts Ave NE, Washington, DC 20002-4999 *Tel:* 202-546-4400 *Toll Free Tel:* 800-544-4843 *Fax:* 202-546-8328 *E-mail:* info@heritage.org *Web Site:* www.heritage.org, pg 98

James, Kristina, MDR, A D&B Co, 6 Armstrong Rd, Suite 301, Shelton, CT 06484 *Tel:* 203-926-4800 *Toll Free Tel:* 800-333-8802 *Fax:* 203-225-4603 *Toll Free Fax:* 866-532-7097 *E-mail:* mdrinfo@dnb.com *Web Site:* mdreducation.com, pg 136

James, Tina, Harlequin Enterprises Ltd, 195 Broadway, 24th fl, New York, NY 10007 *Tel:* 212-207-7000 *Toll Free Tel:* 888-432-4879 *E-mail:* customerservice@harlequin.com *Web Site:* www.harlequin.com, pg 93

James, Tina, Love Inspired Books, 233 Broadway, Suite 1001, New York, NY 10279 *Tel:* 212-553-4200 *Toll Free Tel:* 888-432-4879 *Fax:* 212-227-8969 *E-mail:* customerservice@harlequin.ca *Web Site:* www.harlequin.com, pg 128

Jenkins, Jerrold R, Moonbeam Children's Book Awards, 1129 Woodmere Ave, Suite B, Traverse City, MI 49686 *Tel:* 231-933-0445 *Toll Free Tel:* 800-706-4636 *Fax:* 231-933-0448 *E-mail:* info@moonbeamawards. com *Web Site:* www.moonbeamawards.com, pg 643

Jenkins, John, The MIT Press, One Rogers St, Cambridge, MA 02142 *Tel:* 617-253-5255 *Toll Free Tel:* 800-405-1619 (orders) *Fax:* 617-258-6779; 617-577-1545 (orders) *Web Site:* mitpress.mit.edu, pg 141

Jenkins, Joyce, Northern California Book Awards, c/o Poetry Flash, 1450 Fourth St, Suite 4, Berkeley, CA 94710 *Tel:* 510-525-5476 *Fax:* 510-525-6752 *E-mail:* editor@poetryflash.org; ncbr@poetryflash.org *Web Site:* poetryflash.org, pg 649

Jenkins, Joyce, Poetry Flash Reading Series, 1450 Fourth St, Suite 4, Berkeley, CA 94710 *Tel:* 510-525-5476 *Fax:* 510-525-6752 *E-mail:* editor@poetryflash.org *Web Site:* poetryflash.org, pg 577

Jenkins, Katelyn, Arcadia Publishing Inc, 420 Wando Park Blvd, Mount Pleasant, SC 29464 *Tel:* 843-853-2070 *Toll Free Tel:* 888-313-2665 (orders only) *Fax:* 843-853-0044 *E-mail:* sales@arcadiapublishing. com *Web Site:* www.arcadiapublishing.com, pg 19

Jenks, Carolyn, Carolyn Jenks Agency, 30 Cambridge Park Dr, Suite 3140, Cambridge, MA 02140 *Tel:* 617-233-9130 *E-mail:* queries@carolynjenksagency.com (submissions) *Web Site:* www.carolynjenksagency.com, pg 490

Jennette, Alyssa, Stonesong, 270 W 39 St, Suite 201, New York, NY 10018 *Tel:* 212-929-4600 *E-mail:* editors@stonesong.com *Web Site:* www. stonesong.com, pg 504

Jennings, Randy, SDP Publishing Solutions LLC, 36 Captain's Way, East Bridgewater, MA 02333 *Tel:* 617-775-0656 *Web Site:* www.sdppublishingsolutions.com, pg 470

Jennings, Sharon, Canadian Society of Children's Authors, Illustrators & Performers (CANSCAIP), 720 Bathurst St, Suite 503, Toronto, ON M5S 2R4, Canada *Tel:* 416-515-1559 *E-mail:* office@canscaip. org *Web Site:* www.canscaip.org, pg 530

Jenny, Pat, Oscar Williams/Gene Derwood Award, 909 Third Ave, New York, NY 10022 *Tel:* 212-686-0010 *Fax:* 212-532-8528 *E-mail:* info@nycommunitytrust. org *Web Site:* www.nycommunitytrust.org, pg 678

Jensen, Connie, Saint Mary's Press, 702 Terrace Heights, Winona, MN 55987-1320 *Tel:* 507-457-7900 *Toll Free Tel:* 800-533-8095 *Toll Free Fax:* 800-344-9225 *E-mail:* smpress@smp.org *Web Site:* www.smp.org, pg 191

Jensen, Jack, Princeton Architectural Press, 202 Warren St, Hudson, NY 12534 *Tel:* 518-671-6100 *Toll Free Tel:* 800-722-6657 (dist); 800-759-0190 (sales) *E-mail:* sales@papress.com *Web Site:* www.papress. com, pg 174

Jensen, Jana, Technical Association of the Pulp & Paper Industry (TAPPI), 15 Technology Pkwy S, Suite 115, Peachtree Corners, GA 30092 *Tel:* 770-446-1400 *Toll Free Tel:* 800-332-8686 (US); 800-446-9431 (CN) *Fax:* 770-446-6947 *E-mail:* memberconnection@tappi. org *Web Site:* www.tappi.org, pg 547

Jensen, Jennifer, Chronicle Books, 680 Second St, San Francisco, CA 94107 *Tel:* 415-537-4200 *Toll Free Tel:* 800-759-0190 (cust serv) *Fax:* 415-537-4460 *Toll Free Fax:* 800-858-7787 (orders); 800-286-9471 (cust serv) *E-mail:* frontdesk@chroniclebooks.com *Web Site:* www.chroniclebooks.com, pg 51

Jensen, Joseph, The Astronomical Society of the Pacific, 390 Ashton Ave, San Francisco, CA 94112 *Tel:* 415-337-1100 *Fax:* 415-337-5205 *Web Site:* www. astrosociety.org, pg 24

Jerald, Mike, Pro Lingua Associates Inc, 74 Cotton Mill Hill, Suite A-315, Brattleboro, VT 05301 *Tel:* 802-257-7779 *Toll Free Tel:* 800-366-4775 *Fax:* 802-257-5117 *E-mail:* info@prolinguaassociates.com *Web Site:* www.prolinguaassociates.com, pg 175

Jessen, Eric, Psychological Assessment Resources Inc (PAR), 16204 N Florida Ave, Lutz, FL 33549 *Tel:* 813-449-4065 *Toll Free Tel:* 800-331-8378 *Fax:* 813-961-2196 *Toll Free Fax:* 800-727-9329 *Web Site:* www.parinc.com, pg 177

Jessup, Martha, Lannan Foundation, 313 Read St, Santa Fe, NM 87501-2628 *Tel:* 505-986-8160 *E-mail:* info@ lannan.org *Web Site:* lannan.org, pg 551

Jessup, Martha, Lannan Literary Awards & Fellowships, 313 Read St, Santa Fe, NM 87501-2628 *Tel:* 505-986-8160 *E-mail:* info@lannan.org *Web Site:* lannan.org, pg 631

Jia, Joanna, John Wiley & Sons Inc, 111 River St, Hoboken, NJ 07030-5774 *Tel:* 201-748-6000 *Toll Free Tel:* 800-225-5945 (cust serv) *Fax:* 201-748-6088 *E-mail:* info@wiley.com *Web Site:* www.wiley.com, pg 241

Jiang, Leying, Boyds Mills & Kane, 250 Park Ave, 7th fl, New York, NY 10177 *E-mail:* info@bmkbooks.com *Web Site:* www.boydsmillsandkane.com, pg 39

Jimenez, Anthony, Macmillan, 120 Broadway, 22nd fl, New York, NY 10271 *Tel:* 646-307-5151 *E-mail:* press.inquiries@macmillan.com *Web Site:* www.macmillan.com, pg 130

Jimenez, Kathy, Santillana USA Publishing Co, 2023 NW 84 Ave, Doral, FL 33122 *Tel:* 305-591-9522 *Toll Free Tel:* 800-245-8584 *E-mail:* customerservice@ santillanausa.com *Web Site:* www.santillanausa.com, pg 192

Jimenez, Sandy, Publishers Information Bureau (PIB)®, 757 Third Ave, 11th fl, New York, NY 10017 *Tel:* 212-872-3700 (MPA) *E-mail:* infocenter@ magazine.org *Web Site:* www.magazine.org, pg 545

Jin, Ha, Boston University Creative Writing Program, 236 Bay State Rd, Boston, MA 02215 *Tel:* 617-353-2510 *Fax:* 617-353-3653 *E-mail:* crwr@bu.edu *Web Site:* www.bu.edu/creativewriting, pg 581

Job, Heather, Penguin Random House Audio Publishing, 1745 Broadway, New York, NY 10019 *E-mail:* audio@penguinrandomhouse.com *Web Site:* www.penguinrandomhouseaudio.com, pg 164

Jodoin, Isabelle, Modus Vivendi Publishing Inc, 55, rue Jean-Talon Ouest, Montreal, QC H2R-2W8, Canada *Tel:* 514-272-0433 *Fax:* 514-272-7234 *E-mail:* info@ groupemodus.com *Web Site:* www.groupemodus.com, pg 433

Joel, Jennifer, ICM Partners, 65 E 55 St, New York, NY 10022 *Tel:* 212-556-5600 *Web Site:* www.icmtalent. com, pg 489

Johannesen, Jeremy, Empire State Award for Excellence in Literature for Young People, 6021 State Farm Rd, Guilderland, NY 12084 *Tel:* 518-432-6952 *Toll Free Tel:* 800-252-6952 *Fax:* 518-427-1697 *E-mail:* info@ nyla.org *Web Site:* www.nyla.org, pg 613

Johns, Chelcee, Simon & Schuster, 1230 Avenue of the Americas, New York, NY 10020 *Tel:* 212-698-7000 *Toll Free Tel:* 800-223-2348 (cust serv); 800-223-2336 (orders) *Toll Free Fax:* 800-943-9831 (orders) *Web Site:* www.simonandschuster.com, pg 198

Johns, Christopher, Tuttle Publishing, Airport Business Park, 364 Innovation Dr, North Clarendon, VT 05759-9436 *Tel:* 802-773-8930 *Toll Free Tel:* 800-526-2778 *Fax:* 802-773-6993 *Toll Free Fax:* 800-FAX-TUTL (329-8885) *E-mail:* info@tuttlepublishing. com; orders@tuttlepublishing.com *Web Site:* www. tuttlepublishing.com, pg 222

Johns, Jorun, Ariadne Press, 270 Goins Ct, Riverside, CA 92507 *Tel:* 951-684-9202 *Fax:* 951-779-0449 *E-mail:* ariadnepress@aol.com *Web Site:* www. ariadnebooks.com, pg 19

Johns, Joshua, Little, Brown and Company, 1290 Avenue of the Americas, New York, NY 10104 *Tel:* 212-364-1100 *Fax:* 212-364-0952 *E-mail:* firstname.lastname@ hbgusa.com *Web Site:* www.littlebrown.com; www. hachettebookgroup.com, pg 126

Johnson, Annette R, AllWrite Advertising & Publishing, 3300 Buckeye Rd, Suite 264, Atlanta, GA 30341 *Tel:* 770-284-8983 *Fax:* 770-284-8986 *E-mail:* questions@allwritepublishing.com; support@allwritepublishing.com (orders & returns) *Web Site:* allwritepublishing.com, pg 8

Johnson, Annette R, AllWrite Advertising & Publishing, 3300 Buckeye Rd, Suite 264, Atlanta, GA 30341 *Tel:* 770-284-8983 *Fax:* 770-284-8986 *E-mail:* questions@allwritepublishing.com *Web Site:* allwritepublishing.com, pg 457

Johnson, Bennett J, Path Press Inc, 708 Washington St, Evanston, IL 60202 *Tel:* 847-492-0177 *E-mail:* pathpressinc@aol.com, pg 161

Johnson, Bennie F, AIGA, the professional association for design, 222 Broadway, New York, NY 10038 *Tel:* 212-807-1990 *Fax:* 212-807-1799 *E-mail:* general@aiga.org *Web Site:* www.aiga.org, pg 521

Johnson, Blanche, Wilderness Adventures Press Inc, 45 Buckskin Rd, Belgrade, MT 59714 *Tel:* 406-388-0112 *Toll Free Tel:* 866-400-2012 *E-mail:* books@ wildadvpress.com *Web Site:* store.wildadvpress.com, pg 241

Johnson, Bob, American College, 270 S Bryn Mawr Ave, Bryn Mawr, PA 19010 *Tel:* 610-526-1000 *Toll Free Tel:* 888-263-7265 *Fax:* 610-526-1310 *Web Site:* www.theamericancollege.edu, pg 10

Johnson, Prof Brian, University of Illinois, Department of Journalism, Gregory Hall, Rm 120-A, 810 S Wright St, Urbana, IL 61801 *Tel:* 217-333-0709 *Fax:* 217-333-7931 *E-mail:* journ@uiuc.edu *Web Site:* www. comm.uiuc.edu, pg 586

Johnson, Brianne, Writers House, 21 W 26 St, New York, NY 10010 *Tel:* 212-685-2400 *Web Site:* www. writershouse.com, pg 508

Johnson, Candace, Health Communications Inc, 3201 SW 15 St, Deerfield Beach, FL 33442 *Tel:* 954-360-0909 *Toll Free Tel:* 800-851-9100; 800-441-5569 (cust serv & orders) *Fax:* 954-360-0034 *Toll Free Fax:* 800-424-7652 (cust serv & orders) *E-mail:* customerservice2@hcibooks.com *Web Site:* www.hcibooks.com, pg 96

Johnson, Chuck, Wilderness Adventures Press Inc, 45 Buckskin Rd, Belgrade, MT 59714 *Tel:* 406-388-0112 *Toll Free Tel:* 866-400-2012 *E-mail:* books@ wildadvpress.com *Web Site:* store.wildadvpress.com, pg 241

Johnson, Connie, Double Play, 303 Hillcrest Rd, Belton, MO 64012-1852 *Tel:* 816-651-7118, pg 462

Johnson, Diane E, Livestock Publications Council, 200 W Exchange Ave, Fort Worth, TX 76164 *Tel:* 817-336-1130 *Web Site:* www.livestockpublications.com, pg 536

Johnson, Eric, Redleaf Press, 10 Yorkton Ct, St Paul, MN 55117 *Tel:* 651-641-0508 *Toll Free Tel:* 800-423-8309 *Toll Free Fax:* 800-641-0115 *E-mail:* customerservice@redleafpress.org; sales@ redleafpress.org *Web Site:* www.redleafpress.org, pg 183

Johnson, Erin-Elizabeth, RAND Corp, 1776 Main St, Santa Monica, CA 90407-2138 *Tel:* 310-393-0411 *Fax:* 310-393-4818 *Web Site:* www.rand.org, pg 180

Johnson, George F, Information Age Publishing Inc, PO Box 79049, Charlotte, NC 28271-7047 *Tel:* 704-752-9125 *Fax:* 704-752-9113 *E-mail:* infoage@infoagepub. com *Web Site:* www.infoagepub.com, pg 108

Johnson, Harmony, University of British Columbia Press, 2029 West Mall, Vancouver, BC V6T 1Z2, Canada *Tel:* 604-822-5959 *Toll Free Tel:* 877-377-9378 *Fax:* 604-822-6083 *Toll Free Fax:* 800-668-0821 *E-mail:* frontdesk@ubcpress.ca *Web Site:* www. ubcpress.ca, pg 443

Johnson, Howard Jr, Edgewise Press Inc, 24 Fifth Ave, Suite 224, New York, NY 10011 *Tel:* 212-982-4818 *Fax:* 212-982-1364 *E-mail:* epinc@mindspring.com *Web Site:* www.edgewisepress.org, pg 69

Johnson, Howard, SDP Publishing Solutions LLC, 36 Captain's Way, East Bridgewater, MA 02333 *Tel:* 617-775-0656 *Web Site:* www.sdppublishingsolutions.com, pg 470

Juliar, Troy, Recorded Books Inc, an RBmedia company, 270 Skipjack Rd, Prince Frederick, MD 20678 *Tel:* 410-535-5590 *Toll Free Tel:* 877-732-2898 *Fax:* 410-535-5499 *E-mail:* customerservice@ recordedbooks.com *Web Site:* www.recordedbooks. com, pg 182

Julien, Ria, Frances Goldin Literary Agency, Inc, 214 W 29 St, Suite 410, New York, NY 10001 *Tel:* 212-777-0047 *Fax:* 212-228-1660 *E-mail:* agency@goldinlit. com *Web Site:* www.goldinlit.com, pg 486

Jung, Zaneta, Chronicle Books, 680 Second St, San Francisco, CA 94107 *Tel:* 415-537-4200 *Toll Free Tel:* 800-759-0190 (cust serv) *Fax:* 415-537-4460 *Toll Free Fax:* 800-858-7787 (orders); 800-286-9471 (cust serv) *E-mail:* frontdesk@chroniclebooks.com *Web Site:* www.chroniclebooks.com, pg 52

Junior, Bobbi, InScribe Christian Writers' Fellowship (ICWF), PO Box 6201, Wetaskiwin, AB T9A 2E9, Canada *Tel:* 780-646-3068 *Fax:* 780-635-2190 *E-mail:* inscribe.mail@gmail.com *Web Site:* inscribe. org, pg 535

Junker, Lisa, Entomological Society of America, 3 Park Place, Suite 307, Annapolis, MD 21401-3722 *Tel:* 301-731-4535 *Fax:* 301-731-4538 *E-mail:* esa@ entsoc.org *Web Site:* www.entsoc.org, pg 73

Juodaitis, Thomas W, The Trinity Foundation, PO Box 68, Unicoi, TN 37692-0068 *Tel:* 423-743-0199 *Fax:* 423-743-2005 *Web Site:* www.trinityfoundation. org, pg 220

Jurewicz, Hannah Carlson, Bick Publishing House, 75 Mungertown Rd, Madison, CT 06443 *Tel:* 203-245-0341 *Fax:* 203-208-5253 *E-mail:* bickpubhse@aol.com *Web Site:* www.bickpubhouse.com, pg 33

Jusino, John, HarperCollins General Books Group, 195 Broadway, New York, NY 10007 *Tel:* 212-207-7000 *Web Site:* www.harpercollins.com, pg 93

Jutkowitz, Edward, Camino Books Inc, PO Box 59026, Philadelphia, PA 19102-9026 *Tel:* 215-413-1917 *Fax:* 215-413-3255 *E-mail:* camino@caminobooks. com *Web Site:* www.caminobooks.com, pg 44

Kacian, Jim, Red Moon Press, PO Box 2461, Winchester, VA 22604-1661 *Tel:* 540-722-2156 *Web Site:* www.redmoonpress.com, pg 183

Kadarusman, Michelle, Giller Prize, 543 Logan Ave, Toronto, ON M4K 3B6, Canada *Web Site:* www. scotiabankgillerprize.ca, pg 619

Kadetz, Stuart, Bhaktivedanta Book Trust (BBT), 9701 Venice Blvd, Suite 3, Los Angeles, CA 90034 *Tel:* 310-837-5283 *Toll Free Tel:* 800-927-4152 *Fax:* 310-837-1056 *E-mail:* store@krishna.com *Web Site:* www.krishna.com, pg 33

Kado, Martina PhD, Maryland Historical Society, 201 W Monument St, Baltimore, MD 21201 *Tel:* 410-685-3750 *Fax:* 410-385-2105 *Web Site:* www.mdhs.org, pg 133

Kaeser, Scott, Tide-mark Press, 207 Oakwood Ave, West Hartford, CT 06119 *Tel:* 860-310-3370 *Toll Free Tel:* 800-338-2508 *Fax:* 860-310-3654 *E-mail:* customerservice@tide-mark.com, pg 218

Kagan, Abby, Farrar, Straus & Giroux, LLC, 175 Varick St, 9th fl, New York, NY 10014 *Tel:* 212-741-6900 *E-mail:* fsg.publicity@fsgbooks.com *Web Site:* us. macmillan.com/fsg.aspx, pg 76

Kagan, Heidi, Penguin Group USA, A Penguin Random House Company, 375 Hudson St, New York, NY 10014 *Tel:* 212-366-2000 *Toll Free Tel:* 800-847-5515 (inside sales); 800-631-8571 (cust serv) *Fax:* 212-366-2666; 607-775-4829 (inside sales) *E-mail:* online@ us.penguingroup.com *Web Site:* www.penguin.com, pg 163

Kagan, Ute Wartenberg, American Numismatic Society, 75 Varick St, 11th fl, New York, NY 10013 *Tel:* 212-571-4470 *Fax:* 212-571-4479 *E-mail:* ans@ numismatics.org *Web Site:* www.numismatics.org, pg 13

Kahan, Rachel, HarperCollins General Books Group, 195 Broadway, New York, NY 10007 *Tel:* 212-207-7000 *Web Site:* www.harpercollins.com, pg 93

Kahla, Keith, St Martin's Press, LLC, 120 Broadway, New York, NY 10271 *Tel:* 646-307-5151 *Web Site:* us. macmillan.com/smp, pg 190

Kahn, Jody, Brandt & Hochman Literary Agents Inc, 1501 Broadway, Suite 2310, New York, NY 10036 *Tel:* 212-840-5760 *Fax:* 212-840-5776 *Web Site:* brandthochman.com, pg 477

Kahn, Kenneth F, LRP Publications, 360 Hiatt Dr, Palm Beach Gardens, FL 33418 *Tel:* 561-622-6520 *Toll Free Tel:* 800-341-7874 *Fax:* 561-622-2423 *E-mail:* custserve@lrp.com *Web Site:* www.lrp.com; www.shoplrp.com, pg 129

Kahrizi, Camilia, Marilyn Baillie Picture Book Award, 40 Orchard View Blvd, Suite 217, Toronto, ON M4R 1B9, Canada *Tel:* 416-975-0010 *Fax:* 416-975-8970 *E-mail:* info@bookcentre.ca *Web Site:* www. bookcentre.ca, pg 595

Kahrizi, Camilia, The Geoffrey Bilson Award for Historical Fiction for Young People, 40 Orchard View Blvd, Suite 217, Toronto, ON M4R 1B9, Canada *Tel:* 416-975-0010 *Fax:* 416-975-8970 *E-mail:* info@ bookcentre.ca *Web Site:* www.bookcentre.ca, pg 598

Kahrizi, Camilia, Canadian Children's Book Centre, 40 Orchard View Blvd, Suite 217, Toronto, ON M4R 1B9, Canada *Tel:* 416-975-0010 *Fax:* 416-975-8970 *E-mail:* info@bookcentre.ca *Web Site:* www. bookcentre.ca, pg 530

Kahrizi, Camilia, Norma Fleck Award for Canadian Children's Non-Fiction, 40 Orchard View Blvd, Suite 217, Toronto, ON M4R 1B9, Canada *Tel:* 416-975-0010 *Fax:* 416-975-8970 *E-mail:* info@bookcentre.ca *Web Site:* www.bookcentre.ca, pg 616

Kahrizi, Camilia, Amy Mathers Teen Book Award, 40 Orchard View Blvd, Suite 217, Toronto, ON M4R 1B9, Canada *Tel:* 416-975-0010 *Fax:* 416-975-8970 *E-mail:* info@bookcentre.ca *Web Site:* www. bookcentre.ca, pg 639

Kahrizi, Camilia, John Spray Mystery Award, 40 Orchard View Blvd, Suite 217, Toronto, ON M4R 1B9, Canada *Tel:* 416-975-0010 *Fax:* 416-975-8970 *E-mail:* info@bookcentre.ca *Web Site:* www. bookcentre.ca, pg 669

Kahrizi, Camilia, TD Canadian Children's Literature Award, 40 Orchard View Blvd, Suite 217, Toronto, ON M4R 1B9, Canada *Tel:* 416-975-0010 *Fax:* 416-975-8970 *E-mail:* info@bookcentre.ca *Web Site:* www. bookcentre.ca, pg 672

Kail, Greg, American Water Works Association (AWWA), 6666 W Quincy Ave, Denver, CO 80235-3098 *Tel:* 303-794-7711 *Toll Free Tel:* 800-926-7337 *E-mail:* service@awwa.org (cust serv) *Web Site:* www.awwa.org, pg 15

Kaiman, Ken, Square One Publishers Inc, 115 Herricks Rd, Garden City Park, NY 11040 *Tel:* 516-535-2010 *Toll Free Tel:* 877-900-BOOK (900-2665) *Fax:* 516-535-2014 *E-mail:* sq1publish@aol.com *Web Site:* www.squareonepublishers.com, pg 206

Kain, Amanda, Perseus Books, 1290 Avenue of the Americas, New York, NY 10104 *Tel:* 212-340-8100 *Toll Free Tel:* 800-343-4499 (cust serv) *Fax:* 212-340-8105 *Web Site:* www.perseusbooks.com, pg 168

Kaiser, Cecily, Penguin Workshop, 1745 Broadway, New York, NY 10019 *Tel:* 212-366-2000 *Web Site:* www. penguin.com/publishers/penguinworkshop/, pg 165

Kaiser, Cecily, Penguin Young Readers Group, 345 Hudson St, New York, NY 10014 *Tel:* 212-366-2000; 212-414-3553 *Fax:* 212-414-3340 *Web Site:* www. penguin.com/children, pg 165

Kaiser, Debra, Lorenz Educational Press, 501 E Third St, Dayton, OH 45402 *Tel:* 937-228-6118 *Toll Free Tel:* 800-444-1144 *Fax:* 937-223-2042 *E-mail:* order@ lorenz.com *Web Site:* www.lorenzeducationalpress. com, pg 128

Kaiser, Debra, Milliken Publishing Co, 501 E Third St, Dayton, OH 45402 *Tel:* 937-228-6118 *Toll Free Tel:* 800-444-1144 *Fax:* 937-223-2042 *E-mail:* order@ lorenz.com *Web Site:* www.lorenzeducationalpress. com, pg 140

Kaiser, Debra, Teaching & Learning Co, 501 E Third St, Dayton, OH 45402 *Tel:* 937-228-6118 *Toll Free Tel:* 800-444-1144 *Fax:* 937-223-2042 *E-mail:* info@ lorenz.com *Web Site:* www.lorenzeducationalpress. com, pg 214

Kaiser, Jackie, Westwood Creative Artists Ltd, 138 Sussex Mews, Toronto, ON M5S-2K1, Canada *Tel:* 416-964-3302 *Fax:* 416-964-3302 *E-mail:* wca_office@wcaltd.com *Web Site:* www. wcaltd.com, pg 508

Kaiser, Kathleen, Small Publishers, Artists & Writers Network (SPAWN), 1129 Maricopa Hwy, No 142, Ojai, CA 93023 *E-mail:* info@spawn.org *Web Site:* spawn.org, pg 546

Kaita, Melissa, Second Story Press, 20 Maud St, Suite 401, Toronto, ON M5V 2M5, Canada *Tel:* 416-537-7850 *Fax:* 416-537-0588 *E-mail:* info@ secondstorypress.ca *Web Site:* secondstorypress.ca, pg 439

Kakar, Samir, Aptara Inc, 2901 Telestar Ct, Suite 522, Falls Church, VA 22042 *Tel:* 703-352-0001 *E-mail:* moreinfo@aptaracorp.com *Web Site:* www. aptaracorp.com, pg 458

Kalajian, James, Axiom Business Book Awards, 1129 Woodmere Ave, Suite B, Traverse City, MI 49686 *Tel:* 231-933-0445 *Toll Free Tel:* 800-706-4636 *Fax:* 231-933-0448 *E-mail:* info@axiomawards.com *Web Site:* www.axiomawards.com, pg 595

Kalajian, James, eLit Awards, 1129 Woodmere Ave, Suite B, Traverse City, MI 49686 *Tel:* 231-933-0445 *Toll Free Tel:* 800-706-4636 *Fax:* 231-933-0448 *E-mail:* info@elitawards.com *Web Site:* www. elitawards.com, pg 612

Kalajian, James, Illumination Book Awards, 1129 Woodmere Ave, Suite B, Traverse City, MI 49686 *Tel:* 231-933-0445 *Toll Free Tel:* 800-706-4636 *Fax:* 231-933-0448 *E-mail:* awards@bookpublishing. com *Web Site:* www.illuminationawards.com, pg 625

Kalajian, James, The Independent Publisher Book Awards, 1129 Woodmere Ave, Suite B, Traverse City, MI 49686 *Tel:* 231-933-0445 *Toll Free Tel:* 800-706-4636 *Fax:* 231-933-0448 *E-mail:* awards@bookpublishing.com *Web Site:* www. independentpublisher.com/ipland/ipawards.php, pg 626

Kalajian, James, Jenkins Group Inc, 1129 Woodmere Ave, Suite B, Traverse City, MI 49686 *Tel:* 231-933-0445 *Toll Free Tel:* 800-706-4636 *Fax:* 231-933-0448 *E-mail:* info@bookpublishing.com *Web Site:* www. bookpublishing.com, pg 465

Kalajian, James, Living Now Book Awards, 1129 Woodmere Ave, Suite B, Traverse City, MI 49686 *Tel:* 231-933-0445 *Toll Free Tel:* 800-706-4636 *Fax:* 231-933-0448 *E-mail:* awards@bookpublishing. com *Web Site:* www.livingnowawards.com, pg 634

Kalajian, James, Moonbeam Children's Book Awards, 1129 Woodmere Ave, Suite B, Traverse City, MI 49686 *Tel:* 231-933-0445 *Toll Free Tel:* 800-706-4636 *Fax:* 231-933-0448 *E-mail:* info@moonbeamawards. com *Web Site:* www.moonbeamawards.com, pg 643

Kalett, Alison, Princeton University Press, 41 William St, Princeton, NJ 08540-5237 *Tel:* 609-258-4900 *Fax:* 609-258-6305 *Web Site:* press.princeton.edu, pg 174

Kalish, Ilene, New York University Press, 838 Broadway, 3rd fl, New York, NY 10003-4812 *Tel:* 212-998-2575 (edit) *Toll Free Tel:* 800-996-6987 (orders) *Fax:* 212-995-4798 (orders) *E-mail:* nyupressinfo@nyu.edu; orders@nyupress.org *Web Site:* www.nyupress.org, pg 150

Kallet, Jeff, Ohio University Press, Alden Library, Suite 101, 30 Park Place, Athens, OH 45701-2901 *Tel:* 740-593-1154 *Web Site:* www.ohioswallow.com, pg 155

Kalman, Bobbie, Crabtree Publishing Co, 347 Fifth Ave, Suite 1402-145, New York, NY 10016 *Tel:* 212-496-5040 *Toll Free Tel:* 800-387-7650 *Toll Free Fax:* 800-355-7166 *E-mail:* custserv@crabtreebooks. com *Web Site:* www.crabtreebooks.com, pg 59

Kalman, Bobbie, Crabtree Publishing Co Ltd, 616 Welland Ave, St Catharines, ON L2M 5V6, Canada *Tel:* 905-682-5221 *Toll Free Tel:* 800-387-7650 *Fax:* 905-682-7166 *Toll Free Fax:* 800-355-7166 *E-mail:* custserv@crabtreebooks.com; sales@ crabtreebooks.com; orders@crabtreebooks.com *Web Site:* www.crabtreebooks.com, pg 421

Kalman, Jason, Hebrew Union College Press, 3101 Clifton Ave, Cincinnati, OH 45220 *Tel:* 513-221-1875 *Fax:* 513-221-0321 *Web Site:* press.huc.edu, pg 97

Kalne, Jan, Society for Scholarly Publishing (SSP), 1120 Rte 73, Suite 200, Mount Laurel, NJ 08054 *Tel:* 856-439-1385 *Fax:* 856-439-0525 *E-mail:* info@sspnet.org *Web Site:* www.sspnet.org, pg 546

Kals, Josie, Alfred A Knopf, c/o Penguin Random House Inc, 1745 Broadway, New York, NY 10019 *Tel:* 212-751-2600 *Fax:* 212-572-2662 (foreign rts) *Web Site:* knopfdoubleday.com, pg 118

Kals, Josie, Pantheon Books, c/o Penguin Random House Inc, 1745 Broadway, New York, NY 10019 *Tel:* 212-751-2600 *Fax:* 212-572-2662 (foreign rts) *Web Site:* knopfdoubleday.com, pg 159

Kalweit, Burk, American Academy of Environmental Engineers & Scientists®, 147 Old Solomons Islánd Rd, Suite 303, Annapolis, MD 21401 *Tel:* 410-266-3311 *Fax:* 410-266-7653 *E-mail:* info@aaees.org *Web Site:* www.aaees.org, pg 9

Kalyvas, Adelia, Workman Publishing Co Inc, 225 Varick St, 9th fl, New York, NY 10014-4381 *Tel:* 212-254-5900 *Toll Free Tel:* 800-722-7202 *Fax:* 212-254-8098 *E-mail:* info@workman.com; orders@workman. com *Web Site:* www.workman.com, pg 244

Kam, Kristopher, Random House Children's Books, 1745 Broadway, 10th fl, New York, NY 10019 *Tel:* 212-782-9000 *Web Site:* www.randomhousekids. com, pg 180

Kamin, Hayley, American Psychological Association, 750 First St NE, Washington, DC 20002-4242 *Tel:* 202-336-5510 *Toll Free Tel:* 800-374-2721 *Fax:* 202-336-5502 *E-mail:* order@apa.org *Web Site:* www.apa.org/books, pg 13

Kamin, Rachel, AJL Jewish Fiction Award, PO Box 118, Teaneck, NJ 07666 *Tel:* 201-371-3255 *E-mail:* info@ jewishlibraries.org *Web Site:* jewishlibraries.org/ AJL_Jewish_Fiction_Award, pg 590

Kamin, Sari, Houghton Mifflin Harcourt, 125 High St, Boston, MA 02110 *Tel:* 617-351-5000 *Toll Free Tel:* 855-969-4642; 800-225-5425 (K-12 educ materials); 800-323-9540 (assessment materials); 877-219-1537 (SkillsTutor); 888-242-6747 (Innovation in Educ Group); 800-225-3362 (Trade & Ref Div) *Toll Free Fax:* 800-269-5232 *E-mail:* myhmhco@hmhco. com *Web Site:* www.hmhco.com, pg 103

Kamin, Sari, Houghton Mifflin Harcourt Trade & Reference Division, 125 High St, Boston, MA 02110 *Tel:* 617-351-5000 *Web Site:* www.hmhco.com, pg 104

Kamir, Taeyana, Math Solutions®, One Harbor Dr, Suite 101, Sausalito, CA 94965 *Toll Free Tel:* 877-234-7323 *Toll Free Fax:* 800-724-4716 *E-mail:* info@ mathsolutions.com; orders@mathsolutions. com *Web Site:* www.mathsolutions.com; store. mathsolutions.com, pg 134

Kamoroff, Bernard, Bell Springs Publishing, PO Box 1240, Willits, CA 95490-1240 *Tel:* 707-272-3472 *E-mail:* publisher@bellsprings.com *Web Site:* bellsprings.com; aboutpinball.com, pg 31

Kanagy, Dave, Society for Mining, Metallurgy & Exploration, 12999 E Adam Aircraft Circle, Englewood, CO 80112 *Tel:* 303-948-4200 *Toll Free Tel:* 800-763-3132 *Fax:* 303-973-3845 *E-mail:* cs@ smenet.org; books@smenet.org *Web Site:* www. smenet.org, pg 202

Kane, Adam, Naval Institute Press, 291 Wood Rd, Annapolis, MD 21402-5034 *Tel:* 410-268-6110 *Toll Free Tel:* 800-233-8764 *Fax:* 410-295-1084; 410-571-1703 (cust serv) *E-mail:* webmaster@ navalinstitute.org; customer@navalinstitute.org (cust serv) *Web Site:* www.nip.org; www.usni.org, pg 147

Kane, Barry, Light-Beams Publishing, 36 Blandings Way, Biddeford, ME 04005 *Tel:* 603-659-1300 *E-mail:* info@light-beams.com *Web Site:* www.light-beams.com, pg 124

Kane, Laura, Public Relations Society of America Inc, 120 Wall St, 21st fl, New York, NY 10005-4024 *Tel:* 212-460-1400 *Fax:* 212-995-0757 *E-mail:* memberservices@prsa.org *Web Site:* www. prsa.org, pg 545

Kane, Morgan, Farrar, Straus & Giroux Books for Young Readers, 120 Broadway, New York, NY 10271 *Tel:* 212-741-6900 *Toll Free Tel:* 888-330-8477 (orders) *Fax:* 212-633-9385 *Web Site:* us.macmillan. com/mackids; www.mackidsbooks.com, pg 76

Kane, Morgan, Roaring Brook Press, 120 Broadway, New York, NY 10271 *Tel:* 646-307-5151 *Web Site:* us. macmillan.com/publishers/roaring-brook-press, pg 186

Kane, Roberta, The Write Way, 3048 Horizon Lane, Suite 1102, Naples, FL 34109 *Tel:* 239-273-9145 *E-mail:* darekane@gmail.com, pg 472

Kane, Sonia, Boydell & Brewer Inc, 668 Mount Hope Ave, Rochester, NY 14620-2731 *Tel:* 585-275-0419 *Fax:* 585-271-8778 *E-mail:* boydell@boydellusa.net *Web Site:* www.boydellandbrewer.com, pg 39

Kane, Sonia, University of Rochester Press, 668 Mount Hope Ave, Rochester, NY 14620-2731 *Tel:* 585-275-0419 *Fax:* 585-271-8778 *E-mail:* boydell@boydellusa. net *Web Site:* www.urpress.com, pg 231

Kane, Tracey, Liguori Publications, One Liguori Dr, Liguori, MO 63057-1000 *Tel:* 636-464-2500 *Toll Free Tel:* 800-325-9521 *Toll Free Fax:* 800-325-9526 (sales) *E-mail:* liguori@liguori.org (sales & cust serv) *Web Site:* www.liguori.org, pg 124

Kaneko, Amy, Arcadia Publishing Inc, 420 Wando Park Blvd, Mount Pleasant, SC 29464 *Tel:* 843-853-2070 *Toll Free Tel:* 888-313-2665 (orders only) *Fax:* 843-853-0044 *E-mail:* sales@arcadiapublishing.com *Web Site:* www.arcadiapublishing.com, pg 19

Kanellos, Nicolas, Arte Publico Press, University of Houston, Bldg 19, Rm 100, 4902 Gulf Fwy, Houston, TX 77204-2004 *Tel:* 713-743-2998 (sales) *Toll Free Tel:* 800-633-2783 *Fax:* 713-743-2847 (sales) *E-mail:* appinfo@uh.edu; bkorders@uh.edu *Web Site:* artepublicopress.com, pg 20

Kantor, Emma, The Children's Book Council (CBC), 54 W 39 St, 14th fl, New York, NY 10018 *Tel:* 212-966-1990 *E-mail:* cbc.info@cbcbooks.org *Web Site:* www. cbcbooks.org, pg 531

Kantor, Russell, The Center for Learning, 10200 Jefferson Blvd, Culver City, CA 90232 *Tel:* 310-839-2436 *Toll Free Tel:* 800-421-4246 *Fax:* 310-839-2249 *Toll Free Fax:* 800-944-5432 *E-mail:* access@ socialstudies.com *Web Site:* www.centerforlearning. org, pg 48

Kanya-Forstner, Martha, Doubleday Canada, 320 Front St W, Suite 1400, Toronto, ON M5V 3B6, Canada *Tel:* 416-364-4449 *Fax:* 416-598-7764 *Web Site:* www. penguinrandomhouse.ca, pg 421

Kanya-Forstner, Martha, McClelland & Stewart Ltd, 320 Front St W, Suite 1400, Toronto, ON M5V 3B6, Canada *Tel:* 416-364-4449 *Fax:* 416-598-7764 *E-mail:* customerservicescanada@ penguinrandomhouse.com; publicity@ca.penguingroup. com *Web Site:* penguinrandomhouse.ca/imprints/ mcclelland-stewart, pg 433

Kaplan, Deborah, Puffin Books, 345 Hudson St, New York, NY 10014 *Tel:* 212-366-2000 *Web Site:* www. penguin.com/publishers/puffin, pg 177

Kaplan, Genevieve, Kate Tufts Discovery Award, Harper East, Unit B-7, 160 E Tenth St, Claremont, CA 91711-6165 *Tel:* 909-621-8974 *E-mail:* tufts@cgu.edu *Web Site:* www.cgu.edu/tufts, pg 674

Kaplan, Genevieve, Kingsley Tufts Poetry Award, Harper East, Unit B-7, 160 E Tenth St, Claremont, CA 91711-6165 *Tel:* 909-621-8974 *E-mail:* tufts@cgu.edu *Web Site:* www.cgu.edu/tufts, pg 674

Kaplan, Howard, Silver Gavel Awards, 321 N Clark St, Chicago, IL 60654 *Tel:* 312-988-5719 *Toll Free Tel:* 800-285-2221 (orders) *Fax:* 312-988-5494 *Web Site:* www.ambar.org/gavelawards, pg 667

Kaplan, Joyce, Kensington Publishing Corp, 119 W 40 St, New York, NY 10018 *Tel:* 212-407-1500 *Toll Free Tel:* 800-221-2647 *Fax:* 212-935-0699 *Web Site:* www. kensingtonbooks.com, pg 116

Kaplan, Lawrence D, Alaska Native Language Center, PO Box 757680, Fairbanks, AK 99775-7680 *Fax:* 907-474-6586 *E-mail:* uaf-anlc@alaska.edu (orders) *Web Site:* www.uaf.edu/anlc, pg 6

Kaplan, Linda, DeFiore and Company Literary Management Inc, 47 E 19 St, 3rd fl, New York, NY 10003 *Tel:* 212-925-7744 *Fax:* 212-925-9803 *E-mail:* info@defliterary.com; submissions@ defliterary.com *Web Site:* www.defliterary.com, pg 481

Kaplan, Liza, Philomel, 345 Hudson St, New York, NY 10014 *Tel:* 212-366-2000 *Web Site:* www.penguin. com/publishers/philomel, pg 169

Kaplan, Rebecca, Harry N Abrams Inc, 195 Broadway, 9th fl, New York, NY 10007 *Tel:* 212-206-7715 *Toll Free Tel:* 800-345-1359 *Fax:* 212-519-1210 *E-mail:* abrams@abramsbooks.com *Web Site:* www. abramsbooks.com, pg 3

Kaplan, Stuart R, US Games Systems Inc, 179 Ludlow St, Stamford, CT 06902 *Tel:* 203-353-8400 *Toll Free Tel:* 800-54-GAMES (544-2637) *Fax:* 203-353-8431 *E-mail:* info@usgamesinc.com *Web Site:* www. usgamesinc.com, pg 234

Kaplow, Margaret, National Catholic Educational Association, 1005 N Glebe Rd, Suite 525, Arlington, VA 22201 *Tel:* 571-257-0010 *Toll Free Tel:* 800-711-6232 *Fax:* 703-243-0025 *E-mail:* nceaadmin@ncea.org *Web Site:* www.ncea.org, pg 145

Kaplowitz, Marla, 4A's (American Association of Advertising Agencies), 1065 Avenue of the Americas, 16th fl, New York, NY 10018 *Tel:* 212-682-2500 *Web Site:* www.aaaa.org, pg 534

Kapoor, Prashant, Aptara Inc, 2901 Telestar Ct, Suite 522, Falls Church, VA 22042 *Tel:* 703-352-0001 *E-mail:* moreinfo@aptaracorp.com *Web Site:* www. aptaracorp.com, pg 458

Karagueuzian, Dikran, CSLI Publications, Stanford University, Cordura Hall, 220 Panama St, Stanford, CA 94305-4115 *Tel:* 650-723-1839 *Fax:* 650-725-2166 *E-mail:* pubs@csli.stanford.edu *Web Site:* cslipublications.stanford.edu, pg 61

Karchmar, Dorian, WME, 11 Madison Ave, 18th fl, New York, NY 10010 *Tel:* 212-586-5100 *Web Site:* www. wmeentertainment.com, pg 508

Kardys, Jan L, Unicorn Writers' Conference, 17 Church Hill Rd, Redding, CT 06896 *Tel:* 203-938-7405 *Fax:* 203-938-7405 *E-mail:* unicornwritersconference@gmail.com *Web Site:* unicornwritersconference.com, pg 579

Karl, Laraine, The Rockefeller University Press, 950 Third Ave, 2nd fl, New York, NY 10022 *Tel:* 212-327-7938 *E-mail:* rupress@rockefeller.edu *Web Site:* www. rupress.org, pg 186

Karle, John, St Martin's Press, LLC, 120 Broadway, New York, NY 10271 *Tel:* 646-307-5151 *Web Site:* us. macmillan.com/smp, pg 190

Karp, Jonathan, Simon & Schuster, Inc, 1230 Avenue of the Americas, New York, NY 10020 *Tel:* 212-698-7000 *Toll Free Tel:* 800-223-2336 (orders) *Fax:* 212-698-7007 *Toll Free Fax:* 800-943-9831 (orders) *E-mail:* firstname.lastname@simonandschuster.com; purchaseorders@simonandschuster.com (orders) *Web Site:* www.simonandschuster.com, pg 199

Karpas, Heather, ICM Partners, 65 E 55 St, New York, NY 10022 *Tel:* 212-556-5600 *Web Site:* www. icmtalent.com, pg 489

Karper, Altie, Pantheon Books, c/o Penguin Random House Inc, 1745 Broadway, New York, NY 10019 *Tel:* 212-751-2600 *Fax:* 212-572-2662 (foreign rts) *Web Site:* knopfdoubleday.com, pg 159

Karper, Altie, Schocken Books, c/o Penguin Random House Inc, 1745 Broadway, New York, NY 10019 *Tel:* 212-751-2600 *Fax:* 212-572-2662 (foreign rts) *Web Site:* knopfdoubleday.com, pg 193

Karpfinger, Barney M, The Karpfinger Agency, 357 W 20 St, New York, NY 10011-3379 *Tel:* 212-691-2690 *Fax:* 212-691-7129 *E-mail:* info@karpfinger.com (no queries or submissions) *Web Site:* karpfinger.com, pg 490

Karre, Andrew, Dutton Children's Books, 345 Hudson St, New York, NY 10014 *Tel:* 212-366-2000 *Web Site:* www.penguin.com/publishers/duttonchildrensbooks/, pg 68

Karter, Lucinda, Trident Media Group LLC, 41 Madison Ave, 36th fl, New York, NY 10010 *Tel:* 212-333-1511 *E-mail:* info@tridentmediagroup.com; press@tridentmediagroup.com *Web Site:* www.tridentmediagroup.com, pg 507

Kartsev, Dr Vladimir, Metropolitan Classics, 26 Arthur Place, Yonkers, NY 10701 *Tel:* 914-375-6448 *Web Site:* www.fortrossinc.com, pg 138

Kartsev, Dr Vladimir P, Fort Ross Inc - International Representation for Artists, 26 Arthur Place, Yonkers, NY 10701 *Tel:* 914-375-6448, pg 485, 511

Kartz, Ellen, R Ross Annett Award for Children's Literature, 11759 Groat Rd, Edmonton, AB T5M 3K6, Canada *Tel:* 780-422-8174 *Toll Free Tel:* 800-665-5354 (AB only) *Fax:* 780-422-2663 (attn WGA) *E-mail:* mail@writersguild.ca *Web Site:* writersguild.ca, pg 592

Kartz, Ellen, Georges Bugnet Award for Fiction, 11759 Groat Rd, Edmonton, AB T5M 3K6, Canada *Tel:* 780-422-8174 *Toll Free Tel:* 800-665-5354 (AB only) *Fax:* 780-422-2663 (attn WGA) *E-mail:* mail@writersguild.ca *Web Site:* writersguild.ca, pg 601

Kartz, Ellen, The City of Calgary W O Mitchell Book Prize, 11759 Groat Rd, Edmonton, AB T5M 3K6, Canada *Tel:* 780-422-8174 *Toll Free Tel:* 800-665-5354 (AB only) *Fax:* 780-422-2663 (attn WGA) *E-mail:* mail@writersguild.ca *Web Site:* writersguild.ca, pg 605

Kartz, Ellen, Wilfrid Eggleston Award for Nonfiction, 11759 Groat Rd, Edmonton, AB T5M 3K6, Canada *Tel:* 780-422-8174 *Toll Free Tel:* 800-665-5354 (AB only) *Fax:* 780-422-2663 (attn WGA) *E-mail:* mail@writersguild.ca *Web Site:* writersguild.ca, pg 612

Kartz, Ellen, James H Gray Award for Short Nonfiction, 11759 Groat Rd, Edmonton, AB T5M 3K6, Canada *Tel:* 780-422-8174 *Toll Free Tel:* 800-665-5354 (AB only) *Fax:* 780-422-2663 (attn WGA) *E-mail:* mail@writersguild.ca *Web Site:* writersguild.ca, pg 620

Kartz, Ellen, The Robert Kroetsch City of Edmonton Book Prize, 11759 Groat Rd, Edmonton, AB T5M 3K6, Canada *Tel:* 780-422-8174 *Toll Free Tel:* 800-665-5354 (AB only) *Fax:* 780-422-2663 (attn WGA) *E-mail:* mail@writersguild.ca *Web Site:* writersguild.ca, pg 631

Kartz, Ellen, Howard O'Hagan Award for Short Story, 11759 Groat Rd, Edmonton, AB T5M 3K6, Canada *Tel:* 780-422-8174 *Toll Free Tel:* 800-665-5354 (AB only) *Fax:* 780-422-2663 (attn WGA) *E-mail:* mail@writersguild.ca *Web Site:* writersguild.ca, pg 650

Kartz, Ellen, Gwen Pharis Ringwood Award for Drama, 11759 Groat Rd, Edmonton, AB T5M 3K6, Canada *Tel:* 780-422-8174 *Toll Free Tel:* 800-665-5354 (AB only) *Fax:* 780-422-2663 (attn WGA) *E-mail:* mail@writersguild.ca *Web Site:* writersguild.ca, pg 662

Kartz, Ellen, Stephan G Stephansson Award for Poetry, 11759 Groat Rd, Edmonton, AB T5M 3K6, Canada *Tel:* 780-422-8174 *Toll Free Tel:* 800-665-5354 (AB only) *Fax:* 780-422-2663 (attn WGA) *E-mail:* mail@writersguild.ca *Web Site:* writersguild.ca, pg 670

Kartz, Ellen, Jon Whyte Memorial Essay Prize, 11759 Groat Rd, Edmonton, AB T5M 3K6, Canada *Tel:* 780-422-8174 *Toll Free Tel:* 800-665-5354 (AB only) *Fax:* 780-422-2663 (attn WGA) *E-mail:* mail@writersguild.ca *Web Site:* writersguild.ca, pg 677

Kartz, Ellen, Writers' Guild of Alberta, 11759 Groat Rd, Edmonton, AB T5M 3K6, Canada *Tel:* 780-422-8174 *Toll Free Tel:* 800-665-5354 (AB only) *Fax:* 780-422-2663 (attn WGA) *E-mail:* mail@writersguild.ca *Web Site:* writersguild.ca, pg 549

Kasdorf, Helga, Kindred Productions, 1310 Taylor Ave, Winnipeg, MB R3M 3Z6, Canada *Tel:* 204-669-6575 *Toll Free Tel:* 800-545-7322 *Fax:* 204-654-1865 *E-mail:* kindred@mbchurches.ca *Web Site:* www.kindredproductions.com, pg 431

Kase, Josef, Letterbox/Papyrus of London Publishers USA, 10501 Broom Hill Dr, Suite 1-F, Las Vegas, NV 89134-7339 *Tel:* 702-256-3838 *E-mail:* lb27383@cox.net, pg 123

Kasius, Jennifer, Perseus Books, 1290 Avenue of the Americas, New York, NY 10104 *Tel:* 212-340-8100 *Toll Free Tel:* 800-343-4499 (cust serv) *Fax:* 212-340-8105 *Web Site:* www.perseusbooks.com, pg 167

Kasper, Karl, Crabtree Publishing Co, 347 Fifth Ave, Suite 1402-145, New York, NY 10016 *Tel:* 212-496-5040 *Toll Free Tel:* 800-387-7650 *Toll Free Fax:* 800-355-7166 *E-mail:* custserv@crabtreebooks.com *Web Site:* www.crabtreebooks.com, pg 59

Kasper, Karl, Crabtree Publishing Co Ltd, 616 Welland Ave, St Catharines, ON L2M 5V6, Canada *Tel:* 905-682-5221 *Toll Free Tel:* 800-387-7650 *Fax:* 905-682-7166 *Toll Free Tel:* 800-355-7166 *E-mail:* custserv@crabtreebooks.com; sales@crabtreebooks.com; orders@crabtreebooks.com *Web Site:* www.crabtreebooks.com, pg 421

Kass, Gary, University of Missouri Press, 113 Heinkel Bldg, 201 S Seventh St, Columbia, MO 65211 *Tel:* 573-882-7641; 573-882-3000 (publicity & sales enquiries) *Toll Free Tel:* 800-621-2736 (orders) *Fax:* 573-884-4498 *Toll Free Fax:* 800-621-8476 (orders) *E-mail:* upress@missouri.edu; umpmarketing@missouri.edu (publicity & sales enquiries) *Web Site:* upress.missouri.edu, pg 228

Kastely, Jay, University of Houston Creative Writing Program, 229 Roy Cullen Bldg, Houston, TX 77204-5008 *Tel:* 713-743-2255 *Fax:* 713-743-3697 *E-mail:* cwp@uh.edu *Web Site:* www.uh.edu/cwp, pg 586

Kastenmeier, Edward, Anchor Books, c/o Penguin Random House Inc, 1745 Broadway, New York, NY 10019 *Tel:* 212-572-2420 *E-mail:* vintageanchorpublicity@randomhouse.com *Web Site:* knopfdoubleday.com/imprint/anchor, pg 15

Kastenmeier, Edward, Vintage Books, c/o Penguin Random House Inc, 1745 Broadway, New York, NY 10019 *Tel:* 212-572-2420 *E-mail:* vintageanchorpublicity@randomhouse.com *Web Site:* knopfdoubleday.com/imprint/vintage, pg 236

Kastner, Suzanne, Graphic World Publishing Services, 11687 Adie Rd, St Louis, MO 63043 *Tel:* 314-567-9854 *Fax:* 314-567-7178 *E-mail:* quote@gwinc.com *Web Site:* www.gwinc.com, pg 464

Kasuga, Mika, Random House Publishing Group, 1745 Broadway, New York, NY 10019 *Toll Free Tel:* 800-200-3552 *Web Site:* www.randomhousebooks.com, pg 181

Kater, Julia, The Association of English-Language Publishers of Quebec-AELAQ (Association des Editeurs de Langue Anglaise du Quebec), Atwater Library, 1200 Atwater Ave, Suite 3, Westmount, QC H3Z 1X4, Canada *Tel:* 514-932-5633 *E-mail:* admin@aelaq.org *Web Site:* aelaq.org, pg 526

Katz, Deanne, Chronicle Books, 680 Second St, San Francisco, CA 94107 *Tel:* 415-537-4200 *Toll Free Tel:* 800-759-0190 (cust serv) *Fax:* 415-537-4460 *Toll Free Fax:* 800-858-7787 (orders); 800-286-9471 (cust serv) *E-mail:* frontdesk@chroniclebooks.com *Web Site:* www.chroniclebooks.com, pg 52

Katz, Laurie, Bloom's Literary Criticism, 132 W 31 St, 17th fl, New York, NY 10001 *Toll Free Tel:* 800-322-8755 *Toll Free Fax:* 800-678-3633 *E-mail:* custserv@factsonfile.com *Web Site:* www.infobasepublishing.com, pg 35

Katz, Laurie, Chelsea House, 132 W 31 St, 17th fl, New York, NY 10001 *Toll Free Tel:* 800-322-8755 *Toll Free Fax:* 800-678-3633 *E-mail:* custserv@factsonfile.com; info@infobase.com *Web Site:* www.infobasepublishing.com; www.infobase.com, pg 50

Katz, Laurie, Facts On File, 132 W 31 St, 17th fl, New York, NY 10001 *Tel:* 212-967-8800 *Toll Free Tel:* 800-322-8755 *Toll Free Fax:* 800-678-3633 *E-mail:* custserv@factsonfile.com *Web Site:* infobasepublishing.com, pg 75

Katz, Laurie, Ferguson Publishing, 132 W 31 St, 17th fl, New York, NY 10001 *Tel:* 212-967-8800 *Toll Free Tel:* 800-322-8755 *Toll Free Fax:* 800-678-3633 *E-mail:* custserv@factsonfile.com *Web Site:* infobasepublishing.com, pg 77

Katz, Michael, Tradewind Books, 202-1807 Maritime Mews, Vancouver, BC V6H 3W7, Canada *Tel:* 604-662-4405 *E-mail:* tradewindbooks@yahoo.com; tradewindbooks@gmail.com *Web Site:* www.tradewindbooks.com, pg 442

Katz, Simon, Penguin Random House Audio Publishing, 1745 Broadway, New York, NY 10019 *E-mail:* audio@penguinrandomhouse.com *Web Site:* www.penguinrandomhouseaudio.com, pg 164

Katzenberger, Elaine, City Lights Publishers, 261 Columbus Ave, San Francisco, CA 94133 *Tel:* 415-362-8193 *Fax:* 415-362-4921 *E-mail:* staff@citylights.com *Web Site:* www.citylights.com, pg 53

Katzman, Julie T, Inter-American Development Bank, 1300 New York Ave NW, Washington, DC 20577 *Tel:* 202-623-1000 *Fax:* 202-623-3096 *E-mail:* pic@iadb.org *Web Site:* publications.iadb.org, pg 110

Kauffman, Lisa, Rational Island Publishers, 719 Second Ave N, Seattle, WA 98109 *Tel:* 206-284-0311 *E-mail:* ircc@rc.org *Web Site:* www.rc.org, pg 182

Kaufman, Brian, Anvil Press Publishers, 278 E First Ave, Vancouver, BC V5T 1A6, Canada *Tel:* 604-876-8710 *Fax:* 604-879-2667 *E-mail:* info@anvilpress.com *Web Site:* www.anvilpress.com, pg 415

Kaufman, Gabe, Jump!, 5357 Penn Ave, Minneapolis, MN 55419 *Toll Free Tel:* 888-799-1860 *Toll Free Fax:* 800-675-6679 *E-mail:* customercare@jumplibrary.com *Web Site:* www.jumplibrary.com, pg 115

Kaufman, Jason, Doubleday, c/o Penguin Random House Inc, 1745 Broadway, New York, NY 10019 *Tel:* 212-751-2600 *Fax:* 212-572-2662 (foreign rts) *E-mail:* ddaypub@randomhouse.com *Web Site:* knopfdoubleday.com, pg 66

Kaufmann, Anthony S, Abaris Books, 70 New Canaan Ave, Norwalk, CT 06850 *Tel:* 203-838-8402 *Fax:* 203-857-0730 *E-mail:* abaris@abarisbooks.com *Web Site:* abarisbooks.com, pg 2

Kavaler, Ethan Matt, Centre for Reformation & Renaissance Studies (CRRS), 71 Queen's Park Crescent E, Toronto, ON M5S 1K7, Canada *Tel:* 416-585-4465 *Fax:* 416-585-4430 (attn: CRRS) *E-mail:* crrs.publications@utoronto.ca *Web Site:* crrs.ca, pg 419

Kavonic, Melissa, Bloomsbury Publishing Inc, 1385 Broadway, 5th fl, New York, NY 10018 *Tel:* 212-419-5300 *E-mail:* marketingusa@bloomsbury.com; adultpublicityusa@bloomsbury.com; askacademic@bloomsbury.com *Web Site:* www.bloomsbury.com, pg 35, 36

Kay, Jeremy, Bartleby Press, 8926 Baltimore St, No 858, Savage, MD 20763 *Tel:* 301-589-5831 *Toll Free Tel:* 800-953-9929 *E-mail:* inquiries@bartlebythepublisher.com *Web Site:* www.bartlebythepublisher.com, pg 28

Kaye, David, Anna Zornio Memorial Children's Theatre Playwriting Award, D22 Paul Creative Arts Center, 30 Academic Way, Durham, NH 03824 *Tel:* 603-862-2919 *Fax:* 603-862-0298 *Web Site:* cola.unh.edu/theatre-dance/resource/zornio, pg 682

Kaye, Terry, Behrman House Inc, 11 Edison Place, Springfield, NJ 07081 *Tel:* 973-379-7200 *Toll Free Tel:* 800-221-2755 *Fax:* 973-379-7280 *E-mail:* customersupport@behrmanhouse.com *Web Site:* store.behrmanhouse.com, pg 30

293-6251 *E-mail:* customercare@trustedmediabrands.com; press@trustedmediabrands.com *Web Site:* www.trustedmediabrands.com; www.rd.com, pg 221

Kelley, Claire, Shambhala Publications Inc, 4720 Walnut St, Boulder, CO 80301 *Tel:* 303-222-9598 *Toll Free Tel:* 866-424-0030 (off); 888-424-2329 (cust serv) *E-mail:* customercare@shambhala.com *Web Site:* www.shambhala.com, pg 197

Kelley, Lynn, Kane Miller Books, 4901 Morena Blvd, Suite 213, San Diego, CA 92117 *E-mail:* submissions@kanemiller.com; info@kanemiller.com *Web Site:* www.kanemiller.com, pg 115

Kelley, Mary, Allan Nevins Prize, 2950 Broadway, New York, NY 10027 *Tel:* 212-854-6495 *E-mail:* amhistsociety@columbia.edu *Web Site:* sah.columbia.edu, pg 647

Kelley, Mary, Francis Parkman Prize, 2950 Broadway, New York, NY 10027 *Tel:* 212-854-6495 *E-mail:* amhistsociety@columbia.edu *Web Site:* sah.columbia.edu, pg 652

Kelley, Mary, SAH Prize for Historical Fiction, 2950 Broadway, New York, NY 10027 *Tel:* 212-854-6495 *E-mail:* amhistsociety@columbia.edu *Web Site:* sah.columbia.edu, pg 663

Kelley, Pamela, University of Hawaii Press, 2840 Kolowalu St, Honolulu, HI 96822-1888 *Tel:* 808-956-8255 *Toll Free Tel:* 888-UHPRESS (847-7377) *Fax:* 808-988-6052 *Toll Free Fax:* 800-650-7811 *E-mail:* uhpbooks@hawaii.edu *Web Site:* www.uhpress.hawaii.edu, pg 227

Kelly, Catherine E, Omohundro Institute of Early American History & Culture, Swem Library, Ground fl, 400 Landrum Dr, Williamsburg, VA 23185 *Tel:* 757-221-1110 *Fax:* 757-221-1047 *E-mail:* ieahc1@wm.edu *Web Site:* oieahc.wm.edu, pg 155

Kelly, Claire, NeWest Press, 8540 109 St, No 201, Edmonton, AB T6G 1E6, Canada *Tel:* 780-432-9427 *Fax:* 780-433-3179 *E-mail:* info@newestpress.com; orders@newestpress.com *Web Site:* www.newestpress.com, pg 434

Kelly, Frances, Eye in the Ear Children's Audio, 5 Crescent St, Portland, ME 04102 *Toll Free Tel:* 855-99-STORY (997-8679) *Fax:* 207-699-1380 (attn: Laurence Kelly) *E-mail:* info@eyeintheear.com *Web Site:* www.eyeintheear.com, pg 74

Kelly, Heather, Harry N Abrams Inc, 195 Broadway, 9th fl, New York, NY 10007 *Tel:* 212-206-7715 *Toll Free Tel:* 800-345-1359 *Fax:* 212-519-1210 *E-mail:* abrams@abramsbooks.com *Web Site:* www.abramsbooks.com, pg 3

Kelly, Jean Marie, HarperCollins Publishers, 195 Broadway, New York, NY 10007 *Tel:* 212-207-7000 *Fax:* 212-207-7145 *Web Site:* www.harpercollins.com, pg 94

Kelly, Jim, Aevitas Creative Management, 19 W 21 St, Suite 501, New York, NY 10010 *Tel:* 212-765-6900 *Web Site:* aevitascreative.com, pg 474

Kelly, Jules, Random House Children's Books, 1745 Broadway, 10th fl, New York, NY 10019 *Tel:* 212-782-9000 *Web Site:* www.randomhousekids.com, pg 181

Kelly, Kate, Morgan Gaynin Inc, 149 Madison Ave, Suite 1140, New York, NY 10016 *Tel:* 212-475-0440 *E-mail:* info@morgangaynin.com *Web Site:* www.morgangaynin.com, pg 512

Kelly, Laurence A, Eye in the Ear Children's Audio, 5 Crescent St, Portland, ME 04102 *Toll Free Tel:* 855-99-STORY (997-8679) *Fax:* 207-699-1380 (attn: Laurence Kelly) *E-mail:* info@eyeintheear.com *Web Site:* www.eyeintheear.com, pg 74

Kelly, Margaret, Sourcebooks LLC, 1935 Brookdale Rd, Suite 139, Naperville, IL 60563 *Tel:* 630-961-3900 *Toll Free Tel:* 800-432-7444 *Fax:* 630-961-2168 *E-mail:* info@sourcebooks.com; customersupport@sourcebooks.com *Web Site:* www.sourcebooks.com, pg 204

Kelly, Nancy V, Kinship Books, 305 Cedar Heights Rd, Rhinebeck, NY 12572 *Tel:* 845-876-4592 (orders) *E-mail:* kinship@hvc.rr.com *Web Site:* www.kinshipny.com, pg 117

Kelly, Neil K, F A Davis Co, 1915 Arch St, Philadelphia, PA 19103 *Tel:* 215-568-2270; 215-440-3001 *Toll Free Tel:* 800-523-4049 *Fax:* 215-568-5065; 215-440-3016 *E-mail:* info@fadavis.com; orders@fadavis.com *Web Site:* www.fadavis.com, pg 62

Kelly, Patricia, Lonely Planet, 124 Linden St, Oakland, CA 94607 *Tel:* 510-250-6400 *Toll Free Tel:* 800-275-8555 (orders) *E-mail:* info@lonelyplanet.com *Web Site:* www.lonelyplanet.com, pg 127

Kelly, Robert, Goodheart-Willcox Publisher, 18604 W Creek Dr, Tinley Park, IL 60477-6243 *Tel:* 708-687-5000 *Toll Free Tel:* 800-323-0440 *Toll Free Fax:* 888-409-3900 *E-mail:* custserv@g-w.com; orders@g-w.com *Web Site:* www.g-w.com, pg 87

Kelly, Shannon, Harry N Abrams Inc, 195 Broadway, 9th fl, New York, NY 10007 *Tel:* 212-206-7715 *Toll Free Tel:* 800-345-1359 *Fax:* 212-519-1210 *E-mail:* abrams@abramsbooks.com *Web Site:* www.abramsbooks.com, pg 3

Kelly, Stephanie, Dutton, 1745 Broadway, New York, NY 10019 *Tel:* 212-366-2000 *Fax:* 212-366-2262 *E-mail:* duttonpublicity@us.penguingroup.com *Web Site:* www.penguin.com, pg 68

Kelly, Stephanie, Penguin Group USA, A Penguin Random House Company, 375 Hudson St, New York, NY 10014 *Tel:* 212-366-2000 *Toll Free Tel:* 800-847-5515 (inside sales); 800-631-8571 (cust serv) *Fax:* 212-366-2666; 607-775-4829 (inside sales) *E-mail:* online@us.penguingroup.com *Web Site:* www.penguin.com, pg 163

Kelly, William P, John Simon Guggenheim Memorial Foundation, 90 Park Ave, New York, NY 10016 *Tel:* 212-687-4470 *Fax:* 212-697-3248 *Web Site:* www.gf.org, pg 551

Kelly-Pye, Laurie, Red Wheel/Weiser, 65 Parker St, Suite 7, Newburyport, MA 01950 *Tel:* 978-465-0504 *Toll Free Tel:* 800-423-7087 (orders) *Fax:* 978-465-0243 *E-mail:* info@rwwbooks.com *Web Site:* www.redwheelweiser.com, pg 183

Kelsch, Liz, Sourcebooks LLC, 1935 Brookdale Rd, Suite 139, Naperville, IL 60563 *Tel:* 630-961-3900 *Toll Free Tel:* 800-432-7444 *Fax:* 630-961-2168 *E-mail:* info@sourcebooks.com; customersupport@sourcebooks.com *Web Site:* www.sourcebooks.com, pg 204

Kelsey, Karla, Susquehanna University, Department of English & Creative Writing, 514 University Ave, Selinsgrove, PA 17870 *Tel:* 570-372-0101, pg 585

Keltner, Jennifer, Martingale®, 19021 120 Ave NE, Suite 102, Bothell, WA 98011 *Tel:* 425-483-3313 *Toll Free Tel:* 800-426-3126 *Fax:* 425-486-7596 *E-mail:* info@martingale-pub.com *Web Site:* www.martingale-pub.com, pg 133

Kemp, Jaemellah, Naval Institute Press, 291 Wood Rd, Annapolis, MD 21402-5034 *Tel:* 410-268-6110 *Toll Free Tel:* 800-233-8764 *Fax:* 410-295-1084; 410-571-1703 (cust serv) *E-mail:* webmaster@navalinstitute.org; customer@navalinstitute.org (cust serv) *Web Site:* www.nip.org; www.usni.org, pg 147

Kemp, Steve, Blue Whale Press, 237 Rainbow Dr, No 13702, Livingston, TX 77399-2037 *Toll Free Tel:* 800-848-1631 *E-mail:* info@bluewhalepress.com; sales@bluewhalepress.com *Web Site:* www.bluewhalepress.com, pg 37

Kendall, Grace, Farrar, Straus & Giroux Books for Young Readers, 120 Broadway, New York, NY 10271 *Tel:* 212-741-6900 *Toll Free Tel:* 888-330-8477 (orders) *Fax:* 212-633-9385 *Web Site:* us.macmillan.com/mackids; www.mackidsbooks.com, pg 76

Kendall, Josh, Little, Brown and Company, 1290 Avenue of the Americas, New York, NY 10104 *Tel:* 212-364-1100 *Fax:* 212-364-0952 *E-mail:* firstname.lastname@hbgusa.com *Web Site:* www.littlebrown.com; www.hachettebookgroup.com, pg 125

Keneston, Fran, State University of New York Press, 10 N Pearl St, 4th fl, Albany, NY 12207 *Tel:* 518-944-2800 *Toll Free Tel:* 877-204-6073 (orders) *Fax:* 518-320-1592 *Toll Free Fax:* 877-204-6074 (orders) *E-mail:* info@sunypress.edu (edit off); suny@presswarehouse.com (orders) *Web Site:* www.sunypress.edu, pg 207

Kennedy, Christopher, Syracuse University Creative Writing Program, 401 Hall of Languages, Syracuse, NY 13244-1170 *Tel:* 315-443-2173 *Fax:* 315-443-3660 *Web Site:* english.syr.edu/creative_writing; www.syr.edu, pg 585

Kennedy, Clara-Swan, Black Rose Books Ltd, CP 35788 Succ Leo-Pariseau, Montreal, QC H2X 0A4, Canada *Tel:* 514-844-4076 *E-mail:* info@blackrosebooks.com *Web Site:* blackrosebooks.com, pg 416

Kennedy, Debra, National Coalition for Literacy (NCL), PO Box 2932, Washington, DC 20013-2932 *E-mail:* ncl@ncladvocacy.org *Web Site:* www.national-coalition-literacy.org, pg 539

Kennedy, Mary, Institute of Intergovernmental Relations, Queen's University, Robert Sutherland Hall, Rm 412, Kingston, ON K7L 3N6, Canada *Tel:* 613-533-2080 *Fax:* 613-533-6868 *E-mail:* iigr@queensu.ca *Web Site:* www.queensu.ca/iigr, pg 430

Kennedy, Ryan, Hatherleigh Press Ltd, 62545 State Hwy 10, Hobart, NY 13788 *Toll Free Tel:* 800-528-2550 *E-mail:* info@hatherleighpress.com; publicity@hatherleighpress.com *Web Site:* www.hatherleighpress.com, pg 95

Kennedy, Shane, Lone Pine Publishing, 87 E Pender, Vancouver, BC V6A 1S9, Canada *Tel:* 780-433-9333 *Toll Free Tel:* 800-661-9017 *Fax:* 780-433-9646 *Toll Free Fax:* 800-424-7173 *E-mail:* info@lonepinepublishing.com *Web Site:* www.lonepinepublishing.com, pg 432

Kennedy, Stephen, The Mathematical Association of America, 1529 18 St NW, Washington, DC 20036-1358 *Tel:* 202-387-5200 *Toll Free Tel:* 800-741-9415 *Fax:* 202-265-2384 *E-mail:* maahq@maa.org; advertising@maa.org (pubns) *Web Site:* www.maa.org, pg 134

Kennedy, Tara, Bloomsbury Publishing Inc, 1385 Broadway, 5th fl, New York, NY 10018 *Tel:* 212-419-5300 *E-mail:* marketingusa@bloomsbury.com; adultpublicityusa@bloomsbury.com; askacademic@bloomsbury.com *Web Site:* www.bloomsbury.com, pg 36

Kennedy, Teresa, Winterwolf Press, 1810 E Sahara Ave, Suite 737, Las Vegas, NV 89014 *Toll Free Tel:* 855-ICE-WOLF (423-9653) *E-mail:* info@winterwolfpress.com; questions@winterwolfpress.com; admin@winterwolfpress.com (orders) *Web Site:* winterwolfpress.com, pg 243

Kennedy, Terry, The Robert Watson Literary Prizes in Fiction & Poetry, MFA Writing Program, The Greensboro Review, UNC-Greensboro, 3302 MHRA Bldg, Greensboro, NC 27402-6170 *Tel:* 336-334-5459 *Fax:* 336-256-1470 *Web Site:* www.greensbororeview.org, pg 676

Kennedy, William, New York State Edith Wharton Citation of Merit for Fiction Writers, University at Albany, SL 320, Albany, NY 12222 *Tel:* 518-442-5620 *Fax:* 518-442-5621 *E-mail:* writers@albany.edu *Web Site:* www.albany.edu/writers-inst, pg 648

Kennedy, William, New York State Walt Whitman Citation of Merit for Poets, University at Albany, SL 320, Albany, NY 12222 *Tel:* 518-442-5620 *Fax:* 518-442-5621 *E-mail:* writers@albany.edu *Web Site:* www.albany.edu/writers-inst, pg 648

Kennedy, William, New York State Writers Institute, University at Albany, Science Library 320, 1400 Washington Ave, Albany, NY 12222 *Tel:* 518-442-5620 *Fax:* 518-442-5621 *E-mail:* writers@albany.edu *Web Site:* www.albany.edu/writers-inst, pg 577

Kennelly, Brian, TAN Books, PO Box 269, Gastonia, NC 28053 *Tel:* 704-731-0651 *Toll Free Tel:* 800-437-5876 *Fax:* 815-226-7770 *E-mail:* customerservice@tanbooks.com *Web Site:* www.tanbooks.com, pg 212

Killam, Ray, Business Forms Management Association (BFMA), 1147 Fleetwood Ave, Madison, WI 53716-1417 *Toll Free Tel:* 888-367-3078 *E-mail:* bfma@bfma.org *Web Site:* www.bfma.org, pg 529

Killeen, Valerie, Central Recovery Press (CRP), 3321 N Buffalo Dr, Suite 275, Las Vegas, NV 89129 *Tel:* 702-868-5830 *Fax:* 702-868-5831 *E-mail:* sales@centralrecovery.com *Web Site:* centralrecoverypress.com, pg 48

Killen, Madison, Chronicle Books, 680 Second St, San Francisco, CA 94107 *Tel:* 415-537-4200 *Toll Free Tel:* 800-759-0190 (cust serv) *Fax:* 415-537-4460 *Toll Free Fax:* 800-858-7787 (orders); 800-286-9471 (cust serv) *E-mail:* frontdesk@chroniclebooks.com *Web Site:* www.chroniclebooks.com, pg 51

Killick, Angus, Farrar, Straus & Giroux Books for Young Readers, 120 Broadway, New York, NY 10271 *Tel:* 212-741-6900 *Toll Free Tel:* 888-330-8477 (orders) *Fax:* 212-633-9385 *Web Site:* us.macmillan.com/mackids; www.mackidsbooks.com, pg 76

Killick, Angus, Roaring Brook Press, 120 Broadway, New York, NY 10271 *Tel:* 646-307-5151 *Web Site:* us.macmillan.com/publishers/roaring-brook-press, pg 186

Kilmartin, Kerry, University of British Columbia Press, 2029 West Mall, Vancouver, BC V6T 1Z2, Canada *Tel:* 604-822-5959 *Toll Free Tel:* 877-377-9378 *Fax:* 604-822-6083 *Toll Free Fax:* 800-668-0821 *E-mail:* frontdesk@ubcpress.ca *Web Site:* www.ubcpress.ca, pg 443

Kim, Emily Sylvan, Prospect Agency, 285 Fifth Ave, PMB 445, Brooklyn, NY 11215 *Tel:* 718-788-3217 *Fax:* 718-360-9582 *Web Site:* www.prospectagency.com, pg 499

Kim, Esther, Macmillan, 120 Broadway, 22nd fl, New York, NY 10271 *Tel:* 646-307-5151 *E-mail:* press.inquiries@macmillan.com *Web Site:* www.macmillan.com, pg 129

Kim, Esther, Other Press, 267 Fifth Ave, 6th fl, New York, NY 10016 *Tel:* 212-414-0054 *Toll Free Tel:* 877-843-6843 *Fax:* 212-414-0939 *E-mail:* editor@otherpress.com; marketing@otherpress.com; publicity@otherpress.com *Web Site:* www.otherpress.com, pg 157

Kim, Gail, Judy Lopez Memorial Award For Children's Literature, 1225 Selby Ave, Los Angeles, CA 90024 *Tel:* 310-474-9917 *Fax:* 310-474-6436 *Web Site:* www.wnba-books.org/la; www.judylopezbookaward.org, pg 635

Kim, Hannah, The Museum of Modern Art (MoMA), Publications Dept, 11 W 53 St, New York, NY 10019 *Tel:* 212-708-9443 *E-mail:* moma_publications@moma.org *Web Site:* www.moma.org, pg 144

Kim, Jean H, Stanford University Press, 425 Broadway St, Redwood City, CA 94063-3126 *Tel:* 650-723-9434 *Fax:* 650-725-3457 *E-mail:* info@www.sup.org; publicity@www.sup.org; sales@www.sup.org *Web Site:* www.sup.org, pg 206

Kim, Jennifer, Sandra Dijkstra Literary Agency, 1155 Camino del Mar, PMB 515, Del Mar, CA 92014-2605 *Web Site:* dijkstraagency.com, pg 482

Kim, Dr Jim Yong, World Bank Publications, Office of the Publisher, 1818 "H" St NW, U-11-1104, Washington, DC 20433 *Tel:* 202-458-4497; 202-473-1000 *Toll Free Tel:* 800-645-7247 (cust serv) *Fax:* 202-522-2631 *E-mail:* books@worldbank.org; pubrights@worldbank.org (foreign rts) *Web Site:* www.worldbank.org/en/research, pg 244

Kim, Jisu, The Feminist Press at The City University of New York, 365 Fifth Ave, Suite 5406, New York, NY 10016 *Tel:* 212-817-7915 *Fax:* 212-817-1593 *E-mail:* info@feministpress.org *Web Site:* www.feministpress.org, pg 77

Kim, Kirby, Janklow & Nesbit Associates, 285 Madison Ave, 21st fl, New York, NY 10017 *Tel:* 212-421-1700 *Fax:* 212-355-1403 *E-mail:* info@janklow.com *Web Site:* www.janklowandnesbit.com, pg 490

Kim, Kirsten, Sanford J Greenburger Associates Inc, 55 Fifth Ave, New York, NY 10003 *Tel:* 212-206-5600 *Fax:* 212-463-8718 *Web Site:* greenburger.com; www.sjga.com, pg 487

Kim, Melissa, Islandport Press, 247 Portland St, Bldg C, Yarmouth, ME 04096 *Tel:* 207-846-3344 *Fax:* 207-619-9975 *E-mail:* info@islandportpress.com *Web Site:* www.islandportpress.com, pg 112

Kim, Michelle, Random House Children's Books, 1745 Broadway, 10th fl, New York, NY 10019 *Tel:* 212-782-9000 *Web Site:* www.randomhousekids.com, pg 181

Kim, Sally, GP Putnam's Sons (Hardcover), 375 Hudson St, New York, NY 10014 *Tel:* 212-366-2000 *Fax:* 212-366-2643 *E-mail:* online@penguinputnam.com *Web Site:* www.penguin.com/publishers/gpputnamssons, pg 178

Kim, Sally M, WNBA Pannell Award for Excellence in Children's Bookselling, PO Box 237, FDR Sta, New York, NY 10150-0231 *Toll Free Tel:* 866-610-WNBA (610-9622) *E-mail:* WNBAPannell@gmail.com *Web Site:* www.wnba-books.org; www.NationalReadingGroupMonth.org; www.wnba-books.org/awards, pg 678

Kim, Steve, Chronicle Books, 680 Second St, San Francisco, CA 94107 *Tel:* 415-537-4200 *Toll Free Tel:* 800-759-0190 (cust serv) *Fax:* 415-537-4460 *Toll Free Fax:* 800-858-7787 (orders); 800-286-9471 (cust serv) *E-mail:* frontdesk@chroniclebooks.com *Web Site:* www.chroniclebooks.com, pg 52

Kim, Un Chu, Alfred Music, PO Box 10003, Van Nuys, CA 91410 *Tel:* 818-891-5999 (dealer sales, intl) *Toll Free Tel:* 800-292-6122 (dealer sales, US & CN); 800-628-1528 (cust serv) *Fax:* 818-893-5560 (dealer sales); 818-830-6252 (cust serv) *Toll Free Fax:* 800-632-1928 (dealer sales) *E-mail:* customerservice@alfred.com; sales@alfred.com *Web Site:* www.alfred.com, pg 7

Kimball, David, National Association of Real Estate Editors (NAREE), 1003 NW Sixth Terr, Boca Raton, FL 33486-3455 *Tel:* 561-391-3599 *Fax:* 561-391-0099 *Web Site:* www.naree.org, pg 539

Kimball, Roger, Encounter Books, 900 Broadway, Suite 601, New York, NY 10003 *Tel:* 212-871-6310 *Toll Free Tel:* 800-343-4499 *Fax:* 212-871-6311 *E-mail:* publicity@encounterbooks.com *Web Site:* www.encounterbooks.com, pg 72

Kimbel, Travis, Yale University Press, 302 Temple St, New Haven, CT 06511-8909 *Tel:* 203-432-0960; 203-432-0966 (sales); 401-531-2800 (cust serv) *Toll Free Tel:* 800-405-1619 (cust serv) *Fax:* 203-432-0948; 203-432-8485 (sales); 401-531-2801 (cust serv) *Toll Free Fax:* 800-406-9145 (cust serv) *E-mail:* sales.press@yale.edu (sales); customer.care@triliteral.org (cust serv) *Web Site:* www.yalebooks.com; yalepress.yale.edu/yupbooks, pg 246

Kimberling, Clint, University of Alabama Press, 200 Hackberry Lane, 2nd fl, Tuscaloosa, AL 35487 *Tel:* 205-348-5180 *Fax:* 205-348-9201 *Web Site:* www.uapress.ua.edu, pg 225

Kimzey, Anne, Alabama Artists Fellowship Awards, 201 Monroe St, Suite 110, Montgomery, AL 36130-1800 *Tel:* 334-242-4076 *Fax:* 334-240-3269, pg 590

Kincaid, Christen, New Women's Voices Chapbook Competition, PO Box 1626, Georgetown, KY 40324 *Tel:* 502-603-0670 *E-mail:* finishingbooks@aol.com; flpbookstore@aol.com *Web Site:* www.finishinglinepress.com, pg 647

Kincaid, Christen, Open Chapbook Competition, PO Box 1626, Georgetown, KY 40324 *Tel:* 502-603-0670 *E-mail:* finishingbooks@aol.com; flpbookstore@aol.com *Web Site:* www.finishinglinepress.com, pg 651

Kind, Rachel, Random House Publishing Group, 1745 Broadway, New York, NY 10019 *Toll Free Tel:* 800-200-3552 *Web Site:* www.randomhousebooks.com, pg 181

Kindig, Jessie, Verso, 20 Jay St, Suite 1010, Brooklyn, NY 11201 *Tel:* 718-246-8160 *Fax:* 718-246-8165 *E-mail:* verso@versobooks.com *Web Site:* www.versobooks.com, pg 235

King, Brenda, Yale University Press, 302 Temple St, New Haven, CT 06511-8909 *Tel:* 203-432-0960; 203-432-0966 (sales); 401-531-2800 (cust serv) *Toll Free Tel:* 800-405-1619 (cust serv) *Fax:* 203-432-0948;

203-432-8485 (sales); 401-531-2801 (cust serv) *Toll Free Fax:* 800-406-9145 (cust serv) *E-mail:* sales.press@yale.edu (sales); customer.care@triliteral.org (cust serv) *Web Site:* www.yalebooks.com; yalepress.yale.edu/yupbooks, pg 246

King, Brian B, Appalachian Trail Conservancy (ATC), 799 Washington St, Harpers Ferry, WV 25425 *Tel:* 304-535-6331 *Toll Free Tel:* 888-287-8673 (orders only) *Fax:* 304-535-2667 *E-mail:* publisher@appalachiantrail.org *Web Site:* www.appalachiantrail.org; www.atctrailstore.org, pg 18

King, Eric, Warner Press, 2902 Enterprise Dr, Anderson, IN 46013 *Tel:* 765-644-7721 *Toll Free Tel:* 800-741-7721 (orders) *Fax:* 765-640-8005 *E-mail:* wporders@warnerpress.org *Web Site:* www.warnerpress.org, pg 237

King, Erin, Abrams Learning Trends, 16310 Bratton Lane, Suite 250, Austin, TX 78728-2403 *Toll Free Tel:* 800-227-9120 *Toll Free Fax:* 800-737-3322 *E-mail:* customerservice@abramslearningtrends.com (orders, cust serv); contactus@abramslearningtrends.com *Web Site:* www.abramslearningtrends.com (orders, cust serv), pg 3

King, Georgia Frances, Aevitas Creative Management, 19 W 21 St, Suite 501, New York, NY 10010 *Tel:* 212-765-6900 *Web Site:* aevitascreative.com, pg 474

King, London, Random House Publishing Group, 1745 Broadway, New York, NY 10019 *Toll Free Tel:* 800-200-3552 *Web Site:* www.randomhousebooks.com, pg 181

King, Margaret J PhD, Cultural Studies & Analysis, 1123 Montrose St, Philadelphia, PA 19147-3721 *Tel:* 215-592-8544 *E-mail:* info@culturalanalysis.com *Web Site:* www.culturalanalysis.com, pg 461

King, Margaret Riley, WME, 11 Madison Ave, 18th fl, New York, NY 10010 *Tel:* 212-586-5100 *Web Site:* www.wmeentertainment.com, pg 508

King, Melissa, The University of Arkansas Press, McIlroy House, 105 N McIlroy Ave, Fayetteville, AR 72701 *Tel:* 479-575-7544 *E-mail:* info@uapress.com *Web Site:* www.uapress.com, pg 226

King, Michael, YES New Play Festival, 205 FA Theatre Dept, Nunn Dr, Highland Heights, KY 41099-1007 *Tel:* 859-572-6362 *Fax:* 859-572-6057, pg 681

King, Roger, Center for the Collaborative Classroom, 1001 Marina Village Pkwy, Suite 110, Alameda, CA 94501-1042 *Tel:* 510-533-0213 *Toll Free Tel:* 800-666-7270 *Fax:* 510-464-3670 *E-mail:* info@collaborativeclassroom.org; clientsupport@collaborativeclassroom.org *Web Site:* www.collaborativeclassroom.org, pg 48

King, Stacy, Federal Bar Association, 1220 N Filmore St, Suite 444, Arlington, VA 22201 *Tel:* 571-481-9100 *Fax:* 571-481-9090 *E-mail:* fba@fedbar.org *Web Site:* www.fedbar.org, pg 76

King, Stephen, W W Norton & Company Inc, 500 Fifth Ave, New York, NY 10110-0017 *Tel:* 212-354-5500 *Toll Free Tel:* 800-233-4830 (orders & cust serv) *Fax:* 212-869-0856 *Toll Free Fax:* 800-458-6515 *E-mail:* orders@wwnorton.com *Web Site:* wwnorton.com, pg 152

King, Terry, The Authors Registry Inc, 31 E 32 St, 7th fl, New York, NY 10016 *Tel:* 212-563-6920 *Fax:* 212-564-5363 *E-mail:* staff@authorsregistry.org *Web Site:* www.authorsregistry.org, pg 528

King-Gamble, Marcia, Fun in the Sun Writer's Cruise Conference, PO Box 823414, Pembroke Pines, FL 33082 *E-mail:* frwfuninthesun@yahoo.com *Web Site:* frwfuninthesunmain.blogspot.com/; www.frwriters.org, pg 574

Kingra, Mr Mahinder S, Cornell University Press, Sage House, 512 E State St, Ithaca, NY 14850 *Tel:* 607-253-2338 *Fax:* 607-253-2374 *E-mail:* cupressinfo@cornell.edu; cupress-sales@cornell.edu *Web Site:* www.cornellpress.cornell.edu, pg 57

Kingsley, Jessica, Jessica Kingsley Publishers Inc, 400 Market St, Suite 400, Philadelphia, PA 19106 *Tel:* 215-922-1161 *Toll Free Tel:* 866-416-1078 (cust serv) *Fax:* 215-922-1474 *E-mail:* hello.usa@jkp.com *Web Site:* www.jkp.com, pg 117

Kinman, Gay Toltl, Shamus Awards, 3665 S Needles Hwy, 7G, Laughlin, NV 89029 *Web Site:* www. privateeyewriters.com, pg 666

Kinney, Andrew, Harvard University Press, 79 Garden St, Cambridge, MA 02138-1499 *Tel:* 617-495-2600; 401-531-2800 (intl orders) *Toll Free Tel:* 800-405-1619 (orders) *Fax:* 617-495-5898 (gen); 617-496-4677 (edit & rts); 401-531-2801 (intl orders) *Toll Free Fax:* 800-406-9145 (orders) *E-mail:* contact_hup@ harvard.edu *Web Site:* www.hup.harvard.edu, pg 95

Kinney, Erika, Paul H Brookes Publishing Co Inc, PO Box 10624, Baltimore, MD 21285-0624 *Tel:* 410-337-9580 (outside US & CN) *Toll Free Tel:* 800-638-3775 (US & CN) *Fax:* 410-337-8539 *E-mail:* custserv@brookespublishing.com *Web Site:* www.brookespublishing.com, pg 42

Kinney, Jim, Baker Books, 6030 E Fulton Rd, Ada, MI 49301 *Tel:* 616-676-9185 *Toll Free Tel:* 800-877-2665 (orders) *Fax:* 616-676-9573 *Toll Free Fax:* 800-398-3111 (orders) *E-mail:* media@bakerpublishinggroup. com; orders@bakerpublishinggroup.com; sales@ bakerpublishinggroup.com *Web Site:* www. bakerpublishinggroup.com, pg 27

Kinney, Noreen, Cordon d' Or - Gold Ribbon International Culinary Academy Awards, 7312 Sixth Ave N, St Petersburg, FL 33710 *Tel:* 727-347-2437 *E-mail:* cordonor@aol.com *Web Site:* www.cordonorcuisine.com; www. florida-americasculinaryparadise.com; www. culinaryambassadorofireland.com, pg 606

Kinsella, Bridget, Stanford University Press, 425 Broadway St, Redwood City, CA 94063-3126 *Tel:* 650-723-9434 *Fax:* 650-725-3457 *E-mail:* info@ www.sup.org; publicity@www.sup.org; sales@www. sup.org *Web Site:* www.sup.org, pg 206

Kinter, Marci, PRINTING United Alliance, 10015 Main St, Fairfax, VA 22031-3489 *Tel:* 703-385-1335 *Toll Free Tel:* 888-385-3588 *Fax:* 703-273-0456; 703-691-7492 (membership) *E-mail:* assist@printing.org; info@printing.org *Web Site:* www.printing.org; www. sgia.org, pg 544

Kintigh, Cynthia, ANR Publications University of California, 2801 Second St, Davis, CA 95618 *Tel:* 530-400-0725 (cust serv) *Toll Free Tel:* 800-994-8849 *E-mail:* anrcatalog@ucanr.edu *Web Site:* anrcatalog.ucanr.edu, pg 17

Kintz, Dr Bruce G, Concordia Publishing House, 3558 S Jefferson Ave, St Louis, MO 63118-3968 *Tel:* 314-268-1000; 314-268-1268 (bookshop) *Toll Free Tel:* 800-325-3040 (cust serv) *Toll Free Fax:* 800-490-9889 (cust serv) *E-mail:* order@cph.org *Web Site:* www.cph.org, pg 56

Kintzer, Bonnie, Trusted Media Brands Inc, 750 Third Ave, 3rd fl, New York, NY 10017 *Tel:* 646-293-6299 *Toll Free Tel:* 877-732-4438 (cust serv) *Fax:* 646-293-6251 *E-mail:* customercare@trustedmediabrands. com; press@trustedmediabrands.com *Web Site:* www. trustedmediabrands.com; www.rd.com, pg 221

Kiraz, Christine PhD, Gorgias Press LLC, PO Box 6939, Piscataway, NJ 08854-6939 *Tel:* 732-885-8900 *Fax:* 732-885-8908 *E-mail:* helpdesk@gorgiaspress. com *Web Site:* www.gorgiaspress.com, pg 87

Kiraz, George Anton PhD, Gorgias Press LLC, PO Box 6939, Piscataway, NJ 08854-6939 *Tel:* 732-885-8900 *Fax:* 732-885-8908 *E-mail:* helpdesk@gorgiaspress. com *Web Site:* www.gorgiaspress.com, pg 87

Kirchner, Ann, Perseus Books, 1290 Avenue of the Americas, New York, NY 10104 *Tel:* 212-340-8100 *Toll Free Tel:* 800-343-4499 (cust serv) *Fax:* 212-340-8105 *Web Site:* www.perseusbooks.com, pg 168

Kirchoff, Morris A, Kirchoff/Wohlberg Inc, 897 Boston Post Rd, Madison, CT 06443 *Tel:* 203-245-7308 *Fax:* 203-245-3218 *E-mail:* info@kirchoffwohlberg. com *Web Site:* www.kirchoffwohlberg.com, pg 491

Kirk, Kara, Getty Publications, 1200 Getty Center Dr, Suite 500, Los Angeles, CA 90049-1682 *Tel:* 310-440-7365 *Toll Free Tel:* 800-223-3431 (orders) *Fax:* 310-440-7758 *E-mail:* pubsinfo@getty.edu *Web Site:* www. getty.edu/publications, pg 85

Kirk, Margaret, Copper Canyon Press, Fort Worden State Park, Bldg 313, Port Townsend, WA 98368 *Tel:* 360-385-4925 *Toll Free Tel:* 877-501-1393 (orders) *Fax:* 360-385-4985 *E-mail:* poetry@ coppercanyonpress.org *Web Site:* www. coppercanyonpress.org, pg 56

Kirk, Robert, Princeton University Press, 41 William St, Princeton, NJ 08540-5237 *Tel:* 609-258-4900 *Fax:* 609-258-6305 *Web Site:* press.princeton.edu, pg 174

Kirkey, Jeffrey E, Institute of Continuing Legal Education, 1020 Greene St, Ann Arbor, MI 48109-1444 *Tel:* 734-764-0533 *Toll Free Tel:* 877-229-4350 *Fax:* 734-763-2412 *Toll Free Fax:* 877-229-4351 *E-mail:* icle@umich.edu *Web Site:* www.icle.org, pg 109

Kirkpatrick, Caitlin, Chronicle Books, 680 Second St, San Francisco, CA 94107 *Tel:* 415-537-4200 *Toll Free Tel:* 800-759-0190 (cust serv) *Fax:* 415-537-4460 *Toll Free Fax:* 800-858-7787 (orders); 800-286-9471 (cust serv) *E-mail:* frontdesk@chroniclebooks.com *Web Site:* www.chroniclebooks.com, pg 52

Kirkpatrick, Emily, Charlotte Huck Award, 340 N Neil St, Suite 104, Champaign, IL 61820 *Tel:* 217-328-3870 *Toll Free Tel:* 877-369-6283 (cust serv) *Fax:* 217-328-9645; 217-328-0977 *E-mail:* bookawards@ncte.org *Web Site:* www2.ncte. org/awards, pg 625

Kirkpatrick, Emily, National Council of Teachers of English (NCTE), 340 N Neil St, Suite 104, Champaign, IL 61820 *Tel:* 217-328-3870 *Toll Free Tel:* 877-369-6283 (cust serv) *Fax:* 217-328-9645 *E-mail:* customerservice@ncte.org *Web Site:* www. ncte.org, pg 146, 539

Kirkpatrick, Emily, Orbis Pictus Award, 340 N Neil St, Suite 104, Champaign, IL 61820 *Tel:* 217-328-3870 *Toll Free Tel:* 877-369-6283 (cust serv) *Fax:* 217-328-9645; 217-328-0977 *E-mail:* bookawards@ncte.org *Web Site:* www2.ncte.org/awards, pg 651

Kirkpatrick, Kristin, University Press of Mississippi, 3825 Ridgewood Rd, Jackson, MS 39211-6492 *Tel:* 601-432-6205 *Toll Free Tel:* 800-737-7788 (orders & cust serv) *Fax:* 601-432-6217 *E-mail:* press@ mississippi.edu *Web Site:* www.upress.state.ms.us, pg 233

Kirsch, Julie, Rowman & Littlefield, 4501 Forbes Blvd, Suite 200, Lanham, MD 20706 *Tel:* 301-459-3366 *Toll Free Tel:* 800-462-6420 (ext 3024, cust serv) *Fax:* 301-429-5748 *Web Site:* rowman.com, pg 188

Kirsch, Julie, University Press of America Inc, 4501 Forbes Blvd, Suite 200, Lanham, MD 20706 *Tel:* 301-459-3366 *Toll Free Tel:* 800-462-6420 *Fax:* 301-429-5748 *Toll Free Fax:* 800-338-4550 *Web Site:* univpress.com, pg 232

Kirsch, Julie E, Jason Aronson Inc, 4501 Forbes Blvd, Suite 200, Lanham, MD 20706 *Tel:* 301-459-3366 *Toll Free Tel:* 800-462-6420 ext 3024 (cust serv) *Fax:* 301-429-5748 *Toll Free Fax:* 800-338-4550 (cust serv) *E-mail:* orders@rowman.com; customercare@rowman. com *Web Site:* www.rowman.com, pg 20

Kirschen, Dan, ICM Partners, 65 E 55 St, New York, NY 10022 *Tel:* 212-556-5600 *Web Site:* www. icmtalent.com, pg 489

Kirshbaum, Larry, Waxman Literary Agency, 443 Park Ave S, No 1004, New York, NY 10016 *Tel:* 212-675-5556 *Web Site:* www.waxmanliteraryagency.com, pg 508

Kirsten, Naomi, Chronicle Books, 680 Second St, San Francisco, CA 94107 *Tel:* 415-537-4200 *Toll Free Tel:* 800-759-0190 (cust serv) *Fax:* 415-537-4460 *Toll Free Fax:* 800-858-7787 (orders); 800-286-9471 (cust serv) *E-mail:* frontdesk@chroniclebooks.com *Web Site:* www.chroniclebooks.com, pg 52

Kirtland, Kim-Mei, Howard Morhaim Literary Agency Inc, 30 Pierrepont St, Brooklyn, NY 11201-3371 *Tel:* 718-222-8400 *E-mail:* info@morhaimliterary.com *Web Site:* www.morhaimliterary.com, pg 497

Kiser, Kristin, Perseus Books, 1290 Avenue of the Americas, New York, NY 10104 *Tel:* 212-340-8100 *Toll Free Tel:* 800-343-4499 (cust serv) *Fax:* 212-340-8105 *Web Site:* www.perseusbooks.com, pg 167

Kish, Rudy, Hachette Nashville, 6100 Tower Circle, Room 210, Franklin, TN 37067 *Tel:* 615-221-0996 *Fax:* 615-221-0962 *Web Site:* www.hachettebookgroup. com, pg 91

Kisielewska, Lara, The Graphic Artists Guild Inc, 31 W 34 St, 8th fl, New York, NY 10001 *Tel:* 212-791-3400 *Fax:* 212-791-0333 *E-mail:* admin@graphicartistsguild.org; membership@graphicartistsguild.org *Web Site:* www. graphicartistsguild.org, pg 534, 583

Kisiner, Andrea, Transportation Research Board (TRB), 500 Fifth St NW, Washington, DC 20001 *Tel:* 202-334-3213 (orders); 202-334-3072 (subns) *Fax:* 202-334-2519 *E-mail:* trbsales@nas.edu *Web Site:* trb.org, pg 220

Kispert, Peter, HarperCollins General Books Group, 195 Broadway, New York, NY 10007 *Tel:* 212-207-7000 *Web Site:* www.harpercollins.com, pg 93

Kissner, Matthew S, John Wiley & Sons Inc, 111 River St, Hoboken, NJ 07030-5774 *Tel:* 201-748-6000 *Toll Free Tel:* 800-225-5945 (cust serv) *Fax:* 201-748-6088 *E-mail:* info@wiley.com *Web Site:* www.wiley.com, pg 241

Kistler, Steve, RAND Corp, 1776 Main St, Santa Monica, CA 90407-2138 *Tel:* 310-393-0411 *Fax:* 310-393-4818 *Web Site:* www.rand.org, pg 180

Kitman, Taya, The Ridenhour Book Prize, 116 E 16 St, 8th fl, New York, NY 10003 *Tel:* 212-822-0250 *Fax:* 212-253-5356 *E-mail:* ridenhour@nationinstitute. org *Web Site:* www.ridenhour.org, pg 662

Kitman, Taya, The Ridenhour Courage Prize, 116 E 16 St, 8th fl, New York, NY 10003 *Tel:* 212-822-0250 *Fax:* 212-253-5356 *E-mail:* ridenhour@nationinstitute. org *Web Site:* www.ridenhour.org, pg 662

Kitman, Taya, The Ridenhour Prize for Truth-Telling, 116 E 16 St, 8th fl, New York, NY 10003 *Tel:* 212-822-0250 *Fax:* 212-253-5356 *E-mail:* ridenhour@ nationinstitute.org *Web Site:* www.ridenhour.org, pg 662

Kittelstrom, David, Wisdom Publications Inc, 199 Elm St, Somerville, MA 02144 *Tel:* 617-776-7416 *Toll Free Tel:* 800-272-4050 (orders) *Fax:* 617-776-7841 *E-mail:* info@wisdompubs.org; submission@ wisdompubs.org *Web Site:* www.wisdompubs.org, pg 243

Kiu, Doreen, World Scientific Publishing Co Inc, 27 Warren St, Suite 401-402, Hackensack, NJ 07601 *Tel:* 201-487-9655 *Fax:* 201-487-9656 *E-mail:* wspc_us@wspc.com; sales@wspc.com; mkt@wspc.com; editor@wspc.com *Web Site:* www. worldscientific.com, pg 245

Kiyan, Juliana, The Penguin Press, 375 Hudson St, New York, NY 10014 *Web Site:* thepenguinpress.com, pg 164

Kjeldbjerg, Hanna, Beaver's Pond Press Inc, 939 Seventh St W, St Paul, MN 55102 *Tel:* 952-829-8818 *E-mail:* info@beaverspondpress.com *Web Site:* www. beaverspondpress.com, pg 30

Kjoller, Maria, Carolrhoda Books Inc, 241 First Ave N, Minneapolis, MN 55401 *Tel:* 612-332-3344 *Toll Free Tel:* 800-328-4929 *Fax:* 612-332-7615 *Toll Free Fax:* 800-332-1132 *E-mail:* info@lernerbooks. com; custserve@lernerbooks.com *Web Site:* www. lernerbooks.com; www.facebook.com/lernerbooks, pg 45

Kjoller, Maria, Carolrhoda Lab™, 241 First Ave N, Minneapolis, MN 55401 *Tel:* 612-332-3344 *Toll Free Tel:* 800-328-4929 *Fax:* 612-332-7615 *Toll Free Fax:* 800-332-1132 *E-mail:* info@lernerbooks. com; custserve@lernerbooks.com *Web Site:* www. lernerbooks.com; www.facebook.com/lernerbooks, pg 45

serv) *Fax:* 941-343-9201 *Toll Free Fax:* 866-804-4843 (orders only) *E-mail:* cs@prpress.com *Web Site:* www. prpress.com, pg 176

Knapp, Jamie, Dutton, 1745 Broadway, New York, NY 10019 *Tel:* 212-366-2000 *Fax:* 212-366-2262 *E-mail:* duttonpublicity@us.penguingroup.com *Web Site:* www.penguin.com, pg 68

Knapp, Renee, Between the Lines, 401 Richmond St W, No 277, Toronto, ON M5V 3A8, Canada *Tel:* 416-535-9914 *Toll Free Tel:* 800-718-7201 *Fax:* 416-535-1484 *E-mail:* info@btlbooks.com *Web Site:* btlbooks.com, pg 416

Knauff, Carol, The Massachusetts Historical Society, 1154 Boylston St, Boston, MA 02215-3695 *Tel:* 617-536-1608 *Fax:* 617-859-0074 *E-mail:* publications@masshist.org *Web Site:* www.masshist.org, pg 133

Kneedler, Joel, Thomas Nelson, 501 Nelson Place, Nashville, TN 37214 *Tel:* 615-889-9000 *Toll Free Tel:* 800-251-4000 *Fax:* 615-902-1548 *Web Site:* www.thomasnelson.com, pg 217

Kneerim, Jill, Kneerim & Williams Agency, 90 Canal St, Boston, MA 02114 *Tel:* 617-303-1650 *Web Site:* www. kwlit.com, pg 491

Kniffen, Juliet Viola, Northern California Translators Association, 2261 Market St, Suite 160, San Francisco, CA 94114-1600 *Tel:* 510-845-8712 *E-mail:* administrator@ncta.org *Web Site:* www.ncta.org, pg 542

Knight, Barb, Tiger Tales, 5 River Rd, Suite 128, Wilton, CT 06897-4069 *Tel:* 920-387-2333 *Fax:* 920-387-9994 *Web Site:* www.tigertalesbooks.com, pg 218

Knight, Carol Lynne, Anhinga Press, PO Box 3665, Tallahassee, FL 32315 *Tel:* 850-577-0745 *E-mail:* info@anhinga.org *Web Site:* www. anhingapress.org; www.facebook.com/anhingapress, pg 16

Knight, Chelene, Transatlantic Agency, 2 Bloor St E, Suite 3500, Toronto, ON M4W 1A8, Canada *Tel:* 416-488-9214 *E-mail:* info@transatlanticagency.com *Web Site:* www.transatlanticagency.com, pg 506

Knight, Deidre, The Knight Agency Inc, 232 W Washington St, Madison, GA 30650 *E-mail:* admin@knightagency.net *Web Site:* www.knightagency.net, pg 491

Knight, Judson, The Knight Agency Inc, 232 W Washington St, Madison, GA 30650 *E-mail:* admin@knightagency.net *Web Site:* www.knightagency.net, pg 491

Knight, Margot, Djerassi Resident Artists Program, 2325 Bear Gulch Rd, Woodside, CA 94062 *Tel:* 650-747-1250 *E-mail:* drap@djerassi.org *Web Site:* www.djerassi.org, pg 574

Knight, Tom, Thomas Nelson, 501 Nelson Place, Nashville, TN 37214 *Tel:* 615-889-9000 *Toll Free Tel:* 800-251-4000 *Fax:* 615-902-1548 *Web Site:* www.thomasnelson.com, pg 217

Knight, Tom, Zondervan, 3900 Sparks Dr, Grand Rapids, MI 49546 *Tel:* 616-698-6900 *Toll Free Tel:* 800-226-1122; 800-727-1309 (retail orders) *Fax:* 616-698-3350 *Toll Free Fax:* 800-698-3256 (retail orders) *Web Site:* www.zondervan.com, pg 248

Knight, Tomea, College of Liberal & Professional Studies, University of Pennsylvania, 3440 Market St, Suite 100, Philadelphia, PA 19104-3335 *Tel:* 215-898-7326 *Fax:* 215-573-2053 *E-mail:* lps@sas.upenn.edu *Web Site:* www.sas.upenn.edu/lps, pg 581

Knight, Yolanda, Round Table Companies, 1027 Kenton Rd, Deerfield, IL 60015 *Tel:* 949-375-1006 *Fax:* 815-346-2398 *Web Site:* www.roundtablecompanies.com, pg 187

Knill, Ellen, Bellerophon Books, PO Box 21307, Santa Barbara, CA 93121-1307 *Tel:* 805-965-7034 *Toll Free Tel:* 800-253-9943 *Fax:* 805-965-8286 *E-mail:* sales.bellerophon@gmail.com *Web Site:* www. bellerophonbooks.com, pg 31

Knobloch, Jamie, Thorndike Press®, 10 Water St, Suite 310, Waterville, ME 04901 *Toll Free Tel:* 800-223-1244 (ext 4, cust serv/orders) *Toll Free Fax:* 800-558-

4676 (orders) *E-mail:* gale.printorders@cengage.com; international@cengage.com (cust orders outside US & CN) *Web Site:* www.gale.com/thorndike, pg 217

Knoll, Lori, Governor General's Literary Awards, 150 Elgin St, 2nd fl, Ottawa, ON K2P 1L4, Canada *Tel:* 613-566-4414 *Toll Free Tel:* 800-263-5588 (CN only) *Fax:* 613-566-4390 *E-mail:* info@canadacouncil.ca *Web Site:* canadacouncil.ca/en/council/prizes, pg 620

Knoll, Zach, Simon & Schuster, 1230 Avenue of the Americas, New York, NY 10020 *Tel:* 212-698-7000 *Toll Free Tel:* 800-223-2348 (cust serv); 800-223-2336 (orders) *Toll Free Fax:* 800-943-9831 (orders) *Web Site:* www.simonandschuster.com, pg 198

Knopf, Chris, Second Chance Press, 4170 Noyac Rd, Sag Harbor, NY 11963 *Tel:* 631-725-1101 *E-mail:* info@thepermanentpress.com *Web Site:* www. thepermanentpress.com, pg 196

Knopf, Susan, American Book Producers Association (ABPA), 31 W Eighth St, 2nd fl, New York, NY 10011 *Tel:* 212-675-1363 *Fax:* 212-675-1364 *E-mail:* office@abpaonline.org *Web Site:* www. abpaonline.org, pg 522

Knopf, Susan, WNBA Pannell Award for Excellence in Children's Bookselling, PO Box 237, FDR Sta, New York, NY 10150-0231 *Toll Free Tel:* 866-610-WNBA (610-9622) *E-mail:* WNBAPannell@gmail.com *Web Site:* www.wnba-books.org; www.NationalReadingGroupMonth.org; www.wnba-books.org/awards, pg 678

Knotek, George, Copper Canyon Press, Fort Worden State Park, Bldg 313, Port Townsend, WA 98368 *Tel:* 360-385-4925 *Toll Free Tel:* 877-501-1393 (orders) *Fax:* 360-385-4985 *E-mail:* poetry@coppercanyonpress.org *Web Site:* www. coppercanyonpress.org, pg 56

Knott, Ronald, Andrews University Press, Sutherland House, 8360 W Campus Circle Dr, Berrien Springs, MI 49104-1700 *Tel:* 269-471-6134 *Toll Free Tel:* 800-467-6369 (Visa, MC & American Express orders only) *Fax:* 269-471-6224 *E-mail:* aupo@andrews.edu; aup@andrews.edu; aupress@andrews.edu *Web Site:* www.universitypress.andrews.edu, pg 16

Knowles, Gary, Midwest Travel Journalists Inc, 902 S Randall Rd, Suite C311, St Charles, IL 60174 *Toll Free Tel:* 888-551-8184 *Fax:* 847-622-8015 *E-mail:* admin@mtja.us *Web Site:* www.mtja.us, pg 537

Knowlton, Ginger, Curtis Brown Ltd, 228 E 45 St, 3rd fl, New York, NY 10017 *Tel:* 212-473-5400 *Web Site:* www.curtisbrown.com, pg 478

Knowlton, Timothy F, Curtis Brown Ltd, 228 E 45 St, 3rd fl, New York, NY 10017 *Tel:* 212-473-5400 *Web Site:* www.curtisbrown.com, pg 478

Knutsen, Trond, University of Hawaii Press, 2840 Kolowalu St, Honolulu, HI 96822-1888 *Tel:* 808-956-8255 *Toll Free Tel:* 888-UHPRESS (847-7377) *Fax:* 808-988-6052 *Toll Free Fax:* 800-650-7811 *E-mail:* uhpbooks@hawaii.edu *Web Site:* www. uhpress.hawaii.edu, pg 227

Koball, Heather PhD, National Center for Children in Poverty, 722 W 168 St, New York, NY 10032 *Tel:* 646-284-9600; 212-304-6073 *E-mail:* info@nccp.org *Web Site:* www.nccp.org, pg 146

Kobasa, Paul A, World Book Inc, 180 N LaSalle, Suite 900, Chicago, IL 60601 *Tel:* 312-729-5800 *Toll Free Tel:* 800-967-5325 (consumer sales, US); 800-463-8845 (consumer sales, CN); 800-975-3250 (school & lib sales, US); 800-837-5365 (school & lib sales, CN); 866-866-5200 (web sales) *Fax:* 312-729-5600; 312-729-5606 *Toll Free Fax:* 800-433-9330 (school & lib sales, US); 888-690-4002 (school & lib sales, CN) *E-mail:* customercare@worldbook.com *Web Site:* www.worldbook.com, pg 245

Koch, Bea, The Ripped Bodice Awards for Excellence in Romantic Fiction, 3806 Main St, Culver City, CA 90232 *Tel:* 424-603-4776 *E-mail:* therippedbodicela@gmail.com *Web Site:* www.therippedbodicela.com, pg 662

Koch, Leah, The Ripped Bodice Awards for Excellence in Romantic Fiction, 3806 Main St, Culver City, CA 90232 *Tel:* 424-603-4776 *E-mail:* therippedbodicela@gmail.com *Web Site:* www.therippedbodicela.com, pg 662

Kochan, Susan, GP Putnam's Sons (Children's), 345 Hudson St, New York, NY 10014 *Tel:* 212-366-2000 *Fax:* 212-414-3393 *Web Site:* www.penguin.com/publishers/gpputnamssonsbooksforyoungread, pg 178

Kochman, Charles, Harry N Abrams Inc, 195 Broadway, 9th fl, New York, NY 10007 *Tel:* 212-206-7715 *Toll Free Tel:* 800-345-1359 *Fax:* 212-519-1210 *E-mail:* abrams@abramsbooks.com *Web Site:* www. abramsbooks.com, pg 3

Koehler, Cliff, Andrews McMeel Publishing LLC, 1130 Walnut St, Kansas City, MO 64106-2109 *Toll Free Tel:* 800-851-8923; 800-943-9839 (cust serv) *Toll Free Fax:* 800-943-9831 (orders) *E-mail:* sales@amuniversal.com *Web Site:* www.andrewsmcmeel.com; publishing.andrewsmcmeel.com, pg 16

Koenig, Holly, American Society of Journalists and Authors (ASJA), 355 Lexington Ave, 15th fl, New York, NY 10017-6603 *Tel:* 212-997-0947 *Web Site:* asja.org, pg 524

Koenig, Holly, American Society of Journalists and Authors Annual Writers Conference, 355 Lexington Ave, 15th fl, New York, NY 10017-6603 *Tel:* 212-997-0947 *Web Site:* asja.org, pg 573

Koerner, Darrell, Chelsea Green Publishing Co, 85 N Main St, Suite 120, White River Junction, VT 05001 *Tel:* 802-295-6300 *Toll Free Tel:* 800-639-4099 (cust serv & orders) *Fax:* 802-295-6444 *E-mail:* customerservice@chelseagreen.com; editorial@chelseagreen.com; publicity@chelseagreen.com; rights@chelseagreen.com *Web Site:* www. chelseagreen.com, pg 49

Koester, Robert J, dbS Productions, PO Box 94, Charlottesville, VA 22902 *Tel:* 434-293-5502 *Toll Free Tel:* 800-745-1581 *E-mail:* info@dbs-sar.com *Web Site:* www.dbs-sar.com, pg 63

Koffler, Lionel, Firefly Books Ltd, 50 Staples Ave, Unit 1, Richmond Hill, ON L4B 0A7, Canada *Tel:* 416-499-8412 *Toll Free Tel:* 800-387-6192 (CN); 800-387-5085 (US) *Fax:* 416-499-8313 *Toll Free Fax:* 800-450-0391 (CN); 800-565-6034 (US) *E-mail:* service@fireflybooks.com *Web Site:* www.fireflybooks.com, pg 426

Koh, Becky, Perseus Books, 1290 Avenue of the Americas, New York, NY 10104 *Tel:* 212-340-8100 *Toll Free Tel:* 800-343-4499 (cust serv) *Fax:* 212-340-8105 *Web Site:* www.perseusbooks.com, pg 167

Kohlmeier, Rob, Wilfrid Laurier University Press, 75 University Ave W, Waterloo, ON N2L 3C5, Canada *Tel:* 519-884-0710 *Toll Free Tel:* 866-836-5551 (CN & US) *Fax:* 519-725-1399 *E-mail:* press@wlu.ca *Web Site:* www.wlupress.wlu.ca, pg 445

Kohrs, Sarah, The Sow's Ear Poetry Prize & The Sow's Ear Chapbook Prize, 1748 Cave Ridge Rd, Mount Jackson, VA 22842 *Tel:* 540-477-3257 *E-mail:* sepoetryreview@gmail.com *Web Site:* sowsearpoetry.org, pg 669

Kok, John H, Dordt Press, 700 Seventh St NE, Sioux Center, IA 51250-1671 *Tel:* 712-722-6420 *Toll Free Tel:* 800-343-6738 *Fax:* 712-722-6035 *E-mail:* dordtpress@dordt.edu; bookstore@dordt.edu *Web Site:* www.dordt.edu/about-dordt/publications/dordt-press-catalog, pg 66

Kokko, Larry, Florida Writers Association Conference, PO Box 66069, St Pete Beach, FL 33736-6069 *Web Site:* www.floridawriters.net, pg 574

Kokko, Larry, Florida Writers Association Inc, PO Box 66069, St Pete Beach, FL 33736-6069 *Web Site:* www. floridawriters.net, pg 533

Kokontis, Ellen, Albert Whitman & Co, 250 S Northwest Hwy, Suite 320, Park Ridge, IL 60068 *Tel:* 847-232-2800 *Toll Free Tel:* 800-255-7675 *Fax:* 847-581-0039 *E-mail:* mail@albertwhitman.com *Web Site:* www. albertwhitman.com, pg 6

Kolani, Alison, Random House Children's Books, 1745 Broadway, 10th fl, New York, NY 10019 *Tel:* 212-782-9000 *Web Site:* www.randomhousekids.com, pg 180

Kolbe, Kimberly, The Green Rose Prize in Poetry, c/o Western Michigan University, 1903 W Michigan Ave, Kalamazoo, MI 49008-5463 *Tel:* 269-387-8185 *E-mail:* new-issues@wmich.edu *Web Site:* www.wmich.edu/newissues/sub-guide.html, pg 621

Kolbe, Kimberly, New Issues Poetry & Prose, c/o Western Michigan University, 1903 W Michigan Ave, Kalamazoo, MI 49008-5463 *Tel:* 269-387-8185 *E-mail:* new-issues@wmich.edu *Web Site:* www.wmich.edu/newissues, pg 149

Kolbe, Kimberly, New Issues Poetry Prize, c/o Western Michigan University, 1903 W Michigan Ave, Kalamazoo, MI 49008-5463 *Tel:* 269-387-8185 *E-mail:* new-issues@wmich.edu *Web Site:* www.wmich.edu/newissues, pg 647

Kolby, Jeff, Nova Press, PO Box 692023, West Hollywood, CA 90069 *Tel:* 310-601-8551 *E-mail:* novapress@aol.com *Web Site:* www.novapress.net, pg 153

Kolendo, Kate, Association of University Presses (AUPresses), 1412 Broadway, Suite 2135, New York, NY 10018 *Tel:* 212-989-1010 *Fax:* 212-989-0275 *E-mail:* info@aupresses.org *Web Site:* www.aupresses.org, pg 527

Kolkman, Tammy, Covenant Communications Inc, 1226 S 630 E, Suite 4, American Fork, UT 84003 *Tel:* 801-756-1041 *E-mail:* info@covenant-lds.com *Web Site:* www.covenant-lds.com, pg 59

Kolsrud, Kelli, International Foundation of Employee Benefit Plans, 18700 W Bluemound Rd, Brookfield, WI 53045 *Tel:* 262-786-6700 *Toll Free Tel:* 888-334-3327 *Fax:* 262-786-8780 *E-mail:* editor@ifebp.org *Web Site:* www.ifebp.org, pg 111

Kolwitz, Ok Hee, Penguin Random House Audio Publishing, 1745 Broadway, New York, NY 10019 *E-mail:* audio@penguinrandomhouse.com *Web Site:* www.penguinrandomhouseaudio.com, pg 164

Komie, Michelle, Princeton University Press, 41 William St, Princeton, NJ 08540-5237 *Tel:* 609-258-4900 *Fax:* 609-258-6305 *Web Site:* press.princeton.edu, pg 174

Kompik, Natalie, Wm B Eerdmans Publishing Co, 4035 Park East Ct SE, Grand Rapids, MI 49546 *Tel:* 616-459-4591 *Toll Free Tel:* 800-253-7521 *Fax:* 616-459-6540 *E-mail:* customerservice@eerdmans.com; sales@eerdmans.com *Web Site:* www.eerdmans.com, pg 70

Koncsol, Siena, Little, Brown Books for Young Readers, 1290 Avenue of the Americas, New York, NY 10104 *Tel:* 212-364-1100 *Toll Free Tel:* 800-759-0190 (cust serv) *Web Site:* www.hachettebookgroup.com, pg 126

Konda, Sai, The American Chemical Society, 1155 16 St NW, Washington, DC 20036 *Tel:* 202-872-4600 *Toll Free Tel:* 800-227-5558 (US) *Fax:* 202-872-6067 *E-mail:* help@acs.org *Web Site:* www.acs.org, pg 10

Kondrich, Christopher, Association of Writers & Writing Programs (AWP), University of Maryland, 5245 Greenbelt Rd, Box 246, College Park, MD 20740 *Tel:* 240-696-7700 *E-mail:* awp@awpwriter.org; press@awpwriter.org *Web Site:* www.awpwriter.org, pg 527

Kondrich, Christopher, AWP Award Series, University of Maryland, 5245 Greenbelt Rd, Box 246, College Park, MD 20740 *Tel:* 240-696-7700 *E-mail:* awp@awpwriter.org; press@awpwriter.org *Web Site:* www.awpwriter.org, pg 594

Kondrick, Maureen, Marquette University Press, 1415 W Wisconsin Ave, Milwaukee, WI 53233 *Tel:* 414-288-1564 *Fax:* 414-288-7813 *Web Site:* www.marquette.edu/mupress, pg 132

Konecke, Kaitlin, Health Professions Press, 409 Washington Ave, Suite 500, Towson, MD 21204 *Tel:* 410-337-9585 *Toll Free Tel:* 888-337-8808 *Fax:* 410-337-8539 *Web Site:* www.healthpropress.com, pg 97

Konecky, Sean, Konecky & Konecky LLC, 72 Ayers Point Rd, Old Saybrook, CT 06475 *Tel:* 860-388-0878 *E-mail:* sean.konecky@gmail.com *Web Site:* www.koneckyandkonecky.com, pg 118

Kong, Molly, Disney Press, 1101 Flower St, Glendale, CA 91201 *Web Site:* books.disney.com, pg 65

Konner, Linda, Linda Konner Literary Agency, 10 W 15 St, Suite 1918, New York, NY 10011 *Tel:* 212-691-3419 *Fax:* 212-691-0935 *Web Site:* www.lindakonnerliteraryagency.com, pg 492

Konopinski, Natalie, American Anthropological Association (AAA), 2300 Clarendon Blvd, Suite 1301, Arlington, VA 22201 *Tel:* 703-528-1902 *Fax:* 703-528-3546 *E-mail:* pubs@americananthro.org *Web Site:* www.americananthro.org, pg 9

Konowitch, Paul, Sundance/Newbridge Publishing, 33 Boston Post Rd W, Suite 440, Marlborough, MA 01752 *Toll Free Tel:* 888-200-2720; 800-343-8204 (Sundance cust serv & orders); 800-867-0307 (Newbridge cust serv & orders) *Toll Free Fax:* 800-456-2419 (orders) *E-mail:* info@sundancepub.com; info@newbridgeonline.com *Web Site:* www.sundancepub.com; www.newbridgeonline.com, pg 211

Koohi-Kamali, Dr Farideh, Peter Lang Publishing Inc, 80 Broadway, 5th fl, New York, NY 10004 *Tel:* 703-661-1584 *Toll Free Tel:* 800-770-5264 (cust serv) *Fax:* 703-996-1010 *E-mail:* newyork.editorial@peterlang.com; customerservice@plang.com *Web Site:* www.peterlang.com, pg 119

Kooij, Nina, Arcadia Publishing Inc, 420 Wando Park Blvd, Mount Pleasant, SC 29464 *Tel:* 843-853-2070 *Toll Free Tel:* 888-313-2665 (orders only) *Fax:* 843-853-0044 *E-mail:* sales@arcadiapublishing.com *Web Site:* www.arcadiapublishing.com, pg 19

Kooij, Nina, Pelican Publishing Co, 400 Poydras St, Suite 900, New Orleans, LA 70130 *Tel:* 504-368-1175 *Toll Free Tel:* 800-843-1724 *Fax:* 504-368-1195 *E-mail:* sales@pelicanpub.com (sales); office@pelicanpub.com (permission); promo@pelicanpub.com (publicity) *Web Site:* www.pelicanpub.com, pg 162

Kopelman, Charles, Abrams Artists Agency, 275 Seventh Ave, 26th fl, New York, NY 10001 *Tel:* 646-486-4600 *Fax:* 646-486-0100 *E-mail:* literary@abramsartny.com *Web Site:* www.abramsartists.com, pg 473

Kordic, Lara, Heritage House Publishing Co Ltd, 1075 Pendergast St, No 103, Victoria, BC V8V 0A1, Canada *Tel:* 250-360-0829 *Fax:* 250-386-0829 *E-mail:* heritage@heritagehouse.ca *Web Site:* www.heritagehouse.ca, pg 429

Korman, Keith, Raines & Raines, 103 Kenyon Rd, Medusa, NY 12120 *Tel:* 518-239-8311 *Fax:* 518-239-6029, pg 499

Korn, Linda, Penguin Random House Audio Publishing, 1745 Broadway, New York, NY 10019 *E-mail:* audio@penguinrandomhouse.com *Web Site:* www.penguinrandomhouseaudio.com, pg 164

Korn, Mirabelle, Chronicle Books, 680 Second St, San Francisco, CA 94107 *Tel:* 415-537-4200 *Toll Free Tel:* 800-759-0190 (cust serv) *Fax:* 415-537-4460 *Toll Free Fax:* 800-858-7787 (orders); 800-286-9471 (cust serv) *E-mail:* frontdesk@chroniclebooks.com *Web Site:* www.chroniclebooks.com, pg 52

Korn, Sandra, Duke University Press, 905 W Main St, Suite 18B, Durham, NC 27701 *Tel:* 919-688-5134 *Toll Free Tel:* 888-651-0122 (US) *Fax:* 919-688-2615 *Toll Free Fax:* 888-651-0124 *E-mail:* orders@dukeupress.edu *Web Site:* www.dukeupress.edu, pg 68

Kornbluh, Rena, Hachette Book Group, 1290 Avenue of the Americas, New York, NY 10104 *Tel:* 212-364-1100 *Toll Free Tel:* 800-759-0190 (cust serv) *Fax:* 212-364-0933 (intl orders) *Toll Free Fax:* 800-286-9471 (cust serv) *Web Site:* www.hachettebookgroup.com, pg 91

Kornoelje, Kristin, Revell, PO Box 6287, Grand Rapids, MI 49516-6287 *Tel:* 616-676-9185 *Toll Free Tel:* 800-877-2665; 800-679-1957 *Fax:* 616-676-9573 *Web Site:* www.bakerpublishinggroup.com, pg 185

Koronkiewicz, Juliette, Penguin Random House Audio Publishing, 1745 Broadway, New York, NY 10019 *E-mail:* audio@penguinrandomhouse.com *Web Site:* www.penguinrandomhouseaudio.com, pg 164

Kosiewska, Anthony, Scholastic Trade Division, 557 Broadway, New York, NY 10012 *Tel:* 212-343-6100; 212-343-4685 (export sales) *Fax:* 212-343-4714 (export sales) *Web Site:* www.scholastic.com, pg 194

Koski, Abby, Soho Press Inc, 853 Broadway, New York, NY 10003 *Tel:* 212-614-7900 *E-mail:* soho@sohopress.com; publicity@sohopress.com *Web Site:* sohopress.com, pg 203

Kosmach, Jack, Whole Person Associates Inc, 101 W Second St, Suite 203, Duluth, MN 55802 *Tel:* 218-727-0500 *Toll Free Tel:* 800-247-6789 *Fax:* 218-727-0505 *E-mail:* books@wholeperson.com *Web Site:* www.wholeperson.com, pg 240

Kosmoski, Anne, Avery, 1745 Broadway, New York, NY 10019 *Tel:* 212-366-2000 *Fax:* 212-366-2636 *E-mail:* averypublicity@penguinrandomhouse.com *Web Site:* www.penguin.com/publishers/avery; www.penguinrandomhouse.com, pg 26

Kosmoski, Anne, TarcherPerigee, 375 Hudson St, New York, NY 10014 *Tel:* 212-366-2000 *Fax:* 212-366-2643 *E-mail:* customerservice@penguinrandomhouse.com (cust serv); TarcherPerigeePublicity@penguinrandomhouse.com (media queries) *Web Site:* www.tarcherbooks.com; www.facebook.com/TarcherPerigee/; www.penguin.com/publishers/tarcherperigee, pg 213

Kosowski, Mary Beth, Mercer University Press, 368 Orange St, Macon, GA 31201 *Tel:* 478-301-2880 *Toll Free Tel:* 866-895-1472 *Fax:* 478-301-2585 *E-mail:* mupressorders@mercer.edu *Web Site:* www.mupress.org, pg 138

Kost, Jordan, Sourcebooks LLC, 1935 Brookdale Rd, Suite 139, Naperville, IL 60563 *Tel:* 630-961-3900 *Toll Free Tel:* 800-432-7444 *Fax:* 630-961-2168 *E-mail:* info@sourcebooks.com; customersupport@sourcebooks.com *Web Site:* www.sourcebooks.com, pg 204

Kosztolnyik, Karen, Grand Central Publishing, 1290 Avenue of the Americas, New York, NY 10104 *Tel:* 212-364-1100 *Web Site:* www.hachettebookgroup.com, pg 88

Kot, Rick, Viking, 375 Hudson St, New York, NY 10014 *Tel:* 212-366-2000 *Fax:* 212-243-6002 *Web Site:* penguin.com/publishers/vikingbooks, pg 236

Kotchman, Katie, Don Congdon Associates Inc, 110 William St, Suite 2202, New York, NY 10038-3914 *Tel:* 212-645-1229 *Fax:* 212-727-2688 *E-mail:* dca@doncongdon.com *Web Site:* www.doncongdon.com, pg 480

Kothiwal, Shurti, Independent Institute, 100 Swan Way, Suite 200, Oakland, CA 94621-1428 *Tel:* 510-632-1366 *Toll Free Tel:* 800-927-8733 *Fax:* 510-568-6040 *E-mail:* orders@independent.org *Web Site:* www.independent.org, pg 107

Kotovets, Gary, Dun & Bradstreet, 103 JFK Pkwy, Short Hills, NJ 07078 *Tel:* 973-921-5500 *Toll Free Tel:* 844-869-8244; 800-234-3867 (cust serv) *Web Site:* www.dnb.com, pg 68

Kotsyuba, Oleh, Harvard Ukrainian Research Institute, 34 Kirkland St, Cambridge, MA 02138 *Tel:* 617-495-4053 *Fax:* 617-495-8097 *E-mail:* huri@fas.harvard.edu *Web Site:* www.huri.harvard.edu, pg 95

Kouma, Cecelia, Playwrights Project, 3675 Ruffin Rd, Suite 330, San Diego, CA 92123 *Tel:* 858-384-2970 *Fax:* 858-384-2974 *E-mail:* write@playwrightsproject.org *Web Site:* www.playwrightsproject.org, pg 656

Koundoura, Maria, Emerson College Department of Writing, Literature & Publishing, 180 Tremont St, 10th fl, Boston, MA 02116-4624 *Tel:* 617-824-8750 *Web Site:* www.emerson.edu; www.emerson.edu/writing-literature-publishing, pg 582

Koupal, Nancy Tystad, South Dakota Historical Society Press, 900 Governors Dr, Pierre, SD 57501 *Tel:* 605-773-6009 *Fax:* 605-773-6041 *E-mail:* info@sdshspress.com; orders@sdshspress.com *Web Site:* sdshspress.com, pg 205

Kouts, Barbara S, Barbara S Kouts Literary Agency LLC, PO Box 560, Bellport, NY 11713 *Tel:* 631-286-1278 *Fax:* 631-286-1538 *E-mail:* bkouts@aol.com, pg 492

Kovach, Lynn, Random House Publishing Group, 1745 Broadway, New York, NY 10019 *Toll Free Tel:* 800-200-3552 *Web Site:* www.randomhousebooks.com, pg 181

Kowal, Basia, University of Alberta Press, Ring House 2, Edmonton, AB T6G 2E1, Canada *Tel:* 780-492-3662 *Fax:* 780-492-0719 *Web Site:* www.uap.ualberta.ca, pg 442

Kowal, Rachel, Soho Press Inc, 853 Broadway, New York, NY 10003 *Tel:* 212-260-1900 *E-mail:* soho@sohopress.com; publicity@sohopress.com *Web Site:* sohopress.com, pg 203

Kowalchuk, Tavia, HarperCollins General Books Group, 195 Broadway, New York, NY 10007 *Tel:* 212-207-7000 *Web Site:* www.harpercollins.com, pg 93

Kozlowski, Darrell, DWJ BOOKS LLC, 14 Hill Side Lane, East Hampton, NY 11937 *Tel:* 631-267-8270 *E-mail:* info@dwjbooks.com *Web Site:* www.dwjbooks.com, pg 462

Kracht, Elizabeth, Kimberley Cameron & Associates LLC, 1550 Tiburon Blvd, Suite 704, Tiburon, CA 94920 *Tel:* 415-789-9191 *Fax:* 415-789-9177 *Web Site:* www.kimberleycameron.com, pg 479

Kracht, Peter W, Drue Heinz Literature Prize, 7500 Thomas Blvd, Pittsburgh, PA 15260 *Tel:* 412-383-2456 *Fax:* 412-383-2466 *E-mail:* info@upress.pitt.edu *Web Site:* upittpress.org/prize/drue-heinz-literature-prize/; www.upress.pitt.edu, pg 623

Kracht, Peter W, Agnes Lynch Starrett Poetry Prize, 7500 Thomas Blvd, Pittsburgh, PA 15260 *Tel:* 412-383-2456 *Fax:* 412-383-2466 *E-mail:* info@upress.pitt.edu *Web Site:* upittpress.org/prize/agnes-lynch-starrett-poetry-prize/; www.upress.pitt.edu, pg 670

Kracht, Peter W, University of Pittsburgh Press, 7500 Thomas Blvd, Pittsburgh, PA 15260 *Tel:* 412-383-2456 *Fax:* 412-383-2466 *E-mail:* info@upress.pitt.edu *Web Site:* www.upress.pitt.edu, pg 230

Kral, Steve, Society for Mining, Metallurgy & Exploration, 12999 E Adam Aircraft Circle, Englewood, CO 80112 *Tel:* 303-948-4200 *Toll Free Tel:* 800-763-3132 *Fax:* 303-973-3845 *E-mail:* cs@smenet.org; books@smenet.org *Web Site:* www.smenet.org, pg 202

Kramer, David, United Talent Agency, 9336 Civic Center Dr, Beverly Hills, CA 90210 *Tel:* 310-273-6700 *Fax:* 310-247-1111 *Web Site:* www.unitedtalent.com, pg 507

Kramer, Gary, Temple University Press, 1852 N Tenth St, Philadelphia, PA 19122-6099 *Tel:* 215-926-2140 *Toll Free Tel:* 800-621-2736 *Fax:* 215-926-2141 *E-mail:* tempress@temple.edu *Web Site:* tupress.temple.edu, pg 214

Kramer, Jill, Waterside Productions Inc, 2055 Oxford Ave, Cardiff, CA 92007 *Tel:* 760-632-9190 *Fax:* 760-632-9295 *E-mail:* admin@waterside.com *Web Site:* www.waterside.com, pg 508

Kramp, John, Thomas Nelson, 501 Nelson Place, Nashville, TN 37214 *Tel:* 615-889-9000 *Toll Free Tel:* 800-251-4000 *Fax:* 615-902-1548 *Web Site:* www.thomasnelson.com, pg 217

Krannich, Ronald PhD, Impact Publications/Development Concepts Inc, 7820 Sudley Rd, Suite 100, Manassas, VA 20109 *Tel:* 703-361-7300 *Toll Free Tel:* 800-361-1055 (cust serv) *Fax:* 703-335-9486 *E-mail:* query@impactpublications.com *Web Site:* www.impactpublications.com; www.veteransworld.com, pg 107

Kranz, Deb, Plexus Publishing, Inc, 143 Old Marlton Pike, Medford, NJ 08055 *Tel:* 609-654-6500 *Fax:* 609-654-4309 *E-mail:* info@plexuspublishing.com *Web Site:* www.plexuspublishing.com, pg 170

Kranz, Patricia, Overseas Press Club of America (OPC), 40 W 45 St, New York, NY 10036 *Tel:* 212-626-9220 *Fax:* 212-626-9210 *E-mail:* info@opcofamerica.org *Web Site:* www.opcofamerica.org, pg 543

Kranz, Patricia, The Cornelius Ryan Award, 40 W 45 St, New York, NY 10036 *Tel:* 212-626-9220 *Fax:* 212-626-9210 *E-mail:* info@opcofamerica.org *Web Site:* www.opcofamerica.org, pg 663

Krasner, Emily, Workman Publishing Co Inc, 225 Varick St, 9th fl, New York, NY 10014-4381 *Tel:* 212-254-5900 *Toll Free Tel:* 800-722-7202 *Fax:* 212-254-8098 *E-mail:* info@workman.com; orders@workman.com *Web Site:* www.workman.com, pg 244

Krassner, Kaye, Association of Publishers for Special Sales (APSS), PO Box 715, Avon, CT 06001-0715 *Tel:* 860-675-1344 *Web Site:* www.bookapss.org, pg 527

Krattenmaker, Kathleen, Philadelphia Museum of Art, PO Box 7646, Philadelphia, PA 19101-7646 *Tel:* 215-763-8100 *Fax:* 215-236-4465 *Web Site:* www.philamuseum.org, pg 169

Kraus, Eric, Smith & Kraus Publishers Inc, 177 Lyme Rd, Hanover, NH 03755 *Tel:* 618-783-0519 *Toll Free Tel:* 877-668-8680 *Fax:* 618-783-0520 *E-mail:* editor@smithandkraus.com; info@smithandkraus.com; customerservice@smithandkraus.com *Web Site:* www.smithandkraus.com, pg 201

Krause, Amanda, The University of Arizona Press, 1510 E University Blvd, Tucson, AZ 85721 *Tel:* 520-621-1441 *Toll Free Tel:* 800-426-3797 (orders) *Fax:* 520-621-8899 *Toll Free Fax:* 800-426-3797 *E-mail:* uap@uapress.arizona.edu *Web Site:* www.uapress.arizona.edu, pg 225

Krause, Bill, Llewellyn Publications, 2143 Wooddale Dr, Woodbury, MN 55125 *Tel:* 651-291-1970 *Toll Free Tel:* 800-843-6666 *Fax:* 651-291-1908 *E-mail:* publicity@llewellyn.com; customerservice@llewellyn.com *Web Site:* www.llewellyn.com, pg 127

Krauss, Molly, Chronicle Books, 680 Second St, San Francisco, CA 94107 *Tel:* 415-537-4200 *Toll Free Tel:* 800-759-0190 (cust serv) *Fax:* 415-537-4460 *Toll Free Tel:* 800-858-7787 (orders); 800-286-9471 (cust serv) *E-mail:* frontdesk@chroniclebooks.com *Web Site:* www.chroniclebooks.com, pg 52

Kraut, Diane, DK Research Inc, 9 Wicks Dr, Commack, NY 11725-3921 *Tel:* 631-543-5537 *Fax:* 631-543-5549 *E-mail:* dkresearch@optimum.net *Web Site:* www.dkresearchinc.com, pg 462

Kravitz, Jamie, Aspen Words, 110 E Hallam St, Suite 116, Aspen, CO 81611 *Tel:* 970-925-3122 *Fax:* 970-920-5700 *E-mail:* aspenwords@aspeninstitute.org *Web Site:* www.aspenwords.org, pg 525

Kravitz, Jamie, Aspen Words Literary Prize, 110 E Hallam St, Suite 116, Aspen, CO 81611 *Tel:* 970-925-3122 *Fax:* 970-920-5700 *E-mail:* literary.prize@aspeninstitute.org *Web Site:* www.aspenwords.org/programs/literary-prize/; www.aspenwords.org, pg 594

Kravitz, Jamie, Summer Words Writing Conference & Literary Festival, 110 E Hallam St, Suite 116, Aspen, CO 81611 *Tel:* 970-925-3122 *Fax:* 970-920-5700 *E-mail:* aspenwords@aspeninstitute.org *Web Site:* www.aspenwords.org, pg 579

Kravitz, Jamie, Winter Words Author Series, 110 E Hallam St, Suite 116, Aspen, CO 81611 *Tel:* 970-925-3122 *Fax:* 970-920-5700 *E-mail:* aspenwords@aspeninstitute.org *Web Site:* www.aspenwords.org, pg 579

Krawczyk, Andie, Chronicle Books, 680 Second St, San Francisco, CA 94107 *Tel:* 415-537-4200 *Toll Free Tel:* 800-759-0190 (cust serv) *Fax:* 415-537-4460 *Toll Free Tel:* 800-858-7787 (orders); 800-286-9471 (cust serv) *E-mail:* frontdesk@chroniclebooks.com *Web Site:* www.chroniclebooks.com, pg 51

Krebs, Paula, Modern Language Association of America (MLA), 85 Broad St, Suite 500, New York, NY 10004-2434 *Tel:* 646-576-5000 *Fax:* 646-458-0030 *Web Site:* www.mla.org, pg 141

Krebs, Paula, Modern Language Association of America (MLA), 85 Broad St, Suite 500, New York, NY 10004-2434 *Tel:* 646-576-5000 *Fax:* 646-458-0030 *E-mail:* convention@mla.org *Web Site:* www.mla.org, pg 538

Kregel, Jerold W, Editorial Portavoz, 2450 Oak Industrial Dr NE, Grand Rapids, MI 49505 *Toll Free Tel:* 877-733-2607 (ext 206) *Fax:* 616-493-1790 *E-mail:* portavoz@portavoz.com *Web Site:* www.portavoz.com, pg 69

Kregel, Jerold W, Kregel Publications, 2450 Oak Industrial Dr NE, Grand Rapids, MI 49505 *Tel:* 616-451-4775 *Toll Free Tel:* 800-733-2607 *Fax:* 616-451-9330 *E-mail:* kregelbooks@kregel.com *Web Site:* www.kregel.com, pg 118

Krehbiel, Ken, National Council of Teachers of Mathematics (NCTM), 1906 Association Dr, Reston, VA 20191-1502 *Tel:* 703-620-9840 *Toll Free Tel:* 800-235-7566 *Fax:* 703-476-2970 *E-mail:* nctm@nctm.org *Web Site:* www.nctm.org, pg 146

Kreit, Eileen Bishop, Puffin Books, 345 Hudson St, New York, NY 10014 *Tel:* 212-366-2000 *Web Site:* www.penguin.com/publishers/puffin, pg 177

Kreiter, Lance, Boom! Studios, 5670 Wilshire Blvd, Suite 400, Los Angeles, CA 90036 *Web Site:* www.boom-studios.com, pg 38

Krell, Henry, Springer, 233 Spring St, New York, NY 10013-1578 *Tel:* 212-460-1500 *Toll Free Tel:* 800-SPRINGER (777-4643) *Fax:* 212-460-1700 *E-mail:* customerservice@springer.com *Web Site:* www.springer.com, pg 205

Kremer, John, Open Horizons Publishing Co, PO Box 2887, Taos, NM 87571 *Tel:* 575-751-3398 *E-mail:* books@bookmarketingbestsellers.com *Web Site:* bookmarketingbestsellers.com, pg 156

Kresan, Dawn, Palimpsest Press, 1171 Eastlawn Ave, Windsor, ON N8S 3J1, Canada *Tel:* 519-259-2112 *E-mail:* publicity@palimpsestpress.ca *Web Site:* www.palimpsestpress.ca, pg 435

Kretzschmar, Lauren, Insight Editions, 800 "A" St, San Rafael, CA 94901 *Tel:* 415-526-1370 *Toll Free Tel:* 800-809-3792 *Toll Free Fax:* 866-509-0515 *E-mail:* info@insighteditions.com; marketing@insighteditions.com *Web Site:* insighteditions.com, pg 109

Kreuser, Joe, Bloomsbury Academic, 1385 Broadway, 5th fl, New York, NY 10018 *Tel:* 212-419-5300 *Web Site:* www.bloomsbury.com/us/academic, pg 35

Krichevsky, Stuart, Stuart Krichevsky Literary Agency Inc, 6 E 39 St, Suite 500, New York, NY 10016 *Tel:* 212-725-5288 *Fax:* 212-725-5275 *E-mail:* query@skagency.com *Web Site:* skagency.com, pg 492

Krieger, Ann, Krieger Publishing Co, 1725 Krieger Lane, Malabar, FL 32950 *Tel:* 321-724-9542 *Fax:* 321-951-3671 *E-mail:* info@krieger-publishing.com *Web Site:* www.krieger-publishing.com, pg 119

Krieger, Donald E, Krieger Publishing Co, 1725 Krieger Lane, Malabar, FL 32950 *Tel:* 321-724-9542 *Fax:* 321-951-3671 *E-mail:* info@krieger-publishing.com *Web Site:* www.krieger-publishing.com, pg 119

Krienke, Mary, Sterling Lord Literistic Inc, 115 Broadway, Suite 1602, New York, NY 10006 *Tel:* 212-780-6050 *Fax:* 212-780-6095 *E-mail:* info@sll.com *Web Site:* www.sll.com, pg 504

Krinsky, Santosh, Lotus Press, PO Box 325, Twin Lakes, WI 53181-0325 *Tel:* 262-889-8561 *Toll Free Tel:* 800-824-6396 (orders) *Fax:* 262-889-2461; 262-889-8591 *E-mail:* lotuspress@lotuspress.com *Web Site:* www.lotuspress.com, pg 128

Krise, Matthew, Encyclopaedia Britannica Inc, 325 N La Salle St, Suite 200, Chicago, IL 60654 *Tel:* 312-347-7000 (all other countries) *Toll Free Tel:* 800-323-1229 (US & CN) *Fax:* 312-294-2104 *E-mail:* contact@eb.com *Web Site:* www.britannica.com, pg 72

Krishnan, Karthik, Encyclopaedia Britannica Inc, 325 N La Salle St, Suite 200, Chicago, IL 60654 *Tel:* 312-347-7000 (all other countries) *Toll Free*

Tel: 800-323-1229 (US & CN) *Fax:* 312-294-2104 *E-mail:* contact@eb.com *Web Site:* www.britannica. com, pg 72

Krishnan, Priyanka, Orbit, 1290 Avenue of the Americas, New York, NY 10104 *Tel:* 212-364-1100 *Toll Free Tel:* 800-759-0190 *Web Site:* www.orbitbooks.net, pg 156

Kriss, Miriam, Irene Goodman Literary Agency, 27 W 24 St, Suite 700B, New York, NY 10010 *Tel:* 212-604-0330 *E-mail:* queries@irenegoodman.com *Web Site:* www.irenegoodman.com, pg 486

Krissoff, Derek, West Virginia University Press, West Virginia University, PO Box 6295, Morgantown, WV 26506-6295 *Tel:* 304-293-8400 *Web Site:* www. wvupress.com, pg 239

Kritzmacher, John, John Wiley & Sons Inc, 111 River St, Hoboken, NJ 07030-5774 *Tel:* 201-748-6000 *Toll Free Tel:* 800-225-5945 (cust serv) *Fax:* 201-748-6088 *E-mail:* info@wiley.com *Web Site:* www.wiley.com, pg 241

Kriz, Rebecca, Sunbelt Publications Inc, 1250 Fayette St, El Cajon, CA 92020-1511 *Tel:* 619-258-4911 *Toll Free Tel:* 800-626-6579 (cust serv) *Fax:* 619-258-4916 *E-mail:* service@sunbeltpub.com; info@sunbeltpub. com *Web Site:* sunbeltpublications.com, pg 210

Kroell, Alicia, Counterpoint Press LLC, 2560 Ninth St, Suite 318, Berkeley, CA 94710 *Tel:* 510-704-0230 *Fax:* 510-704-0268 *E-mail:* info@counterpointpress. com *Web Site:* counterpointpress.com; softskull.com, pg 58

Kroger, Rev Dan OFM, Franciscan Media, 28 W Liberty St, Cincinnati, OH 45202 *Tel:* 513-241-5615 *Toll Free Tel:* 800-488-0488 *E-mail:* admin@franciscanmedia. org *Web Site:* www.franciscanmedia.org, pg 81

Kronenberg, Annie, John Hawkins and Associates Inc, 80 Maiden Lane, Suite 1503, New York, NY 10038 *Tel:* 212-807-7040 *E-mail:* jha@jhalit.com *Web Site:* jhalit.com, pg 488

Krones, Christine, Houghton Mifflin Harcourt Trade & Reference Division, 125 High St, Boston, MA 02110 *Tel:* 617-351-5000 *Web Site:* www.hmhco.com, pg 104

Kronzek, Lynn C, Lynn C Kronzek, Richard A Flom & Robert Flom, 145 S Glenoaks Blvd, Suite 240, Burbank, CA 91502 *Tel:* 818-768-7688, pg 466

Krouk, Dean, The Ibsen Society of America (ISA), c/o Indiana University, Global & Intl Studies Bldg 3111, 355 N Jordan Ave, Bloomington, IN 47405-1105 *Web Site:* www.ibsensociety.org, pg 534

Krovitz, Debbie, DeVorss & Co, 553 Constitution Ave, Camarillo, CA 93012-8510 *Tel:* 805-322-9010 *Toll Free Tel:* 800-843-5743 *Fax:* 805-322-9011 *E-mail:* service@devorss.com *Web Site:* www.devorss. com, pg 64

Krowl, Michelle, Abraham Lincoln Institute Book Award, 105 Mount Olive Lane, Ephrata, PA 17522 *E-mail:* secretary@lincoln-institute.org *Web Site:* www.lincoln-institute.org, pg 633

Krueger, Jenny, ediciones Lerner, 241 First Ave N, Minneapolis, MN 55401 *Tel:* 612-332-3344 *Toll Free Tel:* 800-328-4929 *Fax:* 612-332-7615 *Toll Free Fax:* 800-332-1132 *E-mail:* info@lernerbooks. com; custserve@lernerbooks.com *Web Site:* www. lernerbooks.com; www.facebook.com/lernerbooks, pg 69

Krueger, Jenny, First Avenue Editions, 241 First Ave N, Minneapolis, MN 55401 *Tel:* 612-332-3344 *Toll Free Tel:* 800-328-4929 *Fax:* 612-332-7615 *Toll Free Fax:* 800-332-1132 *E-mail:* info@lernerbooks. com; custserve@lernerbooks.com *Web Site:* www. lernerbooks.com; www.facebook.com/lernerbooks, pg 78

Krueger, Jenny, Graphic Universe™, 241 First Ave N, Minneapolis, MN 55401 *Tel:* 612-332-3344 *Toll Free Tel:* 800-328-4929 *Fax:* 612-332-7615 *Toll Free Fax:* 800-332-1132 *E-mail:* info@lernerbooks. com; custserve@lernerbooks.com *Web Site:* www. lernerbooks.com; www.facebook.com/lernerbooks, pg 88

Krueger, Jenny, Lerner Publications, 241 First Ave N, Minneapolis, MN 55401 *Tel:* 612-332-3344 *Toll Free Tel:* 800-328-4929 *Fax:* 612-332-7615 *Toll Free Fax:* 800-332-1132 *E-mail:* info@lernerbooks. com; custserve@lernerbooks.com *Web Site:* www. lernerbooks.com; www.facebook.com/lernerbooks, pg 122

Krueger, Jenny, Lerner Publishing Group Inc, 241 First Ave N, Minneapolis, MN 55401 *Tel:* 612-332-3344 *Toll Free Tel:* 800-328-4929 *Fax:* 612-332-7615 *Toll Free Fax:* 800-332-1132 *E-mail:* info@lernerbooks. com; custserve@lernerbooks.com *Web Site:* www. lernerbooks.com; www.facebook.com/lernerbooks, pg 123

Krueger, Jenny, LernerClassroom, 241 First Ave N, Minneapolis, MN 55401 *Tel:* 612-332-3344 *Toll Free Tel:* 800-328-4929 *Fax:* 612-332-7615 *Toll Free Fax:* 800-332-1132 *E-mail:* info@lernerbooks. com; custserve@lernerbooks.com *Web Site:* www. lernerbooks.com; www.facebook.com/lernerbooks, pg 123

Krueger, Jenny, Millbrook Press, 241 First Ave N, Minneapolis, MN 55401 *Tel:* 612-332-3344 *Toll Free Tel:* 800-328-4929 *Fax:* 612-332-7615 *Toll Free Fax:* 800-332-1132 *E-mail:* info@lernerbooks. com; custserve@lernerbooks.com *Web Site:* www. lernerbooks.com; www.facebook.com/millbrookpress, pg 140

Krueger, Jenny, Twenty-First Century Books, 241 First Ave N, Minneapolis, MN 55401 *Tel:* 612-332-3344 *Toll Free Tel:* 800-328-4929 *Fax:* 612-332-7615 *Toll Free Fax:* 800-332-1132 *E-mail:* info@lernerbooks. com; custserve@lernerbooks.com *Web Site:* www. lernerbooks.com; www.facebook.com/lernerbooks, pg 222

Krueger, Jenny, Zest Books, 241 First Ave N, Minneapolis, MN 55401 *Tel:* 612-332-3344 *Toll Free Tel:* 800-328-4929 *Toll Free Fax:* 800-332-1132 *E-mail:* info@lernerbooks.com; publicity@ lernerbooks.com; custserve@lernerbooks.com (orders) *Web Site:* lernerbooks.com, pg 248

Krueger, Jo Ann, The Aaland Agency, PO Box 849, Inyokern, CA 93527-0849 *Tel:* 760-384-3910 *E-mail:* anniejo41@gmail.com *Web Site:* www.the-aaland-agency.com, pg 473

Krug, Susan, American Medical Writers Association (AMWA), 30 W Gude Dr, Suite 525, Rockville, MD 20850-4357 *Tel:* 240-238-0940 *Fax:* 301-294-9006 *E-mail:* amwa@amwa.org *Web Site:* www.amwa.org, pg 523

Krump, Emily, HarperCollins General Books Group, 195 Broadway, New York, NY 10007 *Tel:* 212-207-7000 *Web Site:* www.harpercollins.com, pg 93

Krumpfer, Jorie, W W Norton & Company Inc, 500 Fifth Ave, New York, NY 10110-0017 *Tel:* 212-354-5500 *Toll Free Tel:* 800-233-4830 (orders & cust serv) *Fax:* 212-869-0856 *Toll Free Fax:* 800-458-6515 *E-mail:* orders@wwnorton.com *Web Site:* wwnorton. com, pg 152

Krup, Agnes, Sanford J Greenburger Associates Inc, 55 Fifth Ave, New York, NY 10003 *Tel:* 212-206-5600 *Fax:* 212-463-8718 *Web Site:* greenburger.com; www. sjga.com, pg 487

Kruse, Katrina, Houghton Mifflin Harcourt, 125 High St, Boston, MA 02110 *Tel:* 617-351-5000 *Toll Free Tel:* 855-969-4642; 800-225-5425 (K-12 educ materials); 800-323-9540 (assessment materials); 877-219-1537 (SkillsTutor); 888-242-6747 (Innovation in Educ Group); 800-225-3362 (Trade & Ref Div) *Toll Free Fax:* 800-269-5232 *E-mail:* myhmhco@hmhco. com *Web Site:* www.hmhco.com, pg 103

Kubie, Greg, Random House Publishing Group, 1745 Broadway, New York, NY 10019 *Toll Free Tel:* 800-200-3552 *Web Site:* www.randomhousebooks.com, pg 181

Kubinec, Jessica, LARB Books, 6671 Sunset Blvd, Suite 1521, Los Angeles, CA 90028 *Tel:* 323-952-3950 *E-mail:* larbbooks@lareviewofbooks.org *Web Site:* larbbooks.org, pg 120

Kubinec, Jessica, LARB/USC Publishing Workshop, 6671 Sunset Blvd, Suite 1521, Los Angeles, CA 90028 *E-mail:* publishingworkshop@lareviewofbooks. org *Web Site:* thepublishingworkshop.com, pg 576

Kuehl, Ashley, Zest Books, 241 First Ave N, Minneapolis, MN 55401 *Tel:* 612-332-3344 *Toll Free Tel:* 800-328-4929 *Toll Free Fax:* 800-332-1132 *E-mail:* info@lernerbooks.com; publicity@ lernerbooks.com; custserve@lernerbooks.com (orders) *Web Site:* lernerbooks.com, pg 248

Kuehl, Kathy, The Guilford Press, 370 Seventh Ave, Suite 1200, New York, NY 10001-1020 *Tel:* 212-431-9800 *Toll Free Tel:* 800-365-7006 *Fax:* 212-966-6708 *E-mail:* info@guilford.com *Web Site:* www.guilford. com, pg 90

Kuehl, Monte, ABDO Publishing Co Inc, 8000 W 78 St, Suite 310, Edina, MN 55439 *Tel:* 952-698-2403 *Toll Free Tel:* 800-800-1312 *Fax:* 952-831-1632 *Toll Free Fax:* 800-862-3480 *E-mail:* customerservice@ abdopublishing.com; info@abdopublishing.com *Web Site:* abdopublishing.com, pg 2

Kuehm, Scot, Princeton University Press, 41 William St, Princeton, NJ 08540-5237 *Tel:* 609-258-4900 *Fax:* 609-258-6305 *Web Site:* press.princeton.edu, pg 174

Kuerbis, Lisa, Syracuse University Press, 621 Skytop Rd, Suite 110, Syracuse, NY 13244-5290 *Tel:* 315-443-5534 *Toll Free Tel:* 800-365-8929 (cust serv) *Fax:* 315-443-5545 *E-mail:* supress@syr.edu *Web Site:* press.syr.edu, pg 212

Kuhn, David, Aevitas Creative Management, 19 W 21 St, Suite 501, New York, NY 10010 *Tel:* 212-765-6900 *Web Site:* aevitascreative.com, pg 474

Kuhne, Chris, The Writer's Lifeline Inc, 400 S Burnside Ave, Suite 11B, Los Angeles, CA 90036 *Tel:* 323-932-1685 *Web Site:* www.thewriterslifeline.com, pg 472

Kujichagulia, Phavia, Media Alliance, 2830 20 St, Suite 102, San Francisco, CA 94110 *Tel:* 415-746-9475 *E-mail:* information@media-alliance.org *Web Site:* www.media-alliance.org, pg 537

Kuka, Ronald, Chris O'Malley Fiction Prize, University of Wisconsin, 6193 Helen C White Hall, English Dept, 600 N Park St, Madison, WI 53706 *E-mail:* madisonrevw@gmail.com *Web Site:* www. themadisonrevw.com, pg 651

Kuka, Ronald, Phyllis Smart-Young Poetry Prize, University of Wisconsin, 6193 Helen C White Hall, English Dept, 600 N Park St, Madison, WI 53706 *E-mail:* madisonrevw@gmail.com *Web Site:* www. themadisonrevw.com, pg 681

Kukafka, Danya, Aevitas Creative Management, 19 W 21 St, Suite 501, New York, NY 10010 *Tel:* 212-765-6900 *Web Site:* aevitascreative.com, pg 474

Kukla, Lauren, Mighty Media Press, 1201 Currie Ave, Minneapolis, MN 55403 *Tel:* 612-455-0252; 612-399-1969 *Fax:* 612-338-4817 *E-mail:* info@mightymedia. com *Web Site:* www.mightymediapress.com, pg 139

Kulick, Gregg, Little, Brown and Company, 1290 Avenue of the Americas, New York, NY 10104 *Tel:* 212-364-1100 *Fax:* 212-364-0952 *E-mail:* firstname.lastname@hbgusa. com *Web Site:* www.littlebrown.com; www. hachettebookgroup.com, pg 126

Kulka, John, The Library of America, 14 E 60 St, New York, NY 10022-1006 *Tel:* 212-308-3360 *Fax:* 212-750-8352 *E-mail:* info@loa.org *Web Site:* www.loa. org, pg 124

Kull, Irene Imperio, Temple University Press, 1852 N Tenth St, Philadelphia, PA 19122-6099 *Tel:* 215-926-2140 *Toll Free Tel:* 800-621-2736 *Fax:* 215-926-2141 *E-mail:* tempress@temple.edu *Web Site:* tupress. temple.edu, pg 214

Kundert, Beth, McGraw-Hill Create, 2 Penn Plaza, New York, NY 10121 *Toll Free Tel:* 800-962-9342 *E-mail:* mhhe.create@mheducation.com *Web Site:* create.mheducation.com; shop.mheducation. com, pg 135

Lakin, Chuck, Zeig, Tucker & Theisen Inc, 2632 E Thomas Rd, Suite 201, Phoenix, AZ 85016 *Tel:* 480-389-4342 *Web Site:* www.zeigtucker.com, pg 248

Lakosil, Natalie, Bradford Literary Agency, 5694 Mission Center Rd, Suite 347, San Diego, CA 92108 *Tel:* 619-521-1201 *E-mail:* queries@bradfordlit.com *Web Site:* www.bradfordlit.com, pg 477

Lalonde, Chantale Gravel, Scholastic Canada Ltd, 604 King St W, Toronto, ON M5V 1E1, Canada *Tel:* 905-887-7323 *Toll Free Tel:* 800-268-3860 (CN) *Toll Free Fax:* 866-387-4944 *E-mail:* custserve@scholastic.ca *Web Site:* www.scholastic.ca, pg 439

Lalwani, R, Laurier Books Ltd, PO Box 8493, Ottawa, ON K1G 3H9, Canada *Tel:* 613-738-2163 *Toll Free Fax:* 855-736-9160 *E-mail:* laurierbooks@yahoo.com, pg 432

Lam, Andrea, Viking, 375 Hudson St, New York, NY 10014 *Tel:* 212-366-2000 *Fax:* 212-243-6002 *Web Site:* www.penguin.com/publishers/vikingbooks, pg 236

Lam, Anna, Alex Awards, 50 E Huron St, Chicago, IL 60611 *Tel:* 312-280-4390 *Toll Free Tel:* 800-545-2433 *Fax:* 312-280-5276 *E-mail:* yalsa@ala.org *Web Site:* www.ala.org/yalsa/alex-awards, pg 591

Lam, Anna, Baker & Taylor/YALSA Conference Grants, 50 E Huron St, Chicago, IL 60611 *Tel:* 312-280-4390 *Toll Free Tel:* 800-545-2433 *Fax:* 312-280-5276; 312-664-7459 *E-mail:* yalsa@ala.org *Web Site:* www.ala.org/yalsa, pg 595

Lam, Anna, Margaret A Edwards Award, 50 E Huron St, Chicago, IL 60611 *Tel:* 312-280-4390 *Toll Free Tel:* 800-545-2433 *Fax:* 312-280-5276 *E-mail:* yalsa@ala.org *Web Site:* www.ala.org/yalsa/edwards, pg 612

Lam, Anna, Frances Henne YALSA/VOYA Research Grant, 50 E Huron St, Chicago, IL 60611 *Tel:* 312-280-4390 *Toll Free Tel:* 800-545-2433 *Fax:* 312-280-5276 *E-mail:* yalsa@ala.org *Web Site:* www.ala.org/yalsa/awardsandgrants/franceshenne, pg 617

Lam, Anna, Nonfiction Award, 50 E Huron St, Chicago, IL 60611 *Toll Free Tel:* 800-545-2433 (ext 4390) *Fax:* 312-280-5276 *E-mail:* yalsa@ala.org *Web Site:* www.ala.org/yalsa/nonfiction-award, pg 649

Lam, Anna, Odyssey Award for Excellence in Audiobook Production, 50 E Huron St, Chicago, IL 60611 *Toll Free Tel:* 800-545-2433 (ext 4390) *Fax:* 312-280-5276 *E-mail:* yalsa@ala.org *Web Site:* www.ala.org/yalsa/odyssey, pg 650

Lam, Anna, Michael L Printz Award, 50 E Huron St, Chicago, IL 60611 *Tel:* 312-280-4390 *Toll Free Tel:* 800-545-2433 *Fax:* 312-280-5276 *E-mail:* yalsa@ala.org *Web Site:* www.ala.org/yalsa/printz, pg 659

Lam, Brian, Arsenal Pulp Press, 211 E Georgia St, No 202, Vancouver, BC V6A 1Z6, Canada *Tel:* 604-687-4233 *Toll Free Tel:* 888-600-PULP (600-7857) *Fax:* 604-687-4283 *E-mail:* info@arsenalpulp.com *Web Site:* www.arsenalpulp.com, pg 415

Lamb, Beth, Anchor Books, c/o Penguin Random House Inc, 1745 Broadway, New York, NY 10019 *Tel:* 212-572-2420 *E-mail:* vintageanchorpublicity@randomhouse.com *Web Site:* knopfdoubleday.com/imprint/anchor, pg 15

Lamb, Beth, Vintage Books, c/o Penguin Random House Inc, 1745 Broadway, New York, NY 10019 *Tel:* 212-572-2420 *E-mail:* vintageanchorpublicity@randomhouse.com *Web Site:* knopfdoubleday.com/imprint/vintage, pg 236

Lamb, Cynthia, Carnegie Mellon University Press, 5032 Forbes Ave, Pittsburgh, PA 15289-1021 *Tel:* 412-268-2861 *Fax:* 412-268-8706 *E-mail:* carnegiemellonuniversitypress@gmail.com *Web Site:* www.cmu.edu/universitypress, pg 45

Lamb, David, Perseus Books, 1290 Avenue of the Americas, New York, NY 10104 *Tel:* 212-340-8100 *Toll Free Tel:* 800-343-4499 (cust serv) *Fax:* 212-340-8105 *Web Site:* www.perseusbooks.com, pg 167

Lamb, Jason, Bread Loaf Writers' Conference, 5525 Middlebury College, 14 Old Chapel Rd, Middlebury, VT 05753 *Tel:* 802-443-5286 *Fax:* 802-443-2087 *E-mail:* blwc@middlebury.edu *Web Site:* www.middlebury.edu/blwc, pg 574

Lamb, Jason, Fellowship, Tuition Scholarship & Work Study Programs for Writers, Middlebury College, 204 College St, Middlebury, VT 05753 *Tel:* 802-443-5286 *Fax:* 802-443-2087 *E-mail:* blwc@middlebury.edu *Web Site:* www.middlebury.edu/blwc, pg 615

Lamb, John D, Lost Lake Writers Retreat, PO Box 304, Royal Oak, MI 48068-0304 *Tel:* 248-589-3913 *Web Site:* www.springfed.org, pg 576

Lamba, Cari, The Jennifer DeChiara Literary Agency, 245 Park Ave, 39th fl, New York, NY 10167 *Tel:* 212-372-8989 *Web Site:* www.jdlit.com, pg 481

Lamba, Marie, The Jennifer DeChiara Literary Agency, 245 Park Ave, 39th fl, New York, NY 10167 *Tel:* 212-372-8989 *Web Site:* www.jdlit.com, pg 481

Lambert, Hannah, Simon & Schuster Children's Publishing, 1230 Avenue of the Americas, New York, NY 10020 *Tel:* 212-698-7000 *Web Site:* www.simonandschuster.com/kids; www.simonandschuster.com/teen; simonandschuster.net; simonandschuster.biz, pg 199

Lambeth, Pike, Foundation Publications, 900 S Euclid St, La Habra, CA 90631 *Tel:* 714-879-2286 *E-mail:* info@foundationpublications.com *Web Site:* www.foundationpublications.com, pg 80

Lambright, Katie, Perseus Books, 1290 Avenue of the Americas, New York, NY 10104 *Tel:* 212-340-8100 *Toll Free Tel:* 800-343-4499 (cust serv) *Fax:* 212-340-8105 *Web Site:* www.perseusbooks.com, pg 167

Lame, Vicki, St Martin's Press, LLC, 120 Broadway, New York, NY 10271 *Tel:* 646-307-5151 *Web Site:* us.macmillan.com/smp, pg 190

Lamkins, Tim, SPIE, 1000 20 St, Bellingham, WA 98225-6705 *Tel:* 360-676-3290 *Toll Free Tel:* 888-504-8171 (orders) *Fax:* 360-647-1445 *E-mail:* help@spie.org; customerservice@spie.org (orders) *Web Site:* www.spie.org, pg 205

Lamm, Gigi, University of Pennsylvania Press, 3905 Spruce St, Philadelphia, PA 19104 *Tel:* 215-898-6261 *Fax:* 215-898-0404 *E-mail:* custserv@pobox.upenn.edu *Web Site:* www.pennpress.org, pg 230

Lamolinara, Guy, The Center for the Book in the Library of Congress, The Library of Congress, 101 Independence Ave SE, Washington, DC 20540-4920 *Tel:* 202-707-5221 *Fax:* 202-707-0269 *E-mail:* cfbook@loc.gov *Web Site:* www.read.gov; www.read.gov/cfb, pg 530

Lamolinara, Guy, Library of Congress Prize for American Fiction, 101 Independence Ave SE, Washington, DC 20540-1400 *Tel:* 202-707-5221 (Center for the Book) *Fax:* 202-707-0269 *Web Site:* www.loc.gov, pg 633

Lamont, Myles, Hancock House Publishers, 4550 Birch Bay Lynden Rd, Suite 104, Blaine, WA 98230-9436 *Tel:* 604-538-1114 *Toll Free Tel:* 800-938-1114 *Fax:* 604-538-2262 *Toll Free Fax:* 800-983-2262 *E-mail:* sales@hancockhouse.com *Web Site:* www.hancockhouse.com, pg 92

Lampack, Andrew, Peter Lampack Agency Inc, 350 Fifth Ave, Suite 5300, New York, NY 10118 *Tel:* 212-687-9106 *Fax:* 212-687-9109 *Web Site:* www.peterlampackagency.com, pg 492

Lampack, Peter A, Peter Lampack Agency Inc, 350 Fifth Ave, Suite 5300, New York, NY 10118 *Tel:* 212-687-9106 *Fax:* 212-687-9109 *Web Site:* www.peterlampackagency.com, pg 492

Lampe, Betsy A, Rainbow Books Inc, PO Box 430, Highland City, FL 33846-0430 *Tel:* 863-648-4420 *Fax:* 863-647-5951 *E-mail:* rbibooks@aol.com *Web Site:* www.rainbowbooksinc.com, pg 179

Lampe, Charles M, Rainbow Books Inc, PO Box 430, Highland City, FL 33846-0430 *Tel:* 863-648-4420 *Fax:* 863-647-5951 *E-mail:* rbibooks@aol.com *Web Site:* www.rainbowbooksinc.com, pg 179

Lancaster, Terri, Chronicle Books, 680 Second St, San Francisco, CA 94107 *Tel:* 415-537-4200 *Toll Free Tel:* 800-759-0190 (cust serv) *Fax:* 415-537-4460

Toll Free Fax: 800-858-7787 (orders); 800-286-9471 (cust serv) *E-mail:* frontdesk@chroniclebooks.com *Web Site:* www.chroniclebooks.com, pg 52

Lance, Dan, Kalmbach Publishing Co, 21027 Crossroads Circle, Waukesha, WI 53186 *Tel:* 262-796-8776 *Toll Free Tel:* 800-533-6644 (cust serv & orders); 800-558-1544 *Fax:* 262-798-6592 *E-mail:* customerservice@kalmbach.com *Web Site:* www.kalmbach.com, pg 115

Lance, James, Cornell University Press, Sage House, 512 E State St, Ithaca, NY 14850 *Tel:* 607-253-2338 *Fax:* 607-253-2374 *E-mail:* cupressinfo@cornell.edu; cupress-sales@cornell.edu *Web Site:* www.cornellpress.cornell.edu, pg 57

Lance, Suzanne, New York State Edith Wharton Citation of Merit for Fiction Writers, University at Albany, SL 320, Albany, NY 12222 *Tel:* 518-442-5620 *Fax:* 518-442-5621 *E-mail:* writers@albany.edu *Web Site:* www.albany.edu/writers-inst, pg 648

Lance, Suzanne, New York State Walt Whitman Citation of Merit for Poets, University at Albany, SL 320, Albany, NY 12222 *Tel:* 518-442-5620 *Fax:* 518-442-5621 *E-mail:* writers@albany.edu *Web Site:* www.albany.edu/writers-inst, pg 648

Lance, Suzanne, New York State Writers Institute, University at Albany, Science Library 320, 1400 Washington Ave, Albany, NY 12222 *Tel:* 518-442-5620 *Fax:* 518-442-5621 *E-mail:* writers@albany.edu *Web Site:* www.albany.edu/writers-inst, pg 577

Land, Bob, Land on Demand, 20 Long Crescent Dr, Bristol, VA 24201 *Tel:* 423-366-0513 *E-mail:* landondemand@gmail.com *Web Site:* boblandedits.blogspot.com, pg 466

Landa, Anne, Walter Foster Publishing Inc, 6 Orchard Rd, Suite 100, Lake Forest, CA 92630 *Tel:* 949-380-7510 *Toll Free Tel:* 800-426-0099; 800-759-0190 (orders) *Fax:* 949-380-7575 *E-mail:* walterfoster@quarto.com *Web Site:* www.quartoknows.com/walter-foster, pg 80

Landauer, Jeramy, Landauer Publishing, 1970 Broad St, East Petersburg, PA 17520 *Tel:* 717-560-4703 *Toll Free Tel:* 800-457-9112 *Fax:* 717-560-4702 *E-mail:* customerservice@foxchapelpublishing.com *Web Site:* landauerpub.com, pg 119

Landers, Sue, Lambda Literary Awards (Lammys), 5482 Wilshire Blvd, No 1595, Los Angeles, CA 90036 *Tel:* 323-643-4281 *E-mail:* admin@lambdaliterary.org *Web Site:* www.lambdaliterary.org, pg 631

Landes, Rachel, Springer Publishing Co, 11 W 42 St, 15th fl, New York, NY 10036-8002 *Tel:* 212-431-4370 *Toll Free Tel:* 877-687-7476 *E-mail:* marketing@springerpub.com; cs@springerpub.com (orders); textbook@springerpub.com; specialsales@springerpub.com *Web Site:* www.springerpub.com, pg 206

Landis, Sarah, Sterling Lord Literistic Inc, 115 Broadway, Suite 1602, New York, NY 10006 *Tel:* 212-780-6050 *Fax:* 212-780-6095 *E-mail:* info@sll.com *Web Site:* www.sll.com, pg 504

Landolf, Diane, Random House Children's Books, 1745 Broadway, 10th fl, New York, NY 10019 *Tel:* 212-782-9000 *Web Site:* www.randomhousekids.com, pg 180

Landskroener, Marcia, Sophie Kerr Prize, c/o College Relations Off, 300 Washington Ave, Chestertown, MD 21620 *Tel:* 410-778-2800 *Toll Free Tel:* 800-422-1782 *Fax:* 410-810-7150 *Web Site:* www.washcoll.edu, pg 669

Landwehr, Kathy, Peachtree Publishing Co Inc, 1700 Chattahoochee Ave, Atlanta, GA 30318-2112 *Tel:* 404-876-8761 *Toll Free Tel:* 800-241-0113 *Fax:* 404-875-2578 *Toll Free Fax:* 800-875-8909 *E-mail:* hello@peachtree-online.com; orders@peachtree-online.com; sales@peachtree-online.com *Web Site:* www.peachtree-online.com, pg 162

Lane, Connor, Ballard Spahr Prize for Poetry, 1011 Washington Ave S, Suite 300, Minneapolis, MN 55415-1246 *Tel:* 612-332-3192 *Toll Free Tel:* 800-520-6455 *Fax:* 612-215-2550 *Web Site:* www.milkweed.org, pg 595

Lang, Adrienne, BenBella Books Inc, 10300 N Central Expwy, Suite 400, Dallas, TX 75231 Tel: 214-750-3600 E-mail: feedback@benbellabooks. com Web Site: www.benbellabooks.com; www. smartpopbooks.com, pg 31

Lang, Amelia, Aperture Books, 547 W 27 St, 4th fl, New York, NY 10001 Tel: 212-505-5555 Toll Free Fax: 888-623-6908 E-mail: customerservice@aperture. org Web Site: aperture.org, pg 17

Lang, Kara, Anvil Press Publishers, 278 E First Ave, Vancouver, BC V5T 1A6, Canada Tel: 604-876-8710 Fax: 604-879-2667 E-mail: info@anvilpress.com Web Site: www.anvilpress.com, pg 415

Lang, Rebecca, St Martin's Press, LLC, 120 Broadway, New York, NY 10271 Tel: 646-307-5151 Web Site: us. macmillan.com/smp, pg 190

Lange, April, W W Norton & Company Inc, 500 Fifth Ave, New York, NY 10110-0017 Tel: 212-354-5500 Toll Free Tel: 800-233-4830 (orders & cust serv) Fax: 212-869-0856 Toll Free Fax: 800-458-6515 E-mail: orders@wwnorton.com Web Site: wwnorton. com, pg 152

Lange, Barbara, Society of Motion Picture & Television Engineers® (SMPTE®), 3 Barker Ave, 5th fl, White Plains, NY 10601 Tel: 914-761-1100 Fax: 914-761-3115 Web Site: www.smpte.org, pg 547

Lange, Heide, Sanford J Greenburger Associates Inc, 55 Fifth Ave, New York, NY 10003 Tel: 212-206-5600 Fax: 212-463-8718 Web Site: greenburger.com; www.sjga.com, pg 487

Lange, Jocelyn, Random House Children's Books, 1745 Broadway, 10th fl, New York, NY 10019 Tel: 212-782-9000 Web Site: www.randomhousekids.com, pg 180

Lange, Marty, McGraw-Hill Science, Engineering, Mathematics, 501 Bell St, Dubuque, IA 52001 Tel: 563-584-6000 Toll Free Tel: 800-338-3987 (cust serv) Fax: 614-755-5645 (cust serv) Web Site: www. mhhe.com, pg 136

Langille, Donald, Palm Island Press, 3607 Maine Ave, Sebring, FL 33870 Tel: 305-296-3102 E-mail: pipress2@gmail.com, pg 159

Langlois, Dennis, Princeton University Press, 41 William St, Princeton, NJ 08540-5237 Tel: 609-258-4900 Fax: 609-258-6305 Web Site: press.princeton.edu, pg 174

Langman, Lucy, Fons Vitae, 49 Mockingbird Valley Dr, Louisville, KY 40207-1366 Tel: 502-897-3641 Fax: 502-893-7373 E-mail: fonsvitaeky@aol.com Web Site: www.fonsvitae.com, pg 79

Langum, David J Sr, Langum Prize in American Historical Fiction, 2809 Berkeley Dr, Birmingham, AL 35242 Tel: 360-809-0465 E-mail: langumtrust@ gmail.com Web Site: www.langumtrust.org, pg 631

Langum, David J Sr, Langum Prize in American Legal History or Biography, 2809 Berkeley Dr, Birmingham, AL 35242 Tel: 360-809-0465 E-mail: langumtrust@ gmail.com Web Site: www.langumtrust.org, pg 631

Langum, David J Sr, Gene E & Adele R Malott Prize for Recording Community Activism, 2809 Berkeley Dr, Birmingham, AL 35242 Tel: 360-809-0465 E-mail: langumtrust@gmail.com Web Site: www. langumtrust.org, pg 637

Lanick, Colleen, The MIT Press, One Rogers St, Cambridge, MA 02142 Tel: 617-253-5255 Toll Free Tel: 800-405-1619 (orders) Fax: 617-258-6779; 617-577-1545 (orders) Web Site: mitpress.mit.edu, pg 141

Lannan, Patrick, Lannan Foundation, 313 Read St, Santa Fe, NM 87501-2628 Tel: 505-986-8160 E-mail: info@ lannan.org Web Site: lannan.org, pg 551

Lannan, Patrick, Lannan Literary Awards & Fellowships, 313 Read St, Santa Fe, NM 87501-2628 Tel: 505-986-8160 E-mail: info@lannan.org Web Site: lannan.org, pg 631

Lansing, Richard, Springer, 233 Spring St, New York, NY 10013-1578 Tel: 212-460-1500 Toll Free Tel: 800-SPRINGER (777-4643) Fax: 212-460-1700 E-mail: customerservice@springer.com Web Site: www.springer.com, pg 205

Lantz, Deb, Christian Schools International, 3350 E Paris Ave SE, Grand Rapids, MI 49512-3054 Tel: 616-957-1070 Toll Free Tel: 800-635-8288 Fax: 616-957-5022 E-mail: info@csionline.org Web Site: www.csionline. org, pg 51

Lape, Todd, University Press of Mississippi, 3825 Ridgewood Rd, Jackson, MS 39211-6492 Tel: 601-432-6205 Toll Free Tel: 800-737-7788 (orders & cust serv) Fax: 601-432-6217 E-mail: press@mississippi. edu Web Site: www.upress.state.ms.us, pg 233

Laperriere, Ginette, Guerin Editeur Ltee, 800, Blvd Industriel, bureau 200, St-Jean-sur-Richelieu, QC J3B 8G4, Canada Tel: 514-842-3481 Fax: 514-842-4923 Web Site: www.guerin-editeur.qc.ca, pg 428

Laplante, Pascal, Canadian Museum of History (Musee canadien de l'histoire), 100 Laurier St, Gatineau, QC K1A 0M8, Canada Tel: 819-776-7000 Toll Free Tel: 800-555-5621 (North American orders only) Fax: 819-776-7187 Web Site: www.historymuseum.ca, pg 419

Laporte, Janine, Doubleday Canada, 320 Front St W, Suite 1400, Toronto, ON M5V 3B6, Canada Tel: 416-364-4449 Fax: 416-598-7764 Web Site: www. penguinrandomhouse.ca, pg 421

Laporte, Janine, Knopf Canada, 320 Front St W, Suite 1400, Toronto, ON M5V 3B6, Canada Tel: 416-364-4449 Toll Free Tel: 888-523-9292 Fax: 416-598-7764 Web Site: www.penguinrandomhouse.ca, pg 431

Laporte, Janine, Penguin Random House Canada, 320 Front St W, Suite 1400, Toronto, ON M5V 3B6, Canada Tel: 416-364-4449 Toll Free Tel: 888-523-9292 (cust serv) Fax: 416-598-7764 Web Site: www. penguinrandomhouse.ca, pg 436

Laporte, Janine, Seal Books, 320 Front St W, Suite 1400, Toronto, ON M5V 3B6, Canada Tel: 416-364-4449 Toll Free Tel: 888-523-9292 (order desk) Fax: 416-598-7764 Web Site: www.penguinrandomhouse.ca, pg 439

Lapp, Alison, Kids Can Press Ltd, 25 Dockside Dr, Toronto, ON M5A 0B5, Canada Tel: 416-479-7000 Toll Free Tel: 800-265-0884 Fax: 416-960-5437 E-mail: info@kidscan.com; customerservice@ kidscan.com Web Site: www.kidscanpress.com; www. kidscanpress.ca, pg 431

Laprairie, Dinah, BrainStorm Poetry Contest for Mental Health Consumers, 36 Elgin St, 2nd fl, Sudbury, ON P3C 5B4, Canada Tel: 705-222-6472 (ext 303) E-mail: openminds@nisa.on.ca Web Site: www. openmindsquarterly.com, pg 600

Lara, Erika, Perseus Books, 1290 Avenue of the Americas, New York, NY 10104 Tel: 212-340-8100 Toll Free Tel: 800-343-4499 (cust serv) Fax: 212-340-8105 Web Site: www.perseusbooks.com, pg 168

Laredo, Sam, Laredo Publishing Co, 465 Westview Ave, Englewood, NJ 07631 Tel: 201-408-4048 E-mail: info@laredopublishing.com Web Site: www. laredopublishing.com, pg 120

Laredo, Sam, Renaissance House, 465 Westview Ave, Englewood, NJ 07631 Tel: 201-408-4048 Web Site: www.renaissancehouse.net, pg 184, 512

Larned, Alex, Penguin Random House LLC, 1745 Broadway, New York, NY 10019 Tel: 212-782-9000 Toll Free Tel: 800-726-0600 Web Site: www. penguinrandomhouse.com, pg 164

LaRocca, Morgan, Graywolf Press, 250 Third Ave N, Suite 600, Minneapolis, MN 55401 Tel: 651-641-0077 Fax: 651-641-0036 E-mail: wolves@graywolfpress. org (no ms queries, sample chapters or proposals) Web Site: www.graywolfpress.org, pg 88

Larochelle, France, Guerin Editeur Ltee, 800, Blvd Industriel, bureau 200, St-Jean-sur-Richelieu, QC J3B 8G4, Canada Tel: 514-842-3481 Fax: 514-842-4923 Web Site: www.guerin-editeur.qc.ca, pg 428

Laroya, Colette, Hippocrene Books Inc, 171 Madison Ave, Suite 1605, New York, NY 10016 Tel: 212-685-4373 E-mail: info@hippocrenebooks.com; orderdept@ hippocrenebooks.com (orders) Web Site: www. hippocrenebooks.com, pg 100

Larsen, David, University of Manitoba Press, University of Manitoba, 301 St Johns College, 92 Dysart Rd, Winnipeg, MB R3T 2M5, Canada Tel: 204-474-9495 Fax: 204-474-7566 E-mail: uofmpress@umanitoba.ca Web Site: uofmpress.ca, pg 443

Larsen, Elizabeth A, Tapestry Press Ltd, 19 Nashoba Rd, Littleton, MA 01460 Tel: 978-486-0200 Toll Free Tel: 800-535-2007 E-mail: publish@tapestrypress.com Web Site: www.tapestrypress.com, pg 213

Larsen, Michael, San Francisco Writers Conference, 1029 Jones St, San Francisco, CA 94109 Tel: 415-673-0939 E-mail: sfwriterscon@aol.com Web Site: www.sfwriters.org, pg 578

Larson, Doran, Hamilton College, English/Creative Writing, English/Creative Writing Dept, 198 College Hill Rd, Clinton, NY 13323 Tel: 315-859-4370 Fax: 315-859-4390 Web Site: www.hamilton.edu, pg 583

Larson, John, Cohesion®, 511 W Bay St, Suite 480, Tampa, FL 33606 Tel: 813-999-3111 Toll Free Tel: 866-727-6800 Web Site: www.cohesion.com, pg 461

Larson, Julie, Sourcebooks LLC, 1935 Brookdale Rd, Suite 139, Naperville, IL 60563 Tel: 630-961-3900 Toll Free Tel: 800-432-7444 Fax: 630-961-2168 E-mail: info@sourcebooks.com; customersupport@ sourcebooks.com Web Site: www.sourcebooks.com, pg 204

Larson, Susan, Pinckley Prizes for Crime Fiction, PO Box 13926, New Orleans, LA 70185 E-mail: pinckleyprizes@gmail.com Web Site: www. pinckleyprizes.org, pg 656

Lasher, Eric, The LA Literary Agency, 1264 N Hayworth Ave, Los Angeles, CA 90046 Tel: 323-654-5288 E-mail: laliteraryagency@mac.com Web Site: www.laliteraryagency.com, pg 492

Lasher, Maureen, The LA Literary Agency, 1264 N Hayworth Ave, Los Angeles, CA 90046 Tel: 323-654-5288 E-mail: laliteraryagency@mac.com Web Site: www.laliteraryagency.com, pg 492

Lasky, Cynthia, Random House Publishing Group, 1745 Broadway, New York, NY 10019 Toll Free Tel: 800-200-3552 Web Site: www.randomhousebooks.com, pg 181

Lasky, Karl, Ravenhawk™ Books, 311 E Drowsey Circle, Payson, AZ 85541 Tel: 520-402-9033 Fax: 520-402-9033 Web Site: www.facebook.com/ 6DOFRavenhawk, pg 182

Lassiter, Steve, APA Talent & Literary Agency, 405 S Beverly Dr, Beverly Hills, CA 90212 Tel: 310-888-4200 Web Site: www.apa-agency.com, pg 474

Laster, Stephen, McGraw-Hill Education, 2 Penn Plaza, New York, NY 10121-2298 Tel: 212-904-2000 E-mail: international_cs@mheducation.com; seg_customerservice@mheducation.com (PreK-12); hep_customerservice@mheducation.com (higher education) Web Site: www.mheducation.com, pg 135

Latham, Adam, Sewanee Writers' Conference, Stamler Ctr, 119 Gailor Hall, 735 University Ave, Sewanee, TN 37383 Tel: 931-598-1141; 931-598-1654 E-mail: swc@sewanee.edu Web Site: www. sewaneewriters.org, pg 578

Latham, Joyce Eileen, JL Communications, 10205 Green Holly Terr, Silver Spring, MD 20902 Tel: 301-593-0640, pg 465

Lathan, Laurie, Thurber Prize for American Humor, 77 Jefferson Ave, Columbus, OH 43215 Tel: 614-464-1032 Fax: 614-280-3645 E-mail: thurberhouse@ thurberhouse.org Web Site: www.thurberhouse.org, pg 673

Latimer, Nicholas, Alfred A Knopf, c/o Penguin Random House Inc, 1745 Broadway, New York, NY 10019 Tel: 212-751-2600 Fax: 212-572-2662 (foreign rts) Web Site: knopfdoubleday.com, pg 118

Latour, Deirdre, Pearson Education Ltd, 225 River St, Hoboken, NJ 07030-4772 *Tel:* 201-236-7000 *Fax:* 201-236-6549 *Web Site:* www.pearsoned.com, pg 162

Latour, Gilles, EdCan Network, 60 St Clair Ave E, Suite 703, Toronto, ON M4T 1N5, Canada *Tel:* 416-591-6300 *Toll Free Tel:* 866-803-9549 *Fax:* 416-591-5345 *Toll Free Fax:* 866-803-9549 *E-mail:* info@edcan.ca *Web Site:* www.edcan.ca, pg 532

Latshaw, Katherine, Folio Literary Management, The Film Center Bldg, 630 Ninth Ave, Suite 1101, New York, NY 10036 *Tel:* 212-400-1494 *Fax:* 212-967-0977 *Web Site:* www.foliolit.com, pg 484

Lattimer, Corinne, Chalice Press, 483 E Lockwood Ave, Suite 100, St Louis, MO 63119 *Tel:* 314-231-8500 *Toll Free Tel:* 800-366-3383 *Fax:* 314-231-8524; 770-280-4039 (orders) *E-mail:* customerservice@chalicepress.com *Web Site:* www.chalicepress.com, pg 48

Lau, Andrea, Random House Children's Books, 1745 Broadway, 10th fl, New York, NY 10019 *Tel:* 212-782-9000 *Web Site:* www.randomhousekids.com, pg 181

Lauber, Kim, Harry N Abrams Inc, 195 Broadway, 9th fl, New York, NY 10007 *Tel:* 212-206-7715 *Toll Free Tel:* 800-345-1359 *Fax:* 212-519-1210 *E-mail:* abrams@abramsbooks.com *Web Site:* www.abramsbooks.com, pg 3

Lauer, Brett Fletcher, George Bogin Memorial Award, 15 Gramercy Park, New York, NY 10003 *Tel:* 212-254-9628 *Web Site:* poetrysociety.org/awards, pg 599

Lauer, Brett Fletcher, Alice Fay Di Castagnola Award, 15 Gramercy Park, New York, NY 10003 *Tel:* 212-254-9628 *Web Site:* poetrysociety.org/awards, pg 609

Lauer, Brett Fletcher, Norma Farber First Book Award, 15 Gramercy Park, New York, NY 10003 *Tel:* 212-254-9628 *Web Site:* poetrysociety.org/awards, pg 614

Lauer, Brett Fletcher, Four Quartets Prize, 15 Gramercy Park, New York, NY 10003 *Tel:* 212-254-9628 *Web Site:* poetrysociety.org/awards, pg 616

Lauer, Brett Fletcher, Frost Medal, 15 Gramercy Park, New York, NY 10003 *Tel:* 212-254-9628 *Web Site:* poetrysociety.org/awards, pg 617

Lauer, Brett Fletcher, Cecil Hemley Memorial Award, 15 Gramercy Park, New York, NY 10003 *Tel:* 212-254-9628 *Web Site:* poetrysociety.org/awards, pg 623

Lauer, Brett Fletcher, Louise Louis/Emily F Bourne Student Poetry Award, 15 Gramercy Park, New York, NY 10003 *Tel:* 212-254-9628 *Web Site:* poetrysociety.org/awards, pg 635

Lauer, Brett Fletcher, Lyric Poetry Award, 15 Gramercy Park, New York, NY 10003 *Tel:* 212-254-9628 *Web Site:* poetrysociety.org/awards, pg 636

Lauer, Brett Fletcher, Lucille Medwick Memorial Award, 15 Gramercy Park, New York, NY 10003 *Tel:* 212-254-9628 *Web Site:* poetrysociety.org/awards, pg 640

Lauer, Brett Fletcher, Poetry Society of America (PSA), 15 Gramercy Park, New York, NY 10003 *Tel:* 212-254-9628 *Web Site:* poetrysociety.org, pg 543

Lauer, Brett Fletcher, Shelley Memorial Award, 15 Gramercy Park, New York, NY 10003 *Tel:* 212-254-9628 *Web Site:* poetrysociety.org/awards, pg 667

Lauer, Brett Fletcher, William Carlos Williams Award, 15 Gramercy Park, New York, NY 10003 *Tel:* 212-254-9628 *Web Site:* poetrysociety.org/awards, pg 678

Lauer, Brett Fletcher, The Writer Magazine/Emily Dickinson Award, 15 Gramercy Park, New York, NY 10003 *Tel:* 212-254-9628 *Web Site:* poetrysociety.org/awards, pg 680

Lauer, Valerie, Hanser Publications LLC, 414 Walnut St, Suite 323, Cincinnati, OH 45202 *Toll Free Tel:* 800-950-8977; 888-558-2632 (orders) *E-mail:* info@hanserpublications.com *Web Site:* www.hanserpublications.com, pg 92

Laughlin, Phil, The MIT Press, One Rogers St, Cambridge, MA 02142 *Tel:* 617-253-5255 *Toll Free Tel:* 800-405-1619 (orders) *Fax:* 617-258-6779; 617-577-1545 (orders) *Web Site:* mitpress.mit.edu, pg 141

Lauletta, Juliana, Boyds Mills & Kane, 250 Park Ave, 7th fl, New York, NY 10177 *E-mail:* info@bmkbooks.com *Web Site:* www.boydsmillsandkane.com, pg 39

Laur, Mary, University of Chicago Press, 1427 E 60 St, Chicago, IL 60637-2954 *Tel:* 773-702-7700; 773-702-7600 *Toll Free Tel:* 800-621-2736 (orders) *Fax:* 773-702-9756; 773-660-2235 (orders); 773-702-2708 *E-mail:* custserv@press.uchicago.edu; marketing@press.uchicago.edu *Web Site:* www.press.uchicago.edu, pg 226

Laurell, David, The Jennifer DeChiara Literary Agency, 245 Park Ave, 39th fl, New York, NY 10167 *Tel:* 212-372-8989 *Web Site:* www.jdlit.com, pg 481

Lauria, Lisa, Simon & Schuster Children's Publishing, 1230 Avenue of the Americas, New York, NY 10020 *Tel:* 212-698-7000 *Web Site:* www.simonandschuster.com/kids; www.simonandschuster.com/teen; simonandschuster.net; simonandschuster.biz, pg 199

Lauterbach, Ellen, Marshall Cavendish Education, 99 White Plains Rd, Tarrytown, NY 10591-9001 *Tel:* 914-332-8888 *Toll Free Tel:* 800-821-9881 *Fax:* 914-332-1082 *E-mail:* mce@marshallcavendish.com; customerservice@marshallcavendish.com *Web Site:* www.mceducation.us, pg 133

Lauzon, Lauren, The Penguin Press, 375 Hudson St, New York, NY 10014 *Web Site:* thepenguinpress.com, pg 164

LaVela, Casey, University of Wisconsin Press, 728 State St, Suite 443, Madison, WI 53706-1418 *Tel:* 608-263-1110; 608-263-0668 (journal orders) *Toll Free Tel:* 800-621-2736 (book orders) *Fax:* 608-263-1173 *Toll Free Fax:* 800-621-2736 (book orders) *E-mail:* uwiscpress@uwpress.wisc.edu *Web Site:* uwpress.wisc.edu, pg 232

Laventhall, Don, Folio Literary Management, The Film Center Bldg, 630 Ninth Ave, Suite 1101, New York, NY 10036 *Tel:* 212-400-1494 *Fax:* 212-967-0977 *Web Site:* www.foliolit.com, pg 484

Lavery, Brittany, Harlequin Enterprises Ltd, Bay Adelaide Centre, East Tower, 22 Adelaide St W, 41st fl, Toronto, ON M5H 4E3, Canada *Tel:* 416-445-5860 *Toll Free Tel:* 888-432-4879; 800-370-5838 (ebook inquiries) *E-mail:* customerservice@harlequin.com *Web Site:* www.harlequin.com, pg 429

Lavoie, Michel, Les Editions Vents d'Ouest, 109, rue Wright, bureau 202, Gatineau, QC J8X 2G7, Canada *Tel:* 819-770-6377 *E-mail:* info@ventsdouest.ca *Web Site:* www.ventsdouest.ca, pg 425

Law, Elizabeth, Holiday House Publishing Inc, 50 Broad St, New York, NY 10004 *Tel:* 212-688-0085 *Fax:* 212-421-6134 *E-mail:* info@holidayhouse.com *Web Site:* www.holidayhouse.com, pg 101

Law, Larry, Great Lakes Independent Booksellers Association (GLIBA), 250 Woodstock Ave, Clarendon Hills, IL 60514 *Tel:* 630-841-8129 *Web Site:* www.gliba.org, pg 534

Law, Larry, Heartland Booksellers Award, 250 Woodstock Ave, Clarendon Hills, IL 60514 *Tel:* 630-841-8129 *Web Site:* www.gliba.org/heartland-booksellers-award.html, pg 622

Lawler, Caitlin, Sourcebooks LLC, 1935 Brookdale Rd, Suite 139, Naperville, IL 60563 *Tel:* 630-961-3900 *Toll Free Tel:* 800-432-7444 *Fax:* 630-961-2168 *E-mail:* info@sourcebooks.com; customersupport@sourcebooks.com *Web Site:* www.sourcebooks.com, pg 204

Lawler, Frank C, Lannan Foundation, 313 Read St, Santa Fe, NM 87501-2628 *Tel:* 505-986-8160 *E-mail:* info@lannan.org *Web Site:* lannan.org, pg 551

Lawler, Frank C, Lannan Literary Awards & Fellowships, 313 Read St, Santa Fe, NM 87501-2628 *Tel:* 505-986-8160 *E-mail:* info@lannan.org *Web Site:* lannan.org, pg 631

Lawler, Kelly, Sourcebooks LLC, 1935 Brookdale Rd, Suite 139, Naperville, IL 60563 *Tel:* 630-961-3900 *Toll Free Tel:* 800-432-7444 *Fax:* 630-961-2168 *E-mail:* info@sourcebooks.com; customersupport@sourcebooks.com *Web Site:* www.sourcebooks.com, pg 204

Lawrence, Eileen, Tom Doherty Associates, LLC, 120 Broadway, New York, NY 10271 *Tel:* 646-307-5511 *Toll Free Tel:* 800-455-0340 *Web Site:* us.macmillan.com/torforge, pg 66

Lawrence, Jessica, St Martin's Press, LLC, 120 Broadway, New York, NY 10271 *Tel:* 646-307-5151 *Web Site:* us.macmillan.com/smp, pg 191

Lawrence, Justin Paul, InterVarsity Press, 430 Plaza Dr, Westmont, IL 60559-1234 *Tel:* 630-734-4000 *Toll Free Tel:* 800-843-9487 *Fax:* 630-734-4200 *E-mail:* email@ivpress.com *Web Site:* www.ivpress.com, pg 112

Lawrence, Merloyd Ludington, Merloyd Lawrence Inc, 102 Chestnut St, Boston, MA 02108 *Tel:* 617-523-5895 *Fax:* 617-263-2749, pg 121

Lawrence, Michael, Orbis Books, PO Box 302, Maryknoll, NY 10545-0302 *Tel:* 914-941-7636 *Toll Free Tel:* 800-258-5838 (orders, Mon-Fri 8AM-4PM EST) *Fax:* 914-941-7005 *E-mail:* orbisbooks@maryknoll.org *Web Site:* orbisbooks.com, pg 156

Lawrence, Richard, Eaton Literary Associates Literary Awards, PO Box 49795, Sarasota, FL 34230-6795 *Tel:* 941-366-6589 *Fax:* 941-365-4679 *E-mail:* eatonlit@aol.com *Web Site:* www.eatonliterary.com, pg 611

Lawrence, Susannah, Akashic Books, 232 Third St, Suite A-115, Brooklyn, NY 11215 *Tel:* 718-643-9193 *Fax:* 718-643-9195 *E-mail:* info@akashicbooks.com *Web Site:* www.akashicbooks.com, pg 6

Lawrie, Colleen, Perseus Books, 1290 Avenue of the Americas, New York, NY 10104 *Tel:* 212-340-8100 *Toll Free Tel:* 800-343-4499 (cust serv) *Fax:* 212-340-8105 *Web Site:* www.perseusbooks.com, pg 167

Laws, Gordon, Lumina Datamatics Inc, 4 Collins Ave, Plymouth, MA 02360 *Tel:* 508-746-0300 *Fax:* 508-746-3233 *Web Site:* luminadatamatics.com, pg 467

Laws, Valerie, The Danuta Gleed Literary Award, 600-460 Richmond St W, Toronto, ON M5V 1Y1, Canada *Tel:* 416-703-8982 *Fax:* 416-504-9090 *E-mail:* info@writersunion.ca *Web Site:* www.writersunion.ca, pg 619

Laws, Valerie, Short Prose Competition for Developing Writers, 600-460 Richmond St W, Toronto, ON M5V 1Y1, Canada *Tel:* 416-703-8982 *Fax:* 416-504-9090 *E-mail:* info@writersunion.ca *Web Site:* www.writersunion.ca, pg 667

Laws, Valerie, The Writers' Union of Canada (TWUC), 600-460 Richmond St W, Toronto, ON M5V 1Y1, Canada *Tel:* 416-703-8982 *Fax:* 416-504-9090 *E-mail:* info@writersunion.ca *Web Site:* www.writersunion.ca, pg 549

Lawson, Alice, The Gersh Agency (TGA), 41 Madison Ave, 33rd fl, New York, NY 10010 *Tel:* 212-997-1818 *Web Site:* gershbooks.com, pg 486

Lawson, Mark, ECS Publishing Group, 1727 Larkin Williams Rd, Fenton, MO 63026 *Tel:* 636-305-0100 *Toll Free Tel:* 800-647-2117 *Web Site:* ecspublishing.com; www.facebook.com/ecspublishing, pg 69

Lawton, Caryn, Washington State University Press, Cooper Publications Bldg, 2300 Grimes Way, Pullman, WA 99164-5910 *Tel:* 509-335-7880 *Toll Free Tel:* 800-354-7360 (orders) *E-mail:* wsupress@wsu.edu *Web Site:* wsupress.wsu.edu, pg 237

Lawton, Wendy, Books & Such, 52 Mission Circle, Suite 122, PMB 170, Santa Rosa, CA 95409-5370 *Tel:* 707-538-4184 *Web Site:* booksandsuch.com, pg 477

Lax, Brian, Henry Holt and Company, LLC, 120 Broadway, 23rd fl, New York, NY 10271 *Tel:* 646-307-5151 *Toll Free Tel:* 888-330-8477 (orders) *Fax:* 646-307-5285 *Web Site:* www.henryholt.com, pg 102

Lee, Joe, McClelland & Stewart Ltd, 320 Front St W, Suite 1400, Toronto, ON M5V 3B6, Canada *Tel:* 416-364-4449 *Fax:* 416-598-7764 *E-mail:* customerservicescanada@penguinrandomhouse.com; publicity@ca.penguingroup.com *Web Site:* penguinrandomhouse.ca/imprints/mcclelland-stewart, pg 433

Lee, Ken, Michael Wiese Productions, 12400 Ventura Blvd, No 1111, Studio City, CA 91604 *Tel:* 818-379-8799 *Toll Free Tel:* 800-833-5738 (orders) *Fax:* 818-986-3408 *E-mail:* mwpsales@earthlink.net; fulfillment@portcity.com *Web Site:* www.mwp.com, pg 241

Lee, Kesha, Hurston/Wright Award for College Writers, 10 "G" St NE, Suite 600, Washington, DC 20002 *Tel:* 202-248-5051 *E-mail:* info@hurstonwright.org *Web Site:* www.hurstonwright.org, pg 625

Lee, Kesha, Hurston/Wright Legacy Awards, 10 "G" St NE, Suite 600, Washington, DC 20002 *Tel:* 202-248-5051 *E-mail:* info@hurstonwright.org *Web Site:* www.hurstonwright.org, pg 625

Lee, Kesha, Hurston/Wright Writers Week, 10 "G" St NE, Suite 600, Washington, DC 20002 *Tel:* 202-248-5051 *E-mail:* info@hurstonwright.org *Web Site:* www.hurstonwright.org, pg 575

Lee, Kesha, The Zora Neale Hurston/Richard Wright Foundation, 10 "G" St NE, Suite 600, Washington, DC 20002 *Tel:* 202-248-5051 *E-mail:* info@hurstonwright.org *Web Site:* www.hurstonwright.org, pg 551

Lee, Linda, Master Point Press, 214 Merton St, Suite 205, Toronto, ON M4S 1A6, Canada *Tel:* 647-956-4933 *E-mail:* info@masterpointpress.com *Web Site:* www.masterpointpress.com; www.ebooksbridge.com (ebook sales), pg 432

Lee, Lisa, Candied Plums, 7548 Ravenna Ave NE, Seattle, WA 98115 *E-mail:* candiedplums@gmail.com *Web Site:* www.candiedplums.com, pg 44

Lee, Lisa, Holiday House Publishing Inc, 50 Broad St, New York, NY 10004 *Tel:* 212-688-0085 *Fax:* 212-421-6134 *E-mail:* info@holidayhouse.com *Web Site:* www.holidayhouse.com, pg 101

Lee, Marie, The MIT Press, One Rogers St, Cambridge, MA 02142 *Tel:* 617-253-5255 *Toll Free Tel:* 800-405-1619 (orders) *Fax:* 617-258-6779; 617-577-1545 (orders) *Web Site:* mitpress.mit.edu, pg 141

Lee, Mark, Doubleday, c/o Penguin Random House Inc, 1745 Broadway, New York, NY 10019 *Tel:* 212-751-2600 *Fax:* 212-572-2662 (foreign rts) *E-mail:* ddaypub@randomhouse.com *Web Site:* knopfdoubleday.com, pg 66

Lee, Min, Hachette Book Group, 1290 Avenue of the Americas, New York, NY 10104 *Tel:* 212-364-1100 *Toll Free Tel:* 800-759-0190 (cust serv) *Fax:* 212-364-0933 (intl orders) *Toll Free Fax:* 800-286-9471 (cust serv) *Web Site:* www.hachettebookgroup.com, pg 90

Lee, Ray, Master Point Press, 214 Merton St, Suite 205, Toronto, ON M4S 1A6, Canada *Tel:* 647-956-4933 *E-mail:* info@masterpointpress.com *Web Site:* www.masterpointpress.com; www.ebooksbridge.com (ebook sales), pg 432

Lee, Ruby Rose, Henry Holt and Company, LLC, 120 Broadway, 23rd fl, New York, NY 10271 *Tel:* 646-307-5151 *Toll Free Tel:* 888-330-8477 (orders) *Fax:* 646-307-5285 *Web Site:* www.henryholt.com, pg 102

Lee, Sonia, William Saroyan International Prize for Writing, Admin, Saroyan Prize Committee, Stanford University Libraries, 557 Escondido Mall, Stanford, CA 94305-6004 *Tel:* 650-736-9538 *Web Site:* library.stanford.edu/saroyan, pg 664

Lee, Spenser, Farrar, Straus & Giroux, LLC, 175 Varick St, 9th fl, New York, NY 10014 *Tel:* 212-741-6900 *E-mail:* fsg.publicity@fsgbooks.com *Web Site:* us.macmillan.com/fsg.aspx, pg 76

Lee, Tiffany Tran, Asian American Writers' Workshop, 112 W 27 St, Suite 600, New York, NY 10001 *Tel:* 212-494-0061 *E-mail:* desk@aaww.org *Web Site:* aaww.org; facebook.com/AsianAmericanWritersWorkshop, pg 525

Lee, Young, Berghahn Books, 20 Jay St, Suite 512, Brooklyn, NY 11201 *Tel:* 212-233-6004 *Fax:* 212-233-6007 *E-mail:* info@berghahnbooks.com; salesus@berghahnbooks.com; editorial@journals.berghahnbooks.com *Web Site:* www.berghahnbooks.com, pg 32

Leep, Jennifer, Revell, PO Box 6287, Grand Rapids, MI 49516-6287 *Tel:* 616-676-9185 *Toll Free Tel:* 800-877-2665; 800-679-1957 *Fax:* 616-676-9573 *Web Site:* www.bakerpublishinggroup.com, pg 185

Lefebvre, Marie-Eve, Editions du CHU Sainte-Justine, 3175, chemin de la Cote-Sainte-Catherine, Montreal, QC H3T 1C5, Canada *Tel:* 514-345-4671 *Fax:* 514-345-4631 *E-mail:* edition.hsj@ssss.gouv.qc.ca *Web Site:* www.editions-chu-sainte-justine.org, pg 423

Lefebvre-Faucher, Valerie, Les Editions du Remue-Menage, La Maison Parent-Roback, 110 rue Sainte-Therese, bureau 303, Montreal, QC H2Y 1E6, Canada *Tel:* 514-876-0097 *Fax:* 514-876-7951 *E-mail:* info@editions-rm.ca *Web Site:* www.editions-rm.ca, pg 423

Leffmann, Laurel, Summertime Publications Inc, 4115 E Palo Verde Dr, Phoenix, AZ 85018 *E-mail:* summertime.publications@gmail.com *Web Site:* www.summertimepublications.com, pg 210

Lefkon, Wendy, Disney Press, 1101 Flower St, Glendale, CA 91201 *Web Site:* books.disney.com, pg 65

Lefkowitz, Jenna, Fairchild Books, 1385 Broadway, 5th fl, New York, NY 10018 *Tel:* 212-419-5300 *Toll Free Tel:* 800-932-4724; 888-330-8477 (orders) *Web Site:* bloomsbury.com/us/academic/fairchildbooks, pg 75

Legault, Claude, Guerin Editeur Ltee, 800, Blvd Industriel, bureau 200, St-Jean-sur-Richelieu, QC J3B 8G4, Canada *Tel:* 514-842-3481 *Fax:* 514-842-4923 *Web Site:* www.guerin-editeur.qc.ca, pg 428

Lehman, Michelle, National Association of Broadcasters (NAB), 1771 "N" St NW, Washington, DC 20036 *Tel:* 202-429-5300 *E-mail:* nab@nab.org *Web Site:* www.nab.org, pg 145, 538

Lehman, Susannah, The Optical Society (OSA), 2010 Massachusetts Ave NW, Washington, DC 20036-1023 *Tel:* 202-223-8130 *Toll Free Tel:* 800-766-4672 *E-mail:* custserv@osa.org *Web Site:* www.osa.org, pg 156

Lehr, Donald, The Betsy Nolan Literary Agency, 112 E 17 St, Suite 1W, New York, NY 10003 *Tel:* 212-967-8200 *Fax:* 212-967-7292 *E-mail:* dblehr@cs.com, pg 498

Lehrman, Maggie, Harry N Abrams Inc, 195 Broadway, 9th fl, New York, NY 10007 *Tel:* 212-206-7715 *Toll Free Tel:* 800-345-1359 *Fax:* 212-519-1210 *E-mail:* abrams@abramsbooks.com *Web Site:* www.abramsbooks.com, pg 3

Lehto, Bill, Polebridge Press, PO Box 346, Farmington, MN 55024 *Tel:* 651-200-2372 *E-mail:* orders@westarinstitute.org *Web Site:* www.westarinstitute.org, pg 172

Leibovitch, Earl, Fitzhenry & Whiteside Limited, 195 Allstate Pkwy, Markham, ON L3R 4T8, Canada *Tel:* 905-477-9700 *Toll Free Tel:* 800-387-9776 *Fax:* 905-477-2834 *Toll Free Fax:* 800-260-9777 *E-mail:* bookinfo@fitzhenry.ca; godwit@fitzhenry.ca *Web Site:* www.fitzhenry.ca, pg 426

Leichum, Laura, University of Chicago Press, 1427 E 60 St, Chicago, IL 60637-2954 *Tel:* 773-702-7700; 773-702-7600 *Toll Free Tel:* 800-621-2736 (orders) *Fax:* 773-702-9756; 773-660-2235 (orders); 773-702-2708 *E-mail:* custserv@press.uchicago.edu; marketing@press.uchicago.edu *Web Site:* www.press.uchicago.edu, pg 226

Leidich, Terri, WriteLife Publishing, 960 Oaktree Blvd, Christianburg, VA 24073 *E-mail:* writelife@boutiqueofqualitybooks.com *Web Site:* www.writelife.com; www.facebook.com/writelife, pg 246

Leifer, Jaime, Perseus Books, 1290 Avenue of the Americas, New York, NY 10104 *Tel:* 212-340-8100 *Toll Free Tel:* 800-343-4499 (cust serv) *Fax:* 212-340-8105 *Web Site:* www.perseusbooks.com, pg 167

Leinberger, Anna, Berrett-Koehler Publishers Inc, 1333 Broadway, Suite 1000, Oakland, CA 94612 *Tel:* 510-817-2277 *Fax:* 510-817-2278 *E-mail:* bkpub@bkpub.com *Web Site:* www.bkconnection.com, pg 32

LeJeune, Becky, Bond Literary Agency, 201 Milwaukee St, Suite 200, Denver, CO 80206 *Tel:* 303-781-9305 *E-mail:* queries@bondliteraryagency.com *Web Site:* bondliteraryagency.com, pg 476

Lellos, Stacy, Klutz, 524 Broadway, 5th fl, New York, NY 10012 *Tel:* 212-343-6360 *Toll Free Tel:* 800-737-4123 (cust serv) *E-mail:* sales@klutz.com (all sales inquires); marketing@klutz.com (all mktg inquiries); publicity@klutz.com (all publicity inquires) *Web Site:* www.klutz.com; store.scholastic.com, pg 117

Lellos, Stacy, Scholastic Trade Division, 557 Broadway, New York, NY 10012 *Tel:* 212-343-6100; 212-343-4685 (export sales) *Fax:* 212-343-4714 (export sales) *Web Site:* www.scholastic.com, pg 194

Lemay, Dominique, Editions Hurtubise, 1815, ave De Lorimier, Montreal, QC H2K 3W6, Canada *Tel:* 514-523-1523 *Toll Free Tel:* 800-361-1664 *Fax:* 514-523-9969 *Web Site:* www.editionshurtubise.com, pg 424

Lemay, Dominique, Editions MultiMondes, 1815, Avenue de Lorimier, Montreal, QC H2K 3W6, Canada *Tel:* 514-523-1523 *Toll Free Tel:* 800-361-1664 *Fax:* 514-523-9969 *Web Site:* www.multim.com, pg 424

Lemieux, Raymond, Editions MultiMondes, 1815, Avenue de Lorimier, Montreal, QC H2K 3W6, Canada *Tel:* 514-523-1523 *Toll Free Tel:* 800-361-1664 *Fax:* 514-523-9969 *Web Site:* www.multim.com, pg 424

Lemmons, Dr Thom, Texas A&M University Press, John H Lindsey Bldg, Lewis St, 4354 TAMU, College Station, TX 77843-4354 *Tel:* 979-845-1436 *Toll Free Tel:* 800-826-8911 (orders) *Fax:* 979-847-8752 *Toll Free Fax:* 888-617-2421 (orders) *E-mail:* bookorders@tamu.edu *Web Site:* www.tamupress.com, pg 215

Lemon, Carolyn, Ignatius Press, 1348 Tenth Ave, San Francisco, CA 94122-2304 *Toll Free Tel:* 800-651-1531 (orders); 888-615-3186 (cust serv) *Fax:* 415-387-0896 *E-mail:* info@ignatius.com *Web Site:* www.ignatius.com, pg 106

Lemon, Faith, Stone Pier Press, PO Box 170572, San Francisco, CA 94117 *Tel:* 415-484-2821 *E-mail:* hello@stonepierpress.org *Web Site:* www.stonepierpress.org, pg 209

Lencicki, Alex, Orbit, 1290 Avenue of the Americas, New York, NY 10104 *Tel:* 212-364-1100 *Toll Free Tel:* 800-759-0190 *Web Site:* www.orbitbooks.net, pg 156

Lengyel, Heather, Paul H Brookes Publishing Co Inc, PO Box 10624, Baltimore, MD 21285-0624 *Tel:* 410-337-9580 (outside US & CN) *Toll Free Tel:* 800-638-3775 (US & CN) *Fax:* 410-337-8539 *E-mail:* custserv@brookespublishing.com *Web Site:* www.brookespublishing.com, pg 42

Lenihan, Kelly, Artisan Bookworks, 921 S Third Ave, No 8, Sequim, WA 98382 *Tel:* 425-954-5277 *E-mail:* books@artisanbookworks.com *Web Site:* www.artisanbookworks.com, pg 21

Lennard, Jeff, Brethren Press, 1451 Dundee Ave, Elgin, IL 60120 *Tel:* 847-742-5100 *Toll Free Tel:* 800-323-8039 *Toll Free Fax:* 800-667-8188 *E-mail:* brethrenpress@brethren.org *Web Site:* www.brethrenpress.com, pg 40

Lennertz, Carl, Children's & Teen Choice Book Awards, 54 W 39 St, 14th fl, New York, NY 10018 *E-mail:* cbc.info@cbcbooks.org *Web Site:* everychildreader.net/choice, pg 604

Lennertz, Carl, The Children's Book Council (CBC), 54 W 39 St, 14th fl, New York, NY 10018 *Tel:* 212-966-1990 *E-mail:* cbc.info@cbcbooks.org *Web Site:* www.cbcbooks.org, pg 531

Leslie, Nathan, Hamilton Stone Editions, PO Box 43, Maplewood, NJ 07040 *Tel:* 973-378-8361 *E-mail:* hstone@hamiltonstone.org *Web Site:* www.hamiltonstone.org, pg 92

Lessne, Donald L, Frederick Fell Publishers Inc, 7519 LaPaz Blvd, Suite C303, Boca Raton, FL 33433 *Tel:* 954-925-5242 *E-mail:* fellpub@aol.com (admin only) *Web Site:* www.fellpub.com, pg 81

Lester, Liz, The University of Arkansas Press, McIlroy House, 105 N McIlroy Ave, Fayetteville, AR 72701 *Tel:* 479-575-7544 *E-mail:* info@uapress.com *Web Site:* www.uapress.com, pg 226

Letourneau, Helene, Association nationale des editeurs de livres, 2514, blvd Rosemont, Montreal, QC H1Y 1K4, Canada *Tel:* 514-273-8130 *Toll Free Tel:* 866-900-ANEL (900-2635) *E-mail:* info@anel.qc.ca *Web Site:* www.anel.qc.ca, pg 526

Lettice, Jenna, Random House Children's Books, 1745 Broadway, 10th fl, New York, NY 10019 *Tel:* 212-782-9000 *Web Site:* www.randomhousekids.com, pg 180

Leung, Mona, McGraw-Hill Higher Education, 1333 Burr Ridge Pkwy, Burr Ridge, IL 60527 *Tel:* 630-789-4000 *Toll Free Tel:* 800-338-3987 (cust serv) *Fax:* 614-755-5645 (cust serv) *Web Site:* www.mhhe.com, pg 135

Leurpecht, Dr Christian, Institute of Intergovernmental Relations, Queen's University, Robert Sutherland Hall, Rm 412, Kingston, ON K7L 3N6, Canada *Tel:* 613-533-2080 *Fax:* 613-533-6868 *E-mail:* iigr@queensu.ca *Web Site:* www.queensu.ca/iigr, pg 430

Levasseur, Stephanie, Sourcebooks LLC, 1935 Brookdale Rd, Suite 139, Naperville, IL 60563 *Tel:* 630-961-3900 *Toll Free Tel:* 800-432-7444 *Fax:* 630-961-2168 *E-mail:* info@sourcebooks.com; customersupport@sourcebooks.com *Web Site:* www.sourcebooks.com, pg 204

Levenstein, Maggie, Inter-University Consortium for Political & Social Research (ICPSR), 330 Packard St, Ann Arbor, MI 48104 *Tel:* 734-647-5000 *Fax:* 734-647-8200 *E-mail:* help@icpsr.umich.edu *Web Site:* www.icpsr.umich.edu, pg 110

Leventhal, Josh, Minnesota Historical Society Press, 345 Kellogg Blvd W, St Paul, MN 55102-1906 *Tel:* 651-259-3205 *Fax:* 651-297-1345 *E-mail:* info-mnhspress@mnhs.org *Web Site:* www.mnhs.org/mnhspress, pg 140

Leventhal, Philip, Columbia University Press, 61 W 62 St, New York, NY 10023 *Tel:* 212-459-0600 *Toll Free Tel:* 800-944-8648 *Fax:* 212-459-3678 *Web Site:* cup.columbia.edu, pg 55

Leverence, John, Television Academy, 5220 Lankershim Blvd, North Hollywood, CA 91601-3109 *Tel:* 818-754-2800 *Fax:* 818-761-2827 *Web Site:* www.emmys.com, pg 547

Leverton, Yossi, Hachai Publishing, 527 Empire Blvd, Brooklyn, NY 11225 *Tel:* 718-633-0100 *Fax:* 718-633-0103 *E-mail:* info@hachai.com *Web Site:* www.hachai.com, pg 90

Levesque, Brigit, Broquet Inc, 97-B, Montee des Bouleaux, St-Constant, QC J5A 1A9, Canada *Tel:* 450-638-3338 *Fax:* 450-638-4338 *E-mail:* info@broquet.qc.ca *Web Site:* www.broquet.qc.ca, pg 417

Levesque, Jennifer, Disney-Hyperion Books, 1101 Flower St, Glendale, CA 91201 *Web Site:* books.disney.com, pg 65

Levi, Katie, The Art Institute of Chicago, 111 S Michigan Ave, Chicago, IL 60603-6404 *Tel:* 312-443-3600; 312-443-3540 (pubns) *Fax:* 312-443-1334 (pubns) *Web Site:* www.artic.edu; www.artinstituteshop.org, pg 20

Levin, Janet, North Atlantic Books, 2526 Martin Luther King Jr Way, Berkeley, CA 94704 *Tel:* 510-549-4270 *Fax:* 510-549-4276 *Web Site:* www.northatlanticbooks.com, pg 151

Levin, Kendra, Simon & Schuster Children's Publishing, 1230 Avenue of the Americas, New York, NY 10020 *Tel:* 212-698-7000 *Web Site:* www.simonandschuster.com/kids; www.simonandschuster.com/teen; simonandschuster.net; simonandschuster.biz, pg 199

Levine, Deborah, The Jeff Herman Agency LLC, 29 Park St, Stockbridge, MA 01262 *Tel:* 413-298-0077 *E-mail:* submissions@jeffherman.com *Web Site:* www.jeffherman.com, pg 488

Levine, Ellen, Trident Media Group LLC, 41 Madison Ave, 36th fl, New York, NY 10010 *Tel:* 212-333-1511 *E-mail:* info@tridentmediagroup.com; press@tridentmediagroup.com *Web Site:* www.tridentmediagroup.com, pg 507

Levine, Jaime, Houghton Mifflin Harcourt Trade & Reference Division, 125 High St, Boston, MA 02110 *Tel:* 617-351-5000 *Web Site:* www.hmhco.com, pg 104

Levine, James, Levine|Greenberg|Rostan Literary Agency, 307 Seventh Ave, Suite 2407, New York, NY 10001 *Tel:* 212-337-0934 *Fax:* 212-337-0948 *Web Site:* lgrliterary.com, pg 493

Levine, Jeffrey, Dorset Prize, 60 Roberts Dr, Suite 308, North Adams, MA 01247 *Tel:* 413-664-9611 *Fax:* 413-664-9711 *E-mail:* info@tupelopress.org *Web Site:* www.tupelopress.org, pg 611

Levine, Jeffrey, Tupelo Press Berkshire Prize for a First or Second Book of Poetry, 60 Roberts Dr, Suite 308, North Adams, MA 01247 *Tel:* 413-664-9611 *Fax:* 413-664-9711 *E-mail:* info@tupelopress.org *Web Site:* www.tupelopress.org, pg 674

Levine, Jeffrey, Tupelo Press Inc, 60 Roberts Dr, Suite 308, North Adams, MA 01247 *Tel:* 413-664-9611 *Fax:* 413-664-9711 *E-mail:* info@tupelopress.org *Web Site:* www.tupelopress.org, pg 222

Levine, Jeffrey, Tupelo Press Snowbound Series Chapbook Award, 60 Roberts Dr, Suite 308, North Adams, MA 01247 *Tel:* 413-664-9611 *Fax:* 413-664-9711 *E-mail:* info@tupelopress.org *Web Site:* www.tupelopress.org, pg 674

Levine, Karen, Getty Publications, 1200 Getty Center Dr, Suite 500, Los Angeles, CA 90049-1682 *Tel:* 310-440-7365 *Toll Free Tel:* 800-223-3431 (orders) *Fax:* 310-440-7758 *E-mail:* pubsinfo@getty.edu *Web Site:* www.getty.edu/publications, pg 85

Levine, Michael, Westwood Creative Artists Ltd, 138 Sussex Mews, Toronto, ON M5S-2K1, Canada *Tel:* 416-964-3302 *Fax:* 416-964-3302 *E-mail:* wca_office@wcaltd.com *Web Site:* www.wcaltd.com, pg 508

Levine, Nathalie, Princeton University Press, 41 William St, Princeton, NJ 08540-5237 *Tel:* 609-258-4900 *Fax:* 609-258-6305 *Web Site:* press.princeton.edu, pg 175

Levine, Ronn, Specialized Information Publishers Association (SIPA), 1090 Vermont Ave NW, 6th fl, Washington, DC 20005-4095 *Tel:* 202-289-7442 *Fax:* 202-289-7097 *Web Site:* www.siia.net/divisions/sipa-specialized-information-publishers-association, pg 547

Levinson, Diane, Chronicle Books, 680 Second St, San Francisco, CA 94107 *Tel:* 415-537-4200 *Toll Free Tel:* 800-759-0190 (cust serv) *Fax:* 415-537-4460 *Toll Free Fax:* 800-858-7787 (orders); 800-286-9471 (cust serv) *E-mail:* frontdesk@chroniclebooks.com *Web Site:* www.chroniclebooks.com, pg 52

Levinson, Meagan, Princeton University Press, 41 William St, Princeton, NJ 08540-5237 *Tel:* 609-258-4900 *Fax:* 609-258-6305 *Web Site:* press.princeton.edu, pg 174

Levinson, Wendy, Harvey Klinger Inc, 300 W 55 St, Suite 11V, New York, NY 10019 *Tel:* 212-581-7068 *Fax:* 212-315-3823 *E-mail:* queries@harveyklinger.com *Web Site:* www.harveyklinger.com, pg 491

Levitan, Jeanie, Bear & Co Inc, One Park St, Rochester, VT 05767 *Tel:* 802-767-3174 *Toll Free Tel:* 800-932-3277 *Fax:* 802-767-3726 *E-mail:* customerservice@InnerTraditions.com *Web Site:* InnerTraditions.com, pg 29

Levitan, Jeanie, Inner Traditions International Ltd, One Park St, Rochester, VT 05767 *Tel:* 802-767-3174 *Toll Free Tel:* 800-246-8648 *Fax:* 802-767-3726 *E-mail:* customerservice@InnerTraditions.com *Web Site:* www.InnerTraditions.com, pg 109

Levithan, David, Scholastic Trade Division, 557 Broadway, New York, NY 10012 *Tel:* 212-343-6100; 212-343-4685 (export sales) *Fax:* 212-343-4714 (export sales) *Web Site:* www.scholastic.com, pg 194

Levitt, Sarah, Aevitas Creative Management, 19 W 21 St, Suite 501, New York, NY 10010 *Tel:* 212-765-6900 *Web Site:* aevitascreative.com, pg 474

Levy, Hope, Counterpoint Press LLC, 2560 Ninth St, Suite 318, Berkeley, CA 94710 *Tel:* 510-704-0230 *Fax:* 510-704-0268 *E-mail:* info@counterpointpress.com *Web Site:* counterpointpress.com; softskull.com, pg 58

Levy, Jeanette, Bloomsbury Publishing Inc, 1385 Broadway, 5th fl, New York, NY 10018 *Tel:* 212-419-5300 *E-mail:* marketingusa@bloomsbury.com; adultpublicityusa@bloomsbury.com; askacademic@bloomsbury.com *Web Site:* www.bloomsbury.com, pg 36

Levy, Michael, Corporation for Public Broadcasting (CPB), 401 Ninth St NW, Washington, DC 20004-2129 *Tel:* 202-879-9600 *Web Site:* www.cpb.org, pg 531

Levy, Roanie, Access Copyright, The Canadian Copyright Licensing Agency, 56 Wellesley St W, Suite 401A, Toronto, ON M5S 2S3, Canada *Tel:* 416-868-1620 *Toll Free Tel:* 800-893-5777 *Fax:* 416-868-1621 *E-mail:* info@accesscopyright.ca *Web Site:* www.accesscopyright.ca, pg 521

Lew, Cheryl, Holiday House Publishing Inc, 50 Broad St, New York, NY 10004 *Tel:* 212-688-0085 *Fax:* 212-421-6134 *E-mail:* info@holidayhouse.com *Web Site:* www.holidayhouse.com, pg 101

Lew, Cindy, Fine Creative Media, Inc, 589 Eighth Ave, 6th fl, New York, NY 10018 *Tel:* 212-595-3500 *Fax:* 212-202-4195 *E-mail:* info@mjfbooks.com *Web Site:* www.mjfbooks.com, pg 78

Lew, Kim, Harry N Abrams Inc, 195 Broadway, 9th fl, New York, NY 10007 *Tel:* 212-206-7715 *Toll Free Tel:* 800-345-1359 *Fax:* 212-519-1210 *E-mail:* abrams@abramsbooks.com *Web Site:* www.abramsbooks.com, pg 3

Lew, Kim, St Martin's Press, LLC, 120 Broadway, New York, NY 10271 *Tel:* 646-307-5151 *Web Site:* us.macmillan.com/smp, pg 191

Lewandoski, Joyce, University of Texas Press, 3001 Lake Austin Blvd, 2.200, Austin, TX 78703 *Tel:* 512-471-7233 *Fax:* 512-232-7178 *E-mail:* utpress@uts.cc.utexas.edu; info@utpress.utexas.edu *Web Site:* utpress.utexas.edu, pg 216

Lewandowski, Lizzie, Sourcebooks LLC, 1935 Brookdale Rd, Suite 139, Naperville, IL 60563 *Tel:* 630-961-3900 *Toll Free Tel:* 800-432-7444 *Fax:* 630-961-2168 *E-mail:* info@sourcebooks.com; customersupport@sourcebooks.com *Web Site:* www.sourcebooks.com, pg 204

Lewin, Arianne, GP Putnam's Sons (Children's), 345 Hudson St, New York, NY 10014 *Tel:* 212-366-2000 *Fax:* 212-414-3393 *Web Site:* www.penguin.com/publishers/gpputnamssonsbooksforyoungread, pg 178

Lewis, Allison, Sourcebooks LLC, 1935 Brookdale Rd, Suite 139, Naperville, IL 60563 *Tel:* 630-961-3900 *Toll Free Tel:* 800-432-7444 *Fax:* 630-961-2168 *E-mail:* info@sourcebooks.com; customersupport@sourcebooks.com *Web Site:* www.sourcebooks.com, pg 204

Lewis, BiBi, Ethan Ellenberg Literary Agency, 155 Suffolk St, Suite 2R, New York, NY 10002 *Tel:* 212-431-4554 *E-mail:* agent@ethanellenberg.com *Web Site:* www.ethanellenberg.com, pg 483

Lewis, Brent, Harlequin Enterprises Ltd, Bay Adelaide Centre, East Tower, 22 Adelaide St W, 41st fl, Toronto, ON M5H 4E3, Canada *Tel:* 416-445-5860 *Toll Free Tel:* 888-432-4879; 800-370-5838 (ebook inquiries) *E-mail:* customerservice@harlequin.com *Web Site:* www.harlequin.com, pg 429

Lewis, Dave, Baker Books, 6030 E Fulton Rd, Ada, MI 49301 *Tel:* 616-676-9185 *Toll Free Tel:* 800-877-2665 (orders) *Fax:* 616-676-9573 *Toll Free Fax:* 800-398-3111 (orders) *E-mail:* media@bakerpublishinggroup.com; orders@bakerpublishinggroup.com; sales@bakerpublishinggroup.com *Web Site:* www.bakerpublishinggroup.com, pg 27

Lewis, Dave, Bethany House Publishers, 11400 Hampshire Ave S, Bloomington, MN 55438 *Tel:* 952-829-2500 *Toll Free Tel:* 800-877-2665 (orders) *Fax:* 952-829-2568 *Toll Free Fax:* 800-398-3111 (orders) *Web Site:* www.bethanyhouse.com; www.bakerpublishinggroup.com, pg 33

Lewis, David, Don Buchwald & Associates Inc, 10 E 44 St, New York, NY 10017 *Tel:* 212-867-1200 *Fax:* 212-867-2434 *E-mail:* info@buchwald.com *Web Site:* www.buchwald.com, pg 478

Lewis, Dottie, National Academies Press (NAP), Lockbox 285, 500 Fifth St NW, Washington, DC 20001 *Toll Free Tel:* 800-624-6242 *Fax:* 202-334-2451 (cust serv); 202-334-2793 (mktg dept) *E-mail:* customer_service@nap.edu *Web Site:* www.nap.edu, pg 145

Lewis, Jack, Hewitt Homeschooling Resources, 8117 N Division, Suite D, Spokane, WA 99208 *Toll Free Tel:* 800-348-1750 *Fax:* 360-835-8697 *E-mail:* sales@hewitthomeschooling.com *Web Site:* hewitthomeschooling.com, pg 98

Lewis, Jennifer, Gryphon House Inc, 6848 Leon's Way, Lewisville, NC 27023 *Toll Free Tel:* 800-638-0928 *Toll Free Fax:* 877-638-7576 *E-mail:* info@ghbooks.com *Web Site:* www.gryphonhouse.com, pg 90

Lewis, Katie, Princeton University Press, 41 William St, Princeton, NJ 08540-5237 *Tel:* 609-258-4900 *Fax:* 609-258-6305 *Web Site:* press.princeton.edu, pg 175

Lewis, Kitty, Brick Books, 22 Spencer Ave, Toronto, ON M6K 2J6, Canada *Tel:* 416-455-8385 *E-mail:* brenda@brickbooks.ca *Web Site:* www.brickbooks.ca, pg 417

Lewis, Kristen, Upper Access Inc, 87 Upper Access Rd, Hinesburg, VT 05461 *Tel:* 802-482-2988 *E-mail:* upperaccessbooks@gmail.com *Web Site:* www.upperaccess.com, pg 234

Lewis, Leigh Zarelli, Houghton Mifflin Harcourt, 125 High St, Boston, MA 02110 *Tel:* 617-351-5000 *Toll Free Tel:* 855-969-4642; 800-225-5425 (K-12 educ materials); 800-323-9540 (assessment materials); 877-219-1537 (SkillsTutor); 888-242-6747 (Innovation in Educ Group); 800-225-3362 (Trade & Ref Div) *Toll Free Fax:* 800-269-5232 *E-mail:* myhmhco@hmhco.com *Web Site:* www.hmhco.com, pg 103

Lewis, Marc, Presbyterian Publishing Corp (PPC), 100 Witherspoon St, Louisville, KY 40202 *Tel:* 502-569-5000 *Toll Free Tel:* 800-523-1631 (US only) *Fax:* 502-569-5113 *E-mail:* customerservice@presbypub.com *Web Site:* www.wjkbooks.com, pg 173

Lewis, Nora, College of Liberal & Professional Studies, University of Pennsylvania, 3440 Market St, Suite 100, Philadelphia, PA 19104-3335 *Tel:* 215-898-7326 *Fax:* 215-573-2053 *E-mail:* lps@sas.upenn.edu *Web Site:* www.sas.upenn.edu/lps, pg 581

Lewis, Stacey, City Lights Publishers, 261 Columbus Ave, San Francisco, CA 94133 *Tel:* 415-362-8193 *Fax:* 415-362-4921 *E-mail:* staff@citylights.com *Web Site:* www.citylights.com, pg 53

Lewis, Stephanie, Sourcebooks LLC, 1935 Brookdale Rd, Suite 139, Naperville, IL 60563 *Tel:* 630-961-3900 *Toll Free Tel:* 800-432-7444 *Fax:* 630-961-2168 *E-mail:* info@sourcebooks.com; customersupport@sourcebooks.com *Web Site:* www.sourcebooks.com, pg 204

Li, Dana, Counterpoint Press LLC, 2560 Ninth St, Suite 318, Berkeley, CA 94710 *Tel:* 510-704-0230 *Fax:* 510-704-0268 *E-mail:* info@counterpointpress.com *Web Site:* counterpointpress.com; softskull.com, pg 58

Li, Johanna, Simon & Schuster, 1230 Avenue of the Americas, New York, NY 10020 *Tel:* 212-698-7000 *Toll Free Tel:* 800-223-2348 (cust serv); 800-223-2336 (orders) *Toll Free Fax:* 800-943-9831 (orders) *Web Site:* www.simonandschuster.com, pg 198

Li, Karen, Groundwood Books, 128 Sterling Rd, Lower Level, Toronto, ON M6R 2B7, Canada *Tel:* 416-363-4343 *Fax:* 416-363-1017 *E-mail:* genmail@groundwoodbooks.com *Web Site:* www.houseofanansi.com, pg 428

Li, Stephanie, National Music Publishers' Association (NMPA), 975 "F" St NW, Suite 375, Washington, DC 20004 *Tel:* 202-393-6672 *E-mail:* members@nmpa.org *Web Site:* nmpa.org, pg 540

Liang, Elysia, Lark Crafts, 1166 Avenue of the Americas, 17th fl, New York, NY 10036 *Tel:* 212-532-7160 *E-mail:* editorial@sterlingpub.com; customerservice@sterlingpublishing.com *Web Site:* larkcrafts.com; www.facebook.com/LarkCrafts; www.sterlingpublishing.com, pg 120

Liao, Tiffany, Henry Holt and Company, LLC, 120 Broadway, 23rd fl, New York, NY 10271 *Tel:* 646-307-5151 *Toll Free Tel:* 888-330-8477 (orders) *Fax:* 646-307-5285 *Web Site:* www.henryholt.com, pg 102

Libby, Lewis, Hudson Institute, 1201 Pennsylvania Ave NW, Suite 400, Washington, DC 20004 *Tel:* 202-974-2400 *Fax:* 202-974-2410 *E-mail:* info@hudson.org *Web Site:* www.hudson.org, pg 104

Liebenow, Aisha, W D Hoard & Sons Co, 28 W Milwaukee Ave, Fort Atkinson, WI 53538 *Tel:* 920-563-5551 *Fax:* 920-563-7298 *E-mail:* hdbooks@hoards.com; editors@hoards.com *Web Site:* www.hoards.com, pg 100

Lieberman, Beth, The Editors Circle, 24 Holly Circle, Easthampton, MA 01027 *Tel:* 862-596-9709 *E-mail:* query@theeditorscircle.com *Web Site:* www.theeditorscircle.com, pg 463

Lieberman, Robert H, Robert Lieberman Agency, 475 Nelson Rd, Ithaca, NY 14850 *Tel:* 607-273-8801 *Web Site:* www.kewgardensmovie.com/CUPeople/users/rhl10, pg 493

Lieberman, Sarah, Simon & Schuster Audio, 1230 Avenue of the Americas, New York, NY 10020 *Web Site:* audio.simonandschuster.com, pg 199

Lieberman, Stefanie, Janklow & Nesbit Associates, 285 Madison Ave, 21st fl, New York, NY 10017 *Tel:* 212-421-1700 *Fax:* 212-355-1403 *E-mail:* info@janklow.com *Web Site:* www.janklowandnesbit.com, pg 490

Liebert, Mary Ann, Mary Ann Liebert Inc, 140 Huguenot St, 3rd fl, New Rochelle, NY 10801-5215 *Tel:* 914-740-2100 *Toll Free Tel:* 800-654-3237 *Fax:* 914-740-2101 *E-mail:* info@liebertpub.com *Web Site:* www.liebertonline.com, pg 124

Liebling, Sara, Disney-Hyperion Books, 1101 Flower St, Glendale, CA 91201 *Web Site:* books.disney.com, pg 65

Liebling, Sara, Disney Publishing Worldwide, 1101 Flower St, Glendale, CA 91201 *Web Site:* books.disney.com, pg 65

Liebmann, Nicholas, Saint Herman Press, 4430 Mushroom Lane, Platina, CA 96076 *Tel:* 530-352-4430 *Fax:* 530-352-4432 *E-mail:* stherman@stherman.com *Web Site:* www.sainthermanmonastery.com, pg 190

Liese, Debra, Princeton University Press, 41 William St, Princeton, NJ 08540-5237 *Tel:* 609-258-4900 *Fax:* 609-258-6305 *Web Site:* press.princeton.edu, pg 175

Liese, Donna, Princeton University Press, 41 William St, Princeton, NJ 08540-5237 *Tel:* 609-258-4900 *Fax:* 609-258-6305 *Web Site:* press.princeton.edu, pg 174

Ligon, Sam, Port Townsend Writers' Conference, 223 Battery Way, Port Townsend, WA 98368 *Tel:* 360-385-3102 *Toll Free Tel:* 800-733-3608 (ticket off) *Fax:* 360-385-2470 *E-mail:* info@centrum.org *Web Site:* centrum.org, pg 577

Likoff, Laurie, Bloom's Literary Criticism, 132 W 31 St, 17th fl, New York, NY 10001 *Toll Free Tel:* 800-322-8755 *Toll Free Fax:* 800-678-3633 *E-mail:* custserv@factsonfile.com *Web Site:* www.infobasepublishing.com, pg 35

Likoff, Laurie, Chelsea House, 132 W 31 St, 17th fl, New York, NY 10001 *Toll Free Tel:* 800-322-8755 *Toll Free Fax:* 800-678-3633 *E-mail:* custserv@factsonfile.com; info@infobase.com *Web Site:* www.infobasepublishing.com; www.infobase.com, pg 50

Likoff, Laurie, Facts On File, 132 W 31 St, 17th fl, New York, NY 10001 *Tel:* 212-967-8800 *Toll Free Tel:* 800-322-8755 *Toll Free Fax:* 800-678-3633 *E-mail:* custserv@factsonfile.com *Web Site:* infobasepublishing.com, pg 74

Likoff, Laurie, Ferguson Publishing, 132 W 31 St, 17th fl, New York, NY 10001 *Tel:* 212-967-8800 *Toll Free Tel:* 800-322-8755 *Toll Free Fax:* 800-678-3633 *E-mail:* custserv@factsonfile.com *Web Site:* infobasepublishing.com, pg 77

Lim, Jasmine, Andrews McMeel Publishing LLC, 1130 Walnut St, Kansas City, MO 64106-2109 *Toll Free Tel:* 800-851-8923; 800-943-9839 (cust serv) *Toll Free Fax:* 800-943-9831 (orders) *E-mail:* sales@amuniversal.com *Web Site:* www.andrewsmcmeel.com; publishing.andrewsmcmeel.com, pg 16

Lin, Jean, Bright Connections Media, A World Book Encyclopedia Company, 180 N LaSalle St, Suite 900, Chicago, IL 60601 *Tel:* 312-729-5800 *Web Site:* www.brightconnectionsmedia.com, pg 41

Lin, Joyce, Chronicle Books, 680 Second St, San Francisco, CA 94107 *Tel:* 415-537-4200 *Toll Free Tel:* 800-759-0190 (cust serv) *Fax:* 415-537-4460 *Toll Free Fax:* 800-858-7787 (orders); 800-286-9471 (cust serv) *E-mail:* frontdesk@chroniclebooks.com *Web Site:* www.chroniclebooks.com, pg 51, 52

Lin, Tricia, Random House Children's Books, 1745 Broadway, 10th fl, New York, NY 10019 *Tel:* 212-782-9000 *Web Site:* www.randomhousekids.com, pg 180

Lindeman, Steve, Creative Writing Day & Workshops, PO Box 801, Abingdon, VA 24212-0801 *Tel:* 276-623-5266 *Fax:* 276-676-3076 *E-mail:* info@vahighlandsfestival.org *Web Site:* vahighlandsfestival.org, pg 574

Lindemer, Christine R, Boston Road Communications, 227 Boston Rd, Groton, MA 01450-1959 *Tel:* 978-448-8133, pg 459

Linden, Brianna, Penguin Books, 375 Hudson St, New York, NY 10014 *Tel:* 212-366-2000 *E-mail:* penguinpublicity@us.penguingroup.com *Web Site:* www.penguinclassics.com; www.penguin.com, pg 163

Linden, Brianna, Viking, 375 Hudson St, New York, NY 10014 *Tel:* 212-366-2000 *Fax:* 212-243-6002 *Web Site:* www.penguin.com/publishers/vikingbooks, pg 236

Linden, Judy, Stonesong, 270 W 39 St, Suite 201, New York, NY 10018 *Tel:* 212-929-4600 *E-mail:* editors@stonesong.com *Web Site:* www.stonesong.com, pg 504

Lindensmith, Chris, Bitingduck Press LLC, 1262 Sunnyoaks Circle, Altadena, CA 91001 *Tel:* 626-507-8033 *E-mail:* notifications@bitingduckpress.com *Web Site:* bitingduckpress.com, pg 34

Lindensmith, Chris, Boson Books™, 1262 Sunnyoaks Circle, Altadena, CA 91001 *Tel:* 626-507-8033 *Fax:* 626-818-1842 *Web Site:* bitingduckpress.com, pg 38

Lindgren, Pat, Lindgren & Smith, 888C Eighth Ave, No 329, New York, NY 10019 *Tel:* 212-397-7330 *E-mail:* info@lindgrensmith.com *Web Site:* lindgrensmith.com, pg 512

Lindner, Stefanie, Harry N Abrams Inc, 195 Broadway, 9th fl, New York, NY 10007 *Tel:* 212-206-7715 *Toll Free Tel:* 800-345-1359 *Fax:* 212-519-1210 *E-mail:* abrams@abramsbooks.com *Web Site:* www.abramsbooks.com, pg 3

Lindquist, Evert A, Institute of Public Administration of Canada, 1075 Bay St, Suite 401, Toronto, ON M5S 2B1, Canada *Tel:* 416-924-8787 *Fax:* 416-924-4992 *E-mail:* ntl@ipac.ca *Web Site:* www.ipac.ca, pg 430

Lindquist, Gina, American Society of Civil Engineers (ASCE), 1801 Alexander Bell Dr, Reston, VA 20191-4400 *Tel:* 703-295-6300 *Toll Free Tel:* 800-548-ASCE (548-2723) *Toll Free Fax:* 866-913-6085 *E-mail:* ascelibrary@asce.org; pubsful@asce.org *Web Site:* www.asce.org, pg 14

Lindquist, Greta, Stanford University Press, 425 Broadway St, Redwood City, CA 94063-3126 *Tel:* 650-723-9434 *Fax:* 650-725-3457 *E-mail:* info@www.sup.org; publicity@www.sup.org; sales@www.sup.org *Web Site:* www.sup.org, pg 206

Lindsay, Diana, Sunbelt Publications Inc, 1250 Fayette St, El Cajon, CA 92020-1511 *Tel:* 619-258-4911 *Toll Free Tel:* 800-626-6579 (cust serv) *Fax:* 619-258-4916 *E-mail:* service@sunbeltpub.com; info@sunbeltpub.com *Web Site:* sunbeltpublications.com, pg 210

Lindsay, Elizabeth, Alfred A Knopf, c/o Penguin Random House Inc, 1745 Broadway, New York, NY 10019 *Tel:* 212-751-2600 *Fax:* 212-572-2662 (foreign rts) *Web Site:* knopfdoubleday.com, pg 118

Lindsay, Lowell, Sunbelt Publications Inc, 1250 Fayette St, El Cajon, CA 92020-1511 *Tel:* 619-258-4911 *Toll Free Tel:* 800-626-6579 (cust serv) *Fax:* 619-258-4916 *E-mail:* service@sunbeltpub.com; info@sunbeltpub.com *Web Site:* sunbeltpublications.com, pg 210

Lindsay, Nick, The MIT Press, One Rogers St, Cambridge, MA 02142 *Tel:* 617-253-5255 *Toll Free Tel:* 800-405-1619 (orders) *Fax:* 617-258-6779; 617-577-1545 (orders) *Web Site:* mitpress.mit.edu, pg 141

Lindsey, Chandler, Gaylord College of Journalism & Mass Communication, Professional Writing Program, c/o University of Oklahoma, 395 W Lindsey St, Rm 3000, Norman, OK 73019-0270 *Tel:* 405-325-2721 *Web Site:* www.ou.edu/gaylord; www.ou.edu/gaylord/undergraduate/professional-writing, pg 582

Ling, Alvina, Little, Brown Books for Young Readers, 1290 Avenue of the Americas, New York, NY 10104 *Tel:* 212-364-1100 *Toll Free Tel:* 800-759-0190 (cust serv) *Web Site:* www.hachettebookgroup.com, pg 126

Ling, Yuyi, Tumblehome Learning Inc, 201 Newbury St, Suite 201, Boston, MA 02116 *E-mail:* info@tumblehomelearning.com *Web Site:* www.tumblehomelearning.com, pg 221

Linick, Andrew S PhD, Copywriters' Council of America™ (CCA), CCA Bldg, 7 Putter Lane, Middle Island, NY 11953-1920 *Tel:* 631-924-3888; 631-775-6075 *Fax:* 631-924-8555, pg 461, 531

Linick, Andrew S PhD, Andrew S Linick PhD, The Copyologist®, Linick Bldg, 7 Putter Lane, Middle Island, NY 11953 *Tel:* 631-924-3888; 631-775-6075 *Fax:* 631-924-8555 *E-mail:* linickgroup@gmail.com *Web Site:* topmarketingadvisor.com, pg 466

Link, Kelly, Small Beer Press, 150 Pleasant St, No 306, Easthampton, MA 01027 *Tel:* 413-203-1636 *Fax:* 413-203-1636 *E-mail:* info@smallbeerpress.com *Web Site:* smallbeerpress.com, pg 201

Link, Maureen, Savvas Learning Co LLC, 15 E Midland Ave, Suite 502, Paramus, NJ 07652 *Toll Free Tel:* 800-848-9500 *Web Site:* www.savvas.com, pg 193

Linke, Megan, Mondo Publishing, 980 Avenue of the Americas, New York, NY 10018 *Tel:* 212-268-3560 *Toll Free Tel:* 888-88-MONDO (886-6636) *Toll Free Fax:* 888-532-4492 *E-mail:* info@mondopub.com *Web Site:* www.mondopub.com, pg 142

Linker, Damon, University of Pennsylvania Press, 3905 Spruce St, Philadelphia, PA 19104 *Tel:* 215-898-6261 *Fax:* 215-898-0404 *E-mail:* custserv@pobox.upenn.edu *Web Site:* www.pennpress.org, pg 230

Linn, Debra, Algonquin Books, 400 Silver Cedar Ct, Suite 300, Chapel Hill, NC 27514-1585 *Tel:* 919-967-0108 *Fax:* 919-933-0272 *E-mail:* inquiry@algonquin.com *Web Site:* www.workman.com/algonquin, pg 7

Liodice, Bob, Association of National Advertisers (ANA), 10 Grand Central, 155 E 44 St, New York, NY 10017 *Tel:* 212-697-5950 *Fax:* 212-302-6714 *Web Site:* www.ana.net, pg 527

Lionetti, Kim, BookEnds Literary Agency, 136 Long Hill Rd, Gillette, NJ 07933 *Web Site:* www.bookendsliterary.com, pg 476

Lipinski, Michelle, University of California Press, 155 Grand Ave, Suite 400, Oakland, CA 94612-3758 *Tel:* 510-883-8232 *Fax:* 510-836-8910 *E-mail:* generalmailbox@ucpress.edu *Web Site:* www.ucpress.edu, pg 226

Lipowski, Vicky, Begell House Inc Publishers, 50 North St, Danbury, CT 06810 *Tel:* 203-456-6161 *Fax:* 203-456-6167 *E-mail:* orders@begellhouse.com *Web Site:* www.begellhouse.com, pg 30

Lippe, James, Savvas Learning Co LLC, 15 E Midland Ave, Suite 502, Paramus, NJ 07652 *Toll Free Tel:* 800-848-9500 *Web Site:* www.savvas.com, pg 193

Lippel, Roz, Scribner, 1230 Avenue of the Americas, New York, NY 10020, pg 195

Lippenholz, Michael, Rowman & Littlefield, 4501 Forbes Blvd, Suite 200, Lanham, MD 20706 *Tel:* 301-459-3366 *Toll Free Tel:* 800-462-6420 (ext 3024, cust serv) *Fax:* 301-429-5748 *Web Site:* rowman.com, pg 188

Lippert, Jennifer, Princeton Architectural Press, 202 Warren St, Hudson, NY 12534 *Tel:* 518-671-6100 *Toll Free Tel:* 800-722-6657 (dist); 800-759-0190 (sales) *E-mail:* sales@papress.com *Web Site:* www.papress.com, pg 174

Lippert, Kevin C, Princeton Architectural Press, 202 Warren St, Hudson, NY 12534 *Tel:* 518-671-6100 *Toll Free Tel:* 800-722-6657 (dist); 800-759-0190 (sales) *E-mail:* sales@papress.com *Web Site:* www.papress.com, pg 174

Lippert, Megan, Hilton Publishing Co, 1630 45 St, Suite B101, Munster, IN 46321 *Tel:* 219-922-4868 *Fax:* 219-924-6811 *E-mail:* info@hiltonpub.com *Web Site:* www.hiltonpub.com, pg 99

Lippincott, Will, Aevitas Creative Management, 19 W 21 St, Suite 501, New York, NY 10010 *Tel:* 212-765-6900 *Web Site:* aevitascreative.com, pg 474

Lipschultz, Margo, Penguin Group USA, A Penguin Random House Company, 375 Hudson St, New York, NY 10014 *Tel:* 212-366-2000 *Toll Free Tel:* 800-847-5515 (inside sales); 800-631-8571 (cust serv) *Fax:* 212-366-2666; 607-775-4829 (inside sales) *E-mail:* online@us.penguingroup.com *Web Site:* www.penguin.com, pg 163

Lipscombe, Trevor C, The Catholic University of America Press, 240 Leahy Hall, 620 Michigan Ave NE, Washington, DC 20064 *Tel:* 202-319-5052 *Toll Free Tel:* 800-537-5487 (orders only) *Fax:* 202-319-4985 *E-mail:* cua-press@cua.edu *Web Site:* cuapress.org, pg 46

Lipskar, Simon, Writers House, 21 W 26 St, New York, NY 10010 *Tel:* 212-685-2400 *Web Site:* www.writershouse.com, pg 508

Liss, Laurie, Sterling Lord Literistic Inc, 115 Broadway, Suite 1602, New York, NY 10006 *Tel:* 212-780-6050 *Fax:* 212-780-6095 *E-mail:* info@sll.com *Web Site:* www.sll.com, pg 504

Liss-Levinson, William PhD, Castle Connolly Medical Ltd, 42 W 24 St, 2nd fl, New York, NY 10010 *Tel:* 212-367-8400 *Fax:* 212-367-0964 *Web Site:* www.castleconnolly.com, pg 46

Litak, Marissa, The Mountaineers Books, 1001 SW Klickitat Way, Suite 201, Seattle, WA 98134 *Tel:* 206-223-6303 *Fax:* 206-223-6306 *E-mail:* mbooks@mountaineersbooks.org; customerservice@mountaineersbooks.org *Web Site:* www.mountaineersbooks.org, pg 143

Lite, Lori, Stress Free Kids®, 2561 Chimney Springs Dr, Marietta, GA 30062 *Tel:* 678-642-9555 *Toll Free Fax:* 866-302-2759 *E-mail:* media@stressfreekids.com *Web Site:* www.stressfreekids.com, pg 210

Lite, Rick, Stress Free Kids®, 2561 Chimney Springs Dr, Marietta, GA 30062 *Tel:* 678-642-9555 *Toll Free Fax:* 866-302-2759 *E-mail:* media@stressfreekids.com *Web Site:* www.stressfreekids.com, pg 210

Lithgow, Angie, Turner Publishing Co, 4507 Charlotte Ave, Suite 100, Nashville, TN 37209 *Tel:* 615-255-BOOK (255-2665) *Fax:* 615-255-5081 *E-mail:* marketing@turnerpublishing.com; submissions@turnerpublishing.com; editorial@turnerpublishing.com *Web Site:* www.turnerpublishing.com; www.facebook.com/turner.publishing, pg 222

Litman, David, Simon & Schuster, 1230 Avenue of the Americas, New York, NY 10020 *Tel:* 212-698-7000 *Toll Free Tel:* 800-223-2348 (cust serv); 800-223-2336 (orders) *Toll Free Fax:* 800-943-9831 (orders) *Web Site:* www.simonandschuster.com, pg 198

Litt, Neil, Princeton University Press, 41 William St, Princeton, NJ 08540-5237 *Tel:* 609-258-4900 *Fax:* 609-258-6305 *Web Site:* press.princeton.edu, pg 174

Littell, Amelie, St Martin's Press, LLC, 120 Broadway, New York, NY 10271 *Tel:* 646-307-5151 *Web Site:* us.macmillan.com/smp, pg 190

Little, Joseph R, American Literacy Council, 1441 Mariposa Ave, Boulder, CO 80302 *Tel:* 303-440-7385 *Web Site:* www.americanliteracy.com, pg 523

Little, Kathryn, Roaring Brook Press, 120 Broadway, New York, NY 10271 *Tel:* 646-307-5151 *Web Site:* us.macmillan.com/publishers/roaring-brook-press, pg 186

Little, Lena, Little, Brown and Company, 1290 Avenue of the Americas, New York, NY 10104 *Tel:* 212-364-1100 *Fax:* 212-364-0952 *E-mail:* firstname.lastname@hbgusa.com *Web Site:* www.littlebrown.com; www.hachettebookgroup.com, pg 126

Little, Stephen, University of Notre Dame Press, 310 Flanner Hall, Notre Dame, IN 46556 *Tel:* 574-631-6346 *Fax:* 574-631-8148 *E-mail:* undpress@nd.edu *Web Site:* www.undpress.nd.edu, pg 230

Littlefield, Alex, Houghton Mifflin Harcourt Trade & Reference Division, 125 High St, Boston, MA 02110 *Tel:* 617-351-5000 *Web Site:* www.hmhco.com, pg 104

Littlefield, Barb, Thorndike Press®, 10 Water St, Suite 310, Waterville, ME 04901 *Toll Free Tel:* 800-223-1244 (ext 4, cust serv/orders) *Toll Free Fax:* 800-558-4676 (orders) *E-mail:* gale.printorders@cengage.com; international@cengage.com (cust orders outside US & CN) *Web Site:* www.gale.com/thorndike, pg 217

Littlefield, Kyle, Texas A&M University Press, John H Lindsey Bldg, Lewis St, 4354 TAMU, College Station, TX 77843-4354 *Tel:* 979-845-1436 *Toll Free Tel:* 800-826-8911 (orders) *Fax:* 979-847-8752 *Toll Free Fax:* 888-617-2421 *E-mail:* bookorders@tamu.edu *Web Site:* www.tamupress.com, pg 215

Littler, Courtney, St Martin's Press, LLC, 120 Broadway, New York, NY 10271 *Tel:* 646-307-5151 *Web Site:* us.macmillan.com/smp, pg 190

Litwack, Lisa, Gallery Books, 1230 Avenue of the Americas, New York, NY 10020 *Toll Free Tel:* 800-456-6798 *Fax:* 212-698-7284 *E-mail:* consumer.customerservice@simonandschuster.com *Web Site:* www.simonandschuster.com, pg 83

Liu, Ingsu, W W Norton & Company Inc, 500 Fifth Ave, New York, NY 10110-0017 *Tel:* 212-354-5500 *Toll Free Tel:* 800-233-4830 (orders & cust serv) *Fax:* 212-869-0856 *Toll Free Fax:* 800-458-6515 *E-mail:* orders@wwnorton.com *Web Site:* wwnorton.com, pg 124

Liu, Kitty, Cornell University Press, Sage House, 512 E State St, Ithaca, NY 14850 *Tel:* 607-253-2338 *Fax:* 607-253-2374 *E-mail:* cupressinfo@cornell.edu; cupress-sales@cornell.edu *Web Site:* www.cornellpress.cornell.edu, pg 57

Liu, Newton, Bridge to Asia, 1505 Juanita Way, Berkeley, CA 94702-1103 *Tel:* 510-665-3998 *E-mail:* asianet@bridge.org *Web Site:* www.bridge.org, pg 551

Liu, Ruby, Penguin Random House Audio Publishing, 1745 Broadway, New York, NY 10019 *E-mail:* audio@penguinrandomhouse.com *Web Site:* www.penguinrandomhouseaudio.com, pg 164

Livingston, Pamela, Goosebottom Books, PO Box 150764, San Rafael, CA 94915-0764 *Tel:* 415-717-6300 *E-mail:* info@goosebottombooks.com *Web Site:* goosebottombooks.com, pg 87

Livingston, Susan, Penguin Random House LLC, 1745 Broadway, New York, NY 10019 *Tel:* 212-782-9000 *Toll Free Tel:* 800-726-0600 *Web Site:* www.penguinrandomhouse.com, pg 164

Lizzi, Marian, TarcherPerigee, 375 Hudson St, New York, NY 10014 *Tel:* 212-366-2000 *Fax:* 212-366-2643 *E-mail:* customerservice@penguinrandomhouse.com (cust serv); TarcherPerigeePublicity@penguinrandomhouse.com (media queries) *Web Site:* www.tarcherbooks.com; www.facebook.com/TarcherPerigee/; www.penguin.com/publishers/tarcherperigee, pg 213

Lloyd, Dennis, University of Wisconsin Press, 728 State St, Suite 443, Madison, WI 53706-1418 *Tel:* 608-263-1110; 608-263-0668 (journal orders) *Toll Free Tel:* 800-621-2736 (book orders) *Fax:* 608-263-1173 *Toll Free Fax:* 800-621-2736 (book orders) *E-mail:* uwiscpress@uwpress.wisc.edu *Web Site:* uwpress.wisc.edu, pg 232

Lloyd, Kate, Scribner, 1230 Avenue of the Americas, New York, NY 10020, pg 195

Lloyd, Kathryn, Texas A&M University Press, John H Lindsey Bldg, Lewis St, Suite 4, 4354 TAMU, College Station, TX 77843-4354 *Tel:* 979-845-1436 *Toll Free Tel:* 800-826-8911 (orders) *Fax:* 979-847-8752 *Toll Free Fax:* 888-617-2421 (orders) *E-mail:* bookorders@tamu.edu *Web Site:* www.tamupress.com, pg 216

Lloyd, Timothy, Opie Prize, Indiana University, Classroom-Off Bldg, 800 E Third St, Bloomington, IN 47405 *Tel:* 812-856-2379 *Fax:* 812-856-2483 *Web Site:* www.afsnet.org, pg 651

Lloyd-Sidle, Elena, Fons Vitae, 49 Mockingbird Valley Dr, Louisville, KY 40207-1366 *Tel:* 502-897-3641 *Fax:* 502-893-7373 *E-mail:* fonsvitaeky@aol.com *Web Site:* www.fonsvitae.com, pg 79

Lo Brutto, Patrick, Philip K Dick Award, PO Box 3447, Hoboken, NJ 07030 *Tel:* 201-876-2551 *Web Site:* www.philipkdickaward.org, pg 609

Lobdell, Jim, Balance Sports Publishing LLC, 195 Lucero Way, Portola Valley, CA 94028 *Tel:* 650-561-9586 *Fax:* 650-391-9850 *E-mail:* info@balancesportspublishing.com *Web Site:* www.balancesportspublishing.com, pg 27

Lochner, Wendy, Columbia University Press, 61 W 62 St, New York, NY 10023 *Tel:* 212-459-0600 *Toll Free Tel:* 800-944-8648 *Fax:* 212-459-3678 *Web Site:* cup.columbia.edu, pg 55

Lockard, Eric, Salina Bookshelf Inc, 1120 W University Ave, Suite 102, Flagstaff, AZ 86001 *Toll Free Tel:* 877-527-0070 *Fax:* 928-526-0386 *Web Site:* www.salinabookshelf.com, pg 191

Locke, Charlene, Davies Publishing Inc, 32 S Raymond Ave, Suites 4 & 5, Pasadena, CA 91105-1961 *Tel:* 626-792-3046 *Toll Free Tel:* 877-792-0005 *Fax:* 626-792-5308 *E-mail:* info@daviespublishing.com *Web Site:* daviespublishing.com, pg 62

Locker, Marilyn, Triumph Learning LLC, 80 Northwest Blvd, Nashua, NH 03063 *Toll Free Tel:* 800-225-5700 (cust serv) *E-mail:* customerservice.eps@schoolspecialty.com *Web Site:* eps.schoolspecialty.com/coach, pg 221

Lockhart, Brianna, Penguin Young Readers Group, 345 Hudson St, New York, NY 10014 *Tel:* 212-366-2000; 212-414-3553 *Fax:* 212-414-3340 *Web Site:* www.penguin.com/children, pg 165

Lockhart, Doug, Thomas Nelson, 501 Nelson Place, Nashville, TN 37214 *Tel:* 615-889-9000 *Toll Free Tel:* 800-251-4000 *Fax:* 615-902-1548 *Web Site:* www.thomasnelson.com, pg 217

Lockhart, Robert, University of Pennsylvania Press, 3905 Spruce St, Philadelphia, PA 19104 *Tel:* 215-898-6261 *Fax:* 215-898-0404 *E-mail:* custserv@pobox.upenn.edu *Web Site:* www.pennpress.org, pg 230

Lockley, Beth, Penguin Random House Canada, 320 Front St W, Suite 1400, Toronto, ON M5V 3B6, Canada *Tel:* 416-364-4449 *Toll Free Tel:* 888-523-9292 (cust serv) *Fax:* 416-598-7764 *Web Site:* www.penguinrandomhouse.ca, pg 436

Locks, Sueyun, Locks Art Publications/Locks Gallery, 600 Washington Sq S, Philadelphia, PA 19106 *Tel:* 215-629-1000 *E-mail:* info@locksgallery.com *Web Site:* www.locksgallery.com, pg 127

Lockwood, Karen, Syracuse University Press, 621 Skytop Rd, Suite 110, Syracuse, NY 13244-5290 *Tel:* 315-443-5534 *Toll Free Tel:* 800-365-8929 (cust serv) *Fax:* 315-443-5545 *E-mail:* supress@syr.edu *Web Site:* press.syr.edu, pg 212

Loder-Kiss, Katie, Amherst Media Inc, PO Box 538, Buffalo, NY 14213 *Tel:* 716-874-4450 *E-mail:* marketing@amherstmedia.com *Web Site:* www.amherstmedia.com, pg 15

Loe, Cheryl, University of Hawaii Press, 2840 Kolowalu St, Honolulu, HI 96822-1888 *Tel:* 808-956-8255 *Toll Free Tel:* 888-UHPRESS (847-7377) *Fax:* 808-988-6052 *Toll Free Fax:* 800-650-7811 *E-mail:* uhpbooks@hawaii.edu *Web Site:* www.uhpress.hawaii.edu, pg 227

Loeb, Sharon, Cengage Learning, 20 Channel Center St, Boston, MA 02210 *Tel:* 617-289-7700 *Toll Free Tel:* 800-354-9706 *Fax:* 617-289-7844 *E-mail:* esales@cengage.com *Web Site:* www.cengage.com, pg 47

Loedel, Daniel, Bloomsbury Publishing Inc, 1385 Broadway, 5th fl, New York, NY 10018 *Tel:* 212-419-5300 *E-mail:* marketingusa@bloomsbury.com; adultpublicityusa@bloomsbury.com; askacademic@bloomsbury.com *Web Site:* www.bloomsbury.com, pg 36

Loehnen, Ben, Avid Reader Press, 1230 Avenue of the Americas, New York, NY 10020 *Web Site:* avidreaderpress.com, pg 26

Loehr, Julie L, Michigan State University Press (MSU Press), Manly Miles Bldg, Suite 25, 1405 S Harrison Rd, East Lansing, MI 48823-5245 *Tel:* 517-355-9543 *Fax:* 517-432-2611 *Web Site:* msupress.org, pg 139

Loehr, Mallory, Random House Children's Books, 1745 Broadway, 10th fl, New York, NY 10019 *Tel:* 212-782-9000 *Web Site:* www.randomhousekids.com, pg 180

Loertscher, David V, Hi Willow Research & Publishing, 123 E Second Ave, Suite 1106, Salt Lake City, UT 84103 *Tel:* 801-755-1122 *E-mail:* lmcsourcesales@gmail.com *Web Site:* www.lmcsource.com; www.davidvl.org, pg 99

Loewen, Darleen, PrairieView Press, 625 Seventh St, Gretna, MB R0G 0V0, Canada *Tel:* 204-327-6543 *Toll Free Tel:* 800-477-7377 *Toll Free Fax:* 866-480-0253 *Web Site:* prairieviewpress.com, pg 437

Loff, Christina, Chronicle Books, 680 Second St, San Francisco, CA 94107 *Tel:* 415-537-4200 *Toll Free Tel:* 800-759-0190 (cust serv) *Fax:* 415-537-4460 *Toll Free Fax:* 800-858-7787 (orders); 800-286-9471 (cust serv) *E-mail:* frontdesk@chroniclebooks.com *Web Site:* www.chroniclebooks.com, pg 51

Loftus, Maria, Bear & Co Inc, One Park St, Rochester, VT 05767 *Tel:* 802-767-3174 *Toll Free Tel:* 800-932-3277 *Fax:* 802-767-3726 *E-mail:* customerservice@InnerTraditions.com *Web Site:* InnerTraditions.com, pg 29

Loftus, Maria, Inner Traditions International Ltd, One Park St, Rochester, VT 05767 *Tel:* 802-767-3174 *Toll Free Tel:* 800-246-8648 *Fax:* 802-767-3726 *E-mail:* customerservice@InnerTraditions.com *Web Site:* www.InnerTraditions.com, pg 109

Logan, Emily, Houghton Mifflin Harcourt, 125 High St, Boston, MA 02110 *Tel:* 617-351-5000 *Toll Free Tel:* 855-969-4642; 800-225-5425 (K-12 educ materials); 800-323-9540 (assessment materials); 877-219-1537 (SkillsTutor); 888-242-6747 (Innovation in Educ Group); 800-225-3362 (Trade & Ref Div) *Toll Free Fax:* 800-269-5232 *E-mail:* myhmhco@hmhco.com *Web Site:* www.hmhco.com, pg 103

Loggia, Wendy, Random House Children's Books, 1745 Broadway, 10th fl, New York, NY 10019 *Tel:* 212-782-9000 *Web Site:* www.randomhousekids.com, pg 180

Loh, Cindy, Bloomsbury Publishing Inc, 1385 Broadway, 5th fl, New York, NY 10018 *Tel:* 212-419-5300 *E-mail:* marketingusa@bloomsbury.com; adultpublicityusa@bloomsbury.com; askacademic@bloomsbury.com *Web Site:* www.bloomsbury.com, pg 35

Lohr, Lece, Highlights for Children Inc, 815 Church St, Honesdale, PA 18431 *Tel:* 570-253-1164 *Toll Free Tel:* 800-490-5111 *Fax:* 570-253-0179 *E-mail:* salesandmarketing@highlightspress.com *Web Site:* www.highlightspress.com; www.highlights.com; www.facebook.com/HighlightsforChildren, pg 99

Lohwater, Tiffany, American Association for the Advancement of Science (AAAS), 1200 New York Ave NW, Washington, DC 20005 *Tel:* 202-326-6400 *E-mail:* media@aaas.org *Web Site:* www.aaas.org, pg 522

Loiselle, Louise, Flammarion Quebec, 375 Ave Laurier W, Montreal, QC H2V 2K3, Canada *Tel:* 514-277-8807 *Fax:* 514-278-2085 *E-mail:* info@flammarion.qc.ca *Web Site:* www.flammarion.qc.ca, pg 426

Loja, Jen, Penguin Group USA, A Penguin Random House Company, 375 Hudson St, New York, NY 10014 *Tel:* 212-366-2000 *Toll Free Tel:* 800-847-5515 (inside sales); 800-631-8571 (cust serv) *Fax:* 212-366-2666; 607-775-4829 (inside sales) *E-mail:* online@us.penguingroup.com *Web Site:* www.penguin.com, pg 163

Loja, Jen, Penguin Young Readers Group, 345 Hudson St, New York, NY 10014 *Tel:* 212-366-2000; 212-414-3553 *Fax:* 212-414-3340 *Web Site:* www.penguin.com/children, pg 165

Lombardini, Kim, Philip G Spitzer Literary Agency Inc, 50 Talmage Farm Lane, East Hampton, NY 11937 *Tel:* 631-329-3650 *Fax:* 631-329-3651 *Web Site:* www.spitzeragency.com, pg 503

London, Essence, Indiana Review Fiction Prize, Ballantine Hall 529, 1020 E Kirkwood Ave, Bloomington, IN 47405 *Tel:* 812-855-3439 *E-mail:* inreview@indiana.edu *Web Site:* indianareview.org, pg 626

Lonesome, Kelly O'Connor, Tom Doherty Associates, LLC, 120 Broadway, New York, NY 10271 *Tel:* 646-307-5511 *Toll Free Tel:* 800-455-0340 *Web Site:* us.macmillan.com/torforge, pg 66

Long, Ben, Dancing Dakini Press, 77 Morning Sun Dr, Sedona, AZ 86336 *Tel:* 505-466-1887 *E-mail:* editor@dancingdakinipress.com *Web Site:* www.dancingdakinipress.com, pg 61

Long, Colton, Insight Editions, 800 "A" St, San Rafael, CA 94901 *Tel:* 415-526-1370 *Toll Free Tel:* 800-809-3792 *Toll Free Fax:* 866-509-0515 *E-mail:* info@insighteditions.com; marketing@insighteditions.com *Web Site:* insighteditions.com, pg 109

Long, Jennifer, Gallery Books, 1230 Avenue of the Americas, New York, NY 10020 *Toll Free Tel:* 800-456-6798 *Fax:* 212-698-7284 *E-mail:* consumer.customerservice@simonandschuster.com *Web Site:* www.simonandschuster.com, pg 83

Long, Karen R, The Anisfield-Wolf Book Awards, 1422 Euclid Ave, Suite 1300, Cleveland, OH 44115 *Tel:* 216-861-3810 *Fax:* 216-861-1729 *E-mail:* awinfo@clevefdn.org *Web Site:* www.anisfield-wolf.org; www.clevelandfoundation.org, pg 592

Long, Thayer, Association for PRINT Technologies (APTech), 1896 Preston White Dr, Reston, VA 20191 *Tel:* 703-264-7200 *Fax:* 703-620-0994 *E-mail:* aptech@aptech.org *Web Site:* www.printtechnologies.org, pg 525

Long, Thayer, Graphic Arts Education & Research Foundation (GAERF), 1899 Preston White Dr, Reston, VA 20191 *Tel:* 703-264-7200 *E-mail:* gaerf@npes.org *Web Site:* www.gaerf.org, pg 551

Longmeyer, Michael, Gallopade International Inc, 611 Hwy 74 S, Suite 2000, Peachtree City, GA 30269 *Tel:* 770-631-4222 *Toll Free Tel:* 800-536-2GET (536-2438) *Fax:* 770-631-4810 *Toll Free Fax:* 800-871-2979 *E-mail:* customerservice@gallopade.com *Web Site:* www.gallopade.com, pg 83

Longo, Edward, Recorded Books Inc, an RBmedia company, 270 Skipjack Rd, Prince Frederick, MD 20678 *Tel:* 410-535-5590 *Toll Free Tel:* 877-732-2898 *Fax:* 410-535-5499 *E-mail:* customerservice@recordedbooks.com *Web Site:* www.recordedbooks.com, pg 182

Lonie, Tonia, University Press of Mississippi, 3825 Ridgewood Rd, Jackson, MS 39211-6492 *Tel:* 601-432-6205 *Toll Free Tel:* 800-737-7788 (orders & cust serv) *Fax:* 601-432-6217 *E-mail:* press@mississippi.edu *Web Site:* www.upress.state.ms.us, pg 233

Loomis, Gloria, Watkins/Loomis Agency Inc, PO Box 20925, New York, NY 10025 *Tel:* 212-532-0080 *Fax:* 646-383-2449 *E-mail:* assistant@watkinsloomis.com *Web Site:* www.watkinsloomis.com, pg 508

Loomis, Michael J, Graphic World Publishing Services, 11687 Adie Rd, St Louis, MO 63043 *Tel:* 314-567-9854 *Fax:* 314-567-7178 *E-mail:* quote@gwinc.com *Web Site:* www.gwinc.com, pg 464

Loose, Emily, Words into Print, 208 Java St, 5th fl, Brooklyn, NY 11222 *E-mail:* query@wordsintoprint.org *Web Site:* wordsintoprint.org, pg 471

Loosvelt, Derek, Vault.com Inc, 132 W 31 St, 16th fl, New York, NY 10001 *Tel:* 212-366-4212 *Toll Free Tel:* 800-535-2074 *Fax:* 212-366-6117 (cust serv) *E-mail:* editors@vault.com; customerservice@vault.com *Web Site:* www.vault.com, pg 235

Loperfido, Olivia, Perseus Books, 1290 Avenue of the Americas, New York, NY 10104 *Tel:* 212-340-8100 *Toll Free Tel:* 800-343-4499 (cust serv) *Fax:* 212-340-8105 *Web Site:* www.perseusbooks.com, pg 167

Lopes, David, Gingko Press Inc, 1321 Fifth St, Berkeley, CA 94710 *Tel:* 510-898-1195 *Fax:* 510-898-1196 *E-mail:* books@gingkopress.com *Web Site:* www.gingkopress.com, pg 86

Lopez, Vanessa, Insight Editions, 800 "A" St, San Rafael, CA 94901 *Tel:* 415-526-1370 *Toll Free Tel:* 800-809-3792 *Toll Free Tel:* 866-509-0515 *E-mail:* info@insighteditions.com; marketing@insighteditions.com *Web Site:* insighteditions.com, pg 109

Lord, Devon, University of Louisiana at Lafayette Press, PO Box 43558, Lafayette, LA 70504-3558 *Tel:* 337-482-6027 *E-mail:* press.submissions@louisiana.edu *Web Site:* ulpress.org, pg 228

Lord, Jacklyn, Indiana University Press, Herman B Wells Library 350, 1320 E Tenth St, Bloomington, IN 47405-3907 *Tel:* 812-855-8817 *Toll Free Tel:* 800-842-6796 (orders only) *Fax:* 812-855-7931; 812-855-8507 *E-mail:* iupress@indiana.edu; iuporder@indiana.edu (orders) *Web Site:* www.iupress.indiana.edu, pg 108

Lord, Sterling, Sterling Lord Literistic Inc, 115 Broadway, Suite 1602, New York, NY 10006 *Tel:* 212-780-6050 *Fax:* 212-780-6095 *E-mail:* info@sll.com *Web Site:* www.sll.com, pg 504

Lord, Tayler, Princeton University Press, 41 William St, Princeton, NJ 08540-5237 *Tel:* 609-258-4900 *Fax:* 609-258-6305 *Web Site:* press.princeton.edu, pg 175

Lord, Wendi, David C Cook, 4050 Lee Vance Dr, Colorado Springs, CO 80918 *Tel:* 719-536-0100 *Toll Free Tel:* 800-708-5550; 800-323-7543 (orders & cust serv) *Toll Free Fax:* 800-430-0726 (cust serv) *Web Site:* www.davidccook.org, pg 56

Lore, Matthew, The Experiment, 220 E 23 St, Suite 600, New York, NY 10010-4658 *Tel:* 212-889-1659 *E-mail:* info@theexperimentpublishing.com *Web Site:* www.theexperimentpublishing.com, pg 74

Lorencz, Amy, Atlantic Provinces Library Association (APLA), Dalhouse University, Kenneth C Rowe Management Bldg, 6100 University Ave, Suite 4010, Halifax, NS B3H 4R2, Canada *Web Site:* www.apla.ca, pg 527

Lorentzen, Allison, Viking, 375 Hudson St, New York, NY 10014 *Tel:* 212-366-2000 *Fax:* 212-243-6002 *Web Site:* www.penguin.com/publishers/vikingbooks, pg 236

Lori, Jennifer, The Pacific Spirit Poetry Prize, University of British Columbia, Buch E462, 1866 Main Mall, Vancouver, BC V6T 1Z1, Canada *Tel:* 778-822-2514 *Fax:* 778-822-3616 *E-mail:* prismwritingcontest@gmail.com *Web Site:* www.prismmagazine.ca, pg 652

Lori, Jennifer, PRISM international Literary Non-Fiction Contest, University of British Columbia, Buch E462, 1866 Main Mall, Vancouver, BC V6T 1Z1, Canada *Tel:* 778-822-2514 *Fax:* 778-822-3616 *E-mail:* prismwritingcontest@gmail.com *Web Site:* www.prismmagazine.ca, pg 659

Lori, Jennifer, The Jacob Zilber Prize for Short Fiction, University of British Columbia, Buch E462, 1866 Main Mall, Vancouver, BC V6T 1Z1, Canada *Tel:* 778-822-2514 *Fax:* 778-822-3616 *E-mail:* prismwritingcontest@gmail.com *Web Site:* www.prismmagazine.ca, pg 681

Lorimer, James, James Lorimer & Co Ltd, Publishers, 117 Peter St, Suite 304, Toronto, ON M5V 0M3, Canada *Tel:* 416-362-4762 *Fax:* 416-362-3939 *Web Site:* www.lorimer.ca, pg 432

Lotis, Christopher, Yale Center for British Art, 1080 Chapel St, New Haven, CT 06510-2302 *Tel:* 203-432-8929 *Fax:* 203-432-1626 *E-mail:* ycba.publications@yale.edu *Web Site:* britishart.yale.edu, pg 246

Lotman, Lynda, A+ English LLC/Book-Editing.com/Book Editing Associates, PO Box 1369, Mansfield, TX 76063 *Tel:* 469-789-3030 *E-mail:* editingnetwork@gmail.com *Web Site:* www.editing-writing.com; www.book-editing.com; www.helpwithstatistics.com; www.apawriting.com; childrensbookeditors.com; www.christianeditorsnetwork.com; dissertationwriting.com; statisticstutors.com, pg 457

Lotowycz, Randall, Algonquin Books, 400 Silver Cedar Ct, Suite 300, Chapel Hill, NC 27514-1585 *Tel:* 919-967-0108 *Fax:* 919-933-0272 *E-mail:* inquiry@algonquin.com *Web Site:* www.workman.com/algonquin, pg 7

Lott, Peter, Lott Representatives Ltd, PO Box 3607, New York, NY 10163 *Tel:* 212-755-5737 *Web Site:* www.lottreps.com, pg 512

Lotto, Elizabeth, Gallery Books, 1230 Avenue of the Americas, New York, NY 10020 *Toll Free Tel:* 800-456-6798 *Fax:* 212-698-7284 *E-mail:* consumer.customerservice@simonandschuster.com *Web Site:* www.simonandschuster.com, pg 83

Lotz, Karen, Candlewick Press, 99 Dover St, Somerville, MA 02144-2825 *Tel:* 617-661-3330 *Fax:* 617-661-0565 *E-mail:* bigbear@candlewick.com; salesinfo@candlewick.com *Web Site:* www.candlewick.com, pg 44

Loughlin, Thomas G, American Society of Mechanical Engineers (ASME), 2 Park Ave, New York, NY 10016-5990 *Tel:* 212-591-7000 *Toll Free Tel:* 800-843-2763 (cust serv-US, CN & Mexico) *Fax:* 973-882-1717 (orders & inquiries) *E-mail:* customercare@asme.org *Web Site:* www.asme.org, pg 14

Loughran, Maggie, Gallery Books, 1230 Avenue of the Americas, New York, NY 10020 *Toll Free Tel:* 800-456-6798 *Fax:* 212-698-7284 *E-mail:* consumer.customerservice@simonandschuster.com *Web Site:* www.simonandschuster.com, pg 83

Loughrey, Mary, Looseleaf Law Publications Inc, 43-08 162 St, Flushing, NY 11358 *Tel:* 718-359-5559 *Toll Free Tel:* 800-647-5547 *Fax:* 718-539-0941 *E-mail:* info@looseleaflaw.com *Web Site:* www.looseleaflaw.com, pg 128

Loughrey, Michael L, Looseleaf Law Publications Inc, 43-08 162 St, Flushing, NY 11358 *Tel:* 718-359-5559 *Toll Free Tel:* 800-647-5547 *Fax:* 718-539-0941 *E-mail:* info@looseleaflaw.com *Web Site:* www.looseleaflaw.com, pg 128

Louie, Karen, Harlequin Enterprises Ltd, Bay Adelaide Centre, East Tower, 22 Adelaide St W, 41st fl, Toronto, ON M5H 4E3, Canada *Tel:* 416-445-5860 *Toll Free Tel:* 888-432-4879; 800-370-5838 (ebook inquiries) *E-mail:* customerservice@harlequin.com *Web Site:* www.harlequin.com, pg 429

Lourie, Dick, Hanging Loose Press, 231 Wyckoff St, Brooklyn, NY 11217 *Tel:* 347-529-4738 *Fax:* 347-227-8215 *E-mail:* print225@aol.com *Web Site:* www.hangingloosepress.com, pg 92

Lourie, Iven, Gateways Books & Tapes, PO Box 370, Nevada City, CA 95959 *Tel:* 530-271-2239 *Toll Free Tel:* 800-869-0658 *E-mail:* info@gatewaysbooksandtapes.com *Web Site:* www.gatewaysbooksandtapes.com; www.retrosf.com (Retro Science Fiction imprint), pg 83

Love, Jennifer J, Bibliographical Society of America, PO Box 1537, Lenox Hill Sta, New York, NY 10021-0043 *Tel:* 212-734-2500 *Fax:* 212-452-2710 *E-mail:* bsa@bibsocamer.org *Web Site:* www.bibsocamer.org, pg 528

Love, Robert, Square One Publishers Inc, 115 Herricks Rd, Garden City Park, NY 11040 *Tel:* 516-535-2010 *Toll Free Tel:* 877-900-BOOK (900-2665) *Fax:* 516-535-2014 *E-mail:* sq1publish@aol.com *Web Site:* www.squareonepublishers.com, pg 206

Lovelace, Mr Plumer, Notable Wisconsin Authors, 4610 S Biltmore Lane, Suite 100, Madison, WI 53718-2153 *Tel:* 608-245-3640 *Fax:* 608-245-3646 *Web Site:* wla.wisconsinlibraries.org, pg 649

Lovelace, Mr Plumer, WLA Literary Award, 4610 S Biltmore Lane, Suite 100, Madison, WI 53718-2153 *Tel:* 608-245-3640 *Fax:* 608-245-3646 *Web Site:* wla.wisconsinlibraries.org, pg 678

Lovell, Deborah, Taylor & Francis Inc, 530 Walnut St, Suite 850, Philadelphia, PA 19106 *Tel:* 215-625-8900 *Toll Free Tel:* 800-354-1420 *Fax:* 215-207-0050; 215-207-0046 (cust serv) *E-mail:* support@tandfonline.com *Web Site:* www.taylorandfrancis.com, pg 213

Lovett, Erin, W W Norton & Company Inc, 500 Fifth Ave, New York, NY 10110-0017 *Tel:* 212-354-5500 *Toll Free Tel:* 800-233-4830 (orders & cust serv) *Fax:* 212-869-0856 *Toll Free Fax:* 800-458-6515 *E-mail:* orders@wwnorton.com *Web Site:* wwnorton.com, pg 152

Lovig, Grant, Company's Coming Publishing Ltd, 87 E Pender St, Vancouver, BC V6A 1S9, Canada *Tel:* 780-450-6223 (orders & inquiries) *Toll Free Tel:* 800-661-9017 (CN); 800-518-3541 (US) *Fax:* 780-450-1857 *E-mail:* info@companyscoming.com *Web Site:* www.companyscoming.com, pg 420

Loving, Lindsey, News Media Alliance, 4401 N Fairfax Dr, Suite 300, Arlington, VA 22203 *Tel:* 571-366-1000 *E-mail:* info@newsmediaalliance.org *Web Site:* newsmediaalliance.org, pg 541

Low, Craig, Children's Book Press, 95 Madison Ave, Suite 1205, New York, NY 10016 *Tel:* 212-779-4400 *Fax:* 212-683-1894 *E-mail:* general@leeandlow.com; orders@leeandlow.com; sales@leeandlow.com *Web Site:* www.leeandlow.com, pg 50

Low, Craig, Lee & Low Books Inc, 95 Madison Ave, Suite 1205, New York, NY 10016 *Tel:* 212-779-4400 *Toll Free Tel:* 888-320-3190 (ext 28, orders only) *Fax:* 212-683-1894 (orders only); 212-532-6035 *E-mail:* general@leeandlow.com *Web Site:* www.leeandlow.com, pg 122

Low, Harriet, Houghton Mifflin Harcourt Trade & Reference Division, 125 High St, Boston, MA 02110 *Tel:* 617-351-5000 *Web Site:* www.hmhco.com, pg 104

Low, Jason, Lee & Low Books Inc, 95 Madison Ave, Suite 1205, New York, NY 10016 *Tel:* 212-779-4400 *Toll Free Tel:* 888-320-3190 (ext 28, orders only) *Fax:* 212-683-1894 (orders only); 212-532-6035 *E-mail:* general@leeandlow.com *Web Site:* www.leeandlow.com, pg 122

Low, Steven D, Parallax Press, 2236B Sixth St, Berkeley, CA 94710 *Tel:* 510-540-6411 *Toll Free Tel:* 800-863-5290 (orders) *Fax:* 510-981-1157 *Web Site:* www.parallax.org, pg 160

Lowe, Amy, Janet B McCabe Poetry Prize, 1041 N Taft Hill Rd, Fort Collins, CO 80521 Tel: 970-449-2726 E-mail: editor@ruminatemagazine.org Web Site: www.ruminatemagazine.com, pg 639

Lowe, Amy, William Van Dyke Short Story Prize, 1041 N Taft Hill Rd, Fort Collins, CO 80521 Tel: 970-449-2726 E-mail: editor@ruminatemagazine.org Web Site: www.ruminatemagazine.com, pg 675

Lowe, Amy, VanderMey Nonfiction Prize, 1041 N Taft Hill Rd, Fort Collins, CO 80521 Tel: 970-449-2726 E-mail: editor@ruminatemagazine.org Web Site: www.ruminatemagazine.com, pg 675

Lowe, Greg, Classical Academic Press, 515 S 32 St, Camp Hill, PA 17011 Tel: 717-730-0711 Toll Free Tel: 866-730-0711 Fax: 717-730-0721 Toll Free Fax: 866-730-0721 E-mail: info@classicalsubjects.com; orders@classicalsubjects.com Web Site: classicalacademicpress.com, pg 53

Lowe, Sandy, Bold Strokes Books Inc, 648 S Cambridge Rd, Bldg A, Johnsonville, NY 12094 Tel: 518-677-5127 E-mail: service@boldstrokesbooks.com Web Site: www.boldstrokesbooks.com, pg 37

Lowenstein, Barbara, Lowenstein Associates Inc, 115 E 23 St, 4th fl, New York, NY 10010 Tel: 212-206-1630 E-mail: assistant@bookhaven.com (queries, no attachments) Web Site: www.lowensteinassociates.com, pg 493

Lowenstein, Elizabeth, The Acheven Book Prize for Young Adult Fiction, c/o Regal House Publishing, 806 Oberlin Rd, No 12094, Raleigh, NC 27605 E-mail: info@regalhousepublishing.com Web Site: regalhousepublishing.com/the-acheven-book-prize-for-young-adult-fiction/, pg 589

Lowenstein, Elizabeth, Fitzroy Books, c/o Regal House Publishing, 806 Oberlin Rd, No 12094, Raleigh, NC 27605 E-mail: info@regalhousepublishing.com Web Site: fitzroybooks.com, pg 78

Lowenstein, Elizabeth, The Kraken Book Prize for Middle-Grade Fiction, c/o Regal House Publishing, 806 Oberlin Rd, No 12094, Raleigh, NC 27605 E-mail: info@regalhousepublishing.com Web Site: regalhousepublishing.com/the-kraken-book-award/, pg 630

Lowery, Andrea Bakewell, Pennsylvania Historical & Museum Commission, State Museum Bldg, 300 North St, Harrisburg, PA 17120-0053 Tel: 717-787-3362; 717-787-5526 (orders) E-mail: ra-shoppaheritage@pa.gov Web Site: www.phmc.pa.gov; www.shoppaheritage.com, pg 166

Lowes, Tara, Broadview Press, 280 Perry St, Unit 5, Peterborough, ON K9J 2J4, Canada Tel: 705-743-8990 Fax: 705-743-8353 E-mail: customerservice@broadviewpress.com Web Site: www.broadviewpress.com, pg 417

Lowman, Sarah, NASW Press, 750 First St NE, Suite 800, Washington, DC 20002 Tel: 202-408-8600 Fax: 203-336-8312 E-mail: press@naswdc.org Web Site: www.naswpress.org, pg 145

Lowry, Monica, BenBella Books Inc, 10300 N Central Expwy, Suite 400, Dallas, TX 75231 Tel: 214-750-3600 E-mail: feedback@benbellabooks.com Web Site: www.benbellabooks.com; www.smartpopbooks.com, pg 31

Lowry, Dr Samuel, Ambassador International, 411 University Ridge, Suite B14, Greenville, SC 29601 Tel: 864-751-4844 E-mail: info@emeraldhouse.com; publisher@emeraldhouse.com (ms submissions); sales@emeraldhouse.com (orders/order inquiries); media@emeraldhouse.com Web Site: ambassador-international.com; www.facebook.com/AmbassadorIntl; twitter.com/ambassadorintl, pg 8

Loyd, Lois, Reporters Committee for Freedom of the Press, 1156 15 St NW, Suite 1250, Washington, DC 20005-1779 Tel: 202-795-9300 Toll Free Tel: 800-336-4243 E-mail: info@rcfp.org Web Site: www.rcfp.org, pg 545

Loyd, Lynn, American Quilter's Society, 5801 Kentucky Dam Rd, Paducah, KY 42003-9323 Tel: 270-898-7903 Toll Free Tel: 800-626-5420 (orders) Fax: 270-898-1173 E-mail: orders@americanquilter.com Web Site: www.americanquilter.com, pg 14

Lozar, Paula, New Mexico Book Association (NMBA), 1219 Luisa St, Suite 1, Santa Fe, NM 87505 Tel: 505-660-6357 E-mail: admin@nmbook.org Web Site: www.nmbook.org, pg 541

Lubell, Lauren Grand, Chronicle Books, 680 Second St, San Francisco, CA 94107 Tel: 415-537-4200 Toll Free Tel: 800-759-0190 (cust serv) Fax: 415-537-4460 Toll Free Fax: 800-858-7787 (orders); 800-286-9471 (cust serv) E-mail: frontdesk@chroniclebooks.com Web Site: www.chroniclebooks.com, pg 52

Lucas, Becky, The Association for Women in Communications, 1717 E Republic Rd, Suite A, Springfield, MO 65804 Tel: 417-886-8606 Fax: 417-886-3685 E-mail: info@womcom.org Web Site: www.womcom.org, pg 573

Lucas, George, InkWell Management, 521 Fifth Ave, 26th fl, New York, NY 10175 Tel: 212-922-3500 Fax: 212-922-0535 E-mail: info@inkwellmanagement.com Web Site: inkwellmanagement.com, pg 489

Lucas, LaBruce M S, Southern Historical Press Inc, 375 W Broad St, Greenville, SC 29601 Tel: 864-233-2346 Toll Free Tel: 800-233-0152 E-mail: southernhistoricalpress@gmail.com Web Site: www.southernhistoricalpress.com, pg 205

Lucas, Paul, Janklow & Nesbit Associates, 285 Madison Ave, 21st fl, New York, NY 10017 Tel: 212-421-1700 Fax: 212-355-1403 E-mail: info@janklow.com Web Site: www.janklowandnesbit.com, pg 490

Lucchese, Iole, Scholastic Inc, 557 Broadway, New York, NY 10012 Tel: 212-343-6100 Toll Free Tel: 800-SCHOLASTIC (724-6527) Web Site: www.scholastic.com, pg 194

Lucero, Seyan, Western States Arts Federation, 1743 Wazee St, Suite 300, Denver, CO 80202 Tel: 303-629-1166 Toll Free Tel: 888-562-7232 Fax: 303-629-9717 E-mail: staff@westaf.org Web Site: www.westaf.org, pg 551

Luchars, Alex, Industrial Press Inc, 32 Haviland St, Suite 3, Norwalk, CT 06854 Tel: 203-956-5593 ext 0 (cust serv) Toll Free Tel: 888-528-7852 ext 0 (cust serv) Fax: 203-354-9391 (cust serv) E-mail: info@industrialpress.com (cust serv) Web Site: books.industrialpress.com; ebooks.industrialpress.com, pg 108

Luciano, Jeannie, W W Norton & Company Inc, 500 Fifth Ave, New York, NY 10110-0017 Tel: 212-354-5500 Toll Free Tel: 800-233-4830 (orders & cust serv) Fax: 212-869-0856 Toll Free Fax: 800-458-6515 E-mail: orders@wwnorton.com Web Site: wwnorton.com, pg 152

Ludlam, Kim, St Martin's Press, LLC, 120 Broadway, New York, NY 10271 Tel: 646-307-5151 Web Site: us.macmillan.com/smp, pg 190

Ludlow, Roberta, Random House Children's Books, 1745 Broadway, 10th fl, New York, NY 10019 Tel: 212-782-9000 Web Site: www.randomhousekids.com, pg 180

Ludwig, Rachel, Georges Borchardt Inc, 136 E 57 St, New York, NY 10022 Tel: 212-753-5785 E-mail: georges@gbagency.com Web Site: www.gbagency.com, pg 477

Ludwin, Corey, Referee Books, 2017 Lathrop Ave, Racine, WI 53405 Tel: 262-632-8855 Toll Free Tel: 800-733-6100 Fax: 262-632-5460 E-mail: customerservice@referee.com Web Site: www.referee.com, pg 183

Lueck, Tristan, little bee books, 251 Park Ave S, 12th fl, New York, NY 10010 Toll Free Tel: 844-321-0237 E-mail: info@littlebeebooks.com Web Site: littlebeebooks.com, pg 125

Luecker, Kristine, Association for Talent Development (ATD) Press, 1640 King St, Box 1443, Alexandria, VA 22313-1443 Tel: 703-683-8100 Toll Free Tel: 800-628-2783 Fax: 703-299-8723; 703-683-1523 (cust care) E-mail: customercare@td.org Web Site: www.astd.org; www.td.org, pg 23

Lugo, Ramon, University of Puerto Rico Press, Edificio La Editorial (level 2), Carr No 1, KM 12.0, Jardin Botanico Norte, San Juan, PR 00927 Tel: 787-250-

0435; 787-250-0550 Toll Free Tel: 877-338-7788 Fax: 787-753-9116 E-mail: info@laeditorialupr.com Web Site: www.laeditorialupr.com, pg 231

Luke, Michelle, Mason Crest Publishers, 450 Parkway Dr, Suite D, Broomall, PA 19008 Tel: 610-543-6200 Toll Free Tel: 866-MCP-BOOK (627-2665) Fax: 610-543-3878 Web Site: www.masoncrest.com, pg 133

Lukk, Howard, Society of Motion Picture & Television Engineers® (SMPTE®), 3 Barker Ave, 5th fl, White Plains, NY 10601 Tel: 914-761-1100 Fax: 914-761-3115 Web Site: www.smpte.org, pg 547

Lum, Robert, PRO-ED Inc, 8700 Shoal Creek Blvd, Austin, TX 78757-6897 Tel: 512-451-3246 Toll Free Tel: 800-897-3202 Fax: 512-451-8542 Toll Free Fax: 800-397-7633 E-mail: info@proedinc.com Web Site: www.proedinc.com, pg 175

Lum, Roxanne, Ignatius Press, 1348 Tenth Ave, San Francisco, CA 94122-2304 Toll Free Tel: 800-651-1531 (orders); 888-615-3186 (cust serv) Fax: 415-387-0896 E-mail: info@ignatius.com Web Site: www.ignatius.com, pg 106

Lumelsky, Irina, United Nations Publications, 300 E 42 St, 9th fl, New York, NY 10017 Tel: 703-661-1571 Fax: 703-996-1010 E-mail: publications@un.org Web Site: shop.un.org, pg 224

Lumsden, Michal, Storey Publishing LLC, 210 MASS MoCA Way, North Adams, MA 01247 Tel: 413-346-2100 Toll Free Tel: 800-441-5700 (orders); 800-827-7444 (cust serv) Fax: 413-346-2199 Toll Free Fax: 800-865-3429 (cust serv) E-mail: sales@storey.com; feedback@storey.com Web Site: www.storey.com, pg 209

Lumsden, Rick, Encyclopaedia Britannica Inc, 325 N La Salle St, Suite 200, Chicago, IL 60654 Tel: 312-347-7000 (all other countries) Toll Free Tel: 800-323-1229 (US & CN) Fax: 312-294-2104 E-mail: contact@eb.com Web Site: www.britannica.com, pg 72

Luna, Andrea, Police Executive Research Forum, 1120 Connecticut Ave NW, Suite 930, Washington, DC 20036 Tel: 202-466-7820 Web Site: www.policeforum.org, pg 172

Luna, Devin, Macmillan, 120 Broadway, 22nd fl, New York, NY 10271 Tel: 646-307-5151 E-mail: press.inquiries@macmillan.com Web Site: www.macmillan.com, pg 129

Lund, Tom, Llewellyn Publications, 2143 Wooddale Dr, Woodbury, MN 55125 Tel: 651-291-1970 Toll Free Tel: 800-843-6666 Fax: 651-291-1908 E-mail: publicity@llewellyn.com; customerservice@llewellyn.com Web Site: www.llewellyn.com, pg 127

Lunghi, Meghan, Merriam-Webster Inc, 47 Federal St, Springfield, MA 01102 Tel: 413-734-3134 Toll Free Tel: 800-828-1880 (orders & cust serv) Fax: 413-731-5979 (sales) E-mail: support@merriam-webster.com Web Site: www.merriam-webster.com, pg 138

Lunn, Jenny, American Geophysical Union (AGU), 2000 Florida Ave NW, Washington, DC 20009 Tel: 202-462-6900 Toll Free Tel: 800-966-2481 (North America) Fax: 202-328-0566 E-mail: service@agu.org (cust serv); earthspacescience@agu.org Web Site: www.agu.org, pg 11

Lunt, Dean, Islandport Press, 247 Portland St, Bldg C, Yarmouth, ME 04096 Tel: 207-846-3344 Fax: 207-619-9975 E-mail: info@islandportpress.com Web Site: www.islandportpress.com, pg 112

Lunzer, Bernard, The NewsGuild - CWA, 501 Third St NW, 6th fl, Washington, DC 20001-2797 Tel: 202-434-7177; 202-434-7162 (The Guild Reporter) Fax: 202-434-1472 E-mail: guild@cwa-union.org Web Site: www.newsguild.org, pg 541

Luongo, Rose, Brill Inc, 2 Liberty Sq, 11th fl, Boston, MA 02109 Tel: 617-263-2323 Toll Free Tel: 800-962-4406; 800-337-9255 (orders - USA & CN) Fax: 617-263-2324 E-mail: sales-us@brill.com Web Site: www.brill.com, pg 41

Lurie, David B, Japan-US Friendship Commission Translation Prize, Columbia University, 507 Kent Hall, MC3920, New York, NY 10027 *Tel:* 212-854-5036 *Fax:* 212-854-4019 *Web Site:* www.keenecenter.org, pg 628

Lurie, Stephanie Owens, Disney-Hyperion Books, 1101 Flower St, Glendale, CA 91201 *Web Site:* books. disney.com, pg 65

Lush, Janette, Penguin Group (Canada), 320 Front St W, Suite 1400, Toronto, ON M5V 3B6, Canada *Tel:* 416-364-4449 *Fax:* 416-598-7764 *E-mail:* customerservicescanada@ penguinrandomhouse.com; publicity@ca.penguingroup. com *Web Site:* penguinrandomhouse.ca/imprints/ penguin-canada, pg 436

Luther, Kay, Ave Maria Press, PO Box 428, Notre Dame, IN 46556 *Toll Free Tel:* 800-282-1865 *Toll Free Fax:* 800-282-5681 *E-mail:* avemariapress.1@ nd.edu *Web Site:* www.avemariapress.com, pg 26

Luttrell, Marsha, Mercer University Press, 368 Orange St, Macon, GA 31201 *Tel:* 478-301-2880 *Toll Free Tel:* 866-895-1472 *Fax:* 478-301-2585 *E-mail:* mupressorders@mercer.edu *Web Site:* www. mupress.org, pg 138

Lutz, Bryan, University Press of Florida, 2046 NE Waldo Rd, Suite 2100, Gainesville, FL 32609 *Tel:* 352-392-1351 *Toll Free Tel:* 800-226-3822 (orders only) *Fax:* 352-392-0590 *Toll Free Fax:* 800-680-1955 (orders only) *E-mail:* press@upress.ufl.edu; orders@ upress.ufl.edu *Web Site:* www.upf.com, pg 232

Lutz, Tom, LARB Books, 6671 Sunset Blvd, Suite 1521, Los Angeles, CA 90028 *Tel:* 323-952-3950 *E-mail:* larbbooks@lareviewofbooks.org *Web Site:* larbbooks.org, pg 120

Lutz, Tom, LARB/USC Publishing Workshop, 6671 Sunset Blvd, Suite 1521, Los Angeles, CA 90028 *E-mail:* publishingworkshop@lareviewofbooks.org *Web Site:* thepublishingworkshop.com, pg 576

Lutzy, Patrick, Cheneliere Education Inc, 5800, rue St Denis, bureau 900, Montreal, QC H2S 3L5, Canada *Tel:* 514-273-1066 *Toll Free Tel:* 800-565-5531 *Fax:* 514-276-0324 *Toll Free Fax:* 800-814-0324 *E-mail:* info@cheneliere.ca *Web Site:* www.cheneliere. ca, pg 420

Lutzy, Patrick, Gaetan Morin Editeur, 5800, rue St-Denis, bureau 900, Montreal, QC H2S 3L5, Canada *Tel:* 514-273-1066 *Toll Free Tel:* 800-565-5531 *Fax:* 514-276-0324 *Toll Free Fax:* 800-814-0324 *E-mail:* info@cheneliere.ca *Web Site:* www.cheneliere. ca, pg 427

Luvaas, William, Joy Harjo Poetry Award, PO Box 2414, Durango, CO 81302 *Tel:* 970-903-7914 *E-mail:* cutthroatmag@gmail.com *Web Site:* www. cutthroatmag.com, pg 622

Ly, Carol, Random House Children's Books, 1745 Broadway, 10th fl, New York, NY 10019 *Tel:* 212-782-9000 *Web Site:* www.randomhousekids.com, pg 181

Lykke, Kristina, Johns Hopkins University Press, 2715 N Charles St, Baltimore, MD 21218-4363 *Tel:* 410-516-6900; 410-516-6987 (journal orders outside US & CN) *Toll Free Tel:* 800-537-5487 (book orders & cust serv); 800-548-1784 (journal orders) *Fax:* 410-516-6968; 410-516-3866 (journal orders); 410-516-6998 (orders) *E-mail:* hfscustserv@press.jhu.edu (cust serv); jrnlcirc@press.jhu.edu (journal orders) *Web Site:* www.press.jhu.edu; muse.jhu.edu, pg 114

Lyman, Joe, Great Lakes Graphics Association, W232 N2950 Roundy Circle E, Pewaukee, WI 53072 *Tel:* 262-522-2210 *Toll Free Tel:* 855-522-2210 *Fax:* 262-522-2211 *E-mail:* admin@glga.info *Web Site:* glga.info, pg 534

Lynch, Amy, Midwest Travel Journalists Inc, 902 S Randall Rd, Suite C311, St Charles, IL 60174 *Toll Free Tel:* 888-551-8184 *Fax:* 847-622-8015 *E-mail:* admin@mtja.us *Web Site:* www.mtja.us, pg 537

Lynch, Catharine, GP Putnam's Sons (Hardcover), 375 Hudson St, New York, NY 10014 *Tel:* 212-366-2000 *Fax:* 212-366-2643 *E-mail:* online@ penguinputnam.com *Web Site:* www.penguin.com/ publishers/gpputnamssons, pg 178

Lynch, Chris, Simon & Schuster Audio, 1230 Avenue of the Americas, New York, NY 10020 *Web Site:* audio. simonandschuster.com, pg 199

Lynch, Chris, Simon & Schuster, Inc, 1230 Avenue of the Americas, New York, NY 10020 *Tel:* 212-698-7000 *Toll Free Tel:* 800-223-2336 (orders) *Fax:* 212-698-7007 *Toll Free Fax:* 800-943-9831 (orders) *E-mail:* firstname.lastname@simonandschuster.com; purchaseorders@simonandschuster.com (orders) *Web Site:* www.simonandschuster.com, pg 199

Lynch, Danielle, Soil Science Society of America (SSSA), 5585 Guilford Rd, Madison, WI 53711-5801 *Tel:* 608-273-8080 *Fax:* 608-273-2021 *Web Site:* www. soils.org, pg 203

Lynch, Jennifer, Society of Environmental Toxicology & Chemistry (SETAC), 229 S Baylen St, 2nd fl, Pensacola, FL 32502 *Tel:* 850-469-1500 *Toll Free Fax:* 888-296-4136 *E-mail:* setac@setac.org *Web Site:* www.setac.org, pg 202

Lynch, John (Jack) J Jr, Houghton Mifflin Harcourt, 125 High St, Boston, MA 02110 *Tel:* 617-351-5000 *Toll Free Tel:* 855-969-4642; 800-225-5425 (K-12 educ materials); 800-323-9540 (assessment materials); 877-219-1537 (SkillsTutor); 888-242-6747 (Innovation in Educ Group); 800-225-3362 (Trade & Ref Div) *Toll Free Fax:* 800-269-5232 *E-mail:* myhmhco@hmhco. com *Web Site:* www.hmhco.com, pg 103

Lynch, John (Jack) J Jr, Houghton Mifflin Harcourt Trade & Reference Division, 125 High St, Boston, MA 02110 *Tel:* 617-351-5000 *Web Site:* www.hmhco. com, pg 104

Lynch, Kelly, Workman Publishing Co Inc, 225 Varick St, 9th fl, New York, NY 10014-4381 *Tel:* 212-254-5900 *Toll Free Tel:* 800-722-7202 *Fax:* 212-254-8098 *E-mail:* info@workman.com; orders@workman.com *Web Site:* www.workman.com, pg 244

Lynch, Patrick, Oxford University Press USA, 198 Madison Ave, New York, NY 10016 *Toll Free Tel:* 800-451-7556 (orders); 800-445-9714 (cust serv) *Fax:* 919-677-1303 *E-mail:* custserv.us@oup.com *Web Site:* global.oup.com, pg 158

Lynell, James, Multicultural Publications Inc, 1939 Manchester Rd, Akron, OH 44314 *Tel:* 330-865-9578 *Fax:* 330-865-9578 *E-mail:* multiculturalpub@prodigy. net *Web Site:* www.multiculturalpub.net, pg 144

Lynley, Cason, Duke University Press, 905 W Main St, Suite 18B, Durham, NC 27701 *Tel:* 919-688-5134 *Toll Free Tel:* 888-651-0122 (US) *Fax:* 919-688-2615 *Toll Free Fax:* 888-651-0124 *E-mail:* orders@dukeupress. edu *Web Site:* www.dukepress.edu, pg 68

Lynn, Kira, Kane Miller Books, 4901 Morena Blvd, Suite 213, San Diego, CA 92117 *E-mail:* submissions@kanemiller.com; info@ kanemiller.com *Web Site:* www.kanemiller.com, pg 115

Lyon, Kevan, Marsal Lyon Literary Agency LLC, 665 San Rodolfo Dr, Suite 124, PMB 121, Solana Beach, CA 92075 *Tel:* 760-814-8507 *Web Site:* www. marsallyonliteraryagency.com, pg 494

Lyons, Brad, Chalice Press, 483 E Lockwood Ave, Suite 100, St Louis, MO 63119 *Tel:* 314-231-8500 *Toll Free Tel:* 800-366-3383 *Fax:* 314-231-8524; 770-280-4039 (orders) *E-mail:* customerservice@chalicepress.com *Web Site:* www.chalicepress.com, pg 48

Lyons, Jed, Rowman & Littlefield, 4501 Forbes Blvd, Suite 200, Lanham, MD 20706 *Tel:* 301-459-3366 *Toll Free Tel:* 800-462-6420 (ext 3024, cust serv) *Fax:* 301-429-5748 *Web Site:* rowman.com, pg 188

Lyons, Jonathan, Curtis Brown Ltd, 228 E 45 St, 3rd fl, New York, NY 10017 *Tel:* 212-473-5400 *Web Site:* www.curtisbrown.com, pg 478

Lyons, Kim, Jason Aronson Inc, 4501 Forbes Blvd, Suite 200, Lanham, MD 20706 *Tel:* 301-459-3366 *Toll Free Tel:* 800-462-6420 ext 3024 (cust serv) *Fax:* 301-429-5748 *Toll Free Fax:* 800-338-4550 (cust serv) *E-mail:* orders@rowman.com; customercare@rowman. com *Web Site:* www.rowman.com, pg 20

Lyons, Lisbeth A, PRINTING United Alliance, 10015 Main St, Fairfax, VA 22031-3489 *Tel:* 703-385-1335 *Toll Free Tel:* 888-385-3588 *Fax:* 703-273-0456; 703-691-7492 (membership) *E-mail:* assist@printing.org; info@printing.org *Web Site:* www.printing.org; www. sgia.org, pg 544

Lyons, Michael, Rowman & Littlefield, 4501 Forbes Blvd, Suite 200, Lanham, MD 20706 *Tel:* 301-459-3366 *Toll Free Tel:* 800-462-6420 (ext 3024, cust serv) *Fax:* 301-429-5748 *Web Site:* rowman.com, pg 188

Lyons, Michael, Tower Publishing Co, 650 Cape Rd, Standish, ME 04084 *Tel:* 207-642-5400 *Toll Free Tel:* 800-969-8693 *E-mail:* info@towerpub.com *Web Site:* www.towerpub.com, pg 219

Lyons, Mike, New City Press, 202 Comforter Blvd, Hyde Park, NY 12538 *Tel:* 845-229-0335 *Toll Free Tel:* 800-462-5980 (orders only) *Fax:* 845-229-0351 *E-mail:* info@newcitypress.com; orders@newcitypress. com *Web Site:* www.newcitypress.com, pg 148

Lyons, Nicole, Wayside Publishing, 2 Stonewood Dr, Freeport, ME 04032 *Toll Free Tel:* 888-302-2519 *E-mail:* info@waysidepublishing.com; support@ waysidepublishing.com *Web Site:* waysidepublishing. com, pg 238

Lyons, Tony, Arcade Publishing Inc, 307 W 36 St, 11th fl, New York, NY 10018 *Tel:* 212-643-6816 *Fax:* 212-643-6819 *E-mail:* info@skyhorsepublishing.com (subs & foreign rts) *Web Site:* www.arcadepub.com, pg 19

Lypen, Krestyna, Algonquin Books, 400 Silver Cedar Ct, Suite 300, Chapel Hill, NC 27514-1585 *Tel:* 919-967-0108 *Fax:* 919-933-0272 *E-mail:* inquiry@algonquin. com *Web Site:* www.workman.com/algonquin, pg 7

Lysaght, Em, Ladderbird Literary Agency, 45 Midland St, Worcester, MA 01602 *Tel:* 508-459-9590 *Web Site:* www.ladderbird.com, pg 492

Ma, Amy, Immedium, 535 Rockdale Dr, San Francisco, CA 94127 *Tel:* 415-452-8546 *Fax:* 360-937-6272 *E-mail:* orders@immedium.com; sales@immedium. com *Web Site:* www.immedium.com, pg 107

Ma, Cindy, House of Anansi Press Inc, 128 Sterling Rd, Lower Level, Toronto, ON M6R 2B7, Canada *Tel:* 416-363-4343 *Fax:* 416-363-1017 *E-mail:* customerservice@houseofanansi.com *Web Site:* www.houseofanansi.com, pg 429

Maaghul, Johanna, Waterside Productions Inc, 2055 Oxford Ave, Cardiff, CA 92007 *Tel:* 760-632-9190 *Fax:* 760-632-9295 *E-mail:* admin@waterside.com *Web Site:* www.waterside.com, pg 508

Maass, Donald, Donald Maass Literary Agency, 1000 Dean St, Suite 252, Brooklyn, NY 11238 *Tel:* 212-727-8383 *E-mail:* info@maassagency.com *Web Site:* www.maassagency.com, pg 493

Mabbot, J D, Histria Books, 7181 N Hualapai Way, Suite 130-86, Las Vegas, NV 89166 *Tel:* 561-299-0802 *E-mail:* info@histriabooks.com; orders@ histriabooks.com; rights@histriabooks.com *Web Site:* histriabooks.com, pg 100

Mabry, John R, The Apocryphile Press, 1700 Shattuck Ave, Suite 81, Berkeley, CA 94709 *Tel:* 510-290-4349 *E-mail:* apocryphile@me.com *Web Site:* www. apocryphilepress.com, pg 17

MacAleese, Michelle, House of Anansi Press Inc, 128 Sterling Rd, Lower Level, Toronto, ON M6R 2B7, Canada *Tel:* 416-363-4343 *Fax:* 416-363-1017 *E-mail:* customerservice@houseofanansi.com *Web Site:* www.houseofanansi.com, pg 429

Macbrien, Nathan, University of Wisconsin Press, 728 State St, Suite 443, Madison, WI 53706-1418 *Tel:* 608-263-1110; 608-263-0668 (journal orders) *Toll Free Tel:* 800-621-2736 (book orders) *Fax:* 608-263-1173 *Toll Free Fax:* 800-621-2736 (book orders) *E-mail:* uwiscpress@uwpress.wisc.edu *Web Site:* uwpress.wisc.edu, pg 232

Macca, Joe, Scholastic International, 557 Broadway, New York, NY 10012 *Tel:* 212-343-6100; 646-330-5288 (intl cust serv) *Toll Free Tel:* 800-SCHOLASTIC (724-6527) *Fax:* 646-837-7878 *E-mail:* international@ scholastic.com, pg 194

Maccarone, Grace, Holiday House Publishing Inc, 50 Broad St, New York, NY 10004 *Tel:* 212-688-0085 *Fax:* 212-421-6134 *E-mail:* info@holidayhouse.com *Web Site:* www.holidayhouse.com, pg 101

Macchiusi, Mary, Pembroke Publishers Ltd, 538 Hood Rd, Markham, ON L3R 3K9, Canada *Tel:* 905-477-0650 *Toll Free Tel:* 800-997-9807 *Fax:* 905-477-3691 *Toll Free Fax:* 800-339-5568 *Web Site:* www.pembrokepublishers.com, pg 436

Maccoby, Gina, Gina Maccoby Literary Agency, PO Box 60, Chappaqua, NY 10514-0060 *Tel:* 914-238-5630 *E-mail:* query@maccobylit.com *Web Site:* www.publishersmarketplace.com/members/GinaMaccoby, pg 494

MacColl, Pamela, Beacon Press, 24 Farnsworth St, Boston, MA 02210-1409 *Tel:* 617-742-2110 *Fax:* 617-723-3097; 617-742-2290 *Web Site:* www.beacon.org, pg 29

Maccoux, Taylor, Sourcebooks LLC, 1935 Brookdale Rd, Suite 139, Naperville, IL 60563 *Tel:* 630-961-3900 *Toll Free Tel:* 800-432-7444 *Fax:* 630-961-2168 *E-mail:* info@sourcebooks.com; customersupport@sourcebooks.com *Web Site:* www.sourcebooks.com, pg 204

MacDonald, Alphonse, National Academies Press (NAP), Lockbox 285, 500 Fifth St NW, Washington, DC 20001 *Toll Free Tel:* 800-624-6242 *Fax:* 202-334-2451 (cust serv); 202-334-2793 (mktg dept) *E-mail:* customer_service@nap.edu *Web Site:* www.nap.edu, pg 145

MacDonald, Brian A, National Braille Press, 88 Saint Stephen St, Boston, MA 02115-4312 *Tel:* 617-266-6160 *Toll Free Tel:* 800-548-7323 (cust serv); 888-965-8965 *Fax:* 617-437-0456 *E-mail:* contact@nbp.org *Web Site:* www.nbp.org, pg 145

MacDonald, Dougald, The American Alpine Club Press, 710 Tenth St, Suite 100, Golden, CO 80401 *Tel:* 303-384-0110 *Fax:* 303-384-0111 *E-mail:* info@americanalpineclub.org *Web Site:* americanalpineclub.org, pg 9

Macdonald, Jane, University of Chicago Press, 1427 E 60 St, Chicago, IL 60637-2954 *Tel:* 773-702-7700; 773-702-7600 *Toll Free Tel:* 800-621-2736 (orders) *Fax:* 773-702-9756; 773-660-2235 (orders); 773-702-2708 *E-mail:* custserv@press.uchicago.edu; marketing@press.uchicago.edu *Web Site:* www.press.uchicago.edu, pg 226

MacDonald, Leo, HarperCollins Canada Ltd, 2 Bloor St E, 20th fl, Toronto, ON M4W 1A8, Canada *Tel:* 416-975-9334 *Fax:* 416-975-5223 *E-mail:* hcorder@harpercollins.com *Web Site:* www.harpercollins.ca, pg 429

MacDonnell, Margo, Rocky Mountain Mineral Law Foundation, 9191 Sheridan Blvd, Suite 203, Westminster, CO 80031 *Tel:* 303-321-8100 *Fax:* 303-321-7657 *E-mail:* info@rmmlf.org *Web Site:* www.rmmlf.org, pg 186

MacFarlane, Fraser, One Act Play Depot, 618 Memorial Dr, PO Box 335, Spiritwood, SK S0J 2M0, Canada *E-mail:* plays@oneactplays.net; orders@oneactplays.net *Web Site:* oneactplays.net, pg 435

MacGregor, Rob, Crabtree Publishing Co Ltd, 616 Welland Ave, St Catharines, ON L2M 5V6, Canada *Tel:* 905-682-5221 *Toll Free Tel:* 800-387-7650 *Fax:* 905-682-7166 *Toll Free Fax:* 800-355-7166 *E-mail:* custserv@crabtreebooks.com; sales@crabtreebooks.com; orders@crabtreebooks.com *Web Site:* www.crabtreebooks.com, pg 421

MacGregor, Robert, Crabtree Publishing Co, 347 Fifth Ave, Suite 1402-145, New York, NY 10016 *Tel:* 212-496-5040 *Toll Free Tel:* 800-387-7650 *Toll Free Fax:* 800-355-7166 *E-mail:* custserv@crabtreebooks.com *Web Site:* www.crabtreebooks.com, pg 59

Mach, Jo Meserve, Finding My Way Books, 3512 SW Huntoon St, Topeka, KS 66604-1748 *Tel:* 785-273-6239 *E-mail:* findingmywaybooks@gmail.com *Web Site:* www.findingmywaybooks.net, pg 78

Machado, Sierra, Perseus Books, 1290 Avenue of the Americas, New York, NY 10104 *Tel:* 212-340-8100 *Toll Free Tel:* 800-343-4499 (cust serv) *Fax:* 212-340-8105 *Web Site:* www.perseusbooks.com, pg 167

Machat, Joshua, Aperture Books, 547 W 27 St, 4th fl, New York, NY 10001 *Tel:* 212-505-5555 *Toll Free Fax:* 888-623-6908 *E-mail:* customerservice@aperture.org *Web Site:* aperture.org, pg 17

Machinist, Alexandra, ICM Partners, 65 E 55 St, New York, NY 10022 *Tel:* 212-556-5600 *Web Site:* www.icmtalent.com, pg 489

MacIlwaine, Paula I, American Water Works Association (AWWA), 6666 W Quincy Ave, Denver, CO 80235-3098 *Tel:* 303-794-7711 *Toll Free Tel:* 800-926-7337 *E-mail:* service@awwa.org (cust serv) *Web Site:* www.awwa.org, pg 15

Macintosh, Adrienne, Harlequin Enterprises Ltd, Bay Adelaide Centre, East Tower, 22 Adelaide St W, 41st fl, Toronto, ON M5H 4E3, Canada *Toll Free Tel:* 888-432-4879; 800-370-5838 (ebook inquiries) *E-mail:* customerservice@harlequin.com *Web Site:* www.harlequin.com, pg 429

Macios, Laurin, George Bogin Memorial Award, 15 Gramercy Park, New York, NY 10003 *Tel:* 212-254-9628 *Web Site:* poetrysociety.org/awards, pg 599

Macios, Laurin, Alice Fay Di Castagnola Award, 15 Gramercy Park, New York, NY 10003 *Tel:* 212-254-9628 *Web Site:* poetrysociety.org/awards, pg 609

Macios, Laurin, Norma Farber First Book Award, 15 Gramercy Park, New York, NY 10003 *Tel:* 212-254-9628 *Web Site:* poetrysociety.org/awards, pg 614

Macios, Laurin, Cecil Hemley Memorial Award, 15 Gramercy Park, New York, NY 10003 *Tel:* 212-254-9628 *Web Site:* poetrysociety.org/awards, pg 623

Macios, Laurin, Louise Louis/Emily F Bourne Student Poetry Award, 15 Gramercy Park, New York, NY 10003 *Tel:* 212-254-9628 *Web Site:* poetrysociety.org/awards, pg 635

Macios, Laurin, Lyric Poetry Award, 15 Gramercy Park, New York, NY 10003 *Tel:* 212-254-9628 *Web Site:* poetrysociety.org/awards, pg 636

Macios, Laurin, Lucille Medwick Memorial Award, 15 Gramercy Park, New York, NY 10003 *Tel:* 212-254-9628 *Web Site:* poetrysociety.org/awards, pg 640

Macios, Laurin, William Carlos Williams Award, 15 Gramercy Park, New York, NY 10003 *Tel:* 212-254-9628 *Web Site:* poetrysociety.org/awards, pg 678

Macios, Laurin, The Writer Magazine/Emily Dickinson Award, 15 Gramercy Park, New York, NY 10003 *Tel:* 212-254-9628 *Web Site:* poetrysociety.org/awards, pg 680

MacIsaac, Tom, Recorded Books Inc, an RBmedia company, 270 Skipjack Rd, Prince Frederick, MD 20678 *Tel:* 410-535-5590 *Toll Free Tel:* 877-732-2898 *Fax:* 410-535-5499 *E-mail:* customerservice@recordedbooks.com *Web Site:* www.recordedbooks.com, pg 182

Mackay, Mary, The American Library Association (ALA), 225 N Michigan Ave, Suite 1300, Chicago, IL 60601 *Tel:* 312-944-6780 *Toll Free Tel:* 800-545-2433 *Fax:* 312-280-5275 *E-mail:* editionsmarketing@ala.org *Web Site:* www.alastore.ala.org, pg 12

MacKeen, Alison, Sterling Lord Literistic Inc, 115 Broadway, Suite 1602, New York, NY 10006 *Tel:* 212-780-6050 *Fax:* 212-780-6095 *E-mail:* info@sll.com *Web Site:* www.sll.com, pg 504

MacKenzie, Joanna, Nelson Literary Agency LLC, 1732 Wazee St, Suite 207, Denver, CO 80202-1284 *Tel:* 303-292-2805 *E-mail:* info@nelsonagency.com *Web Site:* www.nelsonagency.com, pg 497

Mackenzie, Leslie, Grey House Publishing Inc™, 4919 Rte 22, Amenia, NY 12501 *Tel:* 518-789-8700 *Toll Free Tel:* 800-562-2139 *Fax:* 518-789-0556 *E-mail:* books@greyhouse.com; customerservice@greyhouse.com *Web Site:* greyhouse.com, pg 89

Mackey, Zoe, Berrett-Koehler Publishers Inc, 1333 Broadway, Suite 1000, Oakland, CA 94612 *Tel:* 510-817-2277 *Fax:* 510-817-2278 *E-mail:* bkpub@bkpub.com *Web Site:* www.bkconnection.com, pg 32

Mackinnon, Margo, IODE Jean Throop Book Award, 9-45 Frid St, Hamilton, ON L8P 4M3, Canada *Tel:* 905-522-9537 *Fax:* 905-522-3637 *E-mail:* iodeontario@bellnet.ca *Web Site:* www.iodeontario.ca, pg 627

Macklem, Ann, University of British Columbia Press, 2029 West Mall, Vancouver, BC V6T 1Z2, Canada *Tel:* 604-822-5959 *Toll Free Tel:* 877-377-9378 *Fax:* 604-822-6083 *Toll Free Fax:* 800-668-0821 *E-mail:* frontdesk@ubcpress.ca *Web Site:* www.ubcpress.ca, pg 443

Macklem, Michael, Oberon Press, 145 Spruce St, Suite 205, Ottawa, ON K1R 6P1, Canada *Tel:* 613-238-3275 *Fax:* 613-238-3275 *E-mail:* oberon@sympatico.ca *Web Site:* www.oberonpress.ca, pg 435

Macklem, Nicholas, Oberon Press, 145 Spruce St, Suite 205, Ottawa, ON K1R 6P1, Canada *Tel:* 613-238-3275 *Fax:* 613-238-3275 *E-mail:* oberon@sympatico.ca *Web Site:* www.oberonpress.ca, pg 435

Mackwood, Robert, Seventh Avenue Literary Agency, 2052 124 St, South Surrey, BC V4A 9K3, Canada *Tel:* 604-538-7252 *Fax:* 604-538-7252 *E-mail:* info@seventhavenuelit.com *Web Site:* www.seventhavenuelit.com, pg 502

MacLachlan, Christina, Wildflower Press, c/o Oakbrook Press, 3301 S Valley Dr, Rapid City, SD 57703 *Tel:* 605-381-6385 *E-mail:* info@wildflowerpress.org *Web Site:* www.wildflowerpress.org, pg 241

Maclagan, Maral, Scholastic Canada Ltd, 604 King St W, Toronto, ON M5V 1E1, Canada *Tel:* 905-887-7323 *Toll Free Tel:* 800-268-3860 (CN) *Toll Free Fax:* 866-387-4944 *E-mail:* custserve@scholastic.ca *Web Site:* www.scholastic.ca, pg 439

MacLeod, Lauren E, Strothman Agency LLC, 63 E Ninth St, 10X, New York, NY 10003 *E-mail:* info@strothmanagency.com *Web Site:* www.strothmanagency.com, pg 505

MacLeod, Nancy, Short Prose Competition for Developing Writers, 600-460 Richmond St W, Toronto, ON M5V 1Y1, Canada *Tel:* 416-703-8982 *Fax:* 416-504-9090 *E-mail:* info@writersunion.ca *Web Site:* www.writersunion.ca, pg 667

MacLeod, Sam, HRD Press, 22 Amherst Rd, Amherst, MA 01002-9709 *Tel:* 413-253-3488 *Toll Free Tel:* 800-822-2801 *Fax:* 413-253-3490 *E-mail:* info@hrdpress.com; customerservice@hrdpress.com *Web Site:* www.hrdpress.com, pg 104

Macnair, Randal, Oolichan Books, PO Box 2278, Fernie, BC V0B 1M0, Canada *Tel:* 250-423-6113 *E-mail:* info@oolichan.com *Web Site:* www.oolichan.com, pg 435

MacNeil, Mary, The University of Virginia Press, PO Box 400318, Charlottesville, VA 22904-4318 *Tel:* 434-924-3468 (cust serv); 434-924-3469 (cust serv) *Toll Free Tel:* 800-831-3406 (orders) *Fax:* 434-982-2655 *Toll Free Fax:* 877-288-6400 *E-mail:* vapress@virginia.edu *Web Site:* www.upress.virginia.edu, pg 231

MacNevin, James, University of British Columbia Press, 2029 West Mall, Vancouver, BC V6T 1Z2, Canada *Tel:* 604-822-5959 *Toll Free Tel:* 877-377-9378 *Fax:* 604-822-6083 *Toll Free Fax:* 800-668-0821 *E-mail:* frontdesk@ubcpress.ca *Web Site:* www.ubcpress.ca, pg 443

Macris, Natalie, Solano Press Books, PO Box 773, Point Arena, CA 95468 *Tel:* 707-884-4508 *Toll Free Tel:* 800-931-9373 *Fax:* 707-884-4109 *E-mail:* spbooks@solano.com *Web Site:* www.solano.com, pg 203

Madan, Ashish, Aptara Inc, 2901 Telestar Ct, Suite 522, Falls Church, VA 22042 *Tel:* 703-352-0001 *E-mail:* moreinfo@aptaracorp.com *Web Site:* www.aptaracorp.com, pg 458

Madan, Neeti, Sterling Lord Literistic Inc, 115 Broadway, Suite 1602, New York, NY 10006 *Tel:* 212-780-6050 *Fax:* 212-780-6095 *E-mail:* info@sll.com *Web Site:* www.sll.com, pg 504

Madara, James L MD, American Medical Association, AMA Plaza, 330 N Wabash, Suite 39300, Chicago, IL 60611-5885 *Tel:* 312-464-5000 *Toll Free Tel:* 800-621-8335 *Web Site:* www.ama-assn.org, pg 12, 523

Madden, Kyla, McGill-Queen's University Press, 1010 Sherbrooke W, Suite 1720, Montreal, QC H3A 2R7, Canada *Tel:* 514-398-3750 *Fax:* 514-398-4333 *E-mail:* mqup@mqup.ca *Web Site:* www.mqup.ca, pg 433

Madden, Melanie, Diversion Books, 443 Park Ave S, Suite 1008, New York, NY 10016 *Tel:* 212-961-6390 *E-mail:* info@diversionbooks.com *Web Site:* www.diversionbooks.com, pg 65

Maddex, John, Ancient Faith Publishing, 2427 Bond St, University Park, IL 60484 *Tel:* 219-728-2216 *Toll Free Tel:* 800-967-7377 *Toll Free Fax:* 866-599-5208 *E-mail:* info@ancientfaith.com; orders@ancientfaith.com *Web Site:* www.ancientfaith.com/publishing, pg 16

Madhubuti, Haki R, Third World Press, 7822 S Dobson Ave, Chicago, IL 60619 *Tel:* 773-651-0700 *Fax:* 773-651-7286 *E-mail:* twpbooks@thirdworldpressfoundation.org *Web Site:* thirdworldpressfoundation.org, pg 217

Madonia, Nena, Dupree, Miller & Associates Inc, 4311 Oak Lawn Ave, Suite 650, Dallas, TX 75219 *Tel:* 214-559-2665 *Fax:* 214-559-7243 *E-mail:* editorial@dupreemiller.com *Web Site:* www.dupreemiller.com, pg 482

Maeshiro, Jesse, Portfolio, 375 Hudson St, New York, NY 10014 *Web Site:* www.penguin.com/meet/publishers/portfolio, pg 172

Mafchir, James, Sherman Asher Publishing, 126 Candelario St, Santa Fe, NM 87501 *Tel:* 505-988-7214 *E-mail:* westernedge@santa-fe.net *Web Site:* www.shermanasher.com; www.westernedgepress.com, pg 197

Mafchir, James, Western Edge Press, 126 Candelario St, Santa Fe, NM 87501 *Tel:* 505-988-7214 *E-mail:* westernedge@santa-fe.net *Web Site:* www.westernedgepress.com; www.shermanasher.com, pg 239

Maffei, Ms Dorian, Kimberley Cameron & Associates LLC, 1550 Tiburon Blvd, Suite 704, Tiburon, CA 94920 *Tel:* 415-789-9191 *Fax:* 415-789-9177 *Web Site:* www.kimberleycameron.com, pg 479

Magallanes, Anna, Columbia Books & Information Services (CBIS), 4340 East-West Hwy, Suite 300, Bethesda, MD 20814 *Tel:* 202-464-1662 *Fax:* 301-664-9600 *E-mail:* info@columbiabooks.com *Web Site:* www.columbiabooks.com; www.lobbyists.info; www.associationexecs.com, pg 55

Magill, Dr David, John Dos Passos Prize for Literature, Dept of English & Modern Languages, 201 High St, Farmville, VA 23909 *Tel:* 434-395-2155 *Fax:* 434-395-2145 *Web Site:* www.longwood.edu/english/dos-passos-prize, pg 611

Magnani, Enrico MA, Scribendi Inc, 405 Riverview Dr, Chatham, ON N7M 0N3, Canada *Tel:* 519-351-1626 (cust serv) *Fax:* 519-354-0192 *E-mail:* customerservice@scribendi.com *Web Site:* www.scribendi.com, pg 470

Magnone, Sophia Booth, The Feminist Press at The City University of New York, 365 Fifth Ave, Suite 5406, New York, NY 10016 *Tel:* 212-817-7915 *Fax:* 212-817-1593 *E-mail:* info@feministpress.org *Web Site:* www.feministpress.org, pg 77

Magnus, Mary H, Health Professions Press, 409 Washington Ave, Suite 500, Towson, MD 21204 *Tel:* 410-337-9585 *Toll Free Tel:* 888-337-8808 *Fax:* 410-337-8539 *Web Site:* www.healthprops.com, pg 97

Magnus, Dr Sandra, American Institute of Aeronautics & Astronautics (AIAA), 12700 Sunrise Valley Dr, Suite 200, Reston, VA 20191-5807 *Tel:* 703-264-7500 *Toll Free Tel:* 800-639-AIAA (639-2422) *Fax:* 703-264-7551 *E-mail:* custserv@aiaa.org *Web Site:* www.aiaa.org, pg 11

Magowan, Mark, The Vendome Press, 244 Fifth Ave, Suite 2043, New York, NY 10001 *Tel:* 212-737-1857 *E-mail:* info@vendomepress.com *Web Site:* www.vendomepress.com, pg 235

Magruder, Munro, New World Library, 14 Pamaron Way, Novato, CA 94949 *Tel:* 415-884-2100 *Toll Free Tel:* 800-227-3900 (ext 52, retail orders); 800-972-6657 *Fax:* 415-884-2199 *E-mail:* escort@newworldlibrary.com *Web Site:* www.newworldlibrary.com, pg 149

Maguire, Kasey, PEN Canada, 401 Richmond St W, Suite 258, Toronto, ON M5V 3A8, Canada *Tel:* 416-703-8448 *E-mail:* queries@pencanada.ca *Web Site:* www.pencanada.ca, pg 543

Mahajan, Vinod, Nataraj Books, 7967 Twist Lane, Springfield, VA 22153 *Tel:* 703-455-4996 *Fax:* 703-455-4001 *E-mail:* nataraj@erols.com; orders@natarajbooks.com; natarajbooks@gmail.com *Web Site:* www.natarajbooks.com, pg 145

Maharaj, Davan, Los Angeles Times Book Prizes, 2300 E Imperial Hwy, El Segundo, CA 90245 *Tel:* 213-237-5775 *Toll Free Tel:* 800-528-4637 (ext 75775) *Web Site:* www.latimesbookprizes.com, pg 635

Maher, Bess, Colorado Book Awards, 7935 E Prentice Ave, Suite 450, Greenwood Village, CO 80111 *Tel:* 303-894-7951 (ext 19) *Fax:* 303-864-9361 *E-mail:* info@coloradohumanities.org *Web Site:* www.coloradohumanities.org, pg 606

Maher, Sean, Chelsea Green Publishing Co, 85 N Main St, Suite 120, White River Junction, VT 05001 *Tel:* 802-295-6300 *Toll Free Tel:* 800-639-4099 (cust serv & orders) *Fax:* 802-295-6444 *E-mail:* customerservice@chelseagreen.com; editorial@chelseagreen.com; publicity@chelseagreen.com; rights@chelseagreen.com *Web Site:* www.chelseagreen.com, pg 49

Mahler, Cathy, The Edna Staebler Award for Creative Non-Fiction, Office of the Dean, Faculty of Arts, 75 University Ave W, Waterloo, ON N2L 3C5, Canada *Tel:* 519-884-1970 (ext 3361) *E-mail:* staebleraward@wlu.ca *Web Site:* wlu.ca/staebleraward, pg 670

Mahoney, Judy, Teach Me Tapes Inc, 10400 N Enterprise Dr, Mequon, WI 53092 *Toll Free Tel:* 800-456-4656 *E-mail:* marie@teachmetapes.com *Web Site:* www.teachmetapes.com, pg 214

Mahoney, Natasha, Management Sciences for Health, 200 Rivers Edge Dr, Medford, MA 02155 *Tel:* 617-250-9500 *Fax:* 617-250-9090 *E-mail:* bookstore@msh.org *Web Site:* www.msh.org, pg 130

Mahoney, Tyrrell, Chronicle Books, 680 Second St, San Francisco, CA 94107 *Tel:* 415-537-4200 *Toll Free Tel:* 800-759-0190 (cust serv) *Fax:* 415-537-4460 *Toll Free Fax:* 800-858-7787 (orders); 800-286-9471 (cust serv) *E-mail:* frontdesk@chroniclebooks.com *Web Site:* www.chroniclebooks.com, pg 51

Mahorter, Rosie, Bloomsbury Publishing Inc, 1385 Broadway, 5th fl, New York, NY 10018 *Tel:* 212-419-5300 *E-mail:* marketingusa@bloomsbury.com; adultpublicityusa@bloomsbury.com; askacademic@bloomsbury.com *Web Site:* www.bloomsbury.com, pg 36

Maier, Skip, Human Kinetics Inc, 1607 N Market St, Champaign, IL 61820 *Tel:* 217-351-5076 *Toll Free Tel:* 800-747-4457 *Fax:* 217-351-1549 (orders/cust serv) *E-mail:* info@hkusa.com *Web Site:* www.humankinetics.com, pg 105

Maille, Michel, Les Editions Fides, 7333 place des Roseraies, bureau 100, Anjou, QC H1M 2X6, Canada *Tel:* 514-745-4290 *Fax:* 514-745-4299 *E-mail:* editions@groupefides.com *Web Site:* www.editionsfides.com, pg 423

Maillet, Neal, Berrett-Koehler Publishers Inc, 1333 Broadway, Suite 1000, Oakland, CA 94612 *Tel:* 510-817-2277 *Fax:* 510-817-2278 *E-mail:* bkpub@bkpub.com *Web Site:* www.bkconnection.com, pg 32

Maines, Kevin Murphy, New Women's Voices Chapbook Competition, PO Box 1626, Georgetown, KY 40324 *Tel:* 502-603-0670 *E-mail:* finishingbooks@aol.com; flpbookstore@aol.com *Web Site:* www.finishinglinepress.com, pg 647

Maines, Kevin Murphy, Open Chapbook Competition, PO Box 1626, Georgetown, KY 40324 *Tel:* 502-603-0670 *E-mail:* finishingbooks@aol.com; flpbookstore@aol.com *Web Site:* www.finishinglinepress.com, pg 651

Maines, Leah, New Women's Voices Chapbook Competition, PO Box 1626, Georgetown, KY 40324 *Tel:* 502-603-0670 *E-mail:* finishingbooks@aol.com; flpbookstore@aol.com *Web Site:* www.finishinglinepress.com, pg 647

Maines, Leah, Open Chapbook Competition, PO Box 1626, Georgetown, KY 40324 *Tel:* 502-603-0670 *E-mail:* finishingbooks@aol.com; flpbookstore@aol.com *Web Site:* www.finishinglinepress.com, pg 651

Mainhardt, Ricia, RMA, 85 Lincoln St, 1st fl, Meriden, CT 06451 *Tel:* 718-434-1893 *Fax:* 203-440-1013 *Web Site:* www.ricia.com, pg 500

Mainville, Lara MA, University of Ottawa Press (Presses de l'Université d'Ottawa), 542 King Edward Ave, Ottawa, ON K1N 6N5, Canada *Tel:* 613-562-5246 *Fax:* 613-562-5247 *E-mail:* puo-uop@uottawa.ca; acquisitions@uottawa.ca *Web Site:* press.uottawa.ca, pg 444

Maitland, Arnaud, Dharma Publishing, 35788 Hauser Bridge Rd, Cazadero, CA 95421 *Tel:* 707-847-3717 *Fax:* 707-847-3380 *E-mail:* contact@dharmapublishing.com *Web Site:* www.dharmapublishing.com, pg 64

Majczyk, Amy, RAND Corp, 1776 Main St, Santa Monica, CA 90407-2138 *Tel:* 310-393-0411 *Fax:* 310-393-4818 *Web Site:* www.rand.org, pg 180

Majeed, Yasmin Adele, Asian American Writers' Workshop, 112 W 27 St, Suite 600, New York, NY 10001 *Tel:* 212-494-0061 *E-mail:* desk@aaww.org *Web Site:* www.aaww.org; facebook.com/AsianAmericanWritersWorkshop, pg 525

Majumdar, Megha, Counterpoint Press LLC, 2560 Ninth St, Suite 318, Berkeley, CA 94710 *Tel:* 510-704-0230 *Fax:* 510-704-0268 *E-mail:* info@counterpointpress.com *Web Site:* counterpointpress.com; softskull, pg 58

Makanju, Kay, Harry N Abrams Inc, 195 Broadway, 9th fl, New York, NY 10007 *Tel:* 212-206-7715 *Toll Free Tel:* 800-345-1359 *Fax:* 212-519-1210 *E-mail:* abrams@abramsbooks.com *Web Site:* www.abramsbooks.com, pg 3

Makholm, Lauren, The Art Institute of Chicago, 111 S Michigan Ave, Chicago, IL 60603-6404 *Tel:* 312-443-3600; 312-443-3540 (pubns) *Fax:* 312-443-1334 (pubns) *Web Site:* www.artic.edu; www.artinstituteshop.org, pg 20

Makin, Michael F, PRINTING United Alliance, 10015 Main St, Fairfax, VA 22031-3489 *Tel:* 703-385-1335 *Toll Free Tel:* 888-385-3588 *Fax:* 703-273-0456; 703-691-7492 (membership) *E-mail:* assist@printing.org; info@printing.org *Web Site:* www.printing.org; www.sgia.org, pg 544

Makino, Arimichi, The Melville Society, Johns Hopkins University Press, PO Box 19966, Baltimore, MD 21211-0966 *Web Site:* melvillesociety.org, pg 537

Makras, Penny, HarperCollins General Books Group, 195 Broadway, New York, NY 10007 *Tel:* 212-207-7000 *Web Site:* www.harpercollins.com, pg 93

Malak, Stephanie, LARB Books, 6671 Sunset Blvd, Suite 1521, Los Angeles, CA 90028 *Tel:* 323-952-3950 *E-mail:* larbbooks@lareviewofbooks.org *Web Site:* larbbooks.org, pg 120

Malaviya, Nihar, Random House Publishing Group, 1745 Broadway, New York, NY 10019 *Toll Free Tel:* 800-200-3552 *Web Site:* www.randomhousebooks.com, pg 181

Malcolm, Ian, Harvard University Press, 79 Garden St, Cambridge, MA 02138-1499 *Tel:* 617-495-2600; 401-531-2800 (intl orders) *Toll Free Tel:* 800-405-1619 (orders) *Fax:* 617-495-5898 (gen); 617-496-4677 (edit & rts); 401-531-2801 (intl orders) *Toll Free Fax:* 800-406-9145 (orders) *E-mail:* contact_hup@harvard.edu *Web Site:* www.hup.harvard.edu, pg 95

Malcolm, Reed, University of California Press, 155 Grand Ave, Suite 400, Oakland, CA 94612-3758 *Tel:* 510-883-8232 *Fax:* 510-836-8910 *E-mail:* generalmailbox@ucpress.edu *Web Site:* www.ucpress.edu, pg 226

Malcom, Lily, Dial Books for Young Readers, 345 Hudson St, New York, NY 10014 *Tel:* 212-366-2000 *Toll Free Tel:* 800-733-3000 (orders) *Fax:* 212-414-3396 *Web Site:* www.penguin.com/publishers/dialbooksforyoungreaders/, pg 64

Malden, Cheryl, The H W Wilson Library Staff Development Grant, 50 E Huron St, Chicago, IL 60611 *Tel:* 312-280-3247 *Toll Free Tel:* 800-545-2433 (ext 3247) *Fax:* 312-944-3897; 312-440-9379 *E-mail:* awards@ala.org *Web Site:* www.ala.org, pg 678

Malden, Cheryl M, Joseph W Lippincott Award, 225 N Michigan Ave, Suite 1300, Chicago, IL 60601 *Tel:* 312-280-3247 *Toll Free Tel:* 800-545-2433 (ext 3247) *Fax:* 312-944-3897 *E-mail:* awards@ala.org *Web Site:* www.ala.org, pg 634

Malden, Cheryl M, Schneider Family Book Awards, 225 N Michigan Ave, Suite 1300, Chicago, IL 60601 *Tel:* 312-944-6780 *Toll Free Tel:* 800-545-2433 *Fax:* 312-440-9374 *E-mail:* ala@ala.org *Web Site:* www.ala.org/awardsgrants/schneider-family-book-award, pg 666

Maldonado, Ricardo, Discovery/Boston Review Poetry Contest, 1395 Lexington Ave, New York, NY 10128 *Tel:* 212-415-5760 *E-mail:* unterberg@92y.org *Web Site:* www.92y.org/discovery, pg 610

Malec, Erin, Reed Environmental Writing Award, 201 W Main St, Suite 14, Charlottesville, VA 22902 *Tel:* 434-977-4090 *Fax:* 434-977-1483 *Web Site:* www.southernenvironment.org, pg 661

Malek, Nancy, Fernwood Publishing, 32 Oceanvista Lane, Black Point, NS B0J 1B0, Canada *Tel:* 902-857-1388 *Fax:* 902-857-1328 *E-mail:* info@fernpub.ca; roseway@fernpub.ca *Web Site:* fernwoodpublishing.ca, pg 426

Malk, Steven, Writers House, 21 W 26 St, New York, NY 10010 *Tel:* 212-685-2400 *Web Site:* www.writershouse.com, pg 508

Mallardi, Vincent, Printing Brokerage/Buyers Association International (PBBA), 74-5576 Pawai Place, No 599, Kailua Kona, HI 96740 *Tel:* 808-339-0880 *E-mail:* contactus@pbba.org *Web Site:* pbba.org, pg 544

Mallia, Jo, Penguin Group USA, A Penguin Random House Company, 375 Hudson St, New York, NY 10014 *Tel:* 212-366-2000 *Toll Free Tel:* 800-847-5515 (inside sales); 800-631-8571 (cust serv) *Fax:* 212-366-2666; 607-775-4829 (inside sales) *E-mail:* online@us.penguingroup.com *Web Site:* www.penguin.com, pg 163

Mallinson, Margot, Harlequin Enterprises Ltd, Bay Adelaide Centre, East Tower, 22 Adelaide St W, 41st fl, Toronto, ON M5H 4E3, Canada *Tel:* 416-445-5860 *Toll Free Tel:* 888-432-4879; 800-370-5838 (ebook inquiries) *E-mail:* customerservice@harlequin.com *Web Site:* www.harlequin.com, pg 429

Mallory, Erin, Groundwood Books, 128 Sterling Rd, Lower Level, Toronto, ON M6R 2B7, Canada *Tel:* 416-363-4343 *Fax:* 416-363-1017 *E-mail:* genmail@groundwoodbooks.com *Web Site:* www.houseofanansi.com, pg 428

Mallory, Erin, House of Anansi Press Inc, 128 Sterling Rd, Lower Level, Toronto, ON M6R 2B7, Canada *Tel:* 416-363-4343 *Fax:* 416-363-1017 *E-mail:* customerservice@houseofanansi.com *Web Site:* www.houseofanansi.com, pg 429

Malmud, Deborah A, W W Norton & Company Inc, 500 Fifth Ave, New York, NY 10110-0017 *Tel:* 212-354-5500 *Toll Free Tel:* 800-233-4830 (orders & cust serv) *Fax:* 212-869-0856 *Toll Free Fax:* 800-458-6515 *E-mail:* orders@wwnorton.com *Web Site:* wwnorton.com, pg 152

Malnor, Bruce, Dawn Publications Inc, 12402 Bitney Springs Rd, Nevada City, CA 95959 *Tel:* 530-274-7775 *Toll Free Tel:* 800-545-7475 *Fax:* 530-274-7778 *E-mail:* nature@dawnpub.com; orders@dawnpub.com *Web Site:* www.dawnpub.com, pg 63

Malnor, Carol, Dawn Publications Inc, 12402 Bitney Springs Rd, Nevada City, CA 95959 *Tel:* 530-274-7775 *Toll Free Tel:* 800-545-7475 *Fax:* 530-274-7778 *E-mail:* nature@dawnpub.com; orders@dawnpub.com *Web Site:* www.dawnpub.com, pg 63

Malone, Robert Jay, Watson Davis & Helen Miles Davis Prize, 440 Geddes Hall, Notre Dame, IN 46556 *Tel:* 574-631-1194 *E-mail:* info@hssonline.org *Web Site:* www.hssonline.org, pg 609

Malone, Robert Jay, Pfizer Award, 440 Geddes Hall, Notre Dame, IN 46556 *Tel:* 574-631-1194 *E-mail:* info@hssonline.org *Web Site:* www.hssonline.org, pg 655

Malone, Robert Jay, Derek Price/Rod Webster Prize Award, 440 Geddes Hall, Notre Dame, IN 46556 *Tel:* 574-631-1194 *E-mail:* info@hssonline.org *Web Site:* www.hssonline.org, pg 659

Malone, Robert Jay, Nathan Reingold Prize, 440 Geddes Hall, Notre Dame, IN 46556 *Tel:* 574-631-1194 *E-mail:* info@hssonline.org, pg 661

Malone, Robert Jay, Margaret W Rossiter History of Women in Science Prize, 440 Geddes Hall, Notre Dame, IN 46556 *Tel:* 574-631-1194 *E-mail:* info@hssonline.org *Web Site:* www.hssonline.org, pg 663

Maloney, Casey, Avery, 1745 Broadway, New York, NY 10019 *Tel:* 212-366-2000 *Fax:* 212-366-2636 *E-mail:* averypublicity@penguinrandomhouse.com *Web Site:* www.penguin.com/publishers/avery; www.penguinrandomhouse.com, pg 26

Maloney, Casey, TarcherPerigee, 375 Hudson St, New York, NY 10014 *Tel:* 212-366-2000 *Fax:* 212-366-2643 *E-mail:* customerservice@penguinrandomhouse.com (cust serv); TarcherPerigeePublicity@penguinrandomhouse.com (media queries) *Web Site:* www.tarcherbooks.com; www.facebook.com/TarcherPerigee/; www.penguin.com/publishers/tarcherperigee, pg 213

Maloney, Dennis, White Pine Press, PO Box 236, Buffalo, NY 14201 *Tel:* 716-627-4665 *Fax:* 716-627-4665 *E-mail:* wpine@whitepine.org *Web Site:* www.whitepine.org, pg 240

Maloney, Prof Ian, SFC Literary Prize, 180 Remsen St, Brooklyn, NY 11201 *Web Site:* www.sfc.edu/news/sfcliteraryprize, pg 666

Maloney, Joy, Southern Playwrights Competition, 700 Pelham Rd N, Jacksonville, AL 36265-1602 *Tel:* 256-782-5412 *Web Site:* www.jsu.edu/english/southpla.html, pg 669

Malter, Emily, Chronicle Books, 680 Second St, San Francisco, CA 94107 *Tel:* 415-537-4200 *Toll Free Tel:* 800-759-0190 (cust serv) *Fax:* 415-537-4460 *Toll Free Fax:* 800-858-7787 (orders); 800-286-9471 (cust serv) *E-mail:* frontdesk@chroniclebooks.com *Web Site:* www.chroniclebooks.com, pg 52

Maluccio, Paul, Blue Note Publications Inc, 721 North Dr, Suite D, Melbourne, FL 32934 *Tel:* 321-799-2583; 321-622-6289 *Toll Free Tel:* 800-624-0401 (orders) *Fax:* 321-799-1942; 321-622-6830 *E-mail:* bluenotebooks@gmail.com *Web Site:* bluenotepublications.com, pg 36

Malvin, Lisa, University of Chicago, Graham School of General Studies, 1427 E 60 St, Chicago, IL 60637 *Tel:* 773-702-1722 *Fax:* 773-702-6814 *Web Site:* www.grahamschool.uchicago.edu, pg 585

Man, Angela, Orbit, 1290 Avenue of the Americas, New York, NY 10104 *Tel:* 212-364-1100 *Toll Free Tel:* 800-759-0190 *Web Site:* www.orbitbooks.net, pg 156

Man, John, Children's Book Press, 95 Madison Ave, Suite 1205, New York, NY 10016 *Tel:* 212-779-4400 *Fax:* 212-683-1894 *E-mail:* general@leeandlow.com; orders@leeandlow.com; sales@leeandlow.com *Web Site:* www.leeandlow.com, pg 50

Man-Kong, Mary, Random House Children's Books, 1745 Broadway, 10th fl, New York, NY 10019 *Tel:* 212-782-9000 *Web Site:* www.randomhousekids.com, pg 180

Manaktala, Gita, The MIT Press, One Rogers St, Cambridge, MA 02142 *Tel:* 617-253-5255 *Toll Free Tel:* 800-405-1619 (orders) *Fax:* 617-258-6779; 617-577-1545 (orders) *Web Site:* mitpress.mit.edu, pg 141

Manchee, Bill, Top Publications Ltd, 2745 Dallas Pkwy, Suite 420, Plano, TX 75093 *Tel:* 972-628-6414 *Fax:* 972-233-0713 *E-mail:* bill@toppub.com *Web Site:* toppub.com, pg 219

Mancini, Gerard, Puffin Books, 345 Hudson St, New York, NY 10014 *Tel:* 212-366-2000 *Web Site:* www.penguin.com/publishers/puffin, pg 177

Mancini, Gerard, Viking Children's Books, 345 Hudson St, New York, NY 10014 *Fax:* 212-414-3393 *E-mail:* youngreaderspublicity@us.penguingroup.com *Web Site:* www.penguin.com/publishers/vikingchildrensbooks, pg 236

Mancuso, Leslie D PhD, Jhpiego, 1615 Thames St, Baltimore, MD 21231-3492 *Tel:* 410-537-1800 *Fax:* 410-537-1473 *E-mail:* info@jhpiego.net *Web Site:* www.jhpiego.org, pg 113

Mandel, Andrew, Farrar, Straus & Giroux, LLC, 175 Varick St, 9th fl, New York, NY 10014 *Tel:* 212-741-6900 *E-mail:* fsg.publicity@fsgbooks.com *Web Site:* us.macmillan.com/fsg.aspx, pg 76

Mandel, Daniel, Sanford J Greenburger Associates Inc, 55 Fifth Ave, New York, NY 10003 *Tel:* 212-206-5600 *Fax:* 212-463-8718 *Web Site:* greenburger.com; www.sjga.com, pg 487

Mandel, Dr Dena, Mandel Vilar Press, 19 Oxford Ct, Simsbury, CT 06070 *Tel:* 806-790-4731 *E-mail:* info@mvpress.org *Web Site:* mvpress.org, pg 131

Mandel, Jay, WME, 11 Madison Ave, 18th fl, New York, NY 10010 *Tel:* 212-586-5100 *Web Site:* www.wmeentertainment.com, pg 508

Mandel, Jenny, Workman Publishing Co Inc, 225 Varick St, 9th fl, New York, NY 10014-4381 *Tel:* 212-254-5900 *Toll Free Tel:* 800-722-7202 *Fax:* 212-254-8098 *E-mail:* info@workman.com; orders@workman.com *Web Site:* www.workman.com, pg 244

Mandel, Dr Robert A, Mandel Vilar Press, 19 Oxford Ct, Simsbury, CT 06070 *Tel:* 806-790-4731 *E-mail:* info@mvpress.org *Web Site:* mvpress.org, pg 131

Mandeville, Craig, Simon & Schuster, Inc, 1230 Avenue of the Americas, New York, NY 10020 *Tel:* 212-698-7000 *Toll Free Tel:* 800-223-2336 (orders) *Fax:* 212-698-7007 *Toll Free Fax:* 800-943-9831 (orders) *E-mail:* firstname.lastname@simonandschuster.com; purchaseorders@simonandschuster.com (orders) *Web Site:* www.simonandschuster.com, pg 199

Mangan, Joe, Hachette Book Group, 1290 Avenue of the Americas, New York, NY 10104 *Tel:* 212-364-1100 *Toll Free Tel:* 800-759-0190 (cust serv) *Fax:* 212-364-0933 (intl orders) *Toll Free Fax:* 800-286-9471 (cust serv) *Web Site:* www.hachettebookgroup.com, pg 90

Mangol, Lynn, National Association of College Stores (NACS), 500 E Lorain St, Oberlin, OH 44074 *Toll Free Tel:* 800-622-7498 *Fax:* 440-775-4769 *Web Site:* www.nacs.org, pg 539

Mangum, Lisa, Deseret Book Co, 57 W South Temple, Salt Lake City, UT 84101-1511 *Tel:* 801-517-3369; 801-534-1515 (corp) *Toll Free Tel:* 800-453-4532 (orders); 888-846-7302 (orders) *Fax:* 801-517-3126 *E-mail:* service@deseretbook.com *Web Site:* www.deseretbook.com, pg 64

Mangum, Lisa, Shadow Mountain, PO Box 30178, Salt Lake City, UT 84130-0178 *Tel:* 801-534-1515 *Toll Free Tel:* 800-453-3876 *E-mail:* submissions@shadowmountain.com; info@shadowmountain.com *Web Site:* shadowmountain.com, pg 197

Manion, Deborah, Syracuse University Press, 621 Skytop Rd, Suite 110, Syracuse, NY 13244-5290 *Tel:* 315-443-5534 *Toll Free Tel:* 800-365-8929 (cust serv) *Fax:* 315-443-5545 *E-mail:* supress@syr.edu *Web Site:* press.syr.edu, pg 212

Manko, Cliff, Beacon Press, 24 Farnsworth St, Boston, MA 02210-1409 *Tel:* 617-742-2110 *Fax:* 617-723-3097; 617-742-2290 *Web Site:* www.beacon.org, pg 29

Manko, Paul, BLR®—Business & Legal Resources, 100 Winners Circle, Suite 300, Brentwood, TN 37027 *Tel:* 860-510-0100 *Toll Free Tel:* 800-727-5257 *E-mail:* service@blr.com *Web Site:* www.blr.com, pg 36

Manlove, Melissa, Chronicle Books, 680 Second St, San Francisco, CA 94107 *Tel:* 415-537-4200 *Toll Free Tel:* 800-759-0190 (cust serv) *Fax:* 415-537-4460 *Toll Free Fax:* 800-858-7787 (orders); 800-286-9471 (cust serv) *E-mail:* frontdesk@chroniclebooks.com *Web Site:* www.chroniclebooks.com, pg 52

Mann, Carol, Carol Mann Agency, 55 Fifth Ave, 18th fl, New York, NY 10003 *Tel:* 212-206-5635 *Fax:* 212-675-4809 *E-mail:* submissions@carolmannagency.com *Web Site:* www.carolmannagency.com, pg 494

Mann, Jennifer, WNDB Internship Grants, 10319 Westlake Dr, No 104, Bethesda, MD 20817 *Tel:* 701-404-9632 (voicemail only) *E-mail:* internships@diversebooks.org *Web Site:* diversebooks.org/our-programs/internship-grants, pg 679

Mann, Kevin, American Water Works Association (AWWA), 6666 W Quincy Ave, Denver, CO 80235-3098 *Tel:* 303-794-7711 *Toll Free Tel:* 800-926-7337 *E-mail:* service@awwa.org (cust serv) *Web Site:* www.awwa.org, pg 15

Mann, Maria, Houghton Mifflin Harcourt Trade & Reference Division, 125 High St, Boston, MA 02110 *Tel:* 617-351-5000 *Web Site:* www.hmhco.com, pg 104

Mann, Sue, Working With Words, 5320 SW Mayfair Ct, Beaverton, OR 97005 *Tel:* 503-644-4317 *E-mail:* editor@zzz.com, pg 472

Manna, Christine, Association of National Advertisers (ANA), 10 Grand Central, 155 E 44 St, New York, NY 10017 *Tel:* 212-697-5950 *Fax:* 212-302-6714 *Web Site:* www.ana.net, pg 527

Mannheimer, Sarah Murphy, The Tuesday Agency, 132 1/2 E Washington St, Iowa City, IA 52240 *Tel:* 319-338-7080 *E-mail:* trinity@tuesdayagency.com *Web Site:* tuesdayagency.com, pg 516

Manning, Linda, University of Alabama Press, 200 Hackberry Lane, 2nd fl, Tuscaloosa, AL 35487 *Tel:* 205-348-5180 *Fax:* 205-348-9201 *Web Site:* www.uapress.ua.edu, pg 225

Manning, Paul, Walter De Gruyter Inc, 121 High St, 3rd fl, Boston, MA 02110 *Tel:* 857-284-7073 *Fax:* 857-284-7358 *E-mail:* service@degruyter.com *Web Site:* www.degruyter.com, pg 63

Manning, Robert, Adirondack Mountain Club (ADK), 814 Goggins Rd, Lake George, NY 12845-4117 *Tel:* 518-668-4447 *Toll Free Tel:* 800-395-8080 *Fax:* 518-668-3746 *E-mail:* info@adk.org *Web Site:* www.adk.org, pg 5

Manning, Sean, Simon & Schuster, 1230 Avenue of the Americas, New York, NY 10020 *Tel:* 212-698-7000 *Toll Free Tel:* 800-223-2348 (cust serv); 800-223-2336 (orders) *Toll Free Fax:* 800-943-9831 (orders) *Web Site:* www.simonandschuster.com, pg 198

Mannon, Emily, Holiday House Publishing Inc, 50 Broad St, New York, NY 10004 *Tel:* 212-688-0085 *Fax:* 212-421-6134 *E-mail:* info@holidayhouse.com *Web Site:* www.holidayhouse.com, pg 101

Mano, Barry, Referee Books, 2017 Lathrop Ave, Racine, WI 53405 *Tel:* 262-632-8855 *Toll Free Tel:* 800-733-6100 *Fax:* 262-632-5460 *E-mail:* customerservice@referee.com *Web Site:* www.referee.com, pg 183

Manoogian, Daron, Harvard Art Museums, 32 Quincy St, Cambridge, MA 02138 *Tel:* 617-495-9400; 617-496-6529 (edit) *Web Site:* www.harvardartmuseums.org, pg 94

Manos, Wayne, Cold Spring Harbor Laboratory Press, One Bungtown Rd, Cold Spring Harbor, NY 11724 *Tel:* 516-422-4100 *Toll Free Tel:* 800-843-4388 *Fax:* 516-422-4097; 516-422-4092 (submissions) *E-mail:* cshpress@cshl.edu *Web Site:* www.cshlpress.com, pg 54

Mansfield, Katherine, IEEE Computer Society, 2001 "L" St NW, Suite 700, Washington, DC 20036-4928 *Tel:* 202-371-0101 *Toll Free Tel:* 800-678-4333 (memb info) *Fax:* 202-728-9614 *E-mail:* help@computer.org *Web Site:* www.computer.org, pg 105

Mansoor, Leah, Encyclopaedia Britannica Inc, 325 N La Salle St, Suite 200, Chicago, IL 60654 *Tel:* 312-347-7000 (all other countries) *Toll Free Tel:* 800-323-1229 (US & CN) *Fax:* 312-294-2104 *E-mail:* contact@eb.com *Web Site:* www.britannica.com, pg 72

Manston, Freya, Freya Manston Associates Inc, 145 W 58 St, New York, NY 10019 *Tel:* 212-247-3075, pg 494

Manston, Peter B, Travel Keys, PO Box 160691, Sacramento, CA 95816-0691 *Tel:* 916-452-5200 *Fax:* 916-452-5200, pg 220

Mantilla, Tito, Editorial Portavoz, 2450 Oak Industrial Dr NE, Grand Rapids, MI 49505 *Toll Free Tel:* 877-733-2607 (ext 206) *Fax:* 616-493-1790 *E-mail:* portavoz@portavoz.com *Web Site:* www.portavoz.com, pg 69

Manus, Ron, Alfred Music, PO Box 10003, Van Nuys, CA 91410 *Tel:* 818-891-5999 (dealer sales, intl) *Toll Free Tel:* 800-292-6122 (dealer sales, US & CN); 800-628-1528 (cust serv) *Fax:* 818-893-5560 (dealer sales); 818-830-6252 (cust serv) *Toll Free Fax:* 800-632-1928 (dealer sales) *E-mail:* customerservice@alfred.com; sales@alfred.com *Web Site:* www.alfred.com, pg 7

Marbach, Donna M, Poetry Chapbook Contest, 1935 Penfield Rd, Penfield, NY 14526 *Tel:* 585-383-0812 *E-mail:* palettesnquills@gmail.com *Web Site:* www.palettesnquills.com, pg 657

Marbury, Margaret, Harlequin Enterprises Ltd, 195 Broadway, 24th fl, New York, NY 10007 *Tel:* 212-207-7000 *Toll Free Tel:* 888-432-4879 *E-mail:* customerservice@harlequin.com *Web Site:* www.harlequin.com, pg 93

March, Kerstin, RISING STAR Award, PO Box 190, Jefferson, OR 97352 *E-mail:* risingstar@womenfictionwriters.org *Web Site:* wfwa.memberclicks.net/rising-star-award, pg 662

March, Kerstin, STAR Award, PO Box 190, Jefferson, OR 97352 *E-mail:* staraward@womenfictionwriters.org *Web Site:* wfwa.memberclicks.net/star-award, pg 670

March, Kerstin, Women's Fiction Writers Association (WFWA), PO Box 190, Jefferson, OR 97352 *E-mail:* communications@womensfictionwriters.org; membership@womensfictionwriters.org *Web Site:* www.womensfictionwriters.org, pg 549

Marchant, Leigh, Random House Publishing Group, 1745 Broadway, New York, NY 10019 *Toll Free Tel:* 800-200-3552 *Web Site:* www.randomhousebooks.com, pg 181

Marchesano, Michael, Association Media & Publishing (AM&P), 1090 Vermont Ave NW, 6th fl, Washington, DC 20005-4905 *Tel:* 212-784-6398 *E-mail:* info@associationmediaandpublishing.org; sales@associationmediaandpublishing.org *Web Site:* www.siia.net/amp, pg 525

Marchesano, Michael, EXCEL Awards, 1090 Vermont Ave NW, 6th fl, Washington, DC 20005-4905 *Tel:* 212-784-6398 *E-mail:* awards@associationmediaandpublishing.org; info@associationmediaandpublishing.org *Web Site:* www.siia.net/amp; kellencompany.com, pg 614

Marchese, Shannon, Thomas Nelson, 501 Nelson Place, Nashville, TN 37214 *Tel:* 615-889-9000 *Toll Free Tel:* 800-251-4000 *Fax:* 615-902-1548 *Web Site:* www.thomasnelson.com, pg 217

Marchese, Shannon, Tommy Nelson®, 501 Nelson Place, Nashville, TN 37214 *Tel:* 615-889-9000; 615-902-1485 (cust serv) *Toll Free Tel:* 800-251-4000 *Web Site:* www.tommynelson.com, pg 218

Marchese, Stephanie, The Crossroad Publishing Co, 831 Chestnut Ridge Rd, Chestnut Ridge, NY 10977 *Tel:* 845-517-0180 *Toll Free Tel:* 800-888-4741 (orders) *E-mail:* info@crossroadpublishing.com *Web Site:* www.CrossroadPublishing.com, pg 60

Marchini, Tracy, BookEnds Literary Agency, 136 Long Hill Rd, Gillette, NJ 07933 *Web Site:* www.bookendsliterary.com, pg 476

Marciano, Michael, The Connecticut Law Tribune, 201 Ann Uccello St, 4th fl, Hartford, CT 06103 *Tel:* 860-527-7900 *Toll Free Tel:* 877-256-2472 *Web Site:* www.law.com/ctlawtribune/, pg 56

Marcil, Denise, Denise Marcil Literary Agency LLC, 483 Westover Rd, Stamford, CT 06902 *Tel:* 203-327-9970 *Fax:* 203-327-9970 *Web Site:* www.marcilofarrellagency.com, pg 494

Marciniszyn, Alex, Palladium Books Inc, 39074 Webb Ct, Westland, MI 48185 *Tel:* 734-721-2903 (orders) *Web Site:* www.palladiumbooks.com, pg 159

Marcok, Vicki, Vehicule Press, PO Box 42094, CP Roy, Montreal, QC H2W-2T3, Canada *Tel:* 514-844-6073 *E-mail:* vp@vehiculepress.com; admin@vehiculepress.com *Web Site:* www.vehiculepress.com, pg 445

Marcus, Barbara, Penguin Random House LLC, 1745 Broadway, New York, NY 10019 *Tel:* 212-782-9000 *Toll Free Tel:* 800-726-0600 *Web Site:* www.penguinrandomhouse.com, pg 164

Marcus, Barbara, Random House Children's Books, 1745 Broadway, 10th fl, New York, NY 10019 *Tel:* 212-782-9000 *Web Site:* www.randomhousekids.com, pg 180

Marcus, David, Oscar Williams/Gene Derwood Award, 909 Third Ave, New York, NY 10022 *Tel:* 212-686-0010 *Fax:* 212-532-8528 *E-mail:* info@nycommunitytrust.org *Web Site:* www.nycommunitytrust.org, pg 678

Marcus, Karyn, Gallery Books, 1230 Avenue of the Americas, New York, NY 10020 *Toll Free Tel:* 800-456-6798 *Fax:* 212-698-7284 *E-mail:* consumer.customerservice@simonandschuster.com *Web Site:* www.simonandschuster.com, pg 83

Marcus, Kendra, BookStop Literary Agency LLC, 67 Meadow View Rd, Orinda, CA 94563 *E-mail:* info@bookstopliterary.com *Web Site:* www.bookstopliterary.com, pg 477

Marcus, Leonard S, The Carle Honors, 125 W Bay Rd, Amherst, MA 01002 *Tel:* 413-559-6300 *E-mail:* info@carlemuseum.org *Web Site:* www.carlemuseum.org/content/carle-honors, pg 603

Mardak, Keith, Hal Leonard Corp, 7777 W Bluemound Rd, Milwaukee, WI 53213 *Tel:* 414-774-3630 *Fax:* 414-774-3259 *E-mail:* halinfo@halleonard.com *Web Site:* www.halleonard.com, pg 91

Mardon, Austin, Golden Meteorite Press, 11919 82 St NW, Suite 103, Edmonton, AB T5B 2W4, Canada *Tel:* 780-378-0063 *Fax:* 780-378-0063, pg 427

Margolis, Amy, Iowa Summer Writing Festival, 250 Continuing Educ Facility, University of Iowa, Iowa City, IA 52242 *Tel:* 319-335-4160 *E-mail:* iswfestival@uiowa.edu *Web Site:* iowasummerwritingfestival.org, pg 575

Margolis, Wendy, Law School Admission Council, 662 Penn St, Newtown, PA 18940 *Tel:* 215-968-1101 *E-mail:* lsacaccounts@lsac.org *Web Site:* www.lsac.org, pg 120

Marguy, Kathryn, Johns Hopkins University Press, 2715 N Charles St, Baltimore, MD 21218-4363 *Tel:* 410-516-6900; 410-516-6987 (journal orders outside US & CN) *Toll Free Tel:* 800-537-5487 (book orders & cust serv); 800-548-1784 (journal orders) *Fax:* 410-516-6968; 410-516-3866 (journal orders); 410-516-6998 (orders) *E-mail:* hfscustserv@press.jhu.edu (cust serv); jrnlcirc@press.jhu.edu (journal orders) *Web Site:* www.press.jhu.edu; muse.jhu.edu, pg 114

Marin, Joe, Orientation to the Graphic Arts, 10015 Main St, Fairfax, VA 22031-3489 *Tel:* 703-385-1335 *Toll Free Tel:* 888-385-3588 *Fax:* 703-273-0456 *E-mail:* info@printing.org; assist@printing.org *Web Site:* www.printing.org, pg 577

Marin, Joe, PRINTING United Alliance, 10015 Main St, Fairfax, VA 22031-3489 *Tel:* 703-385-1335 *Toll Free Tel:* 888-385-3588 *Fax:* 703-273-0456; 703-

691-7492 (membership) *E-mail:* assist@printing.org; info@printing.org *Web Site:* www.printing.org; www. sgia.org, pg 544

Marinacci, Barbara, The Bookmill, 501 Palisades Dr, No 315, Pacific Palisades, CA 90272-2848 *Tel:* 310-459-0190 *E-mail:* thebookmill1@verizon.net *Web Site:* www.thebookmill.us, pg 459

Marinaccio, Fran, Woodbine House, 6510 Bells Mill Rd, Bethesda, MD 20817 *Tel:* 301-897-3570 *Toll Free Tel:* 800-843-7323 *Fax:* 301-897-5838 *E-mail:* info@ woodbinehouse.com *Web Site:* www.woodbinehouse. com, pg 244

Marinaccio, Fran M, Woodbine House, 6510 Bells Mill Rd, Bethesda, MD 20817 *Tel:* 301-897-3570 *Toll Free Tel:* 800-843-7323 *Fax:* 301-897-5838 *E-mail:* info@ woodbinehouse.com *Web Site:* www.woodbinehouse. com, pg 244

Marini, Victoria, Irene Goodman Literary Agency, 27 W 24 St, Suite 700B, New York, NY 10010 *Tel:* 212-604-0330 *E-mail:* queries@irenegoodman. com *Web Site:* www.irenegoodman.com, pg 486

Marino, Krista, Random House Children's Books, 1745 Broadway, 10th fl, New York, NY 10019 *Tel:* 212-782-9000 *Web Site:* www.randomhousekids.com, pg 180

Marino, Philip, Little, Brown and Company, 1290 Avenue of the Americas, New York, NY 10104 *Tel:* 212-364-1100 *Fax:* 212-364-0952 *E-mail:* firstname.lastname@hbgusa. com *Web Site:* www.littlebrown.com; www. hachettebookgroup.com, pg 125

Mark, P J, Janklow & Nesbit Associates, 285 Madison Ave, 21st fl, New York, NY 10017 *Tel:* 212-421-1700 *Fax:* 212-355-1403 *E-mail:* info@janklow.com *Web Site:* www.janklowandnesbit.com, pg 490

Markel, Jennifer, New England Poetry Club, 46 Wallace St, Somerville, MA 02144 *E-mail:* info@nepoetryclub. org *Web Site:* www.nepoetryclub.org, pg 541

Markell, Rick, Gingko Press Inc, 1321 Fifth St, Berkeley, CA 94710 *Tel:* 510-898-1195 *Fax:* 510-898-1196 *E-mail:* books@gingkopress.com *Web Site:* www.gingkopress.com, pg 86

Markey, Maureen, Association for Information Science & Technology (ASIS&T), 8555 16 St, Suite 850, Silver Spring, MD 20910 *Tel:* 301-495-0900 *Fax:* 301-495-0810 *E-mail:* asist@asist.org *Web Site:* www.asist. org, pg 525

Markfield, Barbara, Association of National Advertisers (ANA), 10 Grand Central, 155 E 44 St, New York, NY 10017 *Tel:* 212-697-5950 *Fax:* 212-302-6714 *Web Site:* www.ana.net, pg 527

Markfield, Sarah, Association for PRINT Technologies (APTech), 1896 Preston White Dr, Reston, VA 20191 *Tel:* 703-264-7200 *Fax:* 703-620-0994 *E-mail:* aptech@aptech.org *Web Site:* www. printtechnologies.org, pg 525

Markland, Marcia, St Martin's Press, LLC, 120 Broadway, New York, NY 10271 *Tel:* 646-307-5151 *Web Site:* us.macmillan.com/smp, pg 190

Markoe, Kaija, Rizzoli International Publications Inc, 300 Park Ave S, 4th fl, New York, NY 10010-5399 *Tel:* 212-387-3400 *Toll Free Tel:* 800-522-6657 (orders only) *Fax:* 212-387-3535 *E-mail:* publicity@rizzoliusa. com *Web Site:* www.rizzoliusa.com, pg 185

Markowitz, Cora, Georges Borchardt Inc, 136 E 57 St, New York, NY 10022 *Tel:* 212-753-5785 *E-mail:* georges@gbagency.com *Web Site:* www. gbagency.com, pg 477

Markowski, Mike, Markowski International Publishers, One Oakglade Circle, Hummelstown, PA 17036-9525 *Tel:* 717-566-0468 *E-mail:* info@possibilitypress. com *Web Site:* www.possibilitypress.com; www. aeronauticalpublishers.com, pg 132

Marks, Corey PhD, Rilke Prize, Auditorium Bldg, Rm 214, 1155 Union Circle, Denton, TX 76203 *E-mail:* untrilkeprize@unt.edu *Web Site:* english.unt. edu/creative-writing/unt-rilke-prize, pg 662

Markson, Todd, Cengage Learning, 20 Channel Center St, Boston, MA 02210 *Tel:* 617-289-7700 *Toll Free Tel:* 800-354-9706 *Fax:* 617-289-7844 *E-mail:* esales@cengage.com *Web Site:* www.cengage. com, pg 47

Marmion, Shane P, William S Hein & Co Inc, 2350 N Forest Rd, Getzville, NY 14068 *Tel:* 716-882-2600 *Toll Free Tel:* 800-828-7571 *Fax:* 716-883-8100 *E-mail:* mail@wshein.com; marketing@wshein.com *Web Site:* www.wshein.com, pg 97

Marmur, Mildred, Mildred Marmur Associates Ltd, 2005 Palmer Ave, PMB 127, Larchmont, NY 10538 *Tel:* 914-834-1170 *Fax:* 914-833-1175 *E-mail:* marmur@westnet.com, pg 494

Marohn, Stephanie, Angel Editing Services, PO Box 752, Mountain Ranch, CA 95246 *Tel:* 209-728-8364 *E-mail:* info@stephaniemarohn.com *Web Site:* www. stephaniemarohn.com, pg 458

Marohn, Stephanie, Elite Books, PO Box 442, Fulton, CA 95439 *Tel:* 707-525-9292 *Toll Free Fax:* 800-330-9798 *E-mail:* support@eftuniverse.com *Web Site:* www.elitebooksonline.com, pg 71

Marohn, Stephanie, Energy Psychology Press, 1490 Mark West Springs Rd, Santa Rosa, CA 95404 *Tel:* 707-525-9292 *Toll Free Tel:* 800-330-9798 *E-mail:* energypsychologypress@gmail. com; support@eftuniverse.com *Web Site:* www. energypsychologypress.com; www.elitebooksonline. com, pg 72

Marolla, Mary, Harry N Abrams Inc, 195 Broadway, 9th fl, New York, NY 10007 *Tel:* 212-206-7715 *Toll Free Tel:* 800-345-1359 *Fax:* 212-519-1210 *E-mail:* abrams@abramsbooks.com *Web Site:* www. abramsbooks.com, pg 3

Marotta, Mary, DK Publishing, 1450 Broadway, Suite 801, New York, NY 10018 *Tel:* 646-674-4000 *Toll Free Tel:* 800-733-3000 *Fax:* 646-674-4020 *E-mail:* marketing@dk.com; publicity@ dk.com; csorders@penguinrandomhouse.com; ecustomerservice@randomhouse.com *Web Site:* www. dk.com; www.penguin.com, pg 65

Marotte, Liz, Chronicle Books, 680 Second St, San Francisco, CA 94107 *Tel:* 415-537-4200 *Toll Free Tel:* 800-759-0190 (cust serv) *Fax:* 415-537-4460 *Toll Free Fax:* 800-858-7787 (orders); 800-286-9471 (cust serv) *E-mail:* frontdesk@chroniclebooks.com *Web Site:* www.chroniclebooks.com, pg 51

Marr, Jill, Sandra Dijkstra Literary Agency, 1155 Camino del Mar, PMB 515, Del Mar, CA 92014-2605 *Web Site:* dijkstraagency.com, pg 482

Marra, Sandra, Appalachian Trail Conservancy (ATC), 799 Washington St, Harpers Ferry, WV 25425 *Tel:* 304-535-6331 *Toll Free Tel:* 888-287-8673 (orders only) *Fax:* 304-535-2667 *E-mail:* publisher@ appalachiantrail.org *Web Site:* www.appalachiantrail. org; www.atctrailstore.com, pg 18

Marrelli, Nancy, Vehicule Press, PO Box 42094, CP Roy, Montreal, QC H2W-2T3, Canada *Tel:* 514-844-6073 *E-mail:* vp@vehiculepress.com; admin@ vehiculepress.com *Web Site:* www.vehiculepress.com, pg 445

Marrow, Linda, Random House Publishing Group, 1745 Broadway, New York, NY 10019 *Toll Free Tel:* 800-200-3552 *Web Site:* www.randomhousebooks.com, pg 181

Marrs, Daniel, Ave Maria Press, PO Box 428, Notre Dame, IN 46556 *Toll Free Tel:* 800-282-1865 *Toll Free Fax:* 800-282-5681 *E-mail:* avemariapress.1@ nd.edu *Web Site:* www.avemariapress.com, pg 26

Mars, Laura, Grey House Publishing Inc™, 4919 Rte 22, Amenia, NY 12501 *Tel:* 518-789-8700 *Toll Free Tel:* 800-562-2139 *Fax:* 518-789-0556 *E-mail:* books@greyhouse.com; customerservice@ greyhouse.com *Web Site:* greyhouse.com, pg 89

Marsal, Jill, Marsal Lyon Literary Agency LLC, 665 San Rodolfo Dr, Suite 124, PMB 121, Solana Beach, CA 92075 *Tel:* 760-814-8507 *Web Site:* www. marsallyonliteraryagency.com, pg 494

Marscola, Kyle, Ave Maria Press, PO Box 428, Notre Dame, IN 46556 *Toll Free Tel:* 800-282-1865 *Toll Free Fax:* 800-282-5681 *E-mail:* avemariapress.1@ nd.edu *Web Site:* www.avemariapress.com, pg 26

Marsh, Amy Rose, Samuel French Inc, 235 Park Ave S, 5th fl, New York, NY 10003 *Tel:* 212-206-8990 *Toll Free Tel:* 866-598-8449 *Fax:* 212-206-1429 *E-mail:* info@samuelfrench.com *Web Site:* www. samuelfrench.com, pg 81

Marsh, Carole, Gallopade International Inc, 611 Hwy 74 S, Suite 2000, Peachtree City, GA 30269 *Tel:* 770-631-4222 *Toll Free Tel:* 800-536-2GET (536-2438) *Fax:* 770-631-4810 *Toll Free Fax:* 800-871-2979 *E-mail:* customerservice@gallopade.com *Web Site:* www.gallopade.com, pg 83

Marsh, Dr Peter, The Mongolia Society Inc, Indiana University, 703 Eigenmann Hall, 1900 E Tenth St, Bloomington, IN 47406-7512 *Tel:* 812-855-4078 *Fax:* 812-855-4078 *E-mail:* monsoc@indiana.edu *Web Site:* mongoliasociety.org, pg 142

Marsh, Rebecca, Penguin Books, 375 Hudson St, New York, NY 10014 *Tel:* 212-366-2000 *E-mail:* penguinpublicity@us.penguingroup.com *Web Site:* www.penguinclassics.com; www.penguin. com, pg 163

Marsh, Rebecca, Penguin Group USA, A Penguin Random House Company, 375 Hudson St, New York, NY 10014 *Tel:* 212-366-2000 *Toll Free Tel:* 800-847-5515 (inside sales); 800-631-8571 (cust serv) *Fax:* 212-366-2666; 607-775-4829 (inside sales) *E-mail:* online@us.penguingroup.com *Web Site:* www. penguin.com, pg 163

Marsh, Rebecca, Viking, 375 Hudson St, New York, NY 10014 *Tel:* 212-366-2000 *Fax:* 212-243-6002 *Web Site:* www.penguin.com/publishers/vikingbooks, pg 236

Marsh, Robert, Rowman & Littlefield, 4501 Forbes Blvd, Suite 200, Lanham, MD 20706 *Tel:* 301-459-3366 *Toll Free Tel:* 800-462-6420 (ext 3024, cust serv) *Fax:* 301-429-5748 *Web Site:* rowman.com, pg 188

Marshall, David, Berrett-Koehler Publishers Inc, 1333 Broadway, Suite 1000, Oakland, CA 94612 *Tel:* 510-817-2277 *Fax:* 510-817-2278 *E-mail:* bkpub@bkpub. com *Web Site:* www.bkconnection.com, pg 32

Marshall, David K, Society for Industrial & Applied Mathematics, 3600 Market St, 6th fl, Philadelphia, PA 19104-2688 *Tel:* 215-382-9800 *Toll Free Tel:* 800-447-7426 *Fax:* 215-386-7999 *E-mail:* siambooks@siam.org *Web Site:* www.siam.org, pg 202

Marshall, Elyse, Penguin Young Readers Group, 345 Hudson St, New York, NY 10014 *Tel:* 212-366-2000; 212-414-3553 *Fax:* 212-414-3340 *Web Site:* www. penguin.com/children, pg 165

Marshall, Evan S, The Evan Marshall Agency, One Pacio Ct, Roseland, NJ 07068-1121 *Tel:* 973-287-6216 *Web Site:* www.evanmarshallagency.com, pg 495

Marshall, Jen, Aevitas Creative Management, 19 W 21 St, Suite 501, New York, NY 10010 *Tel:* 212-765-6900 *Web Site:* aevitascreative.com, pg 474

Marshall, Julie, Island Press, 2000 "M" St NW, Suite 650, Washington, DC 20036 *Tel:* 202-232-7933 *Toll Free Tel:* 800-828-1302 *Fax:* 202-234-1328 *E-mail:* info@islandpress.org *Web Site:* www. islandpress.org, pg 112

Marshall, Kate, University of California Press, 155 Grand Ave, Suite 400, Oakland, CA 94612-3758 *Tel:* 510-883-8232 *Fax:* 510-836-8910 *E-mail:* generalmailbox@ucpress.edu *Web Site:* www. ucpress.edu, pg 226

Marshall, Len, HarperCollins General Books Group, 195 Broadway, New York, NY 10007 *Tel:* 212-207-7000 *Web Site:* www.harpercollins.com, pg 93

Marshall, Thomas, Random House Children's Books, 1745 Broadway, 10th fl, New York, NY 10019 *Tel:* 212-782-9000 *Web Site:* www.randomhousekids. com, pg 181

Marshall, Tim, Thomas Nelson, 501 Nelson Place, Nashville, TN 37214 *Tel:* 615-889-9000 *Toll Free Tel:* 800-251-4000 *Fax:* 615-902-1548 *Web Site:* www. thomasnelson.com, pg 217

Marsham, Nachie, Disney Press, 1101 Flower St, Glendale, CA 91201 *Web Site:* books.disney.com, pg 65

Marshea, Beth, Ladderbird Literary Agency, 45 Midland St, Worcester, MA 01602 *Tel:* 508-459-9590 *Web Site:* www.ladderbird.com, pg 492

Marson, Amy, C&T Publishing Inc, 1651 Challenge Dr, Concord, CA 94520-5206 *Tel:* 925-677-0377 *Toll Free Tel:* 800-284-1114 *Fax:* 925-677-0373 *E-mail:* support@ctpub.com *Web Site:* www.ctpub. com, pg 44

Marte Taveras, Mabel, Simon & Schuster, 1230 Avenue of the Americas, New York, NY 10020 *Tel:* 212-698-7000 *Toll Free Tel:* 800-223-2348 (cust serv); 800-223-2336 (orders) *Toll Free Fax:* 800-943-9831 (orders) *Web Site:* www.simonandschuster.com, pg 198

Martel, Manon, Les Editions Un Monde Different, 3905 Isabelle, bureau 101, Brossard, QC J4Y 2R2, Canada *Tel:* 450-656-2660 *Toll Free Tel:* 800-443-2582 *Fax:* 450-659-9328 *E-mail:* info@umd.ca *Web Site:* www.umd.ca, pg 425

Martell, Alice Fried, The Martell Agency, 1350 Avenue of the Americas, Suite 1205, New York, NY 10019 *Tel:* 212-317-2672 *Web Site:* www.themartellagency. com, pg 495

Martens, Patricia, Boys Town Press, 13603 Flanagan Blvd, 2nd fl, Boys Town, NE 68010 *Tel:* 531-355-1320 *Toll Free Tel:* 800-282-6657 *Fax:* 531-355-1310 *E-mail:* btpress@boystown.org *Web Site:* www. boystownpress.org, pg 39

Martens, Rainer, Human Kinetics Inc, 1607 N Market St, Champaign, IL 61820 *Tel:* 217-351-5076 *Toll Free Tel:* 800-747-4457 *Fax:* 217-351-1549 (orders/cust serv) *E-mail:* info@hkusa.com *Web Site:* www. humankinetics.com, pg 105

Martenz, Arden, MAR*CO Products Inc, PO Box 686, Hatfield, PA 19440 *Tel:* 215-956-0313 *Toll Free Tel:* 800-448-2197 *Fax:* 215-956-9041 *E-mail:* help@ marcoproducts.com; sales@marcoproducts.com *Web Site:* www.marcoproducts.com, pg 131

Marthe, L, Laurier Books Ltd, PO Box 8493, Ottawa, ON K1G 3H9, Canada *Tel:* 613-738-2163 *Toll Free Fax:* 855-736-9160 *E-mail:* laurierbooks@yahoo.com, pg 432

Martin, Andrew, St Martin's Press, LLC, 120 Broadway, New York, NY 10271 *Tel:* 646-307-5151 *Web Site:* us. macmillan.com/smp, pg 190

Martin, Annie, Wayne State University Press, Leonard N Simons Bldg, 4809 Woodward Ave, Detroit, MI 48201-1309 *Tel:* 313-577-6120 *Toll Free Tel:* 800-978-7323 *Fax:* 313-577-6131 *E-mail:* bookorders@wayne. edu *Web Site:* www.wsupress.wayne.edu, pg 238

Martin, Betsy, Skinner House Books, c/o Unitarian Universalist Assn, 24 Farnsworth St, Boston, MA 02210-1409 *Tel:* 617-742-2100 *Fax:* 617-948-6466 *E-mail:* skinnerhouse@uua.org *Web Site:* www. skinnerhouse.org, pg 200

Martin, Courtney J, Yale Center for British Art, 1080 Chapel St, New Haven, CT 06510-2302 *Tel:* 203-432-8929 *Fax:* 203-432-1626 *E-mail:* ycba.publications@ yale.edu *Web Site:* britishart.yale.edu, pg 246

Martin, Denny, Piano Press, 1425 Ocean Ave, Suite 5, Del Mar, CA 92014 *Tel:* 619-884-1401 *Fax:* 858-755-1104 *E-mail:* pianopress@pianopress.com *Web Site:* www.pianopress.com, pg 169

Martin, Emily, Harlequin Enterprises Ltd, Bay Adelaide Centre, East Tower, 22 Adelaide St W, 41st fl, Toronto, ON M5H 4E3, Canada *Tel:* 416-445-5860 *Toll Free Tel:* 888-432-4879; 800-370-5838 (ebook inquiries) *E-mail:* customerservice@harlequin.com *Web Site:* www.harlequin.com, pg 429

Martin, Howard, HeartMath LLC, 14700 W Park Ave, Boulder Creek, CA 95006 *Tel:* 831-338-8500 *Toll Free Tel:* 800-711-6221 *Fax:* 831-338-8504 *E-mail:* info@ heartmath.org; inquiry@heartmath.org *Web Site:* www. heartmath.org, pg 97

Martin, James, PRINTING United Alliance, 10015 Main St, Fairfax, VA 22031-3489 *Tel:* 703-385-1335 *Toll Free Tel:* 888-385-3588 *Fax:* 703-273-0456; 703-691-7492 (membership) *E-mail:* assist@printing.org; info@printing.org *Web Site:* www.printing.org; www. sgia.org, pg 544

Martin, Jennie Taylor, ARE Press, 215 67 St, Virginia Beach, VA 23451 *Tel:* 757-428-3588 *Toll Free Tel:* 800-333-4499 *Web Site:* www.edgarcayce.org, pg 19

Martin, John D, Rod & Staff Publishers Inc, 14193 Hwy 172, Crockett, KY 41413 *Tel:* 606-522-4348 *Fax:* 606-522-4896, pg 186

Martin, Jynne Dilling, Riverhead Books, 375 Hudson St, New York, NY 10014 *Tel:* 212-366-2000 *Web Site:* www.penguin.com/publishers/riverhead, pg 185

Martin, Kelli, Wendy Sherman Associates Inc, 138 W 25 St, Suite 1018, New York, NY 10001 *Tel:* 212-279-9027 *E-mail:* submissions@wsherman.com *Web Site:* www.wsherman.com, pg 502

Martin, Kerry, Holiday House Publishing Inc, 50 Broad St, New York, NY 10004 *Tel:* 212-688-0085 *Fax:* 212-421-6134 *E-mail:* info@holidayhouse.com *Web Site:* www.holidayhouse.com, pg 101

Martin, Lesley, Aperture Books, 547 W 27 St, 4th fl, New York, NY 10001 *Tel:* 212-505-5555 *Toll Free Fax:* 888-623-6908 *E-mail:* customerservice@aperture. org *Web Site:* aperture.org, pg 17

Martin, Lisa Ann PhD, Martin-McLean Literary Associates LLC, 5023 W 120 Ave, Suite 228, Broomfield, CO 80020 *Tel:* 303-465-2056 *Fax:* 303-465-2056 *E-mail:* martinmcleanlit@aol.com *Web Site:* www.martinmcleanlit.com, pg 495

Martin, Marianne K, Bywater Books Inc, PO Box 3671, Ann Arbor, MI 48106-3671 *Tel:* 734-662-8815 *Web Site:* bywaterbooks.com, pg 43

Martin, Matthew, Penguin Random House LLC, 1745 Broadway, New York, NY 10019 *Tel:* 212-782-9000 *Toll Free Tel:* 800-726-0600 *Web Site:* www. penguinrandomhouse.com, pg 164

Martin, Miranda, Columbia University Press, 61 W 62 St, New York, NY 10023 *Tel:* 212-459-0600 *Toll Free Tel:* 800-944-8648 *Fax:* 212-459-3678 *Web Site:* cup. columbia.edu, pg 55

Martin, Patrick, Prometheus Books, 59 John Glenn Dr, Amherst, NY 14228-2119 *Tel:* 716-691-0133 *Fax:* 716-691-0137 *E-mail:* marketing@ prometheusbooks.com; editorial@prometheusbooks. com; rights@prometheusbooks.com *Web Site:* www. prometheusbooks.com, pg 176

Martin, Peter Stanley, G Schirmer Inc/Associated Music Publishers Inc, 180 Madison Ave, 24th fl, New York, NY 10016 *Tel:* 212-254-2100 *Fax:* 212-254-2013 *E-mail:* schirmer@schirmer.com *Web Site:* www. musicsalesclassical.com, pg 193

Martin, Robert, Midwest Bookseller of the Year Award, 1375 St Anthony Ave, Suite 202-3, St Paul, MN 55104 *Tel:* 612-208-6279 *Toll Free Fax:* 844-273-4119 *E-mail:* info@midwestbooksellers.org *Web Site:* www. midwestbooksellers.org/bookseller-of-the-year.html, pg 641

Martin, Robert, Midwest Independent Booksellers Association (MIBA), 1375 St Anthony Ave, Suite 202-3, St Paul, MN 55104 *Tel:* 612-208-6279 *Toll Free Fax:* 844-273-4119 *E-mail:* info@midwestbooksellers. org *Web Site:* www.midwestbooksellers.org, pg 537

Martin, Rux, Houghton Mifflin Harcourt Trade & Reference Division, 125 High St, Boston, MA 02110 *Tel:* 617-351-5000 *Web Site:* www.hmhco.com, pg 104

Martin, Sharlene, Martin Literary Management, 15601 32 Ave SE, Mill Creek, WA 98012 *Tel:* 206-466-1773 (no phone queries) *Fax:* 206-466-1774 *Web Site:* www.martinliterarymanagement.com, pg 495

Martin, Wayne, North Carolina Arts Council Writers Fellowships, 109 E Jones St, Raleigh, NC 27601 *Tel:* 919-807-6500 *Fax:* 919-807-6532 *E-mail:* ncarts@ncdcr.gov *Web Site:* www.ncarts.org, pg 649

Martin-Dent, Ron, BOA Editions Ltd, 250 N Goodman St, Suite 306, Rochester, NY 14607 *Tel:* 585-546-3410 *Fax:* 585-546-3913 *E-mail:* contact@boaeditions.org *Web Site:* www.boaeditions.org, pg 37

Martinek, Jason, William Morris Society in the United States Fellowships, PO Box 53263, Washington, DC 20009 *E-mail:* us@morrissociety.org *Web Site:* www. morrissociety.org, pg 643

Martinelli, Theresa, Wayne State University Press, Leonard N Simons Bldg, 4809 Woodward Ave, Detroit, MI 48201-1309 *Tel:* 313-577-6120 *Toll Free Tel:* 800-978-7323 *Fax:* 313-577-6131 *E-mail:* bookorders@wayne.edu *Web Site:* www. wsupress.wayne.edu, pg 238

Martinet, Caroline L, J Anthony Lukas Book Prize, 2950 Broadway, New York, NY 10027 *Tel:* 212-854-6468 *Web Site:* www.journalism.columbia.edu, pg 636

Martinet, Caroline L, J Anthony Lukas Work-in-Progress Award, 2950 Broadway, New York, NY 10027 *Tel:* 212-854-6468 *Web Site:* www.journalism. columbia.edu, pg 636

Martinet, Caroline L, Mark Lynton History Prize, 2950 Broadway, New York, NY 10027 *Tel:* 212-854-6468 *Web Site:* www.journalism.columbia.edu, pg 636

Martinez, Brabara, United States Holocaust Memorial Museum, 100 Raoul Wallenberg Place SW, Washington, DC 20024-2126 *Tel:* 202-488-0400; 202-314-7837; 202-488-6144 (orders) *Toll Free Tel:* 800-259-9998 (orders) *Fax:* 202-479-9726; 202-488-0438 (orders) *E-mail:* cahs_publications@ushmm.org *Web Site:* www.ushmm.org, pg 224

Martinez, Claudia, Anchor Books, c/o Penguin Random House Inc, 1745 Broadway, New York, NY 10019 *Tel:* 212-572-2420 *E-mail:* vintageanchorpublicity@ randomhouse.com *Web Site:* knopfdoubleday.com/ imprint/anchor, pg 15

Martinez, Claudia, Vintage Books, c/o Penguin Random House Inc, 1745 Broadway, New York, NY 10019 *Tel:* 212-572-2420 *E-mail:* vintageanchorpublicity@ randomhouse.com *Web Site:* knopfdoubleday.com/ imprint/vintage, pg 236

Martinez, Michelle, Tiger Tales, 5 River Rd, Suite 128, Wilton, CT 06897-4069 *Tel:* 920-387-2333 *Fax:* 920-387-9994 *Web Site:* www.tigertalesbooks.com, pg 218

Martinez, Rudy, Soho Press Inc, 853 Broadway, New York, NY 10003 *Tel:* 212-260-1900 *E-mail:* soho@ sohopress.com; publicity@sohopress.com *Web Site:* sohopress.com, pg 203

Martinez Standring, Suzette, National Society of Newspaper Columnists (NSNC), 205 Gun Hill St, Milton, MA 02186 *Tel:* 617-697-6854 *E-mail:* director@columnists.com *Web Site:* www. columnists.com, pg 540

Martinez Standring, Suzette, National Society of Newspaper Columnists Annual Conference, 205 Gun Hill St, Milton, MA 02186 *Tel:* 617-697-6854 *E-mail:* director@columnists.com *Web Site:* www. columnists.com, pg 576

Martino, Alfred C, Listen & Live Audio Inc, 803 13 St, Union City, NJ 07087 *Tel:* 201-558-9000 *Toll Free Tel:* 800-653-9400 (orders) *Fax:* 201-558-9800 *Web Site:* www.listenandlive.com, pg 125

Martino, John B, The Catholic University of America Press, 240 Leahy Hall, 620 Michigan Ave NE, Washington, DC 20064 *Tel:* 202-319-5052 *Toll Free Tel:* 800-537-5487 (orders only) *Fax:* 202-319-4985 *E-mail:* cua-press@cua.edu *Web Site:* cuapress.org, pg 46

Martirano, Erica, St Martin's Press, LLC, 120 Broadway, New York, NY 10271 *Tel:* 646-307-5151 *Web Site:* us. macmillan.com/smp, pg 190

Marton, Meghan, DK Publishing, 1450 Broadway, Suite 801, New York, NY 10018 *Tel:* 646-674-4000 *Toll Free Tel:* 800-733-3000 *Fax:* 646-674-

4020 *E-mail:* marketing@dk.com; publicity@ dk.com; csorders@penguinrandomhouse.com; ecustomerservice@randomhouse.com *Web Site:* www. dk.com; www.penguin.com, pg 65

Martone, Michael, University of Alabama Program in Creative Writing, PO Box 870244, Tuscaloosa, AL 35487-0244 *Tel:* 205-348-5065 *Fax:* 205-348-1388 *E-mail:* english@ua.edu *Web Site:* www.as.ua. edu/english, pg 585

Martone, Robert, F A Davis Co, 1915 Arch St, Philadelphia, PA 19103 *Tel:* 215-568-2270; 215-440-3001 *Toll Free Tel:* 800-523-4049 *Fax:* 215-568-5065; 215-440-3016 *E-mail:* info@fadavis.com; orders@ fadavis.com *Web Site:* www.fadavis.com, pg 62

Martorelli, Nick, Penguin Random House Audio Publishing, 1745 Broadway, New York, NY 10019 *E-mail:* audio@penguinrandomhouse.com *Web Site:* www.penguinrandomhouseaudio.com, pg 164

Martynick, Christine, SLACK® Incorporated, A Wyanoke Group Company, 6900 Grove Rd, Thorofare, NJ 08086-9447 *Tel:* 856-848-1000 *Toll Free Tel:* 800-257-8290 *Fax:* 856-848-6091 *E-mail:* sales@slackinc. com; editor@slackinc.com; customerservice@slackinc. com *Web Site:* www.healio.com/books, pg 201

Marudas, Ashley, Little, Brown and Company, 1290 Avenue of the Americas, New York, NY 10104 *Tel:* 212-364-1100 *Fax:* 212-364-0952 *E-mail:* firstname.lastname@hbgusa. com *Web Site:* www.littlebrown.com; www. hachettebookgroup.com, pg 125

Marun, Serdar, Autism Asperger Publishing Co, 6448 Vista Dr, Shawnee, KS 66218 *Tel:* 913-897-1004 *Toll Free Tel:* 877-277-8254 *Fax:* 913-681-9473 *E-mail:* support@aapcpublishing.net *Web Site:* www. aapcpublishing.net, pg 25

Maruno, Jennifer, Canadian Society of Children's Authors, Illustrators & Performers (CANSCAIP), 720 Bathurst St, Suite 503, Toronto, ON M5S 2R4, Canada *Tel:* 416-515-1559 *E-mail:* office@canscaip. org *Web Site:* www.canscaip.org, pg 530

Marvel, Julia, Chronicle Books, 680 Second St, San Francisco, CA 94107 *Tel:* 415-537-4200 *Toll Free Tel:* 800-759-0190 (cust serv) *Fax:* 415-537-4460 *Toll Free Fax:* 800-858-7787 (orders); 800-286-9471 (cust serv) *E-mail:* frontdesk@chroniclebooks.com *Web Site:* www.chroniclebooks.com, pg 52

Marven, Shannon, Dupree, Miller & Associates Inc, 4311 Oak Lawn Ave, Suite 650, Dallas, TX 75219 *Tel:* 214-559-2665 *Fax:* 214-559-7243 *E-mail:* editorial@dupreemiller.com *Web Site:* www. dupreemiller.com, pg 482

Marvin, Catherine, Macmillan, 120 Broadway, 22nd fl, New York, NY 10271 *Tel:* 646-307-5151 *E-mail:* press.inquiries@macmillan.com *Web Site:* www.macmillan.com, pg 130

Marvin, Sally, Gallery Books, 1230 Avenue of the Americas, New York, NY 10020 *Toll Free Tel:* 800-456-6798 *Fax:* 212-698-7284 *E-mail:* consumer. customerservice@simonandschuster.com *Web Site:* www.simonandschuster.com, pg 83

Marwell, Josh, HarperCollins Publishers, 195 Broadway, New York, NY 10007 *Tel:* 212-207-7000 *Fax:* 212-207-7145 *Web Site:* www.harpercollins.com, pg 94

Marzano, Vincent, John Wiley & Sons Inc, 111 River St, Hoboken, NJ 07030-5774 *Tel:* 201-748-6000 *Toll Free Tel:* 800-225-5945 (cust serv) *Fax:* 201-748-6088 *E-mail:* info@wiley.com *Web Site:* www.wiley.com, pg 241

Masaryk, Hanna, Sanford J Greenburger Associates Inc, 55 Fifth Ave, New York, NY 10003 *Tel:* 212-206-5600 *Fax:* 212-463-8718 *Web Site:* greenburger.com; www.sjga.com, pg 487

Maschino, Matt, Regnery Publishing, 300 New Jersey Ave NW, Washington, DC 20001 *Tel:* 202-216-0600 *Toll Free Tel:* 888-219-4747 *Fax:* 202-393-1795 *Web Site:* www.regnery.com, pg 184

Mascia, Vanisse, Industrial Press Inc, 32 Haviland St, Suite 3, Norwalk, CT 06854 *Tel:* 203-956-5593 ext 0 (cust serv) *Toll Free Tel:* 888-528-7852 ext 0 (cust

serv) *Fax:* 203-354-9391 (cust serv) *E-mail:* info@ industrialpress.com (cust serv) *Web Site:* books. industrialpress.com; ebooks.industrialpress.com, pg 108

Mascone, Cynthia, American Institute of Chemical Engineers (AIChE), 120 Wall St, 23rd fl, New York, NY 10005-4020 *Tel:* 203-702-7660 *Toll Free Tel:* 800-242-4363 *Fax:* 203-775-5177 *E-mail:* customerservice@aiche.org *Web Site:* www. aiche.org, pg 12

Maselli, Elisabeth, Rutgers University Press, 106 Somerset St, New Brunswick, NJ 08901 *Tel:* 848-445-7762; 848-445-7761 (sales) *Fax:* 732-745-4935 *E-mail:* sales@rutgersuniversitypress.org *Web Site:* www.rutgersuniversitypress.org, pg 188

Maslin, Ella, Random House Publishing Group, 1745 Broadway, New York, NY 10019 *Toll Free Tel:* 800-200-3552 *Web Site:* www.randomhousebooks.com, pg 181

Maslow, Zoe, Doubleday Canada, 320 Front St W, Suite 1400, Toronto, ON M5V 3B6, Canada *Tel:* 416-364-4449 *Fax:* 416-598-7764 *Web Site:* www. penguinrandomhouse.ca, pg 421

Masnica, Karen, St Martin's Press, LLC, 120 Broadway, New York, NY 10271 *Tel:* 646-307-5151 *Web Site:* us. macmillan.com/smp, pg 190

Masnik, Julia, Watkins/Loomis Agency Inc, PO Box 20925, New York, NY 10025 *Tel:* 212-532-0080 *Fax:* 646-383-2449 *E-mail:* assistant@watkinsloomis. com *Web Site:* www.watkinsloomis.com, pg 508

Mason, Alane, W W Norton & Company Inc, 500 Fifth Ave, New York, NY 10110-0017 *Tel:* 212-354-5500 *Toll Free Tel:* 800-233-4830 (orders & cust serv) *Fax:* 212-869-0856 *Toll Free Fax:* 800-458-6515 *E-mail:* orders@wwnorton.com *Web Site:* wwnorton. com, pg 152

Mason, Jonathan, Don Buchwald & Associates Inc, 10 E 44 St, New York, NY 10017 *Tel:* 212-867-1200 *Fax:* 212-867-2434 *E-mail:* info@buchwald.com *Web Site:* www.buchwald.com, pg 478

Mason, Rena, Bram Stoker Awards®, PO Box 56687, Sherman Oaks, CA 91413 *Tel:* 818-220-3965 *E-mail:* admin@horror.org *Web Site:* horror.org/ awards/stokers.htm, pg 670

Masquelier, Chelsea, Chronicle Books, 680 Second St, San Francisco, CA 94107 *Tel:* 415-537-4200 *Toll Free Tel:* 800-759-0190 (cust serv) *Fax:* 415-537-4460 *Toll Free Fax:* 800-858-7787 (orders); 800-286-9471 (cust serv) *E-mail:* frontdesk@chroniclebooks.com *Web Site:* www.chroniclebooks.com, pg 52

Massabrook, Jessica, Princeton University Press, 41 William St, Princeton, NJ 08540-5237 *Tel:* 609-258-4900 *Fax:* 609-258-6305 *Web Site:* press.princeton. edu, pg 175

Massey, Jeanne, APC Publishing, PO Box 461166, Aurora, CO 80046-1166 *Tel:* 303-660-2158 *Toll Free Tel:* 800-660-5107 (sales & orders) *E-mail:* mail@4wdbooks.com; orders@4wdbooks.com *Web Site:* www.4wdbooks.com, pg 17

Massey, Peter, APC Publishing, PO Box 461166, Aurora, CO 80046-1166 *Tel:* 303-660-2158 *Toll Free Tel:* 800-660-5107 (sales & orders) *E-mail:* mail@4wdbooks. com; orders@4wdbooks.com *Web Site:* www. 4wdbooks.com, pg 17

Massicotte, Celine, Groupe Sogides Inc, 955 rue Amherst, Montreal, QC H2L 3K4, Canada *Tel:* 514-523-1182 *Fax:* 514-597-0370 *Web Site:* sogides.com, pg 428

Massy, Julie, La Courte Echelle, 4388, rue Saint-Denis, Suite 315, Montreal, QC H2J 2L1, Canada *Tel:* 514-312-6950 *E-mail:* info@courteechelle.com *Web Site:* courteechelle.groupecourteechelle.com, pg 420

Masterson, Amanda, Bureau of Economic Geology, c/o The University of Texas at Austin, 10100 Burnet Rd, Bldg 130, Austin, TX 78758 *Tel:* 512-471-1534 *Fax:* 512-471-0140 *E-mail:* pubsales@beg.utexas.edu *Web Site:* www.beg.utexas.edu, pg 43

Mastrolia, Barbara, Catholic Book Awards, 205 W Monroe St, Suite 470, Chicago, IL 60606 *Tel:* 312-380-6789 *Fax:* 312-361-0256 *E-mail:* cpaawards@ catholicpress.org *Web Site:* www.catholicpress.org, pg 603

Mastrolia, Barbara, Catholic Press Awards, 205 W Monroe St, Suite 470, Chicago, IL 60606 *Tel:* 312-380-6789 *Fax:* 312-361-0256 *E-mail:* cpaawards@ catholicpress.org *Web Site:* www.catholicpress.org, pg 603

Masucci, Diane, Women Who Write Inc, PO Box 652, Madison, NJ 07940-0652 *E-mail:* info@ womenwhowrite.org *Web Site:* womenwhowrite.org, pg 549

Matejovsky, Char, Polebridge Press, PO Box 346, Farmington, MN 55024 *Tel:* 651-200-2372 *E-mail:* orders@westarinstitute.org *Web Site:* www. westarinstitute.org, pg 172

Matheson, Ed, Ampersand Group, 1136 Maritime Way, Suite 717, Kanata, ON K2K 0M1, Canada *Tel:* 613-435-5066, pg 457

Matheson, Laurie, University of Illinois Press, 1325 S Oak St, MC-566, Champaign, IL 61820-6903 *Tel:* 217-333-0950 *Fax:* 217-244-8082 *E-mail:* uipress@uillinois.edu; journals@uillinois.edu *Web Site:* www.press.uillinois.edu, pg 227

Mathews, Lisa Vitarisi, Evan-Moor Educational Publishers, 18 Lower Ragsdale Dr, Monterey, CA 93940-5746 *Tel:* 831-649-5901 *Toll Free Tel:* 800-777-4362 (orders) *Fax:* 831-649-6256 *Toll Free Fax:* 800-777-4332 (orders) *E-mail:* sales@evan-moor.com; marketing@evan-moor.com *Web Site:* www.evan-moor. com, pg 73

Mathews, Richard, The Danahy Fiction Prize, University of Tampa Press, 401 W Kennedy Blvd, Tampa, FL 33606 *Tel:* 813-253-6266 *E-mail:* utpress@ut.edu *Web Site:* tampareview.ut.edu, pg 608

Mathews, Richard, The Tampa Review Prize for Poetry, University of Tampa Press, 401 W Kennedy Blvd, Tampa, FL 33606 *Tel:* 813-253-6266 *E-mail:* utpress@ ut.edu *Web Site:* tampareview.ut.edu, pg 672

Mathis, Catherine J, McGraw-Hill Education, 2 Penn Plaza, New York, NY 10121-2298 *Tel:* 212-904-2000 *E-mail:* international_cs@mheducation.com; seg_customerservice@mheducation.com (PreK-12); hep_customerservice@mheducation.com (higher education) *Web Site:* www.mheducation.com, pg 135

Mathis, Karin, Hachette Nashville, 6100 Tower Circle, Room 210, Franklin, TN 37067 *Tel:* 615-221-0996 *Fax:* 615-221-0962 *Web Site:* www.hachettebookgroup. com, pg 91

Mathoslah, Donna, Romance Writers of America®, 14615 Benfer Rd, Houston, TX 77069 *Tel:* 832-717-5200 *Fax:* 832-717-5201 *E-mail:* info@rwa.org *Web Site:* www.rwa.org, pg 545

Matin, Aref, John Wiley & Sons Inc, 111 River St, Hoboken, NJ 07030-5774 *Tel:* 201-748-6000 *Toll Free Tel:* 800-225-5945 (cust serv) *Fax:* 201-748-6088 *E-mail:* info@wiley.com *Web Site:* www.wiley.com, pg 241

Mativat, Genevieve, Les Editions Pierre Tisseyre, 155, rue Maurice, Rosemere, QC J7A 2S8, Canada *Tel:* 514-335-0777 *Fax:* 514-335-6723 *E-mail:* info@ edtisseyre.ca *Web Site:* www.tisseyre.ca, pg 425

Matloff, Robert, The Guilford Press, 370 Seventh Ave, Suite 1200, New York, NY 10001-1020 *Tel:* 212-431-9800 *Toll Free Tel:* 800-365-7006 *Fax:* 212-966-6708 *E-mail:* info@guilford.com *Web Site:* www.guilford. com, pg 90

Matson, Katinka, Brockman Inc, 260 Fifth Ave, 10th fl, New York, NY 10001 *Tel:* 212-935-8900 *Fax:* 212-935-5535 *E-mail:* rights@brockman.com *Web Site:* www.brockman.com, pg 478

Matson, Peter, Sterling Lord Literistic Inc, 115 Broadway, Suite 1602, New York, NY 10006 *Tel:* 212-780-6050 *Fax:* 212-780-6095 *E-mail:* info@sll.com *Web Site:* www.sll.com, pg 504

Matsuda, Hisae, Parallax Press, 2236B Sixth St, Berkeley, CA 94710 Tel: 510-540-6411 Toll Free Tel: 800-863-5290 (orders) Fax: 510-981-1157 Web Site: www.parallax.org, pg 160

Matsui, Victory, Random House Publishing Group, 1745 Broadway, New York, NY 10019 Toll Free Tel: 800-200-3552 Web Site: www.randomhousebooks.com, pg 181

Matthews, Claire, The Pacific Spirit Poetry Prize, University of British Columbia, Buch E462, 1866 Main Mall, Vancouver, BC V6T 1Z1, Canada Tel: 778-822-2514 Fax: 778-822-3616 E-mail: prismwritingcontest@gmail.com Web Site: www.prismmagazine.ca, pg 652

Matthews, Claire, PRISM international Literary Non-Fiction Contest, University of British Columbia, Buch E462, 1866 Main Mall, Vancouver, BC V6T 1Z1, Canada Tel: 778-822-2514 Fax: 778-822-3616 E-mail: prismwritingcontest@gmail.com Web Site: www.prismmagazine.ca, pg 659

Matthews, Claire, The Jacob Zilber Prize for Short Fiction, University of British Columbia, Buch E462, 1866 Main Mall, Vancouver, BC V6T 1Z1, Canada Tel: 778-822-2514 Fax: 778-822-3616 E-mail: prismwritingcontest@gmail.com Web Site: www.prismmagazine.ca, pg 681

Matthews, Elizabeth, American Society of Composers, Authors & Publishers (ASCAP), 1900 Broadway, New York City, NY 10023 Tel: 212-621-6000 Fax: 212-612-8453 E-mail: info@ascap.com Web Site: www.ascap.com, pg 524

Matthews, Jermey, The MIT Press, One Rogers St, Cambridge, MA 02142 Tel: 617-253-5255 Toll Free Tel: 800-405-1619 (orders) Fax: 617-258-6779; 617-577-1545 (orders) Web Site: mitpress.mit.edu, pg 141

Matthews, Katherine, Lucky Marble Books, 2671 Bristol Rd, Columbus, OH 43221 Tel: 614-264-5588 E-mail: sales@pagespringpublishing.com Web Site: www.luckymarblebooks.com, pg 129

Mattison, Celia, Milkweed Editions, 1011 Washington Ave S, Suite 300, Minneapolis, MN 55415-1246 Tel: 612-332-3192 Toll Free Tel: 800-520-6455 Fax: 612-215-2550 Web Site: milkweed.org, pg 140

Mattura, Cat, McGraw-Hill Create, 2 Penn Plaza, New York, NY 10121 Toll Free Tel: 800-962-9342 E-mail: mhhe.create@mheducation.com Web Site: create.mheducation.com; shop.mheducation.com, pg 135

Matus, Robyn, Seedling Publications Inc, 520 E Bainbridge St, Elizabethtown, PA 17022 Toll Free Tel: 800-233-0759 Toll Free Tel: 888-834-1303 E-mail: edcsr@continentalpress.com Web Site: www.continentalpress.com, pg 196

Matysik, Julie, Perseus Books, 1290 Avenue of the Americas, New York, NY 10104 Tel: 212-340-8100 Toll Free Tel: 800-343-4499 (cust serv) Fax: 212-340-8105 Web Site: www.perseusbooks.com, pg 167

Matysko, Harriet I, Mary Ann Liebert Inc, 140 Huguenot St, 3rd fl, New Rochelle, NY 10801-5215 Tel: 914-740-2100 Toll Free Tel: 800-654-3237 Fax: 914-740-2101 E-mail: info@liebertpub.com Web Site: www.liebertonline.com, pg 124

Matzie, Bridget Wagner, Aevitas Creative Management, 19 W 21 St, Suite 501, New York, NY 10010 Tel: 212-765-6900 Web Site: aevitascreative.com, pg 474

Mauer, Clare, St Martin's Press, LLC, 120 Broadway, New York, NY 10271 Tel: 646-307-5151 Web Site: us.macmillan.com/smp, pg 191

Mauer, Harry, Flashlight Press, 527 Empire Blvd, Brooklyn, NY 11225 Tel: 718-288-8300 Fax: 718-972-6307 Web Site: www.flashlightpress.com, pg 79

Mauer, Tzvi, KTAV Publishing House Inc, 527 Empire Blvd, Brooklyn, NY 11225 Tel: 201-963-9524; 718-972-5449 Fax: 718-972-6307 E-mail: orders@ktav.com Web Site: www.ktav.com, pg 119

Mauer, Tzvi, Urim Publications, 527 Empire Blvd, Brooklyn, NY 11225-3121 Tel: 718-972-5449 Fax: 718-972-6307 E-mail: urimpublisher@gmail.com Web Site: www.urimpublications.com, pg 234

Maurer, Rolf, New Star Books Ltd, 107-3477 Commercial St, Vancouver, BC V5N 4E8, Canada Tel: 604-738-9429 E-mail: info@newstarbooks.com Web Site: www.newstarbooks.com, pg 434

Mavjee, Maya, Penguin Random House LLC, 1745 Broadway, New York, NY 10019 Tel: 212-782-9000 Toll Free Tel: 800-726-0600 Web Site: www.penguinrandomhouse.com, pg 164

Mavreshko, Lana, Business Marketing Association (BMA), 708 Third Ave, New York, NY 10017 Tel: 212-697-5950 Fax: 212-687-7310 E-mail: info@marketing.org Web Site: www.marketing.org, pg 529

Max, P J, Easy Money Press, 82-5800 Napo'opo'o Rd, Captain Cook, HI 96704 Tel: 808-313-2808 E-mail: easymoneypress@yahoo.com, pg 69

Maxfield, Marcela, Stanford University Press, 425 Broadway St, Redwood City, CA 94063-3126 Tel: 650-723-9434 Fax: 650-725-3457 E-mail: info@www.sup.org; publicity@www.sup.org; sales@www.sup.org Web Site: www.sup.org, pg 206

Maxick, Jill, Prometheus Books, 59 John Glenn Dr, Amherst, NY 14228-2119 Tel: 716-691-0133 Fax: 716-691-0137 E-mail: marketing@prometheusbooks.com; editorial@prometheusbooks.com; rights@prometheusbooks.com Web Site: www.prometheusbooks.com, pg 176

Maxwell, Edward, Sanford J Greenburger Associates Inc, 55 Fifth Ave, New York, NY 10003 Tel: 212-206-5600 Fax: 212-463-8718 Web Site: greenburger.com; www.sjga.com, pg 487

Maxwell, Mitchell, The Story Plant, PO Box 4331, Stamford, CT 06907 Tel: 203-742-7920 E-mail: thestoryplant@thestoryplant.com Web Site: www.thestoryplant.com, pg 209

Maxwell, Nancy, Ariel Press, 2317 Quail Cove Dr, Jasper, GA 30143 Tel: 770-894-4226 E-mail: lig201@lightariel.com Web Site: www.lightariel.com, pg 19

May, Christopher, Dufour Editions Inc, PO Box 7, Chester Springs, PA 19425 Tel: 610-458-5005 E-mail: info@dufoureditions.com Web Site: www.dufoureditions.com, pg 67

May, Duncan, Dufour Editions Inc, PO Box 7, Chester Springs, PA 19425 Tel: 610-458-5005 E-mail: info@dufoureditions.com Web Site: www.dufoureditions.com, pg 67

May, Gergana, The Ibsen Society of America (ISA), c/o Indiana University, Global & Intl Studies Bldg 3111, 355 N Jordan Ave, Bloomington, IN 47405-1105 Web Site: www.ibsensociety.org, pg 534

May, Louise, Lee & Low Books Inc, 95 Madison Ave, Suite 1205, New York, NY 10016 Tel: 212-779-4400 Toll Free Tel: 888-320-3190 (ext 28, orders only) Fax: 212-683-1894 (orders only); 212-532-6035 E-mail: general@leeandlow.com Web Site: www.leeandlow.com, pg 122

May, Dr Timothy, The Mongolia Society Inc, Indiana University, 703 Eigenmann Hall, 1900 E Tenth St, Bloomington, IN 47406-7512 Tel: 812-855-4078 Fax: 812-855-4078 E-mail: monsoc@indiana.edu Web Site: mongoliasociety.org, pg 142

Mayer, Dan, Prometheus Books, 59 John Glenn Dr, Amherst, NY 14228-2119 Tel: 716-691-0133 Fax: 716-691-0137 E-mail: marketing@prometheusbooks.com; editorial@prometheusbooks.com; rights@prometheusbooks.com Web Site: www.prometheusbooks.com, pg 176

Mayer, Liese, Bloomsbury Publishing Inc, 1385 Broadway, 5th fl, New York, NY 10018 Tel: 212-419-5300 E-mail: marketingusa@bloomsbury.com; adultpublicityusa@bloomsbury.com; askacademic@bloomsbury.com Web Site: www.bloomsbury.com, pg 36

Mayer, Margery, Houghton Mifflin Harcourt, 125 High St, Boston, MA 02110 Tel: 617-351-5000 Toll Free Tel: 855-969-4642; 800-225-5425 (K-12 educ materials); 800-323-9540 (assessment materials); 877-219-1537 (SkillsTutor); 888-242-6747 (Innovation in Educ Group); 800-225-3362 (Trade & Ref Div) Toll Free Fax: 800-269-5232 E-mail: myhmhco@hmhco.com Web Site: www.hmhco.com, pg 103

Mayer, Tom, W W Norton & Company Inc, 500 Fifth Ave, New York, NY 10110-0017 Tel: 212-354-5500 Toll Free Tel: 800-233-4830 (orders & cust serv) Fax: 212-869-0856 Toll Free Tel: 800-458-6515 E-mail: orders@wwnorton.com Web Site: wwnorton.com, pg 152

Mayers, Aaron, Abrams Learning Trends, 16310 Bratton Lane, Suite 250, Austin, TX 78728-2403 Toll Free Tel: 800-227-9120 Toll Free Fax: 800-737-3322 E-mail: customerservice@abramslearningtrends.com (orders, cust serv); contactus@abramslearningtrends.com Web Site: www.abramslearningtrends.com (orders, cust serv), pg 3

Mayfield, Tyler, Louisville Grawemeyer Award in Religion, 1044 Alta Vista Rd, Louisville, KY 40205-1798 Tel: 502-895-3411 Toll Free Tel: 800-264-1839 Fax: 502-894-2286 E-mail: grawemeyer@lpts.edu Web Site: www.grawemeyer.org, pg 635

Mayland, Chris, Encyclopaedia Britannica Inc, 325 N La Salle St, Suite 200, Chicago, IL 60654 Tel: 312-347-7000 (all other countries) Toll Free Tel: 800-323-1229 (US & CN) Fax: 312-294-2104 E-mail: contact@eb.com Web Site: www.britannica.com, pg 72

Maynard, Gary, The Gary-Paul Agency, 1549 Main St, Stratford, CT 06615 Tel: 203-345-6167 Web Site: www.thegarypaulagency.com; www.nutmegpictures.com, pg 464

Mayotte, Alain, Editions Prise de parole, 109 Elm St, Suite 205, Sudbury, ON P3C 1T4, Canada Tel: 705-675-6491 Fax: 705-673-1817 E-mail: info@prisedeparole.ca Web Site: www.prisedeparole.ca, pg 438

Mays, Wendy, WendyLynn & Co, 504 Wilson Rd, Annapolis, MD 21401 Tel: 410-224-2729; 410-507-1059 Web Site: wendylynn.com, pg 512

Maze, Stephanie, Moonstone Press LLC, 4816 Carrington Circle, Sarasota, FL 34243 Tel: 301-765-1081 Fax: 301-765-0510 E-mail: mazeprod@erols.com Web Site: www.moonstonepress.net, pg 447

Mazer, Cherie, Bisk Education, 9417 Princess Palm Ave, Suite 400, Tampa, FL 33619 Tel: 813-621-6200 Toll Free Tel: 800-280-9718 (cust serv) E-mail: customerservice@bisk.com Web Site: www.bisk.com, pg 33

Mazer, Laura, Wendy Sherman Associates Inc, 138 W 25 St, Suite 1018, New York, NY 10001 Tel: 212-279-9027 E-mail: submissions@wsherman.com Web Site: www.wsherman.com, pg 502

Mazia, Judith, Alan Wofsy Fine Arts, 1109 Geary Blvd, San Francisco, CA 94109 Tel: 415-292-6500 Toll Free Tel: 800-660-6403 Fax: 415-292-6594 (off & cust serv); 510-251-1840 (acctg) E-mail: order@art-books.com (orders); editeur@earthlink.net (edit); beauxarts@earthlink.net (cust serv) Web Site: www.art-books.com, pg 243

Mazurkiewicz, Orchid, UCLA Latin American Center Publications, UCLA Latin American Institute, 10343 Bunche Hall, Los Angeles, CA 90095 Tel: 310-825-4571 Fax: 310-206-6859 E-mail: latinamctr@international.ucla.edu Web Site: www.international.ucla.edu/lai, pg 223

Mazza, Cris, University of Illinois at Chicago, Program for Writers, College of Liberal Arts & Sciences, 2027 University Hall, 601 S Morgan St, Chicago, IL 60607-7120 Tel: 312-413-2200 (Eng dept) Fax: 312-413-1005 Web Site: www.uic.edu, pg 586

McAdam, Elena Goranescu, McGill-Queen's University Press, 1010 Sherbrooke W, Suite 1720, Montreal, QC H3A 2R7, Canada Tel: 514-398-3750 Fax: 514-398-4333 E-mail: mqup@mqup.ca Web Site: www.mqup.ca, pg 433

McAdam, Matthew, Johns Hopkins University Press, 2715 N Charles St, Baltimore, MD 21218-4363 Tel: 410-516-6900; 410-516-6987 (journal orders outside US & CN) Toll Free Tel: 800-537-5487 (book orders & cust serv); 800-548-1784 (journal orders) *Fax:* 410-516-6968; 410-516-3866 (journal orders); 410-516-6998 (orders) *E-mail:* hfscustserv@press.jhu. edu (cust serv); jrnlcirc@press.jhu.edu (journal orders) *Web Site:* www.press.jhu.edu; muse.jhu.edu, pg 114

McAdams, Kevin, Schiavone Literary Agency Inc, 236 Trails End, West Palm Beach, FL 33413-2135 *Tel:* 561-966-9294 *Fax:* 561-966-9294 *E-mail:* profschia@aol.com *Web Site:* www. publishersmarketplace.com/members/profschia, pg 501

McAdoo, Lynne, Andrews McMeel Publishing LLC, 1130 Walnut St, Kansas City, MO 64106-2109 *Toll Free Tel:* 800-851-8923; 800-943-9839 (cust serv) *Toll Free Fax:* 800-943-9831 (orders) *E-mail:* sales@ amuniversal.com *Web Site:* www.andrewsmcmeel.com; publishing.andrewsmcmeel.com, pg 16

McAllister, Casey, PRINTING United Alliance, 10015 Main St, Fairfax, VA 22031-3489 *Tel:* 703-385-1335 *Toll Free Tel:* 888-385-3588 *Fax:* 703-273-0456; 703-691-7492 (membership) *E-mail:* assist@printing.org; info@printing.org *Web Site:* www.printing.org; www. sgia.org, pg 544

McAnarney, Katharine, Little, Brown Books for Young Readers, 1290 Avenue of the Americas, New York, NY 10104 *Tel:* 212-364-1100 *Toll Free Tel:* 800-759-0190 (cust serv) *Web Site:* www.hachettebookgroup. com, pg 126

McAnespia, Elena, University of California Press, 155 Grand Ave, Suite 400, Oakland, CA 94612-3758 *Tel:* 510-883-8232 *Fax:* 510-836-8910 *E-mail:* generalmailbox@ucpress.edu *Web Site:* www. ucpress.edu, pg 226

McArthur, Stephen, Rootstock Publishing, 27 Main St, Suite 6, Montpelier, VT 05602 *Tel:* 802-839-0371 *E-mail:* info@rootstockpublishing.com *Web Site:* www.rootstockpublishing.com, pg 187

McAuley, Genny, Chronicle Books, 680 Second St, San Francisco, CA 94107 *Tel:* 415-537-4200 *Toll Free Tel:* 800-759-0190 (cust serv) *Fax:* 415-537-4460 *Toll Free Fax:* 800-858-7787 (orders); 800-286-9471 (cust serv) *E-mail:* frontdesk@chroniclebooks.com *Web Site:* www.chroniclebooks.com, pg 51

McAuley, Scott, Angel City Press, 2118 Wilshire Blvd, Suite 880, Santa Monica, CA 90403 *Tel:* 310-395-9982 *Toll Free Tel:* 800-949-8039 *Fax:* 310-395-3353 *E-mail:* info@angelcitypress.com *Web Site:* www. angelcitypress.com, pg 16

McAuliffe, Lisa, Houghton Mifflin Harcourt, 125 High St, Boston, MA 02110 *Tel:* 617-351-5000 *Toll Free Tel:* 855-969-4642; 800-225-5425 (K-12 educ materials); 800-323-9540 (assessment materials); 877-219-1537 (SkillsTutor); 888-242-6747 (Innovation in Educ Group); 800-225-3362 (Trade & Ref Div) *Toll Free Fax:* 800-269-5232 *E-mail:* myhmco@hmhco. com *Web Site:* www.hmhco.com, pg 103

McAweeney, Terry, MFA Publications, 465 Huntington Ave, Boston, MA 02115 *Tel:* 617-369-4233 *E-mail:* publications@mfa.org *Web Site:* www.mfa. org/publications, pg 139

McBride, Andre, Penny-Farthing Productions, One Sugar Creek Center Blvd, Suite 820, Sugar Land, TX 77478 *Tel:* 713-780-0300 *Toll Free Tel:* 800-926-2669 *Fax:* 713-780-4004 *E-mail:* corp@pfproductions.com *Web Site:* www.pfproductions.com, pg 166

McBride, David, Oxford University Press USA, 198 Madison Ave, New York, NY 10016 *Toll Free Tel:* 800-451-7556 (orders); 800-445-9714 (cust serv) *Fax:* 919-677-1303 *E-mail:* custserv.us@oup.com *Web Site:* global.oup.com, pg 158

McBride, Margret, Margret McBride Literary Agency, PO Box 9128, La Jolla, CA 92038 *Tel:* 858-454-1550 *E-mail:* staff@mcbridelit.com *Web Site:* www. mcbrideliterary.com, pg 496

McBride, Tammy, Business Forms Management Association (BFMA), 1147 Fleetwood Ave, Madison, WI 53716-1417 *Toll Free Tel:* 888-367-3078 *E-mail:* bfma@bfma.org *Web Site:* www.bfma.org, pg 529

McBroom, Taylor, Houghton Mifflin Harcourt Trade & Reference Division, 125 High St, Boston, MA 02110 *Tel:* 617-351-5000 *Web Site:* www.hmhco.com, pg 104

McCabe, Don, AVKO Educational Research Foundation Inc, 3084 Willard Rd, Birch Run, MI 48415-9404 *Tel:* 810-686-9283 (orders & billing) *Fax:* 810-686-1101 *E-mail:* info@avko.org (gen inquiry) *Web Site:* www.avko.org; www.avko.blogspot.org, pg 26

McCabe, Robert, AVKO Educational Research Foundation Inc, 3084 Willard Rd, Birch Run, MI 48415-9404 *Tel:* 810-686-9283 (orders & billing) *Fax:* 810-686-1101 *E-mail:* info@avko.org (gen inquiry) *Web Site:* www.avko.org; www.avko.blogspot. org, pg 26

McCabe, Sarah, Simon & Schuster Children's Publishing, 1230 Avenue of the Americas, New York, NY 10020 *Tel:* 212-698-7000 *Web Site:* www. simonandschuster.com/kids; www.simonandschuster. com/teen; simonandschuster.net; simonandschuster.biz, pg 199

McCafferty, Taylor, Islandport Press, 247 Portland St, Bldg C, Yarmouth, ME 04096 *Tel:* 207-846-3344 *Fax:* 207-619-9975 *E-mail:* info@islandportpress.com *Web Site:* www.islandportpress.com, pg 112

McCaffrey, Roger A, Roman Catholic Books, PO Box 2286, Fort Collins, CO 80522-2286 *Tel:* 970-490-2735 *Fax:* 904-493-8781 *Web Site:* www.booksforcatholics. com, pg 186

McCaffrey, Tara, Ferguson Publishing, 132 W 31 St, 17th fl, New York, NY 10001 *Tel:* 212-967-8800 *Toll Free Tel:* 800-322-8755 *Toll Free Fax:* 800-678-3633 *E-mail:* custserv@factsonfile.com *Web Site:* infobasepublishing.com, pg 77

McCain, Rev Paul T, Concordia Publishing House, 3558 S Jefferson Ave, St Louis, MO 63118-3968 *Tel:* 314-268-1000; 314-268-1268 (bookshop) *Toll Free Tel:* 800-325-3040 (cust serv) *Toll Free Fax:* 800-490-9889 (cust serv) *E-mail:* order@cph.org *Web Site:* www.cph.org, pg 56

McCall, Jay, The Society of Southwestern Authors (SSA), PO Box 30355, Tucson, AZ 85751-0355 *E-mail:* info@ssa-az.org *Web Site:* www.ssa-az.org, pg 547

McCall, Jay, The Society of Southwestern Authors Writing Contest, PO Box 30355, Tucson, AZ 85751-0355 *E-mail:* info@ssa-az.org *Web Site:* www.ssa-az.org, pg 669

McCall, Jeff, Twenty-Third Publications, One Montauk Ave, Suite 200, New London, CT 06320 *Tel:* 860-437-3012 *Toll Free Tel:* 800-321-0411 (orders) *Toll Free Fax:* 800-572-0788 *E-mail:* resources@ twentythirdpublications.com *Web Site:* www. twentythirdpublications.com, pg 223

McCall, Michael, Country Music Foundation Press, 222 Fifth Ave S, Nashville, TN 37203 *Tel:* 615-416-2001 *Fax:* 615-255-2245 *E-mail:* info@ countrymusichalloffame.org *Web Site:* www. countrymusichalloffame.org, pg 58

McCall, Tim, Dover Publications Inc, 31 E Second St, Mineola, NY 11501-3852 *Tel:* 516-294-7000 *Toll Free Tel:* 800-223-3130 (orders) *Fax:* 516-742-6953 *E-mail:* rights@doverpublications.com; service@doverpublications.com; doversales@ doverpublications.com *Web Site:* store.doverdirect.com; www.doverpublications.com, pg 67

McCann, Peg, American Society of Agricultural & Biological Engineers (ASABE), 2950 Niles Rd, St Joseph, MI 49085-9659 *Tel:* 269-429-0300 *Toll Free Tel:* 800-371-2723 *Fax:* 269-429-3852 *E-mail:* hq@ asabe.org *Web Site:* www.asabe.org, pg 14

McCants, Cassidy, The Pablo Neruda Prize for Poetry, Nimrod International Journal, 800 S Tucker Dr, Tulsa, OK 74104 *Tel:* 918-631-3080 *Fax:* 918-631-3033 *E-mail:* nimrod@utulsa.edu *Web Site:* www.utulsa. edu/nimrod, pg 646

McCants, Cassidy, Katherine Anne Porter Prize for Fiction, Nimrod International Journal, 800 S Tucker Dr, Tulsa, OK 74104 *Tel:* 918-631-3080 *Fax:* 918-631-3033 *E-mail:* nimrod@utulsa.edu *Web Site:* www. utulsa.edu/nimrod, pg 657

McCarren, William, National Press Club (NPC), 529 14 St NW, 13th fl, Washington, DC 20045 *Tel:* 202-662-7500 *Web Site:* www.press.org, pg 540

McCarter, Linda Malnasi, American Psychological Association, 750 First St NE, Washington, DC 20002-4242 *Tel:* 202-336-5510 *Toll Free Tel:* 800-374-2721 *Fax:* 202-336-5502 *E-mail:* order@apa.org *Web Site:* www.apa.org/books, pg 13

McCarthy, Brian, The Library of America, 14 E 60 St, New York, NY 10022-1006 *Tel:* 212-308-3360 *Fax:* 212-750-8352 *E-mail:* info@loa.org *Web Site:* www.loa.org, pg 124

McCarthy, Dan, The Taunton Press Inc, 63 S Main St, Newtown, CT 06470 *Tel:* 203-426-8171 *Toll Free Tel:* 800-477-8727 (cust serv); 800-888-8286 (orders) *Fax:* 203-426-3434 *E-mail:* booksales@taunton.com *Web Site:* www.taunton.com, pg 213

McCarthy, E J, E J McCarthy Agency, 405 Maple St, Suite H, Mill Valley, CA 94941 *Tel:* 415-383-6639 *E-mail:* ejmagency@gmail.com *Web Site:* www. publishersmarketplace.com/members/ejmccarthy, pg 496

McCarthy, Jim, Dystel, Goderich & Bourret LLC, One Union Sq W, Suite 904, New York, NY 10003 *Tel:* 212-627-9100 *Fax:* 212-627-9313 *Web Site:* www. dystel.com, pg 482

McCarthy, Juliana M, Johns Hopkins University Press, 2715 N Charles St, Baltimore, MD 21218-4363 *Tel:* 410-516-6900; 410-516-6987 (journal orders outside US & CN) *Toll Free Tel:* 800-537-5487 (book orders & cust serv); 800-548-1784 (journal orders) *Fax:* 410-516-6968; 410-516-3866 (journal orders); 410-516-6998 (orders) *E-mail:* hfscustserv@press.jhu. edu (cust serv); jrnlcirc@press.jhu.edu (journal orders) *Web Site:* www.press.jhu.edu; muse.jhu.edu, pg 114

McCaskey, Caitlin, Penguin Random House Speakers Bureau, A Penguin Random House Company, 1745 Broadway, Mail Drop 13-1, New York, NY 10019 *Tel:* 212-572-2013 *E-mail:* speakers@ penguinrandomhouse.com *Web Site:* www.prhspeakers. com, pg 515

McCauley, Gerard, Gerard McCauley Agency Inc, PO Box 844, Katonah, NY 10536-0844 *Tel:* 914-232-5700, pg 496

McCauley, Katie, American College of Surgeons, 633 N Saint Clair St, Chicago, IL 60611-3211 *Tel:* 312-202-5000 *Fax:* 312-202-5001 *E-mail:* postmaster@facs.org *Web Site:* www.facs.org, pg 10

McCauley, Kay, Aurous Inc, PO Box 20490, New York, NY 10017 *Tel:* 212-628-9729 *Fax:* 212-535-7861, pg 475

McCauley, Kirby, Aurous Inc, PO Box 20490, New York, NY 10017 *Tel:* 212-628-9729 *Fax:* 212-535-7861, pg 475

McCauley, Patricia, Quincannon Publishing Group, PO Box 8100, Glen Ridge, NJ 07028-8100 *Tel:* 973-380-9942 *E-mail:* editors@quincannongroup.com (query first via e-mail) *Web Site:* www.quincannongroup.com, pg 179

McClain, J Cameron, Cedar Grove Publishing, 3205 Elmhurst St, Rowlett, TX 75088 *Tel:* 415-364-8292 *E-mail:* queries@cedargrovebooks.com *Web Site:* www.cedargrovebooks.com, pg 47

McClanahan, Debbie, Cenveo Publisher Services, 555 Virginia Dr, Fort Washington, PA 19034 *Tel:* 267-470-1590 *Fax:* 215-591-9093 *E-mail:* info.psg@cenveo. com *Web Site:* www.cenveopublisherservices.com, pg 460

McClary, Erin, Sourcebooks LLC, 1935 Brookdale Rd, Suite 139, Naperville, IL 60563 *Tel:* 630-961-3900 *Toll Free Tel:* 800-432-7444 *Fax:* 630-961-2168 *E-mail:* info@sourcebooks.com; customersupport@ sourcebooks.com *Web Site:* www.sourcebooks.com, pg 204

McClay, Ashley Pattison, GP Putnam's Sons (Hardcover), 375 Hudson St, New York, NY 10014 *Tel:* 212-366-2000 *Fax:* 212-366-2643 *E-mail:* online@penguinputnam.com *Web Site:* www. penguin.com/publishers/gpputnamssons, pg 178

McClearn, Lauren, Sourcebooks LLC, 1935 Brookdale Rd, Suite 139, Naperville, IL 60563 *Tel:* 630-961-3900 *Toll Free Tel:* 800-432-7444 *Fax:* 630-961-2168 *E-mail:* info@sourcebooks.com; customersupport@sourcebooks.com *Web Site:* www.sourcebooks.com, pg 204

McClellan, Anita, Anita D McClellan Associates, 464 Common St, Suite 142, Belmont, MA 02478-2704 *Tel:* 617-575-9203 *E-mail:* adm@anitamcclellan.com *Web Site:* www.anitamcclellan.com, pg 496

McClellan, Anita D, Anita D McClellan Associates, 464 Common St, Suite 142, Belmont, MA 02478-2704 *Tel:* 617-575-9203 *E-mail:* adm@anitamcclellan.com *Web Site:* www.anitamcclellan.com, pg 467

McClelland, Anne, Book & Periodical Council (BPC), 192 Spadina Ave, Suite 107, Toronto, ON M5T 2C2, Canada *Tel:* 416-975-9366 *Fax:* 416-975-1839 *E-mail:* info@thebpc.ca *Web Site:* www.thebpc.ca, pg 528

McClelland-Smith, Jennifer, Tom Doherty Associates, LLC, 120 Broadway, New York, NY 10271 *Tel:* 646-307-5511 *Toll Free Tel:* 800-455-0340 *Web Site:* us.macmillan.com/torforge, pg 66

McClenny, Katie, National Music Publishers' Association (NMPA), 975 "F" St NW, Suite 375, Washington, DC 20004 *Tel:* 202-393-6672 *E-mail:* members@nmpa.org *Web Site:* nmpa.org, pg 540

McClure, Cameron, Donald Maass Literary Agency, 1000 Dean St, Suite 252, Brooklyn, NY 11238 *Tel:* 212-727-8383 *E-mail:* info@maassagency.com *Web Site:* www.maassagency.com, pg 493

McClure, John, Signalman Publishing, 3700 Commerce Blvd, Kissimmee, FL 34741 *Tel:* 407-504-4103 *Toll Free Tel:* 888-907-4423 *E-mail:* info@signalmanpublishing.com *Web Site:* www.signalmanpublishing.com, pg 198

McClure, Lauren, Michelin Maps & Guides, One Parkway S, Greenville, SC 29615-5022 *E-mail:* michelin.guides@michelin.com *Web Site:* guide.michelin.com; michelinmedia.com, pg 139

McCollom, Tamar, Scribner, 1230 Avenue of the Americas, New York, NY 10020, pg 195

McConkey, Jill, University of Manitoba Press, University of Manitoba, 301 St Johns College, 92 Dysart Rd, Winnipeg, MB R3T 2M5, Canada *Tel:* 204-474-9495 *Fax:* 204-474-7566 *E-mail:* uofmpress@umanitoba.ca *Web Site:* uofmpress.ca, pg 443

McConnell, David B, Hillsdale Educational Publishers Inc, 39 North St, Hillsdale, MI 49242 *Tel:* 517-437-3179 *Fax:* 517-437-0531 *E-mail:* davestory@aol.com *Web Site:* www.hillsdalepublishers.com; michbooks.com, pg 99

McConnell, Vicki, Geological Society of America (GSA), 3300 Penrose Place, Boulder, CO 80301-1806 *Tel:* 303-357-1000 *Fax:* 303-357-1070 *E-mail:* pubs@geosociety.org (prodn); editing@geosociety.org (edit) *Web Site:* www.geosociety.org, pg 84

McCord, Jennifer, Epicenter Press Inc, 6524 NE 181 St, Suite 2, Kenmore, WA 98028 *Tel:* 425-485-6822 (edit, mktg, busn off) *Fax:* 425-481-8253 *E-mail:* info@epicenterpress.com *Web Site:* www.epicenterpress.com, pg 73

McCord, Luke, Random House Children's Books, 1745 Broadway, 10th fl, New York, NY 10019 *Tel:* 212-782-9000 *Web Site:* www.randomhousekids.com, pg 181

McCormack, Wendy, National Institute for Trial Advocacy (NITA), 1685 38 St, Suite 200, Boulder, CO 80301-2735 *Tel:* 720-890-4860 *Toll Free Tel:* 877-648-2632; 800-225-6482 (orders & returns) *Fax:* 720-890-7069 *E-mail:* customerservice@nita.org; sales@nita.org *Web Site:* www.nita.org, pg 147

McCormick, Tina, Penguin Group USA, A Penguin Random House Company, 375 Hudson St, New York, NY 10014 *Tel:* 212-366-2000 *Toll Free Tel:* 800-847-5515 (inside sales); 800-631-8571 (cust serv)

Fax: 212-366-2666; 607-775-4829 (inside sales) *E-mail:* online@us.penguingroup.com *Web Site:* www.penguin.com, pg 163

McCormick, Wynona, Texas A&M University Press, John H Lindsey Bldg, Lewis St, 4354 TAMU, College Station, TX 77843-4354 *Tel:* 979-845-1436 *Toll Free Tel:* 800-826-8911 (orders) *Fax:* 979-847-8752 *Toll Free Fax:* 888-617-2421 (orders) *E-mail:* bookorders@tamu.edu *Web Site:* www.tamupress.com, pg 215

McCoy, James, Iowa Poetry Prize, 119 W Park Rd, 100 Kuhl House, Iowa City, IA 52242-1000 *Tel:* 319-335-2000 *Fax:* 319-335-2055 *E-mail:* uipress@uiowa.edu *Web Site:* www.uipress.uiowa.edu, pg 627

McCoy, James, Iowa Prize for Literary Nonfiction, 119 W Park Rd, 100 Kuhl House, Iowa City, IA 52242-1000 *Tel:* 319-335-2000 *Fax:* 319-335-2055 *E-mail:* uipress@uiowa.edu *Web Site:* www.uipress.uiowa.edu, pg 627

McCoy, James, University of Iowa Press, 119 W Park Rd, 100 Kuhl House, Iowa City, IA 52242-1000 *Tel:* 319-335-2000 *Toll Free Tel:* 800-621-2736 (orders only) *Fax:* 319-335-2055 *Toll Free Fax:* 800-621-8476 (orders only) *E-mail:* uipress@uiowa.edu *Web Site:* www.uipress.uiowa.edu, pg 228

McCoy, Melody, Jhpiego, 1615 Thames St, Baltimore, MD 21231-3492 *Tel:* 410-537-1800 *Fax:* 410-537-1473 *E-mail:* info@jhpiego.net *Web Site:* www.jhpiego.org, pg 113

McCracken, Elizabeth, University of Texas at Austin, New Writers Project, Dept of English, Calhoun Hall, Rm 226, 204 W 21 St, B-5000, Austin, TX 78712 *Tel:* 512-471-5132; 512-471-4991 *Fax:* 512-471-4909 *Web Site:* newwritersproject.org, pg 586

McCracken, Kelly, Franciscan Media, 28 W Liberty St, Cincinnati, OH 45202 *Tel:* 513-241-5615 *Toll Free Tel:* 800-488-0488 *E-mail:* admin@franciscanmedia.org *Web Site:* www.franciscanmedia.org, pg 81

McCrae, Fiona, Graywolf Press, 250 Third Ave N, Suite 600, Minneapolis, MN 55401 *Tel:* 651-641-0077 *Fax:* 651-641-0036 *E-mail:* wolves@graywolfpress.org (no ms queries, sample chapters or proposals) *Web Site:* www.graywolfpress.org, pg 88

McCreary, Courtney, University Press of Mississippi, 3825 Ridgewood Rd, Jackson, MS 39211-6492 *Tel:* 601-432-6205 *Toll Free Tel:* 800-737-7788 (orders & cust serv) *Fax:* 601-432-6217 *E-mail:* press@mississippi.edu *Web Site:* www.upress.state.ms.us, pg 233

McCrillis, Tara, Fodor's Travel, 909 N Sepulveda Blvd, El Segundo, CA 90245 *E-mail:* marketing@fodors.com *Web Site:* www.fodors.com, pg 79

McCrosky, Judy, SF Canada, 516 Ninth St E, Saskatoon, SK S7N 0B1, Canada *Web Site:* www.sfcanada.org, pg 546

McCue, Mary, Random House Children's Books, 1745 Broadway, 10th fl, New York, NY 10019 *Tel:* 212-782-9000 *Web Site:* www.randomhousekids.com, pg 180

McCullough, Mark S, Wyndham Hall Press, 10372 W Munro Lake Dr, Levering, MI 49755 *Tel:* 419-648-9124 *E-mail:* orders@wyndhamhallpress.com *Web Site:* www.wyndhamhallpress.com, pg 246

McCullough, Robert, Penguin Random House Canada, 320 Front St W, Suite 1400, Toronto, ON M5V 3B6, Canada *Tel:* 416-364-4449 *Toll Free Tel:* 888-523-9292 (cust serv) *Fax:* 416-598-7764 *Web Site:* www.penguinrandomhouse.ca, pg 436

McCune, Sara Miller, SAGE Publishing, 2455 Teller Rd, Thousand Oaks, CA 91320 *Toll Free Tel:* 800-818-7243 *Toll Free Fax:* 800-583-2665 *E-mail:* info@sagepub.com; orders@sagepub.com *Web Site:* www.sagepublishing.com, pg 189

McCurdy, Wendy, Kensington Publishing Corp, 119 W 40 St, New York, NY 10018 *Tel:* 212-407-1500 *Toll Free Tel:* 800-221-2647 *Fax:* 212-935-0699 *Web Site:* www.kensingtonbooks.com, pg 116

McCutcheon, Camille, Southern Books Competition, PO Box 950, Rex, GA 30273 *Tel:* 678-466-4334 *Fax:* 678-466-4349 *Web Site:* selaonline.org, pg 669

McCutcheon, Kathleen, Macmillan, 120 Broadway, 22nd fl, New York, NY 10271 *Tel:* 646-307-5151 *E-mail:* press.inquiries@macmillan.com *Web Site:* www.macmillan.com, pg 130

McDermott, Kathleen, Harvard University Press, 79 Garden St, Cambridge, MA 02138-1499 *Tel:* 617-495-2600; 401-531-2800 (intl orders) *Toll Free Tel:* 800-405-1619 (orders) *Fax:* 617-495-5898 (gen); 617-496-4677 (edit & rts); 401-531-2801 (intl orders) *Toll Free Fax:* 800-406-9145 (orders) *E-mail:* contact_hup@harvard.edu *Web Site:* www.hup.harvard.edu, pg 95

McDonald, Alison, Gagosian Gallery, 980 Madison Ave, New York, NY 10075 *Tel:* 212-744-2313 *Fax:* 212-772-7962 *E-mail:* newyork@gagosian.com *Web Site:* www.gagosian.com, pg 82

McDonald, Brandy, Ozark Mountain Publishing Inc, PO Box 754, Huntsville, AR 72740-0754 *Tel:* 479-738-2348 *Toll Free Tel:* 800-935-0045 *Fax:* 479-738-2448 *E-mail:* info@ozarkmt.com *Web Site:* www.ozarkmt.com, pg 158

McDonald, Caitlin, Donald Maass Literary Agency, 1000 Dean St, Suite 252, Brooklyn, NY 11238 *Tel:* 212-727-8383 *E-mail:* info@maassagency.com *Web Site:* www.maassagency.com, pg 493

McDonald, Erroll, The Center for Fiction, 17 E 47 St, New York, NY 10017 *Tel:* 212-755-6710 *E-mail:* info@centerforfiction.org *Web Site:* centerforfiction.org, pg 530

McDonald, Erroll, Pantheon Books, c/o Penguin Random House Inc, 1745 Broadway, New York, NY 10019 *Tel:* 212-751-2600 *Fax:* 212-572-2662 (foreign rts) *Web Site:* www.knopfdoubleday.com, pg 159

McDonald, Jerry N, The McDonald & Woodward Publishing Co, 695 Tall Oaks Dr, Newark, OH 43055 *Tel:* 740-641-2691 *Toll Free Tel:* 800-233-8787 *Fax:* 740-641-2692 *E-mail:* mwpubco@mwpubco.com *Web Site:* www.mwpubco.com, pg 135

McDonald, Mary, American Philosophical Society, 104 S Fifth St, Philadelphia, PA 19106 *Tel:* 215-440-3425 *Fax:* 215-440-3450 *E-mail:* orders@dianepublishing.net *Web Site:* www.amphilsoc.org, pg 13

McDonald, Scott, Advertising Research Foundation (ARF), 432 Park Ave S, 4th fl, New York, NY 10016-8013 *Tel:* 212-751-5656 *Fax:* 212-689-1859 *E-mail:* help@thearf.org *Web Site:* thearf.org, pg 521

McDonald, Sean, Farrar, Straus & Giroux, LLC, 175 Varick St, 9th fl, New York, NY 10014 *Tel:* 212-741-6900 *E-mail:* fsg.publicity@fsgbooks.com *Web Site:* us.macmillan.com/fsg.aspx, pg 76

McDonnell, Joshua, Perseus Books, 1290 Avenue of the Americas, New York, NY 10104 *Tel:* 212-340-8100 *Toll Free Tel:* 800-343-4499 (cust serv) *Fax:* 212-340-8105 *Web Site:* www.perseusbooks.com, pg 168

McDonnell, Mark, Bloom's Literary Criticism, 132 W 31 St, 17th fl, New York, NY 10001 *Toll Free Tel:* 800-322-8755 *Toll Free Fax:* 800-678-3633 *E-mail:* custserv@factsonfile.com *Web Site:* www.infobasepublishing.com, pg 35

McDonnell, Mark, Chelsea House, 132 W 31 St, 17th fl, New York, NY 10001 *Toll Free Tel:* 800-322-8755 *Toll Free Fax:* 800-678-3633 *E-mail:* custserv@factsonfile.com; info@infobase.com *Web Site:* www.infobasepublishing.com; www.infobase.com, pg 50

McDonnell, Mark, Facts On File, 132 W 31 St, 17th fl, New York, NY 10001 *Tel:* 212-967-8800 *Toll Free Tel:* 800-322-8755 *Toll Free Fax:* 800-678-3633 *E-mail:* custserv@factsonfile.com *Web Site:* infobasepublishing.com, pg 74

McDonnell, Mark, Ferguson Publishing, 132 W 31 St, 17th fl, New York, NY 10001 *Tel:* 212-967-8800 *Toll Free Tel:* 800-322-8755 *Toll Free Fax:* 800-678-3633 *E-mail:* custserv@factsonfile.com *Web Site:* infobasepublishing.com, pg 77

McDonough, Brian, Gale, 27500 Drake Rd, Farmington Hills, MI 48331-3535 *Tel:* 248-699-4253 *Toll Free Tel:* 800-877-4253 *Toll Free Fax:* 800-414-5043 (orders) *E-mail:* gale.customercare@cengage.com *Web Site:* www.gale.com, pg 82

McDonough, Brian, Macmillan Reference USA™, 27500 Drake Rd, Farmington Hills, MI 48331-3535 *Tel:* 248-699-4253 *Toll Free Tel:* 800-877-4253 *Toll Free Fax:* 877-363-4253 *E-mail:* gale.customercare@cengage.com *Web Site:* www.gale.cengage.com/macmillan, pg 130

McDonough, Liz, University of California Extension Professional Sequence in Copyediting & Courses in Publishing, 1995 University Ave, Suite 110, Berkeley, CA 94720-7000 *Tel:* 510-642-6362 *Fax:* 510-643-0216 *E-mail:* letters@unex.berkeley.edu *Web Site:* www.unex.berkeley.edu, pg 585

McDowall, Katy, Prufrock Press, PO Box 8813, Waco, TX 76714-8813 *Tel:* 254-756-3337 *Toll Free Tel:* 800-998-2208 *Fax:* 254-756-3339 *Toll Free Fax:* 800-240-0333 *E-mail:* info@prufrock.com *Web Site:* www.prufrock.com, pg 177

McDowell, Andy, Gulf Energy Information, 2 Greenway Plaza, Suite 1020, Houston, TX 77046 *Tel:* 713-529-4301 *E-mail:* store@gulfpub.com; customerservice@energyinfo.com *Web Site:* www.gulfenergyinfo.com, pg 90

McDuffie, John D, American Psychiatric Association Publishing, 800 Maine Ave SW, Suite 900, Washington, DC 20024 *Tel:* 202-459-9722 *Toll Free Tel:* 800-368-5777 *Fax:* 202-403-3094 *E-mail:* appi@psych.org *Web Site:* www.appi.org; www.psychiatryonline.org, pg 13

McElhinney, Sinead, Kobo Emerging Writer Prize, 135 Liberty St, Suite 101, Toronto, ON M6K 1A7, Canada *E-mail:* pr@kobo.com *Web Site:* www.kobo.com/emergingwriterprize, pg 630

McElhinny, Dan, William H Sadlier Inc, 9 Pine St, New York, NY 10005 *Tel:* 212-227-2120 *Toll Free Tel:* 800-221-5175 (cust serv) *Fax:* 212-312-6080 *E-mail:* customerservice@sadlier.com *Web Site:* www.sadlier.com, pg 189

McElvane, Clyde, Hurston/Wright Award for College Writers, 10 "G" St NE, Suite 600, Washington, DC 20002 *Tel:* 202-248-5051 *E-mail:* info@hurstonwright.org *Web Site:* www.hurstonwright.org, pg 625

McElvane, Clyde, Hurston/Wright Legacy Awards, 10 "G" St NE, Suite 600, Washington, DC 20002 *Tel:* 202-248-5051 *E-mail:* info@hurstonwright.org *Web Site:* www.hurstonwright.org, pg 625

McElvane, Clyde, Hurston/Wright Writers Week, 10 "G" St NE, Suite 600, Washington, DC 20002 *Tel:* 202-248-5051 *E-mail:* info@hurstonwright.org *Web Site:* www.hurstonwright.org, pg 575

McElvane, Clyde, The Zora Neale Hurston/Richard Wright Foundation, 10 "G" St NE, Suite 600, Washington, DC 20002 *Tel:* 202-248-5051 *E-mail:* info@hurstonwright.org *Web Site:* www.hurstonwright.org, pg 551

McEvoy, Nion, Chronicle Books, 680 Second St, San Francisco, CA 94107 *Tel:* 415-537-4200 *Toll Free Tel:* 800-759-0190 (cust serv) *Fax:* 415-537-4460 *Toll Free Fax:* 800-858-7787 (orders); 800-286-9471 (cust serv) *E-mail:* frontdesk@chroniclebooks.com *Web Site:* www.chroniclebooks.com, pg 51

McEwen, Rebecca, Fulcrum Publishing Inc, 4690 Table Mountain Dr, Suite 100, Golden, CO 80403 *Tel:* 303-277-1623 *Toll Free Tel:* 800-992-2908 *Fax:* 303-279-7111 *Toll Free Fax:* 800-726-7112 *E-mail:* info@fulcrumbooks.com; orders@fulcrumbooks.com *Web Site:* www.fulcrumbooks.com, pg 82

McFadden, Daniel, Psychological Assessment Resources Inc (PAR), 16204 N Florida Ave, Lutz, FL 33549 *Tel:* 813-449-4065 *Toll Free Tel:* 800-331-8378 *Fax:* 813-961-2196 *Toll Free Fax:* 800-727-9329 *Web Site:* www.parinc.com, pg 177

McFadden, Trinity, Zondervan, 3900 Sparks Dr, Grand Rapids, MI 49546 *Tel:* 616-698-6900 *Toll Free Tel:* 800-226-1122; 800-727-1309 (retail orders) *Fax:* 616-698-3350 *Toll Free Fax:* 800-698-3256 (retail orders) *Web Site:* www.zondervan.com, pg 248

McFadden, Wendy, Brethren Press, 1451 Dundee Ave, Elgin, IL 60120 *Tel:* 847-742-5100 *Toll Free Tel:* 800-323-8039 *Toll Free Fax:* 800-667-8188 *E-mail:* brethrenpress@brethren.org *Web Site:* www.brethrenpress.com, pg 40

McFarland, Alan, SAMS Technical Publishing LLC, 9850 E 30 St, Indianapolis, IN 46229 *Toll Free Tel:* 800-428-7267 *E-mail:* customercare@samswebsite.com *Web Site:* www.samswebsite.com, pg 191

McFeely, W Drake, W W Norton & Company Inc, 500 Fifth Ave, New York, NY 10110-0017 *Tel:* 212-354-5500 *Toll Free Tel:* 800-233-4830 (orders & cust serv) *Fax:* 212-869-0856 *Toll Free Fax:* 800-458-6515 *E-mail:* orders@wwnorton.com *Web Site:* wwnorton.com, pg 152

McGandy, Michael J, Cornell University Press, Sage House, 512 E State St, Ithaca, NY 14850 *Tel:* 607-253-2338 *Fax:* 607-253-2374 *E-mail:* cupressinfo@cornell.edu; cupress-sales@cornell.edu *Web Site:* www.cornellpress.cornell.edu, pg 57

McGann, Michael, Teachers College Press, 1234 Amsterdam Ave, New York, NY 10027 *Tel:* 212-678-3929 *Fax:* 212-678-4149 *E-mail:* tcpress@tc.edu *Web Site:* www.tcpress.com, pg 214

McGarity, Todd, Hachette Book Group, 1290 Avenue of the Americas, New York, NY 10104 *Tel:* 212-364-1100 *Toll Free Tel:* 800-759-0190 (cust serv) *Fax:* 212-364-0933 (intl orders) *Toll Free Fax:* 800-286-9471 (cust serv) *Web Site:* www.hachettebookgroup.com, pg 91

McGarvey, Joey, Milkweed Editions, 1011 Washington Ave S, Suite 300, Minneapolis, MN 55415-1246 *Tel:* 612-332-3192 *Toll Free Tel:* 800-520-6455 *Fax:* 612-215-2550 *Web Site:* milkweed.org, pg 140

McGauley, Kelly, Random House Children's Books, 1745 Broadway, 10th fl, New York, NY 10019 *Tel:* 212-782-9000 *Web Site:* www.randomhousekids.com, pg 180

McGauley, Sean, Association for Information & Image Management International (AIIM), 1100 Wayne Ave, Suite 1100, Silver Spring, MD 20910 *Tel:* 301-587-8202 *Toll Free Tel:* 800-477-2446 *Fax:* 301-587-2711 *E-mail:* aiim@aiim.org; info@aiim.org *Web Site:* www.aiim.org, pg 525

McGee, Chris, Children's Literature Association Beiter Graduate Student Research Grants, 1301 W 22 St, Suite 202, Oak Brook, IL 60523 *Tel:* 630-571-4520 *Fax:* 708-876-5598 *E-mail:* info@childlitassn.org *Web Site:* www.childlitassn.org, pg 604

McGee, Linda, Bearport Publishing Co Inc, 45 W 21 St, Suite 3B, New York, NY 10010 *Tel:* 212-337-8577 *Toll Free Tel:* 877-337-8577 *Fax:* 212-337-8557 *Toll Free Fax:* 866-337-8557 *E-mail:* service@bearportpublishing.com; info@bearportpublishing.com *Web Site:* www.bearportpublishing.com, pg 30

McGeehon, Allison, Artisan, 225 Varick St, New York, NY 10014-4381 *Tel:* 212-254-5900 *Toll Free Tel:* 800-722-7202 *Fax:* 212-677-6692 *E-mail:* artisaninfo@artisanbooks.com *Web Site:* www.artisanbooks.com; www.workman.com/artisanbooks, pg 21

McGhee, Holly M, Pippin Properties Inc, 110 W 40 St, Suite 1704, New York, NY 10018 *Tel:* 212-338-9310 *E-mail:* info@pippinproperties.com *Web Site:* www.pippinproperties.com; www.facebook.com/pippinproperties, pg 498

McGill, Julia Lee, Scribner, 1230 Avenue of the Americas, New York, NY 10020, pg 195

McGinnis, Claire, Riverhead Books, 375 Hudson St, New York, NY 10014 *Tel:* 212-366-2000 *Web Site:* www.penguin.com/publishers/riverhead, pg 185

McGinnis, Meredith, W W Norton & Company Inc, 500 Fifth Ave, New York, NY 10110-0017 *Tel:* 212-354-5500 *Toll Free Tel:* 800-233-4830 (orders & cust serv) *Fax:* 212-869-0856 *Toll Free Fax:* 800-458-6515 *E-mail:* orders@wwnorton.com *Web Site:* wwnorton.com, pg 152

McGinty, James, Police Executive Research Forum, 1120 Connecticut Ave NW, Suite 930, Washington, DC 20036 *Tel:* 202-466-7820 *Web Site:* www.policeforum.org, pg 172

McGivern, Renee, Society for Advancing Business Editing & Writing (SABEW), Walter Cronkite School of Journalism & Mass Communication, Arizona State University, 555 N Central Ave, Suite 406E, Phoenix, AZ 85004-1248 *Tel:* 602-496-7862 *E-mail:* sabew@sabew.org *Web Site:* sabew.org, pg 546

McGonigle, Michele, Hachette Audio, 1290 Avenue of the Americas, New York, NY 10104 *Tel:* 212-364-1100 *Web Site:* www.hachetteaudio.com, pg 90

McGowan, James, BookEnds Literary Agency, 136 Long Hill Rd, Gillette, NJ 07933 *Web Site:* www.bookendsliterary.com, pg 476

McGowan, Matt, Frances Goldin Literary Agency, Inc, 214 W 29 St, Suite 410, New York, NY 10001 *Tel:* 212-777-0047 *Fax:* 212-228-1660 *E-mail:* agency@goldinlit.com *Web Site:* www.goldinlit.com, pg 486

McGrath, Erinn, Little, Brown and Company, 1290 Avenue of the Americas, New York, NY 10104 *Tel:* 212-364-1100 *Fax:* 212-364-0952 *E-mail:* firstname.lastname@hbgusa.com *Web Site:* www.littlebrown.com; www.hachettebookgroup.com, pg 125

McGrath, Leslie, The Tenth Gate Prize *Tel:* 301-581-9439 *Fax:* 301-581-9443 *E-mail:* editor@wordworksbooks.org *Web Site:* www.wordworksbooks.org, pg 672

McGrath, Sarah, Riverhead Books, 375 Hudson St, New York, NY 10014 *Tel:* 212-366-2000 *Web Site:* www.penguin.com/publishers/riverhead, pg 185

McGrone, Carlton, University Press of Mississippi, 3825 Ridgewood Rd, Jackson, MS 39211-6492 *Tel:* 601-432-6205 *Toll Free Tel:* 800-737-7788 (orders & cust serv) *Fax:* 601-432-6217 *E-mail:* press@mississippi.edu *Web Site:* www.upress.state.ms.us, pg 233

McGuire, Beverly, Coastside Editorial, PO Box 181, Moss Beach, CA 94038 *E-mail:* bevjoe@pacific.net, pg 461

McGuire, Libby, Atria Books, 1230 Avenue of the Americas, New York, NY 10020 *Tel:* 212-698-7000 *Fax:* 212-698-7007 *Web Site:* www.simonandschuster.com, pg 24

McGuire, Libby, Simon & Schuster, Inc, 1230 Avenue of the Americas, New York, NY 10020 *Tel:* 212-698-7000 *Toll Free Tel:* 800-223-2336 (orders) *Fax:* 212-698-7007 *Toll Free Fax:* 800-943-9831 (orders) *E-mail:* firstname.lastname@simonandschuster.com; purchaseorders@simonandschuster.com (orders) *Web Site:* www.simonandschuster.com, pg 199

McGuire, Tim, W W Norton & Company Inc, 500 Fifth Ave, New York, NY 10110-0017 *Tel:* 212-354-5500 *Toll Free Tel:* 800-233-4830 (orders & cust serv) *Fax:* 212-869-0856 *Toll Free Fax:* 800-458-6515 *E-mail:* orders@wwnorton.com *Web Site:* wwnorton.com, pg 152

McGurgan, Diane, Council for the Advancement of Science Writing (CASW), PO Box 910, Hedgesville, WV 25427 *Tel:* 304-754-6786 *Web Site:* www.casw.org, pg 532

McGurk, John, Quirk Books, 215 Church St, Philadelphia, PA 19106 *Tel:* 215-627-3581 *Fax:* 215-627-5220 *E-mail:* general@quirkbooks.com *Web Site:* www.quirkbooks.com, pg 179

McHatton, Ron PhD, Gordon W Dillon/Richard C Peterson Memorial Essay Prize, c/o Fairchild Tropical Botanic Garden, 10901 Old Cutler Rd, Coral Gables, FL 33156 *Tel:* 305-740-2010 *E-mail:* theaos@aos.org *Web Site:* www.aos.org, pg 610

McHugh, Arianne, Saddleback Educational Publishing, 151 Kalmus Dr, Suite J-1, Costa Mesa, CA 92626 *Tel:* 714-640-5200 *Toll Free Tel:* 888-SDLBACK (735-2225); 800-637-8715 *Fax:* 714-640-5297 *Toll Free Fax:* 888-734-4010 *E-mail:* contact@sdlback.com *Web Site:* www.sdlback.com, pg 189

McHugh, Daniel, National Institute for Trial Advocacy (NITA), 1685 38 St, Suite 200, Boulder, CO 80301-2735 *Tel:* 720-890-4860 *Toll Free Tel:* 877-648-2632;

800-225-6482 (orders & returns) *Fax:* 720-890-7069 *E-mail:* customerservice@nita.org; sales@nita.org *Web Site:* www.nita.org, pg 147

McHugh, Elise M, University of New Mexico Press, One University of New Mexico, Albuquerque, NM 87131-0001 *Tel:* 505-272-7777 *Fax:* 505-277-3343 *E-mail:* custserv@unm.edu (order dept) *Web Site:* unmpress.com, pg 229

McHugh, John B, McHugh's Rights/Permissions Workshop™, PO Box 170665, Milwaukee, WI 53217-8056 *Tel:* 414-351-3056 *E-mail:* jack@johnbmchugh. com *Web Site:* www.johnbmchugh.com, pg 576

McInerney, Brittany, Chronicle Books, 680 Second St, San Francisco, CA 94107 *Tel:* 415-537-4200 *Toll Free Tel:* 800-759-0190 (cust serv) *Fax:* 415-537-4460 *Toll Free Fax:* 800-858-7787 (orders); 800-286-9471 (cust serv) *E-mail:* frontdesk@chroniclebooks.com *Web Site:* www.chroniclebooks.com, pg 52

McInerney, Paige, Penguin Group USA, A Penguin Random House Company, 375 Hudson St, New York, NY 10014 *Tel:* 212-366-2000 *Toll Free Tel:* 800-847-5515 (inside sales); 800-631-8571 (cust serv) *Fax:* 212-366-2666; 607-775-4829 (inside sales) *E-mail:* online@us.penguingroup.com *Web Site:* www. penguin.com, pg 163

McInnis, Karen, Association of American Publishers (AAP), 455 Massachusetts Ave NW, Suite 700, Washington, DC 20001-2777 *Tel:* 202-347-3375 *Fax:* 202-347-3690 *E-mail:* info@publishers.org *Web Site:* publishers.org, pg 526

McIntosh, Dorla, Columbia University School of the Arts Creative Writing Program, 609 Kent Hall, New York, NY 10027 *Tel:* 212-854-3774 *Fax:* 212-854-7704 *E-mail:* writingprogram@columbia.edu *Web Site:* www.columbia.edu/cu/writing, pg 582

McIntosh, Joel, Prufrock Press, PO Box 8813, Waco, TX 76714-8813 *Tel:* 254-756-3337 *Toll Free Tel:* 800-998-2208 *Fax:* 254-756-3339 *Toll Free Fax:* 800-240-0333 *E-mail:* info@prufrock.com *Web Site:* www.prufrock. com, pg 177

McIntosh, Kelly, Barbour Publishing Inc, 1810 Barbour Dr, Uhrichsville, OH 44683 *Tel:* 740-922-6045 *Fax:* 740-922-5948 *E-mail:* info@barbourbooks.com *Web Site:* www.barbourbooks.com, pg 27

McIntosh, Madeline, Penguin Random House LLC, 1745 Broadway, New York, NY 10019 *Tel:* 212-782-9000 *Toll Free Tel:* 800-726-0600 *Web Site:* www. penguinrandomhouse.com, pg 164

McIntyre, Jennifer, South Dakota Historical Society Press, 900 Governors Dr, Pierre, SD 57501 *Tel:* 605-773-6009 *Fax:* 605-773-6041 *E-mail:* info@sdshspress.com; orders@sdshspress.com *Web Site:* sdshspress.com, pg 205

McIntyre, Kate, The Jeffrey E Smith Editors' Prize, 357 McReynolds Hall, Columbia, MO 65211 *Tel:* 573-882-4474 *Toll Free Tel:* 800-949-2505 *Fax:* 573-884-4671 *Web Site:* www.missourireview.com, pg 668

McIntyre, Kheil, LearningExpress, 224 W 29 St, 3rd fl, New York, NY 10001 *Toll Free Tel:* 800-295-9556 (ext 2) *Web Site:* learningexpresshub.com, pg 121

McIntyre, Maury, Television Academy, 5220 Lankershim Blvd, North Hollywood, CA 91601-3109 *Tel:* 818-754-2800 *Fax:* 818-761-2827 *Web Site:* www.emmys. com, pg 547

McIntyre, Neil, Dustbooks, PO Box 100, Paradise, CA 95967-0100 *Tel:* 530-877-6110 *Fax:* 530-877-0222 *E-mail:* inquiries@dustbooks.com; info@dustbooks. com *Web Site:* www.dustbooks.com, pg 68

McIntyre, Suzanne Ostiguy, Institute for Research on Public Policy (IRPP), 1470 Peel St, No 200, Montreal, QC H3A 1T1, Canada *Tel:* 514-985-2461 *Fax:* 514-985-2559 *E-mail:* irpp@irpp.org *Web Site:* irpp.org, pg 430

McKay, Angela, Institute of Environmental Sciences & Technology - IEST, 1827 Walden Office Sq, Suite 400, Schaumburg, IL 60173 *Tel:* 847-981-0100 *Fax:* 847-981-4130 *E-mail:* information@iest.org *Web Site:* www.iest.org, pg 109

McKay, John, Association of American Publishers (AAP), 455 Massachusetts Ave NW, Suite 700, Washington, DC 20001-2777 *Tel:* 202-347-3375 *Fax:* 202-347-3690 *E-mail:* info@publishers.org *Web Site:* publishers.org, pg 526

McKay, Matthew (Matt) PhD, New Harbinger Publications Inc, 5674 Shattuck Ave, Oakland, CA 94609 *Tel:* 510-652-0215 *Toll Free Tel:* 800-748-6273 (orders only) *Fax:* 510-652-5472 *Toll Free Fax:* 800-652-1613 *E-mail:* nhhelp@newharbinger.com; customerservice@newharbinger.com *Web Site:* www. newharbinger.com, pg 148

McKay, Sara, Princeton Architectural Press, 202 Warren St, Hudson, NY 12534 *Tel:* 518-671-6100 *Toll Free Tel:* 800-722-6657 (dist); 800-759-0190 (sales) *E-mail:* sales@papress.com *Web Site:* www.papress. com, pg 174

McKean, Claire, Workman Publishing Co Inc, 225 Varick St, 9th fl, New York, NY 10014-4381 *Tel:* 212-254-5900 *Toll Free Tel:* 800-722-7202 *Fax:* 212-254-8098 *E-mail:* info@workman.com; orders@workman. com *Web Site:* www.workman.com, pg 244

McKean, Kate, Howard Morhaim Literary Agency Inc, 30 Pierrepont St, Brooklyn, NY 11201-3371 *Tel:* 718-222-8400 *E-mail:* info@morhaimliterary.com *Web Site:* www.morhaimliterary.com, pg 497

McKee, Christopher, The PRS Group Inc, 5800 Heritage Landing Dr, Suite E, East Syracuse, NY 13057-9358 *Tel:* 315-431-0511 *Fax:* 315-431-0200 *E-mail:* custserv@prsgroup.com *Web Site:* www. prsgroup.com, pg 177

McKee, Katie, Penguin Group USA, A Penguin Random House Company, 375 Hudson St, New York, NY 10014 *Tel:* 212-366-2000 *Toll Free Tel:* 800-847-5515 (inside sales); 800-631-8571 (cust serv) *Fax:* 212-366-2666; 607-775-4829 (inside sales) *E-mail:* online@ us.penguingroup.com *Web Site:* www.penguin.com, pg 163

McKee, Tim, North Atlantic Books, 2526 Martin Luther King Jr Way, Berkeley, CA 94704 *Tel:* 510-549-4270 *Fax:* 510-549-4276 *Web Site:* www.northatlanticbooks. com, pg 151

McKeithen, Madge, St Andrews University Press, 1700 Dogwood Mile, Laurinburg, NC 28352-5598 *Tel:* 910-277-5555 *Toll Free Tel:* 800-763-0198 *Fax:* 910-277-5020 *Web Site:* www.sa.edu/st-andrews-university-press, pg 190

McKenna, Anne, University of Wisconsin Press, 728 State St, Suite 443, Madison, WI 53706-1418 *Tel:* 608-263-1110; 608-263-0668 (journal orders) *Toll Free Tel:* 800-621-2736 (book orders) *Fax:* 608-263-1173 *Toll Free Fax:* 800-621-2736 (book orders) *E-mail:* uwiscpress@uwpress.wisc.edu *Web Site:* uwpress.wisc.edu, pg 232

McKenna, Caitlin, Random House Publishing Group, 1745 Broadway, New York, NY 10019 *Toll Free Tel:* 800-200-3552 *Web Site:* www.randomhousebooks. com, pg 181

McKenna, Gwen, Mountain Press Publishing Co, 1301 S Third W, Missoula, MT 59801 *Tel:* 406-728-1900 *Toll Free Tel:* 800-234-5308 *Fax:* 406-728-1635 *E-mail:* info@mtnpress.com *Web Site:* www.mountain-press.com, pg 143

McKenna, Janine Chiappa, American Anthropological Association (AAA), 2300 Clarendon Blvd, Suite 1301, Arlington, VA 22201 *Tel:* 703-528-1902 *Fax:* 703-528-3546 *E-mail:* pubs@americananthro.org *Web Site:* www.americananthro.org, pg 9

McKenna, Stephanie, Adams Media, 57 Littlefield St, Avon, MA 02322 *Tel:* 508-427-7100 *Web Site:* www. simonandschuster.com, pg 4

McKenzie, Alison Bethel, The Society of Professional Journalists (SPJ), Eugene S Pulliam National Journalism Ctr, 3909 N Meridian St, Suite 200, Indianapolis, IN 46208 *Tel:* 317-927-8000 *Fax:* 317-920-4789 *E-mail:* spj@spj.org *Web Site:* www.spj.org, pg 548

McKenzie, Elle, Ladderbird Literary Agency, 45 Midland St, Worcester, MA 01602 *Tel:* 508-459-9590 *Web Site:* www.ladderbird.com, pg 492

McKenzie, Jean, American Girl Publishing, 8400 Fairway Place, Middleton, WI 53562 *Tel:* 608-836-4848; 608-831-5210 (outside US & CN) *Toll Free Tel:* 800-233-0264; 800-360-1861; 800-845-0005 (US & CN) *Fax:* 608-836-1999 *Web Site:* www. americangirl.com, pg 11

McKenzie, Michael, Algonquin Books, 400 Silver Cedar Ct, Suite 300, Chapel Hill, NC 27514-1585 *Tel:* 919-967-0108 *Fax:* 919-933-0272 *E-mail:* inquiry@ algonquin.com *Web Site:* www.workman.com/ algonquin, pg 7

McKeon, Hilary, Looseleaf Law Publications Inc, 43-08 162 St, Flushing, NY 11358 *Tel:* 718-359-5559 *Toll Free Tel:* 800-647-5547 *Fax:* 718-539-0941 *E-mail:* info@looseleaflaw.com *Web Site:* www. looseleaflaw.com, pg 128

McKie, Ellen, University of Texas Press, 3001 Lake Austin Blvd, 2.200, Austin, TX 78703 *Tel:* 512-471-7233 *Fax:* 512-232-7178 *E-mail:* utpress@uts.cc. utexas.edu; info@utpress.utexas.edu *Web Site:* utpress. utexas.edu, pg 216

McKinney, Anne, PREP Publishing, 3528 Turnberry Circle, Fayetteville, NC 28303 *Tel:* 910-483-6611 *Toll Free Tel:* 800-533-2814 *E-mail:* preppub@aol.com *Web Site:* www.prep-pub.com, pg 173

McKinney, Charlie, Sophia Institute Press®, 18 Celina Ave, Unit 1, Nashua, NH 03063 *Tel:* 603-641-9344 *Toll Free Tel:* 800-888-9344 *Fax:* 603-641-8108 *Toll Free Fax:* 888-288-2259 *E-mail:* orders@ sophiainstitute.com *Web Site:* www.sophiainstitute. com, pg 203

McKinney, Joe, Horror Writers Association (HWA), PO Box 56687, Sherman Oaks, CA 91413 *Tel:* 818-220-3965 *E-mail:* admin@horror.org *Web Site:* horror.org, pg 534

McKinstry, Nancy, Wolters Kluwer US Corp, 2700 Lake Cook Rd, Riverwoods, IL 60015 *Tel:* 847-267-7000 *Fax:* 847-580-5192 *E-mail:* info@wolterskluwer.com *Web Site:* www.wolterskluwer.com, pg 243

McKinzie, Akira, American Booksellers Association, 333 Westchester Ave, Suite S202, White Plains, NY 10604 *Tel:* 914-406-7500 *Toll Free Tel:* 800-637-0037 *Fax:* 914-417-4013 *E-mail:* info@bookweb.org *Web Site:* www.bookweb.org, pg 522

McKitterick, Christopher, John W Campbell Memorial Award, University of Kansas, Wescoe Hall, Rm 3001, Dept of English, 1445 Jayhawk Blvd, Lawrence, KS 66045 *Tel:* 785-864-2518 *Fax:* 785-864-1159 *Web Site:* www.sfcenter.ku.edu/campbell.htm, pg 602

McKitterick, Christopher, Science Fiction Writers Workshop, University of Kansas, Wescoe Hall, Rm 3001, Dept of English, 1445 Jayhawk Blvd, Lawrence, KS 66045 *Tel:* 785-864-2518 *Fax:* 785-864-1159 *Web Site:* www.sfcenter.ku.edu; www.sfcenter.ku. edu/sfworkshop; www.sfcenter.ku.edu/novel-workshop, pg 578

McKusick, Caroline, Stanford University Press, 425 Broadway St, Redwood City, CA 94063-3126 *Tel:* 650-723-9434 *Fax:* 650-725-3457 *E-mail:* info@ www.sup.org; publicity@www.sup.org; sales@www. sup.org *Web Site:* www.sup.org, pg 206

McLain, Casey, Annual Off Off Broadway Short Play Festival, 235 Park Ave S, 5th fl, New York, NY 10003 *Tel:* 212-206-8990 *Toll Free Tel:* 866-598-8449 *Fax:* 212-206-1429 *E-mail:* oobfestival@ samuelfrench.com *Web Site:* www.oobfestival.com; www.samuelfrench.com, pg 650

McLain, Kevin, Perseus Books, 1290 Avenue of the Americas, New York, NY 10104 *Tel:* 212-340-8100 *Toll Free Tel:* 800-343-4499 (cust serv) *Fax:* 212-340-8105 *Web Site:* www.perseusbooks.com, pg 167

McLaughlin, Brenna, Association of University Presses (AUPresses), 1412 Broadway, Suite 2135, New York, NY 10018 *Tel:* 212-989-1010 *Fax:* 212-989-0275 *E-mail:* info@aupresses.org *Web Site:* www.aupresses. org, pg 527

Meacham, Beth, Tom Doherty Associates, LLC, 120 Broadway, New York, NY 10271 *Tel:* 646-307-5511 *Toll Free Tel:* 800-455-0340 *Web Site:* us.macmillan.com/torforge, pg 66

Meade, Michelle, Harlequin Enterprises Ltd, Bay Adelaide Centre, East Tower, 22 Adelaide St W, 41st fl, Toronto, ON M5H 4E3, Canada *Tel:* 416-445-5860 *Toll Free Tel:* 888-432-4879; 800-370-5838 (ebook inquiries) *E-mail:* customerservice@harlequin.com *Web Site:* www.harlequin.com, pg 429

Meader, James, Anchor Books, c/o Penguin Random House Inc, 1745 Broadway, New York, NY 10019 *Tel:* 212-572-2420 *E-mail:* vintageanchorpublicity@randomhouse.com *Web Site:* knopfdoubleday.com/imprint/anchor, pg 15

Meader, James, Vintage Books, c/o Penguin Random House Inc, 1745 Broadway, New York, NY 10019 *Tel:* 212-572-2420 *E-mail:* vintageanchorpublicity@randomhouse.com *Web Site:* knopfdoubleday.com/imprint/vintage, pg 236

Meador, Craig, American Printing House for the Blind Inc, 1839 Frankfort Ave, Louisville, KY 40206 *Tel:* 502-895-2405 *Toll Free Tel:* 800-223-1839 (cust serv) *Fax:* 502-899-2274 *E-mail:* info@aph.org *Web Site:* www.aph.org; shop.aph.org, pg 13

Meadows, Alice, Miles Conrad Memorial Lecture, 3600 Clipper Mill Rd, Suite 302, Baltimore, MD 21211-1948 *Tel:* 301-654-2512 *Fax:* 410-685-5278 *E-mail:* nisohq@niso.org *Web Site:* www.niso.org, pg 606

Meadows, Alice, National Information Standards Organization (NISO), 3600 Clipper Mill Rd, Suite 302, Baltimore, MD 21211-1948 *Tel:* 301-654-2512 *Fax:* 410-685-5278 *E-mail:* nisohq@niso.org *Web Site:* www.niso.org, pg 147, 540

Meadows, Laura, Carl Vinson Institute of Government, University of Georgia, 201 N Milledge Ave, Athens, GA 30602 *Tel:* 706-542-2736 *Fax:* 706-542-9301 *Web Site:* www.cviog.uga.edu, pg 236

Meadows, Rob, Bear & Co Inc, One Park St, Rochester, VT 05767 *Tel:* 802-767-3174 *Toll Free Tel:* 800-932-3277 *Fax:* 802-767-3726 *E-mail:* customerservice@InnerTraditions.com *Web Site:* InnerTraditions.com, pg 29

Means, Allison T, Iowa Poetry Prize, 119 W Park Rd, 100 Kuhl House, Iowa City, IA 52242-1000 *Tel:* 319-335-2000 *Fax:* 319-335-2055 *E-mail:* uipress@uiowa.edu *Web Site:* www.uipress.uiowa.edu, pg 627

Means, Allison T, Iowa Prize for Literary Nonfiction, 119 W Park Rd, 100 Kuhl House, Iowa City, IA 52242-1000 *Tel:* 319-335-2000 *Fax:* 319-335-2055 *E-mail:* uipress@uiowa.edu *Web Site:* www.uipress.uiowa.edu, pg 627

Means, Allison T, University of Iowa Press, 119 W Park Rd, 100 Kuhl House, Iowa City, IA 52242-1000 *Tel:* 319-335-2000 *Toll Free Tel:* 800-621-2736 (orders only) *Fax:* 319-335-2055 *Toll Free Fax:* 800-621-8476 (orders only) *E-mail:* uipress@uiowa.edu *Web Site:* www.uipress.uiowa.edu, pg 228

Mechanic, Joline, Black Mountain Press, PO Box 9907, Asheville, NC 28815 *Tel:* 828-273-3332 *Web Site:* www.theblackmountainpress.com, pg 34

Mechler, Anita, Alex Awards, 50 E Huron St, Chicago, IL 60611 *Tel:* 312-280-4390 *Toll Free Tel:* 800-545-2433 *Fax:* 312-280-5276 *E-mail:* yalsa@ala.org *Web Site:* www.ala.org/yalsa/alex-awards, pg 591

Mechler, Anita, Baker & Taylor/YALSA Conference Grants, 50 E Huron St, Chicago, IL 60611 *Tel:* 312-280-4390 *Toll Free Tel:* 800-545-2433 *Fax:* 312-280-5276; 312-664-7459 *E-mail:* yalsa@ala.org *Web Site:* www.ala.org/yalsa, pg 595

Mechler, Anita, Margaret A Edwards Award, 50 E Huron St, Chicago, IL 60611 *Tel:* 312-280-4390 *Toll Free Tel:* 800-545-2433 *Fax:* 312-280-5276 *E-mail:* yalsa@ala.org *Web Site:* www.ala.org/yalsa/edwards, pg 612

Mechler, Anita, Frances Henne YALSA/VOYA Research Grant, 50 E Huron St, Chicago, IL 60611 *Tel:* 312-280-4390 *Toll Free Tel:* 800-545-2433 *Fax:* 312-280-5276 *E-mail:* yalsa@ala.org *Web Site:* www.ala.org/yalsa/awardsandgrants/franceshenne, pg 616

Mechler, Anita, Nonfiction Award, 50 E Huron St, Chicago, IL 60611 *Toll Free Tel:* 800-545-2433 (ext 4390) *Fax:* 312-280-5276 *E-mail:* yalsa@ala.org *Web Site:* www.ala.org/yalsa/nonfiction-award, pg 648

Mechler, Anita, Odyssey Award for Excellence in Audiobook Production, 50 E Huron St, Chicago, IL 60611 *Toll Free Tel:* 800-545-2433 (ext 4390) *Fax:* 312-280-5276 *E-mail:* yalsa@ala.org *Web Site:* www.ala.org/yalsa/odyssey, pg 650

Mechler, Anita, Michael L Printz Award, 50 E Huron St, Chicago, IL 60611 *Tel:* 312-280-4390 *Toll Free Tel:* 800-545-2433 *Fax:* 312-280-5276 *E-mail:* yalsa@ala.org *Web Site:* www.ala.org/yalsa/printz, pg 659

Mecklenborg, Mark, The American Ceramic Society, 550 Polaris Pkwy, Suite 510, Westerville, OH 43082 *Tel:* 240-646-7054 *Toll Free Tel:* 866-721-3322 *Fax:* 240-396-5637 *E-mail:* customerservice@ceramics.org *Web Site:* ceramics.org, pg 10

Medaille, Jessica, International Society for Technology in Education, 1530 Wilson Blvd, Suite 730, Arlington, VA 22209 *Tel:* 503-342-2848 (intl) *Toll Free Tel:* 800-336-5191 (US & CN) *E-mail:* iste@iste.org *Web Site:* www.iste.org; www.isteconference.org, pg 112

Medeiros, Maria, Novalis Publishing, 10 Lower Spadina Ave, Suite 400, Toronto, ON M5V 2Z2, Canada *Tel:* 416-363-3303 *Toll Free Tel:* 877-702-7773 *Fax:* 416-363-9409 *Toll Free Fax:* 877-702-7775 *E-mail:* books@novalis.ca *Web Site:* www.novalis.ca, pg 434

Medeot, William, Orbis Books, PO Box 302, Maryknoll, NY 10545-0302 *Tel:* 914-941-7636 *Toll Free Tel:* 800-258-5838 (orders, Mon-Fri 8AM-4PM EST) *Fax:* 914-941-7005 *E-mail:* orbisbooks@maryknoll.org *Web Site:* orbisbooks.com, pg 156

Medina, Kate, Random House Publishing Group, 1745 Broadway, New York, NY 10019 *Toll Free Tel:* 800-200-3552 *Web Site:* www.randomhousebooks.com, pg 181

Mednansky, Kristine, Productivity Press, 711 Third Ave, 8th fl, New York, NY 10017 *Tel:* 212-216-7800 *Toll Free Tel:* 800-634-7064 (orders); 800-797-3803 *E-mail:* orders@taylorandfrancis.com *Web Site:* www.crcpress.com, pg 175

Meehan, Emily Thomas, Disney-Hyperion Books, 1101 Flower St, Glendale, CA 91201 *Web Site:* books.disney.com, pg 65

Meehan, Emily Thomas, Disney Publishing Worldwide, 1101 Flower St, Glendale, CA 91201 *Web Site:* books.disney.com, pg 65

Meeropol, Ellen, Chocorua Writing Workshop, PO Box 2280, Conway, NH 03818-2280 *Tel:* 603-447-2280 *E-mail:* reservations@worldfellowship.org *Web Site:* www.worldfellowship.org; www.facebook.com/World.Fellowship.Center, pg 574

Megan, Terry, Remember Point Inc, PO Box 1448, Pacific Palisades, CA 90272 *Tel:* 310-896-8716 *E-mail:* info@rememberpoint.com *Web Site:* www.rememberpoint.com; www.longfellowfindsahome.com, pg 184

Meidenbauer, Edward, American Psychological Association, 750 First St NE, Washington, DC 20002-4242 *Tel:* 202-336-5510 *Toll Free Tel:* 800-374-2721 *Fax:* 202-336-5502 *E-mail:* order@apa.org *Web Site:* www.apa.org/books, pg 13

Meier, Blyth, Porchlight Book Co Business Book Awards, 544 S First St, Milwaukee, WI 53204 *Toll Free Tel:* 800-236-7323 *E-mail:* info@porchlightbooks.com *Web Site:* porchlightbooks.com, pg 657

Meier, Heidi, Simon & Schuster, 1230 Avenue of the Americas, New York, NY 10020 *Tel:* 212-698-7000 *Toll Free Tel:* 800-223-2348 (cust serv); 800-223-2336 (orders) *Toll Free Fax:* 800-943-9831 (orders) *Web Site:* www.simonandschuster.com, pg 198

Meints, Rick, Chaosium Inc, 3450 Wooddale Ct, Ann Arbor, MI 48104 *Tel:* 734-972-9551 *E-mail:* customerservice@chaosium.com *Web Site:* www.chaosium.com, pg 49

Meischeid, Tessa, Penguin Young Readers Group, 345 Hudson St, New York, NY 10014 *Tel:* 212-366-2000; 212-414-3553 *Fax:* 212-414-3340 *Web Site:* www.penguin.com/children, pg 165

Meister, Beth, Doubleday, c/o Penguin Random House Inc, 1745 Broadway, New York, NY 10019 *Tel:* 212-751-2600 *Fax:* 212-572-2662 (foreign rts) *E-mail:* ddaypub@randomhouse.com *Web Site:* knopfdoubleday.com, pg 66

Meister, Beth, Alfred A Knopf, c/o Penguin Random House Inc, 1745 Broadway, New York, NY 10019 *Tel:* 212-751-2600 *Fax:* 212-572-2662 (foreign rts) *Web Site:* knopfdoubleday.com, pg 117

Meister, Beth, Pantheon Books, c/o Penguin Random House Inc, 1745 Broadway, New York, NY 10019 *Tel:* 212-751-2600 *Fax:* 212-572-2662 (foreign rts) *Web Site:* knopfdoubleday.com, pg 159

Meister, Beth, Schocken Books, c/o Penguin Random House Inc, 1745 Broadway, New York, NY 10019 *Tel:* 212-751-2600 *Fax:* 212-572-2662 (foreign rts) *Web Site:* knopfdoubleday.com, pg 193

Meister, Mark, The Ambassador Richard C Holbrooke Distinguished Achievement Award, PO Box 461, Wright Brothers Branch, Dayton, OH 45409-0461 *Tel:* 937-298-5072 *E-mail:* sharon.rab@daytonliterarypeaceprize.org *Web Site:* www.daytonliterarypeaceprize.org/holbrooke.htm, pg 591

Meixelsperger, Wes, Soil Science Society of America (SSSA), 5585 Guilford Rd, Madison, WI 53711-5801 *Tel:* 608-273-8080 *Fax:* 608-273-2021 *Web Site:* www.soils.org, pg 203

Meizlik, Shelby, Penguin Books, 375 Hudson St, New York, NY 10014 *Tel:* 212-366-2000 *E-mail:* penguinpublicity@us.penguingroup.com *Web Site:* www.penguinclassics.com; www.penguin.com, pg 163

Meizlik, Shelby, Penguin Group USA, A Penguin Random House Company, 375 Hudson St, New York, NY 10014 *Tel:* 212-366-2000 *Toll Free Tel:* 800-847-5515 (inside sales); 800-631-8571 (cust serv) *Fax:* 212-366-2666; 607-775-4829 (inside sales) *E-mail:* online@us.penguingroup.com *Web Site:* www.penguin.com, pg 163

Meizlik, Shelby, Viking, 375 Hudson St, New York, NY 10014 *Tel:* 212-366-2000 *Fax:* 212-243-6002 *Web Site:* www.penguin.com/publishers/vikingbooks, pg 236

Mekarnom, Mary, Penguin Young Readers Group, 345 Hudson St, New York, NY 10014 *Tel:* 212-366-2000; 212-414-3553 *Fax:* 212-414-3340 *Web Site:* www.penguin.com/children, pg 165

Melamed, Suzanne Ryan, Oxford University Press USA, 198 Madison Ave, New York, NY 10016 *Toll Free Tel:* 800-451-7556 (orders); 800-445-9714 (cust serv) *Fax:* 919-677-1303 *E-mail:* custserv.us@oup.com *Web Site:* global.oup.com, pg 158

Melancon, Barry C, AICPA Professional Publications, 220 Leigh Farm Rd, Durham, NC 27707 *Tel:* 919-402-4500 *Toll Free Tel:* 888-777-7077 (memb serv ctr) *Fax:* 919-402-4505 *Toll Free Fax:* 800-362-5066 (memb serv ctr) *E-mail:* acquisitions@aicpa.org; service@aicpa.org *Web Site:* www.aicpa.org, pg 6

Melia, James, Henry Holt and Company, LLC, 120 Broadway, 23rd fl, New York, NY 10271 *Tel:* 646-307-5151 *Toll Free Tel:* 888-330-8477 (orders) *Fax:* 646-307-5285 *Web Site:* www.henryholt.com, pg 102

Melillo, Kara, Milady, Executive Woods, 5 Maxwell Dr, Clifton Park, NY 12065-2919 *Tel:* 518-348-2300 *Toll Free Tel:* 800-998-7498 *Fax:* 518-373-6309 *E-mail:* info@milady.com *Web Site:* milady.cengage.com, pg 140

Melnyk, Emma, Canadian Scholars' Press Inc, 425 Adelaide St W, Suite 200, Toronto, ON M5V 3C1, Canada *Tel:* 416-929-2774 *Toll Free Tel:* 800-463-1998 *Fax:* 416-929-1926 *E-mail:* info@cspi.org;

info@canadianscholars.ca; editorial@canadianscholars. ca; orders@canadianscholars.ca *Web Site:* www. canadianscholars.ca; www.womenspress.ca, pg 419

Melnyk, Sarah, St Martin's Press, LLC, 120 Broadway, New York, NY 10271 *Tel:* 646-307-5151 *Web Site:* us. macmillan.com/smp, pg 190

Melo Pienkowski, Larissa, Jill Grinberg Literary Management LLC, 392 Vanderbilt Ave, Brooklyn, NY 11238 *Tel:* 212-620-5883 *E-mail:* info@ jillgrinbergliterary.com *Web Site:* www. jillgrinbergliterary.com, pg 487

Meloche, Luc, LexisNexis® Canada Inc, 111 Gordon Baker Rd, Suite 900, Toronto, ON M2H 3R1, Canada *Tel:* 905-479-2665 *Toll Free Tel:* 800-668-6481; 800-387-0899 (cust care); 800-255-5174 (sales) *E-mail:* service@lexisnexis.ca (cust serv); sales@ lexisnexis.ca *Web Site:* www.lexisnexis.ca, pg 432

Meloto, Charisse, Scholastic Trade Division, 557 Broadway, New York, NY 10012 *Tel:* 212-343-6100; 212-343-4685 (export sales) *Fax:* 212-343-4714 (export sales) *Web Site:* www.scholastic.com, pg 194

Melton, Dianne, Summerthought Publishing, PO Box 2309, Banff, AB T1L 1C1, Canada *Tel:* 403-762-0535 *Fax:* 403-762-3095 *Toll Free Fax:* 800-762-3095 (orders) *E-mail:* info@summerthought.com; sales@ summerthought.com *Web Site:* summerthought.com, pg 441

Meltzer, Kate, GP Putnam's Sons (Children's), 345 Hudson St, New York, NY 10014 *Tel:* 212-366-2000 *Fax:* 212-414-3393 *Web Site:* www.penguin. com/publishers/gpputnamssonsbooksforyoungread, pg 178

Meltzer, Kate, Roaring Brook Press, 120 Broadway, New York, NY 10271 *Tel:* 646-307-5151 *Web Site:* us. macmillan.com/publishers/roaring-brook-press, pg 186

Meltzer, Lauren, Charles Press Publishers, 230 N 21 St, Suite 312, Philadelphia, PA 19103 *Tel:* 215-470-5977 *E-mail:* mail@charlespresspub.com *Web Site:* charlespresspub.com, pg 49

Meltzer, Max, Gallery Books, 1230 Avenue of the Americas, New York, NY 10020 *Toll Free Tel:* 800-456-6798 *Fax:* 212-698-7284 *E-mail:* consumer. customerservice@simonandschuster.com *Web Site:* www.simonandschuster.com, pg 83

Melucci, Giulia, Harper's Magazine Foundation, 666 Broadway, 11th fl, New York, NY 10012 *Tel:* 212-420-5720 *Toll Free Tel:* 800-444-4653 *Fax:* 212-228-5889 *E-mail:* harpers@harpers.org *Web Site:* www. harpers.org, pg 94

Melville, Kirsty, Andrews McMeel Publishing LLC, 1130 Walnut St, Kansas City, MO 64106-2109 *Toll Free Tel:* 800-851-8923; 800-943-9839 (cust serv) *Toll Free Tel:* 800-943-9831 (orders) *E-mail:* sales@ amuniversal.com *Web Site:* www.andrewsmcmeel.com; publishing.andrewsmcmeel.com, pg 16

Melvin, Annette, Random House Publishing Group, 1745 Broadway, New York, NY 10019 *Toll Free Tel:* 800-200-3552 *Web Site:* www.randomhousebooks.com, pg 181

Melvin, Becky, Thomas Nelson, 501 Nelson Place, Nashville, TN 37214 *Tel:* 615-889-9000 *Toll Free Tel:* 800-251-4000 *Fax:* 615-902-1548 *Web Site:* www. thomasnelson.com, pg 217

Melvin, Terrence, The Brookings Institution Press, 1775 Massachusetts Ave NW, Washington, DC 20036-2188 *Tel:* 202-797-6000 *E-mail:* permissions@brookings. edu *Web Site:* www.brookings.edu, pg 42

Mendel, Scott, Mendel Media Group LLC, 115 W 30 St, Suite 209, New York, NY 10001 *Tel:* 646-239-9896 *Web Site:* www.mendelmedia.com, pg 496

Mendelsohn, Aaron, Writers Guild of America Awards, 7000 W Third St, Los Angeles, CA 90048 *Tel:* 323-951-4000; 323-782-4569 *Fax:* 323-782-4800 *Web Site:* www.wga.org, pg 680

Mendelsohn, Aaron, Writers Guild of America, West (WGAW), 7000 W Third St, Los Angeles, CA 90048 *Tel:* 323-951-4000 *Toll Free Tel:* 800-548-4532 *Fax:* 323-782-4800 *Web Site:* www.wga.org, pg 549

Mendelson, John, Candlewick Press, 99 Dover St, Somerville, MA 02144-2825 *Tel:* 617-661-3330 *Fax:* 617-661-0565 *E-mail:* bigbear@candlewick. com; salesinfo@candlewick.com *Web Site:* www. candlewick.com, pg 44

Mendez Berry, Elizabeth, Random House Publishing Group, 1745 Broadway, New York, NY 10019 *Toll Free Tel:* 800-200-3552 *Web Site:* www. randomhousebooks.com, pg 181

Mendez, Maria, Simon & Schuster, 1230 Avenue of the Americas, New York, NY 10020 *Tel:* 212-698-7000 *Toll Free Tel:* 800-223-2348 (cust serv); 800-223-2336 (orders) *Toll Free Fax:* 800-943-9831 (orders) *Web Site:* www.simonandschuster.com, pg 198

Mendola-Hobbie, Jaime, Berkley Publishing Group, 1745 Broadway, 19th fl, New York, NY 10019 *Tel:* 212-366-2000 *Web Site:* www.penguin.com, pg 32

Mendola-Hobbie, Jaime, Dutton, 1745 Broadway, New York, NY 10019 *Tel:* 212-366-2000 *Fax:* 212-366-2262 *E-mail:* duttonpublicity@us.penguingroup.com *Web Site:* www.penguin.com, pg 68

Mendola-Hobbie, Jaime, Plume, 375 Hudson St, New York, NY 10014 *Tel:* 212-366-2000 *Fax:* 212-243-6002 *Web Site:* www.penguin.com/publishers/plume, pg 171

Mendola-Hobbie, Jaime, GP Putnam's Sons (Hardcover), 375 Hudson St, New York, NY 10014 *Tel:* 212-366-2000 *Fax:* 212-366-2643 *E-mail:* online@ penguinputnam.com *Web Site:* www.penguin.com/ publishers/gpputnamssons, pg 178

Mendoza, Isabel, Santillana USA Publishing Co, 2023 NW 84 Ave, Doral, FL 33122 *Tel:* 305-591-9522 *Toll Free Tel:* 800-245-8584 *E-mail:* customerservice@ santillanausa.com *Web Site:* www.santillanausa.com, pg 192

Mendoza, Stephanie, Algonquin Books, 400 Silver Cedar Ct, Suite 300, Chapel Hill, NC 27514-1585 *Tel:* 919-967-0108 *Fax:* 919-933-0272 *E-mail:* inquiry@ algonquin.com *Web Site:* www.workman.com/ algonquin, pg 7

Menick, Jim, Reader's Digest Select Editions, 44 S Broadway, White Plains, NY 10601 *Tel:* 914-238-1000 *Toll Free Tel:* 877-732-4438 (cust serv) *Web Site:* www.facebook.com/selecteditions, pg 182

Menn, Don, Immedium, 535 Rockdale Dr, San Francisco, CA 94127 *Tel:* 415-452-8546 *Fax:* 360-937-6272 *E-mail:* orders@immedium.com; sales@ immedium.com *Web Site:* www.immedium.com, pg 107

Mennel, Timothy, University of Chicago Press, 1427 E 60 St, Chicago, IL 60637-2954 *Tel:* 773-702-7700; 773-702-7600 *Toll Free Tel:* 800-621-2736 (orders) *Fax:* 773-702-9756; 773-660-2235 (orders); 773-702-2708 *E-mail:* custserv@press.uchicago.edu; marketing@press.uchicago.edu *Web Site:* www.press. uchicago.edu, pg 226

Menzies, Tracey, HarperCollins General Books Group, 195 Broadway, New York, NY 10007 *Tel:* 212-207-7000 *Web Site:* www.harpercollins.com, pg 93

Menzies, Tracey, HarperCollins Publishers, 195 Broadway, New York, NY 10007 *Tel:* 212-207-7000 *Fax:* 212-207-7145 *Web Site:* www.harpercollins.com, pg 94

Menzimer, Parker, Princeton Architectural Press, 202 Warren St, Hudson, NY 12534 *Tel:* 518-671-6100 *Toll Free Tel:* 800-722-6657 (dist); 800-759-0190 (sales) *E-mail:* sales@papress.com *Web Site:* www.papress. com, pg 174

Mercado, Jessica, Little, Brown Books for Young Readers, 1290 Avenue of the Americas, New York, NY 10104 *Tel:* 212-364-1100 *Toll Free Tel:* 800-759-0190 (cust serv) *Web Site:* www.hachettebookgroup. com, pg 126

Mercado, Nancy, Dial Books for Young Readers, 345 Hudson St, New York, NY 10014 *Tel:* 212-366-2000 *Toll Free Tel:* 800-733-3000 (orders) *Fax:* 212-414-3396 *Web Site:* www.penguin.com/publishers/ dialbooksforyoungreaders/, pg 64

Mercandetti, Susan, Random House Publishing Group, 1745 Broadway, New York, NY 10019 *Toll Free Tel:* 800-200-3552 *Web Site:* www.randomhousebooks. com, pg 181

Meredith, Leslie, Mary Evans Inc, 242 E Fifth St, New York, NY 10003-8501 *Tel:* 212-979-0880 *Fax:* 212-979-5344 *E-mail:* info@maryevansinc.com *Web Site:* www.maryevansinc.com, pg 484

Merino, Melinda, Harvard Business Review Press, 20 Guest St, Suite 700, Brighton, MA 02135 *Tel:* 617-783-7400 *Fax:* 617-783-7489 *E-mail:* custserv@hbsp. harvard.edu *Web Site:* www.harvardbusiness.org, pg 94

Merkle, Dieter, Springer, 233 Spring St, New York, NY 10013-1578 *Tel:* 212-460-1500 *Toll Free Tel:* 800-SPRINGER (777-4643) *Fax:* 212-460-1700 *E-mail:* customerservice@springer.com *Web Site:* www.springer.com, pg 205

Merkle, Molly, AdventureKEEN, 2204 First Ave S, Suite 102, Birmingham, AL 35233 *Tel:* 763-689-9800 *Toll Free Tel:* 800-678-7006 *Fax:* 763-689-9039 *Toll Free Fax:* 877-374-9016 *E-mail:* info@adventurewithkeen. com *Web Site:* adventurewithkeen.com, pg 5

Merkle, Molly B, Menasha Ridge Press, 2204 First Ave S, Suite 102, Birmingham, AL 35233 *Toll Free Tel:* 888-604-4537 *Fax:* 205-326-1012 *E-mail:* info@ adventurewithkeen.com *Web Site:* www.menasharidge. com; www.adventurewithkeen.com, pg 138

Merola, Marianne, Brandt & Hochman Literary Agents Inc, 1501 Broadway, Suite 2310, New York, NY 10036 *Tel:* 212-840-5760 *Fax:* 212-840-5776 *Web Site:* brandthochman.com, pg 477

Merriam, Ray, Merriam Press, 489 South St, Hoosick Falls, NY 12090 *Tel:* 518-949-0882 *E-mail:* merriampress@gmail.com *Web Site:* www. merriam-press.com, pg 138

Merritt, Jason, Forward Movement, 412 Sycamore St, Cincinnati, OH 45202-4110 *Tel:* 513-721-6659 *Toll Free Tel:* 800-543-1813 *Fax:* 513-721-0729 (orders) *E-mail:* orders@forwardmovement.org (orders & cust serv) *Web Site:* www.forwardmovement.org, pg 80

Mertins, Tyler, National Press Foundation, 1211 Connecticut Ave NW, Suite 310, Washington, DC 20036 *Tel:* 202-663-7280 *Web Site:* nationalpress.org, pg 540

Merz, Kathleen, Wm B Eerdmans Publishing Co, 4035 Park East Ct SE, Grand Rapids, MI 49546 *Tel:* 616-459-4591 *Toll Free Tel:* 800-253-7521 *Fax:* 616-459-6540 *E-mail:* customerservice@eerdmans.com; sales@ eerdmans.com *Web Site:* www.eerdmans.com, pg 70

Messer, Melissa A, Psychological Assessment Resources Inc (PAR), 16204 N Florida Ave, Lutz, FL 33549 *Tel:* 813-449-4065 *Toll Free Tel:* 800-331-8378 *Fax:* 813-961-2196 *Toll Free Fax:* 800-727-9329 *Web Site:* www.parinc.com, pg 177

Messer, Randy, Perfection Learning, 1000 N Second Ave, Logan, IA 51546 *Tel:* 712-644-2831 *Toll Free Tel:* 800-831-4190 *Toll Free Fax:* 800-543-2745 *E-mail:* orders@perfectionlearning.com *Web Site:* perfectionlearning.com, pg 167

Messerli, Douglas, Green Integer, 6210 Wilshire Blvd, Suite 211, Los Angeles, CA 90048 *E-mail:* info@ greeninteger.com *Web Site:* www.greeninteger.com, pg 89

Messersmith, Paul, United States Holocaust Memorial Museum, 100 Raoul Wallenberg Place SW, Washington, DC 20024-2126 *Tel:* 202-488-0400; 202-314-7837; 202-488-6144 (orders) *Toll Free Tel:* 800-259-9998 (orders) *Fax:* 202-479-9726; 202-488-0438 (orders) *E-mail:* cahs_publications@ushmm.org *Web Site:* www.ushmm.org, pg 224

Messick, Mary K, Schoolhouse Network, PO Box 1518, Northampton, MA 01061 *Tel:* 480-427-4836 *E-mail:* schoolhousenetwork@gmail.com, pg 470

Meth, David L, Writers' Productions, PO Box 630, Westport, CT 06881-0630 *Tel:* 203-227-8199, pg 509

Metivier, Michael, Chelsea Green Publishing Co, 85 N Main St, Suite 120, White River Junction, VT 05001 *Tel:* 802-295-6300 *Toll Free Tel:* 800-639-4099 (cust serv & orders) *Fax:* 802-295-6444 *E-mail:* customerservice@chelseagreen.com; editorial@chelseagreen.com; publicity@chelseagreen.com; rights@chelseagreen.com *Web Site:* www.chelseagreen.com, pg 49

Metz, Mary, The Mountaineers Books, 1001 SW Klickitat Way, Suite 201, Seattle, WA 98134 *Tel:* 206-223-6303 *Fax:* 206-223-6306 *E-mail:* mbooks@mountaineersbooks.org; customerservice@mountaineersbooks.org *Web Site:* www.mountaineersbooks.org, pg 143

Metzger, Jennifer, Insight Editions, 800 "A" St, San Rafael, CA 94901 *Tel:* 415-526-1370 *Toll Free Tel:* 800-809-3792 *Toll Free Fax:* 866-509-0515 *E-mail:* info@insighteditions.com; marketing@insighteditions.com *Web Site:* insighteditions.com, pg 109

Metzner, Joerg, Rand McNally, 9855 Woods Dr, Skokie, IL 60077 *Tel:* 847-329-8100 *Toll Free Tel:* 877-446-4863 *Toll Free Tel:* 877-469-1298 *E-mail:* mediarelations@randmcnally.com; tndsupport@randmcnally.com *Web Site:* www.randmcnally.com, pg 180

Meuse, Elena, Random House Children's Books, 1745 Broadway, 10th fl, New York, NY 10019 *Tel:* 212-782-9000 *Web Site:* www.randomhousekids.com, pg 180

Meyer, Caitlin, Beacon Press, 24 Farnsworth St, Boston, MA 02210-1409 *Tel:* 617-742-2110 *Fax:* 617-723-3097; 617-742-2290 *Web Site:* www.beacon.org, pg 29

Meyer, Dan, Doubleday, c/o Penguin Random House Inc, 1745 Broadway, New York, NY 10019 *Tel:* 212-751-2600 *Fax:* 212-572-2662 (foreign rts) *E-mail:* ddaypub@randomhouse.com *Web Site:* knopfdoubleday.com, pg 66

Meyer, Dan, Nan A Talese, c/o Penguin Random House Inc, 1745 Broadway, New York, NY 10019 *Tel:* 212-751-2600 *Fax:* 212-572-2662 (foreign rts) *E-mail:* ddaypub@randomhouse.com *Web Site:* knopfdoubleday.com, pg 212

Meyer, Laura, Groundwood Books, 128 Sterling Rd, Lower Level, Toronto, ON M6R 2B7, Canada *Tel:* 416-363-4343 *Fax:* 416-363-1017 *E-mail:* genmail@groundwoodbooks.com *Web Site:* www.houseofanansi.com, pg 428

Meyer, Laura, House of Anansi Press Inc, 128 Sterling Rd, Lower Level, Toronto, ON M6R 2B7, Canada *Tel:* 416-363-4343 *Fax:* 416-363-1017 *E-mail:* customerservice@houseofanansi.com *Web Site:* www.houseofanansi.com, pg 429

Meyer, Steve, LAMA Books, 2381 Sleepy Hollow Ave, Hayward, CA 94545-3429 *Tel:* 510-785-1091 *Toll Free Tel:* 888-452-6244 *Fax:* 510-785-1099 *Web Site:* www.lamabooks.com, pg 119

Meyers, Catharine A, New Harbinger Publications Inc, 5674 Shattuck Ave, Oakland, CA 94609 *Tel:* 510-652-0215 *Toll Free Tel:* 800-748-6273 (orders only) *Fax:* 510-652-5472 *Toll Free Fax:* 800-652-1613 *E-mail:* nhhelp@newharbinger.com; customerservice@newharbinger.com *Web Site:* www.newharbinger.com, pg 148

Meyers, Katharine, Little, Brown and Company, 1290 Avenue of the Americas, New York, NY 10104 *Tel:* 212-364-1100 *Fax:* 212-364-0952 *E-mail:* firstname.lastname@hbgusa.com *Web Site:* www.littlebrown.com; www.hachettebookgroup.com, pg 125

Meyers, Tona Pearce, New World Library, 14 Pamaron Way, Novato, CA 94949 *Tel:* 415-884-2100 *Toll Free Tel:* 800-227-3900 (ext 52, retail orders); 800-972-6657 *Fax:* 415-884-2199 *E-mail:* escort@newworldlibrary.com *Web Site:* www.newworldlibrary.com, pg 149

Mezhibovskaya, Katya, Bloomsbury Publishing Inc, 1385 Broadway, 5th fl, New York, NY 10018 *Tel:* 212-419-5300 *E-mail:* marketingusa@bloomsbury.com;

adultpublicityusa@bloomsbury.com; askacademic@bloomsbury.com *Web Site:* www.bloomsbury.com, pg 36

Miceli, Jaya, Scribner, 1230 Avenue of the Americas, New York, NY 10020, pg 195

Michaels, Samantha, Wood Lake Publishing Inc, 485 Beaver Lake Rd, Kelowna, BC V4V 1S5, Canada *Tel:* 250-766-2778 *Toll Free Tel:* 800-663-2775 (orders & cust serv) *Fax:* 250-766-2736 *Toll Free Fax:* 888-841-9991 (orders & cust serv) *E-mail:* info@woodlake.com; customerservice@woodlake.com *Web Site:* www.woodlakebooks.com, pg 445

Michailidis, Parisa, Firefly Books Ltd, 50 Staples Ave, Unit 1, Richmond Hill, ON L4B 0A7, Canada *Tel:* 416-499-8412 *Toll Free Tel:* 800-387-6192 (CN); 800-387-5085 (US) *Fax:* 416-499-8313 *Toll Free Fax:* 800-450-0391 (CN); 800-565-6034 (US) *E-mail:* service@fireflybooks.com *Web Site:* www.fireflybooks.com, pg 426

Michalicek, Steven S, Heuer Publishing LLC, PO Box 248, Cedar Rapids, IA 52406 *Tel:* 319-368-8008 *Toll Free Tel:* 800-950-7529 *Fax:* 319-368-8011 *E-mail:* orders@heuerpub.com; customerservice@heuerpub.com *Web Site:* www.hitplays.com, pg 98

Michalski, Chris, Ascension Press, PO Box 1990, West Chester, PA 19380 *Tel:* 610-696-7795; 484-875-4550 (admin) *Toll Free Tel:* 800-376-0520 (sales & cust serv) *Web Site:* ascensionpress.com, pg 21

Michaud, Ann, ALSC Baker & Taylor Summer Reading Grant, 50 E Huron St, Chicago, IL 60611-2795 *Tel:* 312-280-2163 *Toll Free Tel:* 800-545-2433 *Fax:* 312-440-9374; 312-280-5271 *E-mail:* alsc@ala.org *Web Site:* www.ala.org/alsc, pg 591

Michaud, Ann, The May Hill Arbuthnot Honor Lecture Award, 50 E Huron St, Chicago, IL 60611-2795 *Tel:* 312-280-2163 *Toll Free Tel:* 800-545-2433 *Fax:* 312-440-9374; 312-280-5271 *E-mail:* alsc@ala.org *Web Site:* www.ala.org/alsc, pg 592

Michaud, Ann, The Mildred L Batchelder Award, 50 E Huron St, Chicago, IL 60611-2795 *Tel:* 312-280-2163 *Toll Free Tel:* 800-545-2433 *Fax:* 312-440-9374; 312-280-5271 *E-mail:* alsc@ala.org *Web Site:* www.ala.org/alsc, pg 596

Michaud, Ann, The Pura Belpre Award, 50 E Huron St, Chicago, IL 60611-2795 *Tel:* 312-280-2163 *Toll Free Tel:* 800-545-2433 *Fax:* 312-440-9374; 312-280-5271 *E-mail:* alsc@ala.org *Web Site:* www.ala.org/alsc, pg 596

Michaud, Ann, Bound to Stay Bound Books Scholarship, 50 E Huron St, Chicago, IL 60611-2795 *Tel:* 312-280-2163 *Toll Free Tel:* 800-545-2433 *Fax:* 312-440-9374; 312-280-5271 *E-mail:* alsc@ala.org *Web Site:* www.ala.org/alsc, pg 600

Michaud, Ann, The Randolph Caldecott Medal, 50 E Huron St, Chicago, IL 60611-2795 *Tel:* 312-280-2163 *Toll Free Tel:* 800-545-2433 *Fax:* 312-440-9374; 312-280-5271 *E-mail:* alsc@ala.org *Web Site:* www.ala.org/alsc, pg 602

Michaud, Ann, Children's Literature Legacy Award, 50 E Huron St, Chicago, IL 60611-2795 *Tel:* 312-280-2163 *Toll Free Tel:* 800-545-2433 *Fax:* 312-440-9374; 312-280-5271 *E-mail:* alsc@ala.org *Web Site:* www.ala.org/alsc, pg 604

Michaud, Ann, Frederic G Melcher Scholarship, 50 E Huron St, Chicago, IL 60611-2795 *Tel:* 312-280-2163 *Toll Free Tel:* 800-545-2433 *Fax:* 312-440-9374; 312-280-5271 *E-mail:* alsc@ala.org *Web Site:* www.ala.org/alsc, pg 641

Michaud, Ann, John Newbery Medal, 50 E Huron St, Chicago, IL 60611-2795 *Tel:* 312-280-2163 *Toll Free Tel:* 800-545-2433 *Fax:* 312-440-9374; 312-280-5271 *E-mail:* alsc@ala.org *Web Site:* www.ala.org/alsc, pg 648

Michaud, Ann, Robert F Sibert Informational Book Award, 50 E Huron St, Chicago, IL 60611-2795 *Tel:* 312-280-2163 *Toll Free Tel:* 800-545-2433 *Fax:* 312-440-9374; 312-280-5271 *E-mail:* alsc@ala.org *Web Site:* www.ala.org/alsc, pg 667

Michaud, Jacques, Les Editions Vents d'Ouest, 109, rue Wright, bureau 202, Gatineau, QC J8X 2G7, Canada *Tel:* 819-770-6377 *E-mail:* info@ventsdouest.ca *Web Site:* www.ventsdouest.ca, pg 425

Michel, Christie, Other Press, 267 Fifth Ave, 6th fl, New York, NY 10016 *Tel:* 212-414-0054 *Toll Free Tel:* 877-843-6843 *Fax:* 212-414-0939 *E-mail:* editor@otherpress.com; marketing@otherpress.com; publicity@otherpress.com *Web Site:* www.otherpress.com, pg 157

Michels, Anna, Poisoned Pen Press, 4014 N Goldwater Blvd, Suite 201, Scottsdale, AZ 85251 *Tel:* 480-945-3375 *Toll Free Tel:* 800-421-3976 *Fax:* 480-949-1707 *E-mail:* info@poisonedpenpress.com *Web Site:* www.poisonedpenpress.com, pg 171

Michels, Anna, Sourcebooks LLC, 1935 Brookdale Rd, Suite 139, Naperville, IL 60563 *Tel:* 630-961-3900 *Toll Free Tel:* 800-432-7444 *Fax:* 630-961-2168 *E-mail:* info@sourcebooks.com; customersupport@sourcebooks.com *Web Site:* www.sourcebooks.com, pg 204

Michels, Dia L, Platypus Media LLC, 725 Eighth St SE, Washington, DC 20003 *Tel:* 202-546-1674 *Toll Free Tel:* 877-PLATYPS (752-8977) *Fax:* 202-546-2356 *E-mail:* info@platypusmedia.com *Web Site:* www.platypusmedia.com, pg 170

Michels, Dia L, Science, Naturally, 725 Eighth St SE, Washington, DC 20003 *Tel:* 202-465-4798 *Toll Free Tel:* 866-724-9876 *Fax:* 202-558-2132 *E-mail:* info@sciencenaturally.com *Web Site:* www.sciencenaturally.com, pg 195

Michels, Greg, Municipal Analysis Services Inc, PO Box 13453, Austin, TX 78711-3453 *Tel:* 512-704-7194 *E-mail:* munilysis@gmail.com *Web Site:* sites.google.com/site/gregmichels/home, pg 144

Michels, Marie, Wendy Sherman Associates Inc, 138 W 25 St, Suite 1018, New York, NY 10001 *Tel:* 212-279-9027 *E-mail:* submissions@wsherman.com *Web Site:* www.wsherman.com, pg 502

Michelson, David, Artech House®, 685 Canton St, Norwood, MA 02062 *Tel:* 781-769-9750 *Toll Free Tel:* 800-225-9977 *Fax:* 781-769-6334 *E-mail:* artech@artechhouse.com *Web Site:* www.artechhouse.com, pg 21

Miciak, Kate, Random House Publishing Group, 1745 Broadway, New York, NY 10019 *Toll Free Tel:* 800-200-3552 *Web Site:* www.randomhousebooks.com, pg 181

Mickulas, Peter, Rutgers University Press, 106 Somerset St, 3rd fl, New Brunswick, NJ 08901 *Tel:* 848-445-7762; 848-445-7761 (sales) *Fax:* 732-745-4935 *E-mail:* sales@rutgersuniversitypress.org *Web Site:* www.rutgersuniversitypress.org, pg 188

Middlebrook, Ron, Centerstream Publishing LLC, PO Box 17878, Anaheim Hills, CA 92817-7878 *Tel:* 714-779-9390 *E-mail:* centerstrm@aol.com *Web Site:* www.centerstream-usa.com, pg 48

Middleton, Jean F, IndexEmpire Indexing Services, 16740 Orville Wright Dr, Riverside, CA 92518 *Tel:* 951-697-2819 *E-mail:* indexempire@gmail.com, pg 465

Middleton, Kathy, Crabtree Publishing Co, 347 Fifth Ave, Suite 1402-145, New York, NY 10016 *Tel:* 212-496-5040 *Toll Free Tel:* 800-387-7650 *Toll Free Fax:* 800-355-7166 *E-mail:* custserv@crabtreebooks.com *Web Site:* www.crabtreebooks.com, pg 59

Middleton, Kathy, Crabtree Publishing Co Ltd, 616 Welland Ave, St Catharines, ON L2M 5V6, Canada *Tel:* 905-682-5221 *Toll Free Tel:* 800-387-7650 *Fax:* 905-682-7166 *Toll Free Fax:* 800-355-7166 *E-mail:* custserv@crabtreebooks.com; sales@crabtreebooks.com; orders@crabtreebooks.com *Web Site:* www.crabtreebooks.com, pg 421

Middleton, Lydia, Association for Information Science & Technology (ASIS&T), 8555 16 St, Suite 850, Silver Spring, MD 20910 *Tel:* 301-495-0900 *Fax:* 301-495-0810 *E-mail:* asist@asist.org *Web Site:* www.asist.org, pg 23, 525

Middleton, Stephanie, American Law Institute Continuing Legal Education (ALI CLE), 4025 Chestnut St, Philadelphia, PA 19104 *Tel:* 215-243-

1600 *Toll Free Tel:* 800-CLE-NEWS (253-6397) *Fax:* 215-243-1664; 215-243-1608 *Web Site:* www.ali-cle.org, pg 12

Midgley, Peter, University of Alberta Press, Ring House 2, Edmonton, AB T6G 2E1, Canada *Tel:* 780-492-3662 *Fax:* 780-492-0719 *Web Site:* www.uap.ualberta.ca, pg 442

Miers, Charles, Rizzoli International Publications Inc, 300 Park Ave S, 4th fl, New York, NY 10010-5399 *Tel:* 212-387-3400 *Toll Free Tel:* 800-522-6657 (orders only) *Fax:* 212-387-3535 *E-mail:* publicity@rizzoliusa.com *Web Site:* www.rizzoliusa.com, pg 185

Miesionczek, Julie, Words into Print, 208 Java St, 5th fl, Brooklyn, NY 11222 *E-mail:* query@wordsintoprint.org *Web Site:* wordsintoprint.org, pg 471

Migner-Laurin, Anne, Les Editions du Remue-Menage, La Maison Parent-Roback, 110 rue Sainte-Therese, bureau 303, Montreal, QC H2Y 1E6, Canada *Tel:* 514-876-0097 *Fax:* 514-876-7951 *E-mail:* info@editions-rm.ca *Web Site:* www.editions-rm.ca, pg 423

Mihlebach, Ashley, HarperCollins General Books Group, 195 Broadway, New York, NY 10007 *Tel:* 212-207-7000 *Web Site:* www.harpercollins.com, pg 93

Miholer, Sue, Oregon Christian Writers (OCW), 1075 Willow Lake Rd N, Keizer, OR 97303 *Tel:* 503-393-3356 *E-mail:* contact@oregonchristianwriters.org *Web Site:* oregonchristianwriters.org, pg 542

Miholer, Sue, Oregon Christian Writers One-Day Conferences, 1075 Willow Lake Rd N, Keizer, OR 97303 *Tel:* 503-393-3356 *E-mail:* contact@oregonchristianwriters.org *Web Site:* oregonchristianwriters.org, pg 577

Miholer, Sue, Oregon Christian Writers Summer Conference, 1075 Willow Lake Rd N, Keizer, OR 97303 *Tel:* 503-393-3356 *E-mail:* contact@oregonchristianwriters.org *Web Site:* oregonchristianwriters.org, pg 577

Miklos, Lauren, Encounter Books, 900 Broadway, Suite 601, New York, NY 10003 *Tel:* 212-871-6310 *Toll Free Tel:* 800-343-4499 *Fax:* 212-871-6311 *E-mail:* publicity@encounterbooks.com *Web Site:* www.encounterbooks.com, pg 72

Mikula, Catherine, Penguin Random House Speakers Bureau, A Penguin Random House Company, 1745 Broadway, Mail Drop 13-1, New York, NY 10019 *Tel:* 212-572-2013 *E-mail:* speakers@penguinrandomhouse.com *Web Site:* www.prhspeakers.com, pg 515

Mikula, Deborah E, Michigan Library Association (MLA), 3410 Belle Chase Way, Lansing, MI 48911 *Tel:* 517-394-2774 *E-mail:* mla@milibraries.org *Web Site:* www.milibraries.org, pg 537

Mila, Juan, HarperCollins General Books Group, 195 Broadway, New York, NY 10007 *Tel:* 212-207-7000 *Web Site:* www.harpercollins.com, pg 93

Milazzo, Richard, Edgewise Press Inc, 24 Fifth Ave, Suite 224, New York, NY 10011 *Tel:* 212-982-4818 *Fax:* 212-982-1364 *E-mail:* epinc@mindspring.com *Web Site:* www.edgewisepress.com, pg 69

Milford, Brian, Abingdon Press, 2222 Rosa L Parks Blvd, Nashville, TN 37228 *Tel:* 615-749-6000 (academic books) *Toll Free Tel:* 800-251-3320 (orders) *Tel:* 615-749-6056 (academic books) *Toll Free Fax:* 800-836-7802 (orders) *E-mail:* orders@abingdonpress.com; permissions@abingdonpress.com *Web Site:* www.abingdonpress.com, pg 2

Millar, David, Simon & Schuster Canada, 166 King St E, Suite 300, Toronto, ON M5A 1J3, Canada *Tel:* 647-427-8882 *Toll Free Tel:* 800-387-0446; 800-268-3216 (orders) *Fax:* 647-430-9446 *Toll Free Fax:* 888-849-8151 (orders) *E-mail:* info@simonandschuster.ca *Web Site:* www.simonandschuster.ca, pg 440

Millard, Martha, Sterling Lord Literistic Inc, 115 Broadway, Suite 1602, New York, NY 10006 *Tel:* 212-780-6050 *Fax:* 212-780-6095 *E-mail:* info@sll.com *Web Site:* www.sll.com, pg 504

Millen, Tim, Center for the Collaborative Classroom, 1001 Marina Village Pkwy, Suite 110, Alameda, CA 94501-1042 *Tel:* 510-533-0213 *Toll Free*

Tel: 800-666-7270 *Fax:* 510-464-3670 *E-mail:* info@collaborativeclassroom.org; clientsupport@collaborativeclassroom.org *Web Site:* www.collaborativeclassroom.org, pg 48

Miller, Andra, Random House Publishing Group, 1745 Broadway, New York, NY 10019 *Toll Free Tel:* 800-200-3552 *Web Site:* www.randomhousebooks.com, pg 181

Miller, Andrew, Alfred A Knopf, c/o Penguin Random House Inc, 1745 Broadway, New York, NY 10019 *Tel:* 212-751-2600 *Fax:* 212-572-2662 (foreign rts) *Web Site:* knopfdoubleday.com, pg 118

Miller, Anelle, Society of Illustrators (SI), 128 E 63 St, New York, NY 10065 *Tel:* 212-838-2560 *Fax:* 212-838-2561 *E-mail:* info@societyillustrators.org *Web Site:* www.societyillustrators.org, pg 547

Miller, Angela, The Miller Agency Inc, 630 Ninth Ave, Suite 1102, New York, NY 10036 *Tel:* 212-206-0913 *Fax:* 212-206-1473, pg 497

Miller, Fr Byron, Liguori Publications, One Liguori Dr, Liguori, MO 63057-1000 *Tel:* 636-464-2500 *Toll Free Tel:* 800-325-9521 *Toll Free Fax:* 800-325-9526 (sales) *E-mail:* liguori@liguori.org (sales & cust serv) *Web Site:* www.liguori.org, pg 124

Miller, Ceci, CeciBooks Editorial & Publishing Consultation, 7057 26 Ave NW, Seattle, WA 98117 *E-mail:* ceci@cecibooks.com *Web Site:* www.cecibooks.com, pg 460

Miller, David, Evan-Moor Educational Publishers, 18 Lower Ragsdale Dr, Monterey, CA 93940-5746 *Tel:* 831-649-5901 *Toll Free Tel:* 800-777-4362 (orders) *Fax:* 831-649-6256 *Toll Free Fax:* 800-777-4332 (orders) *E-mail:* sales@evan-moor.com; marketing@evan-moor.com *Web Site:* www.evan-moor.com, pg 73

Miller, David, The Garamond Agency Inc, 12 Horton St, Newburyport, MA 01950 *E-mail:* query@garamondagency.com *Web Site:* www.garamondagency.com, pg 485

Miller, David, Island Press, 2000 "M" St NW, Suite 650, Washington, DC 20036 *Tel:* 202-232-7933 *Toll Free Tel:* 800-828-1302 *Fax:* 202-234-1328 *E-mail:* info@islandpress.org *Web Site:* www.islandpress.org, pg 112

Miller, George, Cengage Learning, 20 Channel Center St, Boston, MA 02210 *Tel:* 617-289-7700 *Toll Free Tel:* 800-354-9706 *Fax:* 617-289-7844 *E-mail:* esales@cengage.com *Web Site:* www.cengage.com, pg 47

Miller, Heather, University of British Columbia Creative Writing Program, Buchanan Rm E-462, 1866 Main Mall, Vancouver, BC V6T 1Z1, Canada *Tel:* 604-822-0699 *Web Site:* creativewriting.ubc.ca, pg 585

Miller, Irene, The Edwin Mellen Press, 240 Portage Rd, Lewiston, NY 14092 *Tel:* 716-754-2266; 716-754-2788 (order fulfillment) *Fax:* 716-754-4056 *E-mail:* editor@mellenpress.com *Web Site:* www.mellenpress.com, pg 137

Miller, Jan, Dupree, Miller & Associates Inc, 4311 Oak Lawn Ave, Suite 650, Dallas, TX 75219 *Tel:* 214-559-2665 *Fax:* 214-559-7243 *E-mail:* editorial@dupreemiller.com *Web Site:* www.dupreemiller.com, pg 482

Miller, Jeffrey, Irwin Law Inc, 14 Duncan St, Suite 206, Toronto, ON M5H 3G8, Canada *Tel:* 416-862-7690 *Toll Free Tel:* 888-314-9014 *Fax:* 416-862-9236 *E-mail:* info@irwinlaw.com; contact@irwinlaw.com *Web Site:* www.irwinlaw.com, pg 431

Miller, Jennifer, Utah Geological Survey, 1594 W North Temple, Suite 3110, Salt Lake City, UT 84116-3154 *Tel:* 801-537-3300 *Toll Free Tel:* 888-UTAH-MAP (882-4627, bookstore) *Fax:* 801-537-3400 *E-mail:* geostore@utah.gov *Web Site:* geology.utah.gov, pg 235

Miller, Kathleen, Chronicle Books, 680 Second St, San Francisco, CA 94107 *Tel:* 415-537-4200 *Toll Free Tel:* 800-759-0190 (cust serv) *Fax:* 415-537-4460 *Toll Free Fax:* 800-858-7787 (orders); 800-286-9471 (cust serv) *E-mail:* frontdesk@chroniclebooks.com *Web Site:* www.chroniclebooks.com, pg 52

Miller, Kevin, Atlantic Center for the Arts Master Artist-in-Residence Program, 1414 Art Center Ave, New Smyrna Beach, FL 32168 *Tel:* 386-427-6975 *Toll Free Tel:* 800-393-6975 *Fax:* 386-427-5669 *E-mail:* program@atlanticcenterforthearts.org *Web Site:* atlanticcenterforthearts.org, pg 573

Miller, Kim, Association of University Presses (AUPresses), 1412 Broadway, Suite 2135, New York, NY 10018 *Tel:* 212-989-1010 *Fax:* 212-989-0275 *E-mail:* info@aupresses.org *Web Site:* www.aupresses.org, pg 527

Miller, Kim, AUPresses Book, Jacket & Journal Show, 1412 Broadway, Suite 2135, New York, NY 10018 *Tel:* 212-989-1010 *Fax:* 212-989-0275 *E-mail:* info@aupresses.org *Web Site:* www.aupresses.org, pg 594

Miller, Kristen, Sarabande Books Inc, 822 E Market St, Louisville, KY 40206 *Tel:* 502-458-4028 *Fax:* 502-458-4065 *E-mail:* info@sarabandebooks.org *Web Site:* www.sarabandebooks.org, pg 192

Miller, Lauren, Thames & Hudson, 500 Fifth Ave, New York, NY 10110 *Tel:* 212-354-3763 *Toll Free Tel:* 800-233-4830 *Fax:* 212-398-1252 *E-mail:* bookinfo@thames.wwnorton.com *Web Site:* www.thamesandhudsonusa.com, pg 216

Miller, Lawton, M Lee Smith Publishers, 100 Winners Circle, Suite 300, Brentwood, TN 37027 *Tel:* 615-373-7517 *Toll Free Tel:* 800-274-6774; 800-727-5257 *E-mail:* custserv@mleesmith.com; service@blr.com *Web Site:* www.mleesmith.com; www.blr.com, pg 202

Miller, Leah, Atria Books, 1230 Avenue of the Americas, New York, NY 10020 *Tel:* 212-698-7000 *Fax:* 212-698-7007 *Web Site:* www.simonandschuster.com, pg 24

Miller, Linda Sue, Remember Point Inc, PO Box 1448, Pacific Palisades, CA 90272 *Tel:* 310-896-8716 *E-mail:* info@rememberpoint.com *Web Site:* www.rememberpoint.com; www.longfellowfindsahome.com, pg 184

Miller, Matthew, The Toby Press LLC, PO Box 8531, New Milford, CT 06776-8531 *Tel:* 203-830-8508 *Fax:* 203-830-8512 *E-mail:* toby@tobypress.com; sales@korenpub.com *Web Site:* www.tobypress.com; www.korenpub.com, pg 218

Miller, Melissa, American Society of Agricultural & Biological Engineers (ASABE), 2950 Niles Rd, St Joseph, MI 49085-9659 *Tel:* 269-429-0300 *Toll Free Tel:* 800-371-2723 *Fax:* 269-429-3852 *E-mail:* hq@asabe.org *Web Site:* www.asabe.org, pg 14

Miller, Michelle, Big Apple Conference, 5 Penn Plaza, 19th fl, PMB 19059, New York, NY 10001 *Tel:* 917-720-6959 *E-mail:* iwwgquestions@iwwg.org *Web Site:* www.iwwg.org, pg 573

Miller, Michelle, The International Women's Writing Guild (IWWG), 5 Penn Plaza, 19th fl, PMB 19059, New York, NY 10001 *Tel:* 917-720-6959 *E-mail:* iwwgquestions@iwwg.org *Web Site:* www.iwwg.org, pg 536

Miller, Michelle, IWWG Annual Summer Conference, 5 Penn Plaza, 19th fl, PMB 19059, New York, NY 10001 *Tel:* 917-720-6959 *E-mail:* iwwgquestions@iwwg.org *Web Site:* www.iwwg.org, pg 575

Miller, Miriam, Holiday House Publishing Inc, 50 Broad St, New York, NY 10004 *Tel:* 212-688-0085 *Fax:* 212-421-6134 *E-mail:* info@holidayhouse.com *Web Site:* www.holidayhouse.com, pg 101

Miller, Nancy, Bloomsbury Publishing Inc, 1385 Broadway, 5th fl, New York, NY 10018 *Tel:* 212-419-5300 *E-mail:* marketingusa@bloomsbury.com; adultpublicityusa@bloomsbury.com; askacademic@bloomsbury.com *Web Site:* www.bloomsbury.com, pg 35

Miller, Peter, Global Lion Intellectual Property Management Inc, PO Box 669238, Pompano Beach, FL 33066 *Tel:* 754-222-6948 *Fax:* 754-222-6948 *E-mail:* queriesgloballionmgt@gmail.com *Web Site:* www.globallionmanagement.com, pg 486

Miller, Peter, The Institutes™, 720 Providence Rd, Suite 100, Malvern, PA 19355-3433 *Tel:* 610-644-2100 *Toll Free Tel:* 800-644-2101 *Fax:* 610-640-9576 *E-mail:* customerservice@theinstitutes.org *Web Site:* www.theinstitutes.org, pg 110

Miller, Richard K, Richard K Miller Associates, 2413 Main St, Suite 331, Miramar, FL 33025 *Toll Free Tel:* 888-928-RKMA (928-7562) *Toll Free Fax:* 877-928-7562 *Web Site:* rkma.com, pg 140

Miller, Robert, Paul H Brookes Publishing Co Inc, PO Box 10624, Baltimore, MD 21285-0624 *Tel:* 410-337-9580 (outside US & CN) *Toll Free Tel:* 800-638-3775 (US & CN) *Fax:* 410-337-8539 *E-mail:* custserv@brookespublishing.com *Web Site:* www.brookespublishing.com, pg 42

Miller, Samantha, Sciendex, 1388 Leisure Dr, Summerville, SC 29486 *Tel:* 843-693-6689 *Web Site:* www.sciendex.com, pg 470

Miller, Sarah, Yale University Press, 302 Temple St, New Haven, CT 06511-8909 *Tel:* 203-432-0960; 203-432-0966 (sales); 401-531-2800 (cust serv) *Toll Free Tel:* 800-405-1619 (cust serv) *Fax:* 203-432-0948; 203-432-8485 (sales); 401-531-2801 (cust serv) *Toll Free Fax:* 800-406-9145 (cust serv) *E-mail:* sales.press@yale.edu (sales); customer.care@triliteral.org (cust serv) *Web Site:* www.yalebooks.com; yalepress.yale.edu/yupbooks, pg 246

Miller, Scott, David C Cook, 4050 Lee Vance Dr, Colorado Springs, CO 80918 *Tel:* 719-536-0100 *Toll Free Tel:* 800-708-5550; 800-323-7543 (orders & cust serv) *Toll Free Fax:* 800-430-0726 (cust serv) *Web Site:* www.davidccook.org, pg 56

Miller, Scott, Trident Media Group LLC, 41 Madison Ave, 36th fl, New York, NY 10010 *Tel:* 212-333-1511 *E-mail:* info@tridentmediagroup.com; press@tridentmediagroup.com *Web Site:* www.tridentmediagroup.com, pg 507

Miller, Stephen M, Stephen M Miller Inc, 15727 S Madison Dr, Olathe, KS 66062 *Tel:* 913-768-7997 *Web Site:* www.stephenmillerbooks.com, pg 468

Miller, Sue, Boydell & Brewer Inc, 668 Mount Hope Ave, Rochester, NY 14620-2731 *Tel:* 585-275-0419 *Fax:* 585-271-8778 *E-mail:* boydell@boydellusa.net *Web Site:* www.boydellandbrewer.com, pg 39

Miller, Ted, Human Kinetics Inc, 1607 N Market St, Champaign, IL 61820 *Tel:* 217-351-5076 *Toll Free Tel:* 800-747-4457 *Fax:* 217-351-1549 (orders/cust serv) *E-mail:* info@hkusa.com *Web Site:* www.humankinetics.com, pg 105

Miller, Tom, Liza Dawson Associates, 121 W 27 St, Suite 1201, New York, NY 10001 *Tel:* 212-465-9071 *Web Site:* www.lizadawsonassociates.com, pg 481

Milligan, M, Wings Press, PO Box 591176, San Antonio, TX 78259 *E-mail:* wingspresspublishing@gmail.com *Web Site:* www.wingspress.com, pg 242

Milliken, Jean Mellichamp, Lyric Poetry Prizes, PO Box 110, Jericho, VT 05465 *Tel:* 802-899-3993 *Fax:* 802-899-3993 *E-mail:* themuse@thelyricmagazine.com *Web Site:* thelyricmagazine.com, pg 636

Milliken, Leif, University of Nebraska Press, 1111 Lincoln Mall, Lincoln, NE 68588-0630 *Tel:* 402-472-3581; 919-966-7449 (cust serv & foreign orders) *Toll Free Tel:* 800-848-6224 (cust serv & US orders) *Fax:* 402-472-6214; 919-962-2704 (cust serv & foreign orders) *Toll Free Fax:* 800-526-2617 (cust serv & US orders) *E-mail:* pressmail@unl.edu *Web Site:* www.nebraskapress.unl.edu, pg 229

Millinger, Jenny, Write Now, 900 S Mitchell Dr, Tempe, AZ 85281 *Tel:* 480-921-5700 *Fax:* 480-921-5777 *E-mail:* info@writenow.co *Web Site:* www.writenow.co, pg 680

Millman, Michael, University of New Mexico Press, One University of New Mexico, Albuquerque, NM 87131-0001 *Tel:* 505-272-7777 *Fax:* 505-277-3343 *E-mail:* custserv@unm.edu (order dept) *Web Site:* unmpress.com, pg 229

Millner, Denene, Simon & Schuster Children's Publishing, 1230 Avenue of the Americas, New York, NY 10020 *Tel:* 212-698-7000 *Web Site:* www.

simonandschuster.com/kids; www.simonandschuster.com/teen; simonandschuster.net; simonandschuster.biz, pg 199

Mills, Elizabeth M, Temporal Mechanical Press, 6760 Hwy 7, Estes Park, CO 80517-6404 *Tel:* 970-586-4706 *E-mail:* info@enosmills.com *Web Site:* www.enosmills.com, pg 215

Mills, Eryn, Temporal Mechanical Press, 6760 Hwy 7, Estes Park, CO 80517-6404 *Tel:* 970-586-4706 *E-mail:* info@enosmills.com *Web Site:* www.enosmills.com, pg 215

Mills, Kathleen, Kathleen Mills Editorial Services, 327 E King St, Chardon, OH 44024 *Tel:* 440-285-4347 *E-mail:* mills_edit@yahoo.com, pg 468

Mills, Kevin, The Tuesday Agency, 132 1/2 E Washington St, Iowa City, IA 52240 *Tel:* 319-338-7080 *E-mail:* trinity@tuesdayagency.com *Web Site:* tuesdayagency.com, pg 516

Mills, Megan, Books on Tape™, 1745 Broadway, New York, NY 10019 *Toll Free Tel:* 800-733-3000 (cust serv) *Toll Free Fax:* 800-940-7046 *Web Site:* www.booksontape.com, pg 38

Mills, Pamela, Association of Writers & Writing Programs (AWP), University of Maryland, 5245 Greenbelt Rd, Box 246, College Park, MD 20740 *Tel:* 240-696-7700 *E-mail:* awp@awpwriter.org; press@awpwriter.org *Web Site:* www.awpwriter.org, pg 527

Mills, Pamela, AWP Award Series, University of Maryland, 5245 Greenbelt Rd, Box 246, College Park, MD 20740 *Tel:* 240-696-7700 *E-mail:* awp@awpwriter.org; press@awpwriter.org *Web Site:* www.awpwriter.org, pg 594

Milne, James, The American Chemical Society, 1155 16 St NW, Washington, DC 20036 *Tel:* 202-872-4600 *Toll Free Tel:* 800-227-5558 (US) *Fax:* 202-872-6067 *E-mail:* help@acs.org *Web Site:* www.acs.org, pg 10

Min, Erica, Random House Publishing Group, 1745 Broadway, New York, NY 10019 *Toll Free Tel:* 800-200-3552 *Web Site:* www.randomhousebooks.com, pg 181

Minar, Scott, Marick Press, PO Box 36253, Grosse Pointe Farms, MI 48236 *Tel:* 313-407-9236 *E-mail:* orders@marickpress.com *Web Site:* www.marickpress.com, pg 132

Minchew, Laura, Thomas Nelson, 501 Nelson Place, Nashville, TN 37214 *Tel:* 615-889-9000 *Toll Free Tel:* 800-251-4000 *Fax:* 615-902-1548 *Web Site:* www.thomasnelson.com, pg 217

Minchew, Laura, Zondervan, 3900 Sparks Dr, Grand Rapids, MI 49546 *Tel:* 616-698-6900 *Toll Free Tel:* 800-226-1122; 800-727-1309 (retail orders) *Fax:* 616-698-3350 *Toll Free Fax:* 800-698-3256 (retail orders) *Web Site:* www.zondervan.com, pg 248

Mindlin, Ivy, The Ivy League of Artists Inc, 18 Edgemere Rd, Livingston, NJ 07039 *Tel:* 973-992-4048 *Fax:* 973-992-4049 *E-mail:* ilartists2@gmail.com, pg 511

Minick, James, Sandhills Writers' Series, Dept of English & Foreign Languages, 1120 15 St, Augusta, GA 30912 *Tel:* 706-729-2417, pg 578

Minkin, James, The Dawn Horse Press, 12040 N Seigler Rd, Middletown, CA 95461 *Tel:* 707-928-6590 *Toll Free Tel:* 877-770-0772 *Fax:* 707-928-5068 *E-mail:* dhp@adidam.org *Web Site:* www.dawnhorsepress.com, pg 63

Minnich, Sara, GP Putnam's Sons (Hardcover), 375 Hudson St, New York, NY 10014 *Tel:* 212-366-2000 *Fax:* 212-366-2643 *E-mail:* online@penguinputnam.com *Web Site:* www.penguin.com/publishers/gpputnamssons, pg 178

Mintzer, Conor, Henry Holt and Company, LLC, 120 Broadway, 23rd fl, New York, NY 10271 *Tel:* 646-307-5151 *Toll Free Tel:* 888-330-8477 (orders) *Fax:* 646-307-5285 *Web Site:* www.henryholt.com, pg 102

Miracle, Tracy, Candlewick Press, 99 Dover St, Somerville, MA 02144-2825 *Tel:* 617-661-3330 *Fax:* 617-661-0565 *E-mail:* bigbear@candlewick.com; salesinfo@candlewick.com *Web Site:* www.candlewick.com, pg 44

Miranda, Joseph, Fairchild Books, 1385 Broadway, 5th fl, New York, NY 10018 *Tel:* 212-419-5300 *Toll Free Tel:* 800-932-4724; 888-330-8477 (orders) *Web Site:* bloomsbury.com/us/academic/fairchildbooks, pg 75

Miranda, Lori, Cognizant Communication Corp, 18 Peekskill Hollow Rd, Putnam Valley, NY 10579-0037 *Tel:* 845-603-6440; 845-603-6441 (warehouse & orders) *Fax:* 845-603-6442 *E-mail:* inquiries@cognizantcommunication.com; sales@cognizantcommunication.com *Web Site:* www.cognizantcommunication.com, pg 54

Miranda, Robert N, Cognizant Communication Corp, 18 Peekskill Hollow Rd, Putnam Valley, NY 10579-0037 *Tel:* 845-603-6440; 845-603-6441 (warehouse & orders) *Fax:* 845-603-6442 *E-mail:* inquiries@cognizantcommunication.com; sales@cognizantcommunication.com *Web Site:* www.cognizantcommunication.com, pg 54

Mirolla, Michael, Guernica Editions Inc, 1569 Heritage Way, Oakville, ON L6M 2Z7, Canada *Tel:* 905-599-5304 *E-mail:* info@guernicaeditions.com *Web Site:* www.guernicaeditions.com; www.facebook.com/guernicaed, pg 428

Mishra, Pradeep C, Arkansas State University Graphic Communications Program, PO Box 1930, Dept of Media, State University, AR 72467-1930 *Tel:* 870-972-3114 *Fax:* 870-972-3321 *Web Site:* www.astate.edu, pg 581

Miskin, Michael J, Tapestry Press Ltd, 19 Nashoba Rd, Littleton, MA 01460 *Tel:* 978-486-0200 *Toll Free Tel:* 800-535-2007 *E-mail:* publish@tapestrypress.com *Web Site:* www.tapestrypress.com, pg 213

Mitchell, Brittany, Bloomsbury Publishing Inc, 1385 Broadway, 5th fl, New York, NY 10018 *Tel:* 212-419-5300 *E-mail:* marketingusa@bloomsbury.com; adultpublicityusa@bloomsbury.com; askacademic@bloomsbury.com *Web Site:* www.bloomsbury.com, pg 36

Mitchell, Carine, Cambridge University Press, One Liberty Plaza, 20th fl, New York, NY 10006 *Tel:* 212-924-3900; 212-337-5000 *Fax:* 212-691-3239; 845-353-4141 *E-mail:* newyork@cambridge.org; customer_service@cambridge.org *Web Site:* www.cambridge.org/us, pg 43

Mitchell, Chuck, The Conference Board Inc, 845 Third Ave, New York, NY 10022-6600 *Tel:* 212-759-0900; 212-339-0345 (cust serv) *E-mail:* customer.service@conferenceboard.org; membership@conferenceboard.org *Web Site:* www.conference-board.org; www.linkedin.com/company/the-conference-board, pg 56

Mitchell, David, The Guilford Press, 370 Seventh Ave, Suite 1200, New York, NY 10001-1020 *Tel:* 212-431-9800 *Toll Free Tel:* 800-365-7006 *Fax:* 212-966-6708 *E-mail:* info@guilford.com *Web Site:* www.guilford.com, pg 90

Mitchell, Dr Francis, New World Publishing (Canada), PO Box 36075, Halifax, NS B3J 3S9, Canada *Tel:* 902-576-2055 (inquiries) *Toll Free Tel:* 877-211-3334 (orders) *Fax:* 902-576-2095 *Web Site:* newworldpublishing.com, pg 434

Mitchell, Gwendolyn, Third World Press, 7822 S Dobson Ave, Chicago, IL 60619 *Tel:* 773-651-0700 *Fax:* 773-651-7286 *E-mail:* twpbooks@thirdworldpressfoundation.org *Web Site:* thirdworldpressfoundation.org, pg 217

Mitchell, Jack, Lumina Datamatics Inc, 4 Collins Ave, Plymouth, MA 02360 *Tel:* 508-746-0300 *Fax:* 508-746-3233 *Web Site:* luminadatamatics.com, pg 466

Mitchell, Megan, Random House Children's Books, 1745 Broadway, 10th fl, New York, NY 10019 *Tel:* 212-782-9000 *Web Site:* www.randomhousekids.com, pg 181

Monteith, Barnas, Tumblehome Learning Inc, 201 Newbury St, Suite 201, Boston, MA 02116 *E-mail:* info@tumblehomelearning.com *Web Site:* www.tumblehomelearning.com, pg 221

Montgomery, Heather, Energy Psychology Press, 1490 Mark West Springs Rd, Santa Rosa, CA 95404 *Tel:* 707-525-9292 *Toll Free Fax:* 800-330-9798 *E-mail:* energypsychologypress@gmail. com; support@eftuniverse.com *Web Site:* www. energypsychologypress.com; www.elitebooksonline. com, pg 72

Montgomery, Madeline, Portfolio, 375 Hudson St, New York, NY 10014 *Web Site:* www.penguin.com/meet/ publishers/portfolio, pg 172

Montgomery, Michele, RISING STAR Award, PO Box 190, Jefferson, OR 97352 *E-mail:* risingstar@ womenfictionwriters.org *Web Site:* wfwa. memberclicks.net/rising-star-award, pg 662

Montgomery, Michele, STAR Award, PO Box 190, Jefferson, OR 97352 *E-mail:* staraward@ womenfictionwriters.org *Web Site:* wfwa. memberclicks.net/star-award, pg 670

Montgomery, Michele, Women's Fiction Writers Association (WFWA), PO Box 190, Jefferson, OR 97352 *E-mail:* communications@ womensfictionwriters.org; membership@ womensfictionwriters.org *Web Site:* www. womensfictionwriters.org, pg 549

Monti, Joe, Gallery Books, 1230 Avenue of the Americas, New York, NY 10020 *Toll Free Tel:* 800-456-6798 *Fax:* 212-698-7284 *E-mail:* consumer. customerservice@simonandschuster.com *Web Site:* www.simonandschuster.com, pg 83

Moodie, Matthew, Apress Media LLC, 233 Spring St, 6th fl, New York, NY 10013 *Tel:* 212-460-1500 *E-mail:* editorial@apress.com; customerservice@ springernature.com *Web Site:* www.apress.com, pg 18

Moody, Cindy, The Astronomical Society of the Pacific, 390 Ashton Ave, San Francisco, CA 94112 *Tel:* 415-337-1100 *Fax:* 415-337-5205 *Web Site:* www. astrosociety.org, pg 24

Moody, Jeanne C, Beaver Wood Associates, 655 Alstead Center Rd, Alstead, NH 03602 *Tel:* 603-835-7900 *Web Site:* www.beaverwood.com, pg 459

Moody, Jessica, Grey House Publishing Inc™, 4919 Rte 22, Amenia, NY 12501 *Tel:* 518-789-8700 *Toll Free Tel:* 800-562-2139 *Fax:* 518-789-0556 *E-mail:* books@greyhouse.com; customerservice@ greyhouse.com *Web Site:* greyhouse.com, pg 89

Moody, Rodger, Gerald Cable Book Award, PO Box 3541, Eugene, OR 97403 *Tel:* 541-344-5060 *E-mail:* sfrpress@earthlink.net *Web Site:* www. silverfishreviewpress.com, pg 602

Moog, Bob, BePuzzled, 2030 Harrison St, San Francisco, CA 94110 *Tel:* 415-503-1600 *Toll Free Tel:* 800-347-4818 *Fax:* 415-503-0085 *E-mail:* info@ ugames.com *Web Site:* www.ugames.com, pg 32

Moomaw, Suzanne Morse, The University of Virginia Press, PO Box 400318, Charlottesville, VA 22904-4318 *Tel:* 434-924-3468 (cust serv); 434-924-3469 (cust serv) *Toll Free Tel:* 800-831-3406 (orders) *Fax:* 434-982-2655 *Toll Free Fax:* 877-288-6400 *E-mail:* vapress@virginia.edu *Web Site:* www.upress. virginia.edu, pg 231

Moon, Emily, Houghton Mifflin Harcourt Trade & Reference Division, 125 High St, Boston, MA 02110 *Tel:* 617-351-5000 *Web Site:* www.hmhco.com, pg 104

Mooney, Dr Robert, Etruscan Press, Wilkes University, 84 W South St, Wilkes-Barre, PA 18766 *Tel:* 570-408-4546 *Fax:* 570-408-3333 *E-mail:* books@ etruscanpress.org *Web Site:* www.etruscanpress.org, pg 73

Moore, Allison, Bloomsbury Publishing Inc, 1385 Broadway, 5th fl, New York, NY 10018 *Tel:* 212-419-5300 *E-mail:* marketingusa@bloomsbury.com; adultpublicityusa@bloomsbury.com; askacademic@ bloomsbury.com *Web Site:* www.bloomsbury.com, pg 36

Moore, Berwyn, Gannon University's High School Poetry Contest, Gannon University, 109 University Sq, Erie, PA 16541 *Tel:* 814-871-7504 *Web Site:* www. gannon.edu/departmental/english/poetry.asp, pg 618

Moore, Brian, Houghton Mifflin Harcourt Trade & Reference Division, 125 High St, Boston, MA 02110 *Tel:* 617-351-5000 *Web Site:* www.hmhco.com, pg 104

Moore, David, Dramatists Play Service Inc, 440 Park Ave S, New York, NY 10016 *Tel:* 212-683-8960 *Fax:* 212-213-1539 *E-mail:* postmaster@dramatists. com; orders@dramatists.com; publications@dramatists. com *Web Site:* www.dramatists.com, pg 67

Moore, Dinty W, Ohio University, English Department, Creative Writing Program, Ohio University, English Dept, Ellis Hall, Athens, OH 45701 *Tel:* 740-593-2838 (English Dept) *Fax:* 740-593-2832 *E-mail:* english. department@ohio.edu *Web Site:* www.ohio.edu/cas/ english, pg 584

Moore, George, Cengage Learning, 20 Channel Center St, Boston, MA 02210 *Tel:* 617-289-7700 *Toll Free Tel:* 800-354-9706 *Fax:* 617-289-7844 *E-mail:* esales@cengage.com *Web Site:* www.cengage. com, pg 47

Moore, Heather, Sourcebooks LLC, 1935 Brookdale Rd, Suite 139, Naperville, IL 60563 *Tel:* 630-961-3900 *Toll Free Tel:* 800-432-7444 *Fax:* 630-961-2168 *E-mail:* info@sourcebooks.com; customersupport@ sourcebooks.com *Web Site:* www.sourcebooks.com, pg 204

Moore, John, BNi Building News, 990 Park Center Dr, Suite E, Vista, CA 92081-8352 *Tel:* 760-734-1113 *Toll Free Tel:* 888-BNI-BOOK (264-2665) *Web Site:* www. bnibooks.com, pg 37

Moore, John D, Johns Hopkins University Press, 2715 N Charles St, Baltimore, MD 21218-4363 *Tel:* 410-516-6900; 410-516-6987 (journal orders outside US & CN) *Toll Free Tel:* 800-537-5487 (book orders & cust serv); 800-548-1784 (journal orders) *Fax:* 410-516-6968; 410-516-3866 (journal orders); 410-516-6998 (orders) *E-mail:* hfscustserv@press.jhu.edu (cust serv); jrnlcirc@press.jhu.edu (journal orders) *Web Site:* www.press.jhu.edu; muse.jhu.edu, pg 114

Moore, Joseph, Scarsdale Publishing Ltd, 333 Mamaroneck Ave, White Plains, NY 10607 *E-mail:* scarsdale@scarsdalepublishing.com *Web Site:* scarsdalepublishing.com, pg 193

Moore, Karen, Literary Management Group LLC, 521 Oakley Dr, Nashville, TN 37220 *Tel:* 615-812-4445 *Web Site:* www.literarymanagementgroup.com, pg 493

Moore, Latisha, National Cartoonists Society (NCS), PO Box 592927, Orlando, FL 32859-2927 *Tel:* 407-994-6703 *Fax:* 407-442-0786 *E-mail:* info@reuben.org *Web Site:* www.reuben.org, pg 539

Moore, Lisa, University of Texas at Austin, New Writers Project, Dept of English, Calhoun Hall, Rm 226, 204 W 21 St, B-5000, Austin, TX 78712 *Tel:* 512-471-5132; 512-471-4991 *Fax:* 512-471-4909 *Web Site:* newwritersproject.org, pg 586

Moore, Marvin, Pacific Press® Publishing Association, 1350 N Kings Rd, Nampa, ID 83687-3193 *Tel:* 208-465-2500 *Toll Free Tel:* 800-447-7377 *Fax:* 208-465-2531 *Web Site:* www.pacificpress.com, pg 159

Moore, Mary, Kimberley Cameron & Associates LLC, 1550 Tiburon Blvd, Suite 704, Tiburon, CA 94920 *Tel:* 415-789-9191 *Fax:* 415-789-9177 *Web Site:* www. kimberleycameron.com, pg 479

Moore, Michael, Augsburg Fortress Publishers, Publishing House of the Evangelical Lutheran Church in America, 510 Marquette Ave S, Minneapolis, MN 55402 *Tel:* 612-330-3300 *Toll Free Tel:* 800-426-0115 (ext 639, subns); 800-328-4648 (orders) *Fax:* 612-330-3455 *E-mail:* info@augsburgfortress.org; copyright@ augsburgfortress.org (reprint permission requests); customercare@augsburgfortress.org *Web Site:* www. augsburgfortress.org; www.1517.media, pg 25

Moore, Michele, American Civil Liberties Union, 125 Broad St, 18th fl, New York, NY 10004 *Tel:* 212-549-2500 *E-mail:* media@aclu.org *Web Site:* www.aclu. org, pg 522

Moore, Nancy, Gerald & Cullen Rapp, 41 N Main St, Suite 103, South Norwalk, CT 06854 *Tel:* 212-889-3337 *E-mail:* info@rappart.com *Web Site:* www. rappart.com, pg 512

Moore, Penny, Aevitas Creative Management, 19 W 21 St, Suite 501, New York, NY 10010 *Tel:* 212-765-6900 *Web Site:* aevitascreative.com, pg 474

Moore, Stacey, Zeig, Tucker & Theisen Inc, 2632 E Thomas Rd, Suite 201, Phoenix, AZ 85016 *Tel:* 480-389-4342 *Web Site:* www.zeigtucker.com, pg 248

Moore, Stephen, Paul Kohner Agency, 9300 Wilshire Blvd, Suite 555, Beverly Hills, CA 90212 *Tel:* 310-550-1060 *Fax:* 310-276-1083, pg 492

Moore, Susan, Oregon Book Awards, 925 SW Washington St, Portland, OR 97205 *Tel:* 503-227-2583 *Fax:* 503-241-4256 *E-mail:* la@literary-arts.org *Web Site:* www.literary-arts.org, pg 651

Moore, Tricia J, Lehigh University Press, B-040 Christmas-Saucon Hall, 14 E Packer Ave, Bethlehem, PA 18015 *Tel:* 610-758-3933 *Fax:* 610-758-6331 *E-mail:* inlup@lehigh.edu *Web Site:* lupress.cas2. lehigh.edu, pg 122

Moore-Swafford, Angela, Southern Illinois University Press, 1915 University Press Dr, SIUC Mail Code 6806, Carbondale, IL 62901-4323 *Tel:* 618-453-2281 *Fax:* 618-453-1221 *Web Site:* www.siupress.com, pg 205

Moose, Christina, Davies Publishing Inc, 32 S Raymond Ave, Suites 4 & 5, Pasadena, CA 91105-1961 *Tel:* 626-792-3046 *Toll Free Tel:* 877-792-0005 *Fax:* 626-792-5308 *E-mail:* info@daviespublishing. com *Web Site:* daviespublishing.com, pg 62

Mooser, Stephen, The Don Freeman Memorial Grant-In-Aid, 6363 Wilshire Blvd, Suite 425, Los Angeles, CA 90048 *Tel:* 323-782-1010; 310-403-0675 (cell) *Fax:* 323-782-1892 *E-mail:* grants@scbwi.org; scbwi@scbwi.org *Web Site:* www.scbwi.org, pg 617

Mooser, Stephen, Golden Kite Awards, 6363 Wilshire Blvd, Suite 425, Los Angeles, CA 90048 *Tel:* 323-782-1010; 310-403-0675 (cell) *Fax:* 323-782-1892 *E-mail:* grants@scbwi.org; scbwi@scbwi.org *Web Site:* www.scbwi.org, pg 620

Mooser, Stephen, Magazine Merit Awards, 6363 Wilshire Blvd, Suite 425, Los Angeles, CA 90048 *Tel:* 323-782-1010; 310-403-0675 (cell) *Fax:* 323-782-1892 *E-mail:* grants@scbwi.org; scbwi@scbwi.org *Web Site:* www.scbwi.org, pg 637

Mooser, Stephen, SCBWI Work-In-Progress Grants, 6363 Wilshire Blvd, Suite 425, Los Angeles, CA 90048 *Tel:* 323-782-1010; 310-403-0675 (cell) *Fax:* 323-782-1892 *E-mail:* grants@scbwi.org; scbwi@scbwi.org *Web Site:* www.scbwi.org, pg 665

Mooser, Stephen, Society of Children's Book Writers & Illustrators (SCBWI), 6363 Wilshire Blvd, Suite 425, Los Angeles, CA 90048 *Tel:* 323-782-1010 *E-mail:* membership@scbwi.org *Web Site:* www.scbwi. org, pg 546

Moraleda, Lisa, Simon & Schuster Children's Publishing, 1230 Avenue of the Americas, New York, NY 10020 *Tel:* 212-698-7000 *Web Site:* www.simonandschuster. com/kids; www.simonandschuster.com/teen; simonandschuster.net; simonandschuster.biz, pg 199

Morales, Ruth, University of Puerto Rico Press, Edificio La Editorial (level 2), Carr No 1, KM 12.0, Jardin Botanico Norte, San Juan, PR 00927 *Tel:* 787-250-0435; 787-250-0550 *Toll Free Tel:* 877-338-7788 *Fax:* 787-753-9116 *E-mail:* info@laeditorialupr.com *Web Site:* www.laeditorialupr.com, pg 231

Moran, Bruce, TotalRecall Publications Inc, 1103 Middlecreek, Friendswood, TX 77546 *Tel:* 281-992-3131 *E-mail:* sales@totalrecallpress.com *Web Site:* www.totalrecallpress.com, pg 219

Moran, Michael, Gem Guides Book Co, 1155 W Ninth St, Upland, CA 91786 *Tel:* 626-855-1611 *Toll Free Tel:* 800-824-5118 (orders) *Fax:* 626-855-1610 *E-mail:* info@gemguidesbooks.com; sales@ gemguidesbooks.com (orders) *Web Site:* www. gemguidesbooks.com, pg 84

Moran, Viniita, Chronicle Books, 680 Second St, San Francisco, CA 94107 *Tel:* 415-537-4200 *Toll Free Tel:* 800-759-0190 (cust serv) *Fax:* 415-537-4460 *Toll Free Fax:* 800-858-7787 (orders); 800-286-9471 (cust serv) *E-mail:* frontdesk@chroniclebooks.com *Web Site:* www.chroniclebooks.com, pg 51

Moran, Whitney, Nimbus Publishing Ltd, 3731 Mackintosh St, Halifax, NS B3K 5A5, Canada *Tel:* 902-455-4286 *Toll Free Tel:* 800-NIMBUS9 (646-2879) *Fax:* 902-455-5440 *Toll Free Fax:* 888-253-3133 *E-mail:* customerservice@nimbus.ca *Web Site:* www.nimbus.ca, pg 434

Morano, Nicole, Penguin Random House Audio Publishing, 1745 Broadway, New York, NY 10019 *E-mail:* audio@penguinrandomhouse.com *Web Site:* www.penguinrandomhouseaudio.com, pg 164

Moreau, Deb, Quarto Publishing Group USA Inc, 100 Cummings Ctr, Suite 265D, Beverly, MA 01915 *Tel:* 978-282-9590 *Toll Free Tel:* 800-328-0590 (sales) *Fax:* 978-283-2742 *E-mail:* sales@quartous.com *Web Site:* www.quartoknows.com, pg 179

Moredock, Rebekah, Hachette Nashville, 6100 Tower Circle, Room 210, Franklin, TN 37067 *Tel:* 615-221-0996 *Fax:* 615-221-0962 *Web Site:* www.hachettebookgroup.com, pg 91

Morehouse, Jim, Paradise Cay Publications Inc, 120 Monda Way, Blue Lake, CA 95525 *Tel:* 707-822-9063 *Toll Free Tel:* 800-736-4509 *Fax:* 707-822-9163 *E-mail:* info@paracay.com; orders@paracay.com *Web Site:* www.paracay.com, pg 160

Morel, Madeleine, 2M Communications Ltd, 19 W 21 St, Suite 501, New York, NY 10010 *Tel:* 212-741-1509 *Fax:* 212-691-4460 *Web Site:* www.2mcommunications.com, pg 507

Moreno, Celina, Intercultural Development Research Association (IDRA), 5815 Callaghan Rd, Suite 101, San Antonio, TX 78228 *Tel:* 210-444-1710 *Fax:* 210-444-1714 *E-mail:* contact@idra.org *Web Site:* www.idra.org, pg 110

Moreno, Jennifer, Random House Children's Books, 1745 Broadway, 10th fl, New York, NY 10019 *Tel:* 212-782-9000 *Web Site:* www.randomhousekids.com, pg 181

Moreno, Luis Alberto, Inter-American Development Bank, 1300 New York Ave NW, Washington, DC 20577 *Tel:* 202-623-1000 *Fax:* 202-623-3096 *E-mail:* pic@iadb.org *Web Site:* publications.iadb.org, pg 110

Moreton, Daniel, Penguin Workshop, 1745 Broadway, New York, NY 10019 *Tel:* 212-366-2000 *Web Site:* www.penguin.com/publishers/penguinworkshop/, pg 165

Morgan, Cal, Riverhead Books, 375 Hudson St, New York, NY 10014 *Tel:* 212-366-2000 *Web Site:* www.penguin.com/publishers/riverhead, pg 185

Morgan, Emmanuelle, Stonesong, 270 W 39 St, Suite 201, New York, NY 10018 *Tel:* 212-929-4600 *E-mail:* editors@stonesong.com *Web Site:* www.stonesong.com, pg 504

Morgan, Genevieve, Islandport Press, 247 Portland St, Bldg C, Yarmouth, ME 04096 *Tel:* 207-846-3344 *Fax:* 207-619-9975 *E-mail:* info@islandportpress.com *Web Site:* www.islandportpress.com, pg 112

Morgan, Dr Jean, Castle Connolly Medical Ltd, 42 W 24 St, 2nd fl, New York, NY 10010 *Tel:* 212-367-8400 *Fax:* 212-367-0964 *Web Site:* www.castleconnolly.com, pg 46

Morgan, Jess, James Lorimer & Co Ltd, Publishers, 117 Peter St, Suite 304, Toronto, ON M5V 0M3, Canada *Tel:* 416-362-4762 *Fax:* 416-362-3939 *Web Site:* www.lorimer.ca, pg 432

Morgan, Jill, Purple House Press, 8100 US Hwy 62 E, Cynthiana, KY 41031 *Tel:* 859-235-9970 *Web Site:* www.purplehousepress.com, pg 178

Morgan, Katharine E, ASTM International, 100 Barr Harbor Dr, West Conshohocken, PA 19428-2959 *Tel:* 610-832-9500; 610-832-9585 (intl) *Toll Free*

Tel: 877-909-2786 (sales & cust support) *Fax:* 610-832-9555 *E-mail:* service@astm.org *Web Site:* www.astm.org, pg 23

Morgan, Kristina, Lynx House Press, 420 W 24 St, Spokane, WA 99203 *Tel:* 509-624-4894 *E-mail:* lynxhousepress@gmail.com *Web Site:* www.lynxhousepress.org, pg 129

Morgan, Lael, Epicenter Press Inc, 6524 NE 181 St, Suite 2, Kenmore, WA 98028 *Tel:* 425-485-6822 (edit, mktg, busn off) *Fax:* 425-481-8253 *E-mail:* info@epicenterpress.com *Web Site:* www.epicenterpress.com, pg 73

Morgan, Lauren Diaz, Random House Children's Books, 1745 Broadway, 10th fl, New York, NY 10019 *Tel:* 212-782-9000 *Web Site:* www.randomhousekids.com, pg 181

Morgan, Linda Cicely, The Center for Fiction, 17 E 47 St, New York, NY 10017 *Tel:* 212-755-6710 *E-mail:* info@centerforfiction.org *Web Site:* centerforfiction.org, pg 530

Morgan, Lindsay, University of California Institute on Global Conflict & Cooperation, 9500 Gilman Dr, MC 0518, La Jolla, CA 92093-0518 *Tel:* 858-534-6106 *Fax:* 858-534-7655 *E-mail:* igcc-communications@ucsd.edu *Web Site:* igcc.ucsd.edu, pg 226

Morgan, Michelle, Nicholas Brealey Publishing, 53 State St, 9th fl, Boston, MA 02109 *Tel:* 617-523-3801 *E-mail:* info@nicholasbrealey.com; sales-us@nicholasbrealey.com *Web Site:* www.nicholasbrealey.com, pg 40

Morgan, Stephen, Simon & Schuster, Inc, 1230 Avenue of the Americas, New York, NY 10020 *Tel:* 212-698-7000 *Toll Free Tel:* 800-223-2336 (orders) *Fax:* 212-698-7007 *Toll Free Fax:* 800-943-9831 (orders) *E-mail:* firstname.lastname@simonandschuster.com; purchaseorders@simonandschuster.com (orders) *Web Site:* www.simonandschuster.com, pg 199

Morgan, Thomas, little bee books, 251 Park Ave S, 12th fl, New York, NY 10010 *Toll Free Tel:* 844-321-0237 *E-mail:* info@littlebeebooks.com *Web Site:* littlebeebooks.com, pg 125

Morgan-Sanders, Hayley, Purple House Press, 8100 US Hwy 62 E, Cynthiana, KY 41031 *Tel:* 859-235-9970 *Web Site:* www.purplehousepress.com, pg 178

Morgenfeld, Michael, Perseus Books, 1290 Avenue of the Americas, New York, NY 10104 *Tel:* 212-340-8100 *Toll Free Tel:* 800-343-4499 (cust serv) *Fax:* 212-340-8105 *Web Site:* www.perseusbooks.com, pg 168

Morgenstein, Leslie, Alloy Entertainment LLC, 30 Hudson Yards, 22nd fl, New York, NY 10001 *E-mail:* collaborative@alloyentertainment.com, pg 8

Morgridge, Sally, Holiday House Publishing Inc, 50 Broad St, New York, NY 10004 *Tel:* 212-688-0085 *Fax:* 212-421-6134 *E-mail:* info@holidayhouse.com *Web Site:* www.holidayhouse.com, pg 101

Morhaim, Howard, Howard Morhaim Literary Agency Inc, 30 Pierrepont St, Brooklyn, NY 11201-3371 *Tel:* 718-222-8400 *E-mail:* info@morhaimliterary.com *Web Site:* www.morhaimliterary.com, pg 497

Moriarty, Amy, WordCo Indexing Services Inc, 49 Church St, Norwich, CT 06360 *Tel:* 860-886-2532 *Toll Free Tel:* 877-WORDCO-3 (967-3263) *Fax:* 860-886-1155 *E-mail:* office@wordco.com *Web Site:* www.wordco.com, pg 471

Moriarty, Kerry, Twenty-Third Publications, One Montauk Ave, Suite 200, New London, CT 06320 *Tel:* 860-437-3012 *Toll Free Tel:* 800-321-0411 (orders) *Toll Free Fax:* 800-572-0788 *E-mail:* resources@twentythirdpublications.com *Web Site:* www.twentythirdpublications.com, pg 223

Morin-Spatz, Patrice, MedBooks Inc, PO Box 12805, Dallas, TX 75225 *Tel:* 972-643-1809; 972-643-1802 *Fax:* 972-643-1859 *E-mail:* medbooks@medbooks.com; customerservice@medbooks.com; sales@medbooks.com *Web Site:* www.medbooks.com, pg 137

Morisset, Chantel, Les Editions Goelette Inc, 1350 Marie-Victorin, St-Bruno-de-Montarville, Quebec, QC J3V 6B9, Canada *Tel:* 450-653-1337 *Toll Free*

Tel: 800-463-4961 *Fax:* 450-653-9924 *E-mail:* info@boutiquegoelette.com *Web Site:* www.boutiquegoelette.com, pg 424

Morita, Joe, Springer Publishing Co, 11 W 42 St, 15th fl, New York, NY 10036-8002 *Tel:* 212-431-4370 *Toll Free Tel:* 877-687-7476 *E-mail:* marketing@springerpub.com; cs@springerpub.com (orders); textbook@springerpub.com; specialsales@springerpub.com *Web Site:* www.springerpub.com, pg 206

Morley, Jane, Quirk Books, 215 Church St, Philadelphia, PA 19106 *Tel:* 215-627-3581 *Fax:* 215-627-5220 *E-mail:* general@quirkbooks.com *Web Site:* www.quirkbooks.com, pg 179

Morneau, Claude, Ulysses Travel Guides, 4176, rue Saint-Denis, Montreal, QC H2W 2M5, Canada *Tel:* 514-843-9882 (ext 2232); 514-843-9447 (bookstore) *Toll Free Tel:* 800-748-9171 *Fax:* 514-843-9448 *E-mail:* info@ulysses.ca; st-denis@ulysses.ca *Web Site:* www.ulyssesguides.com, pg 442

Morris, Gary, David Black Agency, 335 Adams St, 27th fl, Suite 2707, Brooklyn, NY 11201 *Tel:* 718-852-5500 *Fax:* 718-852-5539 *Web Site:* www.davidblackagency.com, pg 476

Morris, Heather, Sourcebooks LLC, 1935 Brookdale Rd, Suite 139, Naperville, IL 60563 *Tel:* 630-961-3900 *Toll Free Tel:* 800-432-7444 *Fax:* 630-961-2168 *E-mail:* info@sourcebooks.com; customersupport@sourcebooks.com *Web Site:* www.sourcebooks.com, pg 204

Morris, Natascha, BookEnds Literary Agency, 136 Long Hill Rd, Gillette, NJ 07933 *Web Site:* www.bookendsliterary.com, pg 476

Morris, Paul, The PEN Award for Poetry in Translation, 588 Broadway, Suite 303, New York, NY 10012 *Tel:* 212-334-1660 *Fax:* 212-334-2181 *E-mail:* awards@pen.org *Web Site:* pen.org/pen-award-poetry-translation, pg 653

Morris, Paul, PEN/Bellwether Prize for Socially Engaged Fiction, 588 Broadway, Suite 303, New York, NY 10012 *Tel:* 212-334-1660 *E-mail:* awards@pen.org *Web Site:* pen.org/pen-bellwether-prize, pg 653

Morris, Paul, PEN/Diamonstein-Spielvogel Award for the Art of the Essay, 588 Broadway, Suite 303, New York, NY 10012 *Tel:* 212-334-1660 *E-mail:* awards@pen.org *Web Site:* pen.org/pen-diamonstein-spielvogel-award-for-the-art-of-the-essay, pg 653

Morris, Paul, PEN/E O Wilson Prize for Literary Science Writing, 588 Broadway, Suite 303, New York, NY 10012 *Tel:* 212-334-1660 *E-mail:* awards@pen.org *Web Site:* pen.org/pen-eo-wilson-prize-literary-science-writing, pg 653

Morris, Paul, PEN/ESPN Award for Literary Sports Writing, 588 Broadway, Suite 303, New York, NY 10012 *Tel:* 212-334-1660 *E-mail:* awards@pen.org *Web Site:* pen.org/pen-espn-award, pg 653

Morris, Paul, PEN/ESPN Lifetime Achievement Award for Literary Sports Writing, 588 Broadway, Suite 303, New York, NY 10012 *Tel:* 212-334-1660 *E-mail:* awards@pen.org *Web Site:* pen.org/pen-espn-lifetime-literary-sports-writing, pg 653

Morris, Paul, PEN/Fusion Emerging Writers Prize, 588 Broadway, Suite 303, New York, NY 10012 *Tel:* 212-334-1660 *E-mail:* awards@pen.org *Web Site:* pen.org/literary-awards, pg 654

Morris, Paul, PEN/Jacqueline Bograd Weld Award for Biography, 588 Broadway, Suite 303, New York, NY 10012 *Tel:* 212-334-1660 *E-mail:* awards@pen.org *Web Site:* pen.org/pen-bograd-weld-award-biography, pg 654

Morris, Paul, PEN/Jean Stein Book Award, 588 Broadway, Suite 303, New York, NY 10012 *Tel:* 212-334-1660 *E-mail:* info@pen.org; awards@pen.org *Web Site:* pen.org/pen-jean-stein-book-award, pg 654

Morris, Paul, PEN/Joyce Osterweil Award for Poetry, 588 Broadway, Suite 303, New York, NY 10012 *Tel:* 212-334-1660 *E-mail:* awards@pen.org *Web Site:* pen.org/pen-osterweil-award-for-poetry, pg 654

Morris, Paul, PEN/Nabokov Award for Achievement in International Literature, 588 Broadway, Suite 303, New York, NY 10012 *Tel:* 212-334-1660 *Fax:* 212-334-2181 *E-mail:* awards@pen.org *Web Site:* pen.org/pen-nabokov-award, pg 654

Morris, Paul, PEN Open Book Award, 588 Broadway, Suite 303, New York, NY 10012 *Tel:* 212-334-1660 *E-mail:* awards@pen.org *Web Site:* pen.org/pen-open-book-award, pg 654

Morris, Paul, PEN/Phyllis Naylor Working Writer Fellowship, 588 Broadway, Suite 303, New York, NY 10012 *Tel:* 212-334-1660 *Fax:* 212-334-2181 *E-mail:* awards@pen.org *Web Site:* pen.org/literary-awards/grants-fellowships, pg 654

Morris, Paul, PEN/Ralph Manheim Medal for Translation, 588 Broadway, Suite 303, New York, NY 10012 *Tel:* 212-334-1660 *Fax:* 212-334-2181 *E-mail:* awards@pen.org *Web Site:* pen.org/literary-award/penralph-manheim-medal-for-translation, pg 654

Morris, Paul, PEN/Robert Bingham Prize for Debut Fiction, 588 Broadway, Suite 303, New York, NY 10012 *Tel:* 212-334-1660 *Fax:* 212-334-2181 *E-mail:* awards@pen.org *Web Site:* pen.org/pen-bingham-prize, pg 655

Morris, Paul, PEN/Saul Bellow Award for Achievement in American Fiction, 588 Broadway, Suite 303, New York, NY 10012 *Tel:* 212-334-1660 *Fax:* 212-334-2181 *E-mail:* awards@pen.org *Web Site:* pen.org/pen-saul-bellow-award, pg 655

Morris, Paul, PEN Translation Prize, 588 Broadway, Suite 303, New York, NY 10012 *Tel:* 212-334-1660 *Fax:* 212-334-2181 *E-mail:* awards@pen.org *Web Site:* pen.org/pen-translation-prize, pg 655

Morris, Paul, PEN/Voelcker Award, 588 Broadway, Suite 303, New York, NY 10012 *Tel:* 212-334-1660 *E-mail:* awards@pen.org *Web Site:* pen.org/pen-voelcker-award-poetry, pg 655

Morris, Paul, PEN Writers' Emergency Fund, 588 Broadway, Suite 303, New York, NY 10012 *Tel:* 212-334-1660 *Fax:* 212-334-2181 *E-mail:* feprogram@pen.org *Web Site:* pen.org/writers-emergency-fund, pg 655

Morris, Richard, Janklow & Nesbit Associates, 285 Madison Ave, 21st fl, New York, NY 10017 *Tel:* 212-421-1700 *Fax:* 212-355-1403 *E-mail:* info@janklow.com *Web Site:* www.janklowandnesbit.com, pg 490

Morris, W Travis, William E Colby Award, 158 Harmon Dr, Box 60, Northfield, VT 05663 *Tel:* 802-485-2965 *Web Site:* colby.norwich.edu/award, pg 606

Morrison, Bill, National Cartoonists Society (NCS), PO Box 592927, Orlando, FL 32859-2927 *Tel:* 407-994-6703 *Fax:* 407-442-0786 *E-mail:* info@reuben.org *Web Site:* www.reuben.org, pg 539

Morrison, Charles, Prometheus Awards, 650 Castro St, Suite 120-433, Mountain View, CA 94041 *Tel:* 650-968-6319 *Web Site:* www.lfs.org, pg 659

Morrison, Heath, McGraw-Hill Education, 2 Penn Plaza, New York, NY 10121-2298 *Tel:* 212-904-2000 *E-mail:* international_cs@mheducation.com; seg_customerservice@mheducation.com (PreK-12); hep_customerservice@mheducation.com (higher education) *Web Site:* www.mheducation.com, pg 135

Morrison, Heath, McGraw-Hill School Education Group, 8787 Orion Place, Columbus, OH 43240 *Tel:* 614-430-4000 *Toll Free Tel:* 800-848-1567 *Web Site:* www.mheducation.com, pg 136

Morrison, Henry, Henry Morrison Inc, PO Box 235, Bedford Hills, NY 10507-0235 *Tel:* 914-666-3500 *E-mail:* hmorrison1@aol.com, pg 497

Morrison, Jeff, LexisNexis® Canada Inc, 111 Gordon Baker Rd, Suite 900, Toronto, ON M2H 3R1, Canada *Tel:* 905-479-2665 *Toll Free Tel:* 800-668-6481; 800-387-0899 (cust care); 800-255-5174 (sales) *E-mail:* service@lexisnexis.ca (cust serv); sales@lexisnexis.ca *Web Site:* www.lexisnexis.ca, pg 432

Morrison, Margaret, Harlequin Enterprises Ltd, Bay Adelaide Centre, East Tower, 22 Adelaide St W, 41st fl, Toronto, ON M5H 4E3, Canada *Tel:* 416-445-5860

Toll Free Tel: 888-432-4879; 800-370-5838 (ebook inquiries) *E-mail:* customerservice@harlequin.com *Web Site:* www.harlequin.com, pg 429

Morrison, Megan, American Society of News Editors (ASNE), 209 Reynolds Journalism Institute, Missouri School of Journalism, Columbia, MO 65211 *Tel:* 573-882-2430 *Fax:* 573-884-3824 *Web Site:* asne.org, pg 524

Morrison, Richard, Fordham University Press, Joseph A Martino Hall, 45 Columbus Ave, New York, NY 10023 *Fax:* 347-842-3083 *Web Site:* www.fordhampress.com, pg 79

Morrison, Rusty, Omnidawn Publishing, 2200 Adeline St, Suite 150, Oakland, CA 94607 *Tel:* 510-237-5472 *Toll Free Tel:* 800-792-4957 *Fax:* 510-232-8525 *E-mail:* manager@omnidawn.com *Web Site:* www.omnidawn.com, pg 155

Morrissey, Jake, Riverhead Books, 375 Hudson St, New York, NY 10014 *Tel:* 212-366-2000 *Web Site:* www.penguin.com/publishers/riverhead, pg 185

Morrissey, Robert, Resilient Publishing, 406 S Third St, Boise, ID 83702 *Tel:* 208-258-9544 *E-mail:* submissions@resilientpublishing.com *Web Site:* www.resilientpublishing.com; www.facebook.com/ResilientPub, pg 185

Morrow, Diane, The Barnabas Agency, PO Box 3113, Corsicana, TX 75151-3113 *Tel:* 903-654-1319 *E-mail:* info@barnabasagency.com *Web Site:* www.barnabasagency.com, pg 515

Morrow, Stephen, Dutton, 1745 Broadway, New York, NY 10019 *Tel:* 212-366-2000 *Fax:* 212-366-2262 *E-mail:* duttonpublicity@us.penguingroup.com *Web Site:* www.penguin.com, pg 68

Morse, Garry Thomas, Signature Editions, PO Box 206, RPO Corydon, Winnipeg, MB R3M 3S7, Canada *Tel:* 204-779-7803 *E-mail:* submissions@signature-editions.com; orders@signature-editions.com *Web Site:* www.signature-editions.com, pg 440

Mortensen, Dee, Indiana University Press, Herman B Wells Library 350, 1320 E Tenth St, Bloomington, IN 47405-3907 *Tel:* 812-855-8817 *Toll Free Tel:* 800-842-6796 (orders only) *Fax:* 812-855-7931; 812-855-8507 *E-mail:* iupress@indiana.edu; iuporder@indiana.edu (orders) *Web Site:* www.iupress.indiana.edu, pg 108

Mortimer, Bryce, Cedar Fort Inc, 2373 W 700 S, Springville, UT 84663 *Tel:* 801-489-4084 *Toll Free Tel:* 800-SKY-BOOK (759-2665) *Web Site:* cedarfort.com, pg 47

Mortimer, Michele, Darhansoff & Verrill, 133 W 72 St, Rm 304, New York, NY 10023 *Tel:* 917-305-1300 *E-mail:* permissions@dvagency.com *Web Site:* www.dvagency.com, pg 480

Mortis, Steffanie, Trinity University Press, One Trinity Place, San Antonio, TX 78212-7200 *Tel:* 210-999-8884 *Fax:* 210-999-8838 *E-mail:* books@trinity.edu *Web Site:* www.tupress.org, pg 220

Morton, David, Rizzoli International Publications Inc, 300 Park Ave S, 4th fl, New York, NY 10010-5399 *Tel:* 212-387-3400 *Toll Free Tel:* 800-522-6657 (orders only) *Fax:* 212-387-3535 *E-mail:* publicity@rizzoliusa.com *Web Site:* www.rizzoliusa.com, pg 185

Morton, Larry, Hal Leonard Corp, 7777 W Bluemound Rd, Milwaukee, WI 53213 *Tel:* 414-774-3630 *Fax:* 414-774-3259 *E-mail:* halinfo@halleonard.com *Web Site:* www.halleonard.com, pg 91

Morton, Lisa, Horror Writers Association (HWA), PO Box 56687, Sherman Oaks, CA 91413 *Tel:* 818-220-3965 *E-mail:* admin@horror.org *Web Site:* horror.org, pg 534

Mosberg, Stephen R, College Publishing, 12309 Lynwood Dr, Glen Allen, VA 23059 *Tel:* 804-364-8410 *Fax:* 804-364-8408 *E-mail:* collegepub@mindspring.com *Web Site:* www.collegepublishing.us, pg 55

Mosbrook, Bill, Pathfinder Publishing Inc, 120 S Houghton Rd, Suite 138, Tucson, AZ 85748 *Tel:* 520-647-0158 *Web Site:* www.pathfinderpublishing.com, pg 161

Moschovakis, Anna, Ugly Duckling Presse, The Old American Can Factory, 232 Third St, Suite E303, Brooklyn, NY 11215 *Tel:* 347-948-5170 *E-mail:* office@uglyducklingpresse.org; orders@uglyducklingpresse.org; publicity@uglyducklingpresse.org; rights@uglyducklingpresse.org *Web Site:* uglyducklingpresse.org, pg 223

Moscovich, Rotem, Penguin Random House LLC, 1745 Broadway, New York, NY 10019 *Tel:* 212-782-9000 *Toll Free Tel:* 800-726-0600 *Web Site:* www.penguinrandomhouse.com, pg 164

Moseley, Lauren, Algonquin Books, 400 Silver Cedar Ct, Suite 300, Chapel Hill, NC 27514-1585 *Tel:* 919-967-0108 *Fax:* 919-933-0272 *E-mail:* inquiry@algonquin.com *Web Site:* www.workman.com/algonquin, pg 7

Moselle, Ben, Craftsman Book Co, 6058 Corte Del Cedro, Carlsbad, CA 92011 *Tel:* 760-438-7828 *Toll Free Tel:* 800-829-8123 *Fax:* 760-438-0398 *Web Site:* www.craftsman-book.com, pg 59

Moselle, Gary, Craftsman Book Co, 6058 Corte Del Cedro, Carlsbad, CA 92011 *Tel:* 760-438-7828 *Toll Free Tel:* 800-829-8123 *Fax:* 760-438-0398 *Web Site:* www.craftsman-book.com, pg 59

Moses, Casey, Random House Children's Books, 1745 Broadway, 10th fl, New York, NY 10019 *Tel:* 212-782-9000 *Web Site:* www.randomhousekids.com, pg 181

Moses, James, Primary Research Group Inc, 2585 Broadway, Suite 156, New York, NY 10025 *Tel:* 212-736-2316 *Fax:* 212-412-9097 *E-mail:* primaryresearchgroup@gmail.com *Web Site:* www.primaryresearch.com, pg 174

Moses-Schmitt, Lena, Counterpoint Press LLC, 2560 Ninth St, Suite 318, Berkeley, CA 94710 *Tel:* 510-704-0230 *Fax:* 510-704-0268 *E-mail:* info@counterpointpress.com *Web Site:* counterpointpress.com; softskull.com, pg 58

Mosher, Jessica, Nelson Education Ltd, 1120 Birchmount Rd, Scarborough, ON M1K 5G4, Canada *Tel:* 416-752-9100 *Toll Free Tel:* 800-268-2222 (cust serv) *Fax:* 416-752-8101 *Toll Free Tel:* 800-430-4445 *E-mail:* peopleandengagement@nelson.com *Web Site:* www.nelson.com, pg 434

Moskow, Shirley, Boston Authors Club Inc, 2400 Beacon St, No 208, Chestnut, MA 02467 *Tel:* 617-552-4031 *E-mail:* bostonauthorsclub@gmail.com *Web Site:* bostonauthorsclub.org, pg 529

Moskow, Shirley, Julia Ward Howe Book Awards, c/o Professor Mary Cronin, 2400 Beacon St, Unit 208, Beacon Hill, MA 02467 *Tel:* 617-552-4031 *E-mail:* bostonauthorsclub@gmail.com *Web Site:* bostonauthorsclub.org, pg 624

Mosley, Jody, Harry N Abrams Inc, 195 Broadway, 9th fl, New York, NY 10007 *Tel:* 212-206-7715 *Toll Free Tel:* 800-345-1359 *Fax:* 212-519-1210 *E-mail:* abrams@abramsbooks.com *Web Site:* www.abramsbooks.com, pg 3

Moss, Princess R, National Education Association (NEA), 1201 16 St NW, Washington, DC 20036-3290 *Tel:* 202-833-4000 *Fax:* 202-822-7974 *Web Site:* www.nea.org, pg 146

Moss, Princess R, National Education Association (NEA), 1201 16 St NW, Washington, DC 20036-3290 *Tel:* 202-833-4000 *Fax:* 202-822-7974 *E-mail:* media-relations-team@nea.org *Web Site:* www.nea.org, pg 540

Moss, Stephanie, Random House Children's Books, 1745 Broadway, 10th fl, New York, NY 10019 *Tel:* 212-782-9000 *Web Site:* www.randomhousekids.com, pg 180

Moss, Veronica, Goodreads Choice Awards, 188 Spear St, 3rd fl, San Francisco, CA 94105 *E-mail:* press@goodreads.com *Web Site:* www.goodreads.com/award, pg 620

Mosser, Gianna, Vanderbilt University Press, 2301 Vanderbilt Place, PMB 401813, Nashville, TN 37240-1813 *Tel:* 615-322-3585 *Toll Free Tel:* 800-

E-mail: aabb@aabb.org; sales@aabb.org (ordering); publications1@aabb.org (catalog) *Web Site:* www.aabb. org, pg 9

Munn, Duncan, C D Howe Institute, 67 Yonge St, Suite 300, Toronto, ON M5E 1J8, Canada *Tel:* 416-865-1904 *Fax:* 416-865-1866 *E-mail:* cdhowe@cdhowe.org *Web Site:* www.cdhowe.org, pg 430

Munnelly, Patrick, Bond Literary Agency, 201 Milwaukee St, Suite 200, Denver, CO 80206 *Tel:* 303-781-9305 *E-mail:* queries@bondliteraryagency.com *Web Site:* bondliteraryagency.com, pg 476

Munoz, Gabriela, Artist Research & Development Grants, 417 W Roosevelt St, Phoenix, AZ 85003-1326 *Tel:* 602-771-6501 *Fax:* 602-256-0282 *E-mail:* info@ azarts.gov *Web Site:* www.azarts.gov, pg 593

Munro, Bob, Cengage Learning, 20 Channel Center St, Boston, MA 02210 *Tel:* 617-289-7700 *Toll Free Tel:* 800-354-9706 *Fax:* 617-289-7844 *E-mail:* esales@cengage.com *Web Site:* www.cengage. com, pg 47

Munro, Susan, The Continuing Legal Education Society of British Columbia (CLEBC), 500-1155 W Pender St, Vancouver, BC V6E 2P4, Canada *Tel:* 604-669-3544; 604-893-2121 (cust serv) *Toll Free Tel:* 800-663-0437 (CN) *Fax:* 604-669-9260 *E-mail:* custserv@cle.bc.ca *Web Site:* www.cle.bc.ca, pg 420

Munroe, Sarah, West Virginia University Press, West Virginia University, PO Box 6295, Morgantown, WV 26506-6295 *Tel:* 304-293-8400 *Web Site:* www. wvupress.com, pg 239

Murach, Ben, Mike Murach & Associates Inc, 4340 N Knoll Ave, Fresno, CA 93722 *Tel:* 559-440-9071 *Toll Free Tel:* 800-221-5528 *Fax:* 559-440-0963 *E-mail:* murachbooks@murach.com *Web Site:* www. murach.com, pg 139

Muranaka, Royden, University of Hawaii Press, 2840 Kolowalu St, Honolulu, HI 96822-1888 *Tel:* 808-956-8255 *Toll Free Tel:* 888-UHPRESS (847-7377) *Fax:* 808-988-6052 *Toll Free Fax:* 800-650-7811 *E-mail:* uhpbooks@hawaii.edu *Web Site:* www. uhpress.hawaii.edu, pg 227

Murari, Raj, Disney Publishing Worldwide, 1101 Flower St, Glendale, CA 91201 *Web Site:* books.disney.com, pg 65

Murgolo, Karen, Houghton Mifflin Harcourt Trade & Reference Division, 125 High St, Boston, MA 02110 *Tel:* 617-351-5000 *Web Site:* www.hmhco.com, pg 104

Murkette, Julie, Satya House Publications, 22 Turkey St, Hardwick, MA 01037 *Tel:* 413-477-8743 *E-mail:* info@satyahouse.com; orders@satyahouse. com *Web Site:* www.satyahouse.com, pg 192

Murphy, Bekky, William Holmes McGuffey Longevity Award, PO Box 367, Fountain City, WI 54629 *E-mail:* info@taaonline.net *Web Site:* www.taaonline. net/mcguffey-longevity-award, pg 639

Murphy, Bekky, Most Promising New Textbook Award, PO Box 367, Fountain City, WI 54629 *E-mail:* info@ taaonline.net *Web Site:* www.taaonline.net/promising-new-textbook-award, pg 644

Murphy, Bekky, Ron Pynn Award, PO Box 367, Fountain City, WI 54629 *E-mail:* info@taaonline.net *Web Site:* www.taaonline.net/ron-pynn-award, pg 660

Murphy, Bekky, TAA Council of Fellows, PO Box 367, Fountain City, WI 54629 *E-mail:* info@taaonline. net *Web Site:* www.taaonline.net/council-of-fellows, pg 672

Murphy, Bekky, Textbook Excellence Award, PO Box 367, Fountain City, WI 54629 *E-mail:* info@taaonline. net *Web Site:* www.taaonline.net/textbook-excellence-award, pg 672

Murphy, Christopher, Hachette Book Group, 1290 Avenue of the Americas, New York, NY 10104 *Tel:* 212-364-1100 *Toll Free Tel:* 800-759-0190 (cust serv) *Fax:* 212-364-0933 (intl orders) *Toll Free Fax:* 800-286-9471 (cust serv) *Web Site:* www. hachettebookgroup.com, pg 91

Murphy, Colleen, Houghton Mifflin Harcourt, 125 High St, Boston, MA 02110 *Tel:* 617-351-5000 *Toll Free Tel:* 855-969-4642; 800-225-5425 (K-12 educ materials); 800-323-9540 (assessment materials); 877-219-1537 (SkillsTutor); 888-242-6747 (Innovation in Educ Group); 800-225-3362 (Trade & Ref Div) *Toll Free Fax:* 800-269-5232 *E-mail:* myhmhco@hmhco. com *Web Site:* www.hmhco.com, pg 103

Murphy, Emily, Alfred A Knopf, c/o Penguin Random House Inc, 1745 Broadway, New York, NY 10019 *Tel:* 212-751-2600 *Fax:* 212-572-2662 (foreign rts) *Web Site:* knopfdoubleday.com, pg 118

Murphy, Hugh, Leadership Connect, 1407 Broadway, Suite 318, New York, NY 10018 *Tel:* 212-627-4140 *Toll Free Tel:* 800-627-0311 *Fax:* 212-645-0931 *E-mail:* info@leadershipconnect.io *Web Site:* www. leadershipconnect.io, pg 121

Murphy, Jacqueline, FinePrint Literary Management, 207 W 106 St, Suite 1D, New York, NY 10025 *Tel:* 212-279-6214 *E-mail:* assist@fineprint.com *Web Site:* www.fineprintlit.com, pg 484

Murphy, Jane, BLR®—Business & Legal Resources, 100 Winners Circle, Suite 300, Brentwood, TN 37027 *Tel:* 860-510-0100 *Toll Free Tel:* 800-727-5257 *E-mail:* service@blr.com *Web Site:* www.blr.com, pg 36

Murphy, Jennifer, Quirk Books, 215 Church St, Philadelphia, PA 19106 *Tel:* 215-627-3581 *Fax:* 215-627-5220 *E-mail:* general@quirkbooks.com *Web Site:* www.quirkbooks.com, pg 179

Murphy, John, St Martin's Press, LLC, 120 Broadway, New York, NY 10271 *Tel:* 646-307-5151 *Web Site:* us. macmillan.com/smp, pg 190

Murphy, Kelsey, Philomel, 345 Hudson St, New York, NY 10014 *Tel:* 212-366-2000 *Web Site:* www.penguin. com/publishers/philomel, pg 169

Murphy, Kevin, Soho Press Inc, 853 Broadway, New York, NY 10003 *Tel:* 212-260-1900 *E-mail:* soho@ sohopress.com; publicity@sohopress.com *Web Site:* sohopress.com, pg 203

Murphy, Kim, Coachlight Press LLC, 1704 Craig's Store Rd, Afton, VA 22920-2017 *Tel:* 434-823-1692 *E-mail:* sales@coachlightpress.com *Web Site:* www. coachlightpress.com, pg 54

Murphy, Laurie, Theatre Library Association (TLA), c/o The New York Public Library for the Performing Arts, 40 Lincoln Center Plaza, New York, NY 10023 *E-mail:* TheatreLibraryAssociation@gmail.com *Web Site:* www.tla-online.org/awards/bookawards, pg 548

Murphy, Liza, Bloomsbury Publishing Inc, 1385 Broadway, 5th fl, New York, NY 10018 *Tel:* 212-419-5300 *E-mail:* marketingusa@bloomsbury.com; adultpublicityusa@bloomsbury.com; askacademic@ bloomsbury.com *Web Site:* www.bloomsbury.com, pg 36

Murphy, Michael, Jessie Bernard Award, c/o Governance Off, 1430 "K" St NW, Suite 600, Washington, DC 20005 *Tel:* 202-383-9005 *Fax:* 202-638-0882 *E-mail:* governance@asanet.org *Web Site:* www.asanet. org, pg 597

Murphy, Michael, Distinguished Scholarly Book Award, c/o Governance Off, 1430 "K" St NW, Suite 600, Washington, DC 20005 *Tel:* 202-383-9005 *Fax:* 202-638-0882 *E-mail:* governance@asanet.org *Web Site:* www.asanet.org, pg 610

Murphy, Pat, James Tiptree Jr Literary Award, 173 Anderson St, San Francisco, CA 94110 *Tel:* 415-641-4103 *E-mail:* info@tiptree.org *Web Site:* tiptree.org, pg 673

Murphy, Paul, RAND Corp, 1776 Main St, Santa Monica, CA 90407-2138 *Tel:* 310-393-0411 *Fax:* 310-393-4818 *Web Site:* www.rand.org, pg 180

Murphy, Richard J, BPA Worldwide, 100 Beard Sawmill Rd, 6th fl, Shelton, CT 06484 *Tel:* 203-447-2800 *Fax:* 203-447-2900 *E-mail:* info@bpaww.com *Web Site:* www.bpaww.com, pg 529

Murphy, Ryan, Penguin Books, 375 Hudson St, New York, NY 10014 *Tel:* 212-366-2000 *E-mail:* penguinpublicity@us.penguingroup.com *Web Site:* www.penguinclassics.com; www.penguin. com, pg 163

Murphy, Sean, Schaffner Press, PO Box 41567, Tucson, AZ 85717 *Web Site:* www.schaffnerpress.com, pg 193

Murphy, Suzanne, HarperCollins Children's Books, 195 Broadway, New York, NY 10007 *Tel:* 212-207-7000 *Web Site:* www.harpercollins.com/childrens, pg 93

Murphy, Tessa, Insight Editions, 800 "A" St, San Rafael, CA 94901 *Tel:* 415-526-1370 *Toll Free Tel:* 800-809-3792 *Toll Free Tel:* 866-509-0515 *E-mail:* info@ insighteditions.com; marketing@insighteditions.com *Web Site:* insighteditions.com, pg 109

Murphy, Trace, Paulist Press, 997 Macarthur Blvd, Mahwah, NJ 07430-9990 *Tel:* 201-825-7300 *Toll Free Tel:* 800-218-1903 *Fax:* 201-825-6921 *Toll Free Fax:* 800-836-3161 *E-mail:* info@paulistpress. com; publicity@paulistpress.com *Web Site:* www. paulistpress.com, pg 161

Murray, Brian, HarperCollins Publishers, 195 Broadway, New York, NY 10007 *Tel:* 212-207-7000 *Fax:* 212-207-7145 *Web Site:* www.harpercollins.com, pg 94

Murray, Cindy, Random House Publishing Group, 1745 Broadway, New York, NY 10019 *Toll Free Tel:* 800-200-3552 *Web Site:* www.randomhousebooks.com, pg 181

Murray, David, Piano Press, 1425 Ocean Ave, Suite 5, Del Mar, CA 92014 *Tel:* 619-884-1401 *Fax:* 858-755-1104 *E-mail:* pianopress@pianopress.com *Web Site:* www.pianopress.com, pg 169

Murray, Michael, Cricket Cottage Publishing LLC, 1500 Beville Rd, Suite 606-346, Daytona Beach, FL 32114 *Tel:* 323-207-6213 *E-mail:* thecricketpublishing@ gmail.com *Web Site:* thecricketpublishing.com; www. facebook.com/CricketCottagePublishing, pg 59

Murray, Nancy, Artisan, 225 Varick St, New York, NY 10014-4381 *Tel:* 212-254-5900 *Toll Free Tel:* 800-722-7202 *Fax:* 212-677-6692 *E-mail:* artisaninfo@ artisanbooks.com *Web Site:* www.artisanbooks.com; www.workman.com/artisanbooks, pg 21

Murray, Phyllis, Nimbus Publishing Ltd, 3731 Mackintosh St, Halifax, NS B3K 5A5, Canada *Tel:* 902-455-4286 *Toll Free Tel:* 800-NIMBUS9 (646-2879) *Fax:* 902-455-5440 *Toll Free Fax:* 888-253-3133 *E-mail:* customerservice@nimbus.ca *Web Site:* www. nimbus.ca, pg 434

Murray, Rachael, Sounds True Inc, 413 S Arthur Ave, Louisville, CO 80027 *Tel:* 303-665-3151 *Toll Free Tel:* 800-333-9185 (US); 888-303-9185 (US & CN) *E-mail:* customerservice@soundstrue. com; stpublicity@soundstrue.com *Web Site:* www. soundstrue.com, pg 204

Murray, Rachel, Henry Holt and Company, LLC, 120 Broadway, 23rd fl, New York, NY 10271 *Tel:* 646-307-5151 *Toll Free Tel:* 888-330-8477 (orders) *Fax:* 646-307-5285 *Web Site:* www.henryholt.com, pg 102

Murray, Sean, Sourcebooks LLC, 1935 Brookdale Rd, Suite 139, Naperville, IL 60563 *Tel:* 630-961-3900 *Toll Free Tel:* 800-432-7444 *Fax:* 630-961-2168 *E-mail:* info@sourcebooks.com; customersupport@ sourcebooks.com *Web Site:* www.sourcebooks.com, pg 204

Murray, Tim, little bee books, 251 Park Ave S, 12th fl, New York, NY 10010 *Toll Free Tel:* 844-321-0237 *E-mail:* info@littlebeebooks.com *Web Site:* littlebeebooks.com, pg 125

Musa, Sam, US Government Publishing Office (GPO), Superintendent of Documents, 732 N Capitol St NW, Washington, DC 20401 *Tel:* 202-512-1800 *Toll Free Tel:* 866-512-1800 (orders) *Fax:* 202-512-1998 *E-mail:* contactcenter@gpo.gov *Web Site:* www.gpo. gov; bookstore.gpo.gov (sales), pg 235

Muschett, Jim, Rizzoli International Publications Inc, 300 Park Ave S, 4th fl, New York, NY 10010-5399 *Tel:* 212-387-3400 *Toll Free Tel:* 800-522-6657 (orders only) *Fax:* 212-387-3535 *E-mail:* publicity@rizzoliusa. com *Web Site:* www.rizzoliusa.com, pg 185

Musser, Jacqueline, Adams Media, 57 Littlefield St, Avon, MA 02322 Tel: 508-427-7100 Web Site: www. simonandschuster.com, pg 4

Musser, Jane, Perseus Books, 1290 Avenue of the Americas, New York, NY 10104 Tel: 212-340-8100 Toll Free Tel: 800-343-4499 (cust serv) Fax: 212-340-8105 Web Site: www.perseusbooks.com, pg 167

Musslewhite, Robert, OptumInsight™, 11000 Optum Circle, Eden Prairie, MN 55344 Tel: 952-833-7100 Toll Free Tel: 888-445-8745 Web Site: www.optum. com, pg 156

Musto, Ronald G, Italica Press, 99 Wall St, Suite 650, New York, NY 10005 Tel: 917-371-0563 E-mail: inquiries@italicapress.com Web Site: www. italicapress.com, pg 113

Mutean, Eva, Ignatius Press, 1348 Tenth Ave, San Francisco, CA 94122-2304 Toll Free Tel: 800-651-1531 (orders); 888-615-3186 (cust serv) Fax: 415-387-0896 E-mail: info@ignatius.com Web Site: www. ignatius.com, pg 106

Mutrux, Sarah, Annual & Rolling Grants for Artists, 136 State St, Montpelier, VT 05602 Tel: 802-828-5425 Fax: 802-828-3363 E-mail: info@vermontartscouncil. org Web Site: www.vermontartscouncil.org, pg 592

Muzinic, Jason, Human Kinetics Inc, 1607 N Market St, Champaign, IL 61820 Tel: 217-351-5076 Toll Free Tel: 800-747-4457 Fax: 217-351-1549 (orders/cust serv) E-mail: info@hkusa.com Web Site: www. humankinetics.com, pg 105

Muzzarelli, Linda, Consumer Press, 13326 SW 28 St, Suite 102, Fort Lauderdale, FL 33330-1102 Tel: 954-370-9153 Fax: 954-472-1008 E-mail: info@ consumerpress.com Web Site: www.consumerpress. com, pg 56

Myatovich, Paul, CN Times Books, 100 Jericho Quadrangle, Suite 337, Jericho, NY 11791 Tel: 516-719-0886 E-mail: yanliu@cntimesbooks.com Web Site: www.cntimesbooks.com, pg 54

Myers, Charles, University of Chicago Press, 1427 E 60 St, Chicago, IL 60637-2954 Tel: 773-702-7700; 773-702-7600 Toll Free Tel: 800-621-2736 (orders) Fax: 773-702-9756; 773-660-2235 (orders); 773-702-2708 E-mail: custserv@press.uchicago.edu; marketing@press.uchicago.edu Web Site: www.press. uchicago.edu, pg 226

Myers, Edward, Montemayor Press, 663 Hyland Hill Rd, Washington, VT 05675 Tel: 802-552-0750 E-mail: mail@montemayorpress.com Web Site: www. montemayorpress.com, pg 142

Myers, Kelsey, Reading the West Book Awards, 208 E Lincoln Ave, Fort Collins, CO 80524 Tel: 970-484-3939 Toll Free Tel: 800-752-0249 Fax: 970-484-0037 E-mail: info@mountainsplains.org Web Site: www. mountainsplains.org/reading-the-west-book-awards, pg 661

Myers, Tona Pearce, Publishing Professionals Network, c/o Postal Annex, 274 Redwood Shores Pkwy, Redwood City, CA 94065-1173 E-mail: operations@ pubpronetwork.org Web Site: pubpronetwork.org, pg 545

Nachbaur, Fredric, Fordham University Press, Joseph A Martino Hall, 45 Columbus Ave, New York, NY 10023 Fax: 347-842-3083 Web Site: www. fordhampress.com, pg 79

Nadeau, Jay, Bitingduck Press LLC, 1262 Sunnyoaks Circle, Altadena, CA 91001 Tel: 626-507-8033 E-mail: notifications@bitingduckpress.com Web Site: bitingduckpress.com, pg 34

Nadeau, Jay, Boson Books™, 1262 Sunnyoaks Circle, Altadena, CA 91001 Tel: 626-507-8033 Fax: 626-818-1842 Web Site: bitingduckpress.com, pg 38

Nadeau, Marie, Bitingduck Press LLC, 1262 Sunnyoaks Circle, Altadena, CA 91001 Tel: 626-507-8033 E-mail: notifications@bitingduckpress.com Web Site: bitingduckpress.com, pg 34

Nadell, Bonnie, Hill Nadell Literary Agency, 6442 Santa Monica Blvd, Suite 201, Los Angeles, CA 90038 Tel: 310-860-9605 Fax: 323-380-5206 E-mail: queries@hillnadell.com; rights@hillnadell.com (rts & perms) Web Site: www.hillnadell.com, pg 488

Nagel, Karen, Simon & Schuster Children's Publishing, 1230 Avenue of the Americas, New York, NY 10020 Tel: 212-698-7000 Web Site: www.simonandschuster. com/kids; www.simonandschuster.com/teen; simonandschuster.net; simonandschuster.biz, pg 199

Nagler, Michelle, Random House Children's Books, 1745 Broadway, 10th fl, New York, NY 10019 Tel: 212-782-9000 Web Site: www.randomhousekids. com, pg 180

Naidl, Megan, North Star Editions Inc, 2297 Waters Dr, Mendota Heights, MN 55120 Tel: 651-204-3515 Toll Free Tel: 888-417-0195 Fax: 952-582-1000 E-mail: sales@northstareditions.com Web Site: www. northstareditions.com, pg 152

Nakis, Aleka, Fun in the Sun Writer's Cruise Conference, PO Box 823414, Pembroke Pines, FL 33082 E-mail: frwfuninthesun@yahoo.com Web Site: frwfuninthesunmain.blogspot.com/; www. frwriters.org, pg 574

Nangle, Leslie, Princeton University Press, 41 William St, Princeton, NJ 08540-5237 Tel: 609-258-4900 Fax: 609-258-6305 Web Site: press.princeton.edu, pg 174

Nantier, Terry, NBM Publishing Inc, 160 Broadway, E Wing, Suite 700, New York, NY 10038 Tel: 646-559-4681 Toll Free Tel: 800-886-1223 Fax: 212-643-1545 E-mail: admin@nbmpub.com Web Site: www.nbmpub. com, pg 148

Nantier, Terry, Papercutz, 160 Broadway, E Wing, Suite 700, New York, NY 10038 Tel: 646-559-4681 Toll Free Tel: 800-886-1223 Fax: 212-643-1545 E-mail: papercutz@papercutz.com Web Site: www. papercutz.com, pg 160

Napack, Brian, John Wiley & Sons Inc, 111 River St, Hoboken, NJ 07030-5774 Tel: 201-748-6000 Toll Free Tel: 800-225-5945 (cust serv) Fax: 201-748-6088 E-mail: info@wiley.com Web Site: www.wiley.com, pg 241

Naples, Mary Ann, Perseus Books, 1290 Avenue of the Americas, New York, NY 10104 Tel: 212-340-8100 Toll Free Tel: 800-343-4499 (cust serv) Fax: 212-340-8105 Web Site: www.perseusbooks.com, pg 167

Napolitano, Carrie, Perseus Books, 1290 Avenue of the Americas, New York, NY 10104 Tel: 212-340-8100 Toll Free Tel: 800-343-4499 (cust serv) Fax: 212-340-8105 Web Site: www.perseusbooks.com, pg 167

Napp, Jessica, Rizzoli International Publications Inc, 300 Park Ave S, 4th fl, New York, NY 10010-5399 Tel: 212-387-3400 Toll Free Tel: 800-522-6657 (orders only) Fax: 212-387-3535 E-mail: publicity@rizzoliusa. com Web Site: www.rizzoliusa.com, pg 185

Naqvi, Abigail, Bloomsbury Publishing Inc, 1385 Broadway, 5th fl, New York, NY 10018 Tel: 212-419-5300 E-mail: marketingusa@bloomsbury.com; adultpublicityusa@bloomsbury.com; askacademic@ bloomsbury.com Web Site: www.bloomsbury.com, pg 36

Nara, William, American Society of Civil Engineers (ASCE), 1801 Alexander Bell Dr, Reston, VA 20191-4400 Tel: 703-295-6300 Toll Free Tel: 800-548-ASCE (548-2723) Toll Free Fax: 866-913-6085 E-mail: ascelibrary@asce.org; pubsful@asce.org Web Site: www.asce.org, pg 14

Nardullo, Mike, Levine|Greenberg|Rostan Literary Agency, 307 Seventh Ave, Suite 2407, New York, NY 10001 Tel: 212-337-0934 Fax: 212-337-0948 Web Site: lgrliterary.com, pg 493

Nasrallah, Dimitri, Vehicule Press, PO Box 42094, CP Roy, Montreal, QC H2W-2T3, Canada Tel: 514-844-6073 E-mail: vp@vehiculepress.com; admin@ vehiculepress.com Web Site: www.vehiculepress, pg 445

Natarajan, Jyothi, Asian American Writers' Workshop, 112 W 27 St, Suite 600, New York, NY 10001 Tel: 212-494-0061 E-mail: desk@ aaww.org Web Site: aaww.org; facebook.com/ AsianAmericanWritersWorkshop, pg 525

Nathan, Geetha, American Booksellers Association, 333 Westchester Ave, Suite S202, White Plains, NY 10604 Tel: 914-406-7500 Toll Free Tel: 800-637-0037 Fax: 914-417-4013 E-mail: info@bookweb.org Web Site: www.bookweb.org, pg 522

Nathan, Terry, Benjamin Franklin Awards™, 1020 Manhattan Beach Blvd, Suite 204, Manhattan Beach, CA 90266 Tel: 310-546-1818 E-mail: info@ ibpa-online.org Web Site: www.ibpa-online.org; ibpabenjaminfranklinawards.com, pg 596

Nathan, Terry, The Independent Book Publishers Association (IBPA), 1020 Manhattan Beach Blvd, Suite 204, Manhattan Beach, CA 90266 Tel: 310-546-1818 E-mail: info@ibpa-online.org Web Site: www. ibpa-online.org, pg 535

Nation, Philip, Thomas Nelson, 501 Nelson Place, Nashville, TN 37214 Tel: 615-889-9000 Toll Free Tel: 800-251-4000 Fax: 615-902-1548 Web Site: www. thomasnelson.com, pg 217

Naud, Jocelyne, Les Presses de l'Universite Laval, 2180, Chemin Sainte-Foy, 1st fl, Quebec, QC G1V 0A6, Canada Tel: 418-656-2803 Fax: 418-656-3305 E-mail: presses@pul.ulaval.ca Web Site: www.pulaval. com, pg 437

Nauman-Montana, Beth, Salmon Bay Indexing, PO Box 2362, Vashon, WA 98070 Tel: 206-612-3993 Web Site: salmonbayindexing.com, pg 470

Nava, Michael, Bywater Books Inc, PO Box 3671, Ann Arbor, MI 48106-3671 Tel: 734-662-8815 Web Site: bywaterbooks.com, pg 43

Navarre, Randy, Roncorp Music, PO Box 1210, Coatesville, PA 19320 Tel: 610-679-5400 E-mail: info@nemusicpub.com Web Site: www. nemusicpub.com, pg 186

Navarrete, Vanessa, Chronicle Books, 680 Second St, San Francisco, CA 94107 Tel: 415-537-4200 Toll Free Tel: 800-759-0190 (cust serv) Fax: 415-537-4460 Toll Free Fax: 800-858-7787 (orders); 800-286-9471 (cust serv) E-mail: frontdesk@chroniclebooks.com Web Site: www.chroniclebooks.com, pg 52

Navarro, Cristi, Penguin Young Readers Group, 345 Hudson St, New York, NY 10014 Tel: 212-366-2000; 212-414-3553 Fax: 212-414-3340 Web Site: www. penguin.com/children, pg 165

Nawalinski, Beth, United for Libraries, 859 W Lancaster Ave, Unit 2-1, Bryn Mawr, PA 19010 Tel: 312-280-2161 Toll Free Tel: 800-545-2433 (ext 2161) Fax: 484-698-7868 E-mail: united@ala.org Web Site: www.ala.org/united, pg 548

Nawrocki, Sarah, Trinity University Press, One Trinity Place, San Antonio, TX 78212-7200 Tel: 210-999-8884 Fax: 210-999-8838 E-mail: books@trinity.edu Web Site: www.tupress.org, pg 220

Nayiga, Victoria, Carter G Woodson Book Awards, 8555 16 St, Suite 500, Silver Spring, MD 20910 Tel: 301-588-1800 Toll Free Tel: 800-296-7840 Fax: 301-588-2049 E-mail: excellence@ncss.org; publications@ncss. org Web Site: www.socialstudies.org, pg 679

Naylor, Sherry, Donner Prize, c/o Naylor and Associates, 23 Empire Ave, Toronto, ON M4M 2L3, Canada Tel: 416-368-8253 E-mail: donnerprize@ naylorandassociates.com Web Site: donnerbookprize. com, pg 610

Nazarian, Vera, Norilana Books, PO Box 209, Highgate Center, VT 05459-0209 E-mail: service@norilana.com Web Site: www.norilana.com, pg 151

Neal, Rae, Multicultural Publications Inc, 1939 Manchester Rd, Akron, OH 44314 Tel: 330-865-9578 Fax: 330-865-9578 E-mail: multiculturalpub@prodigy. net Web Site: www.multiculturalpub.net, pg 144

Necarsulmer, Edward IV, Dunow, Carlson & Lerner Literary Agency Inc, 27 W 20 St, Suite 1107, New York, NY 10011 Tel: 212-645-7606 E-mail: mail@ dclagency.com Web Site: www.dclagency.com, pg 482

Neel, Thomas Stephen, Ohio Genealogical Society, 611 State Rte 97 W, Bellville, OH 44813-8813 *Tel:* 419-886-1903 *Fax:* 419-886-0092 *E-mail:* ogs@ogs.org *Web Site:* www.ogs.org, pg 154

Neeley, Donna, Saint Louis Literary Award, Pius XII Memorial Library, 3650 Lindell Blvd, St Louis, MO 63108 *Tel:* 314-977-3100; 314-977-3087 *Fax:* 314-977-3108 *E-mail:* slula@slu.edu *Web Site:* lib.slu.edu/about/associates/literary-award, pg 664

Neesemann, Cynthia, CS International Literary Agency, 43 W 39 St, New York, NY 10018 *Tel:* 212-921-1610; 212-391-9208 *E-mail:* query@csliterary.com; csliterary08@gmail.com *Web Site:* www.csliterary.com, pg 461

Neibauer, Nathan, Neibauer Press, 20 Industrial Dr, Warminster, PA 18974 *Tel:* 215-322-6200 *Toll Free Tel:* 800-322-6203 (orders) *Fax:* 215-322-2495 *E-mail:* info@neibauer.com *Web Site:* www.neibauer.com; www.churchsupplier.com (orders), pg 148

Neimark, Nina, Nina Neimark Editorial Services, 543 Third St, Brooklyn, NY 11215 *Tel:* 718-499-6804 *E-mail:* pneimark@hotmail.com, pg 468

Nellis, Muriel G, Literary & Creative Artists Inc, 3543 Albemarle St NW, Washington, DC 20008-4213 *Tel:* 202-362-4688 *Fax:* 202-362-8875 *E-mail:* lcadc@earthlink.net (queries, no attachments) *Web Site:* www.lcadc.com, pg 493

Nelson, Brian, Nelson Literary Agency LLC, 1732 Wazee St, Suite 207, Denver, CO 80202-1284 *Tel:* 303-292-2805 *E-mail:* info@nelsonagency.com *Web Site:* www.nelsonagency.com, pg 497

Nelson, Dan, Visual Media Alliance (VMA), 665 Third St, Suite 500, San Francisco, CA 94107-1926 *Tel:* 415-495-8242 *Toll Free Tel:* 800-659-3363 *Toll Free Fax:* 800-824-1911 *E-mail:* info@vma.bz *Web Site:* main.vma.bz, pg 548

Nelson, David, Waterside Productions Inc, 2055 Oxford Ave, Cardiff, CA 92007 *Tel:* 760-632-9190 *Fax:* 760-632-9295 *E-mail:* admin@waterside.com *Web Site:* www.waterside.com, pg 508

Nelson, Eric, Penguin Group USA, A Penguin Random House Company, 375 Hudson St, New York, NY 10014 *Tel:* 212-366-2000 *Toll Free Tel:* 800-847-5515 (inside sales); 800-631-8571 (cust serv) *Fax:* 212-366-2666; 607-775-4829 (inside sales) *E-mail:* online@us.penguingroup.com *Web Site:* www.penguin.com, pg 163

Nelson, Erica, Hachette Book Group, 1290 Avenue of the Americas, New York, NY 10104 *Tel:* 212-364-1100 *Toll Free Tel:* 800-759-0190 (cust serv) *Fax:* 212-364-0933 (intl orders) *Toll Free Fax:* 800-286-9471 (cust serv) *Web Site:* www.hachettebookgroup.com, pg 91

Nelson, Kristin, Nelson Literary Agency LLC, 1732 Wazee St, Suite 207, Denver, CO 80202-1284 *Tel:* 303-292-2805 *E-mail:* info@nelsonagency.com *Web Site:* www.nelsonagency.com, pg 497

Nelson, Patricia, Marsal Lyon Literary Agency LLC, 665 San Rodolfo Dr, Suite 124, PMB 121, Solana Beach, CA 92075 *Tel:* 760-814-8507 *Web Site:* www.marsallyonliteraryagency.com, pg 494

Nelson, Priya, Princeton University Press, 41 William St, Princeton, NJ 08540-5237 *Tel:* 609-258-4900 *Fax:* 609-258-6305 *Web Site:* press.princeton.edu, pg 174

Nelson, Sara, HarperCollins General Books Group, 195 Broadway, New York, NY 10007 *Tel:* 212-207-7000 *Web Site:* www.harpercollins.com, pg 93

Nelson, Sarah, Paul Engle Prize, 123 S Linn St, Iowa City, IA 52240 *E-mail:* info@iowacityofliterature.org *Web Site:* www.iowacityofliterature.org/paul-engle-prize, pg 613

Nemeth, Terence, Theatre Communications Group, 520 Eighth Ave, 24th fl, New York, NY 10018-4156 *Tel:* 212-609-5900 *Fax:* 212-609-5901 *E-mail:* info@tcg.org *Web Site:* www.tcg.org, pg 216

Neptune, Alyssa, Alice James Books, 114 Prescott St, Farmington, ME 04938 *Tel:* 207-778-7071 *Fax:* 207-778-7766 *E-mail:* info@alicejamesbooks.org *Web Site:* alicejamesbooks.org, pg 7

Nericcio, Dr Bill, San Diego State University Press, Arts & Letters 283/MC 6020, 5500 Campanile Dr, San Diego, CA 92182-6020 *Tel:* 619-594-6220 (orders); 619-594-1524 (returns) *Fax:* 619-594-4998 (returns) *E-mail:* memo@sdsu.edu *Web Site:* sdsupress.sdsu.edu, pg 191

Nesbit, Lynn, Janklow & Nesbit Associates, 285 Madison Ave, 21st fl, New York, NY 10017 *Tel:* 212-421-1700 *Fax:* 212-355-1403 *E-mail:* info@janklow.com *Web Site:* www.janklowandnesbit.com, pg 490

Netschert, Linda, Farcountry Press, 2750 Broadwater Ave, Helena, MT 59602-9202 *Tel:* 406-422-1263 *Toll Free Tel:* 800-821-3874 (sales off) *Fax:* 406-443-5480 *E-mail:* books@farcountrypress.com; sales@farcountrypress.com *Web Site:* www.farcountrypress.com, pg 75

Nettles, Ms Jordan, University Press of Mississippi, 3825 Ridgewood Rd, Jackson, MS 39211-6492 *Tel:* 601-432-6205 *Toll Free Tel:* 800-737-7788 (orders & cust serv) *Fax:* 601-432-6217 *E-mail:* press@mississippi.edu *Web Site:* www.upress.state.ms.us, pg 233

Nettleton, Kathleen Calhoun, Pelican Publishing Co, 400 Poydras St, Suite 900, New Orleans, LA 70130 *Tel:* 504-368-1175 *Toll Free Tel:* 800-843-1724 *Fax:* 504-368-1195 *E-mail:* sales@pelicanpub.com (sales); office@pelicanpub.com (permission); promo@pelicanpub.com (publicity) *Web Site:* www.pelicanpub.com, pg 162

Neubauer, Erica, Letterbox/Papyrus of London Publishers USA, 10501 Broom Hill Dr, Suite 1-F, Las Vegas, NV 89134-7339 *Tel:* 702-256-3838 *E-mail:* lb27383@cox.net, pg 123

Neubauer, Mrs H, Letterbox/Papyrus of London Publishers USA, 10501 Broom Hill Dr, Suite 1-F, Las Vegas, NV 89134-7339 *Tel:* 702-256-3838 *E-mail:* lb27383@cox.net, pg 123

Neufeld, Jacque, Safari Press, 15621 Chemical Lane, Bldg B, Huntington Beach, CA 92649 *Tel:* 714-894-9080 *Toll Free Tel:* 800-451-4788 *Fax:* 714-894-4949 *E-mail:* info@safaripress.com *Web Site:* www.safaripress.com, pg 189

Neuhaus, Dana, Concordia Publishing House, 3558 S Jefferson Ave, St Louis, MO 63118-3968 *Tel:* 314-268-1000; 314-268-1268 (bookshop) *Toll Free Tel:* 800-325-3040 (cust serv) *Toll Free Fax:* 800-490-9889 (cust serv) *E-mail:* order@cph.org *Web Site:* www.cph.org, pg 56

Neumann, Aki, Chronicle Books, 680 Second St, San Francisco, CA 94107 *Tel:* 415-537-4200 *Toll Free Tel:* 800-759-0190 (cust serv) *Fax:* 415-537-4460 *Toll Free Fax:* 800-858-7787 (orders); 800-286-9471 (cust serv) *E-mail:* frontdesk@chroniclebooks.com *Web Site:* www.chroniclebooks.com, pg 52

Neumann, Grant, Random House Publishing Group, 1745 Broadway, New York, NY 10019 *Toll Free Tel:* 800-200-3552 *Web Site:* www.randomhousebooks.com, pg 181

Neusner, Dena, Behrman House Inc, 11 Edison Place, Springfield, NJ 07081 *Tel:* 973-379-7200 *Toll Free Tel:* 800-221-2755 *Fax:* 973-379-7280 *E-mail:* customersupport@behrmanhouse.com *Web Site:* store.behrmanhouse.com, pg 30

Nevarez, Cecilia, Casa Bautista de Publicaciones, 7000 Alabama St, El Paso, TX 79904 *Tel:* 915-566-9656 *Toll Free Tel:* 800-755-5958 (cust serv & orders) *Fax:* 915-565-9008 (orders) *E-mail:* orders@editorialmh.org *Web Site:* www.editorialmh.org, pg 46

Nevins, Alan, Renaissance Literary & Talent, PO Box 17379, Beverly Hills, CA 90209 *Tel:* 323-848-8305 *E-mail:* query@renaissancemgmt.net *Web Site:* renaissancemgmt.net, pg 499

Nevins, Larry, HarperCollins Publishers, 195 Broadway, New York, NY 10007 *Tel:* 212-207-7000 *Fax:* 212-207-7145 *Web Site:* www.harpercollins.com, pg 94

Nevins, Tyler, Disney-Hyperion Books, 1101 Flower St, Glendale, CA 91201 *Web Site:* books.disney.com, pg 65

New, Sarah, Alfred A Knopf, c/o Penguin Random House Inc, 1745 Broadway, New York, NY 10019 *Tel:* 212-751-2600 *Fax:* 212-572-2662 (foreign rts) *Web Site:* knopfdoubleday.com, pg 118

Newberg, Esther, ICM Partners, 65 E 55 St, New York, NY 10022 *Tel:* 212-556-5600 *Web Site:* www.icmtalent.com, pg 489

Newborn, Sasha "Birdie", Bandanna Books, 1212 Punta Gorda St, No 13, Santa Barbara, CA 93103 *E-mail:* bandanna@cox.net *Web Site:* www.bandannabooks.com; www.mudbornpress.us; www.betabooks.us; www.shakespeareplaybook.com; www.bookdoc.us; catandbirdiebooks.com, pg 27

Newcomb, Doug, Special Libraries Association (SLA), 7918 Jones Branch Dr, Suite 300, McLean, VA 22102 *Tel:* 703-647-4900 *Fax:* 703-506-3266 *Web Site:* www.sla.org, pg 547

Newcomb, Trish, The McDonald & Woodward Publishing Co, 695 Tall Oaks Dr, Newark, OH 43055 *Tel:* 740-641-2691 *Toll Free Tel:* 800-233-8787 *Fax:* 740-641-2692 *E-mail:* mwpubco@mwpubco.com *Web Site:* www.mwpubco.com, pg 135

Newell, Butch, Florida Outdoor Writers Association Inc, 235 Apollo Beach Blvd, Unit 271, Apollo Beach, FL 33572 *Tel:* 813-579-0990 *E-mail:* info@fowa.org *Web Site:* www.fowa.org, pg 533

Newell, Patricia, North Country Press, 126 Main St, Unity, ME 04988 *Tel:* 207-948-2208 *E-mail:* info@northcountrypress.com *Web Site:* www.northcountrypress.com, pg 151

Newell, Terry, Insight Editions, 800 "A" St, San Rafael, CA 94901 *Tel:* 415-526-1370 *Toll Free Tel:* 800-809-3792 *Toll Free Fax:* 866-509-0515 *E-mail:* info@insighteditions.com; marketing@insighteditions.com *Web Site:* insighteditions.com, pg 109

Newens, Jennifer, West Margin Press®, 1700 Fourth St, Berkeley, CA 94710 *Tel:* 510-809-3761 *E-mail:* info-ga@westmarginpress.com *Web Site:* westmarginpress.com, pg 239

Newlin, Bill, Perseus Books, 1290 Avenue of the Americas, New York, NY 10104 *Tel:* 212-340-8100 *Toll Free Tel:* 800-343-4499 (cust serv) *Fax:* 212-340-8105 *Web Site:* www.perseusbooks.com, pg 167

Newlin, Shanta, Penguin Young Readers Group, 345 Hudson St, New York, NY 10014 *Tel:* 212-366-2000; 212-414-3553 *Fax:* 212-414-3340 *Web Site:* www.penguin.com/children, pg 165

Newman, Barbara, Frederick Fell Publishers Inc, 7519 LaPaz Blvd, Suite C303, Boca Raton, FL 33433 *Tel:* 954-925-5242 *E-mail:* fellpub@aol.com (admin only) *Web Site:* www.fellpub.com, pg 81

Newman, Brent, Accuity, 1007 Church St, 6th fl, Evanston, IL 60201 *Tel:* 847-676-9600 *Toll Free Tel:* 800-321-3373 *Fax:* 847-933-8101 *E-mail:* customerservice@accuity.com *Web Site:* www.accuity.com, pg 4

Newman, Carolyn, River City Publishing LLC, 1719 Mulberry St, Montgomery, AL 36106 *Tel:* 334-265-6753, pg 185

Newman, Eric, Fordham University Press, Joseph A Martino Hall, 45 Columbus Ave, New York, NY 10023 *Fax:* 347-842-3083 *Web Site:* www.fordhampress.com, pg 79

Newman, Judy A, Scholastic Inc, 557 Broadway, New York, NY 10012 *Tel:* 212-343-6100 *Toll Free Tel:* 800-SCHOLASTIC (724-6527) *Web Site:* www.scholastic.com, pg 194

Newman, Leigh, Counterpoint Press LLC, 2560 Ninth St, Suite 318, Berkeley, CA 94710 *Tel:* 510-704-0230 *Fax:* 510-704-0268 *E-mail:* info@counterpointpress.com *Web Site:* counterpointpress.com; softskull.com, pg 58

Newman, Megan, Avery, 1745 Broadway, New York, NY 10019 *Tel:* 212-366-2000 *Fax:* 212-366-2636 *E-mail:* averypublicity@penguinrandomhouse.com *Web Site:* www.penguin.com/publishers/avery; www.penguinrandomhouse.com, pg 26

Nisbet, Lynette, Prometheus Books, 59 John Glenn Dr, Amherst, NY 14228-2119 *Tel:* 716-691-0133 *Fax:* 716-691-0137 *E-mail:* marketing@prometheusbooks.com; editorial@prometheusbooks.com; rights@prometheusbooks.com *Web Site:* www.prometheusbooks.com, pg 176

Nishan, Rachel, Twin Oaks Indexing, 138 Twin Oaks Rd, Suite W, Louisa, VA 23093 *Tel:* 540-894-5126 *Web Site:* www.twinoakscommunity.org, pg 471

Nishimoto, Katy, Random House Publishing Group, 1745 Broadway, New York, NY 10019 *Toll Free Tel:* 800-200-3552 *Web Site:* www.randomhousebooks.com, pg 181

Nitz, Caroline, Graywolf Press, 250 Third Ave N, Suite 600, Minneapolis, MN 55401 *Tel:* 651-641-0077 *Fax:* 651-641-0036 *E-mail:* wolves@graywolfpress.org (no ms queries, sample chapters or proposals) *Web Site:* www.graywolfpress.org, pg 88

Niumata, Erin, Folio Literary Management, The Film Center Bldg, 630 Ninth Ave, Suite 1101, New York, NY 10036 *Tel:* 212-400-1494 *Fax:* 212-967-0977 *Web Site:* www.foliolit.com, pg 484

Nivens, Michele R, Beyond the Book, 222 Rosewood Dr, Danvers, MA 01923 *Tel:* 978-750-8400 (sales) *E-mail:* beyondthebook@copyright.com *Web Site:* www.copyright.com; beyondthebookcast.com, pg 573

Noakes-Fry, Kristen, Rothstein Associates Inc, 4 Arapaho Rd, Brookfield, CT 06804-3104 *Tel:* 203-740-7400 *Toll Free Tel:* 888-768-4783 *Fax:* 203-740-7401 *E-mail:* info@rothstein.com *Web Site:* www.rothstein.com; www.rothsteinpublishing.com, pg 187

Noble, Claire, Naval Institute Press, 291 Wood Rd, Annapolis, MD 21402-5034 *Tel:* 410-268-6110 *Toll Free Tel:* 800-233-8764 *Fax:* 410-295-1084; 410-571-1703 (cust serv) *E-mail:* webmaster@navalinstitute.org; customer@navalinstitute.org (cust serv) *Web Site:* www.nip.org; www.usni.org, pg 147

Noble, Katrina, University of Washington Press, 4333 Brooklyn Ave NE, Seattle, WA 98105-9570 *Tel:* 206-543-4050 *Toll Free Tel:* 800-537-5487 (orders) *Fax:* 206-543-3932; 410-516-6998 (orders) *E-mail:* uwapress@uw.edu *Web Site:* uwapress.uw.edu, pg 232

Noble, Nicole, National Braille Press, 88 Saint Stephen St, Boston, MA 02115-4312 *Tel:* 617-266-6160 *Toll Free Tel:* 800-548-7323 (cust serv); 888-965-8965 *Fax:* 617-437-0456 *E-mail:* contact@nbp.org *Web Site:* www.nbp.org, pg 145

Nocera, Bridget, Houghton Mifflin Harcourt Trade & Reference Division, 125 High St, Boston, MA 02110 *Tel:* 617-351-5000 *Web Site:* www.hmhco.com, pg 104

Noh, Chrissy, Simon & Schuster Children's Publishing, 1230 Avenue of the Americas, New York, NY 10020 *Tel:* 212-698-7000 *Web Site:* www.simonandschuster.com/kids; www.simonandschuster.com/teen; simonandschuster.net; simonandschuster.biz, pg 199

Nolan, Betsy, The Betsy Nolan Literary Agency, 112 E 17 St, Suite 1W, New York, NY 10003 *Tel:* 212-967-8200 *Fax:* 212-967-7292 *E-mail:* dblehr@cs.com, pg 498

Nolan, Elizabeth, The Optical Society (OSA), 2010 Massachusetts Ave NW, Washington, DC 20036-1023 *Tel:* 202-223-8130 *Toll Free Tel:* 800-766-4672 *E-mail:* custserv@osa.org *Web Site:* www.osa.org, pg 156

Nolan, Laura, Aevitas Creative Management, 19 W 21 St, Suite 501, New York, NY 10010 *Tel:* 212-765-6900 *Web Site:* aevitascreative.com, pg 474

Nolan, Melanie, Penguin Random House LLC, 1745 Broadway, New York, NY 10019 *Tel:* 212-782-9000 *Toll Free Tel:* 800-726-0600 *Web Site:* www.penguinrandomhouse.com, pg 164

Nolan, Melanie, Random House Children's Books, 1745 Broadway, 10th fl, New York, NY 10019 *Tel:* 212-782-9000 *Web Site:* www.randomhousekids.com, pg 180

Nolan, Patrick, Penguin Books, 375 Hudson St, New York, NY 10014 *Tel:* 212-366-2000 *E-mail:* penguinpublicity@us.penguingroup.com *Web Site:* www.penguinclassics.com; www.penguin.com, pg 163

Nolin, Leslie, Fairwinds Press, PO Box 668, Lions Bay, BC V0N 2E0, Canada *Tel:* 604-913-0649 *E-mail:* orders@fairwinds-press.com *Web Site:* www.fairwinds-press.com, pg 425

Noll, Michael, Writers' League of Texas (WLT), 611 S Congress Ave, Suite 200 A-3, Austin, TX 78704 *Tel:* 512-499-8914 *E-mail:* wlt@writersleague.org *Web Site:* www.writersleague.org, pg 516, 549, 580

Noll, Michael, Writers' League of Texas Book Awards, 611 S Congress Ave, Suite 200 A-3, Austin, TX 78704 *Tel:* 512-499-8914 *E-mail:* wlt@writersleague.org *Web Site:* www.writersleague.org, pg 680

Noms, Kevin A, ProQuest LLC, 789 E Eisenhower Pkwy, Ann Arbor, MI 48108 *Tel:* 734-761-4700 *Toll Free Tel:* 800-521-0600; 877-779-6768 (sales) *E-mail:* sales@proquest.com *Web Site:* www.proquest.com, pg 176

Noonan, Jack, PRINTING United Alliance, 10015 Main St, Fairfax, VA 22031-3489 *Tel:* 703-385-1335 *Toll Free Tel:* 888-385-3588 *Fax:* 703-273-0456; 703-691-7492 (membership) *E-mail:* assist@printing.org; info@printing.org *Web Site:* www.printing.org; www.sgia.org, pg 544

Noonan, Margaret, Fordham University Press, Joseph A Martino Hall, 45 Columbus Ave, New York, NY 10023 *Fax:* 347-842-3083 *Web Site:* www.fordhampress.com, pg 79

Noonan, Robin, Naval Institute Press, 291 Wood Rd, Annapolis, MD 21402-5034 *Tel:* 410-268-6110 *Toll Free Tel:* 800-233-8764 *Fax:* 410-295-1084; 410-571-1703 (cust serv) *E-mail:* webmaster@navalinstitute.org; customer@navalinstitute.org (cust serv) *Web Site:* www.nip.org; www.usni.org, pg 147

Noorda, Rachel, ThunderStone Books, 6575 Horse Dr, Las Vegas, NV 89131 *E-mail:* info@thunderstonebooks.com *Web Site:* www.thunderstonebooks.com, pg 217

Noorda, Robert, ThunderStone Books, 6575 Horse Dr, Las Vegas, NV 89131 *E-mail:* info@thunderstonebooks.com *Web Site:* www.thunderstonebooks.com, pg 217

Nordhaus, Vincent, Rutgers University Press, 106 Somerset St, 3rd fl, New Brunswick, NJ 08901 *Tel:* 848-445-7762; 848-445-7761 (sales) *Fax:* 732-745-4935 *E-mail:* sales@rutgersuniversitypress.org *Web Site:* www.rutgersuniversitypress.org, pg 188

Nordling, Kerry, St Martin's Press, LLC, 120 Broadway, New York, NY 10271 *Tel:* 646-307-5151 *Web Site:* us.macmillan.com/smp, pg 190

Nori, Don, Destiny Image Inc, 167 Walnut Bottom Rd, Shippensburg, PA 17257-0310 *Tel:* 717-532-3040 *Toll Free Tel:* 800-722-6774 (orders only) *Fax:* 717-532-9291 *Web Site:* www.destinyimage.com, pg 64

Norin, Melinda Sue, Book Publicists of Southern California, 714 Crescent Dr, Beverly Hills, CA 90210 *Tel:* 323-461-3921 *Fax:* 323-461-0917 *Web Site:* www.bookpublicists.org, pg 529

Norman, Anne Cole, Words into Print, 208 Java St, 5th fl, Brooklyn, NY 11222 *E-mail:* query@wordsintoprint.org *Web Site:* wordsintoprint.org, pg 471

Norman, Nancy Lowden, Atlantic Center for the Arts Master Artist-in-Residence Program, 1414 Art Center Ave, New Smyrna Beach, FL 32168 *Tel:* 386-427-6975 *Toll Free Tel:* 800-393-6975 *Fax:* 386-427-5669 *E-mail:* program@atlanticcenterforthearts.org *Web Site:* atlanticcenterforthearts.org, pg 573

Norman, Taylor, Chronicle Books, 680 Second St, San Francisco, CA 94107 *Tel:* 415-537-4200 *Toll Free Tel:* 800-759-0190 (cust serv) *Fax:* 415-537-4460 *Toll Free Fax:* 800-858-7787 (orders); 800-286-9471 (cust serv) *E-mail:* frontdesk@chroniclebooks.com *Web Site:* www.chroniclebooks.com, pg 52

Norman, Troy, Pauline Books & Media, 50 Saint Paul's Ave, Boston, MA 02130 *Tel:* 617-522-8911 *Toll Free Tel:* 800-876-4463 (orders); 800-836-9723 (cust serv) *Fax:* 617-541-9805 *E-mail:* editorial@paulinemedia.com (ms submissions); orderentry@pauline.org (cust serv) *Web Site:* www.pauline.org/pbmpublishing, pg 161

Norris, Fran, River City Publishing LLC, 1719 Mulberry St, Montgomery, AL 36106 *Tel:* 334-265-6753, pg 185

Norris, Katie, Hachette Nashville, 6100 Tower Circle, Room 210, Franklin, TN 37067 *Tel:* 615-221-0996 *Fax:* 615-221-0962 *Web Site:* www.hachettebookgroup.com, pg 91

Norton, Debra, Alice James Books, 114 Prescott St, Farmington, ME 04938 *Tel:* 207-778-7071 *Fax:* 207-778-7766 *E-mail:* info@alicejamesbooks.org *Web Site:* alicejamesbooks.org, pg 7

Norton, Jennifer, Penn State University Press, University Support Bldg 1, Suite C, 820 N University Dr, University Park, PA 16802-1003 *Tel:* 814-865-1327 *Toll Free Tel:* 800-326-9180 *Fax:* 814-863-1408 *Toll Free Fax:* 877-778-2665 *E-mail:* orders@psupress.org; orders@eisenbrauns.org *Web Site:* www.psupress.org; www.eisenbrauns.org, pg 166

Norton, Kim, Well-Trained Mind Press, 18021 The Glebe Lane, Charles City, VA 23030 *Tel:* 804-829-5043 *Toll Free Tel:* 877-322-3445 (orders) *Fax:* 804-829-5704 *E-mail:* support@welltrainedmind.com *Web Site:* welltrainedmind.com, pg 238

Norton, Paul, AMMO Books LLC, 5022 N Eagle Rock Blvd, Los Angeles, CA 90041 *Tel:* 323-223-AMMO (223-2666) *Fax:* 323-978-4200 *E-mail:* weborders@ammobooks.com; orders@ammobooks.com *Web Site:* ammobooks.com, pg 15

Nosan, Gregory, The Art Institute of Chicago, 111 S Michigan Ave, Chicago, IL 60603-6404 *Tel:* 312-443-3600; 312-443-3540 (pubns) *Fax:* 312-443-1334 (pubns) *Web Site:* www.artic.edu; www.artinstituteshop.org, pg 20

Nossel, Suzanne, PEN America, 588 Broadway, Suite 303, New York, NY 10012 *Tel:* 212-334-1660 *Fax:* 212-334-2181 *E-mail:* info@pen.org *Web Site:* pen.org, pg 543

Nossel, Suzanne, The PEN Award for Poetry in Translation, 588 Broadway, Suite 303, New York, NY 10012 *Tel:* 212-334-1660 *Fax:* 212-334-2181 *E-mail:* awards@pen.org *Web Site:* pen.org/pen-award-poetry-translation, pg 653

Nossel, Suzanne, PEN/Phyllis Naylor Working Writer Fellowship, 588 Broadway, Suite 303, New York, NY 10012 *Tel:* 212-334-1660 *Fax:* 212-334-2181 *E-mail:* awards@pen.org *Web Site:* pen.org/literary-awards/grants-fellowships, pg 654

Nossel, Suzanne, PEN/Ralph Manheim Medal for Translation, 588 Broadway, Suite 303, New York, NY 10012 *Tel:* 212-334-1660 *Fax:* 212-334-2181 *E-mail:* awards@pen.org *Web Site:* pen.org/literary-award/penralph-manheim-medal-for-translation, pg 654

Nossel, Suzanne, PEN/Robert Bingham Prize for Debut Fiction, 588 Broadway, Suite 303, New York, NY 10012 *Tel:* 212-334-1660 *Fax:* 212-334-2181 *E-mail:* awards@pen.org *Web Site:* pen.org/pen-bingham-prize, pg 655

Nossel, Suzanne, PEN Translation Prize, 588 Broadway, Suite 303, New York, NY 10012 *Tel:* 212-334-1660 *Fax:* 212-334-2181 *E-mail:* awards@pen.org *Web Site:* pen.org/pen-translation-prize, pg 655

Nossel, Suzanne, PEN Writers' Emergency Fund, 588 Broadway, Suite 303, New York, NY 10012 *Tel:* 212-334-1660 *Fax:* 212-334-2181 *E-mail:* feprogram@pen.org *Web Site:* pen.org/writers-emergency-fund, pg 655

Notarantonio, Pam, Harry N Abrams Inc, 195 Broadway, 9th fl, New York, NY 10007 *Tel:* 212-206-7715 *Toll Free Tel:* 800-345-1359 *Fax:* 212-519-1210 *E-mail:* abrams@abramsbooks.com *Web Site:* www.abramsbooks.com, pg 3

Noudehou, Lisa, Barranca Press, 17 Rockridge Rd, Mount Vernon, NY 10552 *Tel:* 347-820-2363 *E-mail:* editor@barrancapress.com *Web Site:* www.barrancapress.com, pg 28

Novack, Matt, Alan Wofsy Fine Arts, 1109 Geary Blvd, San Francisco, CA 94109 Tel: 415-292-6500 Toll Free Tel: 800-660-6403 Fax: 415-292-6594 (off & cust serv); 510-251-1840 (acctg) E-mail: order@art-books.com (orders); editeur@earthlink.net (edit); beauxarts@earthlink.net (cust serv) Web Site: www.art-books.com, pg 243

Novakshonoff, Vasili, Synaxis Press, 37323 Hawkins Rd, Dewdney, BC V0M 1H0, Canada Tel: 604-826-9336 E-mail: synaxis@new-ostrog.org Web Site: synaxispress.ca, pg 441

Novara, Stephanie, Cold Spring Harbor Laboratory Press, One Bungtown Rd, Cold Spring Harbor, NY 11724 Tel: 516-422-4100 Toll Free Tel: 800-843-4388 Fax: 516-422-4097; 516-422-4092 (submissions) E-mail: cshpress@cshl.edu Web Site: www.cshlpress.com, pg 54

Nowak, Emily, Wayne State University Press, Leonard N Simons Bldg, 4809 Woodward Ave, Detroit, MI 48201-1309 Tel: 313-577-6120 Toll Free Tel: 800-978-7323 Fax: 313-577-6131 E-mail: bookorders@wayne.edu Web Site: www.wsupress.wayne.edu, pg 238

Nowak, Wanda, Wanda Nowak Creative Illustrators Agency, 231 E 76 St, Suite 5-D, New York, NY 10021 Tel: 212-535-0438 E-mail: wanda@wandanow.com Web Site: www.wandanow.com, pg 512

Nowicki, Lori, Painted-Words Inc, 310 W 97 St, Suite 24, New York, NY 10025 Tel: 212-663-2311 Fax: 212-663-2891 E-mail: info@painted-words.com Web Site: painted-words.com, pg 512

Noyce, Penny, Tumblehome Learning Inc, 201 Newbury St, Suite 201, Boston, MA 02116 E-mail: info@tumblehomelearning.com Web Site: www.tumblehomelearning.com, pg 221

Noyes, Al, Walch Education, 40 Walch Dr, Portland, ME 04103-1286 Tel: 207-772-2846 Toll Free Tel: 800-558-2846 Fax: 207-772-3105 Toll Free Fax: 888-991-5755 E-mail: customerservice@walch.com Web Site: www.walch.com, pg 237

Nuccio, Colleen, Random House Publishing Group, 1745 Broadway, New York, NY 10019 Toll Free Tel: 800-200-3552 Web Site: www.randomhousebooks.com, pg 181

Nugent, Lynne, The Iowa Review Awards, 308 EPB, Iowa City, IA 52242-1408 E-mail: iowa-review@uiowa.edu Web Site: www.iowareview.org, pg 628

Nunez, Diego, Viking, 375 Hudson St, New York, NY 10014 Tel: 212-366-2000 Fax: 212-243-6002 Web Site: www.penguin.com/publishers/vikingbooks, pg 236

Nunez, Erica, Grove Atlantic Inc, 154 W 14 St, 12th fl, New York, NY 10011 Tel: 212-614-7850 Toll Free Tel: 800-521-0178 Fax: 212-614-7886 E-mail: info@groveatlantic.com; sales@groveatlantic.com; publicity@groveatlantic.com; rights@groveatlantic.com Web Site: www.groveatlantic.com, pg 89

Nurka, Marsida, Ordre des traducteurs, terminologues et interpretes agrees du quebec, 1108-2021 Ave Union, Montreal, QC H3A 2S9, Canada Tel: 514-845-4411 Toll Free Tel: 800-265-4815 Fax: 514-845-9903 E-mail: info@ottiaq.org; direction@ottiaq.org; reception@ottiaq.org Web Site: www.ottiaq.org, pg 542

Nuzman, Rachel, Chronicle Books, 680 Second St, San Francisco, CA 94107 Tel: 415-537-4200 Toll Free Tel: 800-759-0190 (cust serv) Fax: 415-537-4460 Toll Free Fax: 800-858-7787 (orders); 800-286-9471 (cust serv) E-mail: frontdesk@chroniclebooks.com Web Site: www.chroniclebooks.com, pg 52

Nyberg, Karl, Teachers College Press, 1234 Amsterdam Ave, New York, NY 10027 Tel: 212-678-3929 Fax: 212-678-4149 E-mail: tcpress@tc.edu Web Site: www.tcpress.com, pg 214

Nyborg, Randell, University Publishing House, PO Box 1664, Mannford, OK 74044 Tel: 918-865-4726 E-mail: upub5@outlook.com Web Site: www.universitypublishinghouse.net, pg 233

Nys, Claudia, Lynn C Franklin Associates Ltd, 1350 Broadway, Suite 2015, New York, NY 10018 Tel: 212-868-6311 Fax: 212-868-6312 E-mail: agency@franklinandsiegal.com, pg 485

O'Boyle, Jamie, Cultural Studies & Analysis, 1123 Montrose St, Philadelphia, PA 19147-3721 Tel: 215-592-8544 E-mail: info@culturalanalysis.com Web Site: www.culturalanalysis.com, pg 461

O'Brien, Colin D, T H Peek Publisher, PO Box 7406, Ann Arbor, MI 48107 Tel: 734-222-8205 Fax: 734-661-0136 E-mail: info@thpeekpublisher.com Web Site: www.thpeekpublisher.com, pg 162

O'Brien, Daniel, American Booksellers Association, 333 Westchester Ave, Suite S202, White Plains, NY 10604 Tel: 914-406-7500 Toll Free Tel: 800-637-0037 Fax: 914-417-4013 E-mail: info@bookweb.org Web Site: www.bookweb.org, pg 522

O'Brien, Jill, Orbis Books, PO Box 302, Maryknoll, NY 10545-0302 Tel: 914-941-7636 Toll Free Tel: 800-258-5838 (orders, Mon-Fri 8AM-4PM EST) Fax: 914-941-7005 E-mail: orbisbooks@maryknoll.org Web Site: orbisbooks.com, pg 156

O'Brien, John, Dalkey Archive Press, University of Houston-Victoria, 3402 N Ben Wilson, Victoria, TX 77901 E-mail: contact@dalkeyarchive.com Web Site: www.dalkeyarchive.com, pg 61

O'Brien, Julie, Hedgebrook Master Class Retreat Series, PO Box 1231, Freeland, WA 98249 Tel: 360-321-4786 Fax: 360-321-2171 E-mail: hedgebrook@hedgebrook.org Web Site: www.hedgebrook.org; www.facebook.com/hedgebrook, pg 575

O'Brien, Julie, Hedgebrook VORTEXT, PO Box 1231, Freeland, WA 98249 Tel: 360-321-4786 Fax: 360-321-2171 E-mail: hedgebrook@hedgebrook.org Web Site: www.hedgebrook.org; www.facebook.com/hedgebrook, pg 575

O'Brien, Julie, Hedgebrook Writers in Residence Program, PO Box 1231, Freeland, WA 98249 Tel: 360-321-4786 Fax: 360-321-2171 E-mail: hedgebrook@hedgebrook.org Web Site: www.hedgebrook.org; www.facebook.com/hedgebrook, pg 575

O'Brien, Kara L Esq, Practising Law Institute, 1177 Avenue of the Americas, New York, NY 10036 Tel: 212-824-5700 Toll Free Tel: 800-260-4PLI (260-4754, cust serv) Toll Free Fax: 800-321-0093 (local) E-mail: info@pli.edu (cust serv) Web Site: www.pli.edu, pg 173

O'Brien, Kelly, Writers Guild of America, East (WGAE), 250 Hudson St, Suite 700, New York, NY 10013 Tel: 212-767-7800 Fax: 212-582-1909 Web Site: www.wgaeast.org, pg 549

O'Brien, Laura, Gerald Lampert Memorial Award, 2 Carlton St, Suite 1519, Toronto, ON M5B 1J3, Canada Tel: 416-504-1657 E-mail: info@poets.ca Web Site: poets.ca, pg 631

O'Brien, Laura, The League of Canadian Poets, 2 Carlton St, Suite 1519, Toronto, ON M5B 1J3, Canada Tel: 416-504-1657 E-mail: info@poets.ca Web Site: poets.ca, pg 536

O'Brien, Laura, Pat Lowther Memorial Award, 2 Carlton St, Suite 1519, Toronto, ON M5B 1J3, Canada Tel: 416-504-1657 E-mail: info@poets.ca Web Site: poets.ca, pg 636

O'Brien, Laura, Jessamy Stursberg Poetry Contest for Youth, 2 Carlton St, Suite 1519, Toronto, ON M5B 1J3, Canada Tel: 416-504-1657 E-mail: info@poets.ca Web Site: poets.ca, pg 671

O'Brien-Nicholson, Kathleen, Fordham University Press, Joseph A Martino Hall, 45 Columbus Ave, New York, NY 10023 Fax: 347-842-3083 Web Site: www.fordhampress.com, pg 79

O'Cain, Stephanie, Random House Children's Books, 1745 Broadway, 10th fl, New York, NY 10019 Tel: 212-782-9000 Web Site: www.randomhousekids.com, pg 180

O'Callaghan, Katie, HarperCollins General Books Group, 195 Broadway, New York, NY 10007 Tel: 212-207-7000 Web Site: www.harpercollins.com, pg 93

O'Connell, Colleen, HarperCollins Children's Books, 195 Broadway, New York, NY 10007 Tel: 212-207-7000 Web Site: www.harpercollins.com/childrens, pg 93

O'Connell, Tim, Alfred A Knopf, c/o Penguin Random House Inc, 1745 Broadway, New York, NY 10019 Tel: 212-751-2600 Fax: 212-572-2662 (foreign rts) Web Site: knopfdoubleday.com, pg 118

O'Connor, Bland, Catholic Library Association, 8550 United Plaza Blvd, Suite 1001, Baton Rouge, LA 70809 Tel: 225-408-4417 Fax: 225-408-4422 E-mail: cla2@cathla.org Web Site: cathla.org, pg 530

O'Connor, Daniel, Bloomsbury Publishing Inc, 1385 Broadway, 5th fl, New York, NY 10018 Tel: 212-419-5300 E-mail: marketingusa@bloomsbury.com; adultpublicityusa@bloomsbury.com; askacademic@bloomsbury.com Web Site: www.bloomsbury.com, pg 36

O'Connor, Eleanor, Cato Institute, 1000 Massachusetts Ave NW, Washington, DC 20001-5403 Tel: 202-842-0200 Toll Free Tel: 800-767-1241 Fax: 202-842-3490 E-mail: catostore@cato.org Web Site: www.cato.org, pg 46

O'Connor, John, Eastland Press, 2421 29 Ave W, Seattle, WA 98199 Tel: 206-931-6957 (cust serv) Fax: 206-283-7084 (orders) E-mail: info@eastlandpress.com; orders@eastlandpress.com Web Site: www.eastlandpress.com, pg 69

O'Connor, Kevin, Charlotte Sheedy Literary Agency Inc, 928 Broadway, Suite 901, New York, NY 10010 Tel: 212-780-9800 Web Site: www.sheedylit.com, pg 502

O'Connor, Mike, Insomniac Press, 520 Princess Ave, London, ON N6B 2B8, Canada Tel: 519-266-3556 Web Site: www.insomniacpress.com, pg 430

O'Connor, Nichole, Baker & Taylor/YALSA Conference Grants, 50 E Huron St, Chicago, IL 60611 Tel: 312-280-4390 Toll Free Tel: 800-545-2433 Fax: 312-280-5276; 312-664-7459 E-mail: yalsa@ala.org Web Site: www.ala.org/yalsa, pg 595

O'Connor, Nichole, Margaret A Edwards Award, 50 E Huron St, Chicago, IL 60611 Tel: 312-280-4390 Toll Free Tel: 800-545-2433 Fax: 312-280-5276 E-mail: yalsa@ala.org Web Site: www.ala.org/yalsa/edwards, pg 612

O'Connor, Nichole, Frances Henne YALSA/VOYA Research Grant, 50 E Huron St, Chicago, IL 60611 Tel: 312-280-4390 Toll Free Tel: 800-545-2433 Fax: 312-280-5276 E-mail: yalsa@ala.org Web Site: www.ala.org/yalsa/awardsandgrants/franceshenne, pg 617

O'Connor, Nichole, Nonfiction Award, 50 E Huron St, Chicago, IL 60611 Toll Free Tel: 800-545-2433 (ext 4390) Fax: 312-280-5276 E-mail: yalsa@ala.org Web Site: www.ala.org/yalsa/nonfiction-award, pg 648

O'Connor, Nichole, Odyssey Award for Excellence in Audiobook Production, 50 E Huron St, Chicago, IL 60611 Toll Free Tel: 800-545-2433 (ext 4390) Fax: 312-280-5276 E-mail: yalsa@ala.org Web Site: www.ala.org/yalsa/odyssey, pg 650

O'Connor, Nichole, Michael L Printz Award, 50 E Huron St, Chicago, IL 60611 Tel: 312-280-4390 Toll Free Tel: 800-545-2433 Fax: 312-280-5276 E-mail: yalsa@ala.org Web Site: www.ala.org/yalsa/printz, pg 659

O'Connor, Patricia, Eastland Press, 2421 29 Ave W, Seattle, WA 98199 Tel: 206-931-6957 (cust serv) Fax: 206-283-7084 (orders) E-mail: info@eastlandpress.com; orders@eastlandpress.com Web Site: www.eastlandpress.com, pg 69

O'Connor, Siobhan, The Writers' Union of Canada (TWUC), 600-460 Richmond St W, Toronto, ON M5V 1Y1, Canada Tel: 416-703-8982 Fax: 416-504-9090 E-mail: info@writersunion.ca Web Site: www.writersunion.ca, pg 549

O'Donnell, James III, Evan-Moor Educational Publishers, 18 Lower Ragsdale Dr, Monterey, CA 93940-5746 Tel: 831-649-5901 Toll Free Tel: 800-777-4362 (orders) Fax: 831-649-6256 Toll Free Fax: 800-

Obry, Carrie, Midwest Bookseller of the Year Award, 1375 St Anthony Ave, Suite 202-3, St Paul, MN 55104 *Tel:* 612-208-6279 *Toll Free Fax:* 844-273-4119 *E-mail:* info@midwestbooksellers.org *Web Site:* www. midwestbooksellers.org/bookseller-of-the-year.html, pg 641

Obry, Carrie, Midwest Independent Booksellers Association (MIBA), 1375 St Anthony Ave, Suite 202-3, St Paul, MN 55104 *Tel:* 612-208-6279 *Toll Free Fax:* 844-273-4119 *E-mail:* info@midwestbooksellers. org *Web Site:* www.midwestbooksellers.org, pg 537

Ochoa, Gladys, Lectorum Publications Inc, 205 Chubb Ave, Lyndhurst, NJ 07071 *Toll Free Tel:* 800-345-5946 *Fax:* 201-559-2201 *Toll Free Fax:* 877-532-8676 *E-mail:* lectorum@lectorum.com *Web Site:* www. lectorum.com, pg 121

Ochsner, Daniel, University of Minnesota Press, 111 Third Ave S, Suite 290, Minneapolis, MN 55401-2520 *Tel:* 612-301-1990 *Fax:* 612-301-1980 *E-mail:* ump@ umn.edu *Web Site:* www.upress.umn.edu, pg 228

Ode, Jeanne, South Dakota Historical Society Press, 900 Governors Dr, Pierre, SD 57501 *Tel:* 605-773-6009 *Fax:* 605-773-6041 *E-mail:* info@sdshspress.com; orders@sdshspress.com *Web Site:* sdshspress.com, pg 205

Odell, Becky, Dutton, 1745 Broadway, New York, NY 10019 *Tel:* 212-366-2000 *Fax:* 212-366-2262 *E-mail:* duttonpublicity@us.penguingroup.com *Web Site:* www.penguin.com, pg 68

Oden, Kelly, Ballinger Publishing, 314 N Spring St, Suite A, Pensacola, FL 32501 *Tel:* 850-433-1166 *Fax:* 850-435-9174 *E-mail:* info@ballingerpublishing. com *Web Site:* www.ballingerpublishing.com, pg 27

Odiseos, Nikko, Shambhala Publications Inc, 4720 Walnut St, Boulder, CO 80301 *Tel:* 303-222-9598 *Toll Free Tel:* 866-424-0030 (off); 888-424-2329 (cust serv) *E-mail:* customercare@shambhala.com *Web Site:* www.shambhala.com, pg 197

Odiseos, Nikko, Snow Lion, 4720 Walnut St, Boulder, CO 80301 *E-mail:* customercare@shambhala.com *Web Site:* www.shambhala.com/snowlion, pg 202

Odorczyk, Kelsey, Perseus Books, 1290 Avenue of the Americas, New York, NY 10104 *Tel:* 212-340-8100 *Toll Free Tel:* 800-343-4499 (cust serv) *Fax:* 212-340-8105 *Web Site:* www.perseusbooks.com, pg 168

Oefelein, Colleen, The Jennifer DeChiara Literary Agency, 245 Park Ave, 39th fl, New York, NY 10167 *Tel:* 212-372-8989 *Web Site:* www.jdlit.com, pg 481

Oerlemans, Onno, Hamilton College, English/Creative Writing, English/Creative Writing Dept, 198 College Hill Rd, Clinton, NY 13323 *Tel:* 315-859-4370 *Fax:* 315-859-4390 *Web Site:* www.hamilton.edu, pg 583

Oestreich, Julia, University of Delaware Press, 200A Morris Library, 181 S College Ave, Newark, DE 19717-5267 *Tel:* 302-831-1149 *Fax:* 302-831-6549 *E-mail:* ud-press@udel.edu *Web Site:* library.udel. edu/udpress, pg 227

Oey, Eric, Tuttle Publishing, Airport Business Park, 364 Innovation Dr, North Clarendon, VT 05759-9436 *Tel:* 802-773-8930 *Toll Free Tel:* 800-526-2778 *Fax:* 802-773-6993 *Toll Free Fax:* 800-FAX-TUTL (329-8885) *E-mail:* info@tuttlepublishing. com; orders@tuttlepublishing.com *Web Site:* www. tuttlepublishing.com, pg 222

Offit, Sidney, The Authors League Fund, 31 E 32 St, 7th fl, New York, NY 10016 *Tel:* 212-268-1208 *Fax:* 212-564-5363 *E-mail:* staff@authorsleaguefund. org *Web Site:* www.authorsleaguefund.org, pg 527

Ogden, Abraham, American Diabetes Association, 2451 Crystal Dr, Suite 900, Arlington, VA 22202 *Toll Free Tel:* 800-342-2383 *E-mail:* booksinfo@diabetes.org *Web Site:* www.diabetes.org, pg 10

Ogden, Page, McLemore Prize, William F Winter Archives & History Bldg, 200 North St, Jackson, MS 39201 *Tel:* 601-576-6850 *Fax:* 601-576-6975 *E-mail:* mhs@mdah.ms.gov *Web Site:* www.mdah. ms.gov, pg 640

Ogle, Rex, Aevitas Creative Management, 19 W 21 St, Suite 501, New York, NY 10010 *Tel:* 212-765-6900 *Web Site:* aevitascreative.com, pg 474

Ognibene, Peter E, Breakthrough Publications Inc, 3 Iroquois St, Barn, Emmaus, PA 18049 *Toll Free Tel:* 800-824-5001 (ext 12) *Fax:* 610-928-4064 *E-mail:* dot@booksonhorses.com; ruth@ booksonhorses.com *Web Site:* www.booksonhorses. com, pg 40

Ogorek, Keith, AuthorHouse, 1663 Liberty Dr, Bloomington, IN 47403 *Tel:* 812-339-6000 (outside US) *Toll Free Tel:* 888-519-5121 *E-mail:* authorsupport@authorhouse.com *Web Site:* www.authorhouse.com, pg 25

Ohl, Helaine, Macmillan, 120 Broadway, 22nd fl, New York, NY 10271 *Tel:* 646-307-5151 *E-mail:* press. inquiries@macmillan.com *Web Site:* www.macmillan. com, pg 129

Ohlin, Alix, University of British Columbia Creative Writing Program, Buchanan Rm E-462, 1866 Main Mall, Vancouver, BC V6T 1Z1, Canada *Tel:* 604-822-0699 *Web Site:* creativewriting.ubc.ca, pg 585

Ohmart, Ben, BearManor Media, PO Box 71426, Albany, GA 31708 *Tel:* 580-252-3547 *E-mail:* orders@benohmart.com; books@benohmart. com *Web Site:* www.bearmanormedia.com, pg 30

Okun, William, McGraw-Hill Education, 2 Penn Plaza, New York, NY 10121-2298 *Tel:* 212-904-2000 *E-mail:* international_cs@mheducation.com; seg_customerservice@mheducation.com (PreK-12); hep_customerservice@mheducation.com (higher education) *Web Site:* www.mheducation.com, pg 135

Olah, Michael, Dreamscape Media LLC, 1417 Timberwolf Dr, Holland, OH 43528 *Tel:* 419-867-6965 *Toll Free Tel:* 877-983-7326 *E-mail:* info@dreamscapeab.com *Web Site:* www. dreamscapepublishing.com, pg 67

Olander, Rebecca, Perugia Press Prize for a First or Second Book by a Woman, PO Box 60364, Florence, MA 01062 *Web Site:* www.perugiapress. com; perugiapress.org, pg 655

Oldfield, Guy, Macmillan Audio, 120 Broadway, 22nd fl, New York, NY 10271 *Tel:* 646-307-5151 *Toll Free Tel:* 888-330-8477 (cust serv) *Web Site:* www. macmillanaudio.com, pg 130

Oldford, Ed, Flanker Press Ltd, 1243 Kenmount Rd, Unit 1, Paradise, NL A1L 0V8, Canada *Tel:* 709-739-4477 *Toll Free Tel:* 866-739-4420 *Fax:* 709-739-4420 *E-mail:* info@flankerpress.com; sales@flankerpress. com *Web Site:* www.flankerpress.com, pg 427

Olenick, Michelle, Emmaus Road Publishing Inc, 1468 Parkview Circle, Steubenville, OH 43952 *Tel:* 740-283-2880 (outside US) *Toll Free Tel:* 800-398-5470 (orders) *Fax:* 740-283-4011 (orders) *E-mail:* questions@emmausroad.org *Web Site:* www. emmausroad.org, pg 71

Oleniczak, Beth, Sourcebooks LLC, 1935 Brookdale Rd, Suite 139, Naperville, IL 60563 *Tel:* 630-961-3900 *Toll Free Tel:* 800-432-7444 *Fax:* 630-961-2168 *E-mail:* info@sourcebooks.com; customersupport@ sourcebooks.com *Web Site:* www.sourcebooks.com, pg 204

Olinger, Chauncey G Jr, Metropolitan Editorial & Writing Service, 4455 Douglas Ave, Riverdale, NY 10471 *Tel:* 718-549-5518, pg 468

Oliphant, Mike, Annie Dillard Award for Creative Nonfiction, Mail Stop 9053, Western Washington University, Bellingham, WA 98225 *Tel:* 360-650-4863 *E-mail:* bhreview@wwu.edu *Web Site:* www.bhreview. org, pg 610

Oliphant, Mike, 49th Parallel Poetry Award, Mail Stop 9053, Western Washington University, Bellingham, WA 98225 *Tel:* 360-650-4863 *E-mail:* bhreview@ wwu.edu *Web Site:* www.bhreview.org, pg 616

Oliphant, Mike, Tobias Wolff Award for Fiction, Mail Stop 9053, Western Washington University, Bellingham, WA 98225 *Tel:* 360-650-4863 *E-mail:* bhreview@wwu.edu *Web Site:* www.bhreview. org, pg 679

Olisko, Lexy, PRINTING United Alliance, 10015 Main St, Fairfax, VA 22031-3489 *Tel:* 703-385-1335 *Toll Free Tel:* 888-385-3588 *Fax:* 703-273-0456; 703-691-7492 (membership) *E-mail:* assist@printing.org; info@printing.org *Web Site:* www.printing.org; www. sgia.org, pg 544

Olivarez, Enrique, Coffee House Press, 79 13 Ave NE, Suite 110, Minneapolis, MN 55413 *Tel:* 612-338-0125 *Fax:* 612-338-4004 *E-mail:* info@coffeehousepress.org *Web Site:* coffeehousepress.org, pg 54

Oliveira, Josh, Greystone Books Ltd, 343 Railway St, Suite 201, Vancouver, BC V6A 1A4, Canada *Tel:* 604-875-1550 *Fax:* 604-875-1556 *E-mail:* info@ greystonebooks.com *Web Site:* www.greystonebooks. com, pg 427

Oliver, Amber, Dutton, 1745 Broadway, New York, NY 10019 *Tel:* 212-366-2000 *Fax:* 212-366-2262 *E-mail:* duttonpublicity@us.penguingroup.com *Web Site:* www.penguin.com, pg 68

Oliver, Amber, Plume, 375 Hudson St, New York, NY 10014 *Tel:* 212-366-2000 *Fax:* 212-243-6002 *Web Site:* www.penguin.com/publishers/plume, pg 171

Oliver, Becka, Writers' League of Texas (WLT), 611 S Congress Ave, Suite 200 A-3, Austin, TX 78704 *Tel:* 512-499-8914 *E-mail:* wlt@writersleague.org *Web Site:* www.writersleague.org, pg 549, 580

Oliver, Lin, The Don Freeman Memorial Grant-In-Aid, 6363 Wilshire Blvd, Suite 425, Los Angeles, CA 90048 *Tel:* 323-782-1010; 310-403-0675 (cell) *Fax:* 323-782-1892 *E-mail:* grants@scbwi.org; scbwi@scbwi.org *Web Site:* www.scbwi.org, pg 617

Oliver, Lin, Golden Kite Awards, 6363 Wilshire Blvd, Suite 425, Los Angeles, CA 90048 *Tel:* 323-782-1010; 310-403-0675 (cell) *Fax:* 323-782-1892 *E-mail:* grants@scbwi.org; scbwi@scbwi.org *Web Site:* www.scbwi.org, pg 620

Oliver, Lin, Magazine Merit Awards, 6363 Wilshire Blvd, Suite 425, Los Angeles, CA 90048 *Tel:* 323-782-1010; 310-403-0675 (cell) *Fax:* 323-782-1892 *E-mail:* grants@scbwi.org; scbwi@scbwi.org *Web Site:* www.scbwi.org, pg 637

Oliver, Lin, SCBWI Work-In-Progress Grants, 6363 Wilshire Blvd, Suite 425, Los Angeles, CA 90048 *Tel:* 323-782-1010; 310-403-0675 (cell) *Fax:* 323-782-1892 *E-mail:* grants@scbwi.org; scbwi@scbwi.org *Web Site:* www.scbwi.org, pg 666

Oliver, Lin, Society of Children's Book Writers & Illustrators (SCBWI), 6363 Wilshire Blvd, Suite 425, Los Angeles, CA 90048 *Tel:* 323-782-1010 *E-mail:* membership@scbwi.org *Web Site:* www.scbwi. org, pg 546

Oliver, Paul, Soho Press Inc, 853 Broadway, New York, NY 10003 *Tel:* 212-260-1900 *E-mail:* soho@ sohopress.com; publicity@sohopress.com *Web Site:* sohopress.com, pg 203

Oliver, Ramona, National Education Association (NEA), 1201 16 St NW, Washington, DC 20036-3290 *Tel:* 202-833-4000 *Fax:* 202-822-7974 *Web Site:* www. nea.org, pg 146

Olivieri, John, Abbeville Publishing Group, 655 Third Ave, New York, NY 10017 *Tel:* 646-375-2136 *Fax:* 646-375-2359 *E-mail:* abbeville@abbeville.com; marketing@abbeville.com; sales@abbeville.com; rights@abbeville.com *Web Site:* www.abbeville.com, pg 2

Olmanson, Shaina, Twenty-First Century Books, 241 First Ave N, Minneapolis, MN 55401 *Tel:* 612-332-3344 *Toll Free Tel:* 800-328-4929 *Fax:* 612-332-7615 *Toll Free Fax:* 800-332-1132 *E-mail:* info@ lernerbooks.com; custserve@lernerbooks.com *Web Site:* www.lernerbooks.com; www.facebook. com/lernerbooks, pg 222

Olmanson, Shaina, Zest Books, 241 First Ave N, Minneapolis, MN 55401 *Tel:* 612-332-3344 *Toll Free Tel:* 800-328-4929 *Toll Free Fax:* 800-332-1132 *E-mail:* info@lernerbooks.com; publicity@ lernerbooks.com; custserve@lernerbooks.com (orders) *Web Site:* lernerbooks.com, pg 248

Olmo, J Sammi, American Academy of Environmental Engineers & Scientists®, 147 Old Solomons Island Rd, Suite 303, Annapolis, MD 21401 *Tel:* 410-266-3311 *Fax:* 410-266-7653 *E-mail:* info@aaees.org *Web Site:* www.aaees.org, pg 9

Olsen, Eric, Twilight Times Books, PO Box 3340, Kingsport, TN 37664-0340 *Tel:* 423-323-0183 *Fax:* 423-323-0183 *E-mail:* publisher@twilighttimes. com *Web Site:* www.twilighttimesbooks.com, pg 223

Olsen, Kevin, W W Norton & Company Inc, 500 Fifth Ave, New York, NY 10110-0017 *Tel:* 212-354-5500 *Toll Free Tel:* 800-233-4830 (orders & cust serv) *Fax:* 212-869-0856 *Toll Free Fax:* 800-458-6515 *E-mail:* orders@wwnorton.com *Web Site:* wwnorton. com, pg 152

Olsen, William, The Green Rose Prize in Poetry, c/o Western Michigan University, 1903 W Michigan Ave, Kalamazoo, MI 49008-5463 *Tel:* 269-387-8185 *E-mail:* new-issues@wmich.edu *Web Site:* www. wmich.edu/newissues/sub-guide.html, pg 621

Olsen, William, New Issues Poetry & Prose, c/o Western Michigan University, 1903 W Michigan Ave, Kalamazoo, MI 49008-5463 *Tel:* 269-387-8185 *E-mail:* new-issues@wmich.edu *Web Site:* www. wmich.edu/newissues, pg 149

Olsen-Smith, Steven, The Melville Society, Johns Hopkins University Press, PO Box 19966, Baltimore, MD 21211-0966 *Web Site:* melvillesociety.org, pg 537

Olson, Amanda, Annick Press Ltd, 15 Patricia Ave, Toronto, ON M2M 1H9, Canada *Tel:* 416-221-4802 *Fax:* 416-221-8400 *E-mail:* annickpress@annickpress. com *Web Site:* www.annickpress.com, pg 415

Olson, Barbara, Alexander Street, a ProQuest Company, 99 Canal Center Plaza, Suite 200, Alexandria, VA 22314 *Tel:* 703-212-8520 *Toll Free Tel:* 800-889-5937 *Fax:* 703-212-8520 *E-mail:* sales@alexanderstreet.com; marketing@ alexanderstreet.com; info@alexanderstreet.com *Web Site:* alexanderstreet.com, pg 7

Olson, Bianca, Houghton Mifflin Harcourt, 125 High St, Boston, MA 02110 *Tel:* 617-351-5000 *Toll Free Tel:* 855-969-4642; 800-225-5425 (K-12 educ materials); 800-323-9540 (assessment materials); 877-219-1537 (SkillsTutor); 888-242-6747 (Innovation in Educ Group); 800-225-3362 (Trade & Ref Div) *Toll Free Fax:* 800-269-5232 *E-mail:* myhmhco@hmhco. com *Web Site:* www.hmhco.com, pg 103

Olson, Elke, Chronicle Books, 680 Second St, San Francisco, CA 94107 *Tel:* 415-537-4200 *Fax* 415-537-4460 *Toll Free Fax:* 800-858-7787 (orders); 800-286-9471 (cust serv) *E-mail:* frontdesk@chroniclebooks.com *Web Site:* www.chroniclebooks.com, pg 51

Olson, Georgine, Historical Novel Society North American Conference, 400 Dark Star Ct, Fairbanks, AK 99709 *Tel:* 217-581-7538 *Fax:* 217-581-7534 *Web Site:* www.historicalnovelsociety.org/event/hns-north-american-conference; historicalnovelsociety.org, pg 575

Olson, Kaitlin, Atria Books, 1230 Avenue of the Americas, New York, NY 10020 *Tel:* 212-698-7000 *Fax:* 212-698-7007 *Web Site:* www.simonandschuster. com, pg 24

Olson-Getty, Dayna, Herald Press, PO Box 866, Harrisonburg, VA 22803 *Toll Free Tel:* 800-245-7894 (orders) *Fax:* 540-242-4476 *Toll Free Fax:* 877-271-0760 *E-mail:* info@mennomedia.org; customerservice@mennomedia.org *Web Site:* www. heraldpress.com; store.mennomedia.org, pg 98

Olstein, Lisa, University of Texas at Austin, New Writers Project, Dept of English, Calhoun Hall, Rm 226, 204 W 21 St, B-5000, Austin, TX 78712 *Tel:* 512-471-5132; 512-471-4991 *Fax:* 512-471-4909 *Web Site:* newwritersproject.org, pg 586

Olund, Kyle, Thomas Nelson, 501 Nelson Place, Nashville, TN 37214 *Tel:* 615-889-9000 *Toll Free Tel:* 800-251-4000 *Fax:* 615-902-1548 *Web Site:* www. thomasnelson.com, pg 217

Oluwo, Titi, St Martin's Press, LLC, 120 Broadway, New York, NY 10271 *Tel:* 646-307-5151 *Web Site:* us. macmillan.com/smp, pg 191

Omana, Veronica, University of Ottawa Press (Presses de l'Université d'Ottawa), 542 King Edward Ave, Ottawa, ON K1N 6N5, Canada *Tel:* 613-562-5246 *Fax:* 613-562-5247 *E-mail:* puo-uop@uottawa.ca; acquisitions@ uottawa.ca *Web Site:* press.uottawa.ca, pg 444

Onder, Catherine, Houghton Mifflin Harcourt Trade & Reference Division, 125 High St, Boston, MA 02110 *Tel:* 617-351-5000 *Web Site:* www.hmhco.com, pg 104

Onken, Janice, WendyLynn & Co, 504 Wilson Rd, Annapolis, MD 21401 *Tel:* 410-224-2729; 410-507-1059 *Web Site:* wendylynn.com, pg 512

Opsomer, Liliane, AdventureKEEN, 2204 First Ave S, Suite 102, Birmingham, AL 35233 *Tel:* 763-689-9800 *Toll Free Tel:* 800-678-7006 *Fax:* 763-689-9039 *Toll Free Fax:* 877-374-9016 *E-mail:* info@ adventurewithkeen.com *Web Site:* adventurewithkeen. com, pg 5

Ordonez, Alex, Alfred Music, PO Box 10003, Van Nuys, CA 91410 *Tel:* 818-891-5999 (dealer sales, intl) *Toll Free Tel:* 800-292-6122 (dealer sales, US & CN); 800-628-1528 (cust serv) *Fax:* 818-893-5560 (dealer sales); 818-830-6252 (cust serv) *Toll Free Fax:* 800-632-1928 (dealer sales) *E-mail:* customerservice@alfred.com; sales@alfred.com *Web Site:* www.alfred.com, pg 7

Ordower, Patti, Liberty Fund Inc, 11301 N Meridian St, Carmel, IN 46032-4564 *Tel:* 317-842-0880 *Toll Free Tel:* 800-955-8335; 800-866-3520 *Fax:* 317-579-6060 (cust serv); 708-534-7803 *E-mail:* books@libertyfund. org; info@libertyfund.org *Web Site:* www.libertyfund. org, pg 123

Oren, Tiffany, Foster City International Writers Contest, 650 Shell Blvd, Foster City, CA 94404 *Tel:* 650-286-3380 *E-mail:* fostercity_writers@yahoo.com *Web Site:* www.fostercity.org, pg 616

Orlando, Kris, Hendrickson Publishers Inc, PO Box 3473, Peabody, MA 01961-3473 *Tel:* 978-532-6546 *Toll Free Tel:* 800-358-3111 *Fax:* 978-573-8111 *E-mail:* customerservice@hendricksonrose.com; info@ hendricksonrose.com *Web Site:* www.hendricksonrose. com, pg 98

Ornstein, Michael, IET USA Inc, 379 Thornall St, Edison, NJ 08837 *Tel:* 732-321-5575 *Fax:* 732-321-5702 *E-mail:* ietusa@theiet.org *Web Site:* www.theiet. org, pg 106

Orozco, Polo, Random House Children's Books, 1745 Broadway, 10th fl, New York, NY 10019 *Tel:* 212-782-9000 *Web Site:* www.randomhousekids.com, pg 181

Orr, John, Lynx House Press, 420 W 24 St, Spokane, WA 99203 *Tel:* 509-624-4894 *E-mail:* lynxhousepress@gmail.com *Web Site:* www. lynxhousepress.org, pg 129

Orr, Nancy, Art In Literature: The Mary Lynn Kotz Award, 800 E Broad St, Richmond, VA 23219 *Tel:* 804-692-3535 *Web Site:* www.lva.virginia.gov/ public/litawards/kotz.htm, pg 593

Orr, Nancy, Library of Virginia Literary Awards, 800 E Broad St, Richmond, VA 23219 *Tel:* 804-692-3535 *Web Site:* www.lva.virginia.gov/public/litawards/index. htm, pg 633

Orr, Rachel, Prospect Agency, 285 Fifth Ave, PMB 445, Brooklyn, NY 11215 *Tel:* 718-788-3217 *Fax:* 718-360-9582 *Web Site:* www.prospectagency.com, pg 499

Ortile, Matt, Counterpoint Press LLC, 2560 Ninth St, Suite 318, Berkeley, CA 94710 *Tel:* 510-704-0230 *Fax:* 510-704-0268 *E-mail:* info@counterpointpress. com *Web Site:* counterpointpress.com; softskull.com, pg 58

Ortiz, Lukas, Philip G Spitzer Literary Agency Inc, 50 Talmage Farm Lane, East Hampton, NY 11937 *Tel:* 631-329-3650 *Fax:* 631-329-3651 *Web Site:* www. spitzeragency.com, pg 503

Ortiz, Lydia, Chronicle Books, 680 Second St, San Francisco, CA 94107 *Tel:* 415-537-4200 *Toll Free Tel:* 800-759-0190 (cust serv) *Fax:* 415-537-4460 *Toll Free Fax:* 800-858-7787 (orders); 800-286-9471 (cust serv) *E-mail:* frontdesk@chroniclebooks.com *Web Site:* www.chroniclebooks.com, pg 52

Ortiz, Shirley, Workman Publishing Co Inc, 225 Varick St, 9th fl, New York, NY 10014-4381 *Tel:* 212-254-5900 *Toll Free Tel:* 800-722-7202 *Fax:* 212-254-8098 *E-mail:* info@workman.com; orders@workman.com *Web Site:* www.workman.com, pg 244

Ortlund, Dane, Crossway, 1300 Crescent St, Wheaton, IL 60187 *Tel:* 630-682-4300 *Toll Free Tel:* 800-635-7993 (orders); 800-543-1659 (cust serv) *Fax:* 630-682-4785 *E-mail:* info@crossway.org *Web Site:* www. crossway.org, pg 60

Ortman, Tyler, No Starch Press, 245 Eighth St, San Francisco, CA 94103 *Tel:* 415-863-9900 *Toll Free Tel:* 800-420-7240 *Fax:* 415-863-9950 *E-mail:* info@ nostarch.com; sales@nostarch.com *Web Site:* www. nostarch.com, pg 150

Orton, Jeramie, Penguin Group USA, A Penguin Random House Company, 375 Hudson St, New York, NY 10014 *Tel:* 212-366-2000 *Toll Free Tel:* 800-847-5515 (inside sales); 800-631-8571 (cust serv) *Fax:* 212-366-2666; 607-775-4829 (inside sales) *E-mail:* online@us.penguingroup.com *Web Site:* www. penguin.com, pg 163

Orton, Jeramie, Viking, 375 Hudson St, New York, NY 10014 *Tel:* 212-366-2000 *Fax:* 212-243-6002 *Web Site:* www.penguin.com/publishers/vikingbooks, pg 236

Osborn, April, Harlequin Enterprises Ltd, 195 Broadway, 24th fl, New York, NY 10007 *Tel:* 212-207-7000 *Toll Free Tel:* 888-432-4879 *E-mail:* customerservice@ harlequin.com *Web Site:* www.harlequin.com, pg 93

Osman, Chantelle Aimee, Polis Books, 1201 Hudson St, No 211S, Hoboken, NJ 07030 *E-mail:* info@ polisbooks.com; submissions@polisbooks.com *Web Site:* www.polisbooks.com; facebook.com/ PolisBooks; twitter.com/PolisBooks, pg 172

Oster, Seth, United Talent Agency, 9336 Civic Center Dr, Beverly Hills, CA 90210 *Tel:* 310-273-6700 *Fax:* 310-247-1111 *Web Site:* www.unitedtalent.com, pg 507

Ostertag, Genny, ASCD, 1703 N Beauregard St, Alexandria, VA 22311-1714 *Tel:* 703-578-9600 *Toll Free Tel:* 800-933-2723 *Fax:* 703-575-5400 *E-mail:* member@ascd.org *Web Site:* www.ascd.org, pg 21

Osuszek, Alex, Harlequin Enterprises Ltd, Bay Adelaide Centre, East Tower, 22 Adelaide St W, 41st fl, Toronto, ON M5H 4E3, Canada *Tel:* 416-445-5860 *Toll Free Tel:* 888-432-4879; 800-370-5838 (ebook inquiries) *E-mail:* customerservice@harlequin.com *Web Site:* www.harlequin.com, pg 429

Oswald, Denise, HarperCollins General Books Group, 195 Broadway, New York, NY 10007 *Tel:* 212-207-7000 *Web Site:* www.harpercollins.com, pg 93

Otero, Hanna, Lonely Planet, 124 Linden St, Oakland, CA 94607 *Tel:* 510-250-6400 *Toll Free Tel:* 800-275-8555 (orders) *E-mail:* info@lonelyplanet.com *Web Site:* www.lonelyplanet.com, pg 127

Otero, Rosa Vanessa, University of Puerto Rico Press, Edificio La Editorial (level 2), Carr No 1, KM 12.0, Jardin Botanico Norte, San Juan, PR 00927 *Tel:* 787-250-0435; 787-250-0550 *Toll Free Tel:* 877-338-7788 *Fax:* 787-753-9116 *E-mail:* info@laeditorialupr.com *Web Site:* www.laeditorialupr.com, pg 231

Ott, Brian L, Texas Tech University Press, 1120 Main St, 2nd fl, Lubbock, TX 79401 *Tel:* 806-742-2982 *Toll Free Tel:* 800-832-4042 *E-mail:* ttup@ttu.edu *Web Site:* www.ttupress.org, pg 216

Ottaviano, Lia, Diversion Books, 443 Park Ave S, Suite 1008, New York, NY 10016 *Tel:* 212-961-6390 *E-mail:* info@diversionbooks.com *Web Site:* www. diversionbooks.com, pg 65

Otte, Liz, Sourcebooks LLC, 1935 Brookdale Rd, Suite 139, Naperville, IL 60563 *Tel:* 630-961-3900 *Toll Free Tel:* 800-432-7444 *Fax:* 630-961-2168 *E-mail:* info@ sourcebooks.com; customersupport@sourcebooks.com *Web Site:* www.sourcebooks.com, pg 204

Otter, Samuel, The Melville Society, Johns Hopkins University Press, PO Box 19966, Baltimore, MD 21211-0966 *Web Site:* melvillesociety.org, pg 537

Ou, Michelle, Editors' Association of Canada (Association canadienne des reviseurs), 1507-180 Dundas St W, Toronto, ON M5G 1Z8, Canada *Tel:* 416-975-1379 *Toll Free Tel:* 866-CAN-EDIT (226-3348) *Fax:* 416-975-1637 *E-mail:* info@editors. ca; info@reviseurs.ca *Web Site:* www.editors.ca; www. reviseurs.ca, pg 532

Ou, Michelle, Tom Fairley Award for Editorial Excellence, 1507-180 Dundas St W, Toronto, ON M5G 1Z8, Canada *Tel:* 416-975-1379 *Toll Free Tel:* 866-CAN-EDIT (226-3348) *Fax:* 416-975-1637 *E-mail:* fairley_award@editors.ca; info@editors.ca *Web Site:* www.editors.ca; www.reviseurs.ca, pg 614

Ovedovitz, Nancy, Yale University Press, 302 Temple St, New Haven, CT 06511-8909 *Tel:* 203-432-0960; 203-432-0966 (sales); 401-531-2800 (cust serv) *Toll Free Tel:* 800-405-1619 (cust serv) *Fax:* 203-432-0948; 203-432-8485 (sales); 401-531-2801 (cust serv) *Toll Free Fax:* 800-406-9145 (cust serv) *E-mail:* sales. press@yale.edu (sales); customer.care@triliteral.org (cust serv) *Web Site:* www.yalebooks.com; yalepress. yale.edu/yupbooks, pg 246

Owen, Richard C, Richard C Owen Publishers Inc, PO Box 585, Katonah, NY 10536-0585 *Tel:* 914-232-3903 *Toll Free Tel:* 800-336-5588 *Fax:* 914-232-3977 *Web Site:* www.rcowen.com, pg 158

Owens, Alexandra, ASJA Freelance Writer Search, 355 Lexington Ave, 15th fl, New York, NY 10017 *Tel:* 212-997-0947 *E-mail:* asjaoffice@asja.org *Web Site:* www.freelancewritersearch.com, pg 458

Owens, John, Cohesion®, 511 W Bay St, Suite 480, Tampa, FL 33606 *Tel:* 813-999-3111 *Toll Free Tel:* 866-727-6800 *Web Site:* www.cohesion.com, pg 461

Owens, Kimi, Perseus Books, 1290 Avenue of the Americas, New York, NY 10104 *Tel:* 212-340-8100 *Toll Free Tel:* 800-343-4499 (cust serv) *Fax:* 212-340-8105 *Web Site:* www.perseusbooks.com, pg 167

Owens, Mary Ellen, Random House Children's Books, 1745 Broadway, 10th fl, New York, NY 10019 *Tel:* 212-782-9000 *Web Site:* www.randomhousekids. com, pg 180

Owles, John Paul, Joshua Tree Publishing, 3 Golf Ctr, Suite 201, Hoffman Estates, IL 60169 *Tel:* 312-893-7525 *E-mail:* www.joshuatreepublishing.com *Web Site:* www.joshuatreepublishing.com; www. centaurbooks.com (imprint); www.chiralhouse.com (imprint), pg 114

Ozer, Shelby, Harry N Abrams Inc, 195 Broadway, 9th fl, New York, NY 10007 *Tel:* 212-206-7715 *Toll Free Tel:* 800-345-1359 *Fax:* 212-519-1210 *E-mail:* abrams@abramsbooks.com *Web Site:* www. abramsbooks.com, pg 3

Ozturk, Yusuf, Rand McNally, 9855 Woods Dr, Skokie, IL 60077 *Tel:* 847-329-8100 *Toll Free Tel:* 877-446-4863 *Toll Free Fax:* 877-469-1298 *E-mail:* mediarelations@randmcnally.com; tndsupport@randmcnally.com *Web Site:* www. randmcnally.com, pg 180

O'Hayre, Meredith, Adams Media, 57 Littlefield St, Avon, MA 02322 *Tel:* 508-427-7100 *Web Site:* www. simonandschuster.com, pg 4

Pace, Steven, W W Norton & Company Inc, 500 Fifth Ave, New York, NY 10110-0017 *Tel:* 212-354-5500 *Toll Free Tel:* 800-233-4830 (orders & cust serv) *Fax:* 212-869-0856 *Toll Free Fax:* 800-458-6515 *E-mail:* orders@wwnorton.com *Web Site:* wwnorton. com, pg 152

Pace, Zachary, The Experiment, 220 E 23 St, Suite 600, New York, NY 10010-4658 *Tel:* 212-889-1659 *E-mail:* info@theexperimentpublishing.com *Web Site:* www.theexperimentpublishing.com, pg 74

Pachaco, Lisa, Museum of New Mexico Press, 725 Camino Lejo, Suite C, Santa Fe, NM 87505 *Tel:* 505-476-1155; 505-272-7777 (orders) *Toll Free Tel:* 800-

249-7737 (orders) *Fax:* 505-476-1156 *Toll Free Fax:* 800-622-8667 (orders) *Web Site:* www.mnmpress. org, pg 144

Packard, Michael, Binding Industries Association (BIA), 301 Brush Creek Rd, Warrendale, PA 15086-7529 *Tel:* 412-741-6860 *Toll Free Tel:* 800-910-4283 *Fax:* 412-741-2311 *Web Site:* www.printing.org/bia, pg 528

Packard, Mike, Premier Print Awards, 10015 Main St, Fairfax, VA 22031-3489 *Tel:* 703-385-1335 *Toll Free Tel:* 888-385-3588 *Fax:* 703-273-0456 *E-mail:* assist@ printing.org; info@printing.org *Web Site:* www. printing.org/ppa, pg 658

Padakis, Marina, Houghton Mifflin Harcourt Trade & Reference Division, 125 High St, Boston, MA 02110 *Tel:* 617-351-5000 *Web Site:* www.hmhco.com, pg 104

Paddick, Christy, Institute of Public Administration of Canada, 1075 Bay St, Suite 401, Toronto, ON M5S 2B1, Canada *Tel:* 416-924-8787 *Fax:* 416-924-4992 *E-mail:* ntl@ipac.ca *Web Site:* www.ipac.ca, pg 430

Paddio, Martin, Monthly Review Press, 134 W 29 St, Suite 706, New York, NY 10001 *Tel:* 212-691-2555 *E-mail:* mreview@igc.org *Web Site:* monthlyreview. org, pg 142

Padgett, Leslie, Macmillan, 120 Broadway, 22nd fl, New York, NY 10271 *Tel:* 646-307-5151 *E-mail:* press. inquiries@macmillan.com *Web Site:* www.macmillan. com, pg 129

Padilla, Jocelyn, Society of American Travel Writers (SATW), 17W110 22 St, One Parkview Plaza, Suite 800, Oakbrook Terrace, IL 60181 *E-mail:* info@satw. org *Web Site:* www.satw.org, pg 546

Paez, Gabriella, Harry N Abrams Inc, 195 Broadway, 9th fl, New York, NY 10007 *Tel:* 212-206-7715 *Toll Free Tel:* 800-345-1359 *Fax:* 212-519-1210 *E-mail:* abrams@abramsbooks.com *Web Site:* www. abramsbooks.com, pg 3

Paganelli, Courtney, Levine|Greenberg|Rostan Literary Agency, 307 Seventh Ave, Suite 2407, New York, NY 10001 *Tel:* 212-337-0934 *Fax:* 212-337-0948 *Web Site:* lgrliterary.com, pg 493

Page, Lisa, Jenny McKean Moore Writer-in-Washington, English Dept, Rome Hall, 801 22 St NW, Suite 643, Washington, DC 20052 *Tel:* 202-994-6180 *E-mail:* engldept@gwu.edu *Web Site:* english. columbian.gwu.edu, pg 643

Page, Marissa, Houghton Mifflin Harcourt Trade & Reference Division, 125 High St, Boston, MA 02110 *Tel:* 617-351-5000 *Web Site:* www.hmhco.com, pg 104

Page-White, Jenni, National Ten-Minute Play Contest, 316 W Main St, Louisville, KY 40202-4218 *Tel:* 502-584-1265 *Web Site:* actorstheatre.org/national-ten-minute-play-contest/, pg 646

Pagel, Caryl, Cleveland State University Poetry Center Prizes, 2121 Euclid Ave, Cleveland, OH 44115 *Tel:* 216-687-3986 *Toll Free Tel:* 888-278-6473 *Fax:* 216-687-6943 *E-mail:* poetrycenter@csuohio.edu *Web Site:* www.csupoetrycenter.com, pg 605

Paille, Anthony, Association for Information & Image Management International (AIIM), 1100 Wayne Ave, Suite 1100, Silver Spring, MD 20910 *Tel:* 301-587-8202 *Toll Free Tel:* 800-477-2446 *Fax:* 301-587-2711 *E-mail:* aiim@aiim.org; info@aiim.org *Web Site:* www.aiim.org, pg 525

Paine, John, Joelle Delbourgo Associates Inc, 101 Park St, Montclair, NJ 07042 *Tel:* 973-773-0836 (call only during standard business hours) *Web Site:* www. delbourgo.com, pg 481

Paine, John, The Editors Circle, 24 Holly Circle, Easthampton, MA 01027 *Tel:* 862-596-9709 *E-mail:* query@theeditorscircle.com *Web Site:* www. theeditorscircle.com, pg 463

Painter, Benjamin, Schlager Group Inc, 1111 W Mockingbird Lane, Suite 735, Dallas, TX 75247 *Toll Free Tel:* 888-416-5727 *Fax:* 469-325-3700 *E-mail:* info@schlagergroup.com; sales@ schlagergroup.com *Web Site:* www.schlagergroup.com, pg 193

Painter, Jeannie, Mountain Press Publishing Co, 1301 S Third W, Missoula, MT 59801 *Tel:* 406-728-1900 *Toll Free Tel:* 800-234-5308 *Fax:* 406-728-1635 *E-mail:* info@mtnpress.com *Web Site:* www.mountain-press.com, pg 143

Painton, Priscilla, Simon & Schuster, 1230 Avenue of the Americas, New York, NY 10020 *Tel:* 212-698-7000 *Toll Free Tel:* 800-223-2348 (cust serv); 800-223-2336 (orders) *Toll Free Fax:* 800-943-9831 (orders) *Web Site:* www.simonandschuster.com, pg 198

Pak, Eunice, Macmillan, 120 Broadway, 22nd fl, New York, NY 10271 *Tel:* 646-307-5151 *E-mail:* press. inquiries@macmillan.com *Web Site:* www.macmillan. com, pg 130

Palana-Shanahan, Brett, Adams Media, 57 Littlefield St, Avon, MA 02322 *Tel:* 508-427-7100 *Web Site:* www. simonandschuster.com, pg 4

Palermo, Laura, Peachtree Publishing Co Inc, 1700 Chattahoochee Ave, Atlanta, GA 30318-2112 *Tel:* 404-876-8761 *Toll Free Tel:* 800-241-0113 *Fax:* 404-875-2578 *Toll Free Fax:* 800-875-8909 *E-mail:* hello@ peachtree-online.com; orders@peachtree-online.com; sales@peachtree-online.com *Web Site:* www.peachtree-online.com, pg 162

Paley, Lauren, DK Publishing, 1450 Broadway, Suite 801, New York, NY 10018 *Tel:* 646-674-4000 *Toll Free Tel:* 800-733-3000 *Fax:* 646-674-4020 *E-mail:* marketing@dk.com; publicity@ dk.com; csorders@penguinrandomhouse.com; ecustomerservice@randomhouse.com *Web Site:* www. dk.com; www.penguin.com, pg 65

Palisano, John, Horror Writers Association (HWA), PO Box 56687, Sherman Oaks, CA 91413 *Tel:* 818-220-3965 *E-mail:* admin@horror.org *Web Site:* horror.org, pg 534

Palkar, Anuja, Penguin Group USA, A Penguin Random House Company, 375 Hudson St, New York, NY 10014 *Tel:* 212-366-2000 *Toll Free Tel:* 800-847-5515 (inside sales); 800-631-8571 (cust serv) *Fax:* 212-366-2666; 607-775-4829 (inside sales) *E-mail:* online@ us.penguingroup.com *Web Site:* www.penguin.com, pg 163

Palladino, Lily, University of Pennsylvania Press, 3905 Spruce St, Philadelphia, PA 19104 *Tel:* 215-898-6261 *Fax:* 215-898-0404 *E-mail:* custserv@pobox.upenn. edu *Web Site:* www.pennpress.org, pg 230

Palladino, Linda, Random House Children's Books, 1745 Broadway, 10th fl, New York, NY 10019 *Tel:* 212-782-9000 *Web Site:* www.randomhousekids.com, pg 180

Pallante, Maria, Association of American Publishers (AAP), 455 Massachusetts Ave NW, Suite 700, Washington, DC 20001-2777 *Tel:* 202-347-3375 *Fax:* 202-347-3690 *E-mail:* info@publishers.org *Web Site:* publishers.org, pg 526

Palmer, Heather, Jane Addams Children's Book Award, 777 United Nations Plaza, 6th fl, New York, NY 10017 *Tel:* 212-682-8830 *E-mail:* info@janeaddamspeace.org *Web Site:* www. janeaddamspeace.org, pg 590

Palmer, Judd, Bayeux Arts Inc, 2403, 510-Sixth Ave SE, Calgary, AB T2G 1L7, Canada *E-mail:* mail@bayeux. com *Web Site:* bayeux.com, pg 416

Palmer, Michael, Business Marketing Association (BMA), 708 Third Ave, New York, NY 10017 *Tel:* 212-697-5950 *Fax:* 212-687-7310 *E-mail:* info@ marketing.org *Web Site:* www.marketing.org, pg 529

Palmer, Paula, US Games Systems Inc, 179 Ludlow St, Stamford, CT 06902 *Tel:* 203-353-8400 *Toll Free Tel:* 800-54-GAMES (544-2637) *Fax:* 203-353-8431 *E-mail:* info@usgamesinc.com *Web Site:* www. usgamesinc.com, pg 234

Palmquist, Nancy K, W W Norton & Company Inc, 500 Fifth Ave, New York, NY 10110-0017 *Tel:* 212-354-5500 *Toll Free Tel:* 800-233-4830 (orders & cust serv) *Fax:* 212-869-0856 *Toll Free Fax:* 800-458-6515 *E-mail:* orders@wwnorton.com *Web Site:* wwnorton. com, pg 152

Pan, Dr Hui, Information Gatekeepers Inc (IGI), PO Box 606, Winchester, MA 01890 *Tel:* 617-782-5033 *Fax:* 617-507-8338 *E-mail:* info@igigroup.com *Web Site:* www.igigroup.com, pg 108

Panchal-Terhune, Nisha, Little, Brown Books for Young Readers, 1290 Avenue of the Americas, New York, NY 10104 *Tel:* 212-364-1100 *Toll Free Tel:* 800-759-0190 (cust serv) *Web Site:* www.hachettebookgroup.com, pg 126

Pandya-Lorch, Rajul, International Food Policy Research Institute, 1201 Eye St NW, Washington, DC 20005-3915 *Tel:* 202-862-5600 *Fax:* 202-862-5606 *E-mail:* ifpri@cgiar.org *Web Site:* www.ifpri.org, pg 111

Panec, Don, Treasure Bay Inc, PO Box 119, Novato, CA 94948 *Tel:* 415-884-2888 *Fax:* 415-884-2840 *E-mail:* customerservice@treasurebaybooks.com *Web Site:* www.treasurebaybooks.com, pg 220

Panepinto, Lauren, Orbit, 1290 Avenue of the Americas, New York, NY 10104 *Tel:* 212-364-1100 *Toll Free Tel:* 800-759-0190 *Web Site:* www.orbitbooks.net, pg 156

Panetta, Jackie, University Press of Florida, 2046 NE Waldo Rd, Suite 2100, Gainesville, FL 32609 *Tel:* 352-392-1351 *Toll Free Tel:* 800-226-3822 (orders only) *Fax:* 352-392-0590 *Toll Free Fax:* 800-680-1955 (orders only) *E-mail:* press@upress.ufl.edu; orders@upress.ufl.edu *Web Site:* www.upf.com, pg 232

Pangaro, Melissa, little bee books, 251 Park Ave S, 12th fl, New York, NY 10010 *Toll Free Tel:* 844-321-0237 *E-mail:* info@littlebeebooks.com *Web Site:* littlebeebooks.com, pg 125

Pangilinan, Noel T, Asian American Writers' Workshop, 112 W 27 St, Suite 600, New York, NY 10001 *Tel:* 212-494-0061 *E-mail:* desk@aaww.org *Web Site:* aaww.org; facebook.com/AsianAmericanWritersWorkshop, pg 525

Pannenberg, Sarah, Tom Doherty Associates, LLC, 120 Broadway, New York, NY 10271 *Tel:* 646-307-5511 *Toll Free Tel:* 800-455-0340 *Web Site:* us.macmillan.com/torforge, pg 66

Panning, Jeanette, American Geophysical Union (AGU), 2000 Florida Ave NW, Washington, DC 20009 *Tel:* 202-462-6900 *Toll Free Tel:* 800-966-2481 (North America) *Fax:* 202-328-0566 *E-mail:* service@agu.org (cust serv); earthspacescience@agu.org *Web Site:* www.agu.org, pg 11

Pantojan, Marie, Random House Publishing Group, 1745 Broadway, New York, NY 10019 *Toll Free Tel:* 800-200-3552 *Web Site:* www.randomhousebooks.com, pg 181

Panzer, Robert, Visual Artists & Galleries Association Inc (VAGA), 111 Broadway, Suite 1006, New York, NY 10006 *Tel:* 212-736-6666 *Fax:* 212-736-6767 *E-mail:* info@vagarights.com *Web Site:* vagarights.com, pg 548

Papademetriou, Dean, Somerset Hall Press, 416 Commonwealth Ave, Suite 612, Boston, MA 02215 *Tel:* 617-236-5126 *E-mail:* info@somersethallpress.com *Web Site:* www.somersethallpress.com, pg 203

Papadopoulos, Niki, Portfolio, 375 Hudson St, New York, NY 10014 *Web Site:* www.penguin.com/meet/publishers/portfolio, pg 172

Paparozzi, Andrew D, Epicomm, 1800 Diagonal Rd, Suite 320, Alexandria, VA 22314-2862 *Tel:* 703-836-9200 *E-mail:* webmaster@epicomm.org *Web Site:* epicomm.org, pg 533

Pape, Don, NavPress Publishing Group, 3820 N 30 St, Colorado Springs, CO 80904 *Tel:* 719-598-1212 *Toll Free Tel:* 800-323-9400; 855-277-9400 (cust serv) *Toll Free Fax:* 800-684-0247 *Web Site:* www.navpress.com, pg 148

Papin, Jessica, Dystel, Goderich & Bourret LLC, One Union Sq W, Suite 904, New York, NY 10003 *Tel:* 212-627-9100 *Fax:* 212-627-9313 *Web Site:* www.dystel.com, pg 482

Pappas, Cheryl, Harvard Art Museums, 32 Quincy St, Cambridge, MA 02138 *Tel:* 617-495-9400; 617-496-6529 (edit) *Web Site:* www.harvardartmuseums.org, pg 94

Pappas, Joseph J, Consumer Press, 13326 SW 28 St, Suite 102, Fort Lauderdale, FL 33330-1102 *Tel:* 954-370-9153 *Fax:* 954-472-1008 *E-mail:* info@consumerpress.com *Web Site:* www.consumerpress.com, pg 56

Pappenheimer, Andrea, HarperCollins Children's Books, 195 Broadway, New York, NY 10007 *Tel:* 212-207-7000 *Web Site:* www.harpercollins.com/childrens, pg 93

Paprocki, Karin, Simon & Schuster Children's Publishing, 1230 Avenue of the Americas, New York, NY 10020 *Tel:* 212-698-7000 *Web Site:* www.simonandschuster.com/kids; www.simonandschuster.com/teen; simonandschuster.net; simonandschuster.biz, pg 199

Paquin, Valerie, Northwest Independent Editors Guild, 7511 Greenwood Ave N, No 307, Seattle, WA 98103 *E-mail:* info@edsguild.org *Web Site:* edsguild.org, pg 542

Paradis, Anne, Les Editions Chouette, 1001 Lenoir St, Suite B-238, Montreal, QC H4C 2Z6, Canada *Tel:* 514-925-3325 *Fax:* 514-925-3323 *E-mail:* info@editions-chouette.com *Web Site:* www.chouette-publishing.com, pg 422

Paradis, Lucille, Paulines Editions, 5610 rue Beaubien est, Montreal, QC H1T 1X5, Canada *Tel:* 514-253-5610 *Fax:* 514-253-1907 *E-mail:* fsp-paulines@videotron.ca *Web Site:* www.editions.paulines.qc.ca, pg 436

Paradise, Bridgett, Houghton Mifflin Harcourt, 125 High St, Boston, MA 02110 *Tel:* 617-351-5000 *Toll Free Tel:* 855-969-4642; 800-225-5425 (K-12 educ materials); 800-323-9540 (assessment materials); 877-219-1537 (SkillsTutor); 888-242-6747 (Innovation in Educ Group); 800-225-3362 (Trade & Ref Div) *Toll Free Fax:* 800-269-5232 *E-mail:* myhmhco@hmhco.com *Web Site:* www.hmhco.com, pg 103

Paraskevopoulos, Jane, Forward Movement, 412 Sycamore St, Cincinnati, OH 45202-4110 *Tel:* 513-721-6659 *Toll Free Tel:* 800-543-1813 *Fax:* 513-721-0729 (orders) *E-mail:* orders@forwardmovement.org (orders & cust serv) *Web Site:* www.forwardmovement.org, pg 80

Pardo, Wendy, Sounds True Inc, 413 S Arthur Ave, Louisville, CO 80027 *Tel:* 303-665-3151 *Toll Free Tel:* 800-333-9185 (US); 888-303-9185 (US & CN) *E-mail:* customerservice@soundstrue.com; stpublicity@soundstrue.com *Web Site:* www.soundstrue.com, pg 204

Pare, Jean, Guy Saint-Jean Editeur Inc, 4490, rue Garand, Laval, QC H7L 5Z6, Canada *Tel:* 450-663-1777 *E-mail:* info@saint-jeanediteur.com *Web Site:* saint-jeanediteur.com, pg 439

Paredes, Ingrid, Penguin Random House LLC, 1745 Broadway, New York, NY 10019 *Tel:* 212-782-9000 *Toll Free Tel:* 800-726-0600 *Web Site:* www.penguinrandomhouse.com, pg 164

Paredes, Nikay, Academy of American Poets Fellowship, 75 Maiden Lane, Suite 901, New York, NY 10038 *Tel:* 212-274-0343 *E-mail:* academy@poets.org *Web Site:* www.poets.org, pg 589

Paredes, Nikay, The Academy of American Poets Inc, 75 Maiden Lane, Suite 901, New York, NY 10038 *Tel:* 212-274-0343 *E-mail:* academy@poets.org *Web Site:* www.poets.org, pg 521

Paredes, Nikay, Ambroggio Prize, 75 Maiden Lane, Suite 901, New York, NY 10038 *Tel:* 212-274-0343 *E-mail:* awards@poets.org *Web Site:* www.poets.org, pg 591

Paredes, Nikay, James Lauglin Award, 75 Maiden Lane, Suite 901, New York, NY 10038 *Tel:* 212-274-0343 *E-mail:* awards@poets.org *Web Site:* www.poets.org, pg 632

Paredes, Nikay, Lenore Marshall Poetry Prize, 75 Maiden Lane, Suite 901, New York, NY 10038 *Tel:* 212-274-0343 *E-mail:* awards@poets.org *Web Site:* www.poets.org, pg 638

Paredes, Nikay, Harold Morton Landon Translation Award, 75 Maiden Lane, Suite 901, New York, NY 10038 *Tel:* 212-274-0343 *E-mail:* awards@poets.org *Web Site:* www.poets.org, pg 643

Paredes, Nikay, Aliki Perroti & Seth Frank Most Promising Young Poet Award, 75 Maiden Lane, Suite 901, New York, NY 10038 *Tel:* 212-274-0343 *E-mail:* awards@poets.org *Web Site:* www.poets.org, pg 655

Paredes, Nikay, Raiziss/de Palchi Fellowship, 75 Maiden Lane, Suite 901, New York, NY 10038 *Tel:* 212-274-0343 *E-mail:* academy@poets.org *Web Site:* www.poets.org, pg 660

Paredes, Nikay, Wallace Stevens Award, 75 Maiden Lane, Suite 901, New York, NY 10038 *Tel:* 212-274-0343 *E-mail:* awards@poets.org *Web Site:* www.poets.org, pg 670

Paredes, Nikay, Treehouse Climate Action Poem Prize, 75 Maiden Lane, Suite 901, New York, NY 10038 *Tel:* 212-274-0343 *E-mail:* academy@poets.org *Web Site:* www.poets.org, pg 673

Paredes, Nikay, Walt Whitman Award, 75 Maiden Lane, Suite 901, New York, NY 10038 *Tel:* 212-274-0343 *E-mail:* academy@poets.org *Web Site:* www.poets.org, pg 677

Paredez, Deborah, University of Texas at Austin, New Writers Project, Dept of English, Calhoun Hall, Rm 226, 204 W 21 St, B-5000, Austin, TX 78712 *Tel:* 512-471-5132; 512-471-4991 *Fax:* 512-471-4909 *Web Site:* newwritersproject.org, pg 586

Parent, Gilles, Les Editions Vents d'Ouest, 109, rue Wright, bureau 202, Gatineau, QC J8X 2G7, Canada *Tel:* 819-770-6377 *E-mail:* info@ventsdouest.ca *Web Site:* www.ventsdouest.ca, pg 425

Parfrey, Adam, Feral House, 1240 W Sims Way, Suite 124, Port Townsend, WA 98368 *Tel:* 323-666-3311 *E-mail:* info@feralhouse.com *Web Site:* feralhouse.com, pg 77

Parikh, Dhara, Random House Publishing Group, 1745 Broadway, New York, NY 10019 *Toll Free Tel:* 800-200-3552 *Web Site:* www.randomhousebooks.com, pg 181

Parikh, Sudip, American Association for the Advancement of Science (AAAS), 1200 New York Ave NW, Washington, DC 20005 *Tel:* 202-326-6400 *E-mail:* media@aaas.org *Web Site:* www.aaas.org, pg 522

Paris, Shirley, Carroll Publishing, 4701 Sangamore Rd, Suite S-155, Bethesda, MD 20816 *Tel:* 301-263-9800 *Fax:* 301-263-9805 *E-mail:* info@carrollpub.com; customersvc@carrollpub.com *Web Site:* www.carrollpublishing.com, pg 45

Parisi, Anthony, Tom Doherty Associates, LLC, 120 Broadway, New York, NY 10271 *Tel:* 646-307-5511 *Toll Free Tel:* 800-455-0340 *Web Site:* us.macmillan.com/torforge, pg 66

Parisi, Frank, Chronicle Books, 680 Second St, San Francisco, CA 94107 *Tel:* 415-537-4200 *Toll Free Tel:* 800-759-0190 (cust serv) *Fax:* 415-537-4460 *Toll Free Fax:* 800-858-7787 (orders); 800-286-9471 (cust serv) *E-mail:* frontdesk@chroniclebooks.com *Web Site:* www.chroniclebooks.com, pg 52

Park, Ed, The Penguin Press, 375 Hudson St, New York, NY 10014 *Web Site:* thepenguinpress.com, pg 164

Park, Hana, Simon & Schuster, 1230 Avenue of the Americas, New York, NY 10020 *Tel:* 212-698-7000 *Toll Free Tel:* 800-223-2348 *Toll Free Tel:* 800-223-2336 (orders) *Toll Free Fax:* 800-943-9831 (orders) *Web Site:* www.simonandschuster.com, pg 198

Park, Rick, Newbury Street Press, 99-101 Newbury St, Boston, MA 02116 *Tel:* 617-226-1206 *Toll Free Tel:* 888-296-3447 (NEHGS membership) *Fax:* 617-536-7307 *E-mail:* sales@nehgs.org *Web Site:* www.americanancestors.org, pg 150

Parker, Erika, American Psychiatric Association Publishing, 800 Maine Ave SW, Suite 900, Washington, DC 20024 *Tel:* 202-459-9722 *Toll*

Patt, Avinoam PhD, Edward Lewis Wallant Award, Maurice Greenberg Center for Judaic Studies, 200 Bloomfield Ave, Harry Jack Gray E 300, West Hartford, CT 06117 *Tel:* 860-768-4964 *Fax:* 860-768-5044 *E-mail:* mgcjs@hartford.edu *Web Site:* www.hartford.edu/a_and_s/greenberg/wallant, pg 676

Patterson, David, Stuart Krichevsky Literary Agency Inc, 6 E 39 St, Suite 500, New York, NY 10016 *Tel:* 212-725-5288 *Fax:* 212-725-5275 *E-mail:* query@skagency.com *Web Site:* skagency.com, pg 492

Patterson, Elaine, Maryland History Press, PO Box 206, Fruitland, MD 21826-0206 *Tel:* 443-397-0912 *E-mail:* ehpatterson@earthlink.net *Web Site:* www.marylandhistorypress.com, pg 133

Patterson, Emma, Brandt & Hochman Literary Agents Inc, 1501 Broadway, Suite 2310, New York, NY 10036 *Tel:* 212-840-5760 *Fax:* 212-840-5776 *Web Site:* brandthochman.com, pg 477

Patterson, Hallie, Harry N Abrams Inc, 195 Broadway, 9th fl, New York, NY 10007 *Tel:* 212-206-7715 *Toll Free Tel:* 800-345-1359 *Fax:* 212-519-1210 *E-mail:* abrams@abramsbooks.com *Web Site:* www.abramsbooks.com, pg 3

Patterson, James, Fernwood Publishing, 32 Oceanvista Lane, Black Point, NS B0J 1B0, Canada *Tel:* 902-857-1388 *Fax:* 902-857-1328 *E-mail:* info@fernpub.ca; roseway@fernpub.ca *Web Site:* fernwoodpublishing.ca, pg 426

Patterson, Monique, St Martin's Press, LLC, 120 Broadway, New York, NY 10271 *Tel:* 646-307-5151 *Web Site:* us.macmillan.com/smp, pg 190

Patton, Susan, Association of University Presses (AUPresses), 1412 Broadway, Suite 2135, New York, NY 10018 *Tel:* 212-989-1010 *Fax:* 212-989-0275 *E-mail:* info@aupresses.org *Web Site:* www.aupresses.org, pg 527

Paul, Chris, Candlewick Press, 99 Dover St, Somerville, MA 02144-2825 *Tel:* 617-661-3330 *Fax:* 617-661-0565 *E-mail:* bigbear@candlewick.com; salesinfo@candlewick.com *Web Site:* www.candlewick.com, pg 44

Paul, Hannah, Princeton University Press, 41 William St, Princeton, NJ 08540-5237 *Tel:* 609-258-4900 *Fax:* 609-258-6305 *Web Site:* press.princeton.edu, pg 174

Paul, Miranda, Wisconsin Annual Fall Conference, PO Box 1463, Green Bay, WI 54305-1463 *Tel:* 323-782-1010 (corp off) *E-mail:* wisconsin@scbwi.org *Web Site:* www.scbwi.org; www.facebook.com/SCBWIWisconsin, pg 580

Pauley, Arron, Jackie White Memorial National Children's Playwriting Contest, 1400 Forum Blvd, 1C No 214, Columbia, MO 65203 *E-mail:* jwm@cectheatre.org *Web Site:* www.cectheatre.org, pg 628

Paulsen, Nancy, GP Putnam's Sons (Children's), 345 Hudson St, New York, NY 10014 *Tel:* 212-366-2000 *Fax:* 212-414-3393 *Web Site:* www.penguin.com/publishers/gpputnamssonsbooksforyoungread, pg 178

Paulsen, Nancy Rose, Penguin Young Readers Group, 345 Hudson St, New York, NY 10014 *Tel:* 212-366-2000; 212-414-3553 *Fax:* 212-414-3340 *Web Site:* www.penguin.com/children, pg 165

Paulson, Jamis, Turnstone Press, Artspace Bldg, 206-100 Arthur St, Winnipeg, MB R3B 1H3, Canada *Tel:* 204-947-1555 *Toll Free Tel:* 888-363-7718 *Fax:* 204-942-1556 *E-mail:* info@turnstonepress.com *Web Site:* www.turnstonepress.com, pg 442

Paulson, Timothy, Thomas Nelson, 501 Nelson Place, Nashville, TN 37214 *Tel:* 615-889-9000 *Toll Free Tel:* 800-251-4000 *Fax:* 615-902-1548 *Web Site:* www.thomasnelson.com, pg 217

Paustenbach, Anna, HarperCollins General Books Group, 195 Broadway, New York, NY 10007 *Tel:* 212-207-7000 *Web Site:* www.harpercollins.com, pg 93

Pautz, Peter Dennis, World Fantasy Awards, PO Box 43, Mukilteo, WA 98275-0043 *Web Site:* www.worldfantasy.org, pg 679

Pavlin, Jordan, Alfred A Knopf, c/o Penguin Random House Inc, 1745 Broadway, New York, NY 10019 *Tel:* 212-751-2600 *Fax:* 212-572-2662 (foreign rts) *Web Site:* knopfdoubleday.com, pg 117

Pawlak, Kim, William Holmes McGuffey Longevity Award, PO Box 367, Fountain City, WI 54629 *E-mail:* info@taaonline.net *Web Site:* www.taaonline.net/mcguffey-longevity-award, pg 639

Pawlak, Kim, Most Promising New Textbook Award, PO Box 367, Fountain City, WI 54629 *E-mail:* info@taaonline.net *Web Site:* www.taaonline.net/promising-new-textbook-award, pg 644

Pawlak, Kim, Ron Pynn Award, PO Box 367, Fountain City, WI 54629 *E-mail:* info@taaonline.net *Web Site:* www.taaonline.net/ron-pynn-award, pg 660

Pawlak, Kim, TAA Council of Fellows, PO Box 367, Fountain City, WI 54629 *E-mail:* info@taaonline.net *Web Site:* www.taaonline.net/council-of-fellows, pg 672

Pawlak, Kim, Textbook Excellence Award, PO Box 367, Fountain City, WI 54629 *E-mail:* info@taaonline.net *Web Site:* www.taaonline.net/textbook-excellence-award, pg 672

Pawlak, Mark, Hanging Loose Press, 231 Wyckoff St, Brooklyn, NY 11217 *Tel:* 347-529-4738 *Fax:* 347-227-8215 *E-mail:* print225@aol.com *Web Site:* www.hangingloosepress.com, pg 92

Pawlitz, Mr Loren, Concordia Publishing House, 3558 S Jefferson Ave, St Louis, MO 63118-3968 *Tel:* 314-268-1000; 314-268-1268 (bookshop) *Toll Free Tel:* 800-325-3040 (cust serv) *Toll Free Fax:* 800-490-9889 (cust serv) *E-mail:* order@cph.org *Web Site:* www.cph.org, pg 56

Pawluk, Justyna, Facts On File, 132 W 31 St, 17th fl, New York, NY 10001 *Tel:* 212-967-8800 *Toll Free Tel:* 800-322-8755 *Toll Free Fax:* 800-678-3633 *E-mail:* custserv@factsonfile.com *Web Site:* infobasepublishing.com, pg 74

Pawluk, Justyna, Ferguson Publishing, 132 W 31 St, 17th fl, New York, NY 10001 *Tel:* 212-967-8800 *Toll Free Tel:* 800-322-8755 *Toll Free Fax:* 800-678-3633 *E-mail:* custserv@factsonfile.com *Web Site:* infobasepublishing.com, pg 77

Payette, Jacques, Les Editions Heritage Inc, 1101, ave Victoria, St-Lambert, QC J4R 1P8, Canada *Tel:* 514-875-0327, pg 424

Payette, Sylvie, Les Editions Heritage Inc, 1101, ave Victoria, St-Lambert, QC J4R 1P8, Canada *Tel:* 514-875-0327, pg 424

Payne, Bridget Watson, Chronicle Books, 680 Second St, San Francisco, CA 94107 *Tel:* 415-537-4200 *Toll Free Tel:* 800-759-0190 (cust serv) *Fax:* 415-537-4460 *Toll Free Fax:* 800-858-7787 (orders); 800-286-9471 (cust serv) *E-mail:* frontdesk@chroniclebooks.com *Web Site:* www.chroniclebooks.com, pg 51

Payne, Caroline, Dutton, 1745 Broadway, New York, NY 10019 *Tel:* 212-366-2000 *Fax:* 212-366-2262 *E-mail:* duttonpublicity@us.penguingroup.com *Web Site:* www.penguin.com, pg 68

Payne, Courtney, Chronicle Books, 680 Second St, San Francisco, CA 94107 *Tel:* 415-537-4200 *Toll Free Tel:* 800-759-0190 (cust serv) *Fax:* 415-537-4460 *Toll Free Fax:* 800-858-7787 (orders); 800-286-9471 (cust serv) *E-mail:* frontdesk@chroniclebooks.com *Web Site:* www.chroniclebooks.com, pg 51

Payne, Maribeth, W W Norton & Company Inc, 500 Fifth Ave, New York, NY 10110-0017 *Tel:* 212-354-5500 *Toll Free Tel:* 800-233-4830 (orders & cust serv) *Fax:* 212-869-0856 *Toll Free Fax:* 800-458-6515 *E-mail:* orders@wwnorton.com *Web Site:* wwnorton.com, pg 152

Payton, Thomas, Trinity University Press, One Trinity Place, San Antonio, TX 78212-7200 *Tel:* 210-999-8884 *Fax:* 210-999-8838 *E-mail:* books@trinity.edu *Web Site:* www.tupress.org, pg 220

Pazdur, Ryan, Zondervan, 3900 Sparks Dr, Grand Rapids, MI 49546 *Tel:* 616-698-6900 *Toll Free Tel:* 800-226-1122; 800-727-1309 (retail orders) *Fax:* 616-698-3350 *Toll Free Fax:* 800-698-3256 (retail orders) *Web Site:* www.zondervan.com, pg 248

Peabody, William, GP Putnam's Sons (Hardcover), 375 Hudson St, New York, NY 10014 *Tel:* 212-366-2000 *Fax:* 212-366-2643 *E-mail:* online@penguinputnam.com *Web Site:* www.penguin.com/publishers/gpputnamssons, pg 178

Peacock, Hannah, Dorothy Canfield Fisher Book Award, 109 State St, Montpelier, VT 05609-0601 *Tel:* 802-828-2721 *Web Site:* libraries.vermont.gov, pg 610

Peacock, Kathleen, Goose Lane Editions, 500 Beaverbrook Ct, Suite 330, Fredericton, NB E3B 5X4, Canada *Tel:* 506-450-4251 *Toll Free Tel:* 888-926-8377 *Fax:* 506-459-4991 *E-mail:* info@gooselane.com; customerservice@gooselane.com *Web Site:* www.gooselane.com, pg 427

Pearce, Anne, Simon & Schuster, 1230 Avenue of the Americas, New York, NY 10020 *Tel:* 212-698-7000 *Toll Free Tel:* 800-223-2348 (cust serv); 800-223-2336 (orders) *Toll Free Fax:* 800-943-9831 (orders) *Web Site:* www.simonandschuster.com, pg 198

Pearce, John, Westwood Creative Artists Ltd, 138 Sussex Mews, Toronto, ON M5S-2K1, Canada *Tel:* 416-964-3302 *Fax:* 416-964-3302 *E-mail:* wca_office@wcaltd.com *Web Site:* www.wcaltd.com, pg 508

Pearce, Dr Scott, Center for East Asian Studies (CEAS), Western Washington University, 516 High St, Bellingham, WA 98225 *Tel:* 360-650-3339 *Fax:* 360-650-6110 *E-mail:* eas@wwu.edu *Web Site:* www.wwu.edu/eas, pg 48

Pearl, Allyson, Random House Publishing Group, 1745 Broadway, New York, NY 10019 *Toll Free Tel:* 800-200-3552 *Web Site:* www.randomhousebooks.com, pg 181

Pearlman, Robb, BenBella Books Inc, 10300 N Central Expwy, Suite 400, Dallas, TX 75231 *Tel:* 214-750-3600 *E-mail:* feedback@benbellabooks.com *Web Site:* www.benbellabooks.com; www.smartpopbooks.com, pg 31

Pearpoint, Jack, Inclusion Press International, 47 Indian Trail, Toronto, ON M6R 1Z8, Canada *Tel:* 416-658-5363 *Fax:* 416-658-5067 *E-mail:* inclusionpress@inclusion.com *Web Site:* www.inclusion.com, pg 430

Pearson, Lisa, Siglio, PO Box 111, Catskill, NY 12414 *Tel:* 310-857-6935 *E-mail:* publisher@sigliopress.com *Web Site:* sigliopress.com, pg 198

Pearson, Michael, The Mathematical Association of America, 1529 18 St NW, Washington, DC 20036-1358 *Tel:* 202-387-5200 *Toll Free Tel:* 800-741-9415 *Fax:* 202-265-2384 *E-mail:* maahq@maa.org; advertising@maa.org (pubns) *Web Site:* www.maa.org, pg 134

Pearson, Nancy, Scholastic Canada Ltd, 604 King St W, Toronto, ON M5V 1E1, Canada *Tel:* 905-887-7323 *Toll Free Tel:* 800-268-3860 (CN) *Toll Free Fax:* 866-387-4944 *E-mail:* custserve@scholastic.ca *Web Site:* www.scholastic.ca, pg 439

Pearson, Tawny, Michigan Municipal League, 1675 Green Rd, Ann Arbor, MI 48105 *Tel:* 734-662-3246 *Toll Free Tel:* 800-653-2483 *E-mail:* contact@mml.org *Web Site:* www.mml.org, pg 139

Pease, Pamela, Paintbox Press, 275 Madison Ave, Suite 600, New York, NY 10016 *Tel:* 212-878-6610 *E-mail:* info@paintboxpress.com *Web Site:* www.paintboxpress.com, pg 159

Peattie, Gary R, DeVorss & Co, 553 Constitution Ave, Camarillo, CA 93012-8510 *Tel:* 805-322-9010 *Toll Free Tel:* 800-843-5743 *Fax:* 805-322-9011 *E-mail:* service@devorss.com *Web Site:* www.devorss.com, pg 64

Pecorale, Christina, Simon & Schuster Sales Division, 1230 Avenue of the Americas, New York, NY 10020 *Tel:* 212-698-7000, pg 200

Pedersen, Nadine, University of British Columbia Press, 2029 West Mall, Vancouver, BC V6T 1Z2, Canada *Tel:* 604-822-5959 *Toll Free Tel:* 877-377-

Perlee, Mr Christian, McGraw-Hill Contemporary Learning Series, 501 Bell St, Dubuque, IA 52001 *Toll Free Tel:* 800-243-6532 *Web Site:* www.mhcls.com, pg 135

Perlman, Jim, Holy Cow! Press, PO Box 3170, Mount Royal Sta, Duluth, MN 55803 *Tel:* 218-724-1653 *E-mail:* holycow@holycowpress.org *Web Site:* www. holycowpress.org, pg 102

Perlman, Michael, Simon & Schuster, Inc, 1230 Avenue of the Americas, New York, NY 10020 *Tel:* 212-698-7000 *Toll Free Tel:* 800-223-2336 (orders) *Fax:* 212-698-7007 *Toll Free Fax:* 800-943-9831 (orders) *E-mail:* firstname.lastname@simonandschuster.com; purchaseorders@simonandschuster.com (orders) *Web Site:* www.simonandschuster.com, pg 199

Perlmutter, Christie, Texas Tech University Press, 1120 Main St, 2nd fl, Lubbock, TX 79401 *Tel:* 806-742-2982 *Toll Free Tel:* 800-832-4042 *E-mail:* ttup@ttu. edu *Web Site:* www.ttupress.org, pg 216

Perlstein, Jill, American Booksellers Association, 333 Westchester Ave, Suite S202, White Plains, NY 10604 *Tel:* 914-406-7500 *Toll Free Tel:* 800-637-0037 *Fax:* 914-417-4013 *E-mail:* info@bookweb.org *Web Site:* www.bookweb.org, pg 522

Permingeat, Max, Les Editions de Mortagne, CP 116, Boucherville, QC J4B 5E6, Canada *Tel:* 450-641-2387 *Fax:* 450-655-6092 *E-mail:* info@editionsdemortagne. com *Web Site:* www.editionsdemortagne.com, pg 422

Perreault, Diane, Beliveau Editeur, 567 rue Bienville, Boucherville, QC J4B 2Z5, Canada *Tel:* 450-679-1933 *Web Site:* www.beliveauediteur.com, pg 416

Perreault, Melanie, Les Editions Pierre Tisseyre, 155, rue Maurice, Rosemere, QC J7A 2S8, Canada *Tel:* 514-335-0777 *Fax:* 514-335-6723 *E-mail:* info@edtisseyre. ca *Web Site:* www.tisseyre.ca, pg 425

Perreault, Michel, Les Editions Fides, 7333 place des Roseraies, bureau 100, Anjou, QC H1M 2X6, Canada *Tel:* 514-745-4290 *Fax:* 514-745-4299 *E-mail:* editions@groupefides.com *Web Site:* www. editionsfides.com, pg 423

Perri, Trevor, Northwestern University Press, 629 Noyes St, Evanston, IL 60208-4210 *Tel:* 847-491-2046 *Toll Free Tel:* 800-621-2736 (orders only) *Fax:* 847-491-8150 *E-mail:* nupress@northwestern.edu *Web Site:* www.nupress.northwestern.edu, pg 152

Perriello, Rachael, Penguin Random House LLC, 1745 Broadway, New York, NY 10019 *Tel:* 212-782-9000 *Toll Free Tel:* 800-726-0600 *Web Site:* www. penguinrandomhouse.com, pg 164

Perrin, Brian, HarperCollins General Books Group, 195 Broadway, New York, NY 10007 *Tel:* 212-207-7000 *Web Site:* www.harpercollins.com, pg 93

Perrin, Christopher, Classical Academic Press, 515 S 32 St, Camp Hill, PA 17011 *Tel:* 717-730-0711 *Toll Free Tel:* 866-730-0711 *Fax:* 717-730-0721 *Toll Free Fax:* 866-730-0721 *E-mail:* info@ classicalsubjects.com; orders@classicalsubjects.com *Web Site:* classicalacademicpress.com, pg 53

Perrin, Christopher, Plum Tree Books, 2151 Market St, Camp Hill, PA 17011 *Tel:* 717-730-0711 *E-mail:* info@classicalsubjects.com *Web Site:* www. plumtreebooks.com, pg 171

Perrone, Madeline, Literary Artists Representatives, 575 West End Ave, Suite GRC, New York, NY 10024-2711 *Tel:* 212-679-7788 *E-mail:* litartists@aol.com, pg 493

Perry, Bonnie, Beacon Hill Press of Kansas City, PO Box 419527, Kansas City, MO 64141 *Tel:* 816-931-1900 *Toll Free Tel:* 800-877-0700 (cust serv) *Fax:* 816-531-0923 *Toll Free Fax:* 800-849-9827 *E-mail:* orders@thefoundrypublishing. com; customercare@thefoundrypublishing.com *Web Site:* www.thefoundrypublishing.com, pg 29

Perry, David, NYSCA/NYFA Artist Fellowships, 20 Jay St, 7th fl, Brooklyn, NY 11201 *Tel:* 212-366-6900 *Fax:* 212-366-1778 *E-mail:* info@nyfa.org *Web Site:* www.nyfa.org, pg 649

Perry, Hannah, Maine Literary Awards, Glickman Family Library, 314 Forest Ave, Rm 318, Portland, ME 04101 *Tel:* 207-228-8263 *E-mail:* info@mainewriters.org *Web Site:* mainewriters.org/programs/maine-literary-awards, pg 637

Perry, Hannah, Maine Writers & Publishers Alliance, Glickman Family Library, 314 Forest Ave, Rm 318, Portland, ME 04101 *Tel:* 207-228-8263 *E-mail:* info@ mainewriters.org *Web Site:* mainewriters.org, pg 537

Perry, Rochon, Cedar Grove Publishing, 3205 Elmhurst St, Rowlett, TX 75088 *Tel:* 415-364-8292 *E-mail:* queries@cedargrovebooks.com *Web Site:* www.cedargrovebooks.com, pg 47

Perry, Sheila M, Sophia Institute Press®, 18 Celina Ave, Unit 1, Nashua, NH 03063 *Tel:* 603-641-9344 *Toll Free Tel:* 800-888-9344 *Fax:* 603-641-8108 *Toll Free Fax:* 888-288-2259 *E-mail:* orders@sophiainstitute. com *Web Site:* www.sophiainstitute.org, pg 203

Perry, Tom, Random House Publishing Group, 1745 Broadway, New York, NY 10019 *Toll Free Tel:* 800-200-3552 *Web Site:* www.randomhousebooks.com, pg 181

Pershing, John, Hackett Publishing Co Inc, 3333 Massachusetts Ave, Indianapolis, IN 46218 *Tel:* 317-635-9250 (orders & cust serv); 617-497-6303 (edit off & sales) *Fax:* 317-635-9292; 617-661-8703 (edit off) *Toll Free Tel:* 800-783-9213 *E-mail:* customer@ hackettpublishing.com; editorial@hackettpublishing. com *Web Site:* www.hackettpublishing.com, pg 91

Person, Hara, Central Conference of American Rabbis/CCAR Press, 355 Lexington Ave, New York, NY 10017 *Tel:* 212-972-3636 *Fax:* 212-692-0819 *E-mail:* info@ccarpress.org *Web Site:* www.ccarpress. org, pg 48

Pesch, Fran, Dayton Playhouse FutureFest, PO Box 3017, Dayton, OH 45401-3017 *Tel:* 937-424-8477 *Fax:* 937-424-0062 *E-mail:* futurefest@ thedaytonplayhouse.com *Web Site:* wordpress. daytonplayhouse.com, pg 609

Pesek, Diana, Penn State University Press, University Support Bldg 1, Suite C, 820 N University Dr, University Park, PA 16802-1003 *Tel:* 814-865-1327 *Toll Free Tel:* 800-326-9180 *Fax:* 814-863-1408 *Toll Free Fax:* 877-778-2665 *E-mail:* orders@psupress.org; orders@eisenbrauns.org *Web Site:* www.psupress.org; www.eisenbrauns.org, pg 166

Peskin, Elizabeth, little bee books, 251 Park Ave S, 12th fl, New York, NY 10010 *Toll Free Tel:* 844-321-0237 *E-mail:* info@littlebeebooks.com *Web Site:* littlebeebooks.com, pg 125

Peskin, Elizabeth, Random House Children's Books, 1745 Broadway, 10th fl, New York, NY 10019 *Tel:* 212-782-9000 *Web Site:* www.randomhousekids. com, pg 181

Peskin, Joy, Farrar, Straus & Giroux Books for Young Readers, 120 Broadway, New York, NY 10271 *Tel:* 212-741-6900 *Toll Free Tel:* 888-330-8477 (orders) *Fax:* 212-633-9385 *Web Site:* us.macmillan. com/mackids; www.mackidsbooks.com, pg 76

Pester, John, Living Stream Ministry (LSM), 2431 W La Palma Ave, Anaheim, CA 92801 *Tel:* 714-991-4681 *Toll Free Tel:* 800-549-5164 *Fax:* 714-236-6005 *E-mail:* books@lsm.org *Web Site:* www.lsm.org, pg 127

Peters, John G Jr, Palm Springs Writers Guild, PO Box 947, Rancho Mirage, CA 92270-0947 *Web Site:* www. palmspringswritersguild.org, pg 543

Peters, Michelle, Association of Manitoba Book Publishers, 100 Arthur St, Suite 404, Winnipeg, MB R3B 1H3, Canada *Tel:* 204-947-3335 *E-mail:* ambp@ mts.net *Web Site:* ambp.ca, pg 526

Peters, Simone, Tortuga Press, 2777 Yulupa Ave, PMB 181, Santa Rosa, CA 95405 *Tel:* 707-544-4720 *Fax:* 707-595-5331 *E-mail:* info@tortugapress.com *Web Site:* www.tortugapress.com, pg 219

Peterseil, Shlomo, The Toby Press LLC, PO Box 8531, New Milford, CT 06776-8531 *Tel:* 203-830-8508 *Fax:* 203-830-8512 *E-mail:* toby@tobypress.com; sales@korenpub.com *Web Site:* www.tobypress.com; www.korenpub.com, pg 218

Petersell, Linda, BPA Worldwide, 100 Beard Sawmill Rd, 6th fl, Shelton, CT 06484 *Tel:* 203-447-2800 *Fax:* 203-447-2900 *E-mail:* info@bpaww.com *Web Site:* www.bpaww.com, pg 529

Petersen, Alison, Chronicle Books, 680 Second St, San Francisco, CA 94107 *Tel:* 415-537-4200 *Toll Free Tel:* 800-759-0190 (cust serv) *Fax:* 415-537-4460 *Toll Free Fax:* 800-858-7787 (orders); 800-286-9471 (cust serv) *E-mail:* frontdesk@chroniclebooks.com *Web Site:* www.chroniclebooks.com, pg 52

Petersen, Ken, Discovery House Publishers, 3000 Kraft Ave SE, Grand Rapids, MI 49512 *Tel:* 616-942-2803 *Toll Free Tel:* 800-653-8333 (cust serv) *E-mail:* support@dhp.org; customerservice@dhp.org *Web Site:* www.dhp.org, pg 65

Peterson, Carol, Penguin Group USA, A Penguin Random House Company, 375 Hudson St, New York, NY 10014 *Tel:* 212-366-2000 *Toll Free Tel:* 800-847-5515 (inside sales); 800-631-8571 (cust serv) *Fax:* 212-366-2666; 607-775-4829 (inside sales) *E-mail:* online@us.penguingroup.com *Web Site:* www. penguin.com, pg 163

Peterson, Gayla, Foil & Specialty Effects Association (FSEA), 2150 SW Westport Dr, Suite 101, Topeka, KS 66614 *Tel:* 785-271-5816 *Fax:* 785-271-6404 *E-mail:* info@fsea.com *Web Site:* www.fsea.com, pg 533

Peterson, James, Coaches Choice, 5 Harris Ct, Bldg N, Suite 4, Monterey, CA 93940 *Toll Free Tel:* 888-229-5745 *Fax:* 831-372-6075 *E-mail:* info@coacheschoice. com *Web Site:* www.coacheschoice.com, pg 54

Peterson, Jeff, Foil & Specialty Effects Association (FSEA), 2150 SW Westport Dr, Suite 101, Topeka, KS 66614 *Tel:* 785-271-5816 *Fax:* 785-271-6404 *E-mail:* info@fsea.com *Web Site:* www.fsea.com, pg 533

Peterson, Jeff, Search Institute Press®, The Banks Bldg, Suite 125, 615 First Ave NE, Minneapolis, MN 55413 *Tel:* 612-376-8955; 612-692-5520 *Toll Free Tel:* 800-888-7828 *Fax:* 612-692-5553 *E-mail:* si@search-institute.org *Web Site:* www.search-institute.org, pg 196

Peterson, Kathryn, Atlantic Center for the Arts Master Artist-in-Residence Program, 1414 Art Center Ave, New Smyrna Beach, FL 32168 *Tel:* 386-427-6975 *Toll Free Tel:* 800-393-6975 *Fax:* 386-427-5669 *E-mail:* program@atlanticcenterforthearts.org *Web Site:* atlanticcenterforthearts.org, pg 573

Peterson, Laura Blake, Curtis Brown Ltd, 228 E 45 St, 3rd fl, New York, NY 10017 *Tel:* 212-473-5400 *Web Site:* www.curtisbrown.com, pg 478

Peterson, Lowell, Writers Guild of America, East (WGAE), 250 Hudson St, Suite 700, New York, NY 10013 *Tel:* 212-767-7800 *Fax:* 212-582-1909 *Web Site:* www.wgaeast.org, pg 549

Peterson, Mike, The Child's World Inc, 1980 Lookout Dr, North Mankato, MN 56003-1705 *Tel:* 507-385-1044 *Toll Free Tel:* 800-599-READ (599-7323) *Toll Free Fax:* 888-320-2329 *E-mail:* sales@childsworld. com *Web Site:* childsworld.com, pg 51

Peterson, Tom, Creative Editions, PO Box 227, Mankato, MN 56002 *Tel:* 507-388-6273 *Toll Free Tel:* 800-445-6209 *Fax:* 507-388-2746 *E-mail:* info@ thecreativecompany.us; orders@thecreativecompany.us *Web Site:* www.thecreativecompany.us, pg 59

Peterson, Tony, The Society of Professional Journalists (SPJ), Eugene S Pulliam National Journalism Ctr, 3909 N Meridian St, Suite 200, Indianapolis, IN 46208 *Tel:* 317-927-8000 *Fax:* 317-920-4789 *E-mail:* spj@spj.org *Web Site:* www.spj.org, pg 548

Petilos, Randolph, University of Chicago Press, 1427 E 60 St, Chicago, IL 60637-2954 *Tel:* 773-702-7700; 773-702-7600 *Toll Free Tel:* 800-621-2736 (orders) *Fax:* 773-702-9756; 773-660-2235 (orders); 773-702-2708 *E-mail:* custserv@press.uchicago.edu; marketing@press.uchicago.edu *Web Site:* www.press. uchicago.edu, pg 226

Petitt, Tracey, Rizzoli International Publications Inc, 300 Park Ave S, 4th fl, New York, NY 10010-5399 *Tel:* 212-387-3400 *Toll Free Tel:* 800-522-6657 (orders only) *Fax:* 212-387-3535 *E-mail:* publicity@rizzoliusa. com *Web Site:* www.rizzoliusa.com, pg 185

Petrick, Emily, Random House Children's Books, 1745 Broadway, 10th fl, New York, NY 10019 *Tel:* 212-782-9000 *Web Site:* www.randomhousekids.com, pg 181

Petrie, Jeremy, Willow Creek Press, 9931 Hwy 70 W, Minocqua, WI 54548 *Tel:* 715-358-7010 *Toll Free Tel:* 800-850-9453 *Fax:* 715-358-2807 *E-mail:* info@willowcreekpress.com *Web Site:* www. willowcreekpress.com, pg 242

Petrie, Tom, Willow Creek Press, 9931 Hwy 70 W, Minocqua, WI 54548 *Tel:* 715-358-7010 *Toll Free Tel:* 800-850-9453 *Fax:* 715-358-2807 *E-mail:* info@willowcreekpress.com *Web Site:* www. willowcreekpress.com, pg 242

Petrillo, Alan M, Excalibur Publications, PO Box 89667, Tucson, AZ 85752-9667 *Tel:* 520-575-9057 *E-mail:* excaliburpublications@centurylink.net, pg 74

Petrovich, Aaron, Akashic Books, 232 Third St, Suite A-115, Brooklyn, NY 11215 *Tel:* 718-643-9193 *Fax:* 718-643-9195 *E-mail:* info@akashicbooks.com *Web Site:* www.akashicbooks.com, pg 6

Petrowski, Mary Jane, Association of College & Research Libraries (ACRL), 50 E Huron St, Chicago, IL 60611 *Tel:* 312-280-2523 *Toll Free Tel:* 800-545-2433 (ext 2523) *Fax:* 312-280-2520 *E-mail:* acrl@ala. org *Web Site:* www.ala.org/acrl, pg 23

Petrucci, Ashley, Temple University Press, 1852 N Tenth St, Philadelphia, PA 19122-6099 *Tel:* 215-926-2140 *Toll Free Tel:* 800-621-2736 *Fax:* 215-926-2141 *E-mail:* tempress@temple.edu *Web Site:* tupress. temple.edu, pg 214

Petrusewicz, Mary, Wisdom Publications Inc, 199 Elm St, Somerville, MA 02144 *Tel:* 617-776-7416 *Toll Free Tel:* 800-272-4050 (orders) *Fax:* 617-776-7841 *E-mail:* info@wisdompubs.org; submission@ wisdompubs.org *Web Site:* www.wisdompubs.org, pg 243

Pettigrew, Jean, Les Editions Alire, 120 cote du Passage, Levis, QC G6V 5S9, Canada *Tel:* 418-835-4441 *Fax:* 418-838-4443 *E-mail:* info@alire.com *Web Site:* www.alire.com, pg 422

Pettit, Kristen, HarperCollins Children's Books, 195 Broadway, New York, NY 10007 *Tel:* 212-207-7000 *Web Site:* www.harpercollins.com/childrens, pg 93

Pfaff, Eugene E Jr, Tudor Publishers Inc, 3109 Shady Lawn Dr, Greensboro, NC 27408 *Tel:* 336-288-5395 *E-mail:* tudorpublishers@triad.rr.com, pg 221

Pfeifer, Alice, St Martin's Press, LLC, 120 Broadway, New York, NY 10271 *Tel:* 646-307-5151 *Web Site:* us. macmillan.com/smp, pg 190

Pfeiffer, Alice Randal, Syracuse University Press, 621 Skytop Rd, Suite 110, Syracuse, NY 13244-5290 *Tel:* 315-443-5534 *Toll Free Tel:* 800-365-8929 (cust serv) *Fax:* 315-443-5545 *E-mail:* supress@syr.edu *Web Site:* press.syr.edu, pg 212

Pfister, Jenny, The Goddard Riverside Stephan Russo Book Prize, 593 Columbus Ave, New York, NY 10024 *Web Site:* bookprize.goddard.org, pg 619

Pfund, Niko, Oxford University Press USA, 198 Madison Ave, New York, NY 10016 *Toll Free Tel:* 800-451-7556 (orders); 800-445-9714 (cust serv) *Fax:* 919-677-1303 *E-mail:* custserv.us@oup.com *Web Site:* global.oup.com, pg 158

Phair, Sarah, Sanford J Greenburger Associates Inc, 55 Fifth Ave, New York, NY 10003 *Tel:* 212-206-5600 *Fax:* 212-463-8718 *Web Site:* greenburger.com; www. sjga.com, pg 487

Pharand, Ginger, Palimpsest Press, 1171 Eastlawn Ave, Windsor, ON N8S 3J1, Canada *Tel:* 519-259-2112 *E-mail:* publicity@palimpsestpress.ca *Web Site:* www. palimpsestpress.ca, pg 435

Phelan, Shani, IACP Cookbook Awards, 45 Rockefeller Plaza, Suite 2000, New York, NY 10111 *Tel:* 646-358-4957 *Toll Free Tel:* 866-358-4951 *Toll Free Fax:* 866-358-2524 *E-mail:* info@iacp.com *Web Site:* www.iacp. com; www.iacp.com/award/more/cookbook, pg 625

Phelan, Sheila, DK Publishing, 1450 Broadway, Suite 801, New York, NY 10018 *Tel:* 646-674-4000 *Toll Free Tel:* 800-733-3000 *Fax:* 646-674-4020 *E-mail:* marketing@dk.com; publicity@ dk.com; csorders@penguinrandomhouse.com; ecustomerservice@randomhouse.com *Web Site:* www. dk.com; www.penguin.com, pg 65

Phi, Bao, McKnight Artist Fellowship for Writers, Open Book, Suite 200, 1011 Washington Ave S, Minneapolis, MN 55415 *Tel:* 612-215-2575 *Fax:* 612-215-2576 *E-mail:* loft@loft.org *Web Site:* www.loft. org, pg 640

Philips, Ariana, Jean V Naggar Literary Agency Inc (JVNLA), 216 E 75 St, Suite 1-E, New York, NY 10021 *Tel:* 212-794-1082 *E-mail:* jvnla@jvnla.com *Web Site:* www.jvnla.com, pg 497

Philips, Becky, AMWA Annual Conference, 30 W Gude Dr, Suite 525, Rockville, MD 20850-4357 *Tel:* 240-238-0940 *Fax:* 301-294-9006 *E-mail:* amwa@amwa. org *Web Site:* www.amwa.org, pg 573

Phillips, Adam, McFarland, 960 NC Hwy 88 W, Jefferson, NC 28640 *Tel:* 336-246-4460 *Toll Free Tel:* 800-253-2187 (orders) *Fax:* 336-246-5018; 336-246-4403 (orders) *E-mail:* info@mcfarlandpub.com *Web Site:* mcfarlandbooks.com, pg 135

Phillips, Aemilia, Stuart Krichevsky Literary Agency Inc, 6 E 39 St, Suite 500, New York, NY 10016 *Tel:* 212-725-5288 *Fax:* 212-725-5275 *E-mail:* query@ skagency.com *Web Site:* skagency.com, pg 492

Phillips, Andrew V, Windhaven®, 466 Rte 10, Orford, NH 03777 *Tel:* 603-512-9251 (cell) *Web Site:* www. windhavenpress.com, pg 471

Phillips, Barb, The Literary Press Group of Canada, 425 Adelaide St W, Suite 700, Toronto, ON M5V 3C1, Canada *Tel:* 416-483-1321 *Web Site:* www.lpg.ca, pg 536

Phillips, Betsy, Vanderbilt University Press, 2301 Vanderbilt Place, PMB 401813, Nashville, TN 37240-1813 *Tel:* 615-322-3585 *Toll Free Tel:* 800-848-6224 (orders only) *Fax:* 615-343-0308 *E-mail:* vupress@vanderbilt.edu *Web Site:* www. vanderbiltuniversitypress.com, pg 235

Phillips, Frances, Northern California Book Awards, c/o Poetry Flash, 1450 Fourth St, Suite 4, Berkeley, CA 94710 *Tel:* 510-525-5476 *Fax:* 510-525-6752 *E-mail:* editor@poetryflash.org; ncbr@poetryflash.org *Web Site:* poetryflash.org, pg 649

Phillips, Jenna, Vanderbilt University Press, 2301 Vanderbilt Place, PMB 401813, Nashville, TN 37240-1813 *Tel:* 615-322-3585 *Toll Free Tel:* 800-848-6224 (orders only) *Fax:* 615-343-0308 *E-mail:* vupress@vanderbilt.edu *Web Site:* www. vanderbiltuniversitypress.com, pg 235

Phillips, Julie, Andrews McMeel Publishing LLC, 1130 Walnut St, Kansas City, MO 64106-2109 *Toll Free Tel:* 800-851-8923; 800-943-9839 (cust serv) *Toll Free Fax:* 800-943-9831 (orders) *E-mail:* sales@ amuniversal.com *Web Site:* www.andrewsmcmeel.com; publishing.andrewsmcmeel.com, pg 16

Phillips, Kathleen, North American Agricultural Journalists (NAAJ), 6434 Hurta Lane, Bryan, TX 77808 *Tel:* 979-324-4302 *Web Site:* www.naaj.net, pg 542

Phillips, Kirsten, Portage & Main Press, 318 McDermot, Suite 100, Winnipeg, MB R3A 0A2, Canada *Tel:* 204-987-3500 *Toll Free Tel:* 800-667-9673 *Fax:* 204-947-0080 *Toll Free Fax:* 866-734-8477 *E-mail:* customerservice@portageandmainpress.com *Web Site:* www.portageandmainpress.com, pg 437

Phillips, Laura, Bloomsbury Publishing Inc, 1385 Broadway, 5th fl, New York, NY 10018 *Tel:* 212-419-5300 *E-mail:* marketingusa@bloomsbury.com; adultpublicityusa@bloomsbury.com; askacademic@ bloomsbury.com *Web Site:* www.bloomsbury.com, pg 36

Phillips, Meghan, The Vendome Press, 244 Fifth Ave, Suite 2043, New York, NY 10001 *Tel:* 212-737-1857 *E-mail:* info@vendomepress.com *Web Site:* www. vendomepress.com, pg 235

Phinn, Jessica, Nelson Education Ltd, 1120 Birchmount Rd, Scarborough, ON M1K 5G4, Canada *Tel:* 416-752-9100 *Toll Free Tel:* 800-268-2222 (cust serv) *Fax:* 416-752-8101 *Toll Free Fax:* 800-430-4445 *E-mail:* peopleandengagement@nelson.com *Web Site:* www.nelson.com, pg 434

Phirman, James, Houghton Mifflin Harcourt, 125 High St, Boston, MA 02110 *Tel:* 617-351-5000 *Toll Free Tel:* 855-969-4642; 800-225-5425 (K-12 educ materials); 800-323-9540 (assessment materials); 877-219-1537 (SkillsTutor); 888-242-6747 (Innovation in Educ Group); 800-225-3362 (Trade & Ref Div) *Toll Free Fax:* 800-269-5232 *E-mail:* myhmhco@hmhco. com *Web Site:* www.hmhco.com, pg 103

Phua, Max, World Scientific Publishing Co Inc, 27 Warren St, Suite 401-402, Hackensack, NJ 07601 *Tel:* 201-487-9655 *Fax:* 201-487-9656 *E-mail:* wspc_us@wspc.com; sales@wspc.com; mkt@wspc.com; editor@wspc.com *Web Site:* www. worldscientific.com, pg 245

Phuna, K K, World Scientific Publishing Co Inc, 27 Warren St, Suite 401-402, Hackensack, NJ 07601 *Tel:* 201-487-9655 *Fax:* 201-487-9656 *E-mail:* wspc_us@wspc.com; sales@wspc.com; mkt@wspc.com; editor@wspc.com *Web Site:* www. worldscientific.com, pg 245

Picazio, Mr Ryan, Hackett Publishing Co Inc, 3333 Massachusetts Ave, Indianapolis, IN 46218 *Tel:* 317-635-9250 (orders & cust serv); 617-497-6303 (edit off & sales) *Fax:* 317-635-9292; 617-661-8703 (edit off) *Toll Free Fax:* 800-783-9213 *E-mail:* customer@ hackettpublishing.com; editorial@hackettpublishing. com *Web Site:* www.hackettpublishing.com, pg 91

Piche, Mireille, University of Ottawa Press (Presses de l'Université d'Ottawa), 542 King Edward Ave, Ottawa, ON K1N 6N5, Canada *Tel:* 613-562-5246 *Fax:* 613-562-5247 *E-mail:* puo-uop@uottawa.ca; acquisitions@ uottawa.ca *Web Site:* press.uottawa.ca, pg 444

Pickett, Patty, Accuity, 1007 Church St, 6th fl, Evanston, IL 60201 *Tel:* 847-676-9600 *Toll Free Tel:* 800-321-3373 *Fax:* 847-933-8101 *E-mail:* customerservice@ accuity.com *Web Site:* www.accuity.com, pg 4

Pieper, Molly, Plume, 375 Hudson St, New York, NY 10014 *Tel:* 212-366-2000 *Fax:* 212-243-6002 *Web Site:* www.penguin.com/publishers/plume, pg 171

Pierce, Gregory, ACTA Publications, 4848 N Clark St, Chicago, IL 60640 *Toll Free Tel:* 800-397-2282 *E-mail:* actapublications@actapublications.com *Web Site:* www.actapublications.com, pg 4

Pierce, Jennifer Tolo, Chronicle Books, 680 Second St, San Francisco, CA 94107 *Tel:* 415-537-4200 *Toll Free Tel:* 800-759-0190 (cust serv) *Fax:* 415-537-4460 *Toll Free Fax:* 800-858-7787 (orders); 800-286-9471 (cust serv) *E-mail:* frontdesk@chroniclebooks.com *Web Site:* www.chroniclebooks.com, pg 51

Pierce, Valerie, Sourcebooks LLC, 1935 Brookdale Rd, Suite 139, Naperville, IL 60563 *Tel:* 630-961-3900 *Toll Free Tel:* 800-432-7444 *Fax:* 630-961-2168 *E-mail:* info@sourcebooks.com; customersupport@ sourcebooks.com *Web Site:* www.sourcebooks.com, pg 204

Pierpont, Amy, Grand Central Publishing, 1290 Avenue of the Americas, New York, NY 10104 *Tel:* 212-364-1100 *Web Site:* www.hachettebookgroup.com, pg 88

Pierre, Leah, Ladderbird Literary Agency, 45 Midland St, Worcester, MA 01602 *Tel:* 508-459-9590 *Web Site:* www.ladderbird.com, pg 492

Pierson, Caryl K, Math Teachers Press Inc, 4850 Park Glen Rd, Minneapolis, MN 55416 *Tel:* 952-545-6535 *Toll Free Tel:* 800-852-2435 *Fax:* 952-546-7502 *E-mail:* info@movingwithmath.com *Web Site:* www. movingwithmath.com, pg 134

Pierson, Jennifer deForest, Rizzoli International Publications Inc, 300 Park Ave S, 4th fl, New York, NY 10010-5399 *Tel:* 212-387-3400 *Toll Free*

Poster, Kendra, Algonquin Books, 400 Silver Cedar Ct, Suite 300, Chapel Hill, NC 27514-1585 *Tel:* 919-967-0108 *Fax:* 919-933-0272 *E-mail:* inquiry@algonquin. com *Web Site:* www.workman.com/algonquin, pg 7

Poster, Kendra, Workman Publishing Co Inc, 225 Varick St, 9th fl, New York, NY 10014-4381 *Tel:* 212-254-5900 *Toll Free Tel:* 800-722-7202 *Fax:* 212-254-8098 *E-mail:* info@workman.com; orders@workman.com *Web Site:* www.workman.com, pg 244

Posternak, Jeffrey, The Wylie Agency LLC, 250 W 57 St, Suite 2114, New York, NY 10107 *Tel:* 212-246-0069 *Fax:* 212-586-8953 *E-mail:* mail@wylieagency. com *Web Site:* www.wylieagency.com, pg 509

Potash, Dan, Simon & Schuster Children's Publishing, 1230 Avenue of the Americas, New York, NY 10020 *Tel:* 212-698-7000 *Web Site:* www.simonandschuster. com/kids; www.simonandschuster.com/teen; simonandschuster.net; simonandschuster.biz, pg 199

Potorti, David, North Carolina Arts Council Writers Fellowships, 109 E Jones St, Raleigh, NC 27601 *Tel:* 919-807-6500 *Fax:* 919-807-6532 *E-mail:* ncarts@ncdcr.gov *Web Site:* www.ncarts.org, pg 649

Pottebaum, Gerard A, Treehaus Communications Inc, PO Box 249, Loveland, OH 45140-0249 *Tel:* 513-683-5716 *Toll Free Tel:* 800-638-4287 (orders) *Fax:* 513-683-2882 (orders) *E-mail:* treehaus@treehaus1.com *Web Site:* www.treehaus1.com, pg 220

Potter, Dr Beverly, Ronin Publishing Inc, PO Box 3436, Oakland, CA 94609 *Tel:* 510-420-3669 *Fax:* 510-420-3672 *E-mail:* ronin@roninpub.com *Web Site:* www. roninpub.com, pg 187

Potter, Claire, Perseus Books, 1290 Avenue of the Americas, New York, NY 10104 *Tel:* 212-340-8100 *Toll Free Tel:* 800-343-4499 (cust serv) *Fax:* 212-340-8105 *Web Site:* www.perseusbooks.com, pg 167

Potter, Donn King, Elizabeth H Backman, 86 Johnnycake Hollow Rd, Pine Plains, NY 12567 *Tel:* 518-398-9344 *Fax:* 518-398-6368 *E-mail:* bethcountry@fairpoint.net, pg 475

Pottetti, Kathy, Gell: A Finger Lakes Creative Retreat, 740 University Ave, Rochester, NY 14607-1259 *Tel:* 585-473-2590 *Fax:* 585-442-9333 *Web Site:* www. wab.org, pg 574

Potts, Patricia, BuilderBooks, 1201 15 St NW, Washington, DC 20005 *Tel:* 202-822-0200 *Toll Free Tel:* 800-223-2665 *Fax:* 202-266-8096 (edit) *E-mail:* info@nahb.com *Web Site:* builderbooks.com, pg 42

Pound, William T, National Conference of State Legislatures (NCSL), 7700 E First Place, Denver, CO 80230 *Tel:* 303-364-7700 *Fax:* 303-364-7800 *E-mail:* books@ncsl.org *Web Site:* www.ncsl.org, pg 146

Powell, Brenda, The Fairmont Press Inc, 700 Indian Trail, Lilburn, GA 30047 *Tel:* 770-925-9388 *Fax:* 770-381-9865 *Web Site:* www.fairmontpress.com, pg 75

Powell, Judith, Top of the Mountain Publishing, 4837 62 St N, St Petersburg, FL 33709 *Tel:* 727-391-3958, pg 219

Powell, Lynn, Oberlin College Press, 50 N Professor St, Oberlin, OH 44074-1091 *Tel:* 440-775-8408 *Fax:* 440-775-8124 *E-mail:* oc.press@oberlin.edu *Web Site:* www.oberlin.edu/ocpress, pg 154

Powell, Sherri, Contemporary Publishing Co of Raleigh Inc, 5849 Lease Lane, Raleigh, NC 27617 *Tel:* 919-851-8221 *Fax:* 919-851-6666 *E-mail:* questions@ contemporarypublishing.com *Web Site:* www. contemporarypublishing.com, pg 56

Powell, Tag, Top of the Mountain Publishing, 4837 62 St N, St Petersburg, FL 33709 *Tel:* 727-391-3958, pg 219

Power, Daniel, powerHouse Books, 32 Adams St, Brooklyn, NY 11201 *Tel:* 212-604-9074 *E-mail:* info@powerhousebooks.com *Web Site:* www. powerhousebooks.com, pg 172

Power, Nancy, Teachers College Press, 1234 Amsterdam Ave, New York, NY 10027 *Tel:* 212-678-3929 *Fax:* 212-678-4149 *E-mail:* tcpress@tc.edu *Web Site:* www.tcpress.com, pg 214

Powers, April, Society of Children's Book Writers & Illustrators (SCBWI), 6363 Wilshire Blvd, Suite 425, Los Angeles, CA 90048 *Tel:* 323-782-1010 *E-mail:* membership@scbwi.org *Web Site:* www.scbwi. org, pg 546

Powers, David, Pants On Fire Press, 2062 Harbor Cove Way, Winter Garden, FL 34787 *Tel:* 863-546-0760 *E-mail:* submission@pantsonfirepress.com *Web Site:* www.pantsonfirepress.com, pg 159

Powers, Emily, Beacon Press, 24 Farnsworth St, Boston, MA 02210-1409 *Tel:* 617-742-2110 *Fax:* 617-723-3097; 617-742-2290 *Web Site:* www.beacon.org, pg 29

Powers, Jessica, Cinco Puntos Press, 701 Texas Ave, El Paso, TX 79901 *Tel:* 915-838-1625 *Toll Free Tel:* 800-566-9072 *Fax:* 915-838-1635 *E-mail:* info@ cincopuntos.com *Web Site:* www.cincopuntos.com, pg 52

Powers, Joan, Candlewick Press, 99 Dover St, Somerville, MA 02144-2825 *Tel:* 617-661-3330 *Fax:* 617-661-0565 *E-mail:* bigbear@candlewick. com; salesinfo@candlewick.com *Web Site:* www. candlewick.com, pg 44

Powers, Katherine A, Nona Balakian Citation for Excellence in Reviewing, c/o 310 Lewis Ave, Brooklyn, NY 11221 *E-mail:* info@bookcritics.org *Web Site:* bookcritics.org/awards, pg 595

Powers, Marcia, Wilshire Book Co, 22647 Ventura Blvd, No 314, Woodland Hills, CA 91364-1416 *Tel:* 818-700-1522 *E-mail:* sales@mpowers.com *Web Site:* www.mpowers.com, pg 242

Powers, Mark, Apress Media LLC, 233 Spring St, 6th fl, New York, NY 10013 *Tel:* 212-460-1500 *E-mail:* editorial@apress.com; customerservice@ springernature.com *Web Site:* www.apress.com, pg 18

Powers, Retha, Henry Holt and Company, LLC, 120 Broadway, 23rd fl, New York, NY 10271 *Tel:* 646-307-5151 *Toll Free Tel:* 888-330-8477 (orders) *Fax:* 646-307-5285 *Web Site:* www.henryholt.com, pg 102

Powers, Retha, Publishing Certificate Program at City College of New York, Division of Humanities NAC 5225, City College of New York, New York, NY 10031 *Tel:* 212-650-7925 *Fax:* 212-650-7912 *E-mail:* ccnypub@aol.com *Web Site:* www.ccny.cuny. edu/publishing_certificate/index.html, pg 584

Pozier, Bernard, Ecrits des Forges, 992-A rue Royale, Trois-Rivieres, QC G9A 4H9, Canada *Tel:* 819-840-8492 *E-mail:* ecritsdesforges@gmail.com *Web Site:* www.ecritsdesforges.com, pg 421

Pozzuoli, Kristin, DK Publishing, 1450 Broadway, Suite 801, New York, NY 10018 *Tel:* 646-674-4000 *Toll Free Tel:* 800-733-3000 *Fax:* 646-674-4020 *E-mail:* marketing@dk.com; publicity@ dk.com; csorders@penguinrandomhouse.com; ecustomerservice@randomhouse.com *Web Site:* www. dk.com; www.penguin.com, pg 65

Prabhu, Prashant, Lumina Datamatics Inc, 4 Collins Ave, Plymouth, MA 02360 *Tel:* 508-746-0300 *Fax:* 508-746-3233 *Web Site:* luminadatamatics.com, pg 467

Praeger, Marta, Robert A Freedman Dramatic Agency Inc, 1501 Broadway, Suite 2310, New York, NY 10036 *Tel:* 212-840-5760 *Fax:* 212-840-5776, pg 485

Pranzatelli, Robert, Yale University Press, 302 Temple St, New Haven, CT 06511-8909 *Tel:* 203-432-0960; 203-432-0966 (sales); 401-531-2800 (cust serv) *Toll Free Tel:* 800-405-1619 (cust serv) *Fax:* 203-432-0948; 203-432-8485 (sales); 401-531-2801 (cust serv) *Toll Free Fax:* 800-406-9145 (cust serv) *E-mail:* sales. press@yale.edu (sales); customer.care@triliteral.org (cust serv) *Web Site:* www.yalebooks.com; yalepress. yale.edu/yupbooks, pg 246

Prasher, Madhu, Perseus Books, 1290 Avenue of the Americas, New York, NY 10104 *Tel:* 212-340-8100 *Toll Free Tel:* 800-343-4499 (cust serv) *Fax:* 212-340-8105 *Web Site:* www.perseusbooks.com, pg 167

Prato, Cate, Adams Media, 57 Littlefield St, Avon, MA 02322 *Tel:* 508-427-7100 *Web Site:* www. simonandschuster.com, pg 4

Pratt, Beth, Ohio University Press, Alden Library, Suite 101, 30 Park Place, Athens, OH 45701-2901 *Tel:* 740-593-1154 *Web Site:* www.ohioswallow.com, pg 155

Pratt, Beth, Hollis Summers Poetry Prize, Alden Library, Suite 101, 30 Park Place, Athens, OH 45701-2901 *Tel:* 740-593-1154 *Web Site:* www.ohioswallow. com/poetry_prize; ohiouniversitypress.submittable. com/submit (online submissions), pg 671

Pratt, Darrin, University Press of Colorado, 245 Century Circle, Suite 202, Louisville, CO 80027 *Tel:* 720-406-8849 *Toll Free Tel:* 800-621-2736 (orders) *Fax:* 720-406-3443 *Web Site:* www.upcolorado.com, pg 232

Pratt, Darrin, Utah State University Press, 3078 Old Main Hill, Logan, UT 84322-3078 *Tel:* 435-797-1362 *Web Site:* www.usupress.com, pg 235

Pratt, Jane, Association for PRINT Technologies (APTech), 1896 Preston White Dr, Reston, VA 20191 *Tel:* 703-264-7200 *Fax:* 703-620-0994 *E-mail:* aptech@aptech.org *Web Site:* www. printtechnologies.org, pg 525

Pratt, Randy, New Leaf Press, 3142 Hwy 103 N, Green Forest, AR 72638-2233 *Tel:* 870-438-5288 *Toll Free Tel:* 800-999-3777 *Fax:* 870-438-5120 *E-mail:* nlp@ newleafpress.net; submissions@newleafpress.net *Web Site:* www.nlpg.com, pg 149

Prellwitz, Gwendolyn, Coretta Scott King Book Awards, 225 N Michigan Ave, Suite 1300, Chicago, IL 60601 *Tel:* 312-944-6780 *Toll Free Tel:* 800-545-2433 *Fax:* 312-440-9374 *E-mail:* diversity@ala.org *Web Site:* www.ala.org/awardsgrants/coretta-scott-king-book-awards, pg 630

Prentiss, Winnie, Fair Winds Press, 100 Cummings Ctr, Suite 265-D, Beverly, MA 01915 *Tel:* 978-282-9590 *Fax:* 978-282-7765 *E-mail:* sales@quarto.com *Web Site:* www.quartoknows.com, pg 75

Prentiss, Winnie, Harvard Common Press, 100 Cummings Ctr, Suite 265-D, Beverly, MA 01915 *Tel:* 978-282-9590 *Fax:* 978-282-7765 *Web Site:* www. quartoknows.com/harvard-common-press, pg 94

Prescott, Deborah, Creative Writing Day & Workshops, PO Box 801, Abingdon, VA 24212-0801 *Tel:* 276-623-5266 *Fax:* 276-676-3076 *E-mail:* info@ vahighlandsfestival.org *Web Site:* vahighlandsfestival. org, pg 574

Presley, Todd, Chronicle Books, 680 Second St, San Francisco, CA 94107 *Tel:* 415-537-4200 *Toll Free Tel:* 800-759-0190 (cust serv) *Fax:* 415-537-4460 *Toll Free Fax:* 800-858-7787 (orders); 800-286-9471 (cust serv) *E-mail:* frontdesk@chroniclebooks.com *Web Site:* www.chroniclebooks.com, pg 51

Presson, Greg, Psychological Assessment Resources Inc (PAR), 16204 N Florida Ave, Lutz, FL 33549 *Tel:* 813-449-4065 *Toll Free Tel:* 800-331-8378 *Fax:* 813-961-2196 *Toll Free Fax:* 800-727-9329 *Web Site:* www.parinc.com, pg 177

Prestia, Sabrina, Jane Rotrosen Agency LLC, 85 Broad St, 28th fl, New York, NY 10004 *Tel:* 212-593-4330 *Fax:* 212-935-6985 *Web Site:* janerotrosen.com, pg 500

Preston, Douglas, The Authors Guild, 31 E 32 St, 7th fl, New York, NY 10016 *Tel:* 212-563-5904 *Fax:* 212-564-8363 *E-mail:* staff@authorsguild.org *Web Site:* www.authorsguild.org, pg 527

Prevette, Lindsay, Viking, 375 Hudson St, New York, NY 10014 *Tel:* 212-366-2000 *Fax:* 212-243-6002 *Web Site:* www.penguin.com/publishers/vikingbooks, pg 236

Preziosi, Alessandra, Houghton Mifflin Harcourt Trade & Reference Division, 125 High St, Boston, MA 02110 *Tel:* 617-351-5000 *Web Site:* www.hmhco.com, pg 104

Pricci, Linda, Rizzoli International Publications Inc, 300 Park Ave S, 4th fl, New York, NY 10010-5399 *Tel:* 212-387-3400 *Toll Free Tel:* 800-522-6657 (orders only) *Fax:* 212-387-3535 *E-mail:* publicity@rizzoliusa. com *Web Site:* www.rizzoliusa.com, pg 185

Price, Allyssa, Random House Children's Books, 1745 Broadway, 10th fl, New York, NY 10019 *Tel:* 212-782-9000 *Web Site:* www.randomhousekids.com, pg 181

Price, Bernadette B, Orbis Books, PO Box 302, Maryknoll, NY 10545-0302 *Tel:* 914-941-7636 *Toll Free Tel:* 800-258-5838 (orders, Mon-Fri 8AM-4PM EST) *Fax:* 914-941-7005 *E-mail:* orbisbooks@maryknoll.org *Web Site:* orbisbooks.com, pg 156

Price, Bruce, Marathon Press, 1500 Square Turn Blvd, Norfolk, NE 68701 *Tel:* 402-371-5040 *Toll Free Tel:* 800-228-0629 *Fax:* 402-371-9382 *E-mail:* info@marathonpress.net *Web Site:* www.marathonpress.com, pg 132

Price, Jodi, Princeton University Press, 41 William St, Princeton, NJ 08540-5237 *Tel:* 609-258-4900 *Fax:* 609-258-6305 *Web Site:* press.princeton.edu, pg 175

Price, Mathew, Mathew Price International Inc, 2404 W Main St, Wailuku, HI 96793 *Tel:* 808-244-9585 *E-mail:* info@mathewprice.com *Web Site:* www.mathewprice.com, pg 173

Price, Robert, Gatekeeper Press, 2167 Stringtown Rd, Suite 109, Columbus, OH 43123 *Toll Free Tel:* 866-535-0913 *Fax:* 216-803-0350 *E-mail:* info@gatekeeperpress.com *Web Site:* www.gatekeeperpress.com, pg 83

Price, Robert Esq, Price World Publishing, 3971 Hoover Rd, Suite 77, Columbus, OH 43123-2839 *Toll Free Tel:* 888-234-6896 *Fax:* 216-803-0350 *E-mail:* info@priceworldpublishing.com *Web Site:* www.priceworldpublishing.com, pg 174

Price, Todd Alan, Stanley Drama Award, One Campus Rd, Staten Island, NY 10301 *Tel:* 718-390-3223 *Fax:* 718-390-3323 *Web Site:* wagner.edu/theatre/stanley-drama, pg 670

Prichard, Rob, Penguin Group (Canada), 320 Front St W, Suite 1400, Toronto, ON M5V 3B6, Canada *Tel:* 416-364-4449 *Fax:* 416-598-7764 *E-mail:* customerservicescanada@penguinrandomhouse.com; publicity@ca.penguingroup.com *Web Site:* penguinrandomhouse.ca/imprints/penguin-canada, pg 436

Priddis, Ronald L, Signature Books Publishing LLC, 564 W 400 N, Salt Lake City, UT 84116-3411 *Toll Free Tel:* 800-356-5687 *E-mail:* people@signaturebooks.com *Web Site:* www.signaturebooks.com; www.signaturebookslibrary.org, pg 198

Priddle, Clive, Perseus Books, 1290 Avenue of the Americas, New York, NY 10104 *Tel:* 212-340-8100 *Toll Free Tel:* 800-343-4499 (cust serv) *Fax:* 212-340-8105 *Web Site:* www.perseusbooks.com, pg 167

Priddy, Kristine, Southern Illinois University Press, 1915 University Press Dr, SIUC Mail Code 6806, Carbondale, IL 62901-4323 *Tel:* 618-453-2281 *Fax:* 618-453-1221 *Web Site:* www.siupress.com, pg 205

Prielipp, Danielle, St Martin's Press, LLC, 120 Broadway, New York, NY 10271 *Tel:* 646-307-5151 *Web Site:* us.macmillan.com/smp, pg 190

Priest, Aaron M, The Aaron M Priest Literary Agency Inc, 200 W 41 St, 21st fl, New York, NY 10036 *Tel:* 212-818-0344 *Fax:* 212-573-9417 *E-mail:* info@aaronpriest.com *Web Site:* www.aaronpriest.com, pg 498

Prieur, Richard, Association nationale des editeurs de livres, 2514, blvd Rosemont, Montreal, QC H1Y 1K4, Canada *Tel:* 514-273-8130 *Toll Free Tel:* 866-900-ANEL (900-2635) *E-mail:* info@anel.qc.ca *Web Site:* www.anel.qc.ca, pg 526

Prin, Joel, New World Library, 14 Pamaron Way, Novato, CA 94949 *Tel:* 415-884-2100 *Toll Free Tel:* 800-227-3900 (ext 52, retail orders); 800-972-6657 *Fax:* 415-884-2199 *E-mail:* escort@newworldlibrary.com *Web Site:* www.newworldlibrary.com, pg 149

Prince, Danforth, Blood Moon Productions Ltd, 75 Saint Marks Place, Staten Island, NY 10301-1606 *Tel:* 718-556-9410 *E-mail:* danforthprince@gmail.com *Web Site:* bloodmoonproductions.com, pg 35

Pringle, Becky, National Education Association (NEA), 1201 16 St NW, Washington, DC 20036-3290 *Tel:* 202-833-4000 *Fax:* 202-822-7974 *Web Site:* www.nea.org, pg 146

Pringle, Becky, National Education Association (NEA), 1201 16 St NW, Washington, DC 20036-3290 *Tel:* 202-833-4000 *Fax:* 202-822-7974 *E-mail:* media-relations-team@nea.org *Web Site:* www.nea.org, pg 540

Prior, Robert, The MIT Press, One Rogers St, Cambridge, MA 02142 *Tel:* 617-253-5255 *Toll Free Tel:* 800-405-1619 (orders) *Fax:* 617-258-6779; 617-577-1545 (orders) *Web Site:* mitpress.mit.edu, pg 141

Pritchett, Jamie, The Knight Agency Inc, 232 W Washington St, Madison, GA 30650 *E-mail:* admin@knightagency.net *Web Site:* www.knightagency.net, pg 492

Pritzker, Amanda, Grand Central Publishing, 1290 Avenue of the Americas, New York, NY 10104 *Tel:* 212-364-1100 *Web Site:* www.hachettebookgroup.com, pg 88

Proia, Brandon, The University of North Carolina Press, 116 S Boundary St, Chapel Hill, NC 27514-3808 *Tel:* 919-966-3561 *E-mail:* uncpress@unc.edu *Web Site:* www.uncpress.org, pg 229

Pronk, Gord, Pronk Media Inc, PO Box 340, Beaverton, ON L0K 1A0, Canada *Tel:* 416-441-3760 *E-mail:* info@pronk.com *Web Site:* www.pronk.com, pg 469

Pronovost, Nita, Simon & Schuster Canada, 166 King St E, Suite 300, Toronto, ON M5A 1J3, Canada *Tel:* 647-427-8882 *Toll Free Tel:* 800-387-0446; 800-268-3216 (orders) *Fax:* 647-430-9446 *Toll Free Fax:* 888-849-8151 (orders) *E-mail:* info@simonandschuster.ca *Web Site:* www.simonandschuster.ca, pg 440

Prosser, Julia, Simon & Schuster, 1230 Avenue of the Americas, New York, NY 10020 *Tel:* 212-698-7000 *Toll Free Tel:* 800-223-2348 (cust serv); 800-223-2336 (orders) *Toll Free Fax:* 800-943-9831 (orders) *Web Site:* www.simonandschuster.com, pg 198

Prosswimmer, Kate, Simon & Schuster Children's Publishing, 1230 Avenue of the Americas, New York, NY 10020 *Tel:* 212-698-7000 *Web Site:* www.simonandschuster.com/kids; www.simonandschuster.com/teen; simonandschuster.net; simonandschuster.biz, pg 199

Protano, Generosa Gina, GGP Publishing Inc, 105 Calvert St, Suite 201, Harrison, NY 10528-3138 *Tel:* 914-834-8896 *Fax:* 914-834-7566 *Web Site:* www.GGPPublishing.com, pg 464, 486

Proulx, Marc, Editions FouLire, 4339, rue des Becassines, Quebec, QC G1G 1V5, Canada *Tel:* 418-628-4029 *Toll Free Tel:* 877-628-4029 (CN & US) *Fax:* 418-628-4801 *E-mail:* info@foulire.com; edition@foulire.com *Web Site:* www.foulire.com, pg 423

Provost, Cherry, Medal of Honor for Literature, 15 Gramercy Park S, New York, NY 10003 *Tel:* 212-475-3424 *E-mail:* literary@thenationalartsclub.org *Web Site:* www.nationalartsclub.org, pg 640

Pruett, Robert H, Brandylane Publishers Inc, 5 S First St, Richmond, VA 23219 *Tel:* 804-644-3090 *Fax:* 804-644-3092 *Web Site:* brandylanepublishers.com, pg 40

Prunty, Wyatt, Sewanee Writers' Conference, Stamler Ctr, 119 Gailor Hall, 735 University Ave, Sewanee, TN 37383 *Tel:* 931-598-1141; 931-598-1654 *E-mail:* swc@sewanee.edu *Web Site:* www.sewaneewriters.org, pg 578

Prusiewicz, Chloe, Sounds True Inc, 413 S Arthur Ave, Louisville, CO 80027 *Tel:* 303-665-3151 *Toll Free Tel:* 800-333-9185 (US); 888-303-9185 (US & CN) *E-mail:* customerservice@soundstrue.com; stpublicity@soundstrue.com *Web Site:* www.soundstrue.com, pg 204

Pryor, Ann, Kensington Publishing Corp, 119 W 40 St, New York, NY 10018 *Tel:* 212-407-1500 *Toll Free Tel:* 800-221-2647 *Fax:* 212-935-0699 *Web Site:* www.kensingtonbooks.com, pg 116

Pryor, Victoria Gould, Arcadia, 159 Lake Place S, Danbury, CT 06810-7261 *Tel:* 203-797-0993 *E-mail:* arcadialit@gmail.com, pg 475

Pucci, Cameron, Institute of Police Technology & Management, 12000 Alumni Dr, Jacksonville, FL 32224-2678 *Tel:* 904-620-4786 *Fax:* 904-620-2453 *E-mail:* info@iptm.org *Web Site:* www.iptm.org, pg 110

Puckey, Tara, The Society of Professional Journalists (SPJ), Eugene S Pulliam National Journalism Ctr, 3909 N Meridian St, Suite 200, Indianapolis, IN 46208 *Tel:* 317-927-8000 *Fax:* 317-920-4789 *E-mail:* spj@spj.org *Web Site:* www.spj.org, pg 548

Pugh, Marsha, Dog Writers' Association of America Inc (DWAA), PO Box 787, Hughesville, MD 20637 *E-mail:* info@dogwriters.org *Web Site:* dogwriters.org, pg 532

Pugh, Marsha, Dog Writers' Association of America Inc (DWAA) Annual Writing Competition, PO Box 787, Hughesville, MD 20637 *E-mail:* info@dogwriters.org *Web Site:* dogwriters.org, pg 610

Puhalo, Archbishop Lazar, Synaxis Press, 37323 Hawkins Rd, Dewdney, BC V0M 1H0, Canada *Tel:* 604-826-9336 *E-mail:* synaxis@new-ostrog.org *Web Site:* synaxispress.ca, pg 441

Pulice, Mario, Little, Brown and Company, 1290 Avenue of the Americas, New York, NY 10104 *Tel:* 212-364-1100 *Fax:* 212-364-0952 *E-mail:* firstname.lastname@hbgusa.com *Web Site:* www.littlebrown.com; www.hachettebookgroup.com, pg 125

Pullano, Michelle, The MIT Press, One Rogers St, Cambridge, MA 02142 *Tel:* 617-253-5255 *Toll Free Tel:* 800-405-1619 (orders) *Fax:* 617-258-6779; 617-577-1545 (orders) *Web Site:* mitpress.mit.edu, pg 141

Punia, Katherine Fleming, Living Language, c/o Penguin Random House, 1745 Broadway, New York, NY 10019 *Tel:* 212-782-9000 *Toll Free Tel:* 800-733-3000 (orders) *E-mail:* support@livinglanguage.com *Web Site:* www.livinglanguage.com, pg 126

Punia, Katie, Penguin Random House Audio Publishing, 1745 Broadway, New York, NY 10019 *E-mail:* audio@penguinrandomhouse.com *Web Site:* www.penguinrandomhouseaudio.com, pg 164

Puopolo, Kristine, Doubleday, c/o Penguin Random House Inc, 1745 Broadway, New York, NY 10019 *Tel:* 212-751-2600 *Fax:* 212-572-2662 (foreign rts) *E-mail:* ddaypub@randomhouse.com *Web Site:* knopfdoubleday.com, pg 66

Puppa, Brian, TCP Press, 20200 Marsh Hill Rd, Uxbridge, ON L9P 1R3, Canada *Tel:* 905-852-3777 *Toll Free Tel:* 800-772-7765 *E-mail:* tcp@tcpnow.com *Web Site:* www.tcppress.com, pg 441

Purcell, Anita, CAA Award for Canadian History, 6 West St N, Suite 203, Orillia, ON L3V 5B8, Canada *Tel:* 705-325-3926 *E-mail:* admin@canadianauthors.org *Web Site:* www.canadianauthors.org, pg 601

Purcell, Anita, CAA Award for Fiction, 6 West St N, Suite 203, Orillia, ON L3V 5B8, Canada *Tel:* 705-325-3926 *E-mail:* admin@canadianauthors.org *Web Site:* www.canadianauthors.org, pg 602

Purcell, Anita, CAA Emerging Writer Award, 6 West St N, Suite 203, Orillia, ON L3V 5B8, Canada *Tel:* 705-325-3926 *E-mail:* admin@canadianauthors.org *Web Site:* www.canadianauthors.org, pg 602

Purcell, Anita, CAA Poetry Award, 6 West St N, Suite 203, Orillia, ON L3V 5B8, Canada *Tel:* 705-325-3926 *E-mail:* admin@canadianauthors.org *Web Site:* www.canadianauthors.org, pg 602

Purcell, Anita, Canadian Authors Association (CAA), 6 West St N, Suite 203, Orillia, ON L3V 5B8, Canada *Tel:* 705-325-3926 *E-mail:* admin@canadianauthors.org *Web Site:* www.canadianauthors.org, pg 529

Purcell, Jessica, Alfred A Knopf, c/o Penguin Random House Inc, 1745 Broadway, New York, NY 10019 *Tel:* 212-751-2600 *Fax:* 212-572-2662 (foreign rts) *Web Site:* knopfdoubleday.com, pg 118

Purelis, Eileen, Springer, 233 Spring St, New York, NY 10013-1578 *Tel:* 212-460-1500 *Toll Free Tel:* 800-SPRINGER (777-4643) *Fax:* 212-460-1700 *E-mail:* customerservice@springer.com *Web Site:* www.springer.com, pg 205

Purple, Katherine, Purdue University Press, Stewart Ctr 190, 504 W State St, West Lafayette, IN 47907-2058 *Tel:* 765-494-2038 *Fax:* 765-496-2442 *E-mail:* pupress@purdue.edu *Web Site:* www.thepress. purdue.edu, pg 178

Pursiful, Darrell, Smyth & Helwys Publishing Inc, 6316 Peake Rd, Macon, GA 31210-3960 *Tel:* 478-757-0564 *Toll Free Tel:* 800-747-3016 (orders only) *Fax:* 478-757-1305 *E-mail:* information@helwys.com *Web Site:* www.helwys.com, pg 202

Putman, Becca, HarperCollins General Books Group, 195 Broadway, New York, NY 10007 *Tel:* 212-207-7000 *Web Site:* www.harpercollins.com, pg 94

Putnam, Richelle, MWG Writer Workshops & State Conference, 9 Janice Circle, Natchez, MS 39120 *Tel:* 601-442-0980 *E-mail:* mississippi.writersguild@outlook.com *Web Site:* www.mississippiwritersguild. com, pg 576

Putter, Raina, Holiday House Publishing Inc, 50 Broad St, New York, NY 10004 *Tel:* 212-688-0085 *Fax:* 212-421-6134 *E-mail:* info@holidayhouse.com *Web Site:* www.holidayhouse.com, pg 101

Pye, Michael, Red Wheel/Weiser, 65 Parker St, Suite 7, Newburyport, MA 01950 *Tel:* 978-465-0504 *Toll Free Tel:* 800-423-7087 (orders) *Fax:* 978-465-0243 *E-mail:* info@rwwbooks.com *Web Site:* www. redwheelweiser.com, pg 183

Pyland, Mike, Recorded Books Inc, an RBmedia company, 270 Skipjack Rd, Prince Frederick, MD 20678 *Tel:* 410-535-5590 *Toll Free Tel:* 877-732-2898 *Fax:* 410-535-5499 *E-mail:* customerservice@recordedbooks.com *Web Site:* www.recordedbooks. com, pg 182

Qualben, Lois, Langmarc Publishing, 7500 Shadowridge Run, No 28, Austin, TX 78749 *Tel:* 512-394-0989 *Toll Free Tel:* 800-864-1648 (orders) *E-mail:* langmarc@booksails.com *Web Site:* www.langmarc.com, pg 120

Quaranta, Sara, Gallery Books, 1230 Avenue of the Americas, New York, NY 10020 *Toll Free Tel:* 800-456-6798 *Fax:* 212-698-7284 *E-mail:* consumer.customerservice@simonandschuster. com *Web Site:* www.simonandschuster.com, pg 83

Quasha, George, Barrytown/Station Hill Press, 120 Station Hill Rd, Barrytown, NY 12507 *Tel:* 845-758-5293 *E-mail:* publishers@stationhill.org *Web Site:* www.stationhill.org, pg 28

Quasha, Susan, Barrytown/Station Hill Press, 120 Station Hill Rd, Barrytown, NY 12507 *Tel:* 845-758-5293 *E-mail:* publishers@stationhill.org *Web Site:* www. stationhill.org, pg 28

Quatraro, Jenna, Sourcebooks LLC, 1935 Brookdale Rd, Suite 139, Naperville, IL 60563 *Tel:* 630-961-3900 *Toll Free Tel:* 800-432-7444 *Fax:* 630-961-2168 *E-mail:* info@sourcebooks.com; customersupport@sourcebooks.com *Web Site:* www.sourcebooks.com, pg 204

Quattrocchi, John, Albert Whitman & Co, 250 S Northwest Hwy, Suite 320, Park Ridge, IL 60068 *Tel:* 847-232-2800 *Toll Free Tel:* 800-255-7675 *Fax:* 847-581-0039 *E-mail:* mail@albertwhitman.com *Web Site:* www.albertwhitman.com, pg 6

Querido, Levine, Dreamscape Media LLC, 1417 Timberwolf Dr, Holland, OH 43528 *Tel:* 419-867-6965 *Toll Free Tel:* 877-983-7326 *E-mail:* info@dreamscapeab.com *Web Site:* www. dreamscapepublishing.com, pg 67

Quick, Brianna, Wisdom Publications Inc, 199 Elm St, Somerville, MA 02144 *Tel:* 617-776-7416 *Toll Free Tel:* 800-272-4050 (orders) *Fax:* 617-776-

7841 *E-mail:* info@wisdompubs.org; submission@wisdompubs.org *Web Site:* www.wisdompubs.org, pg 243

Quillen, Lida E, Twilight Times Books, PO Box 3340, Kingsport, TN 37664-0340 *Tel:* 423-323-0183 *Fax:* 423-323-0183 *E-mail:* publisher@twilighttimes. com *Web Site:* www.twilighttimesbooks.com, pg 223

Quincannon, Alan, Quincannon Publishing Group, PO Box 8100, Glen Ridge, NJ 07028-8100 *Tel:* 973-380-9942 *E-mail:* editors@quincannongroup.com (query first via e-mail) *Web Site:* www.quincannongroup.com, pg 179

Quinlan, Alex, Southeast Review Narrative Nonfiction Contest, Florida State University, Dept of English, Tallahassee, FL 32306 *E-mail:* southeastreview@gmail.com *Web Site:* www.southeastreview.org, pg 669

Quinlan, Alex, Southeast Review's Gearhart Poetry Contest, Florida State University, Dept of English, Tallahassee, FL 32306 *E-mail:* southeastreview@gmail.com *Web Site:* www.southeastreview.org, pg 669

Quinlan, Alex, World's Best Short-Short Story Contest, Florida State University, Dept of English, Tallahassee, FL 32306 *E-mail:* southeastreview@gmail.com *Web Site:* www.southeastreview.org, pg 680

Quinlin, Margaret, Peachtree Publishing Co Inc, 1700 Chattahoochee Ave, Atlanta, GA 30318-2112 *Tel:* 404-876-8761 *Toll Free Tel:* 800-241-0113 *Fax:* 404-875-2578 *Toll Free Fax:* 800-875-8909 *E-mail:* hello@peachtree-online.com; orders@peachtree-online.com; sales@peachtree-online.com *Web Site:* www.peachtree-online.com, pg 162

Quinn, Katie, Farrar, Straus & Giroux Books for Young Readers, 120 Broadway, New York, NY 10271 *Tel:* 212-741-6900 *Toll Free Tel:* 888-330-8477 (orders) *Fax:* 212-633-9385 *Web Site:* us.macmillan. com/mackids; www.mackidsbooks.com, pg 76

Quinn, Katie, Roaring Brook Press, 120 Broadway, New York, NY 10271 *Tel:* 646-307-5151 *Web Site:* us. macmillan.com/publishers/roaring-brook-press, pg 186

Quinn, Lisa, Wilfrid Laurier University Press, 75 University Ave W, Waterloo, ON N2L 3C5, Canada *Tel:* 519-884-0710 *Toll Free Tel:* 866-836-5551 (CN & US) *Fax:* 519-725-1399 *E-mail:* press@wlu.ca *Web Site:* www.wlupress.wlu.ca, pg 445

Quinn, Martin, St Martin's Press, LLC, 120 Broadway, New York, NY 10271 *Tel:* 646-307-5151 *Web Site:* us. macmillan.com/smp, pg 190

Quinn, Yelba, The Brookings Institution Press, 1775 Massachusetts Ave NW, Washington, DC 20036-2188 *Tel:* 202-797-6000 *E-mail:* permissions@brookings. edu *Web Site:* www.brookings.edu, pg 42

Quinney, Nigel, Roaring Forties Press, 1053 Santa Fe Ave, Berkeley, CA 94706 *Tel:* 510-527-5461 *E-mail:* info@roaringfortiespress.com *Web Site:* www. roaringfortiespress.com, pg 186

Quintanilla, Joseph, National Braille Press, 88 Saint Stephen St, Boston, MA 02115-4312 *Tel:* 617-266-6160 *Toll Free Tel:* 800-548-7323 (cust serv); 888-965-8965 *Fax:* 617-437-0456 *E-mail:* contact@nbp.org *Web Site:* www.nbp.org, pg 145

Quintin, Michel, Editions Michel Quintin, 2259 Papineau Ave, Suite 104, Montreal, QC H2K 4J5, Canada *Tel:* 514-379-3774 *E-mail:* info@editionsmichelquintin.ca *Web Site:* www. editionsmichelquintin.ca, pg 424

Quinton, Sasha, Scholastic Inc, 557 Broadway, New York, NY 10012 *Tel:* 212-343-6100 *Toll Free Tel:* 800-SCHOLASTIC (724-6527) *Web Site:* www. scholastic.com, pg 194

Quon, Felicia, Simon & Schuster Canada, 166 King St E, Suite 300, Toronto, ON M5A 1J3, Canada *Tel:* 647-427-8882 *Toll Free Tel:* 800-387-0446; 800-268-3216 (orders) *Fax:* 647-430-9446 *Toll Free Fax:* 888-849-8151 (orders) *E-mail:* info@simonandschuster.ca *Web Site:* www.simonandschuster.ca, pg 440

Quraishi, Mariam, Chronicle Books, 680 Second St, San Francisco, CA 94107 *Tel:* 415-537-4200 *Toll Free Tel:* 800-759-0190 (cust serv) *Fax:* 415-537-4460

Toll Free Fax: 800-858-7787 (orders); 800-286-9471 (cust serv) *E-mail:* frontdesk@chroniclebooks.com *Web Site:* www.chroniclebooks.com, pg 52

Raagas, Lorna, Financial Executives Research Foundation Inc (FERF), West Tower, 7th fl, 1250 Headquarters Plaza, Morristown, NJ 07960-6837 *Tel:* 973-765-1000 *Fax:* 973-765-1018 *Web Site:* www. financialexecutives.org, pg 77

Raats, Anna, Ambassador International, 411 University Ridge, Suite B14, Greenville, SC 29601 *Tel:* 864-751-4844 *E-mail:* info@emeraldhouse.com; publisher@emeraldhouse.com (ms submissions); sales@emeraldhouse.com (orders/order inquiries); media@emeraldhouse.com *Web Site:* ambassador-international. com; www.facebook.com/AmbassadorIntl; twitter. com/ambassadorintl, pg 8

Rab, Sharon, The Ambassador Richard C Holbrooke Distinguished Achievement Award, PO Box 461, Wright Brothers Branch, Dayton, OH 45409-0461 *Tel:* 937-298-5072 *E-mail:* sharon.rab@daytonliterarypeaceprize.org *Web Site:* www. daytonliterarypeaceprize.org/holbrooke.htm, pg 591

Rab, Sharon, Dayton Literary Peace Prize, 25 Harman Terr, Dayton, OH 45419 *Tel:* 937-298-5072 *Web Site:* daytonliterarypeaceprize.org, pg 609

Rabinovitch, Elana, Giller Prize, 543 Logan Ave, Toronto, ON M4K 3B6, Canada *Web Site:* www. scotiabankgillerprize.ca, pg 619

Raccah, Dominique, Sourcebooks LLC, 1935 Brookdale Rd, Suite 139, Naperville, IL 60563 *Tel:* 630-961-3900 *Toll Free Tel:* 800-432-7444 *Fax:* 630-961-2168 *E-mail:* info@sourcebooks.com; customersupport@sourcebooks.com *Web Site:* www.sourcebooks.com, pg 204

Race, Justin, Purdue University Press, Stewart Ctr 190, 504 W State St, West Lafayette, IN 47907-2058 *Tel:* 765-494-2038 *Fax:* 765-496-2442 *E-mail:* pupress@purdue.edu *Web Site:* www.thepress. purdue.edu, pg 178

Racette, Ann-Christine, Fordham University Press, Joseph A Martino Hall, 45 Columbus Ave, New York, NY 10023 *Fax:* 347-842-3083 *Web Site:* www. fordhampress.com, pg 79

Rach, Beverly, Fernwood Publishing, 32 Oceanvista Lane, Black Point, NS B0J 1B0, Canada *Tel:* 902-857-1388 *Fax:* 902-857-1328 *E-mail:* info@fernpub.ca; roseway@fernpub.ca *Web Site:* fernwoodpublishing.ca, pg 426

Radant, Cyndi, Carolrhoda Books Inc, 241 First Ave N, Minneapolis, MN 55401 *Tel:* 612-332-3344 *Toll Free Tel:* 800-328-4929 *Fax:* 612-332-7615 *Toll Free Fax:* 800-332-1132 *E-mail:* info@lernerbooks. com; custserve@lernerbooks.com *Web Site:* www. lernerbooks.com; www.facebook.com/lernerbooks, pg 45

Radant, Cyndi, Carolrhoda Lab™, 241 First Ave N, Minneapolis, MN 55401 *Tel:* 612-332-3344 *Toll Free Tel:* 800-328-4929 *Fax:* 612-332-7615 *Toll Free Fax:* 800-332-1132 *E-mail:* info@lernerbooks. com; custserve@lernerbooks.com *Web Site:* www. lernerbooks.com; www.facebook.com/lernerbooks, pg 45

Radant, Cyndi, ediciones Lerner, 241 First Ave N, Minneapolis, MN 55401 *Tel:* 612-332-3344 *Toll Free Tel:* 800-328-4929 *Fax:* 612-332-7615 *Toll Free Fax:* 800-332-1132 *E-mail:* info@lernerbooks. com; custserve@lernerbooks.com *Web Site:* www. lernerbooks.com; www.facebook.com/lernerbooks, pg 69

Radant, Cyndi, First Avenue Editions, 241 First Ave N, Minneapolis, MN 55401 *Tel:* 612-332-3344 *Toll Free Tel:* 800-328-4929 *Fax:* 612-332-7615 *Toll Free Fax:* 800-332-1132 *E-mail:* info@lernerbooks. com; custserve@lernerbooks.com *Web Site:* www. lernerbooks.com; www.facebook.com/lernerbooks, pg 78

Radant, Cyndi, Graphic Universe™, 241 First Ave N, Minneapolis, MN 55401 *Tel:* 612-332-3344 *Toll Free Tel:* 800-328-4929 *Fax:* 612-332-7615 *Toll Free Fax:* 800-332-1132 *E-mail:* info@lernerbooks.

com; custserve@lernerbooks.com *Web Site:* www. lernerbooks.com; www.facebook.com/lernerbooks, pg 88

Radant, Cyndi, Lerner Publications, 241 First Ave N, Minneapolis, MN 55401 *Tel:* 612-332-3344 *Toll Free Tel:* 800-328-4929 *Fax:* 612-332-7615 *Toll Free Fax:* 800-332-1132 *E-mail:* info@lernerbooks. com; custserve@lernerbooks.com *Web Site:* www. lernerbooks.com; www.facebook.com/lernerbooks, pg 122

Radant, Cyndi, Lerner Publishing Group Inc, 241 First Ave N, Minneapolis, MN 55401 *Tel:* 612-332-3344 *Toll Free Tel:* 800-328-4929 *Fax:* 612-332-7615 *Toll Free Fax:* 800-332-1132 *E-mail:* info@lernerbooks. com; custserve@lernerbooks.com *Web Site:* www. lernerbooks.com; www.facebook.com/lernerbooks, pg 123

Radant, Cyndi, LernerClassroom, 241 First Ave N, Minneapolis, MN 55401 *Tel:* 612-332-3344 *Toll Free Tel:* 800-328-4929 *Fax:* 612-332-7615 *Toll Free Fax:* 800-332-1132 *E-mail:* info@lernerbooks. com; custserve@lernerbooks.com *Web Site:* www. lernerbooks.com; www.facebook.com/lernerbooks, pg 123

Radant, Cyndi, Millbrook Press, 241 First Ave N, Minneapolis, MN 55401 *Tel:* 612-332-3344 *Toll Free Tel:* 800-328-4929 *Fax:* 612-332-7615 *Toll Free Fax:* 800-332-1132 *E-mail:* info@lernerbooks. com; custserve@lernerbooks.com *Web Site:* www. lernerbooks.com; www.facebook.com/millbrookpress, pg 140

Radant, Cyndi, Twenty-First Century Books, 241 First Ave N, Minneapolis, MN 55401 *Tel:* 612-332-3344 *Toll Free Tel:* 800-328-4929 *Fax:* 612-332-7615 *Toll Free Fax:* 800-332-1132 *E-mail:* info@lernerbooks. com; custserve@lernerbooks.com *Web Site:* www. lernerbooks.com; www.facebook.com/lernerbooks, pg 222

Rade, David, Swan Isle Press, 11030 S Langley Ave, Chicago, IL 60628 *Tel:* 773-728-3780 (edit); 773-702-7000 (cust serv) *Toll Free Tel:* 800-621-2736 (cust serv) *Fax:* 773-702-7212 (cust serv) *Toll Free Fax:* 800-621-8476 (cust serv) *E-mail:* info@ swanislepress.com *Web Site:* www.swanislepress.com, pg 211

Radice, Neal, Maxim Mazumdar New Play Competition, One Curtain Up Alley, Buffalo, NY 14202-1911 *Tel:* 716-852-2600 *E-mail:* publicrelations@alleyway. com *Web Site:* alleyway.com, pg 639

Radich, Anthony, Western States Arts Federation, 1743 Wazee St, Suite 300, Denver, CO 80202 *Tel:* 303-629-1166 *Toll Free Tel:* 888-562-7232 *Fax:* 303-629-9717 *E-mail:* staff@westaf.org *Web Site:* www.westaf.org, pg 551

Radke, Linda F, Dragonfly Book Awards, 4696 W Tyson St, Chandler, AZ 85226-2903 *Tel:* 480-940-8182 *Fax:* 480-940-8787 *E-mail:* info@StoryMonsters.com *Web Site:* www.DragonflyBookAwards.com, pg 611

Radke, Linda F, Story Monsters Approved! Program, 4696 W Tyson St, Chandler, AZ 85226-2903 *Tel:* 480-940-8182 *Fax:* 480-940-8787 *Web Site:* www. StoryMonstersApproved.com, pg 671

Radke, Linda F, Story Monsters LLC, 4696 W Tyson St, Chandler, AZ 85226-2903 *Tel:* 480-940-8182 *Fax:* 480-940-8787 *Web Site:* www.StoryMonsters. com; www.DragonflyBookAwards.com; www. AuthorBookings.com; www.StoryMonstersApproved. com; www.storymonstersink.com, pg 209

Radler, Kyle, W W Norton & Company Inc, 500 Fifth Ave, New York, NY 10110-0017 *Tel:* 212-354-5500 *Toll Free Tel:* 800-233-4830 (orders & cust serv) *Fax:* 212-869-0856 *Toll Free Fax:* 800-458-6515 *E-mail:* orders@wwnorton.com *Web Site:* wwnorton. com, pg 152

Raducanu, Teodor, Teora USA LLC, 9443 Rosehill Dr, Bethesda, MD 20817 *Tel:* 301-986-6990 *E-mail:* teorausa@gmail.com *Web Site:* www.teora. com, pg 215

Raeber, Rick, W W Norton & Company Inc, 500 Fifth Ave, New York, NY 10110-0017 *Tel:* 212-354-5500 *Toll Free Tel:* 800-233-4830 (orders & cust serv)

Fax: 212-869-0856 *Toll Free Fax:* 800-458-6515 *E-mail:* orders@wwnorton.com *Web Site:* wwnorton. com, pg 152

Rafanan, Patrick, Chronicle Books, 680 Second St, San Francisco, CA 94107 *Tel:* 415-537-4200 *Toll Free Tel:* 800-759-0190 (cust serv) *Fax:* 415-537-4460 *Toll Free Fax:* 800-858-7787 (orders); 800-286-9471 (cust serv) *E-mail:* frontdesk@chroniclebooks.com *Web Site:* www.chroniclebooks.com, pg 52

Raffensperger, Daniel, Seedling Publications Inc, 520 E Bainbridge St, Elizabethtown, PA 17022 *Toll Free Tel:* 800-233-0759 *Toll Free Fax:* 888-834-1303 *E-mail:* edcsr@continentalpress.com *Web Site:* www. continentalpress.com, pg 196

Raffio, Michael, Pflaum Publishing Group, 3055 Kettering Blvd, Suite 100, Dayton, OH 45439 *Toll Free Tel:* 800-523-4625; 800-543-4383 (ext 1136, cust serv) *Toll Free Fax:* 800-370-4450 *E-mail:* service@ pflaum.com *Web Site:* www.pflaum.com, pg 168

Rafter, Katherine, Art of Living, PrimaMedia Inc, 1050 Second St Pike, Unit 1373, Southampton, PA 18966 *Tel:* 215-660-5045 *E-mail:* primamedia4@yahoo.com, pg 20

Ragan, Lise B, Course Crafters Inc, 243 Greenleaf Rd, Anson, ME 04911 *Tel:* 207-696-4050 *E-mail:* info@ coursecrafters.com *Web Site:* www.coursecrafters.com, pg 461

Rager, Shari, American Medical Writers Association (AMWA), 30 W Gude Dr, Suite 525, Rockville, MD 20850-4357 *Tel:* 240-238-0940 *Fax:* 301-294-9006 *E-mail:* amwa@amwa.org *Web Site:* www.amwa.org, pg 523

Ragland, Kelley, St Martin's Press, LLC, 120 Broadway, New York, NY 10271 *Tel:* 646-307-5151 *Web Site:* us. macmillan.com/smp, pg 190

Rago, Martha, Random House Children's Books, 1745 Broadway, 10th fl, New York, NY 10019 *Tel:* 212-782-9000 *Web Site:* www.randomhousekids.com, pg 180

Rahaeuser, Alice, Random House Children's Books, 1745 Broadway, 10th fl, New York, NY 10019 *Tel:* 212-782-9000 *Web Site:* www.randomhousekids. com, pg 181

Rahill, Hannah, Random House Publishing Group, 1745 Broadway, New York, NY 10019 *Toll Free Tel:* 800-200-3552 *Web Site:* www.randomhousebooks.com, pg 181

Rahja, John, Augsburg Fortress Publishers, Publishing House of the Evangelical Lutheran Church in America, 510 Marquette Ave S, Minneapolis, MN 55402 *Tel:* 612-330-3300 *Toll Free Tel:* 800-426-0115 (ext 639, subns); 800-328-4648 (orders) *Fax:* 612-330-3455 *E-mail:* info@augsburgfortress.org; copyright@ augsburgfortress.org (reprint permission requests); customercare@augsburgfortress.org *Web Site:* www. augsburgfortress.org; www.1517.media, pg 25

Rahm, Willi, Alan Wofsy Fine Arts, 1109 Geary Blvd, San Francisco, CA 94109 *Tel:* 415-292-6500 *Toll Free Tel:* 800-660-6403 *Fax:* 415-292-6594 (off & cust serv); 510-251-1840 (acctg) *E-mail:* order@art-books. com (orders); editeur@earthlink.net (edit); beauxarts@ earthlink.net (cust serv) *Web Site:* www.art-books.com, pg 243

Rahrig, Jana, Industrial Press Inc, 32 Haviland St, Suite 3, Norwalk, CT 06854 *Tel:* 203-956-5593 ext 0 (cust serv) *Toll Free Tel:* 888-528-7852 ext 0 (cust serv) *Fax:* 203-354-9391 (cust serv) *E-mail:* info@ industrialpress.com (cust serv) *Web Site:* books. industrialpress.com; ebooks.industrialpress.com, pg 108

Raihofer, Susan, David Black Agency, 335 Adams St, 27th fl, Suite 2707, Brooklyn, NY 11201 *Tel:* 718-852-5500 *Fax:* 718-852-5539 *Web Site:* www. davidblackagency.com, pg 476

Railsback, Julie, Andrews McMeel Publishing LLC, 1130 Walnut St, Kansas City, MO 64106-2109 *Toll Free Tel:* 800-851-8923; 800-943-9839 (orders) *Toll Free Fax:* 800-943-9831 (orders) *E-mail:* sales@ amuniversal.com *Web Site:* www.andrewsmcmeel.com; publishing.andrewsmcmeel.com, pg 16

Rainer, Thom S, B&H Publishing Group, One LifeWay Plaza, Nashville, TN 37234 *Toll Free Tel:* 800-251-3225 (retailers); 800-448-8032 (consumers); 800-458-2772 (churches) *Fax:* 615-251-3914 (consumers); 615-251-5933 (churches) *Toll Free Fax:* 800-296-4036 (retailers) *E-mail:* customerservice@lifeway. com; bhcustomerservice@lifeway.com; bhtradesales@ lifeway.com *Web Site:* www.bhpublishinggroup.com, pg 27

Raines, Joan, Raines & Raines, 103 Kenyon Rd, Medusa, NY 12120 *Tel:* 518-239-8311 *Fax:* 518-239-6029, pg 499

Raissian, Katie, Grove Atlantic Inc, 154 W 14 St, 12th fl, New York, NY 10011 *Tel:* 212-614-7850 *Toll Free Tel:* 800-521-0178 *Fax:* 212-614-7886 *E-mail:* info@ groveatlantic.com; sales@groveatlantic.com; publicity@groveatlantic.com; rights@groveatlantic.com *Web Site:* www.groveatlantic.com, pg 89

Rajamani, Madhu, diacriTech Inc, 4 S Market St, 4th fl, Boston, MA 02109 *Tel:* 617-600-3366 *Fax:* 617-848-2938 *Web Site:* www.diacritech.com, pg 462

Rak, Brian, Focus, PO Box 390007, Cambridge, MA 02139-0001 *Tel:* 317-635-9250 *Fax:* 317-635-9292 *E-mail:* customer@hackettpublishing.com; editorial@ hackettpublishing.com *Web Site:* focusbookstore.com; www.hackettpublishing.com, pg 79

Ram, Hari, Chronicle Books, 680 Second St, San Francisco, CA 94107 *Tel:* 415-537-4200 *Toll Free Tel:* 800-759-0190 (cust serv) *Fax:* 415-537-4460 *Toll Free Fax:* 800-858-7787 (orders); 800-286-9471 (cust serv) *E-mail:* frontdesk@chroniclebooks.com *Web Site:* www.chroniclebooks.com, pg 52

Rambo, Cat, Science Fiction & Fantasy Writers of America Inc (SFWA), PO Box 3238, Enfield, CT 06083-3238 *Tel:* 860-698-0536 *E-mail:* office@sfwa. org *Web Site:* www.sfwa.org, pg 545

Rambo, Cat, SFWA Nebula Awards, PO Box 3238, Enfield, CT 06083-3238 *Tel:* 860-698-0536 *E-mail:* office@sfwa.org *Web Site:* www.sfwa.org, pg 666

Rambo, Grace, The Experiment, 220 E 23 St, Suite 600, New York, NY 10010-4658 *Tel:* 212-889-1659 *E-mail:* info@theexperimentpublishing.com *Web Site:* www.theexperimentpublishing.com, pg 74

Ramer, Susan, Don Congdon Associates Inc, 110 William St, Suite 2202, New York, NY 10038-3914 *Tel:* 212-645-1229 *Fax:* 212-727-2688 *E-mail:* dca@ doncongdon.com *Web Site:* www.doncongdon.com, pg 480

Ramondo, Anthony, Berkley Publishing Group, 1745 Broadway, 19th fl, New York, NY 10019 *Tel:* 212-366-2000 *Web Site:* www.penguin.com, pg 32

Ramos, Luis Arturo, University of Texas at El Paso, Department of Creative Writing, MFA/Department of Creative Writing, 901 EDUC, 500 W University Ave, El Paso, TX 79968-9991 *Tel:* 915-747-5713 *Fax:* 915-747-5523 *E-mail:* creativewriting@utep.edu *Web Site:* www.utep.edu/cw, pg 586

Ramos, Mariana, Random House Children's Books, 1745 Broadway, 10th fl, New York, NY 10019 *Tel:* 212-782-9000 *Web Site:* www.randomhousekids.com, pg 181

Ramos, Sophia, Sourcebooks LLC, 1935 Brookdale Rd, Suite 139, Naperville, IL 60563 *Tel:* 630-961-3900 *Toll Free Tel:* 800-432-7444 *Fax:* 630-961-2168 *E-mail:* info@sourcebooks.com; customersupport@ sourcebooks.com *Web Site:* www.sourcebooks.com, pg 204

Ramsess, Akili, National Press Photographers Association Inc (NPPA), 120 Hooper St, Athens, GA 30602 *Tel:* 706-542-2506 *E-mail:* info@nppa.org *Web Site:* nppa.org, pg 540

Ramsey, Mary, International Society of Automation (ISA), 67 T W Alexander Dr, Research Triangle Park, NC 27709-0185 *Tel:* 919-549-8411 *Fax:* 919-549-8288 *E-mail:* info@isa.org *Web Site:* www.isa.org, pg 112

Rand Silverman, Erica, Stimola Literary Studio Inc, 308 Livingston Ct, Edgewater, NJ 07020 *Tel:* 201-945-9353 *Fax:* 201-945-9353; 201-490-5920 *E-mail:* info@stimolaliterarystudio.com *Web Site:* www.stimolaliterarystudio.com, pg 504

Randall, Deidre C, Peter E Randall Publisher, 5 Greenleaf Woods Dr, Suite 102, Portsmouth, NH 03801 *Tel:* 603-431-5667 *Fax:* 603-431-3566 *E-mail:* media@perpublisher.com *Web Site:* www.perpublisher.com, pg 180

Randall, Lee, Oceanview Publishing Inc, 1620 Main St, Suite 11, Sarasota, FL 34236 *Tel:* 941-387-8500 *Web Site:* oceanviewpub.com, pg 154

Randall, Michele E, Bibliographical Society of America, PO Box 1537, Lenox Hill Sta, New York, NY 10021-0043 *Tel:* 212-734-2500 *Fax:* 212-452-2710 *E-mail:* bsa@bibsocamer.org *Web Site:* www.bibsocamer.org, pg 528

Randisi, Robert J, The Private Eye Writers of America (PWA), 3665 S Needles Hwy, 7G, Laughlin, NV 89029 *Web Site:* www.privateeyewriters.com, pg 544

Randolph, Ladette, Ploughshares, Emerson College, 120 Boylston St, Boston, MA 02116 *Tel:* 617-824-3757 *E-mail:* pshares@pshares.org *Web Site:* www.pshares.org, pg 171

Randolph, Ladette, Ploughshares Emerging Writer's Contest, Emerson College, 120 Boylston St, Boston, MA 02116 *Tel:* 617-824-3757 *E-mail:* pshares@pshares.org *Web Site:* www.pshares.org, pg 656

Randolph, Tony, Regular Baptist Press, 3715 N Ventura Dr, Arlington Heights, IL 60004 *Tel:* 847-843-1600 *Toll Free Tel:* 800-727-4440 (cust serv) *Fax:* 847-843-3757 *E-mail:* orders@rbpstore.org *Web Site:* regularbaptistpress.org, pg 184

Rankin, Jenni, Annual Reviews, 4139 El Camino Way, Palo Alto, CA 94306 *Tel:* 650-493-4400 *Toll Free Tel:* 800-523-8635 *Fax:* 650-424-0910; 650-855-9815 *E-mail:* service@annualreviews.org *Web Site:* www.annualreviews.org, pg 17

Rao, Lisa, Simon & Schuster Children's Publishing, 1230 Avenue of the Americas, New York, NY 10020 *Tel:* 212-698-7000 *Web Site:* www.simonandschuster.com/kids; www.simonandschuster.com/teen; simonandschuster.net; simonandschuster.biz, pg 199

Raoult, Marie-Madeleine, Editions de la Pleine Lune, 223 34 Ave, Lachine, QC H8T 1Z4, Canada *Tel:* 514-634-7954 *E-mail:* editpllune@videotron.ca *Web Site:* www.pleinelune.qc.ca, pg 422

Raphel, Neil, Brigantine Media, 211 North Ave, St Johnsbury, VT 05819 *Tel:* 802-751-8802 *Fax:* 802-751-8804 *Web Site:* brigantinemedia.com, pg 41

Rapp, Alan, The Monacelli Press, 65 Bleecker St, 8th fl, New York, NY 10012 *Tel:* 212-229-9925 *E-mail:* contact@monacellipress.com *Web Site:* www.monacellipress.com, pg 141

Rapp, Daniela, St Martin's Press, LLC, 120 Broadway, New York, NY 10271 *Tel:* 646-307-5151 *Web Site:* us.macmillan.com/smp, pg 190

Rappin, Marc, Advertising Research Foundation (ARF), 432 Park Ave S, 4th fl, New York, NY 10016-8013 *Tel:* 212-751-5656 *Fax:* 212-689-1859 *E-mail:* help@thearf.org *Web Site:* thearf.org, pg 521

Raps, Beth, SDP Publishing Solutions LLC, 36 Captain's Way, East Bridgewater, MA 02333 *Tel:* 617-775-0656 *Web Site:* www.sdppublishingsolutions.com, pg 470

Rarick, Ethan, Institute of Governmental Studies, 109 Moses Hall, No 2370, Berkeley, CA 94720-2370 *Tel:* 510-642-1428 *E-mail:* igspress@berkeley.edu *Web Site:* www.igs.berkeley.edu, pg 110

Rasanen, John P, American Geosciences Institute (AGI), 4220 King St, Alexandria, VA 22302-1502 *Tel:* 703-379-2480 (ext 246) *Fax:* 703-379-7563 *E-mail:* agi@americangeosciences.org *Web Site:* www.americangeosciences.org, pg 11

Rasenberger, Mary, The Authors Guild, 31 E 32 St, 7th fl, New York, NY 10016 *Tel:* 212-563-5904 *Fax:* 212-564-8363 *E-mail:* staff@authorsguild.org *Web Site:* www.authorsguild.org, pg 527

Rasi, Cayla, Random House Children's Books, 1745 Broadway, 10th fl, New York, NY 10019 *Tel:* 212-782-9000 *Web Site:* www.randomhousekids.com, pg 180

Raskin, Rebecca, HarperCollins General Books Group, 195 Broadway, New York, NY 10007 *Tel:* 212-207-7000 *Web Site:* www.harpercollins.com, pg 94

Raskin, Sherman, Pace University, Master of Science in Publishing, Dept of Publishing, Rm 805-E, 551 Fifth Ave, New York, NY 10176 *Tel:* 212-346-1431 *Toll Free Tel:* 877-284-7670 *Fax:* 212-346-1165 *Web Site:* www.pace.edu/dyson/mspub, pg 584

Rasmussen, Darin, Capstone Publishers™, 1710 Roe Crest Dr, North Mankato, MN 56003 *Toll Free Tel:* 800-747-4992 (cust serv) *Toll Free Fax:* 888-262-0705 *E-mail:* customer.service@capstonepub.com *Web Site:* www.capstonepub.com, pg 44

Rasmussen, Jim, Bethlehem Books, 10194 Garfield St S, Bathgate, ND 58216 *Toll Free Tel:* 800-757-6831 *Fax:* 701-265-3716 *E-mail:* contact@bethlehembooks.com *Web Site:* www.bethlehembooks.com, pg 33

Ratcliff, Robert A, Westminster John Knox Press (WJK), 100 Witherspoon St, Louisville, KY 40202-1396 *Tel:* 502-569-5052 *Toll Free Tel:* 800-523-1631 (US & CN) *Fax:* 502-569-8308 *Toll Free Fax:* 800-541-5113 (US & CN) *E-mail:* customer_service@wjkbooks.com; orders@wjkbooks.com *Web Site:* www.wjkbooks.com, pg 239

Rath, Morgan, Farrar, Straus & Giroux Books for Young Readers, 120 Broadway, New York, NY 10271 *Tel:* 212-741-6900 *Toll Free Tel:* 888-330-8477 (orders) *Fax:* 212-633-9385 *Web Site:* us.macmillan.com/mackids; www.mackidsbooks.com, pg 76

Rath, Morgan, Roaring Brook Press, 120 Broadway, New York, NY 10271 *Tel:* 646-307-5151 *Web Site:* us.macmillan.com/publishers/roaring-brook-press, pg 186

Rathbun, Jennifer, Ashland Poetry Press, Bixler Center for the Humanities, Ashland University, 401 College Ave, Ashland, OH 44805 *Tel:* 419-289-5098 *E-mail:* app@ashland.edu *Web Site:* www.ashland.edu/aupoetry, pg 22

Rathjen, Melinda, Hachette Nashville, 6100 Tower Circle, Room 210, Franklin, TN 37067 *Tel:* 615-221-0996 *Fax:* 615-221-0962 *Web Site:* www.hachettebookgroup.com, pg 91

Ratliff, Therese, Twenty-Third Publications, One Montauk Ave, Suite 200, New London, CT 06320 *Tel:* 860-437-3012 *Toll Free Tel:* 800-321-0411 (orders) *Toll Free Fax:* 800-572-0788 *E-mail:* resources@twentythirdpublications.com *Web Site:* www.twentythirdpublications.com, pg 223

Rattray, Jessica, Coach House Books, 80 bpNichol Lane, Toronto, ON M5S 3J4, Canada *Tel:* 416-979-2217 *Toll Free Tel:* 800-367-6360 (outside Toronto) *Fax:* 416-977-1158 *E-mail:* mail@chbooks.com *Web Site:* www.chbooks.com, pg 420

Ravenelle, Anna, Houghton Mifflin Harcourt Trade & Reference Division, 125 High St, Boston, MA 02110 *Tel:* 617-351-5000 *Web Site:* www.hmhco.com, pg 104

Rawitch, Jeremy, RAND Corp, 1776 Main St, Santa Monica, CA 90407-2138 *Tel:* 310-393-0411 *Fax:* 310-393-4818 *Web Site:* www.rand.org, pg 180

Rawlings, Jeremy, HarperCollins Canada Ltd, 2 Bloor St E, 20th fl, Toronto, ON M4W 1A8, Canada *Tel:* 416-975-9334 *Fax:* 416-975-5223 *E-mail:* hcorder@harpercollins.com *Web Site:* www.harpercollins.ca, pg 429

Rawlings, Wendy, University of Alabama Program in Creative Writing, PO Box 870244, Tuscaloosa, AL 35487-0244 *Tel:* 205-348-5065 *Fax:* 205-348-1388 *E-mail:* english@ua.edu *Web Site:* www.as.ua.edu/english, pg 585

Rawls, Sue, Houghton Mifflin Harcourt Assessments, One Pierce Place, Itasca, IL 60143 *Tel:* 630-467-7000 *Toll Free Tel:* 800-323-9540 *Fax:* 630-467-7192 (cust serv) *E-mail:* assessmentsorders@hmhco.com *Web Site:* www.hmhco.com/classroom-solutions/assessment, pg 103

Rawn, Nora, Trident Media Group LLC, 41 Madison Ave, 36th fl, New York, NY 10010 *Tel:* 212-333-1511 *E-mail:* info@tridentmediagroup.com; press@tridentmediagroup.com *Web Site:* www.tridentmediagroup.com, pg 507

Ray, Carissa, Houghton Mifflin Harcourt, 125 High St, Boston, MA 02110 *Tel:* 617-351-5000 *Toll Free Tel:* 855-969-4642; 800-225-5425 (K-12 educ materials); 800-323-9540 (assessment materials); 877-219-1537 (SkillsTutor); 888-242-6747 (Innovation in Educ Group); 800-225-3362 (Trade & Ref Div) *Toll Free Fax:* 800-269-5232 *E-mail:* myhmhco@hmhco.com *Web Site:* www.hmhco.com, pg 103

Ray, Jo-Anne, Canadian Institute for Studies in Publishing, Simon Fraser University at Harbour Centre, 515 W Hastings St, Suite 3576, Vancouver, BC V6B 5K3, Canada *Tel:* 778-782-5242 *E-mail:* pub-info@sfu.ca *Web Site:* publishing.sfu.ca, pg 530

Ray, Jody Saunders, Book Industry Guild of New York, PO Box 2001, New York, NY 10113-2001 *E-mail:* admin@bookindustryguildofny.org *Web Site:* bigny.org, pg 528

Ray, Trinity, The Tuesday Agency, 132 1/2 E Washington St, Iowa City, IA 52240 *Tel:* 319-338-7080 *E-mail:* trinity@tuesdayagency.com *Web Site:* tuesdayagency.com, pg 516

Raye, Janis, Brigantine Media, 211 North Ave, St Johnsbury, VT 05819 *Tel:* 802-751-8802 *Fax:* 802-751-8804 *Web Site:* brigantinemedia.com, pg 41

Rayess, Dena, Chronicle Books, 680 Second St, San Francisco, CA 94107 *Tel:* 415-537-4200 *Toll Free Tel:* 800-759-0190 (cust serv) *Fax:* 415-537-4460 *Toll Free Fax:* 800-858-7787 (orders); 800-286-9471 (cust serv) *E-mail:* frontdesk@chroniclebooks.com *Web Site:* www.chroniclebooks.com, pg 52

Raymo, Margaret, Houghton Mifflin Harcourt Trade & Reference Division, 125 High St, Boston, MA 02110 *Tel:* 617-351-5000 *Web Site:* www.hmhco.com, pg 104

Raymond, Andrea, Bear & Co Inc, One Park St, Rochester, VT 05767 *Tel:* 802-767-3174 *Toll Free Tel:* 800-932-3277 *Fax:* 802-767-3726 *E-mail:* customerservice@InnerTraditions.com *Web Site:* InnerTraditions.com, pg 29

Raymond, Andrea, Inner Traditions International Ltd, One Park St, Rochester, VT 05767 *Tel:* 802-767-3174 *Toll Free Tel:* 800-246-8648 *Fax:* 802-767-3726 *E-mail:* customerservice@InnerTraditions.com *Web Site:* www.InnerTraditions.com, pg 109

Raymond, Melissa, Perseus Books, 1290 Avenue of the Americas, New York, NY 10104 *Tel:* 212-340-8100 *Toll Free Tel:* 800-343-4499 (cust serv) *Fax:* 212-340-8105 *Web Site:* www.perseusbooks.com, pg 167

Raymond, Midge, Ashland Creek Press, 2305 Ashland St, Suite C417, Ashland, OR 97520 *Tel:* 760-300-3620 *E-mail:* editors@ashlandcreekpress.com *Web Site:* www.ashlandcreekpress.com, pg 22

Rayner, Terry, Wimmer Cookbooks, 4650 Shelby Air Dr, Memphis, TN 38118 *Toll Free Tel:* 800-548-2537 *Fax:* 901-363-1771 *E-mail:* info@wimmerco.com *Web Site:* www.wimmerco.com, pg 242

Raynor, Bruce, Hillman Prizes for Journalism, 330 W 42 St, Suite 900, New York, NY 10036 *Tel:* 646-448-6413 *Web Site:* www.hillmanfoundation.org, pg 623

Raynor, Jacqueline Hope, The Boston Mills Press, 50 Staples Ave, Unit 1, Richmond Hill, ON L4B 0A7, Canada *Tel:* 416-499-8412 *Toll Free Tel:* 800-387-6192 *Fax:* 416-499-8313 *Toll Free Fax:* 800-450-0391 *E-mail:* service@fireflybooks.com *Web Site:* www.fireflybooks.com, pg 417

Razzouk, Monique, Random House Children's Books, 1745 Broadway, 10th fl, New York, NY 10019 *Tel:* 212-782-9000 *Web Site:* www.randomhousekids.com, pg 181

Rea, Elizabeth R, The Rea Award for the Short Story, 53 W Church Hill Rd, Washington, CT 06794 *Web Site:* reaaward.org, pg 661

Reach, Anna Duke, The Writers Workshop, Finn House, 102 W Wiggin St, Gambier, OH 43022 *Tel:* 740-427-5207 *Fax:* 740-427-5417 *E-mail:* kenyonreview@kenyon.edu *Web Site:* www.kenyonreview.org, pg 580

Reagan, Melissa, Hachette Nashville, 6100 Tower Circle, Room 210, Franklin, TN 37067 *Tel:* 615-221-0996 *Fax:* 615-221-0962 *Web Site:* www.hachettebookgroup.com, pg 91

Real, Jamie, Chronicle Books, 680 Second St, San Francisco, CA 94107 *Tel:* 415-537-4200 *Toll Free Tel:* 800-759-0190 (cust serv) *Fax:* 415-537-4460 *Toll Free Fax:* 800-858-7787 (orders); 800-286-9471 (cust serv) *E-mail:* frontdesk@chroniclebooks.com *Web Site:* www.chroniclebooks.com, pg 52

Reale, Tom, Brown Books Publishing Group, 16250 Knoll Trail, Suite 205, Dallas, TX 75248 *Tel:* 972-381-0009 *Fax:* 972-248-4336 *E-mail:* publishing@brownbooks.com *Web Site:* www.brownbooks.com, pg 42

Ream, Robaire, Polebridge Press, PO Box 346, Farmington, MN 55024 *Tel:* 651-200-2372 *E-mail:* orders@westarinstitute.org *Web Site:* www.westarinstitute.org, pg 172

Reaman, Micki, Oregon State University Press, 121 The Valley Library, Corvallis, OR 97331-4501 *Tel:* 541-737-3166, pg 157

Reamer, Jodi Esq, Writers House, 21 W 26 St, New York, NY 10010 *Tel:* 212-685-2400 *Web Site:* www.writershouse.com, pg 508

Reardon, Emily, Alfred A Knopf, c/o Penguin Random House Inc, 1745 Broadway, New York, NY 10019 *Tel:* 212-751-2600 *Fax:* 212-572-2662 (foreign rts) *Web Site:* knopfdoubleday.com, pg 118

Reardon, Lisa, Chicago Review Press, 814 N Franklin St, Chicago, IL 60610 *Tel:* 312-337-0747 *Toll Free Tel:* 800-888-4741 *Fax:* 312-337-5110 *E-mail:* frontdesk@chicagoreviewpress.com *Web Site:* www.chicagoreviewpress.com, pg 50

Reaume, Julie K, Michigan State University Press (MSU Press), Manly Miles Bldg, Suite 25, 1405 S Harrison Rd, East Lansing, MI 48823-5245 *Tel:* 517-355-9543 *Fax:* 517-432-2611 *Web Site:* msupress.org, pg 139

Reback, Erin, HarperCollins General Books Group, 195 Broadway, New York, NY 10007 *Tel:* 212-207-7000 *Web Site:* www.harpercollins.com, pg 94

Recio, Jamie, International Association of Business Communicators (IABC), 649 Mission St, 5th fl, San Francisco, CA 94105 *Tel:* 415-544-4700 *Toll Free Tel:* 800-776-4222 (US & CN) *Fax:* 415-544-4747 *E-mail:* leader_centre@iabc.com; member_relations@iabc.com *Web Site:* www.iabc.com, pg 535

Redd, Kimberly, LITA/Christian Larew Memorial Scholarship in Library & Information Technology, c/o American Library Association, 50 E Huron St, Chicago, IL 60611-2795 *Toll Free Tel:* 800-545-2433 (ext 4270) *E-mail:* scholarships@ala.org *Web Site:* www.ala.org/lita, pg 634

Redd, Kimberly, LITA/LSSI Minority Scholarship in Library & Information Technology, c/o American Library Association, 50 E Huron St, Chicago, IL 60611-2795 *Toll Free Tel:* 800-545-2433 (ext 4270) *E-mail:* scholarships@ala.org *Web Site:* www.ala.org/lita, pg 634

Redd, Kimberly, LITA/OCLC Minority Scholarship in Library & Information Technology, c/o American Library Association, 50 E Huron St, Chicago, IL 60611-2795 *Toll Free Tel:* 800-545-2433 (ext 4270) *E-mail:* scholarships@ala.org *Web Site:* www.ala.org/lita, pg 634

Redd, Kimberly L, David H Clift Scholarship, 50 E Huron St, Chicago, IL 60611 *Toll Free Tel:* 800-545-2433 (ext 4279) *Fax:* 312-280-3256 *E-mail:* scholarships@ala.org *Web Site:* www.ala.org/scholarships, pg 605

Redkin, Andy, Alan Wofsy Fine Arts, 1109 Geary Blvd, San Francisco, CA 94109 *Tel:* 415-292-6500 *Toll Free Tel:* 800-660-6403 *Fax:* 415-292-6594 (off & cust serv); 510-251-1840 (acctg) *E-mail:* order@art-books.

com (orders); editeur@earthlink.net (edit); beauxarts@earthlink.net (cust serv) *Web Site:* www.art-books.com, pg 243

Redlich, Josh, Random House Children's Books, 1745 Broadway, 10th fl, New York, NY 10019 *Tel:* 212-782-9000 *Web Site:* www.randomhousekids.com, pg 180

Redmon, Hilary, Random House Publishing Group, 1745 Broadway, New York, NY 10019 *Toll Free Tel:* 800-200-3552 *Web Site:* www.randomhousebooks.com, pg 181

Redmond, Robert, Cold Spring Harbor Laboratory Press, One Bungtown Rd, Cold Spring Harbor, NY 11724 *Tel:* 516-422-4100 *Toll Free Tel:* 800-843-4388 *Fax:* 516-422-4097; 516-422-4092 (submissions) *E-mail:* cshpress@cshl.edu *Web Site:* www.cshlpress.com, pg 54

Reed, Adam, The Joy Harris Literary Agency Inc, 1501 Broadway, Suite 2310, New York, NY 10036 *Tel:* 212-924-6269 *Fax:* 212-840-5776 *E-mail:* contact@joyharrisliterary.com *Web Site:* www.joyharrisliterary.com, pg 488

Reed, Alyson, Linguistic Society of America, 522 21 St NW, Suite 120, Washington, DC 20006-5012 *Tel:* 202-835-1714 *Fax:* 202-835-1717 *E-mail:* lsa@lsadc.org *Web Site:* www.linguisticsociety.org, pg 536

Reed, Dwayne, Cenveo Publisher Services, 555 Virginia Dr, Fort Washington, PA 19034 *Tel:* 267-470-1590 *Fax:* 215-591-9093 *E-mail:* info.psg@cenveo.com *Web Site:* www.cenveopublisherservices.com, pg 460

Reed, Frances, The Blackburn Press, PO Box 287, Caldwell, NJ 07006-0287 *Tel:* 973-228-7077 *Fax:* 973-228-7276 *Web Site:* www.blackburnpress.com, pg 34

Reed, Ishmael, American Book Awards, The Raymond House, 655 13 St, Suite 302, Oakland, CA 94612 *Tel:* 916-425-7916 *E-mail:* beforecolumbusfoundation@gmail.com *Web Site:* www.beforecolumbusfoundation.com, pg 592

Reed, Ishmael, Before Columbus Foundation, The Raymond House, 655 13 St, Suite 302, Oakland, CA 94612 *Tel:* 916-425-7916 *E-mail:* beforecolumbusfoundation@gmail.com *Web Site:* www.beforecolumbusfoundation.com, pg 528

Reed, Kathleen, Harlequin Enterprises Ltd, 195 Broadway, 24th fl, New York, NY 10007 *Tel:* 212-207-7000 *Toll Free Tel:* 888-432-4879 *E-mail:* customerservice@harlequin.com *Web Site:* www.harlequin.com, pg 93

Reed, Robert D, Robert D Reed Publishers, PO Box 1992, Bandon, OR 97411-1192 *Tel:* 541-347-9882 *Fax:* 541-347-9883 *E-mail:* 4bobreed@msn.com *Web Site:* rdrpublishers.com, pg 183

Reed, Tyler, Harold W McGraw Jr Prize in Education, 2 Penn Plaza, New York, NY 10121-2298 *Tel:* 646-766-2000 *E-mail:* info@mcgrawprize.com *Web Site:* www.mcgrawprize.com, pg 639

Reed-Morrison, Laura, Penn State University Press, University Support Bldg 1, Suite C, 820 N University Dr, University Park, PA 16802-1003 *Tel:* 814-865-1327 *Toll Free Tel:* 800-326-9180 *Fax:* 814-863-1408 *Toll Free Fax:* 877-778-2665 *E-mail:* orders@psupress.org; orders@eisenbrauns.org *Web Site:* www.psupress.org; www.eisenbrauns.org, pg 166

Reeder, Jen, Dog Writers' Association of America Inc (DWAA), PO Box 787, Hughesville, MD 20637 *E-mail:* info@dogwriters.org *Web Site:* dogwriters.org, pg 532

Reeder, Jen, Dog Writers' Association of America Inc (DWAA) Annual Writing Competition, PO Box 787, Hughesville, MD 20637 *E-mail:* info@dogwriters.org *Web Site:* dogwriters.org, pg 610

Rees, Bonnie G, IODE Violet Downey Book Award, 40 Orchard View Blvd, Suite 219, Toronto, ON M4R 1B9, Canada *Tel:* 416-487-4416 *Toll Free Tel:* 866-827-7428 *Fax:* 416-487-4417 *E-mail:* iodecanada@bellnet.ca *Web Site:* www.iode.ca, pg 627

Rees, Mr Lorin, Rees Literary Agency, 14 Beacon St, Suite 710, Boston, MA 02108 *Tel:* 617-227-9014 *Fax:* 617-227-8762 *Web Site:* www.reesagency.com, pg 499

Rees, Rhonda, Book Publicists of Southern California, 714 Crescent Dr, Beverly Hills, CA 90210 *Tel:* 323-461-3921 *Fax:* 323-461-0917 *Web Site:* www.bookpublicists.org, pg 529

Reese, Bob, Aro Book Publishing Co, 130 S 800 W, Salt Lake City, UT 84104-1120 *Tel:* 801-637-9115 *Fax:* 801-419-0125 *E-mail:* arobook@yahoo.com *Web Site:* www.arobookpublishing.com, pg 20

Reeve, William D, Virginia Kidd Agency Inc, 538 E Harford St, PO Box 278, Milford, PA 18337 *Tel:* 570-296-6205 *Web Site:* vk-agency.com, pg 491

Reeves, Don, Western Heritage Awards (Wrangler Award), 1700 NE 63 St, Oklahoma City, OK 73111 *Tel:* 405-478-2250 *Fax:* 405-478-4714 *E-mail:* info@nationalcowboymuseum.org *Web Site:* nationalcowboymuseum.org, pg 676

Reeves, Howard, Harry N Abrams Inc, 195 Broadway, 9th fl, New York, NY 10007 *Tel:* 212-206-7715 *Toll Free Tel:* 800-345-1359 *Fax:* 212-519-1210 *E-mail:* abrams@abramsbooks.com *Web Site:* www.abramsbooks.com, pg 3

Reeves, Lynn, Jentel Artist Residency Program, 130 Lower Piney Rd, Banner, WY 82832 *Tel:* 307-737-2311 *Fax:* 307-737-2305 *E-mail:* jentel@jentelarts.org *Web Site:* www.jentelarts.org, pg 576

Regala, Jae, Robert F Kennedy Book Awards, 1300 19 St NW, Suite 750, Washington, DC 20036 *Tel:* 646-553-4750 *Fax:* 202-463-6606 *E-mail:* info@rfkhumanrights.org *Web Site:* rfkhumanrights.org, pg 629

Regan, Ann, Minnesota Historical Society Press, 345 Kellogg Blvd W, St Paul, MN 55102-1906 *Tel:* 651-259-3205 *Fax:* 651-297-1345 *E-mail:* info-mnhspress@mnhs.org *Web Site:* www.mnhs.org/mnhspress, pg 140

Regan, Claire, Deadline Club, c/o Salmagundi Club, 47 Fifth Ave, New York, NY 10003 *Tel:* 646-481-7584 *Web Site:* www.deadlineclub.org, pg 532

Regan, Harold, The H W Wilson Foundation, 750 Third Ave, 13th fl, New York, NY 10017 *Tel:* 212-418-8473 *Web Site:* www.thwwf.org, pg 551

Regan, Michael, The H W Wilson Foundation, 750 Third Ave, 13th fl, New York, NY 10017 *Tel:* 212-418-8473 *Web Site:* www.thwwf.org, pg 551

Reggio, Chris, Fox Chapel Publishing Co Inc, 1970 Broad St, East Petersburg, PA 17520 *Tel:* 717-560-4703 *Toll Free Tel:* 800-457-9112 *Fax:* 717-560-4702 *E-mail:* customerservice@foxchapelpublishing.com *Web Site:* www.foxchapelpublishing.com, pg 80

Regimbal, Angelique, ISBN Canada, Library & Archives Canada, 395 Wellington St, Ottawa, ON K1A 0N4, Canada *Tel:* 819-994-6872 *Toll Free Tel:* 866-578-7777 (CN & US) *Fax:* 819-934-7535 *E-mail:* bac.isbn.lac@canada.ca *Web Site:* www.bac-lac.gc.ca/eng/services/isbn-canada/pages/isbn-canada.aspx, pg 536

Regoli, Michael, Indiana University Press, Herman B Wells Library 350, 1320 E Tenth St, Bloomington, IN 47405-3907 *Tel:* 812-855-8817 *Toll Free Tel:* 800-842-6796 (orders only) *Fax:* 812-855-7931; 812-855-8507 *E-mail:* iupress@indiana.edu; iuporder@indiana.edu (orders) *Web Site:* www.iupress.indiana.edu, pg 108

Rehl, Dr Beatrice, Cambridge University Press, One Liberty Plaza, 20th fl, New York, NY 10006 *Tel:* 212-924-3900; 212-337-5000 *Fax:* 212-691-3239; 845-353-4141 *E-mail:* newyork@cambridge.org; customer_service@cambridge.org *Web Site:* www.cambridge.org/us, pg 43

Reichert, Stephen, Erskine J Poetry Prize, PO Box 22161, Baltimore, MD 21203 *E-mail:* smartishpace@gmail.com *Web Site:* www.smartishpace.com, pg 614

Reid, Daniel, Whiting Awards, 16 Court St, Suite 2308, Brooklyn, NY 11241 *Tel:* 718-701-5962 *E-mail:* info@whiting.org *Web Site:* www.whiting.org, pg 677

Reid, Daniel, Whiting Creative Nonfiction Grant, 16 Court St, Suite 2308, Brooklyn, NY 11241 *Tel:* 718-701-5962 *E-mail:* nonfiction@whiting.org; info@whiting.org *Web Site:* www.whiting.org, pg 677

Reid, Daniel, Whiting Literary Magazine Prizes, 16 Court St, Suite 2308, Brooklyn, NY 11241 *Tel:* 718-701-5962 *E-mail:* info@whiting.org *Web Site:* www.whiting.org/writers/whiting-literary-magazine-prizes, pg 677

Reid, Don, Stephen Leacock Memorial Medal for Humour, 149 Peter St N, Orillia, ON L3V 4Z4, Canada *Tel:* 705-326-9286 *Web Site:* www.leacock.ca, pg 632

Reid, Lisa, Broadview Press, 280 Perry St, Unit 5, Peterborough, ON K9J 2J4, Canada *Tel:* 705-743-8990 *Fax:* 705-743-8353 *E-mail:* customerservice@broadviewpress.com *Web Site:* www.broadviewpress.com, pg 417

Reid, Meg, C Michael Curtis Short Story Book Prize, 186 W Main St, Spartanburg, SC 29306 *Tel:* 864-577-9349 *Fax:* 864-577-0188 *E-mail:* info@hubcity.org; submit@hubcity.org *Web Site:* hubcity.org/press/c-michael-curtis-short-story-book-prize, pg 608

Reid, Megan, Sanford J Greenburger Associates Inc, 55 Fifth Ave, New York, NY 10003 *Tel:* 212-206-5600 *Fax:* 212-463-8718 *Web Site:* greenburger.com; www.sjga.com, pg 487

Reid, Rosalind, Council for the Advancement of Science Writing (CASW), PO Box 910, Hedgesville, WV 25427 *Tel:* 304-754-6786 *Web Site:* www.casw.org, pg 532

Reid, Rosalind, Rennie Taylor & Alton Blakeslee Fellowships in Science Writing, PO Box 910, Hedgesville, WV 25427 *Tel:* 304-754-6786 *Web Site:* www.casw.org, pg 672

Reidhead, Julia, W W Norton & Company Inc, 500 Fifth Ave, New York, NY 10110-0017 *Tel:* 212-354-5500 *Toll Free Tel:* 800-233-4830 (orders & cust serv) *Fax:* 212-869-0856 *Toll Free Fax:* 800-458-6515 *E-mail:* orders@wwnorton.com *Web Site:* wwnorton.com, pg 152

Reidy, Kiyoko, Phyllis Smart-Young Poetry Prize, University of Wisconsin, 6193 Helen C White Hall, English Dept, 600 N Park St, Madison, WI 53706 *E-mail:* madisonrevw@gmail.com *Web Site:* www.themadisonrevw.com, pg 681

Reidy, Sarah, Tom Doherty Associates, LLC, 120 Broadway, New York, NY 10271 *Tel:* 646-307-5511 *Toll Free Tel:* 800-455-0340 *Web Site:* us.macmillan.com/torforge, pg 66

Reighard, Jessica, Paul H Brookes Publishing Co Inc, PO Box 10624, Baltimore, MD 21285-0624 *Tel:* 410-337-9580 (outside US & CN) *Toll Free Tel:* 800-638-3775 (US & CN) *Fax:* 410-337-8539 *E-mail:* custserv@brookespublishing.com *Web Site:* www.brookespublishing.com, pg 42

Reilly, Amy, Reader's Digest Select Editions, 44 S Broadway, White Plains, NY 10601 *Tel:* 914-238-1000 *Toll Free Tel:* 877-732-4438 (cust serv) *Web Site:* www.facebook.com/selecteditions, pg 182

Reilly, Cara, Doubleday, c/o Penguin Random House Inc, 1745 Broadway, New York, NY 10019 *Tel:* 212-751-2600 *Fax:* 212-572-2662 (foreign rts) *E-mail:* ddaypub@randomhouse.com *Web Site:* knopfdoubleday.com, pg 66

Reilly, Colleen, Theatre Library Association (TLA), c/o The New York Public Library for the Performing Arts, 40 Lincoln Center Plaza, New York, NY 10023 *E-mail:* TheatreLibraryAssociation@gmail.com *Web Site:* www.tla-online.org/awards/bookawards, pg 548

Reilly, Dan, Templeton Press, 300 Conshohocken State Rd, Suite 550, West Conshohocken, PA 19428 *Tel:* 484-531-8380 *Fax:* 484-531-8382 *E-mail:* tpinfo@templetonpress.org *Web Site:* www.templetonpress.org, pg 215

Reilly, J C, International Poetry Competition, 686 Cherry St NW, Suite 333, Atlanta, GA 30332-0161 *E-mail:* atlantareview@gatech.edu *Web Site:* www.atlantareview.com, pg 627

Reilly, Kevin, St Martin's Press, LLC, 120 Broadway, New York, NY 10271 *Tel:* 646-307-5151 *Web Site:* us.macmillan.com/smp, pg 190

Reilly, Michael, American Association of Collegiate Registrars & Admissions Officers (AACRAO), One Dupont Circle NW, Suite 520, Washington, DC 20036 *Tel:* 202-293-9161 *Fax:* 202-872-8857 *Web Site:* www.aacrao.org, pg 9

Reimer, Marleen, Houghton Mifflin Harcourt, 125 High St, Boston, MA 02110 *Tel:* 617-351-5000 *Toll Free Tel:* 855-969-4642; 800-225-5425 (K-12 educ materials); 800-323-9540 (assessment materials); 877-219-1537 (SkillsTutor); 888-242-6747 (Innovation in Educ Group); 800-225-3362 (Trade & Ref Div) *Toll Free Fax:* 800-269-5232 *E-mail:* myhmhco@hmhco.com *Web Site:* www.hmhco.com, pg 103

Reimer, Marleen, Houghton Mifflin Harcourt Trade & Reference Division, 125 High St, Boston, MA 02110 *Tel:* 617-351-5000 *Web Site:* www.hmhco.com, pg 104

Rein, Jody, Jody Rein Books Inc, 7741 S Ash Ct, Centennial, CO 80122 *Tel:* 303-694-9386 *Web Site:* www.jodyreinbooks.com, pg 490

Reina, Jeanne, HarperCollins General Books Group, 195 Broadway, New York, NY 10007 *Tel:* 212-207-7000 *Web Site:* www.harpercollins.com, pg 93

Reisdorff, James J, South Platte Press, PO Box 163, David City, NE 68632-0163 *Tel:* 402-367-3554 *E-mail:* railroads@windstream.net *Web Site:* www.southplattepress.net, pg 205

Reiser, Annie M, Morton N Cohen Award for a Distinguished Edition of Letters, 85 Broad St, Suite 500, New York, NY 10004-2434 *Tel:* 646-576-5141; 646-576-5000 *Fax:* 646-458-0030 *E-mail:* awards@mla.org *Web Site:* www.mla.org, pg 606

Reiser, Annie M, Katherine Singer Kovacs Prize, 85 Broad St, Suite 500, New York, NY 10004-2434 *Tel:* 646-576-5141; 646-576-5000 *Fax:* 646-458-0030 *E-mail:* awards@mla.org *Web Site:* www.mla.org, pg 630

Reiser, Annie M, Fenia & Yaakov Leviant Memorial Prize in Yiddish Studies, 85 Broad St, Suite 500, New York, NY 10004-2434 *Tel:* 646-576-5141; 646-576-5000 *Fax:* 646-458-0030 *E-mail:* awards@mla.org *Web Site:* www.mla.org, pg 632

Reiser, Annie M, James Russell Lowell Prize, 85 Broad St, Suite 500, New York, NY 10004-2434 *Tel:* 646-576-5141; 646-576-5000 *Fax:* 646-458-0030 *E-mail:* awards@mla.org *Web Site:* www.mla.org, pg 635

Reiser, Annie M, Howard R Marraro Prize, 85 Broad St, Suite 500, New York, NY 10004-2434 *Tel:* 646-576-5141; 646-576-5000 *Fax:* 646-458-0030 *E-mail:* awards@mla.org *Web Site:* www.mla.org, pg 638

Reiser, Annie M, Kenneth W Mildenberger Prize, 85 Broad St, Suite 500, New York, NY 10004-2434 *Tel:* 646-576-5141; 646-576-5000 *Fax:* 646-458-0030 *E-mail:* awards@mla.org *Web Site:* www.mla.org, pg 641

Reiser, Annie M, MLA Prize for a Bibliography, Archive or Digital Project, 85 Broad St, Suite 500, New York, NY 10004-2434 *Tel:* 646-576-5141; 646-576-5000 *Fax:* 646-458-0030 *E-mail:* awards@mla.org *Web Site:* www.mla.org, pg 642

Reiser, Annie M, MLA Prize for a First Book, 85 Broad St, Suite 500, New York, NY 10004-2434 *Tel:* 646-576-5141; 646-576-5000 *Fax:* 646-458-0030 *E-mail:* awards@mla.org *Web Site:* www.mla.org, pg 642

Reiser, Annie M, MLA Prize for a Scholarly Edition, 85 Broad St, Suite 500, New York, NY 10004-2434 *Tel:* 646-576-5141; 646-576-5000 *Fax:* 646-458-0030 *E-mail:* awards@mla.org *Web Site:* www.mla.org, pg 642

Reiser, Annie M, MLA Prize for Independent Scholars, 85 Broad St, Suite 500, New York, NY 10004-2434 *Tel:* 646-576-5141; 646-576-5000 *Fax:* 646-458-0030 *E-mail:* awards@mla.org *Web Site:* www.mla.org, pg 642

Reiser, Annie M, MLA Prize for Studies in Native American Literatures, Cultures & Languages, 85 Broad St, Suite 500, New York, NY 10004-2434 *Tel:* 646-576-5141; 646-576-5000 *Fax:* 646-458-0030 *E-mail:* awards@mla.org *Web Site:* www.mla.org, pg 642

Reiser, Annie M, MLA Prize in United States Latina & Latino & Chicana & Chicano Literary & Cultural Studies, 85 Broad St, Suite 500, New York, NY 10004-2434 *Tel:* 646-576-5141; 646-576-5000 *Fax:* 646-458-0030 *E-mail:* awards@mla.org *Web Site:* www.mla.org, pg 642

Reiser, Annie M, Lois Roth Award, 85 Broad St, Suite 500, New York, NY 10004-2434 *Tel:* 646-576-5141; 646-576-5000 *Fax:* 646-458-0030 *E-mail:* awards@mla.org *Web Site:* www.mla.org, pg 663

Reiser, Annie M, Aldo & Jeanne Scaglione Prize for a Translation of a Literary Work, 85 Broad St, Suite 500, New York, NY 10004-2434 *Tel:* 646-576-5141; 646-576-5000 *Fax:* 646-458-0030 *E-mail:* awards@mla.org *Web Site:* www.mla.org, pg 665

Reiser, Annie M, Aldo & Jeanne Scaglione Prize for a Translation of a Scholarly Study of Literature, 85 Broad St, Suite 500, New York, NY 10004-2434 *Tel:* 646-576-5141; 646-576-5000 *Fax:* 646-458-0030 *E-mail:* awards@mla.org *Web Site:* www.mla.org, pg 665

Reiser, Annie M, Aldo & Jeanne Scaglione Prize for Comparative Literary Studies, 85 Broad St, Suite 500, New York, NY 10004-2434 *Tel:* 646-576-5141; 646-576-5000 *Fax:* 646-458-0030 *E-mail:* awards@mla.org *Web Site:* www.mla.org, pg 665

Reiser, Annie M, Aldo & Jeanne Scaglione Prize for French & Francophone Studies, 85 Broad St, Suite 500, New York, NY 10004-2434 *Tel:* 646-576-5141; 646-576-5000 *Fax:* 646-458-0030 *E-mail:* awards@mla.org *Web Site:* www.mla.org, pg 665

Reiser, Annie M, Aldo & Jeanne Scaglione Prize for Italian Studies, 85 Broad St, Suite 500, New York, NY 10004-2434 *Tel:* 646-576-5141; 646-576-5000 *Fax:* 646-458-0030 *E-mail:* awards@mla.org *Web Site:* www.mla.org, pg 665

Reiser, Annie M, Aldo & Jeanne Scaglione Prize for Studies in Germanic Languages & Literatures, 85 Broad St, Suite 500, New York, NY 10004-2434 *Tel:* 646-576-5141; 646-576-5000 *Fax:* 646-458-0030 *E-mail:* awards@mla.org *Web Site:* www.mla.org, pg 665

Reiser, Annie M, Aldo & Jeanne Scaglione Prize for Studies in Slavic Languages & Literatures, 85 Broad St, Suite 500, New York, NY 10004-2434 *Tel:* 646-576-5141; 646-576-5000 *Fax:* 646-458-0030 *E-mail:* awards@mla.org *Web Site:* www.mla.org, pg 665

Reiser, Annie M, Aldo & Jeanne Scaglione Publication Award for a Manuscript in Italian Literary Studies, 85 Broad St, Suite 500, New York, NY 10004-2434 *Tel:* 646-576-5141; 646-576-5000 *Fax:* 646-458-0030 *E-mail:* awards@mla.org *Web Site:* www.mla.org, pg 665

Reiser, Annie M, William Sanders Scarborough Prize, 85 Broad St, Suite 500, New York, NY 10004-2434 *Tel:* 646-576-5141; 646-576-5000 *Fax:* 646-458-0030 *E-mail:* awards@mla.org *Web Site:* www.mla.org, pg 665

Reiser, Annie M, Mina P Shaughnessy Prize, 85 Broad St, Suite 500, New York, NY 10004-2434 *Tel:* 646-576-5141; 646-576-5000 *Fax:* 646-458-0030 *E-mail:* awards@mla.org *Web Site:* www.mla.org, pg 667

Reisner, Rosalind, AJL Jewish Fiction Award, PO Box 1118, Teaneck, NJ 07666 *Tel:* 201-371-3255 *E-mail:* info@jewishlibraries.org *Web Site:* jewishlibraries.org/AJL_Jewish_Fiction_Award, pg 590

Richmond, Douglas, House of Anansi Press Inc, 128 Sterling Rd, Lower Level, Toronto, ON M6R 2B7, Canada *Tel:* 416-363-4343 *Fax:* 416-363-1017 *E-mail:* customerservice@houseofanansi.com *Web Site:* www.houseofanansi.com, pg 429

Richter, Heidi, HarperCollins General Books Group, 195 Broadway, New York, NY 10007 *Tel:* 212-207-7000 *Web Site:* www.harpercollins.com, pg 93

Richter, Rick, Aevitas Creative Management, 19 W 21 St, Suite 501, New York, NY 10010 *Tel:* 212-765-6900 *Web Site:* aevitascreative.com, pg 474

Rico, Liz, Chronicle Books, 680 Second St, San Francisco, CA 94107 *Tel:* 415-537-4200 *Toll Free Tel:* 800-759-0190 (cust serv) *Fax:* 415-537-4460 *Toll Free Fax:* 800-858-7787 (orders); 800-286-9471 (cust serv) *E-mail:* frontdesk@chroniclebooks.com *Web Site:* www.chroniclebooks.com, pg 51

Ridder, Myles, School Guide Publications, 420 Railroad Way, Mamaroneck, NY 10543 *Tel:* 914-632-1220 *Toll Free Tel:* 800-433-7771 *E-mail:* info@schoolguides.com *Web Site:* www.graduateguide.com; www.schoolguides.com; www.religiousministries.com, pg 195

Ridge, Sam, The University of Arkansas Press, McIlroy House, 105 N McIlroy Ave, Fayetteville, AR 72701 *Tel:* 479-575-7544 *E-mail:* info@uapress.com *Web Site:* www.uapress.com, pg 226

Ridout, Rachel, Harvey Klinger Inc, 300 W 55 St, Suite 11V, New York, NY 10019 *Tel:* 212-581-7068 *Fax:* 212-315-3823 *E-mail:* queries@harveyklinger.com *Web Site:* www.harveyklinger.com, pg 491

Riegert, Keith, Ulysses Press, 195 Montague St, 14th fl, Brooklyn, NY 11201 *Tel:* 510-601-8301 *Toll Free Tel:* 800-377-2542 *Fax:* 510-601-8307 *E-mail:* ulysses@ulyssespress.com *Web Site:* www.ulyssespress.com, pg 223

Riegert, Ray, Ulysses Press, 195 Montague St, 14th fl, Brooklyn, NY 11201 *Tel:* 510-601-8301 *Toll Free Tel:* 800-377-2542 *Fax:* 510-601-8307 *E-mail:* ulysses@ulyssespress.com *Web Site:* www.ulyssespress.com, pg 223

Rienner, Lynne, Kumarian Press, 1800 30 St, Suite 314, Boulder, CO 80301 *Tel:* 303-444-6684 *Fax:* 303-444-0824 *E-mail:* questions@rienner.com *Web Site:* www.rienner.com, pg 119

Rienner, Lynne C, Lynne Rienner Publishers Inc, 1800 30 St, Suite 314, Boulder, CO 80301 *Tel:* 303-444-6684 *Fax:* 303-444-0824 *E-mail:* questions@rienner.com; cservice@rienner.com *Web Site:* www.rienner.com, pg 185

Rieselbach, Erik, New Directions Publishing Corp, 80 Eighth Ave, 19th fl, New York, NY 10011 *Tel:* 212-255-0230 *E-mail:* editorial@ndbooks.com; publicity@ndbooks.com *Web Site:* ndbooks.com, pg 148

Rigas, Maia M, The Art Institute of Chicago, 111 S Michigan Ave, Chicago, IL 60603-6404 *Tel:* 312-443-3600; 312-443-3540 (pubns) *Fax:* 312-443-1334 (pubns) *Web Site:* www.artic.edu; www.artinstituteshop.org, pg 20

Rigaud, Emmanuelle, Les Editions du Ble, 340, blvd Provencher, St Boniface, MB R2H 0G7, Canada *Tel:* 204-237-8200 *Fax:* 204-233-8182 *E-mail:* direction@editionsduble.ca *Web Site:* ble.avoslivres.ca, pg 423

Riggs, Kathryn, Regnery Publishing, 300 New Jersey Ave NW, Washington, DC 20001 *Tel:* 202-216-0600 *Toll Free Tel:* 888-219-4747 *Fax:* 202-393-1795 *Web Site:* www.regnery.com, pg 184

Riley, Elizabeth, W W Norton & Company Inc, 500 Fifth Ave, New York, NY 10110-0017 *Tel:* 212-354-5500 *Toll Free Tel:* 800-233-4830 (orders & cust serv) *Fax:* 212-869-0856 *Toll Free Fax:* 800-458-6515 *E-mail:* orders@wwnorton.com *Web Site:* wwnorton.com, pg 152

Riley, Jocelyn, Her Own Words LLC, PO Box 5264, Madison, WI 53705-0264 *Tel:* 608-271-7083 *Fax:* 608-271-0209 *Web Site:* www.herownwords.com; www.nontraditionalcareers.com, pg 98

Riley, Jovan, National Association of Black Journalists (NABJ), 1100 Knight Hall, Suite 3100, College Park, MD 20742 *Tel:* 301-405-0248 *Fax:* 301-314-1714 *E-mail:* info@nabj.org; press@nabj.org *Web Site:* www.nabj.org, pg 538

Rimas, Ruta, Simon & Schuster Children's Publishing, 1230 Avenue of the Americas, New York, NY 10020 *Tel:* 212-698-7000 *Web Site:* www.simonandschuster.com/kids; www.simonandschuster.com/teen; simonandschuster.net; simonandschuster.biz, pg 199

Rimel, John, Mountain Press Publishing Co, 1301 S Third W, Missoula, MT 59801 *Tel:* 406-728-1900 *Toll Free Tel:* 800-234-5308 *Fax:* 406-728-1635 *E-mail:* info@mtnpress.com *Web Site:* www.mountain-press.com, pg 143

Rimler, Lauri, Information Today, Inc, 143 Old Marlton Pike, Medford, NJ 08055-8750 *Tel:* 609-654-6266 *Toll Free Tel:* 800-300-9868 (cust serv) *Fax:* 609-654-4309 *E-mail:* custserv@infotoday.com *Web Site:* www.infotoday.com, pg 108

Rinaldi, Karen, HarperCollins General Books Group, 195 Broadway, New York, NY 10007 *Tel:* 212-207-7000 *Web Site:* www.harpercollins.com, pg 93

Rinck, Gary M, John Wiley & Sons Inc, 111 River St, Hoboken, NJ 07030-5774 *Tel:* 201-748-6000 *Toll Free Tel:* 800-225-5945 (cust serv) *Fax:* 201-748-6088 *E-mail:* info@wiley.com *Web Site:* www.wiley.com, pg 241

Rinehart, Rick, M Evans & Company, c/o Rowman & Littlefield Publishing Group, 4501 Forbes Blvd, Suite 200, Lanham, MD 20706 *Tel:* 301-459-3366 *Fax:* 301-429-5748 *Web Site:* rowman.com, pg 73

Ringo, Elise, Simon & Schuster, 1230 Avenue of the Americas, New York, NY 10020 *Tel:* 212-698-7000 *Toll Free Tel:* 800-223-2348 (cust serv); 800-223-2336 (orders) *Toll Free Fax:* 800-943-9831 (orders) *Web Site:* www.simonandschuster.com, pg 198

Ringo, Julia, Farrar, Straus & Giroux, LLC, 175 Varick St, 9th fl, New York, NY 10014 *Tel:* 212-741-6900 *E-mail:* fsg.publicity@fsgbooks.com *Web Site:* us.macmillan.com/fsg.aspx, pg 76

Riopel, Patrica, Scribendi Inc, 405 Riverview Dr, Chatham, ON N7M 0N3, Canada *Tel:* 519-351-1626 (cust serv) *Fax:* 519-354-0192 *E-mail:* customerservice@scribendi.com *Web Site:* www.scribendi.com, pg 470

Ripianzi, David, YMAA Publication Center Inc, PO Box 480, Wolfeboro, NH 03894 *Tel:* 603-569-7988 *Toll Free Tel:* 800-669-8892 *Fax:* 603-569-1889 *E-mail:* info@ymaa.com *Web Site:* www.ymaa.com, pg 247

Riske, Kris Brandt, American Federation of Astrologers Inc, 6535 S Rural Rd, Tempe, AZ 85283-3746 *Tel:* 480-838-1751 *Toll Free Tel:* 888-301-7630 *Fax:* 480-838-8293 *Web Site:* www.astrologers.com, pg 11

Riskind, Jon, American Council on Education, One Dupont Circle NW, Washington, DC 20036 *Tel:* 202-939-9300 *Fax:* 202-939-9302 *E-mail:* pubs@acenet.edu *Web Site:* www.acenet.edu, pg 522

Ristau, Todd, Southeastern Theatre Conference New Play Project, 1175 Revolution Mill Dr, Suite 14, Greensboro, NC 27405 *Tel:* 336-272-3645 *Fax:* 336-272-8810 *E-mail:* info@setc.org *Web Site:* www.setc.org, pg 669

Ritchie, Alex, Rocky Mountain Mineral Law Foundation, 9191 Sheridan Blvd, Suite 203, Westminster, CO 80031 *Tel:* 303-321-8100 *Fax:* 303-321-7657 *E-mail:* info@rmmlf.org *Web Site:* www.rmmlf.org, pg 186

Ritchken, Deborah, Marsal Lyon Literary Agency LLC, 665 San Rodolfo Dr, Suite 124, PMB 121, Solana Beach, CA 92075 *Tel:* 760-814-8507 *Web Site:* www.marsallyonliteraryagency.com, pg 494

Rittenberg, Ann, Ann Rittenberg Literary Agency Inc, 15 Maiden Lane, Suite 206, New York, NY 10038 *Tel:* 212-684-6936 *Fax:* 212-684-6929 *E-mail:* info@rittlit.com *Web Site:* www.rittlit.com, pg 499

Riva, Peter, International Transactions Inc, 28 Alope Way, Gila, NM 88038 *Tel:* 845-373-9696 *Fax:* 480-393-5162 *E-mail:* info@internationaltransactions.us *Web Site:* www.intltrans.com, pg 489

Riva, Sandra Anne, International Transactions Inc, 28 Alope Way, Gila, NM 88038 *Tel:* 845-373-9696 *Fax:* 480-393-5162 *E-mail:* info@internationaltransactions.us *Web Site:* www.intltrans.com, pg 489

Rivas, Laura, Candlewick Press, 99 Dover St, Somerville, MA 02144-2825 *Tel:* 617-661-3330 *Fax:* 617-661-0565 *E-mail:* bigbear@candlewick.com; salesinfo@candlewick.com *Web Site:* www.candlewick.com, pg 44

Rivas-Smith, Alexandra, William H Sadlier Inc, 9 Pine St, New York, NY 10005 *Tel:* 212-227-2120 *Toll Free Tel:* 800-221-5175 (cust serv) *Fax:* 212-312-6080 *E-mail:* customerservice@sadlier.com *Web Site:* www.sadlier.com, pg 189

Riven, Judith, Judith Riven Literary Agent LLC, 250 W 16 St, Suite 4F, New York, NY 10011 *Tel:* 212-255-1009 *Fax:* 212-255-8547 *E-mail:* rivenlitqueries@gmail.com *Web Site:* rivenlit.com, pg 469, 499

Rivera, Frank, Adams Media, 57 Littlefield St, Avon, MA 02322 *Tel:* 508-427-7100 *Web Site:* www.simonandschuster.com, pg 4

Rivera, Jacqueline, Santillana USA Publishing Co, 2023 NW 84 Ave, Doral, FL 33122 *Tel:* 305-591-9522 *Toll Free Tel:* 800-245-8584 *E-mail:* customerservice@santillanausa.com *Web Site:* www.santillanausa.com, pg 192

Rivero, Bev, 5 Under 35, 90 Broad St, Suite 604, New York, NY 10004 *Tel:* 212-685-0261 *Fax:* 212-213-6570 *E-mail:* nationalbook@nationalbook.org *Web Site:* www.nationalbook.org, pg 616

Rivero, Bev, Innovations in Reading Prize, 90 Broad St, Suite 604, New York, NY 10004 *Tel:* 212-685-0261 *Fax:* 212-213-6570 *E-mail:* nationalbook@nationalbook.org *Web Site:* www.nationalbook.org/innovations_in_reading, pg 627

Rivero, Bev, Medal for Distinguished Contribution to American Letters, 90 Broad St, Suite 604, New York, NY 10004 *Tel:* 212-685-0261 *Fax:* 212-213-6570 *E-mail:* nationalbook@nationalbook.org *Web Site:* www.nationalbook.org/amerletters.html, pg 640

Rivero, Bev, National Book Awards, 90 Broad St, Suite 604, New York, NY 10004 *Tel:* 212-685-0261 *Fax:* 212-213-6570 *E-mail:* nationalbook@nationalbook.org *Web Site:* www.nationalbook.org, pg 644

Rivero, Bev, National Book Foundation, 90 Broad St, Suite 604, New York, NY 10004 *Tel:* 212-685-0261 *Fax:* 212-213-6570 *E-mail:* nationalbook@nationalbook.org *Web Site:* www.nationalbook.org, pg 551

Rivers, Alena, ALSC Baker & Taylor Summer Reading Grant, 50 E Huron St, Chicago, IL 60611-2795 *Tel:* 312-280-2163 *Toll Free Tel:* 800-545-2433 *Fax:* 312-440-9374; 312-280-5271 *E-mail:* alsc@ala.org *Web Site:* www.ala.org/alsc, pg 591

Rivers, Alena, The May Hill Arbuthnot Honor Lecture Award, 50 E Huron St, Chicago, IL 60611-2795 *Tel:* 312-280-2163 *Toll Free Tel:* 800-545-2433 *Fax:* 312-440-9374; 312-280-5271 *E-mail:* alsc@ala.org *Web Site:* www.ala.org/alsc, pg 592

Rivers, Alena, The Mildred L Batchelder Award, 50 E Huron St, Chicago, IL 60611-2795 *Tel:* 312-280-2163 *Toll Free Tel:* 800-545-2433 *Fax:* 312-440-9374; 312-280-5271 *E-mail:* alsc@ala.org *Web Site:* www.ala.org/alsc, pg 596

Rivers, Alena, The Pura Belpre Award, 50 E Huron St, Chicago, IL 60611-2795 *Tel:* 312-280-2163 *Toll Free Tel:* 800-545-2433 *Fax:* 312-440-9374; 312-280-5271 *E-mail:* alsc@ala.org *Web Site:* www.ala.org/alsc, pg 596

Rivers, Alena, Bound to Stay Bound Books Scholarship, 50 E Huron St, Chicago, IL 60611-2795 *Tel:* 312-280-2163 *Toll Free Tel:* 800-545-2433 *Fax:* 312-440-9374; 312-280-5271 *E-mail:* alsc@ala.org *Web Site:* www.ala.org/alsc, pg 600

Rivers, Alena, The Randolph Caldecott Medal, 50 E Huron St, Chicago, IL 60611-2795 *Tel:* 312-280-2163 *Toll Free Tel:* 800-545-2433 *Fax:* 312-440-9374; 312-280-5271 *E-mail:* alsc@ala.org *Web Site:* www.ala.org/alsc, pg 602

Rivers, Alena, Children's Literature Legacy Award, 50 E Huron St, Chicago, IL 60611-2795 *Tel:* 312-280-2163 *Toll Free Tel:* 800-545-2433 *Fax:* 312-440-9374; 312-280-5271 *E-mail:* alsc@ala.org *Web Site:* www.ala.org/alsc, pg 604

Rivers, Alena, Frederic G Melcher Scholarship, 50 E Huron St, Chicago, IL 60611-2795 *Tel:* 312-280-2163 *Toll Free Tel:* 800-545-2433 *Fax:* 312-440-9374; 312-280-5271 *E-mail:* alsc@ala.org *Web Site:* www.ala.org/alsc, pg 641

Rivers, Alena, John Newbery Medal, 50 E Huron St, Chicago, IL 60611-2795 *Tel:* 312-280-2163 *Toll Free Tel:* 800-545-2433 *Fax:* 312-440-9374; 312-280-5271 *E-mail:* alsc@ala.org *Web Site:* www.ala.org/alsc, pg 648

Rivers, Alena, Robert F Sibert Informational Book Award, 50 E Huron St, Chicago, IL 60611-2795 *Tel:* 312-280-2163 *Toll Free Tel:* 800-545-2433 *Fax:* 312-440-9374; 312-280-5271 *E-mail:* alsc@ala.org *Web Site:* www.ala.org/alsc, pg 667

Rivkin, Charles, Motion Picture Association of America Inc (MPAA), 1301 "K" St NE, Suite 900E, Washington, DC 20005 *Tel:* 202-293-1966 *Fax:* 202-296-7410 *E-mail:* contactus@mpaa.org *Web Site:* www.mpaa.org, pg 538

Rizzo, Adriana, Houghton Mifflin Harcourt Trade & Reference Division, 125 High St, Boston, MA 02110 *Tel:* 617-351-5000 *Web Site:* www.hmhco.com, pg 104

Rizzo, Michael, Deadline Club, c/o Salmagundi Club, 47 Fifth Ave, New York, NY 10003 *Tel:* 646-481-7584 *Web Site:* www.deadlineclub.org, pg 532

Roach, Brian, The Catholic University of America Press, 240 Leahy Hall, 620 Michigan Ave NE, Washington, DC 20064 *Tel:* 202-319-5052 *Toll Free Tel:* 800-537-5487 (orders only) *Fax:* 202-319-4985 *E-mail:* cuapress@cua.edu *Web Site:* cuapress.org, pg 46

Roach, Reginald, Palmetto Bug Books, 1345 NE 105 St, No 2, Miami Shores, FL 33138 *Tel:* 305-531-9813 *E-mail:* palmettobugbooks@gmail.com, pg 159

Roane, Rick, Cherry Hill Publishing LLC, 24344 Del Amo Rd, Ramona, CA 92065 *Tel:* 858-829-5550 *Toll Free Tel:* 800-407-1072 *Fax:* 760-203-1200 *E-mail:* operations@cherryhillpublishing.com; sales@cherryhillpublishing.com *Web Site:* www.cherryhillpublishing.com, pg 50

Roane, Sharon, Cherry Hill Publishing LLC, 24344 Del Amo Rd, Ramona, CA 92065 *Tel:* 858-829-5550 *Toll Free Tel:* 800-407-1072 *Fax:* 760-203-1200 *E-mail:* operations@cherryhillpublishing.com; sales@cherryhillpublishing.com *Web Site:* www.cherryhillpublishing.com, pg 50

Robbins, B J, B J Robbins Literary Agency, 5130 Bellaire Ave, North Hollywood, CA 91607 *E-mail:* robbinsliterary@gmail.com, pg 500

Robbins, Caroline, Trafalgar Square Books, 388 Howe Hill Rd, North Pomfret, VT 05053 *Tel:* 802-457-1911 *Toll Free Tel:* 800-423-4525 *Fax:* 802-457-1913 *E-mail:* contact@trafalgarbooks.com *Web Site:* www.trafalgarbooks.com; www.horseandriderbooks.com, pg 219

Robbins, Christopher, Familius, 1254 Commerce Way, Sanger, CA 93657 *Tel:* 559-876-2170 *Fax:* 559-876-2180 *E-mail:* orders@familius.com *Web Site:* www.familius.com, pg 75

Robbins, Fleetwood, Waxman Literary Agency, 443 Park Ave S, No 1004, New York, NY 10016 *Tel:* 212-675-5556 *Web Site:* www.waxmanliteraryagency.com, pg 508

Robbins, Michele, Familius, 1254 Commerce Way, Sanger, CA 93657 *Tel:* 559-876-2170 *Fax:* 559-876-2180 *E-mail:* orders@familius.com *Web Site:* www.familius.com, pg 75

Robbins, Sandra, See-More's Workshop Arts & Education Workshops, 325 West End Ave, Suite 12-B, New York, NY 10023 *Tel:* 212-724-0677 *Fax:* 212-724-0767 *E-mail:* sbt@shadowboxtheatre.org *Web Site:* www.shadowboxtheatre.org, pg 578

Roberge, Amelie, Kids Can Press Ltd, 25 Dockside Dr, Toronto, ON M5A 0B5, Canada *Tel:* 416-479-7000 *Toll Free Tel:* 800-265-0884 *Fax:* 416-960-5437 *E-mail:* info@kidscan.com; customerservice@kidscan.com *Web Site:* www.kidscanpress.com; www.kidscanpress.ca, pg 431

Roberge, Marian, ProQuest LLC, 789 E Eisenhower Pkwy, Ann Arbor, MI 48108 *Tel:* 734-761-4700 *Toll Free Tel:* 800-521-0600; 877-779-6768 (sales) *E-mail:* sales@proquest.com *Web Site:* www.proquest.com, pg 176

Roberson, Rick, The Barnabas Agency, PO Box 3113, Corsicana, TX 75151-3113 *Tel:* 903-654-1319 *E-mail:* info@barnabasagency.com *Web Site:* www.barnabasagency.com, pg 515

Roberson, Vivian, Penguin Group USA, A Penguin Random House Company, 375 Hudson St, New York, NY 10014 *Tel:* 212-366-2000 *Toll Free Tel:* 800-847-5515 (inside sales); 800-631-8571 (cust serv) *Fax:* 212-366-2666; 607-775-4829 (inside sales) *E-mail:* online@us.penguingroup.com *Web Site:* www.penguin.com, pg 163

Roberson, Vivian, Portfolio, 375 Hudson St, New York, NY 10014 *Web Site:* www.penguin.com/meet/publishers/portfolio, pg 172

Robert, Katie, American Industrial Hygiene Association - AIHA, 3141 Fairview Park Dr, Suite 777, Falls Church, VA 22042 *Tel:* 703-849-8888 *Fax:* 703-207-3561 *E-mail:* infonet@aiha.org *Web Site:* www.aiha.org, pg 11

Roberts, Brian, American Society of Composers, Authors & Publishers (ASCAP), 1900 Broadway, New York City, NY 10023 *Tel:* 212-621-6000 *Fax:* 212-612-8453 *E-mail:* info@ascap.com *Web Site:* www.ascap.com, pg 524

Roberts, Brian, BWL Publishing Inc, 100 Chinook Winds Place SW, Unit 4105, Airdrie, AB T4B-4B4, Canada *Tel:* 403-710-4869 *E-mail:* bwlgeneral@telus.net *Web Site:* bookswelove.net; www.facebook.com/groups/153824114796417, pg 418

Roberts, Dr Catherine A, American Mathematical Society, 201 Charles St, Providence, RI 02904-2213 *Tel:* 401-455-4000 *Toll Free Tel:* 800-321-4267 *Fax:* 401-331-3842; 401-455-4046 (cust serv) *E-mail:* ams@ams.org; cust-serv@ams.org *Web Site:* www.ams.org, pg 12

Roberts, Conrad, University Press of Kansas, 2502 Westbrooke Circle, Lawrence, KS 66045-4444 *Tel:* 785-864-4154; 785-864-4155 (orders) *Fax:* 785-864-4586 *E-mail:* upress@ku.edu; upkorders@ku.edu (orders) *Web Site:* www.kansaspress.ku.edu, pg 233

Roberts, Daniel, Deadline Club, c/o Salmagundi Club, 47 Fifth Ave, New York, NY 10003 *Tel:* 646-481-7584 *Web Site:* www.deadlineclub.org, pg 532

Roberts, Jane F, Literary & Creative Artists Inc, 3543 Albemarle St NW, Washington, DC 20008-4213 *Tel:* 202-362-4688 *Fax:* 202-362-8875 *E-mail:* lcadc@earthlink.net (queries, no attachments) *Web Site:* www.lcadc.com, pg 493

Roberts, Janet, Centering Corp, 7230 Maple St, Omaha, NE 68134 *Tel:* 402-553-1200 *Toll Free Tel:* 866-218-0101 *Fax:* 402-553-0507 *E-mail:* orders@centering.org *Web Site:* www.centering.org, pg 48

Roberts, Jennifer, Candlewick Press, 99 Dover St, Somerville, MA 02144-2825 *Tel:* 617-661-3330 *Fax:* 617-661-0565 *E-mail:* bigbear@candlewick.com; salesinfo@candlewick.com *Web Site:* www.candlewick.com, pg 44

Roberts, Jill, Tachyon Publications LLC, 1459 18 St, No 139, San Francisco, CA 94107 *Tel:* 415-285-5615 *E-mail:* tachyon@tachyonpublications.com *Web Site:* www.tachyonpublications.com, pg 212

Roberts, Laura Weiss MD, American Psychiatric Association Publishing, 800 Maine Ave SW, Suite 900, Washington, DC 20024 *Tel:* 202-459-9722 *Toll Free Tel:* 800-368-5777 *Fax:* 202-403-3094 *E-mail:* appi@psych.org *Web Site:* www.appi.org; www.psychiatryonline.org, pg 13

Roberts, Marc, Centering Corp, 7230 Maple St, Omaha, NE 68134 *Tel:* 402-553-1200 *Toll Free Tel:* 866-218-0101 *Fax:* 402-553-0507 *E-mail:* orders@centering.org *Web Site:* www.centering.org, pg 48

Roberts, Marianne, Write Stuff Enterprises LLC, 1001 S Andrews Ave, Suite 200, Fort Lauderdale, FL 33316 *Tel:* 954-462-6657 *Fax:* 954-462-6023 *E-mail:* info@writestuffbooks.com *Web Site:* www.writestuffbooks.com, pg 245

Roberts, Megan, Sewanee Writers' Conference, Stamler Ctr, 119 Gailor Hall, 735 University Ave, Sewanee, TN 37383 *Tel:* 931-598-1141; 931-598-1654 *E-mail:* swc@sewanee.edu *Web Site:* www.sewaneewriters.org, pg 578

Roberts, Michele, Liberty Fund Inc, 11301 N Meridian St, Carmel, IN 46032-4564 *Tel:* 317-842-0880 *Toll Free Tel:* 800-955-8335; 800-866-3520 *Fax:* 317-579-6060 (cust serv); 708-534-7803 *E-mail:* books@libertyfund.org; info@libertyfund.org *Web Site:* www.libertyfund.org, pg 123

Roberts, Nate, Emmaus Road Publishing Inc, 1468 Parkview Circle, Steubenville, OH 43952 *Tel:* 740-283-2880 (outside US) *Toll Free Tel:* 800-398-5470 (orders) *Fax:* 740-283-4011 (orders) *E-mail:* questions@emmausroad.org *Web Site:* www.emmausroad.org, pg 71

Roberts, Olivia, Chronicle Books, 680 Second St, San Francisco, CA 94107 *Tel:* 415-537-4200 *Toll Free Tel:* 800-759-0190 (cust serv) *Fax:* 415-537-4460 *Toll Free Fax:* 800-858-7787 (orders); 800-286-9471 (cust serv) *E-mail:* frontdesk@chroniclebooks.com *Web Site:* www.chroniclebooks.com, pg 52

Roberts, Paul, George T Bisel Co Inc, 710 S Washington Sq, Philadelphia, PA 19106-3519 *Tel:* 215-922-5760 *Toll Free Tel:* 800-247-3526 *Fax:* 215-922-2235 *E-mail:* gbisel@bisel.com *Web Site:* www.bisel.com, pg 33

Roberts, Sherry, The Roberts Group, 12803 Eastview Curve, Apple Valley, MN 55124 *Tel:* 952-322-4005 *E-mail:* info@editorialservice.com *Web Site:* www.editorialservice.com, pg 470

Roberts, Sian, SAS Press, 100 SAS Campus Dr, Cary, NC 27513-2414 *Tel:* 919-677-8000 *Toll Free Tel:* 800-727-0025 *Fax:* 919-677-4444 *E-mail:* saspress@sas.com *Web Site:* support.sas.com/en/books.html, pg 192

Roberts, Stuart, Simon & Schuster, 1230 Avenue of the Americas, New York, NY 10020 *Tel:* 212-698-7000 *Toll Free Tel:* 800-223-2348 (cust serv); 800-223-2336 (orders) *Toll Free Fax:* 800-943-9831 (orders) *Web Site:* www.simonandschuster.com, pg 198

Roberts, Tim, Counterpath Press, 7935 E 14 Ave, Denver, CO 80220 *E-mail:* counterpath@counterpathpress.org *Web Site:* www.counterpathpress.org, pg 58

Roberts, Tony, The Roberts Group, 12803 Eastview Curve, Apple Valley, MN 55124 *Tel:* 952-322-4005 *E-mail:* info@editorialservice.com *Web Site:* www.editorialservice.com, pg 470

Roberts, Tony, University of Oklahoma Press, 2800 Venture Dr, Norman, OK 73069-8216 *Tel:* 405-325-2000 *Web Site:* www.oupress.com, pg 230

Roberts, U D, Brentwood Christian Press, PO Box 4773, Columbus, GA 31914-4773 *Toll Free Tel:* 800-334-8861 *E-mail:* brentwood@aol.com *Web Site:* www.brentwoodbooks.com, pg 40

Robertson, Alice, Chronicle Books, 680 Second St, San Francisco, CA 94107 *Tel:* 415-537-4200 *Toll Free Tel:* 800-759-0190 (cust serv) *Fax:* 415-537-4460

Root, William Pitt, Joy Harjo Poetry Award, PO Box 2414, Durango, CO 81302 *Tel:* 970-903-7914 *E-mail:* cutthroatmag@gmail.com *Web Site:* www. cutthroatmag.com, pg 622

Roque, Kathryn, Perseus Books, 1290 Avenue of the Americas, New York, NY 10104 *Tel:* 212-340-8100 *Toll Free Tel:* 800-343-4499 (cust serv) *Fax:* 212-340-8105 *Web Site:* www.perseusbooks.com, pg 167

Rosa-Mendoza, Gladys, me+mi publishing inc, 2600 Beverly Dr, Unit 113, Aurora, IL 60502 *Tel:* 630-588-9801 *Toll Free Tel:* 888-251-1444 *Web Site:* www. memima.com, pg 137

Rosado, Adrienne, Stonesong, 270 W 39 St, Suite 201, New York, NY 10018 *Tel:* 212-929-4600 *E-mail:* editors@stonesong.com *Web Site:* www. stonesong.com, pg 504

Rosamilia, Michael, Kensington Publishing Corp, 119 W 40 St, New York, NY 10018 *Tel:* 212-407-1500 *Toll Free Tel:* 800-221-2647 *Fax:* 212-935-0699 *Web Site:* www.kensingtonbooks.com, pg 116

Rosart, Sharyn, Sasquatch Books, 1904 S Third Ave, Suite 710, Seattle, WA 98101 *Tel:* 206-467-4300 *Toll Free Tel:* 800-775-0817 *Fax:* 206-467-4301 *E-mail:* custserv@sasquatchbooks.com *Web Site:* sasquatchbooks.com, pg 192

Rosati, Daniel P, William S Hein & Co Inc, 2350 N Forest Rd, Getzville, NY 14068 *Tel:* 716-882-2600 *Toll Free Tel:* 800-828-7571 *Fax:* 716-883-8100 *E-mail:* mail@wshein.com; marketing@wshein.com *Web Site:* www.wshein.com, pg 97

Rosati, Patty, HarperCollins Children's Books, 195 Broadway, New York, NY 10007 *Tel:* 212-207-7000 *Web Site:* www.harpercollins.com/childrens, pg 93

Rose, Ann, Prospect Agency, 285 Fifth Ave, PMB 445, Brooklyn, NY 11215 *Tel:* 718-788-3217 *Fax:* 718-360-9582 *Web Site:* www.prospectagency.com, pg 499

Rose, Lindsey, Dutton, 1745 Broadway, New York, NY 10019 *Tel:* 212-366-2000 *Fax:* 212-366-2262 *E-mail:* duttonpublicity@us.penguingroup.com *Web Site:* www.penguin.com, pg 68

Rose, Rebecca, Breakwater Books Ltd, One Stamp's Lane, St John's, NL A1C 6E6, Canada *Tel:* 709-722-6680 *Toll Free Tel:* 800-563-3333 (orders) *Fax:* 709-753-0708 *E-mail:* info@breakwaterbooks. com; orders@breakwaterbooks.com *Web Site:* www. breakwaterbooks.com, pg 417

Rose, Verena, Agatha Awards, PO Box 8007, Gaithersburg, MD 20898 *Tel:* 301-730-1675 *E-mail:* mdregservices@gmail.com *Web Site:* malicedomestic.org, pg 590

Roseman, Karl-Heinz, McFarland, 960 NC Hwy 88 W, Jefferson, NC 28640 *Tel:* 336-246-4460 *Toll Free Tel:* 800-253-2187 (orders) *Fax:* 336-246-5018; 336-246-4403 (orders) *E-mail:* info@mcfarlandpub.com *Web Site:* mcfarlandbooks.com, pg 135

Rosen, Joan, Charlotte Sheedy Literary Agency Inc, 928 Broadway, Suite 901, New York, NY 10010 *Tel:* 212-780-9800 *Web Site:* www.sheedylit.com, pg 502

Rosen, Lynn, Yard Dog Press, 710 W Redbud Lane, Alma, AR 72921-7247 *Tel:* 479-632-4693 *Fax:* 479-632-4693 *Web Site:* www.yarddogpress.com, pg 247

Rosen, Mollie, 4A's (American Association of Advertising Agencies), 1065 Avenue of the Americas, 16th fl, New York, NY 10018 *Tel:* 212-682-2500 *Web Site:* www.aaaa.org, pg 534

Rosen, Roger, Enslow Publishing LLC, 101 W 23 St, Suite 240, New York, NY 10011 *Toll Free Tel:* 800-398-2504 *Fax:* 908-771-0925 *Toll Free Fax:* 877-980-4454 *E-mail:* customerservice@enslow.com *Web Site:* www.enslow.com, pg 72

Rosen, Roger, The Rosen Publishing Group Inc, 29 E 21 St, New York, NY 10010 *Toll Free Tel:* 800-237-9932 *Toll Free Fax:* 888-436-4643 *E-mail:* info@rosenpub. com *Web Site:* www.rosenpublishing.com, pg 187

Rosen, Selina, Yard Dog Press, 710 W Redbud Lane, Alma, AR 72921-7247 *Tel:* 479-632-4693 *Fax:* 479-632-4693 *Web Site:* www.yarddogpress.com, pg 247

Rosenbaum, David M, University of Missouri Press, 113 Heinkel Bldg, 201 S Seventh St, Columbia, MO 65211 *Tel:* 573-882-7641; 573-882-3000 (publicity & sales enquiries) *Toll Free Tel:* 800-621-2736 (orders) *Fax:* 573-884-4498 *Toll Free Fax:* 800-621-8476 (orders) *E-mail:* upress@missouri.edu; umpmarketing@missouri.edu (publicity & sales enquiries) *Web Site:* upress.missouri.edu, pg 228

Rosenberg, Barbara Collins, The Rosenberg Group, 23 Lincoln Ave, Marblehead, MA 01945 *Tel:* 781-990-1341 *Fax:* 781-990-1344 *E-mail:* rosenberglitsubmit@ icloud.com *Web Site:* www.rosenberggroup.com, pg 500

Rosenberg, Dan, Harvard Common Press, 100 Cummings Ctr, Suite 265-D, Beverly, MA 01915 *Tel:* 978-282-9590 *Fax:* 978-282-7765 *Web Site:* www. quartoknows.com/harvard-common-press, pg 94

Rosenberg, Jessica, Harlequin Enterprises Ltd, 195 Broadway, 24th fl, New York, NY 10007 *Tel:* 212-207-7000 *Toll Free Tel:* 888-432-4879 *E-mail:* customerservice@harlequin.com *Web Site:* www.harlequin.com, pg 93

Rosenberg, Julie, Disney-Hyperion Books, 1101 Flower St, Glendale, CA 91201 *Web Site:* books.disney.com, pg 65

Rosenberg, Linda, GP Putnam's Sons (Hardcover), 375 Hudson St, New York, NY 10014 *Tel:* 212-366-2000 *Fax:* 212-366-2643 *E-mail:* online@ penguinputnam.com *Web Site:* www.penguin.com/ publishers/gpputnamssons, pg 178

Rosenberg, Liz, Binghamton University Creative Writing Program, c/o Dept of English, PO Box 6000, Binghamton, NY 13902-6000 *Tel:* 607-777-2168 *Fax:* 607-777-2408 *E-mail:* cwpro@binghamton.edu *Web Site:* english.binghamton.edu/cwpro, pg 581

Rosenberg, Tracy, Media Alliance, 2830 20 St, Suite 102, San Francisco, CA 94110 *Tel:* 415-746-9475 *E-mail:* information@media-alliance.org *Web Site:* www.media-alliance.org, pg 537

Rosenberry, Eliza, HarperCollins General Books Group, 195 Broadway, New York, NY 10007 *Tel:* 212-207-7000 *Web Site:* www.harpercollins.com, pg 94

Rosenblum, Batya, The Experiment, 220 E 23 St, Suite 600, New York, NY 10010-4658 *Tel:* 212-889-1659 *E-mail:* info@theexperimentpublishing.com *Web Site:* www.theexperimentpublishing.com, pg 74

Rosenblum, Bruce, Television Academy, 5220 Lankershim Blvd, North Hollywood, CA 91601-3109 *Tel:* 818-754-2800 *Fax:* 818-761-2827 *Web Site:* www. emmys.org, pg 547

Rosenblum, Stefanie, Portfolio, 375 Hudson St, New York, NY 10014 *Web Site:* www.penguin.com/meet/ publishers/portfolio, pg 172

Rosenbush, Ellen, Harper's Magazine Foundation, 666 Broadway, 11th fl, New York, NY 10012 *Tel:* 212-420-5720 *Toll Free Tel:* 800-444-4653 *Fax:* 212-228-5889 *E-mail:* harpers@harpers.org *Web Site:* www. harpers.org, pg 94

Rosenfeld, Dina, Hachai Publishing, 527 Empire Blvd, Brooklyn, NY 11225 *Tel:* 718-633-0100 *Fax:* 718-633-0103 *E-mail:* info@hachai.com *Web Site:* www. hachai.com, pg 90

Rosenfeld, Nancy, AAA Books Unlimited, 3060 Blackthorn Rd, Riverwoods, IL 60015 *Tel:* 847-444-1220 *Fax:* 847-607-8335 *Web Site:* www. aaabooksunlimited.com, pg 473

Rosenfeld, Theodore D, Taplinger Publishing Co Inc, PO Box 175, Marlboro, NJ 07746-0175 *Tel:* 305-256-7880 *Fax:* 305-256-7816 *E-mail:* taplingerpub@yahoo.com (rts & perms, edit, corp only), pg 213

Rosenkranz, Randi, Penguin Random House LLC, 1745 Broadway, New York, NY 10019 *Tel:* 212-782-9000 *Toll Free Tel:* 800-726-0600 *Web Site:* www. penguinrandomhouse.com, pg 164

Rosenkranz, Rita, Rita Rosenkranz Literary Agency, 440 West End Ave, Suite 15D, New York, NY 10024-5358 *Tel:* 212-873-6333 *Fax:* 212-873-5225 *Web Site:* www. ritarosenkranzliteraryagency.com, pg 500

Rosenson, Clare, United States Holocaust Memorial Museum, 100 Raoul Wallenberg Place SW, Washington, DC 20024-2126 *Tel:* 202-488-0400; 202-314-7837; 202-488-6144 (orders) *Toll Free Tel:* 800-259-9998 (orders) *Fax:* 202-479-9726; 202-488-0438 (orders) *E-mail:* cahs_publications@ushmm.org *Web Site:* www.ushmm.org, pg 224

Rosenstreich, Lilian, Eclectic Book Press, 72 Glenmaura National Blvd, Suite 104B, Moosic, PA 18507 *Tel:* 862-251-2296; 570-878-7960 *E-mail:* info@endlessmountainspublishing.com *Web Site:* endlessmountainspublishing.com, pg 69

Rosenstreich, Lilian, Endless Mountains Publishing Co, 72 Glenmaura National Blvd, Suite 104B, Moosic, PA 18507 *Tel:* 862-251-2296; 570-878-7960 *E-mail:* info@endlessmountainspublishing.com *Web Site:* www.endlessmountainspublishing.com, pg 72

Rosenstreich, Lilian, Kalaniot Books, 72 Glenmaura National Blvd, Suite 104B, Moosic, PA 18507 *Tel:* 862-251-2296; 570-878-7960 *E-mail:* info@ endlessmountainspublishing.com *Web Site:* www. endlessmountainspublishing.com, pg 115

Rosenthal, Carole, Hamilton Stone Editions, PO Box 43, Maplewood, NJ 07040 *Tel:* 973-378-8361 *E-mail:* hstone@hamiltonstone.org *Web Site:* www. hamiltonstone.org, pg 92

Rosenthal, David, Houghton Mifflin Harcourt Trade & Reference Division, 125 High St, Boston, MA 02110 *Tel:* 617-351-5000 *Web Site:* www.hmhco.com, pg 104

Rosenthal, Elise, Rosenthal Represents, 23725 Hartland St, West Hills, CA 91307 *Tel:* 818-430-3850 *E-mail:* eliselicenses@earthlink.net, pg 512

Rosenthal, Maggie, Viking Children's Books, 345 Hudson St, New York, NY 10014 *Fax:* 212-414-3393 *E-mail:* youngreaderspublicity@us.penguingroup. com *Web Site:* www.penguin.com/publishers/ vikingchildrensbooks, pg 236

Rosenwald, Robert, Poisoned Pen Press, 4014 N Goldwater Blvd, Suite 201, Scottsdale, AZ 85251 *Tel:* 480-945-3375 *Toll Free Tel:* 800-421-3976 *Fax:* 480-949-1707 *E-mail:* info@poisonedpenpress. com *Web Site:* www.poisonedpenpress.com, pg 171

Rosenwasser, Rena, Kelsey Street Press, 2824 Kelsey St, Berkeley, CA 94705 *E-mail:* info@kelseyst.com *Web Site:* www.kelseyst.com, pg 116

Rosinsky, Lisa, Barefoot Books, 2067 Massachusetts Ave, 5th fl, Cambridge, MA 02140 *Tel:* 617-576-0660 *Toll Free Tel:* 866-215-1756 (cust serv); 866-417-2369 (orders) *Fax:* 617-576-0049 *E-mail:* help@ barefootbooks.com *Web Site:* www.barefootbooks.com, pg 28

Rosoff, Jodi, Grand Central Publishing, 1290 Avenue of the Americas, New York, NY 10104 *Tel:* 212-364-1100 *Web Site:* www.hachettebookgroup.com, pg 88

Rosokoff, Sylvie, Trident Media Group LLC, 41 Madison Ave, 36th fl, New York, NY 10010 *Tel:* 212-333-1511 *E-mail:* info@tridentmediagroup.com; press@tridentmediagroup.com *Web Site:* www. tridentmediagroup.com, pg 507

Ross, Andy, Andy Ross Literary Agency, 767 Santa Ray Ave, Oakland, CA 94610 *Tel:* 510-238-8965 *E-mail:* andyrossagency@hotmail.com *Web Site:* www. andyrossagency.com, pg 474

Ross, Catherine Barbosa, HarperCollins General Books Group, 195 Broadway, New York, NY 10007 *Tel:* 212-207-7000 *Web Site:* www.harpercollins.com, pg 93

Ross, Franz H, Ross Books, PO Box 4340, Berkeley, CA 94704-0340 *Tel:* 510-841-2474 *Fax:* 510-295-2531 *E-mail:* sales@rossbooks.com *Web Site:* www. rossbooks.com, pg 187

Ross, Katelin, Shambhala Publications Inc, 4720 Walnut St, Boulder, CO 80301 *Tel:* 303-222-9598 *Toll Free Tel:* 866-424-0030 (off); 888-424-2329 (cust serv) *E-mail:* customercare@shambhala.com *Web Site:* www.shambhala.com, pg 197

Ross, Maureen, diacriTech Inc, 4 S Market St, 4th fl, Boston, MA 02109 *Tel:* 617-600-3366 *Fax:* 617-848-2938 *Web Site:* www.diacritech.com, pg 462

Ross, Rachel, American Psychological Association, 750 First St NE, Washington, DC 20002-4242 *Tel:* 202-336-5510 *Toll Free Tel:* 800-374-2721 *Fax:* 202-336-5502 *E-mail:* order@apa.org *Web Site:* www.apa.org/books, pg 13

Ross, Whitney, Irene Goodman Literary Agency, 27 W 24 St, Suite 700B, New York, NY 10010 *Tel:* 212-604-0330 *E-mail:* queries@irenegoodman.com *Web Site:* www.irenegoodman.com, pg 486

Rossi, Janet, The MIT Press, One Rogers St, Cambridge, MA 02142 *Tel:* 617-253-5255 *Toll Free Tel:* 800-405-1619 (orders) *Fax:* 617-258-6779; 617-577-1545 (orders) *Web Site:* mitpress.mit.edu, pg 141

Rossi, Janice, Kensington Publishing Corp, 119 W 40 St, New York, NY 10018 *Tel:* 212-407-1500 *Toll Free Tel:* 800-221-2647 *Fax:* 212-935-0699 *Web Site:* www.kensingtonbooks.com, pg 116

Rossi, Stefani, Janet B McCabe Poetry Prize, 1041 N Taft Hill Rd, Fort Collins, CO 80521 *Tel:* 970-449-2726 *E-mail:* editor@ruminatemagazine.org *Web Site:* www.ruminatemagazine.com, pg 639

Rossi, Stefani, William Van Dyke Short Story Prize, 1041 N Taft Hill Rd, Fort Collins, CO 80521 *Tel:* 970-449-2726 *E-mail:* editor@ruminatemagazine.org *Web Site:* www.ruminatemagazine.com, pg 675

Rossi, Stefani, VanderMey Nonfiction Prize, 1041 N Taft Hill Rd, Fort Collins, CO 80521 *Tel:* 970-449-2726 *E-mail:* editor@ruminatemagazine.org *Web Site:* www.ruminatemagazine.com, pg 675

Rossi, Tony, The Christopher Awards, 5 Hanover Sq, 22nd fl, New York, NY 10004-2751 *Tel:* 212-759-4050 *Toll Free Tel:* 888-298-4050 (orders) *Fax:* 212-838-5073 *E-mail:* mail@christophers.org *Web Site:* www.christophers.org, pg 605

Rosso, Don, Waveland Press Inc, 4180 IL Rte 83, Suite 101, Long Grove, IL 60047-9580 *Tel:* 847-634-0081 *Fax:* 847-634-9501 *E-mail:* info@waveland.com *Web Site:* www.waveland.com, pg 238

Rostan, Stephanie, Levine|Greenberg|Rostan Literary Agency, 307 Seventh Ave, Suite 2407, New York, NY 10001 *Tel:* 212-337-0934 *Fax:* 212-337-0948 *Web Site:* lgrliterary.com, pg 493

Rota, Kara, Chicago Review Press, 814 N Franklin St, Chicago, IL 60610 *Tel:* 312-337-0747 *Toll Free:* 800-888-4741 *Fax:* 312-337-5110 *E-mail:* frontdesk@chicagoreviewpress.com *Web Site:* www.chicagoreviewpress.com, pg 50

Rota, Kara, St Martin's Press, LLC, 120 Broadway, New York, NY 10271 *Tel:* 646-307-5151 *Web Site:* us.macmillan.com/smp, pg 190

Roth, Jessica, Gallery Books, 1230 Avenue of the Americas, New York, NY 10020 *Toll Free Tel:* 800-456-6798 *Fax:* 212-698-7284 *E-mail:* consumer.customerservice@simonandschuster.com *Web Site:* www.simonandschuster.com, pg 83

Roth, Laurence, Susquehanna University, Department of English & Creative Writing, 514 University Ave, Selinsgrove, PA 17870 *Tel:* 570-372-0101, pg 585

Roth, Maya E, Jane Chambers Playwriting Award, Georgetown University, 108 David Performing Arts Ctr, Box 571063, 37 & "O" St, NW, Washington, DC 20057-1063 *Web Site:* www.athe.org/?page=Jane_Chambers, pg 604

Roth, Melanie, Fulcrum Publishing Inc, 4690 Table Mountain Dr, Suite 100, Golden, CO 80403 *Tel:* 303-277-1623 *Toll Free Tel:* 800-992-2908 *Fax:* 303-279-7111 *Toll Free Fax:* 800-726-7112 *E-mail:* info@fulcrumbooks.com; orders@fulcrumbooks.com *Web Site:* www.fulcrumbooks.com, pg 82

Roth, Rachel, Transcontinental Music Publications (TMP), 1375 Remington Rd, Suite M, Schaumburg, IL 60173-4844 *Tel:* 847-781-7800 *Fax:* 847-781-7801 *E-mail:* tmp@accantors.org *Web Site:* www.transcontinentalmusic.com, pg 220

Roth, Stefani, ASCD, 1703 N Beauregard St, Alexandria, VA 22311-1714 *Tel:* 703-578-9600 *Toll Free Tel:* 800-933-2723 *Fax:* 703-575-5400 *E-mail:* member@ascd.org *Web Site:* www.ascd.org, pg 21

Rothberg, Adam, Simon & Schuster, Inc, 1230 Avenue of the Americas, New York, NY 10020 *Tel:* 212-698-7000 *Toll Free Tel:* 800-223-2336 (orders) *Fax:* 212-698-7007 *Toll Free Fax:* 800-943-9831 (orders) *E-mail:* firstname.lastname@simonandschuster.com; purchaseorders@simonandschuster.com (orders) *Web Site:* www.simonandschuster.com, pg 199

Rothman, Valinda, Book Publicists of Southern California, 714 Crescent Dr, Beverly Hills, CA 90210 *Tel:* 323-461-3921 *Fax:* 323-461-0917 *Web Site:* www.bookpublicists.org, pg 528

Rothmeyer, Bob, Concordia Publishing House, 3558 S Jefferson Ave, St Louis, MO 63118-3968 *Tel:* 314-268-1000; 314-268-1268 (bookshop) *Toll Free Tel:* 800-325-3040 (cust serv) *Toll Free Fax:* 800-490-9889 (cust serv) *E-mail:* order@cph.org *Web Site:* www.cph.org, pg 56

Rothschild, Eileen, St Martin's Press, LLC, 120 Broadway, New York, NY 10271 *Tel:* 646-307-5151 *Web Site:* us.macmillan.com/smp, pg 190

Rothschild, Richard, American Book Producers Association (ABPA), 31 W Eighth St, 2nd fl, New York, NY 10011 *Tel:* 212-675-1363 *Fax:* 212-675-1364 *E-mail:* office@abpaonline.org *Web Site:* www.abpaonline.org, pg 522

Rothstein, Philip Jan, Rothstein Associates Inc, 4 Arapaho Rd, Brookfield, CT 06804-3104 *Tel:* 203-740-7400 *Toll Free Tel:* 888-768-4783 *Fax:* 203-740-7401 *E-mail:* info@rothstein.com *Web Site:* www.rothstein.com; www.rothsteinpublishing.com, pg 187

Rotor, Elda, Penguin Books, 375 Hudson St, New York, NY 10014 *Tel:* 212-366-2000 *E-mail:* penguinpublicity@us.penguingroup.com *Web Site:* www.penguinclassics.com; www.penguin.com, pg 163

Rotstein, David, St Martin's Press, LLC, 120 Broadway, New York, NY 10271 *Tel:* 646-307-5151 *Web Site:* us.macmillan.com/smp, pg 190

Rounds, John, St Martin's Press, LLC, 120 Broadway, New York, NY 10271 *Tel:* 646-307-5151 *Web Site:* us.macmillan.com/smp, pg 190

Rourke, Kathleen, Candlewick Press, 99 Dover St, Somerville, MA 02144-2825 *Tel:* 617-661-3330 *Fax:* 617-661-0565 *E-mail:* bigbear@candlewick.com; salesinfo@candlewick.com *Web Site:* www.candlewick.com, pg 44

Rouse, Martin, Trident Media Group LLC, 41 Madison Ave, 36th fl, New York, NY 10010 *Tel:* 212-333-1511 *E-mail:* info@tridentmediagroup.com; press@tridentmediagroup.com *Web Site:* www.tridentmediagroup.com, pg 507

Rouse, William R, Capstone Publishers™, 1710 Roe Crest Dr, North Mankato, MN 56003 *Toll Free Tel:* 800-747-4992 (cust serv) *Toll Free Fax:* 888-262-0705 *E-mail:* customer.service@capstonepub.com *Web Site:* www.capstonepub.com, pg 44

Rousseau, Christopher, Practising Law Institute, 1177 Avenue of the Americas, New York, NY 10036 *Tel:* 212-824-5700 *Toll Free Tel:* 800-260-4PLI (260-4754, cust serv) *Toll Free Fax:* 800-321-0093 (local) *E-mail:* info@pli.edu (cust serv) *Web Site:* www.pli.edu, pg 173

Roussopoulos, Dimitrios, Black Rose Books Ltd, CP 35788 Succ Leo-Pariseau, Montreal, QC H2X 0A4, Canada *Tel:* 514-844-4076 *E-mail:* info@blackrosebooks.com *Web Site:* blackrosebooks.com, pg 416

Roux, Michael, University of Illinois Press, 1325 S Oak St, MC-566, Champaign, IL 61820-6903 *Tel:* 217-333-0950 *Fax:* 217-244-8082 *E-mail:* uipress@uillinois.edu; journals@uillinois.edu *Web Site:* www.press.uillinois.edu, pg 227

Rowe, Carol, Waveland Press Inc, 4180 IL Rte 83, Suite 101, Long Grove, IL 60047-9580 *Tel:* 847-634-0081 *Fax:* 847-634-9501 *E-mail:* info@waveland.com *Web Site:* www.waveland.com, pg 238

Rowe, Martin, Lantern Books, 128 Second Place, Garden Suite, Brooklyn, NY 11231 *Tel:* 212-414-2275 *E-mail:* editorial@lanternbooks.com; info@lanternmedia.net *Web Site:* lanternbooks.presswarehouse.com/home/home.aspx, pg 120

Rowe, Neil, Waveland Press Inc, 4180 IL Rte 83, Suite 101, Long Grove, IL 60047-9580 *Tel:* 847-634-0081 *Fax:* 847-634-9501 *E-mail:* info@waveland.com *Web Site:* www.waveland.com, pg 238

Rowland, Melissa, Levine|Greenberg|Rostan Literary Agency, 307 Seventh Ave, Suite 2407, New York, NY 10001 *Tel:* 212-337-0934 *Fax:* 212-337-0948 *Web Site:* lgrliterary.com, pg 493

Roy, Denise, Little, Brown and Company, 1290 Avenue of the Americas, New York, NY 10104 *Tel:* 212-364-1100 *Fax:* 212-364-0952 *E-mail:* firstname.lastname@hbgusa.com *Web Site:* www.littlebrown.com; www.hachettebookgroup.com, pg 126

Roy, Mary Lou, University of Alberta Press, Ring House 2, Edmonton, AB T6G 2E1, Canada *Tel:* 780-492-3662 *Fax:* 780-492-0719 *Web Site:* www.uap.ualberta.ca, pg 442

Roy, Michael, American Psychiatric Association Publishing, 800 Maine Ave SW, Suite 900, Washington, DC 20024 *Tel:* 202-459-9722 *Toll Free Tel:* 800-368-5777 *Fax:* 202-403-3094 *E-mail:* appi@psych.org *Web Site:* www.appi.org; www.psychiatryonline.org, pg 13

Royal, Jaynie, The Acheven Book Prize for Young Adult Fiction, c/o Regal House Publishing, 806 Oberlin Rd, No 12094, Raleigh, NC 27605 *E-mail:* info@regalhousepublishing.com *Web Site:* regalhousepublishing.com/the-acheven-book-prize-for-young-adult-fiction/, pg 589

Royal, Jaynie, The Terry J Cox Poetry Award, 806 Oberlin Rd, No 12094, Raleigh, NC 27605 *E-mail:* info@regalhousepublishing.com *Web Site:* regalhousepublishing.com/the-terry-j-cox-poetry-award/, pg 607

Royal, Jaynie, Fitzroy Books, c/o Regal House Publishing, 806 Oberlin Rd, No 12094, Raleigh, NC 27605 *E-mail:* info@regalhousepublishing.com *Web Site:* fitzroybooks.com, pg 78

Royal, Jaynie, The Kraken Book Prize for Middle-Grade Fiction, c/o Regal House Publishing, 806 Oberlin Rd, No 12094, Raleigh, NC 27605 *E-mail:* info@regalhousepublishing.com *Web Site:* regalhousepublishing.com/the-kraken-book-award/, pg 630

Royal, Jaynie, The Petrichor Prize for Finely Crafted Fiction, 806 Oberlin Rd, No 12094, Raleigh, NC 27605 *E-mail:* info@regalhousepublishing.com *Web Site:* regalhousepublishing.com/the-petrichor-prize-for-finely-crafted-fiction/, pg 655

Royal, Jaynie, Regal House Publishing, 806 Oberlin Rd, No 12094, Raleigh, NC 27605 *E-mail:* info@regalhousepublishing.com *Web Site:* regalhousepublishing.com, pg 184

Royall, John T, Gulf Energy Information, 2 Greenway Plaza, Suite 1020, Houston, TX 77046 *Tel:* 713-529-4301 *E-mail:* store@gulfpub.com; customerservice@energyinfo.com *Web Site:* www.gulfenergyinfo.com, pg 90

Royce, Adam, Penguin Young Readers Group, 345 Hudson St, New York, NY 10014 *Tel:* 212-366-2000; 212-414-3553 *Fax:* 212-414-3340 *Web Site:* www.penguin.com/children, pg 165

Royce, Michael, NYSCA/NYFA Artist Fellowships, 20 Jay St, 7th fl, Brooklyn, NY 11201 *Tel:* 212-366-6900 *Fax:* 212-366-1778 *E-mail:* info@nyfa.org *Web Site:* www.nyfa.org, pg 649

Rozenberg, Rebecca, Johns Hopkins University Press, 2715 N Charles St, Baltimore, MD 21218-4363 *Tel:* 410-516-6900; 410-516-6987 (journal orders outside US & CN) *Toll Free Tel:* 800-537-5487 (book orders & cust serv); 800-548-1784 (journal orders) *Fax:* 410-516-6968; 410-516-3866 (journal orders);

410-516-6998 (orders) *E-mail:* hfscustserv@press.jhu. edu (cust serv); jrnlcirc@press.jhu.edu (journal orders) *Web Site:* www.press.jhu.edu; muse.jhu.edu, pg 114

Rubenstein, Ellis, New York Academy of Sciences (NYAS), 7 World Trade Center, 40th fl, 250 Greenwich St, New York, NY 10007-2157 *Tel:* 212-298-8600 *Toll Free Tel:* 800-843-6927 *Fax:* 212-298-3650 *E-mail:* nyas@nyas.org; annals@nyas.org; customerservice@nyas.org *Web Site:* www.nyas.org, pg 150

Rubie, Peter, FinePrint Literary Management, 207 W 106 St, Suite 1D, New York, NY 10025 *Tel:* 212-279-6214 *E-mail:* assist@fineprint.com *Web Site:* www. fineprintlit.com, pg 484

Rubin, Barry, Lederer Books, 6120 Day Long Lane, Clarksville, MD 21029 *Tel:* 410-531-6644 *Toll Free Tel:* 800-410-7367 (orders) *Fax:* 410-531-9440 *Toll Free Fax:* 800-327-0048 *E-mail:* customerservice@ messianicjewish.net *Web Site:* www.messianicjewish. net, pg 122

Rubin, Barry, Messianic Jewish Publishers, 6120 Day Long Lane, Clarksville, MD 21029 *Tel:* 410-531-6644; 616-970-2449 *Toll Free Tel:* 800-410-7367 (orders) *Fax:* 410-531-9440; 717-761-7273 (orders) *Toll Free Fax:* 800-327-0048 (orders) *E-mail:* editor@messianicjewish. net; customerservice@messianicjewish.net *Web Site:* messianicjewish.net/publish, pg 138

Rubin, Lorna, Triad Publishing Co, PO Box 13355, Gainesville, FL 32604 *Fax:* 304-727-9345 *Toll Free Fax:* 800-854-4947 *E-mail:* orders@triadpublishing. com *Web Site:* www.triadpublishing.com, pg 220

Rubin, Reka, Harlequin Enterprises Ltd, Bay Adelaide Centre, East Tower, 22 Adelaide St W, 41st fl, Toronto, ON M5H 4E3, Canada *Tel:* 416-445-5860 *Toll Free Tel:* 888-432-4879; 800-370-5838 (ebook inquiries) *E-mail:* customerservice@harlequin.com *Web Site:* www.harlequin.com, pg 429

Rubins, Jennifer, Penguin Random House Audio Publishing, 1745 Broadway, New York, NY 10019 *E-mail:* audio@penguinrandomhouse.com *Web Site:* www.penguinrandomhouseaudio.com, pg 164

Rubinstein, Elizabeth Winick, McIntosh and Otis Inc, 207 E 37 St, Suite BG, New York, NY 10016 *Tel:* 212-687-7040 *Fax:* 212-687-6894 *E-mail:* info@ mcintoshandotis.com *Web Site:* www.mcintoshandotis. com, pg 496

Rubinstein, Jordan, Grand Central Publishing, 1290 Avenue of the Americas, New York, NY 10104 *Tel:* 212-364-1100 *Web Site:* www.hachettebookgroup. com, pg 88

Rubsam, Jeannie, Tiger Tales, 5 River Rd, Suite 128, Wilton, CT 06897-4069 *Tel:* 920-387-2333 *Fax:* 920-387-9994 *Web Site:* www.tigertalesbooks.com, pg 218

Ruby-Strauss, Jeremie, Gallery Books, 1230 Avenue of the Americas, New York, NY 10020 *Toll Free Tel:* 800-456-6798 *Fax:* 212-698-7284 *E-mail:* consumer.customerservice@simonandschuster. com *Web Site:* www.simonandschuster.com, pg 83

Rucci, Marysue, Simon & Schuster, 1230 Avenue of the Americas, New York, NY 10020 *Tel:* 212-698-7000 *Toll Free Tel:* 800-223-2348 (cust serv); 800-223-2336 (orders) *Toll Free Fax:* 800-943-9831 (orders) *Web Site:* www.simonandschuster.com, pg 198

Ruchti, Cynthia, Books & Such, 52 Mission Circle, Suite 122, PMB 170, Santa Rosa, CA 95409-5370 *Tel:* 707-538-4184 *Web Site:* booksandsuch.com, pg 477

Ruck, Holly, Macmillan, 120 Broadway, 22nd fl, New York, NY 10271 *Tel:* 646-307-5151 *E-mail:* press. inquiries@macmillan.com *Web Site:* www.macmillan. com, pg 130

Rucker, Sarah, Gibbs Smith Publisher, 1877 E Gentile St, Layton, UT 84041 *Tel:* 801-544-9800 *Toll Free Tel:* 800-748-5439; 800-835-4993 (orders) *Fax:* 801-544-5582 *Toll Free Fax:* 800-213-3023 (orders only) *E-mail:* info@gibbs-smith.com; tradeorders@gibbs-smith.com *Web Site:* www.gibbs-smith.com, pg 85

Ruda, Taneli, John Wiley & Sons Inc, 111 River St, Hoboken, NJ 07030-5774 *Tel:* 201-748-6000 *Toll Free Tel:* 800-225-5945 (cust serv) *Fax:* 201-748-6088 *E-mail:* info@wiley.com *Web Site:* www.wiley.com, pg 241

Rudden, Joe, BuilderBooks, 1201 15 St NW, Washington, DC 20005 *Tel:* 202-822-0200 *Toll Free Tel:* 800-223-2665 *Fax:* 202-266-8096 (edit) *E-mail:* info@nahb.com *Web Site:* builderbooks.com, pg 42

Ruder, Karen, Optometric Extension Program Foundation (OEP), 2300 York Rd, Suite 113, Timonium, MD 21093 *Tel:* 410-561-3791 *E-mail:* admin@oepf.org *Web Site:* www.oepf.org, pg 156

Rudin, Max, The Library of America, 14 E 60 St, New York, NY 10022-1006 *Tel:* 212-308-3360 *Fax:* 212-750-8352 *E-mail:* info@loa.org *Web Site:* www.loa. org, pg 124

Rudman, Michael P, National Learning Corp, 212 Michael Dr, Syosset, NY 11791 *Tel:* 516-921-8888 *Toll Free Tel:* 800-632-8888 *Fax:* 516-921-8743 *E-mail:* info@passbooks.com *Web Site:* www. passbooks.com, pg 147

Rudolph, Janet, Macavity Award, 7155 Marlborough Terr, Berkeley, CA 94705 *Tel:* 510-845-3600 *Web Site:* www.mysteryreaders.org, pg 636

Rudolph, John, Dystel, Goderich & Bourret LLC, One Union Sq W, Suite 904, New York, NY 10003 *Tel:* 212-627-9100 *Fax:* 212-627-9313 *Web Site:* www. dystel.com, pg 482

Rudolph, Kelly, HarperCollins General Books Group, 195 Broadway, New York, NY 10007 *Tel:* 212-207-7000 *Web Site:* www.harpercollins.com, pg 93

Rudy, Caryn Karmatz, DeFiore and Company Literary Management Inc, 47 E 19 St, 3rd fl, New York, NY 10003 *Tel:* 212-925-7744 *Fax:* 212-925-9803 *E-mail:* info@defliterary.com; submissions@ defliterary.com *Web Site:* www.defliterary.com, pg 481

Rue, Robin, Writers House, 21 W 26 St, New York, NY 10010 *Tel:* 212-685-2400 *Web Site:* www.writershouse. com, pg 508

Ruffin, Katherine McCanless, American Printing History Association, PO Box 4519, Grand Central Sta, New York, NY 10163 *E-mail:* secretary@printinghistory.org *Web Site:* printinghistory.org, pg 523

Ruffin, Katherine McCanless, American Printing History Association Award, PO Box 4519, Grand Central Sta, New York, NY 10163 *E-mail:* secretary@ printinghistory.org *Web Site:* printinghistory.org, pg 592

Ruffin, Michael L, Smyth & Helwys Publishing Inc, 6316 Peake Rd, Macon, GA 31210-3960 *Tel:* 478-757-0564 *Toll Free Tel:* 800-747-3016 (orders only) *Fax:* 478-757-1305 *E-mail:* information@helwys.com *Web Site:* www.helwys.com, pg 202

Ruffino, Dan, Simon & Schuster, Inc, 1230 Avenue of the Americas, New York, NY 10020 *Tel:* 212-698-7000 *Toll Free Tel:* 800-223-2336 (orders) *Fax:* 212-698-7007 *Toll Free Fax:* 800-943-9831 (orders) *E-mail:* firstname.lastname@simonandschuster.com; purchaseorders@simonandschuster.com (orders) *Web Site:* www.simonandschuster.com, pg 199

Ruffner, Peter E, Omnigraphics Inc, 615 Griswold, Suite 520, Detroit, MI 48226 *Tel:* 610-461-3548 *Toll Free Tel:* 800-234-1340 (cust serv) *Fax:* 610-532-9001 *Toll Free Fax:* 800-875-1340 (cust serv) *E-mail:* contact@ omnigraphics.com; customerservice@omnigraphics. com *Web Site:* omnigraphics.com, pg 155

Ruggiero, Anthony, Pauline Books & Media, 50 Saint Paul's Ave, Boston, MA 02130 *Tel:* 617-522-8911 *Toll Free Tel:* 800-876-4463 (orders); 800-836-9723 (cust serv) *Fax:* 617-541-9805 *E-mail:* editorial@ paulinemedia.com (ms submissions); orderentry@ pauline.org (cust serv) *Web Site:* www.pauline.org/ pbmpublishing, pg 161

Ruggiero, Greg, City Lights Publishers, 261 Columbus Ave, San Francisco, CA 94133 *Tel:* 415-362-8193 *Fax:* 415-362-4921 *E-mail:* staff@citylights.com *Web Site:* www.citylights.com, pg 53

Ruggiero, Vincenzo, Penguin Group USA, A Penguin Random House Company, 375 Hudson St, New York, NY 10014 *Tel:* 212-366-2000 *Toll Free Tel:* 800-847-5515 (inside sales); 800-631-8571 (cust serv) *Fax:* 212-366-2666; 607-775-4829 (inside sales) *E-mail:* online@us.penguingroup.com *Web Site:* www. penguin.com, pg 163

Ruhl, Peter, American Catholic Press (ACP), 16565 S State St, South Holland, IL 60473 *Tel:* 708-331-5485 *Fax:* 708-331-5484 *E-mail:* acp@acpress.org *Web Site:* www.acpress.org, pg 10

Ruhlig, Steve, Human Kinetics Inc, 1607 N Market St, Champaign, IL 61820 *Tel:* 217-351-5076 *Toll Free Tel:* 800-747-4457 *Fax:* 217-351-1549 (orders/cust serv) *E-mail:* info@hkusa.com *Web Site:* www. humankinetics.com, pg 105

Ruiz, Bea, National Catholic Educational Association, 1005 N Glebe Rd, Suite 525, Arlington, VA 22201 *Tel:* 571-257-0010 *Toll Free Tel:* 800-711-6232 *Fax:* 703-243-0025 *E-mail:* nceaadmin@ncea.org *Web Site:* www.ncea.org, pg 145

Ruiz, Jonathan, Velazquez Press, 9682 Telstar Ave, Suite 110, El Monte, CA 91731 *Tel:* 626-448-3448 *Fax:* 626-602-3817 *E-mail:* info@ academiclearningcompany.com *Web Site:* www. velazquezpress.com, pg 235

Rukkila, Roy, MRTS, PO Box 874402, Tempe, AZ 85287-4402 *Tel:* 480-727-6503 *Toll Free Tel:* 800-621-2736 (orders) *Fax:* 480-965-1681 *Toll Free Fax:* 800-621-8476 (orders) *E-mail:* mrts@asu.edu *Web Site:* acmrspress.com, pg 144

Rule, Megan, Bear & Co Inc, One Park St, Rochester, VT 05767 *Tel:* 802-767-3174 *Toll Free Tel:* 800-932-3277 *Fax:* 802-767-3726 *E-mail:* customerservice@ InnerTraditions.com *Web Site:* InnerTraditions.com, pg 29

Rule, Megan, Inner Traditions International Ltd, One Park St, Rochester, VT 05767 *Tel:* 802-767-3174 *Toll Free Tel:* 800-246-8648 *Fax:* 802-767-3726 *E-mail:* customerservice@InnerTraditions.com *Web Site:* www.InnerTraditions.com, pg 109

Ruley, Meg, Jane Rotrosen Agency LLC, 85 Broad St, 28th fl, New York, NY 10004 *Tel:* 212-593-4330 *Fax:* 212-935-6985 *Web Site:* janerotrosen.com, pg 500

Rulfs, Sarah, Cy Twombly Award for Poetry, 820 Greenwich St, New York, NY 10014 *Tel:* 212-807-7077 *E-mail:* info@contemporary-arts.org *Web Site:* www.foundationforcontemporaryarts.org/ grants/cy-twombly-award-for-poetry, pg 674

Rumberger, Anne, Verso, 20 Jay St, Suite 1010, Brooklyn, NY 11201 *Tel:* 718-246-8160 *Fax:* 718-246-8165 *E-mail:* verso@versobooks.com *Web Site:* www.versobooks.com, pg 235

Rumble, Brant, Perseus Books, 1290 Avenue of the Americas, New York, NY 10104 *Tel:* 212-340-8100 *Toll Free Tel:* 800-343-4499 (cust serv) *Fax:* 212-340-8105 *Web Site:* www.perseusbooks.com, pg 167

Rumsch, BreAnn, ABDO Publishing Co Inc, 8000 W 78 St, Suite 310, Edina, MN 55439 *Tel:* 952-698-2403 *Toll Free Tel:* 800-800-1312 *Fax:* 952-831-1632 *Toll Free Fax:* 800-862-3480 *E-mail:* customerservice@ abdopublishing.com; info@abdopublishing.com *Web Site:* abdopublishing.com, pg 2

Rundall, Nick, Whitecap Books, 314 W Cordova St, Suite 209, Vancouver, BC V6B 1E8, Canada *Tel:* 604-681-6181 *Toll Free Tel:* 800-387-9776 *Toll Free Fax:* 800-260-9777 *Web Site:* www.whitecap.ca, pg 445

Rundle, Lisa, HarperCollins Canada Ltd, 2 Bloor St E, 20th fl, Toronto, ON M4W 1A8, Canada *Tel:* 416-975-9334 *Fax:* 416-975-5223 *E-mail:* hcorder@ harpercollins.com *Web Site:* www.harpercollins.ca, pg 429

Rundquist, Nathan, New Rivers Press, c/o Minnesota State University Moorhead, 1104 Seventh Ave S, Moorhead, MN 56563 *Tel:* 218-477-5870 *Fax:* 218-

477-2236 *E-mail:* nrp@mnstate.edu *Web Site:* www. newriverspress.com; www.mnstate.edu/newriverspress, pg 149

Runge, Gailen, C&T Publishing Inc, 1651 Challenge Dr, Concord, CA 94520-5206 *Tel:* 925-677-0377 *Toll Free Tel:* 800-284-1114 *Fax:* 925-677-0373 *E-mail:* support@ctpub.com *Web Site:* www.ctpub. com, pg 44

Runk, David, FaithWalk Publishing, 5450 N Dixie Hwy, Lima, OH 45807 *Tel:* 419-227-1818 *Toll Free Tel:* 800-537-1030 (orders, non-bookstore mkts) *Fax:* 419-224-9184 *E-mail:* orders@csspub.com *Web Site:* www.faithwalkpub.com, pg 75

Runyon, Ashley, The University Press of Kentucky, 663 S Limestone St, Lexington, KY 40508-4008 *Tel:* 859-257-8400 *Fax:* 859-257-8481 *Web Site:* www. kentuckypress.com, pg 233

Rupnow, Dr John, The Edwin Mellen Press, 240 Portage Rd, Lewiston, NY 14092 *Tel:* 716-754-2266; 716-754-2788 (order fulfillment) *Fax:* 716-754-4056 *E-mail:* editor@mellenpress.com *Web Site:* www. mellenpress.com, pg 137

Rupp, Katherine, American Quilter's Society, 5801 Kentucky Dam Rd, Paducah, KY 42003-9323 *Tel:* 270-898-7903 *Toll Free Tel:* 800-626-5420 (orders) *Fax:* 270-898-1173 *E-mail:* orders@ americanquilter.com *Web Site:* www.americanquilter. com, pg 14

Ruppel, Philip, Phaidon, 65 Bleecker St, 8th fl, New York, NY 10012 *Tel:* 212-652-5400 *Toll Free Tel:* 800-759-0190 (cust serv) *Fax:* 212-652-5410 *Toll Free Fax:* 800-286-9471 (cust serv) *E-mail:* enquiries@phaidon.com *Web Site:* www. phaidon.com, pg 168

Rusch, Vanessa, University of Alabama Press, 200 Hackberry Lane, 2nd fl, Tuscaloosa, AL 35487 *Tel:* 205-348-5180 *Fax:* 205-348-9201 *Web Site:* www. uapress.ua.edu, pg 225

Rusick, Meg, Hendrickson Publishers Inc, PO Box 3473, Peabody, MA 01961-3473 *Tel:* 978-532-6546 *Toll Free Tel:* 800-358-3111 *Fax:* 978-573-8111 *E-mail:* customerservice@hendricksonrose.com; info@ hendricksonrose.com *Web Site:* www.hendricksonrose. com, pg 98

Rusko, Joe, Johns Hopkins University Press, 2715 N Charles St, Baltimore, MD 21218-4363 *Tel:* 410-516-6900; 410-516-6987 (journal orders outside US & CN) *Toll Free Tel:* 800-537-5487 (book orders & cust serv); 800-548-1784 (journal orders) *Fax:* 410-516-6968; 410-516-3866 (journal orders); 410-516-6998 (orders) *E-mail:* hfscustserv@press.jhu.edu (cust serv); jrnlcirc@press.jhu.edu (journal orders) *Web Site:* www.press.jhu.edu; muse.jhu.edu, pg 114

Russ, Susan, Publishers Information Bureau (PIB)®, 757 Third Ave, 11th fl, New York, NY 10017 *Tel:* 212-872-3700 (MPA) *E-mail:* infocenter@magazine.org *Web Site:* www.magazine.org, pg 545

Russell, Kenn, Henry Holt and Company, LLC, 120 Broadway, 23rd fl, New York, NY 10271 *Tel:* 646-307-5151 *Toll Free Tel:* 888-330-8477 (orders) *Fax:* 646-307-5285 *Web Site:* www.henryholt.com, pg 102

Russell, Marisa, Little, Brown Books for Young Readers, 1290 Avenue of the Americas, New York, NY 10104 *Tel:* 212-364-1100 *Toll Free Tel:* 800-759-0190 (cust serv) *Web Site:* www.hachettebookgroup.com, pg 126

Russell, Mary, New Hampshire Literary Awards, 2500 N River Rd, Manchester, NH 03106 *Tel:* 603-314-7980 *E-mail:* info@nhwritersproject.org; awards@ nhwritersproject.org *Web Site:* www.nhwritersproject. org, pg 647

Russell, Pam, Council for Advancement & Support of Education (CASE), 1307 New York Ave NW, Suite 1000, Washington, DC 20005-4701 *Tel:* 202-328-CASE (328-2273) *Fax:* 202-387-4973 *E-mail:* membersupportcenter@case.org *Web Site:* www.case.org, pg 531

Russell, Rick, Naval Institute Press, 291 Wood Rd, Annapolis, MD 21402-5034 *Tel:* 410-268-6110 *Toll Free Tel:* 800-233-8764 *Fax:* 410-295-1084;

410-571-1703 (cust serv) *E-mail:* webmaster@ navalinstitute.org; customer@navalinstitute.org (cust serv) *Web Site:* www.nip.org; www.usni.org, pg 147

Russell, Tom, The Princeton Review, c/o Penguin Random House Inc, 1745 Broadway, MD 16-1, New York, NY 10019 *Toll Free Tel:* 800-273-8439 (orders only) *Web Site:* www.princetonreview.com, pg 174

Russo, Carmine, The Bureau for At-Risk Youth, 40 Aero Rd, Unit 2, Bohemia, NY 11716 *Toll Free Tel:* 800-99YOUTH (999-6884) *Toll Free Fax:* 800-262-1886 *Web Site:* www.at-risk.com, pg 43

Russo, Nicole, Simon & Schuster Children's Publishing, 1230 Avenue of the Americas, New York, NY 10020 *Tel:* 212-698-7000 *Web Site:* www.simonandschuster. com/kids; www.simonandschuster.com/teen; simonandschuster.net; simonandschuster.biz, pg 199

Russo, Olivia, Penguin Young Readers Group, 345 Hudson St, New York, NY 10014 *Tel:* 212-366-2000; 212-414-3553 *Fax:* 212-414-3340 *Web Site:* www. penguin.com/children, pg 165

Russolese, Kaitlin Darcy, Random House Publishing Group, 1745 Broadway, New York, NY 10019 *Toll Free Tel:* 800-200-3552 *Web Site:* www. randomhousebooks.com, pg 181

Rust, Ned, Little, Brown and Company, 1290 Avenue of the Americas, New York, NY 10104 *Tel:* 212-364-1100 *Fax:* 212-364-0952 *E-mail:* firstname.lastname@ hbgusa.com *Web Site:* www.littlebrown.com; www. hachettebookgroup.com, pg 125

Rutenberg, Sara, Spark Award, 6363 Wilshire Blvd, Suite 425, Los Angeles, CA 90048 *Tel:* 323-782-1010 *Fax:* 323-782-1892 *E-mail:* grants@scbwi.org; scbwi@scbwi.org *Web Site:* www.scbwi.org, pg 669

Rutland-Starks, Kimberly, The Mathematical Association of America, 1529 18 St NW, Washington, DC 20036-1358 *Tel:* 202-387-5200 *Toll Free Tel:* 800-741-9415 *Fax:* 202-265-2384 *E-mail:* maahq@maa.org; advertising@maa.org (pubns) *Web Site:* www.maa.org, pg 134

Rutledge, Melanie, Magazines Canada (MC), 555 Richmond St W, Suite 604, Mailbox 201, Toronto, ON M5V 3B1, Canada *Tel:* 416-504-0274 *Fax:* 416-504-0437 *E-mail:* info@magazinescanada.ca *Web Site:* magazinescanada.ca, pg 537

Rutman, Jim, Sterling Lord Literistic Inc, 115 Broadway, Suite 1602, New York, NY 10006 *Tel:* 212-780-6050 *Fax:* 212-780-6095 *E-mail:* info@sll.com *Web Site:* www.sll.com, pg 504

Rutter, Sandy, American Society of Agricultural & Biological Engineers (ASABE), 2950 Niles Rd, St Joseph, MI 49085-9659 *Tel:* 269-429-0300 *Toll Free Tel:* 800-371-2723 *Fax:* 269-429-3852 *E-mail:* hq@ asabe.org *Web Site:* www.asabe.org, pg 14

Ryan, Anthony J, Ignatius Press, 1348 Tenth Ave, San Francisco, CA 94122-2304 *Toll Free Tel:* 800-651-1531 (orders); 888-615-3186 (cust serv) *Fax:* 415-387-0896 *E-mail:* info@ignatius.com *Web Site:* www. ignatius.com, pg 106

Ryan, Becky, DawnSignPress, 6130 Nancy Ridge Dr, San Diego, CA 92121-3223 *Tel:* 858-625-0600 *Toll Free Tel:* 800-549-5350 *Fax:* 858-625-2336 *E-mail:* contactus@dawnsign.com *Web Site:* www. dawnsign.com, pg 63

Ryan, Hampton, Arcadia Publishing Inc, 420 Wando Park Blvd, Mount Pleasant, SC 29464 *Tel:* 843-853-2070 *Toll Free Tel:* 888-313-2665 (orders only) *Fax:* 843-853-0044 *E-mail:* sales@arcadiapublishing. com *Web Site:* www.arcadiapublishing.com, pg 19

Ryan, Joe, Association for Information & Image Management International (AIIM), 1100 Wayne Ave, Suite 1100, Silver Spring, MD 20910 *Tel:* 301-587-8202 *Toll Free Tel:* 800-477-2446 *Fax:* 301-587-2711 *E-mail:* aiim@aiim.org; info@aiim.org *Web Site:* www.aiim.org, pg 525

Ryan, John R, Center for Creative Leadership LLC, One Leadership Place, Greensboro, NC 27410-9427 *Tel:* 336-545-2810; 336-288-7210 *Fax:* 336-282-3284 *E-mail:* info@ccl.org *Web Site:* www.ccl. org/publications, pg 47

Ryan, Michael, Barbara & David Zalaznick Book Prize in American History, 170 Central Park W, New York, NY 10024 *Tel:* 212-873-3400 *Fax:* 212-595-5707 *E-mail:* info@nyhistory.org *Web Site:* www.nyhistory. org/news/book-prize, pg 681

Ryan, Michael T, Bibliographical Society of America, PO Box 1537, Lenox Hill Sta, New York, NY 10021-0043 *Tel:* 212-734-2500 *Fax:* 212-452-2710 *E-mail:* bsa@bibsocamer.org *Web Site:* www. bibsocamer.org, pg 528

Ryan, Mike, McGraw-Hill Humanities, Social Sciences, Languages, 2 Penn Plaza, 21st fl, New York, NY 10121 *Tel:* 212-904-2000 *Toll Free Tel:* 800-338-3987 (cust serv) *Fax:* 614-755-5645 (cust serv) *Web Site:* www.mhhe.com, pg 136

Ryan, Peter K, Stimola Literary Studio Inc, 308 Livingston Ct, Edgewater, NJ 07020 *Tel:* 201-945-9353 *Fax:* 201-945-9353; 201-490-5920 *E-mail:* info@stimolaliterarystudio.com *Web Site:* www.stimolaliterarystudio.com, pg 504

Ryan, Regina, Regina Ryan Books, 251 Central Park W, Suite 7-D, New York, NY 10024 *Tel:* 212-787-5589 *E-mail:* queries@reginaryanbooks.com *Web Site:* www.reginaryanbooks.com, pg 500

Ryan, Regina Sara, Hohm Press, PO Box 4410, Chino Valley, AZ 86323 *Tel:* 928-636-3331 *Toll Free Tel:* 800-381-2700 *Fax:* 928-636-7519 *E-mail:* publisher@hohmpress.com *Web Site:* www. hohmpress.com, pg 101

Ryce, Chris, Pacific Printing Industries Association, 6825 SW Sandburg St, Portland, OR 97223 *Tel:* 503-221-3944 *Toll Free Tel:* 877-762-7742 *Fax:* 503-221-5691 *E-mail:* info@ppiassociation.org *Web Site:* www. ppiassociation.org, pg 543

Saada, Yves, Disney Publishing Worldwide, 1101 Flower St, Glendale, CA 91201 *Web Site:* books.disney.com, pg 65

Saarela, Alexis, Tom Doherty Associates, LLC, 120 Broadway, New York, NY 10271 *Tel:* 646-307-5511 *Toll Free Tel:* 800-455-0340 *Web Site:* us.macmillan. com/torforge, pg 66

Sabia, Mary Ann, Charlesbridge Publishing Inc, 85 Main St, Watertown, MA 02472 *Tel:* 617-926-0329 *Toll Free Tel:* 800-225-3214 *Fax:* 617-926-5720 *Toll Free Fax:* 800-926-5775 *E-mail:* books@charlesbridge.com *Web Site:* www.charlesbridge.com, pg 49

Sablik, Filip, Boom! Studios, 5670 Wilshire Blvd, Suite 400, Los Angeles, CA 90036 *Web Site:* www.boom-studios.com, pg 38

Sablosky, Lindsay, Chronicle Books, 680 Second St, San Francisco, CA 94107 *Tel:* 415-537-4200 *Toll Free Tel:* 800-759-0190 (cust serv) *Fax:* 415-537-4460 *Toll Free Fax:* 800-858-7787 (orders); 800-286-9471 (cust serv) *E-mail:* frontdesk@chroniclebooks.com *Web Site:* www.chroniclebooks.com, pg 51

Sabol, Stephanie, Penguin Young Readers Group, 345 Hudson St, New York, NY 10014 *Tel:* 212-366-2000; 212-414-3553 *Fax:* 212-414-3340 *Web Site:* penguin.com/children, pg 165

Sacca-Schaeffer, Maia, Henry Holt and Company, LLC, 120 Broadway, 23rd fl, New York, NY 10271 *Tel:* 646-307-5151 *Toll Free Tel:* 888-330-8477 (orders) *Fax:* 646-307-5285 *Web Site:* www.henryholt. com, pg 102

Sachs, Cassidy, Dutton, 1745 Broadway, New York, NY 10019 *Tel:* 212-366-2000 *Fax:* 212-366-2262 *E-mail:* duttonpublicity@us.penguingroup.com *Web Site:* www.penguin.com, pg 68

Sachs, Cassidy, Penguin Group USA, A Penguin Random House Company, 375 Hudson St, New York, NY 10014 *Tel:* 212-366-2000 *Toll Free Tel:* 800-847-5515 (inside sales); 800-631-8571 (cust serv) *Fax:* 212-366-2666; 607-775-4829 (inside sales) *E-mail:* online@us.penguingroup.com *Web Site:* www. penguin.com, pg 163

Sacilotto, Loriana, Harlequin Enterprises Ltd, Bay Adelaide Centre, East Tower, 22 Adelaide St W, 41st fl, Toronto, ON M5H 4E3, Canada *Tel:* 416-445-5860 *Toll Free Tel:* 888-432-4879; 800-370-5838 (ebook inquiries) *E-mail:* customerservice@harlequin.com *Web Site:* www.harlequin.com, pg 429

Sacks, Samantha, little bee books, 251 Park Ave S, 12th fl, New York, NY 10010 *Toll Free Tel:* 844-321-0237 *E-mail:* info@littlebeebooks.com *Web Site:* littlebeebooks.com, pg 125

Sadler, Jodell, Transatlantic Agency, 2 Bloor St E, Suite 3500, Toronto, ON M4W 1A8, Canada *Tel:* 416-488-9214 *E-mail:* info@transatlanticagency.com *Web Site:* www.transatlanticagency.com, pg 506

Sadowski, Br Frank, St Pauls, 2187 Victory Blvd, Staten Island, NY 10314-6603 *Tel:* 718-761-0047 (edit & prodn); 718-698-2759 (mktg & billing) *Toll Free Tel:* 800-343-2522 *Fax:* 718-761-0057 *E-mail:* sales@stpauls.us; marketing@stpauls.us *Web Site:* www.stpauls.us, pg 191

Sadowski, Julia, North Atlantic Books, 2526 Martin Luther King Jr Way, Berkeley, CA 94704 *Tel:* 510-549-4270 *Fax:* 510-549-4276 *Web Site:* www.northatlanticbooks.com, pg 151

Safon, Teresa, Corporation for Public Broadcasting (CPB), 401 Ninth St NW, Washington, DC 20004-2129 *Tel:* 202-879-9600 *Web Site:* www.cpb.org, pg 531

Safyan, Susan, Arsenal Pulp Press, 211 E Georgia St, No 202, Vancouver, BC V6A 1Z6, Canada *Tel:* 604-687-4233 *Toll Free Tel:* 888-600-PULP (600-7857) *Fax:* 604-687-4283 *E-mail:* info@arsenalpulp.com *Web Site:* www.arsenalpulp.com, pg 415

Sagalyn, Raphael, ICM Partners, 65 E 55 St, New York, NY 10022 *Tel:* 212-556-5600 *Web Site:* www.icmtalent.com, pg 489

Sagan, Kathy, Harlequin Enterprises Ltd, 195 Broadway, 24th fl, New York, NY 10007 *Tel:* 212-207-7000 *Toll Free Tel:* 888-432-4879 *E-mail:* customerservice@harlequin.com *Web Site:* www.harlequin.com, pg 93

Sagara, Mike, Stanford University Press, 425 Broadway St, Redwood City, CA 94063-3126 *Tel:* 650-723-9434 *Fax:* 650-725-3457 *E-mail:* info@www.sup.org; publicity@www.sup.org; sales@www.sup.org *Web Site:* www.sup.org, pg 206

Sagnette, Lindsay, Atria Books, 1230 Avenue of the Americas, New York, NY 10020 *Tel:* 212-698-7000 *Fax:* 212-698-7007 *Web Site:* www.simonandschuster.com, pg 24

Saikia-Wilson, Becky, Houghton Mifflin Harcourt Trade & Reference Division, 125 High St, Boston, MA 02110 *Tel:* 617-351-5000 *Web Site:* www.hmhco.com, pg 104

Saint-Jean, Marie-Claire, Guy Saint-Jean Editeur Inc, 4490, rue Garand, Laval, QC H7L 5Z6, Canada *Tel:* 450-663-1777 *E-mail:* info@saint-jeanediteur.com *Web Site:* saint-jeanediteur.com, pg 439

Saint-Jean, Nicole, Guy Saint-Jean Editeur Inc, 4490, rue Garand, Laval, QC H7L 5Z6, Canada *Tel:* 450-663-1777 *E-mail:* info@saint-jeanediteur.com *Web Site:* saint-jeanediteur.com, pg 439

Sakalenka, Elvira, Mountain n' Air Books, 2947-A Honolulu Ave, La Crescenta, CA 91214 *Tel:* 818-248-9345 *Toll Free Tel:* 800-446-9696 *Toll Free Fax:* 800-303-5578 *E-mail:* contact@mountain-n-air.com *Web Site:* www.mountain-n-air.com, pg 143

Sakamoto, Dawn, Watermark Publishing, 1000 Bishop St, Suite 806, Honolulu, HI 96813 *Tel:* 808-587-7766 *Toll Free Tel:* 866-900-BOOK (900-2665) *Fax:* 808-521-3461 *E-mail:* info@bookshawaii.net *Web Site:* www.bookshawaii.net, pg 238

Sakuda, Takashi, Kodansha USA Inc, 451 Park Ave S, 7th fl, New York, NY 10016 *Tel:* 917-322-6200 *Fax:* 212-935-6929 *E-mail:* info@kodansha-usa.com *Web Site:* www.kodanshausa.com, pg 118

Sala, Edward, Washington State University Press, Cooper Publications Bldg, 2300 Grimes Way, Pullman, WA 99164-5910 *Tel:* 509-335-7880 *Toll Free Tel:* 800-354-7360 (orders) *E-mail:* wsupress@wsu.edu *Web Site:* wsupress.wsu.edu, pg 237

Salaman, Marisol, Penguin Group USA, A Penguin Random House Company, 375 Hudson St, New York, NY 10014 *Tel:* 212-366-2000 *Toll Free Tel:* 800-847-5515 (inside sales); 800-631-8571 (cust serv) *Fax:* 212-366-2666; 607-775-4829 (inside sales) *E-mail:* online@us.penguingroup.com *Web Site:* www.penguin.com, pg 163

Salaman, Marisol, Portfolio, 375 Hudson St, New York, NY 10014 *Web Site:* www.penguin.com/meet/publishers/portfolio, pg 172

Salane, Jeffrey, Simon & Schuster Children's Publishing, 1230 Avenue of the Americas, New York, NY 10020 *Tel:* 212-698-7000 *Web Site:* www.simonandschuster.com/kids; www.simonandschuster.com/teen; simonandschuster.net; simonandschuster.biz, pg 199

Salayi, Jill, Workman Publishing Co Inc, 225 Varick St, 9th fl, New York, NY 10014-4381 *Tel:* 212-254-5900 *Toll Free Tel:* 800-722-7202 *Fax:* 212-254-8098 *E-mail:* info@workman.com; orders@workman.com *Web Site:* www.workman.com, pg 244

Salazar, Manuel, New City Press, 202 Comforter Blvd, Hyde Park, NY 12538 *Tel:* 845-229-0335 *Toll Free Tel:* 800-462-5980 (orders only) *Fax:* 845-229-0351 *E-mail:* info@newcitypress.com; orders@newcitypress.com *Web Site:* www.newcitypress.com, pg 148

Salcedo, Lyana, Penguin Young Readers Group, 345 Hudson St, New York, NY 10014 *Tel:* 212-366-2000; 212-414-3553 *Fax:* 212-414-3340 *Web Site:* www.penguin.com/children, pg 165

Saleem, Umaima, BookEnds Literary Agency, 136 Long Hill Rd, Gillette, NJ 07933 *Web Site:* www.bookendsliterary.com, pg 476

Salerno, Carey, Alice James Books, 114 Prescott St, Farmington, ME 04938 *Tel:* 207-778-7071 *Fax:* 207-778-7766 *E-mail:* info@alicejamesbooks.org *Web Site:* alicejamesbooks.org, pg 7

Saletan, Rebecca, Riverhead Books, 375 Hudson St, New York, NY 10014 *Tel:* 212-366-2000 *Web Site:* www.penguin.com/publishers/riverhead, pg 185

Salicup, Jim, Papercutz, 160 Broadway, E Wing, Suite 700, New York, NY 10038 *Tel:* 646-559-4681 *Toll Free Tel:* 800-886-1223 *Fax:* 212-643-1545 *E-mail:* papercutz@papercutz.com *Web Site:* www.papercutz.com, pg 160

Salk, Judy, Elsevier Engineering Information (Ei), 230 Park Ave, 8th fl, New York, NY 10169-0123 *Tel:* 212-989-5800 *Fax:* 212-633-3990 *E-mail:* eicustomersupport@elsevier.com *Web Site:* www.elsevier.com/solutions/engineering-village, pg 71

Sallick, Hillary, Barbara Bradley Prize, 46 Wallace St, Somerville, MA 02144 *E-mail:* info@nepoetryclub.org *Web Site:* www.nepoetryclub.org, pg 600

Sallick, Hillary, Der-Hovanessian Translation Prize, 46 Wallace St, Somerville, MA 02144 *E-mail:* info@nepoetryclub.org *Web Site:* www.nepoetryclub.org, pg 609

Sallick, Hillary, Golden Rose Award, 46 Wallace St, Somerville, MA 02144 *E-mail:* info@nepoetryclub.org *Web Site:* www.nepoetryclub.org, pg 620

Sallick, Hillary, Firman Houghton Prize, 46 Wallace St, Somerville, MA 02144 *E-mail:* info@nepoetryclub.org *Web Site:* www.nepoetryclub.org, pg 624

Sallick, Hillary, Sheila Margaret Motton Book Prize, 46 Wallace St, Somerville, MA 02144 *E-mail:* info@nepoetryclub.org *Web Site:* www.nepoetryclub.org, pg 644

Sallick, Hillary, Erika Mumford Prize, 46 Wallace St, Somerville, MA 02144 *E-mail:* info@nepoetryclub.org *Web Site:* www.nepoetryclub.org, pg 644

Sallick, Hillary, New England Poetry Club, 46 Wallace St, Somerville, MA 02144 *E-mail:* info@nepoetryclub.org *Web Site:* www.nepoetryclub.org, pg 541

Sallick, Hillary, May Sarton Award, 46 Wallace St, Somerville, MA 02144 *E-mail:* info@nepoetryclub.org *Web Site:* www.nepoetryclub.org, pg 664

Sallick, Hillary, Daniel Varoujan Award, 46 Wallace St, Somerville, MA 02144 *E-mail:* info@nepoetryclub.org *Web Site:* www.nepoetryclub.org, pg 675

Salo, Gay, Piano Press, 1425 Ocean Ave, Suite 5, Del Mar, CA 92014 *Tel:* 619-884-1401 *Fax:* 858-755-1104 *E-mail:* pianopress@pianopress.com *Web Site:* www.pianopress.com, pg 169

Salpeter, Steven, Curtis Brown Ltd, 228 E 45 St, 3rd fl, New York, NY 10017 *Tel:* 212-473-5400 *Web Site:* www.curtisbrown.com, pg 478

Salser, Mark R, National Book Co, PO Box 8795, Portland, OR 97280-8795 *Tel:* 503-228-6345 *Fax:* 810-885-5811 *E-mail:* info@eralearning.com *Web Site:* www.eralearning.com, pg 145

Saltmarsh, Fiona, Chicago Women in Publishing, PO Box 268107, Chicago, IL 60626 *Tel:* 773-508-0351 *Fax:* 303-942-7164 *E-mail:* info@cwip.org *Web Site:* www.cwip.org, pg 530

Saltus, Iris, University of Nevada Press, c/o University of Nevada, Continuing Educ Bldg, MS 0166, Reno, NV 89557-0166 *Tel:* 775-784-6573 *Fax:* 775-784-6200 *Web Site:* www.unpress.nevada.edu, pg 229

Saltzman, Glenn, Georgetown University Press, 3520 Prospect St NW, Suite 140, Washington, DC 20007 *Tel:* 202-687-5889 (busn) *Fax:* 202-687-6340 (edit) *E-mail:* gupress@georgetown.edu *Web Site:* press.georgetown.edu, pg 85

Salva, Richard, Crystal Clarity Publishers, 14618 Tyler Foote Rd, Nevada City, CA 95959 *Tel:* 530-478-7600 *Toll Free Tel:* 800-424-1055 *Fax:* 530-478-7562 *E-mail:* clarity@crystalclarity.com *Web Site:* www.crystalclarity.com, pg 61

Salvador, Vanda, Paulines Editions, 5610 rue Beaubien est, Montreal, QC H1T 1X5, Canada *Tel:* 514-253-5610 *Fax:* 514-253-1907 *E-mail:* fsp-paulines@videotron.ca *Web Site:* www.editions.paulines.qc.ca, pg 436

Salvadore, Maria, Walter Dean Myers Awards for Outstanding Children's Literature, 10319 Westlake Dr, No 104, Bethesda, MD 20817 *Tel:* 701-404-9632 (voicemail only) *E-mail:* walteraward@diversebooks.org *Web Site:* diversebooks.org/our-programs/walter-award, pg 644

Salvatore, Laurea, Oxford University Press USA, 198 Madison Ave, New York, NY 10016 *Toll Free Tel:* 800-451-7556 (orders); 800-445-9714 (cust serv) *Fax:* 919-677-1303 *E-mail:* custserv.us@oup.com *Web Site:* global.oup.com, pg 158

Salvatore, Ruth, Ucross Foundation Residency Program, 30 Big Red Lane, Clearmont, WY 82835 *Tel:* 307-737-2291 *Fax:* 307-737-2322 *E-mail:* info@ucross.org *Web Site:* www.ucrossfoundation.org, pg 674

Salvi, Erin, Theatre Communications Group, 520 Eighth Ave, 24th fl, New York, NY 10018-4156 *Tel:* 212-609-5900 *Fax:* 212-609-5901 *E-mail:* info@tcg.org *Web Site:* www.tcg.org, pg 216

Salzano, Tammi, Tiger Tales, 5 River Rd, Suite 128, Wilton, CT 06897-4069 *Tel:* 920-387-2333 *Fax:* 920-387-9994 *Web Site:* www.tigertalesbooks.com, pg 218

Salzman, Rachel, W W Norton & Company Inc, 500 Fifth Ave, New York, NY 10110-0017 *Tel:* 212-354-5500 *Toll Free Tel:* 800-233-4830 (orders & cust serv) *Fax:* 212-869-0856 *Toll Free Fax:* 800-458-6515 *E-mail:* orders@wwnorton.com *Web Site:* wwnorton.com, pg 152

Salzman, Richard, Salzman International, 1751 Charles Ave, Arcata, CA 95521 *Tel:* 415-285-8267 *Fax:* 707-822-5500 *Web Site:* www.salzint.com, pg 512

Samms, June, Kids Can Press Ltd, 25 Dockside Dr, Toronto, ON M5A 0B5, Canada *Tel:* 416-479-7000 *Toll Free Tel:* 800-265-0884 *Fax:* 416-960-5437 *E-mail:* info@kidscan.com; customerservice@kidscan.com *Web Site:* www.kidscanpress.com; kidscanpress.ca, pg 431

Samuel, Patrick, Northwestern University Press, 629 Noyes St, Evanston, IL 60208-4210 *Tel:* 847-491-2046 *Toll Free Tel:* 800-621-2736 (orders only) *Fax:* 847-491-8150 *E-mail:* nupress@northwestern.edu *Web Site:* www.nupress.northwestern.edu, pg 152

Samuels, Alicia, Presbyterian Publishing Corp (PPC), 100 Witherspoon St, Louisville, KY 40202 *Tel:* 502-569-5000 *Toll Free Tel:* 800-523-1631 (US only) *Fax:* 502-569-5113 *E-mail:* customerservice@presbypub.com *Web Site:* www.wjkbooks.com, pg 173

Samuels, Alicia, Westminster John Knox Press (WJK), 100 Witherspoon St, Louisville, KY 40202-1396 *Tel:* 502-569-5052 *Toll Free Tel:* 800-523-1631 (US & CN) *Fax:* 502-569-8308 *Toll Free Fax:* 800-541-5113 (US & CN) *E-mail:* customer_service@wjkbooks.com; orders@wjkbooks.com *Web Site:* www.wjkbooks.com, pg 239

Samuelson, Paul, Grand Central Publishing, 1290 Avenue of the Americas, New York, NY 10104 *Tel:* 212-364-1100 *Web Site:* www.hachettebookgroup.com, pg 88

Samulski, Emily, Fairchild Books, 1385 Broadway, 5th fl, New York, NY 10018 *Tel:* 212-419-5300 *Toll Free Tel:* 800-932-4724; 888-330-8477 (orders) *Web Site:* bloomsbury.com/us/academic/fairchildbooks, pg 75

San Filippo, Karen, Association of Manitoba Book Publishers, 100 Arthur St, Suite 404, Winnipeg, MB R3B 1H3, Canada *Tel:* 204-947-3335 *E-mail:* ambp@mts.net *Web Site:* ambp.ca, pg 526

Sanborn, Kat, Llewellyn Publications, 2143 Wooddale Dr, Woodbury, MN 55125 *Tel:* 651-291-1970 *Toll Free Tel:* 800-843-6666 *Fax:* 651-291-1908 *E-mail:* publicity@llewellyn.com; customerservice@llewellyn.com *Web Site:* www.llewellyn.com, pg 127

Sanchez, Irene, Liturgy Training Publications, 3949 S Racine Ave, Chicago, IL 60609-2523 *Tel:* 773-579-4900 *Toll Free Tel:* 800-933-1800 (US & CN only orders) *Fax:* 773-579-4929 *E-mail:* orders@ltp.org *Web Site:* www.ltp.org, pg 126

Sand, Michael, Harry N Abrams Inc, 195 Broadway, 9th fl, New York, NY 10007 *Tel:* 212-206-7715 *Toll Free Tel:* 800-345-1359 *Fax:* 212-519-1210 *E-mail:* abrams@abramsbooks.com *Web Site:* www.abramsbooks.com, pg 3

Sand, Michael, Stewart, Tabori & Chang, 195 Broadway, 9th fl, New York, NY 10007 *Tel:* 212-206-7715 *Fax:* 212-519-1210 *E-mail:* abrams@abramsbooks.com *Web Site:* www.abramsbooks.com/imprints/stc, pg 208

Sanders, Gene, The Society of Naval Architects & Marine Engineers (SNAME), 99 Canal Center Plaza, Suite 310, Alexandria, VA 22314 *Tel:* 703-997-6701 *Toll Free Tel:* 800-798-2188 *Fax:* 703-997-6702 *Web Site:* www.sname.org, pg 203

Sanders, Keith P PhD, Frank Luther Mott-Kappa Tau Alpha Research Award, University of Missouri, School of Journalism, 76 Gannett Hall, Columbia, MO 65211-1200 *Tel:* 573-882-7685 *Fax:* 573-884-1720 *E-mail:* umcjourkta@missouri.edu *Web Site:* www.kappataualpha.org, pg 644

Sanders, Meredith K, Goose River Press, 3400 Friendship Rd, Waldoboro, ME 04572-6337 *Tel:* 207-832-6665 *E-mail:* gooseriverpress@gmail.com *Web Site:* gooseriverpress.com, pg 87

Sanders, Michael, Alpha Books, 6081 E 82 St, 4th fl, Indianapolis, IN 46250 *Tel:* 212-366-2000 *E-mail:* ecommerce@us.penguingroup.com *Web Site:* www.dk.com, pg 8

Sanders, Rachel, Houghton Mifflin Harcourt, 125 High St, Boston, MA 02110 *Tel:* 617-351-5000 *Toll Free Tel:* 855-969-4642; 800-225-5425 (K-12 educ materials); 800-323-9540 (assessment materials); 877-219-1537 (SkillsTutor); 888-242-6747 (Innovation in Educ Group); 800-225-3362 (Trade & Ref Div) *Toll Free Fax:* 800-269-5232 *E-mail:* myhmhco@hmhco.com *Web Site:* www.hmhco.com, pg 103

Sanders, Ray, Purple House Press, 8100 US Hwy 62 E, Cynthiana, KY 41031 *Tel:* 859-235-9970 *Web Site:* www.purplehousepress.com, pg 178

Sanders, Rob, Greystone Books Ltd, 343 Railway St, Suite 201, Vancouver, BC V6A 1A4, Canada *Tel:* 604-875-1550 *Fax:* 604-875-1556 *E-mail:* info@greystonebooks.com *Web Site:* www.greystonebooks.com, pg 427

Sanders, Shelley, Chronicle Books, 680 Second St, San Francisco, CA 94107 *Tel:* 415-537-4200 *Toll Free Tel:* 800-759-0190 (cust serv) *Fax:* 415-537-4460 *Toll Free Fax:* 800-858-7787 (orders); 800-286-9471 (cust serv) *E-mail:* frontdesk@chroniclebooks.com *Web Site:* www.chroniclebooks.com, pg 51

Sanders, Victoria, Victoria Sanders & Associates LLC, 440 Buck Rd, Stone Ridge, NY 12484 *Tel:* 212-633-8811 *E-mail:* queriesvsa@gmail.com *Web Site:* www.victoriasanders.com, pg 501

Sanderson, Cate, City & Regional Magazine Association, 287 Richards Ave, Norwalk, CT 06850 *Tel:* 203-515-9294 *E-mail:* admin@citymag.org *Web Site:* www.citymag.org, pg 531

Sanderson, Whitney, Interlink Publishing Group Inc, 46 Crosby St, Northampton, MA 01060 *Tel:* 413-582-7054 *Toll Free Tel:* 800-238-LINK (238-5465) *Fax:* 413-582-7057 *E-mail:* info@interlinkbooks.com *Web Site:* www.interlinkbooks.com, pg 110

Sandford, Bria, Portfolio, 375 Hudson St, New York, NY 10014 *Web Site:* www.penguin.com/meet/publishers/portfolio, pg 172

Sandler, Neil, Rosenthal Represents, 23725 Hartland St, West Hills, CA 91307 *Tel:* 818-430-3850 *E-mail:* eliselicenses@earthlink.net, pg 512

Sandler, Zoe, ICM Partners, 65 E 55 St, New York, NY 10022 *Tel:* 212-556-5600 *Web Site:* www.icmtalent.com, pg 489

Sandoz, Claude, Galaxy Press, 7051 Hollywood Blvd, Hollywood, CA 90028 *Tel:* 323-466-3310 *Toll Free Tel:* 877-8GALAXY (842-5299) *E-mail:* info@galaxypress.com; customers@galaxypress.com *Web Site:* www.galaxypress.com, pg 82

Sands, Katharine, Sarah Jane Freymann Literary Agency LLC, 59 W 71 St, Suite 9-B, New York, NY 10023 *Tel:* 212-362-9277 *E-mail:* submissions@sarahjanefreymann.com *Web Site:* www.sarahjanefreymann.com, pg 485

Sanfilippo, Tony, The Ohio State University Press, 180 Pressey Hall, 1070 Carmack Rd, Columbus, OH 43210-1002 *Tel:* 614-292-6930 *Fax:* 614-292-2065 *Toll Free Fax:* 800-621-8476 *E-mail:* info@osupress.org *Web Site:* ohiostatepress.org, pg 155

Sanford, Alyssa, Princeton University Press, 41 William St, Princeton, NJ 08540-5237 *Tel:* 609-258-4900 *Fax:* 609-258-6305 *Web Site:* press.princeton.edu, pg 175

Sanford, Bria, Penguin Group USA, A Penguin Random House Company, 375 Hudson St, New York, NY 10014 *Tel:* 212-366-2000 *Toll Free Tel:* 800-847-5515 (inside sales); 800-631-8571 (cust serv) *Fax:* 212-366-2666; 607-775-4829 (inside sales) *E-mail:* online@us.penguingroup.com *Web Site:* www.penguin.com, pg 163

Sanford, Melissa, Random House Publishing Group, 1745 Broadway, New York, NY 10019 *Toll Free Tel:* 800-200-3552 *Web Site:* www.randomhousebooks.com, pg 181

Sangiacomo, Marissa, St Martin's Press, LLC, 120 Broadway, New York, NY 10271 *Tel:* 646-307-5151 *Web Site:* us.macmillan.com/smp, pg 190

Sangrise, Manuel, Penguin Random House LLC, 1745 Broadway, New York, NY 10019 *Tel:* 212-782-9000 *Toll Free Tel:* 800-726-0600 *Web Site:* www.penguinrandomhouse.com, pg 164

Sankaran, Vanitha, Historical Novel Society North American Conference, 400 Dark Star Ct, Fairbanks, AK 99709 *Tel:* 217-581-7538 *Fax:* 217-581-7534 *Web Site:* www.historicalnovelsociety.org/event/hns-north-american-conference; historicalnovelsociety.org, pg 575

Sansigre, Manuel, Random House Publishing Group, 1745 Broadway, New York, NY 10019 *Toll Free Tel:* 800-200-3552 *Web Site:* www.randomhousebooks.com, pg 181

Santamaria, Adrienne, Trident Media Group LLC, 41 Madison Ave, 36th fl, New York, NY 10010 *Tel:* 212-333-1511 *E-mail:* info@tridentmediagroup.com; press@tridentmediagroup.com *Web Site:* www.tridentmediagroup.com, pg 507

Santana, Reina, Springer Publishing Co, 11 W 42 St, 15th fl, New York, NY 10036-8002 *Tel:* 212-431-4370 *Toll Free Tel:* 877-687-7476 *E-mail:* marketing@springerpub.com; cs@springerpub.com (orders); textbook@springerpub.com; specialsales@springerpub.com *Web Site:* www.springerpub.com, pg 206

Santella, Mark, Random House Children's Books, 1745 Broadway, 10th fl, New York, NY 10019 *Tel:* 212-782-9000 *Web Site:* www.randomhousekids.com, pg 180

Santhouse, Paul, Moody Publishers, 820 N La Salle Blvd, Chicago, IL 60610 *Tel:* 312-329-2101 *Toll Free Tel:* 800-678-8812 *Fax:* 312-329-2144 *Toll Free Fax:* 800-678-3329 *E-mail:* mpcustomerservice@moody.edu; mporders@moody.edu; publicity@moody.edu *Web Site:* www.moodypublishers.com, pg 142

Santo, Courtney Miller, The Pinch Writing Awards in Fiction, University of Memphis, English Dept, 435 Patterson Hall, Memphis, TN 38152 *Tel:* 901-678-2651 *Fax:* 901-678-2226 *E-mail:* editor@pinchjournal.com *Web Site:* www.pinchjournal.com, pg 656

Santo, Courtney Miller, The Pinch Writing Awards in Poetry, University of Memphis, English Dept, 435 Patterson Hall, Memphis, TN 38152 *Tel:* 901-678-2651 *Fax:* 901-678-2226 *E-mail:* editor@pinchjournal.com *Web Site:* www.pinchjournal.com, pg 656

Santopolo, Jill, Philomel, 345 Hudson St, New York, NY 10014 *Tel:* 212-366-2000 *Web Site:* www.penguin.com/publishers/philomel, pg 169

Santoro, Jamie, The American Library Association (ALA), 225 N Michigan Ave, Suite 1300, Chicago, IL 60601 *Tel:* 312-944-6780 *Toll Free Tel:* 800-545-2433 *Fax:* 312-280-5275 *E-mail:* editionsmarketing@ala.org *Web Site:* www.alastore.ala.org, pg 12

Santoro, Jed, Merriam-Webster Inc, 47 Federal St, Springfield, MA 01102 *Tel:* 413-734-3134 *Toll Free Tel:* 800-828-1880 (orders & cust serv) *Fax:* 413-731-5979 (sales) *E-mail:* support@merriam-webster.com *Web Site:* www.merriam-webster.com, pg 138

Santucci, Ernest, Agency Chicago, 7000 Phoenix Ave NE, Suite 202, Albuquerque, NM 87110 *E-mail:* agency.chicago@usa.com, pg 474

Saphire-Bernstein, Evie, Jewish Book Council, 520 Eighth Ave, 4th fl, New York, NY 10018 *Tel:* 212-201-2920 *Fax:* 212-532-4952 *E-mail:* jbc@jewishbooks.org *Web Site:* www.jewishbookcouncil.org, pg 536

Saphire-Bernstein, Evie, National Jewish Book Award-Children's Literature, 520 Eighth Ave, 4th fl, New York, NY 10018 *Tel:* 212-201-2920 *Fax:* 212-532-4952 *E-mail:* jbc@jewishbooks.org *Web Site:* www.jewishbookcouncil.org, pg 645

Saphire-Bernstein, Evie, National Jewish Book Award-Natan Book Award, 520 Eighth Ave, 4th fl, New York, NY 10018 *Tel:* 212-201-2920 *Fax:* 212-532-4952 *E-mail:* jbc@jewishbooks.org; natanbookawards@jewishbooks.org *Web Site:* www.jewishbookcouncil.org, pg 645

Saphire-Bernstein, Evie, National Jewish Book Award-Young Adult Literature, 520 Eighth Ave, 4th fl, New York, NY 10018 *Tel:* 212-201-2920 *Fax:* 212-532-4952 *E-mail:* jbc@jewishbooks.org *Web Site:* www.jewishbookcouncil.org, pg 645

Saphire-Bernstein, Evie, National Jewish Book Awards, 520 Eighth Ave, 4th fl, New York, NY 10018 *Tel:* 212-201-2920 *Fax:* 212-532-4952 *E-mail:* jbc@jewishbooks.org *Web Site:* www.jewishbookcouncil.org, pg 645

Web Site: www.tarcherbooks.com; www.facebook. com/TarcherPerigee/; www.penguin.com/publishers/ tarcherperigee, pg 213

Schmalz, Wendy, Wendy Schmalz Agency, 402 Union St, Unit 831, Hudson, NY 12534 Tel: 518-672-7697 E-mail: wendy@schmalzagency.com Web Site: www. schmalzagency.com, pg 501

Schmelzle, Alexandra, New England Book Awards, One Beacon St, 15th fl, Boston, MA 02108 Tel: 617-547-3642 Fax: 617-830-8768 Web Site: www. newenglandbooks.org/bookawards, pg 647

Schmelzle, Alexandra, New England Independent Booksellers Association Inc (NEIBA), One Beacon St, 15th fl, Boston, MA 02108 Tel: 617-547-3642 Fax: 617-830-8768 Web Site: www.newenglandbooks. org, pg 541

Schmid, Gretchen, Penguin Books, 375 Hudson St, New York, NY 10014 Tel: 212-366-2000 E-mail: penguinpublicity@us.penguingroup.com Web Site: www.penguinclassics.com; www.penguin. com, pg 163

Schmidt, Alfred, Windsor Books, 260 W Main St, Suite 5, Bayshore, NY 11706 Tel: 631-665-6688 Toll Free Tel: 800-321-5934 E-mail: windsor.books@att.net Web Site: www.windsorpublishing.com, pg 242

Schmidt, Anja, Tiller Press, 1230 Avenue of the Americas, New York, NY 10020, pg 218

Schmidt, Eric A, University of California Press, 155 Grand Ave, Suite 400, Oakland, CA 94612-3758 Tel: 510-883-8232 Fax: 510-836-8910 E-mail: generalmailbox@ucpress.edu Web Site: www. ucpress.edu, pg 226

Schmidt, Harold D, Harold Schmidt Literary Agency, 415 W 23 St, Suite 6-F, New York, NY 10011 Tel: 212-727-7473, pg 501

Schmidt, Helga, Steerforth Press, 31 Hanover St, Suite 1, Lebanon, NH 03766 Tel: 603-643-4787 Fax: 603-643-4788 E-mail: info@steerforth.com Web Site: www. steerforth.com, pg 207

Schmidt, Jeff, Windsor Books, 260 W Main St, Suite 5, Bayshore, NY 11706 Tel: 631-665-6688 Toll Free Tel: 800-321-5934 E-mail: windsor.books@att.net Web Site: www.windsorpublishing.com, pg 242

Schmidt, Jenny Newton, Green Earth Book Award, 3100 Clarendon Blvd, Suite 400, Arlington, VA 22201 E-mail: info@natgen.org Web Site: www.natgen. org/green-earth-book-awards, pg 621

Schmidt, Jessica, Perseus Books, 1290 Avenue of the Americas, New York, NY 10104 Tel: 212-340-8100 Toll Free Tel: 800-343-4499 (cust serv) Fax: 212-340-8105 Web Site: www.perseusbooks.com, pg 167

Schmidt, Jocelyn, Penguin Young Readers Group, 345 Hudson St, New York, NY 10014 Tel: 212-366-2000; 212-414-3553 Fax: 212-414-3340 Web Site: www. penguin.com/children, pg 165

Schmidt, Randy, University of British Columbia Press, 2029 West Mall, Vancouver, BC V6T 1Z2, Canada Tel: 604-822-5959 Toll Free Tel: 877-377-9378 Fax: 604-822-6083 Toll Free Fax: 800-668-0821 E-mail: frontdesk@ubcpress.ca Web Site: www. ubcpress.ca, pg 443

Schmierer-Lee, Melonie PhD, Gorgias Press LLC, PO Box 6939, Piscataway, NJ 08854-6939 Tel: 732-885-8900 Fax: 732-885-8908 E-mail: helpdesk@ gorgiaspress.com Web Site: www.gorgiaspress.com, pg 87

Schmitz, Elisabeth, Grove Atlantic Inc, 154 W 14 St, 12th fl, New York, NY 10011 Tel: 212-614-7850 Toll Free Tel: 800-521-0178 Fax: 212-614-7886 E-mail: info@groveatlantic.com; sales@groveatlantic. com; publicity@groveatlantic.com; rights@ groveatlantic.com Web Site: www.groveatlantic.com, pg 89

Schmitz, Madeline, GP Putnam's Sons (Hardcover), 375 Hudson St, New York, NY 10014 Tel: 212-366-2000 Fax: 212-366-2643 E-mail: online@ penguinputnam.com Web Site: www.penguin.com/ publishers/gpputnamssons, pg 178

Schneider, Bill, Etruscan Press, Wilkes University, 84 W South St, Wilkes-Barre, PA 18766 Tel: 570-408-4546 Fax: 570-408-3333 E-mail: books@etruscanpress.org Web Site: www.etruscanpress.org, pg 73

Schneider, Carol, Workman Publishing Co Inc, 225 Varick St, 9th fl, New York, NY 10014-4381 Tel: 212-254-5900 Toll Free Tel: 800-722-7202 Fax: 212-254-8098 E-mail: info@workman.com; orders@workman. com Web Site: www.workman.com, pg 244

Schneider, Deborah, Gelfman Schneider/ICM Partners, 850 Seventh Ave, Suite 903, New York, NY 10019 Tel: 212-245-1993 Fax: 212-245-8678 E-mail: mail@ gelfmanschneider.com Web Site: gelfmanschneider. com, pg 486

Schneider, James, Princeton University Press, 41 William St, Princeton, NJ 08540-5237 Tel: 609-258-4900 Fax: 609-258-6305 Web Site: press.princeton.edu, pg 175

Schneider, Jennifer, National Institute for Trial Advocacy (NITA), 1685 38 St, Suite 200, Boulder, CO 80301-2735 Tel: 720-890-4860 Toll Free Tel: 877-648-2632; 800-225-6482 (orders & returns) Fax: 720-890-7069 E-mail: customerservice@nita.org; sales@nita.org Web Site: www.nita.org, pg 147

Schneider, Kathy, Jane Rotrosen Agency LLC, 85 Broad St, 28th fl, New York, NY 10004 Tel: 212-593-4330 Fax: 212-935-6985 Web Site: janerotrosen.com, pg 500

Schneider, Naomi, University of California Press, 155 Grand Ave, Suite 400, Oakland, CA 94612-3758 Tel: 510-883-8232 Fax: 510-836-8910 E-mail: generalmailbox@ucpress.edu Web Site: www. ucpress.edu, pg 226

Schneider, Sam, Encounter Books, 900 Broadway, Suite 601, New York, NY 10003 Tel: 212-871-6310 Toll Free Tel: 800-343-4499 Fax: 212-871-6311 E-mail: publicity@encounterbooks.com Web Site: www.encounterbooks.com, pg 72

Schneider, Sara, Chronicle Books, 680 Second St, San Francisco, CA 94107 Tel: 415-537-4200 Toll Free Tel: 800-759-0190 (cust serv) Fax: 415-537-4460 Toll Free Fax: 800-858-7787 (orders); 800-286-9471 (cust serv) E-mail: frontdesk@chroniclebooks.com Web Site: www.chroniclebooks.com, pg 51

Schneider, Wendy Caruso, New York Academy of Sciences (NYAS), 7 World Trade Center, 40th fl, 250 Greenwich St, New York, NY 10007-2157 Tel: 212-298-8600 Toll Free Tel: 800-843-6927 Fax: 212-298-3650 E-mail: nyas@nyas.org; annals@nyas.org; customerservice@nyas.org Web Site: www.nyas.org, pg 150

Schnell, Judith, Stackpole Books, 31 E Main St, New Kingstown, PA 17072 Tel: 717-590-8974 Web Site: www.stackpolebooks.com, pg 206

Schnitker, Laura, Library of American Broadcasting (LAB), University of Maryland, Hornbake Library, College Park, MD 20742 Tel: 301-405-9160 Web Site: www.lib.umd.edu/special/collections/ massmedia/about-us, pg 536

Schnitzler, Alex, Keller Media Inc, 578 Washington Blvd, No 745, Marina del Rey, CA 90292 Tel: 800-278-8706 E-mail: query@kellermedia.com Web Site: kellermedia.com/query, pg 490

Schoder, Katie, Alfred A Knopf, c/o Penguin Random House Inc, 1745 Broadway, New York, NY 10019 Tel: 212-751-2600 Fax: 212-572-2662 (foreign rts) Web Site: knopfdoubleday.com, pg 118

Schoen, John, SLACK® Incorporated, A Wyanoke Group Company, 6900 Grove Rd, Thorofare, NJ 08086-9447 Tel: 856-848-1000 Toll Free Tel: 800-257-8290 Fax: 856-848-6091 E-mail: sales@slackinc.com; editor@slackinc.com; customerservice@slackinc.com Web Site: www.healio.com/books, pg 201

Schoenborn, Melina, La Courte Echelle, 4388, rue Saint-Denis, Suite 315, Montreal, QC H2J 2L1, Canada Tel: 514-312-6950 E-mail: info@courteechelle.com Web Site: courteechelle.groupecourteechelle.com, pg 420

Schoenwald, Mark, Thomas Nelson, 501 Nelson Place, Nashville, TN 37214 Tel: 615-889-9000 Toll Free Tel: 800-251-4000 Fax: 615-902-1548 Web Site: www. thomasnelson.com, pg 217

Schoenwald, Mark, Tommy Nelson®, 501 Nelson Place, Nashville, TN 37214 Tel: 615-889-9000; 615-902-1485 (cust serv) Toll Free Tel: 800-251-4000 Web Site: www.tommynelson.com, pg 218

Schoenwald, Mark, Zondervan, 3900 Sparks Dr, Grand Rapids, MI 49546 Tel: 616-698-6900 Toll Free Tel: 800-226-1122; 800-727-1309 (retail orders) Fax: 616-698-3350 Toll Free Fax: 800-698-3256 (retail orders) Web Site: www.zondervan.com, pg 248

Schofield, Brianna, Authors Alliance, 2705 Webster St, No 5805, Berkeley, CA 94705 E-mail: info@ authorsalliance.org Web Site: www.authorsalliance.org, pg 527

Schofield, William, Paul Dry Books, 1700 Sansom St, Suite 700, Philadelphia, PA 19103 Tel: 215-231-9939 E-mail: editor@pauldrybooks.com Web Site: www. pauldrybooks.com, pg 161

Scholl, Steve, White Cloud Press, 300 E Hersey St, Suite 11, Ashland, OR 97520 Tel: 541-488-6415 Fax: 541-482-7708 E-mail: info@whitecloudpress.com Web Site: www.whitecloudpress.com, pg 240

Schooler, Marta, HarperCollins General Books Group, 195 Broadway, New York, NY 10007 Tel: 212-207-7000 Web Site: www.harpercollins.com, pg 93

Schor, Lynda, Hamilton Stone Editions, PO Box 43, Maplewood, NJ 07040 Tel: 973-378-8361 E-mail: hstone@hamiltonstone.org Web Site: www. hamiltonstone.org, pg 92

Schorr, Sari, Levy Creative Management LLC, 425 E 58 St, Suite 37F, New York, NY 10022 Tel: 212-687-6463 Fax: 212-661-4839 E-mail: info@levycreative. com Web Site: www.levycreative.com, pg 511

Schoueri, Merjane, Harlequin Enterprises Ltd, Bay Adelaide Centre, East Tower, 22 Adelaide St W, 41st fl, Toronto, ON M5H 4E3, Canada Tel: 416-445-5860 Toll Free Tel: 888-432-4879; 800-370-5838 (ebook inquiries) E-mail: customerservice@harlequin.com Web Site: www.harlequin.com, pg 429

Schrager, Marla, Society of American Travel Writers (SATW), 17W110 22 St, One Parkview Plaza, Suite 800, Oakbrook Terrace, IL 60181 E-mail: info@satw. org Web Site: www.satw.org, pg 546

Schrank, Ben, Boyds Mills & Kane, 250 Park Ave, 7th fl, New York, NY 10177 E-mail: info@bmkbooks.com Web Site: www.boydsmillsandkane.com, pg 39

Schreier, Carl, Homestead Publishing, Box 193, Moose, WY 83012-0193 Tel: 307-733-6248 Fax: 307-733-6248 E-mail: orders@homesteadpublishing.net Web Site: www.homesteadpublishing.net, pg 102

Schroeder, Ben, Centering Corp, 7230 Maple St, Omaha, NE 68134 Tel: 402-553-1200 Toll Free Tel: 866-218-0101 Fax: 402-553-0507 E-mail: orders@centering.org Web Site: www.centering.org, pg 48

Schroeder, Meredith, American Quilter's Society, 5801 Kentucky Dam Rd, Paducah, KY 42003-9323 Tel: 270-898-7903 Toll Free Tel: 800-626-5420 (orders) Fax: 270-898-1173 E-mail: orders@ americanquilter.com Web Site: www.americanquilter. com, pg 14

Schroeder, Sandi, Schroeder Indexing Services, 23 Camilla Pink Ct, Bluffton, SC 29909 Tel: 843-705-9779 E-mail: sanindex@schroederindexing.com Web Site: www.schroederindexing.com, pg 470

Schroeder, Stefanie, Thomas Nelson, 501 Nelson Place, Nashville, TN 37214 Tel: 615-889-9000 Toll Free Tel: 800-251-4000 Fax: 615-902-1548 Web Site: www. thomasnelson.com, pg 217

Schubert, Lori, Quebec Writers' Federation (QWF), 1200 Atwater Ave, Rm 3, Westmount, QC H3Z 1X4, Canada Tel: 514-933-0878 E-mail: info@qwf.org Web Site: www.qwf.org; www.hireawriter.ca, pg 545

Schubert, Lori, QWF Literary Awards, 1200 Atwater Ave, Rm 3, Westmount, QC H3Z 1X4, Canada *Tel:* 514-933-0878 *E-mail:* info@qwf.org *Web Site:* www.qwf.org, pg 660

Schuler, Michael, Northwest Independent Editors Guild, 7511 Greenwood Ave N, No 307, Seattle, WA 98103 *E-mail:* info@edsguild.org *Web Site:* edsguild.org, pg 542

Schulman, Jana K, Medieval Institute Publications, WMU East Campus, 100-E Walwood Hall, Kalamazoo, MI 49008 *Tel:* 269-387-8754 *Fax:* 269-387-8750 *Web Site:* www.wmich.edu/ medievalpublications, pg 137

Schulman, Susan, Susan Schulman Literary Agency LLC, 454 W 44 St, New York, NY 10036 *Tel:* 212-713-1633 *E-mail:* queries@schulmanagency.com; linda@schulmanagency.com (translation & audio rts), pg 501

Schulte, Mary Kate, Adams Media, 57 Littlefield St, Avon, MA 02322 *Tel:* 508-427-7100 *Web Site:* www.simonandschuster.com, pg 4

Schulte-Cooper, Laura, ALSC Baker & Taylor Summer Reading Grant, 50 E Huron St, Chicago, IL 60611-2795 *Tel:* 312-280-2163 *Toll Free Tel:* 800-545-2433 *Fax:* 312-440-9374; 312-280-5271 *E-mail:* alsc@ala. org *Web Site:* www.ala.org/alsc, pg 591

Schulte-Cooper, Laura, The May Hill Arbuthnot Honor Lecture Award, 50 E Huron St, Chicago, IL 60611-2795 *Tel:* 312-280-2163 *Toll Free Tel:* 800-545-2433 *Fax:* 312-440-9374; 312-280-5271 *E-mail:* alsc@ala. org *Web Site:* www.ala.org/alsc, pg 592

Schulte-Cooper, Laura, The Mildred L Batchelder Award, 50 E Huron St, Chicago, IL 60611-2795 *Tel:* 312-280-2163 *Toll Free Tel:* 800-545-2433 *Fax:* 312-440-9374; 312-280-5271 *E-mail:* alsc@ala. org *Web Site:* www.ala.org/alsc, pg 596

Schulte-Cooper, Laura, The Pura Belpre Award, 50 E Huron St, Chicago, IL 60611-2795 *Tel:* 312-280-2163 *Toll Free Tel:* 800-545-2433 *Fax:* 312-440-9374; 312-280-5271 *E-mail:* alsc@ala.org *Web Site:* www.ala. org/alsc, pg 596

Schulte-Cooper, Laura, Bound to Stay Bound Books Scholarship, 50 E Huron St, Chicago, IL 60611-2795 *Tel:* 312-280-2163 *Toll Free Tel:* 800-545-2433 *Fax:* 312-440-9374; 312-280-5271 *E-mail:* alsc@ala. org *Web Site:* www.ala.org/alsc, pg 600

Schulte-Cooper, Laura, The Randolph Caldecott Medal, 50 E Huron St, Chicago, IL 60611-2795 *Tel:* 312-280-2163 *Toll Free Tel:* 800-545-2433 *Fax:* 312-440-9374; 312-280-5271 *E-mail:* alsc@ala.org *Web Site:* www. ala.org/alsc, pg 602

Schulte-Cooper, Laura, Children's Literature Legacy Award, 50 E Huron St, Chicago, IL 60611-2795 *Tel:* 312-280-2163 *Toll Free Tel:* 800-545-2433 *Fax:* 312-440-9374; 312-280-5271 *E-mail:* alsc@ala. org *Web Site:* www.ala.org/alsc, pg 604

Schulte-Cooper, Laura, Frederic G Melcher Scholarship, 50 E Huron St, Chicago, IL 60611-2795 *Tel:* 312-280-2163 *Toll Free Tel:* 800-545-2433 *Fax:* 312-440-9374; 312-280-5271 *E-mail:* alsc@ala.org *Web Site:* www. ala.org/alsc, pg 641

Schulte-Cooper, Laura, John Newbery Medal, 50 E Huron St, Chicago, IL 60611-2795 *Tel:* 312-280-2163 *Toll Free Tel:* 800-545-2433 *Fax:* 312-440-9374; 312-280-5271 *E-mail:* alsc@ala.org *Web Site:* www.ala. org/alsc, pg 648

Schulte-Cooper, Laura, Robert F Sibert Informational Book Award, 50 E Huron St, Chicago, IL 60611-2795 *Tel:* 312-280-2163 *Toll Free Tel:* 800-545-2433 *Fax:* 312-440-9374; 312-280-5271 *E-mail:* alsc@ala. org *Web Site:* www.ala.org/alsc, pg 667

Schultz, Amy, Northwestern University Press, 629 Noyes St, Evanston, IL 60208-4210 *Tel:* 847-491-2046 *Toll Free Tel:* 800-621-2736 (orders only) *Fax:* 847-491-8150 *E-mail:* nupress@northwestern.edu *Web Site:* www.nupress.northwestern.edu, pg 152

Schultz, Brandon, Glitterati Editions, 311 W 43 St, 12th fl, New York, NY 10036 *Tel:* 646-584-6382 *Fax:* 646-607-4433 *E-mail:* media@glitteratieditions. com *Web Site:* glitteratieditions.com, pg 86

Schultz, Jonathan D, Concordia Publishing House, 3558 S Jefferson Ave, St Louis, MO 63118-3968 *Tel:* 314-268-1000; 314-268-1268 (bookshop) *Toll Free Tel:* 800-325-3040 (cust serv) *Toll Free Fax:* 800-490-9889 (cust serv) *E-mail:* order@cph.org *Web Site:* www.cph.org, pg 56

Schultz, Patricia, The Edwin Mellen Press, 240 Portage Rd, Lewiston, NY 14092 *Tel:* 716-754-2266; 716-754-2788 (order fulfillment) *Fax:* 716-754-4056 *E-mail:* editor@mellenpress.com *Web Site:* www. mellenpress.com, pg 137

Schultz, Thom, Group Publishing Inc, 1515 Cascade Ave, Loveland, CO 80538 *Tel:* 970-669-3836 *Toll Free Tel:* 800-447-1070 *E-mail:* puorgbus@group.com (submissions) *Web Site:* www.group.com, pg 89

Schulz, Andrea, Penguin Group USA, A Penguin Random House Company, 375 Hudson St, New York, NY 10014 *Tel:* 212-366-2000 *Toll Free Tel:* 800-847-5515 (inside sales); 800-631-8571 (cust serv) *Fax:* 212-366-2666; 607-775-4829 (inside sales) *E-mail:* online@us.penguingroup.com *Web Site:* www. penguin.com, pg 163

Schulz, Andrea, Viking, 375 Hudson St, New York, NY 10014 *Tel:* 212-366-2000 *Fax:* 212-243-6002 *Web Site:* www.penguin.com/publishers/vikingbooks, pg 236

Schulz, Kristin, Random House Children's Books, 1745 Broadway, 10th fl, New York, NY 10019 *Tel:* 212-782-9000 *Web Site:* www.randomhousekids.com, pg 181

Schulze, Jared, PPI, A Kaplan Company, 332 Front St, Suite 501, La Crosse, WI 54601 *Tel:* 650-593-9119 *Fax:* 650-592-4519 *E-mail:* info@ppi2pass.com *Web Site:* ppi2pass.com, pg 173

Schulze, Karin, Harry N Abrams Inc, 195 Broadway, 9th fl, New York, NY 10007 *Tel:* 212-206-7715 *Toll Free Tel:* 800-345-1359 *Fax:* 212-519-1210 *E-mail:* abrams@abramsbooks.com *Web Site:* www. abramsbooks.com, pg 3

Schumacher, George, Penguin Young Readers Group, 345 Hudson St, New York, NY 10014 *Tel:* 212-366-2000; 212-414-3553 *Fax:* 212-414-3340 *Web Site:* www.penguin.com/children, pg 165

Schumacher, Ryan R, Texas State Historical Association, 3001 Lake Austin Blvd, Suite 3.116, Austin, TX 78703 *Tel:* 512-471-2600 *Fax:* 512-473-8691 *Web Site:* www.tshaonline.org, pg 216

Schuna, Jo Anne, The Schuna Group Inc, 1503 Briarknoll Dr, Arden Hills, MN 55112 *Tel:* 651-631-8480 *Fax:* 651-631-8480 *E-mail:* www.schunagroup.com, pg 512

Schuster, Allison, Random House Publishing Group, 1745 Broadway, New York, NY 10019 *Toll Free Tel:* 800-200-3552 *Web Site:* www.randomhousebooks. com, pg 181

Schutt, David L, SAE (Society of Automotive Engineers International), 400 Commonwealth Dr, Warrendale, PA 15096-0001 *Tel:* 724-776-4841; 724-776-4970 (outside US & CN) *Toll Free Tel:* 877-606-7323 (cust serv) *Fax:* 724-776-0790 (cust serv) *E-mail:* publications@ sae.org; customerservice@sae.org *Web Site:* www.sae. org, pg 189

Schutz, Samantha, Little, Brown Books for Young Readers, 1290 Avenue of the Americas, New York, NY 10104 *Tel:* 212-364-1100 *Toll Free Tel:* 800-759-0190 (cust serv) *Web Site:* www.hachettebookgroup. com, pg 126

Schwacke, Susanna Sharp, Bottom Dog Press, 813 Seneca Ave, Huron, OH 44839 *Tel:* 419-602-1556 *Fax:* 419-616-3966 *Web Site:* smithdocs.net, pg 39

Schwaiger, Elizabeth, University of Ottawa Press (Presses de l'Université d'Ottawa), 542 King Edward Ave, Ottawa, ON K1N 6N5, Canada *Tel:* 613-562-5246 *Fax:* 613-562-5247 *E-mail:* puo-uop@uottawa. ca; acquisitions@uottawa.ca *Web Site:* press.uottawa. ca, pg 444

Schwalb, Jaime, Sounds True Inc, 413 S Arthur Ave, Louisville, CO 80027 *Tel:* 303-665-3151 *Toll Free Tel:* 800-333-9185 (US); 888-303-9185

(US & CN) *E-mail:* customerservice@soundstrue. com; stpublicity@soundstrue.com *Web Site:* www. soundstrue.com, pg 204

Schwalbe, Will, Macmillan, 120 Broadway, 22nd fl, New York, NY 10271 *Tel:* 646-307-5151 *E-mail:* press. inquiries@macmillan.com *Web Site:* www.macmillan. com, pg 129

Schwartz, Anne, Random House Children's Books, 1745 Broadway, 10th fl, New York, NY 10019 *Tel:* 212-782-9000 *Web Site:* www.randomhousekids.com, pg 180

Schwartz, Barry L, Jewish Publication Society, 2100 Arch St, Philadelphia, PA 19103 *Tel:* 215-832-0600 *Toll Free Tel:* 800-234-3151 *Fax:* 215-568-2017 *Web Site:* www.jps.org, pg 113

Schwartz, Dan, Macmillan, 120 Broadway, 22nd fl, New York, NY 10271 *Tel:* 646-307-5151 *E-mail:* press. inquiries@macmillan.com *Web Site:* www.macmillan. com, pg 129

Schwartz, Eric, Columbia University Press, 61 W 62 St, New York, NY 10023 *Tel:* 212-459-0600 *Toll Free Tel:* 800-944-8648 *Fax:* 212-459-3678 *Web Site:* cup. columbia.edu, pg 55

Schwartz, Erika, Random House Children's Books, 1745 Broadway, 10th fl, New York, NY 10019 *Tel:* 212-782-9000 *Web Site:* www.randomhousekids.com, pg 181

Schwartz, Hannah, Stuart Krichevsky Literary Agency Inc, 6 E 39 St, Suite 500, New York, NY 10016 *Tel:* 212-725-5288 *Fax:* 212-725-5275 *E-mail:* query@ skagency.com *Web Site:* skagency.com, pg 492

Schwartz, Justin, Simon & Schuster, 1230 Avenue of the Americas, New York, NY 10020 *Tel:* 212-698-7000 *Toll Free Tel:* 800-223-2348 (cust serv); 800-223-2336 (orders) *Toll Free Fax:* 800-943-9831 (orders) *Web Site:* www.simonandschuster.com, pg 198

Schwartz, Leslie, The Library of America, 14 E 60 St, New York, NY 10022-1006 *Tel:* 212-308-3360 *Fax:* 212-750-8352 *E-mail:* info@loa.org *Web Site:* www.loa.org, pg 124

Schwartz, Matt, Penguin Random House LLC, 1745 Broadway, New York, NY 10019 *Tel:* 212-782-9000 *Toll Free Tel:* 800-726-0600 *Web Site:* www. penguinrandomhouse.com, pg 164

Schwartz, Matt, Random House Publishing Group, 1745 Broadway, New York, NY 10019 *Toll Free Tel:* 800-200-3552 *Web Site:* www.randomhousebooks.com, pg 181

Schwartz, Rebecca, Porchlight Book Co Business Book Awards, 544 S First St, Milwaukee, WI 53204 *Toll Free Tel:* 800-236-7323 *E-mail:* info@ porchlightbooks.com *Web Site:* porchlightbooks.com, pg 657

Schwartz, Rick, HarperCollins Publishers, 195 Broadway, New York, NY 10007 *Tel:* 212-207-7000 *Fax:* 212-207-7145 *Web Site:* www.harpercollins.com, pg 94

Schwartz, Steven, Sarah Jane Freymann Literary Agency LLC, 59 W 71 St, Suite 9-B, New York, NY 10023 *Tel:* 212-362-9277 *E-mail:* submissions@ sarahjanefreymann.com *Web Site:* www. sarahjanefreymann.com, pg 485

Schwartz, Susan, Dutton, 1745 Broadway, New York, NY 10019 *Tel:* 212-366-2000 *Fax:* 212-366-2262 *E-mail:* duttonpublicity@us.penguingroup.com *Web Site:* www.penguin.com, pg 68

Schwartz, Susan, The Editors Circle, 24 Holly Circle, Easthampton, MA 01027 *Tel:* 862-596-9709 *E-mail:* query@theeditorscircle.com *Web Site:* www. theeditorscircle.com, pg 463

Schwartzberg, Noah, Portfolio, 375 Hudson St, New York, NY 10014 *Web Site:* www.penguin.com/meet/ publishers/portfolio, pg 172

Schwartzman, Jill, Dutton, 1745 Broadway, New York, NY 10019 *Tel:* 212-366-2000 *Fax:* 212-366-2262 *E-mail:* duttonpublicity@us.penguingroup.com *Web Site:* www.penguin.com, pg 68

Schwartzman, Jill, Plume, 375 Hudson St, New York, NY 10014 *Tel:* 212-366-2000 *Fax:* 212-243-6002 *Web Site:* www.penguin.com/publishers/plume, pg 171

Schwartzmann, Melissa, Savvas Learning Co LLC, 15 E Midland Ave, Suite 502, Paramus, NJ 07652 *Toll Free Tel:* 800-848-9500 *Web Site:* www.savvas.com, pg 193

Schwarze, Diane, Book Peddlers, 18925 Lake Ave, Deephaven, MN 55391 *Tel:* 952-544-1154 *Web Site:* www.bookpeddlers.com, pg 38

Schweikert, Vincent, New Jersey Business & Industry Association (NJBIA), 10 W Lafayette St, Trenton, NJ 08608-2002 *Tel:* 609-393-7707 *Web Site:* njbia.org, pg 541

Schweitzer, Matt, Houghton Mifflin Harcourt, 125 High St, Boston, MA 02110 *Tel:* 617-351-5000 *Toll Free Tel:* 855-969-4642; 800-225-5425 (K-12 educ materials); 800-323-9540 (assessment materials); 877-219-1537 (SkillsTutor); 888-242-6747 (Innovation in Educ Group); 800-225-3362 (Trade & Ref Div) *Toll Free Fax:* 800-269-5232 *E-mail:* myhmhco@hmhco.com *Web Site:* www.hmhco.com, pg 103

Schweitzer, Matt, Houghton Mifflin Harcourt Trade & Reference Division, 125 High St, Boston, MA 02110 *Tel:* 617-351-5000 *Web Site:* www.hmhco.com, pg 104

Schweitzer, Maxine, Scott Meredith Literary Agency LP, 125 Park Ave, 25th fl, New York, NY 10017 *Tel:* 646-218-9240 *Fax:* 212-977-5997 *E-mail:* info@scottmeredith.com *Web Site:* www.scottmeredith.com, pg 497

Schwoeri, Lindsey, Viking, 375 Hudson St, New York, NY 10014 *Tel:* 212-366-2000 *Fax:* 212-243-6002 *Web Site:* www.penguin.com/publishers/vikingbooks, pg 236

Sciarappa, Matthew, little bee books, 251 Park Ave S, 12th fl, New York, NY 10010 *Toll Free Tel:* 844-321-0237 *E-mail:* info@littlebeebooks.com *Web Site:* littlebeebooks.com, pg 125

Scinta, Sam, Fulcrum Publishing Inc, 4690 Table Mountain Dr, Suite 100, Golden, CO 80403 *Tel:* 303-277-1623 *Toll Free Tel:* 800-992-2908 *Fax:* 303-279-7111 *Toll Free Fax:* 800-726-7112 *E-mail:* info@fulcrumbooks.com; orders@fulcrumbooks.com *Web Site:* www.fulcrumbooks.com, pg 82

Sciortino, Joseph, Editions Mediaspaul, 3965, blvd Henri-Bourassa E, Montreal, QC H1H 1L1, Canada *Tel:* 514-322-7341 *Fax:* 514-322-4281 *E-mail:* editeur@mediaspaul.ca *Web Site:* mediaspaul.ca, pg 424

Scivener, Brian, University of Calgary Press, 2500 University Dr NW, Calgary, AB T2N 1N4, Canada *Tel:* 403-220-7578 *Fax:* 403-282-0085 *E-mail:* ucpress@ucalgary.ca *Web Site:* press.ucalgary.ca, pg 443

Sclama, Nicole, Houghton Mifflin Harcourt Trade & Reference Division, 125 High St, Boston, MA 02110 *Tel:* 617-351-5000 *Web Site:* www.hmhco.com, pg 104

Scognamiglio, John, Kensington Publishing Corp, 119 W 40 St, New York, NY 10018 *Tel:* 212-407-1500 *Toll Free Tel:* 800-221-2647 *Fax:* 212-935-0699 *Web Site:* www.kensingtonbooks.com, pg 116

Scordato, Ellen, Stonesong, 270 W 39 St, Suite 201, New York, NY 10018 *Tel:* 212-929-4600 *E-mail:* editors@stonesong.com *Web Site:* www.stonesong.com, pg 504

Scott, Ardy M, Twilight Times Books, PO Box 3340, Kingsport, TN 37664-0340 *Tel:* 423-323-0183 *Fax:* 423-323-0183 *E-mail:* publisher@twilighttimes.com *Web Site:* www.twilighttimesbooks.com, pg 223

Scott, Craig R, Heritage Books Inc, 5810 Ruatan St, Berwyn Heights, MD 20740 *Toll Free Tel:* 800-876-6103 *Toll Free Fax:* 800-876-6103; 800-297-9954 *E-mail:* orders@heritagebooks.com; submissions@heritagebooks.com *Web Site:* www.heritagebooks.com, pg 98

Scott, Debra Leigh, Hidden River Arts Playwriting Award, PO Box 63927, Philadelphia, PA 19147 *Tel:* 610-764-0813 *E-mail:* hiddenriverarts@gmail.com *Web Site:* www.hiddenriverarts.org; www.hiddenriverarts.com, pg 623

Scott, Debra Leigh, The William Van Wert Memorial Fiction Award, PO Box 63927, Philadelphia, PA 19147 *Tel:* 610-764-0813 *E-mail:* hiddenriverarts@gmail.com *Web Site:* www.hiddenriverarts.org; www.hiddenriverarts.com, pg 675

Scott, Kate, Midwest Bookseller of the Year Award, 1375 St Anthony Ave, Suite 202-3, St Paul, MN 55104 *Tel:* 612-208-6279 *Toll Free Fax:* 844-273-4119 *E-mail:* info@midwestbooksellers.org *Web Site:* www.midwestbooksellers.org/bookseller-of-the-year.html, pg 641

Scott, Kate, Midwest Independent Booksellers Association (MIBA), 1375 St Anthony Ave, Suite 202-3, St Paul, MN 55104 *Tel:* 612-208-6279 *Toll Free Fax:* 844-273-4119 *E-mail:* info@midwestbooksellers.org *Web Site:* www.midwestbooksellers.org, pg 537

Scott, Katherine, Canadian Council on Social Development (Conseil canadien de developpement social), 190 O'Connor St, Suite 100, Ottawa, ON K2P 2R3, Canada *Tel:* 613-236-8977 *Fax:* 613-236-2750 *E-mail:* info@ccsd.ca *Web Site:* www.ccsd.ca, pg 418

Scott, Katie, Kids Can Press Ltd, 25 Dockside Dr, Toronto, ON M5A 0B5, Canada *Tel:* 416-479-7000 *Toll Free Tel:* 800-265-0884 *Fax:* 416-960-5437 *E-mail:* info@kidscan.com; customerservice@kidscan.com *Web Site:* www.kidscanpress.com; www.kidscanpress.ca, pg 431

Scott, Leigh, Arcadia Publishing Inc, 420 Wando Park Blvd, Mount Pleasant, SC 29464 *Tel:* 843-853-2070 *Toll Free Tel:* 888-313-2665 (orders only) *Fax:* 843-853-0044 *E-mail:* sales@arcadiapublishing.com *Web Site:* www.arcadiapublishing.com, pg 19

Scott, Marianne, The Canadian Writers' Foundation Inc (La Fondation des Ecrivains Canadiens), PO Box 13281, Kanata Sta, Ottawa, ON K2K 1X4, Canada *Tel:* 613-256-6937 *Fax:* 613-256-5457 *E-mail:* info@canadianwritersfoundation.org *Web Site:* www.canadianwritersfoundation.org, pg 551

Scott, Michael, Aptara Inc, 2901 Telestar Ct, Suite 522, Falls Church, VA 22042 *Tel:* 703-352-0001 *E-mail:* moreinfo@aptaracorp.com *Web Site:* www.aptaracorp.com, pg 458

Scott, Nita, Educators Award, PO Box 1589, Austin, TX 78767-1589 *Tel:* 512-478-5748 *Toll Free Tel:* 888-762-4685 *Fax:* 512-478-3961 *E-mail:* societyexec@dkg.org *Web Site:* www.dkg.org, pg 612

Scott, Tiffany, BuilderBooks, 1201 15 St NW, Washington, DC 20005 *Tel:* 202-822-0200 *Toll Free Tel:* 800-223-2665 *Fax:* 202-266-8096 (edit) *E-mail:* info@nahb.com *Web Site:* builderbooks.com, pg 42

Scott, Wendy, Winterwolf Press, 1810 E Sahara Ave, Suite 737, Las Vegas, NV 89014 *Toll Free Tel:* 855-ICE-WOLF (423-9653) *E-mail:* info@winterwolfpress.com; questions@winterwolfpress.com; admin@winterwolfpress.com (orders) *Web Site:* winterwolfpress.com, pg 243

Scott, Yolanda, Charlesbridge Publishing Inc, 85 Main St, Watertown, MA 02472 *Tel:* 617-926-0329 *Toll Free Tel:* 800-225-3214 *Fax:* 617-926-5720 *Toll Free Fax:* 800-926-5775 *E-mail:* books@charlesbridge.com *Web Site:* www.charlesbridge.com, pg 49

Scovel, Lauren, Laura Gross Literary Agency Ltd, PO Box 610326, Newton Highlands, MA 02461 *Tel:* 617-964-2977 *Fax:* 617-964-3023 *E-mail:* query@lg-la.com *Web Site:* www.lg-la.com, pg 487

Scriver, Julie, Goose Lane Editions, 500 Beaverbrook Ct, Suite 330, Fredericton, NB E3B 5X4, Canada *Tel:* 506-450-4251 *Toll Free Tel:* 888-926-8377 *Fax:* 506-459-4991 *E-mail:* info@gooselane.com; customerservice@gooselane.com *Web Site:* www.gooselane.com, pg 427

Seager, Deb, Grove Atlantic Inc, 154 W 14 St, 12th fl, New York, NY 10011 *Tel:* 212-614-7850 *Toll Free Tel:* 800-521-0178 *Fax:* 212-614-7886 *E-mail:* info@groveatlantic.com; sales@groveatlantic.com; publicity@groveatlantic.com; rights@groveatlantic.com *Web Site:* www.groveatlantic.com, pg 89

Searle, Linnea, Playwrights Project, 3675 Ruffin Rd, Suite 330, San Diego, CA 92123 *Tel:* 858-384-2970 *Fax:* 858-384-2974 *E-mail:* write@playwrightsproject.org *Web Site:* www.playwrightsproject.org, pg 656

Sears, Rene, Prometheus Books, 59 John Glenn Dr, Amherst, NY 14228-2119 *Tel:* 716-691-0133 *Fax:* 716-691-0137 *E-mail:* marketing@prometheusbooks.com; editorial@prometheusbooks.com; rights@prometheusbooks.com *Web Site:* www.prometheusbooks.com, pg 176

Searson, Lauren, PRINTING United Alliance, 10015 Main St, Fairfax, VA 22031-3489 *Tel:* 703-385-1335 *Toll Free Tel:* 888-385-3588 *Fax:* 703-273-0456 *E-mail:* assist@printing.org; info@printing.org *Web Site:* www.printing.org, pg 175

Seaton, Ann, CALIBA Golden Poppy Awards, 651 Broadway, 2nd fl, Sonoma, CA 95476 *Tel:* 415-561-7686 *Fax:* 415-561-7685 *E-mail:* info@caliballiance.org *Web Site:* www.caliballiance.org/golden-poppy-awards.html, pg 602

Seaton, Ann, California Independent Booksellers Alliance (CALIBA), 651 Broadway, 2nd fl, Sonoma, CA 95476 *Tel:* 415-561-7686 *Fax:* 415-561-7685 *E-mail:* info@caliballiance.org *Web Site:* www.caliballiance.org, pg 529

Secara, Andrea, Algora Publishing, 1732 First Ave, No 20330, New York, NY 10128 *Tel:* 212-678-0232 *Fax:* 212-666-3682 *E-mail:* editors@algora.com *Web Site:* www.algora.com, pg 7

Secara, Claudiu A, Algora Publishing, 1732 First Ave, No 20330, New York, NY 10128 *Tel:* 212-678-0232 *Fax:* 212-666-3682 *E-mail:* editors@algora.com *Web Site:* www.algora.com, pg 7

Sector, Emma, Prospect Agency, 285 Fifth Ave, PMB 445, Brooklyn, NY 11215 *Tel:* 718-788-3217 *Fax:* 718-360-9582 *Web Site:* www.prospectagency.com, pg 499

Sederstrom, Kate, Bloomsbury Publishing Inc, 1385 Broadway, 5th fl, New York, NY 10018 *Tel:* 212-419-5300 *E-mail:* marketingusa@bloomsbury.com; adultpublicityusa@bloomsbury.com; askacademic@bloomsbury.com *Web Site:* www.bloomsbury.com, pg 36

Sedgeley, Carlton, Royce Carlton Inc, 866 United Nations Plaza, Suite 587, New York, NY 10017-1880 *Tel:* 212-355-7700 *Toll Free Tel:* 800-LECTURE (532-8873) *Fax:* 212-888-8659 *E-mail:* info@roycecarlton.com *Web Site:* www.roycecarlton.com, pg 515

Sedita, Francesco, Penguin Workshop, 1745 Broadway, New York, NY 10019 *Tel:* 212-366-2000 *Web Site:* www.penguin.com/publishers/penguinworkshop/, pg 165

Sedita, Francesco, Penguin Young Readers Group, 345 Hudson St, New York, NY 10014 *Tel:* 212-366-2000; 212-414-3553 *Fax:* 212-414-3340 *Web Site:* www.penguin.com/children, pg 165

Sedliar, Renee, Perseus Books, 1290 Avenue of the Americas, New York, NY 10104 *Tel:* 212-340-8100 *Toll Free Tel:* 800-343-4499 (cust serv) *Fax:* 212-340-8105 *Web Site:* www.perseusbooks.com, pg 167

Seegmiller, Tasha, RISING STAR Award, PO Box 190, Jefferson, OR 97352 *E-mail:* risingstar@womenfictionwriters.org *Web Site:* wfwa.memberclicks.net/rising-star-award, pg 662

Seegmiller, Tasha, STAR Award, PO Box 190, Jefferson, OR 97352 *E-mail:* staraward@womenfictionwriters.org *Web Site:* wfwa.memberclicks.net/star-award, pg 670

Seegmiller, Tasha, Women's Fiction Writers Association (WFWA), PO Box 190, Jefferson, OR 97352 *E-mail:* communications@womensfictionwriters.org; membership@womensfictionwriters.org *Web Site:* www.womensfictionwriters.org, pg 549

Seely, Steve, Balance Sports Publishing LLC, 195 Lucero Way, Portola Valley, CA 94028 *Tel:* 650-561-9586 *Fax:* 650-391-9850 *E-mail:* info@balancesportspublishing.com *Web Site:* www.balancesportspublishing.com, pg 27

Seeman, Marsha, Writers Guild of America, East (WGAE), 250 Hudson St, Suite 700, New York, NY 10013 *Tel:* 212-767-7800 *Fax:* 212-582-1909 *Web Site:* www.wgaeast.org, pg 549

Segal, Jonathan, Alfred A Knopf, c/o Penguin Random House Inc, 1745 Broadway, New York, NY 10019 *Tel:* 212-751-2600 *Fax:* 212-572-2662 (foreign rts) *Web Site:* knopfdoubleday.com, pg 118

Segal, Joyce, Pippin Press, 229 E 85 St, New York, NY 10028 *Tel:* 212-288-4920 *Fax:* 908-237-2407, pg 170

Sehlinger, Robert W, AdventureKEEN, 2204 First Ave S, Suite 102, Birmingham, AL 35233 *Tel:* 763-689-9800 *Toll Free Tel:* 800-678-7006 *Fax:* 763-689-9039 *Toll Free Fax:* 877-374-9016 *E-mail:* info@adventurewithkeen.com *Web Site:* adventurewithkeen.com, pg 5

Sehlinger, Robert W, Menasha Ridge Press, 2204 First Ave S, Suite 102, Birmingham, AL 35233 *Toll Free Tel:* 888-604-4537 *Fax:* 205-326-1012 *E-mail:* info@adventurewithkeen.com *Web Site:* www.menasharidge.com; www.adventurewithkeen.com, pg 138

Sehulster, Alexandra, St Martin's Press, LLC, 120 Broadway, New York, NY 10271 *Tel:* 646-307-5151 *Web Site:* us.macmillan.com/smp, pg 190

Seibold, Doug, Surrey Books, 1328 Greenleaf St, Evanston, IL 60202 *Tel:* 847-475-4457 *Toll Free Tel:* 800-326-4430 *Web Site:* agatepublishing.com/surrey, pg 211

Seidlitz, Lauri, Brush Education Inc, 6531-111 St, Edmonton, AB T6H 4R5, Canada *Tel:* 780-989-0910 *Toll Free Tel:* 855-283-0900 *Fax:* 780-989-0930 *Toll Free Fax:* 855-283-6947 *E-mail:* contact@brusheducation.ca *Web Site:* www.brusheducation.ca, pg 418

Seidman, Erika, Farrar, Straus & Giroux, LLC, 175 Varick St, 9th fl, New York, NY 10014 *Tel:* 212-741-6900 *E-mail:* fsg.publicity@fsgbooks.com *Web Site:* us.macmillan.com/fsg.aspx, pg 76

Seidman, Erika, Hill & Wang, 175 Varick St, New York, NY 10014 *Tel:* 212-741-6900 *Fax:* 212-633-9385 *E-mail:* fsg.publicity@fsgbooks.com; fsg.editorial@fsgbooks.com; sales@fsgbooks.com *Web Site:* us.macmillan.com/hillandwang.aspx, pg 99

Seidman, Erika, North Point Press, 18 W 18 St, 8th fl, New York, NY 10011 *Tel:* 212-741-6900 *Toll Free Tel:* 888-330-8477 *Fax:* 212-633-9385 *Web Site:* www.fsgbooks.com, pg 151

Seidman, Yishai, Dunow, Carlson & Lerner Literary Agency Inc, 27 W 20 St, Suite 1107, New York, NY 10011 *Tel:* 212-645-7606 *E-mail:* mail@dclagency.com *Web Site:* www.dclagency.com, pg 482

Seidner, Sophia, Jill Grinberg Literary Management LLC, 392 Vanderbilt Ave, Brooklyn, NY 11238 *Tel:* 212-620-5883 *E-mail:* info@jillgrinbergliterary.com *Web Site:* www.jillgrinbergliterary.com, pg 487

Seigart, Steven, Goldfarb & Associates, 721 Gibbon St, Alexandria, VA 22314 *Tel:* 202-466-3030 *Fax:* 703-836-5644 *E-mail:* rlgawlit@gmail.com *Web Site:* www.ronaldgoldfarb.com, pg 486

Seigel, Jessica, Deadline Club, c/o Salmagundi Club, 47 Fifth Ave, New York, NY 10003 *Tel:* 646-481-7584 *Web Site:* www.deadlineclub.org, pg 532

Seiler, Alice, Chronicle Books, 680 Second St, San Francisco, CA 94107 *Tel:* 415-537-4200 *Toll Free Tel:* 800-759-0190 (cust serv) *Fax:* 415-537-4460 *Toll Free Fax:* 800-858-7787 (orders); 800-286-9471 (cust serv) *E-mail:* frontdesk@chroniclebooks.com *Web Site:* www.chroniclebooks.com, pg 52

Seiler, Maggie, W D Hoard & Sons Co, 28 W Milwaukee Ave, Fort Atkinson, WI 53538 *Tel:* 920-563-5551 *Fax:* 920-563-7298 *E-mail:* hdbooks@hoards.com; editors@hoards.com *Web Site:* www.hoards.com, pg 100

Seitz, Jessica (Pollett), Outdoor Writers Association of America (OWAA), 2814 Brooks St, Box 442, Missoula, MT 59801 *Tel:* 406-728-7434 *E-mail:* info@owaa.org *Web Site:* www.owaa.org, pg 543

Seitz, Jessica (Pollett), Outdoor Writers Association of America Annual Conference, 2814 Brooks St, Box 442, Missoula, MT 59801 *Tel:* 406-728-7434 *E-mail:* info@owaa.org *Web Site:* www.owaa.org, pg 577

Self, Robert, Baby Tattoo Books, 6045 Longridge Ave, Van Nuys, CA 91401 *Tel:* 818-416-5314 *E-mail:* info@babytattoo.com *Web Site:* www.babytattoo.com, pg 26

Self, Ron, Brick Road Poetry Book Contest, 513 Broadway, Columbus, GA 31901-3117 *Web Site:* brickroadpoetrypress.com, pg 601

Selinsky, Page PhD, University of Pennsylvania Museum of Archaeology & Anthropology, 3260 South St, Philadelphia, PA 19104-6324 *Tel:* 215-898-4119; 215-898-4000 *E-mail:* publications@pennmuseum.org *Web Site:* www.penn.museum, pg 230

Sellers, John, Houghton Mifflin Harcourt Trade & Reference Division, 125 High St, Boston, MA 02110 *Tel:* 617-351-5000 *Web Site:* www.hmhco.com, pg 104

Sellers, Scott, Seal Books, 320 Front St W, Suite 1400, Toronto, ON M5V 3B6, Canada *Tel:* 416-364-4449 *Toll Free Tel:* 888-523-9292 (order desk) *Fax:* 416-598-7764 *Web Site:* www.penguinrandomhouse.ca, pg 439

Sellmyer, Charlotte, National Music Publishers' Association (NMPA), 975 "F" St NW, Suite 375, Washington, DC 20004 *Tel:* 202-393-6672 *E-mail:* members@nmpa.org *Web Site:* nmpa.org, pg 540

Sells, Dianna, Texas A&M University Press, John H Lindsey Bldg, Lewis St, 4354 TAMU, College Station, TX 77843-4354 *Tel:* 979-845-1436 *Toll Free Tel:* 800-826-8911 (orders) *Fax:* 979-847-8752 *Toll Free Fax:* 888-617-2421 (orders) *E-mail:* bookorders@tamu.edu *Web Site:* www.tamupress.com, pg 215

Seltz, Martin, Augsburg Fortress Publishers, Publishing House of the Evangelical Lutheran Church in America, 510 Marquette Ave S, Minneapolis, MN 55402 *Tel:* 612-330-3300 *Toll Free Tel:* 800-426-0115 (ext 639, subns); 800-328-4648 (orders) *Fax:* 612-330-3455 *E-mail:* info@augsburgfortress.org; copyright@augsburgfortress.org (reprint permission requests); customercare@augsburgfortress.org *Web Site:* www.augsburgfortress.org; www.1517.media, pg 25

Seltzer, Joyce, Harvard University Press, 79 Garden St, Cambridge, MA 02138-1499 *Tel:* 617-495-2600; 401-531-2800 (intl orders) *Toll Free Tel:* 800-405-1619 (orders) *Fax:* 617-495-5898 (gen); 617-496-4677 (edit & rts); 401-531-2801 (intl orders) *Toll Free Fax:* 800-406-9145 (orders) *E-mail:* contact_hup@harvard.edu *Web Site:* www.hup.harvard.edu, pg 95

Sen, Sharmila, Harvard University Press, 79 Garden St, Cambridge, MA 02138-1499 *Tel:* 617-495-2600; 401-531-2800 (intl orders) *Toll Free Tel:* 800-405-1619 (orders) *Fax:* 617-495-5898 (gen); 617-496-4677 (edit & rts); 401-531-2801 (intl orders) *Toll Free Fax:* 800-406-9145 (orders) *E-mail:* contact_hup@harvard.edu *Web Site:* www.hup.harvard.edu, pg 95

Senders, Marci, Disney-Hyperion Books, 1101 Flower St, Glendale, CA 91201 *Web Site:* books.disney.com, pg 65

Senechal, David, Les Editions Fides, 7333 place des Roseraies, bureau 100, Anjou, QC H1M 2X6, Canada *Tel:* 514-745-4290 *Fax:* 514-745-4299 *E-mail:* editions@groupefides.com *Web Site:* www.editionsfides.com, pg 423

Sengthavy, Khamla, Norma Epstein Foundation Awards in Creative Writing, 15 King's College Circle, UC 165, Toronto, ON M5S 3H7, Canada *Tel:* 416-978-8083 *Fax:* 416-978-8854 *E-mail:* uc.programs@utoronto.ca *Web Site:* www.uc.utoronto.ca/writing-centre, pg 613

Sennholz, Lyn M, Center for Futures Education Inc, 345 Erie St, Grove City, PA 16127 *Tel:* 724-458-5860 *Fax:* 724-458-5962 *E-mail:* info@thectr.com *Web Site:* www.thectr.com, pg 48

Senturk, Huseyin, Tughra Books, 335 Clifton Ave, Clifton, NJ 07011 *Tel:* 646-415-9331 *Fax:* 646-827-6228 *E-mail:* info@tughrabooks.com *Web Site:* www.tughrabooks.com, pg 221

Senz, Lisa, St Martin's Press, LLC, 120 Broadway, New York, NY 10271 *Tel:* 646-307-5151 *Web Site:* us.macmillan.com/smp, pg 190

Seo, Ginee, Chronicle Books, 680 Second St, San Francisco, CA 94107 *Tel:* 415-537-4200 *Toll Free Tel:* 800-759-0190 (cust serv) *Fax:* 415-537-4460 *Toll Free Fax:* 800-858-7787 (orders); 800-286-9471 (cust serv) *E-mail:* frontdesk@chroniclebooks.com *Web Site:* www.chroniclebooks.com, pg 51

Seow, Jackie, Simon & Schuster, 1230 Avenue of the Americas, New York, NY 10020 *Tel:* 212-698-7000 *Toll Free Tel:* 800-223-2348 (cust serv); 800-223-2336 (orders) *Toll Free Fax:* 800-943-9831 (orders) *Web Site:* www.simonandschuster.com, pg 198

Sepehri, Amin, Mage Publishers Inc, 4601 N Park Ave, No 1616, Chevy Chase, MD 20815 *Web Site:* www.mage.com, pg 130

Seplow-Jolley, Elana, Random House Publishing Group, 1745 Broadway, New York, NY 10019 *Toll Free Tel:* 800-200-3552 *Web Site:* www.randomhousebooks.com, pg 181

Serabian, Charlie, Global Lion Intellectual Property Management Inc, PO Box 669238, Pompano Beach, FL 33066 *Tel:* 754-222-6948 *Fax:* 754-222-6948 *E-mail:* queriesgloballionmgt@gmail.com *Web Site:* www.globallionmanagement.com, pg 486

Serafimidis, Sarah, North Atlantic Books, 2526 Martin Luther King Jr Way, Berkeley, CA 94704 *Tel:* 510-549-4270 *Fax:* 510-549-4276 *Web Site:* www.northatlanticbooks.com, pg 151

Seraphim, Clio, Random House Publishing Group, 1745 Broadway, New York, NY 10019 *Toll Free Tel:* 800-200-3552 *Web Site:* www.randomhousebooks.com, pg 181

Sereiko, Claire, NPTA Alliance, 330 N Wabash Ave, Suite 2000, Chicago, IL 60611 *Tel:* 312-321-4092 *Toll Free Tel:* 800-355-NPTA (355-6782) *Fax:* 312-673-6736 *Web Site:* www.gonpta.com, pg 542

Sergel, Christopher III, Dramatic Publishing Co, 311 Washington St, Woodstock, IL 60098-3308 *Tel:* 815-338-7170 *Toll Free Tel:* 800-448-7469 *Fax:* 815-338-8981 *Toll Free Fax:* 800-334-5302 *E-mail:* plays@dramaticpublishing.com; customerservice@dpcplays.com *Web Site:* www.dramaticpublishing.com, pg 67

Sergel, Gayle, Dramatic Publishing Co, 311 Washington St, Woodstock, IL 60098-3308 *Tel:* 815-338-7170 *Toll Free Tel:* 800-448-7469 *Fax:* 815-338-8981 *Toll Free Fax:* 800-334-5302 *E-mail:* plays@dramaticpublishing.com; customerservice@dpcplays.com *Web Site:* www.dramaticpublishing.com, pg 67

Sergel, Susan, Dramatic Publishing Co, 311 Washington St, Woodstock, IL 60098-3308 *Tel:* 815-338-7170 *Toll Free Tel:* 800-448-7469 *Fax:* 815-338-8981 *Toll Free Fax:* 800-334-5302 *E-mail:* plays@dramaticpublishing.com; customerservice@dpcplays.com *Web Site:* www.dramaticpublishing.com, pg 67

Sergio, Christopher, Henry Holt and Company, LLC, 120 Broadway, 23rd fl, New York, NY 10271 *Tel:* 646-307-5151 *Toll Free Tel:* 888-330-8477 (orders) *Fax:* 646-307-5285 *Web Site:* www.henryholt.com, pg 101

Seroy, Jeff, Farrar, Straus & Giroux, LLC, 175 Varick St, 9th fl, New York, NY 10014 *Tel:* 212-741-6900 *E-mail:* fsg.publicity@fsgbooks.com *Web Site:* us.macmillan.com/fsg.aspx, pg 76

Serpe, Sara, The ARF David Ogilvy Awards, 432 Park Ave S, 4th fl, New York, NY 10016-8013 *Tel:* 212-751-5656 *Fax:* 212-689-1859 *E-mail:* help@thearf.org *Web Site:* thearf.org, pg 593

Serrano, Elizabeth, ALSC Baker & Taylor Summer Reading Grant, 50 E Huron St, Chicago, IL 60611-2795 *Tel:* 312-280-2163 *Toll Free Tel:* 800-545-2433 *Fax:* 312-440-9374; 312-280-5271 *E-mail:* alsc@ala.org *Web Site:* www.ala.org/alsc, pg 591

Serrano, Elizabeth, The May Hill Arbuthnot Honor Lecture Award, 50 E Huron St, Chicago, IL 60611-2795 *Tel:* 312-280-2163 *Toll Free Tel:* 800-545-2433 *Fax:* 312-440-9374; 312-280-5271 *E-mail:* alsc@ala.org *Web Site:* www.ala.org/alsc, pg 592

Serrano, Elizabeth, The Mildred L Batchelder Award, 50 E Huron St, Chicago, IL 60611-2795 *Tel:* 312-280-2163 *Toll Free Tel:* 800-545-2433 *Fax:* 312-440-9374; 312-280-5271 *E-mail:* alsc@ala.org *Web Site:* www.ala.org/alsc, pg 596

Serrano, Elizabeth, The Pura Belpre Award, 50 E Huron St, Chicago, IL 60611-2795 *Tel:* 312-280-2163 *Toll Free Tel:* 800-545-2433 *Fax:* 312-440-9374; 312-280-5271 *E-mail:* alsc@ala.org *Web Site:* www.ala.org/alsc, pg 596

Serrano, Elizabeth, Bound to Stay Bound Books Scholarship, 50 E Huron St, Chicago, IL 60611-2795 *Tel:* 312-280-2163 *Toll Free Tel:* 800-545-2433 *Fax:* 312-440-9374; 312-280-5271 *E-mail:* alsc@ala.org *Web Site:* www.ala.org/alsc, pg 600

Serrano, Elizabeth, The Randolph Caldecott Medal, 50 E Huron St, Chicago, IL 60611-2795 *Tel:* 312-280-2163 *Toll Free Tel:* 800-545-2433 *Fax:* 312-440-9374; 312-280-5271 *E-mail:* alsc@ala.org *Web Site:* www.ala.org/alsc, pg 602

Serrano, Elizabeth, Children's Literature Legacy Award, 50 E Huron St, Chicago, IL 60611-2795 *Tel:* 312-280-2163 *Toll Free Tel:* 800-545-2433 *Fax:* 312-440-9374; 312-280-5271 *E-mail:* alsc@ala.org *Web Site:* www.ala.org/alsc, pg 604

Serrano, Elizabeth, Frederic G Melcher Scholarship, 50 E Huron St, Chicago, IL 60611-2795 *Tel:* 312-280-2163 *Toll Free Tel:* 800-545-2433 *Fax:* 312-440-9374; 312-280-5271 *E-mail:* alsc@ala.org *Web Site:* www.ala.org/alsc, pg 641

Serrano, Elizabeth, John Newbery Medal, 50 E Huron St, Chicago, IL 60611-2795 *Tel:* 312-280-2163 *Toll Free Tel:* 800-545-2433 *Fax:* 312-440-9374; 312-280-5271 *E-mail:* alsc@ala.org *Web Site:* www.ala.org/alsc, pg 648

Serrano, Elizabeth, Robert F Sibert Informational Book Award, 50 E Huron St, Chicago, IL 60611-2795 *Tel:* 312-280-2163 *Toll Free Tel:* 800-545-2433 *Fax:* 312-440-9374; 312-280-5271 *E-mail:* alsc@ala.org *Web Site:* www.ala.org/alsc, pg 667

Servant, Sylvie, Les Presses de l'Universite Laval, 2180, Chemin Sainte-Foy, 1st fl, Quebec, QC G1V 0A6, Canada *Tel:* 418-656-2803 *Fax:* 418-656-3305 *E-mail:* presses@pul.ulaval.ca *Web Site:* www.pulaval.com, pg 437

Sery, Douglas, The MIT Press, One Rogers St, Cambridge, MA 02142 *Tel:* 617-253-5255 *Toll Free Tel:* 800-405-1619 (orders) *Fax:* 617-258-6779; 617-577-1545 (orders) *Web Site:* mitpress.mit.edu, pg 141

Seum, Rebecca, Cup of Tea Books, PO Box 21133, Columbus, OH 43221 *E-mail:* sales@pagespringpublishing.com; weditor@pagespringpublishing.com; submissions@pagespringpublishing.com *Web Site:* www.cupofteabooks.com, pg 61

Severini, Giorgia, R Ross Annett Award for Children's Literature, 11759 Groat Rd, Edmonton, AB T5M 3K6, Canada *Tel:* 780-422-8174 *Toll Free Tel:* 800-665-5354 (AB only) *Fax:* 780-422-2663 (attn WGA) *E-mail:* mail@writersguild.ca *Web Site:* writersguild.ca, pg 592

Severini, Giorgia, Georges Bugnet Award for Fiction, 11759 Groat Rd, Edmonton, AB T5M 3K6, Canada *Tel:* 780-422-8174 *Toll Free Tel:* 800-665-5354 (AB only) *Fax:* 780-422-2663 (attn WGA) *E-mail:* mail@writersguild.ca *Web Site:* writersguild.ca, pg 601

Severini, Giorgia, The City of Calgary W O Mitchell Book Prize, 11759 Groat Rd, Edmonton, AB T5M 3K6, Canada *Tel:* 780-422-8174 *Toll Free Tel:* 800-

665-5354 (AB only) *Fax:* 780-422-2663 (attn WGA) *E-mail:* mail@writersguild.ca *Web Site:* writersguild.ca, pg 605

Severini, Giorgia, Wilfrid Eggleston Award for Nonfiction, 11759 Groat Rd, Edmonton, AB T5M 3K6, Canada *Tel:* 780-422-8174 *Toll Free Tel:* 800-665-5354 (AB only) *Fax:* 780-422-2663 (attn WGA) *E-mail:* mail@writersguild.ca *Web Site:* writersguild.ca, pg 612

Severini, Giorgia, James H Gray Award for Short Nonfiction, 11759 Groat Rd, Edmonton, AB T5M 3K6, Canada *Tel:* 780-422-8174 *Toll Free Tel:* 800-665-5354 (AB only) *Fax:* 780-422-2663 (attn WGA) *E-mail:* mail@writersguild.ca *Web Site:* writersguild.ca, pg 620

Severini, Giorgia, The Robert Kroetsch City of Edmonton Book Prize, 11759 Groat Rd, Edmonton, AB T5M 3K6, Canada *Tel:* 780-422-8174 *Toll Free Tel:* 800-665-5354 (AB only) *Fax:* 780-422-2663 (attn WGA) *E-mail:* mail@writersguild.ca *Web Site:* writersguild.ca, pg 631

Severini, Giorgia, Howard O'Hagan Award for Short Story, 11759 Groat Rd, Edmonton, AB T5M 3K6, Canada *Tel:* 780-422-8174 *Toll Free Tel:* 800-665-5354 (AB only) *Fax:* 780-422-2663 (attn WGA) *E-mail:* mail@writersguild.ca *Web Site:* writersguild.ca, pg 650

Severini, Giorgia, Gwen Pharis Ringwood Award for Drama, 11759 Groat Rd, Edmonton, AB T5M 3K6, Canada *Tel:* 780-422-8174 *Toll Free Tel:* 800-665-5354 (AB only) *Fax:* 780-422-2663 (attn WGA) *E-mail:* mail@writersguild.ca *Web Site:* writersguild.ca, pg 662

Severini, Giorgia, Stephan G Stephansson Award for Poetry, 11759 Groat Rd, Edmonton, AB T5M 3K6, Canada *Tel:* 780-422-8174 *Toll Free Tel:* 800-665-5354 (AB only) *Fax:* 780-422-2663 (attn WGA) *E-mail:* mail@writersguild.ca *Web Site:* writersguild.ca, pg 670

Severini, Giorgia, Jon Whyte Memorial Essay Prize, 11759 Groat Rd, Edmonton, AB T5M 3K6, Canada *Tel:* 780-422-8174 *Toll Free Tel:* 800-665-5354 (AB only) *Fax:* 780-422-2663 (attn WGA) *E-mail:* mail@writersguild.ca *Web Site:* writersguild.ca, pg 677

Severini, Giorgia, Writers' Guild of Alberta, 11759 Groat Rd, Edmonton, AB T5M 3K6, Canada *Tel:* 780-422-8174 *Toll Free Tel:* 800-665-5354 (AB only) *Fax:* 780-422-2663 (attn WGA) *E-mail:* mail@writersguild.ca *Web Site:* writersguild.ca, pg 549

Severns, Jennifer, American Marketing Association, 130 E Randolph St, 22nd fl, Chicago, IL 60601 *Tel:* 312-542-9000 *Toll Free Tel:* 800-AMA-1150 (262-1150) *Web Site:* www.ama.org, pg 523

Sevick, Kristin, Tom Doherty Associates, LLC, 120 Broadway, New York, NY 10271 *Tel:* 646-307-5511 *Toll Free Tel:* 800-455-0340 *Web Site:* us.macmillan.com/torforge, pg 66

Sevier, Ben, Grand Central Publishing, 1290 Avenue of the Americas, New York, NY 10104 *Tel:* 212-364-1100 *Web Site:* www.hachettebookgroup.com, pg 88

Sevier, Ben, Hachette Book Group, 1290 Avenue of the Americas, New York, NY 10104 *Tel:* 212-364-1100 *Toll Free Tel:* 800-759-0190 (cust serv) *Fax:* 212-364-0933 (intl orders) *Toll Free Fax:* 800-286-9471 (cust serv) *Web Site:* www.hachettebookgroup.com, pg 90

Sewell, Emily, Bull Publishing Co, PO Box 1377, Boulder, CO 80306 *Tel:* 303-545-6350 *Toll Free Tel:* 800-676-2855 *Fax:* 303-545-6354 *E-mail:* bullpublishing@msn.com *Web Site:* www.bullpub.com, pg 42

Sewell, Vicki, University of South Carolina Press, 1600 Hampton St, Suite 544, Columbia, SC 29208 *Tel:* 803-777-5245 *Toll Free Tel:* 800-768-2500 (orders) *Fax:* 803-777-0160 *Toll Free Tel:* 800-868-0740 (orders) *Web Site:* www.sc.edu/uscpress, pg 231

Sexton, Kim, SDP Publishing Solutions LLC, 36 Captain's Way, East Bridgewater, MA 02333 *Tel:* 617-775-0656 *Web Site:* www.sdppublishingsolutions.com, pg 470

Seyfried, Erika, Random House Publishing Group, 1745 Broadway, New York, NY 10019 *Toll Free Tel:* 800-200-3552 *Web Site:* www.randomhousebooks.com, pg 181

Seymour, Christine, American Institute of Chemical Engineers (AIChE), 120 Wall St, 23rd fl, New York, NY 10005-4020 *Tel:* 203-702-7660 *Toll Free Tel:* 800-242-4363 *Fax:* 203-775-5177 *E-mail:* customerservice@aiche.org *Web Site:* www.aiche.org, pg 12

Sferratore, Nadine, Harry N Abrams Inc, 195 Broadway, 9th fl, New York, NY 10007 *Tel:* 212-206-7715 *Toll Free Tel:* 800-345-1359 *Fax:* 212-519-1210 *E-mail:* abrams@abramsbooks.com *Web Site:* www.abramsbooks.com, pg 3

Shabelman, Doug, Burns Entertainment & Sports Marketing, 820 Davis St, Suite 222, Evanston, IL 60201 *Tel:* 847-866-9400 *Fax:* 847-491-9778 *E-mail:* burnsl@burnsent.com *Web Site:* burnsent.com, pg 515

Shaeffer, Rob, Princeton Architectural Press, 202 Warren St, Hudson, NY 12534 *Tel:* 518-671-6100 *Toll Free Tel:* 800-722-6657 (dist); 800-759-0190 (sales) *E-mail:* sales@papress.com *Web Site:* www.papress.com, pg 174

Shafeyeva, Yelena, Begell House Inc Publishers, 50 North St, Danbury, CT 06810 *Tel:* 203-456-6161 *Fax:* 203-456-6167 *E-mail:* orders@begellhouse.com *Web Site:* www.begellhouse.com, pg 30

Shaffer, Bryan, Purdue University Press, Stewart Ctr 190, 504 W State St, West Lafayette, IN 47907-2058 *Tel:* 765-494-2038 *Fax:* 765-496-2442 *E-mail:* pupress@purdue.edu *Web Site:* www.thepress.purdue.edu, pg 178

Shah, Monica, Harry N Abrams Inc, 195 Broadway, 9th fl, New York, NY 10007 *Tel:* 212-206-7715 *Toll Free Tel:* 800-345-1359 *Fax:* 212-519-1210 *E-mail:* abrams@abramsbooks.com *Web Site:* www.abramsbooks.com, pg 3

Shailor, Barbara A, Bibliographical Society of America, PO Box 1537, Lenox Hill Sta, New York, NY 10021-0043 *Tel:* 212-734-2500 *Fax:* 212-452-2710 *E-mail:* bsa@bibsocamer.org *Web Site:* www.bibsocamer.org, pg 528

Shaine, Ilene, Foster City International Writers Contest, 650 Shell Blvd, Foster City, CA 94404 *Tel:* 650-286-3380 *E-mail:* fostercity_writers@yahoo.com *Web Site:* www.fostercity.org, pg 616

Shallcross, Andrea, Hachette Book Group, 1290 Avenue of the Americas, New York, NY 10104 *Tel:* 212-364-1100 *Toll Free Tel:* 800-759-0190 (cust serv) *Fax:* 212-364-0933 (intl orders) *Toll Free Fax:* 800-286-9471 (cust serv) *Web Site:* www.hachettebookgroup.com, pg 91

Shaloo, Sharon, Massachusetts Book Awards, Simons College - GSLIS, 300 The Fenway, Boston, MA 02115 *Tel:* 617-521-2719 *E-mail:* bookawards@massbook.org *Web Site:* www.massbook.org, pg 638

Shamroe, Amy, Axiom Business Book Awards, 1129 Woodmere Ave, Suite B, Traverse City, MI 49686 *Tel:* 231-933-0445 *Toll Free Tel:* 800-706-4636 *Fax:* 231-933-0448 *E-mail:* info@axiomawards.com *Web Site:* www.axiomawards.com, pg 595

Shamroe, Amy, Illumination Book Awards, 1129 Woodmere Ave, Suite B, Traverse City, MI 49686 *Tel:* 231-933-0445 *Toll Free Tel:* 800-706-4636 *Fax:* 231-933-0448 *E-mail:* awards@bookpublishing.com *Web Site:* www.illuminationawards.com, pg 625

Shamroe, Amy, The Independent Publisher Book Awards, 1129 Woodmere Ave, Suite B, Traverse City, MI 49686 *Tel:* 231-933-0445 *Toll Free Tel:* 800-706-4636 *Fax:* 231-933-0448 *E-mail:* awards@bookpublishing.com *Web Site:* www.independentpublisher.com/ipland/ipawards.php, pg 626

Shamroe, Amy, Living Now Book Awards, 1129 Woodmere Ave, Suite B, Traverse City, MI 49686 *Tel:* 231-933-0445 *Toll Free Tel:* 800-706-4636 *Fax:* 231-933-0448 *E-mail:* awards@bookpublishing.com *Web Site:* www.livingnowawards.com, pg 634

Sheerin, Amber, Michigan Library Association (MLA), 3410 Belle Chase Way, Lansing, MI 48911 *Tel:* 517-394-2774 *E-mail:* mla@milibraries.org *Web Site:* www.milibraries.org, pg 537

Sheinkopf, Barry, The Writing Center, 601 E Palisade Ave, Suite 4, Englewood Cliffs, NJ 07632 *Tel:* 201-567-4017 *Fax:* 201-567-7202 *E-mail:* writingcenter@optonline.net *Web Site:* www.writingcenternj.com, pg 580

Shekari, Lauren, Other Press, 267 Fifth Ave, 6th fl, New York, NY 10016 *Tel:* 212-414-0054 *Toll Free Tel:* 877-843-6843 *Fax:* 212-414-0939 *E-mail:* editor@otherpress.com; marketing@otherpress.com; publicity@otherpress.com *Web Site:* www.otherpress.com, pg 157

Shelton, Darryl, Christian Schools International, 3350 E Paris Ave SE, Grand Rapids, MI 49512-3054 *Tel:* 616-957-1070 *Toll Free Tel:* 800-635-8288 *Fax:* 616-957-5022 *E-mail:* info@csionline.org *Web Site:* www.csionline.org, pg 51

Shelton, Tiffany, St Martin's Press, LLC, 120 Broadway, New York, NY 10271 *Tel:* 646-307-5151 *Web Site:* us.macmillan.com/smp, pg 190

Shen, Tina, Prospect Agency, 285 Fifth Ave, PMB 445, Brooklyn, NY 11215 *Tel:* 718-788-3217 *Fax:* 718-360-9582 *Web Site:* www.prospectagency.com, pg 499

Shepard, Aaron, Shepard Publications, 1117 N Garden St, Apt 302, Bellingham, WA 98225 *Web Site:* www.shepardpub.com, pg 197

Shepard, Christopher, Aurous Inc, PO Box 20490, New York, NY 10017 *Tel:* 212-628-9729 *Fax:* 212-535-7861, pg 475

Shepard, Diane, Bear & Co Inc, One Park St, Rochester, VT 05767 *Tel:* 802-767-3174 *Toll Free Tel:* 800-932-3277 *Fax:* 802-767-3726 *E-mail:* customerservice@InnerTraditions.com *Web Site:* InnerTraditions.com, pg 29

Shepard, Diane, Inner Traditions International Ltd, One Park St, Rochester, VT 05767 *Tel:* 802-767-3174 *Toll Free Tel:* 800-246-8648 *Fax:* 802-767-3726 *E-mail:* customerservice@InnerTraditions.com *Web Site:* www.InnerTraditions.com, pg 109

Shepard, Judith, The Permanent Press, 4170 Noyac Rd, Sag Harbor, NY 11963 *Tel:* 631-725-1101 *Web Site:* www.thepermanentpress.com, pg 167

Shepard, Judith, Second Chance Press, 4170 Noyac Rd, Sag Harbor, NY 11963 *Tel:* 631-725-1101 *E-mail:* info@thepermanentpress.com *Web Site:* www.thepermanentpress.com, pg 196

Shepard, Martin, The Permanent Press, 4170 Noyac Rd, Sag Harbor, NY 11963 *Tel:* 631-725-1101 *Web Site:* www.thepermanentpress.com, pg 167

Shepard, Martin, Second Chance Press, 4170 Noyac Rd, Sag Harbor, NY 11963 *Tel:* 631-725-1101 *E-mail:* info@thepermanentpress.com *Web Site:* www.thepermanentpress.com, pg 196

Sheppard, Christine, Library Association of Alberta (LAA), 80 Baker Crescent NW, Calgary, AB T2L 1R4, Canada *Tel:* 403-284-5818 *Toll Free Tel:* 877-522-5550 *E-mail:* info@laa.ca *Web Site:* www.laa.ca, pg 536

Sheppard, Nancy, Perseus Books, 1290 Avenue of the Americas, New York, NY 10104 *Tel:* 212-340-8100 *Toll Free Tel:* 800-343-4499 (cust serv) *Fax:* 212-340-8105 *Web Site:* www.perseusbooks.com, pg 167

Sheppard, Scott, Quarto Publishing Group USA Inc, 100 Cummings Ctr, Suite 265D, Beverly, MA 01915 *Tel:* 978-282-9590 *Toll Free Tel:* 800-328-0590 (sales) *Fax:* 978-283-2742 *E-mail:* sales@quartous.com *Web Site:* www.quartoknows.com, pg 178

Sherer, John, The University of North Carolina Press, 116 S Boundary St, Chapel Hill, NC 27514-3808 *Tel:* 919-966-3561 *E-mail:* uncpress@unc.edu *Web Site:* www.uncpress.org, pg 229

Sherer, Talia, Macmillan, 120 Broadway, 22nd fl, New York, NY 10271 *Tel:* 646-307-5151 *E-mail:* press.inquiries@macmillan.com *Web Site:* www.macmillan.com, pg 130

Sheridan-Witterschein, Jackie, National Braille Press, 88 Saint Stephen St, Boston, MA 02115-4312 *Tel:* 617-266-6160 *Toll Free Tel:* 800-548-7323 (cust serv); 888-965-8965 *Fax:* 617-437-0456 *E-mail:* contact@nbp.org *Web Site:* www.nbp.org, pg 145

Sherk, Mary Lou, Galen Press Ltd, PO Box 64400-WB, Tucson, AZ 85728-4400 *Tel:* 520-577-8363 *Fax:* 520-529-6459 *E-mail:* sales@galenpress.com *Web Site:* www.galenpress.com, pg 82

Sherman, Amy, University of Pittsburgh Press, 7500 Thomas Blvd, Pittsburgh, PA 15260 *Tel:* 412-383-2456 *Fax:* 412-383-2466 *E-mail:* info@upress.pitt.edu *Web Site:* www.upress.pitt.edu, pg 230

Sherman, Brooks, Janklow & Nesbit Associates, 285 Madison Ave, 21st fl, New York, NY 10017 *Tel:* 212-421-1700 *Fax:* 212-355-1403 *E-mail:* info@janklow.com *Web Site:* www.janklowandnesbit.com, pg 490

Sherman, Cynthia, Association of Writers & Writing Programs (AWP), University of Maryland, 5245 Greenbelt Rd, Box 246, College Park, MD 20740 *Tel:* 240-696-7700 *E-mail:* awp@awpwriter.org; press@awpwriter.org *Web Site:* www.awpwriter.org, pg 527

Sherman, Cynthia, AWP Award Series, University of Maryland, 5245 Greenbelt Rd, Box 246, College Park, MD 20740 *Tel:* 240-696-7700 *E-mail:* awp@awpwriter.org; press@awpwriter.org *Web Site:* www.awpwriter.org, pg 594

Sherman, Ken, Ken Sherman & Associates, 1275 N Hayworth, Suite 103, Los Angeles, CA 90046 *Tel:* 310-273-8840 *E-mail:* kenshermanassociates@gmail.com *Web Site:* www.kenshermanassociates.com, pg 502

Sherman, Rebecca, Writers House, 21 W 26 St, New York, NY 10010 *Tel:* 212-685-2400 *Web Site:* www.writershouse.com, pg 508

Sherman, Stephen, Radix Press, 11715 Bandlon Dr, Houston, TX 77072 *Tel:* 281-879-5688 *Web Site:* www.vvfh.org; www.specialforcesbooks.com, pg 179

Sherman, Wendy, Wendy Sherman Associates Inc, 138 W 25 St, Suite 1018, New York, NY 10001 *Tel:* 212-279-9027 *E-mail:* submissions@wsherman.com *Web Site:* www.wsherman.com, pg 502

Sherr, Roger, Genealogical Publishing Co, 3600 Clipper Mill Rd, Suite 229, Baltimore, MD 21211 *Tel:* 410-837-8271 *Toll Free Tel:* 800-296-6687 *Fax:* 410-752-8492 *Toll Free Fax:* 800-599-9561 *E-mail:* info@genealogical.com; web@genealogical.com *Web Site:* www.genealogical.com, pg 84

Sherrod, Tracy, HarperCollins General Books Group, 195 Broadway, New York, NY 10007 *Tel:* 212-207-7000 *Web Site:* www.harpercollins.com, pg 93

Sherry, Cynthia, Academy Chicago, 814 N Franklin St, Chicago, IL 60610 *Tel:* 312-337-0747 *Toll Free Tel:* 800-888-4741 (orders) *Fax:* 312-337-5110 *E-mail:* frontdesk@chicagoreviewpress.com *Web Site:* www.chicagoreviewpress.com, pg 3

Sherry, Cynthia, Chicago Review Press, 814 N Franklin St, Chicago, IL 60610 *Tel:* 312-337-0747 *Toll Free Tel:* 800-888-4741 *Fax:* 312-337-5110 *E-mail:* frontdesk@chicagoreviewpress.com *Web Site:* www.chicagoreviewpress.com, pg 50

Sherry, Cynthia, Triumph Books, 814 N Franklin St, Chicago, IL 60610 *Tel:* 312-337-0747 *Toll Free Tel:* 800-888-4741 (cust serv) *Fax:* 312-280-5470; 312-337-5985 *Web Site:* www.triumphbooks.com, pg 221

Sheu, Kimberly, Little, Brown and Company, 1290 Avenue of the Americas, New York, NY 10104 *Tel:* 212-364-1100 *Fax:* 212-364-0952 *E-mail:* firstname.lastname@hbgusa.com *Web Site:* www.littlebrown.com; www.hachettebookgroup.com, pg 125

Shewchuk, Alysia, House of Anansi Press Inc, 128 Sterling Rd, Lower Level, Toronto, ON M6R 2B7, Canada *Tel:* 416-363-4343 *Fax:* 416-363-1017 *E-mail:* customerservice@houseofanansi.com *Web Site:* www.houseofanansi.com, pg 429

Shickmanter, Margo, Doubleday, c/o Penguin Random House Inc, 1745 Broadway, New York, NY 10019 *Tel:* 212-751-2600 *Fax:* 212-572-2662 (foreign rts) *E-mail:* ddaypub@randomhouse.com *Web Site:* knopfdoubleday.com, pg 66

Shield, Nina, Avery, 1745 Broadway, New York, NY 10019 *Tel:* 212-366-2000 *Fax:* 212-366-2636 *E-mail:* averypublicity@penguinrandomhouse.com *Web Site:* www.penguin.com/publishers/avery; www.penguinrandomhouse.com, pg 26

Shield, Nina, TarcherPerigee, 375 Hudson St, New York, NY 10014 *Tel:* 212-366-2000 *Fax:* 212-366-2643 *E-mail:* customerservice@penguinrandomhouse.com (cust serv); TarcherPerigeePublicity@penguinrandomhouse.com (media queries) *Web Site:* www.tarcherbooks.com; www.facebook.com/TarcherPerigee/; www.penguin.com/publishers/tarcherperigee, pg 213

Shields, Charlie, The University of Arkansas Press, McIlroy House, 105 N McIlroy Ave, Fayetteville, AR 72701 *Tel:* 479-575-7544 *E-mail:* info@uapress.com *Web Site:* www.uapress.com, pg 226

Shields, Colin, Simon & Schuster Sales Division, 1230 Avenue of the Americas, New York, NY 10020 *Tel:* 212-698-7000, pg 200

Shillingford, Gordon, J Gordon Shillingford Publishing Inc, PO Box 86, RPO Corydon Ave, Winnipeg, MB R3M 3S3, Canada *Tel:* 204-779-6967 *E-mail:* jgshill2@mymts.net *Web Site:* www.jgshillingford.com, pg 440

Shin, Jinna, Random House Children's Books, 1745 Broadway, 10th fl, New York, NY 10019 *Tel:* 212-782-9000 *Web Site:* www.randomhousekids.com, pg 180

Shine, Deborah, Star Bright Books Inc, 13 Landsdowne St, Cambridge, MA 02139 *Tel:* 617-354-1300 *Fax:* 617-354-1399 *E-mail:* info@starbrightbooks.com; orders@starbrightbooks.com *Web Site:* www.starbrightbooks.org, pg 207

Shinsato, David, Savant Books & Publications LLC, 2630 Kapiolani Blvd, Suite 1601, Honolulu, HI 96826 *Tel:* 808-941-3927 (9AM-noon HST) *E-mail:* savantbooks@gmail.com; savantdistribution@gmail.com *Web Site:* www.savantbooksandpublications.com; www.savantdistribution.com, pg 192

Shirley, Melissa, Griffin Poetry Prize, 363 Parkridge Crescent, Oakville, ON L6M 1A8, Canada *Tel:* 905-618-0420 *E-mail:* info@griffinpoetryprize.com; publicity@griffinpoetryprize.com *Web Site:* www.griffinpoetryprize.com, pg 621

Shirley, Melissa, University of Regina Press, 2 Research Dr, Suite 246, Regina, SK S4S 7H9, Canada *Tel:* 306-585-4758 *Fax:* 306-585-4699 *E-mail:* uofrpress@uregina.ca *Web Site:* uofrpress.ca, pg 444

Shirzad, Mr Farhad, Ibex Publishers, PO Box 30087, Bethesda, MD 20824 *Tel:* 301-718-8188 *Toll Free Tel:* 888-718-8188 *Fax:* 301-907-8707 *E-mail:* info@ibexpub.com *Web Site:* ibexpub.com, pg 105

Shoaff, Will Tom, Grand & Archer Publishing, 463 Coyote, Cathedral City, CA 92234 *Tel:* 323-493-2785 *E-mail:* grandandarcher@gmail.com, pg 88

Shoemaker, Jack, Counterpoint Press LLC, 2560 Ninth St, Suite 318, Berkeley, CA 94710 *Tel:* 510-704-0230 *Fax:* 510-704-0268 *E-mail:* info@counterpointpress.com *Web Site:* counterpointpress.com; softskull.com, pg 58

Shoemaker, Susannah, Princeton University Press, 41 William St, Princeton, NJ 08540-5237 *Tel:* 609-258-4900 *Fax:* 609-258-6305 *Web Site:* press.princeton.edu, pg 174

Shokoff, Elisa, Simon & Schuster Audio, 1230 Avenue of the Americas, New York, NY 10020 *Web Site:* audio.simonandschuster.com, pg 199

Shook, Sharon, Harvest House Publishers Inc, PO Box 41210, Eugene, OR 97404-0322 *Tel:* 541-343-0123 *Toll Free Tel:* 888-501-6991 *Fax:* 541-

Silbermann, Chris, ICM Partners, 65 E 55 St, New York, NY 10022 Tel: 212-556-5600 Web Site: www. icmtalent.com, pg 489

Silbersack, Catryn, Henry Holt and Company, LLC, 120 Broadway, 23rd fl, New York, NY 10271 Tel: 646-307-5151 Toll Free Tel: 888-330-8477 (orders) Fax: 646-307-5285 Web Site: www.henryholt.com, pg 102

Silbersack, John, Philip K Dick Award, PO Box 3447, Hoboken, NJ 07030 Tel: 201-876-2551 Web Site: www.philipkdickaward.org, pg 609

Silbersack, John, Trident Media Group LLC, 41 Madison Ave, 36th fl, New York, NY 10010 Tel: 212-333-1511 E-mail: info@tridentmediagroup.com; press@tridentmediagroup.com Web Site: www. tridentmediagroup.com, pg 507

Silburg, Richard, Poetry Flash Reading Series, 1450 Fourth St, Suite 4, Berkeley, CA 94710 Tel: 510-525-5476 Fax: 510-525-6752 E-mail: editor@poetryflash. org Web Site: poetryflash.org, pg 577

Silfin, Beth, HarperCollins General Books Group, 195 Broadway, New York, NY 10007 Tel: 212-207-7000 Web Site: www.harpercollins.com, pg 93

Silva, Filipe, Macmillan, 120 Broadway, 22nd fl, New York, NY 10271 Tel: 646-307-5151 E-mail: press. inquiries@macmillan.com Web Site: www.macmillan. com, pg 130

Silva, Mick, Zondervan, 3900 Sparks Dr, Grand Rapids, MI 49546 Tel: 616-698-6900 Toll Free Tel: 800-226-1122; 800-727-1309 (retail orders) Fax: 616-698-3350 Toll Free Fax: 800-698-3256 (retail orders) Web Site: www.zondervan.com, pg 248

Silva, Pete, McGraw-Hill School Education Group, 8787 Orion Place, Columbus, OH 43240 Tel: 614-430-4000 Toll Free Tel: 800-848-1567 Web Site: www. mheducation.com, pg 136

Silva, Rita, Simon & Schuster Canada, 166 King St E, Suite 300, Toronto, ON M5A 1J3, Canada Tel: 647-427-8882 Toll Free Tel: 800-387-0446; 800-268-3216 (orders) Fax: 647-430-9446 Toll Free Fax: 888-849-8151 (orders) E-mail: info@simonandschuster.ca Web Site: www.simonandschuster.ca, pg 440

Silver, Carly, Harlequin Enterprises Ltd, 195 Broadway, 24th fl, New York, NY 10007 Tel: 212-207-7000 Toll Free Tel: 888-432-4879 E-mail: customerservice@ harlequin.com Web Site: www.harlequin.com, pg 93

Silver, David, YMAA Publication Center Inc, PO Box 480, Wolfeboro, NH 03894 Tel: 603-569-7988 Toll Free Tel: 800-669-8892 Fax: 603-569-1889 E-mail: info@ymaa.com Web Site: www.ymaa.com, pg 247

Silver, Janet, Aevitas Creative Management, 19 W 21 St, Suite 501, New York, NY 10010 Tel: 212-765-6900 Web Site: aevitascreative.com, pg 474

Silver, Joanne S, Beach Lloyd Publishers LLC, 231 Sunnyside Rd, West Grove, PA 19390 Tel: 215-407-4570 (cell) E-mail: beachlloyd@erols.com Web Site: www.beachlloyd.com, pg 29

Silver, Noel, Mazda Publishers Inc, PO Box 2603, Costa Mesa, CA 92628 Tel: 714-751-5252 Fax: 714-751-4805 E-mail: mazdapub@aol.com Web Site: www. mazdapublishers.com, pg 134

Silverstein, Clara, Chautauqua Writers' Workshop, One Ames Ave, Chautauqua, NY 14722 Tel: 716-357-6316; 716-357-6250 Toll Free Tel: 800-836-ARTS (836-2787) Fax: 716-357-9014 Web Site: ciweb.org, pg 574

Silvestri, Charles Anthony, Acroterion Books, 5305 Harvard Rd, Lawrence, KS 66049-4781 Tel: 785-917-0773 E-mail: info@acroterionbooks.com Web Site: www.acroterionbooks.com, pg 447

Silvestro, Denise, Kensington Publishing Corp, 119 W 40 St, New York, NY 10018 Tel: 212-407-1500 Toll Free Tel: 800-221-2647 Fax: 212-935-0699 Web Site: www.kensingtonbooks.com, pg 116

Silvis, Carol, Pennwriters Conference, PO Box 685, Dalton, PA 18414 E-mail: conferencecoordinator@ pennwriters.org; info@pennwriters.org Web Site: pennwriters.org, pg 577

Simard, Camille, Les Editions du Remue-Menage, La Maison Parent-Roback, 110 rue Sainte-Therese, bureau 303, Montreal, QC H2Y 1E6, Canada Tel: 514-876-0097 Fax: 514-876-7951 E-mail: info@editions-rm.ca Web Site: www.editions-rm.ca, pg 423

Simmons, Carolyn, Getty Publications, 1200 Getty Center Dr, Suite 500, Los Angeles, CA 90049-1682 Tel: 310-440-7365 Toll Free Tel: 800-223-3431 (orders) Fax: 310-440-7758 E-mail: pubsinfo@getty. edu Web Site: www.getty.edu/publications, pg 85

Simmons, Zoe, PAGE International Screenwriting Awards, 7190 Sunset Blvd, Suite 610, Hollywood, CA 90046 E-mail: info@pageawards.com Web Site: www. pageawards.com, pg 652

Simms, Maria K, Starcrafts LLC, 68A Fogg Rd, Epping, NH 03042 Tel: 603-734-4300 Toll Free Tel: 866-953-8458 (24/7 message ctr) Fax: 603-734-4311 E-mail: astrosales@astrocom.com Web Site: acspublications.com; www.astrocom.com, pg 207

Simon, Daniel, Neustadt International Prize for Literature, c/o University of Oklahoma, 630 Parrington Oval, Suite 110, Norman, OK 73019-4033 Tel: 405-325-4531 Web Site: www.worldliteraturetoday.org; www.worldlit.org, pg 646

Simon, Daniel, NSK Neustadt Prize for Children's Literature, c/o University of Oklahoma, 630 Parrington Oval, Suite 110, Norman, OK 73019-4033 Tel: 405-325-4531 Web Site: www.worldliteraturetoday.org; www.worldlit.org, pg 649

Simon, Daniel, Seven Stories Press, 140 Watts St, New York, NY 10013 Tel: 212-226-8760 Toll Free Tel: 800-733-3000 (orders) Fax: 212-226-1411 E-mail: seventstories@sevenstories.com Web Site: www.sevenstories.com, pg 197

Simon, Elizabeth, CSWE Press, 1701 Duke St, Suite 200, Alexandria, VA 22314-3457 Tel: 703-683-8080 Fax: 703-683-8493 E-mail: publications@cswe.org; info@cswe.org Web Site: www.cswe.org, pg 61

Simon, Kimberly, Bisk Education, 9417 Princess Palm Ave, Suite 400, Tampa, FL 33619 Tel: 813-621-6200 Toll Free Tel: 800-280-9718 (cust serv) E-mail: customerservice@bisk.com Web Site: www. bisk.com, pg 33

Simon, Peter J, W W Norton & Company Inc, 500 Fifth Ave, New York, NY 10110-0017 Tel: 212-354-5500 Toll Free Tel: 800-233-4830 (orders & cust serv) Fax: 212-869-0856 Toll Free Fax: 800-458-6515 E-mail: orders@wwnorton.com Web Site: wwnorton. com, pg 152

Simon, Robin, Berkley Publishing Group, 1745 Broadway, 19th fl, New York, NY 10019 Tel: 212-366-2000 Web Site: www.penguin.com, pg 32

Simon, Samantha, Houghton Mifflin Harcourt Trade & Reference Division, 125 High St, Boston, MA 02110 Tel: 617-351-5000 Web Site: www.hmhco.com, pg 104

Simon, Tami, Sounds True Inc, 413 S Arthur Ave, Louisville, CO 80027 Tel: 303-665-3151 Toll Free Tel: 800-333-9185 (US); 888-303-9185 (US & CN) E-mail: customerservice@soundstrue.com; stpublicity@soundstrue.com Web Site: www. soundstrue.com, pg 204

Simone, Kyra, Zone Books, 633 Vanderbilt St, Brooklyn, NY 11218 Tel: 718-686-0048 Fax: 718-686-9045 E-mail: info@zonebooks.org Web Site: www. zonebooks.org, pg 248

Simonello, Lorraine, Morehouse Publishing, 19 E 34 St, New York, NY 10016 Tel: 212-592-1800 Toll Free Tel: 800-242-1918 (retail orders only) E-mail: churchpublishingorders@pbd.com Web Site: www.churchpublishing.org, pg 143

Simonoff, Eric, WME, 11 Madison Ave, 18th fl, New York, NY 10010 Tel: 212-586-5100 Web Site: www. wmeentertainment.com, pg 508

Simonoff, Meredith Kaffel, DeFiore and Company Literary Management Inc, 47 E 19 St, 3rd fl, New York, NY 10003 Tel: 212-925-7744 Fax: 212-925-9803 E-mail: info@defliterary.com; submissions@ defliterary.com Web Site: www.defliterary.com, pg 481

Simons, D Brenton, Newbury Street Press, 99-101 Newbury St, Boston, MA 02116 Tel: 617-226-1206 Toll Free Tel: 888-296-3447 (NEHGS membership) Fax: 617-536-7307 E-mail: sales@nehgs.org Web Site: www.americanancestors.org, pg 150

Simons, Jasper, American Psychological Association, 750 First St NE, Washington, DC 20002-4242 Tel: 202-336-5510 Toll Free Tel: 800-374-2721 Fax: 202-336-5502 E-mail: order@apa.org Web Site: www.apa.org/books, pg 13

Simons, Natasha, Gallery Books, 1230 Avenue of the Americas, New York, NY 10020 Toll Free Tel: 800-456-6798 Fax: 212-698-7284 E-mail: consumer.customerservice@simonandschuster. com Web Site: www.simonandschuster.com, pg 83

Simonsen, Reka, Simon & Schuster Children's Publishing, 1230 Avenue of the Americas, New York, NY 10020 Tel: 212-698-7000 Web Site: www. simonandschuster.com/kids; www.simonandschuster. com/teen; simonandschuster.net; simonandschuster.biz, pg 199

Simonson, Emily, Simon & Schuster, 1230 Avenue of the Americas, New York, NY 10020 Tel: 212-698-7000 Toll Free Tel: 800-223-2348 (cust serv); 800-223-2336 (orders) Toll Free Tel: 800-943-9831 (orders) Web Site: www.simonandschuster.com, pg 198

Simpkins, Adam, The Continuing Legal Education Society of British Columbia (CLEBC), 500-1155 W Pender St, Vancouver, BC V6E 2P4, Canada Tel: 604-669-3544; 604-893-2121 (cust serv) Toll Free Tel: 800-663-0437 (CN) Fax: 604-669-9260 E-mail: custserv@cle.bc.ca Web Site: www.cle.bc.ca, pg 420

Simpson, Jeff, Deseret Book Co, 57 W South Temple, Salt Lake City, UT 84101-1511 Tel: 801-517-3369; 801-534-1515 (corp) Toll Free Tel: 800-453-4532 (orders); 888-846-7302 (orders) Fax: 801-517-3126 E-mail: service@deseretbook.com Web Site: www. deseretbook.com, pg 64

Simpson, M Lui, Association of American Publishers (AAP), 455 Massachusetts Ave NW, Suite 700, Washington, DC 20001-2777 Tel: 202-347-3375 Fax: 202-347-3690 E-mail: info@publishers.org Web Site: publishers.org, pg 526

Simpson, Dr Meagan, Peter Lang Publishing Inc, 80 Broadway, 5th fl, New York, NY 10004 Tel: 703-661-1584 Toll Free Tel: 800-770-5264 (cust serv) Fax: 703-996-1010 E-mail: newyork.editorial@ peterlang.com; customerservice@plang.com Web Site: www.peterlang.com, pg 119

Simpson, Michael, Carter G Woodson Book Awards, 8555 16 St, Suite 500, Silver Spring, MD 20910 Tel: 301-588-1800 Toll Free Tel: 800-296-7840 Fax: 301-588-2049 E-mail: excellence@ncss.org; publications@ncss.org Web Site: www.socialstudies. org, pg 679

Simpson-Vos, Mark, The University of North Carolina Press, 116 S Boundary St, Chapel Hill, NC 27514-3808 Tel: 919-966-3561 E-mail: uncpress@unc.edu Web Site: www.uncpress.org, pg 229

Simqu, Blaise R, SAGE Publishing, 2455 Teller Rd, Thousand Oaks, CA 91320 Toll Free Tel: 800-818-7243 Toll Free Fax: 800-583-2665 E-mail: info@ sagepub.com; orders@sagepub.com Web Site: www. sagepublishing.com, pg 189

Sims, Linsey, University of Tennessee Press, 110 Conference Center Bldg, 600 Henley St, Knoxville, TN 37996-4108 Tel: 865-974-3321 Toll Free Tel: 800-621-2736 (orders) Fax: 865-974-3724 Toll Free Fax: 800-621-8476 (orders) E-mail: custserv@utpress. org Web Site: www.utpress.org, pg 231

Sims, Michael, The MIT Press, One Rogers St, Cambridge, MA 02142 Tel: 617-253-5255 Toll Free Tel: 800-405-1619 (orders) Fax: 617-258-6779; 617-577-1545 (orders) Web Site: mitpress.mit.edu, pg 141

Sims-Nichols, Rebecca, Cedar Grove Publishing, 3205 Elmhurst St, Rowlett, TX 75088 *Tel:* 415-364-8292 *E-mail:* queries@cedargrovebooks.com *Web Site:* www.cedargrovebooks.com, pg 47

Sinasac, Joseph, Novalis Publishing, 10 Lower Spadina Ave, Suite 400, Toronto, ON M5V 2Z2, Canada *Tel:* 416-363-3303 *Toll Free Tel:* 877-702-7773 *Fax:* 416-363-9409 *Toll Free Fax:* 877-702-7775 *E-mail:* books@novalis.ca *Web Site:* www.novalis.ca, pg 434

Sinclair, Stephanie, Transatlantic Agency, 2 Bloor St E, Suite 3500, Toronto, ON M4W 1A8, Canada *Tel:* 416-488-9214 *E-mail:* info@transatlanticagency.com *Web Site:* www.transatlanticagency.com, pg 506

Sindler, Jessica, HarperCollins General Books Group, 195 Broadway, New York, NY 10007 *Tel:* 212-207-7000 *Web Site:* www.harpercollins.com, pg 93

Sindwani, PK, American Booksellers Association, 333 Westchester Ave, Suite S202, White Plains, NY 10604 *Tel:* 914-406-7500 *Toll Free Tel:* 800-637-0037 *Fax:* 914-417-4013 *E-mail:* info@bookweb.org *Web Site:* www.bookweb.org, pg 522

Singer, Jeremy, The College Board, 250 Vesey St, New York, NY 10281 *Tel:* 212-713-8000 *Toll Free Tel:* 866-630-9305 *Web Site:* www.collegeboard.com, pg 55

Singerline, Robert, Scepter Publishers, PO Box 360694, Strongsville, OH 44149 *Tel:* 212-354-0670 *Toll Free Tel:* 800-322-8773 *Fax:* 646-417-7707 *E-mail:* info@scepterpublishers.org *Web Site:* www.scepterpublishers.org, pg 193

Singerman, Jerome E, University of Pennsylvania Press, 3905 Spruce St, Philadelphia, PA 19104 *Tel:* 215-898-6261 *Fax:* 215-898-0404 *E-mail:* custserv@pobox.upenn.edu *Web Site:* www.pennpress.org, pg 230

Singh, Archana, John Wiley & Sons Inc, 111 River St, Hoboken, NJ 07030-5774 *Tel:* 201-748-6000 *Toll Free Tel:* 800-225-5945 (cust serv) *Fax:* 201-748-6088 *E-mail:* info@wiley.com *Web Site:* www.wiley.com, pg 241

Singletary, Jennifer, Penn State University Press, University Support Bldg 1, Suite C, 820 N University Dr, University Park, PA 16802-1003 *Tel:* 814-865-1327 *Toll Free Tel:* 800-326-9180 *Fax:* 814-863-1408 *Toll Free Fax:* 877-778-2665 *E-mail:* orders@psupress.org; orders@eisenbrauns.org *Web Site:* www.psupress.org; www.eisenbrauns.org, pg 166

Siniscalchi, Viana, Alloy Entertainment LLC, 30 Hudson Yards, 22nd fl, New York, NY 10001 *E-mail:* collaborative@alloyentertainment.com, pg 8

Sinocchi, Michael, Productivity Press, 711 Third Ave, 8th fl, New York, NY 10017 *Tel:* 212-216-7800 *Toll Free Tel:* 800-634-7064 (orders); 800-797-3803 *E-mail:* orders@taylorandfrancis.com *Web Site:* crcpress.com, pg 175

Sioles, Lee, Louisiana State University Press, 338 Johnston Hall, Baton Rouge, LA 70803 *Tel:* 225-578-6294 *E-mail:* lsupress@lsu.edu *Web Site:* lsupress.org, pg 128

Sipala, Frank, Perseus Books, 1290 Avenue of the Americas, New York, NY 10104 *Tel:* 212-340-8100 *Toll Free Tel:* 800-343-4499 (cust serv) *Fax:* 212-340-8105 *Web Site:* www.perseusbooks.com, pg 168

Sipe, Keith R, Carolina Academic Press, 700 Kent St, Durham, NC 27701 *Tel:* 919-489-7486 *Toll Free Tel:* 800-489-7486 *Fax:* 919-493-5668 *E-mail:* cap@cap-press.com *Web Site:* www.cap-press.com; www.caplaw.com, pg 45

Sipe, Scott, Carolina Academic Press, 700 Kent St, Durham, NC 27701 *Tel:* 919-489-7486 *Toll Free Tel:* 800-489-7486 *Fax:* 919-493-5668 *E-mail:* cap@cap-press.com *Web Site:* www.cap-press.com; www.caplaw.com, pg 45

Sirabian, Stephanie, Tom Doherty Associates, LLC, 120 Broadway, New York, NY 10271 *Tel:* 646-307-5511 *Toll Free Tel:* 800-455-0340 *Web Site:* us.macmillan.com/torforge, pg 66

Sirkin, Jeff, University of Texas at El Paso, Department of Creative Writing, MFA/Department of Creative Writing, 901 EDUC, 500 W University Ave, El Paso, TX 79968-9991 *Tel:* 915-747-5713 *Fax:* 915-747-5523 *E-mail:* creativewriting@utep.edu *Web Site:* www.utep.edu/cw, pg 586

Sirna-Bruder, Anet, Harry N Abrams Inc, 195 Broadway, 9th fl, New York, NY 10007 *Tel:* 212-206-7715 *Toll Free Tel:* 800-345-1359 *Fax:* 212-519-1210 *E-mail:* abrams@abramsbooks.com *Web Site:* www.abramsbooks.com, pg 3

Sirota, Mark, Trusted Media Brands Inc, 750 Third Ave, 3rd fl, New York, NY 10017 *Tel:* 646-293-6299 *Toll Free Tel:* 877-732-4438 (cust serv) *Fax:* 646-293-6251 *E-mail:* customercare@trustedmediabrands.com; press@trustedmediabrands.com *Web Site:* www.trustedmediabrands.com; www.rd.com, pg 221

Siscoe, Nancy, Random House Children's Books, 1745 Broadway, 10th fl, New York, NY 10019 *Tel:* 212-782-9000 *Web Site:* www.randomhousekids.com, pg 180

Sisk, Jonathan, Rowman & Littlefield, 4501 Forbes Blvd, Suite 200, Lanham, MD 20706 *Tel:* 301-459-3366 *Toll Free Tel:* 800-462-6420 (ext 3024, cust serv) *Fax:* 301-429-5748 *Web Site:* rowman.com, pg 188

Sisoler, Suzie, Penguin Random House LLC, 1745 Broadway, New York, NY 10019 *Tel:* 212-782-9000 *Toll Free Tel:* 800-726-0600 *Web Site:* www.penguinrandomhouse.com, pg 164

Sisson, Walter R, American Geosciences Institute (AGI), 4220 King St, Alexandria, VA 22302-1502 *Tel:* 703-379-2480 (ext 246) *Fax:* 703-379-7563 *E-mail:* agi@americangeosciences.org *Web Site:* www.americangeosciences.org, pg 11

Sitzes, Jason, Writers Retreat Workshop (WRW), PO Box 170657, Austin, TX 78717 *E-mail:* info@writersretreatworkshop.com *Web Site:* www.writersretreatworkshop.com, pg 580

Sivasubramaniam, Jeevan, Berrett-Koehler Publishers Inc, 1333 Broadway, Suite 1000, Oakland, CA 94612 *Tel:* 510-817-2277 *Fax:* 510-817-2278 *E-mail:* bkpub@bkpub.com *Web Site:* www.bkconnection.com, pg 32

Sizemore, Terrie, A 2 Z Press LLC, 3670 Woodbridge Rd, Deland, FL 32720 *Tel:* 440-241-3126 *E-mail:* sizemore3630@aol.com *Web Site:* www.a2zpress.com; www.bestlittleonlinebookstore.com, pg 1

Skaj, Paul, ABDO Publishing Co Inc, 8000 W 78 St, Suite 310, Edina, MN 55439 *Tel:* 952-698-2403 *Toll Free Tel:* 800-800-1312 *Fax:* 952-831-1632 *Toll Free Fax:* 800-862-3480 *E-mail:* customerservice@abdopublishing.com; info@abdopublishing.com *Web Site:* abdopublishing.com, pg 2

Skehan, Mary Kate, Penguin Group USA, A Penguin Random House Company, 375 Hudson St, New York, NY 10014 *Tel:* 212-366-2000 *Toll Free Tel:* 800-847-5515 (inside sales); 800-631-8571 (cust serv) *Fax:* 212-366-2666; 607-775-4829 (inside sales) *E-mail:* online@us.penguingroup.com *Web Site:* www.penguin.com, pg 163

Skinner, Heather, University of Minnesota Press, 111 Third Ave S, Suite 290, Minneapolis, MN 55401-2520 *Tel:* 612-301-1990 *Fax:* 612-301-1980 *E-mail:* ump@umn.edu *Web Site:* www.upress.umn.edu, pg 228

Sklena, Jennifer, Institute of Environmental Sciences & Technology - IEST, 1827 Walden Office Sq, Suite 400, Schaumburg, IL 60173 *Tel:* 847-981-0100 *Fax:* 847-981-4130 *E-mail:* information@iest.org *Web Site:* www.iest.org, pg 109

Skokut, Joyce, Educational Book & Media Association (EBMA), 11 Main St, Suite D, Warrenton, VA 20186 *Tel:* 540-318-7770 *Fax:* 202-962-3939 *E-mail:* info@edupaperback.org *Web Site:* www.edupaperback.org, pg 532

Skolek, Amanda, Sourcebooks LLC, 1935 Brookdale Rd, Suite 139, Naperville, IL 60563 *Tel:* 630-961-3900 *Toll Free Tel:* 800-432-7444 *Fax:* 630-961-2168

E-mail: info@sourcebooks.com; customersupport@sourcebooks.com *Web Site:* www.sourcebooks.com, pg 204

Skolkin, David, Museum of New Mexico Press, 725 Camino Lejo, Suite C, Santa Fe, NM 87505 *Tel:* 505-476-1155; 505-272-7777 (orders) *Toll Free Tel:* 800-249-7737 (orders) *Fax:* 505-476-1156 *Toll Free Fax:* 800-622-8667 (orders) *Web Site:* www.mnmpress.org, pg 144

Skrabacz, Anna, Thames & Hudson, 500 Fifth Ave, New York, NY 10110 *Tel:* 212-354-3763 *Toll Free Tel:* 800-233-4830 *Fax:* 212-398-1252 *E-mail:* bookinfo@thames.wwnorton.com *Web Site:* www.thamesandhudsonusa.com, pg 216

Skrabek, Alison, Living Language, c/o Penguin Random House, 1745 Broadway, New York, NY 10019 *Tel:* 212-782-9000 *Toll Free Tel:* 800-733-3000 (orders) *E-mail:* support@livinglanguage.com *Web Site:* www.livinglanguage.com, pg 126

Skurnick, Victoria, Levine|Greenberg|Rostan Literary Agency, 307 Seventh Ave, Suite 2407, New York, NY 10001 *Tel:* 212-337-0934 *Fax:* 212-337-0948 *Web Site:* lgrliterary.com, pg 493

Sky-Peck, Kathryn, Red Wheel/Weiser, 65 Parker St, Suite 7, Newburyport, MA 01950 *Tel:* 978-465-0504 *Toll Free Tel:* 800-423-7087 (orders) *Fax:* 978-465-0243 *E-mail:* info@rwwbooks.com *Web Site:* www.redwheelweiser.com, pg 183

Skyberg, Andrea, Wisconsin Annual Fall Conference, PO Box 1463, Green Bay, WI 54305-1463 *Tel:* 323-782-1010 (corp off) *E-mail:* wisconsin@scbwi.org *Web Site:* www.scbwi.org; www.facebook.com/SCBWIWisconsin, pg 580

Skypeck, Kate, Artech House®, 685 Canton St, Norwood, MA 02062 *Tel:* 781-769-9750 *Toll Free Tel:* 800-225-9977 *Fax:* 781-769-6334 *E-mail:* artech@artechhouse.com *Web Site:* www.artechhouse.com, pg 21

Skyvara, Suzanne, Goodreads Choice Awards, 188 Spear St, 3rd fl, San Francisco, CA 94105 *E-mail:* press@goodreads.com *Web Site:* www.goodreads.com/award, pg 620

Slager, Daniel, Milkweed Editions, 1011 Washington Ave S, Suite 300, Minneapolis, MN 55415-1246 *Tel:* 612-332-3192 *Toll Free Tel:* 800-520-6455 *Fax:* 612-215-2550 *Web Site:* milkweed.org, pg 140

Slager, Daniel, Milkweed National Fiction Prize, 1011 Washington Ave S, Suite 300, Minneapolis, MN 55415-1246 *Tel:* 612-332-3192 *Toll Free Tel:* 800-520-6455 *Fax:* 612-215-2550 *E-mail:* submissions@milkweed.org *Web Site:* www.milkweed.org, pg 641

Slager, Daniel, Max Ritvo Poetry Prize, 1011 Washington Ave S, Suite 300, Minneapolis, MN 55415-1246 *Tel:* 612-332-3192 *Toll Free Tel:* 800-520-6455 *Web Site:* milkweed.org/max-ritvo-poetry-prize, pg 662

Slater, Alex, Trident Media Group LLC, 41 Madison Ave, 36th fl, New York, NY 10010 *Tel:* 212-333-1511 *E-mail:* info@tridentmediagroup.com; press@tridentmediagroup.com *Web Site:* www.tridentmediagroup.com, pg 507

Slesin, Suzanne, Pointed Leaf Press, 136 Baxter St, New York, NY 10013 *Tel:* 212-941-1800 *Fax:* 212-941-1822 *E-mail:* info@pointedleafpress.com *Web Site:* www.pointedleafpress.com, pg 171

Sleven, Paul, Macmillan, 120 Broadway, 22nd fl, New York, NY 10271 *Tel:* 646-307-5151 *E-mail:* press.inquiries@macmillan.com *Web Site:* www.macmillan.com, pg 129

Sloan, Megan, Romance Writers of America®, 14615 Benfer Rd, Houston, TX 77069 *Tel:* 832-717-5200 *Fax:* 832-717-5201 *E-mail:* info@rwa.org *Web Site:* www.rwa.org, pg 545

Sloan, Megan, Romance Writers of America Annual Conference, 14615 Benfer Rd, Houston, TX 77069 *Tel:* 832-717-5200 *Fax:* 832-717-5201 *E-mail:* info@rwa.org *Web Site:* www.rwa.org, pg 577

Slocombe, Kestrel, Wisdom Publications Inc, 199 Elm St, Somerville, MA 02144 *Tel:* 617-776-7416 *Toll Free Tel:* 800-272-4050 (orders) *Fax:* 617-776-

7841 *E-mail:* info@wisdompubs.org; submission@ wisdompubs.org *Web Site:* www.wisdompubs.org, pg 243

Sloma, Stefani, Sourcebooks LLC, 1935 Brookdale Rd, Suite 139, Naperville, IL 60563 *Tel:* 630-961-3900 *Toll Free Tel:* 800-432-7444 *Fax:* 630-961-2168 *E-mail:* info@sourcebooks.com; customersupport@ sourcebooks.com *Web Site:* www.sourcebooks.com, pg 204

Slopen, Beverley, Beverley Slopen Literary Agency, 131 Bloor St W, Suite 711, Toronto, ON M5S 1S3, Canada *Tel:* 416-964-9598 *Fax:* 416-964-9598 *Web Site:* www. slopenagency.com, pg 503

Slovak, Paul, Viking, 375 Hudson St, New York, NY 10014 *Tel:* 212-366-2000 *Fax:* 212-243-6002 *Web Site:* www.penguin.com/publishers/vikingbooks, pg 236

Slutsky, Lorie, Oscar Williams/Gene Derwood Award, 909 Third Ave, New York, NY 10022 *Tel:* 212-686-0010 *Fax:* 212-532-8528 *E-mail:* info@nycommunitytrust.org *Web Site:* www. nycommunitytrust.org, pg 678

Smagler, Alan, Scholastic Trade Division, 557 Broadway, New York, NY 10012 *Tel:* 212-343-6100; 212-343-4685 (export sales) *Fax:* 212-343-4714 (export sales) *Web Site:* www.scholastic.com, pg 194

Small, Ellen, Publishing Synthesis Ltd, 39 Crosby St, New York, NY 10013 *Tel:* 212-219-0135 *E-mail:* mainmail@pubsyn.com *Web Site:* www. pubsyn.com, pg 469

Small, Nick, Sounds True Inc, 413 S Arthur Ave, Louisville, CO 80027 *Tel:* 303-665-3151 *Toll Free Tel:* 800-333-9185 (US); 888-303-9185 (US & CN) *E-mail:* customerservice@soundstrue.com; stpublicity@soundstrue.com *Web Site:* www. soundstrue.com, pg 204

Small, Rachael, Europa Editions, 214 W 29 St, Suite 1003, New York, NY 10001 *Tel:* 212-868-6844 *Fax:* 212-868-6845 *E-mail:* info@europaeditions.com *Web Site:* www.europaeditions.com, pg 73

Smallfield, Edward, Apogee Press, 2308 Sixth St, Berkeley, CA 94710 *E-mail:* editors.apogee@gmail. com *Web Site:* www.apogeepress.com, pg 17

Smallwood, Wendi, Newfoundland and Labrador Book Awards, Haymarket Sq, 223 Duckworth St, St John's, NL A1C 6N1, Canada *Tel:* 709-739-5215 *Toll Free Tel:* 866-739-5215 *E-mail:* wanl@nf.aibn.com *Web Site:* wanl.ca, pg 648

Smallwood, Wendi, Newfoundland and Labrador Credit Union Fresh Fish Award for Emerging Writers, Haymarket Sq, 223 Duckworth St, St John's, NL A1C 6N1, Canada *Tel:* 709-739-5215 *Toll Free Tel:* 866-739-5215 *E-mail:* wanl@nf.aibn.com *Web Site:* wanl. ca, pg 648

Smallwood, Wendi, Writers' Alliance of Newfoundland & Labrador, Haymarket Sq, 223 Duckworth St, Suite 202, St John's, NL A1C 6N1, Canada *Tel:* 709-739-5215 *Toll Free Tel:* 866-739-5215 *E-mail:* info@wanl. ca *Web Site:* wanl.ca, pg 549

Smart, Dan, Twenty-Third Publications, One Montauk Ave, Suite 200, New London, CT 06320 *Tel:* 860-437-3012 *Toll Free Tel:* 800-321-0411 (orders) *Toll Free Fax:* 800-572-0788 *E-mail:* resources@ twentythirdpublications.com *Web Site:* www. twentythirdpublications.com, pg 223

Smetanka, Dan, Counterpoint Press LLC, 2560 Ninth St, Suite 318, Berkeley, CA 94710 *Tel:* 510-704-0230 *Fax:* 510-704-0268 *E-mail:* info@counterpointpress. com *Web Site:* counterpointpress.com; softskull.com, pg 58

Smiley, Matt, University of Minnesota Press, 111 Third Ave S, Suite 290, Minneapolis, MN 55401-2520 *Tel:* 612-301-1990 *Fax:* 612-301-1980 *E-mail:* ump@ umn.edu *Web Site:* www.upress.umn.edu, pg 228

Smirnov, Stephanie, Scholastic Inc, 557 Broadway, New York, NY 10012 *Tel:* 212-343-6100 *Toll Free Tel:* 800-SCHOLASTIC (724-6527) *Web Site:* www. scholastic.com, pg 194

Smist, Erik A, Johns Hopkins University Press, 2715 N Charles St, Baltimore, MD 21218-4363 *Tel:* 410-516-6900; 410-516-6987 (journal orders outside US & CN) *Toll Free Tel:* 800-537-5487 (book orders & cust serv); 800-548-1784 (journal orders) *Fax:* 410-516-6968; 410-516-3866 (journal orders); 410-516-6998 (orders) *E-mail:* hfscustserv@press.jhu.edu (cust serv); jrnlcirc@press.jhu.edu (journal orders) *Web Site:* www.press.jhu.edu; muse.jhu.edu, pg 114

Smith, Allan H, Success Advertising & Publishing, 3419 Dunham Rd, Warsaw, NY 14569 *Tel:* 585-786-5663, pg 210

Smith, Andrew, Harry N Abrams Inc, 195 Broadway, 9th fl, New York, NY 10007 *Tel:* 212-206-7715 *Toll Free Tel:* 800-345-1359 *Fax:* 212-519-1210 *E-mail:* abrams@abramsbooks.com *Web Site:* www. abramsbooks.com, pg 3

Smith, Betty, International Publishers Co Inc, 235 W 23 St, New York, NY 10011 *Tel:* 212-366-9816 *Fax:* 212-366-9820 *E-mail:* service@intpubnyc.com *Web Site:* www.intpubnyc.com, pg 111

Smith, Bradford K, Foundation Center, 32 Old Slip, 24th fl, New York, NY 10005-3500 *Tel:* 212-620-4230 *Toll Free Tel:* 800-424-9836 *Fax:* 212-807-3677 *E-mail:* customerservice@foundationcenter.org *Web Site:* foundationcenter.org, pg 80

Smith, Bryan, Savvas Learning Co LLC, 15 E Midland Ave, Suite 502, Paramus, NJ 07652 *Toll Free Tel:* 800-848-9500 *Web Site:* www.savvas.com, pg 193

Smith, Chris, Penguin Books, 375 Hudson St, New York, NY 10014 *Tel:* 212-366-2000 *E-mail:* penguinpublicity@us.penguingroup.com *Web Site:* www.penguinclassics.com; www.penguin. com, pg 163

Smith, Chris, Viking, 375 Hudson St, New York, NY 10014 *Tel:* 212-366-2000 *Fax:* 212-243-6002 *Web Site:* www.penguin.com/publishers/vikingbooks, pg 236

Smith, David, Practising Law Institute, 1177 Avenue of the Americas, New York, NY 10036 *Tel:* 212-824-5700 *Toll Free Tel:* 800-260-4PLI (260-4754, cust serv) *Toll Free Fax:* 800-321-0093 (local) *E-mail:* info@pli.edu (cust serv) *Web Site:* www.pli. edu, pg 173

Smith, David Cloyce, The Library of America, 14 E 60 St, New York, NY 10022-1006 *Tel:* 212-308-3360 *Fax:* 212-750-8352 *E-mail:* info@loa.org *Web Site:* www.loa.org, pg 124

Smith, Dean, Duke University Press, 905 W Main St, Suite 18B, Durham, NC 27701 *Tel:* 919-688-5134 *Toll Free Tel:* 888-651-0122 (US) *Fax:* 919-688-2615 *Toll Free Fax:* 888-651-0124 *E-mail:* orders@dukeupress. edu *Web Site:* www.dukeupress.edu, pg 68

Smith, Deborah, BelleBooks, PO Box 300921, Memphis, TN 38130 *Tel:* 901-344-9024 *Fax:* 901-344-9068 *E-mail:* bellebooks@bellebooks.com *Web Site:* www. bellebooks.com, pg 31

Smith, Diane E, Baylor University Press, Baylor University, One Bear Place, Waco, TX 76798-7363 *Tel:* 254-710-3164 *Web Site:* www.baylorpress.com, pg 29

Smith, Frederick B, Two Thousand Three Associates, 135 Chilean Ave, Palm Beach, FL 33480 *Tel:* 386-690-2503 *E-mail:* ttta1@att.net *Web Site:* www. twothousandthree.com, pg 223

Smith, George D, Signature Books Publishing LLC, 564 W 400 N, Salt Lake City, UT 84116-3411 *Toll Free Tel:* 800-356-5687 *E-mail:* people@signaturebooks. com *Web Site:* www.signaturebooks.com; www. signaturebookslibrary.org, pg 198

Smith, Ginger B, Success Advertising & Publishing, 3419 Dunham Rd, Warsaw, NY 14569 *Tel:* 585-786-5663, pg 210

Smith, Gordon H, National Association of Broadcasters (NAB), 1771 "N" St NW, Washington, DC 20036 *Tel:* 202-429-5300 *E-mail:* nab@nab.org *Web Site:* www.nab.org, pg 145, 538

Smith, Heather, Accuity, 1007 Church St, 6th fl, Evanston, IL 60201 *Tel:* 847-676-9600 *Toll Free Tel:* 800-321-3373 *Fax:* 847-933-8101 *E-mail:* customerservice@accuity.com *Web Site:* www. accuity.com, pg 4

Smith, Icy, East West Discovery Press, PO Box 3585, Manhattan Beach, CA 90266 *Tel:* 310-545-3730 *Fax:* 310-545-3731 *E-mail:* info@eastwestdiscovery. com *Web Site:* www.eastwestdiscovery.com, pg 68

Smith, Ileene, Farrar, Straus & Giroux, LLC, 175 Varick St, 9th fl, New York, NY 10014 *Tel:* 212-741-6900 *E-mail:* fsg.publicity@fsgbooks.com *Web Site:* us. macmillan.com/fsg.aspx, pg 76

Smith, James Clois Jr, Sunstone Press, PO Box 2321, Santa Fe, NM 87504-2321 *Tel:* 505-988-4418 *Toll Free Tel:* 800-243-5644 *Fax:* 505-988-1025 (orders only) *Web Site:* www.sunstonepress.com, pg 211

Smith, Jeffrey, Bridge to Asia, 1505 Juanita Way, Berkeley, CA 94702-1103 *Tel:* 510-665-3998 *E-mail:* asianet@bridge.org *Web Site:* www.bridge.org, pg 551

Smith, Jessica, Sourcebooks LLC, 1935 Brookdale Rd, Suite 139, Naperville, IL 60563 *Tel:* 630-961-3900 *Toll Free Tel:* 800-432-7444 *Fax:* 630-961-2168 *E-mail:* info@sourcebooks.com; customersupport@ sourcebooks.com *Web Site:* www.sourcebooks.com, pg 204

Smith, Jill, University of Denver Publishing Institute, 2000 E Asbury Ave, Denver, CO 80208 *Tel:* 303-871-2700 *Fax:* 303-871-2501 *Web Site:* www.du. edu/publishinginstitute, pg 585

Smith, Jordan, 5 Under 35, 90 Broad St, Suite 604, New York, NY 10004 *Tel:* 212-685-0261 *Fax:* 212-213-6570 *E-mail:* nationalbook@nationalbook.org *Web Site:* www.nationalbook.org, pg 615

Smith, Jordan, Innovations in Reading Prize, 90 Broad St, Suite 604, New York, NY 10004 *Tel:* 212-685-0261 *Fax:* 212-213-6570 *E-mail:* nationalbook@ nationalbook.org *Web Site:* www.nationalbook.org/ innovations_in_reading, pg 627

Smith, Jordan, Medal for Distinguished Contribution to American Letters, 90 Broad St, Suite 604, New York, NY 10004 *Tel:* 212-685-0261 *Fax:* 212-213-6570 *E-mail:* nationalbook@nationalbook.org *Web Site:* www.nationalbook.org/amerletters.html, pg 640

Smith, Jordan, National Book Awards, 90 Broad St, Suite 604, New York, NY 10004 *Tel:* 212-685-0261 *Fax:* 212-213-6570 *E-mail:* nationalbook@ nationalbook.org *Web Site:* www.nationalbook.org, pg 644

Smith, Jordan, National Book Foundation, 90 Broad St, Suite 604, New York, NY 10004 *Tel:* 212-685-0261 *Fax:* 212-213-6570 *E-mail:* nationalbook@ nationalbook.org *Web Site:* www.nationalbook.org, pg 551

Smith, Jordan, Writers' League of Texas (WLT), 611 S Congress Ave, Suite 200 A-3, Austin, TX 78704 *Tel:* 512-499-8914 *E-mail:* wlt@writersleague.org *Web Site:* www.writersleague.org, pg 549

Smith, Katie Cruice, Ambassador International, 411 University Ridge, Suite B14, Greenville, SC 29601 *Tel:* 864-751-4844 *E-mail:* info@emeraldhouse.com; publisher@emeraldhouse.com (ms submissions); sales@emeraldhouse.com (orders/order inquiries); media@emeraldhouse.com *Web Site:* ambassador-international.com; www.facebook.com/AmbassadorIntl; twitter.com/ambassadorintl, pg 8

Smith, Kelly, Bywater Books Inc, PO Box 3671, Ann Arbor, MI 48106-3671 *Tel:* 734-662-8815 *Web Site:* bywaterbooks.com, pg 43

Smith, Kesley, Greenleaf Book Group LLC, 3 Park Place, 4005 Banister Lane, Suite B, Austin, TX 78704 *Tel:* 512-891-6100 *Fax:* 512-891-6150 *E-mail:* contact@greenleafbookgroup.com *Web Site:* www.greenleafbookgroup.com, pg 89

Smith, Kristi, Thomas Nelson, 501 Nelson Place, Nashville, TN 37214 *Tel:* 615-889-9000 *Toll Free Tel:* 800-251-4000 *Fax:* 615-902-1548 *Web Site:* www. thomasnelson.com, pg 217

Smith, Lance, The Little Entrepreneur, c/o Harper Arrington Media, 18701 Grand River, Suite 105, Detroit, MI 48223 *Toll Free Tel:* 888-435-9234 *Fax:* 248-281-0373 *E-mail:* info@startingaclothingline. com *Web Site:* www.thelittlee.com, pg 126

Smith, Larry, Bottom Dog Press, 813 Seneca Ave, Huron, OH 44839 *Tel:* 419-602-1556 *Fax:* 419-616-3966 *Web Site:* smithdocs.net, pg 39

Smith, Laura, Bottom Dog Press, 813 Seneca Ave, Huron, OH 44839 *Tel:* 419-602-1556 *Fax:* 419-616-3966 *Web Site:* smithdocs.net, pg 39

Smith, Laurie, Dover Publications Inc, 31 E Second St, Mineola, NY 11501-3852 *Tel:* 516-294-7000 *Toll Free Tel:* 800-223-3130 (orders) *Fax:* 516-742-6953 *E-mail:* rights@doverpublications.com; service@doverpublications.com; doversales@ doverpublications.com *Web Site:* store.doverdirect.com; www.doverpublications.com, pg 67

Smith, Lindsey, Redleaf Press, 10 Yorkton Ct, St Paul, MN 55117 *Tel:* 651-641-0508 *Toll Free Tel:* 800-423-8309 *Toll Free Fax:* 800-641-0115 *E-mail:* customerservice@redleafpress.org; sales@ redleafpress.org *Web Site:* www.redleafpress.org, pg 183

Smith, Marisa, Smith & Kraus Publishers Inc, 177 Lyme Rd, Hanover, NH 03755 *Tel:* 618-783-0519 *Toll Free Tel:* 877-668-8680 *Fax:* 618-783-0520 *E-mail:* editor@smithandkraus.com; info@ smithandkraus.com; customerservice@smithandkraus. com *Web Site:* www.smithandkraus.com, pg 201

Smith, Mary Dupuy, Teacher Created Resources Inc, 12621 Western Ave, Garden Grove, CA 92481 *Tel:* 714-891-7895 *Toll Free Tel:* 800-662-4321; 888-343-4335 *Toll Free Fax:* 800-525-1254 *E-mail:* custserv@teachercreated.com *Web Site:* www. teachercreated.com, pg 214

Smith, Mary P, Thorndike Press®, 10 Water St, Suite 310, Waterville, ME 04901 *Toll Free Tel:* 800-223-1244 (ext 4, cust serv/orders) *Toll Free Fax:* 800-558-4676 (orders) *E-mail:* gale.printorders@cengage.com; international@cengage.com (cust orders outside US & CN) *Web Site:* www.gale.com/thorndike, pg 217

Smith, Maxwell, Simon & Schuster, 1230 Avenue of the Americas, New York, NY 10020 *Tel:* 212-698-7000 *Toll Free Tel:* 800-223-2348 (cust serv); 800-223-2336 (orders) *Toll Free Fax:* 800-943-9831 (orders) *Web Site:* www.simonandschuster.com, pg 198

Smith, Melanie, Entangled Publishing LLC, 2614 S Timberline Rd, Suite 105, Fort Collins, CO 80525 *Toll Free Tel:* 877-677-9451 *E-mail:* publisher@ entangledpublishing.com *Web Site:* www. entangledpublishing.com, pg 72

Smith, Michael, East West Discovery Press, PO Box 3585, Manhattan Beach, CA 90266 *Tel:* 310-545-3730 *Fax:* 310-545-3731 *E-mail:* info@eastwestdiscovery. com *Web Site:* www.eastwestdiscovery.com, pg 68

Smith, Michelle, Peter Lang Publishing Inc, 80 Broadway, 5th fl, New York, NY 10004 *Tel:* 703-661-1584 *Toll Free Tel:* 800-770-5264 (cust serv) *Fax:* 703-996-1010 *E-mail:* newyork.editorial@ peterlang.com; customerservice@plang.com *Web Site:* www.peterlang.com, pg 119

Smith, P David, Western Reflections Publishing Co, 951B N Hwy 149, Lake City, CO 81235 *Tel:* 970-944-0110 *E-mail:* publisher@westernreflectionspublishing. com *Web Site:* www.westernreflectionspublishing.com, pg 239

Smith, Paige, Anchor Books, c/o Penguin Random House Inc, 1745 Broadway, New York, NY 10019 *Tel:* 212-572-2420 *E-mail:* vintageanchorpublicity@ randomhouse.com *Web Site:* knopfdoubleday.com/ imprint/anchor, pg 15

Smith, Paige, Vintage Books, c/o Penguin Random House Inc, 1745 Broadway, New York, NY 10019 *Tel:* 212-572-2420 *E-mail:* vintageanchorpublicity@ randomhouse.com *Web Site:* knopfdoubleday.com/ imprint/vintage, pg 236

Smith, Pat, Oolichan Books, PO Box 2278, Fernie, BC V0B 1M0, Canada *Tel:* 250-423-6113 *E-mail:* info@ oolichan.com *Web Site:* www.oolichan.com, pg 435

Smith, Peggy Boulos, Writers House, 21 W 26 St, New York, NY 10010 *Tel:* 212-685-2400 *Web Site:* www. writershouse.com, pg 508

Smith, Piper, Lindgren & Smith, 888C Eighth Ave, No 329, New York, NY 10019 *Tel:* 212-397-7330 *E-mail:* info@lindgrensmith.com *Web Site:* lindgrensmith.com, pg 512

Smith, R Bob III, Psychological Assessment Resources Inc (PAR), 16204 N Florida Ave, Lutz, FL 33549 *Tel:* 813-449-4065 *Toll Free Tel:* 800-331-8378 *Fax:* 813-961-2196 *Toll Free Fax:* 800-727-9329 *Web Site:* www.parinc.com, pg 177

Smith, R T, The James Boatwright III Prize for Poetry, Washington & Lee University, Mattingly House, 204 W Washington St, Lexington, VA 24450-2116 *Tel:* 540-458-8908 *E-mail:* shenandoah@wlu.edu *Web Site:* shenandoahliterary.org, pg 599

Smith, R T, The Carter Prize For The Essay, Washington & Lee University, Mattingly House, 204 W Washington St, Lexington, VA 24450-2116 *Tel:* 540-458-8908 *E-mail:* shenandoah@wlu.edu *Web Site:* shenandoahliterary.org, pg 603

Smith, Rebekah, Ugly Duckling Presse, The Old American Can Factory, 232 Third St, Suite E303, Brooklyn, NY 11215 *Tel:* 347-948-5170 *E-mail:* office@uglyducklingpresse.org; orders@uglyducklingpresse.org; publicity@ uglyducklingpresse.org; rights@uglyducklingpresse.org *Web Site:* uglyducklingpresse.org, pg 223

Smith, Ronald, Oolichan Books, PO Box 2278, Fernie, BC V0B 1M0, Canada *Tel:* 250-423-6113 *E-mail:* info@oolichan.com *Web Site:* www.oolichan. com, pg 435

Smith, Ronnie L, Writer's Relief, Inc, 18766 John J Williams Hwy, Unit 4, Box 335, Rehoboth Beach, DE 19971 *Toll Free Tel:* 866-405-3003 *Fax:* 201-641-1253 *E-mail:* info@writersrelief.com *Web Site:* www. WritersRelief.com, pg 472

Smith, Ruth, Griffin Poetry Prize, 363 Parkridge Crescent, Oakville, ON L6M 1A8, Canada *Tel:* 905-618-0420 *E-mail:* info@griffinpoetryprize.com; publicity@griffinpoetryprize.com *Web Site:* www. griffinpoetryprize.com, pg 621

Smith, Sarah, David Black Agency, 335 Adams St, 27th fl, Suite 2707, Brooklyn, NY 11201 *Tel:* 718-852-5500 *Fax:* 718-852-5539 *Web Site:* www.davidblackagency. com, pg 476

Smith, Stephanie, Zondervan, 3900 Sparks Dr, Grand Rapids, MI 49546 *Tel:* 616-698-6900 *Toll Free Tel:* 800-226-1122; 800-727-1309 (retail orders) *Fax:* 616-698-3350 *Toll Free Fax:* 800-698-3256 (retail orders) *Web Site:* www.zondervan.com, pg 248

Smith, Steve, Steve Smith Autosports, PO Box 11631, Santa Ana, CA 92711-1631 *Tel:* 714-639-7681 *Fax:* 714-639-9741 *Web Site:* www. stevesmithautosports.com, pg 202

Smith, Steven Rathgeb, American Political Science Association, 1527 New Hampshire Ave NW, Washington, DC 20036-1203 *Tel:* 202-483-2512 *Fax:* 202-483-2657 *E-mail:* apsa@apsanet.org; membership@apsanet.org; press@apsanet.org *Web Site:* www.apsanet.org, pg 523

Smith, Sue, Boydell & Brewer Inc, 668 Mount Hope Ave, Rochester, NY 14620-2731 *Tel:* 585-275-0419 *Fax:* 585-271-8778 *E-mail:* boydell@boydellusa.net *Web Site:* www.boydellandbrewer.com, pg 39

Smith, Sue, University of Rochester Press, 668 Mount Hope Ave, Rochester, NY 14620-2731 *Tel:* 585-275-0419 *Fax:* 585-271-8778 *E-mail:* boydell@boydellusa. net *Web Site:* www.urpress.com, pg 231

Smith, Suzanne, Alfred A Knopf, c/o Penguin Random House Inc, 1745 Broadway, New York, NY 10019 *Tel:* 212-751-2600 *Fax:* 212-572-2662 (foreign rts) *Web Site:* knopfdoubleday.com, pg 118

Smith, Victoria L PhD, LD & LaVerne Harrell Clark Fiction Prize, Flowers Hall, Rm 365, 601 University Dr, San Marcos, TX 78666 *Tel:* 512-245-2163 *Fax:* 512-245-8546 *Web Site:* www.english.txstate. edu/clarkfictionprize.html, pg 622

Smith, William, The MIT Press, One Rogers St, Cambridge, MA 02142 *Tel:* 617-253-5255 *Toll Free Tel:* 800-405-1619 (orders) *Fax:* 617-258-6779; 617-577-1545 (orders) *Web Site:* mitpress.mit.edu, pg 141

Smith-Mandell, Barbara, T S Eliot Prize for Poetry, 100 E Normal Ave, Kirksville, MO 63501-4221 *Tel:* 660-785-7336 *Toll Free Tel:* 800-916-6802 *Fax:* 660-785-4480 *E-mail:* tsup@truman.edu *Web Site:* tsup.truman. edu, pg 612

Smith-Mandell, Barbara, Truman State University Press, 100 E Normal Ave, Kirksville, MO 63501-4221 *Tel:* 660-785-7336 *Toll Free Tel:* 800-916-6802 *Fax:* 660-785-4480 *E-mail:* tsup@truman.edu *Web Site:* tsup.truman.edu, pg 221

Smitherman, David, Rand-Smith Publishing, 204 College Ave, Ashland, VA 23005 *Tel:* 804-874-6012 *E-mail:* randsmithllc@gmail.com *Web Site:* www.rand-smith.com, pg 180

Smithers, Westwood Jr, Corporation for Public Broadcasting (CPB), 401 Ninth St NW, Washington, DC 20004-2129 *Tel:* 202-879-9600 *Web Site:* www. cpb.org, pg 531

Smolin, Ronald, Trans-Atlantic Publications Inc, 33 Ashley Dr, Schwenksville, PA 19473 *Tel:* 215-925-2762 *Fax:* 215-925-1912 *Web Site:* www. transatlanticpub.com; www.businesstitles.com, pg 219

Smulski, Lauren, Harlequin Enterprises Ltd, 195 Broadway, 24th fl, New York, NY 10007 *Tel:* 212-207-7000 *Toll Free Tel:* 888-432-4879 *E-mail:* customerservice@harlequin.com *Web Site:* www.harlequin.com, pg 93

Smyk, Dorothy, New Harbinger Publications Inc, 5674 Shattuck Ave, Oakland, CA 94609 *Tel:* 510-652-0215 *Toll Free Tel:* 800-748-6273 (orders only) *Fax:* 510-652-5472 *Toll Free Fax:* 800-652-1613 *E-mail:* nhhelp@newharbinger.com; customerservice@ newharbinger.com *Web Site:* www.newharbinger.com, pg 148

Smyrl, Rebecca, Guild of Book Workers, 521 Fifth Ave, New York, NY 10175 *Tel:* 212-292-4444 *E-mail:* communications@guildofbookworkers.org *Web Site:* www.guildofbookworkers.org, pg 534

Smyth, Sam, StarGroup International Inc, 1194 Old Dixie Hwy, Suite 201, West Palm Beach, FL 33413 *Tel:* 561-547-0667 *Fax:* 561-843-8530 *E-mail:* info@stargroupinternational.com *Web Site:* stargroupinternational.com, pg 207

Snavely, Sheri, W W Norton & Company Inc, 500 Fifth Ave, New York, NY 10110-0017 *Tel:* 212-354-5500 *Toll Free Tel:* 800-233-4830 (orders & cust serv) *Fax:* 212-869-0856 *Toll Free Fax:* 800-458-6515 *E-mail:* orders@wwnorton.com *Web Site:* wwnorton. com, pg 152

Snead, Beth, The Flannery O'Connor Award for Short Fiction, Main Library, 3rd fl, 320 S Jackson St, Athens, GA 30602 *Fax:* 706-542-2558 *Web Site:* www.ugapress.org, pg 650

Snell, Michael, Michael Snell Literary Agency, PO Box 1206, Truro, MA 02666-1206 *Tel:* 508-349-3718 *Web Site:* www.michaelsnellagency.com, pg 503

Snell, Patricia, Michael Snell Literary Agency, PO Box 1206, Truro, MA 02666-1206 *Tel:* 508-349-3718 *Web Site:* www.michaelsnellagency.com, pg 503

Snider, Rebecca, American Printing House for the Blind Inc, 1839 Frankfort Ave, Louisville, KY 40206 *Tel:* 502-895-2405 *Toll Free Tel:* 800-223-1839 (cust serv) *Fax:* 502-899-2274 *E-mail:* info@aph.org *Web Site:* www.aph.org; shop.aph.org, pg 13

Snider, Stephen, St Martin's Press, LLC, 120 Broadway, New York, NY 10271 *Tel:* 646-307-5151 *Web Site:* us. macmillan.com/smp, pg 190

Snodgrass, Jay PhD, Anhinga Press, PO Box 3665, Tallahassee, FL 32315 *Tel:* 850-577-0745 *E-mail:* info@anhinga.org *Web Site:* www. anhingapress.org; www.facebook.com/anhingapress, pg 16

Sottile, Matthew, Novalis Publishing, 10 Lower Spadina Ave, Suite 400, Toronto, ON M5V 2Z2, Canada *Tel:* 416-363-3303 *Toll Free Tel:* 877-702-7773 *Fax:* 416-363-9409 *Toll Free Fax:* 877-702-7775 *E-mail:* books@novalis.ca *Web Site:* www.novalis.ca, pg 434

Soule, Susan, Cambridge University Press, One Liberty Plaza, 20th fl, New York, NY 10006 *Tel:* 212-924-3900; 212-337-5000 *Fax:* 212-691-3239; 845-353-4141 *E-mail:* newyork@cambridge.org; customer_service@cambridge.org *Web Site:* www.cambridge.org/us, pg 43

Soules, Gordon, Gordon Soules Book Publishers Ltd, 2372 Haywood Ave, West Vancouver, BC V7V 1X7, Canada *Tel:* 604-922-6588 *Fax:* 604-922-6574 *E-mail:* books@gordonsoules.com *Web Site:* www.gordonsoules.com, pg 441

Soules, Mike, Corwin, 2455 Teller Rd, Thousand Oaks, CA 91320 *Tel:* 805-499-9734 *Toll Free Tel:* 800-233-9936 *Fax:* 805-499-5323 *Toll Free Fax:* 800-417-2466 *E-mail:* info@corwin.com; order@corwin.com *Web Site:* www.corwin.com, pg 57

Soussan, Lionel, Les Editions Phidal Inc, 5740 Ferrier, Montreal, QC H4P 1M7, Canada *Tel:* 514-738-0202 *Toll Free Tel:* 800-738-7349 *Fax:* 514-738-5102 *E-mail:* info@phidal.com; customer@phidal.com (sales & export) *Web Site:* www.phidal.com, pg 425

Southard, Margaret, Simon & Schuster, 1230 Avenue of the Americas, New York, NY 10020 *Tel:* 212-698-7000 *Toll Free Tel:* 800-223-2348 (cust serv); 800-223-2336 (orders) *Toll Free Fax:* 800-943-9831 (orders) *Web Site:* www.simonandschuster.com, pg 198

Southern, Ed, Doris Betts Fiction Prize, PO Box 21591, Winston-Salem, NC 27120-1591 *Tel:* 336-293-8844 *E-mail:* mail@ncwriters.org; nclrsubmissions@ecu.edu *Web Site:* www.ncwriters.org, pg 597

Southern, Ed, North Carolina Writers' Network, PO Box 21591, Winston-Salem, NC 27120-1591 *Tel:* 336-293-8844 *Web Site:* www.ncwriters.org, pg 542

Southern, Ed, North Carolina Writers' Network Annual Fall Conference, PO Box 21591, Winston-Salem, NC 27120-1591 *Tel:* 336-293-8844 *E-mail:* mail@ncwriters.org *Web Site:* www.ncwriters.org, pg 577

Southern, Ed, Thomas Wolfe Fiction Prize, PO Box 21591, Winston-Salem, NC 27120-1591 *E-mail:* mail@ncwriters.org *Web Site:* www.ncwriters.org, pg 679

Sova, Kathy, Theatre Communications Group, 520 Eighth Ave, 24th fl, New York, NY 10018-4156 *Tel:* 212-609-5900 *Fax:* 212-609-5901 *E-mail:* info@tcg.org *Web Site:* www.tcg.org, pg 216

Sowards, Anne, Berkley Publishing Group, 1745 Broadway, 19th fl, New York, NY 10019 *Tel:* 212-366-2000 *Web Site:* www.penguin.com, pg 32

Spade, Ed, Houghton Mifflin Harcourt, 125 High St, Boston, MA 02110 *Tel:* 617-351-5000 *Toll Free Tel:* 855-969-4642; 800-225-5425 (K-12 educ materials); 800-323-9540 (assessment materials); 877-219-1537 (SkillsTutor); 888-242-6747 (Innovation in Educ Group); 800-225-3362 (Trade & Ref Div) *Toll Free Fax:* 800-269-5232 *E-mail:* myhmhco@hmhco.com *Web Site:* www.hmhco.com, pg 103

Spahr, John F, Teton NewMedia Inc, 90 E Simpson, Suite 110, Jackson, WY 83001 *Tel:* 307-732-0028 *Toll Free Tel:* 877-306-9793 *Fax:* 307-734-0841 *E-mail:* sales@tetonnm.com *Web Site:* www.tetonnm.com, pg 215

Spahr, Welmoed, Apress Media LLC, 233 Spring St, 6th fl, New York, NY 10013 *Tel:* 212-460-1500 *E-mail:* editorial@apress.com; customerservice@springernature.com *Web Site:* www.apress.com, pg 18

Spain, Molly, TCU Press, 3000 Sandage Ave, Fort Worth, TX 76109 *Tel:* 817-257-7822 *Toll Free Tel:* 800-826-8911 (orders) *Fax:* 817-257-5075 *Web Site:* www.prs.tcu.edu, pg 213

Spain, Tom, Simon & Schuster Audio, 1230 Avenue of the Americas, New York, NY 10020 *Web Site:* audio.simonandschuster.com, pg 199

Spaisman, Ben, The Mathematical Association of America, 1529 18 St NW, Washington, DC 20036-1358 *Tel:* 202-387-5200 *Toll Free Tel:* 800-741-9415 *Fax:* 202-265-2384 *E-mail:* maahq@maa.org; advertising@maa.org (pubns) *Web Site:* www.maa.org, pg 134

Spangler, Emily, Teachers College Press, 1234 Amsterdam Ave, New York, NY 10027 *Tel:* 212-678-3929 *Fax:* 212-678-4149 *E-mail:* tcpress@tc.edu *Web Site:* www.tcpress.com, pg 214

Spangler, Stephen, DEStech Publications Inc, 439 N Duke St, Lancaster, PA 17602-4967 *Tel:* 717-290-1660 *Toll Free Tel:* 877-500-4DES (500-4337) *Fax:* 717-509-6100 *E-mail:* info@destechpub.com *Web Site:* www.destechpub.com, pg 64

Sparhawk, Bud, Science Fiction & Fantasy Writers of America Inc (SFWA), PO Box 3238, Enfield, CT 06083-3238 *Tel:* 860-698-0536 *E-mail:* office@sfwa.org *Web Site:* www.sfwa.org, pg 546

Sparhawk, Bud, SFWA Nebula Awards, PO Box 3238, Enfield, CT 06083-3238 *Tel:* 860-698-0536 *E-mail:* office@sfwa.org *Web Site:* www.sfwa.org, pg 666

Sparkes, Kathy, Dumbarton Oaks, 1703 32 St NW, Washington, DC 20007 *Tel:* 202-339-6400 *Fax:* 202-339-6401; 202-298-8407 *E-mail:* doaksbooks@doaks.org; press@doaks.org *Web Site:* www.doaks.org, pg 68

Sparks, Heather, Ladderbird Literary Agency, 45 Midland St, Worcester, MA 01602 *Tel:* 508-459-9590 *Web Site:* www.ladderbird.com, pg 492

Sparks, Kerry, Levine|Greenberg|Rostan Literary Agency, 307 Seventh Ave, Suite 2407, New York, NY 10001 *Tel:* 212-337-0934 *Fax:* 212-337-0948 *Web Site:* lgrliterary.com, pg 493

Sparks, Lee Ann, Trinity University Press, One Trinity Place, San Antonio, TX 78212-7200 *Tel:* 210-999-8884 *Fax:* 210-999-8838 *E-mail:* books@trinity.edu *Web Site:* www.tupress.org, pg 220

Speaker, Mary Austin, Milkweed Fellowship, 1011 Washington Ave S, Suite 300, Minneapolis, MN 55415-1246 *Tel:* 612-332-3192 *Toll Free Tel:* 800-520-6455 *E-mail:* fellowship@milkweed.org *Web Site:* milkweed.org/milkweed-fellowship, pg 641

Spear, Jody, Aaron-Spear, PO Box 42, Brooksville, ME 04617 *Tel:* 207-326-8764, pg 457

Spector, Jon, The Conference Board Inc, 845 Third Ave, New York, NY 10022-6600 *Tel:* 212-759-0900; 212-339-0345 (cust serv) *E-mail:* customer.service@conferenceboard.org; membership@conferenceboard.org *Web Site:* www.conference-board.org; www.linkedin.com/company/the-conference-board, pg 56

Spector, Katelin, Ladderbird Literary Agency, 45 Midland St, Worcester, MA 01602 *Tel:* 508-459-9590 *Web Site:* www.ladderbird.com, pg 492

Spellman-Silverman, Erica, Trident Media Group LLC, 41 Madison Ave, 36th fl, New York, NY 10010 *Tel:* 212-333-1511 *E-mail:* info@tridentmediagroup.com; press@tridentmediagroup.com *Web Site:* www.tridentmediagroup.com, pg 507

Spence, Bill, Information Today, Inc, 143 Old Marlton Pike, Medford, NJ 08055-8750 *Tel:* 609-654-6266 *Toll Free Tel:* 800-300-9868 (cust serv) *Fax:* 609-654-4309 *E-mail:* custserv@infotoday.com *Web Site:* www.infotoday.com, pg 108

Spence, Craig, Federation of BC Writers, PO Box 16028, 617 Belmont St, New Westminster, BC V3M 6W6, Canada *E-mail:* info@bcwriters.ca *Web Site:* bcwriters.ca, pg 533

Spence, Heather, AFB Press, 1401 S Clark St, Suite 730, Arlington, VA 22202 *Tel:* 304-710-3043 *Toll Free Tel:* 800-232-3044 (orders) *Fax:* 917-210-3979 (orders) *E-mail:* afbpress@afb.net *Web Site:* www.afb.org, pg 5

Spence, Marya, Janklow & Nesbit Associates, 285 Madison Ave, 21st fl, New York, NY 10017 *Tel:* 212-421-1700 *Fax:* 212-355-1403 *E-mail:* info@janklow.com *Web Site:* www.janklowandnesbit.com, pg 490

Spence, Thomas, Regnery Publishing, 300 New Jersey Ave NW, Washington, DC 20001 *Tel:* 202-216-0600 *Toll Free Tel:* 888-219-4747 *Fax:* 202-393-1795 *Web Site:* www.regnery.com, pg 184

Spencer, Denise, American Fisheries Society, 425 Barlow Place, Suite 110, Bethesda, MD 20814-2144 *Tel:* 301-897-8616; 703-661-1570 (book orders) *Fax:* 301-897-8096; 703-996-1010 (book orders) *E-mail:* main@fisheries.org *Web Site:* www.fisheries.org, pg 11

Spencer, Elaine, The Knight Agency Inc, 232 W Washington St, Madison, GA 30650 *E-mail:* admin@knightagency.net *Web Site:* www.knightagency.net, pg 491

Sperling, Ehud C, Bear & Co Inc, One Park St, Rochester, VT 05767 *Tel:* 802-767-3174 *Toll Free Tel:* 800-932-3277 *Fax:* 802-767-3726 *E-mail:* customerservice@InnerTraditions.com *Web Site:* InnerTraditions.com, pg 29

Sperling, Ehud C, Inner Traditions International Ltd, One Park St, Rochester, VT 05767 *Tel:* 802-767-3174 *Toll Free Tel:* 800-246-8648 *Fax:* 802-767-3726 *E-mail:* customerservice@InnerTraditions.com *Web Site:* www.InnerTraditions.com, pg 109

Speyer, Anne, Random House Publishing Group, 1745 Broadway, New York, NY 10019 *Toll Free Tel:* 800-200-3552 *Web Site:* www.randomhousebooks.com, pg 181

Spicer, Charles, St Martin's Press, LLC, 120 Broadway, New York, NY 10271 *Tel:* 646-307-5151 *Web Site:* us.macmillan.com/smp, pg 190

Spicer, Ed, Penn State University Press, University Support Bldg 1, Suite C, 820 N University Dr, University Park, PA 16802-1003 *Tel:* 814-865-1327 *Toll Free Tel:* 800-326-9180 *Fax:* 814-863-1408 *Toll Free Fax:* 877-778-2665 *E-mail:* orders@psupress.org; orders@eisenbrauns.org *Web Site:* www.psupress.org; www.eisenbrauns.org, pg 166

Spiegel, Lauren, Gallery Books, 1230 Avenue of the Americas, New York, NY 10020 *Toll Free Tel:* 800-456-6798 *Fax:* 212-698-7284 *E-mail:* consumer.customerservice@simonandschuster.com *Web Site:* www.simonandschuster.com, pg 83

Spieler, Joseph, The Spieler Agency, 27 W 20 St, Suite 302, New York, NY 10011 *Tel:* 212-757-4439 *Fax:* 212-333-2019 *E-mail:* spieleragency@spieleragency.com, pg 503

Spieller, Lauren, TriadaUS Literary Agency, PO Box 561, Sewickley, PA 15143 *Tel:* 412-401-3376 *Web Site:* www.triadaus.com, pg 506

Spinella, Michael, William Holmes McGuffey Longevity Award, PO Box 367, Fountain City, WI 54629 *E-mail:* info@taaonline.net *Web Site:* www.taaonline.net/mcguffey-longevity-award, pg 639

Spinella, Michael, Most Promising New Textbook Award, PO Box 367, Fountain City, WI 54629 *E-mail:* info@taaonline.net *Web Site:* www.taaonline.net/promising-new-textbook-award, pg 644

Spinella, Michael, Ron Pynn Award, PO Box 367, Fountain City, WI 54629 *E-mail:* info@taaonline.net *Web Site:* www.taaonline.net/ron-pynn-award, pg 660

Spinella, Michael, TAA Council of Fellows, PO Box 367, Fountain City, WI 54629 *E-mail:* info@taaonline.net *Web Site:* www.taaonline.net/council-of-fellows, pg 672

Spinella, Michael, Textbook Excellence Award, PO Box 367, Fountain City, WI 54629 *E-mail:* info@taaonline.net *Web Site:* www.taaonline.net/textbook-excellence-award, pg 672

Spinnato, JoAnn, American Water Works Association (AWWA), 6666 W Quincy Ave, Denver, CO 80235-3098 *Tel:* 303-794-7711 *Toll Free Tel:* 800-926-7337 *E-mail:* service@awwa.org (cust serv) *Web Site:* www.awwa.org, pg 15

Spinner, Dianna, The PRS Group Inc, 5800 Heritage Landing Dr, Suite E, East Syracuse, NY 13057-9358 *Tel:* 315-431-0511 *Fax:* 315-431-0200 *E-mail:* custserv@prsgroup.com *Web Site:* www.prsgroup.com, pg 177

Stigler, Laura, Independent Writers of Chicago (IWOC), 332 S Michigan Ave, Suite 1032, Chicago, IL 60604 *Toll Free Tel:* 800-804-IWOC (804-4962) *E-mail:* info@iwoc.org *Web Site:* www.iwoc.org, pg 535

Stillwell, Steph, Harry N Abrams Inc, 195 Broadway, 9th fl, New York, NY 10007 *Tel:* 212-206-7715 *Toll Free Tel:* 800-345-1359 *Fax:* 212-519-1210 *E-mail:* abrams@abramsbooks.com *Web Site:* www. abramsbooks.com, pg 3

Stilson, Joyce, Maxim Mazumdar New Play Competition, One Curtain Up Alley, Buffalo, NY 14202-1911 *Tel:* 716-852-2600 *E-mail:* publicrelations@alleyway.com *Web Site:* alleyway.com, pg 639

Stilwell, Haleh Roshan, Dramatists Play Service Inc, 440 Park Ave S, New York, NY 10016 *Tel:* 212-683-8960 *Fax:* 212-213-1539 *E-mail:* postmaster@dramatists. com; orders@dramatists.com; publications@dramatists. com *Web Site:* www.dramatists.com, pg 67

Stimola, Adriana, Stimola Literary Studio Inc, 308 Livingston Ct, Edgewater, NJ 07020 *Tel:* 201-945-9353 *Fax:* 201-945-9353; 201-490-5920 *E-mail:* info@stimolaliterarystudio.com *Web Site:* www.stimolaliterarystudio.com, pg 504

Stimola, Rosemary B, Stimola Literary Studio Inc, 308 Livingston Ct, Edgewater, NJ 07020 *Tel:* 201-945-9353 *Fax:* 201-945-9353; 201-490-5920 *E-mail:* info@stimolaliterarystudio.com *Web Site:* www.stimolaliterarystudio.com, pg 504

Stine, Jane, Parachute Publishing LLC, 157 Columbus Ave, Suite 518, New York, NY 10023 *Tel:* 212-691-1422, pg 160

Stipp, Horst PhD, Advertising Research Foundation (ARF), 432 Park Ave S, 4th fl, New York, NY 10016-8013 *Tel:* 212-751-5656 *Fax:* 212-689-1859 *E-mail:* help@thearf.org *Web Site:* thearf.org, pg 521

Stitzer, Tina, Fun in the Sun Writer's Cruise Conference, PO Box 823414, Pembroke Pines, FL 33082 *E-mail:* frwfuninthesun@yahoo.com *Web Site:* frwfuninthesunmain.blogspot.com/; www. frwriters.org, pg 574

Stobaugh, Clay, John Wiley & Sons Inc, 111 River St, Hoboken, NJ 07030-5774 *Tel:* 201-748-6000 *Toll Free Tel:* 800-225-5945 (cust serv) *Fax:* 201-748-6088 *E-mail:* info@wiley.com *Web Site:* www.wiley.com, pg 241

Stocke, Todd, Sourcebooks LLC, 1935 Brookdale Rd, Suite 139, Naperville, IL 60563 *Tel:* 630-961-3900 *Toll Free Tel:* 800-432-7444 *Fax:* 630-961-2168 *E-mail:* info@sourcebooks.com; customersupport@ sourcebooks.com *Web Site:* www.sourcebooks.com, pg 204

Stockland, Patricia, Capstone Publishers™, 1710 Roe Crest Dr, North Mankato, MN 56003 *Toll Free Tel:* 800-747-4992 (cust serv) *Toll Free Fax:* 888-262-0705 *E-mail:* customer.service@capstonepub.com *Web Site:* www.capstonepub.com, pg 44

Stocks, John C, National Education Association (NEA), 1201 16 St NW, Washington, DC 20036-3290 *Tel:* 202-833-4000 *Fax:* 202-822-7974 *Web Site:* www. nea.org, pg 146

Stocks, John C, National Education Association (NEA), 1201 16 St NW, Washington, DC 20036-3290 *Tel:* 202-833-4000 *Fax:* 202-822-7974 *E-mail:* media-relations-team@nea.org *Web Site:* www.nea.org, pg 540

Stockton, Hope, MFA Publications, 465 Huntington Ave, Boston, MA 02115 *Tel:* 617-369-4233 *E-mail:* publications@mfa.org *Web Site:* www.mfa. org/publications, pg 139

Stockwell, Diane, Globo Libros Literary Management, 450 E 63 St, New York, NY 10065 *Web Site:* www. globo-libros.com; www.publishersmarketplace.com/ members/dstockwell, pg 486

Stockwell, Gail Provost, Writers Retreat Workshop (WRW), PO Box 170657, Austin, TX 78717 *E-mail:* info@writersretreatworkshop.com *Web Site:* www.writersretreatworkshop.com, pg 580

Stoddard, Bill, Prometheus Awards, 650 Castro St, Suite 120-433, Mountain View, CA 94041 *Tel:* 650-968-6319 *Web Site:* www.lfs.org, pg 659

Stoddard, Brooke C, Archon Editorial LLC, 815 King St, Suite 204, Alexandria, VA 22314 *Tel:* 703-838-1650 *E-mail:* stoddardbc@gmail.com *Web Site:* www. archoneditorial.com, pg 458

Stoeger, Lea, Penguin Random House LLC, 1745 Broadway, New York, NY 10019 *Tel:* 212-782-9000 *Toll Free Tel:* 800-726-0600 *Web Site:* www. penguinrandomhouse.com, pg 164

Stokes, Susan S, Woodbine House, 6510 Bells Mill Rd, Bethesda, MD 20817 *Tel:* 301-897-3570 *Toll Free Tel:* 800-843-7323 *Fax:* 301-897-5838 *E-mail:* info@ woodbinehouse.com *Web Site:* www.woodbinehouse. com, pg 244

Stokes-Peters, Natalie, Black Classic Press, 3921 Vero Rd, Suite F, Baltimore, MD 21203-3414 *Tel:* 410-242-6954 *Toll Free Tel:* 800-476-8870 *Fax:* 410-242-6959 *E-mail:* email@blackclassicbooks.com; blackclassicpress@yahoo.com *Web Site:* www. blackclassicbooks.com; www.bcpdigital.com, pg 34

Stokke, Carol, DK Publishing, 1450 Broadway, Suite 801, New York, NY 10018 *Tel:* 646-674-4000 *Toll Free Tel:* 800-733-3000 *Fax:* 646-674-4020 *E-mail:* marketing@dk.com; publicity@ dk.com; csorders@penguinrandomhouse.com; ecustomerservice@randomhouse.com *Web Site:* www. dk.com; www.penguin.com, pg 65

Stoller, Justin, Simon & Schuster Canada, 166 King St E, Suite 300, Toronto, ON M5A 1J3, Canada *Tel:* 647-427-8882 *Toll Free Tel:* 800-387-0446; 800-268-3216 (orders) *Fax:* 647-430-9446 *Toll Free Fax:* 888-849-8151 (orders) *E-mail:* info@simonandschuster.ca *Web Site:* www.simonandschuster.ca, pg 440

Stolls, Amy, National Endowment for the Arts, 400 Seventh St SW, Washington, DC 20506-0001 *Tel:* 202-682-5400 *Web Site:* www.arts.gov, pg 551

Stoloff, Sam, Frances Goldin Literary Agency, Inc, 214 W 29 St, Suite 410, New York, NY 10001 *Tel:* 212-777-0047 *Fax:* 212-228-1660 *E-mail:* agency@ goldinlit.com *Web Site:* www.goldinlit.com, pg 486

Stoltz, Jamison, Harry N Abrams Inc, 195 Broadway, 9th fl, New York, NY 10007 *Tel:* 212-206-7715 *Toll Free Tel:* 800-345-1359 *Fax:* 212-519-1210 *E-mail:* abrams@abramsbooks.com *Web Site:* www. abramsbooks.com, pg 3

Stoltzfus, Alison, The Princeton Review, c/o Penguin Random House Inc, 1745 Broadway, MD 16-1, New York, NY 10019 *Toll Free Tel:* 800-273-8439 (orders only) *Web Site:* www.princetonreview.com, pg 174

Stone, Crystal, Society for Scholarly Publishing (SSP), 1120 Rte 73, Suite 200, Mount Laurel, NJ 08054 *Tel:* 856-439-1385 *Fax:* 856-439-0525 *E-mail:* info@ sspnet.org *Web Site:* www.sspnet.org, pg 546

Stone, Judi, Artech House®, 685 Canton St, Norwood, MA 02062 *Tel:* 781-769-9750 *Toll Free Tel:* 800-225-9977 *Fax:* 781-769-6334 *E-mail:* artech@artechhouse. com *Web Site:* www.artechhouse.com, pg 21

Stone, Kevin, Cengage Learning, 20 Channel Center St, Boston, MA 02210 *Tel:* 617-289-7700 *Toll Free Tel:* 800-354-9706 *Fax:* 617-289-7844 *E-mail:* esales@cengage.com *Web Site:* www.cengage. com, pg 47

Stone, Kris, Piano Press, 1425 Ocean Ave, Suite 5, Del Mar, CA 92014 *Tel:* 619-884-1401 *Fax:* 858-755-1104 *E-mail:* pianopress@pianopress.com *Web Site:* www. pianopress.com, pg 169

Stone, Madelin, Random House Children's Books, 1745 Broadway, 10th fl, New York, NY 10019 *Tel:* 212-782-9000 *Web Site:* www.randomhousekids.com, pg 181

Stone, Patricia, Chelsea Green Publishing Co, 85 N Main St, Suite 120, White River Junction, VT 05001 *Tel:* 802-295-6300 *Toll Free Tel:* 800-639-4099 (cust serv & orders) *Fax:* 802-295-6444 *E-mail:* customerservice@chelseagreen.com; editorial@chelseagreen.com; publicity@chelseagreen. com; rights@chelseagreen.com *Web Site:* www. chelseagreen.com, pg 49

Stone, Sheryl, Gulf Energy Information, 2 Greenway Plaza, Suite 1020, Houston, TX 77046 *Tel:* 713-529-4301 *E-mail:* store@gulfpub.com; customerservice@ energyinfo.com *Web Site:* www.gulfenergyinfo.com, pg 90

Stone, Suezen, HJ Kramer Inc, PO Box 1082, Tiburon, CA 94920 *Tel:* 415-884-2100 (ext 10) *Toll Free Tel:* 800-972-6657 *Fax:* 415-435-5364 *E-mail:* hjkramer@jps.net *Web Site:* www.hjkramer. com; www.newworldlibrary.com, pg 118

Stookesberry, Tim, State University of New York Press, 10 N Pearl St, 4th fl, Albany, NY 12207 *Tel:* 518-944-2800 *Toll Free Tel:* 877-204-6073 (orders) *Fax:* 518-320-1592 *Toll Free Fax:* 877-204-6074 (orders) *E-mail:* info@sunypress.edu (edit off); suny@presswarehouse.com (orders) *Web Site:* www. sunypress.edu, pg 207

Storch, Maury, Gefen Books, c/o Storch, 255 Central Ave, B-206, Lawrence, NY 11559 *Tel:* 516-593-1234 *Toll Free Tel:* 800-477-5257 *Fax:* 516-295-2739 *E-mail:* gefenny@gefenpublishing.com; info@ gefenpublishing.com *Web Site:* www.gefenpublishing. com, pg 84

Stordahl, Derek, Holiday House Publishing Inc, 50 Broad St, New York, NY 10004 *Tel:* 212-688-0085 *Fax:* 212-421-6134 *E-mail:* info@holidayhouse.com *Web Site:* www.holidayhouse.com, pg 101

Storey, Kendall, Counterpoint Press LLC, 2560 Ninth St, Suite 318, Berkeley, CA 94710 *Tel:* 510-704-0230 *Fax:* 510-704-0268 *E-mail:* info@counterpointpress. com *Web Site:* counterpointpress.com; softskull.com, pg 58

Storrings, Michael, St Martin's Press, LLC, 120 Broadway, New York, NY 10271 *Tel:* 646-307-5151 *Web Site:* us.macmillan.com/smp, pg 190

Story, Elizabeth, Tachyon Publications LLC, 1459 18 St, No 139, San Francisco, CA 94107 *Tel:* 415-285-5615 *E-mail:* tachyon@tachyonpublications.com *Web Site:* www.tachyonpublications.com, pg 212

Stoshak, Joe, Public Citizen, 1600 20 St NW, Washington, DC 20009 *Tel:* 202-588-1000 *Web Site:* www.citizen.org, pg 177

Stouras, Tom, Macmillan, 120 Broadway, 22nd fl, New York, NY 10271 *Tel:* 646-307-5151 *E-mail:* press. inquiries@macmillan.com *Web Site:* www.macmillan. com, pg 129

Stovall, Sierra, Sourcebooks LLC, 1935 Brookdale Rd, Suite 139, Naperville, IL 60563 *Tel:* 630-961-3900 *Toll Free Tel:* 800-432-7444 *Fax:* 630-961-2168 *E-mail:* info@sourcebooks.com; customersupport@ sourcebooks.com *Web Site:* www.sourcebooks.com, pg 204

Strachan, Glenn R, Jhpiego, 1615 Thames St, Baltimore, MD 21231-3492 *Tel:* 410-537-1800 *Fax:* 410-537-1473 *E-mail:* info@jhpiego.net *Web Site:* www. jhpiego.org, pg 113

Strader, Faith, Small Publishers, Artists & Writers Network (SPAWN), 1129 Maricopa Hwy, No 142, Ojai, CA 93023 *E-mail:* info@spawn.org *Web Site:* spawn.org, pg 546

Stramenga, Silvia, Seven Stories Press, 140 Watts St, New York, NY 10013 *Tel:* 212-226-8760 *Toll Free Tel:* 800-733-3000 (orders) *Fax:* 212-226-1411 *E-mail:* sevenstories@sevenstories.com *Web Site:* www.sevenstories.com, pg 197

Strand, Kurt, McGraw-Hill Contemporary Learning Series, 501 Bell St, Dubuque, IA 52001 *Toll Free Tel:* 800-243-6532 *Web Site:* www.mhcls.com, pg 135

Strand, Kurt, McGraw-Hill Higher Education, 1333 Burr Ridge Pkwy, Burr Ridge, IL 60527 *Tel:* 630-789-4000 *Toll Free Tel:* 800-338-3987 (cust serv) *Fax:* 614-755-5645 (cust serv) *Web Site:* www.mhhe.com, pg 135

Strand, Kurt, McGraw-Hill Humanities, Social Sciences, Languages, 2 Penn Plaza, 21st fl, New York, NY 10121 *Tel:* 212-904-2000 *Toll Free Tel:* 800-338-3987 (cust serv) *Fax:* 614-755-5645 (cust serv) *Web Site:* www.mhhe.com, pg 136

Strand, Kurt, McGraw-Hill/Irwin, 1333 Burr Ridge Pkwy, Burr Ridge, IL 60527 *Tel:* 630-789-4000 *Toll Free Tel:* 800-338-3987 (cust serv) *Fax:* 630-789-6942; 614-755-5645 (cust serv) *Web Site:* www.mhhe.com, pg 136

Strand, Kurt, McGraw-Hill Science, Engineering, Mathematics, 501 Bell St, Dubuque, IA 52001 *Tel:* 563-584-6000 *Toll Free Tel:* 800-338-3987 (cust serv) *Fax:* 614-755-5645 (cust serv) *Web Site:* www.mhhe.com, pg 136

Strang, Stephen, Charisma Media, 600 Rinehart Rd, Lake Mary, FL 32746 *Tel:* 407-333-0600 (all imprints) *Toll Free Tel:* 800-283-8494 (Charisma Media, Siloam Press, Creation House); 800-665-1468 *Fax:* 407-333-7100 (all imprints) *E-mail:* charisma@charismamedia.com *Web Site:* www.charismamedia.com, pg 49

Strange, Nancy, Tudor Publishers Inc, 3109 Shady Lawn Dr, Greensboro, NC 27408 *Tel:* 336-288-5395 *E-mail:* tudorpublishers@triad.rr.com, pg 221

Strassner, Amy, Andrews McMeel Publishing LLC, 1130 Walnut St, Kansas City, MO 64106-2109 *Toll Free Tel:* 800-851-8923; 800-943-9839 (cust serv) *Toll Free Tel:* 800-943-9831 (orders) *E-mail:* sales@amuniversal.com *Web Site:* www.andrewsmcmeel.com; publishing.andrewsmcmeel.com, pg 16

Stratton, W K, Carr P Collins Award, PO Box 609, Round Rock, TX 78680 *Tel:* 512-683-5640 *E-mail:* president@texasinstituteofletters.org *Web Site:* www.texasinstituteofletters.org, pg 606

Stratton, W K, Soeurette Diehl Fraser Translation Award, PO Box 609, Round Rock, TX 78680 *Tel:* 512-683-5640 *E-mail:* president@texasinstituteofletters.org *Web Site:* www.texasinstituteofletters.org, pg 617

Stratton, W K, Jesse H Jones Award, PO Box 609, Round Rock, TX 78680 *Tel:* 512-683-5640 *E-mail:* president@texasinstituteofletters.org *Web Site:* www.texasinstituteofletters.org, pg 629

Stratton, W K, Ramirez Family Award, PO Box 609, Round Rock, TX 78680 *Tel:* 512-683-5640 *E-mail:* president@texasinstituteofletters.org *Web Site:* www.texasinstituteofletters.org, pg 660

Stratton, W K, Edwin "Bud" Shrake Award for Best Short Nonfiction, PO Box 609, Round Rock, TX 78680 *Tel:* 512-683-5640 *E-mail:* president@texasinstituteofletters.org *Web Site:* www.texasinstituteofletters.org, pg 667

Stratton, W K, Helen C Smith Memorial Award, PO Box 609, Round Rock, TX 78680 *Tel:* 512-683-5640 *E-mail:* president@texasinstituteofletters.org *Web Site:* www.texasinstituteofletters.org, pg 668

Stratton, W K, Texas Institute of Letters (TIL), PO Box 609, Round Rock, TX 78680 *E-mail:* president@texasinstituteofletters.org; secretary@texasinstituteofletters.org *Web Site:* www.texasinstituteofletters.org, pg 548

Stratton, W K, Texas Institute of Letters Awards, PO Box 609, Round Rock, TX 78680 *Tel:* 512-683-5640 *E-mail:* president@texasinstituteofletters.org *Web Site:* www.texasinstituteofletters.org, pg 672

Straub, Amanda, Association of American Publishers (AAP), 455 Massachusetts Ave NW, Suite 700, Washington, DC 20001-2777 *Tel:* 202-347-3375 *Fax:* 202-347-3690 *E-mail:* info@publishers.org *Web Site:* publishers.org, pg 526

Straub, Peter, The Authors League Fund, 31 E 32 St, 7th fl, New York, NY 10016 *Tel:* 212-268-1208 *Fax:* 212-564-5363 *E-mail:* staff@authorsleaguefund.org *Web Site:* www.authorsleaguefund.org, pg 527

Straus, Jonah, Straus Literary, 77 Van Ness Ave, Suite 101, San Francisco, CA 94102 *Tel:* 646-843-9950 *Web Site:* www.strausliterary.com, pg 505

Straus, Robin, Robin Straus Agency Inc, 229 E 79 St, Suite 5A, New York, NY 10075 *Tel:* 212-472-3282 *Fax:* 212-472-3833 *E-mail:* info@robinstrausagency.com *Web Site:* www.robinstrausagency.com, pg 505

Straus, Robin, The Wallace Literary Agency, 229 E 79 St, No 5A, New York, NY 10075 *Tel:* 212-472-3282 *Fax:* 212-472-3833 *E-mail:* info@wallaceliteraryagency.com, pg 507

Strauss, Dave, Teachers College Press, 1234 Amsterdam Ave, New York, NY 10027 *Tel:* 212-678-3929 *Fax:* 212-678-4149 *E-mail:* tcpress@tc.edu *Web Site:* www.tcpress.com, pg 214

Strauss, Leslie R, Housing Assistance Council, 1025 Vermont Ave NW, Suite 606, Washington, DC 20005 *Tel:* 202-842-8600 *Fax:* 202-347-3441 *E-mail:* hac@ruralhome.org *Web Site:* www.ruralhome.org, pg 104

Strauss, Rebecca, DeFiore and Company Literary Management Inc, 47 E 19 St, 3rd fl, New York, NY 10003 *Tel:* 212-925-7744 *Fax:* 212-925-9803 *E-mail:* info@defliterary.com; submissions@defliterary.com *Web Site:* www.defliterary.com, pg 481

Strauss-Gabel, Julie, Dutton, 1745 Broadway, New York, NY 10019 *Tel:* 212-366-2000 *Fax:* 212-366-2262 *E-mail:* duttonpublicity@us.penguingroup.com *Web Site:* www.penguin.com, pg 68

Strauss-Gabel, Julie, Dutton Children's Books, 345 Hudson St, New York, NY 10014 *Tel:* 212-366-2000 *Web Site:* www.penguin.com/publishers/duttonchildrensbooks/, pg 68

Strecker, Susan, SDP Publishing Solutions LLC, 36 Captain's Way, East Bridgewater, MA 02333 *Tel:* 617-775-0656 *Web Site:* www.sdppublishingsolutions.com, pg 470

Streetman, Ms Burgin, Trinity University Press, One Trinity Place, San Antonio, TX 78212-7200 *Tel:* 210-999-8884 *Fax:* 210-999-8838 *E-mail:* books@trinity.edu *Web Site:* www.tupress.org, pg 220

Strelecki, Heather, AIGA 50 Books|50 Covers, 222 Broadway, New York, NY 10038 *Tel:* 212-807-1990 *Fax:* 212-807-1799 *E-mail:* competitions@aiga.org *Web Site:* www.aiga.org, pg 590

Strickland, Albert Lee, Pacific Publishing Services, PO Box 1150, Capitola, CA 95010-1150 *Tel:* 831-476-8284 *Fax:* 831-476-8294 *E-mail:* pacpubs@attglobal.net, pg 468

Strickland, Jonathan, Black Rabbit Books, 2140 Howard Dr W, North Mankato, MN 56003 *Tel:* 507-388-1609 *Fax:* 507-388-2746 *E-mail:* info@blackrabbitbooks.com; orders@blackrabbitbooks.com *Web Site:* www.blackrabbitbooks.com, pg 34

Stringham, Edward, American Institute for Economic Research (AIER), 250 Division St, Great Barrington, MA 01230 *Tel:* 413-528-1216 *Toll Free Tel:* 888-528-1216 (orders) *E-mail:* info@aier.org *Web Site:* www.aier.org, pg 11

Strittmatter, Aimee, ALSC Baker & Taylor Summer Reading Grant, 50 E Huron St, Chicago, IL 60611-2795 *Tel:* 312-280-2163 *Toll Free Tel:* 800-545-2433 *Fax:* 312-440-9374; 312-280-5271 *E-mail:* alsc@ala.org *Web Site:* www.ala.org/alsc, pg 591

Strittmatter, Aimee, The May Hill Arbuthnot Honor Lecture Award, 50 E Huron St, Chicago, IL 60611-2795 *Tel:* 312-280-2163 *Toll Free Tel:* 800-545-2433 *Fax:* 312-440-9374; 312-280-5271 *E-mail:* alsc@ala.org *Web Site:* www.ala.org/alsc, pg 592

Strittmatter, Aimee, The Mildred L Batchelder Award, 50 E Huron St, Chicago, IL 60611-2795 *Tel:* 312-280-2163 *Toll Free Tel:* 800-545-2433 *Fax:* 312-440-9374; 312-280-5271 *E-mail:* alsc@ala.org *Web Site:* www.ala.org/alsc, pg 596

Strittmatter, Aimee, The Pura Belpre Award, 50 E Huron St, Chicago, IL 60611-2795 *Tel:* 312-280-2163 *Toll Free Tel:* 800-545-2433 *Fax:* 312-440-9374; 312-280-5271 *E-mail:* alsc@ala.org *Web Site:* www.ala.org/alsc, pg 596

Strittmatter, Aimee, Bound to Stay Bound Books Scholarship, 50 E Huron St, Chicago, IL 60611-2795 *Tel:* 312-280-2163 *Toll Free Tel:* 800-545-2433 *Fax:* 312-440-9374; 312-280-5271 *E-mail:* alsc@ala.org *Web Site:* www.ala.org/alsc, pg 600

Strittmatter, Aimee, The Randolph Caldecott Medal, 50 E Huron St, Chicago, IL 60611-2795 *Tel:* 312-280-2163 *Toll Free Tel:* 800-545-2433 *Fax:* 312-440-9374; 312-280-5271 *E-mail:* alsc@ala.org *Web Site:* www.ala.org/alsc, pg 602

Strittmatter, Aimee, Children's Literature Legacy Award, 50 E Huron St, Chicago, IL 60611-2795 *Tel:* 312-280-2163 *Toll Free Tel:* 800-545-2433 *Fax:* 312-440-9374; 312-280-5271 *E-mail:* alsc@ala.org *Web Site:* www.ala.org/alsc, pg 604

Strittmatter, Aimee, Frederic G Melcher Scholarship, 50 E Huron St, Chicago, IL 60611-2795 *Tel:* 312-280-2163 *Toll Free Tel:* 800-545-2433 *Fax:* 312-440-9374; 312-280-5271 *E-mail:* alsc@ala.org *Web Site:* www.ala.org/alsc, pg 641

Strittmatter, Aimee, John Newbery Medal, 50 E Huron St, Chicago, IL 60611-2795 *Tel:* 312-280-2163 *Toll Free Tel:* 800-545-2433 *Fax:* 312-440-9374; 312-280-5271 *E-mail:* alsc@ala.org *Web Site:* www.ala.org/alsc, pg 648

Strittmatter, Aimee, Robert F Sibert Informational Book Award, 50 E Huron St, Chicago, IL 60611-2795 *Tel:* 312-280-2163 *Toll Free Tel:* 800-545-2433 *Fax:* 312-440-9374; 312-280-5271 *E-mail:* alsc@ala.org *Web Site:* www.ala.org/alsc, pg 667

Strobel, Rebecca, Gallery Books, 1230 Avenue of the Americas, New York, NY 10020 *Toll Free Tel:* 800-456-6798 *Fax:* 212-698-7284 *E-mail:* consumer.customerservice@simonandschuster.com *Web Site:* www.simonandschuster.com, pg 83

Strone, Daniel, Trident Media Group LLC, 41 Madison Ave, 36th fl, New York, NY 10010 *Tel:* 212-333-1511 *E-mail:* info@tridentmediagroup.com; press@tridentmediagroup.com *Web Site:* www.tridentmediagroup.com, pg 507

Strong, Laura, University Press of Mississippi, 3825 Ridgewood Rd, Jackson, MS 39211-6492 *Tel:* 601-432-6205 *Toll Free Tel:* 800-737-7788 (orders & cust serv) *Fax:* 601-432-6217 *E-mail:* press@mississippi.edu *Web Site:* www.upress.state.ms.us, pg 233

Strosnider, Ashley, Prairie Schooner Annual Strousse Award, University of Nebraska, 123 Andrews Hall, 625 N 14 St, Lincoln, NE 68508 *Tel:* 402-472-0911 *Fax:* 402-472-9771 *E-mail:* prairieschooner@unl.edu *Web Site:* prairieschooner.unl.edu, pg 657

Strosnider, Ashley, Prairie Schooner Bernice Slote Award, University of Nebraska, 123 Andrews Hall, 625 N 14 St, Lincoln, NE 68508 *Tel:* 402-472-0911 *Fax:* 402-472-9771 *E-mail:* prairieschooner@unl.edu *Web Site:* prairieschooner.unl.edu, pg 657

Strosnider, Ashley, Prairie Schooner Book Prize Contest in Fiction, University of Nebraska, 123 Andrews Hall, 625 N 14 St, Lincoln, NE 68508 *Tel:* 402-472-0911 *Fax:* 402-472-9771 *E-mail:* psbookprize@unl.edu *Web Site:* prairieschooner.unl.edu, pg 658

Strosnider, Ashley, Prairie Schooner Book Prize Contest in Poetry, University of Nebraska, 123 Andrews Hall, 625 N 14 St, Lincoln, NE 68508 *Tel:* 402-472-0911 *Fax:* 402-472-9771 *E-mail:* psbookprize@unl.edu *Web Site:* prairieschooner.unl.edu, pg 658

Strosnider, Ashley, Prairie Schooner Edward Stanley Award, University of Nebraska, 123 Andrews Hall, 625 N 14 St, Lincoln, NE 68508 *Tel:* 402-472-0911 *Fax:* 402-472-9771 *E-mail:* prairieschooner@unl.edu *Web Site:* prairieschooner.unl.edu, pg 658

Strosnider, Ashley, Prairie Schooner Glenna Luschei Award, University of Nebraska, 123 Andrews Hall, 625 N 14 St, Lincoln, NE 68508 *Tel:* 402-472-0911 *Fax:* 402-472-9771 *E-mail:* prairieschooner@unl.edu *Web Site:* prairieschooner.unl.edu, pg 658

Strosnider, Ashley, Prairie Schooner Hugh J Luke Award, University of Nebraska, 123 Andrews Hall, 625 N 14 St, Lincoln, NE 68508 *Tel:* 402-472-0911 *Fax:* 402-472-9771 *E-mail:* prairieschooner@unl.edu *Web Site:* prairieschooner.unl.edu, pg 658

Strosnider, Ashley, Prairie Schooner Jane Geske Award, University of Nebraska, 123 Andrews Hall, 625 N 14 St, Lincoln, NE 68508 *Tel:* 402-472-0911 *Fax:* 402-472-9771 *E-mail:* prairieschooner@unl.edu *Web Site:* prairieschooner.unl.edu, pg 658

Strosnider, Ashley, Prairie Schooner Lawrence Foundation Award, University of Nebraska, 123 Andrews Hall, 625 N 14 St, Lincoln,

NE 68508 *Tel:* 402-472-0911 *Fax:* 402-472-9771 *E-mail:* prairieschooner@unl.edu *Web Site:* prairieschooner.unl.edu, pg 658

Strosnider, Ashley, Prairie Schooner Virginia Faulkner Award for Excellence in Writing, University of Nebraska, 123 Andrews Hall, 625 N 14 St, Lincoln, NE 68508 *Tel:* 402-472-0911 *Fax:* 402-472-9771 *E-mail:* prairieschooner@unl.edu *Web Site:* prairieschooner.unl.edu, pg 658

Strothman, Wendy, Strothman Agency LLC, 63 E Ninth St, 10X, New York, NY 10003 *E-mail:* info@strothmanagency.com *Web Site:* www.strothmanagency.com, pg 505

Stroud, Christine, Autumn House Press, 5530 Penn Ave, Pittsburgh, PA 15206 *Tel:* 412-362-2665 *E-mail:* info@autumnhouse.org *Web Site:* www.autumnhouse.org, pg 25

Stroud, Christine, Coal Hill Review Poetry Chapbook Contest, c/o Autumn House Press, PO Box 5486, Pittsburgh, PA 15206 *E-mail:* reviewcoalhill@gmail.com *Web Site:* www.coalhillreview.com, pg 605

Stroup-Rentier, Vera Lynne PhD, Finding My Way Books, 3512 SW Huntoon St, Topeka, KS 66604-1748 *Tel:* 785-273-6239 *E-mail:* findingmywaybooks@gmail.com *Web Site:* www.findingmywaybooks.net, pg 78

Struna, Barbara, Cape Cod Writers' Center Conference, 919 Main St, Osterville, MA 02655 *Tel:* 508-420-0200 *E-mail:* writers@capecodwriterscenter.org *Web Site:* capecodwriterscenter.org, pg 574

Struna, Barbara, Young Writers' Workshop, 919 Main St, Osterville, MA 02655 *Tel:* 508-420-0200 *E-mail:* writers@capecodwriterscenter.org *Web Site:* capecodwriterscenter.org, pg 580

Stuart, Kari, ICM Partners, 65 E 55 St, New York, NY 10022 *Tel:* 212-556-5600 *Web Site:* www.icmtalent.com, pg 489

Stuart, Kathryn, Writers House, 21 W 26 St, New York, NY 10010 *Tel:* 212-685-2400 *Web Site:* www.writershouse.com, pg 508

Stuart, Kelly, Center for the Collaborative Classroom, 1001 Marina Village Pkwy, Suite 110, Alameda, CA 94501-1042 *Tel:* 510-533-0213 *Toll Free Tel:* 800-666-7270 *Fax:* 510-464-3670 *E-mail:* info@collaborativeclassroom.org; clientsupport@collaborativeclassroom.org *Web Site:* www.collaborativeclassroom.org, pg 48

Stuart, Nancy Rubin, Cape Cod Writers' Center Conference, 919 Main St, Osterville, MA 02655 *Tel:* 508-420-0200 *E-mail:* writers@capecodwriterscenter.org *Web Site:* capecodwriterscenter.org, pg 574

Stuart, Nancy Rubin, Young Writers' Workshop, 919 Main St, Osterville, MA 02655 *Tel:* 508-420-0200 *E-mail:* writers@capecodwriterscenter.org *Web Site:* capecodwriterscenter.org, pg 580

Stubblefield, Terri, Neustadt International Prize for Literature, c/o University of Oklahoma, 630 Parrington Oval, Suite 110, Norman, OK 73019-4033 *Tel:* 405-325-4531 *Web Site:* www.worldliteraturetoday.org; www.worldlit.org, pg 647

Stubblefield, Terri, NSK Neustadt Prize for Children's Literature, c/o University of Oklahoma, 630 Parrington Oval, Suite 110, Norman, OK 73019-4033 *Tel:* 405-325-4531 *Web Site:* www.worldliteraturetoday.org; www.worldlit.org, pg 649

Stubbs, Peter, Fitzhenry & Whiteside Limited, 195 Allstate Pkwy, Markham, ON L3R 4T8, Canada *Tel:* 905-477-9700 *Toll Free Tel:* 800-387-9776 *Fax:* 905-477-2834 *Toll Free Fax:* 800-260-9777 *E-mail:* bookinfo@fitzhenry.ca; godwit@fitzhenry.ca *Web Site:* www.fitzhenry.ca, pg 426

Stueve, Rev Dennis, Lutheran Braille Workers Inc, 13471 California St, Yucaipa, CA 92399 *Tel:* 909-795-8977 *Toll Free Tel:* 800-925-6092 *Fax:* 909-795-8970 *E-mail:* lbw@lbwinc.org *Web Site:* www.lbwinc.org, pg 129

Stufflebean, Nathan, The Donning Company Publishers, 731 S Brunswick St, Brookfield, MO 64628 *Toll Free Tel:* 800-369-2646 (ext 3377) *Web Site:* www.donning.com, pg 66

Stulack, Nancy, Herbert Warren Wind Book Award, 77 Liberty Corner Rd, Far Hills, NJ 07931-0708 *Tel:* 908-234-2300 *Web Site:* www.usga.org, pg 678

Sturdivant, Chris, National Notary Association (NNA), 9350 De Soto Ave, Chatsworth, CA 91311-4926 *Tel:* 818-739-4000 *Toll Free Tel:* 800-876-6827 *Toll Free Fax:* 800-833-1211 *E-mail:* services@nationalnotary.org *Web Site:* www.nationalnotary.org, pg 147

Sturgis, Randy, Copper Canyon Press, Fort Worden State Park, Bldg 313, Port Townsend, WA 98368 *Tel:* 360-385-4925 *Toll Free Tel:* 877-501-1393 (orders) *Fax:* 360-385-4985 *E-mail:* poetry@coppercanyonpress.org *Web Site:* www.coppercanyonpress.org, pg 56

Sturman, Ms Gerrie Lipson, Goldfarb & Associates, 721 Gibbon St, Alexandria, VA 22314 *Tel:* 202-466-3030 *Fax:* 703-836-5644 *E-mail:* rlglawlit@gmail.com *Web Site:* www.ronaldgoldfarb.com, pg 486

Sturmer, Alan, Edward Elgar Publishing Inc, The William Pratt House, 9 Dewey Ct, Northampton, MA 01060-3815 *Tel:* 413-584-5551 *Toll Free Tel:* 800-390-3149 (orders) *Fax:* 413-584-9933 *E-mail:* elgarinfo@e-elgar.com; elgarsales@e-elgar.com; elgarsubmissions@e-elgar.com (edit) *Web Site:* www.e-elgar.com; www.elgaronline.com (ebooks & journals), pg 70

Stutz, Katie, Sourcebooks LLC, 1935 Brookdale Rd, Suite 139, Naperville, IL 60563 *Tel:* 630-961-3900 *Toll Free Tel:* 800-432-7444 *Fax:* 630-961-2168 *E-mail:* info@sourcebooks.com; customersupport@sourcebooks.com *Web Site:* www.sourcebooks.com, pg 204

Stvan, Beck, Random House Publishing Group, 1745 Broadway, New York, NY 10019 *Toll Free Tel:* 800-200-3552 *Web Site:* www.randomhousebooks.com, pg 181

Styler, Lori, The Barbara Hogenson Agency Inc, 165 West End Ave, Suite 19-C, New York, NY 10023 *Tel:* 212-874-8084 *Fax:* 212-595-6748 *E-mail:* bhogenson@aol.com, pg 489

Styles-Hunt, Katrina, Software & Information Industry Association (SIIA), 1090 Vermont Ave NW, 6th fl, Washington, DC 20005-4905 *Tel:* 202-289-7442 *Fax:* 202-289-7097 *Web Site:* www.siia.net, pg 547

Su, Esther, Fodor's Travel, 909 N Sepulveda Blvd, El Segundo, CA 90245 *E-mail:* marketing@fodors.com *Web Site:* www.fodors.com, pg 79

Suciu, Ioan, Georgetown University Press, 3520 Prospect St NW, Suite 140, Washington, DC 20007 *Tel:* 202-687-5889 (busn) *Fax:* 202-687-6340 (edit) *E-mail:* gupress@georgetown.edu *Web Site:* press.georgetown.edu, pg 85

Sugay, Eden, Chronicle Books, 680 Second St, San Francisco, CA 94107 *Tel:* 415-537-4200 *Toll Free Tel:* 800-759-0190 (cust serv) *Fax:* 415-537-4460 *Toll Free Fax:* 800-858-7787 (orders); 800-286-9471 (cust serv) *E-mail:* frontdesk@chroniclebooks.com *Web Site:* www.chroniclebooks.com, pg 52

Sugerman, Andrew, Disney Publishing Worldwide, 1101 Flower St, Glendale, CA 91201 *Web Site:* books.disney.com, pg 65

Sugihara, Kenichi, SelectBooks Inc, 325 W 38 St, Suite 306, New York, NY 10018 *Tel:* 212-206-1997 *Fax:* 212-206-3815 *E-mail:* info@selectbooks.com *Web Site:* www.selectbooks.com, pg 196

Sugihara, Kenzi, SelectBooks Inc, 325 W 38 St, Suite 306, New York, NY 10018 *Tel:* 212-206-1997 *Fax:* 212-206-3815 *E-mail:* info@selectbooks.com *Web Site:* www.selectbooks.com, pg 196

Suilebhan, Gwydion, PEN/Faulkner Award for Fiction, 201 E Capitol St SE, Washington, DC 20003 *Tel:* 202-898-9063 *Fax:* 202-675-0360 *Web Site:* www.penfaulkner.org, pg 653

Suilebhan, Gwydion, PEN/Malamud Award for Excellence in Short Fiction, 201 E Capitol St SE, Washington, DC 20003 *Tel:* 202-898-9063 *Fax:* 202-675-0360 *E-mail:* awards@penfaulkner.org; info@penfaulkner.org *Web Site:* www.penfaulkner.org/pen-malamud-award, pg 654

Suljic, Colleen, Princeton University Press, 41 William St, Princeton, NJ 08540-5237 *Tel:* 609-258-4900 *Fax:* 609-258-6305 *Web Site:* press.princeton.edu, pg 174

Sullivan, Derek, Hazy Dell Press, 1001 SE Water Ave, Suite 132, Portland, OR 97214 *Tel:* 971-279-5779 *E-mail:* info@hazydellpress.com *Web Site:* www.hazydellpress.com, pg 96

Sullivan, Drew, American Program Bureau Inc, One Gateway Center, Suite 751, Newton, MA 02458 *Tel:* 617-614-1600 *Fax:* 617-965-6610 *E-mail:* apb@apbspeakers.com *Web Site:* www.apbspeakers.com, pg 515

Sullivan, Kyle, Hazy Dell Press, 1001 SE Water Ave, Suite 132, Portland, OR 97214 *Tel:* 971-279-5779 *E-mail:* info@hazydellpress.com *Web Site:* www.hazydellpress.com, pg 96

Sullivan, Lisa, Harry S Truman Book Award, 5151 Troost Ave, Suite 300, Kansas City, MO 64110 *Tel:* 816-400-1212 *Toll Free Tel:* 844-358-5400 *Web Site:* trumanlibraryinstitute.org, pg 674

Sullivan, Margaret, University of Washington Press, 4333 Brooklyn Ave NE, Seattle, WA 98105-9570 *Tel:* 206-543-4050 *Toll Free Tel:* 800-537-5487 (orders) *Fax:* 206-543-3932; 410-516-6998 (orders) *E-mail:* uwapress@uw.edu *Web Site:* uwapress.uw.edu, pg 232

Sullivan, Mark, Franciscan Media, 28 W Liberty St, Cincinnati, OH 45202 *Tel:* 513-241-5615 *Toll Free Tel:* 800-488-0488 *E-mail:* admin@franciscanmedia.org *Web Site:* www.franciscanmedia.org, pg 81

Sullivan, Michaela, Houghton Mifflin Harcourt Trade & Reference Division, 125 High St, Boston, MA 02110 *Tel:* 617-351-5000 *Web Site:* www.hmhco.com, pg 104

Sullivan, Patrick, Tiller Press, 1230 Avenue of the Americas, New York, NY 10020, pg 218

Sullivan, Tim, University of California Press, 155 Grand Ave, Suite 400, Oakland, CA 94612-3758 *Tel:* 510-883-8232 *Fax:* 510-836-8910 *E-mail:* generalmailbox@ucpress.edu *Web Site:* www.ucpress.edu, pg 226

Summerfield, Mary, SPIE, 1000 20 St, Bellingham, WA 98225-6705 *Tel:* 360-676-3290 *Toll Free Tel:* 888-504-8171 (orders) *Fax:* 360-647-1445 *E-mail:* help@spie.org; customerservice@spie.org (orders) *Web Site:* www.spie.org, pg 205

Summerhays, Stephanie, Smithsonian Institution Scholarly Press, Aerospace Bldg, 704-A, MRC 957, Washington, DC 20013 *Tel:* 202-633-3017 *Fax:* 202-633-6877 *E-mail:* schol_press@si.edu *Web Site:* scholarlypress.si.edu, pg 202

Summers, Eric, STARbooks Press, PO Box 711612, Herndon, VA 20171 *E-mail:* publish@starbookspress.com; contact@starbookspress.com *Web Site:* www.starbookspress.com, pg 207

Summers, Shauna, Random House Publishing Group, 1745 Broadway, New York, NY 10019 *Toll Free Tel:* 800-200-3552 *Web Site:* www.randomhousebooks.com, pg 181

Sumner, Tom, Franklin, Beedle & Associates Inc, 2154 NE Broadway, Suite 100, Portland, OR 97232 *Tel:* 503-284-6348 *Toll Free Tel:* 800-322-2665 *Fax:* 503-625-4434 *Web Site:* www.fbeedle.com, pg 81

Sun, Amy, Viking, 375 Hudson St, New York, NY 10014 *Tel:* 212-366-2000 *Fax:* 212-243-6002 *Web Site:* www.penguin.com/publishers/vikingbooks, pg 236

Sun, Merry, Penguin Group USA, A Penguin Random House Company, 375 Hudson St, New York, NY 10014 *Tel:* 212-366-2000 *Toll Free Tel:* 800-847-5515 (inside sales); 800-631-8571 (cust serv) *Fax:* 212-366-

2666; 607-775-4829 (inside sales) *E-mail:* online@ us.penguingroup.com *Web Site:* www.penguin.com, pg 163

Sun, Merry, Portfolio, 375 Hudson St, New York, NY 10014 *Web Site:* www.penguin.com/meet/publishers/ portfolio, pg 172

Sundar, Stacey, Random House Children's Books, 1745 Broadway, 10th fl, New York, NY 10019 *Tel:* 212-782-9000 *Web Site:* www.randomhousekids.com, pg 181

Sundaram, Friederike, Stanford University Press, 425 Broadway St, Redwood City, CA 94063-3126 *Tel:* 650-723-9434 *Fax:* 650-725-3457 *E-mail:* info@ www.sup.org; publicity@www.sup.org; sales@www. sup.org *Web Site:* www.sup.org, pg 206

Sundstrom, Allison, Sourcebooks LLC, 1935 Brookdale Rd, Suite 139, Naperville, IL 60563 *Tel:* 630-961-3900 *Toll Free Tel:* 800-432-7444 *Fax:* 630-961-2168 *E-mail:* info@sourcebooks.com; customersupport@ sourcebooks.com *Web Site:* www.sourcebooks.com, pg 204

Supovitz, Elise, Candlewick Press, 99 Dover St, Somerville, MA 02144-2825 *Tel:* 617-661-3330 *Fax:* 617-661-0565 *E-mail:* bigbear@candlewick. com; salesinfo@candlewick.com *Web Site:* www. candlewick.com, pg 44

Sures, Jay, United Talent Agency, 9336 Civic Center Dr, Beverly Hills, CA 90210 *Tel:* 310-273-6700 *Fax:* 310-247-1111 *Web Site:* www.unitedtalent.com, pg 507

Surpin, Jacob, Parallax Press, 2236B Sixth St, Berkeley, CA 94710 *Tel:* 510-540-6411 *Toll Free Tel:* 800-863-5290 (orders) *Fax:* 510-981-1157 *Web Site:* www. parallax.org, pg 160

Sussman, Erica, HarperCollins Children's Books, 195 Broadway, New York, NY 10007 *Tel:* 212-207-7000 *Web Site:* www.harpercollins.com/childrens, pg 93

Sussman, Joni, Kar-Ben Publishing, 241 First Ave N, Minneapolis, MN 55401 *Tel:* 612-332-3344 *Toll Free Tel:* 800-4-KARBEN (452-7236) *Fax:* 612-332-7615 *Toll Free Fax:* 800-332-1132 *Web Site:* www.karben. com, pg 116

Sussman, Linda, Cold Spring Harbor Laboratory Press, One Bungtown Rd, Cold Spring Harbor, NY 11724 *Tel:* 516-422-4100 *Toll Free Tel:* 800-843-4388 *Fax:* 516-422-4097; 516-422-4092 (submissions) *E-mail:* cshpress@cshl.edu *Web Site:* www.cshlpress. com, pg 54

Sutherland, Kari, Bradford Literary Agency, 5694 Mission Center Rd, Suite 347, San Diego, CA 92108 *Tel:* 619-521-1201 *E-mail:* queries@bradfordlit.com *Web Site:* www.bradfordlit.com, pg 477

Sutherland, Victoria, Foreword's INDIES Awards, 413 E Eighth St, Traverse City, MI 49686 *Tel:* 231-933-3699 *Web Site:* www.forewordreviews.com, pg 616

Sutton, Caroline, Avery, 1745 Broadway, New York, NY 10019 *Tel:* 212-366-2000 *Fax:* 212-366-2636 *E-mail:* averypublicity@penguinrandomhouse.com *Web Site:* www.penguin.com/publishers/avery; www. penguinrandomhouse.com, pg 26

Sutton, Caroline, Penguin Group USA, A Penguin Random House Company, 375 Hudson St, New York, NY 10014 *Tel:* 212-366-2000 *Toll Free Tel:* 800-847-5515 (inside sales); 800-631-8571 (cust serv) *Fax:* 212-366-2666; 607-775-4829 (inside sales) *E-mail:* online@us.penguingroup.com *Web Site:* www. penguin.com, pg 163

Sutton, Roger, Boston Globe-Horn Book Award, c/o Book Reviews, The Horn Book Inc, Palace Road Bldg, 300 The Fenway, Suite P-311, Boston, MA 02115-5820 *Tel:* 617-278-0225 *Toll Free Tel:* 888-628-0225 *Fax:* 617-278-6062 *E-mail:* info@hbook.com *Web Site:* www.hbook.com, pg 600

Suvikapakornkul, Shane, Serindia Publications, PO Box 10335, Chicago, IL 60610-0335 *Fax:* 312-664-4389 *E-mail:* info@serindia.com *Web Site:* www.serindia. com, pg 196

Suzanne, Claudia, Wambtac Communications, 1512 E Santa Clara Ave, Santa Ana, CA 92705 *Tel:* 714-954-0580 *Toll Free Tel:* 800-641-3936 *E-mail:* wambtac@ wambtac.com *Web Site:* www.wambtac.com; claudiasuzanne.com (prof servs), pg 471

Svabek, Kaitlin, University of Wisconsin Press, 728 State St, Suite 443, Madison, WI 53706-1418 *Tel:* 608-263-1110; 608-263-0668 (journal orders) *Toll Free Tel:* 800-621-2736 (book orders) *Fax:* 608-263-1173 *Toll Free Fax:* 800-621-2736 (book orders) *E-mail:* uwiscpress@uwpress.wisc.edu *Web Site:* uwpress.wisc.edu, pg 232

Svehla, Gary, Midnight Marquee Press Inc, 9721 Britinay Lane, Baltimore, MD 21234 *Tel:* 410-665-1198 *E-mail:* mmarquee@aol.com *Web Site:* www. midmar.com, pg 139

Svehla, Susan, Midnight Marquee Press Inc, 9721 Britinay Lane, Baltimore, MD 21234 *Tel:* 410-665-1198 *E-mail:* mmarquee@aol.com *Web Site:* www. midmar.com, pg 139

Svetcov, Danielle, Levine|Greenberg|Rostan Literary Agency, 307 Seventh Ave, Suite 2407, New York, NY 10001 *Tel:* 212-337-0934 *Fax:* 212-337-0948 *Web Site:* lgrliterary.com, pg 493

Swail, David, Canadian Publishers' Council (CPC), 3080 Yonge St, Suite 6060, Toronto, ON M4N 3N1, Canada *Tel:* 647-255-8880 *Web Site:* pubcouncil.ca, pg 530

Swaim, Dennis, Viking, 375 Hudson St, New York, NY 10014 *Tel:* 212-366-2000 *Fax:* 212-243-6002 *Web Site:* www.penguin.com/publishers/vikingbooks, pg 236

Swain, Neal, Wales Literary Agency Inc, 1508 Tenth Ave E, No 401, Seattle, WA 98102 *Tel:* 206-284-7114 *E-mail:* waleslit@waleslit.com *Web Site:* www. waleslit.com, pg 507

Swann, Syreeta N, Association of American Publishers (AAP), 455 Massachusetts Ave NW, Suite 700, Washington, DC 20001-2777 *Tel:* 202-347-3375 *Fax:* 202-347-3690 *E-mail:* info@publishers.org *Web Site:* publishers.org, pg 526

Swanson, Haley, HarperCollins General Books Group, 195 Broadway, New York, NY 10007 *Tel:* 212-207-7000 *Web Site:* www.harpercollins.com, pg 93

Swanson, Hilary, HarperCollins General Books Group, 195 Broadway, New York, NY 10007 *Tel:* 212-207-7000 *Web Site:* www.harpercollins.com, pg 93

Swanson, Marit, Coffee House Press, 79 13 Ave NE, Suite 110, Minneapolis, MN 55413 *Tel:* 612-338-0125 *Fax:* 612-338-4004 *E-mail:* info@coffeehousepress.org *Web Site:* coffeehousepress.org, pg 54

Swanson, O'Ryin, Light Technology Publishing LLC, 4030 E Huntington Dr, Flagstaff, AZ 86004 *Tel:* 928-526-1345 *Toll Free Tel:* 800-450-0985 *Fax:* 928-714-1132 *E-mail:* publishing@lighttechnology.net *Web Site:* www.lighttechnology.com, pg 124

Swartz, Kristine, Berkley Publishing Group, 1745 Broadway, 19th fl, New York, NY 10019 *Tel:* 212-366-2000 *Web Site:* www.penguin.com, pg 32

Swauger, Amy, Teachers & Writers Collaborative, 540 Preston St, Booklyn, NY 11215 *Tel:* 212-691-6590 *Fax:* 212-675-0171 *E-mail:* info@twc.org *Web Site:* www.twc.org, pg 547

Swayze, Carolyn, Carolyn Swayze Literary Agency Ltd, 7360 137 St, Suite 319, Surrey, BC V3W 1A3, Canada *Tel:* 604-503-3895 *E-mail:* reception@ swayzeagency.com *Web Site:* www.swayzeagency.com, pg 505

Sweany, Brian, Recorded Books Inc, an RBmedia company, 270 Skipjack Rd, Prince Frederick, MD 20678 *Tel:* 410-535-5590 *Toll Free Tel:* 877-732-2898 *Fax:* 410-535-5499 *E-mail:* customerservice@ recordedbooks.com *Web Site:* www.recordedbooks. com, pg 182

Sweeney, Frances, PREP Publishing, 3528 Turnberry Circle, Fayetteville, NC 28303 *Tel:* 910-483-6611 *Toll Free Tel:* 800-533-2814 *E-mail:* preppub@aol.com *Web Site:* www.prep-pub.com, pg 173

Sweeney, Jillian, The Ned Leavitt Agency, 752 Creeklocks Rd, Rosendale, NY 12472 *Tel:* 845-658-3333 *Web Site:* www.nedleavittagency.com, pg 492

Sweeney, Katie, Fordham University Press, Joseph A Martino Hall, 45 Columbus Ave, New York, NY 10023 *Fax:* 347-842-3083 *Web Site:* www. fordhampress.com, pg 79

Sweeney, Nick, Bloomsbury Publishing Inc, 1385 Broadway, 5th fl, New York, NY 10018 *Tel:* 212-419-5300 *E-mail:* marketingusa@bloomsbury.com; adultpublicityusa@bloomsbury.com; askacademic@ bloomsbury.com *Web Site:* www.bloomsbury.com, pg 36

Sweeney, Renata, Tom Doherty Associates, LLC, 120 Broadway, New York, NY 10271 *Tel:* 646-307-5511 *Toll Free Tel:* 800-455-0340 *Web Site:* us.macmillan. com/torforge, pg 66

Sweeny, Caitlin, Simon & Schuster Children's Publishing, 1230 Avenue of the Americas, New York, NY 10020 *Tel:* 212-698-7000 *Web Site:* www. simonandschuster.com/kids; www.simonandschuster. com/teen; simonandschuster.net; simonandschuster.biz, pg 199

Sweetman, Marie, Wayne State University Press, Leonard N Simons Bldg, 4809 Woodward Ave, Detroit, MI 48201-1309 *Tel:* 313-577-6120 *Toll Free Tel:* 800-978-7323 *Fax:* 313-577-6131 *E-mail:* bookorders@wayne.edu *Web Site:* www. wsupress.wayne.edu, pg 238

Swensen, Evan, Publication Consultants, 8370 Eleusis Dr, Anchorage, AK 99502 *Tel:* 907-349-2424 *Fax:* 907-349-2426 *E-mail:* books@ publicationconsultants.com *Web Site:* www. publicationconsultants.com, pg 177

Swenson, Janine Y, LearningExpress, 224 W 29 St, 3rd fl, New York, NY 10001 *Toll Free Tel:* 800-295-9556 (ext 2) *Web Site:* learningexpresshub.com, pg 121

Sweren, Becky, Aevitas Creative Management, 19 W 21 St, Suite 501, New York, NY 10010 *Tel:* 212-765-6900 *Web Site:* aevitascreative.com, pg 474

Swetonic, Carrie, Penguin Group USA, A Penguin Random House Company, 375 Hudson St, New York, NY 10014 *Tel:* 212-366-2000 *Toll Free Tel:* 800-847-5515 (inside sales); 800-631-8571 (cust serv) *Fax:* 212-366-2666; 607-775-4829 (inside sales) *E-mail:* online@us.penguingroup.com *Web Site:* www. penguin.com, pg 163

Swift, Eliza, Sourcebooks LLC, 1935 Brookdale Rd, Suite 139, Naperville, IL 60563 *Tel:* 630-961-3900 *Toll Free Tel:* 800-432-7444 *Fax:* 630-961-2168 *E-mail:* info@sourcebooks.com; customersupport@ sourcebooks.com *Web Site:* www.sourcebooks.com, pg 204

Swink, Heather, Institute of Environmental Sciences & Technology - IEST, 1827 Walden Office Sq, Suite 400, Schaumburg, IL 60173 *Tel:* 847-981-0100 *Fax:* 847-981-4130 *E-mail:* information@iest.org *Web Site:* www.iest.org, pg 109

Swinwood, Craig, Harlequin Enterprises Ltd, Bay Adelaide Centre, East Tower, 22 Adelaide St W, 41st fl, Toronto, ON M5H 4E3, Canada *Tel:* 416-445-5860 *Toll Free Tel:* 888-432-4879; 800-370-5838 (ebook inquiries) *E-mail:* customerservice@harlequin.com *Web Site:* www.harlequin.com, pg 429

Swinwood, Craig, Love Inspired Books, 233 Broadway, Suite 1001, New York, NY 10279 *Tel:* 212-553-4200 *Toll Free Tel:* 888-432-4879 *Fax:* 212-227-8969 *E-mail:* customerservice@harlequin.ca *Web Site:* www. harlequin.com, pg 128

Swinwood, Susan, Harlequin Enterprises Ltd, Bay Adelaide Centre, East Tower, 22 Adelaide St W, 41st fl, Toronto, ON M5H 4E3, Canada *Tel:* 416-445-5860 *Toll Free Tel:* 888-432-4879; 800-370-5838 (ebook inquiries) *E-mail:* customerservice@harlequin.com *Web Site:* www.harlequin.com, pg 429

Swirsky, Jake, Macmillan, 120 Broadway, 22nd fl, New York, NY 10271 *Tel:* 646-307-5151 *E-mail:* press. inquiries@macmillan.com *Web Site:* www.macmillan. com, pg 130

Switzer, Kristi, Brewers Publications, 1327 Spruce St, Boulder, CO 80302 *Tel:* 303-447-0816 *Toll Free Tel:* 888-822-6273 (CN & US) *Fax:* 303-447-2825 *E-mail:* info@brewersassociation.org *Web Site:* www.brewersassociation.org, pg 40

Swope, Pamela K, Philosophy Documentation Center, PO Box 7147, Charlottesville, VA 22906-7147 *Tel:* 434-220-3300 *Toll Free Tel:* 800-444-2419 *Fax:* 434-220-3301 *E-mail:* order@pdcnet.org *Web Site:* www.pdcnet.org, pg 169

Sybert, Michelle, Indiana University Press, Herman B Wells Library 350, 1320 E Tenth St, Bloomington, IN 47405-3907 *Tel:* 812-855-8817 *Toll Free Tel:* 800-842-6796 (orders only) *Fax:* 812-855-7931; 812-855-8507 *E-mail:* iupress@indiana.edu; iuporder@indiana.edu (orders) *Web Site:* www.iupress.indiana.edu, pg 108

Sye, Stephen, ILA Children's & Young Adults' Book Awards, PO Box 8139, Newark, DE 19714-8139 *Tel:* 302-731-1600 *Toll Free Tel:* 800-336-7323 (US & CN) *Fax:* 302-731-1057 *E-mail:* ilaawards@reading.org *Web Site:* www.literacyworldwide.org, pg 625

Sylbert, John, American Institute for Economic Research (AIER), 250 Division St, Great Barrington, MA 01230 *Tel:* 413-528-1216 *Toll Free Tel:* 888-528-1216 (orders) *E-mail:* info@aier.org *Web Site:* www.aier.org, pg 11

Sylvan, Tanya, Menasha Ridge Press, 2204 First Ave S, Suite 102, Birmingham, AL 35233 *Toll Free Tel:* 888-604-4537 *Fax:* 205-326-1012 *E-mail:* info@adventurewithkeen.com *Web Site:* www.menasharidge.com; www.adventurewithkeen.com, pg 138

Sylve, Elvira C, Clotilde's Secretarial & Management Services, PO Box 871926, New Orleans, LA 70187 *Tel:* 504-242-2912 *E-mail:* elcsy58@att.net, pg 461

Symons, Alan, SAMS Technical Publishing LLC, 9850 E 30 St, Indianapolis, IN 46229 *Toll Free Tel:* 800-428-7267 *E-mail:* customercare@samswebsite.com *Web Site:* www.samswebsite.com, pg 191

Synatschk, Kathy, PRO-ED Inc, 8700 Shoal Creek Blvd, Austin, TX 78757-6897 *Tel:* 512-451-3246 *Toll Free Tel:* 800-897-3202 *Fax:* 512-451-8542 *Toll Free Fax:* 800-397-7633 *E-mail:* info@proedinc.com *Web Site:* www.proedinc.com, pg 175

Szczerban, Michael, Little, Brown and Company, 1290 Avenue of the Americas, New York, NY 10104 *Tel:* 212-364-1100 *Fax:* 212-364-0952 *E-mail:* firstname.lastname@hbgusa.com *Web Site:* www.littlebrown.com; www.hachettebookgroup.com, pg 125

Szekely, Meagan, Naval Institute Press, 291 Wood Rd, Annapolis, MD 21402-5034 *Tel:* 410-268-6110 *Toll Free Tel:* 800-233-8764 *Fax:* 410-295-1084; 410-571-1703 (cust serv) *E-mail:* webmaster@navalinstitute.org; customer@navalinstitute.org (cust serv) *Web Site:* www.nip.org; www.usni.org, pg 147

Szigeti, Helen, Society for Scholarly Publishing (SSP), 1120 Rte 73, Suite 200, Mount Laurel, NJ 08054 *Tel:* 856-439-1385 *Fax:* 856-439-0525 *E-mail:* info@sspnet.org *Web Site:* www.sspnet.org, pg 546

Szost, Bernadette, Portfolio Solutions LLC, 136 Jameson Hill Rd, Clinton Corners, NY 12514 *Tel:* 845-266-1001 *Web Site:* www.portfoliosolutionsllc.com, pg 512

Tackett, Jessica, Bloomsbury Academic, 1385 Broadway, 5th fl, New York, NY 10018 *Tel:* 212-419-5300 *Web Site:* www.bloomsbury.com/us/academic, pg 35

Tackett, Jessica, Princeton Architectural Press, 202 Warren St, Hudson, NY 12534 *Tel:* 518-671-6100 *Toll Free Tel:* 800-722-6657 (dist); 800-759-0190 (sales) *E-mail:* sales@papress.com *Web Site:* www.papress.com, pg 174

Tafolla, Carmen, Carr P Collins Award, PO Box 609, Round Rock, TX 78680 *Tel:* 512-683-5640 *E-mail:* president@texasinstituteofletters.org *Web Site:* www.texasinstituteofletters.org, pg 606

Tafolla, Carmen, Soeurette Diehl Fraser Translation Award, PO Box 609, Round Rock, TX 78680 *Tel:* 512-683-5640 *E-mail:* president@texasinstituteofletters.org *Web Site:* www.texasinstituteofletters.org, pg 617

Tafolla, Carmen, Jesse H Jones Award, PO Box 609, Round Rock, TX 78680 *Tel:* 512-683-5640 *E-mail:* president@texasinstituteofletters.org *Web Site:* www.texasinstituteofletters.org, pg 629

Tafolla, Carmen, Ramirez Family Award, PO Box 609, Round Rock, TX 78680 *Tel:* 512-683-5640 *E-mail:* president@texasinstituteofletters.org *Web Site:* www.texasinstituteofletters.org, pg 660

Tafolla, Carmen, Edwin "Bud" Shrake Award for Best Short Nonfiction, PO Box 609, Round Rock, TX 78680 *Tel:* 512-683-5640 *E-mail:* president@texasinstituteofletters.org *Web Site:* www.texasinstituteofletters.org, pg 667

Tafolla, Carmen, Helen C Smith Memorial Award, PO Box 609, Round Rock, TX 78680 *Tel:* 512-683-5640 *E-mail:* president@texasinstituteofletters.org *Web Site:* www.texasinstituteofletters.org, pg 668

Tafolla, Carmen, Texas Institute of Letters (TIL), PO Box 609, Round Rock, TX 78680 *E-mail:* president@texasinstituteofletters.org; secretary@texasinstituteofletters.org *Web Site:* www.texasinstituteofletters.org, pg 548

Tafolla, Carmen, Texas Institute of Letters Awards, PO Box 609, Round Rock, TX 78680 *Tel:* 512-683-5640 *E-mail:* president@texasinstituteofletters.org *Web Site:* www.texasinstituteofletters.org, pg 672

Tafura, Mariana, Editorial Unilit, 8167 NW 84 St, Medley, FL 33166 *Tel:* 305-592-6136 *Toll Free Tel:* 800-767-7726 *Fax:* 305-592-0087 *E-mail:* info@editorialunilit.com; customerservice@editorialunilit.com *Web Site:* www.editorialunilit.com, pg 224

Tager, Steve, Harry N Abrams Inc, 195 Broadway, 9th fl, New York, NY 10007 *Tel:* 212-206-7715 *Toll Free Tel:* 800-345-1359 *Fax:* 212-519-1210 *E-mail:* abrams@abramsbooks.com *Web Site:* www.abramsbooks.com, pg 3

Tahirkheli, Sharon, American Geosciences Institute (AGI), 4220 King St, Alexandria, VA 22302-1502 *Tel:* 703-379-2480 (ext 246) *Fax:* 703-379-7563 *E-mail:* agi@americangeosciences.org *Web Site:* www.americangeosciences.org, pg 11

Taillon, Peggy, Canadian Council on Social Development (Conseil canadien de developpement social), 190 O'Connor St, Suite 100, Ottawa, ON K2P 2R3, Canada *Tel:* 613-236-8977 *Fax:* 613-236-2750 *E-mail:* info@ccsd.ca *Web Site:* www.ccsd.ca, pg 418

Takes, Bill, Random House Publishing Group, 1745 Broadway, New York, NY 10019 *Toll Free Tel:* 800-200-3552 *Web Site:* www.randomhousebooks.com, pg 181

Takoudes, Emily, Phaidon, 65 Bleecker St, 8th fl, New York, NY 10012 *Tel:* 212-652-5400 *Toll Free Tel:* 800-759-0190 (cust serv) *Fax:* 212-652-5410 *Toll Free Tel:* 800-286-9471 (cust serv) *E-mail:* enquiries@phaidon.com *Web Site:* www.phaidon.com, pg 168

Talbot, Greg, The Lawbook Exchange Ltd, 33 Terminal Ave, Clark, NJ 07066-1321 *Tel:* 732-382-1800 *Toll Free Tel:* 800-422-6686 *Fax:* 732-382-1887 *E-mail:* law@lawbookexchange.com *Web Site:* www.lawbookexchange.com, pg 121

Talbot, Marieve, La Courte Echelle, 4388, rue Saint-Denis, Suite 315, Montreal, QC H2J 2L1, Canada *Tel:* 514-312-6950 *E-mail:* info@courteechelle.com *Web Site:* courteechelle.groupecourteechelle.com, pg 420

Tallberg, Anne Marie, St Martin's Press, LLC, 120 Broadway, New York, NY 10271 *Tel:* 646-307-5151 *Web Site:* us.macmillan.com/smp, pg 190

Tallie, Ekere, Chocorua Writing Workshop, PO Box 2280, Conway, NH 03818-2280 *Tel:* 603-447-2200 *E-mail:* reservations@worldfellowship.org *Web Site:* www.worldfellowship.org; www.facebook.com/World.Fellowship.Center, pg 574

Tallon, Dr Andrew, Marquette University Press, 1415 W Wisconsin Ave, Milwaukee, WI 53233 *Tel:* 414-288-1564 *Fax:* 414-288-7813 *Web Site:* www.marquette.edu/mupress, pg 132

Tamar, Rima, Dharma Publishing, 35788 Hauser Bridge Rd, Cazadero, CA 95421 *Tel:* 707-847-3717 *Fax:* 707-847-3380 *E-mail:* contact@dharmapublishing.com *Web Site:* www.dharmapublishing.com, pg 64

Tamberino, Claire McCabe, Johns Hopkins University Press, 2715 N Charles St, Baltimore, MD 21218-4363 *Tel:* 410-516-6900; 410-516-6987 (journal orders outside US & CN) *Toll Free Tel:* 800-537-5487 (book orders & cust serv); 800-548-1784 (journal orders) *Fax:* 410-516-6968; 410-516-3866 (journal orders); 410-516-6998 (orders) *E-mail:* hfscustserv@press.jhu.edu (cust serv); jrnlcirc@press.jhu.edu (journal orders) *Web Site:* www.press.jhu.edu; muse.jhu.edu, pg 114

Tamminen, Suzanna L, Wesleyan University Press, 215 Long Lane, Middletown, CT 06459-0433 *Tel:* 860-685-7712 *Fax:* 860-685-7712 *Web Site:* www.wesleyan.edu/wespress, pg 239

Tan, Alicia, HarperCollins General Books Group, 195 Broadway, New York, NY 10007 *Tel:* 212-207-7000 *Web Site:* www.harpercollins.com, pg 93

Tan, Cecilia, Circlet Press, 39 Hurlbut St, Cambridge, MA 02138 *Toll Free Tel:* 800-729-6423 *E-mail:* customerservice@riverdaleavebooks.com *Web Site:* www.circlet.com, pg 52

Tanenbaum, Jill, Casemate | publishers, 1950 Lawrence Rd, Havertown, PA 19083 *Tel:* 610-853-9131 *Fax:* 610-853-9146 *E-mail:* casemate@casematepublishers.com *Web Site:* www.casematepublishers.com, pg 46

Tang, Adrienne, Kids Can Press Ltd, 25 Dockside Dr, Toronto, ON M5A 0B5, Canada *Tel:* 416-479-7000 *Toll Free Tel:* 800-265-0884 *Fax:* 416-960-5437 *E-mail:* info@kidscan.com; customerservice@kidscan.com *Web Site:* www.kidscanpress.com; www.kidscanpress.ca, pg 431

Tang, Albert, Grand Central Publishing, 1290 Avenue of the Americas, New York, NY 10104 *Tel:* 212-364-1100 *Web Site:* www.hachettebookgroup.com, pg 88

Tank, David, Planert Creek Press, E4843 395 Ave, Menomonie, WI 54751 *Tel:* 715-235-4110 *E-mail:* publisher@planertcreekpress.com *Web Site:* www.planertcreekpress.com, pg 170

Tannenbaum, Amy, Jane Rotrosen Agency LLC, 85 Broad St, 28th fl, New York, NY 10004 *Tel:* 212-593-4330 *Fax:* 212-935-6985 *Web Site:* janerotrosen.com, pg 500

Tanner, Annette K, Michigan State University Press (MSU Press), Manly Miles Bldg, Suite 25, 1405 S Harrison Rd, East Lansing, MI 48823-5245 *Tel:* 517-355-9543 *Fax:* 517-432-2611 *Web Site:* msupress.org, pg 139

Tanselle, G Thomas, Bibliographical Society of the University of Virginia, c/o Alderman Library, University of Virginia, McCormick Rd, Charlottesville, VA 22904 *Tel:* 434-924-7013 *Fax:* 434-924-1431 *E-mail:* bibsoc@virginia.edu *Web Site:* bsuva.org, pg 528

Tanzer, Steven, TripBuilder Media Inc, 180 Post Rd E, Suite 200, Westport, CT 06880 *Tel:* 203-227-1255 *Toll Free Tel:* 800-525-9745 *Fax:* 203-227-1257 *E-mail:* info@tripbuildermedia.com *Web Site:* www.tripbuildermedia.com, pg 220

Tapia, Miguel A, Santillana USA Publishing Co, 2023 NW 84 Ave, Doral, FL 33122 *Tel:* 305-591-9522 *Toll Free Tel:* 800-245-8584 *E-mail:* customerservice@santillanausa.com *Web Site:* www.santillanausa.com, pg 192

Tapp, Stephen, Institute for Research on Public Policy (IRPP), 1470 Peel St, No 200, Montreal, QC H3A 1T1, Canada *Tel:* 514-985-2461 *Fax:* 514-985-2559 *E-mail:* irpp@irpp.org *Web Site:* irpp.org, pg 430

Tappe, Christian, TAN Books, PO Box 269, Gastonia, NC 28053 *Tel:* 704-731-0651 *Toll Free Tel:* 800-437-5876 *Fax:* 815-226-7770 *E-mail:* customerservice@tanbooks.com *Web Site:* www.tanbooks.com, pg 212

Tapscott, Eleanore, National Council of Teachers of Mathematics (NCTM), 1906 Association Dr, Reston, VA 20191-1502 *Tel:* 703-620-9840 *Toll Free Tel:* 800-235-7566 *Fax:* 703-476-2970 *E-mail:* nctm@nctm.org *Web Site:* www.nctm.org, pg 146

Tarsky, Sue, Albert Whitman & Co, 250 S Northwest Hwy, Suite 320, Park Ridge, IL 60068 *Tel:* 847-232-2800 *Toll Free Tel:* 800-255-7675 *Fax:* 847-581-0039 *E-mail:* mail@albertwhitman.com *Web Site:* www.albertwhitman.com, pg 6

Tart, Brian, Penguin Books, 375 Hudson St, New York, NY 10014 *Tel:* 212-366-2000 *E-mail:* penguinpublicity@us.penguingroup.com *Web Site:* www.penguinclassics.com; www.penguin.com, pg 163

Tart, Brian, Penguin Group USA, A Penguin Random House Company, 375 Hudson St, New York, NY 10014 *Tel:* 212-366-2000 *Toll Free Tel:* 800-847-5515 (inside sales); 800-631-8571 (cust serv) *Fax:* 212-366-2666; 607-775-4829 (inside sales) *E-mail:* online@us.penguingroup.com *Web Site:* www.penguin.com, pg 163

Tart, Brian, Viking, 375 Hudson St, New York, NY 10014 *Tel:* 212-366-2000 *Fax:* 212-243-6002 *Web Site:* www.penguin.com/publishers/vikingbooks, pg 236

Tart, Brian, Viking Studio, 375 Hudson St, New York, NY 10014 *Tel:* 212-366-2000 *Fax:* 212-366-2636 *E-mail:* averystudiopublicity@us.penguingroup.com *Web Site:* www.penguin.com, pg 236

Tart, David, Kendall Hunt Publishing Co, 4050 Westmark Dr, Dubuque, IA 52002-2624 *Tel:* 563-589-1000 *Toll Free Tel:* 800-228-0810 (orders) *Fax:* 563-589-1046 *Toll Free Fax:* 800-772-9165 *E-mail:* orders@kendallhunt.com *Web Site:* www.kendallhunt.com, pg 116

Tasman, Alice, Jean V Naggar Literary Agency Inc (JVNLA), 216 E 75 St, Suite 1-E, New York, NY 10021 *Tel:* 212-794-1082 *E-mail:* jvnla@jvnla.com *Web Site:* www.jvnla.com, pg 497

Tasse, Nathalie, Les Editions XYZ inc, 1815, ave De Lorimier, Montreal, QC H2K 3W6, Canada *Tel:* 514-525-2170 *Fax:* 514-525-7537 *E-mail:* info@editionsxyz.com *Web Site:* www.editionsxyz.com, pg 425

Tassin, Margaret, Business Forms Management Association (BFMA), 1147 Fleetwood Ave, Madison, WI 53716-1417 *Toll Free Tel:* 888-367-3078 *E-mail:* bfma@bfma.org *Web Site:* www.bfma.org, pg 529

Tate, Ben, Princeton University Press, 41 William St, Princeton, NJ 08540-5237 *Tel:* 609-258-4900 *Fax:* 609-258-6305 *Web Site:* press.princeton.edu, pg 174

Tate, Lori, Teachers College Press, 1234 Amsterdam Ave, New York, NY 10027 *Tel:* 212-678-3929 *Fax:* 212-678-4149 *E-mail:* tcpress@tc.edu *Web Site:* www.tcpress.com, pg 214

Taub, Daniel, National Association of Real Estate Editors (NAREE), 1003 NW Sixth Terr, Boca Raton, FL 33486-3455 *Tel:* 561-391-3599 *Fax:* 561-391-0099 *Web Site:* www.naree.org, pg 539

Tauber, Mark, Chronicle Books, 680 Second St, San Francisco, CA 94107 *Tel:* 415-537-4200 *Toll Free Tel:* 800-759-0190 (cust serv) *Fax:* 415-537-4460 *Toll Free Fax:* 800-858-7787 (orders); 800-286-9471 (cust serv) *E-mail:* frontdesk@chroniclebooks.com *Web Site:* www.chroniclebooks.com, pg 51

Taurino, Giuseppe, University of Houston Creative Writing Program, 229 Roy Cullen Bldg, Houston, TX 77204-5008 *Tel:* 713-743-2255 *Fax:* 713-743-3697 pg 586

Taussig, Olivia, Viking, 375 Hudson St, New York, NY 10014 *Tel:* 212-366-2000 *Fax:* 212-243-6002 *Web Site:* www.penguin.com/publishers/vikingbooks, pg 236

Tavani, Mark, GP Putnam's Sons (Hardcover), 375 Hudson St, New York, NY 10014 *Tel:* 212-366-2000 *Fax:* 212-366-2643 *E-mail:* online@penguinputnam.com *Web Site:* www.penguin.com/publishers/gpputnamssons, pg 178

Taveras, Rafael, Simon & Schuster, 1230 Avenue of the Americas, New York, NY 10020 *Tel:* 212-698-7000 *Toll Free Tel:* 800-223-2348 (cust serv); 800-223-2336 (orders) *Toll Free Fax:* 800-943-9831 (orders) *Web Site:* www.simonandschuster.com, pg 198

Tavolacci, Joyce, Bearport Publishing Co Inc, 45 W 21 St, Suite 3B, New York, NY 10010 *Tel:* 212-337-8577 *Toll Free Tel:* 877-337-8577 *Fax:* 212-337-8557 *Toll Free Fax:* 866-337-8557 *E-mail:* service@bearportpublishing.com; info@bearportpublishing.com *Web Site:* www.bearportpublishing.com, pg 30

Taylor, Brent, TriadaUS Literary Agency, PO Box 561, Sewickley, PA 15143 *Tel:* 412-401-3376 *Web Site:* www.triadaus.com, pg 506

Taylor, Carolyn Stanford, Wisconsin Department of Public Instruction, 125 S Webster St, Madison, WI 53703 *Tel:* 608-266-2188 *Toll Free Tel:* 800-441-4563 (US only); 800-243-8782 (US only) *E-mail:* pubsales@dpi.wi.gov *Web Site:* pubsales.dpi.wi.gov, pg 243

Taylor, Dhyana, 5 Under 35, 90 Broad St, Suite 604, New York, NY 10004 *Tel:* 212-685-0261 *Fax:* 212-213-6570 *E-mail:* nationalbook@nationalbook.org *Web Site:* www.nationalbook.org, pg 616

Taylor, Dhyana, Innovations in Reading Prize, 90 Broad St, Suite 604, New York, NY 10004 *Tel:* 212-685-0261 *Fax:* 212-213-6570 *E-mail:* nationalbook@nationalbook.org *Web Site:* www.nationalbook.org/innovations_in_reading, pg 627

Taylor, Dhyana, Medal for Distinguished Contribution to American Letters, 90 Broad St, Suite 604, New York, NY 10004 *Tel:* 212-685-0261 *Fax:* 212-213-6570 *E-mail:* nationalbook@nationalbook.org *Web Site:* www.nationalbook.org/amerletters.html, pg 640

Taylor, Dhyana, National Book Awards, 90 Broad St, Suite 604, New York, NY 10004 *Tel:* 212-685-0261 *Fax:* 212-213-6570 *E-mail:* nationalbook@nationalbook.org *Web Site:* www.nationalbook.org, pg 644

Taylor, Dhyana, National Book Foundation, 90 Broad St, Suite 604, New York, NY 10004 *Tel:* 212-685-0261 *Fax:* 212-213-6570 *E-mail:* nationalbook@nationalbook.org *Web Site:* www.nationalbook.org, pg 551

Taylor, Joe, Livingston Press, University of West Alabama, Sta 22, Livingston, AL 35470 *Tel:* 205-652-3470 *Web Site:* www.livingstonpress.uwa.edu, pg 127

Taylor, Justin, Crossway, 1300 Crescent St, Wheaton, IL 60187 *Tel:* 630-682-4300 *Toll Free Tel:* 800-635-7993 (orders); 800-543-1659 (cust serv) *Fax:* 630-682-4785 *E-mail:* info@crossway.org *Web Site:* www.crossway.org, pg 60

Taylor, Keith, Page Davidson Clayton Prize for Emerging Poets, University of Michigan, 0576 Rackham Bldg, 915 E Washington St, Ann Arbor, MI 48109-1070 *Tel:* 734-764-9265 *E-mail:* mqr@umich.edu *Web Site:* sites.lsa.umich.edu/mqr/, pg 605

Taylor, Keith, Laurence Goldstein Poetry Prize, University of Michigan, 0576 Rackham Bldg, 915 E Washington St, Ann Arbor, MI 48109-1070 *Tel:* 734-764-9265 *E-mail:* mqr@umich.edu *Web Site:* sites.lsa.umich.edu/mqr/, pg 620

Taylor, Marci, American Press, 60 State St, Suite 700, Boston, MA 02109 *Tel:* 617-247-0022 *E-mail:* americanpress@flash.net *Web Site:* www.americanpresspublishers.net, pg 13

Taylor, Mark, Tyndale House Publishers Inc, 351 Executive Dr, Carol Stream, IL 60188 *Tel:* 630-668-8300 *Toll Free Tel:* 800-323-9400; 855-277-9400 *Toll Free Fax:* 866-622-9474 *Web Site:* www.tyndale.com, pg 223

Taylor, Matt, Princeton University Press, 41 William St, Princeton, NJ 08540-5237 *Tel:* 609-258-4900 *Fax:* 609-258-6305 *Web Site:* press.princeton.edu, pg 175

Taylor, Natasha, Macmillan, 120 Broadway, 22nd fl, New York, NY 10271 *Tel:* 646-307-5151 *E-mail:* press.inquiries@macmillan.com *Web Site:* www.macmillan.com, pg 130

Taylor, Nathan, Stephen Leacock Memorial Medal for Humour, 149 Peter St N, Orillia, ON L3V 4Z4, Canada *Tel:* 705-326-9286 *Web Site:* www.leacock.ca, pg 632

Taylor, Ray, Franciscan Media, 28 W Liberty St, Cincinnati, OH 45202 *Tel:* 513-241-5615 *Toll Free Tel:* 800-488-0488 *E-mail:* admin@franciscanmedia.org *Web Site:* www.franciscanmedia.org, pg 81

Taylor, Robert PhD, Institute of Public Administration of Canada, 1075 Bay St, Suite 401, Toronto, ON M5S 2B1, Canada *Tel:* 416-924-8787 *Fax:* 416-924-4992 *E-mail:* ntl@ipac.ca *Web Site:* www.ipac.ca, pg 430

Taylor, Sara, Dumbarton Oaks, 1703 32 St NW, Washington, DC 20007 *Tel:* 202-339-6400 *Fax:* 202-339-6401; 202-298-8407 *E-mail:* doaksbooks@doaks.org; press@doaks.org *Web Site:* www.doaks.org, pg 68

Taylor, Yuval, Chicago Review Press, 814 N Franklin St, Chicago, IL 60610 *Tel:* 312-337-0747 *Toll Free Tel:* 800-888-4741 *Fax:* 312-337-5110 *E-mail:* frontdesk@chicagoreviewpress.com *Web Site:* www.chicagoreviewpress.com, pg 50

Tayman, William P Jr, Corporation for Public Broadcasting (CPB), 401 Ninth St NW, Washington, DC 20004-2129 *Tel:* 202-879-9600 *Web Site:* www.cpb.org, pg 531

Teeple, Charlotte, Marilyn Baillie Picture Book Award, 40 Orchard View Blvd, Suite 217, Toronto, ON M4R 1B9, Canada *Tel:* 416-975-0010 *Fax:* 416-975-8970 *E-mail:* info@bookcentre.ca *Web Site:* www.bookcentre.ca, pg 595

Teeple, Charlotte, The Geoffrey Bilson Award for Historical Fiction for Young People, 40 Orchard View Blvd, Suite 217, Toronto, ON M4R 1B9, Canada *Tel:* 416-975-0010 *Fax:* 416-975-8970 *E-mail:* info@bookcentre.ca *Web Site:* www.bookcentre.ca, pg 598

Teeple, Charlotte, Canadian Children's Book Centre, 40 Orchard View Blvd, Suite 217, Toronto, ON M4R 1B9, Canada *Tel:* 416-975-0010 *Fax:* 416-975-8970 *E-mail:* info@bookcentre.ca *Web Site:* www.bookcentre.ca, pg 530

Teeple, Charlotte, Norma Fleck Award for Canadian Children's Non-Fiction, 40 Orchard View Blvd, Suite 217, Toronto, ON M4R 1B9, Canada *Tel:* 416-975-0010 *Fax:* 416-975-8970 *E-mail:* info@bookcentre.ca *Web Site:* www.bookcentre.ca, pg 616

Teeple, Charlotte, Amy Mathers Teen Book Award, 40 Orchard View Blvd, Suite 217, Toronto, ON M4R 1B9, Canada *Tel:* 416-975-0010 *Fax:* 416-975-8970 *E-mail:* info@bookcentre.ca *Web Site:* www.bookcentre.ca, pg 639

Teeple, Charlotte, John Spray Mystery Award, 40 Orchard View Blvd, Suite 217, Toronto, ON M4R 1B9, Canada *Tel:* 416-975-0010 *Fax:* 416-975-8970 *E-mail:* info@bookcentre.ca *Web Site:* www.bookcentre.ca, pg 669

Teeple, Charlotte, TD Canadian Children's Literature Award, 40 Orchard View Blvd, Suite 217, Toronto, ON M4R 1B9, Canada *Tel:* 416-975-0010 *Fax:* 416-975-8970 *E-mail:* info@bookcentre.ca *Web Site:* www.bookcentre.ca, pg 672

Tegen, Katherine, HarperCollins Children's Books, 195 Broadway, New York, NY 10007 *Tel:* 212-207-7000 *Web Site:* www.harpercollins.com/childrens, pg 93

Teixeira, Ian, Fine Creative Media, Inc, 589 Eighth Ave, 6th fl, New York, NY 10018 *Tel:* 212-595-3500 *Fax:* 212-202-4195 *E-mail:* info@mjfbooks.com *Web Site:* www.mjfbooks.com, pg 78

Telfer, Mekisha, Roaring Brook Press, 120 Broadway, New York, NY 10271 *Tel:* 646-307-5151 *Web Site:* us.macmillan.com/publishers/roaring-brook-press, pg 186

Tell, David, Hudson Institute, 1201 Pennsylvania Ave NW, Suite 400, Washington, DC 20004 *Tel:* 202-974-2400 *Fax:* 202-974-2410 *E-mail:* info@hudson.org *Web Site:* www.hudson.org, pg 104

Tell, Geoffery Crawford, Two Thousand Three Associates, 135 Chilean Ave, Palm Beach, FL 33480 *Tel:* 386-690-2503 *E-mail:* tttta1@att.net *Web Site:* www.twothousandthree.com, pg 223

Temescu, Max, Harry N Abrams Inc, 195 Broadway, 9th fl, New York, NY 10007 *Tel:* 212-206-7715 *Toll Free Tel:* 800-345-1359 *Fax:* 212-519-1210 *E-mail:* abrams@abramsbooks.com *Web Site:* www.abramsbooks.com, pg 3

Tempest, Nephele, The Knight Agency Inc, 232 W Washington St, Madison, GA 30650 *E-mail:* admin@knightagency.net *Web Site:* www.knightagency.net, pg 491

Tempio, Robert, Princeton University Press, 41 William St, Princeton, NJ 08540-5237 *Tel:* 609-258-4900 *Fax:* 609-258-6305 *Web Site:* press.princeton.edu, pg 174

Templar, Kate, Stanford University Press, 425 Broadway St, Redwood City, CA 94063-3126 *Tel:* 650-723-9434 *Fax:* 650-725-3457 *E-mail:* info@www.sup.org; publicity@www.sup.org; sales@www.sup.org *Web Site:* www.sup.org, pg 206

Temple, John F, Guideposts Book & Inspirational Media, 110 William St, Suite 901, New York, NY 10038 *Tel:* 212-251-8100 *Toll Free Tel:* 800-932-2145 (cust serv) *Fax:* 212-587-4282 *E-mail:* gpsprod@cdsfulfillment.com *Web Site:* guideposts.org, pg 90

Temple, Johnny, Akashic Books, 232 Third St, Suite A-115, Brooklyn, NY 11215 *Tel:* 718-643-9193 *Fax:* 718-643-9195 *E-mail:* info@akashicbooks.com *Web Site:* www.akashicbooks.com, pg 6

Temple, Karyn, Motion Picture Association of America Inc (MPAA), 1301 "K" St NE, Suite 900E, Washington, DC 20005 *Tel:* 202-293-1966 *Fax:* 202-296-7410 *E-mail:* contactus@mpaa.org *Web Site:* www.mpaa.org, pg 538

Temple, Sam, North Star Editions Inc, 2297 Waters Dr, Mendota Heights, MN 55120 *Tel:* 651-204-3515 *Toll Free Tel:* 888-417-0195 *Fax:* 952-582-1000 *E-mail:* sales@northstareditions.com *Web Site:* www.northstareditions.com, pg 152

Temple, Travis, Penguin Random House LLC, 1745 Broadway, New York, NY 10019 *Tel:* 212-782-9000 *Toll Free Tel:* 800-726-0600 *Web Site:* www.penguinrandomhouse.com, pg 164

Tenaglia, Lisa, Perseus Books, 1290 Avenue of the Americas, New York, NY 10104 *Tel:* 212-340-8100 *Toll Free Tel:* 800-343-4499 (cust serv) *Fax:* 212-340-8105 *Web Site:* www.perseusbooks.com, pg 167

Tepper, Michael, Genealogical Publishing Co, 3600 Clipper Mill Rd, Suite 229, Baltimore, MD 21211 *Tel:* 410-837-8271 *Toll Free Tel:* 800-296-6687 *Fax:* 410-752-8492 *Toll Free Fax:* 800-99-9561 *E-mail:* info@genealogical.com; web@genealogical.com *Web Site:* www.genealogical.com, pg 84

Terfloth, Caitlin, The Summer Experience, 1831 College Ave, Suite 324, Regina, SK S4P 4V5, Canada *Tel:* 306-537-7243 *E-mail:* sage.hill@sasktel.net *Web Site:* www.sagehillwriting.ca, pg 579

Terraciano, Kevin, UCLA Latin American Center Publications, UCLA Latin American Institute, 10343 Bunche Hall, Los Angeles, CA 90095 *Tel:* 310-825-4571 *Fax:* 310-206-6859 *E-mail:* latinamctr@international.ucla.edu *Web Site:* www.international.ucla.edu/lai, pg 223

Terragni, Emilia, Phaidon, 65 Bleecker St, 8th fl, New York, NY 10012 *Tel:* 212-652-5400 *Toll Free Tel:* 800-759-0190 (cust serv) *Fax:* 212-652-5410 *Toll Free Fax:* 800-286-9471 (cust serv) *E-mail:* enquiries@phaidon.com *Web Site:* www.phaidon.com, pg 168

Terrell, Guy, Laura Day Boggs Bolling Memorial, 900 Timber Creek Place, Virginia Beach, VA 23464 *E-mail:* poetryinva@aol.com *Web Site:* poetrysocietyofvirginia.org, pg 600

Terrell, Guy, Joe Pendleton Campbell Narrative Contest, 900 Timber Creek Place, Virginia Beach, VA 23464 *E-mail:* poetryinva@aol.com *Web Site:* poetrysocietyofvirginia.org, pg 602

Terrell, Guy, Carleton Drewry Memorial, 900 Timber Creek Place, Virginia Beach, VA 23464 *E-mail:* poetryinva@aol.com *Web Site:* poetrysocietyofvirginia.org, pg 611

Terrell, Guy, Alfred C Gary Memorial, 900 Timber Creek Place, Virginia Beach, VA 23464 *E-mail:* poetryinva@aol.com *Web Site:* poetrysocietyofvirginia.org, pg 618

Terrell, Guy, Bess Gresham Memorial, 900 Timber Creek Place, Virginia Beach, VA 23464 *E-mail:* poetryinva@aol.com *Web Site:* poetrysocietyofvirginia.org, pg 621

Terrell, Guy, Loretta Dunn Hall Memorial, 900 Timber Creek Place, Virginia Beach, VA 23464 *E-mail:* poetryinva@aol.com *Web Site:* poetrysocietyofvirginia.org, pg 622

Terrell, Guy, Handy Andy Prize, 900 Timber Creek Place, Virginia Beach, VA 23464 *E-mail:* poetryinva@aol.com *Web Site:* poetrysocietyofvirginia.org, pg 622

Terrell, Guy, Brodie Herndon Memorial, 900 Timber Creek Place, Virginia Beach, VA 23464 *E-mail:* poetryinva@aol.com *Web Site:* poetrysocietyofvirginia.org, pg 623

Terrell, Guy, Judah, Sarah, Grace & Tom Memorial, 900 Timber Creek Place, Virginia Beach, VA 23464 *E-mail:* poetryinva@aol.com; info@poetryvirginia.org *Web Site:* poetrysocietyofvirginia.org, pg 629

Terrell, Guy, Cenie H Moon Prize, 900 Timber Creek Place, Virginia Beach, VA 23464 *E-mail:* poetryinva@aol.com *Web Site:* poetrysocietyofvirginia.org, pg 643

Terrell, Guy, Edgar Allan Poe Memorial, 900 Timber Creek Place, Virginia Beach, VA 23464 *E-mail:* poetryinva@aol.com *Web Site:* poetrysocietyofvirginia.org, pg 657

Terrell, Guy, Miriam Rachimi Memorial, 900 Timber Creek Place, Virginia Beach, VA 23464 *E-mail:* poetryinva@aol.com *Web Site:* poetrysocietyofvirginia.org, pg 660

Terrell, Guy, Ada Sanderson Memorial, 900 Timber Creek Place, Virginia Beach, VA 23464 *E-mail:* poetryinva@aol.com *Web Site:* poetrysocietyofvirginia.org, pg 664

Terrell, Guy, The Robert S Sergeant Memorial, 900 Timber Creek Place, Virginia Beach, VA 23464 *E-mail:* poetryinva@aol.com *Web Site:* poetrysocietyofvirginia.org, pg 666

Terry, Barbara, Waldorf Publishing, 2140 Hall Johnson Rd, No 102-345, Grapevine, TX 76051 *Tel:* 972-674-3131 *E-mail:* info@waldorfpublishing.com *Web Site:* www.waldorfpublishing.com, pg 237

Tesoro, Marisa, Princeton Architectural Press, 202 Warren St, Hudson, NY 12534 *Tel:* 518-671-6100 *Toll Free Tel:* 800-722-6657 (dist); 800-759-0190 (sales) *E-mail:* sales@papress.com *Web Site:* www.papress.com, pg 174

Tessier, Michel, Les Editions Vents d'Ouest, 109, rue Wright, bureau 202, Gatineau, QC J8X 2G7, Canada *Tel:* 819-770-6377 *E-mail:* info@ventsdouest.ca *Web Site:* www.ventsdouest.ca, pg 425

Tessler, Michelle, Tessler Literary Agency LLC, 27 W 20 St, Suite 1003, New York, NY 10011 *Tel:* 212-242-0466 *Web Site:* www.tessleragency.com, pg 506

Thackara, Will, Theosophical University Press, PO Box C, Pasadena, CA 91109-7107 *Tel:* 626-798-3378 *E-mail:* tupress@theosociety.org *Web Site:* www.theosociety.org, pg 217

Thacker, Erin, Chronicle Books, 680 Second St, San Francisco, CA 94107 *Tel:* 415-537-4200 *Toll Free Tel:* 800-759-0190 (cust serv) *Fax:* 415-537-4460 *Toll Free Fax:* 800-858-7787 (orders); 800-286-9471 (cust serv) *E-mail:* frontdesk@chroniclebooks.com *Web Site:* www.chroniclebooks.com, pg 51

Tharcher, Nicholas, The Original Falcon Press, 1753 E Broadway Rd, No 101-277, Tempe, AZ 85282 *Tel:* 602-708-1409 *E-mail:* info@originalfalcon.com *Web Site:* www.originalfalcon.com, pg 157

Tharp, Brent D, Atlas Publishing, 25185 Madison Ave, Suite A, Murrieta, CA 92562 *Tel:* 858-222-3747 *E-mail:* permissions@atlaspublishing.biz *Web Site:* www.atlaspublishing.biz, pg 24

Tharpe, Arthur, Business Marketing Association (BMA), 708 Third Ave, New York, NY 10017 *Tel:* 212-697-5950 *Fax:* 212-687-7310 *E-mail:* info@marketing.org *Web Site:* www.marketing.org, pg 529

Thatcher, Rachael, Adams Media, 57 Littlefield St, Avon, MA 02322 *Tel:* 508-427-7100 *Web Site:* www.simonandschuster.com, pg 4

Thaw, Deborah M, National Notary Association (NNA), 9350 De Soto Ave, Chatsworth, CA 91311-4926 *Tel:* 818-739-4000 *Toll Free Tel:* 800-876-6827 *Toll Free Fax:* 800-833-1211 *E-mail:* services@nationalnotary.org *Web Site:* www.nationalnotary.org, pg 147

Thayer, Henry, Brandt & Hochman Literary Agents Inc, 1501 Broadway, Suite 2310, New York, NY 10036 *Tel:* 212-840-5760 *Fax:* 212-840-5776 *Web Site:* brandthochman.com, pg 477

Thegeby, Sarah, Dutton, 1745 Broadway, New York, NY 10019 *Tel:* 212-366-2000 *Fax:* 212-366-2262 *E-mail:* duttonpublicity@us.penguingroup.com *Web Site:* www.penguin.com, pg 68

Thelander, Jessica, Sourcebooks LLC, 1935 Brookdale Rd, Suite 139, Naperville, IL 60563 *Tel:* 630-961-3900 *Toll Free Tel:* 800-432-7444 *Fax:* 630-961-2168 *E-mail:* info@sourcebooks.com; customersupport@sourcebooks.com *Web Site:* www.sourcebooks.com, pg 204

Theophilus, Gayna, Annick Press Ltd, 15 Patricia Ave, Toronto, ON M2M 1H9, Canada *Tel:* 416-221-4802 *Fax:* 416-221-8400 *E-mail:* annickpress@annickpress.com *Web Site:* www.annickpress.com, pg 415

Theroux, David J, Independent Institute, 100 Swan Way, Suite 200, Oakland, CA 94621-1428 *Tel:* 510-632-1366 *Toll Free Tel:* 800-927-8733 *Fax:* 510-568-6040 *E-mail:* orders@independent.org *Web Site:* www.independent.org, pg 107

Thickstun, Margaret, Hamilton College, English/Creative Writing, English/Creative Writing Dept, 198 College Hill Rd, Clinton, NY 13323 *Tel:* 315-859-4370 *Fax:* 315-859-4390 *Web Site:* www.hamilton.edu, pg 583

Thielen, Joe, American Water Works Association (AWWA), 6666 W Quincy Ave, Denver, CO 80235-3098 *Tel:* 303-794-7711 *Toll Free Tel:* 800-926-7337 *E-mail:* service@awwa.org (cust serv) *Web Site:* www.awwa.org, pg 15

Thies, Sue, Perfection Learning, 1000 N Second Ave, Logan, IA 51546 *Tel:* 712-644-2831 *Toll Free Tel:* 800-831-4190 *Toll Free Fax:* 800-543-2745 *E-mail:* orders@perfectionlearning.com *Web Site:* perfectionlearning.com, pg 167

Thixton, Robert, Pinder Lane & Garon-Brooke Associates Ltd, 159 W 53 St, New York, NY 10019 *Tel:* 212-489-0880 *Fax:* 212-489-7104 *E-mail:* pinderlanegaronbrooke@gmail.com *Web Site:* www.pinderlaneandgaronbrooke.com, pg 498

Thoma, Geri, Writers House, 21 W 26 St, New York, NY 10010 *Tel:* 212-685-2400 *Web Site:* www.writershouse.com, pg 508

Thomas, Alan G, University of Chicago Press, 1427 E 60 St, Chicago, IL 60637-2954 *Tel:* 773-702-7700; 773-702-7600 *Toll Free Tel:* 800-621-2736 (orders); *Fax:* 773-702-9756; 773-660-2235 (orders); 773-702-2708 *E-mail:* custserv@press.uchicago.edu; marketing@press.uchicago.edu *Web Site:* www.press.uchicago.edu, pg 226

Thomas, Christen, The Literary Press Group of Canada, 425 Adelaide St W, Suite 700, Toronto, ON M5V 3C1, Canada *Tel:* 416-483-1321 *Web Site:* www.lpg.ca, pg 536

Thomas, Christy, Highlights for Children Inc, 815 Church St, Honesdale, PA 18431 *Tel:* 570-253-1164 *Toll Free Tel:* 800-490-5111 *Fax:* 570-253-0179 *E-mail:* salesandmarketing@highlightspress.com *Web Site:* www.highlightspress.com; www.highlights.com; www.facebook.com/HighlightsforChildren, pg 99

Thomas, James S, ASTM International, 100 Barr Harbor Dr, West Conshohocken, PA 19428-2959 *Tel:* 610-832-9500; 610-832-9585 (intl) *Toll Free Tel:* 877-909-2786 (sales & cust support) *Fax:* 610-832-9555 *E-mail:* service@astm.org *Web Site:* www.astm.org, pg 23

Thomas, JoAnne C, New Horizon Press, PO Box 669, Far Hills, NJ 07931-0669 *Tel:* 908-604-6311 *E-mail:* nhp@newhorizonpressbooks.com *Web Site:* www.newhorizonpressbooks.com, pg 148

Thomas, John, The Little Entrepreneur, c/o Harper Arrington Media, 18701 Grand River, Suite 105, Detroit, MI 48223 *Toll Free Tel:* 888-435-9234 *Fax:* 248-281-0373 *E-mail:* info@startingaclothingline.com *Web Site:* www.thelittlee.com, pg 126

Thomas, Joy, Chartered Professional Accountants of Canada (CPA Canada), 277 Wellington St W, Toronto, ON M5V 3H2, Canada *Tel:* 416-977-3222 *Toll Free Tel:* 800-268-3793 *Fax:* 416-977-8585 *E-mail:* member.services@cpacanada.ca *Web Site:* www.cpacanada.ca; www.facebook.com/CPACanada/, pg 419

Thomas, Kelly, Society for Industrial & Applied Mathematics, 3600 Market St, 6th fl, Philadelphia, PA 19104-2688 *Tel:* 215-382-9800 *Toll Free Tel:* 800-447-7426 *Fax:* 215-386-7999 *E-mail:* siambooks@siam.org *Web Site:* www.siam.org, pg 202

Thomas, Kelly, University of Pittsburgh Press, 7500 Thomas Blvd, Pittsburgh, PA 15260 *Tel:* 412-383-2456 *Fax:* 412-383-2466 *E-mail:* info@upress.pitt.edu *Web Site:* www.upress.pitt.edu, pg 230

Thomas, Lisa, National Geographic Books, 1145 17 St NW, Washington, DC 20036-4688 *Tel:* 202-857-7000 *Toll Free Tel:* 877-866-6486 *E-mail:* ngbooks@cdsfulfillment.com *Web Site:* www.nationalgeographic.com/books/; ngbooks.buysub.com, pg 146

Thomas, Margaret, Carolrhoda Books Inc, 241 First Ave N, Minneapolis, MN 55401 *Tel:* 612-332-3344 *Toll Free Tel:* 800-328-4929 *Fax:* 612-332-7615 *Toll Free Fax:* 800-332-1132 *E-mail:* info@lernerbooks.com; custserve@lernerbooks.com *Web Site:* www.lernerbooks.com; www.facebook.com/lernerbooks, pg 45

Thomas, Margaret, Carolrhoda Lab™, 241 First Ave N, Minneapolis, MN 55401 *Tel:* 612-332-3344 *Toll Free Tel:* 800-328-4929 *Fax:* 612-332-7615 *Toll Free Fax:* 800-332-1132 *E-mail:* info@lernerbooks.com; custserve@lernerbooks.com *Web Site:* www.lernerbooks.com; www.facebook.com/lernerbooks, pg 45

Thomas, Margaret, ediciones Lerner, 241 First Ave N, Minneapolis, MN 55401 *Tel:* 612-332-3344 *Toll Free Tel:* 800-328-4929 *Fax:* 612-332-7615 *Toll Free Fax:* 800-332-1132 *E-mail:* info@lernerbooks.com; custserve@lernerbooks.com *Web Site:* www.lernerbooks.com; www.facebook.com/lernerbooks, pg 69

Thomas, Margaret, First Avenue Editions, 241 First Ave N, Minneapolis, MN 55401 *Tel:* 612-332-3344 *Toll Free Tel:* 800-328-4929 *Fax:* 612-332-7615 *Toll Free Fax:* 800-332-1132 *E-mail:* info@lernerbooks.com; custserve@lernerbooks.com *Web Site:* www.lernerbooks.com, pg 78

Thomas, Margaret, Graphic Universe™, 241 First Ave N, Minneapolis, MN 55401 *Tel:* 612-332-3344 *Toll Free Tel:* 800-328-4929 *Fax:* 612-332-7615 *Toll Free Fax:* 800-332-1132 *E-mail:* info@lernerbooks.com; custserve@lernerbooks.com *Web Site:* www.lernerbooks.com; www.facebook.com/lernerbooks, pg 88

Thomas, Margaret, Lerner Publications, 241 First Ave N, Minneapolis, MN 55401 *Tel:* 612-332-3344 *Toll Free Tel:* 800-328-4929 *Fax:* 612-332-7615 *Toll Free Fax:* 800-332-1132 *E-mail:* info@lernerbooks.com; custserve@lernerbooks.com *Web Site:* www.lernerbooks.com; www.facebook.com/lernerbooks, pg 122

Thomas, Margaret, Lerner Publishing Group Inc, 241 First Ave N, Minneapolis, MN 55401 *Tel:* 612-332-3344 *Toll Free Tel:* 800-328-4929 *Fax:* 612-332-7615 *Toll Free Fax:* 800-332-1132 *E-mail:* info@lernerbooks.com; custserve@lernerbooks.com *Web Site:* www.lernerbooks.com; www.facebook.com/lernerbooks, pg 122

Thomas, Margaret, LernerClassroom, 241 First Ave N, Minneapolis, MN 55401 *Tel:* 612-332-3344 *Toll Free Tel:* 800-328-4929 *Fax:* 612-332-7615 *Toll Free Fax:* 800-332-1132 *E-mail:* info@lernerbooks.com; custserve@lernerbooks.com *Web Site:* www.lernerbooks.com; www.facebook.com/lernerbooks, pg 123

Thomas, Margaret, Millbrook Press, 241 First Ave N, Minneapolis, MN 55401 *Tel:* 612-332-3344 *Toll Free Tel:* 800-328-4929 *Fax:* 612-332-7615 *Toll Free Fax:* 800-332-1132 *E-mail:* info@lernerbooks.com; custserve@lernerbooks.com *Web Site:* www.lernerbooks.com; www.facebook.com/millbrookpress, pg 140

Thomas, Margaret, Twenty-First Century Books, 241 First Ave N, Minneapolis, MN 55401 *Tel:* 612-332-3344 *Toll Free Tel:* 800-328-4929 *Fax:* 612-332-7615 *Toll Free Fax:* 800-332-1132 *E-mail:* info@lernerbooks.com; custserve@lernerbooks.com *Web Site:* www.lernerbooks.com; www.facebook.com/lernerbooks, pg 222

Thomas, Margaret, Zest Books, 241 First Ave N, Minneapolis, MN 55401 *Tel:* 612-332-3344 *Toll Free Tel:* 800-328-4929 *Toll Free Fax:* 800-332-1132 *E-mail:* info@lernerbooks.com; publicity@lernerbooks.com; custserve@lernerbooks.com (orders) *Web Site:* lernerbooks.com, pg 248

Thomas, Mary Beth, HarperCollins General Books Group, 195 Broadway, New York, NY 10007 *Tel:* 212-207-7000 *Web Site:* www.harpercollins.com, pg 93

Thomas, Michael Payne, Charles C Thomas Publisher Ltd, 2600 S First St, Springfield, IL 62704 *Tel:* 217-789-8980 *Toll Free Tel:* 800-258-8980 *Fax:* 217-789-9130 *E-mail:* books@ccthomas.com *Web Site:* www.ccthomas.com, pg 217

Thomas, Patrick, Milkweed Editions, 1011 Washington Ave S, Suite 300, Minneapolis, MN 55415-1246 *Tel:* 612-332-3192 *Toll Free Tel:* 800-520-6455 *Fax:* 612-215-2550 *Web Site:* milkweed.org, pg 140

Thomas, Patrick, Milkweed National Fiction Prize, 1011 Washington Ave S, Suite 300, Minneapolis, MN 55415-1246 *Tel:* 612-332-3192 *Toll Free Tel:* 800-520-6455 *Fax:* 612-215-2550 *E-mail:* submissions@milkweed.org *Web Site:* www.milkweed.org, pg 641

Thomas, Paul, Crossway, 1300 Crescent St, Wheaton, IL 60187 *Tel:* 630-682-4300 *Toll Free Tel:* 800-635-7993 (orders); 800-543-1659 (cust serv) *Fax:* 630-682-4785 *E-mail:* info@crossway.org *Web Site:* www.crossway.org, pg 60

Thomas, Randolph, Louisiana State University Creative Writing Program MFA, English Dept, 260 Allen Hall, Baton Rouge, LA 70803 *Tel:* 225-578-4086 *Fax:* 225-578-4129 *E-mail:* lsucrwriting@lsu.edu *Web Site:* www.lsu.edu; www.lsu.edu/hss/english/creative_writing, pg 583

Thomas, Rebecca Tarr, Adams Media, 57 Littlefield St, Avon, MA 02322 *Tel:* 508-427-7100 *Web Site:* www.simonandschuster.com, pg 4

Thomas, Rich, HarperCollins Children's Books, 195 Broadway, New York, NY 10007 *Tel:* 212-207-7000 *Web Site:* www.harpercollins.com/childrens, pg 93

Thomas, Sheila, Quail Ridge Press (QRP), 2451 Atrium Way, Nashville, TN 37214 *Toll Free Tel:* 800-358-0560 *Fax:* 615-391-2815 *Web Site:* www.swphbooks.com/quail-ridge-press.html, pg 178

Thomas, Stephanie, BuilderBooks, 1201 15 St NW, Washington, DC 20005 *Tel:* 202-822-0200 *Toll Free Tel:* 800-223-2665 *Fax:* 202-266-8096 (edit) *E-mail:* info@nahb.com *Web Site:* builderbooks.com, pg 42

Thomas, Sue Timmons, Art of Living, PrimaMedia Inc, 1050 Second St Pike, Unit 1373, Southampton, PA 18966 *Tel:* 215-660-5045 *E-mail:* primamedia4@yahoo.com, pg 20

Thomas, William, Abrams Learning Trends, 16310 Bratton Lane, Suite 250, Austin, TX 78728-2403 *Toll Free Tel:* 800-227-9120 *Toll Free Fax:* 800-737-3322 *E-mail:* customerservice@abramslearningtrends.com (orders, cust serv); contactus@abramslearningtrends.com *Web Site:* www.abramslearningtrends.com (orders, cust serv), pg 3

Thomas, William, Doubleday, c/o Penguin Random House Inc, 1745 Broadway, New York, NY 10019 *Tel:* 212-751-2600 *Fax:* 212-572-2662 (foreign rts) *E-mail:* ddaypub@randomhouse.com *Web Site:* knopfdoubleday.com, pg 66

Thompson, Alexander, Cy Twombly Award for Poetry, 820 Greenwich St, New York, NY 10014 *Tel:* 212-807-7077 *E-mail:* info@contemporary-arts.org *Web Site:* www.foundationforcontemporaryarts.org/grants/cy-twombly-award-for-poetry, pg 674

Thompson, Christen, Arcadia Publishing Inc, 420 Wando Park Blvd, Mount Pleasant, SC 29464 *Tel:* 843-853-2070 *Toll Free Tel:* 888-313-2665 (orders only) *Fax:* 843-853-0044 *E-mail:* sales@arcadiapublishing.com *Web Site:* www.arcadiapublishing.com, pg 19

Thompson, Faye, Thompson Educational Publishing Inc, 20 Ripley Ave, Toronto, ON M6S 3N9, Canada *Tel:* 416-766-2763 (admin & orders) *Toll Free Tel:* 877-366-2763 *Fax:* 416-766-0398 (admin & orders) *E-mail:* info@thompsonbooks.com *Web Site:* www.thompsonbooks.com, pg 441

Thompson, Gary, Naval Institute Press, 291 Wood Rd, Annapolis, MD 21402-5034 *Tel:* 410-268-6110 *Toll Free Tel:* 800-233-8764 *Fax:* 410-295-1084; 410-571-1703 (cust serv) *E-mail:* webmaster@navalinstitute.org; customer@navalinstitute.org (cust serv) *Web Site:* www.nip.org; www.usni.org, pg 147

Thompson, Ian M, P & R Publishing Co, 1102 Marble Hill Rd, Phillipsburg, NJ 08865 *Tel:* 908-454-0505 *Toll Free Tel:* 800-631-0094 *Fax:* 908-859-2390 *E-mail:* sales@prpbooks.com; info@prpbooks.com *Web Site:* www.prpbooks.com, pg 158

Thompson, Judy, The Briar Cliff Review Fiction, Poetry & Creative Nonfiction Contest, 3303 Rebecca St, Sioux City, IA 51104-2100 *Tel:* 712-279-1651 *Fax:* 712-279-5486 *Web Site:* www.bcreview.org, pg 601

Thompson, Keith, Thompson Educational Publishing Inc, 20 Ripley Ave, Toronto, ON M6S 3N9, Canada *Tel:* 416-766-2763 (admin & orders) *Toll Free Tel:* 877-366-2763 *Fax:* 416-766-0398 (admin & orders) *E-mail:* info@thompsonbooks.com *Web Site:* www.thompsonbooks.com, pg 441

Thompson, Myles, Columbia University Press, 61 W 62 St, New York, NY 10023 *Tel:* 212-459-0600 *Toll Free Tel:* 800-944-8648 *Fax:* 212-459-3678 *Web Site:* cup.columbia.edu, pg 55

Thompson, Richelle, Forward Movement, 412 Sycamore St, Cincinnati, OH 45202-4110 *Tel:* 513-721-6659 *Toll Free Tel:* 800-543-1813 *Fax:* 513-721-0729 (orders) *E-mail:* orders@forwardmovement.org (orders & cust serv) *Web Site:* www.forwardmovement.org, pg 80

Thompson, Robert, G Schirmer Inc/Associated Music Publishers Inc, 180 Madison Ave, 24th fl, New York, NY 10016 *Tel:* 212-254-2100 *Fax:* 212-254-2013 *E-mail:* schirmer@schirmer.com *Web Site:* www.musicsalesclassical.com, pg 193

Thompson, Rowan, Thompson Educational Publishing Inc, 20 Ripley Ave, Toronto, ON M6S 3N9, Canada *Tel:* 416-766-2763 (admin & orders) *Toll Free Tel:* 877-366-2763 *Fax:* 416-766-0398 (admin & orders) *E-mail:* info@thompsonbooks.com *Web Site:* www.thompsonbooks.com, pg 441

Tomasino, Christine K, The Tomasino Agency Inc, 70 Chestnut St, Dobbs Ferry, NY 10522 *Tel:* 914-674-9659 *Fax:* 914-693-0381 *E-mail:* info@tomasinoagency.com *Web Site:* www.tomasinoagency.com, pg 506

Tomkiw, Beth, Trusted Media Brands Inc, 750 Third Ave, 3rd fl, New York, NY 10017 *Tel:* 646-293-6299 *Toll Free Tel:* 877-732-4438 (cust serv) *Fax:* 646-293-6251 *E-mail:* customercare@trustedmediabrands.com; press@trustedmediabrands.com *Web Site:* www.trustedmediabrands.com; www.rd.com, pg 221

Tomlin, Tiffany, Penguin Random House Speakers Bureau, A Penguin Random House Company, 1745 Broadway, Mail Drop 13-1, New York, NY 10019 *Tel:* 212-572-2013 *E-mail:* speakers@penguinrandomhouse.com *Web Site:* www.prhspeakers.com, pg 515

Tompkins, Amy, Transatlantic Agency, 2 Bloor St E, Suite 3500, Toronto, ON M4W 1A8, Canada *Tel:* 416-488-9214 *E-mail:* info@transatlanticagency.com *Web Site:* www.transatlanticagency.com, pg 506

Tondorf-Dick, Mary, Little, Brown and Company, 1290 Avenue of the Americas, New York, NY 10104 *Tel:* 212-364-1100 *Fax:* 212-364-0952 *E-mail:* firstname.lastname@hbgusa.com *Web Site:* www.littlebrown.com; www.hachettebookgroup.com, pg 125

Tonegutti, Marta, University of Chicago Press, 1427 E 60 St, Chicago, IL 60637-2954 *Tel:* 773-702-7700; 773-702-7600 *Toll Free Tel:* 800-621-2736 (orders) *Fax:* 773-702-9756; 773-660-2235 (orders); 773-702-2708 *E-mail:* custserv@press.uchicago.edu; marketing@press.uchicago.edu *Web Site:* www.press.uchicago.edu, pg 226

Tonetti, Barbara, Princeton University Press, 41 William St, Princeton, NJ 08540-5237 *Tel:* 609-258-4900 *Fax:* 609-258-6305 *Web Site:* press.princeton.edu, pg 175

Tong, Murray, Wilfrid Laurier University Press, 75 University Ave W, Waterloo, ON N2L 3C5, Canada *Tel:* 519-884-0710 *Toll Free Tel:* 866-836-5551 (CN & US) *Fax:* 519-725-1399 *E-mail:* press@wlu.ca *Web Site:* www.wlupress.wlu.ca, pg 445

Tonuzi, Flamur, Grand Central Publishing, 1290 Avenue of the Americas, New York, NY 10104 *Tel:* 212-364-1100 *Web Site:* www.hachettebookgroup.com, pg 88

Toole, Jenny, Mercer University Press, 368 Orange St, Macon, GA 31201 *Tel:* 478-301-2880 *Toll Free Tel:* 866-895-1472 *Fax:* 478-301-2585 *E-mail:* mupressorders@mercer.edu *Web Site:* www.mupress.org, pg 138

Toomer, Sharon, National Association of Black Journalists (NABJ), 1100 Knight Hall, Suite 3100, College Park, MD 20742 *Tel:* 301-405-0248 *Fax:* 301-314-1714 *E-mail:* info@nabj.org; press@nabj.org *Web Site:* www.nabj.org, pg 538

Toppy, Suzanne, Springer Publishing Co, 11 W 42 St, 15th fl, New York, NY 10036-8002 *Tel:* 212-431-4370 *Toll Free Tel:* 877-687-7476 *E-mail:* marketing@springerpub.com; cs@springerpub.com (orders); textbook@springerpub.com; specialsales@springerpub.com *Web Site:* www.springerpub.com, pg 206

Torizzo, Trish, Houghton Mifflin Harcourt, 125 High St, Boston, MA 02110 *Tel:* 617-351-5000 *Toll Free Tel:* 855-969-4642; 800-225-5425 (K-12 educ materials); 800-323-9540 (assessment materials); 877-219-1537 (SkillsTutor); 888-242-6747 (Innovation in Educ Group); 800-225-3362 (Trade & Ref Div) *Toll Free Fax:* 800-269-5232 *E-mail:* myhmhco@hmhco.com *Web Site:* www.hmhco.com, pg 103

Torres, Iris, Perseus Books, 1290 Avenue of the Americas, New York, NY 10104 *Tel:* 212-340-8100 *Toll Free Tel:* 800-343-4499 (cust serv) *Fax:* 212-340-8105 *Web Site:* www.perseusbooks.com, pg 167

Torres, Vanessa, Macmillan, 120 Broadway, 22nd fl, New York, NY 10271 *Tel:* 646-307-5151 *E-mail:* press.inquiries@macmillan.com *Web Site:* www.macmillan.com, pg 130

Tortoroli, Melanie, W W Norton & Company Inc, 500 Fifth Ave, New York, NY 10110-0017 *Tel:* 212-354-5500 *Toll Free Tel:* 800-233-4830 (orders & cust serv) *Fax:* 212-869-0856 *Toll Free Fax:* 800-458-6515 *E-mail:* orders@wwnorton.com *Web Site:* wwnorton.com, pg 152

Tory, Caroline, Aspen Words, 110 E Hallam St, Suite 116, Aspen, CO 81611 *Tel:* 970-925-3122 *Fax:* 970-920-5700 *E-mail:* aspenwords@aspeninstitute.org *Web Site:* www.aspenwords.org, pg 525

Tory, Caroline, Aspen Words Literary Prize, 110 E Hallam St, Suite 116, Aspen, CO 81611 *Tel:* 970-925-3122 *Fax:* 970-920-5700 *E-mail:* literary.prize@aspeninstitute.org *Web Site:* www.aspenwords.org/programs/literary-prize/; www.aspenwords.org, pg 594

Tory, Caroline, Summer Words Writing Conference & Literary Festival, 110 E Hallam St, Suite 116, Aspen, CO 81611 *Tel:* 970-925-3122 *Fax:* 970-920-5700 *E-mail:* aspenwords@aspeninstitute.org *Web Site:* www.aspenwords.org, pg 579

Tory, Caroline, Winter Words Author Series, 110 E Hallam St, Suite 116, Aspen, CO 81611 *Tel:* 970-925-3122 *Fax:* 970-920-5700 *E-mail:* aspenwords@aspeninstitute.org *Web Site:* www.aspenwords.org, pg 580

Toth, Dani, Pantheon Books, c/o Penguin Random House Inc, 1745 Broadway, New York, NY 10019 *Tel:* 212-751-2600 *Fax:* 212-572-2662 (foreign rts) *Web Site:* knopfdoubleday.com, pg 159

Toth, Dani, Schocken Books, c/o Penguin Random House Inc, 1745 Broadway, New York, NY 10019 *Tel:* 212-751-2600 *Fax:* 212-572-2662 (foreign rts) *Web Site:* knopfdoubleday.com, pg 193

Toth, Sara, The Chautauqua Prize, One Ames Ave, Chautauqua, NY 14722 *Toll Free Tel:* 800-836-ARTS (836-2787) *Web Site:* www.ciweb.org/prize, pg 604

Toth, Sarah, Galaxy Press, 7051 Hollywood Blvd, Hollywood, CA 90028 *Tel:* 323-466-3310 *Toll Free Tel:* 877-8GALAXY (842-5299) *E-mail:* info@galaxypress.com; customers@galaxypress.com *Web Site:* www.galaxypress.com, pg 82

Touchie, Rodger, Heritage House Publishing Co Ltd, 1075 Pendergast St, No 103, Victoria, BC V8V 0A1, Canada *Tel:* 250-360-0829 *Fax:* 250-386-0829 *E-mail:* heritage@heritagehouse.ca *Web Site:* www.heritagehouse.ca, pg 429

Toupin, Tom, Blue Book Publications Inc, 8009 34 Ave S, Suite 250, Minneapolis, MN 55425 *Tel:* 952-854-5229 *Toll Free Tel:* 800-877-4867 *Fax:* 952-853-1486 *E-mail:* support@bluebookinc.com *Web Site:* www.bluebookofgunvalues.com; www.bluebookofguitarvalues.com, pg 36

Tourtelot, Nicole, DeFiore and Company Literary Management Inc, 47 E 19 St, 3rd fl, New York, NY 10003 *Tel:* 212-925-7744 *Fax:* 212-925-9803 *E-mail:* info@defliterary.com; submissions@defliterary.com *Web Site:* www.defliterary.com, pg 481

Tourtlotte, Alan N, The Optical Society (OSA), 2010 Massachusetts Ave NW, Washington, DC 20036-1023 *Tel:* 202-223-8130 *Toll Free Tel:* 800-766-4672 *E-mail:* custserv@osa.org *Web Site:* www.osa.org, pg 156

Touvell, Anne, Thurber Prize for American Humor, 77 Jefferson Ave, Columbus, OH 43215 *Tel:* 614-464-1032 *Fax:* 614-280-3645 *E-mail:* thurberhouse@thurberhouse.org *Web Site:* www.thurberhouse.org, pg 673

Tov, Matti Shem, ProQuest LLC, 789 E Eisenhower Pkwy, Ann Arbor, MI 48108 *Tel:* 734-761-4700 *Toll Free Tel:* 800-521-0600; 877-779-6768 (sales) *E-mail:* sales@proquest.com *Web Site:* www.proquest.com, pg 176

Tovbis, Grigory, Henry Holt and Company, LLC, 120 Broadway, 23rd fl, New York, NY 10271 *Tel:* 646-307-5151 *Toll Free Tel:* 888-330-8477 (orders) *Fax:* 646-307-5285 *Web Site:* www.henryholt.com, pg 102

Tower, Carol, SME (Society of Manufacturing Engineers), 1000 Town Ctr, Suite 1910, Southfield, MI 48075 *Tel:* 313-425-3000 *Toll Free Tel:* 800-733-4763 (cust serv) *Fax:* 313-425-3400 *E-mail:* publications@sme.org *Web Site:* www.sme.org, pg 201

Towne, Ashley, University of Chicago Press, 1427 E 60 St, Chicago, IL 60637-2954 *Tel:* 773-702-7700; 773-702-7600 *Toll Free Tel:* 800-621-2736 (orders) *Fax:* 773-702-9756; 773-660-2235 (orders); 773-702-2708 *E-mail:* custserv@press.uchicago.edu; marketing@press.uchicago.edu *Web Site:* www.press.uchicago.edu, pg 226

Townson, Donald, Townson Publishing Co Ltd, PO Box 1404, Sta A, Vancouver, BC V6C 2P7, Canada *Tel:* 604-886-0594 *E-mail:* admin@gpub.com; rights@gpub.ca *Web Site:* generalpublishing.com, pg 441

Tracten, Mark, Crown House Publishing Co LLC, 81 Brook Hills Circle, White Plains, NY 10605 *Tel:* 914-946-3517 *Toll Free Tel:* 877-925-1213 (cust serv) *Fax:* 914-946-1160 *E-mail:* info@chpus.com *Web Site:* www.crownhousepublishing.com, pg 60

Tracy, Kathleen A, SDP Publishing Solutions LLC, 36 Captain's Way, East Bridgewater, MA 02333 *Tel:* 617-775-0656 *Web Site:* www.sdppublishingsolutions.com, pg 470

Tracy, Reid, Hay House Inc, 2776 Loker Ave W, Carlsbad, CA 92010 *Tel:* 760-431-7695 (ext 2, intl) *Toll Free Tel:* 800-654-5126 (ext 2, US) *Toll Free Fax:* 800-650-5115 *E-mail:* info@hayhouse.com; editorial@hayhouse.com *Web Site:* www.hayhouse.com, pg 96

Trainor, Patricia M, BLR®—Business & Legal Resources, 100 Winners Circle, Suite 300, Brentwood, TN 37027 *Tel:* 860-510-0100 *Toll Free Tel:* 800-727-5257 *E-mail:* service@blr.com *Web Site:* www.blr.com, pg 36

Tramble, Madrid, ASM International, 9639 Kinsman Rd, Materials Park, OH 44073-0002 *Tel:* 440-338-5151 *Toll Free Tel:* 800-336-5152; 800-368-9800 (Europe) *Fax:* 440-338-4634 *E-mail:* memberservicecenter@asminternational.org *Web Site:* www.asminternational.org, pg 22

Tran, Jennifer Chen, Bradford Literary Agency, 5694 Mission Center Rd, Suite 347, San Diego, CA 92108 *Tel:* 619-521-1201 *E-mail:* queries@bradfordlit.com *Web Site:* www.bradfordlit.com, pg 477

Tran, Steven, Soho Press Inc, 853 Broadway, New York, NY 10003 *Tel:* 212-260-1900 *E-mail:* soho@sohopress.com; publicity@sohopress.com *Web Site:* sohopress.com, pg 203

Tranen, Joshua Gutterman, Duke University Press, 905 W Main St, Suite 18B, Durham, NC 27701 *Tel:* 919-688-5134 *Toll Free Tel:* 888-651-0122 (US) *Fax:* 919-688-2615 *Toll Free Fax:* 888-651-0124 *E-mail:* orders@dukepress.edu *Web Site:* www.dukepress.edu, pg 68

Tranfaglia, Frank, Piano Press, 1425 Ocean Ave, Suite 5, Del Mar, CA 92014 *Tel:* 619-884-1401 *Fax:* 858-755-1104 *E-mail:* pianopress@pianopress.com *Web Site:* www.pianopress.com, pg 169

Traub, Kevin, Zondervan, 3900 Sparks Dr, Grand Rapids, MI 49546 *Tel:* 616-698-6900 *Toll Free Tel:* 800-226-1122; 800-727-1309 (retail sales) *Fax:* 616-698-3350 *Toll Free Fax:* 800-698-3256 (retail orders) *Web Site:* www.zondervan.com, pg 248

Travaglini, Timothy, Transatlantic Agency, 2 Bloor St E, Suite 3500, Toronto, ON M4W 1A8, Canada *Tel:* 416-488-9214 *E-mail:* info@transatlanticagency.com *Web Site:* www.transatlanticagency.com, pg 506

Travers, Kate, Workman Publishing Co Inc, 225 Varick St, 9th fl, New York, NY 10014-4381 *Tel:* 212-254-5900 *Toll Free Tel:* 800-722-7202 *Fax:* 212-254-8098 *E-mail:* info@workman.com; orders@workman.com *Web Site:* www.workman.com, pg 244

Traversy, Nancy, Barefoot Books, 2067 Massachusetts Ave, 5th fl, Cambridge, MA 02140 *Tel:* 617-576-0660 *Toll Free Tel:* 866-215-1756 (cust serv); 866-417-2369 (orders) *Fax:* 617-576-0049 *E-mail:* help@barefootbooks.com *Web Site:* www.barefootbooks.com, pg 28

Tucher, Andie, Allan Nevins Prize, 2950 Broadway, New York, NY 10027 *Tel:* 212-854-6495 *E-mail:* amhistsociety@columbia.edu *Web Site:* sah.columbia.edu, pg 647

Tucher, Andie, Francis Parkman Prize, 2950 Broadway, New York, NY 10027 *Tel:* 212-854-6495 *E-mail:* amhistsociety@columbia.edu *Web Site:* sah.columbia.edu, pg 652

Tucher, Andie, SAH Prize for Historical Fiction, 2950 Broadway, New York, NY 10027 *Tel:* 212-854-6495 *E-mail:* amhistsociety@columbia.edu *Web Site:* sah.columbia.edu, pg 663

Tucker, Angela, Kensington Publishing Corp, 119 W 40 St, New York, NY 10018 *Tel:* 212-407-1500 *Toll Free Tel:* 800-221-2647 *Fax:* 212-935-0699 *Web Site:* www.kensingtonbooks.com, pg 116

Tucker, Suzi, Zeig, Tucker & Theisen Inc, 2632 E Thomas Rd, Suite 201, Phoenix, AZ 85016 *Tel:* 480-389-4342 *Web Site:* www.zeigtucker.com, pg 248

Tudor, Jeannie, Square One Publishers Inc, 115 Herricks Rd, Garden City Park, NY 11040 *Tel:* 516-535-2010 *Toll Free Tel:* 877-900-BOOK (900-2665) *Fax:* 516-535-2014 *E-mail:* sq1publish@aol.com *Web Site:* www.squareonepublishers.com, pg 206

Tufariello, Frank, Data Trace Publishing Co (DTP), 110 West Rd, Suite 227, Towson, MD 21204-2316 *Tel:* 410-494-4994 *Toll Free Tel:* 800-342-0454 *Fax:* 410-494-0515 *E-mail:* info@datatrace.com; customerservice@datatrace.com; salesandmarketing@datatrace.com; editorial@datatrace.com *Web Site:* www.datatrace.com, pg 62

Tugeau, Nicole, Tugeau 2 Inc, 2231 Grandview Ave, Cleveland Heights, OH 44106 *Tel:* 216-707-0854 *Web Site:* www.tugeau2.com, pg 512

Tull, Katie, Random House Publishing Group, 1745 Broadway, New York, NY 10019 *Toll Free Tel:* 800-200-3552 *Web Site:* www.randomhousebooks.com, pg 181

Tully, Nola, Encounter Books, 900 Broadway, Suite 601, New York, NY 10003 *Tel:* 212-871-6310 *Toll Free Tel:* 800-343-4499 *Fax:* 212-871-6311 *E-mail:* publicity@encounterbooks.com *Web Site:* www.encounterbooks.com, pg 72

Tumambing, Ryan, Hatherleigh Press Ltd, 62545 State Hwy 10, Hobart, NY 13788 *Toll Free Tel:* 800-528-2550 *E-mail:* info@hatherleighpress.com; publicity@hatherleighpress.com *Web Site:* www.hatherleighpress.com, pg 95

Tuminelly, Nancy, Mighty Media Press, 1201 Currie Ave, Minneapolis, MN 55403 *Tel:* 612-455-0252; 612-399-1969 *Fax:* 612-338-4817 *E-mail:* info@mightymedia.com *Web Site:* www.mightymediapress.com, pg 139

Tung, Catherine, Beacon Press, 24 Farnsworth St, Boston, MA 02210-1409 *Tel:* 617-742-2110 *Fax:* 617-723-3097; 617-742-2290 *Web Site:* www.beacon.org, pg 29

Tupholme, Iris, HarperCollins Canada Ltd, 2 Bloor St E, 20th fl, Toronto, ON M4W 1A8, Canada *Tel:* 416-975-9334 *Fax:* 416-975-5223 *E-mail:* hcorder@harpercollins.com *Web Site:* www.harpercollins.ca, pg 429

Tupper Ling, Nancy, Boston Authors Club Inc, 2400 Beacon St, No 208, Chestnut, MA 02467 *Tel:* 617-552-4031 *E-mail:* bostonauthorsclub@gmail.com *Web Site:* bostonauthorsclub.org, pg 529

Turnau, Crystal, Perseus Books, 1290 Avenue of the Americas, New York, NY 10104 *Tel:* 212-340-8100 *Toll Free Tel:* 800-343-4499 (cust serv) *Fax:* 212-340-8105 *Web Site:* www.perseusbooks.com, pg 167

Turner, Erika, Houghton Mifflin Harcourt Trade & Reference Division, 125 High St, Boston, MA 02110 *Tel:* 617-351-5000 *Web Site:* www.hmhco.com, pg 104

Turner, Erin, The Globe Pequot Press, 246 Goose Lane, Guilford, CT 06437 *Tel:* 203-458-4500 *Toll Free Tel:* 800-243-0495 (orders only); 888-249-7586 (cust serv) *Fax:* 203-458-4601 *Toll Free Fax:* 800-820-2329

(orders & cust serv) *E-mail:* editorial@globepequot.com; info@rowman.com; orders@rowman.com *Web Site:* rowman.com, pg 86

Turner, Jessica, Entangled Publishing LLC, 2614 S Timberline Rd, Suite 105, Fort Collins, CO 80525 *Toll Free Tel:* 877-677-9451 *E-mail:* publisher@entangledpublishing.com *Web Site:* www.entangledpublishing.com, pg 72

Turner, Paaige K PhD, National Communication Association, 1765 "N" St NW, Washington, DC 20036 *Tel:* 202-464-4622 *Fax:* 202-464-4600 *E-mail:* inbox@natcom.org *Web Site:* www.natcom.org, pg 539

Turner, Peter, Red Wheel/Weiser, 65 Parker St, Suite 7, Newburyport, MA 01950 *Tel:* 978-465-0504 *Toll Free Tel:* 800-423-7087 (orders) *Fax:* 978-465-0243 *E-mail:* info@rwwbooks.com *Web Site:* www.redwheelweiser.com, pg 183

Turner, T J, Antioch Writers' Workshop, 300 College Park Ave, Suite 200A, Dayton, OH 45469-0001 *Tel:* 937-567-2399 *E-mail:* info@antiochwritersworkshop.com *Web Site:* www.antiochwritersworkshop.com, pg 573

Turney, Cathy, National Society of Newspaper Columnists Annual Conference, 205 Gun Hill St, Milton, MA 02186 *Tel:* 617-697-6854 *E-mail:* director@columnists.com *Web Site:* www.columnists.com, pg 576

Turpin, Molly, Random House Publishing Group, 1745 Broadway, New York, NY 10019 *Toll Free Tel:* 800-200-3552 *Web Site:* www.randomhousebooks.com, pg 181

Tusman, Jordana, Perseus Books, 1290 Avenue of the Americas, New York, NY 10104 *Tel:* 212-340-8100 *Toll Free Tel:* 800-343-4499 (cust serv) *Fax:* 212-340-8105 *Web Site:* www.perseusbooks.com, pg 167

Tutela, Joy, David Black Agency, 335 Adams St, 27th fl, Suite 2707, Brooklyn, NY 11201 *Tel:* 718-852-5500 *Fax:* 718-852-5539 *Web Site:* www.davidblackagency.com, pg 476

Tuttle, Ann Leslie, Dystel, Goderich & Bourret LLC, One Union Sq W, Suite 904, New York, NY 10003 *Tel:* 212-627-9100 *Fax:* 212-627-9313 *Web Site:* www.dystel.com, pg 482

Tuzzo, Kimberly, Printing Industries Alliance, 636 N French Rd, Suite 1, Amherst, NY 14228 *Tel:* 716-691-3211 *Toll Free Tel:* 800-777-4742 *Fax:* 716-691-4249 *E-mail:* info@pialliance.org *Web Site:* pialliance.org, pg 544

Tweed, Charles, Jewel Box Theatre Playwriting Competition, 3700 N Walker, Oklahoma City, OK 73118-7031 *Tel:* 405-521-1786 *Web Site:* jewelboxtheatre.org, pg 628

Tweed, Thomas P, Plowshare Media, 405 Vincente Way, La Jolla, CA 92037 *Tel:* 858-454-5446 *E-mail:* sales@plowsharemedia.com *Web Site:* plowsharemedia.com, pg 171

Twitchell, Betsy, W W Norton & Company Inc, 500 Fifth Ave, New York, NY 10110-0017 *Tel:* 212-354-5500 *Toll Free Tel:* 800-233-4830 (orders & cust serv) *Fax:* 212-869-0856 *Toll Free Fax:* 800-458-6515 *E-mail:* orders@wwnorton.com *Web Site:* wwnorton.com, pg 152

Twombly, Rachel, Jason Aronson Inc, 4501 Forbes Blvd, Suite 200, Lanham, MD 20706 *Tel:* 301-459-3366 *Toll Free Tel:* 800-462-6420 ext 3024 (cust serv) *Fax:* 301-429-5748 *Toll Free Fax:* 800-338-4550 (cust serv) *E-mail:* orders@rowman.com; customercare@rowman.com *Web Site:* www.rowman.com, pg 20

Twomey, Shannon, Penguin Books, 375 Hudson St, New York, NY 10014 *Tel:* 212-366-2000 *E-mail:* penguinpublicity@us.penguingroup.com *Web Site:* www.penguinclassics.com; www.penguin.com, pg 163

Twomey, Shannon, Penguin Group USA, A Penguin Random House Company, 375 Hudson St, New York, NY 10014 *Tel:* 212-366-2000 *Toll Free Tel:* 800-847-5515 (inside sales); 800-631-8571 (cust serv)

Fax: 212-366-2666; 607-775-4829 (inside sales) *E-mail:* online@us.penguingroup.com *Web Site:* www.penguin.com, pg 163

Twomey, Shannon, Viking, 375 Hudson St, New York, NY 10014 *Tel:* 212-366-2000 *Fax:* 212-243-6002 *Web Site:* www.penguin.com/publishers/vikingbooks, pg 236

Tyler, Tracy, Random House Children's Books, 1745 Broadway, 10th fl, New York, NY 10019 *Tel:* 212-782-9000 *Web Site:* www.randomhousekids.com, pg 180

Tyrrell, Bob, Orca Book Publishers, 1016 Balmoral Rd, Victoria, BC V8T 1A8, Canada *Toll Free Tel:* 800-210-5277 *Toll Free Fax:* 877-408-1551 *E-mail:* orca@orcabook.com *Web Site:* www.orcabook.com, pg 435

Tyrrell, Dennis, Penguin Random House Audio Publishing, 1745 Broadway, New York, NY 10019 *E-mail:* audio@penguinrandomhouse.com *Web Site:* www.penguinrandomhouseaudio.com, pg 164

Tyrrell, Jen, Trusted Media Brands Inc, 750 Third Ave, 3rd fl, New York, NY 10017 *Tel:* 646-293-6299 *Toll Free Tel:* 877-732-4438 (cust serv) *Fax:* 646-293-6251 *E-mail:* customercare@trustedmediabrands.com; press@trustedmediabrands.com *Web Site:* www.trustedmediabrands.com; www.rd.com, pg 221

Tysdol, Troy, Faith & Fellowship Publishing, 1020 W Alcott Ave, Fergus Falls, MN 56537 *Tel:* 218-736-7357 *Toll Free Tel:* 800-332-9232 *E-mail:* ffpublishing@clba.org *Web Site:* www.clba.org, pg 75

Tyson, Marie, The Pilgrim Press/United Church Press, 700 Prospect Ave, Cleveland, OH 44115-1100 *Tel:* 216-736-2100 *Toll Free Tel:* 800-537-3394 (orders) *E-mail:* permissions@thepilgrimpress.com; store@ucc.org (orders) *Web Site:* www.thepilgrimpress.com, pg 170

Tzetzo, Liz, Macmillan, 120 Broadway, 22nd fl, New York, NY 10271 *Tel:* 646-307-5151 *E-mail:* press.inquiries@macmillan.com *Web Site:* www.macmillan.com, pg 129

Uddin, Jafreen, Asian American Writers' Workshop, 112 W 27 St, Suite 600, New York, NY 10001 *Tel:* 212-494-0061 *E-mail:* desk@aaww.org *Web Site:* aaww.org; facebook.com/AsianAmericanWritersWorkshop, pg 525

Ude, Wayne, Blue & Ude Writers' Services, 4249 Nuthatch Way, Clinton, WA 98236 *Tel:* 360-341-1630 *E-mail:* blue@whidbey.com *Web Site:* www.blueudewritersservices.com; www.sunbreakpress.com, pg 459

Underwood, April, SLACK® Incorporated, A Wyanoke Group Company, 6900 Grove Rd, Thorofare, NJ 08086-9447 *Tel:* 856-848-1000 *Toll Free Tel:* 800-257-8290 *Fax:* 856-848-6091 *E-mail:* sales@slackinc.com; editor@slackinc.com; customerservice@slackinc.com *Web Site:* www.healio.com/books, pg 201

Underwood, Will, Kent State University Press, 1118 University Library Bldg, 1125 Risman Dr, Kent, OH 44242 *Tel:* 330-672-7913 *Fax:* 330-672-3104 *E-mail:* ksupress@kent.edu *Web Site:* www.kentstateuniversitypress.com, pg 117

Unferth, Deb, University of Texas at Austin, New Writers Project, Dept of English, Calhoun Hall, Rm 226, 204 W 21 St, B-5000, Austin, TX 78712 *Tel:* 512-471-5132; 512-471-4991 *Fax:* 512-471-4909 *Web Site:* newwritersproject.org, pg 586

Ung, Jennifer, Simon & Schuster Children's Publishing, 1230 Avenue of the Americas, New York, NY 10020 *Tel:* 212-698-7000 *Web Site:* www.simonandschuster.com/kids; www.simonandschuster.com/teen; simonandschuster.net; simonandschuster.biz, pg 199

Unger, Andrew, Grove Atlantic Inc, 154 W 14 St, 12th fl, New York, NY 10011 *Tel:* 212-614-7850 *Toll Free Tel:* 800-521-0178 *Fax:* 212-614-7886 *E-mail:* info@groveatlantic.com; sales@groveatlantic.com; publicity@groveatlantic.com; rights@groveatlantic.com *Web Site:* www.groveatlantic.com, pg 89

Unger, David, Publishing Certificate Program at City College of New York, Division of Humanities NAC 5225, City College of New York, New York,

Vananda, Kelsi, American Literary Translators Association (ALTA), University of Arizona, Esquire Bldg, No 205, 1230 N Park Ave, Tucson, AZ 85721 *Tel:* 520-621-1757 *Web Site:* www.literarytranslators. org, pg 523

Vananda, Kelsi, National Translation Award, University of Arizona, Esquire Bldg, No 205, 1230 N Park Ave, Tucson, AZ 85721 *Tel:* 520-621-1757 *Web Site:* www. literarytranslators.org/awards/national-translation-award, pg 646

Vananda, Kelsi, Lucien Stryk Asian Translation Prize, University of Arizona, Esquire Bldg, No 205, 1230 N Park Ave, Tucson, AZ 85721 *Tel:* 520-621-1757 *Web Site:* literarytranslators.org/awards/lucien-stryk-prize, pg 671

Vance, Alexandra (Alix), American Institute of Physics, One Physics Ellipse, College Park, MD 20740-3843 *Tel:* 516-576-2200; 301-209-3100 (orders) *E-mail:* help@aip.org *Web Site:* www.aip.org, pg 12

Vance, Lisa Erbach, The Aaron M Priest Literary Agency Inc, 200 W 41 St, 21st fl, New York, NY 10036 *Tel:* 212-818-0344 *Fax:* 212-573-9417 *E-mail:* info@aaronpriest.com *Web Site:* www. aaronpriest.com, pg 499

Vance, V Ellis, US Board on Books For Young People (USBBY), c/o V Ellis Vance, 5503 N El Adobe Dr, Fresno, CA 93711-2363 *Tel:* 559-351-6119 *Web Site:* www.usbby.org, pg 548

Vandall, Jillian, Random House Children's Books, 1745 Broadway, 10th fl, New York, NY 10019 *Tel:* 212-782-9000 *Web Site:* www.randomhousekids.com, pg 180

VanDam, Arthur, Small Business Advisors Inc, 2005 Park St, Atlantic Beach, NY 11509 *Tel:* 516-374-1387 *Fax:* 516-374-1175 *E-mail:* info@smallbusinessadvice. com *Web Site:* www.smallbusinessadvice.com, pg 201

Vanderlip, Kendra, The Pinch Writing Awards in Fiction, University of Memphis, English Dept, 435 Patterson Hall, Memphis, TN 38152 *Tel:* 901-678-2651 *Fax:* 901-678-2226 *E-mail:* editor@pinchjournal. com *Web Site:* www.pinchjournal.com, pg 656

Vanderlip, Kendra, The Pinch Writing Awards in Poetry, University of Memphis, English Dept, 435 Patterson Hall, Memphis, TN 38152 *Tel:* 901-678-2651 *Fax:* 901-678-2226 *E-mail:* editor@pinchjournal. com *Web Site:* www.pinchjournal.com, pg 656

Vanderslice, Stephanie, Phillip H McMath Post Publication Book Award, Dept of Writing, University of Central Arkansas, 201 Donaghey Ave, Thompson Hall 303, Conway, AR 72035 *Web Site:* arkansaswriters.wordpress.com, pg 640

VanHees, Robert, ProQuest LLC, 789 E Eisenhower Pkwy, Ann Arbor, MI 48108 *Tel:* 734-761-4700 *Toll Free Tel:* 800-521-0600; 877-779-6768 (sales) *E-mail:* sales@proquest.com *Web Site:* www.proquest. com, pg 176

Vann, Kimiko, Chronicle Books, 680 Second St, San Francisco, CA 94107 *Tel:* 415-537-4200 *Toll Free Tel:* 800-759-0190 (cust serv) *Fax:* 415-537-4460 *Toll Free Fax:* 800-858-7787 (orders); 800-286-9471 (cust serv) *E-mail:* frontdesk@chroniclebooks.com *Web Site:* www.chroniclebooks.com, pg 52

Varga, Lisa R, Jefferson Cup Award, c/o Virginia Library Association (VLA), PO Box 56312, Virginia Beach, VA 23456 *Tel:* 757-689-0594 *Fax:* 757-447-3478 *Web Site:* www.vla.org, pg 628

Vargas, Allison Astor, Nuestras Voces National Playwriting Competition, 138 E 27 St, New York, NY 10016 *Tel:* 212-225-9950 *Fax:* 212-225-9085 *Web Site:* www.repertorio.org, pg 649

Vargo, Linda, National Association of College Stores (NACS), 500 E Lorain St, Oberlin, OH 44074 *Toll Free Tel:* 800-622-7498 *Fax:* 440-775-4769 *Web Site:* www.nacs.org, pg 539

Varma, Sarita, Farrar, Straus & Giroux, LLC, 175 Varick St, 9th fl, New York, NY 10014 *Tel:* 212-741-6900 *E-mail:* fsg.publicity@fsgbooks.com *Web Site:* us. macmillan.com/fsg.aspx, pg 76

Varma, Sarita, Hill & Wang, 175 Varick St, New York, NY 10014 *Tel:* 212-741-6900 *Fax:* 212-633-9385 *E-mail:* fsg.publicity@fsgbooks.com; fsg.editorial@ fsgbooks.com; sales@fsgbooks.com *Web Site:* us. macmillan.com/hillandwang.aspx, pg 99

Varma, Sarita, North Point Press, 18 W 18 St, 8th fl, New York, NY 10011 *Tel:* 212-741-6900 *Toll Free Tel:* 888-330-8477 *Fax:* 212-633-9385 *Web Site:* www. fsgbooks.com, pg 151

Varnado, Deb, Ascension Press, PO Box 1990, West Chester, PA 19380 *Tel:* 610-696-7795; 484-875-4550 (admin) *Toll Free Tel:* 800-376-0520 (sales & cust serv) *Web Site:* ascensionpress.com, pg 22

Varner, William, Stenhouse Publishers, One Monument Way, Portland, ME 04101-3400 *Tel:* 207-253-1600 *Toll Free Tel:* 888-363-0566 *Fax:* 207-253-5121 *Toll Free Fax:* 800-833-9164 *E-mail:* customerservice@ stenhouse.com *Web Site:* www.stenhouse.com, pg 208

Varrette, Dan, Insomniac Press, 520 Princess Ave, London, ON N6B 2B8, Canada *Tel:* 519-266-3556 *Web Site:* www.insomniacpress.com, pg 430

Vasquez, Claribel, Random House Children's Books, 1745 Broadway, 10th fl, New York, NY 10019 *Tel:* 212-782-9000 *Web Site:* www.randomhousekids. com, pg 181

Vasquez-Perez, Carmen, Chain Store Guide (CSG), 3710 Corporex Park Dr, Suite 310, Tampa, FL 33619 *Toll Free Tel:* 800-927-9292 (orders) *Fax:* 813-627-6888 *E-mail:* webmaster@csgis.com *Web Site:* www.csgis. com, pg 48

Vaugeois, Denis, Les Editions du Septentrion, 835 Turnbull Ave, Quebec City, QC G1R 2X4, Canada *Tel:* 418-688-3556 *Fax:* 418-527-4978 *E-mail:* info@ septentrion.qc.ca *Web Site:* www.septentrion.qc.ca, pg 423

Vaughan, Brendan, Random House Publishing Group, 1745 Broadway, New York, NY 10019 *Toll Free Tel:* 800-200-3552 *Web Site:* www.randomhousebooks. com, pg 181

Vaughn, Hannah, The Gersh Agency (TGA), 41 Madison Ave, 33rd fl, New York, NY 10010 *Tel:* 212-997-1818 *Web Site:* gershbooks.com, pg 486

Vaysbeyn, Elina, Shambhala Publications Inc, 4720 Walnut St, Boulder, CO 80301 *Tel:* 303-222-9598 *Toll Free Tel:* 866-424-0030 (off); 888-424-2329 (cust serv) *E-mail:* customercare@shambhala.com *Web Site:* www.shambhala.com, pg 197

Vazquez, Shannon Jamieson, Little, Brown and Company, 1290 Avenue of the Americas, New York, NY 10104 *Tel:* 212-364-1100 *Fax:* 212-364-0952 *E-mail:* firstname.lastname@hbgusa. com *Web Site:* www.littlebrown.com; www. hachettebookgroup.com, pg 126

Vega, Javier, School of Visual Arts, 209 E 23 St, New York, NY 10010-3994 *Tel:* 212-592-2100 *Fax:* 212-592-2116 *Web Site:* www.sva.edu, pg 584

Vegso, Peter, Health Communications Inc, 3201 SW 15 St, Deerfield Beach, FL 33442 *Tel:* 954-360-0909 *Toll Free Tel:* 800-851-9100; 800-441-5569 (cust serv & orders) *Fax:* 954-360-0034 *Toll Free Fax:* 800-424-7652 (cust serv & orders) *E-mail:* customerservice2@ hcibooks.com *Web Site:* www.hcibooks.com, pg 96

Veith, Richard, Cengage Learning, 20 Channel Center St, Boston, MA 02210 *Tel:* 617-289-7700 *Toll Free Tel:* 800-354-9706 *Fax:* 617-289-7844 *E-mail:* esales@cengage.com *Web Site:* www.cengage. com, pg 47

Veldran, Richard H, Dun & Bradstreet, 103 JFK Pkwy, Short Hills, NJ 07078 *Tel:* 973-921-5500 *Toll Free Tel:* 844-869-8244; 800-234-3867 (cust serv) *Web Site:* www.dnb.com, pg 68

Velella, Justin, St Martin's Press, LLC, 120 Broadway, New York, NY 10271 *Tel:* 646-307-5151 *Web Site:* us. macmillan.com/smp, pg 191

Velez, Mishell, Hachette Audio, 1290 Avenue of the Americas, New York, NY 10104 *Tel:* 212-364-1100 *Web Site:* www.hachetteaudio.com, pg 90

Veltre, J Joseph III, The Gersh Agency (TGA), 41 Madison Ave, 33rd fl, New York, NY 10010 *Tel:* 212-997-1818 *Web Site:* gershbooks.com, pg 486

Venezia, Angie, Anchor Books, c/o Penguin Random House Inc, 1745 Broadway, New York, NY 10019 *Tel:* 212-572-2420 *E-mail:* vintageanchorpublicity@ randomhouse.com *Web Site:* knopfdoubleday.com/ imprint/anchor, pg 15

Venezia, Angie, Vintage Books, c/o Penguin Random House Inc, 1745 Broadway, New York, NY 10019 *Tel:* 212-572-2420 *E-mail:* vintageanchorpublicity@ randomhouse.com *Web Site:* knopfdoubleday.com/ imprint/vintage, pg 236

VenHuizen, Heather, Sourcebooks LLC, 1935 Brookdale Rd, Suite 139, Naperville, IL 60563 *Tel:* 630-961-3900 *Toll Free Tel:* 800-432-7444 *Fax:* 630-961-2168 *E-mail:* info@sourcebooks.com; customersupport@ sourcebooks.com *Web Site:* www.sourcebooks.com, pg 204

Ventimiglia, Diana, Sounds True Inc, 413 S Arthur Ave, Louisville, CO 80027 *Tel:* 303-665-3151 *Toll Free Tel:* 800-333-9185 (US); 888-303-9185 (US & CN) *E-mail:* customerservice@soundstrue. com; stpublicity@soundstrue.com *Web Site:* www. soundstrue.com, pg 204

Ventura, Susan, Johns Hopkins University Press, 2715 N Charles St, Baltimore, MD 21218-4363 *Tel:* 410-516-6900; 410-516-6987 (journal orders outside US & CN) *Toll Free Tel:* 800-537-5487 (book orders & cust serv); 800-548-1784 (journal orders) *Fax:* 410-516-6968; 410-516-3866 (journal orders); 410-516-6998 (orders) *E-mail:* hfscustserv@press.jhu.edu (cust serv); jrnlcirc@press.jhu.edu (journal orders) *Web Site:* www.press.jhu.edu; muse.jhu.edu, pg 114

Vergilio, Trish, Templeton Press, 300 Conshohocken State Rd, Suite 550, West Conshohocken, PA 19428 *Tel:* 484-531-8380 *Fax:* 484-531-8382 *E-mail:* tpinfo@templetonpress.org *Web Site:* www. templetonpress.org, pg 215

Verhowsky, Victoria, DK Publishing, 1450 Broadway, Suite 801, New York, NY 10018 *Tel:* 646-674-4000 *Toll Free Tel:* 800-733-3000 *Fax:* 646-674-4020 *E-mail:* marketing@dk.com; publicity@ dk.com; csorders@penguinrandomhouse.com; ecustomerservice@randomhouse.com *Web Site:* www. dk.com; www.penguin.com, pg 65

Verma, Monika, Levine|Greenberg|Rostan Literary Agency, 307 Seventh Ave, Suite 2407, New York, NY 10001 *Tel:* 212-337-0934 *Fax:* 212-337-0948 *Web Site:* lgrliterary.com, pg 493

Verma, Mukul, Ernest J Gaines Award for Literary Excellence, 100 North St, Suite 900, Baton Rouge, LA 70802 *Tel:* 225-387-6126 *E-mail:* gainesaward@braf. org *Web Site:* www.ernestjgainesaward.org, pg 618

Vernon, Nancy, Ozark Mountain Publishing Inc, PO Box 754, Huntsville, AR 72740-0754 *Tel:* 479-738-2348 *Toll Free Tel:* 800-935-0045 *Fax:* 479-738-2448 *E-mail:* info@ozarkmt.com *Web Site:* www.ozarkmt. com, pg 158

VernonClark, Kayla, Kane Miller Books, 4901 Morena Blvd, Suite 213, San Diego, CA 92117 *E-mail:* submissions@kanemiller.com; info@ kanemiller.com *Web Site:* www.kanemiller.com, pg 115

Verost, Allison, Farrar, Straus & Giroux Books for Young Readers, 120 Broadway, New York, NY 10271 *Tel:* 212-741-6900 *Toll Free Tel:* 888-330-8477 (orders) *Fax:* 212-633-9385 *Web Site:* us.macmillan. com/mackids; www.mackidsbooks.com, pg 76

Verost, Allison, Roaring Brook Press, 120 Broadway, New York, NY 10271 *Tel:* 646-307-5151 *Web Site:* us. macmillan.com/publishers/roaring-brook-press, pg 186

Verrill, Chuck, Darhansoff & Verrill, 133 W 72 St, Rm 304, New York, NY 10023 *Tel:* 917-305-1300 *E-mail:* permissions@dvagency.com *Web Site:* www. dvagency.com, pg 480

Verses, Judy, John Wiley & Sons Inc, 111 River St, Hoboken, NJ 07030-5774 *Tel:* 201-748-6000 *Toll Free Tel:* 800-225-5945 (cust serv) *Fax:* 201-748-6088 *E-mail:* info@wiley.com *Web Site:* www.wiley.com, pg 241

Vershbow, Sophie, Random House Publishing Group, 1745 Broadway, New York, NY 10019 *Toll Free Tel:* 800-200-3552 *Web Site:* www.randomhousebooks. com, pg 181

Vestal, Rosemary, University of Nebraska Press, 1111 Lincoln Mall, Lincoln, NE 68588-0630 *Tel:* 402-472-3581; 919-966-7449 (cust serv & foreign orders) *Toll Free Tel:* 800-848-6224 (cust serv & US orders) *Fax:* 402-472-6214; 919-962-2704 (cust serv & foreign orders) *Toll Free Fax:* 800-526-2617 (cust serv & US orders) *E-mail:* pressmail@unl.edu *Web Site:* www.nebraskapress.unl.edu, pg 229

Vibbert, Brittany, Sourcebooks LLC, 1935 Brookdale Rd, Suite 139, Naperville, IL 60563 *Tel:* 630-961-3900 *Toll Free Tel:* 800-432-7444 *Fax:* 630-961-2168 *E-mail:* info@sourcebooks.com; customersupport@ sourcebooks.com *Web Site:* www.sourcebooks.com, pg 204

Victor, Nomi, W W Norton & Company Inc, 500 Fifth Ave, New York, NY 10110-0017 *Tel:* 212-354-5500 *Toll Free Tel:* 800-233-4830 (orders & cust serv) *Fax:* 212-869-0856 *Toll Free Fax:* 800-458-6515 *E-mail:* orders@wwnorton.com *Web Site:* wwnorton. com, pg 152

Victorson, Emily, Allium Press of Chicago, 1530 Elgin Ave, Forest Park, IL 60130 *Tel:* 708-689-9323 *E-mail:* info@alliumpress.com *Web Site:* www. alliumpress.com, pg 8

Vigilante, Marisa, Little, Brown and Company, 1290 Avenue of the Americas, New York, NY 10104 *Tel:* 212-364-1100 *Fax:* 212-364-0952 *E-mail:* firstname.lastname@hbgusa. com *Web Site:* www.littlebrown.com; www. hachettebookgroup.com, pg 125

Viktorin, Brian, Greenleaf Book Group LLC, 3 Park Place, 4005 Banister Lane, Suite B, Austin, TX 78704 *Tel:* 512-891-6100 *Fax:* 512-891-6150 *E-mail:* contact@greenleafbookgroup.com *Web Site:* www.greenleafbookgroup.com, pg 89

Vilar, Irene, Mandel Vilar Press, 19 Oxford Ct, Simsbury, CT 06070 *Tel:* 806-790-4731 *E-mail:* info@ mvpress.org *Web Site:* mvpress.org, pg 131

Vilarello, Meredith, Avid Reader Press, 1230 Avenue of the Americas, New York, NY 10020 *Web Site:* avidreaderpress.com, pg 26

Villa-Arce, Jose, Canadian Bookbinders and Book Artists Guild (CBBAG), 180 Shaw St, Unit 102, Toronto, ON M6J 2W5, Canada *Tel:* 416-581-1071 *E-mail:* cbbag@ cbbag.ca *Web Site:* www.cbbag.ca, pg 529

Villalonga, Lionel, Association pour l'Avancement des Sciences et des Techniques de la Documentation, 2065 rue Parthenais, Bureau 387, Montreal, QC H2K 3T1, Canada *Tel:* 514-281-5012 *Fax:* 514-281-8219 *E-mail:* info@asted.org *Web Site:* www.asted.org, pg 527, 573

Villalonga, Lionel, Editions ASTED, 2065 rue Parthenais, Bureau 387, Montreal, QC H2K 3T1, Canada *Tel:* 514-281-5012 *Fax:* 514-281-8219 *E-mail:* editions@asted.org; info@asted.org *Web Site:* www.asted.org, pg 422

Villalonga, Lionel, Prix Alvine-Belisle, 2065 rue Parthenais, Bureau 387, Montreal, QC H2K 3T1, Canada *Tel:* 514-281-5012 *Fax:* 514-281-8219 *E-mail:* info@asted.org *Web Site:* www.asted.org, pg 659

Vinarub, Vanessa, Harvard University Press, 79 Garden St, Cambridge, MA 02138-1499 *Tel:* 617-495-2600; 401-531-2800 (intl orders) *Toll Free Tel:* 800-405-1619 (orders) *Fax:* 617-495-5898 (gen); 617-496-4677 (edit & rts); 401-531-2801 (intl orders) *Toll Free Fax:* 800-406-9145 (orders) *E-mail:* contact_hup@ harvard.edu *Web Site:* www.hup.harvard.edu, pg 95

Vincent, Dorothy, Trident Media Group LLC, 41 Madison Ave, 36th fl, New York, NY 10010 *Tel:* 212-333-1511 *E-mail:* info@tridentmediagroup.com; press@tridentmediagroup.com *Web Site:* www. tridentmediagroup.com, pg 507

Vincent, Eddie, Independent Publishers of New England (IPNE), 10 Court St, No 206, Arlington, MA 02476-0206 *Tel:* 339-368-8229 *E-mail:* talktous@ipne.org *Web Site:* www.ipne.org, pg 535

Vincent, Eddie, Independent Publishers of New England Book Awards, 10 Court St, No 206, Arlington, MA 02476-0206 *Tel:* 339-368-8229 *E-mail:* bookawards@ ipne.org *Web Site:* www.ipne.org/awards, pg 626

Vincent, Heidi M, Johns Hopkins University Press, 2715 N Charles St, Baltimore, MD 21218-4363 *Tel:* 410-516-6900; 410-516-6987 (journal orders outside US & CN) *Toll Free Tel:* 800-537-5487 (book orders & cust serv); 800-548-1784 (journal orders) *Fax:* 410-516-6968; 410-516-3866 (journal orders); 410-516-6998 (orders) *E-mail:* hfscustserv@press.jhu.edu (cust serv); jrnlcirc@press.jhu.edu (journal orders) *Web Site:* www.press.jhu.edu; muse.jhu.edu, pg 114

Vineis, Mark, Mondo Publishing, 980 Avenue of the Americas, New York, NY 10018 *Tel:* 212-268-3560 *Toll Free Tel:* 888-88-MONDO (886-6636) *Toll Free Fax:* 888-532-4492 *E-mail:* info@mondopub.com *Web Site:* www.mondopub.com, pg 142

Vines, Nicole Verlin, Simon & Schuster Sales Division, 1230 Avenue of the Americas, New York, NY 10020 *Tel:* 212-698-7000, pg 200

Vinhateiro, Bethany, Houghton Mifflin Harcourt Trade & Reference Division, 125 High St, Boston, MA 02110 *Tel:* 617-351-5000 *Web Site:* www.hmhco.com, pg 104

Vinson, Arriel, Counterpoint Press LLC, 2560 Ninth St, Suite 318, Berkeley, CA 94710 *Tel:* 510-704-0230 *Fax:* 510-704-0268 *E-mail:* info@counterpointpress. com *Web Site:* counterpointpress.com; softskull.com, pg 58

Vinton, Mary, Society of Motion Picture & Television Engineers® (SMPTE®), 3 Barker Ave, 5th fl, White Plains, NY 10601 *Tel:* 914-761-1100 *Fax:* 914-761-3115 *Web Site:* www.smpte.org, pg 547

Viola, Kieran, Disney-Hyperion Books, 1101 Flower St, Glendale, CA 91201 *Web Site:* books.disney.com, pg 65

Visconti, Max, Grand & Archer Publishing, 463 Coyote, Cathedral City, CA 92234 *Tel:* 323-493-2785 *E-mail:* grandandarcher@gmail.com, pg 88

Viskovic, Hilda, Lectorum Publications Inc, 205 Chubb Ave, Lyndhurst, NJ 07071 *Toll Free Tel:* 800-345-5946 *Fax:* 201-559-2201 *Toll Free Fax:* 877-532-8676 *E-mail:* lectorum@lectorum.com *Web Site:* www. lectorum.com, pg 121

Vitek, John M, Saint Mary's Press, 702 Terrace Heights, Winona, MN 55987-1320 *Tel:* 507-457-7900 *Toll Free Tel:* 800-533-8095 *Toll Free Fax:* 800-344-9225 *E-mail:* smpress@smp.org *Web Site:* www.smp.org, pg 191

Vitola, Krista, Simon & Schuster Children's Publishing, 1230 Avenue of the Americas, New York, NY 10020 *Tel:* 212-698-7000 *Web Site:* www.simonandschuster. com/kids; www.simonandschuster.com/teen; simonandschuster.net; simonandschuster.biz, pg 199

Vitucci, Nancy, Health Administration Press, One N Franklin St, Suite 1700, Chicago, IL 60606-3491 *Tel:* 312-424-2800 *Fax:* 312-424-0014 *E-mail:* hapbooks@ache.org *Web Site:* www.ache. org/hap (orders), pg 96

Vocatura, Jessica Sue, American Literary Translators Association (ALTA), University of Arizona, Esquire Bldg, No 205, 1230 N Park Ave, Tucson, AZ 85721 *Tel:* 520-621-1757 *Web Site:* www.literarytranslators. org, pg 523

Vocatura, Jessica Sue, National Translation Award, University of Arizona, Esquire Bldg, No 205, 1230 N Park Ave, Tucson, AZ 85721 *Tel:* 520-621-1757 *Web Site:* www.literarytranslators.org/awards/national-translation-award, pg 646

Vocatura, Jessica Sue, Lucien Stryk Asian Translation Prize, University of Arizona, Esquire Bldg, No 205, 1230 N Park Ave, Tucson, AZ 85721 *Tel:* 520-621-1757 *Web Site:* literarytranslators.org/awards/lucien-stryk-prize, pg 671

Vogel, Casie, Ulysses Press, 195 Montague St, 14th fl, Brooklyn, NY 11201 *Tel:* 510-601-8301 *Toll Free Tel:* 800-377-2542 *Fax:* 510-601-8307 *E-mail:* ulysses@ulyssespress.com *Web Site:* www. ulyssespress.com, pg 223

Vogel, Chris, National Gallery of Art, Sixth & Constitution Ave NW, Washington, DC 20565 *Tel:* 202-842-6200 *Fax:* 202-408-8530 *E-mail:* publishingoffice@nga.gov *Web Site:* www. nga.gov, pg 146

Vogel, James, Angelus Press, 2915 Forest Ave, Kansas City, MO 64109 *Tel:* 816-753-3150 *Toll Free Tel:* 800-966-7337 *Fax:* 816-753-3557 *E-mail:* support@ angeluspress.org *Web Site:* www.angeluspress.org, pg 16

Vogel, Rachel, Dunow, Carlson & Lerner Literary Agency Inc, 27 W 20 St, Suite 1107, New York, NY 10011 *Tel:* 212-645-7606 *E-mail:* mail@dclagency. com *Web Site:* www.dclagency.com, pg 482

Vogler, Whitley, Gryphon House Inc, 6848 Leon's Way, Lewisville, NC 27023 *Toll Free Tel:* 800-638-0928 *Toll Free Fax:* 877-638-7576 *E-mail:* info@ghbooks. com *Web Site:* www.gryphonhouse.com, pg 90

Vogt, Elizabeth, Penguin Books, 375 Hudson St, New York, NY 10014 *Tel:* 212-366-2000 *E-mail:* penguinpublicity@us.penguingroup.com *Web Site:* www.penguinclassics.com; www.penguin. com, pg 163

Vogt, Morgan, Sourcebooks LLC, 1935 Brookdale Rd, Suite 139, Naperville, IL 60563 *Tel:* 630-961-3900 *Toll Free Tel:* 800-432-7444 *Fax:* 630-961-2168 *E-mail:* info@sourcebooks.com; customersupport@ sourcebooks.com *Web Site:* www.sourcebooks.com, pg 204

Volinsky, Slavik, Milady, Executive Woods, 5 Maxwell Dr, Clifton Park, NY 12065-2919 *Tel:* 518-348-2300 *Toll Free Tel:* 800-998-7498 *Fax:* 518-373-6309 *E-mail:* info@milady.com *Web Site:* milady.cengage. com, pg 140

Volkman, Prof Victor R, Loving Healing Press Inc, 5145 Pontiac Trail, Ann Arbor, MI 48105 *Tel:* 734-417-4266 *Toll Free Tel:* 888-761-6268 (US & CN) *Fax:* 734-663-6861 *E-mail:* info@lovinghealing.com; info@lhpress.com *Web Site:* www.lovinghealing.com; www.modernhistorypress.com (imprint), pg 128

Vollmar, Robert, Neustadt International Prize for Literature, c/o University of Oklahoma, 630 Parrington Oval, Suite 110, Norman, OK 73019-4033 *Tel:* 405-325-4531 *Web Site:* www.worldliteraturetoday.org; www.worldlit.org, pg 647

Vollmar, Robert, NSK Neustadt Prize for Children's Literature, c/o University of Oklahoma, 630 Parrington Oval, Suite 110, Norman, OK 73019-4033 *Tel:* 405-325-4531 *Web Site:* www.worldliteraturetoday.org; www.worldlit.org, pg 649

Volpi, Sara, Kentucky Writers Conference, 1906 College Heights Blvd, Suite 11067, Bowling Green, KY 42101-1067 *Tel:* 270-745-4502 *E-mail:* sokybookfest@wku.edu *Web Site:* www. sokybookfest.org, pg 576

Von Drasek, Lisa, Ezra Jack Keats/Kerlan Memorial Fellowship, University of Minnesota, 113 Andersen Library, 222 21 Ave S, Minneapolis, MN 55455 *Tel:* 612-624-4576 *E-mail:* asc-clrc@umn.edu *Web Site:* www.lib.umn.edu/clrc, pg 629

Von Hertsenberg, Kurt, National Wildlife Federation, 11100 Wildlife Center Dr, Reston, VA 20190-5362 *Toll Free Tel:* 800-477-5034 *Web Site:* www.zoobooks. com, pg 147

Von Hoelscher, Russ, National Association of Book Entrepreneurs (NABE), PO Box 606, Cottage Grove, OR 97424 *Tel:* 541-942-7455 *Fax:* 541-942-7455 *E-mail:* nabe@bookmarketingprofits.com *Web Site:* www.bookmarketingprofits.com, pg 538

von Knorring, John, Stylus Publishing LLC, 22883 Quicksilver Dr, Sterling, VA 20166-2019 *Tel:* 703-661-1504 (edit & sales) *Toll Free Tel:* 800-232-0223 (orders & cust serv) *Fax:* 703-661-1547 *E-mail:* stylusmail@styluspub.com (orders & cust serv); stylusinfo@styluspub.com *Web Site:* styluspub. presswarehouse.com, pg 210 von Mehren, Jane, Aevitas Creative Management, 19 W 21 St, Suite 501, New York, NY 10010 Tel: 212-765-6900 Web Site: aevitascreative.com, pg 474

von Moltke, Nina, Penguin Random House LLC, 1745 Broadway, New York, NY 10019 Tel: 212-782-9000 Toll Free Tel: 800-726-0600 Web Site: www.penguinrandomhouse.com, pg 164

von Moltke, Nina, Random House Publishing Group, 1745 Broadway, New York, NY 10019 Toll Free Tel: 800-200-3552 Web Site: www.randomhousebooks.com, pg 181

von Schilling, Claire, Penguin Random House LLC, 1745 Broadway, New York, NY 10019 Tel: 212-782-9000 Toll Free Tel: 800-726-0600 Web Site: www.penguinrandomhouse.com, pg 164

von Schilling, Claire, Random House Publishing Group, 1745 Broadway, New York, NY 10019 Toll Free Tel: 800-200-3552 Web Site: www.randomhousebooks.com, pg 181

Vondeling, Johanna, Berrett-Koehler Publishers Inc, 1333 Broadway, Suite 1000, Oakland, CA 94612 Tel: 510-817-2277 Fax: 510-817-2278 E-mail: bkpub@bkpub.com Web Site: www.bkconnection.com, pg 32

Vorenberg, Bonnie L, ArtAge Publications, PO Box 19955, Portland, OR 97280 Tel: 503-246-3000 Toll Free Tel: 800-858-4998 Web Site: www.seniortheatre.com, pg 20

Voros, Stephanie, Simon & Schuster Children's Publishing, 1230 Avenue of the Americas, New York, NY 10020 Tel: 212-698-7000 Web Site: www.simonandschuster.com/kids; www.simonandschuster.com/teen; simonandschuster.net; simonandschuster.biz, pg 199

Vosburgh, Andrew R, Graphic World Publishing Services, 11687 Adie Rd, St Louis, MO 63043 Tel: 314-567-9854 Fax: 314-567-7178 E-mail: quote@gwinc.com Web Site: www.gwinc.com, pg 464

Vreeland, Amy, Harry N Abrams Inc, 195 Broadway, 9th fl, New York, NY 10007 Tel: 212-206-7715 Toll Free Tel: 800-345-1359 Fax: 212-519-1210 E-mail: abrams@abramsbooks.com Web Site: www.abramsbooks.com, pg 3

Vreven, Line, Optometric Extension Program Foundation (OEP), 2300 York Rd, Suite 113, Timonium, MD 21093 Tel: 410-561-3791 E-mail: admin@oepf.org Web Site: www.oepf.org, pg 156

Vroegop, Allison, Houghton Mifflin Harcourt Trade & Reference Division, 125 High St, Boston, MA 02110 Tel: 617-351-5000 Web Site: www.hmhco.com, pg 104

Vukov-Kendes, Irena, Anchor Books, c/o Penguin Random House Inc, 1745 Broadway, New York, NY 10019 Tel: 212-572-2420 E-mail: vintageanchorpublicity@randomhouse.com Web Site: knopfdoubleday.com/imprint/anchor, pg 15

Vukov-Kendes, Irena, Vintage Books, c/o Penguin Random House Inc, 1745 Broadway, New York, NY 10019 Tel: 212-572-2420 E-mail: vintageanchorpublicity@randomhouse.com Web Site: knopfdoubleday.com/imprint/vintage, pg 236

Vuong, Kien, Simon & Schuster Canada, 166 King St E, Suite 300, Toronto, ON M5A 1J3, Canada Tel: 647-427-8882 Toll Free Tel: 800-387-0446; 800-268-3216 (orders) Fax: 647-430-9446 Toll Free Fax: 888-849-8151 (orders) E-mail: info@simonandschuster.ca Web Site: www.simonandschuster.ca, pg 440

Vyce, Stephanie, Harvard University Press, 79 Garden St, Cambridge, MA 02138-1499 Tel: 617-495-2600; 401-531-2800 (intl orders) Toll Free Tel: 800-405-1619 (orders) Fax: 617-495-5898 (gen); 617-496-4677 (edit & rts); 401-531-2801 (intl orders) Toll Free Fax: 800-406-9145 (orders) E-mail: contact_hup@harvard.edu Web Site: www.hup.harvard.edu, pg 95

Wachtel, Gina, Penguin Random House LLC, 1745 Broadway, New York, NY 10019 Tel: 212-782-9000 Toll Free Tel: 800-726-0600 Web Site: www.penguinrandomhouse.com, pg 164

Wachtel, Gina, Random House Publishing Group, 1745 Broadway, New York, NY 10019 Toll Free Tel: 800-200-3552 Web Site: www.randomhousebooks.com, pg 181

Wachtell, Diane, The New Press, 120 Wall St, 31st fl, New York, NY 10005 Tel: 212-629-8802 Toll Free Tel: 800-343-4489 (orders) Fax: 212-629-8617 Toll Free Fax: 800-351-5073 (orders) E-mail: newpress@thenewpress.com Web Site: www.thenewpress.com, pg 149

Wackrow, Dan, Harvard University Press, 79 Garden St, Cambridge, MA 02138-1499 Tel: 617-495-2600; 401-531-2800 (intl orders) Toll Free Tel: 800-405-1619 (orders) Fax: 617-495-5898 (gen); 617-496-4677 (edit & rts); 401-531-2801 (intl orders) Toll Free Fax: 800-406-9145 (orders) E-mail: contact_hup@harvard.edu Web Site: www.hup.harvard.edu, pg 95

Wade, Anthony, Letterbox/Papyrus of London Publishers USA, 10501 Broom Hill Dr, Suite 1-F, Las Vegas, NV 89134-7339 Tel: 702-256-3838 E-mail: lb27383@cox.net, pg 123

Wade, Lee, Random House Children's Books, 1745 Broadway, 10th fl, New York, NY 10019 Tel: 212-782-9000 Web Site: www.randomhousekids.com, pg 180

Wadsworth-Booth, Susan, Kent State University Press, 1118 University Library Bldg, 1125 Risman Dr, Kent, OH 44242 Tel: 330-672-7913 Fax: 330-672-3104 E-mail: ksupress@kent.edu Web Site: www.kentstateuniversitypress.com, pg 117

Waechtler, Heidi, Association of Book Publishers of British Columbia, 600-402 W Pender St, Vancouver, BC V6B 1T6, Canada Tel: 604-684-0228 E-mail: admin@books.bc.ca Web Site: www.books.bc.ca, pg 526

Waggner, Jackie, Macmillan, 120 Broadway, 22nd fl, New York, NY 10271 Tel: 646-307-5151 E-mail: press.inquiries@macmillan.com Web Site: www.macmillan.com, pg 130

Waggoner, Lynn, Disney Press, 1101 Flower St, Glendale, CA 91201 Web Site: books.disney.com, pg 65

Waggoner, Lynn, Disney Publishing Worldwide, 1101 Flower St, Glendale, CA 91201 Web Site: books.disney.com, pg 65

Wagner, Amy, Abrams Artists Agency, 275 Seventh Ave, 26th fl, New York, NY 10001 Tel: 646-486-4600 Fax: 646-486-0100 E-mail: literary@abramsartny.com Web Site: www.abramsartists.com, pg 473

Wagner, Chris, Simon & Schuster, Inc, 1230 Avenue of the Americas, New York, NY 10020 Tel: 212-698-7000 Toll Free Tel: 800-223-2336 (orders) Fax: 212-698-7007 Toll Free Fax: 800-943-9831 (orders) E-mail: firstname.lastname@simonandschuster.com; purchaseorders@simonandschuster.com (orders) Web Site: www.simonandschuster.com, pg 199

Wagner, Kyle, University of Chicago Press, 1427 E 60 St, Chicago, IL 60637-2954 Tel: 773-702-7700; 773-702-7600 Toll Free Tel: 800-621-2736 (orders) Fax: 773-702-9756; 773-660-2235 (orders) 773-702-2708 E-mail: custserv@press.uchicago.edu; marketing@press.uchicago.edu Web Site: www.press.uchicago.edu, pg 226

Wagner, Paul, Princeton Architectural Press, 202 Warren St, Hudson, NY 12534 Tel: 518-671-6100 Toll Free Tel: 800-722-6657 (dist); 800-759-0190 (sales) E-mail: sales@papress.com Web Site: www.papress.com, pg 174

Wagshal, Menachem, Moznaim Publishing Corp, 4304 12 Ave, Brooklyn, NY 11219 Tel: 718-438-7680 Fax: 718-438-1305 E-mail: sales@moznaim.com Web Site: www.moznaim.com, pg 144

Wahl, Kate, Stanford University Press, 425 Broadway St, Redwood City, CA 94063-3126 Tel: 650-723-9434 Fax: 650-725-3457 E-mail: info@www.sup.org; publicity@www.sup.org; sales@www.sup.org Web Site: www.sup.org, pg 206

Waintraub, Adrienne, Random House Children's Books, 1745 Broadway, 10th fl, New York, NY 10019 Tel: 212-782-9000 Web Site: www.randomhousekids.com, pg 180

Waintraub, Joanna, The Amy Rennert Agency Inc, 1550 Tiburon Blvd, Suite 302, Tiburon, CA 94920 Tel: 415-789-8955 E-mail: queries@amyrennert.com (no unsol queries) Web Site: amyrennert.com, pg 499

Wait, Candace, Yaddo Artists Residency, 312 Union Ave, Saratoga Springs, NY 12866 Tel: 518-584-0746 Fax: 518-584-1312 E-mail: yaddo@yaddo.org Web Site: www.yaddo.org, pg 580

Wakefield, Julie, Mel Bay Publications Inc, 1734 Gilsinn Lane, Fenton, MO 63026 Tel: 636-257-3970 Toll Free Tel: 800-863-5229 Fax: 800-257-5062 Toll Free Fax: 800-660-9818 E-mail: email@melbay.com Web Site: www.melbay.com, pg 137

Walden, Robert, News Media Alliance, 4401 N Fairfax Dr, Suite 300, Arlington, VA 22203 Tel: 571-366-1000 E-mail: info@newsmediaalliance.org Web Site: www.newsmediaalliance.org, pg 541

Waldman, Brett, TRISTAN Publishing, 2355 Louisiana Ave N, Minneapolis, MN 55427 Tel: 763-545-1383 Toll Free Tel: 866-545-1383 Fax: 763-545-1387 E-mail: info@tristanpublishing.com Web Site: www.tristanpublishing.com, pg 221

Waldman, Sheila, TRISTAN Publishing, 2355 Louisiana Ave N, Minneapolis, MN 55427 Tel: 763-545-1383 Toll Free Tel: 866-545-1383 Fax: 763-545-1387 E-mail: info@tristanpublishing.com Web Site: www.tristanpublishing.com, pg 221

Waldron, Laura, University of Pennsylvania Press, 3905 Spruce St, Philadelphia, PA 19104 Tel: 215-898-6261 Fax: 215-898-0404 E-mail: custserv@pobox.upenn.edu Web Site: www.pennpress.org, pg 230

Waldrup, Jody, Hachette Nashville, 6100 Tower Circle, Room 210, Franklin, TN 37067 Tel: 615-221-0996 Fax: 615-221-0962 Web Site: www.hachettebookgroup.com, pg 91

Wales, Elizabeth, Wales Literary Agency Inc, 1508 Tenth Ave E, No 401, Seattle, WA 98102 Tel: 206-284-7114 E-mail: waleslit@waleslit.com Web Site: www.waleslit.com, pg 507

Walker, Alan F, Ruth & Sylvia Schwartz Children's Book Awards, c/o Ontario Arts Council, 121 Bloor St E, 7th fl, Toronto, ON M4W 3M5, Canada Tel: 416-961-1660 Toll Free Tel: 800-387-0058 (ON) Fax: 416-961-7796 (Ontario Arts Council); 416-969-7450 (Ontario Arts Foundation) E-mail: info@arts.on.ca; foundation@arts.on.ca Web Site: www.arts.on.ca; ontarioartsfoundation.on.ca/pages/ruth-sylvia-schwartz-awards, pg 666

Walker, Amanda, Dutton, 1745 Broadway, New York, NY 10019 Tel: 212-366-2000 Fax: 212-366-2262 E-mail: duttonpublicity@us.penguingroup.com Web Site: www.penguin.com, pg 68

Walker, Andrea, Random House Publishing Group, 1745 Broadway, New York, NY 10019 Toll Free Tel: 800-200-3552 Web Site: www.randomhousebooks.com, pg 181

Walker, Andrew, American Program Bureau Inc, One Gateway Center, Suite 751, Newton, MA 02458 Tel: 617-614-1600 Fax: 617-965-6610 E-mail: apb@apbspeakers.com Web Site: www.apbspeakers.com, pg 515

Walker, Bette, Stephen Leacock Memorial Medal for Humour, 149 Peter St N, Orillia, ON L3V 4Z4, Canada Tel: 705-326-9286 Web Site: www.leacock.ca, pg 632

Walker, Brian, Charlesbridge Publishing Inc, 85 Main St, Watertown, MA 02472 Tel: 617-926-0329 Toll Free Tel: 800-225-3214 Fax: 617-926-5720 Toll Free Fax: 800-926-5775 E-mail: books@charlesbridge.com Web Site: www.charlesbridge.com, pg 49

Walker, Carl, Software & Information Industry Association (SIIA), 1090 Vermont Ave NW, 6th fl, Washington, DC 20005-4905 Tel: 202-289-7442 Fax: 202-289-7097 Web Site: www.siia.net, pg 547

Walter, Timothy M, Catholic Press Awards, 205 W Monroe St, Suite 470, Chicago, IL 60606 *Tel:* 312-380-6789 *Fax:* 312-361-0256 *E-mail:* cpaawards@catholicpress.org *Web Site:* www.catholicpress.org, pg 603

Walters, Ed, Tuttle Publishing, Airport Business Park, 364 Innovation Dr, North Clarendon, VT 05759-9436 *Tel:* 802-773-8930 *Toll Free Tel:* 800-526-2778 *Fax:* 802-773-6993 *Toll Free Fax:* 800-FAX-TUTL (329-8885) *E-mail:* info@tuttlepublishing.com; orders@tuttlepublishing.com *Web Site:* www.tuttlepublishing.com, pg 222

Walters, John P, Hudson Institute, 1201 Pennsylvania Ave NW, Suite 400, Washington, DC 20004 *Tel:* 202-974-2400 *Fax:* 202-974-2410 *E-mail:* info@hudson.org *Web Site:* www.hudson.org, pg 104

Walters, Marthe, University Press of Florida, 2046 NE Waldo Rd, Suite 2100, Gainesville, FL 32609 *Tel:* 352-392-1351 *Toll Free Tel:* 800-226-3822 (orders only) *Fax:* 352-392-0590 *Toll Free Fax:* 800-680-1955 (orders only) *E-mail:* press@upress.ufl.edu; orders@upress.ufl.edu *Web Site:* www.upf.com, pg 232

Walters-Moore, Linda, George Orwell Award, 340 N Neil St, Suite 104, Champaign, IL 61820 *Tel:* 217-328-3870 *Toll Free Tel:* 877-369-6283 (cust serv) *Fax:* 217-328-0977 *E-mail:* publiclangawards@ncte.org *Web Site:* www.ncte.org, pg 651

Walther, Luann, Anchor Books, c/o Penguin Random House Inc, 1745 Broadway, New York, NY 10019 *Tel:* 212-572-2420 *E-mail:* vintageanchorpublicity@randomhouse.com *Web Site:* knopfdoubleday.com/imprint/anchor, pg 15

Walther, LuAnn, Everyman's Library, c/o Penguin Random House Inc, 1745 Broadway, New York, NY 10019 *Tel:* 212-751-2600 *Fax:* 212-572-2662 (foreign rts) *Web Site:* knopfdoubleday.com, pg 74

Walther, Luann, Vintage Books, c/o Penguin Random House Inc, 1745 Broadway, New York, NY 10019 *Tel:* 212-572-2420 *E-mail:* vintageanchorpublicity@randomhouse.com *Web Site:* knopfdoubleday.com/imprint/vintage, pg 236

Waltman, Fran, Edward Lewis Wallant Award, Maurice Greenberg Center for Judaic Studies, 200 Bloomfield Ave, Harry Jack Gray E 300, West Hartford, CT 06117 *Tel:* 860-768-4964 *Fax:* 860-768-5044 *E-mail:* mgcjs@hartford.edu *Web Site:* www.hartford.edu/a_and_s/greenberg/wallant, pg 676

Waltman, Irving, Edward Lewis Wallant Award, Maurice Greenberg Center for Judaic Studies, 200 Bloomfield Ave, Harry Jack Gray E 300, West Hartford, CT 06117 *Tel:* 860-768-4964 *Fax:* 860-768-5044 *E-mail:* mgcjs@hartford.edu *Web Site:* www.hartford.edu/a_and_s/greenberg/wallant, pg 676

Walton, Elysia, Arcadia Publishing Inc, 420 Wando Park Blvd, Mount Pleasant, SC 29464 *Tel:* 843-853-2070 *Toll Free Tel:* 888-313-2665 (orders only) *Fax:* 843-853-0044 *E-mail:* sales@arcadiapublishing.com *Web Site:* www.arcadiapublishing.com, pg 19

Walton, Kathy S, TCU Press, 3000 Sandage Ave, Fort Worth, TX 76109 *Tel:* 817-257-7822 *Toll Free Tel:* 800-826-8911 (orders) *Fax:* 817-257-5075 *Web Site:* www.prs.tcu.edu, pg 213

Wang, Chi, American Psychological Association, 750 First St NE, Washington, DC 20002-4242 *Tel:* 202-336-5510 *Toll Free Tel:* 800-374-2721 *Fax:* 202-336-5502 *E-mail:* order@apa.org *Web Site:* www.apa.org/books, pg 13

Wanger, Shelley, Pantheon Books, c/o Penguin Random House Inc, 1745 Broadway, New York, NY 10019 *Tel:* 212-751-2600 *Fax:* 212-572-2662 (foreign rts) *Web Site:* knopfdoubleday.com, pg 159

Wantland, Clydette, University of Illinois Press, 1325 S Oak St, MC-566, Champaign, IL 61820-6903 *Tel:* 217-333-0950 *Fax:* 217-244-8082 *E-mail:* uipress@uillinois.edu; journals@uillinois.edu *Web Site:* www.press.uillinois.edu, pg 227

Ward, Andy, Random House Publishing Group, 1745 Broadway, New York, NY 10019 *Tel:* 800-200-3552 *Web Site:* www.randomhousebooks.com, pg 181

Ward, Anne C, High Tide Press, 301 Veterans Pkwy, New Lenox, IL 60451 *E-mail:* orders@cherryhillhightide.com *Web Site:* www.cherryhillhightide.com, pg 99

Ward, April, Random House Children's Books, 1745 Broadway, 10th fl, New York, NY 10019 *Tel:* 212-782-9000 *Web Site:* www.randomhousekids.com, pg 180

Ward, Casey, Random House Children's Books, 1745 Broadway, 10th fl, New York, NY 10019 *Tel:* 212-782-9000 *Web Site:* www.randomhousekids.com, pg 180

Ward, Courtney, Pauline Books & Media, 50 Saint Paul's Ave, Boston, MA 02130 *Tel:* 617-522-8911 *Toll Free Tel:* 800-876-4463 (orders); 800-836-9723 (cust serv) *Fax:* 617-541-9805 *E-mail:* editorial@paulinemedia.com (ms submissions); orderentry@pauline.org (cust serv) *Web Site:* www.pauline.org/pbmpublishing, pg 161

Ward, Elizabeth, Random House Children's Books, 1745 Broadway, 10th fl, New York, NY 10019 *Tel:* 212-782-9000 *Web Site:* www.randomhousekids.com, pg 180

Warden, Yorke, Living Stream Ministry (LSM), 2431 W La Palma Ave, Anaheim, CA 92801 *Tel:* 714-991-4681 *Toll Free Tel:* 800-549-5164 *Fax:* 714-236-6005 *E-mail:* books@lsm.org *Web Site:* www.lsm.org, pg 127

Warfield, Marshall, Rosemont College, Graduate Publg Prog, 1400 Montgomery Ave, Rosemont, PA 19010 *Tel:* 610-527-0200 (ext 2431) *Web Site:* www.rosemont.edu, pg 584

Waricha, Joan, Parachute Publishing LLC, 157 Columbus Ave, Suite 518, New York, NY 10023 *Tel:* 212-691-1422, pg 160

Warker, Derek, The New Press, 120 Wall St, 31st fl, New York, NY 10005 *Tel:* 212-629-8802 *Toll Free Tel:* 800-343-4489 (orders) *Fax:* 212-629-8617 *Toll Free Fax:* 800-351-5073 (orders) *E-mail:* newpress@thenewpress.com *Web Site:* www.thenewpress.com, pg 149

Warner, Matt, Gem Guides Book Co, 1155 W Ninth St, Upland, CA 91786 *Tel:* 626-855-1611 *Toll Free Tel:* 800-824-5118 (orders) *Fax:* 626-855-1610 *E-mail:* gemguidesbooks.com; sales@gemguidesbooks.com (orders) *Web Site:* www.gemguidesbooks.com, pg 84

Warnock, Colin, Fine Creative Media, Inc, 589 Eighth Ave, 6th fl, New York, NY 10018 *Tel:* 212-595-3500 *Fax:* 212-202-4195 *E-mail:* info@mjfbooks.com *Web Site:* www.mjfbooks.com, pg 78

Warren, Bruce, Abrams Learning Trends, 16310 Bratton Lane, Suite 250, Austin, TX 78728-2403 *Toll Free Tel:* 800-227-9120 *Toll Free Fax:* 800-737-3322 *E-mail:* customerservice@abramslearningtrends.com (orders, cust serv); contactus@abramslearningtrends.com *Web Site:* www.abramslearningtrends.com (orders, cust serv), pg 3

Warren, Mark, Random House Publishing Group, 1745 Broadway, New York, NY 10019 *Toll Free Tel:* 800-200-3552 *Web Site:* www.randomhousebooks.com, pg 181

Warren, Wenche, YWAM Publishing, PO Box 55787, Seattle, WA 98155-0787 *Tel:* 425-771-1153 *Toll Free Tel:* 800-922-2143 *Fax:* 425-775-2383 *E-mail:* books@ywampublishing.com *Web Site:* www.ywampublishing.com, pg 247

Warschausky, Kara, Macmillan, 120 Broadway, 22nd fl, New York, NY 10271 *Tel:* 646-307-5151 *E-mail:* press.inquiries@macmillan.com *Web Site:* www.macmillan.com, pg 130

Warshenbrot, Amalia, AJL Judaica Bibliography Award, PO Box 1118, Teaneck, NJ 07666 *Tel:* 201-371-3255 *E-mail:* info@jewishlibraries.org *Web Site:* jewishlibraries.org, pg 590

Warshenbrot, Amalia, AJL Judaica Reference Award, PO Box 1118, Teaneck, NJ 07666 *Tel:* 201-371-3255 *E-mail:* info@jewishlibraries.org *Web Site:* jewishlibraries.org, pg 590

Warshenbrot, Amalia, Association of Jewish Libraries (AJL) Inc, PO Box 1118, Teaneck, NJ 07666 *Tel:* 201-371-3255 *E-mail:* info@jewishlibraries.org *Web Site:* jewishlibraries.org, pg 526

Warshenbrot, Amalia, Sydney Taylor Book Awards, PO Box 1118, Teaneck, NJ 07666 *Tel:* 201-371-3255 *E-mail:* chair@sydneytaylorbookaward.org; info@jewishlibraries.org *Web Site:* www.sydneytaylorbookaward.org, pg 671

Warten, Melissa, Farrar, Straus & Giroux Books for Young Readers, 120 Broadway, New York, NY 10271 *Tel:* 212-741-6900 *Toll Free Tel:* 888-330-8477 (orders) *Fax:* 212-633-9385 *Web Site:* us.macmillan.com/mackids; www.mackidsbooks.com, pg 76

Warwick-Smith, Simon, Warwick Associates, 18340 Sonoma Hwy, Sonoma, CA 95476 *Tel:* 707-939-9212 *Fax:* 707-938-3515 *E-mail:* warwick@vom.com *Web Site:* www.warwickassociates.com, pg 507

Wascavage, Matt, American Society of Agronomy, 5585 Guilford Rd, Madison, WI 53711-5801 *Tel:* 608-273-8080 *Fax:* 608-273-2021 *E-mail:* headquarters@sciencesocieties.org *Web Site:* www.agronomy.org, pg 14

Wascavage, Matt, Soil Science Society of America (SSSA), 5585 Guilford Rd, Madison, WI 53711-5801 *Tel:* 608-273-8080 *Fax:* 608-273-2021 *Web Site:* www.soils.org, pg 203

Wasielewski, Leah, HarperCollins General Books Group, 195 Broadway, New York, NY 10007 *Tel:* 212-207-7000 *Web Site:* www.harpercollins.com, pg 93

Wasko, Jim, OCP, 5536 NE Hassalo St, Portland, OR 97213 *Tel:* 503-281-1191 *Toll Free Tel:* 800-548-8749 *Fax:* 503-282-3486 *Toll Free Fax:* 800-843-8181 *E-mail:* liturgy@ocp.org *Web Site:* www.ocp.org, pg 154

Wasserman, Steve, Heyday, 1808 San Pablo Ave, Suite A, Berkeley, CA 94702 *Tel:* 510-549-3564 *E-mail:* heyday@heydaybooks.com *Web Site:* heydaybooks.com, pg 98

Wasserman, Veronica, Houghton Mifflin Harcourt Trade & Reference Division, 125 High St, Boston, MA 02110 *Tel:* 617-351-5000 *Web Site:* www.hmhco.com, pg 104

Wasson, Beth, Eleanor Taylor Bland Crime Fiction Writers of Color Award, PO Box 442124, Lawrence, KS 66044 *Tel:* 785-842-1325 *Fax:* 785-856-6314 *E-mail:* admin@sistersincrime.org *Web Site:* www.sistersincrime.org, pg 599

Waterman, Daniel, University of Alabama Press, 200 Hackberry Lane, 2nd fl, Tuscaloosa, AL 35487 *Tel:* 205-348-5180 *Fax:* 205-348-9201 *Web Site:* www.uapress.ua.edu, pg 225

Waterman, Marisa, American Academy of Environmental Engineers & Scientists®, 147 Old Solomons Island Rd, Suite 303, Annapolis, MD 21401 *Tel:* 410-266-3311 *Fax:* 410-266-7653 *E-mail:* info@aaees.org *Web Site:* www.aaees.org, pg 9

Waterman, Susan, New Mexico Book Association (NMBA), 1219 Luisa St, Suite 1, Santa Fe, NM 87505 *Tel:* 505-660-6357 *E-mail:* admin@nmbook.org *Web Site:* www.nmbook.org, pg 541

Waters, Lindsay, Harvard University Press, 79 Garden St, Cambridge, MA 02138-1499 *Tel:* 617-495-2600; 401-531-2800 (intl orders) *Toll Free Tel:* 800-405-1619 (orders) *Fax:* 617-495-5898 (gen); 617-496-4677 (edit & rts); 401-531-2801 (intl orders) *Toll Free Fax:* 800-406-9145 (orders) *E-mail:* contact_hup@harvard.edu *Web Site:* www.hup.harvard.edu, pg 95

Waters, Michele, New Harbinger Publications Inc, 5674 Shattuck Ave, Oakland, CA 94609 *Tel:* 510-652-0215 *Toll Free Tel:* 800-748-6273 (orders only) *Fax:* 510-652-5472 *Toll Free Fax:* 800-652-1613 *E-mail:* nhhelp@newharbinger.com; customerservice@newharbinger.com *Web Site:* www.newharbinger.com, pg 148

Weidman, Jennifer, Simon & Schuster, Inc, 1230 Avenue of the Americas, New York, NY 10020 *Tel:* 212-698-7000 *Toll Free Tel:* 800-223-2336 (orders) *Fax:* 212-698-7007 *Toll Free Fax:* 800-943-9831 (orders) *E-mail:* firstname.lastname@simonandschuster.com; purchaseorders@simonandschuster.com (orders) *Web Site:* www.simonandschuster.com, pg 199

Weidman, Pamela, Princeton University Press, 41 William St, Princeton, NJ 08540-5237 *Tel:* 609-258-4900 *Fax:* 609-258-6305 *Web Site:* press.princeton. edu, pg 175

Weigl, Charles, AK Press Distribution, 370 Ryan Ave, Unit 100, Chico, CA 95973 *Tel:* 510-208-1700 *Fax:* 510-208-1701 *E-mail:* info@akpress.org *Web Site:* www.akpress.org, pg 6

Weigl, Linda, Weigl Educational Publishers Ltd, 6325 Tenth St SE, Calgary, AB T2H 2Z9, Canada *Tel:* 403-233-7747 *Toll Free Tel:* 800-668-0766 *Fax:* 403-233-7769 *Toll Free Fax:* 866-449-3445 *E-mail:* orders@ weigl.com *Web Site:* www.weigl.ca; av2books.com, pg 445

Weikart, Jim, International Association of Crime Writers Inc, North American Branch, 243 Fifth Ave, Suite 537, New York, NY 10016 *Tel:* 212-243-8966 *Fax:* 815-361-1477 *E-mail:* info@crimewritersna.org *Web Site:* www.crimewritersna.org, pg 535

Weikersheimer, Joshua R, ASCP Press, 33 W Monroe St, Suite 1600, Chicago, IL 60603 *Tel:* 312-541-4999 *Toll Free Tel:* 800-267-2727 *Fax:* 312-541-4998 *Web Site:* www.ascp.org, pg 22

Weil, Elora, GP Putnam's Sons (Hardcover), 375 Hudson St, New York, NY 10014 *Tel:* 212-366-2000 *Fax:* 212-366-2643 *E-mail:* online@penguinputnam. com *Web Site:* www.penguin.com/publishers/ gpputnamssons, pg 178

Weil, Gideon, HarperCollins General Books Group, 195 Broadway, New York, NY 10007 *Tel:* 212-207-7000 *Web Site:* www.harpercollins.com, pg 93

Weil, Joe, Binghamton University Creative Writing Program, c/o Dept of English, PO Box 6000, Binghamton, NY 13902-6000 *Tel:* 607-777-2168 *Fax:* 607-777-2408 *E-mail:* cwpro@binghamton.edu *Web Site:* english.binghamton.edu/cwpro, pg 581

Weil, Robert, W W Norton & Company Inc, 500 Fifth Ave, New York, NY 10110-0017 *Tel:* 212-354-5500 *Toll Free Tel:* 800-233-4830 (orders & cust serv) *Fax:* 212-869-0856 *Toll Free Fax:* 800-458-6515 *E-mail:* orders@wwnorton.com *Web Site:* wwnorton. com, pg 152

Weiland, Matt, W W Norton & Company Inc, 500 Fifth Ave, New York, NY 10110-0017 *Tel:* 212-354-5500 *Toll Free Tel:* 800-233-4830 (orders & cust serv) *Fax:* 212-869-0856 *Toll Free Fax:* 800-458-6515 *E-mail:* orders@wwnorton.com *Web Site:* wwnorton. com, pg 152

Weiman, Mark, Regent Press Publishers & Printers, 2747 Regent St, Berkeley, CA 94705 *Tel:* 510-845-1196 *E-mail:* regentpress@mindspring.com *Web Site:* www. regentpress.net, pg 184

Weimann, Frank, Folio Literary Management, The Film Center Bldg, 630 Ninth Ave, Suite 1101, New York, NY 10036 *Tel:* 212-400-1494 *Fax:* 212-967-0977 *Web Site:* www.foliolit.com, pg 484

Wein, Lauren, Avid Reader Press, 1230 Avenue of the Americas, New York, NY 10020 *Web Site:* avidreaderpress.com, pg 26

Weinbaum, Robyn, Florida Writers Association Conference, PO Box 66069, St Pete Beach, FL 33736-6069 *Web Site:* www.floridawriters.net, pg 574

Weinbaum, Robyn, Florida Writers Association Inc, PO Box 66069, St Pete Beach, FL 33736-6069 *Web Site:* www.floridawriters.net, pg 533

Weinberg, Joy, Jewish Publication Society, 2100 Arch St, Philadelphia, PA 19103 *Tel:* 215-832-0600 *Toll Free Tel:* 800-234-3151 *Fax:* 215-568-2017 *Web Site:* www.jps.org, pg 113

Weinberg, Kathie, Walter Dean Myers Awards for Outstanding Children's Literature, 10319 Westlake Dr, No 104, Bethesda, MD 20817 *Tel:* 701-404-9632

(voicemail only) *E-mail:* walteraward@diversebooks. org *Web Site:* diversebooks.org/our-programs/walter-award, pg 644

Weinberg, Susan, Hachette Book Group, 1290 Avenue of the Americas, New York, NY 10104 *Tel:* 212-364-1100 *Toll Free Tel:* 800-759-0190 (cust serv) *Fax:* 212-364-0933 (intl orders) *Toll Free Fax:* 800-286-9471 (cust serv) *Web Site:* www. hachettebookgroup.com, pg 91

Weinberg, Susan, Perseus Books, 1290 Avenue of the Americas, New York, NY 10104 *Tel:* 212-340-8100 *Toll Free Tel:* 800-343-4499 (cust serv) *Fax:* 212-340-8105 *Web Site:* www.perseusbooks.com, pg 167

Weinberger, Russell, Brockman Inc, 260 Fifth Ave, 10th fl, New York, NY 10001 *Tel:* 212-935-8900 *Fax:* 212-935-5535 *E-mail:* rights@brockman.com *Web Site:* www.brockman.com, pg 478

Weiner, Allison, Chronicle Books, 680 Second St, San Francisco, CA 94107 *Tel:* 415-537-4200 *Toll Free Tel:* 800-759-0190 (cust serv) *Fax:* 415-537-4460 *Toll Free Fax:* 800-858-7787 (orders); 800-286-9471 (cust serv) *E-mail:* frontdesk@chroniclebooks.com *Web Site:* www.chroniclebooks.com, pg 52

Weiner, Andy, Harry N Abrams Inc, 195 Broadway, 9th fl, New York, NY 10007 *Tel:* 212-206-7715 *Toll Free Tel:* 800-345-1359 *Fax:* 212-519-1210 *E-mail:* abrams@abramsbooks.com *Web Site:* www. abramsbooks.com, pg 3

Weiner, Cherry, Cherry Weiner Literary Agency, 925 Oak Bluff Ct, Dacula, GA 30019-6660 *Tel:* 732-446-2096 *Fax:* 732-792-0506 *E-mail:* cherry8486@aol. com, pg 508

Weiner, Ruth, Seven Stories Press, 140 Watts St, New York, NY 10013 *Tel:* 212-226-8760 *Toll Free Tel:* 800-733-3000 (orders) *Fax:* 212-226-1411 *E-mail:* sevenstories@sevenstories.com *Web Site:* www.sevenstories.com, pg 197

Weinfield, Madeline, Four Quartets Prize, 15 Gramercy Park, New York, NY 10003 *Tel:* 212-254-9628 *Web Site:* poetrysociety.org/awards, pg 616

Weinfield, Madeline, Frost Medal, 15 Gramercy Park, New York, NY 10003 *Tel:* 212-254-9628 *Web Site:* poetrysociety.org/awards, pg 617

Weinfield, Madeline, Poetry Society of America (PSA), 15 Gramercy Park, New York, NY 10003 *Tel:* 212-254-9628 *Web Site:* poetrysociety.org, pg 543

Weinfield, Madeline, Shelley Memorial Award, 15 Gramercy Park, New York, NY 10003 *Tel:* 212-254-9628 *Web Site:* poetrysociety.org/awards, pg 667

Weingarden, Matt, American Marketing Association, 130 E Randolph St, 22nd fl, Chicago, IL 60601 *Tel:* 312-542-9000 *Toll Free Tel:* 800-AMA-1150 (262-1150) *Web Site:* www.ama.org, pg 523

Weingarten, Seymour, The Guilford Press, 370 Seventh Ave, Suite 1200, New York, NY 10001-1020 *Tel:* 212-431-9800 *Toll Free Tel:* 800-365-7006 *Fax:* 212-966-6708 *E-mail:* info@guilford.com *Web Site:* www. guilford.com, pg 90

Weingarten, Simone, Harvard Square Editions, Beachwood Terr, Hollywood, CA 90068 *Tel:* 323-203-0233 *E-mail:* submissions@harvardsquareeditions.org *Web Site:* harvardsquareeditions.org, pg 95

Weingel-Fidel, Loretta, The Weingel-Fidel Agency, 310 E 46 St, Suite 21-E, New York, NY 10017 *Tel:* 212-599-2959 *Fax:* 212-286-1986 *E-mail:* queries@ theweingel-fidelagency.com, pg 508

Weinreb, Jenya, Yale University Press, 302 Temple St, New Haven, CT 06511-8909 *Tel:* 203-432-0960; 203-432-0966 (sales); 401-531-2800 (cust serv) *Toll Free Tel:* 800-405-1619 (cust serv) *Fax:* 203-432-0948; 203-432-8485 (sales); 401-531-2801 (cust serv) *Toll Free Fax:* 800-406-9145 (cust serv) *E-mail:* sales. press@yale.edu (sales); customer.care@triliteral.org (cust serv) *Web Site:* www.yalebooks.com; yalepress. yale.edu/yupbooks, pg 246

Weinrich, Curtis, North Star Press of Saint Cloud Inc, 19485 Estes Rd, Clearwater, MN 55320 *Tel:* 320-558-9062 *E-mail:* info@northstarpress.com *Web Site:* www.northstarpress.com, pg 152

Weinstein, Alexander, Summer Writing Seminar, 7 E Pasture Rd, Aquinnah, MA 02535 *Tel:* 954-242-2903 *Web Site:* mvicw.com, pg 579

Weinstein, Dr Cathrin, Thieme Medical Publishers Inc, 333 Seventh Ave, 18th fl, New York, NY 10001 *Tel:* 212-760-0888 *Toll Free Tel:* 800-782-3488 *Fax:* 212-947-1112 *E-mail:* customerservice@thieme. com *Web Site:* www.thieme.com, pg 217

Weinstein, Kenneth R, Hudson Institute, 1201 Pennsylvania Ave NW, Suite 400, Washington, DC 20004 *Tel:* 202-974-2400 *Fax:* 202-974-2410 *E-mail:* info@hudson.org *Web Site:* www.hudson.org, pg 104

Weinstein, Michael, Teachers College Press, 1234 Amsterdam Ave, New York, NY 10027 *Tel:* 212-678-3929 *Fax:* 212-678-4149 *E-mail:* tcpress@tc.edu *Web Site:* www.tcpress.com, pg 214

Weintraub, Dori, St Martin's Press, LLC, 120 Broadway, New York, NY 10271 *Tel:* 646-307-5151 *Web Site:* us. macmillan.com/smp, pg 190

Weintraub, Steve, Lawyers & Judges Publishing Co Inc, 917 N Swan Rd, Suite 300, Tucson, AZ 85711 *Tel:* 520-323-1500 *Fax:* 520-323-0055 *E-mail:* sales@lawyersandjudges.com *Web Site:* www. lawyersandjudges.com, pg 121

Weinzimer, Andrea, Hachette Book Group, 1290 Avenue of the Americas, New York, NY 10104 *Tel:* 212-364-1100 *Toll Free Tel:* 800-759-0190 (cust serv) *Fax:* 212-364-0933 (intl orders) *Toll Free Fax:* 800-286-9471 (cust serv) *Web Site:* www. hachettebookgroup.com, pg 90

Weisberg, Don, Macmillan, 120 Broadway, 22nd fl, New York, NY 10271 *Tel:* 646-307-5151 *E-mail:* press. inquiries@macmillan.com *Web Site:* www.macmillan. com, pg 129

Weisberg, Don, Macmillan Audio, 120 Broadway, 22nd fl, New York, NY 10271 *Tel:* 646-307-5151 *Toll Free Tel:* 888-330-8477 (cust serv) *Web Site:* www. macmillanaudio.com, pg 130

Weisfeld, Jarred, Objective Entertainment, 609 Greenwich St, 6th fl, New York, NY 10014 *Tel:* 212-431-5454 *Fax:* 917-464-6394 *Web Site:* www. objectiveent.com, pg 498

Weisgarber, Ann, Carr P Collins Award, PO Box 609, Round Rock, TX 78680 *Tel:* 512-683-5640 *E-mail:* president@texasinstituteofletters.org *Web Site:* www.texasinstituteofletters.org, pg 606

Weisgarber, Ann, Soeurette Diehl Fraser Translation Award, PO Box 609, Round Rock, TX 78680 *Tel:* 512-683-5640 *E-mail:* president@ texasinstituteofletters.org *Web Site:* www. texasinstituteofletters.org, pg 617

Weisgarber, Ann, Jesse H Jones Award, PO Box 609, Round Rock, TX 78680 *Tel:* 512-683-5640 *E-mail:* president@texasinstituteofletters.org *Web Site:* www.texasinstituteofletters.org, pg 629

Weisgarber, Ann, Ramirez Family Award, PO Box 609, Round Rock, TX 78680 *Tel:* 512-683-5640 *E-mail:* president@texasinstituteofletters.org *Web Site:* www.texasinstituteofletters.org, pg 660

Weisgarber, Ann, Edwin "Bud" Shrake Award for Best Short Nonfiction, PO Box 609, Round Rock, TX 78680 *Tel:* 512-683-5640 *E-mail:* president@ texasinstituteofletters.org *Web Site:* www. texasinstituteofletters.org, pg 667

Weisgarber, Ann, Helen C Smith Memorial Award, PO Box 609, Round Rock, TX 78680 *Tel:* 512-683-5640 *E-mail:* president@texasinstituteofletters.org *Web Site:* www.texasinstituteofletters.org, pg 668

Weisgarber, Ann, Texas Institute of Letters (TIL), PO Box 609, Round Rock, TX 78680 *E-mail:* president@texasinstituteofletters.org; secretary@texasinstituteofletters.org *Web Site:* www. texasinstituteofletters.org, pg 548

Weisgarber, Ann, Texas Institute of Letters Awards, PO Box 609, Round Rock, TX 78680 *Tel:* 512-683-5640 *E-mail:* president@texasinstituteofletters.org *Web Site:* www.texasinstituteofletters.org, pg 672

Weisman, Jacob, Tachyon Publications LLC, 1459 18 St, No 139, San Francisco, CA 94107 *Tel:* 415-285-5615 *E-mail:* tachyon@tachyonpublications.com *Web Site:* www.tachyonpublications.com, pg 212

Weisman, Margaux, Anchor Books, c/o Penguin Random House Inc, 1745 Broadway, New York, NY 10019 *Tel:* 212-572-2420 *E-mail:* vintageanchorpublicity@randomhouse.com *Web Site:* knopfdoubleday.com/imprint/anchor, pg 15

Weisman, Margaux, Penguin Group USA, A Penguin Random House Company, 375 Hudson St, New York, NY 10014 *Tel:* 212-366-2000 *Toll Free Tel:* 800-847-5515 (inside sales); 800-631-8571 (cust serv) *Fax:* 212-366-2666; 607-775-4829 (inside sales) *E-mail:* online@us.penguingroup.com *Web Site:* www.penguin.com, pg 163

Weisman, Steven R, Peterson Institute for International Economics (PIIE), 1750 Massachusetts Ave NW, Washington, DC 20036-1903 *Tel:* 202-328-9000 *Fax:* 202-328-5432 *E-mail:* media@piie.com *Web Site:* piie.com, pg 168

Weiss, Alexandra, The Jennifer DeChiara Literary Agency, 245 Park Ave, 39th fl, New York, NY 10167 *Tel:* 212-372-8989 *Web Site:* www.jdlit.com, pg 481

Weiss, Alison, Sky Pony Press, 307 W 36 St, 11th fl, New York, NY 10018 *Tel:* 212-643-6816 *Fax:* 212-643-6819 *E-mail:* skypony@skyhorsepublishing.com; info@skyhorsepublishing.com; submissions@skyhorsepublishing.com *Web Site:* www.skyponypress.com, pg 200

Weiss, Daniel, The Metropolitan Museum of Art, 1000 Fifth Ave, New York, NY 10028 *Tel:* 212-535-7710 *E-mail:* editorial@metmuseum.org *Web Site:* www.metmuseum.org, pg 139

Weiss, Deborah, Maven House Press, 4 Snead Ct, Palmyra, VA 22963 *Tel:* 610-883-7988 *E-mail:* info@mavenhousepress.com *Web Site:* mavenhousepress.com, pg 134

Weiss, Denise, Cold Spring Harbor Laboratory Press, One Bungtown Rd, Cold Spring Harbor, NY 11724 *Tel:* 516-422-4100 *Toll Free Tel:* 800-843-4388 *Fax:* 516-422-4097; 516-422-4092 (submissions) *E-mail:* cshpress@cshl.edu *Web Site:* www.cshlpress.com, pg 55

Weiss, Dennis, CRC Press, 6000 Broken Sound Pkwy NW, Suite 300, Boca Raton, FL 33487 *Toll Free Tel:* 800-272-7737 (orders) *Toll Free Fax:* 800-374-3401 (orders) *E-mail:* orders@taylorandfrancis.com *Web Site:* www.crcpress.com, pg 59

Weiss, Jodi, Workman Publishing Co Inc, 225 Varick St, 9th fl, New York, NY 10014-4381 *Tel:* 212-254-5900 *Toll Free Tel:* 800-722-7202 *Fax:* 212-254-8098 *E-mail:* info@workman.com; orders@workman.com *Web Site:* www.workman.com, pg 244

Weiss, Kate, Denver Publishing Institute Scholarship, 3135 S State St, Suite 203, Ann Arbor, MI 48108 *Toll Free Tel:* 866-733-9064 *Fax:* 734-477-2806 *E-mail:* info@bincfoundation.org *Web Site:* www.bincfoundation.org/denver-publishing-institute/, pg 609

Weiss, Kate, Carla Gray Memorial Scholarship, 713 W Ellsworth Rd, Suite A, Ann Arbor, MI 48108 *Toll Free Tel:* 866-733-9064 *Fax:* 734-477-2806 *E-mail:* info@bincfoundation.org *Web Site:* bincfoundation.org/carla-gray/, pg 620

Weiss, Kate, Higher Education Scholarship Program, 3135 S State St, Suite 203, Ann Arbor, MI 48108 *Toll Free Tel:* 866-733-9064 *Fax:* 734-477-2806 *E-mail:* info@bincfoundation.org *Web Site:* bincfoundation.org/scholarship, pg 623

Weiss, Kate, Macmillan Booksellers Professional Development Scholarship, 3135 S State St, Suite 203, Ann Arbor, MI 48108 *Toll Free Tel:* 866-733-9064 *Fax:* 734-477-2806 *E-mail:* info@bincfoundation.org *Web Site:* www.bincfoundation.org/scholarship, pg 637

Weiss, Kate, Karl Pohrt Tribute Award, 3135 S State St, Suite 203, Ann Arbor, MI 48108 *Toll Free Tel:* 866-733-9064 *Fax:* 734-477-2806 *E-mail:* info@bincfoundation.org *Web Site:* www.bincfoundation.org/scholarship, pg 657

Weiss, Kim, Health Communications Inc, 3201 SW 15 St, Deerfield Beach, FL 33442 *Tel:* 954-360-0909 *Toll Free Tel:* 800-851-9100; 800-441-5569 (cust serv & orders) *Fax:* 954-360-0034 *Toll Free Fax:* 800-424-7652 (cust serv & orders) *E-mail:* customerservice2@hcibooks.com *Web Site:* www.hcibooks.com, pg 96

Weiss, Kim, Simcha Press, 3201 SW 15 St, Deerfield Beach, FL 33442-8190 *Tel:* 954-360-0909 ext 212 *Toll Free Tel:* 800-851-9100 *Toll Free Fax:* 800-424-7652 *E-mail:* simchapress@hcibooks.com *Web Site:* www.hcibooks.com, pg 198

Weiss, Mitchel, Eclectic Book Press, 72 Glenmaura National Blvd, Suite 104B, Moosic, PA 18507 *Tel:* 862-251-2296; 570-878-7960 *E-mail:* info@endlessmountainpublishing.com *Web Site:* endlessmountainspublishing.com, pg 69

Weiss, Mitchel, Endless Mountains Publishing Co, 72 Glenmaura National Blvd, Suite 104B, Moosic, PA 18507 *Tel:* 862-251-2296; 570-878-7960 *E-mail:* info@endlessmountainpublishing.com *Web Site:* www.endlessmountainspublishing.com, pg 72

Weiss, Mitchel, Kalaniot Books, 72 Glenmaura National Blvd, Suite 104B, Moosic, PA 18507 *Tel:* 862-251-2296; 570-878-7960 *E-mail:* info@endlessmountainpublishing.com *Web Site:* www.endlessmountainspublishing.com, pg 115

Weiss, Sara, Random House Publishing Group, 1745 Broadway, New York, NY 10019 *Toll Free Tel:* 800-200-3552 *Web Site:* www.randomhousebooks.com, pg 181

Weisskopf, Toni, Baen Publishing Enterprises, PO Box 1188, Wake Forest, NC 27588 *Tel:* 919-570-1640 *Fax:* 919-570-1644 *E-mail:* info@baen.com *Web Site:* www.baen.com, pg 26

Weissman, Dana, Writers Guild of America, East (WGAE), 250 Hudson St, Suite 700, New York, NY 10013 *Tel:* 212-767-7800 *Fax:* 212-582-1909 *Web Site:* www.wgaeast.org, pg 549

Weissman, Robert, Public Citizen, 1600 20 St NW, Washington, DC 20009 *Tel:* 202-588-1000 *Web Site:* www.citizen.org, pg 177

Weizenbaum, Pm, Northwest Independent Editors Guild, 7511 Greenwood Ave N, No 307, Seattle, WA 98103 *E-mail:* info@edsguild.org *Web Site:* edsguild.org, pg 542

Welby, Alexis, GP Putnam's Sons (Hardcover), 375 Hudson St, New York, NY 10014 *Tel:* 212-366-2000 *Fax:* 212-366-2643 *E-mail:* online@penguinputnam.com *Web Site:* www.penguin.com/publishers/gpputnamssons, pg 178

Welch, Andrea, Simon & Schuster Children's Publishing, 1230 Avenue of the Americas, New York, NY 10020 *Tel:* 212-698-7000 *Web Site:* www.simonandschuster.com/kids; www.simonandschuster.com/teen; simonandschuster.net; simonandschuster.biz, pg 199

Welch, Jazmin, Arsenal Pulp Press, 211 E Georgia St, No 202, Vancouver, BC V6A 1Z6, Canada *Tel:* 604-687-4233 *Toll Free Tel:* 888-600-PULP (600-7857) *Fax:* 604-687-4283 *E-mail:* info@arsenalpulp.com *Web Site:* www.arsenalpulp.com, pg 415

Welch, Laura, Master Books®, 3142 Hwy 103 N, Green Forest, AR 72638 *Tel:* 870-438-5288 *Toll Free Tel:* 800-999-3777 *E-mail:* sales@masterbooks.com; nlp@nlpg.com; submissions@newleafpress.net *Web Site:* www.masterbooks.com; www.nlpg.com/imprint/master-books, pg 134

Welch, Sally R, Ohio University Press, Alden Library, Suite 101, 30 Park Place, Athens, OH 45701-2901 *Tel:* 740-593-1154 *Web Site:* www.ohioswallow.com, pg 155

Welch, Sally R, Swallow Press, Alden Library, Suite 101, 30 Park Place, Athens, OH 45701-2909 *Tel:* 740-593-1154 *Web Site:* www.ohioswallow.com, pg 211

Welkum, Tara, HarperCollins Children's Books, 195 Broadway, New York, NY 10007 *Tel:* 212-207-7000 *Web Site:* www.harpercollins.com/childrens, pg 93

Welling, Brent, Center for the Collaborative Classroom, 1001 Marina Village Pkwy, Suite 110, Alameda, CA 94501-1042 *Tel:* 510-533-0213 *Toll Free Tel:* 800-666-7270 *Fax:* 510-464-3670 *E-mail:* info@collaborativeclassroom.org; clientsupport@collaborativeclassroom.org *Web Site:* www.collaborativeclassroom.org, pg 48

Wellnitz, Clare, University of California Press, 155 Grand Ave, Suite 400, Oakland, CA 94612-3758 *Tel:* 510-883-8232 *Fax:* 510-836-8910 *E-mail:* generalmailbox@ucpress.edu *Web Site:* www.ucpress.edu, pg 226

Wells, Jason, American Psychological Association, 750 First St NE, Washington, DC 20002-4242 *Tel:* 202-336-5510 *Toll Free Tel:* 800-374-2721 *Fax:* 202-336-5502 *E-mail:* order@apa.org *Web Site:* www.apa.org/books, pg 13

Wells, Jessica, Penguin Random House LLC, 1745 Broadway, New York, NY 10019 *Tel:* 212-782-9000 *Toll Free Tel:* 800-726-0600 *Web Site:* www.penguinrandomhouse.com, pg 164

Wells, Katrina Altersitz, SLACK® Incorporated, A Wyanoke Group Company, 6900 Grove Rd, Thorofare, NJ 08086-9447 *Tel:* 856-848-1000 *Toll Free Tel:* 800-257-8290 *Fax:* 856-848-6091 *E-mail:* sales@slackinc.com; editor@slackinc.com; customerservice@slackinc.com *Web Site:* www.healio.com/books, pg 201

Wells, Phyllis, University of Georgia Press, Main Library, 3rd fl, 320 S Jackson St, Athens, GA 30602 *Fax:* 706-542-2558; 706-542-6770 *Web Site:* www.ugapress.org, pg 227

Wells, Roseanne, The Jennifer DeChiara Literary Agency, 245 Park Ave, 39th fl, New York, NY 10167 *Tel:* 212-372-8989 *Web Site:* www.jdlit.com, pg 481

Wells, Thomas, University of Tennessee Press, 110 Conference Center Bldg, 600 Henley St, Knoxville, TN 37996-4108 *Tel:* 865-974-3321 *Toll Free Tel:* 800-621-2736 (orders) *Fax:* 865-974-3724 *Toll Free Fax:* 800-621-8476 (orders) *E-mail:* custserv@utpress.org *Web Site:* www.utpress.org, pg 231

Welsh, Kara, Penguin Random House LLC, 1745 Broadway, New York, NY 10019 *Tel:* 212-782-9000 *Toll Free Tel:* 800-726-0600 *Web Site:* penguinrandomhouse.com, pg 164

Welsh, Kara, Random House Publishing Group, 1745 Broadway, New York, NY 10019 *Toll Free Tel:* 800-200-3552 *Web Site:* www.randomhousebooks.com, pg 181

Weltz, Jennifer, Jean V Naggar Literary Agency Inc (JVNLA), 216 E 75 St, Suite 1-E, New York, NY 10021 *Tel:* 212-794-1082 *E-mail:* jvnla@jvnla.com *Web Site:* www.jvnla.com, pg 497

Wen, Grace, University of Hawaii Press, 2840 Kolowalu St, Honolulu, HI 96822-1888 *Tel:* 808-956-8255 *Toll Free Tel:* 888-UHPRESS (847-7377) *Fax:* 808-988-6052 *Toll Free Fax:* 800-650-7811 *E-mail:* uhpbooks@hawaii.edu *Web Site:* www.uhpress.hawaii.edu, pg 227

Wendrich, Willeke, Cotsen Institute of Archaeology Press, 308 Charles E Young Dr N, Fowler A163, Box 951510, Los Angeles, CA 90095 *Tel:* 310-206-9384 *Fax:* 310-206-4723 *E-mail:* cioapress@ioa.ucla.edu *Web Site:* www.ioa.ucla.edu, pg 57

Wengerd, Marvin, Carlisle Press - Walnut Creek, 2673 Township Rd 421, Sugarcreek, OH 44681 *Tel:* 330-852-1900 *Toll Free Tel:* 800-852-4482 *Fax:* 330-852-3285, pg 45

Wentworth, Jillian, United for Libraries, 859 W Lancaster Ave, Unit 2-1, Bryn Mawr, PA 19010 *Tel:* 312-280-2161 *Toll Free Tel:* 800-545-2433 (ext 2161) *Fax:* 484-698-7868 *E-mail:* united@ala.org *Web Site:* www.ala.org/united, pg 548

Werden, Barbara, Mandel Vilar Press, 19 Oxford Ct, Simsbury, CT 06070 *Tel:* 806-790-4731 *E-mail:* info@mvpress.org *Web Site:* mvpress.org, pg 131

Werksman, Deb, Sourcebooks LLC, 1935 Brookdale Rd, Suite 139, Naperville, IL 60563 *Tel:* 630-961-3900 *Toll Free Tel:* 800-432-7444 *Fax:* 630-961-2168 *E-mail:* info@sourcebooks.com; customersupport@sourcebooks.com *Web Site:* www.sourcebooks.com, pg 204

Werner, Doug, Tracks Publishing, 458 Dorothy Ave, Ventura, CA 93003 *Tel:* 805-754-0248 *E-mail:* tracks@cox.net *Web Site:* www.startupsports.com, pg 219

Wertheimer, Alice, Akashic Books, 232 Third St, Suite A-115, Brooklyn, NY 11215 *Tel:* 718-643-9193 *Fax:* 718-643-9195 *E-mail:* info@akashicbooks.com *Web Site:* www.akashicbooks.com, pg 6

Wertz, Chloe, University of Pittsburgh Press, 7500 Thomas Blvd, Pittsburgh, PA 15260 *Tel:* 412-383-2456 *Fax:* 412-383-2466 *E-mail:* info@upress.pitt.edu *Web Site:* www.upress.pitt.edu, pg 230

Wescott, T C, New York Academy of Sciences (NYAS), 7 World Trade Center, 40th fl, 250 Greenwich St, New York, NY 10007-2157 *Tel:* 212-298-8600 *Toll Free Tel:* 800-843-6927 *Fax:* 212-298-3650 *E-mail:* nyas@nyas.org; annals@nyas.org; customerservice@nyas.org *Web Site:* www.nyas.org, pg 150

Wesley, Mark, me+mi publishing inc, 2600 Beverly Dr, Unit 113, Aurora, IL 60502 *Tel:* 630-588-9801 *Toll Free Tel:* 888-251-1444 *Web Site:* www.memima.com, pg 137

Wessbecher, Katherine, Bradford Literary Agency, 5694 Mission Center Rd, Suite 347, San Diego, CA 92108 *Tel:* 619-521-1201 *E-mail:* queries@bradfordlit.com *Web Site:* www.bradfordlit.com, pg 477

West, Ann, Mazda Publishers Inc, PO Box 2603, Costa Mesa, CA 92628 *Tel:* 714-751-5252 *Fax:* 714-751-4805 *E-mail:* mazdapub@aol.com *Web Site:* www.mazdapublishers.com, pg 134

West, Dave, Corwin, 2455 Teller Rd, Thousand Oaks, CA 91320 *Tel:* 805-499-9734 *Toll Free Tel:* 800-233-9936 *Fax:* 805-499-5323 *Toll Free Fax:* 800-417-2466 *E-mail:* info@corwin.com; order@corwin.com *Web Site:* www.corwin.com, pg 57

West, J C, Abaris Books, 70 New Canaan Ave, Norwalk, CT 06850 *Tel:* 203-838-8402 *Fax:* 203-857-0730 *E-mail:* abaris@abarisbooks.com *Web Site:* abarisbooks.com, pg 2

West, Krista, University of Alaska Press, Elmer E Rasmuson Library, 1732 Tanana Loop, Suite 402, Fairbanks, AK 99775 *Tel:* 907-474-5831 *Toll Free Tel:* 888-252-6657 (US only) *Fax:* 907-474-5502 *Web Site:* www.alaska.edu/uapress, pg 225

West, Salem, Bywater Books Inc, PO Box 3671, Ann Arbor, MI 48106-3671 *Tel:* 734-662-8815 *Web Site:* bywaterbooks.com, pg 43

Westa, Joel, Christian Schools International, 3350 E Paris Ave SE, Grand Rapids, MI 49512-3054 *Tel:* 616-957-1070 *Toll Free Tel:* 800-635-8288 *Fax:* 616-957-5022 *E-mail:* info@csionline.org *Web Site:* www.csionline.org, pg 51

Westcott, Jean, Stylus Publishing LLC, 22883 Quicksilver Dr, Sterling, VA 20166-2019 *Tel:* 703-661-1504 (edit & sales) *Toll Free Tel:* 800-232-0223 (orders & cust serv) *Fax:* 703-661-1547 *E-mail:* stylusmail@styluspub.com (orders & cust serv); stylusinfo@styluspub.com *Web Site:* styluspub.presswarehouse.com, pg 210

Westermann, Christian, Algonquin Books, 400 Silver Cedar Ct, Suite 300, Chapel Hill, NC 27514-1585 *Tel:* 919-967-0108 *Fax:* 919-933-0272 *E-mail:* inquiry@algonquin.com *Web Site:* www.workman.com/algonquin, pg 7

Westfall, Holly, A 2 Z Press LLC, 3670 Woodbridge Rd, Deland, FL 32720 *Tel:* 440-241-3126 *E-mail:* sizemore3630@aol.com *Web Site:* www.a2zpress.com; www.bestlittleonlinebookstore.com, pg 1

Westfall, William, Barbour Publishing Inc, 1810 Barbour Dr, Uhrichsville, OH 44683 *Tel:* 740-922-6045 *Fax:* 740-922-5948 *E-mail:* info@barbourbooks.com *Web Site:* www.barbourbooks.com, pg 28

Westlund, Laura, University of Minnesota Press, 111 Third Ave S, Suite 290, Minneapolis, MN 55401-2520 *Tel:* 612-301-1990 *Fax:* 612-301-1980 *E-mail:* ump@umn.edu *Web Site:* www.upress.umn.edu, pg 228

Weston, Pamela, Research & Education Association (REA), 258 Prospect Plains Rd, Cranbury, NJ 08512 *Tel:* 732-819-8880 *Fax:* 732-819-8808 (orders) *E-mail:* info@rea.com *Web Site:* www.rea.com, pg 184

Westra, Jessica, Zondervan, 3900 Sparks Dr, Grand Rapids, MI 49546 *Tel:* 616-698-6900 *Toll Free Tel:* 800-226-1122; 800-727-1309 (retail orders) *Fax:* 616-698-3350 *Toll Free Fax:* 800-698-3256 (retail orders) *Web Site:* www.zondervan.com, pg 248

Westwood, Bruce, Westwood Creative Artists Ltd, 138 Sussex Mews, Toronto, ON M5S-2K1, Canada *Tel:* 416-964-3302 *Fax:* 416-964-3302 *E-mail:* wca_office@wcaltd.com *Web Site:* www.wcaltd.com, pg 508

Wetter, Erica, Stanford University Press, 425 Broadway St, Redwood City, CA 94063-3126 *Tel:* 650-723-9434 *Fax:* 650-725-3457 *E-mail:* info@www.sup.org; publicity@www.sup.org; sales@www.sup.org *Web Site:* www.sup.org, pg 206

Wetzel, Deborah, American Society of Mechanical Engineers (ASME), 2 Park Ave, New York, NY 10016-5990 *Tel:* 212-591-7000 *Toll Free Tel:* 800-843-2763 (cust serv-US, CN & Mexico) *Fax:* 973-882-1717 (orders & inquiries) *E-mail:* customercare@asme.org *Web Site:* www.asme.org, pg 14

Wetzel, Liz, Perseus Books, 1290 Avenue of the Americas, New York, NY 10104 *Tel:* 212-340-8100 *Toll Free Tel:* 800-343-4499 (cust serv) *Fax:* 212-340-8105 *Web Site:* www.perseusbooks.com, pg 168

Wetzel, Lucas, Andrews McMeel Publishing LLC, 1130 Walnut St, Kansas City, MO 64106-2109 *Toll Free Tel:* 800-851-8923; 800-943-9839 (cust serv) *Toll Free Fax:* 800-943-9831 (orders) *E-mail:* sales@amuniversal.com *Web Site:* www.andrewsmcmeel.com; publishing.andrewsmcmeel.com, pg 16

Wexler, Chuck, Police Executive Research Forum, 1120 Connecticut Ave NW, Suite 930, Washington, DC 20036 *Tel:* 202-466-7820 *Web Site:* www.policeforum.org, pg 172

Wexler, Daniella, Atria Books, 1230 Avenue of the Americas, New York, NY 10020 *Tel:* 212-698-7000 *Fax:* 212-698-7007 *Web Site:* www.simonandschuster.com, pg 24

Wexler, David, Carolrhoda Books Inc, 241 First Ave N, Minneapolis, MN 55401 *Tel:* 612-332-3344 *Toll Free Tel:* 800-328-4929 *Fax:* 612-332-7615 *Toll Free Fax:* 800-332-1132 *E-mail:* info@lernerbooks.com; custserve@lernerbooks.com *Web Site:* www.lernerbooks.com; www.facebook.com/lernerbooks, pg 45

Wexler, David, Carolrhoda Lab™, 241 First Ave N, Minneapolis, MN 55401 *Tel:* 612-332-3344 *Toll Free Tel:* 800-328-4929 *Fax:* 612-332-7615 *Toll Free Fax:* 800-332-1132 *E-mail:* info@lernerbooks.com; custserve@lernerbooks.com *Web Site:* www.lernerbooks.com; www.facebook.com/lernerbooks, pg 45

Wexler, David, ediciones Lerner, 241 First Ave N, Minneapolis, MN 55401 *Tel:* 612-332-3344 *Toll Free Tel:* 800-328-4929 *Fax:* 612-332-7615 *Toll Free Fax:* 800-332-1132 *E-mail:* info@lernerbooks.com; custserve@lernerbooks.com *Web Site:* www.lernerbooks.com; www.facebook.com/lernerbooks, pg 69

Wexler, David, First Avenue Editions, 241 First Ave N, Minneapolis, MN 55401 *Tel:* 612-332-3344 *Toll Free Tel:* 800-328-4929 *Fax:* 612-332-7615 *Toll Free Fax:* 800-332-1132 *E-mail:* info@lernerbooks.com; custserve@lernerbooks.com *Web Site:* www.lernerbooks.com; www.facebook.com/lernerbooks, pg 78

Wexler, David, Graphic Universe™, 241 First Ave N, Minneapolis, MN 55401 *Tel:* 612-332-3344 *Toll Free Tel:* 800-328-4929 *Fax:* 612-332-7615 *Toll Free Fax:* 800-332-1132 *E-mail:* info@lernerbooks.

com; custserve@lernerbooks.com *Web Site:* www.lernerbooks.com; www.facebook.com/lernerbooks, pg 88

Wexler, David, Lerner Publications, 241 First Ave N, Minneapolis, MN 55401 *Tel:* 612-332-3344 *Toll Free Tel:* 800-328-4929 *Fax:* 612-332-7615 *Toll Free Fax:* 800-332-1132 *E-mail:* info@lernerbooks.com; custserve@lernerbooks.com *Web Site:* www.lernerbooks.com; www.facebook.com/lernerbooks, pg 122

Wexler, David, Lerner Publishing Group Inc, 241 First Ave N, Minneapolis, MN 55401 *Tel:* 612-332-3344 *Toll Free Tel:* 800-328-4929 *Fax:* 612-332-7615 *Toll Free Fax:* 800-332-1132 *E-mail:* info@lernerbooks.com; custserve@lernerbooks.com *Web Site:* www.lernerbooks.com; www.facebook.com/lernerbooks, pg 123

Wexler, David, LernerClassroom, 241 First Ave N, Minneapolis, MN 55401 *Tel:* 612-332-3344 *Toll Free Tel:* 800-328-4929 *Fax:* 612-332-7615 *Toll Free Fax:* 800-332-1132 *E-mail:* info@lernerbooks.com; custserve@lernerbooks.com *Web Site:* www.lernerbooks.com; www.facebook.com/lernerbooks, pg 123

Wexler, David, Millbrook Press, 241 First Ave N, Minneapolis, MN 55401 *Tel:* 612-332-3344 *Toll Free Tel:* 800-328-4929 *Fax:* 612-332-7615 *Toll Free Fax:* 800-332-1132 *E-mail:* info@lernerbooks.com; custserve@lernerbooks.com *Web Site:* www.lernerbooks.com; www.facebook.com/millbrookpress, pg 140

Wexler, David, Twenty-First Century Books, 241 First Ave N, Minneapolis, MN 55401 *Tel:* 612-332-3344 *Toll Free Tel:* 800-328-4929 *Fax:* 612-332-7615 *Toll Free Fax:* 800-332-1132 *E-mail:* info@lernerbooks.com; custserve@lernerbooks.com *Web Site:* www.lernerbooks.com; www.facebook.com/lernerbooks, pg 222

Wexler, David, Zest Books, 241 First Ave N, Minneapolis, MN 55401 *Tel:* 612-332-3344 *Toll Free Tel:* 800-328-4929 *Toll Free Fax:* 800-332-1132 *E-mail:* info@lernerbooks.com; publicity@lernerbooks.com; custserve@lernerbooks.com (orders) *Web Site:* lernerbooks.com, pg 248

Wexler, Leslie, Centre for Reformation & Renaissance Studies (CRRS), 71 Queen's Park Crescent E, Toronto, ON M5S 1K7, Canada *Tel:* 416-585-4465 *Fax:* 416-585-4430 (attn: CRRS) *E-mail:* crrs.publications@utoronto.ca *Web Site:* crrs.ca, pg 419

Wexler, Pearl, Paul Kohner Agency, 9300 Wilshire Blvd, Suite 555, Beverly Hills, CA 90212 *Tel:* 310-550-1060 *Fax:* 310-276-1083, pg 492

Wexler, Tina, ICM Partners, 65 E 55 St, New York, NY 10022 *Tel:* 212-556-5600 *Web Site:* www.icmtalent.com, pg 489

Whalen, John F Jr, Cider Mill Press Book Publishers LLC, 12 Spring St, Kennebunkport, ME 04046 *Tel:* 207-967-8232 *Fax:* 207-967-8233 *Web Site:* www.cidermillpress.com, pg 52

Whalen, Lindsay, The Penguin Press, 375 Hudson St, New York, NY 10014 *Web Site:* thepenguinpress.com, pg 164

Whalen, Will, Alexander Street, a ProQuest Company, 99 Canal Center Plaza, Suite 200, Alexandria, VA 22314 *Tel:* 703-212-8520 *Toll Free Tel:* 800-889-5937 *E-mail:* sales@alexanderstreet.com; marketing@alexanderstreet.com; info@alexanderstreet.com *Web Site:* alexanderstreet.com, pg 7

Whaley, Glenn, STM Learning Inc, 1220 Paddock Dr, Florissant, MO 63033 *Tel:* 314-434-2424 *E-mail:* info@stmlearning.com; orders@stmlearning.com *Web Site:* www.stmlearning.com, pg 208

Whaley, Marianne, STM Learning Inc, 1220 Paddock Dr, Florissant, MO 63033 *Tel:* 314-434-2424 *E-mail:* info@stmlearning.com; orders@stmlearning.com *Web Site:* www.stmlearning.com, pg 208

Whatley, Chris, United Nations Association of the United States of America, 1750 Pennsylvania Ave NW, Suite 300, Washington, DC 20006 *Tel:* 202-887-9040 *Web Site:* www.unausa.org, pg 548

Whatnall, Michaela, Chronicle Books, 680 Second St, San Francisco, CA 94107 *Tel:* 415-537-4200 *Toll Free Tel:* 800-759-0190 (cust serv) *Fax:* 415-537-4460 *Toll Free Fax:* 800-858-7787 (orders); 800-286-9471 (cust serv) *E-mail:* frontdesk@chroniclebooks.com *Web Site:* www.chroniclebooks.com, pg 52

Wheaton, Robert, Doubleday Canada, 320 Front St W, Suite 1400, Toronto, ON M5V 3B6, Canada *Tel:* 416-364-4449 *Fax:* 416-598-7764 *Web Site:* www. penguinrandomhouse.ca, pg 421

Wheaton, Robert, Knopf Canada, 320 Front St W, Suite 1400, Toronto, ON M5V 3B6, Canada *Tel:* 416-364-4449 *Toll Free Tel:* 888-523-9292 *Fax:* 416-598-7764 *Web Site:* www.penguinrandomhouse.ca, pg 431

Wheaton, Robert, Penguin Random House Canada, 320 Front St W, Suite 1400, Toronto, ON M5V 3B6, Canada *Tel:* 416-364-4449 *Toll Free Tel:* 888-523-9292 (cust serv) *Fax:* 416-598-7764 *Web Site:* www. penguinrandomhouse.ca, pg 436

Wheaton, Robert, Seal Books, 320 Front St W, Suite 1400, Toronto, ON M5V 3B6, Canada *Tel:* 416-364-4449 *Toll Free Tel:* 888-523-9292 (order desk) *Fax:* 416-598-7764 *Web Site:* www. penguinrandomhouse.ca, pg 439

Wheeler, Betsy, Juniper Summer Writing Institute, c/o University Conference Services, 810 Campus Center, One Campus Center Way, Amherst, MA 01003 *Tel:* 413-545-5503 *E-mail:* juniperinstitute@hfa.umass. edu *Web Site:* www.umass.edu/juniperinstitute, pg 576

Wheeler, Diane, Kalmbach Publishing Co, 21027 Crossroads Circle, Waukesha, WI 53186 *Tel:* 262-796-8776 *Toll Free Tel:* 800-533-6644 (cust serv & orders); 800-558-1544 *Fax:* 262-798-6592 *E-mail:* customerservice@kalmbach.com *Web Site:* www.kalmbach.com, pg 115

Wheeler, John, Lumina Datamatics Inc, 4 Collins Ave, Plymouth, MA 02360 *Tel:* 508-746-0300 *Fax:* 508-746-3233 *Web Site:* luminadatamatics.com, pg 466

Wheeler, Meg, Westwood Creative Artists Ltd, 138 Sussex Mews, Toronto, ON M5S-2K1, Canada *Tel:* 416-964-3302 *Fax:* 416-964-3302 *E-mail:* wca_office@wcaltd.com *Web Site:* www. wcaltd.com, pg 508

Wheeler, Noa, Bloomsbury Publishing Inc, 1385 Broadway, 5th fl, New York, NY 10018 *Tel:* 212-419-5300 *E-mail:* marketingusa@bloomsbury.com; adultpublicityusa@bloomsbury.com; askacademic@ bloomsbury.com *Web Site:* www.bloomsbury.com, pg 36

Whelan, Maria, Princeton University Press, 41 William St, Princeton, NJ 08540-5237 *Tel:* 609-258-4900 *Fax:* 609-258-6305 *Web Site:* press.princeton.edu, pg 175

Whelan, Michael F, The Baker Street Irregulars (BSI), 7938 Mill Stream Circle, Indianapolis, IN 46278 *Tel:* 317-293-2212; 317-956-6666 (cell) *Web Site:* bakerstreetjournal.com, pg 528

Whelchel, Sandy, Associated Business Writers of America Inc, 10940 S Parker Rd, Suite 508, Parker, CO 80134 *Tel:* 303-841-0246 *E-mail:* natlwritersassn@hotmail.com *Web Site:* www. nationalwriters.com, pg 525

Whelchel, Sandy, National Writers Association, 10940 S Parker Rd, Suite 508, Parker, CO 80134 *Tel:* 303-656-7235 *E-mail:* natlwritersassn@hotmail.com *Web Site:* www.nationalwriters.com, pg 541

Whelchel, Sandy, National Writers Association Novel Contest, 10940 S Parker Rd, Suite 508, Parker, CO 80134 *Tel:* 303-656-7235 *E-mail:* natlwritersassn@ hotmail.com *Web Site:* www.nationalwriters.com, pg 646

Whisler, Kirk, International Latino Book Awards, 3445 Catalina Dr, Carlsbad, CA 92010 *Tel:* 760-434-1223 *Fax:* 760-434-7476 *Web Site:* www.award.news, pg 627

Whisler, Kirk, International Latino Unpublished Book Awards, 3445 Catalina Dr, Carlsbad, CA 92010 *Tel:* 760-434-1223 *Fax:* 760-434-7476 *Web Site:* www. award.news, pg 627

Whisler, Kirk, International Society of Latino Authors, c/o Latino Literacy Now, 3445 Catalina Dr, Carlsbad, CA 92010 *Tel:* 760-434-1223 *Fax:* 760-434-7476, pg 535

Whisler, Kirk, Latino Books Into Movies Awards, 3445 Catalina Dr, Carlsbad, CA 92010 *Tel:* 760-434-1223 *Fax:* 760-434-7476 *Web Site:* www.award.news, pg 631

Whitaker, Ellen, Bloomsbury Publishing Inc, 1385 Broadway, 5th fl, New York, NY 10018 *Tel:* 212-419-5300 *E-mail:* marketingusa@bloomsbury.com; adultpublicityusa@bloomsbury.com; askacademic@ bloomsbury.com *Web Site:* www.bloomsbury.com, pg 36

Whitaker, Theresa, Medieval Institute Publications, WMU East Campus, 100-E Walwood Hall, Kalamazoo, MI 49008 *Tel:* 269-387-8754 *Fax:* 269-387-8750 *Web Site:* www.wmich.edu/ medievalpublications, pg 137

Whitby, Bess, University of North Texas Press, Willis Library, Rm 251P, 1506 Highland St, Denton, TX 76201 *Tel:* 940-565-2142 *Fax:* 940-369-8760 *Web Site:* untpress.unt.edu, pg 229

Whitcher, Sarah, Pegasus Award for Poetry Criticism, 61 W Superior St, Chicago, IL 60654 *Tel:* 312-787-7070 *E-mail:* info@poetryfoundation.org *Web Site:* www. poetryfoundation.org/foundation/criticism-award, pg 653

White, Craig M, EDC Publishing, 5402 S 122 E Ave, Tulsa, OK 74146 *Tel:* 918-622-4522 *Toll Free Tel:* 800-475-4522 *Fax:* 918-665-7919 *Toll Free Fax:* 800-743-5660 *E-mail:* edc@edcpub.com *Web Site:* www.edcpub.com, pg 69

White, Deryck, The Society of Naval Architects & Marine Engineers (SNAME), 99 Canal Center Plaza, Suite 310, Alexandria, VA 22314 *Tel:* 703-997-6701 *Toll Free Tel:* 800-798-2188 *Fax:* 703-997-6702 *Web Site:* www.sname.org, pg 203

White, Don, Oregon Christian Writers (OCW), 1075 Willow Lake Rd N, Keizer, OR 97303 *Tel:* 503-393-3356 *E-mail:* contact@oregonchristianwriters.org *Web Site:* oregonchristianwriters.org, pg 542

White, Don, Oregon Christian Writers One-Day Conferences, 1075 Willow Lake Rd N, Keizer, OR 97303 *Tel:* 503-393-3356 *E-mail:* contact@oregonchristianwriters.org *Web Site:* oregonchristianwriters.org, pg 577

White, Doug, Bloomsbury Publishing Inc, 1385 Broadway, 5th fl, New York, NY 10018 *Tel:* 212-419-5300 *E-mail:* marketingusa@bloomsbury.com; adultpublicityusa@bloomsbury.com; askacademic@ bloomsbury.com *Web Site:* www.bloomsbury.com, pg 36

White, Elizabeth, The Monacelli Press, 65 Bleecker St, 8th fl, New York, NY 10012 *Tel:* 212-229-9925 *E-mail:* contact@monacellipress.com *Web Site:* www. monacellipress.com, pg 141

White, Howard, Douglas & McIntyre (2013) Ltd, 4437 Rondeview Rd, Madeira Park, BC V0N 2H1, Canada *Toll Free Tel:* 800-667-2988 *E-mail:* info@douglas-mcintyre.com *Web Site:* www.douglas-mcintyre.com, pg 421

White, Howard, Harbour Publishing Co Ltd, 4437 Rondeview Rd, Madeira Park, BC V0N 2H0, Canada *Tel:* 604-883-2730 *Toll Free Tel:* 800-667-2988 *Fax:* 604-883-9451 *E-mail:* info@harbourpublishing. com *Web Site:* www.harbourpublishing.com, pg 429

White, Hudson, Ocean Tree Books, 1325 Cerro Gordo Rd, Santa Fe, NM 87501 *Tel:* 505-983-1412 *Fax:* 505-983-0899 *E-mail:* richard@oceantree.com *Web Site:* www.oceantree.com, pg 154

White, Jonathan W, Abraham Lincoln Institute Book Award, 105 Mount Olive Lane, Ephrata, PA 17522 *E-mail:* secretary@lincoln-institute.org *Web Site:* www.lincoln-institute.org, pg 633

White, Katherine, University of New Mexico Press, One University of New Mexico, Albuquerque, NM 87131-0001 *Tel:* 505-272-7777 *Fax:* 505-277-3343 *E-mail:* custserv@unm.edu (order dept) *Web Site:* unmpress.com, pg 229

White, Melissa, Folio Literary Management, The Film Center Bldg, 630 Ninth Ave, Suite 1101, New York, NY 10036 *Tel:* 212-400-1494 *Fax:* 212-967-0977 *Web Site:* www.foliolit.com, pg 484

White, Nancy, The Tenth Gate Prize *Tel:* 301-581-9439 *Fax:* 301-581-9443 *E-mail:* editor@wordworksbooks. org *Web Site:* www.wordworksbooks.org, pg 672

White, Nancy, Word Works Washington Prize, Adirondack Community College, Dearlove Hall, 640 Bay Rd, Queensbury, NY 12804 *Tel:* 301-581-9439 *Fax:* 301-581-9443 *E-mail:* editor@wordworksbooks. org *Web Site:* www.wordworksbooks.org, pg 679

White, Pam, Random House Children's Books, 1745 Broadway, 10th fl, New York, NY 10019 *Tel:* 212-782-9000 *Web Site:* www.randomhousekids.com, pg 180

White, Peter, Begell House Inc Publishers, 50 North St, Danbury, CT 06810 *Tel:* 203-456-6161 *Fax:* 203-456-6167 *E-mail:* orders@begellhouse.com *Web Site:* www.begellhouse.com, pg 30

White, Randall, EDC Publishing, 5402 S 122 E Ave, Tulsa, OK 74146 *Tel:* 918-622-4522 *Toll Free Tel:* 800-475-4522 *Fax:* 918-665-7919 *Toll Free Fax:* 800-743-5660 *E-mail:* edc@edcpub.com *Web Site:* www.edcpub.com, pg 69

White, Travis, Psychological Assessment Resources Inc (PAR), 16204 N Florida Ave, Lutz, FL 33549 *Tel:* 813-449-4065 *Toll Free Tel:* 800-331-8378 *Fax:* 813-961-2196 *Toll Free Fax:* 800-727-9329 *Web Site:* www.parinc.com, pg 177

Whiteside, David, Penguin Group (Canada), 320 Front St W, Suite 1400, Toronto, ON M5V 3B6, Canada *Tel:* 416-364-4449 *Fax:* 416-598-7764 *E-mail:* customerservicescanada@ penguinrandomhouse.com; publicity@ca.penguingroup. com *Web Site:* penguinrandomhouse.ca/imprints/ penguin-canada, pg 436

Whiteway, Doug, Signature Editions, PO Box 206, RPO Corydon, Winnipeg, MB R3M 3S7, Canada *Tel:* 204-779-7803 *E-mail:* submissions@signature-editions. com; orders@signature-editions.com *Web Site:* www. signature-editions.com, pg 440

Whithaus, Carl, Writing Workshops, 1333 Research Park Dr, Davis, CA 95618 *Tel:* 510-642-6362 *E-mail:* extension@ucdavis.edu *Web Site:* extension. ucdavis.edu; writing.ucdavis.edu, pg 580

Whitman, Mara, The Graduate Group/Booksellers, 86 Norwood Rd, West Hartford, CT 06117-2236 *Tel:* 860-233-2330 *E-mail:* graduategroup@hotmail. com *Web Site:* www.graduategroup.com, pg 87

Whitman, Robert, The Graduate Group/Booksellers, 86 Norwood Rd, West Hartford, CT 06117-2236 *Tel:* 860-233-2330 *E-mail:* graduategroup@hotmail. com *Web Site:* www.graduategroup.com, pg 87

Whitney, April, Chronicle Books, 680 Second St, San Francisco, CA 94107 *Tel:* 415-537-4200 *Toll Free Tel:* 800-759-0190 (cust serv) *Fax:* 415-537-4460 *Toll Free Fax:* 800-858-7787 (orders); 800-286-9471 (cust serv) *E-mail:* frontdesk@chroniclebooks.com *Web Site:* www.chroniclebooks.com, pg 52

Whitson, Skip, Sun Publishing Company, PO Box 5588, Santa Fe, NM 87502-5588 *Tel:* 505-471-5177; 505-660-0704 *Toll Free Tel:* 877-849-0051 *E-mail:* info@sunbooks.com *Web Site:* www.sunbooks. com; abooksource.com, pg 210

Whittell, Polly, Deadline Club, c/o Salmagundi Club, 47 Fifth Ave, New York, NY 10003 *Tel:* 646-481-7584 *Web Site:* www.deadlineclub.org, pg 532

Whyte, Debra Jackson, Teachers College Press, 1234 Amsterdam Ave, New York, NY 10027 *Tel:* 212-678-3929 *Fax:* 212-678-4149 *E-mail:* tcpress@tc.edu *Web Site:* www.tcpress.com, pg 214

Wichmann, Sonia, Northern California Translators Association, 2261 Market St, Suite 160, San Francisco, CA 94114-1600 *Tel:* 510-845-8712 *E-mail:* administrator@ncta.org *Web Site:* www.ncta. org, pg 542

Wicks, Erin, HarperCollins General Books Group, 195 Broadway, New York, NY 10007 *Tel:* 212-207-7000 *Web Site:* www.harpercollins.com, pg 93

Wicks, Robert, The Brookings Institution Press, 1775 Massachusetts Ave NW, Washington, DC 20036-2188 *Tel:* 202-797-6000 *E-mail:* permissions@brookings. edu *Web Site:* www.brookings.edu, pg 42

Widdicombe, Elizabeth, Macmillan Learning, 41 Madison Ave, New York, NY 10010 *Tel:* 212-576-9400 *Fax:* 212-689-2383 *Web Site:* www. macmillanlearning.com, pg 130

Wieckowski, Ania, Harvard Business Review Press, 20 Guest St, Suite 700, Brighton, MA 02135 *Tel:* 617-783-7400 *Fax:* 617-783-7489 *E-mail:* custserv@hbsp. harvard.edu *Web Site:* www.harvardbusiness.org, pg 94

Wiegers, Michael, Copper Canyon Press, Fort Worden State Park, Bldg 313, Port Townsend, WA 98368 *Tel:* 360-385-4925 *Toll Free Tel:* 877-501-1393 (orders) *Fax:* 360-385-4985 *E-mail:* poetry@ coppercanyonpress.org *Web Site:* www. coppercanyonpress.org, pg 56

Wieman, Amy, BLR®—Business & Legal Resources, 100 Winners Circle, Suite 300, Brentwood, TN 37027 *Tel:* 860-510-0100 *Toll Free Tel:* 800-727-5257 *E-mail:* service@blr.com *Web Site:* www.blr.com, pg 36

Wiener, Jessica, Harry N Abrams Inc, 195 Broadway, 9th fl, New York, NY 10007 *Tel:* 212-206-7715 *Toll Free Tel:* 800-345-1359 *Fax:* 212-519-1210 *E-mail:* abrams@abramsbooks.com *Web Site:* www. abramsbooks.com, pg 3

Wiener, M Markus, Markus Wiener Publishers Inc, 231 Nassau St, Princeton, NJ 08542 *Tel:* 609-921-1141 *Fax:* 609-921-1140 *E-mail:* publisher@markuswiener. com *Web Site:* www.markuswiener.com, pg 241

Wiener, Robert K, Donald M Grant Publisher Inc, PO Box 187, Hampton Falls, NH 03844-0187 *Tel:* 603-778-7191 *Fax:* 603-778-7191 *E-mail:* office@ grantbooks.com *Web Site:* secure.grantbooks.com, pg 88

Wiese, Michael, Michael Wiese Productions, 12400 Ventura Blvd, No 1111, Studio City, CA 91604 *Tel:* 818-379-8799 *Toll Free Tel:* 800-833-5738 (orders) *Fax:* 818-986-3408 *E-mail:* mwpsales@ earthlink.net; fulfillment@portcity.com *Web Site:* www.mwp.com, pg 241

Wiese, Nancy, Hachette Book Group, 1290 Avenue of the Americas, New York, NY 10104 *Tel:* 212-364-1100 *Toll Free Tel:* 800-759-0190 (cust serv) *Fax:* 212-364-0933 (intl orders) *Toll Free Fax:* 800-286-9471 (cust serv) *Web Site:* www. hachettebookgroup.com, pg 91

Wiese, Nancy, Little, Brown and Company, 1290 Avenue of the Americas, New York, NY 10104 *Tel:* 212-364-1100 *Fax:* 212-364-0952 *E-mail:* firstname.lastname@ hbgusa.com *Web Site:* www.littlebrown.com; www. hachettebookgroup.com, pg 125

Wiess, Kathy, Europa Editions, 214 W 29 St, Suite 1003, New York, NY 10001 *Tel:* 212-868-6844 *Fax:* 212-868-6845 *E-mail:* info@europaeditions.com *Web Site:* www.europaeditions.com, pg 73

Wiewora, Kristen, Perseus Books, 1290 Avenue of the Americas, New York, NY 10104 *Tel:* 212-340-8100 *Toll Free Tel:* 800-343-4499 (cust serv) *Fax:* 212-340-8105 *Web Site:* www.perseusbooks.com, pg 167

Wiggins, Len, Penguin Random House Audio Publishing, 1745 Broadway, New York, NY 10019 *E-mail:* audio@penguinrandomhouse.com *Web Site:* www.penguinrandomhouseaudio.com, pg 164

Wight, Katy, Edward Elgar Publishing Inc, The William Pratt House, 9 Dewey Ct, Northampton, MA 01060-3815 *Tel:* 413-584-5551 *Toll Free Tel:* 800-390-3149 (orders) *Fax:* 413-584-9933 *E-mail:* elgarinfo@e-elgar. com; elgarsales@e-elgar.com; elgarsubmissions@e-elgar.com (edit) *Web Site:* www.e-elgar.com; www. elgaronline.com (ebooks & journals), pg 70

Wilcox, Alana, Coach House Books, 80 bpNichol Lane, Toronto, ON M5S 3J4, Canada *Tel:* 416-979-2217 *Toll Free Tel:* 800-367-6360 (outside Toronto) *Fax:* 416-977-1158 *E-mail:* mail@chbooks.com *Web Site:* www. chbooks.com, pg 420

Wilcox, Diane L, Mazda Publishers Inc, PO Box 2603, Costa Mesa, CA 92628 *Tel:* 714-751-5252 *Fax:* 714-751-4805 *E-mail:* mazdapub@aol.com *Web Site:* www.mazdapublishers.com, pg 134

Wilcox, Jeanne, Quincannon Publishing Group, PO Box 8100, Glen Ridge, NJ 07028-8100 *Tel:* 973-380-9942 *E-mail:* editors@quincannongroup.com (query first via e-mail) *Web Site:* www.quincannongroup.com, pg 179

Wilcox, Lynn, Syracuse University Press, 621 Skytop Rd, Suite 110, Syracuse, NY 13244-5290 *Tel:* 315-443-5534 *Toll Free Tel:* 800-365-8929 (cust serv) *Fax:* 315-443-5545 *E-mail:* supress@syr.edu *Web Site:* press.syr.edu, pg 212

Wilcox, Mary, Houghton Mifflin Harcourt Trade & Reference Division, 125 High St, Boston, MA 02110 *Tel:* 617-351-5000 *Web Site:* www.hmhco.com, pg 104

Wilcoxon, Deborah, Research Press, 2612 N Mattis Ave, Champaign, IL 61822 *Tel:* 217-352-3273 *Toll Free Tel:* 800-519-2707 *Fax:* 217-352-1221 *E-mail:* rp@researchpress.com; orders@researchpress. com *Web Site:* www.researchpress.com, pg 184

Wilderson, Joe, Rocky Mountain Books Ltd (RMB), 103-1075 Pendergast St, Victoria, BC V8V 0A1, Canada *Tel:* 250-360-0829 *Fax:* 250-386-0829 *Web Site:* www.rmbooks.com, pg 438

Wiley, Jesse C, John Wiley & Sons Inc, 111 River St, Hoboken, NJ 07030-5774 *Tel:* 201-748-6000 *Toll Free Tel:* 800-225-5945 (cust serv) *Fax:* 201-748-6088 *E-mail:* info@wiley.com *Web Site:* www.wiley.com, pg 241

Wilhelm, Sharona, Scarsdale Publishing Ltd, 333 Mamaroneck Ave, White Plains, NY 10607 *E-mail:* scarsdale@scarsdalepublishing.com *Web Site:* scarsdalepublishing.com, pg 193

Wilhite, Sue, COVR Visionary Awards, PO Box 1397, Palmer Lake, CO 80133 *Tel:* 719-487-0424 *E-mail:* info@covr.org *Web Site:* covr.org/awards, pg 607

Wilkes, Deborah, Focus, PO Box 390007, Cambridge, MA 02139-0001 *Tel:* 317-635-9250 *Fax:* 317-635-9292 *E-mail:* customer@ hackettpublishing.com; editorial@hackettpublishing. com *Web Site:* focusbookstore.com; www. hackettpublishing.com, pg 79

Wilkes, Deborah, Hackett Publishing Co Inc, 3333 Massachusetts Ave, Indianapolis, IN 46218 *Tel:* 317-635-9250 (orders & cust serv); 617-497-6303 (edit off & sales) *Fax:* 317-635-9292; 617-661-8703 (edit off) *Toll Free Fax:* 800-783-9213 *E-mail:* customer@ hackettpublishing.com; editorial@hackettpublishing. com *Web Site:* www.hackettpublishing.com, pg 91

Wilkie, Craig, The University Press of Kentucky, 663 S Limestone St, Lexington, KY 40508-4008 *Tel:* 859-257-8400 *Fax:* 859-257-8481 *Web Site:* www. kentuckypress.com, pg 233

Wilkie, Devin, Steerforth Press, 31 Hanover St, Suite 1, Lebanon, NH 03766 *Tel:* 603-643-4787 *Fax:* 603-643-4788 *E-mail:* info@steerforth.com *Web Site:* www. steerforth.com, pg 207

Wilkins, Timothy, Princeton University Press, 41 William St, Princeton, NJ 08540-5237 *Tel:* 609-258-4900 *Fax:* 609-258-6305 *Web Site:* press.princeton. edu, pg 174

Wilkinson, Christine, Wilkinson Studios Inc, 2955 Kelly Dr, Elgin, IL 60124-4349 *Tel:* 312-286-3683 *Web Site:* www.wilkinsonstudios.com, pg 513

Wilkinson, Marco, The Field Poetry Prize, 50 N Professor St, Oberlin, OH 44074-1091 *Tel:* 440-775-8408 *Fax:* 440-775-8124 *E-mail:* oc.press@oberlin.edu *Web Site:* www.oberlin.edu/ocpress; www.oberlin. edu/ocpress/prize.htm (guidelines), pg 615

Wilkinson, Marco, Oberlin College Press, 50 N Professor St, Oberlin, OH 44074-1091 *Tel:* 440-775-8408 *Fax:* 440-775-8124 *E-mail:* oc.press@oberlin.edu *Web Site:* www.oberlin.edu/ocpress, pg 154

Wilks, Rick, Annick Press Ltd, 15 Patricia Ave, Toronto, ON M2M 1H9, Canada *Tel:* 416-221-4802 *Fax:* 416-221-8400 *E-mail:* annickpress@annickpress.com *Web Site:* www.annickpress.com, pg 415

Will, Julie, HarperCollins General Books Group, 195 Broadway, New York, NY 10007 *Tel:* 212-207-7000 *Web Site:* www.harpercollins.com, pg 93

Willars-Pirc, Lisa, Writers Retreat Workshop (WRW), PO Box 170657, Austin, TX 78717 *E-mail:* info@ writersretreatworkshop.com *Web Site:* www. writersretreatworkshop.com, pg 580

Willey, Paul, The Book Tree, 3316 Adams Ave, Suite A, San Diego, CA 92116 *Tel:* 619-280-1263 *Toll Free Tel:* 800-700-8733 (orders) *Fax:* 619-280-1285 *E-mail:* orders@thebooktree.com; info@thebooktree. com *Web Site:* thebooktree.com, pg 38

Willey, Susan, New Readers Press, 104 Marcellus, Syracuse, NY 13204 *Tel:* 315-422-9121 *Toll Free Tel:* 800-448-8878 *Toll Free Fax:* 866-894-2100 *E-mail:* nrp@proliteracy.org *Web Site:* www. newreaderspress.com, pg 149

Williams, Angela, Goose Lane Editions, 500 Beaverbrook Ct, Suite 330, Fredericton, NB E3B 5X4, Canada *Tel:* 506-450-4251 *Toll Free Tel:* 888-926-8377 *Fax:* 506-459-4991 *E-mail:* info@gooselane. com; customerservice@gooselane.com *Web Site:* www. gooselane.com, pg 427

Williams, Bob, Burns Entertainment & Sports Marketing, 820 Davis St, Suite 222, Evanston, IL 60201 *Tel:* 847-866-9400 *Fax:* 847-491-9778 *E-mail:* burnsl@ burnsent.com *Web Site:* burnsent.com, pg 515

Williams, Cheyenne, Florida Writers Association Conference, PO Box 66069, St Pete Beach, FL 33736-6069 *Web Site:* www.floridawriters.net, pg 574

Williams, Cheyenne, Florida Writers Association Inc, PO Box 66069, St Pete Beach, FL 33736-6069 *Web Site:* www.floridawriters.net, pg 533

Williams, Dan, Baskerville Publishers Poetry Award, Dept of English, TCU Box 298300, Fort Worth, TX 76129 *Tel:* 817-257-5907 *Fax:* 817-257-5905 *E-mail:* descant@tcu.edu *Web Site:* www.descant.tcu. edu, pg 596

Williams, Dan, Betsy Colquitt Award for Poetry, Dept of English, TCU Box 298300, Fort Worth, TX 76129 *Tel:* 817-257-5907 *Fax:* 817-257-5905 *E-mail:* descant@tcu.edu *Web Site:* www.descant.tcu. edu, pg 606

Williams, Dan, Frank O'Connor Prize for Fiction, Dept of English, TCU Box 298300, Fort Worth, TX 76129 *Tel:* 817-257-5907 *Fax:* 817-257-5905 *E-mail:* descant@tcu.edu *Web Site:* www.descant.tcu. edu, pg 650

Williams, Dan, TCU Press, 3000 Sandage Ave, Fort Worth, TX 76109 *Tel:* 817-257-7822 *Toll Free Tel:* 800-826-8911 (orders) *Fax:* 817-257-5075 *Web Site:* www.prs.tcu.edu, pg 213

Williams, Dan, Gary Wilson Award for Short Fiction, Dept of English, TCU Box 298300, Fort Worth, TX 76129 *Tel:* 817-257-5907 *Fax:* 817-257-5905 *E-mail:* descant@tcu.edu *Web Site:* www.descant.tcu. edu, pg 678

Williams, Heather, Arbordale Publishing, 612 Johnnie Dodds Blvd, Suite A2, Mount Pleasant, SC 29464 *Tel:* 843-971-6722 *Toll Free Tel:* 877-243-3457 *Fax:* 843-216-3804 *E-mail:* info@arbordalepublishing. com *Web Site:* www.arbordalepublishing.com, pg 19

Williams, Jackie, The Knight Agency Inc, 232 W Washington St, Madison, GA 30650 *E-mail:* admin@ knightagency.net *Web Site:* www.knightagency.net, pg 492

Williams, Jan, Jan Williams Indexing Services, 300 Dartmouth College Hwy, Lyme, NH 03768-3207 *Tel:* 603-795-4924 *Web Site:* www. janwilliamsindexing.com, pg 465

Williams, Jane A, Bluestocking Press, 3045 Sacramento St, No 1014, Placerville, CA 95667-1014 *Tel:* 530-622-8586 *Toll Free Tel:* 800-959-8586 *Fax:* 530-642-

9222 *E-mail:* customerservice@bluestockingpress. com; orders@bluestockingpress.com *Web Site:* www. bluestockingpress.com, pg 37

Williams, Jasper, Stellar Publishing, 2114 S Live Oak Pkwy, Wilmington, NC 28403 *Tel:* 910-269-7444 *Web Site:* www.stellar-publishing.com, pg 208

Williams, Jessica, HarperCollins General Books Group, 195 Broadway, New York, NY 10007 *Tel:* 212-207-7000 *Web Site:* www.harpercollins.com, pg 93

Williams, John Taylor "Ike", Kneerim & Williams Agency, 90 Canal St, Boston, MA 02114 *Tel:* 617-303-1650 *Web Site:* www.kwlit.com, pg 491

Williams, Kathy, Brown Books Publishing Group, 16250 Knoll Trail, Suite 205, Dallas, TX 75248 *Tel:* 972-381-0009 *Fax:* 972-248-4336 *E-mail:* publishing@ brownbooks.com *Web Site:* www.brownbooks.com, pg 42

Williams, Kim, Princeton University Press, 41 William St, Princeton, NJ 08540-5237 *Tel:* 609-258-4900 *Fax:* 609-258-6305 *Web Site:* press.princeton.edu, pg 174

Williams, Lindsay, ASM Press, 1752 "N" St NW, Washington, DC 20036-2904 *Tel:* 202-737-3600 *Fax:* 202-942-9342 *E-mail:* books@asmusa.org *Web Site:* www.asmscience.org, pg 22

Williams, Lisa, US Government Publishing Office (GPO), Superintendent of Documents, 732 N Capitol St NW, Washington, DC 20401 *Tel:* 202-512-1800 *Toll Free Tel:* 866-512-1800 (orders) *Fax:* 202-512-1998 *E-mail:* contactcenter@gpo.gov *Web Site:* www.gpo. gov; bookstore.gpo.gov (sales), pg 235

Williams, Matt, Groundwood Books, 128 Sterling Rd, Lower Level, Toronto, ON M6R 2B7, Canada *Tel:* 416-363-4343 *Fax:* 416-363-1017 *E-mail:* genmail@groundwoodbooks.com *Web Site:* www.houseofanansi.com, pg 428

Williams, Matt, House of Anansi Press Inc, 128 Sterling Rd, Lower Level, Toronto, ON M6R 2B7, Canada *Tel:* 416-363-4343 *Fax:* 416-363-1017 *E-mail:* customerservice@houseofanansi.com *Web Site:* www.houseofanansi.com, pg 429

Williams, Megan, Penguin Random House LLC, 1745 Broadway, New York, NY 10019 *Tel:* 212-782-9000 *Toll Free Tel:* 800-726-0600 *Web Site:* www. penguinrandomhouse.com, pg 164

Williams, Megan, Random House Children's Books, 1745 Broadway, 10th fl, New York, NY 10019 *Tel:* 212-782-9000 *Web Site:* www.randomhousekids. com, pg 180

Williams, Michelle, Chicago Review Press, 814 N Franklin St, Chicago, IL 60610 *Tel:* 312-337-0747 *Toll Free Tel:* 800-888-4741 *Fax:* 312-337-5110 *E-mail:* frontdesk@chicagoreviewpress.com *Web Site:* www.chicagoreviewpress.com, pg 50

Williams, Paul, American Society of Composers, Authors & Publishers (ASCAP), 1900 Broadway, New York City, NY 10023 *Tel:* 212-621-6000 *Fax:* 212-612-8453 *E-mail:* info@ascap.com *Web Site:* www. ascap.com, pg 524

Williams, Randall, NewSouth Books, 105 S Court St, Montgomery, AL 36104 *Tel:* 334-834-3556 *E-mail:* info@newsouthbooks.com *Web Site:* www. newsouthbooks.com, pg 150

Williams, Rob, Mountain Press Publishing Co, 1301 S Third W, Missoula, MT 59801 *Tel:* 406-728-1900 *Toll Free Tel:* 800-234-5308 *Fax:* 406-728-1635 *E-mail:* info@mtnpress.com *Web Site:* www.mountain-press.com, pg 143

Williams, Roger S, Roger Williams Agency, 17 Paddock Dr, Lawrence Twp, NJ 08648 *Tel:* 860-973-2439 *E-mail:* roger@rogerwilliamsagency.com *Web Site:* www.rogerwilliamsagency.com, pg 500

Williams, Roslynn, Dun & Bradstreet, 103 JFK Pkwy, Short Hills, NJ 07078 *Tel:* 973-921-5500 *Toll Free Tel:* 844-869-8244; 800-234-3867 (cust serv) *Web Site:* www.dnb.com, pg 68

Williams, Sandra, Mountain Writers Series, 2804 SE 27 Ave, Suite 2, Portland, OR 97202 *Tel:* 503-232-4517 *Fax:* 503-232-4517 *E-mail:* programs@ mountainwriters.org; support@mountainwriters.org *Web Site:* www.mountainwriters.org, pg 576

Williams, Sarah, Penguin Random House LLC, 1745 Broadway, New York, NY 10019 *Tel:* 212-782-9000 *Toll Free Tel:* 800-726-0600 *Web Site:* www. penguinrandomhouse.com, pg 164

Williams, Stephanie, Wayne State University Press, Leonard N Simons Bldg, 4809 Woodward Ave, Detroit, MI 48201-1309 *Tel:* 313-577-6120 *Toll Free Tel:* 800-978-7323 *Fax:* 313-577-6131 *E-mail:* bookorders@wayne.edu *Web Site:* www. wsupress.wayne.edu, pg 238

Williams, Stephen, Indiana University Press, Herman B Wells Library 350, 1320 E Tenth St, Bloomington, IN 47405-3907 *Tel:* 812-855-8817 *Toll Free Tel:* 800-842-6796 (orders only) *Fax:* 812-855-7931; 812-855-8507 *E-mail:* iupress@indiana.edu; iuporder@indiana.edu (orders) *Web Site:* www.iupress.indiana.edu, pg 108

Williams, Suzanne, The Canadian Writers' Foundation Inc (La Fondation des Ecrivains Canadiens), PO Box 13281, Kanata Sta, Ottawa, ON K2K 1X4, Canada *Tel:* 613-256-6937 *Fax:* 613-256-5457 *E-mail:* info@ canadianwritersfoundation.org *Web Site:* www. canadianwritersfoundation.org, pg 551

Williams, Thomas A PhD, Williams & Company Book Publishers, 1317 Pine Ridge Dr, Savannah, GA 31406 *Tel:* 912-352-0404 *E-mail:* bookpub@comcast.net *Web Site:* www.pubmart.com, pg 242

Williams, Tracy, Little, Brown and Company, 1290 Avenue of the Americas, New York, NY 10104 *Tel:* 212-364-1100 *Fax:* 212-364-0952 *E-mail:* firstname.lastname@hbgusa. com *Web Site:* www.littlebrown.com; www. hachettebookgroup.com, pg 125

Williamson, Alain, Editions Le Dauphin Blanc Inc, 825, blvd Lebourgneuf, Suite 125, Quebec, QC G2J 0B9, Canada *Tel:* 418-845-4045 *Fax:* 418-845-1933 *E-mail:* info@dauphinblanc.com *Web Site:* www. dauphinblanc.com, pg 424

Williamson, Iain, OECD Washington Center, 1776 "I" St NW, Suite 450, Washington, DC 20006 *Tel:* 202-785-6323 *Toll Free Tel:* 800-456-6323 (dist ctr/pubns orders) *Fax:* 202-785-0350 *E-mail:* washington. contact@oecd.org; oecdilibrary@oecd.org (sales) *Web Site:* www.oecd-ilibrary.org, pg 154

Williamson, Iain, Productive Publications, 380 Brooke Ave, Lower Level, North York, ON M5M 2L6, Canada *Tel:* 416-483-0634 *Toll Free Tel:* 877-879-2669 (orders) *Fax:* 416-322-7434 *E-mail:* productivepublications@rogers.com *Web Site:* www.productivepublications.ca, pg 438

Williamson, Lesley, Artists & Writers Summer Fellowships, 435 Ellis Hollow Creek Rd, Ithaca, NY 14850 *Tel:* 607-539-3146 *E-mail:* artscolony@ saltonstall.org *Web Site:* www.saltonstall.org, pg 573

Williford, Lex, University of Texas at El Paso, Department of Creative Writing, MFA/Department of Creative Writing, 901 EDUC, 500 W University Ave, El Paso, TX 79968-9991 *Tel:* 915-747-5713 *Fax:* 915-747-5523 *E-mail:* creativewriting@utep.edu *Web Site:* www.utep.edu/cw, pg 586

Willinger, James L, Wide World of Maps Inc, 2133 E Indian School Rd, Phoenix, AZ 85016 *Tel:* 602-279-2323 *Toll Free Tel:* 800-279-7654 *Web Site:* www. maps4u.com, pg 240

Willis, Clarissa, Ozark Creative Writers Inc Annual Conference, 512 Walnut St, Mount Vernon, IN 47620 *E-mail:* ozarkcreativewriters@ozarkcreativewriters.com *Web Site:* www.ozarkcreativewriters.com, pg 577

Willis, Liana, The Experiment, 220 E 23 St, Suite 600, New York, NY 10010-4658 *Tel:* 212-889-1659 *E-mail:* info@theexperimentpublishing.com *Web Site:* www.theexperimentpublishing.com, pg 74

Willis, Meredith Sue, Hamilton Stone Editions, PO Box 43, Maplewood, NJ 07040 *Tel:* 973-378-8361 *E-mail:* hstone@hamiltonstone.org *Web Site:* www. hamiltonstone.org, pg 92

Wills, April, Sourcebooks LLC, 1935 Brookdale Rd, Suite 139, Naperville, IL 60563 *Tel:* 630-961-3900 *Toll Free Tel:* 800-432-7444 *Fax:* 630-961-2168 *E-mail:* info@sourcebooks.com; customersupport@ sourcebooks.com *Web Site:* www.sourcebooks.com, pg 204

Wills, Juliet, Galaxy Press, 7051 Hollywood Blvd, Hollywood, CA 90028 *Tel:* 323-466-3310 *Toll Free Tel:* 877-8GALAXY (842-5299) *E-mail:* info@ galaxypress.com; customers@galaxypress.com *Web Site:* www.galaxypress.com, pg 82

Willshire, Tom, Cambridge University Press, One Liberty Plaza, 20th fl, New York, NY 10006 *Tel:* 212-924-3900; 212-337-5000 *Fax:* 212-691-3239; 845-353-4141 *E-mail:* newyork@cambridge.org; customer_service@cambridge.org *Web Site:* www. cambridge.org/us, pg 43

Wilmoth, Mark, PennWell Books, 1421 S Sheridan Rd, Tulsa, OK 74112 *Tel:* 918-831-9421 *Toll Free Tel:* 800-752-9764 *Fax:* 918-831-9555 *E-mail:* sales@ pennwell.com *Web Site:* www.pennwellbooks.com, pg 166

Wilson, Bev, Information Gatekeepers Inc (IGI), PO Box 606, Winchester, MA 01890 *Tel:* 617-782-5033 *Fax:* 617-507-8338 *E-mail:* info@igigroup.com *Web Site:* www.igigroup.com, pg 108

Wilson, Bob, Sunrise River Press, 838 Lake St S, Forrest Lake, MN 55025 *Tel:* 651-277-1400 *Toll Free Tel:* 800-895-4585 *E-mail:* info@sunriseriverpress. com; sales@sunriseriverpress.com *Web Site:* www. sunriseriverpress.com, pg 211

Wilson, Dr Cheryl, University of Baltimore - Yale Gordon College of Arts & Sciences, Ampersand Institute for Words & Images, 1420 N Charles St, Baltimore, MD 21201-5779 *Tel:* 410-837-6022 *Fax:* 410-837-6029 *E-mail:* scd@ubalt.edu *Web Site:* www.ubalt.edu, pg 585

Wilson, Cristina, Sourcebooks LLC, 1935 Brookdale Rd, Suite 139, Naperville, IL 60563 *Tel:* 630-961-3900 *Toll Free Tel:* 800-432-7444 *Fax:* 630-961-2168 *E-mail:* info@sourcebooks.com; customersupport@ sourcebooks.com *Web Site:* www.sourcebooks.com, pg 204

Wilson, Erika, Authors Alliance, 2705 Webster St, No 5805, Berkeley, CA 94705 *E-mail:* info@ authorsalliance.org *Web Site:* www.authorsalliance.org, pg 527

Wilson, Gary, Green Dragon Books, 2275 Ibis Isle Rd W, Palm Beach, FL 33480 *Tel:* 561-533-6231 *Toll Free Tel:* 800-874-8844 *Fax:* 561-533-6233 *Toll Free Fax:* 888-874-8844 *E-mail:* info@greendragonbooks. com *Web Site:* greendragonbooks.com, pg 88

Wilson, Jaclyn, Wesleyan University Press, 215 Long Lane, Middletown, CT 06459-0433 *Tel:* 860-685-7712 *Fax:* 860-685-7712 *Web Site:* www.wesleyan. edu/wespress, pg 239

Wilson, Jamia, The Feminist Press at The City University of New York, 365 Fifth Ave, Suite 5406, New York, NY 10016 *Tel:* 212-817-7915 *Fax:* 212-817-1593 *E-mail:* info@feministpress.org *Web Site:* www.feministpress.org, pg 76

Wilson, Jamia, Louise Meriwether First Book Prize, 365 Fifth Ave, Suite 5406, New York, NY 10016 *Tel:* 212-817-7915 *E-mail:* louisemeriwetherprize@gmail.com; info@feministpress.org *Web Site:* www.feministpress. org/louise-meriwether-first-book-prize, pg 641

Wilson, Jeff, Simon & Schuster, Inc, 1230 Avenue of the Americas, New York, NY 10020 *Tel:* 212-698-7000 *Toll Free Tel:* 800-223-2336 (orders) *Fax:* 212-698-7007 *Toll Free Fax:* 800-943-9831 (orders) *E-mail:* firstname.lastname@simonandschuster.com; purchaseorders@simonandschuster.com (orders) *Web Site:* www.simonandschuster.com, pg 199

Wilson, Jennifer, Green Dragon Books, 2275 Ibis Isle Rd W, Palm Beach, FL 33480 *Tel:* 561-533-6231 *Toll Free Tel:* 800-874-8844 *Fax:* 561-533-6233 *Toll Free Fax:* 888-874-8844 *E-mail:* info@greendragonbooks. com *Web Site:* greendragonbooks.com, pg 88

Wilson, Jocie, Pacific Northwest Young Reader's Choice Award, Vancouver Mall Community Library, 8700 NE Vancouver Mall Dr, Suite 285, Vancouver, WA 98662 Web Site: www.pnla.org/yrca, pg 652

Wilson, Julie, Penguin Random House Audio Publishing, 1745 Broadway, New York, NY 10019 E-mail: audio@penguinrandomhouse.com Web Site: www.penguinrandomhouseaudio.com, pg 164

Wilson, Lance, Top of the Mountain Publishing, 4837 62 St N, St Petersburg, FL 33709 Tel: 727-391-3958, pg 219

Wilson, Leah, BenBella Books Inc, 10300 N Central Expwy, Suite 400, Dallas, TX 75231 Tel: 214-750-3600 E-mail: feedback@benbellabooks.com Web Site: www.benbellabooks.com; www.smartpopbooks.com, pg 31

Wilson, Martin, HarperCollins General Books Group, 195 Broadway, New York, NY 10007 Tel: 212-207-7000 Web Site: www.harpercollins.com, pg 94

Wilson, Mary Ellen, Quirk Books, 215 Church St, Philadelphia, PA 19106 Tel: 215-627-3581 Fax: 215-627-5220 E-mail: general@quirkbooks.com Web Site: www.quirkbooks.com, pg 179

Wilson, Sr Mary Leonora, Pauline Books & Media, 50 Saint Paul's Ave, Boston, MA 02130 Tel: 617-522-8911 Toll Free Tel: 800-876-4463 (orders); 800-836-9723 (cust serv) Fax: 617-541-9805 E-mail: editorial@paulinemedia.com (ms submissions); orderentry@pauline.org (cust serv) Web Site: www.pauline.org/pbmpublishing, pg 161

Wilson, Megan, Houghton Mifflin Harcourt, 125 High St, Boston, MA 02110 Tel: 617-351-5000 Toll Free Tel: 855-969-4642; 800-225-5425 (K-12 educ materials); 800-323-9540 (assessment materials); 877-219-1537 (SkillsTutor); 888-242-6747 (Innovation in Educ Group); 800-225-3362 (Trade & Ref Div) Toll Free Fax: 800-269-5232 E-mail: myhmhco@hmhco.com Web Site: www.hmhco.com, pg 103

Wilson, Natashya, Harlequin Enterprises Ltd, Bay Adelaide Centre, East Tower, 22 Adelaide St W, 41st fl, Toronto, ON M5H 4E3, Canada Tel: 416-445-5860 Toll Free Tel: 888-432-4879; 800-370-5838 (ebook inquiries) E-mail: customerservice@harlequin.com Web Site: www.harlequin.com, pg 429

Wilson, Olivia, Houghton Mifflin Harcourt Trade & Reference Division, 125 High St, Boston, MA 02110 Tel: 617-351-5000 Web Site: www.hmhco.com, pg 104

Wilson, Pamela, University of Hawaii Press, 2840 Kolowalu St, Honolulu, HI 96822-1888 Tel: 808-956-8255 Toll Free Tel: 888-UHPRESS (847-7377) Fax: 808-988-6052 Toll Free Fax: 800-650-7811 E-mail: uhpbooks@hawaii.edu Web Site: www.uhpress.hawaii.edu, pg 227

Wilson, Stefanya, The Jack London Award, Box 17897, Encino, CA 91416-7897 E-mail: cwcsfv@gmail.com, pg 635

Wilson, Stefanya, Masters Literary Awards, PO Box 17897, Encino, CA 91416-7897 Tel: 818-377-4006 E-mail: titan91416@yahoo.com, pg 639

Wilson, Steve, McFarland, 960 NC Hwy 88 W, Jefferson, NC 28640 Tel: 336-246-4460 Toll Free Tel: 800-253-2187 (orders) Fax: 336-246-5018; 336-246-4403 (orders) E-mail: info@mcfarlandpub.com Web Site: mcfarlandbooks.com, pg 135

Wilson, Steven, Book Sales, 142 W 36 St, 4th fl, New York, NY 10018 Tel: 212-779-4972; 212-779-4971 Fax: 212-779-6058 Web Site: www.quartoknows.com, pg 38

Wilson, Victoria, Alfred A Knopf, c/o Penguin Random House Inc, 1745 Broadway, New York, NY 10019 Tel: 212-751-2600 Fax: 212-572-2662 (foreign rts) Web Site: knopfdoubleday.com, pg 118

Windhorn, Annette, Association of University Presses (AUPresses), 1412 Broadway, Suite 2135, New York, NY 10018 Tel: 212-989-1010 Fax: 212-989-0275 E-mail: info@aupresses.org Web Site: www.aupresses.org, pg 527

Winick, Eugene H, McIntosh and Otis Inc, 207 E 37 St, Suite BG, New York, NY 10016 Tel: 212-687-7400 Fax: 212-687-6894 E-mail: info@mcintoshandotis.com Web Site: www.mcintoshandotis.com, pg 496

Winn, Lisa, American Booksellers Association, 333 Westchester Ave, Suite S202, White Plains, NY 10604 Tel: 914-406-7500 Toll Free Tel: 800-637-0037 Fax: 914-417-4013 E-mail: info@bookweb.org Web Site: www.bookweb.org, pg 522

Winnicki, Ksenia, Bloomsbury Publishing Inc, 1385 Broadway, 5th fl, New York, NY 10018 Tel: 212-419-5300 E-mail: marketingusa@bloomsbury.com; adultpublicityusa@bloomsbury.com; askacademic@bloomsbury.com Web Site: www.bloomsbury.com, pg 36

Winningham, Sharon, School Zone Publishing Co, 1819 Industrial Dr, Grand Haven, MI 49417 Tel: 616-846-5030 Toll Free Tel: 800-253-0564 Fax: 616-846-6181 Web Site: www.schoolzone.com, pg 195

Winns, Nadine, Abbeville Press, 655 Third Ave, New York, NY 10017 Tel: 212-366-5585 Toll Free Tel: 800-ART-BOOK (278-2665); 800-343-4499 (orders) Fax: 646-375-2359 Toll Free Tel: 800-351-5073 (orders) E-mail: abbeville@abbeville.com; sales@abbeville.com; marketing@abbeville.com; rights@abbeville.com Web Site: www.abbeville.com, pg 2

Winns, Nadine, Abbeville Publishing Group, 655 Third Ave, New York, NY 10017 Tel: 646-375-2136 Fax: 646-375-2359 E-mail: abbeville@abbeville.com; marketing@abbeville.com; sales@abbeville.com; rights@abbeville.com Web Site: www.abbeville.com, pg 2

Winslow, Anne, Algonquin Books, 400 Silver Cedar Ct, Suite 300, Chapel Hill, NC 27514-1585 Tel: 919-967-0108 Fax: 919-933-0272 E-mail: inquiry@algonquin.com Web Site: www.workman.com/algonquin, pg 7

Winslow, Susan, Macmillan Learning, 41 Madison Ave, New York, NY 10010 Tel: 212-576-9400 Fax: 212-689-2383 Web Site: www.macmillanlearning.com, pg 130

Winstanley, Nicole, Penguin Group (Canada), 320 Front St W, Suite 1400, Toronto, ON M5V 3B6, Canada Tel: 416-364-4449 Fax: 416-598-7764 E-mail: customerservicescanada@penguinrandomhouse.com; publicity@ca.penguingroup.com Web Site: penguinrandomhouse.ca/imprints/penguin-canada, pg 436

Winstanley, Nicole, Penguin Random House Canada, 320 Front St W, Suite 1400, Toronto, ON M5V 3B6, Canada Tel: 416-364-4449 Toll Free Tel: 888-523-9292 (cust serv) Fax: 416-598-7764 Web Site: www.penguinrandomhouse.ca, pg 436

Winston, Peggy, Association for Information & Image Management International (AIIM), 1100 Wayne Ave, Suite 1100, Silver Spring, MD 20910 Tel: 301-587-8202 Toll Free Tel: 800-477-2446 Fax: 301-587-2711 E-mail: aiim@aiim.org; info@aiim.org Web Site: www.aiim.org, pg 525

Winter, Maureen, Getty Publications, 1200 Getty Center Dr, Suite 500, Los Angeles, CA 90049-1682 Tel: 310-440-7365 Toll Free Tel: 800-223-3431 (orders) Fax: 310-440-7758 E-mail: pubsinfo@getty.edu Web Site: www.getty.edu/publications, pg 85

Winters, Keli, Evan-Moor Educational Publishers, 18 Lower Ragsdale Dr, Monterey, CA 93940-5746 Tel: 831-649-5901 Toll Free Tel: 800-777-4362 (orders) Fax: 831-649-6256 Toll Free Fax: 800-777-4332 (orders) E-mail: sales@evan-moor.com; marketing@evan-moor.com Web Site: www.evan-moor.com, pg 73

Winters, Mr Tracy, Winters Publishing, 705 E Washington St, Greensburg, IN 47240 Tel: 812-663-4948 Toll Free Tel: 800-457-3230 Fax: 812-663-4948 E-mail: winterspublishing@gmail.com Web Site: www.winterspublishing.com, pg 242

Winton, Charlie, Counterpoint Press LLC, 2560 Ninth St, Suite 318, Berkeley, CA 94710 Tel: 510-704-0230 Fax: 510-704-0268 E-mail: info@counterpointpress.com Web Site: counterpointpress.com; softskull.com, pg 58

Winton, Helen M, The Reading Component, 3900 Parkview Lane, 3B, Irvine, CA 92612-2003 Tel: 949-387-6330, pg 469

Wise, Tomas, G Schirmer Inc/Associated Music Publishers Inc, 180 Madison Ave, 24th fl, New York, NY 10016 Tel: 212-254-2100 Fax: 212-254-2013 E-mail: schirmer@schirmer.com Web Site: www.musicsalesclassical.com, pg 193

Wiseman, Paula, Simon & Schuster Children's Publishing, 1230 Avenue of the Americas, New York, NY 10020 Tel: 212-698-7000 Web Site: www.simonandschuster.com/kids; www.simonandschuster.com/teen; simonandschuster.net; simonandschuster.biz, pg 199

Wisenthal, Paul, The Professional Writer, 175 W 12 St, Suite 6D, New York, NY 10011 Tel: 212-414-0188; 917-658-1946 (cell) E-mail: paul@theprofessionalwriter.com, pg 469

Wishard, Tammy, Anson Jones MD Awards, 401 W 15 St, Austin, TX 78701 Tel: 512-370-1300 Fax: 512-370-1693 Web Site: www.texmed.org, pg 629

Wishna, Jennifer, Scholastic Education, 557 Broadway, New York, NY 10012 Tel: 212-343-6100 Fax: 212-343-6189 Web Site: www.scholastic.com, pg 194

Wisler, Wade, OCP, 5536 NE Hassalo St, Portland, OR 97213 Tel: 503-281-1191 Toll Free Tel: 800-548-8749 Fax: 503-282-3486 Toll Free Fax: 800-843-8181 E-mail: liturgy@ocp.org Web Site: www.ocp.org, pg 154

Wispelwey, June C, American Institute of Chemical Engineers (AIChE), 120 Wall St, 23rd fl, New York, NY 10005-4020 Tel: 203-702-7660 Toll Free Tel: 800-242-4363 Fax: 203-775-5177 E-mail: customerservice@aiche.org Web Site: www.aiche.org, pg 12

Wissoker, Ken, Duke University Press, 905 W Main St, Suite 18B, Durham, NC 27701 Tel: 919-688-5134 Toll Free Tel: 888-651-0122 (US) Fax: 919-688-2615 Toll Free Fax: 888-651-0124 E-mail: orders@dukeupress.edu Web Site: www.dukeupress.edu, pg 68

Witcraft, Stacey, Random House Publishing Group, 1745 Broadway, New York, NY 10019 Toll Free Tel: 800-200-3552 Web Site: www.randomhousebooks.com, pg 181

Witherell, Jennifer, InkWell Management, 521 Fifth Ave, 26th fl, New York, NY 10175 Tel: 212-922-3500 Fax: 212-922-0535 E-mail: info@inkwellmanagement.com Web Site: inkwellmanagement.com, pg 489

Witherspoon, Kim, InkWell Management, 521 Fifth Ave, 26th fl, New York, NY 10175 Tel: 212-922-3500 Fax: 212-922-0535 E-mail: info@inkwellmanagement.com Web Site: inkwellmanagement.com, pg 489

Witkin, Karrie, Harry N Abrams Inc, 195 Broadway, 9th fl, New York, NY 10007 Tel: 212-206-7715 Toll Free Tel: 800-345-1359 Fax: 212-519-1210 E-mail: abrams@abramsbooks.com Web Site: www.abramsbooks.com, pg 3

Witte, George, St Martin's Press, LLC, 120 Broadway, New York, NY 10271 Tel: 646-307-5151 Web Site: us.macmillan.com/smp, pg 190

Witzleben, Donna, Society for Industrial & Applied Mathematics, 3600 Market St, 6th fl, Philadelphia, PA 19104-2688 Tel: 215-382-9800 Toll Free Tel: 800-447-7426 Fax: 215-386-7999 E-mail: siambooks@siam.org Web Site: www.siam.org, pg 202

Wofsy, Alan, Alan Wofsy Fine Arts, 1109 Geary Blvd, San Francisco, CA 94109 Tel: 415-292-6500 Toll Free Tel: 800-660-6403 Fax: 415-292-6594 (off & cust serv); 510-251-1840 (acctg) E-mail: order@art-books.com (orders); editeur@earthlink.net (edit); beauxarts@earthlink.net (cust serv) Web Site: www.art-books.com, pg 243

Wojcik, Tim, Levine|Greenberg|Rostan Literary Agency, 307 Seventh Ave, Suite 2407, New York, NY 10001 Tel: 212-337-0934 Fax: 212-337-0948 Web Site: lgrliterary.com, pg 493

Wojtyla, Karen, Simon & Schuster Children's Publishing, 1230 Avenue of the Americas, New York, NY 10020 *Tel:* 212-698-7000 *Web Site:* www.simonandschuster. com/kids; www.simonandschuster.com/teen; simonandschuster.net; simonandschuster.biz, pg 199

Wolf, Ingrid, Wm B Eerdmans Publishing Co, 4035 Park East Ct SE, Grand Rapids, MI 49546 *Tel:* 616-459-4591 *Toll Free Tel:* 800-253-7521 *Fax:* 616-459-6540 *E-mail:* customerservice@eerdmans.com; sales@eerdmans.com *Web Site:* www.eerdmans.com, pg 70

Wolf, Maria, Institute of Governmental Studies, 109 Moses Hall, No 2370, Berkeley, CA 94720-2370 *Tel:* 510-642-1428 *E-mail:* igspress@berkeley.edu *Web Site:* www.igs.berkeley.edu, pg 110

Wolf, Ray, Leisure Arts Inc, 104 Champs Blvd, Suite 100, Maumelle, AR 72113 *Tel:* 501-868-8800 *Toll Free Tel:* 800-643-8030 *Toll Free Fax:* 877-710-5603 (catalog) *E-mail:* customer_service@leisurearts.com *Web Site:* www.leisurearts.com, pg 122

Wolf, Wendy, Viking, 375 Hudson St, New York, NY 10014 *Tel:* 212-366-2000 *Fax:* 212-243-6002 *Web Site:* www.penguin.com/publishers/vikingbooks, pg 236

Wolfe, Alexander, University of Pittsburgh Press, 7500 Thomas Blvd, Pittsburgh, PA 15260 *Tel:* 412-383-2456 *Fax:* 412-383-2466 *E-mail:* info@upress.pitt.edu *Web Site:* www.upress.pitt.edu, pg 230

Wolfe, Gary, New Author Publishing, 4 E Fulford Place, Brockville, ON K6V 2Z8, Canada *Tel:* 613-865-7471 *Web Site:* www.newauthorpublishing.com, pg 434

Wolfe, John, Association of National Advertisers (ANA), 10 Grand Central, 155 E 44 St, New York, NY 10017 *Tel:* 212-697-5950 *Fax:* 212-302-6714 *Web Site:* www.ana.net, pg 527

Wolfe, Margie, Second Story Press, 20 Maud St, Suite 401, Toronto, ON M5V 2M5, Canada *Tel:* 416-537-7850 *Fax:* 416-537-0588 *E-mail:* info@secondstorypress.ca *Web Site:* secondstorypress.ca, pg 439

Wolff, Denise, Aperture Books, 547 W 27 St, 4th fl, New York, NY 10001 *Tel:* 212-505-5555 *Toll Free Fax:* 888-623-6908 *E-mail:* customerservice@aperture.org *Web Site:* aperture.org, pg 17

Wolff, Doug, Workman Publishing Co Inc, 225 Varick St, 9th fl, New York, NY 10014-4381 *Tel:* 212-254-5900 *Toll Free Tel:* 800-722-7202 *Fax:* 212-254-8098 *E-mail:* info@workman.com; orders@workman.com *Web Site:* www.workman.com, pg 244

Wolff, Harvey, Haynes North America Inc, 859 Lawrence Dr, Newbury Park, CA 91320-1514 *Tel:* 805-498-6703 *Toll Free Tel:* 800-4-HAYNES (442-9637) *Fax:* 805-498-2867 *E-mail:* cstn@haynes.com *Web Site:* www.haynes.com, pg 96

Wolff, Rebecca, Fence Books, University at Albany, Science Library 320, 1400 Washington Ave, Albany, NY 12222 *Tel:* 518-567-7006 *Web Site:* www.fenceportal.org, pg 77

Wolff, Rebecca, Fence Modern Poets Series, University at Albany, Science Library 320, 1400 Washington Ave, Albany, NY 12222 *Tel:* 518-567-7006 *Web Site:* www.fenceportal.org, pg 615

Wolff, Rebecca, Ottoline Prize, University at Albany, Science Library 320, 1400 Washington Ave, Albany, NY 12222 *Tel:* 518-567-7006 *Web Site:* www.fenceportal.org, pg 651

Wolff, Rick, Houghton Mifflin Harcourt Trade & Reference Division, 125 High St, Boston, MA 02110 *Tel:* 617-351-5000 *Web Site:* www.hmhco.com, pg 104

Wolford, Henry, Easy Money Press, 82-5800 Napo'opo'o Rd, Captain Cook, HI 96704 *Tel:* 808-313-2808 *E-mail:* easymoneypress@yahoo.com, pg 69

Wolfson, David, HarperCollins Publishers, 195 Broadway, New York, NY 10007 *Tel:* 212-207-7000 *Fax:* 212-207-7145 *Web Site:* www.harpercollins.com, pg 94

Wolfsthal, Bill, Arcade Publishing Inc, 307 W 36 St, 11th fl, New York, NY 10018 *Tel:* 212-643-6816 *Fax:* 212-643-6819 *E-mail:* info@skyhorsepublishing.com (subs & foreign rts) *Web Site:* www.arcadepub.com, pg 19

Wollheim, Elizabeth R, DAW Books Inc, 375 Hudson St, New York, NY 10014 *Tel:* 212-366-2096 *Fax:* 212-366-2090 *E-mail:* daw@penguinrandomhouse.com *Web Site:* www.dawbooks.com; www.penguin.com; www.penguinrandomhouse.com, pg 63

Wolny, Karen, St Martin's Press, LLC, 120 Broadway, New York, NY 10271 *Tel:* 646-307-5151 *Web Site:* us.macmillan.com/smp, pg 190

Wolverton, Man, Fellowships for Creative & Performing Artists & Writers, 185 Salisbury St, Worcester, MA 01609-1634 *Tel:* 508-755-5221 *Fax:* 508-754-9069 *Web Site:* www.americanantiquarian.org, pg 615

Wolverton, Man, Fellowships for Historical Research, 185 Salisbury St, Worcester, MA 01609-1634 *Tel:* 508-755-5221 *Fax:* 508-754-9069 *Web Site:* www.americanantiquarian.org, pg 615

Wolverton, Peter, St Martin's Press, LLC, 120 Broadway, New York, NY 10271 *Tel:* 646-307-5151 *Web Site:* us.macmillan.com/smp, pg 190

Wolverton, Susan, Coe College Playwriting Festival, 1220 First Ave NE, Cedar Rapids, IA 52402 *Tel:* 319-399-8624 *Fax:* 319-399-8557 *Web Site:* www.theatre.coe.edu; www.coe.edu/academics/theatrearts/theatrearts_playwritingfestival, pg 605

Won, Jiyoung, American Society of News Editors (ASNE), 209 Reynolds Journalism Institute, Missouri School of Journalism, Columbia, MO 65211 *Tel:* 573-882-2430 *Fax:* 573-884-3824 *Web Site:* asne.org, pg 524

Wong, Collin, University of Hawaii Press, 2840 Kolowalu St, Honolulu, HI 96822-1888 *Tel:* 808-956-8255 *Toll Free Tel:* 888-UHPRESS (847-7377) *Fax:* 808-988-6052 *Toll Free Fax:* 800-650-7811 *E-mail:* uhpbooks@hawaii.edu *Web Site:* www.uhpress.hawaii.edu, pg 227

Wong, Harry L III, Kumu Kahua/UHM Theatre & Dance Department Playwriting Contest, 46 Merchant St, Honolulu, HI 96813 *Tel:* 808-536-4441 (box off); 808-536-4222 *Fax:* 808-536-4226 *E-mail:* kumukahuatheatre@hawaiiantel.net *Web Site:* www.kumukahua.org, pg 631

Wong, Jaime, Chronicle Books, 680 Second St, San Francisco, CA 94107 *Tel:* 415-537-4200 *Toll Free Tel:* 800-759-0190 (cust serv) *Fax:* 415-537-4460 *Toll Free Fax:* 800-858-7787 (orders); 800-286-9471 (cust serv) *E-mail:* frontdesk@chroniclebooks.com *Web Site:* www.chroniclebooks.com, pg 51

Wong, Jessica, Thomas Nelson, 501 Nelson Place, Nashville, TN 37214 *Tel:* 615-889-9000 *Toll Free Tel:* 800-251-4000 *Fax:* 615-902-1548 *Web Site:* www.thomasnelson.com, pg 217

Wong, Katherine, Encounter Books, 900 Broadway, Suite 601, New York, NY 10003 *Tel:* 212-871-6310 *Toll Free Tel:* 800-343-4499 *Fax:* 212-871-6311 *E-mail:* publicity@encounterbooks.com *Web Site:* www.encounterbooks.com, pg 72

Wong, May, NBM Publishing Inc, 160 Broadway, E Wing, Suite 700, New York, NY 10038 *Tel:* 646-559-4681 *Toll Free Tel:* 800-886-1223 *Fax:* 212-643-1545 *E-mail:* admin@nbmpub.com *Web Site:* www.nbmpub.com, pg 148

Wong, So Lin, Random House Children's Books, 1745 Broadway, 10th fl, New York, NY 10019 *Tel:* 212-782-9000 *Web Site:* www.randomhousekids.com, pg 180

Wong, Valerie, Little, Brown Books for Young Readers, 1290 Avenue of the Americas, New York, NY 10104 *Tel:* 212-364-1100 *Toll Free Tel:* 800-759-0190 (cust serv) *Web Site:* www.hachettebookgroup.com, pg 126

Woo, Wei-Ling, PEN America, 588 Broadway, Suite 303, New York, NY 10012 *Tel:* 212-334-1660 *Fax:* 212-334-2181 *E-mail:* info@pen.org *Web Site:* pen.org, pg 543

Wood, Ann, Penguin Group (Canada), 320 Front St W, Suite 1400, Toronto, ON M5V 3B6, Canada *Tel:* 416-364-4449 *Fax:* 416-598-7764 *E-mail:* customerservicescanada@penguinrandomhouse.com; publicity@ca.penguingroup.com *Web Site:* penguinrandomhouse.ca/imprints/penguin-canada, pg 436

Wood, Eleanor, Spectrum Literary Agency, 320 Central Park W, Suite 1-D, New York, NY 10025 *Tel:* 212-362-4323 *Fax:* 212-362-4562 *Web Site:* www.spectrumliteraryagency.com, pg 503

Wood, Laura, FinePrint Literary Management, 207 W 106 St, Suite 1D, New York, NY 10025 *Tel:* 212-279-6214 *E-mail:* assist@fineprint.com *Web Site:* www.fineprintlit.com, pg 484

Wood, Leighann, Andrew Carnegie Medals for Excellence in Fiction & Nonfiction, 225 N Michigan Ave, Suite 1300, Chicago, IL 60601 *Tel:* 312-944-6780 *Toll Free Tel:* 800-545-2433 *Fax:* 312-440-9374 *E-mail:* ala@ala.org *Web Site:* www.ala.org/awardsgrants/carnegieadult, pg 603

Wood, Michael, Anna Zornio Memorial Children's Theatre Playwriting Award, D22 Paul Creative Arts Center, 30 Academic Way, Durham, NH 03824 *Tel:* 603-862-2919 *Fax:* 603-862-0298 *Web Site:* cola.unh.edu/theatre-dance/resource/zornio, pg 682

Wood, Rick, Rocky Mountain Books Ltd (RMB), 103-1075 Pendergast St, Victoria, BC V8V 0A1, Canada *Tel:* 250-360-0829 *Fax:* 250-386-0829 *Web Site:* www.rmbooks.com, pg 438

Wood, Sara, HarperCollins General Books Group, 195 Broadway, New York, NY 10007 *Tel:* 212-207-7000 *Web Site:* www.harpercollins.com, pg 93

Wooden, Heather, Institute of Environmental Sciences & Technology - IEST, 1827 Walden Office Sq, Suite 400, Schaumburg, IL 60173 *Tel:* 847-981-0100 *Fax:* 847-981-4130 *E-mail:* information@iest.org *Web Site:* www.iest.org, pg 109

Woodford, Charles, Princeton Book Co Publishers, 15 West Front St, Trenton, NJ 08608 *Tel:* 609-426-0602 *Toll Free Tel:* 800-220-7149 *Fax:* 609-426-1344 *E-mail:* pbc@dancehorizons.com *Web Site:* www.dancehorizons.com, pg 174

Woodford, Connie, Princeton Book Co Publishers, 15 West Front St, Trenton, NJ 08608 *Tel:* 609-426-0602 *Toll Free Tel:* 800-220-7149 *Fax:* 609-426-1344 *E-mail:* pbc@dancehorizons.com *Web Site:* www.dancehorizons.com, pg 174

Woodhouse, Sharon, Everything Goes Media LLC, PO Box 1524, Milwaukee, WI 53201 *Tel:* 312-226-8400 *E-mail:* info@everythinggoesmedia.com *Web Site:* www.everythinggoesmedia.com, pg 74

Woodland, Wendy, Texas Library Association (TLA), 3355 Bee Cave Rd, Suite 401, Austin, TX 78746-6763 *Tel:* 512-328-1518 *Fax:* 512-328-8852 *E-mail:* tla@txla.org *Web Site:* www.txla.org, pg 548

Woods, Brian, Cistercian Publications, Saint John's Abbey, PO Box 7500, Collegeville, MN 56321 *Tel:* 320-363-2213 *Toll Free Tel:* 800-436-8431 *Fax:* 320-363-3299 *Toll Free Fax:* 800-445-5899 *E-mail:* sales@litpress.org *Web Site:* www.cistercianpublications.org, pg 52

Woods, Brian, Liturgical Press, PO Box 7500, St John's Abbey, Collegeville, MN 56321-7500 *Tel:* 320-363-2213 *Toll Free Tel:* 800-858-5450 *Fax:* 320-363-3299 *Toll Free Fax:* 800-445-5899 *E-mail:* sales@litpress.org *Web Site:* www.litpress.org, pg 126

Woods, Catherine, Macmillan Learning, 41 Madison Ave, New York, NY 10010 *Tel:* 212-576-9400 *Fax:* 212-689-2383 *Web Site:* www.macmillanlearning.com, pg 130

Woods, Kimberly, Penguin Random House LLC, 1745 Broadway, New York, NY 10019 *Tel:* 212-782-9000 *Toll Free Tel:* 800-726-0600 *Web Site:* www.penguinrandomhouse.com, pg 164

Woods, Ned, Springer, 233 Spring St, New York, NY 10013-1578 *Tel:* 212-460-1500 *Toll Free Tel:* 800-SPRINGER (777-4643) *Fax:* 212-460-1700 *E-mail:* customerservice@springer.com *Web Site:* www.springer.com, pg 205

Woods, Ryan, Newbury Street Press, 99-101 Newbury St, Boston, MA 02116 *Tel:* 617-226-1206 *Toll Free Tel:* 888-296-3447 (NEHGS membership) *Fax:* 617-536-7307 *E-mail:* sales@nehgs.org *Web Site:* www.americanancestors.org, pg 150

Woodward, Charlene, Dogwise Publishing, 403 S Mission St, Wenatchee, WA 98801 *Tel:* 509-663-9115 *Toll Free Tel:* 800-776-2665 *E-mail:* mail@dogwise.com *Web Site:* www.dogwise.com, pg 66

Woodward, Larry, Dogwise Publishing, 403 S Mission St, Wenatchee, WA 98801 *Tel:* 509-663-9115 *Toll Free Tel:* 800-776-2665 *E-mail:* mail@dogwise.com *Web Site:* www.dogwise.com, pg 66

Woodward, Steve, Graywolf Press, 250 Third Ave N, Suite 600, Minneapolis, MN 55401 *Tel:* 651-641-0077 *Fax:* 651-641-0036 *E-mail:* wolves@graywolfpress.org (no ms queries, sample chapters or proposals) *Web Site:* www.graywolfpress.org, pg 88

Woodward, Tessa, HarperCollins General Books Group, 195 Broadway, New York, NY 10007 *Tel:* 212-207-7000 *Web Site:* www.harpercollins.com, pg 93

Woodworth, Bob, Flanker Press Ltd, 1243 Kenmount Rd, Unit 1, Paradise, NL A1L 0V8, Canada *Tel:* 709-739-4477 *Toll Free Tel:* 866-739-4420 *Fax:* 709-739-4420 *E-mail:* info@flankerpress.com; sales@flankerpress.com *Web Site:* www.flankerpress.com, pg 427

Woodworth, Neil, Adirondack Mountain Club (ADK), 814 Goggins Rd, Lake George, NY 12845-4117 *Tel:* 518-668-4447 *Toll Free Tel:* 800-395-8080 *Fax:* 518-668-3746 *E-mail:* info@adk.org *Web Site:* www.adk.org, pg 5

Woolbright, Molly, Sasquatch Books, 1904 S Third Ave, Suite 710, Seattle, WA 98101 *Tel:* 206-467-4300 *Toll Free Tel:* 800-775-0817 *Fax:* 206-467-4301 *E-mail:* custserv@sasquatchbooks.com *Web Site:* sasquatchbooks.com, pg 192

Wooldridge, Andrew, Orca Book Publishers, 1016 Balmoral Rd, Victoria, BC V8T 1A8, Canada *Toll Free Tel:* 800-210-5277 *Toll Free Fax:* 877-408-1551 *E-mail:* orca@orcabook.com *Web Site:* www.orcabook.com, pg 435

Wooldridge, Suzi, Bridge-Logos, 1426W Newberry Rd, No 409, Newberry, FL 32669-2765 *Toll Free Tel:* 800-320-4108 *Web Site:* www.bridgelogos.com, pg 41

Worick, Jennifer, Sasquatch Books, 1904 S Third Ave, Suite 710, Seattle, WA 98101 *Tel:* 206-467-4300 *Toll Free Tel:* 800-775-0817 *Fax:* 206-467-4301 *E-mail:* custserv@sasquatchbooks.com *Web Site:* sasquatchbooks.com, pg 192

Workman, Carolan, Workman Publishing Co Inc, 225 Varick St, 9th fl, New York, NY 10014-4381 *Tel:* 212-254-5900 *Toll Free Tel:* 800-722-7202 *Fax:* 212-254-8098 *E-mail:* info@workman.com; orders@workman.com *Web Site:* www.workman.com, pg 244

Workman, James A, PRINTING United Alliance, 10015 Main St, Fairfax, VA 22031-3489 *Tel:* 703-385-1335 *Toll Free Tel:* 888-385-3588 *Fax:* 703-273-0456; 703-691-7492 (membership) *E-mail:* assist@printing.org; info@printing.org *Web Site:* www.printing.org; www.sgia.org, pg 544

Workman, Mejhann, Chicago Women in Publishing, PO Box 268107, Chicago, IL 60626 *Tel:* 773-508-0351 *Fax:* 303-942-7164 *E-mail:* info@cwip.org *Web Site:* www.cwip.org, pg 530

Worms, William, SSPC: The Society for Protective Coatings, 800 Trumbull Dr, Pittsburgh, PA 15205-4365 *Tel:* 412-281-2331 *Toll Free Tel:* 877-281-7772 (US only) *Fax:* 412-444-3591 *E-mail:* info@sspc.org *Web Site:* www.sspc.org, pg 206

Worrall, Francesca, Institute for Research on Public Policy (IRPP), 1470 Peel St, No 200, Montreal, QC H3A 1T1, Canada *Tel:* 514-985-2461 *Fax:* 514-985-2559 *E-mail:* irpp@irpp.org *Web Site:* irpp.org, pg 430

Worrell, Greg, Scholastic Education, 557 Broadway, New York, NY 10012 *Tel:* 212-343-6100 *Fax:* 212-343-6189 *Web Site:* www.scholastic.com, pg 194

Worrell, Greg, Scholastic Inc, 557 Broadway, New York, NY 10012 *Tel:* 212-343-6100 *Toll Free Tel:* 800-SCHOLASTIC (724-6527) *Web Site:* www.scholastic.com, pg 194

Worrell, Ilana, Farrar, Straus & Giroux Books for Young Readers, 120 Broadway, New York, NY 10271 *Tel:* 212-741-6900 *Toll Free Tel:* 888-330-8477 (orders) *Fax:* 212-633-9385 *Web Site:* us.macmillan.com/mackids; www.mackidsbooks.com, pg 76

Worrell, Ilana, Roaring Brook Press, 120 Broadway, New York, NY 10271 *Tel:* 646-307-5151 *Web Site:* us.macmillan.com/publishers/roaring-brook-press, pg 186

Worthington, Gareth, Vesuvian Books, 2817 West End Ave, No 126-283, Nashville, TN 37203 *E-mail:* info@vesuvianmedia.com *Web Site:* www.vesuvianbooks.com, pg 236

Wortman, Jean, George Washington Book Prize, 101 S Water St, Chestertown, MD 21620 *Tel:* 410-810-7165 *Fax:* 410-810-7175 *Web Site:* starrcenter.washcoll.edu/centers/starr/george-washington-book-prize.php, pg 676

Wowk, Mary, Harry N Abrams Inc, 195 Broadway, 9th fl, New York, NY 10007 *Tel:* 212-206-7715 *Toll Free Tel:* 800-345-1359 *Fax:* 212-519-1210 *E-mail:* abrams@abramsbooks.com *Web Site:* www.abramsbooks.com, pg 3

Wowk, Mary, Stewart, Tabori & Chang, 195 Broadway, 9th fl, New York, NY 10007 *Tel:* 212-206-7715 *Fax:* 212-519-1210 *E-mail:* abrams@abramsbooks.com *Web Site:* www.abramsbooks.com/imprints/stc, pg 208

Wren, Jill Robinson, Adams & Ambrose Publishing, PO Box 259684, Madison, WI 53725-9684 *Tel:* 608-977-1825 *E-mail:* info@adamsambrose.com, pg 4

Wright, Andrew, Harlequin Enterprises Ltd, Bay Adelaide Centre, East Tower, 22 Adelaide St W, 41st fl, Toronto, ON M5H 4E3, Canada *Tel:* 416-445-5860 *Toll Free Tel:* 888-432-4879; 800-370-5838 (ebook inquiries) *E-mail:* customerservice@harlequin.com *Web Site:* www.harlequin.com, pg 429

Wright, Ellen, Orbit, 1290 Avenue of the Americas, New York, NY 10104 *Tel:* 212-364-1100 *Toll Free Tel:* 800-759-0190 *Web Site:* www.orbitbooks.net, pg 156

Wright, J'Nel, Sourced Media Books, 15 Via Picato, San Clemente, CA 92673 *Tel:* 949-813-0182 *E-mail:* editor@sourcedmediabooks.com *Web Site:* sourcedmediabooks.com, pg 204

Wright, Jan C, Wright Information Indexing Services, PO Box 658, Sandia Park, NM 87047 *Tel:* 505-281-2600 *Web Site:* www.wrightinformation.com, pg 472

Wright, Jim, Salem Press, 2 University Plaza, Suite 310, Hackensack, NJ 07601 *Tel:* 201-968-0500 *Toll Free Tel:* 800-221-1592 *Fax:* 201-968-0511 *E-mail:* csr@salempress.com *Web Site:* salempress.com, pg 191

Wright, Ken, Philomel, 345 Hudson St, New York, NY 10014 *Tel:* 212-366-2000 *Web Site:* www.penguin.com/publishers/philomel, pg 169

Wright, Ken, Viking Children's Books, 345 Hudson St, New York, NY 10014 *Fax:* 212-414-3393 *E-mail:* youngreaderspublicity@us.penguingroup.com *Web Site:* www.penguin.com/publishers/vikingchildrensbooks, pg 236

Wright, Michael, W W Norton & Company Inc, 500 Fifth Ave, New York, NY 10110-0017 *Tel:* 212-354-5500 *Toll Free Tel:* 800-233-4830 (orders & cust serv) *Fax:* 212-869-0856 *Toll Free Fax:* 800-458-6515 *E-mail:* orders@wwnorton.com *Web Site:* wwnorton.com, pg 152

Wright, Robert, ABAC/ALAC, 11 Marie St, Ottawa, ON K1N 9M5, Canada *Tel:* 416-364-2376 *E-mail:* info@abac.org *Web Site:* www.abac.org, pg 521

Wright, William, The James Boatwright III Prize for Poetry, Washington & Lee University, Mattingly House, 204 W Washington St, Lexington, VA 24450-2116 *Tel:* 540-458-8908 *E-mail:* shenandoah@wlu.edu *Web Site:* shenandoahliterary.org, pg 599

Wright, William, The Carter Prize For The Essay, Washington & Lee University, Mattingly House, 204 W Washington St, Lexington, VA 24450-2116 *Tel:* 540-458-8908 *E-mail:* shenandoah@wlu.edu *Web Site:* shenandoahliterary.org, pg 603

Wrinn, Julie Kuzneski, Kentucky Women Writers Conference, 232 E Maxwell St, Lexington, KY 40506-0344 *Tel:* 859-257-2874 *E-mail:* kentuckywomenwriters@gmail.com *Web Site:* www.kentuckywomenwriters.org, pg 576

Wrinn, Stephen M, University of Notre Dame Press, 310 Flanner Hall, Notre Dame, IN 46556 *Tel:* 574-631-6346 *Fax:* 574-631-8148 *E-mail:* undpress@nd.edu *Web Site:* www.undpress.nd.edu, pg 230

Wrzesinski, Julie, Michigan State University Press (MSU Press), Manly Miles Bldg, Suite 25, 1405 S Harrison Rd, East Lansing, MI 48823-5245 *Tel:* 517-355-9543 *Fax:* 517-432-2611 *Web Site:* msupress.org, pg 139

Wu, Chih-Yu T, East Asian Legal Studies Program (EALSP), 500 W Baltimore St, Rm 254, Baltimore, MD 21201-1786 *Tel:* 410-706-3870 *Fax:* 410-706-0407 *E-mail:* eastasia@law.umaryland.edu *Web Site:* www.law.umaryland.edu/programs/international/eastasia, pg 68

Wucher, Lisa, Annual Reviews, 4139 El Camino Way, Palo Alto, CA 94306 *Tel:* 650-493-4400 *Toll Free Tel:* 800-523-8635 *Fax:* 650-424-0910; 650-855-9815 *E-mail:* service@annualreviews.org *Web Site:* www.annualreviews.org, pg 17

Wudurski, Tim, Chronicle Books, 680 Second St, San Francisco, CA 94107 *Tel:* 415-537-4200 *Toll Free Tel:* 800-759-0190 (cust serv) *Fax:* 415-537-4460 *Toll Free Fax:* 800-858-7787 (orders); 800-286-9471 (cust serv) *E-mail:* frontdesk@chroniclebooks.com *Web Site:* www.chroniclebooks.com, pg 52

Wuertz von Holt, Mary, Liguori Publications, One Liguori Dr, Liguori, MO 63057-1000 *Tel:* 636-464-2500 *Toll Free Tel:* 800-325-9521 *Toll Free Fax:* 800-325-9526 (sales) *E-mail:* liguori@liguori.org (sales & cust serv) *Web Site:* www.liguori.org, pg 124

Wuest, Dawn, AACC International, 3340 Pilot Knob Rd, St Paul, MN 55121 *Tel:* 651-454-7250 *Fax:* 651-454-0766 *E-mail:* aacc@scisoc.org *Web Site:* www.aaccnet.org, pg 1

Wuest, Dawn, APS PRESS, 3340 Pilot Knob Rd, St Paul, MN 55121 *Tel:* 651-454-7250 *Toll Free Tel:* 800-328-7560 *Fax:* 651-454-0766 *E-mail:* aps@scisoc.org *Web Site:* www.shopapspress.org, pg 18

Wulf, Karen, PEN/New England Awards, MIT, 14N-221A, 77 Massachusetts Ave, Cambridge, MA 02139 *Tel:* 617-324-1729 *E-mail:* pen-newengland@mit.edu; pen-ne@lesley.edu *Web Site:* www.pen-ne.org, pg 654

Wulf, Karin A, Omohundro Institute of Early American History & Culture, Swem Library, Ground fl, 400 Landrum Dr, Williamsburg, VA 23185 *Tel:* 757-221-1110 *Fax:* 757-221-1047 *E-mail:* ieahc1@wm.edu *Web Site:* oieahc.wm.edu, pg 155

Wunderlich, Emily, Viking, 375 Hudson St, New York, NY 10014 *Tel:* 212-366-2000 *Fax:* 212-243-6002 *Web Site:* www.penguin.com/publishers/vikingbooks, pg 236

Wurfbain, Ludo J, Safari Press, 15621 Chemical Lane, Bldg B, Huntington Beach, CA 92649 *Tel:* 714-894-9080 *Toll Free Tel:* 800-451-4788 *Fax:* 714-894-4949 *E-mail:* info@safaripress.com *Web Site:* www.safaripress.com, pg 189

Wybraniec, Barbara, Oscar Williams/Gene Derwood Award, 909 Third Ave, New York, NY 10022 *Tel:* 212-686-0010 *Fax:* 212-532-8528 *E-mail:* info@nycommunitytrust.org *Web Site:* www.nycommunitytrust.org, pg 678

Wyckoff, Joanne, Carol Mann Agency, 55 Fifth Ave, 18th fl, New York, NY 10003 *Tel:* 212-206-5635 *Fax:* 212-675-4809 *E-mail:* submissions@carolmannagency.com *Web Site:* www.carolmannagency.com, pg 494

Wydysh, Martha, Trident Media Group LLC, 41 Madison Ave, 36th fl, New York, NY 10010 *Tel:* 212-333-1511 *E-mail:* info@tridentmediagroup.com; press@tridentmediagroup.com *Web Site:* www.tridentmediagroup.com, pg 507

York, Lynn, Blair, 905 W Main St, Suite 19 D-1, Durham, NC 27701 *Tel:* 919-682-0555 *E-mail:* customersupport@blair.com *Web Site:* www. blairpub.com, pg 35

Yorke, Laura, Carol Mann Agency, 55 Fifth Ave, 18th fl, New York, NY 10003 *Tel:* 212-206-5635 *Fax:* 212-675-4809 *E-mail:* submissions@carolmannagency.com *Web Site:* www.carolmannagency.com, pg 494

Yother, Michele, Gallopade International Inc, 611 Hwy 74 S, Suite 2000, Peachtree City, GA 30269 *Tel:* 770-631-4222 *Toll Free Tel:* 800-536-2GET (536-2438) *Fax:* 770-631-4810 *Toll Free Fax:* 800-871-2979 *E-mail:* customerservice@gallopade.com *Web Site:* www.gallopade.com, pg 83

Younce, Virginia Smith, The Penguin Press, 375 Hudson St, New York, NY 10014 *Web Site:* thepenguinpress. com, pg 164

Younce, Webster, Zondervan, 3900 Sparks Dr, Grand Rapids, MI 49546 *Tel:* 616-698-6900 *Toll Free Tel:* 800-226-1122; 800-727-1309 (retail orders) *Fax:* 616-698-3350 *Toll Free Fax:* 800-698-3256 (retail orders) *Web Site:* www.zondervan.com, pg 248

Young, Courtney, Riverhead Books, 375 Hudson St, New York, NY 10014 *Tel:* 212-366-2000 *Web Site:* www. penguin.com/publishers/riverhead, pg 185

Young, Craig, Little, Brown and Company, 1290 Avenue of the Americas, New York, NY 10104 *Tel:* 212-364-1100 *Fax:* 212-364-0952 *E-mail:* firstname.lastname@ hbgusa.com *Web Site:* www.littlebrown.com; www. hachettebookgroup.com, pg 125

Young, Cyle, Hartline Literary Agency LLC, 123 Queenston Dr, Pittsburgh, PA 15235 *Tel:* 412-829-2483 *Toll Free Fax:* 888-279-6007 *Web Site:* www. hartlineliterary.com, pg 488

Young, David, The Field Poetry Prize, 50 N Professor St, Oberlin, OH 44074-1091 *Tel:* 440-775-8408 *Fax:* 440-775-8124 *E-mail:* oc.press@oberlin.edu *Web Site:* www.oberlin.edu/ocpress; www.oberlin. edu/ocpress/prize.htm (guidelines), pg 615

Young, David, Oberlin College Press, 50 N Professor St, Oberlin, OH 44074-1091 *Tel:* 440-775-8408 *Fax:* 440-775-8124 *E-mail:* oc.press@oberlin.edu *Web Site:* www.oberlin.edu/ocpress, pg 154

Young, Dean, University of Texas at Austin, New Writers Project, Dept of English, Calhoun Hall, Rm 226, 204 W 21 St, B-5000, Austin, TX 78712 *Tel:* 512-471-5132; 512-471-4991 *Fax:* 512-471-4909 *Web Site:* newwritersproject.org, pg 586

Young, Debi, Sunbelt Publications Inc, 1250 Fayette St, El Cajon, CA 92020-1511 *Tel:* 619-258-4911 *Toll Free Tel:* 800-626-6579 (cust serv) *Fax:* 619-258-4916 *E-mail:* service@sunbeltpub.com; info@sunbeltpub. com *Web Site:* sunbeltpublications.com, pg 210

Young, Erin, Dystel, Goderich & Bourret LLC, One Union Sq W, Suite 904, New York, NY 10003 *Tel:* 212-627-9100 *Fax:* 212-627-9313 *Web Site:* www. dystel.com, pg 482

Young, Gretchen, Grand Central Publishing, 1290 Avenue of the Americas, New York, NY 10104 *Tel:* 212-364-1100 *Web Site:* www.hachettebookgroup. com, pg 88

Young, Dr Jeffrey, Dissertation.com, 200 Spectrum Center Dr, 3rd fl, Irvine, CA 92618 *Tel:* 561-750-4344 *Toll Free Tel:* 800-636-8329 *Fax:* 561-750-6797 *Web Site:* www.dissertation.com, pg 65

Young, Jeffrey R, Universal-Publishers Inc, 200 Spectrum Center Dr, 3rd fl, Irvine, CA 92618-5004 *Tel:* 561-750-4344 *Toll Free Tel:* 800-636-8329 (US only) *Fax:* 561-750-6797 *Web Site:* www.universal-publishers.com, pg 225

Young, Marian, The Young Agency, 213 Bennett Ave, No 3H, New York, NY 10040 *Tel:* 212-229-2612, pg 509

Young, Mary, Kent State University Press, 1118 University Library Bldg, 1125 Risman Dr, Kent, OH 44242 *Tel:* 330-672-7913 *Fax:* 330-672-3104 *E-mail:* ksupress@kent.edu *Web Site:* www. kentstateuniversitypress.com, pg 117

Young, Matthew, Oak Knoll Press, 310 Delaware St, New Castle, DE 19720 *Tel:* 302-328-7232 *Toll Free Tel:* 800-996-2556 *Fax:* 302-328-7274 *E-mail:* oakknoll@oakknoll.com; publishing@ oakknoll.com *Web Site:* www.oakknoll.com, pg 153

Young, Sabrina, Perseus Books, 1290 Avenue of the Americas, New York, NY 10104 *Tel:* 212-340-8100 *Toll Free Tel:* 800-343-4499 (cust serv) *Fax:* 212-340-8105 *Web Site:* www.perseusbooks.com, pg 167

Young, Stephen, Pegasus Award for Poetry Criticism, 61 W Superior St, Chicago, IL 60654 *Tel:* 312-787-7070 *E-mail:* info@poetryfoundation.org *Web Site:* www. poetryfoundation.org/foundation/criticism-award, pg 653

Young, Tyler, Pieces of Learning Inc, 1112 N Carbon St, Suite A, Marion, IL 62959-8976 *Tel:* 618-964-9426 *Toll Free Tel:* 800-729-5137 *Toll Free Fax:* 800-844-0455 *E-mail:* info@piecesoflearning.com *Web Site:* piecesoflearning.com, pg 169

Younger, Carol, Smyth & Helwys Publishing Inc, 6316 Peake Rd, Macon, GA 31210-3960 *Tel:* 478-757-0564 *Toll Free Tel:* 800-747-3016 (orders only) *Fax:* 478-757-1305 *E-mail:* information@helwys.com *Web Site:* www.helwys.com, pg 202

Younging, Greg, Theytus Books Ltd, 154 Enowkin Trail, RR 2, Site 50, Comp 8, Penticton, BC V2A 6J7, Canada *Tel:* 250-493-7181 *Fax:* 250-493-5302 *E-mail:* order@theytus.com; marketing@theytus.com *Web Site:* www.theytus.com, pg 441

Yu, Jessica, The New Press, 120 Wall St, 31st fl, New York, NY 10005 *Tel:* 212-629-8802 *Toll Free Tel:* 800-343-4489 (orders) *Fax:* 212-629-8617 *Toll Free Fax:* 800-351-5073 (orders) *E-mail:* newpress@ thenewpress.com *Web Site:* www.thenewpress.com, pg 149

Yu, Jin, Berkley Publishing Group, 1745 Broadway, 19th fl, New York, NY 10019 *Tel:* 212-366-2000 *Web Site:* www.penguin.com, pg 32

Yudelson, Larry, Ben Yehuda Press, 122 Ayers Ct, No 1B, Teaneck, NJ 07666 *E-mail:* orders@ benyehudapress.com; yudel@benyehudapress.com *Web Site:* www.benyehudapress.com, pg 31

Yuhas, Thomas, Random House Publishing Group, 1745 Broadway, New York, NY 10019 *Toll Free Tel:* 800-200-3552 *Web Site:* www.randomhousebooks.com, pg 181

Yukich, Michael, American Catholic Press (ACP), 16565 S State St, South Holland, IL 60473 *Tel:* 708-331-5485 *Fax:* 708-331-5484 *E-mail:* acp@acpress.org *Web Site:* www.acpress.org, pg 10

Yule, Sean, Alfred A Knopf, c/o Penguin Random House Inc, 1745 Broadway, New York, NY 10019 *Tel:* 212-751-2600 *Fax:* 212-572-2662 (foreign rts) *Web Site:* knopfdoubleday.com, pg 118

Yung, Cecilia, GP Putnam's Sons (Children's), 345 Hudson St, New York, NY 10014 *Tel:* 212-366-2000 *Fax:* 212-414-3393 *Web Site:* www.penguin. com/publishers/gpputnamssonsbooksforyoungread, pg 178

Yunker, John, Ashland Creek Press, 2305 Ashland St, Suite C417, Ashland, OR 97520 *Tel:* 760-300-3620 *E-mail:* editors@ashlandcreekpress.com *Web Site:* www.ashlandcreekpress.com, pg 22

Yup, Carline, The New Press, 120 Wall St, 31st fl, New York, NY 10005 *Tel:* 212-629-8802 *Toll Free Tel:* 800-343-4489 (orders) *Fax:* 212-629-8617 *Toll Free Fax:* 800-351-5073 (orders) *E-mail:* newpress@ thenewpress.com *Web Site:* www.thenewpress.com, pg 149

Zabka, Rosanne, Hospital & Healthcare Compensation Service, 3 Post Rd, Suite 3, Oakland, NJ 07436 *Tel:* 201-405-0075 *Fax:* 201-405-2110 *E-mail:* allinfo@hhcsinc.com *Web Site:* www.hhcsinc. com, pg 103

Zaborsky, Katie, Dutton, 1745 Broadway, New York, NY 10019 *Tel:* 212-366-2000 *Fax:* 212-366-2262 *E-mail:* duttonpublicity@us.penguingroup.com *Web Site:* www.penguin.com, pg 68

Zaccaria, Jim, Shambhala Publications Inc, 4720 Walnut St, Boulder, CO 80301 *Tel:* 303-222-9598 *Toll Free Tel:* 866-424-0030 (off); 888-424-2329 (cust serv) *E-mail:* customercare@shambhala.com *Web Site:* www.shambhala.com, pg 197

Zacharius, Adam, Kensington Publishing Corp, 119 W 40 St, New York, NY 10018 *Tel:* 212-407-1500 *Toll Free Tel:* 800-221-2647 *Fax:* 212-935-0699 *Web Site:* www.kensingtonbooks.com, pg 116

Zacharius, Steven, Kensington Publishing Corp, 119 W 40 St, New York, NY 10018 *Tel:* 212-407-1500 *Toll Free Tel:* 800-221-2647 *Fax:* 212-935-0699 *Web Site:* www.kensingtonbooks.com, pg 116

Zachary, Lane, Aevitas Creative Management, 19 W 21 St, Suite 501, New York, NY 10010 *Tel:* 212-765-6900 *Web Site:* aevitascreative.com, pg 474

Zack, Elizabeth, BookCrafters LLC, Box C, Convent Station, NJ 07961 *Web Site:* bookcraftersllc.com, pg 459

Zackheim, Adrian, Penguin Group USA, A Penguin Random House Company, 375 Hudson St, New York, NY 10014 *Tel:* 212-366-2000 *Toll Free Tel:* 800-847-5515 (inside sales); 800-631-8571 (cust serv) *Fax:* 212-366-2666; 607-775-4829 (inside sales) *E-mail:* online@us.penguingroup.com *Web Site:* www. penguin.com, pg 163

Zackheim, Adrian, Portfolio, 375 Hudson St, New York, NY 10014 *Web Site:* www.penguin.com/meet/ publishers/portfolio, pg 172

Zadrozny, Mark, Cambridge University Press, One Liberty Plaza, 20th fl, New York, NY 10006 *Tel:* 212-924-3900; 212-337-5000 *Fax:* 212-691-3239; 845-353-4141 *E-mail:* newyork@cambridge.org; customer_service@cambridge.org *Web Site:* www. cambridge.org/us, pg 43

Zafian, Anne, Simon & Schuster Children's Publishing, 1230 Avenue of the Americas, New York, NY 10020 *Tel:* 212-698-7000 *Web Site:* www.simonandschuster. com/kids; www.simonandschuster.com/teen; simonandschuster.net; simonandschuster.biz, pg 199

Zagat, Nina S, Zagat Inc, 424 Broadway, 5th fl, New York, NY 10013 *Toll Free Tel:* 800-540-9609 *E-mail:* feedback@zagat.com; press@zagat.com *Web Site:* www.zagat.com, pg 247

Zagat, Tim, Zagat Inc, 424 Broadway, 5th fl, New York, NY 10013 *Toll Free Tel:* 800-540-9609 *E-mail:* feedback@zagat.com; press@zagat.com *Web Site:* www.zagat.com, pg 247

Zaidi, Jamil, Chronicle Books, 680 Second St, San Francisco, CA 94107 *Tel:* 415-537-4200 *Toll Free Tel:* 800-759-0190 (cust serv) *Fax:* 415-537-4460 *Toll Free Fax:* 800-858-7787 (orders); 800-286-9471 (cust serv) *E-mail:* frontdesk@chroniclebooks.com *Web Site:* www.chroniclebooks.com, pg 52

Zajdel, George, ASTM International, 100 Barr Harbor Dr, West Conshohocken, PA 19428-2959 *Tel:* 610-832-9500; 610-832-9585 (intl) *Toll Free Tel:* 877-909-2786 (sales & cust support) *Fax:* 610-832-9555 *E-mail:* service@astm.org *Web Site:* www.astm.org, pg 23

Zajechowski, Sheryl, Brilliance Audio, 1704 Eaton Dr, Grand Haven, MI 49417 *Tel:* 616-846-5256 *Toll Free Tel:* 800-648-2312 (orders only) *Fax:* 616-846-0630 *E-mail:* customerservice@brillianceaudio.com *Web Site:* www.brillianceaudio.com, pg 41

Zalewski, Ellen, University of Chicago Press, 1427 E 60 St, Chicago, IL 60637-2954 *Tel:* 773-702-7700; 773-702-7600 *Toll Free Tel:* 800-621-2736 (orders) *Fax:* 773-702-9756; 773-660-2235 (orders); 773-702-2708 *E-mail:* custserv@press.uchicago.edu; marketing@press.uchicago.edu *Web Site:* www.press. uchicago.edu, pg 226

Zamajtuk, Jason, Random House Children's Books, 1745 Broadway, 10th fl, New York, NY 10019 *Tel:* 212-782-9000 *Web Site:* www.randomhousekids.com, pg 180

Zoni, Matthew, American Booksellers Association, 333 Westchester Ave, Suite S202, White Plains, NY 10604 *Tel:* 914-406-7500 *Toll Free Tel:* 800-637-0037 *Fax:* 914-417-4013 *E-mail:* info@bookweb.org *Web Site:* www.bookweb.org, pg 522

Zonnefeld, Courtney, Wm B Eerdmans Publishing Co, 4035 Park East Ct SE, Grand Rapids, MI 49546 *Tel:* 616-459-4591 *Toll Free Tel:* 800-253-7521 *Fax:* 616-459-6540 *E-mail:* customerservice@eerdmans.com; sales@eerdmans.com *Web Site:* www.eerdmans.com, pg 70

Zorian, Lora, Shambhala Publications Inc, 4720 Walnut St, Boulder, CO 80301 *Tel:* 303-222-9598 *Toll Free Tel:* 866-424-0030 (off); 888-424-2329 (cust serv) *E-mail:* customercare@shambhala.com *Web Site:* www.shambhala.com, pg 197

Zoro, Theresa, Random House Publishing Group, 1745 Broadway, New York, NY 10019 *Toll Free Tel:* 800-200-3552 *Web Site:* www.randomhousebooks.com, pg 181

Zschock, Heather, Peter Pauper Press, Inc, 202 Mamaroneck Ave, Suite 400, White Plains, NY 10601-5376 *Tel:* 914-681-0144 *Fax:* 914-681-0389 *E-mail:* customerservice@peterpauper.com; orders@peterpauper.com; marketing@peterpauper.com *Web Site:* www.peterpauper.com, pg 168

Zubal, John T, USBE: United States Book Exchange, 2969 W 25 St, Cleveland, OH 44113 *Tel:* 216-241-6960 *Fax:* 216-241-6966 *E-mail:* usbe@usbe.com *Web Site:* www.usbe.com, pg 548

Zubal, Marilyn, USBE: United States Book Exchange, 2969 W 25 St, Cleveland, OH 44113 *Tel:* 216-241-6960 *Fax:* 216-241-6966 *E-mail:* usbe@usbe.com *Web Site:* www.usbe.com, pg 548

Zucca, Damon, Oxford University Press USA, 198 Madison Ave, New York, NY 10016 *Toll Free Tel:* 800-451-7556 (orders); 800-445-9714 (cust serv) *Fax:* 919-677-1303 *E-mail:* custserv.us@oup.com *Web Site:* global.oup.com, pg 158

Zuccarello, Dasya Anthony, Hohm Press, PO Box 4410, Chino Valley, AZ 86323 *Tel:* 928-636-3331 *Toll Free Tel:* 800-381-2700 *Fax:* 928-636-7519 *E-mail:* publisher@hohmpress.com *Web Site:* www.hohmpress.com, pg 101

Zuccarello, Joe Bala, Hohm Press, PO Box 4410, Chino Valley, AZ 86323 *Tel:* 928-636-3331 *Toll Free Tel:* 800-381-2700 *Fax:* 928-636-7519 *E-mail:* publisher@hohmpress.com *Web Site:* hohmpress.com, pg 101

Zuccaro, Jennifer, Princeton University Press, 41 William St, Princeton, NJ 08540-5237 *Tel:* 609-258-4900 *Fax:* 609-258-6305 *Web Site:* press.princeton.edu, pg 175

Zuch, Franklin Jon, George T Bisel Co Inc, 710 S Washington Sq, Philadelphia, PA 19106-3519 *Tel:* 215-922-5760 *Toll Free Tel:* 800-247-3526 *Fax:* 215-922-2235 *E-mail:* gbisel@bisel.com *Web Site:* www.bisel.com, pg 33

Zucker, Irwin, Book Publicists of Southern California, 714 Crescent Dr, Beverly Hills, CA 90210 *Tel:* 323-461-3921 *Fax:* 323-461-0917 *Web Site:* www.bookpublicists.org, pg 528

Zuckerman, Albert, Writers House, 21 W 26 St, New York, NY 10010 *Tel:* 212-685-2400 *Web Site:* www.writershouse.com, pg 508

Zuckerman, Kathy, Alfred A Knopf, c/o Penguin Random House Inc, 1745 Broadway, New York, NY 10019 *Tel:* 212-751-2600 *Fax:* 212-572-2662 (foreign rts) *Web Site:* knopfdoubleday.com, pg 118

Zuckerman, Phil, Applewood Books Inc, One River Rd, Carlisle, MA 01741 *Tel:* 781-271-0055 *Toll Free Tel:* 800-277-5312 (orders) *Fax:* 781-271-0056 *E-mail:* bookorder@awb.com; customercare@awb.com *Web Site:* www.awb.com, pg 18

Zuckerman, Phil, Commonwealth Editions, One River Rd, Carlisle, MA 01741 *Tel:* 781-271-0055 *Toll Free Tel:* 800-277-5312 *Fax:* 781-271-0056 *E-mail:* customercare@awb.com *Web Site:* www.awb.com, pg 56

Zugschwert, Rachel, Carolrhoda Books Inc, 241 First Ave N, Minneapolis, MN 55401 *Tel:* 612-332-3344 *Toll Free Tel:* 800-328-4929 *Fax:* 612-332-7615 *Toll Free Fax:* 800-332-1132 *E-mail:* info@lernerbooks.com; custserve@lernerbooks.com *Web Site:* www.lernerbooks.com; www.facebook.com/lernerbooks, pg 45

Zugschwert, Rachel, Carolrhoda Lab™, 241 First Ave N, Minneapolis, MN 55401 *Tel:* 612-332-3344 *Toll Free Tel:* 800-328-4929 *Fax:* 612-332-7615 *Toll Free Fax:* 800-332-1132 *E-mail:* info@lernerbooks.com; custserve@lernerbooks.com *Web Site:* www.lernerbooks.com; www.facebook.com/lernerbooks, pg 45

Zugschwert, Rachel, ediciones Lerner, 241 First Ave N, Minneapolis, MN 55401 *Tel:* 612-332-3344 *Toll Free Tel:* 800-328-4929 *Fax:* 612-332-7615 *Toll Free Fax:* 800-332-1132 *E-mail:* info@lernerbooks.com; custserve@lernerbooks.com *Web Site:* www.lernerbooks.com; www.facebook.com/lernerbooks, pg 69

Zugschwert, Rachel, First Avenue Editions, 241 First Ave N, Minneapolis, MN 55401 *Tel:* 612-332-3344 *Toll Free Tel:* 800-328-4929 *Fax:* 612-332-7615 *Toll Free Fax:* 800-332-1132 *E-mail:* info@lernerbooks.com; custserve@lernerbooks.com *Web Site:* www.lernerbooks.com; www.facebook.com/lernerbooks, pg 78

Zugschwert, Rachel, Graphic Universe™, 241 First Ave N, Minneapolis, MN 55401 *Tel:* 612-332-3344 *Toll Free Tel:* 800-328-4929 *Fax:* 612-332-7615 *Toll Free Fax:* 800-332-1132 *E-mail:* info@lernerbooks.com; custserve@lernerbooks.com *Web Site:* www.lernerbooks.com; www.facebook.com/lernerbooks, pg 88

Zugschwert, Rachel, Lerner Publications, 241 First Ave N, Minneapolis, MN 55401 *Tel:* 612-332-3344 *Toll Free Tel:* 800-328-4929 *Fax:* 612-332-7615 *Toll Free Fax:* 800-332-1132 *E-mail:* info@lernerbooks.com; custserve@lernerbooks.com *Web Site:* www.lernerbooks.com; www.facebook.com/lernerbooks, pg 122

Zugschwert, Rachel, Lerner Publishing Group Inc, 241 First Ave N, Minneapolis, MN 55401 *Tel:* 612-332-3344 *Toll Free Tel:* 800-328-4929 *Fax:* 612-332-7615 *Toll Free Fax:* 800-332-1132 *E-mail:* info@lernerbooks.com; custserve@lernerbooks.com *Web Site:* www.lernerbooks.com; www.facebook.com/lernerbooks, pg 123

Zugschwert, Rachel, LernerClassroom, 241 First Ave N, Minneapolis, MN 55401 *Tel:* 612-332-3344 *Toll Free Tel:* 800-328-4929 *Fax:* 612-332-7615 *Toll Free Fax:* 800-332-1132 *E-mail:* info@lernerbooks.com; custserve@lernerbooks.com *Web Site:* www.lernerbooks.com; www.facebook.com/lernerbooks, pg 123

Zugschwert, Rachel, Millbrook Press, 241 First Ave N, Minneapolis, MN 55401 *Tel:* 612-332-3344 *Toll Free Tel:* 800-328-4929 *Fax:* 612-332-7615 *Toll Free Fax:* 800-332-1132 *E-mail:* info@lernerbooks.com; custserve@lernerbooks.com *Web Site:* www.lernerbooks.com; www.facebook.com/millbrookpress, pg 140

Zugschwert, Rachel, Twenty-First Century Books, 241 First Ave N, Minneapolis, MN 55401 *Tel:* 612-332-3344 *Toll Free Tel:* 800-328-4929 *Fax:* 612-332-7615 *Toll Free Fax:* 800-332-1132 *E-mail:* info@lernerbooks.com; custserve@lernerbooks.com *Web Site:* www.lernerbooks.com; www.facebook.com/lernerbooks, pg 222

Zugschwert, Rachel, Zest Books, 241 First Ave N, Minneapolis, MN 55401 *Tel:* 612-332-3344 *Toll Free Tel:* 800-328-4929 *Toll Free Fax:* 800-332-1132 *E-mail:* info@lernerbooks.com; publicity@lernerbooks.com; custserve@lernerbooks.com (orders) *Web Site:* lernerbooks.com, pg 248

Zukergood, Samantha, St Martin's Press, LLC, 120 Broadway, New York, NY 10271 *Tel:* 646-307-5151 *Web Site:* us.macmillan.com/smp, pg 190

Zulli, Jessica, Sourcebooks LLC, 1935 Brookdale Rd, Suite 139, Naperville, IL 60563 *Tel:* 630-961-3900 *Toll Free Tel:* 800-432-7444 *Fax:* 630-961-2168 *E-mail:* info@sourcebooks.com; customersupport@sourcebooks.com *Web Site:* www.sourcebooks.com, pg 204

Zullo, Julia, Jessica Kingsley Publishers Inc, 400 Market St, Suite 400, Philadelphia, PA 19106 *Tel:* 215-922-1161 *Toll Free Tel:* 866-416-1078 (cust serv) *Fax:* 215-922-1474 *E-mail:* hello.usa@jkp.com *Web Site:* www.jkp.com, pg 117

Zurla, Tom, Leadership Connect, 1407 Broadway, Suite 318, New York, NY 10018 *Tel:* 212-627-4140 *Toll Free Tel:* 800-627-0311 *Fax:* 212-645-0931 *E-mail:* info@leadershipconnect.io *Web Site:* www.leadershipconnect.io, pg 121

Zwart, Jeanette, Macmillan, 120 Broadway, 22nd fl, New York, NY 10271 *Tel:* 646-307-5151 *E-mail:* press.inquiries@macmillan.com *Web Site:* www.macmillan.com, pg 130

Zwart, Jeanette, St Martin's Press, LLC, 120 Broadway, New York, NY 10271 *Tel:* 646-307-5151 *Web Site:* us.macmillan.com/smp, pg 190

Zychowicz, James, A-R Editions Inc, 1600 Aspen Commons, Suite 100, Middleton, WI 53562 *Tel:* 608-836-9000 *Toll Free Tel:* 800-736-0070 (North America book orders only) *Fax:* 608-831-8200 *E-mail:* info@areditions.com; orders@areditions.com *Web Site:* www.areditions.com, pg 1

Zyglis, Adam, Association of American Editorial Cartoonists, PO Box 460673, Fort Lauderdale, FL 33346 *Tel:* 954-356-4945 *Web Site:* www.editorialcartoonists.com, pg 526

Publishers Toll Free Directory

Arbordale Publishing, Mount Pleasant, SC *Toll Free Tel:* 877-243-3457, pg 19

Arcadia Publishing Inc, Mount Pleasant, SC *Toll Free Tel:* 888-313-2665 (orders only), pg 19

ARE Press, Virginia Beach, VA *Toll Free Tel:* 800-333-4499, pg 19

Jason Aronson Inc, Lanham, MD *Toll Free Tel:* 800-462-6420 ext 3024 (cust serv) *Toll Free Fax:* 800-338-4550 (cust serv), pg 20

Arsenal Pulp Press, Vancouver, BC Canada *Toll Free Tel:* 888-600-PULP (600-7857), pg 415

Art Image Publications, Derby Line, VT *Toll Free Tel:* 800-361-2598 *Toll Free Fax:* 800-559-2598, pg 20

ArtAge Publications, Portland, OR *Toll Free Tel:* 800-858-4998, pg 20

Arte Publico Press, Houston, TX *Toll Free Tel:* 800-633-2783, pg 20

Artech House®, Norwood, MA *Toll Free Tel:* 800-225-9977, pg 21

Artisan, New York, NY *Toll Free Tel:* 800-722-7202, pg 21

ASCD, Alexandria, VA *Toll Free Tel:* 800-933-2723, pg 21

Ascension Press, West Chester, PA *Toll Free Tel:* 800-376-0520 (sales & cust serv), pg 21

ASCP Press, Chicago, IL *Toll Free Tel:* 800-267-2727, pg 22

ASM International, Materials Park, OH *Toll Free Tel:* 800-336-5152; 800-368-9800 (Europe), pg 22

Aspatore Books, Eagan, MN *Toll Free Tel:* 844-209-1086, pg 23

Association for Computing Machinery, New York, NY *Toll Free Tel:* 800-342-6626, pg 23

Association for Talent Development (ATD) Press, Alexandria, VA *Toll Free Tel:* 800-628-2783, pg 23

Association of College & Research Libraries (ACRL), Chicago, IL *Toll Free Tel:* 800-545-2433 (ext 2523), pg 23

Association of School Business Officials International, Reston, VA *Toll Free Tel:* 866-682-2729, pg 23

Asta Publications LLC, New City, NY *Toll Free Tel:* 800-482-4190, pg 23

ASTM International, West Conshohocken, PA *Toll Free Tel:* 877-909-2786 (sales & cust support), pg 23

Atlantic Law Book Co, West Hartford, CT *Toll Free Tel:* 800-259-5534, pg 24

Atwood Publishing, Madison, WI *Toll Free Tel:* 888-242-7101, pg 24

Augsburg Fortress Publishers, Publishing House of the Evangelical Lutheran Church in America, Minneapolis, MN *Toll Free Tel:* 800-426-0115 (ext 639, subns); 800-328-4648 (orders), pg 25

August House Inc, Atlanta, GA *Toll Free Tel:* 800-284-8784, pg 25

AuthorHouse, Bloomington, IN *Toll Free Tel:* 888-519-5121, pg 25

Autism Asperger Publishing Co, Shawnee, KS *Toll Free Tel:* 877-277-8254, pg 25

Ave Maria Press, Notre Dame, IN *Toll Free Tel:* 800-282-1865 *Toll Free Fax:* 800-282-5681, pg 26

Avery Color Studios, Gwinn, MI *Toll Free Tel:* 800-722-9925, pg 26

Avotaynu Inc, New Haven, CT *Toll Free Tel:* 800-AVOTAYNU (286-8296), pg 26

Baha'i Publishing, Wilmette, IL *Toll Free Tel:* 800-999-9019 (orders), pg 27

Baker Books, Ada, MI *Toll Free Tel:* 800-877-2665 (orders) *Toll Free Fax:* 800-398-3111 (orders), pg 27

B&H Publishing Group, Nashville, TN *Toll Free Tel:* 800-251-3225 (retailers); 800-448-8032 (consumers); 800-458-2772 (churches) *Toll Free Fax:* 800-296-4036 (retailers), pg 27

Banner of Truth, Carlisle, PA *Toll Free Tel:* 800-263-8085 (orders), pg 27

Barefoot Books, Cambridge, MA *Toll Free Tel:* 866-215-1756 (cust serv); 866-417-2369 (orders), pg 28

Barnhardt & Ashe Publishing Inc, Miami, FL *Toll Free Tel:* 800-283-6360 (orders), pg 28

Bartleby Press, Savage, MD *Toll Free Tel:* 800-953-9929, pg 28

Beacon Hill Press of Kansas City, Kansas City, MO *Toll Free Tel:* 800-877-0700 (cust serv) *Toll Free Fax:* 800-849-9827, pg 29

Bear & Bobcat Books, Los Angeles, CA *Toll Free Tel:* 866-918-6173, pg 29

Bear & Co Inc, Rochester, VT *Toll Free Tel:* 800-932-3277, pg 29

Bearport Publishing Co Inc, New York, NY *Toll Free Tel:* 877-337-8577 *Toll Free Fax:* 866-337-8557, pg 30

Behrman House Inc, Springfield, NJ *Toll Free Tel:* 800-221-2755, pg 30

Bella Books, Tallahassee, FL *Toll Free Tel:* 800-729-4992, pg 31

Bellerophon Books, Santa Barbara, CA *Toll Free Tel:* 800-253-9943, pg 31

John Benjamins Publishing Co, Brunswick, ME *Toll Free Tel:* 800-562-5666 (orders), pg 31

Bentley Publishers, Cambridge, MA *Toll Free Tel:* 800-423-4595, pg 32

BePuzzled, San Francisco, CA *Toll Free Tel:* 800-347-4818, pg 32

Bernan, Lanham, MD *Toll Free Tel:* 800-462-6420 (cust serv & orders) *Toll Free Fax:* 800-338-4550, pg 32

Bethany House Publishers, Bloomington, MN *Toll Free Tel:* 800-877-2665 (orders) *Toll Free Fax:* 800-398-3111 (orders), pg 33

Bethlehem Books, Bathgate, ND *Toll Free Tel:* 800-757-6831, pg 33

Between the Lines, Toronto, ON Canada *Toll Free Tel:* 800-718-7201, pg 416

Bhaktivedanta Book Trust (BBT), Los Angeles, CA *Toll Free Tel:* 800-927-4152, pg 33

Big Guy Books, Carlsbad, CA *Toll Free Tel:* 800-536-3030 (booksellers' cust serv), pg 33

George T Bisel Co Inc, Philadelphia, PA *Toll Free Tel:* 800-247-3526, pg 33

Bisk Education, Tampa, FL *Toll Free Tel:* 800-280-9718 (cust serv), pg 33

BJU Press, Greenville, SC *Toll Free Tel:* 800-845-5731, pg 34

Black Classic Press, Baltimore, MD *Toll Free Tel:* 800-476-8870, pg 34

Bloomberg Law Book Division, Arlington, VA *Toll Free Tel:* 800-960-1220, pg 35

Bloom's Literary Criticism, New York, NY *Toll Free Tel:* 800-322-8755 *Toll Free Fax:* 800-678-3633, pg 35

BLR®—Business & Legal Resources, Brentwood, TN *Toll Free Tel:* 800-727-5257, pg 36

Blue Book Publications Inc, Minneapolis, MN *Toll Free Tel:* 800-877-4867, pg 36

Blue Mountain Arts Inc, Boulder, CO *Toll Free Tel:* 800-525-0642 *Toll Free Fax:* 800-545-8573, pg 36

Blue Note Publications Inc, Melbourne, FL *Toll Free Tel:* 800-624-0401 (orders), pg 36

Blue Poppy Press, Boulder, CO *Toll Free Tel:* 800-487-9296, pg 36

Blue Whale Press, Livingston, TX *Toll Free Tel:* 800-848-1631, pg 37

Bluestocking Press, Placerville, CA *Toll Free Tel:* 800-959-8586, pg 37

BNi Building News, Vista, CA *Toll Free Tel:* 888-BNI-BOOK (264-2665), pg 37

BoardSource, Washington, DC *Toll Free Tel:* 877-892-6273, pg 37

The Book Tree, San Diego, CA *Toll Free Tel:* 800-700-8733 (orders), pg 38

BookLogix, Alpharetta, GA *Toll Free Fax:* 888-564-7890, pg 38

Books In Motion, Spokane Valley, WA *Toll Free Tel:* 800-752-3199, pg 38

Books on Tape™, New York, NY *Toll Free Tel:* 800-733-3000 (cust serv) *Toll Free Fax:* 800-940-7046, pg 38

Borealis Press Ltd, Nepean, ON Canada *Toll Free Tel:* 877-696-2585, pg 417

The Boston Mills Press, Richmond Hill, ON Canada *Toll Free Tel:* 800-387-6192 *Toll Free Fax:* 800-450-0391, pg 417

R R Bowker LLC, Ann Arbor, MI *Toll Free Tel:* 888-269-5372 (edit & cust serv, press 2 for returns) *Toll Free Fax:* 877-337-7015 (US & CN), pg 39

Boys Town Press, Boys Town, NE *Toll Free Tel:* 800-282-6657, pg 39

BPC, Summertown, TN *Toll Free Tel:* 888-260-8458, pg 39

Brault & Bouthillier, Montreal, QC Canada *Toll Free Tel:* 800-361-0378 *Toll Free Fax:* 800-361-0378, pg 417

Breakthrough Publications Inc, Emmaus, PA *Toll Free Tel:* 800-824-5001 (ext 12), pg 40

Breakwater Books Ltd, St John's, NL Canada *Toll Free Tel:* 800-563-3333 (orders), pg 417

Brentwood Christian Press, Columbus, GA *Toll Free Tel:* 800-334-8861, pg 40

Brethren Press, Elgin, IL *Toll Free Tel:* 800-323-8039 *Toll Free Fax:* 800-667-8188, pg 40

Brewers Publications, Boulder, CO *Toll Free Tel:* 888-822-6273 (CN & US), pg 40

Brick Tower Press, Shelter Island Heights, NY *Toll Free Tel:* 800-68-BRICK (682-7425), pg 40

Bridge-Logos, Newberry, FL *Toll Free Tel:* 800-320-4108, pg 41

Bridge Publications Inc, Commerce, CA *Toll Free Tel:* 800-722-1733, pg 41

Brill Inc, Boston, MA *Toll Free Tel:* 800-962-4406; 800-337-9255 (orders - USA & CN), pg 41

Brilliance Audio, Grand Haven, MI *Toll Free Tel:* 800-648-2312 (orders only), pg 41

Paul H Brookes Publishing Co Inc, Baltimore, MD *Toll Free Tel:* 800-638-3775 (US & CN), pg 42

Brookline Books, Northampton, MA *Toll Free Tel:* 800-666-2665 (orders), pg 42

Brooklyn Publishers LLC, Cedar Rapids, IA *Toll Free Tel:* 888-473-8521, pg 42

Brush Education Inc, Edmonton, AB Canada *Toll Free Tel:* 855-283-0900 *Toll Free Fax:* 855-283-6947, pg 418

BuilderBooks, Washington, DC *Toll Free Tel:* 800-223-2665, pg 42

Bull Publishing Co, Boulder, CO *Toll Free Tel:* 800-676-2855, pg 42

The Bureau for At-Risk Youth, Bohemia, NY *Toll Free Tel:* 800-99YOUTH (999-6884) *Toll Free Fax:* 800-262-1886, pg 43

Burford Books, Ithaca, NY *Toll Free Fax:* 866-212-7750, pg 43

Business Research Services Inc, Washington, DC *Toll Free Fax:* 877-516-0818, pg 43

Campfield & Campfield Publishing LLC, Philadelphia, PA *Toll Free Tel:* 888-518-2440, pg 44

Canada Law Book®, Toronto, ON Canada *Toll Free Tel:* 800-387-5351 (cust rel, CN & US only); 800-347-5164 (cust rel & orders, CN & US) *Toll Free Fax:* 877-750-9041 (cust rel & orders, CN only), pg 418

Canadian Bible Society, Toronto, ON Canada *Toll Free Tel:* 800-465-2425, pg 418

Canadian Museum of History (Musee canadien de l'histoire), Gatineau, QC Canada *Toll Free Tel:* 800-555-5621 (North American orders only), pg 419

Canadian Scholars' Press Inc, Toronto, ON Canada *Toll Free Tel:* 800-463-1998, pg 419

C&T Publishing Inc, Concord, CA *Toll Free Tel:* 800-284-1114, pg 44

Capitol Enquiry Inc, South Lake Tahoe, CA *Toll Free Tel:* 800-922-7486, pg 44

Capstone Publishers™, North Mankato, MN *Toll Free Tel:* 800-747-4992 (cust serv) *Toll Free Fax:* 888-262-0705, pg 44

Cardiotext Publishing, Minneapolis, MN *Toll Free Tel:* 888-999-9174, pg 44

Cardoza Publishing, Las Vegas, NV *Toll Free Tel:* 800-577-WINS (577-9467), pg 45

Carlisle Press - Walnut Creek, Sugarcreek, OH *Toll Free Tel:* 800-852-4482, pg 45

Carolina Academic Press, Durham, NC *Toll Free Tel:* 800-489-7486, pg 45

Carolrhoda Books Inc, Minneapolis, MN *Toll Free Tel:* 800-328-4929 *Toll Free Fax:* 800-332-1132, pg 45

Carolrhoda Lab™, Minneapolis, MN *Toll Free Tel:* 800-328-4929 *Toll Free Fax:* 800-332-1132, pg 45

Carson Dellosa Publishing LLC, Greensboro, NC *Toll Free Tel:* 800-321-0943 *Toll Free Fax:* 800-535-2669, pg 45

Carswell, Toronto, ON Canada *Toll Free Tel:* 800-387-5164 (CN & US) *Toll Free Fax:* 877-750-9041 (CN only), pg 419

CarTech Inc, Forest Lake, MN *Toll Free Tel:* 800-551-4754, pg 45

Casa Bautista de Publicaciones, El Paso, TX *Toll Free Tel:* 800-755-5958 (cust serv & orders), pg 46

Catholic Book Publishing Corp, Totowa, NJ *Toll Free Tel:* 877-228-2665, pg 46

The Catholic University of America Press, Washington, DC *Toll Free Tel:* 800-537-5487 (orders only), pg 46

Cato Institute, Washington, DC *Toll Free Tel:* 800-767-1241, pg 46

Caxton Press, Caldwell, ID *Toll Free Tel:* 800-657-6465, pg 46

Cedar Fort Inc, Springville, UT *Toll Free Tel:* 800-SKY-BOOK (759-2665), pg 47

CEF Press, Warrenton, MO *Toll Free Tel:* 800-748-7710 (cust serv); 800-300-4033 (USA ministries), pg 47

Cengage Learning, Boston, MA *Toll Free Tel:* 800-354-9706, pg 47

The Center for Learning, Culver City, CA *Toll Free Tel:* 800-421-4246 *Toll Free Fax:* 800-944-5432, pg 48

Center for the Collaborative Classroom, Alameda, CA *Toll Free Tel:* 800-666-7270, pg 48

Centering Corp, Omaha, NE *Toll Free Tel:* 866-218-0101, pg 48

Centre Franco-Ontarien de Ressources en Alphabetisation (Centre FORA), Hanmer, ON Canada *Toll Free Tel:* 888-814-4422 (orders, CN only), pg 419

Chain Store Guide (CSG), Tampa, FL *Toll Free Tel:* 800-927-9292 (orders), pg 48

Chalice Press, St Louis, MO *Toll Free Tel:* 800-366-3383, pg 48

Charisma Media, Lake Mary, FL *Toll Free Tel:* 800-283-8494 (Charisma Media, Siloam Press, Creation House); 800-665-1468, pg 49

Charles Scribner's Sons®, Farmington Hills, MI *Toll Free Tel:* 800-877-4253 *Toll Free Fax:* 800-414-5043, pg 49

Charlesbridge Publishing Inc, Watertown, MA *Toll Free Tel:* 800-225-3214 *Toll Free Fax:* 800-926-5775, pg 49

The Charlton Press Corp, Kitchener, ON Canada *Toll Free Tel:* 866-663-8827, pg 419

Chartered Professional Accountants of Canada (CPA Canada), Toronto, ON Canada *Toll Free Tel:* 800-268-3793, pg 419

Chelsea Green Publishing Co, White River Junction, VT *Toll Free Tel:* 800-639-4099 (cust serv & orders), pg 49

Chelsea House, New York, NY *Toll Free Tel:* 800-322-8755 *Toll Free Fax:* 800-678-3633, pg 50

Cheneliere Education Inc, Montreal, QC Canada *Toll Free Tel:* 800-565-5531 *Toll Free Fax:* 800-814-0324, pg 420

Cheng & Tsui Co Inc, Boston, MA *Toll Free Tel:* 800-554-1963, pg 50

Cherry Hill Publishing LLC, Ramona, CA *Toll Free Tel:* 800-407-1072, pg 50

Chicago Review Press, Chicago, IL *Toll Free Tel:* 800-888-4741, pg 50

Child's Play®, Auburn, ME *Toll Free Tel:* 800-639-6404 *Toll Free Fax:* 800-854-6989, pg 51

The Child's World Inc, North Mankato, MN *Toll Free Tel:* 800-599-READ (599-7323) *Toll Free Fax:* 888-320-2329, pg 51

Chosen Books, Bloomington, MN *Toll Free Tel:* 800-877-2665 (orders only) *Toll Free Fax:* 800-398-3111 (orders only), pg 51

Christian Liberty Press, Arlington Heights, IL *Toll Free Tel:* 800-348-0899, pg 51

Christian Light Publications Inc, Harrisonburg, VA *Toll Free Tel:* 800-776-0478, pg 51

Christian Schools International, Grand Rapids, MI *Toll Free Tel:* 800-635-8288, pg 51

Chronicle Books, San Francisco, CA *Toll Free Tel:* 800-759-0190 (cust serv) *Toll Free Fax:* 800-858-7787 (orders); 800-286-9471 (cust serv), pg 51

Cinco Puntos Press, El Paso, TX *Toll Free Tel:* 800-566-9072, pg 52

Circlet Press, Cambridge, MA *Toll Free Tel:* 800-729-6423, pg 52

Cistercian Publications, Collegeville, MN *Toll Free Tel:* 800-436-8431 *Toll Free Fax:* 800-445-5899, pg 52

Clarion Books, New York, NY *Toll Free Tel:* 800-225-3362 (orders) *Toll Free Fax:* 800-634-7568 (orders), pg 53

Classical Academic Press, Camp Hill, PA *Toll Free Tel:* 866-730-0711 *Toll Free Fax:* 866-730-0721, pg 53

Clear Light Publishers, Santa Fe, NM *Toll Free Tel:* 800-253-2747 (orders), pg 53

Clearfield Co Inc, Baltimore, MD *Toll Free Tel:* 800-296-6687 (orders & cust serv), pg 53

Clinical & Laboratory Standards Institute (CLSI), Wayne, PA *Toll Free Tel:* 877-447-1888 (orders), pg 53

Close Up Publishing, Alexandria, VA *Toll Free Tel:* 800-CLOSE-UP (256-7387), pg 54

Coach House Books, Toronto, ON Canada *Toll Free Tel:* 800-367-6360 (outside Toronto), pg 420

Coaches Choice, Monterey, CA *Toll Free Tel:* 888-229-5745, pg 54

Cold Spring Harbor Laboratory Press, Cold Spring Harbor, NY *Toll Free Tel:* 800-843-4388, pg 54

The College Board, New York, NY *Toll Free Tel:* 866-630-9305, pg 55

The Colonial Williamsburg Foundation, Williamsburg, VA *Toll Free Tel:* 800-HISTORY (447-8679), pg 55

Columbia University Press, New York, NY *Toll Free Tel:* 800-944-8648, pg 55

Commonwealth Editions, Carlisle, MA *Toll Free Tel:* 800-277-5312, pg 55

Company's Coming Publishing Ltd, Vancouver, BC Canada *Toll Free Tel:* 800-661-9017 (CN); 800-518-3541 (US), pg 420

Concordia Publishing House, St Louis, MO *Toll Free Tel:* 800-325-3040 (cust serv) *Toll Free Fax:* 800-490-9889 (cust serv), pg 56

The Connecticut Law Tribune, Hartford, CT *Toll Free Tel:* 877-256-2472, pg 56

The Continuing Legal Education Society of British Columbia (CLEBC), Vancouver, BC Canada *Toll Free Tel:* 800-663-0437 (CN), pg 420

David C Cook, Colorado Springs, CO *Toll Free Tel:* 800-708-5550; 800-323-7543 (orders & cust serv) *Toll Free Fax:* 800-430-0726 (cust serv), pg 56

Copper Canyon Press, Port Townsend, WA *Toll Free Tel:* 877-501-1393 (orders), pg 56

Corwin, Thousand Oaks, CA *Toll Free Tel:* 800-233-9936 *Toll Free Fax:* 800-417-2466, pg 57

Council for Exceptional Children (CEC), Arlington, VA *Toll Free Tel:* 888-232-7733; 866-915-5000 (TTY), pg 57

Council of State Governments, Lexington, KY *Toll Free Tel:* 800-800-1910, pg 58

CQ Press, Washington, DC *Toll Free Tel:* 866-4CQ-PRESS (427-7737), pg 59

Crabtree Publishing Co, New York, NY *Toll Free Tel:* 800-387-7650 *Toll Free Fax:* 800-355-7166, pg 59

Crabtree Publishing Co Ltd, St Catharines, ON Canada *Toll Free Tel:* 800-387-7650 *Toll Free Fax:* 800-355-7166, pg 420

Craftsman Book Co, Carlsbad, CA *Toll Free Tel:* 800-829-8123, pg 59

CRC Press, Boca Raton, FL *Toll Free Tel:* 800-272-7737 (orders) *Toll Free Fax:* 800-374-3401 (orders), pg 59

Creative Editions, Mankato, MN *Toll Free Tel:* 800-445-6209, pg 59

Creative Homeowner, East Petersburg, PA *Toll Free Tel:* 844-307-3677 *Toll Free Fax:* 888-369-2885, pg 59

The Crossroad Publishing Co, Chestnut Ridge, NY *Toll Free Tel:* 800-888-4741 (orders), pg 60

Crossway, Wheaton, IL *Toll Free Tel:* 800-635-7993 (orders); 800-543-1659 (cust serv), pg 60

Crown House Publishing Co LLC, White Plains, NY *Toll Free Tel:* 877-925-1213 (cust serv), pg 60

Crown Publishing Group, New York, NY *Toll Free Tel:* 888-264-1745, pg 60

Crystal Clarity Publishers, Nevada City, CA *Toll Free Tel:* 800-424-1055, pg 61

Cypress House, Fort Bragg, CA *Toll Free Tel:* 800-773-7782, pg 61

John Daniel & Co, McKinleyville, CA *Toll Free Tel:* 800-662-8351, pg 62

The Dartnell Corporation, Durham, NC *Toll Free Tel:* 800-223-8720; 800-472-0148 (cust serv) *Toll Free Fax:* 800-508-2592, pg 62

Data Trace Publishing Co (DTP), Towson, MD *Toll Free Tel:* 800-342-0454, pg 62

Davies Publishing Inc, Pasadena, CA *Toll Free Tel:* 877-792-0005, pg 62

F A Davis Co, Philadelphia, PA *Toll Free Tel:* 800-523-4049, pg 62

The Dawn Horse Press, Middletown, CA *Toll Free Tel:* 877-770-0772, pg 63

Dawn Publications Inc, Nevada City, CA *Toll Free Tel:* 800-545-7475, pg 63

DawnSignPress, San Diego, CA *Toll Free Tel:* 800-549-5350, pg 63

dbS Productions, Charlottesville, VA *Toll Free Tel:* 800-745-1581, pg 63

DC Canada Education Publishing (DCCED), Ottawa, ON Canada *Toll Free Tel:* 888-565-0262, pg 421

Deseret Book Co, Salt Lake City, UT *Toll Free Tel:* 800-453-4532 (orders); 888-846-7302 (orders), pg 64

DEStech Publications Inc, Lancaster, PA *Toll Free Tel:* 877-500-4DES (500-4337), pg 64

Destiny Image Inc, Shippensburg, PA *Toll Free Tel:* 800-722-6774 (orders only), pg 64

DeVorss & Co, Camarillo, CA *Toll Free Tel:* 800-843-5743, pg 64

Dial Books for Young Readers, New York, NY *Toll Free Tel:* 800-733-3000 (orders), pg 64

Discovery House Publishers, Grand Rapids, MI *Toll Free Tel:* 800-653-8333 (cust serv), pg 65

Dissertation.com, Irvine, CA *Toll Free Tel:* 800-636-8329, pg 65

DK Publishing, New York, NY *Toll Free Tel:* 800-733-3000, pg 65

Dogwise Publishing, Wenatchee, WA *Toll Free Tel:* 800-776-2665, pg 66

Tom Doherty Associates, LLC, New York, NY *Toll Free Tel:* 800-455-0340, pg 66

The Donning Company Publishers, Brookfield, MO *Toll Free Tel:* 800-369-2646 (ext 3377), pg 66

Dordt Press, Sioux Center, IA *Toll Free Tel:* 800-343-6738, pg 66

Dorrance Publishing Co Inc, Pittsburgh, PA *Toll Free Tel:* 800-695-9599; 800-788-7654 (gen cust orders), pg 66

Douglas & McIntyre (2013) Ltd, Madeira Park, BC Canada *Toll Free Tel:* 800-667-2988, pg 421

Dover Publications Inc, Mineola, NY *Toll Free Tel:* 800-223-3130 (orders), pg 67

Dramatic Publishing Co, Woodstock, IL *Toll Free Tel:* 800-448-7469 *Toll Free Fax:* 800-334-5302, pg 67

Dreamscape Media LLC, Holland, OH *Toll Free Tel:* 877-983-7326, pg 67

Duke University Press, Durham, NC *Toll Free Tel:* 888-651-0122 (US) *Toll Free Fax:* 888-651-0124, pg 67

Dun & Bradstreet, Short Hills, NJ *Toll Free Tel:* 844-869-8244; 800-234-3867 (cust serv), pg 68

Eakin Press, Fort Worth, TX *Toll Free Tel:* 888-982-8270, pg 68

ECS Publishing Group, Fenton, MO *Toll Free Tel:* 800-647-2117, pg 69

EDC Publishing, Tulsa, OK *Toll Free Tel:* 800-475-4522 *Toll Free Fax:* 800-743-5660, pg 69

ediciones Lerner, Minneapolis, MN *Toll Free Tel:* 800-328-4929 *Toll Free Fax:* 800-332-1132, pg 69

Les Editions Caractere, Montreal, QC Canada *Toll Free Tel:* 855-861-2782, pg 422

Editions FouLire, Quebec, QC Canada *Toll Free Tel:* 877-628-4029 (CN & US), pg 423

Les Editions Goelette Inc, Quebec, QC Canada *Toll Free Tel:* 800-463-4961, pg 424

Editions Hurtubise, Montreal, QC Canada *Toll Free Tel:* 800-361-1664, pg 424

Editions Marie-France, Montreal, QC Canada *Toll Free Tel:* 800-563-6644 (CN), pg 424

Editions MultiMondes, Montreal, QC Canada *Toll Free Tel:* 800-361-1664, pg 424

Les Editions Phidal Inc, Montreal, QC Canada *Toll Free Tel:* 800-738-7349, pg 425

Les Editions Un Monde Different, Brossard, QC Canada *Toll Free Tel:* 800-443-2582, pg 425

Editions Yvon Blais, Montreal, QC Canada *Toll Free Tel:* 800-363-3047, pg 425

Editorial Bautista Independiente, Sebring, FL *Toll Free Tel:* 800-398-7187 (US), pg 69

Editorial Portavoz, Grand Rapids, MI *Toll Free Tel:* 877-733-2607 (ext 206), pg 69

Educational Insights, Gardena, CA *Toll Free Tel:* 800-995-4436 *Toll Free Fax:* 888-892-8731, pg 69

Educator's International Press Inc (EIP), Kingston, NY *Toll Free Tel:* 800-758-3756, pg 70

Edupress Inc, Garden Grove, CA *Toll Free Tel:* 800-662-4321 *Toll Free Fax:* 800-525-1254, pg 70

Wm B Eerdmans Publishing Co, Grand Rapids, MI *Toll Free Tel:* 800-253-7521, pg 70

Eifrig Publishing LLC, Lemont, PA *Toll Free Tel:* 888-340-6543, pg 70

Eisenbrauns, University Park, PA *Toll Free Tel:* 800-326-9180 *Toll Free Fax:* 877-778-2665, pg 70

Edward Elgar Publishing Inc, Northampton, MA *Toll Free Tel:* 800-390-3149 (orders), pg 70

Elite Books, Fulton, CA *Toll Free Fax:* 800-330-9798, pg 71

Elsevier, Health Sciences Division, Philadelphia, PA *Toll Free Tel:* 800-523-1649, pg 71

EMC Publishing LLC, St Paul, MN *Toll Free Tel:* 888-851-7094, pg 71

Emerald Books, Seattle, WA *Toll Free Tel:* 800-922-2143, pg 71

Emmaus Road Publishing Inc, Steubenville, OH *Toll Free Tel:* 800-398-5470 (orders), pg 71

Emond Montgomery Publications Ltd, Toronto, ON Canada *Toll Free Tel:* 888-837-0815, pg 425

Encounter Books, New York, NY *Toll Free Tel:* 800-343-4499, pg 72

Encyclopaedia Britannica Inc, Chicago, IL *Toll Free Tel:* 800-323-1229 (US & CN), pg 72

Energy Psychology Press, Santa Rosa, CA *Toll Free Fax:* 800-330-9798, pg 72

Enslow Publishing LLC, New York, NY *Toll Free Tel:* 800-398-2504 *Toll Free Fax:* 877-980-4454, pg 72

Entangled Publishing LLC, Fort Collins, CO *Toll Free Tel:* 877-677-9451, pg 72

Environmental Law Institute, Washington, DC *Toll Free Tel:* 800-433-5120, pg 73

EPS/School Specialty Literacy & Intervention, Cambridge, MA *Toll Free Tel:* 800-225-5750 *Toll Free Fax:* 888-440-2665, pg 73

Evan-Moor Educational Publishers, Monterey, CA *Toll Free Tel:* 800-777-4362 (orders) *Toll Free Fax:* 800-777-4332 (orders), pg 73

Excelsior Editions, Albany, NY *Toll Free Tel:* 866-430-7869, pg 74

Eye in the Ear Children's Audio, Portland, ME *Toll Free Tel:* 855-99-STORY (997-8679), pg 74

Facts On File, New York, NY *Toll Free Tel:* 800-322-8755 *Toll Free Fax:* 800-678-3633, pg 74

Fairchild Books, New York, NY *Toll Free Tel:* 800-932-4724; 888-330-8477 (orders), pg 75

Faith & Fellowship Publishing, Fergus Falls, MN *Toll Free Tel:* 800-332-9232, pg 75

Faith Library Publications, Tulsa, OK *Toll Free Tel:* 888-258-0999 (orders), pg 75

Faithlife Corp, Bellingham, WA *Toll Free Tel:* 800-875-6467, pg 75

FaithWalk Publishing, Lima, OH *Toll Free Tel:* 800-537-1030 (orders, non-bookstore mkts), pg 75

Farcountry Press, Helena, MT *Toll Free Tel:* 800-821-3874 (sales off), pg 75

Farrar, Straus & Giroux Books for Young Readers, New York, NY *Toll Free Tel:* 888-330-8477 (orders), pg 75

Father & Son Publishing Inc, Tallahassee, FL *Toll Free Tel:* 800-741-2712 (orders only), pg 76

FC&A Publishing, Peachtree City, GA *Toll Free Tel:* 800-226-8024, pg 76

Federal Street Press, Darien, CT *Toll Free Tel:* 877-886-2830, pg 76

Feldheim Publishers, Nanuet, NY *Toll Free Tel:* 800-237-7149 (orders), pg 76

Ferguson Publishing, New York, NY *Toll Free Tel:* 800-322-8755 *Toll Free Fax:* 800-678-3633, pg 77

Fifth Estate Publishing, Blountsville, AL *Toll Free Tel:* 855-299-2160, pg 77

Fifth House Publishers, Markham, ON Canada *Toll Free Tel:* 800-387-9776, pg 426

Filter Press LLC, Palmer Lake, CO *Toll Free Tel:* 888-570-2663, pg 77

Fire Engineering Books & Videos, Tulsa, OK *Toll Free Tel:* 800-752-9764, pg 78

Firefly Books Ltd, Richmond Hill, ON Canada *Toll Free Tel:* 800-387-6192 (CN); 800-387-5085 (US) *Toll Free Fax:* 800-450-0391 (CN); 800-565-6034 (US), pg 426

First Avenue Editions, Minneapolis, MN *Toll Free Tel:* 800-328-4929 *Toll Free Fax:* 800-332-1132, pg 78

Fitzhenry & Whiteside Limited, Markham, ON Canada *Toll Free Tel:* 800-387-9776 *Toll Free Fax:* 800-260-9777, pg 426

FJH Music Co Inc, Fort Lauderdale, FL *Toll Free Tel:* 800-262-8744, pg 78

Flanker Press Ltd, Paradise, NL Canada *Toll Free Tel:* 866-739-4420, pg 427

FleetSeek, Atlanta, GA *Toll Free Tel:* 888-ONLY-TTS (665-9887), pg 79

Flowerpot Press, Oakville, ON Canada *Toll Free Tel:* 866-927-5001, pg 427

Focus on the Family, Colorado Springs, CO *Toll Free Tel:* 800-A-FAMILY (232-6459), pg 79

Forum Publishing Co, Centerport, NY *Toll Free Tel:* 800-635-7654, pg 80

Forward Movement, Cincinnati, OH *Toll Free Tel:* 800-543-1813, pg 80

Walter Foster Publishing Inc, Lake Forest, CA *Toll Free Tel:* 800-426-0099; 800-759-0190 (orders), pg 80

Foundation Center, New York, NY *Toll Free Tel:* 800-424-9836, pg 80

Foundation Press, St Paul, MN *Toll Free Tel:* 877-888-1330, pg 80

Fox Chapel Publishing Co Inc, East Petersburg, PA *Toll Free Tel:* 800-457-9112, pg 80

Franciscan Media, Cincinnati, OH *Toll Free Tel:* 800-488-0488, pg 80

Franklin, Beedle & Associates Inc, Portland, OR *Toll Free Tel:* 800-322-2665, pg 81

Free Spirit Publishing Inc, Minneapolis, MN *Toll Free Tel:* 800-735-7323 *Toll Free Fax:* 866-419-5199, pg 81

Samuel French Inc, New York, NY *Toll Free Tel:* 866-598-8449, pg 81

Fresh Air Books, Nashville, TN *Toll Free Tel:* 800-972-0433 (orders), pg 81

Fulcrum Publishing Inc, Golden, CO *Toll Free Tel:* 800-992-2908 *Toll Free Fax:* 800-726-7112, pg 82

FurnitureCore, Atlanta, GA *Toll Free Tel:* 800-826-8868, pg 82

Future Horizons Inc, Arlington, TX *Toll Free Tel:* 800-489-0727, pg 82

Gaetan Morin Editeur, Montreal, QC Canada *Toll Free Tel:* 800-565-5531 *Toll Free Fax:* 800-814-0324, pg 427

Galaxy Press, Hollywood, CA *Toll Free Tel:* 877-8GALAXY (842-5299), pg 82

Gale, Farmington Hills, MI *Toll Free Tel:* 800-877-4253 *Toll Free Fax:* 800-414-5043 (orders), pg 82

Gallery Books, New York, NY *Toll Free Tel:* 800-456-6798, pg 82

Gallopade International Inc, Peachtree City, GA *Toll Free Tel:* 800-536-2GET (536-2438) *Toll Free Fax:* 800-871-2979, pg 83

Gareth Stevens Publishing, New York, NY *Toll Free Tel:* 800-542-2595 *Toll Free Fax:* 877-542-2596 (cust serv), pg 83

Gatekeeper Press, Columbus, OH *Toll Free Tel:* 866-535-0913, pg 83

Gateways Books & Tapes, Nevada City, CA *Toll Free Tel:* 800-869-0658, pg 83

Gefen Books, Lawrence, NY *Toll Free Tel:* 800-477-5257, pg 84

Gem Guides Book Co, Upland, CA *Toll Free Tel:* 800-824-5118 (orders), pg 84

Genealogical Publishing Co, Baltimore, MD *Toll Free Tel:* 800-296-6687 *Toll Free Fax:* 800-599-9561, pg 84

Genesis Press Inc, Columbus, MS *Toll Free Tel:* 888-463-4461 (orders only), pg 84

GeoLytics Inc, Branchburg, NJ *Toll Free Tel:* 800-577-6717, pg 85

Getty Publications, Los Angeles, CA *Toll Free Tel:* 800-223-3431 (orders), pg 85

GIA Publications Inc, Chicago, IL *Toll Free Tel:* 800-GIA-1358 (442-1358), pg 85

Gibbs Smith Publisher, Layton, UT *Toll Free Tel:* 800-748-5439; 800-835-4993 (orders) *Toll Free Fax:* 800-213-3023 (orders only), pg 85

Global Training Center Inc, El Paso, TX *Toll Free Tel:* 800-860-5030, pg 86

The Globe Pequot Press, Guilford, CT *Toll Free Tel:* 800-243-0495 (orders only); 888-249-7586 (cust serv) *Toll Free Fax:* 800-820-2329 (orders & cust serv), pg 86

Golden West Cookbooks, Phoenix, AZ *Toll Free Tel:* 800-521-9221, pg 87

Goodheart-Willcox Publisher, Tinley Park, IL *Toll Free Tel:* 800-323-0440 *Toll Free Fax:* 888-409-3900, pg 87

Goose Lane Editions, Fredericton, NB Canada *Toll Free Tel:* 888-926-8377, pg 427

Gospel Publishing House, Springfield, MO *Toll Free Tel:* 800-641-4310 *Toll Free Fax:* 800-328-0294, pg 87

Graphic Universe™, Minneapolis, MN *Toll Free Tel:* 800-328-4929 *Toll Free Fax:* 800-332-1132, pg 88

Gray & Company Publishers, Cleveland, OH *Toll Free Tel:* 800-915-3609, pg 88

Green Dragon Books, Palm Beach, FL *Toll Free Tel:* 800-874-8844 *Toll Free Fax:* 888-874-8844, pg 88

Greenhaven Press®, New York, NY *Toll Free Tel:* 800-237-9932 *Toll Free Fax:* 888-436-4643, pg 89

Grey House Publishing Inc™, Amenia, NY *Toll Free Tel:* 800-562-2139, pg 89

Group Publishing Inc, Loveland, CO *Toll Free Tel:* 800-447-1070, pg 89

Groupe Educalivres Inc, Laval, QC Canada *Toll Free Tel:* 800-567-3671 (info serv) *Toll Free Fax:* 800-267-4387, pg 428

Groupe Modulo, Montreal, QC Canada *Toll Free Tel:* 800-565-5531 *Toll Free Fax:* 800-814-0324, pg 428

Grove Atlantic Inc, New York, NY *Toll Free Tel:* 800-521-0178, pg 89

Gryphon Editions, Omaha, NE *Toll Free Tel:* 888-655-0134 (US & CN), pg 90

Gryphon House Inc, Lewisville, NC *Toll Free Tel:* 800-638-0928 *Toll Free Fax:* 877-638-7576, pg 90

Guideposts Book & Inspirational Media, New York, NY *Toll Free Tel:* 800-932-2145 (cust serv), pg 90

The Guilford Press, New York, NY *Toll Free Tel:* 800-365-7006, pg 90

Hachette Book Group, New York, NY *Toll Free Tel:* 800-759-0190 (cust serv) *Toll Free Fax:* 800-286-9471 (cust serv), pg 90

Hackett Publishing Co Inc, Indianapolis, IN *Toll Free Fax:* 800-783-9213, pg 91

Hagstrom Map, Wilmington, DE *Toll Free Tel:* 800-432-MAPS (432-6277) *Toll Free Fax:* 888-210-9654, pg 91

Hameray Publishing Group Inc, Los Angeles, CA *Toll Free Tel:* 866-918-6173, pg 91

Hamilton Books, Lanham, MD *Toll Free Tel:* 800-462-6420 (cust serv) *Toll Free Fax:* 800-388-4550 (cust serv), pg 92

Hampton Press Inc, New York, NY *Toll Free Tel:* 800-894-8955, pg 92

Hampton Roads Publishing, Newburyport, MA *Toll Free Tel:* 800-423-7087 (orders) *Toll Free Fax:* 877-337-3309, pg 92

Hancock House Publishers, Blaine, WA *Toll Free Tel:* 800-938-1114 *Toll Free Fax:* 800-983-2262, pg 92

Hancock House Publishers Ltd, Surrey, BC Canada *Toll Free Tel:* 800-938-1114 *Toll Free Fax:* 800-983-2262, pg 428

Handprint Books Inc, Brooklyn, NY *Toll Free Tel:* 800-722-6657 (orders) *Toll Free Fax:* 800-858-7787 (orders), pg 92

Hanser Publications LLC, Cincinnati, OH *Toll Free Tel:* 800-950-8977; 888-558-2632 (orders), pg 92

Harbour Publishing Co Ltd, Madeira Park, BC Canada *Toll Free Tel:* 800-667-2988, pg 429

Harlequin Enterprises Ltd, New York, NY *Toll Free Tel:* 888-432-4879, pg 93

Harlequin Enterprises Ltd, Toronto, ON Canada *Toll Free Tel:* 888-432-4879; 800-370-5838 (ebook inquiries), pg 429

Harper's Magazine Foundation, New York, NY *Toll Free Tel:* 800-444-4653, pg 94

Hartman Publishing Inc, Albuquerque, NM *Toll Free Tel:* 800-999-9534 *Toll Free Fax:* 800-474-6106, pg 94

Harvard University Press, Cambridge, MA *Toll Free Tel:* 800-405-1619 (orders) *Toll Free Fax:* 800-406-9145 (orders), pg 95

Harvest House Publishers Inc, Eugene, OR *Toll Free Tel:* 888-501-6991, pg 95

Hatherleigh Press Ltd, Hobart, NY *Toll Free Tel:* 800-528-2550, pg 95

Hay House Inc, Carlsbad, CA *Toll Free Tel:* 800-654-5126 (ext 2, US) *Toll Free Fax:* 800-650-5115, pg 95

Haynes North America Inc, Newbury Park, CA *Toll Free Tel:* 800-4-HAYNES (442-9637), pg 96

Hazelden Publishing, Center City, MN *Toll Free Tel:* 800-257-7810; 866-328-9000, pg 96

HCPro, Middleton, MA *Toll Free Tel:* 800-650-6787 *Toll Free Fax:* 800-785-9212, pg 96

Health Communications Inc, Deerfield Beach, FL *Toll Free Tel:* 800-851-9100; 800-441-5569 (cust serv & orders) *Toll Free Fax:* 800-424-7652 (cust serv & orders), pg 96

Health Forum Inc, Chicago, IL *Toll Free Tel:* 800-242-2626, pg 97

Health Professions Press, Towson, MD *Toll Free Tel:* 888-337-8808, pg 97

HeartMath LLC, Boulder Creek, CA *Toll Free Tel:* 800-711-6221, pg 97

Hearts 'n Tummies Cookbook Co, Wever, IA *Toll Free Tel:* 800-571-2665, pg 97

William S Hein & Co Inc, Getzville, NY *Toll Free Tel:* 800-828-7571, pg 97

Heinemann, Portsmouth, NH *Toll Free Tel:* 800-225-5800 (US) *Toll Free Fax:* 877-231-6980 (US), pg 97

Hellgate Press, Ashland, OR *Toll Free Tel:* 800-795-4059, pg 98

Hendrickson Publishers Inc, Peabody, MA *Toll Free Tel:* 800-358-3111, pg 98

Herald Press, Harrisonburg, VA *Toll Free Tel:* 800-245-7894 (orders) *Toll Free Fax:* 877-271-0760, pg 98

Herald Publishing House, Independence, MO *Toll Free Tel:* 800-767-8181, pg 98

Heritage Books Inc, Berwyn Heights, MD *Toll Free Tel:* 800-876-6103 *Toll Free Fax:* 800-876-6103; 800-297-9954, pg 98

The Heritage Foundation, Washington, DC *Toll Free Tel:* 800-544-4843, pg 98

Heuer Publishing LLC, Cedar Rapids, IA *Toll Free Tel:* 800-950-7529, pg 98

Hewitt Homeschooling Resources, Spokane, WA *Toll Free Tel:* 800-348-1750, pg 98

High Plains Press, Glendo, WY *Toll Free Tel:* 800-552-7819, pg 99

Highlights for Children Inc, Honesdale, PA *Toll Free Tel:* 800-490-5111, pg 99

Hillsdale College Press, Hillsdale, MI *Toll Free Tel:* 800-437-2268, pg 99

Himalayan Institute Press, Honesdale, PA *Toll Free Tel:* 800-822-4547, pg 100

Hohm Press, Chino Valley, AZ *Toll Free Tel:* 800-381-2700, pg 101

Henry Holt and Company, LLC, New York, NY *Toll Free Tel:* 888-330-8477 (orders), pg 101

Homa & Sekey Books, Paramus, NJ *Toll Free Tel:* 800-870-HOMA (870-4662 orders), pg 102

Hoover Institution Press, Stanford, CA *Toll Free Tel:* 800-935-2882, pg 102

Hoover's Inc, Austin, TX *Toll Free Tel:* 855-858-5974, pg 102

Hope Publishing Co, Carol Stream, IL *Toll Free Tel:* 800-323-1049, pg 102

Houghton Mifflin Harcourt, Boston, MA *Toll Free Tel:* 855-969-4642; 800-225-5425 (K-12 educ materials); 800-323-9540 (assessment materials); 877-219-1537 (SkillsTutor); 888-242-6747 (Innovation in Educ Group); 800-225-3362 (Trade & Ref Div) *Toll Free Fax:* 800-269-5232, pg 103

Houghton Mifflin Harcourt Assessments, Itasca, IL *Toll Free Tel:* 800-323-9540, pg 103

House to House Publications, Lititz, PA *Toll Free Tel:* 800-848-5892, pg 104

HRD Press, Amherst, MA *Toll Free Tel:* 800-822-2801, pg 104

Human Kinetics Inc, Champaign, IL *Toll Free Tel:* 800-747-4457, pg 104

Humanix Books LLC, New York, NY *Toll Free Tel:* 855-371-7810, pg 105

Huntington Press Publishing, Las Vegas, NV *Toll Free Tel:* 800-244-2224, pg 105

Ibex Publishers, Bethesda, MD *Toll Free Tel:* 888-718-8188, pg 105

IEEE Computer Society, Washington, DC *Toll Free Tel:* 800-678-4333 (memb info), pg 105

Ignatius Press, San Francisco, CA *Toll Free Tel:* 800-651-1531 (orders); 888-615-3186 (cust serv), pg 106

IHS Press, Norfolk, VA *Toll Free Tel:* 877-447-7737 *Toll Free Fax:* 877-447-7737, pg 106

Imagination Publishing Group, Dunedin, FL *Toll Free Tel:* 888-701-6481, pg 106

Impact Publications/Development Concepts Inc, Manassas, VA *Toll Free Tel:* 800-361-1055 (cust serv), pg 107

Incentive Publications by World Book, Chicago, IL *Toll Free Tel:* 800-967-5325; 800-975-3250; 888-482-9764 (trade dept) *Toll Free Fax:* 888-922-3766, pg 107

Independent Institute, Oakland, CA *Toll Free Tel:* 800-927-8733, pg 107

Indiana Historical Society Press, Indianapolis, IN *Toll Free Tel:* 800-447-1830 (orders), pg 107

Indiana University Press, Bloomington, IN *Toll Free Tel:* 800-842-6796 (orders only), pg 107

Industrial Press Inc, Norwalk, CT *Toll Free Tel:* 888-528-7852 ext 0 (cust serv), pg 108

Information Today, Inc, Medford, NJ *Toll Free Tel:* 800-300-9868 (cust serv), pg 108

Inner Traditions International Ltd, Rochester, VT *Toll Free Tel:* 800-246-8648, pg 109

Insight Editions, San Rafael, CA *Toll Free Tel:* 800-809-3792 *Toll Free Fax:* 866-509-0515, pg 109

Institute of Continuing Legal Education, Ann Arbor, MI *Toll Free Tel:* 877-229-4350 *Toll Free Fax:* 877-229-4351, pg 109

Institute of Psychological Research, Inc., Montreal, QC Canada *Toll Free Tel:* 800-363-7800 *Toll Free Fax:* 888-382-3007, pg 430

The Institutes™, Malvern, PA *Toll Free Tel:* 800-644-2101, pg 110

Interlink Publishing Group Inc, Northampton, MA *Toll Free Tel:* 800-238-LINK (238-5465), pg 110

International City/County Management Association (ICMA), Washington, DC *Toll Free Tel:* 800-745-8780, pg 110

International Code Council Inc, Brea, CA *Toll Free Tel:* 888-422-7233 *Toll Free Fax:* 866-891-1695, pg 111

International Foundation of Employee Benefit Plans, Brookfield, WI *Toll Free Tel:* 888-334-3327, pg 111

International Linguistics Corp, Kansas City, MO *Toll Free Tel:* 800-237-1830 (orders), pg 111

International Literacy Association (ILA), Newark, DE *Toll Free Tel:* 800-336-7323 (US & CN), pg 111

International Self-Counsel Press Ltd, North Vancouver, BC Canada *Toll Free Tel:* 800-663-3007, pg 430

International Society for Technology in Education, Arlington, VA *Toll Free Tel:* 800-336-5191 (US & CN), pg 112

International Wealth Success Inc, Merrick, NY *Toll Free Tel:* 800-323-0548, pg 112

InterVarsity Press, Westmont, IL *Toll Free Tel:* 800-843-9487, pg 112

Irwin Law Inc, Toronto, ON Canada *Toll Free Tel:* 888-314-9014, pg 431

ISI Books, Wilmington, DE *Toll Free Tel:* 800-526-7022, pg 112

Island Press, Washington, DC *Toll Free Tel:* 800-828-1302, pg 112

iUniverse, Bloomington, IN *Toll Free Tel:* 800-AUTHORS (288-4677), pg 113

Richard Ivey School of Business, London, ON Canada *Toll Free Tel:* 800-649-6355, pg 431

Jewish Publication Society, Philadelphia, PA *Toll Free Tel:* 800-234-3151, pg 113

JIST Publishing, St Paul, MN *Toll Free Tel:* 800-328-1452 *Toll Free Fax:* 800-328-4564, pg 113

John Deere Publishing, Davenport, IA *Toll Free Tel:* 800-522-7448 (orders), pg 113

Johns Hopkins University Press, Baltimore, MD *Toll Free Tel:* 800-537-5487 (book orders & cust serv); 800-548-1784 (journal orders), pg 113

Jones & Bartlett Learning LLC, Burlington, MA *Toll Free Tel:* 800-832-0034, pg 114

Judaica Press Inc, Brooklyn, NY *Toll Free Tel:* 800-972-6201, pg 114

Judson Press, King of Prussia, PA *Toll Free Tel:* 800-458-3766, pg 114

Jump!, Minneapolis, MN *Toll Free Tel:* 888-799-1860 *Toll Free Fax:* 800-675-6679, pg 115

Just World Books LLC, Charlottesville, VA *Toll Free Tel:* 888-506-3769, pg 115

Kaeden Corp, Rocky River, OH *Toll Free Tel:* 800-890-7323, pg 115

Kalmbach Publishing Co, Waukesha, WI *Toll Free Tel:* 800-533-6644 (cust serv & orders); 800-558-1544, pg 115

Kar-Ben Publishing, Minneapolis, MN *Toll Free Tel:* 800-4-KARBEN (452-7236) *Toll Free Fax:* 800-332-1132, pg 115

J J Keller & Associates, Inc, Neenah, WI *Toll Free Tel:* 877-564-2333 *Toll Free Fax:* 800-727-7516, pg 116

Kendall Hunt Publishing Co, Dubuque, IA *Toll Free Tel:* 800-228-0810 (orders) *Toll Free Fax:* 800-772-9165, pg 116

Kennedy Information Inc, Keene, NH *Toll Free Tel:* 800-531-0140, pg 116

Kensington Publishing Corp, New York, NY *Toll Free Tel:* 800-221-2647, pg 116

Kids Can Press Ltd, Toronto, ON Canada *Toll Free Tel:* 800-265-0884, pg 431

Kindred Productions, Winnipeg, MB Canada *Toll Free Tel:* 800-545-7322, pg 431

Jessica Kingsley Publishers Inc, Philadelphia, PA *Toll Free Tel:* 866-416-1078 (cust serv), pg 117

Kirkbride Bible Co Inc, Indianapolis, IN *Toll Free Tel:* 800-428-4385, pg 117

Klutz, New York, NY *Toll Free Tel:* 800-737-4123 (cust serv), pg 117

Knopf Canada, Toronto, ON Canada *Toll Free Tel:* 888-523-9292, pg 431

HJ Kramer Inc, Tiburon, CA *Toll Free Tel:* 800-972-6657, pg 118

Kregel Publications, Grand Rapids, MI *Toll Free Tel:* 800-733-2607, pg 118

Lake Superior Publishing LLC, Duluth, MN *Toll Free Tel:* 888-BIG-LAKE (244-5253), pg 119

LAMA Books, Hayward, CA *Toll Free Tel:* 888-452-6244, pg 119

Lanahan Publishers Inc, Baltimore, MD *Toll Free Tel:* 866-345-1949, pg 119

Landauer Publishing, East Petersburg, PA *Toll Free Tel:* 800-457-9112, pg 119

Peter Lang Publishing Inc, New York, NY *Toll Free Tel:* 800-770-5264 (cust serv), pg 119

Langmarc Publishing, Austin, TX *Toll Free Tel:* 800-864-1648 (orders), pg 120

Larson Publications, Burdett, NY *Toll Free Tel:* 800-828-2197, pg 120

Laughing Elephant Books, Seattle, WA *Toll Free Tel:* 800-354-0400, pg 120

Laurier Books Ltd, Ottawa, ON Canada *Toll Free Fax:* 855-736-9160, pg 432

The Lawbook Exchange Ltd, Clark, NJ *Toll Free Tel:* 800-422-6686, pg 121

Leadership Connect, New York, NY *Toll Free Tel:* 800-627-0311, pg 121

Leadership Ministries Worldwide, Chattanooga, TN *Toll Free Tel:* 800-987-8790, pg 121

THE Learning Connection®, Orlando, FL *Toll Free Tel:* 800-218-8489, pg 121

Learning Links Inc, Cranbury, NJ *Toll Free Tel:* 800-724-2616 *Toll Free Fax:* 888-960-2508, pg 121

LearningExpress, New York, NY *Toll Free Tel:* 800-295-9556 (ext 2), pg 121

Lectorum Publications Inc, Lyndhurst, NJ *Toll Free Tel:* 800-345-5946 *Toll Free Fax:* 877-532-8676, pg 121

Lederer Books, Clarksville, MD *Toll Free Tel:* 800-410-7367 (orders) *Toll Free Fax:* 800-327-0048, pg 122

Lee & Low Books Inc, New York, NY *Toll Free Tel:* 888-320-3190 (ext 28, orders only), pg 122

Legacy Bound, Ely, MN *Toll Free Tel:* 800-909-9698, pg 122

Leisure Arts Inc, Maumelle, AR *Toll Free Tel:* 800-643-8030 *Toll Free Fax:* 877-710-5603 (catalog), pg 122

Lerner Publications, Minneapolis, MN *Toll Free Tel:* 800-328-4929 *Toll Free Fax:* 800-332-1132, pg 122

Lerner Publishing Group Inc, Minneapolis, MN *Toll Free Tel:* 800-328-4929 *Toll Free Fax:* 800-332-1132, pg 122

LernerClassroom, Minneapolis, MN *Toll Free Tel:* 800-328-4929 *Toll Free Fax:* 800-332-1132, pg 123

LexisNexis®, New York, NY *Toll Free Fax:* 800-437-8674, pg 123

LexisNexis® Canada Inc, Toronto, ON Canada *Toll Free Tel:* 800-668-6481; 800-387-0899 (cust care); 800-255-5174 (sales), pg 432

Liberty Fund Inc, Carmel, IN *Toll Free Tel:* 800-955-8335; 800-866-3520, pg 123

Libraries Unlimited, Santa Barbara, CA *Toll Free Tel:* 800-368-6868 *Toll Free Fax:* 888-873-7017, pg 124

Lidec Inc, Saint-Jean-sur-Richlieu, QC Canada *Toll Free Tel:* 800-350-5991 (CN only), pg 432

Mary Ann Liebert Inc, New Rochelle, NY *Toll Free Tel:* 800-654-3237, pg 124

Life Cycle Books, Fort Collins, CO *Toll Free Tel:* 800-214-5849, pg 124

Life Cycle Books Ltd, Toronto, ON Canada *Toll Free Tel:* 866-880-5860 *Toll Free Fax:* 866-260-8172, pg 432

Light Technology Publishing LLC, Flagstaff, AZ *Toll Free Tel:* 800-450-0985, pg 124

Liguori Publications, Liguori, MO *Toll Free Tel:* 800-325-9521 *Toll Free Fax:* 800-325-9526 (sales), pg 124

Linden Publishing Co Inc, Fresno, CA *Toll Free Tel:* 800-345-4447 (orders), pg 125

Lippincott Williams & Wilkins, New York, NY *Toll Free Tel:* 800-933-6525, pg 125

Listen & Live Audio Inc, Union City, NJ *Toll Free Tel:* 800-653-9400 (orders), pg 125

little bee books, New York, NY *Toll Free Tel:* 844-321-0237, pg 125

Little, Brown Books for Young Readers, New York, NY *Toll Free Tel:* 800-759-0190 (cust serv), pg 126

The Little Entrepreneur, Detroit, MI *Toll Free Tel:* 888-435-9234, pg 126

Liturgical Press, Collegeville, MN *Toll Free Tel:* 800-858-5450 *Toll Free Fax:* 800-445-5899, pg 126

Liturgy Training Publications, Chicago, IL *Toll Free Tel:* 800-933-1800 (US & CN only orders), pg 126

Living Language, New York, NY *Toll Free Tel:* 800-733-3000 (orders), pg 126

Living Stream Ministry (LSM), Anaheim, CA *Toll Free Tel:* 800-549-5164, pg 126

Llewellyn Publications, Woodbury, MN *Toll Free Tel:* 800-843-6666, pg 127

The Local History Co, Pittsburgh, PA *Toll Free Tel:* 866-362-0789 (orders), pg 127

Lone Pine Publishing, Vancouver, BC Canada *Toll Free Tel:* 800-661-9017 *Toll Free Fax:* 800-424-7173, pg 432

Lonely Planet, Oakland, CA *Toll Free Tel:* 800-275-8555 (orders), pg 127

Looseleaf Law Publications Inc, Flushing, NY *Toll Free Tel:* 800-647-5547, pg 128

Lorenz Educational Press, Dayton, OH *Toll Free Tel:* 800-444-1140, pg 128

Lotus Press, Twin Lakes, WI *Toll Free Tel:* 800-824-6396 (orders), pg 128

Love Inspired Books, New York, NY *Toll Free Tel:* 888-432-4879, pg 128

Loving Healing Press Inc, Ann Arbor, MI *Toll Free Tel:* 888-761-6268 (US & CN), pg 128

Loyola Press, Chicago, IL *Toll Free Tel:* 800-621-1008, pg 128

LRP Publications, Palm Beach Gardens, FL *Toll Free Tel:* 800-341-7874, pg 129

LRS, Torrance, CA *Toll Free Tel:* 800-255-5002, pg 129

Lucent Press, New York, NY *Toll Free Tel:* 800-237-9932 *Toll Free Fax:* 888-436-4643, pg 129

Lutheran Braille Workers Inc, Yucaipa, CA *Toll Free Tel:* 800-925-6092, pg 129

Macmillan Audio, New York, NY *Toll Free Tel:* 888-330-8477 (cust serv), pg 130

Macmillan Reference USA™, Farmington Hills, MI *Toll Free Tel:* 800-877-4253 *Toll Free Fax:* 877-363-4253, pg 130

Madonna House Publications, Combermere, ON Canada *Toll Free Tel:* 888-703-7110 *Toll Free Fax:* 877-717-2888, pg 432

Maharishi University of Management Press, Fairfield, IA *Toll Free Tel:* 800-831-6523, pg 130

Mandala Earth, San Rafael, CA *Toll Free Fax:* 866-509-0515, pg 131

MAR*CO Products Inc, Hatfield, PA *Toll Free Tel:* 800-448-2197, pg 131

Marathon Press, Norfolk, NE *Toll Free Tel:* 800-228-0629, pg 132

Maren Green Publishing Inc, Oak Park Heights, MN *Toll Free Tel:* 800-287-1512, pg 132

Marquis Who's Who, Berkeley Heights, NJ *Toll Free Tel:* 844-394-6946, pg 132

Marshall Cavendish Education, Tarrytown, NY *Toll Free Tel:* 800-821-9881, pg 133

Martindale LLC, New Providence, NJ *Toll Free Tel:* 800-526-4902, pg 133

Martingale®, Bothell, WA *Toll Free Tel:* 800-426-3126, pg 133

Mason Crest Publishers, Broomall, PA *Toll Free Tel:* 866-MCP-BOOK (627-2665), pg 133

Master Books®, Green Forest, AR *Toll Free Tel:* 800-999-3777, pg 134

Mastery Education, Saddle Brook, NJ *Toll Free Tel:* 800-822-1080, pg 134

Math Solutions®, Sausalito, CA *Toll Free Tel:* 877-234-7323 *Toll Free Fax:* 800-724-4716, pg 134

Math Teachers Press Inc, Minneapolis, MN *Toll Free Tel:* 800-852-2435, pg 134

The Mathematical Association of America, Washington, DC *Toll Free Tel:* 800-741-9415, pg 134

The McDonald & Woodward Publishing Co, Newark, OH *Toll Free Tel:* 800-233-8787, pg 134

McFarland, Jefferson, NC *Toll Free Tel:* 800-253-2187 (orders), pg 135

McGraw-Hill Career Education, Burr Ridge, IL *Toll Free Tel:* 800-338-3987 (cust serv), pg 135

McGraw-Hill Contemporary Learning Series, Dubuque, IA *Toll Free Tel:* 800-243-6532, pg 135

McGraw-Hill Create, New York, NY *Toll Free Tel:* 800-962-9342, pg 135

McGraw-Hill Higher Education, Burr Ridge, IL *Toll Free Tel:* 800-338-3987 (cust serv), pg 135

McGraw-Hill Humanities, Social Sciences, Languages, New York, NY *Toll Free Tel:* 800-338-3987 (cust serv), pg 136

McGraw-Hill/Irwin, Burr Ridge, IL *Toll Free Tel:* 800-338-3987 (cust serv), pg 136

McGraw-Hill Ryerson, Whitby, ON Canada *Toll Free Tel:* 800-565-5758 (cust serv) *Toll Free Fax:* 800-463-5885, pg 433

McGraw-Hill School Education Group, Columbus, OH *Toll Free Tel:* 800-848-1567, pg 136

McGraw-Hill Science, Engineering, Mathematics, Dubuque, IA *Toll Free Tel:* 800-338-3987 (cust serv), pg 136

MDR, A D&B Co, Shelton, CT *Toll Free Tel:* 800-333-8802 *Toll Free Fax:* 866-532-7097, pg 136

me+mi publishing inc, Aurora, IL *Toll Free Tel:* 888-251-1444, pg 137

R S Means from The Gordian Group, Rockland, MA *Toll Free Tel:* 800-448-8182 (cust serv); 800-334-3509 (sales) *Toll Free Fax:* 800-632-6732, pg 137

Medals of America Press, Fountain Inn, SC *Toll Free Tel:* 800-605-4001 *Toll Free Fax:* 800-407-8640, pg 137

Medical Group Management Association (MGMA), Englewood, CO *Toll Free Tel:* 877-275-6462, pg 137

Medical Physics Publishing Corp (MPP), Madison, WI *Toll Free Tel:* 800-442-5778 (cust serv), pg 137

MedMaster Inc, Fort Lauderdale, FL *Toll Free Tel:* 800-335-3480, pg 137

Mel Bay Publications Inc, Fenton, MO *Toll Free Tel:* 800-863-5229 *Toll Free Fax:* 800-660-9818, pg 137

Menasha Ridge Press, Birmingham, AL *Toll Free Tel:* 888-604-4537, pg 138

MennoMedia, Harrisonburg, VA *Toll Free Tel:* 800-245-7894 (orders & cust serv US) *Toll Free Fax:* 877-271-0760, pg 138

Mercer University Press, Macon, GA *Toll Free Tel:* 866-895-1472, pg 138

Meriwether Publishing, Englewood, CO *Toll Free Tel:* 800-333-7262, pg 138

Merriam-Webster Inc, Springfield, MA *Toll Free Tel:* 800-828-1880 (orders & cust serv), pg 138

Mesorah Publications Ltd, Brooklyn, NY *Toll Free Tel:* 800-637-6724, pg 138

Messianic Jewish Publishers, Clarksville, MD *Toll Free Tel:* 800-410-7367 (orders) *Toll Free Fax:* 800-327-0048 (orders), pg 138

Michigan Municipal League, Ann Arbor, MI *Toll Free Tel:* 800-653-2483, pg 139

Mike Murach & Associates Inc, Fresno, CA *Toll Free Tel:* 800-221-5528, pg 139

Milady, Clifton Park, NY *Toll Free Tel:* 800-998-7498, pg 139

Milkweed Editions, Minneapolis, MN *Toll Free Tel:* 800-520-6455, pg 140

Millbrook Press, Minneapolis, MN *Toll Free Tel:* 800-328-4929 *Toll Free Fax:* 800-332-1132, pg 140

Richard K Miller Associates, Miramar, FL *Toll Free Tel:* 888-928-RKMA (928-7562) *Toll Free Fax:* 877-928-7562, pg 140

Milliken Publishing Co, Dayton, OH *Toll Free Tel:* 800-444-1144, pg 140

The Minerals, Metals & Materials Society (TMS), Pittsburgh, PA *Toll Free Tel:* 800-759-4867, pg 140

The MIT Press, Cambridge, MA *Toll Free Tel:* 800-405-1619 (orders), pg 141

Mitchell Lane Publishers Inc, Hallandale, FL *Toll Free Tel:* 800-223-3251, pg 141

Mondo Publishing, New York, NY *Toll Free Tel:* 888-88-MONDO (886-6636) *Toll Free Fax:* 888-532-4492, pg 142

Moody Publishers, Chicago, IL *Toll Free Tel:* 800-678-8812 *Toll Free Fax:* 800-678-3329, pg 142

Morehouse Publishing, New York, NY *Toll Free Tel:* 800-242-1918 (retail orders only), pg 142

Mountain n' Air Books, La Crescenta, CA *Toll Free Tel:* 800-446-9696 *Toll Free Fax:* 800-303-5578, pg 143

Mountain Press Publishing Co, Missoula, MT *Toll Free Tel:* 800-234-5308, pg 143

MRTS, Tempe, AZ *Toll Free Tel:* 800-621-2736 (orders) *Toll Free Fax:* 800-621-8476 (orders), pg 144

Multnomah, Colorado Springs, CO *Toll Free Tel:* 800-603-7051 (orders) *Toll Free Fax:* 800-294-5686 (orders), pg 144

Museum of New Mexico Press, Santa Fe, NM *Toll Free Tel:* 800-249-7737 (orders) *Toll Free Fax:* 800-622-8667 (orders), pg 144

NACE International, Houston, TX *Toll Free Tel:* 800-797-NACE (797-6223), pg 144

National Academies Press (NAP), Washington, DC *Toll Free Tel:* 800-624-6242, pg 145

National Association of Secondary School Principals (NASSP), Reston, VA *Toll Free Tel:* 800-253-7746; 866-647-7253 (sales), pg 145

National Braille Press, Boston, MA *Toll Free Tel:* 800-548-7323 (cust serv); 888-965-8965, pg 145

National Catholic Educational Association, Arlington, VA *Toll Free Tel:* 800-711-6232, pg 145

National Council of Teachers of English (NCTE), Champaign, IL *Toll Free Tel:* 877-369-6283 (cust serv), pg 146

National Council of Teachers of Mathematics (NCTM), Reston, VA *Toll Free Tel:* 800-235-7566, pg 146

National Geographic Books, Washington, DC *Toll Free Tel:* 877-866-6486, pg 146

National Golf Foundation, Jupiter, FL *Toll Free Tel:* 888-275-4643, pg 147

National Institute for Trial Advocacy (NITA), Boulder, CO *Toll Free Tel:* 877-648-2632; 800-225-6482 (orders & returns), pg 147

National Learning Corp, Syosset, NY *Toll Free Tel:* 800-632-8888, pg 147

National Notary Association (NNA), Chatsworth, CA *Toll Free Tel:* 800-876-6827 *Toll Free Fax:* 800-833-1211, pg 147

National Resource Center for Youth Services, Tulsa, OK *Toll Free Tel:* 800-274-2687, pg 147

National Science Teachers Association (NSTA), Arlington, VA *Toll Free Tel:* 800-277-5300 (orders) *Toll Free Fax:* 888-433-0526 (orders), pg 147

The National Underwriter Co, Erlanger, KY *Toll Free Tel:* 800-543-0874 *Toll Free Fax:* 800-874-1916, pg 147

National Wildlife Federation, Reston, VA *Toll Free Tel:* 800-477-5034, pg 147

Naval Institute Press, Annapolis, MD *Toll Free Tel:* 800-233-8764, pg 147

NavPress Publishing Group, Colorado Springs, CO *Toll Free Tel:* 800-323-9400; 855-277-9400 (cust serv) *Toll Free Fax:* 800-684-0247, pg 148

NBM Publishing Inc, New York, NY *Toll Free Tel:* 800-886-1223, pg 148

Neibauer Press, Warminster, PA *Toll Free Tel:* 800-322-6203 (orders), pg 148

Nelson Education Ltd, Scarborough, ON Canada *Toll Free Tel:* 800-268-2222 (cust serv) *Toll Free Fax:* 800-430-4445, pg 433

New City Press, Hyde Park, NY *Toll Free Tel:* 800-462-5980 (orders only), pg 148

New Forums Press Inc, Stillwater, OK *Toll Free Tel:* 800-606-3766, pg 148

New Harbinger Publications Inc, Oakland, CA *Toll Free Tel:* 800-748-6273 (orders only) *Toll Free Fax:* 800-652-1613, pg 148

New Leaf Press, Green Forest, AR *Toll Free Tel:* 800-999-3777, pg 149

The New Press, New York, NY *Toll Free Tel:* 800-343-4489 (orders) *Toll Free Fax:* 800-351-5073 (orders), pg 149

New Readers Press, Syracuse, NY *Toll Free Tel:* 800-448-8878 *Toll Free Fax:* 866-894-2100, pg 149

New World Library, Novato, CA *Toll Free Tel:* 800-227-3900 (ext 52, retail orders); 800-972-6657, pg 149

New World Publishing (Canada), Halifax, NS Canada *Toll Free Tel:* 877-211-3334 (orders), pg 434

New York Academy of Sciences (NYAS), New York, NY *Toll Free Tel:* 800-843-6927, pg 150

New York State Bar Association, Albany, NY *Toll Free Tel:* 800-582-2452, pg 150

New York University Press, New York, NY *Toll Free Tel:* 800-996-6987 (orders), pg 150

Newbury Street Press, Boston, MA *Toll Free Tel:* 888-296-3447 (NEHGS membership), pg 150

Nimbus Publishing Ltd, Halifax, NS Canada *Toll Free Tel:* 800-NIMBUS9 (646-2879) *Toll Free Fax:* 888-253-3133, pg 434

No Starch Press, San Francisco, CA *Toll Free Tel:* 800-420-7240, pg 150

North Country Books Inc, Utica, NY *Toll Free Tel:* 800-342-7409 (orders), pg 151

North Point Press, New York, NY *Toll Free Tel:* 888-330-8477, pg 151

North River Press Publishing Corp, Great Barrington, MA *Toll Free Tel:* 800-486-2665 *Toll Free Fax:* 800-BOOK-FAX (266-5329), pg 151

North Star Editions Inc, Mendota Heights, MN *Toll Free Tel:* 888-417-0195, pg 152

Northwestern University Press, Evanston, IL *Toll Free Tel:* 800-621-2736 (orders only), pg 152

W W Norton & Company Inc, New York, NY *Toll Free Tel:* 800-233-4830 (orders & cust serv) *Toll Free Fax:* 800-458-6515, pg 152

Norwood House Press, Fairport, NY *Toll Free Tel:* 866-565-2900 *Toll Free Fax:* 866-565-2901, pg 153

Novalis Publishing, Toronto, ON Canada *Toll Free Tel:* 877-702-7773 *Toll Free Fax:* 877-702-7775, pg 434

NRP Direct, New Providence, NJ *Toll Free Tel:* 844-592-4197, pg 153

Nursesbooks.org, The Publishing Program of ANA, Silver Spring, MD *Toll Free Tel:* 800-274-4262; 800-637-0323 (orders), pg 153

Nystrom Education, Culver City, CA *Toll Free Tel:* 800-421-4246 *Toll Free Fax:* 800-944-5432, pg 153

OAG Worldwide, Lisle, IL *Toll Free Tel:* 800-342-5624 (cust serv), pg 153

Oak Knoll Press, New Castle, DE *Toll Free Tel:* 800-996-2556, pg 153

OCP, Portland, OR *Toll Free Tel:* 800-548-8749 *Toll Free Fax:* 800-843-8181, pg 154

OECD Washington Center, Washington, DC *Toll Free Tel:* 800-456-6323 (dist ctr/pubns orders), pg 154

Ohio State University Foreign Language Publications, Columbus, OH *Toll Free Tel:* 800-678-6999, pg 155

The Ohio State University Press, Columbus, OH *Toll Free Fax:* 800-621-8476, pg 155

Omnibus Press, New York, NY *Toll Free Tel:* 800-431-7187 *Toll Free Fax:* 800-345-6842, pg 155

Omnidawn Publishing, Oakland, CA *Toll Free Tel:* 800-792-4957, pg 155

Omnigraphics Inc, Detroit, MI *Toll Free Tel:* 800-234-1340 (cust serv) *Toll Free Fax:* 800-875-1340 (cust serv), pg 155

Open Court Publishing Co, Chicago, IL *Toll Free Tel:* 800-815-2280, pg 156

The Optical Society (OSA), Washington, DC *Toll Free Tel:* 800-766-4672, pg 156

OptumInsight™, Eden Prairie, MN *Toll Free Tel:* 888-445-8745, pg 156

Orbis Books, Maryknoll, NY *Toll Free Tel:* 800-258-5838 (orders, Mon-Fri 8AM-4PM EST), pg 156

Orbit, New York, NY *Toll Free Tel:* 800-759-0190, pg 156

Orca Book Publishers, Victoria, BC Canada *Toll Free Tel:* 800-210-5277 *Toll Free Fax:* 877-408-1551, pg 435

O'Reilly Media Inc, Sebastopol, CA *Toll Free Tel:* 800-998-9938; 800-889-8969, pg 157

Other Press, New York, NY *Toll Free Tel:* 877-843-6843, pg 157

Our Sunday Visitor Publishing, Huntington, IN *Toll Free Tel:* 800-348-2440 (orders) *Toll Free Fax:* 800-498-6709, pg 157

Richard C Owen Publishers Inc, Katonah, NY *Toll Free Tel:* 800-336-5588, pg 158

Oxford University Press USA, New York, NY *Toll Free Tel:* 800-451-7556 (orders); 800-445-9714 (cust serv), pg 158

Ozark Mountain Publishing Inc, Huntsville, AR *Toll Free Tel:* 800-935-0045, pg 158

P & R Publishing Co, Phillipsburg, NJ *Toll Free Tel:* 800-631-0094, pg 158

Pacific Educational Press, Vancouver, BC Canada *Toll Free Tel:* 855-827-2232, pg 435

Pacific Press® Publishing Association, Nampa, ID *Toll Free Tel:* 800-447-7377, pg 158

Papercutz, New York, NY *Toll Free Tel:* 800-886-1223, pg 160

Paraclete Press Inc, Brewster, MA *Toll Free Tel:* 800-451-5006, pg 160

Paradigm Publications, Taos, NM *Toll Free Tel:* 800-873-3946 (US); 888-873-3947 (CN), pg 160

Paradise Cay Publications Inc, Blue Lake, CA *Toll Free Tel:* 800-736-4509, pg 160

Paragon House, St Paul, MN *Toll Free Tel:* 800-447-3709, pg 160

Parallax Press, Berkeley, CA *Toll Free Tel:* 800-863-5290 (orders), pg 160

Parenting Press, Seattle, WA *Toll Free Tel:* 800-99-BOOKS (992-6657), pg 161

Pauline Books & Media, Boston, MA *Toll Free Tel:* 800-876-4463 (orders); 800-836-9723 (cust serv), pg 161

Paulist Press, Mahwah, NJ *Toll Free Tel:* 800-218-1903 *Toll Free Fax:* 800-836-3161, pg 161

Peachpit Press, San Francisco, CA *Toll Free Tel:* 800-283-9444, pg 162

Peachtree Publishing Co Inc, Atlanta, GA *Toll Free Tel:* 800-241-0113 *Toll Free Fax:* 800-875-8909, pg 162

Pearson Allyn & Bacon, Boston, MA *Toll Free Tel:* 800-428-4466, pg 162

Pearson Benjamin Cummings, San Francisco, CA *Toll Free Tel:* 800-922-0579 (orders) *Toll Free Fax:* 800-445-6991 (orders), pg 162

Pearson Education Canada, North York, ON Canada *Toll Free Tel:* 800-567-3800 *Toll Free Fax:* 800-263-7733, pg 436

Pearson ELT, Hoboken, NJ *Toll Free Tel:* 877-202-4572 *Toll Free Fax:* 800-445-6991, pg 162

Pearson ERPI, Montreal, QC Canada *Toll Free Tel:* 800-263-3678 *Toll Free Fax:* 800-643-4720, pg 436

Pearson Learning Solutions, Boston, MA *Toll Free Tel:* 800-428-4466 (orders); 800-635-1579, pg 162

Pelican Publishing Co, New Orleans, LA *Toll Free Tel:* 800-843-1724, pg 162

Pembroke Publishers Ltd, Markham, ON Canada *Toll Free Tel:* 800-997-9807 *Toll Free Fax:* 800-339-5568, pg 436

Pendragon Press, Hillsdale, NY *Toll Free Tel:* 877-656-6381 (orders), pg 163

Penfield Books, Iowa City, IA *Toll Free Tel:* 800-728-9998, pg 163

Penguin Group USA, A Penguin Random House Company, New York, NY *Toll Free Tel:* 800-847-5515 (inside sales); 800-631-8571 (cust serv), pg 163

Penguin Random House Canada, Toronto, ON Canada *Toll Free Tel:* 888-523-9292 (cust serv), pg 436

Penguin Random House LLC, New York, NY *Toll Free Tel:* 800-726-0600, pg 164

Penn State University Press, University Park, PA *Toll Free Tel:* 800-326-9180 *Toll Free Fax:* 877-778-2665, pg 166

PennWell Books, Tulsa, OK *Toll Free Tel:* 800-752-9764, pg 166

Penny-Farthing Productions, Sugar Land, TX *Toll Free Tel:* 800-926-2669, pg 166

Pentecostal Publishing House, Weldon Spring, MO *Toll Free Tel:* 866-819-7667, pg 166

Perfection Learning, Logan, IA *Toll Free Tel:* 800-831-4190 *Toll Free Fax:* 800-543-2745, pg 167

Perseus Books, New York, NY *Toll Free Tel:* 800-343-4499 (cust serv), pg 167

Peterson's, Highlands Ranch, CO *Toll Free Tel:* 800-338-3282, pg 168

Petroleum Extension Service (PETEX), Austin, TX *Toll Free Tel:* 800-687-4132 *Toll Free Fax:* 800-687-7839, pg 168

Pflaum Publishing Group, Dayton, OH *Toll Free Tel:* 800-523-4625; 800-543-4383 (ext 1136, cust serv) *Toll Free Fax:* 800-370-4450, pg 168

Phaidon, New York, NY *Toll Free Tel:* 800-759-0190 (cust serv) *Toll Free Fax:* 800-286-9471 (cust serv), pg 168

Phi Delta Kappa International®, Arlington, VA *Toll Free Tel:* 800-766-1156, pg 169

Philosophy Documentation Center, Charlottesville, VA *Toll Free Tel:* 800-444-2419, pg 169

Pieces of Learning Inc, Marion, IL *Toll Free Tel:* 800-729-5137 *Toll Free Fax:* 800-844-0455, pg 169

The Pilgrim Press/United Church Press, Cleveland, OH *Toll Free Tel:* 800-537-3394 (orders), pg 170

Platypus Media LLC, Washington, DC *Toll Free Tel:* 877-PLATYPS (752-8977), pg 170

Plough Publishing House, Walden, NY *Toll Free Tel:* 800-521-8011, pg 170

Pocket Press Inc, Portland, OR *Toll Free Tel:* 888-237-2110 *Toll Free Fax:* 877-643-3732, pg 171

Poisoned Pen Press, Scottsdale, AZ *Toll Free Tel:* 800-421-3976, pg 171

Pomegranate Communications Inc, Portland, OR *Toll Free Tel:* 800-227-1428 *Toll Free Fax:* 800-848-4376, pg 172

Portage & Main Press, Winnipeg, MB Canada *Toll Free Tel:* 800-667-9673 *Toll Free Fax:* 866-734-8477, pg 437

Pottersfield Press, East Lawrencetown, NS Canada *Toll Free Tel:* 800-646-2879 (orders only), pg 437

Practising Law Institute, New York, NY *Toll Free Tel:* 800-260-4PLI (260-4754, cust serv) *Toll Free Fax:* 800-321-0093 (local), pg 173

PrairieView Press, Gretna, MB Canada *Toll Free Tel:* 800-477-7377 *Toll Free Fax:* 866-480-0253, pg 437

PREP Publishing, Fayetteville, NC *Toll Free Tel:* 800-533-2814, pg 173

Presbyterian Publishing Corp (PPC), Louisville, KY *Toll Free Tel:* 800-523-1631 (US only), pg 173

Price World Publishing, Columbus, OH *Toll Free Tel:* 888-234-6896, pg 174

Princeton Architectural Press, Hudson, NY *Toll Free Tel:* 800-722-6657 (dist); 800-759-0190 (sales), pg 174

Princeton Book Co Publishers, Trenton, NJ *Toll Free Tel:* 800-220-7149, pg 174

The Princeton Review, New York, NY *Toll Free Tel:* 800-273-8439 (orders only), pg 174

PRINTING United Alliance, Fairfax, VA *Toll Free Tel:* 888-385-3588, pg 175

PRO-ED Inc, Austin, TX *Toll Free Tel:* 800-897-3202 *Toll Free Fax:* 800-397-7633, pg 175

Pro Lingua Associates Inc, Brattleboro, VT *Toll Free Tel:* 800-366-4775, pg 175

Productive Publications, North York, ON Canada *Toll Free Tel:* 877-879-2669 (orders), pg 438

Productivity Press, New York, NY *Toll Free Tel:* 800-634-7064 (orders); 800-797-3803, pg 175

Professional Communications Inc, Durant, OK *Toll Free Tel:* 800-337-9838, pg 175

The Professional Education Group LLC (PEG), Wayzata, MN *Toll Free Tel:* 800-229-2531, pg 176

Professional Resource Press, Sarasota, FL *Toll Free Tel:* 800-443-3364 (orders & cust serv) *Toll Free Fax:* 866-804-4843 (orders only), pg 176

ProQuest LLC, Ann Arbor, MI *Toll Free Tel:* 800-521-0600; 877-779-6768 (sales), pg 176

ProStar Publications Inc, Inglewood, CA *Toll Free Tel:* 800-481-6277, pg 177

Prufrock Press, Waco, TX *Toll Free Tel:* 800-998-2208 *Toll Free Fax:* 800-240-0333, pg 177

PSMJ Resources Inc, Newton, MA *Toll Free Tel:* 800-537-PSMJ (537-7765), pg 177

Psychological Assessment Resources Inc (PAR), Lutz, FL *Toll Free Tel:* 800-331-8378 *Toll Free Fax:* 800-727-9329, pg 177

Les Publications du Quebec, Quebec, QC Canada *Toll Free Tel:* 800-463-2100 (Quebec province only) *Toll Free Fax:* 800-561-3479, pg 438

Purple Mountain Press Ltd, Fleischmanns, NY *Toll Free Tel:* 800-325-2665 (orders), pg 178

Quail Ridge Press (QRP), Nashville, TN *Toll Free Tel:* 800-358-0560, pg 178

Quarto Publishing Group USA Inc, Beverly, MA *Toll Free Tel:* 800-328-0590 (sales), pg 178

Quintessence Publishing Co Inc, Batavia, IL *Toll Free Tel:* 800-621-0387, pg 179

Quixote Press, Wever, IA *Toll Free Tel:* 800-571-2665, pg 179

Rand McNally, Skokie, IL *Toll Free Tel:* 877-446-4863 *Toll Free Fax:* 877-469-1298, pg 180

Random House Publishing Group, New York, NY *Toll Free Tel:* 800-200-3552, pg 181

Raven Publishing Inc, Norris, MT *Toll Free Tel:* 866-685-3545, pg 182

Reader's Digest Association Canada ULC (Selection du Reader's Digest Canada SRI), Montreal, QC Canada *Toll Free Tel:* 888-459-3333 (cust serv), pg 438

Reader's Digest Select Editions, White Plains, NY *Toll Free Tel:* 877-732-4438 (cust serv), pg 182

Recorded Books Inc, an RBmedia company, Prince Frederick, MD *Toll Free Tel:* 877-732-2898, pg 182

Red Chair Press, South Egremont, MA *Toll Free Tel:* 800-328-4929 (orders & cust serv), pg 182

Red Deer Press Inc, Markham, ON Canada *Toll Free Tel:* 800-387-9776 (orders), pg 438

Red Wheel/Weiser, Newburyport, MA *Toll Free Tel:* 800-423-7087 (orders), pg 183

Redleaf Press, St Paul, MN *Toll Free Tel:* 800-423-8309 *Toll Free Fax:* 800-641-0115, pg 183

Reedswain Inc, Spring City, PA *Toll Free Tel:* 800-331-5191, pg 183

Referee Books, Racine, WI *Toll Free Tel:* 800-733-6100, pg 183

ReferencePoint Press Inc, San Diego, CA *Toll Free Tel:* 888-479-6436, pg 183

Regal Crest Enterprises, Austin, TX *Toll Free Fax:* 866-294-9628, pg 184

Regnery Publishing, Washington, DC *Toll Free Tel:* 888-219-4747, pg 184

Regular Baptist Press, Arlington Heights, IL *Toll Free Tel:* 800-727-4440 (cust serv), pg 184

Research Press, Champaign, IL *Toll Free Tel:* 800-519-2707, pg 184

Revell, Grand Rapids, MI *Toll Free Tel:* 800-877-2665; 800-679-1957, pg 185

Rio Nuevo Publishers, Tucson, AZ *Toll Free Tel:* 800-969-9558 *Toll Free Fax:* 800-715-5888, pg 185

Rising Sun Publishing, Marietta, GA *Toll Free Tel:* 800-524-2813, pg 185

Rizzoli International Publications Inc, New York, NY *Toll Free Tel:* 800-522-6657 (orders only), pg 185

The Rosen Publishing Group Inc, New York, NY *Toll Free Tel:* 800-237-9932 *Toll Free Fax:* 888-436-4643, pg 187

Rothstein Associates Inc, Brookfield, CT *Toll Free Tel:* 888-768-4783, pg 187

The Rough Notes Co Inc, Carmel, IN *Toll Free Tel:* 800-428-4384 (cust serv) *Toll Free Fax:* 800-321-1909, pg 187

Routledge, New York, NY *Toll Free Tel:* 800-634-7064 (order enquiries, cust serv), pg 187

Rowman & Littlefield, Lanham, MD *Toll Free Tel:* 800-462-6420 (ext 3024, cust serv), pg 188

Russell Sage Foundation, New York, NY *Toll Free Tel:* 800-524-6401, pg 188

Russian Information Services Inc, Montpelier, VT *Toll Free Tel:* 800-639-4301, pg 188

Saddleback Educational Publishing, Costa Mesa, CA *Toll Free Tel:* 888-SDLBACK (735-2225); 800-637-8715 *Toll Free Fax:* 888-734-4010, pg 189

William H Sadlier Inc, New York, NY *Toll Free Tel:* 800-221-5175 (cust serv), pg 189

SAE (Society of Automotive Engineers International), Warrendale, PA *Toll Free Tel:* 877-606-7323 (cust serv), pg 189

Safari Press, Huntington Beach, CA *Toll Free Tel:* 800-451-4788, pg 189

Sagamore Publishing LLC, Champaign, IL *Toll Free Tel:* 800-327-5557 (orders), pg 189

SAGE Publishing, Thousand Oaks, CA *Toll Free Tel:* 800-818-7243 *Toll Free Fax:* 800-583-2665, pg 189

St Andrews University Press, Laurinburg, NC *Toll Free Tel:* 800-763-0198, pg 190

St James Press®, Farmington Hills, MI *Toll Free Tel:* 800-877-4253 (orders) *Toll Free Fax:* 877-363-4253, pg 190

Saint Mary's Press, Winona, MN *Toll Free Tel:* 800-533-8095 *Toll Free Fax:* 800-344-9225, pg 191

Saint Nectarios Press, Seattle, WA *Toll Free Tel:* 800-643-4233, pg 191

St Pauls, Staten Island, NY *Toll Free Tel:* 800-343-2522, pg 191

Salem Press, Hackensack, NJ *Toll Free Tel:* 800-221-1592, pg 191

Salina Bookshelf Inc, Flagstaff, AZ *Toll Free Tel:* 877-527-0070, pg 191

SAMS Technical Publishing LLC, Indianapolis, IN *Toll Free Tel:* 800-428-7267, pg 191

Santa Monica Press LLC, Rancho Santa Fe, CA *Toll Free Tel:* 800-784-9553, pg 191

Santillana USA Publishing Co, Doral, FL *Toll Free Tel:* 800-245-8584, pg 192

Sara Jordan Publishing, St Catharines, ON Canada *Toll Free Tel:* 800-567-7733 *Toll Free Fax:* 800-229-3855, pg 439

SAS Press, Cary, NC *Toll Free Tel:* 800-727-0025, pg 192

Sasquatch Books, Seattle, WA *Toll Free Tel:* 800-775-0817, pg 192

Savvas Learning Co LLC, Paramus, NJ *Toll Free Tel:* 800-848-9500, pg 193

Scepter Publishers, Strongsville, OH *Toll Free Tel:* 800-322-8773, pg 193

Schlager Group Inc, Dallas, TX *Toll Free Tel:* 888-416-5727, pg 193

Scholastic Canada Ltd, Toronto, ON Canada *Toll Free Tel:* 800-268-3860 (CN) *Toll Free Fax:* 866-387-4944, pg 439

Scholastic Inc, New York, NY *Toll Free Tel:* 800-SCHOLASTIC (724-6527), pg 194

Scholastic International, New York, NY *Toll Free Tel:* 800-SCHOLASTIC (724-6527), pg 194

Schonfeld & Associates Inc, Virginia Beach, VA *Toll Free Tel:* 800-205-0030, pg 194

School Guide Publications, Mamaroneck, NY *Toll Free Tel:* 800-433-7771, pg 194

School Zone Publishing Co, Grand Haven, MI *Toll Free Tel:* 800-253-0564, pg 195

Schreiber Publishing Inc, Rockville, MD *Toll Free Tel:* 800-296-1961 (sales), pg 195

Science, Naturally, Washington, DC *Toll Free Tel:* 866-724-9876, pg 195

Seal Books, Toronto, ON Canada *Toll Free Tel:* 888-523-9292 (order desk), pg 439

Search Institute Press®, Minneapolis, MN *Toll Free Tel:* 800-888-7828, pg 196

Seedling Publications Inc, Elizabethtown, PA *Toll Free Tel:* 800-233-0759 *Toll Free Fax:* 888-834-1303, pg 196

Self-Realization Fellowship Publishers, Los Angeles, CA *Toll Free Tel:* 888-773-8680, pg 196

Seven Stories Press, New York, NY *Toll Free Tel:* 800-733-3000 (orders), pg 197

Shadow Mountain, Salt Lake City, UT *Toll Free Tel:* 800-453-3876, pg 197

Shambhala Publications Inc, Boulder, CO *Toll Free Tel:* 866-424-0030 (off); 888-424-2329 (cust serv), pg 197

Signalman Publishing, Kissimmee, FL *Toll Free Tel:* 888-907-4423, pg 198

Signature Books Publishing LLC, Salt Lake City, UT *Toll Free Tel:* 800-356-5687, pg 198

Simcha Press, Deerfield Beach, FL *Toll Free Tel:* 800-851-9100 *Toll Free Fax:* 800-424-7652, pg 198

Simon & Schuster, New York, NY *Toll Free Tel:* 800-223-2348 (cust serv); 800-223-2336 (orders) *Toll Free Fax:* 800-943-9831 (orders), pg 198

Simon & Schuster Canada, Toronto, ON Canada *Toll Free Tel:* 800-387-0446; 800-268-3216 (orders) *Toll Free Fax:* 888-849-8151 (orders), pg 440

Simon & Schuster, Inc, New York, NY *Toll Free Tel:* 800-223-2336 (orders) *Toll Free Fax:* 800-943-9831 (orders), pg 199

Sinauer Associates, Cary, NC *Toll Free Tel:* 800-280-0280, pg 200

SkillPath Publications, Mission, KS *Toll Free Tel:* 800-873-7545, pg 200

SLACK® Incorporated, A Wyanoke Group Company, Thorofare, NJ *Toll Free Tel:* 800-257-8290, pg 201

Sleeping Bear Press™, Ann Arbor, MI *Toll Free Tel:* 800-487-2323, pg 201

SME (Society of Manufacturing Engineers), Southfield, MI *Toll Free Tel:* 800-733-4763 (cust serv), pg 201

Smith & Kraus Publishers Inc, Hanover, NH *Toll Free Tel:* 877-668-8680, pg 201

M Lee Smith Publishers, Brentwood, TN *Toll Free Tel:* 800-274-6774; 800-727-5257, pg 201

Smyth & Helwys Publishing Inc, Macon, GA *Toll Free Tel:* 800-747-3016 (orders only), pg 202

Society for Human Resource Management (SHRM), Alexandria, VA *Toll Free Tel:* 800-283-7476 (orders), pg 202

Society for Industrial & Applied Mathematics, Philadelphia, PA *Toll Free Tel:* 800-447-7426, pg 202

Society for Mining, Metallurgy & Exploration, Englewood, CO *Toll Free Tel:* 800-763-3132, pg 202

Society of American Archivists, Chicago, IL *Toll Free Tel:* 866-722-7858, pg 202

Society of Environmental Toxicology & Chemistry (SETAC), Pensacola, FL *Toll Free Fax:* 888-296-4136, pg 202

The Society of Naval Architects & Marine Engineers (SNAME), Alexandria, VA *Toll Free Tel:* 800-798-2188, pg 203

Solano Press Books, Point Arena, CA *Toll Free Tel:* 800-931-9373, pg 203

Solution Tree, Bloomington, IN *Toll Free Tel:* 800-733-6786, pg 203

Soncino Press Ltd, Brooklyn, NY *Toll Free Tel:* 800-972-6201, pg 203

Sophia Institute Press®, Nashua, NH *Toll Free Tel:* 800-888-9344 *Toll Free Fax:* 888-288-2259, pg 203

Sounds True Inc, Louisville, CO *Toll Free Tel:* 800-333-9185 (US); 888-303-9185 (US & CN), pg 204

Sourcebooks LLC, Naperville, IL *Toll Free Tel:* 800-432-7444, pg 204

South Carolina Bar, Columbia, SC *Toll Free Tel:* 800-768-7787, pg 204

Southern Historical Press Inc, Greenville, SC *Toll Free Tel:* 800-233-0152, pg 205

SPIE, Bellingham, WA *Toll Free Tel:* 888-504-8171 (orders), pg 205

Spinsters Ink, Tallahassee, FL *Toll Free Tel:* 800-729-4992, pg 205

Spizzirri Publishing Inc, Rapid City, SD *Toll Free Tel:* 800-325-9819 *Toll Free Fax:* 800-322-9819, pg 205

Springer, New York, NY *Toll Free Tel:* 800-SPRINGER (777-4643), pg 205

Springer Publishing Co, New York, NY *Toll Free Tel:* 877-687-7476, pg 205

Square One Publishers Inc, Garden City Park, NY *Toll Free Tel:* 877-900-BOOK (900-2665), pg 206

SSPC: The Society for Protective Coatings, Pittsburgh, PA *Toll Free Tel:* 877-281-7772 (US only), pg 206

Standard Publishing, Colorado Springs, CO *Toll Free Tel:* 800-323-7543 *Toll Free Fax:* 800-430-0726, pg 206

Standard Publishing Corp, Boston, MA *Toll Free Tel:* 800-682-5759, pg 206

Starcrafts LLC, Epping, NH *Toll Free Tel:* 866-953-8458 (24/7 message ctr), pg 207

Stargazer Publishing Co, Corona, CA *Toll Free Tel:* 800-606-7895 (orders), pg 207

State University of New York Press, Albany, NY *Toll Free Tel:* 877-204-6073 (orders) *Toll Free Fax:* 877-204-6074 (orders), pg 207

Stenhouse Publishers, Portland, ME *Toll Free Tel:* 888-363-0566 *Toll Free Fax:* 800-833-9164, pg 208

Sterling Publishing Co Inc, New York, NY *Toll Free Tel:* 800-367-9692 *Toll Free Fax:* 800-542-7567, pg 208

Stoneydale Press Publishing Co, Stevensville, MT *Toll Free Tel:* 800-735-7006, pg 209

Storey Publishing LLC, North Adams, MA *Toll Free Tel:* 800-441-5700 (orders); 800-827-7444 (cust serv) *Toll Free Fax:* 800-865-3429 (cust serv), pg 209

Stress Free Kids®, Marietta, GA *Toll Free Fax:* 866-302-2759, pg 210

Stylus Publishing LLC, Sterling, VA *Toll Free Tel:* 800-232-0223 (orders & cust serv), pg 210

Summerthought Publishing, Banff, AB Canada *Toll Free Fax:* 800-762-3095 (orders), pg 441

Sun Publishing Company, Santa Fe, NM *Toll Free Tel:* 877-849-0051, pg 210

Sunbelt Publications Inc, El Cajon, CA *Toll Free Tel:* 800-626-6579 (cust serv), pg 210

Sundance/Newbridge Publishing, Marlborough, MA *Toll Free Tel:* 888-200-2720; 800-343-8204 (Sundance cust serv & orders); 800-867-0307 (Newbridge cust serv & orders) *Toll Free Fax:* 800-456-2419 (orders), pg 210

Sunrise River Press, Forrest Lake, MN *Toll Free Tel:* 800-895-4585, pg 211

Sunstone Press, Santa Fe, NM *Toll Free Tel:* 800-243-5644, pg 211

Surrey Books, Evanston, IL *Toll Free Tel:* 800-326-4430, pg 211

Swan Isle Press, Chicago, IL *Toll Free Tel:* 800-621-2736 (cust serv) *Toll Free Fax:* 800-621-8476 (cust serv), pg 211

Swedenborg Foundation, West Chester, PA *Toll Free Tel:* 800-355-3222 (cust serv), pg 211

Syracuse University Press, Syracuse, NY *Toll Free Tel:* 800-365-8929 (cust serv), pg 212

TAN Books, Gastonia, NC *Toll Free Tel:* 800-437-5876, pg 212

Tanglewood Publishing, Indianapolis, IN *Toll Free Tel:* 800-788-3123 (orders), pg 212

Tantor Media Inc, Old Saybrook, CT *Toll Free Tel:* 877-782-6867 *Toll Free Fax:* 888-782-7821, pg 212

Tapestry Press Ltd, Littleton, MA *Toll Free Tel:* 800-535-2007, pg 213

Taschen America, Los Angeles, CA *Toll Free Tel:* 888-TASCHEN (827-2436), pg 213

The Taunton Press Inc, Newtown, CT *Toll Free Tel:* 800-477-8727 (cust serv); 800-888-8286 (orders), pg 213

Taylor & Francis Inc, Philadelphia, PA *Toll Free Tel:* 800-354-1420, pg 213

TCP Press, Uxbridge, ON Canada *Toll Free Tel:* 800-772-7765, pg 441

TCU Press, Fort Worth, TX *Toll Free Tel:* 800-826-8911 (orders), pg 213

Teach Me Tapes Inc, Mequon, WI *Toll Free Tel:* 800-456-4656, pg 214

Teacher Created Resources Inc, Garden Grove, CA *Toll Free Tel:* 800-662-4321; 888-343-4335 *Toll Free Fax:* 800-525-1254, pg 214

Teacher's Discovery, Auburn Hills, MI *Toll Free Tel:* 800-832-2437 *Toll Free Fax:* 800-287-4509, pg 214

Teaching & Learning Co, Dayton, OH *Toll Free Tel:* 800-444-1144, pg 214

Teaching Strategies LLC, Bethesda, MD *Toll Free Tel:* 800-637-3652, pg 214

Temple University Press, Philadelphia, PA *Toll Free Tel:* 800-621-2736, pg 214

Templegate Publishers, Springfield, IL *Toll Free Tel:* 800-367-4844 (orders only), pg 214

Ten Speed Press, Emeryville, CA *Toll Free Tel:* 800-841-BOOK (841-2665), pg 215

Teton NewMedia Inc, Jackson, WY *Toll Free Tel:* 877-306-9793, pg 215

Texas A&M University Press, College Station, TX *Toll Free Tel:* 800-826-8911 (orders) *Toll Free Fax:* 888-617-2421 (orders), pg 215

Texas Tech University Press, Lubbock, TX *Toll Free Tel:* 800-832-4042, pg 216

Texas Western Press, El Paso, TX *Toll Free Tel:* 800-488-3798 (orders only), pg 216

TFH Publications Inc, Neptune, NJ *Toll Free Tel:* 855-273-7527 (cust serv), pg 216

Thames & Hudson, New York, NY *Toll Free Tel:* 800-233-4830, pg 216

Thieme Medical Publishers Inc, New York, NY *Toll Free Tel:* 800-782-3488, pg 217

Charles C Thomas Publisher Ltd, Springfield, IL *Toll Free Tel:* 800-258-8980, pg 217

Thomas Nelson, Nashville, TN *Toll Free Tel:* 800-251-4000, pg 217

Thompson Educational Publishing Inc, Toronto, ON Canada *Toll Free Tel:* 877-366-2763, pg 441

Thomson West, Eagan, MN *Toll Free Tel:* 844-209-1086 (sales); 800-328-4880 (cust serv), pg 217

Thorndike Press®, Waterville, ME *Toll Free Tel:* 800-223-1244 (ext 4, cust serv/orders) *Toll Free Fax:* 800-558-4676 (orders), pg 217

Tide-mark Press, West Hartford, CT *Toll Free Tel:* 800-338-2508, pg 218

Tilbury House Publishers, Thomaston, ME *Toll Free Tel:* 800-582-1899 (orders), pg 218

Timber Press Inc, Portland, OR *Toll Free Tel:* 800-327-5680, pg 218

TJ Publishers Inc, Dallas, TX *Toll Free Tel:* 800-999-1168, pg 448

Tommy Nelson®, Nashville, TN *Toll Free Tel:* 800-251-4000, pg 218

Tower Publishing Co, Standish, ME *Toll Free Tel:* 800-969-8693, pg 219

Trafalgar Square Books, North Pomfret, VT *Toll Free Tel:* 800-423-4525, pg 219

Trafford, Bloomington, IN *Toll Free Tel:* 888-232-4444, pg 219

Tralco-Lingo Fun, Hamilton, ON Canada *Toll Free Tel:* 888-487-2526, pg 442

Treehaus Communications Inc, Loveland, OH *Toll Free Tel:* 800-638-4287 (orders), pg 220

Triad Publishing Co, Gainesville, FL *Toll Free Fax:* 800-854-4947, pg 220

TripBuilder Media Inc, Westport, CT *Toll Free Tel:* 800-525-9745, pg 220

TriQuarterly Books, Evanston, IL *Toll Free Tel:* 800-621-2736 (orders only), pg 220

TRISTAN Publishing, Minneapolis, MN *Toll Free Tel:* 866-545-1383, pg 221

Triumph Books, Chicago, IL *Toll Free Tel:* 800-888-4741 (cust serv), pg 221

Triumph Learning LLC, Nashua, NH *Toll Free Tel:* 800-225-5700 (cust serv), pg 221

Truman State University Press, Kirksville, MO *Toll Free Tel:* 800-916-6802, pg 221

Trusted Media Brands Inc, New York, NY *Toll Free Tel:* 877-732-4438 (cust serv), pg 221

Tundra Books, Toronto, ON Canada *Toll Free Tel:* 888-523-9292 (orders); 800-588-1074 *Toll Free Fax:* 888-562-9924 (orders), pg 442

Turnstone Press, Winnipeg, MB Canada *Toll Free Tel:* 888-363-7718, pg 442

Tuttle Publishing, North Clarendon, VT *Toll Free Tel:* 800-526-2778 *Toll Free Fax:* 800-FAX-TUTL (329-8885), pg 222

Twenty-First Century Books, Minneapolis, MN *Toll Free Tel:* 800-328-4929 *Toll Free Fax:* 800-332-1132, pg 222

Twenty-Third Publications, New London, CT *Toll Free Tel:* 800-321-0411 (orders) *Toll Free Fax:* 800-572-0788, pg 222

Tyndale House Publishers Inc, Carol Stream, IL *Toll Free Tel:* 800-323-9400; 855-277-9400 *Toll Free Fax:* 866-622-9474, pg 223

Ulysses Press, Brooklyn, NY *Toll Free Tel:* 800-377-2542, pg 223

Ulysses Travel Guides, Montreal, QC Canada *Toll Free Tel:* 800-748-9171, pg 442

Unarius Academy of Science Publications, El Cajon, CA *Toll Free Tel:* 800-475-7062, pg 223

Editorial Unilit, Medley, FL *Toll Free Tel:* 800-767-7726, pg 224

United States Holocaust Memorial Museum, Washington, DC *Toll Free Tel:* 800-259-9998 (orders), pg 224

United States Institute of Peace Press, Washington, DC *Toll Free Tel:* 800-868-8064 (cust serv), pg 224

United States Pharmacopeia, Rockville, MD *Toll Free Tel:* 800-227-8772, pg 224

Universal-Publishers Inc, Irvine, CA *Toll Free Tel:* 800-636-8329 (US only), pg 225

University of Alaska Press, Fairbanks, AK *Toll Free Tel:* 888-252-6657 (US only), pg 225

The University of Arizona Press, Tucson, AZ *Toll Free Tel:* 800-426-3797 (orders) *Toll Free Fax:* 800-426-3797, pg 225

University of British Columbia Press, Vancouver, BC Canada *Toll Free Tel:* 877-377-9378 *Toll Free Fax:* 800-668-0821, pg 443

University of Chicago Press, Chicago, IL *Toll Free Tel:* 800-621-2736 (orders), pg 226

University of Hawaii Press, Honolulu, HI *Toll Free Tel:* 888-UHPRESS (847-7377) *Toll Free Fax:* 800-650-7811, pg 227

University of Iowa Press, Iowa City, IA *Toll Free Tel:* 800-621-2736 (orders only) *Toll Free Fax:* 800-621-8476 (orders only), pg 227

University of Missouri Press, Columbia, MO *Toll Free Tel:* 800-621-2736 (orders) *Toll Free Fax:* 800-621-8476 (orders), pg 228

University of Nebraska Press, Lincoln, NE *Toll Free Tel:* 800-848-6224 (cust serv & US orders) *Toll Free Fax:* 800-526-2617 (cust serv & US orders), pg 229

University of Puerto Rico Press, San Juan, PR *Toll Free Tel:* 877-338-7788, pg 231

University of South Carolina Press, Columbia, SC *Toll Free Tel:* 800-768-2500 (orders) *Toll Free Fax:* 800-868-0740 (orders), pg 231

University of Tennessee Press, Knoxville, TN *Toll Free Tel:* 800-621-2736 (orders) *Toll Free Fax:* 800-621-8476 (orders), pg 231

The University of Virginia Press, Charlottesville, VA *Toll Free Tel:* 800-831-3406 (orders) *Toll Free Fax:* 877-288-6400, pg 231

University of Washington Press, Seattle, WA *Toll Free Tel:* 800-537-5487 (orders), pg 232

University of Wisconsin Press, Madison, WI *Toll Free Tel:* 800-621-2736 (book orders) *Toll Free Fax:* 800-621-2736 (book orders), pg 232

University Press of America Inc, Lanham, MD *Toll Free Tel:* 800-462-6420 *Toll Free Fax:* 800-338-4550, pg 232

University Press of Colorado, Louisville, CO *Toll Free Tel:* 800-621-2736 (orders), pg 232

University Press of Florida, Gainesville, FL *Toll Free Tel:* 800-226-3822 (orders only) *Toll Free Fax:* 800-680-1955 (orders only), pg 232

University Press of Mississippi, Jackson, MS *Toll Free Tel:* 800-737-7788 (orders & cust serv), pg 233

W E Upjohn Institute for Employment Research, Kalamazoo, MI *Toll Free Tel:* 888-227-8569, pg 234

Upper Room Books, Nashville, TN *Toll Free Tel:* 800-972-0433, pg 234

Upstart Books™, Madison, WI *Toll Free Tel:* 800-356-1200 (orders); 800-962-4463 (cust serv) *Toll Free Fax:* 800-245-1329 (orders), pg 234

US Conference of Catholic Bishops, Washington, DC *Toll Free Tel:* 800-235-8722, pg 234

US Games Systems Inc, Stamford, CT *Toll Free Tel:* 800-54-GAMES (544-2637), pg 234

US Government Publishing Office (GPO), Washington, DC *Toll Free Tel:* 866-512-1800 (orders), pg 235

Utah Geological Survey, Salt Lake City, UT *Toll Free Tel:* 888-UTAH-MAP (882-4627, bookstore), pg 235

VanDam Inc, New York, NY *Toll Free Tel:* 800-UNFOLDS (863-6537), pg 235

Vandamere Press, St Petersburg, FL *Toll Free Tel:* 800-551-7776, pg 235

Vanderbilt University Press, Nashville, TN *Toll Free Tel:* 800-848-6224 (orders only), pg 235

Vault.com Inc, New York, NY *Toll Free Tel:* 800-535-2074, pg 235

Voyager Sopris Learning Inc, Dallas, TX *Toll Free Tel:* 800-547-6747 *Toll Free Fax:* 888-819-7767, pg 237

Walch Education, Portland, ME *Toll Free Tel:* 800-558-2846 *Toll Free Fax:* 888-991-5755, pg 237

Warner Press, Anderson, IN *Toll Free Tel:* 800-741-7721 (orders), pg 237

Washington State University Press, Pullman, WA *Toll Free Tel:* 800-354-7360 (orders), pg 237

Water Environment Federation, Alexandria, VA *Toll Free Tel:* 800-666-0206 (cust serv), pg 237

Water Resources Publications LLC, Highlands Ranch, CO *Toll Free Tel:* 800-736-2405 *Toll Free Fax:* 800-616-1971, pg 237

WaterBrook, Colorado Springs, CO *Toll Free Tel:* 800-603-7051 (orders) *Toll Free Fax:* 800-294-5686 (orders), pg 237

Watermark Publishing, Honolulu, HI *Toll Free Tel:* 866-900-BOOK (900-2665), pg 238

Wayne State University Press, Detroit, MI *Toll Free Tel:* 800-978-7323, pg 238

Wayside Publishing, Freeport, ME *Toll Free Tel:* 888-302-2519, pg 238

Weigl Educational Publishers Ltd, Calgary, AB Canada *Toll Free Tel:* 800-668-0766 *Toll Free Fax:* 866-449-3445, pg 445

Well-Trained Mind Press, Charles City, VA *Toll Free Tel:* 877-322-3445 (orders), pg 238

Wesleyan Publishing House, Fishers, IN *Toll Free Tel:* 800-493-7539 *Toll Free Fax:* 800-788-3535, pg 239

West Academic, St Paul, MN *Toll Free Tel:* 877-888-1330, pg 239

Westminster John Knox Press (WJK), Louisville, KY *Toll Free Tel:* 800-523-1631 (US & CN) *Toll Free Fax:* 800-541-5113 (US & CN), pg 239

Whitaker House, New Kensington, PA *Toll Free Tel:* 800-444-4484 (sales), pg 240

Whitecap Books, Vancouver, BC Canada *Toll Free Tel:* 800-387-9776 *Toll Free Fax:* 800-260-9777, pg 445

Whittier Publications Inc, Oceanside, NY *Toll Free Tel:* 800-897-TEXT (897-8398), pg 240

Whole Person Associates Inc, Duluth, MN *Toll Free Tel:* 800-247-6789, pg 240

Wide World of Maps Inc, Phoenix, AZ *Toll Free Tel:* 800-279-7654, pg 240

Michael Wiese Productions, Studio City, CA *Toll Free Tel:* 800-833-5738 (orders), pg 241

Wilderness Adventures Press Inc, Belgrade, MT *Toll Free Tel:* 866-400-2012, pg 241

John Wiley & Sons Canada Ltd, Toronto, ON Canada *Toll Free Tel:* 800-225-5945 (orders only) *Toll Free Fax:* 800-565-6802 (orders), pg 445

John Wiley & Sons Inc, Hoboken, NJ *Toll Free Tel:* 800-225-5945 (cust serv), pg 241

John Wiley & Sons Inc Global Education, Hoboken, NJ *Toll Free Tel:* 800-225-5945 (cust serv), pg 241

John Wiley & Sons Inc Professional Development, Hoboken, NJ *Toll Free Tel:* 800-225-5945 (cust serv), pg 242

Wilfrid Laurier University Press, Waterloo, ON Canada *Toll Free Tel:* 866-836-5551 (CN & US), pg 445

Willow Creek Press, Minocqua, WI *Toll Free Tel:* 800-850-9453, pg 242

Wimmer Cookbooks, Memphis, TN *Toll Free Tel:* 800-548-2537, pg 242

Windsor Books, Bayshore, NY *Toll Free Tel:* 800-321-5934, pg 242

Winters Publishing, Greensburg, IN *Toll Free Tel:* 800-457-3230, pg 242

Winterthur Museum, Garden & Library, Winterthur, DE *Toll Free Tel:* 800-448-3883, pg 242

Winterwolf Press, Las Vegas, NV *Toll Free Tel:* 855-ICE-WOLF (423-9653), pg 243

Wisconsin Department of Public Instruction, Madison, WI *Toll Free Tel:* 800-441-4563 (US only); 800-243-8782 (US only), pg 243

Wisdom Publications Inc, Somerville, MA *Toll Free Tel:* 800-272-4050 (orders), pg 243

Alan Wofsy Fine Arts, San Francisco, CA *Toll Free Tel:* 800-660-6403, pg 243

Wolters Kluwer Law & Business, New York, NY *Toll Free Tel:* 800-234-1660 (cust serv), pg 243

Wood Lake Publishing Inc, Kelowna, BC Canada *Toll Free Tel:* 800-663-2775 (orders & cust serv) *Toll Free Fax:* 888-841-9991 (orders & cust serv), pg 445

Woodbine House, Bethesda, MD *Toll Free Tel:* 800-843-7323, pg 243

Workman Publishing Co Inc, New York, NY *Toll Free Tel:* 800-722-7202, pg 244

World Almanac®, New York, NY *Toll Free Tel:* 800-322-8755, pg 244

World Bank Publications, Washington, DC *Toll Free Tel:* 800-645-7247 (cust serv), pg 244

World Book Inc, Chicago, IL *Toll Free Tel:* 800-967-5325 (consumer sales, US); 800-463-8845 (consumer sales, CN); 800-975-3250 (school & lib sales, US); 800-837-5365 (school & lib sales, CN); 866-866-5200 (web sales) *Toll Free Fax:* 800-433-9330 (school & lib sales, US); 888-690-4002 (school & lib sales, CN), pg 245

World Citizens, Mill Valley, CA *Toll Free Tel:* 800-247-6553 (orders only), pg 245

World Trade Press LLC, Traverse City, MI *Toll Free Tel:* 800-833-8586, pg 245

WorldTariff, San Francisco, CA *Toll Free Tel:* 866-268-7602, pg 245

Worldwide Library, Don Mills, ON Canada *Toll Free Tel:* 888-432-4879, pg 446

Xlibris Corp, Bloomington, IN *Toll Free Tel:* 844-714-8691; 888-795-4274, pg 246

Yale University Press, New Haven, CT *Toll Free Tel:* 800-405-1619 (cust serv) *Toll Free Fax:* 800-406-9145 (cust serv), pg 246

YMAA Publication Center Inc, Wolfeboro, NH *Toll Free Tel:* 800-669-8892, pg 247

YWAM Publishing, Seattle, WA *Toll Free Tel:* 800-922-2143, pg 247

Zagat Inc, New York, NY *Toll Free Tel:* 800-540-9609, pg 247

Zaner-Bloser Inc, Grandview Heights, OH *Toll Free Tel:* 800-421-3018 (cust serv) *Toll Free Fax:* 800-992-6087 (orders), pg 247

Zest Books, Minneapolis, MN *Toll Free Tel:* 800-328-4929 *Toll Free Fax:* 800-332-1132, pg 248

Zondervan, Grand Rapids, MI *Toll Free Tel:* 800-226-1122; 800-727-1309 (retail orders) *Toll Free Fax:* 800-698-3256 (retail orders), pg 248

Index to Sections

Index to Advertisers